WHO WAS WHO

VOL. VII

1971–1980

WHO'S WHO

An annual biographical dictionary
first published in 1849

WHO WAS WHO

VOL. I   1897–1915
VOL. II   1916–1928
VOL. III 1929–1940
VOL. IV   1941–1950
VOL. V   1951–1960
VOL. VI   1961–1970
VOL. VII 1971–1980
A CUMULATED INDEX 1897–1980

Published by
ADAM & CHARLES BLACK

WHO WAS WHO

1971–1980

A COMPANION TO

WHO'S WHO

CONTAINING THE BIOGRAPHIES
OF THOSE WHO DIED DURING
THE DECADE 1971–1980

ADAM AND CHARLES BLACK
LONDON

FIRST PUBLISHED 1981
BY A. & C. BLACK (PUBLISHERS) LIMITED
35 BEDFORD ROW LONDON WC1

COPYRIGHT © 1981 A. & C. BLACK (PUBLISHERS) LTD

ISBN 0–7136–2176–1

DATA PROCESSING AND COMPUTER
TYPESETTING BY
COMPUTAPRINT

PRINTED IN GREAT BRITAIN BY BUTLER & TANNER
LTD, FROME & LONDON

PREFACE

This is the seventh volume of biographies removed from *Who's Who* on account of death, containing the entries of those who died between 1971 and 1980. It also contains, in the two series of Addenda, first the entries of those who died before 31 December 1970, but whose deaths were not known to us until after volume VI of *Who Was Who* was printed; second, the entries of those who died in the decade covered by this volume, whose deaths were not known until after it went to press.

The entries are as they last appeared in *Who's Who*, with the date of death added, and in some cases with a final revision (for example, where posthumous publications have been noted they are included). Where the fact but not the date of death is known, and enquiries have failed to discover it, the editors will welcome information for the next edition of this volume.

For the first time, the appearance of a ten-yearly volume of *Who Was Who* is accompanied by the publication of an index to all seven volumes, giving the names shown in *Who Was Who* from the first volume, with deaths from 1897 onwards; it is hoped that this will make the use of *Who Was Who* a great deal easier for researchers, since it is no longer necessary to search from volume to volume if the year of death is not known.

ADAM AND CHARLES BLACK

CONTENTS

ABBREVIATIONS USED IN THIS BOOK

Some of the designatory letters in this list are used merely for economy of
space and do not necessarily imply any professional or other qualification

A

AA Anti-Aircraft; Automobile Association; Architectural Association; Augustinians of the Assumption
AAA Amateur Athletic Association; American Accounting Association
AAAL American Academy of Arts and Letters (*now see* AAIL)
AA&QMG Assistant Adjutant and Quartermaster-General
AAAS American Association for Advancement of Science
AACCA Associate, Association of Certified and Corporate Accountants; *now see* ACCA
AACE Association for Adult and Continuing Education
AAF Auxiliary Air Force (*now* RAuxAF)
AAG Assistant Adjutant-General
AAI Associate, Chartered Auctioneers' and Estate Agents' Institute; *now (after amalgamation) see* ARICS
AAIL American Academy and Institute of Arts and Letters
AAM Association of Assistant Mistresses in Secondary Schools
AAMC Australian Army Medical Corps
A&AEE Aeroplane and Armament Experimental Establishment
AASA Associate, Australian Society of Accountants
AASC Australian Army Service Corps
AAUQ Associate in Accountancy, University of Queensland
AB Bachelor of Arts (US); able-bodied seaman
ABA Amateur Boxing Association; Antiquarian Booksellers' Association; American Bar Association
ABC Australian Broadcasting Commission
ABCA Army Bureau of Current Affairs
ABCC Association of British Chambers of Commerce
ABCFM American Board of Commissioners for Foreign Missions
Abp Archbishop
ABPsS Associate, British Psychological Society
ABRC Advisory Board for the Research Councils
ABS Associate, Building Societies' Institute (*now see* ACBSI)
ABSI Associate, Boot and Shoe Institution
ABSM Associate, Birmingham and Midland Institute School of Music
ABTAPL Association of British Theological and Philosophical Libraries
AC Companion of the Order of Australia; *Ante Christum* (before Christ)
ACA Associate, Institute of Chartered Accountants
Acad. Academy
ACAS Advisory, Conciliation and Arbitration Service; Assistant Chief of the Air Staff
ACBSI Associate, Chartered Building Societies Institute
ACC Association of County Councils
ACCA Associate, Association of Certified Accountants
ACCM Advisory Council for the Church's Ministry (formerly CACTM)
ACCS Associate, Corporation of Secretaries (formerly of Certified Secretaries)
ACDS Assistant Chief of Defence Staff
ACE Association of Consulting Engineers
ACF Army Cadet Force
ACFA Army Cadet Force Association
ACG Assistant Chaplain-General
ACGI Associate, City and Guilds of London Institute
ACGS Assistant Chief of the General Staff
ACIArb Associate, Chartered Institute of Arbitrators
ACII Associate, Chartered Insurance Institute
ACIS Associate, Institute of Chartered Secretaries and Administrators (formerly Chartered Institute of Secretaries)
ACIT Associate, Chartered Institute of Transport
ACLS American Council of Learned Societies
ACMA Associate, Institute of Cost and Management Accountants
ACNS Assistant Chief of Naval Staff
ACommA Associate, Society of Commercial Accountants; *now see* ASCA
ACOS Assistant Chief of Staff
ACP Association of Clinical Pathologists
ACS American Chemical Society; Additional Curates Society
ACSEA Allied Command SE Asia
ACSM Associate, Camborne School of Mines
ACT Australian Capital Territory; Australian College of Theology; Associate, College of Technology

ACTT Association of Cinematograph, Television and Allied Technicians
ACTU Australian Council of Trade Unions
ACU Association of Commonwealth Universities
ACWA Associate, Institute of Cost and Works Accountants; *now see* ACMA
AD Dame of the Order of Australia; *Anno Domini*
ADB Asian Development Bank
ADC Aide-de-camp
ADCM Archbishop of Canterbury's Diploma in Church Music
AD Corps Army Dental Corps, *now* RADC
ADC (P) Personal Aide-de-camp to HM The Queen
Ad eund *Ad eundem gradum;* and *see under* a e g
ADFManc Art and Design Fellow, Manchester
ADFW Assistant Director of Fortifications and Works
ADGB Air Defence of Great Britain
ADGMS Assistant Director-General of Medical Services
ADH Assistant Director of Hygiene
Adjt Adjutant
ADJAG Assistant Deputy Judge Advocate General
ADK Order of Ahli Darjah Kinabalu (Malaysia)
Adm. Admiral
ADMS Assistant Director of Medical Services
ADOS Assistant Director of Ordnance Services
ADP Automatic Data Processing
ADS&T Assistant Director of Supplies and Transport
Adv. Advisory; Advocate
ADVS Assistant Director of Veterinary Services
ADWE&M Assistant Director of Works, Electrical and Mechanical
AE Air Efficiency Award (changed 1975)
AEA Atomic Energy Authority; Air Efficiency Award (*now see* AE)
AEAF Allied Expeditionary Air Force
AEC Agriculture Executive Council; Army Educational Corps (*now* RAEC)
AEF Amalgamated Union of Engineering and Foundry Workers; American Expeditionary Forces
a e g *ad eundem gradum* (to the same degree—of the admission of a graduate of one university to the same degree at another without examination)
AEGIS Aid for the Elderly in Government Institutions
AEI Associated Electrical Industries
AEM Air Efficiency Medal
AER Army Emergency Reserve
AERE Atomic Energy Research Establishment (Harwell)
AEt., AEtat. *AEtatis* (aged)
AEU Amalgamated Engineering Union
AFA Amateur Football Alliance
AFAIAA Associate Fellow, American Institute of Aeronautics and Astronautics (and *see under* AFIAS)
AFC Air Force Cross; Association Football Club
AFCAI Associate Fellow, Canadian Aeronautical Institute
AFD Doctor of Fine Arts (US)
AFHQ Allied Force Headquarters
AFIA Associate, Federal Institute of Accountants (Australia)
AFIAS (*now under* AFIAAA) (formerly) Associate Fellow, Institute of Aeronautical Sciences (US)
AFICD Associate Fellow, Institute of Civil Defence
AFIMA Associate Fellow, Institute of Mathematics and its Applications
AFM Air Force Medal
AFOM Associate, Faculty of Occupational Medicine
AFRAeS Associate Fellow, Royal Aeronautical Society (*now see* MRAeS)
AFV Armoured Fighting Vehicles
AG Attorney-General
AGARD Advisory Group for Aerospace Research and Development
AGH Australian General Hospital
AGI Artistes Graphiques Internationales; Associate, Institute of Certificated Grocers

9

AGRA	Army Group Royal Artillery
AGSM	Associate, Guildhall School of Music
AHA	Area Health Authority; American Hospitals Association
AHA(T)	Area Health Authority (Teaching)
AHQ	Army Headquarters
AH-WC	Associate, Heriot-Watt College, Edinburgh
ai	*ad interim*
AIA	Associate, Institute of Actuaries; American Institute of Architects
AIAA	American Institute of Aeronautics and Astronautics
AIAL	Associate Member, International Institute of Arts and Letters
AIArb	Associate, Institute of Arbitrators (*now see* ACIArb)
AIAS	Associate Surveyor Member, Incorporated Association of Architects and Surveyors
AIB	Associate, Institute of Bankers
AIBD	Associate, Institute of British Decorators
AIBP	Associate, Institute of British Photographers
AIC	Agricultural Improvement Council; also formerly Associate of the Institute of Chemistry (*see* ARIC)
AICA	Associate Member, Commonwealth Institute of Accountants; Association Internationale des Critiques d'Art
AICC	All-India Congress Committee
AICE	Associate, Institution of Civil Engineers
AICPA	American Institute of Certified Public Accountants
AICTA	Associate, Imperial College of Tropical Agriculture
AIEE	Associate, Institution of Electrical Engineers
AIF	Australian Imperial Forces
AIG	Adjutant-Inspector-General
AIIA	Associate, Insurance Institute of America
AIInfSc	Associate, Institute of Information Scientists
AIL	Associate, Institute of Linguists
AILA	Associate, Institute of Landscape Architects (*now see* ALI)
AILocoE	Associate, Institution of Locomotive Engineers
AIM	Associate, Institution of Metallurgists (*now see* MIM)
AIME	American Institute of Mechanical Engineers
AIMarE	Associate, Institute of Marine Engineers
AInstM	Associate Member, Institute of Marketing
AInstP	Associate, Institute of Physics
AInstPI	Associate, Institute of Patentees and Inventors
AIProdE	Associate, Institution of Production Engineers
AIQS	Associate Member, Institute of Quantity Surveyors
AIS	Associate, Institute of Statisticians; *now see* MIS
AISA	Associate, Incorporated Secretaries' Association
AIStructE	Associate, Institution of Structural Engineers
AJAG	Assistant Judge Advocate General
AJEX	Association of Jewish Ex-Service Men and Women
AK	Knight of the Order of Australia
AKC	Associate, King's College (London)
ALA	Associate, Library Association
Ala	Alabama (US)
ALAA	Associate, Library Association of Australia
ALAM	Associate, London Academy of Music and Dramatic Art
ALCD	Associate, London College of Divinity
ALCM	Associate, London College of Music
ALCS	Authors Lending and Copyright Society
ALFSEA	Allied Land Forces South-East Asia
ALI	Argyll Light Infantry; Associate, Landscape Institute
ALLC	Association for Literary and Linguistic Computing
ALP	Australian Labor Party
ALPSP	Association of Learned and Professional Society Publishers
ALS	Associate, Linnaean Society
Alta	Alberta
AM	Albert Medal; Member of the Order of Australia; Master of Arts (US); Alpes Maritimes
AMA	Association of Metropolitan Authorities; Assistant Masters Association; Associate of the Museums Association; Australian Medical Association
Amb.	Ambulance; Ambassador
AMBIM	Associate Member, British Institute of Management
AMBritIRE	(*now see under* AMIERE) (formerly) Associate Member, British Institution of Radio Engineers
AMC	Association of Municipal Corporations
AMCT	Associate, Manchester College of Technology
AMEME	Association of Mining Electrical and Mechanical Engineers
AMet	Associate of Metallurgy (Sheffield University)
AMF	Australian Military Forces
AMGOT	Allied Military Government of Occupied Territory
AMIAE	Associate Member, Institution of Automobile Engineers
AMIAgrE	Associate Member, Institution of Agricultural Engineers
AMICE	Associate Member, Institution of Civil Engineers (formerly lower rank of corporate membership of Instn, *now see under* MICE; change dated July 1968)
AMIChemE	Associate Member, Institution of Chemical Engineers
AMIE(Aust)	Associate Member, Institution of Engineers, Australia
AMIED	Associate Member, Institution of Engineering Designers
AMIEE	Associate Member, Institution of Electrical Engineers (formerly lower rank of corporate membership of Instn, *now see under* MIEE; change dated Dec. 1966)
AMIE(Ind)	Associate Member, Institution of Engineers, India
AMIERE	Associate Member, Institution of Electronic and Radio Engineers (*and see under* AMBritIRE)
AMIMechE	Associate Member, Institution of Mechanical Engineers (formerly lower rank of corporate membership of Instn, *now see under* MIMechE; change dated April 1968)
AMIMinE	Associate Member, Institution of Mining Engineers
AMIMM	Associate Member, Institution of Mining and Metallurgy
AMInstBE	Associate Member, Institution of British Engineers
AMInstCE	Associate Member, Institution of Civil Engineers (changed 1946 to AMICE)
AmInstEE	American Institute of Electrical Engineers
AMInstR	Associate Member, Institute of Refrigeration
AMInstT	Associate Member, Institute of Transport; *now see* ACIT
AMInstTA	Associate Member, Institute of Traffic Administration
AMINucE	Associate Member, Institution of Nuclear Engineers
AMIStructE	Associate Member, Institution of Structural Engineers
AMP	Advanced Management Program
AMRINA	Associate Member, Royal Institution of Naval Architects
AMS	Assistant Military Secretary; Army Medical Services
AMTE	Admiralty Marine Technology Establishment
ANA	Associate National Academician (America)
ANAF	Arab Non-Arab Friendship
Anat.	Anatomy; Anatomical
ANC	African National Congress
ANECInst	Associate, NE Coast Institution of Engineers and Shipbuilders
ANGAU	Australia New Guinea Administrative Unit
Anon.	Anonymously
ANU	Australian National University
ANZAAS	Australian and New Zealand Association for the Advancement of Science
AO	Officer of the Order of Australia; Air Officer
AOA	Air Officer in charge of Administration
AOC	Air Officer Commanding
AOC-in-C	Air Officer Commanding-in-Chief
AOD	Army Ordnance Department
AOER	Army Officers Emergency Reserve
APA	American Psychiatric Association
APD	Army Pay Department
APEX	Association of Professional, Executive, Clerical and Computer Staffs
APHA	American Public Health Association
APM	Assistant Provost Marshal
APMI	Associate, Pensions Management Institute
APS	Aborigines Protection Society
APsSI	Associate, Psychological Society of Ireland
APSW	Association of Psychiatric Social Workers
APT&C	Administrative, Professional, Technical and Clerical
APTC	Army Physical Training Corps
AQ	Administration and Quartering
AQMG	Assistant Quartermaster-General
AR	Associated Rediffusion (Television)
ARA	Associate, Royal Academy
ARACI	Associate, Royal Australian Chemical Institute
ARAD	Associate, Royal Academy of Dancing
ARAeS	Associate, Royal Aeronautical Society
ARAM	Associate, Royal Academy of Music
ARAS	Associate, Royal Astronomical Society
ARBA	Associate, Royal Society of British Artists
ARBC	Associate, Royal British Colonial Society of Artists
ARBS	Associate, Royal Society of British Sculptors
ARC	Architects' Registration Council; Agricultural Research Council; Aeronautical Research Council
ARCA	Associate, Royal College of Art; Associate, Royal Canadian Academy
ARCamA	Associate, Royal Cambrian Academy of Art (*formerly* ARCA)
ARCE	Academical Rank of Civil Engineers
Archt	Architect
ARCM	Associate, Royal College of Music
ARCO	Associate, Royal College of Organists
ARCO(CHM)	Associate, Royal College of Organists with Diploma in Choir Training
ARCPsych	Associate Member, Royal College of Psychiatrists
ARCS	Associate, Royal College of Science
ARCST	Associate, Royal College of Science and Technology (Glasgow)
ARCUK	Architects' Registration Council of the United Kingdom
ARCVS	Associate, Royal College of Veterinary Surgeons
ARE	Associate, Royal Society of Painter-Etchers and Engravers; Arab Republic of Egypt
ARIAS	Associate, Royal Incorporation of Architects in Scotland
ARIBA	Associate, Royal Institute of British Architects; *and see* RIBA
ARIC	Associate, Royal Institute of Chemistry (*now see* MRIC)
ARICS	Professional Associate of the Royal Institution of Chartered Surveyors
ARINA	Associate, Royal Institution of Naval Architects
Ark	Arkansas (US)
ARLT	Association for the Reform of Latin Teaching
ARMS	Associate, Royal Society of Miniature Painters
ARP	Air Raid Precautions
ARPS	Associate, Royal Photographic Society
ARRC	Associate, Royal Red Cross
ARSA	Associate, Royal Scottish Academy
ARSCM	Associate, Royal School of Church Music
ARSM	Associate, Royal School of Mines
ARTC	Associate, Royal Technical College (Glasgow) (name changed) *see under* ARCST
ARVIA	Associate, Royal Victoria Institute of Architects

ARWA	Associate, Royal West of England Academy
ARWS	Associate, Royal Society of Painters in Water-Colours
AS	Anglo-Saxon
ASA	Associate Member, Society of Actuaries; Associate of Society of Actuaries (US); Australian Society of Accountants; Army Sailing Association
ASAA	Associate, Society of Incorporated Accountants and Auditors
ASAM	Associate, Society of Art Masters
AS&TS of SA	Associated Scientific and Technical Societies of South Africa
ASBAH	Association for Spina Bifida and Hydrocephalus
ASC	Administrative Staff College, Henley
ASCA	Associate, Society of Company and Commercial Accountants
ASCAB	Armed Services Consultant Approval Board
AScW	Association of Scientific Workers
ASD	Armament Supply Department
ASE	Amalgamated Society of Engineers
ASH	Action on Smoking and Health
ASIAD	Associate, Society of Industrial Artists and Designers
ASIA(Ed)	Associate, Society of Industrial Artists (Education)
ASLE	American Society of Lubrication Engineers
ASLEF	Associated Society of Locomotive Engineers and Firemen
ASLIB (Aslib)	Association of Special Libraries and Information Bureaux
ASME	American Society of Mechanical Engineers; Association for the Study of Medical Education
ASO	Air Staff Officer
ASSC	Accounting Standards Steering Committee
ASSET	Association of Supervisory Staffs, Executives and Technicians
AssocISI	Associate, Iron and Steel Institute
AssocMCT	Associateship of Manchester College of Technology
AssocMIAeE	Associate Member, Institution of Aeronautical Engineers
AssocRINA	Associate, Royal Institution of Naval Architects
AssocSc	Associate in Science
Asst	Assistant
ASTMS	Association of Scientific, Technical and Managerial Staffs
Astr.	Astronomy
ASW	Association of Scientific Workers
ATA	Air Transport Auxiliary
ATAE	Association of Tutors in Adult Education
ATAF	Allied Tactical Air Force
ATC	Air Training Corps
ATCDE	Association of Teachers in Colleges and Departments of Education (*now see* NATFHE)
ATCL	Associate, Trinity College of Music, London
ATD	Art Teacher's Diploma
ATI	Associate, Textile Institute
ATII	Associate Member, Institute of Taxation
ato	Ammunition Technical Officer
ATS	Auxiliary Territorial Service (*now see* WRAC)
ATTI	Association of Teachers in Technical Institutions (*now see* NATFHE)
ATV	Associated TeleVision
AUA	American Urological Association
AUCAS	Association of University Clinical Academic Staff
AUEW	Amalgamated Union of Engineering Workers
AUEW(TASS)	Amalgamated Union of Engineering Workers (Technical and Supervisory Section)
AUS	Army of the United States
AUT	Association of University Teachers
AVD	Army Veterinary Department
AVLA	Audio Visual Language Association
AVR	Army Volunteer Reserve
AWA	Anglian Water Authority
AWRE	Atomic Weapons Research Establishment
aws	Graduate of Air Warfare Course

B

b	born; brother
BA	Bachelor of Arts
BAAB	British Amateur Athletic Board
BAAL	British Association for Applied Linguistics
BAAS	British Association for the Advancement of Science
BAB	British Airways Board
BAC	British Aircraft Corporation
BACM	British Association of Colliery Management
BAe	British Aerospace
B&FBS	British and Foreign Bible Society
BAFO	British Air Forces of Occupation
BAFTA	British Academy of Film and Television Arts (formerly SFTA)
BAG	Business Art Galleries
BAI	Bachelor of Engineering (*Baccalarius in Arte Ingeniaria*)
BAIE	British Association of Industrial Editors
BALPA	British Air Line Pilots' Association
BAO	Bachelor of Art of Obstetrics
BAOR	British Army of the Rhine (formerly *on* the Rhine)
BAOS	British Association of Oral Surgeons
BAppSc(MT)	Bachelor of Applied Science (Medical Technology)

BARC	British Automobile Racing Club
Bart or Bt	Baronet
BAS	Bachelor in Agricultural Science
BASc	Bachelor of Applied Science
BASW	British Association of Social Workers
Batt.	Battery
BBA	British Bankers' Association
BB&CIRly	Bombay, Baroda and Central India Railway
BBB of C	British Boxing Board of Control
BBC	British Broadcasting Corporation
BBM	*Bintang Bakti Masharakat* (Public Service Star) (Singapore)
BBS	Bachelor of Business Studies
BC	Before Christ; British Columbia
BCC	British Council of Churches
BCE (Melb)	Bachelor of Civil Engineering (Melbourne Univ.)
BCh or BChir	Bachelor of Surgery
BCL	Bachelor of Civil Law
BCMS	Bible Churchmen's Missionary Society
BCOF	British Commonwealth Occupation Force
BCom	Bachelor of Commerce
BComSc	Bachelor of Commercial Science
BCS	Bengal Civil Service
BCURA	British Coal Utilization Research Association
BCYC	British Corinthian Yacht Club
BD	Bachelor of Divinity
Bd	Board
BDA	British Dental Association
Bde	Brigade
BDS	Bachelor of Dental Surgery
BDSc	Bachelor of Dental Science
BE	Bachelor of Engineering; British Element
BEA	British East Africa; British European Airways; British Epilepsy Association
BEAMA	British Electrical and Allied Manufacturers' Association
BE&A	Bachelor of Engineering and Architecture (Malta)
BEAS	British Educational Administration Society
BEC	Business Education Council
BEc	Bachelor of Economics (Australian)
BEd	Bachelor of Education
Beds	Bedfordshire
BEE	Bachelor of Electrical Engineering
BEF	British Expeditionary Force
BEM	British Empire Medal
BEME	Brigade Electrical and Mechanical Engineer
BEO	Base Engineer Officer
Berks	Berkshire
BFI	British Film Institute
BFMIRA	British Food Manufacturing Industries Research Association
BFPO	British Forces Post Office
BGS	Brigadier General Staff
Bhd	Berhad
BHRCA	British Hotels, Restaurants and Caterers' Association
BHS	British Horse Society
BICC	British Insulated Callender's Cables
BICERA	British Internal Combustion Engine Research Association
BIF	British Industries Fair
BIFU	Banking Insurance and Finance Union
BIM	British Institute of Management
BIR	British Institute of Radiology
BIS	Bank for International Settlements
BISF	British Iron and Steel Federation
BISFA	British Industrial and Scientific Film Association
BISRA	British Iron and Steel Research Association
BJ	Bachelor of Journalism
BJSM	British Joint Services Mission
BKSTS	British Kinematograph, Sound and Television Society
BL	Bachelor of Law
BLA	British Liberation Army
BLE	Brotherhood of Locomotive Engineers; Bachelor of Land Economy
BLESMA	British Limbless Ex-Servicemen's Association
BLitt	Bachelor of Letters
BM	British Museum; Bachelor of Medicine; Brigade Major; British Monomark
BMA	British Medical Association
BMEO	British Middle East Office
BMEWS	Ballistic Missile Early Warning System
BMH	British Military Hospital
BMJ	British Medical Journal
Bn	Battalion
BNAF	British North Africa Force
BNC	Brasenose College
BNEC	British National Export Council
BNOC	British National Oil Corporation; British National Opera Company
BOAC	British Overseas Airways Corporation
BomCS	Bombay Civil Service
BomSC	Bombay Staff Corps
BoT	Board of Trade
Bot.	Botany; Botanical
BOTB	British Overseas Trade Board
Bp	Bishop
BPharm	Bachelor of Pharmacy

BPIF	British Printing Industries Federation
BPsS	British Psychological Society
BR	British Rail
Br.	Branch
BRA	Brigadier Royal Artillery; British Rheumatism & Arthritis Association
BRB	British Railways Board
BRCS	British Red Cross Society
BRE	Building Research Establishment
Brig.	Brigadier
BritIRE	British Institution of Radio Engineers (*now see* IERE)
BRNC	Britannia Royal Naval College
BRS	British Road Services
BS	Bachelor of Surgery; Bachelor of Science
BSA	Bachelor of Scientific Agriculture; Birmingham Small Arms
BSAA	British South American Airways
BSAP	British South Africa Police
BSC	British Steel Corporation; Bengal Staff Corps
BSc	Bachelor of Science
BScA	Bachelor of Science in Agriculture
BSc (Dent)	Bachelor of Science in Dentistry
BSE	Bachelor of Science in Engineering (US)
BSF	British Salonica Force
BSI	British Standards Institution
BSJA	British Show Jumping Association
BSocSc	Bachelor of Social Science
BSRA	British Ship Research Association
BST	Bachelor of Sacred Theology
BT	Bachelor of Teaching
Bt	Baronet; Brevet
BTA	British Tourist Authority (*formerly* British Travel Association)
BTC	British Transport Commission
BTCV	British Trust for Conservation Volunteers
BTh	Bachelor of Theology
Btss	Baroness
BUAS	British Universities Association of Slavists
BUPA	British United Provident Association
BVA	British Veterinary Association
BVM	Blessed Virgin Mary
BVMS	Bachelor of Veterinary Medicine and Surgery
Bucks	Buckinghamshire
BWI	British West Indies (*now* WI: West Indies)
BWM	British War Medal

C

(C)	Conservative; 100
c	Child; cousin
CA	Central America; County Alderman; Chartered Accountant (Scotland and Canada)
CAA	Civil Aviation Authority
CAB	Citizens' Advice Bureau
CACTM	Central Advisory Council of Training for the Ministry (*now see* ACCM)
CALE	Canadian Army Liaison Executive
Cambs	Cambridgeshire
CAMC	Canadian Army Medical Corps
CAMRA	Campaign for Real Ale
CAMW	Central Association for Mental Welfare
Cantab	Of Cambridge University
CARE	Cottage and Rural Enterprises
CARIFTA	Caribbean Free Trade Area
CAS	Chief of the Air Staff
CASI	Canadian Aeronautics and Space Institute
Cav.	Cavalry
CAWU	Clerical and Administrative Workers' Union
CB	Companion of the Bath
CBE	Commander Order of the British Empire
CBI	Confederation of British Industry (*and see under* FBI)
CBIM	Companion, British Institute of Management
CBSA	Clay Bird Shooting Association
CBSI	Chartered Building Societies Institute
CC	Companion of the Order of Canada; City Council; County Council; Cricket Club; Cycling Club; County Court
CCAHC	Central Council for Agricultural and Horticultural Co-operation
CCC	Corpus Christi College; Central Criminal Court; County Cricket Club
CCF	Combined Cadet Force
CCFM	Combined Cadet Forces Medal
CCG	Control Commission Germany
CCH	Cacique's Crown of Honour, Order of Service of Guyana
CChem	Chartered Chemist
CCJ	Council of Christians and Jews
CCPR	Central Council of Physical Recreation
CCRA	Commander Corps Royal Artillery
CCRE	Commander Corps of Royal Engineers
CCRSigs	Commander Corps of Royal Signals
CCS	Casualty Clearing Station; Ceylon Civil Service
CCTA	Commission de Coopération Technique pour l'Afrique
CD	Canadian Forces Decoration; Commander of the Order of Distinction (Jamaica)

CDEE	Chemical Defence Experimental Establishment
CDipAF	Certified Diploma in Accounting and Finance
Cdre	Commodore
CDS	Chief of the Defence Staff
CDU	Christliche Demokratische Union
CE	Civil Engineer
CEDEP	Centre Européen d'Education Permanente
CEE	Communauté Economique Européenne
CEF	Canadian Expeditionary Force
CEGB	Central Electricity Generating Board
CEI	Council of Engineering Institutions
CEIR	Corporation for Economic and Industrial Research
CEMA	Council for the Encouragement of Music and the Arts
CEMS	Church of England Men's Society
CEN	Comité Européen de Normalisation
CEng	Chartered Engineer
Cento	Central Treaty Organisation
CERL	Central Electricity Research Laboratories
CERN	Conseil (*now* Centre) Européen pour la Recherche Nucléaire
CETS	Church of England Temperance Society
CF	Chaplain to the Forces
CFA	Canadian Field Artillery
CFE	Central Fighter Establishment
CFR	Commander of Federal Republic of Nigeria
CFS	Central Flying School
CGA	Community of the Glorious Ascension
CGH	Order of the Golden Heart of Kenya (1st class)
CGIA	City and Guilds of London Insignia Award
CGLI	City and Guilds of London Institute
CGM	Conspicuous Gallantry Medal
CGRM	Commandant-General Royal Marines
CGS	Chief of the General Staff
CH	Companion of Honour
Chanc.	Chancellor; Chancery
Chap.	Chaplain
ChapStJ	Chaplain of Order of St John of Jerusalem (*now* ChStJ)
CHAR	Campaign for the Homeless and Rootless
ChB	Bachelor of Surgery
Ch. Ch.	Christ Church
Ch. Coll.	Christ's College
CHM	Chevalier of Honour and Merit (Haiti)
(CHM)	*See under* ARCO(CHM), FRCO(CHM)
ChM	Master of Surgery
Chm.	Chairman
CHSC	Central Health Services Council
ChStJ	Chaplain of Order of St John of Jerusalem
CI	Imperial Order of the Crown of India; Channel Islands
CIAD	Central Institute of Art and Design
CIAgrE	Companion, Institution of Agricultural Engineers
CIAL	Corresponding Member of the International Institute of Arts and Letters
CIArb	Chartered Institute of Arbitrators
CIBS	Chartered Institution of Building Services (*formerly* IHVE)
CID	Criminal Investigation Department
CIDEC	Conseil International pour le Développement du Cuivre
CIE	Companion of the Order of the Indian Empire; Confédération Internationale des Etudiants
CIFRS	Comité International de la Rayonne et des Fibres Synthétiques
CIGRE	Conférence Internationale des Grands Réseaux Electriques
CIGS	(*formerly*) Chief of the Imperial General Staff (*now* CGS)
CIMarE	Companion of the Institute of Marine Engineers
CIMechE	Companion of the Institution of Mechanical Engineers
CIMGTechE	Companion, Institution of Mechanical and General Technician Engineers
C-in-C	Commander-in-Chief
CINCHAN	Allied Commander-in-Chief Channel
CIPFA	Chartered Institute of Public Finance and Accountancy (*formerly* IMTA)
CIPM	Companion, Institute of Personnel Management
CIR	Commission on Industrial Relations
CIRIA	Construction Industry Research and Information Association
CISAC	Confédération Internationale des Sociétés d'Auteurs et Compositeurs
CIT	Chartered Institute of Transport
CIU	Club and Institute Union
CIV	City Imperial Volunteers
CJ	Chief Justice
CJM	Congregation of Jesus and Mary (Eudist Fathers)
CL	Commander of Order of Leopold
c.l.	*cum laude*
Cl.	Class
CLA	Country Landowners' Association
CLit	Companion of Literature (Royal Society of Literature Award)
CLJ	Commander, Order of St Lazarus of Jerusalem
CLP	Constituency Labour Party
CLRAE	Conference of Local and Regional Authorities of Europe
CM	Member of the Order of Canada; Congregation of the Mission (Vincentians); Master in Surgery; Certificated Master; Canadian Militia
CMA	Canadian Medical Association
CMAC	Catholic Marriage Advisory Council
CMB	Central Midwives' Board

CMF	Commonwealth Military Forces; Central Mediterranean Force
CMG	Companion of St Michael and St George
CMM	Commander, Order of Military Merit (Canada)
CMO	Chief Medical Officer
CMP	Corps of Military Police
CMS	Church Missionary Society
CMT	Chaconia Medal of Trinidad
CNAA	Council for National Academic Awards
CNR	Canadian National Railways
CNRS	Centre National du Recherche Scientifique
CO	Commanding Officer; Commonwealth Office (from Aug. 1966) (*see also* FCO); Colonial Office (before Aug. 1966); Conscientious Objector
Co.	County; Company
C of E	Church of England
C of S	Chief of Staff
COI	Central Office of Information
CoID	Council of Industrial Design (*now* Design Council)
Co.L or Coal.L	Coalition Liberal
Col	Colonel
Coll.	College; Collegiate
Colo	Colorado (US)
Col-Sergt	Colour-Sergeant
Com	Communist
Comd	Command
Comdg	Commanding
Comdr	Commander
Comdt	Commandant
COMEC	Council of the Military Education Committees of the Universities of the UK
COMET	Committee for Middle East Trade
Commn	Commission
Commnd	Commissioned
CompAMEME	Companion, Association of Mining Electrical and Mechanical Engineers
CompICE	Companion, Institution of Civil Engineers
CompIEE	Companion of the Institution of Electrical Engineers
CompIERE	Companion of the Institution of Electronic and Radio Engineers
CompIMechE	Companion, Institution of Mechanical Engineers
CompTI	Companion of the Textile Institute
Comr	Commissioner
Comy-Gen.	Commissary-General
CON	Commander, Order of the Niger
Conn	Connecticut (US)
Const.	Constitutional
COPA	Comité des Organisations Professionels Agricoles de la CEE
COPEC	Conference of Politics, Economics and Christianity
Corp.	Corporation; Corporal
Corr. Mem. or Fell.	Corresponding Member or Fellow
COS	Chief of Staff; Charity Organization Society
COSA	Colliery Officials and Staffs Association
COSIRA	Council for Small Industries in Rural Areas
COSSAC	Chief of Staff to Supreme Allied Commander
COTC	Canadian Officers' Training Corps
Co.U or Coal.U	Coalition Unionist
CP	Central Provinces; Cape Province
CPA	Commonwealth Parliamentary Association; Chartered Patent Agent; *also (formerly)* Certified Public Accountant (Canada) (*now* merged with CA)
CPAS	Church Pastoral Aid Society
CPC	Conservative Political Centre
CPM	Colonial Police Medal
CPR	Canadian Pacific Railway
CPRE	Council for the Protection of Rural England
CPSA	Civil and Public Services Association (*formerly* CSCA)
CPSU	Communist Party of the Soviet Union
CPU	Commonwealth Press Union
CQSW	Certificate of Qualification in Social Work
CR	Community of the Resurrection
cr	created or creation
CRA	Commander, Royal Artillery
CRASC	Commander, Royal Army Service Corps
CRC	Cancer Research Campaign
CRCP(C)	Certificant, Royal College of Physicians of Canada
CRE	Commander, Royal Engineers; Commission for Racial Equality; Commercial Relations and Exports
Cres.	Crescent
CRMP	Corps of Royal Military Police
CRO	Commonwealth Relations Office (before Aug. 1966; *now see* CO and FCO)
CS	Civil Service; Clerk to the Signet
CSA	Confederate States of America
CSB	Bachelor of Christian Science
CSC	Conspicuous Service Cross; Congregation of the Holy Cross
CSCA	Civil Service Clerical Association (*now see* CPSA)
CSCE	Conference on Security and Cooperation in Europe
CSD	Civil Service Department; Cooperative Secretaries Diploma
CSEU	Confederation of Shipbuilding and Engineering Unions
CSG	Companion of the Order of the Star of Ghana
CSI	Companion of the Order of the Star of India

CSIR	Commonwealth Council for Scientific and Industrial Research (re-named; Commonwealth Scientific and Industrial Research Organization; *see* below)
CSIRO	Commonwealth Scientific and Industrial Research Organization (*and see* above)
CSO	Chief Scientific Officer; Chief Signal Officer; Chief Staff Officer
CSP	Chartered Society of Physiotherapists; Civil Service of Pakistan
CSS	Companion of Star of Sarawak
CSSp	Holy Ghost Father
CSSR	Congregation of the Most Holy Redeemer (Redemptorist Order)
CStJ	Commander of the Order of St John of Jerusalem
CSV	Community Service Volunteers
CTA	Chaplain Territorial Army
CTB	College of Teachers of the Blind
CTC	Cyclists' Touring Club
CText	Chartered Textile Technologist
CTR (Harwell)	Controlled Thermonuclear Research
CU	Cambridge University
CUAC	Cambridge University Athletic Club
CUAFC	Cambridge University Association Football Club
CUBC	Cambridge University Boat Club
CUCC	Cambridge University Cricket Club
CUF	Common University Fund
CUHC	Cambridge University Hockey Club
CUP	Cambridge University Press
CURUFC	Cambridge University Rugby Union Football Club
CV	Cross of Valour (Canada)
CVO	Commander of the Royal Victorian Order
CWA	Crime Writers Association
CWS	Co-operative Wholesale Society

D

D	Duke
d	Died; daughter
DA	Diploma in Anaesthesia; Diploma in Art
DAA&QMG	Deputy Assistant Adjutant and Quartermaster-General
DAAG	Deputy Assistant Adjutant-General
DA&QMG	Deputy Adjutant and Quartermaster-General
DACG	Deputy Assistant Chaplain-General
DAD	Deputy Assistant Director
DADMS	Deputy Assistant Director of Medical Services
DADOS	Deputy Assistant Director of Ordnance Services
DADQ	Deputy Assistant Director of Quartering
DADST	Deputy Assistant Director of Supplies and Transport
DAG	Deputy Adjutant-General
DAMS	Deputy Assistant Military Secretary
DAppSc	Doctor of Applied Science
DAQMG	Deputy Assistant Quartermaster-General
DASc	Doctor in Agricultural Sciences
DATA	Draughtsmen's and Allied Technicians' Association
DBA	Doctor of Business Administration
DBE	Dame Commander Order of the British Empire
DC	District Council; District of Columbia (US)
DCAe	Diploma of College of Aeronautics
DCAS	Deputy Chief of the Air Staff
DCB	Dame Commander of the Bath
DCG	Deputy Chaplain-General
DCGRM	Department of the Commandant General Royal Marines
DCGS	Deputy Chief of the General Staff
DCh	Doctor of Surgery
DCH	Diploma in Child Health
DCIGS	(*formerly*) Deputy Chief of the Imperial General Staff (*now* DCGS)
DCL	Doctor of Civil Law
DCLI	Duke of Cornwall's Light Infantry
DCM	Distinguished Conduct Medal
DCMG	Dame Commander of St Michael and St George
DCnL	Doctor of Canon Law
DCP	Diploma in Clinical Pathology
DCS	Deputy Chief of Staff; Doctor of Commercial Sciences
DCSO	Deputy Chief Scientific Officer
DCT	Doctor of Christian Theology
DCVO	Dame Commander of Royal Victorian Order
DD	Doctor of Divinity
DDL	Deputy Director of Labour
DDME	Deputy Director of Mechanical Engineering
DDMI	Deputy Director of Military Intelligence
DDMS	Deputy Director of Medical Services
DDMT	Deputy Director of Military Training
DDNI	Deputy Director of Naval Intelligence
DDO	Diploma in Dental Orthopaedics
DDPR	Deputy Director of Public Relations
DDPS	Deputy Director of Personal Services
DDR	Deutsche Demokratische Republik
DDRA	Deputy Director Royal Artillery
DDS	Doctor of Dental Surgery; Director of Dental Services
DDSc	Doctor of Dental Science
DDSD	Deputy Director Staff Duties

DDSM	Defense Distinguished Service Medal
DDST	Deputy Director of Supplies and Transport
DDWE&M	Deputy Director of Works, Electrical and Mechanical
DE	Doctor of Engineering
DEA	Department of Economic Affairs
Decd	Deceased
DEconSc	Doctor of Economic Science
DEd	Doctor of Education
Del	Delaware (US)
Deleg.	Delegate
DEng	Doctor of Engineering
DenM	Docteur en Médicine
DEOVR	Duke of Edinburgh's Own Volunteer Rifles
DEP	Department of Employment and Productivity; European Progressive Democrats
Dep.	Deputy
DES	Department of Education and Science
DèsL	Docteur ès lettres
DèsS	Docteur ès sciences
DesRCA	Designer of the Royal College of Art
DFA	Doctor of Fine Arts
DFC	Distinguished Flying Cross
DFH	Diploma of Faraday House
DFLS	Day Fighter Leaders' School
DFM	Distinguished Flying Medal
DG	Dragoon Guards
DGAA	Distressed Gentlefolks Aid Association
DGAMS	Director-General Army Medical Services
DGMS	Director-General of Medical Services
DGMT	Director-General of Military Training
DGMW	Director-General of Military Works
DGNPS	Director-General of Naval Personal Services
DGP	Director-General of Personnel
DGS	Diploma in Graduate Studies
DGStJ	(formerly) Dame of Grace, Order of St John of Jerusalem (now DStJ)
DGU	Doctor of Griffith University
DH	Doctor of Humanities
Dhc	Doctor honoris causa
DHEW	Department of Health Education and Welfare (US)
DHL	Doctor of Humane Letters; Doctor of Hebrew Literature
DHM	Dean Hole Medal
DHMSA	Diploma in the History of Medicine (Society of Apothecaries)
DHQ	District Headquarters
DHSS	Department of Health and Social Security
DIAS	Dublin Institute of Advanced Sciences
DIC	Diploma of the Imperial College
DIG	Deputy Inspector-General
DIH	Diploma in Industrial Health
Dio.	Diocese
DipAD	Diploma in Art and Design
DipAe	Diploma in Aeronautics
DipBS	Diploma in Fine Art, Byam Shaw School
DipCAM	Diploma in Communications, Advertising and Marketing
DipCD	Diploma in Civic Design
DipEd	Diploma in Education
DipFE	Diploma in Further Education
DipM	Diploma in Marketing
DipPA	Diploma of Practitioners in Advertising (now see DipCAM)
DipTP	Diploma in Town Planning
DipTPT	Diploma in Theory and Practice of Teaching
DistTP	Distinction Town Planning
Div.	Division; Divorced
DJAG	Deputy Judge Advocate General
DJStJ	(formerly) Dame of Justice of St John of Jerusalem (now DStJ)
DJur	Doctor Juris
DK	Most Esteemed Family Order (Brunei)
DL	Deputy Lieutenant
DLC	Diploma Loughborough College
DLES	Doctor of Letters in Economic Studies
DLI	Durham Light Infantry
DLitt or DLit	Doctor of Literature; Doctor of Letters
DLJ	Dame of Grace, Order of St Lazarus of Jerusalem
DLO	Diploma in Laryngology and Otology
DM	Doctor of Medicine
DMA	Diploma in Municipal Administration
DMD	Doctor of Medical Dentistry (Australia)
DME	Director of Mechanical Engineering
DMet	Doctor of Metallurgy
DMI	Director of Military Intelligence
DMin	Doctor of Ministry
DMJ	Diploma in Medical Jurisprudence
DMO	Director of Military Operations
DMR	Diploma in Medical Radiology
DMRD	Diploma in Medical Radiological Diagnosis
DMRE	Diploma in Medical Radiology and Electrology
DMRT	Diploma in Medical Radio-Therapy
DMS	Director of Medical Services; Decoration for Meritorious Service (South Africa); Diploma in Management Studies
DMT	Director of Military Training
DMus	Doctor of Music
DNB	Dictionary of National Biography
DNE	Director of Naval Equipment
DNI	Director of Naval Intelligence

DO	Diploma in Ophthalmology
DOAE	Defence Operational Analysis Establishment
DObstRCOG	Diploma Royal College of Obstetricians and Gynaecologists
DOC	District Officer Commanding
DocEng	Doctor of Engineering
DoE	Department of the Environment
DoI	Department of Industry
DOL	Doctor of Oriental Learning
Dom.	Dominus
DOMS	Diploma in Ophthalmic Medicine and Surgery
DOR	Director of Operational Requirements
DOS	Director of Ordnance Services
Dow.	Dowager
DPD	Diploma in Public Dentistry
DPed	Doctor of Pedagogy
DPA	Diploma in Public Administration; Discharged Prisoners' Aid
DPEc	Doctor of Political Economy
DPH	Diploma in Public Health
DPh or DPhil	Doctor of Philosophy
DPLG	Diplômé par le Gouvernement
DPM	Diploma in Psychological Medicine
DPR	Director of Public Relations
DPS	Director of Postal Services; also (formerly) Director of Personal Services
DQMG	Deputy Quartermaster-General
Dr	Doctor
DRAC	Director Royal Armoured Corps
DRD	Diploma in Restorative Dentistry
Dr ing	Doctor of Engineering (Germany)
DrŒcPol	Doctor Œconomicæ Politicæ
DS	Directing Staff
DSA	Diploma in Social Administration
DSAO	Diplomatic Service Administration Office
DSC	Distinguished Service Cross
DSc	Doctor of Science
DScA	Docteur en sciences agricoles
DScMil	Doctor of Military Science
DSD	Director Staff Duties
DSIR	Department of Scientific and Industrial Research (now see under SRC)
DSLJ	Dato Seri Laila Jasa Brunei
DSM	Distinguished Service Medal
DSNB	Dato Setia Negara Brunei
DSO	Companion of the Distinguished Service Order
DSocSc	Doctor of Social Science
DSP	Director of Selection of Personnel; Docteur en sciences politiques (Montreal)
d.s.p.	decessit sine prole (died without issue)
DSS	Doctor of Sacred Scripture
DSSc	Doctor of Social Science (USA)
DST	Director of Supplies and Transport
DStJ	Dame of Grace, Order of St John of Jerusalem; Dame of Justice, Order of St John of Jerusalem; and see GCStJ
DTD	Dekoratie voor Trouwe Dienst (Decoration for Devoted Service)
DTech	Doctor of Technology
DTH	Diploma in Tropical Hygiene
DTheol	Doctor of Theology
DThPT	Diploma in Theory and Practice of Teaching (Durham University)
DTI	Department of Trade and Industry
DTM&H	Diploma in Tropical Medicine and Hygiene
DU	Doctor of the University
DUniv	Doctor of the University
DUP	Docteur de l'Université de Paris
DVH	Diploma in Veterinary Hygiene
DVM	Doctor of Veterinary Medicine
DVR	Diploma in Veterinary Radiology
DVSc	Doctor of Veterinary Science
DVSM	Diploma in Veterinary State Medicine

E

£	East; Earl
e	eldest
EAA	Edinburgh Architectural Association
EAHY	European Architectural Heritage Year
EAP	East Africa Protectorate
EAW	Electrical Association for Women
EBC	English Benedictine Congregation
Ebor	(Eboracensis) of York
EBU	European Broadcasting Union
EC	Etoile du Courage (Canada); East Central (postal district); European Commission; Emergency Commission
ECA	Economic Co-operation Administration
ECAFE	Economic Commission for Asia and the Far East (now see ESCAP)
ECE	Economic Commission for Europe
ECGD	Export Credits Guarantee Department
ECLA	Economic Commission for Latin America
ECSC	European Coal and Steel Community

ECU English Church Union
ED Efficiency Decoration; Doctor of Engineering (US); European Democrat
EdB Bachelor of Education
EDC Economic Development Committee
EdD Doctor of Education
Edin. Edinburgh
Edn Edition
EDP Executive Development Programme
Educ Educated
Educn Education
EEC European Economic Community; Commission of the European Communities
EEF Engineering Employers' Federation; Egyptian Expeditionary Force
EETPU Electrical Electronic Telecommunication & Plumbing Union
EETS Early English Text Society
EFTA European Free Trade Association
e.h. *ehrenhalber; see under* h.c.
EI East Indian; East Indies
EICS East India Company's Service
E-in-C Engineer-in-Chief
EIS Educational Institute of Scotland
EIU Economist Intelligence Unit
ELSE European Life Science Editors
EM Edward Medal; Earl Marshal
EMBO European Centre for Molecular Biology
EMS Emergency Medical Service
Ency. Brit. Ecyclopaedia Britannica
Eng. England
Engr Engineer
ENO English National Opera
ENSA Entertainments National Service Association
ENT Ear, Nose and Throat
EOPH Examined Officer of Public Health
EORTC European Organisation for Research on Treatment of Cancer
EPP European People's Party
er elder
ER Eastern Region (BR)
ERA Electrical Research Association
ERC Electronics Research Council
ERD Emergency Reserve Decoration (Army)
ESA European Space Agency
ESCAP Economic and Social Commission for Asia and the Pacific
ESRO European Space Research Organization
E-SU English-Speaking Union
ETH Eidgenössische Technische Hochschule
EUDISED European Documentation and Information Service for Education
Euratom European Atomic Energy Commission
EUW European Union of Women
Ext Extinct

F

FA Football Association
FAA Fellow, Australian Academy of Science; also (*formerly*) Fleet Air Arm
FAAAS Fellow, American Association for the Advancement of Science
FACC Fellow, American College of Cardiology
FACCA Fellow, Association of Certified and Corporate Accountants; *now see* FCCA
FACCP Fellow, American College of Chest Physicians
FACD Fellow, American College of Dentistry
FACDS Fellow, Australian College of Dental Surgeons; *now see* FRACDS
FACE Fellow, Australian College of Education
FACI *now see* FRACI
FACMA Fellow, Australian College of Medical Administrators; *now see* FRACMA
FACOG Fellow, American College of Obstetricians and Gynæcologists
FACP Fellow, American College of Physicians
FACR Fellow, American College of Radiology
FACS Fellow, American College of Surgeons
FACVT Fellow, American College of Veterinary Toxicology
FAGO Fellowship in Australia in Obstetrics and Gynaecology
FAGS Fellow, American Geographical Society
FAHA Fellow, Australian Academy of the Humanities
FAI Fellow, Chartered Auctioneers' and Estate Agents' Institute; *now (after amalgamation) see* FRICS; Fédération Aéronautique Internationale
FAIA Fellow, American Institute of Architects
FAIAA Fellow, American Institute of Aeronautics and Astronautics (*and see under* FIAS)
FAIAS Fellow, Australian Institute of Agricultural Science
FAIEx Fellow, Australian Institute of Export
FAIFST Fellow, Australian Institute of Food Science and Technology
FAIM Fellow, Australian Institute of Management
FAIP Fellow, Australian Institute of Physics

FAMS Fellow, Ancient Monuments Society
FAmSCE Fellow, American Society of Civil Engineers
FANY First Aid Nursing Yeomanry
FANZCP *now see* FRANZCP
FAO Food and Agriculture Organization
FAPA Fellow, American Psychiatric Association
FAPHA Fellow, American Public Health Association
FAPI *now see* FRAPI
FARELF Far East Land Forces
FAS Fellow, Antiquarian Society; Fellow, Nigerian Academy of Science
FASA Fellow, Australian Society of Accountants
FASc Fellow, Indian Academy of Sciences
FASCE Fellow, American Society of Civil Engineers
FASSA Fellow, Academy of the Social Sciences in Australia
FAustCOG Fellow, Australian College of Obstetricians and Gynæcologists
FBA Fellow, British Academy; Federation of British Artists
FBCS Fellow, British Computer Society
FBHI Fellow, British Horological Institute
FBI Federation of British Industries (*see under* CBI, in which now merged)
FBIA Fellow, Bankers' Institute of Australasia
FBIM Fellow, British Institute of Management (*formerly* FIIA)
FBKS Fellow, British Kinematograph, Sound and Television Society
FBOA Fellow, British Optical Association
FBOU Fellow, British Ornithologists' Union
FBritIRE (*formerly*) Fellow, British Institution of Radio Engineers
FBPsS Fellow, British Psychological Society
FBS Fellow, Building Societies Institute (*now see* FCBSI)
FBSI Fellow, Boot and Shoe Institution
FBSM Fellow, Birmingham School of Music
FC Football Club
FCA Fellow, Institute of Chartered Accountants; Fellow, Institute of Chartered Accountants in Australia
FCAI Fellow, New Zealand Institute of Cost Accountants
FCASI (*formerly* FCAI) Fellow of the Canadian Aeronautics and Space Institute
FCBSI Fellow, Chartered Building Societies Institute
FCCA Fellow, Association of Certified Accountants
FCCEA Fellow, Commonwealth Council for Educational Administration
FCCS Fellow, Corporation of Secretaries (*formerly of* Certified Secretaries)
FCEC Federation of Civil Engineering Contractors
FCGI Fellow, City and Guilds of London Institute
FCGP Fellow, College of General Practitioners; *now see* FRCGP
FCH Fellow, Coopers Hill College
FChS Fellow, Society of Chiropodists
FCI Fellow, Institute of Commerce
FCIA Fellow, Corporation of Insurance Agents
FCIArb Fellow, Chartered Institute of Arbitrators
FCIB Fellow, Corporation of Insurance Brokers
FCIBS Fellow, Chartered Institution of Building Services (*formerly* FIHVE)
FCIC Fellow, Chemical Institute of Canada (*formerly* Canadian Institute of Chemistry)
FCII Fellow, Chartered Insurance Institute
FCIPA (*formerly used for*) Fellow, Chartered Institute of Patent Agents (*now see* CPA)
FCIS Fellow, Institute of Chartered Secretaries and Administrators (*formerly* Chartered Institute of Secretaries)
FCIT Fellow, Chartered Institute of Transport
FCM Faculty of Community Medicine
FCMA Fellow, Institute of Cost and Management Accountants
FCO Foreign and Commonwealth Office (departments merged Oct. 1968)
FCOG(SA) Fellow, South African College of Obstetrics and Gynæcology
FCommA Fellow, Society of Commercial Accountants; *now see* FSCA
FCP Fellow, College of Preceptors
FCPath Fellow, College of Pathologists (*now see* FRCPath)
FCPS Fellow, College of Physicians and Surgeons
FCP(SoAf) Fellow, College of Physicians, South Africa
FCPSO(SoAf) Fellow, College of Physicians and Surgeons and Obstetricians, South Africa
FCRA Fellow, College of Radiologists of Australia
FCS Federation of Conservative Students
FCS or Fellow, Chemical Society (now absorbed into Royal
FChemSoc Society of Chemistry)
FCSP Fellow, Chartered Society of Physiotherapy
FCS(SoAf) Fellow, College of Surgeons, South Africa
FCST Fellow, College of Speech Therapists
FCT Federal Capital Territory (*now* ACT)
FCTB Fellow, College of Teachers of the Blind
FCU Fighter Control Unit
FCWA Fellow, Institute of Cost and Works Accountants; *now see* FCMA
FDS Fellow in Dental Surgery
FDSRCPS Glas Fellow in Dental Surgery, Royal College of Physicians and Surgeons of Glasgow
FDSRCS Fellow in Dental Surgery, Royal College of Surgeons of England
FDSRCSE Fellow in Dental Surgery, Royal College of Surgeons of Edinburgh

FEAF   Far East Air Force
FEBS   Federation of European Biochemical Societies
FEIS   Fellow, Educational Institute of Scotland
FEng   Fellow, Fellowship of Engineering
FES   Fellow, Entomological Society; Fellow, Ethnological Society
FF   Field Force
FFA   Fellow, Faculty of Actuaries (in Scotland)
FFARACS   Fellow, Faculty of Anaesthetists, Royal Australian College of Surgeons
FFARCS   Fellow, Faculty of Anaesthetists, Royal College of Surgeons of England
FFARCSI   Fellow, Faculty of Anaesthetists, Royal College of Surgeons in Ireland
FFAS   Fellow, Faculty of Architects and Surveyors, London
FFB   Fellow, Faculty of Building
FFCM   Fellow, Faculty of Community Medicine
FFDRCSI   Fellow, Faculty of Dentistry, Royal College of Surgeons in Ireland
FFF   Free French Forces
FFHom   Fellow, Faculty of Homœopathy
FFI   French Forces of the Interior; Finance for Industry
FFOB   Fellow, Faculty of Building
FFOM   Fellow, Faculty of Occupational Medicine
FFR   Fellow, Faculty of Radiologists (now see FRCR)
FGA   Fellow, Gemmological Association
FGI   Fellow, Institute of Certificated Grocers
FGS   Fellow, Geological Society
FGSM   Fellow, Guildhall School of Music
FGSMT   Fellow, Guildhall School of Music (Music Therapy)
FHA   Fellow, Institute of Health Service Administrators (formerly Hospital Administrators)
FHAS   Fellow, Highland and Agricultural Society of Scotland
FHCIMA   Fellow, Hotel Catering and Institutional Management Association
FHFS   Fellow, Human Factors Society
FHKIE   Fellow, Hong Kong Institution of Engineers
FH-WC   Fellow, Heriot-Watt College (now University), Edinburgh
FIA   Fellow, Institute of Actuaries
FIAAS   Fellow, Institute of Australian Agricultural Science
FIAA&S   Fellow, Incorporated Association of Architects and Surveyors
FIAgrE   Fellow, Institution of Agricultural Engineers
FIAI   Fellow, Institute of Industrial and Commercial Accountants
FIAL   Fellow, International Institute of Arts and Letters
FIAM   Fellow, International Academy of Management
FIArb   Fellow, Institute of Arbitrators (now see FCIArb)
FIAS   (now see under FAIAA) (formerly) Fellow, Institute of Aeronautical Sciences (US)
FIAWS   Fellow, International Academy of Wood Sciences
FIB   Fellow, Institute of Bankers
FIBD   Fellow, Institute of British Decorators
FIBP   Fellow, Institute of British Photographers
FIBiol   Fellow, Institute of Biology
FIBScot   Fellow, Institute of Bankers in Scotland
FIC   See FRIC
FICA   Fellow, Commonwealth Institute of Accountancy; Fellow, Institute of Chartered Accountants in England and Wales (but see FCA)
FICAI   Fellow, Institute of Chartered Accountants in Ireland
FICD   Fellow, Institute of Civil Defence; Fellow of the Indian College of Dentists
FICE   Fellow, Institution of Civil Engineers (see also MICE)
FICeram   Fellow, Institute of Ceramics
FIChemE   Fellow, Institution of Chemical Engineers
FICI   Fellow, Institute of Chemistry of Ireland; Fellow, International Colonial Institute
FICS   Fellow, Institute of Chartered Shipbrokers; Fellow, International College of Surgeons
FICW   Fellow, Institute of Clerks of Works of Great Britain
FIDE   Fédération Internationale des Echecs
FIE(Aust)   Fellow, Institution of Engineers, Australia
FIEE   Fellow, Institution of Electrical Engineers (see also MIEE)
FIEEE   Fellow, Institute of Electrical and Electronics Engineers (NY)
FIEI   Fellow, Institution of Engineering Inspection; now see FIQA
FIEJ   Fédération Internationale des Editeurs de Journaux et Publications
FIERE   Fellow, Institution of Electronic and Radio Engineers
FIES   Fellow, Illuminating Engineering Society; now see FIllumES
FIFA   Fédération Internationale de Football Association
FIFE   Fellow, Institution of Fire Engineers
FIFM   Fellow, Institute of Fisheries Management
FIFor   Fellow, Institute of Forestry
FIFST   Fellow, Institute of Food Science and Technology
FIGasE   Fellow, Institution of Gas Engineers
FIGCM   Fellow, Incorporated Guild of Church Musicians
FIGD   Fellow, Institute of Grocery Distribution
FIGO   International Federation of Gynaecology and Obstetrics
FIH   Fellow, Institute of Housing
FIHE   Fellow, Institute of Health Education
FIHM   Fellow, Institute of Housing Managers (now see FIH)
FIHospE   Fellow, Institute of Hospital Engineering
FIHVE   Fellow, Institution of Heating & Ventilating Engineers (now see FCIBS and MCIBS)

FIIA   Fellow, Institute of Industrial Administration (now see FBIM)
FIIM   Fellow, Institute of Industrial Managers
FIInfSc   Fellow, Institute of Information Scientists
FIInst   Fellow, Imperial Institute
FIIP   Fellow, Institute of Incorporated Photographers
FIIPE   Fellow, Indian Institution of Production Engineers
FIL   Fellow, Institute of Linguists
FILA   Fellow, Institute of Landscape Architects (now see FLI)
FILLM   Fédération Internationale des Langues et Litteratures Modernes
FIllumES   Fellow, Illuminating Engineering Society
FIM   Fellow, Institution of Metallurgists
FIMA   Fellow, Institute of Mathematics and its Applications
FIMarE   Fellow, Institute of Marine Engineers
FIMC   Fellow, Institute of Management Consultants
FIMechE   Fellow, Institution of Mechanical Engineers (see also MIMechE)
FIMGTechE   Fellow, Institution of Mechanical and General Technician Engineers
FIMH   Fellow, Institute of Materials Handling; Fellow, Institute of Military History
FIMI   Fellow, Institute of the Motor Industry (formerly FIMT; Fellow, Institute of Motor Trade)
FIMinE   Fellow, Institution of Mining Engineers
FIMIT   Fellow, Institute of Musical Instrument Technology
FIMLT   Fellow, Institute of Medical Laboratory Technology
FIMM   Fellow, Institute of Mining and Metallurgy
FIMS   Fellow, Institute of Mathematical Statistics
FIMTA   Fellow, Institute of Municipal Treasurers and Accountants (now see IPFA)
FIMunE   Fellow, Institution of Municipal Engineers
FIN   Fellow, Institute of Navigation (now see FRIN)
FInstAM   Fellow, Institute of Administrative Management
FInstB   Fellow, Institution of Buyers
FInstBiol   Fellow, Institute of Biology (now see FIBiol)
FInstD   Fellow, Institute of Directors
FInstE   Fellow, Institute of Energy
FInstF   Fellow, Institute of Fuel (now see FInstE)
FInstFF   Fellow, Institute of Freight Forwarders Ltd
FInstHE   Fellow, Institution of Highways Engineers
FInstLEx   Fellow, Institute of Legal Executives
FInstM   Fellow, Institute of Meat; Fellow, Institute of Marketing
FInstMC   Fellow, Institute of Measurement and Control
FInstMSM   Fellow, Institute of Marketing and Sales Management (formerly FSMA; now see FInstM)
FInstMet   (formerly) Fellow, Institute of Metals (now part of Metals Society)
FInstP   Fellow, Institute of Physics
FInstPet   Fellow, Institute of Petroleum
FInstPI   Fellow, Institute of Patentees and Inventors
FInstPS   Fellow, Institute of Purchasing and Supply (now see FIPS)
FInstSM   Fellow, Institute of Sales Management
FInstW   Fellow, Institute of Welding
FInstWPC   Fellow, Institute of Water Pollution Control
FINucE   Fellow, Institution of Nuclear Engineers
FIOA   Fellow, Institute of Acoustics
FIOB   Fellow, Institute of Building
FIOP   Fellow, Institute of Printing
FIPA   Fellow, Institute of Practitioners in Advertising
FIPHE   Fellow, Institution of Public Health Engineers
FIPlantE   Fellow, Institution of Plant Engineers
FIPM   Fellow, Institute of Personnel Management
FIPR   Fellow, Institute of Public Relations
FIProdE   Fellow, Institution of Production Engineers
FIPS   Fellow, Institute of Purchasing and Supply
FIQ   Fellow, Institute of Quarrying
FIQA   Fellow, Institute of Quality Assurance
FIQS   Fellow, Institute of Quantity Surveyors
FIRA(Ind)   Fellow, Institute of Railway Auditors and Accountants (India)
FIRE(Aust)   Fellow, Institution of Radio Engineers (Australia) (now see FIREE (Aust)
FIREE(Aust)   Fellow, Institution of Radio and Electronics Engineers (Australia)
FIRI   Fellow, Institution of the Rubber Industry (now see FPRI)
FIRTE   Fellow, Institute of Road Transport Engineers
FIS   Fellow, Institute of Statisticians (formerly Association of Incorporated Statisticians)
FISA   Fellow, Incorporated Secretaries' Association
FISE   Fellow, Institution of Sales Engineers; Fellow, Institution of Sanitary Engineers
FIST   Fellow, Institute of Science Technology
FIStructE   Fellow, Institution of Structural Engineers
FISW   Fellow, Institute of Social Work
FITE   Fellow, Institution of Electrical and Electronics Technician Engineers
FIW   Fellow, Welding Institute
FIWE   Fellow, Institution of Water Engineers (now see FIWES)
FIWES   Fellow, Institution of Water Engineers and Scientists
FIWM   Fellow, Institution of Works Managers
FIWPC   Fellow, Institute of Water Pollution Control
FIWSc   Fellow, Institute of Wood Science
FIWSP   Fellow, Institute of Work Study Practitioners (now see FMS)
FJI   Fellow, Institute of Journalists

FJIE	Fellow, Junior Institution of Engineers (*now see* CIMGTechE)
FKC	Fellow, King's College (London)
FLA	Fellow, Library Association
Fla	Florida (US)
FLAI	Fellow, Library Association of Ireland
FLAS	Fellow, Chartered Land Agents' Society (*now* (after amalgamation) *see* FRICS)
FLCM	Fellow, London College of Music
FLHS	Fellow, London Historical Society
FLS	Fellow, Linnaean Society
Flt	Flight
FM	Field-Marshal
FMA	Fellow, Museums Association
FMANZ	Fellow, Medical Association of New Zealand
FMF	Fiji Military Forces
FMS	Federated Malay States; Fellow, Medical Society; Fellow, Institute of Management Services
FMSA	Fellow, Mineralogical Society of America
FNA	Fellow, Indian National Science Academy
FNECInst	Fellow, North East Coast Institution of Engineers and Shipbuilders
FNI	Fellow, Nautical Institute; Fellow, National Institute of Sciences in India (*now see* FNA)
FNZIA	Fellow, New Zealand Institute of Architects
FNZIAS	Fellow, New Zealand Institute of Agricultural Science
FNZIC	Fellow, New Zealand Institute of Chemistry
FNZIE	Fellow, New Zealand Institution of Engineers
FNZIM	Fellow, New Zealand Institute of Management
FO	Foreign Office (*see also* FCO); Field Officer; Flying Officer
FOIC	Flag Officer in charge
FPA	Family Planning Association
FPEA	Fellow, Physical Education Association
FPhS	Fellow, Philosophical Society of England
FPI	Fellow, Plastics Institute (*now see* FPRI)
FPMI	Fellow, Pensions Management Institute
FPRI	Fellow, Plastics and Rubber Institute
FPS	Fellow, Pharmaceutical Society; Fauna Preservation Society
FPhysS	Fellow, Physical Society
f r	fuori ruole
FRACDS	Fellow, Royal Australian College of Dental Surgeons
FRACI	Fellow, Royal Australian Chemical Institute (*formerly* FACI)
FRACMA	Fellow, Royal Australian College of Medical Administrators
FRACO	Fellow, Royal Australian College of Ophthalmologists
FRACP	Fellow, Royal Australasian College of Physicians
FRACS	Fellow, Royal Australasian College of Surgeons
FRAD	Fellow, Royal Academy of Dancing
FRAeS	Fellow, Royal Aeronautical Society
FRAgS	Fellow, Royal Agricultural Societies (*ie* of England, Scotland and Wales)
FRAHS	Fellow, Royal Australian Historical Society
FRAI	Fellow, Royal Anthropological Institute
FRAIA	Fellow, Royal Australian Institute of Architects
FRAIB	Fellow, Royal Australian Institute of Building
FRAIC	Fellow, Royal Architectural Institute of Canada
FRAM	Fellow, Royal Academy of Music
FRAME	Fund for the Replacement of Animals in Medical Experiments
FRANZCP	Fellow, Royal Australian and New Zealand College of Psychiatrists
FRAPI	Fellow, Royal Australian Planning Institute
FRAS	Fellow, Royal Astronomical Society; Fellow, Royal Asiatic Society
FRASB	Fellow, Royal Asiatic Society of Bengal
FRASE	Fellow, Royal Agricultural Society of England
FRBS	Fellow, Royal Society of British Sculptors; Fellow, Royal Botanic Society
FRCGP	Fellow, Royal College of General Practitioners
FRCM	Fellow, Royal College of Music
FRCN	Fellow, Royal College of Nursing
FRCO	Fellow, Royal College of Organists
FRCO(CHM)	Fellow, Royal College of Organists with Diploma in Choir Training
FRCOG	Fellow, Royal College of Obstetricians and Gynaecologists
FRCP	Fellow, Royal College of Physicians, London
FRCP&S (Canada)	Fellow, Royal College of Physicians and Surgeons of Canada
FRCPath	Fellow, Royal College of Pathologists
FRCP(C)	Fellow, Royal College of Physicians of Canada
FRCPE and FRCPEd	Fellow, Royal College of Physicians of Edinburgh
FRCPGlas	Fellow, Royal College (*formerly* Faculty) of Physicians and Surgeons, Glasgow (*and see under* FRFPSG)
FRCPI	Fellow, Royal College of Physicians of Ireland
FRCPS(Hon)	Hon. Fellow, Royal College of Physicians and Surgeons (Glasgow)
FRCPsych	Fellow, Royal College of Psychiatrists
FRCR	Fellow, Royal College of Radiologists
FRCS	Fellow, Royal College of Surgeons of England
FRCSE and FRCSEd	Fellow, Royal College of Surgeons of Edinburgh
FRCSGlas	Fellow, Royal College of Surgeons of Glasgow
FRCSI	Fellow, Royal College of Surgeons in Ireland
FRCSoc	Fellow, Royal Commonwealth Society
FRCUS	Fellow, Royal College of University Surgeons (Denmark)
FRCVS	Fellow, Royal College of Veterinary Surgeons
FREconS	Fellow, Royal Economic Society
FREI	Fellow, Real Estate Institute (Australia)
FRES	Fellow, Royal Entomological Society of London
FRFPSG	(*formerly*) Fellow, Royal Faculty of Physicians and Surgeons, Glasgow (*and see under* FRCPGlas)
FRGS	Fellow, Royal Geographical Society
FRGSA	Fellow, Royal Geographical Society of Australasia
FRHistS	Fellow, Royal Historical Society
FRHS	Fellow, Royal Horticultural Society
FRIAS	Fellow, Royal Incorporation of Architects of Scotland
FRIBA	Fellow, Royal Institute of British Architects (*and see* RIBA)
FRIC	(*formerly* FIC) Fellow, Royal Institute of Chemistry; *now see* FRSC
FRICS	Fellow, Royal Institution of Chartered Surveyors
FRIH	Fellow, Royal Institute of Horticulture (NZ)
FRIN	Fellow, Royal Institute of Navigation
FRINA	Fellow, Royal Institution of Naval Architects
FRIPA	Fellow, Royal Institute of Public Administration (the Institute no longer has Fellows)
FRIPHH	Fellow, Royal Institute of Public Health and Hygiene
FRMCM	Fellow, Royal Manchester College of Music
FRMedSoc	Fellow, Royal Medical Society
FRMetS	Fellow, Royal Meteorological Society
FRMS	Fellow, Royal Microscopical Society
FRNCM	Fellow, Royal Northern College of Music
FRNS	Fellow, Royal Numismatic Society
FRPS	Fellow, Royal Photographic Society
FRPSL	Fellow, Royal Philatelic Society, London
FRS	Fellow, Royal Society
FRSA	Fellow, Royal Society of Arts
FRSAI	Fellow, Royal Society of Antiquaries of Ireland
FRSAMD	Fellow, Royal Scottish Academy of Music and Drama
FRSanI	Fellow, Royal Sanitary Institute (*now see* FRSH)
FRSC	Fellow, Royal Society of Canada; Fellow, Royal Society of Chemistry
FRSCM	Fellow, Royal School of Church Music
FRSE	Fellow, Royal Society of Edinburgh
FRSGS	Fellow, Royal Scottish Geographical Society
FRSH	Fellow, Royal Society for the Promotion of Health (*formerly* FRSanI)
FRSL	Fellow, Royal Society of Literature
FRSM or FRSocMed	Fellow, Royal Society of Medicine
FRSNZ	Fellow, Royal Society of New Zealand
FRSSAf	Fellow, Royal Society of South Africa
FRST	Fellow, Royal Society of Teachers
FRSTM&H	Fellow, Royal Society of Tropical Medicine and Hygiene
FRTPI	Fellow, Royal Town Planning Institute
FRTS	Fellow, Royal Television Society
FRVA	Fellow, Rating and Valuation Association
FRVC	Fellow, Royal Veterinary College
FRVIA	**Fellow, Royal Victorian Institute of Architects**
FRZSScot	**Fellow, Royal Zoological Society of Scotland**
FS	Field Security
fs	**Graduate, Royal Air Force Staff College**
FSA	Fellow, Society of Antiquaries
FSAA	Fellow, Society of Incorporated Accountants and Auditors
FSAE	Fellow, Society of Automotive Engineers
FSAIEE	Fellow, South African Institute of Electrical Engineers
FSAM	Fellow, Society of Art Masters
FSArc	Fellow, Society of Architects (merged with the RIBA 1952)
FSAScot	Fellow, Society of Antiquaries of Scotland
FSASM	South Australian School of Mines
FSBI	Fellow, Savings Banks Institute
fsc	Foreign Staff College
FSCA	Fellow, Society of Company and Commercial Accountants
FSDC	Fellow, Society of Dyers and Colourists
FSE	Fellow, Society of Engineers
FSG	Fellow, Society of Genealogists
FSGT	Fellow, Society of Glass Technology
FSI	Fellow, Royal Institution of Chartered Surveyors (changed Aug. 1947 to FRICS)
FSIAD	Fellow, Society of Industrial Artists and Designers
FSLAET	Fellow, Society of Licensed Aircraft Engineers and Technologists
FSMA	Fellow, Incorporated Sales Managers' Association (*now see* FInstMSM, FInstM)
FSMC	Freeman of the Spectacle-Makers' Company
FSS	Fellow, Royal Statistical Society
FSTD	Fellow, Society of Typographic Designers
FSVA	Fellow, Incorporated Society of Valuers and Auctioneers
FTCD	Fellow, Trinity College, Dublin
FTCL	Fellow, Trinity College of Music, London
FTI	Fellow, Textile Institute
FTII	Fellow, Institute of Taxation
FTP	Fellow, Thames Polytechnic
FTS	Fellow, Australian Academy of Technological Sciences; Flying Training School
FUCUA	Federation of University Conservative and Unionist Associations (*now see* FCS)
FUMIST	Fellow, University of Manchester Institute of Science and Technology

FWA	Fellow, World Academy of Arts and Sciences
FWACP	Fellow, West African College of Physicians
FWeldI	Fellow, Welding Institute
FWSOM	Fellow, Institute of Practitioners in Work Study, Organisation and Method (now see FMS)
FZS	Fellow, Zoological Society
FZSScot	Fellow, Zoological Society of Scotland (now see FRZSScot)

G

Ga	Georgia (US)
GA	Geologists' Association
G&MWU	General and Municipal Workers' Union
GAPAN	Guild of Air Pilots and Air Navigators
GATT	General Agreement on Tariffs and Trade
GB	Great Britain
GBA	Governing Bodies Association
GBE	Knight or Dame Grand Cross Order of the British Empire
GBGSA	Association of Governing Bodies of Girls' Public Schools
GBSM	Graduate of Birmingham and Midland Institute School of Music
GC	George Cross
GCB	Knight Grand Cross of the Bath
GCH	Knight Grand Cross of Hanover
GCHQ	Government Communications Headquarters
GCIE	Knight Grand Commander of the Indian Empire
GCLJ	Grand Cross, St Lazarus of Jerusalem
GCMG	Knight or Dame Grand Cross of St Michael and St George
GCON	Grand Cross, Order of the Niger
GCSG	Knight Grand Cross of the Order of St Gregory the Great
GCSI	Knight Grand Commander of the Star of India
GCStJ	Bailiff or Dame Grand Cross of the Order of St John of Jerusalem
GCVO	Knight or Dame Grand Cross of Royal Victorian Order
GDC	General Dental Council
Gdns	Gardens
GDR	German Democratic Republic
Gen.	General
Ges.	Gesellschaft
GFS	Girls' Friendly Society
g&s	great grandson
GHQ	General Headquarters
Gib.	Gibraltar
GIMechE	Graduate Institution of Mechanical Engineers
GL	Grand Lodge
GLC	Greater London Council
Glos	Gloucestershire
GM	George Medal; Grand Medal (Ghana)
GmbH	Gesellschaft mit beschränkter Hoftung
GMC	General Medical Council; Guild of Memorial Craftsmen
GMIE	Grand Master of Indian Empire
GMSI	Grand Master of Star of India
GNC	General Nursing Council
GOC	General Officer Commanding
GOC-in-C	General Officer Commanding-in-Chief
GOE	General Ordination Examination
Gov.	Governor
Govt	Government
GP	General Practitioner; Grand Prix
GPDST	Girls' Public Day School Trust
GPO	General Post Office
GQG	Grand Quartier Général (French GHQ)
Gr.	Greek
GRSM	Graduate of the Royal Schools of Music
GS	General Staff; Grammar School
gs	Grandson
GSM	General Service Medal; Guildhall School of Music and Drama
GSMD	see GSM
GSO	General Staff Officer
GTCL	Graduate, Trinity College of Music
GTS	General Theological Seminary (New York)
GUI	Golfing Union of Ireland
GWR	Great Western Railway

H

HA	Historical Association
HAA	Heavy Anti-Aircraft
HAC	Honourable Artillery Company
Hants	Hampshire
HARCVS	Honorary Associate, Royal College of Veterinary Surgeons
Harv.	Harvard
HBM	His (or Her) Britannic Majesty (Majesty's); Humming Bird Gold Medal (Trinidad)
hc	honoris causa
HCEG	Honourable Company of Edinburgh Golfers
HCF	Hon. Chaplain to the Forces
HCIMA	Hotel, Catering and Institutional Management Association
HDA	Hawkesbury Diploma in Agriculture (Australian)
HDD	Higher Dental Diploma

HDiplEduc	Honorary Diploma in Education
HE	His Excellency; His Eminence
HEC	Ecole des Hautes Etudes Commerciales
HEH	His Exalted Highness
HEIC	Honourable East India Company
HEICS	Honourable East India Company's Service
Heir-pres.	Heir-presumptive
Herts	Hertfordshire
HFARA	Honorary Foreign Associate of the Royal Academy
HFRA	Honorary Foreign Member of the Royal Academy
HG	Home Guard
HH	His (or Her) Highness; His Holiness; Member, Hesketh Hubbard Art Society
HHD	Doctor of Humanities (US)
HIH	His (or Her) Imperial Highness
HIM	His (or Her) Imperial Majesty
HJ	Hilal-e-Jurat (Pakistan)
HLD	Doctor of Humane Letters
HLI	Highland Light Infantry
HM	His (or Her) Majesty, or Majesty's
HMAS	His (or Her) Majesty's Australian Ship
HMC	Headmasters' Conference; Hospital Management Committee
HMHS	His (or Her) Majesty's Hospital Ship
HMI	His (or Her) Majesty's Inspector
HMOCS	His (or Her) Majesty's Overseas Civil Service
HMS	His (or Her) Majesty's Ship
HMSO	His (or Her) Majesty's Stationery Office
HNC	Higher National Certificate
HND	Higher National Diploma
H of C	House of Commons
Hon.	Honourable; Honorary
HP	House Physician
HPk	Hilal-e-Pakistan
HQ	Headquarters
HQA	Hilal-i-Quaid-i-Azam
(HR)	Home Rule
HRCA	Honorary Royal Cambrian Academician
HRH	His (or Her) Royal Highness
HRHA	Honorary Member of Royal Hibernian Academy
HRI	Honorary Member of Royal Institute of Painters in Water Colours
HROI	Honorary Member of Royal Institute of Oil Painters
HRSA	Honorary Member of Royal Scottish Academy
HRSW	Honorary Member of Royal Scottish Water Colour Society
HS	House Surgeon
HSE	Health and Safety Executive
HSH	His (or Her) Serene Highness
Hum.	Humanity, Humanities (Classics)
Hunts	Huntingdonshire
HVCert	Health Visitor's Certificate
Hy	Heavy

I

I	Island
Ia	Iowa (US)
IA	Indian Army
IAC	Institute of Amateur Cinematographers
IAEA	International Atomic Energy Agency
IAF	Indian Air Force; Indian Auxiliary Force
IAHM	Incorporated Association of Headmasters
IAM	Institute of Advanced Motorists
IAMC	Indian Army Medical Corps
IAMTACT	Institute of Advanced Machine Tool and Control Technology
IAOC	Indian Army Ordnance Control
IAPS	Incorporated Association of Preparatory Schools
IARO	Indian Army Reserve of Officers
IAS	Indian Administrative Service
IASS	International Association for Scandinavian Studies
IATA	International Air Transport Association
IATUL	International Association of Technical University Libraries
ib. or ibid.	Ibidem (in the same place)
IBA	Independent Broadcasting Authority; International Bar Association
IBG	Institute of British Geographers
IBRD	International Bank for Reconstruction and Development (World Bank)
i/c	In charge; in command
ICA	Institute of Contemporary Arts; Institute of Chartered Accountants in England and Wales
ICAA	Invalid Children's Aid Association
ICAI	Institute of Chartered Accountants in Ireland
ICAO	International Civil Aviation Organization
ICBS	Irish Christian Brothers' School
ICC	International Chamber of Commerce
ICCROM	International Centre for Conservation at Rome
ICD	Iuris Canonici Doctor; Independence Commemorative Decoration (Rhodesia)
ICE	Institution of Civil Engineers
ICED	International Council for Educational Development
Icel.	Icelandic

ICF	International Federation of Chemical and General Workers' Unions
ICFC	Industrial and Commercial Finance Corporation
ICFTU	International Confederation of Free Trade Unions
IChemE	Institution of Chemical Engineers
ICI	Imperial Chemical Industries
ICL	International Computers Ltd
ICM	International Confederation of Midwives
ICMA	Institute of Cost and Management Accountants
ICOM	International Council of Museums
ICOMOS	International Council of Monuments and Sites
ICRC	International Committee of the Red Cross
ICS	Indian Civil Service
ICSID	International Council of Societies of Industrial Design
ICSS	International Committee for the Sociology of Sport
ICSU	International Council of Scientific Unions
ICT	International Computers and Tabulators Ltd; *now see* ICL
Id	Idaho (US)
IDA	International Development Association
IDB	Internal Drainage Board
IDC	Imperial Defence College (*now see* RCDS)
idc	Completed a Course at, or served for a year on the Staff of, the Imperial Defence College (*now see* rcds)
IDS	Institute of Development Studies
IEE	Institution of Electrical Engineers
IEEE	Institute of Electrical and Electronics Engineers (NY)
IEETE	Institution of Electrical and Electronic Technician Engineers
IEME	Inspectorate of Electrical and Mechanical Engineering
IERE	Institution of Electronic and Radio Engineers (*and see under* BritIRE)
IES	Indian Educational Service; Institution of Engineers and Shipbuilders in Scotland
IFAC	International Federation of Automatic Control
IFC	International Finance Corporation
IFIP	International Federation for Information Processing
IFL	International Friendship League
IFLA	International Federation of Library Associations
IFPI	International Federation of the Phonographic Industry
IFS	Irish Free State; Indian Forest Service
IG	Instructor in Gunnery
IGasE	Institution of Gas Engineers
IGPP	Institute of Geophysics and Planetary Physics
IGS	Independent Grammar School
IGU	International Geographical Union; International Gas Union
IHA	Institute of Health Service Administrators
IHVE	Institution of Heating and Ventilating Engineers
IInfSc	Institute of Information Scientists
IIS	International Institute of Sociology
IISS	International Institute of Strategic Studies
ILEA	Inner London Education Authority
ILEC	Inner London Education Committee
Ill	Illinois (US)
ILO	International Labour Office; International Labour Organisation
ILP	Independent Labour Party
ILR	International Labour Review
IM	Individual Merit
IMA	International Music Association; Institute of Mathematics and its Applications
IMCO	Inter-Governmental Maritime Consultative Organization
IMEA	Incorporated Municipal Electrical Association
IMechE	Institution of Mechanical Engineers
IMEDE	Institut pour l'Etude des Méthodes de Direction de l'Entreprise
IMF	International Monetary Fund
IMGTechE	Institution of Mechanical and General Technician Engineers
IMinE	Institution of Mining Engineers
IMMLEP	Immunology of Leprosy
IMMTS	Indian Mercantile Marine Training Ship
Imp.	Imperial
IMS	Indian Medical Service; Institute of Management Services
IMTA	Institute of Municipal Treasurers and Accountants; *now see* CIPFA
IMU	International Mathematical Union
IMunE	Institution of Municipal Engineers
IN	Indian Navy
Inc.	Incorporated
INCA	International Newspaper Colour Association
Incog.	*Incognito* (in secret)
Ind.	Independent; Indiana (US)
INSEA	International Society for Education through Art
INSEAD (Insead)	Institut Européen d'Administration des Affaires
Insp.	Inspector
Inst.	Institute
Instn	Institution
InstnMM	Institution of Mining and Metallurgy
InstT	Institute of Transport
IOB	Institute of Building
IODE	Imperial Order of the Daughters of the Empire
I of M	Isle of Man
IOGT	International Order of Good Templars
IOM	Isle of Man; Indian Order of Merit
IOOF	Independent Order of Odd-fellows
IOP	Institute of Painters in Oil Colours
IoW	Isle of Wight

IPCS	Institution of Professional Civil Servants
IPFA	Member or Associate, Chartered Institute of Public Finance and Accountancy
IPI	International Press Institute
IPM	Institute of Personnel Management
IPPF	International Planned Parenthood Federation
IPPS	Institute of Physics and The Physical Society
IProdE	Institution of Production Engineers
IPS	Indian Police Service; Indian Political Service
IPU	Inter-Parliamentary Union
IRA	Irish Republican Army
IRAD	Institute for Research on Animal Diseases
IRC	Industrial Reorganization Corporation
IREE(Aust)	Institution of Radio and Electronics Engineers (Australia)
IRI	Institution of the Rubber Industry (*now see* PRI)
IRO	International Refugee Organization
IRTE	Institute of Road Transport Engineers
Is	Island(s)
IS	International Society of Sculptors, Painters and Gravers
ISC	Imperial Service College, Haileybury; Indian Staff Corps
ISE	Indian Service of Engineers
ISI	International Statistical Institute
ISIS	Independent Schools Information Service
ISM	Incorporated Society of Musicians
ISME	International Society for Musical Education
ISMRC	Inter-Services Metallurgical Research Council
ISO	Imperial Service Order; International Standards Organization
ISTD	Imperial Society of Teachers of Dancing
IStructE	Institution of Structural Engineers
IT	Indian Territory (US)
ITA	Independent Television Authority; *now see* IBA
Ital. or It.	Italian
ITB	Industry Training Board
ITC	International Trade Centre
ITF	International Transport Workers' Federation
ITN	Independent Television News
ITO	International Trade Organization
ITV	Independent Television
IUA	International Union of Architects
IUB	International Union of Biochemistry
IUC	Inter-University Council for Higher Education Overseas
IUCN	International Union for the Conservation of Nature and Natural Resources
IUCW	International Union for Child Welfare
IUGS	International Union of Geological Sciences
IUP	Association of Independent Unionist Peers
IUPAC	International Union of Pure and Applied Chemistry
IUPAP	International Union of Pure and Applied Physics
IUPS	International Union of Physiological Sciences
IVS	International Voluntary Service
IW	Isle of Wight
IWES	Institution of Water Engineers and Scientists
IWGC	Imperial War Graves Commission
IWM	Institution of Works Managers
IWPC	Institute of Water Pollution Control
IWSOM	Institute of Practitioners in Work Study Organisation and Methods (*now see* IMS)
IWSP	Institute of Work Study Practitioners (*now see* IMS)
IY	Imperial Yeomanry
IZ	I Zingari

J

JA	Judge Advocate
JACT	Joint Association of Classical Teachers
JAG	Judge Advocate General
Jas	James
JCB	*Juris Canonici Bachelor* (Bachelor of Canon Law)
JCS	Journal of the Chemical Society
JCD	*Juris Canonici Doctor* (Doctor of Canon Law)
JCL	Licentiate of Canon Law
JCO	Joint Consultative Organisation (of ARC, MAFF, and Department of Agriculture and Fisheries for Scotland)
JD	Doctor of Jurisprudence
JDipMA	Joint Diploma in Management Accounting Services
JG	Junior Grade
JInstE	Junior Institution of Engineers; *now see* IMGTechE
jls	Journals
JMN	*Johan Mangku Negara* (Malaysian Honour)
Joh. or Jno.	John
JP	Justice of the Peace
Jr	Junior
jsc	Qualified at a Junior Staff Course, or the equivalent, 1942–46
JSD	Doctor of Juristic Science
JSLS	Joint Services Liaison Staff
JSM	*Johan Setia Mahkota* (Malaysia)
JSPS	Japan Society for the Promotion of Science
jssc	Joint Services Staff Course
jt, jtly	joint, jointly
JWS or jws	Joint Warfare Staff
JUD	*Juris Utriusque Doctor*, Doctor of Both Laws (Canon and Civil)

Jun.	Junior
Jun. Opt.	Junior Optime

K

Kans	Kansas (US)
KAR	King's African Rifles
KBE	Knight Commander Order of the British Empire
KC	King's Counsel
KCB	Knight Commander of the Bath
KCC	Commander of Order of Crown, Belgium and Congo Free State
KCH	King's College Hospital; Knight Commander of Hanover
KCHS	Knight Commander of the Holy Sepulchre
KCIE	Knight Commander of the Indian Empire
KCL	King's College, London
KCMG	Knight Commander of St Michael and St George
KCSA	Knight Commander, Military Order of the Collar of St Agatha of Paterna
KCSG	Knight Commander of St Gregory
KCSI	Knight Commander of the Star of India
KCSS	Knight Commander of St Silvester
KCVO	Knight Commander of the Royal Victorian Order
KDG	King's Dragoon Guards
KEH	King Edward's Horse
KG	Knight of the Order of the Garter
KGStJ	*formerly* Knight of Grace, Order of St John of Jerusalem (*now* KStJ)
KH	Knight of Hanover
KHC	Hon. Chaplain to the King
KHDS	Hon. Dental Surgeon to the King
KHNS	Hon. Nursing Sister to the King
KHP	Hon. Physician to the King
KHS	Hon. Surgeon to the King; Knight of the Holy Sepulchre
K-i-H	Kaisar-i-Hind
KJStJ	*formerly* Knight of Justice, Order of St John of Jerusalem (*now* KStJ)
KLJ	Knight, St Lazarus of Jerusalem
KM	Knight of Malta
KORR	King's Own Royal Regiment
KOSB	King's Own Scottish Borderers
KOYLI	King's Own Yorkshire Light Infantry
KP	Knight of the Order of St Patrick
KPM	King's Police Medal
KRRC	King's Royal Rifle Corps
KS	King's Scholar
KSC	Knight of St Columba
KSG	Knight of St Gregory the Great
KSLI	King's Shropshire Light Infantry
KSS	Knight of St Silvester
KStJ	Knight of Order of St John of Jerusalem; *and see* GCStJ
KStJ(A)	Associate Knight of Justice, Order of St John of Jerusalem
KT	Knight of the Order of the Thistle
Kt or Knt	Knight
Ky	Kentucky (US)

L

(L)	Liberal
LA	Los Angeles; Literate in Arts; Liverpool Academy
La	Louisiana (US)
(Lab)	Labour
LAC	London Athletic Club
LAMDA	London Academy of Music and Dramatic Art
LAMSAC	Local Authorities' Management Services and Computer Committee
L-Corp. or Lance-Corp.	Lance-corporal
Lancs	Lancashire
LCAD	London Certificate in Art and Design (University of London)
LCC	London County Council (*now see under* GLC)
LCh	Licentiate in Surgery
LCJ	Lord Chief Justice
LCL	Licentiate of Canon Law
LCP	Licentiate of the College of Preceptors
LCST	Licentiate of the College of Speech Therapists
LD	Liberal and Democratic
LDiv	Licentiate in Divinity
LDS	Licentiate in Dental Surgery
LDV	Local Defence Volunteers
LEA	Local Education Authority
LEPRA	British Leprosy Relief Association
LèsL	Licencié ès lettres
LH	Light Horse
LHD	(*Literarum Humaniorum Doctor*) Doctor of Literature
LI	Light Infantry; Long Island
LicMed	Licentiate in Medicine
Lieut	Lieutenant
Lincs	Lincolnshire
LIOB	Licentiate of Institute of Building

Lit.	Literature; Literary
LitD	Doctor of Literature; Doctor of Letters
Lit.Hum.	*Literae Humaniores* (Classics)
LittD	Doctor of Literature; Doctor of Letters
LJ	Lord Justice
LLA	Lady Literate in Arts
LLB	Bachelor of Laws
LLCM	Licentiate London College of Music
LLD	Doctor of Laws
LLL	Licentiate in Laws
LLM	Master of Laws
LM	Licentiate in Midwifery
LMBC	Lady Margaret Boat Club
LMCC	Licentiate of Medical Council of Canada
LMed	Licentiate in Medicine
LMR	London Midland Region (BR)
LMS	London, Midland and Scottish Railway; London Missionary Society
LMSSA	Licentiate in Medicine and Surgery, Society of Apothecaries
LMRTPI	Legal Member, Royal Town Planning Institute
(LNat)	Liberal National
LNER	London and North Eastern Railway
LOB	Location of Offices Bureau
L of C	Lines of Communication
LPTB	London Passenger Transport Board
LRAD	Licentiate of the Royal Academy of Dancing
LRAM	Licentiate of the Royal Academy of Music
LRCP	Licentiate of the Royal College of Physicians, London
LRCPE	Licentiate, Royal College of Physicians, Edinburgh
LRCPI	Licentiate, Royal College of Physicians of Ireland
LRCS	Licentiate of the Royal College of Surgeons of England
LRCSE	Licentiate of the Royal College of Surgeons, Edinburgh
LRCSI	Licentiate, Royal College of Surgeons in Ireland
LRFPS(G)	(*formerly*) Licentiate of the Royal Faculty of Physicians and Surgeons, Glasgow (*now* Royal College of Physicians and Surgeons, Glasgow)
LRIBA	Licentiate, Royal Institute of British Architects
LSA	Licentiate of the Society of Apothecaries
LSE	London School of Economics and Political Science
LSHTM	London School of Hygiene and Tropical Medicine
Lt	Light (*eg* Light Infantry)
Lt or Lieut	Lieutenant
LT	Licentiate in Teaching
LTA	Lawn Tennis Association
LTB	London Transport Board
LTCL	Licentiate of Trinity College of Music, London
Lt-Col	Lieutenant-Colonel
LTE	London Transport Executive
Lt-Gen.	Lieutenant-General
LTh	Licentiate in Theology
(LU)	Liberal Unionist
LUOTC	London University Officers' Training Corps
LWT	London Weekend Television
LXX	Septuagint

M

M	Marquess; Member; Monsieur
m	married
MA	Master of Arts; Military Assistant
MAA	Manufacturers' Agents Association of Great Britain
MAAF	Mediterranean Allied Air Forces
MACE	Member, Australian College of Education; Member, Association of Conference Executives
MACI	Member, American Concrete Institute
MACS	Member, American Chemical Society
MAEE	Marine Aircraft Experimental Establishment
MAF	Ministry of Agriculture and Fisheries
MAFF	Ministry of Agriculture, Fisheries and Food
MAI	Master of Engineering (*Magister in Arte Ingeniaria*)
MAIAA	Member, American Institute of Aeronautics and Astronautics (*and see under* MIAS)
MAICE	Member, American Institute of Consulting Engineers
MAIChE	Member, American Institute of Chemical Engineers
Maj.Gen.	Major-General
Man	Manitoba (Canada)
MAO	Master of Obstetric Art
MAOT	Member, Association of Occupational Therapists
MAOU	Member, American Ornithologists' Union
MAP	Ministry of Aircraft Production
MAPsS	Member, Australian Psychological Society
MArch	Master of Architecture
Marq.	Marquess
MASAE	Member, American Society of Agricultural Engineers
MASCE	Member, American Society of Civil Engineers
MASME	Member, American Society of Mechanical Engineers
Mass	Massachusetts (US)
Math.	Mathematics; Mathematical
MB	Medal of Bravery (Canada); Bachelor of Medicine
MBA	Master of Business Administration
MBASW	Member, British Association of Social Workers
MBCS	Member, British Computer Society
MBE	Member, Order of the British Empire

MBFR	Mutual and Balanced Force Reductions (negotiations)
MBHI	Member, British Horological Institute
MBIM	Member, British Institute of Management (*formerly* MIIA); now *see* FBIM
MBKS	Member, British Kinematograph, Sound and Television Society
MBOU	Member, British Ornithologists' Union
MBritIRE	Member, British Institution of Radio Engineers (*now see* MIERE)
MBS	Member, Building Societies Institute (*now see* MCBSI)
MC	Military Cross
M CAM	Member, CAM Society
MCB	Master in Clinical Biochemistry
MCBSI	Member, Chartered Building Societies Institute
MCC	Marylebone Cricket Club; Metropolitan County Council
MCD	Master of Civic Design
MCE(Melb)	Master of Civil Engineering (Melbourne University)
MCFP	Member, College of Family Physicians (Canada)
MCh or MChir	Master in Surgery
MChE	Master of Chemical Engineering
MChemA	Master in Chemical Analysis
MChOrth	Master of Orthopaedic Surgery
MCIBS	Member, Chartered Institution of Building Services (*formerly* FIHVE or MIHVE)
M.CIRP	Member, International Institution for Production Engineering Research
MCIT	Member, Chartered Institute of Transport
MCL	Master in Civil Law
MCMES	Member, Civil and Mechanical Engineers' Society
MCom	Master of Commerce
MConsE	Member, Association of Consulting Engineers
MCP	Member of Colonial Parliament; Master of City Planning (US)
MCPA	Member, College of Pathologists of Australia (*now see* MRCPA)
MCPath	Member, College of Pathologists (*now see* MRCPath)
MCPS	Member, College of Physicians and Surgeons
MCS	Madras Civil Service; Malayan Civil Service
MCSEE	Member, Canadian Society of Electrical Engineers
MCSP	Member, Chartered Society of Physiotherapy
MD	Doctor of Medicine; Military District
Md	Maryland (US)
MDC	Metropolitan District Council
MDS	Master of Dental Surgery
Me	Maine (US)
ME	Mining Engineer; Middle East
MEAF	Middle East Air Force
MEC	Member of Executive Council
MEc	Master of Economics
MECAS	Middle East Centre for Arab Studies
Mech.	Mechanics; Mechanical
Med.	Medical
MEd	Master of Education
MEF	Middle East Force
MEIC	Member, Engineering Institute of Canada
MELF	Middle East Land Forces
MEng	Master of Engineering
MEP	Member of the European Parliament
MetR	Metropolitan Railway
MetSoc	Metals Society (formed by amalgamation of Institute of Metals and Iron and Steel Institute)
MEXE	Military Engineering Experimental Establishment
MFA	Master of Fine Arts
MFC	Mastership in Food Control
MFCM	Member, Faculty of Community Medicine
MFGB	Miners' Federation of Great Britain
MFH	Master of Foxhounds
MFOM	Member, Faculty of Occupational Medicine
MGA	Major-General in charge of Administration
MGC	Machine Gun Corps
MGDS RCS	Member in General Dental Surgery, Royal College of Surgeons
MGGS	Major-General, General Staff
MGI	Member, Institute of Certificated Grocers
MGO	Master General of the Ordnance; Master of Gynaecology and Obstetrics
Mgr	Monsignor
MHA	Member of House of Assembly
MHK	Member of the House of Keys
MHR	Member of the House of Representatives
MHRA	Modern Humanities Research Association
MHRF	Mental Health Research Fund
MI	Military Intelligence
MIAeE	Member, Institute of Aeronautical Engineers
MIAgrE	Member, Institution of Agricultural Engineers
MIAS	(*now see under* MAIAA)(*formerly*) Member, Institute of Aeronautical Science (US)
MIBF	Member, Institute of British Foundrymen
MIBritE	Member, Institution of British Engineers
MIBS	Member, Institute of Bankers in Scotland
MICE	Member, Institution of Civil Engineers (*formerly* the higher rank of corporate membership of the Institution, now the lower rank; *see also* FICE; change dated July 1968)
MICEI	Member, Institution of Civil Engineers of Ireland
Mich	Michigan (US)

MIChemE	Member, Institution of Chemical Engineers
MIE(Aust)	Member, Institution of Engineers, Australia
MIED	Member, Institute of Engineering Designers
MIEE	Member, Institution of Electrical Engineers (*formerly* the higher rank of corporate membership of the Institution, now the lower rank; *see also* FIEE; change dated Dec. 1966)
MIEEE	Member, Institute of Electrical and Electronics Engineers (NY)
MIEI	Member, Institution of Engineering Inspection
MIE(Ind)	Member, Institution of Engineers, India
MIERE	Member, Institution of Electronic and Radio Engineers (*and see under* MBritIRE)
MIES	Member, Institution of Engineers and Shipbuilders, Scotland
MIEx	Member, Institute of Export
MIFF	Member, Institute of Freight Forwarders
MIFor	Member, Institute of Foresters
MIGasE	Member, Institution of Gas Engineers
MIH	Member, Institute of Housing
MIHM	Member, Institute of Housing Managers (*now see* MIH)
MIHVE	Member, Institution of Heating and Ventilating Engineers (*now see* MCIBS)
MIIA	Member, Institute of Industrial Administration (*now under* MBIM)
MIInfSc	Member, Institute of Information Sciences
Mil.	Military
MILGA	Member, Institute of Local Government Administrators
MILocoE	Member, Institution of Locomotive Engineers
MIM	Member, Institution of Metallurgists
MIMarE	Member, Institute of Marine Engineers
MIMC	Member, Institute of Management Consultants
MIMechE	Member, Institution of Mechanical Engineers (*formerly* the higher rank of corporate membership of the Institution, now the lower rank; *see also* FIMechE; change dated April 1968)
MIMGTechE	Member, Institution of Mechanical and General Technician Engineers
MIMI	Member, Institute of the Motor Industry
MIMinE	Member, Institution of Mining Engineers
MIMM	Member, Institution of Mining and Metallurgy
MIMunE	Member, Institution of Municipal Engineers
Min.	Ministry
MIN	Member, Institute of Navigation (*now see* MRIN)
Minn	Minnesota (US)
MInstAM	Member, Institute of Administrative Management
MInstBE	Member, Institution of British Engineers
MInstCE	Member, Institution of Civil Engineers (changed Feb. 1940 to MICE)
MInstD	Member, Institute of Directors
MInstF	Member, Institute of Fuel
MInstGasE	Member, Institution of Gas Engineers
MInstHE	Member, Institution of Highway Engineers
MInstM	Member, Institute of Marketing
MInstMC	Member, Institute of Measurement and Control
MInstME	Member, Institution of Mining Engineers
MInstMet	(*formerly*) Member of the Institute of Metals (now part of Metals Society)
MInstP	Member, Institute of Physics
MInstPet	Member, Institute of Petroleum
MInstPI	Member, Institute of Patentees and Inventors
MInstPkg	Member, Institute of Packaging
MInstPS	Member, Institute of Purchasing and Supply (*now see* MIPS)
MInstR	Member, Institute of Refrigeration
MInstRA	Member, Institute of Registered Architects
MInstT	Member, Institute of Transport
MInstTM	Member, Institute of Travel Managers in Industry and Commerce
MInstW	Member, Institute of Welding (*now see* MWeldI)
MINucE	Member, Institution of Nuclear Engineers
MIOB	Member, Institute of Building
MIPA	Member, Institute of Practitioners in Advertising
MIPlantE	Member, Institution of Plant Engineers
MIPM	Member, Institute of Personnel Management
MIPR	Member, Institute of Public Relations
MIProdE	(*formerly* MIPE) Member, Institution of Production Engineers)
MIPS	Member, Institute of Purchasing and Supply
MIQ	Member, Institute of Quarrying
MIRE	(*now see under* MIERE) (*formerly*) Member, Institution of Radio Engineers
MIREE(Aust)	Member, Institution of Radio and Electronics Engineers (Australia)
MIRTE	Member, Institute of Road Transport Engineers
MIS	Member, Institute of Statisticians
MIS(India)	Member, Institution of Surveyors of India
MISI	(*formerly*) Member of Iron and Steel Institute (now part of Metals Society)
Miss	Mississippi (US)
MIStructE	Member, Institution of Structural Engineers
MIT	Massachusetts Institute of Technology
MITA	Member, Industrial Transport Association
MITE	Member, Institution of Electrical and Electronics Technician Engineers
MIWE	Member, Institution of Water Engineers (*now see* MIWES)
MIWES	Member, Institution of Water Engineers and Scientists

MIWM		Member, Institution of Works Managers
MIWPC		Member, Institute of Water Pollution Control
MIWSP		Member, Institute of Work Study Practitioners (now see MMS)
MJI		Member, Institute of Journalists
MJIE		Member, Junior Institution of Engineers (now see MIGTechE)
MJr		Magister Juris
MJS		Member, Japan Society
ML		Licentiate in Medicine; Master of Laws
MLA		Member of Legislative Assembly; Modern Language Association; Master in Landscape Architecture
MLC		Member of Legislative Council
MLitt		Master of Letters
Mlle		Mademoiselle (Miss)
MLM		Member, Order of the Legion of Merit (Rhodesia)
MLO		Military Liaison Officer
MM		Military Medal
MMB		Milk Marketing Board
MME		Master of Mining Engineering
Mme		Madame
MMechE		Master of Mechanical Engineering
MMet		Master of Metallurgy
MMGI		Member, Mining, Geological and Metallurgical Institute of India
MMM		Member, Order of Military Merit (Canada)
MMS		Member, Institute of Management Services
MMSA		Master of Midwifery, Society of Apothecaries
MN		Merchant Navy
MNAS		Member, National Academy of Sciences (US)
MNECInst		Member, North-East Coast Institution of Engineers and Shipbuilders
MNI		Member, Nautical Institute
MNSE		Member, Nigerian Society of Engineers
MO		Medical Officer; Military Operations
Mo		Missouri (US)
MoD		Ministry of Defence
Mods		Moderations (Oxford)
MOF		Ministry of Food
MOH		Medical Officer(s) of Health
MOI		Ministry of Information
Mon		Monmouthshire
Mont		Montana (US); Montgomeryshire
MOP		Ministry of Power
Most Rev.		Most Reverend
MoT		Ministry of Transport
MP		Member of Parliament
MPA		Master of Public Administration
MPBW		Ministry of Public Building and Works
MPP		Member, Provincial Parliament
MPS		Member, Pharmaceutical Society
MR		Master of the Rolls; Municipal Reform
MRAC		Member, Royal Agricultural College
MRACP		Member, Royal Australasian College of Physicians
MRACS		Member, Royal Australasian College of Surgeons
MRAeS		Member, Royal Aeronautical Society
MRAIC		Member, Royal Architectural Institute of Canada
MRAS		Member, Royal Asiatic Society
MRC		Medical Research Council
MRCA		Multi-Role Combat Aircraft
MRCGP		Member, Royal College of General Practitioners
MRCOG		Member, Royal College of Obstetricians and Gynaecologists
MRCP		Member, Royal College of Physicians, London
MRCPA		Member, Royal College of Pathologists of Australia
MRCPE		Member, Royal College of Physicians, Edinburgh
MRCPGlas		Member, Royal College (formerly Faculty) of Physicians and Surgeons, Glasgow
MRCPI		Member, Royal College of Physicians of Ireland
MRCPsych		Member, Royal College of Psychiatrists
MRCS		Member, Royal College of Surgeons of England
MRCSE		Member, Royal College of Surgeons, Edinburgh
MRCSI		Member, Royal College of Surgeons in Ireland
MRCVS		Member, Royal College of Veterinary Surgeons
MRES,		Member, Royal Empire Society
MREmpS
MRI		Member, Royal Institution
MRIA		Member, Royal Irish Academy
MRIAI		Member, Royal Institute of the Architects of Ireland
MRIC		Member, Royal Institute of Chemistry; now see MRSC
MRIN		Member, Royal Institute of Navigation
MRINA		Member, Royal Institution of Naval Architects
MRSanI		Member, Royal Sanitary Institute (see MRSH)
MRSC		Member, Royal Society of Chemistry
MRSH		Member, Royal Society for the Promotion of Health (formerly MRSanI)
MRSL		Member, Order of the Republic of Sierra Leone
MRSM,		Member, Royal Society of Medicine
MRSocMed
MRST		Member, Royal Society of Teachers
MRTPI		Member, Royal Town Planning Institute
MRUSI		Member, Royal United Service Institution
MRVA		Member, Rating and Valuation Association
MS		Master of Surgery; Master of Science (US)
MS, MSS		Manuscript, Manuscripts

MSA		Master of Science, Agriculture (US); Mineralogical Society of America
MSAE		Member, Society of Automotive Engineers (US)
MSAICE		Member, South African Institution of Civil Engineers
MSAInstMM		Member, South African Institute of Mining and Metallurgy
MS&R		Merchant Shipbuilding and Repairs
MSAutE		Member, Society of Automobile Engineers
MSC		Manpower Services Commission; Madras Staff Corps
MSc		Master of Science
MScD		Master of Dental Science
MSE		Master of Science in Engineering (US)
MSH		Master of Stag Hounds
MSIAD		Member, Society of Industrial Artists and Designers
MSINZ		Member, Surveyors' Institute of New Zealand
MSIT		Member, Society of Instrument Technology (now see MInstMC)
MSM		Meritorious Service Medal; Madras Sappers and Miners
MSocSc		Master of Social Sciences
MSR		Member, Society of Radiographers
MSTD		Member, Society of Typographic Designers
Mt		Mount, Mountain
MT		Mechanical Transport
MTA		Music Trades Association
MTAI		Member, Institute of Travel Agents
MTB		Motor Torpedo Boat
MTCA		Ministry of Transport and Civil Aviation
MTD		Midwife Teachers' Diploma
MTh		Master of Theology
MTPI		Member, Town Planning Institute (now see MRTPI)
MTS		Master of Theological Studies
MusB		Bachelor of Music
MusD		Doctor of Music
MusM		Master of Music
MV		Merchant Vessel, Motor Vessel (naval)
MVO		Member, Royal Victorian Order
MWA		Mystery Writers of America
MWeldI		Member, Welding Institute
MWSOM		Member, Institute of Practitioners in Work Study Organisation and Methods (now see MMS)

N

(N)		Nationalist; Navigating Duties
N		North
n		Nephew
NA		National Academician (America)
NAACP		National Association for the Advancement of Colored People
NAAFI		Navy, Army and Air Force Institutes
NABC		National Association of Boys' Clubs
NACRO		National Association for the Care and Resettlement of Offenders
NALGO		National and Local Government Officers' Association
(Nalgo)
NAMCW		National Association for Maternal and Child Welfare
NAMH		National Association for Mental Health
NAPT		National Association for the Prevention of Tuberculosis
NASA		National Aeronautics and Space Administration (US)
NAS/UWT		National Association of Schoolmasters/Union of Women Teachers
NATCS		National Air Traffic Control Services
NATFHE		National Association of Teachers in Further and Higher Education (combining ATCDE and ATTI)
NATO		North Atlantic Treaty Organisation
Nat. Sci.		Natural Sciences
NAYC		National Association of Youth Clubs
NB		New Brunswick
NBA		North British Academy
NBC		National Book Council (now National Book League); National Broadcasting Company (of America)
NBL		National Book League (formerly National Book Council)
NBPI		National Board for Prices and Incomes
NC		National Certificate; North Carolina (US)
NCA		National Certificate of Agriculture
NCB		National Coal Board
NCCI		National Committee for Commonwealth Immigrants
NCCL		National Council for Civil Liberties
NCDAD		National Council for Diplomas in Art and Design
NCLC		National Council of Labour Colleges
NCU		National Cyclists' Union
NDA		National Diploma in Agriculture
NDak		North Dakota (US)
ndc		National Defence College
NDD		National Diploma in Dairying; National Diploma in Design
NDH		National Diploma in Horticulture
NDIC		National Defence Industries Council
NE		North-east
NEAC		New English Art Club
NEAF		Near East Air Force
Neb		Nebraska (US)
NEBSS		National Examinations Board for Supervisory Studies

NEC	National Executive Committee
NECCTA	National Educational Closed Circuit Television Association
NECInst	North-East Coast Institution of Engineers and Shipbuilders
NEDC	National Economic Development Council; North East Development Council
NEDO	National Economic Development Office
NEL	National Engineering Laboratory
NERC	Natural Environment Research Council
Nev	Nevada (US)
New M	New Mexico (US)
NFC	National Freight Company (*formerly* Corporation)
NFER	National Foundation for Educational Research
NFS	National Fire Service
NFT	National Film Theatre
NFU	National Farmers' Union
NFWI	National Federation of Women's Institutes
NGO	Non-Governmental Organisation(s)
NH	New Hampshire (US)
NHS	National Health Service
NI	Northern Ireland; Native Infantry
NIAB	National Institute of Agricultural Botany
NIACRO	Northern Ireland Association for the Care and Resettlement of Offenders
NIAE	National Institute of Agricultural Engineering
NICG	Nationalised Industries Chairmen's Group
NICS	Northern Ireland Civil Service
NID	Naval Intelligence Division; National Institute for the Deaf; Northern Ireland District
NIESR	National Institute of Economic and Social Research
NIH	National Institutes of Health (US)
NILP	Northern Ireland Labour Party
NJ	New Jersey (US)
NL	National Liberal
NLF	National Liberal Federation
NNOM	Nigerian National Order of Merit
Northants	Northamptonshire
Notts	Nottinghamshire
NP	Notary Public
NPFA	National Playing Fields Association
NPk	Nishan-e-Pakistan
NPL	National Physical Laboratory
NRA	National Rifle Association; National Recovery Administration
NRD	National Registered Designer
NRDC	National Research Development Corporation
NRPB	National Radiological Protection Board
NRR	Northern Rhodesia Regiment
NS	Nova Scotia; New Style in the Calendar (in Great Britain since 1752); National Society; National Service
ns	Graduate of Royal Naval Staff College, Greenwich
NSA	National Skating Association
NSAIV	Distinguished Order of Shaheed Ali (Maldives)
NSMHC	National Society for Mentally Handicapped Children
NSPCC	National Society for Prevention of Cruelty to Children
NSRA	National Small-bore Rifle Association
N/SSF	Novice, Society of St Francis
NSTC	Nova Scotia Technical College
NSW	New South Wales
NT	New Testament; Northern Territory (Australia); National Theatre; National Trust
NTDA	National Trade Development Association
NUAAW	National Union of Agricultural and Allied Workers
NUBE	National Union of Bank Employees; *now see* BIFU
NUGMW	National Union of General and Municipal Workers; *now see* G&MWU
NUHKW	National Union of Hosiery and Knitwear Workers
NUI	National University of Ireland
NUJ	National Union of Journalists
NUM	National Union of Mineworkers
NUPE	National Union of Public Employees
NUR	National Union of Railwaymen
NUT	National Union of Teachers
NUTG	National Union of Townswomen's Guilds
NUTN	National Union of Trained Nurses
NUU	New University of Ulster
NW	North-west
NWFP	North-West Frontier Province
NWP	North-Western Province
NWT	North-Western Territories
NY	New York
NYC	New York City
NYO	National Youth Orchestra
NZ	New Zealand
NZEF	New Zealand Expeditionary Force
NZIA	New Zealand Institute of Architects

O

O	Ohio (US)
o	only
OA	Officier d'Académie
O & E	Operations and Engineers (US)

O & M	organisation and method
O & O	Oriental and Occidental Steamship Co.
OAS	Organisation of American States; On Active Service
OAU	Organisation for African Unity
ob	died
OBE	Officer Order of the British Empire
OBI	Order of British India
OC	Officer of the Order of Canada (equivalent to former award SM)
o c	only child
OC and o/c	Officer Commanding
OCA	Old Comrades Association
OCDS, ocds Can	Overseas College of Defence Studies (Canada)
OCF	Officiating Chaplain to the Forces
OCSC	Oxford and Cambridge Shakespeare Society
OCTU	Officer Cadet Training Unit
OD	Officer of the Order of Distinction (Jamaica)
ODA	Overseas Development Administration
ODI	Overseas Development Institute
ODM	Ministry of Overseas Development
OE	Order of Excellence (Guyana)
OECD	Organization for Economic Co-operation and Development (*formerly* OEEC)
OEEC	Organization for European Economic Co-operation; *see* OECD
OFEMA	Office Française d'Exportation de Matériel Aéronautique
OFM	Order of Friars Minor (Franciscans)
OFS	Orange Free State
OHMS	On His (or Her) Majesty's Service
O i/c	Officer in charge
OJ	Order of Jamaica
OL	Officer of the Order of Leopold
OLM	Officer of Legion of Merit (Rhodesia)
OM	Order of Merit
OMI	Oblate of Mary Immaculate
OMM	Officer, Order of Military Merit (Canada)
Ont	Ontario
OON	Officer of the Order of the Niger
OP	*Ordinis Praedicatorum*: of the Order of Preachers (Dominican); Observation Post
OPCON	Operational Control
OPCS	Office of Population Censuses and Surveys
OR	Order of Rorima (Guyana); Operational Research
ORC	Orange River Colony
Ore	Oregon (US)
ORS	Operational Research Society
ORSL	Order of the Republic of Sierra Leone
ORT	Organization for Rehabilitation by Training
ORTF	Office de la Radiodiffusion et Télévision Française
o s	only son
OSA	Order of St Augustine (Augustinian); Ontario Society of Artists
OSB	Order of St Benedict (Benedictine)
OSFC	Franciscan (Capuchin) Order
O/Sig	Ordinary Signalman
OSNC	Orient Steam Navigation Co.
o s p	*obiit sine prole*
OSRD	Office of Scientific Research and Development
OSS	Office of Strategic Services
OStJ	Officer of Order of St John of Jerusalem
OSUK	Ophthalmological Society of the United Kingdom
OT	Old Testament
OTC	Officers' Training Corps
OTL	Officer of the Order of Toussaint L'Ouverture (Haiti)
OU	Oxford University; Open University
OUAC	Oxford University Athletic Club
OUAFC	Oxford University Association Football Club
OUBC	Oxford University Boat Club
OUCC	Oxford University Cricket Club
OUDS	Oxford University Dramatic Society
OUP	Oxford University Press; Official Unionist Party
OURC	Oxford University Rifle Club
OURFC	Oxford University Rugby Football Club
Oxon.	Oxfordshire; of Oxford

P

PA	Pakistan Army; Personal Assistant
Pa	Pennsylvania (US)
pac	passed the final examination of the Advanced Class, The Military College of Science
PACE	Protestant and Catholic Encounter
PAg	Professional Agronomist
P&O	Peninsular and Oriental Steamship Co.
P&OSNCo.	Peninsular and Oriental Steam Navigation Co.
PASI	Professional Associate Chartered Surveyors' Institution (changed August 1947 to ARICS)
PBS	Public Broadcasting Service
PC	Privy Councillor; Police Constable; Perpetual Curate; Peace Commissioner (Ireland); Progressive Conservative (Canada)
pc	*per centum* (in the hundred)

PCMO	Principal Colonial Medical Officer	PRUAA	President of the Royal Ulster Academy of Arts
PdD	Doctor of Pedagogy (US)	PRWA	President, Royal West of England Academy
PDSA	People's Dispensary for Sick Animals	PRWS	President of the Royal Society of Painters in Water Colours
PE	Procurement Executive	PS	Pastel Society; Paddle Steamer
PEI	Prince Edward Island	ps	passed School of Instruction (of Officers)
PEN	(Name of Club: Poets, Playwrights, Editors, Essayists, Novelists)	PSA	Property Services Agency
		psa	Graduate of RAF Staff College
PEng	Registered Professional Engineer (Canada)	psc	Graduate of Staff College († indicates Graduate of Senior Wing Staff College)
PEP	Political and Economic Planning (now see PSI)		
PER	Professional and Executive Register	PSD	Petty Sessional Division
PEST	Pressure for Economic and Social Toryism	PSGB	Pharmaceutical Society of Great Britain
PF	Procurator-Fiscal	PSI	Policy Studies Institute
pfc	Graduate of RAF Flying College	PSIAD	President of the Society of Industrial Artists and Designers
PFE	Program for Executives	PSM	Panglima Setia Mahkota
PGA	Professional Golfers' Association	psm	Certificate of Royal Military School of Music
PGCE	Post Graduate Certificate of Education	PSMA	President of Society of Marine Artists
PH	Presidential Order of Honour (Botswana)	PSNC	Pacific Steam Navigation Co.
PHAB	Physically Handicapped & Able-bodied	PSO	Principal Scientific Officer; Personal Staff Officer
PhB	Bachelor of Philosophy	PSSC	Personal Social Services Council
PhC	Pharmaceutical Chemist	PTE	Passenger Transport Executive
PhD	Doctor of Philosophy	Pte	Private (soldier)
Phil.	Philology, Philological; Philosophy, Philosophical	ptsc	passed Technical Staff College
PhL	Licentiate of Philosophy	Pty	Proprietary
PhM	Master of Philosophy (USA)	PUP	People's United Party
PhmB	Bachelor of Pharmacy	PVSM	Param Vishishc Seva Medal (India)
Phys.	Physical	PWD	Public Works Department
PIARC	Permanent International Association of Road Congresses	PWO	Prince of Wales's Own
PIB	Prices and Incomes Board (see NBPI)		
PICAO	Provisional International Civil Aviation Organization (now ICAO)		

Q

pinx.	(He) painted it		
PIRA	Paper Industries Research Association	Q	Queen
Pl.	Place; Plural	QAIMNS	Queen Alexandra's Imperial Military Nursing Service
PLA	Port of London Authority	QALAS	Qualified Associate Chartered Land Agents' Society; now (after amalgamation) see ARICS
Plen.	Plenipotentiary		
PLP	Parliamentary Labour Party	QARANC	Queen Alexandra's Royal Army Nursing Corps
PMG	Postmaster-General	QARNNS	Queen Alexandra's Royal Naval Nursing Service
PMN	Panglima Mangku Negara (Malaysian Honour)	QC	Queen's Counsel
PMO	Principal Medical Officer	QCVSA	Queen's Commendation for Valuable Service in the Air
PMRAFNS	Princess Mary's Royal Air Force Nursing Service	QFSM	Queen's Fire Service Medal for Distinguished Service
PMS	Presidential Order of Meritorious Service (Botswana); President Miniature Society	QGM	Queen's Gallantry Medal
		QHC	Queen's Honorary Chaplain
PNBS	Panglima Negara Bintang Sarawak	QHDS	Queen's Honorary Dental Surgeon
PNEU	Parents' National Educational Union	QHNS	Queen's Honorary Nursing Sister
PNG	Papua New Guinea	QHP	Queen's Honorary Physician
PNP	People's National Party	QHS	Queen's Honorary Surgeon
PO	Post Office	Qld	Queensland
POB	Presidential Order of Botswana	Qly	Quarterly
POMEF	Political Office Middle East Force	QMAAC	Queen Mary's Army Auxiliary Corps
Pop.	Population	QMC	Queen Mary College (London)
POW	Prisoner of War; Prince of Wales's	QMG	Quartermaster-General
PP	Parish Priest; Past President	QOOH	Queen's Own Oxfordshire Hussars
Pp	Pages	Q(ops)	Quartering (operations)
PPCLI	Princess Patricia's Canadian Light Infantry	QPM	Queen's Police Medal
PPE	Philosophy, Politics and Economics (Oxford Univ.)	Qr	Quarter
PPInstHE	Past President, Institution of Highway Engineers	QRV	Qualified Valuer, Real Estate Institute of New South Wales
PPIStructE	Past President, Institution of Structural Engineers	QS	Quarter Sessions
PPRA	Past President of the Royal Academy	qs	RAF graduates of the Military or Naval Staff College (symbol omitted if subsequently qualified psa)
PPRBA	Past President of the Royal Society of British Artists		
PPRBS	Past President, Royal Society of British Sculptors	QSM	Queen's Service Medal (NZ)
PPRE	Past President of the Royal Society of Painter-Etchers and Engravers	QSO	Queen's Service Order (NZ)
		QUB	Queen's University, Belfast
PPRTPI	Past President Royal Town Planning Institute	qv	quod vide (which see)
PPS	Parliamentary Private Secretary		
PPSIAD	Past President of the Society of Industrial Artists and Designers		

R

PQ	Province of Quebec		
PRA	President of the Royal Academy	(R)	Reserve
PRBS	President, Royal Society of British Sculptors	RA	Royal Academician; Royal Artillery
PRCS	President of the Royal College of Surgeons	RAAF	Royal Australian Air Force
PRE	President of the Royal Society of Painter-Etchers and Engravers	RAAMC	Royal Australian Army Medical Corps
		RAC	Royal Automobile Club; Royal Agricultural College; Royal Armoured Corps
Preb.	Prebendary		
PrEng.	Professional Engineer	RACGP	Royal Australian College of General Practitioners
Pres.	President	RAChD	Royal Army Chaplains' Department
PRHA	President of the Royal Hibernian Academy	RACI	Royal Australian Chemical Institute
PRI	President of the Royal Institute of Painters in Water Colours; Plastics and Rubber Institute	RACP	Royal Australasian College of Physicians
		RACS	Royal Australasian College of Surgeons; Royal Arsenal Co-operative Society
PRIA	President of the Royal Irish Academy		
Prin.	Principal	RADA	Royal Academy of Dramatic Art
PRO	Public Relations Officer; Public Records Office	RADC	Royal Army Dental Corps
Proc.	Proctor; Proceedings	RAE	Royal Australian Engineers; Royal Aircraft Establishment
Prof.	Professor	RAEC	Royal Army Educational Corps
PROI	President of the Royal Institute of Oil Painters	RAeS	Royal Aeronautical Society
Pro tem	Pro tempore (for the time being)	RAF	Royal Air Force
Prov.	Provost; Provincial	RAFA	Royal Air Force Association
Prox.	Proximo (next)	RAFO	Reserve of Air Force Officers (now see RAFRO)
Prox.acc.	Proxime accessit (next in order of merit to the winner, or a very close second)	RAFRO	Royal Air Force Reserve of Officers
		RAFVR	Royal Air Force Volunteer Reserve
PRS	President of the Royal Society; Performing Right Society Ltd	RAI	Royal Anthropological Institute
		RAIA	Royal Australian Institute of Architects
PRSA	President of the Royal Scottish Academy	RAIC	Royal Architectural Institute of Canada
PRSE	President of the Royal Society of Edinburgh		
PRSH	President of the Royal Society for the Promotion of Health		
PRSW	President of the Royal Scottish Water Colour Society		

RAM	(Member of) Royal Academy of Music
RAMC	Royal Army Medical Corps
RAN	Royal Australian Navy
R&D	Research and Development
RANR	Royal Australian Naval Reserve
RANVR	Royal Australian Naval Volunteer Reserve
RAOC	Royal Army Ordnance Corps
RAPC	Royal Army Pay Corps
RARDE	Royal Armament Research and Development Establishment
RARO	Regular Army Reserve of Officers
RAS	Royal Astronomical Society; Royal Asiatic Society
RASC	(formerly) Royal Army Service Corps (now see under RCT)
RASE	Royal Agricultural Society of England
RAuxAF	Royal Auxiliary Air Force
RAVC	Royal Army Veterinary Corps
RB	Rifle Brigade
RBA	Member Royal Society of British Artists
RBC	Royal British Colonial Society of Artists
RBK&C	Royal Borough of Kensington and Chelsea
RBS	Royal Society of British Sculptors
RBSA	Royal Birmingham Society of Artists
RBY	Royal Bucks Yeomanry
RC	Roman Catholic
RCA	Member Royal Canadian Academy of Arts; Royal College of Art
RCAC	Royal Canadian Armoured Corps
RCAF	Royal Canadian Air Force
RCamA	Member Royal Cambrian Academy (formerly RCA)
RCAS	Royal Central Asian Society; now see RSAA
RCDS	Royal College of Defence Studies
rcds	Completed a Course at, or served for a year on the Staff of, the Royal College of Defence Studies
RCGP	Royal College of General Practitioners
RCHA	Royal Canadian Horse Artillery
RCHM	Royal Commission on Historial Monuments
RCM	Royal College of Music
RCN	Royal Canadian Navy; Royal College of Nursing
RCNC	Royal Corps of Naval Constructors
RCNR	Royal Canadian Naval Reserve
RCNVR	Royal Canadian Naval Volunteer Reserve
RCO	Royal College of Organists
RCOG	Royal College of Obstetricians and Gynaecologists
RCP	Royal College of Physicians, London
RCPath	Royal College of Pathologists
RCPE and RCPEd	Royal College of Physicians of Edinburgh
RCPI	Royal College of Physicians of Ireland
RCPGlas	Royal College of Physicians and Surgeons, Glasgow
RCR	Royal College of Radiologists
RCS	Royal College of Surgeons of England; Royal Corps of Signals; Royal College of Science
RCSE and RCSEd	Royal College of Surgeons of Edinburgh
RCSI	Royal College of Surgeons in Ireland
RCT	Royal Corps of Transport
RCVS	Royal College of Veterinary Surgeons
RD	Rural Dean; Royal Navy Reserve Decoration
Rd	Road
RDA	Royal Defence Academy
RDC	Rural District Council
RDF	Royal Dublin Fusiliers
RDI	Royal Designer for Industry (Royal Society of Arts)
RDS	Royal Dublin Society
RE	Royal Engineers; Fellow of Royal Society of Painter-Etchers and Engravers
Rear-Adm.	Rear-Admiral
REconS	Royal Economic Society
Reg. Prof.	Regius Professor
Regt	Regiment
REME	Royal Electrical and Mechnical Engineers
REPC	Regional Economic Planning Council
RERO	Royal Engineers Reserve of Officers
RES	Royal Empire Society (now Royal Commonwealth Society)
Res.	Resigned; Reserve; Resident; Research
Rev.	Reverend; Review
RFA	Royal Field Artillery
RFC	Royal Flying Corps (now RAF); Rugby Football Club
RFN	Registered Fever Nurse
RFPS(G)	Royal Faculty of Physicians and Surgeons, Glasgow; now see RCPGlas
RFR	Rassemblement des Français pour la République
RFU	Rugby Football Union
RGA	Royal Garrison Artillery
RGI	Royal Glasgow Institute of the Fine Arts
RGJ	Royal Green Jackets
RGN	Registered General Nurse
RGS	Royal Geographical Society
RGSA	Royal Geographical Society of Australasia
RHA	Royal Hibernian Academy; Royal Horse Artillery; Regional Health Authority
RHB	Regional Hospital Board
RHF	Royal Highland Fusiliers
RHG	Royal Horse Guards
RHistS	Royal Historical Society
RHR	Royal Highland Regiment

RHS	Royal Horticultural Society; Royal Humane Society
RI	Member Royal Institute of Painters in Water Colours; Rhode Island
RIA	Royal Irish Academy
RIAM	Royal Irish Academy of Music
RIAS	Royal Incorporation of Architects in Scotland
RIASC	Royal Indian Army Service Corps
RIBA	Royal Institute of British Architects; also Member of the Institute
RIBI	Rotary International in Great Britain and Ireland
RIC	Royal Irish Constabulary; Royal Institute of Chemistry (now RSC)
RICS	Royal Institution of Chartered Surveyors
RIE	Royal Indian Engineering (College)
RIF	Royal Inniskilling Fusiliers
RIIA	Royal Institute of International Affairs
RIM	Royal Indian Marines
RIN	Royal Indian Navy
RINA	Royal Institution of Naval Architects
RIPA	Royal Institute of Public Administration
RIPH&H	Royal Institute of Public Health and Hygiene
RIrF	Royal Irish Fusiliers
RM	Royal Marines; Resident Magistrate
RMA	Royal Marine Artillery; Royal Military Academy Sandhurst (now incorporating Royal Military Academy, Woolwich)
RMB	Rural Mail Base
RMC	Royal Military College Sandhurst (now Royal Military Academy)
RMCS	Royal Military College of Science
RMedSoc	Royal Medical Society, Edinburgh
RMetS	Royal Meteorological Society
RMFVR	Royal Marine Forces Volunteer Reserve
RMIT	Royal Melbourne Institute of Technology
RMLI	Royal Marine Light Infantry
RMO	Resident Medical Officer(s)
RMPA	Royal Medico-Physchological Association
RMS	Royal Microscopical Society; Royal Mail Steamer; Royal Society of Miniature Painters
RN	Royal Navy; Royal Naval
RNAS	Royal Naval Air Service
RNAY	Royal Naval Aircraft Yard
RNC	Royal Naval College
RNCM	(Member of) Royal Northern College of Music
RNEC	Royal Naval Engineering College
RNIB	Royal National Institute for the Blind
RNID	Royal National Institute for the Deaf
RNLI	Royal National Life-boat Institution
RNR	Royal Naval Reserve
RNS	Royal Numismatic Society
RNT	Registered Nurse Tutor
RNUR	Régie Nationale des Usines Renault
RNVR	Royal Naval Volunteer Reserve
RNVSR	Royal Naval Volunteer Supplementary Reserve
RNZAC	Royal New Zealand Armoured Corps
RNZAF	Royal New Zealand Air Force
RNZIR	Royal New Zealand Infantry Regiment
RNZN	Royal New Zealand Navy
RNZNVR	Royal New Zealand Naval Volunteer Reserve
ROC	Royal Observer Corps
ROF	Royal Ordnance Factories
R of O	Reserve of Officers
ROI	Royal Institute of Oil Painters
RoSPA	Royal Society for the Prevention of Accidents
(Rot.)	Rotunda Hospital, Dublin (after degree)
RP	Member Royal Society of Portrait Painters
RPC	Royal Pioneer Corps
RPMS	Royal Postgraduate Medical School
RPO	Royal Philharmonic Orchestra
RPS	Royal Photographic Society
RRC	Royal Red Cross
RRE	Royal Radar Establishment (formerly TRE)
RRS	Royal Research Ship
RSA	Royal Scottish Academician; Royal Society of Arts; Republic of South Africa
RSAA	Royal Society for Asian Affairs (formerly RCAS)
RSAF	Royal Small Arms Factory
RSAI	Royal Society of Antiquaries of Ireland
RSAMD	Royal Scottish Academy of Music and Drama
RSanI	Royal Sanitary Institute (now see RSH)
RSC	Royal Society of Canada; Royal Society of Chemistry; Royal Shakespeare Company
RSCM	Royal School of Church Music
RSCN	Registered Sick Children's Nurse
RSE	Royal Society of Edinburgh
RSF	Royal Scots Fusiliers
RSFSR	Russian Socialist Federated Soviet Republic
RSGS	Royal Scottish Geographical Society
RSH	Royal Society for the Promotion of Health (formerly Royal Sanitary Institute)
RSL	Royal Society of Literature; Returned Services League of Australia
RSM	Royal School of Mines
RSM or RSocMed	Royal Society of Medicine
RSMA	(formerly SMA) Royal Society of Marine Artists

Rock Valley College - ERC

RSO Rural Sub-Office; Railway Sub-Office; Resident Surgical Officer
RSPB Royal Society for Protection of Birds
RSPCA Royal Society for Prevention of Cruelty to Animals
RSSAILA Returned Sailors, Soldiers and Airmen's Imperial League of Australia; *now see* RSL
RSSPCC Royal Scottish Society for Prevention of Cruelty to Children
RSW Member Royal Scottish Water Colour Society
RTE Radio Telefis Eireann
Rt Hon. Right Honourable
RTO Railway Transport Officer
RTPI Royal Town Planning Institute
RTR Royal Tank Regiment
Rt Rev. Right Reverend
RTS Religious Tract Society; Royal Toxophilite Society
RTYC Royal Thames Yacht Club
RU Rugby Union
RUC Royal Ulster Constabulary
RUI Royal University of Ireland
RUKBA Royal United Kingdom Beneficent Association
RUR Royal Ulster Regiment
RUSI Royal United Services Institute for Defence Studies (*formerly* Royal United Service Institution)
RVC Royal Veterinary College
RWA (RWEA) Member of Royal West of England Academy
RWAFF Royal West African Frontier Force
RWF Royal Welch Fusiliers
RWS Member of Royal Society of Painters in Water Colours
RYA Royal Yachting Association
RYS Royal Yacht Squadron
RZSScot Royal Zoological Society of Scotland

S

(S) (in Navy) Paymaster
S Succeeded; South; Saint
s Son
SA South Australia; South Africa; Société Anonyme
SAAF South African Air Force
SACEUR Supreme Allied Commander (Europe)
SACLANT Supreme Allied Commander Atlantic
SACSEA Supreme Allied Command, SE Asia
SADF Sudanese Auxiliary Defence Force
SADG Société des Architectes Diplômés par le Gouvernement
SAE Society of Automobile Engineers (US)
SAMC South African Medical Corps
Sarum Salisbury
SAS Special Air Service
SASO Senior Air Staff Officer
SB Bachelor of Science (US)
SBAC Society of British Aerospace Companies (*formerly* Society of British Aircraft Constructors)
SBStJ Serving Brother, Order of St John of Jerusalem
SC Star of Courage (Canada); Senior Counsel (Eire, Guyana, South Africa); South Carolina (US)
sc Student at the Staff College
SCAO Senior Civil Affairs Officer
SCAPA Society for Checking the Abuses of Public Advertising
ScD Doctor of Science
SCF Senior Chaplain to the Forces
Sch. School
SCL Student in Civil Law
SCM State Certified Midwife; Student Christian Movement
SCONUL Standing Conference of National and University Libraries
Sculpt. Sculptor
SDak South Dakota (US)
SDB Salesian of Don Bosco
SDF Sudan Defence Force; Social Democratic Federation
SDLP Social Democratic and Labour Party
SE South-east
SEAC South-East Asia Command
SEALF South-East Asia Land Forces
SEATO South-East Asia Treaty Organization
Sec. Secretary
SEE Society of Environmental Engineers
SEN State Enrolled Nurse
SESO Senior Equipment Staff Officer
SFInstE Senior Fellow, Institute of Energy
SFInstF Senior Fellow, Institute of Fuel; *now see* SFInstE
SFTA Society of Film and Television Arts; *now see* BAFTA
SG Solicitor-General
SGA Member Society of Graphic Art
Sgt Sergeant
SHA Secondary Heads Association
SHAEF Supreme Heradquarters, Allied Expeditionary Force
SHAPE Supreme Headquarters, Allied Powers, Europe
SHHD Scottish Home and Health Department
SIAD Society of Industrial Artists and Designers
SIB Shipbuilding Industry Board
SIMA Scientific Instrument Manufacturers' Association of Great Britain
SIME Security Intelligence Middle East

SIMG *Societas Internationalis Medicinae Generalis*
SinDrs Doctor of Chinese
SITA Société Internationale de Télécommunications Aéronautiques
SITPRO Simplification of International Trade Procedures
SJ Society of Jesus (Jesuits)
SJAB St John Ambulance Brigade
SJD Doctor of Juristic Science
SL Serjeant-at-Law
SLA Special Libraries Association
SLAET Society of Licensed Aircraft Engineers and Technologists
SLAS Society for Latin-American Studies
SLP Scottish Labour Party
SM Medal of Service (Canada) (*now see* OC); Master of Science; Officer qualified for Submarine Duties
SMA Society of Marine Artists (*now see under* RSMA)
SME School of Military Engineering
SMIEEE Senior Member of Institute of Electrical and Electronics Engineers (NY)
SMIRE Senior Member Institute of Radio Engineers (New York)
SMMT Society of Motor Manufacturers and Traders Ltd
SMN Seri Maharaja Mangku Negara (Malaysia)
SMO Senior Medical Officer; Sovereign Military Order
SMPTE Society of Motion Picture and Television Engineers (US)
SMRTB Ship and Marine Requirements Technology Board
SNAME Society of Naval Architects and Marine Engineers (US)
SNCF Société Nationale des Chemins de Fer Français
SNP Scottish National Party
SNTS Society for New Testament Studies
SO Staff Officer
SOAS School of Oriental and African Studies
Soc. Society
SocCE(France) Société des Ingénieurs Civils de France
SODEPAX Committee on Society, Development and Peace
SOE Special Operations Executive
SOGAT Society of Graphical and Allied Trades
sowc Senior Officers' War Course
s.p. *sine prole* (without issue)
SP Self-Propelled (Anti-Tank Regiment)
SPAB Society for the Protection of Ancient Buildings
SPCK Society for Promoting Christian Knowledge
SPD Salisbury Plain District
SPG Society for the Propagation of the Gospel (*now* USPG)
SPk Sitara-e-Pakistan
SPMB Seri Paduka Makhota Brunei
SPMO Senior Principal Medical Officer
SPRC Society for Prevention and Relief of Cancer
sprl société de personnes à responsabilité limitée
SPSO Senior Principal Scientfic Officer
SPTL Society of Public Teachers of Law
Sq. Square
SQA Sitara-i-Quaid-i-Azam
Sqdn Squadron
SR Special Reserve; Southern Railway; Southern Region (BR)
SRC Science Research Council (*formerly* DSIR); Students' Representative Council
SRHE Society for Research into Higher Education
SRN State Registered Nurse
SRNA Shipbuilders and Repairers National Association
SRO Supplementary Reserve of Officers
SRP State Registered Physiotherapist
SRY Sherwood Rangers Yeomanry
SS Saints; Straits Settlements; Steamship
SSA Society of Scottish Artists
SS&AFA Soldiers', Sailors', and Airmen's Families Association
SSC Solicitor before Supreme Court (Scotland); Sculptors Society of Canada
SSEB South of Scotland Electricity Board
SSEES School of Slavonic and East European Studies
SSJE Society of St John the Evangelist
SSM Society of the Sacred Mission
SSO Senior Supply Officer
SSRC Social Science Research Council
SSStJ Serving Sister, Order of St John of Jerusalem
St Street; Saint
STB *Sacrae Theologiae Baccalaureus* (Bachelor of Sacred Theology)
STC Senior Training Corps
STD *Sacrae Theologiae Doctor* (Doctor of Sacred Theology)
STh Scholar in Theology
Stip. Stipend; Stipendiary
STL *Sacrae Theologiae Lector* (Reader or a Professor of Sacred Theology)
STM *Sacrae Theologiae Magister* (Master of Sacred Theology)
STP *Sacrae Theologiae Professor* (Professor of Divinity, old form of DD)
STRIVE Society for Preservatiaon of Rural Industries and Village Enterprises
STSO Senior Technical Staff Officer
Supp. Res. Supplementary Reserve (of Officers)
Supt Superintendent
Surg. Surgeon
Surv. Surviving
SW South-west
SWET Society of West End Theatre

SWIA   Society of Wildlife Artists
SWPA South West Pacific Area
Syd.   Sydney

T

T   Telephone; Territorial
TA   Telegraphic Address; Territorial Army
TAA   Territorial Army Association
TA&VRA Territorial Auxiliary and Volunteer Reserve Association
TAF   Tactical Air Force
T&AFA Territorial and Auxiliary Forces Association
T&AVR Territorial and Army Volunteer Reserve
TANS Territorial Army Nursing Service
TANU Tanganyika African National Union
TARO Territorial Army Reserve of Officers
TAS   Torpedo and Anti Submarine Course
TC   Order of the Trinity Cross (Trinidad and Tobago)
TCCB Test and County Cricket Board
TCD   Trinity College, Dublin (University of Dublin, Trinity College)
TCF   Temporary Chaplain to the Forces
TCPA Town and Country Planning Association
TD   Territorial Efficiency Decoration; Efficiency Decoration (T&AVR) (since April 1967); (Teachta Dala) Member of the Dail, Eire
TDD   Tubercular Diseases Diploma
TEAC Technical Education Advisory Council
TEC   Technician Education Council
Tech (CEI) Technician
TEM   Territorial Efficiency Medal
TEMA Telecommunications Engineering Manufacturers' Association
Temp. Temperature; Temporary
TEng (CEI) Technician Engineer
Tenn   Tennessee (US)
TeolD Doctor of Theology
TES   Times Educational Supplement
TET   Teacher of Electrotherapy
Tex   Texas (US)
TF   Territorial Force
TFR   Territorial Force Reserve
TGO   Timber Growers' Organisation
TGWU Transport and General Workers' Union
THELEP Therapy of Leprosy
THES Times Higher Education Supplement
ThL   Theological Licentiate
TIMS The Institute of Management Sciences
TLS   Times Literary Supplement
TMMG Teacher of Massage and Medical Gynmastics
TOSD Tertiary Order of St Dominic
TP   Transvaal Province
TPI   Town Planning Institute (*now see* RTPI)
Trans. Translation; Translated
Transf. Transferred
TRC   Thames Rowing Club
TRE   Telecommunications Research Establishment (*now see* RRE)
TRH   Their Royal Highnesses
Trin.   Trinity
TRRL Transport and Road Research Laboratory
TSB   Trustee Savings Bank
tsc   passed a Territorial Army Course in Staff Duties
TSD   Tertiary of St Dominic
TUC   Trades Union Congress
TV   Television
TYC   Thames Yacht Club (*now see* RTYC)

U

(U)   Unionist
u   Uncle
UAR   United Arab Republic
UAU   Universities Athletic Union
UC   University College
UCCA Universities Central Council on Admissions
UCET Universities Council for Education of Teachers
UCH   University College Hospital (London)
UCL   University College London
UCLA University of California at Los Angeles
UCNS Universities' Council for Non-academic Staff
UCNW University College of North Wales
UCW   University College of Wales; Union of Communication Workers
UDC   Urban District Council
UDF   Union Defence Force; Ulster Defence Force
UDR   Ulster Defence Regiment; Union des Démocrates pour la Vème République (*now see* RFR)
UEA   University of East Anglia
UEFA Union of European Football Associations

UF   United Free Church
UGC   University Grants Committee
UJD   *Utriusque Juris Doctor*, Doctor of both Laws (Doctor of Canon and Civil Law)
UK   United Kingdom
UKAC United Kingdom Automation Council
UKAEA United Kingdom Atomic Energy Authority
UKLF United Kingdom Land Forces
UKSLS United Kingdom Services Liaison Staff
UMIST University of Manchester Institute of Science and Technology
UN   United Nations
UNA   United Nations Association
UNCAST United Nations Conference on the Applications of Science and Technology
UNCIO United Nations Conference on International Organisation
UNCTAD United Nations Commission for Trade and Development
(Unctad)
UNDP United Nations Development Programme
UNDRO United Nations Disaster Relief Organisation
UNECA United Nations Economic Commission for Asia
UNEP United Nations Environment Programme
UNESCO United Nations Educational, Scientific and Cultural
(Unesco) Organisation
UNFAO United Nations Food and Agriculture Organisation
UNHCR United Nations High Commissioner for Refugees
UNICEF United Nations Children's Fund (*formerly* United Nations
(Unicef) International Children's Emergency Fund)
UNIDO United Nations Industrial Development Organisation
UNIDROIT Institut International pour l'Unification du Droit Privé
UNIPEDE Union Internationale des Producteurs et Distributeurs d'Energie Electrique
UNISIST Universal System for Information in Science and Technology
UNITAR United Nations Institute of Training and Research
Univ.   University
UNRRA United Nations Relief and Rehabilitation Administration
UNRWA United Nations Relief and Works Agency
UNSCOB United Nations Special Commission on the Balkans
UP   United Provinces; Uttar Pradesh; United Presbyterian
UPGC University and Polytechnic Grants Committee
UPNI   Unionist Party of Northern Ireland
URC   United Reformed Church
URSI   Union Radio-Scientifique Internationale
US   United States
USA   United States of America
USAAF United States Army Air Force
USAF   United States Air Force
USAID United States Agency for International Development
USAR   United States Army Reserve
USDAW Union of Shop Distributive and Allied Workers
USMA United States Military Academy
USN   United States Navy
USNR   United States Naval Reserve
USPG   United Society for the Propagation of the Gospel (*formerly* SPG)
USS   United States Ship
USSR   Union of Soviet Socialist Republics
UTC   University Training Corps
(UU)   Ulster Unionist
(UUUC) United Ulster Unionist Coalition
(UUUP) United Ulster Unionist Party
UWIST University of Wales Institute of Science and Technology
UWT   Union of Women Teachers

V

V   Five (Roman numerals); Version; Vicar; Viscount; *Vice*
v   *Versus* (against)
v or vid. *Vide* (see)
Va   Virginia (US)
VAD   Voluntary Aid Detachment
V&A   Victoria and Albert
VAT   Value Added Tax
VC   Victoria Cross
VCAS Vice-Chief of the Air Staff
VCDS Vice-Chief of the Defence Staff
VCNS Vice-Chief of Naval Staff
VD   Royal Naval Volunteer Reserve Officers' Decoration (*now* VRD); Volunteer Officers' Decoration; Victorian Decoration
VDC   Volunteer Defence Corps
Ven.   Venerable (of an Archdeacon)
Very Rev. Very Reverend (of a Dean)
Vet.   Veterinary
VG   Vicar-General
VHS   Hon. Surgeon to Viceroy of India
VIC   Victoria Institute of Colleges
Vice-Adm. Vice-Admiral
Visc.   Viscount
VM   Victory Medal
VMH   Victoria Medal of Honour (Royal Horticultural Society)
Vol.   Volume; Volunteers
VP   Vice-President

VPP	Volunteer Political Party
VQMG	Vice-Quartermaster-General
VR	*Victoria Regina* (Queen Victoria)
VRD	Royal Naval Volunteer Reserve Officers' Decoration
VSO	Voluntary Service Overseas
Vt	Vermont (US)
(VUP)	Vanguard Unionist Party

WRAF	Women's Royal Air Force (*formerly* WAAF)
WRNS	Women's Royal Naval Service
WRVS	Women's Royal Voluntary Service (*formerly* WVS)
WS	Writer to the Signet
WSPU	Women's Social and Political Union
WUS	World University Service
WVa	West Virginia (US)
WVS	Women's Voluntary Services (*now see* WRVS)
WWF	World Wildlife Fund
Wyo	Wyoming (US)

W

W	West
WA	Western Australia
WAAF	Women's Auxiliary Air Force (*now* WRAF)
Wash	Washington State (US)
WCC	World Council of Churches
W/Cdr	Wing Commander
WEA	Workers' Educational Association; Royal West of England Academy
WEU	Western European Union
WFTU	World Federation of Trade Unions
WHO	World Health Organization
WhSch	Whitworth Scholar
WI	West Indies (*formerly* BWI: British West Indies); Women's Institute
Wilts	Wiltshire
Wis	Wisconsin (US)
Wits	Witwatersrand
WJEC	Welsh Joint Education Committee
WLA	Women's Land Army
WLF	Women's Liberal Federation
Wm	William
WNO	Welsh National Opera
WO	War Office
Worcs	Worcestershire
WOSB	War Office Selection Board
WR	West Riding; Western Region (BR)
WRAC	Women's Royal Army Corps (*formerly* ATS)

X

X	Ten (Roman numerals)

Y

y	youngest
YC	Young Conservative
YCNAC	Young Conservatives National Advisory Committee
Yeo.	Yeomanry
YHA	Youth Hostels Association
YMCA	Young Men's Christian Association
Yorks	Yorkshire
yr	younger
yrs	years
YVFF	Young Volunteer Force Foundation
YWCA	Young Women's Christian Association

Z

ZANU	Zimbabwe African National Union

ADDENDA I

The following biographies are of those whose deaths occurred before 31 December 1970, but were not reported until after the volume of *Who Was Who* covering the years 1961–1970 had been published.

ROBB, Leonard Arthur, CMG 1933; MVO 1954; JP; retired; *b* 4 Dec. 1891; *s* of David Arthur Robb and Agnes Eliza Allen; *m* 1923; one *s* one *d*. *Educ:* Stratford District High School, NZ. Served with AIF in Gallipoli, Egypt, and France. Retired as Official Secretary to the Governor of New South Wales. *Recreations:* tennis, surfing. *Address:* 1 Wapiti, Superba Parade, Mosman, NSW 2088, Australia. *T:* XM 5803.
[*Died* 7 *Nov.* 1964.

VAILLANCOURT, Hon. Cyrille, CBE 1944; Commandeur, St Grégoire le Grand; Eminent Chevalier, Société du Bon Parler français; Manager: L'Union régionale des Caisses populaires de Quebec, La Caisse Centrale Desjardins de Lévis; La Fédération des Caisses Populaires Desjardins; Les Productions de Sucre d'Erable de Quebec (Co-op. Soc.); Vice President La Société d'Assurance des Caisses Populaires; President: L'Assurance-vie Desjardins; L'Assoc. Co-op. Desjardins; Director: La Caisse populaire de Lévis; Dupuis Frères, Ltée; *b* 17 January 1892; *s* of Dr C. E. and Marie-Louise Larochelle Vaillancourt, Saint-Anselme (Dorchester County), PQ, Canada; *m* 1920, Blanche Lajoie; three *s* five *d*. *Educ:* Lévis Coll.; Laval Univ., Quebec (DSA, Hon.). Clerk at L'Etoile du Nord, Joliette, 1914; Head of Apiculture Service, Dept of Agriculture, Quebec, 1915; Head of Apiculture and Maple Sugar Services, Quebec, 1918. MLC Quebec, 1943-44; Editor of La Revue Desjardins, 1941. Roman Catholic. *Address:* 7 St Mary, Lévis, PQ, Canada. *T:* 837-7285. *Clubs:* Garnison, Club des Journalistes, Cercle Universitaire Laval (Quebec); Saint-Denis (Montreal).
[*Died* 30 *Oct.* 1969.

WEBSTER, Herman Armour, RE 1914; (ARE 1907); painter-etcher; *b* New York City, 6 April 1878; *s* of George Huntingdon Webster and Ellen F. Pickford; *m* 1st, 1909, Doriane Delors (*d* 1950), Paris; one *s*; 2nd, 1951, Charlotte Huard. *Educ:* St Paul's School, Concord; PhB Yale Univ., 1900. Editorial Staff of the Chicago Record-Herald, 1902; began study of art in the Académie Julian under Jean-Paul Laurens, 1904; Mem. Corresp. de la Société des Peintres-Graveurs Français, 1909; Mem. Titulaire, 1953; Associé de la Société Nationale des Beaux-Arts, 1912; Sociétaire, 1933; Mem. Soc. of American Graphic Artists; Gold Medal, San Francisco International Exposition, 1915; Noyes Prize, Brooklyn, USA, 1930; Grand Prix (gravure), Paris Exposition, 1937; Co-founder Société des Amis des Vieux Moulins (France); entered French Army, 1914; American Field Service, 1915; transferred to American Expeditionary Force, 1st Lieut. SC. 1917; Captain, 1918; Major, 1919; Croix de Guerre, Verdun, 1916; Médaille de la France Libérée; Officier de la Légion d'Honneur.
[*Died* 9 *March* 1970.

ADDENDA II

The following biographies are of those whose deaths occurred between 1971 and 1980, but were not reported until after the main part of this volume had gone to press.

ALLAN, Captain John Steele, CBE 1956; company director; *b* 25 Dec. 1889; *s* of late Andrew Allan, JP, Chirnside, Berwickshire; *m* 1915, Margaret (*d* 1978), *d* of late Joseph Mason, Dunbar; one *s. Educ:* Berwickshire High School, Duns. Served War of 1914-18: 1/4 KOSB, Gallipoli, Egypt, and Palestine, 1915-17; wounded in Palestine, 1917. Pres., Aberdeen Chamber of Commerce, 1937-38. Chairman: Technical Section, Paper Makers' Assoc., 1932-34; North of Scotland Bank Ltd, 1942-50 (Director, 1939-50). Dep. Chm., White Fish Authority, 1954-56 (Chm., Scottish Cttee). Director: Home Flax Production, Min. of Supply, 1941-42; Aberdeen Steam Navigation Co. Ltd, 1940-64 (Chm. 1944-64); Burns & Laird Lines Ltd, 1940-64 (Chm., 1944-64); Burns & Laird Lines Ltd, 1955-64; Clydesdale Bank Ltd, 1950-67 (Dep. Chm., 1950-56); Wiggins Teape & Co. Ltd, 193▶-51; Alex. Pirie & Sons Ltd, 1931-51; Dartford Paper Mills, 1931-51; Midland Bank Ltd, 1944-67; Midland Bank Executor and Trustee Co. Ltd, 1944-67. Rector's Assessor, Univ. of Aberdeen, 1949-50. FRIC 1926. DL Aberdeenshire, 1945-70. Chevalier 1st Class Royal Order of Vasa (Sweden), 1950. *Publications:* The Young Angler, 1949; My Picture Gallery of Memory, 1970. *Recreation:* angling. *Address:* Kinord, Links Road, North Berwick. *T:* North Berwick 2868. *Club:* New (North Berwick).
[Died 21 April 1979.

AUSTIN, Sir John Worroker, Kt 1971; CA; Chairman: Blue Metal Industries Ltd, since 1952; Clutha Development Pty Ltd, 1952-76; TRW (Aust.) Ltd, since 1968; Greater Pacific General Insurance Ltd Group, 1970-76; *b* Sydney, New South Wales; *s* of late J. W. Austin; *m* 1948, Doris, *d* of R. Jenkins; one *s. Educ:* Sydney High School; Sydney Univ. Director: Rank Industries Aust. Pty Ltd, 1974-; Greater Union Organisation Pty Ltd, 1974-; George Kent (ANZ) Pty Ltd; Allied Polymer Group (Holdings) Pty Ltd; Ready Mixed Concrete Ltd. Mem. Cttee, Aust. Jockey Club. *Recreations:* farming, breeding racehorses (stud property, Princes Farm); golf, fishing, surfing. *Address:* Toft Monks, 95 Elizabeth Bay Road, NSW 2011, Australia. *Clubs:* Tattersall's, Union, Royal Sydney Yacht Squadron, Elanora Golf (NSW). *[Died 18 Oct. 1980.*

BARBOUR, George Brown; MA, PhD, FRSE, FRGS, FGS, FGSAm; Professor Emeritus of Geology, University of Cincinnati; *b* 22 Aug. 1890; *s* of A. H. F. Barbour, MD, and Margaret Nelson Brown; *m* 1920, Dorothy, *d* of Dr R. L. Dickinson of New York; three *s. Educ:* Merchiston; Marburg Univ.; Edinburgh Univ.; St John's Coll., Cambridge; Columbia Univ., NY. Active Service, FAU and RFA, Sep. 1914-Jan. 1919. Prof. of Applied Geology, Peking Univ., 1920-22; Head of Dept of Geology, Peiyang Univ., Tientsin, 1922-23; Prof. of Geology, Yenching Univ., Peiping, 1923-32; Lecturer, Columbia Univ., 1928-29; Univ. of Cincinnati, 1932-33; Visiting Physiographer, Cenozoic Laboratory, Peiping, 1934; Visiting Prof., Stanford Univ., 1935; Hon. Lecturer, London Univ., 1934-37; Dean of McMicken Coll. of Arts and Science, 1938-58. Academic Coordinator US Army Air-Force College Training Programme, 1943-45. Member Royal Society of South Africa; Hon. Member Société Belge de Géologie, de Paléontologie et d'Hydrologie, 1937; Corresp. Fellow R. Belgian Geog. Soc., 1946; Corresp. Member, Geological Survey of China; Foreign Member, Geolog. Soc. of Finland; Member Soc. géol. de France; Geologist, Univ. of California African Expedition, 1947; Pres. Ohio Academy of Science, 1948-49; Corresp. Mem. Ital. Inst. of Hum. Paleontology, 1955. RGS Gill Memorial Award, 1937; Viking Fund Award, Wenner-Gren Foundation, 1951, 1954. Visiting Professor, Duke Univ., 1961-62, Univ. of Louisville, Ky, 1964-65. George Barbour Collection of letters, photographs, articles etc, in Univ. of Cincinnati Library. *Publications:* Geology of the Kalgan Area, 1928; Physiographic History of the Yangtze, 1935; Ape or Man, 1949; In the Field with Teilhard de Chardin, 1965, paperback, 1975; In China When— (letters 1911-34), 1974; Geological Reports and papers in scientific jls. *Recreations:* mountaineering, music. *Address:* University of Cincinnati, Cincinnati, Ohio 45221, USA; 440 Lafayette Avenue, Cincinnati, Ohio 45220. *Club:* Athenæum. *[Died 1 July 1977.*

BARRINGTON, Sir Charles Bacon, 6th Bt, *cr* 1831; retired Nurseryman (Orchid grower and Carnation specialist); *b* 6 June 1902; *s* of Sir Charles Burton Barrington, 5th Bt, and Mary Rose (*d* 1943), *d* of Sir Henry Hickman Bacon, 10th and 11th Bt; *S* father 1943; *m* 1930, Constance Doris, *d* of E. J. Elkington; two *d. Educ:* Eton. *Recreation:* horticulture. *Heir: b* Capt. Alexander Fitzwilliam Croker Barrington, *b* 19 Nov. 1909. *Address:* Barrihurst, Cranleigh, Surrey GU6 8LQ.
[Died 30 Nov. 1980.

BAUD, Rt. Rev. Joseph A., BA; Former Bishop of Visakhapatnam (RC); *b* Bellevaux (Haute-Savoie, France), 23 July 1890. *Educ:* Evian-les-Bains; Yeovil; Univ. studies at Fribourg (Switzerland). Came to Vizag in 1914; Teacher in St Aloysius' European High-School, Vizagapatam, 1914-30; Principal there, 1930-40; Vicar-General of Diocese of Vizagapatam in 1940; Coadjutor-Bishop of Vizagapatam (British India), 1942-47; Bishop of Visakhapatnam, 1947-66, retired. *Address:* Salesianum, Visakhapatnam 3, India.
[Died 13 March 1980.

BEHAN, Sir Harold Garfield, Kt 1977; CMG 1967; MBE 1958; JP; Grazier; *b* 22 Feb. 1901; *s* of Thomas and Mary Behan, Jericho; *m* 1942, Kathleen, *d* of John Costello; two *s four d. Educ:* Nudgee Coll.; Brisbane Gram. Sch. Member: Jericho Shire Council, 1922-25; Isisford Shire Council, 1926-67 (Chm. 1945-67); Executive Member: Queensland Local Govt Assoc., 1945-67 (Pres. 1952-67); Australian Council of Local Govt Assocs, 1945-67 (Pres. 1967); Graziers' Assoc. of Central and N Queensland, 1942-67 (Pres. 1962-67); Mem. Council and Exec. Council, United Graziers' Assoc. of Queensland, 1939-67. *Address:* Bilbah Downs, Isisford, Qld 4731, Australia. *Clubs:* Longreach, Blackall (Qld). *[Died 7 Aug. 1979.*

BERRY, Prof. Jack; Professor, Department of Linguistics, since 1964, and Director, Program of Oriental and African Languages, 1973-78, Northwestern University, Evanston, Ill, USA; *b* 13 Dec. 1918; *s* of H. and N. Berry; *m* 1942, Winifred Mary; one *s. Educ:* Univ. of Leeds (BA); Univ. of London (PhD). Formerly Reader in West African Languages and subsequently Professor of West African Languages, Oct. 1960-Sept. 1963, at the Sch. of Oriental and African Studies; Prof. of West African Languages at Michigan State Univ., USA, 1963-64. Editor, Journal of African Languages, 1962-64. *Address:* Northwestern University, Evanston, Ill 60201, USA.
[Died 4 Dec. 1980.

BOLTON, Sir John (Brown), Kt 1977; OBE 1973; Member, Legislative Council of Isle of Man, 1962-79; *b* 20 Jan. 1902; *s* of Rev. Richard Bolton and Charlotte Bolton; *m* 1930, Mary Smith; one *s* one *d. Educ:* Hull Grammar Sch.; Keighley Trade and Grammar Sch. Chartered Accountant, 1924, in public practice, IoM, 1928-68. Member: Douglas Corp., 1940-46;

House of Keys, 1946-62; IoM Exec. Council, 1951-62, 1966-79; Chairman: IoM Highway Bd, 1956-61, 1963-66; IoM Finance Bd, 1966-76. Organist, St Andrews Church, Douglas, 1925-46. FRSA. *Recreations:* golf, gardening. *Address:* Amberley, Woodlands Close, Douglas, Isle of Man. *T:* Douglas 3204 and 21267. *Club:* Douglas Golf (Pres.). *[Died* 11 *Sept.* 1980.

BROOME, Francis Napier; retired, 1961, as Judge-President, Natal Provincial Division, Supreme Court of South Africa; *b* 1891; *s* of late William Broome, formerly Judge of Supreme Court of S Africa; *m* 1918, Mary Caroline Jervois; one *s* one *d. Educ:* Hilton College, Natal; Oriel College, Oxford (Rhodes Scholar). BA(Oxon) 1912; Barrister-at-law, Inner Temple, 1913; Advocate of Supreme Court of S Africa, 1914; Natal Carbineers and Royal Field Artillery, 1914-19, SW Africa and France, Captain (MC); KC 1931; MP for Pietermaritzburg District, 1938; Chairman: Natal Education Commission, 1936-38; Indian Penetration Commission, 1940; Natal Indian Judicial Commission, 1944; Durban Native Enquiry Commission, 1947; Stock Exchange Inquiry Commission, 1962; Courts Commn, Rhodesia, 1970. Hon. LLD Natal, 1968. *Publications:* Not the Whole Truth, 1962; Speeches and Addresses, 1973. *Address:* 94 Roberts Road, Pietermaritzburg, South Africa. *Club:* Victoria (Pietermaritzburg). *[Died March* 1980

BROTHERTON, Harry George, CBE 1949; President of the Confederation of Shipbuilding and Engineering Unions, 1948-58; General Secretary of the National Union of Sheet Metal Workers and Braziers, 1941-55; *b* 3 Dec. 1890; *s* of Henry William Brotherton; *m* 1915, Daisy Beatrice (*d* 1953), *d* of Walter Henry King; *m* 1958, May, *d* of John Summers. *Recreation:* reading. *Address:* 18 Cornwallis Gardens, Broadstairs, Kent. *[Died* 5 *Dec.* 1980.

CALDER, Air Vice-Marshal Malcolm Frederick, CB 1957; CBE 1947; Chief of Air Staff, RNZAF, 1958-62; Chairman, New Zealand Chiefs of Staff Committee, 1960–62, retired; *b* 1907; *s* of late Andrew Calder; *m* 1935, Margaret Emily, *d* of Henry Mandeno, architect, Dunedin, NZ; one *s* one *d. Educ:* Christ Church Boys' High Sch., NZ; University Coll., Canterbury, NZ (LLB). Joined RAF, 1931; RNZAF, 1939; served War of 1939-45 in NZ and Pacific; Air Member for Personnel, Air Board, NZ, 1945-47, and 1952-53; Air Cdre 1952; NZ Senior Air Liaison Officer, London, 1954-56; served in Malaya, 1957-58. *Recreations:* fishing and golf. *Address:* Herekiekie Street, Turangi, New Zealand. *Club:* United Services (Wellington, NZ). *[Died* 31 *Aug.* 1978.

CAMERON, Thomas Wright Moir, OC 1972; TD; PhD Edinburgh; HARCVS; MA Edinburgh; DSc Edinburgh; DSc BC; FRSC; Professor Emeritus of Parasitology, McGill University, Montreal; *b* Glasgow, 29 April 1894; *e s* of Hugh Cameron, Edinburgh; *m* Stella Blanche, *y d* of F. H. Hill, Oxford; one *d. Educ:* Allan Glen's Sch., Glasgow; Glasgow, Edinburgh, and London Univs; Royal (Dick) Veterinary Coll., Edinburgh. Commission in HLI 1914-16; RAF 1916-19; in Royal (Dick) Vet. Contingent OTC 1921-23; Major RAVC (TA) London (2nd Div.), 1923-35; McGill COTC 1939-42. Res. Schol., Edinburgh Univ., 1921-23; Min. of Agric. Res. Schol., 1921-23; Sen. Res. Asst, Inst. of Agricultural Parasitology, London, 1923-25; Lecturer and Milner Fellow, Dept of Helminthology, London Sch. of Hygiene and Tropical Medicine, 1925-29; Dir. and Founder, Inst. of Parasitology, 1932-64. Sec., Sect. of Tropical Diseases and Parasitology, Vice-President Sect. of Comparative Medicine, RSM, 1926-29; Lecturer in Helminthology, Univ. of Edinburgh and Royal (Dick) Veterinary Coll., 1929-32; Contrib. on Vet. Diseases to Bull. of Hygiene; Sec., Edin. and Can. Brs, Royal Soc. of Tropical Medicine and Hygiene. President: American Society of Parasitologists, 1949; Sect. V, RSC, 1949-50; RSC, 1957-58; Can. Society of Microbiology, 1959; Can. Society of Zoology, 1960; World Federation of Parasitologists, 1965-; Chairman, Can. Cttee, International Biological Programme; Ed., Canadian Jl Zool. *Publications:* Animal Diseases in Relation to Man; Internal Parasites of Domestic Animals; Principles of Parasite Control; Parasites of Man in Temperate Climates; Early History of Caribe Islands; Parasites and Parasitism; numerous papers on parasitic helminths, and on diseases of animals in relation to man. *Address:* 15300 Wallbrook Court, Apt 304, Silver Spring, Maryland 20906, USA. *[Died* 1 *Jan.* 1980.

CAMPBELL, Arnold Everitt, CMG 1966; retired as Director-General of Education, Department of Education, Wellington, New Zealand (1960-66); *b* 13 Aug. 1906; *s* of Fernly Charlwood and Mabel Annie Campbell; *m* 1934. Louise Annie Combs; one *s* two *d. Educ:* Palmerston North Boys' High Sch.; Wellington Teachers' Coll., Victoria Univ. of Wellington. Primary school teacher, 1926-28; Lecturer in Education, Victoria Univ.

of Wellington, 1929-38; Director, NZ Council for Educational Research, 1939-52; Chief Inspector of Primary Schools, Dept of Education, 1953-58; Asst Director of Education, 1959. Hon. Fellow, NZ Educnl Inst., 1972. *Publication:* Educating New Zealand, 1941: *Address:* 13 Pitt Street, Wellington, New Zealand. *T:* 45-438. *[Died* 2 *July* 1980.

CHAMBERLAIN, Sir Henry Wilmot, 5th Bt, *cr* 1828; *b* 17 May 1899; *o s* of Sir Henry Chamberlain, 4th Bt, and Gwendolen (*d* 1928), *d* of J. Inglis Jones, Royal Horse Guards, Derry Ormond, Cardiganshire, and Lady Elizabeth Inglis Jones. *S* father 1936. *Address:* c/o Church Adams & Co., 23/25 Bell Street, Reigate, Surrey. *[Died* 24 *Dec.* 1980 (*ext*).

DAVIES, Edward Gwynfryn, CBE 1970; JP; DL; Member, Forestry Commission, 1959-73, and Chairman, National Committee for Wales, 1963-73; *b* 28 Nov. 1904; *o s* of Edward and Anne Davies; *m* 1932, Sarah Annie Adams; two *s. Educ:* Cwmavon Elementary Sch., Port Talbot. Mining Industry, 1918-21; Steel Industry, 1921-69; Trade Unionist, 1928-. Mem., Glamorgan CC, 1945-74 (Alderman, 1953-74, Chm., 1969-70); Glamorgan Representative: Glamorgan River Authy, 1956-74; Univ. Cts of Wales, 1957-74; Standing Jt Cttee, later S Wales Police Authy, 1963-74; Welsh Jt Educn Cttee, 1965-74; Glamorgan Magistrates Cts, 1970-74; Mem., Mid-Glamorgan HMC, 1948-69. JP Port Talbot, 1948 (Dep. Chm., Port Talbot Borough Magistrates, 1968-); DL Glamorgan 1972. Chm., Urdd Gobaith Cymru, Cwmavon, 1939-74, Hon. Life Pres., 1975; initiated into Gorsedd of Bards, 1967. Pres., S Glamorgan Welsh Congregational Union, 1970-71. *Recreations:* gardening, local history, music. *Address:* Min-y-Gors, Heol-y-Graig, Cwmavon, Port Talbot, W Glam. *T:* Cwmavon 342. *[Died* 28 *Aug.* 1980.

FARREN, Most Rev. Neil, DD, DCL; *b* 25 March, 1893; *s* of John Farren and Margaret McLaughlin. *Educ:* St Columb's Coll., Derry; University Coll. (NUI) Dublin; Maynooth Coll.; Rome. Prof. St Columb's Coll., Derry, 1920-27 (Maths and Science), Pres., 1927-39; Bishop of Derry, 1939-73. An Asst to Papal Throne. *Publication:* Domicile and Quasidomicile, 1920. *Address:* Mellifont, Grianan Park, Buncrana, Co. Donegal. *T:* Buncrana 66. *[Died* 8 *May* 1980.

FAUTEUX, Rt. Hon. (Joseph Honoré) Gerald, PC (Can.) 1970; CC (Canada) 1974; Counsel, O'Brien, Hall, Saunders, since 1974; Chief Justice of Canada, 1970-73; Judge, Supreme Court of Canada, 1949-73; *b* St Hyacinthe, PQ, 22 Oct. 1900; *s* of Homère Fauteux and Héva Mercier; *m* 1929, Yvette Mathieu. Montreal; two *s* three *d. Educ:* Collège Ste-Marie, Montreal; University of Montreal (law degree). Practised law in Montreal; Crown Attorney, 1929; KC Canada 1933; QC Canada 1952; Asst Chief Crown Counsel, 1930-36; Chief Crown Counsel, 1939-44; Judge of the Superior Court in Montreal, 1947. Life mem. Canadian Bar Assoc., Hon. Sec. of that Assoc. for several years; legal adviser to the Royal Canadian Mounted Police for several years. Prof., 1936-50, Dean, 1949, Law Faculty of McGill Univ.; Univ. of Ottawa: Founder and Dean of Law Faculty, 1953-62; Chm. Bd of Governors (of reorganized Univ.) 1965-67; Chancellor, 1973-. Acted as legal adviser to Royal Commission appointed to investigate spying activities in Canada. Hon. LLD: University of Ottawa, 1953; Laval Univ., Quebec, 1957; University of Sudbury, 1958: University of Montreal, 1962; Hon. DCL McGill Univ., Montreal, 1955. *Recreations:* outdoor sports. *Address:* (home) 937 St Clare Road, Town of Mont Royal, PQ, Canada. *T:* 342-1093; Complexe Desjardins, Montreal, PQ, Canada. *T:* 228-7811. *Club:* Cercle Universitaire (Ottawa).
[Died 14 *Sept.* 1980.

FINLAY, His Honour Bernard, QC 1967; a Circuit Judge (formerly County Court Judge), 1970-79; *b* 4 July 1913. LLB (Hons I); Bar final (Hons I) (certificate of honour); L. J. Holker Scholar. Called to the Bar, Gray's Inn, 1945, Middle Temple, 1966; practised on South-Eastern Circuit. *Address:* Denbigh Lodge, Denbigh Road, Haslemere, Surrey. *[Died* 21 *Oct.* 1980.

GARDNER, Frank Matthias, CBE 1967; Borough Librarian, Luton, 1938-72; *b* 13 Jan. 1908; *s* of Ernest Frank Gardner and Lily Gardner, Sheffield; *m* 1936, Lysobel Margaret Watt Smith (*d* 1966); one *s* one *d. Educ:* Firth Park Grammar Sch., Sheffield. FLA 1932. Unesco Consultant, India, 1950-51; Leader, Seminar on Public Libraries in Asia, Delhi, 1954; Pres., Library Assoc., 1964; Mem., Library Adv. Council, 1965-71; Chm., Books and Libraries Panel, British Council, 1966-72; Chm., Public Libraries Section, Internat. Fedn of Library Assocs, 1969-73. CStJ 1962. *Publications:* (ed) Sequels, 1947, 1955, 1967, 1974; Letters to a Younger Librarian, 1948; Delhi Public Library, Evaluation Report (Unesco), 1955; (with M.

J. Lewis) Reading Round the World, 1969; Public Library Legislation: a comparative study (Unesco), 1971; (with L. C. Persson) Junior Sequels, 1977. *Recreations:* reading, travel, enjoying church architecture and pictures, contract bridge. *Address:* 1 Ryecroft Way, Luton, Beds. *T:* Luton 22795.
[Died 24 July 1980.

GENTNER, Dr Wolfgang; Director of the Max-Planck-Institute for Nuclear Physics, Heidelberg, 1958–74; Vice President, Max-Planck Society, since 1972; Professor of Physics, University of Heidelberg, since 1958; *b* Frankfurt-am-Main, 23 July 1906; *s* of Carl G. Gentner, manufacturer; *m* 1931, Alice Pfaehler; one *s* one *d. Educ:* Universities of Erlangen and
• Frankfurt (PhD). Fellowship at Institut du Radium, Lab. Curie, Paris Univ. (Mme P. Curie), 1933–35; Scientific Asst at Inst. of Physics of Kaiser-Wilhelm-Institut for Med. Research, 1936–46; Lectr in Physics, Univ. of Frankfurt, 1937–41; Fellow, Radiation Lab., Univ. of California (Berkeley), 1938-39; Lectr in Physics, Univ. of Heidelberg, 1941-45, Prof. 1945; Prof. of Physics Freiburg Univ., 1946-58; Dir of CERN, Geneva, 1955-59. Member: Comité des directives scientifiques, CERN, 1959-; Heidelberger Akad. der Wissenschaften (Pres. 1964-67); Bayerische Akad. der Wissenschaften; Akad. Leopoldina; Pontifical Acad. of Science, 1970; Hon. Fellow, Weizmann Inst., Israel, 1965. Order of Merit, Oesterreichische Akad. der Wissenschaften, 1975. Officier, Légion d'Honneur, 1965. *Publications:* on biophysics, radioactivity, nuclear physics; (co-author) Atlas of typical expansion chamber photographs, 1954. *Address:* Im Bäckerfeld 6, Heidelberg, Germany. *T:* 42467.   *[Died 4 Sept.* 1980.

GOUGH, Prof. Jethro; Professor of Pathology, Welsh National School of Medicine, Cardiff, 1948-69, retired; *b* 29 Dec. 1903; *s* of Jabez and Ellen Gough; *m* 1933, Anne (*née* Thomas); two *s. Educ:* Mountain Ash County Sch.; Welsh National Sch. of Medicine, Cardiff. BSc, 1924; MRCS, LRCP, 1926; MB, BCh, 1927; MD, 1930; FRCP 1967; Founder FRCPath (Vice-Pres. 1966-68). Demonstrator in Pathology, Cardiff, 1927, Manchester Univ., 1928; Lecturer in Pathology, Cardiff, 1929; Senior Lecturer, Cardiff, 1933. *Publications:* on several subjects relating to Pathology, but especially silicosis and allied conditions. *Address:* 22 Park Road, Whitchurch, Cardiff CF4 7BQ. *T:* Cardiff 65011.   *[Died 16 Feb.* 1979.

GREENAWAY, Sir Thomas Moore, Kt 1968; Hon. Consulting Physician, Royal Prince Alfred Hospital, since 1930; *b* 1 June 1902; *s* of T. C. Greenaway, Grafton, NSW; *m* 1927, Lavinia, *d* of late G. H. Figtree, Wollongong, NSW; one *s* two *d. Educ:* N Sydney High Sch.; University of Sydney. MB, ChM, 1925; MRCP 1934; FRCP 1950. Foundn Fellow, RACP, 1938; Censor-in-Chief, 1952-56; Pres., RACP, 1960-62. Councillor, BMA (NSW Br.), 1944-48; Mem., NSW Med. Bd, 1963-73; Mem. Bd of Dirs, RPA Hosp., 1953-74. Lectr in Clinical Med., University of Sydney, 1940-62. Hon. Fellow, RACGP, 1968. *Publications:* contribs to various med. jls. *Recreation:* golf. *Address:* 231 Macquarie Street, Sydney, NSW 2000, Australia. *T:* 233-3420. *Club:* Australian (Sydney). *[Died 30 Oct.* 1980.

GREGOR, James Wyllie, CBE 1961; PhD, DSc, FRSE; Director, Scottish Plant Breeding Station, 1950-65; *b* 14 Jan. 1900; *s* of C. E. Gregor, Innerwick, East Lothian; *m* 1929, Mary Joanne Farquharson, *d* of A. Robertson Wilson, MD. *Educ:* St Mary's Sch., Melrose; Edinburgh Univ. *Publications:* scientific papers in various international journals. *Recreations:* various. *Address:* Old Mill House, Balerno, Midlothian. *T:* 031-449 3973.   *[Died 30 Sept.* 1980.

HUNTLEY, Arthur Geoffrey; President, May Acoustics, Ltd, acoustical engineers; *b* 1897; *s* of Rev. A. H. Huntley, Hull; *m;* two *s. Educ:* Hereford Cathedral Sch. Commenced training as chemical engineer, 1913; commissioned to the Royal Engineers (TA), 1914; served in the Royal Engineers in France, Belgium, and India, 1914-19 (1914-15 Star, GS and allied ribbons, despatches, TD); Lieut-Col RA, retd; secured post with large contracting firm and studied sound, 1920; founded the May

Construction Co. Ltd, to undertake the work of acoustical engineers and contractors, 1922; AMIStructE, 1921; Mem. of the Acoustical Soc. of America, 1931. *Publications:* Acoustics, Cantor Lectures, Royal Society of Arts, 1928, and other articles to the technical press; The Acoustics of Structures, paper before the Institute of Structural Engineers, 1925. *Recreation:* bridge. *Adress:* Hill House Farm, 1 School Lane, Netteswell, Harlow, Essex CM20 2QB.   *[Died 30 Sept.* 1980.

JONES, Rev. J(ohn) Ithel; Pastor, Collins Street Baptist Church, Melbourne, since 1970; *b* 1 Jan. 1911; *s* of David Jones and Elizabeth Catherine Jones; *m* 1938, Hannah Mary Rees. *Educ:* Cyfarthfa Castle Sch., Merthyr Tydfil; University Coll., Cardiff; S Wales Baptist Coll. BA (Wales) 1st cl. hons Philosophy and 2nd cl. hons Welsh; BD (Wales); MA (Wales), Theology. Pastorates: Porthcawl, 1936-40; Horfield, Bristol, 1940-50; Haven Green, Ealing, 1950-57; Principal, and Prof. of Theol. and the Philosophy of Religion, S Wales Baptist Coll., 1958-70. Moderator, Free Church Federal Coun. of England and Wales, 1963-64; Dean of Divinity for University of Wales, 1964-67; Pres., Baptist Union of Gt Britain and Ireland, 1967-68. Mem. for Wales on Panel of Religious Advisers, ITA and Welsh Cttee, ITA, 1966-69. Lecture tours in USA, Australia, New Zealand. Guest Chaplain to US Senate, 1978. Hon. DD, Eastern, Pa, 1966; Hon. LLD, Baylor, 1966. *Publications:* Colossians, in New Bible Commentary, 1953; Temple and Town, 1961; The Holy Spirit and Christian Preaching, 1967; Facing the New World, 1968. *Recreations:* golf, music, motoring. *Address:* Suite 43 Rockley Tower, 3 Rockley Road, South Yarra, Vic 3141, Australia.   *[Died 30 Dec.* 1980.

McGUINNESS, Norah Allison; artist; *b* Londonderry; *e d* of late Joseph Allison and Jessie McGuinness; *m* 1925, Geoffrey Phibbs, *e s* of Basil Phibbs, Lisheen, Sligo (marr. diss., 1931). *Educ:* Londonderry High Sch. Studied painting at College of Art, Dublin, Chelsea Polytechnical, London, and with André Lhote, Paris; Illustrated: Sentimental Journey; Stories from Red Hanorhan (W. B. Yeats), etc. Designed for the Abbey Theatre, Dublin; held Exhibitions in London, Dublin, New York, Paris, Holland and Canada, and represented Ireland at Biennial Exhibition, Venice, 1950. Pictures in private collections in many countries. Hon. LittD TCD, 1973. *Recreations:* gardening and bird watching. *Address:* 53 York Road, Dun Laoghaire, Dublin.
[Died 22 Nov. 1980.

STEWART, Sir Bruce Fraser, 2nd Bt *cr* 1920, of Fingask; Chairman, Pigeon Bay Road Board; ex-Flying Officer, New Zealand Air Force; *b* Sept. 1904; *s* of 1st Bt; *S* father, 1924; *m* 1925, Constance, *d* of W. S. Gray, Cambridge; two *d. Educ:* Eton; Cambridge. Past-President, Canterbury Aero Club. *Recreations:* polo, flying, boating, and golf. *Address:* Strathmore, Pigeon Bay, Banks Peninsula, Canterbury, NZ.
[Died 5 Sept. 1979 *(ext).*

OTTLEY, Warner Herbert Taylor, CB 1945; retired; *b* 1889; *m* 1921, Hilda Mary Edwards; two *s. Educ:* Malvern; St John's College, Cambridge. Higher Division Clerk, War Office, 1913; Director of Finance, War Office, 1942; retired, 1949. *Address:* 14 Medlow Court, Eversfield Place, St Leonards-on-Sea, East Sussex.   *[Died 10 Oct.* 1980.

WESTWOOD, Earle Cathers; Agent-General for British Columbia in London, Oct. 1964-Oct. 1968; *b* 13 September 1909; *s* of Joseph Arthur Westwood and Mary Smith; *m* 1956, Sheila Blackwood Maxwell; one *d. Educ:* Nanaimo and Vancouver, BC, Canada. Pres. of Chamber of Commerce, Nanaimo, 1940; Chm. of Sch. Bd, 1942 and 1943; Mem. City Coun., 1944; Finance Chm. for five years; Mayor of City of Nanaimo, 1950, 1951, 1952, 1956. Provincial politics, 1956-63; Minister of Industrial Development, Trade and Commerce; Minister of Recreation and Conservation; Minister of Commercial Transport. *Recreations:* golf, sailing, fishing. *Address:* 71 White Eagle Terrace, Nanaimo, BC V9S 3C5, Canada. *Clubs:* Royal Automobile; Hendon Golf; Nanaimo Yacht; Union (Victoria, BC).   *[Died 14 Aug.* 1980.

A

AALTO, Prof. (Hugo) Alvar (Henrik); Finnish Architect; furniture designer; Founder-Director, Aalto Architectural Office, since 1923; *b* 3 Feb. 1898; *m* 1924 (wife *d* 1949); one *s* one *d* ; *m* 1952. *Educ:* Jyväskylän Lyseo and Univ. of Technology, Helsinki. Architect, 1921. In partnership with wife for twenty years; founded furniture firm; Prof., Massachusetts Institute of Technology, 1946-48. Work in Finland includes: Sanatorium at Paimio, library at Viipuri, factory at Sunila, university buildings at Helsinki and Jyväskylä, concert-hall, government and commercial buildings in Helsinki and many other municipal buildings, country houses, and housing projects, also churches, in Finland. Abroad: dormitory at Massachusetts Institute of Technology, flats in Berlin, Cultural centre and a 22 floor flat-building in Germany, country house in France. Finnish Pavilions at Paris Exhibition, 1937, and New York World Fair, etc, 1939. Member: Finnish Acad. (Pres., 1963-68); Det Kongelige Akademi för de Skønne Kunster; Academie de l'Architecture; Les Congrès Internationaux d'Architecture Moderne; Akademie der Künste, Berlin; Hon. RDI (RSA London); Hon. Member: RCA (London); Associazone per l'Architettura Organica; Instituto de Arquitetos do Brasil; Södra Sveriges Byggnadstekn. Samfund; Assoc. of Finnish Architects; Norske Arkitekters Landsforbund; Accademia di Belle Arti di Venezia; Amer. Acad. of Arts and Sciences; Invited Member: Kungliga Akademin för de Fria Konsterna; Koninklijke Vlaamse Academie; Fell. Mem. World Acad. of Art and Science (Israel); Corresp. Mem. Accademia Nazionale di San Luca; Hon. Corresp. Mem. RIBA; Hon. Fell., Amer. Inst. of Architects. Dr *hc* : Princeton University (US); Univ. of Technology, Helsinki; Inst. of Technology, Trondheim, Norway; Swiss Federal Institute of Technology; Columbia University, New York; Technische Hochschule, Wien; Laurea *hc*, Polytechnic Inst. of Milan. Royal Gold Medal for Architecture, RIBA, 1957; Gold Medal, Amer. Inst. of Architects, 1963; Gold Cube, Svenska Arkitekters Riksförbund, 1963. Chevalier de la Légion d'Honneur; Akademisk Arkitektførenings Aeres-medaille; Prins Eugen medal; Medaglia d'Oro della Città di Firenze; Grande Ufficiale al Merito della Repubblica Italiana; Suomen Leijonan Ritarikunnan Suurristi; Comdr of Dannebrog, etc. *Address:* Tiilimäki 20, 00330 Helsinki 33, Finland. *[Died 11 May 1976.*

ABAYOMI, Sir Kofo Adekunle, Kt 1951; MD, ChB, DTM&H; DOMS (Eng.); FRSA; Member Privy Council, Nigeria, 1951; Chief Ona Ishokun of Oyo since 1949; Chief Baba Isale of Lagos since 1952; is an Eye Specialist; *b* 10 July 1896; *s* of Joseph N. John and Aiyelagbe Davies; *m* 1932, Oyinkan Morenikeji, MBE, *o d* of Sir Kitoyi Ajasa, OBE; five *s* one *d*. *Educ:* Methodist Boys' High School, Lagos; Edinburgh Univ. Served European War, 1914-17 (medals). Pharmacist, 1917-22; Edinburgh Univ., 1922; MB, ChB 1928. Demonstrator in Physiological Methods, Edinburgh Univ., 1927-30; DTM&H Edinburgh 1929; MD with speciality in Tropical Medicine, 1936; FRSA 1934; Rhodes Scholar in Ophthalmology, 1941; studied also at Moorfields Eye Hosp., 1940-41; DOMS England 1941. MLC, Nigeria, 1938-40; MEC, Nigeria, 1949-51; Member: Government and educational committees; Univ. Coll. Council, Ibadan, 1947-; Dep. Chm., Univ. Coll. Hosp., Ibadan, 1953-; Chm. Bd of Management, Univ. Teaching Hosp., Ibadan; President: Nigeria Federal Soc. for the Blind, 1953-; Assoc. of Medical Practitioners, 1946-; Nigeria Br., BMA, 1953-; Nigeria Medical Assoc., 1960; Chm., Lagos Exec. Development Board; Director: Barclays Bank, DCO (Nigeria); ICI (Nigeria); P & Z Co. Ltd; Vice-Chm., British Bata Shoe Co. (Nigeria); Chm. Bd of Trustees, Glover Memorial Hall. Hon. LLD Mount Allison Univ., Canada, 1958;

Hon. LLD Univ. of Ibadan, 1963. *Recreation:* walking. *Address:* 2 Keffi Street, PO Box 300, Lagos, Nigeria. *Clubs:* Royal Commonwealth Society; Dining, Metropolitan, Ikoyi (Lagos). *[Died 1 Jan. 1979.*

ABBOT, Charles Greeley, DSc, LLD; Research Associate, Smithsonian Institution, since 1944; *b* 31 May 1872; *s* of Harris Abbot and Ann Caroline Greeley; *m* 1897, Lillian Elvira Moore (*d* 1944); no *c*; *m* 1954, Virginia Andes Johnston. *Educ:* Massachusetts Inst. of Technology. Continuously employed by Smithsonian Instn of Washington from 1895; Asst, 1895-1906, Director, 1907-44, of Smithsonian Astrophysical Observatory; Asst Sec., 1918-27, Sec., 1928-44, Smithsonian Institution. Research on solar radiation, atmospheric transparency, the weather, applications of solar radiation, stellar radiation; US patents 3,376,165, 1968, 3,654,759, 1972, Unlimited Solar Radiation Power; working on improvements, 1968-. Member Nat. Acad. of Sciences, Am. Assoc. for Advancement of Sciences, and many socs and acads in America and abroad. *Publications:* Vols 1-6 Annals Astrophysical Observatory; The Sun, 1911, 2nd edn 1929; Everyday Mysteries, 1925; The Earth and the Stars, 1926, 2nd edn 1946; The Sun and the Welfare of Man, 1928, 2nd edn 1944; Great Inventions, 1932; Adventures in a World of Science, 1956; Ten Sermons,1940-66; papers on scientific subjects. *Recreations:* reading; music; games, especially golf, tennis, bridge. *Address:* 4409 Beechwood Road, Hyattsville, Md 20782, USA; Smithsonian Institution, Washington, DC 20560. *T:* (301) 927-2046. *Clubs:* Cosmos, Abracadabra (Washington, DC). *[Died 17 Dec. 1973.*

ABBOTT, Hon. Charles Lydiard Aubrey; *b* Sydney, 4 May 1886; *s* of Thomas Kingsmill Abbott, Chief Stipendiary Magistrate at Sydney; *m* Hilda, *d* of John Harnett, Monaro, NSW; two *d*. *Educ:* The King's School, Parramatta. Pastoralist; served with AIF, Aug. 1914-Oct. 1919 (wounded); promoted to commissioned rank, and returned to Australia with rank of captain; Member House of Representatives for Gwydir, NSW, 1925-29 and 1931-37; Minister for Home Affairs, Commonwealth of Australia, 1928-29; Administrator of Northern Territory of Australia, 1937-46. *Publication:* Australia's Frontier Province (The Northern Territory), 1950; addressed RGS on N Territory, 1946. *Recreations:* gardening, writing, historical research. *Address:* Ashdown, 96 Elizabeth Bay Road, Elizabeth Bay, Sydney, NSW 2011, Australia. *T:* 35-3192. *Club:* Imperial Service (Sydney). *[Died 30 April 1975.*

ABBOTT, Claude Colleer, MA London, BA, PhD Cantab; Professor of English Language and Literature in the University of Durham, 1932-54, Emeritus Professor, 1954; *b* 17 April 1889; *er s* of George Henry Abbott and Mary Matilda Colleer; unmarried. *Educ:* King Edward VI Sch., Chelmsford; Gonville and Caius Coll., Cambridge. Asst Master at the Grammar School, Sudbury, Suffolk, and the High School, Middlesbrough; BA London, 1913; MA London, 1915; Artists' Rifles OTC, 1918; Household Brigade OCB; 2nd Lieut Irish Guards (Special Reserve); BA Cantab, 1921; PhD Cantab, 1926; Lecturer in English Language and Literature in the University of Aberdeen, 1921-32; Censor of University College, Durham, 1932-41; Dean of the Faculty of Arts, 1943-45; Chm. Univ. Publications Bd, 1948-50, 1952-54; Editor Durham Univ. Journal, 1939-52. Visited and lectured at many univs in USA, 1949 (Goldwin Smith Lecture at Cornell, Lamont Lecture at Yale); Visiting Professor Univ. of Virginia, Feb.-June 1953; Resident, Yale; lectured at univs in South USA, Oct. 1956-March 1957. Member of Boswell Papers Advisory Committee. *Publications:* Youth and Age, 1918; Nine Songs from the Old French, 1920; Poems, 1921; Miss Bedell and Other Poems, 1924; Life and Letters of George Darley, 1928 (repr. 1967); Ploughed Earth, Poems,

1930; Early Mediæval French Lyrics, 1932; Letters of Gerard Manley Hopkins to Robert Bridges, 1935; Correspondence of Gerard Manley Hopkins and Richard Watson Dixon, 1935; A Catalogue of Papers relating to Boswell, Johnson and Sir William Forbes, 1936; Further Letters of Gerard Manley Hopkins, including his correspondence with Patmore, 1938 (2nd edn revised and enlarged, 1956); Early Verses, 1938; Further Letters of George Darley (Durham University journal, Dec. 1940); The Parents of Thomas Lovell Beddoes (DUJ, June 1942); Versions of Old English Elegies (DUJ, June 1943, June 1944); The Sand Castle and other Poems, 1946; Boswell (Spence Watson Memorial Lecture), 1946; (ed. with introd.) Poems and Plays by Gordon Bottomley, 1953; Poet and Painter: the Correspondence of Gordon Bottomley and Paul Nash, 1955; Summer Love Poems, 1958; Collected Poems, 1963. *Recreations:* walking, book-hunting, gardening. *Address:* 7 Church Street, Durham. *T:* Durham 2853. *Club:* Athenæum.
[*Died* 17 *Sept.* 1971.

ABBOTT, John Sutherland, JP; Chairman, R. Wyliehill Ltd, 1971-75; formerly Director: The Bank of Scotland; Royal Exchange Assurance (Chairman Glasgow Local Board); Glenfield and Kennedy Holdings Ltd, 1952-65, and other Companies; Chairman and Managing Director, Saxone Lilley & Skinner (Holdings) Ltd, 1938-64; Hon. President, Ayrshire Chamber of Industries; Governor, Welbeck College; Member, Scottish National Committee, English-Speaking Union; Vice-Chairman, Kennel Club Cttee, 1973; *b* 24 August 1900; 2nd *s* of late George Sutherland Abbott, JP, Middleton House, Ayr, and Isabel Cathrine Cable; *m* 1928, Winifred May, 2nd *d* of George Thomas, Wolverhampton; one *s*. *Educ:* Bedales School; Pembroke College, Cambridge. JP Ayrshire 1942. *Recreations:* shooting, racing, breeding and exhibiting wire-haired foxterriers. *Address:* 25B Rutland Gate, SW7; Admirals Walk, West Cliff, Bournemouth, Dorset. *Clubs:* East India, Devonshire, Sports and Public Schools, Kennel; Leander; Prestwick Golf.
[*Died* 6 *March* 1979.

ABDOOLCADER, Sir Husein Hasanally, Kt 1948; CBE 1938; LLD (Malaya); Barrister-at-Law, Advocate and Solicitor; formerly Member Advisory Council of Governor of The Malayan Union; *b* Surat, Bombay Presidency, 10 Sept. 1890; *e s* of H. A. Cader, JP, merchant; *m* 1914, Manubai Mohamedally, *yr d* of late Mohamedally Mulla Abdullhusein Hakimji, Surat; five *s* two *d*. *Educ:* Raffles Institution, Singapore; Penang Free School, Penang; County High School, Ilford, Essex; Christ's College, Cambridge; Lincoln's Inn. Indian Member Straits Settlements Legislative Council from 1928 until outbreak of war with Japan; Member of Indian Immigration Cttee, 1935-53; Pres. Third All Malaya Indian Conf., 1929-30; Indian Mem. of Municipal Commn, Georgetown, Penang, 1925-51; Past Pres., Penang Soc. for Prevention of Cruelty to Animals; Past Pres., Mohammedan Football Assoc.; Silver Jubilee Medal, 1935; Coronation Medal, 1937. Hon. LLD Univ. of Malaya, 1963. *Recreations:* tennis, rowing, walking. *Address:* Surat Lodge, 3R Tarjong Tokong Road, Mukim 18, Penang; Georgetown Chambers, 39 Beach Street, Penang. *TA:* Sir Abdoolcader Penang. *T:* 60690, (office) 63275.
[*Died* 16 *June* 1974.

ABDUL RAZAK bin HUSSEIN, Hon. Tun Haji, SMN; Orang Kaya Indera Shahbandar (OKIS) 1950; Prime Minister, Minister of Foreign Affairs and Minister of Defence, Malaysia, since 1970; Chairman: National Action Council; National Security Council; National Unity Advisory Council; *b* Pekan, Pahang, 11 March 1922; *m* Toh Puan Rahah; five *s*. *Educ:* Malay Coll., Kuala Kangsar; Raffles Coll., Singapore. Called to Bar, Lincoln's Inn, London, 1950. Joined Malay Admin. Service, 1939; Malayan Civil Service, 1950; State Sec., Pahang, 1952; Menteri Besar, Pahang, 1955; Minister of Education, in Federal Govt, 1955-57; Dep. Prime Minister and Minister of Defence (after Independence), 1957-59; Prime Minister, Feb.-Aug. 1959; again Dep. Prime Minister and Minister of Defence, Malaya, 1959-63, Malaysia, 1963-70 (also Minister of Rural Development, 1959-69, and Minister of Home Affairs, 1969, incl. Actg Minister of Finance, 1969). Elected, in first Parly Elections, for Pekan, 1959 and subseq. 1964, 1969, 1974. Past Pres., Chm. etc. several public bodies. President: (in Malaysia) UNA; Nat. Olympic Councils; Vice-Pres., Commonwealth Parly Council, etc. Youth Section, United Malays Nat. Org (UMNO) (elected Dep. Pres. yearly, 1951-; Pres. 1971-; Chm. of Alliance, 1971-). As Deputy Prime Minister, rep. Malaysia at various internat. Confs, incl. Tripartite Talks (Malaya, Indonesia and the Philippines) in Manila, Bangkok and Tokyo, 1963, 1964; led Goodwill Missions to: N Africa, 1964; E Africa and Burma, 1965; also rep. Malaysia at various Colombo Plan and other Internat. Economic Develt Confs, and to UN Gen. Assembly; Head, Malaysian Delegn to Bangkok for successful "Bangkok Accord" signed in Jakarta 11 Aug. 1966, ending the

state of confrontation with Indonesia; rep. Malaysia at First Islamic Foreign Ministers' Meeting, Jeddah, 1970; Non-Aligned Nations Conf., Lusaka, 1970, Algiers, 1973; led Malaysian delegn to: Commonwealth Heads of Govts Conf., Singapore, 1971; The Five-Power Defence Talks, London, Apr. 1971; Conf. of Islamic Nations, Lahore, 1974. Received Magsaysay Award, 1967; Hon. LLD Univ. of Malaya; decorations from States in Malaysia; several foreign orders; Associate KStJ. *Recreation:* golf. *Address:* (Office of the Prime Minister) Pejabat Perdana Menteri, Kuala Lumpur, Malaysia. *T:* Kuala Lumpur 84432.
[*Died* 14 *Jan.* 1976.

ABDY, Sir Robert (Henry Edward), 5th Bt, *cr* 1850; late 15th Hussars; *b* 11 Sept. 1896; *s* of 4th Bt and Anna Adele Coronna; *S* father, 1921; *m* 1st, 1923, Iya Jongeyans (who obtained a divorce, 1928); 2nd, 1930, Lady Diana Bridgeman (marr. diss., 1962; she *d* 1967), *e d* of 5th Earl of Bradford; one *s*; 3rd, 1962, Jane Noble (marr. diss. 1973). *Educ:* Sandhurst. *Heir:* s Valentine Robert Duff Abdy, *b* 11 Sept. 1937. *Address:* Newton Ferrers, Callington, Cornwall.
[*Died* 16 *Nov.* 1976.

ABEL, Arthur Lawrence, MS; MD(*hc*); FRCS; Consulting Surgeon: Princess Beatrice Hospital; Gordon Hospital (Westminster Hospital Group); Royal Marsden Hospital and Institute of Cancer Research, Royal Cancer Hospital; Hon. Consulting Surgeon: Woolwich War Memorial Hospital; Wood Green and Southgate Hospital; Hounslow Hospital; Vice-President, British Medical Association; *b* 15 Nov. 1895; *s* of Rev. A. E. Abel; *m* (wife *d* 1963); three *s* one *d*. *Educ:* University Coll., London; University Coll. Hospital. MB, BS 1917; MS Lond. 1921; MRCS, LRCP 1917; FRCS 1920; MD(*hc*) Bristol 1967. Jacksonian Prize 1924 and Hunterian Professor 1926, RCS; Fellowes Silver Medal in Clinical Medicine; First Prize in Clinical Surgery, UCH; Bradshaw Lectr, 1957. Member: Council RCS, 1947-63 (Vice-Pres., 1956-57); Grand Council Cancer Research Campaign; former Member, Bd of Governors: Westminster Hosp.; Royal Marsden Hosp. and Inst. of Cancer Research, Royal Cancer Hospital; Fellow Royal Society of Medicine; Fellow, Chelsea Clinical Soc.; Hon. Fellow, Member Council and Past Pres. Metropolitan Cos Br., BMA; Hon. Fellow and Auditor, Hunterian Soc. (Pres.), 1963; Orator), 1962). Fellow and Past Pres., Harveian Society. Visiting Professor: Royal North Shore Hospital, Sydney; Marquette Univ., Milwaukee; Brooklyn Med. Centre, NY. Lectr, Cook County Graduate Sch. of Medicine, Chicago. Hon. Mem., Soc. of Surgeons of Madrid. Hon. Fellow: Amer. Med. Assoc.; Amer. Soc. of Colon and Rectal Surgs; Argentine Proctol. Soc. Late House Surg. and House Physician, Univ. Coll. Hosp. and Hosp. for Sick Children, Gt Ormond Street; Surg. Registrar (5 years) Cancer Hosp.; Temp. Surg. Lieut RN. Hon. Admiral, Texas Navy. *Publications:* contribs to med. jls. *Address:* 48 Harley Street, W1N 1AD. *T:* 01-580 4118.
[*Died* 18 *Feb.* 1978.

ABEL SMITH, Sir Alexander, KCVO 1980; Kt 1968; TD; JP; retired Merchant Banker; J. Henry Schroder Wagg and Co. Ltd, 1946-67; Chairman: Pressed Steel Co., 1955-65; Provident Mutual Life Assurance Association, 1966-73; Director of other companies; *b* 18 Sept. 1904; *s* of late Lieut-Col Francis Abel Smith, DL; *m* 1st, 1936, Elizabeth (*d* 1948), *d* of David B. Morgan, Biltmore, North Carolina, USA; one *s* one *d*; 2nd, 1953, Henriette Alice (Lady Abel Smith); one *s* one *d*. *Educ:* Eton College; Magdalen College, Oxford. Served War of 1939-45, AA Command and British Army Staff, Washington (hon. Brigadier). Mem., BNEC, 1965-69; Dep. Chm., Export Council for Europe, 1963-69. Chm., Sussex Church Campaign, 1970-; Trustee, Duke of Edinburgh Award Scheme, 1956-79. JP Herts 1949, JP Sussex 1955. Order of Legion of Merit, USA. Knight (1st Class) Order of Dannebrog (Denmark). *Recreations:* shooting and fishing. *Address:* The Garden House, Quenington, Cirencester, Glos. *T:* Coln St Aldwyns 231. *Club:* Buck's.
[*Died* 17 *April* 1980.

ABEL SMITH, Desmond, MC 1916; Major, late Grenadier Guards; Director: Borax Consolidated Ltd, 1937-69; National Westminster Bank Ltd (formerly National Provincial Bank Ltd), 1948-70; Equitable Life Assurance Society, 1930-70, and other companies; *b* 2 Sept. 1892; *e s* of Eustace Abel Smith, Longhills, Lincoln, and Aileen, *d* of Col J. A. Conolly, VC, Coldstream Guards; *m* Elizabeth Barbara Peace, JP Bucks, *d* of General Hon. Sir H. A. Lawrence, GCB; one *s* four *d*. *Educ:* Eton; Trinity College, Cambridge. Served European War, 1914-18, Grenadier Guards, 1918-19; Adjutant Guards Machine Gun Regt (twice wounded, despatches, MC); War of 1939-45, GSO2 London District, 1939-43; Senior Military Liaison Officer, London Region. *Recreations:* shooting, ornithology. *Address:* Hampden Old Rectory, Great Missenden, Bucks; Longhills, Branston, Lincoln. *Club:* Travellers'.
[*Died* 26 *July* 1974.

ABERCORN, 4th Duke of, *cr* 1868; **James Edward Hamilton;** Baron of Paisley, 1587; Baron Abercorn, 1603; Baron Hamilton and Earl of Abercorn, 1606; Baron of Strabane, 1617; Viscount of Strabane, 1701; Viscount Hamilton, 1786; Marquess of Abercorn, 1790; Marquess of Hamilton, 1868; Bt 1660; HM Lieutenant for County of Tyrone since 1951; Captain Grenadier Guards; Member: Tyrone County Council, 1946; of Senate, Government of Northern Ireland, 1949-62; *b* 29 Feb. 1904; *er s* of 3rd Duke of Abercorn, KG, KP, and Lady Rosalind Cecilia Caroline Bingham (*d* 1958, as Dowager Duchess of Abercorn, DBE), *o d* of 4th Earl of Lucan; *S* father, 1953; *m* 1928, Lady Mary Kathleen Crichton (Duchess of Abercorn, DCVO 1969); two *s* one *d*. *Educ:* Eton; RMC Sandhurst. High Sheriff, Co. Tyrone, 1946. Chm. Trustees, Ulster Museum, 1962; Chancellor, New University of Ulster at Coleraine, 1970-. Chm., NI Br., GB-USSR Assoc.; President: Royal Forestry Soc. of England, Wales and N Ireland, 1964; Internat. Dendrological Union, 1964; N Ireland Council of YMCAs; Army Cadet Force Assoc. for N Ireland; Not Forgotten Assoc., N Ireland; RN Lifeboat Inst., N Ireland; Royal UK Beneficent Assoc.; Nat. Playing Fields Assoc., N Ireland; Western Counties NI Assoc., TA&VR; County Pres., Scout Assoc.; Vice-Pres., N Ireland Area, British Legion. Hon. Col, 5th Bn The Royal Inniskilling Fusiliers (TA), 1963. Hon. DLitt Ulster 1970. *Heir: s* Marquess of Hamilton. *Address:* Barons Court, Co. Tyrone, Northern Ireland. *Club:* Turf. [*Died 4 June* 1979.

ABERCROMBIE, George Francis, VRD 1940; MA, MD Cambridge; Surgeon Captain, RNVR, retired; in General Practice, 1924-66; *b* 25 June 1896; *o s* of late George Kennedy Abercrombie, Solicitor, London, and Margaret Jane (*née* Forbes); *m* 1932, Marie, *yr d* of late Frank Underhill, JP, Plympton, S Devon; one *s* two *d*. *Educ:* Charterhouse Sch.; Gonville and Caius Coll., Cambridge. MA, BCh 1922; MB 1924, MD 1935. House Surg. and Resident Midwifery Asst, St Bartholomew's Hosp.; House Phys., Hosp. for Sick Children, Gt Ormond Street. Hon. FRSocMed (first Pres., Sect. of Gen. Practice, 1950); Mem. of Management Cttee, 1963-67, and Chm., Emerg. Bed Service Cttee, King Edward's Hosp. Fund for London, 1951-67; Lectr on Gen. Practice, St Bart's Hosp. Med. Sch., 1953-66. Foundn Mem., Coll. of Gen. Practitioners (Chm. Coun., 1952-55; James Mackenzie Lectr, 1958; Pres., 1959-62). Formerly Surg. Probationer, RNVR (HMS Warwick, Zeebrugge, 1918, despatches); Surg. Lieut 1922; Surg. Comdr 1935. War of 1939-45 (VRD): HMS Birmingham; HMS Anson. Surg. Captain 1948; KHP 1950; retired, 1951. *Publications:* papers in Alpine and med. jls; Joint Editor, The Encyclopædia of General Practice, 1963. *Recreations:* country walking, chess. *Address:* 4 The Barnyard, Ebbisham Lane, Walton-on-the-Hill, Surrey. *T:* Tadworth 2656. [*Died 26 Sept.* 1978.

ABERCROMBIE, Michael, FRS 1958; MA, BSc; Director, Strangeways Research Laboratory, 1970-79; Fellow of Clare Hall, Cambridge, 1970-79; *b* 14 Aug. 1912; *s* of Lascelles and Catherine Abercrombie; *m* 1939, Minnie Louie Johnson; one *s*. *Educ:* Leeds Grammar Sch.; The Queen's Coll., Oxford (Hastings Scholar, 1931; Taberdar, 1935; Junior Research Fellow, 1937). Beit Memorial Fellow for Medical Research, 1940; Lecturer in Zoology, Birmingham University, 1945; Reader in Embryology, UCL, 1950-59, Professor, 1959-62, Jodrell Prof. of Zoology, 1962-70. Mem. Council, Royal Soc., 1967-69. Hon. Fil.Dr. Uppsala, 1977. *Publications:* Dictionary of Biology (with C. J. Hickman and M. L. Johnson), 1951; papers on embryology, tissue culture and wound healing. *Address:* Strangeways Research Laboratory, Wort's Causeway, Cambridge; 2 Bridge Lane, Little Shelford, Cambridge CB2 5HE. [*Died 28 May* 1979.

ABERCROMBY, Sir Robert (Alexander), 9th Bt, *cr* 1636, of Birkenbog; MC 1918; JP; Vice-Lieutenant of Banffshire, 1965-71; *b* (posthumous) 15 Aug. 1895; 2nd *s* of Sir Robert John Abercromby, 7th Bt; *S* brother, Sir George Abercromby, 8th Bt, DSO, 1964; *m* 1st, 1923, Hon. Diamond Hardinge (*d* 1927); 2nd, 1929, Pamela (*d* 1944), *d* of late John Lomax; 3rd, 1951, Elizabeth (*d* 1971), *d* of Major James Corcoran. *Educ:* Eton; RMC. Served European War, 1914-18, France, Belgium, Germany, Scots Guards. Major, retired 1933. Served War of 1939-45, Scots Guards, East Africa, Italy. JP 1940, DL 1947, Banffshire. *Recreations:* fishing, shooting. *Heir: kinsman* Ian George Abercromby [*b* 30 June 1925; *m* 1st, 1950, Joyce Beryl (marr. diss.), *d* of Leonard Griffiths; 2nd, 1959, Fanny Mary, *o d* of Dr Graham Udale-Smith]. *Address:* Dunlugas, Turriff, Aberdeenshire. *Clubs:* Guards, Pratt's; Royal Northern (Aberdeen). [*Died 19 Oct.* 1972.

ABERDEEN and TEMAIR, 3rd Marquis of, *cr* 1916; **Dudley Gladstone Gordon**, DSO 1917; Viscount Formartine, Lord Haddo, Methlic, Tarves and Kellie, Earl of Aberdeen, 1682,

Peerage of Scotland; Viscount Gordon, 1814, and Earl of Haddo, 1916, Peerage of the United Kingdom; Baronet of Nova Scotia, 1642; Hon. LLD (Aberdeen); MIMechE; President: Hadfields Ltd (Chairman 1945-62, Director 1943); Allied Circle; Engineering Section British Association for the Advancement of Science, 1953; Institute of Refrigeration; The Bach Choir; *b* 6 May 1883; 2nd *s* of 1st Marquis of Aberdeen and Temair, KT, PC, GCMG, GCVO; *S* brother, 1965; *m* 1st, 1907, Cécile Elizabeth (*d* 1948), *d* of George Drummond, Swaylands, Penshurst, Kent; three *s* (and one killed in action) one *d*; 2nd, 1949, Margaret Gladys, ARRC, JP, Member East Grinstead UDC, 1947-62 (Chm. 1953, 1960), *d* of late Lieutenant-Colonel R. G. Munn, CMG, East Grinstead. *Educ:* Cargilfield; Harrow. After leaving Harrow served apprenticeship in Hall, Russell & Co.'s shipbuilding yard at Aberdeen, and afterwards to W. H. Allen, Son & Co., engineers, Bedford; joined J. & E. Hall, Ltd, 1907; Past President: British Iron & Steel Research Association; Hall Thermotank Ltd; British Assoc. of Refrigeration; British Engineers Assoc.; FBI; President: Instn of Mech. Engrs Centenary (1847-1947), 1947-48; Highland Society of London, 1955-58. Formerly: Director of British Overseas Fairs; Director, Industrial and Commercial Finance Corp.; Mem. Exec. Cttee British Iron and Steel Federation; Chairman J. & E. Hall Ltd, Engineers, Dartford, 1936-60; Director: Phœnix Assurance Co. Ltd, 1942-59; Barclays Bank, 1943-58; Governor of Harrow School, 1950-65. Hon. Member, Amer. Soc. of Mech. Engrs. Captain 2nd VB Gordon Hldrs, 1902-5; served European War, 1914-18 (DSO); Lieut-Col Comdg 8/10th Bn Gordon Highlanders. Chm., Dartford Urban District Coun., 1924. *Recreations:* choral singing, swimming, golf, shooting. *Heir: s* Earl of Haddo. *Address:* Bullards, East Grinstead, Sussex. *T:* 25446. *Clubs:* Bath, Allied Circle (Pres.); Royal & Ancient Golf, Royal St George's Golf, Royal Ashdown Forest Golf (Pres.). [*Died 16 April* 1972.

ABERDEEN AND TEMAIR, 4th Marquess of, *cr* 1916; **David George Ian Alexander Gordon**, CBE 1963; TD 1946; JP; Bt of Nova Scotia, 1642; Viscount Formatine, Lord Haddo, Methlic, Tarves and Kellie, Earl of Aberdeen, 1682, Peerage of Scotland; Viscount Gordon, 1814, and Earl of Haddo, 1916, Peerage of UK; Lord Lieutenant of Aberdeenshire, since 1973; County Councillor, Aberdeenshire, since 1961, Chairman, Education Committee, since 1970; managing family estate since 1944; *b* 21 Jan. 1908; *e s* of 3rd Marquis of Aberdeen and Temair, DSO, and Cécile Elizabeth (*d* 1948), *d* of George Drummond, Swaylands, Penshurst, Kent; *S* father, 1972; *m* 1939, Beatrice Mary June, MBE, DL, *d* of A. P. Boissier, sometime Headmaster of Harrow Sch.; two adopted *s* two adopted *d*. *Educ:* Harrow; Balliol, Oxford (MA). Chartered Land Agent, 1932; Fellow Chartered Land Agents Soc., 1946-69, FRICS 1969-. Land Agent: to Major W. R. D. Mackenzie, at Fawley Court, Henley-on-Thames and at Carradale, Argyll, 1932-38; to Earl of Derby, at Knowsley, 1938-39; to Lord Aberdeen (transferred Family Estate of Haddo House), Aberdeenshire, 1944. Landowner managing own property, 1944-. Local Dir, Clydesdale Bank, 1968-. DL 1949, JP 1955, Vice-Lieutenant, 1959-73, Aberdeenshire. Brig., Queen's Body Guard for Scotland (Royal Company of Archers), 1971. Chm. County of Aberdeen TAA, 1963-68; Convenor of Scottish Landowners Fedn, 1962-66, Vice-Pres., 1967; Pres. East Aberdeenshire Unionist Assoc., 1959-63; Chm. of various cttees. President: British Assoc. of Experiment in Internat. Living, 1964-; Royal Scottish Agric. Benevolent Instn, 1965-70; Reginald Jacques Orchestra, 1970-. Lay Mem., Provincial Synod. Governor, Robert Gordon's Colls and Inst. Patron, Camphill Village Trust. Served War of 1939-45; 5th Gordons, BEF, 1940 (despatches); 9th Gordons and 2nd London Scottish, Bde Major, 1940-43 (Home Stations); Staff Officer to Provost Marshal, MEF, 1943-45. KStJ, 1964; Prior, Order of St John in Scotland, 1970. *Recreations:* Rugby football (OU Greyhounds RFC, German tour 1930; London Scottish RFC, 1st XV, 1932-38, Captain 1938; Kent RFC, 1933-38; Scottish Trials, 1934-35; Oxfordshire RFC, Captain 1934-38), cricket, swimming, walking, music, model railways. *Heir: b* Lord Archibald Victor Dudley Gordon, *b* 9 July 1913. *Address:* Haddo House, Aberdeenshire. *T:* Tarves 216 and 664. *Clubs:* Bath, MCC; New (Edinburgh); Royal Northern (Aberdeen). [*Died 13 Sept.* 1974.

ABERNETHY, James Smart; *b* 3 Oct. 1907; *s* of J. J. Abernethy, JP, Balmain, Fettercairn; *m* 1st, 1936, Winifred M. J. Marr (*d* 1960); two *d*; 2nd, 1960, Margaret P. Campbell; one *s*. *Educ:* Private Prep. Sch.; Sedbergh, Yorks; Aberdeen Grammar Sch.; Aberdeen and Edinburgh Univs. MA, LLB Aberdeen; WS. Interim Procurator-Fiscal, Portree, 1934; in private practice, Montrose, 1934-36; Legal Adviser, Commissioner of Lands and Protector of Labour, North Borneo (Chartered Co.), 1936; Food Controller, North Borneo, 1941; captured and interned by

Japanese, after 8 months as a fugitive, Sept. 1942, released Sept. 1945; British Military Administration, British Borneo, 1946; actg Attorney-General, 1946, Commissioner of Lands, 1947, Circuit Magistrate and Sessions Judge, 1948, Colony of N Borneo; Resident Magistrate, Tanganyika, 1949; Puisne Judge, Tanganyika Territory, 1951-58; retired. In South Africa and Australia, 1958-61; Town Clerk: Tanga, Tanganyika, 1961-63; Thurso, Caithness, 1963-65; Registrar and Legal Officer, Lands and Surveys Dept, Sarawak, 1965-71, retired. *Recreations:* gardening, cooking. *Address:* Spey Villa, Kingston Fochabers, Moray.   [*Died 25 May 1976.*

ABRAHALL, Sir T. C. H.; *see* Hoskyns-Abrahall.

ABRAHAM, Maj.-Gen. Sir William (Ernest Victor), Kt 1977; CBE 1942; FGS; Lay Member of Restrictive Practices Court, 1961-70, retired; *b* 21 Aug. 1897; *s* of John and Frances Abraham, Enniskillen; *m* 1928, Susan Jeanete Bidwell (*d* 1965), Kinsley, Kansas, USA; one *s* two *d*; *m* 1966, Rosemary Eustace, *d* of Louis H. King, Berrow, Somerset. *Educ:* Methodist Coll., Belfast; Royal Coll. of Science, Dublin. In Burma and India as Geologist, 1920-37. Commanded Upper Burma Bn, Burma Auxiliary Force, 1932-37; rejoined army, 1940, as 2nd Lieut and rose to rank of Major-General, after service in Greece, Middle East (OBE, despatches twice), Burma, Tunisia (CBE), Sicily; Controller General of Mil. Economy, India, 1945. Formerly Managing Director of Burmah Oil Co. Ltd, retd 1955. National Chm., Burma Star Assoc., 1962-77. *Recreations:* until 1967, polo and foxhunting. *Address:* Kencot Manor, Lechlade, Glos GL7 3QU. *T:* Filkins 212. *Clubs:* East India, Devonshire, Sports and Public Schools, Royal Automobile.   [*Died 6 Feb. 1980.*

ABRAHAMS, Gerald; barrister, author, occasional lecturer; *b* 15 April 1907; *s* of Harry and Leah Abrahams; *m* 1971, Elsie Krengel. *Educ:* Liverpool Collegiate Sch.; Wadham Coll., Oxford (Schol., MA). 1st cl. hons PPE, 1928; called to Bar, Gray's Inn, 1931. WEA Lectr, 1930-33; temp. Actg Prof. of Law, Belfast, 1934; lectures to HM Forces, 1940-44. Contested (L) Hallam Div. of Sheffield, 1945. Occasional broadcasts, law, chess, etc; sometime Chess Champion of Oxford Univ., Oxfordshire, Liverpool, Manchester, Lancs, N of England; some internat. chess. *Publications:* Law Affecting Police and Public, 1938; Law Relating to Hire Purchase, 1939; Ugly Angel (fiction), 1940; Retribution, 1941; Day of Reckoning, 1943; World Turns Left, 1943; Conscience Makes Heroes (fiction), 1945; Teach Yourself Chess, 1948; The Chess Mind, 1951; Lunatics and Lawyers (fiction), 1951; The Legal Mind, 1954; La Mediocrazia Contemporanea, 1956; Lo Stato Come Societa Commerciale: e la Irresponsibilita dei Ministri, 1957; Law for Writers and Journalists, 1958; According to the Evidence, 1958; The Jewish Mind, 1961; Technique in Chess, 1961 (trans. Spanish 1965); Brains in Bridge, 1962; Test Your Chess, 1963; Police Questioning: The Judges' Rules, 1964; Pan Book of Chess, 1965; Handbook of Chess, 1965; Let's Look at Israel, 1966; Trade Unions and the Law, 1968; Morality and the Law, 1971; Not only Chess, 1974; Brilliance in Chess, 1977; contrib. Encycl. Judaica, Philosophy, Nat. Review, Courier, Jewish Chronicle, Brit. Chess Magazine, etc. *Recreations:* philosophy, languages, chess, bridge, music, Bible. *Address:* 223 Woolton Road, Liverpool L16 8NA. *T:* 051-722 7712; 21 North John Street, Liverpool L2 5QU. *T:* 051-236 0718; 3 King's Bench Walk, Temple, EC4Y 7DQ. *T:* 01-236 1184. *Club:* Authors'.   [*Died 15 March 1980.*

ABRAHAMS, Harold Maurice, CBE 1957; MA, LLB; Secretary of National Parks Commission, 1950-63; *b* 15 December 1899; *s* of late Isaac Abrahams; *m* 1936, Sybil Marjorie (*d* 1963), *er d* of late C. P. Evers; one adopted *s* one adopted *d. Educ:* Repton; Gonville and Caius Coll., Cambridge. Hons Law Tripos, Cambridge, 1923; called to Bar, 1924; Ministry of Economic Warfare, 1939, Head of Statistics Section, 1941-42; Temp. Asst Sec., 1942-44; Assistant Secretary, Ministry of Town and Country Planning, 1946. Pres. Cambridge Univ. Athletic Club, 1922-23; represented Cambridge against Oxford, 1920-23, winning eight events in all; represented Great Britain in the Olympic Games, 1920 and 1924, winner 100 metres 1924; Captain British Athletic Team Olympic Games, 1928; Mem., Gen. Cttee of Amateur Athletic Assoc., 1926- (Vice-Pres., 1948; Life Vice-Pres., 1958; Pres., 1976); British Amateur Athletic Board: Asst Hon. Sec., 1939-48; Hon. Treas., 1948-68; Chm., 1968-75; 1st Life Vice-Pres., 1975. Hon. Pres., World Assoc. of Track and Field Statisticians, 1950; Athletics Corresp. Sunday Times, 1925-67; first broadcast, on radio, March 1924, on television, 1939. JP Essex, 1956-63. *Publications:* Sprinting, 1925; Athletics, 1926; Training for Athletics (with late A. Abrahams and others), 1928; Oxford *v* Cambridge (with late J. Bruce Kerr), 1931; Training for Health and Athletics (with late A. Abrahams), 1936; Official Records of 1928 and 1936

Olympic Games; Track and Field Olympic Records, 1948; The Olympic Games, 1896-1952, 1956; Empire and Commonwealth Games, 1930-58, 1958; The Rome Olympiad, 1960; Athletics Sportsgraph, 1972. *Recreations:* photography, statistics. *Address:* 42 Orpington Road, N21. *T:* 01-886 6472. *Clubs:* Achilles (Chm., 1947-61), Garrick; Cambridge University Pitt.
                                    [*Died 14 Jan. 1978.*

ACHARD, Marcel; Commandeur de la Légion d'Honneur; dramatic author; Member of the French Academy since 1959; *b* 5 July 1899; *m* 1925, Juliette Marty. Awarded Prix de l'Humour français, 1924. *Publications:* La Messe est dite, 1922; Voulez-vous jouer avec Moâ, 1923; La Femme silencieuse, 1925; Malborough s'en va t'en guerre, 1926; Je ne vous aime pas, 1926; La Vie est belle, 1928; Jean de la Lune, 1929; La Belle Marinière, 1929; Mistigri, 1930; Domino, 1931; La Femme en blanc, 1932; Petrus, 1935; Le Corsaire, 1938; Adam, 1939; Mademoiselle de Panama, 1942; Colinette, 1947; Auprès de ma blonde, 1948; Nous irons à Valparaiso, 1948; La Demoiselle de petite vertu, 1949; Le Moulin de la Galette, 1951; Les Compagnons de la Marjolaine, 1953; Le Mal d'amour, 1955; Patate, 1957; La Bagatelle, 1959; L'Idiote, 1961; Noix de Coco, 1961; La Polka des Lampions, 1962; Turlututu, 1962; Eugène le Mystérieux, 1964; Machin Chouette, 1964; Gugusse, 1968; La Débauche, 1972; the scenarios of 73 films. *Address:* 8 rue de Courty, Paris 7, France.   [*Died 5 Sept. 1974.*

ACHEAMPONG, Ignatius Kutu, CSG 1976; *b* Kumasi, 23 Sept. 1931; *m*; seven *c. Educ:* St Peter's Catholic Sch., Kumasi; Ejisu Roman Catholic Sch.; Central Coll. of Commerce, Agona Swedru (GCE); Mons Officer Cadet Sch., Great Britain; Gen. Staff College, Fort Leavenworth, USA. Has been manual worker, teacher and secretary; Principal, Western Commercial Inst., Achiase, 1951. Enlisted in Army, Ghana, 1953; commissioned in Army, Ghana, 1959; served in the Congo, 1960 and 1962-63 (despatches). Became Chm., West Region Cttee of Admin, and Bde Comdr, 1st Infty Bde Group, Accra. General (Head of State) and Chm., Supreme Military Council, Ghana, 1972-78; Chm., Nat. Redemption Council, and Comr for Defence and Sports, 1972-78.   [*Died 15 June 1979.*

ACHESON, Dean; lawyer, United States of America; *b* 11 April 1893; *s* of Edward Campion Acheson and Eleanor Gooderham; *m* 1917, Alice Stanley; one *s* two *d. Educ:* Groton; Yale (AB 1915); Harvard Law School (LLB 1918). Hon. MA, Yale, 1936; Hon. LLD: Wesleyan Univ., 1947; Harvard, 1950; Cambridge, 1958; Yale, 1962; Johns Hopkins, 1963; Hon. DCL: Oxford, 1952; Michigan, 1967; Hon. LHD, Brandeis Univ., 1956. Private Sec. to Associate Justice Brandeis of US Supreme Court, 1919-21; with law firm Covington, Burling and Rublee, 1921-33; Under-Sec. of Treasury, 1933; Covington, Burling and Rublee, since Jan. 1953; Assistant Sec. of State, 1941-45, Under-Secretary of State, 1945-47, Secretary of State, 1949-Jan. 1953, USA. *Publications:* An American Vista, 1956; A Citizen Looks at Congress, 1957; Power and Diplomacy, 1958; Sketches from Life of Men I Have Known, 1961; Morning and Noon, 1967; Present at the Creation: My Years in the State Department, 1969. *Address:* 2805 P Street, Washington, DC, USA. *Clubs:* Metropolitan (Washington); Century (NYC).
                                    [*Died 12 Oct. 1971.*

ACHESON, Sir James Glasgow, Kt 1945; CIE 1929; ICS (retired); fruit farming, since 1948; *b* 1889; *s* of John Acheson, JP, Portadown, County Armagh; *m* 1917, Violet Catharine French, K-i-H Gold Medal, *d* of Lieut-Col C. W. Field, IA; one *s* one *d* (and one *s* one *d* decd). *Educ:* St Andrew's College and Trinity College, Dublin. BA. Entered ICS, 1913; Political Service, 1917; UP, 1913; Baluchistan, 1917; Anglo-Afghan Conference, 1920; British Mission to Kabul, 1921; Deputy Secretary to Government of India in the Foreign Department, 1927-29 (officiated as Foreign Secretary, 1928, 1931, and 1935); Imperial Defence College, 1929-30; Deputy Commissioner, Peshawar, 1932-34; Resident in Waziristan, 1935-37; Political Resident on the North West Frontier, 1937-39; Revenue and Judicial Commissioner in Baluchistan, 1939-42; Resident in Kashmir, 1943-45; retired from ICS 1945; Control Commission for Germany, Schleswig-Holstein, 1946-48. *Recreations:* fishing, chess. *Address:* Holly Bush House, Much Birch, Hereford. *T:* Wormelow 260.   [*Died 5 Oct. 1973.*

ACKNER, Conrad A.; Knight Commander of Order of St Olav (Norway); Commander of the Crown of Rumania; Mag. Pharm., Vienna, 1902; PhD (Pharmocol), Bern, 1904; LDS, RCS, England (Guy's), 1912; Dental Surgeon to late Queen Maud of Norway and to the late Princess Louise, Duchess of Argyll; naturalised British subject; *m* 1956, Mrs V. Lewis; four *s* by previous marriage. *Educ:* Vienna. Late Dental Radiographer,

Guy's Hosp.; Post-Graduate: Bacteriology, Zürich; Berlin Univ. Hosp. in Radiology and Surgery of the Jaws; Member; BDA; Fédération Dentaire Internationale. FRSocMed. *Publications:* X-Ray Observations on Abscesses, Cysts and Root Resections, 6th International Dental Congress, 1914; A Maxillary Splint, Lancet and Dental Record, 1915. *Recreations:* golf, motoring, photography, and collection of old ivories. *Address:* Yew Tree House, Jordans, Bucks. *Clubs:* Beaconsfield Golf; Wentworth.
                                                                                [Died 24 March 1976.

ACKROYD, Sir Cuthbert (Lowell), 1st Bt, *cr* 1956, of Dewsbury, Co. York; DL; Alderman (Cordwainer Ward) and JP City of London, 1945-70; one of HM Lieutenants for City of London, 1945-70; Commissioner of Assize, City of London, 1945-70; retired; *b* 1892; *y s* of Benjamin Batley Ackroyd and Emily Armitage, Dewsbury, Yorks; *m* 1927, Joyce Wallace Whyte, MA (Cantab); two *s. Educ:* Dewsbury; Univ. of London. Served European War, 1914-19, Hon. Captain RA; HG, 1940-44 and on Advisory Council Eastern Command Welfare of Troops, 1939-44; Veteran, Hon. Artillery Company. Member Corporation of London, 1940-70; Chm. Guildhall Library Cttee and Art Gallery, 1945; Sheriff, City of London, 1945-50; Lord Mayor of London, 1955-56. Underwriting Mem. of Lloyd's; Chm., Licensing Sessions, City of London, 1957-62; Vice-President Victoria League (Chairman, 1958-62); Hon. Treasurer UNICEF, British Section, 1956-59. Visiting Magistrate Holloway Prison, 1945-55. Governor and Almoner, Christ's Hosp. (Blue Coat School), 1945-69; Governor: Charing Cross Hospital; Hospital for Incurables, Putney; Hospital for Sick Children, 1934-47; Royal Hospitals, 1945-48; Royal Bridewell Hospital; Royal Society for Deaf and Dumb; National Corporation for Care of Old People, 1954-63; Trustee: Morden College; Sir John Soane's Museum, 1959-64; Pres., Metropolitan Institute for the Blind; Bromley Churchill Homes for the Aged. Church Commissioner for England, 1947-63; Church Warden Bow Church (Bow Bells); President, Nat. Brotherhood Movement (Inc.), 1947-48; Vice-Pres., British and Foreign Bible Soc.; Vice-Pres., Boys' Brigade; Pres., Nat. Sunday School Union, 1954; Governor: Royal Coll. of Art; RNLBI; The Hon. Irish Society, 1964-67. FRSA; Mem., The Pilgrims of Gt Britain. Past Grand Warden, United Grand Lodge of England; Pres., Ward of Cordwainer Club, 1945-70; Master, Worshipful Co. of Carpenters, 1952-53; Hon. Freeman, Worshipful Co. of Woolmen; Freeman: City of Belfast; City of Washington, USA; Richmond, Virginia. Hon. Colonel 290 Field Regt RA, 1956-. Hon. LLD Leeds University. DL Kent, 1962; High Sheriff of Kent, 1964; Charter Mayor, Greater London Coun. Borough of Bromley (19), 1964. Comdr Royal Order Orange-Nassau; Officer Legion of Honour; Knight Grand Cross Order of El Rafidain, 1st Class, Iraq; 5 Star Bronze Medal, New York City; Grand Officer Order of Merit, Italy. KStJ. *Recreations:* cricket, literature, pictures. *Heir: s* John Robert Whyte Ackroyd [*b* 2 March 1932; *m* 1956, Jennifer, *d* of H. G. S. Bishop; two *s* two *d*]. *Address:* 48 Bow Lane, Cheapside, EC4; Finches, Bromley, Kent. *T:* 01-460 1443. *Clubs:* Athenæum, City Livery, Eccentric.
                                                                                [Died 11 April 1973.

ACLAND, Lieut.-Gen. Arthur N. F.; *see* Floyer-Acland.

ACLAND, Captain Sir Hubert (Guy Dyke), 4th Bt *cr* 1890; DSO 1920; RN; *b* 8 June 1890; *y s* of Sir William Alison Dyke Acland, 2nd Bt; *S* brother, 1970; *m* 1915, Lalage Mary Kathleen (*d* 1961), *e d* of Captain John Edward Acland; two *s.* Lieutenant 1910; Lieutenant Commander, 1918; Commander, 1925; Captain 1932; served European War, 1914-19 (despatches, DSO); commanded 1st Minesweeping Flotilla, 1934-35 and Fishery Protection and Minesweeping Flotilla, 1935-36; lent to Royal Australian Navy, 1937-38, and commanded HMAS Australia, 1937-38 and HMAS Albatross, 1938; Senior Officer of Reserve Fleet, Devonport, 1939; Gunnery School, Chatham, Nov. 1939; commanded HMS Vindictive, 1941-42; retired list, 1942; on staff of C-in-C Rosyth, 1943 and of Flag Officer in Charge N Ireland, 1943-45. *Heir: s* Antony Guy Acland [*b* 17 Aug. 1916; *m* 1st, 1939, Avriel Ann (*d* 1943), *o c* of late Captain Mervyn Edward John Wingfield-Stratford; one *d*; 2nd, 1944, Margaret Joan, *er d* of late Major Nelson Rooke; one *s* one *d*]. *Address:* c/o Sunny Bank, Totland Bay, Isle of Wight.
                                                                                [Died 6 May 1978.

ACTON, Dame (Ellen) Marian, DBE 1951 (CBE 1920; OBE 1918); Deputy Controller from 1921, Comptroller, 1936-63, Forces Help Society and Lord Roberts Workshops: retd Sept. 1963. Formerly Member: Central Adv. Cttee to Ministry of Pensions and National Insurance; Ministry of Labour National Advisory Council on the Employment of the Disabled until 1965. *Address:* c/o Barclays Bank, 137 Brompton Road, SW3.
                                                                                [Died 9 April 1971.

ACTON, Harry Burrows; Professor of Moral Philosophy, University of Edinburgh, since 1964; *b* 2 June 1908; *s* of Henry James Acton and Elizabeth Jane (*née* Burrows); *m* 1938, Barbara James; no *c. Educ:* St Olave's Grammar School, London; Magdalen Coll., Oxford. 1st Cl. Hons PPE 1930; DPhil (Oxon) 1935. Demy, 1927, Senior Demy 1930, Magdalen Coll., Oxford. Asst Lectr in Philosophy, Univ. Coll. of Swansea, 1931; Lectr in Philosophy, Bedford Coll., 1935; Min. of Supply, 1940-45; Prof. of Philosophy, Bedford Coll., Univ. of London, 1945-64. Visiting Professor of Philosophy, University of Chicago, 1949; President, Aristotelian Soc., 1952-53; Editor, Philosophy, 1956-72. Gave Dawes Hicks Lecture, 1959, Comte Meml Lecture, 1973. director, Royal Inst. of Philosophy, 1962-64. *Publications:* The Illusion of the Epoch: Marxism-Leninism as a Philosophical Creed, 1955; What Marx Really Said, 1967; (ed) The Philosophy of Punishment, 1969; Kant's Moral Philosophy, 1970; The Morals of Markets: an ethical exploration, 1971; articles and reviews in Mind, Philosophy, Proc. Aristotelian Soc., etc. *Address:* 5 Abbotsford Park, Edinburgh 10. *T:* 031-447 4026. *Club:* Reform.
                                                                                [Died 16 June 1974.

ACTON, Dame Marian; *see* Acton, Dame E. M.

ACTON, Murray A.; *see* Adams-Acton.

ACTON, Maj.-Gen. Thomas Heward, CBE 1963 (OBE 1957); *b* 12 June 1917; *s* of Lt-Col W. M. Acton, DSO. *Educ:* Eton; RMA Sandhurst. Commissioned Rifle Brigade, 1937; served War of 1939-45 (despatches); Mil. Asst to Governor of Cyprus, 1955-57; Lt-Col, King's Royal Rifle Corps, 1959; Maj.-Gen. 1967; GOC SW District, 1967-70; Dep. Comdr Army in N Ireland, 1970; C of S and Dep. Dir of Operations, NI, 1970-71; retired 1971. *Recreations:* fishing, shooting. *Address:* Gorse Farm, Liverton, S Devon. *Club:* Naval and Military.
                                                                                [Died 22 Jan. 1977.

ADAIR, Gilbert Smithson, FRS 1939; MA; Reader in Biophysics, Physiological Laboratory, Cambridge, 1947-63; *b* 21 Sept. 1896; *s* of Harold Adair, JP; *m* 1931, Muriel Elaine Robinson (*d* 1975); no *c. Educ:* Bootham School, York; King's College, Cambridge. Scholar and Fellow of King's College, Cambridge; Hon. Fellow, 1963; engaged in research on thermodynamical properties of proteins. *Publications:* papers in scientific periodicals. *Address:* 92 Grantchester Meadows, Cambridge. *Club:* Fell and Rock Climbing.
                                                                                [Died 22 June 1979.

ADAM, Captain Charles Keith, DSO 1942; RN (retired); *b* Perth, West Australia, 29 April 1891; 2nd *s* of William Keith Adam and Jane Emily Leake; *m* 1939, Barbara Eunice, *y d* of Maj.-Gen. A. H. Marindin and Gertrude Florence Evelyn Wilmot-Chetwode, Fordel, Glenfarg; one *s* three *d. Educ:* RN Colleges Osborne and Dartmouth. Naval Cadet, 1903; Sub-Lieut, 1911; served European War, 1914-19; commanded destroyers, 1916-19; Brit. Mil. Mission, S. Russia, 1919-20; retd list, rank of Comdr, 1934; Colombian Navy (Capitan di Navio), 1934-37; recalled to RN (staff), 1939; served War of 1939-46, in command: HMS Rion, 1941; HMS Ulster Queen, 1942-43 (DSO); HMS Beachy Head, 1945; HMS Caradoc, 1945; Captain (actg), 1942; Captain, 1946. Convener, Kinross-shire County Council, 1954-60. Mem. of Queen's Body Guard for Scotland (Royal Company of Archers), 1941. JP Kinross-shire, 1937; Lord Lieutenant of County of Kinross, 1955-56. Order of St Anne of Russia, 3rd Class, 1920; Cross of Boyaca (Colombia), 1936. *Recreations:* shooting, fishing, golf. *Address:* Blair Adam, Kinross-shire. *T:* Kelty 239. *Clubs:* Naval and Military; New (Edinburgh).
                                                                                [Died 14 Dec. 1971.

ADAM, Kenneth, CBE 1962; MA; FRSA; Overseas Visitor to Temple University, Philadelphia, since 1969; *b* 1 March 1908; *s* of Edward Percy Adam and Ethel Jane Saunders; *m* 1932, Ruth Augusta King (*d* 1977); three *s* one *d. Educ:* Nottingham High Sch.; St John's Coll., Cambridge (Senior Scholar and Prizeman). Editorial Staff, Manchester Guardian, 1930-34; Home News Editor, BBC, 1934-36; Special Corresp. of The Star, 1936-40; Press Officer, BOAC, 1940-41; Dir of BBC Publicity, 1941-50; Controller, Light Programme, BBC, 1950-55; Gen. Manager (Joint), Hulton Press, 1955-57; Controller of Television Programmes, BBC, 1957-61; Dir of BBC Television, 1961-68. Vis. Prof. of Communications, Temple Univ., Philadelphia, 1968-; Danforth Travelling Fellow, USA, 1970, 1971. Communicating Editor, Jl of Communication Studies, USA, 1974. Chm., NZ Commission on Broadcasting, 1973; Mem., Exec. Cttee, Standing Conference on Broadcasting, UK, 1973. Governor, Charing Cross Hosp., 1960-66; Governor, British Film Inst., 1961; Member: (co-opted), Extra Mural Delegacy, Oxford, 1962; London Topographical Soc., 1962; Brit. Travel Assoc. Council, 1966; Council of Industrial Design, 1967; Council, Nat. Youth Theatre, 1967; Council, Tavistock Inst., 1968; Internat. Broadcasting Inst., 1975. Hon. Mem., Anglo-

Danish Soc., 1952-. FAMS 1962. *Address:* 19 Old Court House, W8 4PD. *T:* 01-937 0369; Tomlinson Hall, Temple University, Philadelphia, Pa 19122, USA. *T:* (215) 787-8421. *Clubs:* Caledonian; Union Society (Cambridge); Diamond (Philadelphia). *[Died* 18 *Oct.* 1978.

ADAM, Neil Kensington, FRS 1935; FRIC; MA, ScD (Cantab); Emeritus Professor of Chemistry, University of Southampton (Professor, 1937-57); formerly Lecturer and Hon. Research Associate, University College, London; *s* of James Adam, MA, LittD and Adela Marion Adam, MA; *m* 1916, Winifred Wright; one *s* one *d. Educ:* Winchester; Trinity College, Cambridge (Fellow, 1915-23). Royal Society Sorby Research Fellow at Sheffield University, 1921-29. *Publications:* The Physics and Chemistry of Surfaces; Physical Chemistry; numerous papers in scientific periodicals. *Recreations:* camping, sailing, ducks. *Address:* 95 Highfield Lane, Southampton SO2 1NN. *Club:* Athenæum. *[Died* 19 *July* 1973.

ADAMS, Captain Bryan Fullerton, DSO 1919; Royal Navy, retired; *b* 22 July 1887; *s* of late G. H. Adams, Portglenone, Co. Down, and Melbourne, Australia; *m* 1st, 1921, Audrey (*d* 1929), *d* of C. E. Marshall, Thurlestone, Devon; one *d*; 2nd, 1937, Pamela Jocelyne, *o d* of late Vice-Adm. Sidney Drury-Lowe, CMG; one *d. Educ:* Sherborne; HMS Britannia. Served European War, 1914-18 (despatches, DSO); Comdr, 1918; retired list, 1933. *Recreation:* gardening. *Address:* Cherry Tree, Hacheston, Suffolk. *Clubs:* United Service and Royal Aero, MCC. *[Died* 22 *Sept.* 1971.

ADAMS, Charles Kingsley, CBE 1954; FSA; Director, Keeper and Secretary of the National Portrait Gallery, 1951-64, retd; *b* 17 June 1899; *s* of late Albert Edward Adams; *m* 1927, Lily Eva Brewer; one *s* two *d. Educ:* King's School, Worcester. Served European War, Temp. 2nd Lieut, E Surrey Regt, 1918-19. Assistant Keeper, National Portrait Gallery, 1919-51. Chairman: National Loan Collection Trust, 1953-; Exec. Cttee, Soc. of Genealogists, 1964-68. *Publications:* compiled Catalogue of Pictures in the Garrick Club, 1936; edited Catalogue of Pictures in the Collection of the Duke of Portland, 1936. *Address:* 9 St Mary Abbots Terrace, W14. *T:* 01-602 3726. *Club:* Athenæum. *[Died* 19 *Jan.* 1971.

ADAMS, Sir Ernest (Charles), Kt 1949; CBE 1945 (MBE 1935); *b* 5 May 1886; *s* of William D. Adams; *m* 1911, Agnes S. Fortune (*d* 1965); one *d. Educ:* Roan Sch., Greenwich. Inland Revenue Dept, 1905; Customs and Excise, 1909; Min. of Pensions, 1919; Export Credits Guarantee Dept, 1928; Comptroller General, Export Credits Guarantee Dept, 1946-49. *Address:* Cleevers, Ham Lane, Shepton Mallet, Somerset. *T:* Shepton Mallet 2646. *[Died* 4 *Aug.* 1974.

ADAMS, Hon. Sir Francis Boyd, Kt 1961; retired as Judge of Supreme Court of New Zealand (1950-60); *b* 25 Nov. 1888; *s* of Hon. Alexander Samuel Adams, Supreme Court Judge; *m* 1st, 1917, Olive Evelyn (*née* Chandler) (*d* 1950); four *d*; 2nd, 1960, Joyce Ellen Gilbert (*née* Terry), Sydney. *Educ:* Otago Boys' High School, Dunedin; Victoria University College, Wellington; University of Otago, Dunedin. BA, LLM. Admitted to Bar, 1911. Served European War, 1914-18, in 1st New Zealand Expeditionary Force, 1916-19 (wounded, 1918). Home Service in War of 1939-45, to rank of Lieut-Colonel. Crown Solicitor and Crown Prosecutor at Dunedin, NZ, 1921-50; occasional service as a Judge of Fiji Court of Appeal, 1960-67. *Publications:* Consulting Editor, Adams' Criminal Law and Practice in NZ, Editor, 2nd edn, 1972; Criminal Onus and Exculpations, 1968; contribs to law jls. *Recreation:* bowls. *Address:* 27 Makora Street, Christchurch 4, New Zealand. *T:* 517-217. *[Died* 24 *April* 1974.

ADAMS, Sir Grantley Herbert, Kt 1957; CMG 1952; QC (Barbados) 1953; *b* 28 April 1898; *s* of Fitzherbert Adams; *m* Grace Thorne; one *s. Educ:* Harrison Coll., Barbados; Oxford University. Called to the Bar, Gray's Inn, 1923. Premier of Barbados, 1954-58; Prime Minister of the West Indies, 1958-62. Formerly: Leader of the House of Assembly and Member of the Executive Committee, Barbados, British West Indies; Mem., Colonial Parlt, 1934-54. Mem., ILO Cttee of Experts, 1949-. Hon. DLitt Mount Allison 1958. *Recreations:* cricket (Barbados XI), gardening. *Address:* Codrington Hill, St Michael, Barbados. *[Died* 28 *Nov.* 1971.

ADAMS, (Harold) Richard; Management Consultant, since 1938; *b* 8 Oct. 1912; *s* of late A. Adams; *m* 1938, Joyce Love (marr. diss. 1955); two *d*; *m* 1956, P. Fribbins; one *s. Educ:* elementary; Emanuel School; London University; Middle Temple. Member Wandsworth Borough Council before War of 1939-45. Served War of 1939-45: joined East Surrey Regt, 1940; with 25 Army

Tank Bde in N Africa and Italy; later, Staff Officer Land Forces Adriatic. Experience as business consultant; one time Asst Comr for National Savings; Lectr in Economics. MP (Lab) Balham and Tooting Div. of Wandsworth, 1945-50, Central Div., 1950-55; Asst Whip (unpaid), 1947-49; a Lord Comr of the Treasury, 1949-51. FIS. Mem., Fabian Soc. *Recreations:* antiques, politics. *[Died* 25 *June* 1978.

ADAMS, Herbert Louis, CMG 1961; TD 1945; Appointments Officer, Overseas Development Administration, Foreign and Commonwealth Office; *b* 29 May 1910; *s* of late Herbert Adams, author, and Jessie Louise Cooper; *m* 1934, Margherita Anna Henley Wareing; one *d. Educ:* Haileybury College. 2nd Lieut, 24th London Regt (The Queen's) TA, 1929. Partner, Adams & Watts, Surveyors and Estate Agents, SW1, 1934-38. Military Service, 1938-45: Staff College, Camberley, War Course; Lt-Col, GSO1, 1945. Joined Colonial Service as Cadet, Kenya, 1946; Sec. for Commerce and Industry, 1949; Economic Sec., E Africa High Commn, 1954; Chief Administrative Secretary, 1958; Permanent Sec., Civil Aviation, E African Common Services Org., 1961-64; Appointments Officer, ODM, 1965. *Recreations:* photography, gardening. *Address:* Corner Cottage, Badlesmere, Faversham, Kent. *Clubs:* East India, Sports and Public Schools; Nairobi. *[Died* 19 *July* 1972.

ADAMS, Paul, CB 1971; TD; Chief Taxing Master of Supreme Court, 1954-72 (Master, 1950-54); *b* 16 March 1903; *s* of late Herbert Adams; *m* 1929, Joan Madeline Corfield; two *s. Educ:* Haileybury College. Admitted Solicitor, 1925; partner in firm of A. J. Adams & Adams, 1935. Lieut-Col TA; commanded, War of 1939-45: 1/7 Bn, then 15th Bn The Queen's Royal Regt; 2nd Bn, Lincolnshire Regt; 13th Infantry Bn Sudan Defence Force. Resumed Practice, Oct. 1945; partner in combined firms of Bridges Sawtell & Co. and A. J. Adams & Adams, 1946; Mem. Lord Chancellor's Advisory Cttee (Legal Aid and Advice Act, 1949), 1961-71; Chairman: MoD Cttee on pay etc of Officers of Army and RAF Legal Services, 1965; Lord Chancellor's Cttee on Civil Judicial Statistics, 1966-68; an Editor of Annual Practice, 1961-71, and Supreme Court Practice, 1967. *Recreations:* growing roses, fly-fishing. *Address:* The Croft, Tangmere, Sussex. *[Died* 10 *Dec.* 1972.

ADAMS, Richard; *see* Adams, (Harold) Richard.

ADAMS, Sydney, MA (Oxon); Headmaster, Bancroft's School, 1944-65, retired; *b* 13 Sept. 1905; *s* of A. S. and H. R. Adams; *m* 1933, Evelyn Mary Evanson; one *d. Educ:* City of Oxford School (Head of School); St John's College, Oxford (Scholar). 1st cl. Maths Mods, 1926; 2nd cl. Maths Finals, 1928; Diploma in Educn, Oxford, 1929. Sixth Form Maths Master: Aldenham, 1929-31; Sedbergh, 1931-44. *Recreations:* walking slowly, watching sport on TV. *Address:* Walden, 28 Roman Way, Glastonbury, Somerset. *T:* Glastonbury 31549
[Died 1 *Aug.* 1980.

ADAMS, Sir Walter, Kt 1970; CMG 1952; OBE 1945; Director, London School of Economics and Political Science, 1967-74, Honorary Fellow, 1975; Fellow, University College, London; *b* 16 Dec. 1906; *m* 1933, Tatiana Makaroff; three *s* one *d. Educ:* Brighton, Hove and Sussex Grammar School; University College, London. Lecturer in History, Univ. Coll., London, 1926-34; Rockefeller Fellow in USA, 1929-30; Organizing Sec., Second International Congress of the History of Science and Technology, 1931; Secretary: Academic Assistance Council, 1933-38; London School of Economics and Political Science, 1938-46. Dep. Head, British Political Warfare Mission, USA, 1942-44; Asst Dep. Director-General, Political Intelligence Dept, Foreign Office, 1945; Secretary, Inter-University Council for Higher Education in the Colonies, 1946-55; Principal, University College of Rhodesia and Nyasaland, 1955-67. Hon. LLD (Malta, Melbourne); Hon. DLit Rhodesia, 1975. *Publication:* (with H. W. Robinson) The Diary of Robert Hooke, 1672-80, 1935. *Address:* 17 Upper Strand Street, Sandwich, Kent. *T:* Sandwich 2339. *Club:* Athenæum. *[Died* 21 *May* 1975.

ADAMS-ACTON, Murray, FIRA, FIAL, FRSA; *b* 1886; godson of Mr and Mrs W. E. Gladstone; *s* of John Adams-Acton, sculptor, and Marion Hamilton, authoress; *m* Ailsa Stevenson (*d* 1955); one *d. Educ:* London, abroad. Authority on art and architecture; exhibited at RA; medal at Salon, 1926; elected to Heraldic and Historical Institute of France; Internat. Inst. of Arts and Letters; late Mem. Architectural Cttee, Royal Soc. of Arts; late Chm., Institute of British Decorators; Member of Committee, The Society for the Preservation of Ancient Cottages; donor of works of art to English and Canadian Museums, etc; held commission in Scots Guards during war. *Publications:* Domestic Architecture and Old Furniture; Portals and Doorways of France; contributor to all leading art journals, England and America, daily Press, etc. *Recreations:* horticulture, fishing, shooting. *Address:* 37 Palace Gate, W8; Beach House, Cooden Beach, Sussex. *Clubs:* Royal London Yacht, Pilgrim's, St John's Wood Arts.   [*Died* 30 *July* 1971.

ADAMS-BECK, John Melliar; Clerk and Solicitor of the Worshipful Company of Ironmongers 1946-72, Hon. Freeman, 1972, Liveryman, 1973; *b* 9 April 1909; *s* of late James Francis Adams Beck and Elsie (*née* Foster-Melliar); *m* 1st, 1939, Doris Elsie Neep (*d* 1966); two *s*; 2nd, 1968, Mrs Mary Elizabeth Helen Coates, widow of Captain Patrick Coates and *e d* of Comdr Sir John Best-Shaw, 9th Bt, RN retd, and of Elizabeth, *e d* of Sir Robert Hughes, 12th Bt. *Educ:* Shrewsbury Sch. Admitted Solicitor, 1932. Served War of 1939-45; joined Hon. Artillery Co., 1939; commissioned RA, 1940; India and Ceylon, 1942; demobilised with rank of Major 1945. Governor of the City and Diocese of London Voluntary Schs Fund, 1947-72; Trustee, City and Metropolitan Welfare Charity, 1968-76. Freeman of the City of London, 1969. *Publication:* The Ironmongers' Company: an historical note, 1954. *Recreations:* shooting, gardening. *Address:* Southfield, Charing, Kent. *T:* Charing 2252.   [*Died* 20 *Dec.* 1979.

ADAMSON, Joy-Friederike Victoria; painter since 1938, research on wild animals since 1956, and author since 1958; *b* 20 Jan. 1910; *d* of Victor and Traute Gessner; *m* 1st, 1935, Victor von Klarwill (Austrian); 2nd, 1938, Peter Bally (Swiss); 3rd, 1943, George Adamson (British). *Educ:* Vienna. Staatspruefung Piano, 1927; Diploma (Gremium) in dress-making, 1928; sculpting, 1929-30; metal work at Kunstgewerbe Schule, 1931-32; graduate course to study medicine, 1933-35; living in Kenya, 1937-; painted indigenous flora, Kenya, 1938-43, about 700 exhibited Nat. Museum, Nairobi; Gold Grenfell Medal, RHS, 1947 (London exhibn); illustrated seven books; painted tribes of Kenya, 1944-52; about 600 paintings in perm. exhbn, Nat. Museum, Nairobi, and State House, Nairobi; Exhibition of water-colours and drawings, Tryon Gall., 1972. Elsa Wild Animal Appeal, UK 1961, USA 1969, Canada 1971. Award for merit (silver medal) Czechoslovakia, 1970; Joseph Wood-Krutsh Medal, Humane Soc. USA, 1971; Cross of Honour for Science and Art, Austria, 1976. *Publications:* Born Free: a lioness of two worlds, 1960, 1964, new edn 1965 (filmed 1966); Elsa, 1961; Living Free, 1961, 1964 (filmed 1971); Forever Free, 1962, 1966 (filmed 1971); Elsa and Her Cubs, 1965; The Story of Elsa, 1966; The Peoples of Kenya, 1967; The Spotted Sphinx, 1969; Pippa and her Cubs, 1970 (filmed 1970); Joy Adamson's Africa, 1972; Pippa's Challenge, 1972; The Searching Spirit (autobiog.), 1978 (filmed as Joy Adamson, 1978); Queen of Shába, 1980; articles in Jl of RGS, Field, Country Life, Blackwood-Magazine, Geographical Jl, German Anthropolog. Jl, E African Annuals, Brit. Geographical Magazine, and in several popular magazines in England, USA and Austria. *Recreations:* riding, ski-ing, tennis, mountaineering, swimming, photography, sketching, painting, playing piano. *Address:* PO Box 60, Isiolo, Kenya. *Clubs:* Nanyuki, Nairobi.
[*Died* 3 *Jan.* 1980.

ADAMSON, Sir Kenneth Thomas, Kt 1968; CMG 1963; Specialist Orthodontic Practice since 1929; Senior Lecturer, Department of Orthodontics, Dental School, University of Melbourne, 1935-68; Hon. Consultant in Orthodontics, Dental Hospital of Melbourne, 1943-68, Hon. Consulting Orthodontist, since 1969; *b* 19 June 1904; *s* of late Thomas Cartwright Adamson, Melbourne; *m* 1932, Jean Isobel, *d* of Dr John Daniel King-Scott; one *s* two *d*. *Educ:* Wesley Coll., Melb.; Univ. of Melbourne. BDSc 1927; DDSc 1929. Hon. Dental Surgeon: Royal Melb. Hosp., 1927-29; Alfred Hosp., 1939-47; Royal Children's, 1927-53. Austr. Dental Assoc. (Victorian Br.): Pres., 1934-35; Vice-Pres., 1962-69; Federal Pres., Austr. Dental Assoc., 1954-60; President: Dental Bd of Victoria, 1964-66; Austr. Soc. of Orthodontists; Austr. Coll. of Dental Surgeons, 1969-70. Mem. Bd, Dental Hosp. of Melbourne. Fellow, Amer. Coll. of Dentists, 1952; FDSRCS 1957; Hon. Life Member: Amer. Dental Assoc., 1964; British Soc. of Orthodontists, 1969. *Publications:* numerous, 1927-62, in various dental jls throughout world. *Recreations:* golf, fishing, gardening. *Address:* 1/589a Toorak Road, Toorak, Victoria 3142, Australia. *T:* 24-2257. *Clubs:* Melbourne, Naval and Military, Frankston Golf (all in Melbourne).   [*Died* 19 *July* 1976.

ADDINGTON, 4th Baron, *cr* 1887; **Raymond Egerton Hubbard;** *b* 11 Nov. 1884; 2nd *s* of 2nd Baron Addington and Mary Adelaide (*d* 1933), *d* of Sir Wyndham S. Portal, 1st Bt; *S* brother, 1966; *m* 1926, Margaret Favre (*d* 1963), widow of Edward Marriott Gibson. *Educ:* Eton; Magdalen College, Oxford (BA). *Heir:* kinsman James Hubbard [*b* 3 Nov. 1930; *m* 1961, Alexandra Patricia, *yr d* of Norman Fordill Mar; two *s*

two *d*]. *Address:* House of Lords, Westminster, SW1; Lesmoyne Hotel, Fleet, Hampshire. *Club:* Bath.   [*Died* 17 *Aug.* 1971.

ADDINSELL, Richard Stewart; composer; *b* London, 13 Jan. 1904. *Educ:* privately; Hertford Coll., Oxford; Royal Coll. of Music. Spent four years in Berlin and Vienna. Contributed to Charlot's Revue, 1926; composed Adam's Opera, 1928. Has since written songs and incidental music for many stage productions including: The Good Companions, Alice in Wonderland, L'Aiglon, The Happy Hypocrite, Trespass, Ring Round the Moon, Penny Plain, Lyric Revue, Globe Revue, Airs on a Shoestring, Joyce Grenfell Requests the Pleasure; Living for Pleasure. Musical scores for films include: South Riding, Good-bye Mr Chips, The Lion Has Wings, Dangerous Moonlight (Warsaw Concerto), Love on the Dole, Blithe Spirit, The Passionate Friends, Under Capricorn, Tom Brown's Schooldays, The Prince and the Showgirl, A Tale of Two Cities, The Greengage Summer, The Roman Spring of Mrs Stone, The Waltz of the Toreadors, The War Lover. During War of 1939-45 wrote music for many documentary films. Also composes for radio and TV. *Address:* 1 Carlyle Mansions, Cheyne Walk, SW3.   [*Died* 14 *Nov.* 1977.

ADDIS, Sir William, KBE 1955; CMG 1948; MA; *b* 5 Sept. 1901; 3rd *s* of late Sir Charles Addis, KCMG, LLD, Woodside, Frant, Sussex; *m* 1929, Rosemary (*d* 1964), *d* of late Rev. R. T. Gardner; four *s*. *Educ:* Rugby; Magdalene College, Cambridge. Mechanical Science Tripos, 1923. Entered Colonial Administrative Service, 1924; served in Zanzibar and Northern Rhodesia; seconded to Dominions Office during 1933; Private Sec. to Sultan of Zanzibar, 1939-45. Served in Zanzibar Naval Volunteer Force, 1939-45. Colonial Secretary, Bermuda, 1945-50; acting Governor, Bermuda, during 1945 and 1946; Deputy Commissioner-General for Colonial Affairs, South-East Asia, 1950-53; Governor and Commander-in-Chief, Seychelles, 1953-58, retired; temporary appointment in Foreign Office, 1958-66. 3rd Class Order of Brilliant Star of Zanzibar, 1945. *Address:* Woodside, Frant, Sussex. *T:* 202.   [*Died* 19 *Nov.* 1978.

ADDISON, 2nd Viscount, *cr* 1945, of Stallingborough; **Christopher Addison;** Baron Addison, 1937; Director of several Companies; *b* 8 Dec. 1904; *s* of 1st Viscount Addison, KG, PC, MD, FRCS, and Isobel (*d* 1934), *d* of late Archibald Gray; *S* father 1951; *m* 1928, Brigit Helen Christine, *d* of Ernest Edwin George Williams, Wimbledon; two *d*. *Educ:* University College School, Hampstead; Newton College, Newton Abbot, Devon. Trained Mechanical Engineering, 1922-27; Automobile Industry, 1927-34 (Past President, Inst. Motor Industry; Hon. Mem. Inst. Auto. Assessors); formerly Member London Stock Exchange, retd 1969. 2nd Lieut, Territorial Army, 1939; served War of 1939-45; discharged, disabled, 1945, with rank of Major. Chm., S-W Metropolitan Regional Hosp. Bd, 1965-68. *Recreations:* formerly boxing, cricket, tennis and sailing. *Heir:* b Hon. Michael Addison [*b* 12 April 1914; *m* 1936, Kathleen, *d* of Rt Rev. and Rt Hon. J. W. C. Wand, PC, KCVO; one *s* two *d*]. *Address:* The Mount, Uffculme, Devon. *T:* Craddock 459. *Clubs:* Naval and Military; (Past Cdre) Birdham Yacht.
[*Died* 18 *Nov.* 1976.

ADDISON, Brig. Leonard Joseph Lancelot, CMG 1952; CBE 1947; *b* 27 Sept. 1902; *s* of Joseph Lancelot Addison; *m* 1928, Phyllis Mabel, *d* of late E. E. Coombs, OBE; one *s* one *d*. *Educ:* Dulwich; RMC Sandhurst. 2nd Lieut The Queen's Own Royal West Kent Regt, 1923; Indian Army, 1926. Served War of 1939-45 (despatches); Brigadier, 1945; retired 1948. Chief Director of Purchase, Dept of Food, Govt of India, 1946; Counsellor, UK High Commn, Calcutta, 1947; Acting Deputy High Commissioner, March-Aug., 1948; Deputy High Commissioner for the UK in India, Calcutta, 1949-52. *Address:* Flat B, 23 Pembroke Gardens, W8.   [*Died* 30 *May* 1975.

ADEANE, Col Sir Robert (Philip Wyndham), Kt 1961; OBE (mil.) 1943; Director: Colonial Securities Trust Co. Ltd; Decca Co. Ltd; Ruberoid and other companies; *b* 1905; 2nd and *o surv. s* of late Charles Robert Whorwood Adeane, CB, Babraham Hall, Cambridge; *m* 1st, 1929, Joyce Violet, *d* of Rev. Cyril Burnett; one *s* one *d* (and one *s* decd); 2nd, 1947, Kathleen, (*d* 1969), *d* of Sir James Dunn, Bt; one *s* one *d*; 3rd, 1971, Mrs Elizabeth Jane Cator. *Educ:* Eton; Trinity Coll., Cambridge. 2nd Lieut RA (TA), 1938; Lt-Col 1941; Temp. Col 1943. Trustee, Tate Gallery, 1955-62. *Address:* Kingston House South, Ennismore Gardens, SW7; Loudham Hall, near Wickham Market, Suffolk. *Clubs:* Brooks's, Bath, Beefsteak.
[*Died* 21 *May* 1979.

ADEREMI I; see Ife.

ADERMANN, Rt. Hon. Sir Charles (Frederick), PC 1966; KBE 1971; Member, House of Representatives, for Fisher, Queensland, 1949-72 (Maranoa, 1943-49); *b* 3 Aug. 1896; *s* of late Charles and Emilie Adermann; *m* 1926, Mildred, *d* of late S. T. and Mrs Turner, Wooroolin, Qld; two *s* two *d.* Chm., Peanut Marketing Bd, 1925-30, 1933-52, retd; Chm., Kingaroy Shire Council, 1939-46, retd; Chm. cttees, House of Reps, 1950-58; Dep. Speaker, periods 1950, 1955, 1956; Minister of State for Primary Industry, in Australian Cabinet, Dec. 1958-Oct. 1967. Dep. Leader, Aust. Country Party, 1964-66. Leader, Aust. Delegn to Commonwealth Parly Conf., Wellington, Nov.-Dec. 1965. *Address:* PO Box 182, Kingaroy, Qld 4610, Australia. *T:* 722112 Kingaroy.   *[Died 9 May 1979.*

ADIE, Edward Percival, MC 1918; *b* 1890; *s* of late W. J. Adie, Voe, Shetland; *m* 1924, Grace Dorothy, *d* of late Thomas Anderson, Hillswick, Shetland. *Educ:* Edinburgh Academy. Served European War, 1914-18, Canadian Scottish Regiment. Convener of Zetland, 1938-44. DL 1939, JP 1951, Zetland; Vice-Lieutenant of Zetland, 1953, retd 1965. *Recreation:* fishing. *Address:* Voe, Shetland. *T:* Voe 202.   *[Died 18 May 1977.*

ADIE-SHEPHERD, His Honour Harold Richard Bowman, QC 1950; a Recorder of the Crown Court, 1972-73; *b* 24 July 1904; *yr s* of late Richard Atkinson Shepherd, Barrister-at-law, and Mabel Shepherd, Cumberland Priory, Headingley, Leeds; *m* 1928, Margaret Rohesia Gundred Mayo, West Lodge, Pinner; two *d; m* 1962, Phyllis Margaret Adie. *Educ:* Uppingham Sch.; Trinity Coll., Oxford. Called to Bar, Inner Temple, 1928; joined North-Eastern Circuit; practised at 39 Park Square, Leeds. Served War of 1939-45, in Army, Aug. 1939-Aug. 1945, including North Africa, Sicily and Italy. Recorder of Pontefract, 1948-50; Recorder of York, 1950-55; Solicitor-General of the County Palatine of Durham, 1950-55; JP Herts, 1952; Dep. Chm., Herts QS, 1953-55; Chm., Cornwall QS, 1966-71 (Dep. Chm., 1955-66); a County Court Judge, 1955-62; a Comr of Assize, 1965-71. Pres., Devon and Cornwall Rent Assessment Panel, 1965-76. *Recreations:* boats, cars, gardening. *Address:* Sealand Court, Newton Ferrers, Plymouth. *T:* Plymouth 872399.   *[Died 11 Aug. 1979.*

ADJAYE, Sir Edward; see Asafu-Adjaye.

ADLAM, Lt-Col Tom Edwin, VC 1916; formerly Headmaster, Blackmoor Church of England School; retired, 1952; late RE; *b* 21 Oct. 1893; *s* of late John Adlam, Salisbury; *m* 1916, Ivy Annette, *y d* of late W. H. Mace, South Farnborough, Hants; two *s* two *d.* Served European War, 1914-18 (VC); awarded the Italian Silver Medal for Military Valour, June 1917 (demobilised 15 Nov. 1919, with hon. rank of Capt.); Army Education Corps; retired March 1923 with hon. rank of Captain. Recalled to Army from RARO, 1939; War of 1939-45; RE (Movement Control Section), 1939-46, Embarkation Comdt Tilbury, and later Glasgow, with rank of Lt-Col; demobilised 1946 with hon. rank of Lt-Col. *Address:* School House, Blackmoor, Liss, Hants. *[Died 28 May 1975.*

ADOO; see Sarkodee-Adoo.

ADRIAN, 1st Baron, *cr* 1955, of Cambridge; **Edgar Douglas Adrian,** OM 1942; FRCP; FRS 1923; Chancellor, University of Cambridge, 1968-75 (Vice-Chancellor, 1957-59); *b* 30 Nov. 1889; *s* of late Alfred Douglas Adrian, CB, KC, of Local Govt Bd; *m* 1923, Hester Agnes, DBE 1965 (*d* 1966), *o d* of late Hume C. and Dame Ellen Pinsent, DBE, Birmingham; one *s* two *d. Educ:* Westminster; Trinity Coll., Cambridge (MA, MD; Fellow, 1913); St Bartholomew's Hosp. Foulerton Res. Prof., Royal Soc., 1929-37; Prof. of Physiology, Cambridge Univ., 1937-51; Master of Trinity Coll., Cambridge, 1951-65. Pres., University Coll. of Leicester, 1955-57; Chancellor, University of Leicester, 1957-71. Romanes Lectr, Oxford Univ., 1960. Royal Society: Foreign Sec., 1946-50; Pres., 1950-55. President: British Assoc. for the Advancement of Science, 1954; RSM, 1960-61. Mem., BBC Gen. Adv. Council, 1952-56. Trustee, Rockefeller Inst., 1962-65. Member: Amer. Philosophical Soc.; Kungl. Vetenskaps-Soc., Uppsala; Royal Acad. of Science, Amsterdam; Royal Danish Acad. of Science and Letters. Foreign Member: Royal Acad. of Lincei; Swedish Royal Acad. of Science; Acad. of Science, Bologna. Foreign Associate: Nat. Acad. of Sci., USA; Acad. Nacional de Medicina, Buenos Aires; Acad. de Médicine, Paris; Soc. Française de Psychologie; Royal Acad., Belgium. Corres. Member: Acad. de Science, Paris; Société de Biologie and Société Philomathique, France. Hon. Member: RSM; Amer. Physiological Soc.; New York Neurological Soc.; Acad. Royale de Médicine Belgique; Amer. Acad. of Arts and Sciences; Sociedad Argentina de Biologia; Deutsche Gesellschaft für Neurol. Hon. Foreign Mem., Royal Flemish Acad. of Medicine. Hon. Life Mem., NY Acad. of Sciences. Hon. Fellow: Darwin Coll., Cambridge, 1966; RSM; RSE; British Psychological Soc.; Soc. Italiana di Biologia; Academia Nacional de Medicina, Mexico. Hon. Liveryman, Dyers Co. Hon. degrees from American, Canadian, British and European universities. Baly Medal, 1929; Nobel Laureate (Medicine), 1932; Royal Medal, Royal Soc., 1934; Copley Medal, 1946; Gold Medal, RSM, 1950; Albert Gold Medal, RSA, 1953; Harben Medal, 1955; Conway Evans Prize, 1956. Chevalier de la Légion d'Honneur. *Publications:* The Basis of Sensation, 1928; The Mechanism of Nervous Action, 1932; The Physical Basis of Perception, 1947; papers on the physiology of the nervous system in Jl of Physiology, Brain, etc. *Heir: s* Hon. Richard Hume Adrian, FRS. *Address:* Trinity College, Cambridge. *Club:* Athenæum. *[Died 4 Aug. 1977.*

ADRIAN, Max; actor; *b* Ireland, 1 Nov. 1903; *s* of Edward Norman Cavendish Bor and Mabel Lloyd Thornton. *Educ:* Portora Royal School, Enniskillen. First appearance on English stage in Katja, the Dancer, 1925; subsequently West End parts and tours; appeared in First Episode, Comedy, 1934, playing same part in New York, 1935; continued in West End. Joined Old Vic, 1939. 1940-56: appearances in London included Haymarket season (Hamlet, A Midsummer Night's Dream, The Circle, The Duchess of Malfi, Love for Love) and Revues: Tuppence Coloured; Oranges and Lemmons; Penny Plain; Airs on a Shoestring; Fresh Airs. Candide, New York, 1956; appeared in America until 1959 (The Would Be Gentleman, No Laughing Matter, Mary Stuart, The Lesson, The Merchant of Venice, The School for Scandal, Pygmalion); Look after Lulu, London, 1959; The Deadly Game, NY, 1960. Joined Royal Shakespeare Company, 1960 (Twelfth Night, Troilus and Cressida, The Duchess of Malfi, The Devils, The Hollow Crown, As You Like It, Romeo and Juliet); played The Hollow Crown in Europe and USA, 1962-63; Chichester Festival, 1963-64 (St Joan, Uncle Vanya) also National Theatre (Hamlet, The Recruiting Officer, The Master Builder, Uncle Vanya, St Joan); Guildford Festival, 1965 (A Month in the Country, Samson Agonistes, Lionel and Clarissa); The Doctor's Dilemma, Guildford and London, 1966; GBS, Edinburgh Festival, London, and tours in England, Northern Ireland, Far and Middle East and US, 1966, 1967, World Tour, 1968; Yvonne Arnaud, Guildford: The Viaduct, 1967; The Cardinal of Spain, 1969; Gilbert and Sullivan, 1969; GBS and Gilbert and Sullivan, World Tour, 1970; E Africa and Far East Tour, 1971; Marching Song, South Africa, 1972; Trelawny of the Wells (musical version), London, 1972. Films include: Kipps, The Young Mr Pitt, Henry V, Pool of London, The Pickwick Papers, Border Story, The Primrose Path, The Music Lovers, The Devils, The Boy Friend. Television in New York, Hollywood and London, from 1937; Delius in Song of Summer, TV film, 1968. Radio from 1933. Recorded verse, prose and plays, 1960-69. *Address:* Smarkham Orchard, Shamley Green, Surrey. *T:* Bramley 2187. *[Died 19 Jan. 1973.*

AGAR, Herbert Sebastian; author; *b* New Rochelle, NY, 29 Sept. 1897; *s* of John Giraud Agar and Agnes Louise Macdonough; *m* 1st, 1918, Adeline Scott; one *s* one *d* ; 2nd, 1933, Eleanor Carroll Chilton (*d* 1949); 3rd, 1945, Mrs Euan Wallace, *widow* of Capt. Euan Wallace and *e d* of late Sir Edwyn Lutyens. *Educ:* Columbia Univ. (BA 1919); Princeton Univ. (MA 1920, PhD 1922). London Correspondent, Louisville Courier-Journal and Louisville Times, 1929-34; Literary Editor, English Review, 1930-34; Editor, Louisville Courier-Journal, 1939-42; Special Assistant to American Ambassador in London, 1942-46; Counsellor for Public Affairs, US Embassy, 1945-46; President of Freedom House, New York, 1941-43; Director: Rupert Hart-Davis Ltd, publishers, 1953-63; TWW Ltd (Independent Television, S Wales and W of England), 1957-68. Served as seaman, later Chief Quartermaster, USNR, 1917-18; Lt-Comdr USNR, 1942. *Publications:* Milton and Plato, 1928; Bread and Circuses, 1930; The Defeat of Baudelaire (trans.), 1932; American Presidents, 1933; What is America, 1936; Pursuit of Happiness, 1938; A Time for Greatness, 1943; The Price of Union, 1950 (Eng. title The United States, 1950); Declaration of Faith, 1952; Abraham Lincoln, 1952; The Unquiet Years, 1957; The Saving Remnant, 1960; The Perils of Democracy, 1965; Britain Alone, 1973. *Address:* Beechwood, Petworth, West Sussex. *T:* Graffham 213. *Clubs:* Savile; National Arts, Century (New York).   *[Died 24 Nov. 1980.*

AGGEY, Most Rev. John Kwao Amuzu, DD, OON; Archbishop of Lagos, since 1965; *b* 5 March 1908. *Educ:* St Gregory's Coll., Lagos. Auxiliary Bishop of Lagos, 1957. Chairman: Bishops' Conference of Nigeria; Welfare Dept., Catholic Secretariat. Mem., Curia for Propaganda Fide, 1968-. *Address:* Holy Cross Cathedral, PO Box 8, Lagos, Nigeria. *T:* 20672. *[Died 14 March 1972.*

AGNEW, Fulque Melville Gerald Noel, 10th Bt, cr 1629 (but discontinued style of Sir and the use of his title); b 1900; s of late Major Charles Hamlyn Agnew, 3rd s of 8th Bt, and Lilian Ann, d of late Lt-Gen. Sir J. Wolfe Murray, KCB; S uncle, 1928; m 1937, Swanzie, d of late Major Esmé Nourse Erskine, CMG, MC; one s. Heir: s Crispin Hamlyn Agnew [b 13 May 1944. Commissioned Royal Highland Fusiliers 1964; Leader, Jt Services Expedn to Patagonia, 1972-73]. Address: Chancellor College, University of Malaŵi, Zomba, Malaŵi.
[Died 28 Aug. 1975.

AGNEW, Commander Hugh Ladas, RN (retired); Chairman of Thos Agnew & Sons Ltd, 1955-65; b 6 June 1894; 4th s of Charles Morland Agnew and Evelyn Mary (née Naylor); m 1st, 1920, Mary Violet Maud Davies (d 1932); one d (one s killed in action, 1943; and one d decd); 2nd, 1934, Gwendolen Ford Low. Educ: Warren Hill, Eastbourne; RN College, Dartmouth. Served RN (including European War, 1914-18), Sub-Lieut and Lieut, 1912-20. Joined Thos Agnew & Sons Ltd (fine art dealers), 1920; Managing Dir, 1931. Lt-Comdr RN, staff of RNC Dartmouth, 1939-45; Comdr RN (retd), 1946. Chm. of Governors, Bloxham School, 1948-60. Address: 59 Cranmer Court, Chelsea, SW3. T: 01-589 1169. Clubs: Bath; Royal Navy Club of 1765 and 1785.
[Died 20 Dec. 1975.

AGNEW, Sir Norris (Montgomery), Kt 1967; CBE 1957; Chairman of Board of Governors of United Manchester Hospitals, 1953-67; Chairman of Manchester Regional Hospital Board, 1953-62; b 2 Dec. 1895; yr s of late Harold Agnew; m 1923, Mona Christine Nimmo Duggan; one s two d. Educ: Wellington College; Brasenose College, Oxford (BA). Practised as Solicitor in Manchester, 1920-52. Hon. LLD Univ. of Manchester, 1968. Recreation: gardening. Address: Yew Tree Cottage, Nether Alderley, Macclesfield, Cheshire. T: Alderley 2320.
[Died 17 Nov. 1973.

AHERN, Maj.-Gen. Timothy Michael Richard, CBE 1959 (OBE 1945); Director of Medical Services, British Army of the Rhine, 1966-69, retired; b 16 Aug. 1908; s of late Lieut-Col M. D. Ahern and late Mrs Ahern, formerly of Glanmire, Co. Cork, Eire; m 1943, Joan Aisne, d of late S. Blencowe, and of Mrs Blencowe, Latmus, Bishopsteignton, S Devon; two s one d. Educ: Ampleforth College; Trinity College, Dublin. ADMS, Eighth Army, 1944-45. Chief of Medical Plans and Ops, SHAPE, 1953-56; Comdt, RAMC Field Training Centre, 1956-59; Exchange Officer, Brooke Army Medical Center, Texas, USA, 1959-60; DDMS: 1 (British) Corps, 1960-63; Eastern Comd, 1965-66. Col Comdt, RAMC, 1969-. Publications: contribs to Proc. Roy. Soc. Med. and Jl of Assoc. of Military Surgeons of USA. Address: c/o Williams & Glyn's Bank Ltd, Kirkland House, 22 Whitehall, SW1. [Died 20 Nov. 1980.

AHLMANN, Prof. Hans Wilhelmson; b 14 Nov. 1889; s of Col W. Ahlmann and Mais Bergqvist; m 1920, Erica (Lillemor) Harloff. Educ: Stockholm and Uppsala Universities. DrPh and Docent Stockholm Univ., 1915; Docent Uppsala Univ., 1920; Prof. and Dir of Geographical Inst., Stockholm Univ., 1929-50; Swedish Ambassador to Norway, 1950-56. Leader of Swedish-Norwegian Arctic Expedn, 1931; leader (with H. U. Sverdrup) of Norwegian-Swedish Spitzbergen Expedn, 1934; leader (with Jón Eythórsson and Sigurdur Thorarinsson) of Swedish-Icelandic Vatnajökull Investigations, 1936-37-38; leader of Swedish glaciological investigations in North-East Greenland, 1939-40; initiator and Swedish representative of board of Norwegian-British-Swedish Antarctic Expedn, 1949-52. Pres., Internat. Geogr. Union, 1956-60; Gold Medallist: Swedish Geographical Soc.; Roy. Geographical Soc.; American Geographical Soc.; Gesellschaft für Erdkunde, Berlin; Tokyo Geographical Soc.; Russian Geographical Soc., Leningrad. Publications: Sommar vid Polhavet, 1931; Land of Ice and Fire, London, 1937; Norge, natur och näringsliv, 1943, 1957; Scientific Results of the Expeditions in 1931, 1934, and 1936-37-38, 39-40, Geografiska Annaler, 1933, 1935-43; Glaciological Research on the North Atlantic Coast; R. Geog. Soc., Research Series I, London, 1948; Glacier Variations and Climatic Fluctuations, Bowman Memorial Lectures, Amer. Geog. Society, New York, 1953. Address: Fregattvägan 6, 11748 Stockholm, Sweden. [Died 10 March 1974.

AHMED, Fakhruddin Ali, Tamra Patra 1974; President of India since 1974; b 13 May 1905; s of late Col Z. A. Ahmed and late Begum Roqaia Sultan; m 1945, Abida Begum; two s one d. Educ: Govt High Schs, Gonda (UP) and Delhi; St Stephen's Coll., Delhi; St Catharine's Coll., Cambridge. BA History Cantab 1927. Called to Bar, Inner Temple, 1928. Advocate, Punjab High Court, 1928; subseq. Advocate, Assam High Court and Sen. Advocate, Supreme Court of India; elected to Assam Assembly, 1935; Mem. Indian Nat. Congress, 1931; Mem.

Assam Pradesh Congress, Working Cttee of Assam Pradesh Congress and All India Congress Cttee, from 1936 (except for short breaks); Minister of Finance and Revenue, 1st Congress Cabinet, Assam, 1938-39; jailed for offering individual Satyagrah, 1940; after release, detained as security prisoner until 1945; Mem. Working Cttee, All India Congress Cttee, 1945-46, 1964-; Advocate General of Assam, 1946-52; Minister of Finance, Law, Community Develt, Panchayats and Local Self-Govt, Assam, 1957-66; Member: Rajya Sabha, 1954-57; Assam Assembly, 1957-62, 1962-66; Rajya Sabha, 1966-67; Mem. Working Cttee and Central Parly Bd, All India Congress Cttee, 1964-74; Cabinet Minister, Govt of India, 1966-74: Min. of Irrigation and Power, Educn, Industry and Agriculture. Led Lawyers Delegn to USSR, 1955; Mem. Indian Delegn to UN, 1957; visited USA on official invitation, 1964; rep. Govt of India at Malaysian Indep. Day celebrations, 1965; many official visits world-wide, and attendance at FAO and other confs. Hon. LLD: Guru Nanak, 1974; Gauhati, 1974; Kurukshetra Univ., 1976. Recreations: golf; formerly hockey (played for College and combined Indian Students team of Oxford and Cambridge), football and tennis; Pres., Assam Football Assoc., Assam Cricket Assoc., for many years; Vice-Chm., Assam Sports Council; Pres., All India Lawn Tennis Assoc. Address: Rashtrapati Bhavan, New Delhi 110004, India. T: 375321. Clubs: Gymkhana (New Delhi); Shillong (Shillong); Delhi Golf.
[Died 11 Feb. 1977.

AIKEN, Conrad Potter; Poet; b Savannah, Georgia, 5 Aug. 1889; s of William Ford and Anna Potter Aitken; m 1st, 1912, Jessie McDonald (marr. diss. 1929); one s two d; 2nd, 1930, Clarice Mary Lorenz (marr. diss. 1937); 3rd, Mary Augusta Hoover. Educ: Middlesex Sch., Concord, Mass; Harvard Coll. (AB). Contributing Editor, The Dial, 1917-19. Library of Congress: Fellow, 1948; Consultant in Poetry, 1950-51, 1951-52. Fellow, Acad. of Amer. Poets, 1957; Mem., Amer. Acad. of Arts and Letters, 1957. Pulitzer Prize for Selected Poems, 1930; Shelley Memorial Award, 1930; Nat. Book Award for Collected Poems, 1954; Bollingen Prize, 1956; Gold Medal for Poetry, Nat. Inst. of Arts and Letters, 1958; Nat. Medal for Literature, 1969. Publications: Poems: Earth Triumphant, 1914; Turns and Movies, 1916; The Jig of Forslin, 1916; Nocturne of Remembered Spring, 1917; The Charnel Rose, 1918; The House of Dust, 1920; Punch, the Immortal Liar, 1921; Priapus and the Pool, 1922; Modern American Poets (ed), 1922; The Pilgrimage of Festus, 1923; Selected Poems of Emily Dickinson (ed), 1924; Senlin: A Biography, 1925; Prose: Scepticisms; Notes on Contemporary Poetry, 1919; Bring!, Bring!, and other Stories, 1925; Blue Voyage, a novel, 1927; Costumes by Eros (short stories), 1928; American Poetry, 1671-1928; A Comprehensive Anthology (ed), 1929; Selected Poems, 1929; John Deth and Other Poems, 1930; The Coming Forth by Day of Osiris Jones, 1931; Preludes for Memnon, 1931; Great Circle, a novel, 1933; Among the Lost People (short stories), 1934; Landscape West of Eden (poem), 1934; King Coffin (novel), 1935; Time in the Rock (poems), 1936; A Heart for the Gods of Mexico (novel), 1939; The Conversation, or Pilgrims' Progress (novel), 1939; And in the Human Heart (poems), 1940; Brownstone Eclogues (poems), 1942; The Soldier (poem), 1944; The Kid (poem), 1947; The Divine Pilgrim (poem), 1949; Skylight One (Poems), 1949; The Short Stories of Conrad Aiken, 1950; Ushant: an Essay (autobiography), 1952; Collected Poems, 1953; A Letter from Li Po (poems), 1955; Mr Arcularis (play), 1957; Sheepfold Hill (poems), 1958; A Reviewer's ABC; Collected Criticism, 1958; Collected Short Stories, 1960; Selected Poems, 1961; The Morning Song of Lord Zero (poems), 1963; The Collected Novels of Conrad Aiken, 1964; A Seizure of Limericks, 1964; Cats and Bats and Things with Wings (poems), 1965; Poets on Poetry (contrib. essay), 1965; Tom, Sue and the Clock (poems), 1966; Preludes (poems), 1966; Collected Criticism (Preface by I. A. Richards), 1967; Thee (poem), 1967; Collected Poems 1916-70, 1971; Ushant: an essay, 1972. Recreations: gardening, tennis, travel, chess. Address: Brewster, Mass, USA. T: Dennis, (Mass) 385. Clubs: Authors'; Harvard (Boston); Oglethorpe (Savannah, Ga).
[Died 17 Aug. 1973.

AIKEN, John Elliott, CB 1973; Deputy Secretary, Ministry (later Department) of Health and Social Services for Northern Ireland, 1970-74, retired; b 1909; s of Thomas John Aiken and Mary Boyton Aiken (née Elliott); m 1939, Isabel Rosaleen (née Hawkesworth); two s. Educ: Dungannon Royal Sch.; Queen's Univ., Belfast (BComSc). Entered Northern Ireland Civil Service, 1926; Ministry of Finance, 1926; Exchequer and Audit Dept, 1936; Ministries of: Public Security, 1941; Home Affairs, 1944; Education, 1948; Labour and National Insurance, 1957; Health and Social Services, 1965. Recreations: sailing, gardening. Address: 8 Rosepark, Belfast BT5 7RG, Northern Ireland. T: Dundonald 2715. Club: Strangford Lough Yacht (Co. Down).
[Died 7 March 1977.

AILESBURY, 7th Marquess of, *cr* 1821; **Chandos Sydney Cedric Brudenell-Bruce,** Bt, 1611; Baron Brudenell, 1628; Earl of Cardigan, 1661; Baron Bruce, 1746; Earl of Ailesbury, 1776; Viscount Savernake, 1821; *b* 26 Jan. 1904; *o s* of 6th Marquess of Ailesbury, DSO, TD, and Sydney (*d* 1941), *o d* of John Madden, Hilton Park, Co. Monagh; *S* father 1961; *m* 1st, 1924, Joan (*d* 1937), *d* of S. Salter, Ryde, Isle of Wight; two *s* ; 2nd, 1944, Mrs Joyce Frances Quennell (marr. diss. 1948), *d* of Charles Warwick-Evans; 3rd, 1950, Jean Frances, *widow* of Sqdn Ldr Williamson, MBE; one *s. Educ:* Eton; Christ Church, Oxford. Served War of 1939-45, RASC and Military Government (prisoner, escaped, despatches). CC Wiltshire, 1961-64. JP Wilts, 1938, DL 1950-69. CStJ 1964. *Publications:* Youth goes East, 1928; Amateur Pilot, 1933; Wardens of Savernake Forest, 1949; I Walked Alone, 1950; Life and Loyalties of Thomas Bruce, 1951. *Heir: s* Viscount Savernake. *Address:* Bel au Vent, St Lawrence, Jersey, Channel Islands. *[Died 15 July 1974.*

AILWYN, 3rd Baron, *cr* 1921, of Honingham, Norfolk; **Eric William Edward Fellowes,** CBE 1962; DL; Captain RN retired; a Deputy Chairman of Committees and a Deputy Speaker, House of Lords, 1957-72; *b* 24 Nov. 1887; 2nd *s* of 1st Baron Ailwyn, PC, KCVO, KBE, 2nd *s* of 1st Baron de Ramsey, and Hon. Agatha Eleanor Augusta Jolliffe, *d* of 2nd Lord Hylton; *S* brother, 1936; *m* 1935, Cecil Lorna, *d* of late Hugh G. Barclay, Colney Hall, Norwich, and *widow* of Col Malise Graham, DSO. *Educ:* Stubbington; HMS Britannia. Entered RN, 1902; served throughout European War, 1914-18, in North Sea; retired 1934 with rank of Captain; War of 1939-45; Member of British Parliamentary Mission to China, 1942; Pres. of China Assoc., 1943-48. DL 1949 and JP 1946, Suffolk. Hon. Col 419 Coast Regt RA (Suffolk TA), 1947-54. Order of Brilliant Star of China. *Heir: b* Hon. Carol Arthur Fellowes, *b* 23 Nov. 1896. *Address:* Sweffling Grange, Saxmundham, Suffolk. *T:* Rendham 496. *Club:* Travellers'. *[Died 23 March 1976.*

AINSCOUGH, Sir Thomas Martland, Kt 1932; CBE 1925 (OBE 1918); MCom; FRGS; *b* 12 Aug. 1886; *e s* of late James M. Ainscough, JP, of Lindley Mount, Parbold, Lancs; *m* 1st, 1918, Mabel (*d* 1956), 3rd *d* of late Wm Lincolne, of Ely, Cambs; one *s* one *d* (and one *s* killed in action, 1941); 2nd, 1956, Mrs Marjorie Jones, Bourne House, 15 Westbourne Grove, W2. *Educ:* Manchester Grammar Sch.; Switzerland; Manchester University. In business in Manchester and China, 1906-12; travelled widely in Western China, 1913; Special Commissioner to the Board of Trade in China, 1914-16; Secretary to the Board of Trade Textile Committee, 1916-17; Secretary to the Empire Cotton Growing Committee, 1917; HM Senior Trade Commissioner in India, Burma, and Ceylon, 1918-44; retired, 1944; Ministry of War Transport Rep. in India, 1942; attached to the Persian Tariff Revision Commission, 1920; attached to the United Kingdom Delegation at the Imperial Economic Conference, Ottawa, 1932. *Address:* Royal Glen Hotel, Sidmouth, Devon. *[Died 15 Oct. 1976.*

AINSLEY, John William; *b* 30 June 1899; *s* of John George and Jane Ainsley, Co. Durham; *m* 1924, Maggie, *d* of Francis Nattrass; two *d. Educ:* elementary school; evening classes; correspondence courses. Enlisted in Durham Light Infantry, 1916. A miner. Labour Party agent at general elections. Chairman Durham County Council, 1952 (Member, 1942); Chairman County Education Committee, Durham; Chairman Northern Advisory Council for Further Education, 1951-55. MP (Lab) North-West Division of Durham, 1955-64. Methodist local preacher. *Address:* 5 Reservoir Road, Wooley Terrace PO, Crook, Co. Durham. *[Died 23 June 1976.*

AINSLIE, James Percival, CMG 1962; Consultant Surgeon, Royal Perth Hospital, Western Australia, since 1952; Consultant Neuro-surgeon, Royal Perth Hospital, since 1959; Consultant Neuro-surgeon, Repatriation Hospital, Perth; *b* 14 Aug. 1899; *s* of James W. Ainslie; *m* 1930, Jean W., *d* of Dr G. E. Clemons; one *s* two *d. Educ:* Hale School, Perth; Univ. of Western Australia; Trinity Coll., Univ. of Melbourne. MB, BS 1923, MD 1924 (Melb.); FRCS 1927, FRACS 1929. Royal Melb. Hosp.: House appts, 1923-24; Med. Supt, 1925-26; Royal Perth Hosp.: Surgeon to out-patients, 1929-35; to in-patients, 1935-51; Neuro-surgeon, 1949-59. Pres. BMA, WA Br., 1941; Mem. of Senate, Univ. of WA, 1933-58; Pres., Medical Bd of WA, 1959- (Mem. 1951-); Mem. Australasian Soc. of Neuro-surgeons (Pres. 1960); Mem. Adv. Med. Council of Australia, 1970; Fellow Aust. Med. Assoc., 1964. Hon. Lt-Col retd list. *Publications:* various to surgical journals. *Recreations:* golf, tennis, fishing. *Address:* 252 St George's Terrace, Perth, WA 6000, Australia. *T:* 214497. *Club:* Weld (Perth). *[Died 14 Jan. 1973.*

AINSWORTH, Mrs Robert; *see* Brunskill, Muriel.

AINSWORTH, Sir Thomas, 2nd Bt, *cr* 1916; late Lieutenant 11th Hussars; *b* 8 Feb. 1886; *s* of 1st Bt and Margaret Catherine (*d* 1918), *d* of Robert Reid Macredie; *S* father, 1923; *m* 1st, 1911, Lady Edina Dorothy Hope (who obtained a divorce, 1925), 4th *d* of 4th Marquess Conyngham; one *s* one *d* ; 2nd, 1925, May Hope Johnstone (*d* 1969), 14 Grove Court, Drayton Gardens, SW; one *s. Heir: s* John Francis Ainsworth [*b* 1912; *m* 1st, 1938, Josephine (marr. diss. 1946), *er d* of Commander W. R. Bernard; 2nd, 1946, Anita, *e d* of late H. A. Lett, Enniscorthy, Co. Wexford]. *Address:* Ballinakill, Kilfinny, Adare, Co. Limerick. *T:* Croom 18. *Clubs:* Cavalry; Kildare Street (Dublin). *[Died 1 March 1971.*

AINSWORTH-DAVIS, John Creyghton, MA, MD, BCh (Cantab); FRCSE; FRCS; LRCP; Consulting Urological Surgeon; Emeritus Consulting Urological Surgeon, Lord Mayor Treloar's Hospital, Alton; Hon. Consulting Urological Surgeon, King Edward VII's Hospital for Officers, Beaumont House; Senior Member British Association of Urological Surgeons; Fellow and late Secretary of Council Royal Society of Medicine (Ex-Vice-President Section of Urology); late President Hunterian Society; Vice-President and Hon. Fellow, Royal Institute of Public Health and Hygiene (late Chairman Executive Council); *b* 23 April 1895; *s* of late Prof. J. R. Ainsworth-Davis; *m* 1920; one *s* two *d* ; *m* 1947, Irene, *d* of late Alfred Hope. *Educ:* Westminster Sch.; Christ's Coll., Cambridge (Closed and Open Exhibition). Served European War 1914-19 as Captain in the Rifle Brigade and RFC, France, Salonica, Palestine, Egypt; World War, 1939-45, as Wing Commander in charge of a Surgical Division, RAFVR Medical Services. Qualified at St Bartholomew's Hospital in 1923, and subsequently held the following appointments: Junior and Senior House-Surgeon, Surgical Registrar and Hon. Asst Surg. to All Saints' Hospital for Genito-Urinary Diseases; Clinical Asst, Hon. Surgical Registrar and Urological Surg. to the Royal Waterloo Hosp. for Women and Children; Clinical Asst, Surgical Registrar and Deputy Surgeon to St Paul's Hospital for Genito-Urinary Diseases. Late Consultant Urological Surg., The Bolingbroke Hospital, Royal Waterloo Hospital, London, Kettering and District General Hospital. *Publications:* Essentials of Urology, 1950; Articles in Postgraduate Surgery, Vol. II, and in Maingot's (1957) Management of Abdominal Operations; many papers contributed to medical journals. *Recreations:* athletics (Olympic Gold Medallist, 1920), gardening. *Address:* Townsend Farmhouse, Stockland, near Honiton, Devon EX14 9DS. *T:* Stockland 257. *[Died 3 Jan. 1976.*

AIRD, Colonel Sir John Renton, 3rd Bt, *cr* 1901; MVO 1936; MC; JP; DL; Extra Equerry to the Queen since 1952 (and to King George VI, 1937-52); *b* 7 Aug. 1898; *e s* of Sir John Aird, 2nd Bt; *S* father 1934; *m* 1939, Lady Priscilla Willoughby, *yr d* of 2nd Earl of Ancaster, GCVO; one *s* three *d. Educ:* Eton; Sandhurst. Served European War, 1917-18; Staff of Governor of Bombay, 1921-23; Staff of High Comr for Egypt, 1926-27; Equerry to the Prince of Wales, 1929-36. Commanded 3rd Bn Grenadier Guards, 1937-40; General Staff, 1940-45. Alderman, Berks CC; Member, Court of Assistants, Drapers' Company; Governor, Queen Mary's Coll., E1. Order of St Olav. *Heir: s* George John Aird [*b* 30 Jan. 1940; *m* 1968, Margaret, *yr d* of Sir John Muir, Bt, TD; two *d*]. *Address:* Forest Lodge, The Great Park, Windsor SL4 2BU. *T:* Windsor 61262; 43 Clabon Mews, SW1. *T:* 01-584 5942. *[Died 20 Nov. 1973.*

AITCHISON, Sir David, KCVO 1954; Captain SS Southern Cross, 1955, retired, 1957; *b* 26 Sept. 1892; *s* of Adam Aitchison and Annie Richardson Aitchison, Sunderland, County Durham; *m* 1924, Mary Alethea, *d* of Samuel William Moscrip, Morebattle, Roxburgh; no *c. Educ:* Sunderland. Commanded: MV Empire Grace, 1941-47; SS Athenic, 1947-50; SS New Australia, 1950-51; MV Dominion Monarch, 1951-53; SS Gothic, 1953-54, including Royal Tour; SS New Australia, 1954. *Publication:* Royal Standard: Red Ensign, 1958. *Address:* The Garth, Great Easton, Dunmow, Essex. *T:* Great Easton 268. *[Died 15 Jan. 1975.*

AKENHEAD, David, OBE 1950; MA Oxon, BSc London; *b* 23 Feb. 1894; *s* of Edmund Akenhead, sometime Prebendary of Lincoln Cathedral, and Lucy Collingwood Akenhead; *m* 1933, Beatrice Carter. *Educ:* Rugby; New College, Oxford; South Eastern Agricultural College, Wye. Served European War, 1914-18. On staff: Royal Agricultural Coll., 1922-24; Internat. Inst. of Agriculture, Rome, 1926-28; helped to start what is now known as the Commonwealth Bureau of Horticulture and Plantation Crops, East Malling, Kent, in 1929, and was Director thereof, 1945-59. *Address:* Three Roods, Offham, Maidstone,

Kent ME19 5NA. *T:* West Malling 842171. *Club:* United Oxford & Cambridge University.   [*Died* 11 *Sept.* 1978.

AKERMAN, Major-General William Philip Jopp, CB 1941; DSO 1918; MC late RA; *b* 16 Jan. 1888; *s* of late W. S. Akerman of the Mount, Burnham, Som; *m* 1st, 1920, Olga Phyllis (*d* 1922), *o d* of late Major-Gen. Sir John Steevens, KCB; one *d*; 2nd, 1925, Annie, *er d* of late Major-Gen. E. W. Alexander, VC, CB, CMG; two *d. Educ:* Oundle School; RMA, Woolwich. Served India, 1908-14; Mesopotamia, 1914-16 (MC); France and Belgium, 1917-18 (DSO and bar); Staff College, Camberley, 1922-23; Imperial Defence College, 1933; Assistant Dir of Artillery, War Office, 1934-36; Assistant Master-General of Ordnance, War Office, 1936-38; Major-Gen. Royal Artillery, AHQ, India, 1939-42; retired pay, 1942. *Address:* Rotherwood, Churt, Surrey.
[*Died* 22 *Feb.* 1971.

AKHURST, Instructor Captain Algernon Frederic, CBE 1944; MA; RN retired; *b* 13 Nov. 1893; *s* of late Herbert Akhurst, Civil Servant, and late Florence Akhurst; unmarried. *Educ:* Merchant Taylors' School, London; Jesus College, Cambridge, Math. Tripos, Wrangler. Joined RN 1915; HMS Minotaur, 1916-19; HMS Cornwall, 1919; HMS Barham, 1920-22; RN Engineering College, 1922-26; RN College, Greenwich, 1926; HMS Warspite, 1926-28; RN College, Greenwich, 1928-31; HMS Nelson, 1931-33; Fleet Education Officer, Home Fleet, 1933-36; RN Engineering College, Keyham, 1936-39; Education Dept, Admiralty, 1939-40; HMS Ganges, 1940; HMS St George, 1940-42. Dean of RNC, Greenwich, 1942-47; HMS Ganges, 1947-48; retired list, 1948. Cravat of the Order of the Cloud and Banner, China. *Recreations:* golf, gardening, walking, music. *Address:* Downscroft, 49 Headland Avenue, Seaford, Sussex. *T:* Seaford 2751. *Club:* United Service and Royal Aero.
[*Died* 28 *March* 1972.

ALANBROOKE, 2nd Viscount, *cr* 1946; **Thomas Brooke;** Baron Alanbrooke, *cr* 1945; *b* 9 Jan. 1920; *e s* of 1st Viscount Alanbrooke, KG, GCB, OM, GCVO, DSO; *S* father, 1963. *Educ:* Wellington College. Served War of 1939-45, RA. *Heir:* half-*b* Hon. Alan Victor Harold Brooke, *b* 24 Nov. 1932. *Address:* c/o Lloyds Bank Ltd, 6 Pall Mall, SW1.
[*Died* 19 *Dec.* 1972.

ALBEMARLE, 9th Earl of, *cr* 1696; **Walter Egerton George Lucian Keppel;** MC; Baron Ashford, 1696; Viscount Bury, 1696; *b* 28 Feb. 1882; *e s* of 8th Earl and Lady Gertrude Lucia Egerton (*d* 1943), *o c* of 1st Earl Egerton of Tatton; *S* father, 1942; *m* 1st, 1909, Lady Judith Sydney Myee Carrington (*d* 1928), 4th *d* of 1st Marquis of Lincolnshire; one *s* two *d* (and two *s* decd); 2nd, 1931, Diana Cicely, DBE 1956, *o c* of late John Archibald Grove; one *d. Educ:* Eton. Late Lieut PWO Norfolk Artillery; ADC to Gov.-Gen. of Canada, 1904-05; to Viceroy of India, 1906-07; to Governor of Orange River Colony, 1907-08; Major Special Reserve Scots Guards, 1918; late commanding PWO Civil Service Rifles; commanded Norfolk Yeo. 108th Brigade RFA until 1926; contested (U) Altrincham Division, Cheshire, 1910; Vice-Lieut County of Norfolk, 1940-44; elected LCC for Central Wandsworth, 1919; elected Norfolk CC and to Church Assembly, 1943; Alderman Norfolk CC, 1957. Formerly: President: St John Amb. Bde, Norfolk (KStJ 1963); Anglo-Netherlands Soc. (1942-65); Norwich Philharmonic Soc.; Tatton Park Gardens Soc.; Vice-Pres. Assoc. of River Authorities. Grand Cross, Order of Orange Nassau. *Heir: g s* Viscount Bury. *Address:* Beacon Hill, Woodbridge, Suffolk.
[*Died* 14 *July* 1979.

ALBERY, Sir Bronson (James), Kt 1949; theatre director; *b* 6 March 1881; *s* of James Albery and Mary Moore, afterwards Lady Wyndham; *m* 1912, Una G. Rolleston; two *s* two *d. Educ:* Uppingham; Balliol Coll., Oxford. Barrister-at-law; Lieut RNVR, 1917-19. Jt Man. Dir (with Howard Wyndham) The Wyndham Theatres Ltd, 1925-47, controlling Criterion, New and Wyndham's Theatres; Man. Dir The Wyndham Theatres Ltd, 1947-50; Jt Man. Dir (with his son, Donald Albery) of The Wyndham Theatres Ltd, 1950-62; appointed Chm., upon resignation of Sir Irving Albery, Jan. 1962; apptd Exec. Dir, upon his resignation as Jt Man. Dir, Sept. 1962; resigned as Chm. and Exec. Dir, Oct. 1965. Governor, Old Vic, 1936-41; Chm., Old Vic Trust, Dec. 1951-Sept. 1959. Presented (in partnership with Lewis Casson and Sybil Thorndyke) Advertising April, Criterion, 1923; Saint Joan, New, 1924 (subsequent revivals); The Lie, New, 1923, and Wyndham's, 1925; 1932-36 (in partnership with John Gielgud) presented: Musical Chairs, Criterion; Richard of Bordeaux, New; Sheppey, Wyndham's; Hamlet, New; Romeo and Juliet, New; The Seagull, New. Presented La Compagnie des Quinze in Noé, New, 1935, Le Viol de Lucrece, and other plays, subsequently. Administrator Sadler's Wells Ballet, 1941-42; Administrator,

jointly with Tyrone Guthrie, of Old Vic and Sadler's Wells, 1942-44; Mem. Exec. Cttee Arts Council of Great Britain and Chm. of Drama Panel, 1948-52, Chm. British Council Drama Advisory Cttee, 1952-61; Pres. Society of West End Theatre Managers, 1941-45 and 1952-53; Chairman Theatres' War Service Council, 1942-46. Pres., Theatrical Traders Assoc.; Vice-Pres., Actors' Benevolent Fund. Chevalier de la Légion d'Honneur. *Recreations:* bridge, maps. *Address:* 8 Lees Place, W1. *T:* 01-629 0901. *Club:* Garrick.   [*Died* 21 *July* 1971.

ALBERY, Michael James, QC 1955; *b* 12 March 1910; *s* of late Sir Irving Albery, MC; *m* 1934, Mary Laughton Isaac; one *s* two *d. Educ:* Uppingham; Exeter Coll., Oxford (Scholar), 1st cl. Jurisprudence, 1933; half-blue for mile. Called to Bar, 1934. Served with Royal Artillery from outbreak of War until discharged on account of wounds in June 1942. Director, The Wyndham Theatres Ltd, 1947-62. Bencher of Lincoln's Inn, 1962. *Publication:* Cellar for Six, 1943. *Recreations:* ski-ing, golf, gardening, bridge. *Address:* 35 Falmouth House, Clarendon Place, W2. *T:* 01-262 3909. *Club:* Garrick.
[*Died* 22 *Sept.* 1975.

ALBRIGHT, Prof. William Foxwell; Professor emeritus of Semitic Languages, Johns Hopkins University, since 1958; W. W. Spence Professor of Semitic Languages, 1929-58; *b* Chile, 24 May 1891; *s* of Rev. Wilbur Finley Albright and Zephine Viola (*née* Foxwell); *m* 1921, Ruth Norton; four *s. Educ:* Upper Iowa Univ. (AB); Johns Hopkins Univ. (PhD). Dir, American Sch. of Oriental Research in Jerusalem, 1920-29, 1933-36; first vice-pres. American Schools of Oriental Research, 1937-65; pres., Internat. Organisation Old Testament Scholars, 1956-59. Jordan Lectr, Univ. of London, 1965. Holds thirty hon. degrees inc. Yale, Harvard, St Andrews, TCD, Utrecht, Oslo, Uppsala, Hebrew Univ. (Jerusalem). Corresp. FBA, 1967. Member: Nat. Acad. of Sciences, Washington; American Philosophical Soc., Philadelphia; American Acad. of Arts and Sciences, Cambridge (Mass); Royal-Danish Acad. (for.); Royal Flemish Acad. (for.); Royal Irish Acad. (hon.). Corr. Member: Inst. of France (Acad. des Inscriptions et Belles Lettres); Austrian Acad. of Sciences. Hon. Fellow, Royal Asiatic Soc. Hon. Member: Société Asiatique; Brit. Soc. for Old Testament Study; Glasgow Oriental Soc., etc. Hon. Fellow German Archaeolog. Inst. *Publications:* Excavations at Gibeah of Benjamin, 1924; The Archaeology of Palestine and the Bible, 1932; The Excavation of Tell Beit Mirsim I-III, 1932-43; The Vocalization of the Egyptian Syllabic Orthography, 1934; From the Stone Age to Christianity, 1940; Archaeology and the Religion of Israel, 1942; The Archaeology of Palestine, 1949; Recent Discoveries in Bible Lands, 1956; The Biblical Period from Abraham to Ezra, 1963; History, Archaeology and Christian Humanism, 1964; The Proto-Sinaitic Inscriptions, 1966; Yahweh and the Gods of Canaan, 1968, etc. *Address:* 3401 Greenway, Baltimore, Md 21218, USA. *T:* Hopkins 7-9859; Johns Hopkins University, Baltimore, Md 21218.   [*Died* 19 *Sept.* 1971.

ALDEN, John Hewlett, MA, DMus (Oxon), FRCO, ARCM; Secretary of the Music Masters' Association, 1956-75; *b* 22 Feb. 1900; *s* of late Herbert E. Alden; *m* 1953, Caroline Patricia, *yr d* of late Lieut-Colonel H. W. Worsley-Gough, CMG; one *s* (one *d* decd). *Educ:* New and Magdalen Coll. Schs, Oxford; New Coll., Oxford. Dir of Music, Diocesan Coll., Capetown, 1923-26; Asst Dir of Music, Harrow Sch., 1927-30; Dir of Music, Bradfield Coll., Berks, 1931-34; Organist, St Martin-in-the-Fields, 1935-38; Acting-Head of Cambridge House, Camberwell, 1939; Director of Music: Eastbourne Coll., 1940-45; RNC, Dartmouth, 1945-46; Chm., Slatter & Rose, Ltd, Oxford, 1942-47; Dir of Music, Bradfield Coll., Berks, 1947-53; part-time Tutor, Education Dept, Reading Univ., 1957-74. *Address:* Lower Lodge, Rowdefield, Rowde, near Devizes, Wilts SN10 2JD. *T:* Devizes 3958.   [*Died* 6 *Nov.* 1976.

ALDERSEY, Captain Ralph, JP; Landowner, Chester; land agent to Col E. Royds, Stubton, Lincolnshire, from 1919; *b* 1890; 2nd *s* of Hugh Aldersey of Aldersey; *m* 1st, 1927, Rachel (*d* 1948), *d* of Commander Gaussen, Brookman's Park, Herts; two *s* two *d*; 2nd, 1949, Beatrice Maude, *e d* of late Charles Stonor, Trearddur Bay, Anglesey; one *s. Educ:* Radley College. Business, 1908-14; Army, 1914-19 (twice wounded, despatches). *Recreations:* hunting, shooting, etc. *Address:* Aldersey, Chester. *TA:* Clutton. *T:* Broxton 265 (Aldersey Estate Office), 279.
[*Died* 12 *Dec.* 1971.

ALDERSON, Sir Harold George, Kt 1956; MBE 1938; Patron of the Olympic Federation of Australia (formerly Chairman for 45 years); Hon. Secretary Anniversary Day Regatta since 1920; Life Member, New South Wales Olympic Council (President, 1926-73); *b* Balmain, NSW, 18 Aug. 1891; *s* of J. B. Alderson, Sydney; *m* 1st, 1915, Rose Stella (*d* 1965), *d* of W. F. Wills; one *d*; 2nd, 1966, Hilda N. Buddee, Mosman, NSW. *Educ:* Mosman Sup. Public School, NSW. Hon. Manager Australian Olympic Team, Berlin, 1936; Member Organising Council, British Empire Games, Sydney, 1938; President Australian Rowing Club, 1928, 1934, 1939-52, 1958, 1964; Chm., NSW Rowing Assoc., 1921-68, Hon. Sec., 1918-20, now Patron; Member Executive Organising Committee Olympic Games, Melbourne, 1956. Member Council National Fitness, NSW; Chm., Rothman Sports Foundn, 1966-; Hon. Treasurer St John Ambulance Assoc. (for 36 years). *Address:* 8/12 Muston Street, Mosman, NSW 2088, Australia. *Clubs:* NSW Sports (President for 45 years, now Patron), Mosman Rowing (50 years, now Patron), Union of Old Oarsmen.   [*Died* 5 *Oct.* 1978.

ALDREN TURNER, Dr J. W.; *see* Turner.

ALDRICH, Winthrop Williams; US lawyer, banker, diplomat; retired; Hon. Trustee: Presbyterian Hospital, New York; Riverside Church, New York; Vice-President and Trustee, The Pilgrims of the United States; Member Advisory Council, School of International Affairs, Columbia University; retired as Member Visiting Committee Harvard Center for International Affairs; Hon. Bencher, Middle Temple, 1953; *b* Providence, Rhode Island, 2 Nov. 1885; *s* of Nelson Wilmarth Aldrich and Abby Pierce Chapman Greene; *m* 1916, Harriet (*d* 1972), *d* of Charles B. Alexander, New York; one *s* four *d* (and one *s* decd). *Educ:* Harvard University (AB); Harvard Law School (JD). Admitted to New York State Bar, 1912; Mem. law firm Byrne, Cutcheon and Taylor, 1916-17; served as Lieut US Naval Reserve, 1917-18; Mem. law firm Murray, Aldrich & Webb, 1919; Pres. Equitable Trust Co., 1929; President, 1930-34, Chairman of Board of Directors, 1934-53, of the Chase National Bank; Ambassador to the Court of St James's, 1953-57. Honorary Degrees: LLD: Colgate University, 1937; Northeastern University, 1938; Washington and Jefferson College, 1939; Brown University, 1944; Lafayette Coll., 1945; Columbia Univ., 1946; Bryant Coll., 1947; Georgetown Univ., 1952; Harvard Univ., 1953; Queen's Univ., Belfast, 1955; Univ. of Liverpool, England, 1956; Univ. of Rhode Island, 1965; Tuskegee Inst., 1967; DBS New York Univ., 1950; DSc Stevens Inst. of Technology, 1957. *Decorations:* Medal for Merit, US; Knight Grand Cross of the Order of the British Empire (Hon. GBE); Associate KStJ; King's Medal for Service in the Cause of Freedom, GB; Comdr Légion d'Honneur, France; Comdr Order of Leopold, Grand Officer of Order of the Crown, Belgium; Grand Officer of the Order of Orange Nassau, Netherlands; Grand Officer of Oak Crown, Luxembourg; Knight Comdr of Order of Pius IX, Vatican. *Clubs:* St James', White's (London); Royal Yacht Squadron (Cowes); Royal and Ancient Golf (St Andrews); Hope (RI), Racquet, Harvard, Pilgrims of the US, Knickerbocker, The Brook, Century, Links, New York Yacht (New York). *Address:* 960 Fifth Avenue, New York, NY 10021, USA.   [*Died* 25 *Feb.* 1974.

ALEXANDER, Conel Hugh O'Donel, CMG 1970; CBE 1955 (OBE 1946); Government Communications Headquarters, Foreign Office, later Foreign and Commonwealth Office, Cheltenham, 1946-71; *b* Cork, 19 April 1909; *s* of late Prof. C. W. L. Alexander and late H. B. Alexander (*née* Bennett); *m* 1934, Enid Constance Crichton Neate; two *s*. *Educ:* King Edward's High Sch., Birmingham; King's Coll., Cambridge. 1st cl. hons Maths 1931. Schoolmaster, Winchester Coll., 1932-38; John Lewis Partnership, 1938-39 and 1945-46; Foreign Office, 1939-45; idc 1956. Chess Correspondent, Sunday Times, Financial Times. British Chess Champion, 1938 and 1956; British team, 1931-58; non-playing Captain, 1964-72. *Publications:* Chess, 1937; Alekhine's Best Games of Chess, Vol. III, 1946; (with T. J. Beach) Learn Chess: a new way for all, 1963; Fischer v Spassky, Rejkyavik 1972, 1972; The Penguin Book of Chess Positions, 1973; A Book of Chess, 1973; Alexander on Chess, 1973. *Recreations:* chess, bridge, croquet, philately, reading. *Address:* Old Bath Lodge, Thirlestaine Road, Cheltenham, Glos. *T:* Cheltenham 59401. *Club:* Savile.
[*Died* 15 *Feb.* 1974.

ALEXANDER, David; Director: National and Commercial Banking Group Ltd, since 1968; The Royal Bank of Scotland Ltd (Vice-Chairman); Brown Brothers & Co. Ltd (Chairman); Life Association of Scotland Ltd; William Bain & Co. Ltd; *b* 26 April 1906; *s* of David Alexander and Helen Burns; *m* 1937, Jessie Paton McMillan; two *d*. *Educ:* The White House Sch., Brampton, Cumberland. Joined service of The National Bank of Scotland Ltd, 1923; Gen. Manager, 1955; Dir, 1958; National Commercial Bank of Scotland Ltd: Gen. Manager, 1959-67; Dir, 1959; Vice-Chm., 1968. *Recreations:* shooting, fishing, gardening. *Address:* The Shieling, Oxton, Lauder, Berwickshire. *T:* Oxton 255. *Club:* Caledonian.   [*Died* 1 *Dec.* 1972.

ALEXANDER, Maj.-Gen. Henry Templer, CB 1961; CBE 1960 (OBE 1942); DSO 1954; *b* 17 May 1911; *s* of Maj.-Gen. H. L. Alexander, CB, CMG, DSO, and Mrs Dorothy Alexander; *m* 1938, Maribel (marr. diss. 1973), *d* of W. A. Sedgwick Rough; one *s* two *d*. *Educ:* Sedbergh School. Gazetted to Cameronians (Scottish Rifles), 1931; served 1st Cameronians (Scottish Rifles), 1931-38; Instructor Royal Military College, Sandhurst, 1938-39. Served War of 1939-45 (despatches, 1941 and 1943, OBE, DSO): saw service in NW Europe, N Africa, Italy, India and Burma, comdg 2nd Cameronians (Scottish Rifles) and serving with General Wingate. Chief Instructor, School of Combined Ops, 1946-48; comdg 1st Cameronians (Scottish Rifles), 1954-55; since War has also commanded 26 Gurkha Bde, 1955-57, and been a Senior Instructor, Staff College; Chief of Defence Staff, Ghana, 1960-61; Chief of Staff, Northern Command HQ, York, 1962-65, retd. Col, The Cameronians (Scottish Rifles), 1969-74. *Publication:* African Tightrope, 1965. *Recreations:* horse racing, hunting. *Address:* 12 Palace Place Mansions, Kensington Court, Kensington, W8. *Club:* White's.   [*Died* 16 *March* 1977.

ALEXANDER, Rt. Hon. Sir James Ulick F. C.; *see* Alexander, Rt Hon. Sir Ulick.

ALEXANDER, Stanley Walter, MBE 1918; Proprietor and Editor, 1951-66, City Press, the City of London Newspaper; Hon. Editor, Free Trader; *b* 16 Nov. 1895; *s* of Walter Henry Alexander; *m* 1919, Doris Emily Kibble; two *s*. *Educ:* Roan School, Greenwich. Entered Lord Beaverbrook's office, 1910; Canadian War Records Office, 1915-17; Ministry of Information, 1918; Financial Editor, Daily Express, Sunday Express, Evening Standard, 1923-46; contested, as Free Trade candidate, City of London, 1945, North Ilford, 1950. One of founders with late Sir Ernest Benn of Soc. of Individualists; President: Free Trade League; Cobden Club; Hon. Treasurer, Anti-Dear Food Campaign. Liveryman, Worshipful Co. of Tallow Chandlers; Mem. Council, Kipling Soc.; a Governor, Cripplegate Foundn, St Giles; Trustee, St Luke's Joint Parochial Charities. Chm., United Reform Party. *Publications:* author of the Hannibal pamphlets (on free trade, sound money, against the coercion of the people by the State, and on the economics of sea power), including The Kingdom of Bevin, The Price We Pay, Tariffs Mean War, 1933-44; Save the Pound—Save the People, 1975. *Recreation:* watching cricket. *Address:* 44 Speed House, Barbican, EC2. *Clubs:* Reform, City Livery.
[*Died* 24 *March* 1980.

ALEXANDER, Rt. Hon. Sir Ulick, PC 1952; GCB 1953 (KCB 1947); GCVO 1948 (KCVO 1937; CVO 1932; MVO 1925); CMG 1934; OBE 1919; an Extra Equerry to the Queen since 1952; Director: Tanganyika Concessions Ltd, 1957-63 (Chairman, 1952-57); The Benguela Railway Co., 1952-64; Union Minière du Haut Katanga, 1954-63; Banque Belge Ltd, 1957-72; *b* 10 Feb. 1889; *e s* of James Dalison Alexander and The Lady Emily Alexander, *e d* of 9th Earl of Cork; *m* 1947, Lady Mary Beatrice (*née* Thynne), *d* of 5th Marquess of Bath, KG, PC, CB (she married 1st, 1927, 3rd Baron Nunburnholme). *Educ:* Eton; Sandhurst. Joined Coldstream Guards, 1909; served European War in France (1914 star), Egypt and Palestine; and on expedition to Darfur, 1916 (medal and clasp); served in Egyptian Army, 1915-21 (Order of the Nile, 4th Class, despatches); Military Secretary, Egyptian Army, 1920-21; Political Secretary to the Governor-General of the Union of South Africa (Lord Athlone), 1923-25; Comptroller of the Household of the Duke and Duchess of Kent, 1928-36; Keeper of the Privy Purse and Extra Equerry to King Edward VIII, 1936; Financial Secretary to the King, 1936-37; Chief of Staff to Prince George during official visit to South Africa, 1934; Keeper of the Privy Purse, 1936-52; Extra Equerry to the King, 1937-52; Keeper of the Privy Purse and Treasurer to the King, 1941-52, to the Queen in 1952. Receiver-General to Duchy of Lancaster, 1936-52; a Trustee of the Ascot Authority, 1939-52. Sec. to Royal Victorian Order, 1942-52. Chairman Rhodesian Board of Standard Bank of South Africa, 1953-57. *Address:* 3 Cadogan Gardens, SW3. *T:* 01-730 6767. *Clubs:* White's, Guards.
[*Died* 4 *April* 1973.

ALEXANDER, Colonel Hon. William Sigismund Patrick, DSO 1917; Irish Guards; *b* 1895; *y s* of 4th Earl of Caledon; *m* 1934, Jane Hermione (*d* 1967), *o d* of late Comdr Bernard Buxton, RN; two *s* one *d*. *Educ:* Harrow; RMC Sandhurst. Served European War, 1914-19 (wounded, despatches, DSO); retired pay, 1936. Served War of 1939-45, Irish Guards and General Staff, 1939-46. DL, Essex, 1956-67. *Address:* Gobions House Farm, Mowsley, near Rugby, Warwickshire. *T:* Fleckney 358.
[*Died* 24 *Dec.* 1972.

ALEXANDROWICZ, Prof. Charles Henry, LLD; Chairman and Director of Studies, Grotian Society; Visiting Fellow,

Centre of International Studies, Cambridge, since 1969; *b* 13 Oct. 1902; *s* of Gen. Francis de Alexandrowicz; *m* 1945, Marguerite Gabrielle Drabble. *Educ:* Scottish Coll., Vienna; Jagellonian Univ., Cracow; Inns of Court Law Sch., London. Barrister-at-Law, Lincoln's Inn. Chm., London Bd of National Econ. Bank of Poland, 1941-46; Chm., European Central Inland Transport Org., 1946-48. Prof. of International Law, Univ. of Madras, Editor of Indian Year Book of International Affairs and Hon. Legal Adviser to Govt of India, 1951-61; Prof., Univ. of Sydney, 1961-68; Visiting Prof.: Sorbonne, 1963; Hague Acad. of Internat. Law, 1960, 1968; Institut des Hautes Etudes Internationales, Paris, 1969; Professorial Fellow, Ecole Pratique des Hautes Etudes, Sorbonne, 1969-70. Grotius Memorial Medal, 1961. *Publications:* International Economic Organisations, 1952; Constitutional Developments in India, 1957; World Economic Agencies- Law and Practice, 1962; History of the Law of Nations in the East Indies, 1967; The Afro-Asian World and the Law of Nations, 1969 (Hague Academy); The Law of Global Communications, 1971; The European-African Confrontation, 1973; The Law Making Functions of the Specialised Agencies of the UN, 1973; articles in BYIL, AJIL, etc. *Recreations:* music, alpinism. *Address:* 8 Rochester Gardens, Croydon, Surrey. *T:* 01-686 2004.
[Died 26 Sept. 1975.

ALFORD, Sir Robert (Edmund), KBE 1960; CMG 1951; *b* 10 Sept. 1904; 2nd *s* of late R. G. Alford and Maud Alford (*née* Griffiths); *m* 1st, 1934, Teresa Margaret Riddell (*d* 1964); one *s* ; 2nd, 1967, Eileen Mary Riddell. *Educ:* Winchester Coll.; University Coll., Oxford. Colonial Administrative Service, Nigeria, 1928; Sen. District Officer, 1946; Financial Sec., Zanzibar, 1947; Chief Secretary, 1952; Governor and C-in-C of St Helena, 1958-62. Served War of 1939-45 in RNVR, 1940-45. Brilliant Star of Zanzibar, 1958. *Address:* The Barn, Staple Cross, Sussex.
[Died 23 Nov. 1979.

ALGIE, Hon. Sir Ronald (Macmillan), Kt 1964; retired; Speaker, House of Representatives, New Zealand, 1961-66; MP (N) for Remuera, 1943-66; *b* 22 Oct. 1888; *s* of John Alexander Algie and Agnes Macmillan Algie; *m* 1st, 1917, Helen Adair McMaster (*d* 1944); 2nd, 1947, Mary Joan Gray Stewart (*d* 1972); one *s* one *d*. *Educ:* primary and secondary schools in NZ; Auckland University College. Barrister, 1913. Auckland University: Lectr in Law, 1913; Prof. of Law, 1919-37. Minister of Education, New Zealand, 1950-57. Hon. LLD Univ. of Auckland, 1968. *Publications:* articles in professional jls. *Recreation:* mountaineering (Mem. Alpine Club). *Address:* 29 Charles Dickens Drive, Howick, Auckland, New Zealand.
[Died 23 July 1978.

ALI; *see* Ameer Ali.

ALI, (Chaudri) Mohamad; politician, Pakistan; *b* Jullundur, India, 15 July 1905; *m* ; four *s* one *d*. *Educ:* Punjab University, Lahore (MSc). Lecturer in Chemistry, Islamia College, Lahore, 1927-28; Indian Audit and Accounting Service, 1928; Accountant-Gen., Bahawalpur, 1932; Private Secretary to Finance Minister, Government of India, 1936; Under Secretary Finance Dept, 1938; Deputy Financial Adviser, 1939; Addtl Financial Adviser, Dept of Supply, 1943; Financial Adviser of War and Supply, 1945; Mem. Steering Cttee of Partition Council, 1947; Secretary-General, Govt of Pakistan, 1947; Minister of Finance, 1951. Alternate Deleg. to UN Security Council. 1948; Deleg. to Commonwealth Consultative Cttee, Colombo Plan Confs, 1951-; Head of Pakistan Delegation to Commonwealth Finance Ministers' Confs, 1952, 1953, 1954; Chairman Bd of Governors of International Monetary Fund and International Bank for Reconstruction and Development, 1953; Prime Minister, Pakistan, 1955-56, resigned, also as Minister of Defence. *Publication:* The Emergence of Pakistan, 1967. *Address:* 86-D/1, Gulberg III, Lahore, Pakistan.
[Died 1 Dec. 1980.

ALLAN OF KILMAHEW, Baron *cr* 1973 (Life Peer), of Cardross, Dunbarton; **Robert Alexander Allan,** DSO 1944; OBE 1942; Chairman, Ladybird Books; Director: Pearson/Longman; Longman/Penguin; Bank of Scotland (Chairman, London Board); H. Clarkson (Holdings) Ltd, and other companies; *b* 11 July 1914; *yr s* of late Claud A. Allan, VL, JP, Kilmahew Castle, Cardross, Dunbartonshire, and of Adeline Allan, OBE; *m* 1947, Maureen, *d* of late Harold Stuart-Clark, Singapore; one *s* one *d*. *Educ:* Harrow (Rothschild Schol.); Clare Coll., Cambridge (Mellon Fellow; ran cross-country for Cambridge, 1935, 1936); Yale University. Served War of 1939-45, mostly in Coastal Forces in Mediterranean until 1946; Lieut RNVR July 1939, Commander, 1943; Senior Officer Inshore Squadron, 1944-45; Dep. Chief of Naval Information, Washington, 1945-46. Pres. Scottish Junior Unionists, 1948-51; contested (U)

Dunbartonshire, 1945 and West Dunbartonshire, general election and bye-election, 1950; MP (C) South Paddington, 1951-66; Assistant Whip, 1953-55; PPS to the Prime Minister, 1955-58; Parly and Financial Sec., Admiralty, Jan. 1958-Jan. 1959; Parly Under-Sec., Foreign Office, 1959-60. A Treasurer, Conservative and Unionist Party Organization, 1960-65; Chm., Conservative Central Board of Finance, 1961-66. A Governor, BBC, 1971-76; a Governor of Harrow School, 1968-; a Trustee and Chm., Lord Mayor Treloar Schools. Commander Légion d'Honneur, 1943;† Croix de Guerre, 1943 (France); Officer of Legion of Merit, 1944 (USA); despatches (5 times). *Publication:* The Open Door Policy in China, 1939. *Recreation:* sailing. *Address:* 5 Campden House Terrace, W8. *T:* 01-727 9515. *Club:* Royal Yacht Squadron.
[Died 4 April 1979.

ALLAN, Prof. Donald James, FBA 1955; Professor of Greek, University of Glasgow, 1957-71; Dean of the Faculty of Arts, 1968-70; *b* 22 Dec. 1907; *s* of J. B. Allan and Ethel Allan (*née* Bullen). *Educ:* Christ's Hospital, Horsham; Christ Church, Oxford. BA 1930, MA 1933. Fellow and Tutor in Classics, Balliol College, 1931-47; Reader in Ancient Philosophy, Edinburgh Univ., 1948-57. Held temporary post at Foreign Office, 1940-45. Pres., Mind Assoc., 1964-65. Hon. DLitt Edinburgh, 1977. *Publications:* Aristotle, de Caelo, 1936; Plato, Republic book I, 1940; The Philosophy of Aristotle, 1952; articles in classical and philosophical journals. *Address:* 83 Bainton Road, Oxford.
[Died 19 June 1978.

ALLAN, Sir Henry Ralph Moreton H.; *see* Havelock-Allan.

ALLAN, Captain Henry Samuel, RD 1929; Commodore, Royal Naval Reserve and Peninsular and Oriental Steam Navigation Co. (retired); *b* 13 Dec. 1892; *o s* of John M. and Beatrice Allan, Saltcoats, Ayrshire, Scotland; *m* 1st, 1916, Ida Mary Poole, Stourbridge, Worcs; one *s* ; 2nd, 1947, Isabel M. A. Fairweather, Cust, NZ. *Educ:* Ardrossan Academy, Ayrshire, Scotland. Apprentice George Smith & Sons, City Line, Glasgow, 1908-13. Joined P & OSN Co., as Junior Officer, Dec. 1913. Served European War, in RN as Sub-Lieut RNR, 1914-19, War of 1939-45 as Comdr., Capt. and Actg Comdr, RNR, 1939-46 (despatches); Commodore of Convoys, Captain HMS Largs, Normandy and South of France landings, and HMS Artifex, British Pacific Fleet. Commander, P&OSN Co., 1946; Command P&O SS Strathaird, 1947-Dec. 1952; Commodore P&OSN Co., Dec. 1951-Dec. 1952 (retd). Order of St Stanislas, 3rd Class, 1915. *Address:* 136 North Road, Hythe, Kent CT21 4AT. *T:* Hythe 66916.
[Died 6 March 1979.

ALLAN, John; Sheriff of Tayside, Central and Fife (formerly of Fife and Kinross) at Kirkcaldy since 1966; *b* 14 Aug. 1927; *s* of Dr John Allan, Cathcart, Glasgow; *m* 1955, Janet Evelyne Geddes; two *s*. *Educ:* Glasgow Academy; Glasgow University. Admitted a Member of the Faculty of Advocates, 1953; Sheriff-Substitute of Inverness, Moray, Nairn and Ross and Cromarty at Stornoway and Lochmaddy, 1961-66. *Recreations:* sailing, fishing. *Address:* Sheriff's Chambers, Kirkcaldy, Fife.
[Died 15 June 1979.

ALLAN, Philip Bertram Murray, MBE 1945; FSA; FRES; Editor-in-chief, The Journal of Criminal Law, 1937-73; *b* 1884; *y s* of Alexander Allan, Bylands, and Frances Ann Hamilton-Beattie; *m* 1914, Elsie Kate, *d* of James Whitehead; one *s* two *d*. *Educ:* Charterhouse; Clare College, Cambridge (MA); Middlesex Hospital. Reader at Smith, Elder & Co., 1912; Asst Editor, Cornhill Magazine, 1912-14. Served European War, 1914-19 (despatches); Staff Captain, Mil. Intell., War Office, 1917-19. Head of Philip Allan & Co., 1919-32. Founded The Police Journal at request of Home Office, 1928, and edited it until Dec. 1958; founded The Journal of Criminal Law, 1937. FSA 1921; FRES 1944. *Publications:* Book-Hunter at Home, 1920; Boy's Book of Verse, 1924; Book of Loneliness, 1926; Prison Breakers, 1927; Golden Ladies of Pampeluna, 1934; Trout Heresy, 1936; Moth-Hunter's Gossip, 1937; Talking of Moths, 1943; Moths and Memories, 1948; other publications under noms-de-plume; edited and annotated many other volumes. *Recreations:* formerly hunting, shooting and fishing; now reading and writing. *Address:* 4 Windhill, Bishop's Stortford, Herts.
[Died 31 Dec. 1973.

ALLAN, Sir Robert George, Kt 1945; CIE 1936; MA Cantab; FRSE; late Indian Agricultural Service; *b* 7 Nov. 1879; *s* of Alexander Allan and Jemina Dalmahoy, Glenmore Estate, Coonoor, S India, and 4 Hillside Crescent, Edinburgh; *m* 1911, Mabel Isabel Anderson; three *d*. *Educ:* Haileybury; Loretto School, Musselburgh; Pembroke College, Cambridge. Principal Agricultural College, Nagpur, CP, 1907; officiating Director of Agriculture, Central Provinces, 1926 and 1930; Director of Agriculture, United Provinces, 1931; retired 1935.

Commissioner of Agriculture, Baroda State, India, 1935-44; Minister for Agriculture and Post-war Development, 1944-46, retired 1946. Services to cultivators of State-commemorated by endowment of a gold medal to be awarded annually under his name at Univ. of Bombay. *Publications:* An Outline of Indian Agriculture; chapters on Indian agriculture in Social Service in India (HMSO); numerous agricultural bulletins and papers. *Address:* 33 Drumsheugh Gardens, Edinburgh. *Club:* Caledonian United Service (Edinburgh). *[Died 4 Jan. 1972.*

ALLEN OF HURTWOOD, Lady, (Marjory), FILA; *b* 10 May 1897; *d* of George and Sarah Shorey Gill; *m* 1921, 1st Baron Allen of Hurtwood (*d* 1939); one *d. Educ:* Bedales School; Reading University. Landscape Architect; Vice-President Institute Landscape Architects, 1939-46; Hon. Vice-President ILA 1962; Governor Bedales School; Chairman Nursery School Assoc. of Great Britain, 1942-48 (Pres., 1948-51); Vice-Pres. British Assoc., 1948; Founder-President World Organisation Early Childhood Education; Member Central Advisory Council for Education (England), 1945-49; Chairman Advisory Council on Children's Entertainment Films, 1944-50; United Nations Children's Fund (Child Welfare in Europe and Middle East), 1950-51; Member Advisory Council Child Care (Home Office); Governor, British Film Institute, 1949-50; Chairman Coronation Planting Committee, 1937-39. Chairman: Lollard Adventure Playground Assoc., 1954-60; London Adventure Playground Association; Handicapped Adventure Playground Assoc. JP Surrey 1946. *Publications:* Gardens, 1953; Whose Children?, 1944; Adventure Playgrounds, 1954; The New Small Garden, 1956 (with Susan Jellicoe); Play Parks, 1960; Design for Play, 1962; New Playgrounds, 1964; Planning for Play, 1968; (with Mary Nicholson) Memoirs of an Uneducated Lady, 1975. *Address:* 10 Selwood Terrace, SW7. *T:* 01-373 4144.
[Died 11 April 1976.

ALLEN, Air Vice-Marshal Charles Edward Hamilton, CB 1945; DFC 1918; *b* 1899; *s* of Edward Allen, Capetown, South Africa, and Louise Henrietta Arendse; *m* 1923, Marion, *d* of Walter Burke, Caythorpe, Lincs; one *s. Educ:* Sea Point Boys' High Sch., Cape Town; St Catharine's Coll., Cambridge. RFC 1917, as a cadet from S Africa; 2nd Lieut Sept. 1917. Permanent commission RAF 1919. Director-General of Technical Services, Air Ministry, 1952-54. Retired, 1954. Lately Liaison Officer, Aviation Division, Dunlop Rubber Company. *Address:* 49a Lillington Road, Leamington Spa, Warwicks.
[Died 27 Oct. 1975.

ALLEN, Charles Peter Selwyn, CMG 1963; MVO 1954; OBE 1959; *b* New Zealand, 29 Sept. 1917; *yr s* of late John Allen; *m* 1947, Joan Audrey Cundall; no *c. Educ:* Wanganui Collegiate Sch., NZ; Gonville and Caius Coll., Cambridge. Administrative Service, Uganda, 1940-63: Dist Officer, 1940-52; Asst Chief Sec., 1952-55. Seconded to British Embassy Washington, 1955-56, Permanent Sec., 1955. Permanent Sec. to Prime Minister of Uganda (Sec. to Cabinet and Head of Uganda Civil Service), 1962-63; Local Director: (Zambia), The British South Africa Company, 1963-65; Anglo American Corporation, Johannesburg, 1965-73. *Address:* Diorama, 19 Rocklands Road, Murdock Valley, Simonstown, Cape, South Africa. *T:* Cape Town 86-1673. *Clubs:* Lansdowne; Clovelly (Cape Town).
[Died 18 March 1977.

ALLEN, Derek Fortrose, CB 1967; FSA 1947; FBA 1963; Treasurer of the British Academy, since 1973 (Secretary, 1969-73); Trustee of the British Museum, since 1972; *b* 29 May 1910; *s* of late Ernest Allen and late Elsie Mackenzie Allen (*née* Skues); *m* 1938, Godyth Winifred (*née* Gell); three *s. Educ:* Wellington Coll., Berkshire; Magdalen Coll., Oxford (MA); British School at Rome. British Museum, Assistant Keeper, Department of Coins and Medals, 1935-39; Min. of Shipping (later War Transport): Dept of Foreign Shipping Relations, 1940-46; marine insurance, 1946-47; UK Shipping Rep., Far East, 1947-52; Min. of Transport (later Min. of Aviation): Asst Sec., Vehicle Regulations, 1952-53, Road Traffic, 1953-58, Aerodrome Lands, 1958-59, Aviation General Policy, 1959-61; Under-Sec., Min. of Aviation, 1961-66, Civil Aviation Div., BoT, 1966-68. Mem., British Library Bd, 1975-. President: Oxford Musical Club, 1932; British Numismatic Soc., 1959-63; Royal Numismatic Soc., 1966-70; Vice-President: Council for British Archaeology, 1972-; Society of Antiquaries, 1973-. Rhind Lectr, 1963-64. Chevalier, Ordre de Mérite Maritime, 1950. *Publications:* Major Ports of Malaya, 1951; British Museum Catalogue of Coins of Henry II, 1952; Minor Ports of Malaya, 1953; Origins of Coinage in Britain, a Reappraisal, 1961; Coins of the Coritani, 1962. Articles in Jl of Walpole Soc., Archaeologia, Proc. of Prehistoric Soc., Numismatic Chronicle, Brit. Numismatic Jl, Revue Numismatique, Jahrb. für Num. und Geldgeschichte, Britannia, Germania, Nordisk

Numismatisk Årsskrift,† etc. *Recreations:* playing string quartets, numismatics. *Address:* Grenna House, Chilson, Oxon. *Clubs:* Athenæum, Savage. *[Died 13 June 1975.*

ALLEN, Frederick Martin Brice, MD, FRCP; *b* 20 June 1898; *m* Anne Evelyn Maud, *d* of James Calvert, Lurgan. Formerly Hospital Officer, Ministry of Home Affairs, Northern Ireland, Member Northern Ireland Hospitals Authority and Northern Ireland Tuberculosis Authority; Fellow of Ulster Med. Society (President 1955-56); Member British Pædiatric Association (President, 1955-56), Hon. Member, The Canadian Pædiatric Society; formerly Chairman Northern Ireland Regional Committee of Inst. of Almoners; Member of: Ministry Advisory Committee on Child Guidance and Speech Therapy; Nuffield Regionalisation Council, and of Medical Planning Commission; Pres., Section Diseases of Children, British Medical Association, 1938 and Northern Ireland Branch, 1951; Pres. Queen's University Association. Surgeon Lieutenant-Comdr RNVR, retd. Emeritus Professor of Child Health, Queen's University, Belfast, 1948-63; Pædiatrician, Royal Belfast Hospital for Sick Children, 1924-63; Physician in charge of Infants to Royal Maternity Hospital, Belfast, 1927-63. Dawson Williams Prize, 1963. *Publications:* Diseases of Children; Aids to Disease of Children; contributions to medical journals. *Address:* Lenaghmore, Cultra, Holywood, Co. Down. *T:* Holywood 3134.
[Died 10 Jan. 1972.

ALLEN, Rev. George Kendall, MA; *b* 15 Feb. 1883; *s* of Rev. Dr Allen, sometime Headmaster, Cranleigh Sch.; *m* 1910, Mary Ellen Blake. *Educ:* Wellington College; Trinity College, Cambridge. Assistant Master, Christ's Hospital, 1906-24; Chaplain to the Forces, 1916-18; Headmaster The London Orphan School, Watford, 1924-30; Rector of Hampton Lovett and Elmley Lovett, 1930-36. *Publication:* Selections from Tennyson. *Recreations:* gardening, walking. *Address:* St Barnabas Homes, Dormans, Lingfield, Surrey.
[Died 15 Nov. 1975.

ALLEN, Harold Major, QC 1965; *b* 2 Oct 1911; *o s* of Arthur Major Allen, journalist, and Minnie Emily (*née* Camfield); *m* 1942, Joan Renée (*née* Boesche); one *d. Educ:* Merchant Taylors' School. Inland Revenue Dept, 1935-50. Called to Bar, Gray's Inn, 1949; practised at Bar, 1950-72. *Recreations:* boats, walking and conversation. *Address:* 9 Harewood Green, Keyhaven, Hants. *Club:* Royal Lymington Yacht.
[Died 24 Dec. 1977.

ALLEN, Brigadier Henry Isherwood, CBE 1943; DSO 1917; Commander, Legion of Merit (USA), 1946; psc; *b* 18 Nov. 1887; *s* of late Rev. Dr George Cantrell Allen; *m* 1921, Rachel Alice Houssemayne, *d* of late Col Woodford George Du Boulay of Cheltenham and *widow* of Capt. William Haire Forster, Royal Irish Fusiliers; (*er s* killed in action, Normandy, 1944 and one *s* decd). *Educ:* Wellington College. Gazetted North Staffordshire Regt, 1908; served European War, France, 1915; Mesopotamia, 1916-19 (DSO, Bt Majority, despatches five times); General Staff, War Office, 1921; transferred to Royal Corps of Signals; Student Staff Coll., Camberley, 1922-23; DAA and QMG 48th Div., 1924-25; GSO2, AHQ, India, 1926-27; Brigade Major 3rd (Jhelum) Infantry Brigade, 1927-29; Bt Lieut-Col 1927; Commandant School of Signals, Catterick, 1930-32; British Military Mission, Iraq Army, 1934-35; General Staff Officer, 1st Grade, War Office, 1936-38; retired pay, 1938; War Service, General Staff, 1939-45. *Address:* Beverley, Dunsfold, Surrey. *T:* Dunsfold 259. *[Died 14 Jan. 1979.*

ALLEN, Dr Norman Percy, CB 1966; FRS 1956; DSc; Deputy Director (A), National Physical Laboratory, 1966-67; *b* 5 June 1903; *s* of Sidney Edward Allen and Emily Eliza Davies; *m* 1929, Olive Gwendolen Williams; two *s* one *d. Educ:* Grammar School, Burton-upon-Trent; Sheffield University. BMet (Sheffield), 1923; MMet (Sheffield), 1924; DSc (Birmingham), 1934. British Non-Ferrous Metals Research Assoc., 1923-28; Lecturer in Metallurgy, Univ. of Birmingham, 1928-35; Senior Research Metallurgist, Research and Development Dept, Mond Nickel Co. Ltd, 1935-44; Supt, Metallurgy Div., National Physical Laboratory, 1944-66. President: Birmingham Metallurgical Soc., 1935-36; Inst. of Metallurgists, 1961; Chm., Inter-Services Metallurgical Council, 1963-69. Osmond Medal Société Française de Métallurgie, 1963; Bessemer Medal Iron and Steel Institute, 1965; Platinum Medal, Inst. of Metals, 1967; Luigi Losana Medal, Associazione Italiana di Metallurgia, 1968. Hon. Dr of Technical Science, Technical Univ. of Prague, 1964; Hon. DMet Sheffield, 1966. *Publications:* papers in Jl of Iron and Steel Institute and Institute of Metals; Hatfield Memorial Lecture (1958). *Address:* 10 Firlands, off Ellesmere Road, Weybridge, Surrey. *T:* Weybridge 49944. *[Died 23 Feb. 1972.*

ALLEN, Raymond Seaforth Stirling, TD; *b* 30 May 1905; *s* of late Ernest Allen, Solicitor, and late Elsie Mackenzie Allen (*née* Skues); unmarried. *Educ:* Wellington College (Scholar); Queens' College, Cambridge (Scholar). MA, LLB. Admitted Solicitor (Hons), 1931. Served Westminster Dragoons (TA) at home, War Office General Staff, Combined Chiefs of Staff, Washington, DC (1939-45); Lieutenant-Colonel 1943; Legion of Merit (US Army), 1945. With E. F. Turner & Sons, Solicitors, 1931-39 and 1955-68; joined Legal Department of National Coal Board on its formation, 1946, Legal Adviser and Solicitor to the Board, 1948-53; Institute of International Air Law, McGill University, Montreal, 1953-54; Legal Consultant to Stock Exchange on Computerisation, 1973. Trustee, Northern Arts and Sciences Foundn, 1965-68. Mem. Internat. Gen. Cttee, Mensa, 1971-. *Publication:* The Legal Relationships of a Nationalised Industry, 1954. *Recreations:* reading, travel, the arts. *Address:* 46 Redhill Drive, Brighton BN1 5FL. *Club:* Royal Automobile.
[*Died* 29 *Oct.* 1974.

ALLEN, Sir Roger, KCMG 1957 (CMG 1950); Director-General Middle East Association, since 1970; *b* 17 Aug. 1909; *s* of late Herbert Charles Goodeve and Winifred Frances Allen; *m* 1954, Jocelyn, *d* of late Comdr A. H. de Kantzow, DSO, RN, and Mrs de Kantzow; one *s* one *d*. *Educ:* Repton; Corpus Christi College, Cambridge. Called to the Bar, Inner Temple, 1937; employed temp. in the Foreign Office, 1940-; transferred to Moscow, April 1946; granted Civil Service Certificate, February 1947, and appointed to be a Foreign Service Officer, Grade 7, January 1946; transferred to the Foreign Office, May 1948; promoted to be a Foreign Service Officer, Grade 6 (Head of United Nations (Political) Department), January 1949; Head of African Dept, 1950; Asst Under Sec. of State, 1953-54; UK Dep. High Comr in Germany, 1954; HM Minister, Bonn, 1955-56; HM Ambassador: to Greece, 1957-61; to Iraq, 1961-65; Dep. Under-Sec. of State, FO, 1965-67; HM Ambassador to Turkey, 1967-69. *Address:* 5 William Street House, William Street, SW1. *Club:* Travellers'.
[*Died* 9 *Feb.* 1972.

ALLEN, Sydney Scholefield, QC 1945; JP; *b* 3 Jan. 1898; *e s* of Joseph William and Annie Edith Scholefield Allen, Birkenhead; *m* 1928, F. Mona Irving, Meols, Wirral; two *s*. *Educ:* Birkenhead Institute; Univ. of Liverpool (LLB 1st cl. Hons 1922). Served European War, 1915-19, first in the ranks and later as an officer in RFA in 55th (West Lancs) Division; called to Bar, Gray's Inn, 1923; joined Northern Circuit practising on that Circuit and in North Wales; Recorder of Blackburn, 1947-69. MP (Lab) Crewe Div. of Cheshire, 1945-74. Pres. Merseyside Fabian Soc.; Chm. Birkenhead Branch, League of Nations Union. Member Manx Bar. Commercial and Insurance Practice. Vice-Chm., Brit. Branch of Inter-Parly Union, 1969-71; Delegate: Inter-Parly Union, Rio de Janeiro, 1958, 1962; Brazilia, 1962; Belgrade, 1963; Copenhagen, 1964; Canada, 1965; Tehran, 1966; Dakar, Senegal, 1968. Member Executive Committee: Commonwealth Parly Assoc. (British Branch), 1960-71; also Jt Treas., Brit. Amer. Parly Gp, 1964-71. Delegate, Council of Europe and Western European Union, 1959-62. Vice-Chm. Legal Cttee, Council of Europe, 1960-62; Mem. Fabian Delegation to Poland (1958), Rumania (1960), Greece (1963), Turkey (1967). JP Lancashire, 1947. Hon. Freeman of Crewe, 1967. *Recreations:* walking, reading, music, drama, politics. *Address:* 2 Romney Close, Hampstead Way, NW11. *T:* 01-455 4385.
[*Died* 26 *March* 1974.

ALLEN, Prof. Thomas Palmer, MSc; CEng; FIEE; Professor of Light Electrical Engineering, The Queen's University, Belfast, 1955-65, Emeritus Professor since 1965; *b* 9 Aug. 1899; *s* of William Palmer Allen and Mary Jane Allen; *m* 1925, Dorothy Margaret Mathews; two *d*. *Educ:* Rosetta School, Belfast; Trades Preparatory School, Belfast; The Queen's University, Belfast. Apprenticeship Elect. Eng, 1914-18; Lectr in Physics and Elect. Eng, Walthamstow Technical Inst., 1922; Asst Lectr in Mathematics, College of Technology, Belfast (CTB), 1923; Asst Lectr in Elect. Eng, CTB, 1924; Extra-Mural Lectr in Wireless Telegraphy and Telephony, QUB, 1927; Lectr in Elect. Eng, CTB, and Extra-Mural Lectr in Elect. Eng, QUB, 1936; Senior Lectr in Elect. Eng, CTB, 1942; Adviser of Studies, Faculty of Applied Science, QUB, 1938-52; Director of Higher Technological Studies, CTB, 1955; Dean of Faculty of Applied Science and Technology, QUB, 1958-61. Chm., N Ireland Centre of IEE, 1946-47. Senator, The Queen's Univ., Belfast, 1964-69; Gov., City of Belfast College of Technology, 1965-. *Publications:* (with R. E. Steven) Selected Calculations in Electric Power, 1979; various contributions to technical press, and many book reviews. *Recreations:* angling, cryptanalysis, amateur radio transmission (call Sign Gi6YW). *Address:* 62 Balmoral Avenue, Belfast BT9 6NY. *T:* Belfast 665982.
[*Died* 19 *March* 1979.

ALLEN, William Edward David, OBE 1948; Chairman of David Allen & Sons Ltd, 1925-70; historian; *b* 6 Jan. 1901; *e s* of William Edward Allen, Commonwood House, Chipperfield, Herts, and *g s* of late David Allen, JP, Belfast; *m* 1922, Lady Phyllis Edith King (marr. diss. 1932; she *d* 1947), 2nd *d* of 3rd Earl of Lovelace; one *d*; *m* 1943, Nathalie (*d* 1966), *e d* of late Maxime Kossovsky, formerly of the Moscow Bar; *m* 1969, Anne, *d* of P. Pentland, Heyfield, Vic, Australia; one *s*. *Educ:* Eton. MP (U) West Belfast, 1929-31; resigned from Unionist Party, 1931. Captain Life Guards, active service Middle East and Africa, 1940-42 (despatches). Press Attaché British Legation, Beirut, 1943-44; Information Officer, N Iraq, 1944; Press Attaché, British Embassy, Angora, 1945. Counsellor (Information), 1947-49. Member Council: Brit. Inst. of Archaeology, Ankara, 1951-67; Hakluyt Soc.; Royal Asiatic Soc.; FSA (Ireland and London); Mem. Société Asiatique (Paris). *Publications:* History of the Georgian People, 1932, repr. 1970; The Ukraine: A History, 1940, repr. 1968; Guerilla War in Abyssinia, 1943; The Russian Campaigns of 1941-45 (2 vols) (with late Paul Muratoff), 1944-46; Caucasian Battlefields, 1953; David Allens: The History of a Family Firm, 1957: The Poet and the Spae-Wife, 1960; Problems of Turkish Power in the Sixteenth Century, 1963; Russian Embassies to the Georgian Kings, 2 vols (for Hakluyt Soc.), 1970. *Address:* Whitechurch House, Cappagh, Co. Waterford, Ireland; 34 Lad Lane, Dublin. *Clubs:* Turf; Kildare Street (Dublin); Cercle d'Orient (Istanbul).
[*Died* 18 *Sept.* 1973.

ALLEN, Sir William (Guilford), Kt 1973; CBE 1970; grazier; Senior Partner, Allen, Allen & Crawshaw, livestock and wool producers, Brisbane; Director, Radio Broadcasting Network of Queensland, etc; Member, Central Council of Australian Country Party; *b* 1898; *s* of R. C. Allen, Goondiwindi, Qld; *m* 1st, 1927, Mona Maree Nolan (*d* 1956), Hughenden, Qld; two *s* one *d*; 2nd, 1961, Josephine Agnes Peacock, Brisbane. *Educ:* Nudgee Coll., Brisbane; Hunters Hill (Christian Brothers' Coll.), Sydney. Dep. Chm., Longreach Shire Council, 1948-58. Mem., Lands Advisory Cttee, Qld Central Council of Country Party. Life Mem., National Party of Queensland (formerly Country Party), 1972. Is a breeder of Poll Shorthorns and Merino sheep. Knighted for services to the Queensland pastoral industry and the community. *Recreations:* horse racing, reading. *Address:* Bexley, Longreach, Queensland 4730, Australia. *Clubs:* Brisbane, Longreach, Flinders, Tattersall's, Huntington, Queensland Turf, Brisbane Amateur Turf (all in Qld).
[*Died* 3 *Jan.* 1977.

ALLERTON, Air Cdre Ord Denny, CB 1960; CBE 1953 (OBE 1945); Royal Air Force; *s* of Charles Hedley and Elizabeth Allerton; *m* 1935, Kathleen Mary Tucker; two *s*. *Educ:* Prof. Ludicker's Private Sch., Felixtowe; Ipswich Sch. Group Captain, 1947; Air Cdre, 1957. Lately Dir of Movements, Air Min. *Address:* Upper Field, Church Hill, Nether Wallop, Stockbridge, Hampshire. *T:* Nether Wallop 276.
[*Died* 22 *Sept.* 1977.

ALLIN, Norman, CBE 1958; Hon. RAM, FRMCM; Professor of Singing at Royal Academy of Music, London, 1935-60; *b* Lancashire, 1884; two *d*. *Educ:* privately; Royal Manchester Coll. of Music. Principal Bass Covent Garden, English and Internat. Seasons, 1918-48; Roles include: Boris, Gurnemanz, Osmin, Mephistopheles, Hagen, Hunding, Sarastro, Baron Ochs, Ramphis, King Mark, etc; Principal Bass at all leading British Musical Festivals, Choral and Orchestral Socs; Principal Bass at Melbourne (Australia) Centenary Season of Grand Opera, 1934-35. *Recreations:* country pursuits. *Address:* Dulas Court, Pontrilas, Hereford. *Club:* Savage. [*Died* 27 *Oct.* 1973.

ALLISON, Sir Charles William, Kt 1966; CBE 1959 (OBE 1947); JP; former Chairman of Tees Valley and Cleveland Water Board; *b* 29 July 1886; *s* of John and Sarah Allison; *m* 1906, Hetty, *d* of William Burn; one *d* (one *s* decd). *Educ:* Stockton Sec. Sch.; Labour College. Trades Union Secretary with late Ernest Bevin for 36 years. JP, Stockton-on-Tees. *Publications:* contrib. to TUC History. *Recreations:* fishing, football and cricket. *Address:* 32 Winston Street, Stockton-on-Tees, Durham. *T:* Stockton 63189.
[*Died* 10 *Sept.* 1972.

ALLISON, James Anthony, CMG 1966; OBE 1960; PH (Botswana); *b* 31 Jan. 1915; *s* of John Schiller Allison, Edinburgh and Union of South Africa, and Anna Elizabeth Christina (*née* van Velden); *m* 1946, Dorothy Patricia Kerr; one *d*. *Educ:* Boys' High School, Pretoria, SA; St John's College, Johannesburg, SA; Witwatersrand University, Johannesburg, SA (BA Hons); Colonial Service Course, Cambridge. Assistant District Officer, Colonial Service, 1938-39; War of 1939-45: Military Service, 3 West African Infantry Brigade, 1939-46 (Major). Asst District Officer and District Officer, Nigeria,

1946-50; District Commissioner, Secretariat, Finance Secretary, Administration Secretary, and Sec. to Cabinet, Bechuanaland, 1950-65; Sen. Permanent Sec. and Sec. to the Cabinet, Botswana (formerly Bechuanaland), 1965-Jan. 1970, retired. *Recreations:* birds, shells, literature, music, travelling. *Address:* 11 Victory Place, Amanzimtoti, Natal, South Africa. *[Died 24 Oct. 1976.*

ALLISON, Prof. Philip Rowland, MA, DM; FRCS, FACS; Nuffield Professor of Surgery, University of Oxford, since 1954; Hon. Consulting Surgeon General Infirmary, Leeds, since 1955; *b* 2 June 1907; *s* of Jesse Rhodes Allison, Selby, and Rhoda Allison; *m* 1937, Kathleen Greaves; two *s* one *d. Educ:* Hymers College, Hull; University of Leeds. MB, BSc, ChM Leeds; MB BS London; MA, DM Oxon. General Infirmary, Leeds: House Surgeon, 1931; Res. Orthop. Officer, 1931-32; Res. Surgical Officer, 1932-33; Hon. Asst Surg., 1936-41, and Senior Thoracic Surgeon, 1941. University of Leeds: Surgical Tutor and Registrar, 1933-36; Clin. Lectr in Surgery, 1936-41; Sen. Lectr in Thoracic Surgery, 1941. Corresp. Mem. Roman Soc. of Surgeons, 1949; Hon. Fellow: Soc. Med. of Pernambuco, 1953; American Surgical Assoc.; American Soc. of Thoracic and Cardiovascular Surgeons; Hon. Mem., Coll. of Surgeons of Brazil, 1953. Hon. DSc Leeds, 1969. *Publications:* chapters contrib. to Textbook of Medicine by Garland and Phillips, 1953; contrib. to surgical and med. jls and text-books. *Address:* Balliol College, Oxford. *T:* Oxford 49601; 31 Over Norton, Chipping Norton, Oxon. *T:* Chipping Norton 3107.

[Died 6 March 1974.

ALLISON, Dr Richard Sydney, VRD; MD (Belfast); FRCP; FRCPI; DPM; Hon. Archivist and Consulting Neurologist (retired) to Royal Victoria and Claremont Street Hospitals, Belfast; *b* 15 May 1899; *s* of William Lowcock and Eliza Russell Allison; *m* 1925, Elizabeth Newett Barnett Steen (*d* 1976); one *s* two *d. Educ:* Royal Belfast Academical Institution; Queen's University, Belfast. RNVR Surg.-Prob. 1918-19; Surg.-Lt 1926, retd 1950 (Surg.-Comdr). Actg Surg.-Capt. and Consultant to SW and W Approaches, 1944-45. Consultant in Medicine to Admiralty, N Ireland. Asst Physician, Ruthin Castle, 1925-30; appointed Asst Physician: Royal Victoria Hospital, 1930; Claremont Street Hospital, 1938. Clinical Examiner in Medicine, Queen's University, Belfast, 1931-64; External Examiner in Neurology, Victoria Univ., Manchester, 1959-62. Visiting Professor: Medical College of South Carolina, 1957; Dalhousie Univ., Nova Scotia, 1958; Visiting Consultant Neurologist to Thailand Govt, 1965. Pres. Ulster Neuropsych. Soc., 1950-52, 1961-63; Pres. Sect. Neurology, RSM, London, 1962-63. Mem. Assoc. of Physicians of GB and Ireland (Pres., 1967); President: Ulster Med. Soc., 1970; Sect. Neurol., Royal Acad. Medicine in Ireland, 1971; Past Pres., Assoc. Brit. Neurologists; For. corresp. Mem., French Soc. of Neurology. *Publications:* Sea Diseases: the story of a great natural experiment in preventive medicine in the Royal Navy, 1943; The Senile Brain, 1962; The Very Faculties, 1969; The Seeds of Time: a history of Belfast General (Royal) Hospital, 1850-1903, 1972; HMS Caroline: a history of the Ulster Division, RNVR, 1974; (Jt) Whitla's Dictionary of Treatment (8th edn), 1938, (ed jtly) *ibid* (9th edn), 1957; papers in scientific jls. *Recreations:* travel, fly fishing, natural history. *Address:* Waringstown, Lurgan, Co. Armagh, Northern Ireland. *T:* Waringstown 353.

[Died 27 April 1978.

ALLITT, Sir (John) William, Kt 1966; MBE 1955; retired Shop Manager; *b* 2 April 1896; *s* of George and Mary Allitt; *m* 1919, Minnie Parker; two *s. Educ:* Village School, Leadenham, Lincs and WEA Classes. Member of Labour Party for 50 years. 40 years public life. *Recreations:* public work; schools and school concerts. *Address:* Lincluden, Crescent Avenue, West Cliff, Whitby, Yorks. *Club:* Newhall Labour. *[Died 15 Dec. 1972.*

ALLNUTT, Colonel Edward Bruce, CBE 1944; MC 1915; late RAMC; *b* Embleton, 16 Sept. 1885; *s* of Rev. W. Bruce Allnutt and Edith Hawks; *m* 1916, Joan Cicely (*d* 1964), *e d* of Rev. G. B. Gainsford, MA, VD; one *s* two *d* (and one *s* decd). *Educ:* Bedford; Alleyne's Sch., Stevenage; St Bartholomew's Hosp. Served in London Scottish Rifles. MRCS; LRCP; DPH (London), 1923. House Physician, Westminster Hospital, 1911; Lieutenant RAMC 1912; De Chaumont Prize, Hygiene, at Royal Army Medical College, 1912. Served European War, 1914-18 (wounded, despatches thrice, MC, OStJ). Served in India; DAD Hygiene and Pathology, Bermuda Command, 1924-28; OC Military Hospital, Gibraltar, 1934-37; ADH Northern Comd, 1937-38. War of 1939-45 (CBE, King Haakon VII Liberty Cross of Norway, 2 Medals). Commandant Army School of Hygiene; Member Army Hygiene Advisory Cttee, War Office, 1939-46; retired, 1947. *Publications:* various articles in Lancet, Journal of RAMC, etc. *Recreations:* rowing, hunting, tennis, hockey, etc (past); music, motoring, watching all forms of

sport (present). *Address:* Woodside, Lynch Road, Farnham, Surrey. *T:* Farnham 5047. *Club:* Leander.

[Died 10 April 1972.

ALLOTT, Eric Newmarch, DM, FRCP; FRIC; Consultant Adviser in Chemical Pathology, Ministry of Health, 1963-68; Director, Group Laboratory, Lewisham Hospital, 1931-64; *b* 28 May 1899; *e s* of Henry Newmarch Allott, Stretford, Manchester; *m* 1930, Edith Mary Kydd (*d* 1974); one *d. Educ:* Manchester Grammar Sch.; Balliol Coll., Oxford (Brackenbury Scholar). St Bartholomew's Hospital, BA 1920; BM Oxford, 1925. Demonstrator in Chemistry, Univ. of Oxford, 1920-22; Beit Memorial Fellow in Medical Research, 1925-27; Asst Physiologist, Sheffield Royal Hosp., 1928; Chief Asst, Medical Professorial Unit, St Barts Hosp., 1929-31. Chm. of Council, 1957-61, and former Pres., Assoc. of Clinical Pathologists; FRSocMed (Sec., 1937-44 Pres., 1944-46, Section of Experimental Medicine); Chm., Section of Chemical Pathology, 1st Internat. Congress of Clinical Pathology, 1951; Mem., Biochemical Soc. (Cttee, 1948-52); Member Council: Royal Institute of Chemistry, 1962-65; College of Pathologists, 1963-66; Member Editorial Board, Journal of Clinical Pathology; Hon. Lecturer in Pathology, KCH and RCS. *Publications:* Richter's Organic Chemistry (3rd English edn), 1934; Section Editor, Recent Advances in Clinical Pathology; papers on medical and chemical pathological subjects. *Recreation:* gardening. *Address:* 27 Ritchie Court, 380 Banbury Road, Oxford OX2 7PW. *T:* Oxford 50496. *[Died 31 Dec. 1980.*

ALLSOP, Kenneth; author, television commentator, journalist with Sunday Times; *b* 29 Jan. 1920; *s* of late John Allsop and Mary Ann Allsop (*née* Halliday); *m* 1942, Betty Ashton Creak; two *s* one *d. Educ:* St Andrew's College. Served RAF, 1940-44. Staff editorial posts: Jun. Reporter, Slough Observer, 1938-39; Sub-Editor, John Bull, 1945; Reporter, Evening Advertiser, Swindon, 1946; Reporter, Sunday Express, 1946-47; Law Courts Reporter, Press Assoc., 1948-50; Feature-writer, Picture Post, 1950-55; Feature-writer, Evening Standard, 1955-56; Literary Editor and Columnist, Daily Mail, 1956-64. Has contrib. to most leading newspapers and periodicals. On television: reporter for ITN, 1955; ed The Bookman for ABC, 1958; presented fortnightly documentary, Searchlight, for Granada, 1959-60; joined BBC as studio interviewer and film reporter for Tonight, 1960; also presented This Nation Tomorrow, 1963, and Life, 1968; presenter: BBC's nightly current affairs programme, Twenty-Four Hours, (from inception) 1965-72; environmental programme, Down to Earth, 1972-; Edition, 1973-. On radio: Mem. The Critics, 1966-67; presented: The World of Jazz, 1963; The World of Books, 1966-67; Wildlife Review, 1967-68; Now Read On, 1970. Elected Vis. Research Fellow of Merton Coll., Oxford, 1968; MA (special status), Oxon, 1969. Mem., Standing Adv. Cttee on Artificial Limbs, 1968-70; Pres., Defenders of W Dorset; Governor, Human Rights Trust; Founder Member, Middle Thames Natural Hist. Soc. (Hon. Life Mem.); Member: British Trust for Conservation Volunteers; CPRE; Dorset Natural History Soc.; Soc. of Dorset Men; Friends of the Earth; Merton Soc.; Society of Authors; Llewellyn Rhys Memorial Prize Cttee, 1958-64. Rector, Edinburgh Univ., 1968-71; Hon. Pres., Edinburgh Univ. Students Rep. Council, 1973. *Publications:* (include): Adventure Lit Their Star, 1949 (John Llewellyn Rhys Memorial Prize for 1950) (repr. 1962 and 1972); The Sun Himself Must Die, 1949; The Daybreak Edition, 1951; The Last Voyages of the Mayflower, 1955 (US only); The Angry Decade, 1958; The Bootleggers, 1961 (repr. 1968); Scan, 1965; Hard Travellin', 1967 (repr. 1972); Fit to Live In?: the Future of Britain's Countryside, 1970; In the Country, 1972. Is incl. in anthologies and collections both Brit. and Amer., 1951-; The Annals of America (Encyc. Brit.), 1968; The Negro in American History (Encyc. Brit.), 1969. *Recreations:* ornithology, walking, music (esp. jazz and folk). *Address:* Milton Mill, West Milton, Bridport, Dorset. *Clubs:* Savile, Ronnie Scott's.

[Died 23 May 1973.

ALLSOPP, Samuel Ranulph, CBE 1954 (MBE 1942); DL; Merchant Banker, Arbuthnot Latham & Co. Ltd, 1929-69; Member, Hops Marketing Board (Chairman, 1947-69); *b* 7 March 1899; *s* of Lt-Col Hon. Ranulph Allsopp, 4th *s* of 1st Baron Hindlip, and Margaret, *d* of William Whitbread; *m* 1923, Hon. Norah Hyacinthe Littleton, *d* of 4th Baron Hatherton; two *s* two *d. Educ:* Eton; King's Coll., Cambridge. Served European War, 1918-19 (2nd Lt); served Home Guard, 1940-44 (Major); Lt-Col OC 12th Essex Cadet Bn, 1945-47; Lt-Col OC 12th Bn Essex Home Guard, 1952-55. Anglo-Austrian Bank, Vienna and London, 1922-28; Hon. Sec. Eton Coll. War Memorial and Bursary Funds, 1943-69. DL Essex, 1946; High Sheriff of Essex, 1955. *Recreation:* shooting. *Address:* Alsa Lodge, Stansted, Essex. *T:* Stansted 3244. *Clubs:* Pratt's, City University.

[Died 10 March 1975.

ALLUM, Sir John (Andrew Charles), Kt 1950; CBE 1946; *b* 27 Jan. 1889; *s* of John Allum, London; *m* Annie, *d* of Thomas William Attwood; two *s* three *d*. Mayor of the City of Auckland, New Zealand, 1941-53. *Address:* 158 Aberdeen Road, Auckland 9, New Zealand. *[Died* 16 *Sept.* 1972.

ALMEDINGEN, Edith Martha; novelist and poet; *b* St Petersburg, 21 July 1898; *y d* of late Prof. A. N. von Almedingen. *Educ:* Xenia Nobility School; The University, Petrograd. Lecturer on English Mediaeval History and Literature, The University, Petrograd, 1920-22; came to England, 1923; has supported herself by writing and lecturing since then. Lecturer on Russian Literature, Univ. of Oxford, 1951. Member Faculty (Historico-Philological), Univ. of Petrograd, 1922. FRSL, 1951. *Publications: poetry:* Rus, 1939; Poloniae Testamentum, 1942; Out of Seir, 1943; Storm at Westminster, 1952; The Unnamed Stream, 1965; *autobiography:* Tomorrow Will Come, 1941; The Almond Tree, 1947; Within the Harbour, 1950; St Petersburg, 1969; *novels:* Frossia, 1943; Dasha, 1945; Stand Fast, Beloved City, 1954; Fair Haven, 1956; Stephen's Light, 1957; The Scarlet Goose, 1958; The Little Stairway, 1960; Dark Splendour, 1961; The Ladies of St Hedwig's, 1965; Too Early Lilac, 1970; *biography:* Life of Many Colours, 1958; So Dark a Stream (a Study of Emperor Paul I). 1959; The Empress Alexandra (1872-1918), 1961; The Emperor Alexander II (1818-1881), 1962; Catherine the Great, 1963; The Emperor Alexander I, 1964; An Unbroken Unity (A Study of Grand-Duchess Serge of Russia), 1964; The Romanovs (1613-1917), 1966; Francis of Assisi, 1967; Charlemagne, 1968; Leonardo Da Vinci: a Portrait, 1969; *children's books:* The Young Pavlova, 1961; The Young Leonardo da Vinci, 1963; The Knights of the Golden Table, 1963; The Treasure of Siegfried, 1964; The Young Catherine the Great, 1965; Little Katia, 1966; The Retreat from Moscow, 1812, 1966; Young Mark, 1967 (1st Prize, Children's Books World Council, USA); Gudrun, 1968; One Little Tree, 1968; A Candle at Dusk, 1969; Fanny, 1969; I Remember St Petersburg, 1969; Ellen, 1970. *Recreations:* reading, embroidery. *Address:* c/o Messrs Anthony Sheil Associates, 47 Dean Street, W1.   *[Died* 5 *March* 1971.

ALSTON ROBERTS WEST, General Sir Michael M.; *see* West.

ALTHAUS, Frederick Rudolph, CBE 1970; Senior Partner, Pember & Boyle, Stockbrokers; *b* 6 Sept. 1895; *s* of late T. F. Althaus, London; *m* 1927, Margaret, *d* of late C. F. Twist, London; two *s* one *d*. *Educ:* Rugby; Balliol College, Oxford. Served Suffolk Regt, 1914-18 (wounded, despatches). Mem. Stock Exchange, London, 1922 (Mem. Council, 1949-73; Deputy-Chairman, 1959-63); London Del. to Conf. of European Stock Exchanges (now Fédération Internationale des Bourses de Valeurs), 1957-, Vice-Pres., 1968-69, Pres., 1970-72; Member Jenkins Cttee on Company Law, 1959; a Comr, Public Works Loan Board, 1965-69. *Publications:* (Originator and Editor) British Government Securities in the Twentieth Century, 1949-72. *Recreations:* music, painting, golf. *Address:* Yew Place, Farnham Royal, Bucks. *T:* Farnham Common 3102. *Clubs:* Oriental, City University.   *[Died* 21 *Aug.* 1975.

ALUWIHARE, Sir Richard, KCMG 1950; Kt 1948; CBE 1945; High Commissioner of Ceylon in India, 1957-63, retired; *b* 23 May 1895; *m* 1921, Lucille Moonemalle (*d* 1961); two *d*. *Educ:* Trinity Coll., Kandy. Served European War, 1914-18, Somme, France (wounded); welfare work with Indian Army (despatches). Joined Ceylon Civil Service, 1920; (appointed by Governor) Actg Police Magistrate, Dandagamuwa, 1923; HM Customs, 1926; District Judge, Kegalle, 1928, Nuwara Eliya, 1931; Class II of Civil Service; Controller of Finance and Supply, General Treasury, 1934; Asst Govt Agent, Kegalle, 1937; Dep. Collector of Customs, 1939; Actg Govt Agent, North Central Prov., 1941; Class I Civil Service; Govt Agent, Central Prov., 1946; Inspector-General of Police, Ceylon, 1947-53, retd. *Recreations:* cricket, Rugby football, swimming, riding. *Address:* Aluwihare, Matale, Sri Lanka. *Clubs:* Singhalese Sports, Orient.   *[Died* 22 *Dec.* 1976.

AMAND de MENDIETA, Rev. Dr Emmanuel Alexandre, DD; Residentiary Canon of Winchester since Oct. 1962; *b* Bouvignes-sur-Meuse, Belgium, 11 Nov. 1907; *e s* of Ludovic Amand de Mendieta and of the Baroness Jeanne de Bonhome; *m* 1956, Ginette Christiane Bosc; one *s*. *Educ:* Coll. Notre-Dame de Bellevue, Dinant; Univ. catholique de Louvain. Entered Benedictine Abbey of Maredsous, Belgium, Oct. 1925; Maredsons and Mont-César, Louvain, 1927-33 (course in philos. and theol.); Priestly ordination in Namur Cathedral, 1932; Univ. of Louvain (courses in Class. Philol., 1933-36); Dr Philosophy and Letters 1939. Regular Contrib. to Revue Bénédictine, 1940-55. Reception into Church of England, 1956; Bye-Fellow of

Gonville and Caius Coll., Cambridge, 1957-62. DD Cambridge 1966. *Publications:* (as Dom David Amand) Fatalisme et liberté dans l'antiquité grecque, 1945 (Louvain); L'ascèse monastique de saint Basile, essai historique, 1949 (Maredsous); (as E. Amand de Mendieta): La Presqu'île des Caloyers, le Mont-Athos, 1955 (Bruges-Paris); (collab. Dr Stig Y. Rudberg) Eustathius, Ancienne version latine des neuf homélies sur l'Hexaéméron de Basile de Césarée, 1958 (Berlin); Rome and Canterbury, A Biblical and Free Catholicism, 1962 (London); contrib. to Biblical and Patristic Studies in Memory of R. P. Casey, 1963; The "Unwritten" and "Secret" Apostolic Traditions in the Theological Thought of St Basil of Caesarea, 1965 (Edinburgh); Anglican Vision, 1971 (London); Mount Athos, The Garden of the Panaghia, 1972 (Berlin); L'art au Mont-Athos, miroir de la mentalité athonite, 1976 (Thessaloniki); (with Prof. S. Y. Rudberg) Basile de Césarée: la tradition manuscrite directe des neuf homélies sur l'Hexaéméron, in preparation (Berlin); contribs to L'Antiquité Classique (Brussels), Jl of Theological Studies (Oxford), Byzantinische Zeitschrift (Munich). *Address:* 1 The Close, Winchester, Hants. *T:* Winchester 61722.   *[Died* 1 *July* 1976.

AMBLER, Air Vice-Marshal Geoffrey Hill, CB 1946; CBE 1944 (OBE 1941); AFC; DL; *b* 1904; *s* of late Fred Ambler; *m* 1940, Phoebe, *d* of Edgar Gaunt, Hawksworth Hall, Guiseley; three *d*. *Educ:* Cambridge University (MA). Joined Auxiliary Air Force, 1931; served in Fighter Command, 1939-42; Comdt, Royal Observer Corps, 1942-43; HQ Fighter Command, 1943-45. Air ADC to the King, 1943-44; Hon. Air Cdre No 609 (W Riding) Sqdn AAF, 1947-57. Hon. LLD Leeds, 1966. DL West Riding, Yorks, 1949.   *[Died* 26 *Aug.* 1978.

AMBROSE, Brig. Robert Denis, CIE 1947; OBE 1938; MC 1917; retired 1961, as Public Relations manager, Smith Kline and French International Company; *b* 3 Feb. 1896; *s* of Dr T. D. Ambrose, Dewsbury, Yorks; *m* 1938, Miriam Tilden, Philadelphia, USA; one *s* two *d*. *Educ:* Mount St Mary's College, Derbyshire; Wellington Military College, India. Commissioned in 104th Wellesley's Rifles, Indian Army, 1916; served European War, 1914-18, Palestine Campaign, 1917-18 (MC); NW Frontier, India, 1923-26 and 1930-38; commanded Tochi Scouts, 1933-36. Served War of 1939-45, in Middle East, Hong Kong and Burma; commanded 5th Bn (Napier's) Rajputana Rifles, 1940-43, Bde Comdr, 1943-45; Inspector Gen., Frontier Corps, 1945-47. *Address:* c/o National Westminster Bank Ltd, 63 Piccadilly, W1. *Club:* Naval and Military.   *[Died* 4 *Nov.* 1974.

AMCOTTS, Lt-Col Sir Weston C.; *see* Cracroft-Amcotts.

AMEER ALI, (Syed) Waris, CIE 1942; Indian Civil Service (retired); *b* 12 Oct. 1886; *e s* of late Rt Hon. Syed Ameer Ali, PC, CIE, and late Isabelle Ida Ameer Ali, 2 Cadogan Place, SW1; *m* 1st, 1918, Anne Marguerite (*d* 1943), *d* of late Walter Thomas Hindmarsh Radford, 25 Park Crescent, Portland Place; no *c*; 2nd, 1951, Lady Eleanor Szanto (*d* 1974), *y d* of 3rd Earl of Dartrey. *Educ:* Wellington College; Balliol College, Oxford. Served in the United Provinces of Agra and Oudh. Closed Indian Service as District and Sessions Judge of Gonda-cum-Bahraich in Oudh; retired, 1929; War Services Adviser to High Commissioner for India, 1939-45. *Publications:* articles, etc. *Recreations:* shooting, golf, target shooting (India Rifle Team, Bisley, 1930-38). *Address:* 1 Alexandra Court, Queen's Gate, SW7. *T:* 01-589 1556. *Club:* Reform.   *[Died* 2 *April* 1975.

AMEER ALI, Sir Torick, Kt 1941; *b* 9 June 1891; *y s* of late Rt Hon. Syed Ameer Ali, PC, CIE, etc, and Isabelle Ida Ameer Ali; *m* 1925, Mary Louise, *d* of late Roderick Edmond Carter, Indian Imperial Service of Engineers; one *s* one *d*. *Educ:* Marlborough; Christ Church, Oxford. Called to Bar Inner Temple; Puisne Judge, High Court, Calcutta, 1931-44; acted as Judge of Federal Court, 1943; acting Chief Justice, Bengal, 1944; an Adviser to Secretary of State for India, 1944. *Publication:* Memoirs of the Chevalier de Melville. *Address:* Gregory Arms, Doccombe, Moretonhampstead, Devon TQ13 8GG.   *[Died* 13 *July* 1975.

AMES, Sir Cecil (Geraint), Kt 1965; *b* 5 Aug. 1897; *s* of late Herbert Edmund Ames, solicitor, Frome; *m* 1938, Jean Munro Miller (*d* 1976); one *d*. *Educ:* Elstree Prep. School; Dover College. Somerset LI, 1916-18. Solicitor, 1921; Nigerian Administrative Service, 1922-33; Registrar, Supreme Court of Nigeria, 1933-34; Asst Judge, High Court of Protectorate of Nigeria, 1934-44; Puisne Judge, Supreme Court of Nigeria, 1944-50; retd 1950. Colonial Magistrate, Gambia, 1953-58; Comr for Law Revision, Sierra Leone, 1958-60; Pres. (part-time) Sierra Leone and Gambia Court of Appeal, 1960-61; Comr for Revision of Laws, Eastern Nigeria, 1960-64; Presiding Judge, Sierra Leone Court of Appeal (part-time), 1961-65; President,

Gambia Court of Appeal (part-time position), 1961-67; Comr for Revision of Laws, Gambia, 1965-67; retd 1967. *Publications*: Gazetteer of the Plateau Province of Nigeria, 1934 (publ. Nigeria). Editor, Nigeria Law Reports, Vols XIV-XVIII. *Address*: 4 Gerrard Buildings, Bath BA2 4DQ. *T*: Bath 64089.
[*Died 17 Aug. 1977*.

AMES, Jennifer; *see* Greig, Maysie.

AMHERST OF HACKNEY, 3rd Baron, *cr* 1892; **William Alexander Evering Cecil,** CBE 1963; Major late Royal Horse Guards; *b* 31 May 1912; *s* of Capt. Hon. William Amherst Cecil, MC (*d* 1914), Grenadier Guards, and Gladys (*d* 1947), *o c* of Col H. C. Baggalay, of Heatherhurst Grange, Frimley; *S* grandmother, 1919; *m* 1939, Margaret E. Clifton, *y d* of late Brig.-Gen. Howard Clifton Brown; two *s* one *d*. *Educ*: Eton; Trinity College, Cambridge. Royal Horse Guards, 1933; served War of 1939-45, MEF, 1940-45. CStJ. *Heir*: *s* Hon. William Hugh Amherst Cecil [*b* 28 Dec. 1940; *m* 1965, Elisabeth, *d* of Hugh H. Merriman; one *s* one *d*]. *Address*: Rudge House, Crondall, Farnham, Surrey. *T*: Aldershot 850450; 29 Eaton Mews South, SW1. *T*: 01-235 1421. *Clubs*: Buck's, Carlton, Royal Yacht Squadron.
[*Died 22 July 1980*.

AMIES, Sir Arthur (Barton Pilgrim), Kt 1957; CMG 1949; Emeritus Professor of Dental Medicine and Surgery, University of Melbourne, 1967; *b* 17 Oct. 1902; *s* of late Arthur P. Amies, Melbourne; *m* 1930, Geraldine C., *d* of Peter Collee, Linlithgow, Scotland. *Educ*: Modern Sch., Perth, Western Australia; Queen's College, Univ. of Melbourne; Edinburgh Royal Colls. DDSc (Melbourne) 1929; DLO Melbourne 1933; FRCSE 1948; FRACS 1934; FDSRCS 1948; FDSRCS Edinburgh, 1950; FRSE 1939. Formerly Member Council and Pro-Vice-Chancellor, University of Melbourne; Hon. Fellow of Queen's College; Hon. Consulting Oral Surgeon, Alfred Hospital, Royal Eye and Ear Hospital, and Royal Dental Hospital, Melbourne; Federal President, Australian Dental Assoc., 1937-39; Hon. Life Member: Austr. Dental Assoc.; British Dental Assoc.; Austr. and NZ Soc. of Oral Surgeons; Patron, Dietetic Assoc. of Victoria. Served War of 1939-45, with 4th Australian General Hospital in Western Desert and Tobruk, and later with Maxillo-Facial and Plastic Surgery Unit, and 2nd AGH Kantara; Patron, Rats of Tobruk Assoc., Vict. Br. Hon. LLD Glasgow, 1963. *Address*: Upper Kinneil, Yarra Glen, Victoria 3775, Australia. *T*: 7301278. *Clubs*: Melbourne, Naval and Military (Melbourne).
[*Died 4 Dec. 1976*.

AMORY, Major Sir John Heathcoat-, 3rd Bt, *cr* 1874; Major Home Guard; *b* 2 May 1894; *e s* of Sir Ian Murray Heathcoat Amory, 2nd Bt, CBE, and Alexandra Georgina, OBE (*d* 1942), *e d* of late Vice-Adm. G. H. Seymour, CB; *S* father 1931; *m* 1937, Joyce, *o d* of Newton Wethered, Brook, Surrey. *Educ*: Christ Church, Oxford. Served European War, 1914-19, with 4th Devon Regt in India and Mesopotamia and in Persia and the Caucasus with the Dunster Force (despatches, two medals); President of John Heathcoat & Co.; High Sheriff of Devon, 1942-43; JP Devon, 1922; DL Devon, 1952. *Recreations*: gardening, shooting. *Heir*: *b* Viscount Amory. *Address*: Knightshayes Court, Tiverton, Devon. *T*: 2438; Glenfernate Lodge, Enochdhu, Blairgowrie, Perthshire. *Club*: Buck's.
[*Died 22 Nov. 1972*.

AMPTHILL, 3rd Baron, *cr* 1881; **John Hugo Russell,** CBE 1945; Captain RN, retired; recalled for Service, 1939; *b* 4 Oct. 1896; *e s* of 2nd Baron and Lady Margaret Lygon, CI, GCVO, GBE (*d* 1957), *d* of 6th Earl Beauchamp; *S* father, 1935; *m* 1st, 1918, Christabel Hulme Hart (who obtained a divorce 1937); one *s*; 2nd, 1937, Sibell Faithfull (*d* 1947), *yr d* of Thomas Wilkinson Lumley; 3rd, 1948, Adeline, *e d* of Canon H. E. Hone; one *s* one *d*. *Heir*: *s* Hon. Geoffrey Denis Erskine Russell [*b* 15 Oct. 1921; *m* 1946, Susan Mary, *d* of Hon. Charles John Frederic Winn; two *s* one *d* (and one *s* decd)]. *Address*: 6 Springfield Road, St John's Wood, NW8. *T*: 01-624 3475. *Clubs*: United Service & Royal Aero, Turf.
[*Died 3 June 1973*.

ANDA, Géza; pianist; Head of Piano Course, within framework of International Master Course in Music, Zürich; *b* Budapest, 19 Nov. 1921; *s* of Géza Anda, Headmaster; became Swiss citizen, 1955; *m* 1964, Hortense Bührle. *Educ*: Budapest Academy of Music. Made début with Mengelberg, 1939; has played with numerous orchestras, including: Berlin Philharmonic; Vienna Philharmonic; New York Philharmonic; Amsterdam Concertgebouw; Philharmonia, London; Paris Conservatoire; Santa Cecilia, Rome; Philadelphia Symphony; Chicago Symphony; San Francisco Symphony, etc. Has played at Salzburg, Lucerne, Edinburgh and Vienna Festivals; makes annual appearances at Festival Hall; frequent tours of United States and Canada. Hon. RAM, 1969. Grand Prix des Disques,

1961, 1962, 1963, 1966; Preis der Deutschen Schallplattenkritik, Berlin; Franz Liszt Prize; Wiener Flötenuhr, 1969-70. Ordre des Arts et des Lettres (France); Professor *hc* (Austrian State), 1974. *Publication*: 13 Cadenzas for Piano Concertos by Mozart, 1972. *Recreations*: bookbinding, sailing, walking tours. *Address*: Zollikerstrasse 178, Zürich, Switzerland. [*Died 14 June 1976*.

ANDERSON, Archibald Stirling Kennedy, DSO 1918; MC; MA, MB, ChB, DPH; retired; *b* 1887; *s* of late Alex. Anderson, Aberdeen; *m* 1925, Joyce (*d* 1954), *e d* of W. S. Wharton, Southtown, Great Yarmouth; twin *s*. *Educ*: Aberdeen Grammar Sch.; Aberdeen Univ. Served European War, 1914-19 (DSO, MC with bar, despatches, Hon. Lieut-Col RAMC). *Address*: 1 Marine Parade, Gorleston, Great Yarmouth, Norfolk. *T*: Great Yarmouth 61438.
[*Died 5 March 1972*.

ANDERSON, Arthur Ingham; Chairman, UAC International Limited (formerly The United Africa Co. Ltd), 1969-76; *b* 4 April 1916; *s* of John Fraser Anderson and Jane (*née* Millie); *m* 1954, Rolande Marie Bois-Meyer; one *s* one *d*. *Educ*: George Watson's Boys' Coll., Edinburgh; Univs of Edinburgh and Glasgow (MA). Joined Unilever, 1935; Management Trainee, 1937-39. Served War of 1939-45, HAC: Captain 19th Field Regt RA, N Africa, Sicily, Italy, Palestine, 1940-46 (despatches). The United Africa Co. Ltd, 1946-76: Germany, 1947; Nigeria, 1948; Company Rep. in US, 1952-54; Merchandise Man., 1955; Dir, 1957; Dep. Chm. and Jt Man. Dir, 1968; Dir, Unilever Ltd, 1970-76. *Recreations*: military history, photography, golf. *Address*: 64 Drax Avenue, West Wimbledon, SW20. *T*: 01-946 3671.
[*Died 10 Oct. 1976*.

ANDERSON, Sir Austin (Innes), Kt 1956; Chairman Orient Line, 1952-60 (Director 1950); Chairman Anderson, Green & Co. Ltd, 1950-63 (Director, 1924); Director: Peninsular and Oriental Steam Navigation Co., 1955-62; University Life Assurance Ltd, 1943-67; Westminster Bank, 1950-68; *b* 16 Mar. 1897; *s* of Sir Hugh Anderson, FRS; *m* Alison Royse, *d* of W. R. Lysaght, CBE; one *s* two *d*. *Educ*: Harrow; King's Coll., Cambridge. Served in Army, 1915-18. Member Food Investigation Board, 1934-38; Assistant Director Liner Division, Ministry of War Transport, 1940-43, and of Sea Transport Division, 1943-45. Chairman, Refrigerated Cargo Research Council, 1946-58; Pres., Chamber of Shipping, 1955; Chm., General Council of British Shipping, 1955; Mem. Cttee Lloyds Register of Shipping, 1951-62; Member: Ministry of Transport Cttee on application of Nuclear Power to Marine Purposes, 1957-62; Air Min. Meteorological Cttee, 1959-65; Central Transport Users Consultative Cttee for Gt Britain, 1952-54. *Address*: Summers, West Clandon, Surrey. *T*: Clandon 512.
[*Died 16 Oct. 1973*.

ANDERSON, Clinton Presba; *b* Centerville, SD, 23 Oct. 1895; *s* of Andrew Jay Anderson and Hattie Belle Presba; *m* 1921, Henrietta McCartney; one *s* one *d*. *Educ*: Dakota Wesleyan University; University of Michigan. Hon. LHD Dakota Wesleyan Univ., 1933; hon. DAgr New Mexico Coll. of Agric. and Mechanic Arts, 1946; hon. LLD: Univ. of Michigan, St Lawrence Univ., Canton, NY, 1946; Missouri Valley Coll., Marshall, Mo., 1949; Univ. of Alaska, 1965. Newspaper reporter and editor, Albuquerque, New Mexico, 1918-22; owner insurance agency, Albuquerque, New Mexico, 1925-63; Treasurer, State of New Mexico, 1933-34; Mem. 77th, 78th and 79th Congresses (1941-45), New Mexico at large. Secretary of Agriculture, United States, 1945-48, when resigned to enter Democratic primary for US Senator; Senator from New Mexico, 1949-73. Member Delta Theta Phi; Democrat; Presbyterian; Mason, Elk. *Address*: (home) 3621 Camino Alameda, SW, Albuquerque, New Mexico 87105, USA; (office) 215-5th Street SW, Albuquerque, New Mexico 87101. *Club*: Rotary (Pres. Rotary Internat., 1932-33).
[*Died 11 Nov. 1975*.

ANDERSON, Sir Colin (Skelton), KBE 1969; Kt 1950; *b* 15 July 1904; *e s* of late Sir Alan Anderson, GBE; *m* 1932, Morna Campbell, 2nd *d* of Sir Alexander MacCormick, KCMG; two *d* (and one *d* decd). *Educ*: Eton; Trinity College, Oxford. Director: Midland Bank Ltd, 1950-74; Marine Insurance Co. Ltd, 1950-70; Orient Steam Navigation Co. Ltd, 1950-69; P&O Steam Navigation Co., 1960-69; Australia & New Zealand Bank Ltd, 1951-70; Royal Opera House, Covent Garden, Ltd, 1961-73; City Arts Trust Ltd, 1962-70; English Opera Group Ltd, 1963-73. Chairman: London Shipowners' Dock Labour Cttee, 1944-45; London Port Employers (and a Member of London Bd of Nat. Dock Labour Bd), 1945-47; Nat. Assoc. of Port Employers, 1947-48, 1950-54; General Council of British Shipping, 1949-50; British Liner Cttee, 1949-50; Internat. Chamber of Shipping, 1949-63; Min. of Transport's Advisory Cttee on Traffic Signs for Motor Roads, 1957-61; Min. of Education's Cttee on Grants to Students, 1958-60; Gray, Dawes, Westray & Co. Ltd, 1960-70;

Trustees of Tate Gall., 1960-67 (Vice-Chm., 1953-59); Ocean Travel Development, 1961-68; Anderson Green & Co. Ltd, 1963-70 (Dir, 1930); HMS Victory Adv. Technical Cttee, 1964-76; Sea Transport Commn of Internat. Chamber of Commerce, 1965-71; Hampstead Heath and Old Hampstead Protection Soc., 1960-67. President: Seamen's Hospital Soc., 1962-78; Chamber of Shipping of the UK, 1949-50 (Vice-Pres., 1948-49); British Employers' Confederation, 1956-58 (Vice-Pres., 1952-56); Hon. Pres., Internat. Chamber of Shipping, 1963-. Member: Min. of Transport's Cttee on the Prevention of Pollution of the Sea by Oil, 1954-64; Commonwealth Office's Oversea Migration Board, 1953-66; Court of Enquiry into National Railway Strike (with Sir J. Cameron and Mr H. Douglas), 1954; Contemporary Art Soc. (Chairman, 1956-60); Council of Royal College of Art (Chairman, 1952-56; Provost, 1967-); National Council of Design and Industries Association (President, 1950-53); Council of Industrial Design, 1951-60; Trustee, Nat. Gall. (representing Tate Gall.), 1963-67. Chm., Royal Fine Art Commn, 1968-76 (Mem., 1959-76). Prime Warden of the Fishmongers' Company, 1963-64. Corres. Mem., Bayerische Akademie der Schönen Künste, 1969-. Hon. ARIBA 1957; Hon. Fellow, Trinity College, Oxford, 1963. Hon. LLD, Aberdeen, 1963. Hon. Designer, RCA, 1953; Hon. Dr, RCA, 1967. Jubilee Medal, RSA, 1954. Officer of the Order of Orange Nassau, 1948. *Recreations:* the home, the arts, the garden. *Address:* Le Val House, St Brelade, Jersey, Channel Islands.
[*Died 16 Oct.* 1980.

ANDERSON, David Dick, CBE 1951; MC 1916 (and Bar, 1918); retired as HM Chief Inspector of Schools, Scottish Education Department, 1954; *b* 26 March 1889; *m* 1930, Catharine Stevenson; three *s*. *Educ:* Glasgow High School and University. Teacher: Queen's Park Senior Secondary School, Glasgow; Madras College, St Andrews; Daniel Stewart's College, Edinburgh. Served European War; officer, 1914-19, in East Yorkshire Regiment; retired with rank of Major. *Recreations:* golf, gardening, foreign travel. *Address:* 12 Ross Road, Edinburgh EH16 5QN. *T:* 031-667 8873. *Clubs:* Royal Over-Seas League; Royal Scots (Edinburgh). [*Died 15 Sept.* 1980.

ANDERSON, Sir Donald (Forsyth), Kt 1954; DL; Chairman and a Managing Director of P&OSN Co., 1960-71 (formerly Deputy Chairman, and a Managing Director); Director: National Westminster Bank Ltd; Australia and New Zealand Bank Ltd; Times Newspapers Ltd; Qantas Ltd; *b* 3 Sept. 1906; 2nd *s* of late Sir Alan Garrett Anderson, GBE; *m* 1935, Margaret Elaine, *e d* of Sir David R. Llewellyn, 1st Bt; four *d*. *Educ:* Eton; Trinity Coll., Oxford (MA). Entered Anderson Green & Co. Ltd; P&OSN Co. in 1934. In Min. of Shipping (subsequently Min. of War Transport), Sept. 1939-June 1943; Washington, DC, with British Merchant Shipping Mission, 1941-43. Chm. Council, Royal Free Hospital Sch. of Medicine; Pres. Seafarers' Education Service; Chm. Shipping Federation, 1950-62 (Pres., 1963-); Joint Chm., National Maritime Board, 1950-62; President International Shipping Federation, 1950-62; Pres. Chamber of Shipping, 1953-54; Chm. General Council of British Shipping, 1953-54; Pres. Inst. of Shipping and Forwarding Agents, 1955; Pres. Inst. of Marine Engineers, 1956; Chm. British Liner Cttee, 1956-58; Pres., Institute of Export, 1961-63. Elder Brother of Trinity House and Hon. Brother of Hull Trinity House. Hon. Captain, RNR; Hon. Mem., Hon. Co. of Master Mariners. DL Glos, 1969. Officer, Order of Orange Nassau; Commendatore, Order Al Merito della Repubblica Italiana. *Address:* Far Upton Wold, Moreton in Marsh, Glos. *T:* Blockley 261. *Clubs:* City of London, Brooks's.
[*Died 20 March* 1973.

ANDERSON, Sir Donald (George), Kt 1967; CBE 1959; Chairman, Qantas, 1973-75; *b* 1 March 1917; *s* of Alick Gibb Anderson and Clara Katherine Anderson; *m* 1941, Monica Mary Porker; two *d*. *Educ:* Adelaide High Sch; Adelaide Teachers' Coll.; Adelaide Univ. Served RAAF, 1940-46, Flt Lt, Pilot (despatches). Asst Dir-Gen., Dept of Civil Aviation, Australia, 1951; Deputy Dir-Gen., 1955, Dir-Gen., 1956-73. *Clubs:* Savage (Melbourne); Imperial Services, University (Sydney). [*Died 30 Nov.* 1975.

ANDERSON, Sir Duncan (Law), KBE 1960 (CBE 1944); TD; CEng, FICE; consulting civil engineer; *b* 10 June 1901; *s* of J. D. Anderson, MA, Aberdeen, and L. Anderson; *m* 1947, Edens Alcyone, *er d* of Wallace McMullen; no *c*. *Educ:* Robert Gordon's Coll., Aberdeen. Practised as Civil Engineer on railway, road, bridge and tunnel construction, 1922-39. TA Officer, 1923-61; served with Royal Engineers, War of 1939-45 (despatches, CBE); Deputy Dir of Works, Gen. Eisenhower's staff, N African Campaign, and Dir of Works (Brig.), and FM Alexander's Staff, Italian Campaign. Concerned latterly with rehabilitation of Italian Industry as Dep. Vice-Pres. Allied

Commn, Rome. Chm. Jt Anglo-American/Jugo-Slav Econ. Commn, Trieste. CCG, 1946-50; Vice-Pres. Econ. Sub-Commn, Berlin, and Dep. Chm. US/UK Control Office, Frankfurt; Mem. two Foreign Office Missions led by Lord Strang to Washington, 1947 (first on rehabilitation of Ruhr coal industry, second, on finance and control of German foreign trade). Gen. Manager, Overseas Food Corp., Southern Prov., Tanganyika, 1950-51; responsible for re-organising and cutting down "Ground-nuts scheme" in that area after its failure. Controller, Caribbean Region, Colonial Development Corp., 1951-53, in charge of the Corporation's interest in Islands of West Indies, Br. Honduras and Br. Guiana; Controller in charge of Corporation's interests in Nyasaland, Rhodesias, Bechuanaland and Swaziland, 1953-55; Chm. Federal Power Bd of Rhodesia and Nyasaland (responsible for construction of Kariba Hydro-electric project on the Zambezi), 1955-61. First Chm., Commn for the New Towns, 1961-64. Director: South Durham Steel and Iron Co., 1961-67; BOAC, 1964-70; British Oxygen Co., 1962-72; Thomas Tilling Ltd, 1965-72. *Address:* Flat 7, 14 Melbury Road, Holland Park, W14. *T:* 01-602 3434. *Club:* Athenæum.
[*Died 28 July* 1980.

ANDERSON, Sir Edward (Arthur), Kt 1952; JP; retired as Director of A. Anderson & Son (Electrical Engineers) Ltd, Middlesbrough; *b* 4 Jan. 1908; *s* of Arthur and Florence Anderson; *m* 1937, Elsa Mary French; no *c*. *Educ:* Middlesbrough High Sch.; South Shields Marine Engineering Coll. Entire working life spent in family business, A. Anderson & Son. AIEE 1937. Councillor for County Borough of Middlesbrough, 1945-56; Chairman Middlesbrough Conservative Assoc., 1947-60; JP Middlesbrough, 1950-. *Recreations:* swimming, walking, reading, music and travel. *Address:* Spring Lodge, Guisborough, North Yorkshire. *T:* Guisborough 2581. *Club:* Cleveland (Middlesbrough).
[*Died 8 Feb.* 1979.

ANDERSON, Major George Denis; *b* 15 Nov. 1885; *s* of George and Alice Anderson; *m* 1926, Mary Myddleton-Evans (*d* 1968); one *d*. *Educ:* Eton; Christ Church, Oxford. High Sheriff of Northumberland, 1935. Dep. Chm. Northumberland QS, 1935-55; Chairman, 1955-60. *Address:* Little Harle Tower, Harle, Northumberland. *T:* Kirkwhelpington 229. *Clubs:* Junior Carlton; Northern Counties (Newcastle upon Tyne).
[*Died 13 Oct.* 1971.

ANDERSON, Sir Gilmour M.; *see* Menzies Anderson.

ANDERSON, James Stirling, MA, MB, ChB, MD, DPH; retired as Physician, St George's Hospital, also Director, Infectious Diseases Unit, Grove Hospital, and External Examiner Epidemiology and Infectious Diseases, University of Edinburgh; *b* 3 Dec. 1891; *s* of William Anderson and Annie Carrie; *m* 1928, Mary Stirk, MRCS, LRCP; one *s* one *d*. *Educ:* Robert Gordon's Coll., Aberdeen; Univ. of Aberdeen. House Physician and House Surg., Aberdeen Royal Infirmary; Resident Physician, City Hospital, Aberdeen; Asst MOH, Aberdeen; Dep. Medical Supt, Monsall Hospital, Manchester; Medical Supt, City Hospitals, Leeds; Lectr in Infectious Diseases, Univ. of Leeds; War service 4th Bn Gordon Highlanders, 1914-16; ed. Aberdeen Univ. Magazine. *Publications:* articles in British Medical Journal, Lancet, Journal of Pathology and Bacteriology, Archives of Disease in Childhood, Public Health and Clinical Journal. *Recreations:* golf, fishing. *Address:* 8 Foxton Road, Barrington, Cambs CB2 5RN. *T:* Cambridge 871012.
[*Died 20 Oct.* 1976.

ANDERSON, Dame Kitty, DBE 1961; BA London; PhD London; Vice-President, Girls' Public Day School Trust, since 1976 (Chairman, 1965-75); President, Schoolmistresses and Governesses Benevolent Institution, since 1972; *b* 4 July 1903; *d* of J. H. Anderson, FCA, and L. Anderson. *Educ:* High Sch. for Girls, Saltburn-by-the-Sea; Royal Holloway Coll., Univ. of London. Head Mistress King's Norton Girls' Grammar Sch., Birmingham, 1939-44; Head Mistress, North London Collegiate Sch., 1944-65. FCP, 1966. Hon. LLD, Hull, 1967; DUniv York, 1971. *Address:* 33 Hutchinson Drive, Northallerton, North Yorks. *Club:* University Women's. [*Died 15 Jan.* 1979.

ANDERSON, Lt-Gen. Sir Richard (Neville), KCB 1961 (CB 1957); CBE 1949; DSO and Bar, 1944; Colonel, The King's Own Royal Border Regiment, 1961-71; Colonel, 10th Princess Mary's Own Gurkha Rifles, 1960-66; *b* 28 April 1907; *s* of Col Sir Neville Anderson, CBE; *m* 1942, Dorrie Norah Wybergh; two *s*. *Educ:* Tonbridge; Royal Mil. Coll., Sandhurst; idc. Served Palestine, 1938-39; War of 1939-45; Italy campaign, 1944-45; Palestine, 1946-48; GOC 17 Gurkha Div., 1955-57; GOC Overseas Forces, Malaya, 1957-58; Vice-Adj.-Gen., War Office, 1958-60; GOC-in-C, MELF, 1960-63; GOC-in-C, NI

Command, 1963-65, retd 1965. Director, Civil Defence for Wales, 1965-68. Hon. Fellow Inst. of Civil Defence, 1966. *Recreation:* golf. *Address:* Tarrant Keynston House, Blandford, Dorset. *[Died 4 Sept.* 1979.

ANDERSON, Roger Charles, LittD; FSA, FRHistS; Chairman of Trustees, National Maritime Museum, 1959-62 (Trustee, 1927-62); *b* 23 July 1883; *o c* of John Rodgerson Anderson, and Edith, *d* of Edward Tayloe; *m* 1916, Romola Urquhart, *d* of Robert Fowler Mackenzie; no *c. Educ:* Winchester; Clare Coll., Cambridge. RNVR as Midshipman and Sub-Lieut, 1905-11; Lieut and Lt-Comdr 1914-19; Hon. Editor The Mariner's Mirror (Soc. for Nautical Research), 1914, 1919-22, 1931-32, and 1939-46; Joint Hon. Gen. Editor Southampton Record Soc., 1930-39; Pres. Soc. for Nautical Research, 1951-60. *Publications:* Naval Wars in the Baltic, 1910; Canoeing and Camping Adventures, 1910; The Naval Pocket Book, 1912-15; The Sailing Ship (with R. U. Anderson), 1926; The Rigging of Ships (1600-1720), 1927; Naval Wars in the Levant, 1952; Catalogue of Ship Models (National Maritime Museum), 1952; Seventeenth Century Rigging, 1955; Oared Fighting Ships, 1962. For Southampton Record Society: Letters of 15th and 16th Centuries, 1921-22; Assize of Bread Book, 1923; Book of Examinations, 1926; Examinations and Depositions, 1931-36. For Navy Records Society: Journal of the Earl of Sandwich, 1929; Journals of Thomas Allin, 1939-40; Journals and Narratives of the Third Dutch War, 1946; A Memoir of James Trevenen (with C. C. Lloyd), 1959. For Society for Nautical Research: A Treatise on Rigging (1625), 1921; Lists of English Men-of-War (1649-1702), 1935; Index to the Mariners' Mirror (Vols 1-35), 1956; List of English Men-of-War (1509-1649), 1959; List of English Naval Captains (1642-60), 1964. *Address:* 9 Grove Place, Lymington, Hants SO4 9SS. *[Died 2 Oct.* 1976.

ANDERSON, Dr Theodore Farnworth, CMG 1956; OBE 1943; HM Overseas Medical Service, retired; *b* 22 Oct. 1901; *s* of Rev. J. F. Anderson; *m* 1928, Isabel Cecile Downey; two *d. Educ:* Rugby Sch.; Trinity Hall, Cambridge; University Coll. Hospital. MA (Cantab), MD, BCh, MRCS, LRCP, DTM & H. General Practice, Kenya, 1925; appointed Medical Officer, Colonial Medical Service, Kenya, 1928. North Persian Forces Memorial Medal, 1930. Commn RAMC, 1939 (despatches); demobilised, 1945, rank of Col. Director of Medical Services, Somaliland Protectorate, 1945-49; Director of Medical Services, HM Overseas Medical Services, Kenya, 1949-57; MLC Kenya, 1950-57, retired. Liveryman Worshipful Soc. of Apothecaries; Freeman, City of London. *Publications:* numerous articles in medical press. *Recreations:* gardening, reading, history, archaeology. *Address:* The Clearing, Hawkhurst, Kent. *T:* Hawkhurst 2217. *Clubs:* Athenæum, Royal Commonwealth Society; Rye Golf; Nairobi; Limuru Country; Muthaiga Country. *[Died 13 June* 1979.

ANDERSON, Maj.-Gen. Thomas Victor, DSO 1918; psc 1920; *b* Ottawa, 4 July 1881; *s* of late Col William P. Anderson, CMG; *m* 1910, Elizabeth Grace, 2nd *d* of late Col W. D. Gordon, Kingston, Canada; three *d. Educ:* Royal Military Coll., Canada; McGill Univ. Graduated with Hons from RMC Canada, 1900; McGill, 1901 (BSc); Instructor in Civil Engineering, RMC, Canada, 1902-06; entered Canadian Permanent Force (Royal Canadian Engineers), 1905; in charge of Military Survey of Canada, 1910-14; served European War in France, Feb. 1915-April 1917; CRE 3rd Canadian Div., 1916-17; Commandant, Canadian Engineers' Training Centre, England, 1917-19; (severely wounded, DSO, Russian Order of St Anne, 2nd class, with swords, despatches four times, 1914-15 Star, British War Medal and Victory Medal, Canadian Volunteer Service Medal, War Medal, 1939-45); GSO, RMC, Kingston, 1921-25; Director Military Training and Staff Duties at National Defence Headquarters, Canada, 1925-29; District Officer Commanding Military District No 10, Winnipeg, 1929-33, Military District No 2, Toronto, 1933-35; Quarter Master General, Canada, 1935-38; Chief of Gen. Staff, Canada, 1938-40; Inspector-Gen. Central Canada, 1940-42, retd 1943. Hon. Col 2nd Fd Eng. Regt Royal Canadian Engineers, 1963-67. DSc Mil., 1963. *Address:* 34 Russell Hill Road, Toronto 7, Ontario. *[Died 8 Nov.* 1972.

ANDERSON, Maj.-Gen. Warren Melville, CBE 1946; DSO 1919; *b* 1894; *e s* of late Marsham Ambrose Anderson, Flowerbank, Singleton, NSW; *m* 1928, Violet, *o d* of Nathaniel Josslyn Clark, Allowah, New Lambton, NSW. *Educ:* RMC Duntroon, Australia. Served European War, 1914-18: with 6th Light Horse Regt, AIF, in Egypt, Gallipoli and Palestine (despatches twice, DSO). Served War of 1939-45, Middle East and SW Pacific. Adjutant-Gen., Australian Military Forces, and Second Mem., Military Board, 1947-51; Maj.-Gen. (retd) Australian Staff Corps. *Address:* 1 Marathon Road, Darling Point, NSW 2027, Australia. *[Died 10 Feb.* 1973.

ANDERSON, William Alexander, CIE 1946; MICE; Parish Councillor, retired; *b* Forfar, Scotland, 29 Jan. 1890; *s* of late W. Anderson, OBE, JP, Aberdeen; *m* 1917, Margaret Grace Dalley; one *s* one *d. Educ:* Robert Gordon's Coll.; Aberdeen Univ. Asst Engineer, Indian State Rlys, 1913, posted NW Rly; Executive Rank, 1920; Administrative Rank, 1938; Gen. Manager, NW Rly, 1944-46; retired finally, from the Railway service, 1948. OStJ. *Publications:* various technical papers and articles. *Recreations:* gardening; organ. *Address:* The Anchorage, 27 Seal Road, Selsey, Sussex. *T:* Selsey 2686. *[Died 27 March* 1971.

ANDERSON, William Galloway Macdonald, CBE 1957; CEng, FICE; Director-General of Works, Air Ministry, 1959-63, retired; *b* 27 Feb. 1905; *s* of late Andrew Syme Anderson, Dundee and of late Mary Anderson (*née* McDonald), Dundee; *m* 1934, Ivy Walker, York; one *s* one *d. Educ:* Dundee High Sch., Dundee; St Andrews Univ. Chief Engineer (Air Ministry) W African Command, 1942-44; Chief Supt Designs, Air Ministry (Works), 1944-46; Chief Engineer (Group Capt.) Far East Command, 1947-48; Deputy Dir of Works, Ministry of Civil Aviation, 1948-52; Dir of Works, Air Ministry, 1952-59. *Recreations:* golfing, motoring and gardening. *Address:* 39 The Barnhams, Bexhill-on-Sea, Sussex. *T:* Cooden 4212. *Clubs:* Devonshire (Eastbourne); Rye Golf. *[Died 30 Jan.* 1978.

ANDERSON, Rt. Rev. William Louis, DD (Lambeth); *b* Tezpur, Assam, India, 11 Feb. 1892; *s* of late James Drummond Anderson, LittD, ICS, and Frances Louisa Cordue; *m* 1st, 1921, Gwendoline Victoria Mary Jones (*d* 1957); two *s*; 2nd, 1963, Jessie Vida Hearn. *Educ:* St Paul's Sch. (Scholar); Gonville and Caius College, Cambridge (Exhibitioner); Ridley Hall, Cambridge. Hon. Fellow, Gonville and Caius Coll., Cambridge, 1950. BA 1914: MA 1920. 1st King Edward's Horse, 1911-16, Squadron Sergeant-Major; Royal Naval Air Service, Flight Lieut; Royal Air Force, 1918-19; Captain (DSC). Deacon, 1920; Priest, 1921; Chaplain of Caius Coll. and Curate of Holy Trinity, Cambridge, 1920; Chaplain, Royal Navy, 1922-28; HMS Antrim, 1922; HMS Thunderer, 1922-24; HMS Royal Oak, 1924-25; HMS Britannia for RNC Dartmouth, 1926-28; Vicar of St John's, Sparkhill, Birmingham, 1928-32; Rural Dean of Bordesley, 1930; Vicar of St John's, Meads, Eastbourne, 1932-37; Rural Dean of Eastbourne, 1937; Bishop Suffragan, Vicar, Rural Dean and Archdeacon of Croydon, 1937-42; Bishop of Portsmouth, 1942-49; Bishop of Salisbury, 1949-62; resigned, Dec. 1962. *Recreations:* sketching, bird-watching. *Address:* Woodriding, Hale Purlieu, Fordingbridge, Hants. *T:* Breamore 279. *Club:* United Service & Royal Aero. *[Died 5 March* 1972.

ANDRADE, Prof. Edward Neville da Costa, FRS 1935; FInstP; DSc London, PhD Heidelberg; Hon. LLD Edinburgh; Hon. DSc Durham, Manchester; Chevalier Légion d'Honneur; Correspondant, Académie des Sciences, Institut de France; Membre d'Honneur, Société Française de Physique; *b* London, 27 Dec. 1887; 2nd *s* of S. H. da C. Andrade; *m* 1st, 1917, Katherine Barbara, *d* of T. T. Evans, Manchester; two *s*; 2nd, 1938, Mona, *widow* of Clennell Wilkinson. *Educ:* St Dunstan's Coll.; University Coll., London; Univ. of Heidelberg; Cavendish Laboratory, Cambridge; Univ. of Manchester. BSc London, 1st class hons physics, 1907; Trouton scholar, Ellen Watson scholar, Jessel scholar, University Coll., London, 1907-10; 1851 Exhibition scholar, 1910-13; Heidelberg Univ. 1910-11; PhD (*summa cum laude*), 1911; Cavendish Lab., Cambridge, 1911-12; University Coll. London, 1912-13; Univ. of Manchester, John Harling Fellow, 1913-14. 2nd Lieut to Captain, RGA, 1914-19; active service, France, 1915-17 (despatches). Fellow of University Coll., London, 1916; Scientific Adviser to Dir of Scientific Research, Min. of Supply, 1939-43, Member Advisory Council of Scientific Research and Technical Development to Ministry of Supply from its inception to 1942; Professor of Physics, Artillery Coll., Woolwich, 1920-28; Quain Prof. of Physics, Univ. of London, 1928-50; Emeritus Prof., 1950; Dir in the Royal Institution, Resident Prof. and Dir of Davy Faraday Research Laboratory, 1950-52. Christmas Lectr, Royal Institution, 1927, 1943 and 1950; Guthrie Lectr, Physical Society, James Forrest Lectr, Institution of Civil Engineers, 1941; Rutherford Memorial Lectr, Royal Society, 1957; President, Physical Society, 1943-45; Council Royal Society, 1942-44; Hon. Mem. Inst. of Metals; Holweck Prizeman, 1947; Grande Médaille Osmond, Société Française de Métallurgie, 1951; Hughes Medallist, Royal Society, 1958. Editor for Physics, Encyclopædia Britannica, Fourteenth Edition. *Publications:* The Structure of the Atom (3rd edn, 1927); Airs; The Atom (Burmese Translation, 1928); Engines (Polish Translation, 1932); The Mechanism of Nature (translated into French, Italian, Polish, Dutch, Danish and Swedish); (with Julian Huxley) Simple Science; The New Chemistry; The Atom and its Energy; Poems and Songs; Isaac Newton; An Approach to Modern Physics (translated into Italian, Dutch and Polish); A

Brief History of the Royal Society; Physics for the Modern World; Rutherford (trans. into German, Norwegian and Japanese); papers on physical and mathematical subjects in Royal Soc. Proceedings and Transactions, Proceedings Physical Society, Philosophical Magazine, Annalen der Physik, and other technical journals; numerous articles in Encyclopædia Britannica and elsewhere. *Recreations:* poetry, collecting old scientific books and useless knowledge. *Address:* Flat 3, 19 The Boltons, SW10. *Clubs:* Athenæum, Savage, Chelsea Arts.
[*Died* 6 *June* 1971.

ANDREW, His Honour William Monro, MBE 1946; BCL, MA Oxon; Judge of Marylebone County Court (Circuit 43), 1958-67; *b* 21 Feb. 1895; *s* of James Andrew, LLD Glasgow, and Jeannie Jackson, *d* of William Monro, MD; unmarried. *Educ:* Glasgow Academy; Oriel Coll., Oxford. Called to Bar, Lincoln's Inn, 1921; joined the Oxford Circuit; Recorder of Dudley, 1934-36; Recorder of Walsall, 1936-46; Judge of County Courts, Circuit No. 58, 1946-50, Circuit No. 40 (Bow), 1950-58. Formerly a mem. of the County Court Rule Cttee. Asst Judge Advocate General, 1944. Served European War in 9th Bn HLI (wounded and prisoner in 1917); War of 1939-45, Squadron Leader in RAF (VR), 1940; Wing Comdr 1944. *Address:* 20 Eaton Mansions, SW1. *T:* 01-730 2860; Crossloan, Gullane, East Lothian. *T:* Gullane 3169.
[*Died* 24 *Dec.* 1973.

ANDREWES, Admiral Sir William (Gerrard), KBE 1951 (CBE 1945); CB 1949; DSO 1944; retired; *b* 3 Nov. 1899; 2nd *s* of late Reverend Canon G. T. Andrewes, Winchester; *m* 1927, Frances Audrey, *e d* of H. G. Welchman, Grove House, Winchester; one *s* one *d*. *Educ:* Twyford Sch., Winchester; RNC, Osborne and Dartmouth. Midshipman and Sub-Lt in European War, 1914-18 (Jutland). Comdr 1932; Capt. 1938; Joint Planning Staff, 1939 and 1940-42. Served War of 1939-45; Atlantic, Mediterranean invasion of Sicily (despatches) and Italy (DSO); Chief Staff Officer for administration and turn round invasion duties to C-in-C Portsmouth, 1944 (CBE); Chief of Staff to Vice-Adm. (Q) Pacific, 1944-45; Chief of Staff to C-in-C Portsmouth, 1947; ADC to the King, 1947; Rear-Adm. 1948; Senior Naval Member directing Staff Imperial Defence Coll., 1948-49; Vice-Admiral, 1951; Flag Officer Commanding 5th Cruiser Squadron and Flag Officer, Second-in-Command, Far East Station, 1950-51; comd British and Commonwealth Naval Forces in Korean war, 1950, and UN Task Force 95, 1951 (KBE); Commander-in-Chief, America and West Indies Station, 1951-53, and Deputy Supreme Allied Commander, Atlantic, 1952-53; Admiral, 1954; Pres., RN Coll., Greenwich, 1954-56; retired Dec. 1956. Officer American Legion of Merit, 1946, and Silver Star, 1950; Greek Military Cross, 1947; Commander, Legion of Merit, 1953; Knight Commander of Royal Order of Sword of Sweden, 1954. CStJ 1964. *Recreations:* gardening and painting. *Address:* Sparkford House, Winchester. *T:* 3977. [*Died* 21 *Nov.* 1974.

ANDREWS, Albert Andrew, CBE 1951 (OBE 1942); *b* 14 July 1896; *s* of late T. F. Andrews, Bath; *m* 1st, 1919, Rose Mabel Nickolds (*d* 1965); one *s* one *d*; 2nd, 1969, Sheila Betty Joyner Mawbey, widow of H. R. Mawbey. *Educ:* Victoria Coll., Bath. Served European War, 1914-18; commissioned 7th (Service) Bn Somerset Light Infantry, 1915; Captain, 1916; invalided, 1919. Joined Soldiers', Sailors' and Airmen's Families Association, 1919 (Asst Secretary); Secretary, 1927; Controller, 1944-61, retired. *Address:* 24 Swan Mill Gardens, Dorking, Surrey RH4 1PN. *T:* Dorking 86197. [*Died* 5 *Oct.* 1976.

ANDREWS, Cyril Frank Wilton, *b* 22 Dec. 1892; *s* of late Robert Parsons and Mariannellen Wilton Gleadhill Andrews; *m* 1929, Dorothy Constance Lascelles (*d* 1976), *d* of late Major George Thomas and Mrs Pickering; no *c*. *Educ:* abroad. Served European War, RE; Foreign Service, 1920; Vice-Consul at Antwerp, 1920-21; Tunis, 1921-23; Paris, 1923-24; Genoa, 1924-28; Montevideo (with rank of 2nd Sec.), 1929; Naples, 1929-30; Katowice, 1930-32; Philadelphia, 1933-35; Consul and 1st Sec. at Panama, 1935-38; Chargé d'Affaires, 1936 and 1938; Consul at Madeira, 1939-42; Minister to Dominican Republic, 1943-45; Special Ambassador for celebration of Centenary of Independence of Dominican Republic, Feb. 1944; Consul-General at Lourenço Marques, 1946-49; Consul-General at Algiers, 1949-53; retired from HM Foreign Service, 1953; Coronation Medal, 1953. Grand Cross of Dominican Order of Merit Juan Pablo Duarte. *Recreation:* reading. *Address:* c/o Lloyds Bank, Ltd, Lansdowne, Bournemouth, Dorset.
[*Died* 7 *Dec.* 1978.

ANDREWS, Sir Edwin Arthur C.; *see* Chapman-Andrews.

ANDREWS, Sir Linton; *see* Andrews, Sir William Linton.

ANDREWS, Norman Roy F.; *see* Fox-Andrews.

ANDREWS, Wilfrid, CBE 1968; Chairman d'Honneur, Royal Automobile Club (Chairman, 1946-72); *b* 15 Jan. 1892; *s* of late Norris Andrews, Sittingbourne, and Harriet, *d* of Chilman Taylor, Sittingbourne; *m* 1917, Ruth Eleanor (*d* 1968), *d* of W. F. Goodhew, Sittingbourne; one *s* two *d*. *Educ:* Wreight's Sch., Faversham. Président d'Honneur, Fédération Internationale de L'Automobile (Pres., 1965-71); Past Pres., Organisation Mondiale de Tourisme et de L'Automobile. Founder and Pres., Roads Campaign Council. Pres., Rotary International Association of Great Britain and Ireland, 1930-31; Chm., Aims and Objects Cttee, 1931-32 and Board of Dirs, 1932-33, Rotary International. Founder Vice-Chm. American British Commonwealth Association. Widely travelled USA and Europe. Order of the Crown of Belgium, 1947; Swedish Royal Order of Vasa, 1947; Danish Order of the Dannebrog, 1948; Royal Order of St Olav, Norway, 1949; Officer, Order of Grimaldi, Monaco. *Publications:* articles upon Rotary, Highways and Motoring. *Recreations:* painting, motoring, yachting, golf. *Address:* c/o Kenneth Large, Cherry Gardens, Goudhurst, Kent; Royal Automobile Club, Pall Mall, SW1Y 5HS. *T:* 01-930 2345. *Clubs:* Royal Automobile, Royal Motor Yacht. [*Died* 18 *Feb.* 1975.

ANDREWS, Sir (William) Linton, Kt 1954; Editor Emeritus, Yorkshire Post, 1968 (Editor, 1939-60 and Director of Yorkshire Post Group, 1950-68); *b* Hull, 1886; *s* of late William Andrews, author; *m* 1915, Gertrude (*d* 1958), *e d* of Alexander Douglas, Dundee. *Educ:* Hull Grammar Sch.; Christ's Hospital. Began journalistic career at Hull and continued it at Huddersfield, Sheffield, Portsmouth, Dundee, Paris, and London. Served in Black Watch throughout World War 1, three years on Western Front. Sub-Editor, Daily Mail, 1919-23; Editor of the Leeds Mercury, 1923-39. President: Guild of British Newspaper Editors, 1952-53; Inst. of Journalists, 1946. Chairman: Brontë Society Council, 1940-70; editorial cttee of Newspaper Soc., etc, 1943-50; Press Council, 1955-59 (Foundation Mem. and first Vice-Chm., 1953); Yorkshire Centre, RSA, 1966-67. Mem. cttee of 6th Imperial Press Conf., and Delegate to Conf. in Canada, 1950; Delegate to Commonwealth Press Union Conf. in India and Pakistan, 1961; helped to set up national scheme of Press training; has often broadcast on North Country and International topics. Pres. Leeds Philosophical and Literary Society, 1948-50, and Bradford English Soc., 1956-57; Vice-Chm. of Leeds Centenary Musical Festival, 1958, and Jt Vice-Chm., 1961 and 1964. Mem. Court and Council, Leeds Univ., 1943-59. Vis. Professor, Southern Illinois Univ., 1967. FRSA; FJI. Hon. LLD, Leeds Univ.; Hon. DLitt, Emerson Coll., Boston, Mass. Médaille d'Argent de la Reconnaissance Française (War of 1939-45). *Publications:* Old English Towns and Picturesque York and the North Riding (with the late W. Andrews); Haunting Years; Wayside Pageant (with A. P. Maguire); Yorkshire Folk; Englands Presserad (Copenhagen); Problems of an Editor; Autobiography of a Journalist; Lords and Labourers of the Press (with H. A. Taylor). Contributor to Has the Church Failed? and If I Had My Time Again. Edited, The Yorkshire Post-Two Centuries. Many articles on humours and pathos of North Country industrial life and English political commentaries for American readers. *Recreations:* books and the country. *Address:* 1 Grosvenor Mount, Leeds 6. *T:* Leeds 52973. *Clubs:* Athenæum, Devonshire, Press, Christ's Hospital; Leeds, Leeds and County Conservative (Leeds); Alwoodley Golf.
[*Died* 27 *Sept.* 1972.

ANDRIC, Ivo; author; *b* Travnik, Bosnia, 10 Oct. 1892; *m* 1959, Milica Babić, painter and theatre designer. *Educ:* secondary sch., Sarajevo; Universities of Zagreb, Vienna, Cracow, Graz. Political prisoner for 3 years during European War, 1914-18. Joined diplomatic service of his country, 1919; served in Rome, Bucharest, Trieste, Graz, Berlin (Ambassador), etc. Deputy to Yugoslav Parl., 1949-55. Pres., Federation of Writers of Yugoslavia, 1946-52. Prize for Life Work, Yugoslavia, 1956; Nobel Prize for Literature, 1961. Dr (*hc*), Kraków University, 1964. *Publications:* Ex Ponto (prison meditations); Gospodjica (Eng. trans. The Woman from Sarajevo, 1966); Travnička hronika (Eng. trans. A Bosnian Story, 1959), Na Drini ćuprija (Eng. trans. The Bridge on the Drina, 1959); Prokleta avlija (Eng. trans. Devil's Yard, 1962); poems, essays, several vols of stories, etc. *Address:* Proleterskih brigada 2, Belgrade, Yugoslavia. [*Died* 13 *March* 1975.

ANGAS, Sir (John) Keith, Kt 1952; Hon. Treasurer of Royal Agricultural Society of South Australia (President 1951-59); Chairman of Council, Institute of Medical and Veterinary Science, 1952-62; Vice-President Royal Zoological Society of South Australia; Former Chairman of Council, St Mark's College, University of Adelaide; *b* 30 Jan. 1900; *s* of Charles H.

Angas, Lindsay Park, Angaston, South Australia; *m* 1924, Gwynnyth Fay, *d* of Dr J. E. Good; one *s* one *d. Educ:* Geelong Grammar Sch., Corio, Victoria. War of 1939-45: Capt. 1st Australian Armoured Div., 1941-42; Staff, 1942-44. Pres., Stockowners Assoc. of SA, 1937-40, 1945-46; Chm., Grazier's Federal Council of Australia, 1939-40; Chm., South Australian Jockey Club, 1940-42, 1947-50; President: Liberal & Country League of SA, 1947-50; Royal Automobile Assoc. of SA, 1973-75. Chairman: Bagots Executor and Trustee Company, 1959-75; Colonial Mutual Life Assce Soc. (SA), 1952-75; Mem. Cttee on Future of Tertiary Educn, Austr. Univs Commn, 1961. *Address:* Bagot House, North Terrace, Adelaide, SA 5000, Australia. *Clubs:* Adelaide, Naval and Military (Adelaide); Melbourne (Melbourne). *[Died* 13 *April* 1977.

ANGAS, Major Lawrence Lee Bazley, MC; MA; Financial Consultant and writer on economic fluctuations; *b* 22 Feb. 1893; *m* Catherine Lowe; one *s* one *d* (and one *d* decd). *Educ:* Charterhouse; Magdalen Coll., Oxford. Major 1st Cheshire Regt; served France and Italy (MC, Croix de Guerre, despatches twice, twice wounded); resigned 1919. Student of unemployment, currency and the Business Cycle. *Publications:* Reparations, Trade and Foreign Exchange; Germany and Her Debts; Investment for Appreciation; L'Art du Placement des Capitaux; The Problems of the Foreign Exchanges; and various other books on economic and Stock Exchange subjects. *Recreations:* rackets, ski-ing, tennis, golf. *Address:* (Private and Office) Academy Avenue, Saxtons River, Vermont, USA. *Clubs:* Bath, Leander; Vincent's (Oxford). *[Died* 20 *Feb.* 1973.

ANNESLEY, 9th Earl, *cr* 1789; **Robert Annesley;** Baron Annesley, 1758; Viscount Glerawly, 1766; Civil Servant, retired; *b* 20 Feb. 1900; *s* of Arthur Albert O'Donel Valentia Annesley (*d* 1947) and Elizabeth Mary (*d* 1909), *d* of late Embertus van Ooms, Consul for the Netherlands; *S* kinsman, 8th Earl of Annesley, 1957; *m* 1922, Nora, *y d* of late Walter Harrison, Sapperton, near Cirencester, Glos; three *s.* Served European War, 1914-18, with Royal Navy; War of 1939-45 with Royal Corps of Signals, France and West Africa. *Heir: s* Viscount Glerawly, *qv. Address:* 67 Vegal Crescent, Englefield Green, Surrey. *T:* Egham 2162. *[Died* 21 *Feb.* 1979.

ANNETT, Engineer-Captain George Lewis, CIE 1941; RIN, retired; *b* 1887; *s* of late George Samuel Annett, MC; *m* 1918, Hessie Mary (*d* 1963), *d* of late Robert Felpts, Ulverston. Arms Traffic Operations, Persian Gulf, 1909-14; served European War, 1914-19 (despatches twice); Head of Engineering Branch, Royal Indian Navy; retired, 1941. CA Lancs. *Address:* Rakehead, Ulverston, Cumbria. *[Died* 24 *Jan.* 1980.

ANNS, Bryan Herbert, QC 1974; a Recorder of the Crown Court, since 1974; *b* 12 March 1929; *e s* of L. J. Anns and D. J. Anns (*née* Gauntlett); *m* 1969, Melanie Elizabeth Mary Brummell; one *s* one *d. Educ:* Wycliffe Coll.; Keble Coll., Oxford. BA Hons Jurisprudence. Called to Bar, Lincolns Inn, 1954. Mem. Council of Justice (British Section of the International Commn of Jurists). *Recreations:* 16th, 17th and 18th century music, burgundy. *Address:* 12 King's Bench Walk, Temple, EC4Y 7EL. *T:* 01-353 5892. *[Died* 8 *July* 1975.

ANSELL, James Lawrence Bunting, MRCS, LRCP; lately Surgeon Apothecary to HM Household at Sandringham. *Educ:* Cambridge Univ.; St Thomas' Hospital. BA Cambridge; MRCS, LRCP, 1940. Formerly: Casualty Officer, Ear, Nose and Throat House Surgeon at St Thomas' Hospital; House Physician and Opthalmic House Surgeon, Royal Hants County Hospital, Winchester; House Physician and Resident Medical Officer, London Chest Hospital. *Address:* The Surgery, Sandringham, Norfolk. *T:* Dersingham 40542. *[Died* 2 *Feb.* 1978.

ANSON, Sir (George) Wilfrid, Kt 1951; MBE 1919; MC 1916; Director of the Imperial Tobacco Co. Ltd, 1941-66, and Deputy Chairman, 1948-58, retired; *b* 2 June 1893; *s* of late G. E. Anson and of Mrs Mabel Anson; *m* 1916, Dinah Maud Lilian, *d* of late A. A. Bourne, Cheltenham; two *s* one *d. Educ:* Winchester; Trinity Coll., Oxford. MA 2nd Class Hons Lit. Hum. Served European War, 1914-18, commissioned in Loyal Regt, 1914; France, 1915-17, Major (wounded). Joined Imperial Tobacco Co. Ltd, 1919, Company's Leaf Manager, 1926, Sec., 1936, Dir, 1941; Mem. of Board of Trade Tobacco Manufacturers' Advisory Cttee, 1940-58. Mem. of Council, Bristol Univ., 1942, Dep. Chm., 1955, Chm., 1956-68, Pro-Chancellor, 1970, Chm. of Appointments Board, 1948-56. Member: Appointments Committee, Oxford Univ., 1943-63; Newson-Smith Cttee on Training for Business Administration, 1945; SW Regional Board for Industry, 1945-48; Council, Public Schools Appointments Bureau, 1950-54 and 1956-58; Council, Outward Bound Trust, 1951; Council, British Institute of Management, 1952-58; Chm.

Oxford Univ. Business Summer Sch. Cttee, 1954-56 and 1959; Pres., Incorporated Association of Preparatory Schools, 1958-64; Mem. Gov. Body BTC Staff Coll., 1959-72; Chm. Advisory Council on Employment for Prisoners, 1960-66. JP Somerset, 1948; High Sheriff, Somerset, 1958. Hon. LLD Bristol, 1963. *Recreations:* mountaineering, ski-ing, shooting, swimming, tennis. *Address:* West Hay, Wrington, Bristol. *T:* Wrington 862274. *Clubs:* Athenæum, Alpine, Alpine Ski. *[Died* 26 *Feb.* 1974.

ANSON, Sir Wilfrid; *see* Anson, Sir G. W.

ANSORGE, Sir Eric Cecil, Kt 1946; CSI 1942; CIE 1937; MA (Oxon); FRES; Fellow, Ancient Monuments Society; Indian Civil Service (retired); *b* 6 March 1887; *s* of late Dr W. J. Ansorge; *m* 1915, Wenonah, *d* of late Major J. W. Leather. *Educ:* St Paul's Sch.; St John's Coll., Oxford (Schol.). Entered ICS 1910 and posted to Bengal, 1911; served under Government of India (Commercial Intelligence Dept, 1918-19, Commerce and Finance Depts, 1919-24); Sec. to Government of Bihar and Orissa, 1926-29; Registrar of Co-operative Societies, 1930-34; Commissioner of Tirhut, 1935-38; revenue Commissioner, Orissa, 1938; Adviser to Governor of Orissa, 1939-Nov. 1941; Chief Commissioner Designate Andaman and Nicobar Islands, 1941; Supervisor ICS Probationers' Training Camp, 1942; Adviser to Governor of Bihar, 1943-46; Mem. Board of Revenue, Bihar, 1946; retired. Employed under Colonial Office in Nyasaland, 1948-50. *Publications:* Silk in India (with late Prof. Maxwell Lefroy); The Macrolepidoptera of Buckinghamshire; Addenda to the Macrolepidoptera of Buckinghamshire; articles in Entomological journals. *Recreations:* entomology, philately. *Address:* Timbers, Welders Lane, Chalfont St Peter, Bucks. *[Died* 3 *Jan.* 1977.

ANSTEY, Gilbert Tomkins, CB 1949; *b* 31 Jan. 1889; *s* of Robert and Elizabeth Mary Anstey; *m* 1914, Eva Alice Simpson; one *s* one *d. Educ:* Sexey's Sch., Blackford, Somerset. Entered Civil Service (Post Office), 1908; Asst Accountant-General, 1940; Dep. Comptroller and Accountant-General, 1945; Comptroller and Accountant-General, 1947-50; Accounting Adviser, S Rhodesian Post Office, 1951-52; representative of Federal Government of Rhodesia and Nyasaland on Commonwealth Telecommunications Board, 1952-63. *Address:* Malham, Hawksfold Lane, Fernhurst, Haslemere, Surrey GU27 3JW. *T:* Fernhurst 340. *[Died* 5 *July* 1974.

ANSTEY, Vera, DSc(Econ.); *b* 1889; 2nd *d* of James and Mary Powell; *m* 1913, Percy L. Anstey (*d* 1920); one *s* one *d. Educ:* Ladies' Coll., Cheltenham; Bedford Coll. for Women; London Sch. of Economics and Political Science. Studied music and German at Frankfurt a/M, 1907-8; Hygiene Diploma, Bedford Coll. for Women, 1910; Gerstenberg Scholar in Economics, 1912; BSc(Econ.) with 1st Class Hons in Economic History, 1913; resided in Bombay, India, 1914-20; Assistant, 1921, Lecturer in Commerce, 1929, London Sch. of Economics and Political Science; Sir Ernest Cassel Reader in Commerce, London Univ., 1941-54 (retired). Part-time Mem. of Academic Staff, London Sch. of Economics, 1954-64, retd 1964. DSc(Econ.) London Univ., 1930, Dean, Faculty of Economics, 1950-54; Mem. of Royal Commission on the Taxation of Profits and Income, Dec. 1950-55. Hon. Fellow, London Sch. of Economics and Political Science, 1964. *Publications:* The Trade of the Indian Ocean, 1929; The Economic Development of India, 1929, revised edn, 1936 and 1952; Introduction to Economics for Students in India and Pakistan, 1964. *Address:* Startforth Mews, The Green, Esher, Surrey. *T:* Esher 63124. *[Died* 26 *Nov.* 1976.

ANSTICE, Vice-Adm. Sir Edmund (Walter), KCB 1953 (CB 1950); retired; *b* 5 May 1899; 2nd *s* of late Major J. C. A. Anstice; *m* 1928, Lesley, *d* of late L. Ritchie, Sydney, NSW; two *s. Educ:* RNC, Osborne and Dartmouth. Lieut, 1920; Comdr, 1932; Capt., 1939; Rear-Adm., 1948; Vice-Adm., 1951. Served European War, 1914-18; specialised Naval Aviation, 1924; War of 1939-45, Admty; comd HMS Fencer; Chief of Staff Flag Officer, Carrier Training; 4th Naval Mem. Australian Naval Board, 1946-48; Flag Officer Training Squadron, 1948-49; Flag Officer Flying Training, 1949-51; a Lord Commissioner of the Admiralty, Fifth Sea Lord and Dep. Chief of Naval Staff (Air), 1951-54; retd 1954. *Recreations:* fishing, shooting. *Address:* Inverdunning House, Dunning, Perthshire. *T:* 207. *Club:* Royal Perth (Perth). *[Died* 30 *Aug.* 1979.

ANSTRUTHER, Sir Windham Eric Francis Carmichael-, 11th Bt, *cr* 1700 and 1798; Hereditary Carver to Royal Household in Scotland; one of the Hereditary Masters of the Household for Scotland; *b* 1900; *s* of late Gerald Yorke Anstruther and Ellen Caroline, *d* of J. Milne, Cradock, Cape Colony; *S* cousin, 1928;

m 1st, 1932, Fay Sibyl Marie (marr. diss.), *o c* of Ernest Rechnitzer, Berkeley Square (she *m* 1948, Capt. Jerzy Bondorowski); 2nd, 1948, Joan Coates (marr. diss.). *Educ:* Marlborough; RMC, Sandhurst. *Heir:* none. *Address:* Carmichael, Thankerton, Biggar, Lanarks.
[*Died 9 April* 1980 (*ext*).

ANTHONY, Irvin; Author; (serving as Lieutenant US Coast Guard Reserve, but placed in inactive duty status); *b* 5 March 1890; *s* of Samuel Anthony and Eliza Conquest; *m* 1918, Eleanor L. Cooper, BS and MA, University of Pennsylvania. *Publications:* Down to the Sea in Ships, 1925; Three Ships in Azure, 1927; Paddle Wheels and Pistols, 1929; Voyagers Unafraid, 1930; Decatur, 1931; Ralegh and His World, 1934; The Saga of the Bounty, 1935; Revolt at Sea, 1937; contributor to The Bookman, Saturday Evening Post, Rudder, Sea Stories, Yachting, Motorboating, etc. *Recreations:* swimming, yachting, travel. *Address:* 45 H Street, Seaside Park, New Jersey 08752, USA. [*Died 6 Dec.* 1971.

ANTONY, Jonquil; author; *b* 5 Oct. 1912; *m* 1941, John Wyse. *Educ:* Worthing High Sch. Began writing for BBC in 1937 and has since written over 4,000 scripts: daily serials, plays, adaptations, features for radio and television; wrote The Robinson Family (jointly) for four years, also initiated Mrs Dale's Diary, 1948 and wrote it (jointly) until 1963. *Publications:* The Robinson Family, 1948; The Malindens, 1951; Mrs Dale's Bedside Book, 1951; Paradise Square, 1952; Mrs Dale At Home, 1952; Mrs Dale, 1958; The Dales of Parkwood Hill, 1959; Hark! Hark! The Ark!, 1960; Mrs Dale's Friendship Book, 1961; Eaglemania, 1966; Dear Dr Dale, 1970. *Recreations:* reading, theatres, the country. *Address:* 142 Foundling Court, Brunswick Centre, WC1N 1AN. *T:* 01-278 4506. [*Died 6 Dec.* 1980.

ANTRIM, 13th Earl of, *cr* 1620; **Randal John Somerled McDonnell,** KBE 1970; JP; DL; Viscount Dunluce, 1785; Vice-Lieutenant, Co. Antrim, 1955-65; Chairman, National Trust, 1965-77; *b* 22 May 1911; *er s* of 12th Earl of Antrim, and Margaret, *y d* of Rt Hon. J. G. Talbot; *S* father, 1932; *m* 1934, Angela Christina, *d* of Sir Mark Sykes, 6th Bt; two *s* one *d*. *Educ:* Eton; Christ Church, Oxford. Served War of 1939-45 in RN. Hon. Attaché, HM Legation, Tehran, 1932; Clerk in the House of Lords, 1933-34; Captain RNVR, i/c Ulster Div., 1954-57, retd. Chairman: Gen. Purposes Cttee, Nat. Trust; Nat. Trust in NI, 1948-64; Ulster Television Ltd; St Peter's Group of Hospitals, London; Mem., Sports Council, 1972-74. Co. Antrim: JP 1934-, DL 1934-. Hon. Col, 429 Coast Regt RA (TA), 1952-58. Hon. DLitt, New Univ. of Ulster, 1972; Hon. FRIBA, 1972. *Heir: s* Viscount Dunluce. *Address:* Glenarm Castle, Ballymena, Co. Antrim, Northern Ireland. *T:* Glenarm 229; 14 Moore Street, SW3. *T:* 01-584 6039. *Clubs:* Beefsteak, Brooks's.
[*Died 26 Sept.* 1977.

ANTROBUS, Lieutenant-Colonel Ronald Henry, MC 1916; DL; *b* 8 Nov. 1891; *s* of John Coutts Antrobus and Mary, *d* of Lieut-Gen. Hon. Sir James Lindsay, KCMG; *m* 1921, Muriel, *d* of R. H. Gosling, Hawthorn Hill, Berks, and *widow* of Capt. Miles Chetwynd Stapylton (killed in action); one *s*. *Educ:* Charterhouse. Royal Artillery Special Reserve, 1910-13; Royal Artillery, 1913-44. DL Cheshire, 1952; High Sheriff of Cheshire, 1960. *Address:* Eaton Hall, Congleton, Cheshire. *T:* Congleton 3123. [*Died 11 June* 1980.

ANWYL-DAVIES, Thomas, MD London; FRCP; Hon. Consulting Physician to St Thomas' Hospital; Member of Lloyd's; *m* 1922, Kathleen Beryl, *o d* of P. G. Oakshott, Barham House, East Hoathly; one *s* ; *m* 1946, Elizabeth, MRCS, LRCP, *e d* of J. S. Counsell, Lympsham Manor, Somerset; one *d*. *Educ:* Bonn; Marburg; Lille; St Thomas' Hospital; University of London (MD, gold Medal). BS 1917 (London); MD 1930; FRCP 1937; FRSocMed; Fellow Med. Soc. of London; Mem. various medical advisory cttees. Formerly: Dir and Physician in Charge of the Dept of Venereal Diseases, St Thomas' Hospital; London University Lecturer at St Thomas's Hospital Medical Sch.; Dir, London Hospital (Whitechapel) Clinic for Venereal Diseases; Lectr on Venereal Diseases to London Hosp. Med. Coll.; Cons. and Venereologist to LCC (which is now GLC); Vice-Pres. Med. Soc. for Study of Venereal diseases; Hon. Sec., Royal Med. Benevolent Fund, 1956-70. Mem. (Pall Mall and St James's) Westminster City Council, 1951-65. Served European War, 1914-18, in RAMC, and was MO with Royal Fusiliers and Field Ambulances. *Publications:* various books and papers on research into therapeutic and administrative problems of venereology; yearly contrib. for venereal diseases to The Medical Annual, 1937-59; articles in med. press and trans of med. socs. *Recreations:* painting, philately. *Address:* 149 Harley Street, W1. *T:* 01-935 4444; Great Buckstepe, Herstmonceux, Sussex.

T: Herstmonceux 3101. *Clubs:* Royal Automobile, 1900.
[*Died 4 Oct.* 1971.

APPLEBY, Lt-Col Charles Bernard, DSO 1944; FSA; FMA; FRAS; first Director, National Army Museum, from 1960 (when founded) until 1966; *b* 4 July 1905; *s* of Alfred James Appleby and Florence Nightingale; *m* 1st, 1937, Hilary Agnes Branch; two *s* one *d* ; 2nd, 1948, Pauline Margaret Brough-Maltby (*d* 1950). *Educ:* Culford Sch. 2nd Lieut 54th Divisional Train, RASC (TA), 1926; RMC Sandhurst; IA, 1928, Burma Rifles; Burma Ops 1930-32 (despatches) Adjt 1936; 1st Cl. Interpr Languages of Burma (the only one); Instructor, Officers' Trng Sch., Maymyo, 1939-40; psc Quetta, 1941; Bde Major, Burma, 1941; Burma Ops, 1941-42 (despatches); Asst Comdt, 1st Punjab Regtl Centre (Lieut-Col), 1943; comd. 2/1st Punjab Regt in Burma Ops, 1944-45 (despatches, DSO); Asst Adjt Gen., Bihar and Orissa Area, 1946; AA&QMG, Malaya, 1947; retired, 1948. Wing Commander RAF Regiment, 1950-55. Curator RMA Sandhurst Museum, 1956. CC Oxon, 1967-70. *Publications:* Victoria Crosses and George Crosses of the Honourable East India Company and the Indian Army, 1962; Culford School History and Roll 1873-1973, 1974; articles on military history, genealogy and museum technique, TV and radio broadcasts. *Address:* The Old Malt House, Middle Barton, Oxford. *T:* Steeple Aston 252. *Club:* United Service & Royal Aero. [*Died 5 March* 1975.

ARBUTHNOT, Clifford William Ernest, CIE 1930; ED 1945; Superintending Engineer (retired) Bombay Public Works Department; *s* of late William H. Arbuthnot, Belfast; *m* 1921, Josephine Turton (*d* 1922). *Educ:* Campbell Coll., Belfast; Queen's University, Belfast, BA, BE. Entered Indian Service of Engineers, 1908; served European War, 1914-18, Lieut, 53rd Sikhs (FF), Capt., 3rd Sappers and Miners, Egypt, Aden, Mesopotamia and India; Member Bombay and Sind Public Service Commn 1937-42; Rent Controller, Bombay, 1942-47. *Clubs:* East India, Sports and Public Schools; Royal Bombay Yacht; Sind (Karachi). [*Died 4 March* 1974.

ARBUTHNOTT, Robert, MBE 1945; TD 1941; HM Lord-Lieutenant of the County of Dunbarton, 1968-75; *b* 22 Sept. 1900; *s* of Hugh Corsar Arbuthnott and Marianne Arbuthnott (*née* Gibson); unmarried. *Educ:* Cheltenham Coll. Served War of 1939-45: The Manchester Regt; RAC; REME. Mem., Iron and Steel Consumers' Council, 1951; Dep. Leader, UK Heavy Engineering Mission to India, 1956; Pres., Inst. of Locomotive Engrs, 1958-59. Mem. Queen's Body Guard for Scotland, Royal Company of Archers. CEng, FICE; FIMechE. DL Dunbartonshire, 1961. *Address:* Ardmory, Rhu, Dunbartonshire G84 8NH. *T:* Rhu 820230. *Clubs:* New (Edinburgh); Royal Northern and Clyde Yacht. [*Died 29 Nov.* 1980.

ARCHDALL, Rev. Canon Henry Kingsley, MA, ThD; Chancellor, St David's Cathedral, 1940-56; Canon Emeritus, 1956; *b* Balmain, Sydney, 1886; *s* of late Rev. Canon Mervyn Archdall, MA, Sydney; *m* Laura Madden (*d* 1953), one *s* (and two lost in War of 1939-45) one *d*. *Educ:* Sydney Grammar Sch.; Sydney Univ. (First class honours in philosophy and classics, Woolley Travelling Scholarship); Trinity Coll., Cambridge, MA (First Class, philosophy of religion Tripos); Fellow and Lectr, Corpus Christi Coll., Cambridge, 1911-15; Dean 1915; Dean of Newcastle, NSW, 1915-19; Fellow Australian Coll. of Theology (ThD), 1916; Headmaster, Armidale School, NSW, 1919-26; Headmaster King's Coll., Auckland, NZ, 1926-35; Chaplain, Wellington Coll., Berks, 1935-38; Principal and Professor of Theology, St David's Coll., Lampeter, Cards, 1938-53; Fellow of Jesus Coll., Oxford, 1941. Select Preacher, Cambridge, 1940, Oxford, 1947-48. Visiting Fellow, Yale Univ., USA, 1954-55; Visiting Prof., Berkeley Divinity Sch., New Haven, USA, 1954-57. Episcopal Chaplain, Heidelberg, 1957-59. Hon. LLD Wales, 1971. *Publication:* A Christian Instruction, 1933. *Address:* 51 Victoria Avenue, Porthcawl, South Wales. [*Died 27 Feb.* 1976.

ARCHER, William George, OBE 1947; MA; DLitt; Keeper Emeritus, Indian Section, Victoria and Albert Museum, since 1959; *b* 11 Feb. 1907; *s* of William Archer; *m* 1934, Mildred Agnes Archer; one *s* one *d*. *Educ:* Strand Sch.; Emmanuel Coll., Cambridge. Entered ICS, 1930; posted Bihar, 1931; District Magistrate, Purnea, 1938-39; Superintendent of Census Operations, Bihar, 1939-41; Dist Magistrate Patna, 1941-42; Dep. Comr, Santal Parganas, 1942-45; Special Officer, Santal Law, 1945-46; Addtl Dep. Comr, Naga Hills, 1946-48; retired ICS, 1948; Keeper, Indian Section, Victoria and Albert Museum, 1949-59; re-visited India, 1954, as lecturer (Indian Painting), Govt of India, British Council; research tours India, Ceylon, 1960, 1966, 1968, 1973, 1976; Vis. Lectr, USA, 1958, 1963, 1970, 1977. Editor, Man in India, 1942-49; Contrib. Editor, Marg, 1956-75; Mem. Editorial Bd, Roopa Lekha, 1959-.

Hon. DLitt Punjab Univ., Chandigarh, 1968; Hon. DLit Guru Nanak Dev Univ., Amritsar, 1976. *Publications:* The Blue Grove, 1940; The Vertical Man, 1947; The Plains of the Sun, 1948; The Dove and the Leopard, 1948; Forty Thousand Years of Modern Art (with Robert Melville), 1948; Indian Painting in the Punjab Hills, 1952; Kangra Painting, 1952; Bazaar Paintings of Calcutta, 1953; Garhwal Painting, 1954; Indian Painting for the British (with Mildred Archer), 1955; Indian Painting, 1957; The Loves of Krishna, 1957; Indian Paintings from Rajasthan, 1957; Ceylon: Paintings from Temple, Shrine and Rock, 1958; Central Indian Painting, 1958; India and Modern Art, 1959; Indian Painting in Bundi and Kotah, 1960; Indian Miniatures, 1960; Kalighat Drawings, 1962; The Kama Sutra (ed), 1963; Love Songs of Vidyapati (jt), 1963; Kangra Paintings of the Gita Govinda (jt), 1964; The Rose Garden of Sa'di (ed), 1964; The Koka Shastra (preface), 1964; Paintings of the Sikhs, 1966; Rajput Miniatures, 1968; Kalighat Paintings, 1971; Indian Paintings from the Punjab Hills (2 vols), 1973; The Hill of Flutes, 1974; Pahari Miniatures: a concise history, 1975; Visions of Courtly India, 1976. *Recreations:* films, foreign travel. *Address:* 18 Provost Road, NW3 4ST. *T:* 01-722 2713.
[*Died 6 March* 1979.

ARCHER HOUBLON, Mrs Doreen, CVO 1969 (MVO 1954); *b* 1899; *d* of Lt-Col Walter Charles Lindsay, MVO, and Lady Kathleen Lindsay, OBE, *d* of 6th Earl of Carrick; *m* 1929, Major Richard Archer Houblon, DSO (*d* 1957); no *c.* Spent many years training and remaking horses with her father, and studying in depth the art of horsemanship and adapting it to the side saddle. Has lectured with films, and officiated as a judge at Internat. Horse Shows at Olympia, etc. Farms 300 acres organically and biodynamically. Member: Soil Assoc.; Bio-Dynamic Agric. Assoc. *Publication:* Side Saddle, 1938. *Address:* Kilmurry, Thomastown, Co. Kilkenny, Ireland. *T:* Kilkenny 24130. *Club:* English-Speaking Union. [*Died 1 Dec.* 1977.

ARCHEY, Sir Gilbert (Edward), Kt 1963; CBE 1958 (OBE 1919); retired; *b* York, England, 4 Aug. 1890; *s* of late Thomas Archey, Christchurch, New Zealand; *m* 1915, Myrtle, *d* of William Gee, Christchurch NZ; three *d. Educ:* West Christchurch Sch.; Canterbury Coll., Univ. of New Zealand. MA 1914; DSc 1940. Lecturer, Canterbury Coll. and Asst Curator, Canterbury Museum, 1914-24; Dir, Auckland Institute and Museum, 1924-64, retd. Mem. of Senate, Univ. of New Zealand, 1940-61; Mem., Univ. Grants Committee, 1948-51 and 1954-60; Fellow, Royal Soc. of New Zealand (Pres., 1941-42); Mem. Auckland Cathedral Chapter; President, Auckland Branch of Royal Commonwealth Soc., 1956-59. Served European War, 1916-18 (OBE), Captain, New Zealand Field Artillery; War of 1939-45: CO (Lt-Col) 4 Bn Auckland Regt, NZ Service; Staff Officer, (Lt-Col) British Military Admin., Malaya. *Publications:* South Sea Folk; Sculpture and Design, An Outline of Maori Art; Art Forms of Polynesia, 2nd edn, 1974; contributions to Trans. Royal Society of New Zealand, Journal Polynesian Soc., Records (also Bulletin) Auckland Inst. and Museum. *Recreation:* gardening. *Address:* 20 Bassett Road, Remuera, Auckland 5, New Zealand. *T:* 502.262. *Club:* Northern (Auckland). [*Died 20 Oct.* 1974.

ARCHIBALD, 1st Baron, *cr* 1949, of Woodside in the City of Glasgow; **George Archibald,** CBE 1968; Chairman, Anvil Film and Recording Group Ltd, since 1968; *b* 21 July 1898; *m* 1st, 1926, Dorothy Holroyd Edwards (*d* 1960); one *s;* 2nd, 1961, Mrs Catherine Edith Mary Colwell, *d* of late Rt Hon. Andrew Bonar Law, MP. *Educ:* elementary and secondary schs. Deputy Regional Commissioner for the Midlands, 1941-42; Director Films Div., British Information Services, New York, 1942-44; Controller MOI, 1944-45. Mem. Cinematograph Films Council, 1963-67. Labour Mem. of Glasgow City Council, 1920-28; Magistrate of the City of Glasgow, 1925-28; contested (Lab) South Aberdeen, 1924, Sparkbrook, Birmingham, 1931; Capt. of HM Bodyguard of the Yeomen of the Guard, June-Oct. 1951. Was Asst Government Whip, House of Lords, June-Oct. 1951. Formerly Director: J. Arthur Rank Productions Ltd; This Modern Age Ltd. Chm. Fedn of British Film Makers, 1957-66; Dep. Pres., Film Production Assoc. of GB, 1967-68. *Heir: s* Hon. George Christopher Archibald [*b* 30 Dec. 1926; *m* 1951, Liliana Barou (marr. diss., 1964); *m* 1971, Daphne May Vincent]. *Address:* 3 Martlett Lodge, Oak Hill Park, Frognal, NW3. [*Died 25 Feb.* 1975.

ARDIZZONE, Edward Jeffrey Irving, CBE 1971; RA 1970 (ARA 1962); RDI 1974; Hon. ARCA; Artist; *b* 16 Oct. 1900; *s* of Auguste Ardizzone and Margaret Irving; *m* 1929, Catherine Berkley Anderson; one *s* one *d* (and one *s* decd). *Educ:* Clayesmore Sch. Worked for 6 years for Eastern Telegraph Co.; studied art at Westminster and Central Schools of Art; Official War Artist, 1940-46; pictures purchased by Tate Gallery,

Sheffield, Leeds and Liverpool Art Galleries and Contemporary Art Society. First retrospective exhibn, V&A Museum, 1973. *Publications:* Little Tim and the Brave Sea Captain, 1936; Lucy Brown and Mr Grimes, 1937; Tim and Lucy go to Sea, 1938; Baggage to the Enemy, 1941; Nicholas and the Fast Moving Diesel, 1947; Paul the Hero of the Fire, 1947; Tim to the Rescue, 1949; Tim and Charlotte, 1951; Tim in Danger, 1953; Tim All Alone, 1956 (Kate Greenaway medal of Library Association, for best illustrated children's book in 1956); Johnny the Clockmaker, 1960; Tim's Friend Towser, 1962; Peter the Wanderer, 1963; Diana and Her Rhinoceros, 1964; Tim and Ginger, 1965; Sarah and Simon and No Red Paint, 1965; Tim to the Lighthouse, 1968; Tim's Last Voyage, 1972; Ship's Cook Ginger, 1977; *illustrated:* more than 170 books which include: In a Glass Darkly, 1929; My Uncle Silas, 1939; The Local, 1939; Peacock Pie, 1947; The Poems of François Villon, 1947; The Pilgrim's Progress, 1947; The Blackbird in the Lilac, 1952; The Warden, 1952; The Little Bookroom, 1955; Henry Esmond, 1956; Ding Dong Bell, 1957; Titus in Trouble, 1959; More Prefabulous Animiles, 1975; The James Reeves Story Book, 1978; contrib. Oxford Illustrated Old Testament, 1968; The Young Ardizzone: an autobiographical fragment, 1970; Diary of a War Artist, 1974. *Address:* 5 Vine Cottages, Rodmersham Green, Sittingbourne, Kent. [*Died 8 Nov.* 1979.

ARGENTI, Philip Pandely, Hon. CVO 1963; Hon. MBE (mil.) 1920; formerly Cultural Counsellor at the Royal Greek Embassy in London; Commander, Order of George I (Greece); Commander, Order of Phoenix (Greece); Commander, Order of Merit (Italy); 4th *s* of late Pandely Leonidas Argenti and late Fanny, 3rd *d* of late John Stephen Schilizzi; *m* 1930, Alexandra Helen Schilizzi (Grand Officer of the Holy Sepulchre; Officer Order of Ευπομας; Greek Commemorative Naval Medal), 3rd *d* of late Stephen John Schilizzi, formerly of Loddington Hall, and Julia, 2nd *d* of Sir Lucas Ralli, 1st Bt; one *s* two *d. Educ:* Winchester Coll.; Christ Church, Oxford; Athens Univ. BA, MA 1919, and DLitt 1941 (Oxon); LLB 1920 (Athens); Silver Medallist, Athens Academy, 1938; Corresp. Mem. Athens Academy, 1947; Barrister-at-law, 1922, Athens. Entered Greek Diplomatic Service, 1923; Counsellor to Greek Legations to exiled Govts of Poland, Belgium and Luxemburg. Served European War, 1914-18, in 3rd Greek cavalry regt and as Adj. to GOC 2nd Greek Army Corps (despatches, Greek MC and Greek MM, 1919), and Asia Minor Campaign. Freeman of town of Chios, 1920 and 1953; Gold Medal of town of Chios. Grand Officer, Order of Holy Sepulchre, 1928, Cross of Mount Athos, etc. *Publications:* Massacres of Chios, 1822, 1932; The Expedition of Colonel Fabvier to Chios, 1827, 1933; Chius Liberata, 1912, 1933; The Expedition of the Florentines to Chios, 1599, 1934; The Occupation of Chios by the Venetians, 1694, 1935; Bibliography of Chios, 1940; Chius Vincta, 1566, 1941; (with Prof. Stilpon Kyriakides) 'Η Χίος παρὰ τοῖς Γεωγράφοις καὶ Περιηγηταῖς (Chios according to the Geographers and Travellers) (3 vols, Athens), 1946; (with Prof. H. J. Rose) The Folklore of Chios, 1949; The Costumes of Chios, 1953; Diplomatic Archive of Chios 1577-1841 (2 vols), 1954; Libro d'Oro de la Noblesse de Chio (2 vols), 1955; The Occupation of Chios by the Genoese, 1346-1566 (3 vols), 1958; ed The Architecture of Chios, by Arnold Smith, 1962; The Occupation of Chios by the Germans and Their Administration of the Island, 1966; The Religious Minorities of Chios, 1970. *Recreations:* riding, travelling. *Address:* 16 via Tevere, Rome, Italy; Argentikon, Campos, Chios. *Clubs:* Turf, St James'; Athénien (Athens); La Caccia (Rome). [*Died 14 April* 1974.

ARGYLL, 11th Duke of, *cr* 1701 (Scotland), 1892 (UK); **Ian Douglas Campbell,** TD; DL; Marquess of Lorne and Kintyre; Earl of Campbell and Cowal; Viscount Lochow and Glenisla; Baron Inveraray, Mull, Morvern, and Tiry, 1701; Baron Campbell, 1445; Earl of Argyll, 1457; Baron Lorne, 1470; Baron Kintyre, 1633 (Scotland); Baron Sundridge, 1766; Baron Hamilton, 1776; Baronet, 1627; 35th Baron and 45th Knight of Lochow; Celtic title, Mac Cailein Mòr, Chief of Clan Campbell (from Sir Colin Campbell, knighted 1286); Hereditary Master of the Royal Household, Scotland; Hereditary High Sheriff of the County of Argyll; Admiral of the Western Coast and Isles; Keeper of the Great Seal of Scotland and of the Castles of Dunstaffnage, Dunoon, and Carrick and Tarbert; formerly Capt. Argyll and Sutherland Highlanders; *b* Paris, 18 June 1903; *s* of late Douglas Walter Campbell (*gs* of 8th Duke) and Aimée, 3rd *d* of John Lawrence, New York; *S* cousin 1949; *m* 1st, 1927, Hon. Janet Gladys Aitken (who obtained a divorce, 1934), *d* of 1st Baron Beaverbrook, CD; one *d;* 2nd, 1935, Hon. Mrs Louise Vanneck (who obtained a divorce, 1951, and *m* 3rd, 1954, Robert C. L. Timpson, New York, and *d* 1970), *o d* of Henry Clews; two *s;* 3rd, 1951, Margaret (marr. diss., 1963), *d* of George Hay Whigham; 4th, 1963, Mrs Mathilda Coster Mortimer. *Educ:* Milton, Massachusetts; Christ Church,

Oxford. Served War of 1939-45 (prisoner). FRSA 1953. DL Argyllshire, 1950. KStJ. *Heir:* s Marquess of Lorne. *Address:* Inveraray Castle, Argyll. *T:* Inveraray 2275. *Clubs:* MCC, Pratt's; New (Edinburgh); Travellers' (Paris).
[Died 7 April 1973.

ARKELL, Rev. Anthony John, MBE 1928; MC 1918; DLitt; FSA; Vicar of Cuddington with Dinton, in the Diocese of Oxford, 1963-71; Reader in Egyptian Archæology, University of London, 1953-63; Curator of the Flinders Petrie Collection of Egyptian Antiquities at Univ. Coll., London, 1948-63; Hon. Asst Curate, Great Missenden, 1960-63; *b* Hinxhill, Kent, 29 July 1898; *s* of late Rev. John Norris Arkell and late Eleanor Jessy (*née* Bunting); *m* 1st, 1928, Dorothy (*d* 1945), *d* of late John Davidson; one *s* one *d*; 2nd, 1950, Joan Margaret Burnell, *d* of late Col Louis James Andrews, Indian Army. *Educ:* Bradfield Coll. (Schol.); Queen's Coll., Oxford (Jodrell Schol. in Classics). DLitt. (Oxon) 1955; Cuddesdon Coll.; deacon, 1960, priest, 1961. Served European war: RFC 1916-18; RAF 1918-19. Joined Sudan Political Service, 1920; Asst Dist Commr, Darfur Province, 1921-24; Actg Res., Dar Masalit, 1925-26; Dist Comr, Kosti (White Nile Province), 1926-29; Sennar (Blue Nile Province), 1929-32; Actg Dep.-Governor, Darfur Province, 1932-37; Comr for Archæology and Anthropology, Sudan Govt, 1938-48; Chief Transport Officer, Sudan Govt, 1940-44; Ed., Sudan Notes and Records, 1945-48; Archæological Adviser to Sudan Govt, 1948-53; Lecturer in Egyptology, Univ. Coll., London, 1948-53. British Ennedi Expedition, 1957. First Pres., Philosophical Soc. of Sudan, 1947 (Hon. Life Mem., 1949); Hon. Mem., German Archæological Inst., 1953; Mem. Council, Soc. of Antiquaries, 1956-57; Mem. Cttee Egypt Exploration Soc. Order of the Nile, 4th Class (Egypt), 1931. *Publications:* Early Khartoum, 1949; The Old Stone Age in the Anglo-Egyptian Sudan, 1949; Shaheinab, 1953; The History of the Sudan from the earliest times to 1821, 1955, 2nd rev. edn, 1961; Wanyanga, 1964; The Prehistory of the Nile Valley, 1975; articles in Enc. Britannica; numerous articles in Sudan Notes and Records and other learned jls. *Recreations:* travel, photography, natural history and gardening. *Address:* Cuddington, Colam Lane, Little Baddow, Chelmsford, Essex. *T:* Danbury 4221.
[Died 26 Feb. 1980.

ARKLE, Harry; *b* 7 April 1893; *m* 1928, Nell V. Coventry; no *c*. *Educ:* various schools and privately. Freight Traffic Department, Canadian Pacific Railway, Winnipeg, 1912; General Freight Traffic Manager, Canadian Pacific Railway, Montreal, Que., 1953; European General Manager, Canadian Pacific Railway Co., London, 1954; Managing Director, Europe, Canadian Pacific Railway Co., London, and Chairman, Canadian Pacific Steamships Ltd, 1961-63. *Recreation:* golf. *Clubs:* Travellers'; Denham; Hurlingham; Manitoba (Winnipeg).
[Died 11 March 1973.

ARKWRIGHT, Maj.-Gen. Robert Harry Bertram, CB 1945; DSO 1943; *b* 30 July 1903; *s* of late Bertram Harry Godfrey Arkwright; *m* 1927, Kathleen Gladys, *d* of late Major E. E. Hanbury, Scots Gds; one *s* one *d* (and one *s* decd). *Educ:* Eton; RMC, Sandhurst. Joined 11th Royal Lancers, 1924; Staff Coll., Camberley, 1934-35; Bde Major 1st Cavalry Bde, 1936-39; GSO2 War Office, June-Dec. 1939; DAAG 1st Armoured Div., 1940 (France); GSO1 8th Armoured Div., 1940-42; Brig. AFV Eighth Army, 1942-43; Comdr 23rd Armoured Bde, 1943-46 (DSO and Bar, CB); Comdr 2nd Div., 1946; DRAC War Office, 1947-48; Comdr, 56th (London) Armoured Div., TA, 1948-49; Comdr 7th Armoured Div., 1949-51. *Recreations:* hunting, fishing. *Address:* The Nether House, Poulton, Cirencester, Glos. *Club:* Cavalry.
[Died 14 Nov. 1971.

ARLEN, Stephen Walter, (*né* Badham), CBE 1968; theatre manager; Managing Director, Sadler's Wells Opera, since 1967; *b* Birmingham, 31 Oct. 1913; *s* of Walter Cyril Badham and Annie Sophia Earnshaw; *m* Iris Kells; one *d*. Formerly actor and stage director; General Manager, the Old Vic, 1946-51; Administrative Dir. Sadler's Wells Opera, 1951. Chm., British Centre of the International Theatre Inst.; Governor, London Opera Centre. London Representative for consortium of six Australian drama rep. cos. *Address:* 10 The Terrace, Woodford Green, Essex. *T:* 01-504 0064.
[Died 19 Jan. 1972.

ARMAND, Louis, KBE (Hon.), 1957; Grand Officier de la Légion d'Honneur, 1956; Compagnon de la Libération, 1944; Membre de l'Académie Française, 1963; Membre de l'Académie des Sciences Morales et Politiques, 1960; *b* 17 Jan. 1905; *m* 1925; two *s* two *d*. *Educ:* Ecole Polytechnique. Mining Engineer, Clermont-Ferrand, 1926; Engineer, PLM Railways Company, 1934; Director of Works, SNCF, 1944; Director-Gen., SNCF, 1946; President: Board of Directors, SNCF, 1955; European Atomic Energy Commission, 1958-59; Ecole Polytechnique,

1956-68. Past Pres. and Gen. Sec. of Internat. Union of Railways, 1961; Pres. Channel Tunnel Company, 1957; Vice-Pres. European Foundation of Culture, 1961; Director, number of Companies. Medal of Freedom (US), 1946; Comdr of the Order of Leopold (Belgium), 1952; Comdr of the Order of Orange-Nassau (Netherlands), 1953; Comdr of the Order of San Tiego (Portugal), 1958. *Publications:* Plaidoyer pour l'Avenir; Simples Propos, 1968; Le Pari européen, 1968; Propos ferroviaires, 1970; various papers on mineral waters, on the treatment of feed waters for boilers, on the direct utilisation of the industrial current for electric propulsion, on the building of Europe, on education, on perspective thought, etc. *Recreations:* reading, walking. *Address:* 30 Avenue de Villiers, Paris 17e.
[Died 30 Aug. 1971.

ARMFIELD, Maxwell Ashby, RWS; Writer, Lecturer, Designer and Painter; *s* of Joseph J. Armfield and Margaret Maxwell; *m* Constance Smedley (*d* 1941). *Educ:* Sidcot and Leighton Park; Birmingham Sch. of Art; Paris; Italy. Exhibitor, RA, Salons NEAC, Venice International, Berlin, New York, Chicago, and all principal exhibitions; Lectures on Design and Stage Decoration at the Univs of Columbia, California, New Mexico, etc; Special Studies, Esoteric Symbolism, Design, Tempera Painting; represented: National Collection, Paris, British Museum, Bath, Bournemouth, Derby, Nottingham, etc. *Publications:* The Hanging Garden, 1914; White Horses; An Artist in America, 1925; An Artist in Italy, 1926; (technical) Rhythmic Shape; Stencil-Printing; A Manual of Tempera Painting, 1930; Tempera Painting Today, 1946; 3 Rhythmic Plays: Homage to Masters, 1949; Hermes in the Zodiac; articles in art journals. *Recreation:* musical composition. *Address:* Teddington House, Warminster, Wilts. *[Died 23 Jan. 1972.*

ARMITAGE, Bernard William Francis, MA Cambridge; FBPsS; MRCS, LRCP; *b* 6 July 1890; *s* of William Armitage, FZS, and Clara, *niece* of late Sir Jonathan Hutchinson of Inval, Haslemere, Surrey; *m* 1938, Lucy Mitchell, *d* of late John Charles Molteno, MP (SA) and of Mrs Molteno, Virginia, USA, and *gd* of late Sir John Molteno, Prime Minister of Cape Colony. *Educ:* Gresham's Sch., Holt; St John's Coll., Cambridge; St Bartholomew's Hosp., London. Fellow and Tutor of St John's Coll., Cambridge, 1919-25; Demonstrator of Anatomy, Cambridge Univ., 1919-23; Director of Psychotherapy, Bethlem Royal Hospital, 1935-41; Medico-Psychological Dept, St Bartholomew's Hospital; Mem. of the British Repatriation Commission, 1918; Medical Adviser, Olympic Games, Antwerp, 1920; FRSocMed, Mem. Council and Chm. Parly Cttee of Royal Medico-Psychological Assoc.; Has represented British Psychiatry abroad. Freeman of the City of London. *Publications:* occasional articles. *Recreations:* represented Cambridge in 3 miles *v.* Oxford, 1910-12, and Oxford and Cambridge *v.* Harvard and Yale, USA; Past Pres. Cambridge Univ. Ski and Ice Hockey Club; painting, music, field sports and country pursuits, travel. *Clubs:* Athenæum, Savage; University Pitt, Hawks, Alverstone, Cambridge University Cruising.
[Died 25 Aug. 1976.

ARMITAGE, Gen. Sir (Charles) Clement, KCB 1938 (CB 1933); CMG 1918; DSO 1916; DL; Colonel Commandant, RA; *b* 12 Dec. 1881; *s* of late C. I. Armitage of High Royd, Honley, Yorks; *m* 1st, 1915, Hilda Caroline (*d* 1931), *d* of late T. J. Hirst, Meltham Hall, Yorks; two *s* one *d*; 2nd, 1933, Eileen, *widow* of Lieut-Col F. A. W. Armitage. Served South African War, 1901-2; European War, 1914-18 (Croix de Guerre, DSO and bar, CMG, Chevalier of the Legion of Honour, Officer of the Order of Leopold, despatches seven times); Comdt Sch. of Artillery, 1927-29; Comdr 7th Inf. Bde, 1929-32; ADC to King George V, 1930-32; Comdt Staff Coll., Camberley, 1934-36; Comdr 1st Div., 1936-38; Master General of the Ordnance, India, 1938-42; retired, 1942. DL Glos, 1950. *Address:* Downington House, Lechlade, Glos.
[Died 15 Dec. 1973.

ARMITAGE, John; editor and bookseller; *b* 25 Sept. 1910; *s* of C. V. and C. C. Armitage, Lincoln; *m* 1934, Margaret Rosa, *y d* of W. G. Watkins; three *s*. *Educ:* Bedford Sch; Emmanuel Coll., Cambridge. Editor Rackets Publications Ltd, 1932-39; Asst Editor, The Fortnightly, 1937-39, Editor, 1939-54; RAF 1942, Educational Service, Squadron Leader, 1943-46; Times Educational Supplement, 1946-49; Editor, Encyclopædia Britannica Ltd, 1949-67. Councillor, Surbiton Borough Council, 1942-46; Chairman: Education Advisory Cttee, Liberal Party, 1948-56; The Norton Sch., 1964-76; Letchworth Adult Settlement. Pres. Rugby Fives Assoc., 1956-60; Dir, David's Bookshops (Letchworth) Ltd. *Publications:* A History of Ball Games and Rugby Fives (Lonsdale Library), 1934; To Christian England, 1942; Europe in Bondage, 1943; Our Children's Education, 1960; Man at Play, 1977; contributor to: Partnership in Education, 1948; The Unservile State, 1957; The Oxford

Companion to Sports and Games, 1975; Times Lit. Supp., 1947-74; Encyc. Britannica, 14th and 15th edns. *Address:* 100 Wilbury Road, Letchworth, Herts. *[Died 1 Feb. 1980.*

ARMOUR, William, RSA 1966 (ARSA 1958); RSW; RGI 1977; painter; formerly Head of Drawing and Painting, School of Art, Glasgow, retired; *b* 1903; *s* of Hugh T. Armour; *m* 1927, Mary Nicol Neill, RSA, RSW, RGI, *d* of William Steel. *Educ:* Camphill Sch., Paisley. Has exhibited: RSA, RSW, etc. *Address:* Kilbarchan, Renfrewshire. *Club:* Glasgow Art.
[Died 20 Jan. 1979.

ARMSTRONG, 2nd Baron, *cr* 1903, of Bamburgh and Cragside; **William John Montagu Watson-Armstrong;** late Captain 7th Battalion Northumberland Fusiliers (TF); *b* 10 Oct. 1892; *o* surv. *c* of 1st Baron Armstrong (2nd *cr* 1903) and Winifreda, *d* of late Sir John Adye, GCB; *S* father 1941; *m* 1917, Zaida Cecile, *e d* of Cecil Drummond-Wolff, Caplanne, Billere, Pau, France; one *s. Educ:* Eton College; Trinity Coll., Cambridge; MA, first-class honours Historical Tripos, 1914; Bowen Modern History Prize, etc. Contested Berwick-on-Tweed Division as Independent Candidate, 1918; obtained commission in 7th NF (TF), 1913; served abroad France, and Belgium (severely wounded, April 1915, 2nd battle, Ypres, despatches); invalided home, Nov. 1917; served in India, 1918-19; Siamese Consul in Canada, 1924-29; Siamese Consul-General in Canada, 1929-42; Consul of the Netherlands for British Columbia and Yukon Territory, 1942-46; Commander of the Order of the Crown of Siam; Commander of the Order of the White Elephant; Commander Order of Orange-Nassau (Netherlands). *Publications:* various articles in the Press; My First Week in Flanders (2nd battle Ypres), etc. *Recreations:* travel and exploration; fishing, motoring, cricket. *Heir: s* Hon. William Henry Cecil John Robin Watson-Armstrong [*b* 6 Mar. 1919; *m* 1947, Baroness Maria-Teresa du Four Chiodelli Manzoni, *o c* of late Mme Paul J. Ruegger]. *Address:* Cragside, Rothbury, Morpeth, Northumberland. *T:* Rothbury 333; Bamburgh Castle, Bamburgh, Northumberland. *T:* Bamburgh 245. *Clubs:* MCC; Canadian, Vancouver (Vancouver); Surrey County Cricket.
[Died 6 July 1972.

ARMSTRONG OF SANDERSTEAD, Baron *cr* 1975 (Life Peer), of the City of Westminster; **William Armstrong,** PC 1973; GCB 1968 (KCB 1963; CB 1957); MVO 1945; Chairman, Midland Bank Ltd, since 1975 (Dep. Chm., 1974-75); *b* 3 March 1915; *s* of William Armstrong, Stirling, Scotland; *m* 1942, Gwendoline Enid Bennett; one *s* one *d. Educ:* Bec Sch., London; Exeter Coll., Oxford. Asst Principal, Board of Educn, 1938; Asst Private Sec. to Pres. of Board of Educn, 1940; Private Sec. to Sec. of War Cabinet, 1943-46; Prin. Private Sec. to successive Chancellors of the Exchequer, 1949-53; Under-Sec., Overseas Finance Div., HM Treasury, 1953-57, and Home Finance Div., 1957-58; Third Sec. and Treasury Officer of Accounts, 1958-62; Jt Permanent Sec., 1962-68; Permanent Sec., Civil Service Dept, and Official Head of Home CS, 1968-74. Chm., Midland and International Banks Ltd, 1976-; Chm., Cttee of London Clearing Bankers, 1978-80 (Dep. Chm., 1976-78). Dir, Shell Transport & Trading Co. Ltd, 1976-. Hon. Fellow, Exeter Coll., Oxford, 1963; Visiting Fellow, Nuffield Coll., Oxford, 1964-72; Hon. Fellow, Imperial Coll. of Science and Technology, 1977. Pres., Manpower Soc., 1970-73. Chm. Council, Mansfield Coll., Oxford; Member: Governing Body, London Business Sch., 1970-74; Council, Manchester Business Sch., 1970-74; Council, Oxford Centre for Management Studies, 1970-. Governor, Abingdon Sch., 1979-. Trustee: Wellcome Trust, 1974 (Chm., 1981-); Civic Trust, 1975. Hon. Liveryman, Salters' Co., 1974. Hon. FICE 1973. Hon. DCL Oxford, 1971; Hon. DLitt: City Univ., 1974; Heriot-Watt, 1975; other Hon. degrees: Open Univ., 1974; Cranfield Inst of Technol., 1975; Sheffield Univ., 1975. *Recreations:* reading, walking, talking. *Address:* Midland Bank Ltd, 27-32 Poultry, EC2P 2BX. *Club:* City Livery.
[Died 12 July 1980.

ARMSTRONG, Anthony, (A. A.); *see* Willis, A. A.

ARMSTRONG, His Honour Arthur Henry; *b* 19 Dec. 1893; *s* of Rev. W. D. H. Armstrong, Ilchester, Somerset; *m* 1917, Monica Clare (*d* 1969), *d* of Rev. C. F. Benthall, Cofton, Devon; one *s* two *d. Educ:* Eton; Christ Church, Oxford. Somerset LI and MGC, 1914-18. Called to Bar, 1919; Western Circuit. Wiltshire Regt, 1940-45. Judge of County Courts, Dorset Circuit, 1946-63; Dep. Chm. Dorset QS, 1953-71. *Recreations:* "The meanest chares". *Address:* The Old Vicarage, Queen Camel, Som. *T:* Marston Magna 210. *[Died 12 Jan. 1972.*

ARMSTRONG, Arthur Leopold, CMG 1944; OBE 1939; *b* 1888. Cadet, Fiji, 1915; Principal Assistant Colonial Secretary, 1936; Agent and Consul, Tonga, 1937; Commissioner for

Reconstruction, Fiji, 1943; retired, 1946. *Address:* Bexley, Selwyn Corner, Howich, Auckland, New Zealand.
[Died 11 Nov. 1973.

ARMSTRONG, George James, CMG 1953; CBE 1946 (OBE 1942; MBE 1938); *b* 15 June 1901; *s* of late P. G. Armstrong, Magistrate, Union of South Africa Public Service; *m* 1936, Viva Pearl Rhodes Forrester; three *s* one *d. Educ:* St Andrew's Coll., Grahamstown. Entered South-West Africa Protectorate Admin., Jan. 1920; Colonial Service, Basutoland, July 1920; District Commissioner, Basutoland, 1938; Financial Secretary, Swaziland, 1940; Dep. Resident Commissioner and Govt Sec., Swaziland, 1943-48; Deputy Resident Commissioner and Government Secretary, Basutoland, 1948-53; Retired, 1953, and re-appointed as Agent for the High Commission Territories at Johannesburg, S Africa. Retired, 1963. Coronation Medal, 1953. *Recreations:* fishing, conchology. *Address:* Glengariff Hotel, PO Box 709, East London, S Africa. *[Died 29 March 1972.*

ARMSTRONG, Hamilton Fish; Editor of Foreign Affairs since 1928; Writer; *b* New York, 7 April 1893; *s* of late David Maitland Armstrong and Helen Neilson; *m* 1st, 1918, Helen Macgregor Byrne (divorced 1938); one *d*; 2nd, 1945, Carman Barnes; 3rd, 1951, Christa von Tippelskirch. *Educ:* Princeton Univ. 1st Lieut US Army, 1917; Acting Military Attaché, American Legation, Belgrade, Serbia, 1918-19; Member of Editorial Staff of New York Evening Post, 1919-22; Managing Editor of Foreign Affairs, 1922-28; Director, Council on Foreign Relations; Member, Advisory Cttee on Post-war Problems, State Dept, 1942-44; Special Assistant to Mr Winant, 1944; Special Adviser to Secretary of State, USA, 1944-45; Adviser to US Delegation, San Francisco Conference, 1945; Vice-Pres., Woodrow Wilson Foundation, 1928-30; Pres., 1935-37; Trustee, New York Society Library; Member of President's Advisory Cttee on Political Refugees; BA Princeton, 1916; Hon. LLD, Brown Univ., 1942; Hon. LittD, Yale Univ., 1957; Hon. Dr rer. pol., Univ. of Basel, 1960; Hon. LittD Princeton Univ., 1961; Hon. LLD, Columbia Univ., 1963; Hon. LittD, Harvard Univ., 1963. Order of White Eagle (Serbian), 1919; Legion of Honour (French), Officer 1937, Commander 1947; Order of the White Lion (Czechoslovakia), 1937. *Publications:* The New Balkans, 1926; Where the East Begins, 1929; Hitler's Reich; The First Phase, 1933; Europe Between Wars?, 1934; Can We Be Neutral? (with A. W. Dulles), 1936; We or They, 1937; When There is no Peace, 1939; Can America Stay Neutral? (with A. W. Dulles), 1939; Chronology of Failure, 1940; The Calculated Risk, 1947; Tito and Goliath, 1951; Those Days, 1963; Peace and Counterpeace: from Wilson to Hitler, 1971; Fifty Years of Foreign Affairs, 1973. *Address:* 58 East 68th Street, New York, NY 10021, USA. *TA:* Foraffairs, New York. *T:* Lehigh 5-3300. *Club:* Century (NY). *[Died 24 April 1973.*

ARMSTRONG, James Shelley Phipps; Director, Imperial Life Assurance Co. of Canada, since 1968; *b* 28 Dec. 1899; *s* of Joseph E. Armstrong, MP, Petrolia, Ontario, and Margaret Phipps Armstrong, Petrolia and Philadelphia; *m* 1924, Helen Strawn, *d* of late C. W. I. Woodland, Toronto; one *s* one *d*; *m* 1948, Eileen Mary, *widow* of Harry Lascelles Carr, and *d* of Sir Bracewell Smith, 1st Bt, KCVO; one *d. Educ:* Ashbury Coll., Ottawa; Univ. of Toronto Schools. Superintendent of Agencies, Norwich Union Fire Insurance Soc., 1922-29; Agency Manager of Dominion of Canada General Insurance Company and Casualty Company of Canada, 1930-39; Agent-Gen. for Ontario in UK, 1944-67. Past President: Life Underwriters Assoc. of Toronto; Canadian Veterans' Assoc. in UK; Canadian Ch. of Commerce in UK; Vice-President: Insurance Inst., Toronto; Empire Club; Past Hon. Sec. Canada Club. Member, Canada Committee, BNEC, 1968. Hon. Life Mem. The Board of Trade of Metropolitan Toronto. AIIA. Major, 48th Highlanders of Canada. *Address:* 14 Ennismore Gardens, SW7; National Trust Company, Toronto, Canada. *[Died 3 Dec. 1971.*

ARMSTRONG, John, ARA 1966; painter; *b* Nov. 1893; *s* of Rev. W. A. Armstrong and E. M. Cripps; *m* Benita Jaeger; one *s* one *d*; *m* Veronica Sibthorp; *m* Annette Heaton; one *d. Educ:* St Paul's Sch.; St John's Coll., Oxford. Has had one-man exhibitions during many years at Leicester and Lefevre Galleries, the most recent being at Leicester Galls., 1957. Designer of costumes, etc. for numerous films, theatrical productions and ballet; paintings in the Tate Gallery, Birmingham, Newport (Mon), Aberdeen, Preston, Glasgow and Newcastle galleries, etc. Murals in Festival of Britain Exhibn, ceiling of Bristol Council Chamber, Shell Centre, etc. Paintings purchased by V&A, Arts Council, and Chantrey Bequest. *Address:* 40 Erpingham Road, SW15. *T:* 01-788 5959.
[Died 19 May 1973.

ARMSTRONG, Hon. John Ignatius, AC 1977; High Commissioner for Australia in the United Kingdom, 1972-Jan. 1975; *b* 6 July 1908; *m* 1945, Joan Curran; one *s* four *d. Educ:* Marist Bros High Sch., Sydney. Elected Commonwealth Senate, 1937; Minister for Munitions, then Minister for Supply and Develt in Chifley Govt, 1946-49; Deputy Leader of Opposition in Senate, 1951-56. Member: Rationing Commn, 1942-46; Film Board, 1942-46. Alderman, Sydney City Council, 1934-47; Chm., Sydney County Council, 1963-65; Lord Mayor of Sydney, 1965-67. *Recreations:* bowls, swimming. *Address:* 47 Beach Road, Collaroy, Sydney, NSW, Australia.
[Died 10 March 1977.

ARMSTRONG, Louis Daniel; jazz musician; trumpeter, singer and bandleader; composer; *b* New Orleans, 4 July 1900; *s* of Willie and Mary Ann Armstrong; *m* 1st, 1917, Daisy Parker (marr. diss.); 2nd, 1924, Lillian Hardin (marr. diss.); 3rd, Alpha Smith (marr. diss.); 4th, Lucille Wilson. *Educ:* Coloured Waifs' Home, Louisiana. Began professional career with Kid Ory's Band in the United States, 1917; formed own band, 1925; has since toured USA and Europe, and has made two tours for the State Department of the USA, in Africa and South America. *Film appearances:* Every Day's a Holiday, Going Places, 1938; Cabin in the Sky, 1943; Jam Session, 1944; Doctor Rhythm, Glory-Alley, The Strip, Glen Miller Story, 1953; High Society, 1956; The Five Pennies, 1959; Hello Dolly, 1970. Has made very numerous recordings, particularly as trumpeter and singer. *Publication:* Swing that Music (auto-biography), 1936. *Recreations:* writing, eating Creole food. *Address:* 445 Parkhouse, New York City, NY 10022, USA.
[Died 6 July 1971.

ARMSTRONG, Martin Donisthorpe; author; *b* Newcastle upon Tyne, Oct. 1882; *s* of late Charles Armstrong, Brisco Hill, Carlisle; *m* 1930, Jessie McDonald Aiken (*d* 1970); one *s. Educ:* Charterhouse Sch.; Pembroke Coll., Cambridge (BA). Private in 2nd Batt. Artists Rifles, 1914-15; Commissioned in 8th Batt. Middlesex Regt, 1915-19; served in France; Associate Literary Editor of The Spectator, 1922-24. *Publications:* Exodus, and other poems, 1912; Thirty New Poems, 1918; The Buzzards, 1921; The Puppet Show, 1922; Jeremy Taylor, a Selection from his Works, 1923; The Bazaar, 1924; The Goat and Compasses, 1925; Desert, 1926; Sir Pompey and Madame Juno, 1927; The Stepson, 1927; Saint Hercules, 1927; St Christopher's Day, 1928; The Birdcatcher (poems) and The Sleeping Fury, 1929; Adrian Glynde, 1930; Collected Poems, Mr Darby, and The Paintbox, 1931; Lover's Leap, 1932; The Foster-Mother and Fifty Four Conceits, 1933; General Buntop's Miracle, 1934; (ed) The Major Pleasures of Life, 1934; Venus over Lannery, 1936; A Case of Conscience, 1937; Spanish Circus (1788-1808), 1937; The Snake in the Grass, 1938; Victorian Peep-Show, 1938; Simplicity Jones, 1940; The Butterfly, 1941; Chichester Concert (An Ode), 1944; Said the Cat to the Dog, 1945; Said the Dog to the Cat, 1948; George Borrow, 1950; Selected Stories, 1951. *Address:* Sutton, near Pulborough, Sussex.
[Died 24 Feb. 1974.

ARMSTRONG, Thomas; Author; *b* 3 Sept. 1899; *s* of late Charles Plaxton and late Alice Lily Armstrong, Airedale, Yorks; *m* 1930, Una Dulcie, er *d* of late Edgar and late Amy Jane Bray, Huddersfield. *Educ:* Queen Elizabeth's Sch., Wakefield; Royal Naval Coll., Keyham. Served in Royal Navy during European War, 1914-19. *Publications:* The Crowthers of Bankdam, 1940 (filmed as Master of Bankdam); Dover Harbour, 1942; King Cotton, 1947; Adam Brunskill, 1952; Pilling Always Pays, 1954; A Ring Has No End, 1958; Sue Crowther's Marriage, 1961; The Face of a Madonna, 1964; Our London Office, 1966. *Recreations:* reading, mediæval architecture, outdoor constructional work, country pursuits, any ball game, racing. *Address:* Lawn House, Low Row, Swaledale, North Yorks. *T:* Gunnerside 247.
[Died 2 Aug. 1978.

ARMSTRONG, Prof. Wallace Edwin, MA Cantab; Professor Emeritus since 1961; *b* 24 Feb. 1896; *s* of William Wallace Armstrong and Alice Imeson; *m* 1928, Mary Agnes Canavan; one *s* one *d. Educ:* Dulwich Coll.; (Exhibitioner) Sidney Sussex College, Cambridge. Volunteered as Private in RAMC, 1914 (wounded, 1915, with loss of leg). BA Cantab Moral Sciences Tripos, 1918; Anthony Wilkin Studentship for ethnological research in New Guinea, 1919-22; Asst Anthropologist in Papuan Govt, 1921-22; Lecturer in Social Anthropology, Cambridge, 1922-26; Supervisor and occasional lecturer in Economics, Cambridge, 1926-39; Lecturer in Economics, University Coll., Southampton, 1939, Senior Lecturer, 1949; Reader, Univ. of Southampton, 1953; Professor of Economic Theory, Univ. of Southampton, 1958-61. *Publications:* Rossel Island, 1928; Saving and Investment, 1936. Numerous articles in: Man, Anthropos, Economic Journal, Oxford Economic Papers, Review of Economic Studies. *Recreations:* gardening,

building. *Address:* Ballards Wood, Straight Mile, Ampfield, near Romsey, Hants. *T:* Romsey 513234.
[Died 10 March 1980.

ARMSTRONG COWAN, Sir Christopher; see Cowan, Sir C. G. A.

ARNASON, Frú Barbara; see Moray Williams, B.

ARNOLD, Sir William (Henry), KBE 1973 (CBE 1955); Kt 1963; Bailiff of Guernsey since 1960; *b* 5 Aug. 1903; *s* of William John Arnold and Emma Elizabeth Le Patourel; *m* 1933, Christine Beryl Carré; two *s* one *d. Educ:* Guernsey Gram. Sch.; Univ. of Caen. Bachelier en Droit, Caen, 1923; Barrister-at-Law, Gray's Inn, 1926; Advocate of the Royal Court, Guernsey, 1927; HM Attorney-General for the Bailiwick of Guernsey, 1946-60. Docteur en Droit (*hc*), Caen, 1967; Hon. LLD: Brock Univ., Canada, 1969; Southampton, 1973. KStJ. *Recreation:* gardening. *Address:* The Royal Court House, Guernsey. *T:* Guernsey 26161 and 55812. *Clubs:* Savage; Royal Guernsey Golf, Royal Channel Islands Yacht.
[Died 21 July 1973.

ARNOTT, Maj.-Gen. Stanley, CB 1948; CBE 1944; DSO 1937; MD; County Director and Hon. Secretary City of Edinburgh Branch of British Red Cross Society, 1956-64; retired; *b* 16 Dec. 1888; British. *Educ:* Durham Sch., Edinburgh Univ. MB, ChB 1913; MD 1920, Edin. Lieut RAMC 1913. Served throughout European War, 1914-18, in France and Egypt (despatches); Soudan Service, 1918 for 4 years (despatches, 4th Order of Nile); served North West Frontier, India (DSO); 13 years (on and off) in India; War of 1939-45 (despatches, CBE): ADMS, 4th Div., in France (Dunkirk); War Office; then DDMS, 13th Corps (Sicily and Italy); DDMS, 8th Army (Italy); DMS, Southern Army, India, as Maj.-Gen., 1944; retired 1948, after 36 years' service. Formerly Medical Superintendent, Borders Hospitals Board of Management. *Clubs:* New, Royal Scots (Edinburgh); Hon. Company of Edinburgh Golfers (Muirfield); Gullane Golf.
[Died 27 Oct. 1972.

ARON, Robert; Chevalier, Légion d'Honneur; French author; Member, Académie Française, since 1974; *b* Vesinet, S-et-O, 25 May 1898; *s* of Georges Aron and Louise Aron (*née* Lippmann); *m* 1929, Sabine Pelletier (nom de plume Sabine Berritz). *Educ:* Lycée Condorcet; Faculty of letters, Sorbonne, Paris. Served European War, 1914-18 (Croix de Guerre). Founder (with Arnaud Dandieu) of Personalist Movement (Ordre Nouveau), 1930. In War of 1939-45, escaped to Algeria, 1943, after arrest by forces of occupation, and worked with govts of Giraud and de Gaulle, 1943-44. Dir of Theoretical Studies, in Mouvement Fédéraliste Français and La Fédération, 1946-; Literary Dir, Librairie Fayard. Prix Femina-Vacaresco, 1961; Prix Eve-Delacroix, 1967. *Publications:* La Révolution nécessaire (with A. Dandieu), 1934; Victoire à Waterloo, 1937, new edn 1968; Le Piège où nous a pris l'Histoire, 1950; Histoire de Vichy, 1954; Ce que je crois, 1955; Histoire de la Libération de la France, 1959; Les Années obscures de Jésus, 1960 (Eng. trans: Jesus of Nazareth: The Hidden Years, 1962); Les Grands Dossiers de l'Histoire contemporaine, 1962; Les Nouveaux Grands Dossiers de l'Histoire contemporaine, 1963; Le Dieu des origines des cavernes du Sinaï, 1964; Charles de Gaulle, 1964; Histoire de l'épuration, 1967; Ainsi priait Jésus enfant, 1968; Discours contre la Méthode, 1973; Lettre ouverte à l'église de France, 1975. *Address:* 2 rue Michel-Ange, Paris 16e, France.
[Died 19 April 1975.

ARROWSMITH, Hugh, CBE 1953; *b* 2 June 1888; *s* of late P. R. Arrowsmith; *m* 1914, Edith (*d* 1963), *d* of John Jaques; no *c. Educ:* Marlborough. Cotton Broker, 1910-40; Asst Controller, Min. of Supply, 1940-47; Independent Mem., Raw Cotton Commission, 1951-54. *Recreation:* gardening. *Address:* Ribby Cottage, Wood Lane, Neston, Wirral, Cheshire. *T:* Neston 1355.
[Died 25 Aug. 1972.

ARTEMUS JONES, Sir Thomas; see Jones.

ARTHUR, Sir (Oswald) Raynor, KCMG 1957 (CMG 1953); CVO 1953; JP; retired as Governor and Commander-in-Chief, The Bahamas (1957-60); *b* 1905; *s* of late Sigismund Raynor Arthur, ICS, and of Constance Eleanor (*née* Hobhouse); *m* 1935, Mary Elizabeth, *d* of late Rt Hon. Sir Cecil Spring Rice, PC, GCMG, GCVO; one *s* one *d. Educ:* Charterhouse; Corpus Christi Coll., Cambridge. Entered Nigerian Political Service, 1928; transferred to Cyprus as administrative officer, 1937; Commissioner, 1947; Chief Commissioner, 1948. Colonial Sec., Bermuda, 1951; Governor and Commander-in-Chief, Falkland Islands, 1954. JP East Sussex, 1962. *Recreations:* tennis, hunting. *Address:* 36 Argyll Road, W8. *T:* 01-937 5912; The Glebe House, Burwash, Sussex. *T:* Burwash 224. *Club:* East India, Sports and Public Schools.
[Died 4 Dec. 1973.

ARWYN, Baron, *cr* 1964 (Life Peer); **Arwyn Randall Arwyn;** Chairman, Atkinson Electrical Engineering, Penryn, Cornwall, since 1976; Director of various companies; Chartered Mining Engineer and Industrial Consultant; *b* 17 April 1897; *s* of Rev. William Davies, Congregational Minister, Glamorgan; changed name by deedpoll from Davies to Arwyn, 1964; *m* 1st, 1929, Norah Gwynne (marr. diss. 1945), *d* of Ernest Watkins, Swansea; two *d*; 2nd, 1946, Beatrix Emily Bassett, *d* of Capt. F. H. Organ, St Austell; one *s*. *Educ:* Ystalyfera Grammar Sch.; Swansea Technical Coll. Served Wars of 1914-18 and 1939-45: Army, Air Force, and specialist duties. Member: Mineral Develt Cttee, 1946-49; China Clay Council, 1948-71; Mil., Sci. and Tech. Cttees, North Atlantic Assembly, 1967-73. Dep. Chm., Bath and Portland Group, 1926-75, now Gp Consultant. Past Pres., Inst. of Cornish Mining Engrs. CEng, FIMinE. *Address:* Ormonde, Lostwithiel, Cornwall. *Clubs:* Reform; Royal Automobile; Royal Cornwall Yacht, House of Lords Yacht, Flushing Sailing. *[Died 23 Feb. 1978.*

ASAFU-ADJAYE, Sir Edward (Okyere), Kt 1960; Fellow of University College, London, since 1959; formerly Member, Ghana Board, Barclays Bank DCO; *b* 1903; *m* 1930, Martha Violet Randolph; several *s* and *d*. *Educ:* Kumasi Government Primary Boys' Sch.; SPG Grammar Sch. (now Adisadel Coll.), Cape Coast; University Coll., London Univ. Hons Philosophy, 1925; Law, 1926. Profumo prize, Inner Temple; called to Bar, Inner Temple, 1927; enrolled as member Gold Coast Bar (now the Bar of Ghana), 1927. Practised principally in Accra Courts until 1934, when Kumasi Courts were opened and his Accra Chambers moved to Kumasi. Formerly: Dir Ghana Commercial Bank; Councillor in the old Kumasi Town Council; Mem. Asantenhan Council; Mem. Council University Coll. of Ghana. Served on CNC delegation to London, 1934; a representative of the Gold Coast at the Coronations: of King George VI, 1937; and of Queen Elizabeth II, 1953; attended Commonwealth Parly Conf., Ottawa, 1949. MLC 1946; MLA 1951; Minister of Local Govt, 1951-55 (MLA as Convention People's Party candidate, 1954); Minister of Trade and Labour, 1955: did not seek election in 1956, and resumed his legal practice until his appt as Ghana's first High Commissioner to the UK; also first Ambassador of Ghana to France; High Commissioner for Ghana in London, 1957-61. Director, Consolidated African Selection Trust, 1961-66. *Recreations:* golf and walking. *Address:* c/o Standard Bank Ltd, 73/79 King William Street, EC4N 7AB. *[Died 27 Feb. 1976.*

ASH, Graham Baron; *b* 18 Aug. 1889; *s* of Alfred James Ash, OBE. *Educ:* Radley. Served European War with RFC and RAF, and with RAF, 1939-40; High Sheriff of Warwickshire, 1938-39. *Recreation:* shooting. *Address:* Wingfield Castle, Diss, Norfolk. *[Died 20 Feb. 1980.*

ASHBRIDGE, Sir Noel, Kt 1935; BSc; MICE; MIEE; FKC; FIRE; Knight of Royal Order of Dannebrog (Danish); *b* 10 Dec. 1889; 4th *s* of John Ashbridge, Wanstead; *m* 1926, Olive Maude (*d* 1948), *d* of Rowland Strickland, Erith; two *d*. *Educ:* Forest Sch.; King's Coll., London. Engineering training with Yarrow and Co., Ltd, and British Thomson-Houston Co., Ltd; served European War, 1914-19, Royal Fusiliers and RE; six years Marconi's, at Writtle Experimental Station; joined BBC 1926 as Assistant Chief Engineer; late Controller of Engineering, BBC; Deputy Dir-Gen., BBC, 1943-48; Dir of Technical Services, BBC, 1948-52; Chm., Radio Research Bd, 1952-57. President Institution of Electrical Engineers, 1941-42; Member of Television Cttee, 1934 and 1943, and Television Advisory Cttee, 1935; Vice-Pres. Inst. of Radio Engineers, 1947; Pres. Junior Inst. of Engineers, 1949-50. *Publications:* various technical and scientific papers. *Address:* Tyneham, Highview Road, Sidcup, Kent. *Club:* Athenæum. *[Died 4 June 1975.*

ASHDOWN, Baron *cr* 1974 (Life Peer); **Arnold Silverstone,** Kt 1964; Director of Companies; *b* 28 Sept. 1911; *y s* of late Henry and Rebecca Silverstone; *m* 1937, Lillian King (CBE 1971); no *c*. *Educ:* Llanelly County Intermediate School; University College, Swansea. Served with HM Forces, 1940-45; Major, 1944. Called to the Bar, Middle Temple, 1953. Contested (C) East Ham North, 1955; Joint Treasurer, Conservative Party, 1974- (Greater London Area, 1963-74). Governor, Queen Charlotte's and Chelsea Hosps; Member: Cttee of Management Inst of Obstetrics and Gynæcology; Roy. Homeopathic Hosp. Management Cttee, 1964-65. Freeman of City of London; Master, Worshipful Company of Needlemakers, 1975. *Address:* 45 Lowndes Square, SW1. *T:* 01-235 3097; Gale, Chelwood Gate, Haywards Heath, West Sussex. *T:* Chelwood Gate 208. *Clubs:* Carlton, Junior Carlton. *[Died 23 July 1977.*

ASHDOWN, Rt. Rev. Hugh Edward, MA, DD; *b* 5 July 1904; *s* of William Edward and Sarah Annie Constance Ashdown; *m*

1937, Georgina Sylvia (*née* Battye); one *s* two *d*. *Educ:* St John's, Leatherhead; Keble College, Oxford; Lincoln Theological College. Deacon, 1929; priest, 1930; Curate of St Mary, Portsea, 1929-34; Chaplain and Lecturer, Lincoln Theol Coll., 1934-37; Exam. Chaplain to Bishop of Ripon, 1935-46; Perpetual Curate of St Aidan's, West Hartlepool, 1937-43; Rector of Houghton-le-Spring, 1943-48; Rector of St Saviour with St Peter, Southwark, and Provost of Southwark, 1948-57; Bishop of Newcastle, 1957-72. *Address:* Manor Cottage, Misterton, near Crewkerne, Somerset. *[Died 26 Dec. 1977.*

ASHER, Florence May, RBA; FRSA 1950; figure and landscape painter; *b* Nottingham, 2 May 1888; 2nd *d* of Joseph William and Ruth Asher. *Educ:* Nottingham. Studied at the Royal Academy Schs (Silver Medallist and Landseer Scholarship); exhibited Royal Academy, International Exhibition, America, Stockholm, Toronto, Paris Salon, Australia, New Zealand; sold picture, In the Tyrol, to Canadian Government for permanent collection at Toronto. *Recreations:* reading, gardening, and scientific interests. *Address:* 2 Yorke Gardens, Reigate, Surrey. *[Died 22 Jan. 1977.*

ASHER, Mrs Peter; *see* Shuard, Amy.

ASHKANASY, Maurice, CMG 1961; QC (Victoria); LLM; *b* 16 Oct. 1901; *s* of late Aaron Solomon Ashkanasy and Annie Ashkanasy; *m* 1927, Heather Helen Epstein; two *s* one *d*. *Educ:* South Melbourne Coll.; Melbourne High Sch.; Melbourne Univ. Admitted to Victorian Bar, 1924; KC Victoria, 1940, NSW, 1949; QC Tasmania, 1959. Served War of 1939-45 (despatches): Lieut-Col, AAG, AIF, Malaya, 1st Aust. Corps, 2nd and 3rd Aust. Corps and New Guinea Forces. Past Chm. Victorian Bar Council, 1952-55. Pres. Melbourne High School Old Boys, 1924-28. Past Pres. Victorian Jewish Board of Deputies; Dep. Pres. Executive Council of Australian Jewry; Vice-Pres. Aust. Section Internat. Commn of Jurists. *Recreation:* fishing. *Address:* 205 William Street, Melbourne, Victoria 3000, Australia. *T:* BL 7161. *Clubs:* Naval and Military; Constitutional (Melbourne) (Pres. 1958). *[Died 2 April 1971.*

ASHLEY; *see* Havinden, A. E.

ASHLEY, Francis Noel, CMG 1937; Squadron Leader RAFVR; *b* 11 Dec. 1884; *s* of Frederick Moorewood Ashley and Edith, *d* of J. O. Hodges, Penny Hill Park, Bagshot; *m* 1913, Marjorie, *d* of James Wills Robinson, Barrister-at-law; one *d*. *Educ:* Westminster. Sussex Militia Artillery, 1902-04; Cape Colonial Mounted Forces, 1904-08; Cadet, Political Service, Nigeria, 1908; West Africa Frontier Force, 1915; Resident, Southern Provinces, Nigeria, 1924-28; Resident Commissioner British Solomon Islands Protectorate, 1929-39; RAFVR, 1940-44; employed by Bahamas Government, 1944-46. *Recreations:* cricket, golf. *Address:* Flat 21, Southbury, Lawn Road, Guildford. *T:* Guildford 62480. *[Died 28 May 1976.*

ASHLEY-SCARLETT, Lt-Col Henry, DSO 1918; JP; Past Councillor Hampstead Borough Council (which is now in Camden Borough Council); *b* Jan. 1886; *m* 1928, Marjorie Laird, *d* of Percy Collins, JP, Frinton-on-Sea, Essex. *Educ:* Berkhampstead Sch.; Lycée Carnot, Paris. Capt. and Adjutant, 13th Royal Fusiliers; Major, 2nd in Command, 9th Royal Fusiliers; Lieut-Col, 7th Norfolk Regt; Lt-Col, Royal Fusiliers (Reserve of Officers); served European War, 1914-19 (despatches thrice, DSO); War of 1939-45, attached to RAF, 1943-45; formerly: Sch. Manager, Fitzjohns, Fleet and New End Primary Schs; Governor of Royal Soldiers' Daughters' Sch.; ex-Council Royal Society St George; Mayor, Borough of Hampstead, 1957-59 (Deputy Mayor, 1959-61, 1962-63); Member: London Magistrates Club; past Chairman, HM Prison, Wormwood Scrubs; past Visiting Magistrate, HM Prison, Wandsworth; Trustee, Smoothfield Old People's Home; President, Hampstead Old People's Homesteads. Vice-President: Hampstead Cons. Assoc; Hampstead Young Cons. Assoc. Managing Director: Tuberfield Ltd; Hillpath Ltd; Trowchurch Ltd. JP London. *Address:* 43 Ferncroft Avenue, NW3. *[Died 11 May 1976.*

ASHMORE, Vice-Adm. Leslie Haliburton, CB 1947; DSO 1944; *b* 21 Feb. 1893; *e s* of late Arthur Haliburton Ashmore, Shanklin, IoW; *m* 1919, Tamara Vasilevna Shutt (*d* 1972), Petrograd; two *s*. *Educ:* Sandroyd; RN Colleges, Osborne and Dartmouth. Lieut 1915; European War, 1914-18: served in submarines; commanded HM Submarines C35, V3, E46, and subsequently L52. Comdr 1928; RN Staff Coll.; commanded HM ships Wallflower and Cyclamen; Capt. 1934; Imperial Defence Coll.; commanded HM ships Kent, Valiant and Malaya; Rear-Admiral, 1944; Flag Officer commanding Reserve Fleet, 1945-47; retired list, 1947; Vice-Adm. retd, 1948. *Address:*

Godden Green Lodge, Godden Green, near Sevenoaks, Kent. *T:* Sevenoaks 61594. *[Died 10 Jan. 1974.*

ASHTON, Lt-Col Edward Malcolm, CIE 1947; OBE 1945; Indian Army (retired); *b* 21 May 1895; 3rd *s* of late H. Bankes Ashton, Bury St Edmunds; *m* 1927, Gwyneth Ena Darcy Smith; one *s* two *d*. *Educ:* Falconbury Sch.; Purley; King Edward VI Sch., Bury St Edmunds. Indian Army; Mil. Officer in Civil Employ; Dir Military Lands and Cantonments; Defence Dept, Govt of India. Served European War, 1914-18 (despatches). *Recreations:* fishing, shooting, tennis. *Address:* 34 Well Street, Bury St Edmunds. *T:* Bury St Edmunds 63937. *Club:* National Liberal. *[Died 20 June 1978.*

ASHTON, Sir Hubert, KBE 1959; MC; MA Cantab; Third Church Estates Commissioner, 1962-72; *b* 13 Feb. 1898; *s* of late H. S. Ashton, Trueloves, Ingatestone, Essex, and Mrs V. A. Ashton; *m* 1927, Dorothy Margaret Gaitskell; one *s* two *d* (and one *s* decd). *Educ:* Winchester Coll.; Trinity Coll., Cambridge (Blues for cricket (captain), football and hockey). Royal Field Artillery, 1916-19. Burmah Oil Co., 1922-45; Underwriter at Lloyd's, 1936. MP (C) Chelmsford Division of Essex, 1950-64; Parliamentary Private Secretary to the Chancellor of the Exchequer, 1951-55, to the Lord Privy Seal, Oct. 1955 and to Lord Privy Seal and Home Sec., 1957; Second Church Estates Comr, 1957-62. Governor: Brentwood Sch., 1948- (Chm., 1962-76); London Hosp., 1948-70 (Dep. Chm., 1967-70; Vice-Patron, 1970-); Mem. GBA, 1963-, Vice-Chm. 1966-76. Cttee Mem., MCC, 1947-50, 1952-55 and 1957-64, Pres. 1961; Pres., Essex CCC, 1948-70. Church Warden, St Peter's Church, S Weald, 1940-70. DL Essex, 1942-78; High Sheriff of Essex, 1943; Essex County Councillor, 1946, Vice-Chm., 1949-52; Alderman Essex CC, 1950-61. Dir of public companies. *Recreations:* walking, grandchildren. *Address:* Wealdside, South Weald, Brentwood, Essex. *T:* Coxtie Green 72324. *Clubs:* City of London, Oriental, MCC. *[Died 17 June 1979.*

ASHTON-GWATKIN, Frank Trelawny Arthur, CB 1939; CMG 1933; *b* 14 April 1889; *s* of late Rev. Canon W. H. T. Ashton-Gwatkin; *m* Nancy Violet Butler (*d* 1953), Melbourne, Australia. *Educ:* Eton; Balliol Coll., Oxford. Entered HM Consular Service (Far East), 1913; 2nd Sec., Foreign Office, 1921; 1st Sec., 1924; Acting Counsellor of Embassy, Moscow, 1929; 1st Sec., Foreign Office, 1930; Counsellor, 1934; attached to suite of Crown Prince of Japan on his visit to England, 1921; attached to United Kingdom Delegation, Disarmament Conference at Washington, 1921-22; Imperial Economic Conference at Ottawa, 1932; World Monetary and Economic Conference at London, 1933; Lord Runciman's Mission to Czecho-Slovakia, 1938; Policy Adviser, Min. of Economic Warfare, 1939; Asst Under-Sec. and Chief Clerk, Foreign Office, 1940; Sen. Insp. of Diplomatic Missions (with rank of Minister), 1944; Asst Under-Sec. FO, 1947; retired on pension, 1947; Associate Director of Studies, Royal Institute of International Affairs, 1947-52. FSA. *Publications:* Michelangelo (Newdigate Prize Poem for English verse, 1909); The British Foreign Service (Syracuse Univ. lectures, USA 1949); contributions to the RIIA History of The War; (under *nom de plume* of John Paris) Kimono, 1921; Sayonara, 1924; Banzai, 1925; A Japanese Don Juan (poems), 1926; The Island beyond Japan, 1930; Matsu, 1932. *Address:* 9 Barton Close, Nyetimber, Sussex. *T:* Pagham 2058. *Club:* Brooks's. *[Died 29 Jan. 1976.*

ASHTOWN, 5th Baron *cr* 1800; **Dudley Oliver Trench,** OBE 1961; retired as Assistant Chief Constable, War Department Constabulary, 1964; late KRRC; *b* 11 July 1901; *yr s* of 3rd Baron Ashtown (*d* 1946), and Violet Grace (*d* 1945), *d* of Col R. G. Cosby; *S* brother, 1966; *m* 1st, 1932, Ellen Nancy (*d* 1949), *y d* of late William Garton, Brixedone, Bursledon, Hants; two *d*; 2nd, 1955, Sheelah A. S. (*d* 1963), *yr d* of late Brig.-Gen. L. F. Green-Wilkinson, OBE; 3rd, 1966, Natalie, *widow* of Major James de Sales La Terrière. *Educ:* Wellington Coll.; RMC Sandhurst. Adjutant 11th London Regt, 1934-35, and Queen's Westminsters, 1936-38; retd pay, 1939. Served War of 1939-45 (despatches). *Heir: kinsman* Christopher Oliver Trench, *b* 23 March 1931. *Address:* Woodlawn, King's Somborne, Near Stockbridge, Hants. *T:* King's Somborne 333.
[Died 19 Aug. 1979.

ASHWIN, Sir Bernard Carl, KBE 1956; CMG 1946; company director, retired; *b* Paeroa, NZ, 1896; *s* of Manley John Ashwin; *m* 1926, Rachel Robinson, *d* of William Turnbull; one *s* two *d*. *Educ:* Cambridge Dist High Sch.; Victoria University Coll. (MCom Hons). Cadet Educ. Dept, 1912; served European War, 1914-18, with NZEF; qualified as public accountant 1921; transferred to Treasury, 1922; Sec. to Treasury, and Director, Reserve Bank of NZ, 1939-55, retired. Director: Reid NZ Rubber Mills Ltd, 1959-70; Colonial Mutual Life Assurance

Soc. Ltd, 1964-71; C. & A. Odlin Timber and Hardware Co. Ltd, 1965-69; BP (New Zealand) Ltd, 1946-66; Coulls, Somerville, Wilkie Ltd, 1955-73; Thomas Ballinger & Co. Ltd, 1955-73; Holland and Hannen and Cubitts (NZ) Ltd, 1959-71. *Recreation:* golf. *Address:* 122 Woburn Road, Lower Hutt, New Zealand. *[Died 12 Feb. 1975.*

ASHWORTH, Harold Kenneth, TD and Clasp 1951; Hon. Consultant Anaesthetist, Charing Cross and Moorfields Hospitals, since 1968; *b* 16 May 1903; *s* of Dr J. H. Ashworth, Manchester. *Educ:* Sedbergh; Manchester Univ. MB, ChB (Vic) 1925; MRCS, LRCP 1925; DA 1934; FFARCS 1948. Formerly: Visiting Anaesthetist, Royal Infirmary, Manchester; Clinical Lecturer in Anaesthesia, Univ. of Manchester; Senior Anaesthetist, Charing Cross and Moorfields Hosps; Director, Dept of Anaesthesia, Charing Cross Hosp. Med. Sch., 1956-68; Consulting Anaesthetist to the Kingdom of Libya, 1968-69. RAMC (TA) 1939-45, BEF France, 1940; Brig., Cons. Anaesthetist, India Command, 1944-45. Councillor: St Marylebone Borough Council, 1949-65; Westminster City Council, 1964-68. Examiner for DA (RCP & S), 1962-68. Sen. Mem., Assoc. of Anæsthetists of Great Britain and Ireland, 1968. *Publications:* Practical Points in Anaesthesia, 1936. Contributions to Medical Journals. *Recreations:* watching cricket; formerly Rugby football (Manchester Univ. XV, 1922-26). *Address:* 1 Quelland, Beverley Close, East Ewell, Surrey KT17 3HB. *T:* 01-393 9032. *Clubs:* MCC; XXI (Manchester University). *[Died 4 Sept. 1978.*

ASHWORTH, Hon. Sir John (Percy), Kt 1954; MBE 1944; DL; Hon. Mr Justice Ashworth; Judge of Queen's Bench Division, High Court of Justice, since Oct. 1954; *b* 3 Feb. 1906; *s* of Percy Ashworth, Ollerton, Bolton; unmarried. *Educ:* Winchester; Christ Church, Oxford. Junior Counsel: to the Post Office, 1936; to the Treasury (Common Law), 1950-54. Staffs QS, Dep. Chm., 1951-63, Chm., 1963-71; Presiding Judge, Midland and Oxford Circuit, 1970-74. Chancellor of Diocese: of Rochester, 1943-54; of London, 1944-54; of Lichfield, 1947-54. Served War of 1939-45, Intelligence Corps, 1940-45 (despatches). DL Stafford, 1973. *Address:* Royal Courts of Justice, Strand, WC2; Fradswell Hall, Stafford. *T:* Weston (Staffs) 270210; 26 Stourcliffe Close, W1. *T:* 01-723 3766. *[Died 26 Sept. 1975.*

ASHWORTH, Air Commandant Dame Veronica Margaret, DBE 1964; RRC 1959 (ARRC 1944); Air Commandant-Matron-in-Chief, PMRAFNS, 1963-66; *b* 25 Dec. 1910; *d* of late Dr and Mrs F. H. S. Ashworth. *Educ:* St Katharine's Sch., Wantage, Berks. Trained at St Bartholomew's Hosp., London, 1930-34 (SRN); Midwifery Training, Leeds Maternity Hosp., 1935 (SCM). Joined Princess Mary's Royal Air Force Nursing Service, 1936; Group Officer-Principal Matron, PMRAFNS, 1960-63. QHNS, 1963-66. *Recreation:* music.
[Died 12 Jan. 1977.

ASKWITH, Arthur Vivian, CSI 1945; CIE 1941; *b* 16 Nov. 1893; *s* of Preb. Henry Askwith, Ripon and Hereford; *m* 1926, Kathleen Margaret, *d* of Archibald Murray-Macvicar, Aberdeen. *Educ:* Bedford Sch. Joined India Police, 1913; War of 1914-18, served with 28th Light Cavalry and on General Staff; joined Indian Civil Service, 1921; Sec. to Government of the Punjab, Home Dept, 1935-40; Chief Commissioner, Delhi, 1940-45. *Address:* 13 Loder Drive, Aylestone Hill, Hereford. *T:* Hereford 67958; c/o Lloyds Bank Ltd (Cox and King's Branch), 6 Pall Mall, SW1. *[Died 25 April 1971.*

ASPINALL, Arthur, CVO 1965; MA, DLitt; Professor of Modern History, University of Reading, 1947-65; Professor Emeritus since 1965; *b* 11 July 1901; *m* 1st, 1931, Gladys Shaw (*d* 1965); one *s* one *d*; 2nd, 1968, Beryl Johnson. *Educ:* Manchester Univ. Lecturer in History, Univ. of Rangoon, 1925-31; Lecturer in Modern History, Univ. of Reading, 1931-47. Raleigh Lecturer, British Academy, 1952. External Examiner in Final Hon. Sch. of Mod. Hist., Oxford Univ., 1947-49. *Publications:* Lord Brougham and the Whig Party, 1927; Cornwallis in Bengal, 1931; The Formation of Canning's Ministry, 1937; The Letters of King George IV, 1812-1830 (3 vols), 1938; (with the Earl of Bessborough) Lady Bessborough and her Family Circle, 1940; The Correspondence of Charles Arbuthnot, 1941; The Diary of Henry Hobhouse, 1820-1827, 1947; Politics and the Press, *c* 1780-1850, 1949; The Letters of Princess Charlotte, 1811-1817, 1949; The Early English Trade Unions, 1949; Mrs Jordan and her Family, 1951; Three Early Nineteenth Century Diaries, 1952; The Cabinet Council, 1783-1835, 1954; The reporting of the House of Commons' Debates, 1771-1834, in Essays presented to Sir Lewis Namier, 1956; English Historical Documents, Vol. XI, 1783-1832 (with E. A. Smith), 1959; The Later Correspondence of George III, Vols I-V, 1962-70; Parliament through Seven Centuries: Reading and its MPs (with others), 1962; The Correspondence of George, Prince of Wales, Vols I-VIII, 1963-71; articles in the Eng. Hist. Review, etc. *Address:* Highlands, Belle Vue, Maughold, Isle of Man. *T:* Ramsey 3343. *[Died* 2 *May* 1972.

ASTBURY, Arthur Ralph, CSI 1933; CIE 1928; FInstCE; *b* 5 June 1880; *o s* of Arthur Kingsby Astbury; *m* 1908, Friede Hildegard von Schoenberg (*d* 1972); one *s* one *d*. *Educ:* Westminster; Royal Indian Engineering College, Coopers Hill. Assistant Engineer, Indian Public Works Dept, 1900; Superintending Engineer, 1920; Chief Engineer and Sec. to Government, 1925; retired, 1935; Ministry of Home Security, 1938; Ministry of Works, 1945-50, retired, 1950. *Address:* Hampdenleaf, Dunsmore, Aylesbury, Bucks. *Club:* Athenæum. *[Died* 26 *Nov.* 1973.

ASTERLEY JONES, Philip; *see* Jones, P. A.

ASTLEY, Mrs Reginald, CBE 1920; Kathleen Mary, *e d* of Thomas Mercer Cliffe Vigors, Burgage, Co. Carlow; *m* 1st, 1909, Hon. Wilfred Thesiger, DSO (*d* 1920); three *s* (and one *s* killed on active service, 1942); 2nd, 1931, Reginald Basil Astley (*d* 1942). *Address:* 15 Shelley Court, Tite Street, Chelsea, SW3. *T:* 01-352 7213. *Club:* Guards. *[Died* 28 *Oct.* 1973.

ASTOR OF HEVER, 1st Baron, *cr* 1956, of Hever Castle; **Colonel John Jacob Astor;** Chief Proprietor of The Times Newspaper, 1922-66; *b* 20 May 1886; *y s* of 1st Viscount Astor; *m* 1916, Lady Violet May Elliot, (DStJ) (*d* 1965), *y d* of 4th Earl of Minto, and *widow* of Major Lord Charles Mercer Nairne, *s* of 5th Marquess of Lansdowne; three *s*. *Educ:* Eton Coll. Joined 1st Life Guards, 1906; ADC to Viceroy of India, 1911-14; served European War, 1914-18; commanded Household Siege Battery; Hon. Colonel: 23rd London Regt (TA), 1928-49; Kent and Sussex RGA (TA), 1927-46; Lieut-Col 5th Bn City of London Home Guard, 1940-44. MP (U) Dover Division of Kent, 1922-45. Director: GWR, 1929-48; Barclays Bank, 1942-52; Hambros Bank, 1934-60. Dir until Oct. 1962 when resigned: The Times Publishing Co., Phoenix Assurance Co. (Dep. Chm., 1941-52, Chm. 1952-58), and London Guarantee and Accident Co. Ltd. Member: Govt Broadcasting Cttee, 1923; Gen. Advisory Council, BBC, 1937; Council, St Dunstan's, 1922-62. President: Press Club; Commonwealth Press Union; Nat. Assoc. for Employment of Regular Sailors, Soldiers and Airmen, 1936-62; Kent Council, British Legion, 1934-62; MCC, 1937; Kent County Cricket Club, 1929. Past Pres., Newspaper Press Fund. Vice-Pres., Royal Coll. of Music, 1934-62. Chairman: 4th, 5th, 6th and 7th Imperial Press Confs; Middlesex Hosp., 1938-62; Middlesex Hosp. Medical Sch., 1945-62; Old Etonian Assoc., 1939-49; Hurlingham Club, 1929-49. Master of Guild, St Bride's Church (Fleet Street), 1955-62. DL, Kent, 1936-62, JP, Kent, 1929-62. Hon. Freeman, Borough of Dover. Holds hon. degrees at Univs of Perth (Australia), 1925, London, 1939, McGill, 1950. Chevalier, Legion of Honour, 1918. Recreations: Eton XI, 1904-05; Public Sch. Racquets, 1904-05 (winner); Army Racquets, 1908 (singles and doubles). *Heir: e s* Hon. Gavin Astor. *Address:* Les Terres Blanches, Pegomas, (AM), France. *Club:* Royal Yacht Squadron. *[Died* 19 *July* 1971.

ASTOR, Hon. Michael Langhorne; *b* 10 April 1916; *s* of 2nd Viscount Astor; *m* 1st, 1942, Barbara Mary Colonsay (marr. diss., 1961; she *m* 1962, 1st Viscount Ward of Witley, PC), *o d* of late Capt. Ronald Fitzroy Rous McNeill; two *s* two *d*; 2nd, 1961, Mrs Pandora Jones (marr. diss. 1968), *d* of late Sir Bede Clifford, GCMG, CB, MVO; 3rd, 1970, Judy, *d* of Paul Innes; one *s* one *d*. *Educ:* Eton; New College, Oxford. Served in Berkshire Yeomanry TA and GHQ Liaison Regt Sept. 1939-June 1945. MP (C) Eastern Division of Surrey, 1945-51. Chm., The London Library; Mem., Arts Council, 1968-71. Mem. Exec., Nat. Trust, 1978-. *Publications:* Tribal Feeling (biog.), 1963; Brand (novel), 1967. *Clubs:* White's, Brooks's. *[Died* 28 *Feb.* 1980.

ASTURIAS, Miguel Angel; Guatemalan writer and diplomat; Guatemalan Ambassador in Paris, 1966-70; *b* 19 Oct. 1899. *Educ:* Instituto Nacional de Guatemala, University of Guatemala. Cultural Attaché, Guatemalan Embassy, Mexico, 1946-47; Counsellor, 1947-52; Minister, Paris, 1952-53; Ambassador to El Salvador, 1953. Founder, General Students' Association, and Popular Univ., Guatemala. Prizes: Sylla Monsegur, Paris, 1931; du Meilleur Roman Etranger, Paris, 1952; Lenin Peace Prize, 1966; Nobel Prize for Literature, 1967. *Publications:* El Problema Social del Indio, 1923; Arquitectura de la Vida Nueva (Lectures), 1928; Leyendas de Guatemala, 1930; El Señor Presidente, 1946; Sien de Alondra (anthology of poetry 1918-48), 1948; Hombres de Maiz, 1949; Viento Fuerte, 1950; El Papa Verde, 1953 (The Green Pope, 1971); Week-end

en Guatemala, 1955; Los Ojos de los Enterrados, 1960; El Alhajadito, 1961; Mulata de Tal, 1963; Antologia Teatral, 1964; Clarivigilia Primaveral (poems), 1965; Le Miroir de Lida Sal, 1967; (with Pablo Neruda) Comiendo en Hungria, 1969; Maladron (novel), 1969; Tres de cuatro Soles, 1971; Viernes de Dolores (novel), 1972; Amanecer en el delta del Parana (poem), 1972. *Address:* 27 rue Saint Ferdinand, Paris 17, France. *[Died* 9 *June* 1974.

ATHENAGORAS, Spyrou; Oecumenical Patriarch, also Archbishop of Constantinople and New Rome, since Nov. 1948; *b* 1886. *Educ:* Theological Academy of Halki, Istanbul, Turkey. Metropolitan of Corfu, 1923-30; Archbishop of North and South America, 1930-48. *Address:* Rum Ortodoks Patrikhanesi, Fener, Istanbul, Turkey. *T:* 212532-211921. *[Died* 7 *July* 1972.

ATHENAGORAS, Theodoritos, (*né* Theodoros G. Kokkinakis), STM, MA, STD; Archbishop Athenagoras, Metropolitan of Thyateira and Great Britain, since 1964; Exarch of Sweden, Norway, Ireland, Iceland, and Malta; *b* Patmos, Dodecanese, 1912. *Educ:* schs in Patmos and Cyprus; Patriarchal Theological Seminary; Gen. Theolog. Seminary, NY; Northwestern Univ., Chicago. Went to USA 1936. Priest, Greek Orthodox Church, 1940. Formerly: served Patriarchal Church of St Sava, Alexandria, St Andrew's Church, Chicago and St Demetrios Church, Astoria, NY; taught theology at Acad. of Pomfret, Conn. and at Acad. of St Basil; Dean and then Pres., Holy Cross Theolog. Sch., Brookline, Mass; rep. The Ecumenical Patriarchate of Constantinople at World Council of Churches Conferences: Amsterdam, Evanston, New Delhi, Uppsala; Bishop, Western States Dio., 1950; Metropolitan Bishop of Canada, 1960-63. Pres. 4th Panorthodox Conference, Belgrade, 1967. Editor, Orthodox Herald; past Editor, Orthodox Observer and Greek Orthodox Theolog. Review. Hon. DD Edinburgh, 1970. *Publications:* several books in English and in Greek. *Address:* Greek Archdiocese, 5 Craven Hill, W2. *T:* 01-723 4787. *[Died* 9 *Sept.* 1979.

ATKINS, Alexander Robert; *see* Atkins, R.

ATKINS, Ian Robert, OBE 1963; Controller, Programme Services, Television, BBC, 1963-72; *b* 22 Jan. 1912; *s* of late Robert Atkins, CBE, and Mary (*née* Sumner); *m* 1939, Freda Bamford; one *s* one *d*. *Educ:* St Paul's Sch. Film cameraman, 1930-33; theatre stage manager, 1934-36; asst film dir, 1936-37; theatre stage manager, 1937-39. Royal Artillery, 1939-46; seconded to Min. of Supply, 1942-46. Television, BBC: Television Studio Manager, BBC, 1939 and 1946; Producer, Drama Dept, 1946-58; Asst to Controller, Programme Services, 1958-62; Asst Controller, Programme Services, 1962-63. *Recreations:* gardening, fishing. *Address:* Ash Cottage, Blacksmith Lane, London Street, Chertsey, Surrey. *T:* Chertsey 63161. *[Died* 10 *March* 1979.

ATKINS, Robert, CBE 1949; actor and producer; *b* Dulwich, 10 Aug. 1886; *s* of Robert Atkins and Annie Evans; *m* 1st, Mary Sumner (marr. diss.); one *s*; 2nd, Ethel Davey. *Educ:* privately; Academy of Dramatic Art. First appearance His Majesty's, 1906; three years with Sir Herbert Tree; one season with Glasgow Repertory Company; with Martin Harvey on tour and at Lyceum, 1911; with Forbes Robertson on tour, at Drury Lane, 1913, and in America; toured with Sir Frank Benson's Shakespearean Companies; joined Old Vic Company, 1915; war service; after demobilisation, 1919, toured with Ben Greet's Company; Dir of the Plays at Old Vic, 1920-25; produced and appeared in many plays since 1926 at London Theatres; took his own Shakespearean Repertory Company to Egypt, 1927 and 1928; Dir of British Empire Shakespeare Society, 1927; produced and played lead in Mussolini's Napoleon, New Theatre, 1932 (Cavaliere of Order of Crown of Italy); produced plays at Open Air Theatre, 1933-39, and appeared in many of them; managed and produced the plays in Regent's Park during war years including 1944, also subsequently, continuing annual seasons of producing and playing in Shakespearean and other productions there. Produced Henry V at Stratford-on-Avon, 1934; Dir of Stratford-on-Avon Shakespeare Memorial Theatre Festival Company, 1944-45; produced adaptation of an Elizabethan masque, in the hall of Gray's Inn, 1956. First appeared in films, 1935, in Peg of Old Drury. *[Died* 10 *Feb.* 1972.

ATKINSON, Rt. Hon. Sir Fenton, PC 1968; Kt 1960; a Lord Justice of Appeal, 1968-71; *b* 6 Jan. 1906; *s* of late Hon. Sir Cyril Atkinson; *m* 1929, Margaret Mary, *d* of James Edward and Mary Roy, Scotscraig, Radlett; one *s* two *d*. *Educ:* Winchester; New Coll., Oxford (MA). Called to Bar, 1928; Bencher of Lincoln's Inn, 1958. Joined Northern Circuit and practised in Manchester, 1928-39. Served War of 1939-45: 2/Lieut Royal

Norfolk Regt, 1939; Staff Captain and DAAG Madras District, 1940-42; AAG Southern Army, India, 1943; AAG, GHQ, India, 1944; Pres. Military Govt Court, Germany, 1945; released with rank of Colonel, 1945. QC 1953; Judge of the Salford Hundred Court of Record, 1953-60; Deputy Chm., Hertfordshire Quarter Sessions, 1958-60; Judge of High Court, Queen's Bench Div., 1960-68. Member, Royal Commn on Assizes and Quarter Sessions, 1966-67. *Recreations:* gardening, golf and reading. *Address:* Dalbeathie House, Dunkeld, Perthshire. *T:* 230.
[*Died* 28 *March* 1980.

ATKINSON, Frank Stuart, MEng, MInstCE, MIMinE; Professor of Mining, Sheffield University, 1954-65, retired; Emeritus Professor, 1965; Dean of the Faculty of Engineering, 1963-65; *b* 3 Oct. 1899; *s* of Thomas Henry and Ettie Atkinson; *m* 1925, Winifred Sarah Routledge; two *s* one *d. Educ:* Chesterfield Grammar Sch.; Sheffield Univ. Articled pupil to Dr J. H. W. Laverick, JP; Asst Manager of Frickley Colliery, 1924-27; Manager of the Hatfield Main Colliery of the Carlton Main Group, 1927-35; Professor of Mining, Univ. of Leeds, 1936-41; Gen. Manager Upton Colliery of Dorman, Long & Co. Ltd, 1941-46; Shaw, Wallace & Co. Ltd, India, 1946-49; Asst Production Dir, NE Div. Nat. Coal Bd, 1949-54. *Publications:* contributed many papers to technical press. *Address:* 15 Blenheim Chase, Leigh-on-Sea, Essex. [*Died* 21 *Jan.* 1971.

ATTENBOROUGH, Frederick Levi, MA; Principal of University College, Leicester, 1932-51; *b* 4 April 1887; *s* of Frederick and Mary Attenborough, Stapleford, Notts; *m* 1922, Mary (*d* 1961), *d* of Samuel and Mary Clegg, New Sawley, Notts; three *s. Educ:* County Schs, Long Eaton; Emmanuel Coll., Cambridge. Entered Normal Coll., Bangor, 1906; Schoolmaster in Liverpool and Long Eaton, 1908-15; entered Emmanuel Coll., 1915: Foundation Scholar and Choral Exhibitioner; First Class Hons Modern and Medieval Languages Tripos; Research Student, 1918-20; Fellow, 1920-25; Principal, Borough Road Training Coll., Isleworth, 1925-32. *Publication:* The Laws of the Earliest English Kings, 1922. *Recreations:* photography, music. *Address:* 22 Marchmont Road, Richmond, Surrey. *T:* 01-940 0237. [*Died* 20 *March* 1973.

ATTEWELL, Humphrey Cooper; National Organiser, National Union of Boot and Shoe Operatives, 1950-59, retired; *b* 1894; *m* 1915, Rose, *d* of David Brazier; one *s.* European War, 1914-18, served overseas (Meritorious Service Medal). Mem. Middlesex County Council, 1940-49; MP (Lab) Harborough Div. of Leicestershire, 1945-50. *Address:* 32 Cornbrook Road, Selly Oak, Birmingham 29. [*Died* 15 *Oct.* 1972.

AUBIN, Charles Walter Duret, CBE 1945; *b* St Helier, Jersey, 22 May 1894; *o s* of late Walter Duret Aubin, MB, CM Edinburgh, and of Catherine Francesca Murrow; *m* 1919, Isabel Mary, 2nd *d* of George Touzel; two *d. Educ:* Victoria Coll., Jersey, and privately. Called to Jersey Bar, 1920; English Bar (Middle Temple), 1923; Solicitor-Gen. for Jersey, 1931; Attorney-Gen. for Jersey, 1936-48; retired 1948. *Address:* Belfontaine, La Rocque, Jersey. *T:* Jersey, Eastern 449. [*Died* 22 *March* 1972.

AUDEN, Wystan Hugh; poet; *b* 21 Feb. 1907; 3rd *s* of George Augustus Auden, MD. *Educ:* Gresham's Sch., Holt; Christ Church, Oxford (exhibitioner). Associate Prof. of English Literature, Ann Arbor Univ., Michigan; Guggenheim Research Fellowship, 1942; Prof. of Poetry, Univ. of Oxford, 1956-61. Hon. Student of Christ Church, Oxford, 1962. King George's Gold Medal for Poetry, 1937; Pulitzer Prize, 1948; Feltrinelli Prize, 1957; National Medal for Literature, USA, 1967. Mem., American Acad. of Arts and Letters, 1954; Hon. Pres., Associated Socs of Edinburgh Univ. Hon. DLitt Oxon, 1971; Hon. DLit London, 1972. *Publications:* Poems, 1930; The Orators, 1932; The Dance of Death, 1933; (with Christopher Isherwood) The Dog Beneath the Skin, 1935; (with John Garrett) The Poet's Tongue, 1935; (with Christopher Isherwood) The Ascent of F6, 1936; Look Stranger, 1936; (with Louis MacNeice) Letters from Iceland, 1937; Oxford Book of Light Verse (ed), 1938; (with Christopher Isherwood) On the Frontier, 1938, and, Journey to a War, 1939; Selected Poems, 1940; Another Time, 1940; New Year Letter, 1941; For the Time Being, 1944; Tennyson, 1946; Nones, 1951; (with Chester Kallman) Libretto of the Rake's Progress (music by Igor Stravinsky), 1951; ed (with Norman Holmes Pearson) Poets of the English Language, 5 vols, 1952; 50 Selections from Kierkegaard, 1952; The Knights of the Round Table (from French Play of Jean Cocteau), 1954; Kierkegaard (selections and introduction), 1955; The Shield of Achilles, 1955; ed The Faber Book of Modern American Verse, 1956; ed (with Chester Kallman) An Elizabethan Song Book, 1957; trans. (with Chester Kallman) The Magic Flute, 1957; ed The Selected Writings of Sydney Smith, 1957; Homage to Clio, 1960; (with Chester

Kallman) Libretto of Elegy for Young Lovers (Music by Hans Werne Henze), 1961; The Dyer's Hand, 1963; ed (with L. Kronenberger) The Faber Book of Aphorisms, 1964; trans. (with Leif Sjöberg) Markings (by Dag Hammerskjöld), 1964; About the House, 1966; Collected Shorter Poems, 1927-57, 1966; (ed) Nineteenth-Century Minor Poets, 1967; Collected Longer Poems, 1968; Secondary Worlds (T. S. Eliot Lectures), 1968; City without Walls, 1969; G. K. Chesterton: a selection from his non-fictional prose, 1969; A Certain World: a commonplace book, 1971; Academic Graffiti, 1971; Epistle to a Godson and Other Poems, 1972; (with Chester Kallman) Libretto of Love's Labours Lost (music by Nicholas Nabakov), 1973; Forewords and Afterwords, 1973; A Choice of Dryden's Verse, 1973; *posthumous publications:* (with Chester Kallman) Libretto of the Entertainment of the Senses; Thank You, Fog, 1974. *Address:* Christ Church, Oxford. [*Died* 28 *Sept.* 1973.

AUDLAND, Brig. Edward Gordon, CB 1950; CBE 1943; MC 1917; DL; JP; late RHA and RA; *b* 30 Dec. 1896; *s* of William Edward Audland, MBE, KStJ, Wellingborough; *m* 1923, Violet Mary, *d* of late Herbert Shepherd-Cross, MP, JP, Hamels Park, Herts; two *s* one *d. Educ:* Winchester. Served European War, 1914-19, France, Belgium (despatches, MC); War of 1939-45 (despatches thrice, CBE); France, 1939-40; 5th Corps, N Africa and Italy, 1942-44; Land Forces, Greece, 1944-46; Comd W Lancs Area, 1947, Cyrenaica Dist, 1948-51, retd 1951. Served on Cttees in Westmorland and N Lancs, including County Council Planning, Hosp. Management, Prison Bd, Carlisle Dio., British Legion; County Hon. Sec., SSAFA. Westmorland: JP 1954; DL 1957. CStJ; Cmdr, Order of George I with Swords (Greece). *Address:* Ackenthwaite, Milnthorpe, Cumbria LA7 7DH.
[*Died* 22 *Oct.* 1976.

AUDLEY, Baroness (24th in line), *cr* 1312-13; **Rosina Lois Veronica Macnamee;** *b* 10 July 1911; *o d* of Thomas Touchet Tuchet-Jesson (*d* 1939), and *sister* of 23rd Baron Audley; granted title, rank and precedence as *d* of a baron, 1946; *S* brother, 1963; *m* 1943, John Archibald Joseph Macnamee (*d* 1969), MA, journalist, *yr s* of late Bernard Macnamee, Glasgow; no *c.* Heir: kinsman Richard Michael Thomas Souter [*b* 31 May 1914; *m* 1941, Lily Pauline, *d* of D. L. Eskell; three *d*]. *Address:* House of Lords, SW1. [*Died* 24 *Oct.* 1973.

AUDSLEY, Matthew Thomas, CMG 1949; retired from Civil Service 1956; *b* 15 Oct. 1891; *s* of late Matthew Robert Audsley, 54 Spur Road, Orpington, Kent; *m* 1919, Florence (*d* 1948), *d* of late Henry Moody, 44 Broadwood Avenue, Ruislip; one *s* two *d* ; *m* 1952, Hilda Margaret, *d* of late John Fairless, Blyth, Northumberland. *Educ:* privately. Entered Civil Service, 1912. Min. of Labour: Asst Regional Controller, 1941; Dep. Regional Controller, 1947; Counsellor (Labour), British Embassy, Cairo and Labour Adviser to Middle East Development Div., 1945-56. *Recreations:* motoring and music. *Address:* 8 Nevill Park, Tunbridge Wells, Kent. *T:* Tunbridge Wells 21749.
[*Died* 9 *Feb.* 1975.

AUSTEN, Harold Cholmley Mansfield, CBE 1935; MInstCE; *b* 21 Nov. 1878; 4th *s* of Rev. George Austen, late Chancellor of York Minster; *m* 1st, Annie Alice Mary, *d* of Henry Maclean of Kingairloch; two *d* ; 2nd, 1966, Helena Frances Kerslake. *Educ:* Repton; King's Coll., London. Pupil in grandfather's firm (James Abernethy, FRSE, Past Pres. InstCE), Westminster; Asst Engineer Midland Railway, 1898-1901; Asst and Resident Engineer Bristol Docks, 1901-07; Miller Prizeman, InstCE, 1902; elected 1904; 2 cross-Channel ferry schemes, Dover Harbour, 1908; Engineer and Agent for Perry & Co. (Bow) Ltd, Contractors, 1909-15; served during European War as Supt Engineer, Ministry of Munitions, Yorkshire (OBE); Harbour Engineer, Mauritius, 1923-31; Gen. Manager of Railways and Harbour Engineer, Mauritius; designed, constructed, and supervised traffic of new deep-water quay; dredged harbour and constructed Granary to contain whole rice supply of Colony; Cons. Engineer to Colonial Govt; Retired 1940; Dep. Area Officer Ministry of Supply, Bristol, 1940; Dep. Regional Controller, 1942; Regional Controller, 1943; retired 1945. *Publications:* Modern Development of British Fishery Harbours; Sea Fights and Corsairs of the Indian Ocean (The Naval History of Mauritius from 1715-1810). *Recreations:* history, walking. *Address:* Delabole Cottage, Minehead, Som.
[*Died* 15 *Aug.* 1975.

AUSTIN, George Wesley, OBE 1935; MA, MSc; FIM; Goldsmiths' Professor of Metallurgy, University of Cambridge, 1945-58; sometime Fellow of Trinity Hall, Cambridge; *b* 1 March 1891; *s* of Edwin and Marie Austin; *m* 1933, Isabella Mary Murray; one *s. Educ:* Friends Sch., Sibford; Queens Coll., Taunton. Metallurgical training Univ. of Birmingham (1851 Exhibitioner) and Royal Technical High Sch., Aachen.

Successively Metallurgist, Principal Scientific Officer and Superintending Scientist RN Torpedo Factory and Torpedo Experimental Establishment, Greenock. Vice-Pres. Institute of Metals and Institution of Metallurgists; Chm. Home Office Cttee on Gas Cylinders and Containers; Research Supervisor, Metallurgy Div., BISRA; Chm. ISMRC; OECD Consultant. *Publications:* trans. Modern Open Hearth Steelworks, 1924; Effect of Molten Solder on some Stressed Materials, Burnt Alloy Steels (in technical journals), 1936. *Recreations:* art and travel. *Address:* New Barn House, Lindsell, Essex. *T:* Great Easton 242; Cove Castle, Cove, Dunbartonshire. *T:* Kilcreggan 2311. *Clubs:* Savage, National Liberal; Royal Scottish Automobile (Glasgow).									*[Died 5 March 1975.*

AUSTIN, Robert Sargent, RA 1949 (ARA 1939); RWS 1934 (ARWS, 1930); RE 1928 (ARE 1921); Professor of Engraving, Royal College of Art; President: Royal Society of Painters in Water Colours, 1956; Royal Society of Painter-Etchers and Engravers, 1962; *b* Leicester, 23 June 1895; *s* of Robert Austin and Elizabeth Smith, both of Leicester; *m* 1924, Ada (*d* 1958), *d* of Henry Harrison; one *s* two *d. Educ:* Sch. of Art, Leicester; Royal College of Art, South Kensington. Active Service, 1915-19; Rome Scholar, 1922. *Recreation:* bird-watching. *Address:* Lingard House, Chiswick Mall, W4. *T:* 01-994 4852.
									[Died 18 Sept. 1973.

AUSTIN, Roland Gregory, MA; Professor of Latin, University of Liverpool, 1954-68, now Emeritus; *b* Gloucester, 19 Feb. 1901; *s* of late Roland Austin; *m* 1931, Violet Margerie, *y d* of late Robert Wilson Dron, Prof. of Mining, Univ. of Glasgow. *Educ:* Crypt Sch., Gloucester; Balliol Coll, Oxford (Exhibitioner in Classics). First Class, Classical Hon. Moderations, 1921; 2nd Class, Literae Humaniores, 1923; *prox acc.,* Gaisford prize for Greek verse, 1923; Asst to Prof. of Humanity (Prof. J. S. Phillimore), Univ. of Glasgow, 1923-26; Lecturer in Humanity, 1926-37; Prof. of Latin, University Coll. of South Wales and Monmouthshire, 1937-54. Leverhulme Research Fellow, 1960-61, Emeritus Fellow, 1972-73; Public Orator, Liverpool Univ., 1965-68. A Vice-President: Soc. for the Promotion of Roman Studies, 1964; Classical Assoc., 1966. Mem. Classical Journals Bd, 1947-68. Hon. DLitt, Glasgow, 1960; Dr *hc* Besançon, 1961. *Publications:* Arma, in Glossaria Latina, vol. II, 1926 (with W. M. Lindsay); Cicero, pro M. Cælio (ed), 1933, new edn, 1960; (ed) Quintilian Inst. Or. XII, 1948; (ed) Virgil, Aeneid IV, 1955; (ed) Virgil, Aeneid II, 1964; (ed) Virgil, Aeneid I, 1971; articles and reviews in classical and archæological periodicals. *Address:* Utica, Stanton, Broadway, Worcs. *T:* Stanton (Glos) 350.
									[Died 5 Oct. 1974.

AUSTIN, Sir Thomas, KCIE 1945 (CIE 1941); *b* 20 July 1887; *e s* of Rev. T. Austin, RN; *m* 1915, Christina Wilson, MB (*d* 1960); *m* 1961, Mrs Cecile Rosemary Macann (*née* Stallard). *Educ:* Plymouth Coll.; Jesus Coll., Cambridge. Entered ICS, 1910, and posted to Madras, 1911; Asst Resident in Travancore and Cochin, 1915-17; military duty, 1918-19; Collector, C and M Station, Bangalore, 1922-24; Chm., Assam Labour Board, 1924-28; called to Bar, Gray's Inn, 1931; Dewan of Travancore, 1932-34; Registrar of Co-operative Societies, Madras, 1934-38; Mem., Board of Revenue, 1938-40; Chief Sec. to Government of Madras, 1940; Adviser to Governor of Madras, 1941-46; retired from ICS 1946; Prime Minister of Kolhapur State, 1946-47. *Recreations:* reading, fishing. *Address:* 29 Chivelston, Wimbledon Parkside, SW19. *T:* 01-788 3240.
									[Died 27 June 1976.

AUTY, Prof. Robert, MA (Cantab and Oxon); DrPhil (Münster); DLitt (Oxon); FBA 1976; Professor of Comparative Slavonic Philology, University of Oxford, and Fellow of Brasenose College, since 1965; *b* Rotherham, 10 Oct. 1914; 2nd *s* of George Auty, schoolmaster, and Martha Louise Richards; *m* 1944, Kathleen Marjorie Milnes-Smith (marr. diss.); one *s* one *d. Educ:* Rotherham Grammar School; (Scholar) Gonville and Caius Coll., Cambridge; Münster Univ. Tiarks German Schol., Cambridge Univ., 1935; Faculty Asst Lectr in German, 1937; Univ. Lectr (in German), 1945, (in German and Czech), 1948, (in Slavonic Studies), 1957-62; Head of Dept of Other Languages, 1948-56; Sen. Proctor, 1949-50; Fellow and Coll. Lectr in Modern Langs, Selwyn Coll., 1950-62; Dean of Selwyn Coll., 1953-56; Professor of Comparative Philology of the Slavonic Languages, Univ. of London, and Head of Dept of Languages and Literature, Sch. of Slavonic and East European Studies, 1962-65. War work with Czechoslovak authorities in London, 1939-43, attached to the Foreign Office, 1944-45. Visiting Prof. Slavic Languages, Univ. of California, Los Angeles, 1968; de Carle Lectr, Univ. of Otago, 1975. Sec. Assoc. Internationale des Langues et Littératures Slaves, 1957-60, Pres. 1966-72, Vice-Pres., 1972; Sec., British Univs Assoc. of Slavists, 1957-63, Pres., 1964-67, Vice-Pres., 1967-72; Treas.,

Philological Society, 1962-65; Vice-Pres., Fédération Internationale des Langues et Littératures Modernes, 1966-72, Hon. Vice-Pres., 1976. Pres., Assoc. of Teachers of Russian, 1967-69; Chm., Modern Humanities Research Assoc., 1968-73; Member: International Cttee of Slavists, 1965 (Vice-Pres., 1966); Exec., Internat. Cttee for Soviet and E European Studies, 1974; Governing Body, GB-E Europe Centre, 1970 (Vice-Chm., 1976); Chm. Council, SSEES, 1977; Editorial Board of Slavonic and East European Review (Chm., 1963-65); Ed. Board, International Journal of Slavic Linguistics and Poetics, 1965; Slavonic Editor, Modern Language Review, 1966-78; Editor, Oxford Slavonic Papers, 1968; Hon. Member: Slovak Linguistic Soc., 1971; Aust. and NZ Slavists Assoc., 1975; Vice-President: British-Yugoslav Soc.; Anglo-Byelorussian Soc.; Corresp. Mem., Austrian Acad. of Sciences, 1975. Josef Dobrovský Gold Medal, Czechoslovak Acad. of Sciences, 1968. *Publications:* Old Church Slavonic Texts and Glossary, 1960; (adviser and contrib.) Cassell's Encyclopædia of World Literature, 1973; (ed and contrib.) Cambridge Companion to Russian Studies, 1976-77. Articles in Brit. and foreign learned jls and encyclopædias. *Recreation:* travel, especially in Central and South-Eastern Europe. *Address:* Brasenose College, Oxford. *T:* Oxford 48641. *Clubs:* Athenæum, United Oxford & Cambridge University.
									[Died 18 Aug. 1978.

AVEBURY, 3rd Baron, *cr* 1900; **John Lubbock,** Bt *cr* 1806; *b* 13 May 1915; *o s* of late Capt. Harold Fox Pitt Lubbock, 4th *s* of 1st Baron Avebury, and Dorothy Charlotte, *d* of 1st Baron Forster (she *m* 2nd, 1st Baron Wardington); *S* uncle, 1929; *m* 1st, 1938, Cecily Kathleen (who obtained a divorce 1945), *d* of late Dr N. A. K. Sparrow and of Mrs M. H. Ormsby, Bosworth House, Woodbridge; 2nd, 1946, Diana Mary Margaret (marr. diss. 1955), *d* of late Capt. Edward Westcott King, RA: one *d* ; 3rd, 1956, Betty Gay, *d* of late William Oscar Ingham, Poulton-le-Fylde. *Educ:* Eton. *Heir: cousin* Eric Reginald Lubbock. *Address:* Yacht Kailva, Royal Gibraltar Yacht Club, Gibraltar. *Club:* Royal Yacht Squadron.					*[Died 21 June 1971.*

AVON, 1st Earl of, *cr* 1961; **Robert Anthony Eden,** KG 1954; PC 1934; MC 1917; Viscount Eden, *cr* 1961; Hon. DCL, Oxford and Durham; Hon. LLD: Birmingham, Bristol, Cambridge, Leeds, Sheffield, Belfast, Toronto, California, McGill, Columbia, Denver; *b* 12 June 1897; only surv. *s* of Sir William Eden, 7th and 5th Bt; *m* 1st, 1923, Beatrice Helen (marr. diss. 1950; she *d* 1957), *d* of Hon. Sir Gervase Beckett, 1st Bt; one *s* (and *er s,* Pilot Officer Simon Eden, RAF, killed in Burma, 1945); 2nd, 1952, Clarissa Anne, *d* of late Major John Spencer Churchill and Lady Gwendeline Spencer Churchill. *Educ:* Eton; Christ Church, Oxford. BA First Cl. Hons (Oriental langs), 1922. Formerly Capt. KRRC; served European War, 1915-19, with his regt and as GSO3, also as Bde Major (MC). Contested Spennymoor Division of Durham, 1922; MP (C) Warwick and Leamington, 1923-57. Attended Imperial Press Conference, Melbourne, 1925; Parliamentary Private Sec. to Sec. of State for Foreign Affairs (Sir Austen Chamberlain, KG), 1926-29; Parliamentary Under-Sec., Foreign Office, 1931-33; Lord Privy Seal, 1934-35; Minister without Portfolio for League of Nations Affairs, 1935; Sec. of State: for Foreign Affairs, 1935-38; for Dominion Affairs, 1939-40; for War, 1940; for Foreign Affairs, 1940-45, also Leader of House of Commons, 1942-45; Dep. Leader of the Opposition, 1945-51; Sec. of State for Foreign Affairs and Deputy Prime Minister, 1951-April 1955; Prime Minister and First Lord of the Treasury, April 1955-Jan. 1957. Chm. of OEEC, 1952-54. Hon. Master of the Bench, Middle Temple, 1952; Hon. Mem. Salters' Company, 1946, and of Fishmongers' Company, 1955. Trustee of National Gallery, 1935-49; Chancellor of Univ. of Birmingham, 1945-73; Elder Brother of Trinity House, 1953; Wateler Peace Prize, Carnegie Foundation, 1954. Pres. of Royal Shakespeare Theatre, Stratford-on-Avon, 1958-66. JP (Hon.) Co. Durham; Freeman of Durham, Leamington Spa, Warwick, Perth, Athens. Hon. Col Queen's Westminsters, KRRC, 1952-60, Queen's Royal Rifles, 1960-62; Hon. Air Cdre No 500 (Co. Kent) Squadron, RAF, 1943-57. Hon. Life Patron, Young Cons. Organisation; Pres., Anglo-Ethiopian Soc., 1966-; Patron, Hereford Herd Book Soc., 1968-. Hon. FRIBA, 1955. *Publications:* Places in the Sun; Foreign Affairs, 1939; Freedom and Order; Days for Decision (selected speeches), 1949; The Eden Memoirs: Full Circle, 1960; Facing the Dictators, 1962; The Reckoning, 1965; Towards Peace in Indo-China, 1966; Another World 1897-1917 (autobiog.), 1976. *Heir: s* Viscount Eden, OBE, TD. *Address:* Manor House, Alvediston, Salisbury, Wilts. *Clubs:* Carlton, Buck's.									*[Died 14 Jan. 1977.*

AXON, Sir Albert (Edwin), KBE 1959; consulting engineer in private practice, Australia, 1929-72, retired; Chairman: Queensland Cement & Lime Co. Ltd; Central Queensland Cement Pty Ltd; Director: Walkers Ltd; South Brisbane Gas &

Light Co. Ltd; North Australian Cement Ltd; *b* 21 Dec. 1898; *s* of Herbert Fisher Axon, Lancashire, England and Florence Emily (*née* Parker), Galway, Ire.; *m* 1926, Hilda Harris Withecombe; one *s* one *d. Educ:* Brisbane Grammar Sch.; Univ. of Queensland. Master of Engrg, Qld, 1928; Dr of Engrg, Melbourne Univ., 1961; Dr of Science, Univ. of New England, 1962. Mem. Royal Commn on Electricity, Qld, 1936; part-time Mem. State Electricity Commn of Qld, 1938-47. Mem. of Senate, Univ. of Qld, 1935-66; Chancellor of Univ. of Qld, 1957-66; Mem., Commonwealth Banking Corp. Bd, 1959-64. Hon. DrEng Queensland, 1972. Peter Nicol Russell Memorial Medal of Instn of Engrs, Aust., 1960. *Recreations:* fishing, gardening, conchology. *Address:* 25 Stafford Street, Clayfield, Qld 4011, Australia. *T:* 6-2729. *Club:* United Service (Brisbane).
[*Died* 17 Feb. 1974.

AYKROYD, Wallace Ruddell, CBE 1943; MD, ScD; *b* 30 July 1899; *e s* of Alfred Constantine Aykroyd, Bradford and Dublin; *m* 1931, Freda Kathleen Buttery; one *s* two *d. Educ:* The Leys Sch., Cambridge; Trinity Coll., Dublin (Vice-Chancellor's Prizeman in English Prose). MB, BCh 1924; MD 1928; ScD 1938; after various hospital appts Beit Memorial Research Fellow, 1928; Mem. of Health Section, League of Nations, 1931-35; Dir, Nutrition Research Laboratories, Coonoor, S India, 1935-45; Delegate of Govt of India to League of Nations Intergovernmental Conference on Rural Hygiene, Bandoeng, 1937; Far Eastern Representative, 1938, of League of Nations Technical Commission on Nutrition; Delegate to United Nations Conference on Food and Agriculture, Hot Springs, Virginia 1943; Dir, Nutrition Div., FAO, 1946-60; Senior Lectr, Dept of Human Nutrition, London Sch. of Hygiene and Tropical Medicine, 1960-66. Hon. Fellow, Amer. Public Health Assoc., 1954; Hon. Mem. American Nutrition Soc., 1960. *Publications:* Vitamins and other Dietary Essentials, 1933; Three Philosophers, 1935; Nutrition and Public Health, 1935 (with Et. Burnet); Sweet Malefactor: Sugar, Slavery and Human Society, 1967; The Conquest of Famine, 1974; numerous scientific papers on various aspects of nutrition. *Recreations:* reading, walking, gardening. *Address:* Queen Anne House, Charlbury, Oxon.
[*Died* 7 Feb. 1979.

AYLEN, Rt. Rev. Charles Arthur William; Assistant Bishop in Diocese of Peterborough, 1950-63; *b* 12 Mar 1882; *s* of late John Robert Aylen, Lieut RN; *m* 1932, Elisabeth Margaret Anna, *er d* of late Judge Eustace Hills; two *s* one *d. Educ:* Bradfield; Keble Coll., Oxford; Cuddesdon Theol. Coll. BA, 3rd Cl. Mod. History, 1904; MA. Curate, Henley-on-Thames, 1905-12; Vicar of Shiplake, Oxon, 1913-25; Chaplain, HMS St Vincent, Grand Fleet, 1916-19; Mission Priest, Empangeni District, Zululand, 1926-30; Bishop of Zululand, 1930-35; Bishop of St Helena, 1935-39; Rector of Aston Tirrold, Berkshire, 1939-45; Vicar of Flore, Northants, 1945-58. Non-residentiary Canon, Peterborough, 1946-61; Rural Dean of Weedon, 1947-51. *Recreation:* scoutmaster since 1913 (District Commissioner for Zululand, 1927). *Address:* 40 Latimer Road, Oxford. *T:* 61911.
[*Died* 15 Aug. 1972.

AYLMER, 10th Baron *cr* 1718; **Kenneth Athalmar Aylmer;** Bt 1662; *b* 23 June 1883; 2nd *s* of 8th Baron Aylmer and Amy Gertrude (*d* 1935), *d* of Hon. John Young; *S* brother, 1970; *m* 1924, Eleanor Katharine (*d* 1970), 3rd *d* of late John Francis Rogers, Swannington, Norfolk. *Heir: b* Hon. Basil Udolphus Aylmer [*b* 20 May 1886; *m* 1st, 1916, Bessie Irving, ARRC (*d* 1956), *d* of late Joseph Watson; (one *s* killed in action, 1944); 2nd, 1960, Helen Cooper, *widow* of Frederick Gordon Riseborough and *d* of late Thomas Hogg, Toronto, Canada]. *Address:* Queen's Bay, Kootenay Lake, BC, Canada.
[*Died* 1 May 1974.

AYLMER, 11th Baron *cr* 1718; **Basil Udolphus Aylmer;** Bt 1662; *b* 20 May 1886; *s* of 8th Baron Aylmer and Amy Gertrude (*d* 1935), *d* of Hon. John Young; *S* brother, 1974; *m* 1st, 1916, Bessie Irving, ARRC (*d* 1956), *d* of late Joseph Watson; (one *s* killed in action, 1944); 2nd, 1960, Helen Cooper, *widow* of Frederick Gordon Riseborough and *d* of late Thomas Hogg, Toronto, Canada. Served European War, 1914-18 with Canadian Expeditionary Force. *Heir:* kinsman Hugh Yates Aylmer [*b* 5 Feb. 1907; *m* 1939, Althea, *e d* of late Lt-Col John Talbot; one *d*]. *Address:* Queen's Bay, Kootenay Lake, BC, Canada.
[*Died* 13 March 1977.

AYLMER, Sir Felix, (Sir Felix Edward Aylmer-Jones), Kt 1965; OBE 1950; Actor; *b* 21 Feb. 1889; *s* of Lieut-Col T. E. Aylmer-Jones, RE, and Lilian Cookworthy; *m* Cecily Byrne (*d* 1975); one *d* (and two *s* decd). *Educ:* Magdalen Coll. Sch.; Exeter Coll., Oxford. First stage appearance, Coliseum, with Seymour Hicks, 1911; Birmingham Rep. Theatre, 1913. Served European War, 1914-18, RNVR. Pres., British Actors' Equity Assoc., 1949-69.

Principal London appearances: R. E. Lee, 1923; The Terror, 1927; Bird in Hand, 1928; The Nelson Touch, 1931; The Voysey Inheritance, St Joan, 1934; Heroes Don't Care, Waste, 1936; Yes and No, 1937; The Flashing Stream, 1938; Scandal at Barchester, 1944; Daphne Laureola, 1949; Spider's Web, 1955; The Chalk Garden, 1956. New York: 1922, 1925, 1939; The Prescott Proposals, 1953-54. Numerous films and broadcasts. *Principal films:* Tudor Rose, Victoria the Great, The Demi-Paradise, Henry V, Mr Emmanuel, The Ghosts of Berkeley Square, Hamlet, Prince of Foxes, Quo Vadis, The Lady With a Lamp, Ivanhoe, The Knights of the Round Table, The Angel Who Pawned Her Harp, St Joan, Separate Tables, The Doctor's Dilemma, The Mummy, Never Take Sweets from a Stranger, From the Terrace, Exodus, The Chalk Garden. *Publications:* Dickens Incognito, 1959; The Drood Case, 1964. *Address:* 6 Painshill House, Cobham, Surrey. *Clubs:* Garrick, Green Room, Beefsteak.
[*Died* 2 Sept. 1979.

AYLMER-JONES, Sir Felix Edward; *see* Aylmer, Sir Felix.

AYLWARD, Prof. Francis; Professor and Head of Department of Food Science, University of Reading, 1968-76, now Emeritus; *b* Liverpool, 21 July 1911; *e s* of J. F. and Margaret Aylward, Liverpool; *m* 1947, Nora Gunter, Warwickshire; two *d. Educ:* Univ. of Liverpool. BSc 1st cl. Hons Chem.; PhD Biochem.; DSc; Johns Hopkins University, 1935-37; Commonwealth Fund Fellow and Univ. Fellow in Paediatrics. ICI Ltd, 1941-44. Teaching and research posts, 1937-41, 1944-60: at Univ. of Liverpool; Manchester; Borough Polytechnic, London. Field staff, FAO, 1960-65: in Ghana, Scientific Adviser, food and nutrition, Min. of Agric., also Prof. and Head of Dept of Nutrition and Food Science at Univ. of Ghana; in Poland, Dir FAO/UNDP project; Consultant, 1968-, for internat. bodies (inc. FAO, UNESCO, Protein Adv. Gp UN, OECD, EEC) and UK bodies (ODM, IUC), mainly Africa and ME; Hon. Consultant, Nestle Foundn. Dir, Campden Food Preserv. Res. Assoc., 1965-68; Member Council: Nutrition Soc., 1975-; Soc. Chem. Ind., 1975-; former Vice-Pres. Council and Chm., Food Gp; Chm., Overseas Cttee, Univ. of Reading, 1968-76; Mem., IUC Acad. Policy Cttee, 1974-. FRIC; CChem.; FRSM; FRSA; FIFST. Hon. Mem., Agric. Univ., Warsaw, 1965; Internat. Award (US), Inst. of Food Tech., 1973. KSG. *Publications:* (jtly) Protein and Nutrition Policy in Low Income Countries, 1975; research papers and reviews in scientific and other jls. *Recreation:* travel. *Address:* Four Corners, Upper Warren Avenue, Mapledurham, near Reading. *T:* Reading 472 308. *Club:* Athenæum.
[*Died* 28 Sept. 1978.

AYRE, Captain Leslie Charles Edward, CBE 1941 (OBE 1919); RN, retired; *b* 30 May 1886; *er s* of late Rev. H. E. Ayre, Rector of Brendon, North Devon; *m* 1911, Dorothy Beatrice Agnes, *e d* of late Rev. J. F. Vallings, Vicar of Sopley, Hants; (one *s* killed on active service, Dec. 1941) one *d. Educ:* St John's Sch., Leatherhead. Entered Royal Navy, 1904; Paymaster of Royal Yacht Alexandra, 1913-14; HMS Agincourt (Grand Fleet), 1914-15; Secretary to: Admiral Commanding Coastguard, 1917-21; to Rear-Admiral Commanding Destroyer Flotillas, 1922-23; to Asst Chief of Naval Staff, 1923-24; to Rear-Admiral Commanding First Cruiser Squadron, 1924-26; to Commander-in-Chief, China Station, 1928-31; to Commander-in-Chief, Portsmouth, 1931-34; Deputy Paymaster Dir-Gen., 1935-37; Command Accountant Officer, Plymouth Command, 1939-43. Polonia Restituta, 1942. *Recreations:* gardening; played football (Association) for navy. *Address:* 38 Chapel Street, Ely, Cambs. *T:* Ely 2704.
[*Died* 29 Jan. 1979.

AYRE, Sir Wilfrid, Kt 1945; JP Fife; *b* 12 April 1890; *s* of late Amos Lowery Ayre, JP South Shields; *m* 1914, Mary Johnson; one *d. Educ:* S Shields; King's Coll., Newcastle upon Tyne (Hons Final Degree in Naval Architecture). First place in Final Exam. Naval Architecture, Co. of Shipwrights; Apprenticeship, Wood, Skinner & Co. Ltd, Newcastle; subseq. served in exec. capacity with Jos. T. Eltringham & Co. Ltd, Newcastle, John Lewis & Sons Ltd, Aberdeen; then, with (brother) late Sir Amos L. Ayre, KBE, DSc, founded The Burntisland Shipbuilding Co. Ltd, 1918; Dir, Allen Lithographic Co. Ltd. Past President: The Shipbuilding Conference and The Shipbuilding Employers Federation; Past Chairman, British Shipbuilding Research Assoc.; Underwriting Mem. of Lloyd's; Chm., Fife Emergency Reconstruction Panel, Min. of Aircraft Production and Admiralty, 1940-45; Leader of Admiralty Shipbuilding Mission to USA and Canada, 1942, and of Government Shipbuilding Trade Mission to S American countries, 1946; Chm., Scottish Cttee of Board of Trade Wool Working Party, 1946; Member: Special Cttee of Advisory Council on Technical Education in Scotland, 1943-46; Census of Production Cttee, 1945-51; Iron and Steel Bd, 1946-48 and of Railway Executive, 1947-50; Pres. Inst. of Engineers and Shipbuilders in Scotland, 1939-41. Mem.

Royal Inst. of Naval Architects; Mem. NE Coast Inst. Engineers and Shipbuilders; Mem. Inst. Marine Engineers; Freeman and Liveryman of City of London; Past Prime Warden of Worshipful Co. of Shipwrights. *Recreations:* shooting, angling. *Address:* Priory House, Aberdour, Fife, Scotland. *T:* Aberdour 396.   *[Died 11 Aug. 1971.*

AYRTON, Michael; painter, sculptor, author, theatre designer and illustrator; *b* 20 Feb. 1921; *s* of late Gerald Gould, poet and critic, and late Barbara Ayrton Gould; *m* 1951, Elisabeth (*née* Walshe). *Educ:* London, Vienna and Paris. Hon. DLitt Exeter, 1975. Exhibitions: Leicester Galls 1942, Redfern Gallery 1943, 1945, 1947, 1949, 1951, 1952, 1953 and 1959, Arts Council 1946 and 1952, Hanover Gallery, 1948, Wakefield City Art Gallery (retrospective), 1949, Milan 1950, Rome, 1950, Zürich 1951, Paris, 1952, Whitechapel Gall. (retrospective), 1955, Leicester Galls. 1957, 1959 (sculpture), Chicago (sculpture), 1960, 1967, 1969, 1970, 1971, 1972, 1975, Matthiesen Gall., 1961, Grosvenor Gall., 1964, 1966, 1967, Athens (Greece), 1966, Buffalo (USA), Toronto, 1966, Santa Barbara, 1968, Hamet Gall., 1969, Reading Museum (retrospective), 1969, Detroit, 1970, Bruton Gall., 1971, Penn University Museum (retrospective), 1973, 'Maze and Minotaur', W of England Museums (retrospective), 1973, Birmingham Art Gall. (retrospective), 1976. Décor for theatrical productions: John Gielgud's revival of Macbeth, 1942; Sadler's Wells Ballet Le Festin de l'Araignée, 1944; Covent Garden revival of Purcell's Fairy Queen, 1946 and 1951. Constructions: Arkville Maze, 1969. Art critic of The Spectator, 1944-46. Documentary Films: The Drawings of Leonardo da Vinci, 1953; Greek Sculpture, 1960; Maze Maker 1972. *Publications:* British Drawings, 1946; Hogarth's Drawings, 1948; Tittivulus, 1953; Golden Sections, 1957; The Testament of Daedalus, 1962; Drawings and Sculpture, 1962, new edn, 1966; The Maze Maker, 1967 (Heinemann Award for Literature, 1968); Berlioz, a Singular Obsession, 1969; Giovanni Pisano, 1970; The Rudiments of Paradise, 1971; Fabrications, 1972; The Midas Consequence, 1974; A Meaning to the Maze, 1974. Illustrator of: Poems of Death, 1945; The Duchess of Malfi, 1945; Summers Last Will and Testament, 1946; The Unfortunate Traveller, 1948; Macbeth, 1951; The Human Age, 1956; The Golden Ass, 1961; The Oresteia, 1961; Three Plays of Euripides, 1967; The Trial and Execution of Socrates, 1972; Femmes, Hombres, 1972. *Recreation:* conversation. *Address:* Bradfields, Toppesfield, near Halstead, Essex. *T:* Great Yeldham 228. *Club:* Savile.
                                               [Died 17 Nov. 1975.

AYUB KHAN, Field-Marshal Mohammad; *see* Khan, M. A.

AZCARATE y FLOREZ, Pablo de, MA, DCL; Spanish diplomat; *b* Madrid (Spain), 30 July 1890; *s* of Cayo de Azcarate, Colonel of Military Engineers, and Delfina Florez; *m* 1915, Amelia Diz (*d* 1944); two *s* two *d*; *m* 1948, Frida Herter. *Educ:* Institución Libre de Enseñanza, Madrid; Univs of Madrid, Zaragoza, and Paris. Professor of Administrative Law, Univ. Santiago de Compostela, 1913; Prof. Administrative Law, Univ. Granada, 1915; Mem. of Spanish Parliament, 1918-19; Mem. of Secretariat of League of Nations, 1922; Dir of its Minorities Section, 1929-33; Deputy Sec.-Gen. of League of Nations, 1933-36; Spanish Ambassador in London, 1936-39; Chm. of Servicio para la Emigración de Republicanos Españoles, Paris, 1939-40; Hon. Sec. Juan Luis Vives Scholarship Trust, 1942-43; Dir and Founder Instituto Español, London; Vice-Sec. UNO Palestine Commission and Head of its advance Mission in Palestine, 1948; Sec. of Consular Truce Cttee, Jerusalem; Principal Sec. United Nations Palestine Conciliation Commission, 1949-52. *Publications:* El Regimen Parroquial en Inglaterra, 1912; La Intervención Administrativa del Estado en los Ferrocarriles, 1917; La Guerra y los Servicios Públicos de Caracter Industrial (vols I and II), 1921; Report on Minorities in Encyclopædia Britannica; League of Nations and National Minorities: an Experiment (Carnegie Endowment for International Peace, Washington, 1944); Memoria sobre los Vaughan papers; Boletin de la Real Academia de la Historia (Vol. CXLI), Madrid, 1957; La Nota de la Junta Suprema de Sevilla al Zar Alejandro I de Rusia; Boletin de la Real Academia de la Historia (Vol. CXLIV), Madrid, 1959; La Guerra Hispano-Americana: Estudio de Historia Diplomatica, 1960; Wellington y España, 1961; Apunte biográfico de D. Patricio de Azcárate (Boletin de la Real Academia de la Historia (Vol. CLI, 1962)); Mission to Palestine 1948-1952, 1966 (Spanish edn, 1968); Protection of National Minorities, UN, 1967; La guerra del 98, Madrid, 1969; Gumersindo de Azcárate: estudio biográfico-documental, Madrid, 1969; Protection de Minorités, Genève, 1969; I Sanz del Rio, 1969. *Recreation:* walking. *Address:* 19 Rue Ferdinand Hodler, Geneva, Switzerland. *T:* 36.98.81. *[Died Dec. 1971.*

B

BABINGTON, Rt. Hon. Sir Anthony Brutus, PC (N Ire.) 1926; Kt 1937; QC 1917; *b* 1877; *e s* of Hume Babington Londonderry; *m* 1907, Ethel Vaughan Hart; one *s* two *d*. *Educ:* Glenalmond; Trinity Coll., Dublin. Called to the Bar, 1900; MP South Belfast in Northern Parliament, 1925-29, Cromac, 1929-37; Attorney-Gen. for Northern Ireland, 1925-37; Lord Justice of Appeal for Northern Ireland, 1937-49; retired 1949. *Recreations:* golf and fishing. *Address:* Creevagh, Portrush, Co. Antrim. *T:* Portrush 2738. *Club:* Northern Counties (Londonderry).
                                               [Died 10 April 1972.

BABINGTON, Air Marshal Sir John T.; *see* Tremayne, Air Marshal Sir J. T.

BACHAUER, Gina, (Mrs Alec Sherman); concert pianist; *b* Athens, Greece, 21 May 1913; *d* of John and Ersilia Bachauer; *m* 1st, 1937, John Christodoulo; 2nd, 1951, Alec Sherman, British conductor. *Educ:* Athens Conservatoire (studied with Woldemar Freeman); Ecole Normale, Paris (studied with Alfred Cortot); worked later with Sergei Rachmaninoff; Gold Medal of Athens Conservatoire, 1929; Prix d'Honneur, Internat. Music Competition, Vienna, 1933. Début in Athens with Nat. Symphony Orchestra of Athens, 1935; toured Europe, 1937, 1938 and 1939; resided in Egypt during War, 1940-45, giving more than 600 concerts for Allied Forces in Base Camps and Hospitals. Début in London, Royal Albert Hall, with the London Orchestra, 1947, in New York, Carnegie Hall, with the New York Philharmonic Symphony Orchestra, 1950. Visited USA annually, 1951- for coast to coast concert tours; has also made concert tours in Canada, S America, Australia, New Zealand, South, East and West Africa, France, Holland, Germany, Austria, Italy, Greece, Israel, Norway, Sweden, Portugal, Cuba, Puerto Rica, Honolulu, Belgium, Hong Kong, Yugoslavia, Finland, Roumania, Poland, Spain, Switzerland and Czechoslovakia. Founding Artist, Kennedy Center for the Performing Arts, Washington, 1971. Hon. Dr Humanities Utah, 1971. Comdr, Order of Golden Phœnix (Greece), 1948; Comdr of Order of Welfare (Greece), 1951. *Recreations:* swimming, cooking, reading. *Address:* 6 Cumberland Terrace, Regent's Park, NW1 4HS. *T:* 01-935 0182. *Club:* Cosmopolitan (New York City, USA).   *[Died 22 Aug. 1976.*

BACKHOUSE, Col (Hon. Brig.) Edward Henry Walford, CBE 1961; Vice-Lieutenant of Suffolk since 1965; *b* 7 Feb. 1895; *er s* of Rev. E. B. Backhouse, Northwood, Middx; *m* 1920, Eileen Noël Newby Jenks, Colchester; one *s* one *d*. *Educ:* St Lawrence Coll.; RMC Sandhurst. Commnd into Suffolk Regt, 1914; wounded and POW, Le Cateau, Aug. 1914. Staff Coll., Camberley, 1927-28; Staff Capt. and Bde Major, 1929-33; comd Depot Suffolk Regt, 1934-35; War Office, 1936-38; comd 1st Bn Suffolk Regt, 1938-39; comd 54 Inf. Bde, 1939-42; POW, Singapore, 1942. Bt Major 1932; Bt Lieut-Col 1937; Brig. 1948, retired. Col Suffolk Regt, 1947-57; Chm. Suffolk TA Assoc., 1953-59. DL Suffolk, 1949; Mem. W Suffolk CC, 1958-70. *Recreations:* shooting, fishing. *Address:* Rowen House, Stonebridge Avenue, Bury St Edmunds, Suffolk. *T:* 4028. *Club:* Army and Navy.   *[Died 20 Nov. 1973.*

BADDELEY, Angela; *see* Clinton-Baddeley, Madeline A.

BADDELEY, Sir John Beresford, 3rd Bt, *cr* 1922; Managing Director of Baddeley Bros (London) Ltd 1929-70; *b* 23 Nov. 1899; *er s* of Sir William Baddeley, 2nd Bt, and Kate (*d* 1956), *d* of Matthew Shaw, Clapton; *S* father, 1951; *m* 1929, Nancy Winifred, *d* of Thomas Wolsey; one *s* two *d*. *Educ:* Lancing Coll. *Heir:* *s* John Wolsey Beresford Baddeley [*b* 27 Jan. 1938; *m* 1962, Sara Rosalind, *o d* of Colin Crofts, Scarborough, and Mrs John Holman, Ferring, Sussex; three *d*]. *Address:* Street Cottage, Bury, Sussex. *T:* Bury 442. *Club:* Royal Automobile.
                                               [Died 27 Jan. 1979.

BADDELEY, John Halkett, CMG 1970; HM Diplomatic Service; Counsellor, HM Embassy, Washington, since 1972; *b* 30 April 1920; *s* of late Lt-Col Sydney Baddeley; *m* 1st, 1941, Barbara, *d* of Henry Maine, CMG (marr. diss.); one *s* one *d*; 2nd, 1949, Maria, *d* of Adm. Pericles Roussen, Royal Hellenic Navy; one *s* three *d*. *Educ:* Winchester; Magdalen Coll., Oxford. Served War, Coldstream Guards, 1940-45. Entered Foreign Service, 1945: 3rd Sec., Athens, 1947; 2nd Sec., Singapore, 1952; 2nd Sec., Rangoon, 1954; 1st Sec., Brussels, 1957; Counsellor, Foreign and Commonwealth Office, 1970. *Address:* Larkhams Farm, Sutton Mandeville, near Salisbury, Wilts. *T:* Fovant 235; c/o British Embassy, Washington DC, USA. *Clubs:* Garrick; City Tavern (Washington).   *[Died 23 Oct. 1972.*

BADEN-POWELL, Olave, Lady; (Olave St Clair), GBE 1932; World Chief Guide, since 1930; *b* 22 Feb. 1889; *yr d* of Harold Soames, Lilliput, Dorset; *m* 1912, 1st Baron Baden-Powell, OM, GCMG, GCVO, KCB; two *d* (one *s*, 2nd Baron Baden-Powell, *d* 1962). County Commissioner for Girl Guides of Sussex, 1916; Chief Commissioner for the Girl Guides of Great Britain and Empire; elected World Chief Guide, 1930. 1914-18 War Medal. Order of Merit (Poland), 1933; Order of White Rose (Finland) 1934; Order of Silver Phœnix (Greece), 1949; Order of Honour and Merit (Haiti), 1951; Order of St Bernard (Chile), 1959; Order of the Sun (Peru), 1959; Order of Vasco de Balboa (Panama), 1959; Order of Cedars of Lebanon, 1960; Order of the Sacred Treasure (Japan), 1963. *Publication:* (with Mary Drewery) Window on my Heart (autobiog.), 1973; *relevant publication:* Wade, Olave Baden-Powell, 1971. *Address:* c/o The General Secretary, The Girl Guides Association, 17-19 Buckingham Palace Road, SW1W 0PT. *[Died 25 June 1977.*

BADENOCH, Sir (Alexander) Cameron, KCIE 1944 (CIE 1931); Kt 1941; CSI 1937; KStJ 1941; *b* Torphins, Aberdeenshire, 2 July 1889; *s* of Rev. Alexander Badenoch; *m* 1914, Jess Greg (*d* 1972), *d* of P. Fraser Mackenna, Procurator-Fiscal, Ayrshire; two *s* one *d*. *Educ:* Dunfermline High Sch.; Edinburgh Univ.; Balliol Coll., Oxford. Entered Indian Civil Service, 1912; various posts in Punjab, 1912-19; Accountant Gen., Central Provinces, 1919-21; Accountant Gen., Posts and Telegraphs, 1923-28; various posts, 1928-32 (including Mem. Frontier Defence Cttee, 1931); Dep. Auditor-Gen. of India, 1932-40; Auditor-Gen. of India, 1940-45, retired, 1945; Controller, Finance Div., British Council, 1947-49. *Address:* Pedlar's Way, Gifford, East Lothian. *T:* Gifford 209. *[Died 14 Aug. 1973.*

BADHAM, Rev. Leslie (Stephen Ronald); Vicar of Windsor, 1958-72; Chaplain to the Queen since 1964; *b* 1908; *s* of late Stephen Badham and Elizabeth (*née* Lewis); *m* 1938; Effie Garratt, BSc, *y d* of David and Nellie Garratt; two *s* two *d*. *Educ:* St David's Coll., Lampeter; Jesus Coll., Oxford. BA(Eng), Senior Scholar, St David's Coll., 1931; BA (Theol) Oxon. 1931; MA Oxon. 1935. Curate of: Pembroke Dock, 1933-37; Tenby, 1937-39; Rector of Walton West, with Talbenny, 1939; Chaplain, RAFVR, 1940-46 (despatches; 1939-45 Star; France and Germany Star); Rector of Rotherfield Peppard, 1946-58. Chaplain, Edward VII Hospital, 1958-72. *Publications:* These Greatest Things, 1942; Verdict on Jesus, 1950, 2nd edn 1972; Love Speaks from the Cross, 1956. *Recreations:* motoring, writing. *Address:* 4 Cheynies Court, Arundel Way, Highcliffe-on-Sea, Christchurch, Dorset. *T:* Highcliffe 6750.
[Died 3 July 1975.

BAERLEIN, Edgar Max, BA (Cantab); MICE; *b* Manchester, 13 Dec. 1879; 2nd *s* of M. Baerlein, The Grange, Withington, Manchester; *m* 1909, Dorothy, *d* of R. A. Dixon, Cottingham, E Yorks; one *s* (*yr s* killed in action, RAF 1941), two *d*. *Educ:* Eton; Cambridge. Open Rackets Champion of Great Britain, 1910; open Tennis Champion, 1931; won amateur Rackets Championships (singles) first in 1903, and 9 times in all; won amateur Tennis Championship first in 1912, and 13 times in all; won many other prizes at tennis, including MCC Gold Racket (9 years in succession); French amateur Championship (4 times); Olympic Games Tennis (1924) and at rackets, golf, lawn tennis, etc. *Publications:* in Lonsdale Library, Rackets, Squash Rackets, Tennis, Fives, and Badminton. *Recreations:* shooting, fishing, and various games. *Address:* The White House, Whytings, Sedgwick Lane, Horsham, Sussex. *T:* Horsham 62446. *Clubs:* Queen's, Royal Automobile, MCC, Oxford and Cambridge Golfing Society. *[Died 3 June 1971.*

BAGENAL, (Philip) Hope (Edward), OBE 1956; DCM; FRIBA; architect and writer on architectural subjects; consultant in the acoustics of buildings; *b* 11 Feb. 1888; *s* of Philip Henry Bagenal; *m* 1914, Alison Mary, *d* of Stuart Hogg; two *s* one *d*. *Educ:* Uppingham Sch.; Leeds Univ.; Architectural Assoc. Sch. Articled to Niven & Wigglesworth, FFRIBA. War Service, France, RAMC 27th F. Ambulance. RIBA Prize Essay and Silver Medal; holder of Athens Bursary, etc. Acoustic Consultant for: Free Trade Hall, Manchester; Guild Hall, Portsmouth; Coventry Hippodrome; Fairfield Halls, Croydon; Royal Festival Hall, etc. Hon. Mem., Inst. of Acoustics, 1976. *Publications:* Fields and Battlefields, 1918; Sonnets in War and Peace, 1940; Practical Acoustics and Planning against Noise; (With Robert Atkinson) Theory and Elements of Architecture, 1926; (with late Dr Alex. Wood) Planning for Good Acoustics, 1931. *Address:* Leaside, Hertingfordbury, Hertford.
[Died 20 May 1979.

BAGGALEY, Ernest James; Bursar of Chichester Theological College, 1968-77, retired; *b* 2 June 1900; *er s* of A. H. Baggaley, Wokefield, Mortimer, Berks; *m* 1929, Sylvia Austen Bell,

LRAM; one *s* one *d*. *Educ:* University Coll., Reading (BSc London). Asst Master (later Second Master), Bembridge Sch., IOW, 1923-41; Asst Master (later Second Master) Queen Elizabeth Grammar Sch., Wakefield, 1941-56, Headmaster, 1956-64. Former Mem. of Selection Board, Voluntary Service Overseas. *Publication:* A Geography of New Zealand, 1967. *Recreations:* walking, gardening, writing autobiography of early years, 1910-20. *Address:* 57 Cedar Drive, Chichester, West Sussex. *T:* Chichester 82624. *[Died 6 March 1978.*

BAGGALLAY, Lt-Col Richard Romer Claude, DSO 1919; MC 1917; *b* 4 May 1884; *s* of late Claude Baggallay, KC, 20 Elvaston Place, SW, and Wilderwick, East Grinstead; *g s* of Rt Hon. Sir Richard Baggallay, PC; *m* 1910, Kathleen Constance Charlotte Murphy; one *s*; *m* 1922, Phyllis Legge. *Educ:* Marlborough Coll.; RMC Sandhurst. Lieut-Col (retired) Irish Guards; served European War, 1914-19, commanded 1st Bn Irish Guards France and Germany, 1918-19 (wounded, despatches twice, DSO, MC, 1914 Star); Military Sec. to Lord Lieut of Ireland, April-July 1919. Asst Military Sec. to Viscount Allenby and Egyptian Expeditionary Force, Aug. 1919-May 1920; Asst District Commissioner Sudan, 1920-22; served in Constantinople, 1922-23; commanded Men's Alien Internment Camps, Isle of Man, 1940-42; Capt. Derbyshire County Cricket, 1913-14 and 1919. *Recreations:* cricket, riding, ski-ing, all games. *Club:* Guards. *[Died 12 Dec. 1975.*

BAGNALL, Sir Arthur; *see* Bagnall, Sir W. A.

BAGNALL, Hon. Sir (William) Arthur, Kt 1970; MBE 1945; **Hon. Mr Justice Bagnall;** a Judge of the High Court of Justice, Family Division (formerly Probate, Divorce and Admiralty Division), since 1970; Member Restrictive Practices Court, since 1971; *b* 24 March 1917; *s* of late William Brookes Bagnall and Mary Bagnall (*née* Wood), Wolverhampton; *m* 1955, Margaret Jean, *er d* of John Robert Kerr Tyre and late Dora Tyre (*née* Smyth); one *s* one *d*. *Educ:* Wolverhampton Grammar Sch.; Univ. Coll., Oxford (MA). Served in War of 1939-45: RA in Malta, 1940-44; DAAG Land Forces, Adriatic (despatches), 1944-45. Called to Bar, Lincoln's Inn, 1946; QC 1961; Bencher, 1968. Junior Counsel to Registrar of Restrictive Trading Agreements, 1959-61. Mem. Review Body on Doctors' and Dentists' Remuneration, 1964-70. Mem. Council, Univ. of Kent, 1972-. *Recreation:* golf. *Address:* Yew Tree House, Rotherfield, Sussex. *T:* Rotherfield 2408. *Clubs:* Garrick, Beefsteak, MCC.
[Died 21 Oct. 1976.

BAGOT, 7th Baron, *cr* 1780; **Harry Eric Bagot;** Bt 1627; *b* 4 Feb. 1894; *s* of late Charles Frederick Heneage Bagot (4th *s* of *g s* of 1st Baron) and late Florence Eleanor (*née* Bagot); *S* kinsman, 1961; *m* 1st, 1951, Kathleen Elizabeth Saddler (*d* 1972), widow of Noel Murray Puckle, Melbourne, Australia; 2nd, 1972, Mrs Mary Hewitt. *Educ:* Marlborough. Served European War, 1914-19, as Captain RFA, also RFC (severely wounded). Heir: *b* Reginald Walter Bagot, Major (retired) Royal Marines [*b* 24 Aug. 1897; *m* 1st, 1922, Winifred Gwyneth Bowen (marr. diss., 1934); 2nd, 1934, Millicent Brenda Bowden].
[Died 20 June 1973.

BAGOT, 8th Baron *cr* 1780; **Reginald Walter Bagot;** Bt 1627; *b* 24 Aug. 1897; *s* of Charles Frederick Heneage Bagot (*d* 1939) (4th *s* of *g s* of 1st Baron) and Florence Eleanor (*née* Bagot) (*d* 1940); *S* brother, 1973; *m* 1st, 1922, Winifred Gwyneth Bowen (marr. diss. 1934); 2nd, 1934, Millicent Brenda, *o d* of late Henry White Bowden. *Educ:* Wellington. Major, Royal Marines, retired. Heir: *half-b* Heneage Charles Bagot [*b* 11 June 1914; *m* 1939, Muriel Patricia Moore, *y d* of late Maxwell James Moore Boyle; one *s* one *d*]. *Address:* Tower House, Clarendon Gardens, Southsea, Hants. *[Died 2 Oct. 1979.*

BAGRIT, Sir Leon, Kt 1962; Chairman, Elliot-Automation Ltd, 1963-73 (Deputy Chairman from its formation, 1957, until 1962); Director, Technology Investments Ltd, since 1963; *b* 13 March 1902; *s* of Manuel and Rachel Bagrit; *m* 1926, Stella Feldman; two *d*. *Educ:* St Olave's; London Univ. Organised the first company in Europe devoted to automation. Mem., Council for Scientific and Industrial Research, 1963-65; Mem., Advisory Council on Technology, 1964-. Dir, Royal Opera House, Covent Garden, 1962-70; Founder, Friends of Covent Garden, Chm., 1962-69. Reith Lecturer, 1964. RSA Albert Medal, 1965. DUniv. Surrey, 1966; DSc Univ. Reading, 1968. *Publication:* The Age of Automation, 1966. *Recreations:* music and visual arts. *Address:* 80F Eaton Square, SW1W 9AP. *Club:* East India, Devonshire, Sports and Public Schools. *[Died 22 April 1979.*

BAGSHAWE, Thomas Wyatt, FSA, FRHistS; *b* 18 April 1901; *yr s* of late Arthur Bagshawe, The Grove House, Dunstable, Beds; *m* Grace Geering; two *s*. *Educ:* Rugby School; Gonville and Caius Coll., Cambridge. Geologist, Expedition to Graham Land (Antarctica), 1920-22. Dir, Bagshawe & Co., Ltd, Dunstable, 1925-47. Hon. Curator, later Hon. Dir, Luton Museum, 1928-47. Liveryman, Curriers' Company, 1936, also Past-Master. Served War of 1939-45, RAFVR and Combined Operations, 1940-45. High Sheriff of Beds, 1949; Trustee, Cecil Higgins Museum, Bedford, 1951-56; Hon. Adviser, The Moot Hall, Elstow, Bedford, 1952-58; Vice-Pres., Royal Anthropological Institute, 1952-55. Name given to Bagshawe Glacier, Danco Coast, Antarctica, 1958. *Publications:* Notes on the Habits of the Gentoo and Ringed or Antarctic Penguins, 1938; Two Men in the Antarctic, 1939; Pompey was a Penguin, 1940; numerous articles and notes in jls relating to antiquarian matters, folk life, early furniture, sculpture, etc. *Recreations:* the study of the history of trades; collecting antiques. *Address:* 95 Orchard Avenue, Worthing, Sussex BN14 7QD. *Club:* Antarctic. [*Died 28 Jan.* 1976.

BAHADUR SHAMSHER JANG BAHADUR RANA, **Commanding-General,** (retired); GBE (Hon.), 1934; and Mil., 1938; KCB (Hon.), 1945; Nepalese Army, retired: Hon. Colonel British Army, 1942; *b* 1892; *e surv. s* of H. H. Maharaja Joodha Shamsher Jang Bahadur Rana of Nepal, GCB, GCSI, GCIE; *m* 1st, 1906, Chandra Rajya Lakshmi (*d* 1934); one *s* three *d* ; 2nd, 1937, Lakshmi Kumari Devi; one *s* two *d.* In command Patan Bde, 1910-29; led 1st Nepalese Contingent to India, 1915-16 (British War Medal); present during Prince of Wales's visit to Nepal, 1921; Rotary Judge of Supreme Court of Appeal, Nepal, 1922-29; Dir-Gen. of Public Instruction, Nepal, 1924-29; Pres. of Development Bd, 1935-40; Dir-Gen., Nepal Bank Ltd, 1937-40; First Nepalese Minister at the Court of St James's, 1934-35; head of First Special Nepalese Missions to present Decorations to King George V and others; visited India and concluded agreement between India and Nepal Govts in connection with Nepalese Contingent for India on outbreak of War, 1939; GOC-in-C Nepalese Contingent in India, 1940-43; Chief Justice Supreme Court of Nepal, 1943-45 (KCB). In charge of 8 provinces of Nepal Terai, 1946-47; Dir-Gen. of Foreign Aff., 1937-40, and again from 1943; Pres. Cttee to negotiate with Goodwill Mission of USA, 1947; Pres. Constitutional Reforms Cttee set up in Kathmandu under order of Maharaja of Nepal, 1947; Eastern Comg Gen. and Act. Senior Gen., 1948; has Order of Star of Nepal 1st Class (with title of Supradipta Manyabara), and Nepalese Orders of Gorkha Dashina Bahu 1st Class (with title of Prasidha Pravala Gorkha Dakshina Bahu), 1935, and of Trishakti Patta, 1st Class (with the title of Subikhyat-Trishakti-Patta), 1939; Om Rama Patta, 1948. Hon. Grand Cross, Crown of Italy, 1934, and Legion of Honour (France), 1939. *Recreations:* riding, shikar, lawn tennis. *Address:* Bahadur Bhavan, Nepal, *via* India. [*Died 19 May* 1977.

BAILEY, Arthur, OBE 1945; FRIBA 1946; Architect; *s* of Charles Hill and Winnifred Bailey; *m* 1930, Phyllis, *d* of William and Harriet Martin; one *s.* Consulting Architect to: King George's Fields Foundn; London Dio.; Rochester Dio.; Min. of Transport (Bridges); GLC (Housing); Worshipful Co. of Vintners; London Electricity Bd; Nat. Council of Social Service; Church Pastoral-Aid Soc; Lloyds Bank Ltd; Hambros Bank Ltd; Nat. Deposit Friendly Soc.; ICAA; Commissions include: remodelling and extensions, Sheffield Cath. (Civic Trust Award, 1969); rebuilding St Nicholas Cole Abbey (Wren) London (Civic Trust Award, 1967); re-building and remodelling St George-in-the-East (Hawksmoor), Stepney (Civic Trust Award, 1967); Churches: New Dutch, Austin Friars, EC2; St James-the-Less, Bethnal Green; St Mary's, Shortlands, Kent; Holy Trinity, Gillingham (Civic Trust Award, 1969); Baptist, Norwood and Paddington; London Electricity Bd: Divl Offices, Ilford and Bexleyheath; Meter Test Stn and Labs, Bexleyheath, also Stores; Offices: Austin Friars; Holborn Circus; St Peter's Square, Manchester; Church Pastoral-Aid Soc., Fleet Street; Divl Offices for Nat. Deposit Friendly Soc. in various cities; new HQ, CMS, SE1; Bridges: Stratford-upon-Avon; Ross-on-Wye; Maidstone By-Pass; M4, Maidenhead; M6, Cheshire and Westmorland; Housing for: LCC, Mortimer Crescent, Tower Hamlets, Hawgood Street; West Ham Corp.; Sevenoaks RDC; Brit. Drug Houses Ltd; Tower Court Flats, Bournemouth; Convalescent Home, Portal House, Bournemouth; Arts Block, Highgate Sch.; Pilgrims Sch., Seaford, and Edith Edwards House Sch., Banstead, ICAA; Highgate Sch. Swimming Bath; many private commissions. Min. of Lab. and Nat. Service, 1940-45; Chief Inspector, Building Labour Supply, and Advisor on War Building Programme. Prize Winner of Open Architectural Competitions: Swansea City Hall, Coun. Offices and Law Cts; Wimbledon Town Hall; Wiggeston Gram. Sch., Leicester; Bradford Civic Centre Improvement Scheme; Wolverhampton Town Hall; Overhead Motorway; Liverpool RC Cathedral. Member: Architects' Registration Coun. (RIBA Rep.); and Finance Cttee (Vice-Chm.); RIBA Practice Cttee (Vice-Chm.

and Past Chm.); Councillor, Artists General Benevolent Instn; Hon. Architect to: ICAA; Nat. Council of Social Service; Queen Alexandra's House; Exhibitor, Royal Academy (Water Colours and Architecture). President's Certificate, 1970, for work with Nat. Playing Fields Assoc. Officer, Order of Orange Nassau, 1954. *Publications:* papers in learned jls. *Recreations:* water colours, fly-fishing. *Address:* 48 Tower Court, West Cliff Road, Bournemouth, Dorset BH2 5HA. *T:* Bournemouth 23991. *Club:* Athenæum. [*Died 9 June* 1979.

BAILEY, Air Cdre George Cyril, CB 1944; DSO 1917; BSc; MICE; RAF, retired; *b* 15 July 1890; *s* of Dr Bailey; *m* 1st, 1918, Phyllis (*d* 1927), *y d* of late Sir John Foster Stevens; one *s* ; 2nd, 1944, Mary Ellen Goldney (*d* 1970), *o d* of late Dr Frederick St John Kemm and Mrs Kemm, Bristol. *Educ:* King Edward VI Sch., Stratford-on-Avon; Manchester Univ. Served European War, 1914-18 (despatches, DSO). Joined Royal Flying Corps, 1916; psa 1925; Group Capt., 1935; Air Commodore, 1939; retired from Royal Air Force, 1944. *Address:* Stockland, Honiton, Devon. [*Died 1 June* 1972.

BAILEY, George Leo, CBE 1952; MSc, FIM; Director, British Non-Ferrous Metals Research Association, 1944-66; *b* 1 July 1901; *s* of late Charles and Annie Bailey; *m* 1925, Blanche Joy, *d* of late J. A. Pearce; one *s* one *d. Educ:* King Edward VI Grammar Sch., Birmingham; Birmingham Univ. Metallurgist, Research Dept, Woolwich, 1922; Chief Development Officer, BNFMRA, 1930-44. Past-Pres. Inst. of Metals and of Instn of Metallurgists. Hon. DMet (Sheffield). *Publications:* The Casting of Brass Ingots (with R. Genders). Papers on metallurgical and related subjects in Jl of Inst. of Metals and other scientific instns. *Recreations:* walking and bridge. *Address:* 77 River Park, Kingsland Road, Hemel Hempstead, Herts. *T:* Hemel Hempstead 52488. [*Died 2 April* 1979.

BAILEY, Sir Kenneth (Hamilton), Kt 1958; CBE 1953; QC; Special Adviser in International Law to the Departments of the Attorney General and of Foreign Affairs, Canberra, since 1969; *b* 1898; *e s* of late E. T. Bailey, Melbourne; *m* 1925 (Editha Olga) Yseult (OBE 1961), *d* of late Frank S. Donnison of Blewbury, Berks; three *s. Educ:* Wesley Coll., Melbourne; Queen's Coll., Univ. of Melbourne; Corpus Christi Coll., Oxford. 2nd Divn Australian Field Artillery, 1918-19; Victorian Rhodes Scholar for 1918; BA Oxon (Mod. Hist.), 1921; MA 1927; Bachelor of Civil Law, Oxon, 1923; called to Bar, Gray's Inn, 1924; Bencher, 1961. Prof. of Jurisprudence, 1928-30, of Public Law, 1931-46 Univ. of Melbourne; consultant, Commonwealth Attorney-Gen.'s Dept, 1943-46. Solicitor-Gen. and Sec. of the Attorney-Gen.'s Department of the Commonwealth of Australia, 1946-64; Australian High Comr in Canada, 1964-69. Mem. of Australian Delegations, League of Nations Assembly, 1937 and 1946 United Nations Conference on Internat. Organisation, San Francisco, 1945, United Nations Preparatory Commn and Gen Assembly, 1945-46, and many later years; Leader of Australian Delegation and Chm. First Cttee, United Nations Conf. on Law of the Sea, 1958. Hon. Fellow, Corpus Christi Coll., Oxford Hon. LLD: Dalhousie, 1966; ANU, 1970; Melbourne, 1972 *Publications:* articles on constitutional and international matters. *Address:* c/o Department of Foreign Affairs, Canberra ACT 2600, Australia. [*Died 3 May* 1972

BAILEY, Sidney Alfred, CB 1946; MBE 1918; *b* 16 Sept. 1886; *m* 1912, Ethel Alice Towse; three *s* one *d.* Entered Civil Service Board of Education, 1906; Insurance Commission, 1912 Ministry of Health, 1919, Principal, 1931, Senior Deputy Chie Inspector, 1937; Ministry of Transport, Asst Sec., 1937 Principal Asst Sec., 1941, Under-Sec., 1946; Dir of Studies Administrative Staff Coll., 1950-51. *Address:* Milestone, Th Fair Mile, Henley on Thames, Oxon. *T:* Henley 5170. [*Died 14 Nov.* 1972

BAILEY, Prof. Stanley John, LLD; Rouse Ball Professor o English Law in the University of Cambridge, 1950-68; Fellow o St John's College, Cambridge, since 1931; Barrister-at-Law Inner Temple, 1924; *b* 19 June 1901; *o s* of John Bailey an Evelyn Mary Bailey (*née* Campkin); *m* 1st, 1926, Kathleen Aimée (*d* 1949), *d* of late Rev. F. J. Hamilton, DD; 2nd, 1952 Wilhelmina, *d* of late Dr H. W. Leeksma, The Hague, Holland one *s. Educ:* Queen's Coll., Taunton; St John's Coll., Cambridge Lecturer in Univ. Coll. of Wales, Aberystwyth, 1926; Reader i English Law in Univ. of Birmingham, 1930; Coll. Lecturer at S John's Coll., Cambridge, 1931-50; Lecturer in Univ. o Cambridge, 1934, Senior Proctor, 1936-37; Tutor of St John' Coll., 1939-46; Reader in Law, Cambridge, 1946-50. Edito Cambridge Law Jl, 1948-54. *Publications:* Law of Wills, 193 (6th edn, 1967); contrib. to Law Quarterly Review, Cambridg Law Journal, The Conveyancer. *Address:* St John's Colleg Cambridge. *T:* Cambridge 61621. [*Died 16 Aug.* 198

BAILLIE, Lady Maud L. E., CBE 1945; JP; *b* 20 April 1896; *e d* of 9th Duke of Devonshire; *m* 1st, 1917, Captain Angus Alexander Mackintosh, RHG (*d* 1918); one *d*; 2nd, 1928, Brig. Hon. G. E. M Baillie, MC (*d* on active service, 1941); two *s* one *d*. *Educ:* privately. Master High Peak Harriers, 1922-47. Served ATS, 1938-45. JP Derbys, 1932. *Address:* Ballindarroch, Inverness. *T:* Scaniport 208. *[Died 30 March 1975.*

BAILLIE-GROHMAN, Vice-Admiral Harold Tom, CB 1941; DSO 1917; OBE 1922; RN retired; *b* Victoria, British Columbia, 16 Jan. 1888; *o s* of late W. A. Baillie-Grohman, Kootenay pioneer, author and sportsman; *m* 1915, Evelyn, *e d* of Arthur S. Taylor, MD, FRCS; one *s* (and one *s* decd). Joined HMS Britannia, 1903; Lieut 1909; Lt-Com. 1917; Captain 1930; Rear-Adm. 1941; Vice-Admiral, 1943 (retd). Served European War, 1914-18, with Grand Fleet, in Dover Patrol in destroyers and minesweepers (DSO, OBE, Chevalier of Order of Leopold, Star of Ethiopia, Order of the Brilliant Jade); in Persian Gulf and Red Sea, 1922-23; as SO 1st Minesweeping Flotilla, 1923-24; and as ACNS and DNI in Navy Office, Melbourne, 1925-27; Military Staff Coll., Camberley, 1928; Head of British Naval Mission to China, 1931-33; in command First Destroyer Flotilla, Mediterranean, 1934-36; in command HMS St Vincent and in charge Boys' Training Establishment, 1936-38; commanded HMS Ramillies, 1st Battle Squadron, Mediterranean, 1939-40; attached to Staff of GOC Mid. East, 1941 (chiefly responsible for shore to ship arrangements, evacuation of British Forces from Greece, 1941); Rear-Admiral Combined Operations, 1942; FOIC, Harwich, 1944, Kiel and Schleswig-Holstein, 1945-46, to eliminate the remains of the German naval forces; hoisted White Ensign over German Naval HQ, Kiel, 8 May 1945. *Publication:* (with A. Heckstall-Smith) Greek Tragedy, 1941. *Address:* 6 St Martin's Square, Chichester, West Sussex. *T:* Chichester 82753. *Clubs:* Naval and Military, Alpine Ski; (Naval Member) Royal Yacht Squadron; RN Sailing Assoc. *[Died 23 Sept. 1978.*

BAILLIE REYNOLDS, Paul Kenneth; *see* Reynolds.

BAILLIEU, 2nd Baron, *cr* 1953, of Sefton, Australia, and Parkwood, Co. Surrey; **William Latham Baillieu;** Assistant Master, St Peter's Sch., Seaford, Sussex; *b* 10 Dec. 1915; *s* of 1st Baron Baillieu, KBE, CMG and Ruby (*d* 1962), *d* of late William Clark; *S* father 1967; *m* 1st, 1945, Anne Bayliss (marriage dissolved, 1961) *d* of Leslie William Page, Southport, Queensland; two *s*; 2nd, 1962, Mrs Delia Muriel Champion. *Educ:* Winchester; Magdalen Coll., Oxford (MA). *Recreations:* gardening, and fishing. *Heir:* s Hon. James William Latham Baillieu, *b* 16 Nov. 1950. *Address:* The Oast House, Park Farm, Chiddingly, Lewes, Sussex. *T:* Chiddingly 319. *Clubs:* Bath; Leander (Henley-on-Thames); Melbourne (Melb.). *[Died 18 April 1973.*

BAILY, Leslie; freelance writer; *b* 14 Dec. 1906; *s* of James T. Baily and Lucy Allott; *m* 1928, Margaret Jesper; one *s* one *d*. *Educ:* Friends Sch., Sibford, near Banbury; Cheltenham Grammar Sch. Editorial staff, Yorks Ev. News, Leeds, 1924; Radio Editor, Sunday Referee, London, 1932; started writing for BBC features, plays, revues, talks, 1924, esp. pioneering techniques for historical documentaries, first in Leeds and Manchester studios; in London from 1933 when created Scrapbook series. Took part in TV programme experiments, 1936. Joined BBC, 1937, as staff writer, later producer (radio); freelance, 1946-; continued scripting Scrapbooks until 1966; writer of many other programmes involving original research, incl.: South with Shackleton, The Schubert Discoveries, Lives of Gilbert and Sullivan, Trial of William Penn, Rise of the Labour Party. Ran series for BBC, incl.: Travellers' Tales, Dear Sir, Leslie Baily's Log Book; also scripts for TV and Cinema, incl.: Lives of Gilbert and Sullivan for London Film Productions. Founder-Member, Radiowriters Assoc.; FRHistS. *Publications:* The BBC Scrapbooks, 1937; Travellers' Tales, 1945; The Gilbert and Sullivan Book, 1952; (ed with James T. Baily) A Crafts Anthology, 1953; Scrapbook 1900-1914, 1957; Craftsman and Quaker, 1959; Scrapbook for the Twenties, 1959; Leslie Baily's BBC Scrapbooks: Vol.i, 1966; Vol.ii, 1968; Gilbert and Sullivan and Their World, 1973. *Recreations:* music, reading, escaping to undesecrated countryside (if any) and uncorrupted sea. *Address:* The Granary, New Parks, Shipton-by-Beningbrough, York YO6 1BD. *T:* Beningbrough 369. *[Died 21 Feb. 1976.*

BAILY, Robert Edward Hartwell, CBE 1932; retired from Sudan Political Service; Chairman, Herefordshire Scout Council since October 1960 (County Commissioner, Herefordshire Boy Scouts, 1939-60); *b* 6 June 1885; *s* of E. P, Baily, Hazelwood, Limpsfield; *m* 1920, Brenda (*d* 1962), *d* of H. A. Wadworth and *widow* of Captain G. E. Lea, Worcestershire Regt. *Educ:* Harrow; Cambridge. Captain Harrow Cricket XI, 1903-4; Cambridge Cricket XI, 1908. Sudan Political Service, 1909-32;

Governor Kassala Province, 1926-32. Secretary, Roy. Empire Soc., 1935-38. *Address:* Castle Pool Hotel, Hereford. *T:* Hereford 3551. *Clubs:* Travellers', Royal Commonwealth Society, Chatham House, MCC, Free Foresters.
[Died 19 Sept. 1973.

BAIN, William Alexander; formerly Professor of Pharmacology, University of Leeds; *b* Dunbar, 20 Aug. 1905; *o s* of late Rev. Alex. Wright Bain and late Grace Martin, *e d* of James Brough, JP, Inveresk; *m* 1st, 1929, Bessie Beveridge Smith (*d* 1961), Uphall; one *s* one *d*; 2nd, 1962, Freda Dratman, Philadelphia, Pa, USA. *Educ:* Broxburn High Sch.; Bathgate Academy (John Newland Bursar); Univ. of Edinburgh. BSc, 1st Cl. Hons Physiol., and Wellcome Gold Medallist, History of Medicine, 1928; Ellis Prizeman, 1930; Crichton Research Scholar, 1930 and 1931; FRSE, 1931; PhD, Faculty of Medicine, 1932; DSc, 1953. Asst to Sir E. Sharpey Schafer, FRS, 1928; Lecturer in Experimental Physiology, Univ. of Edin., 1931; Lecturer in Physiol., Univ. of Leeds, 1934; Reader in Pharmacology, Univ. of Leeds, 1935; Professor of Pharmacology, Univ. of Leeds, 1946-59; Dir, Smith Kline and French Research Inst., Welwyn Garden City, Herts, 1959-66. Academic Sub-Dean, Faculty of Medicine, Leeds, 1943-48; Hon. Treas., Brit. Pharmacological Soc., 1947-64; Mem. Brit. Nat. Cttee for Physiological Sciences, 1955-60, 1967-; Assessor Univ. Grants Cttee, 1958-69; Member: Physiolog. Soc.; Soc. for Experimental Biol.; Biometric Soc.; Royal Med. Soc. (Edin.); Royal Soc. Med.; Institute of Biology (Fellow). Sometime Examiner in Pharmacology, Univs of Cambridge, Aberdeen, Durham and London and for the Pharmaceutical Society of Great Britain. Press Editor, British Journal of Pharmacology and Chemotherapy, 1953-57. Hon. ScD (TCD), 1967, Hon. Mem. Brit. Pharmacol. Soc., 1967 (Mem. 1939-67). *Publications:* articles in medical and scientific journals on autonomic nerves, adrenaline, histamine antagonists, quantitative human pharmacology etc. *Recreations:* music, gardening, reading dictionaries. *Address:* Oakdene, Digswell, Welwyn, Herts. *T:* Welwyn 4119. *Club:* Royal Societies.
[Died 24 Aug. 1971.

BAINES, Rt. Rev. Henry Wolfe; Bishop of Wellington, New Zealand, since 1960; *b* 7 Feb. 1905; *y c* and 3rd *s* of Talbot and Caroline Agnes Baines; *m* 1944, Natalie Elizabeth Bartlett; two *s*. *Educ:* Repton; Balliol Coll., Oxford; Cuddesdon Theological College. Travelling Secretary of Student Christian Movement in England, 1927-29; Deacon, 1930; Asst Curate, St Mary the Virgin, Oxford, 1930; Priest, 1931; Asst Chaplain, later Chaplain-in-Charge, St John's Cathedral, Hongkong, 1934-38; Vicar of St Nicholas, Radford, Coventry, 1938-41; Rector of Rugby (St Andrew), 1941-49; Bishop of Singapore, 1949-60. Hon. Canon of Coventry Cathedral, 1947; Proctor in Convocation, 1946. *Recreations:* cricket, music, bird watching. *Address:* Bishopscourt, 28 Eccleston Hill, Thorndon, Wellington 1, NZ. *Clubs:* Travellers', MCC, Student Movement House, Wellington.
[Died 29 Nov. 1972.

BAIRD, James Craig, CB 1967; retired Civil Servant, now farming; *b* 4 Nov. 1906; *s* of John Jackson and Martha Baird; *m* 1934, Janet Gentiles McFarlane; two *d* (two *s* decd). *Educ:* Methodist Coll., Belfast; Queen's Univ., Belfast (BSc, BAgr). Agricl Chem. Dept, QUB, 1927-38; Min. of Agric., NI, 1927-66; Chief Inspector, 1948; Asst Sec., 1955; Perm. Sec., 1963; retired, 1966. *Recreation:* Rugby football. *Address:* Holestone, Doagh, Co. Antrim, N Ireland. *T:* Doagh 232. *[Died 14 Oct. 1973.*

BAIRD, William George, CMG 1949; JP; MA, LLB; Transport Licensing Authority, Otago Province, 1950-60; *b* East Taieri, 1889; *s* of Robert Baird, farmer. *Educ:* Allanton; Mosgiel; Victoria Coll. Entered Public Trustee Office as clerical cadet, 1906; Asst District Public Trustee, Christchurch; Controller of Estates Div., Head Office; Asst Public Trustee, 1931, Public Trustee, 1942, Wellington, NZ; retired, 1949. JP, Wellington, 1932-. *Address:* 101 Highgate, Dunedin, NZ. *Clubs:* Wellesley (Wellington); University (Dunedin). *[Died 2 Nov. 1975.*

BAKER, Air Marshal Sir Brian Edmund, KBE 1944; CB 1943; DSO 1918; MC; AFC; *b* 31 Aug. 1896; *m* 1926, Jaimsie Derby Robinson (*d* 1979); two *d*. *Educ:* Haileybury. Served European War, 1914-18 (despatches, MC, DSO, AFC); Chief Flying Instructor, RAF Training Base, Leuchars, 1932-34; HMS Eagle, 1934; HMS Courageous, 1936; commanded RAF Station, Gosport, 1937-38; RAF Station, Leuchars, 1938; No 51 Group, 1940-41; RAF Iceland, 1941; No 16 Group, 1941-42; No 19 Group, 1943-44; AOC East Africa, 1945; Senior Air Staff Officer, HQ, Middle East, 1945; AOC-in-C, Transport Command, 1947-50; retd 1950. Hon. Life Governor, RNLI, 1971. *Address:* 3 Howard Place, St Andrews, Fife.
[Died 8 Oct. 1979.

BAKER, Charles E. S.; see Smalley-Baker.

BAKER, Doris Manning, MD, FRCP; Physician Elizabeth Garrett Anderson Hospital and South London Hospital; Physician, Arthur Stanley Institute, Middlesex Hospital, retired. *Educ:* London Univ. MRCS; LRCP 1924; MB, BS 1925; DOMS 1927; MD London 1927; MRCP 1927; FRCP 1952; late Major RAMC. FRSocMed. *Publications:* Cardiac Symptoms in the Neuroses, 1942; articles in medical journals. *Address:* 132 Richmond Hill, Richmond, Surrey. *T:* 01-940 0412.
[*Died* 17 *Sept.* 1971.

BAKER, Rev. Dr Eric Wilfred, MA; Secretary of the Methodist Conference, 1951-71; *b* 17 Feb. 1899; *s* of Alfred and Eliza Baker, Birmingham; *m* 1934, Winifred Mary, *o d* of Thomas Laban and Mary Thorne, Ilfracombe; one *s* one *d. Educ:* King Edward's Sch., Birmingham; Christ's Coll., Cambridge; Wesley House, Cambridge. Served European War, 1914-18; Second Lieut, Norfolk Regt, 1917; Egypt, 1918-19. Classical and Theological Triposes, Carus Greek Testament Prize, Cambridge; MA (Cantab.), 1925; PhD (Edin.), 1941. Minister: Hall Green Methodist Church, Birmingham, 1923-27; King Street Methodist Church, Derby, 1927-31; Harrow-on-the-Hill Methodist Church, 1931-35; Edinburgh Central Hall, 1935-44; Bowes Park Methodist Church, London, 1944-46; Chm., London North Dist Methodist Church, 1945-51; Sec., Methodist Education Cttee, 1946-51; Pres. of the Methodist Conference, 1959-60; Moderator, Free Church Federal Council, 1964-65. Delegate to: Second Assembly, World Council of Churches, Chicago, 1954; Third Assembly, New Delhi, 1961; Mem. World Council of Churches Central Cttee, 1954-68; Vice-Pres., World Methodist Council (Mem., 1947-); Vice-Pres., British Council of Churches, 1962-65; Vice-Pres. British and Foreign Bible Soc.; Hon. Vice-Pres., The Boys' Brigade; Gov. of The Leys Sch., Cambridge; Chm. of Govs, Farringtons Sch., Chislehurst, 1960-65; Gov. of Kingswood Sch., Bath; Gov. of Queenswood Sch.; Willson Lecturer, Southwestern Univ., Texas, 1950; Fernley-Hartley Lecturer, 1958; Cambridge Univ. Select Preacher, 1960; Fondren Lectr, Southern Methodist Univ., Texas, 1963; Brown Lectr, Randolph-Macon Coll., Ashland, Virginia, 1963; Willson Lectr, Nashville, Tenn, 1963; Cato Lectr, Australia, 1963; Visiting Professor: Claremont Sch. of Theology, California, 1971-72; Iliff Sch. of Theology, Denver, Colorado, 1972. Hon. DD Randolph-Macon, Virginia, 1956; Hon. LLD Mount Union, Ohio. *Publications:* He Shall Suffice Me, 1947; A Herald of the Evangelical Revival, 1948; From the Church in the Orchard, 1949; Belief and Behaviour, 1950; Preaching Theology, 1954; John Scott Lidgett (part author), 1957; The Faith of a Methodist, 1958; The Neglected Factor, 1963. *Recreations:* tennis, golf. *Address:* 21 Walnut Tree Walk, Ratton Manor, Eastbourne, Sussex. *T:* Eastbourne 54197. *Club:* Athenæum.
[*Died* 19 *Sept.* 1973.

BAKER, Field-Marshal Sir Geoffrey Harding, GCB 1968 (KCB 1964; CB 1955); CMG 1957; CBE 1946 (OBE 1943); MC 1941; Constable of the Tower of London, since 1975; *b* 20 June 1912; *s* of late Col Cecil Norris Baker, CIE, IA, and Ella Mary Baker; *m* 1946, Valerie, *d* of late Major J. L. Lockhart and Mrs Lockhart; two *s* one *d. Educ:* Wellington Coll.; RMA Woolwich (Sword of Honour). Commnd RA, 1932; India, with 11th Field Bde, RA, 1935; "F" (Sphinx) Battery, RHA, 1937 (Egypt, 1939); Middle East Staff Coll., 1940; Bde Major RA, 4th Indian Div., Western Desert and Eritrea, 1940, 1941; Instructor ME Staff Coll., 1942; GSO1, HQ Eighth Army, 1942-43; CO 127th Field Regt, 51st Highland Div., Sicily, 1943. BGS, HQ 21st Army Gp, North West Europe, 1944; Dep. Dir, War Office, 1947; Commanding Officer 3rd Regt RHA, 1950-52; Dir War Office, 1952-54; Dir of Operations and Chief of Staff to Governor of Cyprus, Nov. 1955-Feb. 1957; CRA, 7th Armd and 5 Divs, BAOR, 1957-59; Asst C of S, HQ, Northern Army Gp, Germany, 1959; Chief of Staff, HQ Southern Command, 1960-61; Chief of Staff, Contingencies Planning, Supreme HQ, Allied Powers Europe, 1961-63; Vice-Chief of the General Staff, 1963-66; GOC-in-C, Southern Command, 1966-68; CGS, 1968-71; Field-Marshal, 1971. Director: Grindlays Bank, 1972-; Central London Reg. Bd, Lloyds Bank; Consolidated Safeguards Ltd, 1977-; Cititel Consultancy Ltd, 1979-. Colonel Commandant: RA, 1964-; RMP, 1968-71; RHA, 1970-. Master Gunner, St James's Park, 1970-76. President: Officers' Assoc., 1972-80; Army Benevolent Fund, 1971-. Vice-Pres., Wellington Coll., 1976; Mem. Council, Radley Coll., 1973-. Hon. Liveryman, Haberdashers' Co.; Freeman, City of London. US Legion of Merit (Comdr), 1946. *Address:* Broomden Oast, Ticehurst, Sussex. *Club:* Army and Navy.
[*Died* 8 *May* 1980.

BAKER, George (Arthur), CBE 1971; FRCM; Hon. RAM; baritone singer, adjudicator, lecturer and journalist; *b* 10 Feb. 1885; *e s* of Walter and Elizabeth Baker, Birkenhead; *m* 1st,

Kathlyn Hilliard (*d* 1933); 2nd, 1936, Olive Groves (*d* 1974). *Educ:* privately; Birkenhead Inst.; Royal College of Music. Organist Woodchurch Parish Church, Cheshire, at the age of 16; subsequently held similar appointments at St Matthew's and St Michael's Churches, Birkenhead; won open scholarship for singing at the Royal College of Music, 1908; studied in Milan with Thomas Blackburn, 1914; has sung at all the principal concerts in Great Britain; played in opera and musical comedy; toured Australia, 1922-23; The Beggar's Opera in USA and Canada, 1927-28, and played in New York, 1928; toured South Africa, 1937; Holland, 1937 and 1947; USA 1939-40; Overseas Music Dir, BBC, 1944-47; Hon. Mem. Royal Philharmonic Society; Mem. Incorporated Soc. of Musicians; Vice-Pres., Catholic Stage Guild. *Publications:* This Singing Business, 1947; The Common Sense of Singing, 1963; musical and miscellaneous journalism. *Address:* Dulas Court, Pontrilas, Herefordshire. *T:* Pontrilas 458. *Clubs:* Savage (Trustee); Salmagundi (New York).
[*Died* 8 *Jan.* 1976.

BAKER, Henry, PhD, MSc, CEng, MICE, MIMechE; Principal Nottingham and District Technical College, 1946-55; *b* 22 June 1893; *s* of Alfred Baker; *m* 1918, Constance Mary Lightbown; one *s. Educ:* The Fielden Sch.; University of Manchester. MSc Manchester, PhD Birmingham. Experience in Industry, subsequently Lecturer, University of Birmingham, 1920-23, and Armstrong (now King's) Coll., University of Durham, 1923-29; Head of Dept of Civil and Mechanical Engineering, Sunderland Tech. Coll., 1929-34; Principal, Tech. Colls of Norwich, 1934-36, West Ham, 1936-46. *Address:* 7 Cissbury Drive, Findon Valley, Worthing, West Sussex BN14 0DT. *T:* Findon 2241.
[*Died* 21 *Sept.* 1975.

BAKER, Air Chief Marshal Sir John (Wakeling), GBE 1954; KCB 1949 (CB 1942); MC 1918; DFC 1925; RAF retired; *b* Winnipeg, Canada, 23 Oct. 1897; *er s* of late Rev. F. V. Baker, DD, BA; *m* 1927, Hilary, *o d* of late Lieut-Col H. Bonham-Carter; three *s* one *d. Educ:* Eastbourne Coll.; RMA Woolwich. Commissioned RA, 1916; transferred RFC 1917; RAF 1918 (MC); 60 Sqdn, India, NWF, 1923-28 (DFC); RAF Staff Coll. 1931; 33 Sqdn, Middle East, 1935-36; Imperial Defence Coll. 1938; Director of Bomber Operations, Air Ministry, 1942 (CB); SASO Air Command, SE Asia, 1943-44 (despatches); AOC 12 (Fighter) Group, 1945-46; Dir-Gen. of Personnel, Air Ministry, 1946-48; AOC-in-C, Coastal Command, 1948-49 (KCB); C-in-C MEAF, 1950-52; DCAS then VCAS, Air Ministry, 1952-53 Controller of Aircraft, Min. of Supply, 1953-56 (GBE). Air ADC to the Queen, 1952-56. *Address:* 10 The Glebe, Chislehurst, Kent BR7 5PX.
[*Died* 10 *March* 1978

BAKER, Mrs Noel John Horne; see Scott-Moncrieff, J. C.

BAKER, Olive Katherine Lloyd L.; see Lloyd-Baker.

BAKER, Reginald George Gillam, CBE 1945; retired; *b* 1 Feb 1887; *s* of John Edward Baker; *m* 1st, 1915, Dora Winifred Withycombe, Kaisar-i-Hind Silver Medal, 1945 (*d* 1947); no *c* 2nd, 1951, Pamela Mary, *d* of Stanley Johnson; one *s.* British American Tobacco Co., Oct. 1910; landed India, March 1911 retired, 1945. Served India 34 years, 21 years as Dir, last 9 years as Chm. Imperial Tobacco Co. of India. Interested in Agriculture. Pres. Calcutta Club, 1944; British War Saving Cttee in India; Red Cross work for Bengal. *Address* Rivermeadow, Harlyn Bay, Padstow, Cornwall. *T:* St Merryn 270. *Club:* Oriental.
[*Died* 5 *May* 1971

BAKER, Sir Stanley, Kt 1976; actor/producer; Director, HTV Limited, since 1968; *b* 28 Feb. 1928; *s* of late John Henry and Elizabeth Louise Baker; *m* 1950, Ellen Martin; three *s* one *d. Educ:* Ferndale, S Wales. Served in Army, 1946-48. Screen debut in Undercover, 1942; stage debut, Druid's Rest; subseq two yrs at Birmingham Rep. Theatre. Frequent TV appearances Rudolf Valentino Award, 1974. *Films include:* The Cruel Sea Knights of the Round Table; Hell Below Zero; The Red Beret Richard the Third; Alexander The Great; A Hill in Korea Checkpoint; Hell Drivers; Campbell's Kingdom; Violen Playground; Sea Fury; Blind Date; The Angry Hills; Hell is City; The Guns of Navarone; The Criminal; Sodom an Gomorrah; Eve; Prize of Arms; In the French Style; Zulu (als produced); Dingaka; Sands of Kalahari (also produced Accident; Robbery (also produced); Girl with a Pistol; Where Jack? (also produced); The Games; The Last Grenade; Perfec Friday; Popsy Pop; Innocent Bystanders; Zorro; Pepita Jimenez Orzowei; appears in TV films. *Recreation:* golf. *Address:* 9 Albert Embankment, SE1 7TY. *T:* 01-735 7141. *Club* Wentworth Golf (Virginia Water); Coombe Hill Golf (Kingston Hill).
[*Died* 28 *June* 1976

BAKER, Prof. Stephen Leonard; Professor Emeritus, Manchester University; *b* 24 Oct. 1888; *s* of Arthur de Chair Baker and Sophia Baker (*née* Sandes); *m* 1921, Georgina Mary (*née* Barnes); five *s. Educ:* Whitgift Grammar Sch.; London Hospital Medical Sch. Temp. Surgeon Lieut RN, 1915-18; Pathologist to King Edward VII Sanatorium, Midhurst, 1919-21; Chief Asst, Bland-Sutton Institute, Middlesex Hospital, 1922-31; Proctor Prof. of Pathology, Manchester Univ., 1931-50; Professor of Osteo-pathology, Manchester Univ., 1950-55. John Hunter Medal and Triennial Prize, Royal Coll. of Surgeons, 1955. *Publications:* numerous publications in medical journals. *Recreations:* gardening, photography, geology. *Address:* Sea Winds, Orford, Woodbridge, Suffolk.   *[Died 17 April 1978.*

BAKER, Col Thomas MacDonald, CBE 1951; TD 1931; DL; retired as Solicitor, Metropolitan Police, (1934-60), also as Solicitor, Central Criminal Court, Court Prosecutions, County of London Sessions and County of Middlesex Sessions; Legal Member, London Rent Assessment Panel, 1966; *b* 1 Aug. 1894; *s* of late Thomas John Baker, Castle Hotel, Lynton, and of Margaret Grant Baker (*née* MacDonald), Forres, Scotland; *m* 1926, Vera Evelyn, *d* of late Philip Smith, Solihull, Warwickshire; one *s* one *d. Educ:* Radley Coll. Inspector of Taxes, Inland Revenue, 1920-24; Asst Solicitor, Inland Revenue, Somerset House, 1924-34; set up new Solicitor's Dept, and became first Solicitor, Met. Police, 1934. 6th Bn, E Surrey Regt, TA, 1911-32, Lt-Col comdg, 1928-32; Col, TA, 1933-54; served European War overseas, with 6th Bn, E Surrey Regt, 1914-19, (Hon. Col, 1949-61); Ft-Lieut, RAFVR, 1941-46; founder and first Comdg Officer, 1349 Woking Sqdn, ATC, and 167 Gliding Sch., 1942-46; mem. of Surrey T&AFA, 1928-63. DL Surrey, 1949. *Publications:* on Taxation and on Criminal Law. *Recreations:* motoring, gardening. *Address:* Netley, Hurst Close, Hook Heath Road, Woking, Surrey.
[Died 31 Dec. 1976.

BAKER WILBRAHAM, Sir Randle John; *see* Wilbraham.

BALCON, Sir Michael, Kt 1948; Film Producer since 1920; Director of Border Television Ltd, from formation until 1971, now Consultant; *b* 19 May 1896; *s* of Laura and Louis Balcon, Birmingham; *m* 1924, Aileen, MBE, 1946, *d* of H. Leatherman, Johannesburg; one *s* one *d. Educ:* George Dixon Sch., Birmingham. Founder and Dir of Gainsborough Pictures Ltd, 1928; subsequently (1931) Dir of Production for Gaumont-British Picture Corporation Ltd; Dir and Producer Ealing Films Ltd, 1938-59; Chairman: British Lion Films Ltd and of British Lion Films (Holdings) Ltd, 1964-65. Fellow, British Film Academy; Governor, British Film Institute; Chairman, Film Production Board (BFI), 1963-71. Hon. Fellow, British Kinematograph Soc.; a Sen. Fellow, Royal Coll. of Art. Hon. DLitt: Birmingham 1967; Sussex 1975. Chevalier des Arts et des Lettres, 1977. Knight First Class of Order of St Olav (Norway). *Films* include: (1945-): The Captive Heart; The Overlanders; It Always Rains on Sunday; Scott of the Antarctic; Kind Hearts and Coronets; Whisky Galore; The Blue Lamp; The Lavender Hill Mob; The Man in the White Suit; Where No Vultures Fly; The Cruel Sea; The Maggie; The Divided Heart; The Ladykillers; The Long Arm; The Man in the Sky; The Shiralee; Dunkirk; The Scapegoat; The Siege of Pinchgut; The Long and the Short and the Tall; Sammy Going South. *Publication:* A Lifetime of Films, 1969. *Recreation:* walking. *Address:* Upper Parrock, Hartfield, East Sussex. *T:* Forest Row 2370. *Clubs:* Garrick, MCC.   *[Died 17 Oct. 1977.*

BALDWIN OF BEWDLEY, 3rd Earl, *cr* 1937; **Arthur Windham Baldwin;** Viscount Corvedale, 1937; *b* 22 March 1904; 2nd *s* of 1st Earl Baldwin of Bewdley, KG, PC, FRS, and Lucy, GBE 1937, DGStJ (*d* 1945), *e d* of late Edward Lucas J. Ridsdale, The Dene, Rottingdean, Sussex; *S* brother 1958; *m* 1936, Joan Elspeth, *y d* of late C. Alexander Tomes, New York, USA; one *s. Educ:* Eton; Trinity Coll., Cambridge. Served War of 1939-45, in the Royal Air Force, 1941-45. Formerly a Dir of the Great Western Railway Company. *Publications:* My Father: The True Story, 1956; The Macdonald Sisters, 1960; A Flying Start (autobiog.), 1967. *Recreations:* none. *Heir: s* Viscount Corvedale. *Address:* Bushey House, Apperley, Glos. *Club:* Reform.   *[Died 5 July 1976.*

BALDWIN, Air Marshal Sir John Eustace Arthur, KBE 1943 (CBE 1942; OBE 1919); CB 1938; DSO 1918; DL Lincolnshire; JP Rutland; High Sheriff of Rutland, 1955; Hon. Air Cdre, R Aux. AF; *b* 13 April 1892; *e s* of late J. H. L. Baldwin; *m* Kathleen Betsy, *y d* of T. W. L. Terry, York; one *d. Educ:* Rugby; Sandhurst. Gazetted to 8th (KRI) Hussars, 1911; ADC to the King, 1931-33; Dir of Personal Services, Air Min., 1935-36; Comdt RAF Coll., Cranwell, 1936-39; AOC, 3 Gp, 1939-42; Dep. AOC-in-C India, 1942-43; commanded No 3 Tactical Air

Force, 1943-44. Col 8th King's Royal Irish Hussars, 1948-58; Dep. Col, Queen's Royal Irish Hussars, 1959-60. KStJ, 1962. Officer of Crown of Belgium; Belgian Croix de Guerre; White Lion 2nd Class; American Air Medal; Czech War Cross. *Address:* Park Farm, Ketton, Stamford, Lincs. *T:* Ketton 256. *Clubs:* Cavalry, Royal Air Force.   *[Died 28 July 1975.*

BALDWIN, Nelson Mills, OBE 1977; Chairman, RAC Motoring Services, since 1979; Director: Automobile Proprietary Ltd, since 1979; RAC Insurance Ltd; RAC Travel and Brokerage; *b* 17 March 1923; *s* of Nelson Baldwin and Alice (*née* Mills); *m* 1950, Cynthia Agnes Kienel; three *d. Educ:* Tonbridge Sch.; St John's Coll., Cambridge. Admitted as a Solicitor of the Supreme Court, 1948. Chairman, Speedway Control Board, 1964; Secretary-General, later Director General, RAC, 1971-79. Member of Court of Assistants, Guild of Loriners. *Recreation:* golf. *Address:* 29 Hurlingham Gardens, SW6. *T:* 01-736 1538; Sarne, Greenway, Frinton-on-Sea, Essex. *T:* Frinton 2729. *Clubs:* Royal Automobile; Hawks, Frinton-on-Sea Golf.
[Died 18 April 1980.

BALFOUR, Patrick; *see* Kinross, Baron.

BALFOUR, Lieut-Gen. Sir Philip Maxwell, KBE 1950 (CBE 1944); CB 1946; MC 1917; late RA; *b* 10 March 1898; *s* of late C. F. Balfour, ICS; *m* 1930, Catharine Marjorie, *d* of Lieut-Col Sir Charles Frederick Rugge-Price, 7th Bt. *Educ:* Wellington Coll.; RMA, Woolwich. 2nd Lieut RA 1915; served European War, 1916-18, France and Belgium (MC and Bar); War of 1939-45 (despatches, CBE, CB); Comdr 2nd Infantry Div., 1947-49; Gen. Officer, Commanding-in-Chief, N Command, 1949-53; retired from Army, 1953. Col Commandant RA, 1950-60. *Address:* Little Wincombe House, Donhead St Mary, Shaftesbury, Dorset. *Club:* Naval and Military.
[Died 4 Feb. 1977.

BALL, Air Vice-Marshal Sir Benjamin, (Ben), KBE 1969 (CBE 1946; OBE 1943); CB 1963; Chairman: Chelton (Holdings) Ltd, since 1972 (Director since 1970); Chelton (Electrostatics) Ltd, since 1972 (Director since 1970); *b* 6 Sept. 1912; *s* of late John William Ball, Barrister-at-Law, Kingstown, Co. Dublin; *m* 1938, Pamela, *d* of late Captain W. E. Caldbeck, Beds and Herts Regt; three *s. Educ:* Trinity Coll., Dublin. De Havilland Sch. of Flying, 1933-34; BA Dublin, 1934; RAF Coll., Cranwell, 1934-35; No 209 (FB) Sqdn, RAF, 1935-38; Signals Specialist Course, 1938-39; RAF Bircham Newton, 1939; CSO of: Reserve Comd, RAF, 1939-40; No 1 Trg Comd, RCAF, 1940-42; No 2 Trg Comd, RCAF, 1942-43; Gp Captain Ops No 26 Gp, RAF, 1943-46 (despatches); RAF Staff Coll., 1946; CSO, Bomber Comd, RAF, 1946-48; Dir of Signals, Air Force Staff, BJSM, Washington, USA, 1948-51; Comd, RAF Debden, 1951-53; DDOR, Air Min., 1953-56; CSO Bomber Comd, RAF, 1957-60; DCSO, SHAPE, 1960-63; SASO, Technical Training Cmd, RAF, 1963-66; AOC-in-C, RAF Signals Comd, 1966-68; retired 1969. Chm. Exec. Cttee, RAFA, 1972-. Dir, Festiniog Rly Co., 1973-; Pres., British Motor Cycle Racing Club, 1971-. *Recreation:* sport. *Address:* c/o Lloyds Bank Ltd, 6 Pall Mall, SW1. *Club:* Royal Air Force.   *[Died 24 Jan. 1977.*

BALL, Major Charles James Prior, DSO 1918; MC 1916; FRAeS 1938; *b* 15 Feb. 1893; *s* of George William Ball, JP; *m* 1920, Eva (*d* 1964), *d* of Herbert Lucas, Shepleigh Court, Devon; two *s* one *d. Educ:* Charterhouse; London Univ. Royal Artillery, 1914-23; served European War, 1914-18 (despatches, DSO, MC); Military Inter-Allied Commission of Control (disarming Germany), 1919-23. Fellow of University Coll., London, 1959; Fellow of Institute of Metals, 1960. *Publication:* The Campaign in Gallipoli. *Address:* The Nursing Home, Sarum Road, Winchester, Hants. *Clubs:* Army and Navy, Royal Thames Yacht.   *[Died 15 Oct. 1973.*

BALL, Sir Edmund Lancaster, Kt 1941; *b* 1883; *s* of William Edmund Ball, LLD, Barrister-at-law; *m* 1911, Harriet Estelle (*d* 1963), *d* of Capt. Hugo Beaumont Burnaby, RN; two *s. Educ:* City of London Sch.; Christ Church, Oxford. 1st Class Classical Hon. Mods, 1904; 1st Class Lit. Hum., 1906; MA. Auditor of India Home Accounts, India Audit Office, 1934-43. *Address:* Clavell Edge, 12 Ballard Estate, Swanage, Dorset. *Club:* United University.   *[Died 19 June 1971.*

BALL, Sir Nigel Gresley, 3rd Bt, *cr* 1911; MA, ScD, FLS; *b* 27 Aug. 1892; *s* of late Sir Charles Bent Ball, Bt, MD; *S* brother, 1945; *m* 1922, Florine Isabel, *d* of late Col Herbert Edwardes Irwin; two *s* one *d. Educ:* St Columba's Coll., Rathfarnham, Co. Dublin; Trinity Coll., Dublin. Received commission in 8th (S) Bn Royal Dublin Fusiliers, Nov. 1914; demobilised March 1919; Asst to the University Prof. of Botany, Trinity Coll., Dublin, 1920-24; Prof. of Botany, University Coll., Colombo, 1924-43;

Lecturer in Botany, University of London, King's Coll., 1944-55, Reader, 1955-57, Special lecturer, 1957-59. *Publications:* chapters on physiology of plant movements in: Vistas in Botany, vol. 3 (ed Turrill), 1963; Plant Physiology, vol. 5A (ed Steward), 1969; Physiology of Plant Growth and Development (ed Wilkins), 1969; various papers on plant physiology in scientific jls. *Heir: s* Charles Irwin Ball. *Address:* 19 Bernard Road, West Worthing, West Sussex. *T:* Worthing 47155.

[*Died* 1 *July* 1978.]

BALL, William Antony, TD; MRCS, LRCP, MB, BS London; retired Medical Practitioner; late Temporary Lt-Col RAMC, TA (despatches for service in Italy); *b* 9 April 1904; *s* of late Arthur Franklin and Edith Mary Ball; *m* 1933, Barbara Pauline Johnston. *Educ:* King's Coll. Sch., Wimbledon; King's Coll., London; King's Coll. Hospital. House appointments at King's Coll. Hosp., Westminster Hosp., Belgrave Hosp. for Children. *Publications:* in Practitioner, Lancet, BMJ, Medical Press and Circular, American Year Book of Surgery for 1940. *Recreations:* old Sussex maps, touring in France and her vineyards. *Address:* Ivy House, Tillington, Petworth, Sussex. *T:* Petworth 42558. *Clubs:* Carlton; Royal Tennis (Hampton Court).

[*Died* 18 *Oct.* 1973.]

BALLANCE, Rear-Adm. Frank Arthur, CB 1953; DSO 1944; Royal Navy, retired; *b* 16 Nov. 1902; *s* of Sydney Ballance, Sandon, Herts; *m* 1st, 1930, Marie Arundell (*d* 1972), *d* of Reavely Maitland, Loughton, Essex; one *s* ; 2nd, 1972, Sybil, *d* of E. C. Lee, Petersfield, and *widow* of Comdr G. P. U. Morris, DSC, RN. *Educ:* Royal Naval Colls Osborne and Dartmouth. Commander, 1939; HMS Phoebe; HMS Gosling; Capt., 1943; took part in Invasion of Normandy; Admiralty, 1944-46; Ordnance Board, 1946-48; HMS Jamaica, 1949-50; Chief of Naval Staff, New Zealand, 1950-53; Flag Officer Flotilla, Indian Fleet, 1953-55; Rear-Admiral, 1953; Admiralty, 1955; retired, 1957. *Recreation:* shooting. *Address:* Malthouse Cottage, Rogate, Petersfield, Hants. *T:* Rogate 338. [*Died* 6 *Feb.* 1978.]

BALLANTRAE, Baron *cr* 1972 (Life Peer), of Auchairne and The Bay of Islands; **Bernard Edward Fergusson,** KT 1974; GCMG 1962; GCVO 1963; DSO 1943; OBE 1950; Chairman, London Board, Bank of New Zealand, since 1968; Chancellor, University of St Andrews, since 1973; Registrar, Order of St Michael and St George, since 1979; *b* 6 May 1911; *y s* of Gen. Sir Charles Fergusson of Kilkerran, 7th Bt, GCB, GCMG, DSO, MVO, and of Lady Alice Boyle (*d* 1958), *d* of 7th Earl of Glasgow; *m* 1950, Laura Margaret (*d* 1979), *y d* of Lieut-Col A. M. Grenfell, DSO; one *s*. *Educ:* Eton; RMC Sandhurst. Joined The Black Watch, 1931; Lieut 1934, Capt. 1939; ADC to Maj.-Gen. (later F.-M.) Wavell, 2nd Div. Aldershot, 1935-37; served Palestine, 1937 (medal and clasp); Instructor RMC, 1938-39; served War of 1939-45 (wounded, despatches twice, DSO); Staff Coll., 1940; Bde Major 46th Inf. Bde, 1940; Middle East, 1941; GSO1 Joint Plans India, 1942; Wingate Expeditions into Burma, 1943-44; comd 16th Inf. Bde in 1944 Expedition; Dir of Combined Ops (Military), 1945-46. Asst Inspector-Gen., Palestine Police, 1946-47; commanded 1st Bn The Black Watch, 1948-51; Col Intelligence, Supreme HQ, Allied Powers, Europe, 1951-53; idc 1954; Comdr, 153rd Highland Bde, TA, 1955-56; Allied Force HQ Port Said Operations, 1956; Comdr, 29th Infantry Bde, 1957-58, retd. Governor-General and C-in-C of New Zealand, 1962-67. Internat. Observer Team, Nigeria, Oct. 1968-March 1969. Mem., Cttee to review Defamation Act, 1952, 1971-74; Chm., Scottish Trust for the Physically Disabled, 1971-. Chm., British Council, 1972-76. Lord High Comr to Gen. Assembly of Church of Scotland, 1973, 1974. Col The Black Watch (Royal Highland Regt), 1969-76. Hon. DCL Canterbury, 1965; DUniv Waikato, 1967; Hon. LLD: Strathclyde, 1971; Dundee, 1973; Hon. DLitt St Andrews, 1974. *Publications:* Eton Portrait, 1937; Beyond the Chindwin, 1945; Lowland Soldier (verse), 1945; The Wild Green Earth, 1946; The Black Watch and the King's Enemies, 1950; Rupert of the Rhine, 1952; The Rare Adventure, 1954; The Watery Maze: The Story of Combined Operations, 1961; Wavell: Portrait of a Soldier, 1961; Return to Burma, 1962; The Trumpet in the Hall, 1970; Captain John Niven, 1972; Hubble-Bubble (light verse), 1978; Travel Warrant, 1979. *Address:* Auchairne, Ballantrae, Ayrshire. *T:* Ballantrae 344. *Clubs:* White's; New (Edinburgh).

[*Died* 28 *Nov.* 1980.]

BALLANTYNE, Archibald Morton, OBE 1966; TD 1951; Secretary, Royal Aeronautical Society, 1951-73; *b* 1908; *o s* of late Archibald Morton Ballantyne and of Janet Ballantyne, Pollokshields, Glasgow; *m* 1941, Catherine Mary, 2nd *d* of J. Warner Crofts, Kilsby Grange, Rugby; one *s* one *d*. *Educ:* Hutchesons' Grammar Sch.; Glasgow Univ. BSc (Eng) 1930; PhD 1936; Diploma in Town Planning; FAIAA. Senior Lecturer in Civil and Municipal Engineering Department,

University College, London, 1936-51. Served War of 1939-45, in Royal Artillery, attached to Inspector-Gen. of Armaments; Captain Royal Artillery, TA. Hon. FCASI; Hon. FRAeS, 1973. *Recreations:* golf, writing. *Address:* 27 Clifton Lawns, Chesham Bois, Bucks. *T:* Amersham 3711. [*Died* 3 *Dec.* 1977.]

BALLARD, Lieut-Col Basil W.; *see* Woods-Ballard.

BALLARD, Bristow Guy, OBE 1946; retired; President: Canadian Patents and Development Ltd, 1967-70; National Research Council of Canada, Ottawa, 1963-67; *b* 19 June 1902; *s* of Charles Ballard and Etta Moffat; *m* 1928, Irene Foreman; no *c*. *Educ:* Queen's Univ., Kingston, Ont (BSc). Electrical Engineering, Westinghouse Electric & Manufacturing Co., East Pittsburgh, Pa, 1925-30; Div. of Physics, National Research Council of Canada, 1930-46; Asst Dir, Div. of Physics and Elect. Engrg, NRC, 1946-48; Dir, Radio & Electrical Engrg Div., NRC, 1948-63; Vice-Pres. (Scientific), NRC, 1954-63. Fellow Inst. of Electrical and Electronic Engrs, 1955; Hon. Member: Engrg Inst. of Canada, 1960; Instrument Soc., America, 1964. Coronation Medal, 1953. Fellow, Royal Soc. of Canada, 1963. Hon. DSc: Queen's Univ., 1956; Assumption Univ. of Windsor, 1961; Memorial Univ., Newfoundland, 1964; Hon. DEng, Nova Scotia Tech. Coll., 1964; Hon. LLD, Univ. of Victoria, 1965. *Publications:* articles in technical jls. *Recreations:* nature study, camping. *Address:* 390 Cloverdale Road, Rockcliffe Park, Ottawa, Ont K1M 0X3, Canada. *T:* 749-9744.

[*Died* 22 *Sept.* 1975.]

BALLARD, Brig. (Retd) James Archibald William, CBE 1957 (MBE 1940); DSO 1943; *b* 31 July 1905; *s* of late Admiral G. A. Ballard, CB and Mrs M. F. H. Ballard (*née* Paterson); *m* 1st, 1939, Helen Mary (*d* 1941), *d* of late F. Longdon; 2nd, 1945, Ursula Mary (*d* 1962), *d* of late Rev. F. Icely, Naval Chaplain. *Educ:* Rugby. Joined Northamptonshire Regiment, 1925; psc 1939; HQ 2 Corps, BEF, 1940; Military mission to S Africa, 1941-42; in command 2nd Bn Northamptonshire Regt, 1942-43 and 1944; USA, 1943-44; SHAEF Mission to Denmark, 1945; BGS British Troops, Egypt, 1946-48; in comd 2nd Bn Northamptonshire Regt, 1948-50; Chief of Staff British Forces, Trieste, 1950-52; in comd 133 Inf. Bde (TA), 1952-54. War Office, 1954-57. *Address:* Laundry Cottage, Hanmer, Whitchurch, Salop. *Club:* Naval and Military.

[*Died* 19 *Dec.* 1978.]

BALMFORTH, Rev. Canon Henry, MA; Residentiary Canon and Chancellor in Exeter Cathedral, 1956-73; Lecturer in Theology, Exeter University, 1959-73; *b* 2 Oct. 1890; *s* of William Albert Balmforth and Sarah Crowther; *m* 1916, Helen Haigh (*d* 1971); two *d*. *Educ:* Manchester Grammar Sch.; Corpus Christi Coll., Oxford (Open Classical Scholar), 1st Class Honours Classical Moderations, 2nd Class Final Classical Sch. Attached to General Manager's Staff, Parr's Bank, 1913-15; Lower Sixth Form Master, Manchester Grammar Sch., 1916; Sixth Form Master and Librarian of Repton Sch., 1916-32; Headmaster of St Edmund's Sch., Canterbury, 1932-41; Deacon, 1916; Priest, 1917; Asst Priest, St Werburgh's, Derby, 1920-25; Reader in Derby Cathedral, 1929-32; Examining Chaplain to the Bishop of Derby, 1931-32; Select Preacher, Oxford, 1934-35; Cambridge, 1938 and 1949; Examining Chap. to Archbishop of Canterbury, 1936; to Bishop of Bath and Wells, 1946-60; to Bishop of Exeter, 1956; Dir, Archbishop's Examination in Theology, 1947-64; Six-Preacher in Canterbury Cathedral, 1938-41; Canon of Ely and Principal of Ely Theological Coll., 1941-56. *Publications:* Is Christian Experience an Illusion?, 1923; editor, Gospel according to St Luke (Clarendon Bible), 1930; (joint), Introduction to Pastoral Theology, 1937; The Christ of God, 1938; The Christian Religion: A Brief Account, 1945; The Royal Priesthood, 1956; Christian Priesthood, 1963; contributor to Theology and other journals. *Recreations:* walking, painting. *Address:* 8 Greenway Crescent, Taunton, Som. *Club:* Oxford Union. [*Died* 9 *Feb.* 1977.]

BALSDON, John Percy Vyvian Dacre, DLitt Oxon; FBA 1967; *b* 4 Nov. 1901; *e s* of late Robert Percy (farmer). *Educ:* Exeter Sch.; Exeter Coll., Oxford (MA). Stapeldon Scholar, Exeter Coll., 1920; Literae Humaniores, 1924. Asst Master, Sedbergh Sch., 1924-26; Tutor, Keble College, Oxford, 1926-27; Junior Proctor, 1940; Fellow, Exeter Coll., Oxford, 1927-69. Ministry of Labour and National Service, 1940-45. Vice-Pres., Soc. for the Promotion of Roman Studies. Hon. LLD Dalhousie, 1964; Hon. DLitt Exeter, 1975. *Publications:* The Emperor Gaius (Caligula), 1934 (reprinted 1965); Oxford Life, 1957 (new edition, 1962); Roman Women: their History and Habits, 1962; Julius Caesar and Rome, 1967 (in USA, Julius Caesar: a Political Biography); Life and Leisure in Ancient Rome, 1969; Oxford Now and Then, 1970; Rome: the story of an Empire, 1970; Romans and Aliens, 1978; and various novels. Contributor

to Cicero, 1964; Editor, The Romans, 1965. Papers and reviews (mainly on Roman History). *Address:* The Orchard, Great Haseley, Oxford OX9 7JQ. *T:* Great Milton 275.
[*Died* 18 *Sept.* 1977.

BAMBER, John; Stipendiary Magistrate, Metropolitan County of Greater Manchester (formerly City of Manchester), since 1965; *b* 10 Aug. 1915; *s* of John and Ada Helen Bamber; *m* 1947, Jean Buchanan Love; one *s* one *d. Educ:* Manchester Gram. Sch.; Wadham Coll., Oxford. Called to Bar, Gray's Inn, 1938. Practised on Northern Circuit. Served in Manchester Regt in England and in Staff appts, SE Asia Comd, 1939-46. *Recreations:* association football, cricket. *Address:* 108 Radcliffe New Road, Whitefield, Manchester. *T:* 061-766 2572. *Club:* Reform (Manchester). [*Died* 27 *April* 1976.

BANDON, 5th Earl of, *cr* 1880; **Percy Ronald Gardner Bernard,** GBE 1961 (KBE 1957); CB 1945; CVO 1953; DSO 1940; Baron Bandon, 1793; Viscount Bandon, 1795; Viscount Bernard, 1800; Air Chief Marshal, Royal Air Force, retired; *b* 30 Aug. 1904; *s* of late Lt-Col Ronald P. H. Bernard and Lettice Mina, *yr d* of late Captain Gerald C. S. Paget (she *m* 2nd, late Hon. Charles C. J. Littleton, DSO); *S* cousin, 1924; *m* 1st, 1933, Elizabeth (marr. diss., 1946; she *m* 1965, Sir Reginald Holcroft, 2nd Bt, TD), 2nd *d* of R. W. Playfair; two *d*; 2nd, 1946, Lois White, *d* of Francis Russell, Victoria, Australia. *Educ:* Wellington; RAF Coll., Cranwell. RAF Staff Coll., 1938; served War of 1939-45; commanded No 82 Squadron, 1939-40; commanded RAF Station, West Raynham, 1941-42; AOC No 224 Group, South-East Asia, 1945 (despatches thrice, American DFC and Bronze Star); Commandant, ROC, 1945-48; idc 1949; AOC No 2 Group, BAFO, Germany, 1950-51, No 11 Group, 1951-53; ACAS (Trg), Air Ministry, 1953-Dec. 1955; C-in-C, 2nd Tactical Air Force, and Comdr, 2nd Allied Tactical Air Force, 1955-57; C-in-C, Far East Air Force, 1957-60; Comdr, Allied Air Forces, Central Europe, 1961-63. *Heir:* none. *Address:* Castle Bernard, Bandon, Co. Cork. *Club:* Royal Air Force.
[*Died* 8 *Feb.* 1979 (*ext*).

BANERJEA, A. C., CIE 1943; DrPH; *b* 5 Feb. 1894; *s* of late A. T. Banerjea; *m* 1917, Prabhabati; one *s* four *d. Educ:* India, England and USA. MB, BS 1920; DPH 1922; DrPH 1928; Malariologist, UP Govt for ten years. Dir of Public Health, UP, India, 1939; Dir of Medical and Health Services, 1948; retired, 1950. *Publications:* In official files and records. *Address:* 31 Station Road, Lucknow, UP, India. *T:* 2686.
[*Died* 2 *Aug.* 1979.

BANKES, Robert Wynne, CBE 1929; *b* 23 June 1887; *s* of late Rt Hon. Sir John Bankes, PC, GCB; *m* Mabel Elizabeth, 2nd *d* of Major H. Pelham Burn; two *s* one *d. Educ:* Eton; University College, Oxford (BA). Called to Bar, Inner Temple, 1911; on active service European War, 1914; Captain, Montgomeryshire Yeomanry, 1914-17; ADC to Brig.-Gen. C. A. C. Godwin, 6th Mounted Brigade, EEF, 1917-18; ADC FM Lord Allenby, 1918-19 (despatches); Private Sec. to successive Lord Chancellors, 1919-29; Asst Sec., Institute of Chartered Accountants, 1929-35, Sec., 1935-49. JP 1912, High Sheriff, Flintshire, 1945; Comr, Flints St John Ambulance Bde, 1952-62; KStJ 1960. *Address:* Soughton Hall, Northop, Mold, Clwyd. *Club:* Anglo-Belgian. [*Died* 18 *July* 1975.

BANKES-WILLIAMS, Ivor Maredydd; Headmaster, Wellington School, Somerset, 1945-April 1957; *b* 10 June 1896; *s* of late Rev. W. Bankes-Williams, MA, JP; *m* 1924, Winifred Mary Grellier Barnes. *Educ:* Radley Coll.; CCC, Cambridge. BA 1923; MA 1931; served in Gallipoli and France, 1914-19. Capt. RFA. Classical Scholar CCC, Cambridge, 1914; Hons Natural Sciences Tripos, 1922. Asst Master, Harrow Sch., 1923-41. Chm. of Cttee, Science Masters' Assoc., 1931. Dir of Training, St Dunstan's, for Men and Women blinded on war service, 1941-44. *Recreations:* sketching, gardening. *Address:* Greenway Cottage, Kington Magna, Gillingham, Dorset. *TA* and *T:* East Stour 286. [*Died* 2 *May* 1974.

BANKS, Sir Donald, KCB 1935 (CB 1933); DSO 1918; MC 1917; TD 1942; *b* 31 March 1891; *m* 1921, Dorothy (*d* 1947), *d* of late Dr Norman Webster, Guernsey; one *d*; *m* 1948, Elizabeth, 2nd *d* of Lt-Col R. W. Bradley, DSO, Lymington; one *s* one *d. Educ:* Elizabeth Coll., Guernsey. Exchequer and Audit Dept, 1909, Private Sec. to the Sec. GPO, and to four Postmasters-General, 1920-23; Deputy Controller, Post Office Savings Bank, 1924, Controller, 1931; First Dir-Gen. of Post Office, 1934-36; Transatlantic Air Mission to Ottawa and Washington, 1935; Permanent Sec. to the Air Ministry, 1936-38; First Permanent Under Sec. of State for Air, 1938-39; Air Mission to Australia and New Zealand, 1939; Mem. of National Savings Cttee, 1931-39; of Import Duties Advisory Cttee, 1939; JP (London), 1936-

42; London Yeomanry, 1910-14; served European War in France, 1915-18; commanded 10th (Service) Bn Essex Regt and 8th (Service) Bn Royal Berkshire Regt (DSO, MC, Fr. Croix de Guerre; despatches twice); commanded Princess Louise's Kensington Regt TA, 1927-31; Asst Adjutant and Quartermaster General 50th (Northumbrian) Div. 1939; Temp. Brig., 1940; Maj.-Gen., 1943; Deputy Adjutant-Gen. GHQ BEF 1940 (despatches); Local Defence Area Commander for Hampshire, 1940; Dir-Gen. Petroleum Warfare Dept (involving operations Pluto, Fido, etc.), 1940-45. (Commander, US Legion of Merit); Chm. Anglo-Chinese Chamber of Commerce, 1946-54; Head of UK delegation to first Assembly International Civil Aviation Organisation, Montreal, 1946; Deputy Chm., Air Transport Advisory Council, 1947-51. *Publications:* With the Tenth Essex in France; Flame over Britain. *Address:* Cadnam Lodge, Hants. *Club:* Reform. [*Died* 11 *July* 1975.

BANKS, Sir John (Garnett), Kt 1956; CBE 1953; LLD; DL; JP; *b* 9 May 1889; *s* of John Garnett Banks and Elizabeth Forrest Grieve; *m* 1st 1923, Gertrude Rosamond Marshall Symonds (*d* 1941); one *s*; 2nd, 1952, Margaret Wallace Macdonald. *Educ:* Leith Walk Public Sch., Edinburgh. Edinburgh Town Council: Member, 1936; Treasurer, 1950-53; Lord Provost, City of Edinburgh, 1954-57. DL Edinburgh, 1958. Hon. LLD Edinburgh, 1956. OStJ 1958. *Recreations:* music and travel. *Address:* Cairn Lodge, 48 Duddingston Road West, Edinburgh. *T:* 031-661 2146. [*Died* 2 *Jan.* 1974.

BANKS, Sir Thomas Macdonald; *see* Banks, Sir Donald.

BANNERMAN, David Armitage, OBE 1961 (MBE 1918); MA, ScD, Hon. LLD; FRSE; *b* 27 Nov. 1886; *o s* of late David Alexander Bannerman; *m* 1911, Muriel (*d* 1945), 2nd *d* of T. R. Morgan of Las Palmas, Grand Canary; twin *d* (one *s* decd); *m* 1952, Winifred Mary (Jane), OBE, *e d* of David Holland, Cardiff. *Educ:* Wellington College; Pembroke College, Cambridge. Graduated 1909; joined temp. Staff Natural History Museum, 1910; travelled extensively West Indies, N, S, and W Africa, S America, Atlantic Isles and Europe; carried out Zoological Survey of Canary Islands, 1908-13. Served with BEF (Europe), first as Ambulance driver, then, as Staff Officer, on HQ Staff BRCS (France), 1915-18 (MBE; OStJ 1919); British and French War Medals, Mons Star; after Armistice rejoined staff of Natural History Museum; Leader, British Museum Expedition to Tunisia, 1925. Assistant Editor, Ibis, 1931-41. On outbreak of Second World War, 1939, appointed Deputy Assistant Censor (Liaison Branch) on Staff of Controller of Postal and Telegraph Censorship, War Office; Assistant Censor, IRB Censorship Hqrs, 1940-42; Sgt in Home Guard. Retd from Natural History Museum, 1952, to take up book-writing and stock-breeding in Kirkcudbrightshire. Carried out ornithological surveys of Morocco, 1950-52, Cyprus, 1954, Madeira and Azores, 1960-64, Cape Verde Islands, 1966. Chairman, British Ornithologists' Club, 1932-35; Brit. representative Internat. Council Bird Preservation, Vienna, 1937, Rouen, 1938; MBOU (Vice-Pres., 1943-45); Member Council: RGS, 1935-38; Zoological Soc., 1943-50; RSPB, 1938-52 (Vice-Pres., 1961); Hon. Associate, British Museum (Natural History), 1950; Hon. Curator, Royal Scottish Museum (Edinburgh), 1971; Hon. Pres., Scottish Ornithologists' Club; Hon. Member: Société Ornithologique de France; Soc. Española de Ornitologia (Madrid); Les Naturalistes de Mons et du Borinage (Belgium); Ornithological Society of: Cyprus; Gambia; Mallorca (Balearic Islands); Hon. Fellow, Amer. Ornith. Union. Hon. LLD Glasgow, 1964. Gold Medal of British Ornithologists' Union, 1959. *Publications:* The Canary Islands, their History, Natural History and Scenery, 1922; Reports on numerous British Museum Expeditions for the advancement of ornithological knowledge; The Birds of Tropical West Africa, by order of the Secretary of State for the Colonies, vols i-viii, 1930-51; The Birds of West and Equatorial Africa (2 vols), 1953; The Birds of the British Isles Vols 1-12 1953-63; The Larger Birds of West Africa, 1958, in Penguin series; (by request of Government) The Birds of Cyprus (in conjunction with W. Mary Bannerman), 1958; Birds of the Atlantic Islands (with W. Mary Bannerman): Vol. 1, Canary Islands, 1963; Vol. 2, Madeira, 1965; Vol. 3, Azores, 1966; Vol. 4, Cape Verde Islands, 1968; Handbook of the Birds of Cyprus and Migrants of the Middle East, 1971; (with Joseph A. Vella) Birds of the Maltese Archipelago. *Recreations:* natural history and travel. *Address:* Bailiff's House, Slindon, by Arundel, West Sussex. *T:* Slindon 212. *Club:* Athenæum. [*Died* 6 *April* 1979.

BANNISTER, Prof. Frank Kenneth, CBE 1971; PhD, CEng, FIMechE; Professor of Thermodynamics, Department of Mechanical Engineering, University of Birmingham, since 1952; *b* Colne, Lancs, 29 June 1909; *s* of late Frank Foulds Bannister; *m* 1937, Alice Mary, *d* of late Clement Turner, Halifax, Yorks;

one s two d. Educ: Grammar Sch., Colne, Lancs; University of Leeds. BSc Hons Physics Leeds 1930; BSc (Eng) Hons London 1937; PhD Mech Eng Birmingham, 1946. Lecturer in Mechanical Engineering, Municipal Coll., Burnley, 1937-40; Lecturer in Mechanical Engineering, University of Birmingham, 1941-51; Reader in Thermodynamics, University of Birmingham, 1951-52. *Publications:* papers in Proc. Instn Mech. Engineers. *Address:* 401 Heath Road South, Northfield, Birmingham 31. *T:* 021-475 1081.   *[Died 26 Jan. 1975.*

BANTING, Air Vice-Marshal George Gaywood, CB 1946; CBE 1943; RAF; retired; *b* 25 Feb. 1898; *s* of G. F. Banting, Roehampton; *m* Helen Margaret Ramsay, MBE 1920. *Educ:* Emanuel Sch.; RMC Sandhurst. Served European War, 1914-18, E Surrey Regt and RFC; RAF, 1918-51; War of 1939-45 (despatches, CBE, CB); Air Officer Commanding Rhodesian Air Training Group, 1946-49; Air Officer Commanding No 21 Group, Flying Training Command, 1949-51; Wing Cdr 1937; Air Commodore, 1947; retired, 1951, with rank of Air Vice-Marshal. *Address:* Ridgeway, St Margaret's Bay, Dover, Kent. *Club:* Royal Air Force.   *[Died 27 Dec. 1973.*

BARBER, Elizabeth; see Barber, M. E.

BARBER, Sir Herbert (William), Kt 1952; *b* 8 Nov. 1887; *m* 1912, Annie Nora Heys (*d* 1953); one *s*. *Educ:* Salford Technical Coll. Mem. of Southport County Borough Council, 1931-62; Mayor, 1937-39 and 1943-44; Freeman of Southport, 1962. *Recreations:* Rugby Union football and cricket. *Address:* 40 Hesketh Road, Southport, Merseyside. *T:* Southport 31837.
                [Died 23 Feb. 1978.

BARBER, Prof. Horace Newton, FAA 1958; FRS 1963; Professor of Botany, University of New South Wales, since 1964; *b* Warburton, Cheshire, 26 May 1914; *s* of H. M. Barber, Bowdon, Cheshire; *m* 1946, Nancy P., *d* of late Mr and Mrs F. J. O'Grady, Sydney, NSW; one *s* one *d*. *Educ:* Manchester Grammar Sch.; Emmanuel Coll., Cambridge. MA Cantab. 1941; PhD London 1942; ScD, Cantab, 1963. Scientific Officer, John Innes Inst., London, 1936-40; Scientific Officer, TRE, 1940-45. Flt-Lieut (Hon.) RAFVR, 1943-45. Lecturer, Univ. of Sydney, 1946-47. Rockefeller Foundation Fellow at California Inst. of Technology, 1953-54; Professor of Botany, Univ. of Tasmania, 1947-63. Royal Society Vis. Prof., Ibadan Univ., Nigeria, 1967. *Publications:* Papers in scientific jls. *Recreations:* wandering around Australia and the rest of the world. *Address:* University of NSW, PO Box 1, Kensington, NSW 2033, Australia. *T:* Sydney 663-0351. *Club:* Tasmanian (Hobart).
                [Died 17 April 1971.

BARBER, (Mary) Elizabeth, OBE 1968; MA; General Secretary, Society of Authors, 1963-71; *b* 14 March 1911; *yr d* of Frederic Viccars and Margaret Filmer Barber; unmarried. *Educ:* St Swithun's Sch., Winchester; Somerville Coll., Oxford. Called to the Bar, Gray's Inn, 1935. Asst-Sec., then Sec., Society of Authors, 1936-63. *Publications:* Contrib. on copyright and allied subjects to British and foreign books and periodicals. *Address:* Warren Corner, Froxfield, Petersfield, Hants GU32 1BJ.
                [Died 3 June 1979.

BARBER, Philip Stanley, CBE 1949; DSO 1919; MC; Director of Edward Barber & Son, Ltd, London, EC4; *b* Ravenscroft, South Norwood, Surrey, 12 June 1895; 2nd *s* of Herbert H. Barber; *m* 1921, Iris, 2nd *d* of late E. C. S. Baker, CIE, OBE; one *s* (and *er s* killed as Pilot Royal Air Force, War of 1939-45). *Educ:* King's Sch., Canterbury. Served European War, 1914-19; Private, HAC 1914; Commission, Dorset Regt, Dec. 1914; General Staff, 1916; Brigade Major, 1917-19 (DSO, MC and bar, despatches five times). *Publication:* History of the 50th Infantry Brigade, 1914-19. *Address:* Brooks House, 48 Upper Thames St, EC4. *Club:* Bath.   *[Died 9 Aug. 1973.*

BARBERTON, Ivan Graham Mitford-; ARCA (Sculptor); ARBS; KLJ; *b* 1 Feb 1896; *e s* of late Henry Mitford Barberton and Mary, *d* of Thomas H. Bowker, MLA; *m* 1st, 1921, Cecile, *d* of late T. T. Hoole, Atherstone, Cape Province; two *s* one *d*; 2nd, 1939, Pamela, *d* of Harold Gibbs, Romford, Essex; one *s* one *d*. *Educ:* St Andrew's Coll., Grahamstown. Emigrated to British East Africa, 1912; served German East African Campaign, 1915-19; presented the Barberton Duiker, a new antelope from Mt Elgon, Kenya, to the British Museum; first studied art in Grahamstown, 1919; entered Royal College of Art, 1923; Diploma, ARCA; studied in Italy, 1926, and later in Paris, returning to Kenya, 1927; settled in Cape Town, 1930; has various sculptural works in leading South African galleries; completed large bronze statue of J. Smuts for Capetown, 1972. *Publications:* The Barbers of the Peak, 1935; The Bowkers of Tharfield, 1952; Ivan Mitford-Barberton, Sculptor, 1962; Some

Frontier Families, 1968; Comdt Holden Bowker, 1970. *Address:* Castleton, Hout Bay, Cape, Republic of South Africa.
                [Died 9 June 1976.

BARCLAY, Brig. Cyril Nelson, CBE 1945; DSO 1940; Cameronians (Scottish Rifles); free-lance writer; Military Adviser and Contributor to the Encyclopædia Britannica; *b* 20 Jan. 1896; *o s* of late E. J. Barclay; *m* 1934, Margaret (*d* 1976), *d* of G. Roberts; one *d*. *Educ:* Thanet Coll., St Peter's, Kent; Elstow Sch., Beds. Commissioned in Cameronians (Scottish Rifles), 1915; served European War, 1914-18, France and Mesopotamia; 3rd Afghan War, 1919; War of 1939-45: Dunkirk, Holland, Germany and South-East Asia; retired, 1946. Editor, Army Quarterly, 1950-66; Jt Editor, Brassey's Annual, 1950-69. *Publications:* History of The Cameronians (Scottish Rifles), 1933-46; Part-Time Farmer; History of the London Scottish, 1939-45; History of the Royal Northumberland Fusiliers in the Second World War; History of the 3rd QAO Gurkha Rifles, 1927-47; The New Warfare; History of the Duke of Wellington's Regiment, 1919-52; The First Commonwealth Division, Korea, 1950-53; Against Great Odds; History of the 53rd (Welsh) Division in the Second World War; History of the Sherwood Foresters, 1919-57; History of the 16th/5th The Queen's Royal Lancers, 1963; On Their Shoulders, 1964; Battle 1066, 1966; Armistice 1918, 1968. *Recreation:* bridge. *Address:* York House, 35 South Side, Clapham Common, SW4 9BS. *T:* 01-720 5922. *Club:* Army and Navy.   *[Died 30 Jan. 1979.*

BARCLAY, Prof. William, CBE 1969; Professor of Divinity and Biblical Criticism, University of Glasgow, 1963-74; *b* Wick, 5 Dec. 1907; *m* Katherine Barbara Gillespie; one *s* two *d*. *Educ:* Dalziel High Sch., Motherwell; Univs of Glasgow and Marburg; Trinity Coll., Glasgow. Minister, Trinity Church, Renfrew, 1933-46; Lectr in New Testament Language and Literature, Univ. of Glasgow, 1946-63. Vis. Prof., Univ. of Strathclyde, 1975. External Examiner: Edinburgh, St Andrews, Aberdeen, Leeds. Lectures: Bruce, 1935; Croall, 1955; Kerr, 1956; Baird, 1969-70; Sir David Owen Evans, Aberystwyth, 1969; James Reid Memorial, 1969, 1970. Member: Joint Cttee, New English Bible; Soc. of New Testament Studies; Soc. of Old Testament Studies. Hon. Pres., Glasgow YMCA; Hon. Vice-Pres., Boys Bde. *Publications:* Ambassador for Christ, 1950; And Jesus Said, 1953; The Daily Study Bible, 1953-59; And He had Compassion on Them, 1955; A New Testament Word Book, 1955; The Mind of Paul, 1957; Letters to the Seven Churches, 1957; More New Testament Words, 1958; Educational Ideas in the Ancient World, 1959; The Plain Man's Book of Prayers, 1959; The Master's Men, 1959; The Mind of Jesus, 1960; The Promise of the Spirit, 1960; Crucified and Crowned, 1961; Flesh and Spirit, 1962; Jesus as they saw Him, 1962; More Prayers for the Plain Man, 1962; Prayers for the Young People, 1962; Many Witnesses, One Lord, 1963; Turning to God, 1963; The All-Sufficient Christ, 1964; New Testament Words, 1964; The Plain Man Looks at the Lord's Prayer, 1964; Prayers for the Christian Year, 1964; Prayers for Help and Healing, 1968; The New Testament: a new translation, 1969; Ethics in a Permissive Society, 1972; The Plain Man's Guide to Ethics, 1973; Jesus of Nazareth, 1977; Men and Affairs, ed Clive Rawlins, 1977; contribs to learned journals. *Address:* 32 Holmhead Road, Cathcart, Glasgow G44 3AR. *T:* 041-637 4917. *Club:* Royal Scottish Automobile (Glasgow).   *[Died 24 Jan. 1978.*

BARCLAY-SMITH, (Ida) Phyllis, CBE 1971 (MBE 1958); Ornithologist; 2nd *d* of late Prof. Edward Barclay-Smith, MD. *Educ:* Church House Sch., Worthing; Blackheath High Sch.; King's Coll., London. Asst Sec. Royal Society for the Protection of Birds, 1924-35; Asst Sec. Internat. Cttee for Bird Preservation, 1935-46; Foreign Office, 1939-42; Sec. to Business Manager, Bristol Aeroplane Shadow Factory, Corsham, 1942-43; Specialist Local Welfare Officer (Transport Workers), SW Region, Min. of Labour, 1943-45; Hon. Sec. British Ornithologists' Union, 1945-51; Member: Home Office Advisory Cttee on Wild Birds, 1948-53; Exec. Bd of Internat. Union for Protection of Nature, 1950-56; Council, Royal Geographical Soc., 1970-73. Sec. Internat. Council for Bird Preservation, 1946-78 (Vice-Pres., 1978-); Editor Avicultural Magazine, 1939-73; Jt Hon. Sec. Internat. Wildfowl Research Bureau, 1948-69, Sec. of Honour, 1969-; Hon. Sec. Advisory Cttee on Oil Pollution of the Sea, 1952-71; Organising Sec., Internat. Conferences on Prevention of Oil Pollution of the Sea: London, 1953; Copenhagen, 1959; Rome, 1968; Mem. Home Office, later DoE Advisory Cttee on Protection of Birds for England and Wales, 1954-; Vice-Pres. Commn on Migratory Game-birds of Conseil Internat. de la Chasse, 1950-61, Hon. Vice-Pres. 1965-; Vice-President: British Ornithologists' Union 1957-60; Avicultural Soc., 1970-; Pheasant Trust, 1972-; Hon. Vice-Pres., Soc. for the Promotion of Nature Reserves, 1971-. Mem. of Honour, Internat. Union for Conservation of Nature and Natural Resources, 1978. Hon. Member: Avicultural Soc.; British Falconers' Club; Fauna Preservation Soc.; Corresp. Mem. Bavarian, German, Netherlands, S African Ornithological Unions and Hungarian Inst. of Ornithology. Gold Medal, Sveriges Djurskyddsforenigars Riksforbund, 1954; Isidore Geoffroy St Hilaire Gold Medal of Société Nationale de Protection de la Nature et d'Acclimatation de France, 1963; Delacour Gold Medal of the Internat. Council for Bird Preservation, 1970; Gold Medal, Svenska Kvinnors Djurskyddsforening, 1970; Gold Medal, World Wildlife Fund, 1971; Gold Medal, RSPB, 1973; Silver Medals: Soc. d'Acclimatation de France, 1951; RSPB, 1951; V. v. Heidenstams Fond (Sweden), 1958; President's Medal, Avicultural Soc., 1960. Coronation Medal, 1953; Ridder, Most Excellent Order of Golden Ark, Netherlands, 1973. *Publications:* British Birds on Lake, River and Stream, 1939; (with Hugh Pollard) British and American Game Birds, 1939; Garden Birds, 1945; A Book of Ducks, 1951; Woodland Birds, 1955; (trans. from German) The Bird (by Gertrude Hess), 1951; (trans. from French) Birds of the World (by P. Barruel), 1954, 2nd edn, 1973; (trans. from French) Water Birds with Webbed Feet (by P. Géroudet), 1965. *Recreations:* bird-watching, travelling. *Address:* 5 Eton Avenue, NW3. *[Died 2 Jan. 1980.*

BARFF, Stafford (Edward Douglas), OBE 1954; HM Diplomatic Service, retired; Head of Anglo-American Scholarships Section, Association of Commonwealth Universities, since 1970; *b* 26 Dec. 1909; *s* of late Capt. Arthur Douglas Barff, RN, OBE and Ellen Barff; *m* 1937, Hélène Iost, Geneva; no *c. Educ:* Highfield Sch., Liphook, Hants; Brentwood Coll., Victoria, BC, Canada. Bank of Montreal and Vancouver Stock Exchange, 1928-30; returned to England, 1931; employed by British Gas Light Co. and Philips Lamps Ltd, 1932-39. Civil Defence forces, 1939-40. Min. of Information, 1940-45. Asst-Dir, British Information Services, Chicago, 1945-46; Dir, 1947-56; UK High Commission, New Delhi, 1956-58; First Sec., British Embassy, Washington, DC, 1958-60; Dir, Press Division, British Information Services, New York, 1960-62; temp. appt, Brussels, 1962; Consul, St Louis, 1962-64; Consul-Gen., New Orleans, 1964-69. *Recreations:* travel, fishing, reading, gardening. *Address:* 15 Palmeira Avenue, Hove, East Sussex. *T:* Brighton 735164. *Clubs:* Travellers'; Pickwick, Plimsoll, (New Orleans). *[Died 28 Nov. 1976.*

BARFOOT, Most Rev. Walter Foster, DD (Hon.) 1937; DD (Lambeth), 1958; Primate of All Canada, 1951-Dec. 1958; *b* 17 Oct. 1893; *m* 1942. *Educ:* Wycliffe Coll., Toronto, BA 1923; Univ. of Toronto, MA 1930. Deacon, 1922; priest 1923; Tutor at Em. Coll., Saskatoon, 1926-33, Prof., 1933-34; Prof. of St John's Coll., Winnipeg, 1934-35. Warden, 1935-41; Canon of St John's Cathedral, Winnipeg, 1934-41; Bishop of Edmonton 1941-51, Archbishop, 1951-53; Archbishop and Metropolitan of Rupert's Land. 1953-60; retired Dec. 1960. Served European War, 1915-19. Capt. 2nd Royal Sussex Regt (Croix de Guerre). *Address:* 2803 West 41st Avenue, Suite 235, Vancouver, BC V6N 4B4, Canada. *[Died 28 June 1978.*

BARFORD, Edward, MC 1918; Landowner; *b* 23 April 1898; *m* 1st, 1928, Hon. Grace Lowrey Stanley (from whom he obtained a divorce, 1940), *yr d* of 1st and last Baron Ashfield; one *s* two *d*; 2nd, 1944, Mrs June Johnstone (marr. diss. 1963); one *s*; 3rd, 1964, Hon. Mrs Marian Hubbard (marr. diss. 1970), *er d* of 1st and last Baron Ashfield. *Educ:* Rugby. Enlisted, European War, 1915 (wounded twice, despatches twice), Acting Major 1918. Founded Aveling-Barford Ltd, 1933; Chm., 1933-68. Under-writing Member of Lloyd's. *Publication:* Reminiscences of a Lance Corporal of Industry, 1972. *Address:* 29 Kingston House North, SW7. *T:* 01-584 4425. *Clubs:* Buck's, Boodle's. *[Died 11 July 1979.*

BARGE, Lieut-Col Kenneth, DSO 1918; MC; psc; DL; JP; late 17th Cavalry Indian Army; *b* 1883; *s* of Robert Henry Barge; *m* 1915, Debonnaire Eva Ruth (*d* 1959), *o c* of late Maj.-Gen. Sir Herbert Mansfield, KCB; one *s* two *d* (and one *s* killed in action). *Educ:* Larchfield; Trinity Coll., Glenalmond. Served in S Africa with 3rd Argyll and Sutherland Highlanders, 1901 (Queen's medal two clasps); Cameronians, India, 1903-5; joined 17th Cavalry Indian Army, 1905; served European War, 1914-18 (despatches thrice, MC, DSO); The Order of the Serbian White Eagle while serving in the Balkans at the end of the War; ADC, OC Northern Army, 1909-10; ADC, C-in-C India, 1911-12; Adjutant, Imperial Cadet Corps, 1913-14; GSO3, Brigade Major, GSO2, GSO1, 1914-18; retired, 1922; Mem. of Queen's Body Guard for Scotland, Royal Company of Archers. *Recreation:* active farmer still! *Address:* Armadale, Rhu, Dunbartonshire. *T:* Rhu 202. *TA:* Rhu; Evanachan Farm, Otter Ferry, Argyll. *T:* Kilfinan 214.   *[Died 7 Jan. 1971.*

BARHAM, Rt. Rev. E(dward) Lawrence; an Assistant Bishop of Southwark, 1967-71; Incumbent of Emmanuel Church, Wimbledon, 1967-71; *b* 25 June 1901; *s* of Harold and Florence Barham; *m* 1931, Julia Mary Bazett Leakey; three *s* two *d. Educ:* Merchant Taylors' Sch.; Gonville and Caius Coll., Cambridge; Ridley Hall, Cambridge. Deacon, 1925; Priest, 1926. Curate of St James', Hatcham (Southwark), 1925-28; CMS Missionary: Uganda, 1928-38; Ruanda-Urundi, 1938-57; Canon of Uganda, 1939; Archdeacon of Nkore-Kigezi (Uganda), 1957-59; General Sec., Ruanda Mission (CMS), London, 1959-64; Bishop of Rwanda and Burundi, 1964-66; Examining Chaplain to the Bishop of Southwark, 1968-71. Médaille D'Or, Ordre Royal du Lion (Belgium), 1955. *Address:* 1 Gloucester Avenue, Bexhill-on-Sea, Sussex. *T:* Bexhill 217462.   *[Died 5 June 1973.*

BARKER, Cecil; see Barker, H. C. J.

BARKER, Sir (Charles Frederic) James, Kt 1970; MBE 1944; Chairman, Unigate Ltd, 1970-77 (Chief Executive, 1970-72; Joint Chief Executive, 1972-73); *b* 17 Feb. 1914; *s* of Charles F. J. Barker and Ethel (*née* Brooke), Walton-on-the-Naze; *m* 1940, Thora Daphne (*d* 1978), *d* of Amos Perry and Nancy (*née* Aspland); two *s. Educ:* Royal Grammar Sch., Colchester. Served War of 1939-45, Wilts Regt (Major): Staff Coll., 1943; GSO2, 43rd Wessex Division. L. Rose & Co. Ltd, 1934-39 and 1948; Man. Dir, 1957; Schweppes Ltd, 1958-69: Dir, 1962; Man. Dir, 1969; Dir, Cadbury Schweppes Ltd, 1962-71. Mem., Central London Regional Board, Lloyds Bank, 1976-. Chairman: CCAHC, 1975-80; CBI Employment Policy Cttee, 1976-77. FBIM, 1965; Fellow, Inst. Grocery Distribution, 1973. President: Food Manufacturers Fedn, 1967-70; Dairy Trade Fedn, 1973-75; British Food Manufacturing Industries Res. Assoc., 1974-. Croix de Guerre, 1944. *Recreations:* sailing, reading, family. *Address:* New Hall, Thorpe-le-Soken, Essex. *T:* Thorpe-le-Soken 507. *Clubs:* Carlton, Farmers'; Walton and Frinton Yacht.   *[Died 29 April 1980.*

BARKER, Air Vice-Marshal Clifford Cockcroft, CBE 1960; AFC 1944; MB, ChB; Principal Medical Officer, Training Command, 1968-69 (Technical Training Command, 1966-68), retired; *b* 19 Sept. 1909; *s* of late Dr A. C. Barker, Hull; *m* 1939, Diana (*née* Coxhead), Exmouth, Devon; one *s* one *d. Educ:* Trent Coll.; Edinburgh Univ. Joined RAF, 1936; Iraq, 1937-39; PMO Ferry Comd, Canada, 1943-44 (King's Commendation); India, 1944-45 (despatches); Flying Personnel MO in UK, 1945-50; Aden, 1950-52; CO Headley Court, 1952-54; SHAPE, 1954-57; CO, RAF Hosp., Wroughton, 1957-61; CO, RAF Hosp., Halton, 1961-62; PMO Bomber Comd, 1962-63; Far East Air Force, 1963-65. QHP 1966-69. *Recreation:* formerly Rugby football (Capt. Edinburgh Univ., 1932-33). *Address:* 34 Greenway Lane, Budleigh Salterton, Devon. *Club:* Royal Air Force.   *[Died 10 April 1977.*

BARKER, Douglas William Ashley, CMG 1966; Secretary to the Treasury, New Zealand, 1965-66; *b* 19 Sept. 1905; *s* of John Joseph and Annie Barker; *m* 1934, Elsie May Owen; one *s* one *d. Educ:* Palmerston North Boys' High Sch.; Victoria Univ. Coll., Wellington; LSE. Joined NZ Treasury, 1922; seconded NZ High Comr's Office, London, 1934; Treasury, NZ, 1937. Dir, Cable Price Downer Ltd, 1967. *Recreations:* bowls, golf, gardening. *Address:* 7 Amritsar Street, Wellington, NZ. *T:* 797151. *Club:* Civil Service (Wellington, NZ).   *[Died 17 Jan. 1978.*

BARKER, (Harold) Cecil (James), CMG 1949; retired; *b* 27 May 1893; *s* of late Harold Hastings Barker, MBE; *m* 1922, Sylvia Mary Stanford; one *s* one *d. Educ:* Woolwich. Farming in S Rhodesia, 1912-14. Served European War, 1914-18, German SW Africa, in Imperial Light Horse, 1914-15; E Africa, in Rhodesian Service Column, attached BSAP, 1915-16; commissioned in 1/1 KAR, 1916-18. Nyasaland Administration (Provincial Commissioner), 1919-52; seconded as Political Liaison Officer, Staff HQ, Nairobi, 1939-40. *Address:* 83 Westcliff Road, Hermanus, CP, South Africa. *T:* 31.
[Died 1 Jan. 1974.

BARKER, Sir James; see Barker, Sir C. F. J.

BARKER, Lancelot Elliot; Metropolitan Stipendiary Magistrate since 1960; *b* 29 Feb. 1908; *s* of Elliot Francis Barker and Margaretha Maria (*née* Walker); *m* 1937, Sylvia Marvell Haworth-Booth. *Educ:* Westminster Sch.; Trinity Coll., Cambridge (MA). BA Hons in Law, 1929. Admitted Solicitor of Supreme Court, Dec. 1932. Partner in firm of Wontner & Sons, solicitors, 1935-60. *Recreations:* riding; photography; formerly athletics (University Relay Team *v* Oxford, 1928). *Address:* The Walled House, 87 Christ Church Road, East Sheen, SW14. *T:* 01-876 6956. *Clubs:* United Oxford & Cambridge University; MCC.   *[Died 4 July 1972.*

BARKER, Ronald Ernest, OBE 1968; author; Joint Secretary The Publishers Association; Director: Book Development Council Ltd; Standard Book Numbering Agency Ltd; Publishers' Information Cards Services Ltd; Vice-Chairman, British Copyright Council; *b* 22 Dec. 1920; *s* of Charles Jacob and Margaret Grace Barker; *m* 1941, Joyce Edith Wynne; one *s* one *d* (and one *s* decd). *Educ:* largely war-time reading. Served War of 1939-45, demobilized as Captain (non-med.) RAMC, 1946. Publishers Assoc.: apptd Asst Sec. (Export), 1947; Dep. Sec., 1950; Secretary, 1958-. Curtis Brown Ltd, Literary Agents, 1956-58. Mem., Crime Writers' Assoc.; Hon. Mem., Soc. of Bookmen. Koninklijke Nederlandsche Uitgeversbond Medal of Honour, 1968. *Publications:* Books for All: a study of international book trade, 1956; (ed jtly) Books Are Different: the defence of the Net Book Agreement, 1966; Photocopying Practices in the United Kingdom, 1970; (ed jtly) The Book Hunger, 1973; *novels:* Tendency to Corrupt, 1957; The Days are Long, 1959; *thrillers:* Clue for Murder, 1962; and, as E. B. Ronald (*pseudonym*): Cat and Fiddle Murders, 1954; Death by Proxy, 1956; A Sort of Madness, 1958; contributor to The Bookseller, The Author, etc. on copyright and other book trade subjects. *Recreations:* cooking, swimming, listening to music. *Address:* Desmond House, Romanhurst Avenue, Bromley, Kent BR2 0PF. *T:* 01-464 2885.   *[Died 22 May 1976.*

BARKER, Dame Sara Elizabeth, DBE 1970; *b* 15 Feb. 1904; *d* of late George Barker and late Ethel Barker (*née* Brier). *Educ:* Siddal Elementary Sch., Halifax; Halifax Technical Coll. Sec.-Agent to Halifax Labour Party, 1935-42; Woman Organiser of Labour Party for Yorks, 1942-52; Labour Party: Asst Nat. Agent, 1952-60; Sen. Asst Nat. Agent and Chief Woman Officer, 1960-62; Nat. Agent, 1962-69. *Publication:* (pamphlet) How the Labour Party Works, 1946. Editor, Labour Organiser. *Recreations:* reading, music, walking. *Address:* 4 Chevin Edge Crescent, Exley, Halifax, Yorks. *T:* Halifax 535917.
[Died 19 Sept. 1973.

BARLEY, Lieut-Col Leslie John, DSO 1917; late Royal Engineers and Cameronians; *b* Gosport, 7 July 1890; *s* of Rev. A. G. Barley; *m* 1915, Muriel More (*d* 1978), *d* of James Kerr Love, LLD, MD, Glasgow; two *d. Educ:* Taunton Sch.; University Coll., Southampton; Kiel Univ.; Queen's Coll., Oxford. MA (Hons Chemistry) Oxon; BSc (London); Commissioned The Cameronians, June 1913; 1st Batt. France, Dec. 1914; when first gas attack occurred made one of first efficient respirators, instituted the gas-proof dugout and other methods of protection and training of troops in anti-gas measures; Army Chemical Adviser, June 1915; Asst Dir and Head, Gas Services, Italy, Nov. 1917; Superintendent Anti-Gas Dept (Ministry of Munitions), 1919 (despatches thrice, DSO; Croix de Guerre, 1918; Cavalier of the Order of St Maurice and St Lazarus of Jerusalem, 1918; brevet majority, 1918; Officer of the Order of the Crown of Italy, 1919); Head of Development Dept of Nobel Industries Ltd, 1919, and of ICI Ltd, 1926 (ICI Ltd was founded on his Memoranda to Sir Harry McGowan which he now has permission to publish); re-employed with RE, 1939-43, served in most Overseas Commands and USA with Chemical Warfare Liaison Mission, 1942. Pacific Relations Conf., 1947. Overseas Development Controller of ICI Ltd until retirement, 1952. *Publications:* Set of Lectures on Chemical Defence, 1915; Use of Smoke in Mountain Warfare, 1918; The Riddle of Rationalisation, 1932; (part) A Food Plan for India, 1945; working on autobiography (section relating to Chemical Defence in First World War is on tape at Imperial War Museum) and on publication on world food and population problem. *Address:* 12 Dore Road, Dore, Sheffield S17 3NB.
[Died 7 Sept. 1979.

BARLOW, Sir Frank (Herbert),Kt 1979; CBE 1965; Secretary, Parliamentary Labour Party, since 1959; *b* 14 Jan. 1918; *s* of Charles and Emma Barlow; *m* 1946, Diana, *yr d* of Harold and Ethel Kippin. *Educ:* John Ruskin Grammar Sch., Croydon, Surrey. Joined staff of PLP, 1937; Cttee Clerk, 1944; Asst Sec., 1947. *Recreations:* philately, studying Parliamentary Labour history, art. *Address:* The Bungalow, Convent Lane, Burwood, Cobham, Surrey. *T:* 01-266 2695.   *[Died 14 Aug. 1979.*

BARLOW, James; Novelist; *b* 1 Dec. 1921; *s* of late Stanley Barlow and of Gladys Barlow; *m* 1949, Joyce Margaret Everiss, *d* of Alfred and Lily Everiss; three *s* one *d. Educ:* schools at Leamington Spa, Potteries, North Wales. Joined City of Birmingham Water Dept, 1939; joined RAF, 1940, invalided out, 1941; returned after illness to City of Birmingham Water Dept; retired 1960, to follow writing career full time. Wrote articles for Aeroplane and Flight, 1944; for Punch, 1948-53 then began writing novels. *Publications:* The Protagonists, 1956; One Half of the World, 1957; The Man with Good Intentions, 1958; The Patriots, 1960; Term of Trial, 1961; The Hour of Maximum

Danger, 1962; This Side of the Sky, 1964; One Man in the World, 1966; The Love Chase, 1968; The Burden of Proof, 1968; Goodbye, England, 1969; Liner, 1970; Both your Houses, 1971; In all Good Faith, 1971. *Recreations:* photography, motoring, collecting beer and wine labels, watching, listening and reading. *Address:* c/o Charles Lavell Ltd, 176 Wardour Street, W1V 3AA.   *[Died 30 Jan. 1973.*

BARLOW, Ralph Mitford Marriott, MA Cantab; *b* 3 Jan. 1904; *s* of late H. G. Barlow, late of Clifton College, Bristol; *m* 1934, Agnes Margaret, 2nd *d* of late G. M. Carey, Sherborne; one *s* two *d. Educ:* Clifton College; Corpus Christi College, Cambridge (Choral Scholar). Assistant Master and House Master, Sherborne School, Dorset, 1926-48; Warden of Trinity College, Glenalmond, 1948-64. *Recreations:* fishing, walking, gardening; formerly Rugby football (Cambridge University XV, 1925; English Trial Cap, 1926). *Address:* Brook House, Chew Stoke, Bristol. *T:* Chew Magna 2488.   *[Died 1 Feb. 1977.*

BARLOW, Sir Robert, Kt 1944; President of the Metal Box Company since 1961 (formerly Chairman); *b* 1 September 1891; *s* of Edward Charles and Annie Eleanor Barlow; *m* 1942, Margaret Rawlings, actress; one *d. Educ:* Grocer's Company's School. *Address:* Rocketer, Wendover, Bucks. *T:* Wendover 2234.   *[Died 30 Sept. 1976.*

BARMAN, Christian August, OBE 1963; RDI; Past President, Society of Industrial Artists; *b* 1898. *Educ:* University of Liverpool School of Architecture. Editor, the Architect's Journal and the Architectural Review; Publicity Officer, London Passenger Transport Bd, 1935-41; was generally responsible for the visual presentation of the undertaking to the public; Asst Dir of Post-War Building, Min. of Works, 1941-45; Public Relations Adviser, GWR, 1945-47; Chief Publicity Officer, British Transport Commn, 1947-62; Exec. Mem., BTC Design Panel, 1956-62. *Publications:* Sir John Vanbrugh, 1924; edition of James Gibbs, Rules for Drawing the various Parts of Architecture, 1925; Balbus, or the Future of Architecture, 1926; Architecture: An Introduction for the General Reader, 1927; Next Station, 1947 (repr. as The Great Western Railway's Last Look Forward, 1972); Public Transport (The Things We See Series), 1949; Early British Railways, 1950; Introduction to Railway Architecture, 1950; The Man who built London Transport, 1979; under pseudonym Christian Mawson: Ramping Cat (a novel), 1941; Portrait of England (an anthology), 1941. *Address:* 12a Hillbrow, Reading, Berks.
[Died 5 Oct. 1980.

BARNARD, Beverley Gayer, CMG 1959; consultant on Middle East Affairs, since 1959; *b* 4 Aug. 1916; *s* of late Frederick William Barnard, Thursley, Surrey; *m* 1945, Joan Anne Mary (*née* Fernandes); three *s. Educ:* Imperial Coll. of Science and Technology, London. Television research, Scophony Ltd, 1938-40; Westland Aircraft Ltd, Yeovil, 1940-41; Royal Aircraft Establishment, Farnborough, 1941-44; CCG, Advance Element, 1944-46; Civil Air Attaché at Baghdad, Teheran and Persian Gulf, 1947-52; Civil Air Attaché in the Middle East (resident at Cairo and Beirut), 1952-59. *Recreations:* painting, making films, golf. *Address:* 46 New Dover Road, Canterbury, Kent.
[Died 5 Sept. 1973.

BARNARD, Eric, CB 1951; CBE 1943; DSO 1917; MA (Oxon), Deputy Secretary, Department of Scientific and Industrial Research, 1945-55; *b* 19 Sept. 1891; *s* of Edward John Barnard, Exmouth, Devon; *m* 1923, Marjorie Cecil, *d* of Hugh Walters; one *s* one *d. Educ:* University Coll., Oxford. Gloucestershire Regt, 1914-19 (DSO, despatches twice). Entered Civil Service, 1919. *Address:* Milland Place Hotel, Liphook, Hants.
[Died 11 Oct. 1980.

BARNARD, Vice-Adm. (Retd) Sir Geoffrey, KCB 1957 (CB 1953); CBE 1943; DSO 1941, Bar, 1945; Légion d'Honneur; Croix de Guerre (with Palm); *b* 12 Nov. 1902; *s* of T. H. Barnard, JP, Banker, Bedford and Bertha Mary Lambton; *m* 1926, Julyan Frances Crawley; one *s* two *d. Educ:* Cheam Sch.; RNC Dartmouth. Specialised in Gunnery, 1927; Fleet Gunnery Officer, Africa Station; Comdr, 1935; commanded HMS Daring, China Station; Staff Course, 1937; Fleet Gunnery Officer, Mediterranean (HMS Warspite), 1939-41; Capt. 1942; Dep. Chief of Staff to Naval C-in-C for North African landings, 1942, and subsequently to C-in-C Mediterranean, 1942-43; commanded HMS Aurora, Mediterranean 1944-45; Chief Staff Officer to Flag Officer (Air), 1946-47; Dir Royal Naval Tactical Sch., 1948-49. Lent to Indian Navy for command of IN Squadron, 1950-51; Rear-Adm, 1951; Asst Chief of Naval Staff (Warfare), 1952-53; a Lord Commissioner of the Admiralty and Deputy Chief of Naval Staff, 1953-54; Admiral, British Joint Services Mission, Washington, 1954-56; Pres. of the Royal

Naval Coll., Greenwich, 1956-Dec. 1958; retired, 1959. *Recreations:* gardening and fishing. *Address:* 109 Sussex Road, Petersfield, Hants. *T:* Petersfield 4327. *Club:* English-Speaking Union.   *[Died 19 Dec. 1974.*

BARNELL, Herbert Rex, MA, PhD (Cantab); BSc (London); Chief Scientific Adviser (Food), Ministry of Agriculture, Fisheries and Food, 1959-68, retired; *b* 8 Nov. 1907; *o s* of Herbert Joseph Barnell, Luton, Beds.; *m* 1933, Elsie Eileen, 3rd *d* of D. McCullough, Capetown. *Educ:* Luton Modern Sch.; Downing Coll., Cambridge. 1st Class Hons Pt II Nat. Sci. Tripos (Botany); Frank Smart Univ. Prize (Botany) and Univ. Studentship (Botany). Research Asst and Lectr in Plant Physiology, Sch. of Agric., Cambridge, 1932-37; Plant Biochemist on staff of Imperial Coll. of Trop. Agric., Trinidad (Low Temperature Research Stn, Research on storage and transport of trop. fruits and vegs), 1937-43. Various scientific posts in Min. of Food and in combined Min. of Agric., Fisheries and Food. FIBiol; Fellow, Institute of Food Science and Technology. *Publications:* papers on plant physiology, plant biochem. and food technology in various scientific jls. *Recreations:* sea fishing; reading. *Address:* 22b Radnor Cliff, Folkestone, Kent. *T:* Folkestone 38484. *Clubs:* Athenæum, Authors', New Arts Theatre, Royal Commonwealth Society.
                                                      [Died 26 May 1973.

BARNES, Rt. Hon. Alfred; PC 1945; a Designer by trade; *b* North Woolwich, 1887. *Art Educ:* Northampton Institute; LCC Sch. of Arts and Crafts. MP (Lab-Co-op) South East Ham, 1922-31 and 1935-55; Lord Commissioner of the Treasury, 1929-30; Minister of War Transport, 1945-46, Minister of Transport, 1946-51; Chairman of the Co-operative Party, 1924-45. *Address:* Eastcliffe Hotel, Walton-on-the-Naze, Essex.
                                                      [Died 26 Nov. 1974.

BARNES, Anthony Charles, DSO 1916; OBE 1943; Past Director of Barclays Bank DCO (Deputy Chairman, 1947-59), and of Barclays Bank Ltd. (Vice-Chairman, 1951-56); *yr s* of late Sir George Barnes, KCB, KCSI; *b* 13 October 1891; *m* 1920, Honor Dorothea, *d* of late Stanley V. Coote, JP; one *s* two *d. Educ:* Eton; New Coll., Oxford (BA). Served with 9th Batt. Yorkshire Regt, Sept. 1914-April 1918; commanded 4th (Territorial) Batt. Yorkshire Regt, June 1918-Oct. 1918, and 15th Batt. the Durham Light Infantry, Oct. 1918-April 1919 (DSO and bar, despatches thrice). Mem. Joint Anglo-Egyptian Cotton Commn, 1941; a Trustee of the Whiteley Homes; Chm. Guildford Diocesan Bd of Finance, 1961-64. *Recreation:* gardening. *Address:* Foxholm, Cobham, Surrey KT11 1EF. *T:* Byfleet 45183. *Club:* Brooks's.   *[Died 11 Sept. 1974.*

BARNES, Dr John Morrison, CBE 1962; Director, Toxicology Unit, Medical Research Council Laboratories, Carshalton, since 1947; *b* 11 Jan. 1913; *s* of Dr A. E. Barnes, Sheffield; *m* 1941, Ruth Eleanor, *d* of Rev. Edward Joseph Northcote-Green, Oxford; two *s* one *d. Educ:* Repton; Trinity Hall, Cambridge. BA 1933; MB, BCh, MRCS, LRCP, 1936. Served War of 1939-45; RAMC, 1942-45 (Lieut-Col). *Recreations:* none. *Address:* 16 Holmwood Gardens, Wallington, Surrey. *T:* 01-647 1388.
                                                      [Died 24 Sept. 1975.

BARNETT, Sir Ben L(ewis), KBE 1952; CB 1948; MC 1918; MA; *b* London 20 July 1894; *s* of Isaac and Eva Barnett. *Educ:* Christ's Hospital; Trinity Coll., Cambridge. Entered GPO, 1920; Principal, 1930; Telecoms Controller, Scotland, 1935; Asst Sec. (HQ), 1939; Reg. Dir, Home Counties Region, 1945; Dir Inland Telecommunications, 1946; Dep. Dir-Gen., GPO, 1949-56. Chm., Commonwealth Telecommunications Board, 1956-62. Director: Pye Ltd; Telephone Manufacturing Co. Ltd; Unidare Ltd (Dublin); Adviser to: ATV Ltd; Western Union International, 1958-69. Served European War, 1914-18. Lieut RE (TA) (despatches twice, MC). OStJ 1959. Hon. FIEE, 1973. *Address:* c/o Barclays Bank Ltd, 110 Bishopsgate, EC2.
                                                      [Died 25 Nov. 1979.

BARNETT, Rev. Dr Maurice; Minister, Westminster Central Hall, London, since 1964; *b* Coppenhall, Crewe, 21 March 1917; *s* of Edward Percy and Beatrice Barnett; *m* 1943, Margaret Brown, Chester; one *s. Educ:* Crewe Grammar Sch.; Hartley Victoria Coll., The University, Manchester. BA Manchester, 1939, BD 1941, MA 1946; PhD Sheffield, 1960. Minister, East Ham Central Hall, 1941-43; Eden Grove Methodist Church, Bristol, 1943-46; Tutor, Cliff Coll., Derbyshire, 1946-47; Minister, Eastbrook Hall, Bradford, 1947-64. Hon. FLCM, 1973. *Publications:* The Living Flame, 1953; This Concerns You, 1954; What Next?, 1954; New Life Now, 1976; The Divine Invasion, 1976; articles, etc. *Recreations:* organ and piano. *Address:* Westminster Central Hall, SW1. *T:* 01-930 1801.
                                                      [Died 9 April 1980.

BARNIE, Mrs Donald; *see* Veitch, Marian.

BARNS, Rev. Prof. John Wintour Baldwin, MA, DPhil; (Queen's) Professor of Egyptology, Oxford University, since 1965; *b* 12 May 1912; *o s* of late William Henry Barns and of Helen Maria (*née* Baldwin), Bristol; *m* 1954, Dorothy Eileen Constance, *e d* of late Col W. E. Sturges, Clevedon. *Educ:* Fairfield Sch., Bristol; Bristol Univ.; Corpus Christi Coll., Oxford. BA Bristol, 1932; Classical Scholar Corpus Christi Coll., Oxford, 1933; BA 1937; MA 1942; DPhil 1947. Foreign Office, 1940-45; Lady Wallis Budge Research Fellow in Egyptology at university Coll., Oxford, 1945-53; Lectr in Papyrology in Univ. of Oxford, 1953-65. S Stephen's House, Oxford; deacon, 1955; priest, 1956. British Academy award, 1963. *Publications:* The Ashmolean Ostracon of Sinuhe, 1952; Five Ramesseum Papyri, 1956; Part XXIV of Oxyrhynchus Papyri (with E. Lobel, E. G. Turner, C. H. Roberts), 1957; Merton Papyri, vol. II (with Sir Harold Idris Bell and B. R. Rees), 1959; Part II of Antinoopolis Papyri (with H. Zilliacus), 1960; Part XXXI of Oxyrhynchus Papyri (with P. J. Parsons, J. Rea, E. G. Turner), 1966; Part III of Antinoopolis Papyri (with H. Zilliacus), 1967; Four Martyrdoms from the Pierpont Morgan Coptic Codices (with E. A. E. Reymond), 1973; articles in Journal of Egyptian Archaeology, Classical Quarterly, Chronique d'Egypte, Journal of Theological Studies, etc. *Recreations:* preservation of tradition, antiquities and nature; church music and madrigals; cats. *Address:* 23 Victoria Road, Abingdon, Berks. *T:* Abingdon 711. *Club:* United Oxford & Cambridge University.   *[Died 23 Jan. 1974.*

BARON, Cyril Faudel Joseph, MRCS, LRCP; Barrister-at-law; HM Coroner for County of Greater London (Western District), 1965-68 (Surrey, 1939-64); *b* 22 Jan. 1903; *s* of John and Lily Baron; *m* 1933, Kathleen Julia, *d* of Henry and Hilda Jacob; one *d. Educ:* Owen's Sch.; University Coll., London; St Bartholomew's Hospital (Wix Prize, 1923), MRCS, LRCP, 1924; Bar Final (1st Class Criminal Law), 1926. Practised medicine, 1924-36; called to Bar Middle Temple, 1936; practised at Bar (Common Law) from 1936. Pres., Coroners' Soc. of England and Wales; Vice-Pres., Medico-legal Soc.; Hon. Sec., Association of Whole-time Coroners. *Publications:* Doctor at the Bar, 1977; various articles on medico-legal subjects in learned journals. *Recreations:* tennis, swimming, foreign travel. *Address:* The Spinney, More Lane, Esher, Surrey. *T:* Esher 64240.   *[Died 12 July 1978.*

BARRACLOUGH, Frank, CBE 1951; Secretary for Education, North Riding of Yorkshire, 1934-65; *b* 22 March 1901; *yr s* of George and Eleanor Barraclough, Bradford; *m* 1930, Barbara, *y d* of Samuel and Mary Clegg, New Sawley, Long Eaton; one *s. Educ:* Bradford Grammar Sch.; Queen's Coll., Oxford. Hon. Scholar, Queen's Coll., Oxford, 1919; MA 1926. Tutor, Borough Road Training Coll., Isleworth, 1925-28; Asst Master, Clifton Coll., Bristol, 1928-31; Technical Officer, Leeds Education Cttee, 1931-32; Vice-Principal, Leeds Technical Coll., 1932-34; Asst Sec., North Riding Education Cttee, 1934. Hon. Treasurer, Association of Education Cttees, 1948-65; Member: Burnham Cttees, 1948-65; Loveday Cttee on Agricultural Education, 1944; Cttee on Cadet Entry to Royal Navy, 1952; Pres., Assoc. of Education Officers, 1954. *Address:* 72 Thirsk Road, Northallerton, Yorks. *T:* Northallerton 2286. *Club:* United Oxford & Cambridge University.   *[Died 26 Nov. 1974.*

BARRAN, Sir John (Leighton), 3rd Bt, *cr* 1895; *b* 24 March 1904; *e s* of Sir John Barran, 2nd Bt and Alice Margarita (*d* 1939), *d* of Rev. Leighton Parks, DD, New York City; *S* father 1952; *m* 1929, Hon. Alison Mary Hore-Ruthven (*d* 1973), 3rd *d* of 9th Baron Ruthven, CB, CMG, DSO; one *s. Educ:* Winchester Coll.; Trinity Coll., Cambridge. BA (Cambridge), 1925. Served War of 1939-45, Lieut Royal Naval Volunteer Reserve, 1939; Comdr, 1945. CC for Pateley Bridge, West Riding of Yorks, 1952; JP W Riding, Yorks, 1952. *Heir: s* John Napoleon Ruthven Barran [*b* 14 Feb. 1934; *m* 1965, Jane Margaret, *d* of Sir Stanley Hooker, CBE, FRS; one *s*]. *Address:* The Hermitage, East Bergholt, near Colchester, Essex. *T:* East Bergholt 236. *Club:* Bath.
                                                      [Died 28 Dec. 1974.

BARRATT, Sir Charles, Kt 1966; LLB; Town Clerk and Clerk of the Peace for the City of Coventry, 1946-70; *b* Huddersfield, 27 May 1910; *s* of late H. T. Barratt; *m* 1938, Kathleen Mary, *d* of late E. M. Johnson; two *d. Educ:* Royds Hall Grammar Sch.; Leeds Univ. Articled pupil, Huddersfield County Borough Council; Asst Solicitor, Halifax County Borough Council, 1931-35; Dep. Town Clerk: Rochdale County Borough Council, 1935-41; Coventry City Council, 1941-46. Univ. of Warwick: Sec., Promotion Cttee, 1961-65; Sec., Academic Planning Bd, 1961-65; Mem. Council, 1965-. Council for National Academic Awards: Mem. Legal Studies Board, 1966-; Mem., Public

Administration Bd, 1968-. President: Coventry Sch. of Music, 1964- (Chm., Management Cttee, 1950-63); Coventry and Warwicks Council on Alcoholism, 1969-; Soc. of Town Clerks, 1969-70; Chm., Crafts Council of Great Britain, 1969-; Member: Cttee on Local Authority and Allied Personal Social Services (Seebohm Cttee), 1965-68; Exec. Council, Town Clerks' Soc., 1963-70; Local Authorities' Management Services and Computer Cttee, 1966-70 (Chm., Technical Adv. Sub-Cttee, 1966-70); AMC Law Cttee, 1965-70; AMC Management Techniques Gp, 1965-70; Local Govt Training Bd, 1967; Adv. Council, Civil Service Coll., 1970-. *Publications:* Your Local Authority; numerous articles and reviews in technical jls. *Recreations:* travel, music, gardening, sailing (Cdre, Banbury Sailing Club, 1962-64; Chm., Draycote Water Steering Cttee, 1967-69; Cdre, Draycote Water Sailing Club, 1969-). *Address:* Kenilworth Lodge, Kenilworth, Warwicks. *T:* Kenilworth 54317.   *[Died 10 Feb. 1971.*

BARRATT, Major Stanley George Reeves E.; *see* Elton-Barratt.

BARRATT, Sir Sydney, Kt 1961; Chairman, Albright & Wilson Ltd, 1958-67, retired; *b* 11 Aug. 1898; *s* of Peter Barratt; *m* 1927, Isabel Vaughan Lucas; one *s* one *d. Educ:* Clifton Coll., Bristol; Balliol Coll., Oxford. BA 1920. Lecturer in Chemistry, University of Leeds, 1922-24, UCL 1924-32; Asst Dir of Research, Albright & Wilson Ltd, 1932; Director: Albright & Wilson Ltd, 1938; Joseph Lucas Ltd, 1959-68. Pres., Soc. of Chemical Industry, 1963-65. A Pro-Chancellor of Bath Univ., 1970-; Chairman: Clifton Coll. Council, 1958-67 (Pres., 1967-72); Ramsay Memorial Fellowships Trustees, 1954. Hon. Fellow, UCL, 1960. Hon. LLD Manchester, 1964; Hon. DSc Bath, 1972. *Address:* Thalatta, Higher Sea Lane, Charmouth, Dorset.   *[Died 28 Aug. 1975.*

BARRETT, Col John Cridlan, VC 1918; TD; DL; FRCS 1928; Emeritus Surgeon, Leicester Royal Infirmary (Senior Surgeon, 1945-62); *b* 10 Aug. 1897; *er s* of late Josephus Teague and Fanny Ada Barrett; *m* 1935, Ernestine Helen, *o c* of late Ernest and Edith Wright, Leics. *Educ:* Merchant Taylors' Sch.; St Thomas' Hosp. LRCP 1924; MB, BS (London) 1925. Joined Army, Jan. 1916; served in France (VC for 24 Sept. 1918; thrice severely wounded). Commanded 5th Bn, Royal Leics Regt, 1937-39 (Hon. Col, 1953-58). Formerly Consulting Surgeon: Leicester Isolation Hosp. and Sanatorium; City Gen. Hosp., Leicester; formerly Surgeon, Hinckley and District Hosp. Pres., Provincial Surgical Club of Great Britain, 1961-63; Hon. Vice-Pres., Leics Br. of BRCS, 1971- (Dir, 1962-67, Dep. Pres., 1967-71); Mem. Council, RCS, 1958-66. DL Leics, 1951. *Recreations:* swimming, philately. *Address:* Selby Lodge, 11 Southernhay Road, Leicester. *T:* 708309.   *[Died 7 March 1977.*

BARRETT, Norman Rupert, CBE 1969; FRCS 1930; retired 1970; Surgeon to King Edward VII Sanatorium, Midhurst, 1938-70; Consulting Thoracic Surgeon to Royal Navy and to Ministry of Social Security, 1944-70; Lecturer in Surgery, University of London, 1935-70; Formerly: Senior Surgeon, St Thomas' Hospital; Surgeon, Brompton Hospital; *b* Adelaide, Australia, 16 May 1903; *o s* of late Alfred Barrett, Sussex; *m* 1931, Elizabeth, *d* of late H. Warington Smyth, CMG; two *d. Educ:* Eton Coll., Trinity Coll., Cambridge (1st class Hons Natural Science Tripos, 1925, MA 1930); St Thomas' Hosp. (MB 1928, MChir 1931). Rockefeller Travelling Fellowship, 1935; Visiting Professor of Surgery: Royal North Shore Hosp., Sydney, 1963; Cleveland Metropolitan Gen. Hosp., USA. Formerly Examiner in Surgery: Univs of Cambridge, Oxford, Birmingham, London, Khartoum; RCS. Hunterian Prof., RCS, 1955, and Arris and Gale Lectr, RCS, 1957, 1959; Thomas Vicary Lectr, 1970; Tudor Edwards Lectr, 1970. President: Thoracic Surgeons of Great Britain and Ireland, 1962; The Thoracic Soc., 1963. Fellow, Assoc. of Surgeons of Great Britain and Ireland. Member: Council, RCS, 1962-74, Vice-Pres., 1972; Tuberculosis Assoc. Hon. Mem., Amer. Assoc. for Thoracic Surgery. Editor of Thorax, 1946-71. *Publications:* many papers on surgical and historical subjects; contribs to many textbooks of surgery. *Recreation:* yacht cruising. *Address:* Old Palace Place, Richmond Green, Surrey. *T:* 01-940 3834. *Club:* Royal Corinthian Yacht.   *[Died 8 Jan. 1979.*

BARRETT-LENNARD, Sir (Thomas) Richard F.; *see* Lennard.

BARRINGTON, His Honour John Harcourt, TD; County Court Judge, 1955-70, retired; *b* 3 March 1907; *s* of late George Harcourt Barrington, Great Missenden, Bucks; *m* 1st, 1934, Margaretta Rowena Marion Whitfield Hayes (*d* 1962); one *s* one *d*; 2nd, 1963, Virginia Beatrice Cunard, OBE. *Educ:* Clifton; Trinity Coll., Cambridge. Called to the Bar, 1930. Served War of 1939-45 in Royal Artillery (despatches). Staff Coll., Camberley, 1942; Normandy Landing 1944. *Recreation:* fishing. *Address:* 13

The Terrace, Barnes, SW13. *Club:* Athenæum.
                                                [Died 20 April 1973.

BARRINGTON, Hon. Rupert Edward Selborne, DSO 1918; *b* 10 Dec. 1877; *y s* of 9th Viscount Barrington, and *heir-presumptive* of 11th Viscount Barrington; *m* 1903, Mary Georgina (*d* 1971), *d* of Lieut-Col G. A. Ferguson; one *s. Educ:* Cheam; Charterhouse. Served South African War, 1900-1; South African Constabulary, 1901-7; European War, 1914-18, Gallipoli, Egypt, Salonika and France (wounded, DSO, despatches thrice). *Address:* Walhatch Hotel, Forest Row, Sussex.   *[Died 7 Aug. 1975.*

BARRINGTON-WARD, Sir (Victor) Michael, KCVO 1952; CBE 1945; DSO 1916; FCIT; CStJ; Colonel, retired, Railway Staff Corps, RE; *b* 17 July 1887; 3rd *s* of late Canon M. J. Barrington-Ward, DD, Rector of Duloe; *m* 1st, 1920, Barbara (marr. diss. 1938, she *d* 1972), *o d* of late J. T. Pilling, Wolverley Court, Worcester; three *d*; 2nd, 1938, Isobel, *er d* of late Dr S. J. Kerfoot, Clifton, Bristol; one *d. Educ:* Westminster; Edinburgh. Formerly an Asst Engineer on the staff of W. B. Worthington, MInstCE, Engineer-in-Chief, Midland Railway; an Asst to General Superintendent, Midland Railway; Dir Railway Operations, Ministry of Transport, 1919-21; General Manager's Staff, NER, 1922; District Supt, LNER, Middlesbrough, 1923-27; Supt, LNER (Western Section), 1927-39; Supt, LNER, Southern Area, 1939-42; Asst Gen. Man., LNER, 1942-45; Divisional General Manager, LNER, 1945-47; Mem. of Railway Exec., 1947-53. BSc (Engineering) Edinburgh; Miller Prizeman, Institution of Civil Engineers; Operations Gold Medal, Institute of Transport, 1938; at beginning of 1914-18 war Captain, South Lancashire Regt; transferred and promoted Major in Royal Engineers, 1915, for duty with the Railway Operating Division, and commanded a large group of Railway Operating Companies (despatches four times, DSO, Bt Lt-Col; citation, French Army and Croix de Guerre with Palm); Lieut-Col Comdg Headquarters Railway Operating Group Supp. Reserve RE, 1924-28; Vice-Pres. Inst. Transport, 1945-48; Chm. Operating Cttee, REC, 1938-45; Chm. Rly Clearing House, 1948-53. Medal of Freedom with Silver Palm (USA). *Publications:* contributions Proceedings of Institution of Civil Engineers, Institute of Transport, and several lectures on transport subjects. *Address:* Beverley, Ledborough Lane, Beaconsfield, Bucks. *T:* Beaconsfield 3211.   *[Died 28 July 1972.*

BARRON, Donovan Allaway, CBE 1962; MIEE; Engineer-in-Chief of the Post Office, 1965-67; *b* 1907; *s* of late George Barron; *m* 1941, Margaret Kathleen, *d* of Percival Aylwin Selfe; one *d. Educ:* Bristol Grammar Sch.; Bristol Univ. BSc 1927, MSc 1936. General Post Office: Asst Engineer, 1927-35; Area Engineer, 1936-40; Asst Staff Engineer, 1941-48; Staff Engineer, 1949-53; Asst Engineer-in-Chief, 1954-59; Deputy Engineer-in-Chief, 1960-65. Formerly Member of the Council of the Institution of Electrical Engineers. *Publications:* various contributions to learned journals. *Recreations:* music, gardening, philately. *Address:* 30 Cadogan Close, Beckenham, Kent BR3 2XY. *T:* 01-460 1781.   *[Died 24 March 1980.*

BARRON, Wilfrid P. S.; *see* Shepherd-Barron.

BARROW, Hon. Sir Malcolm (Palliser), Kt 1953; CBE 1946 (OBE 1942); Deputy Prime Minister, Defence, Economic Affairs and Power, Federation of Rhodesia and Nyasaland, 1962-63; Tea and Tung Planter; *b* 1900; *s* of late Sir Samuel Barrow; *m* 1927, Frances Teresa (*d* 1972), *d* of F. E. Richards, Coombe Hall, East Grinstead, Sussex. *Educ:* Malvern Coll., Clare College, Cambridge (BA). Chm., Tea Res. Foundation of Central Africa; Mem., Agricultural Res. Council of Malawi. *Address:* Namingomba Estate, Thyolo, Malawi. *Club:* Salisbury (Rhodesia).   *[Died 9 June 1973.*

BARROWCLOUGH, Rt. Hon. Sir Harold (Eric), PC 1954; KCMG 1954; CB 1944; DSO 1919; MC; ED; Chief Justice of New Zealand, 1953-65; *b* 1894; *s* of late A. E. Barrowclough, Dunedin; *m* 1921, Mary Ogilvy (*d* 1964), *d* of James S. Duthie, Dunedin; two *s* one *d. Educ:* Palmerston N High Sch.; Otago Univ., LLB. Served European War, 1914-18, France, Belgium and Egypt, eventually commanding 4th Bn NZ Rifle Brigade, and as Asst Dir Education for NZ Division (despatches, MC, DSO, French Croix de Guerre); formerly Lecturer on Procedure, Faculty of Law and Commerce, Otago Univ.; commanding 1st Bn Otago Regt NZ Military Forces, 1924-29; commanded 3rd New Zealand Infantry Brigade, 1930-31; Comdr 6th NZ Infantry Brigade, 2nd NZ Expeditionary Force, 1940-42 (despatches, Bar to DSO, Greek Military Cross, Class A); Comdr 1st NZ Div., Apr.-Sept. 1942; commanded 3rd NZ Div. and 2nd NZ Expeditionary Force in the Pacific, 1942-44, as Maj.-Gen. (CB). Comdr Legion of Merit (US). LLD *hc* Otago,

1969. *Address:* 29 Salamanca Road, Kelburn, Wellington, New Zealand. *T:* Wellington 43.377. *Clubs:* Northern; Royal New Zealand Yacht Squadron (Auckland); Wellington (Wellington).
[Died 4 March 1972.

BARROWS, William Leonard, JP; formerly Partner, Price Waterhouse & Co., retired 1970, and Howard Smith Thompson & Co., 1931-70, Chartered Accountants, Birmingham and London; *b* 13 July 1905; *s* of Rev. F. W. Barrows; *m* 1929, Elizabeth Goodman; two *s* two *d. Educ:* Marlborough. Qualified as Chartered Accountant, 1929; Dir 1942-71, Chm. 1954-71, Evered & Co. Hldgs Ltd; Dir and Chm., Duport Ltd, 1947-73; Dir, 1941-74, Chm., 1957-74, Averys, Ltd; Chm., Firmin & Sons Ltd, 1950-75. Member: Council of Inst. of Chartered Accountants, 1941-66 (Pres., 1958-59); Excess Profits Tax Advisory Panel, 1947-56; Board of Referees, 1953-70; Geddes Cttee on Carriers' Licensing, 1963; Board of United Birmingham Hospitals, 1953-68; Life Governor, Birmingham Univ. Hon. LLD Birmingham, 1958. JP City of Birmingham. *Recreations:* shooting and gardening. *Address:* Wakeley Cottage, The Green, Tanworth-in-Arden, Solihull B94 5AL. *T:* Tanworth-in-Arden 2476. *Clubs:* Reform; Conservative (Birmingham).
[Died 4 June 1976.

BARRY, Rt. Rev. (Frank) Russell, DSO 1916; MA; Hon. DD (St Andrews) 1936, Nottingham 1951; DD (Lambeth) 1947; Hon. Fellow of Oriel College, Oxford, 1943; Hon. STD Gen. Theological Seminary, New York, 1952; FKC, London, 1929; *b* 28 Jan. 1890; *e s* of Rev. George Duncan Barry, formerly Rector of Bratton Fleming, Barnstaple; *m* 1929, Lilian Janet, *o d* of late Dr G. Buchanan Gray; one *d. Educ:* Bradfield; Oriel Coll., Oxford (Scholar). 1st Class Mods. and Lit. Hum.; Passmore Edwards Prize; Hall Greek Testament Prize; Denyer Johnson Scholarship; Fellow and Lecturer of Oriel, 1913-19; TCF, 1915-19 (DSO, despatches, Montenegrin medal); Hon. CF 2nd Class; Principal of Ordination Test Sch., Knutsford, 1919-23; Archdeacon of Egypt and Chaplain of All Saints, Cairo, 1923; Prof. of New Testament Interpretation at King's Coll., London, 1923-28; Vicar of St Mary the Virgin (the University Church), and Fellow and Tutor of Balliol Coll., Oxford, 1928-33; Canon of Westminster and Rector of St John's, Smith Square, 1933-41; Sub-Dean of Westminster, 1940-41; Bishop of Southwell, 1941-63. Canon Theologian of Liverpool Cathedral, 1932-33; Examining Chaplain to the Bishop of Southwark, 1920-32, of Salisbury, 1928-33, of Winchester, 1932-34; Select Preacher: Cambridge, 1921, 1934, 1936 and 1939; Oxford, 1927-29 and 1938; Chaplain to the King, 1940-41; Moorhouse Lecturer, St Paul's Cathedral, Melbourne, 1934; Lectr, St Michael, Cornhill, EC4, 1967. *Publications:* One Clear Call, 1922; St Paul and Social Psychology, 1923; Christianity and Psychology, 1923; contributor to the Church in the Furnace, 1917; A Philosophy from Prison, 1926; The Relevance of Christianity, 1931; The Relevance of the Church, 1935; What has Christianity to say?, 1937; Contributor, Christianity and the Crisis, 1933; The Christian Faith, 1936; Convictions, 1939; I heard a Voice, 1940; Faith in Dark Ages, 1940; Church and Leadership, 1945; Recovery of Man, 1948; Vocation and Ministry, 1958; Asking The Right Questions, 1960; Mervyn Haigh, 1964; Questioning Faith, 1965; Christian Ethics and Secular Society, 1966; The Atonement, 1968; Weep not for me, 1968; Secular and Supernatural, 1969; Period of My Life, 1970; To Recover Confidence, 1974. *Recreations:* indescribable. *Address:* The Coppice, Manesty, Keswick, Cumbria. *T:* Borrowdale 252; 26 Tufton Court, SW1. *T:* 01-222 2505. *Club:* Athenæum.
[Died 24 Oct. 1976.

BARRY, Geraldine Mary; retired; late Senior Surgeon, Royal Free Hospital, and Senior Surgeon, London Homœopathic Hospital; Examiner in Surgery, University of London; *b* 4 Oct. 1897; *d* of Rev. Walter George and Anna Barry. *Educ:* Queen Anne's Sch., Caversham; London (Royal Free Hosp.); Sch. of Medicine for Women, MRCS, LRCP 1921; MB, BS London Univ. Gold Medal, Distinction Medicine and Surgery, 1922; FRCS, 1926; MS London, 1929; Asst Surgeon, London Homœopathic Hospital, 1929; Asst Surgeon, Royal Free Hospital, 1930; EMS, Surgeon to Three Counties Emergency Hospital, Arlesey, Beds, 1940. *Address:* Three Hedges, Dungells Lane, Yateley, near Camberley, Surrey. *T:* Yateley 873187.
[Died 1 July 1978.

BARRY, Rt. Rev. Hugh Van Lynden O.; *see* Otter-Barry.

BARRY, Sir Patrick (Redmond), Kt 1950; MC; Judge of Queen's Bench Division of the High Court of Justice, 1950-66; Chairman of Advisory Council on the Treatment of Offenders, 1958-66; *b* 4 Sept. 1898; *o s* of late Rt Hon. Redmond Barry, PC, Lord Chancellor of Ireland, 1911-13, and late Mrs Redmond Barry, 6 Bushell Place, Preston; *m* 1933, Ruth Marion, *o d* of late Ernest

Agnew and late Mrs Agnew, of Westwood, Alderley Edge, Cheshire; one *d. Educ:* Downside; RMC Sandhurst; Balliol Coll., Oxford. Joined Irish Guards, 1917; served with 1st Bn in France and Germany, 1918-19. Lieut, a/Adjutant (MC); transferred to Reserve of Officers, 1919. BA Oxford, 1922; called to Bar, 1923; joined Northern Circuit; contested (L) Bolton, 1928. KC 1938; Bencher, Inner Temple, 1946. Recorder of Oldham, 1942-50; Judge of Appeal, Isle of Man, 1946-50; Dep. Chm., Wilts QS, 1964-71. Mem., Radcliffe Tribunal, 1962-63. Recalled to Irish Guards, Aug. 1939; Capt. and Adjutant, 1939-40; transferred to General Staff, 1940; Lt-Col 1942. *Recreations:* fishing and gardening. *Address:* Apsehill House, Chicksgrove, Tisbury, Wilts. *T:* Fovant 662. *Clubs:* White's, Army and Navy.
[Died 6 May 1972.

BARRY, Sir Rupert (Rodney Francis Tress), 4th Bt *cr* 1899; MBE 1945; *b* 6 Dec. 1910; *s* of Sir (Claude) Francis Barry, 3rd Bt and Angela Doris Manners (*d* 1960), *er d* of Herbert Charles Hume-Spry; *S* father, 1970; *m* 1st, 1936, Diana Madeline (*d* 1948), *o d* of R. O'Brien Thompson; one *s* one *d*; 2nd, 1951, Sheila Georgina Veronica, *o d* of Major George Joseph Francis White, MBE; three *s* two *d. Educ:* King's School, Canterbury; RMC. Major, retd, Oxfordshire and Bucks LI; served War, 1939-40. *Heir: s* Lawrence Edward Anthony Tress Barry, *b* 1 Nov. 1939. *Address:* Brisley Rise, Willesborough Lees, Ashford, Kent. *Club:* Army and Navy. *[Died 9 March 1977.*

BARRY, Rt. Rev. Russell; *see* Barry, Rt Rev. F. R.

BARRY, William Whitmore O.; *see* Otter-Barry.

BARSON, Derek Emmanuel; Director General, British Red Cross Society, 1976-80; *b* 31 Jan. 1922; *s* of Horace Barson and Phyllis Edna (*née* Hathaway); *m* 1948, Maya Renwick; two *s* one *d. Educ:* Westminster Abbey Choir Sch.; The King's Sch., Ely; Downing Coll., Cambridge. FCIS. Served War, UK, ME, E Africa, Burma, Ethiopia; Major, King's Shropshire LI (despatches, Burma, 1944), 1942-47. Cambridge, 1947-49; HM Colonial Admin. Service, Nyasaland, 1949-64. Asst Sec., Royal Nat. Life-Boat Instn, 1964-69; Sec., British Red Cross Soc., 1970-75. OStJ 1977. *Recreations:* music (esp. choral), conducting, country walking. *Address:* Willow Cottage, Slines Oak Road, Woldingham, Surrey. *T:* Woldingham 2381. *Clubs:* Royal Over-Seas League, Anglo-Belgian. *[Died 25 Sept. 1980.*

BARTER, Sir Percy, Kt 1951; CB 1947; Chairman of the Board of Control and Under Secretary, Ministry of Health, 1945-52, retired; *b* 27 April 1886; *yr s* of late Frank Barter, Plymouth; *m* 1928, Doris Sheriff; one *d. Educ:* Dulwich Coll.; Jesus Coll., Oxford. Entered Local Government Board, 1910; Sec. to Departmental Cttee on the Blind, 1915; Private Sec. to Rt Hon. C. Addison, Minister of Reconstruction and Minister of Health, 1918-21; Secretary, to Cttee on Asylum Administration, 1921-22, to Royal Commission on Lunacy and Mental Disorder, 1924-26, to Royal Commission on Local Government, 1928-29; Sec. of the Board of Control, 1930-39; Principal Officer, SW Region, Civil Defence, 1939-40; Principal Asst Sec., Ministry of Health, 1940-45. *Address:* Trenant, The Highway, Sutton, Surrey. *[Died 8 May 1975.*

BARTLETT, Rt. Rev. David Daniel, DD (Lambeth); *b* 5 Nov. 1900. *Educ:* St David's College, Lampeter; St John's College, Oxford. BA 1920, BD 1930, Lloyd Williams Fellow, 1927, St David's College; late Casberd Scholar, BA (1st Cl. Theology), 1922. MA 1926, St John's Coll. Deacon, 1923; Priest, 1924. Chaplain and Lecturer in Theology, St David's College, Lampeter, 1923-31; Vicar of Pembroke Dock with Nash and Upton, 1931-46; Examining Chaplain to the Bishop of St David's from 1938, to the Bishop of Monmouth from 1947; Professor of Hebrew and Theology, St David's College, Lampeter, and licensed preacher, Diocese of St David's, 1946; Bishop of St Asaph, 1950-71. Chaplain and Sub-Prelate, Order of St John of Jerusalem, 1965. Hon. DD Wales, 1971. *Publication:* (ed) Book of Numbers in A New Commentary, 1931. *Address:* 18 Conwy Avenue, Rhuddlan, Clwyd. *T:* Rhuddlan 590850. *[Died 10 April 1977.*

BARTON, Dr Arthur Willoughby; Member, London Diocesan Board of Education; *b* 14 Sept. 1899; *yr s* of late Professor E. H. Barton, FRS, and Mary Ann Barton, Nottingham; *m* 1935, Alison Mary, 2nd *d* of Colin Read Shaw, Bolton, Lancs; no *c. Educ:* Nottingham High Sch.; Trinity Coll. Cambridge. Served European War, 1914-18, 2nd Lieut RE, 1918. Research Asst, Cavendish Lab., Cambridge, 1922-25; Chief Physics Master, Repton Sch., 1925-39; Head Master, King Edward VII Sch., Sheffield, 1939-50; Head Master, City of London Sch., 1950-65; Schs Liaison Officer, UCL, 1965-71. *Publications:* Text Book on Heat, 1933; Text Book on Light, 1939. *Recreations:* refereeing at football and umpiring at cricket; Hon. Member, Repton Pilgrims Cricket Club; lawn tennis, squash, mountaineering. *Address:* 2 Stone Road, Bromley, Kent. *T:* 01-460 2372. *Clubs:* Alpine, MCC. *[Died 24 Aug. 1976.*

BARTON, Cecil James Juxon Talbot, CMG 1937; OBE 1932; MA 1921; *b* 13 April 1891; *e s* of late Rev. R. C. E. Barton, MA, and Emma Isabella Talbot; *m* 1926, Cicely (*d* 1940), *y d* of Lt-Col F. E. Bradshaw, DSO; one *s* one *d* ; *m* 1945, Sheila Jean, *d* of A. Macgregor, Dannevirke, NZ. *Educ:* Denstone; Downing Coll., Cambridge, BA 1913. Asst District Comr, E African Protectorate (Kenya), 1914; served in various administrative posts; Asst for Native Affairs, 1923; acted in various Secretariat posts; Senior Asst Colonial Sec. Kenya, 1933; MLC 1934 and 1935; Colonial Sec. Fiji, 1936-41; MLC; Chm. Public Service Reorganisation Cttee, 1936; Administered Government of Fiji and acted as High Commissioner and as Consul General for the Western Pacific in 1936, 1938, 1939; Chief Sec. Nyasaland, 1941; MLC; Mem. Central African Council; Chm. Development Cttee; Administered Government of Nyasaland in 1942, 1944; retired 1945. Employed in Colonial Office, 1945-58. *Publications:* various papers on East African tribes and local history. *Recreations:* formerly Rugby, cricket, polo, shooting; now grandchildren, repairing education, stamps, walking. *Address:* The Old Coach House, Rye, East Sussex.
[Died 29 Sept. 1980.

BARTON, Guy Trayton, CMG 1960; OBE 1957; retired from HM Overseas Civil Service; *b* 7 June 1908; *s* of late Canon H. Barton; *m* 1946, Sybil Maud Seddon, *d* of late Canon G. E. W. Holmes; one *s* one *d.* *Educ:* Weymouth Coll.; Selwyn Coll., Cambridge. Nigerian Administrative Service, 1931-46; Asst Chief Sec., Barbados, 1946-58; Chief Sec., Barbados, 1958-61; was acting Governor of Barbados for periods during 1958 and 1959. *Publication:* The Prehistory of Barbados, 1953 (Barbados). *Recreations:* gardening, golf, archaeology. *Address:* 108 Hazelton Road, Parson's Heath, Colchester, Essex.
[Died 22 April 1977.

BARTON, Rt. Rev. Mgr. Canon John Mackintosh Tilney, DD; Priest-in-charge, SS Peter and Edward's, Palace Street, SW1, 1950-75; Canon of Westminster Cathedral, since 1971; *b* 20 May 1898; *o c* of Tilney Wallace Barton and Marian Barton (*née* Jowitt). *Educ:* Harrow (Entrance Scholar); St Edmund's Coll., Ware; Angelico Univ., Rome; Ecole Biblique, Jerusalem. Priest, 1921; DD (magna cum laude), 1922; LSS 1928. Prof. of Holy Scripture, Hebrew and Liturgy, St Edmund's, Ware, 1924-36; Warden of Edmonton House of Studies, 1936-37; Administrator of St Catherine's Parish and House of Studies, West Drayton, 1937-50. Named Consultor of Pontifical Biblical Commn and *ex-officio* examiner for Papal degrees, 1935 (jubilarian, 1960, emeritus, 1972); Privy Chamberlain to HH, 1936; Prelate of Honour to HH, 1952. Pres. Soc. for OT Study, 1952. Chairman: Catholic Biblical Assoc., 1942-57; Soc. of S John Chrysostom, 1959-65 (Vice-Pres., 1965-); Pro-Synodal Judge, Westminster Metropolitan Tribunal, 1944-46 and 1963-; Promoter of justice and Defender of the Bond, 1946-63; Dir of Diploma Course in Theology, 1943-72; a diocesan censor. FSA 1944; FRSA 1945. Mem., Newman Assoc. *Publications:* The Holy Ghost, 1930; Semitic Religions, 1933; The Religion of Israel, 1934; The Phases of the Sacred Passion, 1954; Penance and Absolution, 1961; Our Lord's Last Farewells before His Passion, 1967. Edited: D. Buzy's St John the Baptist, 1933; Cardinal Wiseman's Lectures on the Blessed Eucharist, 1933; Abbot Chapman's Matthew, Mark and Luke, 1937; S Salaville's Introduction to Eastern Liturgies, 1938; J. Bonsirven's Theology of the New Testament; P. Drijvers, On the Psalms; Scripture Textbooks for Catholic Schools; Studies in Comparative Religion; articles in Clergy Review, Tablet, Theology, etc. *Recreations:* swimming and criminology. *Address:* St John's Convent, Kiln Green, Twyford, Reading, Berks RG10 9XP. *[Died 16 April 1977.*

BARTON, Robert Childers; *b* 1881; *e s* of Charles William Barton, JP, DL; *m* 1950, Rachel Warren Lothrop (*d* 1973), Cambridge, Mass, *d* of late Fiske Warren, Boston, Mass. *Educ:* Rugby; Christ Church, Oxford. Chm. of Wicklow County Council, 1920; a farmer in Co. Wicklow; served European War; MP (S Fein) West Wicklow, Dec. 1918-22; Mem. of Dail Eireann for Cos Kildare and Wicklow, 1921-23; Minister of Agriculture, 1919-21; Sec. for Economic Affairs, 1921-22; an Irish Peace Delegate to London Conference, 1921; Chm. Agricultural Credit Corporation, 1934-59; Chm. Turf Development Board (now Bord Na Mona), 1935-60. *Address:* Glendalough House, Annamoe, Co. Wicklow.
[Died 10 Aug. 1975.

BARWELL, Prof. Claud Foster, MA, MD; Goldsmiths' Company's Professor of Bacteriology, University of London, at

London Hospital, since 1952; *b* 12 Nov. 1912; *s* of late Harold Barwell; *m* 1938, Joanna O'Toole; no *c.* *Educ:* Marlborough Coll.; Trinity Hall, Cambridge. Qualified at St George's Hosp., London, 1938; Asst Bacteriologist, London Hosp., 1938; Asst Pathologist, EMS, at Colchester, 1940, and Epping, 1942; Pathologist at Epping, 1943, and Sector Pathologist for Essex Div., 1944; Lecturer in Bacteriology, London Hosp. Medical Coll., 1946; Reader in Bacteriology, 1949. *Publications:* experimental work on viruses of the psittacosis group, in Nature, British Jl of Experimental Pathology, Jl of Clinical Pathology. *Recreations:* gardening, fly fishing. *Address:* 17 Holly Walk, NW3. *T:* 01-435 4747. *[Died 3 July 1971.*

BARWICK, Sir Richard (Llewellyn), 3rd Bt, *cr* 1912; *b* 4 Nov. 1916; *o surv. s* of Sir John Storey Barwick, 2nd Bt, and Gwladys Jessie (*d* 1949), 3rd *d* of George William Griffith Thomas, Ystrad Mynach, Co. Glamorgan; *S* father 1953; *m* 1st, 1948, Valerie Maud (Ward) (marr. diss.), *d* of Robert J. Skelton, Nairobi, Kenya Colony; three *d* ; 2nd, 1968, Mrs Denise Radcliffe, *widow* of Hugh Christian Radcliffe. *Educ:* Harrow; Christ's Coll., Cambridge. Served Royal Air Force, 1940-46. *Heir:* none. *Address:* Thimbleby Hall, Northallerton, North Yorks. *T:* Osmotherly 212. *Club:* Northern Counties (Newcastle upon Tyne). *[Died 16 June 1979 (ext).*

BASKETT, Sir Ronald (Gilbert), Kt 1966; OBE 1947; BSc (London), MSc (Reading); FRIC; Secretary, Agricultural Research Council, since 1971; Director of the National Institute for Research in Dairying and Research Professor, Reading University, 1959-67, now Professor Emeritus; *b* 30 Oct. 1901; *s* of Charles Henry Baskett, RE, and Florence Maud Baskett; *m* 1927, Joan Shirley Staples Firth; three *s.* *Educ:* King Edward VI Grammar Sch., Chelmsford; University Coll., Reading. Demonstrator in Agricultural Chemistry, University Coll., Reading, 1923-24; Asst to Head of Chemical and Animal Nutrition Div., Ministry of Agriculture, Northern Ireland, 1924, and Asst Agricultural Chemistry Dept, Queen's Univ.; Lecturer in charge of Agricultural Chemistry Dept, 1928; Head of Chemical and Animal Nutrition Div., Ministry of Agriculture for Northern Ireland, 1928; Prof. of Agricultural Chemistry, Queen's Univ. of Belfast, 1935-59. Chief Scientific Officer, Ministry of Agriculture for Northern Ireland, 1947-59; Agricultural Attaché, British Embassy, Washington DC, 1950-52. Hon. DSc (Belfast). *Publications:* Scientific papers to agricultural journals. *Recreations:* sailing; gardening. *Address:* 15 The Brae, Groomsport, Bangor, Co. Down, Northern Ireland. *Club:* Athenæum. *[Died 24 Nov. 1972.*

BASON, Fred, (Frederick Thomas Bason); bookseller since 1922; author since 1931; Lecturer on authors, books and collecting books since 1941; *b* Southwark, 29 Aug. 1907; *s* of William Bason and Annie (*née* Blount), Southwark; bachelor. *Educ:* Westmorland Road LCC Sch. Became a bookseller at age of 15; journalist, 1924. Many broadcasts for BBC and appearances on TV; frequent broadcasts to Australia and America; has given over 800 lectures in Gt Britain and abroad. *Publications:* The W. Somerset Maugham Bibliography (introd by Somerset Maugham), 1931 (2 edns); Gallery Unreserved (introd by Somerset Maugham), 1931; The Cigarette Card Hand Book and Guide to Values, 1938; Toys for Nothing, 1941; More Toys for Nothing, 1942; Fred Bason's Diary (introd by N. Bentley), 1951 (2nd edn 1952); Fred Bason's Second Diary (introd by L. A. G. Strong), 1952; The Third Diary of Fred Bason (introd etc by Michael Sadleir), 1955; The Last Bassoon, A Cockney's Diary (ed and introd by Sir Noël Coward), 1960; Fishing, 1960; Fred Bason Has A Picnic, 1961; Spring, 1962 (ltd edn); Summer, 1963 (ltd edn); contribs to The Saturday Book, vols 5-32; contribs to all leading magazines etc in which there is an interest in authors, books or collecting books; has had over 2,000 articles published all over the world. *Recreations:* meeting people and making them laugh; encouraging writers by lecturing; visitors welcomed any Thursday. *Address:* Four, Broadmayne, Portland Street, Walworth, SE17. *T:* none. *Clubs:* none. *[Died 2 July 1973.*

BASSET, Ronald Lambart; *b* 30 Nov. 1898; *s* of late Arthur Francis Basset; *m* 1931, Lady Elizabeth Legge (Extra Woman of the Bedchamber to Queen Elizabeth the Queen Mother), 2nd *d* of 7th Earl of Dartmouth; one *s* (and one *s* decd). *Educ:* Eton; RMC Sandhurst. 2nd Lieut Royal Scots Greys; served European War, France, 1918; Partner Reeves Whitburn and Co., 1923, Chm., 1932-38; Emergency Commission Welsh Guards, 1940; Temp. Lieut-Col 1942. *Recreations:* shooting; fishing. *Address:* The Lodge House, Hatfield Park, Hatfield, Herts. *T:* 2150. *Clubs:* Turf, White's; Travellers' (Paris). *[Died 24 Sept. 1972.*

BASSETT, George Arthur, CB 1945; *b* 3 Aug. 1884; *s* of late George Bassett; *m* 1907, Mabel Alice (*d* 1957), *d* of late John Gransden, Luton, Chatham; one *s* three *d.* *Educ:* Mathematical

Sch., Rochester; RN Coll., Greenwich. Royal Corps of Naval Constructors, 1907; Asst Constructor Admiralty and Overseeing HM Submarines, Vickers, Barrow, 1911-18; Constructor Commander Naval Armistice Commission and Naval Inter-Allied Commission of Control, Germany, 1919-20; Chief Constructor, HM Dockyard, Gibraltar, 1932-35; Superintendent of Repairs by Contract, Admiralty, 1940; Dep. Dir of Dockyards, Admiralty, 1941-46. *Recreation:* books. *Address:* 115 Farnaby Road, Bromley, Kent. *T:* 01-460 0704.
[*Died 29 Jan.* 1971.

BASSETT, His Honour John Harold, QC 1951; a County Court Judge, Circuit 58, Ilford, etc., 1955-65; called to the Bar, Middle Temple, 1931. South Eastern Circuit; South London Sessions; Central Criminal Court. *Address:* 2 Garden Court, Temple, EC4.
[*Died 9 Feb.* 1974.

BASSETT, Sir Walter (Eric), KBE 1959; MC; FIEAust; Consultant to W. E. Bassett & Partners Pty Ltd, Consulting Engineers; *b* Melbourne, 19 Dec. 1892; *m* 1923, Marnie, *d* of late Sir David Orme Masson; one *s* one *d. Educ:* Wesley Coll., Melbourne; Melbourne Univ. (MMechE, BEE). Served European War, 1914-18, with AIF; Lieut 5th Field Co. Engineers and Australian Flying Corps. Senior Lecturer, Mechanical Engineering and Aerodynamics, Melbourne Univ., 1919-28; Mt Lyell M. & R. Co., Australia: Dir, 1948-74; Chm., 1951-68; Pres., 1969-74; Director: Gas and Fuel Corp., Victoria, 1951-75; Renison Ltd, 1958-74 (Chm., 1958-68). Pres. Instn Engrs Australia, 1942. Kernot Memorial Medal, 1948; Peter Nicol Russell Memorial Medal, 1958; James Harrison Medal, 1976. Hon. DrEng Monash, 1970; Hon. LLD Melbourne, 1974. *Recreations:* fishing, sailing, woodwork. *Address:* 133 Kooyong Road, Armadale, Victoria 3143, Australia. *Clubs:* Melbourne, Royal Melbourne Golf (both Melbourne).
[*Died 8 March* 1978.

BASTYAN, Lt-Gen. Sir Edric (Montague), KCMG 1962; KCVO 1963; KBE 1957 (CBE 1943; OBE 1942); CB 1944; *b* 5 April 1903; *s* of late Lt-Col S. J. Bastyan, Ferndown, Dorset; *m* 1944, Victoria Eugénie Helen (*née* Bett), DStJ 1969; one *s. Educ:* West Buckland; RMC, Sandhurst. 2nd Lieut Sherwood Foresters, 1923; Capt. West Yorks Regt, 1935; Staff Coll., 1936-37; Royal Irish Fusiliers, 1937; Major, 1940; Temp. Lt-Col 1941; Temp. Brigadier, 1942; Acting Maj.-Gen, 1944; Col, 1945; Maj.-Gen. (with seniority, 1946), 1948. Served Palestine, 1938-39 (despatches); War of 1939-45, Africa, Italy, SEAC (despatches, OBE, CBE, CB). Chief Admin. Officer, Eighth Army, 1943; Maj.-Gen. i/c Administration Allied Land Forces, SE Asia, 1944-45. Imperial Defence Coll., 1946. Maj.-Gen. i/c Administration, British Army of the Rhine, 1946-48; employed in special duties, War Office, 1949; Chief of Staff Eastern Command, 1949-50; Dir of Staff Duties, WO 1950-52; Comdr 53rd (Welsh) Infantry Div. (TA) and Mid-West District, 1952-55; Vice Adjutant Gen., War Office, 1955-57; Lieut-Gen., 1957; Comdr, British Forces, Hongkong, 1957-60; retired, 1960. Governor of: South Australia, 1961-68; Tasmania, 1968-74. Exhibn of drawings and paintings, Hahndorf Gall., 1974. Assoc. Mem., Royal S Aust. Soc. of Arts. KStJ, 1961. *Recreations:* golf; tennis; painting. *Address:* Flat 42, 52 Brougham Place, North Adelaide, SA 5006, Australia. *Club:* Adelaide (Adelaide).
[*Died 6 Oct.* 1980.

BASTYAN, Maj.-Gen. Kenneth Cecil Orville, CB 1959; CBE 1953 (OBE 1943); *b* 10 Dec. 1906; *s* of late Lieut-Col S. J. Bastyan, OBE, Ferndown, Dorset; *m* 1934, Patricia, *e d* of Major P. B. Riley, MRCVS; one *s. Educ:* Bedford Sch. 2nd Lieut, Royal Signals, 1926; served War of 1939-45 in India, Iraq and Burma (OBE); Malaya, 1951-53; Chief Signal Officer, FARELF, 1953-54; Dep. Signal Officer in Chief at the War Office, 1954-57; Chief Signal Officer, BAOR and Northern Army Group, 1957-60. *Address:* 23 Brownsea View Avenue, Lilliput, Poole, Dorset.
[*Died 21 March* 1975.

BATCHELOR, Col Gordon Guthrie Malcolm, JP; Lord-Lieutenant for Stewartry District of Dumfries and Galloway, since 1975; *b* 2 May 1908; *o s* of Francis Malcolm Batchelor, Kellyfield, Dundee; *m* 1935, Lettice, *d* of Adam Darling, Bondington, Berwick-on-Tweed; two *d. Educ:* Trinity Coll., Glenalmond; Jesus Coll., Cambridge (BA). King's Own Scottish Borderers: 2nd Lieut 1930; Lieut 1932; Captain 1938; Major 1944; Lt-Col 1945; retd 1947; 5th TA Bn, King's Own Scottish Borderers: Lt-Col 1947; Brevet Col 1951. Served in Palestine, 1936 (medal and clasp); served War of 1939-45, NW Europe, 1940 and 1944-45 (despatches). Chm., T&AFA of Stewartry of Kirkcudbright, 1956-63; Pres. Assoc. of County Councils in Scotland, 1964-66; Vice-Chm., Bd of Management, Crichton Royal Hosp., 1958-70. JP 1957, DL 1960, Convener of County Council 1964-73, Vice-Lieutenant 1972-75, Stewartry of

Kirkcudbright. Order of Bronze Lion, Netherlands, 1945. *Address:* Crochmore, Irongray, Dumfries. *T:* Lochfoot 238.
[*Died 16 Nov.* 1976.

BATE, Maj.-Gen. (Alfred) Christopher, OBE 1968 (MBE 1960); Signal Officer in Chief (Army), since 1980; *b* 18 Aug. 1927; *y s* of late S. C. C. Bate, Dulwich; *m* 1954, Patricia Mary Stuart Bell; twin *s* two *d. Educ:* Alleyn's Sch. Commnd Royal Signals, 1949; served Middle East, BAOR, 1949-56; Staff Coll., 1957; HQ Northern Army Gp, 1958-61; 19 Airportable Bde, Cyprus, Kenya, Kuwait, 1961-63; 99 Gurkha Bde, Borneo, 1963-65 (despatches); JSSC, 1965; 7 Armoured Bde, BAOR, 1965-67; Comd 9th Signal Regt, Cyprus, 1967-69; DS, IDC and RCDS, 1969-71; Comdt, Sch. of Signals, 1971-74; Dir, Defence Operational Requirements Staff, 1974-75; MoD (Army), 1975-77; Comdt, Nat. Defence Coll., 1977-80. *Recreations:* philately, industrial archaeology. *Address:* 1 Courtney Close, Shroton, Blandford Forum, Dorset.
[*Died 3 Sept.* 1980.

BATEMAN, Rev. Arthur Fitzroy Dobbie-: see Dobbie-Bateman.

BATEMAN, Lt-Col (Hon. Brig.) Harold Henry, CBE 1945 (OBE 1942); DSO, 1917; MC; *b* 3 July 1888; *s* of late Robert Edward Bateman of Brighton; *m* 1920, Eileen (*d* 1972), *d* of late Henry Boyd, CBE; one *s* two *d. Educ:* Cheltenham Coll.; RMA Woolwich. Entered Royal Engineers, 1908; Captain, 1914; Bt. Major, 1919; Major, 1925; Bt. Lieut-Col, 1929; Lieut-Col 1933; served European War, 1914-18 (despatches four times, Bt. Major, DSO, MC); retired pay, 1935; rejoined 1939; relegated to unemployment, 1945; Dir of Works, Prison Commission, 1945-53. Croix de Guerre (Belgium), 1919; Legion of Merit (USA), 1945. *Address:* Redwell Mount, Ightham, Kent.
[*Died 6 May* 1974.

BATES, Sir Alfred, Kt 1952; MC 1918; DL; Solicitor; *b* 3 July 1897; *s* of Alfred Bates (Solicitor) and Agnes Bates; *m* 1925, Margaret, *d* of the Rev. J. H. Clarke, MSc, Heywood; three *s* one *d. Educ:* Royal Grammar Sch., Lancaster (Scholar). Member Lancs CC 1931-74; Chm., 1949-52, 1955-58 and 1961-64; CA 1949-74; Chairman: Planning Cttee of County Councils Assoc., 1948-68; Lancs Police Cttee, 1952-74; North West Police Training Centre, 1952-74; Governor, Police Coll., 1957-74. Served on W Lancs T&AFA 1949-61. Deputy Pro-Chancellor, Lancaster Univ., 1964-75. DL 1951. Hon. FRTPI(MTPI 1959); Hon. LLD (Lancaster), 1964. *Address:* 191 Coleherne Court, SW5. *T:* 01-373 4799. *Club:* Royal Automobile.
[*Died 2 Feb.* 1979.

BATES, Air Vice-Marshal Eric Cecil, CB 1958; CBE 1945; AFC 1941; RAF retired; Principal of the College of Air Training, Hamble, Hants, 1960-71; *b* 9 June 1906; *s* of late R. J. Bates, Perth, Western Australia; *m* 1938, Kathleen May Norminton; one *s. Educ:* Perth Modern Sch.; Univ. of W Australia. Cadetship, RAAF, 1929; Commissioned RAF, 1930; Iraq, 1936-38; Australia, 1939-41; Canada, 1941-43; Bomber Command 1943-45; Pacific, 1945-46; Flying Training Command, 1947-50; Imperial Defence Coll., 1951; Singapore, 1952-53; Dir of Intelligence, Air Ministry, 1953-55; Air Officer i/c Administration, Far East Air Force, 1955-58, retired. *Address:* 27 Benyon Court, Bath Road, Reading. *T:* Reading 585974.
[*Died 23 March* 1975.

BATES, Herbert Ernest, CBE 1973; author; former Squadron Leader in RAF; *b* 16 May 1905; *s* of Albert Ernest Bates and Lucy Elizabeth Lucas; *m* 1931, Marjorie Helen Cox; two *s* two *d. Educ:* The Grammar Sch., Kettering. Worked as a provincial journalist and clerk before publishing first novel at the age of 20; subsequently became known both as a novelist and short story writer in England and America; his stories are widely anthologised; his novels have been translated into sixteen languages; has also written plays and many essays on country life. *Publications: novels:* The Two Sisters; Catherine Foster; Charlotte's Row; The Fallow Land; The Poacher; A House of Women, 1936; Spella Ho, 1938; Fair Stood the Wind for France, 1944; The Purple Plain, 1947; The Jacaranda Tree, 1949; Dear Life, 1950; The Scarlet Sword, 1951; Love for Lydia, 1952; The Feast of July, 1954; The Sleepless Moon, 1956; The Darling Buds of May, 1958 (play: A Breath of French Air, 1959); When the Green Woods Laugh, 1960; The Day of the Tortoise, 1961; A Crown of Wild Myrtle, 1962; Oh! To Be In England, 1963; A Moment in Time, 1964; The Distant Horns of Summer, 1967; The Wild Cherry-Tree, 1968; The Triple Echo, 1970; *short stories:* Day's End, Seven Tales and Alexander; The Black Boxer; The Woman who had Imagination; Cut and Come again; Something Short and Sweet; The Flying Goat; My Uncle Silas; Country Tales; The Beauty of the Dead; The Bride Comes to Evensford; Colonel Julian, 1951; The Nature of Love, 1953; The Daffodil Sky, 1955; Death of a Huntsman, 1957; Sugar for the

Horse, 1957; The Watercress Girl, 1959; An Aspidistra in Babylon, 1960; Now Sleeps the Crimson Petal, 1961; The Four Beauties, 1968; A Little of What You Fancy, 1969; The Song of the Wren, 1972; *autobiography:* The Vanished World, 1969; The Blossoming World, 1971; The World in Ripeness, 1972; *miscellaneous:* Flowers and Faces; Through the Woods; Down the River; The Seasons and the Gardener; The Last Bread; The Modern Short Story; The Heart of the Country; The Day of Glory (play); The Country of White Clover; A Love of Flowers, 1971; The White Admiral (for children), 1968; as Flying Officer X: The Greatest People in the World, 1942; How Sleep the Brave, 1943; The Face of England, 1952. *Recreations:* gardening and fishing. *Address:* The Granary, Little Chart, Kent. *T:* Pluckley 255.   [*Died 29 Jan.* 1974.

BATES, Leslie Fleetwood, CBE 1966; FRS 1950; BSc Bristol, PhD Cambridge, DSc London; FInstP; Emeritus Professor of Physics, Nottingham University (formerly University College, Nottingham), since 1964 (Lancashire-Spencer Professor, 1936-64); Deputy Vice-Chancellor, University of Nottingham, 1953-56; *b* 7 March 1897; *e s* of late W. F. Bates, Kingswood, Bristol; *m* 1925, Winifred Frances Furze Ridler, MSc, (*d* 1965), *o d* of late F. Ridler, Bristol; one *s* one *d. Educ:* Merchant Venturers' Sch., Bristol; University of Bristol; Trinity Coll., Cambridge. Served as radiographer, Capt. Unattached List, i/c X-Ray Laboratory IX Division, Secunderabad, Deccan, India, 1916-20; Research at University of Bristol, 1920-22, and Cavendish Laboratory, 1922-24; Lecturer in Physics, University Coll., London, 1924-30, Reader in Physics, 1930-36; Pres. of Physical Soc., 1950-52; Holweck Prizeman (French and English Physical Socs), 1949; Mem. of Board of Institute of Physics, 1947-49; Pres. Association of University Teachers, 1938-39. Consultant to Inter-Services Research Bureau, 1941-45; Vice-Principal, University Coll. Nottingham, 1944-46; Vice-Pres., Lace Research Association, 1955-63; Senior Scientific Adviser for Civil Defence, North Midland Region (No 3), 1951-72. May Lecture, Inst. of Metals, 1954; Rippon Lectures University of Calcutta, 1960; Guthrie Lecture, 1963. Hon. DSc: Nottingham, 1972; Durham, 1975. *Publications:* Modern Magnetism, 1939, 1948, 1951, 1961, 1963; Sir Alfred Ewing, 1946; Recent Advances in Physics, Science Progress, 1928-36; Research publications mainly on electricity and magnetism in various journals. *Address:* Flat 2, Castlethorpe, Newcastle Circus, The Park, Nottingham NG7 1BJ. *T:* Nottingham 42135. *Club:* Athenæum.   [*Died 20 Jan.* 1978.

BATES, Ven. Mansel Harry, MA; Archdeacon of Lindisfarne and Vicar of Eglingham, Diocese of Newcastle, since 1970; *b* 4 Aug. 1912; *s* of Rev. John Handel Greenhalgh and Alice Bates; *m* 1939, Queenie Mary Fraser Campbell; one *s* three *d. Educ:* Liverpool Institute; Brasenose Coll., Oxford; Wycliffe Hall. BA 1934; Dip. in Theol., 1935; MA 1938. Deacon, 1935, Priest, 1936, Dio. Liverpool. Curate, SS John and James, Litherland, 1935-38; Curate in Charge of Netherton, 1938-41; Vicar: St Saviour, Everton, 1941-47; Jesmond, Newcastle upon Tyne, 1947-59 (Proctor in Convocation, 1950-59); Great Crosby, Liverpool, 1959-70. Hon. Canon of Liverpool Cath., 1964-70. *Address:* Eglingham Vicarage, Alnwick, Northumberland. *T:* Powburn 250.   [*Died 14 Dec.* 1980.

BATESON, Lieut.-Col David Mayhew, DSO 1944; TD 1941; DL, JP; Deputy Chairman, Wrexham & East Denbighshire Water Co.; *b* 3 March 1906; *s* of Ernest Bateson, Pant-y-Ochin Hall, Gresford, N Wales; *m* 1948, Ursula Mary Browne, *d* of Major A. S. C. Browne; one *s* one *d. Educ:* Eton; University Coll., Oxford. Joined Denbighshire Yeomanry (61 Medium Regt RA), 1925; Comd, 1943-45. Served with BEF, 1939-40, and with BLA, 1944-45 (despatches, DSO). Master of Border Counties (NW) Otter Hounds, 1946-50. JP, 1946, DL, 1947, Clwyd (formerly Denbighshire); High Sheriff of Cheshire, 1961. *Address:* Cherry Hill, Malpas, Cheshire. *T:* Malpas 355. *Clubs:* Cavalry; Palatine (Liverpool).   [*Died 21 May* 1975.

BATESON, Frederick Wilse; Fellow and Tutor in English Literature, Corpus Christi College, Oxford, 1946-69, now Emeritus; *b* 25 Dec. 1901; *s* of Alfred Bateson, Styal, Cheshire; *m* 1931, Jan Cancellor, JP; one *s* one *d. Educ:* Charterhouse; Trinity Coll., Oxford. Commonwealth Fellow, Harvard Univ., 1927-29. Editor of Cambridge Bibliography of English Literature, 1930-40; Lecturer WEA, 1935-40; Statistical Officer, Bucks War Agric. Exec. Cttee, 1940-46; Agricultural correspondent, The Observer and The New Statesman, 1944-48; Founder and Editor of Essays in Criticism (Quarterly), 1951-74. Visiting Professor: Cornell Univ., USA, 1955, California Univ. (Berkeley), 1958; Pennsylvania State Univ., 1960, 1962 and 1964. *Publications:* English Comic Drama, 1700-1750, 1929; English Poetry and the English Language, 1934, rev. edn 1973; Towards a Socialist Agriculture, 1946; Mixed Farming and

Muddled Thinking, 1946; English Poetry; a Critical Introduction, 1950 (rev. 1966); Pope's Epistles to Several Persons, 1951 (rev. 1961); Wordsworth: a Re-interpretation, 1954; Selected Poems of William Blake, 1957; A Guide to English Literature, 1965, rev. edn 1977; Brill: a Short History, 1966; Essays in Critical Dissent, 1972; The Scholar Critic, 1972. *Recreation:* local history. *Address:* Temple House, Brill, Bucks HP18 9SX. *T:* Brill 255.   [*Died 16 Oct.* 1978.

BATESON, Margaret, (Mrs Gregory Bateson); *see* Mead, Dr M.

BATESON, Rear-Adm. Stuart Latham, CB 1950; CBE 1948; MIEE; retired; *b* 7 July 1898; *twin s* of late Sir Alexander Dingwall Bateson, Judge of the High Court, and Isabel Mary (*née* Latham); *m* 1923, Marie Elphinstone Fleming Cullen; one *s* one *d. Educ:* Lockers Park; Rugby; RNC Keyham. Joined Navy, 1916; specialised in Torpedo, 1923; Comdr, 1934; Capt., 1939; Rear-Admiral (L), 1949, the first holder of the rank. Served War of 1939-45; Commanded HMS Latona, 1941; HMS Ajax, 1941-42; HMS London, 1944-46; Dir of Naval Electrical Department, Admiralty, 1946-51; retd, 1951. County Comr for Boy Scouts of Rutland, 1953-66. Chm. and Sec. Rutland Historic Churches Preservation Trust, 1954-. Sheriff of Rutland, 1958; DL 1957, Vice-Lieut Co. Rutland, 1963-72. *Recreation:* shooting. *Address:* Ridlington, Leics.   [*Died 17 April* 1980.

BATEY, Rowland William John S.; *see* Scott-Batey.

BATSON, Prof. Reginald George, MEng, FKC, CEng, FICE, FIMechE; Professor of Civil Engineering, University of Liverpool, 1936-50 (Dean, Faculty of Engineering, 1938-48), Emeritus since 1950; *b* 1885; *m* 1914, Nellie Eva Seal; one *s. Educ:* Tiffins Boys' Sch., Kingston-on-Thames; King's Coll., Univ. of London. Building Works Department of Woolwich Arsenal, 1904-8; Principal Scientific Officer Engineering Dept. of National Physical Laboratory, 1908-33; Principal Scientific Officer in charge of Road Research Laboratory of Department of Scientific Industrial Research, 1933-36. *Publications:* Mechanical Testing; Roads, 1950; numerous technical papers to Institution of Civil Engineers, Institution of Mechanical Engineers, Iron and Steel Institute, British Association, Soc. of Chemical Industry, etc. *Recreations:* gardening, motoring and cricket. *Address:* Trelawney, Bradshaw Lane, Mawdesley, Ormskirk, Lancs. *T:* Mawdesley 692.   [*Died 27 Dec.* 1974.

BATT, Lt-Col William Elliott, CMG 1918; late RFA, TF; a Metropolitan Magistrate, retired 1956; Stipendiary Magistrate of East Ham, 1939 and West Ham, 1943-46; *b* 6 Dec. 1882; 2nd *s* of late Capt. H. E. Batt, Heavitree, Exeter; *m* 1st, 1912, Gladys Edith (*d* 1918), *o c* of E. E. Hopewell, Rugby; one *d* ; 2nd, 1925, Dorothy Anne (marriage dissolved), *e d* of Charles Manville, Northumberland; 3rd, Joan, *d* of Rev. Bruce Mackay, Sutton Courtney, Berks. *Educ:* Heles Sch., Exeter; privately. Articled to R. Tapley, Solicitor, Exeter, 1900; admitted Solicitor, 1905; called to Bar, Gray's Inn, 1920; practised in London; joined 1st Devon Volunteer RGA, 1904; transferred to 1st London Brigade RFA; TF, 1908; served throughout European War (Lieut-Col 1916). Major, Home Guard, War of 1939-45. Freeman, City of London. *Recreations:* cooking, crosswords. *Address:* 27 Strand Court, Topsham, Devon. *T:* Topsham 4247.
                                    [*Died 4 Dec.* 1971.

BATTEN, Maj.-Gen. Richard Hutchison, CB 1961; CBE 1953 (OBE 1945); DSO 1943; DL; Colonel, Royal Hampshire Regiment, 1964-71; *b* 1908; *s* of Charles Henry Batten; *m* 1931, Betty Mary, *d* of Edward Andrews. *Educ:* Cheltenham; RMC, Sandhurst; Caius Coll., Cambridge. Served in Palestine, 1936-39; War of 1939-45, N Africa, Sicily, Italy, France and Germany (DSO, OBE, North Africa Star with 8th Army, Clasp); Korea, 1953 (CBE), Chief of Staff, HQ, Eastern Command, 1959-60; Chief of Staff, HQ, Northern Army Group, 1960-63; retd, 1964. DL Hants, 1967. *Recreations:* sailing, golf, fishing. *Address:* Godshill Wood, Fordingbridge, Hants. *T:* Fordingbridge 52238. *Clubs:* United Service & Royal Aero; Royal Yacht Squadron, Royal Lymington Yacht.   [*Died 15 June* 1972.

BATTERBEE, Sir Harry Fagg, GCMG 1946 (KCMG 1931; CMG 1918); KCVO 1927 (CVO 1918); *b* 1880; *s* of N. S. Batterbee, Faversham; *m* 1909, Eleanor Laura (*d* 1950), *d* of Rev. John Harding; *m* 1972, Mrs Dagmar Hayes. *Educ:* Queen Elizabeth's Grammar Sch., Faversham; Hertford Coll., Oxford; MA; Hon. Fellow, 1956. Entered the Colonial Office in 1905; Private Sec. to Sec. of State for the Colonies (Rt Hon. Walter H. Long, MP), 1916-19; Political Sec. to Vice-Admiral Commanding Special Service Squadron, Empire Cruise, 1923-24; Asst Sec. Dominions Office, 1925-30; Asst Under-Sec. of State, Dominions Office, 1930-38; Political Sec. to HRH Duke of York during Australian and New Zealand Tour, 1927;

Registrar of the Order of St Michael and St George, 1930-38; Deputy Sec., Imperial Conferences, 1930 and 1937; High Comr for UK in New Zealand, 1939-45. A Governor: London House Trust, London; Queen Elizabeth's Sch. Faversham. A Vice-Pres., Royal Commonwealth Society. *Address:* 63 The Ridgeway, Chatham, Kent ME4 6PB. *T:* Medway 42537. *Club:* United Oxford & Cambridge University. *[Died 25 Aug. 1976.*

BATTERSBY, Edmund James, FRICS; formerly Senior Partner, Edmund Kirby & Sons, Architects and Surveyors, Liverpool; *b* Knowsley, Lancs, 1911; *m* 1942, Mary, *y d* of J. F. W. Ravenhill; one *s* one *d.* Served War of 1939-45: Corps of Royal Engineers; during part of that time commanded Battle Wing of Sapper OCTU; demobilised in rank of Major. Was trained, and has spent whole career, with Edmund Kirby & Sons. Royal Institution of Chartered Surveyors: Council (Branch Rep.), 1960-; Vice-Pres., 1966; Sen. Vice-Pres., 1969; Pres., 8 June 1970-28 June 1971. Past service to the Institution includes many cttees, post-war rehabilitation of Chartered Surveyors, etc. Chm., Unification Cttee of the three Chartered Land Societies (united June 1970). Formerly Member: Bd, Runcorn New Town Development Corp.; Property Cttee, Nat. Freight Corp.; Court, Lancaster Univ. Formerly Governor and Dep. Treas., Liverpool Blue Coat School. Interested in youth and social welfare. Past Mem., Liverpool Regional Hosp. Bd; Past Chm., House Cttee of Liverpool Ear, Nose and Throat Hosp. *Recreations:* gardening, shooting. *Address:* Hornby Castle, near Lancaster. *T:* Hornby 21670.   *[Died 6 Feb. 1978.*

BATTEY, Mrs E. J.; *see* White, E. Evelyne McI.

BATTY, Tom, FRVA; Chairman, West Yorkshire Metropolitan County Council, 1978-79; *b* 4 March 1906; *s* of Robert Batty and Ada Louise Batty; *m* 1937, Mona Nicholson; one *s* one *d. Educ:* Jesmond Sch., West Hartlepool. Served Civil Defence, 1939-45; DM 1945. Local govt officer, 1926-52; private practice as valuer and rating surveyor, 1952-78. Elected to: W Riding CC, 1961 (Alderman, 1968); W Yorks Metrop. CC, 1973; Chm., Finance Cttee, 1967-74; Leader of Council, 1970-73 and 1977-78; Leader of Opposition, 1974-77; Chm., Policy and Finance Cttee, 1977-78. President: Valuers Inst., 1963-64; N Cheshire Br., Nalgo, 1947-48. Mem., Conservative National Adv. Cttee; Vice-Chm., Cons. Yorks Area Local Govt Adv. Cttee. *Publications:* papers on rating and local govt finance to Rating and Valuation Assoc. Confs, 1971 and 1974. *Recreation:* interest in all forms of sport, particularly cricket. *Address:* 21 Bankfield Road, Nab Wood, Shipley, W Yorks. *T:* Shipley 54961. *Clubs:* Bingley; Wilsden Conservative; Denholme Conservative.   *[Died 9 Nov. 1979.*

BATY, Charles Witcomb; *b* 1900; *e s* of late Wm Baty and late Margarette Ballinger; *m* 1923, Edith Halina, *d* of late Robert Bevan; one *s* two *d. Educ:* Westminster Sch. (King's Scholar); Christ Church, Oxford (Scholar). Asst Master, later sixth form Master, Bedford Sch. 1923-29; Head Master of the King's Sch., Chester, 1930-46; Dir, Education Div., Allied Commn for Austria, 1946-48; one of Her Majesty's Inspectors of Schools, 1949-62 (Staff Inspector, 1954), retd, 1962. A Vice-Pres., The Classical Assoc., 1966. *Address:* Greenbank, West Street, Mayfield, East Sussex TN20 6DS. *T:* Mayfield 2273.
                                                    [Died 27 March 1979.

BAULKWILL, Sir (Reginald) Pridham, Kt 1960; CBE 1955 (OBE 1950); Solicitor; Public Trustee, 1956-61; *b* 1895. *Educ:* Shebbear College, North Devon. LLB (Hons) 1914. Served with London Rifle Brigade in European War, 1914-18. Qualified as Solicitor, 1918. Previously asst Public Trustee. Mem. of the Egyptian Loans Advisory Board, 1962-; a Governor of Shebbear Coll. *Address:* 5 Derncleugh Gardens, Holcombe, Dawlish, S Devon. *T:* Dawlish 3169.   *[Died 11 Nov. 1974.*

BAWDEN, Sir Frederick (Charles), Kt 1967; FRS 1949; FRSA 1959; Director of Rothamsted Experimental Station, Harpenden, since 1958; *b* 18 Aug. 1908; *s* of George Bawden and Ellen Balment; *m* 1935, Marjorie Elizabeth Cudmore; two *s. Educ:* Emmanuel Coll., Cambridge (Hon. Fellow 1967). Research Asst, Potato Virus Research Station, Cambridge, 1930-36; Virus Physiologist, Rothamsted Experimental Station, 1936-40; Deputy Dir, Rothamsted Experimental Station, 1950-58; Head of Plant Pathology Dept, 1940-58. Leeuwenhoek Lectr, Royal Soc. 1959; Vis. Prof., Imperial Coll., London Univ., 1971; Hon. Life Member: New York Academy of Sciences, 1959; Indian Botanical Soc., 1960; Association Applied Biologists, 1966; Indian Phytopathological Soc., 1967; Foreign Mem. Royal Netherlands Academy of Sciences, 1960; President: Society of General Microbiology, 1959-61; Association Applied Biologists, 1965; British Insecticide and Fungicide Council, 1966-68; Internat. Congress of Plant Pathology, 1968; British Crop Protection Council; Inst. of Biology; a Vice-Pres. and Treasurer,

Royal Soc., 1968-. Chm., Agricultural Research Council of Central Africa. Mem., Natural Environment Research Council. Hon. DSc: Hull, 1964; Bath, 1969; Reading, 1970; Hon. DTech Brunel, 1967. Research Medal, Royal Agricultural Soc. of England, 1955; Elvin C. Stakman Award, Univ. of Minnesota, 1968. *Publications:* Plant Viruses and Virus Diseases, 1939, 4th edn 1964; Plant Diseases, 1948, 2nd edn 1950; many papers on viruses and virus diseases in scientific journals. *Address:* 1 West Common, Harpenden, Herts. *T:* Harpenden 2264.
                                                    [Died 8 Feb. 1972.

BAXTER, Frederick William; Professor of English Language and Literature in The Queen's University of Belfast, 1949-58, retired (Professor of English Literature, 1930-49); *b* Auckland New Zealand, 29 April 1897; *m* 1925, Marjorie Newsam Coles (*d* 1978), Newbury, Berks. *Educ:* Auckland Grammar Sch.; Auckland Univ. Coll.; Worcester Coll., Oxford. Divisional Signal Company, New Zealand Engineers, 1917-19; King's Coll., London, 1921-24; McGill Univ., Montreal, Canada, 1924-26; The University of Leeds, 1926-30. *Address:* Amberley Nursing Home, Clarence Square, Cheltenham, Glos.
                                                    [Died 12 March 1980.

BAXTER, His Honour Herbert James, OBE 1946; A Circuit Judge (formerly County Court Judge), 1955-73; *b* 6 March 1900; *s* of James Baxter; *m* 1931, Mary Kathleen Young; one *s* two *d. Educ:* Bishop Wordsworth Sch., Salisbury; Exeter Coll., Oxford (BA Modern History). Inns of Court OTC, and No. 7 Officers Cadet Bn, 1918; 2nd Lieut 1919. Called to Bar, Inner Temple, 1927 (Certificate of Honour); South Eastern Circuit, Kent Sessions. Civil Asst, War Office, 1939; Major, Intelligence Corps, 1940-43; Lieut-Col, 1943-45. Commander Order of Orange Nassau, 1946. *Recreations:* reading, golf, gardening. *Address:* Many Trees, Packhorse Road, Bessels Green, Sevenoaks, Kent. *T:* Sevenoaks 54512. *Clubs:* Reform; Wildernesse (Sevenoaks).   *[Died 3 May 1974.*

BAXTER, James Houston, MA, BD; FRSE; Regius Professor of Ecclesiastical History, University of St Andrews, 1922-70, now Emeritus; *b* Glasgow, 23 Feb. 1894; *y s* of James Baxter and Mary Houston; *m* 1919, Helen (*d* 1970), 2nd *d* of late A. K. Robertson, Kilmarnock; one *s. Educ:* Whitehill Sch., Glasgow Univ. (First Class Hons, Classics; Prize for Essay; Ramsay Memorial Medal; Logan Medal and Prize; Geo. A. Clarke Scholar in Classics; Faulds Fellow in Arts; MA 1918); Aberdeen Univ. (Asst to Prof. of Humanity, 1918-20; BD 1920). Instructor Commander, RN, 1943-45. Ordained to Ministry of Church of Scotland, 1921; Parish Minister of Ballantrae, 1921-22. Excavated Byzantine Imperial Palace, Istanbul, 1933-39. Sec., British Acad. Cttee on New Dictionary of Medieval Latin; Trustee, Scottish National Library, 1927-47. Member: Scottish Records Commission; Scottish Dictionaries Council. Corr. Member: Vereeniging voor de uitgave van Grotius, The Hague; Société de l'Histoire du Protestantisme français. Associate Member, Royal Belgian Acad. Associate: Royal Flemish Acad; Naples Acad.; Hon. Mem., Royal Geographical Soc., Antwerp, 1952. Officier de l'Instruction Publique. Hon. DLitt: St Andrews, 1930; Louvain, 1956; Hon. DD Glasgow, 1932; Hon. LLD St Andrews, 1971. Cross of St Mark, 1970. *Publications:* Contrib. to: Dictionnaire d'Histoire et de Géographie ecclésiastiques (Louvain), Chambers's Encyclopaedia and Bibliotheca Sanctorum; (Ed) A Dictionary of Later Latin, AD 125-750; (Co-Ed) Bulletin Du Cange; Bibliography of St Andrews, 1926; History of the Church, 312-800 (in History of Christianity), 1928; Select Letters of St Augustine, 1930; Copiale Prioratus S Andree, 1930; (Co-Ed) Books printed abroad by Scotsmen to 1700, 1932; Index to Scottish Historical Review, vols 13-25, 1932; A St Andrews Music Manuscript, 1932; (Ed) R. F. Murray, The Scarlet Gown, 1932, 1955; (Co-Ed) Index of British and Irish Latin Writers, 1933, and A Word List of Medieval Latin, 1934 (and later edns); Turkey and the Middle East, 1943; The Reformation in Dundee, 1960. *Address:* 41 South Street, St Andrews. *T:* 4230. *Club:* National Liberal.
                                                    [Died 1 April 1973.

BAXTER, William; JP; *b* 4 Dec. 1911; *s* of William Baxter, Kilsyth; *m* 1938, Margaret, *d* of Anthony Bassy, Kilsyth; one *s. Educ:* Banton Public Sch. County Councillor, Stirlingshire, Dec. 1931; Vice-Convener Stirling CC, 1957-; MP (Lab) West Stirlingshire, 1959-Oct. 1974. JP 1952; Stirling Representative, County Councils Association. *Address:* Gateside Farm, Kilsyth, by Glasgow. *T:* Kilsyth 2167.   *[Died 20 April 1979.*

BAYLEY, Victor, CIE 1917; CBE 1926; FICE; Indian State Railways, retired; *b* 1880. *Educ:* University Coll. Sch. *Publications:* Permanent Way Through the Khyber, 1934; Carfax of the Khyber, 1935; Liquid Fury, 1936; Nine Fifteen from Victoria, 1937; Frontier Fires, 1937; Pathan Treasure,

1937; Khyber Contraband, 1938; City of Fear, 1938; Indian Artifex, 1939; North-West Mail, 1939; Is India Impregnable?, 1942. *Address:* Plumptree Cottage, Naphill, Bucks.
[Died 5 Nov. 1972.

BAYLIS, Harry Arnold, MA, DSc (Oxon.); *b* 1889; *s* of late Rev. F. Baylis and Ellen Husbands; *m* 1915, Edith Baylis; one *d.* *Educ:* Epsom Coll.; Jesus Coll., Oxford. BA (Oxon.) 1912; MA, 1918; DSc (Oxon.) 1921; Asst Keeper, Dept of Zoology, British Museum (Natural History) 1912; Protozoologist, Royal Naval Hospital, Haslar, 1916-18; Deputy Keeper, Dept of Zoology, British Museum (Natural History), 1936-49. *Publications:* A Manual of Helminthology, Medical and Veterinary, 1929; Fauna of British India, Nematoda, Vol. 1, 1936; Vol. 2, 1939; various articles in Encyclopædia Britannica (14th ed.), 1929; A Synopsis of the Families and Genera of Nematoda (with R. Daubney), 1926; many papers on zoological subjects, chiefly systematic helminthology. *[Died 13 July 1972.*

BAYLISS, Edwin, OBE 1960; Member: the National Assistance Board and Board of Social Security, 1961-67; LCC for East Islington, 1946-65 (Chairman, LCC, 1952-53); GLC for Islington, 1964-67; Chairman, North Thames Gas Consultative Council, 1949-69; *b* 1894; *s* of Edwin Bayliss, Wolverhampton; *m* 1st, 1913, Lily Smithers (*d* 1948), Windsor, Berks.; (two *s* decd); 2nd, 1949, Constance Shipley (*d* 1965), London. *Educ:* Wolverhampton; WEA; Nottingham Coll. Served European War, 1914-18 (wounded, Mons star, war medals). Founder Mem. British Legion, 1921, served Area Councils, etc.; Vice-Pres. and Founder Anglo-Turkish Soc.; Vice-Chm., Northern Polytechnic; served LCC cttees; Chm. Gen. Purposes Cttee, 1948-52; Chm. LCC Parks Cttee, 1955-58. JP 1950, DL 1951, County of London. KStJ 1966 (CStJ 1959). Vice-Pres. London District St John Ambulance Brigade. *Address:* 48 Biddestone Road, N7. *T:* 01-607 4351. *[Died 30 March 1971.*

BAYNE, Rt. Rev. Stephen Fielding, Jr; Professor of Christian Mission, since 1970, Dean, since 1972, General Theological Seminary, New York; *b* New York, NY, 21 May 1908; *s* of Stephen Fielding Bayne and Edna Mabel (*née* Ashley); *m* 1934, Lucie Culver Gould; four *s* one *d.* *Educ:* Trinity Sch., NY; Amherst Coll. (BA); General Theological Seminary, NY (STM). Fellow and Tutor, Gen. Theological Seminary, 1932-34; Rector, Trinity Church, St Louis, Mo, 1934-39; Rector, St John's Church, Northampton, Mass, 1939-42; Chaplain, Columbia Univ., 1942-47. Chaplain USNR, 1944-45. Bishop of Olympia, 1947-59; Anglican Executive Officer and Bishop-in-charge, Amer. Churches in Europe, 1960-64; Dir, Overseas Dept, Episcopal Church, USA, 1964-68; 1st Vice-Pres. and Deputy for Program, Episcopal Church, USA, 1968-70. Hon. degrees: STD: Gen. Theol. Sem. 1947; Columbia Univ. 1952; DD: Amherst Coll. 1948; Whitman Coll., 1952; Anglican Theol. Coll., 1954; St Paul's, Tokyo, 1960; Harvard Univ., 1961; Huron Coll., 1963; Cuttington Coll., 1967; Trinity Coll., 1969; LLD, Mills Coll., 1951; DLitt: Hobart Coll., 1957; Kenyon Coll., 1960; LHD, Univ. Puget Sound, 1959; ThD, Australian Coll. of Theology, 1962. *Publications:* Gifts of the Spirit, 1943; The Optional God, 1953; Christian Living, 1957; In the Sight of the Lord, 1958; Enter with Joy, 1961; Mindful of the Love, 1962; An Anglican Turning-Point, 1964. *Address:* Chelsea Square, 175 Ninth Avenue, New York, NY 10011, USA. *Clubs:* Athenæum; Century (New York); University (Seattle). *[Died 18 Jan. 1974.*

BAYNES, Dorothy Julia C.; *see* Colston-Baynes.

BAYNES, Edward Stuart Augustus, OBE 1950; United Kingdom Trade Commissioner in Dublin, 1946-54; *b* 25 June 1889; *s* of Edward Neil Baynes and Charlotte Augusta Baynes, OBE, *d* of Hon. Augustus Anthony Frederick Irby; *g s* of Sir William J. W. Baynes, 3rd Bart; *m* 1918, Helen Mary, *widow* of J. S. White, and *d* of G. A. Meredith; one *s*. *Educ:* Cheam Sch. and Radley Coll. Served European War, 1914-18, 11th Bn KRRC; Capt. 1916 (wounded twice, 1914-15 Star). Foreign Office 1918; Dept of Overseas Trade, 1919-41; Asst to British Trade Comr in NZ, 1920-22; visited Canada on official business, 1929; Dep. Comr Gen. for UK at British Empire Exhibition, Johannesburg, 1936; Official organizer, British Pavilion, Glasgow Exhibition, 1938; Dep. Comr Gen. for British Pavilion, New York World's Fair, 1939 (Hon. Citizen, New York, 1940). Dominions Office, 1942-45. *Publication:* A Revised Catalogue of Irish Macrolepidoptera. *Recreation:* entomology (FRES 1912). *Address:* Sandford, Adelaide Road, Glenageary, Co. Dublin. *T:* Dublin 805087. *Clubs:* Green Jackets (Winchester); Kildare Street (Dublin); Royal Irish Yacht (Kingstown). *[Died 14 May 1972.*

BAYNES, Keith Stuart; artist; *b* 1887; *s* of Rev. M. C. Baynes and Margaretha, *d* of Rev. Canon Arthur Cazenove. *Educ:* Harrow; Trinity Coll., Cambridge; Slade Sch. Held exhibitions at the Independent Gallery, London Artists Association, Lefevre Gallery and Agnew's Gallery; exhibn, 50 Years of Painting, England, France and Portugal, Colchester, 1969; retrospective exhibn, Harvane Gallery, 1973; exhibited France, Denmark, Germany, Italy, USA, Canada, Australia. *Publications:* (illustrated) Vineyards of France, 1950; (illustrated) English Channel, 1952. *Address:* 6 Catherine Place, Bath BA1 2PR. *Club:* Athenæum. *[Died 17 April 1977.*

BAYNES, Sir Rory (Malcolm Stuart), 6th Bt *cr* 1801; retired; *b* 16 May 1886; *s* of Rev. Malcolm Charles Baynes, MA (4th *s* of 3rd Bt) (*d* 1941), and Margaretha (*d* 1936), *d* of Rev. Arthur Cazenove; *S* cousin, 1971; *m* 1925, Ethel Audrey (*d* 1947), *d* of Edward Giles, CIE; one *s*. *Educ:* Harrow School. 3rd Bedford Militia, 1905-08; commissioned in The Cameronians (Scottish Rifles), 1908; served European War, 1914-18; commanded 2nd Bn The Cameronians (Scottish Rifles), 1933-37; served war of 1939-45. County Councillor, Somerset, 1946-58, County Alderman, 1958-68. *Recreations:* fishing, golf (until eight lost). *Heir: s* Lt-Col John Christopher Malcolm Baynes [*b* 24 April 1928; *m* 1955, Shirley Maxwell, *o d* of late Robert Allan Dodds; four *s*]. *Address:* Lake Vyrnwy Hotel, via Oswestry, Salop SY10 0LY. *T:* Llanwddyn 244. *[Died 29 April 1979.*

BAYNES, Sir William Edward Colston, 5th Bt, *cr* 1801; MC; *b* 23 Feb. 1876; *er s* of Sir Christopher W. Baynes, 4th Bt; *S* father, 1936. *Educ:* Harrow; Trinity Coll., Cambridge (MA, LLM). Barrister-at-Law Inner Temple, 1900; Licencié en droit, Paris, 1905; Egyptian Civil Service, 1906-22; Judge, Egyptian Native Courts, 1913; Chief Inspector of Justice, 1919; Coldstream Guards, 1915-19 (Capt., MC). *Heir: c* Rory Malcolm Stuart Baynes [Lt-Col late Cameronians; *b* 16 May 1886; *m* 1925, Audrey (*d* 1947), *d* of late Edward Giles, CIE; one *s*]. *Club:* Brooks's. *[Died 17 Sept. 1971.*

BEACH, Major William Whitehead H.; *see* Hicks Beach.

BEACHCOMBER; *see* Morton, J. C. A. B. M.

BEADLE, Sir Gerald (Clayton), Kt 1961; CBE 1951; retired from BBC in 1961 after 38 years' service in broadcasting; Vice-President, Bath and West Society; *b* 17 April 1899; *e s* of late Clayton Beadle; *m* Jocelyn Corinne, *d* of late Hugh Rae; two *s*. *Educ:* Tonbridge Sch.; Pembroke Coll., Cambridge. Subaltern RA, 1917-19. With BBC 1923-61 during which period held office as: Dir of Broadcasting, Durban, S Africa; Controller N Ireland; Asst Director of Programmes, London; Head of Staff Training, London; Controller, West Region; wartime Dir of Administration and Principal Asst to Jt Dirs Gen., London; Dir of BBC Television, London. *Publication:* Television: a Critical Review, 1963. *Recreations:* fishing, golf. *Address:* Little Priory, Bathwick Hill, Bath, Avon. *TA* and *T:* Bath 5388. *Clubs:* Savile; Bath and County. *[Died 6 Nov. 1976.*

BEADLE, Rt. Hon. Sir (Thomas) Hugh (William), PC 1964; Kt 1961; CMG 1957; OBE 1946; QC 1946; Chief Justice, Rhodesia, 1961-77, retired; *b* 6 Feb. 1905; *s* of late A. W. Beadle, OBE, Sec. to Southern Rhodesia Treasury; *m* 1st, 1934, Leonie Barry (*d* 1953); two *d*; 2nd, 1954, Olive Staley Jackson (*d* 1974); 3rd, 1976, Pleasance Johnson. *Educ:* Salisbury Boys' High Sch.; Diocesan Coll., Rondebosch; University of Cape Town (BA, LLB); Queen's Coll., Oxford (BCL, Hon. Fellow). Advocate, Bulawayo, 1930-39; Seconded Royal WAfFF, Gold Coast, 1939-40; Deputy Judge Advocate-Gen., S Rhodesia Forces, and Parliamentary Sec. to Prime Minister, 1940-46; MP Bulawayo North (United Party), 1939-50; Southern Rhodesia, 1946-50: Minister of Justice; of Internal Affairs; of Health; of Education; Judge of the High Court, Rhodesia, 1950-61. Cross of the Grand Commander of Royal Hellenic Order of the Phœnix (Greece), 1950. Hon. Fellow Queen's Coll., Oxford, 1966. *Recreations:* shooting, fishing, Boy Scouts, care of physically handicapped. *Address:* 63 Leander Avenue, Hillside, Bulawayo, Rhodesia. *Clubs:* Bulawayo, Salisbury (Rhodesia). *[Died 14 Dec. 1980.*

BEAGLEHOLE, John Cawte, OM 1970; CMG 1958; FRSNZ 1967; Professor of British Commonwealth History, Victoria University of Wellington, New Zealand, 1963-66, Emeritus 1967; *b* 13 June 1901; *s* of David Ernest Beaglehole and Jane Butler; *m* 1930, Elsie Mary Holmes; three *s*. *Educ:* Wellington Coll., NZ; Victoria Univ. Coll.; University of London. MA (New Zealand), 1924; PhD (London), 1929. Asst in History Department, Victoria Univ. Coll., 1924-26; Post-graduate travelling scholarship, 1926-29; WEA Tutor-organiser, 1930-31; lecturer in history, Auckland Univ. Coll., 1932; odd jobs, 1933-35; Lecturer in History, Victoria Univ. Coll., 1936-47, senior lecturer, 1947-48; Senior Research Fellow and Lecturer in Colonial History, 1949-63; Historical Adviser, NZ Department of Internal Affairs, 1938-52. Chm. of Board of Management, NZ

University Press, 1947-61. Pres., NZ Council for Civil Liberties, 1952-; Member: NZ Historic Places Trust, 1955-; NZ Arts Advisory Council, 1960-64. Hon. Fellow, Australian Acad. of the Humanities, 1969. Univ. Canterbury Condliffe Memorial Award, 1952; Royal Geographical Society's Gill Memorial Award for contributions to biography of Capt. Cook, 1957; University of Melbourne Ernest Scott Prize, 1962. Hon. DLitt: Oxford, 1966; Sydney, 1970; Hon. LitD Wellington, 1968; Hon. LittD Otago, 1969. Mueller Medal, ANZAAS, 1969. *Publications:* Captain Hobson and the New Zealand Company, 1928; The Exploration of the Pacific, 1934, 3rd edn 1966; New Zealand, A Short History, 1936; The University of New Zealand, 1937; The Discovery of New Zealand, 1939, 2nd edn 1961; Victoria University College, an Essay towards a History, 1949; (Ed.) Abel Janszoon Tasman and the Discovery of New Zealand, 1942; New Zealand and the Statute of Westminster, 1944; The Journals of Captain James Cook on his Voyages of Discovery, 3 Vols, 1955-67; The *Endeavour* Journal of Joseph Banks, 1962; articles and reviews; *posthumous publication:* The Life of Captain James Cook, 1974. *Recreations:* books, typography, music. *Address:* 6 Messines Road, Wellington, W3, New Zealand.   *[Died 10 Oct. 1971.*

BEALE, Dame Doris Winifred, DBE 1944; RRC 1941 (and Bar 1944); OStJ, *b* 9 Aug. 1889; *o d* of late George Beale, Forest Hill. *Educ:* Prendergast Sch., Lewisham. Trained at London Hospital; joined QARNNS, 1917; served at Royal Naval Establishments at Chatham, Haslar, Dartmouth, Malta, Gibraltar and Plymouth; Superintending Sister, 1933; Matron, 1937; Matron-in-Chief, Queen Alexandra's Royal Naval Nursing Service, 1941-44; Deputy-Matron-in-Chief, Joint War Organization of the Red Cross Soc. and Order of St John, 1944-46. A Governor of Lewisham Prendergast Sch., 1945-64. Florence Nightingale Medal by ICRC, 1951. *Recreations:* travel and gardening. *Address:* Trinity Lodge, London Road, Forest Hill, SE23. *Club:* United Nursing Services. *[Died 14 Jan. 1971.*

BEALE, Sir Louis (Bernhardt George Stephen), KCMG 1937; CBE 1929; *b* 28 Nov. 1879; *s* of Louis S. and Mary A. Beale; *m* 1902, May A., *d* of T. N. and Mary Marr; two *s. Educ:* Skinners' Sch., Tunbridge Wells. HM Trade Comr: Canada, 1919-25; New Zealand, 1926-28; on special mission to British Malaya, 1928-29; Trade Comr Overseas Trade Development Council, Dept of Overseas Trade; Commercial Counsellor British Embassy, Shanghai, 1932-37; Commissioner-Gen. for HM Govt in the UK, New York World's Fair, 1939-40; Mem. of Anglo-French Purchasing Board, New York, 1940. *Address:* 1 Wall Street, New York, USA. *Clubs:* Devonshire; Union (Victoria, BC); Vancouver (Vancouver).   *[Died 25 May 1971.*

BEALES, Arthur Charles Frederick, MA, DLit (London); Professor Emeritus of History of Education, King's College, University of London, 1972; FKC 1966; *b* 24 Jan. 1905; *er s* of Arthur Beales and Elizabeth (*née* Matthews), Kensington; *m* 1936, Freda, *er d* of Augustine Coleman Morris, Enniskillen; no *c. Educ:* Latymer Upper Sch.; King's Coll., University of London. BA, 1st cl. Hons, Hist., 1925; MA (dist.) 1927; University of London Teacher's Dipl., 1928; DLit 1964. Asst Master, Haberdashers' Askes' Hampstead Sch., 1928-31; Lectr in History, University Coll., Swansea, 1931-32; Lectr in Education, 1933-34; Lectr in Education, King's Coll. University of London, 1935-53, Reader, 1953-64, Prof. 1964-72. Talks Producer, Religious Broadcasting Dept, BBC, 1941-45. Received into Catholic Church, 1935; Cross, Pro Ecclesia et Pontifice, 1960. Mem. Council Historical Association, 1939-50; Chm. Editorial Bd Catholic Record Soc., 1948-55; Hon. Sec., Sword of the Spirit Movement, intermittently, 1941-47 (Chm. 1949). On British Delegation to 1st World Congress of UNESCO, Paris, 1947; Brit. deleg. internat. Educ. Conf., Santander, 1949; Mem. Catholic Educ. Council; Editor, Brit. Jl of Educational Studies, 1952-. *Publications:* The History of Peace: a Short Account of the Movements for International Order, 1931; A Guide to the Teaching of History in Schools, 1937; The Catholic Church and International Order, 1941 (Penguin); Education under Penalty: the Education of English Catholics, 1547-1689, 1963. Articles in Journal of Education, Dublin Review, The Tablet, and foreign educl jls. *Address:* 18 Grosvenor Court, Rayners Road, SW15. *T:* 01-788 5343.   *[Died 16 Aug. 1974.*

BEALES, Reginald Edwin, CBE 1961; Deputy Director, Central Statistical Office, Cabinet Office, 1957-72; *b* 16 Sept. 1909; *s* of Charles Neslen Beales, Norwich; *m* 1938, Margaret Alice Poulton (*d* 1964); one *s* one *d. Educ:* City of Norwich Sch. Norwich Union Life Ins. Soc., 1926; Northern Assce Co., 1931; Central Statistical Office, 1943; Chief Statistician, Inland Revenue, 1949; Dir of Statistics and Intell., Inland Revenue, 1952-57. FIA 1934, FSS 1947. Mem. Coun., 1965-69; Vice-

Pres., 1967-68). *Publications:* articles in: Jl of Royal Statistical Soc.; Review of Income and Wealth. *Recreations:* tennis, gardening. *Address:* 5 The Meadows, Chelsfield, Orpington, Kent BR6 6HS. *T:* Farnborough (Kent) 56070.
                                        [Died 22 Sept. 1980.

BEALS, Carlyle Smith, OC (Canada) 1970; FRS 1951; FRSC 1933; Private Scientific Consultant in Celestial and Earth Sciences, 1964-77; *b* 29 June 1899; *s* of Rev. F. H. Beals, Inglisville, NS, and Annie F. N. Smith, Albert, NB; *m* 1931, Miriam White Bancroft; one *d. Educ:* Acadia Univ., NS (BA 1919); Toronto Univ. (MA (Physics), 1923); Imperial Coll. of Science and Technology (DIC 1925); London Univ. (PhD 1926, DSc 1934); DSc hon.: Acadia Univ, 1951; Univ. of New Brunswick, 1956; Queen's Univ., 1960; Pittsburgh Univ., 1963. Tory Medal, RSC 1957; Gold Medal of Professional Inst. of the Public Service of Canada, 1958; F. C. Leonard Medal of Meteoritical Soc., 1966. Asst Prof. of Physics, Acadia Univ., 1926-27; Astronomer, Dominion Astrophysical Observatory, Victoria, BC, 1927-40; Asst Dir, 1940-46; Dominion Astronomer, Ottawa, 1946-64. *Publications:* about 87 papers in astronomical and physical journals on analysis of line spectra, emission line stars, interstellar matter, terrestial and lunar impact craters, and the development of scientific instruments. *Recreations:* wild life study, the study of lunar photographs, geology. *Address:* Manotick, Ont KOA 2NO, Canada. *T:* Manotick 692-3247.   *[Died 2 July 1979.*

BEAN, Sir Edgar Layton, Kt 1955; CMG 1937; MA (Oxon), LLB; Parliamentary Draftsman, State of South Australia, 1926-58; *b* Melbourne, 15 Oct. 1893; *m* Constance Mary, *d* of William James Greenlees, Adelaide; two *s. Educ:* Scotch Coll., Western Australia; Adelaide Univ.; Merton Coll., Oxford. BA 1st Class Hons Classics, Adelaide, 1913; Exhibitioner Merton Coll., Oxford, 1914; served BEF France, 1916-19; BA Oxford, 1919; MA Oxford, 1922; LLB Adelaide, 1922; twice awarded Stow Prize for Law; admitted to Bar of South Australia, 1922; Chm., Local Government Commission, 1929-34; Editor, South Australian Statutes, 1934; Mem. SA Public Service Board, 1942-51; Chm., Education Enquiry Cttee, 1943-45; Chm., Teachers' Salaries Bd, 1946-64. *Publications:* South Australian Statutes, with notes, etc (8 vols). *Recreations:* fishing, history, literature. *Address:* 51 Godfrey Terrace, Leabrook, South Australia 5068. *T:* 30 4551. *Clubs:* Naval Military and Air Force, Royal South Australia Yacht Squadron (Adelaide). *[Died 28 July 1977.*

BEAN, Hon. Sir George (Joseph), Kt 1970; OBE 1945; Hon. Mr Justice Bean; a Judge of the High Court, Queen's Bench Division, since 1969; *b* 19 Sept. 1915; *s* of late George and Phoebe Bean; *m* 1953, Zdenka White; one *s. Educ:* Liverpool Institute; Liverpool Univ. Pres. Liverpool Univ. Union, 1937-38. Served in Army, 1939-46 (despatches). Col RASC. Called to Bar, Middle Temple, 1940; Bencher, 1969. QC 1963; Recorder of Carlisle, 1965-69. Mem., Parole Bd, 1972-. *Recreations:* gardening, reading. *Address:* 27 Seymour Road, SW19 5JL. *T:* 01-947 1706.   *[Died 19 Nov. 1973.*

BEARD, Maj.-Gen. (Hon.) Edmund Charles, CB 1947; CBE 1940; MC; *b* 21 April 1894; *s* of late C. T. Beard, CB, ISO, and Gertrude, *y d* of late E. J. Figgis, JP, Dublin; *m* 1922, Helen Beatrice Beryl (*d* 1968), *yr d* of late Percy Barlow, JP, Acton, W3; one *s* two *d* (and *er s* killed in Malaya, Dec. 1952). *Educ:* Marlborough; Brasenose Coll., Oxford (BA). Commissioned The Royal Irish Regiment, 1914; served European War in Gallipoli, Salonika, Palestine and France (despatches, wounded, MC); transferred to South Lancs Regt, 1922; SSO and Staff Capt. India, 1922-26; Staff Coll., Camberley, 1927-28; Gen. Staff, S Command, 1929-30; Bde Major 9th Inf. Bde, 1930-33; Brevet Major 1930; GSO 2, War Office, 1933-38; Brevet Lieut-Col 1935; transferred to Duke of Wellington's Regt, 1937, and commanded 1st Bn 1939. AA and QMG 44 Div., France and Belgium, 1940; commanded 133 Inf. Bde, 1940-42; Brig. GS Home Forces, 1942-43; Area commd (Maj.-Gen.) India, 1943-46. ADC to the King, 1946; retired pay, 1946. Col S Lancs Regt, 1948-57. *Recreation:* golf. *Address:* Nutcombe Height, Hindhead, Surrey. *Clubs:* Golfers'; MCC. *[Died 20 Jan. 1974.*

BEARDS, Samuel Arthur, MS; Hon. Surgeon, Royal National Ear, Nose and Throat Hospital; formerly Consulting Laryngologist St Mary Abbots Hospital, W8. MRCS, LRCP 1924; MB, BS, 1926; MS London 1929. Late Surgical Registrar and Senior House Surgeon, Hospital for Diseases of the Throat, Golden Square; Hon. Assistant, Bacteriological Department, London Hospital; House Surgeon, West London Hospital. *Address:* 14 Endsleigh Street, WC1. *[Died 2 March 1975.*

BEATON, Sir Cecil (Walter Hardy), Kt 1972; CBE 1957; photographer and designer; *b* London, 14 Jan. 1904; *s* of late

Ernest Walter Hardy Beaton and Etty Sisson. *Educ:* Harrow; Cambridge. Exhibitions of photographs: Cooling Gallery, 1930; Nat. Portrait Gallery, 1968. Exhibitions of painting and stage designs: Redfern Gallery, 1936, 1958, 1965; Lefevre Gallery, 1966; Wright Hepburn Gallery, 1968; Parkin Gallery, 1976. Writer; Photographer for Min. of Information; Designer of scenery and costumes for ballet and opera, and for many theatrical productions (London and New York stage); including sets and costumes for Lady Windermere's Fan, Quadrille, The Grass Harp; The School for Scandal (Comédie Française); costumes for: My Fair Lady (New York, London); *films:* Gigi, The Doctor's Dilemma, My Fair Lady. Légion d'Honneur, 1960. *Publications:* The Book of Beauty, 1930; Cecil Beaton's Scrapbook, 1937; Cecil Beaton's New York, 1939; My Royal Past, 1939 (rev. 1960); (with P. Quennell) Time Exposure, 1941; Air of Glory, 1941; Winged Squadrons, 1942; Near East, 1943; British Photographers, 1944; Far East, 1945; Time Exposure, 1946; Portrait of New York, 1949; Ashcombe, 1949; Ballet, 1951; Photobiography, 1951; (with Kenneth Tynan) Persona Grata, 1953; The Glass of Fashion, 1954; It Gives me Great Pleasure, 1955; The Face of the World, 1957; Japanese, 1959; The Wandering Years, 1961; Quail in Aspic, 1962; Royal Portraits, 1963; Images, 1963; Cecil Beaton's Fair Lady 1964; The Years Between, 1965; The Best of Beaton, 1968; My Bolivian Aunt, 1971; The Happy Years, 1972; The Strenuous Years, 1973; The Magic Image, 1975; The Restless Years, 1976; The Parting Years, 1978. Photograph illustrations and drawings for many books including: History Under Fire (James Pope Hennessy), Bomber Command, The Importance of Being Earnest (Folio Society) 1960; author of play The Gainsborough Girls. *Recreations:* diaries, scrap-books, decoration, travel. *Address:* Reddish House, Broadchalke, near Salisbury. *T:* Broadchalke 211.   *[Died 18 Jan. 1980.*

BEATTIE, John, MD, DSc; *b* 30 June 1899; *s* of James and M. Beattie, Dunmurry, Co. Antrim, N Ireland; *m* 1926, Elizabeth Hall Price, MB; two *s* one *d. Educ:* Royal Academical Institute, Belfast; Queen's Univ., Belfast; University Coll., London. Demonstrator of Embryology, Queen's Univ., Belfast, 1923-24; Research Associate and Demonstrator of Anatomy, University Coll., London, 1924-27; Anatomist to Zoological Soc. of London, 1926-27; Asst Prof. of Anatomy, 1927-30, Assoc. Prof. of Anatomy, 1930-33, McGill Univ., Canada; Conservator of Museum and Dir of Research, Royal College of Surgeons, 1933-42; Prof. of Experimental Surgery, Royal College of Surgeons, 1938-42; Bernhard Baron Research Prof., Royal College of Surgeons, 1942-50; Col AMS, Dir Army Blood Transfusion Service, 1939-40; Consultant, Surg.-Gen. US Army, 1948-50; Arris and Gale Lecturer, Royal College of Surgeons, 1935-42; Henderson Trust Lecturer, University of Edinburgh, 1936; Banting Memorial Lecturer, University of Toronto, 1949; Research Associate Physiology Dept and Low Temperature Research Station, Cambridge, 1950-58; Physiologist, Houghton Poultry Research Station, Houghton, Hunts, 1958-66; Consultant: Asbestos Research Council, 1958-66; Inst. of Occupational and Environmental Health, Montreal, 1966-73. Vis. Prof., Univ. of California, 1963, 1964, 1965. *Publications:* articles in scientific journals. *Address:* Queens' College, Cambridge. *T:* Swavesey 30284.   *[Died 17 Oct. 1976.*

BEATTIE, Captain Stephen Halden, VC 1942; Royal Navy, retired; *b* 29 March 1908; *s* of Rev. Prebendary E. H. Beattie, MC; *m* 1933, Philippa Mary Blanchflower; four *s. Educ:* Abberley Hall; Rugby. Joined Royal Navy, 1926; Captain, 1951. Senior Officer, 1st Australian Frigate Squadron, 1952-54. Senior Naval Officer, Persian Gulf, 1956-58; in command HMS Birmingham, 1958; retd 1960. Naval Adviser to Ethiopian Govt, 1965. Chevalier Légion d'Honneur, 1947; Croix de guerre with palms, 1947; Officer, Order of Menelik, 1969. *Address:* Salt House, Mullion, Cornwall. *Club:* Army and Navy.
                                                      [Died 24 April 1975.

BEATTY, 2nd Earl, *cr* 1919, of the North Sea and of Brooksby; **David Field Beatty,** DSC 1942; Commander RN (retired); *b* 22 Feb. 1905; *er s* of 1st Earl and Ethel (*d* 1932), *o d* of Marshall Field, sen., of Chicago; *S* father 1936; *m* 1st, 1937, Dorothy Power Sands (marriage dissolved, 1945; she *m* 1954, 6th Baron Brownlow); 2nd 1946, Mrs Dorothy Rita Bragg (marriage dissolved, 1950; she *m* 1951, Abram Stevens Hewitt, New York); one *s*; 3rd, 1951, Mrs Adelle O'Connor (marriage dissolved, 1958), New York; one *d*; 4th, 1959, Diane, *d* of Mrs Duncan Kirk and step *d* of Capt. Duncan Kirk, Sheaves Farm, Loxwood, Sussex; one *s* one *d.* MP (U) Peckham Div. of Camberwell, 1931-36; PPS to Financial Secretary to the Admiralty, 1931-36; Joint Parliamentary Sec., Air Ministry, 1945; Mem. LCC for Peckham, 1937-46; Chm. of Navy League, 1937-41, Pres., 1941-44; served War of 1939-45 with Royal Navy; commanded: HMS Puffin, Buxton and Boreas, 1940-41;

Combined Operations Dieppe and Sicily, 1942-43; Dep. Dir Combined Operations Dept, Admiralty, 1944-45. Chm., British Empire Games (England), 1950-. Chm., Home Oil of Canada Limited, 1966-. *Heir: s* Viscount Borodale. *Recreations:* shooting and fishing. *Address:* Regency Cottage, 5 Rutland Gardens, SW7. *T:* 01-589 5093; Chicheley Hall, Newport Pagnell, Bucks. *T:* North Crawley 252. *Clubs:* White's; Royal Yacht Squadron (Cowes).   *[Died 10 June 1972.*

BEAUCHAMP, 8th Earl, *cr* 1815; **William Lygon,** DL, JP; Baron Beauchamp, 1806; Viscount Elmley, 1815; *b* 3 July 1903; *e s* of 7th Earl and Lady Lettice Grosvenor (*d* 1936), *d* of late Earl Grosvenor and *sister* of 2nd Duke of Westminster, GCVO, DSO; *S* father, 1938; *m* 1936, Else Doronville de la Cour, MBE 1944, Order of the Dannebrog (RDI) 1964, Grand Commander of the Dannebrog, 1970, DStJ 1957, *widow* of Director C. de la Cour. *Educ:* Eton; Magdalen Coll., Oxford. MP (L) Norfolk E, 1929-31 (LNat), 1931-38. Parliamentary Private Sec. to late Lord Hore-Belisha, in four Government Departments, 1931-38; DL 1948, JP 1941, CC 1940-52, Worcs. Pres., Three Counties Show, 1964. Served in RAOC Aug. 1941-45 at home and in Italy. *Heir:* none. *Address:* Madresfield Court, Great Malvern, Worcs. *T:* Malvern 3024; 8 Halkin Place, SW1. *T:* 01-235 5665.
                                                      [Died 3 Jan. 1979 (ext).

BEAUCHAMP, Sir Brograve (Campbell), 2nd Bt, *cr* 1911; *b* 5 May 1897; *s* of 1st Bt and Betty Campbell, *d* of late Archibald Woods, Columbus, Ohio, USA; *S* father, 1925; *m* 1923, Lady Evelyn Leonora Alima Herbert, *e d* of 5th Earl of Carnarvon; one *d.* MP (U) Walthamstow East, 1931-45. *Heir:* none. *Address:* 19 Kingston House, Princes Gate, SW7. *Club:* White's.
                                                      [Died 25 Aug. 1976 (ext).

BEAUCHAMP, Rev. Sir Ivor Cuthbert Proctor-, 8th Bt, *cr* 1744; MA; MB, BCh; late Medical Missionary of the China Inland Mission; *b* 19 Aug. 1900; *s* of Rev. Sir Montagu Proctor-Beauchamp, 7th Bt and Florence (*d* 1955), *d* of Robert Barclay of Reigate; *S* father 1939; *m* 1933, Caroline Muriel (of the same Mission), *d* of Frank Densham, Stoneygate, Leicester; two *s* one *d. Educ:* Marlborough; King's Coll., Cambridge. *Heir: s* Christopher Radstock Proctor-Beauchamp [*b* 30 Jan. 1935; *m* 1965, Rosalind Emily Margot, 3rd *d* of G. P. Wainwright, St Leonards-on-Sea; one *s* one *d. Educ:* Rugby. Trinity College, Cambridge (MA)]. *Address:* 335 Springfield Road, Chelmsford, Essex. *T:* Chelmsford 58216.   *[Died 8 Aug. 1971.*

BEAUMAN, Brig.-Gen. Archibald Bentley, CBE 1937; DSO 1916; *b* 30 Nov. 1888; *e s* of Bentley Martin Beauman; *m* 1923, Eva Dorothy (*d* 1949), *d* of Albert E. Pullar Durn, Perth; one *d* (one *s* decd); *m* 1952, Barbara Arnold. *Educ:* Malvern Coll.; Sandhurst. Joined 2nd South Staffs. Regt, 1908; served South Africa and England prior to War; landed in France, Aug. 1914, with original Expeditionary Force; invalided home Nov. 1914; rejoined in France, Jan. 1915; served as Staff Capt., DAA and QMG, and acting Lieut-Col 1st battalion S Staffs. Regt; Brig.-Gen., 26 May 1918, and commanded 69th Infantry Brigade in Italy until 6 April 1919; Bt Lieut-Col Jan. 1919 (DSO and bar, Bt Major, despatches six times, Italian Silver Medal for Valour and Italian Croce di Guerra); Staff Coll., Camberley, 1920; Gen. Staff Officer, 2nd Grade, Baluchistan District, India, 1921-25; Chief Instructor RMA Woolwich, 1926-27; commanded 1st Battalion The York and Lancaster Regiment 1928-32; Asst Commandant, and Chief Instructor, Netheravon Wing, Small Arms School, 1932-34; Comdr 15th Infantry Bde 1934-38; ADC to the King, 1938; retired pay, 1938; commanded a Division, 1940 (despatches twice); Comdr North Riding District, 1943; reverted to retired pay, 1944. Vice-Chm., Racehorse Owners' Assoc., 1959. *Publications:* Common Mistakes in the Solution of Tactical Problems; A Short Outline of Modern Tactics, 1939; Then a Soldier, 1960. *Recreations:* fishing, shooting, racing. *Address:* The Flat, Orwell, Walton-on-the-Hill, Surrey.
                                                      [Died 22 March 1977.

BEAUMARCHAIS, Jacques Delarüe Caron de; Hon. GCVO 1976; Commandeur de la Légion d'Honneur 1976; Commandeur de l'Ordre National du Mérite 1968; Ambassadeur de France; French Ambassador to the Court of St James's, 1972-77; *b* Bayonne (Pyrénées Atlantiques), 16 April 1913; *s* of Maurice Delarüe Caron de Beaumarchais, diplomat, and Louise Lagelouze; *m* 1944, Marie-Alice Le Couteulx de Caumont; one *s. Educ:* Ecole des Roches; Faculty of Law, Paris Univ. Licencié en droit, Diplômé de l'Ecole Libre des Sciences Politiques. Attaché d'Ambassade, 1942; Mem. French Delegn to Germany Armistice Commn for Economic Affairs, 1942; escaped from France, 1942; Head of section, Foreign Affairs Commissariat, Algiers, 1943; Second Sec., Rome (Quirinal), 1945; seconded to Commissariat-Général for German and Austrian Affairs, 1946; First Secretary, 1951; Counsellor, 1952;

Counsellor, French Embassy, London, 1953; Private Sec. to Minister of Foreign Affairs, 1958; Minister Plenipotentiary, 1959; Minister-Counsellor, Moscow, 1962; Head of European Dept, Min. of Foreign Affairs, 1962; Principal Private Sec. to Minister of Foreign Affairs, 1964; Head of Political Affairs Dept, Min. of Foreign Affairs, 1965. Hon. Fellow, St Antony's Coll., Oxford, 1972. Officier de la Légion d'Honneur 1965. *Address:* 5 Avenue Franklin-Roosevelt, 75008 Paris, France.
[Died 11 Nov. 1979.

BEAUMONT, Baroness, 11th in line, *cr* 1309; **Mona Josephine Tempest Fitzalan-Howard,** *née* Stapleton; OBE 1946; *b* Broughton Hall, Skipton, 1 Aug. 1894; *e d* of 10th Baron and late Ethel Mary, *d* of Sir Charles H. Tempest, 1st and last Bt of Heaton; *s* father, 1896; *m* 1914, 3rd Baron Howard of Glossop; four *s* four *d.* Roman Catholic. *Heir: s* Maj.-Gen. Hon. Miles Francis Fitzalan-Howard. *Address:* 23 Lennox Gardens, SW1. *T:* 01-589 2824; Carlton Towers, York. *[Died 31 Aug. 1971.*

BEAUMONT, Cyril William, OBE 1962; FRSL; FRSA; bookseller, publisher, writer on Theatre and Dance, particularly the Classical Ballet; Hon. Fellow, Imperial Society of Teachers of Dancing (Chairman, 1958-70); Editor of Dance Journal 1924-70; *b* 1 Nov. 1891; *e s* of Frederick John Beaumont (inventor, mechanical and electrical engineer) and Mary Henrietta Balchin; *m* 1914, Alice Mari Beha; no *c. Educ:* Stationers' Company's Sch.; privately. Antiquarian bookseller, 1910-65; in 1910 saw the dancing of Pavlova and Mordkin and developed interest in Ballet, intensified by visits to the Diaghilev Ballet in 1912; founded the Beaumont Press, 1917; codified Cecchetti's method of training in Classical Ballet for benefit of future dancers, 1918-22; Ballet Critic to Dancing World, 1921-24; Sunday Times, 1950-59; initiated foundation of Cecchetti Soc., 1922, which amalgamated with Imperial Soc. of Teachers of Dancing, 1924. Pres., Critics' Circle, 1957. Gold Medal, Inst. Historique et Héraldique de France, 1934; Officier d'Académie, 1934; Gold Medal, Renaissance Française, 1938; Chevalier de la Légion d'Honneur, 1950; Imperial Society's Imperial Award, 1961; Royal Academy of Dancing's Queen Elizabeth II Coronation Award, 1962; Kt Officer, Order of Merit (Italy), 1962. *Publications:* as Author: Impressions of the Russian Ballet, 12 parts, 1914-21; The Art of Lydia Lopokova, 1920; The Art of Lubov Tchernicheva, 1921; A Manual of the Theory and Practice of Classical Theatrical Dancing (with Stanislas Idzikowsky), 1922; The Mysterious Toyshop, 1924; A Burmese Pwé at Wembley, 1925; The Art of Stanislas Idzikowsky, 1926; The Strange Adventures of a Toy Soldier, 1926; The History of Harlequin, 1926; The First Score, an Account of the Beaumont Press, 1927; The Wonderful Journey, 1927; Sea Magic, 1928; Serge Lifar, 1928; Enrico Cecchetti, a Memoir, 1929; A Bibliography of Dancing, 1929; The Theory and Practice of Allegro in Classical Ballet (with Margaret Craske), 1930; Toys, 1930; A History of Ballet in Russia (1613-1881), 1930; Flashback, 1931; A French-English Dictionary of Technical Terms used in Classical Ballet, 1931; Fanny Elssler, 1931; Anna Pavlova, 1932; Vaslav Nijinsky, 1932; A Short History of Ballet, 1933; Serge Diaghilev, 1933; A Miscellany for Dancers, 1934; Three French Dancers of the 18th Century, 1934; The Monte Carlo Russian Ballet, 1934; Three French Dancers of the 19th Century, 1935; Alicia Markova, 1935; The Vic-Wells Ballet, 1935; Michel Fokine and his Ballets, 1935; A Primer of Classical Ballet for Children, 1935; A Second Primer of Classical Ballet for Children, 1935; Design for the Ballet, 1937; The Complete Book of Ballets, 1937; The Romantic Ballet in Lithographs of the Time (with Sacheverell Sitwell), 1938; Puppets and the Puppet Stage, 1938; Five Centuries of Ballet Design, 1939; The Diaghilev Ballet in London, 1940; A Third Primer of Classical Ballet for Children, 1941; Supplement to the Complete Book of Ballets, 1942: The Ballet called Giselle, 1944; The Sadler's Wells Ballet, 1946; The Sleeping Beauty, 1946; Margot Fonteyn, 1948; Dancers under my Lens, 1949; The Swan Lake, 1949; The Ballet called Swan Lake, 1952; Antonio, 1952; Ballets of Today, 1954; Ballets Past and Present, 1955; Puppets and Puppetry, 1958; (ed) A Bibliography of the Dance Collection of Doris Niles and Serge Leslie, Part I, 1966, Part II, 1968, Part III, 1974; Bookseller at the Ballet, 1975; has translated and edited classic French and other works on the technique and history of the dance, etc. Contributions to specialist jls. *Recreations:* Research work in British Museum Library, reading, music, searching for material relative to the history of Ballet. *Address:* 68 Bedford Court Mansions, Bedford Avenue, WC1B 3AD. *T:* 01-636 6487.
[Died 24 May 1976.

BEAUMONT, George Ernest, MA, DM (Oxon), FRCP; DPH London; Consulting Physician, Middlesex Hospital and Hospital for Consumption, Brompton; Physician, Royal Masonic Hospital, 1925-43; *b* 16 July 1888; *s* of late E. T. Beaumont, JP, Oxford; *m* 1917, Norah (*d* 1969), *y d* of late

Philip Hamill; one *d. Educ:* Magdalen Coll. Sch., Oxford; University Coll., Oxford (scholar). 1st cl. Final Hon. Sch. of Physiology, Oxford, 1910; University scholar, Middlesex Hospital, 1910; Theodore Williams Pathology scholar, 1912; Temp. Capt. RAMC, 1914 (Mons Star); Radcliffe Travelling Fellow, 1916; Fellow of Royal College of Physicians, 1920; Fellow of the Royal Soc. of Medicine, 1925; Examiner in Medicine, University of Oxford; Censor, Royal College of Physicians, London, 1938-40. President, Section of Medicine: BMA, 1954; Royal Soc. of Medicine, 1955-57. *Publications:* Applied Medicine, 1950, reprinted 1950 and 1951; The Clinical Approach in Medical Practice, 1956; Medicine: Essentials for Practitioners and Students, 9th edn; Recent Advances in Medicine (jointly), 13th edn; A Pocket Medicine, 5th edn; Scientific and Clinical Medicine of Today, 1968; articles, Diseases of the Lungs; Price's Text-Book of Medicine (10th edn); Diseases of the Adrenals and Pituitary, Dictionary of Medicine; Haemoglobinuria, and Ascites, British Encyclopædia of Medical Practice; Bronchiectasis, Current Therapy, 1969; various articles in the medical journals. *Address:* 1 Hamilton Terrace, NW8. *T:* 01-286 6973. *[Died 23 April 1974.*

BEAUMONT, Hugh; Managing Director H. M. Tennent Ltd and of Tennent Productions Ltd; Director, London Pavilion; Governor, Shakespeare Memorial Theatre since 1950; Member, National Theatre Board, 1962-68; *b* 27 March 1908. *Educ:* privately. *Recreation:* gardening. *Address:* 14 Lord North Street, SW1. *T:* 01-222 5216. *[Died 22 March 1973.*

BEAUMONT, James Buchan; Under-Secretary, Scottish Development Department, since 1968; *b* 29 Sept. 1925; *s* of late James Beaumont and Jessie Bruce, Edinburgh; *m* 1952, Irene Alexandria Dow; one *s* one *d. Educ:* Royal High Sch., Edinburgh; Glasgow Univ.; Edinburgh Univ. Asst Lecturer Glasgow Univ., 1949; Scottish Education Dept, 1950; Under-Sec., Scottish Development Dept, 1968. *Recreations:* golf, music. *Address:* Topgates, 93 Ravelston Dykes, Edinburgh 12. *T:* 031-337 4635. *[Died 13 Sept. 1973.*

BEAUMONT, Rt. Hon. Sir John William Fisher, PC 1944; Kt 1931; QC 1930; a Member of the Judicial Committee of the Privy Council since 1944; *b* 4 Sept. 1877; *s* of late Edward Beaumont of the Chancery Bar and Elizabeth Helen Beaumont; *m* 1904, Mabel Edith (*d* 1958), *d* of late William Wallace; one *s* decd. *Educ:* Winchester Coll.; Pembroke Coll., Cambridge; 1st Cl. History Tripos, 1899; Hon. Fellow of Pembroke Coll., 1946; Called to Bar, Lincoln's Inn, 1901; practised at Chancery Bar; Lieut RGA, 1916-19; Chief Justice of Bombay, 1930-43; acting Judge of Federal Court of India, 1942-43; Bencher of Lincoln's Inn, 1943 (Treasurer 1963). Master Cutlers' Co., 1951-52. *Address:* 52 Dorset House, Gloucester Place, NW1. *Clubs:* Athenæum, Alpine. *[Died 8 Feb. 1974.*

BEAUMONT, Hon. Ralph Edward Blackett, CBE 1967; TD; JP; Vice-Lieutenant of Montgomeryshire, 1962-74; *b* 12 Feb. 1901; 2nd *s* of 1st Viscount Allendale; *m* 1926, Helena Mary Christine (*d* 1962), *yr d* of late Brig.-Gen. Cecil Wray, CB, CMG, CVO; two *s* one *d. Educ:* Eton; Christ Church, Oxford (MA). MP (U) Portsmouth Central, 1931-45; Parliamentary Private Sec.: To Postmaster-Gen., 1935-40; To Sec. of State for War, 1942-45; Chm. of Montgomeryshire County Agricultural Executive Cttee, 1948-69. PSC 1940; Lieut-Col 636 Lt AA Regt RA (RWF) TA, 1947-51. A Development Commissioner, 1952-69. Member: Council on Tribunals, 1958-70; Welsh Economic Council, 1965-68; Welsh Council, 1968-71; Council of Management, Council for Small Industries in Rural Areas, 1968-77. Pres., Welsh Weavers' Assoc., 1973-. JP 1932, High Sheriff, 1957, DL 1961, Montgomeryshire. *Recreations:* fishing, gardening. *Address:* Bron-y-Wennol, Pantperthog, Machynlleth, Powys. *T:* Machynlleth 2491. *Club:* Carlton.
[Died 18 Sept. 1977.

BEAUMONT-NESBITT, Maj.-Gen. Frederick George, CVO 1938; CBE 1945; MC; retired; *b* 26 March 1893; *s* of late E. J. Beaumont-Nesbitt, JP, Lord Lieutenant of King's Co. and late of Tubberdaly, Edenderry, King's Co., and Helen Thomas, *sister* of 1st Marquis of Willingdon; *m* 1st, Lavinia (*d* 1920), *d* of Maj.-Gen. Hon. Sir C. Bingham, GCVO, KCMG, CB; one *d* (and one *s* decd); 2nd, 1928, Hon. Ruby Hardinge, *d* of 3rd Visc. Hardinge; two *s* one *d. Educ:* Eton Coll.; RMC Sandhurst. Joined Grenadier Guards 1912; served European War; Commanding 2nd Bn Grenadier Guards, 1932-35; Military Attaché, Paris, 1936-38; Dep. Dir Military Intelligence, 1938-39; Dir of Military Intelligence, War Office, 1939-40; Military Attaché, Washington, 1941; Maj.-Gen., Gen. Staff, 1941-45; ADC to King George VI 1944-45; retd pay, 1945. Gentleman Usher to the Queen, 1959-67; Extra Gentleman Usher, 1967. *Address:* 53 Melton Court, SW7. *Club:* Turf.
[Died 14 Dec. 1971.

BEAVIS, Maj.-Gen. Leslie Ellis, CB 1952; CBE 1942; DSO 1918; Australian Staff Corps; *b* 1895; *s* of late H. C. Beavis, Bathurst, New South Wales; *m* Ethel (decd), *d* of L. Blumer, Hunter's Hill, NSW; one *s* one *d.* Served European War, 1915-18 (despatches twice, DSO); psc, pac; War of 1939-45, DOS, AIF, Middle East, 1940-42 (CBE); Master General of the Ordnance HQ, AMF, 1942-46; Defence Dept, 1946-52; High Commissioner for Australia in Pakistan, 1952-54. *Club:* Naval and Military (Melbourne). *[Died 27 Sept. 1975.*

BEBBINGTON, Bernard Nicolas, CBE 1969 (OBE 1955); QPM 1962; Adviser to Home Office Community Development Project, 1970-72; *b* 23 Nov. 1910; *yr s* of Canon John Henry and Mabel Edith Bebbington; *m* 1936, Daphne Frizelle Drury; two *s.* *Educ:* Sutton Valence Sch.; Jesus Coll., Cambridge. Joined Metropolitan Police, 1932; attended Hendon Police Coll., 1935-36; apptd Chief Constable of Cambridge, 1944; Sec. of Assoc. of Chief Police Officers, 1961-63; HM Inspector of Constabulary, 1963-70; Dir, Home Office Police Research and Develt Branch, 1965-69; Home Office Adviser on Police Management Services, 1969-70; retd, 1970. Hon. MA Cantab 1963. OStJ 1959. *Publications:* articles and broadcasts on Police. Several children's books including The Policeman, 1952. *Recreations:* painting, writing. *Address:* 21 Riverside, Shoreham-by-Sea, East Sussex BN4 5RU; 24600 Vanxains, Dordogne, France. *Club:* Pitt (Cambridge). *[Died 1 April 1980.*

BECH, Joseph; Grande Croix, Ordre de la Couronne de Chêne (Luxembourg); Président d'Honneur de la Chambre des Députés du Luxembourg (Président, 1959-64); Ministre d'état honoraire; *b* 17 Feb.1887; *m* 1918, Georgette Delahaye; one *s* one *d.* *Educ:* Universities of Fribourg and Paris. Mem. (PSC) Chamber of Deputies, 1914; Minister Interior and Education, 1921-25; Minister of State, President of the Government and Minister of Foreign Affairs, 1926-37; leading Luxembourg Delegate to League of Nations, 1926-39; Vice-Pres., League of Nations, 1929; Chief of Luxembourg Deleg. to San Francisco Conf., 1945; Pres., Political and General Affairs Cttee, UNO, 1946; Minister of Foreign Affairs, 1926-58 (Minister of State, President of the Government, 1954-57). Dr *(hc):* University Louvain, 1954; University Innsbruck, 1968. Knight Grand Cross British Empire (Hon. GBE 1959); Grand' Croix de la Légion d'Honneur, Grand' Croix Ordre de Léopold (Belgium), Grand Cross, Order of Netherlands Lion, etc. *Publication:* Statut International du Luxembourg. *Address:* 34 Avenue Monterey, Luxembourg. *T:* 242-24. *[Died 8 March 1975.*

BECHER, Rear-Adm. Otto Humphrey, CBE 1961; DSO 1950; DSC 1940, and Bar, 1944; retd; *b* 13 Sept. 1908; *m* 1935, Valerie Chisholm Baird; three *s.* *Educ:* Harvey State Sch.; RAN Coll. Served War of 1939-45 (DSC and Bar): in Norwegian waters, Atlantic, Mediterranean, Indian and Pacific Oceans. Capt. of HMAS: Quickmatch, 1944-45; Warramunga, 1950-51; Vengeance, 1954-55; idc 1956; Capt. of HMAS Melbourne, 1957-58; Deputy Chief of Naval Staff, Australia, 1959-61; Head of Australian Joint Services Staff, London, 1962-63; Flag Officer Comdg Australian Fleet, 1964; Flag Officer in Charge, East Australian Area, 1965-66; Dir-Gen. of Recruiting, 1966-69. Officer, Legion of Merit (USA), 1950. *Address:* 3 Moore Street, Vaucluse, NSW 2030, Australia. *Recreations:* gardening, golf, tennis. *Club:* Royal Sydney Golf. *[Died 15 June 1977.*

BECK, Maj.-Gen. Edward Archibald, CB 1938; DSO 1916; *b* 16 March 1880; *o s* of Col. C. E. Beck; *m* 1912, Mary, *o d* of late Rt Rev. H. R. Wakefield, late Bishop of Birmingham; two *d.* *Educ:* Wellington; Sandhurst. Joined RS Fusiliers, 1900; served S Africa with 2nd Bn and with 12th Bn Mounted Infantry (Queen's Medal 3 clasps, King's Medal 2 clasps); with Egyptian Army, 1909-12; Capt., 1910; Major, 1915; served European War, 1914-18, (despatches, 6 times, DSO Brevet Lieut-Col); Lieut-Col King's Own Yorkshire Light Infantry, 1929; Col, 1923; Chief Instructor, Small Arms Sch., Hythe, 1925-29; Operations NW Frontier, India, 1930-31; Instructor, Senior Officers' Sch., Sheerness, 1932-33; Gen. Staff Officer, 1st Grade, Scottish Command, 1933-34; Commander 2nd Infantry Brig. Aldershot, 1935-36; ADC to the King, 1935-36; Maj.-Gen., 1936; Dir of Personal Services, War Office, 1938-40; Comdr 9th (High.) Div., 1940; retd pay, 1940. Comdr Perthshire Home Guard, 1940-45; Country Comdt Perthshire Cadets, 1943-50; Hon. Col 4/5th Bn Royal Scots Fusiliers, 1942-49. Order of SS Maurice and Lazarus (Italy), 1918; Croix de Guerre (France), 1918; Croix de Guerre (Belgium), 1918. *Recreations:* shooting, fishing. *Club:* Army and Navy. *[Died 11 July 1974.*

BECK, Most Rev. George Andrew, AA; *b* 28 May 1904; 2nd *s* of late P. T. Beck, journalist. *Educ:* Clapham Coll. and St Michael's Coll., Hitchin. Priest, 1927; BA Hons (History), London, 1934. Staff St Michael's Coll., Hitchin, until 1941,

Headmaster, 1941-44; Headmaster, The Becket Sch., Nottingham, 1944-48. Consecrated Titular Bishop of Tigia and Coadjutor Bishop of Brentwood by Cardinal Griffin, 1948; Bishop of Brentwood, 1951-55; Bishop of Salford, 1955-64; Archbishop of Liverpool and Metropolitan of Northern Province, 1964-76. Chm. Catholic Education Council, 1949-70. Hon. LLD Manchester, 1967. *Publications:* Assumptionist Spirituality, 1936; The Family and the Future, 1948; (ed. with A. C. F. Beales) Eng. translation of Gonella's The Papacy and World Peace, 1944; (ed) The English Catholics 1850-1950, 1950; occasional contributions to the Tablet and Clergy Review. *Address:* Upholland Northern Institute, Upholland College, Skelmersdale, Lancs WN8 0PZ. *T:* Upholland 622286. *Clubs:* Athenæum, Royal Automobile. *[Died 13 Sept. 1978.*

BECK, John Melliar A.; see Adams-Beck.

BECKER, Sir Ellerton; see Becker, Sir J. E.

BECKER, Harry (Thomas Alfred); Publishers' Representative, occupied in encouraging UK imports into USA; *b* Wadsworth, 16 June 1892; *e s* of late Sir Frederick Becker; *m* 1st, 1912; one *d* ; 2nd, 1926; one *s* one *d* ; 3rd, 1939 (marr. diss., Reno, Nevada, USA, 1952), *d* of John Henry and Elizabeth Newman; one *d* ; 4th, 1952, in USA, Mary Beth, *d* of Clyde and Mae Browder, Tenn, USA. *Educ:* Colet Court; Uppingham; Bristol Univ. Served European War, 1914-18; was invalided from the Service through wounds; retd with rank of 2nd Lieut Suffolk Regt, 1918 (medals, 1914-15 Star, etc.); many years spent in newspaper production in Fleet Street; MP Richmond (Ind) 1922-23, (Ind C) 1923-24; contested W Bermondsey, 1918, as ex-Servicemen's candidate. USA Naturalization Certificate, 8 July 1955. *Recreation:* swimming. *Address:* 300 West Franklin Street, Richmond, Va 23220, USA. *[Died 6 March 1980.*

BECKER, Sir (Jack) Ellerton, Kt 1962; FAA; retired; formerly Chairman of Directors of private pastoral companies from 1929; *b* 4 Oct. 1904; *s* of Percy Harold and Mabel Martha Becker, Adelaide, S Australia; *m* 1928, Gladys Sarah, *d* of Percival John and Mary Elizabeth Duggan, Adelaide, S Australia. *Educ:* Unley High Sch.; Adelaide Sch. of Technology and Univ. Manufacturing jeweller, 1920; commenced teaching music, 1926. Founded Adelaide Coll. of Music and, as Principal, built it up to 5000 students and 30 teachers; three world tours; organised Music League of S Australia and directed for charity, theatrical productions. Retired from music 1943, to farm scientifically in S Australia. FAA (special election), 1961 (the fourth Australian non-scientist elected) between Sir R. Menzies, 1958 and Lord Casey, 1966; Academy Building Auditorium named Becker Hall in 1962. Mem. Council of Australian Academy of Science, 1965-68. Acquired important stud cattle and sheep properties, Hereford, England, and NSW, Australia, 1962 and 1964. Fellow: Intercontinental Biographical Assoc., 1975; Internat. Inst. Community Service, 1976. Mem., Imperial Soc. of Knights Bachelor. *Recreations:* overseas travel, antique collecting. *Address:* Palomera, Fairylands, Pembroke, Bermuda. *T:* 5.0439. *[Died 9 May 1979.*

BECKETT, Maj.-Gen. Clifford Thomason, CB 1945; CBE 1943; MC; Chevalier Légion d'Honneur, 1951; *b* 9 Nov. 1891; *e s* of late Brig.-Gen. W. T. C. Beckett, CBE, DSO; *m* Winifred Mary Ackerley (*d* 1960), *d* of late C. A. W. Chichester; one *s* two *d.* *Educ:* Tonbridge; RMA Woolwich. 2nd Lieut RA 1911; served European War, 1914-18, Gallipoli, France, Salonika, Palestine (wounded MC); Iraq Rebellion, 1919-21; Persia, Egypt, Turkey, 1922; Staff Capt., War Office, 1926-30. Special Award War Office Cttee on Awards to Inventors, 1929; Major, 1928; travelled in Afghanistan and Australia. Employed on Strategic Reconnaissances in Western Europe, 1929, 1931; served in Lahore, 1935-36 (suppressed riots; organised Military Jubilee Tattoo). Gold Staff Officer at Coronation 1937; served frequently with French Army and in 1937 with German Army; Lieut-Col, 1938; Comd 12th Field Regt, RA, 1938-39, 1st Survey Regt, RA, 1939-40; CRA 15th Scottish Div., 1940-41; Flanders campaign, 1939-40 (despatches); Col, 1941; commanded the Artillery of the Fortress of Malta, 1941-43; Acting GOC Troops, Malta, July-Aug. 1942; Maj.-Gen. RA 1942; commanded 4th and 5th AA Groups, 1943-46; retired pay with hon. rank of Maj.-Gen., 1946; DL for Somerset, 1952-67. Hon. Fellow and Pres. Emeritus, Huguenot Soc. of London (Pres. 1949-52 and subseq., a Vice-Pres.). Dir, French Hospital of La Providence; Pres. SSAFA, Somerset, 1949-58; Executive Cttee, Squash Rackets Assocn, 1928-31. Judged at Rhône and Delhi Horse Shows. Hereditary Keeper, Inchgaw Castle, Fife. *Publications:* The Yeomanry of Devon (with Comdr W. Benson Freeman); numerous contributions to military jls and Jl of Huguenot Soc. of London. *Recreations:* the study of history, travel; formerly: rackets, squash rackets, polo, hunting, fencing,

fishing. *Address:* 36 Belvedere Court, Upper Richmond Road, Putney, SW15. *Clubs:* Athenæum, Army and Navy; Jesters.
[Died 8 July 1972.

BECKETT, Sir Eric (Frederick), Kt 1964; CBE 1956, FRCVS; *b* Nov. 1895; *s* of late F. L. and Jane Louise Beckett; *m* 1932, Margaret Patricia, *d* of late John J. Jones, The Teak House, Bournemouth; no *c. Educ:* Liverpool Coll.; Liverpool Univ. MRCVS 1924. Served European War, 1914-18: BEF, RFA, France, 1915-18 (wounded). Chm. of the North Dorset Conservative Assoc., 1947-67. MFH The Portman Hounds, 1944 (Master or Joint Master for 12 seasons). *Recreations:* foxhunting, shooting. *Address:* Blandford, Dorset. *T:* Blandford 2494. *Club:* British Legion (Blandford).
[Died 24 Sept. 1971.

BECKWITH, Air Vice-Marshal William Flint, CBE 1954; RAF retired; Director, Seaglider Ltd, since 1970; *b* 21 April 1913; *s* of Harold Beckwith, MIChemE, Leeds and Ilminster, and Lillie Hewitt Beckwith; *m* 1938, Helen Zina Yeo; one *d. Educ:* Bishops Stortford Coll.; Univ. of London. BSc (Eng) 1933. Entered RAF, 1934. Served War of 1939-45 in UK, West Africa and Air Ministry. Command Engineer Officer, Far East AF, 1951-54; Asst Commandant, RAF Technical Coll., 1954-57; Senior British Rep., Cape Canaveral, 1957-60; Dir of Weapons Engineering, Air Min., 1960-63; Student IDC, 1963-64; Dir-Gen., Ground Training, Air Min., 1964-66; Vice-Pres., Ordnance Board, 1966-68, Pres., 1968-69. *Recreations:* water ski-ing, building, shooting, olive growing. *Address:* Benchmark, Little Hatherden, Andover, Hants. *T:* Hatherden 262; La Bergerie Sclos de Contes, AM, France. *Club:* Royal Air Force.
[Died 20 Sept. 1971.

BEDDALL, Maj.-Gen. Walter Samuel, CBE 1954; OBE 1941; Director of Army Education, 1952-57, retired; *b* 7 Feb. 1894; *s* of late W. Beddall; *m* 1937, Alice May, *d* of Henry Greaves, London; one *d. Educ:* Kelham Coll., Notts; Cambridge Univ. Served European War, 1916-18, in France, with MGC; AEC 1920; Instructor, WO Sch. of Educ., 1920-24 (Capt.); Dist. Educ. Officer, NWFP, India, 1924-30; Officer, RMC Sandhurst, 1930-37; Chief Educ. Officer, E Comd, India, 1937-45; Comdt, Army Schs of Educ., 1945-49; Chief Educ. Officer, GHQ, Far East Land Forces, Singapore, 1949-52; Dir Army Educ., WO, 1952. Lieut-Col, 1949; Col, 1949; Brig., 1952; Maj.-Gen., 1954. *Publications:* articles on educn in Times Educnl Supp., Army Educ. *Recreations:* golf, tennis. *Address:* Crown Villa, Halstead, Sevenoaks, Kent. *Club:* Army and Navy. *[Died 7 March 1973.*

BEDDINGTON, Maj.-Gen. William Richard, CBE 1941; Major-General, retired; *b* 8 Oct. 1893; *s* of late Gerald Ernest Beddington, CBE; *m* 1946, Elizabeth Rees, *d* of Sir Guy Fison, 3rd Bt, MC; one *s* (and one *s* decd). *Educ:* Eton; New Coll., Oxford. Served European War, 2nd Lieut 2nd Co. of London Yeomanry, Egypt, Gallipoli, Macedonia, 1914-16; The Queen's Bays, France, 1916-18 (wounded); Staff Coll., 1927-28; Staff Capt., 1930-32; Bde Major, 1932-34; GSO2 Southern Command, 1936-38; commanded the Queen's Bays, 1939; GSO1 Palestine, 1940; Brig., Middle East, Persia-Iraq, Mediterranean, France, and Germany, 1941-45; Acting Maj.-Gen. 1945; temp. Maj.-Gen., 1945-47; retired pay, 1947. Comdr, Legion of Merit (US) and Chevalier, Légion d'Honneur, 1945. *Recreation:* hunting. *Address:* The Old Rectory, Winterbourne Stickland, Blandford, Dorset. *Clubs:* Cavalry, Shikar, MCC.
[Died 7 Dec. 1975.

BEDDY, James Patrick, DEconSc; MRIA; Consultant, The Industrial Credit Company Ltd, since 1972; *b* Cobh, County Cork, 1900. *Educ:* O'Connell Schs Dublin; National Univ. of Ireland, University Coll., Dublin. Inspector of Taxes, 1927-33; Sec., Industrial Credit Co. Ltd, 1933-49; Dir, The Industrial Credit Co. Ltd, 1949-52, Man. Dir 1952-69, Chm., 1952-72; Chm., Mergers Ltd, 1969-72. Lectr in Commerce, University Coll., Dublin, 1936-51. Pres., Statistical and Social Inquiry Soc. of Ireland, 1954-56; Council Mem., Economic and Social Res. Inst., 1960-75. Chairman: Commn on Emigration and Other Population Problems, 1948-54; Cttee of Inquiry into Internal Transport, 1956-57; An Foras Tionscail, 1952-65; The Industrial Development Authority, 1949-65. Member: Tribunal of Inquiry into Public Transport, 1939; Industrial Res. Cttee of Inst. for Industrial Res. and Standards, 1946-60. LLD (*hc* Dublin). *Publications:* Profits, Theoretical and Practical Aspects, 1940. Various articles on matters of economic interest. *Address:* 15 Spencer Villas, Glenageary, County Dublin. *T:* Dublin 801542. *Club:* Royal Irish Yacht (Dun Laoghaire).
[Died 28 Sept. 1976.

BEDFORD, D(avis) Evan, CBE 1963; MD, FRCP, London; FACP (Hon.); MD (Hon.) Cairo; retired; Hon. Consultant

Physician, Middlesex, National Heart and Connaught Hospitals; Consultant Emeritus in Cardiology to the Army, 1976; Hon. Civil Consultant in Cardiology, RAF; formerly Chairman Council, British Heart Foundation; *b* 1898; *s* of William Bedford, JP, Boston, Lincs; *m* 1935, Audrey Selina North, *e d* of Milton Ely, CBE; two *s. Educ:* Epsom Coll.; Middlesex Hospital. Medical Registrar, Middlesex Hospital, 1923-25; Paterson Research Scholar, London Hospital Cardiographic Dept, 1926-27; Medical Officer in Charge Cardiac Wards, Ministry of Pensions Hospital, Orpington, 1922; studied in Paris and Lyons, 1926; Surg.-Sub-Lieut RNVR, 1918, 20th Destroyer Flotilla. Served in RAMC, 1939-45, Brig. Cons. Physician, MEF (despatches). Late Pres. British Cardiac Soc.; Corresp. mem., Soc. Française de Cardiologie, Soc. Belge de Cardiologie, Soc. Suisse de Cardiologie; Hon. Member: Cardiac Soc. of Australia and NZ, Brazilian Soc. of Cardiology and Egyptian Cardiological Soc.; Hon. Pres., European Soc. of Cardiology; late Vice-Pres. International Soc. of Cardiology; Corresp. Acad. of Med., Rome. Carey Coombs Lectr, 1963. *Publications:* articles on Diseases of Coronary Arteries, Angina Pectoris and Congenital Heart Disease, in Lancet, Heart, etc, and other papers and addresses on Diseases of the Heart; Strickland Goodall Memorial Lecture, 1939; Bradshaw Lecture, RCP, 1946; St Cyres' Lecture, 1947; Lumleian Lectures, RCP 1960; Harveian Oration, RCP 1968. *Recreation:* gardening. *Address:* 118 St Pancras, Chichester, W Sussex. *T:* Chichester 83993. *[Died 24 Jan. 1978.*

BEDFORD, John, OBE 1948 (MBE 1944); Director: Commercial Union Assurance Co. Ltd, 1959-73; National Building Agency, 1964-77 (Deputy Chairman of Board and Chairman, Finance Committee, 1967-77); Governor, The Leys School, Cambridge; Trustee, The Cottage Homes for Old People; *b* 16 Jan. 1903; *o s* of John and Rosalind Bedford; *m* 1930, Florence Mary Oddy; one *d.* Chm., Debenhams Ltd, 1956-71 (also Man. Dir, 1956-70); Mem., Banwell Cttee to look at Contractual matters in the Construction Industries for MPBW, 1962; Part-time Mem., London Transport Bd, 1962-68. FRSA 1976. *Recreations:* golf, reading, walking. *Address:* 23 Kepplestone, Staveley Road, Eastbourne, East Sussex BN20 7JY. *T:* Eastbourne 26689. *Club:* MCC. *[Died 11 Nov. 1980.*

BEDOYERE, Count Michael de la; *see* de la Bedoyere.

BEESLY, Lewis Rowland, CB 1966; CEng, FIMechE, FIProdE; industrial consultant; Head of Engineering Staff, 1962-73, and Director-General of Aircraft Production, 1960-73, Ministry of Defence; *b* 1 May 1912; *s* of Edward Rowland Beesly, Derby; *m* 1936, Kathleen Lilian, *d* of late Rev. S. Ivan Bell, Glasgow; four *d. Educ:* Bemrose Sch., Derby. Various managerial positions in Royal Ordnance Factories, 1935-49; Asst Dir, Longterm Production Planning (Air), Ministry of Supply, 1950; Dir, Engine Production, Ministry of Supply, 1951-59; Superintendent-Dir, Royal Small Arms Factory, Enfield, 1959-60; Min. of Aviation, 1960. Treasurer, London Derbyshire Soc. *Address:* 58 Wood Ride, Petts Wood, Kent. *T:* Orpington 21185. *[Died 27 Feb. 1978.*

BEESON, Cyril Frederick Cherrington, CIE 1941; *b* 10 Feb. 1889; *s* of Walter Thomas Beeson, Oxford, and Rose Eliza Clacy; *m* 1st 1922, Marion Cossentine Fitze (*d* 1946); one *d*; 2nd, 1971, Margaret Athalie Baldwin Carbury. *Educ:* City of Oxford Sch.; St John's Coll., Oxford. BA (Oxon.) Geology; DSc (Oxon.) Entomology; Indian Forest Service, 1911-42, Conservator of Forests and Forest Entomologist; Dir, Imperial Forestry Bureau, Oxford, 1945-47. Medals: General Service, Victory, Jubilee, Coronation. *Publications:* The Ecology and Control of the Forest Insects of India and the neighbouring countries, 1941; Clockmaking in Oxfordshire, 1400 to 1850, 1967; English Church Clocks, 1280-1850, 1971; from 1910 many publications in various journals, or separately, on taxonomy, ecology, and control of insect pests, on forest protection, and on horology. *Recreation:* horology. *Address:* Sundial, School Lane, Appleford, Oxon OX14 4NY. *T:* Sutton Courtenay 637.
[Died 3 Nov. 1975.

BEETHAM, Sir Edward (Betham), KCMG 1955 (CMG 1950); CVO 1947; OBE 1946; retired as Governor and Commander-in-Chief, Trinidad and Tobago (1955-60); *b* 19 Feb. 1905; *s* of late Dr Beetham, Red House, Knaresborough; *m* 1933, Eileen Joy Parkinson, CStJ; one *d. Educ:* Charterhouse; Lincoln Coll., Oxford. District Officer, Kenya, 1928-38; seconded to Colonial Office, 1938; District Commissioner, Sierra Leone, 1938-40; Chief Asst Colonial Sec., Sierra Leone, 1940-46; acted as Colonial Sec. and Governor's Deputy, Sierra Leone, on many occasions; Resident Commissioner of Swaziland, 1946-50; of the Bechuanaland Protectorate, 1950-53; Governor and C-in-C, Windward Is, 1953-55. Chm. Texaco Ltd, and Chief Exec.

Officer, Texaco Gp of Cos in UK, 1963-70; Chm., Oaklife Assurance Ltd. KStJ 1953. *Address:* Millstream, Mill End, Hambleden, Henley-on-Thames, Oxon. *Clubs:* Army and Navy; Phyllis Court (Henley-on-Thames). *[Died* 19 *Feb.* 1979.

BEETON, William Hugh, CMG 1954; *b* 14 Oct. 1903; *s* of late E. H. and late Mrs F. E. Beeton, Oulton Broad, Suffolk; *m* 1932, Mary Alice (*d* 1959), *d* of late F. H. and A. C. Wagstaff, Croydon, Surrey; one *s*; *m* 1962, Margaret Rachel Frances Crowley. *Educ:* Strathallan Sch.; London Sch. of Economics, University of London. Colonial Administrative Service, Gold Coast, 1926-54; Asst District Comr, 1926-32; District Comr, 1932-43; Dep. Provincial Comr, 1943-46; Asst Chief Comr, 1946-50; Chief Comr Ashanti, 1950; title changed to Chief Regional Officer, 1952; retd, 1954. Training Officer, Oversea Service, 1954-68. Mem. Council, Polytechnic of the South Bank, 1970-. Vice-Pres., Royal African Soc. 1966-. *Recreation:* golf. *Address:* 28 Bench Field, South Croydon, Surrey. *T:* 01-688 2002. *Clubs:* Travellers', Royal Commonwealth Society; Croham Hurst Golf (Croydon). *[Died* 26 *March* 1976.

BEGBIE, Rt. Rev. Herbert Gordon Smirnoff; retired; *b* 28 Oct. 1905; *s* of Herbert Smirnoff Begbie and Emily Augusta (*née* Miller); *m* 1932, Gwendoline Dean; one *s* one *d. Educ:* Trinity Gram. Sch. and C of E Gram. Sch., Sydney; University of Sydney; Mooore Theol Coll. BA (Sydney) 1927. Deacon 1928; Priest, 1929. Curate: Eastwood, Dio. of Sydney, 1929-31; St George's, Hobart, Dio. of Tasmania, 1931-34; Rector: Narrabeen, 1934-37; Moss Vale, 1937-47; Campsie, 1947-49; Wollongong, 1949-60; Archdeacon of: Camden, 1949-54; Wollongong, 1954-62; Cumberland, 1962-67 (all Dio. of Sydney); Registrar, Diocese of Sydney, 1960-69; Asst Bishop of Sydney, resident in Parramatta, 1967-72. *Recreation:* gardening. *Address:* 39 George Street, Springwood, NSW 2777. *T:* 51.1136. *[Died* 7 *June* 1973.

BEGG, Jean, CBE 1948 (OBE 1946; MBE 1943); *b* 7 Oct. 1887; *d* of John Begg, Dunedin, NZ. *Educ:* Girls' High Sch.; Teachers' Training Coll.; Otago Univ., Dunedin, NZ. Teacher, London Missionary Soc., Tutuila, Samoa, 1910-19; graduate, Sch. of Social Work, New York, and executive sec. of Inwood House for Delinquent Girls, New York City, 1919-23; Investigator, Child Welfare Dept, Govt of NZ, Organizer, Women's Section, NZ and South Seas Exhibition, NZ, 1924-26; Gen. Sec., YWCA, Auckland, NZ; Leader NZ deleg. to Pan Pacific Conf., Honolulu, 1926-31; Nat. Gen. Sec., YWCA of India, Burma and Ceylon, 1931-40; Dir, YWCA Welfare, with British and Allied Servicewomen of the Forces, Middle East, Central Mediterranean, India, SE Asia, Japan, 1940-48 (despatches); Head Warden, YWCA Residence, Helen Graham House, London, 1948-51; Pres. YWCA, Dunedin, 1957; Organiser, Council of Organisations for Relief Services Overseas, Wellington, NZ; Pres. United Nations Assoc. (Otago), 1960; Field Vice-Pres., YWCA of NZ. *Address:* 3 Queen's Drive, Dunedin, C2, NZ. *[Died* 15 *Feb.* 1971.

BEHARRELL, Sir (George) Edward, Kt 1961; Chairman, The Dunlop Co. Ltd, 1957-67; President, Dunlop Holdings Ltd, since 1968; *b* 26 May 1899; *e s* of late Sir George Beharrell; *m* 1921, Barbara (*d* 1970), *yr d* of late Walter Waddington, York; two *s* two *d. Educ:* Wellingborough. Served European War, 1914-18, in Inns of Court Regt and RE. Early training in Shipping business. Joined Dunlop Rubber Co. Ltd, 1928; various executive appointments; Dir, 1942; Joint-Managing Dir, 1943; Managing Dir, 1945; Deputy Chm., 1949; Chm., 1957. Chm., Internat. Synthetic Rubber Co. Ltd, 1955. Member: Pres. of Board of Trade's Informal Advisory Group on Exports, 1955-59; Iron & Steel Bd, 1953-58; President: Federation of British Rubber Manufacturers Assocns, 1948-50; Tyre Manufacturers' Conference, 1947-56; Soc. of Motor Manufacturers and Traders, 1951-52; Instn of the Rubber Industry, 1962-64. *Recreations:* golf, literature. *Address:* Carinya, Priory Road, Sunningdale, Berks. *T:* Ascot 23278. *[Died* 6 *June* 1972.

BEHRENS, Edgar Charles, CBE 1951 (OBE 1919); JP West Riding Yorks; FRSA; Chairman, Craig Convalescent Home for Children, Morecambe, 1927-67; Director (previously Chairman): Sir Jacob Behrens & Sons Ltd, Bradford, Manchester and Hong Kong; Francis Willey (British Wools, 1935) Ltd, Bradford, and other textile companies in Manchester; *b* 13 May 1885; 3rd *s* of late Gustav and Fanny Behrens, Manchester; *m* 1926, Winifred, *o d* of late Charles Luckhurst, Coneysthorpe, near York; one *s* one *d. Educ:* Rugby Sch. Served European War, RASC (Capt.), and on Staff (despatches twice, OBE). Chm. National Wool Textile Export Group, 1942-58 (Vice-Chm. 1958-65); President, Bradford Chamber of Commerce, 1938-40; mem. of NE Tribunal for Conscientious Objectors, 1939-57. *Address:* Norwood House, Ilkley, Yorks. *T:* Ilkley 3518. *[Died* 4 *Feb.* 1975.

BEHRENS, Sir Leonard (Frederick), Kt 1970; CBE 1956; MCom; Vice-President, Liberal Party Organisation; Hon. Member, Royal Manchester College of Music; Member of Court, Manchester University; Vice-President, UN Association; Hon. President, World Federation of UN Associations and acting President, Stockholm, 1951; New York, 1963; *b* 15 Oct. 1890; *y s* of late Gustav Behrens; *m* 1920, Beatrice Mary, *y d* of late Dr W. Sandham Symes, Maryborough, Queen's Co. and Chesterfield; two *d. Educ:* Ladybarn House Sch.; Manchester Grammar Sch.; Rugby Sch.; Manchester Univ. Partner Sir Jacob Behrens and Sons, 1920-48; Dir Sir Jacob Behrens and Sons Ltd. 1948-54, Dep.-Chm. Cotton and Rayon Merchants' Assoc., 1939-42 and 1954. JP City of Manchester, 1940. Chm. Manchester Information Cttee, and Lecturer to HM Forces, 1940-45; Royal Observer Corps. 1941-52 (now Hon. Mem.). Pres., Manchester Statistical Soc., 1942-44; Dir, Manchester Chamber of Commerce, 1923-67, now Emeritus. Liberal Candidate, Withington, 1945 and 1950; Pres. Liberal Party Org., 1955-57; Chm. of Exec., 1959-61. Pres. Manchester Reform Club, 1956-57; Pres. Manchester Liberal Fedn, 1947-49; Chm. Hallé Concerts Soc., 1952-59 (Cttee Mem., 1932, Hon. Life Cttee Mem., 1974). Order of St Sava (Jugoslavia), 1919; Brilliant Star with Ribbon (China), 1949. *Publications:* pamphlets, articles and letters to the Press. *Recreations:* music and crossword puzzles. *Address:* Netherby, 119 Barlow Moor Road, Didsbury, Manchester M20 8TS. *T:* 061-445 3600. *Clubs:* National Liberal, English-Speaking Union; Manchester (Manchester). *[Died* 12 *March* 1978.

BEHRMAN, S. N.; Playwright; *b* 9 June 1893; *s* of Joseph Behrman and Zelda Feingold; *m* 1936, Elza Heifetz; one *s. Educ:* Harvard Coll., AB 1916; Columbia Univ., MA 1918. Brandeis Univ. Creative Arts Award, Theatre Medal, 1962. First play, The Second Man, Prod. in New York, 1927 with Alfred Lunt and Lynn Fontanne, prod. London, 1928, with Noel Coward. Subsequent productions: Serena Blandish, 1928; Meteor, 1929; Brief Moment, 1932; Biography, 1933; Love Story, 1934; Rain from Heaven, 1935; End of Summer, 1936; Amphitryon (adapted from French), 1937; Wine of Choice, 1938; No Time for Comedy, 1939; The Talley Method, 1941; The Pirate, 1942; Jacobowsky and the Colonel (with Franz Werfel), 1944; Dunnigan's Daughter, 1945; Jane (from Somerset Maugham), 1946; I Know my Love (from Achard), 1949; Fanny (with Joshua Logan), 1954; The Cold Wind and the Warm, 1959; Lord Pengo, 1962; But for Whom Charlie, 1964. *Publications:* Duveen, 1952, new edn, 1972; The Worcester Account, 1954; Portrait of Max (USA edn, 1960), Conversation with Max (GB, 1960); The Suspended Drawing Room, 1965; The Burning Glass, 1968; People in a Diary, 1972 (in UK as Tribulations and Laughter); also plays. *Address:* 1185 Park Avenue, New York, NY 10028, USA. *[Died* 9 *Sept.* 1973.

BEINART, Prof. Ben Zion; Barber Professor of Jurisprudence, University of Birmingham, since 1975; Dean, Faculty of Law, 1976-79; *b* 21 Oct. 1914; *s* of Woolf Beinart and Gitel Apter; *m* 1945, Gladys Beryl Levy; one *s* two *d. Educ:* Boys' High Sch., Malmesbury, Cape Province; Univ. of Cape Town (BA, LLB; Hon. LLD, 1979); Univ. of London (LLM). Barrister-at-Law, Gray's Inn, 1940; Advocate, Supreme Ct of SA. War Service, S Af. Def. Force, 1941-45; Lieut. Advocate, Grahamstown, 1945-49; Prof. of Law, Rhodes University Coll., Grahamstown, 1945-49; Dean, Faculty of Law, Univ. of SA, 1948-49; Univ. of Cape Town: W. P. Schreiner Prof. of Roman and Comparative Law, 1950-74; Dean, Faculty of Law, 1953-56 and 1963-66; Asst-Principal, 1969-74; Fellow, 1960-74; Prof. Emeritus, 1975-. Gen. Editor, Acta Juridica, 1958- (Cape Town). *Publications:* (ed and trans. with P. van Warmelo) D. G. van der Keessel, Praelectiones ad Jus Criminale, 5 vols, 1969-78; Dictata ad Institutiones, 2 vols, 1965-67; (ed) S. Groenewegen van der Made, De Legibus abrogatis, 2 vols, 1974-75; (with Riccobono and Wylie) Stipulation and the Theory of Contract, 1957; articles and revs in Mod. Law Rev., SA Law Jl, Tydskrif vir HRHReg and Acta Juridica. *Relevant Publication:* Essays in Honour of Ben Beinart, 3 vols, 1978-79. *Address:* 54 Hamilton Avenue, Harborne, Birmingham B17 8AR. *T:* 021-427 4314, (univ.) 021-472 1301. *Clubs:* Royal Commonwealth Society; Owl (Cape Town); Albany (Grahamstown).

[Died 2 *Nov.* 1979.

BÉKÉSY, Dr Georg von; Professor of Sensory Sciences, University of Hawaii, since 1966; *b* 3 June 1899; *s* of Alexander von Békésy and Paula (*née* Mazaly). *Educ:* University of Berne; University of Budapest (PhD). Research Laboratory, Hungarian Telephone System, 1923-26; Central Lab., Siemens & Halske, Berlin, 1926-27. University of Budapest: Privatdozent, 1932-39, Ausserordentlicher Prof., 1939-40, Ordentlicher Prof., 1940-46; Karolinski Inst, Stockholm, 1946-47, Research Prof., 1947-49; Research Lectr, Harvard, 1947-49; Sen. Research Fellow in

Psychophysics, Harvard, 1949-66. Member: Nat. Acad. of Science; Amer. Acad. of Science; Akad. Leopoldina; Corres. Mem., Akad. der Wissenschaften, Mainz; Hon. Mem. of various assocs. Hon. MD: Wilhelm Univ., Münster, 1955; Univs Berne, 1959, Padua, 1962, Budapest, 1969; Hon. DSc: Gustavus Adolphus Coll. 1963; Pennsylvania 1965; Cordoba 1968; Buenos Aires 1968; Hawaii, 1969. Nobel Prize in Medicine and Physiology, 1961. *Publications:* Experiments in Hearing, 1960; Sensory Inhibition, 1967; articles in scientific publications. *Address:* Laboratory of Sensory Sciences, 1993 East-West Road, University of Hawaii, Honolulu, Hawaii 96822, USA.
[Died 13 June 1972.

BELGION, (Harold) Montgomery; author; *b* Paris, 28 Sept. 1892, British subject by birth; *m* 1945, Gladys Helen, *e d* of late J. R. Mattock, Headington. Editor-in-charge, New York Herald (European edition), Paris, 1915-16; private, HAC, 1916-18; commissioned July 1918 to The Dorsetshire Regt; BEF, France, 1916 and 1918-19; foreign sub-editor, London Daily Mail, 1919-21 and 1922-24; editorial staff of the New York World, New York, 1921-22; chief sub-editor. Westminster Gazette, 1924-25; with Harcourt, Brace and Co., publishers, New York, 1925-28; Daily Mirror, 1935-37; Daily Sketch, 1939. Capt. Royal Engineers, 1940-45; BEF France, 1940; Greece, 1941 (prisoner of war). Sec. of Westwood House Sch. Trust, 1950-61. *Publications:* Our Present Philosophy of Life, 1929 (translated into French as Notre Foi Contemporaine, 1934); The Human Parrot, 1931; News of the French, 1938 (translated into German as Neues aus Frankreich, 1939); Reading for Profit, 1945 (translated into French, 1947, expanded version, USA, 1950, Britain, 1951); Introduction to Cresset Press Moby Dick, 1947; Epitaph on Nuremberg, 1947; (new and exp. version, Victors' Justice, USA, 1949); Lydgate and Dorothea in New Road No. 6, 1949; A Selection of Poe's Poems with Introduction, 1948; A Man After My Own Heart (USA), 1949; H. G. Wells, 1953 and David Hume, 1965 (British Council booklets); Contrib. to Promise of Greatness, 1968; The Worship of Quantity: a Study of Megalopolitics, 1969; André Malraux in the Politics of 20th Century Novelists, 1971; contributions to numerous reviews and other periodicals. *Address:* Highfield, Titchmarsh, Kettering, Northants. *Club:* Athenæum.
[Died 29 Oct. 1973.

BELISARIO, Dr John Colquhoun, CMG 1968; CBE 1945 (OBE 1942); ED 1946; *b* Sydney, 30 April 1900; *s* of Guy Alexander Fernandez Belisario and Isobel Colquhoun Fraser; *m* 1930, Freda Adele Sauber; two *d*. *Educ:* King's Sch., Parramatta; University of Sydney. MB, ChM 1926; DDM Sydney 1947; MD Sydney 1950; FRACP 1959; MACD 1966; Hon. Mem. Sect. of Dermatology, RSM, 1966. Post-grad. study in dermatology, London, Edinburgh, Paris and Breslau. Served War of 1939-45, AAMC, commanding 2/3 CCS, 1940-41 (Lt-Col) and 2/5 AGH, 1941-44 (Col). Royal Prince Alfred Hosp., Sydney: RMO 1926; Registrar, 1927-28; Hon. MO Venereal Dept, 1929-41; Hon. Asst Physician, Diseases of the Skin, 1932-44, Hon. Physician, 1944-60, Hon. Cons. Physician, 1960-; Mem., Board of Dirs, 1955-. Lectr in Dermatology, Univ. of Sydney, 1945-61 (founder and supervisor of Course, DDM). Holds hon. consultancies in many other hosps. Charter Mem., Bd of Dirs, Internat. Soc. of Tropical Dermat., 1962, Vice-Pres. 1964, Pres., 1969; 1st President: Dermatological Assoc. of Australia, 1949-50; Australasian Coll. of Dermatologists, 1967-68. Hon. Mem. and Corres. Mem. of Dermatological and other Medical Societies throughout the world; Mem. Editorial Bds, 6 overseas dermat. jls. *Publications:* Cancer of the Skin, 1959; many contribs to symposia and journals. *Recreations:* surfing, gardening. *Address:* 193 Macquarie Street, Sydney, New South Wales 2000, Australia. *T:* 36-6536. *Clubs:* Union, American National, Tattersall's, Royal Sydney Golf (Sydney).
[Died 3 Aug. 1976.

BELL, Adrian Hanbury; author; Compiler of the Times Crosswords, since 1930; *b* 4 Oct. 1901; *e s* of Robert Bell and Frances Hanbury; *m* 1931, Marjorie Gibson; one *s* two *d*. *Educ:* Uppingham. After leaving school went as pupil on a Suffolk farm, and has farmed in West and East Suffolk. *Publications:* Corduroy, 1930; Silver Ley, 1931; The Cherry Tree, 1932; Folly Field, 1933; The Balcony, 1934; Poems, 1935; By-Road, 1937; Shepherd's Farm, 1939; Men and the Fields, 1939; Apple Acre, 1942, repr. 1964; Sunrise to Sunset, 1944; The Budding Morrow, 1947; The Black Donkey, 1949; The Flower and the Wheel, 1949; The Path by the Window, 1952; Music in the Morning, 1954; A Young Man's Fancy, 1955; A Suffolk Harvest, 1956; The Mill House, 1958; My Own Master, 1961; A Street in Suffolk, 1964; A Countryman's Notebook, 1975; The Green Bond, 1976; (ed) The Open Air, 1936. [Died 5 Sept. 1980.

BELL, Sir Arthur (Capel Herbert), Kt 1963; FRCS, FRCOG; Past President of the Royal College of Obstetricians and Gynæcologists; Consultant Gynæcological Surgeon: Westminster Hospital; Chelsea Hospital for Women; Consultant Surgeon, Queen Charlotte's Maternity Hospital; Consulting Gynæcological Surgeon, Thames Ditton Cottage Hospital and Edenbridge Memorial Hospital; *b* 18 Sept. 1904; *o s* of late J. H. Bell; *m* 1933, Hilda, *d* of late H. M. F. Faure; three *s* two *d*. *Educ:* Marlborough Coll.; St Bartholomew's Hosp. MRCS Eng, LRCP London 1927; MB, BS London 1930; FRCS Eng 1930; FRCOG 1946; Hon. MMSA; Hon. FRCPSG. Formerly: House Surgeon to Surg. Prof. Unit, and Obstetric House Surg., St Bartholomew's Hosp.; Obstetric House Surg., Liverpool Royal Infirmary; Obstetric and Gynæcological Registrar and Tutor, Charing Cross Hosp. and Westminster Hosp.; Obstetric Surgeon, Westminster Hosp.; Gynæcological Surgeon, Chelsea Hosp. for Women. Hon. Adviser on Obstetrics and Gynæcology to the Army, 1963-70. Sometime Examr to the Univs of London, Glasgow, Belfast, Durham, Birmingham, Oxford, Conjoint Board of RCP and RCS, RCOG, Soc. of Apothecaries, Central Midwives Board. *Publications:* A Pocket Obstetrics; (jointly) Queen Charlotte's Practice of Obstetrics; Hysterectomy; Total and Subtotal (Jl of Obst. and Gynec. of Br. Empire). *Recreations:* gardening, shooting, fishing, tennis and golf. *Address:* Garden End, Orchard Way, Esher, Surrey. *T:* Esher 62455. [Died 24 Nov. 1977.

BELL, Captain Charles Leigh de Hauteville, DSC 1943; RD 1938; Commodore Captain, Canadian Pacific Steamships Ltd, 1961-63, retired; *b* 24 March 1903; *s* of Commander Charles de H. Bell, RNR, and Ethel Maud Bell (*née* Legg); *m* 1938, Hilda Olga Ottilie Kohn Speyer; one *s* two *d*. *Educ:* St Bees; HMS Conway. Joined Canadian Pacific Steamships as cadet, 1918; commissioned as Sub-Lieut, RNR, 1925. Served Comdr, RNR, in comd of destroyers, 1940-43; Commodore of convoys, 1944; Capt. RNR, 1945; HMS Palomares, 1946; subsequently rejoined CPS in command. Mem. Hon. Company of Master Mariners. *Recreations:* golf, philately. *Address:* Mogador Point, Lower Kingswood, Surrey. *T:* Reigate 42909. *Club:* Walton Heath Golf. [Died 1 June 1972.

BELL, Sir Douglas (James), Kt 1966; CBE 1962; *b* 16 June 1904; *s* of William and Helen Bell, Glasgow; *m* 1936, Phyllis Maude Jones; one *s* one *d*. *Educ:* Allan Glen's Sch., Glasgow. Resident Dir in India, Indian Steelworks Construction Co., 1958-62; Gen. Man., Hindustan Steel Ltd, Durgapur Steel Plant, Bengal, 1962-65; Chairman: British Steelworks Equipment Ltd, 1965-67; Davy-Ashmore Ltd, 1969-70, retired. *Address:* Casa Nova Esperança, Cerro, São Miguel, Silves, Algarve, Portugal. *Clubs:* Oriental; Bengal, Calcutta (Calcutta); Royal British (Lisbon). [Died 21 July 1974.

BELL, Sir Frederick (Archibald), Kt 1947; OBE 1943; MC 1918; Farmer; Chairman of Herring Industry Board, 1944-61, retired; *b* 19 Sept. 1891; *s* of Robert King Bell, Paisley; *m* 1917, Lilian Hunter Wilson (*d* 1948); two *s* three *d*; *m* 1950, Marjory Helen, MB, ChB, DPH, widow of Charles G. Kennaway, WS, Auchterarder. *Educ:* Loretto. Royal Engineers (TF), European War, 1914-18, Capt. (MC); commanded 3rd Perthshire Battalion Home Guard, War of 1939-45, Lieut-Col (OBE). Vice-Chm., Scottish Milk Marketing Board, 1935-38; Mem. of Herring Industry Board, 1938, Chm., 1944. *Address:* 39 Pickletullum Road, Perth. *T:* Perth 28397. *Clubs:* Farmers'; Royal (Perth). [Died 5 Jan. 1972.

BELL, Col Frederick Charles, CMG 1919; retired; late Canadian Army Medical Corps; *b* 1883; *s* of Charles Napier Bell, LLD, Winnipeg; *m* 1916, Dorothy Gladys, *d* of late John Nairn; *m* 1957, Marcella Ellen, *d* of late Lieut-Col W. H. Moodie, Kelowna, BC, Canada. BA Queen's Univ., Kingston, Ont., 1905; MD University of Manitoba, 1909. Served European War, 1914-19 (despatches, CMG). *Address:* Tyndrum, 6015 Eagle Ridge Drive, West Vancouver, British Columbia. *Club:* Alpine of Canada. [Died 27 June 1971.

BELL, Capt. Frederick Secker, CB 1939; RN retired; *b* 17 Aug. 1897; *y s* of late Col F. B. Bell, HAC; *m* Dulcie, *d* of Nahun Barnet, FRIBA, Melbourne, Aust. *Educ:* Matfield Grange, Kent; RN Colls, Osborne and Dartmouth. Served in HMS Cumberland in Cameroons campaign, 1914-15; HMS Canada (Grand Fleet and Jutland); Submarines, 1916-23; lent to RAN, 1930-32; Comdr, 1931; RN Staff Coll., 1933; Executive Officer, HMS Repulse, 1935-38; Capt., 1938; Exeter in command, 1939; served in battle with Graf Spee, 1939 (CB). Retired list, 1948; ADC to the King, 1947-48. [Died 23 Nov. 1973.

BELL, Grace Effingham Laughton, CBE 1946; *y d* of late Sir John Knox Laughton, RN; *m* 1st, 1915, John Russell Little (killed in action May 1917); 2nd, 1918, Harry Graham Bell (*d* 1950); two *s*. *Educ:* Convent Schs; King's Coll., London Univ. Women's

Forestry Corps (Travelling Officer for Wales and West of England), 1915-19; Women's Royal Naval Service, Sept. 1939-Jan. 1946; Superintendent, WRNS: The Nore, 1942; Western Approaches, 1944. *Recreations:* painting, gardening. *Address:* Apart: Yuca 12, Fuengirola, Spain. *Clubs:* Service Women's; Royal Burnham Yacht (Burnham-on-Crouch).
[Died 10 Dec. 1975.

BELL, Harold Arthur; Chairman, Gateway Building Society, since 1974; *b* 13 Sept. 1918; *s* of Anthony Bell and Emily Bell (*née* Johnson); *m* 1946, Barbara Joyce Copp; four *s* one *d. Educ:* Westminster City School. Solicitor in private practice, 1940-; Dir, Temperance Permanent Building Soc., 1958, Vice-Chm., 1961; Chm., Jan.-July 1974; merged with Bedfordshire Building Soc., July 1974, to become Gateway Building Soc. Vice-Pres., Metropolitan Assoc. of Building Societies, 1976-; Hon. Solicitor: Baptist Missionary Soc., 1950-67; Home Counties Baptist Assoc., 1958-. *Recreations:* charitable works, golf, reading. *Address:* Bickwell House, Sidmouth, Devon. *T:* Sidmouth 4663; Devon House, 172-174 Kingston Road, Ewell, Surrey. *T:* 01-393 0231. *Club:* Royal Automobile.   *[Died 27 June 1978.*

BELL, Mrs Harry Graham; *see* Bell, G. E. L.

BELL, Julia, MA; FRCP; retired; *b* 28 Jan. 1879; unmarried. *Educ:* Nottingham Girls' High Sch.; Girton Coll., Cambridge; London Sch. of Medicine for Women; St Mary's Hospital. Mathematical Tripos, Cambridge. Hon. aegrotat degree, 1901; MA granted by Trinity Coll. Dublin (Cambridge degree not then given to women). Research into Solar Parallax, Cambridge Observatory, 1902-08; Statistical Asst, UC London, 1908-14; medical student and research (with Karl Pearson, FRS), 1914-20; MRCS, LRCP; research asst under Med. Res. Council (during much of time on permanent Acad. Staff), working in Galton Lab., University Coll., 1920-65; Hon. Research Associate at University Coll., London, 1944-65; MRCP (on basis of research work), Galton Research Fellow, 1920; FRCP 1938. Weldon Medal and Prize, Oxford Univ., 1941. *Publications:* in Treasury of Human Inheritance, Vol. II, 6 Monographs on Hered. Diseases of the Eye, 1922-33; Vol. IV, 4 monographs on Nerv. Disease and Muscular Dystrophies, 1934-48; Vol. V, Pts 1 and 2, monographs on Digital Anomalies, 1951-53; Pt 3, on the Lawrence-Moon Syndrome, 1958. A number of papers in Biometrika and Annals of Eugenics, etc. *Recreations:* reading, delights of friendship; chief interests Applied Statistics and Historical side of Medicine and Science.
[Died 26 April 1979.

BELL, Sir Stanley, Kt 1954; OBE 1943; JP; DL; Director (formerly Chairman), Astley Industrial Trust Ltd, Manchester; *b* 30 Oct. 1899; *s* of Thomas George Bell, Wigan, Lancs; *m* 1923, Margaret Frances, *d* of James Slevin, Wigan; one *d.* Served European War, 1914-19, with RASC and RAF; 2nd Lieut 1918. Col 1944. Director of Companies; Pres. N-W Provincial Area Council, Conservative Party, 1956-60; Chm., National Union of Conservative Associations, 1958. Contested Westhoughton and West Salford divs, 1945 and 1950. JP Lancs, 1942; DL, Co. Palatine of Lancaster, 1967. *Recreations:* golf, shooting. *Address:* Euxton Hall, Euxton, near Chorley, Lancs. *T:* Chorley 3359. *Clubs:* Carlton; St James's (Manchester).
[Died 23 July 1972.

BELLAMY, Brig. Robert Hugh, CBE 1956; DSO 1944 (and Bar 1945); *b* 8 Dec. 1910; *yr s* of late Lieut-Col Robert Bellamy, DSO, St Leonards-on-Sea, and late Mrs Constance Gwendoline Stephenson Clarke, Knightsbridge Court, Sloane Street, SW1; *m* 1940, Kathleen Louisa Isabel (marriage dissolved, 1953), *d* of late Sir Alfred Lascelles, Terrington, Yorks; one *s* one *d. Educ:* Sherborne; RMC, Sandhurst. 2nd Lieut DCLI, 1930; Lieut-Col 1943; Brig. 1945. Served in France, 1940 (despatches), Adjt DCLI; NW Europe, 1944-45; Palestine, 1945-46 (despatches); comd Air Landing Brigade, 1945; comd Parachute Brigade, 1946-48; Dep. Dir of Weapons Development, 1950-52; Imperial Defence Coll., 1953; Dep. Comdr, Hong Kong, and Comdr 40 Infantry Div., 1954-56; Chief of Staff, 1 Corps, 1956-58; retired, 1958. psc; idc. *Recreations:* yachting, shooting. *Address:* 7 Eaton Place, SW1. *T:* 01-235 7187. *Clubs:* Bath, Royal Ocean Racing; Royal Yacht Squadron.   *[Died 27 Nov. 1972.*

BELLERBY, Rev. Alfred Courthope Benson, MA Cantab; Headmaster, King Edward School, Witley, Surrey, 1926-51; retired, 1951; *b* 26 Jan. 1888; *s* of late E. J. Bellerby, MusDoc Oxon., LRAM, and Charlotte Bellerby; *m* 1922, Enid Florence Apperly (*d* 1979). *Educ:* St Lawrence Coll., Ramsgate; Emmanuel Coll., Cambridge; Ridley Hall, Cambridge. Cambridge Univ. Athletic Blue, 1907, 1908, 1909, 1910; Pres. Cambridge Univ. Athletic Club, 1910; Holder of Univ. Gold Medal for 3 wins in succession against Oxford; Cambridge Univ.

Hockey Blue, 1909-10; International Hockey Trials, 1909-10; represented United Kingdom in Olympic Games, 1908 (High Jump). Deacon, 1911; Priest, 1913; Chaplain, Games Master and Senior House Master, St Lawrence Coll., 1911-26. *Publication:* The Lonely Dog. *Recreations:* gardening, lecturing. *Address:* Redcot, Three Gates Lane, Haslemere, Surrey.
[Died 10 April 1979.

BELLERBY, Major John Rotherford, MC; author; editor; trustee of Education Services, since 1930; *b* 25 May 1896; *e s* of George A. Bellerby, York; *m* 1st, 1929, Mary Eirene Frances (marr. diss. 1949), *o d* of Rev. F. Talbot Parker, Winchester; 2nd, 1961, Rosalind Winifred, *e d* of late Frederick Arthur James, Olton, Warwicks. *Educ:* Archbishop Holgate's Grammar Sch., York; Leeds Univ.; Harvard Univ. Served in 8 W York R and Machine Gun Corps, 1914-19; Leeds Univ., BCom 1920; MA 1924; ILO, League of Nations, 1921-27; Commonwealth Fund Fellow, Harvard, 1925-26; Technical adviser, British Delegation to the International Economic Conference, Geneva, 1927; Fellow of Gonville and Caius Coll., Cambridge, 1927-30; Brunner Prof. of Economic Science, University of Liverpool, 1930-32; Leverhulme Research Fellow, 1940-42; Lecturer, University of Glasgow, 1942; Ministry of Food, 1943-47; Oxford Institute of Agricultural Economics Research, 1947-61; University Demonstrator, 1951-61; Dir, Hunter and Smallpage Ltd, York, 1965-69. *Publications:* Control of Credit as a Remedy for Unemployment, 1924; Monetary Stability, 1925; Stabilisation of Employment in the United States, 1925; Coalmining, a European Remedy, 1928; A Contributive Society, 1931; The Conflict of Values, 1933; (with others): Industrial Survey of Merseyside, 1932; Economic Reconstruction, 1943; Agriculture and Industry, Relative Income, 1956; Agricultural Economic Theory and the Indian Economy, 1961; (ed and contrib.) Factory Farming, 1970; Human Ecology and Human Values, 1972; Britain in Debt?, 1975. *Address:* 19 Norham Road, Oxford.   *[Died 1 April 1977.*

BELLEW, 5th Baron, *cr* 1848; **Edward Henry Bellew,** Bt 1688; MBE 1919; late Captain RAF; *b* 6 Feb. 1889; *e s* of late Hon. R. E. Bellew, 4th *s* of 2nd Baron; *S* uncle 1935; *m* 1912, Barbara Helen Mary (*d* 1967), *d* of late Sir Henry Farnham Burke, KCVO. *Heir:* b Hon. Bryan Bertram Bellew, MC [*b* 11 June 1890; *m* 1918, Jeanie Ellen Agnes (*d* 1973), *d* of late James O. Jameson; one *s*]. *Address:* Barmeath Castle, Co. Louth. *Clubs:* Turf, Pratt's; Kildare Street (Dublin).   *[Died 8 Aug. 1975.*

BELLINGHAM, Sir Roger Carroll Patrick Stephen, 6th Bt (2nd creation), *cr* 1796; Physician; *b* 23 April 1911; *s* of Capt. Roger Charles Noel Bellingham, RFA, 2nd *s* of 4th Bt (*d* 1915), and Alice Ann Naish (*d* 1949); *S* uncle, Brig.-Gen. Sir Edward Henry Charles Patrick Bellingham, 5th Bt, CMG, DSO, 1956; *m* 1941, Mary, *d* of late William Norman; two *s. Educ:* France; Edinburgh Univ. MB, ChB Edinburgh 1936; DA England 1956. Served as Flight-Lieut RAFVR, 1941-46. Knight of the Sovereign Order of Malta. *Recreation:* travel. *Heir:* s Noel Peter Roger Bellingham, *b* 4 Sept. 1943. *Address:* 1 Adswood Lane West, Stockport, Cheshire. *T:* Stockport 2564; Castle Bellingham, Co. Louth, Ireland.   *[Died 6 Feb. 1973.*

BEN-GURION, David; Israeli statesman; past Prime Minister and Minister of Defence, Government of Israel; *b* Plonsk, 16 Oct. 1886; *m* 1917, Paula Mounvas (*d* 1968); one *s* two *d. Educ:* privately; Constantinople Univ. (Faculty of Law). Active in Zionist Labour Movement from early youth; settled in Israel, 1906; exiled as Zionist by Turkish admin., 1915; went to USA; founded Hechalutz organization there; helped raise Jewish Legion and served in its ranks under Gen. Allenby; Mem. Gen. Council, Zionist Organization, 1920; co-organizer, Jewish Labour Party (Mapai) and Gen. Fedn of Jewish Labour (Histadruth); Sec.-Gen. of Fedn, 1921-35; political missions abroad; Mem. Exec. Jewish Agency for Palestine, 1933; Chm., Jewish Agency for Palestine, 1935-48; following UN Partition Resolution, 1947, elected Chm. Nat. Council (in charge of security and defence); proclaimed Independence of State of Israel, May 1948; Prime Minister and Minister of Defence: (Provisional Govt), 1948-49; also 1949-53; resigned, 1953; Minister of Defence, 1955; Prime Minister and Minister of Defence, Nov. 1955-June 1963. Dr *hc* of Hebrew Letters, Jewish Theological Seminary of America; Bialik Literary Prize for Judaica, 1952; Dr *hc* of Philosophy, Hebrew Univ., Jerusalem, 1957; Hon. LLD: Brandeis Univ., Boston, 1960; Rangoon Univ., 1961. *Publications:* (in Hebrew) Self-Government of Villayets, 1914; Eretz Israel, 1918; We and Our Neighbours, 1920; The Labour Movement and Revisionism, 1933; From Class to Nation, 1933 (new edn 1955); Mishmarot (essays on Labour Zionism), 1935; The Struggle (5 vols), 1947-50; Israel at War, 1950 (in Yiddish, NY, 1951); Vision and Implementation (5 vols), 1951-57; Mima-amed Leam, 1955; Rebirth and Destiny of

Israel, 1954; Nezach Israel (in Yiddish), 1953 (Buenos Aires); En la Patria Libre (Buenos Aires), 1954; The Sinai Campaign (Hebrew), 1959; Israel: Years of Challenge (in English), 1963; Ben-Gurion looks back, 1965; Dvarim Kehavayatam; (ed) The Jews in their Land, 1966; Talks with Arabs; Michtavim LePaula, 1969; The Restored State of Israel (2 vols), 1969; Iyunim Batanach, 1969; Israel: a personal history, 1971; Igrot David Ben-Gurion, 1971; Zichronot, vol. 1, 1971, vol. 2, 1972, vol. 3, 1973; Yehud Veye'ud, 1971; Ben-Gurion Looks at the Bible, 1972; essays and articles. *Address:* Sdeh-Boker, Israel.
[Died 1 Dec. 1973.

BENCE-JONES, Col Philip Reginald, MC; MA Hons (Cantab.), MInstCE, MICEI, MIMechE; *b* 12 Jan. 1897; *s* of late Reginald Bence-Jones, DL, JP, Lisselane, Co. Cork, and late Ethel Da Costa; *m* 1925, Victoria May, *d* of William Thomas, Alexandria, Egypt; one *s*. *Educ:* Rugby; Pembroke Coll., Cambridge; Bonn; Paris. Served with Royal Engineers in France, Belgium and Germany, 1914-19; Pembroke Coll., Cambridge, 1919-22, taking 1st Cl. Hons Mechanical Sciences Tripos and post-graduate Engineering Scholarship; Construction of Blue Nile Dam and Gezira Irrigation Project for Sudan Govt, 1922-26; Principal Asst to Chief Engineer to the London County Council, and other engineering work in UK, 1926-34; Punjab Govt service, 1934-46; Col Comdt, Punjab Univ. OTC, Indian Territorial Force, 1936-45; Staff Officer RE First Grade, GHQ, India, 1941-44. *Recreations:* country life. *Address:* Glenville Park, Glenville, Co. Cork, Ireland. *T:* Cork 880103. *Club:* Leander; Cork and County (Cork).
[Died 2 June 1972.

BENDIT, Gladys; *see* Presland, John.

BENIN, Oba of; Akenzua II; Godfrey Okoro, CMG 1946; *b* 1899; *e s* of Oba Eweka II and *o s* of Queen Ariowa (titled Queen Ezon); *S* father 1933; first marriage, 1922; over 50 *s* and *d*. *Educ:* Government Sch., Benin City; King's Coll., Lagos. Transport Clerk, 1922; Private Sec. and Clerk to Oba Eweka II and to Benin Judicial Council, 1924-25; Administrative Training, Abeokuta, 1926-27; District Head, Ekiadolor District in Benin Div., 1928-33. Minister Without Portfolio, Western Nigeria, 1955-60. Chancellor, Ahmadu Bello University, 1966-70. JP 1960. Jubilee medal, 1935; Coronation medal, 1937; Medal for African Chiefs. *Recreations:* snooker, etc. *Heir:* *s* Solomon Igbinoghodua Aisiokuoba Akenzua, *b* 22 June 1923. *Address:* PO Box 12, Benin City, Western Nigeria. *T:* 1 Benin City.
[Died 1978.

BENNET, Edward Armstrong, MC; MD; FRCPsych; Consultant Physician Emeritus, Bethlem Royal and Maudsley Hospital; occasional Lecturer, Institute of Psychiatry, University of London; Patron C. G. Jung-Inst. Zürich; *s* of late William Boyd Bennet and Marion McCaldin; *m* 1st, 1926, Flora (*d* 1952), *d* of late Rev. Alex Wylie, Edinburgh; two *s*; 2nd, 1958, Frances Eveline, *d* of late Rev. R. F. R. Routh. *Educ:* Campbell Coll., Belfast; Trinity Coll., Dublin. Stewart Sch. in Mental Disease, Moderator Mental and Moral Science; MB, BCh, BAO, 1925; DPM England 1926; MA, MD 1930; ScD 1939. Fellow Royal Society of Medicine; Fellow Brit. Psychological Soc. (Past Chm. Med. Sect.). War of 1939-45: Major RAMC, 1940; Command Psychiatrist Aldershot Command, 1940-42; Brigadier, RAMC, 1942; Consultant in Psychiatry, India Command, and 11th Army Group, 1942-45. Formerly Consulting Psychiatrist, India and Burma Office. *Publications:* C. G. Jung, 1961; The Freud-Janet controversy: an unpublished letter, British Medical Journal, 1965; What Jung Really Said, 1966; etc. *Address:* 2 St Katharine's Precinct, Regent's Park, NW1 4HH. *T:* 01-935 6252; Underwood Cottage, Langrish, Hants. *T:* Petersfield 3972. *Club:* Oriental.
[Died 7 March 1977.

BENNET, Maj.-Gen. John; *b* 12 Feb. 1893; *s* of late John R. and Elizabeth S. Bennet, Hillwood, Ratho; *m* 1926, Margaret Scott, *d* of late Samuel S. Tanner, Hillwood Mains, Ratho; two *s*. *Educ:* George Heriot's Sch.; Edinburgh Univ. MB, ChB (Hons) University of Edinburgh, 1916; DPM London, 1926; MD Edinburgh, 1935; DTM&H London, 1938; FRCP 1948 (Member 1937). Joined RAMC 1916; regular commission, 1920; served Salonika, Egypt, China, India, Malaya; Medical Specialist, 1928. Consulting Physician, Malaya Command, 1941-42; PoW in Malaya, Formosa and Manchuria, 1942-45; despatches (Malaya), 1946; Dir of Medicine and Consulting Physician to the Army, Jan. 1947-51. Col 1947; Brig. 1947; Maj.-Gen., 1950; KHP, 1947-51. Medical Superintendent, East Fife Hospital Group, 1951-59, retd. *Publications:* contribution to Medical History of World War II; Nutrition POW Camps Far East (MRC). *Recreation:* golf. *Address:* 21 Esslemont Road, Edinburgh 9. *T:* 031-667 2407.
[Died 4 March 1976.

BENNET-CLARK, Thomas Archibald, CBE 1966; FRS 1950; BA, PhD (Cantab.), MA (Dublin); Professor Emeritus of Biology, University of East Anglia, Norwich, since 1967 (Professor of Biology and Dean of School of Biological Sciences, 1962-67); Fellow of King's College, University of London; *b* 13 Jan. 1903; *s* of Thomas Bennet-Clark, CA, JP, and Anne Chalmers (*née* Hanna), 32 Buckingham Terrace, Edinburgh; *m* 1926, Elizabeth Constance, *d* of Rev. James Haythornthwaite, Dublin; one *s* one *d*. *Educ:* Marlborough Coll., Wilts; Trinity Coll., Cambridge (Sen. Scholar). Natural Sciences Tripos, 1923; Frank Smart Prize; Asst to Prof. of Botany in Trinity Coll., Dublin, 1924-30; Lectr, Univ. of Manchester, 1930-36; Prof. of Botany, University Coll., Nottingham, 1936-44; Prof. of Botany, King's Coll., University of London, 1944-62. Mem., ARC, 1957-67. Formerly Editor, Jl of Experimental Botany. FRSA, 1959; Hon. FRSE, 1969. Hon. ScD, E Anglia, 1968; Hon. DSc, Leicester, 1968. *Publications:* papers in scientific journals. *Address:* c/o 23 Warriston Crescent, Edinburgh EH3 5LB.
[Died 24 Nov. 1975.

BENNETT, Sir Albert (Edward), Kt 1965; JP; Member Midlands Electricity Board, 1950-71; *b* 1 Oct 1900; *s* of Wm Bennett, coalminer; *m* 1923, Minnie Smith; one *s* two *d*. *Educ:* Elem. Sch. Colliery Blacksmith, until 1926; Labour Party Agent, 1929-35; full-time Trade Union Officer, 1935-48; Councillor (Leader) and Alderman, Stoke on Trent City Council, 1944-74. JP Stoke on Trent, 1948. *Recreations:* bowls, horticulture. *Address:* 7 Milnes Close, Blurton, Stoke on Trent ST3 2HB. *T:* Stoke on Trent 35265.
[Died 6 July 1972.

BENNETT, Engr-Rear-Adm. Cecil Reginald Percival, CBE 1952 (OBE 1943); retired; *b* Morchard Bishop, Devon, 29 July 1896; *s* of Albert Webber Bennett; *m* 1923, Ethel Elizabeth (*née* Bartlett) (*d* 1975); two *d*. *Educ:* Crediton Grammar Sch., Devon. Boy Artificer, HMS Indus, Devonport, 1912-16; served European War in HMS Iron Duke, Grand Fleet, 1916-18; HMS Courageous, 1918-19; HMS Calcutta, 1919-20; commissioned as Mate (E), 1921; RN Colls Greenwich and Keyham, 1921-22; Eng.-Lieut, 1923; Eng.-Lieut-Comdr, 1931; Eng.-Comdr, 1935; served in HMS Formidable, War of 1939-45, 1939-42 (despatches, OBE); Eng.-Capt, 1944; served with Royal Canadian Navy, 1944-45; Chief Engineer, Sheerness Yard, 1945-47; Manager, Engineering Dept: Malta, 1947-50; HM Dockyard, Devonport, 1950-54; retd 1954. AMIMechE, 1930, MIMechE, 1947, FIMechE, 1970. *Recreation:* gardening. *Address:* The Maples, Goats Hill, Northam, North Devon.
[Died 29 Jan. 1976.

BENNETT, Cyril; Controller of Programmes, London Weekend Television, 1967-70; re-appointed 1971; *b* 23 April 1928; *e s* of Harry and Golda Bennett; *m* 1959, Shirley Berry; one *s* two *d*. *Educ:* Fleet Street. Beaverbrook Newspapers, 1943; Bedfordshire Times, 1944; re-joined Beaverbrook Newspapers, 1945; Lobby Correspondent, Commonwealth Press Union, 1947-48; Odhams Press, 1950; joined Rediffusion Television, 1955; wrote and produced range of television programmes; Producer 'This Week', 1961; Head of Current Affairs, 1963; Controller of Programmes, Rediffusion Television, 1965-67. Managing Director, Talent Associates-Norton Simon Inc., 1970. *Recreations:* kibbitzing, mirth. *Address:* London Weekend Television, South Bank Television Centre, SE1. *T:* 01-261 3434.
[Died 7 Nov. 1976.

BENNETT, Henry Stanley, FBA; Life Fellow, Emmanuel College, Cambridge (Librarian, 1934-59); Emeritus University Reader in English; Vice-President of The British Academy, 1959-60; *b* 15 Jan. 1889; *e s* of William Henry Bennett, Hastings; *m* 1919, Joan, MA, *d* of Julia Frankau (Frank Danby); one *s* three *d*. *Educ:* Emmanuel Coll., Cambridge. Entered S Mark's Coll., Chelsea, 1907; Elementary Schoolmaster in London, 1909-15; invalided from Army, 1918; entered Emmanuel Coll., 1918. Mem. of Council of the Senate, Cambridge, 1943-50; Mem., of Bd of Advisers in English in University of London, 1942-50; Pres. 1958-60, and Trustee, 1965-, Bibliographical Soc. Chm. Cambridge Univ. Press Syndicate, 1952-64; Visiting Prof. University of Chicago, 1931, 1948, 1952, 1955, and 1958-; Leverhulme Research Fellow, 1947-49; Sandars Reader in Bibliography, 1951; Gregynog Lectr, University Coll. of Wales, Aberystwyth, 1953. Fellow, Folger Library, 1958 and 1961. Hon. DHL (Chicago), 1955. *Publications:* The Pastons and their England, 1922; England from Chaucer to Caxton, 1928; Marlowe's Jew of Malta and The Massacre at Paris, edited for the definitive edition of the Works and Life of Christopher Marlowe, 1931; Life on the English Manor, 1937; Quia Amore Langueo (edition of), 1937; The Author and his Public in the Fourteenth and Fifteenth Centuries, and Medieval Literature and the Modern Reader (Essays and Studies of English Assoc.), 1938 and 1945; Vol. II Part I, The Oxford History of English

Literature, 1947; English Books and Readers: Vol. I, 1475 to 1557, 1952; Six Medieval Men and Women, 1955; English Books and Readers: Vol. II, 1558-1603, 1965; Vol. III, 1603-1640, 1970. *Recreation:* travel in Austria and Switzerland. *Address:* Church Rate Corner, Cambridge. *T:* Cambridge 53571.
[*Died 6 June* 1972.

BENNETT, Prof. James Allan Jamieson, DSc, PhD; Hon. FRAeS, FAIAA; Professor Emeritus, Cranfield Institute of Technology, since 1969; helicopter consultant (attached to US Navy); *b* 1 July 1903; *m* Elizabeth Roxburgh Hodge (*d* 1972); one *s* one *d. Educ:* Universities of Glasgow, London and Göttingen. The College of Aeronautics: Prof. of Aerodynamics, 1954-69; Deputy Principal, 1960-61 and 1965-68. Vis. Prof., US Naval Postgraduate Sch., Monterey, Calif, 1967, 1969-72. Engaged in development of rotary-wing aircraft since 1930; designed first production direct take-off aircraft (C40 Autogiro) and first compound helicopter (Gyrodyne); originator of helicopter which established International Speed Record for helicopters, 1948; originator of rotorcraft which established Internat. Speed Record for rotorcraft, 1959; originator of numerous patents relating to rotary-wing aircraft. Royal Aeronautical Society: Vice-Pres., 1966-69; Pres. Elect, 1969-70; Hon. Fellow 1968. Hon. Fellow American Helicopter Soc., 1968. Hon. LLD Glasgow, 1970. American Helicopter Soc. Award, 1947; Louis Breguet Memorial Trophy, 1959. *Publications:* many papers published in technical journals (mainly on rotary-wing aircraft). *Address:* Box 2473, Carmel-by-the-Sea, Calif 93921, USA; 59a High Street, Stotfold, Hitchin, Herts. *T:* Hitchin 730757. *Clubs:* Caledonian; Royal Scottish Automobile (Glasgow); Convivium (Carmel-by-the-Sea).
[*Died 26 Feb.* 1973.

BENNETT, John; Hon. Mr Justice Bennett; Justice of Appeal, Courts of Appeal for the Seychelles, St Helena, The Falkland Islands Colony and Dependencies, and The British Antarctic Territory, since 1965; Vice-President, Immigration Appeal Tribunal, since 1975; *b* 20 July 1909; 2nd *s* of late John and Mary Bennett, Armagh, NI; *m* 1953, Rachael Kathleen, *o d* of late Major John Watson Laidlay, the Royal Scots, and late Hilda Eleanor Laidlay, Edinburgh. *Educ:* Royal School, Armagh; Queen's Univ., Belfast. Solicitor, Supreme Court of N Ireland, 1932; Asst Administrator-Gen. and Dep. Public Trustee, Zanzibar, 1934; Land Officer, Zanzibar, 1938; Registrar, Supreme Court and Registrar-Gen., Fiji Islands, 1940; Resident Magistrate, 1943, Chief Magistrate, 1945; Chm., Commission on Juvenile Delinquency, Fiji, 1944; Chm., European Civil Servants Assoc., Fiji and W Pacific, 1946; Magistrate, Nigeria, 1949, Chief Magistrate, Nigeria, 1951; Judge of the High Court of Lagos and the Southern Cameroons, 1956-62. Called to Bar, Gray's Inn, 1952. Chairman: S Mddx Rent Tribunal, 1964-70; Industrial Tribunals, England and Wales, 1966-70; Temporary Deputy Chm., Greater London QS, 1967-70; Chief Adjudicator, Immigration Appeals, 1970-75. Served Fiji Infantry Regt, 1940-43, Capt. 3 Bn. *Recreations:* fishing, travel. *Address:* Flat F, 21 Cadogan Gardens, SW3 2RW. *T:* 01-730 0323. *Club:* Chelsea Arts.
[*Died 16 Sept.* 1975.

BENNETT, John Reginald William, MA (Oxon); late ICS; *b* 18 Oct. 1888; *s* of John Bennett and Elizabeth Mary Balfour; *m* 1922, Margaret Winifred Seabrook; two *s* one *d. Educ:* Warwick Sch.; Worcester Coll., Oxford (Hons Classical Moderations and History). Entered Indian Civil Service after 1911 examination; Judge, Chief Court of Oudh, 1940-44; Judge, High Court of Allahabad, 1945-47; retired, 1947. *Recreation:* reading. *Address:* Beechurst, Shaftesbury Road, Woking. *T:* Woking 60216.
[*Died 27 Sept.* 1971.

BENNETT, Sir John W. W.; *see* Wheeler-Bennett.

BENNETT, Kenneth Geoffrey, CMG 1966; Puisne Judge, Kenya, 1968; *b* 15 Jan. 1911; *er s* of late Wallace Bennett and Beatrice Norman Jeffery; unmarried. *Educ:* Clifton Coll. and privately. Called to the Bar (Middle Temple), 1932; Western Circuit; Resident Magistrate, Tanganyika, 1938; Crown Counsel, Tanganyika, 1946; Solicitor-Gen., Nyasaland, 1948. Acting Attorney-Gen., various occasions, 1949-53; Puisne Judge, Uganda, 1953; Acting Chief Justice, various occasions, 1955-65. Chairman: Uganda Immigration Appeals Tribunal, 1954-60; Commn of Inquiry into disturbances in Eastern Province of Uganda, 1960. *Recreation:* fishing. *Address:* PO Box 30041, Nairobi, Kenya. *Club:* Kampala.
[*Died 3 Jan.* 1974.

BENNETT, Rex George, CB 1946; *b* 11 April 1885; *s* of Rex Bennett and Charlotte Heath, Hildenborough, Kent; *m* 1909, Maud Louise Emmoney; one *s* one *d. Educ:* Bancroft's Sch., Woodford Green. Entered GPO, 1904; Asst Controller, Stores Dept, 1935; Vice-Controller, 1939; Controller, 1940; Dir of

Contracts, 1941-46; Mem. Forests Products Research Board, Dept of Scientific and Industrial Research, 1947-52, Chm., 1952-58. Seconded to Federated Malay States Post Office, 1920-24, and to Ministry of Home Security, 1939. *Publications:* various papers on Wood Preservation to British Wood Preserving Association and Soc. of Chemical Engineering, 1935-52. *Recreations:* philately, local history. *Address:* 70 Hervey Road, Blackheath, SE3. *T:* 01-856 0055. [*Died 27 Sept.* 1972.

BENNETT, Maj.-Gen. Roland Anthony, CB 1959; MD, FRCPE; Physician, Royal Hospital, Chelsea, 1959-69; *b* 10 April 1899; *s* of late Roland Ponsonby Bennett and of Johanna Morrison; *m* 1937, Constance Elizabeth Nanette Stokes; one *d* (and one *d* decd). *Educ:* Stornoway; Edinburgh Univ. MD (Edin) 1936; FRCP (Edin) 1947. Joined Seaforth Highlanders, 1917; served France, 1918 (wounded). Graduated, Edinburgh Univ., 1924; joined RAMC, 1925. Medical Officer, Houston Mount Everest Expedition, 1933. Served in France, Egypt, Palestine, India, Burma, 1939-45; Consulting Physician: Far East Land Forces, 1946-49; BAOR, 1950-55; Hon. Physician to the Queen, 1955-59; Dir of Medicine and Consulting Physician to the Army, 1955-59, retired. *Publications:* articles in RAMC Jl and BMJ. *Address:* c/o Williams & Glyn's Bank Ltd, Kirkland House, Whitehall, SW1.
[*Died 10 Nov.* 1974.

BENNETT, Rev. Canon Ronald D. G.; *see* Grange-Bennett.

BENNETT, Sir Thomas (Penberthy), KBE 1954 (CBE 1942); Kt 1946; FRSA; FRIBA; Hon. FIOB; Hon. FIBD; Chairman: New Town of Crawley, 1947-60; Stevenage Development Corporation, 1951-53; *b* 14 Aug. 1887; *s* of Thomas William Bennett and Anne Frances Penberthy; *m* 1916, Mary Langdon Edis (*d* 1976); one *s. Educ:* Royal Academy Schs; Heatherleys, etc. Architectural Staff of LNWR; Staff of HM Office of Works; Head of Northern Polytechnic Sch. of Architecture, Surveying and Building, 1920-28; Dir of Bricks, 1940, Dir of Works, 1941-44, and Controller of Temporary Housing, Min. of Works, 1944-45; Chm., Bd of Trade Boot and Shoe Working Party, 1945; Lecturer, Board of Education; Private Practice as Architect: *theatres:* including Saville; *cinemas:* including several Odeons; *offices:* incl. Diamond Corp.; Rank Organisation; Anglo-American: Metal Box; Marks & Spencer; Pearl Assurance; Portman Building Soc.; Esso House, Iraq Petroleum Company; Ford Motor Co.; Rugby Portland Cement; Norwich Union Insurance Co.; South Bank Estates; Hill, Samuel & Co. Ltd; *flats:* incl. Eyre Court; Westminster Gardens; Marsham Court; Caroline House; Campbell Court; Queensmead, St John's Wood; *factories:* for Smiths (Eng.); Kodak; *department stores:* Hammonds, Hull; Harrods (Rackhams); Bentalls; Fenwicks; Grants; stores in Africa for United Africa Co.; *hospital work at:* King Edward VII Hosp. for Officers; London Hosp.; Middlesex Hosp.; Westminster Hosp.; *air terminal and offices* for BOAC; Mormon Temple, chapels (Church of Christ Scientist); *synagogues:* St John's Wood; Great Cumberland Pl.; *banks:* for Westminster; Barclay's; Bank of Ireland; *hotel:* The Royal Lancaster. Liveryman and Mem. Court of Assts, Painter-Stainers Co. *Publications:* The Relation of Sculpture and Architecture; Architectural Design in Concrete; articles in Architectural Press, etc. *Recreations:* architecture, golf. *Address:* The Sycamores, 19 North Road, Highgate Village, N6 4BD. *T:* 01-340 6081. *Clubs:* Reform; Highgate Golf.
[*Died 29 Jan.* 1980.

BENNETT, Sir William James, Kt 1966; CBE 1953; DL; JP; CA; Member Eastern Electricity Board since 1948 and Chairman Eastern Electricity Consultative Council; Railway Clerk (consecutively LNWR, LMS, LMR) since 1912; *b* 30 March 1896; *s* of James William Cator Bennett and Marion Blanche Pearson; *m* 1916, Juliet Emily, *d* of John William Watkins, engraver; one *s* one *d. Educ:* elementary sch.; Mr Fegan's Orphanage; London Sch. of Economics. Chm. Tilbury Electricity Undertaking, 1929-49. Formerly Tilbury (subseq. Thurrock) UDC (Chm. 1931-32, 1932-33); CC Essex, 1934-, CA 1946- (Vice-Chm. CC, 1948-49, Chm. 1952-55, 1958-60). DL County of Essex, 1962-; JP Essex 1937-. FRSA 1950. *Recreations:* music, operatics (amateur), astronomy, chess. *Address:* 26 Ruskin Road, Chadwell St Mary, Grays, Essex. *T:* Tilbury 2911.
[*Died 3 May* 1971.

BENNION, Claud; Director British United Shoe Machinery Co. Ltd (formerly Chairman and Managing Director); *b* 12 June 1886; *s* of late Charles Bennion, The Grange, Thurnby, Leics; *m* 1912, Nora Grace (*d* 1967), *d* of late W. G. Jarvis, Leicester; two *s* (one *d* decd). *Educ:* Uppingham; Pembroke Coll., Cambridge. BA, LLB (Cantab.), 1907; Solicitor, 1910; High Sheriff, Leics, 1938-39. *Recreations:* reading, walking, golf. *Address:* Billesdon Coplow, Leics. *T:* Billesdon 208.
[*Died 27 May* 1976.

BENOY, Brig. James Francis, CMG 1951; CBE 1944; Brigadier (retired) late South Staffordshire Regiment; *b* 10 July 1896; *s* of late Rev. J. Benoy, Asst Chaplain-Gen. to the Forces; *m* 1923, Margery Frances Stewart (*d* 1969), *d* of late H. C. Stewart, Jersey; one *s*. *Educ:* St John's Coll., Cambridge. Served European War, 1914-19, France, Belgium (wounded, despatches, 1914-15 star, 2 medals). GSO, Aldershot Comd, 1932-35; DAAG, China Comd, 1936-40; AQMG, BEF, 1940; AQMG, Home Forces, 1941; Brig. i/c Admin West Africa, 1942-43; DA & QMG SE Asia Comd, 1944-45; Head of Lord Mountbatten's Liaison Staff in Australia, 1945-46; Dep.-Dir of Civil Affairs, War Office, 1947-49; Dep. Dir-Gen., Foreign Office Administration of African Territories, 1949-52. Comdr Legion of Merit (USA), 1946. *Address:* The Old Bank House, Wickham Brook, near Newmarket, Suffolk. *Club:* Army and Navy.   [*Died* 14 *Oct.* 1972.

BENOY, Maj.-Gen. John Meredith, CBE 1943 (OBE 1931); Major-General Retired; *b* 13 July 1896; *s* of late Rev. J. Benoy; *m* 1920, Ursula Hulme Cox; one *s* one *d*. *Educ:* Denstone Coll., Staffs; Felsted Sch., Essex; RMC, Sandhurst. 2nd Lieut, South Staffs Regt, 1914; served European War, 1914-18, in France and Belgium with South Staffs and Royal Warwicks Regts (wounded twice); GSO3 Supreme War Council, Versailles and Peace Conference, Paris, 1918-20; Internal Security, S Ireland, 1920-21. Palestine Riots, 1929-30 (OBE); Staff Coll., Camberley, 1932-33; GSO3 War Office, 1934-36; Brigade Major, Aldershot, Palestine, and Transjordan, 1936-39; Bt Lieut-Col, 1940; AA&QMG, BEF, France and Belgium, 1940; Dep. Dir, War Office, 1941-42; Col, 1942; Brig., DA&QMG. First Army, BNAF, 1942-43; DA&QMG Second Army, 1943-44; Maj.-Gen. i/c Administration, Anti-Aircraft Command, 1944-45; Chief Administrator, Eritrea, 1945-46. Mem. Council of Industrial Design, 1949-66; Controller, Association of Socs of Art and Design, 1966-70. Consultant, UN Develt Prog., Thailand, 1971. *Address:* c/o National Westminster Bank, 208 Piccadilly, W1.
                                                   [*Died Aug.* 1977.

BENSKIN, Gladys, (Mrs Joseph Benskin), CBE 1918; *d* of Michael Paul Grace, 40 Belgrave Square, SW; *m* 1st, 1912, Major Raymond Sheffield Hamilton-Grace (*d* 1915); 2nd, 1919, Col Joseph Benskin, DSO, OBE (*d* 1953). Was Sec. to Mesopotamian Relief Fund. Owner and breeder of race-horses. *Address:* Knowle, Frant, near Tunbridge Wells, Kent.
                                                   [*Died* 31 *May* 1978.

BENSON, Rear-Adm. Cyril Herbert Gordon, DSO 1918; RN, retired; *b* 17 Feb. 1884; *s* of late James Bourne Benson; *m* 1919, May (*d* 1951), *d* of late James Boyd. *Educ:* Winchester; HMS Britannia. Lieut, 1906; Shadwell Testimonial Prize, 1910; Comdr, 1917; Capt. 1924; Rear-Adm., 1936; served European War, 1914-18 (despatches, DSO and bar); commanded 4th Destroyer Flotilla, 1926-28; commanded Royal Australian Naval Coll. at Captain's Point, Jervis Bay, 1929-31; Capt.-Superintendent of Training at Flinders Naval Depôt, Vic; 2nd Naval Mem. Royal Australian Naval Board, 1930-32; HMS Cumberland, 1933-35; retired list, 1936; Hon. Wing Comdr RAFVR, 1937-39; Commodore M/S, 1940; HMS Cochrane, 1940-43; Commodore of Convoys, 1943-45; HMS Valkyrie, 1945-47. Royal Humane Society's bronze medal, 1915. *Recreations:* golf and fishing. *Address:* Granny's Cottage, 348 Sea Front, Hayling Island. *Clubs:* Royal and Ancient Golf (St Andrews), Hon. Co. of Edinburgh Golfers.
                                                   [*Died* 17 *March* 1974.

BENSON, Sir George, Kt 1958; estate agent and valuer; *b* 3 May 1889; *s* of Thomas Duckworth Benson; *m* 1919, Marjorie Lodge; one *s* one *d*. *Educ:* Manchester Grammar Sch. MP (Lab) Chesterfield Div., 1929-31 and 1935-50, Chesterfield, 1950-64. *Publication:* History of Socialism. *Address:* c/o G. M. Russell, Grove House, 140 Salmons Lane, Whyteleafe, Surrey.
                                                   [*Died* 17 *Aug.* 1973.

BENSON, Guy Holford; Partner and Director, Robert Benson & Co., 1913-60; Director of London Assurance, 1927-60; *b* 1888; *e s* of late R. H. Benson; *m* 1921, Lady Violet (*d* 1971), 2nd *d* of 8th Duke of Rutland, *widow* of Lord Elcho; three *s*. Served in Gallipoli and France. *Educ:* Eton; Balliol Coll., Oxford. *Address:* Stanway, Winchcomb, Glos. *T:* Stanton 208. *Clubs:* Brooks's, Bath.   [*Died* 30 *April* 1975.

BENSON, Rev. Niale Shane Trevor, AFC 1942; MA; *b* Johannesburg, SA, 14 Dec. 1911; *s* of late Rev. A. H. T. Benson, Vicar of Ilam, Staffs, formerly of Castle Connell, Co. Limerick and of St Saviour's, Johannesburg, and late Emily Maud Malcolmson, Woodlock, Portlaw, Co. Waterford; *m* 1939, Helen Marjorie, *d* of late Air Chief Marshal Sir John Miles Steel, GCB, KBE, CMG; two *s* one *d*. *Educ:* Wolverhampton Grammar Sch.; St John's Coll., Oxford (Open Classical Scholar). BA 1934; MA 1945. Asst Master, Shrewsbury Sch., 1934; Giggleswick Sch., 1935-39. Served War of 1939-45, RAF (AFC); Sqdn-Ldr, 1941; Dep. Chief-Instructor, Empire Central Flying Sch., 1942-43. Giggleswick Sch., 1945-47; Headmaster: Queen Elizabeth's Grammar Sch., Blackburn, 1948-56; Giggleswick Sch., 1956-60; The Cathedral Sch., Salisbury, 1963-70. Deacon, 1968; priest, 1969; Vicar of Broadchalke with Bowerchalke, 1970-80; RD of Chalke, 1974-80; also Priest-in-Charge of Berwick St John and Ebbesbourne Wake with Fifield Bavant and Alvediston, 1979-80. *Address:* 149 Bridge Street, Wye, Ashford, Kent.   [*Died* 28 *Oct.* 1980.

BENSON, Preston; journalist, retired; *b* Kendal, Westmorland, 4 April 1896; *s* of W. P. Benson, journalist; *m* 1932, Winifred Frances Gadd; two *s*. *Educ:* village sch., Orton, Westmorland; King Edward VII Sch., Sheffield. Middlesex and Bucks Advertiser, 1912-16; Navy, 1916-19; Daily News, 1919-23; Daily Chronicle, 1923-30; Star, 1930-60. *Publications:* Unknown Country, 1941; various pamphlets. *Recreations:* playing piano and recorder; painting, gardening. *Address:* 7 Groveland Avenue, SW16 3BD. *T:* 01-679 3017.
                                                   [*Died* 2 *Dec.* 1975.

BENSTEAD, Sir John, Kt 1953; CBE 1946; DL; Member British Transport Commission, 1947-61 (Deputy Chairman); *b* 10 Jan. 1897; *m* 1922, Gladys Mary Palmer (*d* 1965); one *d*; *m* 1967, Catherine Ferguson McCabe. *Educ:* King's Sch., Peterborough. RN, 1915-19. Gen. Sec., National Union of Railwaymen, 1943-47; Pres., International Transport Workers' Federation, 1946; Member: Advisory Council for Scientific and Industrial Research, 1943-48; Colonial and Economic Development Council, 1947-48; Royal Commission on Press, 1946; FCIT. DL Cambridgeshire (formerly Huntingdon and Peterborough), 1967. *Address:* 98a Lincoln Road, Peterborough. *T:* Peterborough 62072.   [*Died* 24 *Jan.* 1979.

BENTALL, Gerald Chalmers, CBE 1950; Chairman, 1942-68, and Managing Director, 1942-63, Bentalls Ltd, Kingston-on-Thames; *b* 17 Feb. 1903; *s* of late Leonard Hugh Bentall and Winifred Ivy Bentall; *m* 1945, Marjorie Sydney Meller; *m* 1959, Sybil Brett; one *s* (by a former marriage). *Educ:* Tonbridge. *Recreation:* agriculture. *Address:* Witley Park, Brook, Godalming, Surrey.   [*Died* 17 *Sept.* 1971.

BENTHALL, Michael Pickersgill, CBE 1960; Theatrical Producer and Company Director; *b* 8 Feb 1919; *s* of late Sir Edward Charles Benthall, KCSI. *Educ:* Eton; Christ Church, Oxford. Actor, 1938-39. Joined RA, Oct. 1939; served War of 1939-45 (despatches), demobilised with rank of Major (Royal Artillery), May 1946. Co-produced with Tyrone Guthrie, Hamlet, for Old Vic Company, New Theatre, 1944. Wrote scenarios for two Sadler's Wells Ballets, Miracle in the Gorbals, 1944, Adam Zero, 1946. *Produced operas:* Don Pasquale, Cambridge Theatre, 1946; Turandot, Covent Garden, 1947; Aida, Covent Garden, 1948; Queen of Spades, Covent Garden, 1950; Macbeth, Royal Opera House, 1960. *Produced plays:* The White Devil, Duchess, 1947; The Wild Duck, St Martin's, 1948; Master of Arts, Strand, 1949; She Stoops to Conquer, Old Vic Co., New, 1949; (at Stratford-on-Avon) Merchant of Venice, 1947, King John, Merchant of Venice (revival), Hamlet, Taming of the Shrew, 1948, A Midsummer Night's Dream, Cymbeline, 1949; As You Like It, Cort Theatre, New York, 1950; Golden City, Adelphi, 1950; Cæsar and Cleopatra, Antony and Cleopatra, St James's, 1951, and Ziegfeld Theatre, New York, 1951; The Tempest, Stratford-on-Avon, 1951 and 1952; The Millionairess, New, London and Shubert Theatre, New York, 1952; A Woman of No Importance, Savoy, 1953; Hamlet, Edinburgh Festival and Old Vic. 1953; All's Well that Ends Well, Old Vic, 1953; Coriolanus, Old Vic, 1954; Macbeth, Edinburgh Festival and Old Vic, 1954; A Midsummer Night's Dream, Edinburgh Festival and Metropolitan Opera House, New York, 1954; Richard II, 1955; The Merchant of Venice, Measure for Measure, The Taming of the Shrew, Old Vic Australian Tour, 1955; Julius Caesar, Edinburgh Festival and Old Vic, 1955; A Winter's Tale, Henry V, Old Vic, 1955; Othello, Old Vic, 1956; Revival of Richard II and Macbeth for Old Vic American Tour, 1956; Timon of Athens, Cymbeline, Merchant of Venice, Old Vic, 1956; Hamlet, A Midsummer Night's Dream, Old Vic, 1957; Twelfth Night, Henry VIII, Old Vic, 1958; Revival of Hamlet, Henry V, Twelfth Night, for Old Vic American Tour, 1958; The Cenci, Old Vic, 1959; The Double Dealer, Edinburgh Festival and Old Vic, 1959; The Importance of Being Earnest, Old Vic, 1959; Macbeth (Verdi), Covent Garden, 1960; Revival of Macbeth, and the Importance of Being Earnest, for Russian tour, 1961; Doctor Faustus, Edinburgh Festival and Old Vic, 1961; Man and Boy, Queen's 1963, and Brooks Atkinson Theatre, New York, 1963; Macbeth,

Lisbon, 1964 (and Chichester, 1966); Romeo and Juliet, Tokyo, 1965; Katharine Hepburn in Coco, New York, 1969. Directed, A Man and his Wife (Churchill Centenary Production), 1974. Director of Old Vic Theatre, 1953-62. *Address:* 72 Eaton Square, SW1.   *[Died 6 Sept. 1974.*

BENTLEY, Frederic Herbert, OBE 1944; *b* 1905; *e s* of Fred Bentley, JP, and Laura Evelyn Bentley; *m* 1946, Radmila Novakovic, of Belgrade. *Educ:* Church Institute Sch., Bolton; University of Manchester. BScManch. 1926; MB, ChB, 1929; FRCS 1932; MD Manchester, 1946; FACS 1955. Bradley Memorial Schol. Clinical Surgery, Manchester Royal Infirmary, 1928. Formerly House Surgeon, Asst RSO; First Asst and Tutor, Manchester Royal Infirmary; formerly House Surg. and Res. Surg. Off., St Mark's Hospital, London; formerly Hon. Surgeon various hospitals in Manchester area. Hunterian Prof., Royal College of Surgeons, England, 1936 and 1937; Prof. of Surgery, the University of Durham, 1945-52; formerly: Mackenzie Mackinnon Research Fellow, RCP London and RCS England; Bernhard Baron Scholar RCS Eng; Dickinson Scholar and Demonst. Anatomy, University of Manchester; Sommer Meml Fellow, Instructor in Surgery, Portland, Oregon, 1953-75; Chm., Oregon State Health Commn, 1972-75; Prof. of Surgery, Univ. of Jordan, 1975-79; Medical Dir, North Lincoln Hosp., 1969-75. On Active Service with RAMC 1942-45, rank Lieut-Col. First as Officer in charge a Surgical Division and later OC Penicillin Control Team in Mediterranean area; separate mission to Russian Army in Rumania, and Partisan Army in Yugoslavia. *Publications:* various contributions to Medical and Physiological Journals since 1936. *Recreations:* angling, music. *Address:* Box 192, Route 2, Newberg, Oregon 97132, USA. *Clubs:* Waverley, Arlington (Portland); Reform (London, England).   *[Died 4 Nov. 1980.*

BENTLEY, Nicolas Clerihew, FRSA, FSIA; Publisher, Artist, and Author; *b* Highgate, London, 14 June 1907; *yr s* of late Edmund Clerihew Bentley; *m* 1934, Barbara, *e d* of late Sir Patrick Hastings, QC; one *d. Educ:* University Coll. Sch., London; Heatherley Sch. of Art. Dir, André Deutsch Ltd. *Publications:* Die, I Thought I'd Laugh, 1936; Ballet-Hoo, 1937; The Time of My Life, 1937; Gammon and Espionage, 1938; Le Sport, 1939; Second Thoughts, and other poems, 1939; Animal, Vegetable and South Kensington, 1940; The Tongue-Tied Canary, 1948; The Floating Dutchman, 1950; Third Party Risk, 1953; How Can You Bear to be Human?, 1957; A Version of the Truth, 1960; The Victorian Scene, 1968; Golden Sovereigns, 1970; Tales from Shakespeare, 1972; The Events of That Week, 1972; An Edwardian Album, 1974; Inside Information, 1974, etc.; *edited:* The Pick of Punch, 1955-56, 1956-57, 1957-58, 1959-60; A Choice of Ornaments, 1959; Dispatches from the Crimea 1854-56 by Sir W. H. Russell, 1966; The Reminiscences of Captain Gronow, 1977; *illustrated:* New Cautionary Tales by H. Belloc, 1930; More Than Somewhat by Damon Runyon, 1937; Old Possum's Book of Practical Cats by T. S. Eliot, 1939; Baseless Biography by E. C. Bentley, 1940; How to be an Alien by G. Mikes, 1946; Stiff Upper Lip by L. Durrell, 1958; On Drink by Kingsley Amis, 1973, etc. *Address:* The Old School, Downhead, Shepton Mallet, Somerset. *Club:* Garrick.
                                                  [Died 14 Aug. 1978.

BENTLEY, Phyllis Eleanor, OBE 1970; BA; Hon. LittD Leeds, 1949; FRSL 1958; Author; *b* Halifax, Yorks, 19 Nov. 1894; *d* of Joseph Edwin and Eleanor Bentley; unmarried. *Educ:* Halifax; Cheltenham Ladies' Coll. *Publications:* The World's Bane, 1918; Pedagomania, 1918; Environment, 1922; Cat-in-the-Manger, 1923; The Spinner of the Years, 1928; The Partnership, 1928; Carr, 1929; Trio, 1930; Inheritance, 1932; A Modern Tragedy, 1934; The Whole of the Story, 1935; Freedom, Farewell!, 1936; Sleep in Peace, 1938; Take Courage, 1940; Manhold, 1941; Here is America, 1941; The English Regional Novel, 1942; The Rise of Henry Morcar, 1946; Some Observations on the Art of Narrative, 1946; Colne Valley Cloth, 1947; The Brontës, 1947; Life Story, 1948; Quorum, 1950; Panorama, 1952; The House of Moreys, 1953; Noble in Reason, 1955; Love and Money, 1957; Crescendo, 1958; Kith and Kin, 1960; The Young Brontës, 1960; O Dreams, O Destinations (autobiography), 1962; Committees, 1964; Public Speaking, 1964; The Adventures of Tom Leigh, 1964; Tales of the West Riding, 1965; A Man of His Time, 1966; Ned Carver in Danger, 1967; Gold Pieces, 1968; The Brontës and their World, 1969; Ring in the New, 1969; Sheep May Safely Graze, 1972; The New Venturers, 1973; More Tales of the West Riding, 1974; (ed) Heather Edition of the Works of the Brontës, 1949. *Recreation:* reading. *Address:* Ing Royde, Broomfield Avenue, Halifax, W Yorks. *T:* Halifax 54508. *Club:* PEN.   *[Died 27 June 1977.*

BENTLEY, Walter Owen, MBE 1919; retired; MIME; *b* 16 Sept. 1888; *s* of Alfred Bentley and Emily, *d* of Thomas Waterhouse;

m 1934, Margaret Roberts Hutton, *d* of Thomas Roberts and Ann Murray; no *c. Educ:* Lambrook; Clifton Coll. Premium Apprentice, Great Northern Railway Loco. Works, Doncaster, 1905-10; Served in RNVR, attached RNAS, 1915-18. Originated use of aluminium for pistons in internal combustion engines, 1913. Responsible for design of: BR1 and BR2 rotary aero engines; all Bentley cars, 1919-31; 12 cylinder 4+ litre and 2+ litre Lagondas, 1935-46; 2+ litre Lagonda engine used later in Aston Martin. *Publications:* "W.O.", 1958; Cars in My Life, 1961; Illustrated History of the Bentley Car, 1964; My Life and my Cars, 1967. *Address:* Little Garden Cottage, Shamley Green, near Guildford, Surrey. *T:* Bramley 2136. *[Died 13 Aug. 1971.*

BENTON, William; Chairman and Publisher, Encyclopædia Britannica, Inc., since 1943; *b* Minneapolis, Minn., 1 April 1900; *s* of Charles William Benton and Elma Caroline Hixson; *m* 1928, Helen Hemingway; two *s* two *d. Educ:* Shattuck Sch., Faribault, Minn.; Carleton Coll. BA Yale Univ., 1921. Hon. Degrees: LLD: Louisville Univ., 1948, Bard Coll., 1951, Montana State Coll., 1957; Knox Coll., 1960; Carleton Coll. 1961; Univ. of Notre Dame, 1968; Brandeis Univ., 1968; Dartmouth Coll., 1968. With advertising agencies, 1922-36; Co-founder Benton & Bowles. University of Chicago: Vice-Pres., 1937-45; Asst Chancellor, 1945, Trustee, 1946-65. Asst Sec. of State of US, Washington, DC, 1945-47; US Senator from Connecticut, 1949-53. Chm. Encyclopædia Britannica Education Corporation (formerly Encyclopædia Britannica Films), 1943-; Founding Vice-Chm., Bd Trustees, Cttee for Economic Development, 1942-45, Mem. Exec. Cttee, Bd Trustees, 1958-63; Vice-Chm. US Commn of Inter-Amer. Devel., 1943-45; Mem. Adv. Cttee. Coordinator of Inter-Amer. Affairs, 1939-45; Has Served 18 times as US Chm. of US Delegns at UNESCO and other international confs. US Mem., Executive Board of Unesco, 1963-68, with rank of Ambassador; Trustee: Univs Chicago (Life); Connecticut; Bridgeport; Brandeis; Hampton Inst. (Hon.); Carleton Coll. (Hon.); Shattuck Sch. (Emeritus). Contributor to Magazines. Hon. Fellow, Weizmann Inst. of Science, Israel, 1970. Has received many decorations and awards, US and foreign. *Publications:* This Is the Challenge, 1958; The Voice of Latin America, 1961; The Teachers and the Taught in the USSR, 1966. *Address:* (home) Southport, Conn. 06490; (office) 342 Madison Avenue, New York 10017.
                                              [Died 17 March 1973.

BENTWICH, Helen Caroline, (Mrs Norman Bentwich), CBE 1965; *b* 6 Jan. 1892; *yr d* of Arthur and Caroline Franklin; *m* 1915, Norman Bentwich, *qv. Educ:* St Paul's Girls' Sch.; Bedford Coll., London. Hon. Secretary: Palestine Council of Women, 1921-30; Movement of Children from Germany, 1939-40; Parliamentary Candidate, 1932 and 1935; co-opted LCC Education Cttee, 1934 (Chm. 1947-50); LCC Mem. for N Kensington, 1937-46, for NE Bethnal Green, 1946-49, for Stoke Newington and N Hackney, 1955-58; Vice-chm. LCC, 1950-51; Chm. of the Council, 1956-57. Alderman of LCC, 1949-55 and 1958-65. Governor: Bedford Coll.; Haberdashers' Aske's Schs; N London Polytechnic; Dartford Physical Training Coll.; Central Sch. of Arts and Crafts; Almoner, Christs's Hosp. *Publications:* Our Councils, 1962; The Vale of Health on Hampstead Heath, 1777-1967, 1968; History of Sandwich in Kent, 1971; (with Norman Bentwich), Mandate Memories, 1965. *Recreations:* gardening, travel. *Address:* Hollycot, Vale of Health, Hampstead, NW3. *T:* 01-435 2881; 17 Upper Strand Street, Sandwich. *Club:* Royal Commonwealth Society.
                                              [Died 26 April 1972.

BENTWICH, Norman, OBE; MC; LLD (Hon.) Aberdeen and Melbourne; PhD (Hon.) Jerusalem; Barrister-at-law, Lincoln's Inn, 1908; *b* 1883; *e s* of late Herbert Bentwich; *m* 1915, Helen (*see* H. C. Bentwich), *y d* of Arthur E. Franklin. *Educ:* St Paul's Sch.; Trinity Coll., Cambridge. Members' Essay Prize, Whewell Scholarship for International Law, and Yorke Prize. Called to Bar, 1908: Co-editor of the Jewish Review, 1910-13 and 1932-34; Ministry of Justice, Cairo, 1912-15; Major, Camel Transport, 1916-18. Lectr at Hague Academy of International Law, 1929, 1934 and 1955. Dir of High Commission for Refugees from Germany, 1933-35; Attorney-General, Government of Palestine, 1920-31; Prof. of International Relations, Jerusalem Univ. 1932-51; Vice-Pres. Jewish Cttee for Relief Abroad; Chm. National Peace Council, 1944-46; Chm. United Restitution Office, 1948-; Foreign Office Cttee on Restitution in British Zone of Germany, 1951; Pres., Jewish Historical Soc., 1960-62; Chm., Friends of Hebrew Univ., Jerusalem. *Publications:* Philo-Judæus; Josephus; Hellenism; The Declaration of London; Domicile and Succession; The Practice of the Privy Council; The Mandates System, 1930; England in Palestine, 1932; A Wanderer in the Promised Land, 1932; The Religious Foundations of Internationalism, 1933; Palestine, 1934; The Jews, 1934; The Refugees from Germany, 1936; Wanderer

Between Two Worlds, 1941; Judea Lives Again, 1943; Jewish Youth Comes Home, 1944; Wanderer in War, 1946; From Geneva to San Francisco, 1946; I Understand the Risks, 1950; (with A. Martin) A Commentary on the Charter, 1950; Israel, 1952; The Rescue and Achievement of Refugee Scholars, 1953; Life of Judah Magnes, 1954; Israel and Her Neighbours, 1955; They Found Refuge, 1956; The Jews in Our Time, 1960; Israel Resurgent, 1960; The New-Old Land of Israel, 1960; The Hebrew University, 1961; My 77 Years, 1962; (with Helen Bentwich) Mandate Memories, 1965; (with Michael Kisch) Biography of Brigadier Fred Kisch, 1966; Israel: Two Fateful Years 1967-69, 1970. *Recreations:* music, travel. *Address:* Hollycot, Vale of Health, NW3. *T:* 01-435 2881; University, Jerusalem. *Clubs:* Reform, Maccabæans. *[Died 8 April 1971.*

BERENDSEN, Sir Carl August, KCMG 1946 (CMG 1936); LLM; *s* of Ferdinand and Fannie Berendsen; *m* 1917, Nellie Ellis Brown; two *s. Educ:* Gore District High Sch.; Victoria Univ. Coll., Wellington. Civil Service, 1906; Chief Clerk Labour Department and Deputy Registrar of Industrial Unions, 1916. Permanent Head, Prime Minister's Department, Wellington, NZ, 1932-43; Sec. of External Affairs, 1928-43; New Zealand High Commissioner in Australia, 1943-44; Minister of New Zealand in the USA, 1944-48, Ambassador, 1948-52. *Address:* 16 Waiteata Road, Kelburn, Wellington, NZ.
[Died 12 Sept. 1973.

BERESFORD, Jack, CBE 1960; Member, British Olympic Council, since 1936; Member, Council for England, British Empire and Commonwealth Games (BE & CG) 1931-74; *b* 1 Jan. 1899; *s* of Julius and Ethel Mary Beresford; *m* 1st, 1940, Mary Leaning (marr. diss.); one *s* one *d* ; 2nd, 1958, Stroma Jean Margaret Morrison; two *d. Educ:* Bedford Sch. Served, European War of 1914-18: enlisted Artists' Rifles, 1917; commissioned. Liverpool Scottish Regiment; served 1917-19, Northern France; wounded, 1918. Champion Sculler of Great Britain, 1920-26; winner of Diamond Sculls, 1920, 1924, 1925, 1926; only winner of all five principal events, Henley Royal Regatta; Grand (twice), Stewards, Silver Goblets (twice), Diamonds (four times), Double Sculls; Olympic Games: (Brussels) 1920 silver medal Olympic Sculls, (Paris) 1924 gold medal Olympic Sculls, (Amsterdam) 1928 silver medal Olympic Eights, (Los Angeles) 1932 gold medal Olympic Fours, (Berlin) 1936 gold medal Olympic Double Sculls; 1930 British Empire Games (Canada) silver medal Empire Sculls. Philadelphia Gold Cup, World Amateur Sculling Championship, 1924-25; Helms Athletic Foundn (USA) Helms World Trophy, Europe, 1926. Leader of British Olympic team, Berlin, 1936; coach and manager, English oarsmen in Argentina and Uruguay, 1947; awarded gold medal of honour of the Fédération Internationale des Sociétés d'Aviron (FISA), Lucerne, 1947; Organising Cttee, Olympic Games, London, 1948; Olympic diploma of merit, Amsterdam, 1949; coach and manager, English crews to New Zealand and Australia, British Empire and Commonwealth Games, 1950; coach and manager, British rowing team, Olympic Games, Finland, 1952; Pres., Bucks, Berks and Oxon branch, British Olympic Assoc., 1971-76; Founder Mem. of the Furniture Makers' Guild; Liveryman of Painter Stainers' Company; Member: Council, National Playing Fields Assoc., British Field Sports Assoc.; Greater London and South East Sports Council, 1966-73; Council, Amateur Rowing Assoc., 1932-67; Selection Cttee for British crews, 1938-64; Steward and Mem. Cttee of Management, Henley Royal Regatta, 1946-73. Mem., Court of Worshipful Co. of Furniture Makers, Master 1971-72. Rowing correspondent of The Field, 1966-71. Played Umpire in film "Half a Sixpence". Freeman of City of London, 1952. *Recreations:* family life, beagling, rowing, and swimming. *Address:* Highlands House, Shiplake-on-Thames, Oxon. *T:* Wargrave 2346. *Clubs:* Thames Rowing (Pres. 1971), Kingston Rowing, Leander; British Sportsman's; Christchurch and Farley Hill Beagles; Remenham; Old Bedfordians. *[Died 3 Dec. 1977.*

BERESFORD-PEIRSE, Sir Henry (Campbell de la Poer), 5th Bt, *cr* 1814; CB 1957; BA; Director-General of the Forestry Commission, 1962-68, and Deputy Chairman 1965-68 (seconded for 1960-62, as Deputy Director of Forestry Division of Food and Agriculture Organisation of UN, Rome); *b* 24 April 1905; *er s* of Sir Henry Beresford-Peirse, 4th Bt, DSO, and Lady Mabel M. Campbell (*d* 1966), *d* of 3rd Earl Cawdor; *S* father, 1949; *m* 1932, Margaret, *d* of F. M. S. Grant, Knockie, Inverness-shire; one *s* (and one *s* decd); one adopted *d. Educ:* Eton; Magdalen Coll., Oxford (BA). Served War of 1939-45, with Lovat Scouts, 1939-40. Gold Medal, Royal Forestry Society, 1963. Hon. Mem., Soc. of American Foresters, 1967. *Heir: s* Henry Grant de la Poer Beresford-Peirse [*b* 7 Feb. 1933; *m* 1966, Jadranka Njers, Zagreb, Yugoslavia; one *s*]. *Address:* Bedall Manor, Bedale, Yorks. *T:* Bedale 2811. *[Died 11 Aug. 1972.*

www—4

BERKIN, John Phillip, CBE 1952; Director: "Shell" Transport & Trading Co. 1957-76; Shell Petroleum Co., 1953-76; Grindlays Bank, 1966-76; Grindlays Holdings Ltd, 1969-76; retired 1976; *b* 23 Oct. 1905; *s* of John Berkin and Leila Louise (*née* Doolittle); *m* 1st, 1934, Elizabeth Mary Joseph Arnold (*d* 1967); one *s* ; 2nd, 1968, Mrs Lilian Ivy Beatrice Chisholm, *widow* of Lieut W. B. Chisholm, RNVR. *Educ:* Taunton Sch.; Sidney Sussex Coll., Cambridge. BA 1927, MA 1956. Joined Royal Dutch/Shell Group of Cos, 1927 and served in Far East, US and London; a Man. Dir, Royal Dutch/Shell Group, 1957-66; Dir, Shell Petroleum NV (formerly Bataafse Petroleum Maatschappij), 1957-68. Part-time Mem., IRC, 1966-68. *Address:* Oriel, Fairfield Road, Southdown, Shawford, Winchester, Hants. *T:* Twyford (Hants) 712331. *Club:* Carlton. *[Died 8 Sept. 1979.*

BERLE, Adolf Augustus; Senior Partner of Berle & Berle, USA; *b* Boston, Mass, 29 Jan. 1895; *s* of Rev. A. A. Berle and Mary Augusta, *d* of Prof. G. Frederick Wright; *m* 1927, Beatrice Bend Bishop; one *s* two *d. Educ:* Harvard (AB 1913, AM 1914, LLB 1916). Lawyer; Prof. Emer. of Law, Columbia University; US Govt, Asst Secretary of State, 1938-44; US Ambassador to Brazil, 1945-46. Holds hon. doctorates. Commander, Order of Southern Cross (Brazil), 1948; Ordine "Al Merito della Repubblica Italiana", 1949. *Publications:* Studies in the Law of Corporation Finance, 1928; Cases and Materials in the Law of Corporation Finance, 1930; The Modern Corporation and Private Property (with Dr G. C. Means), 1932; Liquid Claims and National Wealth (with V. J. Pederson), 1934; New Directions in the New World, 1940; Business Organizations: (with Prof. Wm C. Warren) Corporations, 1948; The Twentieth Century Capitalist Revolution, 1955; Tides of Crisis, 1957; Power without Property, 1959; Latin America: Diplomacy and Reality, 1962; The American Economic Republic, 1963; Power, 1969. *Address:* 70 Pine Street, New York, USA. *Clubs:* Century, Harvard, Players (NY); Army and Navy (Washington).
[Died 17 Feb. 1971.

BERNAL, John Desmond, FRS 1937; MA Cantab; Professor of Crystallography, Birkbeck College, University of London, 1963-68, now Emeritus Professor; Hon. Fellow, Emmanuel College, Cambridge, 1965; Fellow, Birkbeck College, 1969; *b* Nenagh, Ireland, 10 May 1901; *m* 1922; two *s. Educ:* Stonyhurst Coll.; Bedford Sch.; Emmanuel Coll., Cambridge (Scholar). Research at Davy Faraday Laboratory, 1923-27; Lectr and later Asst Dir of Research in Crystallography, Cambridge, 1934-37; Prof. of Physics, Birkbeck Coll., 1937-63. Royal Medal, Royal Society, 1945; Mem. Hungarian Academy of Sciences, 1954; Mem. Polish Acad. of Sciences, 1954. Hon. Prof. Moscow Univ., 1956; Mem. Rumanian Acad. of Sciences, 1957; Mem. Bulgarian Acad. of Sciences, 1958; For. Mem. Acad. of Sciences, USSR, 1958; Regular Mem. Czechoslovak Acad. of Sciences, 1960; Corresponding Mem. German Acad. of Sciences, Berlin, 1962; Mem. Acad. of Sciences, Norway, 1966. Lenin Peace Prize, 1953; Grotius Medal, 1959. *Publications:* The World, The Flesh, and the Devil, 1929 (repr. 1969); The Social Function of Science, 1939 (repr. 1967); The Freedom of Necessity, 1949; The Physical Basis of Life, 1951; Marx and Science, 1952; Science and Industry in the Nineteenth Century, 1953 (repr. 1969); Science in History, 1954 (revised edns 1957, 1965; illus. edn 1969); World without War, 1958 (revised edn, 1960); The Origin of Life, 1967; various scientific papers on crystallographical, physical and biochemical subjects; contributions on scientific, philosophical and social questions; *posthumous publication:* The Extension of Man, 1972. *Address:* Department of Crystallography, Birkbeck College, Malet Street, WC1.
[Died 15 Sept. 1971.

BERNARD, Hon. Charles Brodrick Amyas, CBE 1962; Chairman, Suffolk County Council, 1973-76 (Chairman, East Suffolk County Council, 1968-73, Vice-Chairman 1964-68); *b* 30 Aug. 1904; *twin s* of late Lt-Col Ronald P. H. Bernard and Lettice Mina, *yr d* of late Capt. Gerald C. S. Paget; *twin b* and *heir-pres.* of 5th Earl of Bandon; granted rank and precedence of an earl's son, 1925; *m* 1937, Hon. Ursula Margaret Vivian (*d* 1963), *d* of 3rd Baron Swansea, DSO, MVO, TD. *Educ:* Wellington Coll., RMC. Lieut, Oxford and Bucks LI 1926, ADC to Comdr 2nd Div., 1937-39, Major 1940 (despatches). Chm., Eye Div., Conservative Assoc., 1957-66. County Councillor, East Suffolk, 1952-. High Sheriff Suffolk, 1976. *Recreations:* hunting, shooting. *Address:* By the Crossways, Kelsale, Saxmundham, Suffolk. *T:* Saxmundham 2044.
[Died 28 Feb. 1977.

BERNARD, Sir Dallas (Gerald Mercer), 1st Bt, *cr* 1954; Lieutenant of the City of London; *b* 22 March 1888; *s* of late Edmund Bowen Bernard, JP, of Snakemoor, Botley, Hants; *m* 1922, Betty, *e d* of late Sir Charles Addis, KCMG; one *s* two *d. Educ:* Stubbington House, Fareham, Hants; HMS Britannia.

Left the Navy as a midshipman, 1906; Man. Dir of Jardine Matheson & Co. Ltd (Hong-Kong, China and Japan), 1922-28; mem. of Exec. Council of Hong-Kong, 1927-28, and Legislative Council, 1926-28; Chm., Hong-Kong General Chamber of Commerce, 1923, 1926-27; Chm., Court of Directors Hong-Kong and Shanghai Banking Corporation, 1924, 1926-27; Dir, Matheson & Co. Ltd, 1928-42; Alliance Assurance Co. Ltd, 1931-42; Mem. of London Consultative Cttee of Hong-Kong and Shanghai Banking Corporation, 1929-42, and 1960-64. Dir, Bank of England, 1936-49; Dep. Governor, Bank of England, 1949-54; Chairman: Courtaulds Ltd, 1962-64; British Bank of the Middle East, 1954-65 (Dir, 1965-67). Dir, The Proprietors of Hay's Wharf Ltd, 1961-69. Sheriff of County of London, 1942. *Heir: s* Dallas Edmund Bernard. *Address:* 7 Nun's Walk, Virginia Water, Surrey.   *[Died 26 Nov. 1975.*

BERNARD, Rt. Rev. Canon Eustace A. M.; *see* Morrogh Bernard.

BERNARD, Francis Georgius; Chartered Accountant, since 1931; Publishing Consultant, since 1974; *b* 20 Jan. 1908; *m* 1st, 1934, Muriel Florence Bealer; two *s* one *d*; 2nd, 1954, Eileen Theresa Richley; one *s* one *d*. *Educ:* St Edmund's Coll., Ware. Served War, RAPC (Lt-Col), 1939-46. Kelly-Iliffe Holdings: Dir, 1954; Asst Man. Dir, 1961. Associated Iliffe Press Ltd, Jt Man. Dir, Kelly Iliffe Holdings, 1963, and dir of many other cos in UK and abroad; Financial Dir, IPC Business Press Ltd, 1966; Dir, two publishing cos abroad, 1971. *Recreations:* gardening, bee-keeping, photography. *Address:* 52 Manor Road South, Esher, Surrey. *T:* 01-398 1929.   *[Died 18 June 1978.*

BERNARD, Jean-Jacques; auteur dramatique et homme de lettres; *b* 30 juillet 1888; *s* of late Tristan Bernard and Suzanne Bomsel; *m* 1911, Georgette Fray; two *s* one *d*. *Educ:* Paris. *Théâtre:* Le Voyage à deux; la Joie du Sacrifice; la Maison Epargnée; le Feu qui reprend mal; Martine; le Printemps des autres; l'Invitation au Voyage; Denise Marette; l'Ame en peine; le Secret d'Arvers; le Roy de Malousie; la Louise; A la Recherche des Cœurs; les Sœurs Guédonec; Jeanne de Pantin; Nationale 6; le Jardinier d'Ispahan; Louise de la Vallière; Marie Stuart Reine d'Ecosse; la Librairie Jalin; Notre-Dame d'en haut; la Route de France; Mon grand ami; De Tarse, en Cilicie. *Pièces jouées à Londres* (tr J. Leslie Frith): The Springtime of others; The Sulky Fire (Le Feu qui reprend mal); The Unquiet Spirit (l'Ame en peine); Martine; l'Invitation au Voyage; le Secret d'Arvers; Nationale 6; Madeleine (Le Jardinier d'Ispahan); The Clay and the Flame (Notre Dame d'en haut). *Romans, contes, nouvelles, récits:* l'Epicier, nouvelles; les Enfants jouent... récits de guerre; les Tendresses menacées, contes; le Roman de Martine; Madeleine Landier; New Chicago, nouvelle; Le Camp de la Mort Lente, souvenirs de captivité Compiègne, 1941-42; Le Pain rouge, récits de l'occupation; Marie et le vagabond, roman; Mon Père Tristan Bernard; Mon Ami le théâtre; Saint Paul ou la Fidélité. *Address:* 22 rue Eugène Flachat, Paris 17e. *T:* Etoile 29-00; Loguivy-de-la-Mer (Côtes-du-Nord), France.
                                              [Died 14 Sept. 1972.

BERNAYS, Lewis Edward, OBE 1929; *b* 27 May 1886; *s* of late Henry Arthur Bernays, of Rochester and Chatham and later of Moscow, and Alice Mary Hardy; *m* 1st, 1915, Alida Winona (*d* 1940), *d* of late Andrew McDermid, AM, MD, Winnipeg and Chicago; three *s*; 2nd, 1953, Jeanne Françoise Foss (*née* Beurton) (marr. diss.). Passed a competitive examination and appointed a Vice-Consul in the Consular Service, 1910; Vice-Consul, New Orleans, 1911-12; Portland, Oregon, 1913; Lobito, San Thomé, and Fernando Po, 1913; Chicago, 1914-18; Philadelphia, 1919-20; Consul, New York, 1920-29; Danzig, 1930; Liège, 1931; Consul-Gen., Chicago, 1932-42; retired from the Career Service, 1944; Consul-Gen. in charge of the Vice-Consulate at Dallas, Texas, 1945-50. Since retirement has lectured in Political Science at Northwestern Univ., Evanston; at MacMurray Coll., Jacksonville, Ill; at Rockford Coll., Rockford, Ill; and at Univ. of Plano, Plano, Texas. *Recreations:* fishing, walking, cycling. *Address:* c/o Richard Bernays, Attorney-at-Law, 2500 Fidelity Union Tower, Dallas, Texas 75201, USA.   *[Died 31 March 1972.*

BERNEY, Captain Sir Thomas Reedham, 10th Bt, *cr* 1620; MC; late Royal Norfolk Regiment; *e s* of Captain Thomas Hugh Berney and Fridzwede Katherine, *d* of Lieut-Col F. W. Bell, of Fermoy; *b* 6 July 1893; *S* grandfather, 1907; *m* 1st, 1921, Estelle Irene (who obtained a divorce, 1927), *yr d* of R. Norton Dawson, Remony, Watford; one *d*; 2nd, 1927, Marjorie Agnew Erskine Gill; two *d* (one *s* decd); 3rd, 1947, Peggie, *yr d* of late Howard M. Page, The Elms, Ewell, Surrey. *Educ:* Wellington Coll.; Trinity Hall, Cambridge. ADC to Governor of Southern Rhodesia, 1925-26. *Heir: g s* Julian Reedham Stuart Berney [*b* 26 Sept. 1952 (posthumous); *s* of Lieut John Reedham Erskine

Berney, Royal Norfolk Regt (killed on active service in Korea, 1952) and Jean Davina, *o d* of 1st Viscount Stuart of Findhorn, PC, CH, MVO, MC]. *Address:* St George's Cottage, Downton, Wilts.   *[Died 5 Jan. 1975.*

BERRY, Sir (Henry) Vaughan, Kt 1949; *b* 28 March 1891; *s* of late John Henry Berry; *m* 1st, 1921, Dorothy Loveday (*d* 1959), *d* of late Charles Baldwin, Bath, Somerset; (two *s* decd); 2nd, 1960, Mrs Joan Ogilvie Kirke, *d* of Percy Lachlan, Wadhurst, Sussex. *Educ:* City of London Sch.; Caius Coll., Cambridge. Somerset Light Infantry and Intelligence Corps, 1914-18; on staff of Inter-Allied Rhineland High Commission, 1919-25; Mem. Union Discount Company of London Ltd, 1925-45; Chm. Southern Region Manpower Board, 1941-44; Mem. Capital Issues Cttee, 1946; Regional Commissioner Hamburg, CCG, 1946-49; British delegate to the Internat. Authority for the Ruhr, 1949-50; Full-time Mem., Iron and Steel Corporation of Great Britain, 1950-53. Hon. Senator, University of Hamburg. *Address:* Dutch House, College Road, Bath, Avon. *T:* Bath 314879.   *[Died 27 Feb. 1979.*

BERRY, John Stanley; Chief Highway Engineer, Department of the Environment, since 1974; *b* 9 Dec. 1915; *m* 1938, Eileen Muriel Langhorne. *Educ:* University Sch., Hastings; London Univ. (BSc). Middx County Council, 1936-37; Admty Civil Engr in Chief Dept, 1937-41, Lieut RNVR 1941-46. Joined Min. of Transport as Asst Engr, 1946; Divisional Road Engr, Midlands, 1963-64; Dep. Chief Engr, 1968-71; Under-Sec., 1971-74. MICE, FIStructE, MInstHE. *Publications:* in technical jls. *Address:* 17 Manor Close, Tunbridge Wells, Kent. *Club:* Naval.   *[Died 2 Oct. 1975.*

BERRY, John William Edward, CBE 1943; FRSA; AMInstT; Partner, Kilburn & Co., Ltd, Calcutta, 1945; Senior Managing Director, Kilburn & Co. (Pakistan) Ltd, Agents, India General Navigation & Railway Co. Ltd; *b* 27 Sept. 1901; *s* of late Rev. P. E. FitzPatrick Berry, Mallow, Co. Cork, and Hayle, Cornwall; *m* 1932, Marie Griffin, *d* of late W. E. Ranson, Needham Market, Suffolk, and *widow* of R. H. Read, The Beeches Hayle; no *c*. *Educ:* St John's Sch., Leatherhead. George Henderson & Co., Ltd, Calcutta, 1920-32; India General Navigation & Railway Co. Ltd, Calcutta, 1933-45 (Sen. Exec. Officer, 1939-45). Chm. East Bengal Branch European Assoc., 1935-38; Adviser on Inland Water Transport to Govt of India Defence Dept since 1941; Mem. Calcutta Traffic Advisory Bd and E Bengal Labour Advisory Bd; Lieut Calcutta Scottish Emergency Reserve Co. AF (1), 1941. Mem. Calcutta Diocesan Council, 1939-; Bengal Provincial Bd of Communications, 1940-; Pilots "A" Licence, 1929; Gliding "B" Cert., 1949. *Publication:* Report on Inland Water Transport in Iraq, 1941. *Recreations:* fishing, flying, sailing, swimming, golf. *Address:* 5 Peter Road, Narayanganj, Bengal; Parc Sparbles, Carbis Bay, Cornwall. *TA:* Mindaros. *T:* Calcutta 5502, St Ives 516. *Clubs:* Oriental, Royal Automobile; Bengal (Calcutta); West Cornwall Golf (Lelant).
                                              [Died 14 Jan. 1971.

BERRY, Sir Vaughan; *see* Berry, Sir H. V.

BERRYMAN, Prof. John; poet; Regents' Professor of Humanities, University of Minnesota, USA, since 1969; *b* 25 Oct. 1914; *s* of John Allyn Smith Berryman and Martha Little; *m* 1st, 1942, Eileen Patricia Mulligan; 2nd, 1956, Ann Levine; one *s*; 3rd, 1961, Kate Donahue; two *d*. *Educ:* Columbia Univ., USA (AB); Clare Coll., Cambridge (BA, MA). Taught at Harvard, 1940-43, and (at intervals) at Princeton, for next ten years (when moved to Univ. of Minnesota); Rockefeller Fellow, 1944-46; Guggenheim Fellow, 1952-53 and 1964-65. US Specialist, State Dept, India, 1957. Visiting Prof., Univs: Berkeley, Brown, etc. Shelley Memorial Award, 1948; Harriet Monroe Award, 1957; Pulitzer Prize, 1964; Bollingen Award, 1967; National Book Award, 1968. Congressional grant, 1969. Member: Nat. Inst. Arts and Letters; Amer. Acad. Arts and Sciences; Acad. of American Poets (Chancellor); Mark Twain Soc.; Phi Beta Kappa, etc. Hon. LittD Drake, 1971. *Publications: poetry:* (contribs to) Five Young American Poets, 1940 (USA); Poems, 1942 (USA); The Dispossessed, 1948 (USA); Homage to Mistress Bradstreet, 1956 (USA), 1959 (GB); His Thought made Buckets and the Plane Buckt, 1958 (USA); 77 Dream Songs, 1964 (USA), 1964 (GB); Berryman's Sonnets, 1967 (USA), 1968 (GB); Short Poems, 1968 (USA); His Toy, His Dream, His Rest (308 dream songs), 1968 (USA), 1969 (GB); The Dream Songs (77 Dream Songs, and His Toy, His Dream, His Rest), 1969 (USA); Love and Fame, 1970 (USA), 1971 (GB); also wrote, Stephen Crane, 1950 (USA), 1951 (GB); (ed) (T. Nash's) The Unfortunate Traveller (or The Life of Jack Wilton), 1960 (USA); contribs to: TLS, Partisan Rev., New Yorker, etc.; *posthumous publication:* Recovery (novel), 1973. *Recreations:* chess, art history, dream-analysis, fatherhood, stargazing, prayer and self-flagellation. *Address:* 33 Arthur Avenue SE, Minneapolis, Minnesota, USA. *T:* (612) 338-3353. *Club:* AA (American and Internat.).   *[Died 7 Jan.* 1972.

BERRYMAN, His Honour Montague Levander, QC 1945; JP; Chairman, Kent County Quarter Sessions, 1962-71, retired; *b* 21 July 1899; *er s* of late Frederic John Berryman, LLB, Great Chesterford, Essex; *m* Marjorie Myhill; one *s* two *d. Educ:* Westminster Sch. Called to Bar, Middle Temple, 1921; Mem. of Middle and Inner Temple; Bencher, Middle Temple, 1953-66; Bencher Emeritus, 1966. Served Royal Sussex Regt and attached RAF, 1917-18. Contested (C) Romford, 1945; Recorder of Gravesend, 1945-47, Dover, 1947-62; Dep. Chm., 1950-59, Chm., 1959-63, Herts QS. JP Herts and Kent. Admitted to Hon. Freedom of Borough of Dover, 1963. *Recreations:* anything connected with the theatre and ships; books and print collecting. *Address:* Fairycroft, Great Chesterford, Saffron Walden, Essex. *T:* Great Chesterford 237. *Club:* Garrick. *[Died 25 June* 1974.

BERTRAM, Anthony, MA; author and lecturer; Editor, History of Art, for Visual Publications; *b* London, 19 Nov. 1897; *s* of Ernest Bertram; *m* 1929, Barbara Randolph; two *s. Educ:* Douai Abbey; Pembroke Coll., Oxford. Served in Army, 1915-19 (wounded) and 1940-45 (Legion of Honour and Croix de Guerre); Art Critic to Spectator, 1922-24; to Saturday Review, 1924-27; Lectr to National Portrait Gallery, 1922-24; Stipendiary Lectr to Extramural Delegacy, Oxford, 1927-68; Ed., Design for To-day, 1934; Lectr in Fine Arts, Queen's Univ. Belfast, 1938-39; Dep.-Dir of British Council in France, 1945-46. Vis. Prof., Elmira Coll., NY, USA, 1958. *Publications:* English Portraiture in National Portrait Gallery, 1924; The Pool, 1926; Here We Ride, 1927; Life of Rubens, 1928; The Sword Falls, 1929; To the Mountains, 1929; The Man who made Gottlieb, 1930; They Came to the Castle, 1931; Three Meet, 1932; Pavements and Peaks, 1933; Men Adrift, 1935; The House, 1935; The King Sees Red, 1936; Design in Daily Life, 1937; Design, 1938; Contemporary Painting, 1939; Bright Defiler, 1940; Pleasures of Poverty, 1950; A Century of British Painting, 1951; Paul Nash, 1955; Michelangelo, 1964; 1000 Years of Drawing, 1966; Florentine Sculpture, 1969; various small monographs on artists. *Recreations:* gardening, reading. *Address:* Coates Castle, Fittleworth, Sussex. *T:* Fittleworth 213.   *[Died 2 Aug.* 1978.

BERTRAM, Neville Rennie, CMG 1960; MBE 1941; retired; *b* 13 March 1909; *s* of late C. F. Bertram, 1890 Rhodesian Pioneer; *m* 1935, Eve Cook; one *s* one *d. Educ:* Chaplin High Sch., Gwelo; Univ. of Witwatersrand. Southern Rhodesia Civil Service: Treasury, 1926; Under-Sec., Treasury, 1943; Under-Sec., Internal Affairs, 1946; Asst Sec., Treasury, 1947; Sec. for Trade and Industrial Development, 1948; Federal Govt of Rhodesia and Nyasaland: Sec. for Commerce and Industry, 1953-59, retired. Director of numerous companies, 1959-70. Central African Air Transport Authority, 1949-53; Rhodesian Iron and Steel Commn, 1952-54; Tobacco Export Promotion Council of Rhodesia, 1959-60; represented S Rhodesia and subsequently the Federation at numerous international and Commonwealth conferences, 1948-58. Pres., Automobile Assoc. of Rhodesia; Prov. Pres., Boy Scouts' Assoc; Past Pres., Rhodesian Economic Soc. City Councillor, 1961-62. *Publications:* Strange Instrument, 1948; various economic and commercial publications. *Recreations:* fishing, bridge, Africana and Rhodesiana. *Address:* 16 Mountfield, Goring-on-Thames, Oxon. *Clubs:* Royal Commonwealth Society; Salisbury, Automobile Association.   *[Died 20 July* 1974.

BERTRAND, Cavalier Léon; Professor at the London Fencing Club, retired; British; father of French extraction; *b* 10 July 1897; unmarried. *Educ:* St George's Coll., Wimbledon; Grenoble Univ. Diplomé L'Accademia Nazionale di Scherma, Naples; studied fencing under Profs Georges and Adolphe Rouleau, Paris, and Maestro Commendatore Guiseppe Nadi, Leghorn; served European War, Artists' Rifles; active service, commnd in RFC and RAF; War of 1939-45: commnd in RAFVR, 1939, and served until Nov. 1945 in France, Middle East, Italy, home stations (African Star with clasp, etc). Past Pres., British Academy of Fencing. Awarded (twice) Gold Medal of the Amateur Fencing Assoc. Order of the Crown of Italy, 1938. *Publications:* Cut and Thrust; The Subtlety of the Sabre; The Fencer's Companion, 1935. *Recreations:* billiards and snooker. *Address:* 3 The Villas, Cutcombe Road, SE5 9RT. *T:* 01-274 8168. *Club:* London Sketch. *[Died 12 March* 1980.

BEST, Charles Herbert, CC (Canada) 1967; CH 1971; CBE 1944; FRS 1938; MA, MD, DSc; FRSC, FRCP(C); Professor of Physiology and Director of Department, University of Toronto, 1929-65, Director Emeritus, 1966; Director of Banting-Best Department of Medical Research, University of Toronto, 1941-

67, Director Emeritus, 1967; *b* West Pembroke, Maine, USA, 27 Feb. 1899 (parents both Canadian); *s* of Herbert Huestis Best, MD, and Luella May Best; *m* 1924, Margaret Hooper Mahon; two *s. Educ:* Univ. of Toronto; Univ. of London. BA 1921, MA 1922, MD 1925, Toronto; DSc 1928, London. FRCP 1961. Went overseas with 70th Battery (2nd Canadian Tanks Corps section), serving as Driver and Sergeant, 1918-19; Surg. Lt-Comdr, RCNVR, 1941; Surg.-Comdr 1942; Surg.-Capt. 1943. Co-discoverer of insulin with late Sir Frederick Banting in 1921; in charge of production of insulin, Connaught Laboratories, Univ. of Toronto, 1922-41. Hon. Mem., American Diabetes Assoc., 1940 (Past Pres., 1948-49; Hon. Pres., 1960); Vice-Pres., British Diabetic Assoc., 1934; Hon. Pres., Internat. Diabetes Fedn, 1949; Hon. Dir, Muscular Dystrophy Assoc. of Canada, 1964; Hon. Mem., European Assoc. for the Study of Diabetes, 1965. Initiated Canadian Serum Project for securing dried human serum for military use, 1939; Dir, RCN Med. Res. Unit 1941-; Scientific Dir, Internat. Health Div., Rockefeller Foundn, 1941-43, re-appointed 1946; Consultant to Nat. Inst. of Health, US Public Health Service, 1946; Member: Research Defence Board, Dept Nat. Defence, Canada, 1946-65; Nat. Research Council of Canada, 1947; Interim Cttee, Nat. Cancer Inst. of Canada, 1947. Mem., Paris Acad. of Medicine, 1945; Hon. Mem., Royal Acad. of Sciences, Amsterdam, 1946; For. Corresp., Académie Royale de Médecine de Belgique, 1946; Corresp. Fellow, NY Acad. of Medicine, 1947; Hon. Life Mem., NY Acad. of Sciences, 1950; For. Assoc., Nat. Acad. of Sciences, 1950; Mem., Amer. Philosophical Soc., 1950; Hon. FRSocMed, 1951; Hon. FRCPE, 1953; Hon. FRSE, 1972; First Pres., Internat. Union of Physiological Sciences, 1953; Mem., Pontifical Acad. of Sciences, 1955; Mem., Royal Danish Acad. of Sciences and Letters, 1956. Hon. Mem., Ont. Med. Assoc., 1959; For. Mem., Royal Swedish Acad. of Science, 1961; Adv. Vice-Pres., Pan American Med. Assoc., 1961; Adv. Cttee on Medical Research, WHO, 1963. Croonian Lectr, Royal Soc., 1955; Hon. DSc: Chicago, 1941; Oxford, 1947; Laval, 1952; Maine, 1955; Northwestern, 1959; Laurentian, 1971; Hon. ScD Cambridge, 1946; Hon. Doctor of Medicine: Amsterdam, 1947; Louvain, 1947; Liège, 1947; Freie Univ. of Berlin, 1966; Zagreb, 1976; Hon. LLD: Dalhousie, 1949; Queen's, 1950; Melbourne, 1952; Edinburgh, 1959; Toronto, 1970; Ottawa, 1972; Hon. Degrees, Univs of Chile, Uruguay, San Marcos (Peru), 1951; Hon. PhD Jerusalem, 1971; Hon. Doctorate: Paris, 1945; Central Univ. of Venezuela, 1958; Aristotelian Univ. of Thessaloniki, 1963. Holds many medals from Canadian, American and European instns; first Brazil Science biennial award, Sao Paulo Biennial Foundn, 1971. Legion of Merit, US, 1947; King Haakon VI Liberty Cross, Norway, 1947; Comdr of Order of the Crown, Belgium, 1948. *Publications:* (with F. G. Banting) original publication on insulin, 1922; Co-author books: The Human Body, 1932; Physiological Basis of Medical Practice, 1937 (9th edn, 1973); Selected Papers of Charles H. Best, 1963; numerous articles on insulin, carbohydrate and fat metabolism, muscular exercise, heparin, histamine, etc. *Recreations:* riding, golf. *Address:* The Charles H. Best Institute, University of Toronto, Toronto, Ontario M5G 1L6, Canada. *T:* 978-2586. *Clubs:* Athenæum; (Hon. Life) Canadian (Toronto); York Downs Golf (Toronto); Faculty (Univ. of Toronto).   *[Died 31 March* 1978.

BEST, Edna; actress, stage and films; *b* 3 March 1900; *d* of Leonard William Best and Claire Romaire; *m* 1st, 1920, Seymour Beard (marr. diss., 1928); twin *s*; 2nd, 1928, Herbert Marshall (*d* 1966); one *d*; 3rd, 1940, Nat Wolff. First appeared on stage at Grand Theatre, Southampton, 1917; Peter in Peter Pan, 1920; Teresa Sanger in The Constant Nymph, 1926; Leonora Perrycoste in There's Always Juliet, 1931; many subsequent appearances in London; also Played in US where appearances include: Mary Adams in Yankee Point, 1942; Millie Crocker-Harris in The Browning Version, 1949; Edna Selby in Harlequinade, 1949; Lady Cicely Waynflete in Captain Brassbound's Conversion, 1950; Jane, 1952; Mme Alexandra in Mademoiselle Colombe, 1954. *Films:* began career, 1929; successes in South Riding, Prison Without Bars, etc. *Address:* c/o Actors' Equity Association, 45 West 47th Street, New York, NY 10036, USA.   *[Died 18 Sept.* 1974.

BEST, Sir John Victor Hall, Kt 1956; BDS, DMD, FDSRCS, FACD; President of the Australian Dental Association, 1940-44 and 1950-54 (Vice-President, 1948-50); *s* of Rev. John Hall Best, MA, Greenwich, NSW; *m* 1927, Marion E., *d* of Dr E. H. Burkitt; one *s* one *d.* Pres., NSW Branch of Australian Dental Association, 1935-37; Lt-Col AA Dental Corps, Consulting Dental Surg. LHQ, 1942-44; Chm. Central Dental Advisory Cttee, Directorate of Manpower, 1943-45. Pres., 12th Australian Dental Congress, 1950. Foundn Fellow, Aust. Coll. of Dental Surgeons. *Address:* 3 The Grove, 153a Queen Street, Woollahra, NSW 2025. Australia. *Club:* Australian. *[Died 27 Feb.* 1972.

BESTERMAN, Theodore Deodatus Nathaniel, Hon. DLitt: Oxford; Case Western Reserve; Hon. LLD St Andrews, DèsL hc Geneva; Director, Voltaire Foundation; b 18 Nov. 1904; y s of B. J. N. Besterman, Bradford, and Augusta (née Cringle); m 1st, Evelyn, y d of Arthur Mack, New York; one s; 2nd, Marie-Louise van Muyden. Educ: privately; Lycée de Londres; Oxford (extra-mural). Chm., British Federation of Youth Movements, 1925-26; Investigation Officer, etc of Soc. for Psychical Research, 1927-35; Special Lectr in Univ. of London Sch. of Librarianship, 1931-38. Served 1939-45 in CD, RA (Field), and Army Bureau of Current Affairs. Joint Editor, Oxford Books on Bibliography; Gen. Editor, Assoc. of Special Libraries and Information Bureaux, 1942-46; Ed. and Exec. Officer, British Union Catalogue of Periodicals, 1944-46; founded and ed Journal of Documentation, 1945-47; Chm., St Martin's Sch. of Art, 1946; Head, Dept for the Exchange of Information, UNESCO, 1946-49; founded and directed Institut et Musée Voltaire, 1952-73; President: Internat. Congress on the Enlightenment, 1963-71; Internat. Soc. for 18th century studies, 1967-71. Corresp. Member: Institut de France; Académies de Dijon, de Lyons, de Marseille; Hon. FLA; FRSL. Hon. Member: Soc. for French Studies; Société d'Histoire littéraire de la France; British Soc. for 18th Century Studies, etc. Chevalier de la Légion d'Honneur. *Publications:* A Bibliography of Annie Besant, 1924; Crystal-Gazing: a Study in the History, etc, of Scrying, 1924; The Divining-Rod: an Experimental and Psychological Investigation (with Sir William Barrett, FRS), 1926; Library Catalogue of the Society for Psychical Research, 1927; supplements, 1928, 1929, 1931, 1934; The Mind of Annie Besant, 1928; Some Modern Mediums, 1930; Men against Women; a Study of Sexual Relations, 1934; A Bibliography of Sir James George Frazer, OM, 1934; Mrs Annie Besant: a Modern Prophet, 1934; ed. and contributor to Inquiry into the Unknown (BBC Talks), 1934; The Druce-Portland Case, 1935; A Bibliography of Sir Oliver Lodge, FRS, 1935; The Beginnings of Systematic Bibliography, 1935, 3rd edn (in French, Les Débuts de la Bibliographie Méthodique), 1950; The Publishing Firm of Cadell and Davis, 1793-1836, 1938; Water-Divining, 1938; The Travellings and Sufferings of Father Jean de Brébeuf among the Hurons of Canada, 1938; The Pilgrim Fathers, 1939; A World Bibliography of Bibliographies, two vols, 1939-40; 2nd edn, three vols, 1947-49; 3rd edn, four vols, 1955-56; 4th edn, five vols, 1965-66; Early Printed Books to the End of the Sixteenth Century, 1940, 2nd edn 1961; British Sources of Reference and Information, 1948; Unesco: Peace in the Minds of Men, 1951; Index Bibliographicus, two vols, 1952; Voltaire's Notebooks, two vols, 1952, 2nd edn 1968; Voltaire's Correspondence, 107 vols, 1953-65, definitive edn 1968-; founded and edited Studies on Voltaire and the eighteenth century, Vols I-CLXII 1955-; Le Goût des manuscrits, 1956; Lettres de la Marquise Du Châtelet, two vols, 1958; Lettres d'amour de Voltaire à sa nièce, 1958; Voltaire Essays and another, 1962; Select Letters of Voltaire, 1963; Flaubert's Théâtre de Voltaire, two vols, 1967; Voltaire on Shakespeare, 1967; Collected Papers on the Paranormal, 1968; Voltaire's Household Accounts, 1760-1778, 1968; jt editor, Complete Works of Voltaire, 1968-; Voltaire (biography), 1969, 3rd edn 1976; The Besterman Bibliographies, 25 vols, 1971; Voltaire's Philosophical Dictionary, 1971; (ed) The Printed Sources of Western Art, 29 vols, 1972; Some Eighteenth-Century Voltaire Editions unknown to Bengesco, 1973; Voltaire on the Arts (Zaharoff Lecture), 1974; A World Biography of Oriental Bibliographies, 1975; A World Bibliography of African Bibliographies, 1975; Old Art Books, 1975; edited several works by E. Crawley, translations from French and German. *Recreations:* The Guyon House Press, for the printing and binding of fine books (until completely destroyed by enemy action, Dec. 1940); collecting English drawings, etc. *Address:* Thorpe Mandeville House, near Banbury, Oxfordshire. *Clubs:* Reform; Century (New York). [Died 10 Nov. 1976.

BETTS, Edward William; journalist and critic; b London, 27 March 1881; e s of late Edward Betts, London and Tunbridge Wells; m 1904, Elizabeth Annie (d 1945), 2nd d of late William West, Tunbridge Wells. Educ: privately. Began journalistic career on Kent and Sussex Courier; afterwards on editorial staff of Sussex Daily News; Actg Ed., Malton Gazette, 1904-12; Asst Ed. and Dramatic Critic, Birmingham Gazette, 1912-19; Asst London Editor and Dramatic Critic, Birmingham Gazette and associated papers, 1919-21; Dramatic and Film Critic, Westminster Gazette, 1921-28; Editor, The Era, to 1939; Associate Editor, Daily Film Renter, retd 1951. Founder, 1955, Pres., 1973, Pinner Gramophone Soc. Mem. of Council, Critics' Circle; contributor to Daily Telegraph, Stage, Weekly Westminster, Theatre and Stage, and other periodicals on theatrical and kinema subjects. *Recreations:* music, seeing and reading plays. *Address:* 24 Chiltern House, Hillcrest Road, Ealing W5 1HL. T: 01-997 1071. *Club:* National Liberal. [Died 4 June 1980.

BETTS, Prof. James Anthony; Professor of Fine Art, University of Reading, 1934-63; Emeritus since 1963; b 28 Dec. 1897; s of James and Ellen Betts; m 1925, Nellie Serena Flexen; one s. Educ: St Stephens, Skipton; Bradford Coll. of Art; Royal Coll. of Art. Head, Sch. of Painting, Sheffield Coll. of Art, 1926-30; Principal, Kingston-on-Thames Sch. of Art, 1930-34. Address: Norfolk House, 28 Kidmore Road, Caversham, Reading, Berks. T: Reading 471600. Club: Athenæum. [Died 27 Sept. 1980.

BETUEL, Herbert William Norman; Assistant Legal Officer, Foreign Compensation Commission, 1965-75; b Johannesburg, 9 July 1908; s of Leon Louis Betuel, solicitor and advocate of self-governing Colony of the Transvaal (as it was then known), and Christina Ferran, d of a planter, both of Port Louis, Mauritius; m 1938, Kathleen Harriette Meredith Welsh, MBE, Dublin. Educ: Ecole Publique St Julien, Marseilles; Wandsworth Technical Coll., University Tutorial Coll., University Coll., London; Gray's Inn, London. Lee Prizeman, Gray's Inn, 1932; Barrister, 1933; LLB, London, 1934. Magistrate, 1939, Chief Magistrate, 1953, Nigeria; Judge of the High Court of Eastern Nigeria, 1958-65, retd. Chm. Arbitral Tribunal (arrears of overtime among Maritime Workers), 1941. Fellow, Royal Commonwealth Soc. (formerly Royal Empire Soc.), 1939; FRSA 1969. *Recreations:* walking, travelling, literature, history and Contract Bridge. Address: 28 Ashfield Road, W3. T: 01-743 7439. Clubs: Gray's Inn, Royal Commonwealth Society. [Died 11 April 1980.

BEVAN, Sir David Martyn E.; see Evans Bevan.

BEVAN, John Henry, CB 1945; MC 1917; b 5 April 1894; y s of late David Augustus Bevan and late Hon. Dame Maud Bevan, DBE; m 1927, Lady Barbara Bingham (d 1963), d of 5th Earl of Lucan, PC, GCVO, KBE, CB; one s two d. Educ: Eton Coll.; Christ Church, Oxford. Served European War, 1914-19, with the Herts Regt; Capt., 1916; Major, 1918; TARO General List, recalled, 1939. Address: 232 Cranmer Court, Sloane Avenue, SW3 3HD. T: 01-589 9302. Club: Brooks's. [Died 3 Dec. 1978.

BEVAN, John Sage; Managing Director, The Union-Castle Mail Steamship Co. Ltd, 1956-65; b 29 Nov. 1900; er s of E. H. Bevan, Southampton; m 1953, Lilian Ellen, d of C. Channing, Exeter; no c. Educ: King Edward VI Sch., Southampton. Joined Union-Castle Co., 1917; Chairman's Private Sec., 1932; Asst Head, Freight Dept, 1934; Asst Manager, 1946; Asst Man. Dir, 1953; Dep. Man. Dir, 1955. Ministry of Shipping and War Transport, 1939-46. Chairman: South and East African Confs, 1954-66; Delagoa Bay Agency Co., 1955-66; King Line, 1956-58; London General Shipowners Soc. Cttee, 1958-60; Dir, British and Commonwealth Shipping Co., 1956-66; Member: Chamber of Shipping Council, 1953-66; Shipping Fedn Council, 1953-66; Lloyds Register Gen. Cttee, 1958-66; Port of London Authority 1958-67 (Chm., Docks and Warehouse Cttee, 1964-67); South Africa Club Cttee, 1953-; Old Edwardians Assoc., Southampton (Pres., 1959-60, and Chm., London Br.); Governor, King Edward VI Sch., Southampton. Retired Mem., Baltic Mercantile and Shipping Exchange. FCIS. *Recreations:* gardening, writing, reading. Address: Redlands, Rewe, Exeter, Devon EX5 4ES. T: Stoke Canon 329. Clubs: Royal Commonwealth Society, Royal Over-Seas League; South Africa. [Died 17 July 1978.

BEVAN, Lawrence Emlyn Douglas, CBE 1960; banker; b 7 Jan. 1903; o s of late Herbert Spencer Bevan and late Jennie Douglas, d of Gen. J. R. Williams; unmarried. Educ: Lancing. Entered Barclays Bank Ltd as junior clerk, 1922, and after serving various capacities apptd a local Dir at 54 Lombard Street, 1929; Director, 1938; Vice-Chm., 1961-68. director: Barclays Bank SA; Barclays Bank (London & International) Ltd; National Provident Instn (Chm., 1953-67); Banque de Bruxelles; Credit Congolais; Yorkshire Bank Ltd; and other Companies. Pres., St Peter's, St Paul's and St Philip's Hospitals Board; Treas., British Post-graduate Medical Federation and Queen's Inst. of District Nursing. Officers' Emergency Reserve, 1938; commissioned Scots Guards, 1940; Staff Capt., London District, 1941. Officer de la Couronne (Belgium), 1966. *Recreations:* fishing, gardening. Address: Troston Cottage, Bury St Edmunds, Suffolk. Clubs: Carlton, Guards, White's, Pratt's. [Died 17 Feb. 1972.

BEVAN, Rear-Adm. Sir Richard Hugh Loraine, KBE 1946; CB 1942; DSO 1916; MVO 1923; DL; b 10 July 1885; s of late Capt. Eustace B. L. Bevan, Royal West Kent Regt, and Mary, d of late Rev. Dr G. W. Hill, for many years Vicar of Halifax, NS, and g s of late Richard Lee Bevan, Brixworth Hall, Northampton; m 1934, Frances Anne Beckford, o surv. d of late Algernon Beckford Bevan, JP, Bury St Edmunds. Educ: Foster's,

Stubbington House; Britannia. Midshipman in Implacable, 1901-04; Sub-Lieut in Drake, 1905-06; Lieut in Aboukir, 1907-09; Signal Sch., and in command of TBD Express, 1911; Lieut of HMS Medina when their Majesties went to Bombay for Durbar; Flag-Lieut to Vice-Adm. Sir Rosslyn Wemyss in Orion, 1912-13, and on his staff during the European War; promoted Commander, 1918; Capt., 1923; landed at Cape Helles in charge of signal stations during occupation of Gallipoli; present at evacuation of Suvla and Anzac (DSO); Comdr HM Yacht Victoria and Albert, 1921-23; Flag Capt. Africa Station, 1923-26; Naval Attaché to HM Missions in Italy, Greece, etc, 1928-31; commanded HMS York, 1932-33; comdg HM Signal Sch., Portsmouth, 1934-35; Rear-Adm. and retired list, 1935; rejoined Navy, 1939; Naval Attaché, Rome, Feb.-June 1940; Senior British Naval Officer, North Russia, 1941-42; Flag Officer, in charge Northern Ireland, 1942-45. DL Glos 1946; County Councillor, Glos, 1949; County Alderman, 1952. Order of the Nile, 4th Class, 1917; Legion of Honour, Chevalier, 1918; Officer of Legion of Merit (USA), 1946. *Address:* Greylands, Minchinhampton, Glos. *T:* Brimscombe 3215.

[Died 10 May 1976.

BEVAN, Robert Alexander Polhill, CBE 1963 (OBE 1941); Chairman, S. H. Benson Ltd, 1954-64; *b* 15 March 1901; *s* of late Robert Polhill Bevan and late Stanislawa, *d* of Alexander de Karlowski; *m* 1946, Natalie, *d* of Court Denny. *Educ:* Westminster (King's Scholar); Christ Church, Oxford (Scholar). Joined S. H. Benson Ltd, 1923. Dir of General Production, Ministry of Information, 1940; RNVR 1940-45; Dep. Chief of Naval Information, Washington, 1944-45; UK representative on UN Cttee on Public Information, 1958. Member: Advisory Council on Middle East Trade, 1958-63; Export Publicity Council, 1959-63; National Advisory Council on Art Education, 1960-64; Advertising Standards Authority, 1962-66. FIPA (Pres., 1961). *Recreations:* sailing, travel. *Address:* Boxted House, Colchester, Essex. *T:* Boxted 254. *Clubs:* Garrick, Royal Ocean Racing.   *[Died 20 Dec. 1974.*

BEVERLEY, Frank; Barrister-at-law, North-Eastern Circuit; Recorder of Bradford, 1926-55; *o s* of late Walter Beverley, Barrister-at-law, Bramley, Leeds; *b* 27 Aug. 1880; *m* 1934, Lucy, *d* of late Norman McDougall, Winnipeg, widow of Allan J. Kerr, Quebec. *Educ:* Shrewsbury; London Univ. (LLB). Called to Bar, 1908; served European War, Capt. RGA, France, Flanders, Italy (MC, Italian Croce di Guerra). *Recreations:* fly-fishing, motoring, empire travel. *Address:* Low Hall, Travers Farm Road, St Brelade, Jersey, Channel Islands.

[Died 16 Jan. 1972.

BEVIR, Sir Anthony, KCVO 1952 (CVO 1946); CBE 1944; *b* 7 Nov. 1895; 4th *s* of late Ernest Bevir, Hendon; *m* 1935, Noël Sidney, *d* of late Dominick Sidney Browne, Breaghwy, Co. Mayo. *Educ:* Eton; Hertford Coll., Oxford. Served European War, 1915-18, 7th Bn King's Liverpool Regt (despatches twice); Colonial Office, 1921-39; Private Sec. to Rt Hon. W. G. A. Ormsby Gore, Parly Under-Sec. of State for the Colonies, 1926-29; Sec. to Colonial Office Conference, 1930; Asst Sec., War Cabinet Office, 1939; Private Sec. to Rt Hon. Neville Chamberlain, 1940, Rt Hon. Winston Churchill, 1940-45, Rt Hon. C. R. Attlee, 1945-51, Rt Hon. Winston Churchill, 1951-55, Rt Hon. Anthony Eden, 1955-56; Sec. for Appointments to the Prime Minister, 1947-Feb. 1956. *Recreation:* reading. *Address:* Bleanaskill Lodge, Achill Sound, Co. Mayo. *Clubs:* United Oxford & Cambridge University; Kildare Street and University (Dublin).   *[Died 17 Jan. 1977.*

BEWLEY, William Fleming, CBE 1935; DSc; VMH; Scientific Horticultural Consultant since 1956; *b* Newcastle upon Tyne, 1891; *s* of late William Bewley, Maryport, Cumberland; *m* Olive Mary, *d* of late Richard Price, MBE, Woolwich; one *d*. *Educ:* Univ. of Durham. Served overseas in Royal Field Artillery during European War. Dir of Experimental and Research Station, Cheshunt, 1921; Dir of Glasshouse Crops Research Inst., Littlehampton, from its inception, 1954-56, retired. Veitch Memorial Gold Medal, RHS, 1956. *Publications:* Diseases of Glasshouse Plants; The Cultivation of Mushrooms; Commercial Glasshouse Crops; Science has Green Fingers; various publications on horticulture and related sciences in scientific journals and the Press. *Recreations:* local government (RD and Parish Councils), golf, fishing. *Address:* Brayton, The Thatchway, Angmering, Sussex. *T:* Rustington 3836.

[Died 11 Dec. 1976.

BEYEN, Dr Johan Willem; banker and diplomat, Netherlands; Chairman, Wm H. Müller & Co., Rotterdam; *b* 2 May 1897; *m* 1922; two *s* one *d* ; *m* 1945, Margaretha Antonia Lubinka. *Educ:* Utrecht, Holland. Treasury of the Netherlands, 1918-23; Legal Adviser, Phillips Incandescent Lamp Works, Eindhoven,

Holland, 1924-25; representative at Amsterdam of Javasche Bank, Batavia, Dutch East Indies, 1925-27; Man. Dir, Rotterdamsche Bankvereeniging, 1927-35. Alternate Pres. of Bank for International Settlements, Basle, 1935-37, Pres., 1937-40; Director: Lever Bros and Unilever Ltd, 1940-46; Flag Investment Co; Irish Investment Co.; formerly Executive Dir, International Bank for Reconstruction and Development; Executive Dir, Internat. Monetary Fund, Washington, DC. Minister of Foreign Affairs, Netherlands, 1952-56; Netherlands Ambassador in Paris, 1958-63. *Publications:* Money in a Maelstrom (New York) 1949, (London) 1950; Helspel en de Knikkus (Rotterdam), 1968. *Address:* Ridderlaan 14, Wassenaar, Holland. *Club:* Witte Societeit (The Hague).

[Died 29 April 1976.

BEYNON, Albert Gwyn, CB 1972; Chief Veterinary Officer, Ministry of Agriculture, Fisheries and Food, 1970-73; *b* 11 Feb. 1908; *s* of Daniel and Jane Beynon; *m* 1st, 1935, Margaret Markillie, Diss, Norfolk (*d* 1972); one *s* one *d* ; 2nd, 1975, Nicolette Hamilton Rice, Houghton in the Dale, Norfolk. *Educ:* Llanelli Gram. Sch.; Royal Veterinary College, London; Manchester Univ. Joined Animal Health staff of Min. of Agric., Fisheries and Food, 1932; Divisional Veterinary Officer, 1938-52; Regional Vet. Off. for Wales, 1952-60; Dep. Chief Vet. Off., 1960-64; Director of Vet. Field Service, 1965-70. Chairman: European Foot and Mouth Disease Commn, 1971-73; Adv. Cttee, IRAD, 1974-; Pigs Cttee ARC/MAFF: JCO. Mem., ARC, 1970-73. President: Brit. Vet. Assoc., 1961-62; RCVS, 1975-76, Sen. Vice-Pres., 1976-77, Mem. Council, 1976-. Dalrymple-Champneys Award, for services to animal welfare and health both nationally and internationally, 1967. *Publications:* several contribs to veterinary jls on animal disease and control. *Recreations:* travel, golf, gardening. *Address:* Buckland, Houghton in the Dale, Walsingham, Norfolk NR22 6AQ. *T:* Walsingham 312.   *[Died 10 June 1978.*

BHAGAT, Lt-Gen. Premindra Singh, VC 1941; PVSM 1972; Chairman, Damodar Valley Corporation; *b* 14 Oct. 1918; *s* of S. S. Bhagat, ISE; *m* 1942, Mohini, *d* of Col M. G. Bhandari; one *s* one *d*. *Educ:* Royal Indian Mil. Coll. and Indian Mil. Acad., Dehra Dun. Under Officer in 1939. Joined Royal Bombay Sappers and Miners as Company Officer and proceeded overseas, 1940; served with Indian Divs in Abyssinia, Eritrea and North Africa (VC). psc 1945. Has held staff appts including: Commandant, Royal Bombay Sappers and Miners; Dep. Commandant and Chief Instructor, Staff Coll., Wellington; Brigade Comdr; Dir of Military Intelligence; Commandant, Indian Military Academy; Chief of Staff, Divl Comdr; Corps Comdr; GOC-in-C, Central Comd, 1970-72; GOC-in-C Northern Comd, Indian Army, 1972-74. *Publications:* Forging the Shield, 1965; The Shield and the Sword, 1968; contributions to The Statesman (Indian newspaper). *Recreations:* tennis, squash, golf, shooting. *Address:* c/o Grindlays Bank Ltd, 'E' Block, Connaught Place, New Delhi, India.

[Died 23 May 1975.

BHUTTO, Zulfikar Ali, HPK 1964; politician and lawyer, Pakistan; Prime Minister of Pakistan, 1973-77 (President of Pakistan, Dec. 1971-73); Minister for Foreign Affairs and Defence, 1971-77; Founder and Chairman, Pakistan People's Party, 1967, Life President, 1978; *b* 5 Jan. 1928; *s* of late Sir Shahnawaz Khan Bhutto; *m* ; two *s* two *d*. *Educ:* Univ. of California, Berkeley (grad. Hons Pol. Sci.); Christ Church, Oxford (MA with dist. Jurisprudence). Called to Bar, Lincoln's Inn, 1953. Lectr in Internat. Law, Univ. of Southampton, 1952; Legal Practice, West Pakistan High Court, Karachi, 1953-58; taught Constitutional Law, Sind Muslim Law Coll., Karachi, 1956-58. Elected Mem., Nat. Assembly of Pakistan for Larkana, 1962; Minister: for Commerce, Pakistan, 1958-60; of Minority Affairs and Nat. Reconstruction and Information, 1960-62, also of Fuel, Power and Nat. Resources and of Kashmir Affairs, April 1960-62; and of Industries and Natural Resources, 1962-63; for Foreign Affairs and Atomic Energy, 1963-66; resigned from Govt, June 1966, returned to legal profession; imprisoned, Sept. 1968; released Feb. 1969; elected Mem., Nat. Assembly, Dec. 1970; Dep. Prime Minister and Foreign Minister of Pakistan, Dec. 1971; Chief Martial Law Administrator, Dec. 1971- April 1972. Sec.-Gen., Pakistan Muslim League, 1964. Mem. Pakistan Delegn to Gen. Assembly, UN, 1957; Leader of various Delegns and Special Missions, including UN Conf. on Law of the Sea, Geneva, 1958, and UN General Assembly, 1959, 1960, 1963, 1965 and 1966. Hon. LLD Sind Univ., 1966. Hilal-i-Pakistan, 1964; holds foreign orders. *Publications:* The Myth of Independence, 1968; The Great Tragedy, 1971. *Recreations:* studies and big game. *Address:* Al-Murtaza, Larkana, Pakistan.

[Died 4 April 1979.

BICKERSTETH, Rev. Canon Edward Monier, OBE 1962; MA; Licensed to preach, Diocese of Sarum, since 1959; *b* 20 Nov. 1882; *e s* of late Rev. Samuel Bickersteth, DD; *m* 1911, Inez Katharine (*d* 1936), 3rd *d* of late Rev. Dr G. E. Jelf; two *s* two *d*. *Educ:* Rugby; Christ Church, Oxford; Wells Theological Coll. Deacon, 1907; Priest, 1908; Curate, Lambeth Parish Church, 1907-09; Bedale, 1909-10; Leeds Parish Church, 1910; Rector, Castle Bromwich, 1911-15; Sec. of Jerusalem and the East Mission, 1915-35; Rector, Chiddingstone, 1935-50; Hon. Canon Rochester, 1946-50; Rector of The Orchestons, Salisbury, 1950-59; Hon. Canon, St George's Collegiate Church, Jerusalem, 1953. Commissary to: Archbishop in Jerusalem, 1919-74, Bishop in Egypt, 1920-74, and Bishop in the Sudan, 1945-74; to Vicar General in Jerusalem, 1974-76. Editor, Bible Lands, 1930-63. *Address:* Ivy House, Worton, Devizes, Wilts. *T:* Devizes 3727.   *[Died 24 July 1976.*

BICKERSTETH, Geoffrey Langdale; Emeritus Professor in the University of Aberdeen; *b* 1884; 2nd *s* of late Rev. Samuel Bickersteth, DD; *m* 1918, Jean, *d* of late Prof. W. R. Sorley; one *s* two *d* (and two *s* decd). *Educ:* Charterhouse (scholar); Christ Church, Oxford, BA (2nd class Lit Hum), 1907; MA 1910. Asst master, Marlborough Coll., 1909-13; studied philology, Munich and Heidelberg universities, 1913-14; on staff of War Trade Intelligence Dept, 1915-18; Naval Staff, ID, 1918-19; Senior Lecturer in English Language and Literature, Glasgow Univ., 1919-38; Regius (Chalmers) Prof. of English Literature, Aberdeen Univ., 1938-54; Taylorian Lectr, Oxford Univ., 1933; W. P. Ker Lectr, Glasgow Univ., 1950. Hon. LLD (Aberdeen), 1955. Commenda. Ord. al Merito della Repub. Ital., 1960. *Publications:* Carducci, a selection of his poems, with verse translations and three introductory essays, 1913; The Poems of Leopardi, edited with introduction and notes and verse translation in the metres of the original, 1923; Leopardi and Wordsworth, 1927; The Paradiso of Dante Alighieri, with a translation into English triple rhyme, 1933; Form, Tone and Rhythm in Italian Poetry, 1934; The Golden World of King Lear, 1947; Dante's Virgil, 1951; Dante's Divine Comedy trans. into English triple rhyme, 1955; the same, facing Ital. text, 1965, 2nd (rev.) edn, 1972. *Address:* 2 St Martin's Square, Chichester, Sussex. *T:* Chichester 82520.   *[Died 29 March 1974.*

BICKERSTETH, John Burgon, MC 1918; CM (Canada) 1974; MA; FSA; *b* 1888; 4th *s* of late Rev. Samuel Bickersteth, DD. *Educ:* Charterhouse; Christ Church, Oxford; University of Paris. Gained Blue for Association football, 1908 (Capt., Oxford Univ. AFC 1910-11); in Western Canada as mem. of the Archbishops' Mission, 1911-13; served European War with The Royal Dragoons, 1914-19 (MC and Bar); on staff of University of Alberta, 1919-21; Warden of Hart House, University of Toronto, 1921-47; served War of 1939-45; Personal Asst and Adviser (Educn) to GOC Canadian Corps and then to GOC-in-C First Canadian Army, 1940-42; Dir of Army Education, War Office, 1942-44. Hon. LLD Toronto. *Publications:* The Land of Open Doors (Letters from Western Canada); The History of the 6th Cavalry Brigade. *Address:* 11a The Precincts, Canterbury, Kent.   *[Died 1 Feb. 1979.*

BICKERTON, John Myles; Wing Commander RAFVR (retired); late Surgeon Lieutenant RN; late Ophthalmic Surgeon, King's College Hospital; London Specialist; Ophthalmic Surgeon, Denham; Chairman, Bickerton's Aerodromes Ltd; *b* 1894; *y s* of Thomas Herbert and Mary Jessie Bickerton, Liverpool; *m* 1st, 1926, Margaret Alsager, *d* of Col Hawdon; one *s* four *d*; 2nd, 1936, Eva Griffiths; one *d*. *Educ:* Leas Sch., Hoylake; Leighton Park, Reading; Pembroke Coll., Cambridge; King's Coll. Hosp. (Burney Yeo Scholar). MRCS, LRCP, 1919; BA (Hons), BCh Cantab, 1919; FRCS 1923; MA Cantab, 1924. Late Ophthalmic Surg., King's Coll. Hosp.; late Ophthalmic Consultant, LCC, Board of Education; Ophthalmic Surg., Royal Eye, St Olave's and Lewisham Hosps and Dean Royal Eye Hosp.; Surg. Prob. RNVR, 1916-17, HMS Lawford and Sybille; Surg. Lieut RN, HMS Royal Oak, 1918-19; Surgical Specialist to Sir R. Houston Bt Yacht Cruise, 1921. *Publications:* Clinical Ophthalmology, 1933; A Modern Treatment of Squint, 1934; Welfare of the Blind and National Economy, BMJ, 1932; The Inheritance of Blindness, Eugenics Review 1932 and 1933; Eye Diseases in General Practice, Med. Press, 1935; The Bespectacled Pilot and the Air Forces, Aeroplane, 1937. *Recreations:* ski-ing, flying. *Address:* Owls Oak, Denham, Bucks. *T:* Denham 2060. *Clubs:* Denham Golf, Denham Aero (Denham).   *[Died 13 March 1977.*

BICKET, Brig.-Gen. William Neilson, C.B.E. 1919; late R.E.; retired; *b* 1883; *m*. 1951, Mrs. Frances Howard Braham (marr. diss. 1969); two *s*. Served European War, 1914-18, France, Mesopotamia, Egypt, Palestine, with Royal Engineers (despatches four times, C.B.E., Bt. Lt.-Col.). *Address:*

Rippington's, Willingdon, Sussex; 50 St. James' Street, S.W.1.   *[Died 3 Jan. 1978.*

BICKLEY, Francis (Lawrance); author; *b* London, 11 June 1885; *o s* of Francis Bridges Bickley, late Asst Keeper of MSS, Brit. Mus.; *m* Nora Magdalen, MBE (*d* 1962), *y d* of Comdr Edward Phillips Statham, RN. *Educ:* Merchant Taylors' Sch. Sub-editor, Victoria County Histories, 1905-08; Editor under Historical MSS. Commission from 1910; War Trade Intelligence Dept, 1915-19; Postal Censorship Dept, 1939-45 (Bermuda, 1940-44). *Publications:* Kings' Favourites, 1910; The Cavendish Family, 1911; Matthew Arnold and his Poetry, 1911; The Story of Marie Antoinette, 1911; Where Dorset Meets Devon, 1911; John Millington Synge and the Irish Dramatic Movement, 1912; The Life of Matthew Prior, 1914; The Adventures of Harlequin, 1923; Lord Maida Vale, 1932; The Pre-Raphaelite Comedy, 1932; The Leiths of Harthill, 1937; (Ed) An English Letter Book, 1925; True Dialogues of the Dead, 1925; Diaries of Sylvester Douglas, Lord Glenbervie, 1928; various reports for Historical MSS. Commission; contributions to the Quarterly, Punch, etc, Dictionary of National Biography, Encyclopædia Britannica, etc. *Address:* Charterhouse, EC1.   *[Died 29 Dec. 1976.*

BIDDULPH, 3rd Baron *cr* 1903; **Michael William John Biddulph;** *b* 6 March 1898; *e s* of 2nd Baron and Marjorie Caroline Susan (*d* 1961), *d* of Col W. Mure, Caldwell; *S* father, 1949; *m* 1925, Lady Amy Agar, *d* of 4th Earl of Normanton; two *s* two *d*. *Educ:* Eton; RMC Sandhurst. Late Lieut Coldstream Guards. *Recreations:* fishing, golf, shooting, tennis. *Heir: s* Hon. Robert Michael Christian Biddulph [*b* 6 Jan. 1931; *m* 1958, Lady Mary Maitland, *d* of late Viscount Maitland (*o s* of 15th Earl of Lauderdale), and of Viscountess Maitland, Chelsea; two *s* one *d*]. *Address:* Under Down, Ledbury, Herefordshire. *TA:* Ledbury. *T:* Ledbury 2669. *Club:* Kennel.   *[Died 21 July 1972.*

BIDDULPH, Sir Francis (Henry), 9th Bt *cr* 1664; Grazier, Queensland; *b* Mount Playfair, 8 June 1882; *s* of late Walter John Biddulph and Harriette Sophia Biddulph (*née* Foot); *S* kinsman, Sir Theophilus George Biddulph, 8th Bt, who died 1948 (the title became dormant in that year; succ. proved, 1956); *m* 1907, Janet (*d* 1956), *d* of late Walter Bain Hannah, Brisbane; two *s* (one *d* decd). *Educ:* Mount Playfair. *Heir: er s* Stuart Royden Biddulph [*b* 24 June 1908; *m* 1939, Muriel Margaret, 3rd *d* of Angus Harkness, Hamley Bridge, S Australia; one *s* two *d*]. *Address:* Mount Playfair, Tambo, Qld 4478, Australia. *T:* 4.9U Tambo.   *[Died 7 Jan. 1980.*

BIGGART, Sir John Henry, Kt 1967; CBE 1948; DSc, MD; FRCP, FRCPath; Director of Institute of Pathology, Queen's University, Belfast, 1948-71; Dean of Faculty of Medicine, 1943-71; Professor of Pathology, 1937-71; Pro-Vice-Chancellor, 1967-71; Pro-Chancellor, 1972; *b* 17 Nov. 1905; *s* of John Henry Biggart and Mary Gault; *m* 1934, Mary Isobel Gibson, Knock, Belfast; one *s* one *d*. *Educ:* Royal Belfast Academical Instn; Queen's Univ., Belfast; Johns Hopkins Medical Sch. MB (Hons) 1928; MD (Gold Medal), 1931; DSc 1937; MRCP 1952; FRCP 1957; FCPath 1964; Hon. FRCPI 1969. Commonwealth Fellowship, Johns Hopkins, 1931-33; Pathologist to Scottish Asylums Board, 1933-37; Lecturer in Neuropathology, Edinburgh Univ., 1933-37; Regional Dir, Blood Transfusion Service, 1939-46. Robert Campbell Orator, 1948; Mem., University Senate, 1948; Chm., Laboratory Services Cttee, Hospitals Authority, 1948-54; Chm., Medical Education and Research Cttee, Hospitals Authority, 1950-64; Gen. Med. Council, 1951; Gen. Dental Council, 1959; Chm., Standing Med. Adv. Cttee, Min. of Health, NI, 1967-73; Council, Brit. Empire Cancer Campaign, 1968; Council, Coll. of Pathologists, 1968; Chairman: NI Council for Postgraduate Med. Educn, 1971-79; Irish br. Council, GMC, 1971-; Belfast Home for the Blind, 1972-; Marie Curie Beaconfield Home, 1969-; Age Action Year (NI), 1976; Vice-President: NI Mental Assoc.; NI Br., British Empire Cancer Campaign; Pres., NI Muscular Dystrophy Assoc., 1972-. Hon. FRCGP, 1971; MD (*hc*) Dublin, 1957; Hon. LLD QUB, 1971; Hon. DSc NUI, 1973. *Publications:* Text Book of Neuropathology, 1936; papers on general and nervous pathology in Brain, Jl Pathology and Bacteriology, Ulster Med. Jl, and Johns Hopkins Bulletin. *Recreations:* reading, writing, gardening, music. *Address:* 64 King's Road, Belfast. *T:* Belfast 653107.   *[Died 21 May 1979*

BIGGE, Sir John Amherst S.; *see* Selby-Bigge.

BIGGS, Christopher Thomas Ewart E.; *see* Ewart-Biggs.

BIGGS, Vice-Adm. Sir Hilary Worthington, KBE 1958; CB 1955; DSO 1940 (Bar 1941); RN retired; *b* 15 Jan. 1905; *s* of late Lieut-Col C. W. Biggs; *m* 1934, Florence, *d* of late Adm. of the

Fleet Sir Roger Backhouse, GCB, and of Lady Backhouse, MBE; two *s* two *d. Educ:* RNC Osborne and Dartmouth. Midshipman, 1923; Sub-Lieut 1925; Lieut 1926; Lieut-Comdr 1934; Comdr 1938; Capt. 1943; Rear-Adm. 1952; Vice-Adm. 1956. War Service: HMS Revenge (Exec. Officer), 1939-40; HMS Hero (in command), 1940-42, Norwegian Campaign and Mediterranean; Admiralty, 1942-44; Capt.(D) 11th Destroyer Flotilla, Eastern Fleet, 1944-45; Deputy Chief of Naval Personnel (Personal Services), 1953-55; Flag Officer, Home Fleet Training Squadron, 1955-56; Comdr-in-Chief, East Indies Station, 1956-58; with John Tyzack & Partners, 1959-74. *Address:* Hill House, Meonstoke, Southampton SO3 1NH. *T:* Droxford 409.   *[Died 2 Jan. 1976.*

BILLINGS, Rear-Adm. Frederick Stewart, CBE 1953; CEng; FIMechE; *b* 11 Aug. 1900; *s* of F. W. Billings, Cheltenham; *m* 1933, Mary Sheila (*née* Howell); two *s* two *d. Educ:* Royal Naval Colls, Osborne and Dartmouth. As Capt. (E): Fleet Engineer Officer on staff of C-in-C, Mediterranean, 1945-47; Asst Engineer-in-Chief (Personnel) at Admiralty, 1947-48; Fleet Engineer Officer (Submarines), 1948-50; Manager, Engineering Dept, HM Dockyard, Portsmouth, 1950-54; retd list, 1954. Local Dir and Chief Engineer, the Consett Iron Co., County Durham, 1956-62. Chilean Order Al Merito, 1932. *Address:* Sideways, Bredon, near Tewkesbury, Glos. *T:* Bredon 72313.   *[Died 25 Oct. 1980.*

BINDOFF, Prof. Stanley Thomas; Professor of History, Queen Mary College, University of London, 1951-75; *b* 8 April 1908; 2nd *s* of late Thomas Henry and Mary Bindoff, Brighton; *m* 1936, Marjorie (*d* 1979), *d* of William George and Helen Blatcher, New Malden; one *s* one *d. Educ:* Brighton Grammar Sch.; University Coll., London. BA (History Hons), 1929; MA (with mark of distinction), 1933; Alexander Medallist of the RHistS, 1935. Research Asst, Inst. of Historical Research, 1930-33; Sec., Netherlands Information Bureau, 1933-34; successively Asst Lectr and Lectr in History, University Coll., London, 1935-45; service in Naval Intelligence Div., Admty, 1942-45; Reader in Modern History, University Coll., London, 1945-51. Visiting Prof. in History: Columbia Univ., NY, 1960; Claremont Graduate Sch., Calif., 1966; Wellesley Coll., Mass., Harvard Univ., 1968; Cornell Vis. Prof., Swarthmore Coll., Pa, 1973. FRHistS, 1946; Vice-Pres., 1967. Fellow: University Coll., London, 1958; Queen Mary Coll., London, 1977. Member: Utrecht Historical Soc., 1947; Royal Dutch Soc. of Literature, 1950; Senate, Univ. of London, 1966. *Publications:* (with E. F. Malcolm Smith and C. K. Webster) British Diplomatic Representatives, 1789-1852, 1934; The Scheldt Question to 1839, 1945; Ket's Rebellion (Hist. Assoc. Pamphlet), 1949; Tudor England, 1950; (ed jtly) Elizabethan Government and Society, 1961; articles and reviews in historical journals. *Recreations:* walking and climbing; watching games which he has grown too old to play. *Address:* 2 Sylvan Gardens, Woodlands Road, Surbiton, Surrey. *T:* 01-399 4880. *Club:* Reform.   *[Died 23 Dec. 1980.*

BING, Geoffrey Henry Cecil, CMG 1960; QC 1950; Barrister; Legal Adviser to ASTMS, since 1971; *b* 24 July 1909; *s* of Geoffrey Bing, Rockport, Craigavad, Co. Down; *m* 1940, Christian Frances, *d* of Sir Ralph Blois, 9th Bt; two *s* ; *m* 1956, Eileen Mary, *d* of late Alderman Frederick Cullen; one *s* (adopted). *Educ:* Tonbridge Sch.; Lincoln Coll., Oxford. Jane Eliza Proctor Visiting Fellow, Princeton Univ., USA, 1932-33. Called to Bar, Inner Temple, 1934, Gibraltar, 1937, Gold Coast, 1950, Nigeria, 1954. Joined Royal Signals, 1941; commissioned, 1943; GSO2 Airborne Forces Development Centre, 1943; British North Africa Forces, 1943; Major, BLA, 1944-45 (despatches). MP (Lab) Hornchurch Div. of Essex, 1945-50, Hornchurch, 1950-55; Asst Govt Whip, 1945-46. Constitutional Adviser to Prime Minister of Ghana, 1956-57; Attorney-Gen. of Ghana, 1957-61; Adviser to Pres. Nkrumah, 1961-66. Fellow, Ghana Academy of Sciences. Consultant to Irish University Press, 1970-74. *Publications:* (as Henry Blythe) Spain over Britain, 1937; John Bull's Other Ireland, 1950; Reap the Whirlwind-an account of Kwame Nkrumah's Ghana, 1950-66, 1967; (editor) The Family Lawyer, new rev. edn, 1970. *Address:* 11 Clarendon Gardens, Maida Vale, W9 1AY.   *[Died 24 April 1977.*

BINGEN, Sir Eric Albert, Kt 1966; *b* 12 April 1898; *yr s* of late Max and Leily Bingen; *m* 1st, 1928, Peggy Ida (*d* 1964), *d* of late Arthur M. Lawrence; one *d* ; 2nd, 1967, Eileen Peel, *widow* of T. Ainslie Robertson. *Educ:* Cheltenham Coll.; St John's Coll., Oxford (Classical Scholar). Served European War, France and Flanders, Lieut, Royal Sussex Regt and RAF (wounded), 1917-18. MA (Oxon) 1st class Final Honours Sch. of Jurisprudence, 1921; Solicitor, 1924 (Law Society's Prizeman); Imperial Chemical Industries Ltd: Legal Dept, 1927-51; Dir, 1951-63;

Deputy Chm., 1959-63; retd, 31 March 1963. Chm., Remploy Ltd, 1963-69. Member: Advisory Cttee on Commercial Information Overseas, 1957-59; Departmental (Jenkins) Cttee on Company Law, 1959-62; Restrictive Practices Court, 1963-70. Pres., Cheltonian Soc., 1965-66. Leader, UK Delegation to UN Industrial Develt Organisation Symposium, Athens, Dec. 1967. *Address:* Kingsclere House, Kingsclere, near Newbury, Berks. *T:* Kingsclere 395. *Club:* Royal Air Force.   *[Died 10 Aug. 1972.*

BINGHAM, Lt-Col Ralph Charles, CVO 1953; DSO 1917; *b* 1885; *m* 1913, Dorothy Louisa (*d* 1967), *d* of late Edward Roger Murray Pratt; one *s* one *d. Educ:* Eton. Served European War, 1914-18 (DSO, Italian Silver Medal, despatches thrice); commanded 4th Bn City of London Regt (The Royal Fusilliers), 1934-37; Sec. The Order of St John of Jerusalem, 1927-37; Exon in the Yeoman of the Guard, 1938; Clerk of the Cheque and Adjutant of the Yeoman of the Guard, 1950-55. *Recreations:* sailing (passed Board of Trade Yacht Master (Coastal) Exam., 1945); bookbinding and calligraphy. *Address:* 10 Evelyn Gardens, SW7. *T:* 01-373 5543.   *[Died 4 Nov. 1977.*

BINGLEY, Adm. Sir Alexander Noel Campbell, GCB 1962 (KCB 1959; CB 1956); OBE 1943; Rear-Admiral of the United Kingdom and of the Admiralty, 1966-68; *b* 15 Feb. 1905; *s* of R. N. G. Bingley; *m* 1948, Juliet Martin, *d* of late R. M. Vick, OBE; one *s* two *d. Educ:* RN Colls Osborne, Dartmouth and Greenwich. Naval Observer, 1929; commanded HM Ships: Slinger, 1943; Biter, 1944; Nabaron, 1945; Eagle, 1952-53; Fifth Sea Lord and Deputy Chief of Naval Staff (Air), 1954-57; Flag Officer, Aircraft Carriers, 1958-59; Commander-in-Chief, Mediterranean, 1959-61; Commander-in-Chief, Portsmouth, and Allied Commander-in-Chief, Channel, 1961-63; retd list 1963. Rear-Adm. 1954; Vice-Adm. 1957; Actg Adm. 1959; Adm. 1960. Pres. Royal Naval Benevolent Trust, 1963-70; Sec., SEMBAL Trust, 1964-. *Recreation:* gardening. *Address:* Hoddesdonbury Farm, Hoddesdon, Herts. *T:* Hoddesdon 63238. *Club:* Naval and Military.   *[Died 28 Sept. 1972.*

BINGLEY, Col Robert Albert Glanville, CVO 1954; DSO 1944; OBE 1946; retired; *b* 15 Nov. 1902; *s* of R. Noel G. Bingley, OBE, and Mrs Bingley, Notley Abbey, Thame, Oxon, Braisewerth, Suffolk; *m* 1st, 1933, Sybil Gladys Rodney Duff; one *s* one *d* ; 2nd, 1941, May Olivia Lenox-Conyngham; one *d. Educ:* Charterhouse; RMC Sandhurst. Joined 11th Hussars, 1923; ADC to GOC-in-C, Aldershot, 1930-31; Adjt, 11th Hussars, 1933-35; Adjt Inns of Court Regt, 1936-40; served War of 1939-45; raised and commanded Inns of Court Armoured Car Regt, 1940-45 (DSO); Asst Mil. Sec. to Field-Marshal Viscount Montgomery, 21 Army Group and BAOR, 1945-46 (OBE); Head of Brit. Mil. Mission, Luxembourg, 1946-47; Military Attaché, Brit. Embassy, The Hague, 1947-51; Asst Mil. Sec. to: Gen. Sir Gerald Templer, 1951-52; Gen. Sir George Erskine, 1952-53; Lt-Gen. G. K. Bourne, 1953-54. Dir, St John Ambulance Assoc., Glos. Landowner and farmer. Commander Order of Orange Nassau, 1950. CStJ. *Address:* Higher Eggbeer, Cheriton Bishop, Exeter, Devon. *Club:* Cheltenham Steeplechase.   *[Died 5 July 1976.*

BINNALL, Rev. Canon Peter Blannin Gibbons, FSA; *b* 5 Jan. 1907; *s* of late Rev. R. G. Binnall and Geraldine (*née* Pearson); *m* 1936, Stephanie, *d* of late Rev. W. Goss; one *s. Educ:* Worksop Coll.; Lichfield Theological Coll. Deacon, Grantham for Lincoln, 1932; priest, Lincoln, 1933. Curate of Caistor with Holton le Moor and Clixby, 1932-36; Vicar of Holland Fen with Amber Hill, 1936-45; Rector of East and West Barkwith with S Willingham, 1945-61; Hon. Canon of Lincoln, 1956; Canon Residentiary, Sub-Dean and Treasurer of Lincoln Cathedral, 1961-75. Hon. Sec., Lincs Old Churches Trust, 1952-68; Pres., Lincs Soc. for History and Archaeology, 1975-78; Chairman: Lincoln Dio. Adv. Cttee, 1963-76; Local Cttee, Nat. Trust for Tattershall Castle; Heritage Panel, Lincs and Humberside Arts; Vice-Chm., Historic Bldgs Jt Cttee for Lincs and Humberside; Vice-Pres., Tennyson Soc.; Mem., British Soc. of Master Glass-Painters. FSA 1944; MA (Lambeth) 1962. *Publications:* contribs to: Collins' Guide to English Parish Churches; Antiquaries Jl, Jl Brit. Soc. Master Glass Painters, Hibbert Jl, various archæological transactions etc, Folklore. *Recreations:* history, folklore, ornithology. *Address:* Elm Cottage, Hemswell, Gainsborough, Lincs DN21 5UN. *T:* Hemswell 264.   *[Died 29 Nov. 1980.*

BINNEY, Anthony Lockhart, CSI 1945; CIE 1939; *b* 1890; 5th *s* of T. G. Binney, late of Guisnes Court, Tolleshunt D'Arcy, Essex; *m* 1919, Dorothy Margery, *d* of late J. H. Cox, CIE, CBE, ICS; one *s* two *d. Educ:* Rugby. Entered ICS, 1914; served European war, 1915-19 (RFA (T) and RHA in Mesopotamia and Afghanistan, Capt., 1918); on deputation in Hyderabad, Dir

Gen. Revenue, Controller to the Princes, 1928-34; Financial Sec. to Govt, CP, 1935; Chief Sec. (offg), 1936; Financial Com, 1940; Adviser to Governor, 1944-46. *Address:* Crossland, Copthorne, Sussex.   *[Died 7 Dec. 1973.*

BINNEY, Sir (Frederick) George; see Binney, Sir G.

BINNEY, Sir George, Kt 1941; DSO 1944; MA; FRGS; *b* 23 Sept. 1900; *s* of late Rev. M. F. B. Binney and late Emily Blinkhorn; *m* 1946, Evelyn Mary (marr. diss., 1955), *er d* of T. G. Marriott; *m* 1955, Sonia, *widow* of Lt-Col F. Simms and *d* of late Paymaster Rear-Adm. Sir William Beresford-Whyte, KCB, CMG. *Educ:* Eton Coll. (scholar); Merton Coll., Oxford (Chambers Postmastership). Ed. of Isis, 1920; Organiser and Sec., Oxford Univ. Spitzbergen Expedition, 1921; Leader, Merton Coll. Arctic Expedition, 1923; Leader, Oxford Univ. Arctic Expedition, 1924; received Back Award of RGS and Gold Medal de la Roquette of Geographical Society of Paris for his journey across North East Land; Founder's Gold Medal, Royal Geographical Society, 1957. Served Hudson's Bay Company, 1926-31, spending much time in Canadian Arctic. Joined United Steel Companies Ltd, 1931; seconded from United Steel Cos for service with Iron and Steel Control, Min. of Supply, 1939; Asst Commercial Attaché, Stockholm, 1940-42; Comdr RNVR, 1942-45 (retired, 1945). Led United Kingdom Trade and Industrial Mission to Ghana, 1959. Dir, Hambro's (Finance) Co. Ltd, Jersey, 1971. *Publications:* With Seaplane and Sledge in the Arctic, 1925; The Eskimo Book of Knowledge, 1931. *Recreations:* shooting, antique collecting, travel. *Address:* Domaine des Vaux, St Lawrence, Jersey, CI. *T:* Jersey North 529. *Clubs:* White's, Garrick.   *[Died 27 Sept. 1972.*

BINNS, Sir Arthur (Lennon), Kt 1954; CBE 1945; MC 1916; *b* 31 March 1891; *er s* of John Binns, Grimsby; *m* 1915, Florence Gertrude Coggon; two *d. Educ:* Wintringham Grammar Sch.; St John's Coll., Cambridge. Lincolnshire Regt and Gen. Staff, 1914-19. Chief Education Officer: West Riding of Yorks, 1936-45; Lancs, 1945-47. Mem. Fleming Cttee on Public Schs, 1944; Mem. Colonial Office Advisory Cttee, 1945-53; Special Commissioner in Sierra Leone, 1949; Mem. Beveridge Cttee on BBC, 1940; Chm. Colonial Office Mission to East and Central Africa, 1951-52; Pres. Section L, British Association, 1952; Governor: Welbeck Coll., 1953-57; Sedbergh Sch., 1954-62; Royal Lancaster Grammar Sch., 1958-62; King Edward Sch., Lytham, 1958-62; Chm. Standing Conference of Regional Examining Unions, 1957-60; Visiting Lecturer, University of British Columbia, 1958; Pres. North of England Educational Conference, 1962; Mem. of several other Govt Departmental Cttees. *Address:* The Firs, Woodville Terrace, Lytham, Lancs. *T:* Lytham 7310. *Club:* Lytham Yacht.   *[Died 23 Sept. 1971.*

BINNS, Joseph, CBE 1961; Consulting Engineer; Chairman of Public Works Loans Board, 1970-72 (Deputy Chairman, 1958-70); *b* 19 March 1900; *s* of Alderman Joseph Binns (a former Lord Mayor of Manchester); *m* 1924, Daisy Graham; two *s. Educ:* Primary and Secondary Sch., Manchester; Manchester Coll. of Technology. MP (Lab) Gillingham Div. of Rochester, 1945-50; PPS to Minister of Supply, 1946-47; Chm. Metropolitan Boroughs Standing Joint Cttee, 1945-49. *Address:* 4 Sycamore Close, Dymchurch, Romney Marsh, Kent. *T:* Dymchurch 3068. *Club:* Reform.   *[Died 23 April 1975.*

BINYON, Basil, OBE; MA; CEng, FIEE, FIEEE, AFRAeS; *b* 1885; *s* of Brightwen Binyon; *m* Gladys (*d* 1960), *o d* of late J. Howard Keep; one *s* (and one killed in action, Arnhem, 24 Sept. 1944) one *d*; *m* 1962, V. M. Hibbert. *Educ:* Leighton Park Sch.; Trinity Coll., Cambridge. War Service, Flight-Comdr RNAS; Major RAF, 1914-18; Group Comdt No. 19 Group Royal Observer Corps, rank Observer Comdr, 1939-47; retired 1947. Past Chm. Electronics Section, IEE; Dir, British Broadcasting Co., 1922-26. *Address:* Longridge, The Glen, Farnborough Park, Kent. *T:* Farnborough 54371. *Clubs:* Royal Air Force; Itchenor Sailing.   *[Died 4 April 1977.*

BIRCH-REYNARDSON, Lieut-Col H. T.; see Reynardson.

BIRCHENOUGH, Charles, MA; FCP; *b* 8 Aug. 1882; *s* of late Samuel Birchenough, Stockport; *m* 1910, Gertrude Mary Elizabeth Angel (*d* 1947), *d* of late James Thomas, Cardiff; one *d* (one *s* decd); *m* 1964, Rhoda Mary, *d* of late Philip Taylor, Street. *Educ:* Balliol Coll., Oxford. Asst Lecturer in Education, University Coll. of South Wales, Cardiff, 1905-09; Lecturer in Education and Master of Method, Sheffield Univ., 1909-19; County Inspector of Education, Kent Education Cttee, 1919-27; Asst for Further Education, 1925-27; Chief Inspector of Education, 1927-47; Commissioned RGA 1916; served with 105 Siege Battery, RGA, France, Belgium, 1917, Italy, 1917-18 (despatches); Chief Educn Officer, Heavy Artillery, Italy, 1918-

19. Examiner in Educn for Univ. of Wales, etc; advised on the reorganisation of education, Borough of Chesterfield; Vice-Pres., Coll. of Preceptors, 1952-65; Asst Ed., Journal of Education, 1947-55. *Publications:* A Primer of Teaching Practice (with J. A. Green), 1911; History of Elementary Education in England and Wales since 1800, 1914 (enlarged, 1925, 1939); Report on Elementary Education in the Borough of Chesterfield, 1927; Articles in the Encyclopædia and Dictionary of Education, Journal of Education, etc. *Address:* Montrose, 1 Brooks Road, Street, Somerset.   *[Died 5 Jan. 1973.*

BIRD, Sir Francis Hugh William S.; see Stonehewer Bird.

BIRD, Terence Frederick, CB 1954; Executive Director, P&O, 1965-71; Chairman, Committee of European Shipowners, 1968-71; *b* 29 Sept. 1906; *s* of F. J. Bird and G. M. Bird (*née* Caulfeild); *m* 1939, Prudence Ann Hutton Moss; one *s* one *d. Educ:* Southern Rhodesia; Balliol Coll., Oxford; Harvard Univ. Zoologist and Surveyor to Oxford Univ. Expedition to New Hebrides, 1933-34; Sec., Aerodromes Advisory Board, 1934-35. Entered Civil Service, 1935; Home Civil Service Commonwealth Fellow, 1947-48; Under-Sec., Min. of Transport, 1951-65; Under-Sec., BoT, 1965. Chm., Royal Nat. Inst. for the Deaf, 1972-75. *Address:* 12 Ardleigh Court, Ardleigh, Colchester, Essex CO7 7LA. *Club:* Athenæum.   *[Died 12 Aug. 1979.*

BIRKBECK, Harold Edward; Secretary of the Headmasters' Conference and Incorporated Association of Headmasters, 1965-69; *b* 1902. *Educ:* Bradford Grammar Sch.; Queen's Coll., Oxford. Asst Master, Edinburgh Academy, 1925-35; Headmaster of Barnard Castle School, 1935-64. *Address:* 65 Parkside Drive, Watford, Herts.   *[Died 24 Sept. 1977.*

BIRKBECK, Maj.-Gen. Theodore Henry, CB 1963; CBE 1958; DSO 1945 and Bar, 1948; JP; DL; *b* 17 Nov. 1911; *s* of late Maj.-Gen. Sir William Henry Birkbeck, KCB, CMG, Settle, Yorks and Lady Mabel (*née* Shaw), New York, USA; *m* 1939, Rozanne Elizabeth Wyatt (*née* Metcalfe) (marr. diss., 1961); two *s*; *m* 1962, Moyra L. M. Hewitt. *Educ:* Oundle Sch. 2nd Lieut, Border Regt, 1932; seconded to King's African Rifles, 1935-46; ADC to Governor and C-in-C, Nyasaland, 1937-39. Served War of 1939-45 (despatches thrice) with KAR in Ethiopia, Eritrea, Somaliland, Ceylon and Burma; commanded 11 KAR, 1944-46; seconded to Parachute Regt, 1947-50; OC 3rd Bn, Palestine, 1947-48; GSO1 (Trg) Eastern Comd, 1950-51; GSO1 (SD) Northern Comd, 1951-52; commanded New Coll., RMA, Sandhurst, 1952-55; commanded 70th Inf. Bde (KAR), Kenya, 1955-58; Dep. Military Sec. (A), War Office. 1958-60; GOC North Midland Area and 49th Div., TA, 1960-62; Dir, TA Cadets, War Office, 1962-66; Dir of Civil Defence, NE Region, 1966-68. Hon. Colonel: Cumbria (formerly Cumberland and Westmorland) ACF, 1971-; The Northumbrian Volunteers, T&AVR, 1972-75. Chm., N of England TA&VRA, 1971-. JP W Riding of Yorks, 1967; DL N Yorks, 1976. *Address:* Anley, Settle, N Yorks. *Club:* Army and Navy.   *[Died 2 Aug. 1976.*

BIRKENHEAD, 2nd Earl of, *cr* 1922; **Frederick Winston Furneaux Smith,** TD; Viscount Furneaux, 1921; Baron Birkenhead, 1919; Bt 1919; High Steward of HM Manor of the Savoy, London, since 1942; *b* 7 Dec. 1907; *o s* of 1st Earl and Margaret Eleanor, 2nd *d* of late Rev. H. Furneaux, Fellow of Corpus Christi Coll., Oxford; *S* father, 1930; *m* 1935, Hon. Sheila Berry (author of Against Oblivion, 1943, Peace in Piccadilly, 1958, Illustrious Friends, 1965) (temporary Lady-in-Waiting to the Duchess of Kent, 1949-53), 2nd *d* of 1st Viscount Camrose; one *s* one *d. Educ:* Eton; Christ Church, Oxford. Parliamentary Private Sec. to Sec. of State for Foreign Affairs, 1938-39. A Lord-in-Waiting to King George VI, 1938-40 and 1951-52, to the Queen, 1952-55. Joined 53 (Oxfordshire Yeomanry) Anti-Tank Regt, 1938; served War of 1939-45, Capt. 1940, Staff Coll., 1941, Major, 1942; attd Pol. Intelligence Dept, Foreign Office, 1942; attd Brit. Mil. Mission to Yugoslav Partisans, 1944-45. *Publications:* Frederick Edwin, 1st Earl of Birkenhead: 2 vols, 1933, 1935; Strafford, 1938; Lady Eleanor Smith-a Memoir, 1953; FE, 1959; The Prof. in Two Worlds, 1961; Halifax, 1965; Walter Monckton, 1969; *posthumous publication:* Rudyard Kipling, 1978. *Recreations:* lawn tennis, golf. *Heir:* *s* Viscount Furneaux. *Address:* Charlton, Banbury, Oxon; 24 Wilton Street, SW1. *Clubs:* Beefsteak, Buck's, White's; Royal Yacht Squadron (Cowes).   *[Died 10 June 1975.*

BIRKINSHAW, Air Commodore George William, CB 1946; *b* 17 June 1896; *m* 1923; three *s* one *d. Educ:* Downing Coll., Cambridge (BA 1927). RFC and RAF from 1915; served European War, 1914-18, France; India and Iraq, 1920-24; Egypt and Palestine, 1933-38; Dir, Repair and Maintenance, Ministry of Supply, 1943-46; Senior Technical Staff Officer, RAF HQ, India, 1946-47; retired, 1947. Freeman of York, Freeman of

London. *Clubs:* Royal Air Force, Pathfinder.
[*Died* 22 *Oct.* 1977.

BIRLEY, Norman Pellew, DSO 1918; MC 1916; *b* Pelton Vicarage, Co. Durham, 29 April 1891; *s* of Rev. Hugh Hornby Birley and Florence Lydia Birley; *m* 1919, Eileen Alice Morgan, Underwood, Mumbles, Glamorgan; two *s. Educ:* Repton Sch.; New Coll., Oxford. Served European War, 1914-19. History Master, Gresham's Sch., Holt, 1919; Asst Master, Marlborough Coll., 1922-27; Headmaster, King's Sch., Canterbury, 1927-35; Headmaster, Merchant Taylors' Sch., 1935-46; retired, 1946; Mem., Wiltshire Education Cttee, 1948-66. *Recreations:* fishing and gardening. *Address:* Hyde Leaze, Hyde Lane, Marlborough, Wilts. [*Died* 29 *June* 1980.

BIRNIE, Col Eugene St John, OBE 1965; FRGS; The Guides Cavalry (QVOFF); *b* 18 March 1900; *s* of Cyril Montague Birnie and Margaret Dannatt; *m* 1933, Lady Marguerite Kathleen Courtenay, 3rd *d* of Rev. 16th Earl of Devon; two *d. Educ:* Charterhouse. Commissioned to 25th Cavalry (Frontier Force) now Sam Browne's Cavalry (12th FF), 1919; transferred to Guides Cavalry, 1937; served 3rd Afghan War, 1919; Capt., 1925; Major, 1937; ADC to Governor of Bengal, 1929-30; Adjutant to Governor of Bengal's Body Guard, 1930-32; AMS, AHQ India, 1939-41; DAMS, GHQ Middle East, 1941 (despatches); Private Secretary to C-in-C India, 1941-42; AAG, MEF, 1942; AAG Paiforce, 1942-43; Commandant Hyderabad Lancers, 1943-44; HQ CMF, Italy, 1944-45; Director AWS Alfsea, SEAC, 1946; Military Secretary to Governor-General of Pakistan, 1947-48; Secretary, Church of England Children's Soc., 1949-65. "A" Pilot's Certificate, 1930; Kamet Expedition, 1931; MacGregor Memorial Medal for 1932 by the C-in-C and Council of the United Services Institution of India for Reconnaissances in Tehri Garhwal during 1931; Everest Expedition, 1933. *Address:* The Cottage, Longparish, Hants.
[*Died* 31 *Jan.* 1976.

BIRT, Guy Capper, CVO 1935; MRCS, LRCP, LDS; retired; Extra Surgeon-Dentist to Queen Mary, 1949; *b* 6 Aug. 1884; *s* of Daniel Birt and Mary Ella Capper; *m* 1913, Roberta Ross; two *s. Educ:* Wellington Coll.; St Thomas's and Royal Dental Hospitals. Practised dentistry in Cavendish Square, 1910; Asst in Dental Dept, St Thomas's Hospital, 1910-14; Surgeon Dentist to King George V, 1925-36; to Queen Mary, 1925-49; Dental Surgeon to Metropolitan Police, 1910-34; Capt. (Plastic Surgeon) in RAMC, European War, 1914-18; member Board of Governors of and Hon. Consulting Dental Surgeon to St Thomas's Hospital. *Recreations:* Caravanning and yachting. *Address:* Merlebank, Moulsford, Wallingford, Berks. *T:* Cholesey 347. *Club:* Lansdowne House. [*Died* 11 *June* 1972.

BIRT, Rev. Canon Roderick Harold Capper, MA Oxon; Canon Emeritus of St George's Cathedral, Cape Town; *b* 24 Oct. 1882; *s* of Daniel and M. E. Birt; *m* 1st, 1909, Sophie (*d* 1942), *o d* of Walter Kidd, MD, formerly of Blackheath; no *c*; 2nd, 1944, Mary, *widow* of Frank Goch, SAAF, and *er d* of Canon T. Gerald Le Mesurier, Cape Town. *Educ:* Wellington Coll.; New Coll., Oxford. Deacon, 1907; Priest, 1908; Asst Master, Radley Coll., 1906-18; Principal of the Diocesan Coll., Rondebosch, Cape Town, 1919-43; Canon of St George's Cathedral, Cape Town, 1940-51; Honorary Canon, 1951; Asst Priest, St Saviour's, Claremont, Cape, 1944-60. *Recreation:* gardening. *Address:* 14 Penrith Road, Wynberg, Cape Town, S Africa. *Club:* Leander. [*Died* 19 *Oct.* 1975.

BIRTWISTLE, Ivor Treharne, OBE 1951; literary editor and cadet counsellor, The West Australian, Perth, WA, 1945-57; *b* Beaumaris, Victoria, Australia, 8 April 1892; *s* of James Birtwistle, architect, Perth, and Emily, *d* of David Davies, Daylesford, Victoria; *m* 1925, Kathleen Winifred, *d* of late James Herbert Broadley, North Perth, WA, formerly of Bath, England; one *s* one *d. Educ:* State Sch., Claremont, WA. Studied for Presbyterian ministry, but joined literary staff Melbourne Age, 1913; enlisted AIF 1915, serving Egypt, Gallipoli and France; Publicity Officer, National Cttee Australian YMCA, 1918; Peace Loan Campaign (Victoria), 1919; National Campaign Council, Federal elections (Victoria), 1920; Vice-Chairman, State Repatriation Board (Victoria), 1919-20; joined literary staff The West Australian, Perth, 1920; Editor, The Western Mail, 1924-45; State President Boy Scouts' Assoc., 1938-50; State President Surf Life Saving Assoc., 1929-37; Dir, Studies in Journalism, University of W. Australia, 1930-40; President: Perth Legacy, 1930 and 1937; Royal WA Historical Soc., 1945-65; WA Regional YMCA Council, 1964-67; Perth YMCA, 1951-63; Gallipoli Legion of Anzacs of WA, 1970-72; Mem., Armadale-Kelmscott Shire Council, 1964-69. *Recreations:* gardening, historical research. *Address:* Greenway, Peet Road, Roleystone, West Australia. *T:* Roleystone 955333. *Club:* Legacy (Perth, WA). [*Died* 15 *June* 1976.

BISAT, William Sawney, FRS 1947; DSc, MSc, FGS; retired civil engineer and surveyor, lately engaged on construction of large civil engineering works and gravel and sand quarries for H. Arnold & Son Ltd, Public Works Contractors, Doncaster and Leeds 1903; *b* 19 Oct. 1886; *s* of Charles Edward Bisat, bookseller, Doncaster; *m* 1st, 1915, Enid Alice, *d* of Rev. T. Powell, MA; 2nd, 1940, Mary St Agnes, *d* of Rev. W. H. Stansfield; one *d* (and two *s* one *d* decd); 3rd, 1971, Irene, *d* of John Wilkinson, RN. *Educ:* Grammar Sch., Doncaster. Hon. MSc Leeds, 1938; Hon. DSc Durham, 1963. Lyell Medal, Geol. Soc. London, 1942; Silver Medal, Liverpool Geol. Soc., 1954; Clough Medal, Edinburgh Geol. Soc., 1960; Sorby Medal, Yorkshire Geol. Soc., 1961. Hon. Member: Belgian Geol. Soc.; Yorkshire Geol. Soc.; Doncaster Sci. Soc. *Publications:* many geological treatises on fauna of carboniferous rocks and their stratigraphical succession; also the drift deposits (gravels and boulder-clays) of Yorkshire. *Recreation:* geological research. *Address:* Leighton, Crabtree Hill, Collingham, Wetherby, Yorkshire. *T:* Collingham Bridge 2365. [*Died* 14 *May* 1973.

BISHOP, Sir (Frank) Patrick, Kt 1964; MBE 1945; Barrister-at-Law; Director, Rediffusion Ltd; *b* 7 March 1900; *m* 1st, Vera (*d* 1953), *d* of late Arthur Drew, Coulsdon, Surrey; one *s* two *d*; 2nd, 1955, Ella Mary Hunt. *Educ:* Tottenham Grammar Sch.; King's Coll., London. Called to the Bar, Gray's Inn, 1923; practised as a barrister-at-law, 1924-29; joined the staff of The Times, Asst Manager, 1937-45; Gen. Man. Newsprint Supply Co., 1947-57. MP (C) Harrow Central, 1950-64. Formerly Chairman: Advertisement Cttee, Newspaper Proprietors' Assoc.; Advertisement Cttee, Internat. Chamber of Commerce; Exec. Cttee, Advertising Assoc. Served European War, 1914-18, in RAF, 1918; War of 1939-45, Second in Command, 5th City of London (Press Battalion) of the Home Guard. *Publications:* Advertising and the Law, 1928; The Economics of Advertising, 1944; The Ethics of Advertising, 1949. *Address:* Scotland Street, Stoke-by-Nayland, Suffolk. *Clubs:* Carlton, Devonshire.
[*Died* 5 *Oct.* 1972.

BISHOP, Sir Patrick; *see* Bishop, Sir F. P.

BISHOP, Peter Maxwell Farrow, DM (Oxon); FRCP; FRCOG; Endocrinologist Emeritus, Guy's Hospital; Hon. Consulting Endocrinologist, Chelsea Hospital for Women; late Medical Consultant, Family Planning Association; Past Master, Society of Apothecaries; *b* 14 Aug. 1904; *o s* of late Dr T. H. Bishop; *m* 1937, (Winifred) Phyllis, *o d* of Lt-Col E. O. Thurston, IMS; one *s* two *d. Educ:* Berlin; Charterhouse; Trinity Coll., Oxford. Guy's Hosp. Medical Sch.: Senior Demonstrator in Physiology, 1930-33; Lectr in Physiological Chemistry, 1933-38; Lectr in Applied Physiology and Pharmacology, 1938; Warden of the College, 1938-47; Dep. Supt, 1938-45; MO in charge (EMS), Guy's Hosp., 1939-45. First Treas., Member Editorial Board and one of founders of Journal of Endocrinology, 1939; Member Council of Management, Soc. for Endocrinology, 1947, Hon. Mem. 1973; one of first two Hon. Co-Secretaries Section of Endocrinology, Royal Society Medicine, 1946 (Pres. 1955, Hon. Mem. 1973); Hon. Sec. 1959, Chm. 1960-63, Hon. Mem. 1971, Soc. for Study of Fertility. Hon. Dipl. Acad. of Med., Barcelona, 1949; Chm. Council of Management, Jl of Reproduction and Fertility, 1960-63; Ayerst Lectr, 1958, and Hon. Mem., American Soc. for Study of Sterility; Hon. Librarian, Royal Soc. Med., 1963-69. Sir Arthur Sims Commonwealth Travelling Prof., 1964. Hon. Mem., Endocrine Soc., Madrid, 1965; Mem., Torquay Med. Soc., 1973; H. D. Rolleston Lecturer, RCP, 1965; Litchfield Lecturer, Oxford Univ., 1967. *Publications:* Gynæcological Endocrinology, Recent Advances in Endocrinology; Chemistry of the Sex Hormones; various articles on endocrine subjects. *Address:* Moorhaven, Bovey Tracey, Devon TQ13 9HE. *T:* Bovey Tracey 833264.
[*Died* 19 *Jan.* 1979.

BISHOP, Sir William (Poole), Kt 1961; CMG 1947; AASA; Auditor-General, State of South Australia, 1946-59, retired; *b* 8 Aug. 1894; *s* of Henry Bishop, Adelaide, South Australia; *m* 1st, 1922, Leira Viola (*d* 1967); one *s* two *d*; 2nd, 1968, Daphne Rhea, *widow* of Walter Richard Birks. *Educ:* Adelaide High Sch. Official appts: Comr of Taxes for State of South Australia and Federal Dep. Comr of Taxation, 1935-46; Trustee Savings Bank of S Australia, 1946-; Director: Adelaide Cement Co. Ltd (Chm. 1965-70); Johnson & Sons (S Australia) Ltd; Santos Ltd; Chairman City Bricks (Holdings) Ltd., 1963-71. Charitable organisations: Member Exec. and Chairman Finance Cttee, Fighting Forces Comforts Fund (S Australia Div. of Australian Fund), 1939-46; Member Board of Management and Chairman of Finance Cttee, Legacy Club of Adelaide, 1944-56; Member AIF Cemetery Trust, 1928-67 (Chm. 1958-67); Member Exec. War Veterans' Home, Myrtle Bank Inc., 1933-67; Mem. Board of Governors, Burnside War Memorial Hosp., 1959-63; Dir, .

Nat. Heart Foundn of Australia (and the SA Div.), 1961-70. Served European War, 1914-18, AIF, 1915-19; War of 1939-45, Volunteer Defence Corps, 1942-45. *Address:* 90 Devereux Road, Beaumont, SA 5066, Australia. *T:* 79 5294. *Clubs:* Naval, Military and Air Force (S Australia); Glenelg Golf.
[Died 13 Aug. 1977.

BLACK, Donald Harrison, CMG 1956; PhD, MSc, FInstP; *b* 18 June 1899; *s* of Robert Black, Nelson, NZ; *m* 1927, Winifred Maida Robertson; two *s* one *d*. *Educ:* Nelson Coll., New Zealand; Canterbury University Coll., New Zealand; Emmanuel Coll. and Cavendish Laboratory, Cambridge. Standard Telephones and Cables Ltd (and associates), 1925-39; Supt of Research, Radar Research and Development Establishment, Min. Supply, 1939-43 and 1945-47; Admiralty Liaison Officer in USA, 1943-45; Asst Director Telecommunication Research and Development, Ministry of Supply, 1947-49; Director, Electronics Research and Development, Ministry of Supply, 1949-53; Head of UK Ministry of Supply Staff, Australia, 1953-56; Director-General of Electronics Research and Development, Ministry of Supply, 1956-58; Director, Royal Armament Research and Development Establishment, WO, Fort Halstead, Sevenoaks, Kent, 1958-62; Electronics Adviser to Chief Scientist, WO, 1962-66. *Publications:* contributions to Proc. Royal Society, Phil. Mag., Proc. Cambridge Phil. Soc., Jl Sci. Inst. *Recreations:* gardening, woodworking. *Address:* 8 Little Green, Alverstoke, Gosport, Hants PO12 2EU.
[Died 7 July 1978.

BLACK, Hugo LaFayette; Associate Justice, United States Supreme Court, 1937-71, retired; Harlan, Clay County, Alabama, 27 Feb. 1886; *s* of William LaFayette Black and Martha Ardellah Toland; *m* 1st, 1921, Josephine Foster (*d* 1952); two *s* one *d*; 2nd, 1957, Elizabeth Seay. *Educ:* Public Sch., Ashland, Alabama. LLB University of Alabama, 1906; began practice at Ashland, Ala, 1906; moved to Birmingham, Ala, and began practice there, 1907; Police Judge, 1910-11; Solicitor (Prosecuting Attorney) Jefferson County, Alabama, 1915-17; in general practice, Birmingham, 1919-27; US Senator from Alabama 2 terms, 1927-37. Entered 2nd OTC, Fort Oglethorpe, Ga, 1917; Comd Capt. FA; served European War, 1917-18; 81st FA and Adjt 19th Army Bde. *Recreation:* tennis. *Address:* Supreme Court Building, Washington, DC, USA.
[Died 25 Sept. 1971.

BLACK, Sir Misha, Kt 1972; OBE 1946; RDI 1957; FSIAD, MInstRA, Hon. Dr (RCA); Hon. DTech Bradford; Architect and Industrial Designer; Senior Partner, Design Research Unit, since 1946; Professor of Industrial Design, Royal College of Art, 1959-75, Professor Emeritus, 1975; Industrial Design Consultant to London Transport Executive, since 1964; *b* 16 Oct. 1910; *m* 1935, Helen Lillian Evans (marr. diss., 1952); one *s* one *d*; *m* 1955, Edna Joan Fairbrother; one *s*. Coordinating Architect, Mars Exhibition, 1938; Designer, interior British Pavilion, World's Fair, NY, 1939; Principal Exhibition Architect to Ministry of Information, 1940-45; Exhibition Consultant to UNESCO, 1947 and 1953; Co-ordinating Architect to South Bank Exhibition, Festival of Britain, 1951 and Co-Architect for Regatta Restaurant; Industrial Design Consultant to: Gas Light and Coke Co., 1946-48; BOAC for Headquarters Bldg, London Airport, 1951-56; Vickers Ltd, 1968-71; Turner & Newall Ltd, 1969-71; Hong Kong Rapid Transit System, 1969-; Consultant to Govt of Ceylon for Colombo Exhibition, 1952 and also Architect UK Pavilion there; Architect UK Pavilion, Rhodes Centenary Exhibition, Bulawayo, 1953; Design Consultant to British Transport Commn for Diesel and Electric Locomotive programme, 1956-66; Joint Interior Architect to Orient Line, 1957-61. Architect to Civic Trust for Norwich and Burslem Projects, 1959-60; Consultant: Beagle Aircraft, 1961-65; Indian Inst. of Technology, 1971; Architect to Zoological Society for small Mammal House, 1967; Consultant to Westminster CC for Piccadilly Circus develt, 1972; Member: Advisory Council Inst. of Contemporary Art, 1951-67; Council Soc. of Industrial Artists, 1933-52, 1954-57 (Pres. 1954-56); Council of Industrial Design, 1955-64; Nat. Adv. Council on Art Education, 1959-72; Adv. Council to Science Museum, 1966-; UK Nat. Commn for UNESCO, 1971- (Chm., Culture Adv. Cttee, 1973-); Pres., Engrg Section, Brit. Assoc. Advancement of Sci., 1973-74; Master, Fac. of Royal Designers for Industry, 1973-75; Vice-President: Internat. Council of Socs of Industrial Design, 1957-59 (Pres., 1959-61); Modular Soc., 1965-; Nat. Union of Students (Hon.), 1967-; Member, Internat. Jury for: Compasso d'Oro, 1957 and 1964; Signe d'Or, 1958; Triennale, 1960; Delta d'Oro, 1970; Trustee, British Museum, 1968-. Medal of Soc. of Industrial Artists and Designers, 1965. CompIMechE, 1969. *Publications:* Public Interiors, 1959; (ed) Exhibition Design, 1950; contributions to: Physical Planning, 1945; Architects'

Year Book, 1945; The Practice of Design, 1946; Group Practice in Design, 1968; and architectural press. *Address:* 32 Aybrook Street, W1M 4BB; 160 Gloucester Road, SW7 Fife; St Michael's, 40 Buchanan Gardens, St Andrews, Fife. *Club:* Athenæum.
[Died 11 Aug. 1977.

BLACK, Sir Robert Andrew Stransham, 2nd Bt *cr* 1922; ED 1942; JP; *b* 17 Jan. 1902; *s* of 1st Bt and Ellen Cecilia, 2nd *d* of late Gen. W. P. La Touche, IA; *S* father, 1925; *m* 1927, Ivy, *o d* of late Brig.-Gen. Sir Samuel Wilson, GCMG, KCB, KBE; one *s*. *Educ:* Eton; Cambridge Univ. JP 1934, High Sheriff 1934, Berks. *Heir: s* Robert David Black [*b* 29 March 1929; *m* 1953, Rosemary Diana (marr. diss. 1972), *d* of Sir Rupert Hardy, 4th Bt; three *d*]. *Address:* Elvendon Priory, Goring, near Reading, Berks. *T:* Goring 160. *Club:* Bath.
[Died 14 Dec. 1979.

BLACKBURN, Lt-Col Sir Charles Bickerton, KCMG 1960; Kt, 1936; OBE 1919; BA, MD, ChM; FRCP, FRCPE (Hon.), FRACP, FRSM; Hon. LLD, Melbourne and Western Australia; Hon. DSc, Tasmania, Queensland and NSW; Physician engaged in consulting practice; Hon. Consulting Physician, Royal Prince Alfred Hospital, Sydney; Consulting Physician, Commonwealth Repatriation Department, New South Wales; Chancellor, Sydney University, 1941-64; Member of Council of New South Wales Branch of BMA, 1910-58; Vice-President, AMA, 1967; *b* Greenhithe, Kent, England, 1874; *s* of Rev. Thomas Blackburn and Jessie Anne Wood; *m* 1910, Vera Louise Le Patourel (*d* 1936); one *s* one *d*. *Educ:* St Peters Collegiate Sch., Adelaide; Adelaide Univ.; Univ. of Sydney. Engaged in practice of medicine since qualification in 1898 (retired); Member of Hon. Staff, Royal Prince Alfred Hosp., 1904-; Australian Army Medical Corps, 1916; Lieut-Col 14th Australian General Hospital, 1916-19 (despatches twice, OBE); AAMC, 1941, Lieut-Col (Home Service). *Publications:* various medical papers including Lister Oration, Adelaide, Bancroft Memorial Oration, Brisbane, Sir Richard Stawell Oration, Melbourne. *Recreations:* golf, trout, and game fishing. *Address:* 152/177 Bellevue Road, Double Bay, NSW 2028, Australia. *Clubs:* Union, University, Royal Sydney Golf (Sydney).
[Died 20 July 1972.

BLACKBURN, Sir Thomas, Kt 1968; Chairman, Beaverbrook Newspapers Ltd, 1955-68; Director, British Printing Ink Co. Ltd; Hon. Treasurer, Institute of Child Health. *Educ:* University College, Nottingham. Served European War, 1914-18: Seaforth Highlanders. FRSA; Hon. LLD New Brunswick, 1969. *Recreations:* cattle breeding, motor racing. *Address:* Beaverbrook Newspapers Ltd, 121 Fleet Street, EC4.
[Died 10 March 1974.

BLACKBURNE, Sir Kenneth (William), GCMG 1962 (KCMG 1952; CMG 1946); GBE 1962 (OBE 1939); *b* 12 Dec. 1907; *er s* of late Very Rev. H. W. Blackburne; *m* 1935, Bridget Senhouse Constant, *d* of James Mackay Wilson, DL, Currygrane, Co. Longford; one *s* one *d*. *Educ:* Marlborough; Clare Coll., Cambridge. Asst District Officer, Nigeria, 1930; Asst District Comr, Nazareth, Palestine, 1935; Actg District Comr, Galilee District, Palestine, May-Sept. 1938; Actg Asst Princ. and Princ., CO, 1938; Colonial Sec., The Gambia, 1941; Administrative Sec. to the Comptroller for Development and Welfare in the West Indies, 1943-47 (Actg Comptroller, 1944 and 1946); Dir of Information Services, CO, 1947-50; Governor and C-in-C of the Leeward Islands, 1950-56; Capt.-General and Governor-in-Chief, Jamaica, 1957-62; Governor-General of Jamaica, 1962; retd 1963. Chm., Sussex Church Campaign, 1963-70. KStJ, 1952. *Publication:* Lasting Legacy: a story of British Colonialism, 1976. *Recreations:* sailing, gardening. *Address:* Garvagh, Ballasalla, Isle of Man. *T:* Castletown (IoM) 3640.
[Died 4 Nov. 1980.

BLACKER, Carlos Paton, MC, GM; MA, MD (Oxford); FRCP; Hon. Consultant, Royal Bethlem Hospital and The Maudsley Hospital; *b* 8 Dec. 1895; *e s* of Carlos Blacker and Caroline Frost; *m* 1923, Helen Maud, *d* of Major A. J. Pilkington; one *s* two *d*. *Educ:* Eton. Coldstream Guards, 1915-19 (Captain, MC, despatches twice, wounded); Balliol, Oxford, 1919-22 (Distinction shortened course Natural Science, Zoology); Capt. OU Boxing Club, 1920 and 1922; represented University foil, 1920. Registrar, Dept Psychological Medicine, Guy's Hosp., 1927-36; Regimental MO 2nd Bn Coldstream Guards, 1940-42. Formerly: Hon. Sec., Population Investigation Cttee; Consultant, Ex-Services Mental Welfare Soc. Galton Medal 1959. *Publications:* Neurosis and the Mental Health Services; Eugenics: Galton and After; The Chances of Morbid Inheritance; Human Values in Psychological Medicine; Voluntary Sterilization; papers on psychological medicine, birth control, eugenics, and population. *Address:* Pasturewood, Shamley Green, Surrey. *T:* Bramley 3081. *Clubs:* United Oxford & Cambridge University; Vincent's (Oxford).
[Died 21 April 1975.

BLACKER, Maj.-Gen. George Patrick Demaine, CB 1957; CBE 1944; *b* 21 Feb. 1906; *s* of late Sir George Blacker, CBE, MD, FRCS, FRCP; *m* 1939, Marion, *d* of H. Kinahan, Belfast; one *s* one *d*. *Educ:* Cheltenham Coll.; RMA Woolwich. 2nd Lieut RA, 1926; NW Frontier of India, 1930-31; psc 1938; served BEF, France, 1939-40; Sicily and Italy, 1943-44; NW Europe, 1944-45; HQ SACSEA, 1945; DAG BAOR, 1947; Student US National War Coll., 1949-50; Chief of Staff, AA Command, 1952-54; Director, Mobile Defence Corps, 1955; Chief of Staff, HQ, UK Land Forces, 1956-59; retired 1959. Officer Legion of Merit (USA), 1945. *Recreation:* gardening. *Address:* Sandheys, Tekels Avenue, Camberley, Surrey. *T:* Camberley 63752. *Club:* Army and Navy.   *[Died 14 July 1974.*

BLACKETT, Baron *cr* 1969 (Life Peer), of Chelsea; **Patrick Maynard Stuart Blackett,** OM 1967; CH 1965; FRS 1933; MA; Professor Emeritus and Senior Research Fellow, Imperial College of Science and Technology, since 1965, Fellow since 1967; lately Scientific Adviser (part-time), Ministry of Technology; President of the Royal Society, 1965-70; *b* 18 Nov. 1897; *s* of Arthur Stuart Blackett; *m* 1924, Costanza Bayon; one *s* one *d*. *Educ:* RNC, Osborne and Dartmouth; Magdalene Coll., Cambridge. Served with RN, 1914-19. Fellow, King's Coll., Cambridge, 1923-33, Hon. Fellow, 1949. Prof. of Physics, Birkbeck Coll., 1933-37; Langworthy Prof. of Physics, Univ. of Manchester, 1937-53; Pro-Vice-Chancellor, Univ. of Manchester, 1950-52; Prof. of Physics, Imperial Coll. of Science and Technology, 1953-65; Dean, RCS, Imperial Coll., 1955-60; Pro-Rector, Imperial Coll., 1961-64. Member: Bd of National Res. Development Corp., 1949-64; Scientific Policy Cttee, European Organisation for Nuclear Res., 1954-58; Governing Bd, National Inst. for Res. in Nuclear Science, 1957-60; Council, DSIR, 1955-60 (Chm., Res. Grants Cttee, 1956-60); Council, Overseas Development Inst., 1960-; Council for Scientific Policy, 1955-60. Pres., British Assoc. for the Advancement of Science, 1957-58; Trustee, British Museum, 1963-65. Member: Berlin Acad. of Science, 1950; Soviet Acad. of Sciences, 1966. Corr. Mem., Acad. of Sciences, Inst. of France. Foreign Mem., Accademia Nazionale dei Lincei, Rome, 1965. Rede Lectr, Cambridge Univ., 1969. Hon. Fellow: Magdalene Coll., Cambridge, 1948; Indian Acad. of Sciences, 1949; Weizmann Inst. of Science, Israel, 1954; Inst. of Physics, 1962; Manchester Coll. of Technology, 1966; Fellow, Birkbeck Coll., University of London, 1970. Foreign Associate, Nat. Acad. of Sciences, Washington, 1966. Hon. DSc: New Delhi, Strasbourg, 1947; Reading, 1948; QUB, 1953; Leeds, Durham, Manchester, 1962; Oxon, 1963; Exeter, Bristol, York, Hull, Sussex, 1966; Chicago, 1969; Hon. ScD Cantab, 1954; Hon. LLD: Glasgow, 1955; Dalhousie (Halifax), 1960; St Andrews, 1962. Royal Medal of Royal Soc., 1940, Copley Medal, 1956; Nobel Prize for Physics, 1948. American Medal for Merit, 1946. *Publications:* scientific papers on nuclear and atomic physics, cosmic rays and rock magnetism; Rayons Cosmiques, 1934; Military and Political Consequences of Atomic Energy, 1948; Lectures on Rock Magnetism, 1956; Atomic Weapons and East-West Relations, 1956; Studies of War, 1962. *Address:* 806 Nelson House, Dolphin Square, SW1. *Club:* Athenæum. *[Died 13 July 1974.*

BLACKFORD, 2nd Baron *cr* 1935, of Compton Pauncefoot; **Col Glyn Keith Murray Mason,** CBE 1962; DSO 1916 and Bar, 1918; JP; Bt 1918; late 14th (King's) Hussars; a Deputy Speaker, House of Lords, 1949-66; Deputy Chairman, Midland Bank, 1960-67 (Director, 1932-67); Chairman, Guardian Assurance Co., 1950-67 (Hon. President, 1967-); a Lieutenant of the City of London; *b* 29 May 1887; *s* of 1st Baron Blackford and Edith (*d* 1958), *d* of late Alexander Murray Affleck of Dumfries; *S* father, 1947; *m* 1918, Grace Ellinor, 2nd *d* of N. Keen; one *s* (and one killed on Active Service). *Educ:* Eton; Sandhurst. Served in India until 1914; France, 1914-15 (wounded); Salonika, 1915-17 (DSO); Comd Dorset Yeo. in Palestine, 1917-18 (wounded, bar to DSO); Sector Comdr London Home Guard, 1940-44. MP (C) North Croydon, 1922-40. JP Somerset, 1946. *Heir: s* Hon. Keith Alexander Henry Mason, DFC [*b* 3 Feb. 1923; *m* 1957, Sarah Worthington-Evens (marr. diss. 1971), *er d* of late Sir (William) Shirley (Worthington) Worthington-Evans, 2nd Bt; one *s* one *d*]. *Address:* 17 Ennismore Gardens, SW7. *Clubs:* Brooks's, Hurlingham.   *[Died 31 Dec. 1972.*

BLACKFORD, 3rd Baron *cr* 1935, of Compton Pauncefoot; **Keith Alexander Henry Mason,** DFC 1943; Bt 1918; Chairman, City of London Brewery and Investment Trust Ltd, and other companies; *b* 3 Feb. 1923; *s* of 2nd Baron Blackford, CBE, DSO, and of Grace Ellinor, *d* of late Nimrod Keen; *S* father, 1972; *m* 1957, Sarah (marr. diss. 1971), *d* of Sir Shirley Worthington-Evans, 2nd Bt; one *s* one *d*. *Educ:* Eton. Served War of 1939-45 (DFC), N Africa and NW Europe; Wing Commander, RAF. Barrister, Middle Temple, 1947. Chairman: Bankers' Investment Trust Ltd; Hour Glass Investment Co. Ltd; Cedar Investment Trust Ltd; Dep. Chm., Rickmansworth and Uxbridge Water Co.; Director: Atlas Electric and General Trust Ltd; British and Foreign General Securities and Investment Trust Ltd; Altifund Ltd; Tragan Finance Co. Ltd. *Recreation:* shooting. *Heir: s* Hon. William Keith Mason, *b* 27 March 1962. *Address:* Third Floor, Winchester House, 77 London Wall, EC2N 1BH. *Clubs:* White's, Portland.   *[Died 21 April 1977.*

BLACKLOCK, Prof. John William Stewart, MD; FRCPGlas; retired as Professor of Pathology, University of London, at St Bartholomew's Hospital Medical College, 1962, now Emeritus. *Educ:* University of Glasgow. MB, ChB (Hons) 1920, MD (Hons) 1937, FRCPGlas 1933. Formerly: Prof. of Pathology, University of Glasgow; Pathologist, Royal Infirmary, and Royal Hospital for Sick Children, Glasgow. Member Path. Soc. Gt Britain; FRSM. *Publications:* contribs to medical jls, etc. *Address:* 18 Hill Head Road, Hill Head, Fareham, Hants. *T:* Stubbington 3063.   *[Died 7 April 1973.*

BLACKMAN, Prof. Geoffrey Emett, FRS 1959; Sibthorpian Professor of Rural Economy, University of Oxford, 1945-70, now Emeritus Professor, and Director of Agricultural Research Council Unit of Experimental Agronomy, 1950-70; *b* 17 April 1903; *er s* of late Prof. V. H. Blackman, FRS, and Edith Delta Emett; *m* 1931, Audrey Babette, *o d* of Richard Seligman and Hilda McDowell; no *c*. *Educ:* King's College Sch.; St John's Coll., Cambridge. Head of Botany Section, Jealott's Hill Agricultural Research Station, Warfield, Berks, 1927-35; Lecturer in Ecology, Imperial Coll. of Science and Technology, London, 1935-45; Dir, APV Holdings, 1937-73. Directed research under the aegis of Agricultural Research Council on introduction of new crops, principles of selective toxicity and development of selective herbicides, 1941-70. Delegate of the Clarendon Press, 1950-70; Secretary of the Biology War Cttee, 1942-46. Chairman Advisory Cttee enquiring into Production Development and Consumption Research, in Natural Rubber Industry, 1956. Member, Sub-Cttees, UGC: Technology, 1960-68, Biological Sciences, 1968-70; Mem., Nat. Acad. of Sciences Cttee on the effects of herbicides in Vietnam, 1971-74. President, Institute of Biology, 1963-64; Vice-President, Royal Society, 1967-68; Fellow, Imperial Coll. of Science and Technology, 1968-. *Publications:* papers in scientific jls on agricultural, ecological, physiological and statistical investigations. *Recreations:* gardening with the Ericaceae, collecting water-colours. *Address:* Woodcroft, Foxcombe Lane, Boars Hill, Oxford. *Club:* Athenæum.   *[Died 8 Feb. 1980.*

BLACKMORE, Col Lindsay William Saul, CB 1960; TD 1935; DL; Chairman, Territorial and Auxiliary Forces Association of Hampshire and the Isle of Wight, 1956-61; Member of T&AFA since 1930; *b* 24 May 1896; *s* of Major Charles Nelson Lindsay Blackmore, MBE, and Lucy Blackmore; *m* 1921, Katherine May Lacey; one *s* one *d* (and one *s* decd). *Educ:* Eastmans Naval Acad., Southsea; Churchers Coll., Petersfield. Gazetted 2nd Lieut 6th (DCO) Bn, The Hampshire Regt (TA), 1915; Bn and Machine-Gun Corps, 1915-19; Lt-Col i/c Bn, 1932-39; Bt-Col 1936; Southampton Home Guard, 1939-45. Lloyds Bank Ltd, 1912-56, Manager: Portswood, Southampton Branch, 1938-47; Albert Road, Southsea Branch, 1947-50; Kings Road and Clarendon Road, Southsea Branches, 1950-56. DL Hampshire, 1952. *Address:* 3 Solent Gate, Craneswater Park, Southsea, Hants PO4 0NJ. *T:* Portsmouth 36407. *Club:* Nuffield United Service Officers, Royal Naval and Royal Albert Yacht (Portsmouth).   *[Died 25 Sept. 1973.*

BLACKSHAW, Maurice Bantock, CBE 1953; MA Cantab; RIBA; retired Civil Servant, formerly Deputy Chief Architect, Ministry of Housing and Local Government; UK Technical Representative to Housing Committee of Economic Commission for Europe, 1947-62; Chairman, Association of Civil Service Art Clubs, 1947-64; *b* 1903; *s* of Rev. William Blackshaw; *m* 1929, Elena Mary, *d* of A. E. Pater. *Educ:* Rossall; Corpus Christi Coll., Cambridge. *Address:* The Coach House, Grovehurst, Pembury Road, Tunbridge Wells, Kent.
                                        [Died 10 Oct. 1975.

BLACKWELL, John Humphrey, CBE 1937; MC; *b* 25 April 1895; *e s* of John Thomas Blackwell, Architect, Kettering, Northants; *m* 1922, Jessie Pauline Luard Pears (*d* 1979); one *s* two *d*. *Educ:* Bedford Sch. Served European War (France), Bedfordshire Regt, 1914-18 (despatches, MC and Bar); Beds and Herts Regt, India, 1919-20; joined staff of Asiatic Petroleum Co. (India) Ltd, 1920; MLA (Central), 1935; Chairman, Karachi Chamber of Commerce, 1939-40 and 1943-44; Trustee, Karachi Port Trust. Director, Burmah-Shell (India) Ltd (Pakistan) Ltd, 1946-50; Resident Manager, Shell Training Centre, Teddington, Middlesex, 1951-54. *Address:* The Rafters, Drury Lane, Ridgewell, Essex CO9 4SJ. *T:* Ridgewell 681.
                                        [Died 27 Nov. 1979.

BLACKWELL, Richard, DSC 1944; Chairman: B. H. Blackwell Ltd, since 1969; Basil Blackwell, Publisher, since 1976; *b* 5 Jan. 1918; *s* of Sir Basil Blackwell, and late Marion Christine (*née* Soans); *m* 1942, Marguerite, *d* of late Major L. B. Holliday, Copgrove Hall, Yorks; two *s. Educ:* Winchester; New Coll., Oxford (MA). War-time service in Royal Navy, 1939-46 (Lieut (S) RNVR). Concerned with expansion of the family group in Britain, USA, Denmark, Holland and Austria, serving on boards of companies involved, 1946-. Fellow, St Cross Coll., Oxford, 1978. Hon. DLitt York (Toronto), 1971. *Recreations:* sailing, shooting, swimming. *Address:* Tubney House, near Abingdon, Oxon OX13 5QH. *T:* Frilford Heath 390444. *Clubs:* Athenæum; Leander (Henley-on-Thames). *[Died 26 Feb.* 1980.

BLACKWOOD, Sir Francis Elliot Temple, 6th Bt, *cr* 1814; Assistant Vice-President, retired, Crocker-Citizens National Bank, San Francisco; *b* 11 March 1901; *s* of late Henry Robert Temple Blackwood (*e s* of 4th Bt) and Rebecca Paffard (she *m* 2nd, 1930, Walter G. C. Stevenson), *d* of J. Scullard; *S* brother, 1948; *m* 1921, Lily M. *d* of H. F. MacGougan. *Heir: cousin,* Francis George Blackwood [*b* 10 May 1916; *m* 1941, Margaret, *d* of Hector Kirkpatrick, Lindfield, NSW; two *s* one *d*]. *Address:* 114-1050 West Capitol Avenue, West Sacramento, Calif 95691, USA. *[Died 2 March* 1979.

BLADIN, Air Vice-Marshal Francis Masson, CB 1950; CBE 1943; *b* 26 Aug. 1898; *s* of F. W. Bladin, Melbourne, Victoria; *m* 1927, Patricia Mary (decd), *d* of P. J. Magennis, Jeir Station, Yass, NSW; one *s* two *d. Educ:* Melbourne; RMC, Duntroon. Attached Royal Field Artillery, 1920-22; joined Royal Australian Air Force, 1923; served War of 1939-45, in Pacific and North-West Europe (despatches, CBE, American Silver Star); AOC North Australia, 1942; SASO, 38 Group, Royal Air Force, 1943-44; Chief of Staff, British Commonwealth Occupation Forces, Japan, 1946-47; Air Member for Personnel, RAAF, 1949-53, retired 1953. Hon. National Treasurer, Returned Servicemen's League of Australia, 1951-69. *Address:* 1 Dale Street, Deepdene, Vic. 3103, Australia.
[Died 2 Feb. 1978.

BLAIKLEY, John Barnard, CBE 1967; FRCS, FRCOG; Consultant Emeritus since 1971, Obstetric and Gynæcological Surgeon, 1941-71, and Medical Superintendent, 1958-67, Guy's Hospital; Consultant Emeritus since 1971, Surgeon, 1936-71, Chelsea Hospital for Women; Consultant Emeritus since 1971, Gynæcological Surgeon, 1944-71, Royal Marsden Hospital; Hon. Consultant: in Gynæcology, to Queen Alexandra Military Hospital, Millbank, 1954-71; in Obstetrics and Gynæcology, to the Army, 1969-71, Consultant Emeritus since 1972; *b* 21 Sept. 1906; *s* of late Alex. J. Blaikley; *m* 1932, Vivien Maude Johnson; two *s. Educ:* Christ's Coll., Finchley; Guy's Hospital. LRCP, MRCS 1928; MB, BS, London, 1932; FRCS 1931; MRCOG 1933; FRCOG 1944. Sometime Examiner in Obstetrics and Gynæcology for Universities of Oxford, London, Birmingham, Bristol, and for RCOG (Vice-Pres., 1964-67); Member Council and Chairman of Examination Cttee, RCOG, 1955-58; Sims-Black Travelling Prof., RCOG, 1958. Joseph Price Orator, American Assoc. Obstetricians and Gynæcologists, 1964. Member Gynæcological Visiting Soc. of Great Britain. Hon. Member: American Gynæcological Club; American Assoc. of Obstetricians and Gynæcologists; Pres., Section of Obstetrics and Gynæcology, Royal Soc. of Medicine, 1964-65, Hon. Mem., 1974. Various appts at Guy's Hosp.; Pathologist, Chelsea Hosp. for Women, 1933. Mem. Scientific Adv. and Pathology Cttees, RCOG, 1959-67. Governor: Guy's Hosp. Med. Sch., 1963-71; Guy's Hosp., 1969-72. *Publications:* contributor to British Gynæcological Practice (3rd edn), 1963; various articles in medical jls. *Recreations:* golf, gardening, etc. *Address:* 8 Tollgate Drive, College Road, Dulwich SE21 7LS. *T:* 01-693 7901. *Club:* Royal Automobile. *[Died 21 Oct.* 1975.

BLAIR, David, CBE 1964; Premier Dancer, Royal Ballet at Covent Garden, 1955-73; remains connected with Royal Ballet, teaching the company, from 1973; *b* 27 July 1932; *m* 1957, Maryon Lane; twin *d. Educ:* Trinity Sch., Halifax; Royal Ballet Sch. Joined Sadler's Wells Theatre Ballet, 1948, and became principal dancer of that company, 1950; toured USA, Canada, Holland, Belgium, Germany and Rhodesia; created rôle of Capt. Belaye in Pineapple Poll and Harlequin in Harlequin in April; danced all leading classical and character rôles in repertoire. Joined Royal Ballet at Covent Garden, 1953. Has danced all classical and many leading character rôles; created rôles include: the Prince in The Prince of the Pagodas; Colas in Frederick Ashton's production of La Fille Mal Gardée. Danced as guest artist at La Scala, Milan, May 1957. Has appeared on TV in USA and England. Toured Australia with Royal Ballet, 1958; danced in: Turkey and Spain, 1959; Leningrad, Moscow, USA and Canada, 1961; Australia, New Zealand, Manila and Hong Kong, 1962; USA, 1963. Principal Productions for Amer. Ballet Theatre, NY: Swan Lake, 1967; Giselle, 1968; Sleeping Beauty. Directed and choreographed Giselle, Hong Kong, 1973 (first full length ballet in Colony). Member: Controlling Body, Royal Acad. of Dancing; Council, British Equity; Executive, British Theatre Museum; Artistic Dir for Ballet, Internat. Youth Festival, Aberdeen and London, 1973-. Directed film, Giselle, 1968-69. *Address:* 19 Holland Park Road, Kensington, W14.
[Died 1 April 1976.

BLAIR, Oliver Robin; HM Diplomatic Service; Head of Consular Department, Foreign and Commonwealth Office, since 1973; *b* 7 Oct. 1925; *s* of late Lt-Col A. C. Jaffe and late Frances Evelyn Swann (*née* Harbord); changed surname to Blair 1935; *m* 1964, Brigid Emily Philomena, *d* of late Lt-Col B. L. Franklin; one *s* one *d. Educ:* Winchester; King's Coll., Cambridge. Called to Bar, Middle Temple, 1959. Served War, RN (Petty Officer) June 1944; Coldstream Guards (Lieut), 1944-47. HM Oversea Civil Service, Ghana (retd as Administrative Officer Class II), 1949-58. Entered Commonwealth Relations Office, 1959; First Sec.: Calcutta, 1960; Karachi, 1962; Commonwealth Office, 1965; Budapest (sometime Chargé d'Affaires), 1968-71; Counsellor: Senior Officers' War Course, Greenwich, 1972; FCO, 1972. *Recreations:* gardening, tennis, skiing, shooting. *Address:* Wellclose House, Bradford-on-Avon, Wiltshire. *T:* Bradford-on-Avon 3121; 2 Hamston House, Kensington Court Place, W8. *T:* 01-937 1094. *Club:* United Oxford & Cambridge University.
[Died 24 Nov. 1975.

BLAIR, Col Sir Patrick James, KBE 1958 (CBE 1943); DSO 1919; TD; DL; *b* 1891; 2nd *s* of Hugh Blair, CA Edinburgh; *m* 1930, Dorothy Leslie, OBE (*d* 1966), *er d* of late Lt-Col J. Leslie Findlay. *Educ:* Edinburgh Acad.; Balliol Coll., Oxford (MA). Served European War, 1914-19 (France and Belgium, 1915-19), with 9th (Highrs) Bn The Royal Scots, as Bde Major 44th Inf. Bde, and temp. Lieut-Col commanding 13th (Scottish Horse) Bn the Black Watch, 1918; Lieut-Col comdg 9th and 7th/9th Bns (Highrs) The Royal Scots, 1920-27 (DSO, French Croix de Guerre, despatches twice); Bt Col 1924; Col (TA), 1924; Hon. Col 7th/9th (Highrs) Bn The Royal Scots, 1945-55. Mem. of Queen's Body Guard for Scotland, Royal Company of Archers. Admitted to Faculty of Advocates, 1921; Political Sec. to Chm. of Unionist Party in Scotland, 1922-60. *Address:* 9 Magdala Crescent, Edinburgh. *Club:* New (Edinburgh).
[Died 10 Dec. 1972.

BLAKE, Lt-Col Arthur O'Brien ffrench, TD; DL; *b* 22 Feb. 1879; *e s* of late Rev. Robert ffrench Blake of Staple Rectory, Canterbury, Kent and Kilnock, Co. Mayo; *m* 1910, Laura Iris, *d* of late C. H. Walker of Muckridge, Co. Cork; one *s* three *d. Educ:* Eton; Christ Church, Oxford. Master of West Street Harriers, 1905-10 (Jt Master, 1902-03); Jt Master of Wilton Hounds, 1922-26; Jt Master of the Grove Hounds, 1926-30; Master of the East Kent Hounds, 1930-32 (Jt Master, 1932-33); Master of South Shropshire Hounds, 1938-46. Served European War in Gallipoli, Egypt, Palestine, Syria, 1914-19. DL Kent, 1955. *Recreations:* hunting, cricket, shooting. *Address:* 5 South Close, The Precincts, Canterbury, Kent. *T:* Canterbury 62424. *Clubs:* MCC; Free Foresters. *[Died 28 Oct.* 1973.

BLAKE, Comdr Sir Cuthbert Patrick, 6th Bt *cr* 1772, of Langham; DSO 1916; late RN; *b* 2 Jan. 1885; *o s* of 5th Bt and Emma Gertrude (*d* 1924), *o d* of late T. P. Dawson; *S* father, 1930; *m* 1916, Florence Wilhelmina (*d* 1958), *d* of late Engr-Capt. W. R. Apps, MVO; one *d.* Served European War, including Battle of Jutland (despatches, DSO, Russian Order of St Anne); retired list, 1928; recalled, 1939-45. *Heir:* none. *Address:* Poplar House, Beyton, Bury St Edmunds, Suffolk.
[Died 27 June 1975 (*ext*).

BLAKE, Maj.-Gen. Gilbert Alan, CB 1944; MB; *b* 9 Jan. 1887; *s* of Edgar Frederick Blake, Grove Park, Lee, SE; *m* 1925, Margaret Brooke, *d* of H. A. Eastwood, Fleet, Hants. *Educ:* Eastbourne Coll.; Guy's Hospital. European War, 1914-18, Indian Frontier, Afghanistan, East Persia. Service: Egypt, Soudan and India; Norway, 1940. Retired, 1946. *Address:* Field House, Hartley Wintney, Hants. *T:* 2512. *[Died 7 Aug.* 1971.

BLAKE, Nicholas; see Day-Lewis, Cecil.

BLAKELEY, Hon. Arthur; retired; *b* Gilberton, S Australia, 3 July 1886; *s* of Simeon Blakeley; *m* 1914, Ruby Pauline McCarroll; two *s* two *d. Educ:* North Broken Hill Convent Sch. Organiser, Sec., Gen. Pres., Australian Workers' Union, 1910-21; Federal mem. for Darling, 1917-34; Sec. to Federal Parliamentary Labour Party, 1920-28 and 1932-34; Dep. Leader of Federal Parliamentary Labour Party, 1928-29; Minister for Home Affairs, Commonwealth of Australia, 1929-31;

Commonwealth Arbitration Inspector, 1935-40; Senior Commonwealth Arbitration Inspector, 1940-47; Conciliation Comr, 1941-52, retired. Mem. Cttee Public Works, 1922-25. *Recreations:* fishing, billiards, reading. *Address:* c/o Oranje Private Hospital, 1565 Malvern Road, Glen Iris, Victoria 3146, Australia. *Club:* Commercial Travellers of Australia.
[*Died 27 June 1972.*

BLAKEMAN, Joan, (Mrs L. T. Blakeman); *see* Woodward, Joan.

BLAKEMAN, Leslie Thompson, CBE 1968; Member of Commission on Industrial Relations, 1969-74; *b* 11 July 1904; *m* 1951, (Dorothy) Joan Woodward (*d* 1971); one *d* of former marriage. *Educ:* Wallasey Grammar School. Senior Labour Manager, Min. of Supply, 1941-52; Director of Labour Relations, Ford Motor Co, 1952-69. Fellow, Inst. of Personnel Management; President, 1965-67. Member: SE Economic Planning Council, 1966-69; Race Relations Bd, 1969-. Governor, SE Essex Technical Coll., 1959-69. *Recreations:* music, photography, golf. *Address:* Fishponds Farm, Brook, Ashford, Kent. *T:* Wye 812514; 71 Roebuck House, Stag Place, SW1. *T:* 01-828 6203. *Club:* Junior Carlton.
[*Died 11 April 1975.*

BLAKER, Sir Reginald, 2nd Bt *cr* 1919; TD 1942; *b* 27 April 1900; *s* of 1st Bt and Lily (she *m* 2nd, 1928, Lieut Arthur D. Cutts), *d* of Sam. Cowell; *S* father, 1926; *m* 1930, Sheila Kellas, 3rd *d* of Dr Alexander Cran, Little Court, Merrow; one *s* one *d.* *Educ:* Charterhouse. MP (U) Spelthorne Div. of Middx, 1931-45. *Heir: s* John Blaker [*b* 22 March 1935; *m* 1st, 1960, Catherine Ann (marr. diss. 1965), *o d* of late F. J. Thorold, Tye Farm, Hartfield, Sussex; 2nd, 1968, Elizabeth Katherine, *d* of late Col John Tinsley Russell, DSO]. *Address:* Knowles, Ardingly, Sussex. *T:* Ardingly 217.   [*Died 3 Jan. 1975.*

BLAKISTON, Sir Arthur Frederick, 7th Bt *cr* 1763; MC; farmer; *b* 16 June 1892; *s* of late F. T. Blakiston, *y b* of 5th Bt, and Mrs Blakiston, Aspley Guise, Bucks; *S* uncle, 1941; *m* 1915, May Walton (marr. diss. 1954), *d* of Frederick Walton Fuller, West Didsbury, Manchester; *m* 1954, Ann Hope, *yr d* of Purcell Jeans, Cortington Grange, Warminster, Wilts. *Educ:* Bedford Sch.; Trent Coll.; Emmanuel Coll., Cambridge. Served European War, 1914-18, King Edward's Horse and RFA (MC). *Recreation:* fox-hunting. *Heir: kinsman* Arthur Norman Hunter Blakiston [*b* 26 April 1899; *m* 1962, Mary Ferguson, *d* of late A. E. Gillingham, NZ; two *s*]. *Address:* Higher Wyke Farm, Wyke Road, Trowbridge, Wilts.   [*Died 31 Jan. 1974.*

BLAKISTON, Sir (Arthur) Norman (Hunter), 8th Bt *cr* 1763; solicitor; *b* 26 April 1899; *s* of Reginald Norman Blakiston (*d* 1946) (*g s* of 3rd Bt) and Annie Constance (*d* 1955), *d* of late William Henry Hunter; *S* kinsman, Sir Arthur Frederick Blakiston, 7th Bt, MC, 1974; *m* 1962, Mary Ferguson, *d* of late Alfred Ernest Gillingham, Cave, S Canterbury, NZ; two *s.* *Educ:* Christ's Coll., Christchurch, NZ; Victoria Univ., Wellington, NZ. Barrister and solicitor, Supreme Court of NZ, 1921-. *Recreations:* general. *Heir: s* Ferguson Arthur James Blakiston, *b* 19 Feb. 1963. *Address:* 28 McKenzie Street (or Box 55), Geraldine, South Canterbury, New Zealand. *T:* 160 Geraldine.   [*Died 1977.*

BLAND, Sir (George) Nevile (Maltby), KCMG 1947 (CMG 1927); KCVO 1937; Comdr Order of Leopold, 1930; Kt Grand Cross Order of Orange-Nassau, 1950; King of Arms, Order of St Michael and St George, 1952-61; *b* 6 Dec. 1886; *y s* of late Francis Maltby Bland, DL, JP, Inglethorpe Manor, Emneth, Norfolk; *m* 1919, Portia (*d* 1968), *y d* of late Canon Edward Bickersteth Ottley; one *s* (and one *s* killed in action, 1943, one *d* decd). *Educ:* Eton; King's Coll., Cambridge. Rowed in Eton eight, 1905. Entered FO, 1911; served on Peace Delegation in Paris, 1919; Private Sec. to Lord Hardinge of Penshurst, Under-Sec. of State for Foreign Affairs, 1919; to Sir Eyre Crowe, 1920; to Sir William Tyrrell, 1925; to Sir Ronald Lindsay, 1928; to Sir Robert Vansittart, 1930; Counsellor of Embassy, Brussels, 1930-35; Counsellor in FO, 1935-38; Envoy Extraordinary and Minister Plenipotentiary to Netherlands, 1938-42, Ambassador, 1942-48; Special Ambassador to Pres. of Malagasy Republic, July 1960; reapptd to Foreign Service, as Special Representative of Sec. of State, Nov. 1960-70. Chairman: Anglo-Netherlands Soc., 1949-63; Children's Aid Soc., 1952-67; Royal Surgical Aid Society, 1959-69. Consultant, Abbott Laboratories (England). Vice-Pres., Amateur Orchestral Soc. *Publication:* (ed) 4th edn of Satow's Guide to Diplomatic Practice. *Address:* 164 Ebury Street, SW1. *Clubs:* United Oxford & Cambridge University; Leander; Royal Fowey Yacht.   [*Died 19 Aug. 1972.*

BLAND, Lieut-Col John Edward Michael, OBE 1945; DL; JP; late Scots Guards; *b* 25 Oct. 1899; *s* of late Francis Lawrence

Bland, JP, Copdock, near Ipswich, and Mabel Barbara Gooch, Bracknell; *m* 1933, Nancy Mary, *d* of late Major H. Bull, RHA; two *s* one *d* (and one *s* decd). *Educ:* Cheam Sch.; Eton Coll. Scots Guards, 1918-47: Adjt 2nd Bn (China), 1927-29; Regimental Adjt, 1932-35; Comd Holding Bn, 1942-43. Served War, 1939-45, in UK, 1939-43, in Italy, 1944-45; retired 1947. Asst Sec., Suffolk Territorial Assoc., 1948-52; Comdt, Suffolk Army Cadet Force, 1952-55; Area Comr, St John Ambulance Brigade, 1954-60. Member: East Suffolk CC, 1951-67; Samford RDC. High Sheriff of Suffolk, 1958; DL, Suffolk, 1958; JP, 1949. OStJ. *Recreations:* shooting, boating, tennis. *Address:* Little Hall, Stutton, near Ipswich. *T:* Holbrook 357. *Clubs:* Guards; County (Ipswich).   [*Died 14 Feb. 1976.*

BLAND, Sir Nevile; *see* Bland, Sir G. N. M.

BLEDISLOE, 2nd Viscount, *cr* 1935; **Benjamin Ludlow Bathurst,** QC 1952; *b* 2 Oct. 1899; *er s* of 1st Viscount Bledisloe, PC, GCMG, KBE, and Hon. Bertha Susan Lopes (*d* 1926), *y d* of 1st Baron Ludlow, PC; *S* father 1958; *m* 1933, Joan Isobel Krishaber; two *s.* *Educ:* Eton; Magdalen Coll., Oxford (BA). Served European War, 1914-18, 2nd Lieut RA. Called to Bar, Inner Temple, 1927. War of 1939-45: Squadron Leader, RAF, 1939-40; Senior Comdr, ATA, 1940-45. Bencher, Lincoln's Inn, 1956. Late Chm., Plant Variety Rights Tribunal; Vice-President: West London Flying Club; British Light Aviation Centre. Past-Pres., St Moritz Tobogganing Club; Gen. Council and Register of Osteopaths; Verderer of Forest of Dean. *Recreations:* mountaineering, ski-ing, tobogganing, shooting, flying, rowing, gardening, photography. *Heir: s* Hon. Christopher Hiley Ludlow Bathurst, QC. *Address:* 14 Mulberry Walk, SW3. *T:* 01-352 7533; 4 Stone Buildings, Lincoln's Inn, WC2. *T:* 01-242 5524; Lydney Park, Glos. *T:* Lydney 2538. *Clubs:* Garrick, Green Room, Portland, Alpine, Alpine Ski; Vincent's (Oxford); Leander (Henley-on-Thames); West London Aero (White Waltham).   [*Died 17 Sept. 1979.*

BLEE, David, CBE 1955; FCIT; retired 1961; *b* 7 Aug. 1899; *m* 1926, Catharine Rosetta Vaughan (*d* 1972); one *s.* Served European War, 1917-19, France, Belgium, Germany. Apptd Chief Goods Manager, GWR, 1946; Mem. of Railway Executive, 1947-53; Chief of Commercial Services, British Transport Commission, 1953-55; becoming Traffic Adviser, 1955; Gen. Manager of the London Midland Region of British Railways, 1956-61. Col, Eng. & Rly Staff Corps RE (TA). Former Mem. Council and Vice-Pres., Institute of Transport. Director: Atlantic Steam Navigation Co.; Birmingham & Midland Motor Omnibus Co. Member: Permanent Commn of Internat. Rly Congress Assoc.; Internat. Chamber of Commerce. *Publications:* papers and lectures on transport subjects. *Recreations:* walking, travel. *Address:* 1 Hull Place, Sholden, near Deal, Kent. *T:* Deal 5260. [*Died 26 Sept. 1979.*

BLEGEN, Carl William; Professor of Classical Archæology, University of Cincinnati, from 1927 (and Head of Department of Classics, 1950-57), Emeritus, since 1957, Distinguished Service Professor Emeritus, 1969; Fellow of Graduate School of Arts and Sciences; *b* 27 Jan. 1887; *s* of Prof. John H. Blegen and Anna B. (*née* Olsen); *m* 1924, Elizabeth Denny (*d* 1966), *d* of William L. and Flora McKnight Pierce, Englewood, NJ. *Educ:* Augsburg Seminary; University of Minn; Yale Univ.; Amer. Sch. of Classical Studies, Athens. Sec., Amer. Sch. of Classical Studies, Athens, 1913-20; Asst Dir, 1920-26; Actg Dir, 1926-27; Dir, 1948-49; Field Dir, Archeol Expedn of University of Cincinnati, 1932-; Excavations at Troy, 1932-38, at ancient PYlos, 1939, 1952-. With office of Strategic Services, Washington, 1942-45; Cultural Relations Attaché, Amer. Embassy, Athens, 1945-46. Hon. Degrees: MA Yale, 1927; PhD Oslo, 1951; Thessaloniki, 1951; DLitt Oxford, 1957; LLD Cincinnati, 1958; DHL, Hebrew Union Coll., Jewish Inst. of Religion, 1963; LittD Cambridge, 1963; Doctorate, Univ. of Athens, 1963. Fellow Amer. Academy of Arts and Sciences; Corr. Fellow British Acad.; Member: Royal Society of Letters of Lund; Swedish Royal Acad. of Letters, History and Antiquities (Stockholm); Acad. of Science and Letters, Oslo; Arch. Soc. of Athens; Amer. Philosoph. Soc.; Hon. Mem. Soc. for Promotion of Hellenic Studies. Kenyon Medal, British Academy, 1963. First Gold Medal of Archæological Inst. of America, 1965; Gold Medal of the Soc. of Antiquaries of London. 1966; Gold Medal, Cincinnati Univ., 1969. *Publications:* Korakou, 1921; Zygouries, 1927; Acrocorinth (with others), 1934; Prosymna (with Elizabeth Blegen), 1937; Troy, Vols I-IV (with others), 1950, 1951, 1953, 1958; Troy and the Trojans, 1963; The Palace of Nestor at Pylos, Vol. I (with Marion Rawson), 1966. *Recreations:* travel and reading. *Address:* 9 Plutarch Street, Athens 139, Greece; Department of Classics, University of Cincinnati, Cincinnati 21, Ohio, USA. *Clubs:* University; Literary (Cincinnati); Yale (NY); Cosmos (Washington).
[*Died 24 Aug. 1971.*

BLENKINSOP, Arthur; *b* 30 June 1911; *s* of John Matthewson Blenkinsop and Anne Douglas Rowell; *m* 1939, Mary Norman Harrold; two *s* one *d. Educ:* Newcastle Royal Grammar Sch. MP (Lab) for Newcastle upon Tyne East, 1945-59; MP (Lab) South Shields, 1964-79; Parly Sec., Min. of Health, 1949-51; former Mem., Chairmen's Panel, House of Commons; former Chm., Shipping Gp, Parly Lab Party. Vice-President, Health Inspectors Assoc.; Delegate to Council of Europe, 1966-70 (Pres. Social Commission, 1968-70). Member, Exec. Cttee, National Trust; Chm., Council, Town and Country Planning Assoc. *Recreations:* walking and reading. *Address:* 233 Wingrove Road, Newcastle upon Tyne NE4 9DD. *T:* Newcastle 35187.   *[Died* 23 *Sept.* 1979.

BLIGH, Sir Edward Clare, Kt 1949; Chief Officer of Welfare Department, London County Council, 1932-51; *b* 1887; *s* of James Blight, Doncaster; *m* 1915, Patricia Greville (*d* 1941); one *s* (and two *s* decd). *Educ:* Doncaster; Balliol Coll., Oxford. Resident, Toynbee Hall; served in 8th Bn London Regt (Captain); Assistant General Inspector, Ministry of Health. *Address:* Pinehurst, Broad Way, Fairlight, Sussex. *T:* Pett 2123.
[Died 27 *Dec.* 1976.

BLISS, Sir Arthur, CH 1971; KCVO 1969; Kt 1950; composer; Master of the Queen's Musick since 1953; *b* London, 2 Aug. 1891; *m* 1925, Gertrude Hoffmann, Santa Barbara, California; two *d. Educ:* Rugby; Pembroke Coll., Cambridge (BA, MusBac). Served European War (wounded), despatches; Prof. of Music, University of California, 1940; Asst Overseas Music Director, BBC, 1941-42; Director of Music, BBC, 1942-44; Chairman Music Cttee, British Council, 1946-50; President: Western Orchestral Soc. Ltd, 1954-; Performing Right Soc., 1954-; Internat. Confederation of Authors' and Composers' Societies, 1964-; Hon. President, London Symphony Orchestra, 1956-. Hon. MusD: Edinburgh; London; Cambridge; Lancaster; Hon. DMus Bristol; Hon. LLD Glasgow; Hon. DFA Westminster Coll., Princeton, USA. Hon. FRCM, Hon. RAM; Hon. FTCL; FRCO; Hon. Fellow, Pembroke Coll., Cambridge, 1953; Hon. Freeman Worshipful Company of Musicians, 1954. Gold Medal, Royal Philharmonic Society, 1963. Commander of the Order of Leopold II. *Compositions:* Madam Noy, 1918; Rhapsody, 1919; Rout, 1920; Conversations, 1920; Concerto, 1920; Two Studies for Orchestra, 1920; Mêlée Fantasque for Orchestra, 1920; Two Nursery Rhymes, 1920; Music to the Tempest, 1921; A Colour Symphony, 1922; Introduction and Allegro for Orchestra, 1926; Hymn to Apollo, 1927; Pastoral; Oboe Quintet; Morning Heroes, 1930; Clarinet Quintet, 1932; Viola Sonata, 1933; Film Music to Things to Come, 1935; Music for Strings, 1935; Ballet, Checkmate, 1937; Film Music to Conquest of the Air; Piano Concerto, 1939; String Quartet, 1941; Ballet, Miracle in the Gorbals, 1944; Film Music to Men of Two Worlds, 1945; Ballet, Adam Zero, 1946; Opera, The Olympians, 1948; Film Music to Christopher Columbus, 1949; 2nd String Quartet, 1950; Scena, The Enchantress; Piano Sonata, 1951; Film Music to The Beggar's Opera, 1953; Song of Welcome, 1954; Violin Concerto, 1955; Meditations on a Theme of John Blow, 1955; Overture 'Edinburgh', 1956; Discourse for Orchestra, 1957; Ballet, The Lady of Shalott, 1958; Television Opera, Tobias and the Angel, 1960; Cantata, The Beatitudes, 1962; A Knot of Riddles, 1963; Golden Cantata, 1964; (song cycle) Angels of the Mind, 1969; (cantata) The World is Charged, 1969; Cello Concerto, 1970; Variations for Orchestra, 1973. *Publication:* As I Remember, 1970. *Address:* 8 The Lane, Marlborough Place, NW8. *Clubs:* Athenæum (elected under rule 2), Garrick.   *[Died* 27 *March* 1975.

BLIVEN, Bruce; editor and author; *b* Emmetsburg, Iowa, 27 July 1889; *s* of Charles F. and Lilla C. Bliven; *m* 1913, Rose F. Emery; one *s. Educ:* public schools in Emmetsburg; Stanford Univ. Editorial staff, San Francisco Bulletin, 1909-12; magazine contributor and advertising writer, 1912-14; Director, Dept of Journalism, University of Southern California, 1914-16; editorial staff, Printer's Ink Magazine, 1916-18; Member: Editorial Board, New York Globe, 1919-23; Editorial Board, New Republic, 1923-54; New York correspondent Manchester Guardian, 1927-47; Lecturer in Communication and Journalism, Stanford Univ., 1957-; Trustee, Twentieth Century Fund, 1922-57. *Publications:* The Men Who Make the Future, 1942; Preview for Tomorrow: The Unfinished Business of Science, 1953; The World Changers, 1965; Five Million Words Later (autobiog.), 1970; A Mirror for Greatness, 1975. Edited: What the Informed Citizen Needs to Know, 1945; Twentieth Century Unlimited, 1950. Contributor to about 20 American magazines. *Recreations:* reading, music, the theatre. *Address:* Kingscote Gardens, Lagunita Drive, Stanford, California 94305, USA.   *[Died* 27 *May* 1977.

BLOCK, Brig. Allen Prichard, CB 1945; CBE 1944; DSO 1943; retired; *b* 13 Jan. 1899, British; *m* 1924, Loveday Glasgow; one *s* one *d. Educ:* Repton; Royal Military College, Sandhurst. Served European War, France, May-Nov. 1918; India, 1919-27 and 1938-39; Service NWFP, India, 1920-21; Home Service, 1927-38; War of 1939-45, CO Queen's Bn, 1940-43; Brig., 139 Infantry Bde, 1943-45; Service North Africa with 8th Army, Italy and Greece (DSO, CBE, CB); retired May 1953. *Address:* Creek Cottage, 41 Beach Road, Emsworth, Hants. *T:* Emsworth 2599. *Club:* Army and Navy.   *[Died* 22 *May* 1973.

BLOCK, His Honour Commander Leslie Kenneth Allen, DSC 1945; DL; Commissioner, Central Criminal Court, 1955-69; *b* 9 Aug. 1906; *s* of Harry Allen Block, Esher; *m* 1930, Maud Marion (*née* Hicks) (*d* 1980); two *s* one *d. Educ:* RN Colleges Osborne and Dartmouth. Joined Royal Navy, 1920; Emergency List, RN, 1933; called to Bar, Inner Temple, 1936; served War of 1939-45; Navigating Officer, HMS Hermes, 1939-42; Rosyth Escort Force, 1942-43; HMS Duke of York, 1943-44; Fleet Navigating Officer, Home Fleet, 1944-45; Commander, 1945. Chairman Agricultural Land Tribunal, SE Area, 1948-54; Asst Judge of Mayor's and City of London Court, 1954-69; Dep. Chm., 1955-67, Chm., 1967-71, W Sussex QS. Freeman, City of London; Liveryman, Tallowchandlers Co. (Master, 1971-72). JP 1947, DL 1960, Sussex. *Address:* Shiprods, Henfield, West Sussex. *T:* Henfield 2004.   *[Died* 13 *Sept.* 1980.

BLODGET, Mrs A. S.; *see* Skinner, Cornelia O.

BLOMFIELD, Douglas John, CIE 1941; ACGI; Regional Technical Adviser, Home Office, 1941-52; *b* 20 Dec. 1885; *s* of Charles Edward Blomfield; *m* 1915, Coralie (*d* 1967), *d* of F. H. Tucker, Indian Police; one *s* one *d. Educ:* St Dunstan's Coll.; City and Guilds Central Technical Coll. Joined Indian Service of Engineers, 1908; retired as Chief Engineer (Communications and Works Branch), Bengal, 1940. *Address:* c/o Grindlay's Bank Ltd, 13 St James's Square, SW1.   *[Died* 6 *Feb.* 1979.

BLOMFIELD, Maj.-Gen. Valentine, CB 1947; DSO 1944; *b* 29 March 1898; *e s* of late Frederick Charles Blomfield; *m* 1925, Gladys Edith, *d* of late Col A. M. Lang, CB, RE; three *s. Educ:* Rugby; RMC, Sandhurst. Commissioned Border Regt, 1916; served in France, 1916-18 (despatches); NWF India, 1922-23; graduated Staff Coll., Camberley; served in France, 1939-40 (despatches) and 1944 (DSO). Director of Prisoners of War, Aug. 1945-47; Director of Personal Services, War Office, 1947-50; Commander, North-West District and 42nd (Lancs) Div., TA, 1950-53; retired pay, 1954. Col The Border Regt, 1954-59; Col The King's Own Royal Border Regt, 1959-61. *Address:* c/o Lloyds Bank Ltd, 6 Pall Mall, SW1. *Club:* Naval and Military.
[Died 11 *Jan.* 1980.

BLOOD, Brig. William Edmund Robarts, CBE 1943; MC 1918; late RE; *b* 20 Feb. 1897; *s* of late Col William Persse Blood, Shankill, Co. Dublin, and Marienne Frances Robarts; *m* 1st, 1919, Eva Gwendoline Harrison; one *s*; 2nd, 1945, Janet, *d* of Col W. W. Edwards, US Army. *Educ:* Imperial Service Coll.; RMA, Woolwich. 2nd Lieut, RE, 1915; Capt., 1917; retired 1925; Director, William Blood Ltd, Building and Civil Engineering Contractors; recalled to military service, Sept. 1939-45. Croix de Guerre (France), 1917; Legion of Merit (USA), 1945. *Address:* 39 Hans Place, SW1. *T:* 01-584 0170.
[Died 14 *March* 1976.

BLOOD, Brig. William Holcroft, MVO 1922; Indian Army (retired); *b* 29 May 1887; *s* of late John Blood, Ballykilty, Quin, Co. Clare, Ireland; *m* 1st, 1920, Ierne Cecilia (against whom he obtained a divorce, 1935), *d* of late Capt. H. Montgomery Hawkins, Holme Lodge, Dorchester, Dorset; one *s* one *d*; 2nd, 1936, Helen, widow of Col J. D. Crawford, Indian Army. *Educ:* Clifton Coll. Indian Army, 1905; NW Frontier, India, 1915; European War, Mesopotamia (despatches); Afghan War, 1919; Bt Major, 1920; Bt Lieut-Col 1931; Commandant QVO Corps of Guides (Cavalry), 1932-36. Re-employed 1940-42, Administrative Comdt Delhi Area; Chief Administrative Officer, GHQ, India, 1942-44; Dep. Secretary, Defence Dept, Govt of India, 1944-45. *Recreations:* shooting, fishing. *Address:* Pear Tree Cottage, near Burwash, Sussex. *[Died* 27 *Jan.* 1976.

BLOSSE, Sir David Edward L.; *see* Lynch-Blosse.

BLOUNT, Sir Edward Robert, 11th Bt, *cr* 1642; retired; *b* 2 Dec. 1884; *s* of Sir Walter Blount, 9th Bt; *S* brother (Sir Walter Blount, 10th Bt) 1958; *m* 1914, Violet Ellen (*d* 1969), *d* of Alpin Grant Fowler; one *s* one *d. Educ:* Convent, Bath; Wimbledon Coll. (RC). Lieut RFC and RAF, 1914-18. British Sugar Corporation Ltd, 1924-50. *Recreation:* sailing. *Heir:* *s* Walter Edward Alpin Blount, DSC, MA [*b* 31 Oct. 1917; *m* 1954,

Eileen Audrey, *o d* of late Hugh B. Carritt; one *d*]. *Clubs:* Seaview Yacht Club, Seaview, Isle of Wight; Island Sailing (Cowes). *[Died 21 Jan. 1978.*

BLUNDELL, Lionel Alleyne, QC 1959; *b* 30 Dec. 1910; *s* of John Joseph and Florence Blundell; *m* 1935, Muriel Theresa Timson. *Educ:* King's Norton and George Dixon Grammar Schools; Birmingham Univ.; Gray's Inn. Certificate of Honour, Bar Final Examinations, 1932; Arden Scholar and Sen. Holker Scholar, Gray's Inn. Called to the Bar, Gray's Inn, 1933; LLM, Birmingham Univ., 1934. Royal Air Force, 1940-45. Bencher, Gray's Inn, 1965. Practice, specialising in: landlord and tenant, town planning, compensation and other branches of law affecting property. *Publications:* Rent Restrictions Guide, four editions, 1943-56; Rent Restrictions Cases, three editions, 1944-55; (with V. G. Wellings): The Landlord and Tenant Acts 1927 and 1954, two editions; The Complete Guide to the Rent Acts, 1958; (with G. Dobry) Town and Country Planning, 1963. Editor, Woodfall, Law of Landlord and Tenant, 24th edition 1939, 25th edition 1954, 26th and 27th editions (with V. G. Wellings), 1960, 1968; Joint Contributor Landlord and Tenant Title, Encyclopædia of Forms and Precedents, 4th edition, 1966. *Recreations:* cycling (Pres. Cyclists' Touring Club, 1963-72), walking, photography, hi-fi. *Address:* 11 King's Bench Walk, The Temple, EC4. *T:* 01-353 2484. *[Died 18 July 1975.*

BLUNDEN, Edmund Charles, CBE 1951; MC; MA; CLit; LittD (Leeds, Leicester); FRSL; Professor of Poetry, University of Oxford, 1966-68; Hon. Member of the Japan Academy; *b* 1 Nov. 1896; *m* 1945, Claire Margaret Poynting; four *d*. *Educ:* Christ's Hospital; Queen's Coll., Oxford. Prof. of English Literature, Tokyo Univ., 1924-27; served in France and Belgium, 1916-19, with the Royal Sussex Regt. Awarded the Hawthornden Prize, 1922. Fellow and Tutor in English Literature, Merton Coll., Oxford, 1931-43; on staff of Oxford Univ. Senior Training Corps, 1940-44; with UK Liaison Mission, Tokyo, 1948-50; Emeritus Prof. at the University of Hong Kong. Queen's Gold Medal for Poetry, 1956; Benson Medallist, RSL; Midsummer Prize, Corporation of London, 1970. Order of the Rising Sun, 3rd Class (Japan), 1963. *Publications: poetry:* Poems, 1914-1930; second series, 1930-1940; Shells by a Stream, 1944; After the Bombing, 1948; Poems of Many Years, 1957; A Hong Kong House, 1962; Eleven Poems, 1966; (with Bernard Mellor) Wayside Poems of the Seventeenth Century (anthology), 1963; *prose:* The Bonadventure, 1922; On the Poems of Henry Vaughan, 1927; Undertones of War, 1928, new editions, 1956, 1964; Nature in English Literature, 1929; Life of Leigh Hunt, 1930; The Face of England, 1932; Charles Lamb and His Contemporaries, 1934; The Mind's Eye, 1934; Keats's Publisher, 1936; English Villages, 1941; Thomas Hardy, 1942; Cricket Country, 1944; Shelley, a Life-Story, 1946. *Editorship:* has edited Clare, Collins, Smart, Keats, Shelley, Wilfred Owen, Ivor Gurney. *Address:* Hall Mill, Long Melford, Sudbury, Suffolk. *[Died 20 Jan. 1974.*

BLUNT, Sir Richard David Harvey, 11th Bt *cr* 1720; *b* 22 Oct. 1912; *s* of Sir John Blunt, 9th Bt, and Maud Julia (*d* 1935), *e d* of late Sir David Lionel Goldsmid-Stern-Salomons, 2nd Bt; *S* brother, 1969; *m* 1st, 1936, Elisabeth Malvine Ernestine, *er d* of Comdr F. M. Fransen van de Putte, Royal Netherlands Navy (retd); one *s* ; 2nd, 1943, Margaret, *e d* of John Dean, Nutbean, Cirencester; two *d*. *Recreations:* racing, shooting, stud management. *Heir: s* David Richard Reginald Blunt, *b* 8 Nov. 1938. *Address:* Diana Lodge Stud, Purton, Wilts. *[Died 13 Feb. 1975.*

BLYTH, 3rd Baron, *cr* 1907; **Ian Audley James Blyth;** Bt, *cr* 1895; *s* of late Hon. James Audley Blyth (2nd *s* of 1st Baron); *b* 28 Oct. 1905; *S* uncle, 1943; *m* 1928, Edna Myrtle (*d* 1952), *d* of Ernest Lewis, Wellington, NZ; two *s* three *d*. *Heir: s* Hon. Anthony Audley Rupert Blyth [*b* 3 June 1931; *m* 1st, 1954, Elizabeth Dorothea (marr. diss. 1962), *d* of R. T. Sparrow, Vancouver, BC; one *s* one *d* ; 2nd, 1963, Oonagh Elizabeth Ann, *yr d* of late W. H. Conway, Dublin; one *s* one *d*]. *Address:* Rockfield House, Athenry, Co. Galway. *[Died 29 Oct. 1977.*

BLYTHE, Ernest; Director of Abbey Theatre, Dublin (Managing Director, 1943-67); Member of Royal Irish Academy; *b* 13 April 1889; *s* of James Blythe, Magheragall, Lisburn, Co. Antrim; *m* 1919, Annie McHugh; one *s*. MP (S Fein) N Monaghan 1918-21; Mem. of Dail Eireann for Co. Monaghan, 1921-33; Mem. of Seanad Eireann, 1934-36. Minister: for Trade and Commerce in Provisional Government, 1921-22; for Local Government, 1922-23; Minister of Finance, 1923-32, and Minister of Posts and Telegraphs, 1927-32; Vice-Pres. of Executive Council, 1927-32; Mem. of Radio Eireann Authority, 1961-65; sometime Editor of the Southern Star Skibbereen; Mem. of Church of Ireland. *Publications:* Fraoch is Fothannáin, a volume of Gaelic verse,

1938; Briseadh Na Teorann, a study in Gaelic of Irish Partition, 1955; Trasna na Bóinne (Across the Boyne), vol. I of autobiography in Gaelic, 1957; Slán le Ultaibh (Good-bye to Ulster), vol. II of autobiography, 1970; Gaeil á Móscailt (Irishmen Awakening), Vol. III of autobiography, 1973. *Address:* 50 Kenilworth Square, Rathmines, Dublin. *[Died 23 Feb. 1975.*

BLYTHE, Wilfred Lawson, CMG 1953; *b* 9 Nov. 1896; *s* of late Joseph Blythe; *m* 1925, Muriel Gertrude Woodward (*d* 1969); one *d*. *Educ:* Universities of Liverpool and Grenoble. Served European War, 1915-19, Capt. RFA (despatches). Malayan Civil Service, 1921; studied Chinese at Canton, 1922-24; Protector of Chinese, various parts of Malaya, 1924-36; Dep. Pres., Municipality, Penang, 1936-37 and 1939-40; Dep. Controller of Labour (Chinese), 1941-42; served with Army in Malaya, 1942; interned, 1942-45; Sec. for Chinese Affairs, Federation of Malaya, 1946-48; Pres. Municipal Commission, Singapore, 1948-50; Colonial Sec., Singapore, 1950-53. *Publications:* The Impact of Chinese Secret Societies in Malaya, 1969; articles on Chinese Secret Societies and Chinese Labour. *Address:* Le Grand Pré, Grouville, Jersey, Channel Islands. *T:* Jersey 51962. *Club:* Royal Commonwealth Society. *[Died 6 Nov. 1975.*

BOARD, Air Cdre Andrew George, CMG 1919; DSO 1918; DL; *b* 11 May 1878; 3rd *s* of late Major John Board, JP, of Farley, Westerham, Kent; *m* 1932, Phyllis, *widow* of Capt. V. C. W. Agnew, 2nd *d* of late Claude Baggallay, KC. *Educ:* Charterhouse. Formerly Major and Temporary Lieut-Col South Wales Borderers; served in India and South Africa; Aviators Royal Aero Club Certificate No 36, Nov. 1910; Seconded to RFC, 1912; served European War, 1914-18 (despatches, DSO, CMG); Major S Wales Borderers, 1915; Col RFC, 1917; Wing Comdr RAF, 1919; Group Capt, 1923; Air Cdre, 1928; Dep. Dir Personnel, Air Ministry, 1922-23; served in Iraq, 1923-26; Chief Staff Officer, HQ RAF Middle East, Cairo, 1927-31; retired list, 1931; Dir of Egyptian Military Aviation, 1931-32 (El Lewa, Pasha); re-employed Air Min., 1939-45. DL (Caerns) 1943. *Clubs:* Army and Navy, Royal Air Force, United Service & Royal Aero; Royal Welsh Yacht (Caernarvon). *[Died 25 Feb. 1973.*

BOARD, Sir (Archibald) Vyvyan, Kt 1941; DSO 1918; MC 1916; *b* Bristol, 5 Feb. 1884; *s* of Alderman Joseph Thomas Board; *m* 1908, Isobel Phyllis (*d* 1968), *er d* of Dr G. G. Willett, Keynsham, Somerset; one *s* one *d*. *Educ:* Clifton Coll. Served European War in 3rd Bn Essex Regt, Machine Gun Corps and Gen. Staff; War of 1939-45, at Ministry of Supply: Controller, Industrial Alcohol Molasses, 1939, Plastics, 1941, Rubber, 1944; Dir of Economy, 1942; Chm. Salvage Bd. Dir, Distillers Co. Ltd, 1924, retd 1946. Late Dir, Hector Whaling Ltd. Retired, 1965. *Address:* Clevedon House, Hillhead, near Fareham, Hants. *[Died 10 Jan. 1973.*

BOASE, Thomas Sherrer Ross, MC; MA; FBA 1961; Chairman, British School at Rome, 1965-72; *b* 31 Aug. 1898; *s* of late Charles Millet Boase and Anne Malcolm Ross. *Educ:* Rugby Sch.; Magdalen Coll., Oxford. Served European War, 1914-18: Oxford and Bucks Lt Infantry, France, 1917-19 (MC). Fellow and Tutor, Hertford Coll., Oxford, 1922-37; Prof. of History of Art, Univ. of London, and Dir, Courtauld Inst. of Art, 1937-47. Temp. Civil Servant, Air Min., Cairo and UK, 1939-43; Chief Representative, British Council, Middle East, 1943-45. Pres., Magdalen Coll., Oxford, 1947-68; Vice-Chancellor, Oxford Univ., 1958-60. Trustee: National Gall., 1947-53 (Chm., 1951-53); Shakespeare Birthplace Trust, 1949-; British Museum, 1950-69. Member: Adv. Council of V & A Museum, 1947-70; Council, Royal Albert Hall, 1968-. Governor: Rugby Sch., 1951-65; Royal Shakespeare Theatre, 1952-. Comr for Exhibition of 1851, 1956-. Pres., British Archæological Assoc., 1969-72. Hon. Fellow: Hertford Coll., 1947; St Mark's Coll., Adelaide, 1956; Magdalen Coll., Oxford, 1968. Foreign Member, Amer. Philosophical Soc. Hon. DCL Oxon; Hon. LLD: St Andrews; Melbourne; Rockefeller Inst.; Hon. DLitt: Durham; Reading. Grosses Verdienstkreuz der Bundesrepublik Deutschland, 1958. *Publications:* Boniface VIII, 1933; St Francis of Assisi, 1936 (new edn, 1968); English Art, 1100-1216, 1953; English Art, 1800-70, 1959; The York Psalter, 1962; Castles and Churches of the Crusading Kingdom, 1967; Kingdoms and Strongholds of the Crusaders, 1971; (with A. Boyd) Nebuchadnezzar, 1972; Death in the Middle Ages: Mortality, Judgement and Remembrance, 1972; articles in the Jl of the Warburg and Courtauld Insts; (ed) Oxford History of English Art. *Address:* 6 Atherton Drive, Wimbledon Common, SW19. *T:* 01-946 1131. *Club:* United Oxford & Cambridge University. *[Died 14 April 1974.*

BODY, Maj.-Gen. Kenneth Marten, CB 1942; CMG 1918; OBE 1919; *b* 9 June 1883; *s* of H. M. Body, Crediton, Devon; *m* 1907, Isabel (*d* 1971), *d* of W. Fell-Smith, Deer Park, Honiton, Devon; four *d*. *Educ:* Blundell's Sch., Tiverton. Royal Military Academy, Woolwich. Commission in Royal Field Artillery, 1900; Instructor RAOC Sch. of Instruction, 1931-34; Dir of Army Ordnance Services, War Office, 1939; retired pay, 1942; Capt. 1913; Major, 1915; Bt Lieut-Col 1916; Lieut-Col 1928; Col 1934; Maj.-Gen. 1939. Col Comdt RAOC, 1942-51. Ordre de la Couronne (Belgium), 1919. *Recreations:* Capt. of Coventry Rugby FC, 1907-08; played hockey for Midlands, 1904-05. *Address:* Cranhill, Weston Road, Bath.   *[Died 23 Dec. 1973.*

BOHLEN, Charles Eustis; Deputy Under-Secretary of State for Political Affairs, USA, 1968-Jan. 1969, retired; *b* 30 Aug. 1904; *m* Avis Howard Thayer; one *s* two *d*. *Educ:* Harvard Univ. AB 1927. Entered Foreign Service, 1929; Vice-Consul, Prague, 1929-31; Paris, 1931-34; Moscow, 1934; Dept of State, 1935; Second Sec., Moscow, 1937, Consul, 1938; Second Sec., Tokyo, 1941-42; Dept of State 1942; Asst Chief, Div. of European Affairs, 1943; First Sec., Moscow, 1943-44; Chief, Div. of Eastern European Affairs, 1944; Asst to Sec. of State for White House Liaison, 1944; Special Asst to Sec. of State, 1946; Counsellor, Dept of State, 1947; Minister, US Embassy, Paris, 1949; Counsellor, Dept of State, 1951-53; US Ambassador to the USSR, 1953-57; to the Philippines, 1957-59. Asst to Sec. of State of the United States, in the field of Soviet Affairs, 1959-62; US Ambassador to France, 1962-68. Has attended many internat. confs, etc. *Address:* 2811 Dumbarton Avenue NW, Washington, DC 20007, USA. *T:* 338-3051.   *[Died 1 Jan. 1974.*

BOILEAU, Sir Edmond (Charles), 7th Bt *cr* 1838; *b* 28 May 1903; 2nd *s* of Sir Francis James Boileau, 5th Bt, and Wilhelmina, *d* of George Lyon; *S* brother, 1978; *m* 1933, Marjorie Lyle, *d* of Claude Monteath D'Arcy; two *s*. *Educ:* Xavier College, Melbourne. Served as Captain, Australian Military Forces, 1939-45; now retired. *Recreations:* punting, reading. *Heir: s* Lt-Col Guy Francis Boileau [*b* 23 Feb. 1935; *m* 1962, Judith Frances, *d* of George Conrad Hannan; two *s* three *d*]. *Address:* 61 Erica Avenue, Glen Iris, Victoria, Australia. *T:* (03) 509 7047.   *[Died 6 Feb. 1980.*

BOILEAU, Sir Gilbert George Benson, 6th Bt, *cr* 1838; MOH for City of Dandenong; *b* 13 Feb. 1898; *e s* of Sir Francis James Boileau, 5th Bt; *S* father 1945; *m* 1st, 1924, Chica Patricia, *d* of late J. L. Edgeworth-Somers; two *d*; 2nd, 1941, Mary Catherine, *d* of late Lawrence Riordan; three *d*. *Educ:* Xavier Coll., Kew, Vic; Newman Coll., University of Melbourne. MB, BS, Melbourne 1923. Service with rank of Major, 1940-44, AAMC Australian Military Forces, now on Reserve. *Recreation:* Turf. *Heir: b* Edmond Charles Boileau, Capt. AIF [*b* 28 May 1903; *m* 1933, Marjorie, *d* of late C. M. D'Arcy, Launceston, Tasmania; two *s*]. *Address:* Minto Lodge, 1480 Heatherton Road, Dandenong, Vic 3175, Australia. *T:* 792 2853. *Clubs:* Athenæum, Naval and Military, Savage (Melbourne).   *[Died 31 March 1978.*

BOLAND, Sir (Edward) Rowan, Kt 1964; CBE 1945 (OBE 1941); MD; FRCP; Physician Emeritus, Guy's Hospital, SE1; Consulting Physician, Hospital of St John and St Elizabeth; Hon. Consulting Physician to the Army, 1945-70, Emeritus 1971; *b* 9 March 1898; *s* of John Patrick and Margaret Boland, Broughty Ferry, Scotland; *m* 1931, Barbara Scott; no *c*. *Educ:* Stonyhurst; Wimbledon Coll.; Caen, France, 2nd Lieut London Rifle Brigade, France and Flanders, 1916-18, discharged owing to wounds. Entered Guy's, 1915. MRCS, LRCP 1921; MRCP 1925; DPH 1928; FRCP 1934. Asst Physician Guy's Hospital, 1934. Lt-Col RAMC 1940; Egypt, 1940-42; Brig., Consulting Physician Allied Force Headquarters, 1942-45, North Africa, Sicily, Italy and Greece (despatches); Dean of Faculty of Medicine, University of London, 1948-52; Dean of Medical and Dental Sch., Guy's Hospital, 1945-65; late Mem. of Senate, University of London; Mem. Gen. Med. Council (Treas.); Chm., Army Medical Advisory Board; Chm., Central Medical Recruitment Cttee. Hon. FRCPS Canada; Corresp. FACP; MD (*hc*): University Algiers, 1944; TCD, 1956. Officier Legion of Merit. *Recreation:* gardening. *Address:* Guy's Hospital, SE1. *T:* 01-407 0082; Hill House, Stowting, Kent. *T:* Lyminge 87329.   *[Died 24 Aug. 1972.*

BOLAND, Sir Rowan; *see* Boland, Sir E. R.

BOLINGBROKE and ST JOHN, 6th Viscount *cr* 1712; **Vernon Henry St John;** Bt 1611; Baron St John of Lydiard Tregoze, 1712; Viscount St John and Baron St John of Battersea, 1716; *b* 15 March 1896; *s* of 5th Viscount and Mary Emily Elizabeth Howard (*d* 1910); *S* father, 1899. Owns about 4000 acres. *Heir: cousin* Kenneth Oliver Musgrave St John [*b* 22 March 1927; *m*

1st, 1953, Patricia Mary (marr. diss. 1972), *d* of B. J. McKenna; one *s*; 2nd, 1972, Jainey Anne, *d* of late Alexander Duncan and of Desborough McRae; one *s*]. *Address:* Moorhayes, Crow Hill, Ringwood, Hants.   *[Died 1 May 1974.*

BOLITHO, (Henry) Hector; author; *b* Auckland, New Zealand, 1897; *s* of Henry and Ethelred Frances Bolitho. Travelled in South Sea Islands, 1919; through New Zealand with the Prince of Wales, 1920; came to England, 1922; travelled in Africa, Australia, Canada, America, and Germany, 1923-24; lecture tours, USA, 1938-39, 1947, 1948, and 1949. Served War of 1939-45, Sqdn Ldr RAFVR; Editor RAF Journal. *Publications:* With the Prince in New Zealand, 1920; The Islands of Wonder, 1920; Solemn Boy, a novel, 1927; The Letters of Lady Augusta Stanley, 1927; Thistledown and Thunder, 1928; The New Zealanders, 1928; Judith Silver, a novel, 1929; The New Countries, 1929; The Later Letters of Lady Augusta Stanley, 1929; The Glorious Oyster, 1929; (with Very Rev. A. V. Baillie) A Victorian Dean: A Memoir of Arthur Stanley, 1930; The Flame on Ethirdova, 1930; Albert the Good, a Life of the Prince Consort, 1932; Alfred Mond: First Baron Melchett, a biography, 1933; Beside Galilee: a diary in Palestine, 1933; The Prince Consort and his Brother, 1934; Victoria, the Widow and her Son, 1934; Older People, 1935; The House in Half Moon Street, 1936; James Lyle MacKay, First Earl of Inchcape, 1936; Marie Tempest, a biography, 1936; Edward VIII, his life and reign, 1937; Royal Progress, 1937; George VI, 1937; Victoria and Albert, 1938; (ed) Further Letters of Queen Victoria, 1938; Victoria and Disraeli, a play for the radio, performed 1938; (with John Mulgan) The Emigrants, 1939; Roumania under King Carol, 1939; America Expects, 1940; War in the Strand, 1942; Combat Report, 1943; No Humour in My Love, 1946; Task for Coastal Command, 1946; The Romance of Windsor Castle, 1947; The Reign of Queen Victoria, 1949; A Biographer's Notebook, 1950; A Century of British Monarchy, 1951; Their Majesties, 1951; (with Derek Peel) Without the City Wall, 1952; Jinnah, Creator of Pakistan, 1954; A Penguin in the Eyrie, 1955; The Wine of the Douro, 1956; The Angry Neighbours, 1957; No 10, Downing Street, 1957; My Restless Years, 1962; The Galloping Third, 1963; Albert, Prince Consort, 1964, rev. edn, 1970; (with Derek Peel) The Drummonds of Charing Cross, 1967. *Address:* 1 St Nicholas Road, Brighton, Sussex.   *[Died 12 Sept. 1974.*

BOLLAND, Robert William, PhD, FRIC, MBIM; Director, Bristol Polytechnic, since 1969; *b* 30 Sept 1915; *s* of George James Bolland and Margaret Bolland (*née* Ditchburn); *m* 1943, Eunice Olive Mack; one *s* one *d*. *Educ:* Rutherford Coll. of Technology, Newcastle upon Tyne. BSc, PhD (London External). Analytical Chemist, Brady and Martin Ltd, Newcastle upon Tyne, 1932-43; Experimental Officer, Armaments Research, Royal Arsenal, Woolwich, 1943-45; Lectr, Leeds Coll. of Technology, 1945-46; Lectr, Makerere Univ. Coll., Uganda, EA, 1947-52; Sen. Lectr, Rutherford Coll. of Technology, Newcastle upon Tyne, 1952-55; Head, Chemistry and Biology Dept: Bristol Coll. of Science and Technology, 1955-60; Bristol Coll. of Advanced Technology, 1960-64; Prof. of Chemistry and Head of Sch. of Chemistry and Chemical Engineering, Bath Univ. of Technology, 1964-69. Mem. Council, Royal Inst. of Chemistry, 1960-63 (Vice-Pres. 1963-65); Visiting Prof., Natal Univ., SA, 1968, Founder Governor, Further Educn Staff Coll.; Lectr, Bristol Univ., 1970-. *Recreations:* walking, reading, travel, study of European and African affairs. *Address:* Makerere, Sham Castle Lane, Bath, Somerset BA2 6JL. *T:* Bath 5568; Polytechnic, Ashley Down Road, Bristol BS7 9BU. *T:* Bristol 41241. *Club:* Royal Commonwealth Society.   *[Died 6 June 1974.*

BOLT, George Thomas, CMG 1955; Chairman, Public Service Commission, New Zealand, 1953-58; *b* 16 June 1900; *s* of late George Henry and Emma Sarah Bolt; *m* 1925, Linda May, *d* of late S. Roberts; one *s*. *Educ:* Wellington Coll., New Zealand. Joined NZ Public Service, 1917; Sec., Public Service Commissioner's Office, 1936; Asst Public Service Comr, 1944; Mem. and Dep. Chm., Public Service Commission, 1946. *Address:* 305 The Parade, Island Bay, Wellington 2, New Zealand.   *[Died 20 March 1971.*

BOLTON, Lt-Col Edward Frederick, DSO 1940; The Queen's Royal Regiment (retired); *b* 27 Aug. 1897; 2nd *s* of late E. C. Bolton, Bibbenluke Estate, Mysore, India; *m* 1926, Alice Joy Tillie; no *c*. *Educ:* Haileybury Coll.; RMC, Sandhurst. Commissioned 1915; served European War, 1914-18, Mesopotamia, 1917-18; in Ireland, 1920-23; Nigeria Regt, Royal West African Frontier Force, 1924-30; India, 1937-39; commanded 2/6th Bn, Queen's Royal Regt, 1940-42 (in BEF, France, April-June 1940); OC 70th Bn Queen's Royal Regt, Aug.-Nov. 1942; Instructor Senior Officers School, Nov. 1942;

GSO1 Aldershot District, 1944-45. *Publication:* Horse Management in West Africa. *Recreations:* cricket (Haileybury XI, Member of MCC, Free Foresters CC and Grasshoppers CC), racquets (Captain of Haileybury), fives (Haileybury team). *Address:* Roeheath, North Chailey, Lewes, East Sussex. *Club:* Army and Navy. *[Died 3 March 1977.*

BOLTON, Guy; Playwright; *b* Broxbourne, Herts, 23 Nov. 1884; *o s* of Reginald Pelham Bolton and Katherine Behenna; *m* 1st, Julia Currie; one *s* one *d*; 2nd, Marguerite Namara; one *s* one *d*; *m* Virginia De Lanty (*d* 1979). *Educ:* Private tutors; Ecole des Beaux Arts. Started life as an architect practising in NY City; engaged by War Dept for special work on the rebuilding of West Point; concurrently wrote magazine stories, the first being published when the writer was 19; in 1913, started career as a playwright and is the author of more than fifty plays and musical comedies; among these are: Polly-with-a-Past, Sally, Kissing-Time, The Dark Angel, Tiptoes, Lady Be Good, Polly Preferred, Oh Boy, Song of the Drum, Anything Goes, Who's Who, Seeing Stars, Swing Along, This'll Make You Whistle, Going Greek, The Fleet's Lit Up, Magyar Melody, Hold On To Your Hats, Follow the Girls, Don't Listen Ladies, Larger than Life (adapted from W. Somerset Maugham's Theatre), The Shelley Story, Music at Midnight, Anastasia, Child of Fortune, Guardian Angel, Fireworks in the Sun. Author of films: Transatlantic, The Love Parade, Words and Music, 'Til the Clouds Roll By, Weekend at the Waldorf, A Man and his Wife, Jennie Kissed Me, Very Good Eddie. *Publications:* (joint autobiography with P. G. Wodehouse) Bring on the Girls, 1954; The Olympians (novel); 1961; The Enchantress (novel); Gracious Living (novel), 1965; Anya (musical play), 1965; A Man and his Wife, 1970; Jeeves, a musical (with P. G. Wodehouse). *Recreation:* travelling. *Address:* Remsenburg, Long Island, USA.
[Died 4 Sept. 1979.

BONCOUR, J. P.; *see* Paul-Boncour.

BOND, Maj.-Gen. Richard Lawrence, CB 1943; CBE 1937; DSO 1915; MC 1918; Hon. FRAM 1954; *b* 10 June 1890; *s* of late Maj.-Gen. Sir F. G. Bond, KBE; *m* Isabelle Helewise (*d* 1943), *y d* of late Col T. J. R. Mallock; one *d* (one *s* killed in action, 1941); *m* 1949, Dorothy Mary, *d* of late Sydney How. Entered Army, 1910; Major, 1926; Bt Lieut-Col, 1931; Lieut-Col, 1934; Col, 1937; Maj.-Gen., 1940; served European War, 1914-19 (despatches, DSO for gallantry in the successful attack on the Railway Embankment at Cuinchy); Waziristan Operations, 1936-37 (CBE); GSO 2nd Grade, War Office, 1930-31; Imperial Defence Coll., 1933; CRE India, 1934-37; AQMG, War Office, 1937-39; Chief Engineer, Aldershot Command, 1939; Chief Engineer, 1 Corps BEF, 1939-40, Maj.-Gen. i/c Administration, 1940; Deputy Quartermaster-General in India, 1941-42; Engineer-in-Chief in India, 1942-43; Commander, 1943 and 1944-46; retired pay, 1946. *Address:* 3 Angel Court, Compton, Guildford, Surrey GU3 1EF. *[Died 13 May 1979.*

BOND, Walter Fitzgerald; *see* Fitzgerald, Walter.

BONE, Phyllis Mary, RSA 1944 (ARSA, 1939); animal sculptor; *b* Hornby, Lancs, 1894; *d* of Dr Douglas John Mayhew Bone. *Educ:* St George's High Sch. for Girls, Edinburgh. Studied sculpture at the Edinburgh College of Art (Sculpture Diploma), Paris and Italy; exhibited in Royal Scottish Academy, Edinburgh; Paris Salon, Royal Academy, Walker Art Gallery, Liverpool, and Royal Glasgow Institute; Aberdeen Art Gallery purchased two bronzes, 1930, and Glasgow Corporation one, 1942; executed all the animal sculpture on the Scottish National War Memorial; the animal sculpture in the New Zoology Buildings, Edinburgh Univ.; sculpture on New Government Buildings, Edinburgh; other work: in St Peter's RC Church, Edinburgh; St John's Church, Perth; Stowe Chapel, Buckinghamshire; St Winifred's Church, Welbeck; Preening and Drying (bronze group) 1952 (bought by Min. of Works for a scheme for decorating British Embassies throughout the World). Shere Khan, bronze (diploma work at Royal Scottish Academy); Shelties, bronze, to private collection, NSW. *Publication:* (for children) Deer Talk, 1962. *Address:* Hillview, Barrhill Road, Kirkcudbright. *Club:* Ladies' Caledonian (Edinburgh).
[Died 12 July 1972.

BONE, Group Captain Reginald John, CB 1934; CBE 1919; DSO 1916; *b* Dorking, Surrey, 2 Oct. 1888; *m* Sylvia Joan Mary (*née* Fitzpatrick), *widow* of Douglas A. Payne. *Educ:* Ripley Court, Ripley, Surrey. Service in Royal Navy in destroyers and in submarines. Learned to fly at Eastbourne Aviation Company Sch., 1912, and at Central Flying Sch., Upavon, 1913. Served in Naval Wing, RFC, RNAS and RAF, 1913-34. Director-General of Civil Aviation under Egyptian Government, 1936-39; commanded RAF base, Pembroke Dock, 1939-41; Civil Air

Attaché, Far East, 1948-51. *Address:* 8 Mark House, Wake Green Road, Moseley, Birmingham B13 4EZ.
[Died 29 Aug. 1972.

BONFIELD, John Martin; General Secretary, National Graphical Association, since 1969 (Joint General Secretary, 1964-69); Part-time Member, Eastern Electricity Board, since 1968; *b* 1 May 1915; *s* of Harry Bonfield; *m* 1946, Anne Brierley; one *s*. *Educ:* British and Wilshere-Dacre Schs, Hitchin, Herts. Trained with Lawrence & Sons, Welwyn; thereafter with various printing firms. Nat. Asst Sec., Typographical Assoc., 1948-55; Gen. Pres., 1955-57 and Gen. Sec., 1957-63; Mem. Exec. Cttee, Internat. Graphical Fedn, 1957-67; Pres., Printing and Kindred Trades Fedn, 1961-74; Mem., Printing and Publishing EDC, 1965-71; Pres., Internat. Graphical Fedn, 1967-; Mem., Printing and Publishing Industry Trng Bd, 1968-74. *Address:* 53 Larkway, Bedford. *T:* Bedford 67856. *[Died 9 Jan. 1976.*

BONHAM CARTER, Rear-Adm. Sir Christopher Douglas, GCVO 1970 (KCVO 1968; CVO 1962); GB 1959; an Extra Equerry to the Duke of Edinburgh, since 1970; Secretary and Registrar of the Order of Merit, since 1971; *b* 3 Nov. 1907; *e s* of Captain A. E. Bonham Carter, 60th Rifles, and Margaret (*née* Malcolm of Poltalloch); *m* 1931, Maryanne M. H. Taylor, Glasgow, and Ardgarten, Argyll; one *s*. *Educ:* Elstree Sch.; RNC Dartmouth. Served War of 1939-45 (despatches, 1943); Captain RN 1948; Commanded Second Frigate Flotilla, 1949-51; Naval Attaché, Rome, 1951-53; Admiralty, 1953-55; Commanded HMS Glasgow, 1955-56; Rear-Adm. 1957; Chief of Staff, Mediterranean, 1957-59; Treasurer to the Duke of Edinburgh, 1959-70, Treasurer and Private Secretary, 1970. Comdr, Legion of Honour. *Recreations:* shooting and fishing. *Address:* The Cottage, Horringer, Bury St Edmunds, Suffolk. *T:* Horringer 221. *Club:* White's. *[Died 3 June 1975.*

BONHAM-CARTER, Air Commodore David William Frederick, CB 1950; DFC 1945; psa 1933; *b* 22 Feb. 1901; *s* of late Walter Henry Bonham-Carter, Solicitor, and late Anita Bonham-Carter (*née* Heuer); *m* 1927, Joyce Angela Palmer; three *s* one *d*. *Educ:* Winchester Coll.; RAF Coll., Cranwell (first term). Seconded to RCAF, 1940-43; with No 5 (Bomber) Group, 1943-45 (despatches); Officer Commanding No 45 Wing, RAF Dorval, PQ, Canada, 1946; seconded to Ministry of Civil Aviation, 1947-49; AOC, RAF Hong Kong, 1951-53; retired 1953. Member of Council, Nightingale Fund, 1947-; Vice-Pres., Anglo-Belgian Union, 1967; Pres., Newark (Notts and Lincs) Air Museum. *Recreation:* photography. *Address:* Mariner's Cottage, Felixstowe Ferry, Suffolk. *T:* Felixstowe 3511. *Clubs:* United Service & Royal Aero; Royal Channel Islands Yacht. *[Died 17 May 1974.*

BONHAM-CARTER, Adm. Sir Stuart Sumner, KCB 1943 (CB 1941); CVO 1934; DSO 1918; RN; *b* 1889; *yr s* of late Lothian George Bonham-Carter, Buriton House, Petersfield, and Emily Maud, *d* of Rev. J. M. Sumner; *m* 1933, Eve, *widow* of Brig. C. R. Lloyd, Indian Army, and *d* of late Donald Shaw; one *d*. Served European War, 1914-18 (despatches, DSO, Legion of Honour, French Croix de Guerre, with Palm, Italian Silver Cross for Valour, Belgian Croix de Guerre); commanded HMS Intrepid at Zeebrugge. Asst Director of Naval Equipment, 1932-34; Commodore Royal Naval Barracks, Chatham, 1937-39; Naval Secretary to first Lord of the Admiralty, 1939; RA 3rd BS 1940; Rear-Adm. 18th Cruiser Squadron, 1944; Vice-Adm. Malta, 1943; retired 1944; Commodore of Convoys, 1944-45. *Address:* Ardmoy, 76 Heath Road, Petersfield, Hants. *T:* Petersfield 4154. *[Died 5 Sept. 1972.*

BONHOTE, Rev. Edward Frederic, MA; Canon of Rochester, 1953 (Emeritus, 1961); *b* 13 Oct. 1888; *s* of late Thomas T. and late Marie Rose Bonhote; unmarried. *Educ:* Merchant Taylors' Sch.; Clare Coll., Cambridge (Scholar). 1st Class Hons in Mathematics, 10th Wrangler, 1910; Deacon, 1912; Priest, 1913; Asst Master at Rugby Sch., 1911-14 and 1919-34; CMS Missionary at St John's Coll., Agra, 1914-17; served in ranks with 58th and 59th Divisions, MGC, 1917-19; Housemaster at Rugby Sch., 1925-34; Master of Haileybury Coll. (now Haileybury and Imperial Service Coll.), 1934-48; Hon. Canon of St Albans, 1935-48; Vicar of St Thomas', Southborough, 1949-61. *Address:* 27 Sondes Place Drive, Dorking, Surrey.
[Died 25 Dec. 1972.

BONNET, Georges, Hon. GCMG 1938; Deputy for Dordogne, France, 1924-40, 1956-68; Conseiller-Général de la Dordogne, 1951-68; *b* 1889. *Educ:* Ecole des Hautes Etudes; Ecole des Sciences Politiques. Held Cabinet rank from 1925; President French delegation to London Economic and Monetary Conference, 1934; Ambassador to USA, 1937; Minister of Foreign Affairs, Daladier Cabinet, 1938-39; Minister of Justice,

1939-40. Président, Union Mondiale des Intellectuels. *Publications:* Défense de la paix, 1950; De Washington au Quai d'Orsay, 1961; Le Quai d'Orsay sous Trois Républiques, 1965; Miracles de la France, 1965; De Munich à la Guerre, 1967. *Address:* 94 Boulevard Flandrin, Paris 16e.
[Died 18 June 1973.

BONSER, Wilfrid; Librarian, University of Birmingham, 1929-52; *b* 1887; *s* of A. E. Bonser; *m* Madoline Carrie, *d* of Henry Davis, Beckenham. *Educ:* Highgate Sch.; University Coll., London. BA London, 1914; PhD London, 1927; Fellow, Library Assoc.; Sub-Librarian of University College, London, till 1928; Member of Council of Folklore Society till 1928 and 1953-; Hon. Secretary, Birmingham Library, 1939-40, 1944-45; President 1941. *Publications:* Catalogue of the Geological Books in the Library of University College, London, 1927; Proverb Literature (General Editor), 1930; Union Catalogue of Periodical Publications in University Libraries of British Isles (Co-Editor), 1937; An Anglo-Saxon and Celtic Bibliography (450-1087), 1957; A Bibliography of Folklore, 1961; The Medical Background of Anglo-Saxon England, 1963; A Romano-British Bibliography, 1964; articles and reviews in Folklore, Antiquity, The Library, Library Association Record, Man, Nature, etc. *Recreations:* folklore and archæology. *Address:* 1 Parkwood, Beckenham, Kent BR3 1TR. *T:* 01-650 2467.
[Died 23 Nov. 1971.

BONSOR, Sir Bryan Cosmo, 3rd Bt, *cr* 1925; MC 1945; TD; DL; Director of Watney Mann, 1958-69 (Watney's, 1947-58), retired; *b* 26 Aug. 1916; *er s* of Major Sir Reginald Bonsor, Bt; *S* father 1959; *m* 1942, Elizabeth Hambro; two *s*. *Educ:* Eton. Served War of 1939-45 with Bucks Yeomanry (despatches, MC). Major RA. DL Bucks, 1973. *Recreations:* shooting, fishing, sailing. *Heir: s* Nicholas Cosmo Bonsor [*b* 9 Dec. 1942; *m* 1969, Hon. Nadine Marisa Lampson, *d* of 2nd Baron Killearn; one *s* one *d*. *Educ:* Eton; Christ Church, Oxford (BA). Called to Bar, Inner Temple, 1967]. *Address:* Liscombe, Leighton Buzzard, Bedfordshire. *Clubs:* White's, Pratt's.   *[Died 5 March 1977.*

BOORD, Sir Richard (William), 3rd Bt, *cr* 1896; late RAFVR; *b* 9 Nov. 1907; *o s* of late Alexander Edgar Boord, 3rd *s* of 1st Bt, and Coralie Mary, *y d* of late Herman Hoskier; *S* uncle, 1928; *m* 1st, 1933, Yvonne Swingler (from whom he obtained a divorce, 1944), *o d* of J. A. Hubert Bird; two *s*; 2nd, 1944, Ethel El Marie (*d* 1973), *d* of Herman Moline, Duluth, Minnesota, USA. *Educ:* Marlborough; Lincoln Coll., Oxford. *Heir: s* Nicolas John Charles Boord [*b* 10 June 1936; *m* 1st, 1960, Françoise (marr. diss. 1965), *d* of Guiseppe Tempra, Pas de Calais; 2nd, 1965, Françoise Renée, *d* of M. C. Mouret, Marseilles]. *Address:* 4 Trumpeters House, Old Palace Yard, Richmond, Surrey.
[Died 12 Dec. 1975.

BOOS, Sir Werner (James), Kt 1965; CBE 1961; Chairman, Public Service and Police Service Commissions and Member, Judicial and Legal Service Commission of Trinidad and Tobago, since 1960 (relinquished positions temporarily to act as Governor-General of Trinidad and Tobago, 15 May-15 Sept. 1964 and April-July 1967); *b* 25 July 1911; *s* of late Julius Edward Boos, and late Audrey (*née* Hobson); *m* 1932, Alisa (*née* Pasea); two *s* two *d*. *Educ:* St Mary's Coll., Trinidad; Oxford Univ. Various appointments Trinidad and Tobago Civil Service, 1928-60; retired, 1960, as Dep. Chief Sec.; acted on various occasions as Chief Sec., Financial Sec., Governor's Deputy. *Recreations:* gardening, fishing, swimming, reading. *Address:* (home) 7 Fondes Amandes, St Ann's, Trinidad. *T:* 42692; Service Commissions' Offices, 151B Charlotte Street, Port of Spain, Trinidad. *T:* 38916 or 32971. *Club:* Trinidad Country (Maraval).   *[Died 4 May 1974.*

BOOSEY, Leslie Arthur; Hon. President: International Confederation of Societies of Authors and Composers; Performing Right Society; President, Boosey & Hawkes Ltd; *b* 26 July 1887; *s* of Arthur and Lucy Ashton Boosey; *m* 1921, Ethel Torfrida, *d* of Frank Marchant; three *s* one *d*. *Educ:* Malvern Coll.; abroad. Served with 22nd London Regt The Queens, 1908-19; France, 1915-18. Chevalier, Légion d'Honneur. *Address:* Meadowlands, Hambledon Road, Denmead, Portsmouth PO7 6HB. *T:* Waterlooville 55995. *Clubs:* Savile, Oriental.   *[Died 5 Sept. 1979.*

BOOTH, Dame Edith; *see* Evans, Dame Edith.

BOOTH, Sir (George) Arthur (Warrington), KBE 1935; *b* 28 Oct. 1879; *e s* of Frank H. A. Booth, of Sydenhurst, Chiddingfold, Surrey, and Florence Eliza, *d* of E. Giffard, late of the Admiralty; *m* 1925, Claire, *d* of John Sibley. *Educ:* Bradfield; New Coll., Oxford. Called to the Bar, Middle Temple, 1905; practised in London and at Alexandria, Egypt; Legal Adviser to

Custodian of Enemy Property in Egypt, 1916-18; Judge of the Mixed Tribunal, Cairo, 1918; Royal Counsellor Egyptian State Legal Dept, 1926; Judicial Adviser to the Egyptian Government, 1928-37; Grand Cordon, Order of the Nile, Egypt, 1936. *Address:* Little Shalwyn, Three Gates Lane, Haslemere, Surrey. *T:* Haslemere 2885.   *[Died 22 March 1972.*

BOOTH, George Macaulay; *b* 22 Sept. 1877; 2nd *s* of late Rt Hon. Charles Booth and Mary Catherine, *o d* of Charles Zachary Macaulay; *m* 1906, Margaret (*d* 1959), 2nd *d* of late Daniel Meinertzhagen; three *s* three *d*. *Educ:* Harrow; Trinity Coll., Cambridge. Served War of 1914-18. Past Director: White Drummond & Co.; Municipal and General Securities Co. Ltd; Manaos Harbour Ltd; Manaos Tramway and Light Co. Ltd; CAC Ltd. Dep. Dir-Gen., Min. of Munitions, 1914-19; Dir Bank of England, 1915-47; first Chm. Brazilian Chamber of Commerce and Economic Affairs in Great Britain, 1942-45. One of HM Lieuts of the City of London; High Sheriff, City of London. The Order of Stanislov, 1st Class (Russia); Cross of Chevalier of Legion of Honour (France), 1919; Order of the Southern Cross (Brazil), 1947. *Relevant Publication:* A Man of Push and Go: George Macaulay Booth, by Duncan Crow, 1965. *Address:* Funtington Lodge, Chichester, Sussex. *T:* West Ashling 205. *Club:* Reform.   *[Died 10 March 1971.*

BOOTH, William Sykes; retired as Headmaster of the Borlase School, Marlow, Bucks (1927-56); *b* 1896. *Educ:* Manchester Grammar Sch.; Manchester Univ. Former Senior Classical Master Blackburn Grammar Sch. *Address:* 24 Burford Road, Stratford-on-Avon.   *[Died 28 Sept. 1972.*

BOOTH-GRAVELY, Sir Walter, KCMG 1939; CSI 1936; CIE 1931; late ICS; *b* 22 May 1882; *m* 1939, Dorothy Faickney. *Educ:* Daniel Stewart's Coll. and Univ., Edinburgh; Trinity Coll., Oxford. Entered Indian Civil Service, 1906; Chief Sec. to Government, Burma, 1932; Governor's Counsellor, Burma, 1937-40. *Address:* 11 Elliot Place, Edinburgh 11. *T:* 031-441 3215.   *[Died 1 Jan. 1971.*

BOR, Max; *see under* Adrian, Max.

BOR, Norman Loftus, CIE 1945; OBE 1957; MA; DSc; FNI; FLS; FRSE; Assistant Director, Royal Gardens, Kew, retired; formerly Indian Forest Service (Conservator of Forests), retired; *b* 2 May 1893; 2nd *s* of late E. N. C. Bor and Mabel Thornton, Kilcoran House, Callan, County Kilkenny, Eire (of Dutch descent); *m* 1931, Eleanor Constance (*d* 1957), *d* of late Rev. J. W. Rundall, St Ninian's, Moffat; no *c*. *Educ:* Kilkenny Coll.; Mountjoy Sch., Dublin; Dublin and Edinburgh Univs. Served European War, 1914-18, in Connaught Rangers, Capt. (wounded). Indian Forest Service, 1921, Assam; Forest Botanist, Forest Research Institute, Dehra Dun, UP, 1937-42. Chief Refugee Administrator, Assam, 1943-46; in charge rehabilitation, Naga Hills and Manipur State, 1944-46. Pres., Botany Sect., Indian Science Congress, 1942; Pres., Indian Botanical Soc., 1945. Paul Johannes Brühl Medal, Royal Asiatic Society of Bengal, 1945; Linnean Gold Medal, 1962. *Publications:* Manual of Indian Forest Botany; Some Beautiful Indian Climbers and Shrubs (with M. B. Raizada), 1954; Grasses of Burma, Ceylon, India and Pakistan, 1960; contribs on Gramineae to: Rechinger, Flora of Lowland Iraq; vol. 9, Flora of Iraq; Flora Iranica; over 130 papers on botanical subjects. *Recreations:* botany and walking. *Address:* 20 Royston Court, Lichfield Road, Kew, Richmond, Surrey. *T:* 01-940 5838; Lloyds Bank, Cox's and King's Branch, 6 Pall Mall, SW1.
[Died 22 Dec. 1972.

BORG OLIVIER, George, LLD; Prime Minister and Minister of Commonwealth and Foreign Affairs, Malta, 1965-71; Leader of the Nationalist Party, Malta, 1950-76; *b* 5 July 1911; *s* of Oliviero Borg Olivier, Architect and Civil Engineer; *m* 1943, Alexandra (*née* Mattei); two *s* one *d*. *Educ:* Lyceum and Royal University of Malta. Mem. of Council of Government, Malta, 1939-45; Mem. of Legislative Assembly, 1947; Minister of Works and Reconstruction, 1950-55; Minister of Education, and of Justice, 1950-51; Prime Minister, 1950-55; Leader of the Opposition, 1955-58; Minister of Economic Planning and Finance, 1962-65. Hon. DLitt, Royal University Malta, 1964. Kt Grand Cross: Order of St Sylvester, 1962; Order of Pope Pius IX, 1964. *Adddress:* 55 Victoria Avenue, Sliema, Malta. *T:* 30393; 27 St Paul by the Sea, St Paul's Bay, Malta. *T:* 73471.
[Died 29 Oct. 1980.

BORSCHETTE, Albert; Member of Commission of European Communities, 1970-76; *b* 14 June 1920. *Educ:* Aix-en-Provence, Munich, Erlangen, Paris. Dr en Phil. et Lettres. Press Attaché, Min. of State, Luxembourg, 1945-47; Head of Liaison Mission, French Headquarters in Germany, 1947-49; Mem. Luxembourg

Mission, Allied Control Council, Berlin, 1948-50; Legation Sec., Luxembourg Legation, Bonn, 1950-53; Sec., then Counsellor, Luxembourg Embassy, Brussels, 1953-57; Dep. Head of Delegn, Intergovtl Cttee for Common Market and Euratom, 1956-57; Ambassador and Perm. Rep. of Grand-Duchy of Luxembourg to European Communities, 1958-70. Holds numerous foreign orders. *Publications:* Journal Russe, 1946; Literatur und Politik, 1951; Itinéraires, 1952; Continuez à mourir, 1957; Itinéraires soviétiques, 1971. *[Died 8 Dec. 1976.*

BORTHWICK, Algernon Malcolm, MC; TD; Chairman, Thomas Borthwick & Sons, since 1949; *b* 22 March 1907; *m* 1935, Edith Wylde Addison (*d* 1975); one *s* two *d* (and one *s* one *d* decd). *Educ:* Harrow; Christ Church, Oxford (MA). With Thomas Borthwick & Sons, meat importers, 1928-39; served War of 1939-45, officer in London Scottish, England, Middle East, Italy, 1939-44 (wounded, MC); subsequently comd London Scottish 1949-52; returned to civil life with Thomas Borthwick & Sons, 1946. *Recreations:* shooting, ski-ing, painting. *Address:* Flat 11, Campbell Court, Gloucester Road, SW7 5LY. *T:* 01-584 1547. *Clubs:* Caledonian, Boodle's; Australian (Melbourne). *[Died 6 Jan. 1975.*

BORTHWICK, Brig.-Gen. Francis Henry, CMG 1919; DSO 1918; *b* 1883; *s* of Alexander Borthwick; *m* 1929, Gertrude Anne Frances, *o d* of Milne Keay, Edinburgh. Served European War, 1914-19 (despatches four times, DSO with bar, CMG). *Address:* The Langham Hotel, Valley Drive, Harrogate, N Yorks. *[Died 12 Feb. 1977.*

BOSE, Prof. Satyendranath, FRS 1958; Emeritus Professor of Physics in the University of Calcutta; National Professor, 1958; *b* 1894. *Educ:* Calcutta Univ. (MSc). Came to Europe, 1924; collaborated with Einstein in discovery of Bose-Einstein law of quantum mechanics. Reader in Physics, later Prof. and Head of Dept, Dacca Univ., 1927-46; Khaira Prof. of Physics, Calcutta Univ., 1946-56. Formerly Vice-Chancellor, Visa-Bharati Univ., India. Chm. Nat. Inst. of Sciences of India, 1948-50; Mem. Governing Body, CSIR, India, 1948-. *Publications:* numerous scientific papers. *Address:* 92 Acharyya Prafullachandra Road, Calcutta 9, India. *[Died 4 Feb. 1974.*

BOSTOCK, John, CBE 1972; Business Consultant; Director: British Hartford Fairmont Ltd; British Hartford Fairmont Investments Ltd; Unibin Ltd; *b* 30 Sept. 1916; *s* of William Bostock and Lucy (*née* Booth); *m* 1942, Sybil Field; one *s*. *Educ:* Sheffield Univ. CEng, MIEE. Exper. Officer, Admty Engrg Labs, W Drayton, 1942-45; Develt Engr, English Electric Co. Ltd, Preston and Bradford, 1945-48; Engrg and Project Man., Sperry Gyroscope Div., Brentford, 1948-62; Gen. Man. 1962-67, Man. Dir 1967-71, Sperry Gyroscope Div., Sperry Rand Ltd. *Recreations:* music, painting, Stock Exchange activities. *Address:* Dial House, 25 Sutton Avenue, Slough, Berks. *T:* Slough 21733. *[Died 26 Oct. 1977.*

BOSTON, 8th Baron *cr* 1761; **Bt** 1704; **Cecil Eustace Irby,** MC 1917; DL; *b* 14 July 1897; *yr s* of Hon. Cecil Saumares Irby (*s* of 5th Baron); *S* brother 1958. *Educ:* Eton; RMC Service European War (MC). Grenadier Guards, 1916-35; R of O, 1935-39; Gren. Gds, 1939-48. Major (Retd). DL Anglesey, 1960. *Heir:* cousin Gerald Howard Boteler Irby, MBE [*b* 29 Aug. 1897; *m* 1st, 1926 (marr. diss.); one *d* ; 2nd, 1936, Erica Hill; one *s*]. *Address:* Cae'r Borth, Moelfre, Anglesey. *T:* Moelfre 249. *Clubs:* Guards, Royal Automobile. *[Died 12 Oct. 1972.*

BOSTON, 9th Baron *cr* 1761; **Gerald Howard Boteler Irby, MBE** 1918; Bt 1704; *b* 29 Aug. 1897; *s* of Leonard Paul Irby, OBE (*g g s* of 2nd Baron) (*d* 1936), and Ethel Maud (*d* 1957), *d* of Captain William John Casberd Boteler, RN; *S* cousin, 1972; *m* 1st, 1926, Katherine Gertrude (marr. diss. 1931), *d* of Captain C. M. H. Edwards; one *d* ; 2nd, 1936, Erica, *d* of T. H. Hill; one *s*. Served European War, 1914-18 as Lieutenant, KRRC (MBE); War of 1939-45 as Major, RASC. *Heir:* *s* Hon. Timothy George Frank Boteler Irby [*b* 27 March 1939; *m* 1967, Rhonda Anne, *d* of R. A. Bate, Sydney, Australia; two *s* one *d*]. *Address:* Flat 11, Gunters Mead, Copsem Lane, Esher, Surrey. *[Died 17 Feb. 1978.*

BOSWELL, Captain Lennox Albert Knox, DSO 1940; RN (retired); fruit farmer since 1950; *b* 18 May 1898; 3rd *s* of William Albert Boswell and Florence Helen Rotch; *m* 1942, Diana de Lacy Bacon; three *s* (and one *d* decd). *Educ:* RN Colleges, Osborne and Dartmouth. Cadet and Midshipman HMS Irresistible, 1914-15, Belgian Coast and Dardanelles; Midshipman and Sub-Lieut HMS Queen Elizabeth, 1915-19, Flagship of Admiral Sir D. Beatty; surrender of High Sea Fleet, Nov. 1918; Trinity Coll., Cambridge, 1919, First Trinity VIII Henley; qualified in Gunnery, 1923; Comdr 1933; Comdr "G"

HMS Excellent, 1933-35; Fleet Gunnery Officer, Home Fleet, 1936-37; RN Staff Coll., 1935; RAF Staff Coll., 1938; War of 1939-45, commanded HMS Pelican, 1939-41; Captain 1940; Ordnance Board and Gunnery Div. Admiralty, 1941-43; Hedgehog and VT Fuse Trials; commanded aircraft carriers HMS Dasher and HMS Biter, 1943-44; Chief of Staff to Flag Officer Western Mediterranean and BNLO, Algiers, 1944-45; commanded RN Air Station Halesworth (HMS Sparrowhawk), 1945-46; commanded HMS Kenya (A and WI Station), 1946-48; Chief of Staff to C-in-C, The Nore, 1948-49; retired 1950. *Recreations:* gardening, music, colour cinematography. *Address:* Holts, Bosham, Chichester, W Sussex. *T:* Bosham 573092. *Club:* United Service & Royal Aero.
[Died 19 April 1975.

BOSWORTH, George Herbert; retired; *b* 17 May 1896; *s* of John Henry Bosworth. *Educ:* Peter Symonds, Winchester; University of Southampton. Served European War: RNAS and RAF; Air Ministry, 1919; Private Secretary to Marshal of RAF Sir Cyril (later Lord) Newall, 1932; Asst Secretary, 1939; Dir of Housing, Ministry of Aircraft Production, 1940; Asst Secretary Min. of Works, 1944; Under Secretary, 1952-59. *Publications:* How To Be Happy in France, 1930; Prelude (novel), 1932; Where Shall We Go?, 1939. *Recreations:* music, salmon fishing. *Address:* 31 Church Street, Willingdon, Eastbourne, E Sussex. *Club:* National Liberal. *[Died 21 July 1979.*

BOTHA, Colin Graham, VD; MA, LLD; FSA; FRHistS; Lieut-Col retired list; formerly Chief Archivist for Union of South Africa; *b* Knysna, Cape Colony, 15 Aug. 1883; *y s* of late Rev. Michiel Christiaan Botha and Elizabeth Mary Young; *m* ; two *s* one *d*. *Educ:* Cape Town. Entered Civil Service of the Cape Colony, 1901; Keeper of Archives of Cape Province, 1912; first Chief Archivist, 1919; retired, 1944; Member of the Archives Commn, 1922-; President: SA National Soc. for preservation of hist. objects; The Heraldry Soc. of Southern Africa; Member War Histories Cttee Union; Past President SA Assoc. for Advancement of Science; Fellow Huguenot Soc., London; Fellow Genealogical Soc., London; Member of various South African and Dutch literary societies, etc; sent by Union Government of South Africa to Europe, USA, and Canada, 1920-21, to examine into system of keeping Archives; visited Europe, USA and Canada again in 1938 to examine into archival systems; was at first Assembly League of Nations, 1920; was OC Duke of Edinburgh's Own Rifles; served South African War, 1901; 1914-18; Chief Recruiting Officer, Cape Fortress Command, War of 1939-45; over 42 years service with Volunteers and Active Citizen Force. KJStJ; awarded Carnegie Visitors' Grant, 1938. Hon. LLD: Cape Town, 1943; Witwatersrand, 1952. *Publications:* Place Names in Cape District, 1917; A Brief Guide to the Documents in the Cape Archives, 1652-1806, 1918; The French Refugees at the Cape, 1919 (3rd edn, 1970, Afrikaans translation, 1939); Report of a Tour to various Archives in Europe, Canada and USA, 1921; Social Life in the Cape Colony in the 18th Century, 1927 (2nd edn, 1970); Place Names in the Cape Province, 1927; The Public Archives of South Africa, 1652-1910, 1928; Our South Africa, Past and Present, 1938; Collected Writings (from 1912, 3 vols), 1962; edited 5th vol. of van Riebeeck Society Publications; articles in SA Law Journal and Science Journal; contributor to various magazines, and newspapers. *Recreations:* reading, writing. *Address:* Alameda Hotel, Talana Road, Newlands, CP, S Africa. *Clubs:* Authors' (London); Civil Service (Cape Town).
[Died 1 Feb. 1973.

BOUCHIER, Air Vice-Marshal Sir Cecil Arthur, KBE 1953 (CBE 1941; OBE 1936); CB 1945; DFC 1918; *b* 14 Oct. 1895, British; *m* 1st, 1927, Gladys Dorothy Sherwood (*d* 1964); one *s* ; 2nd, 1968, Isabella Dorothy Guyver, *d* of Frank Guyver Britton, Yokohama. *Educ:* Chichester; RAF Staff Coll. Served in "A" Battery HAC, 1915-17, in Palestine; commissioned RFC 1918; served with RAF in Middle East and N Russia, 1918-19; India and Iraq, 1920-21; RAE Experimental Pilot, Farnborough, 1922-25; No 41 (F) Squadron, 1926-28; Test Pilot, Egypt, 1929; graduated RAF Staff Coll., Andover, 1930; HQ RAF India, 1931-32; formed and commanded Indian Air Force, 1932-35; commanded: No 54 (F) Sqdn, 1936-37; No 11 Group, 1938-39; commanded RAF Sector, Hornchurch (Battle of Britain), 1940 (CBE and despatches); No 11 Group and RAF Station, Kenley, 1941; Air Ministry, 1942; No 11 (F) Group, 1943-45 (in control Fighter "umbrella" at Normandy Beach landings) (CB); AOC No 221 Group in Burma, 1945; AOC, British Commonwealth Air Forces of Occupation, Japan, 1945-48; AOC No 21 Group, Swinderby, Lincs, 1948-49; retired list, 1949; re-instated on active list, 1950; Personal Representative of British Chiefs of Staff to Generals MacArthur, Ridgway and Mark Clark throughout Korean War, 1950-53; retired list 1953. Order of St Anne (Russia), 1919; Legion of Merit (Commander), USA,

1945. *Recreations:* golf, chess. *Address:* 2275 Isshiki, Hayama, Kanagawa-ken, Japan. *T:* 0468-75-1217. *Club:* Royal Air Force.
[Died 15 June 1979.

BOUGHEY, Sir Richard (James), 10th Bt, *cr* 1798; JP; DL; *b* 30 July 1925; *s* of Sir George Menteth Boughey, 9th Bt; *m* 1st, 1950, Davina Julia (marr. diss. 1975), 2nd *d* of Fitzherbert Wright; two *s* three *d*; 2nd, 1976, Gillian Claire, *d* of late Major Robert Moubray. *Educ:* Eton. Served with Coldstream Guards, 1943-46, in France and Germany, Lieut. Chairman, Apple and Pear Development Council, 1967-72; Liaison Officer to Minister of Agriculture, Fisheries and Food, 1965-71; Chairman, East Sussex Agricultural Exec. Cttee, 1958-67; Pres., Nat. Fedn of Young Farmers Clubs, 1970; Mem., Adv. Council for Agriculture and Horticulture in England and Wales, 1973-. High Sheriff of Sussex, 1964; DL, Sussex, 1970-. OStJ. *Heir:* s John George Fletcher Boughey, *b* 12 Aug. 1959. *Address:* The Old Rectory, Quarley, Andover, Hants. *Club:* Boodle's.
[Died 3 Oct. 1978.

BOULANGER, Nadia (Juliette), Hon. CBE; Grand Officier de la Légion d'Honneur; teacher of composition; conductor; lecturer; *b* Paris, 16 Sept. 1887; *d* of Ernest and Raïssa (Princess Mychetsky) Boulanger. Studied at Paris Nat. Conservatory. Formerly head of theory dept, Ecole Normale de Musique, Paris. Went to US in 1924, 1935, 1940, 1958, 1962; was faculty member in many American Schools. Now Conservatory of Music, Paris (Hon. Prof.); Prof. and Director, Conservatoire Americain, Fontainebleau; Guest Conductor: Boston Symphony Orchestra; Royal Philharmonic, London; NY Philharmonic; Philadelphia Orchestra; Washington Symphony. Maître de Chapelle to the Prince of Monaco. Has lectured and conducted in many European countries and in US. Has made numerous recordings. FRCM. Dr *hc:* Oxford; Harvard, Newcastle, etc; holds several other hon. doctorates. Gold Medal, Acad. des Beaux Arts. Commander, Arts et Lettres (France); Commander: Order of Polonia Restituta (Poland); Ordre de la Couronne (Belgium); Commander of St Charles (Monaco). *Address:* 3 Place Lili Boulanger (anciennement 36 Rue Ballu), Paris IXe, France.
[Died 22 Oct. 1979.

BOULTER, Robert, CMG 1923; OBE 1947; *b* 6 April 1885; *s* of H. J. Boulter, Brook Vale, Rattlesden, Bury St Edmunds; *m* 1914, Ethel Marie Brazier; one *s*. *Educ:* Framlingham Coll. Entered British Consular Service in Japan, 1907; Commercial Secretary, British Embassy, Tokio, 1925-29; Trade Commissioner, Singapore, 1929-34; Trade Commissioner, Wellington, 1934-49; Economic Adviser to High Commissioner for the United Kingdom in New Zealand, 1944-49; given title of Senior Trade Commissioner, 1946; retired, 1949. *Recreations:* walking, bridge. *Address:* Carey's Manor Hotel, Brockenhurst, Hants. *Clubs:* East India, Sports and Public Schools; Lymington (Lymington).
[Died 3 Nov. 1973.

BOUQUET, Rev. Alan Coates, DD; Honorary CF; *b* 26 May 1884; *o c* of late Robert Coates Bouquet of The Laurel House, Padbury, Buckingham, and Elizabeth, *d* of John Stow, Sepham Court, Shoreham, Kent; *m* 1910, Edith Gertrude (*d* 1952), *d* of late G. W. Sayer of London; no *c*. *Educ:* St Dunstan's Coll., London; Trinity Coll., Cambridge (Scholar); Jesus Coll., Cambridge (Scholar); Westcott House, Cambridge. Bowen Prize for Modern History, 1903; Corrie Prize for Greek Testament, 1907; Winchester Reading Prize, 1907; 1st Class Theological Tripos, Part I, 1907; BA 1905; MA 1910; BD 1918; DD 1922. Asst Curate of Putney, 1907-12; Lecturer in Church History, Deaconesses' Institution, 1911-12; Senior Curate, St Margaret's, Altrincham, 1912-14; Army Chaplain, 1914-1919 (despatches); Member Archbishop's No 1 Cttee of Reform, 1917; Central Organising Secretary SPCK, 1919-22; Hon Asst Curate St Martin-in-the-Fields, 1920-22; Vicar of All Saints, Cambridge, 1922-45. Recognised Lecturer in Theology in University of Cambridge, 1914-36, and in the History and Comparative Study of Religions, 1934-44; Select Preacher, University of Cambridge, 1917, 1923, 1931, and 1942; Hulsean Lecturer, Cambridge Univ., 1924-25; Stanton Lecturer in the Philosophy of Religion, Cambridge Univ., 1931-34; OCF Anti-Aircraft Troops, Cambridge Area, 1942-45; Lectr in the History and Comparative Study of Religion, Univ. of Cambridge, 1945-54; Lecturer on Upton Foundation, Michaelmas Term, Oxford, 1946. Has given lectures at Harvard, Princeton, New York, University of California, Delhi and Andhra Universities, 1955-65. *Publications:* A Point of View, 1913; Christian Reunion, 1914; A Man's Pocket-Book of Religion, 1916; When He is Come, 1917; The Greatest Relationship, 1919; Is Christianity the Final Religion?, 1921; The Christian Religion and its Competitors Today (Hulsean Lectures, 1924-25), 1925; The Real Presence, 1928; Modern Handbooks of Religion, vols 1-4, 1932-33; Man and Deity, 1933; Jesus (A New Outline and Estimate), 1933; The Doctrine of God, 1934; Translation of Przywara's Philosophy of Religion (Polarity), 1935; A Lectionary of Christian Prose, 1939 (3rd edn enlarged, 1965); Comparative Religion (in Pelican Books), 1941, 8th edn 1973; Hinduism (University Series), 1949, 4th edn 1969; Everyday Life in New Testament Times, 1953, 2nd edn, 1956 (and numerous foreign edns); Sacred Books of the World, 1953, 4th edn, 1967; contrib. to Encyclopædia Britannica (new edn); Chambers's Encyclopædia (new edn); Oxford Encyclopædia for Schools, 1948; Old Monumental Brasses in Great Britain, 1956; Christianity and Non-Christian Faiths (in Library of Constructive Theology), 1958; contrib. to Telugu Encyclopædia, 1960, to Encyclopædia Americana, 1963; Studies in The Problems of Peace (with Prof. K. S. Murty), 1960; European Brasses (with Dr M. J. Waring), 1967; Religious Experience: Its nature, types, and validity, 2nd edn 1968. *Recreations:* bird-watching; Hon. Vice-President Cambridge Univ. Judo Club. *Address:* Gilling House, Cambridge. *T:* 53119.
[Died 4 March 1976.

BOURDILLON, Robert Benedict, CBE 1946; MC 1917; AFC 1918; retired; *b* 8 Sept. 1889; *s* of Francis William Bourdillon, Buddington, Midhurst, Sussex; *m* 1922, Harriet Ada, *d* of Henry Broughton Barnes, Henley, Sussex; one *s* (and one *s* decd). *Educ:* Balliol Coll., Oxford; St Mary's Hospital, London. BA (Nat. Science) 1912 Oxon.; MA 1919; BM, BCh, 1925; DM, 1935; Lecturer in Chemistry Balliol Coll., Oxford, 1912-14; Fellow and Praelector in Chemistry, University Coll., Oxford, 1913-21; Dean, University Coll., Oxford, 1920-21; Ho. Physician and later Asst Medical Unit, St Mary's Hospital, London, 1925-26; National Institute for Medical Research, Hampstead, 1926-46; Director, Electro-medical Research Unit, Stoke Mandeville Hospital (Ministry of Health and Medical Research Council, 1946-54). War Service, 1914-19, Intelligence Corps, RFC and RAF. *Publications:* various papers in scientific journals. *Recreations:* mountaineering and walking. *Address:* Ganges, British Columbia, Canada. *Club:* Athenæum.
[Died 3 March 1971.

BOURKE, Major Sir (Edward Alexander) Henry L.; *see* Legge-Bourke.

BOURKE-WHITE, Margaret; on staff of Life Magazine since 1936; *b* 14 June 1906; *d* of Joseph White and Minnie Elizabeth Bourke; *m* 1st, 1925, Everett Chapman; 2nd, 1939, Erskine Caldwell (marr. diss., 1942); no *c*. *Educ:* Universities of Columbia, Michigan and Cornell. Industrial photographer, 1927-. Has taken photographs in various countries. Associate editor: Fortune Magazine, 1929-33; Life Magazine, 1936- (UN War corresp. in Korea, 1952; accredited War corresp.-photographer to US Air Forces in Great Britain, N. Africa and Europe, 1942-45). Has executed photo-murals for firms. Is represented in Library of Congress and in notable museums. Holds numerous awards. AFD (hon.) Michigan, 1951; LittD (hon.) Rutgers, 1949. *Publications:* Eyes on Russia, 1931; USSR, A Portfolio of Photographs, 1934; You Have Seen Their Faces (with Erskine Caldwell), 1937; North of the Danube (with Erskine Caldwell), 1939; Say! Is This The USA? (with Erskine Caldwell), 1941; Shooting the Russian War (text and photographs), 1942; Purple Heart Valley, 1944; Dear Fatherland, Rest Quietly, 1946; Halfway to Freedom, A Study of the New India, 1949; A Report on the American Jesuits (with Father John LaFarge, SJ), 1956; Portrait of Myself, 1963. *Recreation:* gardening. *Address:* Life Magazine, Time and Life Building, Rockefeller Center, New York, NY 10020, USA. *T:* Judson 6-1212. *Club:* Overseas Press (New York).
[Died 27 Aug. 1971.

BOURNE, Aleck William, MA, MB, BCh Cantab, FRCS, FRCOG; retired; formerly Consulting Obstetrical Surgeon, Queen Charlotte's Hospital, St Mary's Hospital; Consulting Surgeon, Samaritan Hospital; *b* 4 June 1886; *o s* of Rev. W. C. Bourne, formerly of Barnet; *m* 1912, Bessie, *e d* of G. W. Hayward, Barnet; three *d*. *Educ:* Rydal Sch., Colwyn Bay; Downing Coll., Cambridge (open scholar). 1st Class Nat. Science Tripos, 1908; Senior Univ. Scholar, St Mary's Hosp., 1908; War Service as Surgical Specialist, Egypt and France, 1914-17; filled resident and other appointments at St Mary's, Queen Charlotte's, and Samaritan Hospitals, 1910-14; former Examiner, University of Cambridge; former Mem. of Central Health Services Council (1948); Pres. Obstetrical and Gynæcological Section, Royal Society of Medicine, 1938-39. Hon. FRSM 1973. *Publications:* Recent Advances in Obstetrics and Gynæcology, 12th edn, 1962; Synopsis of Midwifery and Gynæcology, 13th edn, 1965; A Doctor's Creed, 1962; (Jt Ed.) British Practice of Obstetrics and Gynæcology, 3rd edn, 1963, and various papers in periodical medical journals. *Address:* The Red House, Skinners Lane, Ashtead, Surrey.
[Died 27 Dec. 1974.

BOURNE, Prof. Edward John, FRIC; PhD, DSc Birmingham; Professor of Chemistry in the University of London, Royal Holloway College, since 1956; *b* 1 Jan. 1922; *s* of Arthur John and Florence Grace Bourne, Cannock, Staffs; *m* 1947, Kathleen Joyce, *d* of James and Ellen Cryer; one *s*. *Educ:* Rugeley Grammar Sch., Staffs; University of Birmingham. Lecturer in Chemistry, University of Birmingham, 1944-50; Senior Lecturer, 1950-55; Reader in Organic Chemistry, 1955-56; Vice-Principal, Royal Holloway Coll., Univ. of London, 1967-69. Council of Chemical Soc., 1954-56. Joint Library Cttee, 1959-63. Chairman: Board of Studies in Chemistry, University of London, 1959-63; Downland Section, Royal Institute of Chemistry, 1966-67. *Publications:* scientific papers mainly in Journal of Chemical Society. *Address:* Royal Holloway College, Englefield Green, Surrey. *T:* Egham 5351. *Club:* Wentworth (Virginia Water, Surrey).   *[Died 30 Nov. 1974.*

BOURNE, Sir Frederick Chalmers, KCSI 1946 (CSI 1944); CIE 1941; late ICS; *b* 12 Aug. 1891; *s* of late Sir Frederick Bourne, CMG, Mayfield, Sussex; *m* 1918, Heather Frances, *d* of late Lieut-Col F. W. Burbury. *Educ:* Rugby; Christ Church, Oxford, MA. Served in 4th Bn Queen's Own (RW Kent Regt), 1910-20. Entered Indian Civil Service, 1920; Sec. to Government, Punjab, Electricity and Industries Dept, 1934-37; Dep. Commissioner, Lahore, 1937-40; Sec. to Government of Punjab, Home Dept, 1940-41; Chief Sec. to Govt, Punjab, 1941-45; Acting Governor Central Provinces and Berar, May-Oct, 1945; Acting Governor of Assam, 1946; Governor of Central Provinces and Berar, 1946-47; Governor of East Bengal, Aug. 1947-50. Appointed as Adviser, Gold Coast, 1955. *Address:* Eachen Hill, Buxted, Sussex. *T:* Buxted 3108.   *[Died 3 Nov. 1977.*

BOUSFIELD, Guy William John, MD, BS London; *b* 20 Oct. 1893; *s* of Edward Collins Bousfield, MRCS, LRCP, DPH Cantab.; *m* 1923, Phyllis Doyle; one *s*. *Educ:* St Olaves; St Thomas's Hospital. Formerly Dir of Public Health Laboratory (MRC) Denmark Hill, and of Camberwell Laboratories; Immunological Specialist to LCC and Middx. CC; Ho. Physician, Ho. Surg. and Clinical Asst. of Electrocardiograph Dept, St Thomas's Hosp. (publ. first tracings ever recorded of changes during and after an attack of Angina pectoris, Lancet 1918); Pathologist to St Giles and Dulwich Hosp., LCC; Dep. Principal MO, St John Amb. Assoc., and County Surg., St John Amb. Bde; Supt (Surg.) City of London Special Constabulary. Commissioned Infantry, Oct. 1914; served with Oxon and Bucks Light Infantry; Commissioned Royal Air Force Medical Service, 1918; Capt. 1919; Awarded Pilot's Certificate of Fédération Aéronautique Internationale, 1918. Major (Medical Officer) 44th Co. of London Bn Home Guard. (With Dr W. W. King-Brown) made 1st British Diptheria Immunisation propaganda film The Empty Bed, 1934. OStJ. *Publications:* A Practical Guide to the Schick Test and Diphtheria and Scarlet Fever Immunisation, 1929; A Preliminary Course of Hygiene, 1953; numerous technical articles. Children's book: In Search of Alice, 1949. *Recreations:* yachting, amateur cinema film production, engineering, winter sports, bowls, etc. *Address:* Well Cottage, Goose Green, Warnham, Sussex. *T:* Horsham 5324. *Clubs:* Savage, Chelsea Arts.   *[Died 14 Aug. 1974.*

BOUSSAC, Marcel; French industrialist, retired; President and Director-General, Société des parfums Christian Dior, 1970-72; *b* Châteauroux, Indre, 17 April 1889; *s* of Louis-Alexandre Boussac and Primitive Jeanne (*née* Mette); *m* 1939, Margarita Deceuninck (Fanny Heldy), Chevalier de la Légion d'Honneur (*d* 1973); one *d*. Since 1917 has been Dir, Managing Dir, Chm., and Dir-Gen. of many companies (dealing in textiles, chemicals, dyes, printing, sizing, etc.). Founder and proprietor, Christian Dior; Chm. and Dir-Gen. of the Comptoir de l'Industrie Cotonnière, 1963-70, Pres., 1970-74, Pres. supervisory council, 1974-75. Is a leading racehorse owner and his horses have won numerous international trophies. *Address:* (business) 21 rue Poissonnière, 75002 Paris, France; (home) 74 boulevard Maurice-Barrès, 92200 Neuilly-sur-Seine, France.
                    [Died 21 March 1980.

BOUSTEAD, Col Sir (John Edmund) Hugh, KBE 1965 (OBE 1934); CMG 1954; DSO 1941; MC and Bar; Vladimir with cross swords; St George's Military Medal with one Palm (Ethiopia); FRGS; late Gordon Highlanders; British Political Agent, Abu Dhabi, Nov. 1961-May 1965, retired; Development Secretary to Sultanate of Muscat and Oman, Oct. 1958-Oct. 1961; Resident Adviser, Hadhramaut States and British Agent, East Aden Protectorate, Southern Arabia, Oct. 1949-Oct. 1958; *b* 14 April 1895; *s* of Lawrence Twentyman Boustead and Ethel Margaret Alers-Hankey; unmarried. *Educ:* RNC Osborne and Dartmouth; HMS Cornwall; Oxford Univ. Midshipman and acting Sub Lieut, 1913-15; Royal Navy, German East and German South West Africa and Cape Station; S African Bde,

Egypt, Western Desert and France, 1915-19; Capt. S African Brigade attached General Denikin's Army in South Russia, 1919; Worcester Coll., Oxford (while still serving in South African Brigade), 1920; appointed Gordon Highlanders, Malta, Constantinople, Chanak and Eastern Thrace, 1921-24; Sudan Camel Corps, 1924-29; Gen. Staff SDF, Khartoum, 1930; commanded Sudan Camel Corps, 1931; retired from Army 1935 to Sudan Political Service; District Commissioner Western District, Darfur, 1935-40; recalled to service with temp. rank of Lieut-Col 1940, raised and trained Sudan Frontier Bn SDF and commanded it, Jan.-July 1941, in operations in Central Abyssinia against the Italians (despatches, DSO); 2nd in command SDF Bde, Eritrea, 1943, with temp. rank of Col; Commanded 2nd SDF Brigade, April 1945; recalled to Political Service, Aug. 1945; late District Commissioner Sudan Political Service; Hon. rank of Col on ceasing to belong to R of O. Captained British Olympic Team Modern Pentathlon, Antwerp, and winner Army Lightweight Championships, 1920; Mem. of Fourth Everest Expedition, 1933. BBC TV programme, The World About Us, 1972. Awarded Lawrence of Arabia Memorial Medal by Royal Central Asian Society, 1966. *Publication:* The Wind of Morning, 1971. *Recreations:* riding, shooting, mountaineering, and ski-ing. *Clubs:* Athenæum, Naval and Military.   *[Died 3 April 1980.*

BOVELL, Sir (Conrad Swire) Kerr, Kt 1961; CMG 1958; Bursar, Radley College, since 1968; *b* St Leonards-on-Sea, Sussex, 9 Sept. 1913; *s* of late C. W. K. Bovell, MBE, Colonial Police Service, and of Edith Margaret Bovell (*née* Haughton); *m* 1941, Ethne Jane, *d* of late A. V. Perrin; two *d*. *Educ:* Bradfield Coll., Berks. Appointed to Colonial Police Service as a Probationary Asst Supt of Police. Federated Malay States, 1934; served in Malaya until outbreak of Pacific War; interned in Singapore, 1942-45; returned to Malaya; served until 1956; apptd Inspector-Gen. of Police, Federation of Nigeria, 1956; served until retirement in 1962. Bursar, Worksop Coll., 1963-68. Colonial Police Medal, 1951; Queen's Police Medal, 1954; OStJ 1957. *Recreation:* golf. *Address:* Radley College, Abingdon, Berkshire. *T:* Abingdon 1272. *Clubs:* East India, Sports and Public Schools; MCC.   *[Died 29 Sept. 1973.*

BOVENSCHEN, Sir Frederick Carl, KCB 1943 (CB 1927); KBE 1938; *s* of late C. and Mrs Bovenschen; *m* Mabel Alice (*d* 1975), *o d* of the late Right Hon. Sir A. H. D. Acland, 13th Bart; one *d*. *Educ:* King's Sch., Canterbury; Corpus Christi Coll., Oxford (Scholar). 1st Class Classical Mods, 1905; 1st Class Lit. Hum., 1907. Asst Private Sec. to Viscount Haldane, Sec. of State for War, 1908-12; Private Sec. to Sir Charles Harris, KCB, 1912-15; Principal, War Office, 1920; Asst Sec., 1921; lent to Government of India to serve on Army Retrenchment Cttee, 1931; Dir of Army Contracts, 1932; Dir of Finance, 1936; Dep. Under-Sec. of State for War, 1936-42; Joint Permanent Under-Sec. of State for War, and Mem. of the Army Council, 1942-45. Chevalier Légion d'Honneur, 1920. A Governor of Westminster Hospital and Chm. of its Finance Cttee, 1948-60; a Governor of King's Sch., Canterbury; Mem. Kent County Council, 1949-55; Councillor, Hythe Town Council; Baron of the Cinque Ports, 1953. *Address:* Dunkery, Church Road, Hythe, Kent. *T:* Hythe 67854. *Club:* Athenæum.   *[Died 9 Nov. 1977.*

BOWATER, Sir Dudley; *see* Bowater, Sir T. D. B.

BOWATER, Sir (Thomas) Dudley (Blennerhassett), 3rd Bt, *cr* 1914; *b* 29 Sept. 1889; 2nd *s* of Sir T. Vansittart Bowater, 1st Bt, MP; *S* brother 1945; *m* 1916, Kathleen Mary (*d* 1921), *o d* of A. A. Frost, Rugby; one *d*; *m* 1948, Mrs Jessie F. Bowater. *Educ:* Whitgift; Maison-de-Melle, Belgium. Liveryman of the Gardeners Company. Capt. 2/2nd County of London (Westminster Dragoons) Yeomanry, 1914-18. Capt. TF Reserve; Chief Observer, Royal Observer Corps, 1940-44. *Recreations:* tennis, golf and the garden. *Heir: nephew* John Vansittart Bowater [*b* 6 June 1918; *m* 1943, Joan Kathleen, *d* of late W. E. H. Scullard; one *s* one *d*]. *Address:* 15 Encombe, Sandgate, Kent.   *[Died 3 March 1972.*

BOWDEN, Rev. Canon Guy Arthur George; Vicar of All Saints, Highbrook in Diocese of Chichester, since 1965; *b* 19 April 1909; *s* of Arthur Ashfordby and Ellen Louisa Bowden; *m* 1942, Jessie Margaret Guild; two *s* one *d*. *Educ:* Haileybury Coll.; Magdalene Coll., Cambridge; Westcott House, Cambridge. Cambridge Mission to Delhi, 1931-34; Westcott House, 1934-36; Curate, St Mary and St John's, Birmingham, 1936-39; Curate, Hatfield, Herts, 1939-40; Instructor and officiating Chaplain, RAF, 1940-43; Chaplain, RAF, 1943-46; Chaplain and Lecturer in Divinity, King Alfred's Coll., Winchester, 1946-51; Canon and Chancellor, Truro Cathedral, 1951-60, and Diocesan Dir of Religious Education, Canon Emeritus, 1972; Warden of the SPG Coll. of the Ascension, Selly Oak, Birmingham, 1960-64.

Publication: The Dazzling Darkness, 1950. *Recreation:* golf. *Address:* Lucaslands, Highbrook, Ardingly, Sussex.
[*Died* 1 *April* 1974.

BOWEN, Arthur C. M.; *see* Mainwaring-Bowen, A. C.

BOWEN, Catherine Drinker; author; *b* Haverford, Pa; *d* of Henry Sturgis Drinker and Aimée Ernesta (*née* Beaux); *m* 1st, Ezra Bowen; one *s* one *d* ; 2nd, 1939, Thomas McKean Downs. *Educ:* Peabody Institute; Juilliard Music Conservatory. Fellow: Royal Society of Literature; Royal Society of Arts; World Acad. of Art and Science; Mem. Amer. Philosophical Soc. Holds hon. degrees from Amer. Univs, and several Amer. awards. *Publications:* numerous books, including: Friends and Fiddlers (essays), 1935; (with Barbara Von Meck) Beloved Friend, biography of Tchaikowsky, 1937; Free Artist, biography of Anton and Nicolas Rubinstein, 1939; Yankee from Olympus, biography of Justice Holmes, 1944; John Adams and the American Revolution, 1950; The Lion and the Throne, biography of Sir Edward Coke, 1957; Adventures of a Biographer, 1960; Francis Bacon, The Temper of a Man, 1963; Miracle at Philadelphia, 1966; Biography: the craft and the calling, 1968; Family Portrait, 1970. *Address:* 260 Booth Lane, Haverford, Pa 19041, USA. *T:* Midway 9-4975. [*Died* 1 *Nov.* 1973.

BOWEN, Edmund John, FRS 1935; MA, DSc Oxon; Hon. Fellow of University College, Oxford; lately Aldrichian Praelector in Chemistry; *b* 29 April 1898; *s* of Edmund Riley Bowen and Lilias Kamester; *m* 1924, Edith Moule; one *s* one *d.* *Educ:* Royal Grammar Sch., Worcester; Balliol Coll., Oxford (Brackenbury Scholar). BA, 1920; MA, 1922; Fellow of University Coll., Oxford, 1922; Junior Proctor, 1935-36; Lieut 13th Siege Battery, RGA (France), 1917-18. Davy Medal, Royal Society, 1963; Niels Finsen Medal, 1968. *Publications:* The Chemical Aspects of Light, 1942; papers on physical chemical subjects in scientific journals. *Address:* 10 Park Town, Oxford. *T:* Oxford 57631. [*Died* 19 *Nov.* 1980.

BOWEN, Elizabeth (Dorothea Cole), CBE 1948; Hon. DLitt: TCD 1949; Oxon 1956; CLit 1965; *o c* of Henry Cole Bowen, Bowen's Court, Co. Cork, and Florence Isabella Pomeroy Colley; *m* 1923, Alan Charles Cameron (*d* 1952). *Educ:* Downe House, Downe, Kent. *Publications:* Encounters (short stories), 1923; Ann Lee's (short stories), 1926, The Hotel, 1927; The Last September, 1929; Joining Charles (short stories), 1929; Friends and Relations, 1931; To the North, 1932; The Cat Jumps (short stories), 1934; The House in Paris, 1935; The Death of the Heart, 1938; Look at All those Roses (short stories), 1941; Bowen's Court, 1942; Seven Winters, 1943; The Demon Lover (short stories), 1945; The Heat of the Day, 1949; Collected Impression (essays), 1950; The Shelbourne, 1951; A World of Love, 1955; A Time in Rome, 1960; After-thought (essays), 1962; The Little Girls, 1964; A Day in the Dark, 1965; Eva Trout, 1969. *Address:* Carbery, Church Hill, Hythe, Kent.
[*Died* 22 *Feb.* 1973.

BOWEN, Ira Sprague; astrophysicist; Distinguished Service Member, Carnegie Institution of Washington, 1964-73; *b* New York, 21 Dec. 1898; *s* of James Henry Bowen and Philinda May Sprague; *m* 1929, Mary Jane Howard. *Educ:* Oberlin Coll., Oberlin, Ohio (BA). Asst in physics, University of Chicago, further study, 1919-21; Calif. Institute of Technology, Pasadena: Instructor, 1921; PhD 1926; Hon. PhD University of Lund, 1950; Hon. ScD: Oberlin Coll., 1948; Princeton Univ., 1953. Asst Prof., 1926; Associate Prof., 1928; Prof., 1931-45; Director: Mount Wilson Observatory, 1946-64; Palomar Observatory, 1948-64 (Observatories maintained jtly by Carnegie Instn and Calif. Inst. of Technology); Morrison Research Associate at Lick Observatory, Mount Hamilton, Calif, 1938-39; associated with Office of Scientific Research and Development during War of 1939-45, specialising in rockets and in new types of cameras, etc. Mem. National Academy of Sciences, and of several scientific societies. Medals for work on nebulæ, 1942, 1946, 1949, 1957, 1966. *Address:* Hale Observatories, Pasadena, Calif 91101, USA; 2388 North Altadena Drive, Altadena, Calif 91001. [*Died* 6 *Feb.* 1973.

BOWEN-DAVIES, Alan, FRCS; Senior Consulting Surgeon, Ear, Nose and Throat Department, The London Hospital, since 1946; *b* 26 July 1907; *s* of Dr W. L. Bowen-Davies and Mrs H. A. Bowen-Davies (*née* Burton); *m* 1944, Irené Maude Atkinson; one *s* two *d.* *Educ:* Harrow Sch.; Pembroke Coll., Cambridge; Guy's Hospital. MA, MB, BChir Cantab 1933; FRCS 1936. Wing Comdr, RAFVR (retired), 1942-46. *Publications:* contributions to Scott-Brown's Diseases of the Ear, Nose and Throat, Proc. Royal Society Med., Lancet, Guy's Hospital reports. *Recreations:* tennis, shooting, fishing. *Address:* 34 Kensington Mansions, SW5 9TB. *T:* 01-370 2721. *Clubs:* East India, Sports and Public Schools; MCC. [*Died* 19 *Feb.* 1974.

BOWER; *see* Nott-Bower.

BOWER, Commander Robert Tatton; *b* 9 June 1894; *o s* of late Sir Robert Lister Bower, KBE, CMG, and Annette Norah, *d* of late Henry Head, Thornhill, Bray, Co. Wicklow; *m* 1922, Henrietta, 4th *d* of 1st Baron Strickland, GCMG; one *s* seven *d.* *Educ:* Cheam Sch.; RN Colleges Osborne and Dartmouth. Joined RN 1907; served throughout European War; present at Battle of Jutland in HMS Inconstant; in submarines, 1916-18; Flag-Lieut to C-in-C, Portsmouth (Hon. Sir S. C. Colville), 1918-19; in HMS Iron Duke (Turkey and South Russia), 1919-21; psc (RN), 1925; attached RAF Staff Coll., 1928, retired, 1931; returned to service at the outbreak of War of 1939-45, with RAF Coastal Command and at sea escorting convoys; MP (U) Cleveland, Yorks, 1931-45. Chairman Exec. Cttee Society for Individual Freedom, 1950-53. *Publications:* memoirs and occasional contributions to Reviews and Press. *Recreations:* racing, sailing. *Address:* Gatto-Murina Palace, Mdina, Malta. *T:* 74370. *Club:* Royal Yacht Squadron (Cowes). [*Died* 5 *July* 1975.

BOWERING, John; *b* 29 Oct. 1894; *s* of late Thomas Bowering, Axbridge, Somerset; *m* 1931, Sylvia Elizabeth, *d* of Ernest Hobbs, Santiago, Chile; one *s* one *d.* *Educ:* Clifton; abroad. Served European War, 1914-18 (despatches). During career in the Foreign Service has been stationed at Berlin, Stuttgart, New York, Santo Domingo, Magallanes, Brussels, Antofogasta, Reykjavik and Monrovia; Envoy Extraordinary and Minister Plenipotentiary to the Republic of Liberia, 1946-49; Consul-General at Nice, France, 1949-52; retired 1952. *Recreations:* country pursuits and fishing. *Address:* Ringmere, Town Hill, Lingfield, Surrey. *T:* 307. [*Died* 8 *Jan.* 1973.

BOWES-LYON, Maj.-Gen. Sir (Francis) James (Cecil), KCVO 1973; CB 1970; OBE 1972; MC and Bar, 1944; a Gentleman Usher to the Queen, 1974-76, an Extra Gentleman Usher, since 1976; *b* 19 Sept. 1917; *o s* of Capt. Geoffrey Bowes-Lyon; *m* 1941, Mary, 2nd *d* of Sir Humphrey de Trafford, 4th Bt, MC; two *s* one *d.* *Educ:* Eton; Royal Military Coll., Sandhurst. Commissioned into Grenadier Guards, 1938; served War of 1939-45, Guards Armoured Division; Commandant, Guards Depot, 1955-57; comd 2nd Bn Grenadier Guards, 1957-59; Mil. Assistant (GSO1) to CIGS, 1960-62; comd 157 Lowland Bde (Scotland), 1963; GOC 52nd Lowland Division District, 1966-68; GOC Berlin (British Sector), 1968-70; GOC London District, and Maj-Gen. commanding Household Div., 1971-73. Pres., Nat. Small Bore Rifle Assoc., 1974-; Chm. Bd of Governors, The Queen Alexandra Hospital Home for Disabled Sailors, Soldiers and Airmen, 1974-. *Recreations:* shooting, gardening, racing. *Address:* Beltingham House, Bardon Mill, Northumberland. *Clubs:* White's, Pratt's. [*Died* 18 *Dec.* 1977.

BOWLE, Horace Edgar; Consul-General in HM's Foreign Service (retired); *b* 13 Aug. 1886; *y s* of late Edward Bowle, Salisbury, Wilts; *m* 1917, Letitia Constance, *y d* of late Charles Penruddocke, Compton Park, Wilts. *Educ:* Pembroke Coll., Cambridge (BA 1908); abroad. Served in USA, Colombia (Chargé d'Affaires, 1914), France, Belgium, Argentina and Portuguese E Africa; retired on pension, Nov. 1944. *Address:* 23 Merrywood Park, Reigate, Surrey RH2 9PA. *T:* Reigate 46103. [*Died* 5 *March* 1978.

BOWLER, Air Vice-Marshal Thomas Geoffrey, CB 1951; CBE 1944; RAF, retired; *b* 1 March 1895; 2nd *s* of Thomas William Bowler; *m* 1924, Evelyn Mary, *o d* of Charles Luxon, MVO; one *s* one *d.* *Educ:* Bloxham Coll. Commissioned Dorset Regt, 1914; served European War, 1914-18, Captain, 1915; Suvla Bay landing, Gallipoli, 1915 (wounded); transferred to RFC and RAF, 1918; Sqdn Ldr, 1924; RAF Staff Coll., psa, 1930; Wing Comdr, 1938; Group Capt., 1940; Air Commodore, 1942; Air Vice-Marshal, 1947; retired 1951. *Address:* Westwards, Hook Hills Road, Paignton, Devon. *Club:* Royal Dart Yacht. [*Died* 5 *Sept.* 1974.

BOWLING, Air Vice-Marshal Victor Swanton, CB 1958; CBE 1948; DL; *b* 3 July 1908; *s* of Lieut-Col William Henry Bowling, TD, Pembroke Dock, South Wales; *m* 1936, Margaret Jennette, *d* of late Rev. R. T. Jones, Hope, Wrexham, Denbighshire; one *s* two *d.* *Educ:* Haverfordwest Grammar Sch.; St Lawrence Coll., Ramsgate. Entered RAF, 1927; served War of 1939-45 in Egypt, Iraq, North Africa, Norway (despatches); Senior Air Staff Officer, 11 Group, 1946-48; Group Capt., Operations Central Fighter Establishment, 1948-50; OC 323 Wing Canal Zone, 1950-51; Senior Air Staff Officer, Air Headquarters Iraq, 1951-52; Air Officer Commanding, Cyprus, 1952-54; Sector Comdr, Northern Fighter Sector, 1954-56; Air Officer Commanding 11 Group, 1956-59; Asst Chief of Staff (Air Defence), Supreme Headquarters, Allied Powers, Europe, Paris, 1959-61; Group-Capt. 1947; Air Commodore, 1952; Air Vice-Marshal, 1956;

Retired, 1961. DL Pembrokeshire, 1967. Freedom Cross of King Haakon VII, Norway. *Recreations:* ski-ing, sailing. *Address:* Old Chimneys, St Florence, Tenby, Pembrokeshire. *T:* Manorbier 205. *Clubs:* Royal Air Force, Ski Club of Great Britain. *[Died 27 Dec. 1971.*

BOWMAN, Sir James, 1st Bt *cr* 1961; KBE 1957 (CBE 1952); JP; DCL; *b* 8 March 1898; *m* 1922, Jean, *d* of Henry Brook, Ashington, Northumberland; one *s* one *d.* Served European War, 1914-18, Royal Marines. Gen. Sec., Northumberland Miners' Association (later National Union of Mineworkers, Northumberland Area), 1935-49; Vice-Pres., National Union of Mineworkers, 1938-49; Mem. of Gen. Council of TUC, 1945-49; Chm., National Coal Board Northern (N & C) Div., 1950-55; Dep. Chm., National Coal Board, 1955-56; Chm., National Coal Board, 1956-61. JP, Northumberland, 1935. Mem., Court of Governors of Administrative Staff Coll., 1957-. Former member: National Miners' Welfare Joint Council; DSIR; Royal Commission on the Press. *Heir: s* George Bowman [*b* 2 July 1923; *m* 1960, Olive (*née* Case); three *d*]. *Address:* Woodlands, Killingworth Drive, Newcastle upon Tyne NE12 0ES. *T:* Newcastle 661252. *Club:* Reform. *[Died 25 Sept. 1978.*

BOWRA, Sir (Cecil) Maurice, CH 1971; Kt 1951; FBA 1938; Warden of Wadham College, University of Oxford, 1938-70; *b* 8 April 1898; *y s* of late Cecil A. V. Bowra, Chinese Customs Service. *Educ:* Cheltenham Coll. (Scholar); New Coll., Oxford (Scholar). 1st class Hons Mods, 1920; 1st class Literae Humaniores, 1922; MA 1923; DLitt 1937. Joined RFA, 1917; served in France, 1917-18. University of Oxford: Fellow and Tutor, Wadham Coll., 1922-38; Prof. of Poetry, 1946-51; Vice-Chancellor, 1951-54; Romanes Lectr, 1966. Pres., British Acad., 1958-62. Hon. Fellow, New Coll., Oxford, 1946. Hon. Member: Amer. Acad. of Arts and Letters; Royal Irish Acad. Hon. LittD: Dublin; Hull; Wales; Harvard; Columbia; Hon. LLD St Andrews; Hon. DCL Oxford; Docteur hc: Paris; Aix; Teheran. Conington Prize, Univ. of Oxford, 1930; Kenyon Medal for Classical Studies, 1966. Commandeur de la Légion d'Honneur; Kt-Comdr, Royal Order of Phoenix (Greece); Pour le Mérite (W Germany). *Publications:* (trans. with H. T. Wade-Gery) Pindar's Pythian Odes, 1928; (co-Ed.) Oxford Book of Greek Verse, 1930; Tradition and Design in the Iliad, 1930; Ancient Greek Literature; Pindari Carmina, 1935; Greek Lyric Poetry, 1936; rev. edn 1961; (co-Ed.) Oxford Book of Greek Verse in Translation, 1937; Early Greek Elegists, 1938; The Heritage of Symbolism, 1943; A Book of Russian Verse, 1943; Sophoclean Tragedy, 1944; From Virgil to Milton, 1945; The Creative Experiment, 1949; The Romantic Imagination, 1950; Heroic Poetry, 1952; Problems in Greek Poetry, 1954; Inspiration and Poetry, 1955; The Greek Experience, 1957; Primitive Song, 1962; In General and Particular, 1964; Pindar, 1964; Landmarks in Greek Literature, 1966; Poetry and Politics, 1900-1960, 1966; Memories, 1898-1939, 1966; (trans.) The Odes of Pindar, 1969; On Greek Margins, 1970; Periclean Athens, 1971; articles in learned jls. *Recreations:* none. *Address:* Wadham College, Oxford. *T:* Oxford 44045. *[Died 4 July 1971.*

BOWYER, John Francis, CB 1966; Lieutenant-Commander RN; lately Chief Registrar of the High Court in Bankruptcy; *b* 11 Jan. 1893; *s* of Col W. G. Bowyer, RE, and Eva Mary (formerly Lane); *m* 1919, Violet Wright (*d* 1974) (widow; *née* Shakespeare); four *s* one *d.* *Educ:* Royal Naval Colls, Osborne and Dartmouth. Served in Royal Navy as Midshipman, Sub-Lieut, Lieut, 1910-19, and as Captain of HM Destroyer Nonsuch, 1918-19; Lieut-Cmdr (Emergency List), 1922. Called to Bar, Inner Temple, 1928; joined Lincoln's Inn, 1934; Bencher, Lincoln's Inn, 1952. Apptd Registrar of the High Court in Bankruptcy, Dec. 1953; Chief Registrar, 1957. *Recreations:* golf, painting. *Address:* Little Park House, Brimpton, near Reading Berks. *Clubs:* United Service & Royal Aero; Seaford Golf. *[Died 7 May 1974.*

BOWYER-SMYTH, Captain Sir Philip Weyland; *see* Smyth.

BOYCE, Air Cdre George Harold, CB 1945; AFC; late RAF; *b* 1894; *s* of late John Boyce, Ottawa; *m* 1921, Constance Browning (*d* 1974), Carnoustie, Scotland; one *d.* Served European War, 1914-19; Senior Air Staff Officer, No 15 Group, 1939; Air Commodore, 1941; retired list, 1946. *[Died 24 Sept. 1975.*

BOYCOTT, Rev. D. M.; *see* Morse-Boycott.

BOYD, Prof. Alexander Michael, FRCS; Professor of Surgery, University of Manchester, 1947-70, Emeritus Professor since 1970; *b* 5 March 1905; *s* of Henry Strene Boyd and Beatrice Kate Boyd (*née* Tatham). *Educ:* Haileybury. MRCS, LRCP, MB, BS London, 1929; FRCS 1931. Senior Demonstrator of Anatomy,

St Bartholomew's Hosp., 1933; 1st Asst Surg. Professional Unit, Bart's, 1934-39. War Service RAMC, 1940-45, principally in Egypt; Lieut-Col; O/C Surgical Div., 63rd Gen. Hospital, Cairo, Hon. Asst Surg. and Asst Dir Surgical Professional Unit, Bart's, 1946; MSc (Hon.) University of Manchester, 1950. Comdr Order of the Phœnix, Greece, 1942. *Publications:* numerous, upon surgery of peripheral vascular disease in all Med. Jls. *Recreations:* fishing, shooting. *Address:* 64 Platt Lane, Rusholme, Manchester. *T:* 061-224 4180. *[Died 7 April 1973.*

BOYD, Maj.-Gen. Ian Herbert Fitzgerald, CB 1962; CBE 1957 (OBE 1950); *b* 21 Dec. 1907; *s* of late Sir Donald James Boyd, KCIE, Indian Civil Service, Punjab, and late Laura Caroline (*née* Hope); *m* 1931, Dorothy Margaret, *d* of Lewis French, CIE, CBE, ICS; two *s* one *d.* *Educ:* Fettes; RMA, Woolwich; Christ's Coll., Cambridge (BA). Commissioned RE 1927; served Mohmand, 1933; Waziristan, 1936 (despatches); Instr Staff Coll., Quetta, 1943-44; served Burma and Malaya, 1944-45 (despatches 4 times). Chief Instr SME, 1946-47; AA and QMG, War Office, 1948-50 (OBE); Col, Q (Movements), Far ELF, 1950-53; DQMG, BAOR, 1954-57; Chief Engineer, Far ELF, 1957-59; Chief Engineer, Northern Army Group and BAOR, 1959-62; retd, 1963. Col Comdt, Corps of Royal Engineers, 1966-72. Chm., Lewes Div., Cons. Assoc., 1972-75. *Recreations:* sailing, shooting, fishing, horology. *Address:* Primrose Hill, Barcombe, Lewes, E Sussex. *T:* Barcombe 203.
[Died 6 Jan. 1978.

BOYD, Lachlan Macpherson, CMG 1955; *b* 29 Sept. 1904; *s* of late Hugh Boyd, S Uist; *m* 1936, Betty Pinkerton, MBE 1958, *d* of late Dr Robert Scott, Exeter. *Educ:* Portree Secondary Sch.; Edinburgh Univ. Colonial Administrative Service, Uganda, 1930-46; Resident, Buganda, 1947-51; Sec. for African Affairs, 1951-55; Minister of Local Government, Uganda, 1955-60; retired, 1960. *Address:* Devoran, 33 Granary Lane, Budleigh Salterton, Devon. *T:* Budleigh Salterton 2452. *Clubs:* Royal Commonwealth Society, East Africa House.
[Died 2 Dec. 1980.

BOYD, Martin à Beckett; Author; *b* Lucerne, Switzerland, 10 June 1893; *s* of late Arthur M. Boyd and Emma, *d* of Hon. William à Beckett, Penleigh, Wilts, and Melbourne, Vic. Served European War as Lieut The Buffs, Observer, RFC and Pilot, RAF. Trained as architect. Began to write, 1925. Reviewed for Times Literary Supplement, 1930-40. *Publications:* Fourteen novels, including: The Lemon Farm, 1935; Lucinda Brayford, 1946; The Cardboard Crown, 1952; A Difficult Young Man, 1954; Outbreak of Love, 1957; When Blackbirds Sing, 1962; The Tea-Time of Love, 1969. Autobiography, Day of my Delight, 1965. Travel book, Much Else in Italy, 1958. *Address:* c/o Australia and New Zealand Bank, Ltd, 71 Cornhill, EC3.
[Died 3 June 1972.

BOYD, Prof. Maurice James; Professor of Latin, Queen's University, Belfast, 1939-76, now Emeritus; Chairman, N Ireland GCE Examinations Board; *b* 7 Jan. 1911; *s* of James Boyd, MA, LLB, Londonderry and Belfast; *m* 1936, Constance Eveline, *d* of Harry Marlow, JP, Croydon; two *s* one *d.* *Educ:* Royal Academical Instn, Belfast; Queen's Univ., Belfast (BA 1931); Trinity Coll., Oxford (MA). Asst and Junior Lecturer in Latin, Queen's Univ., Belfast, 1933-39; Dean of the Faculty of Arts, 1944-47 and 1956-57; Dean of the Faculty of Theology, 1962-68; Editor of Annual Record of QUB, 1940-49, 1959-71; Pres. QU Assoc., 1954; Chm. of Convocation, QUB, 1956-65. Mem., Belfast Educn and Library Bd, 1976-; Chm., Belfast Library Cttee, 1977-. MRIA 1968. *Publications:* articles in Classical Periodicals. *Address:* 8 Maryville Park, Belfast BT9 6LN. *T:* Belfast 665610. *[Died 20 Aug. 1979.*

BOYD, Thomas J. L. Stirling; Barrister-at-law; *b* Edinburgh, 23 Oct. 1886; *o c* of late P. J. Stirling Boyd, DL, *y s* of late Sir Thomas Boyd, Lord Provost of Edinburgh, and late Beatrice Rachel, OBE, *d* of late Prof. Thomas Laycock, MD, Edinburgh. *Educ:* Edinburgh Academy; Trinity Coll., Oxford (MA 1915; Hon. Fellow, 1969). Asst Paymaster, RNVR, 1914; Lieut, RAF, 1918; Barrister, Inner Temple, 1919. Chief Justice, Sarawak, 1930-39. Air Ministry, 1939-43. Mem. Westminster City Council, 1945-65. Mem. Special Cttee for Province of Canterbury, constituted under Reorganisation Areas Measure, 1944, 1947-60. Chairman: Works and Traffic Cttee, Westminster CC, 1952-55; Westminster Health Soc., 1956-59. *Publications:* The Web (play), 1925; The Laws of Sarawak, 1936. *Address:* 16/17 Pall Mall, SW1. *T:* 01-839 5332; 11 King's Bench Walk, Temple, EC4. *Clubs:* Athenæum, MCC.
[Died 1 Jan. 1973.

BOYD ORR, 1st Baron, *cr* 1949, of Brechin Mearns in the County of Angus; **John Boyd Orr,** CH 1968; Kt 1935; DSO

1917; MC; FRS 1932; LLD; Director of several cos; Rector of Glasgow University, 1945, Chancellor, 1946; *b* Kilmaurs, Ayrshire, 23 Sept. 1880; *s* of late R. C. Orr of Holland Green, Kilmaurs; *m* Elizabeth Pearson, *d* of late John Callum, West Kilbride; two *d* (and one *s* killed in action). *Educ:* University, Glasgow; MA, MD, DSc; Bellahouston Gold Medallist. Hon. Graduate St Andrews, Edinburgh, Glasgow, Aberdeen, Princeton USA, Santiago Chile, Brazil, Groeningen Holland, Manchester, Vollebach Norway, Delhi India, Uppsala Sweden; Hon. Fellow New York Academy of Medicine; Harben Medal, Royal Inst. of Public Health, 1949; Borden Medal (USA), 1958; Gold Medal, NFU of USA; Gold Medal, Internat. League of Agric. Producers. Hon. FRCS Dublin. Served European War 1914-18, RAMC (MC, DSO, despatches); Member: Reorganisation Commission for Fat Stock Industry, 1932; Reorganisation Commission for Milk, 1935-36; Cattle Cttee (Ministry of Agriculture); Colonial Advisory Council of Agriculture and Animal Health; Advisory Cttee on Nutrition (Ministry of Health); Technical Commission on Nutrition, League of Nations; Chm. Scottish Scientific Advisory Cttee; Prof. of Agriculture, University of Aberdeen, 1942-45; MP (Ind.) Scottish Universities, 1945-46; late Dir of Rowett Research Inst., Aberdeen; formerly Dir of Imperial Bureau of Animal Nutrition; Joint Editor Nutrition Abstracts and Reviews; Dir-Gen. United Nations Food and Agricultural Organisation, 1945-48; Nobel Peace Prize, 1949. Comdr Légion d'Honneur; Comdr and Cross with Star, Polonia Restituta. *Publications:* History of Scotch Church Crisis of 1904; Minerals in Pastures and their relation to Animal Nutrition, 1928; Food, Health and Income, 1936; Fighting for What, 1943; Food and the People, 1944; The White Man's Dilemma, 1952; Feast and Famine, 1960; As I Recall, 1966; several papers on physiological subjects in scientific journals. *Recreation:* farming. *Heir:* none. *Address:* Newton, by Brechin, Angus. *T:* Edzell 294. *Clubs:* Farmers'; Royal Automobile (Glasgow); Strathcona (Aberdeen). 					*[Died 25 June 1971 (ext.).]*

BOYD-WILSON, Edwin John, MA, BSc (NZ), BA (Cantab); Professor of Modern Languages, Victoria University College, Wellington, New Zealand, 1920-54, retired; *b* 1886; *m* 1910, Helen Walker, Hobart; two *s* two *d. Educ:* Nelson Coll., NZ; Canterbury Univ. Coll., NZ; Emmanuel Coll., Cambridge. *Recreations:* Rugby football, tramping, shooting. *Address:* 44 Pukatea Street, Eastbourne, Wellington, New Zealand.
					[Died 2 July 1973.]

BOYLE, Prof. John Andrew; Professor of Persian Studies, University of Manchester, since 1966; *b* Worcester Park, Surrey, 1916; *e s* of William Andrew and Florence May Boyle; *m* 1945, Margaret Elizabeth, *er d* of Charles and Rose Dunbar; three *d. Educ:* Univs of Birmingham, Göttingen, Berlin and London. BA 1st cl. hons Birmingham 1936; PhD London 1947. Service with Royal Engrs, 1941; seconded to a special dept of FO, 1942-50; Manchester Univ.: Sen. Lectr in Persian Studies, 1950-59; Reader, 1959-66. Vis. Prof. of Persian, Univ. of California, Berkeley, 1959-60. Member: Governing Council, British Inst. of Persian Studies, 1964-; Editorial Bd, Cambridge History of Iran, 1966-; Adv. Bd, Iran-Shenasi (Tehran), 1969-; Gibb Memorial Trust, 1970-; Council, British Soc. for Middle Eastern Studies, 1973-; Cttee, Folklore Soc., 1973-; Editorial Bd, Central Asiatic Jl, 1978-; Chairman: Anglo-Mongolian Soc., 1970-; Greater Manchester Folklore Soc., 1977-. Hon. Fellow, Körösi Csoma Soc., 1973. Hon. MA Manchester, 1970. Order and Decoration of Sepass, Iran, 1958. *Publications:* A Practical Dictionary of the Persian Language, 1949; (trans.) Juvaini: History of the World-Conqueror, 1958; Modern Persian Grammar, 1966; (ed and contrib.) Cambridge History of Iran, Vol. V, 1968; (with Karl Jahn) Rashid al-Din Commemoration Volume (1318-1968), 1970; (trans.) Rashid al-Din: The Successors of Genghis Khan, 1971; The Mongol World Empire 1206-1370, 1977; (trans.) Farid al-Din 'Attar: The Ilahi-nama or Book of God, 1977; (ed) Persia: History and Heritage, 1978; contrib. learned jls and encyclopaedias on Persian history and literature and the Mongol world empire. *Recreation:* motoring. *Address:* 266 Rye Bank Road, Manchester M21 1LY. *T:* 061-881 1161.
					[Died 19 Nov. 1978.]

BOYLE, Air Commodore Hon. John David, CBE 1919; DSO 1917; late RAF; *b* 8 July 1884; 4th *s* of 7th Earl of Glasgow; *m* 1st, 1913, Ethel (*d* 1932), *d* of Sir Henry A. Hodges, Judge of the Supreme Court, Victoria, Australia; *er s* Major, The Black Watch, killed in action, 1945; *yr s* Sqdn-Ldr, RAF, killed on flying duty, 1960; 2nd, 1935, Marie (JP, Co. Councillor for Wigtownshire), *d* of John Gibb, Chillesford, Orford, Suffolk. *Educ:* Winchester. Gazetted 2nd Lieut Rifle Brigade, 1906; Lieut 1910; Seconded to Royal Flying Corps, 1912; Wing-Comdr in Royal Air Force on formation, 1918; Group-Capt., 1922; Air Commodore, 1929. Served European War, 1914-18

(despatches twice, Brevet-Major, Italian Order of St Maurice and St Lazarus); Chief Air Staff Officer, Air Defence of Great Britain, 1929-30; Air Officer Commanding Fighting Area, 1930-31; retired list, 1932; Aerodrome Board, Air Ministry, 1934-36; Commandant, RAFVR, Glasgow, 1936-39; re-employed active list Sept. 1939; retired list, 1941. Formerly JP Counties of Ayr and Kirkcudbright. *Address:* Dinvin, Portpatrick, Wigtownshire. *Clubs:* United Service & Royal Aero; Royal Scottish Automobile (Glasgow). 			*[Died 25 Sept. 1974.]*

BOYS, Rt. Rev. John, DLitt, MA, LTh; Provincial Commissary to the Archbishop of Cape Town, since 1961; Assistant Bishop of Southwark, since 1968; *b* 17 Jan. 1900; *s* of Walter and Frances Boys. *Educ:* S Olave's Grammar Sch., Southwark; Hatfield Coll., Durham; S Boniface Theological Coll., Warminster. Service with BRCS in France, 1916-19. In business in Athens (Greece), 1919-21; in business in London, 1921-28; Sec., Guildford YMCA, 1929-30; Reader in Diocese of Salisbury, 1930-31; Deacon, 1935; priest, 1936; Asst Curate at S Paul's, Egham Hythe (Guildford), 1935-36; Personal Chaplain to Bishop of Gibraltar, 1936-38; Missionary in Diocese of Lebombo, 1938-47; Archdeacon of Lebombo, 1947; Bishop of Lebombo, 1948-51; Bishop of Kimberley and Kuruman, 1951-60; Asst Bp and Canon of St Albans, 1961-68; Dir of S African Church Inst., London, 1961-69. *Recreations:* chess, travelling. *Address:* 41 Elm Bank Gardens, SW13 0NX. *T:* 01-878 0770.
					[Died 26 Dec. 1972.]

BOZMAN, Geoffrey Stephen, CSI 1946; CIE 1938; ICS (retired); *b* 1896; *s* of late Samuel Bozman; *m* 1927, Kathleen Hilary (marr. diss.), *d* of late Sir Percy Rothera; one *s. Educ:* Whitgift Sch.; Brasenose Coll., Oxford. Served European War, 1914-18, 2nd Lieut, 4th Queens Royal West Surrey Regt, 1915; transferred to RFC, 1916; joined ICS Madras, 1922; Settlement Officer, 1924; Under Secretary, Govt of Madras, 1927; Secretary, Indian Tariff Board, 1930; Secretary Agent General for India in S. Africa, 1932; Commissioner of Coorg, 1935; Dep. Secretary and Joint Secretary, Govt of India, Education, Health and Lands Dept, 1936; Secretary, Govt of India, Indians Overseas Dept, 1941; Secretary, Govt of India, Information and Broadcasting Dept, 1943-47. *Address:* Shawside, Hosey Hill, Westerham, Kent. *T:* Westerham 3377. *Club:* Oriental.
					[Died 23 Feb. 1973.]

BRABANT, Rev. Frank Herbert, DD; *b* 22 May 1892; *s* of Frederick and Augusta Brabant, Oxford. *Educ:* Winchester; Balliol Coll., Oxford (MA, DD). BD and DD by accumulation, 1952. Ordained, 1920; Chaplain of Wadham Coll., 1920-31; Diocese of Zululand, 1931-37; Canon Residentiary of Winchester Cathedral, 1938-42; Asst Master, Winchester Coll., 1942-46; Principal, St Patrick's Coll., Gwelo, Southern Rhodesia, 1946; Principal of St Bede's Coll., Umtata, 1948; Lecturer in Philosophy at Fort Hare African Coll., 1949-56; Curate of Ferreira's Town, Johannesburg, 1956-63. Examining Chaplain to Bishop of Kimberley and Kuruman, 1952-61. *Publications:* Faith and Truth (with Rev. P. Hartill); Prayer; Religion and the Mysterious; Time and Eternity in Christian Thought (Bampton Lecture for 1936); The Beginning of the Third Republic in France; Neville Stuart Talbot, 1879-1943, A Memoir, 1949. *Address:* Homes of St Barnabas, Dormans, Lingfield, Surrey. 				*[Died 28 Oct. 1972.]*

BRABAZON OF TARA, 2nd Baron, *cr* 1942, of Sandwich; **Derek Charles Moore-Brabazon,** CBE 1960; Member of the Stock Exchange, London; associated with Read, Hurst-Brown & Co.; *b* 24 Dec. 1910; *er* and *o* surv. *s* of 1st Baron Brabazon of Tara, PC, GBE, MC, and Hilda Mary Krabbé, Buenos Aires; *S* father 1964; *m* 1939, Mrs Henriette Mary Krabbé, *d* of late Sir Rowland Clegg; one *s. Educ:* Harrow; Trinity Coll., Cambridge. BA 1931. National Fire Service, 1939-45. Member, Kensington Borough Council, 1948-52. Chairman: South Kensington Conservative Assoc., 1952-54; London Conservative Union, 1957-58. President: Kensington (formerly N Kensington) Conservative Assoc., 1966-; St Moritz Tobogganning Club, 1964-68; Commodore: Bembridge Sailing Club, 1970-71; Redwing Club, 1971-. *Heir:* s Hon. Ivon Anthony Moore-Brabazon [*b* 20 Dec. 1946. *Educ:* Harrow. Mem., Stock Exchange]. *Address:* 28 Lansdowne Road, W11. *T:* 01-727 5638; The Watch House, Bembridge, Isle of Wight. *T:* Bembridge 2258. *Clubs:* White's, City of London; Royal Yacht Squadron.
					[Died 11 Dec. 1974.]

BRABIN, Hon. Sir Daniel James, Kt 1962; MC 1945; Hon. Mr Justice Brabin; Judge of High Court, Queen's Bench Division, since 1962; *b* 14 Aug. 1913; *yr s* of late William Henry and Sarah Brabin; *m* 1949, Mary, *y d* of late John McParland and Mrs McParland. *Educ:* Douai Sch.; Trinity Hall, Cambridge. Called to the Bar, Inner Temple, 1936; Master of the Bench, 1960.

Joined Northern Circuit, 1937. Served War of 1939-45, in RA. QC 1951; Recorder of Bolton, 1953-62; Judge of Appeal, Isle of Man, 1960-62. *Address:* Royal Courts of Justice, WC2; 4 Kidderpore Avenue, NW3. *T:* 01-435 1081. *Club:* Liver.
[Died 22 Sept. 1975.

BRADDOCK, Thomas, FRIBA; *b* 1887; British; *s* of Henry William Braddock, Bolton, Lancs; *m* 1910, Betty Dolleri, *d* of Henry Parker Houghton; one *s*. *Educ:* Rutlish Sch., Merton, Surrey. Member: Surrey County Council, 1934-46; Wimbledon Borough Council, 1936-45; LCC 1958-61. Contested: Wimbledon, 1929, 1931, 1935, 1966; Kingston-upon-Thames, 1964. MP (Lab) Mitcham, 1945-50. *Address:* 8 Coastguard Cottages, South Strand, East Preston, Sussex.
[Died 9 Dec. 1976.

BRADFORD, Ven. Richard Bleaden; Archdeacon of Carlisle, 1970-78, Archdeacon Emeritus, 1978; Chaplain to The Queen, since 1973; *b* 12 Jan. 1913; *s* of Percival Richard and May Anne Bradford; *m* 1939, Beryl Elizabeth Stanley; two *s* three *d*. *Educ:* LSE. BA London, 1st cl. hons Med. and Mod. History. Vicar: of St Luke, Barrow-in-Furness, 1942; of St Aidan, Carlisle, 1951; Chaplain to Bp of Carlisle, 1946-66; Proctor in Convocation, 1951-67; Vicar: of Ainstable and Armathwaite, 1957; of Penrith, 1960; Residentiary Canon, Carlisle Cathedral, 1966-78; Church Comr, 1968-73; Mem., General Synod, 1971-78. *Address:* The Mews, Vicarage Hill, Keswick, Cumbria. *T:* Keswick 73823.
[Died 4 Jan. 1980.

BRADFORD, William Vincent, CB 1942; until 1943 a Commissioner of Inland Revenue and a Secretary to the Board; *b* 14 May 1883; *s* of William Masters Bradford; *m* 1st, 1914, Lizzie (*d* 1962), 4th *d* of James Bowman; 2nd, 1962, Kathleen Winifred Peacock. *Educ:* Christ's Hospital; Oxford. *Address:* Ringmore, The Street, Washington, Pulborough, Sussex. *Club:* United Oxford & Cambridge University. *[Died 15 Nov. 1974.*

BRADLEY, Albert James, FRS 1939; MA, DSc; *b* 5 Jan. 1899; *s* of Thomas Henry and Amy Bradley; *m* 1929, Marjorie Dinnis; one *s*. *Educ:* Chesterfield Grammar Sch.; Manchester Univ. 1851 Senior Exhibitioner, 1926-28; Royal Society Warren Research Fellow, 1932-38; formerly Asst Dir of Research in Crystallography, Cavendish Laboratory, Cambridge. Associate Mem. Royal Aubomobile Club. *Publications:* various publications on x-ray crystallography. *Address:* 169 Ashgate Road, Chesterfield, Derbyshire. *T:* Chesterfield 2081.
[Died 4 Sept. 1972.

BRADLEY, Gladys Lilian; Head Mistress, Fairfield High School for Girls, Droylsden, Manchester, 1941-60; *d* of late T. R. Bradley. *Educ:* The Cowley Sch. for Girls, St Helens; Chester City and County High Sch. for Girls (now City High Sch. for Girls, Chester); Manchester Univ. (Scholar). BA (Hons Eng.). Asst Mistress: Withington Girls' Sch., Manchester; Havergal Coll., Toronto; Miss Edgar's and Miss Cramp's Sch., Incorp., Montreal; Gunnerside Sch., Plymouth; Head of English Dept, Cowley Sch. for Girls, St Helens; Head Mistress, Farringtons Sch., Chislehurst, Kent (at Trecarn, Babbacombe, S Devon) Sept. 1939-Dec. 1940 (closed for duration of War). *Publications:* Punctuation Hints and Exercises, 1934; sundry articles on youth and Girl Guide work, 1925-30. *Recreations:* walking, boating, swimming, riding, travelling. *Address:* 6 Belvedere Court, Mooragh Promenade, Ramsey, Isle of Man. *T:* Ramsey 814049. *Club:* University Women's. *[Died 30 Sept. 1978.*

BRADLEY, Sir Kenneth (Granville), Kt 1963; CMG 1946; Director of the Commonwealth Institute, 1953-69, a Trustee, since 1971; *b* 5 Jan. 1904; *s* of Major H. V. Bradley, 9th Gurkha Rifles and Norah Foster; *g s* of Very Rev. G. G. Bradley, sometime Dean of Westminster; *m* 1926, Emily Guyon Rea (*d* 1972), Cleveland, Ohio; two *s*. *Educ:* Wellington Coll., Berks; University Coll., Oxford. District Officer Northern Rhodesia, 1926-39; Information Officer Northern Rhodesia, 1939-42; Colonial and Financial Sec., Falklands Islands, 1942-46; Under-Sec., Gold Coast, 1946-49, actg Colonial Sec., 1946 and 1947; retd, 1949; first Editor, Corona, Colonial Service Journal, 1948-53. Chm., League for the Exchange of Commonwealth Teachers, 1962-74; a Vice-Pres., Royal African Society. *Publications:* Africa Notwithstanding, 1928; Hawks Alighting, 1930; Lusaka, 1936; Story of Northern Rhodesia, 1942; Native Courts and Authorities in Northern Rhodesia, 1942; Diary of a District Officer, 1942; The Colonial Service as a Career, 1950; Copper Venture, 1952; Britain's Purpose in Africa, 1955; Once a District Officer, 1966; (Ed.) The Living Commonwealth, 1961. *Recreation:* golf. *Address:* 10 Benson Place, Norham Road, Oxford. *T:* 54581. *Club:* Royal Commonwealth Society.
[Died 6 Feb. 1977.

BRADLEY, Prof. Peter Colley S.; see Sylvester-Bradley.

BRADLEY, Reginald Livingstone, CBE 1955; MC 1916; Commissioner of Prisons, 1949-57, retired; *b* 9 Aug. 1894; *s* of Frederick L. and Florence Bradley; *m* 1920, Phyllis Mary Richardson; one *s* three *d*. *Educ:* Repton; Oriel Coll., Oxford (MA). Oxford, 1913-14 and 1919-20. Served European War, 1914-18 (despatches, MC); 22nd London Regt, The Queen's; Capt. Sec., Oxford and Bermondsey Club, SE1, 1920-21; Prison Service: Dep. Governor, 1922-26, HM Borstal, Portland; Dep. Governor, 1926-29, Governor, 1929-36, HM Borstal, Rochester; Governor Cl. II, 1936-38, HM Prison, Wormwood Scrubs; Asst Commissioner, Prison Commission, 1938-52; Dir of Borstal Administration, 1948-57; Commissioner and Dir of Borstal Administration, 1952-57. Coronation Medal, 1953. *Recreations:* walking, reading, chores. *Address:* Avonmore, 4 Malbrook Road, Putney, SW15 6UF. *T:* 01-788 9768. *Clubs:* United Oxford & Cambridge University; Vincent's (Oxford); Surrey County Cricket. *[Died 8 Dec. 1977.*

BRADLEY, Prof. William, PhD, DSc (Manchester); FRIC; Professor of Colour Chemistry and Dyeing, University of Leeds, 1948-63; Emeritus Professor, since 1963; *b* 24 July 1903; *s* of John T. and Mary A. Bradley, Leigh, Lancs; *m* 1932, Charlotte, *d* of J. E. Dolman, Brightwell, Berks; one *s*. *Educ:* Leigh Grammar Sch.; Manchester Univ. University Awards: Woodiwis Exhib. in Chemistry, 1922, Dalton Chemical Scholarship, 1925, Darbishire Fellowship, 1925, Beyer Fellowship, 1926, Sir Clement Royds Mem. Scholarship in Chemistry, 1927. Research Asst, University Coll., London, 1927-29; Research Asst, Dyson Perrins Lab., Oxford, 1929-31; Lecturer in Tinctorial Chemistry and Dyestuffs, Coll. of Technology, Manchester, 1931-42; Research in industry, 1942-48. DSIR Visitor to The British Hat and Allied Feltmakers' Research Association, 1956-62; Gold Medal for services to Soc. of Dyers and Colourists, 1959; Mem. of Council Royal Inst. of Chemistry, 1959-63; Mem. Bd of Studies, Nat. Council for Technological Awards, 1961-63. *Publications:* papers on organic chemistry mainly in Journal of Chem. Soc. *Address:* Rosedale, Broadsands Park Road, Paignton, Devon. *T:* Churston 2440.
[Died 20 Sept. 1972.

BRADNACK, Brian Oswald, MC; MA; Headmaster, College for the Blind, Worcester, 1938-59, retired; *b* 3 March 1898; *s* of Oswald H. Bradnack, Combe Down, Bath; *m* 1929, Doris (*d* 1945), *d* of D. M. Milne, JP, of Gosforth, Newcastle upon Tyne; two *s*; *m* 1947, Margaret, *d* of H. E. Tringham, Great Crosby, Lancs. *Educ:* Repton Sch.; Brasenose Coll., Oxford. Served European War, France, with RGA 1917-18; Intercollegiate Sec. of Student Christian Movement in Northumberland and Durham, 1921-23; Asst Master at Dean Close Sch., Cheltenham, 1923-38. *Recreations:* various. *Address:* Merry Mead, 90 Bowes Hill, Rowlands Castle, Hants. *T:* Rowlands Castle 2431.
[Died 8 Jan. 1973.

BRADSHAW, Brig. George Rowley, CB 1953; CBE 1946; *b* 1 July 1898; *s* of Surg.-Comdr F. Bradshaw, OBE, RN, and Mrs Bradshaw, Malahide, County Dublin; *m* 1928, Mary Constance, *d* of W. T. Ford, Malpas, Mon; one *s* two *d*. *Educ:* King's Sch., Rochester; RMA, Woolwich. Commissioned into Royal Artillery, 1917; Served European War, 1917-18; Iraq, 1921-22; Staff Coll., 1934-35; Served War of 1939-45, NW Europe, 1944-45; Col 1944; Brig. 1946. Dep. District Comdr, 1950-53; retired, 1953. Comdr Order of Orange Nassau, 1946. *Recreations:* tennis, cricket, riding. *Address:* Kingswood, St George's Hill, Weybridge, Surrey KT13 0LD. *T:* Weybridge 42876. *Club:* Naval and Military. *[Died 7 June 1976.*

BRADWELL, Baron *cr* 1975 (Life Peer), of Bradwell juxta Mare, Essex; **Thomas Edward Neil Driberg;** journalist, lecturer and broadcaster; *b* Crowborough, Sussex, 22 May 1905; 3rd *s* of John James Street Driberg and Amy Mary Irving Bell; *m* 1951, Mrs Ena Mary Binfield. *Educ:* Lancing; Christ Church, Oxford. On editorial staff of the Daily Express, 1928-43. Contributor since 1943 to Reynolds News and other periodicals; television and radio critic, New Statesman, 1955-61. War Correspondent, War of 1939-45 and in Korea. Nat. Exec. Cttee of Labour Party 1949-72, Chm. 1957-58. MP Maldon Div. of Essex, 1942-55 (Ind. 1942-45; Lab. 1945-55); MP (Lab) Barking, 1959-Feb. 1974; Chairman: House of Commons Select Cttee on Publications and Debates Reports, 1964-65; Select Cttee on Broadcasting of Proceedings in Parliament, 1965-67; Commonwealth and Colonies Gp, Parly Labour Party, 1965-68; Leader, Parly Delegn to Sarawak and Sabah, 1966. Select Preacher before the University of Oxford, 1965; Comr, Churches' Commn on Internat. Affairs, Uppsala, 1968-75. Mem. Historic Buildings Council, 1966-. Finalist (bronze medal) in first Nat. Crossword Championship, 1970. *Publications:* Colonnade, 1949; The Best

of Both Worlds, 1953; Beaverbrook: a Study in Power and Frustration, 1956; Guy Burgess: a Portrait with Background, 1956; The Mystery of Moral Re-Armament: a Study of Frank Buchman and his Movement, 1964; Swaff: the life and times of Hannen Swaffer, 1974; *Posthumous publication:* Ruling Passions, 1977. *Address:* House of Lords, SW1.
[Died 12 Aug. 1976.

BRAGG, Sir (William) Lawrence, CH 1967; Kt 1941; OBE 1918; MC 1918; FRS 1921; MA Cantab; Hon. DSc Dublin, Leeds, Manchester, Lisbon, Paris, Brussels, Liège, Durham; Hon. PhD Cologne, Cantab; Hon. LLD St Andrews; Fullerian Professor of Chemistry, Royal Institution, 1953-66, and Director of the Royal Institution, 1954-66; *b* Adelaide, South Australia, 31 March 1890; *s* of late Sir William Henry Bragg, OM, KBE, FRS; *m* 1921, Alice Grace Jenny, *er d* of the late Albert Hopkinson; two *s* two *d. Educ:* St Peter's Coll., Adelaide; Adelaide Univ.; Trinity Coll., Cambridge (Allen Scholar). Fellow and Lecturer in Natural Sciences, Trinity Coll. Cambridge, 1914; awarded Barnard Medal, 1914, and Nobel Prize for Physics, 1915, for work on X-Rays and Crystal Structure done with Sir W. H. Bragg; Hughes Medal of Royal Society, 1931; Royal Medal of Royal Society, 1946; Copley Medal of Royal Society, 1966; Roebling Medal of Min. Soc. of America, 1948; Technical Adviser on Sound Ranging to Map Section, GHQ, France, 1915-19; Langworthy Prof. of Physics, Victoria Univ. of Manchester, 1919-37; Dir of National Physical Laboratory, 1937-38; Cavendish Prof. of Experimental Physics, Cambridge, 1938-53; Chm., Frequency Advisory Cttee, 1958-60. Hon. FInstP; Hon. FRIC; Hon. FRSE; Hon. MRIA; Hon. MInstMet; Foreign Associate, Acad. Sciences, Paris; Hon. Mem., Swedish Acad. of Sciences; Mem. American Philosophical Soc.; Hon. Mem., New York Mineralogical Club; Chinese Phys Soc.; For. Hon. Mem. Amer. Acad. of Arts and Sciences; For. Associate, Nat. Acad. Sci. Washington; For. Mem., Dutch Acad. Sci.; Associate, Royal Acad. Belgium; Membre d'Honneur de la Soc. française de Minéralogie et Cristallographie. Comdr of the Order of Leopold of Belgium. *Publications:* various scientific papers on Crystal Structure; (with Sir W. H. Bragg), X-Rays and Crystal Structure, 1915; The Crystalline State, 1934; Electricity, 1936; Atomic Structure of Minerals, 1937; Crystal Structures of Minerals (with W. F. Claringbull), 1965; Ideas and Discoveries in Physics, 1970. *Recreations:* painting, bird-watching. *Address:* 6 The Boltons, SW10.*T:* 01-370 5189; Quietways, Waldringfield, near Woodbridge, Suffolk. *T:* Waldringfield 220. *Club:* Athenæum. *[Died 1 July 1971.*

BRAIN, Sir Hugh (Gerner), Kt 1972; CBE 1959 (OBE 1919; MBE 1918); Chairman, T. & G. Mutual Life Society, 1957-69, retired; *b* 3 Dec. 1890; *s* of William Joseph Brain, Malvern, Vic, and Florence (*née* Payne); *m* 1920, Monica Eva Futcher, Southsea; one *s* two *d. Educ:* State Sch., Armadale; University High Sch., Melbourne. War Service, 1915-19 (Captain and DAAG); Hon. Business Mem., Australian Naval Bd, 1941-46. Victorian Public Service, Premier's Office, 1907-13; Commonwealth Public Service, Inter-State Commn, 1913-19; with Edward H. Shackell & Co., Melbourne, 1919-32; Director: Secretariat Pty Ltd, Melb., 1932-60; T. & G. Mutual Life Soc., and subsids, 1943-72; Metal Manufactures Ltd, Austral Bronze Co. Pty Ltd, Cable Makers Australia Pty Ltd, Austral Standard Cables Pty Ltd, until 1960. Father of the Year, Victoria, 1959. Past Chairman: Melbourne Univ. Appts Bd; Melbourne Lord Mayor's Fund Appeal Cttee for Hosps and Charities. Hon. Mem., Australasian Inst. of Mining and Metallurgy. *Recreations:* music, reading. *Address:* 415 Kooyong Road, Elsternwick, Victoria 3185, Australia. *T:* 53-5158. *Clubs:* Athenæum (Life Mem.), Melbourne Legacy (Pres. 1935), Sciences, Beefsteak (all Melbourne). *[Died 31 Dec. 1976.*

BRAIN, Dr Reginald Thomas, MD, BS, FRCP; Hon. Consulting Physician: Royal Free Hospital; The Hospital for Sick Children, Great Ormond Street; St John's Hospital for Diseases of the Skin; Corresponding Member: American Dermatological Association; La Société Dermatologique Danoise; La Société Française de Dermatologie et de Syphiligraphie; Australasian College of Dermatologists; Hon. Member, Sociedad Venezolana de Dermatologia, Venereologia e Leprologia; *b* 6 Jan 1894; *s* of Robert Brain and Mary Elizabeth Kimberlin; *m* 1928, Hallie Frances Weir; two *s* one *d. Educ:* Queen Elizabeth's Grammar Sch., Tamworth; London Hospital Medical Coll. Served European War BEF, RAMC, 1914-19; past appointments at The London Hospital, the British Post-Graduate Medical Sch., The Evelina Hospital for Sick Children. Prosser White Orator, 1961. Past. Pres. Section Derm., RSM and BMA. Retired. *Publications:* Sequeira's Diseases of the Skin (Ingram & Brain), 1957, Skin Diseases (Modern Health Series), 1955; papers on Biochemistry, Pathology (Virus Diseases), and Skin Diseases. *Recreations:* electrical engineering, fishing, gardening. *Address:* Home Wood, Loudwater, Herts. *[Died 10 Dec. 1971.*

BRAIS, François Philippe, CBE 1943; QC (Quebec) 1927; Hon. LLD: University of Montreal 1945, Laval University, Quebec, 1953; MLC Quebec since 1940; Senior Partner, Brais, Campbell, Pepper & Durand, Place Ville Marie, Dorchester Blvd W, Montreal, Quebec; *b* Montreal, Que., 18 Oct. 1894; *s* of N. E. Brais and Blanche (*née* Brunet); *m* 1925, Louise, *d* of J. E. Doré; one *s* five *d. Educ:* Montreal High Sch.; Ste Marie de Monnoir Coll., St John's Que.; McGill Univ., Montreal. Pres. Canadian Bar Association, 1944-45; mem. of Provincial Cabinet, Quebec, and Government Leader in Legislative Council, 1940-42; Sec. Montreal Bar Association, 1920-21; Bâtonnier, Montreal Bar Assoc., 1949; Bâtonnier Gen., Quebec Bar Assoc., 1949-1950; Director: Sun Life Assurance Co. of Canada, Montreal Trust Company, Canadian Pacific Railway; Canadian Investment Fund Ltd; Canadian Fund Inc.; Woods Manufacturing Co.; Chm., Board of Banque Canadienne Nationale; Pres., Les Cinémas Odéon Ltée; Canada Iron Foundries Ltd; Wabasso Cotton Co. Ltd; Golden Eagle Refining Co. of Canada Ltd; Seigniory Club Community Assoc., Ltd; Chm. Rediffusion Inc.; Mem. Canadian Advisory Bd, Sun Alliance and London Insurance Group, of London, England; Vice-Chm., Canadian Disaster Relief Fund, Inc.; Pres., Donor's Cttee, University of Montreal; Hon. Life Member: Montreal Board of Trade; American Bar Association; Governor: Montreal Children's Hospital; Children's Memorial Hospital; Royal Edward Laurentian Hospital; mem. of Dominion executive and Joint Chm., Quebec Div., National War Finance Cttee, 1941-45; Vice-Chm. Wartime Information Board, 1941-45. Mem. Nat. Board, Canadian Council of Christians and Jews; Roman Catholic. *Recreations:* riding and hunting. *Address:* 21 Roskilde Avenue, Outremont, PQ. *Clubs:* Mount Royal, St Denis, Montreal Reform; Seigniory, Quebec Reform, Garrison (Quebec).
[Died 2 Jan. 1972.

BRAITHWAITE, Sir John (Bevan), Kt 1953; *b* 22 Nov. 1884; *s* of late Joseph Bevan Braithwaite and Anna Sophia (*née* Gillett); *m* 1908, Martha Janette (*d* 1972), *d* of late Joseph Allen Baker, MP and Elizabeth B. Baker; two *s* one *d. Educ:* Leighton Park Sch., Reading; Owens Coll., Manchester (now Manchester Univ.). Mem. of Stock Exchange, 1907; Mem. of Cttee, 1937; Joint Chm. Cttee on Quotations, 1946-49; Dep. Chm. of Council, 1946-49. Chm. City of Montreal British Stockholders' Cttee, 1942-44; Director: City of London Electric Lighting Co., 1934-48 (Chm. 1943-48); Victoria Falls and Transvaal Power Co., 1937-49; County of London Electric Supply Co., 1939-48; South London Elec. Supply Corp. Ltd, 1943-48. Chm., Council of the Stock Exchange, 1949-59. Governor of LSE, 1953-64. *Recreations:* English literature, music, photography. *Address:* 85 Hampstead Way, NW11 7LG. *T:* 01-455 3570. *Club:* Garrick. *[Died 5 April 1973.*

BRAITHWAITE, Warwick, FRAM; Conductor, Australian National Opera Co.; *b* 9 Jan. 1896; *s* of Joseph and Mary Braithwaite, Dunedin, NZ; *m* 1931, Lorna, *d* of Ewart Davies, Dinas Powis, Cardiff; two *s* one *d. Educ:* Selwyn Coll., Dunedin, NZ; Royal Academy of Music, London. Conductor O'Mara Opera Co., 1919; Repetiteur BNOC, 1921; Asst Musical Dir, BBC, 1922; Musical Dir, BBC Western Regional, 1922; Conductor Cardiff Musical Soc. and National Orchestra of Wales till 1930; Conductor Sadler's Wells Opera Co., 1932-40; Conductor Robert Mayer Children's Concerts, season, 1934; Conductor Opera at RAM, 1937-38; Conductor all important orchestras in Great Britain, recording HMV, Decca, Columbia; Conductor of Scottish Orchestra, 1940-46; Principal Conductor of Sadler's Wells Ballet, 1948; Conductor, Opera, Covent Garden, 1949-53; Conductor National Orchestra of New Zealand, 1953-54; Artistic Director, National Opera of Australia, 1954-55; Musical Dir, Welsh National Opera Co.; Conductor, Sadler's Wells Opera, 1960-68. *Publications:* The Conductor's Art. *Recreations:* drama, literature, composition. *Address:* 23 Linden Lea, N2. *T:* 01-455 9570.
[Died 18 Jan. 1971.

BRAMWELL, John Crighton, MA Camb; MD, Manchester; FRCP, London; Hon. FRCP Ed; Professor Emeritus, University of Manchester; Consulting Physician, Manchester Royal Infirmary; *b* 4 March 1889; *y s* of late Sir Byrom Bramwell, MD, LLD, DCL, FRCP; *m* 1929, Elsa, 2nd *d* of James Risk, Gogarbank House, Midlothian; two *s* one *d. Educ:* Cheltenham Coll.; Trinity Coll., Cambridge (Exhibitioner, 1st Class Natural Science Tripos); Manchester Univ. (Entrance Scholar, MD, Gold Medal). Rockefeller Fellow, Medical Research Council, 1923; Lumleian Lecturer Royal College of Physicians of London, 1937; Gibson Lectr, Royal College of Physicians of Edinburgh, 1939; Finlayson Memorial Lecture, Royal Fac. of Physicians and Surgeons of Glasgow, 1941; St Cyres Lecturer, 1945; Carey Coombs Memorial Lecture, University of Bristol, 1954; First John Hay Memorial Lecture, University of

Liverpool, 1965; Harveian Orator, Royal College of Physicians, 1956; Ramsden Memorial Lecture, Manchester Literary and Philosophical Society, 1949; Professor of Systematic Medicine, Manchester Univ., 1942-46; Professor of Cardiology, Manchester Univ., 1946-54; Senior Editor, Quarterly Journal of Medicine; Member of Editorial Board, British Heart Journal; President Assoc. Physicians of Great Britain and Ireland, 1955-56. Hon. Member of British Cardiac Society, 1956; Senior Censor, 1949, Councillor, 1945-48, and Member of Science Cttee, Royal College of Physicians; President Manchester Medical Soc., 1952-53; Member Physiological Soc.; Member of Medical Priority Cttee of Ministry of Health, 1941-48; Member of Grading Cttee, Central Medical War Cttee, 1941. Late Examiner in Medicine, Universities of Cambridge, Aberdeen, Sheffield, Edinburgh, Durham and St Andrews. Served European War, 1914-19, in Egypt, France, Italy. Temp. Capt. RAMC; DADMS, GHQ, Italy, 1918. *Publications:* Heart Disease, Diagnosis and Treatment, 1932; Heart Disease and Pregnancy (jointly), 1938; Principles and Practice of Cardiology (jointly), 1941; The Approach to Cardiology, 1951; A Clinical Introduction to Heart Disease, 1959; numerous papers to Medical and Scientific Journals. *Recreations:* fishing and gardening. *Address:* Orchard Cottage, Outgate, near Ambleside, Cumbria. *T:* Hawkshead 233.   [*Died 8 Sept.* 1976.

BRAMWELL DAVIS, Maj.-Gen. Ronald Albert, CB 1957; DSO and bar, 1945; GOC Aldershot District, 1957-60, retired; *b* 8 Oct. 1905; *s* of late Capt. P. Bramwell Davis, The Highland Light Infantry, and of late Mrs E. M. Bramwell Davis, Crookham House, Newbury; *m* 1942, Lorna Winifred Hobling; one *s* one *d. Educ:* Wellington Coll.; RMC, Sandhurst. Joined HLI, 1925, as 2nd Lieut; Instructor, RMC Sandhurst, 1937-39; Company Comdr, OCTU, 1939-40; Staff Coll., student, 1940; Bde Major, 1940-41; Joint Staff Mission, Washington (Lieut-Col), 1941-42; CO 5th HLI (UK) (Lieut-Col), 1943; Joint Staff Mission, Washington (Col), 1943-44; CO 10th HLI (NW Europe) (Lieut-Col), and BAOR Training Centre, 1945; Bde Comdr, 146 Infantry Bde (49 WR Div.), 1945-46; BGS (Training) GHQ, MELF, 1946-49; Lieut-Col, Black Watch, 1948; Col, 1949; Bde Comdr 153 Infantry Bde (51st Highland Div.), 1950-51; Canadian National Defence Coll., student, 1951-52; Chief of Staff, Scottish Command, 1953-54; Brig. 1953; Maj.-Gen. 1955; Chief of Staff, Southern Command, 1955-56. Col, The Highland Light Infantry, 1957-59; Col, The Royal Highland Fusiliers, 1959-63. Pres., Modern Pentathlon Assoc. of GB, 1967-73 (Chm., 1963). USA Legion of Merit (Degree of Officer), 1944. *Recreations:* field sports. *Address:* Hamilton House, Downton, near Salisbury, Wilts. *T:* Downton 510. *Clubs:* Army and Navy, MCC; I Zingari, Free Foresters.
[*Died 12 May* 1974.

BRAND, Hon. Sir David, KCMG 1969; *b* Dongara, WA, 1 Aug. 1912; *s* of late Albert John Brand and late Hilda (*née* Mitchell), Dongara, WA; *m* 1944, Doris Elspeth, *d* of H. McNeill, Arrino, WA; two *s* one *d. Educ:* Mullewa Sch., WA. Joined AIF, 1939; served in Middle East and Greece (wounded, 1941, and discharged on med. grounds, 1942); joined Volunteer Defence Force, 1942, and apptd Chief Instr, Geraldton Area, WA. Member, WA Legislative Assembly (for Greenough), 1945-75; Junior Minister for Housing, Local Govt and Forests, 1949; Minister for Works and Water Supplies, 1950-53; Leader of Opposition, 1957-59 and 1971-72; Premier, Treasurer and Minister for Tourists, 1959-71. Hon. LLD (Univ. of WA). *Recreations:* golf, tennis. *Address:* 24 Ednah Street, Como, WA, Australia. *T:* 67.2906. *Club:* West Australian (Perth).
[*Died 15 April* 1979.

BRANDER, George Maconachie, CIE 1946; ICS retired; *b* 12 Oct. 1906; *s* of late J. P. Brander, ICS; *m* 1936, Joan (*née* Darley); three *d. Educ:* Edinburgh Academy; Exeter Coll., Oxford. Entered Indian Civil Service, 1930; Secretary to HE the Governor of Punjab, 1942; Additional Commissioner, Lahore, 1947; retired 1947. *Address:* 58 College Road, Dulwich, SE21. *T:* 01-693 5373.   [*Died 11 Feb.* 1977.

BRANDER, Maj.-Gen. Maxwell Spieker, CB 1937; OBE 1925; MIMechE; Col Comdt RASC, 1942-49; *b* 11 Oct. 1884; *s* of late Lt-Col William Maxwell Brander; *m* 1919, Mary Frances Alice, *d* of late Campbell Fortescue Stapleton Sanctuary, Bridport, Dorset; one *s. Educ:* Bedford Sch.; RMC, Sandhurst. Commissioned ASC 1906; served European War, 1914-18 (despatches, Bt Maj. and Bt Lieut-Col); Capt. 1914; Maj. 1925; Lieut-Col 1933; Col 1933; Maj.-Gen. 1936; Inspector, RASC, 1936-37; Director of Supplies and Transport, War Office, 1937-40; Maj.-Gen., i/c Administration, Eastern Command, 1940-41; Deputy Director-Gen. of Mechanization, Ministry of Supply, 1941-47. *Address:* Vincent Lodge, Bishopsteignton, Devon. *T:* Teignmouth 5200. *Clubs:* United Service & Royal Aero, Royal Automobile.   [*Died 30 Oct.* 1972.

BRANDON, Rev. Prof. Samuel George Frederick, MA, DD Leeds; MA Manchester 1955; Hon. CF; Professor of Comparative Religion in the University of Manchester since 1951, and Pro-Vice-Chancellor of the University, 1967-70; *b* 2 Oct. 1907; *s* of Samuel James and Lilian Emily Brandon; *m* 1934, Ivy Ada Miles; one *s* (and one *s* decd). *Educ:* College of the Resurrection, Mirfield; University of Leeds. Curate of St Mark's, Ford, Devonport, 1932-36; Curate-in-Charge of Westward Ho!, N. Devon, 1936-39; Chaplain to the Forces: Aldershot, 1939; BEF, 1939-40; Home Forces, 1940-42; Senior Chaplain to the Forces: North Africa, 1942-44; Italy, 1944-45 (despatches); Catterick, 1945-47; Austria, 1947-51. Wilde Lecturer in Natural and Comparative Religion, Oxford Univ., 1954-57; Forwood Lecturer in Philosophy and History of Religion, Liverpool Univ., 1964. Examiner in History and Philosophy of Religion, University of Wales, 1957-59; Dean of Faculty of Theology, University of Manchester, 1959-60, 1967-69. Sec.-Gen., Internat. Assoc. for History of Religions, 1970-. *Publications:* Time and Mankind, 1951; The Fall of Jerusalem and the Christian Church, 1951; The Formation of Christian Dogma (trans. from the German of M. Werner), 1957; Man and his Destiny in the Great Religions, 1962; Creation Legends of the Ancient Near East, 1963; The Saviour God (ed. and contrib.), 1963; History, Time and Deity, 1965; Jesus and the Zealots, 1967; The Judgement of the Dead, 1967; The Trial of Jesus of Nazareth, 1968; Religion in Ancient History, 1969; (ed and contrib.) Dictionary of Comparative Religion, 1970; Man and God in Art and Ritual, 1971; contributions to: Myth, Ritual and Kingship, 1958; The Voices of Time, 1965; The Hibbert Journal, Folklore, The Modern Churchman, Numen, History Today, Encyclopædia Judaica, Dictionary of the History of Ideas, Encyclopædia Britannica, etc. *Address:* Ewen, 18 Woodvale Road, Knutsford, Cheshire. *T:* 2370.
[*Died 29 Oct.* 1971.

BRANNIGAN, Owen, OBE 1964; Bass Singer; *b* 10 March 1908; *s* of Owen Brannigan and Sarah (*née* Connelly); *m* 1933, Mary Ashley; one *s. Educ:* privately; Guildhall School of Music. Studied with Walter Hyde and George Baker; Principal Bass: Glyndebourne, Covent Garden, Sadler's Wells Opera; first performance of Britten's Peter Grimes (later at Covent Garden), at 1958 Centenary Gala Performance before the Queen, Paris Opera, La Monnaie Brussels; and in Vienna, Prague, Hamburg and Geneva Opera Houses, 1965; created Collatinus in Rape of Lucretia, Glyndebourne, afterwards in Amsterdam, The Hague, etc.; original Dr Coutras in Moon and Sixpence, Sadler's Wells, 1957; created rôle of Noah in Britten's Noyes Fludde at Aldeburgh Festival, 1958, and of Bottom in Britten's Midsummer Night's Dream, Aldeburgh Festival, 1960 (re-created at Montreal Expo '67, and in San Francisco, 1971); Hasselbacher in Our Man in Havana, Sadler's Wells, 1963. Edinburgh International Festival, 1947, 1948, 1951, 1954; Lucerne and Brussels Festivals, 1969; leading Festivals in Great Britain, including Three Choirs, Leeds Triennial, Bath, Canterbury, Malvern; soloist with Royal Philharmonic, Royal Choral and Hallé Societies, and regular appearances at Promenade Concerts, BBC recitals and Television. Films include: The Gilbert and Sullivan Story, The Tales of Hoffmann. President Northumberland and Durham Association in London. Repr. Incorp. Society of Musicians, Catholic Stage Guild; Vice-Pres., Northern Arts Assoc. (formerly N Eastern Assoc. of the Arts). FGSM; Hon. RAM 1967; FIAL. Hon. MA Newcastle upon Tyne, 1969. Worshipful Company of Musicians' Award, Oct. 1943, and Liveryman, 1963; Sir Charles Santley Memorial Award, 1969. Papal Cross, Pro Ecclesia Pontifice, 1958. *Recreations:* golf and joinery. *Address:* 9 Lauradale Road, E Finchley, N2 9LT. *T:* 01-883 6368. *Clubs:* Savage, City Livery.
[*Died 10 May* 1973.

BRASHER, William Kenneth, CBE 1951; MA, FIEE; Secretary, The Institution of Electrical Engineers, 1939-62 (Hon. Secretary, 1962-63); *b* 31 March 1897; *e s* of late Dr C. W. J. Brasher, Clifton, and late Mabel M. Westlake, Bristol; *m* 1922, Katie Howe Howe; two *s* two *d. Educ:* Clifton Coll.; St John's Coll., Cambridge. Served European War, 1914-18, commission in Royal Engineers (TF) Signals, France, 1915-18. Asst Engineer, Marconi's Wireless Telegraph Co., 1921; Asst Engineer, Post Office, British Guiana, 1922, Chief Engineer, 1927; Senior Executive Engineer Posts and Telegraphs, Iraq 1929; Engineer-in-Chief, Posts and Telegraphs, Palestine, 1933. Hon. Associate, College of Technology, Aston, 1959. Chairman, Advisory Cttee, Conference of Engineering Societies of Western Europe and the USA (EUSEC), 1960-63; Secretary Exec. Cttee, Conference of Engineering Institutions of the Commonwealth, 1950-62. Al Rafidain, 5th Class, 1937; Commander Order of King Leopold II, 1963. *Recreations:* motoring and gardening. *Address:* 10 Kensington Mansions, SW5. *T:* 01-373 9999. *Club:* Athenæum.   [*Died 24 May* 1972.

BRAY, Frederick, CB 1949; MA Oxon; Consultant to the City and Guilds of London Institute, 1959-70; *b* 1895; *y s* of late Herbert James Bray; *m* 1926, Emily Lloyd, *d* of Richard Poole; two *s. Educ:* Queen Elizabeth's, Tamworth; Pembroke Coll., Oxford. War Service, 1914-18. Master, Clifton Coll., 1922-25; Asst Director of Education, Leeds, 1925-28; Board of Education: HM Inspector of Schools, 1928-38; Staff Inspector, 1938-40; Divisional Inspector, 1940-45; Ministry of Education; Principal Asst Secretary, 1945-46, Under-Secretary, 1946-56. Technical Adviser to City and Guilds of London Institute; Educational Adviser to the British Assoc. for Commercial and Industrial Education, 1956; Dean of College of Preceptors, 1957; Adviser on Technical Education to the Federal Govt of Rhodesia and Nyasaland and to the Govt of Southern Rhodesia, 1957-63. *Publications:* Light, 1927; General Science, 1928. *Recreation:* golf. *Address:* 24 Pall Mall, 97 Third Street, Salisbury, Rhodesia. *Clubs:* Chelsea Arts; Royal Salisbury Golf.
[Died 22 Dec. 1977.

BRAYLEY, Baron *cr* 1973 (Life Peer), of the City of Cardiff; **(John) Desmond Brayley,** Kt 1970; MC; DL, JP; *b* 29 Jan. 1917; *s* of Frederick and Jennie Brayley; *m* 1945, Q. E. S. Bee (marr. diss. 1960); two *d. Educ:* privately; grammar sch.; military. FICA 1958. Regular Army, 1934-45 (MC, despatches; Lt-Col). Joined Phoenix Glass Co. Ltd, 1946; Chm., Canning Town Glass Works Group, 1961-73; Parly Under-Sec. for Defence (Army), March-Sept. 1974. Hon. Col Comdt, Royal Regt of Artillery, June 1970-June 1975. Pres., Pontypridd Soc. of Mentally Handicapped Children; Patron, Inst. of Engineers and Technicians. Pres., Pontypridd Boys' Amateur Boxing Club. Patron, Masonic Hosp.; Vice-Patron, Masonic Schs. Companion, Grand Order of Water Rats. Freeman, City of London, 1961; Freeman, Worshipful Co. of Barber-Surgeons. DL Greater London, 1970; JP Middlesex Area of Greater London, 1968. FRSA 1973. *Recreations:* politics, books and letters, charities, flying (holds private pilot's licence); boxing (pre-war International, ISBA, and Army representative); yachting, shooting, fishing, horse-racing. *Address:* Arlington House, St James's, SW1; House of Lords, SW1. *Clubs:* Eccentric, Saints and Sinners (past Chm. and Trustee); Bristol, University (Bristol).
[Died 16 March 1977.

BREBNER, Sir Alexander, Kt 1938; CIE 1920; BSc Edinburgh; Indian Service of Engineers, retired; Member of Council and Executive of National Trust for Scotland, retired 1961; Board of Scottish Special Housing Association (appointed by Secretary of State for Scotland), 1954-61; Acting Secretary, Royal Scottish Academy, Edinburgh, 1954-55, retired; *b* 19 Aug. 1883; *s* of R. C. Brebner, Edinburgh; *m* 1911, Margaret Patricia (*d* 1974), *d* of W. Cunningham, Edinburgh; two *d* (one *s* decd). *Educ:* George Watson's Coll., Edinburgh; Edinburgh Univ. Asst Engineer, PWD, 1906; Executive Engineer, 1912; Under-Secretary, Bihar and Orissa, 1919; Under-Secretary to Govt of India, 1919-23; Superintending Engineer, 1923. Consulting Engineer to Govt of India, 1927 and 1929; Chief Engineer, Govt of India, 1931-38, retired, 1938; one-time Member Council of State; employed in Chief Divisional Food Office for Scotland, Ministry of Food, 1940-42; Ministry of Works (Licensing Officer, Scotland), 1942-54. *Recreation:* golf. *Address:* 4 Ainslie Place, Edinburgh. *T:* 031-225 1991. *Clubs:* New (Edinburgh); Hon. Co. Edinburgh Golfers; Royal and Ancient (St Andrews).
[Died 5 March 1979.

BRECHIN, Sir Herbert Archbold, KBE 1971 (CBE 1961; OBE 1952); Kt 1968; JP; DL; Lord Provost of the City of Edinburgh, 1966-69; Lord Lieutenant, County of the City of Edinburgh, 1966-69; Chartered Quantity Surveyor; *b* 3 Nov. 1903; *s* of late David Brechin and Katharine Mary (*née* O'Brien); *m* 1934, Jane Richmond Cameron; two *s. Educ:* Edinburgh. Senior Partner, H. A. Brechin & Co., FRICS, Chartered Quantity Surveyors, Edinburgh, Kelso, Rothesay, Isle of Bute and Hang Lung Centre, Patterson Street, Hong Kong. Chm. 9th British Commonwealth Games, 1955-70. Dist. Comr, Scout Assoc.; Holder of Scout Wood Badge, 1944; Scout Medal of Merit; and awarded Scout Silver Acorn by Chief Scout (1962); retired from Movement 1962 after 45 years' service; awarded Silver Wolf, 1969, by Chief Scout, in recognition of services of exceptional character in Edinburgh. Chairman: Scottish Br., RICS, 1948; Scottish Cttee for Award of Nat. Certs in Bldg; Scottish Bldg and Engrg Services Cttee, BSI; Scottish Codes of Practice Cttee on Bldg (Min. of Works); Mem., Bldg Industry Working Party set up by Govt in 1948. Member Edinburgh Town Council, 1949-69; City Treasurer, 1962-65. Chm. Bd of Governors, Heriot-Watt Coll., 1966, Chm. Ct, Heriot-Watt Univ., 1972-78. Chm., Edinburgh Festival Soc, 1966-69; Hon. President: The Bohemians Lyric Opera Co; The Scottish Paraplegic (Spinal Injuries) Assoc.; Hon. Vice-President: Commonwealth Games Council for Scotland; Scout Assoc. of Scotland; Scout Assoc. of

Edinburgh Area Scout Council; Gilbert and Sullivan Assoc.; Scottish Amateur Boxing Assoc.; Scottish Badminton Union; Royal Scottish Country Dance Soc.; Mem., Co. of Merchants of City of Edinburgh (Master's Court, 1969-72). FRSE 1969; FRICS; FH-WC (*hc*) 1962. Hon. DLitt Heriot-Watt, 1967. JP 1966, DL 1970, City of Edinburgh. Grand Officer, Order of Al-Kawkab Al-Urduni, Jordan, 1966; Grand Ufficiale dell' Ordine al Merito della Repubblica Italiana, 1969; Hon. Citizen, Dallas, Texas, 1966; Hon. Cedar Rapidian, 1966. *Address:* The Garth, Colinton, Edinburgh EH13 0DN. *T:* 031-441 2226; 13 Great King Street, Edinburgh EH3 6QP. *T:* 031-556 5441.
[Died 25 Jan. 1979.

BRECON, 1st Baron, *cr* 1957; **David Vivian Penrose Lewis,** PC 1960; JP; Director: A. B. Electronic Components Ltd (Chairman); Aberthaw & Bristol Channel Portland Cement Co.; United Capitals Investment Trust (Chairman); formerly a Proprietor of Quarries; *b* 14 Aug. 1905; *s* of late Alfred William and Elizabeth Mary Lewis, Craiglas, Talybont-on-Usk; *m* 1933, Mabel Helen (CBE 1964; JP; High Sheriff of Breconshire, 1971-72), 2nd *d* of late John McColville and late Mrs McColville, Abergavenny; two *d. Educ:* Monmouth Sch. Governor: Christ Coll., Brecon. Held various political offices in Wales including: Chairman, Conservative Party in Wales and Monmouthshire, 1956-58; Minister of State for Welsh Affairs, 1957-64; Mem., British delegn to European Parlt, 1973. Mem., Brecon CC, 1946-58; Mem. Brecon RDC, 1938-49; Chm., Breconshire County Planning Cttee (4 yrs). Ex-Chm., Jt Industrial Council for Quarrying Industry; Chm., Welsh Nat. Water Develt Authority, 1973; President, Brecknock Agricultural Soc., 1957. *Recreations:* trout fishing; Pres., Newport Athletic Club; formerly Rugby football (G. Crawshay's Welsh XV, etc.) and cricket (Capt. of Crickhowell CC 16 yrs). *Address:* (private) Greenhill, Cross Oak, Brecon. *T:* Talybont-on-Usk 247. *Clubs:* Carlton, MCC; Cardiff and County (Cardiff).
[Died 10 Oct. 1976 (ext).

BREECH, Ernest Robert; Chairman, Ford Motor Company, 1955-60; Honorary Chairman and Director Emeritus, Trans World Airlines Inc. (Chairman, 1961-69); *b* Lebanon, Missouri, 24 Feb. 1897; *s* of Joseph F. E. Breech; *m* 1917, Thelma Rowden; two *s. Educ:* Drury Coll., Springfield, Mo; Walton Sch. of Commerce. Accountant, Fairbanks, Morse & Co., 1917-20; Auditor, Adams & Westlake, 1920-22; Comptroller, Yellow Cab Mfg Co., 1923-29; Dir Yellow Truck & Coach Mfg Co., Chicago, 1927-33; Gen. Asst Treas., Gen. Motors Corp., NYC, 1929-33, Vice-Pres. i/c household appliance div. and aviation subsids, also Mem. administration cttee, 1939-42; Dir N Amer. Aviation Inc., 1933-1946 (Chm., 1933-42); Pres., and Dir Bendix Aviation Corp., 1942-46; with Ford Motor Co. as Exec. Vice-Pres., 1946-55; Dir, 1946-67; Chm. Finance Cttee, 1960-61. *Address:* 12723 Telegraph Road, Detroit, Michigan 48239, USA.
[Died 3 July 1978.

BREENE, Very Rev. Richard Simmons, MA, LLD; Rector, St Peter's, Belfast, from 1926, Dean of Connor, 1956-63, retd from active ministry, 1963; *b* Co. Clare, 25 June 1886; 2nd *s* of late T. J. Breene, formerly HMCS, Belfast; *m* 1st, 1913, Louise (*d* 1957), *e d* of late Robert Denison, Belfast; one *s* one *d*; 2nd, 1958, Mrs Vera Elizabeth Capper, *d* of late David Clugston Hutchinson, Belfast. *Educ:* Privately; Royal Univ.; and Queen's Univ. of Belfast. BA Hons 1910; MA Hon. School of Modern History, 1914; LLB 1918; LLD 1919; Universities Theological Examination, 1911; Deacon, 1911; Priest, 1912; Curate of Ballynure, Co. Antrim, till 1913; Glenavy, 1913-15; Chaplain to the Forces, 1915-19 (despatches); served in Mediterranean, Egypt, etc (1914-15 Star, King's and Victory medals); Hon. Chaplain to the Forces, 1920; Rector, Killinchy Union, 1920-26; Editor, The Irish Churchman, 1920-34; Member of General Synod, 1924-63; Rural Dean, North Belfast, 1931-47; Domestic Chaplain to the Bishop of Down, 1935; Examining Chaplain to the Bishop of Down, 1938; Examining Chaplain and Domestic Chaplain to the Bishop of Connor, 1945; Chancellor of Connor Cathedral, 1941-56, and Diocesan Registrar, 1941-63. Select Preacher (Trinity College, Dublin), 1941. Member of Faculty of Theology, QUB, 1944. Pres., Belfast Nat. History and Philosophical Soc., 1969. *Publications:* numerous short stories, literary sketches, theological articles, reviews, and essays. *Recreations:* antiquities, archæology, literature. *Address:* 2 Mount Pleasant, Belfast 9. *T:* Belfast 660494.
[Died 4 Feb. 1974.

BRENAN, Terence Vincent, CBE 1948 (OBE 1921); *b* 29 Nov. 1887; *s* of late Edward Vincent Brenan and Rose Peyton; *m* 1925, Marjorie Winifrede, *d* of late Thomas Draper Harrison; no *c. Educ:* King William's College, Isle of Man; Switzerland and Germany. Business; HM Land Forces, 1915-18, as an Officer; Vice-Consul at Birjand, Persia, 1917; Acting Consul at Sistan,

Persia, 1920; Vice-Consul, Levant Consular Service, 1921; Vice-Consul, Resht, 1921-23, Teheran, 1924-32; Consul at Teheran, 1932-35; in FO, 1936-38; attached to Representative of Iran at Coronation of King George VI, May 1937; Consul to Sofia, 1938; in charge of Consulate at Mersin, Turkey, May-Oct. 1941; Consul, Shiraz, Nov. 1941-Oct. 1943 when transferred to Damascus as Consul and Political Officer to Spears Military Mission; Consul-General at Tunis, 1944-46; at Rabat, 1946-47; retired, 1947; Director of Middle East Centre for Arab Studies, Beirut, 1948-53. *Address:* Champlins, Ewhurst, Robertsbridge, East Sussex.   *[Died 2 Nov. 1974.*

BRENNAN, Charles John, OBE 1949; MA (*hc*), QUB; MusB, FRCO, LRAM; Organist and Director of Choir, Belfast Cathedral, 1904-64; City Organist; Examiner in Music to Ministry of Education, and other examining authorities; *b* Gosport, 25 Oct. 1876; *m* 1903; three *s*. *Educ:* privately. Organist and Choirmaster, Clifton, Beds, 1892; Fellowship of Royal College of Organists, 1897; Organist and Choirmaster, Parish Church, Strabane, Co. Tyrone, 1897; Elmwood Church, Belfast, 1901. Conductor of the Ulster Male Choir, the Queen's Island Operatic Society and the Belfast City Amateur Operatic Society; Conductor of the Belfast Professional Orchestra; PPGO of Masonic Province of Down; President, Ulster Society Organists and Choirmasters; Past President, Society of Professional Musicians of Ulster; ex-Captain Royal Irish Fusiliers. *Publications:* Four Traditional Irish Songs; Words in Singing, a Handbook on Pronunciation for Singers. *Address:* Belgravia Hotel, Belfast, BT9 7AP.   *[Died 8 May 1972.*

BRENNAN, Joseph; *b* 1887; *e s* of late Joseph Brennan, Kilbrogan House, Bandon, Co. Cork; *m* 1918, Evelyn, *d* of late James Simcox, Cork; one *s* two *d*. *Educ:* Clongowes Wood Coll., Co. Kildare; Univ. College, Dublin; Christ's College, Cambridge. Hon. LLD National University of Ireland; Board of Customs and Excise, London, 1911; Chief Secretary's Office, Dublin Castle, 1912; Deputy Clerk, Irish Privy Council, 1917. Comptroller and Auditor-General of the Provisional Government, Irish Free State, 1922; Secretary of the Department of Finance, 1923-27; Chairman of the Irish Currency Commission, 1927-43; Chairman, Commission of Inquiry into Civil Service, 1932-34; Chairman, Investments Advisory Committee, 1933; Chairman, Commission of Inquiry into Banking, Currency and Credit, 1934-38; President, Statistical and Social Inquiry Society of Ireland, 1934-38; President, Institute of Bankers in Ireland, 1946; Governor of Central Bank of Ireland, 1943-53. *Recreations:* golf, travel. *Address:* Clancool, Shrewsbury Road, Dublin. *T:* 691540.
[Died 3 March 1976.

BRENNAN, Maj.-Gen. William Brian Francis, CB 1966; RAMC; retired; *b* 23 May 1907; *s* of late Captain C. J. Brennan, OBE, MA, Belfast; *m* 1943, Margaret Patricia, *d* of late A. B. Miners, MC, Essex; two *d*. *Educ:* Campbell College; Queen's University, Belfast. MB, BCh, BAO, Belfast, 1930. Lieut RAMC, 1930. Served NW Frontier, India, 1932-37 (Mohmand, Loë Agra and Waziristan campaigns). Served War of 1939-45, Middle East and Europe. Deputy DMS: Scottish Command, 1960; 17 Gurkha Division, and Overseas Commonwealth Land Forces, 1962-63; Southern Command, 1963-67. QHP 1962-67. Lieut-Col 1942; Col 1952; Brig. 1960; Maj.-Gen. 1963. Hon. Mem., Soc. of Medical Consultants to the Armed Forces (US). Officer, Legion of Merit (US), 1946. *Address:* Clifton Cottage, Broughton, Hants. *T:* Broughton 294.   *[Died 1 July 1977.*

BRETSCHER, Egon, CBE 1966; PhD; retired as Head of Nuclear Physics Division, AERE (1948-66), now Consultant; *b* 23 May 1901; 2nd *s* of Julius Bretscher and Anna Martin; *m* 1931, Hanna Greminger; three *s* two *d*. *Educ:* Gymnasium Zürich; Federal Inst. of Technology (ETH). Dipl. in Chem. Engineering, 1925; PhD (Edinburgh Univ.), 1927. Asst and Privat Dozent für Physik, Eidgenössisch Technische Hochschule, 1929-36; Fellow, Rockefeller Foundn, 1934-35; Clerk Maxwell School, Cavendish Lab., Cambridge, 1936-39; Lectr in Nuclear Physics, Cambridge Univ., 1939-44; Mem., Maud Cttee; Mem., Brit. Mission to Los Alamos Lab., New Mexico, 1944-46; Head of Chemistry Div., AERE, 1947-48. *Publications:* papers in various scientific jls. *Recreations:* maltreating piano, climbing mountains. *Address:* Salix, Conduit Head Road, Cambridge. *T:* Cambridge 59529.
[Died 16 April 1973.

BRETT, James; see Brett, L. J.

BRETT, (Louis) James; Principal Assistant Treasury Solicitor, 1969-72, Under Secretary (Legal), HM Procurator-General and Treasury Solicitor's Department, 1971-72; *b* 16 Jan. 1910; *er* surv. *s* of Alfred Bretzfelder and Raie Bretzfelder (*née* Prince);

m; two *d*; *m* 1962, Mary, *d* of late Frederick Thomas Tanner and of Mary Tanner (*née* Thomas). *Educ:* St Paul's Sch.; LLB (London); John Mackrell Prizeman and Hons (Law Society). Admitted Solicitor, 1931; private practice, 1931-36; Asst Solicitor, Epsom and Ewell Borough, 1936-41; Asst Divl Food Officer (Enforcement), London Div., Min. of Food, 1941-46; joined Treasury Solicitor's Dept, 1946; Asst Treasury Solicitor, 1959-69. *Recreations:* theatre, travel, reading. *Address:* 8 Hayes Court, Sunnyside, Wimbledon, SW19 4SH. *T:* 01-946 9409.
[Died 10 Aug. 1975.

BRETTON, Very Rev. William Frederick; Dean of Nelson, New Zealand, 1956-70, Dean Emeritus 1970; Vicar of Christ Church Cathedral, 1956-70; *b* 2 May 1909; *s* of William and Alice Bretton; *m* 1934, Mary Hope Rokeby Robinson; two *s* two *d*. *Educ:* Downing College, Cambridge; Ridley Hall, Cambridge. BA, 1931; MA, 1935. Deacon 1933; Priest, 1935; Curate: St Andrew's, Watford, 1933-35; St John's, Sparkhill, 1936-39; Vicar: St Cuthbert's, Birmingham, 1939-42; St John the Evangelist, Sandown, 1942-46; Johnsonville, NZ, 1946-50; Lower Hutt, NZ, 1950-56. Hon. Canon, Wellington, NZ, 1953-57. Examining Chaplain to Bishop of Nelson, 1965-. Coronation Medal, 1953. *Publication:* ABC of Our Religion. *Address:* 1 Marybank Road, Atawhai, Nelson, New Zealand.
[Died 4 Nov. 1971.

BREWIN, Elizabeth Maud, (Mrs P. K. Brewin); see Pepperell, E. M.

BREWIS, Rev. John Salusbury, MA; Rector of St James's, Piccadilly, 1954-67; *m* 1935, Lady Anne Beatrice Mary Palmer, *e d* of 3rd Earl of Selborne, PC, CH; two *s* two *d*. *Educ:* Eton; Hertford College, Oxford (Scholar), 1st Class Final Honour School of Modern History; Princeton Univ. (Henry P. Davison Scholar); Cuddesdon College. Assistant Master at Eton, 1927-29; Examining Chaplain to the Bishop of Carlisle, 1929-46; Vice-Principal and Tutor of St Edmund Hall, Oxford, 1929-37 (Fellow Emeritus, 1956); Examining Chaplain to the Bishop of Durham, 1937-47; Principal, St Chad's Coll., Durham, 1937-47; Vicar, Melton-on-the-Hill, Yorks, 1947-54. Hon. Canon of Durham, 1947. Archdeacon, 1947-54, and Rural Dean, 1947-54, of Doncaster. Examining Chaplain to the Bishop of London, 1956. *Address:* Benhams House, Benhams Lane, Blackmoor, Liss, Hants.   *[Died 1 March 1972.*

BRIAN, Prof. Percy Wragg, CBE 1975; FRS 1958; Professor of Botany, University of Cambridge, 1968-77, now Emeritus Professor; Fellow of Queens' College, Cambridge, 1968-77; *b* 5 Sept. 1910; *s* of Percy Brian, Macclesfield, and Adelaide Wragg, Shirley, nr Birmingham; *m* 1st, 1935, Iris Neville Hunt (marr. diss. 1947); one *s* two *d*; 2nd, 1948, Margaret Audrey Gilling. *Educ:* King Edward's School, Birmingham; King's College, Cambridge. Univ. of Cambridge. Frank Smart Univ. Student in Botany, 1933-34; PhD 1936; ScD 1951. Assistant Mycologist, Long Ashton Research Station, 1934; Mycologist, Jealott's Hill Research Station, ICI Ltd, 1936; Head of Dept of Microbiology, Akers Research Labs ICI Ltd, Welwyn, 1946; Associate Research Manager, Pharmaceuticals Div., 1961-62; Regius Prof. of Botany, Glasgow Univ., 1962-68; Clive Behrens Lectr in Agric., Leeds Univ., 1964-65. Mem., ARC, 1966-76. President: British Mycological Society, 1959, 1965; Assoc. of Applied Biologists, 1961; Society for General Microbiology, 1965; Cambridge Philosophical Soc., 1978-. Leeuwenhoek Lectr, Royal Soc., 1966; Mem. Council, Royal Soc., 1968-70. Hon. DSc Hull, 1978. *Publications:* many in learned journals on subjects concerned with plant pathology, microbiology and plant physiology. *Recreation:* gardening. *Address:* Walkers Field, Kingston, Cambridge CB3 7NG. *T:* Comberton 2200.
[Died 17 Aug. 1979.

BRICKMAN, Brig. Ivan Pringle, CB 1949; CBE 1942 (OBE 1929); Regular Army retired; *b* 14 May 1891; *s* of Francis Brickman, Edinburgh, and Eliza Macdonald; *m* 1920, Mildred Ducker (*d* 1977); one *d*. *Educ:* Edinburgh Academy; Bowdon College. Served European War, 1914-18, France (despatches); War of 1939-45; ME, 1941 (despatches); BNAF, 1943; CMF, 1944 (despatches), Bronze Star (USA), 1946. *Recreations:* fishing, golf. *Address:* 10 Brynllys East, Meliden, Clwyd. *T:* Prestatyn 3442.   *[Died 16 June 1980.*

BRICKWOOD, Sir Rupert Redvers, 2nd Bt, *cr* 1927; Director of Brickwoods Ltd, brewers, Portsmouth; *b* 18 Feb. 1900; *e s* of Sir John Brickwood, 1st Bt, and Jessie (*d* 1917), *d* of John Cooper of Burghfield, Berks; *S* father 1932; *m* 1932, Rachel Neale (*d* 1972), *o d* of late Dr M. W. Shutte, Newnham, Oatlands Chase, Weybridge; two *d*. *Educ:* Twyford School; Cheltenham College; RMC Sandhurst. *Heir: half-b* Basil Greame Brickwood, *b* 21 May 1923. *Address:* 2 Solent Gate, Craneswater Park, Southsea, Hants. *Club:* Royal Automobile.   *[Died 29 April 1974.*

BRIDGE, Ann, (Lady O'Malley); author; *b* 1891; *d* of James Harris Sanders and Marie Louise, *d* of James Ingersoll Day; *m* 1913, Sir Owen St Clair O'Malley, *qv* ; two *d* (one *s* decd). *Educ:* Home; London School of Economics. *Publications:* Peking Picnic, 1932 (Atlantic Monthly Prize); The Ginger Griffin, 1934 (Book Society Choice); Illyrian Spring, 1935 (Book Society Choice); The Song in the House (short stories), 1936; Enchanter's Nightshade, 1937 (Book Society Choice); Four-Part Setting, 1939; Frontier Passage, 1942; Singing Waters, 1945 (Book Society Choice and Choice of the Literary Guild of America); And Then You Came, 1948; (with Susan Lowndes) The Selective Traveller in Portugal, 1949; The House at Kilmartin (for children), 1951; The Dark Moment 1952 (Choice of the Literary Guild of America); A Place to Stand, 1953; Portrait of my Mother, 1955; The Light-Hearted Quest, 1956; The Portuguese Escape, 1958 (Choice of the Literary Guild of America); The Numbered Account, 1960; The Tightening String, 1962; The Dangerous Islands, 1964; Emergency in the Pyrenees, 1965; The Episode at Toledo, 1966; Facts and Fictions, 1968; The Malady in Madeira, 1969; Moments of Knowing, 1970; Goings-on in the Corridors of Power, 1971; Permission to Resign, 1972. *Recreations:* sailing, botany, archæology. *Address:* c/o A. D. Peters, 10 Buckingham Street, Adelphi, WC2. *[Died 9 March 1974.*

BRIDGE, Admiral Sir (Arthur) Robin (Moore), KBE, 1950 (CBE 1940); CB 1948; *b* 15 Feb. 1894; *s* of late Robert Moore and Mary Frances Bridge; *m* 1933, Ida Nancy, *e d* of George Tulk Shepherdson, Santiago, Chile; one *s* one *d*. *Educ:* RN Colleges, Osborne and Dartmouth. Comd. HMS Eagle, 1939-41; Dir, Naval Air Div., Admiralty, 1941-43; Chief of Staff to Flag Officer, Carrier Training, 1943-44 Commodore 1st Class, Comdg Northern Naval Air Stations, 1944-45; Rear-Adm., 1945; Flag Officer (Air) East Indies, 1945-46; Flag Officer (Air) British Pacific Fleet and East Indies, 1946-47. Senior Naval Representative, British Element of Joint Chiefs of Staff Cttee, Australia, 1947-48; Vice-Adm., 1948; Flag Officer Commanding Reserve Fleet, 1948-50; retired list, 1951; adm., retired list, 1952. *Address:* Greengates, Emsworth, Hants. *T:* Emsworth 2752. *[Died 19 Feb. 1971.*

BRIDGE, George Wilfred; Deputy Chairman, Legal and General Assurance Society Ltd and associated societies; *b* 1 Jan. 1894; *s* of Josiah and Mary Bridge; *m* 1st, 1920, Minna (*d* 1962); one *s* one *d*; 2nd, Neta Margaret, *widow* of Alec Aldridge. *Educ:* Westoe Road Secondary School, South Shields. Joined Legal and General Assurance Soc. Ltd, 1919; General Manager, 1946-58; Executive Vice-Chairman, 1958-59. President, Insurance Institute of London, 1951-52; President, Chartered Insurance Institute, 1954-55. Governor, Stowe School and Queenswood School. FCII. *Recreation:* golf. *Address:* Hazel Croft, Deans Lane, Walton-on-the-Hill, Tadworth, Surrey. *T:* Tadworth 2846. *Club:* Reform. *[Died 22 March 1971.*

BRIDGE, Adm. Sir Robin; *see* Bridge, Adm. Sir A. R. M.

BRIDGE, Roy Arthur Odell, CMG 1967; Director (since 1970): Bank Julius Baer International Ltd, London; Bär Holding A. G. Zürich; Scandinavian Bank Ltd, London; *b* 27 June 1911; *s* of late A. S. W. Bridge and late Mary E. Bridge; *m* 1st, 1938, Mary Ethel (*d* 1972), *d* of late E. N. Ruddock; two *s* two *d* (and one *d* decd); 2nd, 1974, Jane Catliffe Glover. *Educ:* Dulwich College. Bank of England, 1929-69: UK Alternate on Managing Bd of European Payments Union, Paris, 1950-52; Dep. Chief Cashier, Bank of England, 1957-63; Adviser to the Governors, 1963-65; Asst to the Governors, 1965-69; Advisor to the Chm., Mellon Bank NA, Pittsburgh, 1970-77. Pres., Assoc. Cambiste Internationale, Paris, 1962-67 (Hon. Pres., 1967). FRSA 1969. *Recreations:* people, music, eating and drinking. *Address:* 16 St Leonard's Court, West Hill Road, St Leonards-on-Sea, E Sussex. *T:* Hastings 433098. *Clubs:* Bath, Overseas Bankers; Forex (Paris). *[Died 14 Sept. 1978.*

BRIDGEFORD, Lt.-Gen. Sir William, KBE 1956 (CBE 1941); CB 1945; MC; Australian Military Forces, retired; *b* 28 July 1894; *s* of George Bridgeford; *m* 1922, Phyllis W., *d* of Walter Frederico; one *s*. *Educ:* High School, Ballarat; Duntroon Royal Military College. Served European War, 1914-18 (MC); Instructor, Duntroon, 1925; Staff College, Quetta, 1926-27; Bde Major, 6th Cavalry Bde, Adelaide, 1928-31; Training Directorate, Army HQ, 1932-34; GSO 1, 2nd Cavalry Div., Victoria, 1934-38; Instructor Army Command and Staff School, 1938; Imperial Defence College, London, 1939; War of 1939-45 (despatches, CBE, CB). Formerly GOC Eastern Command, Australia; C-in-C British Commonwealth Forces in Korea; retired, 1953. *Address:* c/o Navy and Military Club, Alfred Place, Melbourne, Australia. *[Died 21 Sept. 1971.*

BRIDGEMAN, Hon. Geoffrey John Orlando, MC; MB, FRCS; *heir-pres.* to 2nd Viscount Bridgeman, KBE, CB, DSO, MC; *b* 3 July 1898; 2nd son of 1st Viscount Bridgeman; *m* 1929, Mary Talbot (*d* 1974); one *s* two *d*. *Educ:* Èton; Trinity College, Cambridge. Served European War, RFA, 1917-19; and as Brig. RAMC, 1940-45. Consulting Surgeon, Western Ophthalmic Hospital; Consulting Ophthalmic Surgeon, St George's Hospital; formerly: Classical Exhibitioner, Trinity College, Cambridge; Hon. Consultant Ophthalmologist to India and Burma Offices. Fellow of Royal Society of Medicine; Member of British Medical Association. *Recreations:* cricket, shooting, skiing. *Address:* Watley House, Sparsholt, Winchester, Hants. *T:* Sparsholt 297. *Club:* Travellers'. *[Died 15 Oct. 1974.*

BRIDGEMAN, Col Hon. Henry George Orlando, DSO, 1918; MC; JP and DL Northumberland; Late RFA; 3rd *s* of 4th Earl of Bradford; *b* 15 Aug. 1882; *m* 1930, Joan, *y d* of late Hon. Bernard Constable Maxwell; two *s* two *d*. *Educ;* Harrow; Royal Military Academy, Woolwich. Entered Royal Field Artillery, 1901; ADC to Field-Marshal Lord Grenfell, then Commander of the Forces in Ireland, 1905-8; for six months to Gen. Hon. Sir N. G. Lyttelton, in the same office; served in India in Royal Horse Artillery, 1908-14; Captain, 1914; Major, 1915; Lt-Col 1918; Commanded a Battery of Field Artillery in France, Sept. 1914-Jan. 1917, when posted as Brigade Major, 47th Divisional Artillery; Commanded Brigade RFA, Oct. 1918 to end of War (DSO, MC, Order of Danilo of Montenegro, despatches five times); retired, June 1919. *Recreations:* shooting, fishing, big-game shooting, and travel. *Address:* Fallodon Hall, Embleton, Alnwick, Northumberland. *T:* Embleton 252. *Club:* Turf. *[Died 19 May 1972.*

BRIDGEMAN, Hon. Sir Maurice (Richard), KBE 1964 (CBE 1946); Chairman of British Petroleum Company, 1960-69; Member, Industrial Reorganisation Corporation, 1969-71; *b* 26 Jan. 1904; 3rd *s* of 1st Viscount Bridgeman; *m* 1933, Diana Mary Erica Wilson (*d* 1979); four *d*. *Educ:* Eton; Trinity Coll., Cambridge. Joined Anglo-Persian Oil Co., 1926; Petroleum Adviser Ministry of Economic Warfare, 1939; Asst Secretary Petroleum Dept and Joint Secretary Oil Control Board, 1940; temporarily loaned as Petroleum Adviser Govt of India, 1942; Principal Assistant Secretary Petroleum Division, Ministry of Fuel and Power, 1944-46; Mem. Advisory Council on Middle East Trade, 1958-63; Pres., Middle East Assoc., 1965-76. Hon. Fellow, Fitzwilliam Coll., Cambridge, 1967. Hon. LLD Leeds Univ., 1969. Cadman Memorial Medal, 1969. KStJ 1961 (CStJ 1957). Knight Grand Cross of the Italian Republic, 1966; Grand Officer, Order of Orange Nassau, 1968; Order of Homayun (Iran), 2nd Class, 1968. *Address:* The Glebe House, Selham, Petworth, West Sussex. *T:* Lodsworth 205. *Club:* White's. *[Died 18 June 1980.*

BRIDGES, Daisy Caroline, CBE 1954; RRC 1943; General Secretary, International Council of Nurses, 1948-61; *b* 7 April 1894; *d* of late John Henry Bridges, JP and late Edith Isabella Bridges. *Educ:* Heathfield School, Ascot; Ladies' College, Cheltenham. British Red Cross Society, 1914-19 (despatches 1918); Nightingale School, St Thomas' Hosp., 1919-23; Staff, St Thomas' Hosp., 1925-36; Rockefeller Fellowship, US and Canada, 1937-38. TANS. Served War of 1939-45: France, Egypt and India; retired with rank of Prin. Matron; Min. of Health Working Party on Recruitment and Training of Nurses, 1946-47; Fellow Royal Soc. of Health, 1959. Florence Nightingale Medal (awarded by Internat. Red Cross Cttee), 1953; Coronation Medal, 1953. *Publication:* A History of the International Council of Nurses, 1967. *Recreations:* reading, chess. *Address:* 60 Burton Court, Chelsea, SW3. *T:* 01-730 7622. *Club:* Royal Commonwealth Society. *[Died 29 Nov. 1972.*

BRIDGMAN, Leonard Logoz; AMRAeS; *b* 15 Feb. 1895; *o s* of late A. H. Bridgman, ISO; unmarried. *Educ:* Cambridge House; Strand School; King's Coll., London. Hon. Artillery Company, 1915-18 and 1921-; Royal Air Force, 1918-19; Editorial Staff, The Aeroplane, 1919-34; Joint Editor and Compiler, All the World's Aircraft, 1923-40, Editor, 1941-60; International Aviation Associates, 1939-47; Esso Export Ltd, 1947-60; Executive Editor, Esso Air World, 1939-60, Advisory Editor, 1960-66. FAI Paul Tissandier Diploma, 1956, in recognition of 35 years' work on All the World's Aircraft. *Publications:* Aircraft of the British Empire, 1935-1939; The Clouds Remember, 1935, (with O. Stewart) new edn 1972; also illustrated several air historical books. *Address:* Danny, Hurstpierpoint, Hassocks, Sussex BN6 9BB. *T:* Hurstpierpoint 833212. *Club:* Naval and Military. *[Died 19 Dec. 1980.*

BRIERCLIFFE, Sir Rupert, Kt 1939; CMG 1936; OBE 1919; MD, FRCP, DPH, etc; *b* 27 January 1889. *Educ:* Bolton Grammar School; University of Manchester. Resident Medical

Officer Manchester Children's Hospital, 1910; House Physician Manchester Royal Infirmary, 1911; Assistant Manchester Public Health Laboratories, 1912; Assistant MOH Manchester, 1913; RAMC (TF), 1914-20; served Egypt, Gallipoli, Palestine (despatches); demobilized with rank of Major; Principal Medical Officer, Haifa, 1919; DADMS Occupied Enemy Territory (South), 1920; Deputy Director of Health, Palestine, 1920-1930; Director of Medical and Sanitary Services, Ceylon, and Principal, Ceylon Medical College, 1930-36; Director of Medical Services, Nigeria, 1936-40; OC 1st WA Bde Field Amb., The Nigeria Regt, 1939-40; Medical Adviser to Comptroller for Development and Welfare in West Indies, 1940-46, and Medical Adviser, British Section, Anglo-American Caribbean Commission, 1942-46. Hon. Col Trinidad Local Forces, 1944. Esquire, Order of St John of Jerusalem, 1926. *Recreation:* sailing. *Address:* Pasea Estate, Tortola, British Virgin Islands. *Club:* Royal Thames Yacht. *[Died 2 Dec. 1975.*

BRIGGS, Alderman Albert William; Chairman, South East Metropolitan Regional Hospital Board, since 1968; *b* 30 Dec. 1900; *s* of John Henry Briggs and Lydia Briggs; *m* 1930, Anne Counter; two *s* one *d*. *Educ:* West Ham Central Secondary School. Chairman: Briggs & Son Ltd (trading as Kensington Press), 1924-; Raystede Centre for Animal Welfare, 1965-; Dir, Brighton Internat. Trade Fairs Ltd, 1965-. Brighton CB Council, 1936-; Mem. Court, Sussex Univ., 1965-. Contested (Lab) Lewes, 1950 and 1951. Lessee, Brighton Racecourse. *Address:* 186 Bevendean Crescent, Brighton, Sussex. *T:* Brighton 66913. *[Died 30 May 1971.*

BRIGGS, Sir (Alfred) George (Ernest), Kt 1953; Chairman: John Scott and Partners; Unit Trusts Information and Broking Service; The Bedwin Organisation; Director: Gulf Development Co. Ltd; *b* 12 Feb. 1900; *s* of Alfred Briggs, Nottingham; *m* 1924, Kathlene Margaret, *d* of Peter MacGregor, JP, Sheffield; one *s*. *Educ:* Oundle. Served European War, Royal Naval Air Service, 1918. Deputy-Controller Iron and Steel Supplies, Ministry of Supply, 1942-45; Deputy-Controller of Supplies (Munitions Production) Ministry of Supply, March 1951-Dec. 1952. Member: Royal Ordnance Factories Board, 1952-59; European Purchasing Commission, 1951-52; Government Cttee on Steel and Tinplate Redundancies, West South Wales, 1953-55; London Electricity Board, 1959-. AMIMechE. *Address:* Courtyard House, Lavershot Hall, London Road, Windlesham, Surrey. *T:* Ascot 20144. *[Died 30 Nov. 1976.*

BRIGGS, Donald Henry Currer, MBE 1944; retired; *b* 28 April 1893; *s* of Arthur Currer Briggs; *m* 1917, Elizabeth, *d* of Dr James Denniston, MD, Dunoon and Altrincham; one *s* three *d*. *Educ:* Charterhouse School; Trinity College, Oxford. Mining Engineer in charge of Collieries in the Wakefield and Castleford district of Yorkshire, 1920-47. *Recreations:* shooting, fishing. *Address:* 7 North Hill Road, Headingley, Leeds 6, Yorks. *T:* Leeds 52727. *[Died 29 Sept. 1974.*

BRIGGS, Sir George; *see* Briggs, Sir A. G. E.

BRIGGS, Martin Shaw, FRIBA; *b* Otley, 1882; *e s* of late Rev. G. S. Briggs, Congregational minister; *m* 1910, Constance (*d* 1954), *d* of Prof. J. Holland Rose, of Cambridge; one *s* one *d*. *Educ:* Mill Hill School; Leeds University. Practised as an architect in London. *Principal works:* Keyston Manor; Surbiton Housing Scheme; Golderbrock House (Gt Titchfield Street); Otford Vicarage; the McClure Music School and Winterstoke House, Mill Hill School; houses at Mill Hill and elsewhere. Served in Egypt and Palestine, 1916-19; lecturer in London University School of Architecture, 1919-23, 1947-57; HM Inspector of Technical Schools, Board of Education, 1923-45; Member of RIBA Council, 1929-31, 1933-35, 1948-53; Vice-President 1952-53. *Publications:* In the Heel of Italy, 1910 (Italian translation, 1913); Baroque Architecture, 1913 (German translation, 1914); Through Egypt in Wartime, 1919; Muhammadan Architecture in Egypt and Palestine, 1924; A Short History of the Building Crafts, 1925; Rusticus, 1927; The Architect in History, 1927; English Architecture: an Outline, 1928; The Homes of the Pilgrim Fathers in England and America, 1932; Middlesex, Old and New, 1934; Freiburg and the Black Forest, 1936; How to Plan Your House, 1937; Building To-Day, 1944; Round the Shires, 1945; Puritan Architecture, 1946; Men of Taste, 1947; Architecture (Home University Library), 1947; The Approach to Architecture, 1948; Town and Country Planning, 1948; Down the Thames, 1949; Christopher Wren, 1951; Goths and Vandals, 1952; Wren the Incomparable, 1953; The English Farmhouse, 1953; Everyman's Concise Encyclopædia of Architecture, 1959; Architecture in Italy, 1961; contributions to many other books; numerous illustrated articles and reviews. *[Died 13 Oct. 1977.*

BRIGGS, Percy, CBE 1966; Member, Electricity Council, 1962-66; *b* 4 Sept. 1903; *s* of late Alfred and late Caroline Briggs; *m* 1927, Annie M. Folker; one *s*. *Educ:* Deacon's School, Peterborough; Northampton Polytechnic. Supt, Fulham Power Station, 1945; Chief Generation Engr, SE Div., British Elect. Authy, 1948-53; Controller, Merseyside and N Wales Div., 1954-56, Yorks Div., 1957; Regional Dir, NE Region, CEGB, 1958-61. CEng, FIMechE; MInstF. *Recreations:* gardening, fishing. *Address:* 7 Thackers Close, Wansford, Peterborough PE8 6LD. *T:* Stamford 782248. *[Died 1 Sept. 1980.*

BRIGSTOCKE, Geoffrey Reginald William; Under-Secretary, Department of Trade and Industry, since 1970; *b* 4 Aug. 1917; *s* of late C. R. Brigstocke, CB, and late Dora Constance Bowen-Davies; *m* 1952, Heather Renwick Brown; three *s* one *d*. *Educ:* Charterhouse School; Magdalene College, Cambridge. Served Army, 1939-47. Secretary, Transport Directorate, Berlin, CCG, 1946-48; Asst Principal, Foreign Office (German Section), 1948-50; Principal, Ministry of Transport, 1950-60; Assistant Secretary, 1960; Shipping Attaché, Washington, 1960-64; Board of Trade, 1964-67; Under-Sec., Min. of Transport, 1967-70. *Address:* 41 Moore Street, SW3. *T:* 01-589 2560.
[Died 3 March 1974.

BRIGSTOCKE, George Edward; *m* 1942, Mary Sandford; two *s*. *Educ:* Marlborough; Keble College, Oxford; Wells Theological College. BA 1913; MA 1923. Deacon, 1914; Priest, 1915; Provost of St Nicholas Cathedral and Vicar of Newcastle upon Tyne, 1938-47; Principal, College of the Venerable Bede, Durham, 1947-59; Canon Residentiary, Durham Cathedral, 1959-61. Examining Chaplain to the Archbishop of Canterbury, 1961-65. Received into the Roman Catholic Church, 1965. *Address:* The Barn House, Elofts, Thorner, Leeds.
[Died 25 Oct. 1971.

BRILLANT, Jules-André; CBE 1944; ED; Hon. Colonel, St Lawrence Fusiliers; MLC, Province Quebec 1942-68; *b* St Octave de Métis, 30 June 1888; *s* of Joseph Brillant and Rose Raiche; *m* 1st, 1923, Rose Coulombe (*d* 1933); three *s* two *d*; 2nd, 1940, Agnes Villeneuve. *Educ:* University of St Joseph, NB. President: The Canada & Gulf Terminal Railway Co. Ltd, 1947; The Bonaventure and Gaspe Telephone Co., 1953; Chairman, Les Prévoyants du Canada, 1965-70; Hon. President and Director, Québec-Téléphone, 1967, Trust Général du Canada, 1971; Vice-President and Founder, Rimouski Technical and Marine Schools, 1936; Director, Canada Wire & Cable Co. Ltd, 1961-69. Prominent in industrial and commercial affairs for many years; Co-ordinator in Committee of Reconstruction at Ottawa; Director of Communications for defence of Country (War of 1939-45); President Conseil d'Orientation Economique du Québec, 1943-46; Hon. Member Red Cross Society (Quebec Provincial Division); Member, Newcomen Society of England. Bachelor in Commercial Sciences (*hc*), St Joseph University, Memramcook, NB, 1939; LLD (*hc*), St Joseph University, 1942; Doctor in Commercial Sciences (*hc*): Montreal Univ., 1943; Univ. of Moncton, NB, 1967; Dr in Social Sciences (*hc*), St Louis Univ., Edmundston, NB; Dr of The University, Montreal University, 1959. Liberal. Roman Catholic; Commander Order of St Grégoire le Grand, 1949; Knight of Honor, and Devotion, Sovereign Military Order of Malta (Canada Assoc.). *Address:* Rimouski, PQ, Canada. *[Died May 1973.*

BRINDLE, Prof. Harry; Professor of Pharmacy, Manchester University, 1946-55; Professor Emeritus, 1955; *m* Ellen Warburton; no *c*. *Educ:* Accrington Secondary School; King's College, London. Served European War, 1916-19, RAMC and RE. Principal, Manchester School of Pharmacy, 1920-28; Lecturer in Pharmaceutical Chemistry, Manchester University, 1928. Chairman British Pharmaceutical Conference, 1944, 1945. Examiner to Pharmaceutical Society of Gt Britain and a number of Universities, from 1925. *Publications:* many papers in Jl of Pharmacy and Pharmacology, Pharmaceutical Jl, Lancet, Analyst, British Medical Jl, etc. *Recreations:* golf, gardening. *Address:* 35 Delahays Drive, Hale, Cheshire. *T:* 061-980 2996.
[Died 30 Jan. 1976.

BRINK, Lt.-Gen. George Edwin, CB 1941; CBE 1942; DSO 1917; South African Permanent Force (retired list); *b* Jagersfontein, OFS, 27 Sept. 1889; *m* 1919, Lilian Alice de Villiers; three *d*. *Educ:* Grey College, Bloemfontein. Served European War, 1914-18 in German South-West Africa and in German East Africa (despatches thrice, DSO, French Croix de Guerre); War of 1939-45, served Abyssinia, Egypt, and Cyrenaica as GOC, 1st SA Division (CB, CBE); GOC Inland Area, South Africa, 1942-43; Director-General of Demobilisation, South Africa, 1944-48. Chm., SA Ex-Services National Council; Mem., SA War Histories Adv. Cttee. KStJ 1944. *Address:* PO Box 101, St Michaels-on-Sea, South Coast, Natal, South Africa.
[Died 30 April 1971.

BRINSON, Derek Neilson, CMG 1973; MC 1944; HM Diplomatic Service; Head of Guidance and Information Policy Department, Foreign and Commonwealth Office, since 1970; *b* 23 June 1921; 2nd *s* of late H. N. Brinson, DSO, OBE and of Mrs V. M. Brinson; *m* 1st, 1954, Muna Samy; 2nd, 1958, Prudence Elizabeth Wheeler. *Educ:* Bradfield Coll.; Hertford Coll., Oxford. Welsh Guards, 1941-46. FO, 1949; 2nd Sec., Rome, 1951; FO, 1953; 1st Sec., 1954; 1st Sec. and Head of Chancery, Saigon, 1957 (acted as Chargé d'Affaires, 1958 and 1959); 1st Sec., later Head of Chancery, UK Delegns Nuclear Tests, Laos and Disarmament Confs, Geneva, 1960-64; FO, 1964; Counsellor, 1964; Counsellor and Head of Chancery, Caracas, 1965 (acted as Chargé d'Affaires, 1968). *Address:* 1 Sloane Square, SW1. *T:* 01-730 5689. *Clubs:* Guards, Pratt's.
[Died 28 Dec. 1974.

BRISSON, Mrs F.; *see* Russell, Rosalind.

BRISTOL, Major Everett, CMG 1918; QC (Ont), 1928; *b* Hamilton, Ontario, 21 Oct. 1888; *s* of late George Everett Bristol and Margaret White; *m* 1919, Helen Francis, *o d* of late F. H. and Mrs Mathewson, Montreal; two *d. Educ:* Royal Military College of Canada; University of Toronto (BA); Osgoode Hall Law School, Toronto. On Reserve of Officers, Canada, 1908; called to Bar, Ontario, 1914, and practised till outbreak of war; 2nd Lieut 13th Hussars (Imperials), 7 Sept. 1914; Lieut, 15th Batt. 48th Highlanders (Canadian Infantry) June 1915; Capt. Aug. 1915; wounded, Dec. 1915; Major, Dec. 1916; retired from Canadian Forces, Aug. 1919, and practised as barrister in Toronto until 1970; was Military Secretary to Minister of Overseas Military Forces of Canada. *Recreations:* golf, riding. *Address:* University Club, 380 University Avenue, Toronto, Ontario. *Clubs:* University, Toronto Golf (Toronto).
[Died 17 Feb. 1976.

BRISTOWE, William Syer, MA, ScD Cantab; *b* 1 Sept. 1901; *s* of Bertram Arthur Bristowe and Mary Rosa (*née* Johnston), Stoke d'Abernon, Surrey; *m* 1934, Helen Mary Harper (marr. diss. 1962); three *d* (and one *d* decd); *m* 1964, Jean Kiddle. *Educ:* Wellington Coll; Cambridge. Cambridge Scientific Expeditions to Jan Mayen, 1921, and Brazil, 1923. Joined Brunner Mond, 1925, subsequently merged in ICI 1926; Head of Far East Department, 1936, and Director of Eastern subsidiary companies; Head of Central Staff Department, 1948-62. Member ECA special productivity mission to USA studying education and the employment of graduates, 1950; Member FBI cttee studying shortage of science teachers, 1954. Pres. Ray Society, 1959-62; Master of Armourers and Braziers, 1965-66; Member, Court of City University. Stamford Raffles Award for Zoology, 1961. *Publications:* The Comity of Spiders, 2 vols, 1939-41; Spiders, 1947; The World of Spiders, 1958; Victorian China Fairings, 1964; Natural History of the Garden of Buckingham Palace (pt author), 1964; Emma, the Resolute Queen, 1966; A Book of Islands, 1969; Louis and the King of Siam, 1976; occasional papers on athletics, explorations, early naturalists, giants, Sherlock Holmes and staff management. *Recreations:* lawn tennis, visiting small islands, studies of Viking and Saxon history, Siamese history, Arctic Exploration, genealogy, folklore and curios, biological research; formerly athletics (Camb. Blue, 1922-24; Pres. CUAC, 1924; Capt. Jt Oxf. and Camb. Team to USA, 1924). Rugby football (Harlequins and Sale). *Address:* Mill House, Whatlington, Battle, East Sussex.
[Died 11 Jan. 1979.

BRITTAIN, Sir Harry E., KBE 1918; CMG 1924; LLD, MA; DL; Barrister-at-Law; *b* 24 Dec. 1873; *e s* of late W. H. Brittain, Storth Oaks, Sheffield; *m* 1st 1905, Alida Luisa, DBE (*d* 1943), *o d* of Sir Robert Harvey; one *s* one *d;* 2nd, 1961, Muriel Leslie, *d* of H. Leslie Dixon. *Educ:* Repton; Worcester Coll, Oxford, BA 1896 (hons in Law), MA 1898. Went through business trng in Sheffield; late Lieut 4th W. York Volunteer Artillery; called to Bar, Inner Temple, 1897, practised successfully for one week, then retd from the Law; former Dir numerous daily and weekly newspapers and other business concerns; First MP (U), Acton, 1918-29; since foundn in 1902, active head of The Pilgrims' Club for 17 years; resigned Chairmanship, 1918; now Sen. Vice-Pres., Pilgrim Emeritus on 70th Anniversary; Co-Chm. with US Chm., Internat. Cttee to commemorate 100 yrs of Peace between Gt Britain and the USA, 1912-14; formerly Mem., Sulgrave Manor Bd; joined Sir C. Arthur Pearson and worked with him in formation of Tariff Reform League, and creation of Tariff Commn, also joining staff of Standard and Evening Standard, 1902; Chm. Political Cttee Constitutional Club, 1920-21; Chm. Middx. Div. of Conservative Assoc., 1926; Vice-Pres. 1927 and Hon. Mem., 1961, Royal Commonwealth Soc.; a founder and Mem. Coun., Oxford Soc., 1932; originated and organised first Imperial Press Conf., 1909; presentation portrait by Sir Wm Orpen from UK Press; Founder and Hon. Life Mem. Empire

(now Commonwealth) Press Union. Opened Golden Jubilee Conf., 1959. Hon. LLD McGill for Service to Empire. In Rio on Mission to Brazilian Government, Dec. 1912 to Feb. 1913. Member Canadian and Australian War Contingent Committees, and Chairman Belgium Finance Committee, 1914; British Representative on Amer. Citizens Emergency Cttee, Aug. 1914; on special mission throughout the USA, 1915; Capt. Co. of London Vol. Regt, 1916, on staff Gen. Lloyd; Dir Intell. Nat. Service Dept; Founder and Chm. Amer. Officers' Club in London, 1917-19; Originator, and Hon. Life Mem., Assoc. of Amer. Correspondents in London, 1919; Coun. Brit. Olympic Assoc., British Rep. and British Ski Club Rep. at Chamonix, 1924; President, Anglo-Amer. delegation to Holland for celebrations of Pilgrim Fathers Tercentenary 1920; Pres., British Internat. Association of Journalists, 1920-22, and took delegates to Czecho-Slovakia, Holland, Belgium, and Roumania as guests of respective States; Pres., Press Golfing Soc., 1953; Patron, Soc. of Women Writers and Journalists, 1925-; Mem. Exec. and Publicity Coun., Brit. Empire Exhibn, representing House of Commons, and Chm. Press Hospitality Cttee, 1924; originator and Chm. Reception Cttee, 1st Conf. Students of Univs of the Empire, 1924; Mem. Exec., Empire Parly Assoc., 1919-29, Mem., Commonwealth Parly Assoc., 1929-. For protection of British Birds, steered through Parliament the Brittain Act, passed May, 1925; subseq. (with Prime Minister Baldwin), unveiled Hudson Memorial in Bird Sanctuary, Hyde Park. Started ski-ing in Norway; rep. Pres., British Ski Club, and House of Commons, in Paris and in Winter Sports Section of Olympic Games, Chamonix, 1923. A Founder and Mem. Coun., British Travel Assoc., and Chm. Publicity Cttee, 1929-31, Travel Cttee, 1939-45, Membership Cttee, 1947; London Chamber of Commerce: Mem. Coun., 1930-51; 1st Chm. Civil Aviation Sect., 1929; Deleg. of Brit. Nat. Cttee, on subject of Air Transport at Congress of Internat. Chambers of Commerce, Washington, 1931, and Vienna, 1933; Co-founder and Hon. Pres., McGill Soc. of GB, 1936-50; Hon. Pres., Friends of Italy, 1936-39; Pres., Schoolboys' Exhibn, Olympia, 1936-62; President Incorporated Sales Managers' Association (now Institute of Marketing), 1938-44; Vice Pres., Inst. of Export; Chm. Bd St George's School, Harpenden, 1938-47; Chm., Open Air Theatres Cttee, 1939; Mem., Central Council of Welfare, ATC, 1941-62; Mem., Inter-Parly Union, 1942-; Hon. Life Mem., Canadian Legion, 1958, for Service to Canada; Founder, Canada Masonic Lodge of Freemasons; Mem., Apollo Lodge, Oxford; Hon. Mem. Soc. of Americans in London; Trustee, Westminster Fund (responsible for Churchill Club, Dean's Yard, and weekly courses for Overseas Service personnel at Balliol Coll., Oxford, 1943-48); Mem., Anglo-Amer. Brains Trust, 1942-44; Chm. Appeal Cttee to save Gilbert White's home at Selborne, 1953; responsible for saving of Moor Park Coll., Farnham, and Sulgrave Manor, Northants. Frequent Broadcaster in GB, US and Commonwealth; awarded Silver Medal of Merit and Diploma, by Poor Richard Club of Philadelphia for his lifelong services to Anglo-American fellowship and understanding, 1958; Mem. Council Economic League, until 1946; President, Old Reptonian Soc. 1950-51; Pres. Yorkshire Soc., and Soc. of Yorkshiremen in London, 1956-57; Hon. Member Inst. of Journalists, 1963-; Hon. Member Foreign Press Assoc., 1963-; Astor Award, CPU, 1973; admitted to Barbados Bar, 1969. First Hon. Life Mem., Inst. of Dirs, 1973; Hon. Life Mem., Royal Horticultural Soc. Gold Staff Officer at Coronation, 1937; Freeman, City of London, 1938; Cross of Officer, Order of the Crown, for Services to Belgium during War of 1914-18; Comdr, White Lion of Czecho-Slovakia; Comdr, Star of Roumania (with Gold Medallion). *Publications:* Canada: There and Back, 1908; To Verdun from the Somme, 1916; America and the German Menace, 1917; The ABC of the BBC, Romance of British Wireless, 1932; By Air, 1933; Wings of Speed, 1934; Austria Invites, 1936; Come the Three Corners, 1940; Pilgrim Partners, Forty Years of British American Fellowship, 1942; Pilgrims and Pioneers, an Autobiography, 1945; Happy Pilgrimage, Autobiography, 2nd vol., 1949; articles in London and other periodicals. *Recreations:* friends and happy memories; avoiding retirement. *Address:* 88 St James's Street, SW1. *T:* 01-839 3222; Flat 124, Marine Court, St Leonards-on-Sea, Sussex. *T:* Hastings 32397. *Clubs:* (Hon. Life Member of all): Carlton, Bath, Pilgrims, Queen's, American, Wig and Pen, 1900, Royal Commonwealth Society, English-Speaking Union, Royal Over-Seas League, Dinosaurs, Caravan, Clambake (Newport, RI).
[Died 9 July 1974.

BRITTAIN, Rear-Admiral Wilfred Geoffrey, CB 1956; CBE 1945; *b* 19 June 1903; *m* 1st, 1935, May Russell Shorto (*d* 1964); two *d;* 2nd, 1968, Mary Clifton (*d* 1977), *d* of late Dennis Hughes. *Educ:* RNC Osborne and Dartmouth. Joined Royal Navy, 1917; Comdr 1939; Captain 1944; Rear-Adm. 1954; Retired 1957. Last appointment Flag Officer, Malta, and Admiral Superintendent, HM Dockyard, Malta, 1954-57. Dir,

Nat. Trade Develt Assoc., 1957-67. Officer, Legion of Merit, 1946. *Address:* 1 Little Stodham House, Liss, Hants. *T:* 3189.
[Died 10 May 1979.

BRITTAIN, William James; Chairman: Brittain Publishing Co. (London) Ltd; Brittain Publishing Co. (Canada) Ltd; London and Local Newspapers Ltd; Brittain Newspapers Ltd; Latin-American Trade Ltd; World Trade Publishing Co. Ltd; Indicator Newspapers Ltd; West London Chronicle Ltd; Practical Banking Ltd; *b* 22 July 1905; *s* of late William James and Eliza Brittain; *m* 1929, Janet Carrick; one *d.* Hull Daily Mail; Liverpool Daily Courier; Night News Editor, Daily Mail, Manchester; Montreal Daily Star; Asst City Ed., Toronto Daily Star; Science Dir, Pall Mall Magazine; Evening News, London; Asst Ed., Sunday Express; Editor, Sunday Dispatch; Dir, Time & Tide Ltd (Chm. 1962-72), formerly Editor, Time & Tide. *Publications:* This Man Beaverbrook; articles television and photo-telegraphy, Universal Encyclopædia; papers in scientific and other journals. *Address:* 5 Brocket Hall, Welwyn, Herts. *T:* Welwyn Garden 26440; 15 Byron Court, Mecklenburgh Square, WC1. *T:* 01-837 6007.   [Died 12 July 1977.

BRITTEN, Baron *cr* 1976 (Life Peer), of Aldeburgh, Suffolk; **(Edward) Benjamin Britten,** OM 1965; CH 1953; composer; *b* Lowestoft, England, 22 Nov. 1913; *s* of Robert Victor and Edith Rhoda Britten. *Educ:* South Lodge Preparatory School; Gresham's School, Holt; Royal Coll. of Music, London; privately with Frank Bridge, Harold Samuel. Artist Dir, Aldeburgh Festival. Worked with GPO film unit, 1935-37. Worked in America, 1939-42; Coolidge medal, 1941; founded, 1948, Aldeburgh Festival, with Peter Pears and Eric Crozier. Freedom of: Borough of Lowestoft, 1953; Borough of Aldeburgh 1962; Worshipful Co. of Musicians, 1965; Hon. Fellow, Magdalene Coll., Camb., 1965; Fellow, Royal Coll. of Music, London; Hon. Member: Accademia Nazionale di Santa Cecilia, Rome; Academie Royale des Sciences, des Lettres et des Beaux-Arts de Belgique; Royal Academy of Music, London; Akademie der Künste in Hamburg; Svenska Musicaliska Academiens, Vagnar; Amer. Acad. of Arts and Letters; National Institute of Arts and Letters. MusDoc (*hc*): Univs of: Belfast, 1954; Cambridge, 1959; Nottingham, 1961; Hull, 1962; Oxford, 1963; Manchester, 1964; London, 1964; Leicester, 1965; East Anglia, 1967; Wales, 1975; Warwick, 1975. Awarded Hanseatic Goethe Prize, for 1961; Aspen Award, Colorado, USA, 1964; Royal Philharmonic Society's Gold Medal, 1964; Sibelius Prize, 1965; Mahler Medal of Honour (Bruckner and Mahler Soc. of America), 1967; Leonie Sonning Prize (Denmark), 1968; Ernst von Siemens Prize, 1973; Ravel Prize, 1974. Commander of Royal Order of the Pole Star (Sweden), 1962. *Publications include:* On Receiving the First Aspen Award, 1964; *Operas:* Paul Bunyan (operetta), Peter Grimes, The Rape of Lucretia, Albert Herring, The Beggar's Opera (new version), The Little Sweep, Billy Budd, Gloriana, The Turn of the Screw, Noye's Fludde, A Midsummer Night's Dream, The Golden Vanity (vaudeville for boys and piano), Three Church Operas (Curlew River, The Burning Fiery Furnace, The Prodigal Son), Owen Wingrave, Death in Venice; *Choral works:* A Boy was Born, Ballad of Heroes, Hymn to St Cecilia, Ceremony of Carols, Rejoice in the Lamb, Saint Nicolas, Spring Symphony, Cantata Academica, Missa Brevis, War Requiem, Psalm 150, Cantata Misericordium, Voices for Today, Children's Crusade, Sacred and Profane; *Orchestral Works:* Simple Symphony, Sinfonietta, Soirées Musicales, Variations on a Theme of Frank Bridge, Mont Juic (with Lennox Berkeley), Piano Concerto No 1, Violin Concerto No 1, Matinées Musicales, Sinfonia da Requiem, Kermesse Canadienne, Diversions, Scottish Ballad, Young Person's Guide to the Orchestra, Prelude and Fugue, Prince of the Pagodas (ballet), Cello Symphony, The Building of the House; Suite on English Folk Tunes: *Chamber music:* Phantasy (Oboe Quartet), Violin Suite, 4 String Quartets, Lachrymae (Viola and Piano), Ovid Metamorphoses (Oboe Solo), Cello Sonata, Nocturnal after Dowland (for Guitar), 3 Suites for Cello, Gemini Variations, Harp Suite; *Song Cycles, etc:* Friday Afternoons, Our Hunting Fathers, On this Island, Holy Sonnets of John Donne, Les Illuminations, Seven Sonnets of Michelangelo, Serenade, 5 Canticles, Charm of Lullabies, Winter Words (Hardy), Sechs Hölderlin Fragmente, Songs from the Chinese, Nocturne, Songs and Proverbs of William Blake, Poet's Echo (Pushkin), Who are these children? (Soutar), A Birthday Hansel (Burns), Phaedra; Piano Music; Anthems; Part-songs; Incidental music to plays and films; folk song arrangements; Purcell realisations, etc. *Recreation:* watching-particularly birds. *Address:* The Red House, Aldeburgh, Suffolk IP15 5PZ. *Clubs:* Athenæum; Aldeburgh Festival.
[Died 4 Dec. 1976.

RITTEN, Benjamin; *see* Britten, Baron.

BRITTEN, (Forester Richard) John, CBE 1970; AFRAeS; *b* 27 May 1928; *s* of late Lt-Col F. C. R. Britten and of E. Z. R. James; unmarried. *Educ:* Royal Naval Coll., Dartmouth; de Havilland Aeronautical Technical Sch. Managing Director of family cinema and theatre business, 1950-53; Founder of Britten-Norman Ltd, with N. D. Norman, 1954; Jt Man. Dir, Britten-Norman Ltd, 1954-71; Director: Fairey Britten-Norman, 1972-76 (Chief Exec., 1973-76); Fairey SA, 1972-76. High Sheriff, Isle of Wight, 1976. *Recreation:* sailing. *Address:* St Denis, High Street, Bembridge. *T:* Bembridge 2167. *Club:* Royal Yacht Squadron (Cowes).   [Died 7 July 1977.

BRITTOROUS, Brig. Francis Gerard Russell, CBE 1964; DSO 1940; MC 1917; late Manchester Regiment; *b* 1 Feb. 1896; *s* of Francis Patrick Brittorous, of Barna, Co. Galway, and Mary Josephine, *d* of John Russell, Londonderry; *m* 1925, Ilynne, *d* of Ernest Chambers Hitchmough, of Co. Cork; two *d. Educ:* Ushaw. 2nd Lieut Manchester Regt, 1915; Captain, 1926; Major, 1938; Lt-Colonel 1940; Brigadier, 1940; Staff Captain, India, 1922-26; Staff Captain, Egypt, 1937-38; served European War, 1915-19, France and Belgium (despatches twice, British War Medal, Victory Medal, MC); Iraq, 1919-20 (Medal and Clasp); Palestine, 1938 (Medal and Clasp); France, 1940 (DSO); commanded Lancashire Fusiliers, 1940-41; Maj.-General GOC Aegean, 1943. Retired pay, 1946. Chm., North West Hants Conservative Assoc., 1952-68, Pres. 1968-72. *Recreations:* hunting, cricket, golf. *Address:* Longhouse Farm, St Mary Bourne, Hants. *T:* St Mary Bourne 224. *Clubs:* Army and Navy, MCC.   [Died 25 March 1974.

BROAD, Lt-Gen. Sir Charles (Noel Frank), KCB 1941 (CB 1938); DSO 1917; *b* 29 Dec. 1882; *s* of Major C. H. Broad, 5th Fusiliers, and Ann Paul; *m* 1st, 1915, Lillian Mary (*d* 1942), *d* of Edwin Mackintosh; one *d* ; 2nd, 1944, Diana Myrtle, *yr d* of Col. Philip R. Bald; two *s* one *d* (and one *s* decd). *Educ:* Wellington College; Pembroke College, Cambridge. Entered RA 1905; Staff College, 1914; Captain, 1914; Major, 1916; Bt.-Lieut-Colonel, 1919; Colonel, 1923; Maj.-General, 1936; Lieut-General, 1940; served S. African War, 1902; European War, 1914-18 (1914 Star, Legion of Honour, Belgian Croix de Guerre); War service, 1939-42; Maj.-General in charge of Administration, Aldershot Command, 1937-39; GOC-in-C Aldershot Command, 1939-40; GOC-in-C, Eastern Army, India, 1940-42; retired pay, 1942; Col Comdr Rl T. R., 1939-47. *Address:* The Old Flax Mill, Beaminster, Dorset.   [Died 23 March 1976.

BROAD, Charlie Dunbar, MA, LittD Cantab; Hon. LLD Aberdeen, Bristol, Dublin; Hon. ScD Cantab; Hon. Doctor of Philosophy Uppsala; FBA; Fellow of Royal Swedish Academy of Science; Hon. Member of Stockholms Nation (Uppsala); Fellow, Societas Scientiarum Fennica; Fellow, Amer. Acad. of Arts and Sciences; Knightbridge Professor of Moral Philosophy, Cambridge University, 1933-53; *b* London, 30 Dec. 1887; *o c* of late Charles Stephen Broad and Emily Gomme; unmarried. *Educ:* Dulwich College; Trinity College, Cambridge (Major Scholar in Natural Science); first class Nat. Sci. Trip. Part I; first class, with special distinction in metaphysical and ethical philosophy, Moral Sci. Trip. Part II; Arnold Gerstenberg Studentship in philosophy; Burney Prizeman; Fellow of Trinity College, Cambridge. Assistant to Professor of Logic, University of St Andrews; Lecturer on Logic, University College, Dundee; Professor of Philosophy, University of Bristol; Fellow and Lecturer in Moral Science, Trinity College, Cambridge; Sidgwick Lecturer in Moral Science, University of Cambridge; Tarner Lecturer in the Philosophy of Science, 1923-24; Donnellan Lecturer, Trinity College, Dublin, 1929; President of the Society for Psychical Research, 1935-36 and 1959-60; Pres. of the Aristotelian Society, 1927-28, 1954-55. Visiting Professor in Philosophy, University of Michigan, 1953-54; Flint Professor of Philosophy, University of Calif., in Los Angeles, 1954. Nicholas Murray Butler gold medal, Columbia University, 1960. *Publications:* Perception, Physics, and Reality; Scientific Thought; Mind and its Place in Nature; The Philosophy of Francis Bacon; Five Types of Ethical Theory; Examination of McTaggart's Philosophy; Ethics and the History of Philosophy (Selected Essays); Psychical Research, Religion and Philosophy (Selected Essays); Lectures on Psychical Research; numerous contributions on philosophical subjects to Mind, the Hibbert Journal, Proceedings of the Aristotelian Society, Philosophy, and the International Journal of Ethics. *Recreation:* model engineering. *Address:* Trinity College, Cambridge. *Club:* United University.   [Died 11 March 1971.

BROADBRIDGE, 2nd Baron, *cr* 1945, of Brighton; **Eric Wilberforce Broadbridge,** Bt, *cr* 1937; Company Director; *b* 22 Dec. 1895; *e s* of 1st Baron Broadbridge, KCVO, and Fanny Kathleen (*d* 1928), *d* of late Richard Brigden; *S* father 1952; *m* 1924, Mabel Daisy (*d* 1966), *o d* of Arthur E. Clarke,

Carshalton, Surrey; one s. *Educ:* Hurstpierpoint College. Commissioned in Machine Gun Corps, 1914; served European War, 1914-18, in France, Salonika, Egypt and Palestine (despatches). After end of war studied and became fully qualified mechanical engineer; Director of several Trust Companies; acquired business of A. J. Barton and Co. (Timber Brokers) and is now Managing Director. Liveryman of Worshipful Company of Woolmen. *Recreations:* shooting, golf. *Heir: s* Hon. Peter Hewett Broadbridge, MA, BSc (Oxon) [*b* 19 Aug. 1938; *m* 1967, Mary, *o d* of W. O. Busch, Germany; one *d*]. *Address:* Beach Rise, Westgate-on-Sea, Kent; St Stephen's House, Westminster, SW1. *Club:* City Livery.
[*Died* 18 *Nov.* 1972.

BROADBRIDGE, Stanley Robertson; General Secretary, National Association of Teachers in Further and Higher Education (NATFHE), since 1977; *b* 16 April 1928; *s* of Robert Harriss Broadbridge and Lily May Broadbridge; *m* 1951, Eva Bollington; two *d. Educ:* Queen Elizabeth's Sch., Barnet; Univ. of Manchester (MA Econ). National Service, RAF, 1950-52; Sen. Econs Master, Boteler Grammar Sch., Warrington, 1952-57; Lectr, Leigh Tech. Coll., Lancs, 1957-64; Lectr, subseq. Principal Lectr, N Staffs Polytechnic (formerly Staffs Coll. of Technology), 1965-77. *Publications:* Birmingham Canal Navigations 1768-1846, 1974; articles in Transport Hist. and Jl Indust. Archaeol. *Recreations:* collecting antiques, canals, English Baroque music. *Address:* c/o NATFHE, Hamilton House, Mabledon Place, WC1H 9BH. *T:* 01-387 6806.
[*Died* 22 *Nov.* 1978.

BROADMEAD, Sir Philip Mainwaring, KCMG, *cr* 1952 (CMG 1944); MC; retd; *b* 3 Dec. 1893; *s* of late Colonel Henry Broadmead. *Educ:* Wellington College; Christ Church, Oxford. Served European War, 1914-19, with KRRC; Staff Capt. 1918. Third Secretary in Diplomatic Service, 1920; 2nd Secretary 1923; 1st Secretary 1929; Counsellor of Embassy, 1940. Ambassador to Colombia, 1945-47; Minister at Damascus, 1947-50; Ambassador to Czechoslovakia, 1950-53. *Address:* 26 Devonshire Place, W1. *Club:* Brooks's. [*Died* 23 *May* 1977.

BROADWAY, Leonard Marsham; *b* 29 Nov. 1903; *m* 1928, Edith Emily Ayckbourn; one *s* two *d. Educ:* privately. Joined Castrol Ltd (then C. C. Wakefield & Co. Ltd), 1920; apptd Company Secretary, 1938; Director, 1947; Asst Managing Director, 1951; Deputy Chairman, 1957-62 and Managing Director, 1954-62, Castrol World Gp of Companies. Member Port of London Authority, 1955-58; Member Petroleum Industry Advisory Cttee; Patron, College of Aeronautical and Automobile Engineering. *Recreations:* tennis, swimming, gardening, clay pigeon shooting. *Address:* Long Meadow, Cokes Lane, Chalfont St Giles, Bucks. *T:* Little Chalfont 2815. [*Died* 23 *Dec.* 1974.

BROADWOOD, Captain Evelyn Henry Tschudi, MC 1915; Chairman, John Broadwood & Sons Ltd; Senior Governor of Old Vic and of Sadler's Wells, since 1937; *b* 17 March 1889; *o s* of late James Henry Tschudi Broadwood, and late Margaret Evelyn, *d* of T. F. Maitland, JP, Garth, Breconshire. *Educ:* Wellington. Captain Norfolk Regt, 1909; served European War, 1914-19 (MC, Mons Star, despatches twice). Past Master of Worshipful Co. of Musicians. Chm., Dorking and Horley District Council, 1949-50, 1951-52. CC 1944, CA 1959, Surrey; JP 1949, High Sheriff 1957, Surrey. A Governor of the Old Vic, and Old Vic Member of Governing Body of Sadler's Wells, 1937-; Governor's Representative, Cttee of Vic-Wells Assoc., 1953-; Founder-Mem., Old Vic Trust, 1946-65. Royal Warrant Holder to the Queen; Royal Warrant Holder to Queen Elizabeth the Queen Mother. Pres., Sussex Unitarian Union, 1967-. Governor, Royal Normal College for the Blind; Mem. Exec. Council of London Society; Vice-Pres. Royal Hospital and Home for Incurables, Putney, 1960-; Founder Mem. and Vice-Pres. Institute of Music Instrument Technology, 1961-. Rep. Great Britain on Internat. Congress for Standardisation of Concert Pitch, 1939-. Pres., Shakespearean Authorship Soc. FIMIT. *Address:* Lyne, Capel, Surrey; 9 Hanover Street, W1. *Clubs:* Athenæum, Army and Navy. [*Died* 24 *June* 1975.

BROCK, Baron, *cr* 1965 (Life Peer), of Wimbledon; **Russell Claude Brock;** Kt 1954; Director, Department of Surgical Sciences, Royal College of Surgeons, since 1968; Surgeon to: Guy's Hospital, 1936-68; Brompton Hospital, 1936-68; *b* 24 Oct. 1903; *s* of Herbert and Elvina Brock; *m* 1927, Germaine Louise Ladevèze (*d* 1978); two *d* (and one *d* decd); *m* 1979, Chrissie Palmer Jones. *Educ:* Christ's Hospital; Guy's Hospital (Schol.). MB, BS London, Hons med. surg. and anat., 1927; MS London 1932. Rockefeller Travelling Fellow, 1929-30; Demonstrator in Pathology and Anatomy, Surgical Registrar and Tutor, Guy's Hospital, 1932; Research Fell., Assoc. Surg. of Great Britain, 1932; Hunterian Prof., RCS, 1938; Cons. Thoracic Surgeon,

LCC, 1935-46; Surgeon, Min. of Pensions (Queen Mary's, Roehampton), 1936-45; Thoracic Surgeon and Regional Adviser in Thoracic Surgery, EMS, 1939-46; Exchange Prof. of Surgery, Johns Hopkins Hospital, Baltimore, 1949. MRCS 1926; FRCS 1928; Member Council RCS, 1949-67; a Vice-Pres., RCS, 1956-58; Pres., 1963-66. President, Thoracic Society of Great Britain and Ireland, 1952; Med. Society London, 1968. LRCP 1926; FRCP 1965; FACS 1949; Hon. FRACS 1957; Hon. ScD Cantab., 1968; Hon. LLD Leeds 1965; Hon. MD: Hamburg, 1962; Munich, 1972. Hon. Fellow: Surgical section of RSM, 1951; Brazilian College of Surgeons, 1952; RCSEd 1966; RCSI, 1966; RCSCan. 1966. Hon. Mem., AU-Union Soviet Soc. of Surgeons, 1974. Lectures: Lettsomian, Med. Soc. London, 1952; Bradshaw, RCS, 1957; Tudor Edwards Memorial, 1963; Hunterian Orator, RCS, 1961; Lister Orator, 1967; Astley Cooper Orator, 1968; BMA Prize Essay, 1926; Jacksonian Prize Essay, RCS, 1935; Julius Mickle Prize, London Univ., 1950-51; Cameron Prize, Edinburgh Univ., 1954; Gairdner Award, 1960-61. Treasurer's Gold Medal for Clin. med. and Clin. Surg., 1926; Golding Bird Gold Medal for Pathology, 1926; Fothergillian Gold Medal, Med. Soc. London, 1953; Leriche Medal, Internat. Soc. Surg., 1953; Gold Medal, Soc. Apoth., 1955; Gold Medal W. London Med.-Chir. Soc., 1955; Lannelongue Medal, Acad. de Chirurgie, 1963; Bronze Medal of City of NY, 1965; Lister Medal, RCS, 1966. KStJ. *Publications:* Anatomy of the bronchial tree, 1946; Life and Work of Astley Cooper, 1952; Lung Abscess, 1952; Anatomy of Pulmonary Stenosis, 1957; numerous articles in surgical and medical journals. *Recreations:* writing, reading, antiquities and topography of London. *Address:* 3 Parkside Gardens, Wimbledon, SW19. *T:* 01-946 5634. *Club:* Athenæum. [*Died* 3 *Sept.* 1980.

BROCK, Prof. Alan Francis C.; *see* Clutton-Brock.

BROCKBANK, Russell Partridge; free-lance artist; *b* Niagara Falls, Canada, 15 April 1913; *s* of Clarence and Caroline Brockbank; *m* 1933, Eileen Hames; one *s* one *d. Educ:* Ridley College, Ontario; Chelsea School of Art, London. Came to England, 1929, and studied Art; forsook Art for Industry, 1932 forsook Industry for Art, 1936; Free-lance until 1941. Served War of 1939-45, Lieut RNVR, Northern Convoys, British Pacific Fleet; demobilised, 1946. Free-lanced until 1949; Art Editor of Punch, 1949-60. *Publications:* Round the Bend, 1948 Up the Straight, 1953; Over the Line, 1955; The Brockbank Omnibus, 1957; Manifold Pressures, 1958; Move Over, 1963 The Penguin Brockbank, 1963; Motoring Through Punch, 1900 1970, 1970; Brockbank's Grand Prix, 1973; The Best o Brockbank, 1975. *Recreations:* motoring, sport. *Address* Zephyrs, 14 Goulds Ground, Frome, Somerset.
[*Died* 14 *May* 1979

BROCKHURST, Gerald Leslie, RA 1937 (ARA 1928, now Hon Retired Senior Member of Royal Academy); *m* 1947, Kathleen Nancy Woodward; no *c*. Painter, chiefly of portraits; exhibited at the Royal Academy, 1915-49; portrait of Bishop Fulton J Sheen exhibited 1949. Has been living in the United States since 1939. *Address:* 239 Woodside Avenue, Franklin Lakes, N. 07417, USA. [*Died* 4 *May* 1978

BROCKIE, Thomas, CVO 1967; Under Secretary, Ministry of Public Building and Works, 1956-66 (Under Secretary fo Scotland, 1962-66); retired; *b* 9 June 1906; *o s* of Thomas Brockie, Peebles, Scotland; *m* 1936, Phyllis, *e d* of Austin Godson, Edinburgh; no *c. Educ:* Ayr Academy; Glasgow University (MA). Entered Civil Service, 1928; Ministry of Labour, 1928-33; Assistance Board, 1934-41 (Principal 1939) HM Treasury, 1942-43; MPBW, 1944; Asst Sec., 1944; Under Sec., 1956. *Recreations:* reading, motoring. *Address:* 19 Gaytor Court, Gayton Road, Harrow, Mddx HA1 2HB. *T:* 01-42 3944. *Club:* Devonshire. [*Died* 11 *April* 1976

BROCKLEBANK, Sir John Montague, 5th Bt, *cr* 1885; TD; *b* Sept. 1915; *s* of 3rd Bt and Hon. Grace Mary Jackson (*d* 1940), *d* of 1st Baron Allerton; *S* brother 1953; *m* 1950, Pamela Sue, of W. H. Pierce, OBE, JP; one *s. Educ:* Eton; Cambridge. *Heir:* Aubrey Thomas Brocklebank, *b* 29 Jan. 1952. *Address:* Palazz, Zejtun, Malta GC. [*Died* 13 *Sept.* 1974

BROCKLEHURST, Charles Douglas, F. P.; *see* Phillip Brocklehurst.

BROCKLEHURST, Sir Philip Lee, 2nd Bt, *cr* 1903; *b* 7 March 1887; *s* of 1st Bt and Annie (*d* 1951), *d* of Samuel Dewhurst; father, 1904; *m* 1st, 1913, Gwladys, MBE 1946 (who obtained divorce, 1947), *d* of late Colonel Gostling Murray of Whittle Park, Hounslow; two *d*; 2nd, 1952, Mrs Audrey Evely Mackenzie, *e d* of Hugh Miller Macmillan, Ferniegair Helensburgh, Dunbartonshire. *Educ:* Eton; Trinity Hall

Cambridge. Accompanied British Antarctic Expedition, 1907; received medal from Royal Geographical Society, 1909; Derbyshire IY, 1904; Bt Lt-Col 1924; served European War with 1st Life Guards, 1914-17 (wounded); Egyptian Army, 1918-20; commanded 2nd Regt Arab Legion Desert Mechanised Bde, 1941-42; British Council, Palestine-Trans-Jordan, 1943-44; is Lord of Manor of Heaton, Swythamley. *Heir: n* John Ogilvy Brocklehurst, *b* 6 April 1926. *Address:* Swythamley Park, near Macclesfield, Cheshire. [Died 28 Jan. 1975.

BROCKMAN, Edward Phillimore, MChir Cantab; FRCS; Retired; Hon. Consulting Orthopædic Surgeon to: Westminster Hosp.; Royal National Orthopædic Hosp. and St Vincent's Orthopædic Hosp., Northwood Hills. *Educ:* Cambridge University; St Thomas's Hospital, London University. BA Cantab; MRCS, LRCP 1919; MB, BCh 1921; FRCS 1924; MChir Cantab 1925. Fellow British Orthopædic Association. *Address:* Hook Cottage, Askett, near Aylesbury, Bucks. [Died 27 Jan. 1977.

BROCKMAN, Ralph St Leger, MA, MChir Cantab, FRCS; formerly Professor of Surgery, Sheffield University; Hon. Surgeon, Royal Infirmary, Sheffield; Consulting Surgeon, City General Hospital, Sheffield; Member of Court of Examiners, Royal College of Surgeons; Examiner to Gen. Nursing Council; *b* 3 June 1889; *s* of Ralph Thomas Brockman and Anna Sheldrake; *m* 1915, Estelle Wilson (*d* 1964); one *s* one *d*; *m* 1965, Elizabeth Ritchie, *widow* of Dr Alexander Ritchie. *Educ:* Liverpool Coll.; Gonville and Caius Coll., Camb. (Nat. Science Tripos); St Bartholomew's Hosp. Brackenbury Surgical Scholarship, Willett Medal for Operative Surgery, Walsham Prize for Surgical Pathology; Temp. Surgeon, RN; Hunterian Professor, Royal Coll. of Surgeons: Arris and Gale Lecturer, Royal Coll. of Surgeons; Erasmus Wilson Lecturer, Royal College of Surgeons; late Surgeon to Children's Hospital, Sheffield. *Publications:* various scientific. *Recreations:* shooting and fishing. [Died 21 Oct. 1975.

BRODERICK, Brigadier Ralph Alexander, DSO 1919; MC 1916; TD 1934; DL; Hon. Consulting Dental Surgeon, Children's Hospital and Ear and Throat Hosp., Birmingham; Consulting Dental Surgeon to Ministry of Health; Consulting Dental Surgeon to Birmingham Hospital Regional Board; Director Post Graduate Bureau of General Dental Council; *b* Dorking, Surrey, 17 March 1888; *y s* of George Alexander and Annie Elizabeth Broderick; *m* 1914, Dulcie, 4th *d* of Richard Lunt, Edgbaston; one *s* two *d*. *Educ:* King Edward's School, Birmingham; Berkhamsted School; Birmingham University. LDS, RCS, 1911; MB, ChB Birmingham, 1912; MDS, Birmingham, 1924; FDS RCS, 1947. Commenced practice as Dental Surgeon, 1913; joined RAMC, TF, Aug. 1914; Lieut-Col, 1917; commanded 2nd South Midland Field Ambulance till 1922; ADMS 48th South Midland Div., 1935; Col 1935; Mobilised Aug. 1939 as ADMS 48th Div.; Cons. Dental Surg. to Army, 1944-52; KHDS, 1948; Councillor, Lawn Tennis Assoc. of Great Britain. Vice-Dean, Faculty of Dental Surgery, RCS, 1959-. *Publications:* Dental Bacteriology; various articles in British Dental Journal and Lancet. *Recreations:* shooting, lawn tennis. *Address:* 33 Mackenzie Road, Birmingham 11. *T:* 021-449 0636. *Clubs:* United Service; Union, Edgbaston Lawn Tennis (Birmingham); All England Lawn Tennis.

[Died 8 March 1971.

BRODEUR, Rear-Admiral Victor Gabriel, CB 1946; CBE 1943; Rear-Adm. (retd), Royal Canadian Navy; Commanding Officer Pacific Coast, Canada, 1938-40 and 1943-46; *b* 17 Sept. 1892; *s* of Hon. L. P. Brodeur, PC, KC, LLD; *m* 1st, 1915, Doris Fages (decd); two *s*; 2nd, 1938, Dorothy Whitfield Kennard. *Educ:* Montreal. Entered RCN 1909; Sub-Lieut 1913; Lieut 1915; Lieut-Cdr 1923; Qualified Gunnery at Whale Island, 1921; Comdr 1927; Capt. 1936; Rear-Adm. 1942. Imperial Defence College, 1936; Canadian Naval Attaché, Washington, 1940-42; Naval Member Canadian Joint Staff, US, 1942-43; 16 years on loan to RN. *Recreations:* golf, fishing, shooting, gardening. *Address:* 702-1025 Gilford Street, Vancouver 5, BC, Canada. [Died 6 Oct. 1976.

BRODIE, Captain Sir Benjamin Collins, 4th Bt, *cr* 1834; *b* 6 March 1888; *o s* of Sir Benjamin Vincent Sellon Brodie, 3rd Bt, DL, JP; *S* father, 1938; *m* 1924, Mary Charlotte (*d* 1940), *e d* of R. E. Palmer, Ballyheigue, Co. Kerry; two *s* one *d*. *Educ:* Eton College; Magdalen College, Oxford. BA, 1911, Honour School of Modern History; served European War, Lieut Surrey Yeomanry, MEF (Gallipoli) 29th Division; Captain and Adjutant, 4th Bn The Gordon Highlanders, 51st (Highland) Division, BEF; Staff Captain, 1st Highland Bde British Army of the Rhine (despatches twice, MC and Bar); Officer of Company GCs; Royal Military College, Sandhurst, 1922-27; Headmaster

(with L. T. Prosser Evans) Holyrood School, Bognor Regis, 1927-40; Governor of Tonbridge School, 1939- (Chm. of Governors, 1944-45 and 1950-51); Governor Reigate Grammar School, 1938-49, and Chairman Judd School, Tonbridge, 1945-60; Master of the Skinners' Company, 1944-45 and 1950-51; Assistant Commandant, Special Constabulary, 1940-46. *Recreations:* formerly shooting, fishing, riding, photography. *Heir: s* Benjamin David Ross Brodie, *b* 29 May 1925. *Address:* Betchworth Lodge, Betchworth, Surrey. *T:* Betchworth 3265. *Club:* Athenæum. [Died 2 Aug. 1971.

BRODIE, Rabbi Sir Israel, KBE 1969; BA, BLitt, Hon. DD; Hon. DCL; Chief Rabbi of the United Hebrew Congregations of the British Commonwealth of Nations, 1948-65, now Emeritus Chief Rabbi; *b* 10 May 1895; *s* of Aaron Brodie, Newcastle upon Tyne; *m* 1946, F. Levine. *Educ:* Rutherford Coll., Newcastle upon Tyne; Jews' Coll., London; Univ. Coll., London; Balliol Coll., Oxford. CF, 1917-19; Social Service, East End, London, 1921-23; Rabbi, Melbourne, Australia, 1923-37; Lecturer and Tutor, Jews' Coll., 1939-48; Pres., Jews' Coll.; CF, Army and RAF, 1940-44; Senior Jewish Chaplain, 1944-48; Fellow, University College, London; Hon. officer of several public bodies. *Publications:* A Word in Season, 1958; (ed) The Etz Hayyim by Rabbi Jacob ben Jehuda Hazan of London, Vols 1, 2, 3, 1962, 1964, 1967. *Address:* Flat R, 82 Portland Place, W1N 3DH. [Died 13 Feb. 1979.

BRODIE, Thomas Vernor Alexander; Attorney-General, Federation of Malaya, Nov. 1955-Nov. 1959; *b* 9 Oct. 1907; *s* of late Norman Somerville Brodie, formerly ICS; *m* 1947, Mollie Frances (*née* Chubb); one *d*. *Educ:* Marlborough College; Brasenose College, Oxford. Called to Bar, Middle Temple, 1931; Assistant Legal Adviser, FMS, 1938; Federated Malay States Volunteer Force, 1941-45 (POW, 1942-45). Solicitor-General, Federation of Malaya, 1950: QC (Federation of Malaya), 1952. *Recreations:* reading, gardening. *Address:* Lychett Glade, Upton, Poole, Dorset. *T:* Lychett Minster 2348.

[Died 13 Nov. 1975.

BRODRICK, Alan Houghton; *b* Kensington; *o c* of Alan Brodrick of Wooder Manor, South Devon, and Katherine, *d* of Thomas Houghton and Elizabeth, *g d* of George Moore of Moore Hall; *m* 1923, Hon. Hester Astley, *d* of 20th Lord Hastings; one *s*. *Educ:* privately and abroad. Member of British Military Mission to the French Government, 1917-20; Joint Secretary-General of the International Congress of Anthropological and Ethnological Sciences, 1934-38; has orders of the Legion of Honour, Black Star, Dragon of Annam, Croix de Guerre, Crown of Roumania, White Eagle; Nichan Iftikhar, etc. *Publications:* Little China, 1942; North Africa, 1942; Parts of Barbary, 1944; Beyond the Burma Road, 1945; Cross Channel, 1946; Early Man-a Survey, 1948 (Spanish Edition 1955); Prehistoric Painting, 1948 (Spanish Edition 1950); Lascaux, 1949; Little Vehicle, 1949; Chinese Painting, 1949 (Spanish Edition 1954); Pillars of Hercules, 1950; Danger Spot of Europe, 1951; The Tree of Human History, 1951; Prospect of France, Breuil, mirage of Africa, 1953; Persona, 1955; Casual Change, 1961; Man and his Ancestry, 1961 (American Edn, 1964); The Abbé Breuil, 1963; The Father of Prehistory, 1963; Near to Greatness, 1965; Man and His Ancestors, 1970; (ed) Animals in Archaeology, 1972; Editor, The People's France Series: Normandy, 1947; Touraine, 1948; Paris, 1949; Brittany, 1950; Provence, 1952; Greater Paris and the Ile-de-France, 1953. *Translations:* Life the Great Adventure, 1955; On the Track of Prehistoric Man, 1955; The Rock-Pictures of Europe, 1956; The Prehistory of Africa, 1956: The Inhabited Planet, 1957; Man and Mammoth, 1957; We Come from the Sea, 1958; The Galapagos, 1960; The Mandala, 1961, and other works from French, German, Spanish, Italian, Swedish, Dutch, etc. *Address:* 9 Weymouth Street, Portland Place, W1; 24 rue Barbet-de-Jouy, Paris VIIe. [Died 19 July 1973.

BRODRICK, Brig. William Le Couteur, CIE 1940; Indian Army, retired; *b* 27 Jan. 1888; *m* 1st, 1915, Ora Maxwell; two *d*; 2nd, 1934, Evelyn Ballantyne Wishart. *Educ:* Blundell's School, Tiverton. Joined Indian Army, 1908; in 27th Light Cavalry till 1914, then was in Royal Indian Army Service Corps till 1931; joined Contracts Directorate Army Headquarters and from 1936 to 1940 was Director of Contracts, Army Headquarters, India; served Aden, 1915-16; Sistan, 1916-17; Malabar, 1921-22; Waziristan, 1921-24. *Address:* 18 Grange Terrace, Edinburgh 9. *T:* 031-667 1169. [Died 23 May 1973.

BROGAN, Colm, MA Glasgow; journalist; *b* 20 Oct. 1902; *s* of Denis Brogan and Elizabeth Toner, Glasgow; *m* Helena Rogers, MA (*d* 1967); two *d*. *Educ:* St Columcille's School, Rutherglen; St Aloysius College, Glasgow; Glasgow University. Engaged in teaching and journalism in Glasgow till 1946; from then journalism and political study in London. Editor of monthly magazine, Round the World, 1945-46. *Publications:* Who Are the People? 1943; The Democrat at the Supper Table, 1945; Our New Masters, 1947; Patriots My Foot, 1949; Fifty Years On, 1949; Glasgow Story, 1952; The Educational Revolution, 1955; The Nature of Education, 1962. *Address:* 28 Ridgmount Gardens, WC1. *T:* 01-580 7804; 16 Athole Gardens, Glasgow. *T:* 041-334 7896. *[Died 28 Jan. 1977.*

BROGAN, Sir Denis (William), Kt 1963; MA; FBA 1955; Professor of Political Science, Cambridge, 1939-68, now Emeritus Professor, and Fellow of Peterhouse (Hon. Fellow, 1967); Director, Hamish Hamilton Ltd; *b* 11 Aug. 1900; *e s* of Denis Brogan and Elizabeth Toner, Glasgow; *m* Olwen Phillis Frances Kendall, MA, FSA; three *s* one d. *Educ:* St Columcille's School; Rutherglen Acad.; Glasgow University; Balliol College, Oxford; Harvard. Lectr, University Coll., London, and at the London School of Economics; Hon. Fellow, Corpus Christi College, Oxford, formerly Fellow and Tutor. Foreign Member: Mass Historical Society; Institut de France; Amer. Acad. of Arts and Sciences; Amer. Philosophical Soc. Hon. DèsL: Algiers, 1943; Clermont, 1947; Besançon, 1950; Hon. LLD: Glasgow, 1946; British Columbia, 1952; Lehigh, 1966; Hon. DLitt Oxon 1969. Benjamin Franklin Medal, Royal Society of Arts, 1966. Chevalier de la Légion d'Honneur; Comdr, Order of Orange-Nassau. *Publications:* The American Political System, 1933; Proudhon, 1934; Abraham Lincoln, 1935; The Development of Modern France, 1870-1939, 1940; USA: An Outline; Is Innocence Enough?; Politics and Law in the United States, 1941; The English People, 1943; The American Problem, 1944; The Free State, 1945; French Personalities and Problems, 1946; American Themes, 1948; Stop on the Green Light, 1950; The Price of Revolution, 1951; The Era of Franklin D. Roosevelt (Eng. edn Roosevelt and the New Deal), 1952; Introduction to American Politics, 1955; The French Nation, 1957; America in The Modern World, 1961; (with Douglas Verney) Political Patterns in Today's World, 1963; American Aspects, 1964; Worlds in Conflict, 1967; numerous articles in British, French, and American journals. *Address:* 1 Hedgerley Close, Cambridge CB3 0EW. *Clubs:* Reform; Lotos (New York); National Press (Washington). *[Died 5 Jan. 1974.*

BROMLEY-DAVENPORT, Dame Lilian (Emily Isabel Jane), DBE 1954; JP; *d* of late Lieut-Colonel John Henry Bagot Lane, King's Bromley, Staffordshire; *m* 1902, Walter Arthur Bromley-Davenport (*d* 1942); three *s* (and one *s* died of wounds, in Holland, 1944). Alderman and JP Cheshire. *Address:* The Kennels, Capesthorne, Macclesfield, Ches. *[Died 2 May 1972.*

BROMMAGE, Joseph Charles, CIE 1947; OBE 1945 (MBE 1921); *b* 4 Feb. 1897; *m* 1926, Edith Marie Neilson, MB, ChB, DPH. Served European War, 1914-18, operations France and Belgium; operations Waziristan, Tochi and Derajat columns. 1919-20 (Mahsud Clasp, MBE). Entered service of Govt of India, 1923; various appts in Govt of India, Fin. Dept, until 1940; Joint Financial Adviser, Munitions Production, India, 1940-44 (OBE); Additional Financial Adviser, Military Finance, and ex-officio Joint Secretary to Govt of India Finance Dept, 1944-47; Military Accountant General, India, 1947 (CIE); Chief Bipartite Finance Group, Frankfurt/Main, Germany, 1947-50. *Address:* Les Champignons, Alderney, CI. *Clubs:* Oriental; Royal Calcutta Turf. *[Died 15 Feb. 1972.*

BRONK, Detlev Wulf, OBE 1947 (Hon.); Foreign Member Royal Society 1948; AB, MS, PhD; President: Johns Hopkins University, 1940-53; Rockefeller University, 1953-68; National Academy of Sciences, 1950-62; *b* 13 Aug. 1897; *s* of Mitchell Bronk and Marie Wulf; *m* 1921, Helen Ramsey; three *s.* *Educ:* Swarthmore Coll.; Univ. of Michigan. Ensign US Naval Aviation Corps, 1918-19; Instructor in Physics, Univ. of Pennsylvania, 1921; Univ. of Michigan, 1921-24; Instructor in Physiology, 1924-26; Assistant Prof. of Physiology, 1926; Assistant Prof. of Physiology and Biophysics, Swarthmore Coll., 1926-27; Associate Prof. of Physiology and Biophysics, 1927-28; Prof. of Physiology and Biophysics, 1928-29; Dean of Men, Swarthmore Coll., 1927-29; Prof. of Physiology, Cornell, 1940-41; Dir, Johnson Research Foundation and Prof. of Biophysics, also Dir Inst. of Neurology, Univ. of Pennsylvania, 1929-49; Chm., Nat. Research Council, 1946-50; Mem., Inter-American Cttee on Science and Technology, Orgn of American States, 1969-; Fellow in Medicine of the Nat. Research Council at Cambridge and London, 1928-29; Lectures: Weir Mitchell, Philadelphia Coll. of Physicians, 1938; Hughlings Jackson, McGill, 1938; Vanuxem, Princeton, 1939; Priestley, Pennsylvania State Coll., 1941; Herter, New York Univ. Medical Coll., 1943; Colver, Brown Univ., 1946; A. D. Little, MIT, 1949; Louis H. Bauer, 1960; Gideon Seymour, 1960; Robert Kennedy Duncan Meml, 1960; First Annual William

Bartram, Florida State, 1974. Managing Editor, Journal of Cellular and Comparative Physiology and Associate Editor o several specialist journals; SAAAS (Pres. 1952); Member: Amer Acad. Arts and Sciences; World Acad. of Art and Science (Pres 1971-); French Acad. of Sciences; Roy. Danish Acad. o Sciences and Letters; Roy. Swedish Acad. of Science; Acad. o Sciences, USSR; Brazilian Acad. of Sciences; Swiss Acad. o Sciences; American Philosophical Soc.; Chm., NY State Science and Technology Foundn; Hon. Member: British Physiologica Soc., Royal Institution and of numerous scientific socs Advisory Cttee for Biology and Medicine, US Atomic Energy Commission, 1946-50; US National Commission for UNESCO Sci. Advisory Board, Army Air Forces; National Advisory Committee for Aeronautics; National Science Foundatior Board; President's Science Advisory Committee. Trustee: John Hopkins Univ., Univ. of Pennsylvania, Bucknell Univ. Rockefeller Fund, Rockefeller Univ., Rensselaer Polytechni Inst.; Rockefeller Brothers Fund, Sloan Kettering Inst., etc Presidential Medal of Freedom, 1964; Benjamin Franklin Meda (RSA), 1967; Nat. Medal of Science, 1968. Holds 57 hor degrees in Law, Science, etc., from Cambridge, Londor Harvard, etc. *Publications:* articles in Astrophysical Journa Journal of the Optical Society, Journal of Physiology, America Journal of Physiology, etc. *Recreation:* sailing. *Address:* The Rockefeller University, New York, NY 10021, USA. *T:* 360 1000. *Clubs:* Athenæum (London); Century, University, Nev York Yacht (New York); Rittenhouse (Philadelphia); Cosmo (Washington); Maryland (Baltimore). *[Died 17 Nov. 1975*

BRONOWSKI, Jacob, MA, PhD; Senior Fellow, since 1964, an Director of the Council for Biology in Human Affairs, sinc 1970, Salk Institute for Biological Studies; *b* 18 Jan. 1908; *e s* o Abram and Celia Bronowski; *m* 1941, Rita Coblentz; four d *Educ:* Central Foundation School; Jesus College, Cambridg (Hon. Fellow, 1967). Sr Lecturer at University College, Hul 1934-42; seconded to Govt service, 1942; Joint Target Grou Washington, and Chiefs of Staff Mission to Japan, 194 statistical research into economics of building and othe industries, Ministry of Works, 1946-50; seconded to UNESC as Head of Projects, 1948; Carnegie Visiting Professo Massachusetts Institute of Technology, 1953; Director of Co Research Establishment, National Coal Board, 1950-5 Director-General of Process Development Department o National Coal Board, 1959-64. Lectures: inaugural Man an Nature, Amer. Mus. Nat. History, 1965; Blashfield, Amer Acad. Arts and Letters, 1966; Condon, Univ. Oregon, 196 Silliman, Yale, 1967; Mellon, Nat. Gallery of Art, Washingto DC, 1969; Bampton, Columbia Univ., 1969. Foreign Ho Member, American Acad. of Arts and Sciences, 1960; Fello Member, World Acad. of Art and Science. *Publications:* Th Poet's Defence, 1939 and 1966; William Blake, a Man without Mask, 1944; The Common Sense of Science, 1951; radio play including The Journey to Japan, 1948, and The Face of Violenc (Italia Prize, 1951), 1954 and 1967; Science and Human Value 1958; Selection of William Blake's Poems, 1958; The Wester Intellectual Tradition, 1960; Insight, 1964; The Abacus and th Rose: A New Dialogue on Two World Systems, 1965; Willia Blake and the Age of Revolution, 1965, 2nd edn, 1972; Th Identity of Man, 1965; Nature and Knowledge, 1969; The Ascent of Man, 1973; numerous papers in mathematic *Recreations:* squash rackets and chess. *Address:* PO Box 180 San Diego, California 92112, USA. *Club:* Athenæum. *[Died 22 Aug. 197*

BROOK, Clive; Actor; *b* 1 June, 1887; *s* of George Alfred an Charlotte Mary Brook; *m* 1920, Charlotte Elizabeth Mildre (*née* Evelyn); one *s* one d. *Educ:* privately. Served Europea War, 1914-18; Artists Rifles, 1914-15; Machine Gun Corps 1915-18. Stage plays, 1919-23: Over Sunday, Harbury Poin James the Less, Just Like Judy, Clothes and the Woman; *Film in England,* 1920-24: Trent's Last Case, Kissing Cup's Rac Sportsman's Wife, Daniel Deronda, Loudwater Mystery, H Penalty, Christine Johnson, Married to a Mormon, Reverse the Medal, Through Fire and Water, Sonia, Out to Win, Shirle This Freedom, Woman to Woman; *Films in America,* 1924-(Silent): Christine of the Hungry Heart, Enticement, T Mirage, Playing with Souls, Declasse, If Marriage Fails, Huma Desires, Woman Hater, The Homemaker, Pleasure Buye Seven Sinners, Compromise, Three Faces East, When Lo Grows Cold, Why Girls Go Back Home, You Never Kno Women, For Alimony Only, Popular Sin, Barbed Wire, Afra to Love, Underworld, Hula, Devil Dancer, French Dressin Midnight Madness, Yellow Lily, Perfect Crime, Heliotrop (Talking): Interference, Four Feathers, Dangerous Woma Charming Sinners, Sherlock Holmes, Laughing Lady, Sligh Scarlet, Sweethearts and Wives, Anybody's Woman, Scand Sheet, East Lynne, Tarnished Lady, Lawyer's Secret, Silenc Twenty-four Hours, Husband's Holiday, Shanghai Expre

Man from Yesterday, The Night of June 13th, Return of Sherlock Holmes, Cavalcade, Midnight Club, If I Were Free, Gallant Lady, Dover Road, Let's Try Again; The Dictator (England), 1934; Dressmaker of Luneville (America), 1935; *Films in England*, 1935-43: Love in Exile, Lonely Road, Action for Slander, The Ware Case, Return to Yesterday, Convoy, Freedom Radio, The Shipbuilders, Flemish Farm, Breach of Promise, On Approval (also produced, adapted and directed). Returned to stage in England, 1944; appeared in: The Years Between, Play's The Thing, Gioconda Smile, Stratton; Second Threshold, New York, 1950-51; Vaudeville, London, 1952; A Woman of No Importance, London, 1953; The Count of Clérambard, London, 1955; One Bright Day, London, 1956; Judge's Story, 1963. *Film in Hollywood*, 1962: List of Adrian Messenger. Has appeared on television from 1956. Wrote stage play, That's What Victor Hugo Said, prod 1968. *Address:* 95 Eaton Square, SW1. *T:* 01-235 7110. *Club:* Garrick.
[Died 17 Nov. 1974.

ROOK, Donald Charles; Chartered Accountant, 1922; Company Director; *b* 31 May 1894; *e s* of late Walter Henry Brook and of Emily Brook; *m* Doris Emmett; one *s* one *d. Educ:* High School and Technical College, Newport. Served European War 1914-18, France and Egypt; War of 1939-45, Upper Thames Patrol, 1941-44. With Peat Marwick Mitchell & Co., London, 1918-26; assisted in formation in 1926 and subseq. development of Perak River Hydro-Electric Co. Ltd, Malaya (Vice-Chm., 1950-72); Vice-Chm., Nigerian Electricity Corp., 1944-66; Exec. Member London Boards of: E African Power & Lighting Co. Ltd, 1942-66; Kenya Power Co. Ltd (1954-66); Dir, Balfour, Beatty & Co. Ltd, 1944-66; Dir and Vice-Chm., Jerusalem Electric & Public Service Corp., 1942-57; Dir and Chm. British Central Africa Co. Ltd, 1943-63. Exec. Mem. Council, Jt African Bd, 1942- (Vice-Chm. 1963-66); Mem., Council, Exec. Cttee and Finance and General Purposes Cttee, Organisation of Employers' Federations and Employers in Developing Countries, 1958-68. Corporate Mem., RIIA, 1949-59. Mem., Nyasaland Tea Assoc. London Cttee, 1950-63; Mem., Cttee, E Africa Dinner Club, 1963-. Mem., Royal Nat. Rose Soc. FRSA; FSAA; FRHS; FCA. *Recreations:* fishing, gardening; Cdre, British Motor Yacht Club, 1947 and 1948. *Address:* 7 Hamble Court, Broom Park, Teddington, Mddx TW11 9RW. *T:* 01-977 2875. *Clubs:* East India, Sports and Public Schools, Royal Automobile, East Africa House, Royal Commonwealth Society; Muthaiga Country (Nairobi). [Died 11 March 1976.

ROOK, Sir Dryden, Kt 1965; wool merchant; Member Halifax County Borough Council; *b* 25 Aug. 1884; *s* of James Brook. MP (Lab) Halifax, 1945-55. Freeman of County Borough of Halifax, 1964. *Address:* Flat 15, Old Well Head, Halifax, Yorks. *T:* Halifax 52166. [Died 31 Jan. 1971.

ROOK, Commodore James Kenneth, CBE 1942; DSO 1918; RD; RNR; retired; Master in the Mercantile Marine; *b* 1889; *s* of late James Alfred Brook, Barnsley Farm, Isle of Wight; *m* 1942, Betty, *d* of late H. L. Brook, AMIEE; one *d. Educ:* Isle of Wight College, Ryde; HMS Worcester (Training Ship). Served in square-rigged sailing ships Ladye Doris and Marian Woodside, 1906-11; in Tramp steamers, 1912-14; in HM ships on active service, 1914-19; served in Armed Merchant cruisers, in Grand Fleet (HMS Conqueror) and later in Q and Mystery ships (despatches, DSO for sinking U34 when in command of HMS Privet, Q19); after demobilising joined Andrew Weir & Co. as Chief Officer and 2 years later in command of various Company's Ships until retirement; 1939-44, served as Commodore in various convoys (despatches, CBE); ADC to the King, 1942-43. *Recreations:* stroked Worcester-Conway boat-race, 1905; walking, swimming; music lover (amateur). *Address:* West Hill, Seaview, Isle of Wight. *T:* Seaview 3294.
[Died 16 Dec. 1976.

ROOK, Rev. Victor John Knight, MA; Chaplain of All Souls College, 1935; Fellow, 1938-59; *b* 22 June 1887; *s* of Richard Brook and Emma Knight; *m* 1st, 1914, Marie (*d* 1963), *d* of W. Groux; one *s* one *d*; 2nd, 1965, Janet, *d* of George Swift. *Educ:* Bradford Grammar School; Queen's College, Oxford (Exhibitioner). 1st class Lit. Hum.; 1st class Theology. Curate, Wakefield Cathedral, 1912-15; St James's, Piccadilly, 1915-16; Assistant Master, Charterhouse, 1916-21; Fellow and Chaplain, Lincoln College, Oxford, 1921-30; Prebendary of Lincoln, 1927-33; Senior Proctor, University of Oxford, 1922; Select Preacher, University of Oxford, 1928-30; University of Cambridge, 1938; University Lecturer in Reformation Theology, 1929-34; Member of Hebdomadal Council, 1926-49; Censor St Catherine's Society, Oxford, 1930-52. Hon. Fellow, St Catherine's College, 1963. *Publications:* The Claims of Duty; Divine Justice; John Whitgift and the English Church; A Life of Archbishop Parker. *Recreation:* walking. *Address:* Stonefield, Burford, Oxford. [Died 1 July 1974.

BROOKE, Brigadier Walter Headfort, CBE 1938; MC; DL; *b* 13 Jan. 1887; *s* of late John Monck Brooke; *m* 1st, 1920, Mary S. G., *d* of late Henry Dawson-Greene, Whittington Hall, Kirkby Lonsdale; (one *s* decd); 2nd, 1923, Lady Edith Mary Stopford, *d* of 6th Earl of Courtown; one *d. Educ:* Haileybury Coll. Served European War 1914-19, in France and Belgium (despatches four times, Brevet Major, MC, 4th Class Order of Crown of Roumania). DL Devon, 1942. *Publication:* Gladeye the War Horse, 1939. *Recreations:* polo, hunting, shooting, fishing. *Address:* 12 Roborough Lane, Ashburton, Devon. *T:* Ashburton 367. [Died 25 Nov. 1975.

BROOKEBOROUGH, 1st Viscount, *cr* 1952 of Colebrooke; **Basil Stanlake Brooke**, 5th Bt, *cr* 1882; KG 1965; PC Northern Ireland, 1933; CBE 1921; MC 1916; 10th Hussars; Prime Minister of Northern Ireland, 1943-63, resigned; MP (U) Lisnaskea Division, Parliament of Northern Ireland, 1929-68; Vice-Admiral of Province of Ulster since 1961; HM Lieutenant of Fermanagh, 1963-69; *b* 9 June 1888; *s* of 4th Bt and Gertrude Isabella, *o d* of S. R. Batson; *S* father, 1907; *m* 1st, 1919, Cynthia (Mary) (*d* 1970), DBE 1959, *d* of late Captain and Hon. Mrs Sergison of Cuckfield Park, Sussex; one *s* (and two *s* killed in action); 2nd, 1971, Sarah Eileen Bell Calvert, widow of Cecil Armstrong Calvert, FRCS, Dir of Neurosurgery, Royal Victoria Hospital, Belfast. *Educ:* Winchester; RMC, Sandhurst. Served European War, 1914-19 (Dardanelles) (despatches, MC, Croix de Guerre with Palm); Minister of Agriculture, Northern Ireland, 1933-41; Minister of Commerce, 1941-45 (jointly with Premiership from 1943). Chairman, Carreras of Northern Ireland Ltd; Director, Devenish Trade; President Institute of Directors, Northern Ireland. Hon. Capt. RNVR; Hon. Air Commodore, RAuxAF. KStJ; LLD, Queen's Univ., Belfast. *Recreation:* fishing. *Heir: s* Rt Hon. John Warden Brooke. *Address:* Colebrooke, Brookeboro', Northern Ireland. *T:* Brookeboro' 204. *Clubs:* (Hon.) Junior Carlton, (Hon.) Constitutional, (Hon.) Cavalry, (Hon.) Buck's; Ulster, (Hon.) Ulster Reform (Belfast). [Died 18 Aug. 1973.

BROOKES, Hon. and Rev. Edgar Harry, MA, DLitt; Hon. LLD; Author; late Senator representing the natives of Natal and Zululand in the Union of South Africa Parliament; late Professor of Public Administration and Political Science, University of Pretoria, and Principal, Adams College, Natal; *b* Smethwick, England, 4 Feb. 1897; *s* of J. H. Brookes and E. E. Thomas; *m* 1st, 1925, Heidi Genevieve, *d* of Rev. C. Bourquin, Mission Suisse, Pretoria; three *s* two *d*; 2nd, Edith Constance Moe. *Educ:* Pietermaritzburg College; University of South Africa; London School of Economics. Professor of Public Administration and Political Science, Transvaal University College (later University of Pretoria), 1924; SA Delegate to the League of Nations Assembly, 1927; Observer for Union Government at World Population Conference, 1927; President of SA Institute of Race Relations, 1932 and 1946; Member of Union Social and Economic Planning Council, 1942-52; Member, Native Affairs Commission, 1945-50; Professor of History and Political Science, University of Natal, 1959-62. *Publications:* History of Native Policy in South Africa, 1923; Native Education in South Africa, 1929; A Retrospect and a Forecast; History of the Swiss Mission in South Africa, 1875-1925, 1926; The Colour Problems of South Africa, 1934; South Africa in a Changing World, 1954; The Native Reserves of Natal, 1957; The Commonwealth, 1959, 1959; The City of God and the Politics of Crisis, 1959; Power, Law, Right, and Love: A Study in Political Values, 1963; The History of Natal, 1965; Freedom, Faith and the Twenty-First Century, 1966; A History of the University of Natal, 1967; Apartheid: a Documentary Study of Modern South Africa, 1968; White Rule in South Africa 1830-1910, 1974; collaborated in: Coming of Age: Studies in South African Citizenship and Politics, 1930; Western Civilisation and the Bantu of South Africa, 1934; Civil Liberty in South Africa, 1958; White Rule in South Africa 1830-1910, 1976; A South African Pilgrimage, 1977. *Address:* PO Box 222, Gillitts, Natal, 3603, South Africa. *T:* Durban 7411 88.
[Died 22 April 1979.

BROOKES, Ernest Roy, CB 1954; *b* 25 Aug. 1904; *m* 1938, Margaret, *d* of J. T. Reeve; no *c. Educ:* Heath Grammar School, Halifax; Magdalene College, Cambridge, Lecturer at St David's College Lampeter, 1926-28; entered Inland Revenue Department, 1929; Sec., Committee on Taxation of Trading Profits, 1949-51; Secretary, Royal Commission on Taxation of Profits and Income, 1951-52; Commissioner of Inland Revenue, 1952-65; Deputy Chairman, Board of Inland Revenue, 1965-67. Mem. E. Africa Commn of Enquiry on Income Tax, 1956. *Recreation:* music. *Address:* 9 Netherhall Gardens, NW3. *T:* 01-435 7254. *Clubs:* Reform, Oxford and Cambridge Musical.
[Died 25 Aug. 1972.

BROOKES, Lady; Mabel Balcombe, DBE 1955 (CBE 1933); Chevalier de la Légion d'Honneur; *d* of late Harry Emmerton, solicitor, South Yarra, and Alice Mabel Maud Emmerton, CBE; *m* 1911, Sir Norman Everard Brookes (*d* 1968). President, Cttee of Management, Queen Victoria Meml Hosp., Melbourne, from 1924. Hon. LLD Monash, 1967. *Publications:* Broken Idols, 1916; Old Desires, 1918; Crowded Galleries, 1956; St Helena Story, 1960; Riders of Time, 1967. *Address:* 237 Domain Road, South Yarra, Vic 3141, Australia; Brookwood, Mount Eliza, Victoria, Australia. *[Died 30 April 1975.*

BROOKFIELD, G. Piers, Mem. AIA, FRIBA; Practising Architect, 1929-42, and since 1946; *b* Halifax, NS, 9 Jan. 1894; *s* of late Walter G. Brookfield and Edith Harrington Piers; *m* 1924, Martha Johnstone Balfour Forgie, *d* of late James Forgie, MICE, Cons. Eng., NYC; one *d. Educ:* Dalhousie Univ. (BSc); MIT (SB); Oxford Univ. (BLitt); Atelier Gromort, Ecole des Beaux Arts, Paris. Officer, Canadian Artillery, 1916-18. Architectural draftsman, 1920-28; Bellows and Aldrich, Strickland, Blodget and Law, Boston; Sir Aston Webb & Son, London; Sir Alfred Bossom and Th. Engelhardt, New York; Lend Lease Procurement, British Min. of Supply, Washington, 1942-46; Principal, own office, NYC. Delegate Fine Arts Federation of New York, 1941-42, 1955-57, 1957-61. Trustee: Kew-Forest School; Theodore Roosevelt Associaton. *Recreations:* tennis, golf, ski-ing. *Address:* 724 Burns Street, Forest Hills Gardens, LI, NY, USA. *T:* BO 8-3578; (office) 10 West 33rd Street, New York, NY 10001, USA. *T:* PE 6-1759. *Clubs:* West Side Tennis (Forest Hills, LI); British Schools and Universities (NYC) (Past Pres.). *[Died 28 March 1975.*

BROOKING, Allan John; Administrator, South Western Regional Health Authority, since 1973; *b* 28 March 1934; *s* of Harold Nicholas Brooking and Margaret Ethel Brooking; *m* 1957, Audrey Irene (*née* Walton); two *s* one *d. Educ:* Okehampton Grammar Sch.; University Coll., Oxford (MA). FHA. Sec., Salisbury General Infirmary, 1959-62; Dep. Sec., Lewisham HMC, 1962-65; Group Sec., Lewisham HMC, 1965-70; Sec., Bd of Governors, United Liverpool Hosps, 1971-73. Mem., NHS Nat. Training Council, 1975-. *Recreations:* singing, walking, surfing. *Address:* Black Wicket, 128 Westbury Road, Westbury-on-Trym, Bristol BS9 3AR. *T:* Bristol 624825. *[Died 30 Dec. 1980.*

BROOKS, Rt. Rev. Gerald Henry; Vicar of St Thomas, New Groombridge, Sussex, since 1967; *b* 11 Feb. 1905; *s* of Capt. Percy Wilmot Brooks and Florence Maud Haward. *Educ:* Tonbridge School, Kent; Keble College, Oxford; Ely Theological College. Deacon, 1930; Priest, 1931; Assistant Priest, St Saviour's, Poplar, 1930-32; Domestic Chaplain to Bishop of Nassau and Priest-in-Charge of St Barnabas, Nassau, Bahamas, 1932-34; Priest-in-Charge of All Saints, Andros, Bahamas, 1934-40; Priest-in-Charge of St Stephen's, Grand Bahama, 1940-45; General Missionary and Diocesan Treasurer of Diocese of Nassau, 1945-46; Archdeacon of Nassau, 1946-50; Bishop of British Honduras, 1950-66. *Address:* St Thomas' Vicarage, New Groombridge, Sussex. *Club:* United Oxford & Cambridge University. *[Died 12 Dec. 1974.*

BROOKS, Iris Mary, MA Cantab; Lecturer and Member of the Guild of Drama Adjudicators, since 1954. *Educ:* Bromley High School (GPDST); Girton College, Cambridge. Headmistress, Malvern Girls' College, Worcs, 1928-54, retired 1954. *Address:* 10 Greenacres, The Avenue, Branksome Park, Dorset. *Club:* English-Speaking Union. *[Died 12 May 1971.*

BROOKS, Ronald Clifton, OBE 1944; MC 1918; Chairman, Commercial Union Assurance Co. Ltd, 1959-72; retired; *b* 3 March 1899; 2nd *s* of Robert Brooks; *m* 1928, Iris Winifred (*d* 1978), *er d* of M. W. Payne; two *s* one *d. Educ:* Haileybury College; Trinity College, Cambridge. Joined The Queen's (Royal West Surrey) Regt, with rank 2nd Lieut, 1917 (MC). Cambridge (BA), 1919-20. Partner, Robert Brooks & Co., Merchants, 1924-68; Chm., Crosby House Group, retd 1972; Director: Dalgety Ltd, retd 1972; Yeoman Investment Trust Ltd, retd 1973. DAG, SHAEF, 1945. Legion of Merit, USA, 1945; Chevalier, Légion d'Honneur, 1945. *Recreations:* fishing, shooting, golf. *Address:* 14 Whitelands House, Chelsea, SW3. *T:* 01-730 1950. *Clubs:* Bath, City of London. *[Died 14 Aug. 1980.*

BROSIO, Manlio; *b* 10 July 1897; *s* of late Edoardo Brosio and Fortunata Curadelli; *m* 1936, Clotilde Brosio. *Educ:* Turin University (graduated in Law), Officer in Alpine Troops, European War, 1915-18 (Silver Medal and Cross for Valour). Young political leader, Member of Liberal Party, Central Secretary of "Rivoluzione Liberale" movement, Turin, 1922-25; retired from politics after Fascism took power. Barrister in Turin, in continuous contact with anti-fascist groups, 1926-43;

Member of Nat. Liberation Cttee in Rome under German occupation, 1943-44; General Sec. of Liberal Party, 1944-45. Minister without portfolio in Bonomi Cabinet, 1944; Vice-President of Cabinet in De Gasperi Govt, 1945; Minister of War in De Gasperi Govt, 1945-46; Ambassador: in Moscow, Jan. 1947-Dec. 1951; in London, 1952-54; in Washington, 1955-61; in Paris, 1961-64; Sec.-Gen. of NATO, 1964-71; Senator of Italian Republic for Turin, 1972-76, retired. *Publications:* juridical and political articles. *Address:* Corso Re Umberto 29 bis, Torino, Italy. *T:* 532441, 548597 *[Died 14 March 1980.*

BROUGHTON, Sir Alfred Davies Devonsher, Kt 1969; DL; MP (Lab) for Batley and Morley, Yorkshire, since Feb. 1949; retired physician; *b* 18 Oct. 1902; *s* of A. G. S. Broughton, MB, JP; *m* 1st, 1930, Dorothy, MA, PhD (marr. diss. 1967), *d* of late Commander W. D. Parry Jones, RD, RNR; one *s* one *d*; 2nd, 1967, Joyce Diana, *d* of H. S. Denton, Leeds. *Educ:* Rossall School; Cambridge Univ.; London Hosp. MRCS (Eng.), LRCP (Lond.), 1929; MA, MB, BChir (Cantab.), 1936; DPM (Leeds), 1936; DPH (Leeds), 1937; Casualty Officer at Poplar Hospital, 1929-30. Receiving Room Officer at London Hospital, 1930; Resident MO at Rossall School, 1930-32; Medical Practitioner in Batley, 1932-40 and 1945-50. Served War of 1939-45, RAFVR (Squadron Leader), 1940-45. Member of Batley Borough Council, 1946-49. Opposition Whip, 1960-64. UK delegate to Council of Europe and to Assembly of WEU, 1956-58. Member of Speaker's Panel of Chairmen, 1964-76. Hon Treasurer, Commonwealth Parly Assoc., 1969-70. Vice-Pres. Leeds Trustee Savings Bank, 1974-. DL W Yorks, 1971. Hon. Freeman of Morley, 1972, of Batley, 1973. SBStJ 1946, OStJ 1951. *Publication:* Clean Handling of Food, 1953. *Address* Stockwell Shay Farm, Batley, W Yorkshire. *T:* 474321. *[Died 2 April 1979*

BROWDER, Earl (Russell); Author, Lecturer; *b* Wichita Kansas, 20 May 1891; *s* of William and Martha (Hankins) Browder; *m* 1926, Raissa Berkmann (*d* 1955); three *s. Educ:* self educated. Candidate for Pres. Communist Party, 1936 and 1940 Sec., 1930-45; Member Exec. Cttee Communist International 1935-40; Director of Pan-Pacific Trade Union Secretariat Shanghai, 1926-29; Member Exec. Cttee Red International of Labor Unions, 1921-30. Served prison terms 1917-20 and 1941-42 in connection with conflicts over war policy. Expelled from Communist Party, 1946, for upholding policies of President Roosevelt. No present organisational activities or connections *Publications:* Communism in US, 1935; What is Communism? 1936; People's Front, 1938; Fighting for Peace, 1939; Second Imperialist War, 1940; Way Out, 1941; Victory and After, 1942 Teheran, 1944; American Marxists and War, 1945; War o Peace with Russia, 1947; Marx and America, 1959; over 100 pamphlets, circulation 8,000,000 copies. *Recreation:* music *Address:* 20 Maple Street, Princeton, NJ. USA. *[Died 27 June 1973*

BROWN, Alan Brock; Emeritus Fellow, Worcester College Oxford; Hon. Bencher, Inner Temple, since 1972; *b* 30 Apr 1911; *s* of Harold Rinder Brown and Elsie Clara Burnet Brown (*née* Lord), Brisbane; *m* 1940, Elizabeth Muriel McCarthy Moss Vale, NSW; four *s. Educ:* Geelong Grammar Sch.; New Coll., Oxford (BCL, MA). Vinerian Law Scholar, Oxford, 1935 called to Bar, Inner Temple, 1935; admitted to Bar of NSW 1936. Commnd into Scots Guards, 1940; served in UK, N Africa, Italy (Captain, wounded, despatches). Worcester College: Fellow, 1937; Domestic Bursar, 1947-58; Estate Bursar, 1957-66; Senior Tutor, 1961-66; Vice-Provost, 1967-7 Supernumerary Fellow, 1971-78. University Member, Oxfor City Council, 1939-65; Mayor of Oxford, 1953-54. Sen Procto Oxford Univ., 1950-51; Mem. Hebdomadal Council, 1951-65 Sen. Mem., Oxford Univ. Law Soc., 1945-65; Hon. Treasure Oxford Univ. Athletic Club, 1945-54; Oxford Univ. Boxin Club, 1945-53; Sen. Mem., Oxford Univ. Penguins Lawn Tenn Club, 1945-65 and Oxford Univ. Australian Club, 1945-6 Pres., Oxford Consumers Group; Pres., UK Br. Old Geelon Grammarians. *Recreations:* gardening, music, reading, talkin making speeches. *Address:* Mole End, Burcot, Abingdon, Oxc OX14 3DP. *T:* Clifton Hampden 7910. *Club:* Vincent (Oxford). *[Died 25 Dec. 198*

BROWN, Alan Grahame; *b* Wood Green, N22, 23 Oct. 1913; *o* of late Alexander Harris Brown, Bedford, and Blanche Loui Brown, Whitehill, Hitchin, Herts; *m* 1937, Joan Emily Maxe Bedford; two *s. Educ:* Bedford School; College of t Pharmaceutical Society, University of London. Served wit Beds & Herts Regt, 5th Bn 1932-37, 4th Bn 1940-44, rank Lieu Member Socialist Party, 1937-62; Chm. S Tottenham Co-op Party, 1957-60; Mem. Exec. Cttee Tottenham Trades Counc 1958-; MP Tottenham: (Lab) 1959-61; (Ind) 1961-62; (C) 196 64; resigned Labour Party March 1962, following difference

opinion on fundamental policies; rejoined Labour Party April 1966. Member, Middlesex County Council, 1956-65. Specialises in Welfare of Children and Young Persons, in Juvenile Delinquency and in Prison, Borstal and Approved School Administration; formerly Member County of Middlesex Approved Schools Sub-cttee and of Children's Cttee; introduced Restriction of Imprisonment of Children Bill, in House of Commons, 1960; introduced Nursing Homes Act in House of Commons, 1963. PhC, FCS, MPS. *Recreations:* motoring, and sailing (Yachting). *Address:* 77 Fitzjohn's Avenue, Hampstead, NW3.
[Died 5 Jan. 1972.

BROWN, Brig. Alan Ward, CBE 1955; DSO 1943; MC 1935; retired; *b* 8 July 1909; *s* of Hugh Ward Brown, Dublin, and Gertrude Corisande Brown (*née* Bean, now Stephens); *m* 1936, Pamela Margaret (*née* Preston); one *s. Educ:* Bromsgrove Sch., Worcs. Commissioned Royal Tank Corps, 1930; posted 5 RTR, 1931; 2nd Armoured Car Company (India/Pakistan), 1931-35; 2nd Bn RTC, 1936-38; Staff College, 1940; Comd 147 RAC and 3 RTR in NW Europe, 1943-44; Comd 31 Armoured Bde, 1944-45; GSO1 79 Armoured Div., 1942-43; Comd Specialised Armour Establishment, 1948-49; idc 1949-50; Comd 25 Armoured Bde, 1953-56. Croix de Guerre, Chevalier of the Order of Leopold (Belgium). *Address:* Medleys Farm, High Hurstwood, Sussex.
[Died 1 Sept. 1971.

BROWN, Anthony Geoffrey Hopwood G.; *see* Gardner-Brown.

BROWN, Prof. Arthur; Professor of English, Monash University, since 1973; *b* 8 March 1921; *s* of Herbert Brown and Edith Mary Honour; *m* 1946, Eudora Margaret Whitehead (marr. diss. 1975); four *s* one *d. Educ:* Urmston Grammar Sch.; University Coll. London. BA 1947, MA 1949, DLit 1965. Undergraduate, Dept of English, UCL, 1939-41, 1946-47. Served RAF, 1941-46. Dept of English, UCL: Quain Student, 1947-50; Lectr, 1950-56; Commonwealth Fund Fellow, 1953-54 (held mainly at Folger Shakespeare Library, Washington, Huntington Library, Calif, libraries of Harvard and Yale and Univs of Texas and Virginia.); Foyle Research Fellow, Shakespeare Inst., Stratford-upon-Avon (Univ. of Birmingham), 1958-59; Reader in English, UCL, 1956-62 (by conferment of title); Prof. of English, UCL, 1962-69 (by conferment of title); Prof. of Library Studies and Dir of Sch. of Library, Archive and Inf. Studies, UCL, 1969-73. Sen. Fellow, South Eastern Inst. of Medieval and Renaissance Studies, Duke Univ., North Carolina, Summer 1966; Commonwealth Vis. Prof. of English, Sydney Univ., 1972. Gen. Editor, The Malone Society, 1961-71. Pres., Bibliographical Soc. of Aust. and NZ, 1974-76. Fellow of UCL, 1971. *Publications:* Editor (alone and in collab.) of numerous vols for Malone Society; A Whole Theatre of Others (anthology of Elizabethan and Jacobean Drama), 1960; ed (with P. G. Foote) Early English and Norse Studies, 1963; Edmond Malone and English Scholarship, 1963; articles and studies in Mod. Lang. Review, Mod. Lang. Quarterly, Shakespeare Survey, The Library, Studies in Bibliography, Year's Work in English Studies, Philological Quarterly, etc. *Recreations:* taking snuff, walking, talking, reading booksellers' catalogues, amateur printing, maps. *Address:* Department of English, Monash University, Clayton, Victoria 3168, Australia. *Clubs:* Athenæum; United Arts (Dublin).
[Died 28 July 1979.

BROWN, Edward Percy, CB 1971; Commissioner, HM Customs and Excise, 1970-72; *m* 20 Dec. 1911; *s* of Percy Brown and Lilian Brown (*née* Gibbs), Wanstead, Essex; *m* 1938, Kathleen Julia Gale (*d* 1967); one *s*; *m* 1971, Barbara Kathleen Howe. *Educ:* Loughton Sch., Loughton, Essex. Career Civil Servant, Oct. 1931-; in Customs and Excise Dept, successively as Officer, Surveyor, Inspector, Collector, Chief Inspector, and Commissioner. *Recreations:* hockey, tennis, ale-conning. *Address:* Barrowfield, Chestnuts, Hutton, Essex.
[Died 7 March 1972.

BROWN, Frank Leslie, CMG 1945; OBE 1938; MC 1916 (and Bar, 1919); *b* 15 Dec. 1896; *s* of late W. F. Brown; *m* 1927, Edith Mary, *yr d* of late S. J. Sandle, Alderman and DL of City of London; one *s* one *d. Educ:* Wilson's Grammar School. Sizarship, St John's College, Cambridge, 1915; served European War, 1915-19, KRRC, Captain (MC and bar, despatches); District Administration, Northern Rhodesia, 1919-35; Asst Colonial Secretary, Jamaica, 1935; Deputy Colonial Secretary, Jamaica, 1942-45; Chief Secretary, Nyasaland, 1945-51; retired 1951. *Address:* 1 Church Lane, Hellingly, East Sussex.
[Died 11 Sept. 1977.

BROWN, Rear-Adm. George Herbert Hempson, CBE 1948; *b* 23 July 1893; *s* of H. S. Brown, Commander RNR, Madras Port Department, and Anna Brown (*née* Hempson); *m* 1919, Ida Mary, *d* of George Hempson, Bradfield, Essex; one *s* three *d.*

Educ: RN Colleges Osborne and Dartmouth. Midshipman HM Ships Bellerophon, Defence, Indomitable, 1910-12; Acting Sub-Lieut and Sub-Lieut HMS Indomitable, Ajax, Arab, 1912-14; promoted Lieut RN, HMS Adventure, 1914, in command HMS Iris, 1915; appointed Lieut (E) HMS Hercules, 1915; HMS Liverpool, 1917; RN Engineering College, Keyham, 1919-20; Advanced Engineering Course, RN College, Greenwich, 1920-22; Lieut-Comdr (E), Engineer-in-Chief Dept, Admiralty, 1922-25; HMS Warspite, 1925-27; Comdr (E) Engineer-in-Chief Dept, Admiralty, 1927-31; HMS Sussex, 1931-33; HM Dockyard, Portsmouth, 1934-38; HMS Furious, 1938; Captain (E), Engineer-in-Chief Dept, Admiralty, 1939-45. Rear-Admiral (E) 1945; Deputy Engineer-in-Chief of the Fleet, 1947-50; retired 1950. *Recreation:* gardening. *Address:* Robin Hill, 112 Coombe Lane, Westbury-on-Trym, Bristol. *T:* Bristol 683250.
[Died 3 June 1977.

BROWN, Sir (George) Lindor, Kt 1957; CBE 1947; FRS 1946; FRCP 1958; Principal, Hertford College, Oxford, since 1967; Waynflete Professor of Physiology, Oxford University, and Fellow of Magdalen College, 1960-67; Biological Secretary, Royal Society, 1955-63 (Vice-President, 1957-63); *b* 9 Feb. 1903; *o s* of late G. W. A. Brown and Helen Brown, Warrington, Lancs; *m* 1930, Jane Rosamond, *d* of late Prof. C. H. Lees, FRS, and late Mrs E. M. Lees, Tonbridge; three *s* one *d. Educ:* Boteler Grammar Sch., Warrington. Univ. of Manchester, 1921-28; BSc (Hons Physiology) 1924; Platt Physiological Scholar, 1924; MSc, 1925; MB, ChB, 1928; Bradley Surgical Prize, Medal in Operative Surgery, 1928. Lectr in Physiology, Univ. of Leeds, 1928; Mem. Scientific Staff of MRC, National Institute for Medical Research, 1934-49; Jodrell Prof. of Physiology, University Coll., London, 1949-60. Medical Research Council: Secretary RN Personnel Research Cttee, 1942-49, Chm., 1949-69; Mem. Council, 1951-55; Assessor, 1961-63. Hon. Sec. Physiological Soc., 1941-49, Foreign Sec., 1949-61; Mem. Editorial Board of Journal of Physiology, 1940-47; President, Internat. Union of Physiological Sciences, 1962-68. Mem. Council for Scientific and Industrial Research, 1963-65; Chm., Lister Inst., 1968-71. Pres. ASLIB, 1961-63. Feldberg Prize Lectr, Heidelberg, 1961. Mem., Royal Danish Acad. of Science. Officer of Order of Southern Cross of Brazil; Foreign Member Brazilian Academy of Sciences. Hon. LLD St Andrews; Hon. DSc: Leicester; Monash; Hon. D de l'Univ. Liège; Hon. Dr Univ. do Brasil. *Publications:* Papers in Journal of Physiology, and Proc. Royal Soc. *Recreations:* gardening, engraving. *Address:* Hertford College, Oxford. *T:* Oxford 41434. *Club:* Athenæum.
[Died 22 Feb. 1971.

BROWN, His Honour Harold John, MC; QC 1955; Judge of County Courts, Circuit No 50 (Sussex), 1959-71; *s* of Charles Edward Brown; *m* 1929, Isabel Margaret Sefton; one *s* two *d. Educ:* Chesterfield; Corpus Christi College, Cambridge. Barrister, Middle Temple, 1930. Recorder of King's Lynn, 1958-59, Norwich, 1959. Dep. Chm. W Sussex QS, 1955-60. *Address:* Fairlawn, Warden Court, Cuckfield, Sussex. *T:* Haywards Heath 4268.
[Died 27 Dec. 1975.

BROWN, Ivor John Carnegie, CBE 1957; Hon. LLD; FRSL; author and journalist; *b* Penang, 25 April 1891; 2nd *s* of late Dr W. Carnegie Brown; *m* Irene, *e d* of Carl Hentschel; no *c. Educ:* Cheltenham College; Balliol College, Oxford. Entered Home Civil Service, 1913, but resigned to take up literary work; London dramatic critic and leader-writer for the Manchester Guardian, 1919-35; dramatic critic to Saturday Review, 1923-30; Observer, 1929-54; Week End Review, 1930-34; Sketch, 1935-39; Punch, 1940-42. Shute Lecturer in the Art of the Theatre at Liverpool Univ., 1926; Prof. of Drama, Royal Soc. of Literature, 1939; Director of Drama, Council for Encouragement of Music and the Arts, 1940-42; Editor of the Observer, 1942-48 Associate Editor and hon. director, 1948-54. Chm., The British Drama League, 1954-65; Governor: Old Vic; Royal Shakespeare Theatre. Hon. LLD: St Andrews, Aberdeen, 1950; Fell. Inst. of Journalists, 1951. Knight of Dannebrog, Denmark, 1949. *Publications:* (novels) Years of Plenty, 1915; Security, 1916; Lighting-up Time, 1920; Marine Parade, 1932; (politics) The Meaning of Democracy, 1919; English Political Theory, 1920; (essays) H. G. Wells, 1922; Masques and Phases, 1926; First Player, 1927; Parties of the Play, 1928; Now on View, 1929; Brown Studies, 1930; I Commit to the Flames, 1934; Master Sanguine, 1934; The Heart of England, 1935; The Great and the Goods, 1937; Life Within Reason, 1939; Amazing Monument (part author), 1939; A Word in Your Ear, 1942; Just Another Word, 1943; I Give You My Word, 1945; Say the Word, 1947; No Idle Words, 1948; Shakespeare, 1949; Having the Last Word, 1950; Winter in London, 1951; I Break My Word, 1951; Summer in Scotland, 1952; A Word in Edgeways, 1953; The Way of My World, 1954; Balmoral, 1955; Chosen Words, 1955; Theatre (1955), 1956; Theatre (1956), 1957; Dark

Ladies, 1957; Words in Our Time, 1958; London 1960; Shakespeare in His Time, 1960; Words in Season, 1961; Mind Your Language, 1962; How Shakespeare Spent the Day, 1963; Dickens in His Time, 1963; (ed) A Book of Marriage, 1963; Shakespeare and His World, 1964; What is a Play?, 1964; Bernard Shaw in His Time, 1965; Dr Johnson and His World, 1965; A History of London (illustrated) 1965; A Ring of Words, 1967; The Women in Shakespeare's Life, 1968; A Rhapsody of Words, 1969; Shakespeare and the Actors, 1970; Somerset Maugham: a Profile, 1970; Dickens and His World, 1970; Old and Young: a personal summing up, 1971; Conan Doyle and Sherlock Holmes, 1972; A Charm of Names, 1972; Words on the Level, 1973. *Address:* 20 Christchurch Hill, NW3. *Clubs:* Garrick, Savile.   [Died 22 April 1974.

BROWN, J. H.; *see* Hullah-Brown.

BROWN, Dr James Arthur Kinnear, CMG 1967; Senior Consultant, Uganda, since 1951; Grantee, Medical Research Council, since 1963; *b* 2 Sept. 1902; *s* of Arthur Kinnear Brown and Ethel (*née* Payling); *m* 1929, Hilda Kirkland, SRN, SCM; one *s* one *d. Educ:* Hymers Coll., Hull; Manchester and Liverpool Universities. BSc Hons Chem., Manchester, 1924; MRCS England, LRCP London, 1929; MB, ChB, Manchester, 1929; DTM&H, Liverpool, 1930; MD, Manchester, 1934. Actg Supt, Itu Leprosy Settlement, Nigeria, 1930; Founder, Uzuakoli Leprosy Settlement, Nigeria, 1930, Supt 1930-36; clinical practice, Altrincham, Ches., 1937-51; Sen. Specialist Leprosy, Uganda, 1951; Mem. WHO Expert Cttee, 1957; Hon. Life Mem., Brit. Red Cr., 1946. FRSTM&H, 1930. *Publications:* chapter in Diseases of Children in Tropics and Subtropics (by Trowell and Jelliffe), 1957; Leprosy (Techn. Information Series, Uganda), 1962; about 60 papers in Internat. Jl Leprosy, Leprosy Review, Central Afr. Jl Medicine, E. African Med. Jl, Lancet, BMJ. *Recreations:* golf, bridge. *Address:* Leicester Road, Hale, Ches. *T:* Altrincham 4470. *Club:* (Life Mem.) Manchester University Union.   [Died 28 Sept. 1971.

BROWN, Sir James (Raitt), Kt 1948; Third Church Estates Commissioner, 1954-62, retired; a Vice-Patron SPCK, since 1973 (Vice-President and Member, Board of Governors, 1958-72); a Trustee of Toc H since 1954; *b* 9 May 1892; *s* of James Brown and Margaret Laing (*d* 1971), *d* of David Raitt; *m* 1926, Joanna Martin (*d* 1971), *d* of late Lewis Bennett. *Educ:* Merchant Taylors' School, London. Junior Clerk, Ecclesiastical Commission, 1912; Secretary, 1937; Steward of the Manors, 1937; Financial Adviser, 1944; Secretary of Church Comrs for England, 1948-54. Member, Church Assembly (co-opted), 1955-65. Chm., Ecclesiastical Insurance Office Ltd, 1961-71. A Governor, Westfield Coll., Univ. of London, 1954-69; Trustee, City Parochial Foundn, 1963-69; Trustee, Highgate Literary and Scientific Instn (Pres., 1954-73), and Trustee of other local educnl trusts. Served European War, 1914-19, First Surrey Rifles (TA) and Oxford and Buckinghamshire LI (despatches twice). LLD (Lambeth), 1962. *Publication:* Number One, Millbank, 1944. *Address:* Homfray House, 4 Broadlands Road, Highgate, N6 4AS. *T:* 01-340 6147. *Clubs:* Athenæum; Highgate Golf (Highgate).   [Died 29 Dec. 1979.

BROWN, John, CBE 1955 (MBE 1918); MC 1917; retired; *b* 29 March 1890; *s* of Hugh Brown and Maggie Gibb; *m* 1919. *Educ:* Universities of Glasgow and Göttingen MA, BSc 1911; LLD (Glasgow) 1953. Assistant to the Professor of Natural Philosophy, Glasgow University, 1912; Assistant Master, Bellahouston Academy, Glasgow, 1913-19; District Inspector, LCC, 1919-25; Assistant Education Officer, LCC, 1925-36; Chief Inspector, LCC, 1936-47; Deputy Education Officer, LCC, 1947-51; Education Officer, LCC, 1951-Sept. 1956. Served European War, 1915-19 (despatches twice); in Royal Flying Corps and Royal Air Force, in France, Egypt and Palestine. *Publication:* Teaching Science in Schools, 1926. *Recreations:* golf, bowls, gardening. *Address:* 74 Ryecroft Road, SW16. *T:* 01-670 4542. *Club:* Royal Commonwealth Society.
[Died 24 Aug. 1977.

BROWN, Sir Kenneth (Alfred Leader), Kt 1963; *b* 26 Jan. 1906; *s* of late Henry Robert Brown; *m* 1st, 1931, Emily Agnes (*d* 1967), *d* of W. J. Pugsley; two *s* one *d*; 2nd, 1977, Mrs Michael Mary Turpin, widow, York House, Druids Lodge, Salisbury. *Educ:* Worcester Cathedral King's School. Marine Engineer and Surveyor; Company Director. Mem., Guild of Air Pilots and Navigators. *Recreations:* shooting, fishing. *Address:* Knowle House, Freshford, Bath BA3 6ED. *Clubs:* Constitutional, Bristol, University (all Bristol).   [Died 5 July 1978.

BROWN, Air Vice-Marshal Sir Leslie Oswald, KCB 1948 (CB 1945); CBE 1941; DSC 1916; AFC 1918; *b* Durban, 11 June 1893; *m* 1926, P. M. Widowson (whom he divorced); one *s*; *m*

1945, Irene, *widow* of H. F. Seymour, MD, FRCS, FRCOG. *Educ:* Hilton College, Natal, South Africa. South African Defence Force (Artillery) commencement of 1914-18 war served in German West Africa, 1914-15; commissioned Royal Naval Air Service, Oct. 1915; served in France and East Africa (DSC, despatches, AFC); RAF Staff College, 1929; served in India commanding 20 Squadron and at Karachi, 1930-35 commanded first Reconnaissance Wing at Odiham, 1936-38 Group Captain, 1939; served Middle East, Western Desert, Sept 1939-April 1941 (despatches); Air Commodore, 1941; AOC Levant, 1941, 1942 (despatches twice, Commander Greek Order of George I with cross swords); Acting Air Vice-Marshal, 1943 AOC No. 84 Group AEAF, 1943-44; Air Vice-Marshal, 1944 Commandant School of Land/Air Warfare, RAF, Old Sarum 1944-49; retired, 1949. King Haakon VII Liberty Medal *Address:* 149 North Ridge Road, Durban, S Africa. *T:* 882794 *Clubs:* RAF; Durban (Durban).   [Died 28 June 1978

BROWN, Sir Lindor; *see* Brown, Sir G. L.

BROWN, Lieut-Col Sir Norman S. S.; *see* Seddon-Brown.

BROWN, Pamela Mary; actress; *b* 8 July 1917; *d* of late George Edward Brown and of Helen Blanche Ellerton; *m* 1941, Peter Copley (marr. diss.). *Educ:* St Mary's Convent, Ascot; Royal Academy of Dramatic Art. First appearance Stratford Memorial Theatre (Juliet, Cressida, Jessica), then London, in The King and Mistress Shore, Little Theatre, 1936; toured S Africa, then at Open Air Theatre (Hermia), 1937; Rep. Oxford Playhouse and Perranporth Summer Theatre, then in The Heart was no Burned (Fanny Brawne), Gate Theatre, 1938; joined Old Vic (Constance Neville in She Stoops to Conquer, Bianca in The Taming of the Shrew); then Perranporth, 1939; Oxford Playhouse (Hedda Gabler, Nina in The Seagull, Ann Pedersdotter in The Witch, Lady Teazle, Juliet), 1940-41; toured in Golden Boy, then Claudia in Claudia, St Martin's, 1942 Ophelia in Hamlet, New, then Madeleine in Madeleine, Lyric Hammersmith, 1944; Theatre Royal, Bristol, (Lady Macbeth) 1946; Goneril in King Lear, New, 1946; toured America with John Gielgud, 1947; Janet Spence in The Gioconda Smile, New 1948; Jennet in The Lady's Not for Burning, Globe, and Royale (New York), 1949-51; Marie Chassaigne in The River Line Edinburgh Festival, 1952; Rachel Gardiner in A Question of Fact, Piccadilly, 1953; Miss Madrigal in The Chalk Garden Haymarket, 1956; Heartbreak House, 1959; This Year, Next Year, Vaudeville, 1960. *Films include:* One of Our Aircraft is Missing, 1941; I Know Where I'm Going, 1943; Tales of Hoffmann, 1950; Personal Affair, 1953; Richard III, 1955; Now and Forever, 1956; Lust for Life, 1957; Cleopatra, 1963; Becke 1964; A Funny Thing Happened on The Way to the Forum 1966; Secret Ceremony, 1969; Lady Caroline Lamb, 1972. BBC TV Series, Six Faces, 1972.   [Died 18 Sept. 197

BROWN, Prof. Robert J.; *see* Jardine-Brown.

BROWN, Robson Christie, MB, MS, FRCS, FRCOG; retire from practice; Hon. Consulting Gynæcologist: St Mary's Group of Hospitals, W2; Samaritan Hospital, W1; City of London Maternity Hospital, N7; Metropolitan Hospital, N8; Trustee, C B. Medical Research Fund; *b* 13 July 1898; *o* *s* of late Robson Brown and Ann H. Christie; *m* Mildred (*d* 1970), *d* of late J. H Warrington, Redbourn; one *s. Educ:* Royal Kepier Grammar School; Durham University. MB, BS (Hons.) 1920, Goyder Scholar, Phillipson Scholar, Gibson Prize; MS, FRCS 1924 Formerly: Obstetric Tutor: Leeds University; London Hospital Medical School; Demonstrator in Pharmacology, London Hospital Medical School; late Cons. Gynæcologist, West End Hospital for Nervous Diseases; Examiner to Central Midwive Board; Examiner to Royal College of Obstetricians and Gynæcologists. Foundation Member of College Obstetrician and Gynæcologists. *Publications:* Textbook on Midwifery (jointly); Common Gynæcological Conditions and The Treatment, 1935; Reproduction and Survival, 1948; articles in professional journals. *Recreations:* photography and entomology. *Address:* 15 Rothesay Drive, Highcliffe-on-Sea Christchurch, Hants. *T:* Highcliffe 3540. [Died 13 Dec. 197

BROWN, Spencer C.; *see* Curtis Brown.

BROWN, William, FRS 1938; MA (Edinburgh), DSc (London Emeritus Professor of Plant Pathology, University of London since 1953; *b* Dumfriesshire, 1888; *s* of Gavin and Margaret Brown; *m* Lucy Doris Allen (*d* 1966); one *s* three *d. Educ* Annan Academy; Edinburgh University. After graduation, did research at Imperial College of Science. Subsequently carried c investigations for Department of Scientific and Industria Research and for Ministry of Agriculture; Assistant Professor Imperial College, 1923; Professor, 1928-53, and Head

Botanical Dept, 1938-53. *Publications:* Papers in various scientific journals; article, Plant Pathology, in Encyclopædia Britannica. *Recreation:* gardening. *Address:* 93 Church Road, Hanwell, W7. *[Died 18 Jan. 1975.*

BROWN, William John, MC 1943; Vice President of the Law Society, 1977; Partner, Bristows Cooke & Carpmael; *b* 18 July 1911; *s* of John Brown and Edith Mary Stevens; *m* 1950, Jenifer Chesterman; one *s* two *d. Educ:* Magdalen Coll. Sch., Oxford. Solicitor. Employed by Westminster Bank, 1928-30; taught in prep. school while reading for the Bar, 1931-34; called to the Bar, Gray's Inn, 1934; Asst to J. W. Robertson-Scott on the Countryman, 1935; produced Law Journal, 1935-39. War of 1939-45: served in 2nd Bn Scots Guards (Major), N Africa and Italy. Qualified as Solicitor and joined firm of Bristows Cooke & Carpmael, 1946. Mem., Scott-Henderson Cttee on Cruelty to Wild Animals, 1949. Mem. Council, Law Soc., 1962; Dep. Chm., Council of Law Reporting, 1967; Chm. Governors, Coll. of Law, 1972-77. Dir, BPB Industries Ltd. *Publications:* The Gods had Wings, 1936, 1938; Cartel Law of the EEC, 1963; contribs to The Field as legal correspondent. *Recreations:* reading, hill-walking, growing vegetables. *Address:* The Vane, The Avenue, Northwood, Middlesex. *T:* Northwood 26494. *Club:* Bath. *[Died 4 Dec. 1977.*

BROWN, Sir William R.; see Robson Brown.

BROWNE, E(lliott) Martin, CBE 1952; FRSL 1955; DLitt Lambeth, 1971; *b* 29 Jan. 1900; *s* of Lieut-Col Percy J. Browne, CB, and Bernarda Gracia (*née* Lees); *m* 1st, 1924, Henzie Raeburn (*d* 1973); two *s*; 2nd, 1974, Audrey (*née* Tuck), widow of John Rideout. *Educ:* Eton; Christ Church, Oxford. Warden of Educational Settlement, Doncaster, 1924-26; Assistant Professor of Drama, Carnegie Institute of Technology, Pittsburgh, Pa, 1927-30; first Director of Religious Drama, Diocese of Chichester, 1930-34; Producer (London and New York), including all the plays of T. S. Eliot and many of Christopher Fry, since 1934; Director, the Pilgrim Players, including three seasons of New Plays by Poets at Mercury Theatre, 1939-48; Director, British Drama League, 1948-57; revived York Cycle of Mystery Plays at York, 1951-54-57-66; Visiting Professor in Religious Drama, Union Theological Seminary, New York, 1956-62; Hon. Drama Adviser to Coventry Cathedral, 1962-65. Danforth Visiting Lecturer to American Colleges, 1962-65. Directed Murder in the Cathedral, Canterbury Cathedral, 1970. President, RADIUS (The Religious Drama Society of Great Britain), 1960-80. *Publication:* The Making of T. S. Eliot's Plays, 1969. *Address:* 20 Lancaster Grove, NW3 4PB. *T:* 01-794 4322. *Club:* Garrick. *[Died 27 April 1980.*

BROWNE, Prof. John Campbell McClure, CBE 1975; FRCOG, FRCSE; retired; *b* 7 Feb. 1912; *s* of late Prof. F. J. Browne; *m* 1940, Veronica Evelyn Partridge; one *s* one *d. Educ:* Edinburgh Academy; University College, London University (BSc Hons 1934; MB, BS 1938). MRCOG 1948; FRCOG 1954; FRCSEd 1948. Qualified 1937; served War of 1939-45; RAFVR, 1939-46 (despatches twice). Asst Lectr, 1948; Prof. of Obstetrics and Gynaecology, Univ. of London, at Royal Postgraduate Medical Sch. and Inst. of Obstetrics and Gynæcology, 1952-77; Consultant Obstetrician and Gynæcologist, Hammersmith Hosp., 1948-77. Hon. Fellow: American Assoc. of Obstetricians and Gynæcologists (Joseph Price Orator, 1962); Finnish Gynæcological Assoc.; Hon. Mem. Ankara Gynæcological Assoc.; Hon. For. Mem., Royal Belgian Soc. of Obstetricians and Gynæcologists. *Publications:* Co-author Antenatal and Postnatal Care, 11th edn 1978; Postgraduate Obstetrics and Gynæcology, 4th edn 1973; numerous articles in medical jls. *Address:* Barn End, Castle Lane, Bramber, Steyning, West Sussex BN4 3FB. *Clubs:* Royal Air Force, Anglo-Belgian. *[Died 23 July 1978.*

BROWNE, John Edward Stevenson, CBE 1969; QPM 1959; Chief Constable, Nottinghamshire Combined Constabulary, 1968-70, retired; *b* 27 June 1910; *s* of late Edward Dennis Browne, OBE; *m* 1st, 1936, Muriel May (*d* 1966), *d* of late William Ashcroft Lambert, Sheffield; two *s*; 2nd, 1966, Mrs Sylvia Millicent Goodhew. *Educ:* Imperial Service Coll., Windsor. Joined Sheffield Police, 1930; Chief Constable, Scarborough, 1943-47; Asst Chief Constable, North Riding of Yorks, 1947-49; Chief Constable, Nottinghamshire, 1949-68 (seconded as Chief Constable, Cyprus, 1958-59). *Recreations:* gardening, shooting. *Address:* Wheathill, Goathland, near Whitby, North Yorks. *T:* Goathland 303. *Club:* Forty. *[Died 29 Oct. 1976.*

BROWNE, Martin; see Browne, E. M.

BROWNE, Most Rev. Michael, DD, DCL, LLD; *s* of Michael Browne, Westport, Co. Mayo. *Educ:* St Jariath's Coll., Tuam; St Patrick's Coll., Maynooth. BA Hons Classics, National Univ. of Ireland, 1916; ordained, 1920; DD Rome, 1921; DCL 1924; Prof. of Theology, Maynooth, 1921-37; Sec. Maynooth Union, 1929-37; Mem. of Senate, Nat. University of Ireland, 1934-76; Bishop of Galway and Kilmacduagh, 1937-76; Apostolic Administrator of Kilfenora, 1937-76. Hon. LLD Nat. Univ. of Ireland, 1971. Freedom of Galway City, 1973. Retired, 1976. *Publications:* various articles in Irish Ecclesiastical Record on Theological subjects. *Address:* St Anne's, Maunsell's Road, Galway. *[Died 23 Feb. 1980.*

BROWNE, Cardinal, His Eminence Michael (David), DD; LLD; OP; *b* Grangemockler, Co. Tipperary, 6 May 1887; *s* of Maurice Browne and Catherine Browne (*née* Fitzgerald). *Educ:* Rockwell College, Cashel, Ireland; St Mary's, Tallaght, Ireland; Collegio S. Tommaso, Rome; the Angelicum, Rome; University of Fribourg, Switzerland. Master of Novices, St Mary's, Tallaght, 1915-19; Professor of Philosophy, the Angelicum, Rome, 1919-32; Rector of the Angelicum, 1932-41; Professor of Theology, the Angelicum, Rome, 1932-51; Master of the Sacred Palace, Vatican City, Rome, 1951-55; Master General of Order of Preachers, 1955-62. Grand Chancellor, the Angelicum, Rome, 1955-62; Cardinal, 1962; consecrated as titular Archbishop of Idelbesso, 1962. Hon. LLD; National University of Ireland, 1954; Univ. of Ottawa, 1955; of Lauras Coll., Dubuque, 1955; Hon. DD, Santo Tomás, Manila, 1958. *Publications:* Contributions to Revue Thomiste, Angelicum, Sapienza, on questions of philosophy and theology. *Address:* Piazza del S. Uffizio 11, Rome (Borghi), Italy. *[Died 31 March 1971.*

BROWNE, Prof. Richard Charles, MA, DM, FRCP; Nuffield Professor of Industrial Health, University of Newcastle upon Tyne, 1946-76, retired; Chairman, Division of Social Medicine, University of Newcastle upon Tyne, 1970-75; Consultant Physician, Department of Industrial Health, Royal Victoria Infirmary, Newcastle upon Tyne; *b* 6 May 1911; *s* of Dr Frederick William and Edith Maud Darvel Browne; *m* 1941, Barbara, *o d* of late Ebenezer Cunningham, Fellow of St John's Coll., Cambridge, and Ada Collins; one *s* three *d. Educ:* Clifton; Wadham College, Oxford; Oxford and Bristol Medical Schools. BA honours in human physiology, 1934; Theodore Williams Scholar in Pathology, 1935-36; BM and MA 1937; House Appts, Depts of Medicine, Univs of Oxford and Bristol; MRCP 1940; FRCP 1964; DM Oxon, 1946. Hon. FFOM. Research Asst and Registrar, Dept of Medicine, Oxford; MRC Grant, 1940; Sqdn Ldr (Research Specialist), RAF Medical Br. Nuffield Visitor in Industrial Health to East and Central Africa, 1949 and 1952. Regional Med. Adviser, CEGB, 1948-77; Main Bd Med. Industrial Consultant, CEGB, 1970-77. Dir, N of England Industrial Health Service, 1960-76. Council of Europe Fellow in Medicine, 1961; WHO Consultant, 1965. British Editor, Internat. Archives of Occupational Health, 1974-. Lectures: Ernestine Henry, RCP, 1964; John Holmes Meml, Univ. of Newcastle upon Tyne, 1969; Apothecaries', Soc. of Occupational Medicine, 1972; Pres., Sect. of Occupational Medicine, RSM, 1970. Church Warden, 1966-68, and Vice-Chm., 1976-78, Parochial Church Council, St Andrews, Corbridge, 1966-68. *Publications:* Health in Industry, 1961; Chemistry and Therapy of Industrial Pulmonary Disease, 1965; articles in British Medical Jl, Lancet and British Journal of Industrial Medicine. *Recreations:* fell walking, swimming, gardening, photography. *Address:* Sele House, Dunkirk Terrace, Corbridge on Tyne NE45 5AQ. *[Died 3 March 1980.*

BROWNE, Ven. Thomas Robert; Archdeacon of Ipswich, 1946-63, now Archdeacon Emeritus; *b* 15 June 1889; *s* of Horace Browne, London, and Jessie Drury; *m* 1915, Ellen Gertrude Fowler. *Educ:* King's College, University of London. Captain 3rd Battalion Dorsetshire Regt, 1914-19; Deacon, 1919; Priest, 1920; Curate of Christ Church, West Green, Tottenham, 1919-23; Vicar of Edwardstone, Suffolk, 1923-28; Rector of Earl Soham, Suffolk, 1928-36; Vicar of All Saints, Newmarket, Suffolk, 1936-46; Rector of Elmsett and Aldham, Suffolk, 1946-56. Canon of St Edmundsbury, Ipswich, 1936-46; Rural Dean of Hadleigh, 1946-49; Rector of Shotley, Suffolk, 1956-64. FKC, 1957. *Recreations:* tennis and bowls. *Address:* Manormead, Nursing Home Wing, Tilford Road, Hindhead, Surrey GU26 6RA. *[Died 13 Aug. 1978.*

BROWNE, Lt-Col William Percy, MC; DL; *b* 22 March 1893; *s* of Col Percy Browne, CB, Fifehead Magdalen, Dorset; *m* 1st, 1921, Richenda Margaret (*d* 1953), 2nd *d* of Basil Hoare, Sutton Veny, Wilts, and 6 Lowndes Street, SW; three *s*; 2nd, 1954, Sheelagh, *d* of John McClintock, Willey Place, Farnham, Surrey. *Educ:* Eton; Sandhurst. Joined The Royals, 1913; served European War with the Regiment (wounded at Ypres, 1914, despatches, MC); MFH The Portman, 1920-30 and 1932-39; MFH Stevenstone, 1946-49. DL Dorset, 1957. *Recreation:* fox-hunting. *Address:* Higher Houghton, Blandford, Dorset. *TA* and *T:* Milton-Abbas 256. *[Died 6 Jan. 1972.*

BROWNING, Amy Katherine, RP, ROI, ARCA; 2nd *d* of J. D. Browning; *m* 1916, T. C. Dugdale, RA, RP (*d* 1952). *Educ:* Privately. Studied painting, Royal College of Art and Paris; exhibits regularly in Royal Academy, New English Art Club, and other London Exhibitions; one-man show Fine Art Society, 1925; Smiths Gallery, Manchester, 1935; leading provincial exhibitions; Pittsburgh; Salon des Artistes Français, Silver Medal, Gold Medal, HC, two pictures purchased by Luxembourg Gallery; represented in permanent collections, Glasgow, Southport, Manchester, Wolverhampton, National Gallery, Wellington, NZ, Luton; figure subjects, plein air, portraits, flowers. *Recreations:* gardening and open air. *Address:* 58 Glebe Place, SW3. *T:* 01-352 9969. *[Died 27 Jan. 1978.*

BROWNING, Professor Andrew, MA Glasgow and Oxon, DLitt Glasgow, FBA 1955; Professor of History, Glasgow University, 1931-Sept. 1957, retired; *b* 28 March 1889. *Educ:* Glasgow Univ. and Balliol College, Oxon. *Publications:* Thomas Osborne, Earl of Danby and Duke of Leeds, 1944-51, etc. Editor of Memoirs of Sir John Reresby, 1936; English Historical Documents, Vol. VIII (1660-1714), 1953. *Address:* Durie House, Helensburgh, Dunbartonshire. *[Died 8 May 1972.*

BROWNING, Prof. Carl Hamilton, FRS 1928; MD; LLD; FRCP (Glas.); FRCPath; *b* 1881. *Educ:* Glasgow Academy and University. MB, ChB with honours, 1903; Carnegie Travelling Fellowship in Pathology, 1904; MD with honours (Bellahouston gold medal for Thesis), 1907 (Glasgow); DPH (Oxon), 1913, LLD, 1935 (St Andrews), 1952 (Glasgow). Official Asst to Prof. Ehrlich, Frankfurt-am-Main, 1906-07; Director of the Bland-Sutton Institute of Pathology, the Middlesex Hosp., 1914-19; Prof. of Bacteriology, Univ. of London; Gardiner Professor of Bacteriology, Glasgow University and Western Infirmary, 1919-51; Cameron prize, Edinburgh University, 1936. *Publications:* Chemotherapy in Trypanosome Infections, 1908; Studies in Immunity (jointly), 1909; Recent Advances in the Diagnosis and Treatment of Syphilis (jointly), 1924; Applied Bacteriology, 1918; Immunochemical Studies, 1925; Textbook of Bacteriology (11 edn. of Muir and Ritchie's Manual) (jointly), 1949; Chemotherapy with Antibacterial Dyestuffs in Experimental Chemotherapy, vol. 2, 1964; studies on chemotherapy, etc., in various scientific journals, etc. *Address:* c/o Bacteriological Laboratory, Shelley Road, Glasgow, W2. *[Died 22 Jan. 1972.*

BROWNING, Maj.-Gen. Langley, CB 1944; OBE 1919; MC 1915; psc; *b* 28 July 1891; *s* of late Lieut-Col W. B. Browning, CIE, IMS, Cregg, Fermoy, Co. Cork; *m* 1915, Violet, *d* of Alan Thomas Cairnes, The Glen, Drogheda, Co. Meath; one *s* one *d*. *Educ:* Tonbridge (scholar); RMA Woolwich. Joined RA 1911; served European War, 1914-19 (despatches, Croce di Guerra); NW Frontier Campaign, 1930; Brevet Lieut-Col 1933; Instructor Staff College, 1933-35; Colonel, 1936; GSO1, 1938-39; Acting Maj.-Gen., Inspector of the Royal Artillery, 1939-40; Maj.-Gen. 1941; GOC 10 AA Div., 1940-42; GOC RA Training Establishments and MGRA Training, 1942-44; GOC military mission to the Italian Army, 1944-46; retired pay, 1946. Hon. Citizen of Texas, 1946; USA Legion of Merit (Commander), 1946; Knight Grand Cross of the Crown of Italy, 1946; Cross of Merit, 1st Cl., Sovereign Military Order of Malta, 1946; despatches. *Recreations:* fishing, shooting, golf. *Address:* c/o Bank of Ireland, Ballsbridge, Dublin 4. *[Died 19 April 1974.*

BROWNING, Robert, CBE 1961; President, Institute of Chartered Accountants of Scotland, 1965-66 (Vice-President 1964-65); Partner John E. Watson & Co., CA, Glasgow, 1927-69, retired; *b* 26 Aug. 1902; *s* of George Browning and Helen Macmillan; *m* 1932, Christina Wallace Freebairn; one *s* one *d*. *Educ:* Glasgow High Sch.; Univ. of Glasgow. MA (1923) LLB (1925), CA (1926). Mem. Chartered Accountants of Scotland General Examining Board, 1938-44. Member Council of Institute of Chartered Accountants of Scotland, 1952-56; Member Cumbernauld Development Corporation, 1956-58; Chairman, East Kilbride Development Corporation, 1958-69; Director: Clydesdale Bank Ltd, 1957-69; Malcolm Campbell Ltd, 1940-69. Chairman: Glasgow Univ. Graduates Assoc., 1947-52; Glasgow County Scout Council, 1947-52 (and Pres., 1965-69); Member, Royal Commission on the Press, 1961-62; Professor of Accountancy, University of Glasgow, 1950-64. *Publication:* Legal Notes for CA Students, 1931. *Recreations:* golf, fishing. *Address:* 16 West Chapelton Avenue, Bearsden, Glasgow G61 2DQ. *T:* 041-942 0108. *[Died 7 Aug. 1974.*

BROWNJOHN, General Sir Nevil (Charles Dowell), GBE 1957 (OBE 1941); KCB 1951 (CB 1944); CMG 1949; MC 1917; *b* 25 July 1897; *s* of Arthur Dowell Brownjohn, Richmond, Surrey, and Repton; *m* 1929, Isabelle White; one *s*. *Educ:* Malvern Coll.; RMA, Woolwich. Commissioned in RE, 1915. Served European War, 1916-18, with RE Signals (MC); Palestine, 1938; Dep. Military Governor, Control Commission for Germany (British Element), 1947-49; Vice-Quarter-Master-General, War Office, 1949-50; Vice-Chief of the Imperial General Staff, War Office, 1950-52; Chief Staff Officer, Ministry of Defence, Dec. 1952-55; QMG, WO, 1956-58, retd; ADC Gen. to the Queen, 1957-58; Chm. Crawley Development Corp., 1960-62; Member, Commission for the New Towns, 1962-65; President, Malvernian Society, 1964-67; Council, Trust Houses Group Ltd; Chm. Housing Assoc. for Officers' Families. Col Commandant, RE, 1955-62. US Legion of Merit (Comdr) and Medal of Freedom. *Club:* Naval and Military. *[Died 21 April 1973.*

BROWNLOW, 6th Baron, *cr* 1776; **Peregrine Francis Adelbert Cust;** Bt 1677; *b* 27 April 1899; *o s* of 5th Baron and Maud, *d* of Capt. S. Buckle, RE; *S* father, 1927; *m* 1st, 1927, Katherine Hariot (*d* 1952), *y d* of Brig.-Gen. Sir David Kinloch, 11th Bt; one *s* one *d*; 2nd 1954, Mrs Dorothy Power Beatty (*d* 1966), Broomfield House, Ashford, Co. Wicklow; 3rd, 1969, Leila, widow of 2nd Baron Manton. *Educ:* Eton; Royal Military College, Sandhurst. Served European War, 1918; entered Grenadier Guards 1918; Adjutant of the 3rd Battalion, 1923-26; sometime ADC to the GOC London District; resigned, 1926; joined Royal Air Force VR as Flight Lieut, 1939; Parliamentary Private Secretary to Lord Beaverbrook, Minister of Aircraft Production, 1940; attached Bomber Command, 1941; Staff Officer to Air Vice-Marshal J. Slessor, Assistant Chief of Air Staff, 1942, and to Deputy Chief of Staff 8th US Air Force, 1943; resigned comm. with rank of Sqn Leader, 1944. Personal Lord in Waiting to King Edward VIII, 1936; Lord Lieut and Custos Rotulorum of Lincolnshire, 1936-50; JP and DL for Lincs; Mayor of Grantham, 1934-35. *Heir:* s Hon. Edward John Peregrine Cust [*b* 25 March 1936; *m* 1964, Shirlie, *d* of John Yeomans, Upton-on-Severn, Worcs; one *s*]. *Address:* 2 Belgrave Mews West, SW1; Belton House, Grantham, Lincs. *T:* Grantham 3278; The Great House, Roaring River, Jamaica, West Indies; Sagesse Estates, St Davids, Grenada, West Indies. *Clubs:* White's; Travellers' (Paris). *[Died 28 July 1978.*

BRUCE, David (Kirkpatrick Este); US Ambassador to NATO, 1974-76; *b* 12 Feb. 1898; *s* of William Cabell Bruce and Louise Este Bruce (*née* Fisher); *m* 1st, 1926, Ailsa Mellon (*d* 1969); one *d* (decd); 2nd, 1945, Evangeline Bell; two *s* (and one *d* decd). *Educ:* Princeton Univ.; Univ. of Virginia; Univ. of Maryland. Served in US Army, 1917-19 and 1942-45. Admitted to Maryland Bar, 1921; Member Maryland House of Delegates, 1924-26; practised law in Baltimore, Md, 1921-25; Amer. Vice-Consul, Rome, 1926-28; engaged in business and farming, 1928-40; Mem. Virginia House of Delegates, 1939-42; Chief Rep. in Gt Brit. for Amer. Red Cross, 1940; with Office of Strategic Services, 1941-45 (Dir European Theater of Ops, 1943-45); Asst Sec. of Commerce, 1947-48; Chief, Econ. Co-op. Admin. to France, 1948-49; US Ambassador to France, 1949-52; Under Secretary of State, 1952-53; apptd Special US Observer at interim cttee of European Defense Community, 1953; Special Amer. Rep. to European High Authority for Coal and Steel, 1953-54; US Ambassador to: Federal Republic of Germany, 1957-59; UK, 1961-69; US Rep., Vietnam Peace Talks, Paris, 1970-71; Chief, US Mission to Peoples' Republic of China, 1973-74. Hon. CBE (mil.) 1945; military decorations from USA, France, Poland, Norway, Czechoslovakia, Denmark. *Publication:* Sixteen American Presidents, 1938. *Address:* 1405 34th Street NW, Washington, DC 20007, USA. *Clubs:* Buck's, White's, Brooks's, Turf; Jockey (Paris), Travellers' (Paris); various (USA). *[Died 5 Dec. 1977.*

BRUCE, George Gordon, MB, ChB Aberdeen, LRCP, FRCS, FRCSE; Extra Surgeon to the Queen in Scotland since 1961 (formerly Surgeon to King George VI, and to the Queen, 1952-61, in Scotland); Surgeon, EMS; retd as Surgeon Aberdeen Royal Infirmary, 1957; *b* 25 Aug. 1891; *s* of George Bruce, Tochineal, Cullen; *m* 1st, 1917; one *d*; 2nd, 1947, Jane Ann Gill (*d* 1973), Glenlea, Hopeman, Morayshire. *Educ:* Fordyce Academy; Aberdeen University; St Mary's and St Bartholomew's Hospitals, London. MB, ChB, with Distinction and Keith Gold Medallist in Surgery in 1915; House Surgeon, Aberdeen Royal Infirmary: Active Service, 1915-19 (despatches); FRCS (Eng.), 1921; University Assistant in Surgery, 1929-33; Surgeon to Royal Aberdeen Hospital for Sick Children until 1950; Lecturer and Examiner in Clinical Surgery, University of Aberdeen. *Publications:* numerous papers on surgical subjects. *Recreations:* shooting, fishing. *Address:* 5 Rubislaw Place, Aberdeen AB1 1XN. *T:* Aberdeen 23028. *Club:* University (Aberdeen). *[Died 6 June 1976.*

BRUCE, Mrs H. J.; *see* Karsavina, Tamara.

BRUCE, Captain Sir Hervey John William, 6th Bt, *cr* 1804; late Royal Scots Greys; *b* 29 June 1919; *s* of 5th Bt and Margaret Florence (she *m* 2nd, 1925, Lieut-Col C. O. Morris), *d* of Rev. Robert Jackson, Rector of Little Thurlow, Newmarket; *S* father, 1924; *m* 1949, Mrs Innes Ker; one *s* one *d. Educ:* Eton; RMC. *Heir: s* Hervey James Hugh Bruce, *b* 4 Sept. 1952. *Address:* Boyarin Lodge, Newmarket, Suffolk.   [*Died* 20 *June* 1971.

BRUCE, Sir John, Kt 1963; CBE 1945; TD 1946; FRSE 1963; FRCSE 1931; Honorary Surgeon to the Queen in Scotland, since 1960; Emeritus Professor of Clinical Surgery, Edinburgh University; Consultant Emeritus to the Army, 1971; *b* 6 March 1905; *m* 1935, Mary Whyte Craig. *Educ:* Edinburgh Univ. (MB, ChB Hons 1928). Served War of 1939-45 with RAMC: Norway, 1940 (despatches); Brig.-Consulting Surgeon, 14th Army, SEAC, 1943; Burma, 1945 (despatches). Asst Surgeon, Royal Infirmary, Edinburgh, 1935-46; Lectr on Surgery, Edinburgh Univ., and Surgeon, Western Gen. Hosp., 1946-56; Regius Prof. of Clinical Surgery, Edinburgh Univ., 1956-70. Consulting Surgeon, Scottish Comd; Member: Army Med. Adv. Bd; RAF Med. Adv. Bd. Editor, Jl of RCSE. President: RCSE, 1957-62; Assoc. of Surgeons of Great Britain and Ireland, 1965; (also Archivist) James IV Assoc. of Surgeons, 1966-69; British Cancer Council, 1968-; Eastern Surgical Soc. of America, 1966-67; Internat. Fedn of Surgical Colls. Visiting Professor: (Naffziger) Univ. of California, San Francisco, 1961; Univ. of Copenhagen, 1961; Univ. of Ohio, 1963; (Gunderson) Univ. of Wisconsin, 1964; Univ. of Cincinnati, 1964; (Sir Arthur Sims Commonwealth) Australasia, 1966. Lectures: Francis Shepherd, Montreal, 1951; Donald Balfour, Toronto, 1957; Mayo Foundn, Rochester, 1957; McMurray, Liverpool, 1960; Colles', RCSI, 1960; Phemister, Chicago, 1963; Sir John Marnoch, Aberdeen, 1964; Willis, Richmond, Va, 1964; Sir Gordon Gordon-Taylor, Edinburgh, 1965; Kenelm Digby, Hong Kong, 1969; McCombe, 1972, Thom, 1973, Fraser, 1975 (all Edinburgh). External Examiner in Surgery: NUI; Univs of Wales, Glasgow, Liverpool, Oxford, St Andrews, Hong Kong; formerly: RCSI; Coll. of Surgeons in Africa. Hon. Col, 205 (Scottish) Gen. Hosp. RAMC (Volunteers), T&AVR (formerly 205 Army Gen. Hosp.) 1967-71. Fellow, Assoc. of Surgeons of Great Britain and Ireland; FRSM. Hon. FACS 1957; Hon. FRCS 1960; Hon. FRACS; Hon. FRCPS; Hon. FRCSI; Hon. FCPSO(So. Af.); Hon. FRCS Canada; Hon. Fellow, Royal Coll. of Univ. Surgeons of Denmark. Hon. Member: Acad. of Medicine, Malaya, 1960 (AM Malaya); Amer. Surgical Assoc., 1961; Eastern Surgical Assoc., USA, 1964. Hon. DSc Pennsylvania; Hon. LLD Alberta, 1970. *Publications:* Manual of Surgical Anatomy, 2nd edn, 1964; contribs to surgical literature. *Recreation:* fishing. *Address:* St Bernard's Cottage, 11 Mackenzie Place, Edinburgh. *T:* 031-225 1426. *Clubs:* Athenæum, Royal Commonwealth Society; New (Edinburgh).   [*Died* 30 *Dec.* 1975.

BRUCE, Major-General (retired) John Geoffrey, CB 1944; DSO 1938; MC 1923; *b* 4 Dec. 1896; *s* of late Colonel Sir Gerald Bruce, KCB, CMG, DSO; *m* 1932, Marjorie Isabel Crump; two *d. Educ:* Rugby School. 2nd Lieut Glamorgan Yeomanry, Aug. 1914; served in Egypt and Palestine to 1918. Transferred to 6th Gurkha Rifles; served 3rd Afghan War, 1919; NW Frontier expeditions, 1920-23 and 1937-38; passed Staff College course, Quetta, 1927-28, RAF Staff College course, Andover, 1932, and Imperial Defence College, London, 1939. Instructor at Staff College, 1933-36; commanded 2nd Bn 6th Gurkha Rifles, 1937-38; Brig. General Staff, Norwegian Exped. Force and in France, 1940; commanded Infantry Brigade in India, 1940-41; Deputy Director of Military Operations, India, 1941-42; Maj.-General i/c British Military Mission to China, 1942; Maj.-General command in India, 1942-44; Deputy Chief General Staff, Indian Army, 1944-46; GOC Lahore District, 1946-47; retired 1948. Commandant Civil Defence Staff College, 1952-56. Member of Mount Everest Expeditions of 1922 and 1924 (MacGregor Memorial Medal and Olympic Gold Medal). Order of Star of Nepal (2nd class), 1946. *Recreations:* riding, shooting, tennis, mountaineering, and travel. *Address:* Queen's Haye, Colyton, Devon. *T:* Colyton 554. *Club:* United Service and Royal Aero.   [*Died* 31 *Jan.* 1972.

BRUCE, Robert Elton Spencer; Editor, Woman's Own, 1968-70; *b* 8 Feb. 1936; *s* of F. S. Bruce and A. B. Bruce (*née* Clarke); *m* 1961, Frances Ann Rosemary (*née* Marshall); two *s* one *d. Educ:* Christ's Hospital. Editor, Literary Quarterly, New Chapter, 1957-58. *Publications:* Escape and Surrender (poems) 1956; Permissive Paradise (with F. Habicht and H. Cremonesi), 1969. Contributor Contemporary Review. *Recreation:* philately. *Address:* Tauntons, 2 Whyteleafe Road, Caterham, Surrey. *T:* Caterham 45202.   [*Died* 22 *March* 1971.

BRUCE MITFORD, Terence; *see* Mitford, T. B.

BRUNDAGE, Avery; Engineer; Executive; amateur sportsman; President, Comité International Olympique, 1952-72; Chairman, President and Director of various corporations; *b* 28 Sept. 1887; *s* of Charles and Amelia Lloyd Brundage; *m* 1st, 1927, Elizabeth Dunlap (*d* 1971); 2nd, 1973, Princess Marianne Reuss. *Educ:* University of Illinois. Founder and President, Avery Brundage Company, 1915-47; President: US Olympic Association, 1929-53; Amateur Athletic Union of the US, 1928-37; Comité Deportivo Panamericano, 1940-52. Holds various awards from US organizations and many foreign decorations. *Publications:* numerous articles on Amateur Sport and the Olympic Movement, *Recreations:* Amateur All-around Champion of America, 1914-16-18; US Olympic Team, 1912. Collector of Oriental Art (Trustee, Art Institute of Chicago). *Address:* 10 North La Salle Street, Chicago, Illinois 60602, USA. *T:* State 2-6168. *Clubs:* Chicago Athletic Association, Chicago Engineers.   [*Died* 8 *May* 1975.

BRUNDRETT, Sir Frederick, KCB 1956 (CB 1946); KBE 1950; MA; retired as Scientific Adviser to Ministry of Defence and Chairman Defence Research Policy Committee (1954-Dec. 1959); Chairman, Air Traffic Control Board, since Nov. 1959; a Civil Service Commissioner, 1960-67; Chairman Naval Aircraft Research Committee, Aeronautical Research Council, 1960-66; *b* 25 Nov. 1894; *s* of Walter Brundrett, lately of Hinxhill, Kent, and Ada, *d* of James Richardson, Chorlton-cum-Hardy; *m* 1920, Enid, *d* of late George R. James, Cambridge; (only son killed in Italy 1944). *Educ:* Rossall School; Sidney Sussex College, Cambridge. Served in RNVR in European War, 1914-18. Joined Scientific Staff of Admiralty in 1919 and served in HM Signal School, Portsmouth, until 1937 when transferred to Headquarters. Chief of Royal Naval Scientific Service, 1947-50; Dep. Scientific Adviser, Ministry of Defence, 1950-54. Hon. Scientific Adviser to Ministry of Civil Aviation, 1953-59; Chairman, Civil Aviation Radio Advisory Cttee, 1958-60. Hon. Fellow, Sidney Sussex College, Cambridge, 1955. Governor: Rossall School, 1957-66; Prebendal School, Chichester, 1960; Navy League, 1960; Chairman of Trustees, Rural Industries Bureau, 1961-66; Member, White Fish Authority, 1961-73; Hon. Vice-Pres., Soc. for Underwater Technology, 1972; Chm. Board of Governors, Houghton Poultry Research Station, 1962-68; President, Agricultural Co-operative Assoc.; Chm., Council of Red and White Friesian Cattle Soc., 1967-; Director, Thames Valley Egg Ltd. Hon. DSc Manchester, 1967. *Recreations:* games of all kinds. Captain Hampshire County Hockey for many years. Captain British CS Hockey before the war and also played for Civil Service at cricket; farming and particularly animal breeding-Red and White Friesian cattle; Agricultural Co-operation; philately. *Address:* Field Side, Prinsted, Emsworth, Hants. *T:* and *TA:* Emsworth 5038. *Club:* United Oxford & Cambridge University.   [*Died* 1 *Aug.* 1974.

BRUNE, Sir Humphrey I. P.; *see* Prideaux-Brune.

BRUNSKILL, Muriel; contralto; *b* 18 Dec. 1899; *d* of Edmund Capstick Brunskill; *m* 1925, Robert Ainsworth (*d* 1947), conductor, pianist; two *s. Educ:* Kendal High School. Studied in London and Germany, pupil of Blanche Marchesi; debut, Aeolian Hall, 1920; sang with British National Opera Company at Covent Garden, His Majesty's Theatre, and provincial theatres, 1922-27; has sung regularly at Three Choirs, Handel, Norwich, and Leeds Festivals, etc., Royal Choral, Royal Philharmonic, Liverpool Philharmonic, and Hallé Societies, etc.; Toronto Symphony Orchestra and Canadian Tour, 1930; Cincinatti May Festival, 1931; Canadian Recitals, Chicago Symphony Orchestra and New York, 1932; Opera Seasons in Melbourne and Sydney and Concert Tour in Australia and New Zealand, 1934-35; frequent appearances in Holland; sang Tanta in Golden City, Adelphi Theatre, 1950. Gilbert and Sullivan Film, 1952; Gilbert and Sullivan Tour in Australia and New Zealand, 1956-57. *Address:* Downrew House, Bishops Tawton, Devon. *T:* Barnstaple 2497.   [*Died* 18 *Feb.* 1980.

BRUNTON, John Stirling, CB 1960; *b* 8 May 1903; *s* of John Brunton, Glasgow; *m* 1934, Mary G. Cameron, Bo'ness; one *s* one *d. Educ:* Albert Road Academy, Glasgow; Glasgow University. Appointed HM Inspector of Schools, 1932; seconded to Dept of Health for Scotland, for work on Emergency Hospital Scheme, 1939-42; HM Inspector in charge of counties of Stirling, Perth and Kinross, 1942-48; HM Inspector in charge of Glasgow, 1948-50; Assistant Secretary, Scottish Education Department, 1951-55; HM Senior Chief Inspector of Schools, Scottish Education Department, 1955-66, retd. Hon. Scottish Nat. Camps Assoc. *Recreations:* golf, motoring. *Address:* 1/12 Pentland Drive, Edinburgh EH10 6PU. *T:* 031-445 2848.   [*Died* 22 *Oct.* 1977.

BUCCLEUCH, 8th Duke of, *cr* 1663, 10th Duke of **QUEENSBERRY** (*cr* 1684); **Walter John Montagu-Douglas-Scott,** KT 1949; GCVO 1935; PC 1937; Baron Scott of Buccleuch, 1606; Earl of Buccleuch, Baron Scott of Whitchester and Eskdaill, 1619; Earl of Doncaster and Baron Tynedale (Eng.), 1662; Earl of Dalkeith, 1663; Marquis of Dumfriesshire, Earl of Drumlanrig and Sanquhar, Viscount of Nith, Torthorwold, and Ross, Baron Douglas, 1684; Lord Clerk Register of Scotland and Keeper of the Signet since 1956; HM Lieutenant of County of Roxburgh since 1932; Chancellor, Order of the Thistle, since 1966; DL Dumfriesshire; DL Selkirkshire; JP Roxburghshire and Dumfriesshire; Captain-General Royal Company of Archers; President: St Andrew's Ambulance Association; Scottish Landowners' Federation; Animal Diseases Research Association; Royal Scottish Agricultural Benevolent Institution; Commonwealth Forestry Association; Scottish Woodland Owners' Association; *b* 30 Dec. 1894; *e s* of 7th Duke and late Lady Margaret Alice Bridgeman, 2nd *d* of 4th Earl of Bradford; *S* father, 1935; *m* 1921, Vreda Esther Mary, *er d* of late Major W. F. Lascelles and Lady Sybil Lascelles, *d* of 10th Duke of St Albans; one *s* two *d*. *Educ:* Eton; Christ Church, Oxford. European War, 1914-18; Royal Scots, 1914; Grenadier Guards, 1914-21; ADC to Governor-General of Canada, 1920; Reserve of Officers, 1921; Colonel late commanding 4th KOSB's, 1923-29; MP (U) Roxburgh and Selkirk, 1923-35; Lord Steward of HM Household, 1937-40. Ex-Governor, Royal Bank of Scotland; Ex-President: Royal Scottish Forestry Society; Dock & Harbour Authorities' Association; The Earl Haig Fund (Scottish Branch); Nat. Playing Fields Association (Scottish Branch); Freeman of Hawick and Selkirk. Hon. LLD Edin. and St Andr. *Heir: s* Earl of Dalkeith. *Recreations:* farming, forestry, shooting. *Address:* Bowhill, Selkirk. *T:* Selkirk 2732; Drumlanrig Castle, Thornhill, Dumfriesshire. *T:* Thornhill 248; 15 Grosvenor Square, W1. *T:* 01-629 6985; Boughton House, Geddington, Kettering, Northants. *T:* Kettering 82248. *Clubs:* Turf, White's; New (Edinburgh). *[Died 4 Oct. 1973.*

BUCHAN, Hon. Alastair Francis, CBE 1968 (MBE 1944); MA Oxon; Montague Burton Professor of International Relations, University of Oxford, since 1972; *b* 9 Sept. 1918; 3rd *s* of 1st Baron Tweedsmuir, and of Susan Charlotte Grosvenor; *m* 1942, Hope Gordon Gilmour, Ottawa, Canada; two *s* one *d*. *Educ:* Eton College; Christ Church, Oxford. Junior Fellow, University of Virginia, 1939. Commissioned Canadian Army, 1939; Dieppe Raid, 1942; Staff College, 1943; Major, 14th Canadian Hussars, 1944; North-west Europe Campaign, 1944-45. Asst Editor, The Economist, 1948-51; Washington Correspondent, The Observer, 1951-55; Diplomatic and Defence Correspondent, The Observer, 1955-58; Dir, Inst. for Strategic Studies, 1958-69; Comdt, Royal Coll. of Defence Studies (formerly IDC), 1970-71. Reith Lectr, 1973. *Publications:* The Spare Chancellor: the Life of Walter Bagehot, 1959; NATO in the 1960's, 1960 (rev. edn, 1963); The United States, 1963; (part-author) Arms and Stability in Europe, 1963; (ed) China and the Peace of Asia, 1965; War in Modern Society, 1966; (ed) A World of Nuclear Powers?, 1966; (ed) Europe's Futures: Europe's Choices, 1969; (ed) Problems of Modern Strategy, 1970; Power and Equilibrium in the 1970s, 1973; The End of a Postwar Era, 1974; Change without War (Reith lectures), 1974; articles in: Foreign Affairs, etc. *Recreations:* gardening, reading. *Address:* 40 Wellington Square, Oxford OX1 2JF. Waterloo House, Brill, Bucks. *T:* Brill 212. *Club:* Brooks's. *[Died 3 Feb. 1976.*

BUCHAN, Priscilla Jean Fortescue; *see* Baroness Tweedsmuir of Belhelvie.

BUCHANAN, Brig. Edgar James Bernard, DSO 1918; retired; *b* 1892; *s* of Robert Eccles Buchanan, of Templemore Park, Londonderry; *m* 1st, 1923, Evelyn Constance (*d* 1970), *d* of Richard Charles Holland, of Glanty House, Egham, Surrey; one *s*; 2nd, 1971, Kathleen Hannah Frances, *d* of S. Crosby Halahan, Chiddingford. Served European War, 1914-18; commanded 1st Bn RE, 1918 (wounded, DSO); Bt Lt-Col 1935. Served War of 1939-45; Senior Royal Engineer, Allied Force HQ, 1943; Director of Fortification and Works, War Office, 1945 (despatches); retired 1946. Officer of Legion of Merit, USA. *Address:* Bridge Meadow, Harting, Petersfield, Hants GU31 5LS. *[Died 13 Sept. 1979.*

BUCHANAN, Sir George H. M. Leith; *see* Leith-Buchanan.

BUCHANAN, Sir John (Cecil Rankin), KCMG 1961 (CMG 1948); MD, FRCP(E), FRACP, DTM&H; Chief Medical Officer, Colonial Office, 1960 (Department of Technical Co-operation, 1961-62), retired; *b* 18 June 1896; *s* of late John Buchanan, CMG, Blantyre, Nyasaland; *m* 1931, Eileen, *e d* of late J. D. Robertson, JP, Redhurst, Ravelston, Dykes,

Edinburgh; no *c. Educ:* Stewart's College; Edinburgh University. Colonial Medical Service, 1925; Medical Officer Tanganyika and British Somaliland, 1925-35; Senior Medical Officer, British Somaliland, 1935; Aden, 1936; DDMS, Uganda, 1943; Inspector-General, South Pacific Health Service, 1945. Served European War, 1914-18, The Black Watch, 1915-19 (despatches); War of 1939-45, RAMC (rank of Colonel), 1940-43 (despatches). Scottish Rugby XV, 1921-25 (Captain Scottish XV, 1924). KStJ. *Publications:* Guide to Pacific Island Dietaries, 1948; many contributions to scientific journals. *Address:* Broomwood, Woodland Rise, Sevenoaks, Kent. *Club:* East India, Sports and Public Schools. *[Died 19 Feb. 1976.*

BUCHANAN, Maj.-Gen. Sir Kenneth Gray, Kt, *cr* 1946; CB 1934; CMG 1919; DSO 1916; Seaforth Highlanders; *b* 1880; *m* 1911, Muriel-Kate (*d* 1948), *d* of T. F. Cumming, Melbourne; two *d*; *m* 1952, Mrs A. G. Marr, *widow* of Capt. A. M. Marr, MBE, DCM, The Seaforth Highlanders. *Educ:* Harrow; RMC, Sandhurst. Entered Army, 1900; Major, 1915; Lieut-Colonel, 1923; Colonel, 1927; Maj.-General, 1932; served NW Frontier of India, 1908 (despatches, medal and clasp); European War, 1914-18 (wounded thrice, despatches, DSO, Bt. Lieut-Colonel); GSO 1 Northern Command, 1928-30; Commanded 2nd Infantry Brigade, Aldershot, 1930-32; Commander, 42nd (East Lancashire) Division, TA, 1934-38; retired, pay, 1938. *Address:* High Fields, Far Oakridge, Stroud, Glos. *Club:* Army and Navy. *[Died 7 June 1973.*

BUCHANAN, Prof. Robert Ogilvie; Emeritus Professor, University of London; *b* 12 Sept. 1894; *s* of Duncan and Janet Buchanan; *m* 1931, Kathleen Mary Parnell; one *s* two *d*. *Educ:* University of Otago, New Zealand; University of London. Served European War, 1914-18, NZEF (Otago Regt), 1915-19, in France. Mount Albert Grammar School, Auckland, NZ, 1922-25; student at London School of Economics, 1925-28. University College, University of London; Asst Lecturer in Geography, 1928. Lecturer, 1930. Reader in Economic Geography, 1938-49; Prof. of Geography, London School of Economics, 1949-61; Hon. Fellow, 1970. War of 1939-45, RAF, maps organisation, Air Ministry and War Office. Member Senate, University of London, 1951-67; President: Section E (Geography) British Assoc. for the Advancement of Science, 1952; Inst. of British Geographers, 1953; Geographical Association, 1958. Member Nature Conservancy, 1965-71. *Publications:* Pastoral Industries of New Zealand, 1935; An Economic Geography of the British Empire, 1936; (with R. C. Estall) Industrial Activity and Economic Geography, 1961; articles on various topics in economic geography in geographical periodicals in UK, USA, NZ and India. *Address:* 13B Westleigh Avenue, Putney, SW15 6RF. *T:* 01-789 4350.

[Died 9 July 1980.

BUCHANAN-WOLLASTON, H. A.; *see* Wollaston, H. A. B.

BUCHER, Gen. Sir Francis Robert Roy; *see* Bucher, Gen. Sir Roy.

BUCHER, General Sir Roy, KBE 1948 (OBE 1943); CB 1945; MC 1919; DL; psc; *b* 1895; *m* 1922, Edith Margaret Reid (*d* 1944); one *d*; *m* 1946, Maureen, OBE (*d* 1978), *e d* of late Captain Thomas George Gibson, DL, Welham Hall, Malton, Yorks. *Educ:* Edinburgh Academy; RMC Sandhurst. Served European War, 1914-19, with 1st Bn The Cameronians (wounded 1915, France); India, 1915, attached 55th Coke's Rifles (FF); transferred 31st Duke of Connaught's Own Lancers, 1916; Mahsud, 1917; Afghanistan, Waziristan, 1919-20; Staff Coll., Camberley, 1926-27; DAAG, Deccan District, 1930-32; Bt. Lieut-Colonel 13 Duke of Connaught's Own Lancers, 1937; Comdt Sam Browne's Cav., Nov. 1939-Feb. 1940; Colonel, 1940; Comdt No. 2 ACTC, Lucknow, 1940; AAG, GHQ, Jan.-June 1941; AQMG, Iraq, 1941; Major-General in charge Administration, Southern Army, India, 1942-45; GOC Bengal and Assam Area, 1946; officiating GOC-in-C Eastern Command, 1946-Jan. 1947; Chief of Staff, AHQ, India, Aug.-Dec. 1947; C-in-C, Army of India, 1948-49; Officer on special duty, Indian Defence Ministry, 1949; retired, 1949. Past National Chairman, The Royal British Legion (Life Member, Nat. Exec. Council); Member of Council of Officers' Association; Vice-President Not-Forgotten Association; Chm., Yorkshire Area Council, Royal Society of St George. Chairman, Anglo Polish Society. DL, NR Yorks, 1962. Order of Star of Nepal Class I; Order of Polonia Restituta 1st Cl. *Address:* Normanby House, Sinnington, York Y06 6RH. *T:* Kirkby Moorside 31483. *Club:* Army and Navy. *[Died 5 Jan. 1980.*

BUCK, Pearl Sydenstricker; *b* Hillsboro, W Va, USA, 26 June 1892; *d* of American missionaries; *m* 1st, a teacher of Nanking University; two *d*; 2nd, 1935, Richard J. Walsh (*d* 1960)

Awarded: Pulitzer Prize, 1932; 1938 Nobel Prize for Literature. *Publications:* The Good Earth (William Dean Howells Medal, 1935); East Wind-West Wind; Sons; The First Wife and other Stories, 1933; All Men are Brothers, a translation of the Old Chinese Classic Shui hu Chuan; The Mother, 1934; A House Divided, 1935; The Exile, 1936; Fighting Angel, 1936; This Proud Heart, 1938; The Patriot, 1939; Other Gods, 1940; Dragon Seed, 1942; The Promise, 1943; What America Means to Me, 1944; Portrait of a Marriage, 1945; Pavilion of Women, 1946; Peony, 1948; Kinfolk, 1949; Far and Near, 1949; God's Men, 1951; The Hidden Flower, 1952; Come My Beloved, 1953; My Several Worlds, 1955; Imperial Woman, 1956; Letter from Peking, 1958; American Triptych, 1958; (with Carlos P. Romulo), Friend to Friend, 1958; Command the Morning, 1959; Fourteen Stories, 1961; A Bridge for Passing, 1962; With a Delicate Air (short stories), 1962; The Living Reed, 1963; Welcome Child, 1964; Joy of Children, 1965; The Gifts They Bring, 1965; Death in the Castle, 1965; The Time is Noon, 1967; The New Year, 1968; The People of Japan, 1968; The Good Deed and Other Stories of Asia, Past and Present, 1969; The Three Daughters of Madame Liang, 1969; The Kennedy Women, 1970; China as I See It, 1970; Mandala, 1970; The Goddess Abides, 1971; The Story Bible, 1971; *posthumous:* The Woman Who Was Changed, 1980; also books for children and collections of essays. *Address:* Main Street, Danby, Vermont 05739, USA. 　　　　　　　　　　*[Died 6 March 1973.*

BUCKLE, Col Cuthbert, CB 1931; CBE 1919; TD 1931; retired; *s* of Henry Rogers Buckle and Emily Hotine; *m* 1st, 1909, Edith Marion (*d* 1949), *d* of John Kennedy Barlow; one *s* ; 2nd, 1950, Letty Iris, *d* of J. R. T. Nind. *Educ:* Univ. Coll., London; City and Guilds of London Institute. Air Defence Commander Sheppey and Grain, 1916; Air Defence Commander, London Air Defences, 1917-18; raised and commanded 53rd (City of London) Anti-Aircraft Brigade, RA, TA, 1921-27; commanded 27th (London) Air Defence Brigade, TA, 1927-31; elected to Lloyd's, 1920, and is Chartered Adjuster to the Fire Offices and Underwriters. *Publications:* several papers on technical matters connected with insurance. *Recreation:* yachting. *Address:* Galiots, West Mersea, Essex. *T:* West Mersea 2897. *Club:* Royal Artillery Yacht. 　　　　　　　　　　　　　*[Died 3 June 1971.*

BUCKLEY, Howard; *see* Buckley, W. H.

BUCKLEY, Professor John Joseph Cronin, DSc (NUI); Professor Emeritus of Helminthology in the University of London at the London School of Hygiene and Tropical Medicine, since 1967; *b* Dublin, 29 May 1904; *s* of late John Joseph Buckley and late Ellen Mary Cronin, Dublin; unmarried. *Educ:* Catholic University Sch., Dublin; National Univ. of Ireland. Wandsworth Research Scholar, 1931-34; Milner Research Fellow, 1934-38; Lecturer in Helminthology, 1938-40; William Julian Courtauld Professor of Helminthology, University of London, 1947-67. Research expeditions to: British West Indies, 1931; Assam, 1933; Malaya, 1935, 1955, 1956; Kenya, 1941, 1957, 1958; Northern Rhodesia, 1944; Ceylon, 1956; Uganda, 1959. Mem., (Expert) panel of Parasitic Diseases of WHO; Reference Expert in Helminthology to Public Health Laboratory Service; Examiner for higher degrees in Science at London and other British and foreign Universities. FIBiol. *Publications:* Editor, Jl of Helminthology, 1947-; numerous papers on Parasitology in various scientific jls. *Recreation:* helminthology. *Address:* London School of Hygiene and Tropical Medicine, Keppel Street, WC1. *T:* 01-636 8636. 　　　　　　　　　　　　*[Died 12 April 1972.*

BUCKLEY, (William) Howard; retired; Director, Oxford Polytechnic, 1970; *b* 3 Nov. 1909; *s* of Thomas Buckley and Minnie Buckley (*née* Russell); *m* 1937, Margaret Schaeffer; one *s* one *d.* *Educ:* John Ruskin Sch., Croydon; Croydon Sch. of Art; Royal Coll. of Art (ARCA). Principal: Lydney Sch. of Art, Glos, 1938; Shipley Sch. of Art and Technical Inst., 1940. Served War, 1941-45, Navigator, RAF. Principal: Northampton Sch. of Art, 1946; Derby Coll. of Art, 1948; Oxford Coll. of Technology, 1956-70. Hon. MA Oxford Univ. 1969. *Publications:* book reviews and articles on art and technical educn. *Recreations:* motoring, gardening. *Address:* Kiln Cottage, 25 Westfield Road, Wheatley, Oxford OX9 1NG. *T:* Wheatley 2909. 　　　　　　　　　　　*[Died 21 March 1974.*

BUCKMASTER, 2nd Viscount, *cr* 1933; **Owen Stanley Buckmaster,** Baron of Cheddington, *cr* 1915; an Underwriting Member of Lloyd's; Vice-Chairman, London County Freehold and Leasehold Properties Ltd, 1952-68; *b* 24 Sept. 1890; *o s* of 1st Viscount and Edith Augusta (*d* 1935), *d* of Spencer Robert Lewin of Widford, Ware; *S* father 1934; *m* 1st, 1916, Joan (marr. diss., 1944), 2nd *d* of Dr Garry Simpson, 89 Lancaster Gate, W2; two *s* ; 2nd, 1961, Mrs D. C. Vane-Tempest (*née* Seth-

Smith). *Educ:* Winchester; Christ Church, Oxford, MA (Law). Called to Bar, Inner Temple, 1913; served European War, 1914-18, Captain Duke of Cornwall's Light Infantry (wounded, 1914-15 Star). Member of Committee of London Stock Exchange, 1938-42; Member of House of Lords Cttee on Gas, Electricity and Water Holding Cos, 1939; Pres. Assoc. of Land and Property Owners, 1946-57; Pres. Nat. Fed. of Property Owners, 1947-50; Chairman, Friends of Stowe Trust, 1939-59; Pres., Arundel and Shoreham Div. Conservative Assoc., 1951-61. Major, 16th Sussex Home Guard, 1941-44. Resigned from Liberal Party to join Conservative Party, 1947. *Publication:* Roundabout (memoirs), 1970. *Heir: s* Hon. Martin Stanley Buckmaster [*b* 11 April 1921; Capt. Royal Sussex Regt, 1939-46; HM Diplomatic Service, 1946-]. *Address:* Furzefield House, Wineham, Henfield, East Sussex BN5 9BS. *T:* Partridge Green 710380. 　　　　　　　　　　　　*[Died 25 Nov. 1974.*

BUCKNALL, Lt-Gen. Gerard Corfield, CB 1943; MC; psc; ns; lately Colonel, The Middlesex Regiment; Assistant Lieutenant for Greater London, 1965-70; *b* 14 Sept. 1894; *s* of Harry Corfield Bucknall and Alice Oakshott; *m* 1925, Kathleen Josephine Moore-Burt; two *s* one *d. Educ:* Repton; Sandhurst. Commissioned 1st Battalion Middlesex Regiment, 1914; served throughout European War, 1914-18, France and Flanders, latterly on General Staff (wounded, MC and Bar, despatches, Bt Major); in Sudan with Egyptian Army, 1920-21; Brevet Lieut-Colonel 1936; General Staff Canadian Forces, 1937-38; commanded 2nd Bn Middx, 1939; Colonel on Staff, War Office, 1939; commanded 5th Div. in Sicily and Italy, and 30th Corps in Army of Invasion, 1944; GOC N Ireland, 1945-47; Lord Lieut of Middlesex, 1963-65. *Address:* c/o 19 Model Cottages, East Sheen, SW14. *Clubs:* Army and Navy, MCC; Royal Wimbledon Golf. 　　　　　　　　　　　　　　*[Died 7 Dec. 1980.*

BUCKTON, Baron *cr* 1966 (Life Peer), of Settrington; **Samuel Storey;** Bt, *cr* 1960; *b* 1896; *er s* of late Frederick George Storey, JP; *m* 1929, Elisabeth, JP (*d* 1951) *d* of late Brig.-Gen. W. J. Woodcock, DSO; one *s* one *d. Educ:* Haileybury Coll.; Trinity Coll., Cambridge, MA. Barrister, Inner Temple, 1919; MP (C) Sunderland, 1931-45 and Stretford, 1950-66; Chairman of Ways and Means, and Dep. Speaker, House of Commons, 1965-66; (Dep. Chm. of Ways and Means, 1964-65); Member Chairman's Panel, House of Commons, 1957-64. E Riding CC, 1946-64. *Heir* (to Baronetcy only): *s* Hon. Richard Storey [*b* 23 Jan. 1937; *m* 1961, Virginia Anne, 3rd *d* of Sir Kenelm Cayley, 10th Bt; one *s* two *d*]. *Address:* Settrington House, Settrington, Malton, North Yorks YO17 8NP. *T:* North Grimston 200. *Club:* Carlton. 　　　　　　　　　　　　　*[Died 17 Jan. 1978.*

BUCKTON, Ernest James, BSc Eng (Lond.); MICE; MIMechE; Fellow of Queen Mary College, London; retired; *b* 1 July 1883; *m* 1920, Joyce Ethel Pym (*d* 1933), *y d* of Captain Riall Sankey, CB, RE; one *d. Educ:* Drapers' Company School and College (now Queen Mary College), London; Whitworth Exhibitioner. Engineering pupil, London & India Docks Company, 1904; Assistant Engineer, 1907; Assistant Engineer, Port of London Authority, 1909; European War, served 1914-18 in Gibraltar and France; hon. rank of Major on relinquishing Commission; Resident Engineer, New Works, Port of London Authority, 1918; Deputy Resident Engineer, New Port Works, Buenos Aires, Argentine, 1920; Agent and Chief Engineer, Loanda Harbour Works, Portuguese West Africa, 1924; Engineer-in-Charge, Rendel, Palmer & Tritton, Consulting Engineers, 1925, Partner, 1929-47, Consultant, 1947-51, retired, 1951. *Publications:* The Construction of Haifa Harbour, Palestine, 1936; The Demolition of Waterloo Bridge (joint), 1936; The Reconstruction of Chelsea Bridge (joint), 1937; The New Waterloo Bridge (joint), 1943. *Recreations:* riding and golf. *Address:* 11 St Aubin's Court, Sea Lane, Ferring, Sussex. T: Worthing 40434. *Club:* Royal Automobile.
　　　　　　　　　　　　　　　[Died 30 Nov. 1973.

BUCKWORTH-HERNE-SOAME; *see* Soame.

BUDD, Hon. Sir Harry Vincent, Kt 1970; President of the Legislative Council of New South Wales, 1966-78 (MLC 1946-78); *b* 18 Feb. 1900; *s* of Arthur Eames Budd and Anne (*née* Knight); *m* 1930, Colina Macdonald White, *d* of Alfred White; one *s* two *d* (and one *s* decd). *Educ:* privately. Editor, Tweed Daily, Murwillumbah, 1921-23; Editorial Staff, Sydney Daily Telegraph, 1923-30; Managing Editor, The Land, 1930-70. *Recreations:* music, gardening. *Address:* 26 Mistral Avenue, Mosman, Sydney, NSW 2088, Australia. *T:* 969-4810. *Clubs:* Australian, American. 　　　　　　　　　　　　*[Died 8 March 1979.*

BUDGE, Rev. Ronald Henderson Gunn, MVO 1971; MA; Extra Chaplain to Her Majesty the Queen in Scotland, since 1972; Parish Minister of Crathie, Aberdeenshire, and Domestic

Chaplain to Her Majesty the Queen in Scotland, 1964-71; *b* 4 Oct. 1909; *o s* of late Ex-Provost R. Gunn Budge, Moffat; *m* 1940, Maisie, *o d* of late Very Rev. Prof. Archibald Main, DD, DLitt, LLD. *Educ:* Ashville Coll., Harrogate; Glasgow Univ. (MA). Ordained and inducted to Selkirk West Church, 1938. Served with Church of Scotland Huts and Canteens in France and Scotland, 1939-44. Inducted to Troon Old Church, 1944; inducted to Murrayfield Church, Edinburgh, 1953; Convener of the General Assembly's Stewardship and Budget Committee, 1959-64; Chaplain in attendance to HM the Queen at Gen. Assembly of Church of Scotland, 1969. Guest Preacher in the Scots Church: Sydney, 1951-52; Staunton, Virginia, 1958; Toronto, 1967. Member of the Baird Trust. 1945-71. *Recreations:* fishing, gardening. *Address:* Mote Yett, Alton, Moffat, Dumfriesshire DG10 9LB.   *[Died 22 Nov. 1976.*

BULGANIN, Marshal Nikolai Alexandrovich; Hero of Socialist Labour; 2 Orders of Lenin, Order of Red Banner, Order of Suvorov (1st and 2nd class), 2 Orders of Kutuzov, 2 Orders of Red Star; Chairman of the State Bank, USSR, 1958; Chairman, Stavropol Economic Region, 1958-62; *b* Nizhne-Novgorod, 1895. *Educ:* at technical secondary school, Nizhne-Novgorod. Joined Communist Party, 1917; worked in Cheka, 1918-22; held responsible posts in Supreme Economic Council, 1922-27; director Moscow Electrical Works, 1927-30; Chm. Moscow City Soviet, 1931-37; Chm. Council of People's Commissars of RSFSR, 1937-38; Dep. Chm. Council of People's Commissars of USSR, 1938-41; head of board of USSR State Bank, 1938-41; Mem. Military Council, various fronts, 1941-44; Mem. State Cttee of Defence, 1944-45; Dep. People's Commissar of Defence of USSR, 1944-47; Minister of Defence of USSR, 1947-49 and 1953-55; Dep. Chm. USSR Council of Ministers, 1947-49; 1st Dep. Chm. USSR Council of Ministers, 1949-55; Chm. of Council of Ministers of USSR, 1955-58; Mem. Central Cttee, USSR Communist Party, 1934; Mem. Politburo, 1948-52; Mem. Praesidium Central Cttee, Communist Party, 1952; Dep. to Supreme Soviet of USSR, 1937. Marshal of the Soviet Union, 1947. *Address:* c/o Ministry of Social Security of the RSFSR, 14 Shabolovka, Moscow, USSR.   *[Died 24 Feb. 1975.*

BULL, George Lucien, CBE 1920; Officier de la Légion d'Honneur; Hon. director of the Marey Institute, Paris; *b* Dublin, 5 Jan. 1876; *s* of C. Bull, Bedford, and G. Jouve, Paris; unmarried. *Educ:* Belvedere Coll., Dublin; Faculté des Sciences, Paris Univ. Graduated in Paris Univ. (Zoology, Botany, Geology); retired. Work, principally technical research for new methods of investigation of phenomena in Natural Science, high speed cinematography, sound registering, optical illusions, etc. *Publications:* Various communications to the French Academy of Science and other scientific Societies. *Address:* 14 Rue du Général Delestraint, Paris, 16e. *T:* Jasmin 08.62.
          [Died 25 Aug. 1972.

BULLARD, Sir Edward (Crisp), Kt 1953; FRS 1941; MA, PhD, ScD; Fellow of Churchill College, Cambridge, since 1960; Professor, University of California at San Diego, 1963-79, now Emeritus; *b* 21 Sept. 1907; *s* of Edward John Bullard and Eleanor Howes Crisp; *m* 1st, 1931, Margaret Ellen Thomas; four *d* ; 2nd, 1974, Mrs Ursula Curnow, *d* of late Dr E. J. Cooke, Christchurch, NZ, and Mrs E. J. Cooke. *Educ:* Repton; Clare Coll., Cambridge. Research in Physics, 1929-31; Geophysics, 1931-; Demonstrator in Geodesy at Cambridge Univ., 1931-35; Smithson Research Fellow of Royal Society, 1936-43; Experimental Officer HMS Vernon and Admiralty, 1939-45; Asst Dir of Naval Operational Research, 1944-45; Fellow of Clare, 1943-48 and 1956-60; Reader in Experimental Geophysics at Cambridge Univ., 1945-48; Prof. of Physics at Univ. of Toronto, 1948-49; Director National Physical Laboratory, 1950-55; Fellow of Caius Coll., Cambridge, 1956; Asst Dir of Research, Cambridge Univ., 1956-60; Reader in Geophysics, 1960-64, Prof., 1964-74. Centennial Prof., Univ. of Toronto, 1967; Hitchcock Prof., Univ. of California, Berkeley, 1975; Vis. Prof., Univ. of Alaska, 1978-. Formerly Director: IBM UK; Bullard & Sons. Foreign Corresp. Geol. Soc. Amer., 1952; Foreign Hon. Mem. Amer. Acad. Arts and Sci., 1954; Foreign Assoc. US Nat. Acad. Sci., 1959; Foreign Mem., Amer. Philos. Soc., 1969. Segdwick Prize, 1936; Hughes Medal of Royal Soc., 1953; Chree Medal of Physics Soc., 1956; Day Medal of Geol. Soc. Amer., 1959; Gold Medal, Royal Astronomical Soc., 1965; Agassiz Medal, US Nat. Acad. of Sci., 1965; Wollaston Medal of Geol. Soc. of London, 1967; Bakerian Lecturer of the Royal Society, 1967; Vetlesen Prize, 1968; Bowie Medal, 1975, Ewing Medal, 1978, Amer. Geophysical Union; Royal Medal of Royal Soc., 1975. *Publications:* scientific papers. *Address:* 2491 Horizon Way, La Jolla, Calif 92037, USA. *Club:* Athenæum.   *[Died 3 April 1980.*

BULLARD, Sir Reader (William), KCB 1944; KCMG 1936 (CMG 1933); CIE 1916; *b* 5 Dec. 1885; *s* of late Charles Bullard and Mary Bullard, of Walthamstow; *m* 1921, Miriam (*d* 1973), 4th *d* of late Arthur Lionel Smith, Master of Balliol Coll., Oxford; four *s* one *d.* Acting Vice-Consul, Beirout, 1909-10; Vice-Consul, Bitlis, 1910-11; 3rd Dragoman, 1911-13; Acting Consul, Trebizond, 1912; Acting Consul, Erzerum, 1913; Acting Consul, Basra, 1914; Civil Adviser to Principal Military Governor, Basra, 1914; Political Officer, Kifri, 1918; Dep. Revenue Sec., Mesopotamia, 1919; Military Governor, Baghdad, 1920; Middle East Dept, Colonial Office, 1921; HBM Agent and Consul, Jedda, 1923-25; Consul at Athens, 1925-28; Consul, Addis Ababa, 1928; Consul-General, Moscow, 1930; Leningrad, 1931-34; Rabat, 1934; Minister, Jedda, 1936-39; Minister (later Ambassador), Tehran, 1939-46; retired, 1946. Director of the Institute of Colonial Studies, Oxford, 1951-56; Member of Governing Body of the School of Oriental and African Studies, Univ. of London, 1953-65. Hon. Fellow: Queens' Coll., Cambridge; Sch. of Oriental and African Studies, Univ. of London; Lincoln Coll., Oxford. Sir Percy Sykes Memorial Medal, 1962. *Publications:* Britain and the Middle East, 1964; The Camels Must Go (Autobiog.), 1961. *Address:* 46 Plantation Road, Oxford. *T:* Oxford 59259. *Club:* Athenæum.
          [Died 24 May 1976.

BULLEN, Keith Edward, FRS 1949; PhD, ScD; Professor of Applied Mathematics, University of Sydney, 1946-71, now Emeritus; *b* Auckland, NZ, 29 June 1906; *s* of George S. and Maud H. Bullen; *m* 1935, Florence Mary Pressley, MA, Auckland, NZ; one *s* one *d. Educ:* Auckland Grammar Sch. and Auckland Univ. Coll., NZ; St John's Coll., Cambridge, England. MA 1928, BSc 1930, New Zealand; MA 1945 Melbourne; PhD, ScD 1946 Cambridge. Premium in pure mathematics, Auckland Univ. Coll., 1923; Senior Scholar in Mathematics, Univ. of NZ, 1925; Strathcona exhibition, St John's Coll., Cambridge, 1932-33. Foundn Fellow, Aust. Acad. of Sci., 1954; elected Correspondent of Geol. Soc. of Amer., 1959, Hon. Fellow, 1963; For. Mem. Amer. Acad. of Arts and Sci., 1960; For. Assoc. US Nat. Acad. of Sci., 1961; Fellow Amer. Geophys Union, 1962; Hon. Fellow: Royal Soc. of NZ, 1963; Geol. Soc. of London, 1967; Pontifical Academician, 1968; Hon. Fellow, Royal Soc. of NSW, 1974. Master, Auckland Grammar Sch., New Zealand, 1926-27; Lectr in Mathematics, Auckland Univ. Coll., 1928-31 and 1934-40; Special Lectureship, Hull Univ. Coll., England, 1933; Senior Lecturer in mathematics, Univ. of Melbourne, 1940-45; Senior Consultant, Internat. Inst. of Seismology and Earthquake Engrg, Tokyo, 1969-72. Lectures: Einstein Meml, Inst. of Physics, SA, 1959; Harricks, Australian Inst. of Engrs, 1963; Zipora Alterman Meml, Israel, 1975; Gilbert Archey, Auckland, NZ, 1975. President Internat. Assoc. of Seismology and Physics of Interior of Earth, 1954-57; Council Member, Australian Acad. of Science, 1955-57; Chm. Australian Nat. Cttee. for Internat. Geophysical Year, 1955-60; Vice-Pres., Scientific Cttee (of Internat. Council of Scientific Unions) on Antarctic Research, 1958-62; Vice-Pres. Internat. Union of Geodesy and Geophys, 1963-67. Chm., Internat. Cttee, Standard Earth Model, 1971-75; Mem., Governing Council, Internat. Seismological Centre, 1973-. Hon. DSc: Auckland, 1963; Sydney, 1976. Lyle Medallist, Aust., 1949; Hector Medallist, NZ, 1952; Walter Burfitt Prize, Royal Soc. of NSW, 1953; Bicentennial Medal, Columbia Univ., NY 1954; William Bowie Medal, Amer. Geophys. Union, 1961; Day Medal, Geol. Soc. of America, 1963; Research Medal, Royal Soc. of Vic., 1965; Flinders Lectr and Medallist, Australian Acad. of Sci., 1969; Gold Medal, RAS, 1974. *Publications:* Introduction to the Theory of Seismology, Cambridge, 1947 (3rd edn, 1963); Introduction to the Theory of Mechanics, Sydney, 1949 (8th edn, 1971); Seismology, 1954; The Earth's Density, 1975; papers in scientific journals. *Recreation:* numismatics. *Address:* c/o Department of Applied Mathematics, University of Sydney, NSW 2006, Australia.   *[Died 23 Sept. 1976.*

BULLERWELL, Dr William, FRS 1972; FRSE 1973; Deputy Director, Institute of Geological Sciences, since 1976 (Chief Geophysicist (Assistant Director), 1967-76); *b* Newcastle-on-Tyne, 27 Sept. 1916; *s* of John William Bullerwell and Alice Bullerwell (née Wilkinson); *m* 1942, Eileen Nora Field; no *c. Educ:* Rutherford Coll., Newcastle-on-Tyne; Armstrong Coll. (later King's Coll.), Newcastle-on-Tyne (Univ. of Durham). BSc (Physics) 1937, BSc (Geology) 1939, PhD (Mining Geophysics) 1951. Served War, 1940-46: with Min. of Supply, RAOC and REME. Geological Survey of Gt Britain: Geologist, 1946; Chief Geophysicist, 1962. *Publications:* scientific papers on geophysical exploration and geological structure of UK land mass and continental shelf. *Recreations:* music, travel. *Address:* Institute of Geological Sciences, Exhibition Road, SW7 2DE. *T:* 01-589 3444.   *[Died 25 Nov. 1977.*

BULLOCK, Sir Christopher (Llewellyn), KCB 1932 (CB 1929); CBE 1926 (OBE 1919); MA; *b* 10 Nov. 1891; 2nd *s* of Rev. Ll. C. W. Bullock, Rector of Great and Little Wigborough, Essex; *m* 1917, Barbara May, *d* of Henry Lupton, Torquay; two *s. Educ:* Rugby (Captain of Running Eight); Trinity Coll., Cambridge (Scholar). Abbott and Porson Univ. Scholarships; Charles Oldham Shakespeare Scholarship; Whewell Scholarship in International Law (re-elected, 1921); member's Latin Essay prize; Browne Medals for Latin Ode (twice) and Greek Epigram, etc.; BA 1913; MA 1919; 1st Division 1st Class Classical Tripos; took first place in the open competitive examination for the Home and Indian Civil Services, 1914; selected the ICS and appointed as a probationer to the United Provinces, 1915; Principal, Air Ministry, 1920; late Captain The Rifle Brigade (Special Reserve), and Major, Royal Air Force; served European War, 1915-19 (with 1st Battalion Rifle Brigade in France, 1915; seconded to Royal Flying Corps Oct. 1915, first as Observer and subsequently as Pilot; with RFC in Egypt, 1916; on Air Staff at Air Ministry, 1917-18; (wounded, despatches, OBE); Principal Private Sec. to the Rt Hon. Winston Churchill as Secretary of State for Air, 1919; served in same capacity 1923-30 with successive Secretaries of State, the Rt Hon. Sir Samuel Hoare and the Rt Hon. Lord Thomson, whom he accompanied on tours of inspection by air in Egypt, Palestine, Transjordania and Iraq in 1924 and 1925, to India in 1927, and to the Sudan in 1929; Asst Secretary, Air Ministry, 1929-30; Permanent Secretary, Air Ministry and Member of Air Council, 1931-36; was in 1935 deputed by HM Government to negotiate with the Union of South Africa and other African administrations in connection with the Empire Air Mail Scheme. Subsequently Director, Eagle Star Insurance Co., British Metal Corp., Strong & Co. of Romsey, and other public cos, and Chairman, Beralt Tin & Wolfram, Cox & Wyman, James Norris (Burslem), etc; now retired. *Publication:* The Law of Angary in British Year Book of International Law, 1922. *Recreations:* books, bird-watching, fly-fishing. *Address:* Flat 16, 39 Hyde Park Gate, SW7. *T:* 01-584 6961. *Club:* United Oxford & Cambridge University.   *[Died 16 May 1972.*

BULLOCK, Sir Ernest, Kt 1951; CVO 1937; MusD (Dunelm); Hon. LLD (Glasgow, 1955); FRCM; FRCO; FRSCM; FRSAMD; Hon. RAM; Director of the Royal College of Music, 1953-60; *b* 15 Sept. 1890; *y s* of late Thos Bullock, Wigan, Lancs; *m* 1919, Margery, *d* of late George H. Newborn, Epworth, Lincolnshire; two *s* one *d. Educ:* Wigan Grammar Sch.; privately; musically under Sir E. C. Bairstow, MusD, at Leeds Parish Church; Asst Organist, Leeds Parish Church, and Organist of St Mary, Micklefield and Adel Church, 1906-12; Sub-organist of Manchester Cathedral, 1912-15; served in HM Forces as Captain and Adjutant, 1915-19; Organist of St Michael's Coll., Tenbury, 1919; of Exeter Cathedral, 1919-28; of Westminster Abbey, 1928-41. Joint Musical Director and Conductor of the Coronation Service, 1937. Professor of Music, Glasgow Univ. and Principal Royal Scottish Academy of Music and Drama, Glasgow, 1941-52. Pres. Incorporated Assoc. of Organists, 1946-48; Pres. Incorporated Soc. of Musicians, 1947; Pres. Royal Coll. of Organists, 1951-52; Pres. Union of Graduates in Music, 1947-48. *Publications:* Church and organ music, songs, part-songs, etc. *Address:* Welby Cottage, Long Crendon, Aylesbury, Bucks.   *[Died 23 May 1979.*

BULLOCK-MARSHAM, Brigadier F. W.; *see* Marsham.

BULMAN, Oliver Meredith Boone, FRS 1940; ScD Cambridge; PhD London; ARCSc; FGS; FLS; Woodwardian Professor of Geology, University of Cambridge, 1955-66, now Emeritus; Fellow of Sidney Sussex College; *b* 20 May 1902; *y s* of late Henry H. Bulman, RBA, and Beatrice E. Bulman (*née* Boone); *m* 1938, Marguerite, *e d* of late William George Fearnsides, FRS; one *s* three *d. Educ:* Battersea Grammar Sch.; Chelsea Polytechnic; Imperial Coll. of Science and Technology; Sidney Sussex Coll., Cambridge. Beit Scientific Research Fellowship, 1923-25; 1851 Senior Studentship, 1925-28; Huxley Memorial Medal, Imperial Coll., 1928; Demonstrator in Zoology, 1928-29, Demonstrator in Geology, Imperial Coll., 1929-31; Univ. Demonstrator in Geology, 1931-34; Univ. Lecturer in Palæozoology, 1934-44; Reader in Palæozoology, Cambridge, 1944-45. Pres. Sect. C (Geology) British Assoc., 1959. Pres. Geological Society London, 1962-64, Vice-Pres. 1953-57, 1964-66, 1967-68, Foreign Secretary, 1964-67; Lyell Medallist, 1953; President: Palæont. Assoc., 1960-62; Palæont. Soc., 1971-. Trustee of the British Museum (Natural History), 1963-70. Editor, Geological Magazine, 1934-72. Foreign Mem., Royal Physiogr. Soc. Lund; Corresponding Mem., Geol. Soc. Stockholm; Hon. Fellow Pal. Soc. India; Hon. DrPhil (Oslo), 1965; Fellow, Imperial Coll. of Science and Technology, 1961. *Publications:* numerous papers on Lower Palæozoic rocks and fossils. *Address:* The Sedgwick Museum, Cambridge CB2 3EQ.   *[Died 18 Feb. 1974.*

BUNBURY, Brigadier Noël Louis St Pierre, DSO 1937; psc; *b* Woolwich, 25 Dec. 1890; *s* of Lieut-Col William St Pierre Bunbury, S Farnborough; *m* 1923, Iris Graham (*d* 1965), *d* of J. B. Whitelaw, North Berwick; one *s. Educ:* Bedford; RMC Sandhurst. Served European War, Mesopotamia and Siberia; Waziristan, 1920-21; NW Frontier, 1930; Waziristan, 1936-37 (DSO); Commandant 6th Royal Bn (Scinde) 13th Frontier Force Rifles, 1934-38; Gen. Staff, India Office, 1938-40; Brigade Comdr in India, 1941-44; ADC to the King, 1943-44; retired, 1944. OC 12th County of London Home Guard Bn, 1952-55. *Address:* 1 Hazelwood Road, Hale, Cheshire.

[Died 31 Jan. 1971.

BUNCHE, Ralph Johnson, PhD; Under Secretary-General, United Nations, 1968-71 (Under Secretary for Special Political Affairs, 1954-67); *b* 7 Aug. 1904; *s* of Fred Bunche and Olive Bunche (*née* Johnson); *m* 1930, Ruth Harris; one *s* one *d* (and one *d* decd). *Educ:* Univ. of California, Los Angeles (AB); Harvard Univ., (AM, PhD). Howard Univ., Washington, DC; Chm., Dept of Political Science, 1928-50, Prof. of Political Science, 1937-50; Asst to Pres., 1931-32. Co-Director, Inst. of Race Relations, Swarthmore, Pa., 1936; Staff Member, Carnegie Corp. of New York-Myrdal Survey of Negro in America, 1938-40. Senior Social Science Analyst (Africa and Far East), Office of Co-ordinator of Information, 1941-42; Principal Research Analyst (Africa and the Far East), Office of Strategic Services, 1942-43; Chief, Africa Section, Research and Analysis Branch, Office of Strategic Services, 1943-44; Dept of State, 1944-47: as expert on colonial problems and Africa, held posts of Area Specialist, Associate Chief and Acting Chief of Division, (seconded to UN, May 1946-March 1947); United States Commissioner, Anglo-American Caribbean Commission, Sept. 1945-June 1947 (Presidential Appt); Director, Div. of Trusteeship, UN, 1946-47; Principal Director, Department of Trusteeship, 1947-54; Actg UN Mediator on Palestine, Sept. 1948-Aug. 1949; UN Special Representative in the Congo, 1960; Supervisory responsibilities over UN peacekeeping operations in Kashmir, Near East, Cyprus and Dominican Republic. Prof. of Govt, Harvard, 1950-52. Holds numerous hon. degrees from univs in USA, Brazil, Canada, Scotland and India. Nobel Prize for Peace, 1950. Grand Cross: of National Order of Honor and Merit, Haiti, 1949; of Order of Merit Carlos Miguel de Cespedes, Cuba, 1951. US Presidential Medal of Freedom, 1963. *Publications:* A World View of Race, 1936; (jointly) An American Dilemma, 1944; Africa: The War and Peace Aims, 1942. Numerous articles in scholarly journals. *Recreations:* baseball, football enthusiast, fishing, theatre, billiards. *Address:* 115-24 Grosvenor Road, Kew Gardens, NY 11418, USA. *T:* Virginia 9-8269.   *[Died 9 Dec. 1971.*

BUNT, Rev. F(rederick) Darrell, CB 1958; OBE 1950; retired as Chaplain of the Fleet and Archdeacon of the Royal Navy (1956-60); Hon. Chaplain to the Queen, 1952-60; *b* 3 July 1902; *o s* of F. W. M. Bunt; *m* 1960, Marianne E. Watson; one *d. Educ:* City of London Sch.; St Chad's Coll., Durham (BA 1923, DipTh 1924, MA 1926). Deacon, 1926; Priest, 1927, Diocese of Chelmsford; St Luke's, Victoria Docks, 1926; St Augustine's, Wembley Park, 1928; Chaplain, Royal Navy, 1930. Served in various ships from 1930; HMS President (Asst to Chaplain of the Fleet), 1948-50; HMS Excellent, 1950-51; RN College, Dartmouth, 1951-53; HM Dockyard, Portsmouth, 1953-56. *Recreations:* golf, sailing. *Address:* Ringer's Plat, Lymore, Milford-on-Sea, Hants. *T:* Milford-on-Sea 3213.

[Died 31 Oct. 1977.

BURBIDGE, Sir John (Richard Woodman), 4th Bt, *cr* 1916; Director, Charta Cards Co. Ltd, since 1964; *b* 5 Oct. 1930; *s* of Sir Richard Grant Woodman Burbidge, 3rd Bt, CBE, and Gladys (*d* 1967), *d* of late C. F. Kearley; *S* father, 1966; *m* 1956, Benita Roxane Mosselmans; no *c. Educ:* Rugby Sch. Harrods Ltd, Knightsbridge, 1952-64. *Heir: cousin* Herbert Dudley Burbidge [*b* 13 Nov. 1904; *m* 1933, Ruby, *d* of Charles Ethelbert Taylor, Vancouver I.; one *s*]. *Address:* Albury Farmhouse, Tiddington, Oxon. *Clubs:* MCC; Huntercombe Golf.

[Died 31 May 1974.

BURCH, Maj.-Gen. Frederick Whitmore, CSI 1946; CIE 1944; MC 1916; DL; late Indian Army; *b* 1 Nov. 1893; 2nd *s* of late Major Frederick Burch, Elvington, York; *m* 1929, Marigold (*d* 1977), 2nd *d* of P. U. Allen, late ICS; one *s* one *d. Educ:* Framlingham Coll. Served European War, 1914-19, in Egypt, France, Belgium with E Yorks Regt, and India (wounded, despatches, MC, 1914-15 Star, 2 War Medals, Afghanistan, 1919); Indian Army: 7th Gurka Rifles and Royal Garhwal Rifles; held various staff appointments including AMS (Personal) to C-in-C India, DSD, GHQ, India; War of 1939-45, India and Italy (4 war medals); Bt Major 1930; Bt Lt-Col 1938; Maj.-Gen. 1942; organised India's Victory Celebrations, New

Delhi, 1946; Chief of Staff and C-in-C Baroda State Forces, 1946; retired, 1949. Raised and commanded NE Sector Essex Home Guard (5 Bns), 1951; Area Controller, Civil Defence, NE Essex, 1950-64. DL Essex, 1956; Chm., Lexden and Winstree Rural District Council, 1959-63. Hon. Treasurer, Chelmsford Diocesan Bd of Finance, 1968-73. *Recreations:* golf, tennis, fishing, polo. *Address:* The Well House, Dedham, Colchester, Essex CO7 6AB. *T:* Colchester 322223. *Club:* Army and Navy.
[*Died 20 Dec.* 1977.

BURCHNALL, Professor Joseph Langley, OBE 1956; MC 1918; MA (Oxon); FRSE; Emeritus Professor of Mathematics in University of Durham since 1958; *b* 8 Dec. 1892; *s* of Henry Walter and Ann Newport Burchnall; *m* 1917, Gertrude Frances Rollinson; two *s* one *d. Educ:* Boston Gram. Sch.; Christ Church Oxford. Open Exhibn, 1911, Hon. Scholar, 1913, Univ. Jun. Mathematical Exhibn, 1913; BA 1914, MA 1922. Served European War, 1914-18, France and Belgium, officer in RA, 1915-19. Lecturer and Reader in Mathematics in Univ. of Durham, 1919-39, Prof., 1939-58; Sec., Durham Colls Council, 1926-38. *Publications:* papers in mathematical journals. *Address:* 58 Pier Avenue, Southwold, Suffolk.
[*Died 29 April* 1975.

BURCKHARDT, Charles James; Swiss historian, diplomat and author; *b* Basle, Switzerland, 10 Sept. 1891; *s* of Charles Chr. Burckhardt and Hélène Aline (*née* Schazmann); *m* 1926, Elizabeth de Reynold; two *d. Educ:* Basle Coll.; Glarisegg Coll.; Univs of Basle, Munich, Göttingen, Zürich and Paris. Attaché Swiss Legation, Vienna, 1918-22; Chief Delegate of International Committee of Red Cross in Turkey, 1923; Prof. of Modern History at the Univ., Zürich, 1923; Prof. Post-graduate Sch. of International Studies, Geneva, 1932; High Commissioner of League of Nations for Free City of Danzig, 1937-39; Pres. of the Mixed Relief Commission of Internat. Red Cross, 1939; Pres. of the Cttee of Internat. Red Cross, 1944-49; Swiss Minister in Paris, 1945-49. Associate Member: Acad. of Salamanca, 1945; Institut des Sciences morales et politiques de l'Acad. Française, 1947; Acad. of Montpelier, 1947; Bavarian Acad. of Fine Arts, 1950; Acad. of Arts, Berlin, 1961. Hon. Mem., Austrian Acad. of Science and Art, 1965. Dr *hc*: Basle, 1939; Lille, 1947; Grenoble, 1947; Rehovot, 1963. Hon. Citizen: Lille, 1947; Lübeck, 1950; Vinzel, 1966. Kt, Pour le Mérite, Germany, 1955; Grand Officier de la Légion d'Honneur, France, 1950. *Publications:* Charles Chr. Burckhardt (biography), 1916; Travel in Asia Minor, 1924; Maria Theresa (biography), 1931; The Cardinal Richelieu, Vol. I, 1934 (trans. in English, French, Italian and Spanish); Correspondence H. v. Hofmannsthal- C. J. Burckhardt, 1956; My Mission at Danzig, 1960; The Cardinal Richelieu, Vols II, III and IV, 1965-67; Correspondence C. J. Burckhardt- Max Rychner, 1970; Gesammelte Werke (6 vols), 1971; many other novels, essays and publications. *Address:* Château de Vinzel, La Bâtie, 1181 VINZEL/VD, Switzerland.
[*Died 3 March* 1974.

BURDEN, Frederick Parker, BA, BCLS; Consulting Engineer; Partner, Burden, Duffy & Usher, Engineers and Surveyors, since 1958; *b* Queensbury, New Brunswick, 28 Dec. 1874; *s* of Stephen Pharel Burden and Ruth Ann Hagerman; *m* 1908, Jane Burgess Payson; two *s* one *d. Educ:* Common schs; Fredericton High and Normal Schools; Univ. of New Brunswick. Went to British Columbia, 1901; became British Columbia Land Surveyor; practised as such until 1928; elected a member for Fort George Riding in 1928 and became Minister of Lands; resigned 1930; Agent-Gen. for British Columbia, 1930-34; conducted Special Surveys for Canadian Govt on Alaska Highway, 1942-46; special survey of Pacific Great Eastern Railway Right-of-way, 1950-52. *Recreations:* played baseball, football, hockey, and has indulged in horse-racing in an amateur way. *Address:* 910 Alward Street, Prince George, BC, Canada. [*Died Jan.* 1971.

BURET, Captain Theobald J. C. P.; *see* Purcell-Buret.

BURGESS, Clarkson Leo, CBE 1951; Clerk of the Peace for the County of London, 1941-68; *b* 7 Sept. 1902; *er s* of late T. C. J. Burgess; *m* 1929, Marie Louise, *d* of late Capt. H. W. Prendergast; one *s* one *d. Educ:* Beaumont; Trinity Coll., Cambridge. Called to the Bar, Middle Temple, 1927. Knight of the Holy Sepulchre (KHS), 1963. *Recreations:* following outdoor sports of all kinds. *Address:* 17 Hillview, Cottenham Park Road, SW20. *T:* 01-947 0668. *Clubs:* Hurlingham; Essex County Cricket. [*Died 15 July* 1975.

BURGESS, Geoffrey, CMG 1955; CIE 1946; OBE 1942; *b* 29 April 1906; *s* of Charles R. Burgess, Bucknall, Staffs; *m* 1933, Jill Margaret, *d* of John Hope-Almond, Cambridge; one *s* one *d. Educ:* Hanley High Sch.; Emmanuel Coll., Cambridge (MA). Served in ICS, 1928-47. Home Office until 1949. Mem. British

Board of Film Censors, 1949-51; Dir, Civil Service Academy, Lahore, Pakistan, 1951-59; UN Advisor to Govt of Ghana, 1959-61; to Govt of the Somali Republic, 1961-63; Div. of Public Administration, UN, 1963-68; Advisor to Govt of Iran, 1968-69. *Address:* La Maison des Landes, St Brelade, Jersey, CI.
[*Died 19 May* 1972.

BURGESS, Russell Brian, MBE 1975; Director of Music, Wandsworth School, since 1954; Associate Chorus Master, New Philharmonia Chorus, since 1971; *b* 3 July 1931. *Educ:* Royal Academy of Music, London. GRSM(Lond), ARAM 1973, LRAM, ARCM. Founder, Wandsworth School Boys' Choir which has made numerous broadcasts and TV programmes (including BBC's Omnibus, The Wandsworth Sound) and records for every major company. Asst to Wilhelm Pitz, 1964-71, and succeeded him as Associate Chorus Master. He was closely associated with the music of Lord Britten (*d* 1976), and with performances of Bach and Purcell; he conducted the world première of Britten's Children's Crusade, in St Paul's Cathedral, 1969. Has taken choirs to Holland, Spain, Sweden, France; conducted at: Henry Wood Promenade Concerts; Royal Festival Hall; the Maltings, Snape. *Recreations:* cricket, studying cooking and wine, photography; exploring his beloved Scotland. *Address:* 60 Sandringham Road, Leyton, E10. *T:* 01-539 7119.
[*Died 31 Aug.* 1979.

BURGESS, His Honour Sir Thomas (Arthur Collier), Kt 1972; DL; Vice-Chancellor, County Palatine of Lancaster, 1963-73, resigned; *b* 14 April 1906; 3rd *s* of Arthur Henry Burgess, FRCS, and Elspeth Burgess; *m* 1935, Anne Marian Mortimer Hunt, 2nd *d* of Wilfred and Henrietta Hunt. *Educ:* Charterhouse; Lincoln Coll., Oxford (MA). Called to Bar, 1928. RAFVR, 1940-45. Bar Council, 1953-57; Bencher, Lincoln's Inn, 1957. Mem. Council, Duchy of Lancaster, 1966-73. DL Lancs 1974. Legion of Merit (Officer), 1946. *Recreation:* music. *Address:* Tatham Old Rectory, Lancaster. *T:* Hornby 21381.
[*Died 19 June* 1977.

BURGIS, Lawrence Franklin, CMG 1927; CVO 1938 (MVO 1925); *b* 1892; *e s* of late J. F. Burgis, FCA, and Mary Franklin, Leamington; *m* 1914, Lorna, *d* of late Arthur Herbert, Whyteleafe, Surrey; one *d. Educ:* King's Sch., Worcester. Private Secretary to Viscount Esher, GCB, 1909-13; Asst Secretary, County of London TF Association, 1913-14; joined 6th Bn The Black Watch, 1913; Captain, 1917; served European War (despatches, Legion of Honour); Asst Secretary, War Cabinet, 1918 and 1939-45; Military Asst Secretary, Cttee of Imperial Defence, 1919-21; late Asst Secretary, Cabinet Office. An Esquire of the Order of St John of Jerusalem. *Address:* The Old Malt House, Steeple Aston, Oxon. *T:* Steeple Aston 353.
[*Died 8 Dec.* 1972.

BURHOP, Prof. Eric Henry Stoneley, FRS 1963; MSc, PhD; Professor of Physics, University College, London, 1960-78, now Emeritus Professor; *b* 31 Jan. 1911; *s* of Henry A. and Bertha Burhop, Melbourne, Australia; *m* 1936, Winifred, *d* of Robert Stevens, Melbourne, Australia; two *s* one *d. Educ:* Ballarat and Melbourne High Schools, Australia; Melbourne Univ.; Trinity Coll., Cambridge. BA 1932, MSc 1933, Melbourne; PhD 1937, Cambridge. Exhibition of 1851 Schol., 1933-35; Research at Cavendish Laboratory, Cambridge, 1933-35; Research Physicist and Lecturer, Univ. of Melbourne, 1935-45; Dep. Dir., Radio Research Laboratory, Melbourne, 1942-44; Technical Officer, DSIR Mission to Berkeley, California, 1944-45; University Coll., London: Lectr in Mathematics, 1945-49; Reader in Mathematics, 1949-50; Reader in Physics, 1950-60. Sen. Vis. Scientist, CERN, 1962-63 and 1978-79. Pres., World Fedn of Scientific Workers, 1971. Foreign Mem., Acad. of Science, German Democratic Republic, 1974. Hon. DUniv: Open Univ., 1975; Warsaw, 1979. Joliot-Curie Medal, 1966; Lenin Peace Prize, 1972. *Publications:* The Challenge of Atomic Energy, 1951; The Auger Effect, 1953; Electronic and Ionic Impact Phenomena (with H. S. W. Massey), 1953; High Energy Physics (ed), vols I, II, 1967, vols III, IV, 1969, vol. V, 1972. Various publications on atomic and nuclear physics. *Recreation:* furtherance of international scientific co-operation. *Address:* 206 Gilbert House, Barbican, EC2. *T:* 01-638 8816.
[*Died 22 Jan.* 1980.

BURKITT, Miles Crawford, JP, MA, FSA, FGS; University Lecturer at Cambridge in the Faculty of Archæology and Anthropology, 1926-58; County Councillor, Cambridgeshire, 1939-64 (Vice-Chairman, 1958-61; Chairman, 1961-64); Alderman, 1964-65; Chairman, Town and Country Planning Committee, 1949-56; Chairman, Children's Committee, 1947-60; *b* Cambridge, 27 Dec. 1890; *o s* of late Prof. F. C. Burkitt, DD, FBA, and Amy Persis, *d* of Rev. W. Parry, DCL; *m* 1923, Margaret Isobel, *d* of Sir John Fry, 2nd Bt; two *s* one *d. Educ:*

Eton; Trinity Coll., Cambridge. Has Travelled extensively on archæological work in Spain, N Russia, Africa, Turkey, etc.; Past Chairman of the Prehistoric Soc. of East Anglia, Cambridge Antiquarian Soc., Section H of British Association, 1949. Lieut (Signals Officer) 4th Cambs. Home Guard, 1941-45; Lieut-Colonel Army Cadet Force, 1942-46. JP 1942, High Sheriff of Counties of Cambridge and Huntingdon, 1960-61. *Publications:* Prehistory, 1921, 2nd Edn 1925; Our Forerunners, 1923; Our Early Ancestors, 1926; South Africa's Past in Stone and Paint, 1928; The Old Stone Age, 1933, 3rd Edn 1955, 4th Edn USA paperback, 1963; Rock Paintings of Southern Andalusia (with Professor Breuil); contributed to Man, Antiquaries Journal, Antiquity, Proc. Prehistoric Society, Nature, Scientia, etc. *Recreation:* travel. *Address:* Merton House (South Wing), Grantchester, Cambs. *T:* Trumpington 2205.
[*Died* 22 *Aug.* 1971.

BURKITT, Robert William; retired; Principal Officer, UK Atomic Energy Authority, 1958-73; *b* 3 March 1908; *s* of late R. F. Burkitt, MC and Alice, *d* of R. Leighton, MA; *m* 1938, Bridget, *d* of Hugh Barber, MD, FRCP; four *s* two *d. Educ:* Bedford Sch.; Pembroke Coll., Cambridge. Kitchener Scholar; MA. MIMechE. Employed in industry, 1930-42 and 1943-44; Ministry of Production, 1942-43; Asst Secretary, Board of Trade, 1944-52; Student, Imperial Defence Coll., 1953; Asst Secretary Monopolies and Restrictive Practices Commn, 1954-55; Dep. Comptroller General, Export Credits Guarantee Dept., 1955-58. Reserve of Air Force Officers, 1928-33; Aux. Air Force (600 City of London Sqdn), 1933-35. *Address:* 26 Charlwood Road, SW15 1PW. *T:* 01-788 9513. *Clubs:* Athenæum; London Rowing, Leander.
[*Died* 7 *Feb.* 1976.

BURNABY, Rev. Prof. John; Regius Professor of Divinity (Emeritus), Cambridge University; *b* 28 July 1891; 2nd *s* of Rev. J. C. W. Burnaby and Ina, *d* of Maj.-Gen. J. P. Battersby; *m* 1922, Dorothy Helen (*d* 1971), *d* of Rev. J. B. Lock, and widow of Capt. W. Newton; one *s* one *d* (one step-*d*) (and one *s* decd). *Educ:* Haileybury Coll.; Trinity Coll., Cambridge. Craven Univ. Scholar, 1912; Chancellor's Classical Medalist, 1914. Served European War, 1914-19, 1st Bn The London Regt, Gallipoli and France. Fellow of Trinity Coll., Cambridge, 1915; Junior Dean, 1919; Steward and Prælector, 1921; Junior Bursar, 1921-31; Tutor, 1931-38; Senior Tutor, 1938-45; Dean of Chapel, 1943-58; Hulsean Lecturer, 1938; College Lecturer in Theology, 1939-51; University Lecturer in Divinity, 1945-52; Regius Professor of Divinity, 1952-58. Deacon, 1941; Priest, 1942. *Publications:* Amor Dei: a study in the religion of St Augustine, 1938; Is the Bible Inspired?, 1949; Later Works of St Augustine (trans. and ed) in Library of Christian Classics, 1955; Christian Words and Christian Meanings, 1955; The Belief of Christendom, 1959. *Recreation:* reading aloud. *Address:* 6 Hedgerley Close, Cambridge. *T:* 50395.
[*Died* 6 *March* 1978.

BURNE, Sir Lewis (Charles), Kt 1959; CBE 1955; *b* West Leederville, WA, 14 Jan. 1898; *s* of late William Charles and Sarah Ellen Burne; *m* 1922, Florence Mary Stafford; two *s* two *d. Educ:* Xavier Coll., Melbourne. President: Master Builders Assoc. of Victoria, 1941-44; Master Builders' Federation of Australia, 1947; Victorian Employers' Federation, 1948-50 and 1953-61; Australian Council of Employers' Federations, 1957-58. Pres. Royal Melbourne Inst. of Technology, 1961; Chairman: Federation Insurance Ltd, 1956-; VEF Corporate Investments Ltd, 1958. Australian Employers' Deleg. at ILO, 1950-52-55-57-66; Australian Employers' Rep. Asian Advisory Cttee of ILO, 1951-66; Employer Member at Governing Body meetings of ILO, 1950-66, and elected Member Governing Body, 1957-66. Fellow Australian Inst. of Builders (Foundation Member). Australian Flying Corps, 1918. *Recreations:* golf and bowls. *Address:* 20 Rockingham Street, Kew, Vic. 3101, Australia. *T:* 86-8354. *Clubs:* Victoria Racing, RAC of Victoria (all in Melbourne).
[*Died* 22 *Feb.* 1978.

BURNETT, Maj.-Gen. Edward John Sidney, CB 1975; DSO 1964; OBE 1965 (MBE 1955); MC 1945; *b* 8 Feb. 1921; *s* of Dr A. H. Burnett; *m* 1967, Christine Adrienne de Jenner; two *d* (and two *s* one *d* by a previous *m*). *Educ:* Kelly Coll., Tavistock. Commissioned into Indian Army, 1941; served with 4th PWO Gurkha Rifles until 1947; transferred to 10th PMO Gurkha Rifles, 1948; served in Hong Kong and Malaya. Military Attaché, Katmandu, 1957-58; College Commander, RMAS, 1967; commanded 48 Gurkha Inf. Bde in Hong Kong, 1968-70; commanded Gurkha L of C, in Nepal, 1970-71; Dep. Comdr Land Forces and Maj.-Gen. Brigade of Gurkhas, in Hong Kong, 1971-75. Col, 10 PMO Gurkha Rifles, 1975-77. Managing Dir, Tehran Racing, PO Box 12/1635 Iran. Star of Nepal, 1954. *Recreations:* golf, shooting. *Address:* c/o Lloyds Bank, 6 Pall Mall, SW1; Whitehouse Farm, near Shaftesbury, Dorset. *Club:* Naval and Military.
[*Died* 19 *Nov.* 1978.

BURNETT, Prof. George Murray; Principal and Vice-Chancellor, Heriot-Watt University, since 1974; *b* 12 July 1921; *s* of G. Burnett, Messina, South Africa; *m* 1946, Anne Edith, *d* of S. M. Bow, Aberdeen; one *s* three *d. Educ:* Robert Gordon's Coll., Aberdeen; Aberdeen Univ. DSIR Senior Fellow, 1947-48. Lectr, Birmingham Univ., 1949-55; Prof. of Chemistry, Univ. of Aberdeen, 1955-74, Vice-Principal, 1966-69. Member: Science Bd, SRC, 1975-78; Council, Open Univ., 1975-78; Council for Applied Scis in Scotland, 1978-; Scottish Nat. Cttee, English Speaking Union, 1979-; Council for Tertiary Educn in Scotland, 1979-. FRSE 1957; FRIC 1961. Hon. LLD Strathclyde, 1979. JP Aberdeen 1967-74. Commander of Royal Order of St Olav (Norway), 1979. *Publications:* Mechanism of Polymer Reactions, 1954; contrib. to Proc. Royal Society, Trans. Faraday Soc., etc. *Address:* Hermiston House, Hermiston, Edinburgh EH14 4AQ. *T:* 031-449 5595. *Clubs:* Caledonian; New (Edinburgh).
[*Died* 4 *Sept.* 1980.

BURNETT, Lt-Col Robert Richardson, CMG 1951; CIE 1944; OBE 1932; *b* 22 Oct. 1897; *s* of late Alexander Burnett, JP, Haddington, Scotland; *m* 1927, Dorothy Mary Laetitia, *d* of late Col J. Anderson; one *s* one *d. Educ:* George Watson's Coll., Edinburgh. 2nd Lieut Royal Scots (TF), 1915; Lieut Machine-Gun Corps, 1916; served in Belgium, France, and Mesopotamia, 1917-18; Indian Army (27th Punjabis), 1918; Zhob Militia, 1922-25; Indian Political Service, 1925-47; Lt-Col 1944; Resident for Rajputana, 1946-47; Dep. High Commissioner for the UK in Pakistan (Karachi), 1947-52; British Member of Sudanisation Cttee, Khartoum, 1954-55. Gen. Sec. for Scotland, Royal Over-Seas League, 1956-64. *Recreations:* fishing and golf. *Address:* Inverdruie, Gullane, East Lothian. *T:* North Berwick 2271.
[*Died* 3 *Nov.* 1975.

BURNETT, William George Esterbrooke, CB 1946; Commissioner of Inland Revenue and Secretary, Board of Inland Revenue, 1942-49, retired; *b* 1886; *s* of late William Burnett, Belturbet, Co. Cavan; *m* 1918, Dorothea (*d* 1978), *y d* of late J. E. Kingsbury, Crawley Down, Sussex; two *s. Educ:* Royal School, Cavan; Trinity Coll., Dublin. *Address:* c/o Brian W. Burnett, White Lodge, 2 Rose Walk, Purley, Surrey. *T:* 01-668 2002.
[*Died* 19 *Nov.* 1978.

BURNHAM, (Marie) Enid, CBE 1957; (Enid Lady Burnham); Vice-President, Girl Guides Association for England, since 1971 (President, 1961-71); President, Buckinghamshire Red Cross, 1936-64; *d* of Hugh Scott Robson, Buenos Aires; *m* 1920, 4th Baron Burnham, CB, DSO, MC, TD; two *s* one *d. Educ:* Heathfield Sch., Ascot. Pres. Bucks Federation of Women's Institutes, 1947-52; Chief Commissioner for England, Girl Guides, 1951-60. Vice-Pres., Bucks County CPRE, 1969. *Publication:* (with Geoffrey Toye) Military Menus. *Recreations:* riding, country life, dogs. *Address:* Wycombe End House, Beaconsfield, Bucks. *Club:* Guide.
[*Died* 29 *July* 1979.

BURNIE, James, MC 1918; *b* Bootle, 10 May 1882; *s* of Joseph Burnie; *m* 1910, Ruth E. Thornton (*d* 1939); one *s* one *d. Educ:* St John's, Bootle; Merchant Taylors', Crosby. Mobilised as Sergeant at outbreak of war; retired as Major in Bootle Battalion, 7th King's Liverpool Regt (MC). MP (L) Bootle, 1922-24; Mayor of Bootle, 1936-37. *Address:* High Beech, 48 Beaconsfield Road, Liverpool L25 6EL. *T:* 051-428 2145. *Club:* National Liberal.
[*Died* 15 *May* 1975.

BURNS, Sir Alan Cuthbert, GCMG 1946 (KCMG 1936; CMG 1927); Knight of Order of St John of Jerusalem, 1942; *b* 9 Nov. 1887; *s* of James Burns, Treas. of St Christopher-Nevis; *m* 1914, Kathleen Hardtman, CStJ (*d* 1970); two *d. Educ:* St Edmund's Coll., Ware. Colonial Civil Service, Leeward Islands, 1905-12; Nigeria, 1912-24; Colonial Sec., Bahama Islands, 1924-29; administered Govt of Bahamas, May-Oct. 1924, Sept.-Nov. 1925, Sept. 1926-March 1927, June-Sept. 1928; Member Bahamas House of Assembly, 1925-28; Dep. Chief Sec. to Govt of Nigeria, 1929-34; Governor and C-in-C of British Honduras, 1934-40; Assistant Under-Sec. of State for the Colonies, 1940-41; Governor and C-inC, Gold Coast, 1941-47; Acting Governor of Nigeria, 1942; Permanent UK Representative on Trusteeship Council of United Nations, 1947-56. Represented Bahamas at West Indies Conference in London, 1926; served with Cameroons Expeditionary Force, 1914-15, and during Egba rebellion, 1918. Chm., Commission of Enquiry into Land and Population Problems, Fiji, 1959-60. *Publications:* Index to Laws of Leeward Islands (joint compiler); Nigeria Handbook 1917-23; History of Nigeria, 1929 (rev. and enl. edn, 1978); Colour Prejudice, 1948; Colonial Civil Servant, 1949; History of the British West Indies, 1954; In Defence of Colonies, 1957; Fiji, 1963. *Address:* 16 Pall Mall, SW1. *T:* 01-839 4258. *Club:* Athenæum.
[*Died* 29 *Sept.* 1980.

BURNS, Hendry Stuart Mackenzie; b 28 April 1900; s of John Stuart Burns and Anne Mackenzie Burns, Aberdeen, Scotland; m 1929, Dorcas Jackson, San Francisco, Calif; two s. *Educ:* Robert Gordon's Coll., Scotland; Aberdeen Univ. (BSc); Cambridge Univ. (BA). Geophysicist, Shell Oil Co., Calif, 1926; transferred to mfg and supplies dept, 1927; asst to div. man., Seattle, 1928-32; asst gen sales mgr, 1932-34, gen. sales mgr, 1934-36; gen. mgr Shell Co. of Colombia, SA, 1936-46; senior vice-pres., Shell Oil Co., Inc., NY, 1946-47, director 1947-60, Pres., 1947-60. Director: American Petroleum Institute; Gen. Dynamics Corporation; Ampex Corporation. Member' St Andrew's Soc.; Metropolitan Opera Assoc. (New York); Burns Soc. hon. LLD Aberdeen Univ., 1956; Hon. DSc St Louis Univ. 1957. *Recreations:* golf, photography. *Address:* 485 Park Avenue, New York 22, NY, USA. *T:* Eldorado 5-0351. *Clubs:* White's; Pacific Union (San Francisco); Racquet and Tennis, etc (NY); Piping Rock, etc (LI).   *[Died* 20 *Oct.* 1971.

BURNS, Robert, CB 1961; CMG 1952; Deputy Secretary, Department of Trade and Industry, since 1970; b 31 Oct. 1912; s of Robert and Jessie V. Burns; m Mary, d of C. H. Goodland, MBE, TD; three s one d. *Educ:* Hamilton Academy; Glasgow Univ. (MA). Asst Principal Dominions Office, 1936; transferred to Colonial Office, 1937; seconded to Ministry of Supply, 1940; Private Sec. to Lord Beaverbrook and Mr Lyttelton, 1941; Asst Sec., Min. of Production, 1944; Board of Trade, 1945; Counsellor Commercial HM Embassy, Washington, 1949-52; Asst Sec., Board of Trade, 1952-53; Under Sec.; Ministry of Supply, 1953-59; Ministry of Aviation, 1959-63 (Dep. Sec. 1963-66); Second Sec., BoT, 1966-70. *Address:* 90 Cromwell Avenue, N6. *Club:* Reform.   *[Died* 13 *July* 1971.

BURNS, William Alexander, RSA 1970 (ARSA 1955); RSW 1956; Principal Lecturer in Art, College of Education, Aberdeen, since 1967; b 31 May 1921; s of James Burns and Marion Maclean. *Educ:* Hyndland; Glasgow Sch. of Art. DA Glasgow. Pilot, RAF, 1939-42; Glasgow Sch. of Art, 1944-48; Hospital-field Art Coll., Arbroath, 1948-49; taught in schools in Glasgow, Argyll, E Lothian; Lectr, Coll. of Educn, Aberdeen, 1955. Four one-man shows, Edinburgh, incl. Festival Exhibn 1968. Paintings in Arts Council collection and collections of British Embassies, Nuffield Foundn, Glasgow Art Gallery, Aberdeen, Dundee, etc. *Recreation:* flying. *Address:* Grianan, Whitecairns, Balmedie, Aberdeenshire. *T:* Newmachar 339. *Clubs:* Art (Glasgow); Art (Edinburgh); Pegasus Flying (Aberdeen).   *[Died* 15 *Oct.* 1972.

BURRA, Edward John, CBE 1971; painter; b London, 1905. *Educ:* Chelsea Sch. of Art; Royal College of Art. First one-man show, Leicester Galleries, London, 1929; subsequent shows there: May 1932, June 1947, and June 1949; Lefevre Galleries, 1952, 1955, 1957, 1959, 1961, 1963, 1965, 1967, 1969, 1971, 1973; retrospective exhibn, Tate Gallery, 1973. Has designed scenery and costumes for the ballet and opera. Works bought by Tate Gallery, etc. Travels include: the United States, Mexico, Spain, France. Gaetano Marzotto Prize, 1967. *Address:* c/o Lefevre Galleries, 30 Bruton Street, W1. *[Died* 22 *Oct.* 1976.

BURRELL, John Percy; Theatrical Producer; Director, Training Academy of American Shakespearean Theatre, since 1955; b 6 May 1910; s of late Prof. P. S. Burrell, CIE; m 1936, Margaret Souttar; two s. *Educ:* Shrewsbury Sch.; Royal Coll. of Art, London. Studied painting, sculpture and stage designing, being at the same time occupied with production, 1928-34; joined Michel St Denis at London Theatre Studio as Producer and Dir of Decor, 1937; War Office, 1939-41; Drama Producer, BBC, 1941-44; programmes included: Marriage of St Francis, Pilgrim's Progress, The Rescue, Don Quixote. Produced Heartbreak House, at Cambridge Theatre, for H. M. Tennent, Ltd, 1942. Chm. of Dirs of the Old Vic Theatre Co., 1944-49. Productions for Old Vic, at New Theatre: Richard III, Arms and the Man, Uncle Vanya, 1944; Henry IV, Part I, Henry IV, Part II, 1945; The Alchemist, 1946; The Taming of the Shrew, 1947; Saint Joan, 1947; The Government Inspector (Gogol), 1948; The Tragical History of Doctor Faustus (Marlowe), 1948; The Way of the World (Congreve), 1948. *Recreations:* drawing, painting, boating. *Address:* 37 Ladbroke Road, W11. *T:* 01-727 7616.   *[Died* 28 *Sept.* 1972.

BURROUGH, Admiral Sir Harold Martin, GCB 1949 (KCB 1944; CB 1939); KBE 1942; DSO 1942 (and Bar 1943); DSM (USA), 1943; Legion of Merit (USA), 1946; Knight Grand Cross Orange Nassau (Netherlands), 1947; Grand Officer, Legion of Honour (France), 1949; b 4 July 1888; s of Rev. Charles Burrough, MA; m 1914, Nellie Wills Outhit (d 1972), Halifax, Nova Scotia; two s three d. *Educ:* St Edward's Oxford; HMS Britannia. Gunnery Officer of HMS Southampton at the Battle of Jutland; Comdr, 1922; Capt., 1928; commanded HMS

London, 1930-32; 5th Destroyer Flotilla, 1935-37; HMS Excellent, 1937-38; served War of 1939-45 (DSO and Bar, KBE); Assistant Chief of Naval Staff, Admiralty, 1939-40; commanding Cruiser Squadron, 1940-42; commanding Naval Forces, Algiers, 1942; Flag Officer Commanding, Gibraltar and Mediterranean Approaches, 1943-45; Allied Naval C-in-C. Expeditionary Force, 1945; British Naval C-in-C, Germany, 1945-46; C-in-C The Nore, 1946-48. Rear-Admiral, 1939; Vice-Admiral, 1942; Admiral, 1945; retired list, 1949. *Address:* Barn House, Aldbourne, Marlborough, Wilts. *Club:* Naval and Military.   *[Died* 22 *Oct.* 1977.

BURROUGHS, Ronald Arthur, CMG 1966; HM Diplomatic Service, retired; company director; b 4 June 1917; s of Rev. Henry Frederick Burroughs and Ada Burroughs; m 1st, 1947, Jean Valerie McQuillen; two d; 2nd, 1971, Audrey Cunha. *Educ:* St John's Sch., Leatherhead; Trinity Coll., Cambridge. Fleet Air Arm, 1940-45. FO, 1946; 2nd Sec., HM Embassy, Rio de Janeiro, 1947-49; HM Consul, Marseilles, 1949-50; 1st Sec., HM Embassy, Cairo, 1950-53; FO, 1953-55; Canadian National Defence Coll., 1955-56; 1st Sec., HM Embassy, Vienna, 1956-59; Counsellor, FO, 1959-62; Counsellor and Head of Chancery, Rio de Janeiro, 1962-64; Counsellor, HM Embassy, Lisbon, 1964-67; British Chargé d'Affaires, South Yemen, 1967-68; Assistant Under-Sec. of State, FCO, 1968-71, seconded to Home Office as UK Rep. to NI Govt, March 1970-April 1971; Ambassador to Algeria, 1971-73. *Recreations:* reading, fishing. *Address:* The Post House, Graffham, near Petworth, W Sussex. *Club:* Travellers'.   *[Died* 24 *May* 1980.

BURROWS, Albert; Director-General, Merseyside Passenger Transport Executive, since 1969; b 3 Nov. 1919; s of John Joseph Burrows and Ada Wainwright; m 1944, Blodwen Megan Evans; one s one d. *Educ:* Warrington Grammar Sch.; Manchester Coll. of Commerce. Armed Forces, 1939-46. Service in transport at: Warrington, 1937-39 and 1948-49; Nottingham, 1949-53; Portsmouth, 1953-56; Gen. Manager, Transport Undertaking: Lancaster, 1956-61; Barrow-in-Furness, 1961-63; Chesterfield, 1963-66; Liverpool City, 1966-69. *Recreation:* golf. *Address:* 24 Hatton Garden, Liverpool, L3 2AN. *T:* 051-236 7411 (Ext. 1). *Clubs:* National Liberal; West Lancashire Golf.
                    [Died 23 *Dec.* 1972.

BURROWS, Sir Frederick (John), GCSI 1947; GCIE 1945; DL, JP; Chairman of Wye River Authority, since 1965; b 1887; s of John Burrows; m 1912, Dora Beatrice (Kaisar-i-Hind Gold Medal) (d 1968), d of G. Hutchings, Hereford; one s one d. Served European War, 1914-19, Company Sergeant-Major, Grenadier Guards (Meritorious Service Medal). Pres. Nat. Union of Railwaymen, 1942-44; Member Soulbury Commission on Constitutional Reform, Ceylon, 1945; Governor of Bengal, 1946-47. Chairman of the Agricultural Land Commission, 1948-63 (Commn abolished); Member Governing Body of Sch. of Oriental and African Studies, London Univ., 1951-63; Member Royal Commn on Marriage and Divorce, 1951; formerly a Director Lloyds Bank Ltd until 1958 and of S Wales Local Cttee of Lloyds Bank until Dec. 1962. DL, JP Herefordshire; High Sheriff, Herefordshire, 1955. *Address:* Thrushes Nest, Rope Walk, Ross-on-Wye. *T:* Ross 2693. *Club:* Oriental.
                    [Died 20 *April* 1973.

BURROWS, Comdr Henry Montagu, CB 1964; CBE 1956; Royal Navy (retired); Clerk-Assistant of the Parliaments, House of Lords, 1961-63, retired (Reading-Clerk and Clerk of the Journals, 1959-61; Principal Clerk of Public Bills, 1950-59); b 24 March 1899; er s of late Rev. Montagu John Burrows; m 1939, Harriet Elizabeth, o d of late Ker George Russell Vaizey, Star Stile, Halstead, Essex; one s one d. *Educ:* RNC Osborne and Dartmouth. Went to sea at outbreak of European War, 1914-18, as a midshipman in HMS Benbow and served in her at Battle of Jutland. Transferred to RAF, 1923, Flt-Lt in No 1 (Fighter) Sqdn in Irak. Appointed a Clerk in the House of Lords, 1925. Rejoined Royal Navy as Lieut-Comdr at outbreak of War of 1939-45 and commanded a motor boat at Dunkirk evacuation; later appointed 1st Lieut of HMS Argus (despatches while serving in her in N African landings, 1942); Comdr 1945. Trustee, Attlee Meml Foundn, 1969. Royal Humane Society's bronze medal for life saving, 1920. *Recreation:* golf. *Address:* East House, Long Crendon, near Aylesbury, Bucks. *T:* Long Crendon 208 498. *Club:* Travellers'.   *[Died* 16 *Aug.* 1979.

BURROWS, Rev. Millar; Winkley Professor of Biblical Theology, Yale University, 1934-58; Member of the Standard Bible Committee since 1938, Vice-Chairman, 1954-63; b 26 Oct. 1889; s of Edwin Jones Burrows and Katharine Millar Burrows; m 1915, Irene Bell Gladding (d 1967); one s. *Educ:* Cornell Univ. (BA 1912), Union Theological Seminary (BD 1915), Yale Univ. (PhD 1925). Rural Pastor in Texas, 1915-19; Rural survey

supervisor for Texas, Interchurch World Movement, 1919-20; College pastor and professor of Bible, Tusculum Coll., 1920-23; Asst Professor, Assoc. Professor, and Professor of Biblical Literature and Hist. of Religions, Brown Univ., 1925-34; Visiting Professor of Religion, Amer. Univ. of Beirut, 1930-31; Director, Amer. Sch. of Oriental Research, Jerusalem, 1931-32 and 1947-48; Chm. Dept. of Near Eastern Languages and Literatures, Yale Univ. 1950-58. Pres., Amer. Schools of Oriental Research, 1934-48. Pres., Amer. Middle East Relief, 1954-56. Fellow Amer. Academy of Arts and Sciences, 1949. Hon. DD: Oberlin Coll., 1960; Brown Univ.; Yale Univ., 1961. *Publications:* Founders of Great Religions, 1931; Bible Religion, 1938; Basis of Israelite Marriage, 1938; What Mean These Stones?, 1941; Outline of Biblical Theology, 1946; Palestine is Our Business, 1949; The Dead Sea Scrolls, 1955; More Light on the Dead Sea Scrolls, 1958 (1955 and 1958 titles repr. 1978 as Burrows on the Dead Sea Scrolls); Diligently Compared— The Revised Standard Version and the King James Version of the Old Testament, 1964; Jesus in the First Three Gospels, 1977. Editor, The Dead Sea Scrolls of St Mark's Monastery, 1950-51. Articles in many learned journals. *Address:* 1670 Woodland Avenue, Winter Park, Florida 32789, USA. *T:* 1-305-647-0070.
[Died 29 April 1980.

BURT, Professor Alfred LeRoy; *b* Listowel, Ont., Canada, 28 Nov. 1888; *e s* of C. K. Burt; *m* 1915, Dorothy, *d* of J. M. M. Duff, Montreal; one *s* three *d. Educ:* Toronto Public Schools; Univ. of Toronto, BA 1910; Corpus Christi Coll., Oxford, BA 1912, MA 1916. Rhodes Scholar for Ontario, 1910; divided Beit Prize, Robert Herbert Memorial Prize, 1913, FRHistS. Lecturer, 1913; Asst Prof. of History, Univ. of Alberta, Canada, 1916; Lieut Canadian Tank Batt., CEF, 1918; Associate Prof., 1920; Prof. and Head of History Dept, Univ. of Alberta, 1921; Prof., Univ. of Minnesota, 1930-57, Emeritus Professor of Univ., 1957-. Visiting Professor: Carleton Univ., Canada, 1957-58; Univ. of Chicago, 1959-60; Univ. of Manitoba, 1960-61. Royal Society of Canada Tyrrell Medal, 1946; Canada Centennial Medal, 1967. Hon. Dr Laws, Univ. of Alberta, 1966. *Publications:* Imperial Architects, 1913; A Short History of the League of Nations, 1924; edited vol. 3, Makers of Canada Series, 1926; High School Civics, 1928; Romance of the Prairie Provinces, 1930; The Old Province of Quebec, 1933; The Romance of Canada, 1937; The United States, Great Britain, and British North America from the Revolution to the Establishment of Peace after the War of 1812, 1940; A Short History of Canada for Americans, 1942; (in part) The United States and Its Place in World Affairs, 1943; The Evolution of the British Empire and Commonwealth from the American Revolution, 1956; contributor to various journals and to Cambridge History of the British Empire. *Recreations:* music, gardening, golf. *Address:* 39 Crown Ridge Road, Wellesley, Mass. 02181, USA. *[Died 21 June 1971.*

BURT, C. K. J.; *see* Johnstone-Burt.

BURT, Sir Cyril Lodowic, Kt 1946; MA, DSc Oxon; Hon. LLD Aberdeen; Hon. DLitt Reading; FBA; Hon. Fellow, Jesus College, Oxford; Professor of Psychology, University College, London, 1931-50. Emeritus Professor since 1950; *b* 3 March 1883; *s* of Dr C. Barrow Burt, JP, of Snitterfield, Stratford-on-Avon; *m* Joyce, *d* of late P. F. Woods. *Educ:* Christ's Hospital (Charles Lamb Medallist); Jesus Coll., Oxford (Classical Scholar); Post-graduate Research Scholar; Würzburg Univ. John Locke Scholar in Mental Philosophy in the Univ. of Oxford, 1908; Lecturer in Experimental Psychology and Asst Lecturer in Physiology, Univ. of Liverpool, 1909-13; Asst Lecturer, Psychological Laboratory, Univ. of Cambridge, 1912-13; Psychologist to the London County Council (Education Dept), 1913-32; Professor of Education in the Univ. of London, 1924-31; Pres. Psychological Section, British Assoc., 1923; Pres. British Psychological Soc., 1942; Chm. of the Psychological Cttee of the Industrial Health Board (Medical Research Council); Governor and Almoner of Christ's Hospital; Member of: Nat. Inst. of Industrial Psychology, Industrial Health Research Board; Advisory Cttee to War Office on Personnel Selection; Psychological Consultant to Civil Service Commission. Editor, British Journal of Statistical Psychology. *Publications:* The Distribution of Educational Abilities, 1917; Mental and Scholastic Tests, 1921; Handbook of Tests, 1923; The Young Delinquent, 1925; The Measurement of Mental Capacities, 1927; How the Mind Works, 1933; The Subnormal Mind, 1935; The Backward Child, 1937; Factors of the Mind, 1940; The Causes and Treatment of Backwardness, 1952; A Psychological Study of Typography, 1959; various articles in scientific periodicals. *Address:* 9 Elsworthy Road, Hampstead, NW3. *T:* 01-722 0233.   *[Died 10 Oct. 1971.*

BURT, Hugh Armitage, MA Cantab; FRCP; Director, Department of Physical Medicine, University College Hospital, since 1947; Hon. Consultant in Physical Medicine to Army, since 1954; *b* 16 March 1911; *e s* of late J. Barnes Burt, MD, and Dorothy Armitage. *Educ:* Westminster Sch.; Trinity Coll., Cambridge (Westminster Sch. Exhibitioner); UCH. BA Cantab 1932; MB, BCh Cantab 1937; MRCS 1935; FRCP 1952. Late House Physician, House Surgeon and Asst on the Medical Unit, UCH, and Chief Asst, Dept for Chronic Rheumatic Diseases, West London Hosp. War of 1939-45, Lt-Col RAMC and Adviser in Physical Medicine to WO. Examiner in Physical Medicine, RCP. Pres. of the British Assoc. of Physical Medicine, 1959-62 (Member Council 1945-71; Vice-President 1956-59, 1968-71); Member Army Health Advisory Cttee; Mem. Council for Professions Supplementary to Medicine; Mem. Bd of Govs, UCH, 1962-71. Former Pres. Section of Physical Medicine, Royal Society of Medicine; ex-Member of Executive and Educational Cttees, Arthritis and Rheumatism Council. Former Editor of Annals of Physical Medicine. *Publications:* various articles and chapters in medical journals and textbooks. *Address:* 44 Wimpole Street, W1M 7DG. *T:* 01-935 0788. *Club:* Athenæum.   *[Died 12 March 1976.*

BURTON, Prof. Alan Chadburn, MBE 1947; FRSC 1952; FRSA (UK) 1954; formerly Professor of Biophysics, University of Western Ontario, Canada, now Professor Emeritus; *b* 18 April 1904; *s* of Frank Burton, Dental Surgeon, and Annie Grey (*née* Tyrrell), N Ireland; *m* 1933, Clara Ballard, Niagara Falls, Ontario; one *s. Educ:* Strand Sch., Streatham Hill; Univ. Coll., London (Fellow, 1917). BSc Physics and Maths, UCL, 1925. Demonstrator in Physics, Univ. Coll., 1925-26; Science Master, Liverpool Collegiate Sch., 1926-27; Demonstrator and lecturer, Univ. of Toronto, Physics Dept, 1927-32; Fellow of Nat. Res. Council, Canada, 1930-32; PhD Physics, Univ. of Toronto, 1932; Research Asst, Dept of Vital Economics, Univ. of Rochester, NY, 1932-34; Rockefeller Gen. Ed. Board Fellow, Univ. of Pennsylvania, 1934-36; Fellow, Johnson Foundation for Medical Physics, 1936-40; Research Assoc., Nat. Research Council of Canada, 1941-46. War Research on Protective Clothing and Equipment for RCAF. Asst Prof., 1946, later Assoc. Prof. of Biophysics, Univ. of W. Ontario. President: American Physiological Soc., 1956-57; Canadian Physical Soc., 1962-63; Biophysical Soc., 1958. Hon. LLD Alberta, 1963; Hon. DSc Western Ontario, 1974. Gairdner Internat. Award for Cardiovascular Research, 1961. *Publications:* The Science of Field Testing of Clothing and Equipment (Monograph of Defence Research Board of Canada), 1947; (with O. G. Edholm) Man in a Cold Environment, 1955; The Physiology and Biophysics of the Circulation, 1965; about 170 publications in journals of Physiology and Biophysics, 12 in Journals of Physics. *Recreations:* formerly Rugby and tennis, now golf; interested in penal reform and prisoner rehabilitation (John Howard Society). *Address:* 243 Epworth Avenue, London, Ontario, Canada. *T:* 434-9938.   *[Died 27 June 1979.*

BURTON, Sir Geoffrey Pownall, KCSI 1946; KCIE 1937 (CIE 1935); DL; MA; *b* 19 Nov. 1884; *s* of John Albert Burton, JP, and Anne Sophia Hadfield; *m* 1914, Doris Hargreaves Speight; one *s* one *d. Educ:* Bradford Grammar Sch.; Queen's Coll., Oxford (Hastings Exhibitioner). Entered Indian Civil Service as Asst Commissioner, 1909; Under Secretary to Government, CP, 1913; Deputy Commissioner, 1918; Excise Commissioner, 1927; Revenue Secretary to Government, CP, 1929; Commissioner, Berar, 1932; Commissioner, Jubbulpore Division, 1933; Revenue and Finance Member of Govt, CP, 1936-37; Financial Commissioner, CP AND Berar, 1937; Adviser to Governor of Central Provinces, 1939-45. DL Yorkshire, West Riding, 1954. *Address:* 8 Park View Road, Heaton, Bradford 9. *T:* Bradford 44995.   *[Died 8 April 1972.*

BUSH, Raymond G. W.; Horticultural consultant and author, retired; *b* 30 Mar. 1885; *s* of Robert Francis Evans Bush and Grace Marion Bush; *m* 1911, Audrey Elizabeth Cobb (*d* 1947); one *s* one *d. Educ:* Rugby Sch. Fruitgrower, 1915-38. *Publications:* Soft Fruit Growing, 1942; (with G. H. T. Kimble) The Weather, 1943; Tree Fruit Growing; Frost and the Fruitgrower, 1945; Fruitgrowing Outdoors, 1947; Harvesting and Storing Garden Fruits; A Fruitgrower's Diary; Fruit Salad; Pruning; (with Prof. T. Wallace) Commercial Fruit Growing. *Recreations:* gardening, travelling, painting, swimming and basking in the sun. *Address:* Rock Cottage, Ocho Rios, Jamaica.
[Died 15 Sept. 1972.

BUSH, Dr Vannevar, Hon. KBE 1948; Hon. Chairman of the Corporation, Massachusetts Institute of Technology, since 1959 (Chairman 1957-59); Chairman of Board of Graphic Arts Research Foundation; Trustee, The George Putnam Fund; Trustee, Carnegie Institution of Washington; *b* 11 Mar. 1890; *s* of Richard Perry Bush and Emma Linwood Paine; *m* 1916, Phoebe Davis; two *s*. *Educ:* Tufts Coll. (now Tufts Univ.), Medford, Mass; Harvard, Cambridge, Mass; Massachusetts Inst. of Technology. BS and MS (Tufts Coll.), 1913; EngD Harvard, 1916; EngD Mass Inst. of Tech., 1916; Test Dept, Gen. Electric Co., 1913; Inspection Dept US Navy 1914; Instr in Maths, Tufts Coll., 1914-15; Asst Prof. of Elec. Eng, Tufts Coll., 1916-17; Research, US Navy, in connection with submarine detection, 1917-18; Mass Inst of Technology: Associate Prof. of Electric Power Transmission, 1919-23, Prof. 1923-32; Vice-Pres. and Dean of Engineering, 1932-38; Hon. Chm. Corp., 1959-; Pres., Carnegie Instn of Washington, 1939-56, Trustee, 1939-; Chm. Nat. Defense Research Cttee, US Govt 1940, 1941; Dir, Office of Scientific Research and Development, US Govt, 1941-46; Chm. Jt Research and Development Board, US Govt, 1946-47; Chairman, Research and Development Board, National Military Establishment, US Government, Washington, DC, 1947-48; Mem. Council on Foreign Relations, 1953; Mem. Nat. Science Foundation Advisory Cttee, on Govt-Univ. Relationships, 1953. Trustee Emeritus, Johns Hopkins Univ. Hon Fellow, American Coll., of Surgeons. Hon. Member: American Society of Mechanical Engineers, American Society of Naval Architects and Marine Engineers; Inst. of Electrical and Electronics Engineers. Holds many medals, awards, and hon. degrees, inc. Atomic Pioneer Medal, awarded by Pres. Nixon, 1970. Officer, Légion d'Honneur, France. *Publications:* (with William H. Timble) Principles of Electrical Engineering (NY and London), 1922; Operational Circuit Analysis (NY and London), 1929; Endless Horizons (Washington), 1946; Modern Arms and Free men, New York, 1949; Science Is Not Enough, 1967; Pieces of the Action (NY and London), 1970, 1971. *Address:* Massachusetts Institute of Technology, Cambridge, Mass 02139, USA; 304 Marsh Street, Belmont, Mass, USA. *Club:* St Botolph (Boston, Mass). *[Died 28 June 1974.*

BUSHELL, Warin Foster; retired; *b* Harrow, 1885; *s* of William Done Bushell, for 50 years assistant master and Hon. chaplain at Harrow School and Lord of the Manor of Caldey Island, Pembrokeshire; unmarried. *Educ:* Charterhouse; King's Coll., Cambridge. Asst Master, Gresham's Sch., Holt, 1907-12; Head of Modern Side and Housemaster, Rossall Sch., 1912-20; Headmaster of Solihull Sch., 1920-27; Rector of Michaelhouse, Natal, 1927-30; Headmaster of Birkenhead Sch., 1930-46. Pres., Mathematical Assoc., 1946-47. Served in the Herefordshire Regiment in European War, 1914-18; saw service in Palestine and France. *Publications:* miscellaneous articles of an educational and archaeological nature; School Sermons, 1950; School Memories, 1952. *Recreation:* travelling. *Address:* Colonsay, Talbot Road, Birkenhead, Cheshire. *T:* 051-652 2713. *Clubs:* Royal Over-Seas League, Royal Commonwealth Society. *[Died 21 Nov. 1974.*

BUSHNELL, Geoffrey Hext Sutherland, MA, PhD, FBA 1970; Fellow of Corpus Christi College, Cambridge, since 1969; author; Curator, University Museum of Archaeology and Ethnology, Cambridge, 1948-70, retd; Reader in New World Archaeology, 1966-70, now Emeritus; *b* 31 May 1903; *s* of Rev. G. D. S. Bushnell and Mildred Mary (*née* Earle); *m* 1936, Patricia Louise Egerton Ruck; four *s*. *Educ:* Wellington; Downing Coll., Cambridge. Geologist, Anglo-Ecuadorian Oilfields Ltd, in Ecuador, 1926-38. Served War: Lincolnshire Regt, 1940, RE 1941-46, Major 1946. Asst Curator, Cambridge Univ. Museum of Archaeology and Ethnology, 1947; Curator, 1948; FSA 1934, Vice-Pres., 1961-65. Mem., Cathedrals Advisory Cttee, 1955-; Trustee, Historic Churches Preservation Trust, 1964-. Comendador, Al Mérito of Ecuador, 1971. *Publications:* Archaeology of the Santa Elena Peninsula, SW Ecuador, 1951; Ancient American Pottery (with A. Digby), 1955; Peru (Ancient Peoples and Places), 1956, 2nd edn 1963; Ancient Arts of the Americas, 1965; The First Americans, 1968. *Recreations:* gardening, visiting ancient buildings. *Address:* 4 Wordsworth Grove, Cambridge CB3 9HH. *T:* Cambridge 59539. *[Died 26 Dec. 1978.*

BUSHNELL, George Herbert; author; retired as Librarian of the University of St Andrews (1924-61); *b* Wolverhampton, 26 July 1896; 2nd *s* of late George Bushnell and late Bertha Mary Jupp, Moseley, Birmingham; *m* 1922, Elizabeth, *d* of late Thomas Bladon, Birmingham; three *d*. *Educ:* Waverley Sch., Small Heath; Birmingham Sch. of Art; privately. Served in Cavalry; RAMC, 1914-19; Member of League of Interpreters during the European War; Regimental Instructor in French; War Artist. Formerly mem. council, Scottish Library Association. Examiner in Anglo-Saxon, 1955-57. Hon. Corr. mem., Ecole Palatine d'Avignon; D. d'Hon. S. Int. d. Philol.; FLA. *Publications:* Emptyings of my Ashtray (miscellaneous poems), 1917; Library Manual; The Libraries of Shem; The Productions of the Early Presses at St Andrews, 1926; Scottish Entries for Bibl Soc. Dicty

of Printers, etc, 1726-76, 1932; University Librarianship, 1930; Diane de Poitiers, 1927; Scottish Bookbindings and Bookbinders, 1450-1800, 1927; The Alexandrian Library, translated and published in Japanese, 1932; Life and Work of Edward Raban; Scottish Hist. Research Series, I-VII; The St Andrews Type-Foundry; The World's Earliest Libraries, 1929, translated and published in Japanese, 1936; Dictionary of Scottish Engravers of Eighteenth Century, 1929, supplement, 1931; Fulke Fitzwarin, 1933; Sindbad the Sailor (in Braille), 1928; The Three Wise Men, 1935; Sir Richard Grenville, 1936; Patrick Bower, 1942; Kościuszko, 1943; Sir Henry Babington Smith (with Lady Elisabeth Babington Smith), 1943; Ghost Stories, 1945; From Papyrus to Print, 1947; From Bricks to Books, 1949; Scottish Engravers, 1949; contributor to Encyclopædia Britannica; editor of Andrew Lang's History of St Andrews; joint-editor, 1916-18, of The Linseed Lance (trench magazine); contributor to numerous magazines, etc; exhibitor various galleries. *Recreations:* gardening, painting. *Address:* The Shielin, Wormit-on-Tay, Fife. *[Died 12 Aug. 1973.*

BUSIA, Dr Kofi Abrefa, GM; Prime Minister of Ghana, 1969-72; *b* 11 July 1913; *m* 1950; two *s* two *d*. *Educ:* Mfantsipim Sch., Gold Coast (Methodist Synod Schol., 1927-30); Achimota Coll.; Oxford Univ. (Achimota Council Schol., 1935-36, 1939-41). Carnegie Res. Student, Oxford, 1941-42, 1945-47; Nuffield Coll. Student Oxford, 1946-47. BA London; MA, DPhil Oxon. Mem. Staff: Wesley Coll., Kumasi, 1932-34; Achimota Coll., Accra, 1936-39; Admin. Officer (District Comr), Govt of Gold Coast, 1942-49; Officer i/c Sociological Surveys, 1947-49; UC Gold Coast: Res. Lectr in African Studies, 1949-51; Sen. Lectr in Sociology, 1952-54; Prof. of Sociology, 1954-59; Prof. of Sociology, Inst. of Social Studies, The Hague, 1959-62; Prof. of Sociology and Culture of Africa, Univ. of Leiden, 1960-62; Dir of Studies for World Council of Churches, Birmingham, 1962-64; Prof. of Sociology, St Antony's Coll., Oxford, 1964-66. Vis. Professor: Northwestern Univ., Ill, 1954; Nuffield Coll., Oxford, 1955; Agricultural Univ. of Wageningen, Holland, 1956; El Colegio de México, 1962; Univ. of York. Member: Exec. Cttee, Internat. Sociological Assoc., 1953-62; Internat. Social Science Council (Unesco), 1955-61. Mem., Nat. Assembly of Ghana, 1951-59 (Leader of Parly Opposition, 1956-59). Chairman: Nat. Adv. Cttee, NLC, 1967; Centre for Civic Educn, 1967. Hon. DLitt Ghana, 1970. *Publications:* The Position of the Chief in the Modern Political System of Ashanti, 1951; The Challenge of Africa, 1962; Purposeful Education for Africa, 1964; Urban Churches in Britain, 1966; Africa in Search of Democracy, 1967, etc. *Recreations:* music, walking. *Address:* 93 Abingdon Road, Standlake, Witney, Oxon OX8 7QN. *[Died 28 Aug. 1978.*

BUSTAMANTE, Rt. Hon. and Exc. Sir (William) Alexander, PC 1964; GBE 1967; Kt 1955; National Hero (Jamaica) 1969; Planter, Penkeeper, Trade Unionist; Prime Minister of Jamaica and Minister of External Affairs and Defence, 1962-67, retired; MHR, 1944-67 (for W Kingston, 1944-49, for S Clarendon, 1949-67); *b* Blenheim, Hanover, Jamaica, 24 Feb. 1884; *s* of late Robert Constantine Clarke, planter, and Mary (*née* Wilson); *m* 1962, Gladys Longbridge, JP. *Educ:* elem. schs and by private studies; La Salle Univ., USA (certif. in Commercial Spanish). Left Jamaica in youth and travelled in Latin America, Spain, USA, Canada. Was Inspector of Police in Havana, Cuba; formerly Traffic Manager, NY Bond & Share Co. tramway system, in Panama; served for several years as dietitian in a New York hosp. Returned to Jamaica from USA, 1934, and began taking interest in public affairs; wrote letters in the press exposing economic and social conditions of the people; when strikes took place throughout Jamaica, May 1938, assumed leadership of masses and was arrested, charged with sedition, refused bail, but was subseq. released and charge withdrawn; called gen. strike, 1939; was interned under Defence Regulations, 1940-42; after his release, started reorganization of Bustamante Industrial Trade Union and membership grew to several thousands; formed Jamaica Labour Party, 1943; won 22 seats out of 32 to the House of Representatives under universal adult suffrage, 1944; 18 of 32 in second election, 1949. Leader of Govt Business and Minister of Communications, 1945-53; Chief Minister of Jamaica, 1953-55, also Minister of Local Govt; Leader of Opposition, 1955-62; led opposition to Jamaica remaining in West Indies Federation; won Referendum 1961 and Gen. Elecs, 1962; again Chief Minister, Apr.-Aug. 1962; became first Prime Minister, Aug. 1962. Founder (1938) and Pres., Bustamante Industrial Trade Union; Founder-Leader (1943) Jamaica Labour Party; Mayor of Kingston, 1947-48; Mem. Caribbean Commn, 1950-55; Jamaica's Representative at Coronation of HM Queen Elizabeth II, June 1953; Founder-Pres., West Indies Democratic Labour Party, 1957; resigned, 1960; Jamaica's Rep. several Bds, Cttees, Delegns abroad, re. banana, citrus, sugar, etc; Sole Proprietor Loan & Securities Co., 1934-39. Hon. Dr of Laws: Fairfield Univ., USA, 1963; Univ. of the West Indies, 1966. Religion: Roman Catholic. Nat. Order of Cedars, Lebanon; Distinguished Order of Brilliant Star with Special Grand Cordon, Repub. of China; Grand Gold Cross, Order Gran Heraldica de Cristobal Colon, Dominican Repub.; Gran Cordon, Order of Liberatador, Venezuela. *Recreations:* farming, swimming, motoring. *Address:* 24 Tucker Avenue, Kingston 6, Jamaica; Irish Town PO, Jamaica.

[Died 6 Aug. 1977.

BUTCHART, Brevet Lt-Col Henry Jackson, DSO 1918; OBE 1951; Hon. LLD Aberdeen 1952; DL, JP County and City of Aberdeen; Secretary to University of Aberdeen, 1919-52; Member: Education Committee of the City of Aberdeen, 1955-66; Valuation Appeal Committee for the City of Aberdeen, 1957-66; President Aberdeen Branch Red Cross Society, 1958-65; Law Agent to University of Aberdeen, 1952-67; *b* 18 April 1882; 4th *s* of James S. Butchart, Advocate in Aberdeen; *m* 1912, Catherine (*d* 1969), 2nd *d* of Alexander Johnston, Aberdeen; four *d. Educ:* Aberdeen Grammar Sch.; Univs of Aberdeen and Edinburgh. BL with distinction, Aberdeen Univ., 1905; admitted member of the Society of Advocates in Aberdeen, 1908; commissioned 1st VB Gordon Highlanders, 1907; transferred to Scottish Horse, 1908; Capt. 1913; Major, 1916; served European War, 1914-18 (despatches, DSO); Territorial War Medal for voluntary service overseas, Star of Roumania; held following appointments, 1916-19: A/DAA and QMG, No. 3 Section Canal Defences, EEF; Div. Intelligence Officer, 52nd (Lowland) Division; DAAG Australian and New Zealand Training Centre; DAA and QMG, Imperial Mounted Division; DAA and QMG and DAAG 74th (Yeomanry) Division; transferred to 2nd Highland Scouts (Scottish Horse) Reserve, 1919; Commanded Aberdeen University contingent OTC, 1925-33; TD 1927; Bt Lieut-Col 1930; in ranks of LDV and Home Guard, 1940-45. Member of City of Aberdeen Territorial Army Assoc., 1919-50, Chm., 1947-50; Hon. Col, Aberdeen Contingent OTC, 1951-52; Pres. North District (Scotland) Rugby Union, 1952-54; Pres. Scottish Ski Club, 1950-56, Hon. Mem., 1956; Pres. Society of Advocates in Aberdeen, 1954-56; Hon. Sheriff-Substitute, County of Aberdeen; County Comr Boy Scouts, Aberdeen, 1937-57; Pres. Aberdeen Grammar Sch. Former Pupils' Club, 1955-56. *Recreations:* walking, ski-ing. *Address:* Willowwood, 626 King Street, Aberdeen. *T:* 43020. *Club:* Caledonian. *[Died 30 Aug. 1971.*

BUTCHER, Rt. Rev. Reginald Albert Claver; Domestic Prelate to HH Paul VI; Hon. Canon of Westminster (RC) since 1952; *b* 9 Sept. 1905; *e s* of Albert George Butcher and Mary Dore. *Educ:* Downside; Allen Hall, St Edmund's, Ware; Christ's Coll., Cambridge (Scholar). MA History Tripos (1st Class Parts 1 and 2). Headmaster Cardinal Vaughan Sch., Kensington, 1948-52; Pres., St Edmund's Coll., Ware, 1952-64. Mem., Old Brotherhood of English Secular Clergy. *Address:* St Edmund's College, Old Hall, Ware, Herts. *T:* Puckeridge 821504, ext. 57. *Club:* United Oxford & Cambridge University.

[Died 22 Nov. 1975.

BUTLER, Colonel Arnold Charles Paul, CBE 1943; attached General Staff, War Office, 1926-50; *b* 24 March 1890; *e s* of late Col L. W. G. Butler, KRRC, and Adelaide, *d* of late John Bulteel; *m* 1916, Violet Frances Gertrude, *d* of late Col Abel H. Smith and Hon. Mrs Abel Smith; one *s* one *d. Educ:* Wellington Coll.; RMC Sandhurst. KRRC, 1909-20; R of O, 1920. *Address:* 11 Manor Court, Grange Road, Cambridge. *T:* Cambridge 62962. *Club:* MCC. *[Died 7 Dec. 1973.*

BUTLER, Harold Edwin, CIE 1944; OBE 1937; OStJ 1947; *b* 1 April 1893; *s* of late Harold Shaw Butler, Newcastle upon Tyne; *m* Winifride Jean, MBE, *d* of late Charles Eglinton; two *d. Educ:* Worcester Royal Grammar Sch. Joined Indian Police, 1913; IARO 1917-19; District Supt of Police, 1920; Dep. Comr of Police, Bombay, 1928-36; Comr of Police, Bombay, 1942-46; retired 1948. *Recreations:* golf, shooting. *Address:* Belle Causey, Barnstaple, Devon. *Club:* Royal Bombay Yacht.

[Died 12 May 1973.

BUTLER, Herbert William; Member, North-East Regional Hospital Board; *b* 1897; *s* of Frank Butler, London; *m* 1926, Nellie, *d* of H. W. Bingley, London. Served European War, 1914-19, with Royal Navy. Member Hackney Borough Council, 1928-60; Mayor of Hackney, 1936-37. MP (Lab): S Hackney, 1945-55; Hackney Central, 1955-70; PPS to Civil Lord of Admiralty and Parly Sec., Admiralty, 1950-51. JP London, 1929. *Address:* 214 Well Street, Hackney, E9.

[Died 16 Nov. 1971.

BUTLER, Hugh Montagu, MA; *b* 24 Jan. 1890; *s* of Rev. Montagu Russell and Mary Elizabeth Butler; *m* 1919, Annie Isabel Wiltshire; two *s* one *d. Educ:* Denstone Coll.; Magdalene

Coll., Cambridge (Latimer Neville Exhibitioner). 2nd Class Historical Tripos. Asst Master, Ardingly Coll., 1911-12; Worksop Coll., 1912-15; Denstone Coll., 1915-20; St George's Sch., Harpenden, 1923; Headmaster, Govt English Sch., Batu Pahat, Malaya, 1920-22; Hexham Grammar Sch., 1923-30; Queen Mary's Grammar Sch., Walsall, 1931-51. Member House of Laity, Church Assembly, 1945-51. Assoc. Guild of Drama Adjudicators, 1952-60. FRHistS, 1923-68. *Publications:* A First Sketch of Empire History; Shakespeare Plays in Schools; articles in many journals; *plays:* Trixie; Sunset at Croxden; The Goose Girl. *Recreations:* travel, painting, play production. *Address:* Meadow Cottage, Station Road, Churchdown, Gloucester. *T:* Churchdown 2755. *[Died 24 April 1972.*

BUTLER, Sir James Ramsay Montagu, Kt 1958; MVO 1920; OBE 1919; MA; Fellow of Trinity College, Cambridge, since 1913; Chief Historian for the Official Military Histories of War of 1939-45; *b* 1889; *s* of late Rev. Henry Montagu Butler, DD, and late Agnata Frances, *d* of Sir J. H. Ramsay, 10th Bt. *Educ:* Harrow; Trinity Coll., Cambridge. President of the Union, 1910; served in European War, 1914-18, Scottish Horse (despatches twice); MP (Ind) Cambridge Univ., 1922-23; served in War of 1939-45, Intelligence Corps (Chevalier Legion of Honour). Regius Professor of Modern History, Univ. of Cambridge, 1947-54. *Publications:* The Passing of the Great Reform Bill, 1914; Henry Montagu Butler: a Memoir, 1925; History of England, 1815-1918, 1928; Grand Strategy, Vol. II (Sept. 1939-June 1941), in the Official History, 1957; Lord Lothian, 1960; (with J. M. A. Gwyer) Grand Strategy, Vol. III (June 1941-Aug. 1942), 1964. *Address:* Trinity College, Cambridge. *Clubs:* United Oxford and Cambridge University, Alpine.

[Died 2 March 1975.

BUTLER, Prof. John Alfred Valentine, FRS 1956; DSc; FRIC; Emeritus Professor of Physical Chemistry, University of London; *b* 14 Feb. 1899; *s* of Alfred and Mary Ann Butler; *m* 1929, Margaret Lois Hope; two *s* one *d. Educ:* Cheltenham Grammar Sch.; Birmingham Univ. Asst Lecturer, Univ. Coll. of Swansea, 1922-26; Lecturer, Univ. of Edinburgh, 1927-39; Rockefeller Fellow, 1939-41; Exec. Officer, British Commonwealth Scientific Office, Washington, 1941-44; Courtauld Research Fellow (Courtauld Institute of Biochemistry, London), 1946-49; Chester Beatty Research Institute, 1949-66; Prof. of Physical Chemistry, London Univ., 1952-66. Editor, Progress in Biophysics and Molecular Biology, 1950-. *Publications:* Chemical Elements and their Compounds, 1927; Chemical Thermodynamics, 1928, 5th edn 1965; Electrocapillarity, 1940; Electrical Phenomena at Interfaces, 1951; Science and Human Life, 1957; Inside the Living Cell, 1959; The Life of the Cell, 1964; Gene Control in the Living Cell, 1968; The Life Process, 1970; Modern Biology and its Human Implications, 1976; papers in Proc. Royal Soc., Jl Chem. Soc., Trans. Faraday Soc., Biochemical Jl, etc. *Recreations:* gardening, painting. *Address:* Nightingale Corner, Rickmansworth, Herts. *T:* Rickmansworth 72938.

[Died 16 July 1977.

BUTLER, Gen. Sir Mervyn (Andrew Haldane), KCB 1968 (CB 1964); CBE 1957; DSO 1945, and Bar, 1957; MC 1940; Commandant, Royal College of Defence Studies, 1972, retired; *b* 1 July 1913; *s* of late Major James Dickson Butler, MBE, Rathgar, Dublin; *m* 1941, Marjorie Millicent, *d* of Frederick G. Dann, Hove, Sussex. *Educ:* St Columba's Coll., Rathfarnham, Eire; RMC Sandhurst. Commissioned South Lancashire Regt, 1933. Served War of 1939-45: BEF, 1939-40, France (MC); N Africa, 1942-43; NW Europe, 1944-45 (DSO); Lt-Col 1944; transferred to Suffolk Regt, 1945. Commanded 16 Independent Parachute Bde, 1955-57; Suez Ops, 1956 (Bar to DSO, French Croix de Guerre); Cyprus, 1957 (CBE); GOC 2 Div., 1962-64; Asst Chief of the Defence Staff (Jt Warfare), MoD, 1964-66; Comdt, Staff Coll., Camberley, 1966-67; GOC 1 (Br) Corps, 1968-70; GOC-in-C, Army Strategic Comd, 1970-71. Col Comdt, The Parachute Regt, 1967-. Brig. 1961; Maj.-Gen. 1961; Lt-Gen. 1968; Gen. 1972. Chm., Army Rugby Union, 1965-. *Recreations:* climbing, tennis, bird-watching, cricket; assisting in Rugby football. *Address:* c/o Lloyds Bank Ltd, 6 Pall Mall, SW1; Lane Lodge, South Harting, Sussex; 56 Grosvenor Road, Rathgar, Co. Dublin, Eire. *Club:* Naval and Military.

[Died 3 Jan. 1976.

BUTLER, Hon. Sir Milo (Broughton), GCMG 1973; GCVO 1975; Kt 1973; Governor-General, The Commonwealth of the Bahamas, since 1973; *b* 11 Aug. 1906; *s* of George Raleigh and Frances M. Butler; *m* Caroline Lorette (*née* Watson), Morrisville, Long Island, Bahamas; seven *s* three *d. Educ:* George Washington Sch., Florida, USA; a Public Sch., Rum Cay, Bahamas; Central Sch., Nassau Court, Bahamas, Formerly candidate at various elections and a harbinger of the Progressive

Liberal Party. Became an Independent Mem., Bahamas Legislative Council. Recent government posts included: Minister of Labour, Welfare, Agriculture and Fisheries, 1968-72; Minister without Portfolio, 1972. Finally Member for Bains Town, New Providence Constituency, after representing other areas. Was Pres., Milo B. Butler and Sons Ltd. Member, Synod of Anglican Church; interested in hospital welfare, etc. Became Governor-General (Independence Day, 10 July), Aug. 1973. *Address:* Highland Park, PO Box N712, Nassau, Bahamas.
[Died 22 Jan. 1979.

BUTLER, Sir Nevile Montagu, KCMG 1947 (CMG 1942); CVO 1933; *b* 20 Dec. 1893; *s* of late Very Rev. Henry Montagu Butler, DD, sometime Headmaster of Harrow and Master of Trinity Coll., Cambridge, and late Agnata Frances, *d* of Sir James Henry Ramsay, 10th Bt; *m* 1923, Oonah Rose, *d* of late Col John McNeile, Kippilaw, St Boswells, Roxburgh; two *d. Educ:* Harrow; Trinity Coll., Cambridge. Served European War, 1916-18, Scottish Horse, Household Bn, Intelligence Corps; entered Foreign Office, May 1920; Private Secretary to successive Parliamentary Under-Secretaries of State for Foreign Affairs, Feb. 1924-June 1927; to Viscount Cecil of Chelwood, June-Aug. 1927, and to Lord Cushendun, Oct. 1927-June 1929; a Private Secretary to the Prime Minister, 1930-35; Counsellor at Legation, Tehran, 1936-39; Berne, Sept.-Dec. 1939; Counsellor at Embassy, Washington, 1940, and Minister there, 1940-41; Head of North American Dept in Foreign Office, 1941; an Asst Under-Secretary of State, Foreign Office, 1944-47; Ambassador to Brazil, 1947-51; Ambassador to the Netherlands, 1952-54; Pres., Internat. Inst. of Differing Civilisations, 1956. *Recreations:* walking, lawn tennis, golf. *Address:* North Lodge, Newick, Lewes, Sussex. *T:* Newick 2020. *Clubs:* Travellers', Hurlingham.   *[Died 11 Nov. 1973.*

BUTLER, Theobald Richard Fitzwalter; *b* 24 May 1894; *o s* of late Theobald Butler, 28 Molyneux Park, Tunbridge Wells; *m* 1948, Laura Rachel, *d* of late Sir Vincent Nash, DL, Shannon View House, Kilmurry, Co. Limerick. *Educ:* Charterhouse; University Coll., Oxford. Called to the Bar, Inner Temple, 1921; Master of the Bench, 1960. Recorder of Newark, 1945-62, of Derby, 1962-63. Dep. Chm. Notts QS, 1951-54, Chm., 1954-63 (also of Notts Adjourned QS); Dep. Chm., Middlesex QS, 1960-65; Dep. Chm., Kent QS, 1963; Chm., South East Area, Greater London Quarter Sessions, 1965-67. Chancellor, Diocese of Peterborough, 1962-. *Publication:* Senior Editor, Archbold's Criminal Pleading, 38th edn 1973, etc. *Recreations:* bridge, archæology. *Address:* Flat 1, 70 Shepherds Hill, Highgate, N6. *T:* 01-348 0954. *Club:* Reform.   *[Died 9 March 1976.*

BUTLIN, Sir William (Edmund), Kt 1964; MBE 1944; Chairman and Joint Managing Director of Butlin's Ltd and Butlin Properties Ltd, 1935-68; retired, 1968; President, since 1972; *b* 29 Sept. 1899; *s* of William Butlin, an engineer, and Bertha; *m* 1927, Dorothy Cheriton (*d* 1958); *m* 1959, Norah Faith Butlin (*née* Cheriton) (marr. diss.; she *d* 1976); one *s* one *d* (and two *d* decd); *m* 1976, Sheila Devine. *Educ:* Canada and Bristol. Founder of Butlin's Ltd, holiday camp proprietors. Three times President of Variety Club of Great Britain. Member, Worshipful Companies of Gardeners and Gold and Silver Wyre Drawers. *Recreations:* President Vaudeville Golfing Society; Companion of the Water Rats; Vice-Pres., Variety Club International. *Address:* c/o 439-441 Oxford Street, W1. *T:* 01-629 6616. *Clubs:* Eccentric, Saints and Sinners, Variety Club of Great Britain; National Sporting; Anglo-American Sporting; World Sporting.
[Died 12 June 1980.

BUTT, Charles Sinclair, CMG 1962; Director (formerly Chairman), Olympic Consolidated Industries Ltd and its subsidiary companies; Director, Guthrie & Co. (Aust.) Pty Ltd; *b* Warrnambool, Victoria, 28 July 1900; *s* of late Charles H. S. Butt, Melbourne; *m* 1927, Cicely E. M., *d* of late H. F. Lloyd; two *d. Educ:* Melbourne Church of England Grammar Sch. Hon. War-time Controller of Rubber for Commonwealth of Australia, 1942-45. Chm., Commonwealth Serum Laboratories Commn, 1961-67. FAIM. *Recreation:* golf. *Address:* 19 Hamilton Road, Malvern, Victoria 3144, Australia. *T:* 20.3992. *Clubs:* Athenæum, Royal Automobile of Victoria (Melbourne); Royal Melbourne Golf.   *[Died 21 Feb. 1973.*

BUTTERFIELD, Sir Harry (Durham), Kt 1963; CBE 1953; MSM 1917; Chairman, Bank of N. T. Butterfield & Son Ltd, since 1966 (Managing Director, 1957-66); *b* 1 Sept. 1898; *s* of Hon. Harry Durham Butterfield and Anna Maria Butterfield; *m* 1925, Florence Blair Heywood; three *s. Educ:* Saltus Grammar Sch., Bermuda; McGill Univ., Montreal; University Coll., Oxford. Served as Signal Sgt, 7th Canadian Siege Battery, 1916-18, France and Belgium; Lieut, 2nd Canadian Div. Signals, 1918-19. BA Jurisprudence, Oxford, 1921; Barrister, Middle

Temple, 1922. Member, Colonial Parliament, Bermuda, 1937-56; MEC, 1947-56; MLC, 1956-68. Chairman: Hospital Board, 1940-46; Board of Health, 1941-42, 1944-47; Board of Education, 1942; Board of Works, 1947-56. *Recreations:* sailing, golf. *Address:* Sundown, Pembroke, Bermuda. *T:* 1-1315. *Clubs:* Royal Thames Yacht; Royal and Ancient (St Andrews); Canadian Club of New York (New York); Royal Bermuda Yacht, Royal Hamilton Dinghy, Mid Ocean Golf, Riddels Bay Golf, Coral Beach (all in Bermuda).   *[Died 21 May 1976.*

BUTTERFIELD, Sir Herbert, Kt 1968; FBA 1965; MA; Hon. LLD, Aberdeen, 1952; Hon. DLitt: UC, Dublin, 1954; Hong Kong, 1961; Sheffield, 1962; Hull, 1963; Warwick, 1967; Bonn, 1968; Hon. DLit: Belfast, 1955; London, 1968; Hon. LittD: Harvard and Columbia, 1956; Manchester, 1966; Bradford, 1973; Cambridge, 1974; Master of Peterhouse, 1955-68; Professor of Modern History, University of Cambridge, 1944-63, Regius Professor, 1963-68 (now Emeritus), and Fellow of Peterhouse, 1923-55 (now an Hon. Fellow); *b* 7 Oct. 1900; *e s* of Albert Butterfield and Ada Mary Buckland; *m* 1929, Edith Joyce (Pamela) Crawshaw; two *s* (and one *s* decd). *Educ:* Trade and Grammar Sch., Keighley; Peterhouse, Cambridge (Scholar). Jane Eliza Procter Visiting-Fellow, Univ. of Princeton, NJ, 1924-25; Lecturer in History, Peterhouse, Cambridge, 1930-44; Editor, Cambridge Historical Journal, 1938-52; President, Historical Assoc., 1955-58; Chm., British Cttee on Theory of Internat. Politics, 1958-68; Member, Administrative Board of International Association of Universities, 1960-65; Commn on Higher Education in Ireland, 1960-67; Court of Governors, LSE, 1961-68; Adv. Council on Public Records, 1962-72; Inst. of Historical Research Cttee, 1963-68. Vice-Chancellor, Univ. of Cambridge, 1959-61; Fellow, Center for Advanced Studies, Wesleyan Univ., Middletown, Conn., 1965. Gifford Lecturer, Glasgow Univ., 1965-67. Hon. Vice-Pres., RHistS, 1968-. Foreign Hon. Mem., American Acad. of Arts and Sciences, 1967; Hon. MRIA, 1967; Hon. Mem., American Historical Assoc., 1968. Pres., Bd of Dirs, Jl of the History of Ideas, 1974-75. *Publications:* The Historical Novel, 1924; The Peace-tactics of Napoleon, 1806-8, 1929; The Whig Interpretation of History, 1931; (ed.) Select Documents of European History, Vol. III, 1715-1920, 1931; Napoleon (Great Lives), 1939; The Statecraft of Machiavelli, 1940; The Englishman and his History, 1944; Inaugural Lecture on The Study of Modern History, 1944; George III, Lord North and the People, 1949; The Origins of Modern Science, 1949; Christianity and History, 1949; History and Human Relations, 1951; Christianity in European History, 1951; Christianity, Diplomacy and War, 1953; Man on his Past, 1955; George III and the Historians, 1957; International Conflict in the Twentieth Century, 1960; The University and Education Today, 1962; Inaugural Lecture on The Present State of Historical Scholarship, 1965; (jt ed. with Martin Wight) Diplomatic Investigations, 1966; Sincerity and Insincerity in Charles James Fox, 1972; The Discontinuities between the Generations in History (Rede Lecture), 1972. *Address:* 26 High Street, Sawston, Cambridge CB2 4BG.   *[Died 20 July 1979.*

BUTTERWORTH, Hon. W. Walton; United States Ambassador to Canada, 1963-68; *b* 7 Sept. 1903; *s* of William W. Butterworth, MD, and Maud Ravencamp Campbell; *m* 1928, Virginia Parker; one *s* one *d. Educ:* New Orleans Acad.; Lawrenceville Sch.; Princeton Univ.; Rhodes Scholar, Worcester Coll., Oxford Univ., 1925-27. American Foreign Service, 1928; Vice-Consul, Singapore, 1929-31; Dept of State, 1931; Third Secretary of Legation, Ottawa, 1932; Second Secretary of Embassy and Special Rep. Treasury Dept, London, 1934-41; Dept of Commerce, 1941; Member Commn on Trade policy in relation to Lend-Lease Programme, 1942; First Secretary of Embassy, Lisbon and Madrid (in charge of economic and financial affairs) and Dir-General of United States Commercial Corporation, 1942-44; Counselor of Embassy, Madrid, 1944; American Minister, Nanking, 1946; Director, Office of Far Eastern Affairs, 1947; Asst Secretary of State, US, 1949; American Ambassador to Sweden, 1950-53; American Minister, London, 1953-55; United States Representative to the European Communities (US Representative to the European Coal and Steel Community, 1956-63, and to the European Economic and European Atomic Energy Communities) 1958-63, with the rank of Ambassador. *Recreations:* shooting, tennis, golf. *Address:* 30 Battle Road, Princeton, NJ 08540, USA. *Clubs:* White's (London); Metropolitan (Washington, DC); Century (NY); University Cottage, Nassau (Princeton, NJ).
[Died 31 March 1975.

BUXTON, Gladys, CBE 1958; JP; *b* 7 Nov. 1891; *d* of Thomas Edwin and Annie Eliza Stocks; *m* 1919, Frederick Buxton. *Educ:* West Riding Secondary Sch.; Penistone Grammar Sch.; Lincoln Training Coll. for Teachers. Teachers' Certificate, 1913. Mem., Sheffield Regional Hospital Board, 1947-63; Chm.,

Derby No 3 Hosp. Management Cttee; Member: Council for the Professions Supplementary to Medicine, 1961; Adv. Council for Child Care, 1967. Derbyshire County Council: Mem., 1943; Vice-Chm. 1949; Chm. 1957-62; CA 1952. Chm. Derbyshire Educn Cttee, 1962. Vice-Pres., County Councils Assoc., 1970. Hon. MA Nottingham, 1961. JP County of Derby, 1944. *Recreations:* reading; listening to orchestral music; house and garden. *Address:* The Gables, 17 Quarry Hill Road, Ilkeston, Derbys. *T:* Ilkeston 5536. *[Died 20 Sept. 1971.*

BUXTON, Rt. Rev. Harold Jocelyn; *b* 1880; 4th *s* of Sir Thomas Fowell Buxton, 3rd Bt, Warlies, Waltham Abbey, Essex; unmarried. *Educ:* Harrow; Trinity Coll., Cambridge. Vicar of Horley with Hornton, Oxon, 1913; temp. Chaplain in France, 1915; Head of Medical Unit (Lord Mayor's Fund) with Russian Army in the Caucasus, 1916-17; Archdeacon in Cyprus, 1928-33; Bishop of Gibraltar, 1933-47; Rector of Launton, Oxford, 1949-52; Sub-Prelate, Order of St John of Jerusalem; Order of King George I of Greece, 1944; Royal Order of Saint Sava, Yugoslavia, 1945. *Publications:* Travel and Politics in Armenia (part), 1913; Transcaucasia, 1926; Substitution of Law for War, 1925; A Mediterranean Window, 1954. *Address:* c/o Morden College, Blackheath, SE3 0PW. *Club:* Royal Commonwealth Society. *[Died 13 March 1976.*

BUXTON, Captain Richard Gurney, JP Norfolk; *b* 6 May 1887; *s* of S. Gurney Buxton, Catton Hall, Norwich; *m* 1914, Mary Primrose (*d* 1972), *d* of late Major A. S. Ralli, 12th Lancers; two *d. Educ:* Eton; Trinity Coll., Cambridge. *Address:* Wiveton Hall, Holt, Norfolk. *T:* Cley 207. *Club:* Boodle's.
[Died 26 Dec. 1972.

BUZZARD, Rear-Adm. Sir Anthony Wass, 2nd Bt *cr* 1929; CB 1953; DSO 1940; OBE 1941; RN (retired); with International Department, British Council of Churches; *b* 28 April 1902; *er s* of Sir E. Farquhar Buzzard, 1st Bt, KCVO, and May, *d* of late E. Bliss; *S* father, 1945; *m* 1932, Margaret Elfreda, *o d* of late Sir Arthur Knapp, KCIE, CSI, CBE; two *s* one *d. Educ:* RN Colls, Osborne and Dartmouth. Director of Naval Intelligence, 1951-54. *Heir: s* Anthony Farquhar Buzzard, *b* 28 June 1935. *Address:* Todd House, West Clandon, Surrey. *T:* Clandon 597.
[Died 10 March 1972.

BYASS, Bt Col Sir Geoffrey Robert Sidney, 2nd Bt *cr* 1926; TD; DL; *b* Port Talbot, 30 Sept. 1895; *e s* of 1st Bt and Eveline (*d* 1951), *d* of T. L. Stratton, Turweston House, Brackley; *S* father, 1929; *m* 1919, Marian (*d* 1968), *d* of Col Sir Gerald Trevor Bruce, KCB; five *d; m* 1972, Winifred Gillespie-Hill (*née* Paton). *Educ:* Winchester. Glamorgan Yeomanry 1914 onwards; served Palestine, Egypt and France (wounded); Major RA (TA) 1922; Lt-Col 1933; commanded 81st (Welsh) Field Brigade RA, TA, 1933-38; Bt Col 1938. Mayor of Port Talbot, 1937-38. DL Glamorgan, 1936. *Recreation:* golf. *Address:* Normanswood, Charles Hill, Tilford, Farnham, Surrey.
[Died 29 Oct. 1976 (ext).

BYERS, Joseph Austen; Judge of the Provincial Court of British Columbia, 1969-70; retired; *b* 1 Oct. 1895; *er s* of Joseph and Sarah Dalton Byers, Newcastle upon Tyne; *m* 1934, Sheila Margaret O'Neill; one *d. Educ:* King's Sch., Chester; Balliol Coll., Oxford. Military Service, 1914-19 with Cheshire Regiment and Army Signal Service in Mediterranean, Egypt, Mesopotamia, and India, NWF; Balliol, 1914-21; MA 1921; Indian Civil Service, 1921. Held various executive posts, 1921-28; joined judicial branch 1928, and served as District and Sessions Judge in various districts in Madras and Orissa, 1930-41; Additional Judge, Madras High Court, Jan. 1942; Puisne Judge, High Court of Judicature, Madras, 1942-47. Called to Bar, Inner Temple, 1936; to Bar of British Columbia, Canada, 1948; Judge of Family Court, Greater Victoria, and Stipendiary Magistrate, BC, 1960-69. *Address:* J. A. Byers, Barrister and Solicitor, Post Box 33, Victoria, BC, Canada. *Club:* Union (Victoria, BC). *[Died 18 May 1977.*

BYRNE, Rt. Rev. Herbert Kevin, OSB, MA; Abbot of Ampleforth Abbey, 1939-63; *b* 7 Sept. 1884; 3rd *s* of late Andrew Byrne, Croney Byrne, Co. Wicklow. *Educ:* Ampleforth Coll. Joined Benedictine Order, 1902; at the Ampleforth House of Studies, Oxford, 1905-09; Classical Master, Ampleforth Coll., 1909-35; priest, 1911; parish work at St Peter's, Liverpool, 1935-39. *Address:* Ampleforth Abbey, York. *[Died 26 Oct. 1978.*

BYRNE, Prof. Patrick Sarsfield, CBE 1975 (OBE 1966); FRCGP; Professor and Director of Department of General Practice, University of Manchester, 1969-78, now Emeritus; *b* 17 April 1913; *s* of John Stephen Byrne and Marie Anne Byrne; *m* 1937, Dr Kathleen Marianne Pearson; two *s* four *d. Educ:* St Edward's Coll., Liverpool; Liverpool Univ. (State Scholarship;

MB, ChB 1936). MSc Manchester, 1976; FRCGP 1967. GP, Milnthorpe, Cumbria, 1936-68. Pres., RCGP, 1973-76; Chm., Armed Services Gen. Practice Approval Bd, MoD, 1973-79; Cons. Adviser in Gen. Practice to DHSS, 1973-78; Mem., Jt Trng Cttee in Gen. Practice (UK), 1976-. Visitor, Jt Trng Cttee for Gen. Practice, 1976-. Chm., Adv. Cttee, MSD Foundn, 1978-. Fellow, RSocMed; Hon. Fellow, Coll. of Medicine of SA, 1975; Hon. Mem., Canadian Coll. of Family Physicians, 1976. Sesquicentennial Medal, Med. Univ. of SC, 1974; Hippocratic Medal, SIMG, 1974. *Publications:* Learning to Care—person to person (with B.E.L. Long), 1973 (2nd edn 1975); (with J. Freeman) Assessment of Postgraduate Training for General Practice, 1972 (2nd edn 1973); (with B. E. L. Long) Doctors talking to Patients, 1976; (ed with H. W. Proctor) A Handbook of Medical Treatment, 1976; (with J. Freeman) Assessment of Vocational Training in General Practice, 2nd edn 1976 (Report from General Practice no 17, Jl RCGP 1976); various papers; chapters in books; pubns in med. jls in Britain and overseas. *Recreations:* fishing and wine. *Address:* Grievegate, Leasgill, Milnthorpe, Cumbria. *T:* Milnthorpe 3121.
[Died 25 Feb. 1980.

BYRNES, James Francis; lawyer and politician, USA; *b* Charleston, SC, 1879; *m* 1906, Maude Busch. Admitted to Bar, 1903; Editor Journal and Review, Aiken, 1903-07; official Court Reporter, 2nd Circuit, South Carolina, 1900-08; Solicitor, 2nd Circuit, South Carolina, 1908-10; Mem. of Congress, 1911-25; in practice of law, Spartanburg, 1925-31; US Senator, 1931; Associate Justice, US Supreme Court, 1941-42; Director of Economic Stabilisation, 1942-43; Director Office of War Mobilisation, 1943-45; Sec. of State, United States, 1945-47; Governor of State of South Carolina, 1951-55. *Publications:* Speaking Frankly, 1947; All in One Lifetime, 1958.
[Died 9 April 1972.

BYRNES, Hon. Sir Percy (Thomas), Kt 1965; Member of the Legislative Council for North-Western Province, Victoria, Australia, 1942-69; Country Party Leader in the Legislative Council, 1952-69; JP; *b* Eidsvold, Queensland, 28 Jan. 1893; *s* of Thomas Byrnes, Swan Hill, Victoria; *m* 1918, Dorothy, *d* of W. J. Judd; one *s* three *d. Educ:* Wesley Coll., Melbourne; Queen's Coll., Univ. of Melbourne. Served European War, 1914-18, with 1st Australian Imperial Forces, in France. Hon. Minister, 1948; Minister for Public Works, Victoria, 1950-52. Director, Woorinen Cooperative Packing Company. *Recreation:* shooting. *Address:* Box 378, Swan Hill, Vic. 3585, Australia. *Club:* Commercial Travellers' Association (Melbourne).
[Died 5 March 1973.

BYWATER, Thomas Lloyd, BSc, MS; Emeritus Professor, University of Leeds; *b* 19 Aug. 1905; *m* 1935, Ishobel McL. Millar; two *s* one *d. Educ:* Lucton Sch.; University Coll. of North Wales; Univ. of Wisconsin, USA. Lecturer in Agriculture, Univ. of Leeds, 1929-46; Prof. of Agriculture: Aberdeen Univ., 1946-53; Leeds Univ., 1953-69. *Address:* 1 Balmoral Terrace, Shaw Lane, Leeds LS6 4EA.
[Died 3 June 1979.

C

CABOT, Sir Daniel Alfred Edmond, Kt 1943; MRCVS; company director; *m* 1949, Anne Le Cornu Blampied, l'Abri, La Rocque. Late Chief Veterinary Officer, Ministry of Agriculture and Fisheries; Veterinary Adviser, 1948. Hon. Pres., Office International des Epizooties (Pres., 1948-51); Member: Académie Vétérinaire de France; American Veterinary Medical Assoc.; Corresp. Mem., Sociedad veterinaria de zootecnia; late Jurat of Royal Court, Lt Bailiff, Jersey. *Address:* Le Bernage, Longueville, Jersey, CI. *[Died 16 March 1974.*

CACOYANNIS, Hon. Sir Panayotis (Loizou), Kt 1936; LLB; Advocate; Member of Town School Committee, Limassol (Cyprus), since 1925, Chairman, 1946-61; *b* 20 Sept. 1893; *s* of Loizos Cacoyannis, Limassol, Cyprus; *m* 1915, Angeliki, *d* of George M. Efthyvoulos and Zoe Constantinides, Limassol, Cyprus; two *s* two *d.* MLC, Cyprus, 1925-30; MEC, Cyprus, 1929-46; Mem. of Advisory Council, 1933-46; Mem. of Council of Cyprus Anti-Tuberculosis League until 1946. Attended the Coronation Ceremony of King George VI and Queen Elizabeth as representative of Cyprus, 1937. *Address:* POB 122, Limassol, Cyprus. *[Died 9 Dec. 1980.*

CADBURY, Henry Joel; Professor Emeritus, Harvard Divinity School, 1954 (Hollis Professor Divinity, 1934-54); Lecturer, Pendle Hill, 1954-72, and Temple University, 1962-66; *b* 1 Dec. 1883; *s* of Joel Cadbury and Anna Kaighn Lowry; *m* 1916, Lydia Caroline Brown; two *s* two *d. Educ:* William Penn Charter Sch.; Haverford Coll.; Harvard Univ. Teacher, Haverford Coll., 1910-19, Lecturer, 1955-64; Harvard Divinity Sch., 1919-26; Andover Theological Seminary, 1919-26; Prof., Bryn Mawr Coll., 1926-34. Mem. Translation Cttee of Revised Standard Version of the Bible, 1929-70; Dir, Andover-Harvard Theol. Library, 1938-54. Chm., American Friends Service Cttee, 1928-34 and 1944-60, Hon. Chm. 1960-; Chm., Board of Directors of Bryn Mawr Coll., 1956-68. Mem. several learned societies; Mem. Studiorum Novi Testamenti Societas (Pres. 1958); Fellow American Academy of Arts and Sciences. Hon. degrees: LittD Haverford Coll., 1933; DD Glasgow Univ., 1937; LLD Whittier Coll., 1951, Swarthmore Coll., 1954; LHD Howard Univ., 1959, Earlham Coll., 1967. *Publications:* The Style and Literary Method of Luke, 1920; National Ideals in the Old Testament, 1920; The Making of Luke-Acts, 1927 (and 1958); (with K. Lake) Beginnings of Christianity, Vols IV and V, 1933 (and 1966); The Peril of Modernizing Jesus, 1937 (and 1962); Jesus What Manner of Man, 1947 (and 1962); George Fox's Book of Miracles, 1948, 1972; The Book of Acts in History, 1955; Quakerism and Early Christianity, 1957; The Eclipse of the Historical Jesus, 1964; John Woolman in England, 1971; Friendly Heritage, 1972; Narrative Papers of George Fox, 1972. *Recreations:* Quaker history, camping. *Address:* 774 Millbrook Lane, Haverford, Pa 19041, USA.   *[Died 7 Oct. 1974.*

CADE, Sir Stanford, KBE 1946; CB 1944; FRCS, FRCP, FRCOG; Hon. DSc (Brit. Columbia); Hon. FRCSE; Hon. FRCSI; Hon. FACS; Hon. FFR; Hon. Consultant Surgeon, Westminster Hospital and Mount Vernon Hospital and Radium Institute; late Civilian Consultant in Surgery RAF; Consultant in Radiotherapeutics to the Army, 1951-65, now Consultant Emeritus; Past Member: National Radium Commission; Grand Council and Vice-Chairman Executive Committee, British Empire Cancer Campaign; Chairman, Cancer and Radiotherapy Committee and late Member Standing Medical Advisory Committee, Ministry of Health; Member RAF Medical Advisory Board; *b* 22 March 1895; *y s* of Samuel Kadinsky, St Petersburgh, assumed name of Cade by deed poll, 1924; *m* 1920, Margaret Hester (*d* 1951), *e d* of late William Agate, MusB, FRCO, Paisley; three *d. Educ:* Bruxelles; King's Coll., London. Westminster Hospital Entrance Scholarship in Anatomy and Physiology, 1916; Bird Prize and Gold Medal and Chadwick Prize, 1917; MRCS, LRCP 1917; held all the resident appts and Surg. Registrar Westminster Hospital; FRCS 1923; MRCP 1941; FRCP 1960; FRCOG 1954. Hunterian Prof., RCS of England, 1925, 1933 and 1954; Arris and Gale Lectr, 1926; Bradshaw Lectr, 1960; Hunterian Orator, 1963; Walker Prize, RCS, 1966; late Mem. Council (Vice-Pres., Mem. Ct of Examiners and Dir of Surgical Studies), RCS. FRSocMed (Mem. Council, Pres. Surgical Section, 1950-51, and United Services Section, 1952-54, Hon. Fellow 1961, Nuffield Lectr 1962); Fellow Medical Soc. of London (Fothergillian Gold Medal, 1959) and Assoc. of Surgeons of Great Britain and Ireland. Formerly Examr in Surgery: Univs of Edinburgh, London, Bristol and Cambridge; Faculty of Radiology. Hon. Member: Assoc. Military Surgeons, USA; American Radium Soc. (Janeway Medal, 1948); New York Cancer Soc. and Soc. Head and Neck Surgeons, USA; Cancer Soc. of Chile; Société de Chir. de Lyon; Skinner Lectr, Faculty of Radiology, 1948; Crookshank Lectr, 1965; Blair-Bell Memorial Lectr, Liverpool, 1950; Mackenzie-Davidson Lectr and Medal, British Inst. Radiology, 1951; Dorothy Platt Lectr, King's College Hosp., London, 1956; Moynihan Lectr, Univ. of Leeds, 1957; Colles' Lectr and Medal, RCSI, 1960; Honeyman Gillespie Lectr, Edinburgh, 1961; Vis. Prof. of Surgery, Sheffield Univ., 1962; Frazer Lectr, Univ. of Edinburgh, 1966; Hon. Gold Medal, RCS, 1968. Pres., 7th Internat. Cancer Congress, London, 1958. Air Vice-Marshal RAFVR; Hon. Air Commodore Central Medical Estabt, RAF. Grand Officier, Order George I (Greece). *Publications:* numerous papers and articles and several books on cancer and various surgical subjects. *Address:* 102 Parkside House, Clarendon Gardens, Southsea, Hants. *T:* Portsmouth 27416.   *[Died 19 Sept. 1973.*

CAFFERY, Jefferson; diplomat; Honorary Chamberlain to the Pope; *b* Lafayette, La, USA, 1 Dec. 1886; *s* of Charles Duval Caffery and Mary Catherine Parkerson; *m* 1937, Gertrude McCarthy. *Educ:* Tulane Univ., New Orleans (BA 1906; LLD 1968). Studied law privately, 1907-08; admitted to Bar of Louisiana, 1909. Sec. of Legation, Caracas, 1911; Dept of State, 1913; Sec. of Legation, Stockholm, 1913; Teheran, 1916 (i/c Turkish and German interests, July, British and Italian interests, August); accompanied Special Kerensky Russian Mission to US,

1917; Embassy, Paris, 1917; special rep. of State Dept. on Permanent Inter-allied Commn on treatment and training disabled soldiers and sailors, 1917-22; Head American delegn to Internat. Conf., London, 1918; Sec., American section at Paris, 1919-22; detailed to Dept of State, 1919, for visits of foreign royalty; Counsellor of Embassy, Madrid, 1919; Mem. Board Examiners, Diplomatic Service Exam., Paris, 1919; Chargé d'Affaires *ad interim,* Athens, 1922; helped in assisting Greek refugees from Asia Minor, 1922; Counsellor of Embassy, Tokyo, 1923; Chm. American Red Cross earthquake relief, Japan, 1923-24; Counsellor of Embassy, Berlin, 1925; Minister to El Salvador, 1926; to Columbia, 1928; Rep. of Dept of State, El Salvador, 1931-32; Asst Sec. of State, 1933; Mem. Personnel Board of Foreign Service and Foreign Service Schools Board, 1933; US Ambassador: to Cuba, 1934; to Brazil, 1937; to France, 1944-49; to Egypt, 1949-55; attended Potsdam Conf., 1945; US Delegn, Paris Peace Conf., 1946; Rep. of US Govt, European Recovery Plan, 1948. acting Dep. US Rep. on UN Security Council, 1948; several times special rep. of President or Govt of US (often with rank of Ambassador); has attended many conferences and has signed various treaties and international agreements; retd from Foreign Service, 1955. Holds several hon. degrees and hon. memberships; Hon. Dr of Laws, (and Meml Plaque **·**erected by Alumni Assoc.), Univ of Southwestern Louisiana, Lafayette, La, 1971. has received numerous US awards and medals, also foreign honours, citizenships, and decorations; Catholic Action medal for 1944; State Dept's Distinguished Service Award, 1950; American Foreign Service Cup, 1971. *Recreations:* mountain climbing and riding. *Address:* c/o Fendrich Industries Inc., PO Box 3645, Evansville, Indiana 47701, USA. *Clubs:* Metropolitan, Dacor and Dacor House (Washington, DC); Jockey (Paris); Boston (New Orleans).
          [Died 13 April 1974.

CAFFYN, Sir Sydney (Morris), Kt 1972; CBE 1959; Chairman, Caffyns Ltd, since 1942 (Joint Managing Director, 1938-72); *b* 22 July 1901; *s* of Percy Thomas Caffyn, Hay Tor, Eastbourne; *m* 1925, Annie, *d* of Alex Dawson, Turriff, Aberdeenshire; three *s* one *d. Educ:* Eastbourne Grammar Sch.; Royal Sch. of Mines, Imperial Coll. of Science and Technology, London Univ. Mem., Eastbourne Town Council, 1937-74; Alderman, 1944, Mayor, 1956-58 and 1973-74; Hon. Freeman. Raised and commanded Sussex Recovery Company, HG, 1940-45, Major. Member: Gen. Purposes Cttee and Coun., British Employers Confedn, 1948-58; Nat. Jt Adv. Coun., Min. of Labour, 1951-59; Nat. Arbitration Tribunal, 1951-59; Civil Service Arbitration Tribunal, 1951-63; Industrial Court, 1959-71; many *ad hoc* Tribunals and Courts of Enquiry; EDC for Retail Motor Trade, 1966-71. Cttee on Training and Educn of Young Workers, 1956-58; Central Adv. Coun. for Educn (Eng.), 1957-63; Gas Industry Training Coun., 1965-66. Pres., Motor Agents, Assoc., 1948-50; Pres., British Motor Trade Assoc., 1953-54. Chm. of Council and Pro-Chancellor Univ. of Sussex; Chm. Governors: Chelsea Coll. of Physical Education, 1947-76; Eastbourne Coll. of Education, 1948-76. Convener, Finance and Administration Cttee of Presbyterian Church of England, 1966-72; Treasurer, Nat. Free Church Federal Council, 1969-77; Mem., British Council of Churches, 1974-77. Liveryman, Coachmakers and Coachharness Makers Company. Hon. DSc Sussex, 1963. *Recreations:* book-collecting, reading, concert and theatre going. *Address:* 11 Tavistock, 12/14 Devonshire Place, Eastbourne. *T:* Eastbourne 31118. *Clubs:* Athenæum, Royal Automobile.
          [Died 26 Sept. 1976.

CAHILL, Most Rev. Thomas Vincent, CBE 1972; DD, PhD; Archbishop of Canberra, since 1967; *b* 22 Feb. 1913; *s* of Patrick Cahill and Elizabeth Cavagna. *Educ:* Marist Brothers' Coll., Bendigo, Victoria, Australia; Propaganda Coll., Rome. Ordained Priest, Rome, 1935; Asst Priest, Sacred Heart Cathedral, Bendigo, Diocese of Sandhurst, Victoria, Australia, 1936-39; Secretary, Apostolic Delegation, Sydney, 1939-48; Chancellor, Diocese of Sandhurst, 1948; Bishop of Cairns, Queensland, 1948-67; appointed Archbishop of Canberra and Goulburn, 1967. *Address:* Archbishop's House, Commonwealth Avenue, Canberra, ACT 2600, Australia. *T:* Canberra 486411.
          [Died 16 April 1978.

CAIN, Major Robert Henry, VC 1944; late South Staffordshire Regiment; *b* 2 Jan. 1909; *s* of Robert James Cain, Douglas, Isle of Man; *m* 1941, Mary Denise Addison; one *s* three *d. Educ:* King William's Coll., Isle of Man. Served War of 1939-45 in N Africa, Sicily, Italy, Arnhem (VC) and Norway. *Address:* The Rock, Castletown, Isle of Man.   *[Died 2 May 1974.*

CAINE, Sir Derwent Hall, 1st Bt *cr* 1937; Kt 1933; *b* 12 Sept. 1891; *s* of late Sir Hall Caine, CH, KBE. *Educ:* Isle of Man; Eastbourne. Subsequently Chairman, News Letter Ltd; also Argosy and Sundial Libraries Ltd; Founder and late Man. Dir,

The Readers' Library Publishing Co. Ltd; contested Parliamentary Divisions of Reading 1922, Clitheroe 1924, and Everton (Nat Lab) 1931; MP (Lab) Everton Division of Liverpool, 1929-31. *Recreations:* motoring, golf, flying. *Address:* Greeba Castle, Isle of Man. *[Died 2 Dec.* 1971 *(ext)*

CAKOBAU, Ratu Sir Etuate Tui-Vanuavou Tugi, KBE 1971 (CBE 1966, OBE 1954); MC; ED; Deputy Prime Minister, Fiji, since 1971; also Minister of Labour; Member, Legislative Council, since 1942; *b* 1908; *s* of Adi L. Cakobau; *m* Adi Vasemaca, *d* of Ratu Marika Toroca. *Educ:* Queen Victoria Sch.; Wanganui Tech. Coll., NZ; Wadham Coll., Oxford. Served War 1939-45, Captain Fijian Military Forces; Lt-Col Malaya, 1952-53. Mem., Council of Chiefs, Fiji, 1938-. *Address:* Ministry of Labour, Suva, Fiji.   *[Died 25 June* 1973.

CALDER, Alexander; sculptor; *b* 22 July 1898; *s* of A. Stirling Calder and Nanette Lederer; *m* 1931, Louisa James; two *d*. *Educ:* Putney Sch., Putney, Vermont, USA. Graduated as Mech. Engineer, Stevens Inst. of Technology, 1919; various engineering jobs, 1923; Art Students' League, NYC, 1924; lived in Paris, on and off, 1926-33; subsequently domiciled in France. Retrospective exhibn, Gimpel Fils, 1969. Sculpture Award, Venice Biennale, 1952; several architectural medals, etc. *Publications:* Fables d'Æsop, 1931; Three Young Rats, 1944; also Ancient Mariner; Fables de la Fontaine; Bestiary. *Recreations:* swimming, dancing, drinking. *Address:* Roxbury, Conn, USA; Saché, 37190 Azay-le-Rideau, France.
[Died 11 Nov. 1976.

CALDER, James William, CB 1973; OBE 1957; CEng, FIMinE; HM Chief Inspector of Mines and Quarries, 1970-75; *b* Hamilton, Lanarkshire, 20 June 1914; *s* of late Henry Stewart Calder and late Mary McKinlay Calder; *m* 1941, Eileen Elizabeth McLeod; one *d*. *Educ:* Dunfermline; Edinburgh Univ. BSc Hons, Mining and Metallurgy, 1938; 1st cl. Colliery Manager's Certif., 1939. Served with Fife Coal Co. Ltd and Lochgelly Iron and Coal Co. Ltd, HM Junior Inspector of Mines and Quarries, North Staffordshire, 1941; served in N Wales and Yorkshire; Dist. Inspector, 1946; Sen. Dist. Inspector, 1950; Divisional Inspector: NW Div., 1962; E Midlands Div., 1963; Dep. Chief Inspector of Mines and Quarries, Headquarters, 1967-70. *Publications:* Divisional Inspector's Annual Reports, 1963-66 (inclusive); Chief Inspector's Annual Report, 1969-74; Report on Inrush at Lofthouse Colliery, Yorks; Report on Extensive Fall at Seafield Colliery, Fife; Report on Accident at Markham Colliery, Derbyshire. *Recreations:* farming, bird watching, walking, golf. *Address:* 56 Belgravia Court, Ebury Street, SW1. *T:* 01-730 1318; Keith Hills, Fossoway, Kinross, Scotland. *T:* Fossoway 317.   *[Died 28 May* 1975.

CALDER, Sir John Alexander, KCMG 1947 (CMG 1939); MA; *b* 20 Oct. 1889; *s* of Robert Calder, ISO, JP, HM Inspector of Schools, and May Drummond Alexander; *m* 1st, 1915, Phoebe Robertson McCartney Stuart (*d* 1964); no *c*; 2nd, 1966, Mrs Mary E. Saville. *Educ:* Grove and Harris Academies, Dundee; Edinburgh Univ. (MA). 1st Class Hons History, 1911; 1st Class Hons Philosophy, 1912. Appointed to Colonial Office 1912; military service Sept.-Dec. 1918; Sec. to E African Parliamentary Commn, Aug.-Dec. 1924; Asst Sec., Colonial Office, 1933; Principal Asst Sec., Min. of Supply, 1942; Third Crown Agent for the Colonies, 1942-43; Second Crown Agent, 1943; Senior Crown Agent for the Colonies, 1943-53; retired 1953. *Recreations:* golf, chess. *Address:* Gordon House, Ridgemount Road, Sunningdale, Ascot SL5 9RL. *T:* Ascot 21405. *Club:* Sunningdale Golf.   *[Died 28 Sept.* 1974.

CALDWELL, Prof. John, OBE 1971; PhD, DSc; Head of Department of Botany, University College and University of Exeter, 1935-69; Director, Hatherly Biological Laboratories 1952-69; Dean of Science, 1938-42 and 1951-54; Deputy Vice-Chancellor, 1957-59; *b* 8 May 1903; *s* of late Peter and Emily Caldwell, Ayr; *m* 1941, Christine Natalie, 2nd *d* of J. H. Hayes, East Harting, Sussex; three *d*. *Educ:* Kilmarnock Acad.; Univ. of Glasgow (Robert Donaldson Student); Univ. of Cambridge. PhD 1929, DSc 1935, Glasgow; PhD Cantab, 1931. Virus Physiologist, Rothamsted Experimental Station, Harpenden, 1929-35; Min. of Agriculture Travelling Fellow, Canada and USA, 1935. Chm., SW Region Careers Advisory Council (Min. of Labour), 1952-71; Chm. Management Cttee, Nat. Allotments and Gardens Soc., 1956-62. President: Devonshire Assoc., 1969; SW Naturalists' Union, 1969. Formerly Governor: Long Ashton and National Vegetable Research Stations. *Publications:* numerous papers on plant physiology and virus studies in scientific jls. *Recreations:* gardening, bee-keeping. *Address:* St Germans Lodge, St Germans Road, Exeter. *T:* Exeter 55675.
[Died 26 Aug. 1974.

CALDWELL, Prof. Peter Christopher, FRS 1975; Professor of Zoology (Biochemistry), University of Bristol, since 1977; *b* 25 Jan. 1927; *s* of Bernard Caldwell and Dr Margaret Joyce Caldwell, JP; *m* 1955, Phoebe-Ann, *d* of Air Chief Marshal Sir Roderic Hill, KCB, MC, AFC; two *s* three *d*. *Educ:* Ampleforth; Trinity Coll., Oxford (Millard Scholar; MA, DPhil). ICI Res. Fellow in Biophysics Res. Unit, UCL, 1951-54; Asst Lectr, Dept of Biophysics, UCL, 1954-55; Beit Meml Res. Fellow, 1955-57 and Johnston, Lawrence and Moseley Res. Fellow of Royal Soc., 1957-60, Marine Biol Assoc.'s Lab., Plymouth; Lectr in Zoology (Biochem.), Univ. of Bristol, 1960-66, Reader in Zoology, 1966-77. Mem. Editorial Bd, Jl of Physiology, 1973-; Mem. Council, Marine Biological Assoc., 1974-77. *Publications:* sci. papers on nucleic acids, muscle contraction, intracellular pH and movt of substances across cell membranes, mainly in Jl Physiology. *Recreations:* composing, performing and listening to music; farming. *Address:* White Oak House, Youngwood Lane, Nailsea, Bristol BS19 2NS. *T:* Nailsea 2436. *Club:* Oxford and Cambridge Musical.   *[Died 7 June* 1979.

CALEDON, 6th Earl of, *cr* 1800; **Denis James Alexander;** Baron Caledon, 1789; Viscount Caledon, 1797; DL; *b* 10 Nov. 1920; *s* of late Lieut-Col Hon. Herbrand Charles Alexander, DSO (*b* of 5th Earl of Caledon), and Millicent Valla (*d* 1979), *d* of Sir Henry Bayly Meredyth, 5th Bt; *S* uncle, 1968; *m* 1st, 1943, Ghislaine Dresselhuys (marr. diss. 1948); one *d*; 2nd, 1952, Baroness Anne de Graevenitz (*d* 1963); one *s* one *d*; 3rd, 1964, Marie Elisabeth Erskine (*née* Allen). *Educ:* Eton; RMC. Major, Irish Guards; Ulster Defence Regt, 1970-78, retired (Bt Lt-Col). Chm., Foyle Fisheries Adv. Council, 1973-. Governor, The Royal Sch., Armagh, 1978. DL Co. Tyrone, 1974. *Heir: s* Viscount Alexander. *Address:* Caledon Castle, Caledon, Co. Tyrone, Northern Ireland. *Club:* Turf.   *[Died 20 May* 1980.

CALLANDER, Lt-Gen. Sir Colin (Bishop), KCB 1955 (CB 1945); KBE 1952; MC; *b* 13 March 1897; *y s* of late W. W. Callander, Ilminster, Som.; *m* 1923, Mary Charteris Stather Dunn; one *s* one *d*. *Educ:* West Buckland Sch.; RMC Sandhurst. 2nd Lieut Royal Munster Fusiliers, 1915; Leicestershire Regt 1922; Capt. 1925; Major 1936; Temp. Lt-Col 1940; Col 1944; Temp. Maj.-Gen. 1944; Maj.-Gen. 1946; Lt-Gen. 1951. Served European War, 1916-17 (wounded thrice, MC); NW Frontier, India, 1938-39 (despatches); War of 1939-45 (CB); GOC 4th Div. (Greece), 1945-46; Dir-Gen. of Military Training, 1948; GOC 2nd Div. (BAOR), 1949-51; Dir-Gen. of Military Training, 1952-54; Military Sec. to the Sec. of State for War, 1954-56; retired 1957. Col Royal Leicestershire Regt, 1954-63. *Address:* Rolvenden Lane, Cranbrook, Kent. *T:* Rolvenden 436. *Club:* Army and Navy.   *[Died 31 May* 1979.

CALLAS, Maria; soprano; *b* New York, 2 Dec. 1923; *d* of Greek parents; *m* 1947, Giovanni Battista Meneghini (marr. diss., 1971). *Educ:* New York, USA; Royal Conservatory, Athens. Italian début in Gioconda (Verona), 1947; South American tour, 1949; Has sung in major rôles at La Scala, Covent Garden, the Metropolitan Opera House, the Vienna State Opera House, Mexico, at Edinburgh Festival, and in other cities in Europe and N and S America. Chief rôles in: Madame Butterfly, Aida, Norma, I Puritani, Pagliacci, Rigoletto, Cavalleria Rusticana, Anna Bolena, Lucia, Medea, Tosca, etc: Resumed concert singing, 1973. Produced I Vespri Siciliani, Turin, 1973. Has recorded most of main parts. Played Medea in film (from Euripides) directed by Pier Paolo Pasolini, 1969. *Relevant publication:* Callas, by George Jellinek, 1961. *Address:* 36 Avenue Georges Mandel, Paris 16e, France.
[Died 16 Sept. 1977.

CALLAWAY, Air Vice-Marshal William Bertram, CBE 1942; AFC; DL; Polonia Restituta (1945); *b* 15 Oct. 1889; *s* of Engineer Capt. R. G. Callaway, RN; *m* 1925, Evelyn Winifred Trim; one *d*. *Educ:* privately. Royal Navy, 1907-16; Royal Naval Air Service, 1916-18 (AFC); Royal Air Force, 1918-45. Air Vice-Marshal, 1942. Commandant, Midland Command, Air Training Corps, 1945-46; Divisional Controller, SW Div., Min. of Civil Aviation, 1947-53. DL Co. Gloucester, 1953. *Address:* Greathed Manor, Lingfield, Surrey. *T:* Lingfield 588. *Club:* Royal Air Force.   *[Died 28 Aug.* 1974.

CALVERLEY, 2nd Baron *cr* 1945; **George Raymond Orford Muff;** *b* 1 May 1914; *s* of 1st Baron Calverley, JP, DL and Ellen, *e d* of Charles and Mary Orford; *S* father, 1955; *m* 1940, Mary, *d* of Arthur Farrar, Halifax; two *s*. *Educ:* Bradford Grammar Sch. Formerly Capt., Royal Indian Ordnance Corps. *Heir: s* Hon. Charles Rodney Muff, *b* 2 Oct. 1946. *Address:* 77 Cecil Avenue, Great Horton, Bradford 7, Yorks.   *[Died 4 June* 1971.

CALVERT, Edwin George Bleakley, MD, FRCP; Hon. Consultant Physician, Royal Northern Hospital, London; Hon.

Consultant Physician to St Paul's Hospital for Genito-Urinary Diseases (Institute of Urology), Samaritan Hospital for Women, City of London Maternity Hospital, National Temperance Hospital, London; practised at 132 Harley Street for over 50 years to 1972; *e s* of late James and Anne (*née* Armstrong) Calvert, Lyndhurst, Lurgan, Co. Armagh; *m* 1928, Nancy, *yr d* of late Charles W. Marsden, Sydney, NSW; one *s* two *d. Educ:* Methodist Coll., Belfast; Queen's Univ., Belfast; Dublin; St Mary's Hosp., London; Paris; Vienna. MD Belfast (Gold Medal), 1920; FRCP 1941; MRCP 1923; DPH 1920; MB, BCh, BAO Belfast (1st Class hons, and Schol. and Special Schol.), 1915; also four other Clinical Schols, Juliet-Symington Gold Medal and two additional 1st Schols in Medicine. Temp. Capt. RAMC, BEF, France, 1915-19; Demonstrator in Physiology, Queen's Univ., Belfast, 1919-20; RMO, Hosp. for Nervous Diseases, Maida Vale, 1920; Asst to Dir of Medical Clinical Unit, St Mary's Hosp., 1920-25; Physician, EMS London, 1939-45. *Publications:* Kidney Function Tests and Examination of the Urine, Pye's Surgical Handicraft, 11th-18th edns, 1939-63; Estimation of Sugar in the Blood, Biochemical Jl, 1923-24; Function Tests in Kidney Disease, BMJ, 1925; various papers in leading med. jls on diabetes, acidosis, kidney disease, diseases of lymphatic glands, endocrine glands, rheumatoid arthritis (lectures given: Internat. Soc. of Internal Med., Philadelphia, and at Harvard Univ.). *Recreation:* golf. *Address:* 1 Solent Drive, Barton-on-Sea, Hants. *T:* New Milton 61 3434.
[Died 3 Aug. 1976.

CALVERT, Rt. Rev. George Reginald; *b* 11 Oct. 1900; *s* of William John Calvert and Mary (*née* Young); *m* 1925, Kate Verona, *d* of William Alexander Moir; one *d. Educ:* Univ. of Toronto (BA); Wycliffe Coll., Toronto (LTh). Hon. DD Wycliffe Coll., Toronto, Univ. of King's Coll., Halifax and Univ. of Emmanuel Coll., Saskatoon. Deacon, 1924; Priest, 1925; Incumbent of Snowflake, Manitoba, 1924; Rector: Holland, Man., 1926; Killarney, Man., 1928; St Anne's, West Kildoran, Man., 1932; St Matthew's, Winnipeg, Man., 1933; Hon. Canon, St John's Cathedral, Winnipeg, 1940; Archdeacon of Winnipeg, 1945; Dep. Prolocutor of Gen. Synod of C of E in Canada, 1946, Prolocutor, 1949; Prolocutor of Provincial Synod of Rupert's Land, 1947; Dean and Rector of Christ Church Cathedral, Victoria, British Columbia, 1949-52; Bishop of Calgary, 1952-67, retired. Grand Master, Grand Lodge, Manitoba, Ancient Free and Accepted Masons, 1941. LLD Alberta, 1963. *Address:* 303 Camosack Manor, 1035 Belmont Avenue, Victoria, BC V8S 3T5, Canada.
[Died 18 March 1976.

CALVERT-JONES, Maj.-Gen. Percy George, CB 1948; CBE 1945; DSO 1943; MC 1917; *b* 24 April 1894; *s* of James George Calvert-Jones and Mary Louisa Saundry; *m* 1936, Jean Stevenson Binning, JP, DL; one *s* one *d. Educ:* S Wales Univ. TA Commn, 1915; Regular Commn, 1916; served European War, 1914-18; France, Belgium, Egypt, Palestine, 1915-18; N Russia, 1919; India, 1920-24 and 1930-35. Staff Coll., Camberley, 1928-29; SORA Western Comd, India, 1931-34; Air Staff Officer, HQ Fighter Comd, RAF, 1936-39; served War of 1939-45 (despatches thrice); France, Syria, Western Desert, Italy, 1940-43; France, Belgium, 1944-45; BRA Southern Comd, 1945-46; GOC 4AA Group, Warrington, 1946-49; retired pay, 1949. Comdr American Legion of Merit. Recreations: golf, sailing. *Address:* Little Brooke, Brooke, Isle of Wight. *T:* Brighstone 740369. *Clubs:* Naval and Military; Royal Solent Yacht.
[Died 1 Jan. 1977.

CALWELL, Rt. Hon. Arthur Augustus, PC 1967; Leader of Federal Parliamentary Labour Party, Australia, 1960-67 (Deputy Leader, 1951-60); MHR Melbourne, 1940-72; *b* 28 Aug. 1896; *s* of A. A. Calwell; *m* 1932, Elizabeth Marren; one *d. Educ:* Christian Brothers' Coll., N Melbourne. Dept of Agriculture, Vic., 1913-23; Victorian Treasury, 1923-40. Pres. Vic. Australian Labour Party (ALP), 1931; Vic. Delegate to Fed. Confs of ALP, 1930-51; Mem. Fed. Executive, ALP, 1931-50; Mem. Melbourne City Council, 1939-45; Commissioner, Melbourne and Metropolitan Bd of Works, 1939-45; Mem. Jt Parl. Cttee on Broadcasting, 1941-43; Mem. Central Med. Co-ordination Cttee, 1942-44; Chm. Aliens Classification and Advisory Cttee, 1942-46; Minister for Information, Australia, 1943-49, and for Immigration, 1945-49. Mem. Exec. Cttee of Organising Cttee, 1956 Olympic Games; Chm. Melbourne Cricket Ground Trust, 1952- (Trustee, 1931-). Nat. Vice-Pres., Winston Churchill Meml Trust, 1965-. KCSG with Grand Silver Star, 1964. Hon. LLD Melbourne, 1970. *Publications:* Labour's Role in Modern Society, 1963; Be Just and Fear Not, 1972. *Address:* 30 Baroda Street, Flemington, Melbourne, Vic., Australia. *Clubs:* Green Room, Celtic (Melbourne); Tattersall's, Catholic (Sydney); Irish (London); Darwin (Northern Territory).
[Died 8 July 1973.

CAMERON, Mrs Alan Charles; *see* Bowen, Elizabeth D. C.

CAMERON, Basil; *see* Cameron, G. B.

CAMERON, Sir Cornelius, Kt 1968; CBE 1960; DL, JP, FCA; *b* 21 Nov. 1896; *s* of late John Martin Cameron and Elizabeth Roxburgh Cameron, Lutterworth; *m* 1923, Beatrice M., *d* of George Edward Nicholls, Coventry; two *s. Educ:* Trinity Academy, Edinburgh. Served European War, 1914-18, Sub-Lieut, RNVR. CA, 1920. Organised Greek Relief Fund Appeal, Nottingham, during War, 1939-45 (Greek Red Cross Medal, 1946). Jt Man. Dir, William Hollins & Co. Ltd, Nottingham, until retirement in 1961; Mem., East Midlands Gas Board, and Chm., East Midlands Gas Consultative Council, 1961-67. Chm., City of Nottingham Magistrates, 1958-68 (JP 1947); Sheriff of Nottingham, 1960-61, and Lord Mayor, 1963-64; Hon. Alderman. DL Co. Notts, 1963. Hon. Vice-Pres., Nottingham Chamber of Commerce, 1962; Hon. Treas. and Dep. Chm., City of Nottingham Conservative Assoc., 1958-61 (Hon. Sec., 1950-58), etc. Life Mem., Court of Nottingham Univ. *Address:* Bramble Cottage, Red Lane, Lowdham, Notts. *T:* Lowdham 2691. *Club:* Dorchester (Nottingham). *[Died 5 May 1975.*

CAMERON, Vice-Adm. Cyril St Clair, CBE 1919; Royal Navy, retired; *b* 22 July 1879; 4th *s* of late Col A. S. Cameron, VC, CB; *m* 1909, Isabel Edith (*d* 1955), *d* of late Peter Hordern, late Director of Public Instruction, Burmah; two *s* three *d. Educ:* private sch. Joined HMS Britannia as Naval Cadet, 1893; Lieut 1901; Comdr 1913; Capt. 1918; served as 2nd in comd HMS Agamemnon during the operations off the Dardanelles, and subsequent operations in the Mediterranean, 1915-17; employed in anti-submarine work in the Mediterranean, 1917 till the Armistice, Oct. 1918; Dir of Torpedo Div. of Naval Staff, 1926-28; Rear-Adm. retired list, 1930; Vice-Adm. retired, 1935. *Recreation:* gardening. *Address:* Whatley Combe House, Whatley, near Frome, Somerset. *[Died 18 Sept. 1973.*

CAMERON, (George) Basil, CBE 1957; conductor; *b* Reading, 18 Aug. 1884; unmarried. *Educ:* Grammar Sch., Tiverton; Hochschule für Musik, Berlin. First Conductor of Torquay Municipal Orchestra (Wagner Centenary Festival, 1913, Strauss Festival, 1914); Conductor, Hastings Municipal Orchestra, 1923-30; Harrogate Municipal Orchestra, 1924-30; San Francisco Symphony Orchestra, 1930-32; Seattle Symphony Orchestra, 1932-38. Since 1940 one of principal conductors of Henry Wood Promenade Concerts. Guest conductor BBC Symphony Orchestra, London Symphony Orchestra, Royal Philharmonic, London Philharmonic and Philharmonia Orchestras; Berlin Philharmonic, Amsterdam Concertgebouw, Budapest Symphony and Belgian National Symphony Orchestra. *Address:* 30 Ingelow House, Holland Street, W8.
[Died 26 June 1975.

CAMERON, Maj.-Gen. (retired) Roderic Duncan, CB 1952; CBE 1948 (OBE 1945); MC 1918; CStJ 1947; psc; *b* 16 Feb. 1893; *s* of late William Cameron, JP, and Johanna Macdonald, Inverness-shire; *m* 1953, Morva, *d* of late J. H. Nicholson, Loanend, Berwick-upon-Tweed. *Educ:* Glen Urquhart Sch.; George Watson's Coll.; Edinburgh Univ. (MB, ChB). Lieut RAMC, SR, 1914; Lieut RAMC, 1916. Served in Egypt, Greece, Turkey, China, India, UK and North-West Europe (wounded). Major-General, 1950; KHS 1951; QHS 1952-53; DMS, BAOR, 1950-53; Col Comdt RAMC, 1953-58. *Address:* c/o Williams & Glyn's Bank Ltd, Kirkland House, Whitehall, SW1; Ardochy, Furze Hill, Farnham, Surrey GU10 1PS. *T:* Runfold 2465.
[Died 23 April 1975.

CAMERON-RAMSAY-FAIRFAX-LUCY; *see* Fairfax-Lucy.

CAMOYS, 6th Baron *cr* 1264 (called out of abeyance, 1839); **Ralph Robert Watts Sherman Stonor,** DL; land manager (independent); Vice-Chairman, Joint Sun Alliance and London Group Chancery Lane; Director, Robert Jackson Ltd; *b* 5 July 1913; *s* of 5th Baron; *S* father, 1968; *m* 1938, Mary Jeanne Stourton; two *s* three *d. Educ:* privately, mostly self taught. Served 4 Bn Oxfordshire and Buckinghamshire LI; 2nd Lieut 1939; Capt. 1940; Major 1941; retired (ill health) 1944. Has served in local government at various levels since 1938; member of many cttees and sub-cttees; Oxfordshire CC: past Chm., County Records Cttee; Past Chm., Henley Area Planning Cttee. DL Oxon, 1953. *Recreations:* the arts, architecture and church crawling; botany especially wild orchids, ornithology, lepidoptera; member CPRE. *Heir: s* Hon. (Ralph) Thomas Campion George Sherman Stonor [*b* 16 April 1940; *m* 1966, Elizabeth Mary Hyde, *d* of late Sir William Stephen Hyde Parker, 11th Bt; one *s* three *d*]. *Address:* Stonor Park, Henley-on-Thames, Oxon. *T:* Turville Heath 300. *Clubs:* Brooks's, Pratt's, British Parachute; Huntercombe Golf.
[Died 9 March 1976.

CAMPBELL, Brigadier Alexander Donald Powys, CB 1945; late Indian Army, 3rd Gurkha Rifles; *b* 6 July 1894; *s* of General A. A. E. Campbell, IA; *m* 1929; one *s*. *Educ:* Dover Coll.; RMC Sandhurst. 2nd Lieut Indian Army, 1914; Captain 1918; Major 1932; Lieut-Colonel 1936; Colonel 1939; Brigadier 1940; retired 1947. *Address:* Meadowlands, Nutley, Sussex. *Club:* Army and Navy. [*Died* 31 *March* 1974.

CAMPBELL, Maj.-Gen. Sir (Alexander) Douglas, KBE 1956 (CBE 1945); CB 1949; DSO 1943; MC 1918; MA (Cantab); Colonel Commandant Royal Engineers, 1958-64; *b* 20 June 1899; *s* of late Colonel Alan James Campbell, DSO; *m* 1923, Patience Loveday Carlyon; three *s* one *d* (one *s* killed in action, 1945). *Educ:* Aravon Sch.; Bray; Cheltenham Coll.; RMA Woolwich; Queens' Coll., Cambridge. Served European War, 1914-18, France 1918; DADFW War Office, 1933-39; War of 1939-45 (despatches); France, 1940; Asst Dir, Bomb Disposal, 1940; Chief Engr 9 Corps, N Africa, 1943; Chief Engr 1 Corps, Normandy, June 1944; Chief Engr Second Army, 1944-45; Chief Engr Fourteenth Army, June-Nov. 1945; Dep. Dir Tactical Investigation, 1945-46; Chief Engr MELF, 1947-48. E-in-C War Office, 1948-52; Vice-Adjt General to the Forces, 1952-54; Comdr Aldershot District, 1954-57, retired. Lieut Governor, Royal Hospital, Chelsea, 1957-62. Pres., Instn of Royal Engineers, 1957-61; Pres., Assoc. of Service Newspapers, 1957-74. Vice-Chm., Council of Voluntary Welfare Work, 1956-62; Member: Army Benevolent Fund Control Board, 1958-62; ATS Benevolent Fund Cttee, 1953-57 and 1959-63; Soldiers' and Airmen's Scripture Readers' Assoc. (SASRA), 1934-73. Vice-President: Officers' Christian Union, 1958-71; Sandes Soldiers' Homes; Pres., Cheltonian Soc., 1963-64; Governor and Vice-Chm., Royal Sch. for Daughters of Army Officers, 1958-74; Mem. Exec. Cttee, Gordon Boys' Sch., 1959-73; Chm., Newells and Desmoor Sch., 1968-75; Pres., Handcross Park Sch., 1976-. Dir, Taylor Woodrow Industrial Estates, 1962-65. Hon. Colonel, Queen's Univ., Belfast OTC, 1959-64. Commander USA Legion of Merit, 1946. *Address:* Green Bough Cottage, Shipley, Horsham, W Sussex. *T:* Coolham 291. *Club:* Army and Navy. [*Died* 3 *April* 1980.

CAMPBELL, Major-General Alfred Edward, CB 1957; MD, DPH; late RAMC; *b* 21 May 1901; *s* of Rev. J. W. R. Campbell, MA, Stephen's Green, Dublin; *m* 1938, Hilda, *d* of Dr Henry, Clones, Co. Monaghan; three *d*. *Educ:* Methodist Coll. and Queen's Univ., Belfast. Lieut, RAMC, 1924; Captain 1928; Major 1934; Lieut-Colonel 1945; Colonel 1949; Brigadier 1953; Maj.-Gen. 1956. Served in general medical and Army Health duties, UK, India, Norway, Iceland, Germany and Malaya. Dep. Dir of Army Health, 1945; Dir of Army Health, 1953; Dep. Director-General of Army Medical Services, 1956-60; Director of Physiological and Biological Research, War Office, 1960-63; Regimental Headquarter Duties, RAMC, 1963-67. QHP 1953-60. Retired 1960. CStJ 1958. Col Comdt, RAMC, 1961-64. Representative Col Comdt, RAMC, 1962-63. *Address:* 6 West Hill Avenue, Epsom, Surrey. *T:* Epsom 22500. [*Died* 1 *March* 1973.

CAMPBELL, Alistair; Rawlinson and Bosworth Professor of Anglo-Saxon, University of Oxford, and Fellow of Pembroke College, Oxford, since Oct. 1963; *b* 12 Dec. 1907; *s* of Lauchlan and Sarah Campbell, Birmingham; *m* 1935, Kathleen Le Pelley Blackmore; three *s*. *Educ:* Malvern Coll.; Birmingham Univ.; Balliol Coll., Oxford. BA Birm. 1929; BLitt 1932, MA 1940, Oxford. Lectr in English Language, Balliol Coll., 1946-53; Univ. Lectr in Mediaeval English, Oxford, 1949-63. Sen. Research Fellow, Balliol Coll., 1953-63. *Publications:* The Battle of Brunanburh, 1938; Gysbert Japicx: The Oxford Text of Four Poems, 1948; Encomium Emmae Reginae, 1949; Frithegodi Monachi Breuiloquium et Wulfstani Cantoris Narratio Metrica, 1950; Thet Freske Riim; Tractatus Alvini, 1952; The Tollemache Orosius, 1953 (Early English Manuscripts in Facsimile, vol. iii); An Old English Grammar, 1959; The Chronicle of Aethelweard, 1962; Aethelwulf: De Abbatibus, 1967; An Anglo-Saxon Dictionary (Addenda and Corrigenda), 1972; many articles on linguistic and historical subjects. *Address:* 11 Marston Ferry Road, Oxford. *T:* Oxford 55519. [*Died* 5 *Feb.* 1974.

CAMPBELL, Archibald Duncan, CBE 1972; Chief Executive, Sidlaw Industries Ltd, since 1974 (Director, since 1969); *b* 22 Jan. 1919; *s* of late Duncan Alexander and Catherine Anne Campbell; *m* 1950, Mary Elizabeth McFarlane Wilson; one *s* two *d*. *Educ:* Allan Glen's Sch.; Univ. of Glasgow. Served with Royal Engineers (Major 1945), 1940-45; Lectr and Senior Lectr, in Political Economy, Univ. of Glasgow, 1945-55; Prof. of Applied Economics: Univ. of St Andrews, 1955-67; Univ. of Dundee, 1967-74. Economic Consultant to Sec. of State for Scotland, 1962-74; Part-time Member: Scottish Gas Board,

1966-72; British Gas Corporation, 1973-. Member: Fleck Cttee on the Fishing Industry, 1959-60; Boundary Commn for Scotland, 1961-; Econ. Development Cttee for Building, 1967-; Rochdale Cttee on Shipping, 1967-70; Scottish Economic Council, 1971-74; Chm., Econ. Develt Cttees for Building and Civil Engineering, 1973-. Companion IGasE, 1973. *Publications:* articles in economic and other jls. *Recreation:* golf. *Address:* 23 Strathern Road, West Ferry, Dundee. *T:* Dundee 79030. *Clubs:* Caledonian; New (Edinburgh); Royal and Ancient (St Andrews). [*Died* 6 *Jan.* 1975.

CAMPBELL, Rt. Rev. Archibald Rollo G.; *see* Graham-Campbell.

CAMPBELL, Charles Arthur; Emeritus Professor since 1961 (Professor of Logic and Rhetoric, Glasgow University, 1938-61); *b* 13 Jan. 1897; *s* of John Munro Campbell and Rose Jane Arthur; *m* 1926, Ruth Stewart, *y d* of Claud Bald; one *s* one *d*. *Educ:* Glasgow Academy; Glasgow Univ.; Balliol Coll., Oxford. Served European War, 2nd Lieut in 10th Border Regt at home and in Egypt, Jan. 1915-Oct. 1917 (invalided out); Asst in Moral Philosophy at Glasgow, 1924; Lecturer, 1925; Professor of Philosophy, University Coll. of North Wales, Bangor, 1932; Gifford Lectr, St Andrews Univ., 1953-54-55. Hon. DLitt, QUB, 1950-. *Publications:* Scepticism and Construction, 1931; Defence of Free Will (Collected Essays), 1967; Moral Intuition and the Principle of Self-realisation (British Academy Lecture), 1948; On Selfhood and Godhood (Gifford Lectures), 1957; papers in Mind, Philosophy, Proc. Aristotelian Soc., etc. *Address:* 11 Lubnaig Drive, Callander, Perthshire. [*Died* 17 *March* 1974.

CAMPBELL, Charles Douglas, CB 1961; *b* 8 Oct. 1905; *s* of Charles Edward Campbell; *m* 1932, Margaret Stevenson Miller; no *c*. *Educ:* William Hulme Grammar Sch.; Univ. of Manchester. Asst Lectr in Economics, Manchester Univ., 1927-31; Rockefeller Fellow, USA, 1931-32; Lectr in Commerce, Liverpool Univ., 1932-40; Min. of Supply, 1940-42; British Raw Materials Mission, USA, 1942-47; Board of Trade, 1947-. Under-Sec., 1956-62; Principal Asst Registrar, Office of Restrictive Trading Agreements, 1962-65; Chm., Timber Trade Fedn of UK, 1966-69. idc 1950. *Publications:* British Railways in Boom and Depression, 1932; (with M. S. Miller) Financial Democracy, 1933; various papers in learned jls, etc. *Recreations:* reading; pottering about. *Address:* 4 Belltrees Grove, SW16. *T:* 01-769 7936. *Club:* Royal Automobile. [*Died* 28 *May* 1975.

CAMPBELL, Charles Graham; *er s* of late Colin Campbell of Jura and Frances Monteath Sidey (*d* 1925); *b* 3 June 1880; *m* 1930, Debora Sylvester Fane, *d* of late William Gore Lambarde, Beechmont, Sevenoaks; no *c*. *Educ:* St Paul's Sch. Served Royal Field Artillery, 1915-19 (despatches); Station owner, NSW, Australia. *Recreations:* hunting, stalking, shooting. *Address:* 2 Campden Hill Gate, Duchess of Bedford's Walk, W8. *T:* 01-937 6795. *Clubs:* Boodle's; New (Edinburgh). [*Died* 18 *Nov.* 1971.

CAMPBELL, Sir Colin, Kt 1952; OBE 1941; Town Clerk, Plymouth, 1935-53; *b* 1891; *m* 1923, Matilda Hopwood (*d* 1955); two *d*. *Educ:* Burnley Grammar Sch. Town Clerk, Burnley, 1923-35. ARP Controller of Plymouth, 1939-45. *Recreation:* golf. *Address:* Reedley Hallows, Delgany, Plymouth, Devon. *T:* Plymouth 772115. [*Died* 12 *Oct.* 1979.

CAMPBELL, Sir David, Kt 1953; MC 1918; MA, BSc, MD, LLD (Glasgow, Dublin, Liverpool, Aberdeen); DCL (Durham); FRCPG; FRSE; FRCP; Regius Professor of Materia Medica and Therapeutics, University of Aberdeen, 1930-59; Dean of the Faculty of Medicine, 1932-59; President, General Medical Council, 1949-61; *b* 6 May 1889; *m* 1921, Margaret, *o d* of Alexander Lyle of Kerse. *Educ:* Ayr Academy; Univ. of Glasgow; Johns Hopkins Univ. MA (Hons) 1911; BSc 1911; MB, ChB (Hons) 1916; MD (Hons and Bellahouston Gold Medal), 1924; LLD 1950. Captain (a/Major) RAMC (TF), 1916-19; Univ. Asst to Prof. of Materia Medica and Therapeutics, Glasgow Univ., 1919-21; Pollok Lectr in Materia Medica and Pharmacology, 1921-30; Resident Physician, 1915-16; Physician to Out-Patients, 1920-29; Asst Physician to Western Infirmary, Glasgow, 1929-30; Extra-Hon. Physician, Aberdeen Royal Infirmary, 1930-59; Rockefeller Medical Fellow in Pharmacology and Therapeutics, 1925-26. *Publications:* Handbook of Therapeutics; papers on pharmacological and therapeutic subjects in various medical and scientific jls. *Recreations:* golf, motoring. *Address:* Carskeoch, Milltimber, Aberdeenshire. *T:* Culter 733335. *Clubs:* Athenæum; Royal Northern (Aberdeen). [*Died* 30 *May* 1978.

CAMPBELL, Maj.-Gen. Sir Douglas; *see* Campbell, Sir Alexander Douglas.

CAMPBELL, Douglas Mason, CBE 1978; QC (Scotland) 1953; Hon. Sheriff (Sheriff-Principal and Sheriff, 1958-74) of Inverness, Moray, Nairn, and Ross and Cromarty; Chairman; Medical Appeal Tribunal, Industrial Injuries Scheme, Scotland; *b* 14 Nov. 1905; *s* of late David C. Campbell, Glasgow; *m* 1955, Alice Barbara Chalmers, *d* of late W. G. Chalmers Hanna, OBE, MC, CA, Edinburgh. *Educ:* Sedbergh; Worcester Coll., Oxford. BA Oxford, 1928; LLB Glasgow, 1931. Admitted to Scottish Bar, 1931. Served RA, 1940-45. Advocate-Depute, 1951-53 and 1957-58. Chm., Workmen's Compensation and Pneumoconiosis, Byssinosis and Misc. Diseases Benefit Bds, until 1977. *Recreations:* fishing, shooting, golf. *Address:* 10 Forres Street, Edinburgh EH3 6BJ. *T:* 031-225 3150. *Clubs:* United Oxford & Cambridge University; New (Edinburgh); Highland (Inverness).
[Died 16 July 1978.

CAMPBELL, Colonel (Hon. Brigadier, retired) Edmund George, CBE 1943; *b* 3 April 1893; *e s* of late Brig.-General G. P. Campbell, CBE, CIE; *m* 1918, Esmé, *d* of late H. A. Rose, ICS; no *c. Educ:* Mount St Mary's Coll.; RMA, Woolwich. 2nd Lieut RA 1912. Served European War, 1914-18; passed Staff College, Quetta, and RAF Staff College; Colonel 1939; Temp. Brigadier 1940. Served War of 1939-45 (despatches, CBE); retired 1946. *Recreations:* bridge, and gardening. *Address:* Half Acre, Fleet, Hants. *T:* Fleet 6115. *[Died 22 Nov. 1972.*

CAMPBELL, Evan Roy, CBE 1958; Chairman: Rhodesia Fertilizer Corporation Ltd; Albatros Fisons Fertilizers Holdings Ltd; Fisons Pest Control (CA) (pvt) Ltd; Commercial Union Assurance Co. of Rhodesia (pvt) Ltd; Murray and Roberts Rhodesia Ltd; Central African Branch of Institute of Directors; Manica Freight Services (Rhodesia) Ltd; Standard Finance Ltd, and other companies; Director: Discount Co. of Rhodesia Ltd; Messina Rhodesia Investments Ltd; M. T. D. (Mangula) Ltd; Sable Chemical Industries Ltd, and other companies; *b* 2 Sept. 1908; *m* 1934, Norah May Vaughan; one *s* one *d. Educ:* St Andrew's Coll., Grahamstown, S Africa; Potchefstroom Agricultural Coll. Started farming in Umvukwes, S Rhodesia, 1931; farmed in Inyazura, 1935-65. Enlisted in Rhodesia Regt, 1940; seconded to King's African Rifles (Abyssinia, Burma and India); Staff Coll., Quetta, 1944 (psc); GSO 2, 11 (E Africa) Div.; Bde Major 25 (E Africa) Infantry Bde. High Comr in London for Southern Rhodesia, 1964-65; Chm., Rhodesian Bd, Standard Bank Ltd, 1965-79. Rhodesia Tobacco Assoc.: Mem., 1946; Vice-Pres., 1947; Pres., 1952-58, now Life Vice-Pres.; Chm. Makoni Br., and Mem. Nat. Council, British Empire Service League, 1947; Mem., Tobacco Marketing Board, 1950; Chm., Tobacco Export Promotion Council, 1958; Chm., Gwebi Agric. Coll. Council, 1963; Pres., First Internat. Tobacco Congress; Life Vice-Pres., Manicaland Agricultural Show Society. Governor, Peterhouse Sch. Farmers' Oscar for outstanding services to agriculture and British Empire Service League meritorious service medal, 1962. *Recreations:* riding, croquet, yachting. *Address:* (business) Standard Bank, PO Box 373, Salisbury, Rhodesia; (private) 5 Fenton Close, PO Chisipite, Salisbury, Rhodesia. *Clubs:* MCC; Salisbury Umtali (Rhodesia). *[Died 20 Aug. 1980.*

CAMPBELL, Ewen, CMG 1946; MBE 1926; MC 1917; Member of Council, British Red Cross Society, 1970-74, Chairman, Executive Committee, Scottish Branch, 1962-70; Secretary, South-Eastern Regional Hospital Board, Scotland, 1948-62; Sudan Political Service (retired); Member Queen's Body Guard for Scotland, Royal Company of Archers; *b* 13 Aug. 1897; *er s* of late Colonel Ewen Campbell, VD, JP; *m* 1929, Evelyn Winifred, *o d* of late Philip Robertson, NSW, Australia; three *d. Educ:* Edinburgh Academy; Oriel Coll., Oxford. European War, commissioned RFA 1915; served in France (MC) and North Russia; entered Oxford, 1919; played Rugby football for Oxford Univ., 1919, 1920 and captained the XV in 1921; BA Hons 1921; joined Sudan Political Service, 1921; served as Asst District Commissioner in Kassala and Darfur Provinces; Deputy-Governor Kassala Province, 1935-36; Deputy Civil Secretary, Khartoum, 1936-38; Governor of Kordofan Province, Sudan, 1938-47. Order of the Nile 4th Class 1933, 3rd Class 1941; despatches 1943. *Address:* 8 Succoth Gardens, Edinburgh EH12 6BS. *Club:* New (Edinburgh). *[Died 5 Nov. 1975.*

CAMPBELL, Engineer Captain George Douglas, CBE 1944; DSO 1918; Royal Navy, retired; *b* 10 March 1884; *m* 1944, Ruth Evelyn, *d* of F. J. Misselbrook, Southampton. *Educ:* private; abroad. Joined RNE College, 1900; served European War, 1914-18 (despatches, DSO); Engineer Captain, 1931; retired list, 1937. Served War of 1939-45 (CBE). *Club:* Royal Naval and Royal Albert Yacht (Portsmouth). *[Died 8 April 1972.*

CAMPBELL, Harold Ernest, CBE 1974; *b* 28 May 1902; *s* of W. W. Campbell and Emma Campbell; *m* 1929, Marion Fordyce

Wheeler; one *s* one *d. Educ:* Belfast Royal Academy; Trinity Coll., Dublin. MA, MAI, CEng, FICE. Asst Engr, S. Pearson & Son (Contracting Dept) Ltd, 1923-32; Civil Engr, T. J. Moran & Co. Ltd, 1932-34; McLaughlin & Harvey Ltd: Civil Engr, 1934; Dir, 1944-78; Chm., 1954-75. Dir, Bank of Ireland, 1960-75; Chm., NI Airports Ltd, 1970-77; Belfast Harbour Comr, 1955-77. *Recreation:* golf. *Address:* Rockmore, Newcastle, Co. Down, N Ireland. *T:* Newcastle (Down) 22295. *Clubs:* Ulster Reform (Belfast); Royal Belfast Golf, Royal County Down Golf.
[Died 1 Feb. 1980.

CAMPBELL, Brigadier Hector, CB 1933; DSO 1918; MVO 1906; Colonel Queen Victoria's Own Corps of Guides (Cavalry and Infantry), 1935; *b* 24 Oct. 1877; *s* of late Major-General R. B. P. P. Campbell, CB, and Ada, *d* of late L. G. A. Campbell, of Fairfield, Ayrshire; *m* 1956, Gertrude Eunice Cowman. *Educ:* Haileybury Coll.; RMC, Sandhurst. Entered Army, 1897; Captain, 1906; Major, 1915; Lieut-Colonel, 1921; Colonel, 1925; Brigadier, 1931; with 1st Gordon Highlanders during Tirah Expedition, 1897-98, present at action of Dargai (medal and 2 clasps); China Expeditionary Force, 1900 (medal); European War, 1914-18, Egypt, Gallipoli, Egypt and Palestine (despatches twice, 1914-15 Star, two medals, DSO); Military Adviser-in-Chief, Indian States Forces, 1931-34; retired 1934. *Recreations:* polo, riding, shooting; in winning team Indian Championship Polo Tournament, 1909-10. *Address:* c/o National and Grindlay's Bank, 13 St James's Square, SW1. *Club:* United Service & Royal Aero. *[Died 18 April 1972.*

CAMPBELL, Vice-Admiral Sir Ian Murray Robertson, KBE 1955; CB 1951; DSO 1942, Bar 1943; *b* 8 Aug. 1898; 2nd *s* of Brig. A. A. E. Campbell, Indian Army; *m* 1929, Marjorie Mary McCreath, Looseleigh, Tamerton Foliot, Devon; two *s. Educ:* Dover Coll. Junior Sch.; Osborne; Dartmouth; Cambridge. Service in N Sea, Adriatic and Eastern Baltic, 1914-19; Captain, Naval Staff, 1940; Comd 3rd Destroyer Flotilla, HMS Milne, 1942-44; Naval Staff, and Comd HMS Jamaica, E Indies Squadron, 1945-47; Rear-Adm. 1950; Vice-Adm., 1953; Commander-in-Chief, South Atlantic Station, 1954-56; retd list, 1956. *Publication:* (jointly) The Kola Run, 1958. *Address:* Ivy Cottage, Sapperton, Glos. *[Died 15 April 1980.*

CAMPBELL, Sir Ian (Vincent Hamilton), 7th Bt *cr* 1831, of Barcaldine and Glenure; CB 1951; Assistant Under-Secretary of State, Air Ministry, 1945-55, retired 1955; *b* 1895; *e* surv. *s* of Richard Hamilton Campbell, CIE, ICS (retd) (*d* 1923); *S* cousin, Captain Sir (Francis) Eric Dennistoun Campbell, 6th Bt, 1963; *m* 1st, Madeline (*d* 1929), *e d* of late H. Anglin Whitelocke, FRCS, Oxford; one *s*; 2nd, Iris Constance (marr. diss., 1942), *d* of late Lt-Col Ronald Charles Gibb, CBE; 3rd, Agnes Louise, *e d* of late William Henry Gerhardi, and *widow* of Vsevolod Victor Watson, MBE. *Educ:* Cheltenham; Corpus Christi Coll., Oxford. Served European War, 1914-18 as Lieut The King's (Liverpool Regt); severely wounded in Battle of the Somme, 1916, and invalided from Army, May 1918. Entered Home Civil Service, 1919, as Asst Principal, Air Ministry; Priv. Sec. to Chief of Air Staff (late Marshal of the RAF Lord Trenchard), 1926-27; Private Sec. to Permanent Sec. of the Air Ministry (late Sir Walter Nicholson), 1927-30; Asst Private Sec. to successive Secs of State for Air (late Lord Thomson, late Lord Amulree, and, late Marquess of Londonderry), 1930-34; Principal, Air Ministry, 1934; Asst Sec. 1939. *Heir: s* Niall Alexander Hamilton Campbell [*b* 7 Jan. 1925; *m* 1st, 1949, Patricia Mary (marr. diss., 1956), *d* of R. Turner; 2nd, 1957, Norma Joyce, *d* of W. N. Wiggin; two *s* two *d* (including twin *s* and *d*)]. *Address:* White Rose, Hawkhurst, Kent. *T:* Hawkhurst 2268.
[Died 14 April 1978.

CAMPBELL, Mrs John; *see* Campbell, May Eudora.

CAMPBELL, (John) Maurice (Hardman), OBE; MD Oxon; FRCP; formerly: Consulting Physician to Guy's Hospital; Consulting Physician, National Hospital for Diseases of the Heart; Consulting Editor, British Heart Journal; *b* 1891; *s* of J. E. Campbell, FRS; *m* 1924, Ethel Mary, *d* of Captain Chrimes, CBE; two *s* three *d. Educ:* Winchester (Scholar); New Coll., Oxford. 1st Class Physiology, Oxford and Senior Demyship, Magdalen Coll.; Captain RAMC (SR), Mesopotamia and North Persia, 1916-19; Beit Memorial Research Fellow, 1923-27; Past Pres., British Cardiac Soc.; Past Chm., British Heart Foundn. *Publications:* various papers on heart disease and goitre in medical journals. *Recreations:* ornithology and Sherlock Holmes. *Address:* 47 Arkwright Road, Hampstead, NW3.
[Died 7 Aug. 1973.

CAMPBELL, J(ohn) Menzies, (retired), DDS (cum laude), Toronto University; Hon. FDS (RCS) (1st award to a dentist); FDS (RCS Edin.); LDS (RCDS Ont.); LDS (RFPS Glas.);

FRSE; FICD; FACD (Life); FRSM (Section of Odontology) (Council, 1931-34, a Vice-President, 1950-53); Dental Historian; a Vice-President of the Ivory Cross; British Correspondent to Journal of Canadian Dental Association; *b* 1887; *s* of John Menzies Campbell; *m* Margaret Williamson, MB, ChB, *d* of James Shirlaw. *Educ:* George Watson's Coll., Edinburgh; Anderson's and St Mungo's Medical Colls, Glasgow; Univ. of Toronto; Royal Coll. of Dental Surgeons of Ontario. LLD (Tor.) was offered, 1952, but unconferred owing to ill-health. Hon. Visiting Dental Surgeon, Woodside and Springburn Red Cross Hospitals, Glasgow (awarded British Red Cross War Medal). Hon. Mem.: Canadian Dental Assoc.; Amer. Acad. of History of Dentistry; Pierre Fauchard Academy; Société Française de l'Histoire de l'Art Dentaire; Royal Odonto-Chirurgical Soc. of Scotland; Dental Students' Soc., St Andrews Univ.; The Lindsay (Dental history) Club; Corr. Mem., Svenska Tandläkare-Sällskapet; Mem.: British Dental Association (Pres., 1938, West of Scotland Branch); Odonto-Chirurgical Soc. of Scotland (Pres., 1939-45); Glasgow Odontological Soc.; Secours Dentaire International (Exec.); Scottish Soc. of the History of Medicine (Council, 1950-53); Glasgow Royal Institute of Fine Arts; Foreign Correspondent, Revista da Associacão Paulista de Cirurgiões Dentistas (Brazil). Adviser, Sub-cttee on dental history, International Dental Federation, American Coll. of Dentists. Delivered John Smith Centenary Oration, RCS Edinburgh, 1956. Menzies Campbell Triennial Lecture on Dental History instituted, RCS Eng., 1958. Collections of early dentistry exhibited in Glasgow Art Galleries and Museum, 1949, and Hunterian Library, Univ. of Glasgow, 1955. Presented Menzies Campbell collection of dental pictures, instruments, appliances, ornaments, etc. to RCS Edinburgh, 1964; presented Menzies Campbell Library of early dental books and pamphlets to RCS Eng, 1969. Hon. Lecturer in History of Dentistry, Edin. Univ., 1960-. *Publications:* Those Teeth of Yours: A Popular Guide to Better Teeth, 1929, rev. and enl. 2nd edn 1931; A Dental Bibliography, British and American, 1682-1880, 1949; Dentistry as practised, 1800-1921, 1955; From a Trade to a Profession: Byways in Dental History, 1958; Dentistry Then and Now, 1963; Foreword to Edward Samson's Men, Manners and Molars, 1963; Catalogue of the Menzies Campbell Collection, RCS Edin., 1966; numerous contributions to dental historical literature. *Recreations:* collecting early dental books and instruments, dental history. *Address:* 70 Great George Street, Glasgow G12 8RU. *T:* 041-339 0011. *[Died 27 June 1974.*

CAMPBELL, Maurice; see Campbell, J. M. H.

CAMPBELL, May Eudora, (Mrs John Campbell), CBE 1952 (OBE 1944); JP; *d* of Henry Moncreiff Horsbrugh, CA, Edinburgh; *m* 1st, 1910, Kenneth Mackenzie (*d* 1918), Dolphinton; three *s* one *d*; 2nd, 1922, John Campbell (*d* 1943), WS, Edinburgh; one *d*. *Educ:* Lansdowne House, Murrayfield. Women's Voluntary Services, 1938-52 (Chm for Scotland, 1946-52); Mem.: Furnished Rents Tribunal for Lothians and Peebles, 1944-68; Royal Commission on Scottish Affairs, 1952; Gen. Advisory Council, BBC 1959-62; Vice-Pres., Women's Advisory Council on Solid Fuel, 1963-70. JP, County of Lanark, 1920. *Address:* Meadowhead, Dolphinton, Lanarkshire. *T:* Dolphinton 210. *Club:* Queen's (Edinburgh).
[Died 1 May 1975.

CAMPBELL, Mrs Mungo; see McCracken, Esther.

CAMPBELL, Patrick; see Glenavy, 3rd Baron.

CAMPBELL, Richard Mitchelson, CMG 1953; retired as Deputy High Commissioner for New Zealand, London, 1958; *b* Maungatapere, New Zealand, 28 Aug. 1897; *y s* of Norman Campbell; *m* 1935, Mary, *y d* of John Campbell, Glendale, Isle of Skye; one *s* two *d*. *Educ:* Whangarei High Sch.; Victoria Univ., NZ; London Sch. of Economics. LLB NZ 1922; MA Hons NZ 1925; PhD Econ. London, 1929. In NZ Public Service (Educn Dept), 1914-26; Private Sec. to Prime Minister, 1926-27; Travelling Schol. Univ. NZ, 1927-29; Harkness Fund Fellow, USA, 1929-31; Sec. to Min. of Finance, 1931-35; NZ Govt in London: Economic Adviser, 1935-40; Official Sec., 1940-46 and 1953-58. Chm. Public Service Commn, NZ, 1946-53. NZ Trustee, Commonwealth Foundn, 1966-73. *Address:* 10 King Edward Parade, Devonport, Auckland, NZ.
[Died 17 Nov. 1974.

CAMPBELL, Robert Richmond, CMG 1967; OBE 1958; artist; writer, lecturer and broadcaster on art; Director, National Gallery of South Australia, 1951-67; Member, Commonwealth Art Advisory Board, since 1953; *b* Edinburgh, Scotland, 18 July 1902; *s* of A. R. Campbell, Tynemouth, England; *m* 1933, Jean E., *d* of J. Young; one *s* three *d*. *Educ:* George Watson's Academy, Edinburgh; Wallasey Grammar Sch., Ches. Arrived

Australia 1916; first show, Melbourne, 1928; 4 years travelling and painting in Europe; exhibitions in Melbourne, Sydney, Brisbane, Adelaide; represented in all Australian State and Provincial Galleries; Head, Dept of Art, Launceston Technical Coll., 1941-47; Curator of Art Gallery, W Australia, 1947-49; First Dir, Queensland Art Gallery, 1949-51. Mem., Aust. Watercolour Inst.; Past Pres., Perth Soc. of Artists. *Publications:* Paintings of Tom Roberts, 1963; many articles on art subjects. *Recreations:* walking, sketching, reading. *Address:* Innisfail, Gorge Road, Athelstone, SA 5076, Australia. *T:* 37-4702. *[Died 30 Sept. 1972.*

CAMPBELL, Dr Sidney Scholfield, MVO 1972; Organist, and Master of the Choristers, St George's Chapel, Windsor Castle, since 1961; *b* 7 June 1909. DMus Dunelm, 1945; FRCO 1931; Organist, St Peter's Collegiate Church, Wolverhampton, 1943-47. Sub-Warden, Royal School of Church Music, 1947-49; Organist, Ely Cathedral, 1949-53; Organist and Master of the Music, Southwark Cathedral, 1953-56; Organist, Canterbury Cathedral, 1956-61. Dir of Musical Studies, Royal Sch. of Church Music, 1954-55. *Address:* 23 The Cloisters, Windsor Castle. *T:* Windsor 64529. *[Died 4 June 1974.*

CAMPBELL, Sybil, OBE 1942; MA; Metropolitan Magistrate, Tower Bridge, 1945-61, retired; *b* 1889; *d* of late Neill Graeme Campbell (Auchendarroch), and Maude Georgiana, *d* of late Sir William Bovill, Chief Justice of Common Pleas. *Educ:* Dunardarigh, North Berwick; Girton Coll., Camb. (Nat. Sciences Tripos Pt I; Economics Tripos Pt II). Inspector under Trade Boards Act, 1914-18; Assistant Enforcement Officer, Min. of Food, Midland Div., 1918-21; Called to Bar, Middle Temple, 1922; a Metropolitan Chm., Courts of Referees, 1930-39; Asst Div. Food Officer (Enforcement), London div., Ministry of Food, 1939-44. *Address:* c/o Sisters of Bon Secours, 40 Mansion House Road, Langside, Glasgow. *T:* 041-632 0390.
[Died 29 Aug. 1977.

CAMPBELL, Hon. Thane Alexander, QC 1974; MA, LLD; Chief Commissioner, Foreign Claims Commission (Canada), 1970-74; Chief War Claims Commissioner (Canada), 1952-74; Adviser on claims under agreement with Bulgaria, 1967; *b* 7 July 1895; *s* of Alexander and Clara Tremaine Campbell; *m* 1st, 1930, Cecilia Lillian Bradshaw (*d* 1968); two *s* two *d*; 2nd, 1970, Paula Champ. *Educ:* Prince of Wales Coll., Charlottetown, PEI; Dalhousie Univ. Halifax, NS; Corpus Christi Coll., Oxford. Admitted to Bar of PEI 1927; Attorney-Gen. of PEI 1930-31 and 1935-43; Mem. of Legislative Assembly, 1931-43; Premier and Provincial Sec.-Treasurer, PEI, 1936-43; Chief Justice, Prince Edward Island, 1943-70. Chancellor, Univ. of Prince Edward Island, 1970-74. Member: Historical Sites and Monuments Bd of Canada, 1948-59; Nat. Library Adv. Council, 1949-59; Bd of Governors of: Dalhousie Coll., 1950-; St Dunstan's Univ., 1964-. Pres., Dominion Curling Assoc., 1942; Vice-Pres., Royal Caledonian Curling Club of Scotland, 1945; admitted to Curling Hall of Fame for Canada, 1975. Chm., Brier Trustees, 1963-. Holds hon. doctorates. *Address:* Box 1358, Summerside, PEI, Canada. *T:* (office) Ottawa 995-8702, (residence) 436-2556. *[Died 28 Sept. 1978.*

CAMPBELL, Lt-Col Sir Walter Fendall, KCIE, *cr* 1946 (CIE 1941); *b* 20 May 1894; 2nd *s* of late Brig-Gen. G. P. Campbell, CIE, CBE, RE; *m* 1920, Ann (*d* 1969), *d* of late T. McLaughlin, Roscommon, Ireland; four *d*. *Educ:* Mount St Mary's Coll., Derbys. Entered Indian Army, 1914; seconded, Civil Administration, Iraq, 1919-20 (despatches, Iraq Rebellion, 1920); Joined Indian Political Dept, 1921; held various posts in Districts and Agencies of Baluchistan and NWFP, 1921-33; Sec. to Agent to Governor-Gen. in states of Western India, 1933; Prime Minister, Alwar, 1935-36; Political Agent, Bundelkhand, 1937; Resident in Waziristan, 1939-40; Adviser to Governor, NWFP, 1941-42; Resident for Central India, 1942-46; Resident in Mysore, 1946-47. *Address:* 2 Clarendon Court, Granville Road, Sevenoaks, Kent. *T:* Sevenoaks 58833.
[Died 15 May 1973.

CAMPBELL, William, CBE 1959; General Secretary, Educational Institute of Scotland, 1952-60, retired; *b* 1 June 1895; *e s* of James Campbell, Auchinleck, Ayrshire; *m* 1925, Agnes Wightman, *d* of Thomas Boyd Stirling, JP, Alexandria, Dunbartonshire; two *s* one *d*. *Educ:* Auchinleck Sch.; Cumnock Academy; Kilmarnock Academy; Glasgow Univ. MA Glasgow 1920; BL Glasgow 1940. Teacher in Glasgow, 1920-45; Asst Sec., Educational Institute of Scotland, 1945-48; Dep. Sec., 1948-52. Fellow of Educational Institute of Scotland (FEIS) 1945. Hon. Mem., Nat. Union of Teachers, 1960. Pres. Educational Institute of Scotland, 1961-62. *Recreations:* bowling, reading. *Address:* 3 Rosebank Road, Edinburgh 5. *T:* 031-552 2664. *Club:* Scottish Liberal (Edinburgh).
[Died 31 March 1976.

CAMPBELL, William Gordon; Chartered Accountant; partner in Josolyne Miles & Company, London, Manchester and Paris, 1924-58; *b* Glasgow, 3 Oct. 1891; *er s* of Duncan Macalpine Campbell (BISN Co. Ltd, Calcutta and London); *m* 1919, Ena Clarissa (*d* 1962), *d* of George Henry Castle, Stoke-by-Nayland, Suffolk; one *d*. (one *s* decd). *Educ:* Morrison's Academy, Crieff; Mill Hill Sch.; Trinity Coll., Cambridge. BA, Nat. Sci. Tripos, 1912. Served European War, 1914-18, Lieut, 2/1 Sussex Yeomanry and attached 8th Queens (RWS) Regiment. Mem. of Central Price Regulation Cttee of Board of Trade, 1946-49; Mem. Council Institute of Chartered Accountants in England and Wales, 1947-58; Mem. of Gen. Nursing Council for England and Wales, 1953-58; Lay mem. of the Restrictive Practices Court, 1958-62. *Recreations:* books, gardening, fishing. *Address:* Hillstead, Cornsland, Brentwood, Essex. *T:* Brentwood 1019.
[Died 11 Jan. 1974.

CAMPBELL SWINTON; *see* Swinton, Brigadier A. H.

CAMPBELL-WALTER, Rear-Adm. (retired) Keith McNeil, CB 1957; *b* 31 Aug. 1904; *s* of Alexander McNeil Walter; *m* 1930, Frances Henriette, FSA Scot., *e d* and senior co-heir of Sir Edward Taswell Campbell of Airds Bay, 1st Bt, MP (*d* 1945); two *s* two *d*. *Educ:* RN Colls, Osborne and Dartmouth. Comdr, 1938; Captain, 1945; Commodore, 1953; Rear-Adm., 1955. ADC to the Queen 1954; Flag Officer, Germany, and Comdr Allied Naval Forces Northern Area, Central Europe, 1955-58, retd. Legion of Merit, USA, 1946. *Recreation:* fishing. *Address:* 19a Princes Gate Mews, SW7 2PS. *T:* 01-589 0897; 10 Ellenabeich, Isle of Seil by Oban, Argyll PA34 4RQ. *T:* Balvicar 202. *Clubs:* Naval and Military; Puffins (Edinburgh).
[Died 24 April 1976.

CAMPION, Cecil; *see* Campion, J. C.

CAMPION, (John) Cecil; Magistrate of the Magistrates' Courts of the Metropolis, 1955-70; *b* 8 Aug. 1907; *s* of Bernard Campion and Rose (*née* Lees); *m* 1932, Constance Mary Doggart (*d* 1953); two *d*; *m* 1959, Diana Jacqueline Rodwell; one *d*. *Educ:* Marlborough; Magdalen Coll., Oxf. Called to the Bar, Gray's Inn, 1932; Central Criminal Court, Midland Circuit. Served RASC, 1939-45 (invalided out as Major). *Address:* 111 Crabtree Lane, Harpenden, Herts. *T:* Harpenden 3144.
[Died 9 March 1971.

CAMPION, Sidney Ronald, OBE 1953; FRSA; FJI 1950; Author, Barrister, Journalist, Schoolmaster, Lecturer, Sculptor, and from 1940 until retirement in 1957, Head of the Press and Broadcast Division, GPO Headquarters; *b* Coalville, Leics, 30 June 1891; *e s* of Chelsea Pensioner, late Walter Campion and late Martha Robinson, Leicester; *m* 1912, Claire (*d* 1968), *y d* of late Horatio and Elizabeth Armitage, Cotebrook, Tarporley, Cheshire; one *d*; *m* 1971, Margery, widow of Stanley Ainsworth, Southport. *Educ:* Charnwood Street Elementary Sch., Leicester; Vaughan Working Men's Coll., Leicester; Chester Diocesan Teachers' Training Coll.; Gray's Inn; Morley Coll., London; Wimbledon School of Art; Regent Street Polytechnic School of Art; St Martin's School of Art; Southport Coll. of Art. Street newspaper seller in Leicester from 11 to 14. Worked in factories, workshops and woodmills in Leicester for three years. Assisted by late Rt Hon. J. Ramsay MacDonald, late Sir Edward Wood (Chm. Freeman Hardy & Willis, Ltd), and late Thomas Adcock, MA, was privately educated and joined editorial staff of Leicester Pioneer. Later worked on Wilmslow Express (Cheshire), Leeds Weekly Citizen, Daily Citizen, Chorley Guardian, Bradford Daily Telegraph, Daily News, London, and served as chief of the Allied (Kemsley) (now Thomson's Allied) Newspapers; Parliamentary Press Gallery staff, 1933-40; Chief Press and Broadcasting Officer to General Post Office, 1940-57. Town Councillor and Poor Law Guardian, Chorley, 1920-23; Parliamentary Labour Candidate, Oswestry, 1923; qualified as schoolmaster with First Class teaching certificate, Liverpool Univ.; admitted Gray's Inn, 1927, honours in Final and called to Bar, 1930; member South-Eastern Circuit; holder bronze medal of Royal Life Saving Society and hon. instructor in life saving; Madden Prizeman, Chester Coll. Life Member: National Union of Journalists, 1957; Newspaper Press Fund; Life Fellow RSA, 1975; Member: of Francis Bacon Society; Society of Civil Service Authors; Cttee of Post Office Art Club of Great Britain; William Morris Society; League for Abolition of Cruel Sports; Royal National Institute for the Deaf; travelled Scandinavia, Russia (1935 and 1960), Germany, Turkey, etc. European War, 1914-18, served in RFC, RAF, IAF. *Publications:* Sunlight on the Foothills, 1941; Towards the Mountains, 1943; Reaching High Heaven, 1944; Only the Stars Remain, 1946; The World of Colin Wilson: a Biographical Study, 1962; Adventures Under the Sycamore Tree, 1964; contributor to home and overseas newspapers, magazines and

periodicals, and to Central Office of Information. *Recreations:* experimenting in literary forms; picture painting, sculpture, modelling (portrait busts, etc., exhibitor: London galleries; Morden public library; Society of British Portrait Sculptors; Paris, 1963-70; Madrid, 1965; one-man exhibitions: London, 1960, Astley Hall, Chorley, Lancs, 1962; Tower Gallery, City of London, 1964); searching for the Shakespeare MSS, chess and golf. *Address:* 13 Argyle Court, Argyle Road, Southport, Merseyside PR9 9LQ. *T:* Southport 33047. *Club:* Press (became Life Member 1958). *[Died 29 Dec. 1978.*

CAMPLING, Rev. Canon William Charles, MA; Hon. CF; Canon Emeritus of Southwark, 1960 (Hon. Canon, 1944-60); *b* 13 July 1888; 2nd *s* of late Thomas Campling and Kate Augusta Campling; *m* 1919, Phyllis Russell, 3rd *d* of Francis Henry and Margaret Colet Webb of Backsett, Horsham, Sussex; three *s* one *d*. *Educ:* William Ellis' Sch., Gospel Oak; Trinity Coll., Cambridge; Bishops' Coll., Cheshunt. Curate of St Mary's, Wimbledon, 1914-18; Chaplain to the Forces, BEF, 1918-19 (attached to the 59th Div., France, 1918); Tutor at Ordination Test Sch., Knutsford, 1919; Principal of St Francis' Coll., Nundah, Brisbane, 1919-26; Canon Residentiary of St John's Cathedral, Brisbane, 1919-26; Vicar of St Augustine's, Honor Oak Park, SE, 1926-30; Vicar of St Andrews, Coulsdon, 1930-40; Rector of Charlton, 1940-45; Vicar of Roehampton, 1945-60; Rural Dean of Richmond and Barnes, 1946; Proctor in Convocation, 1944; Priest-in-charge of St Leonard and St James, Rousham, 1960-69. *Address:* Netherlea, Gig Bridge Lane, Pershore, Worcs. *T:* Pershore 3384. *[Died 23 Feb. 1973.*

CAMPS, Francis Edward, MD, FRCP, FRCPath, DMJ; Professor of Forensic Medicine, in the University of London, at the London Hospital Medical College, 1963-70, now Emeritus (Reader, 1954-63); Hon. Consultant to the Army in Forensic Medicine since 1964; *b* 28 June 1905; *s* of late P. W. L. Camps, FRCS; *m*; one *s* one *d*; *m* 1942, Mary Ross Mackenzie, MB, ChB Aberdeen (decd); one *s* one *d*; *m* 1972, Dr Ann E. Camps. *Educ:* Marlborough Coll.; Guy's Hosp. Med. Sch.; Sch. of Trop. Med., Liverpool; Neuchâtel Univ., Switzerland. Late House Physician, Guy's Hospital; Pathologist, Chelmsford and Essex Hospital; Cons. Pathologist to Essex County Council; Travelling Fellowship of the Kellogg Foundation; late Examiner in Forensic Medicine, St Andrews Univ. and Univs. of Bristol, Durham, Sheffield and London. Member: BMA Special Cttee on the Recognition of Intoxication and the Relation of Alcohol to Road Accidents, 1951; Coroners Rules Cttee, Home Office, 1953; Mortuaries Cttee, Ministry of Housing and Local Govt, 1955; Home Office Scientific Advisory Council, 1965; Past President British Assoc. Forensic Medicine; Vice-President Medico-Legal Society; Secretary-General of British Academy of Forensic Sciences; Hon. Member: Harvard Associates in Police Science; Pharmaceutical Soc. of GB; Member American Acad. of Forensic Sciences. Swiney Prize for Med. Jurisprudence, 1969. *Publications:* Medical and Scientific Investigations of the Christie Case, 1953; Practical Forensic Medicine, 1st edn (with Sir Bentley Purchase), 1956, 2nd edn (with J. M. Cameron), 1971; (with Richard Barber) The Investigation of Murder, 1966; (ed) Medicine, Science and Law, 1964; (ed) Gradwohl's Legal Medicine, 2nd edn, 1968; (ed) Recent Advances in Forensic Pathology, 3rd edn, 1969; numerous papers on pathological and medico-legal subjects. *Recreation:* fishing. *Address:* 190 Andrewes House, Barbican, EC2. *T:* 01-638 8204; The Limes, Purleigh, Essex. *Clubs:* Savage, Savile. *[Died 8 July 1972.*

CANDY, Major-General Ronald Herbert, CIE 1937; IMS, retired; *s* of late Professor Hugh Candy; *m* 1912, Lilian Amy (*d* 1944), *d* of late W. Sutherland; no *c*. *Educ:* City of London Sch.; London Hospital. Hon. Surgeon to the King, 1940-44. *Address:* c/o National and Grindlay's Bank Ltd, 13 St James's Square, SW1. *[Died 11 Dec. 1972.*

CANE, Robert Alexander Gordon, BSc London; *b* Dulwich, 11 Feb. 1893; *s* of late Robert Coats Cane; *m* 1924, Ida Mary, *d* of Brook Bray, Dulwich and S. Rhodesia; no *c*. *Educ:* Alleyn's Sch., Dulwich; University Coll., London; Bishop's Coll., Cheshunt. House tutor and science master, Saffron Walden Sch., Essex, 1923-24; Headmaster, 1924-29; temp. master, Oratory Sch., Caversham, Oxon, 1929; Headmaster of Kinmel Sch., Abergele, N. Wales, 1929-33; Temp. 2nd Lieut, 11th Batt., KO Yorks LI, 19 Sept. 1914; promoted Captain commanding A Coy 28 Nov. 1914; served with Mediterranean EF (May-Aug. 1915); severely wounded, Gallipoli when attached 1st Royal Dublin Fusiliers; invalided from service, July 1916. *Recreations:* travel, rifle shooting. *Address:* 22 Manscombe Road, Torquay, Devon. *T:* Torquay 67452. *[Died 10 Sept. 1975.*

CANN, Percy Walter; *b* 20 June 1884; *m* 1909, Ellen Beatrice Blackburn; no *c*. *Educ:* St Gabriel's Church Sch. and North

Street Higher Grade Sch., Bristol. Learning the boot trade, then Commercial Traveller, 1904-22; Director, Haynes & Cann Ltd, Northampton, 1922. Served European War, 1914-18, RASC 1916-18 (Mech. Staff Sergeant; Commandant of Special Constabulary, Bristol, 1939-49 (Special Constab. Police Medal and Bar for long service, 1938-49). Member of Bristol City Council, 1930; Alderman, 1946-74; Lord Mayor, 1949-50; served on many Committees of the Council as Chairman or Vice-Chairman, 1959-74. Chairman: North Bristol Boy Scouts' Association, 1946-57; North Bristol Nat. Liberal Assoc., 1932-48. President: Rotary Club of Bristol, 1942; Anchor Society, 1951, 1952; National President English Nat. Council of Development Boards, 1947-55; Chairman Bristol Light Opera Co., 1950-; Vice-Chairman, Bristol Branch, Empire Soc., 1952-; Chairman BBC West of England's Appeals Cttee, 1953-; Member BBC UK Appeals Advisory Cttee, 1952-; Chairman and Founder, Bristol Elderly Peoples Assoc. for Permanent Daily Clubs; founded Bristol Branch of Incorp. Sales Managers Assoc. FSMA (Past Sec., Chairman and Pres.). Chm., Bristol Safety First Cttee, 1967-; Vice-Chm., South Western Safety First, 1967-; Mem., Nat. Safety First, RoSPA, 1967-. Free Mason, Methodist. Grand Governor, Loyal Order of Moose, 1929, and Senior Past Governor of GB. Meritorious Service Medal, 1919; Defence Medal, 1939-45. *Recreations:* bowls, golf, gardening and cinematograph photography; music (plays organ and piano; choirmaster and organist). *Address:* Cliftonia, Walsingham Road, Bristol 6. *T:* 44486. *Club:* Royal Commonwealth Society (London and Bristol).

[Died 30 Dec. 1973.

CANNAN, Maj.-Gen. James Harold, CB 1915; CMG 1918; DSO 1919; VD; late Manager for NSW, The Insurance Office of Australia, Ltd; *b* Townsville, Queensland, 29 Aug. 1882; *s* of John Kearsey Cannan and Bessie Constance Hodson; *m* Eileen Clair Ranken; no *c. Educ:* Brisbane State Sch. and Grammar Sch. Four years in wholesale ironmongers and importers, three years clerk New Zealand Insurance Company, five years manager Patriotic Insurance Company, thirty years manager Insurance Office of Australia in Australia; retired, 1946. Lieut in 1st Queenslanders (Infantry), 1903; merged into 9th Infantry Commonwealth; Adjutant of that batt. for five years; Captain, 1907; Major, 1910; on formation of compulsory service transferred as 2nd in Command of 8th (Oxley) Infantry batt.; Lieut-Colonel, and commanded this batt., 1914; served European War (Dardanelles), 1914-16 (despatches, CB); Colonel and Temp. Brig.-General 30 Aug. 1916; commanded 11th Australian Infantry Brigade (CMG, DSO, despatches 7 times; Command of 2/15th Infantry, Commonwealth Military Forces, 1918-20; commanded 2nd Infantry Brigade, 1920-21 and 11th Infantry Brigade, 1921-25; Inspector-General of Administration under Board of Business Administration, Commonwealth of Australia, Jan.-July 1940; GOC 2nd Australian Div., July-Oct., 1940; Quarter Master General, Army HQ, Australia, 1940-46; Maj.-General 1942; retired list, 1946; Founder and 1st President, Brisbane Legacy, 1924; President, Queensland State Returned Servicemen's League, 1919-20; Director SW Pacific Area (Sydney) of UNRRA, 1946-47. *Recreations:* Inter-State rowing (8 oar), lacrosse, sailing (12-footer and 16-footer), golf, horse racing. *Address:* Flat 7, Craigston, 217 Wickham Terrace, Brisbane, Queensland 4000, Australia. *Clubs:* Pioneers' (Sydney); Queensland (Brisbane).

[Died 24 May 1976.

CANTLIE, Sir Keith, Kt 1944; CIE 1939; *s* of Sir James Cantlie, KBE, FRCS; *b* 6 Feb. 1886; *m* May, *d* of James Walker, Lord Provost of Aberdeen; *one s* one *d. Educ:* Robert Gordon's Coll. Aberdeen; Universities of Aberdeen and Oxford. Indian Civil Service, 1910; Commissioner, Assam Valley, 1937; Member Revenue Tribunal, 1942, Chairman Public Service Commission, Assam, 1945-47. *Publications:* Notes on Khasi Law; Notes on Revenue Law; Assam in Former Times; entomological papers in Bombay Nat. History Soc. Journal. *Address:* 5 Upper Wimpole Street, W1.

[Died 29 April 1977.

CANTLIE, Lt-Gen. Sir Neil, KCB 1952 (CB 1946); KBE 1949; MC; MB, ChB; FRCS; late RAMC; House Governor and Medical Superintendent, King Edward VII Convalescent Home for Officers, Osborne, IW, 1952-58; *b* 11 Dec. 1892; 3rd *s* of late Sir James Cantlie; *m* 1930, Alice Mary Irene, *d* of Rev. R. H. Lucas; one *s. Educ:* Robert Gordon's Coll.; Aberdeen Univ (MB, ChB, 1914 with 2nd class Hons). Entered RAMC July 1914; Captain 1915; European War, 1914-18, France and Flanders; FRCS 1920; Seconded for service, Egyptian Army, 1920-24; Sudan Defence Force, 1924-25; Major, 1924; Lt-Col 1935; War of 1939-45; ADMS 46 Div., DDMS 5 Corps, N. Africa and Italy; Colonel 1941; Maj.-Gen. 1944; DDMS Southern Command, 1946-48; Lt-Gen. 1948; Director-General Army Medical Services, 1948-52; KHS 1950-52. *Publications:*

(joint) Life of Sir James Cantlie, 1939; An History of the Army Medical Department, 1974; Diseases of Mongalla (Journal Tropical Medicine and Hygiene, 1921); Treatment of Malaria by Intravenous Quinine (Journal of Tropical Medicine and Hygiene, 1923); Treatment of Injuries of Knee Joint (RAMC Journal, 1939). *Recreation:* sailing. *Address:* Timbers, 25 Manor Road, Milford-on-Sea, Hants SO4 0RG. *T:* Milford-on-Sea 3185.

[Died 16 May 1975.

CAPEL, Air Vice-Marshal Arthur John, CB 1943; DSO 1925; DFC; JP; DL; *b* 1894; *s* of late Arthur Capel, JP, Bulland Lodge, Wiveliscombe, Somerset; *m* 1934, Austin Robina, *y d* of late Charles Austin Horn, and *widow* of Flight Lieut H. M. Moody, MC; one *d. Educ:* Marlborough Coll.; Trinity Coll., Oxford; Royal Military Coll., Sandhurst. Was Lieut, Somerset Light Infantry; served European War, RFC and RAF, France, 1914-18 (despatches twice); Waziristan, 1924-25 (DFC, DSO); Commandant School of Army Co-operation, Old Sarum, 1936-38; at Imperial Defence Coll., 1939; War of 1939-45, served France, UK, and Middle East (despatches thrice, CB); retired from RAF Nov. 1945. JP Somerset, 1946; DL Somerset, 1952; High Sheriff of Somerset, 1952. Member Somerset County Council, 1962-64. *Address:* Bulland Lodge, Chipstable, Wiveliscombe, Somerset. *T:* Wiveliscombe 23346. *Club:* Royal Air Force.

[Died 18 April 1979.

CAPENER, Norman (Leslie), CBE 1966; FRCS; Chairman, Medical Commission on Accident Prevention, since 1967; Consultant Orthopædic Surgeon Emeritus, South Western Regional Hospital Board, since 1963; Member of Council, University of Exeter, since 1966; *b* 4 May 1898; *s* of Alick Wellstead Capener, Freeman of City of London, and Ada Isabella Tree; *m* 1st, 1922, Marion Constance Vera Clarke (*d* 1970), *d* of Captain J. Stanhope Clarke, RN; one *s* three *d*; 2nd, 1970, Elsa May Batstone. *Educ:* City of London Sch.; The Temple Choir, London; St Bartholomew's Hospital. Surg. Sub-Lt RNVR, 1918. Res. MO, Hospital of St John and St Elizabeth, 1922; House Surg. and Chief Asst, St Bartholomew's Hospital, 1926; Instructor in Anatomy and Asst Prof. of Surgery, Univ. of Michigan, 1926-31; Senior Orthopædic Surg., Princess Elizabeth Orthopædic Hospital, Exeter, 1931-63; Cons. Orthopædic Surg., Royal Devon and Exeter Hospital, and other hospitals in Plymouth and Devon, 1934-63; Cons. Adviser (Orthopædics), Min. of Health, 1964-71. Hunterian Prof., RCS, 1941; Arris and Gale Lectr, RCS, 1947; Robert Jones Lectr, RCS, 1958; Thomas Vicary Lectr, RCS, 1971. Robert Jones Lectr, NY Hosp. for Joint Diseases, 1947. President: Orthopædic Sect., Royal Society Med., 1951; Devon and Exeter Medico-Chirurg. Society, 1955; British Orthopædic Assoc., 1957-59; Devonshire Assoc., 1965; Mem. Council, RCS, 1961-73, Vice-Pres., 1971-73; Vice-Press., Anatomical Soc. of GB, 1967; Sectional Vice-Pres., British Assoc. for the Advancement of Science, 1969; Chairman: Inst. of Sports Medicine, 1967-69; BSI Cttee on Surgical Implants, 1956-70; Cttee for Research into Appliances for Disabled, 1960-72; Northcott Devon Health Foundn, 1964-73. *Publications:* many articles on orthopædics, bio-mechanics, and historical medical subjects; critical reviews, especially relating to surgery. *Recreations:* art and music; a weekend sculptor. *Address:* Webberton Meadows, Dunchideock, Exeter EX2 9TX. *T:* Exeter 832240.

[Died 30 March 1975.

CAPON, Norman Brandon, MD Liverpool; FRCP; FRCOG London; Professor Emeritus of Child Health, University of Liverpool; Hon. Consultant Pædiatrician, Liverpool Regional Hospital Board; and United Liverpool Hospitals; President, Liverpool Pædiatric Club; *b* 14 June 1892; *s* of Robert M. and Agnes Capon; *m* 1924, Dorothy (*d* 1966), *d* of W. H. Packer, MD. *Educ:* Liverpool Coll.; Univ. of Liverpool. MB, ChB with First Class Hons and Distinction in Medicine, Obstetrics and Gynæcology, 1916; MD (Special Merit), 1921; MRCP 1922; FRCP 1931; FRCOG 1957; Dawson Williams Prize, 1955; Lloyd Roberts Lect. (Manchester), 1954. Blackham Memorial Lecturer, 1955. Temp. Lieut and Capt. RAMC 1916-19. Formerly Prof. of Child Health, Univ. of Liverpool, 1944-57, External Examiner in Pædiatrics, Univ. of Birmingham; Examiner for DCH. Past-Pres., Liverpool Medical Institution; Original Mem. and Past-Pres. British Pædiatric Association; Charles West Lecturer, Royal Coll. of Physicians; Fellow of the Royal Society of Medicine, and Past-Pres. Section of Pædiatrics; Past-Pres. Section of Child Health, BMA and Section of Maternal and Child Health, Royal Society of Health; Convocation Lecturer, National Children's Home. *Publications:* contribs to British Encyclopædia of Medicine; Diseases of Children, 5th edn (Moncrieff and Evans); Text-Book of Children's Diseases (Parsons & Barling). Various papers on diseases of children in medical journals. *Address:* Gray Gables, Llanbedr, Ruthin, Clwyd LL15 1UT. *T:* Ruthin 2060.

[Died 7 Jan. 1975.

CAPPELL, Daniel Fowler, CBE 1958; Professor of Pathology, Glasgow University, 1945-67; *b* 28 Feb. 1900; *s* of Robert Cappell and Annabella Fowler; *m* 1927, Isabella Audrey, *yr d* of Charles A. Griffin, Glasgow; no *c. Educ:* Hillhead High Sch.; Glasgow Acad.; Univ. of Glasgow. MB, ChB with Hons, 1921; Struthers Medal and Prize, 1919, McCunn Research Scholar, 1921-23; Asst to Prof. of Pathology, Univ. of Glasgow, 1923-28; Lecturer in Pathological Histology, 1928-31; Prof. of Pathology, Univ. of St Andrews, 1931-45; Dean of the Faculty of Medicine, St Andrews, 1939. Mem., Gen. Med. Council, 1940, re-elected 1960; Adviser, Commonwealth Scholarship and Fellowship Plan, 1962; Mem., Scientific Advisory Cttee, Dept of Health for Scotland, 1944; Mem. Scottish Health Services Advisory Council, 1948; Mem. Scottish Advisory Cttee on Medical Research, Dept of Health for Scotland, 1952; Pathologist, Royal Infirmary, Dundee; Dir, East of Scotland Blood Transfusion Service. MD with Hons, 1929; Bellahouston Gold Medal, 1930; FRCP 1960; FRCPGlas 1962; FRCPE; FRSE; FRSM. Hon. Mem. of Pathological Soc. of Gt Britain and Ireland, 1922; Founder Fellow, Hon. Fellow and former Vice-Pres. Royal Coll. of Pathologists; Past-Pres. Royal Glasgow Medico-Chirurgical Soc.; Past-Pres. and Hon. Mem., Association Clinical Path. and Chm. of Council. Hon. Fellow, Brit. Soc. Haematol., Hon. FRCP Glas. Hon LLD St Andrews, 1966. Mem., Angus CC. *Publications:* Intra-vitam Staining, in Journal of Pathology and Bacteriology, 1929 et seq.; The Blood Group Rh, 1946; Muir's Textbook of Pathology, 9th edn, 1971; Blood Groups, in Chambers's Encyclopædia; and numerous scientific papers in various medical journals. *Recreation:* fishing. *Address:* Heathcote, Edzell, Angus DD9 7TT. *[Died* 13 Feb. 1976.

CAPPER, Sir (William) Derrick, Kt 1968; QPM 1962; Chief Constable of West Midlands, 1974-75; *b* 3 Jan. 1912; *s* of James Herman Capper, Upton Magna, Shrewsbury; *m* 1939, Muriel Woodhouse, Shrewsbury; two *d. Educ:* Priory Sch., Shrewsbury; Birmingham Univ. Constable, Metropolitan Police, 1935-37; Police Coll., Hendon, 1937-39; Jun. Station Insp. and Station Insp., Met. Police, 1939-44; Asst Supt, Nigeria Police, 1944-46; Metropolitan Police: Station Insp., 1946-49; Chief Insp., 1949-51; Supt, 1951-57; Chief Supt, 1957-58; Birmingham: Asst Chief Constable, Jan.-April 1959; Dep. Chief Constable, 1959-63; Chief Constable, 1963-74. CStJ 1974. *Recreations:* golf, athletics, Rugby football. *Address:* 18 Sandiway, Radbrook, Shrewsbury. *[Died* 21 *March* 1977.

CARCANO, Miguel Angel; Hon. KCMG; Hon. KBE; Presidente de la Academia National de la Historia, 1968-70; *b* 18 July 1889; *s* of Ramón J. Cárcano, sometime Governor of Cordoba and Ambassador, and of Ana Saenz de Zumarán; *m* Stella, *d* of Marqueses de Morra; one *s* two *d. Educ:* Faculty of Law, Univ. of Buenos Aires. Prof. of Political Economy and Admin. Law, Univ. of Buenos Aires: National Deputy, 1930-36. Minister in London on special mission for negotiation of Anglo-Argentine Treaty, 1936; Delegate Pan-American Congress, Buenos Aires, 1937; Minister of Agriculture, Industry and Commerce, Argentina, 1936-38; Ambassador of Argentina in France 1938-42, in London, 1942-46; Pres., Argentine Delegn to UN, 1946; Minister of Foreign Affairs and Worship, 1961, 1962. Member: Acad. of Letters; Acad. of Economics; Academia Nacional de la Historia; Corresp. Fellow, RHistS. Grand Cross of: Legion of Honour; Pius IX; Leopold II. Knight Comdr Order of British Empire (Hon. KBE). Knight Comdr, Order of St Michael and St George (Hon. KCMG), 1933. *Publications:* Evolución Histórica de la Tierra Pública (Premio Nacional en Letras); Organización de la Producción; Alberdi, su doctrina Económica, 1934; Dos Años en la Cámara, 1934; Memoria del Ministerio de Agricultura (6 vol.), 1939; Realidad de una Política, 1938; Hommage A Sarmiento, 1938; British Democracy Retains its Prestige, 1942; Victoria Sin Alas, 1949; Fortaleza de Europa, 1951; La Sexta Republica, 1958; Recuerdos del Viejo Congreso, 1960; Travesía Española, 1961; Argentina y Brasil, 1961; Saenz Peña, 1963; Churchill, Kennedy, 1967; La Presidencia de Pellegrini, 1968; Estilo de Vida Argentino, 1969; Modos de ver la Historia, 1971; La Política Internacional en la Historia Argentina (6 vols), 1973; El Mar de las Cicladas, 1974. *Address:* Centeno 3131, Buenos Aires, Argentina. *Clubs:* Athenæum; Circulo de Armas, Jockey (Buenos Aires). *[Died* 9 *May* 1978.

CARDEN ROE, Brigadier William, CB 1950; CBE 1944; MC 1915; retired 1949; *b* 8 Dec. 1894; *s* of Charles Edward Liesching, Tiverton, Devon; assumed surname of Carden Roe in lieu of his patronymic, 1915; *m* 1915, Rosalie (*d* 1967), *d* of David Babington, Londonderry. *Educ:* Blundell's; Royal Military Coll., Sandhurst. 2nd Lieut 1913, Capt. 1917, Royal Irish Fusiliers. Served European War, France and Belgium, 1914-19 (wounded thrice, despatches thrice); Bt Major, Staff Coll., psc 1925-26. Lieut-Col Comdg 2nd Bn Royal Irish Fusiliers, 1937-39; Col, 1939; Brig., 1940; BGS 4th Corps, 1940-41; Bde Comdr 1941-45; Comdr Southern Area, E Africa, 1946; Comdr British Advisory Staff to Polish Resettlement Corps, 1947-49; Home Guard Adviser HQ Western Command, 1951-54. ADC to the King, 1946-49. Chevalier, Légion d'Honneur, 1914. *Recreations:* gardening, fishing. *Address:* Lawnside, Gordon Avenue, Foxrock, Co. Dublin. *T:* Dublin 894301. *Club:* Kildare Street and University (Dublin). *[Died* 22 *March* 1977.

CARDUS, Sir Neville, Kt 1967; CBE 1964; music critic and cricket writer; *b* Manchester, 2 April 1889; *m* 1921, Edith Honorine King (*d* 1968). *Educ:* Manchester; abroad. Music critic to Daily Citizen, 1913, after studying singing with Charles Egan in Manchester; contributed to various musical journals, 1912-14; joined staff of Manchester Guardian, 1916; wrote in most parts of the paper-descriptive articles to leaders; asst to Samuel Langford in music criticism; first contributed cricket articles to that paper, 1919; cricket coach at Shrewsbury Sch., 1912-16; was also sec. to the Headmaster the Rev. C. A. Alington; Music Critic and Cricket Writer: The Manchester Guardian; Sydney Morning Herald, 1941-47; visited Australia to broadcast on music one hour weekly for seven years; on staff of Sunday Times, 1948-49; London music critic of Manchester Guardian, 1951-. Wagner Medal, City of Bayreuth, 1963; Special Press Award, IPC, 1970. *Publications:* A Cricketer's Book, 1921; Days in the Sun, 1924; The Summer Game, 1929; ed, Musical Criticisms of Samuel Langford, 1929; Cricket, 1930; Good Days, 1934; Australian Summer; Ten Composers, 1945 (trans. into Swedish, 1947, into Japanese, 1964); Autobiography, 1947; Second Innings: More Autobiography, 1950; Cricket All the Year, 1952; ed, Kathleen Ferrier Memorial Book, 1954; Close of Play, 1956; Talking of Music, 1957; A Composer's XI, 1958 (German trans. 1961); Komponisten und Dirigenten (German trans.), 1959; Sir Thomas Beecham: A Portrait, 1961; The Playfair Cardus, 1963; Gustav Mahler: His Mind and his Music, Vol. I, 1965; The Delights of Music, 1966; (with John Arlott) The Noblest Game, 1969; Full Score, 1970; *posthumous publications:* Cardus on Cricket, 1977; A Fourth Innings with Cardus, 1981. *Recreations:* conversation, walking, and anything not in the form of a game or sport. *Address:* 112 Bickenhall Mansions, Baker Street, W1. *Clubs:* National Liberal, Garrick. *[Died* 28 *Feb.* 1975.

CARE, Henry Clifford, CB 1948; *b* 1892; *s* of William John Care and Alice Mary Allen; *m* 1923, Helen Ivy May, *d* of late Col James Cameron and Mrs M. I. Cameron, Blackheath. *Educ:* Univ. Coll. Sch., Hampstead; St John's Coll., Cambridge. Higher Div. Clerk, War Office, 1915; Principal, 1923; Asst Sec. 1937; Director of Finance (with rank of Under-Sec.), 1945-54. *Address:* Old Orchard, Little Bedwyn, Marlborough, Wilts SN8 3JP. *T:* Great Bedwyn 288. *[Died* 11 *Nov.* 1979.

CAREW, Sir Thomas Palk, 10th Bt, *cr* 1661; *b* 1 March 1890; *o s* of Sir Henry Palk Carew, 9th Bt and Frances Gertrude (*d* 1955), *y d* of late Robert Lock-Roe, JP, of the Manor House, Lynmouth, N Devon; *S* father 1934; *m* 1st, 1913, cousin Ivy Madeleine Laura (whom he divorced, 1920), *d* of late Col Arthur John Breakey, OBE; one *d*; 2nd, 1927, Phyllis Evelyn (*d* 1976), *o c* of late Neville Mayman, Sydney, NSW; one *s* one *d. Educ:* Wellington; Pembroke Coll., Oxford. Served European War in Indian Army. *Recreation:* solitude. *Heir: s* Rivers Verain Carew, MA, BAgr(Hort) Dublin [*b* 17 Oct. 1935; *m* 1969, Susan Babington, *yr d* of late H. B. Hill, London; three *d*]. *Address:* Killyon Manor, Hill of Down, Co. Meath, Eire.
[Died 6 *April* 1976.

CAREW HUNT, Rear-Adm. Geoffrey Harry, CB 1967; Chairman, Joseph Barber & Co. Ltd; *b* 6 April 1917; *s* of late Captain Roland Cecil Carew Hunt, CMG, Royal Navy retd and Mrs Thelma Reay Carew Hunt; *m* 1st, 1939, Diana (*d* 1969), *er d* of late Rear-Adm. J. F. C. Patterson, OBE; no *c*; 2nd, 1971, Elizabeth Frances Mary Adams, 2nd *d* of late J. Hunter, MP. *Educ:* Winchester Coll. Joined RN, 1934; Midshipman on China Station, 1935-37; served in Submarines, HMS Snapper, Mediterranean and North Sea, 1939-40 (despatches twice); qualified Gunnery Officer, 1941; Home Fleet Destroyers 1942-43; HMS Diadem, Home Station, 1943-45 (despatches three times); HMS Kenya, West Indies, 1947; HMS Vanguard, Mediterranean and Home Station, 1949-50; British Naval Staff, Washington, DC, 1951-53; HMS Theseus, 1953-56; Imperial Defence Coll., 1958; HMS Defender, 1959-60; Admiralty, 1945-47, 1950-51, 1956-57, 1962-65; Admiral Commanding Reserves, 1965-68; retired from Royal Navy. *Recreations:* sailing, shooting, golf. *Address:* Mill House, Abbots Worthy, Winchester, Hants. *T:* Winchester 882115. *Clubs:* Army and Navy, MCC; Royal Naval Sailing Association.
[Died 11 *Aug.* 1979.

CAREY, Cecil William Victor; retired; formerly Supreme Court Judge, Colonial Service; *b* 6 Oct. 1887; 2nd *s* of late William Percival Carey, Solicitor, Dublin; *m* 1st, Lucy Kathleen (*d* 1922), *d* of late Rev. W. T. Stokes, MA; two *d*; 2nd, Isabella Morrison (*d* 1932), *d* of late John Anderson, Perthshire. *Educ:* Trinity Coll., Dublin Univ. (BA, LLB). Barrister-at-Law (King's Inns, Dublin); practised at Irish Bar, 1910-15; Asst District Officer, Uganda, 1915; Magistrate, 1919; transferred to Nigeria as Crown Counsel, 1921; Judge, Supreme Court, Nigeria, 1930-40; Judge, Supreme Court, SS, 1940-46 (interned in Malaya, 1942-45); acting Chief Justice, Singapore, April-June 1946; Judge, Supreme Court, Malayan Union, 1946-48; retired, 1948. *Address:* Trendle, Bere Alston, Yelverton, Devon.
[*Died* 29 *Oct.* 1976.

CAREY, Rt. Rev. Kenneth Moir, MA; Non-stipendiary Bishop in the diocese of Moray, since 1975; *b* 6 April 1908; *s* of late Godfrey Mohun Carey and Agnes Charlotte Milligan; unmarried. *Educ:* Marlborough; Exeter Coll., Oxford; Westcott House, Cambridge. Chaplain of Oxford House, Bethnal Green, 1932-36; Curate of St Andrew's, Handsworth, Birmingham, 1936-38; Vicar of Whitworth with Spennymoor, 1939-44; Gen. Sec., Central Advisory Council of Training for the Ministry, 1944-48; Principal of Westcott House, Cambridge, 1947-61; Hon. Canon of Portsmouth Cathedral, 1956-61; Bishop of Edinburgh, 1961-75. Chaplain to the Queen, 1957-61. Hon. DD Edinburgh, 1964. *Publication:* (ed) The Historic Episcopate, 1955. *Address:* Morven, Kincraig, by Kingussie, Inverness-shire PH21 1NA. [*Died* 3 *Jan.* 1979.

CAREY, Major-General Laurence Francis de Vic, CB 1959; CBE 1955; Jurat of the Royal Court, Guernsey, 1963; Chairman, British Channel Island Airways; *b* 5 June 1904; *s* of late Sir Victor Carey, and late Adelaide, *d* of late Julius Jeffreys, FRS; *m* 1928, Alicia Frances Liebe, *d* of late Col C. E. Phipps, CB, Blackheath; three *s*. *Educ:* Elizabeth Coll., Guernsey; Royal Naval Coll., Osborne and Dartmouth; Royal Military Academy, Woolwich. Commissioned in Royal Engineeers, 1924; served in RE field units, Madras Sappers and Miners and in various appointments in Ordnance Survey and Military Survey; Director of Military Survey, War Office, 1953; Brig., 1955; Temp. Maj.-Gen. and Maj.-Gen., 1957. Dir-Gen., Ordnance Survey, 1957-61, retd. Mem. Council, RGS, 1957-60; Chm., Joint Advisory Survey Bd, 1957-61; Chm., Field Survey Assoc., 1960-61. *Address:* Courtil Desperques, St Martin, Guernsey. *T:* Guernsey 37565. *Clubs:* Army and Navy; Royal Channel Islands Yacht (Guernsey). [*Died* 30 *Sept.* 1972.

CAREY TAYLOR, Alan; see Taylor, A. C.

CARGILL THOMPSON, Prof. William David James, MA, PhD; Professor of Ecclesiastical History, University of London King's College, since 1976; *b* Rangoon, Burma, 17 Dec. 1930; *e s* of late William David David Cargill Thompson and of Helen Mary Sutherland Cargill Thompson (*née* Reed); *m* 1966, Jennifer Anketell Williams Warren, *er d* of Rt Rev. A. K. Warren, CMG, MC, and of Doreen Eda (*née* Laws); two *s*. *Educ:* Harrow Sch.; King's Coll., Cambridge (Scholar). BA 1954, MA 1959, PhD 1960; 1st Cl. Hist. Tripos Pt I 1953, Pt II 1954; Members' English Essay Prize, 1952; Lightfoot Scholar, 1955. Fellow of King's Coll., Cambridge, 1956-65, Dean, 1959-64; Lectr in History, Univ. of Sussex, 1965-69; Lectr in Ecclesiastical Hist., Univ. of London King's Coll., 1969-75, Reader, 1975-76, Dean of Faculty of Theology, 1976-78. Visiting Lectr, University Coll. of Rhodesia and Nyasaland, 1962. Commonwealth Fund Fellowship, Harvard and Huntington Library, 1957-58; Alexander von Humboldt Fellowship, Göttingen, 1964-65. Governor, Harrow Sch., 1962-; Asst Editor, Jl of Eccles. History; FRHistS 1972. *Publications:* contrib. to: Political Ideas (ed D. Thomson), 1966; Essays in Modern English Church History in Memory of Norman Sykes (ed G. V. Bennett and J. D. Walsh), 1966; Studies in Richard Hooker (ed W. S. Hill), 1972; The Dissenting Tradition (ed C. R. Cole and M. E. Moody), 1975; articles in Jl of Eccles. Hist., Jl of Theol Studies, Studies in Church History, etc. *Address:* Department of Ecclesiastical History, University of London King's College, Strand, WC2R 2LS. *T:* 01-836 5454. [*Died* 21 *Feb.* 1978.

CARLETON, John Dudley; Headmaster of Westminster School, 1957-70; *b* 29 Aug. 1908; *y s* of late Brig.-Gen. Frederick Montgomerie Carleton, DSO, HM Hon. Corps of Gentlemen-at-Arms, and Emma Gwendoline Priscilla Lloyd; *m* 1965, Janet Adam Smith. *Educ:* Westminster; Merton Coll., Oxford. Assistant Master, Westminster Sch., 1932-41 and 1945-49. War Office (attached Special Forces), 1941-45. Under Master and Master of the Queen's Scholars, Westminster, 1949-57. *Publications:* Westminster, 1938; Westminster School: a history, 1965. *Recreation:* travel. *Address:* 57 Lansdowne Road, W11. *T:* 01-727 9324. *Club:* Athenæum. [*Died* 6 *Nov.* 1974.

CARLISLE, Lt-Col (John Charles) Denton, DSO 1918; OBE 1944; MC; *b* 15 June 1888; *m* 1922, Elsie Hope (*d* 1970), *d* of Sir C. F. Gill, KC, and *widow* of Hubert Stewart Smiley; one *d*. Served European War, 1914-18 (despatches, DSO, MC); Served War of 1939-45 (OBE). Order of Polonia Restituta (Polish); Order of St Olaf, Knight First Class (Norwegian); Order of the White Lion, Third Class (Czech); Commander Order of Orange Nassau, with Swords (Netherlands); Medal of Military Merit (Brazil). *Address:* The Lodge, Braunstow, Oakham, Rutland. *T:* Oakham 2134. [*Died* 13 *March* 1972.

CARMICHAEL, Edward Arnold; CBE 1942; FRCP; Hon. Consulting Physician, National Hospital, Queen Square; formerly Director of Neurological Research Unit and Physician National Hospital for Nervous Diseases, Queen Square, London; *b* 25 March 1896; *y s* of late Edward Carmichael, MD, Edinburgh; *m* 1927, Jeanette Marie Montgomerie; two *s*. *Educ:* Edinburgh Academy; Edinburgh Univ. MB, ChB, Annandale Gold Medal, 1921; FRCPE 1926, FRCP 1932. Served European War, 1914-19. President Royal Medical Society, 1921-22; Morrison Lecturer, RCP Edin., 1938; Oliver Sharpey Lecturer, 1933, Lumleian Lecturer, 1953, RCP (Lond.); Bramwell Memorial Lecturer, Edinburgh, 1963; Wall Memorial Lecturer, Washington, 1963; Visiting Professor of Neurology, Columbia Univ., New York, 1964; Visiting Scientist, Nat. Inst. of Health, Bethesda, USA, 1964-66; Visiting Professor, Montreal Neurological Inst., 1966; Visiting Professor of Neurology, Univ. of Pennsylvania, 1966-67; Milton Shy Meml Prof., Univ. of Pennsylvania, 1970; Rockefeller Foundation Travelling Fellow, 1934; Hon. Member: Society for Psychiatry and Neurology, Vienna, 1948; American Neurological Assoc., 1952; Philadelphia Neurological Society, 1967; Hon. Foreign Member, French Neurological Society, 1949; Corresp. Member German Neurological Society, 1954; President, Neurological Section, Royal Society Medicine, London, 1953-54; President EEG Society, 1963-64. Hon. DSc, Edinburgh Univ., 1963; Gold Medal, Graz Univ., 1963; Honorary Alumnus, Neurological Inst., NY, 1966. *Publications:* The Cerebrospinal Fluid (with Dr J. G. Greenfield), 1925; articles in physiological, clinical and neurological journals. *Address:* 20 Lucastes Avenue, Haywards Heath, West Sussex. *T:* Haywards Heath 54598.
[*Died* 9 *Feb.* 1978.

CARMICHAEL, James, CMG 1950; DSc, MRCVS, Dip. Bact.; Chairman: Murphy Chemical Co. Ltd, 1955-68; Murphy & Son Ltd, Wheathampstead, since 1955; *s* of James Carmichael; *m* 1930, Kathleen Jackson, Scarborough, Yorks; one *s* one *d*. *Educ:* Denstone Coll.; Univ. of Edinburgh; Univ. of London. Veterinary Officer, Colonial Service, Uganda Protectorate, 1923; Veterinary Research Officer, 1930; Senior Veterinary Research Officer, 1937; retired from Colonial Service, 1945; Member various Scientific Advisory Cttees, Colonial Office, 1946-58. Member Council of Royal Society of Tropical Medicine and Hygiene, 1950-65. *Publications:* numerous publications in scientific journals on tropical veterinary medicine, tsetse fly problem, etc. *Recreations:* fishing, shooting, hunting, tennis, golf, etc. *Address:* Boarded Barns Farm, Ongar, Essex. *T:* Ongar 2573. *Club:* East India and Sports. [*Died* 24 *March* 1972.

CARMICHAEL, Leonard; Vice-President for Research and Exploration, National Geographic Society, since 1964 (Trustee, National Geographic Society, since 1957); *b* Philadelphia, Pennsylvania, 9 Nov. 1898; *s* of Thomas Harrison Carmichael and Emily Henrietta Leonard; *m* 1932, Pearl Kidston; one *d*. *Educ:* Germantown Friends Sch., Philadelphia; Tufts Coll. (BS 1921); Harvard Univ. (PhD 1924); Univ. Berlin. Instructor in Psychology, Princeton Univ. 1924-26; Asst Professor, 1926-27; Assoc. Professor of Psychology, Brown Univ., 1927-28; Professor, 1928-36; Director of Psychological Laboratory, 1927-36, and Director of Laboratory of Sensory Physiology, 1934-36; Chairman, Dept of Psychology, and Dean, Faculty of Arts and Science, Univ. of Rochester, 1936-38; President, Tufts Coll., and Director, Laboratory of Sensory Psychology and Physiology, 1938-52; Secretary (Director), Smithsonian Inst., 1953-64 (now Director Emeritus). Director, Nat. Roster of Scientific and Specialized Personnel, 1940-44; Chairman, American Council on Education, 1947-48; Member: Naval Res. Advisory Cttee, 1947-52; Advisory Cttee to Nat. Scientific Register; Nat. Advisory Cttee for Aeronautics, 1952-58; Nat. Acad. of Sciences; American Philosophical Soc., Philadelphia (Pres. 1970-73); American Acad. of Arts and Sciences; American Psychological Assoc.; Hon. LLD Harvard Univ., 1952; also 22 Hon. Degrees from other Universities. Hartley Public Welfare Medal, Nat. Acad. of Scis, 1972; Decorated by the Governments of Spain, Denmark, Italy and Germany. *Publications:* (with Dearborn and Lord) Special disabilities in learning to read and write, 1925; (with Warren) Elements of human psychology, 1930; The response mechanism (chapter in Boring, Langfeld and

Weld, Introduction to Psychology), 1939; The Onset and early development of behaviour (Chapter in Carmichael L. (ed.), Manual of child psychology), 1946 (2nd edn, 1954; 3rd edn, ed Mussen, 1970); (with Dearborn) Reading and Visual Fatigue, 1947; Basic Psychology, 1957. Editorial Rep. of British Journal of Educational Psychology; many articles. *Address:* The National Geographic Society, 17th and M Streets, NW, Washington, DC 20036, USA. *Clubs:* St Botolph, Alfalfa, Algonquin (Boston); Century Association (New York); Cosmos, Chevy Chase, Metropolitan (Washington).
[Died 16 Sept. 1973.

CARMICHAEL-ANSTRUTHER, Sir W. E. F.; *see* Anstruther.

CARNAC, Sir Henry George Crabbe R.; *see* Rivett-Carnac.

CARNEGY of Lour, Lt-Col (Ughtred) Elliott (Carnegy), DSO 1919; MC; DL, JP Angus; Baron of Lour; late 3rd Dragoon Guards; *b* 13 June 1886; *o s* of late Major Francis Edward Joseph and late Isabella Carnegy, 10th of Lour, *o c* of Patrick Carnegy, CIE; by deed poll assumed the name of Carnegy, 1915, on his mother succeeding to the estate of Lour; *m* 1919, Violet (MBE, Order of Mercy) (*d* 1965), *y d* of late H. W. Henderson, West Woodhay, Berks; two *d* (and one *d* decd). *Educ:* Wellington Coll.; RMC, Sandhurst. Entered Army, 1907; Captain, 1914; Major, 1921; served European War as ADC to Maj.-General Hon. Sir Julian Byng, commanding 3rd Cavalry Division, and GSO 3rd Grade 3rd Cavalry Division in France; Staff Captain 22nd Mounted Brigade in Palestine (wounded 27 Nov. 1917); GSO 2nd Grade 21st Army Corps in Palestine and Syria, 1918; attached Staff of Gen. Sir R. Wingate, Residency, Cairo, 1919 (despatches twice, 1914 Star, MC and bar, DSO); Chevalier of Order of the Star of Roumania with Swords, 1920; served on General Staff, War Office, 1919-22; retired, 1922; commanded 20th (Fife and Forfar Yeomanry) Armoured Car Company, 1929-33; Member of HM's Bodyguard (Hon. Corps of Gentlemen-at-Arms), 1931-56; Bt Lt-Col, TA, 1932; County Director, Angus Branch British Red Cross, 1934-40; Member of Angus County Council, 1937-55; Member King's Body Guard for Scotland (the Royal Company of Archers), 1940-49; on outbreak of War joined volunteer Reserve of Royal Air Force and posted to Staff of late Air Vice-Marshal C. D. Breese, CB, AFC, commanding 18 Group, Coastal Command; Wing Comdr, 1941, commanded Central Area, Scotland, Air Training Corps, 1941-45. King's Jubilee Medal, 1935; Coronation Medal, 1937. *Recreation:* shooting. *Address:* Lour, Angus. *T:* Inverarity 237. *Clubs:* Cavalry, Pratt's, MCC; New (Edinburgh).
[Died 1 Feb. 1973.

CARPENTER, Sir Eric (Ashton), Kt 1951; OBE 1948; *b* 12 Nov. 1896; *s* of Richard and Annie Carpenter; *m* 1951, Edith Elizabeth Mary, *d* of late William and Edith Sansom. *Educ:* Cheadle Hulme School. Chm. and Man. Dir, Greg Bros & Co Ltd, 1929-69; Director: Williams Deacon Bank Ltd, 1949-70 (Chm. 1952-64); Yorkshire Bank Ltd, 1952-64 (Chm. 1964-70); Industrial and General Trust Ltd, 1953-71; Manchester Ship Canal Co., 1956-70; Lloyds Packing Warehouses (Holdings) Ltd (Chm. 1950-56); London & Lancashire Insurance Co. Ltd, 1951-70; Royal Insurance Co. Ltd, 1962-70; Liverpool & London & Globe Insurance Co. Ltd, 1962-70; Royal Bank of Scotland, 1952-68; British Wagon Co. 1958-64; Member: North Western Gas Board, 1949-67; General Council, Anglo-Dutch Trade, 1958-71; Chm. Cotton and Rayon Merchants Assoc., 1942-45; President Manchester Chamber of Commerce, 1948-50; President Association of British Chambers of Commerce, 1954-56 (Vice-Pres. 1951-54); Member Dollar Exports Council, 1949-60; British Member, Council of International Chamber of Commerce, 1949-61; President, The Inst. of Bankers, 1960-62. High Sheriff of Lancashire, 1959-60; JP City of Manchester, 1945-62. *Address:* Burrows Cross House, Gomshall, Guildford, Surrey. *T:* Shere 2441. *Club:* St James's (Manchester).
[Died 2 Aug. 1973.

CARPENTER, Rhys, MA Oxon, PhD, LittD; *b* Cotuit, Mass, USA, 5 Aug. 1889; *s* of William Henry Carpenter and Anna Morgan Douglass; *m* 1918, Eleanor Houston Hill, Evanston, Ill., USA; no *c. Educ:* Columbia Univ.; Balliol Coll., Oxford. Instructor in classical archæology in Bryn Mawr Coll., Penna, USA, 1913-15; Associate, 1915-16; Associate Professor, 1916-18; Professor, 1918-55; Professor Emeritus, 1955-. Attached to the American Commission to Negotiate Peace at Paris, 1918-19, as expert on Greco-Albanian territorial problems; Annual Prof. at American Acad., Rome, 1926-27; Director, American Sch. for Classical Studies at Athens, 1927-32 and 1946-48; Professor-in-charge, Classical School, American Academy in Rome, 1939-40; Sather Professor, Univ. of California, 1944-45; Member: Hispanic Society of America, Pontifical Roman Academy of Archæology; Greek Archæological Society, German

Archæological Institute, Austrian Archæological Institute, American Philosophical Society. Gold Medal, Amer. Inst. of Archaeology, 1969. *Publications:* Tragedy of Etarre, 1912; The Sunthief, and other Poems, 1914; The Plainsman, and other Poems, 1920; The Land Beyond Mexico, 1921; The Esthetic Basis of Greek Art, 1921 (2nd ed. 1959); The Greeks in Spain, 1925; The Sculpture of the Nike Temple Parapet, 1929; The Humanistic Value of Archæology, 1933; The Defenses of Acrocorinth, 1936; Folk Tale, Fiction and Saga in the Homeric Epics, 1946; Greek Sculpture: A Critical Review, 1960; Greek Art: A Study in the Evolution of Style, 1963; Discontinuity in Greek Civilization, 1966; Beyond the Pillars of Heracles, 1966; The Architects of the Parthenon, 1970; numerous articles on Greek Art in American Journal of Archæology and elsewhere. *Recreation:* archæological exploration. *Address:* Devon Manor, Devon, Pa 19333, USA.
[Died 2 Jan. 1980.

CARPENTIER, Général d'Armée Marcel Maurice; Grand Croix de la Légion d'Honneur, 1956; Croix de Guerre (1914-18, 1939-45; Théâtres d'opérations extérieures) (thirteen times); Director and Editor-in-Chief of the General Military Review; *b* 2 March 1895; *m*; one *s. Educ:* Tours; Saint-Cyr. 2nd Lieut French Army, Aug. 1914; Lieut Nov. 1914; Captain 1915; Pilot's Certificate, 1916. Served European War, 1914-18 (wounded, Legion of Honour, Croix de Guerre, five citations). Instructor, Saint-Cyr, 1919-23; Ecole de Guerre Supérieure, 1924; Military Attaché, Rio de Janeiro, and Inf. Prof., Brazilian War Academy, 1930-35; Chef de Bataillon, 1933; comd. Bn in Syria, 1936; Staff of HQ Levant Troops, Beyrouth, 1937; served War 1940-44 (Commander Legion of Honour, Croix de Guerre, seven citations); Chef de Cabinet Militaire, French High Comr, Levant States, 1939; Lt-Col, Staff of C-in-C French N. Africa, 1940; Colonel 1942; Comd. 7th Moroccan Tirailleurs Regt, N. Africa, 1942-43; Général de Brigade, 1943; Chief of Staff, French Exped. Corps, Italy, 1943-44; Chief of Staff, First French Army, 1944; Comdr. 2nd Moroccan Inf. Div. in liberation of Alsace and Rhine crossings, 1944-45; Général de Division, 1944. Comdr. XV Region, Marseille, 1945-46; C-in-C French Forces in Morocco, 1946-49; Général de Corps d'Armée, 1946; Member Conseil Supérieur de Guerre, since 1947; C-in-C French Forces, Indo-China, 1949-50 (Croix de Guerre); Dep. Chief of Staff, SHAPE, 1951-52; Inspector-General of French Inf. and Comdr of Strategic Reserves, Central Europe, 1952-53; Général d'Armée, 1953; Commander Allied Land Forces Central Europe, 1953-56. Vice-President Atlantic Treaty Association. American Legion of Merit, 1946; Commander Order of Leopold of the Belgians, 1948; Hon. CBE, 1949; Grand Officer, Portuguese Order of Military Merit, 1952; many other foreign decorations. *Publications:* Les Forces alliées en Italie, 1949; Un Cyrard au Feu, 1964; articles in military and academic journals. *Recreations:* fishing, swimming. *Address:* 1 Rue Blaise Desgoffe, 75006 Paris, France. *Club:* Cercle Internallié (Paris).
[Died 14 Sept. 1977.

CARPMAEL, Kenneth Sydney, QC; *b* 12 July 1885; *s* of late Ernest Carpmael, KC, MA, Sutton, Surrey. *Educ:* Dulwich Coll. Entered Accountant Branch, Royal Navy, 1903; HMS Canterbury, Battle of Jutland; granted temporary commission as Sub-Lt, Dec. 1916, for period of hostilities; Lieut, 1917; retired as Paymaster Lt-Comdr, 1920; Paymaster Comdr (retired list), 1924; restored to active list RN, Sept. 1940 with rank of temp. Lt-Comdr, acting Comdr, Nov. 1940; on panel of Wreck Comrs (Eng.) under Merchant Shipping Acts, 1938-65. Reverted to retired list, March 1942, at own request; Mem. Admiralty Ferry Crew Organisation, 1943-60. Barrister, Middle Temple, 1919; Junior Counsel to Admiralty (Admiralty Court), 1931-35; KC 1935; Bencher of Middle Temple, 1942; Lent Reader, 1954; Treasurer, 1961; Governor of Dulwich Coll. (Lord Chancellor's representative), 1942; Estates Governor Dulwich, 1943; Governor James Allen's Girls' Sch., Dulwich, 1946-58. Barrister and KC (N Ire.), 1948. *Recreation:* yachting. *Address:* c/o Mrs A. Klouda, 20 Fitz James Avenue, W14 0RP. *T:* 01-603 3078. *Clubs:* Bath, Royal Cruising.
[Died 26 Nov. 1975.

CARR, Air Marshal Sir (Charles) Roderick, KBE, 1945 (CBE 1941); CB 1943; DFC; AFC; King of Arms, Order of British Empire, 1947-68; *b* 31 Aug. 1891; *s* of Charles Carr, Feilding, New Zealand; *m* Phyllis Isabel (*d* 1969), *d* of C. S. Elkington, Amersham; one *s. Educ:* Wellington Coll., NZ. Served European War, 1914-18, with NZ Forces, RNAS and RAF; North Russian Expedition, 1919; Chief of Air Staff, Lithuania, 1920; Shackleton's Antarctic Expedition, 1921-22; First RAF Long Distance Flight, England to Persian Gulf non-stop, 1927; RAF Egypt, 1929-33; HMS Eagle (Aircraft Carrier), China, 1936-39; Advanced Air Striking Force, RAF, France, 1939-40; AOC RAF in Northern Ireland, 1940-41; AOC No. 4 Group Bomber Command, 1941-45 (despatches); Deputy Chief of Staff (Air), Supreme HQ, Allied Exped. Force, 1945; AOC-in-C, India,

1946; retired list, 1947. Croix de Guerre (France); Commander: Legion of Honour (France); Order of St Anne, Order of St Stanislav (Russia). *Address:* Leighton Cottage, Bampton, Oxford. *Club:* Royal Air Force. *[Died* 15 *Dec.* 1971.

CARR, Prof. Charles Telford, MA Manchester, DLitt St Andrews; Professor of German Language and Literature, University of St Andrews, 1948-73; *b* 1905; *m* 1929, Marian Frances Hilton Roscoe (*d* 1948); one *s*; *m* 1952, Jean Margaret Berneaud; one *d. Educ:* Manchester Grammar Sch.; Univs of Manchester, Zürich and Vienna. Lectr in German: Birkbeck Coll., London, 1925-26; Univ. of Manchester, 1926-29; Univ. of of St Andrews, 1929-48; Dean of the Faculty of Arts, Univ. of St Andrews, 1955-59; Master of St Salvator's Coll., 1968-72. General editor, Forum for Modern Language Studies, 1974-. *Publications:* Von Unsers Herren Liden, 1929; The German Influence on the English Vocabulary, 1934; Nominal Compounds in Germanic, 1939; contribs to modern languages jls. *Recreations:* golf, chess. *Address:* 21 Hepburn Gardens, St Andrews, Fife. *T:* St Andrews 2764. *[Died* 10 *March* 1976.

CARR, John Dickson; author. *Publications:* The Wax Works Murder; The Eight of Swords; The Arabian Nights Murder; Black Spectacles; To Wake the Dead; The Burning Court; The Case of the Constant Suicides; The Four False Weapons; The Blind Barber; The Problem of the Wire Cage; Seat of the Scornful; Poison in Jest; The Man Who Could Not Shudder; The Emperor's Snuff Box; Till Death Do Us Part; He Who Whispers; The Hollow Man; The Sleeping Sphinx; The Crooked Hinge; Death Watch; The Life of Sir Arthur Conan Doyle; The Bride of Newgate; The Devil in Velvet, 1951; The Lost Gallows, 1952; The Nine Wrong Answers, 1952; Captain Cut-Throat, 1955; Patrick Butler for the Defence, 1956; Fire, Burn!, 1957; The Dead Man's Knock, 1958; Scandal at High Chimneys, 1959; A Dr Fell Omnibus, 1959; In Spite of Thunder, 1960; The Witch of the Low Tide, 1961; The Demoniacs, 1962; The Men Who Explained Miracles, 1964; Most Secret, 1964; The House at Satan's Elbow, 1965; The Third Bullet and other Stories, 1965; Panic in Box C, 1966; Dark of the Moon, 1968; The Mad Hatter Mystery, 1968; The Black Spectacles, 1969; Papa La-Bas, 1969; The Ghost's High Noon, 1970; The Hungry Goblin, 1972. *Address:* c/o Hamish Hamilton Ltd, 90 Great Russell Street, WC1. *[Died* 27 *Feb.* 1977.

CARR, Air Marshal Sir Roderick; *see* Carr, Air Marshal Sir C. R.

CARR, Rupert Ellis; Chairman: The Associated Biscuit Manufacturers Ltd, 1963-69; Peek, Frean & Co. Ltd, 1963-68; Meltis Ltd, 1963-68; *b* 16 Feb. 1910; *s* of Philip and Marjorie Carr; *m* 1949, Anna Louise Roncallo; one *s* one *d. Educ:* Rugby. Joined Peek, Frean & Co. Ltd, 1928; Dir, 1933; Man. Dir, 1940-63. Hon. Treas., Royal Warrant Holders' Assoc. (Pres., 1958); Pres., Cake and Biscuit Alliance Ltd, 1950-53; Chm. Standing Cttee and Mem. Council, Nat. Assoc. of Biscuit Manufacturers. *Recreations:* boats, gardening. *Address:* Bembridge Lodge, Bembridge, IoW. *Club:* Royal Thames Yacht. *[Died* 14 *May* 1974.

CARR, Sir William (Emsley), Kt 1957; FRSA; Chairman: News of the World Organisation, 1960-69; News of the World Ltd, 1952-69 (now Life President of the Companies (called News International Ltd) and Consultant to the Board); Bees, Ltd, 1970-73; *b* 30 May 1912; *y s* of late Sir Emsley and Lady Carr; *m* 1938, Jean Mary Forsyth; one *s* one *d. Educ:* Clifton Coll.; Trinity Coll., Cambridge (BA). News of the World, 1937-. Vice-Patron, Amateur Athletic Assoc.; President: Artisan Golfers' Assoc.; Press Golfing Soc.; London Newspapers Golf Soc.; Counties Athletic Union; Vice-President: Professional Golfers' Assoc.; Llangollen Eisteddfod; Cartoonists Club. *Recreation:* sport. *Address:* Cliveden House, Cliveden Place, SW1; Bentley Wood, Halland, Sussex. *Clubs:* Buck's, Crockford's; Lucifer Golfing Society; Walton Heath Golf (Chm. 1948); Royal and Ancient Golf; Oxford and Cambridge Golfing Society. *[Died* 14 *Nov.* 1977.

CARRIER, Philippe Leslie Caro, CBE 1955; MD; *b* 14 Oct. 1893; *s* of Rev. E. T. Carrier; *m* 1925, Edith Gertrude Craig (*d* 1970); one *d. Educ:* Kingswood Sch., Bath; King's Coll., London. MRCS, LRCP 1916; MB, BS (London) 1922; MD (London) 1936; MRCP 1946. House Surgeon and Physician, Charing Cross Hosp., 1916. Capt. RAMC (SR), 1916-19. Private practice, 1919-27; Dist Med. Officer, Burma Rlys, 1927-36; Chief Med. Officer, 1936-48; Lieut-Col, RAMC, 1941-46, service in Burma and India. Home Office: Med. Officer, 1948-50; Principal Med. Officer, 1950-62. *Recreations:* fishing and sailing. *Address:* Ashdown House, St Ann's Hill, Lewes, Sussex. *T:* Lewes 2531. *Club:* East India, Sports and Public Schools. *[Died* 21 *June* 1975.

CARRINGTON, Most Rev. Philip, MA, LittD, STD, DCL; Archbishop of Quebec and Metropolitan of the Province of Canada, 1944-60; *b* Lichfield, England, 6 July 1892; *s* of late Very Rev. Charles Walter Carrington; *m* 1919, Gwendolen Smith; no *c. Educ:* Christ's Coll., New Zealand; Canterbury Univ. Coll., NZ; Selwyn Coll., Cambridge (Hon. Fellow, 1958). Chancellor's Gold Medal for English Verse, Carus, Member's, Hulsean Prizes; Deacon, 1918; Priest, 1919; specialised in boys' work; Boy Scout Commissioner for Canterbury; developed Soldiers of the Cross Scheme for children; Rector of Lincoln, NZ, 1922; Warden of St Barnabas Theological Coll., North Adelaide, South Australia, 1924-27; Speaker at Melbourne Church Congress, 1925; Dean of Divinity Bishop's Univ., Lennoxville, Quebec, 1927; Bishop of Quebec, 1935-44. Hon. STD Seabury-Western Seminary, Evanstown, Ill., 1933; Hon. DCL Lennoxville, 1933; LittD in course of New Zealand, 1934; Hon. DD: Durham; King's Coll., NS; Trinity Coll., Toronto; Wycliffe Coll., Toronto; Hon. D ès Lettres, Université de Laval, 1959. *Publications:* The Boy Scouts Camp Book, 1918; Christian Apologetics in the Second Century, 1921; Scoutcraft in the Church, 1921; The Soldier of the Cross, 1925; The Sign of Faith, 1930; The Meaning of the Revelation, 1931; The Road to Jerusalem, 1933; The Pilgrim's Way, 1937; The Primitive Christian Catechism, 1941; A Church History for Canadians, 1947; The Story of the Christ, 1957; The Early Christian Church, 1957; According to Mark, 1960; The Anglican Church in Canada, 1963. *Recreations:* cinephotography, literary. *Address:* Quebec Lodge, Little Somerford, Chippenham, Wilts. *[Died* 3 *Oct.* 1975.

CARRINGTON, Richard; author and biologist; *b* 10 June 1921; *s* of late Murray Carrington, actor, and Ethel McDowall, actress; *m* 1st, 1946, Audrey Barringer Sloan (marr. diss. 1952); 2nd, Mary Eden, *e d* of late C. O. Ellis. *Educ:* The Hall Sch., Hampstead; privately. Served War of 1939-45: Merchant Service, 1940; RAF, Britain and Far East, 1941-46. British Council, 1946-47; BBC, 1947-50; writing, scientific educn, and field work in biology, 1950-; res. on elephants in E Africa, 1955-56. Scientific FZS; FRAI; FRGS. Member: Internat. Oceanographic Foundn; Inst. of Archæology; Fauna Preservation Soc.; Egypt Exploration Soc. Founder and Editor of: The World Naturalist Series; The Advancement of Science Series; The Weidenfeld and Nicolson Natural History (Associate Editors: Dr L. Harrison Matthews and Prof. J. Z. Young); Manuals in Biology (Co-Editor, Dr L. Harrison Matthews). Founder and Director, Internat. Communications Centre, Nice, France, 1969. *Publications:* A Guide to Earth History, 1956; Mermaids and Mastodons, 1957; East from Tunis, 1957; Elephants, 1958; The Tears of Isis, 1959; A Biography of the Sea, 1960; The Mammals, 1963; A Million Years of Man, 1963; Great National Parks, 1967; The Mediterranean, 1971; (with Mary Eden) The Philosophy of the Bed, 1961; (with Dr A. d'A. Bellairs) The World of Reptiles, 1966; (ed, with Dr L. Harrison Matthews, and contrib) The Living World of Mammals, 1970; many foreign and braille edns. Educational books for children: The Dawn of History, 1955-61 (six titles): How Life Began, 1955; The Early Days of Man, 1955; Ancient Egypt, 1959; Ancient Sumer, 1959; Ancient Greece, 1961; Ancient Rome, 1961. Numerous articles and broadcasts. *Recreations:* music, friends. *Address:* c/o Royal Geographical Society, 1 Kensington Gore, SW7. *[Died* 24 *Sept.* 1971.

CARRINGTON, Roger Clifford, MA, DPhil (Oxon); FRSA; Headmaster, St Olave's School, 1937-70; *b* 16 Nov. 1905; *s* of Albert Carrington, Hastings; *m* Charlotte, *d* of Alexander Chalmers, Glasgow; one *s* one *d. Educ:* Wakefield Grammar Sch.; Queen's Coll., Oxford. Barclay Head Prize for Ancient Numismatics, 1930; Rome Student in Archæology at British Sch. at Rome, 1928-30; Asst Master, Haileybury Coll., 1930-34; Head of Classical Side, Dulwich Coll., 1934-37. *Publications:* Pompeii, 1936; Pompéi, 1937; Caesar's Invasions of Britain, 1938; Caesar's Gallic War, Book V, 1939; Two Schools, 1962; various articles. *Recreations:* walking, gardening, archæology. *Address:* St Olave's, Goddington Lane, Orpington, Kent. *[Died* 10 *July* 1971.

CARRINGTON, Sir William (Speight), Kt 1958; Partner, Whinney Murray & Co., Chartered Accountants, 1932-70; Member of Council, Institute of Chartered Accountants in England and Wales, 1942-68 (President, 1955-56); *b* 20 Feb. 1904; *s* of William Carrington, Blackpool; *m* 1932, Dorothy Mary, *d* of T. W. Fabian, Finchley; one *s. Educ:* Hebden Bridge, Yorks; Manchester Grammar Sch. Mem. Central Valuation Board and Panel of Referees Coal Nationalisation Act, 1946. Mem. Royal Commission on Taxation, 1951-55 and Millard Tucker Cttees, on Taxation of Trading Profits, 1949-51, and on Taxation treatment of provisions for Retirement, 1950-53; Chm. Dental Rates Study Group, 1961-. Younger Brother of Trinity

House, 1952. *Publications:* various papers in professional journals at home and overseas. *Address:* 17 Polwithen Road, Penzance, Cornwall TR18 4JW. *T:* Penzance 3534. *Clubs:* Junior Carlton, MCC. *[Died 6 May* 1975.

CARROLL, Sir Alfred Thomas, (Sir Turi Carroll), KBE 1962 (OBE 1950); farmer, New Zealand, since 1912; Patron, New Zealand Maori Council (President, 1962-67); *b* 24 Aug. 1890; *s* of Thomas Carroll and Mako Kaimoana; *m* 1922, Parehuia Shrimpton (*d* 1965); one *d. Educ:* Te Aute Coll.; Wanganui Collegiate; Lincoln Agricultural Coll. Chm., Wairoa CC, 1938-59 (Mem., 1924-59); Past Chairman: Wairoa Co-op. Dairy Co. Ltd; Wairoa A. & P. Assoc.; East Coast Maori Trust Council; Maori Incorporated Blocks; Kahungunu Tribal Exec.; Wairoa Maori Trust; Wairoa Farmers' Union; and various sporting associations. Formerly Member: NZ Tuberculosis Assoc.; Wairoa Hosp. and Harbour Bd; Bd of Govs Wairoa Coll.; Wairoa Power Bd; Maori Educn Foundation. Bledisloe Medal, 1940. *Address:* Huramua Station, RD Wairoa, Hawkes Bay, New Zealand. *T:* 7431. *Club:* Wairoa Gentlemen's County.
[Died 11 Nov. 1975.

CARROLL, Sir John (Anthony), KBE 1953; MA, PhD; retired as Chief Scientist (Royal Navy); *b* 1899; *m* 1st, 1930; one *d*; 2nd, 1951, Jean Leslie, *d* of late W. Tudor Pole, OBE; one *d. Educ:* King's Sch., Chester; Sidney Sussex Coll., Cambridge. Isaac Newton Student, 1922-25; Research Fellow, Sidney Sussex Coll., 1922-25; Asst Dir of Solar Physics Observatory, Cambridge, and Univ. Lectr in Astrophysics, 1924-30; Prof. of Natural Philosophy, Univ. of Aberdeen, 1930-45; Deputy for Research and Development to Controller of the Navy, and Scientific Adviser to Bd of Admiralty, 1946-64; Chief Scientist (RN), 1964, retd. Gresham Prof. in Astronomy, 1964-68. Eclipse-observing expeditions to California, Norway, Malay, Canada, and Siberia. Fellow: (sometime mem. Council) Royal Astronomical Soc.; Royal Society of Edinburgh; Cambridge Philosophical Soc.; American Physical Soc. Sometime Member: Board of Governors, Aberdeen Royal Infirmary; Aberdeen Univ. Court; Aberdeen Education Cttee. Mem. of various national and international scientific cttees; sometime Pres. of Commission on Instruments of International Astronomical Union. *Publications:* on mathematical, physical and astrophysical topics in journals of learned societies and technical publications. *Recreation:* golf. *Address:* 72 Marryat Road, Wimbledon, SW19 5BN. *T:* 01-947 1801. *Club:* Athenæum.
[Died 2 May 1974.

CARROLL, Sir Turi; *see* Carroll, Sir Alfred Thomas.

CARROW, Comdr John Hinton, CMG 1943; DSC; RN, retired; Senior Resident, Nigeria, retired; *b* 1890; *m* 1936, Gladys Lilian (Michael), MA Oxon, (marr. diss. 1963), *o d* of Anstruther Cardew-Rendle, MD (Cantab), DPH. *Educ:* Clifton Coll. Entered Royal Navy, 1905; served Battle of Jutland (DSC); invalided out, 1919; Colonial Administrative Service, Nigeria, 1919-47. *Address:* 40 Dorchester Road, Weymouth, Dorset DT4 7JZ. *Club:* East India, Sports and Public Schools.
[Died 27 Oct. 1973.

CARTER; *see* Bonham Carter and Bonham-Carter.

CARTER, Arthur Herbert, JP; Council of Royal Agricultural Society of England (Vice-President); Council of Lincolnshire Agricultural Society (Chairman, 1946-47); *b* 1 June 1890; *er s* of Arthur Henry Carter, Wiggenhall, St Mary Magdalen, Norfolk; *m* 1916, Edith Mary Tindall; two *s*. Farmer and landowner in Lincolnshire and Cambridgeshire; High Sheriff Cambridgeshire and Huntingdon, 1940; Mem. Isle of Ely CC, 1922-47; Alderman 1933, resigned 1948; Council of Cambridgeshire and Isle of Ely Agricultural Society, 1923-48; Deeping Fen Drainage Board. Chairman County Civil Defence Cttee; Chairman Theatres and Cinemas Cttee; Vice-Chairman Finance Cttee; Member Holland (Lincs) War Agricultural Executive Cttee; Dep. Chairman HAEC and Chairman Labour Sub-Cttee and Housing; RASE representative on Rothamsted Trust Cttee. Freeman, City of London. *Recreations:* shooting, cricket. *Address:* The Manor House, Tydd St Giles, Wisbech, Cambs. *TA* and *T:* Newton 555. *[Died 7 Sept.* 1979.

CARTER, Francis Edward, OBE 1937; Bailiff of the Royal Parks, 1928-47; *b* 18 Oct. 1886; *e s* of Francis Joseph Carter, Bristol; *m* 1917, Winifred, *d* of H. H. Stunt; two *s* one *d. Educ:* Colston Sch., Bristol. Entered Civil Service, 1907, retired 1947. Secretary, Government Hospitality Fund, 1914-16; Private Secretary to six successive First Commissioners of Works. *Recreation:* gardening. *Address:* 1 Grangelands, Knowle Drive, Sidmouth, Devon. *T:* Sidmouth 3452. *[Died 16 Oct.* 1977.

CARTER, John (Waynflete), CBE 1956; bibliographical consultant; Director: Sotheby Publications Ltd, since 1968; The Collector Ltd, since 1966; Parke-Bernet Galleries, Inc., New York, since 1964; *b* 10 May 1905; *s* of Thomas Buchanan Carter and Margaret Teresa (*née* Stone), Eton; *m* 1936, Ernestine Marie Fantl, OBE; no *c. Educ:* Eton (King's Scholar; Keeper of the Wall); King's Coll., Cambridge (1st Cl. Classical Tripos). European representative of Scribners (New York) Rare Book Dept, 1927-39; Min. of Information, 1939-43; British Information Services, New York, 1944-45; Managing Director of Charles Scribners' Sons Ltd, London, 1946-53. Personal Asst to HM Ambassador and Counsellor, British Embassy, Washington, 1953-55. Associate Dir, Sotheby & Co., 1955-72. Sandars Reader in Bibliography in the University of Cambridge, 1947. London Rose Bearer to Provost of King's Coll., Cambridge, 1947-. Member of Council, Arts Council of Great Britain, 1951-53. Member Court of Governors, University College of North Staffordshire, 1957-62. President, Bibliographical Society, 1968-69. Hon. Colonel, Commonwealth of Kentucky, 1963. Fellow of Eton Coll., 1967. *Publications:* Binding Variants in English Publishing 1820-1900, 1932; (anonymously) Victory in Burma, 1945; Taste and Technique in Book-collecting, 1948, repr. 1970; ABC for Book Collectors, 1952 (5th edn, 1972); Books and Book Collectors, 1956; Edited: Sir T. Browne, Urne Buriall and the Garden of Cyrus, 1932, repr. 1958; A Handlist of the Writings of Stanley Morison, 1950; Selected Prose of A. E. Housman, 1962; A. E. Housman, The Confines of Criticism, 1969; (with Graham Pollard): An Enquiry into the Nature of Certain Nineteenth Century Pamphlets, 1934; The Firm of Charles Ottley, Landon & Co., 1948; (with John Sparrow) A. E. Housman, an annotated handlist, 1952; (with Percy H. Muir) Printing and the Mind of Man, 1967 (German trans. 1968, Japanese trans. 1971). *Address:* 113 Dovehouse Street, Chelsea, SW3. *T:* 01-352 6336. *Clubs:* Garrick, Beefsteak, Double Crown, Eton Ramblers; Grolier (New York); Rowfant (Cleveland); Barclay (Chicago).
[Died 18 March 1975.

CARTER, W. Horsfall, MA Oxon; writer and lecturer on international political questions; retired European civil servant; *b* 25 March 1900; *s* of William Beazley Carter and Frances Esther Horsfall Rydal; *m* 1st, 1927, Doris Golby (*d* 1939); one *d*; 2nd, 1941, Esther Elizabeth Way Thacker (*d* 1942); one *s*; 3rd, 1944, Ethel Mary Mabbott (*d* 1970); 4th, 1971, Phoebe Grizel Ashburner Latham. *Educ:* Hurstpierpoint Coll., Sussex; St John's Coll., Oxford (Casberd Scholar). Heath Harrison Travelling Scholarship French, 1921, German, 1923; First Class Hons School of Modern Languages, 1922; Pres., Oxford Univ. French Club, 1922; Laming Travelling Fellow, Queen's Coll., Oxford, 1924-26; League of Nations Secretariat, Geneva, temporarily, 1924, 1928, 1930, 1937; on staff of The Spectator as assistant to the Editor and assistant leader-writer, 1928-30; on editorial staff of the Christian Science Monitor, 1931; Sec. of The New Commonwealth Soc., 1932-33; Editor: The New Commonwealth, 1932-36; The Fortnightly Review, 1937-39; leader-writing staff of The Manchester Guardian, 1940-42; European Publicity Officer, BBC, 1942-43; Foreign Office Research Dept, 1943-51; Head of Western Europe Section, 1947-51; Head of Publications Div., Secretariat, Council of Europe, Strasbourg, 1951-63. Contributor to all principal newspapers and periodicals; broadcasts on Spain. *Publications:* (with Mrs Krassin) The Life of Leonid Krassin, 1928; Speaking European, 1966; several translations from French, German and Spanish; numerous articles in monthly reviews. *Recreations:* talking foreign languages, lawn tennis, bridge. *Address:* 11 Port Hill, Hertford. *Club:* Savile. *[Died 9 June* 1976.

CARTER, Walter, CBE 1943; Chevalier of the Order of Vasa (Sweden); Chairman of London Committee of Management Board of Trade (War Damage Claims) and Hon. Adviser Board of Trade; *b* 9 April 1873; *s* of Charles Frederick Carter, Grimsby, Lincs; *m* 1st, Annie Elizabeth (*d* 1926), *d* of Henry Kelly, Cleethorpes, Lincs; one *s*; 2nd, 1931, Elsie Mary (*d* 1968), *d* of Alfred John Francis, Clifton, Bristol. Manager London Head Office, Royal Insurance Co. Ltd, to 1932. *Recreations:* golf, fishing. *Address:* The Grange, High Halden, Kent. *[Died 9 Feb.* 1975.

CARTMEL, Lt-Col Alfred Edward, CIE 1937; MM; late 20th Lancers; *b* 1893; *s* of Alfred Cartmel; *m* 1920, Flora May Macdonald; two *s* one *d. Educ:* St Albans Sch. Served European War, 1914-18, Egypt, Gallipoli, NWF, Egypt, Iraq with Herts Yeomanry (despatches, MM); transferred to Indian Army, 1918; served Afghanistan, 1919; Waziristan, 1919-20; NWF India, 1930-31; Burma, 1930-32; King's Police Medal, 1936; Major, 1936; Battalion Commandant: Burma Military Police, Lashio, 1931-36; Burma Frontier Force, Lashio, 1937; Remount Department, India, 1942-47; Lieut-Col 1944; Asst Director,

Remounts, Eastern Command, 1944-46; retd, 1948. *Recreation:* golf. *Address:* 29 Fanshawe Street, Hertford. *T:* Hertford 2414.

[Died 7 June 1974.

CARTWRIGHT, Rev. Canon James Lawrence, FSA 1958; Canon Emeritus since 1966 (Residentiary Canon and Chancellor of Peterborough Cathedral, and Chapter Librarian, 1952-66); *b* Loughborough, 8 June 1889; *s* of James Cartwright and Harriet Macaulay Todd; *m* 1918, Ruth, *o d* of William Frederick Buck; two *d. Educ:* Loughborough Grammar Sch.; King's Coll., Cambridge. BA 1917 (2nd Class Hist. Tripos, Parts I and II); MA 1921. Admitted a Solicitor, 1911. Served European War, 1918-19, in France, Temp. 2nd Lieut Royal Sussex Regt. Deacon, 1919; Priest, 1920; Curate: St Peter's and Thorpe Acre, Loughborough, 1919-22; St John Baptist, Knighton, Leicester, 1922-25; Vicar: Christ Church, Northampton, 1925-33; Oundle with Ashton, 1933-52; Rural Dean Oundle I, 1937-52; Non-Residentiary Canon of Peterborough, 1946-52; Select Preacher, University of Cambridge, 1964. *Recreation:* reading. *Address:* 129 Park Road, Peterborough. *T:* Peterborough 68396.

[Died 4 March 1978.

CARUS-WILSON, Eleanora Mary, FBA 1963; Emeritus Professor of Economic History in the University of London since 1965 (Professor, 1953-65); *b* Montreal, 27 Dec. 1897; *d* of late Prof. Charles Ashley Carus-Wilson and Mary L. G. Petrie, BA (London). *Educ:* St Paul's Girls' Sch.; Westfield Coll., London. BA 1921; MA with Distinction, 1926; Leverhulme Research Fellow, 1936-38; Head of Branch, Min. of Food, 1940-45; Lecturer at the London Sch. of Economics and Political Science, 1945; Reader in Economic History in the University of London, 1948. Trustee, Cassel Educational Trust, 1963; Ford's Lecturer in English History, University of Oxford, 1964-65; Pres., Economic History Soc., 1966-69; Pres., Medieval Archæology Soc., 1966-69; Assoc. Mem. Royal Academy of Belgium, 1961. Hon. Fellow, LSE, 1969. Hon. LLD Smith Coll., 1968. *Publications:* The Overseas Trade of Bristol in the later Middle Ages, 1937; chapters on The Trade of Bristol and on The Iceland Trade in Studies in English Trade in the Fifteenth Century, 1933; Chapter on The Woollen Industry in the Cambridge Economic History of Europe, Vol. II, 1952; Medieval Merchant Venturers, 1954; (ed) Essays in Economic History, 1954, 1962; England's Export Trade, 1275-1547, 1963; The Expansion of Exeter at the Close of the Middle Ages, 1963; (with M. D. Lobel) Historic Towns: Bristol, 1975; contributions to Medieval England, 1958, and to Victoria History of the County of Wiltshire, 1959; articles and reviews in the Economic History Review and other historical journals. *Recreations:* music, mountains. *Address:* 14 Lansdowne Road, W11.

[Died 1 Feb. 1977.

CARVELL, John Eric Maclean, CBE 1950; *b* 12 Aug. 1894; *s* of John Maclean Carvell, MBE, MRCS, and Euphemia Sarah Avery; *m* 1918, Cicely Lilian, *y d* of F. S. Garratt, Reigate, Surrey; one *d. Educ:* Berkhamsted. Served European War, 2nd Lieut Queen's Westminster Rifles, 1914; France, 1915 (twice wounded); Instructor to Portuguese Army, 1917-18; Staff Capt., HQ London District, 1918-19; Vice-Consul, Lisbon, 1919, Cadiz, 1921; Chargé d'Affaires, Port-au-Prince, 1922; Consul (Local Rank), Brest, 1925; Vice-Consul, Munich, 1929; Consul, Porto Alegre, 1932, New York, 1934; Consul-General, Munich, 1938-39; Algiers, 1942-45; Los Angeles, 1945-47; Ambassador to Ecuador, 1950-51 (Minister, 1947-50); Minister to Bulgaria, 1951-54, retd from Foreign Service, 1954.

[Died 29 April 1978.

CARVER, David Dove, OBE 1967; Secretary General, International PEN, since 1951; *b* 10 Aug. 1903; *s* of Henry George Dove and Alice Mary Carver; *m* 1945, Violet Blanche Hall (née Parlby), *widow* of Sir Gerald Boles, 2nd Bt; no *c. Educ:* Emanuel School, London. After short period as business executive studied singing (baritone) with Alfredo Morelli, Reinhold von Warlich and John Goss; recitals, Wigmore Hall, BBC, etc. War Service, Squadron-Leader RAFVR, 1940-45 (despatches); ADC to HRH the Duke of Windsor, Governor of the Bahamas, 1942-44. Resumed singing career, 1946. Director, Singers in Consort Male Voice Quintet, 1948-53. Secretary General, English Centre PEN and International PEN. Hon. DLitt Chung Ang Univ., Seoul, 1970. *Publications:* various songs and part songs, carols, etc. *Recreations:* music, travel, theatre. *Address:* 7 Wadham Gardens, Hampstead, NW3. *T:* 01-722 6772. *Clubs:* Savile, Savage, English-Speaking Union.

[Died 10 May 1974.

CARY, Sir (Arthur Lucius) Michael, GCB 1976 (KCB 1965; CB 1964); Permanent Under-Secretary of State, Ministry of Defence, since 1974; *b* 3 April 1917; *e s* of late Joyce Cary; *m* 1946, Isabel Margaret Leslie; four *s* one *d. Educ:* Eton, Trinity Coll., Oxford. 1st Class Hon. Mods, 1st Class Litt. Hum.; Hon. Fellow, 1973. Asst Principal, Air Min., 1939. Joined RNVR, 1940; Radar Officer, HMS Illustrious, 1942-43. Principal, Air Min., 1945; Asst Sec., 1951. Counsellor UK Delegation to NATO, 1956-58; Asst Under Sec., Air Min., 1958-61; Dep. Sec. of the Cabinet, 1961-64; Second Permanent Under Sec. of State (RN), Min. of Defence, 1964-68; Permanent Sec., MPBW, 1968-70; Sec., Housing and Construction, DoE, Oct. 1970-Apr. 1971; Sec., 1971-72, Chief Exec., 1972-74, MoD (PE). CompIEE 1967; Pres., Instn of General Technician Engrs, 1972. Governor, Dragon Sch., 1965 (Chm., 1973). Commodore, Civil Service Sailing Assoc., 1971. Fellow: RCA, 1973 (Mem. Council, 1968); Eton Coll., 1967. *Recreation:* making clavichords and harpsichords. *Address:* Huntswood House, Harpsden, near Henley-on-Thames, Oxon. *T:* Henley 3308. *Club:* Brooks's.

[Died 6 March 1976.

CARY, Sir Robert (Archibald), 1st Bt, *cr* 1955; Kt 1945; *b* 25 May 1898; *s* of Robert Cary; *m* 1924, Hon. Rosamond Mary Curzon, *d* of late Col Hon. Alfred Nathaniel Curzon and *sister* of 2nd Viscount Scarsdale, TD; one *s. Educ:* Ardingly; Royal Military Coll., Sandhurst. Served European War, 1916-18; 4th Dragoon Guards, 1916-23; Gen. Staff, Iraq, 1920; North Persia, 1921; rejoined 4th/7th Royal Dragoon Guards, Sept. 1939, and reappointed to Gen. Staff; MP (U) Eccles, 1935-45; PPS to Civil Lord of Admiralty, 1939; PPS to Sec. of State for India, 1942-44; a Lord Commissioner of the Treasury, 1945; MP (C) Withington, Manchester, 1951-Feb. 1974; PPS to Min. of Health, 1951-52; PPS to Lord Privy Seal and Leader of the House, 1951-64. Mem. of House of Commons Select Cttee on National Expenditure, 1941. *Heir: s* Roger Hugh Cary. *Address:* Wrotham Water, Wrotham, Kent. *T:* Fairseat 822476. *Clubs:* Carlton, Turf, Pratt's.

[Died 1 Oct. 1979.

CARY, Maj.-Gen. Rupert Tristram Oliver, CB 1948; CBE 1943 (MBE 1919); DSO 1943; late Royal Corps of Signals; *b* 17 Aug. 1896; *m* Dorothy Violet (*d* 1974); one *d* of former marriage. Served European War, 1916-19, France, Belgium, India (wounded, MBE, 3 medals); Persia and Iraq, 1941-43 (despatches, CBE); signal officer Eighth Army, 1943; Maj.-Gen. 1944; Commandant Sch. of Signals, 1945-46; ADC to the King, 1946-47; Comdr of Catterick sub-district, 1946-49; retired pay, 1949. *Address:* Etable du Porc, Little Sark, CI.

[Died 23 Sept. 1980.

CASADESUS, Robert; concert pianist and composer; *b* Paris, 7 April 1899; *m* Gaby Lhote; two *s* one *d.* Studied harmony and piano, Paris Conservatory (first prize, piano, 1913, first prize, harmony, 1919; Diémer prize, 1921). Since 1921 has performed as soloist with orchestras in all principal cities in Europe and USA; has also given recitals throughout Europe, N Africa, Egypt, Brazil, Argentina, Mexico and the United States. Made American concert début with NY Philharmonic Symphony Orchestra (Arturo Toscanini, conductor), 1935. Director of American Conservatory of Fontainebleau, France, 1946-47 (Dir-Gen., 1948-). Composer of: numerous quartettes, trios, sonatas, concertos and pieces for piano; four orchestral suites; four symphonies. Awarded Gold Medal, World's Fair, Paris, 1937; Grand Prix du Disque, 1955; Brahms Medal, Hamburg, 1958; Gold Medal, City of Paris, 1959. Comdr of Legion of Honour, France; Comdr of Order of Orange-Nassau, Netherlands. *Address:* 54 rue Vaneau, Paris 7; Berwyn, Penn, USA.

[Died 19 Sept. 1972.

CASALS, His Excellency Pablo, violoncellist; composer, conductor; *b* Vendrell, Tarragona, 29 Dec. 1876; *m* 1914, Susan Metcalfe (decd); *m* 1957, Marta Montanez. *Educ:* Municipal School of Music, and Madrid Conservatoire; Barcelona Conservatoire (1st prize). Made début in England at Crystal Palace, 1898; Conductor of the Pau Casals Symphony Orchestra of Barcelona, Spain, founded, 1920; Founder Workers' Concert Soc. (Barcelona), 1923; Doctor Honoris Causa of The University of Edinburgh, 1934; Barcelona, 1939; Montpellier, 1946; Citizen of Honour of Barcelona; Citizen of Honour of Madrid, 1935; of Prades, 1941; of Perpignan, 1945; of Béziers, 1946; of Foix, 1947; of Narbonne, 1948; Mem. of Honour of the Spanish Academy, 1935; Mem. Academy Sciences et Lettres of Montpellier, 1947. Corresponding Mem. of The Hispanic Soc., New York. Beethoven gold medal: of Philharmonic Soc. of London; of Friends of Music, Vienna; Hon. Mem. of Friends of Music Soc. of Vienna (founded 1812), 1930; Hon. Mem. of Royal Philharmonic Soc. FRCM 1937; Gold Medal of the Worshipful Company of Musicians, London, 1937; Grand Cross of Isabella the Catholic; Grand Cross for services to the Republic of Austria; Grand Cross of the Republic of Spain; Grand Officer Legion of Honor, 1946; Medal of City of Toulouse, 1946; US Presidential Medal of Freedom, 1963. Holds Hon. Doctorates in Music and in Letters; Citizen of honour of

several cities in Central America. *Publications:* symphonic and choral works, chamber music, etc. *Relevant Publications:* (by Lillian Littlehales) Pablo Casals (English-Spanish); (by Dr Rudolf von Jabel) Pablo Casals (German, French, etc.); (by Arthur Compte) Legende de Pablo Casals; (by Jose M. Corredor) Conversations with P. Casals, 1955 (German, English, French, Spanish, etc.); (by Bernard Gavoty) Pablo Casals, 1955 (French, German, Spanish); (by Joan Llangeres) Pau Casals (Catalan); (by Emil Ludwig) Galerie des Portraits; (by Navarro Costabella) Pablo Casals; Joys and Sorrows, as told to A. E. Kahn, 1970. *Address:* San Juan, Puerto Rico, USA.
[*Died 22 Oct.* 1973.

CASEY, Baron *cr* 1960 (Life Peer); **Richard Gardiner Casey**, KG 1969; PC 1939; GCMG 1965; CH 1944; DSO 1918; MC; Governor-General of Australia, 1965-69; *b* 29 Aug. 1890; *s* of Richard Gardiner Casey, Shipley House, Melbourne, Australia; *m* 1926, Ethel Marian Sumner, *d* of Maj.-Gen. Sir Charles Ryan, KBE, CB; one *s* one *d*. *Educ:* Melbourne Church of England Grammar Sch.; Melbourne Univ.; Trinity Coll., Cambridge (BA 1913). Served European War, 1914-18, in Gallipoli and France (despatches, DSO, MC); Foreign Affairs Officer, Canberra, 1927; Liaison officer between the Australian Government and the Foreign Office, 1924-27 and 1927-31; Mem. of House of Representatives for Corio, 1931-40; and for Latrobe, 1949-60; Asst Federal Treasurer, 1933-35; Federal Treasurer, 1935-39; Minister in charge of Development, 1937-39; Minister for Supply and Development, 1939-40; Australian Minister to USA, 1940-42; Minister of State Resident in the Middle East and Mem. of War Cabinet of the UK, 1942-43; Governor of Bengal, 1944-46; Federal President, Liberal Party of Australia, 1947-49; Minister of Works and Housing, Australia, 1949-51 and of National Development, 1950-51 (Supply and Development 1949-50); Minister in Charge of the Commonwealth Scientific and Industrial Research Organisation, 1950-60; Minister for External Affairs, Australia, 1951-60. Represented Australia at Coronation and Imperial Conf. 1937 and at London Conf. on Conduct of the War, Nov. 1939. Freeman, City of Melbourne, 1969. Hon. degrees from a number of Univs. KStJ. *Publications:* An Australian in India, 1947; Double or Quit, 1949; Friends and Neighbours, 1954; Personal Experience, 1939-46, 1962; The Future of the Commonwealth, 1963; Australian Father and Son, 1966; Australian Foreign Minister: the diaries of R. G. Casey, 1951-60, 1972. *Address:* Edrington, Berwick, Vic. 3806, Australia. *Clubs:* Athenæum, United Oxford & Cambridge University; Athenæum, Melbourne (Melbourne); Union (Sydney). [*Died 17 June* 1976.

CASH, Sir Thomas James, KBE 1946; CB 1939; *b* 5 July 1888; *s* of late Thomas Cash; *m* 1929, Gladys Ann, *d* of late Charles Hopkins, Beckenham, Kent; one *s* one *d*. *Educ:* St Ignatius' Coll., Stamford Hill; Univ. Coll., London; Malden medal and Schol.; Hollier Scholarship in Greek; Bunnell Lewis Prizes for Latin verse. BA (Hons Classics), 1909; Fellow of University Coll., London. Barrister, Middle Temple, 1924. Entered War Office as Higher Div. Clerk, 1912; Principal, 1920; Asst Sec., 1925; Director of Finance and Assistant Under-Secretary of State, 1936; Deputy Under-Sec. of State for War, 1945-54; retired 1954. Chevalier, Legion of Honour, 1920; Comdr, Czechoslovakian Order of the White Lion, 1947. *Address:* 1 Lincoln Court, Old Avenue, Weybridge, Surrey. *T:* Weybridge 47617. [*Died 22 Jan.* 1978.

CASHMAN, Rt. Rev. David (John); Bishop of Arundel and Brighton (RC), since 1965; *b* 27 Dec. 1912; *s* of Philip and Norah Cashman (*née* McSwiney). *Educ:* Cotton Coll., North Staffordshire; English Coll., Rome. Assistant, St Mary and Angels, Stoke on Trent, 1939; Sec., Apostolic Delegation, London, 1940; Parish Priest, Arundel, and Chaplain to Duke of Norfolk, 1956-58; Parish Priest, St Mary's Cadogan Street, SW3, 1958-65; Auxiliary Bishop of Westminster, (RC), 1958-65, and Titular Bishop of Cantano. Canon Metropolitan Chapter of Westminster and Canon Theologian, 1961. Commander Polonia Restituta (Poland), 1945; Knight of Malta (Sovereign Military Order), 1947; Commander Order of Holy Sepulchre, 1952; Cruz Distinguida San Ramón de Peñafort (Spain), 1956. *Recreation:* shooting. *Address:* St Joseph's Hall, Greyfriars Lane, Storrington, Pulborough, Sussex. *T:* Storrington 2172. *Clubs:* Royal Automobile, Turf. [*Died 14 March* 1971.

CASHMORE, Herbert Maurice, MBE 1948; FLA; Emeritus City Librarian, Birmingham; *b* London, 29 Jan. 1882; *s* of Herbert Henry Cashmore and Ellen Eliza Morris: unmarried. *Educ:* King Edward's Sch., Aston, Birmingham. Employed Birmingham Public Libraries since leaving sch.; Deputy Chief Librarian, 1912-28; City Librarian, 1928-47; war service 8th Royal Warwicks Regt, 1915-19; Vice-Pres. Internat. Federation of Library Assocs, 1947-; Past President: Birmingham and

District Library Assoc.; Assoc. of Asst Librarians; Central Literary Assoc.; Midlands Arts Club (Hon. Treas., 1955-69); Délégué Touring Club de France; Fellow of Library Assoc. and mem. of its Council, 1928- (Hon. Treas. 1936-45; Pres. 1946; Hon. Fellow, 1947; Hon. Vice-Pres. 1964); Hon. Sec. and Treasurer, Regional Library Bureau (W Midland); Life Governor of Birmingham Univ.; Governor of Birmingham and Midland Institute (Vice-Pres. 1955-59); formerly Chm. Birmingham Sch. of Music; Mem. BBC Midland Area Council; Mem., Council of the Dugdale Soc.; Vice-President: Council of the British Records Assoc. and Business Archives Council; Unesco National Co-operating Body for Libraries; Coun. of Brit. Union Catalogue of Periodicals; Bryony House Management Cttee; Hon. Sec. and Treasurer of the Shakespeare Memorial Library Cttee, 1928-48, Chm., 1963-; Surveyed the Libraries of Eastern Europe for Library Association and Rockefeller Foundation, 1936; delegate to American Library Association Conference and toured USA and Canada at request of Foreign Office, 1941; Coronation Medal, 1937; Defence medal, 1946. *Publications:* Libraries of North-Eastern Europe, including Russia, 1938; compiled Birmingham Book of Remembrance, 1939-45; various contributions to the Central Literary Magazine and professional (library) periodicals, etc. *Recreations:* reading, philately. *Address:* 17 Greswolde Park Road, Acock's Green, Birmingham 27. *T:* 021-706 0042. [*Died 25 June* 1972.

CASLON, Vice-Adm. Clifford, CB 1949; CBE 1942; RN (retired); *b* 11 May 1896; *s* of Sydney Herbert Caslon and Edith Elizabeth Thorpe; *m* 1930, Laurie Kathleen Walch; two *s*. *Educ:* Royal Naval Colls, Osborne and Dartmouth. Served in battleships Monarch and Malaya, European War, 1914-18. Qualified in Signals and W/T, 1920; Flag-Lieut and Signal Officer in cruisers Cardiff (Med.) and Hawkins (China) and battle-cruiser Hood (Empire cruise), 1921-28; Fleet Signal Officer, Med. Fleet, 1929-30; Comdr 1930; Commanded destroyers Thruster, Viceroy and Blanche; Capt. 1937; qualified RN Staff Coll. and Imperial Defence Coll.; commanded 4th, 18th and 6th destroyer flotillas, 1938-42; Chief of Staff, Plymouth, 1943-44; commanded HMS Nelson, 1945-46; Naval ADC to the King, 1946-47; Rear-Adm. 1947; Flag Officer, Malaya, 1947-50; Vice-Adm. 1950; retd list, 1950. *Address:* 1 Maltravers Drive, Littlehampton, Sussex. *T:* 3119. *Club:* United Service & Royal Aero. [*Died 8 Feb.* 1973.

CASSELS, Sir James Dale, Kt 1939; Judge of Queen's Bench Division, High Court of Justice, 1939-61, retired; *b* 22 March 1877; *o s* of Robert Cassels; *m* 1900, Alice Jessie (*d* 1904), *d* of Josiah Stone; no *c*; *m* 1906, Bertha Frances (*d* 1957), *d* of Alfred Terry; one *s* (and two *s* decd) one *d*; *m* 1958, Mrs Deodora Croft, OBE, widow of Hon. Col C. M. Croft, DL, MICE, MIME. *Educ:* Westminster City Sch. MP (U) West Leyton, 1922-29; MP (U) NW Camberwell, 1931-35; Called to Bar, Middle Temple, 1908; KC 1923; Recorder of Guildford, 1927-29; of Brighton, 1929-39; Bencher of the Middle Temple since 1929; Treasurer, 1947. [*Died 7 Feb.* 1972.

CASSIDY, Sir Jack Evelyn, Kt 1968, BA, LLB, QC (NSW); *b* 12 June 1894; *s* of J. W. Cassidy, Mudgee, NSW; *m* 1928, Gwynneth (MBE 1964), *d* of Dr G. A. Waterhouse; one *s*. *Educ:* Mudgee Sch.; University of Sydney. Barrister-at-law, 1923; KC 1938. Vice-Pres., NSW Liberal Party, 1945-56. *Address:* 3/2 Aston Gardens, Bellevue Hill, NSW 2023, Australia. *Clubs:* Australian (Sydney); Royal Sydney Golf. [*Died 11 June* 1975.

CASSIN, Prof. René, Grand Croix Légion d'Honneur; Compagnon de la Libération; Médaille Militaire; Croix de Guerre; Judge (formerly President), European Court of Human Rights; President, International Institute of Human Rights, Strasbourg; Member of the French Institute since 1947; *b* Bayonne, 5 Oct. 1887; *s* of Henri Cassin; *m* 1917, Simone Yzombard; no *c*. *Educ:* Lycée de Nice; Facultés, Aix (Licencié ès lettres. Licencié en droit); Paris (Docteur ès Sciences juridiques, politiques et économiques); Agrégé des Facultés de Droit, 1919; Prof. of Civil Law, Lille, 1920-29; Agrégé then Prof., Faculty of Law, Paris, 1929-60; Prof. Hague Academy of Internat. Law, 1930, 1934, 1951; French Delegate to the League of Nations, 1924-38, and to Gen. Conference on disarmament, 1932-34; Legal Counsellor to Gen. de Gaulle, 1940; Permanent Sec. de Gaulle's Council of Defence of the Empire, 1940-41; Nat. Commr for Justice and Public Education, 1941-43; Prés. du Comité Juridique, 1943-45; Pres. legisl. sect. of Cons. Assembly, Algiers, 1944; Pres. Prov. Constitutional Cttee, 1958-59; French Delegate: to Conf. of Allied Ministers of Education, 1942-43; to UN Commission on War Crimes, 1943-45; to UN Assemblies, 1946-51, 1968, and to UNESCO, 1945-52-58-60-62; Membre du Conseil Constitutionnel, 1960-71; Hon. Pres., retired, Conseil d'Etat (Vice-Pres., 1944-60); Mem. (ex-Pres.) Human Rights Commn of UN, 1946-72, and first Reporter of the Universal

Declaration. Founder, President and Hon. President Union Fédérale des Mutilés et Anciens Combattants; Hon. Pres., French Union of Ex-servicemen; Founder, International Confederation of Wounded (CIAMAC). President: Supreme Court of Works Disputes, 1950-60; Soc. of Comparative Law, 1952-55; Internat. Institute of Administrative Sciences 1953-56; Institut d'études des relations internationales, 1955-; Alliance israélite universelle, 1943-; Friends of Paris Univ., 1952. Nobel Peace Prize, 1968; UN Human Rights prize, 1968; Goethe prize, 1973. Hon. DCL: Oxford; Mainz; Jerusalem; London; Brandeis Univ., Boston. Corresp. Fellow, British Acad, 1971; Fellow: Bologne Acad; New Orleans Acad.; Belgrade Acad. *Publications:* L'Exception d'inexécution dans les rapports synallagmatiques, 1914; Les Droits de l'Etat dans les successions d'après le code civil, suisse, 1914; L'Interdiction du commerce avec l'ennemi (1917-19); La Nouvelle Conception du domicile dans le règlement des conflits de loi, 1931; La Déclaration universelle et la mise en œuvre des Droits de l'Homme, 1951; Le Conseil d'Etat, 1952; Pensée et Action, 1972; Les hommes partis de rien, 1975; Founder of Etudes et Documents du Conseil d'Etat, and Human Rights International Review; numerous articles on civil, public and international law. *Address:* 36 Quai de Béthune, Paris IVe, France.   *[Died 20 Feb. 1976.*

CASSON, Dame Sybil; see Thorndike.

CASTAING, J. C. de; see Chastenet de Castaing.

CASTELLANI, Professor Marchese Count Aldo, DSC; Hereditary Count of Kisymaio; MD, FRCP; FACP; Hon. FRMS; FAmAcDerm; MD, Cairo (Hon.); Physician to Royal Houses of Savoy and of Aosta; Italian Medals (one silver, two bronze) for bravery on the Field; Italian Military Cross; Grand Cross, Crown of Italy; also Grand Cross: Order of Civil Merit (Spain); Order of George I (Greece); Order of the Nile (Egypt); Sovereign Order of Malta; Order of St Sava; Knight Officer Legion of Honour (France) and Serbian White Eagle; Comm. Polish Order Odrodzenia; Commander Order of Santiago de Espada (Portugal); Professor of Tropical Medicine, Lisbon Institute for Tropical Diseases; Emeritus Professor of Tropical Medicine, Ceylon Medical School; late Professor of Tropical Medicine Tulane University and Louisiana State University, New Orleans, USA, also Rome University and Naples University, Italy; late Director of Mycology, London School of Hygiene and Tropical Medicine; late Physician Italian Hospital, London; concerned with Sir William Simpson in foundation of Ross Institute; (Ross thanked them both in a letter to the Times, 18 Oct. 1928); *b* Florence, 8 Sept. 1877; *s* of Ettore Castellani; *m* Josephine, *d* of George Ambler Stead; one *d. Educ:* Univs of Florence and Bonn. Qualified 1899 (MD, highest honours); MRCP 1916. Mem. British Foreign Office and Royal Society's Commission on Sleeping Sickness in Uganda, 1902-03. Dir Govt Clinique for Tropical Diseases, and Physician Seamen's Ward, Gen. Hospital, Colombo, 1903-15. Milroy Lecturer, RCP, London, 1920; Gehrmann Lecturer, University of Illinois, 1926; Royal Italian Academy prize for Science, 1932; Bernhardt Nocht Medal for Tropical Med.; Pres. Internat. Soc. of Tropical Dermatology, 1960. Lieut-Col Royal Italian Med. Service (Balcanic zone, 1915-18) and Mem. Interallied Sanitary Commission; during Ethiopian War, 1935-36, Surgeon-Gen. to Italian Forces (Count of Kisymaio). Senator of the Kingdom of Italy, 1929-46. Fellow: Accademia Nazionale dei Lincei; Accad. dei Quaranta; Accad. Pontificia. Chiefly known for his discovery of the etiological agents of sleeping sickness and yaws, for the elucidation of the etiology of several other diseases, and for description of new tropical diseases and their causes; also for original work in dermatology (parasitic skin diseases) and bacteriology (absorption test, dilution method, combined vaccines, gas-fermentation, symbiotic phenomenon, new species of bacteria, fungi and protozoa). *Publications:* Manual of Tropical Medicine (with Dr A. J. Chalmers); Fungi and Fungal Diseases, 1928; Climate and Acclimatisation (2nd edn), 1938; Manuale di Clinica Tropicale (with Prof. Jacono), 1938; Malattie dell' Africa, 1947; Little Known Tropical Diseases, 1954 (Lisbon); Microbes, Men and Monarchs, 1960 (London) (3rd edn 1968), 1961 (New York, as: A Doctor in Many Lands); numerous scientific articles; formerly Ed. Jl Trop. Med. *Address:* Institute for Tropical Diseases, Junqueira, Lisbon, Portugal; Villa Azzurra, Cascais, Portugal. *Clubs:* Authors' (London); Caccia (Rome); Rotary (Lisbon).
                                                              [Died 3 Oct. 1971.

CASTLE, Baron *cr* 1974 (Life Peer), of Islington; **Edward Cyril Castle;** journalist; Member, European Parliament, 1975-79; *b* 5 May 1907; *m* 1944, Barbara Anne Betts (Rt Hon. Barbara Castle, PC). *Educ:* Abingdon and Portsmouth Grammar Schools; served on newspapers in Portsmouth, Southampton, Newcastle, 1925-31; News Editor, Manchester Evening News,

1932; Asst Editor, Daily Mirror, 1943; Asst Editor, Picture Post, 1944-50; Editor of Picture Post, 1951-52. Alderman, GLC 1964-70, Islington, 1971-. *Recreation:* gardening. *Address:* House of Lords, SW1; Hell Corner Farm, Grays Lane, Ibstone, Bucks.   *[Died 26 Dec. 1979.*

CASTLE, Edgar Bradshaw, MA Oxon; Professor Emeritus, University of Hull; *b* 23 Dec. 1897; *s* of Frederick and Ellen Castle; *m* 1923, Mignon Marrable (*d* 1959); one *s* one *d; m* 1962, E. Ann Hodgkin. *Educ:* Bemrose Sch., Derby; Lincoln Coll., Oxford. Asst Master, Mill Hill Sch., 1923-28; Headmaster, Leighton Park Sch., Reading, 1928-47; Prof. of Education, University of Hull, 1948-61, Pro-Vice-Chancellor, 1956-59; Visiting Prof., University Coll. of Makerere, Uganda, 1961-65. Chm., Uganda Education Commission, 1963. *Publications:* Fathers and Sons, 1932; The Undivided Mind, 1941; Building the New Age, 1945; People in School, 1954; Moral Education in Christian Times, 1958; Ancient Education and To-Day, 1961; Approach to Quakerism, 1961; Principles of Education for Teachers in Africa, 1965; Growing Up in East Africa, 1966; Parents' Guide to Education, 1968; The Teacher, 1970; Education for Self-Help, 1972. *Address:* 12 Mead Road, Corfe Castle, Wareham, Dorset.   *[Died 10 Sept. 1973.*

CASTLEMAINE, 7th Baron, *cr* 1812; **John Michael Schomberg Staveley Handcock;** Chairman, Mancunian Building Society, since 1967 (Director since 1957); Director, Irish International Bank Ltd, since 1967; *b* 10 March 1904; *s* of Robert John Handcock (*d* 1951), and Eleanoré Annie Esther Staveley; *S* kinsman 1954; *m* 1930, Rebecca Ellen, *d* of William T. Soady, RN; one *s* two *d. Educ:* The Abbey, Tipperary. Joined Provincial Bank of Ireland Ltd, 1923, retired 1957. Served with Irish Defence Forces, Adjutant, 1939-45. *Recreations:* all sports, particularly sailing, shooting and fishing; gardening and all forms of agriculture. *Heir: s* Captain Hon. Roland Thomas John Handcock, Army Air Corps [*b* 22 April 1943; *m* 1969, Pauline Anne, *e d* of John Taylor Bainbridge, Exeter]. *Clubs:* University, Bankers (Dublin).   *[Died 31 July 1973.*

CATARINICH, John, CMG 1952; Consultant Psychiatrist; *b* Melbourne, 13 Nov. 1882; *s* of Capt. J. Catarinich, Dalmatia; *m* 1909, Nora J., *d* of J. Mouat; three *s* five *d. Educ:* St Patrick's Coll.; Melbourne Univ. (MB, BS). Joined Mental Hygiene Dept, State of Victoria, 1907; Medical Supt, Beechworth Mental Hospital, 1915-22, of Mont Park Mental Hospital, 1922-37; Director of Mental Hygiene, Victoria, 1937-51. *Address:* 18 Bradford Avenue, Kew, Melbourne, Victoria, Australia.
                                                              [Died 8 Oct. 1974.

CATCHPOOL, Egerton St John Pettifor, CBE 1951; Member Workers Travel Association Management Committee, since its foundation, 1921; Chairman, Firbank Housing Society, since 1957; *b* 22 Aug. 1890; 4th *s* of Thomas K. Catchpool, Colchester; *m* 1920, Ruth Allason, 2nd *d* of Henry Lloyd Wilson, Birmingham; one *s* three *d* (and one *d* decd). *Educ:* Sidcot Sch.; Woodbrooke Quaker Coll.; Birmingham Univ. Secretary of Friends' Social Service Union, 1913-14; with Friends' War Victims Relief Cttee, 1915-19; Sub-Warden Toynbee Hall, first University Social and Educational Settlement, London, E1, 1920-29; First Secretary Youth Hostels Association England and Wales, 1930-50 (Vice-Pres. 1951-); retired 1950. Warden of Toynbee Hall, 1963-64. President Internat. Federation of Youth Hostels, 1938-50; Vice-President Internat. Friendship League; Member Society of Friends, Elder, 1946-. Co-opted Member LCC Education Cttee, 1925-31; Member Catering Wages Commn, 1947-50. Invited to Delhi by Govnt of India to advise on Social Service development, 1951. 15,000-mile tour of Africa, at invitation of British Council, advising on youth welfare, 1957. Fellow, Woodbrooke Coll., Birmingham, 1957. Royal Society of Arts Lecture, Leisure in an Affluent Society, 1964. Pres., Adventure Playpark Assoc., Welwyn Garden City, 1967-. Chevalier Order of Orange Nassau, 1948. *Publications:* Uniting Nations by means of Youth Hostels and International Work Camps; Candles in the Darkness, 1966. *Recreations:* walking, travelling and work camps. *Address:* Meadow Cottage, Welwyn Garden City, Herts. *T:* Welwyn Garden 22657.   *[Died 13 March 1971.*

CATLIN, Sir George (Edward Gordon), Kt 1970; MA, PhD; FRSL; Concerned with Atlantic Community policy, since 1925; Founder, Movement for Atlantic Union (UK); *b* 29 July 1896; *s* of late Rev. George E. Catlin, sometime Vicar of St Luke's, Kew Gardens, Surrey, and of late Mrs Catlin, *née* Orton; godson of George Edward Gordon, incumbent of New Old South Church, Boston, Mass; *m* 1925, Vera Brittain (*d* 1970); one *s* one *d; m* 1971, Delinda (*née* Tassi), *widow* of Lt-Comdr Victor Gates. *Educ:* Warwick; St Paul's Sch.; New Coll., Oxford (Exhibitioner in Modern History, 1914). Subsequently London Rifle Brigade.

Oxford Modern History Sch. *cum laude*; Chancellor's English Essayist; *prox. accessit* Lothian Prize, 1920; Gladstone Prizeman, Matthew Arnold Memorial Prizeman, Oxford, 1921; Professor of Politics, Cornell Univ., 1924-35 (PhD Cornell); acting Head of Dept, 1928. Associated with Clarence Streit and Walter Lippmann, 1938-, and Jean Monnet, 1950-, in propaganda for Atlantic Union; draftsman of Constitution of Atlantic Inst., Paris. Foundation Lecturer: Yale Univ., 1938; Calcutta Univ., 1947; Lecturer: Peking Univ., Columbia Univ., University of California (Berkeley), Bologna, Cologne, etc.; Goethe Bicentenary Lecturer, Heidelberg Univ.; Kierkegaard Commemoration Address, University of Copenhagen, 1949; Weil Lecturer, University of N Carolina, 1957; Tagore Centenary Lecturer, Royal Society of Arts, 1961; Provost Mar Ivanios Coll., S India, 1951; Bronman Professor of Political Science, McGill Univ., 1956-60; Chairman of Dept; Walker-Ames Lecturer, University of Washington, 1964. Churchill Memorial Lectr, Fulton, Mo, 1969. Fellow and Vice-President of the World Academy of Arts and Sciences; Medallist, Soc. de l'Encouragement au Progrès (France); Vice-President and founder, Anglo-German Assoc.; Director, Investigation into Eighteenth Amendment, US Constitution, under Rockefeller Foundation, 1926; editorial writer to Yorkshire Post, 1927-28, editor of People and Freedom, and special foreign correspondent, inc. Reuters, Germany, Russia, Spanish Civil War, Italy and India; co-founder, Realist Magazine, with H. G. Wells, Arnold Bennett and others. Contested (Lab.) Brentford Div., 1931, Sunderland Div., 1935; sometime Member Executive Cttee, Fabian Soc.; joint founder, America and British Commonwealth Assoc. (now E-SU); Technical adviser to Rt Hon. Arthur Greenwood, 1939-40; Temp. adviser to Wendell Wilkie on Presidential election campaign, 1940; Member Internat. Executive Cttee of Nouvelles Equipes Internationales (Internat. Cttee of Christian Socialist Parties) and rapporteur on European Union. Mem., FCO Liaison Cttee re US Bicentary Celebration. Vice-Pres., War on Want; British Atlantic Unity Cttee. Sponsor, Martin Luther King Foundn. Mem., Inst. for Strategic Studies; Mem., Adv. Council, E-SU. Draftsman of Internat. Declaration in Support of Indian Independence, 1943. LDV, 1940. Comdr, Grand Cross, Order of Merit (Germany). *Publications:* Thomas Hobbes, 1922; The Science and Method of Politics, 1926, repr. 1964; Mary Wollstonecraft's Vindication: introd., 1928; Study of the Principles of Politics, 1929, repr. 1967; Liquor Control, 1931; Preface to Action, 1934; New Trends in Socialism, ed 1935; War and Democracy, ed 1938; (ed. and introd.) Durkheim's Rules of Sociological Method, 1938; Anglo-Saxony and its Tradition, 1939; The Story of the Political Philosophers, 1939; (8th edn, published in Britain as A History of the Political Philosophers, 1950); One Anglo-American Nation: The Foundation of Anglo-Saxony, 1941; Anglo-American Union as Nucleus of World Federation, 1942; The Unity of Europe, 1945; Above All Nations (jtly), 1945; Mahatma Gandhi, 1948; What Does the West Want?, 1957; The Atlantic Community, 1959; Systematic Politics, 1962; Rabindranath Tagore centenary lectures, 1964; Political and Sociological Theory and its Applications, 1964; The Grandeur of England and the Atlantic Community, 1966; The Atlantic Commonwealth, 1969; For God's Sake, Go (autobiography), 1972; Atlanticism, 1973; Kissinger's Atlantic Charter, 1974; Détente, 1975; trans of above into various languages. *Address:* Corner Cottage, Allum Green, near Lyndhurst, Hants. *Clubs:* Pilgrims, National Liberal, Institute of Directors.
[*Died 7 Feb.* 1979.

CATNACH, Agnes, CBE 1952; BA; *b* 8 Dec. 1891; *d* of Charles Burney Catnach, Newcastle upon Tyne. *Educ:* Polam Hall, Darlington; Royal Holloway Coll. Headmistress of Wallasey High Sch., 1926-34, of Putney County Sch., Mayfield, 1934-51. President of Assoc. of Headmistresses, 1942-44; Chairman of Joint Cttee of Four Secondary Associations, 1944-46; Member of Secondary Schools' Examinations Council, 1946-52; Member of General Nursing Council, 1943-58. *Address:* 3 Rusper House, Michel Grove, Eastbourne, E Sussex. *T:* Eastbourne 31014.
[*Died 15 Aug.* 1979.

CATOR, Sir Geoffrey (Edmund), Kt 1946; CMG 1936; *b* 14 Aug. 1884; *s* of Robert Cator and Evelyn Susan Sotheron Estcourt; *m* 1922, Elizabeth Margaret Wynne Mostyn (*d* 1967); one *s* one *d*. *Educ:* Bruton; Cambridge. BA 1906; Malayan CS 1907; various appointments in the Colonial Administrative Service, Agent for Malaya. Retired, 1948. *Address:* The Grange, Goring on Thames, Oxon. [*Died 21 April* 1973.

CATTON, Bruce; Senior Editor, American Heritage Magazine, since 1959 (Editor, 1954-59); *b* 9 Oct. 1899; *s* of George R. Catton; *m* 1925, Hazel Cherry; one *s*. *Educ:* Oberlin Coll. Newspaper Reporter in Cleveland, Boston and Washington, 1920-41. Asst Director of Information, US War Production Board, 1942-43, Director, 1944-45; Director of Information, US Dept of Commerce, 1945-47; Special Assistant, Secretary of Commerce, 1948; Asst Director of Information, US Dept of the Interior, 1950-52. Mem., Amer. Acad. of Arts and Letters. Pulitzer Prize for history, 1954; National Book Award, 1954; Presidential Medal of Freedom, 1977. Hon. degrees from various colleges and univs, inc. Oberlin, Harvard, Columbia, Michigan and Northwestern. *Publications:* The War Lords of Washington, 1948; Mr Lincoln's Army, 1951; Glory Road, 1952; A Stillness at Appomattox, 1953; U. S. Grant and the American Military Tradition, 1954; Banners at Shenandoah, 1955; This Hallowed Ground, 1956; America Goes to War, 1958; Grant Moves South, 1960; The American Heritage Picture History of the Civil War, 1960; The Coming Fury, 1961; Terrible Swift Sword, 1963; Never Call Retreat, 1965; Grant Takes Command, 1969; Waiting for the Morning Train, 1972; Gettysburg: the Final Fury, 1975. *Recreations:* virtually none, except for unadorned loafing in the north woods of Michigan every summer. *Address:* American Heritage, 10 Rockefeller Plaza, New York, NY 10020, USA. *Clubs:* Players, Century, Lotos (New York). [*Died 28 Aug.* 1978.

CAULTON, Rt. Rev. Sidney Gething, MA; *b* 24 Aug. 1895; *s* of John Caulton, Ripley, Derby; *m* 1933, Beryl, *d* of Joseph Guylee, Feilding, New Zealand; one *s*. *Educ:* St Chad's Coll. Durham (Exhibitioner). BA (2nd class Th.), 1922; MA 1927. Deacon, 1922; Priest, 1923; Curate of St Dunstan, Liverpool, 1922-29; Missionary in Diocese of Melanesia, 1927-37; Vicar of Whakatane, 1937-43; of Onehunga, 1943-46; of St Mary's Cathedral, Auckland, and Dean of Auckland, 1946-47; Bishop of Melanesia, 1947-54; Vicar of Northcote, 1954-57; Asst Bishop of Auckland, NZ, 1955-64; Vicar of St George, Epsom, NZ, 1957-62; Asst Bishop of Southwark, 1964-68. *Address:* 12 Rookery Close, Gillingham, Dorset. [*Died 23 Aug.* 1976.

CAWADIAS, Alexander Pocnagioti, Hon. OBE; MD; FRCP; Knight Commander Royal Greek Order of Phoenix: Chairman Editorial Board, British Journal of Clinical Practice; Hon. Physician St John Clinic and Institute of Physical Medicine; Professor Emeritus of Medicine, Athens University (lecturing at the University, 1963); Fellow Academy of Athens; FRSM; *s* of Professor P. Cawadias, Gen. Dir of Antiquities and Fine Arts, Greece; *m* 1914, Sophie (*d* 1967), *d* of C. Constantinides, Alexandria; one *s* one *d*. *Educ:* Gymnasium, Athens; Universities of Paris, Bonn, and Heidelberg; Post-Graduate studies, London. Asst Physician, Paris teaching hospitals, 1910; Chief of Medical Clinic and Lecturer on Internal Diseases, Paris Univ., 1912; Senior Physician and Lecturer on Internal Diseases, Evangelismos Hospital, Athens, 1914; Mem. International Health Board, 1920; Pres. Royal Society of Medicine, Section of History, 1937-39; Pres. International Congress of Neo-Hippocratic Medicine, 1938; Thomas Vicary Lecturer, Royal College of Surgeons, 1941; during European War, 1914-18, Consulting Physician to the Greek Army, and major with Forces on Macedonian Front in charge of epidemics (Greek Military Cross, despatches); during War of 1939-45, Pres. Greek Red Cross. *Publications:* Diseases of the Intestines, 1927; Modern Therapeutics of Internal Diseases, 1931; Hermaphroditos, The Human Inter-sex, 1943; Clinical Endocrinology, 1947; and numerous papers on internal and constitutional diseases. *Recreations:* music and ballet. *Address:* 22 Academy Street, Athens, Greece. [*Died 20 Nov.* 1971.

CAWLEY, Rev. Dr Frederick; Principal Emeritus, Spurgeon's College, London, since Sept. 1955 (Principal, 1950-55); *b* Sept. 1884; *s* of S. R. and S. A. Cawley; *m* 1917, Mary Gold Coutts. *Educ:* Spurgeon's Coll., London; New Coll., Edinburgh. BA, BD (London); PhD (Edinburgh). Missionary: Baptist Missionary Soc., India, 1912-22 and Trinidad, West Indies, 1922-26. Baptist Minister: Falkirk, Scotland, 1926-35 and Camberwell, London, 1935-38; Penge, 1940-46. Senior Tutor, Spurgeon's Coll., London, 1938-47; Vice-Principal, 1947-50. Senator, University of London, 1951-56. *Publication:* The Transcendence of Jesus Christ, 1933. *Address:* The Tor, 30 Corstorphine Road, Edinburgh EH12 6HP. *T:* 031-337 7702.
[*Died 12 June* 1978.

CAZALET, Peter Victor Ferdinand, DL; trainer of racehorses; *b* 15 Jan. 1907; *s* of late William Marshal Cazalet; *m* 1st, 1932, Leonora (*d* 1944), *o d* of Leonard Rowley; one *s* one *d*; 2nd, 1949, Zara (who *m* 1st, 1940, Major Hon. Alexander R. G. Strutt, now 4th Baron Belper; one *s*), *yr d* of late Sir Harry Mainwaring, Bt; two *s* (and one *s* decd). *Educ:* Eton; Christ Church, Oxford. Amateur rider, 1930-38; trainer, 1939; served War of 1939-45; RA 1939-40. Welsh Guards, 1940-45. JP 1954-69, High Sheriff, 1960, DL 1961, Kent. *Recreations:* ball games. *Address:* Fairlawne, Tonbridge, Kent. *T:* Plaxtol 326; 14 Eaton Row, SW1. *T:* 01-235 1826. *Clubs:* White's, Buck's.
[*Died 29 May* 1973.

CAZENOVE, Philip Henry de Lerisson, TD 1944; Major, Northamptonshire Yeomanry (retired); Stockbroker (retired); *b* 21 Dec. 1901; *yr s* of late Major Edward Cazenove; *m* 1942, Aurea Ethelwyn, *d* of C. I. L. Allix; three *s* one *d*. *Educ:* Eton. High Sheriff of Northants, 1949. *Recreations:* hunting, shooting, rackets, squash rackets, tennis, lawn tennis, golf. *Address:* Cottesbrooke, Northampton. *T:* Creaton 203. *Clubs:* White's, MCC, All England Lawn Tennis.   [*Died* 17 *Jan.* 1978.

CEADEL, Eric Bertrand, MA; University Librarian, University of Cambridge, since 1967; Fellow of Corpus Christi College, Cambridge, since 1962; *b* London, 7 Feb. 1921; *o s* of late Albert Edward Ceadel, FSS, and of Bertha Margaret (*née* Blackall); *m* 1946, Pamela Mary Perkins; three *s. Educ:* Bec Sch., London; Christ's Coll., Cambridge (Entrance Schol.). 1st cl. hons Class. Tripos, Pts I and II; BA 1941, MA 1945; Charles Oldham Class. Schol., 1941. Suffolk Regt, then Intelligence Corps, Capt., 1941-45. A. H. Lloyd Research Schol., Christ's Coll., 1945-47; Univ. Lectr in Japanese, University of Cambridge, 1947-67; Vis Prof. of Japanese, University of Michigan, 1960, 1961; Sen. Tutor, Corpus Christi Coll., Cambridge, 1962-66; Sec., 1948-52, and Chm., 1963-65, Faculty Bd of Oriental Studies; Mem. Coun. of Senate, 1965-68; Curator in Oriental Literature, Univ. Library, Cambridge, 1954-67; Syndic of Univ. Library, 1961-67; Mem., British Library Organising Cttee, 1971-73; Chm., British Library Bibliog. Services Div. Adv. Cttee, 1975-. *Publications:* (contrib. and ed) Literatures of the East, 1953; Classified Catalogue of Modern Japanese Books in Cambridge University Library, 1962; articles in Class. Quarterly, Asia Major and other jls. *Address:* 20 Porson Road, Cambridge. *T:* 50053.
                    [*Died* 1 *June* 1979.

CECIL, Henry; *see* Leon, H. C.

CECIL, Rev. Canon Philip Henry; Residentiary Canon and Treasurer of Peterborough Cathedral, since 1972; *b* 27 July 1918; *s* of Rev. Henry Cecil and Elizabeth Cecil (*née* Spall); *m* 1945, Jessie Marie Barrick; one *s* four *d. Educ:* King Edward VII Sch., Sheffield; City of London Sch.; King's Coll., London (BD 2nd Class Hons, AKC 1940); Westcott House, Cambridge. University Prizes: Junior Wordsworth Prize for Latin, 1938; Bishop Collins Memorial Prize for Ecclesiastical History, 1939; Plumptre Prize for English Literature, 1940. Curate, Leeds Parish Church, 1941-45; Precentor and Sacrist, Durham Cath., 1945-48; Dean of Belize, Brit. Honduras, 1948-52; Rector, St Luke's, Old Street, 1952-54; Rector, Wormley, Herts, 1956-60; Vicar, Bushey Heath, Herts, 1960-63; Principal, Bishops' Coll., Cheshunt, and Public Preacher, Dio. St Albans, 1963-67; Vicar of Potton with Cockayne Hatley, 1967-72. Proctor in Convocation, 1959-64, and 1970-72; Exam. Chap. to Bp of St Albans 1960-72; Dir Ordinands, dio. St Albans, 1960-63; Hon. Canon of St Albans, 1965-72. Lectr, St Olave's, Hart Street, 1953-63, 1968-; Limborough Lectr, St Botolph's, Aldgate, 1960-68; Queen's Chapel of the Savoy, 1969-71, 1974-. *Recreations:* listening to music, motoring, reading and writing comic verse. *Address:* Canonry House, Minster Precincts, Peterborough PE1 1XX. *T:* Peterborough 62125.   [*Died* 11 *March* 1977.

CECIL, V. A. G.; *see* Gascoyne-Cecil.

CERAM, C. W.; *see* Marek, K. W.

CERF, Bennett; Founder of Random House Inc. and President until 1965; *b* 25 May 1898; *s* of Gustave Cerf and Fredericka Wise; *m* 1940, Phyllis Fraser; two *s. Educ:* Columbia Sch. of Journalism. BA Columbia Univ.; BLit Columbia Sch. of Journalism. Columnist for King Features, 1946-; Lecturer, 1946-. Panelist on American "What's My Line". Hon. Dr Lit: Coll. of Puget Sound, 1958; W Maryland Coll., 1966; Pace Univ., 1971. *Publications:* Try and Stop Me, 1945; Encyclopædia of Modern American Humor, 1955; Reading for Pleasure, 1957; Treasury of Atrocious Puns, 1968; The Sound of Laughter, 1970, etc. *Recreations:* golf, tennis. *Address:* 201 E 50 Street, New York, USA. *T:* Plaza 1-2600. *Clubs:* Dutch Treat, Overseas Press, Raffles (New York).   [*Died* 27 *Aug.* 1971.

CHADWICK, Sir James, CH 1970; Kt 1945; FRS 1927; FRSE; MSc (Vict); PhD (Cantab); Hon. DSc Reading, Dublin, Leeds, Oxford, Birmingham, Exeter, McGill; Hon. LLD Liverpool, Edinburgh; Fellow of Gonville and Caius Coll., Cambridge; *b* 20 Oct. 1891; *e s* of J. J. Chadwick; *m* 1925, Aileen, *e d* of H. Stewart-Brown, Liverpool; *twin d. Educ:* Manchester Secondary Sch.; Universities of Manchester, Berlin, and Cambridge. Formerly Lyon Jones Prof. of Physics in the University of Liverpool; Master of Gonville and Caius Coll., Camb., 1948-58. Mem., Pontifical Academy of Sciences; Assoc. Acad. Royal Belgium; Foreign Member; German Order Pour le Mérite; K. Ned Akad.Wet., Amsterdam; K. Danske Vid. Selskab.; Corr.

Mem. Sächs. Akad. Wiss., Leipzig; Hon. Fellow: Inst. of Physics; Manchester Coll. of Science and Technology; Hospital Physicists Assoc.; Franklin Inst.; Amer. Philosophical Soc.; Amer. Physical Soc. Awarded Hughes Medal of Royal Society, 1932; Mackenzie Davidson Medal, 1932; Copley Medal, 1950; Nobel Laureate (Physics), 1935; US Medal for Merit, 1946; Trasenster Medal, 1946; Melchett Medal, 1946; Faraday Medal, 1950; Franklin Medal of Franklin Institute, Philadelphia, 1951; Guthrie Medal, IPPS, 1967. *Publications:* Radioactivity and Radioactive Substances, 1921; Radiations from Radioactive Substances (with Lord Rutherford and C. D. Ellis), 1930; various papers on radio-activity and connected problems, on the neutron and its properties. *Address:* 16 Grange Court, Pinehurst, Cambridge CB3 9BD. *T:* Cambridge 59326. *Club:* Athenæum.   [*Died* 24 *July* 1974.

CHADWICK, Nora Kershaw, CBE 1961; MA, FSA; FBA 1956; DLitt (Hon. Wales), 1958; DLitt (Hon., National University of Ireland), 1959; LLD (Hon., University of St Andrews), 1963; Hon. Life Fellow Newnham College, Cambridge, since 1958; *b* 28 Jan. 1891; *e d* of James Kershaw and Emma Clara Kershaw (*née* Booth); *m* 1922, Professor Hector Munro Chadwick (*d* 1947), Prof. of Anglo-Saxon, University of Cambridge; no *c. Educ:* Private School in Southport, Lancs; Newnham Coll., Cambridge. Medieval and Modern Langs. Tripos, Cl. II, 1913; Medieval and Modern Langs Tripos, (Part II, English Literature), Cl. I, 1914. Temp. post as Lecturer in English Language and Asst Lecturer in English Literature, University of St Andrews, 1914-19; returned to Cambridge, 1919, research work as a private student until marriage; continued writing and research work till the present day. Research Fellow, Newnham Coll., 1941-44; University Lecturer in the Early History and Culture of the British Isles, University of Cambridge, 1950-58. Director of Studies in Anglo-Saxon and Celtic subjects, in Newnham Coll., 1950-59, Girton Coll., 1951-62, Cambridge; O'Donnell Lecturer in Celtic Studies, Universities of Edinburgh, 1959, Wales, 1960, Oxford, 1961; Riddell Memorial Lecturer, University of Durham, 1960; Lecturer to British Academy, The Colonization of Brittany from Celtic Britain, 1965 (publ. 1966). *Publications:* Stories and Ballads of the Far Past, 1921; Anglo-Saxon and Norse Poems, 1922; an Early Irish Reader, 1927; Russian Heroic Poetry, 1932; Poetry and Prophecy, 1942; The Beginnings of Russian History, 1945; Poetry and Letters in Early Christian Gaul, 1955. (Ed. and contributor) Studies in Early English History, 1954; (Ed. and contributor) Studies in the Early British Church, 1958; (Ed. and contributor) Celt and Saxon: Studies in the Early British Border, 1963; Celtic Britain, 1963; The Age of the Saints in the Early Celtic Church, 1964; The Druids, 1966; The Celtic Realms (with Myles Dillon), 1967; Early Brittany, 1969; The Celts, 1970; (in collaboration with Professor H. M. Chadwick) The Growth of Literature, 3 vols, 1932-40; contributor to The Heritage of Early Britain, 1952; Irish Sagas (ed. Myles Dillon), 1959 (Dublin); Wales Through the Ages (ed A. J. Roderick), 1959; contrib. to learned journals. *Recreation:* exploring pre-Conquest Britain. *Address:* 7 Causewayside, Cambridge. *T:* Cambridge 55550.
                    [*Died* 24 *April* 1972.

CHADWYCK-HEALEY, Sir Edward Randal, 3rd Bt, *cr* 1919; MC 1917, bar to MC 1943; *b* 23 Jan. 1898; *e s* of Sir Gerald Chadwyck-Healey, 2nd Bt, CBE, and Mary Verena, *d* of G. A. Watson, East Court, Finchampstead, Berks; *S* father 1955; *m* 1924, Rachel Margaret, TD, formerly Chief Commander, ATS (*d* 1978), *d* of L. C. W. Phillips, Unsted Park, Godalming. *Educ:* Eton; RMA, Woolwich. Commissioned RA, 1916; served European War, 1916-18; France, RFA and RHA. Served War of 1939-45: Field Artillery (France, North Africa, Italy); Major 1942; wounded twice. Chairman of Charrington & Co. (Brewers), 1949-59. A Trustee, City Parochial Foundation, 1943-72; Prime Warden, Fishmongers' Company, 1953; President London Chamber of Commerce, 1955-57; President Freshwater Biological Assoc., 1960-77; a Vice-Pres., Marine Biological Assoc., 1969-. Belgian Croix de Guerre, 1917. *Recreation:* fishing. *Heir b* Charles Arthur Chadwyck-Healey, OBE [*b* 27 May 1910; *m* 1939, Viola, *d* of late Chadwick Lubbock; three *s* two *d*]. *Address:* The Mill House, Hook, Basingstoke. *T:* Hook 2436. *Clubs:* Bath; Leander.   [*Died* 22 *Aug.* 1979.

CHAIN, Prof. Sir Ernst (Boris), Kt 1969; FRS 1949; FRSA 1963; MA Oxon; DrPhil Berlin; PhD Cambridge; DPhil Oxon; Professor of Biochemistry, University of London at Imperial College, 1961-73, now Professor Emeritus; Fellow, 1978 (Senior Research Fellow, 1973-76); *b* Berlin, Germany, 19 June 1906; *s* of Dr Michael Chain, chemist and industrialist (of Russian origin) and Margarete Eisner; *m* 1948, Dr Anne Beloff, *y d* of S. Beloff, NW3; two *s* one *d. Educ:* Luisengymnasium, Berlin; Friedrich-Wilhelm Univ., Berlin (Graduate in chemistry and physiology, 1930). Research in chemical dept of Institute of

Pathology, Charité Hospital, Berlin, 1930-33; emigrated from Germany to England in 1933 because of racial persecution; research in the School of Biochemistry, Cambridge, under Sir Frederic Gowland Hopkins, OM, 1933-35; research in the Sir William Dunn School of Pathology, Oxford, since 1935. University Demonstrator and Lecturer in Chemical Pathology, University of Oxford, 1936-48; Scientific Director of International Research Centre for Chemical Microbiology, Istituto Superiore di Sanità, Rome, 1948-64. Initiated, jointly with Prof. H. W. Florey (later Lord Florey), work on penicillin that led to the remarkable curative properties of this substance; Nobel Prize for Physiology and Medicine, 1945; Harmsworth Memorial Fund, 1946; Berzelius Medal in silver of Swedish Med. Soc., 1946; Pasteur Medal of Institut Pasteur, Paris, 1946; Pasteur Medal of Société de Chimie biologique, 1946; Paul Ehrlich Centenary Prize, 1954; Gold Medal in Therapeutics, Worshipful Soc. of Apothecaries of London, 1957; Marotta Medal, Società Chimica Italiana; Carl Neuberg Medal; Hanbury Meml Medal, 1972. Heymans Meml Medal, 1974. Member Société Philomathique, Paris; Hon. Member New York Academy of Medicine; Foreign Member Accademia dei Lincei, Rome, Accademia dei XL; For. Associate, Acad. des Sciences, Inst de France; Associé Etranger, Académie Nationale de Médecine, Paris; Foreign Member, Real Acad. de Ciencias, Madrid; Hon. Life Member, New York Acad. of Science; Foreign Mem., USSR Acad. of Scis, 1976. Dr hc Université de Liège, 1946, Université de Bordeaux, 1947, University of Turin, 1954, University of Paris, 1959; Albert Einstein College of Medicine, Yeshiva Univ., 1961; Universities of La Plata, Cordoba (Argentina), Montevideo (Uruguay), Brasil, 1962, Chicago, 1965, Bar-Ilan 1974, Santiago de Compostela, 1977, Ramat-Gan; Philadelphia College of Pharmacy. Hon. Fellow: Royal College of Physicians; Royal Society of Medicine; Institute of Biology; Weizmann Institute of Science, Rehovot, Israel; National Institute of Sciences, India; Società Chimica Italiana; Microbiological Society of Israel; Finnish Biochemical Society; Fitzwilliam Coll., Cambridge; Società delle Scienze Farmaceutiche, Milan; Deutsche Pharmazeutische Gesellschaft; Wiener Aerztegesellschaft. Commandeur de la Légion d'Honneur; Grande Ufficiale al merito della Repubblica Italiana; Grand Decoration of Honour in Gold (Austria); Order of Rising Sun, 2nd degree (Japan), 1976. *Publications:* numerous on biochemical and chemical subjects in scientific journals. *Recreation:* music. *Address:* Department of Mechanical Engineering, Imperial College of Science, Imperial Institute Road, SW7. *T:* 01-589 5111; 9 Northview, Wimbledon Common, SW19. *Club:* Athenæum.   *[Died 12 Aug. 1979.*

CHALLE, Général d'Armée Aérienne Maurice; President and Director-General, European Society of Transport and Freight, since 1969; *b* Le Pontet, Vaucluse, France, 5 Sept. 1905; *m* 1927, Madeleine Mollard; two *s. Educ:* Ecole Spéciale Militaire de Saint-Cyr, France. Pilot, 1925; Lieut, 1927; Captain, 1932. Ecole Supérieure de Guerre Aérienne, 1937-39. Served War of 1939-45; Sqdn Leader, with 8th Army, 1939-40; GHQ Air, 1940; Comdr, Reconnaissance Group 2/14, Avignon, Sept.-Dec. 1942; organised networks for the Resistance Movement. Lieut-Colonel 2nd Bde de Bombardement "Les Maraudeurs". 1945; Colonel, 1945; attached to Chief of Staff (Air), Cabinet, 1945; Deputy Chief of Staff (Air), 1946; Brig.-General (Air), Moroccan Air Command, 1949; Special Chief of Staff of Secretary of State for Air, 1951; Director, Centre d'Enseignement Supérieur Aérien and Comdr Ecole Supérieure de Guerre Aérienne, 1953; Lieut-General, Chief of Staff of Armed Forces, 1955; General, Flying Corps, 1957; Air Chief Marshal, Asst Chief of Staff of the Army, 1958; Asst C-in-C, Algeria, and Comdr 5th Aerial Region, Oct. 1958; C-in-C, Algeria, Dec. 1958. Member Conseil Supérieur de l'Air, 1958, 1960 (Secretary, 1951, 1952, 1953). Commander-in-Chief, Allied Forces Central Europe (NATO), May 1960-March 1961; led French Army revolt in Algeria, April 1961. Political prisoner, June 1961, sentenced to 15 years imprisonment; freed 1966, amnestied 1968. Grand Cross of Legion of Honour, 1960 (Grand Officer, 1952, Officer, 1945, Chevalier, 1940). War of 1939-45 (French Croix de Guerre). Holds several foreign decorations. *Publication:* Notre Révolte, 1968. *Address:* 63 avenue Raymond-Poincaré, 75116 Paris, France.
          [Died 19 Jan. 1979.

CHALMERS, Archibald MacDonald, MC; Sheriff Substitute of Argyll at Oban, 1933-55, retired; Hon. Sheriff (formerly Hon. Sheriff Substitute) of Perthshire since 1956; *b* 26 Sept. 1883; *s* of James Chalmers and Caroline Berry Honey; *m* 1921, Mary, *o d* of late William T. Procter, DL Clackmannanshire; no *c. Educ:* Perth Academy; Glasgow Univ. Partner of firm of Robertson, Chalmers, Auld and Hunter, Solicitors, Glasgow; served European War, 1915-19, Major MGC (MC); Chairman, Court of Referees, Falkirk and Glasgow, 1927-30; Lecturer, Court Procedure and Negligence, Glasgow Atheneum, 1923-24.

President Boy Scouts, Stirling, 1958-64. Hon. Vice-President, 1964-. *Recreations:* golf, fishing, etc. *Address:* Kilrock, Bridge of Allan. *T:* Bridge of Allan 2341. *Club:* Conservative (Glasgow).
          [Died 9 Aug. 1977.

CHALMERS, Rev. Canon Reginald, TD 1943; MA; Vicar of Great Bowden and Welham 1948-65; Canon Residentiary of Leicester Cathedral, 1954-65, Canon Emeritus since 1965; Member of Canterbury Convocation 1955-65; Rural Dean of Gartree, 1957-63; licensed to officiate on Carlisle Diocese; *b* 5 June 1893; *s* of Thomas William Chalmers, Ryde, IOW; *m* 1st, 1915, Gladys Lee Saunders, Hull (*d* 1944); one *s* one *d*; 2nd 1949, Mary Barron Robinson, Sunderland. *Educ:* Durham Univ. (MA 1920). Officer, E. Yorks Regt, 1915-18. Ordained deacon, 1918, priest, 1919; Curate of Drypool, Hull, 1918-20; Vicar of St Luke's, Hull, 1920-24; CMS Staff, 1924-27; Vicar of St Paul, Newcastle upon Tyne, 1927-31; CMS, HQ London, 1931-35; Vicar of Holy Trinity, Leicester, 1935-48. CF (TA) 1927; on active service, 1939-45 (despatches, TD); DACG, 1943-45. Hon. Canon, Leicester Cathedral, 1945-54. *Recreations:* gardening, golf. *Address:* White Bridge, Grasmere, Westmorland. *T:* Grasmere 430.   *[Died 31 Jan. 1974.*

CHALMERS, Rear-Admiral William Scott, CBE 1939; DSC; retired; *b* 1 May 1888; *m* 1921, Muriel Violet Frances, *d* of Hon. Francis Agar; two *s. Educ:* Glasgow Academy; HMS Britannia; Dartmouth. Served European War, 1914-18, Royal Naval Siege Guns, Belgium (Croix de Guerre, France, DSC); HMS Lion and Queen Elizabeth, Battle of Jutland (despatches, British once, French twice); in command HMAS Australia, 1929-32, HMS Delhi, 1934-36; Director RN Staff Coll., 1937; Rear-Admiral and retired, 1939, and re-employed Admiralty Staff. *Publications:* The Life and Letters of David Beatty, 1951; Max Horton and the Western Approaches, 1954; Full Cycle (the biography of Admiral Sir B. H. Ramsay), 1959. *Address:* Guessens, Titchfield, Hants. *T:* Titchfield 3144. *Club:* United Service.   *[Died 11 June 1971.*

CHAMBERLAIN, Rt. Rev. (Frank) Noel, CB 1953; OBE 1949; MA (Lambeth), 1953; Hon. Assistant Bishop in the diocese of Portsmouth, since 1963 (Assistant Bishop, 1961-63); *b* 25 Dec. 1900; *y s* of late A. H. Chamberlain, Highgate; unmarried. *Educ:* Haberdashers' Sch.; King's Coll., London; AKC 1925; Fellow, King's Coll., London, 1953; Wells Theological Coll. Deacon, 1925; Priest, 1926; Curate Eton Mission, Hackney Wick, 1925-28; Chaplain, Royal Navy, 1928; Chaplain of the Fleet and Archdeacon of the Royal Navy, 1952-56; Hon. Chaplain to the Queen, 1952-56; Bishop of Trinidad and Tobago, 1957-61, resigned. Honorary Canon, Portsmouth Cathedral, 1962-64. *Recreation:* walking. *Address:* 1 Pembroke Chambers, Penny Street, Portsmouth. *Clubs:* Army and Navy; Royal Naval and Royal Albert Yacht (Portsmouth).   *[Died 17 July 1975.*

CHAMBERLAIN, Rt. Rev. Noel; see Chamberlain, Rt Rev. F. N.

CHAMBERLAYNE, Air Commodore Paul Richard Tankerville James Michael Isidore Camille, CBE 1945; AFC 1918; RAF, retired; *b* 15 May 1898; 2nd and *o surv. s* of late Major Tankerville James Chamberlayne, Chamberlainstown, Kells, Meath, Ireland, and late Donna Leopoldina, Princess Ruspoli; *m* 1935, Euphemia Caldwell Kerr; one *s* one *d*. 11th Hussars SR 1914; attached RFC 1915, RAF 1918; Wing Comdr 1937; Asst Air Attaché, Paris, 1937; Air Attaché, Lisbon, 1938; Group Captain, 1940; AOC 25 Group S Africa, 1943; AOC Training Delegation, Bordeaux, 1944-45; retired list, 1946. Order of Leopold (Belgium). *Recreation:* yachting. *Address:* Chamberlainstown House, Navan, Co. Meath, Eire.
          [Died 3 May 1972.

CHAMBERLIN, Sir Michael, Kt 1964; OBE 1955; Chairman, National Trustees Executors and Agency Company Australasia Ltd, Melbourne, since 1933 (General Manager, 1933-67); *b* 30 Aug. 1891; *e s* of Richard Chamberlin, Essendon, Victoria, Australia; *m* 1924, Veronica Christina (née Erck). *Educ:* Christian Brothers and Central Coll., Geelong, Australia. Dep. Chancellor, Monash Univ., Vic., 1962-68. Hon. LLD Monash, 1969. Kt of Order of Pius. *Recreation:* work. *Address:* 31 Studley Park Road, Kew, Victoria 3101, Australia; Monash University, Clayton, Victoria, Australia. *T:* 81-4817. *Club:* Athenæum (Melbourne).   *[Died 16 March 1972.*

CHAMBERLIN, Peter Hugh Girard, CBE 1974; ARA 1975; FRIBA 1959, RIBA DistTP 1963; architect and planner in private practice with Geoffry Powell and Christoph Bon, since 1952; *b* 31 March 1919; *m* 1940, Jean Bingham. *Educ:* Bedford Sch.; Pembroke Coll., Oxford; Kingston Sch. of Art. Member: Ancient Monuments Bd for England, 1976-; Central Housing

Adv. Cttee, 1960-66. Governor, Thames Polytechnic, 1971-. *Planning work* includes development plans: for Barbican district in City of London; for expansion of Univ. of Leeds; for King's Coll. and New Hall, Cambridge; for Science area in Oxford; for central area of Peterborough; for new civic centre, Leicester. *Architectural commissions* include: Residential Community, Golden Lane, for City of London; Barbican redevelopment scheme for City of London (2000 flats, garages, shops, City of London Sch. for Girls, Guildhall Sch. of Music and Drama, Arts Centre with theatre for RSC, concert hall for LSO, cinema, lending library and art gallery, restaurants, etc); 13 teaching and research depts, block of lecture theatres, library, Senior Common Room, Sports Hall, hall of residence, and student flats for Univ. of Leeds; physical educn centre for Univ. of Birmingham; New Hall, Cambridge; Bousfield Sch. and Trinity Sch. for LCC; Cheltenham Grammar Sch.; industrial building in Witham, Essex, etc. *Awards* include: RIBA Bronze Medals for Bousfield Sch., Kensington, and Cooper Taber, Witham; Min. of Housing and Local Govt Medal for Golden Lane Estate; 1973 RIBA Regional Award for Chancellor's Court, Univ. of Leeds; 1974 RIBA Regional Award for St Giles' Square, Barbican; Civic Trust Commendation for St George's Fields, Univ. of Leeds. *Recreations:* travel, reading, enjoying the arts. *Address:* c/o Chamberlin, Powell & Bon, 1 Lamont Road Passage, King's Road, SW10 0HW. *T:* 01-352 2841.   *[Died 23 May 1978.*

CHAMIER, Air Cdre Sir John Adrian, Kt 1944; CB 1925; CMG 1919; DSO 1917; OBE 1918; Indian Army, retired; late RAF; *b* 1883; *s* of late Maj.-General F. E. A. Chamier; *m* 1918, Edwina Ratcliff, *d* of E. Lordly, Chester, Canada; one *s* (and one *s* decd). *Educ:* St Paul's Sch.; Royal Military Coll., Sandhurst. Served Somaliland, 1904; European War, 1914-18 (despatches, DSO); Dir of Technical Development, Air Ministry, 1927-28; Technical Dir Vickers and Supermarine Aviation Companies, 1929-32; recalled to RAF Sept. 1939; Commandant Air Training Corps, 1941. *Publication:* The Birth of the Royal Air Force, 1944. *Address:* Fairwater, Hill Head, Hants. *Clubs:* Special Forces; Royal Thames Yacht.   *[Died 3 May 1974.*

CHAMIER, Lt-Col (Hon. Col) Richard Outram, CIE 1928; late Indian Army; *b* 24 Aug. 1888; *s* of late Maj.-General F. E. A. Chamier, CB, CIE, formerly of the Bengal Staff Corps. *Educ:* Woodcote House, Windlesham, Surrey; St Paul's Sch.; RM Coll., Sandhurst. Joined Indian Army, 1909; served European War, 1914-18, Mesopotamia; Private Secretary to the Governor of Assam, 1922, to Governor of the United Provinces, India, 1924-27. *Address:* Woodlands House, Ashurst, Hants SO4 5GL.
                    [Died 19 March 1980.

CHAMPION, Prof. Frank Clive; Professor of Experimental Physics, University of London, King's College, since 1959; Fellow of King's Coll., 1970; *b* 2 Nov. 1907; *s* of Frank Charles Champion and Alice Champion (*née* Killick); *m* 1936, Joan Mingay (marr. diss., 1951). *Educ:* Royal Grammar Sch., Guildford; St John's Coll., Cambridge. (Scholar; Double 1st Class Natural Sciences Tripos (Physics); BA 1929, MA 1930, PhD 1932). Hockin Physics Prize and Hughes Prizeman, 1929. Asst Demonstrator, Cavendish Laboratory, 1929-32; Asst Lecturer in Physics, Nottingham Univ., 1932-34; Lecturer in Physics, King's Coll., London, 1934-48; Reader in Physics, 1941-59. Royal Society Visiting Professor, Malaysia, 1947. Scientific Adviser, Civil Defence, SE Div., 1946-51. Hon. Secretary, Atomic Scientists Assoc., 1945-48. FInstP 1932. FKC, 1970. *Publications:* (with N. Davy) Properties of Matter, 1936, 3rd edn 1959; University Physics, 1946, new edn 1960; Electronic Properties of Diamonds, 1963; research papers in nuclear physics and solid state physics in Proc. Royal Society, Proc. Physical Society, Physical Review, 1931-. *Recreations:* tennis, swimming, travel, music, literature (English and Spanish). *Address:* Physics Department, King's College, Strand, WC2. *T:* 01-836 5454.   *[Died 24 Feb. 1976.*

CHAMPION, Sir Harry George, Kt 1956; CIE 1941; MA, DSc; Professor Emeritus, Oxford University, since 1959; Emeritus Fellow, St John's College, Oxford; *b* 17 Aug. 1891. *Educ:* New Coll., Oxford. BA 1912; MA 1924; DSc 1950. Joined Indian Forest Service, 1915; Conservator of Forests, United Provinces, 1938; Professor of Forestry, Oxford Univ., 1940-59. *Address:* Windrush, Boars Hill, Oxford. *T:* 735240.
                    [Died 20 June 1979.

CHAMPNEYS, Captain Sir Weldon D.; *see* Dalrymple-Champneys.

CHANCE, Kenneth Miles, DSO 1916; DL; *b* 27 Jan. 1893; *y s* of late Sir F. W. Chance, KBE; *m* 1924, D. R. Shaw; two *d. Educ:* Repton; Hertford Coll., Oxford. High Sheriff, Cumberland, 1949; DL Cumberland, 1961. *Recreations:* shooting; golf.

Address: The Glebe House, Wreay, Carlisle.
                    [Died 7 April 1980.

CHANDLER, Hon. Sir Gilbert (Lawrence), KBE 1972; CMG 1958; Minister of Agriculture, Victoria, Australia, 1955-73; MLC (L), Boronia Province, since 1967; Government Leader, Legislative Council, since 1962; nurseryman; *b* N Melbourne, 29 Aug. 1903; *s* of Hon. A. E. Chandler; *m* 1930, Thelma A., *d* of J. Coon; two *s. Educ:* The Basin State Sch.; Scotch Coll., Melbourne. Asst Minister, Dunstan-Hollway Govt, 1943-45; MLC: SE Province, 1935-37; S Province, 1937-67. Chm., Churchill Nat. Park Cttee of Management, 1960-; Member: Healesville Wildlife Sanctuary Cttee of Management, 1944-; Ferntree Gully Nat. Park Cttee of Management, 1941-; Chm., Govt Bush Fires Relief Cttee, 1944-46; Municipal Rep., Olympic Games Organisation Cttee, 1950-57; Co-founder and Pres., William Angliss Hosp., Ferntree Gully, 1939-; Trustee, Melbourne Cricket Ground. SBStJ 1971. *Recreations:* horticulture; formerly cricket and football (Senior cricket, Richmond CC, 1927-33; League football, Hawthorn FC, 1928-29; ex-Captain, ex-Pres., Life Mem., Bayswater FC; ex-Captain, Bayswater-Boronia FC; ex-Captain, ex-Pres., Life Mem., Boronia FC; ex-Pres., Croydon-Ferntree Gully Football League; Life Member: Eastern Districts Football League; Ringwood District Cricket Assoc.). *Address:* 34 Boronia Road, Boronia, Victoria 3155, Australia. *Club:* MCC.   *[Died 8 April 1974.*

CHANDOS, 1st Viscount, *cr* 1954, of Aldershot; **Oliver Lyttelton,** KG 1970; PC 1940; DSO 1916; MC; late Grenadier Guards; President, Governing Body of Queen Elizabeth House, Oxford, 1955-69; Chairman, Northern Ireland Development Council, 1955-65; a Trustee of the National Gallery, 1958-65; A Trustee of Churchill College, Cambridge, since 1958; *b* 15 March 1893; *o s* of late Right Hon. Alfred Lyttelton and late Hon. Mrs Alfred Lyttelton, GBE; *m* 1920, Lady Moira Godolphin Osborne, 4th *d* of 10th Duke of Leeds and Lady Katherine Frances Lambton (*d* 1952), *d* of 2nd Earl of Durham; two *s* (and one killed in action) one *d. Educ:* Eton; Trinity Coll., Cambridge. Joined army at outbreak of War, and Grenadier Guards, Dec. 1914; served continuously on active service, 1915-18; Adjutant 3rd Battalion, 15 Oct. 1915-18; Brigade Major 4th Guards Brigade, Feb. 1918; 2nd Guards Brigade, Sept. 1918 (despatches thrice, DSO, MC); Managing Dir, of the British Metal Corporation, Ltd; Controller of Non-Ferrous Metals, 1939-40. MP (U) Aldershot Div. of Hants 1940-54; Pres. of Board of Trade, 1940-41; Minister of State and Mem. of War Cabinet, 1941-42; Minister of Production and Member of War Cabinet, 1942-45; Pres. of Board of Trade and Minister of Production, May-July 1945; Chm. Associated Electrical Industries Ltd, 1945-51; Sec. of State for the Colonies, 1951-54; Chm., Associated Electrical Industries Ltd and subsidiaries, 1954-63; Director: Alliance Assurance Co. Ltd, 1954-69; I.C.I. Ltd, 1954-68. Pres. Institute of Directors, 1954-63; Pres., Manchester Coll. of Science and Technology, 1956-61; Chm., Nat. Theatre Bd, 1962-71, Pres., 1971-; Mem., S Bank Theatre Bd. *Publications:* The Memoirs of Lord Chandos, 1962; From Peace to War: a study in contrast, 1857-1918, 1968. *Recreations:* golf, cricket, shooting; played golf for Cambridge Univ. 1913. *Heir: s* Hon. Antony Alfred Lyttelton [*b* 23 Oct. 1920; *m* 1949, Caroline Mary, *d* of Rt Hon. Sir Alan Lascelles; two *s* two *d. Educ:* Eton; Trinity Coll., Cambridge. Served War of 1939-45 (despatches)]. *Address:* Trafalgar House, Downton, near Salisbury, Wilts; Chesham House, 30/31 Chesham Place, SW1. *Clubs:* Buck's; St James'; Grillions.   *[Died 21 Jan. 1972.*

CHANDOS, 2nd Viscount *cr* 1954, of Aldershot; **Antony Alfred Lyttelton;** *b* 23 Oct. 1920; *s* of 1st Viscount Chandos, KG, PC, DSO, MC, and of Lady Moira (Lady Moira Lyttelton) (*d* 1976), *d* of 10th Duke of Leeds; *S* father, 1972; *m* 1949, Caroline Mary, *d* of Rt Hon. Sir Alan Lascelles, GCB, GCVO, CMG, MC, PC; two *s* two *d. Educ:* Eton; Trinity College, Cambridge (MA Hons). Served General Staff, Mediterranean, 1942-45 (despatches). Partner, Panmure Gordon & Co., 1950-75; Member of London Stock Exchange, 1950-75; Publisher, 1976-. *Heir: s* Hon. Thomas Orlando Lyttelton, *b* 12 Feb. 1953. *Address:* The Vine, Sherborne St John, Basingstoke, Hampshire. *T:* Bramley Green 227.   *[Died 28 Nov. 1980.*

CHANNON, Harold John, CMG 1946; DSc London, BA London; FRIC; Fellow of University College, London; *b* 7 March 1897; *s* of W. J. Channon; *m* 1925, Hilda Alice Bond, MB, BS, DPH, Mem. Commn on Higher Educn in Malaya, 1938. *Educ:* Leathersellers Company Sch.; University Coll., London. Research Asst, Bio-chemical Dept, University Coll., London, 1922-24; Beit Memorial Fellow for Medical Research, 1923-26; Asst Biochemical Dept, University Coll., London, 1925-27; Biochemist, Dept of Experimental Pathology and Cancer Research, University of Leeds, 1927-31; Prof. of

Biochemistry University of Liverpool, 1932-43; Research Manager, Unilever Ltd, 1943-55. Mem. Commission on Higher Education in the Colonies; Mem. Commission on Higher Education in West Africa, 1944; Mem. of Advisory Cttee on Education in the Colonies, 1939-44. Mem. Colonial Products Council, 1956-59. *Publications:* scientific papers mainly in The Biochemical Journal. *Recreations:* gardening; fishing. *Address:* Dunwood, Southway, Sidmouth, Devon. *T:* Sidmouth 2921.
[Died 7 April 1979.

CHAPLIN, Sir Charles (Spencer), KBE 1975; producer, and actor in films; *b* London, 16 April 1889; both parents (deceased) in theatrical profession; *s* of Charles Chaplin, variety comedian and Hannah (Lily Harley), singer; *m* 1st, 1918, Mildred Harris (marr. diss.); 2nd, 1924, Lolita McMurry (Lita Grey) (marr. diss.); one *s* (and one *s* decd); 3rd, 1936, Paulette Goddard (marr. diss.); 4th, 1943, Oona, *d* of late Eugene O'Neill; three *s* five *d.* Formed his own producing organisation and built Chaplin Studios, Hollywood, California, 1918. Was a founder of United Artists' Corporation (with Mary Pickford, Douglas Fairbanks, and D. W. Griffith) with British affiliation Allied Artists. Member, American Academy of Arts and Sciences, 1970. Films Include: Shoulder Arms, The Kid, The Gold Rush, The Circus, City Lights, Modern Times, The Great Dictator, Monsieur Verdoux, Limelight (Oscar, 1973), A King in New York, A Countess from Hong Kong. Erasmus Prize, 1965; Creative Arts Award, Brandeis Univ., Mass, 1971; Hon. Oscar award, 1972. Fellow, British Acad. of Film and Television Arts, 1976. Hon. Member: AAAL, 1976; Nat. Inst. of Arts and Letters, 1976. Hon. DLitt: Oxford, 1962; Durham, 1962. Officier de l'instruction Publique, République Française; Commander, Legion of Honour, 1971. *Publications:* My Autobiography, 1964; My Life in Pictures, 1974. *Address:* c/o United Artists Ltd, 142 Wardour Street, W1.
[Died 25 Dec. 1977.

CHAPLIN, Frederick Leslie; Chairman, F. W. Woolworth & Co. Ltd, 1961-69; Director, F. W. Woolworth, USA, 1961-69; *b* 6 Dec. 1905; *s* of late Frederick and Marion Chaplin; *m* 1934, Vera Irene Townes; two *s.* *Educ:* St Osyth's Sch., Clacton. Joined Woolworth Company, 1928; Director, 1957; Managing Dir, 1960. *Recreations:* gardening; fishing; shooting. *Address:* Links View, 5 Broad Walk, Winchmore Hill, N21. *T:* 01-886 0244.
[Died 25 Dec. 1977.

CHAPLIN, Sir George (Frederick), Kt 1962; CBE 1958; DL; JP; FRICS; Chairman of Essex County Council, 1961-65 (Member 1944-46; Vice-Chairman 1955-58); *b* 1900; *s* of late Jesse Chaplin, Leicester; *m* 1928, Doris Evelyn, *d* of William Henry Lee; one *s* two *d.* *Educ:* Leicester. Chm. Romford Divl Conservative Assoc., 1945-52 (Pres., 1952-66); Member: Romford Borough Council, 1937-52 (Mayor, 1946-47). Regional Dir, Lloyds Bank. Mem. Council of Govs for University of Essex; Gov., Brentwood Sch. Mem., Ct of Worshipful Co. of Innholders. JP 1952, DL 1963, Essex. *Recreation:* golf. *Address:* Great Ropers, Great Warley, Brentwood, Essex. *T:* Brentwood 2514. *Club:* Constitutional.
[Died 22 April 1975.

CHAPLIN, William Robert, CBE 1958; *b* 4 Feb. 1888; *s* of late William Robert Chaplin; *m* 1917, Tereora, *d* of Rev. J. J. Hutchin, Raratonga, Cook Islands; one *d.* Apprenticeship and Officer in sailing ships, Australian Naval Transport Service, 1914-18; commanded ships of the Australian Commonwealth Line, 1918-28. Elected an Elder Brother of Trinity House, 1928; retired, 1958. Member, Royal Commonwealth Society; FRGS. *Address:* c/o Trinity House, EC3N 4DH. [Died 21 Feb. 1974.

CHAPMAN, Fitzroy Tozer, CBE 1942; DSc(Eng); BSc; MICE; FIEE; retired; *b* 6 Oct. 1880; *s* of Frederic Chapman; *m* 1906, Beatrice Maude Briggs (*d* 1968); *m* 1968, Amy Thomas (*d* 1976). *Educ:* Leeds Modern Sch.; Leeds Univ. Electrical Designer, Greenwood & Batley Ltd, Leeds, 1901-11; Sen. Lectr and Supt, Testing Dept, Faraday House, London, 1911-20; District Technical Inspector, Board of Education, 1920-23; Divisional Inspector, 1933-36; Staff Inspector, 1936-39; seconded to War Office as temp. Brig., 1939-46; retired 1946. *Publications:* A Study of the Induction Motor, 1933; Electrical Engineering, 1956; miscellaneous papers on electrical subjects. *Recreation:* gardening. *Address:* 37 Military Road, Sandgate, Kent. *T:* Folkestone 39229. *Club:* Reform. [Died 21 Dec. 1976.

CHAPMAN, Lt-Col Frederick S.; *see* Spencer Chapman.

CHAPMAN, Prof. Guy Patterson, OBE 1919; MC 1918; MA Oxon; BSc (Econ.) London; *b* 11 Sept. 1889; *o s* of George Walter Chapman, Beechwood, Cookham Dean, Berks, late Official Receiver in Bankruptcy; *m* 1926, Margaret Storm

Jameson, *qv. Educ:* Westminster Sch.; Christ Church, Oxford; London Sch. of Economics, Barrister-at-Law, 1914. Served Royal Fusiliers, 1914-20, in France and Belgium, 1915-18 (despatches twice, OBE, MC), Major. Engaged in book-publishing, 1920-40. Served War of 1939-45, in Army Educational Corps, 1941-45; Lieut-Col Commandant Army Sch. of Education (Army Bureau of Current Affairs), 1943; Prof. of Modern History in the University of Leeds, 1945-53; Visiting Prof., University of Pittsburgh, Pa., 1948-49; Mem., Institute for Advanced Study, Princeton, NJ, 1957. FRSL. *Publications:* A Passionate Prodigality, 1933; Beckford, a biography, 1938; A Bibliography of the Works of William Beckford, 1931; Culture and Survival, 1940; The Dreyfus Case: A Reassessment, 1955 (rewritten as The Dreyfus Trials, 1972); The Third Republic of France: the First Phase, 1963; Why France Collapsed, 1968. *Recreation:* travel. *Club:* Savile. [Died 30 June 1972.

CHAPMAN, Mrs Hester Wolferstan, (Mrs R. L. Griffin); *b* 26 Nov. 1899; *d* of T. Pellatt, Durnford Preparatory Sch., Dorset; *m* 1st, 1926, N. K. Chapman; 2nd, 1938, R. L. Griffin; no *c.* *Educ:* privately. Subsequently became mannequin in Paris; later in London, secretary, telephone operator, typist, companion, daily governess, schoolmistress. War of 1939-45: worked for Fighting French, American Red Cross and as waitress in a canteen at Combined Operations. *Publications:* novels: She Saw Them Go By, 1932; To Be a King, 1934; Long Division, 1943; I Will Be Good, 1945; Worlds Apart, 1947; Ever Thine, 1951; Falling Stream, 1954; The Stone Lily, 1957; Eugénie, 1961; Fear No More, 1968; Limmerston Hall, 1972; *biographies:* Great Villiers, 1949; Mary II, Queen of England, 1953; Queen Anne's Son, 1954; The Last Tudor King, 1958; Two Tudor Portraits, 1960; Lady Jane Grey, 1962; The Tragedy of Charles II, 1964; Lucy, 1965; Privileged Persons, 1966; The Sisters of Henry VIII, 1969; Caroline Matilda, Queen of Denmark 1751-1775, 1971; Anne Boleyn, 1974; *posthumous publication:* Four Fine Gentlemen, 1977. *Recreations:* foreign travel, cinema and theatre, dress, interior decoration. *Address:* 13 Conway Street, W1. *T:* 01-636 3260. [Died 6 April 1976.

CHAPMAN, Air Vice-Marshal Hubert Huntlea, CB 1958; CBE 1952; *b* 20 Feb. 1910; *s* of late Major George James Chapman, OBE, Bournemouth; *m* 1937, Phyllis Mary, *d* of late Cyril Smith Owbridge, Parkstone, Dorset; one *s.* *Educ:* Bedford Sch. Joined RAF, 1928; Fighter and Army Co-operation Squadrons and Signals Appointments, 1928-39; Signals Staff Appointments, 1940-43; Chief Telecommunications Officer, MAAF, 1944-45 (despatches twice); Dep. Dir of Signals Training, 1945-47; Chief Signals Officer, Air Command, Far East, 1947-48; Student, Jt Services Staff Coll., 1948; Sen. Air Staff Officer, HQ 43 Group, 1949-50; AOC, 43 Group, 1950-51; Dir of Signals Policy, 1952-53; Student, idc, 1954; Senior Air Staff Officer, Headquarters 90 (Signals) Group, RAF Medmenham, 1955-58; Dir-Gen. of Technical Services, Air Min., 1958-61; Air Officer-in-charge of Administration, Maintenance Command, 1961-63, retired, 1963. CEng, MIEE. Bronze Star (US), 1946. *Recreation:* photography. *Address:* Spencer Cottage, Spencer Road, Canford Cliffs, Dorset. *T:* Canford Cliffs 77830. *Clubs:* Royal Air Force; Parkstone Yacht (Dorset). [Died 10 April 1972.

CHAPMAN, Mrs Murray, (Olive); FRGS; *d* of late G. A. Garry Simpson, MRCS, and of Ethel Maud (*née* Gibbon); *m* C. H. Murray Chapman, Flt-Lt RN (*d* 1916). *Educ:* Queen's Coll.; Heatherley's Art Sch., London. Extensive travels both in the Artic and the East, including journey on horseback across Iceland; winter sledge journey through Lapland; and a journey among primitive tribes in Madagascar; has lectured on her expeditions before Royal Geog. Soc., Royal Scottish Geog. Soc., Royal Asiatic Soc., etc, and also in America; has held three one-man shows in Bond Street of her water-colour paintings and in 1933 produced a short sound travel film-Winter with the Laps-shown at the Academy Cinema, London, etc. *Publications:* Across Iceland, 1930; Across Lapland, 1932, in Penguin series 1939 (new edn 1947); Across Cyprus, 1937; Across Madagascar, 1943. [Died 11 June 1977.

CHAPMAN, Mrs Olive M.; *see* Chapman, Mrs Murray.

CHAPMAN, Oscar Littleton; attorney-at-law; *b* Omega, Virginia, 22 Oct. 1896; *s* of James Jackson Chapman and Rosa Archer Blount; *m* 1st, 1920, Olga Pauline Edholm (*d* 1932); 2nd, 1940, Ann Kendrick; one *s.* *Educ:* public schs, Va.; Randolph Macon Acad., Bedford, Va.; Univ. of Denver; Westminster Law Sch. (LLB). Enlisted in US Navy, 1918, served until 1920. Served for five years as asst and chief probation officer of Juvenile Court of Denver. Admitted to law practice, 1929; Mem. of Dist of Columbia Bar: admitted to practice before Supreme Court of US, 1934. Asst-Sec. of the Interior, 1933-46; Under-Sec. of the Interior, 1946-49; Sec. of the Interior, USA, 1949-53.

Active in civic, political, and veterans' affairs, both in Denver and in Washington; has served at request of President, as head of Govt div. of Red Cross, Community Fund, and War Fund drives; appointed by late President Roosevelt to Interdepartmental Cttee to coordinate Health and Welfare Services of Govt, 1935; Cttee on Vocational Education, 1936; mem. of President's Advisory Cttee on Management Improvement in Govt; director: Franklin D. Roosevelt Foundation; Harry S. Truman Library. Has received several citations for service to US. Hon. Dr of Laws; Augustana Coll., 1934; Colorado State Coll. of Education, 1940; Howard Univ., 1949, Univ. of Denver, 1951; Western State Coll. of Colorado, 1961. Mem. American Judicature Soc. and of Phi Alpha Delta Law Fraternity. *Address:* 1730 Pennsylvania Avenue, NW, Suite 1200, Washington, DC 20006, USA; 4975 Hillbrook Lane, Washington, DC. *[Died 8 Feb. 1978.*

CHAPMAN, Air Chief Marshal Sir Ronald I.; *see* Ivelaw-Chapman.

CHAPMAN-ANDREWS, Sir Edwin Arthur, KCMG 1953 (CMG 1948); OBE 1936; retired as British Ambassador at Khartoum (1956-61); *b* 9 Sept. 1903; *er s* of Arthur John Chapman-Andrews and Ada Allen, Exeter; *m* 1931, Sadie Barbara Nixon, London; two *s* two *d. Educ:* Hele's Sch., Exeter; University College, London (Fellow, 1952); Sorbonne; St John's Coll., Cambridge (while a probationer Vice-Consul, to study oriental languages). Probationer Vice-Consul, Levant Consular Service, 1926; Actg Vice-Consul, Port Said, Cairo and Suez, 1928-29; Actg Vice-Consul, Addis Ababa, 1930; FO, 1931-32; Vice-Consul at Kirkuk, Iraq and at Rowanduz, 1933-35; Actg Consul at Harar, 1935-36; Foreign Office, 1937; Asst Oriental Sec., Cairo, 1937-40. Hon. Commission in Royal Sussex Regt, 1940; Liaison Officer on staff of C-in-C, Middle East, with Emperor Haile Selassie; Foreign Office, 1942; Head of Personnel Dept, 1945; Inspector of Overseas Establishments, 1946; British Minister at Cairo, 1947-51; at Beirut, 1951; Ambassador, 1952. Adviser, Massey-Ferguson (Holdings) Ltd, 1962-77; Director: Massey-Ferguson (Export), 1964-77; Mitchell Cotts (Export), 1965-73; John Carrington & Co. Ltd, 1972-77. Member: Council of Lord Kitchener National Memorial Fund; British Nat. Export Council, 1965-68; Cttee for Middle East Trade (COMET), 1963-65 (Chm. 1965-68). Member Council: Anglo-Arab Assoc.; Royal Albert Hall; Royal Central Asian Soc., 1962-69. KStJ; KCSG (Papal). *Recreation:* any change of occupation handy. *Address:* 2 The Leys, Brim Hill, N2 0HE. *Clubs:* Athenæum, Oriental. *[Died 10 Feb. 1980.*

CHARLEMONT, 11th Viscount *cr* 1665 (Ireland); **Charles St George Caulfeild;** Baron Caulfeild of Charlemont, 1620 (Ireland); retired as Manager of Bank of NSW, Cambooya, Queensland, 1945; *b* 23 Nov. 1884; *s* of Henry St George Caulfeild (*d* 1943) and Jane (*d* 1924), *d* of William Goldsmith; *S* brother, 1967; *m* 1915, Lydia Clara Kingston; two *d. Educ:* Private Grammar Sch., Bundaberg, Queensland. *Recreations:* gardening, stamp collecting. *Heir: b* Richard William St George Caulfeild [*b* 13 March 1887; *m* 1914, Dorothy Laura (*d* 1961), *d* of late Frank Giles; two *d*]. *Address:* 45 Amelia Street, Coorparoo, Brisbane, Queensland, Australia. *T:* Brisbane 97-1798. *[Died 18 Nov. 1971.*

CHARLEMONT, 12th Viscount *cr* 1665 (Ireland); **Richard William St George Caulfeild;** Baron Caulfeild of Charlemont, 1620 (Ireland); retired from Air Ministry, 1950; *b* 13 March 1887; 4th *s* of Henry St George Caulfeild (*d* 1943) and Jane (*d* 1924), *d* of William Goldsmith; *S* brother 1971; *m* 1914, Dorothy Laura (*d* 1961), *d* of late Frank Giles, ICS; two *d. Educ:* Schultz Private School, Bundaberg, Queensland. Malayan Govt Service, 1906-20; Straits Settlements Govt Service as Resident Engineer in charge construction Singapore Airport, 1931-37; Air Ministry, 1940-50; Resident Engineer, Gambia, Sierra Leone, Gold Coast, Nigeria, 1940-42; Liaison Officer, 8th and 9th US Army Air Force, 1942-45. USAAF Medal of Freedom with palm, 1945. *Recreations:* long past it. *Heir: cousin* Charles Wilberforce Caulfeild [*b* 10 March 1899; *m* 1930, Dorothy Jessie, *d* of late Albert A. Johnston]. *Address:* Lane End, Elmstead, Colchester, Essex. *T:* Wivenhoe 2826. *Club:* Royal Over-Seas League. *[Died 18 June 1979.*

CHARLES, Enid, MA Cantab, PhD Cape Town; FRSE; Regional Adviser in Health Statistics, 1955-59, Consultant, 1961-64, WHO, South-East Asia; *b* Dec. 1894; *o d* of Rev. James Charles, Denbigh; *m* 1918, Lancelot Hogben (marr. diss. 1957); two *s* two *d. Educ:* Newnham Coll., Cambridge; Univ. of Liverpool. Leverhulme Research Fellow, 1937-39; Census Research Specialist, Dominion Bureau of Statistics, Ottawa, 1942-47; Chief Statistical Officer to the City Corporation, Birmingham, 1949-52. *Publications:* The Practice of Birth

Control, 1932; The Twilight of Parenthood, 1935; The Changing Size of the Canadian Family, 1948; on comparative physiology, and mathematical genetics in Proc. Royal Soc. B, Quart. Jl Exper. Physiol., Jl Genetics, Jl Exper. Biol., etc; on vital statistics in London and Cambridge Economic Service Monographs, Economica, Sociological Review, Proc. Royal Soc. Edinburgh, and in Political Arithmetic. *Address:* 605 Greenwood Avenue, Iowa City, Iowa, USA. *[Died 26 March 1972.*

CHARLES, Sir John Alexander, KCB 1955; Kt 1950; MD, FRCP, DPH; Chief Medical Officer to Ministry of Health, Ministry of Education and Home Office, 1950-60; *m* 1947, Madeleine Frances, *d* of late Sir W. E. Hume; one *s* one *d.* MB, BS (1st Class Hons.) 1916; DPH Cantab 1925; MD (Durham) 1930; FRCP 1935. Harveian Orator, Royal College of Physicians, 1955. (First) Rock Carling Fellow, 1962. President, 12th World Health Assembly, 1959. Jacques Parisot Lectr, WHO, 1970. Hon. DHY Durham. Leon Bernard Prize, WHO, 1962. *Address:* 25 Campden Hill Road, W8. *T:* 01-937 4527. *Club:* Athenæum. *[Died 6 April 1971.*

CHARLES, Sir Noel Hughes Havelock, 3rd Bt *cr* 1928; KCMG 1941 (CMG 1937); MC; HM Ambassador to Turkey, 1949-51; *b* 20 Nov. 1891; 2nd *s* of Sir Richard Havelock Charles, 1st Bt, GCVO, KCSI; *S* brother, 1936; *m* 1st, Grace (*d* 1955), *d* of J. L. Bevir; 2nd, 1957, Gipsy Joan, 2nd *d* of late Sir Walter Lawrence, Hyde Hall, Sawbridgeworth, Herts. *Educ:* Rugby; Christ Church, Oxford, (MA). Served European War, 1914-18: France, 1915-18 (MC, despatches twice). Entered Diplomatic Service as 3rd Sec. at Brussels, 1919; 2nd Sec., 1920; 1st Sec., 1925; Bucharest; Tokyo, 1926; FO, 1929; Stockholm, 1931; Moscow, 1933; Counsellor, Brussels, 1936-37; Counsellor, Rome, 1937-39, Minister there, 1939-40; Minister at Lisbon, 1940-41; British Ambassador to Brazil, 1941-44; High Comr in Italy with rank of Ambassador, 1944-47; FO, 1947-49; retired, 1951. KStJ; 3rd Class Rising Sun. *Heir:* none. *Address:* c/o Coutts & Co., 440 Strand, WC2; St Christophe, Chateauneuf-de-Grasse, AM, France. *Club:* Royal Automobile. *[Died 8 Sept. 1975 (ext).*

CHARLES, Robert Lonsdale, MC 1942; MA; FMA; JP; Keeper, Department of Art, National Museum of Wales; *b* 19 Aug. 1916; *s* of late Robert Henry Charles, CBE; *m* 1946, Margaret Joy, *d* of late A. C. R. Stephenson; one *s* two *d. Educ:* Aysgarth Sch., Yorks; Shrewsbury; Corpus Christi Coll., Oxford. Royal Artillery, 1939-46; Control Commission for Germany, 1945-46. Assistant Keeper, National Museum of Wales, 1946; Keeper, 1952. Member: British Council Fine Arts Cttee, 1958; British Council Welsh Cttee, 1959; Welsh Arts Council, 1976. JP Dynaspowis 1971. *Publications:* Continental Porcelain of the 18th Century, 1964; articles and reviews. *Address:* National Museum of Wales, Cardiff. *T:* 26241. *[Died 8 March 1977.*

CHARLESWORTH, John Kaye, CBE 1957; DSc Leeds, PhD Breslau, MRIA, FRSE, FRGS, FGS; Professor of Geology, Queen's University, Belfast, 1921-54; Professor Emeritus, 1954; *b* 3 Jan. 1889; *e s* of late George Charlesworth, Burley, Leeds; *m* Janet Cumming, *e d* of late Rev. Alex. Gibson, MA, BD, Tarbolton; one *s* one *d. Educ:* Univs of Leeds, London, Breslau, Munich. Geologist on Scottish Spitsbergen Expedition of 1919; Senior Lectr in Geology in Univ. of Manchester, 1919-21; Member Senate, Queen's Univ., 1938-54; Member Charlemont Cttee on Industrial and Mineral Resources, NI, 1924-26; Mem. Scientific Research Grants Advisory Board, NI, 1929-32 (Chm. Board, 1935-41); Indep. Member several Trade Boards, NI, and Chairman several Wages Councils, NI, 1945-; Apptd Member Nat. Arbitration Tribunal, NI, 1941-59; Chairman, Sen. Certificate Examination enquiry, NI, 1948-50; Geological Adviser to Ministries of Agriculture, Commerce and Finance, NI, 1924-47; Mem. Unemployment Insurance Statutory Cttee, 1944-47; Mem. Nat. Insurance Advisory Cttee, 1947-60. Neill Prize Royal Society Edin., 1954; Prestwich Medal, Geological Soc., London, 1957. Hon. DSc Queen's Univ., Belfast, 1957. *Publications:* The Geology of Ireland: an introduction, 1953 (reprint 1966); The Quaternary Era, 1957 (reprint 1966); Historical Geology of Ireland, 1963; geological papers. *Address:* Corrig, Ballycastle, Co. Antrim, Northern Ireland. *[Died 26 Jan. 1972.*

CHARLEY, Sir Philip (Belmont), Kt 1968; President, Royal Agricultural Society of NSW, 1965-69, Vice-Patron, 1969; *b* Richmond, NSW, 28 Dec. 1893; *s* of late P. Charley, Richmond, NSW; *m* 1st, 1923, N. M. Nivison; one *s* three *d*; 2nd, 1957, Myfanwy Rickard. *Educ:* Barker Coll., Hornsby, Sydney. Farming and dairying, Clarendon Park, from 1919. Served European War, 1914-18, as Gunner 5 Bde, AFA; served War of 1939-45: Lieut in AFC, Flt-Lieut ATC, RAAF, 1943-45. *Recreations:* racing, Rugby, cricket, swimming. *Address:* 59

Junction Road, Wahroonga, NSW 2076, Australia. *T:* Sydney 482000. *Clubs:* Union, Air Force Officers' (Sydney); Ex-Servicemen (Richmond). *[Died* 7 *Feb.* 1976.

CHARLTON, George James; artist; Member of Staff of Slade School of Art, 1919-62; examiner for General School Examinations, University of London since 1931 and Associated Examining Board since 1959; *b* 1899; *s* of James William Charlton, London; *m* 1929, Daphne, *d* of Conrad Gribble, MICE, Weybridge. Student, Slade School, 1914, at age of fifteen (Slade and Robert Ross Scholarships). Served European War, 1917-19. Senior Lecturer in charge of Slade School, 1948-49; examiner for Board of Education Art Examinations, 1932-45, 1949-50-51; member of staff of Willesden School of Art, 1949-59; exhibitor at New English Art Club from 1915, member 1925-45, 1950-, Hon. Treasurer, 1958; works purchased by Tate Gallery, Contemporary Art Society and Bradford Art Gallery; exhibitor at London, provincial and overseas galleries. Formerly Governor: Camberwell School of Art; Trent Park Coll.; Farnham School of Art, 1950-60. *Publications:* Illustration for Wolff's Anatomy for Artists; for T. F. Powys' Mr Weston's Good Wine, 1st edn; for Richard Hughes' The Spider's Palace; articles on Prof. Henry Tonks and on Prof. Frederick Brown in Dictionary of National Biography. *Address:* 40 New End Square, Hampstead, NW3. *[Died* 12 *Sept.* 1979.

CHARQUES, Mrs Dorothy, (Mrs S. A. G. Emms); novelist since 1937; *b* 4 June 1899; *d* of Benjamin and Florence Margaret Taylor, Arrow, Alcester, Warwicks; *m* 1929, Richard Charques, author and critic; no *c*; *m* 1964, S. A. G. Emms, inventor and consultant engineer. *Educ:* Alcester Grammar Sch.; Sheffield Univ. BA Hons. Econ. (Sheffield); MA History. *Publications:* with Richard Charques, 2 novels: Above and Below, 1929, After The Party, 1933; alone: The Tramp and His Woman, 1937; Between Sleeping and Waking, 1938; Time's Harvest (a trilogy comprising: Time's Harvest, 1940, The Returning Heart, 1943, Between the Twilights, 1946); Men Like Shadows, 1952; The Valley, 1954; The Dark Stranger, 1956; The Nunnery, 1959; A Wind from the Sea, 1971. *Recreations:* reading, walking; looking and seeing, generally out of doors. *Address:* 159 Banbury Road, Stratford upon Avon, Warwicks. *T:* Stratford upon Avon 5648. *[Died* 20 *March* 1976.

CHARRINGTON, Sir John, Kt 1949; President, Charrington, Gardner, Locket & Co. Ltd, since 1964 (Chairman, 1940-64); *b* 1886; *s* of late John Charrington, Shenley, Herts, and Rose Georgiana Elizabeth Grainger; *m* 1912, Elizabeth Mary Dalbiac (*d* 1977); two *s* three *d*. *Educ:* Haileybury. Served European War, 1914-18 (despatches). President: Coal Merchants Federation of Great Britain, 1930-31 and 1947-49; National Society for Clean Air; Coal Utilisation Council, 1967-68. *Address:* Bay Tree House, Aston Rowant, Oxford. *T:* Kingston Blount 51335. *Club:* Carlton. *[Died* 16 *July* 1977.

CHARRINGTON, John Arthur Pepys; late President, Bass Charrington Ltd (formerly Chairman Charrington United Breweries Ltd from formation; previously Chairman Charrington & Co. Ltd); *b* 17 Feb. 1905; *s* of Arthur Finch Charrington and Dorothea Lethbridge; *m* 1st, Barbara Haliburton Cunard (marr. diss); three *s* two *d*; 2nd, Daphne Coleman. *Educ:* Eton; New College, Oxford. *Address:* Netherton House, Andover, Hampshire. *T:* Linkenholt 230. *Club:* Bath. *[Died* 23 *Oct.* 1979.

CHASE, Rt. Rev. George Armitage, MC; DD (*hc*), Cambridge, Leeds; STD (*hc*), Ripon College, USA; Bishop of Ripon, 1946-April 1959, retired; Fellow of Selwyn College, Cambridge; Hon. Fellow of Trinity Hall and Queens' College; *b* 3 Sept. 1886; 3rd *s* of late Rt Rev. Frederic Henry Chase. *Educ:* Rugby School; Queens' Coll., Cambridge (Carus Prize, 1909; Crosse Schol., 1910; Hulsean Prize, 1911). Ordained, 1911; Curate of Portsea, 1911-13; Fellow and Dean of Trinity Hall, 1913-34; Tutor, 1919-34; Master of Selwyn Coll., Cambridge, 1934-46; Univ. Lectr in Divinity, 1926-46; TCF, 1914-19; MC, 1917; Hon. Canon of Ely Cathedral, 1945-46. Examining Chaplain to Bishop of Ely, 1914-24 and 1935-46, to Bishop of Southwark, 1919-32, to Bishop of Winchester, 1932-42, to Archbishop of York, 1942-46. *Publication:* A Companion to the Revised Psalter, 1963. *Address:* 36 Millington Road, Cambridge.

[Died 30 *Nov.* 1971.

CHASE, Mary Ellen, PhD; Professor of English Literature, Smith College, Northampton, Mass, 1929-55, now Emeritus Professor; *b* 24 Feb. 1887; *d* of Edward Everett Chase and Edith Lord. *Educ:* Blue Hill Academy, Blue Hill, Maine; Univ. of Maine (BA 1909); Univ. of Minnesota (MA 1918, PhD 1922). Asst Prof., 1922-26, Associate Prof., 1926-29, Smith Coll. Hon. LittD: Univ. of Maine, 1928; Bowdoin Coll., 1933; Hon. LHD:

Colby Coll., 1937; Northeastern Univ., 1948; Smith Coll., 1949; Wilson Coll., 1957; Hon. LLD: Goucher Coll., 1960. Phi Beta Kappa, 1920. *Publications:* Mary Christmas (novel), 1927; A Goodly Heritage, 1932; Mary Peters (novel), 1934; Silas Crockett (novel), 1935; Dawn in Lyonnesse (novel), 1937; A Goodly Fellowship, 1939; Windswept (novel), 1941; The Bible and the Common Reader, 1944; Jonathan Fisher: Maine Parson, 1948; The Plum Tree (novel), 1949; The White Gate, 1955; Life and Language in the Old Testament, 1956; The Edge of Darkness (novel), 1957; The Lovely Ambition (novel), 1960; The Psalms for the Common Reader, 1963; A Journey to Boston, 1965; A Walk on an Iceberg, 1966. *Address:* 16 Paradise Road, Northampton, Mass 01060, USA. *[Died* 28 *July* 1973.

CHASTENET de CASTAING, Jacques, CBE 1938; Croix de Guerre, 1916; Grand Officier de la Légion d'Honneur, 1968; Grand Croix, Ordre du mérite, 1974; LLD Paris; historian and journalist; member of Académie française, 1956, and of Académie des Sciences morales et politiques, 1947; *b* 20 April 1893; *s* of G. Chastenet de Castaing, a French Senator; *m* 1919, Germaine Saladin; two *s*. *Educ:* Université de Paris. Served European War, 1914-19; Liaison officer with the American EF, 1918; French Diplomatic Service, 1919; Attaché, 1919; General Secretary, Rhineland inter-allied High Commission, 1920; Secrétaire d'Ambassade, 1921; diplomatic correspondent, L'Opinion, 1926; Editor of Le Temps, 1931; Major, French Military Mission in Egypt, 1945. *Publications:* Du Sénat, 1919; William Pitt, 1941; Godoy, 1943; Wellington, 1945; Vingt Ans d'histoire diplomatique (1920-1940), 1945; Le Siècle de Victoria, 1947; Poincaré, 1948; La France de M. Fallieres, 1949; Histoire de la IIIe République, 7 Vols, 1952-62; Elizabeth the 1st, 1953; Winston Churchill et l'Angleterre du XX Siècle, 1956; Vie quotidienne au début du règne de Victoria, 1961; L'Angleterre d'aujourd'hui, 1965; En avant vers l'Ouest, 1967; Léon Gambetta, 1968; De Pétain à de Gaulle, 1970; Cent ans de République (9 vols), 1970; Quatre Fois Vingt Ans, 1974; Une Epoque de Contestation, 1976; contribs to l'Opinion, le Figaro, la Revue de Paris, le Temps, Paris-Presse, L'Aurore, La Revue des Deux-Mondes, etc. *Address:* 14 rue d'Aumale, Paris 9e; Château de Carles, Saillans, Gironde, France. *Club:* L'Union (Paris). *[Died* 7 *Feb.* 1978.

CHATER, Maj.-Gen. Arthur Reginald, CB 1941; CVO 1966; DSO 1918; OBE 1931; *b* 7 Feb. 1896; *s* of Thomas Addison Chater and Gertrude Lockyer Peel; *m* 1954, Diana, *o d* of late Edward Charles Daubeny, and *widow* of Maj.-Gen. Archibald Maxwell Craig. *Educ:* Aldenham. Entered Royal Marines as 2nd Lieut, 1913; served with RM Brigade in Flanders, 1914 (wounded at Antwerp); Gallipoli, 1915 (despatches, French Croix de Guerre); Grand Fleet, 1916-17; was Adjt of RM Bn which landed from HMS Vindictive at Zeebrugge on 23 April 1918 (DSO, Bt Major); served in Egyptian Army, 1921-25, and Sudan Defence Forces, 1925-31; commanded Sudan Camel Corps, 1927-30; commanded Military Operations in Kordofan, 1929-30 (despatches); Senior RM Officer, East Indies Station, 1931-33; Home Fleet, 1935-36; commanded Somaliland Camel Corps, 1937-40; commanded defence of British Somaliland, 1940 (despatches, CB); Military Governor and comd Troops, British Somaliland, 1941-43; comd Portsmouth Div. Royal Marines, 1943-44; Director of Combined Operations, India and SE Asia, 1944-45; MGGS, 1945-46, comd Chatham Group, Royal Marines, 1946-48; retired pay, 1948. One of HM's Body Guard of Hon. Corps of Gentlemen-at-Arms, 1949-66 and Harbinger, 1952-66; Col Comdt Somaliland Scouts, 1948-58. Member Berkshire CC, 1955-61. *Address:* Copford Place, Copford, near Colchester, Essex. *T:* Colchester 210042. *Club:* Naval and Military. *[Died* 3 *Jan.* 1979.

CHAU TSUN-NIN, Sir, Kt 1956; CBE 1938; *b* 22 Oct. 1893; *s* of late Hon. Chau Siu Ki and of Mrs Chau; *m* 1931, Elaine Leung; four *s* one *d*. *Educ:* St Stephen's Coll., Hong Kong; The Queen's Coll., Oxford (MA). Barrister-at-law, Middle Temple. Unofficial Member of Legislative Council, Hong Kong, 1931-53; Unofficial MEC, Hong Kong, 1946-59. Hon. LLD Univ. of Hong Kong. *Address:* No. 8, Queen's Road West, Hong Kong. *[Died* 27 *Jan.* 1971.

CHAUVEL, Jean Michel Henri, GCMG (Hon.) 1960; GCVO (Hon.) 1957; Grand Croix de la Légion d'Honneur; Grand Croix de l'Etoile Noire; Grand Croix de Malte; Hon. DCL Internat. Oxford; *b* Paris, 16 April 1897; *s* of Ferdinand Chauvel and Mme Chauvel (*née* Derrien); *m* 1926, Diane de Warzee d'Hermalle; two *s* two *d*. *Educ:* Université de Paris (Licencié en Droit). Foreign Affairs, 1921-40; subsequently, consecutively, Third, Second and First Secretary, Consul-General, and Minister. Founder of Study Group, Foreign Affairs (Resistance); Delegate in France of Commn of Foreign Affairs of Algiers, 1944; acting Sec.-Gen., Foreign Affairs Commn,

Algiers, 1944; Ambassador of France and Sec.-Gen. of Foreign Affairs, 1945; Perm. Representative of France at Security Council, United Nations, 1949; Ambassador of France at Berne, 1951; Delegate at Conference of Geneva, 1954; Delegate at Manila Conference, 1954; Ambassador of France and High Commissioner in Austria, 1954; Ambassador of France in London, 1955-62; Delegate at the Geneva Conference (Laos), 1961-62; Diplomatic Counsellor of Govt, 1962-63. *Publications:* Préludes, 1945; D'une eau profonde, 1948; Labyrinthe, 1950; Infidèle, 1951; Imaginaires, 1952; Clepsydre, 1958; Sables, 1963; Commentaire, 1971; L'aventure terrestre de Jean Arthur Rimbaud, 1971; Commentaire II, 1972; Commentaire III, 1973. *Address:* 123 Rue de la Tour, 75016 Paris; Le Ruluet, Combrit, Finistère. *Clubs:* Union, Union Interalliée (Paris).
[Died 31 *May* 1979.

CHAYTOR, Sir William Henry Clervaux, 7th Bt *cr* 1831; *b* 4 May 1914; *o s* of Sir Edmund Hugh Chaytor, 6th Bt and Isobel (who *m* 2nd, 1935, Edwin Burton Fiske, and died 1968), *d* of Thomas Scott, Darlington; *S* father, 1935; *m* 1947, Mrs Patricia Alderman; one *d. Educ:* Chillon Coll., Switzerland. *Heir: kinsman* George Reginald Chaytor, *b* 1913. *Address:* Flat 3, Bridlemere, Newmarket, Suffolk. *T:* 2491. *[Died* 5 *Sept.* 1976.

CHENEVIX-TRENCH, Anthony, MA (Oxon); FRSE 1978; Head Master, Fettes College, Edinburgh, since 1971; *b* 10 May 1919; *s* of late C. G. Chenevix-Trench, CIE; *m* 1953, Elizabeth Chalmers, *e d* of late Capt. Sir Stewart Spicer, 3rd Bt, RN retd, and Lady Spicer, Chichester, Sussex; two *s* twin *d. Educ:* Shrewsbury Sch.; Christ Church, Oxford. Classical Schol. Christ Church, 1st Cl. Hon. Mods, De Paravicini Schol. Served War of 1939-45; joined RA 1939: seconded Indian Artillery (4th Hazara Mountain Battery, Frontier Force), 1940; served Malaya (Capt.), POW Singapore, 1942, released 1945). 1st Class Lit. Hum., and Prox. Acc., Craven and Ireland Scholarships, 1948. Asst Master, Shrewsbury Sch., 1948; Tutor in Classics, Christ Church, Oxford, 1951; House Master, Shrewsbury Sch. (Sch. House), 1952; Headmaster, Bradfield Coll., Berks, 1955-63; Head Master, Eton College, 1964-70. Mem., Robbins Cttee on Higher Education, 1961. FRSA. JP Berks, 1960-71. OStJ (Scotland) 1974. *Recreations:* shooting and general outdoor activities. *Address:* The Lodge, Fettes College, Edinburgh EH4 1QX. *T:* 031-332 2281; Penn Cottage, Watlington, near King's Lynn, Norfolk. *T:* King's Lynn 810673. *Clubs:* East India, Devonshire, Sports and Public Schools; Vincent's (Oxford).
[Died 21 *June* 1979.

CHENEVIX-TRENCH, Brig. Ralph, CB 1940; OBE 1919; MC; *b* 15 Dec. 1885; *s* of Col C. Chenevix-Trench; *m* 1916, Meriel Edith Jelf; one *s* one *d* (and one *s* killed in action, 1943). *Educ:* Wellington Coll.; RMA Woolwich. Commissioned Royal Engineers, 1905; Asst Dir Posts and Telegraphs, Sudan, 1913-16; Darfur Campaign, 1916 (MC); European War in France and North Russia, 1917-19 (despatches thrice, OBE); transferred to Royal Signals, 1920; GSO1 and Dep. Dir Staff Duties, War Office, 1934-37; Comdt Signal Training Centre, 1938-39; Maj.-Gen. BEF, 1939-40 (CB); Signal Officer-in-Chief, Home Forces, 1940; retired pay, 1941. *Publications:* Gold Medal Essay of Royal United Service Institution, 1921; Bertrand-Steward Essay in Army Quarterly, 1931. *Recreation:* gardening. *Address:* Little Westport, Westport Road, Wareham, Dorset.
[Died 1 *May* 1974.

CHERRY, Prof. (Edward) Colin; Henry Mark Pease Professor of Telecommunication at Imperial College, University of London, since 1958; *b* 23 June 1914; *s* of Arthur and Margaret Cherry; *m* 1956, Heather Blanche White; two *d. Educ:* St Alban's; University of London. Student, with General Electric Company (Research Laboratories), 1932-36; studied for London BSc at the same time (as evening student at Northampton Polytechnic). BSc 1936, MSc 1940, DSc 1955. Research Staff of General Electric Company, 1936-45, being seconded during part of War years to Min. of Aircraft Production for radar research. Lectr, College of Technology, Manchester, 1945-47; Reader in Telecommunication, Imperial Coll. of Science and Technology, 1949-58. Marconi International Fellowship Award, 1978. Hon. ACGI. *Publications:* On Human Communication, 1957; World Communication-Threat or Promise?, 1971; numerous scientific papers on theory of electric circuits, on telecommunication principles and on the psychology of speech and hearing. *Recreations:* gardening, foreign travel, watercolour. *Address:* Combe House, Chichester Road, Dorking, Surrey. *T:* Dorking 882021. *[Died* 23 *Nov.* 1979.

CHESHIRE, Geoffrey Chevalier, FBA 1945; DCL; Barrister-at-Law; Hon. Fellow of Merton College and of Exeter College, Oxford; Hon. Master of the Bench of Lincoln's Inn; Hon. LLD: Manchester University; London University; Jadavpur

University, Calcutta; *b* Hartford, Ches, 27 June 1886; 2nd *s* of Walter Christopher Cheshire, Solicitor and Registrar of Northwich County Court, Ches; *m* 1st, 1915, Primrose Barstow (*d* 1962), 2nd *d* of Col T. A. A. Barstow, Seaforth Highlanders; two *s*; 2nd, 1963, Dame Mary (Kathleen) Lloyd, DBE (*d* 1972). *Educ:* Denstone Coll.; Merton Coll., Oxford. 1st Class Hon. Sch. of Jurisprudence, 1908; 2nd Cl. BCL 1910; Inns of Court Studentship, 1911. Lectr at University Coll. of Wales, Aberystwyth, 1909 and 1910; Fellow of Exeter Coll., Oxford, 1912-44; Bursar, 1919-33; All Souls Lecturer in Private International Law, 1922-33; All Souls Reader in English Law, 1933-44; Vinerian Prof. of English Law, Oxford, and Fellow of All Souls Coll., 1944-49; Mem. of Lord Chancellor's Cttee on Foreign Marriages, 1939; Deleg. to Hague Conf. on Codification of Private Internat. Law, 1951; Mem. Lord Chancellor's Cttee on Private Internat. Law, 1952-57; Mem. of the Inst. of Internat. Law, 1950-65. Served European War, Cheshire Regt, 1914-16; RFC (Kite-Balloon Section), 1916-18, Capt; Home Guard, 1940. *Publications:* Investigation of Charges in the RAF, 1919; Modern Law of Real Property, 1925, 11th and 12th edns, ed by E. H. Burn, 1972 and 1976; Private International Law, 1935, 9th edn by P. M. North, 1974; (with C. H. S. Fifoot) The Law of Contract, 1945, 9th edn (ed M. P. Furmston), 1976; International Contracts, 1948; (Gen. Ed.) Stephen's Commentaries, 19th edn; The Private International Law of Husband and Wife, 1963. *Address:* Laundry Cottage, Empshott, Liss, Hants. *[Died* 27 *Oct.* 1978.

CHESHIRE, Commandant Dame Mary (Kathleen), DBE 1952 (OBE 1946); *b* 31 May 1902; *d* of late A. J. Lloyd and late Mrs Lloyd; *m* 1963, Geoffrey Chevalier Cheshire. *Educ:* Ursuline Convent, Wimbledon. Joined WRNS, 1939; served as motor transport driver, and a writer, while a rating. Commissioned, 1940; Actg Supt, WRNS Portsmouth Command, 1946; Asst Dir Women's Royal Naval Service, 1948; Superintendent, Training and Drafting, HM Training Establishment Dauntless, Burghfield, near Reading, Berks; Superintendent, 1949; Dir Women's Royal Naval Service, 1950-54; Hon. Naval ADC to the Queen, 1952-54. *Address:* Laundry Cottage, Empshott, Liss, Hants. *[Died* 3 *April* 1972.

CHESHIRE, Air Chief Marshal Sir Walter (Graemes), GBE 1965 (CBE 1949); KCB 1959 (CB 1955); idc; psa; Member, Commonwealth War Graves Commission, 1968-74, Vice-Chairman, 1970-74; *b* 21 March 1907; *s* of late John F. Cheshire, Beckenham, Kent; *m* 1940, Mary, *d* of late Col E. W. Chance, OBE, TD; two *s. Educ:* Ipswich Sch.; Downing Coll., Cambridge. Commnd into RAF, 1926; Sqdn Ldr, 1937; RAF Staff Coll., 1938; various appts, Bomber Command; Air Attaché, Moscow; on staff HQ, ACSEA, 1939-45; AOC French Indo-China, 1945-46; idc 1949; AOC Gibraltar, 1950-52; Comdt RAF Staff Coll., Andover, 1952-53; Air Officer in charge of Administration, HQ 2nd TAF, 1953-55; AOC No 13 Group, Fighter Command, 1955-57; RAF Instructor at Imperial Defence Coll., 1957-59; AOC, RAF Malta, and Dep. C-in-C (Air), Allied Forces, Mediterranean, 1959-61; Mem. for Personnel, Air Council, 1961-64; Air ADC to the Queen, 1963-65; Air Mem. for Personnel, Min. of Defence, 1964-65; retired, 1965. *Address:* 30 Courtenay Place, Belmore Lane, Lymington, Hants. *Club:* Royal Air Force. *[Died* 10 *Dec.* 1978.

CHESNEY, Kathleen, MA, DPhil, DLitt; Principal, Westfield College (University of London), 1951-62; *b* 26 April 1899; *d* of Edward Shuldham Chesney. *Educ:* The Manor House, Brondesbury; Lady Margaret Hall, Oxford. MA 1926; DPhil Oxon, 1929; DLitt Oxon, 1953. Tutor in Modern Languages, St Hilda's Coll., Oxford, 1923, Fellow, 1924; University Lecturer in French, 1937; Vice-Principal of St Hilda's, 1941. Hon. Fellow of St Hilda's Coll., 1951, of Lady Margaret Hall, 1962, of Westfield Coll., 1963. *Publications:* Oeuvres Poétiques de Guillaume Crétin (Paris), 1932; Fleurs de Rhétorique, from Villon to Marot (Oxford), 1950; Poèmes de Transition, Medium Ævum Monographs VIII, 1965; articles in Medium Ævum, French Studies, etc. *Address:* Barber's Cross, Watlington, Oxford. *Club:* University Women's. *[Died* 12 *April* 1976.

CHESSER, Eustace; lecturer and consulting psychiatrist; *b* Edinburgh, 22 March 1902; 2nd *s* of Arthur Chesser; *m* 1st, 1926, Rose Morris, Durham (*d* 1960); one *s* one *d*; 2nd, 1961, Sheila Blayney-Jones. *Educ:* George Watson's, Edinburgh; Royal Colleges. LRCP, LRCS, LRFPS, 1926. Hon. Sec. Soc. for Sex Education and Guidance (from inception until Dec. 1953). Member: The Royal Institution; Medico-Legal Council; Abortion Law Reform Assoc.; Married Women's Assoc.; Marriage Law Reform Soc. (Sponsor); Royal Medico-Psychological Soc.; Assoc. for Advancement of Psychotherapy; Brit. Exec. Cttee Internat. Union of Family Organizations; Brit. Social Biology Council; Soc. for Study of Addiction;

International Cttee for Sexual Equality, Amsterdam (Mem. Council). Research Director, Research Council into Marriage and Human Relationships; Hon. Surgeon Dilke Mem. Hosp. FRSocMed. *Publications:* Love Without Fear, 1941; Marriage and Freedom, 1943; Unwanted Child, 1945; Grow Up-And Live, 1949; Successful Living, 1950; Cruelty to Children, 1951; Unquiet Minds, 1952; How to Make a Success of your Marriage, 1952; Humanly Speaking, 1954; The Sexual, Marital and Family Relationships of the English Woman, 1956; Live and Let Live, 1958; Psychology of Everyday Living, 1958; Woman, 1959; Outline of Human Relationships, 1959; Odd Man Out, 1959; Life is for Living, 1962; Woman and Love, 1962; Is Chastity Outmoded?, 1962; When and How to Stop Smoking, 1963; The Cost of Loving, 1964; Challenge of the Middle Years, 1964; Shelley and Zastrozzi: Self-revelation of a Neurotic, 1965; Unmarried Love, 1965; Living with Suicide, 1967; Sex and the Married Woman, 1969; Who Do You Think You Are?, 1970; The Human Aspects of Sexual Deviation, 1971; contributor, Chambers's Encyclopædia. *Recreations:* ideas, places, people and things. *Address:* 17 Wimpole Street, W1. *T:* 01-580 4707.
[Died 5 Dec. 1973.

CHETHAM-STRODE, Warren, MC 1916; author and playwright since 1932; *b* 28 Jan. 1896; *yr s* of Dr Chetham-Strode; *m* 1927, Moira Hamilton Verschoyle; (one *s* decd). *Educ:* Sherborne Sch. Served War of 1914-18, Capt., 3rd Bn The Border Regt, 2nd Bn, and Tank Corps. British American Tobacco Co., 1919-22, USA and S India. In business, 1922-32. Attached Military Affairs Branch, MOI and WO, 1939; Commercial Relations Div. and Overseas General Div., MOI, 1940-45. *Publications: novels:* Mice and Management, 1932; Three Men and a Girl, 1958; Top of the Milk, 1959; The Years of Alison (USA), 1961; A Cat Called Tootoo (a book for children), 1966; Tootoo's Friends at the Farm, 1967; Tootoo the Travelling Cat, 1968; A Short Walk: an autobiography of youth; *plays:* Sometimes Even Now, Embassy, 1933; Man Proposes, Wyndhams, 1933; Heart's Content, Shaftesbury, 1936; The Day is Gone, Embassy, 1937; Strangers Road, on tour, 1942; Young Mrs Barrington, Winter Garden, 1945; The Guinea-Pig, Criterion, 1946; A Play for Ronnie, on tour, 1946; The Gleam, Globe, 1946; Background, Westminster, 1950; The Pet Shop, St Martin's, 1954; Silver and Gold, Connaught, Worthing, 1954; The Stepmother, St Martin's, 1958; *radio serial play:* The Barlowes of Beddington; *TV serial play:* The Happy Man; Sinister Street (adapted from the novel by Compton Mackenzie); *films:* Return to Night; The Gay Pursuit; The Guinea-Pig; Odette; The Lady with a Lamp; Background. *Address:* The Oast House, Playden, near Rye, Sussex. *T:* Iden 254. *Club:* Rye Dormy House.   *[Died 26 April 1974.*

CHETWYND, Sir (Arthur Henry) Talbot, 7th Bt *cr* 1795; OBE 1919; MC; late Captain, 9th Lancers; *b* 13 April 1887; *s* of late Arthur Chetwynd; *S* cousin, 1938; *m* 1st, 1914, Evelyn Margaret (who obtained a divorce, 1940), *d* of late Leonard Andrews; 2nd, 1940, Violet Mary (*d* 1955), *d* of William Charles Cripps, Camden Park, Tunbridge Wells; 3rd, 1956, Frances Audrey Boumphrey, *o d* of late Dr Flawith-Smith. *Educ:* Wellington Coll., Berks. Served European War, 1914-19 (despatches twice, OBE, MC); Colonel Commanding Frontiers Camel Corps and Cars Patrols, 1924-30; War of 1939-45, Commandant War Reserve and Special Constabulary and Police Staff Officer for the County of Monmouthshire. 4th Class, Order of Nile, 1930. *Heir: n* Arthur Ralph Talbot Chetwynd [*b* 28 Oct. 1913; *m* 1940, Marjory May MacDonald, *e d* of late Robert Bruce Lang, Vancouver, BC; two *s*]. *Address:* Firs Cottage, Belmore Lane, Lymington, Hants. *T:* Lymington 4238. *Clubs:* Naval and Military; Royal Lymington Yacht.   *[Died 24 July 1972.*

CHETWYND, Sir Talbot; *see* Chetwynd, Sir A. H. T.

CHEVALIER, Maurice; Officier, Légion d'Honneur, 1969; stage and film actor; *b* 12 Sept. 1888; *m* 1926, Yvonne Vallée (marr. diss. 1935); no *c. Educ:* Menilmontant Primary Sch., Paris. From small cafés in Paris at the age of twelve to a one-man show in the greatest theatres in the whole world. Croix de Guerre; Legion of Honour. *Films include:* The Innocents of Paris, The Love Parade, Merry Widow, I have Seven Daughters, Love in the Afternoon, Gigi, etc. *Publications:* Ma Route et Mes Chansons (ten books of autobiography); I Remember It Well, 1971. *Recreations:* walking, writing. *Address:* La Louque, Marnes-La-Coquette 92, France.   *[Died 1 Jan. 1972.*

CHEVASSÛT, Rev. Canon Frederick George; Canon Emeritus, Manchester, 1968; *b* 28 Jan. 1889; *e s* of late Rev. Canon Frederick George Chevassût; unmarried. *Educ:* Manchester Univ. (BSc); Trinity Coll., Cambridge (Exhibitioner, æq. Abbott Scholarship, BA, Senior Optime, 1912; 2nd Class Theological Tripos Part 2, 1913; MA 1919; Ridley Hall, Cambridge. Asst

Curate, Bolton Parish Church, 1913-15; served in Army (Lieut RFA), 1915-19; Warden of St Anselm Hall, Manchester Univ., 1919-22; Special Service Priest, Manchester Diocese, 1922-26; Rector of St George's, Hulme, Manchester, 1926-68; Hon. Canon of Manchester, 1955-68. Warden Toc H Hostel, Hulme, 1926; Sec. Manchester Corp. Advisory Cttee on Hulme Clearance, 1934-35. *Publications:* occasional articles and reviews. *Recreations:* general reading, mountain walking. *Address:* 155 Chester Road, Manchester M15 4JB.
[Died 2 Jan. 1974.

CHEYLESMORE, 4th Baron (UK) *cr* 1887; **Francis Ormond Henry Eaton,** DSO 1917; Lieut-Colonel; late Captain 3rd Battalion Grenadier Guards; *b* 19 June 1893; *e s* of 3rd Baron and Elizabeth Richardson (*d* 1945), *d* of late F. O. French, New York; *S* father, 1925; *m* 1929, Pearl Margaret, *d* of late A. J. Sundberg, Alix, Alberta, Canada. *Educ:* Eton; Trinity Coll., Cambridge; RMC Sandhurst. Served European War, 1914-19 (DSO); served War of 1939-45, RCOC (CA), 1941-45. *Heir:* none. *Address:* Happy Valley Ranch, Alix, Alberta, Canada.
[Died 21 April 1974 (ext).

CHEYNE, James, CMG 1950; *b* 7 Oct. 1894; *s* of late James Cheyne, Umtali, Rhodesia; *m* 1923, Minnie Mary Elizabeth Gordon, *d* of late George Barron Beattie, Aberdeen; one *d. Educ:* Robert Gordon's Coll., Aberdeen. Served European War, 1917-18; entered Colonial Service, Administrative Officer in Tanganyika Territory, 1918; Provincial Commissioner, 1941; Secretary for African Affairs, 1948; Mem. for Local Govt, Tanganyika Territory, 1950; retd 1951. *Address:* Glenwood, West Moors, Dorset. *T:* Ferndown 3102.
[Died 2 March 1973.

CHIANG, Yee, BSc; LHD; DLit; FRSA; FAAS; Professor of Chinese, Columbia University, USA, 1970-72; now Emeritus Professor; *b* 19 May 1903; *s* of Chiang Ho-an and Tsai Hsiang-Lin. *Educ:* Nat. South-Eastern Univ., Nanking. Teacher of Chemistry in two different middle schools; Lecturer in Chemistry at National Chi-Nan Univ.; soldier in the Chinese Army for one year; Asst Editor of a daily newspaper at Hangchow in Chekiang province; District Governor of four districts, Kiukiang, Yushan, Tangtu, and Wuhu in Kiangsi and Anhui provinces; Lecturer in Chinese at Sch. of Oriental Studies, London Univ., 1935-38; in charge of Chinese Section at Wellcome Historical Medical Museum, 1938-40. Designed the décor and costumes for the Sadler's Wells Ballet, The Birds, 1942; Curator of Chinese Ethnology, Peabody Museum, Salem, Massachusetts, USA, 1956-; Ralph Waldo Emerson Fellow in Poetry, Harvard Univ., 1958-59; Vis. Prof. of Chinese, ANU, 1972-73. Mem. Sub-Cttee on New Art Center for Univ. of Virginia, 1962; Senior Specialist, East-West Center, 1967. Hon. LHD Hofstra; Hon. LittD ANU; Hon. DArt, Rider; Hon. DLitt Hong Kong. *Publications:* a Book of poems in Chinese, 1935; The Chinese Eye, 1935; The Silent Traveller in Lakeland, 1937; Chinese Calligraphy, 1938; The Silent Traveller in London, 1938; Birds and Beasts, 1939; Chinpao and the Giant Panda, 1939; The Silent Traveller in Wartime, 1939; A Chinese Childhood, 1940; The Silent Traveller in the Yorkshire Dales, 1941; Lo Cheng, the Boy who wouldn't keep still, 1941; Chinpao at the Zoo, 1941; The Men of the Burma Road, 1942; The Story of Ming, 1943; The Silent Traveller in Oxford, 1944; Dabbitse, 1944; Yebbin, 1947; The Silent Traveller in Edinburgh, 1948; The Silent Traveller in New York, 1950; Chinese Painting, 1953; The Silent Traveller in Dublin, 1955; The Silent Traveller in Paris, 1956; The Silent Traveller in Boston, 1959; The Silent Traveller in San Francisco, 1964; Chinese Ch'an Poetry, 1966; The Silent Traveller in Japan, 1971; China Revisited, 1977; contributed many articles to various English and American papers and magazines. *Recreations:* calligraphy, painting, walking, travelling and climbing. *Address:* c/o W. W. Norton Co., 500 Fifth Avenue, New York, NY 10036, USA; c/o Methuen & Co. Ltd, 11 New Fetter Lane, EC4.
[Died 17 Oct. 1977.

CHIANG KAI-SHEK, Generalissimo, Hon. GCB 1942; *b* 31 Oct. 1887; *s* of Chiang Sohan, Chekiang Province; *m* 1927, Mayling Soong, Chinese sociologist; (two *s* by a previous marriage). Visited Japan 1906, where he first met Dr Sun Yat-Sen and other revolutionary leaders; studied at National Military Acad., Paoting, North China, 1906, and at Tokyo Military Acad.; joined Dr Sun's revolutionary party, 1907; joined revolutionary army, Shanghai, on outbreak of Chinese Revolution, Oct. 1911; followed Dr Sun to Canton and attached to Gen. Headquarters, 1918-20; sent by Dr Sun to Soviet Russia to study military and social System, 1923; founder and principal, Whampoa Military Acad., Canton, 1924, which provided all officers to Northern Expeditionary Forces; elected member of Central Exec. Cttee of Kuomintang, 1926; C-in-C Northern Expeditionary Forces,

1926-28; Chairman of State Council and Generalissimo of all fighting services, 1928, following establishment of National Govt at Nanking; resigned both posts, 1931; inaugurated New Life Movement, 1934; Tsungtsai (Director-General) of Kuomintang Party, Republic of China, 1938; Chairman of Supreme National Defence Council, 1939-47; Chairman of National Military Affairs Council, 1932-46; Chairman of People's Political Council (war-time parliament), 1939-40; Pres. of Executive Yuan, 1935-38 and 1939-45; Head of Supreme Policy Council, Canton, 1949. Chairman National Govt of Republic of China, 1943; elected President of Republic of China, 1948, under new constitution; retired, 1949; resumed Presidency (in Taiwan), 1950; elected for second term, 1954; re-elected President, 1960, 1966, 1972, Dir-Gen., Kuomintang Party, 1969. Chm. National Security Council, 1967. Hon. PhD St John's Univ., NY, 1971. Holds many foreign orders and decorations, incl. Croix de Guerre. *Publications:* China's Destiny, 1943; Soviet Russia in China, 1957; chap. on National Fecundity; Social Welfare, Education, Health and Happiness. *Address:* Office of the President, Taipei, Taiwan (Formosa). *T:* 313731.   *[Died 5 April 1975.*

CHICHESTER, Lieut-Col Arthur O'Neill Cubitt, OBE 1941; MC 1918; *b* 14 July 1889; *s* of Canon E. A. Chichester and Hon. Mrs M. A. Chichester; *m* 1924, Hilda Grace, *d* of Rt Hon. W. R. Young, Galgorm Castle, Ballymena; three *d. Educ:* Wellington Coll.; Trinity Coll., Cambridge. Served European War, 1914-18, Surrey Yeomanry; Clerk, House of Lords, 1919-21; Clerk of Parliaments, N Ireland, 1928-45; served War, 1939-41, comdg 102 HAA Regts, RA; Director: Braidwater Spinning Co., Ballymena; Stevenson & Son, Dungannon; Chairman: Moygashel Ltd, 1952-63; County Cttee on Training and Employment, 1955-61; Pres., County Antrim Agricultural Assoc., 1957-64; Chairman and Vice-Chairman Co. Antrim Territorial Force Assoc., 1938-55; Mayor, Ballymena, 1948-52. Mem. ITA, 1955-59. *Recreation:* field sports. *Address:* Galgorm Castle, Ballymena, N Ireland. *T:* Ballymena 2365. *Clubs:* Royal Automobile; Ulster (Belfast).   *[Died 9 March 1972.*

CHICHESTER, Sir Francis, KBE 1967 (CBE 1964); FIN; Chairman, Francis Chichester Ltd, Map and Guide Publishers since 1945; air navigator and pilot; yachtsman; *b* 17 Sept. 1901; *m* 1st, 1923, Muriel Eileen Blakiston (*d* 1929); (one *s* decd); 2nd, 1937, Sheila Mary Craven; one *s. Educ:* Marlborough Coll. Emigrated to NZ, 1919; Dir, Godwin Chichester Aviation Co. Ltd, 1927-30; second pilot to fly solo, England-Australia, 1929; NZ (Territorial) AF, 1930; first E to W solo flight from New Zealand to Australia across Tasman Sea, 1931 (Johnston Memorial Trophy for 1931, for navigation); first long-distance solo seaplane flight (NZ-Japan), 1931; cruising flight in Puss Moth with one passenger Sydney to London *via* Peking, 1936. Served in RAF, 1941-45, as Sen. Navigation Officer, Empire Central Flying Sch., 1943-45. Director, Straight Aviation Training Ltd, 1946-49. Ex-Warden, Guild of Air Pilots and Air Navigators; winner of first Single-handed Trans-Atlantic Yacht Race, Plymouth-New York, 1960; awarded Yachtsman of the Year Trophy, 1960; record solo East-West Crossing, Plymouth-New York, 1962; 2nd in Second Solo Trans-Atlantic Yacht Race, 1964; First solo circumnavigation of world via Capes of Good Hope, Leeuwin and the Horn, 1966-67 (fastest true circumnavigation port to port by any small boat: 29,600 miles in 226 days sailing time, Plymouth-Sydney-Plymouth); world speed records for long distance solo sailing: 1966, in Gipsy Moth IV; 1971, in Gipsy Moth V (1,017.75 miles in 5 days). Trustee, Nat. Maritime Museum, 1965-70; Vice-Pres., RGS, 1970; Hon. Vice.Pres., Cutty Sark Soc., 1967. Freeman of Barnstaple, Devon. Vice-Pres., Inst. of Navigation, 1964; Younger Brother of Trinity House, 1968. Membre d'Honneur, Yacht Club de France, 1967 (Special Centenary Award, 1967). Hon. Master of Bench, Middle Temple, 1967. Special Gold Medal, RGS; Institute of Navigation Gold Medal, 1961; Special Award, Inst. of Navigation; Superior Achievement Award, American Inst. of Navigation; Aust. Inst. of Navigation Gold Medal, 1967. Marconi Memorial Medal of Honour, NY, 1967; Italian Polhena da Bravura, San Remo, 1967; Capitani Coraggiosi, Riposto, Sicily; Blue Water Medal (Cruising Club of America), 1960 and 1967; Special Bronze Medal, and Chichester Award, Royal Yacht Squadron, 1967. Gold Medal, Guild of Yachting Writers, 1967; Medal for Seamanship, Royal Cruising Club, 1967; Livingstone Gold Medal, Royal Scottish Geographical Soc., 1969. *Publications:* Navigation Notes for Instructors and Students (Air Ministry), 1941-43; Solo to Sydney, 1930; Seaplane Solo, 1932 (republished as Alone Over the Tasman Sea, 1946, and in Aviation Classics series, 1965); Ride on the Wind, 1937; Spotters' Hand Book, 1940; Astro-Navigation, 1940 (4 parts); Pocket Planisphere, 1941; Pinpoint the Bombers, 1941; Star Recognition, 1941; The Star Compass, 1961; The Sun Compass, 1961; Alone Across the Atlantic, 1961 (published in

France, Seul en Course, 1962); Atlantic Adventure, 1962; The Lonely Sea and the Sky, 1964 (trans. 8 languages); Along the Clipper Way, 1966; Gipsy Moth Circles the World, 1967 (trans. 13 languages); How to Keep Fit, 1969; The Romantic Challenge, 1971. *Address:* 9 St James's Place, SW1A 1PE. *T:* 01-493 0931. *Clubs:* United Service and Royal Aero, Royal Yacht Squadron, Royal Ocean Racing, Ocean Cruising, Royal Cruising, RAF Yacht, Royal Thames Yacht, Royal London Yacht, Royal Western Yacht (Plymouth), Royal Cork Yacht, Royal St George Yacht, Royal Sydney Yacht, Beaulieu River Sailing, Bosham Sailing, North Devon Sailing.   *[Died 26 Aug. 1972.*

CHICK, Sir (Alfred) Louis, KBE 1952; *b* 19 Jan. 1904; *s* of late Alfred Y. Chick; *m* 1948, Betty, *d* of Col C. J. D. Freeth, Lymington, Hants; one *s* three *d. Educ:* King's Sch., Canterbury; London School of Economics, London Univ. Entered Sudan Civil Service, 1930; Asst Financial Secretary, 1943-46; Dep. Financial Secretary, 1947-48; Financial Secretary, 1948-53; Fiscal Comr, Nigeria, 1953; Chief of Mission, International Bank Mission to Malaya, 1954; Chairman, White Fish Authority, 1954-63. *Address:* Upper Bolney Cottage, Harpsden, Henley-on-Thames, Oxon. *T:* Henley 4784.
                    [Died 29 April 1972.

CHICK, Dame Harriette, DBE 1949 (CBE 1932); DSc London; Hon. DSc Manchester; Fellow of University College, London; Member of the Scientific Staff of the Lister Institute, 1905-46, Hon. Member, 1946-70; *b* 6 Jan. 1875; 3rd *d* of Samuel and Emma Chick, Ealing and Branscombe, Devon. *Educ:* Notting Hill High Sch.; University Coll., London (1851 Exhibitioner); University of Vienna. Engaged in researches on nutrition in Vienna, 1919-22. *Publications:* numerous papers on physiological and biochemical subjects in the Journal of Hygiene, Journal of Physiology, Biochemical Journal, British Journal of Nutrition. *Recreation:* walking. *Address:* 34 Storeys Way, Cambridge.   *[Died 9 July 1977.*

CHICK, Sir Louis; *see* Chick, Sir A. L.

CHIESMAN, Sir Walter (Eric), Kt 1960; CB 1955; MD, FRCP; Treasury Medical Adviser, 1945-65, retired; *b* July 1900; *m* 1930, Feodora Rennie; one *s* two *d. Educ:* Whitgift Sch.; Corpus Christi Coll., Cambridge; St Thomas's Hospital. MD Cambridge, 1934; FRCP 1947. Resident Asst Physician, 1928, 1st Asst, Medical Unit, 1929-33, St Thomas's Hospital; Medical Adviser to ICI, 1933-45; KHP 1950, QHP 1951. Past President Assoc. of Industrial Medical Officers. *Recreations:* gardening, fishing. *Address:* Little Prettymans, Edenbridge, Kent. *T:* Four Elms 237. *Club:* United Oxford & Cambridge University.
                    [Died 13 Aug. 1973.

CHILD, Major Sir (Coles) John, 2nd Bt *cr* 1919, of Bromley Palace, Kent; DL; *b* 11 Feb. 1906; *o s* of 1st Bt and Eliza Caroline, *d* of late R. B. Barton, LLD; *S* father, 1929; *m* 1933, Sheila (*d* 1964), *e d* of Hugh Mathewson, 1570 Pine Avenue, Montreal; one *s* two *d.* ADC to Governor-Gen. of Dominion of Canada, 1931-33. Lieut Coldstream Guards R of O, re-employed 1939; Capt. 1940, Maj. 1941. DL Surrey, 1960. Lord of the Manor of Bromley. *Recreation:* won the Canadian Amateur Rackets, 1932, 1933, Singles and Doubles, and Doubles in 1934. *Heir: s* Coles John Jeremy Child [*b* 20 Sept. 1944; *m* 1971, Deborah Jane, *d* of H. P. Snelling]. *Address:* 33 First Avenue, Mortlake, SW14. *Clubs:* Guards, Pratt's. *[Died 26 May 1971.*

CHILD, Rev. Robert Leonard, MA, BD, BLitt; Principal-Emeritus of Regent's Park College, Oxford; *b* 28 March 1891; *s* of Joseph Colin Child and Mary Ellen Sargent; unmarried. *Educ:* Chepstow Grammar Sch.; Newport Intermediate Boys' Sch. Civil Service as Second Division Clerk, and Officer of Customs and Excise, 1909-19. In training for Min. at Regent's Park Coll., London, Mansfield Coll., Oxford, and Marburg Univ. (Germany), 1919-26. Minister of St Andrew's Street Baptist Church, Cambridge, 1926-34; Minister of Broadmead Baptist Church, Bristol, 1934-42; Principal of Regent's Park Coll., Oxford, 1942-58; President, Baptist Union, 1954. *Publication:* A Conversation about Baptism, 1963. *Address:* 34 Lonsdale Road, Oxford. *T:* 59546.   *[Died 2 Jan. 1971.*

CHILDERS, Erskine Hamilton; President of Ireland, since 25 June 1973; *b* London, 11 Dec. 1905; *s* of Robert Erskine Childers and Mary Alden Childers (*née* Osgood); *m* 1st, 1925, Ruth Dow (decd); two *s* three *d* ; 2nd, 1952, Margaret Dudley; one *d. Educ:* Gresham Sch.; Trinity Coll., Cambridge. BA Hist. Tripos (hons). Advertisement Manager, The Irish Press Ltd, 1932-35; Sec., Fedn of Irish Manufacturers, 1936-44. Mem. Dáil Eireann, 1938-73 (Athlone-Longford 1938-48, Longford-Westmeath 1948-61, Monaghan 1961-73); Parly Sec. to Minister for Local Govt and Public Health, 1944-47, to Minister for Local Govt,

1947-48; Minister for: Posts and Telegraphs, 1951-54; Lands, Forestry and Fisheries, 1957-59; Transport and Power, 1959-69, Posts and Telegraphs, 1966-69; Health, 1969-73; Tánaiste (Deputy Prime Minister), 1969-73. LLD (*hc*) Nat. Univ. of Ireland; MRIA; Hon. Bencher, Hon. Soc. of the King's Inns. Spanish Grand Order of Merit, 1958. *Recreations:* walking, gardening. *Address:* Aras an Uachtaráin, Dublin 8.
[*Died* 17 *Nov.* 1974.

CHILTON, Donovan; retired as Keeper, Department of Electrical Engineering and Communications, Science Museum, London (1960-74); *b* 24 Feb. 1909; 5th *s* of Percy Chilton and Ada Grace Ryall; *m* 1937, Jane Margaret Saunders; two *s* (one *d* decd). *Educ:* Latymer Upper Sch.; Royal College of Science (Royal Scholar); University of Göttingen, Germany. BSc 1931; ARCS 1930; DIC 1931. Works physicist, Ilford Ltd, 1932-38; entered Science Museum, 1938; Dep. Keeper, 1949; Keeper, 1960-74. Air Ministry, Meteorological Office, 1939-45. FInstP. *Address:* 33 Park Avenue, Hutton, Brentwood, Essex CM13 2QL. *T:* Brentwood 210775. [*Died* 17 *Jan.* 1978.

CHIMAY, Lt-Col Prince Alphonse de; Alphonse Marcel Jules Matteo Joseph de Riquet, Comte de Caraman; TD; *b* 23 June 1899; *m* Brenda, *er d* of late Lord Ernest Hamilton; one *d*. *Educ:* Eton; RMC Sandhurst. Late Lieut Scots Guards; served European War, 1916-18; R of O 1920; Major TA 1939; Lt-Col 1942; commanded 2/7th Bn Middx Regt (DCO), 1942-45; AAG, AFHQ, CMF, 1945; served France, 1940, Africa, Sicily, Italy, 1943-45 (despatches). *Recreations:* sailing, golf, shooting. *Address:* The Garden House, Arrow, Alcester, Warwicks. *T:* Alcester 2513. *Club:* Guards. [*Died* 1 *Oct.* 1973.

CHINA, William Edward, CBE 1959; MA, ScD, FIBiol; DipAgric Cantab; FRES; Keeper, Department of Entomology, British Museum (Natural History), 1955-61; Deputy Chief Scientific Officer, 1957-61; *b* 7 Dec. 1895; 2nd *s* of William Edwin China, London; *m* 1922, Lita Frances Gaunt, *d* of late A. R. Gaunt, Birmingham; one *s* twin *d*. *Educ:* Battersea Polytechnic; Trinity Hall, Cambridge (Open Scholar 1914). Entered British Museum as Asst, 1922; Asst Keeper, 1927; Dep. Keeper, 1944; Keeper, 1955. World authority on Hemiptera. Scientific Controller, International Trust, 1959-70, and Sec., International Commn, 1962-70, on Zoological Nomenclature. Foreign Mem. Soc. pro Faun. Flor. Fennica; Corresponding Mem. Entomological Soc. of Egypt. Served in France in Special Brigade (Poison Gas), RE, 1915-17; in 52 Squadron (Observer), RAF, 1918. Home Guard, 1940-45. *Publications:* over 200 scientific papers on the structure, taxonomy, evolution and zoogeography of the insect order Hemiptera. *Recreation:* gardening. *Address:* Chy-an-Cloam, Gwelenys Road, Mousehole, Penzance, Cornwall TR19 6PY. *T:* Mousehole 516.
[*Died* 17 *Sept.* 1979.

CHINNERY, E. W. Pearson; teaching and research since 1949; *b* Waterloo, Vic., Australia, 5 Nov. 1887; *m* 1919, Sarah Johnston Neill, Belfast (*d* 1970); four *d*. *Educ:* various schools; Christ's Coll., Cambridge; Diploma Anthropology Cantab. Magistrate British New Guinea, 1909-21; Government Anthropologist, New Guinea, 1924-32; Dir of District Services and Native Affairs, and Mem. of the Legislative and Executive Councils, New Guinea, 1932-38; Dir of Native Affairs, Northern Territory, 1938-46; Official Adviser in Native Matters to Commonwealth of Australia, 1938-47; explored new districts in Owen Stanley Range, British New Guinea, between Mt Obree and Mt Chapman, and took a leading part in the discovery and pacification of tribes and cannibals and head-hunters in various parts of the interior of New Guinea; Lieut AIF (Australian Flying Corps, observer); Medal Royal Humane Society; awarded Cuthbert Peek Grant, 1920, Royal Geographical Society; lectured in England, 1919-20, and in USA, England, Geneva, and Australia, 1930, 1934, 1947 and 1948. Delegate to Pan Pacific Science Congress, Australia, 1923, and International Pacific Health Conference, 1926; an Australian delegate to League of Nations (Permanent Mandates Commission) 18th Session Geneva, 1930 and 22nd Session, 1934; Delegate New Guinea and Australia International Anthropological Conf., London, July-Aug. 1934; Pres. Section Anthropology Australian and New Zealand Association for Advancement of Science, Sydney, 1932; an Australian Delegate to Trusteeship Council, United Nations, Lake Success, 1947; a mem. UN visiting mission to Ruanda Urundi and Tanganyika, 1948; Anthropologist, External Territories Dept, 1948-49. *Publications:* numerous papers and reports. [*Died Dec.* 1972.

CHIRICO, Giorgio de; Italian artist; painter, theatrical designer and writer; *b* Greece, 10 July 1888; *s* of Evaristo and Gemma de Chirico; *m* Isabella Far. *Educ:* Polytechnic Institute, Athens; Academy of Fine Arts, Munich. During early career as a painter

in Italy and Paris, began series of Italian townscapes; launched metaphysical School, Italy, 1917; has designed scenery and costumes for ballet and operatic productions; other work includes murals, lithographs, book illustrations, designs etc. Known for his compositions of horses, gladiators, archaeological subjects, scenes of Greek mythology, portraits, still life. Since 1968, he has carried out his characteristic subjects in sculpture. Hon. RBA 1949. *Publications:* Hebdomeros, 1929; (with Isabella Far) Commedia dell' arte moderna, 1945, and other volumes of art criticism; Memorie della mia vita, 1945. *Address:* Piazza di Spagna 31, Rome, Italy. [*Died* 18 *Nov.* 1978.

CHISHOLM, Ven. Alexander, MA; Prebendary of Combe VI in Wells Cathedral since 1959; retired as Archdeacon of Carlisle (1947-Oct. 1958), also as Canon Residentiary of Carlisle Cathedral and Examining Chaplain to the Bishop of Carlisle; Archdeacon Emeritus, 1958; *b* 21 Jan. 1887; *s* of Alexander Chisholm, The Bank, Dolphinton. *Educ:* Hatfield Coll., Durham Univ. Curate of St Luke's, Bath, 1911-18; Vicar of Wedmore, 1918-36; Vicar of Yeovil with Preston Plucknett and Yeovil Marsh, 1936-40; Rector of Weston-super-Mare, 1940-47; Preb. of Whitchurch in Wells Cathedral, 1935-47; Sub-Dean of Wells Cathedral, 1946-47; Examining Chaplain to Bishop of Bath and Wells, 1938-47; OCF, 1939-47; Hon. Chaplain to Bishop of Bath and Wells, 1947-60. *Recreation:* music. *Address:* Abbey Close, Ditcheat, Shepton Mallet, Somerset BA4 6RE. *T:* Ditcheat 314. [*Died* 17 *Dec.* 1975.

CHISHOLM, Alexander Hugh, OBE 1958; Chief Editor, Australian Encyclopædia; *b* Maryborough, Vic., 28 March 1890, of Scottish parents; *m* 1923, Olive Hackin; Brisbane; one *d*. *Educ:* State Sch., Maryborough Bushland. Sometime hon. lecturer in nature study in schools of Victoria and Queensland; Pres., Queensland Bird Lovers' League, 1919-22; Editor: Queensland Naturalist, 1920-22; The Emu, 1926-28; Victorian Naturalist, 1939-48; late Editor, The Australasian, Melbourne; Editor, The Argus, Melbourne, 1937-38; Adviser on Fauna Protection to Queensland Government; President: Field Naturalists' Club of Victoria; Royal Australasian Ornithologists' Union; Royal Australian Historical Soc.; holds honours from British, American, and Australian Ornithologists' Unions, Zoological Soc. of London, etc; Australian Nat. Hist. Medallion, 1940; Press Liaison Officer, March-July 1945, to the Duke of Gloucester. *Publications:* Bird Seeking in Queensland, 1922; Mateship with Birds, 1922; Feathered Minstrels of Australia, 1926; Birds and Green Places, 1929; Nature Fantasy in Australia, 1932; Bird Wonders of Australia, 1934; Strange New World, 1942; The Incredible Year, 1944; The Story of Elizabeth Gould, 1944; An Explorer and His Birds, 1945; The Making of a Sentimental Bloke, 1946; Fairy Wrens, 1948; News from Nature, 1948; Scots Wha Hae, 1950; The Romance of the Lyrebird, 1960; Ferdinand von Mueller, 1962; Australian Wild Life, 1966; The Joy of the Earth, 1969. *Recreation:* idling in green places. *Address:* History House, 133 Macquarie Street, Sydney, Australia. [*Died* 10 *July* 1977.

CHISHOLM, (George) Brock, CC (Canada) 1967; CBE 1943; MC (and Bar); ED; MD; *b* 18 May 1896; *s* of Frank Herbert and Lisbeth McCraney Chisholm; *m* 1924, Grace McLean Ryrie; one *s* one *d*. *Educ:* Univ. of Toronto, Yale, etc. Psychiatrist, Toronto, Canada; OC Lorne Scots; OC 5th Infantry Bde; Comdt Northern Area, Military District 2; served 1940-45: GSO1; Dir of Personnel Selection; Deputy Adjt-Gen.; Dir-Gen. of Medical Services, Canadian Army, rank of Maj.-Gen.; Dep. Minister of Health, Department of National Health and Welfare, Canadian Government, 1945-46; Executive Sec., Interim Commission of the World Health Organisation, United Nations, 1946-48; Dir-Gen., WHO, 1948-53, United Nations, Palais des Nations, Geneva. Pres., World Federation for Mental Health, Aug. 1957-58; Vice-Pres., World Assoc. of World Federalists; Hon. Pres., World Federalists of Canada. Holds numerous hon. degrees, decorations and awards from organisations throughout the world. *Publications:* Prescription for Survival, 1957 (USA); Can People Learn to Learn?, 1958 (USA), 1959 (Eng.). *Address:* Apartment 202, 1400 Newport Avenue, Victoria, BC, Canada. *Club:* Union (British Columbia). [*Died* 2 *Feb.* 1971.

CHISHOLM, Most Rev. John Wallace; Archbishop of Melanesia, since 1975; *b* 14 Sept. 1922; *y s* of James and Eleanor Chisholm. *Educ:* Trinity Coll., University of Melbourne (Kew Schol.). BA 1942; Dipl. Educn 1943; Bromby Greek Prize, 1944; Leeper Prize, 1945. Curate, St Stephen's, Rochester Row, Westminster, 1947-51; Sub-Dean, Cathedral of St Peter and St Paul, Dogura, Papua and New Guinea, 1953, Canon, 1954; Auxiliary Bishop of New Guinea, 1964-67; Bishop of Melanesia, 1967 until 1975 when the Diocese of Melanesia became a Province. *Recreations:* gardening, music. *Address:* Archbishop's House, Honiara, British Solomon Islands Protectorate. *Club:* Royal Commonwealth Society. [*Died* 24 *May* 1975.

CHISHOLM, Roderick William; HM Diplomatic Service, retired; *b* 18 July 1925; *s* of late William Andrew Chisholm, Fort Augustus, and Kathleen Winifred (*née* Hart), Dumbarton; *m* 1954, Janet Anne, *d* of late Lt-Col G. R. H. Deane, OBE, RE; two *s* two *d. Educ:* Salesian Coll., Farnborough, St Catharine's Coll., Cambridge (2nd Cl. Hons Mod. Langs, 1951). Served War of 1939-45: Inf., 1943-48; commnd The Buffs, 1944; demobilised 1948 (Captain). Entered Foreign (later Diplomatic) Service, 1951; served in: Control Commn for Germany, 1951-53; Berlin, 1953-55; FO, 1955-57; Singapore, 1958-59; Moscow, 1960-62; FO, 1962-64; Singapore, 1964-65; FCO, 1965-70; Pretoria, 1970-74; FCO, 1974-77; Pretoria, 1977-79. *Publication:* Ladysmith, 1979. *Recreations:* most outdoor activities, military history. *Address:* Ringden Wood, Flimwell, Wadhurst, E Sussex. *T:* Flimwell 431. *Clubs:* Royal Commonwealth Society; Lamberhurst Golf (Kent); Bewle Valley Sailing (Sussex).
[Died 22 Sept. 1979.

CHISHOLM, Ronald George, TD 1944; late of HM Diplomatic Service; *b* 26 Jan. 1910; *s* of William Alexander Chisholm and Elizabeth George, both of Inverness; *m* 1st, 1937, Hilda (decd), *yr d* of James Gray, Aberdeen; 2nd, 1956, Elsie Mabel (Susan) (*d* 1972), *yr d* of James John Craik, Lewes; one *s* three *d. Educ:* Inverness High Sch.; Peterhead Acad. Sheriff Court Service, Scotland, 1929. Commnd in N Scottish Heavy Bde, RA, TA, 1929; TA Staff Coll. course, Camberley, 1939 (tsc); Staff appts, Scottish Comd, GHQ Home Forces and GHQ Middle East; demobilised, 1945, with rank of Major. Principal, Burma Office, 1945; transferred to India Office, 1946, and to Commonwealth Relations Office, 1947; First Sec., UK High Commission, Karachi, 1951; Actg Dep. High Commissioner for the UK in Peshawar, 1951-52, and in Dacca, 1952-53; UK Deleg. to Internat. Sugar Conf., 1953, Internat. Conf. on Polution of the Sea by Oil, 1954, and Volta River Conf., 1955; Dep. High Comr for the UK in Madras, 1957-60; CRO, 1960-63; British Dep. High Comr in Eastern Nigeria, 1963-65; London Secretariat, SEATO Ministerial Council Meeting, London, 1965. FSA Scot. 1954. Haakon VI Frihetsmedalji (Norway), 1945. *Recreation:* golf. *Address:* Little Buntings, Balcombe Road, Haywards Heath, Sussex. *T:* 50161. *Club:* Madras (Madras).
[Died 8 July 1972.

CHITHAM, Sir Charles Carter, Kt 1936; CIE 1934; JP; *b* 13 Sept. 1886. Joined Indian Police, 1906; Inspector-General of Police, Central Provinces, 1931; Federal Public Service Commissioner, Delhi, 1937, 1939; Acting Inspector of Constabulary, SW Region, 1940-45; King's Police Medal, 1931. *Address:* c/o Lloyds Bank, 6 Pall Mall, SW1; The Old Rectory, Great Cheverell, Devizes, Wilts. *T:* Lavington 2335.
[Died 25 Sept. 1972.

CHITTY, Anthony Merlott, MA; FRIBA; AADipl.; MRTPI; architect and town-planning consultant since 1936, now retired; *b* 10 Dec. 1907; *s* of Rev. G. J. Chitty, Eton Coll., and Mary Dyson Hort, Cambridge; *m* 1938, Elizabeth Davis; two *s. Educ:* Eton; Trinity Coll., Cambridge. Chm. Board of Architectural Education, 1952-54; mem. of Sec. of State for the Colonies Advisory Cttee on Colonial Colleges of Art, Science and Technology, 1955-62; Mem. Governing Council, Kumasi Coll., Ghana, 1956-59; Architect Planner to new Universities at Nairobi, Kenya, and Lusaka, Zambia, 1965-70. Pres. Architectural Assoc., 1950-51. *Publications:* Curvature Refinements in Greek Architecture, 1932; Houses, Permanence and Prefabrication, 1945; Audio-visual aids in American Universities, 1966; Space Use Surveys in Universities, 1967. *Recreations:* gardening, knocking the Government. *Address:* Collapit Creek House, Kingsbridge, Devon. *Club:* Leander.
[Died 21 Oct. 1976.

CHIVERS, Edgar Warren, CB 1963; BSc; Director, Royal Armament Research and Development Establishment, 1962-67; *b* 7 Dec. 1906; *s* of E. Norton Chivers and Rose Chivers (*née* Warren); *m* 1934, Ruth, *d* of Rev. W. Simons; one *s* one *d. Educ:* Hampton Grammar Sch.; Queen Mary Coll., University of London. Joined Research Dept, Woolwich (War Office), 1928; Air Defence Experimental Establishment, 1931-40; Radar Research and Development Establishment, 1940-53; Supt of Ground Radar, 1947; Royal Radar Establishment, 1953-54; Head of Ground Radar Dept, 1953; Min. of Supply, Dir of Atomic Weapons (Development and Production), 1954-56; War Office, Royal Armament Research and Development Estabt, 1956-; Head of Guided Weapons and Electronics, 1956; Dep. Dir, 1957. *Publications:* various in technical journals. *Recreations:* gardening, music, bee-keeping. *Address:* Nomads, Church Road, Crowborough, East Sussex. *[Died 27 July 1979.*

CHIVERS, Stephen Oswald, CBE 1945; MA; formerly Chairman, Chivers & Sons Ltd; former Member of Cambridgeshire and Isle of Ely CC; *b* 1899; *s* of John Chivers; *m* 1926, Marjorie Clarke; one *s. Educ:* Mill Hill Sch.; Christ's Coll., Cambridge. *Address:* Cawcutts, Impington, Cambridge. *T:* Histon 2553.
[Died 21 Aug. 1975.

CHOPRA, Iqbal Chand, CBE 1958 (OBE 1946); QC (Tanganyika) 1951; *b* 1 Dec. 1896; *s* of late Lala Ganga Ram; *m* 1919, Thelma Florence Campbell; two *s. Educ:* King's Inns, Dublin; Middle Temple, London. Practised at Lahore High Court, 1919-28, at Mwanza, Tanganyika, from 1928; MLC 1945-59, MEC 1953-59, Tanganyika. Mem., Tanganyika Railway Council, until 1941; Mem., East Africa Railway Cttee until 1959; Mem., Makerere Coll. Council until 1959. A Founder Member, and (with the late Dr Williamson) only other shareholder of Williamson Diamonds until his death in Jan. 1958; thereafter Executor and Managing Director until the company was acquired by Govt of Tanganyika and Diamond Corp., and a Director until 1970. *Address:* 69 Chemin de Ruth, Cologny, Geneva, Switzerland. *T:* 521500. *[Died 16 July 1976.*

CHORLEY, 1st Baron *cr* 1945, of Kendal; **Robert Samuel Theodore Chorley,** QC 1961; JP; *b* Kendal, 1895; *e s* of late R. F. Chorley; *m* Katharine Campbell, *d* of late Edward Hopkinson, DSc; two *s* one *d. Educ:* Kendal Sch.; Queen's Coll., Oxford (Hastings Exhibitioner, Robert Herbert prize, MA). During European War served in Foreign Office; Cheshire Regt (HS), and Min. of Labour; called to Bar, 1920 (certificate of Honour); Pres. Hardwicke Soc., 1921-22; Tutor at the Law Society's School of Law, 1920-24; Lectr in Commercial Law, 1924-30; Sir Ernest Cassel Prof. of Commercial and Industrial Law in the Univ. of London, 1930-46; Dean of Faculty of Laws, London Univ., 1939-42; temporarily employed in Home Office, 1940-41; Acting Asst Sec., Min. of Home Security, 1941; Dep. Regional Comr for Civil Defence, NW Region, 1942-44; Chm. of Westmorland QS, 1944-68. Contested (Lab) Northwich Div., 1945. Lord in Waiting to the King, 1946-50. Member: Hobhouse Cttee (National Parks), 1945; Parly Delegn to India, 1945; Mocatta Cttee (Indorsements on Cheques), 1955. Former Mem. Council and Vice-Chm., National Trust; Hon. Sec. of Council for Preservation of Rural England, 1935-67, a Vice-Pres., 1969-; Pres., Fell Rock Climbing Club of English Lake District, 1935-37. Assoc. of University Teachers: Mem. Coun. and Exec. Cttee, 1938-; Vice-Pres., 1945-47; Pres., 1947; Hon. Gen. Sec., 1953-65; President: Nat. Council for the Abolition of the Death Penalty, 1945-48; Sheffield and Peak District Branch, CPRE, 1946-75; Friends of the Lake District, 1961-69 (Vice-Pres., 1946-56 and 1969-); Fire Service Research and Training Trust, 1946-73; Pres., Holiday Fellowship, 1947-57; a Vice-Pres. of Howard League for Penal Reform, 1948-; Chm., Inst. for Study and Treatment of Delinquency, 1950-56 (Pres., 1956-72); Pres., British Mountaineering Council, 1950-53; Pres., Ethical Union, 1950-54; Pres., Soc. of Public Teachers of Law, 1954-55; Vice-Pres., Alpine Club, 1956-58; Pres., Haldane Soc., 1957-72; Pres., Commons and Footpaths Preservation Soc., 1961-75. Hon. Fellow: Inst. of Bankers, 1960; LSE 1970. *Publications:* (jointly) Leading Cases in Mercantile Law; (jointly) Shipping Law; Law of Banking; (jointly) Leading Cases in the Law of Banking; (ed.) Arnould's Law of Marine Insurance (13th, 14th and 15th edns); General Editor Modern Law Review, 1937-71; various articles in the Law Quarterly Review, Modern Law Review, and elsewhere. *Recreations:* gardening, mountaineering and travel. *Heir:* s Hon. Roger Richard Edward Chorley, FCA. *Address:* The Rookery, Stanmore, Mddx; House of Lords, SW1. *Club:* Alpine.
[Died 27 Jan. 1978.

CHOU EN-LAI; Premier, State Council of the People's Republic of China since 1958; *b* Hwaiyin, Central Kiangsu, East China, 1898; *m* 1925, Teng Ying-ch'ao. *Educ:* Nankai High Sch. and Nankai Univ., China. Became active worker for Communist Party, 1921. Took part in Chinese National Revolution, 1924-27; mem. of Central Cttee of Chinese Communist Party, 1926-. Premier of Government Administration Council, Vice-Chm. People's Revolutionary Cttee, and Minister for Foreign Affairs, 1949-58. Has represented Chinese People's Republic at conferences abroad. *Address:* The Office of the Prime Minister, Peking, China. *[Died 8 Jan. 1976.*

CHRIMES, Sir (William) Bertram, Kt 1945; CBE 1939 (OBE 1930); JP; Chairman of Cooper's Stores, Grocers and Provision Merchants, Glasgow, Liverpool and London; *b* 6 Dec. 1883; *s* of Captain Henry Chrimes; *m* Mary (*d* 1952), *d* of John Holder, Liverpool; one *s* one *d.* Chm., Liverpool Cttee King's National Roll for Disabled Ex-Servicemen, 1922-45; Dir of War-time Meals Div., Min. of Food, 1940-47. Trustee, Bluecoat Hosp.; Mem., Liverpool Univ. Court; Vice-Pres., Liverpool Child Welfare Assoc.; Chm., Liverpool Advisory Cttee to Assistance Board, 1935-49; Liverpool Employment Cttee, 1937-56; Liverpool Disablement Advisory Cttee, 1945-55; Mem., Nat.

Advisory Council on the employment of the disabled, 1951-55; Poppy Day Appeal, 1934-47. *Address:* 12 Church Street, Liverpool; Bryn y Glyn, Nantyglyn, Colwyn Bay, N Wales. *Clubs:* University, Athenæum, Lyceum (Liverpool).
[*Died* 14 *Dec.* 1972.

CHRIST, George Elgie, CBE 1955; Parliamentary Liaison Officer, Conservative Party, and Editor Weekly News Letter, 1945-65; *b* 26 May 1904; *s* of late H. G. Christ, BSc, Dulwich Coll.; *m* 1938, Marianne Evans (*d* 1966). *Educ:* Christ's Hosp.; King's Coll., London Univ. Political Correspondent, Daily Telegraph, 1940-45; Governor of Christ's Hosp., 1937, and Almoner, 1945. *Recreations:* gardening, cricket. *Address:* 5 Winterstoke Crescent, Ramsgate, Kent. *T:* Thanet 53736. *Clubs:* Savage, MCC. [*Died* 24 *May* 1972.

CHRISTELOW, Allan, CMG 1950; Executive Vice-President and Director, Esso Standard Sekiyu KK; Director, TOA Nenryo KK; Director and Officer General, Sekiyu KK and General Gas KK; *b* 31 Jan. 1911; *s* of Joseph Christelow and Louisa Bateman, Bradford, Yorks; *m* 1942, Dorothy Beal; one *s* one *d. Educ:* Heckmondwike Sch.; Univ. of Leeds; Queen's Coll., Oxford; Princeton Univ.; Univ. of California at Berkeley. Asst Sec., War Cabinet Secretariat, 1944-45; Asst Sec. 1945-48, Under-Sec., 1948, HM Treasury Delegation to Washington, also Financial Counsellor, British Embassy, Washington, 1948. Acting Exec. Dir, Internat. Bank for Reconstruction and Development, 1948, Dir, 1953. Treasurer, Standard Vacuum Oil Co., 1959; disabled and retired, 1963. *Address:* 34 Toquam Road, New Canaan, Conn 06840, USA. *Clubs:* American (Tokyo), Country (New Canaan), Tokyo Lawn Tennis.
[*Died* 8 *Aug.* 1975.

CHRISTIE, Dame Agatha (Mary Clarissa), DBE 1971 (CBE 1956); Hon. DLitt; FRSL; *b* Torquay, 15 Sept. 1890; *yr d* of Frederick Alvah Miller, New York; *m* 1st, 1914, Col Archibald Christie, DSO (from whom she obtained a divorce, 1928; he *d* 1962); one *d*; 2nd, 1930, Sir Max Mallowan, CBE, FBA. *Educ:* home. *Publications: books:* The Mysterious Affair at Styles, 1920; The Secret Adversary, 1922; The Murder on the Links, 1923; The Man in the Brown Suit, 1924; Poirot Investigates, 1924; The Secret of Chimneys, 1925; The Murder of Roger Ackroyd, 1926; The Big Four, 1927; The Mystery of the Blue Train, 1928; The Seven Dials Mystery, 1929; Partners in Crime, 1929; The Mysterious Mr Quin, 1930; Murder at the Vicarage, 1930; The Sittaford Mystery, 1931; Peril at End House, 1932; The Thirteen Problems, 1932; Lord Edgware Dies, 1933; The Hound of Death, 1933; Murder on the Orient Express, 1934; The Listerdale Mystery, 1934; Why Didn't They Ask Evans?, 1934; Parker Pyne Investigates, 1934; Three Act Tragedy, 1935; The A. B. C. Murders, 1935; Death in the Clouds, 1935; Murder in Mesopotamia, 1936; Cards on the Table, 1936; Dumb Witness, 1937; Death on the Nile, 1937; Murder in the Mews, 1937; Appointment with Death, 1938; Hercule Poirot's Christmas, 1938; Murder is Easy, 1939; Ten Little Niggers, 1939; Sad Cypress, 1940; One Two Buckle My Shoe, 1940; Evil Under the Sun, 1941; N or M, 1941; The Body in the Library, 1942; Five Little Pigs; The Moving Finger, 1943; Towards Zero, 1944; Death comes as the End, 1945; Sparkling Cyanide, 1945; The Hollow, 1946; The Labours of Hercules, 1947; Taken at the Flood, 1948; Crooked House, 1949; A Murder is Announced, 1950; They Came to Baghdad, 1951; Mrs McGinty's Dead, 1952; They Do It With Mirrors, 1952; After the Funeral, 1953; A Pocket full of Rye, 1953; Destination Unknown, 1954; Hickory Dickory Dock, 1955; Dead Man's Folly, 1956; 4.50 from Paddington, 1957; Ordeal by Innocence, 1958; Cat among the Pigeons, 1959; The Adventure of the Christmas Pudding, 1960; The Pale Horse, 1961; The Mirror Crack'd from Side to Side, 1962; The Clocks, 1963; The Caribbean Mystery, 1964; At Bertram's Hotel, 1965; Third Girl, 1966; Endless Night, 1967; By the Pricking of my Thumbs, 1968; Hallowe'en Party, 1969; Passenger to Frankfurt, 1970; Nemesis, 1971; Elephants can Remember, 1972; Akhnaton, 1973; Poems, 1973; Postern of Fate, 1973; Poirot's Early Cases, 1974; Curtain, 1975; as Agatha Christie Mallowan: Come Tell Me How You Live, 1947; Star Over Bethlehem, 1965; as Mary Westmacott: Giant's Bread, 1930; Unfinished Portrait, 1934; Absent in the Spring, 1944; The Rose and the Yew Tree, 1948; A Daughter's a Daughter, 1953; The Burden, 1956; *Plays:* Alibi, 1928; Black Coffee, 1934; Love From a Stranger, 1936; Peril at End House, 1940; Ten Little Niggers, 1943; Appointment with Death, 1945; Murder on the Nile, 1946; Murder at the Vicarage, 1950, 1975; The Hollow, 1951; The Mousetrap, 1952 (has run for a record 24 years); Witness for the Prosecution, 1953; Spider's Web, 1954; Towards Zero, 1956; Verdict, 1958; The Unexpected Guest, 1958; Go Back for Murder, 1960; Rule of Three, 1962; *posthumous publications:* Sleeping Murder, 1976; An Autobiography, 1977. *Recreations:* reading, travelling,

bathing. *Address:* Winterbrook House, Wallingford, Oxon.
[*Died* 12 *Jan.* 1976.

CHRISTIE, Hon. Sir Harold George, Kt 1964; CBE 1949; real estate broker; Principal Partner, H. G. Christie, Real Estate; company director; *b* 31 May 1896; *e s* of H. Christopher and Margaret Alice Christie; *m* 1959, Virginia (*née* Campbell), Palm Beach, Fla, USA. *Educ:* Nassau Gram. Sch. General Electric Company, Schenectady, NY, 1916; Canadian Air Force, 1917-18; Knickerbocker Press, Albany, NY, 1918-21; H. G. Christie, Real Estate, Nassau, NP, 1921-. Elected Bahamas House of Assembly, 1927; returned in all subsequent General Elections; mem. Governor's Exec. Council, 1939; retired, 1948, after being re-appointed three terms; permission to retain title as Honourable. Mem. Bahamas Air Board during War of 1939-45, a dep. Commissioner of Currency. President: Eleuthera Land Co. Ltd; Bahamas Land and Finance Co. Ltd, etc; Dir, Trust Corp. of Bahamas Ltd. Pres., Bahamas Hist. Soc. *Recreations:* flying, sailing. *Address:* (office) PO Box 164, Bay Street, Nassau, Bahamas; Cascadilla, Nassau, NP, Bahamas. *T:* 2-2020. *Clubs:* Royal Nassau Sailing, Bahamas Country, Lyford Cay (Nassau).
[*Died* 25 *Sept.* 1973.

CHRISTIE, John Traill; Principal of Jesus College, Oxford, 1950-67, Hon. Fellow, 1967; Assistant Master, Westminster School, 1967-69; *b* 1899; 4th *s* of late C. H. F. Christie, DL, JP; *m* 1933, Lucie Catherine, *o d* of late T. P. Le Fanu, CB; two *d. Educ:* Winchester; Trinity Coll., Oxford (Scholar). 1st Class Class. Mods, 1920; 1st Class Lit. Hum., 1922. Sixth Form Master, Rugby Sch., 1922-28; Fellow and Tutor, Magdalen Coll., Oxford, 1928-32; Headmaster of Repton Sch., 1932-37; Headmaster of Westminster Sch., 1937-49. *Recreation:* walking. *Address:* Great Henny, Sudbury, Suffolk. *Club:* Athenæum.
[*Died* 8 *Sept.* 1980.

CHRISTIE, Group-Captain Malcolm Grahame, CMG 1919; DSO 1917; MC 1916; Doktor-Ingenieur, Aachen; Consultant to Otto Simon-Carves Chemical Engineering Group, since 1950; *b* Edgbaston, Warwicks, 1881; 3rd *s* of J. A. Christie, banker, London; unmarried. *Educ:* Leamington; Malvern Coll.; Aachen Univ. (1st cl. hons). Became Gen. Manager and Dir, Otto Cokeoven Co. of Leeds and Pres., Otto Coking Corp., New York; Hon. Lecturer to Leeds Univ.; Royal Flying Corps, 1914-18; Royal Air Force, 1919-30; Air Attaché, Washington, USA, 1922-26, and Berlin, 1927-30; retired, 1930. *Publication:* The Nitrogen Compounds in Coal. *Recreations:* mountaineering, travel, aviation. *Address:* 58 Cranmer Court, Sloane Avenue, SW3. *Club:* Travellers'. [*Died* 3 *Nov.* 1971.

CHRISTOFFELSZ, Arthur Eric, CMG 1949; BA, LLB Cantab; Barrister-at-Law, Gray's Inn; *b* 22 Aug. 1890; *s* of James Edwin Christoffelsz, ISO, and Eugenie Julia Weinman; *m* 1927, Edith Muriel Daniels. *Educ:* Royal College, Colombo; Queen's Coll., Cambridge. Called to the Bar, Gray's Inn, 1915; entered Ceylon Civil Service, 1915, and held various judicial and administrative appointments chief of which were: Govt Agent, North-Central Province, Ceylon, 1938-41; Comr of Labour, 1942-46; Principal Collector of Customs, 1947-49; Permanent Sec. to Minister of Labour and Social Services, 1949-51. *Address:* 8 Galle Face Court, Colombo 3, Sri Lanka. *T:* Colombo 25761.

CHRISTOPHER, Sir George Perrin, Kt 1946; Member of Council, Chamber of Shipping, since 1927; *b* 1 July 1890; *s* of Henry Boase Christopher, St Ives, Cornwall; *m* 1915, Violet Elsie Liscombe, Bristol. Formerly held the following positions: Dir, Peninsular & Oriental Steam Navigation Co.; Chm., Hain Steamship Co. Ltd; Chm. and Man. Dir, Union-Castle Mail Steamship Co. Ltd; Mem. General Cttee of Lloyd's Register of Shipping; Mem. Exec. Council of Shipping Federation Ltd; Mem. Gen. Council, King George's Fund for Sailors; Mem. Cttee, HMS Worcester. Chm. Tramp Shipping Administrative Cttee, 1939, and London Gen. Shipowners' Soc., 1939; Dir of Commercial Services, Ministry of War Transport, 1941-45 (Dep.-Dir, 1939-41); Pres. of the Chamber of Shipping of the United Kingdom, 1948-49 (Vice-Pres., 1947-48); Jt Vice-Chm. of General Council of British Shipping, 1947-49; Liveryman Worshipful Co. of Shipwrights. *Address:* Trencrom, Raglan Road, Reigate, Surrey. *T:* Reigate 42530. [*Died* 24 *Nov.* 1977.

CHRISTOPHERS, Brevet Col Sir (Samuel) Rickard, Kt 1931; CIE 1915; OBE 1918; FRS 1926; MB; IMS retired; *b* 27 Nov. 1873; *s* of Samuel Hunt Christophers, Liverpool; *m* 1902, Else Emma (*d* 1963), *d* of FitzRoy Sherman; one *s* one *d*. Member Malaria Commission, Royal Society and Colonial Office, 1898-1902; joined Indian Medical Service, 1902; Officer in Charge Central Malaria Bureau, India, 1910-22; Director Central Research Inst., Kasauli, India, 1922-32; KHP 1927-30; Professor of Malarial Studies, Univ. of London; Leverhulme

Fellow, MRC, in charge Experimental Malaria Unit at the London School of Hygiene and Tropical Medicine, 1932-38. Buchanan Medal of Royal Society, 1952. *Publications:* Practical Study of Malaria; Reports to the Malaria Committee of the Royal Society; various publications on malaria, kalaazar and medical zoology, etc. *Address: c/o* Lloyds Bank Ltd, Cox's and King's Branch, PO Box 220, 6 Pall Mall, SW1Y 5NH; Cluanie House, 18 Ridgeway, Broadstone, Dorset. *[Died* 19 *Feb.* 1978.

CHURCH, Eric Edmund Raitt, CMG 1967; CBE 1959; retired; *b* 18 Sept. 1907; *s* of James and Catherine Church, Chelsworth, Suffolk; *m* 1948, Diana Mary Lloyd Mawson; no *c. Educ:* Sudbury Gram. Sch.; Lincoln Coll., Oxford. Teaching appts in England, India and Brazil, 1928-36; Lectr, Univ. of Brazil, 1937; British Council: Rep., Brazil, 1939; Dir, Latin-American Dept, 1943; Asst Rep., Greece, 1947; Dir, Personnel Dept, 1948; Controller: Establishments Div., 1954; Overseas Div. B, 1962; Finance Div., 1964. *Address:* 31 Station Road, Sawbridgeworth, Herts. *T:* Bishop's Stortford 723023. *[Died* 23 *June* 1972.

CHURCH, Brig. Sir Geoffrey Selby, 2nd Bt *cr* 1901; CBE 1940; MC; DL, JP; *b* 11 Jan. 1887; 2nd *s* of Sir William Selby Church, Bt, KCB, and Sybil Constance, *d* of Charles John Bigge, Linden, Northumberland; *S* father, 1928; *m* 1st, 1913, Doris Louise (*d* 1917), *d* of late Sir W. Somerville, KBE; 2nd, 1920, Helene Elizabeth (*d* 1962), *d* of John L. Trayner, Mich., USA; no *c. Educ:* Winchester; University Coll., Oxford. Sheriff of Herts, 1936; JP 1927, DL 1931, Herts. ADC (Additional) to King George VI, 1941-51. *Recreations:* outdoor sports. *Heir:* none. *Address:* St Michaels, Hatfield, Herts. *T:* Hatfield 62115. *Club:* United Oxford & Cambridge University.
[Died 8 *Oct.* 1979 (*ext*).

CHURCH, Richard (Thomas), CBE 1957; FRSL; Vice-President, Royal Society of Literature; Past President: English Association; PEN; poet, novelist, and literary critic; *b* London, 26 March 1893; 2nd *s* of Thomas John Church and Lavinia Annie, *d* of Benjamin Orton; *m* 1st, Caroline Parfett; 2nd, Catherina Anna (*d* 1965), *d* of Carl Otto Schimmer; one *s* three *d* ; 3rd, Dorothy Beale. *Educ:* Dulwich Hamlet Sch. *Publications: poetry:* Flood of Life, 1917; Hurricane, 1919; Philip, 1923; Portrait of the Abbot, 1926; The Dream, 1927; Theme and Variations, 1928; Mood without Measure, 1928; The Glance Backward, 1930; News from the Mountain, 1932; Twelve Noon, 1936; The Solitary Man, 1941; 20th Century Psalter, 1943; Poems of Our Time (Everyman's), 1945; The Lamp, 1946; Collected Poems, 1948; Poems for Speaking, 1949; Selected Lyrical Poems, 1951; The Prodigal, 1953; The Inheritors (winner of Foyle's Poetry Prize), 1957; North of Rome, 1960; The Burning Bush, 1967; *prose:* Mary Shelley, 1928; Oliver's Daughter, 1930; High Summer, 1931; The Prodigal Father, 1933; Apple of Concord, 1935; The Porch, 1937 (Femina-Vie Heureuse Prize); The Stronghold, 1939; Calling for a Spade, 1939; The Room Within, 1940; Eight for Immortality, 1941; Rufus, 1941; Plato's Mistake, 1941; The Sampler, 1942; Some Modern British Authors (for British Council), 1943; Green Tide, 1944; Kent, 1948; The Cave, 1950; The Growth of the English Novel, 1950; A Window on a Hill, 1951; The Nightingale, 1952; Portrait of Canterbury, 1953; Dog Toby, 1953; Over the Bridge, 1955 (awarded Sunday Times Prize for Literature, 1955); Small Moments, 1956; The Dangerous Years, 1956; The Golden Sovereign, 1957; Down River, 1958; A Country Window, 1958; The Crabapple Tree, 1959; The Bells of Rye, 1960; Calm October, 1961; Prince Albert, 1963; The Little Kingdom, 1964; The Voyage Home, 1964; A Stroll Before Dark, 1965; London: Flower of Cities All, 1966; Speaking Aloud, 1968; The White Doe, 1968; Little Miss Moffatt, 1969; The Wonder of Words, 1970; A Harvest of Mushrooms (essays), 1970; The French Lieutenant, 1971; London in Colour, 1971; *posthumous publication:* Kent's Contribution, 1972. *Address:* The Priest's House, Sissinghurst Castle, Cranbrook, Kent. *Clubs:* Athenæum, Savile.
[Died 4 *March* 1972.

CHURCHILL, 2nd Viscount *cr* 1902; Victor Alexander Spencer; Baron 1815; Prince of the Holy Roman Empire; *b* 1 Aug. 1890; *s* of 1st Viscount and Lady Verena Maud Lowther, VA (*d* 1938), *d* of 3rd Earl of Lonsdale; godson of Queen Victoria; *S* father, 1934; *m* 1916, Kathleen (*d* 1943), *d* of Hon. Robert Beaven; *m* 1949, Joan (*d* 1957), *d* of Joseph Baron Black. *Educ:* Eton; Sorbonne, Paris. Page of Honour to King Edward VII, 1901-07; War of 1914-18, Major GSO (despatches); War of 1939-45, Staff Sergeant (1942-45), US Air Force. *Publication:* All My Sins Remembered. *Heir: half-b* Hon. Victor George Spencer, *b* 31 July 1934. *Address: c/o* National City Bank of New York, 17 Bruton Street, W1. *[Died* 21 *Dec.* 1973.

CHURCHILL, Clementine Ogilvy S.; *see* Spencer-Churchill, Baroness.

CHURCHILL, George Percy, CBE 1924; *b* 14 Aug. 1877; *s* of Henry A. Churchill, CB; *m* 1906, Muriel (*d* 1967), *d* of Sir Alfred East, RA; two *s. Educ:* privately. Oriental Sec. to HM Legation at Teheran, with a Royal Commission, and given local rank of a 3rd Sec. in the Diplomatic Service, 1903: 2nd Sec., 1916; served in Persia until the end of European War; transferred to the Eastern Dept of the Foreign Office, 1919-24; British Consul-Gen. at Algiers, 1924-27; retired, 1937; employed by Home Office, 1939-41, as Sec. of Advisory Cttee, Defence Regulations 18B. Attached to the English Suite of the Shah of Persia during HM's State Visit to England in 1919, and was given the First Class of the Order of the Lion and the Sun of Persia. *Address:* 20 Abbey Road, NW8. *[Died* 15 *March* 1973.

CHURCHILL, Peter Morland, DSO 1946; *b* 14 Jan. 1909; *s* of late W. A. Churchill, Consul General; *m* 1947, Mrs Odette Sansom (marr. diss. 1955); *m* 1956, Jane Hoyle. *Educ:* Malvern; Caius Coll., Cambridge (BA mod. langs, French, Spanish, Italian). Served War of 1939-45, in French Resistance; Capt., DSO, Croix de Guerre, 1946. Author; estate agent on the Riviera. *Publications:* Of their own Choice, 1952; Duel of Wits, 1953; Spirit in the Cage, 1954; By Moonlight, 1959; All about the French Riviera, 1960. *Recreations:* swimming, golf; formerly ice-hockey (Capt. Cambridge Univ. Ice Hockey Team, 1932; International, 12 caps). *Address:* 06-Le Rouret, France. *T:* (93) 67.60.49. *[Died* 1 *May* 1972.

CLANCARTY, 6th Earl of, *cr* 1803; Richard Frederick John Donough Le-Poer-Trench; Viscount Dunlo, 1801; Baron Kilconnel of Garbally, Co. Galway, 1797; Baron Trench (UK), 1815; Viscount Clancarty (UK), 1823; Marquess of Heusden in Kingdom of the Netherlands; *b* 27 Dec. 1891; *e s* of 5th Earl and Isabel Maude Penrice (*d* 1906), *d* of John G. Bilton, Charlton, Kent; *S* father, 1929; *m* 1st, 1915, Edith Constance (from whom he obtained a divorce, 1918), *d* of Major Alexander Albemarle Rawlinson; 2nd, 1918, Cora, *e d* of late H. H. Spooner and Mrs Philip Lindoe, Bourne Court, Bourne End; three *d.* Was in Royal Naval Air Force. *Heir: b* Hon. Greville Le-Poer-Trench, *b* 10 Dec. 1902. *Address:* Flint Place, Earnley, near Chichester, West Sussex. *T:* Birdham 512337. *[Died* 5 *June* 1971.

CLANCARTY, 7th Earl of, *cr* 1803; Greville Sidney Rochfort Le Poer Trench; Baron Kilconnel, 1797; Viscount Dunlo, 1801; Baron Trench (UK), 1815; Viscount Clancarty (UK), 1823; Marquess of Heusden (Kingdom of the Netherlands), 1818; *b* 10 Dec. 1902; 4th *s* of 5th Earl of Clancarty and Isabel Maude Penrice (*d* 1906), *d* of John G. Bilton; *S* brother, 1971; *m* 1926, Beatrice Georgiana, *y d* of Captain James Gordon-Miller, Thurlow Park, Little Thurlow, Suffolk. *Educ:* RN Colleges, Osborne and Dartmouth. *Recreations:* yachting, fishing, archaeology, restoration of old buildings. *Heir presumptive: half-brother* Hon. William Francis Brinsley Le Poer Trench [*b* 18 Sept. 1911; *m* 1st, 1940, Diana Joan (marr. diss. 1947), *yr d* of Sir William Younger, 2nd Bt; 2nd, 1961, Mrs Wilma Dorothy Millen Belknap (marr. diss. 1969), *d* of S. R. Vermilyea, USA; 3rd, 1974, Mrs Mildred Alleyn Spong (*d* 1975)]. *Address:* Rivey House, Buckland, near Faringdon, Oxon. *T:* Buckland 205.
[Died 15 *Sept.* 1975.

CLAPPEN, Air Commodore Donald William, CB 1946; RAF retired; *b* 30 June 1895; 2nd *s* of late E. S. Clappen and of Mrs F. Clappen, Westcliff-on-Sea; *m* 1917, Kathleen Mary Broughton Knight; one *s. Educ:* St John's Coll., Westcliff-on-Sea; Hurstpierpoint; University Coll., London. Joined Bleriot Aviation Co. as apprentice, 1911; flying pupil, 1912, gaining Pilot's Certificate No 591 Aug. 1913, on Bleriot Monoplane; Flying Instructor, Hendon, until outbreak of war; joined 1st Bn London Scottish (14th Bn Territorials), 1914; Commission Royal Flying Corps, 1915 (despatches); subsequently RAF, 1918; passed University and Engineer Course, 1922; various appointments including two overseas tours, Iraq prior to outbreak of war. Middle East, 1939-42; Officer Commanding RAF Cosford, near Wolverhampton, 1942-43; Senior Engineer Officer, Army Co-operation Command, 1943; Senior Air Staff Officer HQ 24 Gp, 1943-44; Air Officer Commanding RAF Station, St Athan, Wales, 1944-46; Senior Technical Staff Officer, HQ Bomber Command, 1946; retd 1949. *Recreations:* tennis, winter sports (ski-ing), forestry, cine-photography. *Address:* Three, The Garth, Great Missenden, Bucks. *T:* Great Missenden 4667. *Clubs:* Royal Air Force; Ski Club of Gt Britain.
[Died 30 *Nov.* 1978.

CLARABUT, Maj.-Gen. Reginald Blaxland, CB 1945; Indian Army, retired; *b* 7 Aug. 1893. Lieut Indian Army, 1917; Capt. 1919; Major, 1933; Bt Lieut-Col 1936; Lieut-Col 1939; Col 1940. AQMG Eastern Command, India, 1940-41; Deputy Dir, Supplies and Transport, India, 1941-44; Comd Nagpur District, 1944-45. *Address:* Oak Bank, Woodlands Close, Ottershaw, Surrey. *[Died* 18 *March* 1977.

CLARK, Alec Fulton Charles, CB 1960; Under-Secretary, Scottish Home and Health Department (retired); *b* 17 Dec. 1898; *yr s* of Charles and Mary Clark; *m* 1926, Mary, *er d* of David and Janet Watson; one *s* one *d. Educ:* Dunfermline High Sch.; Edinburgh Univ.; Lincoln Coll., Oxford. Asst Principal, Ministry of Agriculture and Fisheries, 1925; Principal, Ministry of Agriculture and Fisheries, 1934; Principal, Scottish Home Dept, 1939; Asst Sec. in Scottish Home Dept, 1942; promoted Under-Sec., 1953; retd 1963. *Recreation:* music. *Address:* 22 Warrender Park Terrace, Edinburgh EH9 1EF. *T:* 031-229 1020. *[Died 8 Aug. 1979.*

CLARK, Sir Andrew Edmund James, 3rd Bt *cr* 1883; MBE 1941; MC; QC 1943; *b* 18 July 1898; *o s* of Sir James Clark, 2nd Bt, CB, CMG, and Lilian Margaret, 2nd *d* of Robert Hopkins, Tidmarsh Manor, Berks; *S* father, 1948; *m* 1st, 1921, Angelica (*d* 1922), *d* of James Taylor, Strensham, Worcs; 2nd, 1924, Adeline Frances, *o d* of late Col A. D. Derviche-Jones, DSO; two *d. Educ:* Eton. 2nd Lieut Regular Army, RFA, 1916; served France and Belgium, 1916-18 (MC); Order of St John of Jerusalem; retd, 1921. Called to Bar, Inner Temple, 1928, Lincoln's Inn, 1930; called up for service with Regular Army, 1939-45; Lieut-Col and Hon. Brigadier RARO. Bencher of Inner Temple, 1951; conducted Crichel Down Inquiry, 1954. *Publications:* The Way of Lucifer; God's Children; Selected Poems. *Recreations:* shooting, fishing, gardening. *Heir:* none. *Address:* 45 Victoria Road, Kensington, W8. *T:* 01-937 7008. *Clubs:* Boodle's, MCC. *[Died 19 May 1979 (ext).*

CLARK, Arthur Campbell S.; *see* Stuart-Clark.

CLARK, Sir George (Norman), Kt 1953; DLitt, MA; Hon. LLD, Aberdeen; Hon. LitD, Utrecht; Hon. DLitt, Durham, Sheffield, Hull, Columbia; Hon. LittD, Dublin and Cambridge; Hon. Fellow: Trinity College, Dublin, 1953; Trinity College, Cambridge, 1955; Balliol and Oriel Colleges, Oxford, 1957; All Souls College, Oxford, 1975; Trustee, British Museum, 1949-60; Member, University Grants Committee, 1951-58; President of the British Academy, 1954-58; President, Northamptonshire Record Society, 1958-65; *b* 27 Feb. 1890; *s* of late J. W. Clark, CBE, JP; *m* 1919, Barbara, *e d* of W. B. Keen; one *s* one *d. Educ:* Bootham Sch.; Manchester Grammar Sch.; Balliol Coll., Oxford; Brakenbury Scholar, 1908. 1st Cl. Lit. Hum., 1911; 1st Cl. Modern History, 1912; Fellow of All Souls Coll., 1912; 2nd Lieut Post Office Rifles, Aug. 1914; served in France; retd with rank of Capt., 1920; Fellow and Lectr of Oriel Coll., 1919-31; Tutor, 1922; Librarian, 1930; joined staff of English Historical Review, 1919; Editor, 1920-25; Joint Editor, 1925-26 and 1938-39; Univ. Lectr in Modern History, 1927-31; Proctor, 1929-30; Chichele Prof. of Economic History and Fellow of All Souls Coll., 1931-43; Regius Prof. of Modern History, and Fellow of Trinity Coll., Cambridge, 1943-47; Provost of Oriel Coll., Oxford, 1947-57, retd. Fellow of All Souls Coll., Oxford, 1961-75. Creighton Lectr, London Univ., 1948; Ford's Lectr, Oxford Univ., 1949-50; Murray Lectr, Glasgow Univ., 1952; Wiles Lectr, Queen's Univ., Belfast, 1956; Donnellan Lectr, Trinity Coll., Dublin, 1960; Whidden Lectr, McMaster Univ., 1960; Leslie Stephen Lectr, Cambridge Univ., 1965. FBA 1936; FRCP (Hon.) 1965. Mem., Royal Danish Acad. of Sciences; Foreign Mem., Royal Netherlands Academy of Sciences; Foreign Hon. Mem., American Acad. of Arts and Sciences and Amer. Historical Assoc. Comdr Order of Orange-Nassau. *Publications:* The Dutch Alliance and the War against French Trade, 1923; (with F. W. Weaver) Churchwarden's Accounts of Marston, etc, 1925; The Seventeenth Century, 1929; The Later Stuarts, 1934; Science and Social Welfare in the Age of Newton, 1937; Guide to English Commercial Statistics (1696-1782), 1938; (with W. J. M. van Eysinga) The Colonial Conferences between England and the Netherlands, 2 vols, 1940, 1951; The Wealth of England, 1946; Early Modern Europe, 1957; War and Society in the Seventeenth Century, 1958; The Campden Wonder, 1959; History of the Royal College of Physicians, 2 vols, 1964-66; English History, a survey, 1971. *Address:* 7 Ethelred Court, Headington, Oxford OX3 9DA. *T:* Oxford 61028. *Club:* Athenæum. *[Died 6 Feb. 1979.*

CLARK, Brig. George Philip, CBE 1945; DSO 1940; *b* 25 March 1901; *e s* of late Rev. G. W. Clark; *m* 1st, 1936, Susan Caroline (*d* 1967), *o d* of late Major T. Close-Smith; one *s* one *d*; 2nd, 1969, Margaret Wheeler. *Educ:* Worcester; RMC Sandhurst. Joined Northamptonshire Regt, 1921; service in India and Sudan with Regiment; Capt. 1932; Major, 1938; Temp. Lieut-Col 1940; Temp. Col 1942; Temp. Brig. 1944; Col 1945; Hon. Brig. Served War of 1939-45 (despatches, DSO, CBE); retd pay, 1947. DL Suffolk, 1966-69. *Recreation:* hunting. *Address:* Stonehouse, Whitchurch, Aylesbury, Bucks. *T:* Whitchurch (Bucks) 555. *[Died 24 Aug. 1977.*

CLARK, George Sidney R. K.; *see* Kitson Clark.

CLARK, Sir Henry Laurence; *see* Urling Clark.

CLARK, John, OBE 1969; TD 1942; Chartered Surveyor; Partner in J. M. Clark & Partners, since 1925; *b* 11 June 1903; *s* of J. M. Clark, Haltwhistle, and Mrs Clark (*née* Jackson); *m* 1928, Audrey Irwin; one *s* three *d. Educ:* Oundle. Served 4th Bn, Royal Northumberland Fusiliers, 1922-43; retd as Lt-Col. President: Chartered Land Agents Soc., 1956; Royal Instn of Chartered Surveyors, 1969. *Recreation:* shooting. *Address:* Featherstone Castle, Haltwhistle, Northumberland. *Clubs:* National; Northern Counties (Newcastle upon Tyne). *[Died 18 Dec. 1977.*

CLARK, Brig.-Gen. John Arthur, CMG 1919; DSO 1917; VD 1922; CD 1955; KC 1932; LLD 1952; Member, Advisory Board, Canada Trust Co. Ltd; Director, Stock Exchange Building Corp. Ltd; Hon. Member: American Bar Assoc.; Bar of Mons, Belgium; *b* Dundas, Ontario; *s* of William and Frances J. Clark; *m* Jean Abercrombie, *d* of late Donald McGillivray, Vancouver, BC; two *s* two *d. Educ:* Toronto Univ. (BA, LLB); Osgoode Hall. Called to Bar, Ontario 1909, British Columbia 1910. Practises Law, Clark, Wilson & Co., Vancouver, BC; Dominion Vice-Pres., Canadian Bar Assoc., 1950-51; Pres., Canadian Bar Assoc., 1951-52, Vancouver Bar Assoc., 1936-37. Hon. Life Dir., Mutual Life Assurance Company, Canada, 1974 (Dir, 1952-66). Commanded 72nd Seaforth Highlanders of Canada, 1915-18; commanded 7th Canadian Infantry Brigade, 1918, to demobilisation; Canadian Representative, British Mission to Italy, 1917 (CMG, DSO and two bars, despatches five times); Hon. Col Seaforth Highlanders of Canada; Citoyen d'Honneur: City of Mons; Province of Hainaut. Mem. Canadian House of Commons for Vancouver-Burrard, 1921-30; a Conservative. Chm., Canadian Nat. Inst. for the Blind, 1949-53, Hon. Counsel, 1953-; Hon. Solicitor, Vancouver Red Cross, 1941-56. Gov., St George's Sch. *Recreation:* golf. *Address:* 475 Howe Street, Vancouver, BC. *Clubs:* Vancouver; Capilano Golf and Country. *[Died 18 Jan. 1976.*

CLARK, Mrs Margaret; *see* Storm, Lesley.

CLARK, Philip Lindsey, DSO; FRBS; sculptor; *b* 1889; *m* 1917, Truda Mary Calnan (*d* 1952); six *s*; *m* 1962, Monica Mary Hansford. *Educ:* Douglas House Sch., Cheltenham. Studied sculpture at the Royal Academy Schs, London; served European War, 1914-18, Artists' Rifles, Royal Sussex Regt, rank of Capt. (despatches, DSO); War of 1939-45, Cameronians (Scottish Rifles), RAF Regt and RNVR, 1940-45. First exhibited sculpture at Royal Academy, 1920; Paris Salon, 1921. *Works:* The Cameronians (Scottish Rifles) War Memorial (1914-18), Glasgow; St Saviour's (Southwark) War Memorial, Boro High Street; sculpture on Belgian Soldiers' Memorial (1914-18), Kensal Green, awarded Palm of Order of Crown of Belgium, 1932; sculpture in wood, stone and bronze works in Westminster Cathedral, Aylesford Priory, English Martyrs Church, Wallasey, and in and on many other churches and public buildings. *Address:* Flat 2, 6 Douglas Avenue, Exmouth, Devon. *T:* Exmouth 3570. *[Died 25 Dec. 1977.*

CLARK, Sir Stewart S.; *see* Stewart-Clark.

CLARK, Sir Thomas, 3rd Bt *cr* 1886; DL; FRSE 1932; late senior partner, publishing firm of T. & T. Clark, Edinburgh; Major, late 7th Battalion Royal Scots (the Royal Regiment); *b* 30 March 1886; *s* of 2nd Bt and Helen (*d* 1942), *d* of Rev. H. M. Douglas; *S* father, 1924; *m* 1914, Ellen Mercy, *o d* of late Francis Drake; two *s* two *d. Educ:* Edinburgh Academy; University Coll., Oxford. Chm., City of Edinburgh Territorial and Auxiliary Forces Assoc., 1947-50; late Hon. Col 414 (Forth) Coast Regt, RA TA; DL Edinburgh 1955. *Heir: s* John Douglas Clark [*b* 9 Jan. 1923; *m* 1969, Anne, *d* of late Angus Gordon Beauly, Inverness-shire]. *Address:* 23 Wester Coates Avenue, Edinburgh EH12 5LS. *T:* 031-337 1913. *Club:* Caledonian (Edinburgh). *[Died 21 April 1977.*

CLARK, Thomas Archibald B.; *see* Bennet-Clark.

CLARK, Thomas Campbell, (Tom C. Clark); a Justice of the Supreme Court, US, 1949; retired, 1967; former Director, Federal Judicial Center, Washington, DC; *b* 23 Sept. 1899; *s* of William H. Clark and Jennie Falls; *m* 1924, Mary Ramsey; one *s* one *d* (and one *s* decd). *Educ:* Grade Sch. and High Sch., Dallas, Texas; Virginia Military Inst.; Univ. of Texas (AB, LLB). Associated with Clark and Clark, Dallas, Texas, 1922-27; served European War, 1917-18, 153rd Inf. US Army. Civil District Attorney for Dallas County, Texas, 1927; Asst Attorney-Gen. in charge of Anti-trust Div., Dept of Justice, 1943; Asst Attorney-

Gen. in charge of Criminal Div., Dept of Justice, 1943-45; Attorney-Gen., 1945-49. Fraternities: Delta Tau Delta, Phi Alpha Delta, Order of Coif. Holds numerous hon. doctorates in Law from Amer. Univs and Colls; Distinguished Alumnus Award, Univ. of Texas, 1962; Amer. Bar Assoc. Gold Medal, 1962, and other medals. *Address:* 2101 Connecticut Avenue, NW, Washington, DC. *T:* Decatur 2-2101; (business) Supreme Court Building, Washington, DC. *T:* Executive 3-1640. *Clubs:* Chevy Chase (Md); Burning Tree; Alfalfa; University, National Lawyers' (Washington, DC). *[Died 13 June 1977.*

CLARK, Tom C.; *see* Clark, Thomas Campbell.

CLARK, Prof. Sir Wilfrid (Edward) Le Gros, Kt 1955; FRS 1935; MA, DSc, Hon. DSc (Durham, Manchester, Edinburgh, Witwatersrand, S Africa); Hon. MD (Melbourne, Oslo); Hon. LLD (Malaya); FRCS; Professor of Anatomy, Oxford University, 1934-Oct. 1962; Director, MRC Unit for Research on Climatic and Working Efficiency, 1948-62; *b* Hemel Hempstead, 5 June 1895; *s* of Rev. Travers Clark; *m* 1st, 1923, Freda Constance Giddey (*d* 1963); two *d*; 2nd, 1964, Violet, *widow* of late Leonard Browne, MD. *Educ:* Blundell's Sch., Tiverton; St Thomas's Hospital. Capt. RAMC, 1918; Principal Medical Officer of Sarawak, Borneo, 1920-23; Reader in Anatomy, Univ. of London, 1924-27; Prof. of Anatomy, at St Bartholomew's Hosp., 1927-29, at St Thomas's Hosp., 1929-34; Mem., Anat., Physiol. and Zool. Soc. (Vice-Pres., Zool. Soc., 1942-44); Vice-Pres., Royal Anthropological Inst., 1939-42, 1947-52; Council, Royal Society, 1942-44; Mem., Medical Research Council, 1950-54; Pres. Anthropology Sect., British Assoc., 1939; Pres., Internat. Anat. Congress, 1950; Pres., British Assoc., 1961; Pres., Anatomical Soc., 1952-53; Mem., Norwegian Academy of Art and Science; For. Mem., Kungl. Vetenshaps. Soc. Uppsala; For. Assoc. Acad. Nacional Med. Buenos Aires; Hon. Mem., Royal Society New Zealand, 1954; Mem., Amer. Phil. Soc., Hon. Life Mem., NY Acad. Scis; Mem., Nat. Acad. Science, Washington. Doyne Memorial Medal, 1942; Triennial Prize, RCS, 1947; Viking Medal, 1956; Royal Medal, Royal Society, 1961; Lashley Prize, Amer. Phil. Soc., 1971. Hunterian Prof., RCS, 1934, 1945; Lectures: Henderson, Edinburgh, 1936; Robert Boyle, 1947; William Smith, 1949; Earl Grey Meml, 1949; Hunter Meml, Sydney Univ., 1952; Munro, Edinburgh, 1953; Lady Jones, 1953; Ferris, Yale Univ., 1956; Ferrier, Royal Society, 1956; Maudsley, 1957; Edridge-Green, RCS, 1961; Harvey, NY Acad. of Medicine. Past Examiner in Anatomy for RCS, and Univs of London, Durham, Wales and Bristol. Master Salters' Company, 1954. Hon. Fellow Hertford Coll., Oxford, 1962. *Publications:* Early Forerunners of Man, 1934; Morphological Aspects of the Hypothalamus, 1936; The Tissues of the Body, 1939, 6th edn 1970; Central Nervous System (Cunningham's Anatomy), 1943, 1956; History of the Primates, 1949, 8th edn 1962; The Fossil Evidence for Human Evolution, 1955, 2nd edn 1964; The Antecedents of Man, 1959, 3rd edn 1970; Chant of Pleasant Exploration, 1968; numerous papers in Phil. Trans Royal Society and other scientific journals on neurology, anatomy, anthropology and palæontology; Editor, Jl Anat., 1940-45. *Address:* 16 Park Close, Templar Road, Oxford. *T:* Oxford 52716.
[Died 28 June 1971.

CLARKE, Austin, MA; poet; *b* 1896; *s* of late Augustine Clarke and Ellen Patten Browne, Dublin. *Educ:* Belvedere Coll., Dublin; University Coll., Dublin. English Lectr at University Coll., Dublin, 1917-21; Asst Examiner in Matriculation, National Univ. of Ireland; Asst Editor of The Argosy Magazine during 1929; National Award for Poetry, Tailteann Games, 1932; Foundation Mem. of the Irish Academy of Letters, 1932, Pres., 1952-54; Pres., Irish PEN, 1939-42 and 1946-49; Chairman: Dublin Verse Speaking Soc.; Lyric Theatre Co. *Publications:* The Vengeance of Fionn (poems), 1917; The Fires of Baal (poems), 1920; The Sword of the West (poems), 1921; The Cattle-drive in Connaught (poems), 1925; The Son of Learning (a poetic comedy), 1927; Pilgrimage (poems), 1929; The Flame (a verse play), 1930; The Bright Temptation (novel), 1932; The Singing-Men at Cashel (novel), 1936; Collected Poems, 1936; Night and Morning (poems), 1938; Sister Eucharia (a verse play), 1939; Black Fast (a verse play), 1941; As the Crow Flies (a radio verse play), 1943; The Viscount of Blarney and other plays, 1944; First Visit to England (essays), 1945; The Second Kiss (a poetic comedy), 1946; The Plot Succeeds (a poetic comedy), 1950; Poetry in Ireland (a prose study), 1950; The Sun Dances at Easter (novel), 1952; The Moment Next to Nothing (a verse play), 1953; Ancient Lights (poems), 1955; Too Great a Vine (poems), 1957; The Horse-Eaters (poems), 1960; Collected Later Poems, 1961; Twice Round the Black Church (memoirs), 1962; Forget-me-not (verse), 1962; Collected Plays (verse), 1963; Flight to Africa (verse), 1963; Mnemosyne (verse), 1965; Two Interludes (Verse), 1966; Beyond the Pale (memoirs),

1967; Old-Fashioned Pilgrimage (verse), 1967; St Patrick's Purgatory, The Frenzy of Sweeney, The Silent Lover (all verse plays), 1967; The Third Kiss (a poetic comedy), 1967; A Penny in the Clouds (memoirs), 1968; The Echo at Coole (verse), 1968; A Sermon on Swift (verse), 1968; The Celtic Twilight and the Nineties (essays), 1969; Orphide (verse), 1970; Tiresius (verse), 1972; St Patrick's Purgatory (trans. from Calderón), 1972; *posthumous:* Liberty Lane (verse play), 1978; numerous reviews in daily, weekly, monthly press and quarterlies, and broadcasts. *Address:* Bridge House, Templeogue, Co. Dublin.
[Died 19 March 1974.

CLARKE, Rev. Basil Fulford Lowther; Hon. Canon of Christ Church, Oxford, since 1970; *b* 6 March 1908; *s* of late Rev. W. K. L. Clarke; *m* 1939, Eileen Noël Coates; one *s* two *d*. *Educ:* St John's Sch., Leatherhead; St John's Coll., Durham (BA 1930; MA 1933); Cuddesdon Theological Coll. Deacon 1932; Priest 1933. Curate of: St Andrew's, Coulsdon, Surrey, 1932-35; St Mary's, Monmouth, 1935-38; St James's, Watford, 1938-39; SS Philip and James's, Oxford, 1939-44; Vicar of Knowl Hill, Berks, 1944-74. Member: Exec. Cttee, Council for Places of Worship, 1972; Adv. Bd for Redundant Churches, 1969; Westminster Abbey Arch. Adv. Panel, 1973. *Publications:* Church Builders of the 19th Century, 1938; Lesson Notes on the Prayer Book, 1943; My Parish Church, 1943; Clement Joins the Church, 1944; Anglican Cathedrals outside the British Isles, 1958; The Building of the 18th Century Church, 1963; (with Sir John Betjeman) English Churches, 1964; Parish Churches of London, 1966. *Recreations:* visiting churches, and research in connexion with them. *Address:* 220 Henley Road, Caversham, Reading, Berks. *T:* Reading 471750. *[Died 27 Jan. 1978.*

CLARKE, Maj.-Gen. Sir Campbell; *see* Clarke, Maj.-Gen. Sir E. M. C.

CLARKE, Brig. Dudley Wrangel, CB 1945; CBE 1943 (OBE 1942); *b* 27 April 1899; *s* of late Sir Ernest Michael Clarke; unmarried. *Educ:* Charterhouse; RMA Woolwich. Royal Artillery, 1916-36; Gen. Staff, 1936-47; retired, 1947. With RFC and RAF, European War, 1914-18 (War and Victory Medals); Iraq Rebellion, 1920 (Medal and clasp); Palestine Rebellion, 1936 (Bt Major, Medal and clasp); Middle East Forces, 1939-40; Norway, 1940; Med. Theatre, 1940-45 (despatches, OBE, CBE, CB, Africa Star, Italy medal, US Legion of Merit). Head of Public Opinion Research Dept at Conservative Central Office, 1948-52. *Publications:* Seven Assignments, 1948; The Eleventh at War, 1952; Golden Arrow, 1955. *Recreations:* travel and the theatre. *Address:* 802 Raleigh House, Dolphin Square, SW1. *Club:* Cavalry. *[Died 7 May 1974.*

CLARKE, Maj.-Gen. Sir (Edward Montagu) Campbell, KBE 1946 (CBE 1942); CB 1944; *b* 20 Nov. 1885; *m* 1914, Nancy (*d* 1948), *d* of S. M. Sheppard; one *s*. *Educ:* Rugby; RMA Woolwich. 2nd Lieut RA, 1905; Capt., 1914; Bt Major, 1917; Major, 1925; Bt Lt-Col, 1929; Col, 1933; Maj.-Gen., 1938; Dep. Supt, Design Dept, Royal Arsenal, 1933-36; Mem. Ordnance Cttee, 1936-37; Vice-Pres., 1938; Dir of Artillery, 1938; Dir-Gen. of Artillery, 1942-45; retired pay, 1946. *Address:* c/o Lloyds Bank, 6 Pall Mall, SW1. *Club:* United Service & Royal Aero. *[Died 4 Nov. 1971.*

CLARKE, Ernest Meredyth H.; *see* Hyde-Clarke.

CLARKE, Brig. Frederick Arthur Stanley, DSO 1918; psc†; late The Essex Regiment; *b* 3 Oct. 1892; *s* of F. W. Clarke, Bushey, Herts, and A. E. Crees, Prittlewell, Essex; *m* 1917, Millicent, *d* of W. Charity, Wallington, Surrey; one *s* one *d* (and one *s* decd). *Educ:* Loughborough Sch.; abroad. Served 10th Bn London Regt, 1912; Lieut Essex Regt, 1916; Major TA, 1916-20; Capt. Essex Regt, 1925; Bt Major, 1933; Major, 1936; Bt Lt-Col, 1939; Lt-Col, 1942; Temp. Brig., 1940-41; Temp. Col., 1943; Temp. Brig., 1943-47; psc† 1929; GSO, Small Arms Sch., 1930-32; DAAG, HQ Western Commd, 1932-34; GSO2, Nigeria, 1935-38 (Local Lt-Col); Asst Comdt, Nigeria, 1938-39 (Local Col); DAAG, BEF, 1939-40; GSO2 and 1, BEF, 1940; DA & QMG, W Africa, 1940-41; Comdr, W Africa, 1941; AQMG, BNAF, 1942-43; ADQMG, BNAF, 1943; Comdr, BNAF, 1943-44; Comdr, CMF, 1944-45; Comdr, Home Forces, 1945-46; retired, 1947. Served European War, 1914-17, Gallipoli, Egypt, Palestine, India (1917-19 Star, British War Medal, Victory Medal, DSO, despatches); attached 57th Wildes Rifles, Frontier Force, 1918; served War of 1939-45, France, W Africa, N Africa, Italy (1939-45 Star, Africa Star (First Army Clasp), Italy Star, Defence Medal, War Medal). *Publications:* The History of the Royal West African Frontier Force, Part II, 1920-1961; articles in Service Journals; Bertrand Stewart Prize Essay, 1926; Gold Medal, Royal United Service Institution Essay, 1933. *Recreations:* various. *Address:* Ratcliffs, Black Notley, Essex.
[Died 3 Jan. 1972.

CLARKE, Very Rev. (Harold George) Michael, MA 1925; FRSA; *b* 1898; *s* of George Herbert Clarke, then second master of Hymer's Coll., Hull; *m* 1923, Katharine Beryl, *d* of late Barry Edward Girling, Algiers; two *s* one *d. Educ:* St Paul's Sch. (scholar); Trinity Coll., Cambridge (scholar). Served with 2nd Field Company RE in France, 1918. 1st Class Hons Mathematical Tripos, Pt 1, 1919, 2nd Class Hons History Tripos, Pt 2, 1921. Deacon, 1938; Priest, 1939. Asst Master at Winchester Coll., 1921-32; Headmaster of Rossall Sch., 1932-37; Headmaster of Repton Sch., 1937-44; Rector of Holy Trinity, St Marylebone, 1945-51. Chm., Standing Joint Cttee Public and Preparatory Schs, 1940-43; lectured in Canada, 1945, at invitation of Canadian Council of Churches; one of founders, and till 1961 Governor, of Administrative Staff Coll., Greenlands, Henley-on-Thames; Chm., Marriage Welfare Cttee of Family Welfare Assoc., 1948-51; Advisory Sec. to Bishop of London on Religious Drama, 1949-51; Rural Dean of St Marylebone, 1950-51; Provost of Birmingham, 1951-61. Master of the Glovers' Company, 1960. Chm. Home Cttee, SPG, 1961-64. Rector of Westonbirt with Lasborough, and Chaplain to Westonbirt Sch., 1961-68. Sub-Warden, Servants of Christ the King, 1963-70; Chaplain to Haberdashers' Co., 1970. *Address:* Flint Cottage, Chipperfield, Herts.   *[Died 19 Aug. 1978.*

CLARKE, Sir Humphrey (Orme), 5th Bt *cr* 1831; *b* 6 July 1906; *e s* of Sir Orme Bigland Clarke, 4th Bt, CBE, and Elfrida, *e d* of Alfred Roosevelt, New York; *S* father, 1949; *m* 1st, 1931, Frances Mary Powys, *d* of late Major Powys Sketchley, DSO; 2nd, 1938, Elisabeth, *d* of Dr W. A. Cook, Santa Barbara, Calif.; one *s* ; 3rd, 1947, Constance Elizabeth, *d* of late Herbert Gibbs and of Mrs Gibbs, 32 Brechin Place, SW7; one *s. Educ:* Eton; Christ Church, Oxford. *Heir: er s* Charles Mansfield Tobias Clarke [*b* 8 Sept. 1939; *m* 1971, Charlotte, *e d* of Roderick Walter. *Educ:* Eton; Christ Church, Oxford]. *Address:* 18 Walton Street, SW3. *T:* 01-589 4738; The Church House, Bibury, Glos. *T:* Bibury 225. *Clubs:* Boodle's; Travellers'; Jockey (Paris).   *[Died 22 Jan. 1973.*

CLARKE, Mary Gavin, MA (Cantab and TCD), LLD (Aberdeen); *b* 29 Dec. 1881; *d* of late John Clarke, Lecturer in Education, Aberdeen Univ.; unmarried. *Educ:* Aberdeen High Sch. for Girls; Aberdeen Univ.; Girton Coll., Cambridge (Class I Med. and Mod. Langs Tripos); Cambridge Training Coll. After completion of training held research scholarship at Girton Coll. for two periods of a year each; Gamble Prize; taught Modern Languages for two years at Roedean Sch., Brighton; acted as Asst to Prof. of English Language and Literature in Aberdeen Univ., and as Asst Examiner to the Central Welsh Board in same subjects; Chief English Mistress, St Leonard's Sch., St Andrews; Headmistress of Edinburgh Ladies' Coll. (Mary Erskine Sch. for Girls), 1914-24; Headmistress of Manchester High Sch. for Girls, 1924-45. Special Lectr, Manchester Univ. Dept of Educn, 1948-53; Examiner, Manchester Univ. Sch. of Educn, 1949-59. Mem. Bd of Educn Investigation panel for Higher Sch. Certificate examination, 1937-38; Mem. of Board of Education Cttee (Norwood Cttee), 1941-43, on Secondary Sch. Examinations and Curriculum; special Lecturer for British Council in China, 1947; Mem. of Education Board, Edinburgh Merchant Company, 1955-67. *Publications:* Sidelights on Teutonic History during the Migration Period; The Headmistress Speaks (joint); Manchester and Salford Shaftesbury Society Lecture on Religious Education; A Short Life of Ninety Years. *Address:* 3 Gordon Road, Edinburgh EH12 6NB. *T:* 031-334 2616.   *[Died 12 Feb. 1976.*

CLARKE, Very Rev. Michael; *see* Clarke, Very Rev. H. G. M.

CLARKE, Rear-Adm. Noel Edward Harwood, CB 1959; *b* 21 Oct. 1904; *s* of Henry Trevisa Clarke and Margaret Evelyn Sale; *m* 1942, Katherine Miller, *d* of Harman Visger, France Lynch, near Stroud; two *s. Educ:* RN Colleges, Osborne and Dartmouth. RNEC Keyham, 1923-27; HMS Marlborough, 1927-29; HMS Kent, 1930-33; HMS Cairo, 1933-34; HM Dockyard, Portsmouth, 1934-36; HMS Sheffield, 1936-39; Admty, 1939-41; HMS Cumberland, 1942-43; HMS Excellent, 1943-47; HM Dockyard, Singapore, 1947-49; Admty, 1949-52; HM Dockyard, Gibraltar, 1952-56; Admty, 1957; Dir of Fleet Maintenance, Admty, 1958; Command Engineer Officer and Chief Staff Officer (Technical), on staff of C-in-C, Portsmouth, Nov. 1958-July 1960, retd; worked with Nat. Economic Development Office, 1963-68. Mem. Isle of Wight County Council, 1967-74. *Recreation:* golf. *Address:* Seamark House, St Helens, Isle of Wight. *T:* Bembridge 2866. *Club:* Royal Naval and Royal Albert Yacht (Portsmouth). *[Died 27 April 1980.*

CLARKE, Rt. Rev. Norman Harry, MA; LLD (Hon.) Sheffield, 1956; Assistant Bishop, Canterbury Diocese, since 1962; Canon Emeritus of Southwark Cathedral since 1945; *b* Sheffield, 31

July 1892; *s* of Henry Stockdale Clarke; *m* 1919, Muriel, *d* of W. R. Locke; three *d* (one *s* decd). *Educ:* Sheffield Univ. (BA 1st Class Hons Maths 1912); Ridley Hall, Cambridge. Diocesan Inspector of Schs, 1930-35; Canon Residentiary and Treasurer of Southwark Cathedral, 1940-45; Vicar of St Andrew's, Plymouth, 1945-51; Archdeacon of Plymouth, 1950-62; Suffragan Bishop of Plymouth, 1950-62. *Publication:* Thine is the Kingdom, 1941. *Address:* 4 Nailbourne Close, Kingston, Canterbury, Kent. *T:* Barham 202.   *[Died 18 Feb. 1974.*

CLARKE, Sir Richard (William Barnes), KCB 1964 (CB 1951); OBE 1944; Chairman, Stothert and Pitt, since 1971; Director: Courtaulds, since 1971; EMI, since 1971; Guest Keen & Nettlefolds, since 1971; Orion Insurance Co., since 1971; Guiness Peat Group, since 1973; *b* 13 Aug. 1910; *s* of late William Thomas Clarke, schoolmaster, and late Helen Barnes; *m* 1950, Brenda Pile (*née* Skinner); three *s. Educ:* Christ's Hospital; Clare Coll., Cambridge. BA; Wrangler, 1931; Frances Wood Prizeman, Royal Statistical Society, 1932. British Electrical and Allied Manufacturers' Association, 1932-33; Financial News, 1933-39; Visiting Lecturer, Cambridge Univ., 1935-36; Ministries of Information, Economic Warfare, Supply and Production, 1939-45: Combined Production and Resources Board (Washington), 1942-43; Asst Sec., HM Treasury, 1945; Under-Sec., 1947; Third Sec., 1955-62; Second Sec., 1962-66; Permanent Secretary: Min. of Aviation, 1966; Min. of Technology, 1966-70. Member: Council, Manchester Business Sch., 1969-; Council of Industry for Management Educn, 1971-; Vice-Pres., Royal Instn, 1973-; Chm., Internat. Panel, BSI, 1973-. FBIM. *Publications:* The Economic Effort of War, 1939; The Management of the Public Sector of the National Economy (Stamp Memorial Lecture, 1964); New Trends in Government, 1971; (jtly) Taxation Policy, 1973. *Address:* 3 Meadway Close, NW11. *T:* 01-455 7863. *Club:* Reform.   *[Died 21 June 1975.*

CLARKE, Sir Selwyn S.; *see* Selwyn-Clarke.

CLARKE, Rev. Sydney Herbert; *b* 7 May 1894; *s* of late Joseph Clarke; unmarried. *Educ:* Leeds Grammar Sch.; Trinity Coll., Cambridge (Senior Scholar); Cuddesdon Theological Coll. Preparatory Schoolmaster, 3 years; Deacon, 1919; Priest, 1920; Asst Master and Chaplain, Tonbridge Sch., Kent, 1919-34; Headmaster, St John's Coll., Johannesburg, 1935-54. Mem. Jt Matriculation Bd, Univ. of S Africa, 1936-54; Chm., 1943-44. Asst Master, Diocesan Coll., Rondebosch, Cape Town, 1955-62; Chaplain, Ardingly Coll., Sussex, 1963-64. Asst Priest (Hon.), St Saviour's Church, Eastbourne, 1964-. *Recreations:* walking, cricket, etc. *Address:* 10 Ripley Chase, The Goffs, Eastbourne, Sussex. *T:* Eastbourne 33966.   *[Died 11 Sept. 1974.*

CLARKE, Col Thomas Cecil Arthur, DSO 1941; OBE 1945; MIMechE; late Royal Tank Regt; Secretary Royal Armoured Corps War Memorial Benevolent Fund, and Royal Tank Regt Assoc. and Benevolent Fund, 1951-62; *b* 24 Nov. 1898; *s* of Cecil Clarke, Hampstead; *m* 1932, Dorothy Leslie-Spinks, Bournemouth; one *s* one *d. Educ:* Dover Coll.; RMC Sandhurst. In Regular Army from 1917; served European War, 1917-19 (wounded); War of 1939-45 (DSO, OBE, despatches thrice, wounded); commanded 46th (Liverpool Welsh) RT Regt; retired 1951. *Address:* 8 The Pines, The Avenue, Branksome, Poole, Dorset.   *[Died 9 Jan. 1979.*

CLARKE, Brig. William Stanhope, CBE 1945; DSO 1944; psc; *b* 29 Dec. 1899; *s* of Capt. J. S. Clarke, RN, Dublin; *m* 1929, Roslyn Stewart, *d* of Dr E. S. Littlejohn, Sydney; two *s. Educ:* Wellington Coll. Joined RA, 1919; transferred to Royal Tank Corps, 1923; Major, Royal Tank Regt, 1938; served War of 1939-45, NW Europe (CBE, DSO); Lt-Col 1945; Col 1946; ADC to the Queen, 1952-54; retired, 1954. *Address:* Clint House, Ellisfield, Basingstoke, Hants. *Club:* Army and Navy.
                                                     [Died 4 March 1973.

CLARKE HALL, Lady, (Edna); artist; *d* of late Rev. B. Waugh, founder of the NSPCC; *m* 1898, Sir W. Clarke Hall (*d* 1932); two *s. Educ:* The Slade Sch. (Slade Scholarship). Drawings, water-colours, etchings and lithographs. Represented at the Tate Gallery, British, Victoria and Albert and Fitzwilliam Museums and Manchester City Art Gallery. Exhibition, d'Offay Couper Gallery, London, 1971. *Publications:* Poems, 1926; Facets, 1930. *Address:* Upminster Common, Essex.   *[Died 16 Nov. 1979.*

CLARKE TAYLOR, Air Vice-Marshal James; *see* Taylor, Air Vice-Marshal J. C.

CLARKSON, Anthony; *see* Clarkson, G. W. A.

CLARKSON, (George Wensley) Anthony; Chairman, Reveille Newspapers Ltd, 1967-72; Director, Daily Mirror Newspapers

Ltd, 1967-72; *b* Christchurch, NZ, 21 April 1912; *s* of George Wensley and Nan O'Keeffe Clarkson, and *step s* of Percy Crisp; *m* 1st, 1935, Olive Oxley; 2nd, 1940, Pamela Minck; three *s*. *Educ:* St Bede's, Christchurch, NZ; King's Coll., Auckland, NZ. Reporter Auckland Sun, 1928-30; Founder-Editor, Challenge, 1933-35; Features Editor, Daily Mirror, 1937-40; served War of 1939-45, RN, 1940-46; Asst Editor, John Bull, 1946-49, Associate Editor, 1949-52, Editor, 1952-53; Editor: Illustrated, 1953-55; Odhams Magazine Unit, 1955-57; Reveille, 1957-70; Dir, Reveille Newspapers Ltd, 1962-. *Recreation:* swimming. *Address:* 80 Warwick Gardens, W14. *T:* 01-603 3682; 51 New Road, Shoreham-by-Sea, Sussex. *T:* Shoreham-by-Sea 4316. *Clubs:* Press, Burma, Royal Automobile. *[Died 17 April 1977.*

CLARKSON, Rt. Rev. George William, MA; *b* 13 Dec. 1897; *s* of William and Eliza Medley Clarkson. *Educ:* New Coll., Oxford. Deacon 1926, Priest 1927, Diocese of Liverpool; Curate of Wigan, 1926-30; Vicar of St Elizabeth, Aspull, 1930-33; Fleetwood, 1933-36; Sub-Dean and Hon. Canon of John de Wheathampstead, Abbot, in St Albans Cathedral, 1936-39; Rector of Dunstable, 1939-44; Skegness, 1944-48; Vicar of Newark with Codington, Diocese of Southwell, 1948-54; Rural Dean of Dunstable, 1940-44; of Candleshoe, 1947-48; of Newark, 1948-54; Hon. Canon of Southwell Minster, 1952-54; Bishop Suffragan and Archdeacon of Pontefract, 1954-61; Dean of Guildford, 1961-68, retd; an Asst Bishop, Diocese of Lincoln, 1968-. *Address:* 4 Syne Avenue, Skegness, Lincs.
[Died 15 Aug. 1977.

CLAUSON, Sir Gerard Leslie Makins, KCMG 1945 (CMG 1933); OBE 1919; Grand Officer, Order of Orange Nassau, 1947; Hon. Vice-President, Royal Archæological Institute; Past President, Royal Asiatic Society; *b* 28 April 1891; *e s* of late Major Sir John Eugene Clauson, KCMG, CVO; *m* 1918, Honor Emily Mary, *d* of late Ernest Innis Husey, MVO; one *s* one *d* (and one *s* decd). *Educ:* Eton (Scholar); Corpus Christi Coll., Oxford (Scholar). Boden Sanskrit Scholar, 1911; Hall-Houghton Syriac Prizeman, 1913; James Mew Arabic Scholar, 1920; 2nd Lieut 7th Som. LI 1914; transferred to General List, 1915; served in Gallipoli, Egypt, Mesopotamia; Capt. Gen. Staff (despatches twice, French Croix de Guerre with Palms); 2nd Class Clerk, Board of Inland Revenue, Sept. 1914; transferred to Colonial Office on retirement from Army, 1919; Principal, 1920; Asst Sec., 1934; Asst Under-Sec. of State, 1940-51; retired, 1951. Mem. UK Delegn to: Imperial Economic Conference, Ottawa, 1932; Monetary and Economic Conference, London, 1933; Imperial Conf., 1937; Hot Springs Conf., 1943, and various other internat. meetings; Chm., Pirelli Ltd, 1960-69; Chm., Internat. Wheat Conf., 1947; and International Rubber Conf., 1951. FSA. Indiana Univ. Prize for Altaic Studies, 1969; Sesquicentenary Commemorative Gold Medal, RAS, 1973. *Publications:* Sanglax by Muhammad Mahdi Xan, 1960; Turkish and Mongolian Studies, 1962; An Etymological Dictionary of Pre-Thirteenth Century Turkish, 1972; papers on Turkish languages and history. *Recreations:* archæology and Oriental languages. *Address:* 28 Kensington Court Gardens, W8. *T:* 01-937 0378. *Club:* Athenæum.   *[Died 1 May 1974.*

CLAVERING, Sir Albert, Kt 1935; OBE 1941; an hon. adviser, National Savings Committee; *b* 17 April 1887; *s* of Isaac Clavering; *m* 1913, May Muriel Harris; one *s* two *d*. *Educ:* private. Dir of Companies, now retired. Mem. LCC, SE St Pancras, 1931-34. Hon. Organising Dir, Conservative and Unionist Films Assoc., 1930-45. *Address:* 2 Courtenay Gate, Kingsway, Hove BN3 2WJ. *Clubs:* St Stephen's; Hove (Hove).
[Died 7 June 1972.

CLAY, Sir Charles Travis, Kt 1957; CB 1944; Hon. LittD; FSA; FBA 1950; Librarian, House of Lords, 1922-56; *b* 30 July 1885; *y s* of late John William Clay of Rastrick House, Yorks; *m* 1913, Hon. Violet (*d* 1972), 2nd *d* of late Lord Robson; three *d*. *Educ:* Harrow; Balliol Coll., Oxford, 1st Class History. Asst private sec. to Marquess of Crewe at Colonial Office, 1909-10, and at India Office, 1910-14; Asst Librarian, House of Lords, 1914-22; Lieut Devon Yeo.; Major, Territorial Army Reserve; served European War (despatches twice, DAQMG); Pres., Yorks Archæological Soc., 1953-56. *Address:* 30 Queen's Gate Gardens, SW7. *T:* 01-584 0205. *Club:* Brooks's.
[Died 31 Jan. 1978.

CLAY, Gen. Lucius DuBignon; US Army (retd); Senior Partner, Lehman Brothers, 1963-73; Director, Chase International Investment Corp., 1963-72; Chairman, Continental Can Company, 1950-62; *b* 23 April 1897; *s* of Alexander Stephen and Francis White Clay; *m* 1918, Marjorie McKeown; two *s*. *Educ:* USMA, West Point, New York. Instructor, Officers' Training Camp, 1918-19; Engr Sch. of Application, 1919-20; Asst Prof. Mil. Science and Tactics, Alabama Poly. Inst., 1920-21; Constr

Quartermaster and Post Engr Ft Belvoir, Va, 1921-24; Instr Dept Civil Engr, USMA, 1924-27; 11th Engrs Canal Zone, Field Mapping, 1927-30; Asst to Dist Engr Pittsburgh, in charge Construction Lock and Dam No. 2, Allegheny River, 1930-33; Asst to Chief of Engrs in River and Harbor Sec., 1933-37; Consultant on Devel. of Water Resources to Nat. Power Corp., Philippine Commonwealth, 1937-38; in charge constr. of Denison Dam, 1938-40; Asst to Administrator Civil Aeronautics Admin. on Airport Program, 1940-41; Dir of Matériel, ASF, 1942-44; commanded Normandy Base, 1944; Dep. Dir War Mobilization and Reconversion, 1945; Dep. Mil. Gov. of Germany, 1945-47; C-in-C, European Comd, and Military Governor of US Zone of Germany, 1947-49; retired, 1949. Personal Representative of the President, with rank of Ambassador, in Berlin, Aug. 1961-May 1962. Numerous hon. degrees, civic hons, medals, foreign decorations. Trustee: Presbyterian Hosp. of NY. *Publication:* Decision in Germany, 1950. *Recreations:* fishing, golf. *Address:* 633 Third Avenue, New York, NY 10017, USA. *Clubs:* Army and Navy (Washington DC); University, Links, Pinnacle, Blind Brook (all NY); Bohemian (San Francisco).   *[Died 16 April 1978.*

CLAYE, Sir Andrew (Moynihan), Kt 1960; Emeritus Professor of Obstetrics and Gynæcology, University of Leeds; *b* Brigg, Lincs, 18 July 1896; *o s* of Rev. Arthur Needham Claye and late Ada Augusta, *d* of Capt. Andrew Moynihan, VC; *m* 1928, Marjorie Elaine, MB, ChB, Leeds (1st Class Hons, Gold Medal), BA London, DCH, *yr d* of late Dr C. H. Knowles, Garforth, Leeds; two *d*. *Educ:* Lancing; Univ. of Leeds. Lieut 4th Dorset Regt, 1915-19; MRCS, LRCP, 1924; MB, ChB Leeds, 1924; MD Leeds, 1926; FRCS 1928; FRCOG 1934; BA London, 1964; MPhil Leeds, 1967. Formerly: Obstetric Surg., Leeds Maternity Hosp., and Surg., Hosp. for Women at Leeds; Hon. Consultant Surg., Royal Women's Hosp., Melbourne; MD Melbourne (*hc*), 1956; Sims-Black Travelling Prof. (Australia and New Zealand), RCOG, 1956; late Examiner, Univs of Oxford, Cambridge, Aberdeen, Belfast, Manchester and Conjoint Board in England; Pres., 1957-60, and late Examr, RCOG; Mem. of Council RCS (co-opted), 1950-55; late Mem., Central Midwives Board; Pres., 13th British Congress of Obstetrics and Gynæcology, 1952; Hon. Fellow and late Pres., North of England Obst. and Gynæcol. Soc.; Hon. Fellow, Edinburgh Obst. Soc.; Ed., British Obstetric Practice. *Publications:* The Evolution of Obstetric Analgesia, 1939; Management in Obstetrics, 2nd edn, 1956; (with Canon Adam Fox) English Well Used, 1968; articles on obstetric and gynæcological subjects. *Recreations:* reading the classics and music. *Address:* 6 Amhurst Court, Cambridge CB3 9BH. *T:* Cambridge 65050.   *[Died 25 Feb. 1977.*

CLAYSON, Rev. Canon Jesse Alec Maynard, AKC; Chaplain, HM's Household, since 1965; *b* 12 June 1905; *s* of Jesse and Lilian Clayson. St Margaret-at-Cliffe, Kent; *m* 1934, Gwendoline Mary, *d* of William and Olive Reed, Streatham; two *s* two *d*. *Educ:* Dover County Sch.; King's Coll., London. Deacon, 1934; Priest, 1935; Curate of St Stephen, Norbury, 1934-37; Chaplain RN (HMS Newcastle), 1937-38; Vicar of Holy Trinity, Dover, 1938-40; Vicar of St Stephen, Norbury, 1940-45; Sec., Canterbury Diocesan Bd of Finance, 1945-67; Archdeacon of Croydon, 1957-67; Hon. Canon of Canterbury Cathedral, 1951; Vicar of Bisley, 1967-69. *Address:* 27 Gorselands, Sedlescombe, Battle, Sussex. *T:* Sedlescombe 550.
[Died 21 Aug. 1971.

CLAYTON, Colin, MA, LLB Cantab; Barrister-at-Law; a Master of the Supreme Court, Queen's Bench Division, 1951-67; *b* 13 Aug. 1895; 2nd *s* of Wheeler Welland Fielden Clayton, Morecambe and West Worthing; *m* 1937, Doris Marion (*d* 1971), MBE, widow of Will. H. Moore and *d* of John Minshall. *Educ:* Brighton Grammar Sch.; Christ's Coll., Cambridge. Held commission in Royal Sussex Regt; served European War in France, 1915-18. Called to the Bar, Middle Temple, 1921. Law corresp. of The Times, 1926-51, and Editor of The Times Law Reports, 1934-51. *Address:* Cloisters, Temple, EC4. *T:* 01-353 7818. *Club:* United Oxford & Cambridge University.
[Died 19 Nov. 1975.

CLAYTON, Edwin, ISO 1950; *b* 18 Sept. 1887; *s* of Henry Bell Clayton, Solicitor, Nottingham; *m* 1935, Gwendoline Douglas, *d* of Arthur Douglas Hay; one *s*. *Educ:* Nottingham; Huntingdon. Admitted a Solicitor, 1910; joined staff of Dir of Public Prosecutions, 1919; Asst Dir of Public Prosecutions, 1945-52; retired 1952. Served European War, 1914-18; joined RA, Aug. 1914; commissioned Dec. 1914, with the RFA; served overseas in France and Belgium; wounded at Passchendaele, 1917; Army of Occupation in Germany until 1919. *Recreations:* rowing, football, walking. *Address:* 128 Kenilworth Court, SW15. *T:* 01-788 2208.   *[Died 26 Feb. 1973.*

CLAYTON, Col Hon. Sir Hector (Joseph Richard), Kt 1968; ED; BA, LLB; MLC, NSW, 1937-73; Upper House Opposition Leader, 1960-62; Chairman, Australian Guarantee Corp. Ltd, 1942-72; *b* Sydney, 3 June 1885; *s* of late J. H. Clayton, Sydney, NSW; *m* 1917, Phyllis E., *d* of late A. R. Midwood; two *s* two *d*. *Educ:* Sydney Grammar Sch.; Univ. of Sydney. Admitted Solicitor, 1911; Mem. Clayton, Utz & Co., Sydney. AIF, overseas, 1914-19; AMF, 1939-45; Col comdg 1st Austr. Movement Control Gp; Hon. Col, retd. *Recreations:* bowls, gardening. *Address:* 283 Edgecliff Road, Woollahra, NSW 2025, Australia. *Clubs:* Australian, University, Royal Sydney Golf (all Sydney). *[Died 18 July 1975.*

CLAYTON, Rev. Philip Thomas Byard, CH 1933; MC; DD (Lambeth); MA; FSA; an Extra Chaplain to the Queen (formerly Chaplain to King George V, to King George VI, and to the Queen); Chaplain to British Petroleum Oil Co.; Founder Padre of Toc H, when Toc H (Talbot House) began in Ypres Salient, 1915; Vicar, 1922-63, of All Hallows, Barking-by-the-Tower (bombed and burnt, 1940), the Guild Church of Toc H; *b* Queensland, 12 Dec. 1885; *y s* of late R. B. B. Clayton, JP; unmarried. *Educ:* St Paul's Sch. (Scholar); Exeter Coll., Oxford (Scholar). 1st Cl. Theological Final, 1909. Curate of Portsea, 1910-14; Temp. CF 1915; Chaplain, 16th Gen. Hosp.; 16th Inf. Bde; Bde Chaplain, 6th Div.; opened Talbot House in Poperinghe, which was named after Gilbert Talbot, *y s* of the Bishop of Winchester, Dec. 1915; Chaplain and Tutor of Service Candidates' Sch. at Knutsford, 1919; refounded Talbot House, 1920, as Toc H (Royal Charter, 1922)-a movement to teach younger generation racial reconciliation and unselfish service; first planned and launched Tower Hill Improvement, 1926; secured opening of Tower Beach for children, 1934; brought Toc H to support Leprosy Relief; inaugurated Winant Volunteers (1948) and Osler Volunteers (1950) to help East End Clubs and Settlements. Toured the Empire, US, S America, on behalf of Toc H, 1922, 1925, 1927, 1952, 1956, 1963, 1966; Persia, 1932; Gold Coast and Nigeria, 1933; S Africa, 1934; India, 1925, 1934, 1939; US, 1947, 1949, 1959, 1961; Middle East, 1950-51. Mediterranean Fleet, 1935-37; Chaplain of Anglo-Saxon Tanker Fleet, 1941-43; Chaplain MN in Indian Ocean and Mediterranean, 1942-45. Awarded special Salvation Army Diploma, 1971, to recognise exceptional service to mankind in forming Toc H, and also for his spiritual support of Salvation Army. Order of the Crown of Belgium, 1965; Hon. Freeman of Poperinghe and Ypres. *Publications:* Encaustic Mediæval Tiles, 1910; The Work of a Great Parish, 1912; Tales of Talbot House, 1919; Plain Tales from Flanders, 1929; Earthquake Love, 1932; Letters from Flanders, 1932; Pageant of Tower Hill, 1963; much current, social, and religious writing, etc; *relevant publication:* Clayton of Toc H, by Sir Tresham Lever, 1972. *Recreation:* seafaring. *Address:* Wakefield House, 41 Trinity Square, Tower Hill, EC3. *T:* 01-488 3333. *Club:* Press. *[Died 15 Dec. 1972.*

CLEARY, Sir William Castle, KBE 1947; CB 1945; *b* 14 March 1886; *s* of Rev. Augustus Castle Cleary and Kate Wyon; *m* 1914, Rosalind Clara Gwendoline Crosbie (*d* 1965); one *s* one *d*. *Educ:* Bedford Sch.; Trinity Coll., Cambridge. Junior Inspector of Elementary Schs, Board of Education, 1910; Principal Private Sec. to H. B. Lees Smith, Sir Donald Maclean and Lord Halifax, Presidents of Board, 1931-35; Principal Asst Sec., Elementary Education, 1940; Dep. Sec., Min. of Education, 1945-50. *Address:* 29 Denbigh Gardens, Richmond, Surrey. *T:* 01-940 3397. *[Died 19 Jan. 1971.*

CLEE, Sir Charles (Beaupré Bell), Kt 1947; CSI 1944; CIE 1938; *b* 5 Feb. 1893; *s* of J. B. B. Clee; *m* 1931, Rosemary Margaret Meredydd, *d* of late H. P. M. Rae; one *s*. *Educ:* Cambridge Univ. Nominated to Indian Civil Service, 1919, after serving with Suffolk Regt during European War; arrived India, 1919; Asst Collector and Magistrate, Bombay; Acting Dir of Information, 1924; Sec., Indian Tariff Board, 1925; Dep. Sec. to Govt Finance Dept, Bombay, 1928; Officiating Sec. to Govt, Home and Ecclesiastical Dept, Bombay, 1932; Officiating Sec. to Govt Finance Dept, 1933; Collector and Magistrate, 1935; Officiating Sec. to Govt Finance Dept, Bombay, 1936; Sec. to Govt Finance Dept, Sind, 1936; Officiating Chief Sec., 1938; Fin. Sec., 1939; Chief Sec. to Govt of Sind, 1940; Revenue Comr for Sind, 1943; retired, 1950. *Recreations:* shooting, cricket, golf. *Address:* c/o Lloyds Bank Ltd, Cox's & King's Branch, 6 Pall Mall, SW1. *[Died 28 May 1980.*

CLEEVE, Brig. Francis Charles Frederick, CBE 1945; DSO 1940; MC; *b* 26 June 1896; *e s* of late Maj.-Gen. W. F. Cleeve, CB, and late Mrs Cleeve, Ty Gwyn, Abergavenny; *m* 1st, 1934, Vera (*d* 1949), 2nd *d* of James T. Daly, Raford, Leamington; 2nd, 1951, Helen (*d* 1974), *d* of Mrs Arthur West. *Educ:* Cheltenham; Royal Military Academy, Woolwich. Entered Royal Artillery, 1914; served European War, 1915-18, Egypt,

Balkans, France (MC, 1914-15 Star, Gen. Service and Allied War Medals); War of 1939-45, France (despatches twice, DSO, CBE). Retired, 1948, with hon. rank of Brig. *Address:* Throop Farm, Horsington, Templecombe, Som. *T:* Templecombe 349. *Club:* Naval and Military. *[Died 21 Nov. 1975.*

CLELAND, Brig. Sir Donald Mackinnon, Kt 1961; CBE 1945; Administrator, Territory of Papua and New Guinea, 1953-66, and President Executive and Legislative Councils of Papua and New Guinea, 1951-64; *b* 28 June 1901; *m* 1928, Rachel Evans (CBE 1966); two *s*. *Educ:* Guildford Grammar Sch., Western Australia. Barrister and Solicitor, Western Australia, 1925-39. Served War of 1939-45: Middle East, Greece, Crete, Syria, New Guinea; Capt. 1939, Brig. 1942; Chief of Staff, Military Administration, Papua and New Guinea, and Chm. Australian-New Guinea Production Control Board, 1943-45. Dir, Federal Secretariat of Australian Liberal Party, 1945-51; Asst Administrator, Papua-New Guinea, 1951; Acting Administrator, 1952-53. Chancellor, Anglican Diocese of New Guinea, 1968; Pro-Chancellor, Univ. of Papua and New Guinea, 1969. Hon. Col of the Pacific Islands Regt, 1953-66. CStJ 1967. *Recreations:* gardening, golf. *Address:* Chester Street, Box 358, PO Port Moresby, Papua. *Clubs:* Australian, Royal Sydney Golf (Sydney); Weld (WA); Papua (Port Moresby). *[Died 27 Aug. 1975.*

CLELAND, Sir John (Burton), Kt 1964; CBE 1949; MD, ChM; Professor of Pathology, University of Adelaide, 1920; retd, 1948; *b* 22 June 1878; *e s* of late Dr Wm Lennox Cleland, of the Clelands of that ilk, and Matilda Lauder, *d* of late Dr John Hill Burton, Historiographer Royal for Scotland; *m*; one *s* four *d*. *Educ:* Univs of Adelaide and Sydney. House Surg., etc, PA Hospital, Sydney, 1900, and Resident Pathologist, 1901; visited China and Japan, 1903; Examin. with distinction London Sch. of Tropical Medicine, 1904; Cancer Research Scholar, London Hosp., 1904-05; Govt Pathologist and Bacteriologist, W Australia, 1906-09; Principal Asst Microbiologist, Govt Bureau of Microbiol. NSW, 1909-13; Principal Microbiol., Dept of Public Health, NSW, 1913-19; President: Royal Society of NSW, 1917; Royal Society of South Australia, 1928 and 1941. *Publications:* many papers in medical and scientific journals; Dengue and Papataci Fevers, in A System of Bacteriology in Relation to Medicine, Medical Research Council, 1930; Toadstools and Mushrooms and other Larger Fungi of South Australia, Part I, 1934, Part II, 1935; (with R. V. Southcott) Injuries to Man from Marine Invertebrates in the Australian Region, 1965; Ecology, Environment and Diseases in Aboriginal Man in South and Central Australia, 1966. *Recreations:* ornithology and botany. *Address:* 1 Dashwood Road, Beaumont, Adelaide, S Australia. *[Died 11 Aug. 1971.*

CLEVELAND, Sydney Dyson, OBE 1955; FMA; Director of Manchester City Art Galleries, 1952-62; *b* 11 April 1898; *m* 1923, Helen Plant; two *s*. *Educ:* Manchester Central Grammar Sch.; Regional College of Art. Hon. Sec., Arundel Soc. of Manchester, 1922-34; Keeper, Rutherston Loan Collection, 1927-37; Dep. Dir, Manchester City Art Galleries, 1937-52; Pres., North Western Fedn of Museums and Art Galleries, 1939; Hon. Treas., Museums Assoc., 1942-50; Pres., Museums Assoc., 1950-52; Mem., Arts Council art panel, 1953-55; Mem. British National Cttee of International Council of Museums. Hon. DA (Manchester) 1958; Hon. MA (Manchester) 1963, *Publications:* Guide to the Manchester Art Galleries: Arundel Soc. of Manchester Transactions; History of the Royal Manchester Institution; Heaton Hall, Heaton Park; Presidential Addresses to Museums Association; contribs to Studio, Connoisseur, Museums Journal, etc. *Recreation:* golf. *Address:* 6 Highfield Park, Heaton Mersey, Stockport, Cheshire. *[Died 11 Nov. 1975.*

CLEWORTH, Ralph, QC 1947; MA, LLB (Cantab); *b* 31 Oct. 1896; *s* of late Rev. William Enoch Cleworth, MA (Cantab), AKC London, Vicar of Hanging Heaton, Dewsbury, Yorks, and late Jane Emily Burbey; *m* 1928, Eleanore (*d* 1975), *d* of late George S. Greenwood, Batley, Yorks; one *s*. *Educ:* Wheelwright Grammar Sch., Dewsbury; Christ's Coll., Cambridge. Served European War, 1914-18, KOYLI. Called to Bar, Middle Temple, 1924; practice on NE Circuit. Parliamentary Candidate West Leeds, 1929. Last Recorder of Berwick-upon-Tweed, 1947-51. Stipendiary Magistrate of Leeds, 1950-65. *Address:* 124 Micklegate, York. *[Died 22 Oct. 1975.*

CLIFDEN, 8th Viscount *cr* 1781 (Ireland); **(Arthur) Victor Agar-Robartes**, MC; Baron Clifden (Ireland), 1776; Baron Mendip (Great Britain), 1794; Baron Robartes, 1869; Major (retd) Grenadier Guards; *b* 9 June 1887; *o* surv. *s* of Thomas Charles Agar-Robartes, 6th Viscount Clifden (*d* 1930) and of Mary (*d* 1921), *d* of late Francis Henry Dickinson, Kingweston, Som; *S*

brother, 1966; *m* 1st, 1920, Patience Mary (*d* 1956), *d* of A. F. Basset; one *d*; 2nd, 1948, Margaret, *d* of L. Ray Carter. *Educ:* Eton; Brasenose Coll., Oxford. Served European War, 1914-18, Grenadier Guards, retiring with rank of Major (thrice wounded, MC). Partner, Roger Cunliffe Sons & Co., 1920, till amalgamation with Cater, Brightwen & Co. in 1941; Dir of Cater, Brightwen & Co., 1941-63, retired. *Recreations:* shooting and fishing. *Heir:* (to Viscountcy) none; (to Barony of Mendip in remainder) 6th Earl of Normanton. *Address:* La Vielle Demeure, Beaumont, Jersey, CI. *T:* Jersey Central 31192.
[Died 22 Dec. 1974 (*ext*).

CLIFFORD, Prof. James Lowry; William Peterfield Trent Professor of English, Columbia University, 1964-69 (Professor of English, 1946-69), now Emeritus Professor; President, Lichfield Johnson Society, 1958-59; *b* Evansville, Ind., USA, 24 Feb. 1901; *s* of George S. and Emily Orr Clifford; *m* 1940, Virginia Iglehart; two *s* one *d*. *Educ:* Wabash Coll. (AB); Massachusetts Inst. of Tech. (BS); Columbia Univ. (PhD). Manager, Young Car Co., Evansville, Indiana, 1926-28; English Master, Evans Sch., Tucson, Ariz., 1929-32; Graduate student, Columbia Univ., 1932-35; Travelling Fellow, Columbia Univ., 1935-36; Dept of English, Lehigh Univ., Bethlehem, Pa, 1938-44, Instructor to Associate Prof.; Associate Prof. of English, Barnard Coll., 1944-46; Guggenheim Fellowship, 1951-52 and 1965-66. Mem. Gen. Advisory Editorial Cttee, Yale Boswell Edition and Yale Edition of the Works of Samuel Johnson, also Mem. Adv. Cttee, Wesleyan Univ. Fielding Edn. Pres., Amer. Soc. for Eighteenth Century Studies, 1972-73; Hon. Vice-Pres., Johnson Soc. of London; Hon. Mem., The Johnson Club, London and Johnson Soc., Oslo, Norway; Mem., The Johnsonians, NY. Hon. LittD Evansville Coll., 1955; Hon. LHD: Wabash Coll., 1956; Indiana Univ., 1963; Lehigh Univ., 1972. Phi Beta Kappa. PEN; FRSL 1956; FRSA 1970. *Publications:* Hester Lynch Piozzi (Mrs Thrale), 1941; Dr Campbell's Diary (edn), 1947; Pope and his Contemporaries (ed with Louis A. Landa), 1949; Johnsonian Studies, 1887-1950: a Survey and Bibliography, 1951 (rev. edn 1970); Young Samuel Johnson, 1955; Eighteenth Century English Literature: Modern Essays in Criticism (ed), 1959; Biography as an Art (ed), 1962; Smollett's Peregrine Pickle (ed), 1964; Man versus Society in 18th Century Britain (ed), 1968; From Puzzles to Portraits: problems of a literary biographer, 1970; Editor, Johnsonian News Letter, 1940-; various other editions for the Augustan Reprint Soc., and articles in scholarly jls; Festschrift, English Writers of the Eighteenth Century, ed J. H. Middendorf, 1971. *Recreations:* baseball, music and theatre. *Address:* 25 Claremont Avenue, New York, New York, NY 10027, USA. *T:* New York-Monument 3-2233. *[Died 7 April* 1978.

CLIFTON, Leon James Thomas; Under-Secretary, Department of Trade and Industry (formerly Ministry of Technology), 1967-72, retired; *b* 17 May 1912; *s* of William Clifton and Helen Florence Clifton (*née* Holloway); *m* 1937, Doris Camp; one *s* one *d*. *Educ:* Fulham Central. Air Min., 1929; Min. of Aircraft Production, 1940; Min. of Supply, 1946; Min. of Aviation, 1959 (Dir of Contracts, 1960-67). *Recreations:* bowls, gardening. *Address:* 9 Evans Gardens, Hunstanton, Norfolk. *T:* Hunstanton 2057. *[Died 9 Aug.* 1978.

CLINTON, David Osbert F.; see Fynes-Clinton.

CLINTON, Michael Denys Arthur, CMG 1971; GM 1942 and Bar 1943; Deputy Colonial Secretary, Hong Kong, since 1969; *b* 9 Oct. 1918; *s* of late Frederick William Gregory Clinton and Dorothy Violet Clinton (*née* Hasluck); *m* 1953, Rosemary Anita (*née* Home-Douglas); one *s* four *d*. *Educ:* Beaumont Coll.; London Univ. (Imperial Coll. and LSE). Intermediate BSc (Eng). Served RE 1939-46 (Major). Hong Kong Govt: Administrative Officer, 1946; Asst Dir of Commerce and Industry, 1952; Dep. Financial Sec., 1957; Dep. Economic Sec., 1966; Actg Financial Sec. at various times, 1961-68; Dep. Colonial Sec., 1969, Actg Colonial Sec. on various occasions. *Recreations:* tennis, furniture design and construction. *Address:* c/o Colonial Secretariat, Lower Albert Road, Hong Kong. *T:* 95568; Higher Sweetwell House, Sedgehill, Shaftesbury, Dorset. *Club:* Hong Kong (Hong Kong). *[Died 31 May* 1976.

CLINTON-BADDELEY, Madeline Angela, (Angela Baddeley), CBE 1975; actress since 1915; *b* 4 July 1904; 3rd *d* of William Herman Clinton-Baddeley and Louise Bourdin; *m* 1st, 1921, Stephen Kerr Thomas (marr. diss.); one *d*; 2nd, 1929, Glencairn Alexander Byam Shaw, CBE; one *s* one *d*. *Educ:* privately. First stage appearance, Old Vic, 1913, in Richard III and frequently on London stage until 1926; went to Australia with Dion Boucicault, 1926, during which tour parts included Mary Rose in the play of that name; reappeared in London, 1927, and continued on London stage in various parts including Katheryn

Howard in The Rose Without a Thorn, Duchess, 1932, and Florrie in Sheppey, Wyndhams, 1933; played Olivia Grayne in Night Must Fall, Duchess, 1935, and the same part as her first appearance in New York, Barrymore Theatre, 1936. More recent London appearances include: Grace Fenning in Dear Octopus, Queen's, 1938; Cecily Cardew in The Importance of Being Earnest, 1939; Cattrin in The Light of Heart, Apollo, 1940, Globe, 1941; Miss Prue in Love for Love, Phoenix, 1943; Catherine Winslow in The Winslow Boy, Lyric, 1946; The Madwoman of Chaillot, St James's, 1951; Mrs Moxton (Moxie) in Relative Values, Savoy, 1951; Gina in The Wild Duck, Saville, 1955. Mem. Old Vic Company for 1949-50 season, New Theatre; Mem. Festival Company, Stratford, for 1955, 1958, 1959 seasons; Russian tour with Festival Company, 1958-59; Mae Peterson in Bye Bye Birdie, Her Majesty's, Haymarket, 1961-62; Mum in Day of the Prince, Royal Court, 1963; Lady Bracknell in The Importance of Being Earnest, 1964, and Madame Ranevsky in The Cherry Orchard, 1965, Playhouse, Nottingham; Zozyushka Savishna in Ivanov, Phœnix, 1965. TV Series include: Mrs Gamp in Martin Chuzzlewit, 1965; Mrs Bridges in Upstairs Downstairs, 1973-75. *Recreation:* swimming. *Address:* 169 Ashley Gardens, SW1.
[Died 22 Feb. 1976.

CLISSITT, William Cyrus, OBE 1968; TD; JP; Editor, Evening Express, Liverpool, 1928-54; Secretary of the Press Council, 1960-68; *b* 1898; *o s* of late Cyrus Thomas Clissitt, JP, Newport, Mon; *m* 1923, Antoinette Mary (marr. diss. 1972), *e d* of late Joseph Herbert Canning, OBE, JP (Knight of Papal Order of St Gregory), Newport, Mon; one *s* two *d*. Editor Torbay Herald, Torquay, 1924; active service with Artists' Rifles OTC, European War, 1914-18; and Royal Artillery, 1939-45 (Lt-Col); commanded Sudan Artillery in the rank of Kaimakam; inaugurated Weekly Wireless Talks on Sport for BBC at Cardiff, 1923; Founder Mem. Guild of British Newspaper Editors; selected Military Mem. West Lancs T & AFA; Hon. Col 626 (Liverpool Irish) HAA Regt RA, TA, 1950-55. JP Liverpool. *Publications:* Knowsley Hall; numerous newspaper articles on wide variety of subjects. *Recreation:* aerophilately. *Address:* 150 Stow Hill, Newport, Gwent. *T:* Newport 65516.
[Died 13 Dec. 1977.

CLOETE, (Edward Fairly) Stuart (Graham), CIAL; *b* Paris, 23 July 1897; *s* of Laurence Cloete, Cape Town, and Edith Margaret Park, London; divorced; no *c* ; *m* 1914, Mildred West, Elizabeth, New Jersey. *Educ:* Lancing Coll. 2nd Lieut Sept. 1914 (wounded twice); retired from Coldstream Guards, 1925; farmed in South Africa, 1925-35 and 1949-53. *Publications:* Turning Wheels, 1937; Watch for the Dawn, 1939; Yesterday is Dead, 1940; The Old Men and the Young (Poems), 1941; The Hill of Doves, 1941; Christmas in Matabeleland, 1942; Congo Song, 1943; Against These Three, 1945; The Third Way, 1946; The Curve and the Tusk, 1953; The African Giant, 1955; Mamba, 1956; Storm over Africa, 1956; The Mask, 1957; Gazella, 1958; The Soldiers' Peaches, 1959; The Fiercest Heart, 1960; The Silver Trumpet, 1961; West With the Sun, 1962; The Looking Glass, 1963; Rags of Glory, 1963; The Honey Bird, 1964; The 1001 Nights of Jean Macaque, 1965; The Abductors, 1966; The Writing on the Wall, 1968; South Africa: the land and peoples, 1969; How Young They Died, 1969; Three White Swans, 1971; A Victorian Son, 1971; The Company with a Heart of Gold, 1973; The Gambler, 1973; More Nights of Jean Macaque, 1975; Canary Pie, 1976; stories, poems and articles to Saturday Evening Post, Collier's, Ladies' Home Journal, Argosy, Vogue, Saturday Review of Literature, Life and others. *Recreations:* farming, horses, cattle, painting, natural history. *Address:* c/o Curtis Brown Ltd, 1 Craven Hill, W2; Box 164, Hermanus, S Africa. *Clubs:* Guards, Savage; Coffee House, Explorers, National Arts, Overseas Press (New York).
[Died 20 March 1976.

CLORE, Sir Charles, Kt 1971; President: Sears Engineering Ltd; Sears Holdings Ltd; former Chairman: British Shoe Corporation Ltd; Lewis's Investment Trust Ltd; Selfridges Ltd; Sears Industries Inc.; Scottish Motor Traction Co. Ltd; Mappin & Webb Ltd; Princes Investments Ltd; *b* 26 Dec. 1904; *m* 1943, Francine Rachel Halphen (marr. diss.); one *s* one *d*. *Educ:* London. Is also Dir of a number of other public companies engaged in commercial and industrial enterprises. *Address:* 22 Park Street, Park Lane, W1Y 4AE. *T:* 01-499 3821.
[Died 26 July 1979.

CLOUTMAN, His Honour Sir Brett (Mackay), VC; Kt 1957; MC; QC; Senior Official Referee of the Supreme Court of Judicature, 1954-63; of Gray's Inn and Western Circuit; *b* 7 Nov. 1891; *s* of late Alfred B. Cloutman; *m* Margaret Hunter; two *d*. *Educ:* Berkhamsted Sch.; Bishops Stortford Coll.; London Univ. Served 1914-18 and 1939-45 Wars in France,

Belgium, Syria, Egypt and Italy, in Royal Engineers; VC and MC while comdg 59th Field Co. RE in 5th Div., 1918; despatches, 1944. Called to Bar, 1926; KC 1946; Sen. Chm. War Pensions (Special Review) Tribunals, 1947; Official Referee, 1948. Master Worshipful Co. of Glass Sellers of London, 1939-40, 1965-66. Pres., Hornsey (N London) YMCA; Chm., Metropolitan Union of YMCA. Governor, Eltham Coll. *Publications:* (joint) The Law Relating to Authors and Publishers; The Law Relating to Printers. *Address:* 2 The Old Hall, Highgate, N6. *T:* 01-340 8205. *Club:* Athenæum.
[Died 15 Aug. 1971.

CLOWES, Maj.-Gen. Norman, CBE 1943; DSO 1918; MC; ADC to the King, 1946-49; retired Sept. 1949; *b* 7 Oct. 1893; *s* of late Albert Clowes, Warwick, Queensland; *m* 1918, Vera Elizabeth Ingleby (marr. diss. 1954), 2nd *d* of Sir Alexander Pengilly; one *s. Educ:* Toowoomba Grammar Sch.; RMC Duntroon. Commissioned Australian Staff Corps, 1914; served with AIF, 1914-18, in Egypt, Gallipoli, France, Belgium; Grad. Staff Coll., Camberley, 1920; exchange duty Indian Army, 1927-30; transf. British Army, 1931; Comdg 1st Bn Manchester Regt, 1937-39, served during Palestine Rebellion, 1937-38. Col, 1939; Brig. 1941; temp. Maj.-Gen. 1943. Despatches 5 times; Croix de Guerre, France; Medal of Freedom, USA. *Address:* Tanglin, Harefield Road, Middleton-on-Sea, Sussex.
[Died 2 March 1980.

CLUNIE, James; *b* 20 March 1889; *m* 1912, Elizabeth Stewart. *Educ:* Lundin Links, Lower Largo. House painter and decorator. Mem. Exec. of Scottish Painters' Soc. for 18 years (Chm. three times). Mem. of Dunfermline Town Council, 1933-50; Magistrate 6 years. MP (Lab) Dunfermline, 1950-Sept. 1959. *Publications:* First Principles of Working Class Education, 1920; The Autobiography of a House Painter: Labour is my Faith, 1954; The Voice of Labour, 1958; Literature of Labour, 1966. *Recreations:* reading and book reviewing. *Address:* c/o Mrs Brown, Craigie Lea, Balcurvie, Windygates, Fife.
[Died 25 Feb. 1974.

CLUTTERBUCK, Sir Alexander; *see* Clutterbuck, Sir P. A.

CLUTTERBUCK, Sir (Peter) Alexander, GCMG 1952 (KCMG 1946; CMG 1943); MC; *b* 27 March 1897; *e s* of late Sir Peter Clutterbuck, CIE, CBE, formerly Inspector Gen. of Forests, India and Burma; *m* 1921, Dorita, *y d* of Francis Seymour Weldon; one *d. Educ:* Malvern Coll. (Scholar); Pembroke Coll., Cambridge (Scholar). Served European War, Coldstream Guards, 1916-19 (despatches, MC); entered Civil Service as Asst Principal GPO, 1919; Colonial Office, 1922; additional Private Sec. to Parly Under-Sec. for the Colonies, 1924; Sec., Donoughmore Commn on Ceylon Constitution, 1927-28; Private Sec. to Permanent Under-Sec. of State, Dominions Office, 1928-29; Principal, Dominions Office, 1929; Mem. of UK Delegation to League of Nations Assembly, 1929, 1930, and 1931, negotiations with Egypt, 1930, and Reparations Conferences, London, 1931, Lausanne, 1932; Sec., Newfoundland Royal Commn, 1933; Dep. High Comr for UK, Union of South Africa, 1939-40; Asst Sec., Dominions Office, 1940; Asst Under-Sec. of State, 1942-46; High Comr for the UK in Canada, 1946-52, in India, 1952-55; HM Ambassador to the Republic of Ireland, 1955-59; Permanent Under-Sec. of State, CRO, 1959-61. Governor, Malvern Coll. Hon. DCL: Bishop's Univ., Quebec; Queen's Univ., Ont; Univ. of BC. *Address:* Upperton Farmhouse, Bury, Sussex. *T:* Bury 640. *Club:* Travellers'.
[Died 29 Dec. 1975.

CLUTTON-BROCK, Prof. Alan Francis; *m* 1936, Barbara Foy Mitchell; one *d. Educ:* Eton; King's College, Cambridge. Art Critic, The Times; Trustee of the National Gallery. Slade Professor of Fine Art, Univ. of Cambridge, 1955-58. *Address:* Chastleton House, Moreton-in-Marsh, Glos.
[Died 18 Dec. 1976.

CLYDE, Rt. Hon. Lord; Rt. Hon. James Latham McDiarmid Clyde, PC 1951; LLD, Edinburgh 1954, St Andrews 1955, Aberdeen 1960; DL; Lord Justice-General of Scotland and Lord President of the Court of Session, 1954-72; *b* 30 Oct. 1898; *e s* of late Lord Clyde, PC; *m* 1928, Margaret Letitia Du Buisson (*d* 1974); one *s* one *d. Educ:* Edinburgh Academy; Trinity Coll., Oxford; Edinburgh Univ. Called to Scots Bar, 1925; KC (Scotland) 1936. Lord Advocate, 1951-54; Hon. Bencher, Middle Temple, 1958. MP (C) North Edinburgh, 1950-54. DL County of Kinross, 1965. *Address:* Briglands, Rumbling Bridge, Kinross. *T:* Fossoway 205. *Club:* New (Edinburgh).
[Died 30 June 1975.

CLYDE, Dr William McCallum, CMG 1948; Senior Lecturer in English, Avery Hill College, 1958-70, retired; *b* 23 June 1901; *e s*

of Rev. William A. Clyde; *m* 1931, Catherine Grace, *d* of Rev. D. D. Rees, Saltcoats, Scotland; four *s. Educ:* King Edward VII's Sch., Sheffield; St Andrews Univ. MA, 1st Class Hons, Eng. Lang. and Lit., St Andrews, 1925; Carnegie Research Fellowship, 1927-29; PhD St Andrews, 1929; Lectr in Eng. Lang. and Lit., St Andrews, 1929; Head of Dept of Eng. Lang. and Lit., University Coll., Dundee, 1935; Asst Div. Food Officer, East Scotland, 1939; Dep. Div. Food Officer, East Scotland, 1941; Adviser to Sec. of State for Colonies on wartime food supplies, 1942; Chm. of Nutrition, Food and Agricultural Unit to study food situation in Malaya in post-liberation period, 1945; Food Adviser to Special Commissioner in SE Asia, 1946; Leader, UK Delegn to UN FAO Meetings: Trivandrum, India, 1947; Baguio, Philippines, 1948; Singapore and Bangkok, 1949; Bandung, Indonesia, 1952; Tokyo and Rangoon, 1954; Dir of Economic Activities for Commissioner-Gen. for UK in SE Asia, Singapore, 1948-51; Vice-Chm., International Rice Commission, 1949, 1954; Rice Adviser to Foreign Office, 1951-56. Professor of English, Baghdad, 1956-58. *Publications:* The Freedom of the Press from Caxton to Cromwell, 1934; AE (George W. Russell): Poet, Essayist and Painter, 1935. *Recreation:* sketching. *Address:* 79 Queens Park Rise, Brighton, Sussex.
[Died 10 July 1972.

COAD, Maj.-Gen. Basil Aubrey, CB 1953; CBE 1950; DSO 1944 (Bar 1945); DL; *b* 27 Sept. 1906; *s* of late Engineer-Capt. H. J. Coad, RN, and Mrs E. M. Coad; *m* 1st, 1935, Janet Octavia (*d* 1954); no *c*; 2nd, 1955, Mrs Clare Henley; one *d. Educ:* Felsted; RMC Sandhurst. Commissioned into Wilts Regt, 1926; served in India, 1926-28; Shanghai, 1929-30; Adjutant 2nd Bn Wilts Regt, 1934-37; Palestine, 1935-36; Adjt 4th Bn Wilts Regt, 1937-39; comd 5th Bn Dorsetshire Regt, 1942-44; Comdr 130 Infantry Bde, 1944-46; Staff Coll., 1946; comd 2nd Bn Wilts Regt, Dec. 1946-48; formed and comd 27 Infantry Bde, 1948-51; Hong Kong, 1949-50; Korea, 1950-51; Comdr 2nd Infantry Div., 1951-54; Pres., Regular Commissions Board, Westbury, Wilts, 1954-57, retired. Col The Wilts Regt (Duke of Edinburgh's), 1954-59; Col The Duke of Edinburgh's Royal Regt (Berks and Wilts), 1959-64. Mem., Cttee to write Official History of Korean War, 1978-. DL Wilts 1963. Officer, US Legion of Merit, 1954; American Silver Star, 1950. *Recreation:* gardening. *Address:* Nursteed House, Devizes, Wilts. *[Died 26 March 1980.*

COATES, Sir Albert (Ernest), Kt 1955; OBE 1946; MD, MS; LLD (*hc*); FRCS; FRACS; retired Consulting Surgeon, Melbourne, Australia; Consulting Surgeon: Royal Melbourne, Royal Women's Hospital, Melbourne; *b* 28 Jan. 1895; *s* of Arthur Coates, Ballarat, Vic.; *m* 1st, 1921, Harriet Josephine (*d* 1934), *d* of Elisha Hicks, Melbourne; 2nd, 1936, Catherine Martha, *d* of Alfred Anderson, Dunedin, NZ; two *s* three *d. Educ:* Ballarat; Univ. of Melbourne. MB, BS, Melbourne, 1924; MD 1926; MS 1927; FRACS 1932; FRCS (by election) 1953. Served European War, 1914-18: AIF, Gallipoli and France; Surg., Royal Melbourne Hosp., 1927-55. War Service, 1941-46 (despatches, OBE): Senior Surg. (Lt-Col) to AIF, Malaya; POW 1942; Chief MO in POW Hosp., Siam, 1944-45. Stewart Lectr in Surgery, Univ. of Melbourne, 1949-56. Mem. Dental Board, Vic., 1936-49; Pres. BMA, Vic., 1941 and 1947; Foundation Fellow, AMA; Mem. Council, Univ. of Melbourne, 1951-57; Pres., Nurses Memorial Centre, Melbourne, 1955-62; Chm. Board of Management, Fairfield Hosp., 1956-73; Pres. Rotary Club, Melbourne, 1954-55; Mem. Olympics Civic Cttee, 1955-56. Hon. LLD, Melbourne, 1962. *Publications:* contribs on surgical subjects in Australian and other jls. *Address:* 2 Chastleton Avenue, Toorak, Vic 3142, Australia. *Clubs:* Melbourne, Athenæum (Melbourne). *[Died 8 Oct. 1977.*

COATES, Captain Sir Clive Milnes-, 2nd Bt *cr* 1911; OBE 1919; *b* 21 May 1879; *s* of 1st Bt and Edith, *e d* of Capt. Philip Woolley, Gravenhurst, Sussex; *S* father, 1921; changed names by deed poll to Sir Clive Milnes-Coates, 1946; *m* 1906, Lady Celia Hermione Crewe Milnes, 2nd *d* of 1st Marquis of Crewe, KG, PC; one *s* two *d* (and *yr s* killed in Normandy, 1944). *Educ:* Charterhouse; Exeter Coll., Oxford. Late 15th Hussars; Patron of one Living. *Heir:* *s* Robert Edward James Clive Milnes-Coates, Lt-Col Coldstream Guards, DSO [*b* 27 Sept. 1907; *m* 1945, Lady Patricia Milnes-Gaskell, *er d* of 4th Earl of Listowel and *widow* of Lt-Col Charles Milnes-Gaskell, Coldstream Guards; one *s* (*b* 8 Dec. 1948), one *d*]. *Address:* 13 Hyde Park Gate, SW7. *T:* 01-584 8434; Helperby Hall, Helperby, York YO6 2QP. *T:* Helperby 204. *[Died 4 Sept. 1971.*

COATES, Joseph Edward, OBE 1919; DSc, FRIC; *b* 6 May 1883; *e s* of W. and M. J. Coates, Oakamoor, N Staffs; *m* 1915, Ada Maria Finney, MSc, FRIC (*d* 1968); two *s. Educ:* Alleyne's Grammar Sch., Uttoxeter; University Coll. of N Wales, Bangor. Fellow of Univ. of Wales, 1906-08; Research Asst to Prof. Haber, Karlsruhe, 1908-09; Lecturer in Chemistry, Univ. of

Birmingham, 1910-20; Prof. of Chemistry, University Coll. of Swansea (University of Wales), 1920-48; retired 1948. Senior Technical Officer, RN Experimental Station, Stratford, London with rank of Lieut-Comdr, RNVR, 1915-19. *Publications:* papers in chemical journals. *Address:* Sabinal, Lucklands Road, Weston Park, Bath. *T:* Bath 23377.   *[Died 20 Sept.* 1973.

COATS, Air Cdre Rowland, CB 1954; RAF retd; ICT 1958-65; *b* 26 May 1904; *m* 1959, Eva Gertrud Truemer; two *s* one *d* (triplets). *Educ:* Emmanuel Coll., Cambridge (MA); RAF Coll., Cranwell. 7 Squadron, 1925-28; spec. in Engrg; India, 1934-37; Staff Coll., 1938; War of 1939-45: Air Min.; Bomber Comd, Egypt; Stn Comdr, Bridgnorth, 1947-49; Air Cdre, 1949; AOC: Record Office, 1949-51; 62 Gp, 1951-53; AOA 205 Group, 1953-56; AOC 205 Group, 1956. *Address:* Lower Ebford, Barton, Topsham, Exeter. *T:* Topsham 3109.   *[Died 3 March* 1974.

COBB, Hon. Sir John Francis Scott, Kt 1975; **Hon. Mr Justice Cobb;** a Judge of the High Court, Queen's Bench Division, since 1975; Presiding Judge, North Eastern Circuit, since 1976; *b* 15 Dec. 1922; *o s* of late J. H. Cobb, FRCS and Mrs E. M. Cobb (*née* Davidson); *m* 1951, Joan Mary, *o d* of W. H. Knapton, Whitgift, near Goole, Yorks, and of Mrs E. M. Knapton (*née* Silvester); two *s* two *d. Educ:* Winchester Coll.; Trinity Coll., Oxford. Commissioned Royal Artillery, 1942; Staff Capt. (Civil Affairs), Trieste, 1945-46; MA Oxon 1947; called to Bar, Inner Temple, 1948, Master 1969; QC 1962. Recorder of: Doncaster, 1961-64; Bradford, 1964-69; Hull, 1969-70; Sheffield, 1970-71; a Recorder, and Hon. Recorder of Sheffield, 1972-75. Leader of NE Circuit, 1971-75. Asst Boundary Comr, 1965. Chancellor, Dio. of Bradford, 1971-75. *Recreations:* golf and gardening. *Address:* The Priory, Follifoot, near Harrogate, N Yorks. *T:* Harrogate 871537; 2 King's Bench Walk, Temple, EC4. *T:* 01-353 2411. *Clubs:* Garrick; Vincent's (Oxford).
                                              [Died 7 Feb. 1977.

COBB, John Leslie; Executive Director, National and Commercial Development Capital Ltd, since 1971; Director, Nicholas Lane Management Services Ltd, since 1975; *b* 25 Sept. 1923; *yr s* of late Rev. John E. Cobb, Meltham, Huddersfield; *m* 1949, Pamela Teresa, *d* of late Arthur John Bareham, Chelmsford, Essex; one *d. Educ:* Burnage High Sch., Manchester; Thornes House, Wakefield. Served War of 1939-45: Ordinary Seaman, 1941; Midshipman, RNVR, 1943; Sub-Lieut, 1944; Lieut, 1945. Daily Express, 1949-52; Investors Chronicle, 1952-67, apptd Dep. Ed., 1957; Ed., Investors Chronicle and Stock Exchange Gazette following merger, 1967-70. *Address:* The Colnes, Coppins Close, Springfield, Chelmsford, Essex. *T:* Chelmsford 62454. *Club:* Reform.   *[Died 14 Jan.* 1977.

COBB, Rear-Adm. Robert Harborne, CBE 1953 (OBE 1941); retired; *b* 18 Sept. 1900; *s* of late Lieut-Col Cobb; *m* 1930, Honor, *d* of late Sir C. Aubrey Smith; one *s* one *d. Educ:* All Saints, Bloxham; RN Colls, Osborne and Dartmouth. Joined Osborne, 1914; Midshipman, 1917; Comdr (E), 1934; Asst Naval Attaché, Europe, 1935-37; Capt. (E), 1944; Rear-Adm. (E), 1951; retired list 1954. War of 1939-45 (despatches twice, OBE). With British Council, 1954-59. *Address:* Hill Farm Cottage, 18 Highlands Road, Fareham, Hants. *T:* Fareham 80286.   *[Died 10 March* 1978.

COBHAM, 10th Viscount *cr* 1718; **Charles John Lyttelton,** KG 1964; PC 1967; GCMG 1957; GCVO 1972; TD; Baron Lyttelton, 1756 (renewed 1794); Baron Westcote, 1776; Bt 1618; Lord Lieutenant of Worcestershire 1963-74; Chancellor, Order of the Garter, since 1972; *b* 8 Aug. 1909; *s* of 9th Viscount, KCB and Violet Yolande (*d* 1966), *yr d* of Charles Leonard, Gloria, Cape Province; *S* father, 1949; *m* 1942, Elizabeth Alison, *yr d* of J. R. Makeig-Jones, Southerton House, near Ottery St Mary, Devon; four *s* four *d. Educ:* Eton; Trinity Coll., Cambridge. BA (Hons) Law Cambridge, 1932. Joined 100th (Worcs Yeo.) Fd Bde RA, TA, 1933; Capt. Worcs County Cricket Team, 1936-39; Vice-Capt., MCC New Zealand Tour, 1935-36. Served War of 1939-45, 53rd (Worcs Yeo.) Anti-Tank Regt RA, France, 1940; seconded to 3rd Maritime Regt, RA, 1941; commanded 5th Regt Maritime RA, 1943-45. Parly Candidate (C) for Dudley and Stourbridge, 1948, but relinquished appointment upon death of his father, 1949. Governor-Gen. and C-in-C of New Zealand, 1957-62. Lord Steward of HM Household, 1967-72. President, MCC, 1954, Treasurer, 1963-64. Director: Lloyds Bank (and Chm., Birmingham Cttee); National Bank of New Zealand; Eagle Star Insurance Co.; Monks Investment Trust; John Brockhouse Ltd. DL, Co. of Worcester, 1952-57 and 1963. Hon. Col The Queen's Own Warwicks and Worcs Yeomanry, TA, 1963-69. Trustee, Nat. Portrait Gall., 1972-. Pres., RNIB, 1964-75. *Recreations:* shooting, cricket, golf. *Heir: s* Hon. John William Leonard Lyttelton [*b* 5 June 1943; *m* 1974, Penelope Ann, *er d* of Roy Cooper]. *Address:* Hagley Hall, Stourbridge,

West Midlands. *T:* Hagley 2408. *Clubs:* White's, MCC.
                                              [Died 20 March 1977.

COBHAM, Sir Alan (John), KBE 1926; AFC 1926; pioneer aviator; *b* 6 May 1894; *s* of Frederick Cobham and Elizabeth Burrows; *m* 1922, Gladys Lloyd (*d* 1961); two *s. Educ:* Wilson Grammar Sch. Pupilled, farming, 1912; commercial career, City, 1913; served European War, Aug. 1914 to Jan. 1919; served three years in France; commissioned 1917, RFC, later RAF; on demobilisation entered Civil Aviation; carried 5,000 passengers in 1919; joined the Aircraft Manufacturing Co. for aerial photography work, 1920; joined De Havilland Aircraft Co., 1921; did much aerial photography; Aug., flew 5,000 miles round Europe; started Spanish Air Line to Morocco, Nov. 1921; another 8,000 mile tour round Europe and North Africa, 1922; flew Belgrade-London in day, June 1922; flew 12,000 miles Europe, N Africa, Egypt, Palestine 1923; awarded Britannia Trophy, first Britisher to cross Channel in light aeroplane; flew London-Brussels with 6-hp engine; won King's Cup Race, 1924; flew London-Rangoon and back, 1924, 1925; awarded Britannia Trophy for 1925: flew London-Cape Town and back (AFC) 1925-26; awarded Royal Aero Club Gold Medal, Simms Gold Medal by Royal IAE, Aviation Gold Medal from Institute of Transport, 1926; flew from England to Australia and back, Summer 1926; won Britannia Trophy, 1926; Comdr Pilot of flying boat expedition, flying round entire African continent for first time in history; promoter of Through African Air Route scheme, 1927-28; organised Municipal Aerodrome Campaign, 1929; survey flight for Imperial Airways to Rhodesia, 1929; Air Ministry flight of survey with multi-engine seaplane, up Nile to Congo, 1931; organised National Aviation Day Ltd touring the British Isles, 1932 and 1933; organised National Aviation Displays Ltd, 1934, 1935, 1936 (1250 Air Displays carrying 900,000 people, 1932-36); Pioneer of refuelling in the air; development and experimental work, 1936-46; introduced Cobham system of refuelling in flight into USAF, 1948; introduced Probe and Drogue System of Refuelling in flight to USAF, US Navy and Royal Air Force, 1951. Chm., Bournemouth Symphony Orchestra, 1956-67; Master, Guild of Air Pilots and Air Navigators, 1964-65. Hon. FRAeS, 1927. *Films:* With Cobham to the Cape and Back, With Cobham Round Africa, The Flight Commander, Cobham to Kivu and Back, The King's Cup. Has appeared on television, notably in series called The Flying Years. *Publications:* Skyways; My Flight to the Cape and Back; Australia and Back; Twenty Thousand Miles in a Flying Boat; numerous articles. *Recreations:* yachting, gardening. *Address:* PO Box 313, Tortola, British Virgin Islands. *T:* 52351. *Clubs:* United Service & Royal Aero, Royal Air Force.   *[Died 21 Oct.* 1973.

COCHRANE, Sir Desmond Oriel Alastair George Weston, 3rd Bt *cr* 1903; Consul-General of Ireland to the Republics of Syria and The Lebanon since 1949; *b* 22 Oct. 1918; 2nd *s* of Sir Ernest Cochrane, 2nd Bt, and Elsa, *y d* of Erwin Schumacher, 1952; *m* 1946, Yvonne, *o c* of late Alfred Bey Sursock and of Donna Maria Sursock; three *s* one *d. Educ:* Eton. Served War of 1939-45; Staff Captain: Northern Command, 1941; War Office, AG 12, 1942; GHQ Middle East Forces (Mil. Sec. Branch), 1943; Military Sec. to GOC 9th Army, 1944. *Heir: s* Henry Mark Sursock Cochrane [*b* 23 Oct. 1946; *m* 1969, Hala, *d* of Fuad Es Said; one *s* one *d*]. *Address:* Maison Sursock, Beyrouth, Lebanon. *Club:* Carlton.   *[Died 12 March* 1979.

COCHRANE, Rear-Adm. Sir Edward Owen, KBE 1943; *b* 17 Aug. 1881; *s* of Vice-Adm. Basil E. Cochrane and Cornelia Ramsay Robinson Owen; *m* 1908, Mary Lucy George (*d* 1955); (*s* Major RA, killed in Tunisia) one *d. Educ:* HMS Britannia. Midshipman, 1897; qualified as a Gunnery Lieut, 1905; Comdr, 1915; Capt., 1920; served at Admiralty as Asst Dir Gunnery Div. and Asst then Deputy Dir Naval Intelligence Div., 1921-24; Capt. of HMS Cairo, East Indies Station, 1924-26; of Devonport Gunnery Sch., 1927-29; Dir of Training and Staff Duties, 1929-31; Capt., HMS Repulse, 1931-32; Rear-Adm., 1933; retired list, 1933; employed as a Convoy Commodore with the rank of Commodore RNR, 1939-45. *Recreations:* interest: has been connected with work of Moral Re-Armament for many years. *Address:* 5 St George's Square, SW1. *T:* 01-828 5460. *Club:* United Service & Royal Aero.   *[Died 27 Jan.* 1972.

COCHRANE, Maj.-Gen. James Rupert, CB 1951; CBE 1947; retired; *b* 28 Nov. 1904; *s* of Brig.-Gen. J. K. Cochrane, CMG; *m* 1937, Hilary, *d* of H. W. Standen, Westways, Sevenoaks; one *s* one *d. Educ:* Charterhouse; RMA Woolwich. Commissioned Royal Artillery, 1925; Staff Coll., Camberley, 1939; Imperial Defence Coll., 1948. Served War of 1939-45 (despatches): in NW Europe, Italy and Middle East, on Staff and Commanding 191 (Herts and Essex) Yeomanry Fd Regt. Chief of Staff, HQ British troops in Palestine and Transjordan, 1945-47 (despatches).

Commanded HAA Regt, 1947; Chief of Staff, HQ East Africa Command, 1949-52; Comd 51 (U) AA Brigade, 1952-53; Deputy Chief of Staff HQ Allied Land Forces, Central Europe, 1953-56; Principal Staff Officer to Deputy Supreme Allied Commander (Viscount Montgomery), Allied Powers in Europe, 1956-58; retired, 1959. *Recreation:* fishing. *Address:* Plestor House, Selborne, Alton, Hants. *Club:* Army and Navy.
[*Died* 13 *June* 1978.

COCHRANE, Hon. Lady, (Julia Dorothy), CBE 1952; Chief Commissioner for England, Girl Guides Association, 1941-51, President, 1951-61; *e d* of 1st Baron Cornwallis, CBE, TD, DL, JP (*d* 1935); *m* 1926, Capt. the Hon. Sir Archibald Douglas Cochrane, GCMG, KCSI, DSO (*d* 1958); one *s* one *d.* Commander Sister of the Order of St John of Jerusalem. Red Cross Long Service Medal and clasp. *Address:* 17 Morpeth Mansions, Morpeth Terrace, SW1. *T:* 01-834 5700. *Club:* Guide.
[*Died* 15 *June* 1971.

COCHRANE, Air Chief Marshal Hon. Sir Ralph (Alexander), GBE 1950 (KBE 1945); KCB 1948; AFC 1919; FRAeS; *b* 24 Feb. 1895; *y s* of 1st Baron Cochrane of Cults; *m* 1930, Hilda Frances Holme Wiggin; two *s* one *d.* *Educ:* Osborne and Dartmouth. Entered Navy, 1912; transferred to newly created Airship branch 1915 and to RAF 1919; served in Egypt and Iraq, 1920-23, and at Aden, 1928-29; on the directing staff RAF Staff Coll., Andover, 1930-31, and at Air Ministry, 1932-33; Imperial Defence Coll., 1934. Seconded to New Zealand Govt to advise on air defence and became first Chief of the Air Staff of the Royal New Zealand Air Force, 1936-39. ADC to the King, 1939-40. Held various appointments covering intelligence and training, 1939-42; commanded Nos 3 and 5 Bomber Groups, 1942-45; AOC-in-C Transport Command, 1945-47; AOC-in-C Flying Training Command, 1947-50; Vice-CAS, Air Ministry, 1950-52; retd Nov. 1952. Air ADC to the King, 1949; ADC to the Queen, 1952. Joint Man. Dir Atlantic Shipbuilding Co., 1953-56; Rolls Royce Ltd, 1956-61; Chairman: RJM Exports Ltd, 1962; Cochrane's of Oxford Ltd, 1973-. RUSI Gold Medal Essay, 1935; Edward Busk Meml Prize, RAeS, 1948; Triennial Award of Merit, InstT, 1958-61. *Address:* Grove Farmhouse, Shipton-under-Wychwood, Oxford OX7 6DG. *T:* 830253. *Clubs:* Brooks's, Royal Air Force. [*Died* 17 *Dec.* 1977.

COCK, Gerald, MVO 1935; *b* 1887; *yr s* of late Alfred Cock, QC, Elm Court, Temple; unmarried. *Educ:* Tonbridge Sch.; Seafield Park. Travelled USA, British Columbia, Mexico, etc, 1909-15; returned to England, 1915; commissioned Royal Engineers, BEF, France and Belgium, 1915-20 (Captain 1917); business in London, 1920-24; joined BBC, 1925 as first Dir of Outside Broadcasts; first Dir of Television, 1935; organised and directed the first television service to be established in Europe or America; North American representative of BBC, 1940-41; Pacific Coast representative of BBC, 1942-45; retired, 1946. *Publications:* articles on broadcasting and television. *Recreations:* travel, walking, riding. *Club:* Reform.
[*Died* 10 *Nov.* 1973.

COCKBURN, Very Rev. James Hutchison, DD; Minister of Dunblane Cathedral (Church of Scotland), 1918-45; Director, Department of Reconstruction and Inter-Church Aid, World Council of Churches, Geneva, 1945-48; Chaplain to King George VI, 1944-52, and to the Queen, 1952; now an Extra Chaplain to the Queen; *b* Paisley, 29 Oct. 1882; *s* of late George Hannah Cockburn, FEIS, schoolmaster, and late Isabella Brodie Marshall; *m* 1912, Amy Macloy; one *s* one *d.* *Educ:* Paisley Grammar Sch.; Glasgow Univ. (MA, BD, DD). Ministries: Mearns, 1908-14; Battlefield (Glasgow), 1914-18; War Service in France with YMCA and as Chaplain in Egypt and in East Africa; Offices held in Church of Scotland: Clerk, Union Cttee, 1927-29; Convener, Church and Nation Cttee, 1929-35; Clerk, Cttee on Restatement of Church's Faith, 1930-35; Convener of Business Cttee of the Gen. Assembly, 1936; Moderator of Gen. Assembly, 1941; Chm., Eastern Section of Presbyterian Alliance, 1939-44; Lecturer on Pastoral Theology, St Mary's Coll., St Andrews, 1931-34; Convener, Cttee on Inter-Church Relations, 1941-44; founded Society of Friends of Dunblane Cathedral, 1929; visited Canada and United States, 1942, during Moderatorship, speaking on spiritual issues of the war, and frequently since; Vice-Chm., British Council of Churches, 1942-44; William Belden Noble Lecturer, Harvard, 1942; Warrack Lecturer, Edinburgh, 1944-45; Hon. Prof., Buda-Pest Univ., 1946; DTh Prague, 1948; DD Yale, 1948, and Occidental, USA, 1950; LHD Wooster Coll., Ohio, 1953; Otts Lecturer, Davidson Coll., North Carolina, 1951; Mem. Royal Commission on Scottish Affairs, 1952-54. Order of White Lion (Czechoslovakia), 1948. *Publications:* Religious Freedom in Eastern Europe, 1951 (USA); The Celtic Church in Dunblane, 1954; The Medieval Bishops of Dunblane and their Church,

1959. *Recreation:* fishing. *Address:* The Cathedral, Dunblane, Perthshire. [*Died* 20 *June* 1973.

COCKELL, Seton F.; see Forbes-Cockell.

COCKEY, Air Cdre Leonard Herbert, CB 1945; Royal Air Force (retired); *b* 1893; *s* of late Rev. H. A. Cockey, Oldland Vicarage, Glos; *m* 1942, Eileen Anne, *d* of James A. Hogan, Tipperary; one *s* two *d.* *Educ:* Bristol Univ. Served European War, 1914-18 (French Croix de Guerre avec Palme, 1916). Qualified RAF Staff Coll. and idc. Served War of 1939-45 in Bomber Command and Southern Rhodesia; retired, 1945. *Address:* Sprayside, Banks Road, Sandbanks, Dorset. *T:* Canford Cliffs 707485. *Club:* Royal Air Force. [*Died* 29 *Dec.* 1978.

CODE HOLLAND, R. H.; see Holland, R. H. C.

CODRINGTON, Sir Christopher William Gerald Henry, 2nd Bt *cr* 1876; *b* 6 Oct. 1894; *s* of late Sir Gerald William Henry Codrington, 1st Bt, and Lady Edith Sybil Henrietta Denison (*d* 1945), *d* of 1st Earl of Londesborough; *S* father, 1929; *m* 1st, 1921, Joan (*d* 1961), 2nd *d* of T. Reginald Hague-Cook; one *s*; 2nd, 1963, Henrietta Desirée Moutray Read (*d* 1979), *d* of late Major Beresford Moutray Read. *Educ:* Uppingham. Joined 19th Royal Hussars, 1914; served with 19th Hussars in France, 1914-18 (wounded); High Sheriff for Co. of Glos, 1938. *Recreations:* cricket, shooting, hunting. *Heir: s* Simon Francis Bethel Codrington [*b* 14 Aug. 1923; *m* 1959, Pamela Joy Halliday, *d* of Major G. W. B. Wise, MBE; three *s.* Late Coldstream Guards]. *Address:* Castle Grove, Bampton, Tiverton, Devon.
[*Died* 10 *Nov.* 1979.

CODRINGTON, Col Sir Geoffrey Ronald, KCVO 1953 (CVO 1948); CB 1932; CMG 1951; DSO 1918; OBE 1919; TD; Extra Gentleman Usher to the Queen since 1967 (Gentleman Usher, 1952-66); *b* 13 May 1888; *s* of late Lt-Gen. Sir A. E. Codrington, GCVO, KCB; *m* 1923, Cecilia, *y d* of late Ernest James Wythes, CBE; two *s* two *d.* *Educ:* Harrow; Christ Church, Oxford (MA). Late The Leics Yeomanry. Served European War, 1914-18 (wounded, DSO, OBE, Order of SS Maurice and Lazarus, Italy), War of 1939-45 (American Bronze Star Medal). High Sheriff of Wilts, 1955-56. *Publication:* The Territorial Army, 1937. *Address:* Roche Court, Winterslow, Salisbury, Wilts. *T:* Winterslow 204. *Clubs:* Travellers'; Leander.
[*Died* 18 *June* 1973.

COFFEY, Christopher, JP; *b* 8 Dec. 1902; *s* of Bernard and Thirza Coffey; *m* 1922, Doris May Coffey (*née* Scott); four *s* two *d.* *Educ:* St Catherine's, Sheffield. Employed in Railway Industry, Traffic Grade; NUR Trade Union Sec. (Branch); Nat. Conf. Sec.; Approved Soc. Branch Sec.; District Council Pres.; represented NUR at TUC and Labour Party Annual Conference, 1918-49; City Councillor, Nottingham, 1945-, Lord Mayor, 1953-54; JP 1947; Alderman, 1954; Hon. Alderman, 1975; Labour Party Organising Sec., 1949-53. *Recreations:* fishing, football (soccer). *Address:* 55 Glapton Road, Nottingham. *T:* 865818. [*Died* 8 *May* 1976.

COGHILL, Prof. Nevill Henry Kendal Aylmer, MA; Merton Professor of English Literature, Oxford, 1957-66; Fellow and Tutor in English Literature, Exeter College, Oxford, 1925-57; Emeritus Fellow: Exeter College, Oxford, 1957; Merton College, Oxford, 1966; *b* 19 April 1899; 2nd *s* of Sir Egerton Bushe Coghill, 5th Bt, and Elizabeth Hildegarde Augusta, *d* of late Col Thomas Henry Somerville, Drishane, Skibbereen; *m* 1927, Elspeth Nora (marr. diss. 1933), *d* of Dr Harley, Inchture, Perthshire; one *d.* *Educ:* Haileybury; Exeter Coll., Oxford. Stapeldon Scholar (History), Exeter Coll., Oxford, 1916. Served European War, from 1917; 2nd Lieut RFA (BSF), 1918-19. Research Fellow, Exeter Coll., 1924, Official Fellow, 1925, and Tutor in English Literature; Sub-Rector, 1940-45; Dean of Degrees, 1940; Clark Lecturer, Trinity Coll., Cambridge, 1959. Mem. Oxford University Drama Commission, 1945; Dir, Friends of OUDS, 1940-47; produced: A Midsummer Night's Dream, Haymarket, 1945; Pilgrim's Progress, Covent Garden, 1951; Dr Faustus, University Theatre, Oxford, 1966; jt dir, Dr Faustus (film), 1967. FRSL 1950. Governor of Shakespeare Memorial Theatre, Stratford-upon-Avon, 1956. Pres., Poetry Soc., 1964-66. Hon. DLitt, Williams Coll., Mass, 1966; Hon. LLD St Andrews, 1971. Has broadcast on Chaucer, Langland, etc. *Play:* (with Martin Starkie) Canterbury Tales, Phœnix Theatre, 1968. *Publications:* The Pardon of Piers Plowman (Gollancz Mem. Lecture, Br. Acad., 1945); Visions from Piers Plowman, 1949; The Poet Chaucer, 1949; The Canterbury Tales (in modern English), 1951; Geoffrey Chaucer, 1956; Shakespeare's Professional Skills, 1964; Troilus and Criseyde (in modern English), 1971; (ed) A Choice of Chaucer's Verse, 1972; Chaucer's Idea of What is Noble, 1972. *Recreations:* producing

Shakespearian and other plays; music, etc. *Address:* Savran House, Aylburton, near Lydney, Glos. *T:* Dean 42240; c/o Merton College, Oxford. *Club:* Travellers'.
[Died 6 Nov. 1980.

COHEN, Baron (Life Peer) *cr* 1951, of Walmer; **Lionel Leonard Cohen,** PC 1946; Kt 1943; a Lord of Appeal in Ordinary, 1951-60; *b* 1 March 1888; *s* of late Sir Leonard Lionel Cohen, KCVO; *m* 1918, Adelaide (*d* 1961), *y d* of late Sir Isidore Spielmann, CMG; two *s* one *d. Educ:* Eton; New Coll., Oxford. 1st class history, 1909, law 1910; called to Bar, Inner Temple, 1913; KC 1929; Bencher, Lincolns Inn, 1934 (Treasurer 1954); served in Min. of Economic Warfare, 1939-43; Judge of Chancery Div. of High Court of Justice, 1943-46; Lord Justice of Appeal, 1946-51. Chm., Company Law Amendment Cttee, 1943-45; Chm. of Royal Commission on awards to Inventors, 1946-56; Chm., Council on Prices, Productivity and Incomes, 1957-59. Hon. Fellow of New Coll., Oxford, 1946; Hon. Fellow University Coll., London, 1955; Hon. LLD London Univ., 1962; Fellow of Eton Coll., 1950-60; Chm. College Cttee, UC London, 1953-63; Capt. Royal and Ancient, St Andrews, 1960-61. Mem. of Council, St Mary's Hospital Medical Sch. (Pres., 1961-66). Served European War, 1914-18, with 13th Princess Louise's Kensington Bn the London Regt and Staff. *Recreation:* golf. *Address:* 55 Porchester Terrace, W2. *T:* 01-723 5057. *Clubs:* White's, St James'.
[Died 9 May 1973.

COHEN OF BIRKENHEAD, 1st Baron *cr* 1956, of Birkenhead; **Henry Cohen,** CH 1974; Kt 1949; MD, ChB (Liverpool); FRCP; P and Hon. FRSH; Hon. FRCPE; Hon. FRCPI; Hon. FRCPGlas; Hon. FRCS; Hon. FRCOG; Hon. FRCGP; Hon. FDSRCS; Hon. FFARCS; Hon. FRIC; Hon. FACP; Hon. FRSM; Hon. FCS; Hon. DSc (NUI, Sussex, Nott.); Hon. ScD (Cambridge, Union Univ. of New York); Hon. LLD (Liverpool, London, Manchester, Hull, TCD, Wales); Hon. DCL Oxford; Hon. FRCR; Hon. FBPsS; Hon. FAPHA; Hon FPS; Hon. FChS; FSA; FRSA; DL Lancs, JP; Chancellor of Hull University since 1970; Hon. Fellow, Jesus College, Cambridge; Hon. Master of the Bench, Inner Temple; Professor of Medicine, University of Liverpool, 1934-65; Consulting Physician, Royal Infirmary, Liverpool, since 1924; President: Royal Society of Health, since 1958; Assoc. Study of Med. Educn; Internat. Acad. Hist. of Med.; (Life), Inst. of Health Education; Liverpool Playhouse, since 1961; Nat. Children's Bureau, since 1965; Children's Research Fund; (Life) Brit. Soc. History of Medicine; Assoc. of Sea and Airport Health Authorities, since 1965; Assoc. of Medical Secretaries, UK, since 1968; Hon. Pres., Internat. Congress of History and Medicine, 1972; Vis. Prof. of Med., NY State Univ., 1958; McGill Univ., Montreal, 1959; Chairman: Central Health Services Council, 1957-63; Standing Medical Advisory Cttee, Ministry of Health, 1948-63; several cttees and jt-cttees (Min. of Health), including Gen. Practice, Prescribing, Mental Nursing, Epilepsy, Welfare Foods, Poliomyelitis, Health Educn, Operational Research in Pharmaceutical Service, Safety of Drugs; Flour Panel, Ministry of Food, 1955; Jt-Cttee MRC and Nuffield Trust on Cortisone; RCP on Nomenclature; UK Foundation WHO; Advisory Res. Bd, Spastics Soc.; Advisory Panel on Medical History, Wellcome Trust; *b* 1900. *Educ:* Birkenhead; Univs of Liverpool and Paris. MB, ChB (1st Cl. Hons) 1922, MD (Special Merit), 1924, FRCP 1934. Several prizes, medals, fellowships, scholarships, etc. Beit Fellow, 1924. Editor-in-Chief, British Encyclopædia Medical Practice, 1955-70. Past Chairman: Min. of Health cttee on Rheumatism, Definition of Drugs and Food, etc; BMA cttees on Trng of a Doctor, and Gen. Practice; President: 5th British Congress on History of Medicine and Pharmacy, 1960; 10th European Institute on Alcoholism, 1964; King David Sch., Liverpool; Home for Aged; Nat. Soc. for Clean Air, 1961-63; BECC (SW Lancs); Brit. Diabetic Assoc.; Nat. Polio Foundn (Liverpool); Merseyside Multiple Sclerosis Soc.; E-SU Merseyside; Merseyside Council on Alcoholism; Wirral Assoc. for Mental Health; BMA Student's Trust, 1961-; Past President: BMA, 1950-52 (Gold Medal, 1967); 7th Internat. Congress of Biological Standards, 1961; RSM (Sect. of Medicine, 1953-55; Sect. History Medicine, 1966); Liverpool Medical Inst., 1954-55; Heberden Soc., 1950-53; Gen. Med. Council, 1961-73; RSM, 1964-66; Assoc. of Physicians of GB and Ireland, 1968-69; University Club, 1952-54; First World Conf. on Med. Educn, 1952, resigned; Jt Meeting BMA-CMA, Toronto (Section of Medicine), 1955. Vice-Pres., BMA, 1953-; National Assoc. for Mentally Handicapped Children; Imperial Cancer Res. Fund; Inst. of Welfare Officers; Crown Rep. GMC, 1945-73 (mem. deleg. to USA and Canada, 1946); Governing Trustee, Nuffield Provincial Hospitals Trust; Member: United Liverpool Teaching Hospitals and Liverpool Regional Hospitals Board, 1947-71; Assoc. Brit. Neurologists (Council, 1938-46); Physiological Soc.; Soc. Internat. de Médecine Interne; Soc. Internat. de Gastro-

entérologie; Soc. Internat. d'Histoire de la Médicine; Expert Advisory Panel on Professional Educ., WHO; Br. Pharmacopœia Commn, 1948-53; Med. Adv. Cttee, Min. of Health, 1941-48; Councillor, RCP, 1943-46; rep. RCP on Negotiating Cttee for NHS; Examiner, RCP and Clinical Research Bd, MRC, 1954-57; Hon. Member: Assoc. of Phys., Gt Brit. and Ire.; York Med. Soc.; Harveian Soc.; Heberden Soc.; Montreal Clin. Soc.; Ophthalmological Soc.; Birkenhead Med. Soc.; Liverpool Arch. Soc.; New York Acad. Science; British Geriatric Soc.; Bedford Med. Inst.; RSM (Sect. Med. Educn); Liverpool Med. Inst. Lectures: Bradshaw, RCP, 1940; Skinner, Faculty of Radiologists, 1942; Lettsomian, Med. Soc., London, 1944; John Burns and Finlayson, RFPSG 1944; Samuel Hyde, RSM, 1947; Moynihan, RCS, 1949; Newsholme, Univ. of London, 1950; Harveian, 1950; Manson, Royal Inst. of Philosophy, 1951; Coronation, ERC, 1953; John Tate, Middx County Med. Soc., 1954; Sherrington, Univ. of Liverpool, 1955; Sydney Body, 1955; Hunterian Oration, 1955; Sir Charles Hastings, 1956; Henry Cavendish, 1956; Maurice Bloch, Glasgow Univ., 1957; Isaac Gilchrist, Aberdeen Univ., 1957, 1968; Paget, RDS, 1957; Crookshank (and Medallist), FAC. Radiol., 1958; Henry Wyld, 1958; Charles Tomes, RCS, 1959; Watson-Jones, RCS, 1959; Louis Gross, Montreal, 1959; Gilbert Scott, CRC, 1960; Founder's, RCN, 1960; Wilkinson, London Univ., 1960; Frederick William Price, RCPE, 1960; Founders and Benefactors, Univ. of Durham Dental Sch., 1960; Chadwick (and gold medal), RSH, 1961; Heberden (and medallist), 1961; Gideon de Laune (and medal), Soc. Apoth., 1962; John Snow, Assoc. of Anæsth., 1962; Osler Oration, CMA, 1963; Albee Memorial, USA, 1963; Croonian, RCP, 1964; Bowman Medal, Ophth. Soc., 1964; Lloyd-Roberts, RSM, 1964; Alpha Omega Alpha, Johns Hopkins, USA, 1964; Bengué, RIPHH, 1965; Winchester Address, BMA, 1965; Annual Oration, Med. Soc. London, 1966; Hastings Memorial, BMA, 1966; Astor, Middx Hosp., 1966; John Ash, Birmingham Univ., 1966; Abrahamson, RCSI, 1966; Nuffield Lectr and Medal, RSM, 1966; Trevor Lloyd Hughes, 1967; Ludwig Hektoen, Chicago, 1967; Wood Jones, Univ. of Manchester, 1967; Thomas Vicary, RCS, 1968; Roscoe, 1969; Upjohn, Univ. Sheffield, 1969; Kate Harrower Memorial, Med. Women's Fedn, 1969; Wiles, QUB, 1969; Harveian Oration, RCP, 1970; Rickards, S Staffs Med. Inst., 1971; Wade, N Staffs Med. Inst., 1971; Arthur Hall, Sheffield, 1972; Henry Cohen, Liverpool, 1972; Woodhull, Royal Instn, 1973. Gold Medal, RSM, 1971. Hon. Freeman: Liverpool; Birkenhead; Soc. Apothecaries. Coronation Medal, 1953. Associate KStJ. *Publications:* New Pathways in Medicine, 1935; Nature, Method and Purpose of Diagnosis, 1943; Sherrington: Physiologist, Philosopher and Poet, 1958; The Evolution of Modern Medicine, 1958; contribs to many books, and medical and scientific journals. *Recreations:* theatre (President of Board, Liverpool Repertory Theatre; Chm., 1948-61), music, the arts. *Address:* Cornercroft, Glendyke Road, Liverpool 18. *T:* 051-724 1981. *Clubs:* Athenæum, Savage (Hon. Life Mem.).
[Died 7 Aug. 1977 (*ext*).

COHEN, His Honour Clifford Theodore, MC 1945; TD 1946; DL; a Circuit Judge (formerly County Court Judge), 1953-72; *b* 26 June 1906; *er s* of R. Cohen, Registrar, Stockton County Court; *m* 1961, Mrs Gladys Eileen Fielding, *yr d* of late Charles Allaun. *Educ:* Clifton Coll., Bristol; Magdalene Coll., Cambridge (MA). Called to Bar, Inner Temple, 1929. Practised on North-Eastern Circuit as barrister until Aug. 1939. Served War of 1939-45: 2nd Lieut with 1st Tyneside Scottish, The Black Watch, Royal Highland Regt; POW in Germany from May 1940 for nearly 5 years. Returned to work as barrister until July 1953. Hon. Col, 17 Bn The Parachute Regt, TA, 1963-67. DL Durham, 1958. *Recreation:* gardening. *Address:* Tanton Hall, Stokesley, North Yorks. *T:* Stokesley 300.
[Died 23 Aug. 1972.

COHEN, Sir Edgar (Abraham), KCMG 1955 (CMG 1951); retired civil servant; *b* 5 Dec. 1908; *s* of late J. B. Cohen and Marthe Lewié; *m* 1967, Lillian Kathleen Langham. *Educ:* Manchester Grammar Sch.; Balliol Coll., Oxford (Scholar). 1st class Classical Hon. Mods., 1929, and Greats, 1931. Entered Board of Trade, 1932; Under-Sec., 1947; Second Sec. (Overseas), 1952; Permanent Deleg., with rank of Ambassador: to EFTA and GATT, Geneva, 1960-65; to OECD, Paris, 1965-68. *Address:* Heath Ridge, Graffham, Petworth, Sussex.
[Died 30 Jan. 1973.

COHEN, Sir John (Edward), Kt 1969; Founder of Tesco Stores (Holdings) Limited and associated companies; First Life President since 1969 (formerly Chairman); *b* 6 Oct. 1898; *m* 1924, Sarah Fox; two *d. Educ:* Rutland Street LCC Sch. Served with RFC, 1917-19, in France, Egypt, Palestine. Commenced in business on own account, 1919. Master, Worshipful Company of Carmen, 1976-77. FGI. *Recreations:* bridge, world travel. *Address:* 22 Cumberland Terrace, Regent's Park, NW1. *Clubs:* Royal Automobile, City Livery.   *[Died 24 March 1979.*

COHEN, Sir Karl Cyril, Kt 1968; CBE 1963; *s* of Solomon Cohen, Leeds. *Educ:* Leeds University (LLB Hons 1935). Solicitor, 1940 (Partner, K. C. Cohen & Rhodes, Leeds). Councillor, later Alderman, Leeds City Council, 1952-. *Address:* Century House, South Parade, Leeds 1; 22 Gledhow Park Avenue, Leeds LS7 4JH.   *[Died 8 June 1973.*

COHEN, Marcel; Directeur d'études à l'Ecole pratique des Hautes Etudes, 1919-55, retired 1955; Professeur à l'Ecole nationale des Langues Orientales Vivantes, 1911-50 (Hon. Prof. 1955); Directeur de recherches, 1937, 1938; Chargé de cours Institut d'ethnologie, Paris, 1926-59; *b* 6 Feb. 1884; *s* of Benjamin Cohen and Anna Bechmann; *m* 1913, Marguerite Bloch; three *c. Educ:* Paris. Agrégé de L'Université (Grammaire), 1908; Chargé de mission en Abyssinie, 1910-11; Docteur ès Lettres, 1924; Membre étranger de l'Académie des Sciences de Berlin; Docteur *hc* Univs: Warsaw, Manchester, Prague. Membre d'honneur de l'Association phonétique internationale et de la Société de linguistique américaine; Lauréat du prix international Haile Selassie Ier, pour les études éthiopiennes, 1964. Chevalier de la Légion d'Honneur; Croix de Guerre, 1914-18, and 1939-45. *Publications:* Le Parler arabe des juifs d'Alger, 1912 (prix Volney); Le Système verbal sémitique et l'expression du temps, 1924 (prix Volney); Les Langues du Monde (direction avec A. Meillet), 1924 (1952); Instructions d'enquête linguistiques et questionnaires linguistiques, 1928 (1951); Etudes d'éthiopien méridional, 1931; Traité de langue amharique, 1936 (1970); Nouvelles études d'éthiopien méridional, 1939; Le français en 1700 d'après le témoignage de Gile Vaudelin, 1946; Essai comparatif sur le vocabulaire et la phonétique du chamito-sémitique, 1947 (1969); Histoire d'une langue: le français, 1947 (1950, 1967, 1973); Linguistique et matérialisme dialectique, 1948; Grammaire française en quelques pages, 1948 (1966); Regards sur la langue française, 1950; Le Langage (Structure et évolution), 1950 (English trans. 1970); Sur l'étude du langage enfantin, 1952, nos 3, 4, 1969; L'écriture, 1953; Grammaire et Style, 1954; Cinquante années de recherches (bibliographie complète), 1955; (avec un groupe de linguistes) Français élémentaire? Non, 1955; Pour une Sociologie du langage, 1956, new edn, as Matériaux pour une sociologie du langage, 1971; Notes de méthode pour l'histoire du français, 1958; La grande invention de l'écriture et son évolution, 1958; Le subjonctif en français contemporain, 1960 (1965); Etudes sur le langage de l'enfant (in collab.), 1962; Nouveaux regards sur la langue française, 1963; Encore des regards sur la langue française, 1966; Toujours des regards sur la langue française, 1970; Mélanges Marcel Cohen, 1970; Une fois de plus des regards sur la langue française, 1972; (jtly) Dictionnaire du français vivant, 1972; Œuvres complètes, vol. I, 1974; numerous articles and mémoires. *Address:* 26 Rue Joseph Bertrand, 78220 Viroflay, Yvelines, France. *T:* 926.5152. *Club:* Comité national des écrivains (Paris).   *[Died 5 Nov. 1974.*

COKE WALLIS, Leonard George, CMG 1960; CIE 1945; late ICS; *b* 12 March 1900; *s* of late G. C. Wallis; *m* 1932, Frances Chieveley, *d* of late C. H. Coke; two *s* one *d. Educ:* University Coll., London; Christ's Coll., Cambridge. 1st class, BA Hons History, London; double first in Historical Tripos, Cambridge. Entered ICS 1924; Asst Magistrate and Sub-divisional Officer, Bengal, 1924-29; entered Political Service, 1929; served successively in NWF Province, on special duty in Political Dept Secretariat, in Eastern States Agency, Cooch Behar State, Central India, Hyderabad; Punjab Hill States; Resident for the Eastern States, 1944; Political Agent in Jaipur; Resident at Baroda and for Western India States, 1947; Dep. High Commissioner for UK in Pakistan, 1947-52; with National Savings Cttee, 1953-55; Chairman: Public Service Commission, Ibadan, W Region, Nigeria, 1956; Overseas Public Service Board, Nigeria House (West), London, 1961-66; London Selection Panel, Nigeria High Commission, 1966-67. *Publications:* articles on Nigerianisation of Public Services, and the Public Service Commission in Jl of African Administration, 1959, Incidi, 1960, Jl of Royal African Society, 1961. *Recreation:* golf. *Address:* 14 King's Close, Lyndhurst, Hants. *T:* Lyndhurst 2543. *Club:* Oriental.   *[Died 14 July 1974.*

COLBERT, John Patrick, MSc (Econ.); economist; *b* 12 Feb. 1898; *s* of late William Colbert, JP; *m* 1927, Helena, *d* of Hermann von Campe, Nachod, Czechoslovakia; one *s* two *d. Educ:* Rockwell Coll.; National Univ. of Ireland (University Coll., Cork). Joined staff of The Statist, 1920; Ed., 1923-28; first Chm. and Managing Dir, The Agricultural Credit Corporation Ltd, 1928-33; first Chm. and Man. Dir, The Industrial Credit

Co. Ltd, 1933-52; formerly Lecturer on Banking and Finance at University Coll., Dublin. *Publication:* Commentary on Misconceptions regarding Money and Bank Credit, 1942 (two edns). *Address:* Carysfort House, Grove Avenue, Blackrock, Co. Dublin. *T:* 881064.   *[Died 20 Sept. 1975.*

COLBORNE, Surgeon Rear-Adm. William John, CB 1950; FRCS; Royal Navy, Retired, and an Hon. Surgeon to HM. MRCS, LRCP 1916; FRCS 1943; retired 1951. *Address:* Croft House, Yealmpton, Devon.   *[Died 3 Nov. 1971.*

COLDRICK, William; Ex-Chairman of the Co-operative Party; Ex-Member of National Council of Labour, now retired; *b* 19 Feb. 1896; two *s* one *d. Educ:* Elementary and Continuation Classes and Labour Coll., London. MP (Lab. and Co-op.) Bristol North, 1945-50, North-East, 1950-Sept. 1959. Ex-Mem. Monmouthshire County Council. Trustee, Bristol Trustee Savings Bank; Mem. Central Exec., Co-op. Union; Mem. Advisory Cttee, Govt Dept of Technical Co-operation. Lecturer for National Council of Labour Colls. Sheriff of the City and County of Bristol, 1964. *Publications:* articles in various journals. *Recreations:* football, cricket. *Address:* 52 The Crescent, Sea Mills, Bristol BS9 2JS. *T:* Bristol 682174.   *[Died 15 Sept. 1975.*

COLE, Baron *cr* 1965, of Blackfriars (Life Peer); **George James Cole,** GBE 1973; Chairman, Unilever Ltd, 1960-70 (Director, 1948; Vice-Chairman, 1956); Vice-Chairman, Unilever NV, 1960-70; Chairman, Leverhulme Trust; *b* 3 Feb. 1906; *s* of late James Francis Cole; *m* 1940, Ruth (*d* 1978), *d* of late Edward Stanley Harpham; one *s* one *d. Educ:* Raffles Inst., Singapore. Joined a Lever Brothers Ltd subsidiary, The Niger Co. Ltd (later merged into The United Africa Co. Ltd), 1923; various positions in London and Africa till 1939 when appointed Controller for British West Africa; Staff of Resident Minister, W Africa, as Commercial Mem. at Supply Centre, 1941; Director: The United Africa Co. Ltd, 1945-63 (Joint Man. Dir, 1952-55); Taylor Woodrow (West Africa) Ltd, 1947-55; Finance Corp. for Industry Ltd, 1965-73; Chm., Palm Line Ltd, 1952-55 (Dir, 1949); on European Continent for Unilever Ltd, 1955; Chm., Rolls-Royce (1971) Ltd, 1970-72; Chm., Govt Advisory Cttee on Appointment of Advertising Agents, 1962-70; Pres., Advertising Assoc., 1970-73; Mem. Council: RIIA; Royal African Society; UK South Africa Trade Assoc.; Vice-Pres., Hispanic Council; Vice-Pres., Luso-Brazilian Council; Mem. Internat. Adv. Cttee, Chase Manhattan Bank, 1965-73; FRSA; FZS; Corresp. Emeritus, The Conf. Bd (New York). Comdr, Order of Orange Nassau, 1963. *Address:* 50 Victoria Road, W8. *T:* 01-937 9085. *Clubs:* Athenæum, Hurlingham.
                    [Died 29 Nov. 1979.

COLE, Charles Woolsey, MA, LHD, PhD, ScD, LittD, LLD; President Emeritus, Amherst College; *b* 8 Feb. 1906; *s* of Bertha Woolsey Dwight and Charles Buckingham Cole; *m* 1st, 1928, Katharine Bush Salmon (decd); two *d*; 2nd, 1974, Marie Greer Donahoe. *Educ:* Montclair (New Jersey) High Sch.; Amherst Coll., Amherst, Mass; Columbia Univ., NY, Univ. Fellow, Columbia, 1928-29; Instr History, Columbia Coll., 1929-35; Travelling Fellow of Social Science Research Council in Paris, 1932-33; Assoc. Prof. Economics, Amherst Coll., 1935-37; Prof. Economics, Amherst Coll., 1937-40; Prof. Hist. in graduate faculty, Columbia, 1940-46; Pres., Amherst Coll., 1946-60. Vice-Pres., Rockefeller Foundn, 1960-61; US Ambassador to Chile, 1961-64. Chief, Service Trades Branch, Office of Price Administration, Washington, DC, 1942; Regional Price Exec., New York Office of Price Administration, 1942-43; Columbia's Navy Sch. of Military Govt and Administration in addition to lecturing at Army Sch. of Mil. Govt in Charlottesville, Va, 1943-45; Vis. Lectr in Economics at Yale Univ., New Haven, Conn., 1938-39. Trustee, Merrill Trust. Grand Cross, Order of Merit (Chile); Grand Officer, Order of Morazán (Honduras). *Publications:* French Mercantalist Doctrines Before Colbert, 1931; Colbert and a Century of French Mercantilism, 1939; Economic History of Europe (with S. B. Clough), 1941; French Mercantilism, 1683-1700, 1943; (with C. J. H. Hayes and M. Baldwin) History of Europe, 1949; History of Western Civilization, 1967; (with H. W. Bragdon and S. P. McCutchen): A Free People: the United States in the Formative Years, 1970; A Free People: the United States in the Twentieth Century, 1970; History of a Free People, 1973; edited Macmillan Career Books. *Recreation:* fly fishing for trout. *Address:* The Highlands, Seattle, Washington 98177, USA. *Clubs:* Century, Anglers' (New York); University (Seattle), Seattle Golf.
                    [Died 20 Feb. 1978.

COLE, Edward Nicholas; Chairman of the Board, International Husky, Inc., since 1974; President and Chief Operating Officer, General Motors Corporation, 1967-74; *b* Marne, Michigan,

USA, 17 Sept. 1909; *s* of Franklin Benjamin Cole and Lucy Catherine Cole (*née* Blasen); *m* 1964, Dollie Ann McVey; one *s*; one *s* one *d* adopted; and one *s* one *d* by a previous marriage. *Educ:* Berlin (now Marne) High Sch., Marne, Mich; Pre-Law Course, Grand Rapids Junior Coll.; General Motors Inst., Flint, Mich (BSME). General Motors, Cadillac Motor Car Div.: Cooperative Student (Gen. Motors Inst.), 1930; various posts, 1933-42; then Chief Design Engr, 1943; Asst Chief Engr, 1944; Chief Engr, 1946; Works Manager, 1950; Plant Manager, Cadillac-Cleveland Tank Plant, 1950; Chief Engr, Chevrolet Motor Div., 1952, Gen. Manager, 1956. General Motors Corporation: Vice-Pres., 1956; Director, 1961; Gp Vice-Pres. in charge of Car and Truck Divs, 1961; Exec. Vice-Pres. in charge of Ops Staff Activities, 1965. Member: Soc. of Automotive Engrs; Nat. Acad. of Engineering; Pi Tau Sigma; Delta Sigma Pi; Sigma Xi; Tau Beta Pi; etc. Numerous other social and educational activities. Holds 12 hon. degrees from US univs and colls. *Address:* International Husky, Inc., 10 West Long Lake Road, Bloomfield Hills, Michigan 48013, USA. *Clubs:* Detroit Athletic, Detroit, Recess (all Detroit); Bloomfield Hills Country. *[Died 2 May 1977.*

COLE, Lt-Gen. Sir George Sinclair, KCB 1965 (CB 1962); CBE 1953; Vice-Chief of the Defence Staff, 1966-67, retired; *b* 12 March 1911; *s* of Capt. A. V. Cole, Fen Farm, Elmstead; *m* 1943, Sybil Irene Russell, *d* of W. R. Stoneham, RN; one *s* one *d*. *Educ:* Wellington Coll.; RMA Woolwich. Commissioned RA 1931; served War of 1939-45, BEF 1939-40; GSO1, Mil. Ops, WO, 1943-44; OC 58 LAA Regt RA, 21 Army Group, 1945; Military Assistant: to CIGS, 1946-48; to Chm. Western Europe Comdrs-in-Chief, 1949; jssc, Latimer, 1950; Dep. Chief of Staff, ALFCE, 1950-51; Head, Exercise Planning Staff, SHAPE, 1951-52; idc, 1953; OC 40 Fd Regt RA, Egypt and Cyprus, 1954-55; CRA 1 Inf. Div., 1956-59; Sec., Chiefs of Staff Cttee, 1959-61; Dir of Staff Duties, War Office, 1961-64; GOC-in-C, Eastern Command, 1965-66. Col Comdt, RA, 1965-70. *Recreations:* golf, fishing, bridge. *Address:* Moy Lodge, Old Avenue, West Byfleet, Surrey. *T:* Byfleet 46376. *Clubs:* Army and Navy; Jesters; Royal and Ancient, Rye Golf, New Zealand Golf. *[Died 2 March 1973.*

COLE, John, ROI; RBA; NEAC; **(Reginald John Vicat Cole);** landscape painter, especially of old shop fronts; *b* 2 Nov. 1903; *s* of late Rex Vicat Cole, ROI, RBC. Mem. Council, Artists' Gen. Benevolent Instn; Mem. Council of Management, Byam Shaw Sch. of Drawing and Painting Ltd; Chm., St James Art Soc. (for the Deafened); Chm., The Campden Hill Club. Paris Salon Silver Medal, 1952; Paris Salon Gold Medal, 1954. Works in public collections: Aberdeen; Manchester; Salford; Eastbourne; Greenock; Paisley; Newport (Mon.); Nat. Gall., Wellington, NZ; Hastings Corporation Art Gall.; Kensington (Leighton House). *Address:* The Duke of Sussex Studios, 44 Uxbridge Street, Kensington, W8 7TG. *T:* 01-727 4526.
[Died 5 Sept. 1975.

COLE, Dame Margaret Isabel, DBE 1970 (OBE 1965); author and lecturer; *b* Cambridge, 1893; *d* of Prof. J. P. Postgate, LittD, Prof. of Latin, Univ. of Liverpool, and Edith Allen; *m* 1918, G. D. H. Cole (*d* 1959); one *s* two *d*. *Educ:* Roedean Sch., Brighton; Girton Coll., Cambridge (1st class Hons Classical Tripos). Classical Mistress, St Paul's Girls' Sch., 1914-16; Asst Sec., Labour Research Dept, 1917-25; Lectr for Univ. Tutorial Classes, London, 1925-49, Cambridge, 1941-44; Contributor to Evening Standard, New Statesman, Guardian, Listener, Socialist Commentary, etc; Hon. Sec., New Fabian Research Bureau, 1935-39; of Fabian Soc., 1939-53; Chm., 1955; Pres., 1963-; Mem., LCC Education Cttee, 1943-65; Alderman, 1952-65; Chm., Further Education Cttee, 1951-60 and 1961-65; Mem., ILEA Educn Cttee, 1965-67; Vice-Chm., Further and Higher Education Sub-Cttee, 1965-67. Hon. Fellow, LSE, 1977. FRHistS. Hon. Daughter of Mark Twain, 1978. *Publications:* The Bolo Book (with G. D. H. Cole), 1923; Twelve Studies in Soviet Russia (ed), 1932; Roads to Success (ed), 1936; Women of To-Day, 1937; Marriage Past and Present, 1938; Books and the People, 1938; Democratic Sweden (ed.), 1938; Evacuation Survey (ed), 1940; Our Soviet Ally (ed), 1943; Beatrice Webb: a Memoir, 1945; Our Partnership (part Editor), 1948; Makers of the Labour Movement, 1948; The Webbs and Their Work (ed), 1949; Growing up into Revolution, 1949; The Diaries of Beatrice Webb (ed), 1952; Robert Owen of New Lanark, 1953; The Diaries of Beatrice Webb II (ed), 1956; Servant of the County, 1956; The Story of Fabian Socialism, 1961; Life of G. D. H. Cole, 1971; also detective novels and works on politics, etc, jointly with late G. D. H. Cole, for many years. *Recreations:* reading, looking at own and other countries. *Address:* 4 Ashdown, Cliveden Court, Clevelands, W13 8DR. *T:* 01-997 8114. *Clubs:* Arts Theatre, English-Speaking Union.
[Died 7 May 1980.

COLE, Sir Noel, Kt 1971; Governing Director, N. Cole Ltd, Builders and Contractors, since 1913; *b* 8 Nov. 1892; both parents from Lancashire, England; *m* 1938, Doreen Joyce Aiken. *Educ:* Onehunga District High Sch., Auckland, NZ. Served European War, Captain, NZ Field Engineers, 1917-18. Full life of building and contracting, carrying out major construction works for industry in New Zealand and Australia. Vice-Patron, Auckland Anniversary Regatta Cttee. Fellow, Inst. of British Builders. *Recreations:* boating, racing, trotting. *Address:* Le Nid, 42 Curran Street, Auckland 2, New Zealand. *T:* 761-207; Moose Lodge, Rotorua, New Zealand. *Clubs:* White Elephant, Royal Yachting Association (London); Lions' (Charter Mem.), Richmond Yacht (Patron), Kohimarama Yacht (Patron), Ponsonby Cruising (Vice-Patron), Point Chevalier Yacht, Royal NZ Yacht Squadron, Officers', Avondale Jockey, Auckland Trotting (all Auckland); (Hon. Life Mem. and Patron) Civil Service, Royal Port Nicholson Yacht (all Wellington); Masonic, Balgowlah Bowling (Sydney).
[Died 14 Oct. 1975.

COLE, Norman John, VRD; *b* 1 June 1909; *s* of Walter John Cole and Maud Mary (*née* Thomas); *m* 1935, Margaret Grace, *d* of Arthur James Potter, Buxton, Derbyshire; one *s* two *d*. *Educ:* St John's Coll., Southsea. Served abroad War of 1939-45, with Royal Navy; RNVR, 1934-54 (Lt-Comdr). Formerly held offices in Conservative Associations in Barnet Vale and Potters Bar. Mem. of Potters Bar Urban District Council, 1947-48. MP (L and C) South Division of Bedfordshire, 1951-66; sponsored Private Member's Bill which became Children and Young Persons (Amendment) Act, 1952. Has served for many years on numerous youth, health, welfare and church cttees; retired 1974. *Recreations:* formerly Association football, cricket, tennis, rowing. *Address:* Derwent House, 30 Warwick Road, New Barnet, Herts. *T:* 01-449 5076. *[Died 22 Jan. 1979.*

COLEBROOK, Edward Hilder, CIE 1946; MC 1918; KPM 1924; Indian Police, retired; *b* 16 Oct. 1898; *s* of Edward Colebrook. Served European War, 1914-18, East Surrey Regt; Lieut, 1917-20; Indian Police, 1921-49, retired as Dep. Inspector-Gen. Indian Police Medal, 1936. Mem. Guildford Borough Council, 1956-68. *Address:* Holly Mount, 21a Austen Road, Guildford, Surrey. *T:* Guildford 67727. *Club:* East India, Sports and Public Schools. *[Died 4 Jan. 1977.*

COLEMAN, Lt-Gen. Sir (Cyril Frederick) Charles, KCB 1957 (CB 1950); CMG 1954; DSO 1945; OBE 1944; Lieutenant-Governor and C-in-C of Guernsey, 1964-69; *b* Plymouth; *s* of late A. E. Coleman, Downderry, Cornwall; *m* 1935, Margaret Mary, *d* of late Bruce Petrie, Singapore; three *d*. *Educ:* Plymouth Coll.; RMC Sandhurst. 2nd Lieut The Welch Regt, 1923; Adjt 2nd Bn The Welch Regt, 1932-35; Service in China, Malaya, India; OC 4th Bn The Welch Regt, 1941-44; comd 160th Inf. Bde, 1944-46, in NW Europe (despatches); Staff Coll., 1946; comd 160th Inf. Bde, 1947-48; GOC South-Western District and 43rd (Wessex) Inf. Div., 1949-51; GOC Berlin (British Sector), 1951-54; Chief of Staff, Northern Army Group, BAOR, 1954-56; GOC-in-C Eastern Comd, 1956-59; retd 1959. Col The Welch Regt, 1958-65. Militaire Willemsorde (Netherlands), 1947. KStJ 1964. *Recreations:* shooting, hockey (Wales). *Address:* Greensleeves, Bentworth, Alton, Hants. *T:* Medstead 2126. *Club:* Army and Navy. *[Died 17 June 1974.*

COLERAINE, 1st Baron *cr* 1954, of Haltemprice; **Richard Kidston Law,** PC 1943; High Steward of Kingston-upon-Hull; *b* Helensburgh, 27 Feb. 1901; *y s* of late Rt Hon. Andrew Bonar Law and Annie Pitcairn Robley; *m* 1929, Mary Virginia (*d* 1978), *y d* of late A. F. Nellis, Rochester, NY; two *s*. *Educ:* Shrewsbury Sch.; St John's Coll., Oxford. Travelled in Asia Minor, India, Canada, United States, and South America; editorial staff, Morning Post, 1927; New York Herald-Tribune, 1928; Philadelphia Public Ledger, 1929; MP (U) SW Hull, 1931-45; (C) South Kensington Div., Nov. 1945-Feb. 1950; Haltemprice Div. of Kingston-on-Hull, 1950-54. Financial Sec., War Office, 1940-41; Parly Under-Sec. of State, Foreign Office, 1941-43; Minister of State, 1943-45; Minister of Education, 1945. Leader, UK Delegn Hotsprings Conf. on Food and Agriculture, 1943. Mem., Medical Research Council, 1936-40; Mem., Industrial Health Research Board, 1936-40; Chm. of Council of British Socs for Relief Abroad, 1945-49-54; Chm., Nat. Youth Employment Council, 1955-62; Chm., Central Transport Consultative Cttee, 1955-58; Chm., Mansfield House Univ. Settlement, 1953-66; Hon. Treas., British Sailors Soc., 1955-74; Chm., Marshall Scholarship Commn, 1956-65; Chm., Standing Advisory Cttee on Pay of Higher Civil Service, 1957-61. Chm., Royal Postgraduate Medical Sch. of London, 1958-71, Fellow 1972. Hon. LLD New Brunswick, 1951. *Publications:* The Individual and the Community in Ernest Barker's The Character of England, 1947; Return from Utopia, 1950; For

Conservatives Only, 1970. *Recreations:* sailing, walking. *Heir: s* Hon. (James) Martin (Bonar) Law [*b* 8 Aug. 1931; *m* 1st, 1958, Emma Elizabeth (marr. diss. 1966), *o d* of late Nigel Richards and of Mrs H. C. C. Batten; two *d*; 2nd, 1966, Patricia, *yr d* of Maj.-Gen. Ralph Farrant, CB; one *s* two *d*]. *Address:* 52 Holland Park Avenue, W11.   [*Died* 15 *Nov.* 1980.

COLES, Sir George (James), Kt 1957; CBE 1942; Founder and Director, G. J. Coles & Co.; *b* 28 March 1885; *s* of George Coles, Horsham, and Elizabeth Coles (*née* Scouler); *m* 1920, Margaret Gertrude, *d* of C. Herbert; one *s* three *d* (and one *d* decd). *Educ:* Beechworth Grammar Sch. Served War as L-Corp. 60th Bn AIF, 1916-18. Founded G. J. Coles and Co., 1914; Man. Dir, 1923-31; Chm., 1923-56. *Publication:* Chain Store Economics, 1927. *Recreations:* golf, bowls. *Address:* 28 St George's Road, Toorak, Vic 3142, Australia. *T:* 24-4901. *Clubs:* Athenæum (Melbourne); Peninsula Country Golf.   [*Died* 4 *Dec.* 1977.

COLES, Gordon Robert; Development Officer, Antrim and Ballymena, since 1973; *b* 24 Nov. 1913; *s* of late Major Ernest A. Coles, MC, and Florence L. B. Coles; *m* 1939, Georgina Elizabeth, *d* of late George Canning and Agnes Canning (*née* Watson), of Belfast; two *s* one *d*. *Educ:* St Albans Sch.; Imperial Coll., London Univ. DIC, BSc(Eng), ACGI. Civil Engineer, LMS Railway, 1935-37; HM Inspector of Factories, Home Office, 1937-39. Served War of 1939-45: Royal Engineers (Lt Col), England, Middle East (despatches), and India. HM Inspector of Factories, Min. of Labour, 1945-49; Principal, 1949, Asst Sec., 1956, Min. of Housing and Local Govt, 1949-68. Gen. Manager, Antrim and Ballymena Develt Commn, 1968-73. *Recreations:* boats, golf, rifle shooting. *Address:* Foresight, 4 Ballyloughan Brow, Ballymena, Co. Antrim, Northern Ireland BT43 6PW. *T:* Ballymena 43921.
                                                    [*Died* 23 *Aug.* 1975.

COLES, Air Marshal Sir William (Edward), KBE 1967 (CBE 1952); CB 1963; DSO 1944; DFC and Bar; AFC; Member of Council, Royal Air Force Benevolent Fund and Royal Air Force Association, since 1975; Director, Argyle Building Society, since 1977; *b* 1913; *s* of late George Frederick Coles, Shenington, Banbury; *m* 1945, Eileen Marjorie, *d* of Ernest Wilberforce Hann; two *s*. *Educ:* Tysoe Secondary Sch. Entered Royal Air Force, 1938; served in 216, 233 and 117 Squadrons, Middle East, N Africa, Italy, Burma and European theatres, 1939-44; RAF Staff Coll., 1945; Air Min., 1946-48; Empire and Central Flg Sch., 1948-50; Comd RAF Middleton St George, 1950; Chief Instr CFS, 1951-53; Sen. RAF Liaison Officer and Air Advisor to UK High Comr in Austr., 1953-55; HQ, Flg Trg Comd, 1956; idc 1957; SASO, HQ No 3 Bomber Gp, RAF Mildenhall, Suffolk, 1957-60; AOC No 23 Gp, RAF Flg Trg Comd, 1960-63; Dir-Gen. of Personal Services (RAF), Min. of Defence, 1963-66; AOC-in-C, RAF Technical Training Comd, 1966-68. Controller, RAF Benevolent Fund, 1968-75. DFC (US) 1944. *Recreations:* golf, winter sports. *Address:* 3 Walpole Road, Surbiton, Surrey. *T:* 01-399 4625; Top Farm House, Shenington, Banbury, Oxon. *Club:* Royal Air Force.   [*Died* 7 *June* 1979.

COLGRAIN, 2nd Baron *cr* 1946, of Everlands; Donald Swinton Campbell, MC 1917; JP; *b* 6 Nov. 1891; *e s* of 1st Baron Colgrain and Lady Angela Mary Alice, 2nd *d* of 4th Earl of Harrowby; *S* father, 1917, Margaret Emily, *d* of P. W. Carver; three *s* one *d*. *Educ:* Eton Coll.; Trinity Coll., Cambridge. Served with West Kent Yeomanry, 1914-19, and with 8th Bn Royal West Kent Regt, 1940-41. JP Kent, 1942. *Recreation:* shooting. *Heir: s* Hon. David Colin Campbell [*b* 24 April 1920; *m* 1st, 1945, Veronica Margaret Webster (marr. diss. 1964); one *s* one *d*; 2nd, 1973, Mrs Sheila Hudson]. *Address:* Everlands, Sevenoaks, Kent. *T:* Sevenoaks 53303. *Clubs:* City University; Bombay Yacht.   [*Died* 20 *Oct.* 1973.

COLLES, Comdr Sir Dudley, KCB 1953; KCVO 1949 (CVO 1943; MVO 1936); OBE 1919; RN (retd); Extra Equerry to The Queen since 1958; Deputy Treasurer to The Queen and Assistant Keeper of the Privy Purse, 1952-58 (Secretary, HM Privy Purse, 1932-52, and Deputy Treasurer to King George VI, 1941-52); *b* 1889; *s* of late Richard and late Selina Colles; *m* 1920, Jacqueline (*d* 1959), *d* of H. G. Norman, Gloucester; one *d* (decd). *Educ:* Arnold House, Llandullas; Eastman's, Winchester. Royal Navy, 1906; Paymaster Comdr, 1928; Sec. to 3rd and 2nd Sea Lords and to Comdr-in-Chief America and West Indies Station; retired, 1932. *Address:* Wren House, Kensington Palace, W8 4PY.   [*Died* 13 *July* 1976.

COLLETT, Sir Henry Seymour, 2nd Bt *cr* 1934, of Bridge Ward in the City of London; Member for Bridge Ward, Court of Common Council, 1958-70; *b* 14 Feb. 1893; *e s* of Sir Charles Collett, 1st Bt (Lord Mayor of London, 1933-34); *S* father, 1938; *m* 1920, Ruth Mildred, *e d* of late William Thomas Hatch,

MICE; one *s* one *d* (and *er s* decd). *Educ:* Bishop's Stortford Coll. Textile Trade, London and Belgium; served European War: UPS Corps 1914; Lieut Suffolk Regt, 1915-16 (wounded); Lieut RFC France (wounded, prisoner 1918); Freedom of City of London, 1920; Liveryman, Worshipful Company of Glovers. Retail distributing trade, America, London and Provinces; retired as Dir of Colletts Ltd, 1964; Past Pres., City of London Retail Traders' Assoc.; FRSA. Comdr, Ordre National du Côte d'Ivoire, 1962; Comdr, Royal Order of the Phœnix (Greece), 1963. *Recreations:* gardening, riding, swimming, etc. *Heir: g s* Ian Seymour Collett, *b* 5 Oct. 1953. *Address:* The Knoll, Stone Road, Bromley, Kent. *T:* 01-460 3068. *Clubs:* United Wards, Bridge Ward.   [*Died* 6 *Jan.* 1971.

COLLEY, David Isherwood, MA, FLA; MBIM; Director, Cultural Services, City of Manchester, since 1974; *b* 5 July 1916; *s* of Squire Colley and Ethel Isherwood; *m* 1947, Barbara Mary, *d* of Canon T. A. Child, Lincoln; four *d*. *Educ:* Holt Sch., Liverpool. Served Royal Corps of Signals, 1940-46. FLA 1947. City Librarian, Manchester, 1955-74. Pres., NW Branch Library Assoc., 1963; Hon. Sec., NW Regl Library System, 1955-74; Mem., Min. of Education Working Party on Public Libraries, 1961-62; Mem., Cons. Cttee for Nat. Library for Science and Technology, 1959-65; Hon. Librarian and Curator of Ancient Monuments Soc., 1955-; Hon. Librarian of Manchester Statistical Soc., 1955-; Mem., Manchester and Dist Advisory Council for Further Education, 1956-; Adviser to Libraries, Museums and Arts Cttee of AMC, 1957-74; Mem., Youth Development Coun., 1963-66; Hon. Sec., Manchester Soc. of Book Collectors, 1955-. MA (*hc*) Manchester, 1962. *Publications:* various articles in learned periodicals. *Recreations:* libraries, photography, young people; YMCA; Stretford Athletic Club. *Address:* 5 Dalton Gardens, Davyhulme, Urmston, Manchester. *T:* 061-748 6626.   [*Died* 17 *Jan.* 1975.

COLLIER, Maj.-Gen. Angus Lyell, CBE 1943; MC 1917; DL; JP; psc; *b* 10 Nov. 1893; *e s* of late Thomas Edward Collier; *m* 1922, Edith Dorothea Margaret, *yr d* of late George Edward Herne; one *s* one *d*. *Educ:* Sedbergh; Oriel Coll., Oxford (BA). 2nd Lieut Queen's Own Cameron Highlanders (Special Reserve), 1914; regular commission as Capt., 1917; served European War, 1914-19, in Belgium, France, Balkans and S Russia (MC, despatches twice, White Eagle of Serbia). Staff Coll., Camberley, 1927-28; Bt Major, 1930; Bt Lt-Col, 1936; Bt Col, 1938. War of 1939-45: GSO1 Scottish Comd; Infantry Bde Comdr; Mil. Sec., GHQ, Middle East Forces; Dist Comdr Cyrenaica, 1943; Dist Comdr, Italy, 1944; Dist Comdr, Home Forces, 1944-46 (CBE, despatches twice, French Légion d'Honneur, Officer, and Croix de Guerre avec palme). ADC to the King, 1945-46. DL Inverness-shire, 1950; JP 1953. *Address:* Glassburn, by Beauly, Inverness-shire. *Clubs:* United Service and Royal Aero; Highland (Inverness).   [*Died* 7 *Sept.* 1971.

COLLIER, Dorothy Josephine, MA, BM, BCh Oxon; FRCS; retired, formerly Consultant Surgeon, Ear, Nose and Throat Department, Royal Free Hospital; Emeritus Consultant Surgeon, Ear, Nose and Throat Department, South London Hospital, formerly Associate Lecturer, Institute of Laryngology and Otology; Hunterian Professor, RCS, 1939; *b* 8 March 1894; *d* of late John Collier and late Agnes Mullins, Liverpool. *Educ:* Convent of Notre Dame, Southport; Oxford University; University Coll. Hosp. House Surgeon, King Edward VII Hosp., Windsor; House Surgeon, Registrar, and First Asst, Ear, Nose and Throat Dept, University Coll. Hosp.; Registrar, Central London Throat and Ear Hosp.; late Temp. Major, RAMC (Specialist Otologist); served in N Africa and Italy. Fellow Royal Soc. of Medicine, late Pres., Section of Otology; late Sec. Section of Laryngology; Mem., late Mem. Council, Med. Women's Federation. *Publications:* (with J. D. MacLaggan) Diseases of the Ear, Nose and Throat, 1952 (trans. Spanish Mexican Edn, 1955); articles on facial paralysis and other contribs to medical jls in England and USA. *Recreations:* travel in Spanish America and Middle East; orchid growing gardening. *Address:* 25 Blenheim Road, St John's Wood, NW8 *T:* 01-624 6733.   [*Died* 6 *Feb.* 1972

COLLIER, Air Commodore Kenneth Dowsett Gould, CBE 1945 *b* 4 April 1892; *m* 1917; no *c*. *Educ:* privately. RFC 1915-18 RAF 1918 (despatches); India and Egypt, 1921-25; HM Glorious, 1929-31; Admiralty, 1938-41; Air Ministry, 1941-47 Principal Scientific Officer, Ministry of Supply, 1947-53. Retired with the rank of Air Commodore, 1947. Bronze Star, USA 1946. *Recreations:* sailing, garden. *Address:* Robin Hill Fritham, New Forest, Hants. *T:* Cadnam 2312. *Club:* Naval and Military.   [*Died* 24 *April* 197

COLLIER, Sir Laurence, KCMG 1944 (CMG 1934); *b* 13 Jun 1890; *s* of late Hon. John Collier and Ethel Gladys Huxley; *r*

1917, Eleanor Antoinette (*d* 1975), *o d* of late William Luther Watson; one *s*. *Educ:* Bedales Sch.; Balliol Coll., Oxford (Brackenbury Scholar; 1st Class Modern History 1912). Clerk in Foreign Office, 1913; 2nd Sec. to HM Embassy, Tokyo, 1919; returned to Foreign Office, 1921; 1st Sec., 1923; Counsellor, 1932; Minister to Norway, 1941; British Ambassador to the Norwegian Govt, 1942-50; retired, 1951. *Publication:* Flight from Conflict, 1944. *Address:* Monkswell Gate, 37 Granville Road, Limpsfield, Surrey. *T:* Oxted 3552. *Club:* Athenæum.

[*Died* 20 *Oct.* 1976.

COLLIER, Marie Elizabeth; soprano; *b* Ballarat, Australia, 16 April 1927; *d* of Thomas Robinson Collier and Ann-Marie Bechaz; *m* 1952; three *s* one *d*. *Educ:* High Sch., Melbourne. Australian debut, 1952; Covent Garden, 1957; South America, 1961; USA, 1962; Italy, 1964; Germany, 1969; S Africa, 1971. *Recreations:* conversation, food and wine, sunshine. *Address:* (home) 45 Burnt Oak, Cookham, Berks. *T:* Cookham 23745; Leicester Square Chambers, 42 Leicester Square, WC2.

[*Died* 8 *Dec.* 1971.

COLLINGWOOD, Rt. Rev. Mgr. Canon Cuthbert; retired; *b* 26 May 1908; *s* of late Austin Vincent Collingwood. *Educ:* St Edmund's College, Ware. Ordained by His Eminence Cardinal Bourne, 1934; Chaplain of Westminster Cathedral and Asst Master of Ceremonies, 1934-44, Master of Ceremonies, 1945-49; Editor of Westminster Cathedral Chronicle, 1940-45; Private Sec. to HE Cardinal Griffin, 1944-47; Administrator of Westminster Cathedral, 1947-54; Canon of Metropolitan Chapter of Westminster, 1948; Parish Priest of Staines, 1954-73. Privy Chamberlain to HH the Pope, 1946, Domestic Prelate, 1968. Chm. of Catholic Truth Soc., 1948-71; Pres. of Metropolitan and City Catholic Police Guild, 1948-73. *Address:* 7 Overton Court, Overton Park Road, Cheltenham, Glos GL50 3BW. *T:* Cheltenham 519239.   [*Died* 11 *Sept.* 1980.

COLLINS, Brig. Arthur Francis St Clair, CBE (OBE 1918); MC; *b* 10 March 1892; *s* of late Dr A. H. Collins, Edinburgh; one *d*. *Educ:* Bedford Sch. 3rd Bn Beds Regt, 1911-13; ASC 1913; Temp. Capt., 1914; Adjt, 1917-18; Acting Major, 1918-19; Adjt, 1927-28; Major, 1933; Lt-Col, 1939; Temp. Col, 1940; Col, 1943; Brig., 1941-46; served France and Belgium, 1914-21 (despatches twice, 1914 Star, MC, OBE); Germany and Upper Silesia, 1919-21; India, 1926; Shanghai, 1927; BEF France, 1939-40 and 1945 (CBE); retired pay, 1946; AMIME 1933. *Recreations:* Rugby, tennis, golf, rowing. *Address:* 17 Ingles Road, Folkestone, Kent. *Club:* Army and Navy.

[*Died* 9 *Feb.* 1980.

COLLINS, Arthur Jefferies; President, Henry Bradshaw Society; *b* 30 Sept. 1893; *e s* of late Arthur and Beatrice Agnes Collins; *m* 1st, Winifred Alice (*d* 1924), *d* of D. Edward Higham; one *d*; 2nd, Mary Tindall, *d* of Robert Thornhill Harris; one *s*. *Educ:* Merchant Taylors' Sch.; Magdalene Coll., Cambridge (Exhibnr). BA (War Degree) 1915; MA 1961. European War, 1914-19; Capt. and Adjt, Royal North Devon Hussars; severely wounded with Devon Regt, 1917. Asst, British Museum, 1919; Dep. Keeper of Manuscripts, 1944-47; Lecturer in Palaeography to Sch. of Librarianship, London, 1947-55. Keeper of Manuscripts and Egerton Librarian, British Museum, 1947-55. *Publications:* Legal and Manorial Formularies (with B. Schofield), 1933; The Documents of the Great Charter of 1215 (Proc. Brit. Acad.); An Inventory of the Jewels and Plate of Queen Elizabeth I, 1574; Manuale ad usum Sarum (Henry Bradshaw Soc.); Bridgettine Breviary of Syon Abbey (Henry Bradshaw Soc.); articles in Antiquaries' Jl, History, Times, etc. *Address:* Broughton Gorse, Hale Purlieu, near Fordingbridge, Hants. *T:* Downton 20376.   [*Died* 13 *May* 1976.

COLLINS, Douglas; perfumer and seedsman; Founder and Chairman: Goya Ltd; Chairman: National Seed Development Organisation; Suttons Seeds Ltd; *b* 31 Aug. 1912; *s* of Richard Johnson Douglas Collins, Renfrew and Anascaul, Co. Kerry; *m* 1st, 1938, Patricia Backhouse (marr. diss. 1961); two *s* three *d*; 2nd, 1962, Elisabeth Worswick; one *s* two *d*. *Educ:* private schs, Sussex; state schs, Canada; Vevey; Zürich; Hanover; University, Perugia. Office boy in French hotels, 1928; clerk in paint works and stockbrokers, 1929-33; started unsuccessful businesses, 1933-36; started Goya Ltd, 1937. RNVR 1939; Navigator, HMS Gardenia; in command escort vessels; retd as Lt-Comdr, 1945. Chairman: British Lion Films Ltd and British Lion Studio Co. Ltd, 1958-61; Dir, National Film Finance Corporation, 1955-61. Owns and farms 500 acres at Great Missenden (cereals and pigs). *Publications:* Sailing in Helen, 1946; Mr Mole series of Children's Books, 1947-50; A Nose for Money, 1963. *Recreations:* ocean sailing, ski-ing, writing; repairing old furniture. *Address:* 14 Bourdon Street, W1. *T:* 01-629 4971. *Club:* Royal Cruising.   [*Died* 4 *March* 1972.

COLLINS, Victor John; *see* Stonham, Baron.

COLLINS, Sir William (Alexander Roy), Kt 1970; CBE 1966; Chairman and Managing Director, William Collins Sons & Co. Ltd, Publishers; *b* 23 May 1900; *s* of late William Alexander Collins, CBE, DSO and Grace Brander; *m* 1924, Priscilla Marian, *d* of late S. J. Lloyd, Pipewell Hall, Kettering; two *s* one *d* (and one *d* decd). *Educ:* Harrow; Magdalen Coll., Oxford. Hon. LLD Strathclyde, 1973. *Address:* 14 St James's Place, SW1. *T:* 01-493 5321; Hayle Farm House, Horsmonden, Tonbridge, Kent. *T:* Brenchley 2564. *Clubs:* MCC, All England Lawn Tennis; Rye Golf.   [*Died* 21 *Sept.* 1976.

COLLIS, Maurice; ICS, retired; historian, biographer, novelist, dramatist, critic and art critic, formerly contributing to The Observer and Time and Tide and now occasionally to The Arts Review, The Sunday Telegraph, and to other publications; Founder Member, International Association of Art Critics; *b* 10 Jan. 1889; *s* of late W. S. Collis, JP, Kilmore, Killiney, Co. Dublin, Ireland, and Edith Barton; *m* 1912, Dorothy (marr. diss. 1917), *d* of Arthur Tilney-Bassett; two *s*; *m* 1922, Eleanor (*d* 1967), *d* of late Arthur Bourke; two *s* one *d*. *Educ:* Rugby Sch.; Corpus Christi Coll., Oxford. First class in Final Hons Sch. of Modern History; passed into Indian Civil Service in 1911 and was posted to Burma in 1912; served in Burma in various administrative and secretarial appointments for twenty-three years, being District Magistrate, Rangoon, in 1930, and Excise Commissioner in 1931; military service with the 35th Scinde Horse in India and active service with 1/70th Burma Rifles in Palestine, 1917-18; retired, 1936, when immediately began literary career. Took up painting, 1957; one man exhibition of gouaches, Kaplan Gallery, W1, Dec. 1959; exhibition of tempera paintings and stone figures at Gallery One, W1, April 1962. *Publications: on oriental subjects:* Siamese White, 1936; She was a Queen, 1937; Trials in Burma (autobiog.), 1938; Lords of the Sunset, 1938; Sanda Mala, 1939; The Dark Door, 1940; The Great Within, 1941; British Merchant Adventurers, 1942; The Land of the Great Image, 1943; The Motherly and Auspicious, 1943; The Burmese Scene, 1944; White of Mergen, 1945; Quest for Sita, 1946; Foreign Mud, 1946; Lord of the Three Worlds, 1947; The First Holy One, 1948; The Descent of the God, 1948; The Grand Peregrination, 1949; Marco Polo, 1950; The Mystery of Dead Lovers, 1951; The Journey Outward, 1952 and Into Hidden Burma, 1953 (two vols of autobiography); Last and First in Burma, 1956; Wayfoong, 1965 (centenary vol. of Hongkong and Shanghai Banking Corp., commissioned, 1962); *on Mexico:* Cortés and Montezuma, 1954; *on English History and biography:* The Hurling Time, 1957; Nancy Astor, an informal biography, 1960; Stanley Spencer, a biography, 1962; Raffles (biography of Sir Stamford Raffles), 1966; Somerville and Ross, 1968; (many of above have been translated into one or more of following languages: Norwegian, Swedish, German, Danish, Dutch, French, Italian, Spanish, Portuguese, Rumanian, Bulgarian, Hindi, Tamil, Burmese, Siamese, Japanese, or publ. in America); *on art:* Alva, an introduction to his paintings, 1942; Introduction to the Drawings of Feliks Topolski, 1946; Alva, 1951; The Discovery of L. S. Lowry, 1951; Nicholas Egon; Some Beautiful Women of Today, 1952; *general:* The Three Gods, 1970; The Journey Up: Reminiscences 1934-68 (autobiog.), 1970. *Address:* 65 Cornwall Gardens, SW7. *T:* 01-937 1950.

[*Died* 12 *Jan.* 1973.

COLLIS, William Robert FitzGerald, MA, MD, FRCP, FRCPI, DPH; Retired; Professor of Pædiatrics, Medical College, Ahmadu Bello University, Zaria, N Nigeria, and Clinical Dean of Medical School, 1967-70; *b* 16 Feb. 1900; *s* of William Stewart Collis and Edith Barton; *m*; four *s*, and one *s* one *d* adopted. *Educ:* Rugby Sch.; Trinity Coll., Cambridge; Yale Univ. (Davison scholar); King's Coll. Hosp., London (Burney Yeo scholar); Johns Hopkins Hosp., Baltimore (Rockefeller fellowship). Entered army, 1918; obtained commission in Irish Guards; graduated medical sch., 1924; held resident medical officer appts King's Coll. Hosp. and Hosp. for Sick Children, Great Ormond Street, 1924-27; Sec., Research Dept, Hosp. for Sick Children, Great Ormond Street, 1929-32; Dir, Dept of Pædiatrics, Rotunda Hosp., Physician to the National Children's Hosp., Dublin, 1932-57; Dir of Pædiatrics, University Coll. Hosp., Ibadan, Nigeria, 1959-61; Prof. of Pædiatrics, and Dir, Inst. of Child Health, Lagos, 1962-67. *Publications:* The Silver Fleece, an Autobiography, 1936; Clinical Pædiatrics (The Baby), Text Book, 1938; Straight On, 1947; Modern Methods of Infant Management, 1948; Ultimate Value, 1951; The Lost and the Found; Fanconi and Wallgren's Textbook of Pædiatrics; African Encounter; A Doctor's Nigeria, 1960; Nigerians in Conflict, 1970; To Be a Pilgrim, 1975; papers in medical journals; *plays:* Marrowbone Lane; The Barrel Organ. *Recreations:* Rugby International, Ireland, 1924-26; riding. *Address:* Bo Island, Newtownmountkennedy, Co.

Wicklow, Ireland; Park House, Abinger Common, Surrey.
[Died 27 May 1975.

COLLISHAW, Air Vice-Marshal Raymond, CB 1941; DSO 1917; OBE (mil.), 1920; OBE (civil), 1946; DSC, DFC; *b* Canada, 22 Nov. 1893; *s* of John Edward Collishaw, Nanaimo, BC, Canada; *m* Juanita Eliza Trapp, New Westminster, BC; two *d. Educ:* Naval Coll. and Staff Coll. Royal Canadian Navy (Fishery Protection Service), 1908-14; entered the RNAS 1915; commanded a number of squadrons in France, 1916-18; reached second place (with total of 60) in records for pilots of British Empire in number of hostile aircraft destroyed during Great War (despatches four times, DSO and bar); posted to Egypt, 1919; commanded RAF detachment with South Russian Expedition, 1919-20 (despatches); commanded RAF detachment with British Forces, North Persia, 1920; served in Iraq, 1921-23 (despatches); Senior Royal Air Force Officer, HMS Courageous, 1929-32; commanded RAF Stations, Bircham Newton, 1932-35, Upper Heyford, 1935, RAF in the Sudan, 1935-36, and Heliopolis, 1936-38; Air Officer commanding Egypt Group, RAF, 1939; retired, 1943; holds French Croix de Guerre with two palms, and Russian Orders St Stanislaus, St Anne, and St Vladimir. *Publication:* (with R. V. Dodds) Air Command, 1973. *Address:* 2627 Ottawa Avenue West, Vancouver, BC, Canada. *[Died 29 Sept. 1976.*

COLMAN, Grace Mary, MA; *b* 1892; *d* of Canon F. S. Colman. *Educ:* Newnham Coll., Cambridge. Formerly Tutor, Ruskin Coll., Oxford, and Staff Tutor, London Univ.; formerly Ed. of Educational Publications, Labour Party. MP (Lab.) Tynemouth, 1945-50. *Address:* 5 West Ford Road, Stakeford, Northumberland. *[Died 7 July 1971.*

COLQUHOUN, (Cecil) Brian (Hugh), BSc (Eng) (London); FKC; FICE, FIStructE, MConsE, FASCE, MAmIConsE, MEIC, MSocCE (France); Senior Partner, Brian Colquhoun & Partners, Consulting Engineers and Chartered Civil Engineers, Upper Grosvenor Street, London W1, and at Manchester, Liverpool, Abu Dhabi, Dubai, Saudi Arabia, Sultanate of Oman, Kuwait, The Sudan, Ecuador and Paraguay; seconded for 2 years as Engineering Adviser to the International Bank for Reconstruction and Development, Sept. 1954; Engineering Adviser to Parliamentary Channel Tunnel Committee, 1956-57; *b* 13 Nov. 1902; *yr s* of late Arthur Hugh Colquhoun, OBE; *m* 1936, Beryl Marquis, *y d* of late Lieut-Col H. G. Cowan, MBE, late of 22nd (Cheshire) Regt; two *s. Educ:* Felsted Sch.; London Univ., King's Coll. Joined Muirhead, Macdonald Wilson & Co. Ltd, Civil Engineering Contractors. Then joined C. H. Lobban, MInstCE. Spent four years in Mexico with Mexican Eagle Oil Co. Resident Engineer of Mersey Tunnel, 1930, and Resident Engineer-in-Charge, 1933-36. Engineer-in-Chief, Royal Ordnance Factories at Chorley, Risley and Kirkby, 1936-40, also Adviser on Maas (Rotterdam) tunnel, Tamar (Plymouth) tunnel and Rossall sea wall, 1935-39. Rehabilitation of war production factories in main industrial centres, 1940; Dir-Gen. of Aircraft Production Factories, 1941-44. Founded Brian Colquhoun and Partners, 1944. *Address:* 24 Eaton House, Upper Grosvenor Street, W1. *T:* 01-499 4350; Mill Farm, Milland, West Sussex. *T:* Milland 314. *Clubs:* Royal Thames Yacht, Caledonian. *[Died 26 Sept. 1977.*

COLSON, Phyllis Constance, CBE 1964; retired; *b* 24 June 1904; *d* of late Charles Henry Colson, CBE, sometime Dep. Civil Engr-in-Chief, Admty and late Isabel Maude Colson. *Educ:* Huyton Coll. for Girls; Bedford Coll. of Physical Education. Teacher of Physical Educn, 1926-30; Organiser of Physical Educn, Nat. Assoc. of Girls' Clubs, 1930-33; Gen. Sec. (and Founder), Central Council of Physical Recreation, 1935-63 (Hon. Life Vice-Pres., 1966); Hon. Life Mem., Physical Education Assoc. of GB and NI. Le Titre Honorifique de la Féd. Internat. d'Educn Physique, 1945; King Gustavus Gold Medal, 1945; William Hyde Award for services to physical educn, 1953. *Recreations:* painting; interest in care of handicapped children and young adults. *Address:* 2 Forset Court, Edgware Road, W2. *Club:* English-Speaking Union. *[Died 26 June 1972.*

COLSTON-BAYNES, Dorothy Julia; author; *d* of Sir Christopher Baynes, 4th Bt; assumed by deed poll, 1946, additional surname of Colston. *Publications:* Enter a Child; Andromeda in Wimpole Street; The Regent and his Daughter; Fountains of Youth (a Life of Marie Bashkirtseff); In Search of Two Characters (Book Society Recommendation; Royal Society of Literature Award); The Youthful Queen Victoria; (trans.) Poems from Paul Verlaine; work included in Lord David Cecil's Anthology of Modern Biography. *Address:* c/o Lt-Col J. C. M. Baynes, West Grindon, by Norham, Berwick-on-Tweed.
[Died 14 April 1973.

COLUM, Padraic; author; *b* Longford, Ireland, 8 Dec. 1881; *m* 1912, Mary Maguire (*d* 1957). Associated with W. B. Yeats and Lady Gregory at beginning of Irish Theatre movement, 1902; wrote for Irish Theatre The Land, The Fiddler's House, Thomas Muskerry; went to America, 1914, lectured; invited by Hawaiian Legislature to make survey of native myth and folk-lore, and to make same over into stories for children of Hawaiian islands; went to Hawaii, 1923. First production of Balloon, 1946, Summer Theatre. Mem. of Irish Academy of Literature and American Academy of Arts and Letters. *Publications:* Three Plays: Wild Earth (poems); Dramatic Legends (poems); Castle Conquer (novel); many books for children, including The Adventures of Odysseus and The Tale of Troy; The King of Ireland's Son; The Golden Fleece; The Children of Odin; The Girl who Sat by the Ashes; The Boy Apprenticed to an Enchanter; The Children who Followed the Piper; The Voyagers; The Forge in the Forest; Hawaiian Tales and Legends; At the Gateways of the Day, The Bright Islands, The Road Round Ireland; The Fountain of Youth (Stories); Orpheus, or Stories from the Mythologies of the World; Balloon, a comedy in three acts; Cross Roads in Ireland; Collected Poems (1932); A Half-day's Ride, or Estates in Corsica (Essays), 1932; The Big Tree of Bunlahy: stories of my own countryside; The Legend of Saint Columba; The Story of Lowry Maen (narrative poem), 1937, Ten Poems, 1958; Our Friend James Joyce (with Mary Colum), 1959; Arthur Griffith, 1960; The Poet's Circuits, 1960; The Flying Swans (novel); Images of Departure (poems), 1968. *Recreation:* walking. *Address:* 11 Edenvale Road, Ranelagh, Dublin; 415 Central Park W, New York City 25.
[Died 11 Jan. 1972.

COLVILL, Lt-Col David Chaigneau, DSO 1940; MC 1918; Queen's Messenger, 1946-63, retd; late Oxfordshire and Bucks LI; *b* 4 July 1898; *y s* of late Robert Frederick Steuart Colvill, Coolock, Co. Dublin, and Sophia Maconchy; *m* 1954, Kathleen, *widow* of Paul Boissier. *Educ:* Winchester; RMC Sandhurst. 2nd Lieut, Oxon and Bucks Light Infantry, 1916; Capt., 1925; Major, 1938; Temp. Lt-Col, 1940; served European War, France, 1917-18 (wounded, MC); N Russia, 1919; India and Burma, 1926-35 (India General Service Medal with Clasp, Burma, 1931); BEF, France and Belgium, 1939-40 (wounded DSO); commanded 1st Bn (43rd Light Infantry), 1940-42; BLA, Normandy and Belgium, 1944-45; retired, 1946. *Address:* Jacobs, Boxford, Suffolk CO6 5NZ. *Club:* Naval and Military.
[Died 2 Oct. 1979.

COLVILLE, Norman Robert; *b* 11 Sept. 1893; *o surv. s* of late David Colville, JP, Jerviston House, Lanarkshire; *m* 1st, 1915 Marjorie Southworthe (*d* 1937), 2nd *d* of late P. H. Edelston, Penwortham House, Lancs; (one *s* killed in action, 1941) one *d* 2nd, 1938, Audrey Manuella Alexandre Joaquina (*d* 1940) formerly wife of Raymond Cecil Parr, and *d* of late Germain Bapst, Paris; 3rd, 1951, Diana Evelyn (she *m* 1st, 1945, 4th Earl of Kimberley, from whom she obt. a divorce, 1948), *o d* of late Lt-Col Hon. Sir Piers Walter Legh, GCVO, KCB, CMG, CIE OBE; one *s. Educ:* Fettes; Clare Coll., Cambridge. Served European War, 1914-18, with Argyll and Sutherland Highlanders (MC, despatches twice); Capt. 1917; retd 1919 Group Comdr Home Guard, 1940-41. High Sheriff of Cornwall 1940-41. FSA 1968. *Recreations:* hunting, shooting, golf, travel *Address:* Penheale Manor, Launceston, Cornwall. *T:* North Petherwin 241; 11 Kensington Square, W8. *T:* 01-937 8942 *Club:* Travellers'. *[Died 26 Aug. 1974*

COLVILLE, Comdr Sir Richard, KCVO 1965 (CVO 1953; MVO 1950); CB 1960; DSC 1943; Royal Navy retd; Extra Equerry to the Queen since 1968; *b* 26 Sept. 1907; *3rd s* of late Adm. Hon Sir Stanley Colville, GCB, GCMG, GCVO; *m* 1933, Dorothy (*d* 1972), *d* of late Brig.-Gen. Halhed B. Birdwood; one *s* two *d Educ:* Harrow. Joined Royal Navy, 1925. Served War of 1939-45, Mediterranean. Comdr (S), 1944. Press Secretary to King George VI, 1947-52, to the Queen, 1952-68. *Address:* Inchreed Jarvis Brook, East Sussex. *[Died 14 June 1975*

COLYER, Air Marshal Sir Douglas, CB 1942; CMG 1958; DFC 1918; MA; *b* 1 March 1893; *y s* of Henry Charles Colyer, HM Customs, and Charlotte, *d* of Owen Hill, Greenhithe, Kent; *m* Violet (*d* 1977), *d* of Charles Zerenner. *Educ:* St Dunstan's Coll and St Catharine's Coll., Cambridge. 2nd Lieut Lincolnshir Regt, 1915; transf. to RFC, 1916; permanent commission i Royal Air Force, 1919; Air Adviser, Latvian Govt, 1930-31; Ai Attaché Paris, Madrid, Lisbon, 1936-40; RAF Mem., Combine Chiefs of Staff, Washington, 1945-46; Civil Air Attaché, Pari 1947-52; Civil Aviation Representative, Western Europe, 1952 60; retd, 1960. Officer of Legion of Honour, 1938; Order Polonia Restituta, 2nd Class, 1941; Commander of Legion Merit (USA), 1946; Grand Officer, Order of Orange-Nassa (Holland), 1946. *Address:* c/o National Westminster Ban Cambridge. *[Died 23 Feb. 1978*

COMBE, Air Vice-Marshal Gerard, CB 1946; retired; *b* 15 Feb. 1902; 3rd *s* of late Percy Combe, Cobham, Surrey; *m* 1930, Brenda Mary, *er d* of Capt. Hugh Bainbridge, Killeen, Bournemouth; two *s. Educ:* King's College Sch.; RAF Coll., Cranwell. Flying duties in No 31 Sqdn India (NWFP), 1922-26; on return to UK in 1926 specialised in Armament; Armament Staff duties until 1932; Flying duties in No 30 Sqdn, Iraq, 1932-33 (Barzan Operations, Northern Kurdistan); Staff Coll. (psc), 1934; Armament and Chemical Warfare duties, 1935-38; commanded No 52 (Bomber) Sqdn, 1939; Armament Staff duties, Advanced Air Striking Force, 1939-40 (despatches). During 1941-45: Vice-Pres. (Air) Ordnance Board; Chief Superintendent Chemical Defence Experimental Station, Porton; Dir of Armament Development (MAP); Dir-Gen. of Armament, Air Ministry, 1945-47; Senior Air Staff Officer, RAF, HQ MEAF, 1947-49; Pres. of The Ordnance Board, 1950-51; AOA, HQ Maintenance Command, 1951-52; Air Officer Commanding, No 41 Group, 1953-55, retd 1955. United States Legion of Merit, Degree of Commander, 1946. *Recreation:* sailing. *Address:* Caley Cottage, Meysey Hampton, Cirencester, Glos GL7 5JU. *T:* Poulton 367. *Club:* Royal Lymington Yacht.
[*Died* 15 Dec. 1979.

COMPTON, Edward (Robert Francis); DL; late Major Royal Scots Greys; *b* 14 Dec. 1891; *e s* of late Lord Alwyne Compton; *m* 1st, 1918, Sylvia (*d* 1950), *y d* of late A. H. Farquharson; two *s* one *d*; 2nd, 1952, Mrs Allan Wilson (*d* 1957), Little Court, Bracknell, Berks; 3rd, 1958, Lady Sysonby, Kitale, Kenya. DL N Yorks (formerly WR Yorks), 1926. *Address:* Newby Hall, Ripon, Yorks; Torloisk, Aros, Isle of Mull, Scotland. *Clubs:* Bath; Muthaiga (Nairobi). [*Died* 7 Feb. 1977.

COMPTON, Fay, CBE 1975; *b* London, 18 Sept. 1894; *d* of Edward Compton and Virginia Bateman; *m* 1st, Harry Gabriel Pélissier (*d* 1913); one *s*; 2nd, Lauri de Freece (*d* 1921); 3rd, 1922, Leon Quartermaine (marr. diss., 1942; he died 1967); 4th, 1942, Ralph Champion Shotter (marr. diss., 1946). *Educ:* Leatherhead Court, Surrey. First appearance on stage, 1911; America, 1914; London music-hall stage (Coliseum), 1939. Has played Titania, Ophelia, Calpurnia, Paulina, and other Shakespearean parts, and had many successes in leading rôles of great variety, including: name part in Mary Rose, 1920 and 1926; Fanny Grey in Autumn Crocus, Lyric, 1931 (subsequently on tour); Dorothy Hilton in Call it a Day, Globe, 1935-37 (subsequently touring in the same part); Mary in Family Portrait, on tour 1940, and Strand, 1948 (Ellen Terry Award); Ruth in Blithe Spirit, Piccadilly, 1941-42; Martha Dacre in No Medals, Vaudeville, 1944-46; name part in Candida, Piccadilly, 1947; Gina Ekdal in The Wild Duck, St Martin's, 1948, etc. Old Vic Company, 1953-54 (having first appeared at Edinburgh Festival of 1953 with the Company): Gertrude in Hamlet; Countess of Rossillion in All's Well That Ends Well; Constance of Bretagne in King John; Volumnia in Coriolanus; Juno in The Tempest. Lady Bracknell in The Importance of Being Earnest, Old Vic, 1959; visited USA, 1959, playing lead in God and Kate Murphy; Comtesse de la Brière in What Every Woman Knows, Old Vic, 1960; Acted, Chichester Festival Theatre, 1962, 1963; A Month in the Country, Guildford (Yvonne Arnaud), 1965. Film career began 1917; has appeared in several notable films including, more recently, The Story of Esther Costello; Town on Trial; The Virgin and the Gipsy; has broadcast, and first appeared on television, 1952, since when has played numerous important rôles in plays and serials (including The Forsyte Saga, 1967). *Publication:* Rosemary: Some Remembrances, 1926. *Address:* 10 Eaton Gardens, Hove, East Sussex.
[*Died* 12 Dec. 1978.

COMPTON, Maurice; Adviser on the Budget to the Government of Singapore, 1970-71; *b* 26 March 1908; *s* of late S. Compton; *m* 1936, Maureen Ebie Reed; one *s. Educ:* Liverpool Univ.; King's Coll., Cambridge. Family Business, 1924-29; Universities, 1929-34; Min. of Agriculture, 1934-39; Min. of Food, 1939-51; Asst Sec., Min. of Agric., Fisheries and Food, 1951-62; Under-Sec. and Comr for Administration and Finance, Forestry Commn, 1962-69; retd. Engaged in research in Dept of Develt Studies, Univ. of Sussex, 1969-70. *Publications:* (with Hugh Bott) British Industry, 1940; contrib. to Economic Reconstruction, by J. R. Bellerby, 1943; FAO and the United Kingdom: a study of an association between an international agency and a government, 1971; articles in economic periodicals. *Recreations:* reading, gardening, the theatre, bowls. *Address:* 42 Whittingehame Gardens, Surrenden Road, Brighton, Sussex. *Club:* Royal Automobile. [*Died* 29 March 1974.

CONACHER, Mungo, OBE 1971; retired as Director and Chief General Manager, Martins Bank Ltd (1955-66); *b* 24 March 1901; *o s* of late Thomas and Margaret Conacher, Luss, Dunbartonshire; *m* 1930, Florence Victoria Fuller; two *d. Educ:*

mainly in Scotland. Entered Bank of Liverpool at Newcastle upon Tyne, 1917; Joint Gen. Manager, Martins Bank Ltd, 1945; Dep, Chief Gen. Manager, 1950; Chief Gen. Manager, 1955; Dir, 1965. Mem. Court, Univ. of Liverpool. Dir, Wyresdale Anglers Ltd. *Recreations:* foreign travel, golf, gardening, fishing. *Address:* Arden, 4 Ringwood Talbot Road, Oxton, Birkenhead, Merseyside L43 2LT. *T:* 051-653 7519. *Clubs:* Caledonian; Royal Liverpool Golf. [*Died* 15 Sept. 1977.

CONANT, James Bryant, Hon. CBE 1948; PhD; Author and Educational Consultant, in US, since 1965; President Emeritus, Harvard University; *b* 26 March, 1893; *s* of James Scott Conant and Jennet Orr Bryant; *m* 1921, Grace Thayer Richards; two *s. Educ:* Roxbury Latin Sch.; Harvard, AB, 1913, PhD, 1916; Instructor in Chemistry, Harvard, 1916-17; Lieut Sanitary Corps, USA, 1917; Major, Chemical Warfare Service, 1918; Asst Prof., Harvard, 1919-25; Assoc. Prof., 1925-27; Sheldon Emery Prof., Organic Chemistry, 1928-33; Chm., Dept of Chemistry, 1931-33; Pres., 1933-53, retired. US High Commissioner, 1953-55, Ambassador, 1955-57, Federal Republic of Germany. *Hon. degrees:* LLD: Chicago, 1933, New York, 1934, Princeton, 1934, Yale, 1934, Amherst, 1935, Coll. of Charleston, 1935, Coll. of William and Mary, 1936, Williams, 1938, Dartmouth, 1938, Tulane, 1939, Calif, 1940, Pa, 1940, Bristol (England), 1941, Queen's, 1941, Jewish Theol Seminary, 1951, NC, 1945, Toronto, 1945, Baylor, Ill., State of New York, 1947, Northeastern, Mass, 1948, Michigan, Yeshiva, Wesleyan, 1949, Swarthmore Coll., 1950, Jewish Theol Seminary, 1951, Birmingham (England), 1954; Harvard, Edinburgh, and Michigan State Univs, 1955, Leeds, 1956; New Hampshire, 1966; LHD, Boston, 1934; ScD: Columbia, Stevens Inst., Tufts Coll., 1934, Wisconsin, 1935, Cambridge (England), 1941, McGill, 1945, Free Univ. of Berlin, 1954; DCL: Oxford (England), 1936, Colgate, 1952; LittD: Algiers, 1944, Hamilton Coll., 1947; DSc: London, 1946 Lyons (France), 1947, Canterbury University Coll., NZ, 1951; FEIS 1947; admitted to Univ. of Adelaide ad eundem gradum, 1951. Lectures: Univ. of Calif, 1924; Sachs, Teachers' Coll., 1945; Terry, Yale, 1946; Stafford-Little, Princeton, 1957; Godkin, Harvard, 1958; Stimpson, Goucher Coll., 1951; Page Barbour, Univ. Va, 1952, Stevenson, LSE, 1952; Morrow, Smith Univ., 1959; Inglis, Harvard, 1959; Pollack, Harvard, 1959; Jefferson, Univ. of Calif, 1960. Research Associate California Technical, 1927. Mem. Educational Policies Commn of NEA, 1941-46, 1947-50, 1957-63; Chairman: National Defence Research Cttee and Dep. Dir, Office of Scientific Research and Development, 1941-46; Steering Cttee for Manhattan Dist charged with production of atomic bombs, 1942-45; Gen. Advisory Cttee of AEC, 1947-52. Member: Nat. Acad. of Sciences; Amer. Chem. Soc.; Mass. Historical Soc.; Amer. Acad. of Arts and Sciences, Amer. Philosophical Soc.; Nat. Science Foundation, 1950-53; Science Advisory Cttee, 1951-53. For. Member: Royal Society; Royal Institute of Chemistry; RSE; Hon. FCS; awarded Chandler Medal, Columbia Univ., 1932; Nichols Medal, 1932; Priestley Medal, Amer. Chem. Soc., 1944; Medal of Merit with Oak Leaf Cluster, 1948; Woodrow Wilson Award for Distinguished Service, 1959; Presidential Medal of Freedom, 1963; Great Living American Award, 1965; Sylvanus Thayer Award, 1965; Arches of Science Award, 1967; Atomic Pioneer Award, 1970. Hon. Fellow, Emmanuel Coll., Cambridge. Comdr, Legion of Honor. *Publications:* Practical Chemistry (with N. H. Black); Organic Chemistry; Chemistry of Organic Compounds; Our Fighting Faith, 1942; On Understanding Science, 1947; Education in a Divided World, 1948 (Gleichkeit der Chancen, 1955); Fundamentals of Organic Chemistry (with A. H. Blatt), 1950; Science and Common Sense, 1951; Modern Science and Modern Man, 1952; Education and Liberty, 1953; The Citadel of Learning, 1956; Germany and Freedom, 1958; The American High School Today, 1959; The Child, The Parent, and the State, 1959; Education in the Junior High School Years, 1960; Slums and Suburbs, 1961; Thomas Jefferson and the Development of American Public Education, 1962; The Education of American Teachers, 1963; Two Modes of Thought, 1964; Shaping Educational Policy, 1964; The Comprehensive High School, 1967; Scientific Principles and Moral Conduct, 1967; My Several Lives, 1970; Editor: Vols II and IX Organic Syntheses; Harvard Case Histories in Experimental Science; papers in scientific journals on researches in organic chemistry. *Address:* (home) 200 East 66th Street, New York, NY10021. *Clubs:* Athenæum; Tavern, Harvard; Century, Chemists, Harvard (New York); Cosmos (Washington). [*Died* 11 Feb. 1978.

CONANT, Sir Roger John Edward, 1st Bt *cr* 1954; CVO 1953; *b* 28 May 1899; *e s* of late E. W. P. Conant, Lyndon Hall, Oakham; *m* 1920, Daphne, *d* of A. E. Learoyd; three *s*; *m* 1972, Mrs Mary Buchanan. *Educ:* Eton; RMC Sandhurst. Grenadier Guards, 1917-21 and 1939-45; served European War (wounded); MP (C) Chesterfield, 1931-35, Bewdley Div. of Worcs, 1937-50,

Rutland and Stamford, 1950-Sept. 1959. Comptroller of HM Household, 1951-54. *Heir: s* John Ernest Michael Conant [*b* 24 April 1923; *m* 1950, Periwinkle Elizabeth, *d* of late Dudley Thorp, Kimbolton, Hunts; two *s* two *d* (and one *s* decd)]. *Address:* Manor House, Harringworth, Corby, Northants. *Club:* Carlton.						[*Died* 30 *March* 1973.

CONDON, Prof. Edward Uhler, PhD; Professor of Physics, University of Colorado, Boulder, Colorado, 1963-70, now Emeritus Professor; Editor, Reviews of Modern Physics, 1957-68; *b* 2 March 1902; *s* of late William Edward Condon, civil engineer; *m* 1922, Emilie Honzik; two *s* one *d*. *Educ:* Univ. of Calif, Berkeley, Calif. National Research Fellow, Göttingen and Munich, 1926-27; Lectr in Physics, Columbia Univ., 1927-28; Asst Prof. of Physics, Princeton Univ., 1928-29; Prof. of Theoretical Physics, Univ. of Minn., 1929-30; Assoc. Prof. of Physics, Princeton Univ., 1930-37; Assoc. Dir of Research, Westinghouse Electric Corp., 1937-45; Dir, National Bureau of Standards, US Dept of Commerce, Washington, DC, 1945-51. Dir of Research and Development, Corning Glass Works, 1951-54; Prof. of Physics, Washington Univ., St Louis, Mo, 1956-63. Scientific Adviser to US Senate Special Cttee on Atomic Energy 79th Congress. President: American Physical Soc., 1946; Amer. Assoc. for Advancement of Science, 1953; Amer. Assoc. of Physics Teachers, 1964; Soc. for Social Responsibility in Science, 1968-69. Visiting Prof. of Physics: Univ. of Pa, 1955-56; Oberlin Coll., 1962-63. DSc (hon.): Delhi (India); New Mexico Sch. of Mines; American Univ.; Alfred Univ.; Univ. of Chicago. *Publications:* Quantum Mechanics (with P. M. Morse), 1929; The Theory of Atomic Spectra (with G. H. Shortley), 1935; Handbook of Physics (with H. Odishaw), 1958; Scientific Study of Unidentified Flying Objects, 1969; numerous research papers, mostly published in Physical Review. *Address:* 761 Cascade Avenue, Boulder, Colo, USA. *Clubs:* Cosmos (Washington, DC); University (Boulder).				[*Died* 25 *March* 1974.

CONESFORD, 1st Baron, *cr* 1955, of Chelsea; **Henry George Strauss,** QC 1946; *b* London, 1892; *o s* of late A. H. Strauss; *m* 1927, Anne, *yr d* of late J. Bowyer Nichols, Lawford Hall, Manningtree. *Educ:* Rugby (Scholar); Christ Church, Oxford (Scholar). MA (1st class Classical Hon. Mods; 1st class Lit. Hum.). Junior Treasurer, Oxford Union Soc., 1914; enlisted, 1914; invalided; served in Government Depts; called to Bar, Inner Temple, 1919; Hon. Bencher, 1969. MP (C) Norwich, 1935-45, Combined English Universities, 1946-50, Norwich South, 1950-April 1955. Parliamentary Private Sec. to the Attorney-Gen., 1936-42; Joint Parliamentary Sec., Ministry of Works and Planning, 1942-43; Parliamentary Sec., Ministry of Town and Country Planning, 1943-45, when he resigned office in disagreement with the decisions of the Crimea Conference; Parliamentary Sec., Board of Trade, 1951-55; Past Pres.: Architecture Club; Design and Industries Assoc; London Soc.; Hon. FRIBA, 1965. *Publication:* Trade Unions and the Law, 1946. *Heir:* none. *Address:* 25 Cheyne Walk, SW3. *T:* 01-352 1984. *Clubs:* Carlton, Beefsteak, Pratt's; Norfolk (Norwich).
						[*Died* 28 *Aug.* 1974 (*ext*).

CONNELL, Sir Charles, Kt 1956; DL; Chairman, Charles Connell & Co. Ltd, since 1949; *b* 15 May 1900; *s* of late Charles Broadfoot Connell; *m* 1924, Audrey Menzies Raymond; one *s* two *d*. *Educ:* Fettes; Clare Coll., Cambridge. Joined Charles Connell & Co. Ltd, 1921, Dir, 1930. Chairman: Alscot Shipping Co.; Iron Trades Employers' Insurance Assoc. Ltd; Scottish Ore Carriers Ltd, etc. President: Clyde Shipbuilders Assoc., 1949; Shipbuilding Employers' Federation, 1950-51; Shipbuilding Conference, 1952-53; British Employers' Confederation, 1954-56. Mem., Anglo-American Council of Productivity, 1951-53; Vice-Pres., British Productivity Council, 1955; Joint Chm., Technical Cttee, Lloyd's Register of Shipping, 1955-65. Mem., Admiralty Shipbuilding Advisory Cttee, 1953-54; Chm. of Council, British Shipbuilding Research Assoc., 1954-56, and again 1957, 1959; Mem., Iron and Steel Board, 1953-62; Chm., Scottish Cttee, Council of Industrial Design, 1958-61; Mem., Royal Fine Art Commission for Scotland, 1964-; Vice-Pres., Royal Highland and Agricultural Soc. of Scotland, 1969-70. Prime Warden, Shipwrights' Co., 1965-66. MA, MRINA, MIES; Hon. Comdr, RNR; DL Dunbartonshire, 1957. Comdr Royal Norwegian Order of St Olav, 1958. *Address:* Colquhalzie, Auchterarder, Perthshire. *T:* Auchterarder 59; 42 Upper Brook Street, W1. *T:* 01-629 8628. *Clubs:* Travellers'; Western (Glasgow).					[*Died* 29 *Oct.* 1972.

CONNELLY, Marc; playwright; *b* 13 Dec. 1890; *s* of Patrick Joseph Connelly and Mabel Louise Fowler Cook. *Educ:* Trinity Hall, Washington, PA. Member of Authors' League of America (Past Pres.) and of National Inst. of Arts and Letters (Past Pres.). Prof. of Playwriting, Yale (retired). LittD (Hon.) Bowdoin. *Publications:* Plays: The Wisdom Tooth, The Green

Pastures (awarded Pulitzer Prize, 1930), and others; co-author: Dulcy, Merton of the Movies, Beggar on Horseback, To the Ladies, Farmer Takes a Wife, and others; several musical comedies; A Souvenir from Qam (novel), 1965; Voices Offstage (memoirs), 1968; contributor of verse, articles and fiction to magazines, including Coroner's Inquest (awarded O. Henry short-story prize). *Address:* 25 Central Park West, New York City, NY 10023, USA. *TA:* Marconel NY. *T:* Circle 7-2147. *Clubs:* Savage; Players' (New York).			[*Died* 21 *Dec.* 1980.

CONNOLLY, Cyril (Vernon), CBE 1972; CLit 1972; FRSL; Author and Journalist; Chevalier de la Légion d'Honneur; *b* 10 Sept. 1903; *o s* of Major Matthew Connolly, Bath, and Muriel Vernon; *m* 1930, Frances Jean Bakewell; *m* Barbara Skelton; *m* 1959, Deirdre, *o c* of Hon. P. W. D. Craig, MBE, and Mrs Aline Hanbury; one *s* one *d*. *Educ:* Eton (scholar): Balliol Coll., Oxford (Brackenbury Scholar). Has written for New Statesman and other periodicals, 1927-; founded Horizon, 1939, and ed, 1939-50; Literary Editor, Observer, 1942-43; contributes weekly to Sunday Times. Hon. Mem., Amer. Acad. and Nat. Inst. of Arts and Letters, 1974. *Publications:* The Rock Pool (fiction), 1935; Enemies of Promise, 1938; The Unquiet Grave, 1944-45; The Condemned Playground, 1944; Put Out the Light (translation), 1944; Ideas and Places, 1953; The Missing Diplomats, 1953; (ed) The Golden Horizon, 1953; (ed) Great English Short Novels, 1953; (with Jerome Zerbe) Les Pavillons, 1962; Previous Convictions, 1963; The Modern Movement, 1965; The Evening Colonnade, 1973. *Recreation:* travel. *Address:* 48 St John's Road, Eastbourne, East Sussex. *Clubs:* White's, Pratt's, Beefsteak.			[*Died* 26 *Nov.* 1974.

CONROY, Sir Diarmaid (William), Kt 1962; CMG 1960; OBE 1955; TD 1946; QC (Gibraltar) 1953; (Kenya) 1956; Chairman, Industrial Tribunals (Southampton), since 1974; President, Industrial Tribunals for England and Wales, 1965-74; *b* 22 Dec. 1913; *m* 1939, Alice Lilian Elizabeth Craig; one *s* two *d*. *Educ:* Mount St Mary's; Gray's Inn. Practised at Bar, 1935-39; served War, 1939-46, with London Irish Rifles (Major, wounded); Crown Counsel, N Rhodesia, 1946; Legal Draftsman, N Rhodesia, 1949; Attorney-Gen., Gibraltar, 1952; Permanent Sec. of Ministry of Legal Affairs, Solicitor-Gen. and Dep.-Speaker, Kenya, 1955-61; Chief Justice, N Rhodesia, 1961-65. *Recreations:* sailing, fishing. *Address:* 26 Ward Avenue, Cowes, Isle of Wight PO31 8AY. *T:* Cowes 5949. *Club:* Royal London Yacht (Cowes).				[*Died* 8 *Aug.* 1978.

CONRY, Brigadier John de Lisle, CIE 1937; Indian Army, retired; *b* 14 April 1882; *y s* of late Thomas Conry, Staff Surgeon, RN, Clonryn, Longford, Ireland, and late Isabella Mary Conry, later of Spestos Grange, Bow, Devon; *m* 1921, Dorothy, *o d* of late Rev. G. H. Marwood, Royal Navy, Plymouth, Devon; (one *s* killed in action, 1945). *Educ:* Mannamead Sch., Plymouth; Royal Naval Sch.; Eltham; Sandhurst. 1st Bn The Dorset Regt, 1901; transferred 96th Berar Inf., Indian Army, 1903; Adjt and CO; served 3+ years in Burma Military Police, NE frontier of India; Instructor, later Senior Instructor, Senior Officers Sch., Belgaum; Comdr, Mhow Brigade Area; late Col 2/19th Hyderabad Regt; served European War, Mesopotamia (despatches twice). *Address:* Brook House, Dawlish, Devon.			[*Died* 11 *Oct.* 1971.

CONSTABLE, Sir Henry Marmaduke S.; *see* Strickland-Constable.

CONSTABLE, William George; MA, Hon. DCL Durham; Hon. LittD Nottingham, New Brunswick; FSA; Curator of Paintings Boston Museum of Fine Arts, 1938-57; late Director, Courtauld Institute of Art, London University; Barrister-at-law; Chevalier Legion of Honour; Commendatore of Crown of Italy Corresponding Member, Academy of Fine Arts, Brussels Officier de l'Ordre des Arts et des Lettres; Hon. Phi Beta Kappa Fellow: American Academy of Arts and Sciences; International Institute for Conservation of Museum Objects (President 1958) Hon. Fellow, St John's College, Cambridge, 1956; *b* Derby 1887; *m* Olivia, *d* of A. Carson Roberts; two *s*. *Educ:* Derby Sch.; St John's Coll., Cambridge (Fellow; Whewell Scholar in the University); Slade Sch. In the Army, 1914-18, Major, 16th Sherwood Foresters; 2 i/c, 11th Lancs Fusiliers (despatches) Lecturer, Wallace Collection; Asst, National Gallery, 1923-28 Lecturer in Art, Bristol University, 1928; Ferens Lecturer in Fine Art, University Coll., Hull, 1929-30; Asst Dir, National Gallery, 1929-31; Slade Prof. of Fine Art, Cambridge Univ 1935-37; Sydney Jones Lecturer in Art, Liverpool Univ Ryerson Lecturer, Yale Univ. *Publications:* Contributions to Essays in Adult Education, 1919; Catalogue of British Primitives Exhibition, 1924; Catalogue of the Marlay Bequest Fitzwilliam Museum, 1927; Catalogue of Italian Pictures in the W. H. Woodward Collection, 1928; John Flaxman, 1928

Commemorative Catalogue of the Dutch Exhibition, 1929 (pictures: with Dr H. Schneider); Commemorative Catalogue of the Italian Exhibition, 1930 (with Lord Balniel and K. Clark); English Painting 1500-1700, 1930 (with C. H. Collins Baker); general editor Commemorative Catalogue; French Exhibition, 1932; British Exhibition (with Charles Johnson and others); contrib. to Cambridge Medieval History; Mantegna (W. H. Charlton lecture), 1936; Art History and Connoisseurship; Catalogue of English XII Cent. Mural Paintings (with E. W. Tristram), 1944; Venetian Painting, 1949; Richard Wilson, 1953; The Painter's Workshop, 1954; Canaletto, 1962; Art Collecting in the United States, 1964; contributions to the principal art periodicals. Was art critic of New Statesman and Saturday Review, and is on the consultative cttee of Burlington Magazine. *Address:* 23 Craigie Street, Cambridge, Mass, USA. *Club:* Athenæum.   *[Died 3 Feb. 1976.*

CONSTANTINE, Baron *cr* 1969 (Life Peer), of Maraval and Nelson; **Learie Nicholas Constantine**, Kt 1962; MBE 1945; Member, Race Relations Board, since 1966; *b* 21 September 1901; *s* of Lebrun Constantine and Anna Pascal; *m* 1927, Norma Agatha Cox, Port of Spain, Trinidad; one *d*. *Educ:* St Ann's RC, Trinidad. Solicitor's Clerk, 1917-22; Civil Servant, 1922-25; Clerk, Oil Company, 1925-29; Professional Cricketer, 1929-40; ARP Equipment Clerk, Nelson, Lancs, also Billeting Officer, 1940-42; Welfare Officer, Min. of Labour and Nat. Service, 1942-47 (MBE); broadcast during War, including several times, BBC Brains-Trust. Lecturer, HM Forces, NW Region. Student, Middle Temple, 1949 (Hon. Master of the Bench, 1963); qualified in Law, Sept. 1954; called to Trinidad Bar, 1955. Asst to Legal Adviser, Oil Co., Trinidad, 1955-56. Entered local politics; fought election Tunapuna constituency; became Minister of Works and Transport in first Party Government, 1956; High Commissioner for the Government of Trinidad and Tobago, in London, 1962-64. Member: Sports Council, 1965-; General Adv. Council of BBC; a Governor of BBC, 1968-. Honorary Freedom of Nelson, Lancashire, 1963. Rector of Univ. of St Andrews, 1968- (Hon. LLD 1968). *Publications:* Cricket and I; Cricket in the Sun; How to play Cricket; Cricketers' Carnival; Cricket Crackers; Colour Bar: The Young Cricketer's Companion; (with Denzil Batchelor) The Changing Face of Cricket. Contributions to The Listener, John Bull, and leading papers and magazines in London. *Recreations:* cricket, football. *Address:* 11 Kendal Court, Shoot-up Hill, Hampstead, NW2. *T:* 01-452 8462. *Clubs:* MCC, Lord's Taverners'; The XL; Esher (Surrey) Cricket; Bootle (Liverpool); Fulwood and Broughton (Preston); Windhill (Shipley, Yorks); Chinghoppers (Chingford).   *[Died 1 July 1971.*

CONWAY, Brig. **Albert Edward**, CB 1945; OBE 1940; New Zealand Forces (retired list); *b* 7 April 1891; *s* of Edward J. J. P. and Ann J. Conway; *m* 1916, Alice Rose Hinemoa Francis; two *s* one *d*. *Educ:* Reefton District High School. NZ Volunteers, 1907 and NZ Territorial Force, 1911; commissioned 12th (Nelson) Regt 1911, 13th (NC & W) Regt 1912; Canterbury Regt 1st NZEF, European War, incl. landing at Gallipoli, 1914-19 (twice wounded, despatches); NZ Staff Corps, 1919. Comdt, Central Military Dist Sch. of Instruction, Trentham, 1937; Dir of Mobilization, 1939; Dir of Military Training, May 1940. Capt. 1914; Major, 1927; Lt-Col, 1939; Temp. Col, 1940; Temp. Brig., 1941; Col, 1946; Brig., 1947; Adjt-Gen., NZ Military Forces and 2nd Military Mem., NZ Army Board, 1940-46; Hon. ADC to Governor-Gen., 1940-46; retired list, 1947. Councillor, NZ Golf Assoc., 1925-26-27, Vice-Pres., 1961. Sec.-Treas., Bay of Plenty District Golf Assoc., 1951-61. Patron, Bay of Plenty Eagles Golfing Soc., 1962-73; Mem. Cttee, Manawatu Golf Club, 1964; Hon. Life Mem., Manawatu Officers' Club, 1972. American Legion of Merit (Officer), 1946. *Recreations:* golf, sea fishing. *Address:* 51 Te Awe Awe Street, Palmerston North, New Zealand. *T:* 76-832.   *[Died 7 Aug. 1974.*

CONWAY, **James**; General Secretary, Amalgamated Union of Engineering Workers, since 1964 (Assistant General Secretary, 1962-64); *b* 7 Oct. 1915; British; *m* 1951, Sylvia; one *s*. Became Gen. Sec., AEU, later Amalgamated Union of Engineering and Foundry Workers. Member: Machine Tools Cttee; Machine Tools EDC, 1966-; Chm., TUC General Purpose Cttee. Director: Cooperative Press; Ditchley Foundn. Governor, Ruskin Coll. *Publications:* articles in newspapers and AEU Jl; Editor: AEU Journal; The Way (AEU). *Recreation:* golf. *Address:* Camden Cottage, Wilderness Road, Chislehurst, Kent BR7 5EY.   *[Died 3 March 1974.*

CONWAY, His Eminence Cardinal **William**; Archbishop of Armagh and Primate of All Ireland (RC), since 1963; *b* 22 Jan. 1913; *s* of Patrick Joseph and Annie (*née* Connelly) Conway. *Educ:* Christian Brothers, Belfast; Queen's Univ., Belfast; St Patrick's Coll., Maynooth; Gregorian Univ., Rome. Prof. of

Moral Theology and Canon Law, Maynooth, 1942; Vice-Pres., Maynooth, 1957; Auxiliary Bishop to the Archbishop of Armagh, 1958. Cardinal, 1965. *Publications:* Problems in Canon Law, 1956; The Child and the Catechism, 1959; articles in Irish Theological Quarterly, Irish Ecclesiastical Record, Christus Rex, The Furrow, etc. *Recreations:* walking; local history and archaeology. *Address:* Ara Coeli, Armagh, Ireland. *T:* Armagh 522045.   *[Died 17 April 1977.*

CONYNGHAM, 6th Marquess, *cr* 1816; **Frederick William Burton Conyngham**; Baron Conyngahm, 1780; Viscount Conyngham, 1789; Earl Conyngham, Viscount Mount-Charles, 1797; Earl of Mount-Charles, Viscount Slane, 1816; Baron Minster (UK), 1821; *b* 24 June 1890; *s* of 4th Marquess and Hon. Frances Eveleigh de Moleyns (who *m* 2nd, 1899, J. R. B. Cameron; she *d* 1939), *e d* of 4th Baron Ventry; *S* brother, 1918; *m* 1st, 1914, Elizabeth Alice Tobin (marr. diss. 1921); 2nd, 1922, Antoinette Winifred (*d* 1966), *er d* of late J. W. H. Thompson; one *s* (one *s* one *d* decd); 3rd, 1966, Stella, *d* of Francis Barrallier Thompson, and *widow* of Robert Newton Tory. Late Inniskilling Fusiliers and Westmorland and Cumberland Yeomanry and served in the North Irish Horse; Capt. commanding No. 1 Independent Platoon. 1st Ross-shire Home Guard in war of 1939-45. *Heir: s* Earl of Mount Charles. *Address:* Les Prés, St Lawrence, Jersey, CI.   *[Died 1 April 1974.*

COOK, Air Vice-Marshal **Albert Frederick**, CBE 1955 (OBE 1946); *b* 26 Aug. 1901; *s* of Charles Neville Cook, Dun Laoghaire, Co. Dublin; *m* 1st, 1929, Cecil Phyllis (*d* 1967), *d* of Lionel McEnnery, Dublin; two *d*; 2nd, 1969, Penelope, *d* of late K. B. Anderson, Weybridge. *Educ:* Kingstown Sch.; Royal College of Surgeons, Dublin. LRCP, LRCS, Ireland, 1924; DPH 1935. Joined RAF, 1925; seconded to Transjordan Frontier Force, 1928-30; served War of 1939-45 (despatches): Middle East, France and Germany; Principal Medical Officer, BAFO, Germany, 1949-51; PMO, Flying Trg Comd, 1951-55; PMO, Bomber Comd, 1955-56. QHP 1956; PMO, MEAF, 1957-59; retired, 1959. *Address:* 9 Freshborough Court, Guildford, Surrey. *Club:* Royal Air Force.   *[Died 27 Aug. 1980.*

COOK, Ven. **Edwin Arthur**, MA; Archdeacon of Bath, 1947-62, now Emeritus; Prebendary of Whitelackington, 1947-62; Rector of Bath Abbey, 1947-60, retired; *b* 9 July 1888; *s* of George Thomas and Mary Ann Cook; *m* 1920, Marion Elliott; one *s* one *d*. *Educ:* Maidstone Grammar Sch.; Queens' Coll. and Ridley Hall, Cambridge. Curate, Holy Trinity, Margate, 1911; CMS Missionary Western China, 1913; Rector, St James's, Dover, 1926; Vicar, Holy Trinity, Margate, 1929; Vicar, Christ Church, Folkestone, 1939; Vicar (in Plurality), Holy Trinity, Folkestone, 1942; Rural Dean of Elham, 1943; Proctor in Convocation, 1945; Hon. Canon of Canterbury, 1946. *Address:* 1 Cranhill Road, Bath, Somerset. *T:* 22368.   *[Died 15 Sept. 1972.*

COOK, Sir **Francis Ferdinand Maurice**, 4th Bt, *cr* 1886; *b* 21 Dec. 1907; *s* of Sir H. F. Cook, 3rd Bt, and Hon. Mary Hood, *e d* of 2nd Viscount Bridport; *S* father, 1939, also as Visconde de Monserrate in Portugal; *m* 3rd, 1937, Joan Loraine Ashton-Case (marr. diss. 1942), *d* of late Hon. Mrs Herbert Eaton; one *s*; *m* 6th, 1951, Jane Audrey Nott (marr. diss., 1956), *er d* of Mrs Turnbull and step *d* of late Lieut-Comdr S. G. L. Turnbull, RN (retd); one *d*; *m* 7th, 1956, Mrs Bridget Brenda Polland (*née* Lynch), *d* of Thomas David Lynch. *Educ:* Bradfield Coll., Berks, and privately. Musician, composer, organist; reconstructive scientist on mediums and methods of the old masters. FRSA; Member: Chelsea Art Soc., 1938-; Royal Cornish Soc., Truro; Jersey Artists' Group; St Ives Soc. of Artists, Cornwall; Assoc. Mem., Royal Soc. of British Artists, 1938-48; Patron and Mem., British Picture Restorers Assoc. Gold Medallist, 1934. Exhibited works at RA, RBA, London Portrait Soc., London Group, etc., and provinces. Represented in the permanent collections Walker Art Gall., Liverpool, Manchester, Northampton. *Recreation:* architecture. *Heir: s* Christopher Wymondham Rayner Herbert Cook [*b* 24 March 1938; *m* 1975, Mrs Margaret Miller, *d* of late John Murray (one *s* one *d* of previous marriage)]. *Address:* Le Coin, La Haule, St Aubin, Jersey, CI. *T:* Jersey Central 41234; (Studio) The Studio, Augres Galleries, Augres, Trinity, Jersey, CI. *T:* Jersey Central 63333. *Clubs:* Arts, Royal Automobile; Victoria (St Helier).   *[Died 12 Sept. 1978.*

COOK, **Frank**, BSc, MB, BS London, FRCS, FRCOG; Consulting Obstetric Surgeon Emeritus, Guy's Hospital; Consulting Surgeon, Chelsea Hospital for Women; Hon. Consulting Gynæcologist and Obstetrician to Orpington and Sevenoaks Hospitals; Fellow of Royal Society of Medicine; Freeman of the Society of Apothecaries; *b* 6 Nov. 1888; *o s* of late Frank Plant Cook of Mansfield Woodhouse, Notts; *m* 1917,

Edith Harriette Wallace, yr d of late Rev. James Reid, Co. Clare; one s. Educ: Bedford Modern Sch.; Guy's Hospital; University of London; Scholarship and Research Studentship in Physiology, University of London; First Class Hons in BSc (Physiology); Beit Memorial Research Fellow; Dean of the Institute of Obstetrics and Gynæcology; Examiner in Obstetrics and Gynæcology to the Universities of Cambridge, London, Glasgow and Bombay, and to the Royal College of Obstetricians and Gynæcologists; Mem., SW Metropolitan Regional Hosp. Board; Member: Boards of Governors, St Thomas' Hosp., and Queen Charlotte's and Chelsea Hosps. Col RAMC. Served in both Great Wars; France, Belgium and Mesopotamia (1914 Star with Bar); Palestine, Greece, Sudan, Egypt and India. Hunterian Prof., Royal College of Surgeons, 1917 and 1924: Consulting Gynæcologist to Queen Alexandra Military Hosp., Millbank and to King Edward VII Sanatorium, Midhurst; Medical Inspector of the High Court, Divorce Division; Demonstrator of Pathology, Surgical Registrar and tutor, etc., Guy's Hosp. Publications: Midwifery, 1948; (joint) Diseases of Women, 1949; various papers on physiological, surgical, and obstetric subjects. Address: 21 Hamilton Court, Chilston Road, Tunbridge Wells, Kent. T: Tunbridge Wells 22038. [Died 25 Feb. 1972.

COOK, Frank Allan Grafton, CBE 1959 (OBE 1942); retired; b 13 June 1902; s of George and Lucy Cook; m 1934, Phyllis Mary, y d of H. W. Blunt, MA, of Oxford; three d. Educ: Nottingham High Sch.; Gonville and Caius Coll., Cambridge. Entered the Levant Consular Service, 1924; served in Egypt, Hejaz, Morocco, Greece; Consul at Mosul, 1939; served in Persia and Abyssinia; Chargé d'Affaires at Addis Ababa, 1945-46; Consul-Gen., Berlin, 1947; Counsellor and Consul-Gen., Rangoon, 1948-49; Consul-Gen., Basra, 1949-53; Antwerp, 1953-57; Izmir, 1957-59; retired, 1959. Address: 409 The Ridge, Hastings, Sussex. [Died 18 July 1973.

COOK, Sir James (Wilfred), Kt 1963; FRS 1938; DSc, PhD (London); FRIC; Vice-Chancellor, University of East Africa, 1966-70; b 10 Dec. 1900; s of late Charles William and late Frances Cook; m 1st, 1930, Elsie Winifred (d 1966), d of late Major Griffiths; three s; 2nd, 1967, Vera Elizabeth Ford. Educ: Sloane Sch., Chelsea; University Coll., London (Tuffnell Scholar). Lectr in Organic Chemistry, The Sir John Cass Tech. Inst., 1920-28; Research Chemist, DSIR, 1928-29; Research Chemist, The Royal Cancer Hosp. (Free), 1929-39; Reader in Pathological Chemistry, University of London, 1932-35; Prof. of Chemistry, Univ. of London, 1935-39; Professorial Lectr in Chemistry, Chicago Univ., 1938; Regius Prof. of Chemistry, Glasgow Univ., 1939-54; Principal, University Coll. of the South West, Exeter, 1954-55; Vice-Chancellor, Exeter Univ., 1955-66. Member: University Grants Cttee, 1950-54; Cttee on cost of Nat. Health Service, 1953-56; Cttee of Enquiry into Pharmaceutical Ind., 1965-66; Member Council: DSIR, and Chm. Post-graduate Training Awards Cttee, 1960-65; University Coll. of Rhodesia, 1955-68. Hon. Dir, MRC Carcinogenic Substances Res. Unit, 1956-66; Chairman: Chemical Council, 1959-63; Cttee on Composition of Milk, 1958-60; Advisory Cttee on Pesticides and other Toxic Chemicals, 1962-66; Advisory Cttee on Scientific and Technical Information, 1965-66; Academic Adv. Cttee, New Univ. of Ulster, 1971-. President: Royal Inst. of Chemistry, 1949-51; Section B, British Assoc., 1957, Section X, 1966; Hon. Member: Polish Chem. Soc.; Chilean Chem. Soc.; Corr. Mem. Nat. Acad. of Exact Sciences of Buenos Aires. Awarded, jointly with Prof. Sir Ernest Kennaway, prize of Union Internationale contre le Cancer, 1936; part recipient of first award of Anna Fuller Memorial Prize, 1939; recipient of Katherine Berkan Judd Prize (Mem. Hosp., New York) for 1940; Davy Medallist, Royal Society, 1954; Pedler Lectr., Chem. Soc., 1950. Fellow, University Coll., London, 1950. Hon. ScD Dublin, 1948; Hon. DSc Nigeria, 1961; Ulster, 1970; Hon. D de l'U Rennes, 1960; Hon. LLD Exeter, 1967. Officier de l'Ordre de Léopold. Publications: numerous papers on organic chemistry, especially in relation to cancer, hormones, polycyclic compounds, bile acids, etc., published mainly in the Journal of the Chemical Society and the Proceedings of the Royal Society. Ed Progress in Organic Chemistry, Vols I-VII. Address: The Burn, 15a Knowle Road, Budleigh Salterton, Devon EX9 6AR. T: Budleigh Salterton 2813. Club: Athenæum. [Died 21 Oct. 1975.

COOK, John Gilbert, CVO 1970; CBE 1963; HM Treasury Valuer, 1950-69, retd; b 16 May 1911; s of late John Andrew Cook; m 1st, 1937, Doreen Violet Mary Harrington (d 1973); two s two d; 2nd, 1973, Hilda Joan (Bunty) Plewman (née Braggins). Educ: Bedford Sch. Articled to Sir H. Trustram Eve, 1929-32. FRICS. Recreations: Rugby football (English International and Barbarian; Captain of Bedford, 1936-39), golf, cricket. Address: Sleepers, 6 Highfield Road, Overstrand, Norfolk. T: Overstrand 561. Clubs: MCC, Pathfinder; Royal Cromer Golf. [Died 10 Sept. 1979.

COOKE, Sir Charles (Arthur John), 11th Bt, cr 1661; b 12 Nov. 1905; yr s of 10th Bt and Lady Mildred Adelaide Cecilia Denison; S father, 1964; m 1932, Diana, o d of late Maj.-Gen. Sir Edward Maxwell Perceval, KCB, DSO, JP; one s one d. Educ: Wellington Coll.; RMC Sandhurst. Served War of 1939-45, 4/7th Dragoon Guards, France (prisoner, 1940). Capt., 1945, Major, 1952, 4/7th Dragoon Guards; retired from Army, 1953. Recreations: shooting and fishing. Heir: s David William Perceval Cooke [b 28 April 1935; m 1959, Margaret Frances, d of Herbert Skinner, Knutsford, Cheshire; three d]. Address: 15 Esplanade, Fowey, Cornwall PL23 1HY. [Died 5 July 1978.

COOKE, Christopher Herbert, CIE 1946; b 29 May 1899; s of late F. J. Cooke, ICS (retired); m 1929, Beryl Gourley Ainsley; one s one d. Educ: Clifton; Christ Church, Oxford (MA). Indian Civil Service (United Provinces), 1922; Joint Magistrate, Collector, Settlement Officer, 1922-39; Revenue Sec., Finance Sec., Settlement Commissioner, 1939-44; Commissioner, Lucknow Division, 1945-47; retired from ICS, 1947; Settlement Commissioner for Forest Reserves, Ghana, 1951-57. Recreation: golf. Address: Redholme, Great Missenden, Bucks. T: Great Missenden 2580. [Died 3 April 1979.

COOKE, Air Marshal Sir Cyril Bertram, KCB 1947 (CB 1945); CBE 1941; retired; b 28 June 1895; s of late John Cooke, Chalkcliffe, Dorking; m 1918, Elizabeth Amelia Phyllis, d of John Benjamin Davies, Bank House, Pembroke; one s one d. Educ: Dorking High Sch.; Northampton Engineering Coll., London. Temp. 2nd Lieut RGA, 1914; transferred to RFC, 1915; Flight-Comdr and Temp. Capt., 1916: Sqdn Comdr and Acting Major, 1918; Permanent Commission RAF as Flight-Lieut, 1919; Squadron Leader, 1924; Wing-Comdr, 1935; Group Capt., 1939; Acting Air Cdre, 1940; Temp. Air Cdre, 1941; Subst. Air Cdre, 1944; Acting Air Vice-Marshal, 1944; Air Vice-Marshal, 1946; Actg Air Marshal, 1947; Air Marshal, 1947. Served European War, 1914-18, in Egypt, Sudan, Salonika and Home Defence; India, 1922-25; NW Frontier, 1925; Iraq, 1931-33; War of 1939-45, served in Middle East, 1941-42, North Africa and Italy, 1944-45 (despatches, CBE, CB); commanded No 206 Group in Middle East, 1941-42; Chief Maintenance Staff Officer, MAAF, 1944-45; AOC No 43 Group, Maintenance Command, RAF, 1945-46; Dir-Gen., Servicing and Maintenance, Air Min., 1946-47; AOC-in-C Maintenance Command, 1947-49, retd. Recreation: represented RAF at cricket, 1927-37. Address: North Barn, Old Manor Road, Rustington, Sussex. T: 4831. [Died 27 Sept. 1972.

COOKE, Deryck Victor; Music Presentation Editor, BBC, since 1965; b 14 Sept. 1919; s of Henry Victor Cooke and Mabel Cooke (née Judd); m 1966, Jacqueline Etienne. Educ: Selwyn Coll., Cambridge. ARCM 1937; BA 1940, MA 1943, Cantab; ARCO 1946. Gunner, RA, 1940-45. Asst. Music Div., BBC, 1947-59; Free-lance Writer, 1959-65. Responsible for Realisation of Mahler's Tenth Symphony, first performed London, 1964. Kilenyi Mahler Medal, 1964. Publications: The Language of Music, 1959; Mahler 1860-1911, 1960. Address: 207 Melfort Road, Thornton Heath, Surrey. T: 01-689 7719. [Died 27 Oct. 1976

COOKE, Sir Henry Frank, Kt 1969; Chairman, Western Australian Division, Australian Red Cross, since 1961; b 10 Oct. 1900; s of F. V. Cooke; m 1926, Jean, d of B. L. Clarkson; two s three d. Educ: Hale School. Chairman: W Aust. Bd, Commercial Union Assurance Co.; Terrace Arcade Ltd. Vice Chairman, Chamberlain Industries. Member of Senate, Univ. of W Aust. Hon. Treasurer, Pastoralists' and Graziers' Assoc. Address: 5 Brae Road, Claremont, W Australia 6010, Australia [Died 22 Feb. 1973.

COOKE, Rear-Adm. John Ernest, CB 1955; CEng, FIMechE Royal Navy, retired; b 1899; s of Arthur Cockerton Cooke; m 1923, Kathleen Mary (d 1976), d of Walter James Haward; one one d. Educ: Owen's Sch. Entered Royal Navy, 1915; serve War of 1939-45, HMS Furious and HMS Anson; Capt., 1946 Manager of the Engineering Dept, HM Dockyard, Malta, 1950 53; Rear-Adm., 1953; Manager of the Engineering Dept, HM Dockyard, Portsmouth, 1954-57; retired. General Manager Production, Messrs Bailey (Malta) Ltd, 1959-61. Address: Kells Glen Dale, Rowlands Castle, Hants. Clubs: Roya Commonwealth Society; Royal Naval and Royal Albert Yach Union (Malta). [Died 8 Oct. 1980

COOKE, Rear-Adm. (John) Gervaise (Beresford), CB 1965; CBC 1940; Naval Secretary, 1966-67, retired; b 19 Oct. 1911; s of lat (Judge) John Fitzpatrick Cooke, Londonderry, Northerr Ireland, and Eleanora Lucia Caroline Macky; m 1941, Hele Beatrice Cameron; three s one d. Educ: Royal Naval Coll Dartmouth. Entered Navy, 1925; served in Destroyers; qualifie

in gunnery, 1938; Commanded HM Ships Modeste and Finisterre, 1947; Comdr 1947; Admiralty, 1948-49; commanded HM Ships Broadsword and Battleaxe, 1950-51; Staff of C-in-C Med., 1952-54. Capt., 1954; Admiralty, 1955-57; idc 1958; commanded Admiralty Surface Weapons Establishment, 1959-60; Chief of Staff to Commander, British Navy Staff and Asst Naval Attaché, Washington, 1961-63; Rear-Adm., 1963; Asst Chief of Naval Staff (Warfare), 1963-66. *Recreations:* tennis, golf, shooting, fishing. *Address:* Downstead House, Twyford, Hants. *T:* Owslebury 209. *Club:* Naval and Military.
[Died 30 Jan. 1976.

COOKE, John Sholto Fitzpatrick, CBE 1971; DL; Clerk of the Parliaments in Northern Ireland, 1962-71; *b* 21 July 1906; *s* of late H. J. Cooke, Londonderry; *m* 1st, 1934, Phoebe Maxwell Hamilton (marr. diss. 1946); two *s* one *d*; 2nd, 1946, Elizabeth Anne Nugent; three *d*. *Educ:* Harrow Sch.; Magdalen Coll., Oxford. BA Mod. Hist. 1927. Barrister-at-Law: Inner Temple, 1930; NI, 1931. Law practice, Belfast, 1931-39. Served War, RNVR (Lt-Comdr), 1939-45. Parliamentary Staff, NI, 1948; Clerk Asst, 1952-62. DL (Co. Down), 1966. *Publication:* The Maiden City and the Western Ocean, 1956. *Recreations:* sailing, gardening, local history. *Address:* The Watch House, Strangford, Downpatrick, Co. Down, Northern Ireland. *T:* Strangford 654. *Clubs:* Army and Navy, Naval.
[Died 15 Aug. 1975.

COOKE, Sir Leonard, Kt 1965; OBE 1951; President and Chairman, Co-operative Wholesale Society Ltd, 1960-66; *b* 6 May 1901; *s* of late Ernest Llewellyn Cooke and of Elizabeth Anne Cooke; *m* 1927, Florence Ellen Nunn; one *d*. *Educ:* Bishop Wordsworth Sch., Salisbury. Managing Sec., Macclesfield Co-operative Soc., 1933-38; Director: Co-operative Wholesale Soc., 1938-66; Co-operative Insurance Soc., 1945-66. Chm., NW Passenger Transport Co-ordinating Cttee, 1966-69; Vice-Chairman: Sugar Bd, 1969- (Mem., 1967-); SE Lancs and NE Cheshire Passenger Transport Authority, 1969-72; Member: BR (London Midland) Board, 1955-73; North Western Regional Economic Planning Council, 1965-71; Board of BTA, 1965-70; NW Gas Board, 1967-71; Merseyside Passenger Transport Authority, 1969-72. Comdr, Order of the Dannebrog, 1962. *Recreations:* gardening, bridge. *Address:* Sunning Hey, Tytherington, Macclesfield, Cheshire. *T:* Macclesfield 22524. *Club:* Royal Commonwealth Society. *[Died 1 May 1976.*

COOKE, Col Philip Ralph D.; *see* Davies-Cooke.

COOKE, Robert Victor, FRCS 1929; Sheriff of Bristol, 1971-72; retired from National Health Service, 1967, when Senior Surgeon: Bristol Royal Hospital; Bristol Homoeopathic Hospital; Tetbury and Almondsbury District Hospitals; *b* Berkeley, Glos, 17 May 1902; *e s* of John Cooke and Rose Eva (*née* O'Neill); *m* 1st, 1929, Elizabeth Mary (*d* 1964), MD, MRCP, *d* of Hugh Gordon Cowie, MD, Banff, Scotland; two *s*; 2nd, 1970, Dr Mavis Coutts. *Educ:* Lydney Grammar Sch., Glos; Bristol Univ.; Bristol Gen. Hosp. (ChM 1930); Middlesex Hosp.; Guy's Hosp. House appointments in Bristol and London; Asst to Prof. of Surgery, Univ. of Wales, 1929-33; Hon. Asst Surgeon, Bristol Gen. Hosp. and Bristol Children's Hosp., 1933-. Royal College of Surgeons: Mem. Council, 1949-75; Mem. Court of Examiners; Hunterian Prof.; Vice-Pres., Central Consultants and Specialists Cttee, 1969-71). British Medical Association: Mem.; Pres., Section of Surgery, Oxford, 1963; Pres., 1967-68. Pres., Proctological and Surgical Sections, RSM. Formerly Examiner in Surgery, Univs of Glasgow, Birmingham, Wales, Bristol, Oxford, Liverpool, Lahore, Cairo, Khartoum, Nairobi, Ceylon, Hong Kong. Lectures: A. B. Mitchell Meml, Belfast, 1966; Bradshaw, RCS, 1970; (first) De Silva Meml, Colombo, 1970; Sheen Meml, 1975. Mem., Bd of Governors, Bristol Royal Hosp. Hon. Secretary: Bristol Medico-Chirurgical Soc., 1935-46; Moynihan Chirurgical Club, 1950-59; Pres., Anchor Soc., 1971-72. FRSM; Fellow, Assoc. of Surgeons of Great Britain and Ireland. Liveryman, Soc. of Apothecaries of London. Hon. MD 1967. Cecil Joll Award, RCS, 1963; Lawrence Abel Cup, BMA, 1965. *Publications:* papers on intravenous pyelography, blood vessel injuries, goitre surgery, surgery of colon and biliary tract; chapter on intestinal resection and anastomosis in Textbook of British Surgery, 1956. *Recreations:* golf, gardening (FRHS, and Mem. Iris, Rose and Delphinium Socs); Antiquary (Collector of English furniture; Mem., Bristol and Glos Archaeological Soc.). *Address:* Litfield House, Clifton Down, Bristol BS8 3JU. *T:* Bristol 36363.
[Died 17 Jan. 1978.

COOKE, Maj.-Gen. Ronald Basil Bowen Bancroft, CB 1950; CBE 1943; DSO 1944; *b* 1 Sept. 1899; *s* of late Lieut-Col Sydney Cooke, Orwell Lodge, Horsham, and Alice Elizabeth Bancroft; *m* 1933, Joan, *d* of late Major Claude Chichester, Tunworth

Down House, Basingstoke; two *s* one *d* (one *s* decd). *Educ:* Charterhouse; RMC. 2nd Lieut 17th Lancers, 1918; Major, 1937; Chief Instr, RAC Tactical Sch., 1939; CO, E Riding Yeomanry, 1940; AQMG, GHQ Home Forces, 1941; GSO1, 6 Armd Div. and 1st Armd Gp, 1941-42; Brig. RAC 1st Army, 1942; Brig.-Gen. Staff, 10 Corps, 1943-44; Comdr 9 Armd Bde, 1944-45; Lieut-Col and Col, 1945; Chief of Staff, Allied Commn, Austria, 1946-47; Comdr, 8 Armd Bde, 1948; Maj.-Gen., 1949; Comdr 49 Armd Div. and North Midland District, 1949-52; Dir of the Royal Armoured Corps, War Office, 1952-55; Dir of Civil Defence for Wales, 1956-60; Comdt Civil Defence Staff Coll., Sunningdale, 1960. High Sheriff of Hampshire, 1966. Mem., Hampshire CC, 1967. Comdr US Legion of Merit, 1944 and 1946. *Recreations:* polo, hunting and shooting. *Address:* Poland Court, Odiham, Hants; 13 Bolton Gardens, SW5. *Club:* Cavalry.
[Died 26 March 1971.

COOKE, Rupert C.; *see* Croft-Cooke.

COOKE, Hon. Sir Samuel Burgess Ridgway, Kt 1967; Hon. Mr Justice Cooke; Judge of the High Court of Justice, Queen's Bench Division, since 1967; Chairman of the Law Commission, since 1973; *b* 16 March 1912; *o s* of Samuel and Jessie Lennox Cooke; *m* 1st, Isabel Nancy, *d* of late E. F. Bulmer, Adams Hill, Hereford; 2nd, Diana, *d* of late George Witherby, Burley, Hants. *Educ:* Gonville and Caius Coll., Cambridge (schol.). 1st Class Hons Classical Tripos Pt I, 1932, 1st cl. Hons, Law Tripos Pt II, 1934; Pres., Cambridge Union Soc., 1934. Cholmeley Schol., Lincoln's Inn; called to Bar (cert. of honour), 1936; Asst to Parly Counsel to Treasury, 1938-45; Parly Counsel, 1945-46; private practice, 1946; Jun. Counsel to Min. of Lab. and Nat. Service, 1950-60; QC 1960. Bencher of Lincoln's Inn; Mem., Senate of the Four Inns of Court, 1966-68; Vice-Chm., Statute Law Cttee, 1973-. *Address:* 3 Well Road, Hampstead, NW3. *T:* 01-435 1282; Rectory Farm, Plumpton, Northants. *T:* Blakesley 271.
[Died 12 April 1978.

COOKE, Maj.-Gen. Sidney Arthur, CB 1953; OBE 1943; retired; *b* 21 July 1903; *s* of late Major Arthur Cooke, 13th Hussars, and late Mrs Kezia Cooke; unmarried. *Educ:* Warwick; RMC Sandhurst. British Army: Gazetted to Lincolnshire Regt, 1924; Lieut, 1926; Capt., 1935; Major, 1941; Lieut-Col, 1948; Maj.-Gen., 1951; retired, 1957. Order of Al Istiqlal (First Class) Jordan, 1953; Order of Al Kawkab (First Class) Jordan, 1957. *Address:* The Wilderness, 62 Grove Lane, Holt, Norfolk NR25 6ED. *T:* Holt 3258. *[Died 25 March 1977.*

COOKSON, Clive; *b* 16 Sept. 1879; 3rd *s* of Norman Charles Cookson; *m* 1913, Marion Amy James (*d* 1961); two *s* one *d*. *Educ:* Harrow. A Vice-Pres., FBI (now CBI). Hon. DCL Durham. *Recreations:* gardening, shooting, fishing. *Address:* Nether Warden, Hexham, Northumberland. *T:* 3277. *Clubs:* Brooks's; Northern Counties, Union (Newcastle upon Tyne).
[Died 14 Feb. 1971.

COOLIDGE, William David, BS, PhD, DSc, MD, LLD, DEng; Director Emeritus of the Research Laboratory, General Electric Co., Schenectady, New York; *b* 23 Oct. 1873; *s* of Albert E. Coolidge and Martha Alice; *m* 1st, 1908, Ethel Westcott Woodard (*d* 1915); one *s* one *d*; 2nd, 1916, Dorothy Elizabeth MacHaffie (*d* 1969). *Educ:* Massachusetts Institute of Technology; University of Leipzig. Instructor Phys. Chem., Mass. Inst. of Tech., 1901-03; Asst Prof. Phys. Chem. Research, Mass. Inst. of Tech., 1904-05; Phys. Chem., Research Lab., GE(USA), 1905-07; Asst Dir, 1908-28; Assoc. Dir, 1928-32; Dir, 1932-40; Vice-Pres. and Dir of Research, 1940-44. Member: Nat. Acad. of Sciences; Amer. Acad. of Arts and Sciences, etc; Honorary or Corresponding Mem. numerous Socs both in USA and abroad. *Medals and Awards:* Rumford Medal, 1914; Howard N. Potts Medal, 1926; Louis Edward Levy Gold Medal, 1926; Gold Medal (Amer. Coll. of Radiology), 1927; Hughes Medal, 1927; Edison Medal, 1927; John Scott Award, 1937; Faraday Medal, 1939; Duddell Medal, 1942; Franklin Medal, 1944; K. C. Li Medal and Award (Columbia Univ.), 1952 (first recipient). Orden al Merito, Chilean Government, 1942. Roentgen Medal, 1963. *Publications:* articles in specialist journals. *Recreations:* photography and travel. *Address:* 1480 Lenox Road, Schenectady, NY 12308, USA. *Club:* Mohawk (Schenectady). *[Died 3 Feb. 1975.*

COOLS-LARTIGUE, Alexander Raphael, QC (Windward Islands), 1945; *b* 25 Oct. 1899; *e s* of Theodore Cools-Lartigue and Emily Cools-Lartigue (*née* Giraud); *m* 1927, Alexandra Sybil Potter; two *s* four *d*. *Educ:* St Mary's Coll., St Lucia; Dominica Grammar Sch., WI. Called to the Bar, Gray's Inn, 1924; practised at the Bar of the Leeward Islands, 1924-35. Crown Attorney, Dominica, 1935; Attorney-General: St Lucia, 1938; Windward Islands, 1942; Puisne Judge, Supreme Court of the Windward Islands and Leeward Islands, 1949-53; Senior Puisne Judge, Jamaica, 1958-64 (Puisne Judge, 1953-64), retd 1964. *Recreations:* tennis and golf. *Address:* 43 Glendon Circle, Kingston, Jamaica. *Clubs:* various in St Vincent, Grenada and St Lucia, WI.   [*Died* 25 *April* 1973.

COOMARASWAMY, Sir Velupillai, Kt, *cr* 1952; CMG 1947; High Commissioner for Ceylon in Canada, 1958-61; *b* 25 Sept. 1892; *s* of late S. Velupillai, Vaddukoddai, Jaffna, Ceylon; *m* 1926, Nesamany (*d* 1971), *d* of W. H. T. Bartlett, formerly Asst Supt of Surveys, Ceylon; one *s* one *d. Educ:* Victoria Coll., Jaffna; Trinity Coll., Kandy. Entered CCS, 1913; formerly Registrar-Gen., Dir of Commercial Intelligence, Food Controller, Controller of Imports, Exports and Exchange, Dir of Food Supplies and Control, Govt Agent, Western and Eastern Provinces, Permanent Sec. to Ministry of Home Affairs and Rural Development, Ceylon; Dep. High Comr for Ceylon in UK, 1948-53; Minister Plenipotentiary and Envoy Extraordinary for Ceylon in Burma, 1953-54; Chm., Ceylon prohibition commn, 1955-57; Delegate of Ceylon to 14th Gen. Assembly of the United Nations, 1959. *Address:* Kalpaka 16/2, Albert Crescent, Colombo, Sri Lanka. *Clubs:* Orient (Colombo), Colombo (Colombo).   [*Died* 13 *Nov.* 1972.

COOPER, Captain Archibald Frederick, CBE 1944 (OBE 1919); Royal Navy; *b* 7 March 1885; 3rd *s* of Major T. F. Cooper, Royal Artillery. *Educ:* abroad; Brighton Grammar Sch. Sec. to Naval Sec. to First Lord of the Admiralty, 1927-29; Sec. to C-in-C, East Indies, 1929-32; to C-in-C, Plymouth, 1932-35. Deputy Judge-Advocate of the Fleet, 1935-46; retired, 1946. Special Service in Germany, Oct.-May 1947. Naval Gen. Service Medal Bar, 1909-14 (Persian Gulf), 1914-15 Star, British and Allied war medals; Officer of the Crown of Belgium, 1918; Star of Ethiopia 3rd Class, 1930; Jubilee Medal, 1935; Coronation Medal, 1937; France and Germany War Medal; Defence Medal; British War Medal. *Recreations:* ski-ing and gardening. *Address:* Horns Hill Lodge, Squerryes Park, near Westerham, Kent. *T:* Westerham 63114.   [*Died* 13 *April* 1975.

COOPER, Dame Gladys, DBE 1967; (Dame Gladys Merivale); actress; *b* 18 Dec. 1888; *m* 1st, H. J. Buckmaster (marr. diss.) one *s* one *d* ; 2nd, 1928, Sir Neville Pearson, 2nd Bt (marr. diss.); one *d* ; 3rd, 1937, Philip Merivale (*d* 1946). First appearance on stage, Theatre Royal, Colchester, Dec. 1905; first London appearance, Vaudeville Theatre, 1906; subsequent successes at London theatres, notably as: Paula in revival of The Second Mrs Tanqueray, 1922; Magda in revival of Magda, 1923; Peter Pan, 1923 and 1924; Dora, in revival of Diplomacy, 1924; Mrs Cheyney in The Last of Mrs Cheyney, 1925; Leslie Crosbie in The Letter, 1927; Felicity, Countess of Marshwood, in Relative Values, Savoy, 1951; Grace Smith in A Question of Fact, Piccadilly, 1953; Lady Yarmouth in The Night of the Ball, New, 1955; Mrs Gantry in The Bird of Time, Savoy, 1961. Conducted management of Playhouse, 1927-33. First New York appearance, as Marcelle Linden in The Shining Hour, 1934; also, in New York: Lady Macbeth in Macbeth, 1935; Tiny Fox Collier in Spring Meeting, 1938; Mrs Parrilow in The Morning Star, 1942; Mrs St Maugham in The Chalk Garden, 1955, and again in 1971; A Passage to India, 1962; The Sacred Flame, 1967; Out of the Question, 1968; His, Hers and Theirs, 1969. *Films include:* Rebecca; That Hamilton Woman; Now, Voyager; The Song of Bernadette; Mrs Parkington; The White Cliffs of Dover; Love Letters; The Green Years; Green Dolphin Street; The Bishop's Wife; Madame Bovary. *Relevant Publications:* Gladys Cooper, 1931; Without Veils, 1953. *Address:* Barn Elms, Henley-on-Thames, Oxon.   [*Died* 17 *Nov.* 1971.

COOPER, Sir Guy; *see* Cooper, Sir H. G.

COOPER, Harold H.; *see* Hinton-Cooper.

COOPER, Sir (Harold) Stanford, Kt 1945; FCA; retired; *b* 26 Aug. 1889; *s* of late Rev. James Rides Cooper, Wimbledon, and Bessie Pomeroy; *m* 1st, 1916 (decd); two *d* ; 2nd, 1939; 3rd, 1952, Joan Bretten. *Educ:* private tuition. Served in RNVR, 1916-19. Member: Scott Cttee on Land Utilisation in Rural Areas, 1941-42. Vice-President: Royal Society of St George; Brit. Soc. for Internat. Understanding; Brit. Atlantic Cttee; Member: Council in England of Council of Christians and Jews; World Brotherhood, Europe. Formerly: Permanent Lay Mem. of Restrictive Practices Court; Vice-Chm., Ford Motor Co. Ltd; Chm. of various European Ford Cos. FRGS. Liveryman, Glaziers' and Coachmakers' Cos; Knight of the Round Table; Premier Comdr of Finnish Lion Order; Knight of Swedish North Star; Comdr of Order of Dannebrog; Knight of Order of Leopold. *Recreation:* country life. *Address:* 22 Kepplestone, Eastbourne, East Sussex BN20 7JZ. *Clubs:* Carlton, Pilgrims, MCC, Anglo-Belgian.   [*Died* 11 *Nov.* 1976.

COOPER, Sir (Henry) Guy, Kt 1941; MC; DCM; *b* 1890; *s* of late Rev. H. S. Cooper, MA Oxon; *m* 1922, Charlotte (Kaisar-i-Hind Gold Medal, 1941), *e d* of late William Meek, OBE, St Andrews, Fife; two *d. Educ:* St Edmunds, Canterbury; Keble Coll., Oxford. Served European War, 1914-18, with Royal Corps of Signals and 130th KGO Baluchis, IA (despatches thrice, DCM, MC); Pres., Karachi Chamber of Commerce, 1930; Bengal Legislative Assembly, 1934-35; Bengal Chamber of Commerce Cttee, 1936-42; Gen. Manager of Burmah-Shell, India, 1936-44. Chm., Indian Petroleum Industry Cttee, 1939-44; British Petroleum Co., 1945-56; Dir, National and Grindlay's Bank, 1954-67. *Address:* Priory Acres, Boscombe Village, near Salisbury, Wilts. *Club:* Oriental.
                                                              [*Died* 20 *Nov.* 1975.

COOPER, James Lees; President and Publisher, The Globe and Mail, Toronto, 1963-74; Director, The Globe and Mail Ltd; *b* Darwen, Lancs, 6 March 1907; *s* of James William and Alice (Lees) Cooper; *m* 1930, Ruby Smith; one *d. Educ:* Darwen Grammar Sch. Articled to Darwen News as journalist; worked as reporter, Ashton-under-Lyne; Allied Newspapers, Manchester, and Daily Express, London. War Correspondent, 1941-45: Malta Convoys, Western Desert, Madagascar, Sicily, Italy campaigns. First staff correspondent in Canada for Daily Express, 1947-55; Chief of New York Bureau, 1955-57; organized Overseas Edn of Globe and Mail and its printing and distribution by The Times of London (first overseas edn of a Canadian newspaper), 1958; returned to Canada as Asst to Editor and Publisher, 1959. Dir, Imperial Trust, Montreal; Hon. Chm., Canadian Section, Commonwealth Press Union; led Canadian delegn to Commonwealth Press Union Quinquennial Conf., 1970, in Gibraltar, Malta, Cyprus and Scotland. *Address:* 140 King Street West, Toronto 1, Ont, Canada. *T:* 361 5100.
                                                              [*Died* 9 *April* 1980.

COOPER, Lance Harries, MBE 1944; FCA; retired; Chairman, Mond Nickel Company, Ltd, 1951-59; *b* 7 May 1890; *o s* of late William White and late Edith Lydia Cooper; *m* 1st, 1920, Mary (*d* 1933), *e d* of late Nathaniel Kinch; one *s* one *d* ; 2nd, 1937, Greta Mary, *o d* of late Walter Roff. *Educ:* University Coll. Sch., London; University Coll., Reading. Served European War, 1914-18, RFA. Accountant at Guest, Keen & Nettlefolds, Ltd, Dowlais Works & Collieries, Merthyr Tydfil, Glam., 1920-26; The Mond Nickel Company, Ltd: Chief Accountant, 1926; Sec., 1928; Dir, 1945; Vice-Pres., International Nickel Co. of Canada Ltd, 1954, Dir, 1958-61; retd, 1961. Formerly Mem., Internat. Nickel Adv. Cttees, New York and London. OStJ. *Recreations:* cricket and other games; the theatre and music. *Address:* Newlands, 10 Grove End Road, NW8. *T:* 01-286 0344. *Club:* MCC.   [*Died* 12 *Dec.* 1972.

COOPER, Malcolm Edward, CBE 1974; Chairman and Managing Director, Allied Suppliers Ltd (formerly The Home and Colonial Stores Ltd), 1959-72, later first President; Solicitor; *b* 21 Nov. 1907; *m* 1935, Christine Joan Metcalfe (*d* 1967); two *d.* Joined Allied Suppliers Group, Jan. 1931, on the legal side; transferred to Secretarial side, 1934, and to Management, 1946. *Address:* Cavenham House, Millington Road, Hayes UB3 4AY.
                                                              [*Died* 17 *Feb.* 1977.

COOPER, Sir Stanford; *see* Cooper, Sir H. S.

COOPER, Hon. Sir Walter (Jackson), Kt 1959; MBE 1918; Member Australian Country Party; *b* 23 April 1892; *s* of Joseph Pollitt Cooper; *m* 1918, Louie Dorothy Marion Crick; no *c. Educ:* John Wyggeston Sch., Leicester; University of Leeds. Arrived Australia from England, 1910; acquired grazing property NW Qld, 1914. Served War, Australian Forces, 1914-18 (wounded, losing leg, France); subseq. joined Australian sect., RFC, 1917; served England, France, Germany (despatches); discharged rank Capt. Senator for Queensland, 1928-32 and 1934-68; Mem., Public Works Cttee, 1937-47; Jt Cttee on Social Security; Temp. Chm. of Cttees, 1938-47; Mem., Standing Cttee on Broadcasting, 1942-47; Jt Cttee on War Gratuity, 1944-45-48; Historic Memorials Cttee, 1947, 1948. Leader of Opposition in the Senate, 1947-49; Minister for Repatriation, Dec. 1949-Dec. 1960. Member: Empire Parly Assoc. Delegn to UK, 1948; Jt Parly Cttee on Foreign Affairs, 1962-68; Printing Cttee, 1962-68; Cttee of Disputed Returns and Qualifications, 1962-68. *Recreations:* gardening, fishing, swimming. *Address:* Molena, Gordon Parade, Manly, Qld 4179, Australia. *T:* 96.1417. *Clubs:* Royal Automobile of Queensland, Royal Queensland Aero, Brisbane Legacy (all in Brisbane).   [*Died* 22 *July* 1973.

COOPLAND, George William, MA; BSc(Econ.); LittD; Hon. LittD Fouad I University; Emeritus Professor, 1940; *b* 8 July 1875; *m* 1902; one *d. Educ:* University Coll., Liverpool. Various Secondary Schs., 1896-1913; Lecturer in Mediæval History,

University of Liverpool, 1913; Lecturer in charge of Dept of Mediæval History, 1914-37; Prof. of Mediæval History, Egyptian University, Cairo, 1929-30; Prof. of Mediæval History, University of Liverpool, 1937-40; in charge of Dept of Mediæval History, University of Liverpool, 1940-45; Lecturer in Dept Mediæval History, University of Liverpool, 1945-46; retired, 1946; Visiting Prof., Farouk I University, Alexandria, 1946-47, 1948, 1954-55, Fouad I Univ., Cairo, 1949, 1950-51. Sometime Sec. to University Extension Board, Liverpool, Chm. of Faculty of Arts, Examiner for Matriculation, Higher Sch. Certificate etc. *Publications:* The Abbey of St Bertin and its Neighbourhood, 900-1350, 1914 (Oxford Studies in Social and Legal History, ed Vinogradoff); Notes on Domanial Administration (Mackay Miscellany), 1914; The Franco-Belgian Frontier, (Geographical Teacher, 1916); The Tree of Battles and some of its Sources (Revue d'Histoire du Droit, 1923); An Unpublished Work of John of Legnano, The Somnium of 1372 (Nuovi Studi Medievali, 1925); Eustache Deschamps and Nicholas Oresme (Romania, 1926); Nicholas Oresme's Livre Contre Divinacion (The Monist, 1927); Serfdom and Feudalism, Harmsworth Universal History, 1928; The Tree of Battles, 1949; Nicole Oresme and the Astrologers, 1952; Le Jouvencel Revisited (Symposium, 1951); Le Songe du Vieil Pèlerin of Philippe de Mézières, 1969; Articles and Reviews on Mediæval Life and Thought in Manchester Guardian, Liverpool Post, etc. *Recreations:* travel, country life. *Address:* Fairholme, Broad Oak, Rye, Sussex TN31 6DG.
[Died 31 March 1975.

COORAY, Edmund Joseph, CMG 1955; OBE 1952; Officier, Légion d'Honneur, 1961; Chairman, Browns Group, Colombo; *b* 16 Nov. 1907; 2nd *s* of M. E. Cooray, Wadduwa, Ceylon; *m* 1933, Eileen de S. Wijeyeratne; two *s* two *d. Educ:* St Joseph's Coll., Colombo, Ceylon; University of London (BA Hons 1927; LLB Hons 1930; LLM 1931). Barrister-at-Law, Lincoln's Inn, 1931; passed Ceylon Civil Service Examination, 1931 (1st in order of merit); served in Ceylon Civil Service, 1931-53; Senator, Ceylon, 1955-61; Minister of Justice, 1960. *Recreations:* tennis, gardening. *Address:* 14 Dawson Road, Colombo 5, Sri Lanka. *T:* Colombo 88203. *Club:* 80 (Colombo).   *[Died 6 Nov. 1979.*

COOTE, Captain Sir Colin (Reith), Kt 1962; DSO 1918; journalist; Managing Editor of the Daily Telegraph and Morning Post 1950-64 (deputy editor, 1945-50); *b* 18 Oct. 1893; *er s* of late Howard Coote. *Educ:* Chilverton Elms, Dover; Rugby; Balliol Coll., Oxford. BA 1914. Served European War, 1914-18 (wounded and gassed). MP (CL) Isle of Ely Division, 1917-22. Legion of Honour, 1958. *Publications:* Italian Town and Country Life, 1925; In and About Rome, 1926; Maxims and Reflections of The Rt Hon. Winston Churchill, 1948; (with R. H. Mottram) Through Five Generations: The History of the Butterley Company, 1950; (with P. D. Bunyan) Sir Winston Churchill: A Self-Portrait, 1954; A Companion of Honour: The Story of Walter Elliot, 1965; Editorial, 1965; The Government We Deserve, 1969; The Other Club, 1971. *Address:* 16 Bigwood Road, NW11.   *[Died 8 June 1979.*

COOTE, Rear-Adm. Sir John Ralph, 14th Bt, *cr* 1621; CB 1957; CBE 1946; DSC; RN retired; *b* 10 Jan. 1905; *s* of Sir Ralph Coote, 13th Bt, and Alice (*d* 1975), *y d* of late Thomas Webber of Kellyville, Queen's Co.; *S* father 1941; *m* 1927, Noreen Una, JP Wilts 1950, *o d* of late Wilfred Tighe of Rossanagh, Ashford, Co. Wicklow; two *s. Educ:* Royal Naval Colls, Osborne and Dartmouth. Retired 1958. *Heir: s* Christopher John Coote [*b* 22 Sept. 1928; *m* 1952, Anne Georgiana, *d* of Lt-Col Donald Handford, Guyers House, Corsham, Wilts; one *s* one *d*]. *Address:* Monkton House, near Melksham, Wilts. *T:* Melksham 702286.   *[Died 23 Jan. 1978.*

COPE, Sir Mordaunt (Leckonby), 16th Bt *cr* 1611; MC 1915; retired; *b* 12 Feb. 1878; 4th *s* of Sir Anthony Cope, 13th Bt; *S* nephew, 1966; *m* 1st, 1917, Frances Muriel (*d* 1935), *o surv c* of A. E. W. Darby, DL, JP, of Shropshire; 2nd, 1936, Eveline, *d* of late Alfred Bishop, Gloucester; no *c. Educ:* Prior Park Coll., Bath. Captain, late Rifle Brigade; formerly Egyptian Camel Corps. Served European War, 1914-18 (wounded, despatches, MC). *Recreations:* one-time polo, tennis and usual general sports. *Heir:* none. *Address:* 41 Grove End Gardens, St John's Wood, NW8.   *[Died 7 Nov. 1972 (ext).*

COPE, Sir (Vincent) Zachary, Kt 1953; BA, MD, MS London, FRCS; Hon. FRSM; Consulting Surgeon to St Mary's Hospital, Paddington, and to Bolingbroke Hospital, Wandsworth Common; Vice-President, BMA; *b* Hull, 14 Feb. 1881; *m* 1st, 1909, Agnes Dora (*d* 1922), *d* of late James Newth; 2nd, 1923, Alice May (*d* 1944), *d* of late J. Watts and Ellen Watts, King's Lynn; one *d. Educ:* Westminster City Sch.; St Mary's Hospital Medical Sch. MB, BS with distinction in Surgery and Forensic Medicine, 1905; Hunterian Prof., Royal Coll. of Surgeons, 1916,

1920, 1925, and 1927; Arris and Gale Lecturer, RCS, 1922; Bradshaw Lecturer, 1949; Tomes' Lecturer and Vicary Lecturer, 1952; served as Capt. and temp. Major RAMCT, attached to 3rd London General Hospital, and saw active service in Mesopotamia, 1916-18 (despatches); formerly: Sector Hospital Officer, EMS; Hon. Librarian, Royal Society of Medicine; President, Lettsomian Lecturer and Orator, Medical Soc. of London; Chm., National Medical Manpower Cttee; Vice-Pres. and Mem. of Council (ex-Court of Examiners), RCS; Examiner at London, Manchester, and Birmingham Universities. *Publications:* The Surgical Aspect of Dysentery, 1921; The Early Diagnosis of the Acute Abdomen, 1st edn 1922, 14th edn 1972; Clinical Researches in Acute Abdominal Disease, 2nd edn, 1927; The Treatment of the Acute Abdomen, 2nd edn, 1928; Human Actinomycosis, 1938; The Versatile Victorian (the life of Sir Henry Thompson, Bt), 1951; William Cheselden, 1953; Florence Nightingale and the Doctors, 1958; Editor, the two clinical volumes, Official History of War of 1939-45; A History of the Royal College of Surgeons of England, 1959; A History of the Acute Abdomen, 1965; Almroth Wright, 1966; various articles in medical journals. *Address:* Endsleigh, 13 Blandford Avenue, Oxford OX2 8EA. *T:* Oxford 58464.
[Died 28 Dec. 1974.

COPLAND, Sir Douglas Berry, KBE 1950; CMG 1933; MA, DSc (NZ); LittD, Melbourne, Queensland, Harvard; LLD McGill, Carleton, Clark, BC, Adelaide, Tasmania, Melbourne, Australian National University; DCL Bishop's University; Economic Consultant and Company Director; Founder, Committee for Economic Development of Australia, 1960-67; *b* Timaru, New Zealand, 24 Feb. 1894; *s* of Alexander Copland; *m* 1919, Ruth Victoria, *y d* of F. W. S. Jones, Waimate, NZ; two *d. Educ:* Waimate District High Sch.; Canterbury Coll. MA with first-class honours in Economics, 1915; DSc for research in Currency and Finance, 1925; Lecturer in History and Economics and Dir of Tutorial Classes, University of Tasmania, 1917; Prof. of Economics, University of Tasmania, 1920-24; Sidney Myer Prof. of Commerce and Dean of the Faculty of Commerce, University of Melbourne, 1924-44; Truby Williams Prof. of Economics, University of Melbourne, 1944-45, Prof. Emeritus, 1946; Commonwealth Prices Commr, 1939-45; Econ. Consultant to Prime Minister, 1941-45; Australian Minister in China, 1946-48; First Vice-Chancellor, Australian Nat. Univ., Canberra, 1948-53. Editor, Economic Record, 1925-45; Commr, Victorian State Savings Bank, 1940-45; Chm., State Econ. Cttee of Victoria, 1938-45; served on many govtl cttees, Australia and NZ, and was Chm., Cttee of Economists and Under Treasurers which reported to Australian Loan Council 1931 and initiated Premiers' Plan; Marshall Memorial Lecturer, Cambridge Univ., 1933; Godkin Lecturer. Harvard, 1945; Sidney Ball Lecturer, Oxford, 1953; Finlay Lecturer, University Coll., Dublin, 1953; Beatty Lecturer, McGill Univ., 1961; Shann Memorial Lecturer, Univ. of Western Australia, 1962. High Comr for Australia in Canada, 1953-56; First Principal, Australian Administrative Staff Coll. (Founded 1956), 1956-60; Leader, Australian Trade Mission to Canada, 1960. Mem., Amer. Philosophical Soc., 1948. Mem., ANZAAS (President, 1952). *Publications:* Monetary Policy and its Application to Australia, 1926; Australia in the World Crisis- 1929-33, 1934; The Australian Economy, Sixth Edition, 1947; Towards Total War, 1942; The Road to High Employment, 1945; Report to Prime Minister on Economic Conditions in United Kingdom, United States and Canada, 1945; Back to Earth in Economics; Australia, 1948; Inflation and Expansion, 1951. With E. O. G. Shann: The Crisis in Australian Finance, 1931; The Battle of the Plans, 1931; The Australian Price Structure, 1933. With C. V. Janes: Cross Currents in Australian Finance, 1937; Australian Marketing Problems, 1938; Australian Trade Problems, 1938. With R. H. Barback, The Conflict of Expansion and Stability, 1957. The Adventure of Growth, 1960; The Changing Structure of the Western Economy (Beatty Lectures, McGill Univ.), 1963; numerous articles in Economic Journals. *Recreations:* golf and tennis. *Address:* Mount Macedon, Victoria 3441, Australia. *Club:* Melbourne (Melbourne).   *[Died 27 Sept. 1971.*

COPLAND, Harold W.; *see* Wallace-Copland.

COPLAND SIMMONS, Rev. F. P.; *see* Simmons.

COPNALL, (Edward) Bainbridge, MBE 1944; FRBS 1948; President, Royal Society of British Sculptors, 1961-66; *b* 29 Aug. 1903; *s* of E. W. Copnall, photographer, and Emily Bainbridge, Wellington, NZ; *m* 1927, Edith Muriel Dancy, LRAM; one *s* one *d* (and one *s* decd). *Educ:* Goldsmiths' Coll.; Royal Academy Schs. Served War of 1939-45: (rank Major, GS; Western Desert and Italy with 8th Army). First exhibited Royal Academy, 1924, as painter; exhibited Royal Scottish Acad., Paris Salon, and at most London Galls and Provincial Galls;

many portraits painted until 1928; became sculptor, 1929; master: Liverpool Coll. of Art, 1928-30; Rochester Coll. of Art, 1935-38; Headmaster, Sir John Cass Coll. of Art, 1945-53. One-man Exhibitions: Horsham, Worthing, Folkestone, Liverpool, Wertheim, Goupil, Alwin and Maidstone Galls, Rangoon, and Toronto. Sculptures: RIBA, 1930-34; Queen ships, 1938 and 1946; many sculptures for London buildings; Liverpool (3 churches); Luton; Southampton; Plymouth; Portsmouth; Cardiff; Sunderland; Hull; Billingham, etc; statue of Gen. Aung San (Burma, 1954; Bronze); figure of Ven. Nynaung Sayadaw (Burma, 1955; bronze); statue of Dr Mallinal, Mauritius; again architectural sculpture, London; fountains at Victoria Park and Crawley New Town; Stag in Stag Pl., London; group in fibre glass for Dudley, Worcs; Glass Screen for Dudley (Churchill Memorial); Growing Family, Billingham, 1970; large figure, Sir Thomas Becket, bought from RA Exhibn by City of London Corp. for St Paul's Precincts, 1971; fibre glass figure of David for Chelsea Embankment. Founder Mem., Soc. of Portrait Sculptors, 1947; Mem., Art Workers Guild, 1968; Hon. Member: Nat. Soc., 1968; Liverpool Artists Club, 1969; Hon. Corresp. Mem., Nat. Soc. of Sculptors of America, 1967. Master Glass Painter, 1968. FRSA 1968. Broadcasts on BBC (TV) experiences and work. Winner, Constance Fund, 1949. Silver Medal, RBS, 1962. *Publications:* A Sculptor's Manual, 1971; articles and reproductions in most architectural journals and Listener (mainly sculpture); paper, RSA, 1966, etc. *Recreations:* painting and Rugby football. *Address:* Lee Priory, Littlebourne, Canterbury, Kent. *Clubs:* Chelsea Arts, Architectural Association; Artists' (Liverpool); Richmond RFC; Liverpool RFC. *[Died 18 Oct. 1973.*

COPPEL, Dr Elias Godfrey, CMG 1965; QC (at the Bar of Victoria and Tasmania); *b* 7 Oct. 1896; *s* of Albert Coppel; *m* 1925, Marjorie Jean Service (*d* 1970); two *s* (and one *s* decd). *Educ:* Melbourne Grammar Sch.; Melbourne Univ. Served European War, 1st Australian Imperial Force, France, 1915-19. Admitted to the Bar, 1922; LLD 1936; KC 1945. Acting Justice, Supreme Court, Victoria, 1950-52; Acting Justice, Supreme Court, Tasmania, 1956 and 1958; Warden of Convocation, University of Melbourne, 1950-59; Mem. of University Council, 1959-67. *Publication:* The Law Relating to Bills of Sale, 1935. *Address:* 14 Ailsa Avenue, East Malvern, Victoria 3145, Australia. *[Died 4 Oct. 1978.*

COPPOCK, Sir Richard, Kt 1951; CBE 1942; Hon. ARIBA; retired as General Secretary, National Federation of Building Trades Operatives, 1961; *b* 21 Feb. 1885; *s* of Joseph Coppock and Hannah Woodward; *m* 1st, 1908; 2nd, 1926, Ursula M'Loughlin; one *s* one *d*. *Educ:* Didsbury National Sch.; Manchester Technical Sch. Bricklayer and Trade Union Official; International work for the trade unions in the Building trade; Pres. of same for many years; has travelled extensively throughout Europe and America; Mem. of Manchester City Council, 1919-21; Alderman, London County Council, and also Councillor and Chm. of Parks, Highways, and Parliamentary Cttees, 1925-52; Chm. of LCC, 1943-44 (Vice-Chm. 1939-40); Chm., Fire Bde Cttee, 1951-58. *Publications:* many pamphlets dealing with organisation of Building Trade, Workmen and Rationalisation, etc. *Recreations:* reading, music, and propaganda. *Address:* Little Wanborough, Wanborough Lane, Cranleigh, Surrey. *T:* 4391. *[Died 4 Feb. 1971.*

COPSON, Prof. Edward Thomas, MA Oxford, DSc Edinburgh, FRSE; Emeritus Professor of Mathematics, St Andrews University; *b* 21 Aug. 1901; *s* of late T. C. Copson; *m* 1931, Beatrice Mary, *er d* of late Prof. Sir Edmund Whittaker, FRS; two *d*. *Educ:* King Henry VIII Sch., Coventry; St John's Coll., Oxford. Lecturer, University of Edinburgh, 1922-29; St Andrews, 1930-34; Asst Prof., RNC, Greenwich, 1934-35; Prof. of Mathematics, University Coll., Dundee, 1935-50; Regius Prof. of Mathematics, St Andrews Univ., 1950-69. Keith Prize, Royal Society of Edinburgh, 1939-41. Master of St Salvator's Coll., St Andrews, 1954-57. Hon. LLD St Andrews, 1971. *Publications:* The Theory of Functions of a Complex Variable, 1935; The Mathematical Theory of Huygens' Principle (with Prof. Bevan Baker), 1939; Asymptotic Expansions, 1965; Metric Spaces, 1968; Partial Differential Equations, 1975; papers in various mathematical periodicals. *Address:* 42 Buchanan Gardens, St Andrews, Fife. *T:* St Andrews 72708. *Club:* Royal and Ancient (St Andrews). *[Died 16 Feb. 1980.*

CORAH, Sir John (Harold), Kt 1952; Chairman, N. Corah & Sons Ltd, Leicester, 1954-64 (Deputy Chairman, 1924-54); *b* 25 Dec. 1884; *s* of Alfred Corah of Scraptoft Hall, Leicestershire; *m* 1st, 1913, Vivienne Woodhouse (*d* 1942); one *d*; 2nd, 1951, Edmée Pattera. *Educ:* Marlborough. JP 1924; High Sheriff of Leicestershire, 1933; Dep. Chm., County Bench, 1942-51. *Recreations:* sailing and cruising. *Address:* Gayhurst, Fernside

Lane, Sevenoaks, Kent. *T:* Sevenoaks 56501. *Club:* Royal Motor Yacht (Sand Banks, Dorset). *[Died 27 May 1978.*

CORBISHLEY, Rev. Thomas, SJ; *b* 30 May 1903; *s* of William and Catherine Corbishley. *Educ:* Catholic Coll., Preston; Campion Hall, Oxford. 1st in Mods; 1st in Greats. Entered Soc. of Jesus, 1919; Priest, 1936; Master of Campion Hall, 1945-58; Superior of Farm Street Church, W1, 1958-66. *Publications:* Agnosticism, 1936; The Divine Majesty (trans. from German), 1948, 2nd edn 1971; Roman Catholicism, 1950; Religion is Reasonable, 1960; Spiritual Exercises of St Ignatius (trans.), 1963; Ronald Knox the Priest, 1964; The Contemporary Christian, 1966; The Spirituality of Teilhard de Chardin, 1971; One Body, One Spirit, 1973; contributed to: Catholic Commentary on Holy Scripture, 1953; Religion in the Modern World, 1952; We believe in God, 1968; contributions to Journal of Roman Studies, Journal of Theological Studies, Klio, Month, Dublin Review, etc. *Address:* 114 Mount Street, W1. *T:* 01-493 7811. *[Died 11 March 1976.*

CORDIER, Dr Andrew Wellington; President, Columbia University, 1969-70 (Acting President, 1968-69) and Dean, School of International Affairs, 1962-72; *b* 3 March 1901; *s* of Wellington J. Cordier and Ida May Anstine; *m* 1924, Dorothy Elizabeth Butterbaugh; one *s* one *d*. *Educ:* Hartville High Sch.; Manchester Coll., Indiana; Univ. of Chicago; Graduate Inst. of Internat. Studies, Geneva. BA Manchester, 1922; MA 1923, PhD 1926, Chicago. Teacher, Greentown High Sch., 1919-21; Chm., Dept of History and Polit. Sci., Manchester Coll., 1927-44, and Lectr in Social Scis for Indiana Univ. Extension Div., 1929-44; travelled extensively, 1928-41; US Dept of State, 1944-46 (drafting new Charter for UN); Techn. Expert, US Delegn at founding conf., San Francisco; Exec. Asst to Sec.-Gen. of UN, 1946-61 (Under-Sec.); Under-Sec. i/c General Assembly and Related Affairs, 1961-62; Principal Adviser to all Presidents of Gen. Assembly of UN since inception; Special Rep. of Sec.-Gen.: Korea, 1952; in connection with Mount Scopus problem, 1958; Congo, 1960. Consultant to Dept of State; Mem., Council on Foreign Relations; Trustee: Carnegie Endowment for Internat. Peace; Internat. House; Manchester College. Holds numerous hon. degrees, medals and awards incl.: Alumni Medal, Chicago Univ.; Ohioan Career Medal for 1959; Walter W. Van Kirk Award; Ohio Governor's Award, 1962; Mayor's Award of City of New York; Alexander Hamilton Award, Columbia Univ.; Charles Evans Hughes Medal. Order of the Sacred Treasure, First Class (Japan); Comdr's Cross, Order of Merit, Fed. Republic of Germany; Kt Comdr, first class, Royal Order of the North Star, Sweden. *Publications:* (ed jtly) The Quest for Peace, 1965; (with K. L. Maxwell) Paths to World Order, 1967; (ed) Columbia Essays in International Affairs: The Dean's Papers, vols 3-7, 1969-72; (ed, jtly) Public Papers of the Secretaries-General of the United Nations, vols 1-2, 1968-72. *Address:* Columbia University, New York, NY 10027, USA. *T:* 212-280-4601; 6 Merrivale Road, Great Neck, NY 11021, USA. *T:* 516-487-6120. *Club:* Century Association. *[Died 11 July 1975.*

CORDINGLEY, Air Vice-Marshal Sir John (Walter), KCB 1946 (CB 1943); KCVO 1962; CBE 1937 (OBE 1919); RAF, retd; *b* 10 Dec. 1890; *m* 1st, 1913, Elizabeth Ruth Carpenter (*d* 1938); one *s*; 2nd, 1944, Mrs Joan Isabel Morton. RNVR 1905-13; RND 1914-17; Air Bd 1918; Air Ministry, 1918-22; Admiralty and Air Ministry mentions for service, European War, 1914-18. Officer-in-Charge Records, RAF, 1922-39; Dir-Gen. of Manning, Air Ministry, 1939-47; Controller, RAF Benevolent Fund, 1947-62; Wing Comdr, 1924; Group Capt., 1931; Air Commodore, 1941 (Acting, 1939); Air Vice-Marshal, 1947 (Acting 1943); retired list, 1947. Dep. Chm., Royal Mutual Building Soc., 1962-71. Vice-Patron of National Association for Employment of Regular Sailors, Soldiers and Airmen; a Dir of United Services Trustee, 1947-72; a Vice-President: Officers' Assoc.; Royal Wolverhampton Sch.; Jamaica Legion; Star and Garter Home (Governor, 1955-70); RAF Benevolent Fund; Member Councils of: League of Remembrance, 1961-72; British Commonwealth Ex-Service League, 1950-63 and 1971-74; Mem., BBC Appeals Advisory Cttee, 1957-60. *Address:* 147b Ashley Gardens, SW1. *T:* 01-828 8916. *Club:* Royal Thames Yacht. *[Died 5 Jan. 1977.*

CORDINGLY, Rt. Rev. Eric William Bradley, MBE 1946; Bishop Suffragan of Thetford, since 1963; Archdeacon of Norfolk since 1962; *b* 17 May 1911; 2nd *s* of Charles and Edith Maud Phillips; *m* 1937, Mary Eileen Mathews; three *s* one *d*. *Educ:* King's Coll., London, 1930-33 (AKC 1933); St Stephen's House, Oxford, 1933-34. Ordained Deacon, 1934; Priest, 1935; Curate: St Peter-le-Poer, Friern Barnet, 1934-36; Holy Trin., Minchinhampton, Dio. Gloucester, 1936-38; Rector: Stanton with Snowshill, Glos., 1938-41; Leckhampton, Cheltenham, 1941-55; Stevenage 1955-62. CF, 1940-46; France and Belgium,

1940; Malaya, Siam and Burma Rly (POW), 1942-45. Hon. CF, 1946-. Bishop's Chaplain for Youth (Glos). 1946-55. Chaplain to the Queen, 1960-63; Residentiary Canon and Librarian of Norwich Cathedral, 1962-63. Governing Body of SPCK, 1958-. Mem. Stevenage Development Corp., 1960-62. Member: Council, Univ. of E Anglia, 1972-; BBC E Anglia Adv. Council; BBC Gen. Adv. Council, 1976-. *Address:* The Rectory, Caistor St Edmunds, Norwich NOR 52W. *T:* Framingham Earl 2490.
[*Died* 13 Aug. 1976.

CORFIELD, Sir Conrad Laurence, KCIE 1945 (CIE 1937); CSI 1942; MC; ICS (retired); *b* 15 Aug. 1893; *s* of late Rev. Egerton Corfield, MA, Rector of Finchampstead, Berks; *m* 1922, Phyllis Betha (*d* 1932), *d* of late L. P. E. Pugh, KC; one *s* one *d*; *m* 1961, Mrs Sylvia Daunt (*d* 1977), *widow* of Lt-Col C. O'B. Daunt, OBE, MC, Central India Horse. *Educ:* St Lawrence; St Catharine's Coll., Cambridge. Capt. 1st Cambridgeshire Regt; served European War, France; joined ICS 1920; Asst Comr Punjab; Asst Private Sec. to the Viceroy, 1921-22; joined Political Dept 1925; served in Kathiawar, Baluchistan, Rajputana, Central India, and Hyderabad; Vice-Pres., Rewa State Council, 1933-34; Joint Sec., Political Dept, Simla, 1934-38; Officiating Political Sec., June-Sept. 1937; Resident at Jaipur, 1938-40; officiating Resident for Rajputana, May-Oct. 1939; Resident for the Punjab States, 1941-45; Political Adviser to the Viceroy as Crown Representative, 1945-47. Governor and Vice-Pres., St Lawrence Coll. Chm., Wokingham Div. Conservative Assoc., 1950-54 (Pres. 1954-62). Chm. Wessex Area, 1960-63; former Chairman: Yateley Industries for Disabled Girls, 1954-64; St John Council for Berks, 1944-62; St Crispin's Sch., Wokingham, 1954-67; Finchampstead Parish Council, 1955-61. CStJ. *Publication:* The Princely India I Knew, 1975. *Recreations:* (past) Captain, Cambridge Univ. Hockey, 1919-20; English Hockey International, 1920; gardening. *Address:* Warren Lodge, Warren Lane, Finchampstead, Berks.
[*Died* 3 Oct. 1980.

CORMACK, Prof. James Maxwell Ross, MA; Regius Professor of Greek, University of Aberdeen, since 1965; *b* 20 July 1909; *s* of Benjamin Cormack and Frances Helen Ross; *m* 1st, 1938, Isabel Ogg Catto, MA (*d* 1968); 2nd, 1968, Sybil Phyllis Dadley, BA; one *s*. *Educ:* Robert Gordon's Coll., Aberdeen; Aberdeen Univ. (1st Cl. Hons in Classics, 1932); Trinity Coll., Cambridge (Senior Scholar and Research Scholar); Vienna Univ.; British Sch. at Athens. Cambridge Classical Tripos: 1st Cl. Pt I, 1933, 1st Cl. Part II, with distinction in Literature, 1935; Fullerton Scholar and Wilson Fellow of Aberdeen Univ., 1935-37; Lecturer in Classics, University of Reading, 1937-46; Prof. of Classics, University of Reading, 1946-65; Dean of Faculty of Letters, 1948-54; Dep. Vice-Chancellor, 1954-64; Acting Vice-Chancellor, Oct. 1963-March 1964. Review Editor of Jl of Hellenic Studies, 1948-51. FRNS. *Publications:* The Inscribed Monuments of Aphrodisias, 1955; Monumenta Asiae Minoris Antiqua, vol. viii (jt editor), 1962; articles on Greek Epigraphy, with particular reference to Asia Minor and Macedonia, in Journal of Roman Studies, Annual of the British Sch. at Athens, American Journal of Archæology, Harvard Theological Review, Proceedings of British Academy, Klio, and Hesperia, 1940 onwards. *Address:* The Department of Greek, King's College, Aberdeen AB9 2UB.
[*Died* 4 June 1975.

CORNELL, Katharine; Actress-Manager, Producer, Actress; retired; *b* 16 Feb. 1898; *d* of Peter C. Cornell, MD, and Alice Gardner Plimpton; *m* 1921, Guthrie McClintic (*d* 1961); no *c*. *Educ:* Private schs in Buffalo, NY; Oaksmere, Mamaroneck, NY. Made her debut, 1916, with Washington Square Players in Bushido, and remained with this company two years, following which she spent two seasons with Jessie Bonstelle stock company at Buffalo and Detroit. Her first and only appearance on the London stage was as Jo in Little Women, New Theatre, 1919. Subsequently, in America, appeared in Nice People, A Bill of Divorcement, Will Shakespeare, The Enchanted Cottage, Casanova, The Way Things Happen, The Outsider, Tiger Cats, Candida, The Green Hat (in which she became a star), The Letter, The Age of Innocence, Dishonored Lady; became America's only actress-manager, with her presentation of The Barretts of Wimpole Street, 1931; since then she has produced and appeared in Lucrece, Alien Corn, Romeo and Juliet, Flowers of the Forest, Saint Joan, The Wingless Victory, Candida, Herod and Mariamne, No Time for Comedy, The Doctor's Dilemma, Rose Burke, The Three Sisters, Lovers and Friends, Antigone, Antony and Cleopatra, That Lady, Captain Carvallo, The Constant Wife, The Prescott Proposals, The Dark is Light Enough, The Firstborn (Habimah Theatre, Tel Aviv, Israel, July 1958), Dear Liar. Her late husband, a producer in his own right, directed all her plays since The Green Hat (exc. Prescott Proposals; directed by a co-author, Howard Lindsay). Television debut in The Barretts of Wimpole Street, 1956, There

Shall be No Night, 1957. Holds numerous hon. degrees and awards. Medals include: Medal of Merit (US Govt); Medal, Amer. Academy of Arts and Letters. *Publications:* I wanted to be an Actress, the autobiography of Katharine Cornell, 1938; Curtain Going Up, 1941. *Recreations:* music, reading. *Address:* Palisades, New York, USA. *Clubs:* Colony, Cosmopolitan (New York); Garrett (Buffalo, NY).
[*Died* 9 June 1974.

CORNWALL-JONES, Brig. Arthur Thomas, CMG 1949; CBE 1945 (OBE 1943); *b* 21 July 1900; *s* of Rev. E. Cornwall-Jones (sometime Canon of Aberdeen); *m* 1929, Marie Evelyn Joan, *d* of late Lieut-Col R. H. Hammersley-Smith, CBE; four *s*. *Educ:* Trinity Coll., Glenalmond. IA, 1920-47; 2nd Bn 5th Royal Gurkha Rifles (FF); Asst Sec. Offices of War Cabinet and Minister of Defence, 1939-41 and 1943-44; Sec. Middle East Defence Cttee, 1941-43; British Sec. Combined Chiefs of Staff, 1944-46; Senior Asst Sec. (Military) of the Cabinet, 1946-50. British Army since Aug. 1947 (Gen. List, Supernumerary); retired pay, 1950. Served with British, Australian and Pakistan Administrative Staff Colls and Philippine Executive Academy, 1950-68. US Legion of Merit (Comdr) 1946. *Address:* Snowball Hill, Russells Water, Henley-on-Thames, Oxon. *T:* Nettlebed 641309.
[*Died* 6 Aug. 1980.

CORNWELL, Ven. Leonard Cyril, MA, BD, Hon. CF; Archdeacon of Swindon, 1947-63, now Emeritus; *b* 28 March 1893; 2nd *s* of T. E. D. Cornwell and Alice Warner; *m* 1927, Grace Annie, *d* of R. E. D. Rudman and Alice Pike; four *s*. *Educ:* Fitzwilliam House and Ridley Hall, Cambridge. BA Cambridge, 1914; MA 1918; BD London, 1921. Curate St Augustine, Plymouth, 1916-18; Temp. Army Chaplain, 1918-21; Curate of St Paul, Chippenham, 1921-26; Curate-in-Charge, St Christopher, Brislington, Bristol, 1926-31, and first Vicar, 1931-36; Rector of St Paul, Chippenham, Wilts, 1936-50; Rector of Brinkworth, Wilts, 1950-60. Hon. Clerical Sec., Bristol Diocesan Conf., 1928-47; Editor, Bristol Diocesan Directory, 1929-32; Hon. Chaplain to Bishop of Bristol, 1942-47; Hon. Canon of Bristol Cathedral, 1945-47, and 1962-63. Sub-Chaplain of Order of St John of Jerusalem, 1954-63. *Address:* Causeway House, Brinkworth, Chippenham, Wilts. *T:* Brinkworth 202.
[*Died* 16 March 1971.

CORRIGAN, Rev. Terence Edward; Secretary to Trustees for Roman Catholic Purposes Registered, since 1972; *b* Brislington, Bristol, 30 Sept. 1915; *s* of Joseph Corrigan and Ann (*née* Tunks). *Educ:* Christian Brothers. Ordained priest, 1948. Master at Stonyhurst Coll., 1944-46, 1951-52; Procurator and Bursar at Stonyhurst Coll., 1952-59; Regular Superior of Salisbury Mission of Soc. of Jesus in S Rhodesia, 1959-64; Provincial, Soc. of Jesus in Eng., 1964-70. *Address:* 114 Mount Street, W1.
[*Died* 8 May 1975.

CORRY, Lt-Col Sir Henry Charles L.; *see* Lowry-Corry.

CORSON, Rear-Adm. Eric Reid, MVO 1922; DSC 1914; Commander Greek Order of the Redeemer, 1933; Royal Navy (retired); *b* 1887; *s* of late George Corson, Dumfries and Leeds; *m* 1924, Marjorie (*d* 1969), *d* of late James Winants, New Jersey, USA; three *s*. *Address:* 17 Lowndes Close, Belgravia, SW1. *T:* 01-235 7221.
[*Died* 17 Aug. 1972.

CORTLANDT, Lyn, BA; FIAL, FRSA; artist, United States; *b* 7 Jan. 1926; *d* of late Graf Karl Gustav von Lubieński and late Mrs Elinor Ernestine (Thiel) Cortlandt. *Educ:* Los Angeles: Chouinard and Jepson Art Insts; New York: Art Students' League of NY; Art Sch. of Pratt Inst.; Columbia Univ. Sch. of Painting and Sculpture; Hans Hofmann Sch. of Fine Arts; China Inst. in America followed by private instruction. Phi Beta Kappa, Phi Kappa Phi. National exhibitions in USA include: Pennsylvania Academy of Fine Arts, National Academy of Design, Brooklyn Museum and many others; also numerous exhibitions in Europe, India, Japan, S America. Represented in Collections: Metropolitan Museum of Art, New York; Museum of Fine Arts, Boston; Fogg Museum of Art; Art Inst. of Chicago; Brooklyn Museum; Baltimore Museum of Art; Cincinnati Art Museum; Springfield Museum of Fine Arts, Mass; Musée National d'Art Moderne, Paris, France; Stedelijk Museum, Amsterdam, Netherlands; New York Public Library, Boston Public Library; and other important public and private collections. Titles of Major Paintings: Echo Through the Ages; Corridors of Time; Towards Tomorrow; Doorway in the Distance; Voyage to Yesterday; The Force of Destiny; Discovery; Stardust to Stardust; The Earliest Time; The Spark of Life. Toured extensively in Brazil and Argentina by invitation, 1963. Solo exhibitions, Museums in São Paulo, Buenos Aires, etc, 1964-65. Radio: Moderator, Panel Forums on Art Subjects. Lectured on Contemporary Art and on various National Ideologies, in foreign countries. Member: Allied Artists of

America; The Painters' and Sculptors' Soc. of NJ; Creative Club; Philadelphia Water Color Club; Internat. Platform Assoc.; Amer. Acad. of Political and Social Science; Acad. of Political Science; Center for the Study of Democratic Institutions; Amer. Judicature Soc.; UN/USA; Nat. Trust for Historic Preservation; Nat. Soc. of Literature and the Arts; Knight of Mark Twain; Comitato Internazionale: Centro Studi e Scambi Internazionali; Accademia Internazionale Leonardo da Vinci; New York Zoological Soc. Adv. Mem., Marquis Biographical Library Soc., etc. Recipient of numerous awards. CSSI Medal of Honor. *Recreations:* reading, music, travel, tennis. *Address:* 1070 Park Avenue, New York, NY 10028, USA. *T:* Atwater 9-6370. *Clubs:* Pen and Brush; Le Cercle d'Or.
[Died 30 Jan. 1979.

CORY, Ven. Alexander; Archdeacon Emeritus (retired, 1961); *b* 19 March 1890; *s* of Rev. Alexander Arthur Cory, Vicar of Tipton, Staffs; *m* 1st, 1917, Dorothy Frances Barnard (*d* 1958); one *s* one *d*; 2nd, 1958, Kathleen, *d* of J. A. Emily, Vancouver, BC. *Educ:* S John's Sch., Leatherhead; Keble Coll., Oxford (MA); Cuddesdon Theological Coll., Oxford. Curate of Portsea, 1914-17; TCF, 1917-19; Rector of Burton Overy, Leics, 1919-23; Vicar of S Mary's, Far Cotton, Northampton, 1923-28; Vicar of Fareham, Hants, 1928-38; Vicar of Hayling Island, 1938-46; Rural Dean of Havant, 1943-46; Vicar of All Saints, Ryde, IW, 1946-52; Rural Dean of East Wight, 1948-51; Hon. Canon of Droxford in Portsmouth Cathedral, 1948-52; Archdeacon of the Isle of Wight, 1952-61; Hon. Canon of Portsmouth Cathedral 1961. *Recreations:* gardening and handicrafts. *Address:* Four Hedges, 171 Golf Links Road, Ferndown, Dorset BH22 8BX. *T:* Ferndown 4717. *Club:* (Hon. Mem.) Royal Victoria Yacht (Ryde, IW). *[Died 7 April 1973.*

COSGRAVE, Rev. Francis Herbert, MA; DCL (Hon.) Bishop's University, Lennoxville, PQ, 1927; LLD (Hon.) Queen's University, Kingston, 1929, McMaster University, Hamilton, 1933, University of Toronto, 1945; DD (Hon.) Victoria University, Toronto, 1936; formerly Provost and Vice-Chancellor of the University of Trinity College, Toronto; *b* 11 July 1880; 5th *s* of late Frederick Cosgrave, JP, Glebelands, Kilsallaghan, Co. Dublin; *m* Annie Leila, *d* of late Dr J. Metcalf, Kingston, Ont. *Educ:* Corrig Sch., Kingstown, Co. Dublin; Trinity Coll., Dublin. *Address:* 561 Avenue Road, Toronto 7, Canada. *T:* WA 1.6821. *Clubs:* Royal Canadian Yacht: Faculty of University (Toronto). *[Died 31 Jan. 1971.*

COSGRAVE, Col L. Moore, DSO 1916; ED; retired as Economic Adviser, Mercantile Bank of Canada, Montreal; *b* Toronto, 28 Aug. 1890; *s* of Lawrence Joseph Cosgrave, Toronto, and Kate Ellen Forbes, Port Hope, Ont; *m* 1916, Beryl Hunter Jones, Windsor, Canada, and Honolulu; one *s* one *d. Educ:* St Michael's Coll., Toronto; Royal Military Coll., Kingston; McGill Univ., Montreal. Commissioned rank, Canadian Field Artillery, 1914; Capt. 1915; Major, 1916 (DSO and bar, despatches thrice, ED (Canada), French Croix de Guerre); Lieut-Col and OC 1st Can. Arty Bde, 1918; Canadian Govt Trade Comr, Wembly Exhibition, England, 1922-24; Canadian Govt Trade Commissioner to China, 1925-35; Group Comr Shanghai Volunteer Corps, 1932-35; Senior Canadian Government Trade Commissioner to Australia, 1935-42; Canadian Military Attaché South-West Pacific area attached High Commissioner for Canada in Australia, 1942; Official Signatory for Canada at surrender of Japan on Board USS Missouri, 2 Sept. 1945; Mem. Canadian Delegation, Far East Advisory Council to Japan, Jan. 1946; Commercial Counsellor Canadian Embassy, China, 1947; Western Representative, Foreign Trade Service, 1949-52; Chargé d'Affaires *ad interim,* Canadian Legation, Lisbon, Aug. 1952-June 1956, retired. *Publication:* Afterthoughts of Armaggeddon, 1919. *Recreations:* golf and hunting. *Address:* Mercantile Bank of Canada, Montreal, Quebec, Canada. *Clubs:* Royal Commonwealth Society; United Services, English-Speaking Union (Montreal); University (Toronto, Ont); Royal British (Lisbon).
[Died 28 July 1971.

COSTELLO, John Aloysius, SC; *b* Dublin, 20 June 1891; *s* of John Costello and Rose Callaghan; *m* 1919, Ida Mary O'Malley (*d* 1956); three *s* two *d. Educ:* Christian Brothers' Schs and University Coll., Dublin. BA 1911, LLB 1914; called to Bar, 1914; called to Inner Bar, 1925; Senior Bencher of Honourable Soc. of King's Inns; Mem. of Royal Irish Academy, 1948. Hon. LLD: University of Montreal, Ottawa Univ. and Fordham Univ., 1948; Catholic Univ. of America, St John's Univ., NY, and Iona Coll., New Rochelle, NY, 1956. Hon. Life Member Canadian Bar Association. Asst to Law Officer, Provisional Govt, 1922; Asst to Attorney-Gen., Irish Free State, 1922-26; Attorney-Gen. IFS, 1926-32; Taoiseach, 1948-51 and Minister for Health, April-June, 1951; Leader of the Opposition in Dáil

Eireann, 1951-54, Taoiseach, 1954-57; again Leader of the Opposition in Dáil Eireann, 1957-59. TD, Co. Dublin, 1933-37, Dublin Townships, 1937-43 and 1944-48, Dublin South (East), 1948-69. *Address:* 20 Herbert Park, Ballsbridge, Dublin 4.
[Died 5 Jan. 1976.

COSTELLO, Sir Leonard (Wilfred James), Kt 1935; CBE 1946; JP; President, Devon Old Peoples Welfare Committee; Commissioner of Income Tax for E Exminster Division of Devon; Vice-President and Member of Committees, Devon Community Council; Vice-President, Devon Branch of Forces Help Society and Lord Roberts Workshops; Member Council, Alexandra Rose Day (Hon. Treasurer, 1941-48); Chairman, Lumley Memorial Trust, since 1950; President, Local Committee, Cancer Campaign for Research, since inception; *b* London, 25 Aug. 1881; *e s* of late James Edward and late Alice Eliza Costello; *m* 1st, 1907, Winifred Avery (*d* 1950), *e d* of Thomas and Sarah Belgrave; two *d*; 2nd, 1952, Joan Barbara Alice Piper, *d* of George Earle Hewitt. *Educ:* Dulwich Coll.; Peterhouse, Cambridge. BA, LLB, 1902; MA 1906. Called to Bar, Inner Temple, 1903; practised in London and on Midland Circuit, 1903-26; Lectr in Common Law, University Coll., Nottingham, 1906-08; served European War, 1916-18, Capt. RASC; Judge, High Court, Calcutta, 1926-40; Acting Chief Justice of Bengal, May-Aug. 1937, and July-Aug. 1939; Chm. of a Home Office Advisory Cttee on Aliens in the Isle of Man, 1941; Mem. Managing Cttee of Elizabeth Garrett Anderson Hospital, 1941-50; Pres. of All India and of Calcutta Societies for the Prevention of Cruelty to Animals, 1933-41; Pres. of Soc. for the Protection of Children in India, 1927-37; twice Pres. of Bengal Flying Club, Calcutta. Mem., first Exec. Cttee of League of Young Liberals, 1907, and later Chm. of London Council and Mem. of London Liberal Council; President: Devon and Cornwall Liberal Fedn, 1968-71; Tiverton Div., Liberal Assoc., 1968-71, Pres. Emeritus, 1971; Prospective Lib Candidate, N Islington, 1912-14; contested (L) Strand Div. of Westminster, Jan. 1910; Exeter, 1918 and 1922; MP (L) Huntingdonshire, 1923-24; contested Huntingdon, 1924. High Sheriff of Devon, 1945-46; Hon. Legal Adviser Devon County Army Welfare Services, 1941-46 (Defence Medal); Dep. Chm. Devon QS, 1940-47, Chm., 1947-56; Mem. Rating Appeal Cttee, 1940-50; Dep. Chm. County Justices Cttee, 1941-46 (Chm. 1946-56); Mem. Devon Standing Joint Cttee, 1946 (Vice-Chm., 1952-56); Chairman: Gen. Comrs of Income Tax for E Budleigh and Clifton Div. of Devon, 1954-64; Devon Br., Magistrates Assoc., 1954-63 (Past Mem. Council, and also of Exec. Legal and Mental Health Cttees); Past Mem. Council, Jt Cttee of Magistrates Assoc., and BMA; Member: Exeter Cathedral Restoration Fund Cttee, 1946-66; Central Exec. Cttee and Chm., Exeter, Mid and E Devon Br., NSPCC, 1949-70; Bd of Visitors, HM Prison, Dartmoor, 1950-61; Chm. County Confirming and Compensation Cttees, 1951-56; Mem. Exeter Prison Visiting Justices Cttee, 1946-56 and for five years Pres. Conf. of Prison and Borstal Visiting Justices; Member: Devon Magistrates Courts Cttee from its inception until 1956; Devon Agricultural Wages Cttee, 1956-62; JP Devon, 1940-. Chm. Agric. Land Tribunal for SW Region of England, 1948-58. Has given evidence before various Royal Commissions. Past Chm., Dirs Exeter Theatre Co. Ltd. *Publications:* articles on policies and economics; Law relating to Enquiries Profiteering Act, 1919. *Recreations:* formerly golf and tennis, now croquet and studying foreign languages. *Address:* Grantlands, Uffculme, Devon. *T:* Cradock 418. *Clubs:* National Liberal; Royal Calcutta Turf (Calcutta). *[Died 2 Dec. 1972.*

COSTIGAN, Rev. John, SJ; MA; Superior, St Aloysius, Oxford, since 1971; *b* Feb. 1916. *Educ:* Stonyhurst; Oxford. Joined the Soc. of Jesus, 1934; ordained, 1949. Rector of: Beaumont Coll., 1958-64; St Aloysius' Coll., Glasgow, 1964-70. *Address:* St Aloysius, 25 Woodstock Road, Oxford OX2 6HA.
[Died 9 Nov. 1978.

COSTIN, Maj.-Gen. Eric Boyd, DSO 1917; late Royal Canadian Regiment, West yorkshire Regiment and Manchester Regiment; *b* 1889; *yr s* of late Capt. Charles Costin, 14th Foot (W Yorks Regt); *m* 1922, Violet Constance, *e d* of late Sir George Saltmarsh; one *s* one *d. Educ:* Christ's Hospital, Hertford, London and Horsham. Served European War, 1914-18 (despatches, DSO, Chevalier Légion d'Honneur, Brevet of Major); psc; Brevet Lieut-Col, 1934; commanded 2nd Bn The Manchester Regt, 1935-38; served War of 1939-45; retired, 1946. Col The Manchester Regt, 1948-54. *Address:* Bessborough House, St Mawes, Cornwall. *T:* St Mawes 220. *Club:* Royal Cornwall Yacht (Falmouth). *[Died 24 Feb. 1971.*

COSTLEY-WHITE, Cyril Grove, CMG 1953; *b* 30 Oct. 1913; *s* of late Very Rev. H. Costley-White, DD; *m* 1st, 1938, Elizabeth Delmore (marr. diss. 1955); two *s* one *d*; 2nd, 1955, Elisabeth

Marianne, *d* of late Rev. Noel Braithwaite Chard and of late Lady Janet Chard; two *s*. *Educ*: Eton; Balliol Coll., Oxford. Joined Colonial Office (after competitive examination), 1937; transferred, 1940, to Dominions Office. Served on Staff of UK High Commissioner in Canada, 1941-44, and New Zealand, 1944-46; Deputy United Kingdom High Commissioner in Ceylon, 1949-50; Asst Sec., CO (formerly CRO), 1951-68; retd 1968 and re-employed as a disestablished officer in Historical Section,, India Office Library and Records, 1968-78. *Address*: Middle Farm Cottage, Dinder, Wells, Somerset. *T*: Wells 72120; 129a Ashley Gardens, SW1P 1HL. *T*: 01-828 8159.
[Died 27 Aug. 1979.

COT, Pierre Donatien Alphonse, Commander Legion of Honour; Croix de Guerre; President-Director-General, Société Générale d'Entreprises, since 1974; *b* 10 Sept. 1911; *s* of late Donatien Cot, Engr-Gen. and Naval Hydrographer, Membre de l'Institut, and Yvonne (*née* Bunout); *m* 1939, Claude Bouguen; two *s* two *d*. *Educ*: Lycée Louis-le-Grand, Paris; Ecole Polytechnique, Paris. Licencié ès Sciences. Govt Civil Engr, Paris, 1936; Chief Executive of Port of Le Havre, 1945; Techn. Manager, 1951, and Pres., 1955-67, Paris Airport Authority; Pres., Air France, 1967-74. Chm., National Geographic Inst., 1967-75. Médaille de l'Aéronautique; Officier du Mérite Touristique. Hon. MVO. *Address*: (office) 21 rue du Pont-des-Halles, 94536 Rungis, France. *T*: 687-22-36; (home) 2 avenue Emile Bergerat, 75016 Paris, France. *T*: 527-08-59.
[Died 21 Aug. 1977.

COTTERELL, Lt-Col Sir Richard (Charles Geers), 5th Bt, *cr* 1805; CBE 1965; Lord Lieutenant and Custos Rotulorum for County of Hereford, 1945-57; a Forestry Commissioner (unpaid), 1945-64; *b* 1 June 1907; *s* of Sir J. R. G. Cotterell, 4th Bt, and Lady Evelyn Amy Gordon Lennox, *e d* of 7th Duke of Richmond and Gordon; *S* father, 1937; *m* 1st, 1930, Lady Lettice Lygon (marr. diss. 1958), *e d* of 7th Earl Beauchamp; two *s* two *d*; 2nd, 1958, Patricia Lady Sherwood, *d* of 1st Viscount Camrose. *Educ*: Eton; Sandhurst. Entered Royal Horse Guards, 1927; retd on to Reserve of Officers, 1932; entered Shropshire Yeo., 1935; Major, 1937; commanded 76th Shropshire Yeomanry Medium Regt RA in Middle East and Italy, 1943-45 (despatches). Chm., Wye River Authority, 1968-74. JP 1938. *Heir*: *s* John Henry Geers Cotterell [*b* 8 May 1935; *m* 1959, Vanda Alexandra Clare Bridgewater; three *s* one *d*]. *Address*: Garnons, Hereford. *T*: Bridge Sollers 232. *Club*: White's.
[Died 5 Dec. 1978.

COTTINGHAM, Dame Margaret; *see* Teyte, Dame Maggie.

COTTRELL, Sir Edward (Baglietto), Kt 1957; CBE 1946 (OBE 1943); JP; Chairman of Saccone & Speed Ltd, 1938-71; retired as British Consul, Algeciras, Spain, 1970; *b* 5 May 1896; *s* of late Capt. William Henry Cottrell, CMG, OBE, RNVR; *m* 1926, Josephine, *o d* of late Dr J. Baggetto; two *s* two *d*. *Educ*: King's Sch., Canterbury. Dir Gibraltar Chamber of Commerce, 1923, Vice-President, 1943; Authorised Officer Exports and Imports, 1939; Chm. and Officer Administration City Council, 1940-45; Chm. Evacuation Cttee, 1940; Unofficial Mem. Executive Council, 1941-51. JP Gibraltar, 1939. Life Patron, Sandpits Lawn Tennis Club. *Recreations*: shooting, tennis. *Address*: 4 Library Street, Gibraltar. *T*: A4571. *Club*: Royal Gibraltar Yacht.
[Died 14 July 1976.

COTTRELL, Leonard; author; writer and producer for radio and television; *b* Tettenhall Staffs, 21 May 1913; *s* of William and Beatrice Cottrell; *m* 1940, Doris Swain (marr. diss., 1960); no *c*; *m* 1965, Diana, *d* of Roy and Deidre Randolph. *Educ*: King Edward's Grammar Sch., Birmingham. Worked first in manufacturer's advertising dept and as free-lance writer for BBC. Joined BBC as writer/producer (Features), 1942. War Correspondent, 1944-45; Sen. Producer, 1946; seconded UNESCO, 1951-53; joined BBC Television (Drama) as writer/producer, 1956; resigned to concentrate on authorship and free-lance radio and television writing, 1960. *Publications*: All Men are Neighbours, 1947; The Lost Pharaohs, 1950; The Bull of Minos, 1953; Madame Tussaud, 1954; Life under the Pharaohs, 1955; Seeing Roman Britain, 1956; The Mountains of Pharaoh, 1956; Lost Cities, 1957; The Great Invasion, 1958; Anvil of Civilisation, 1958; Concise Encyclopaedia of Archæology (ed), 1960; Land of the Pharaohs, 1960; Enemy of Rome, 1961; Wonders of Antiquity, 1961; The Tiger of Ch'in, 1962; Lost Worlds, Land of the Two Rivers, 1962; The Lion Gate, 1963; Guide to Egypt, Digs and Diggers, Tutankhamun, 1964; Land of Shinar, 1965; Queens of the Pharaohs, 1966; The Warrior Pharaohs, 1968; Reading the Past, 1969; Lost Civilisations, 1973; In Search of the Pharaohs, 1973; Up in a Balloon, 1974. *Recreations*: archæology, music, history, fast cars. *Address*: Beach Helm, Redhills Road, Arnside, via Carnforth, Lancs. *Club*: Saville.
[Died 6 Oct. 1974.

COTTRELL, Tom Leadbetter; first Principal and Vice-Chancellor of Stirling University since 1965; *b* 8 June 1923; *s* of late Allin Cottrell and of Mrs Lily Cottrell; *m* 1950, Marie, *e d* of E. A. Findlay, Fairlie; two *s*. *Educ*: George Watson's Boys' Coll.; Edinburgh Univ. BSc 1943, DSc 1958. Joined Research Dept ICI (Explosives) Ltd, 1943; seconded to do research at the Physical Chemistry Laboratory, Oxford, 1946-48; research on Physical Chemistry and Blasting Explosives with Nobel Division of ICI, 1948-58; on Directorate Staff of ICI, 1958-59; Prof. of Chem., University of Edinburgh, 1959-66. Member: Council for Scientific Policy, 1969-72; Scottish Economic Planning Council, 1969-71; Bd of Scottish Opera, 1971-. Meldola Medalist, 1952. *Publications*: The Strengths of Chemical Bonds, 1954, 2nd edn 1958; (with J. C. McCoubrey) Molecular Energy Transfer in Gases, 1961; Chemistry, 1963; Dynamic Aspects of Molecular Energy States, 1965; papers in various scientific jls. *Recreations*: yacht racing, looking at pictures. *Address*: The University of Stirling, Stirling. *Clubs*: Scottish Arts (Edinburgh); Royal Forth Yacht.
[Died 2 June 1973.

COUCH, William Charles Milford, CB 1956; CBE 1946; FIEE; Deputy Director of Electrical Engineering, Admiralty, 1941-59; *b* 24 Aug. 1894; *s* of Samson H. E. Couch, RN; *m* 1919, Dorothy, *d* of Henry Charles Mosson, Gillingham, Kent; one *s* one *d*. *Educ*: Mathematical Sch., Rochester; HM Dockyard Sch., Chatham; RN Coll., Greenwich. Dockyard apprentice, 1909-14; Admiralty Scholarship, RN Coll., Greenwich, 1914-16; sea service, 1920-22; successive ranks in electrical engineering dept, serving at Admiralty Engineering Laboratory, West Drayton, Chatham and Malta; at Admiralty as Asst Dir of Electrical Engineering, 1937-41. *Address*: 33 Woodcock Road, Norwich NR3 3TT. *T*: Norwich 45254. *[Died 26 Nov. 1975.*

COUDENHOVE-KALERGI, Richard Nicolaus, DrPhil, Count; President Paneuropean Union; formerly Professor at New York University; *b* 16 Nov. 1894; *s* of Count Henri Coudenhove-Kalergi and Mitsou Aoyama; *m* 1st, Ida Roland (*d* 1951); 2nd, 1952, Countess Alix Tiele-Bally (*d* 1968); 3rd, 1969, Melanie Benatzky. *Educ*: Theresianic Acad., Vienna, DrPhil; founded Paneuropean Union and started PE Movement, 1923; Paneuropean Congresses: first, Vienna, 1926; second, Berlin, 1929; third, Basel, 1932; fourth, Vienna, 1935; fifth, New York, 1943; sixth, Baden Baden, 1954; seventh, Baden Baden, 1955; eighth, Bad Ragaz, 1957; ninth, Nice, 1960; tenth, Vienna, 1966; founded European Parliamentary Union, 1947; European Parliamentary Congresses: first, Gstaad, 1947; second, Interlaken, 1948; third, Venice, 1949; fourth, Constance, 1950. Awarded first Charlemagne Prize (with gold medal), by City of Aachen, 1950; Sonning Prize, Copenhagen University, 1965; Japanese Peace Prize, 1967. Hon. Citizen of Frankfurt Univ., 1953; Hon. Chairman: European Movement, 1952; Yuai Movement, Tokyo, 1954. Hon Dr Nihon Univ., Tokyo. French Legion of Honour, 1954 (officer, 1963); Grand Cross of Merit, 1955; Grand Silver Decoration with star (Austria), 1962; Italian Grand Cross of Merit, 1970; Japanese Order of the Sacred Treasure (First Class), 1970. *Publications*: Ethik U Hyperethik; Krise der Weltanschauung; Praktischer Idealismus; Paneuropa; Held oder Heiliger; Los vom Materialismus; Kampf um Paneuropa; Gebote des Lebens; Stalin and Co.; Revolution durch Technik; Europa Erwacht!, 1934; Europa ohne Elend, 1936; The Totalitarian State Against Man, 1938; Europe Must Unite, 1939; Crusade for Pan Europe, 1943; Europe seeks Unity, 1949; Kampf um Europa, 1949; An Idea conquers the World, 1953; In Memoriam Ida Roland, 1951; Die Europaeische Nation, 1953; Vom ewigen Krieg zum grossen Frieden, 1956; Eine Idee erobert Europa, 1958; From War to Peace, 1959; Die Wiedervereinigung Europas, 1964; Weltmacht Europa, 1971. Revue: (1924-38) Paneuropean (in French and German). *Address*: 8053 Zürich, Wehrenbachhalde 47, Switzerland.
[Died 27 July 1972.

COULDREY, Robert Charles, CBE 1942; *b* 5 June 1890; *e s* of late Henry Robert and Josephine Couldrey; *m* 1931, Honorine Oonagh (*d* 1971), *o d* of late Travers Blackley; one *s* one *d*. *Educ*: United Services Coll., Windsor. Served European War, France, 1915-18; Capt. RFA 1917 (despatches); seconded Egyptian Army, 1918; Sudan Government, 1918; Dir Commercial Intelligence Board, 1931; Dir of Customs, 1935; Pres. Sudan Resources Board, 1940; Mem. of Governor-General's Council, 1940-44; Controller-Gen. of War Supply, Sudan Government, 1941-44 (despatches); Ministry of Supply, 1944; Board of Trade, 1947; retired 1953. Order of the Nile, 1936. *Address*: Sparks Cottage, Northiam, Sussex. *T*: Staplecross 352. *Club*: Sudan (Khartoum). *[Died 13 March 1974.*

COULSON, Charles Alfred, FRS 1950; MA, PhD Cantab; DSc St Andrews; FRSE; FInstP; FIMA; Professor of Theoretical

Chemistry, Oxford University, since 1972; Fellow of Wadham College, Oxford, since 1952; *b* 1910; *m* 1938, Eileen Florence Burrett; two *s* two *d* (and one *s* decd). Formerly: Fellow of Trinity Coll., Cambridge; Lecturer, Department of Mathematics, University of St Andrews, at University Coll., Dundee; College Lecturer in Mathematics, University Coll., Oxford; ICI Fellow in Chemistry, Physical Chemistry Laboratory, Oxford; Prof. of Theoretical Physics, King's Coll., University of London, 1947-52; Rouse Ball Prof. of Mathematics, Oxford, 1952-72. Firth Vis. Prof., Sheffield, 1969. Lectures: Tilden, Chem. Soc., 1951; Riddell, Newcastle, 1953; Rede, Cambridge, 1954; McNair, Chapel Hill, NC, USA, 1954; Douglas Lea Meml, Hosp. Physicists Assoc., 1954; Bruce Preller, Royal Society of Edinburgh, 1956; Firth, Nottingham, 1957; Scott Lidgett, 1957; Eddington Memorial, 1958; Fisher Baker, Cornell Univ., 1959; Beckly, 1960; George B. Pegram, Brookhaven, 1961; Peter Ainslie Meml, Rhodes, 1962; Silvanus Thompson, 1963; Tawney, 1965; Sir D. Owen Evans, Aberystwyth, 1966; Faraday, Chem. Soc., 1967; Freemantle, Oxford, 1968; Burton Meml, London, 1972; Farkas Meml, Jerusalem, 1973. Chm. of Oxfam, 1965-71; Member: Council, Royal Society, 1964-65; Central Cttee, World Council of Churches, 1962-68; President: Mathematical Assoc., 1968-69 (Hon. Life Mem. 1971); Inst. of Mathematics and its Applications, 1972-73; Vice-Pres., Methodist Conference, 1959. Hon. Member: American Academy of Arts and Sciences, 1963; New York Academy of Sciences, 1956; Royal Socs of Liège and Brussels; Foreign Mem., Mathematics and Physics Section, Societas Scientiarum Fennica, 1971; Hon. Fellow, Croatian Chem. Soc., 1972. FKC 1973. Hon. DSc: E Anglia, 1969; Leicester, 1969; Otago, 1969; Cantab, 1971; Manchester, 1972; Hull, 1972; Kent, 1972; Hebrew Univ. of Jerusalem, 1973; Hon. DTech Bradford, 1970; Hon. DLitt Sheffield, 1971; Hon. Fil. Dr Stockholm, 1971; Hon. DD St Andrews, 1973. Pierre Lecomte de Nouy Prize, 1955; Davy Medal, Royal Soc., 1970. *Publications:* five scientific textbooks and about 350 research papers, chiefly in the fields of quantum theory and theoretical chemistry; 3 general books and many articles on relation between science and religion. *Address:* Department of Theoretical Chemistry, 1 South Parks Road, Oxford OX1 3TG. *T:* Oxford 53303; Wadham College, Oxford; The Merbles, Bayswater Road, Headington, Oxford OX3 9RZ. *T:* Stanton St John 625. [*Died 7 Jan.* 1974.

COULTAS, William Whitham, CBE 1943; *b* 17 Feb. 1890; *s* of Rev. G. W. Coultas; *m* 1919, Joyce Visger Lloyd; one *s* (one *d* decd). *Educ:* St Lawrence Coll.; Sidney Sussex Coll., Cambridge. Student interpreter in Thailand, 1913; Consul at Medan, 1930; Chiengmai, 1933; Consul-Gen., Saigon, 1937-38; Counsellor of Legation and HBM Consul-Gen. at Bangkok, 1938-41. *Address:* Ockenden Manor Hotel, Cuckfield, Sussex.
[*Died 10 Nov.* 1973.

COUPER, Sir George Robert Cecil, 5th Bt *cr* 1841; *b* 15 Oct. 1898; *s* of James Robert Couper (*d* 1917) (4th *s* of 2nd Bt) and Jessie (*d* 1922), *d* of John Kissock; *S* kinsman, Sir Guy Couper, 4th Bt, 1973; *m* 1941, Margaret Grace, *d* of late Robert George Dashwood Thomas; one *s* one *d* (twins). *Educ:* Uppingham. Served European War, 1914—18; War of 1939-45 (despatches); Major, 1st Royal Dragoons. *Heir:* *s* Robert Nicholas Oliver Couper, *b* 9 Oct. 1945. *Address:* Annery Barton, Monkleigh, Bideford, N Devon. [*Died 26 May* 1975.

COUPER, Sir Guy, 4th Bt, *cr* 1841; *b* 12 March 1889; *s* of Sir Ramsay Couper, 3rd Bt and Norah (*d* 1925), *d* of Horatio Wilson Scott; *S* father, 1949. Served European War, 1916-18. *Heir:* kinsman George Robert Cecil Couper [*b* 15 Oct. 1898; *m* 1941, Margaret Grace, *d* of late R. G. D. Thomas; one *s* one *d* (twins)]. *Address:* 350 Station Street, Box Hill, Melbourne, Vic, Australia. [*Died 30 Nov.* 1973.

COURT, William Henry Bassano; FBA 1968; Professor of Economic History, University of Birmingham, 1947-70; *b* Cirencester, Glos, 12 Oct. 1904; *m* 1940, Audrey Kathleen, *d* of Rev. A. E. Brown, CIE; three *d*. *Educ:* Cirencester and Newbury Grammar Schs; Downing Coll., Cambridge. Choate Fellow and Rockefeller Fellow, Harvard Univ., 1927-29; AM (Harvard), 1928. Successively Lecturer, Reader, and Prof. of Economic History at University of Birmingham; Dean of the Faculty of Commerce and Social Science, 1956-59; Acting Dean, Feb.-July, 1960; Dep. Dean, May-Sept. 1970. Temporary Civil Servant, 1941-45, attached to Ministry of War Transport, later to Historical Section, War Cabinet Office. Pres., Economic History Soc., 1969. Visiting Fellow: Institute of Advanced Studies, Princeton, NJ, USA, 1954; Australian National Univ., 1959. Hon. Fellow Downing Coll., Cambridge, 1965. *Publications:* The Rise of the Midland Industries, 1938; Coal (History of the Second World War, United Kingdom Civil Series), 1951;

Concise Economic History of England from 1750 to recent times, 1954; contrib. Economic History, to Approaches to History, by H. P. R. Finberg, 1962; British Economic History, 1870-1914: Commentary and Documents, 1965; Scarcity and Choice in History, 1970; articles in learned jls. *Address:* 113 Selly Park Road, Birmingham 29. *T:* 021-472 1758.
[*Died 30 Sept.* 1971.

COURTNEIDGE, Dame Cicely, DBE 1972 (CBE 1951); *b* Sydney, NSW, 1 April, 1893; *d* of late Robert Courtneidge and Rosaline May Adams; *m* Jack Hulbert, actor (*d* 1978); one *d*. First appearance on stage, Prince's Theatre, Manchester, 1901; on London stage, Apollo, 1907; appeared in variety theatres with great success, from 1916; has made popular broadcasts; Gaiety Theatre, New York, 1925; commenced film career, 1929; *Films include:* Ghost Train; Jack's The Boy; Aunt Sally; Soldiers of the Queen; The L-shaped Room; Wrong Box; Things are Looking Up; Imperfect Gentleman; *Revues include:* Little Revue; House That Jack Built; Folly to be Wise; By the Way; Over the Moon; *Plays include:* Hide and Seek, Hippodrome. 1937; Under Your Hat, Palace, 1938; Full Swing, Palace, 1942; Under the Counter, Phoenix, 1945, New York, 1947, Australia, 1947-48; Her Excellency, Hippodrome, 1949; Gay's the Word, Saville, 1951; The Bride and the Bachelor, Duchess, 1956; Fool's Paradise, Apollo, 1959; The Bride Comes Back, Vaudeville, 1960; High Spirits, Savoy, 1964; Dear Octopus, Haymarket, 1967; Move Over Mrs Markham, Vaudeville, 1971. *Publication:* *autobiography:* Cicely, 1953. *Address:* c/o Herbert de Leon (Management) Ltd, Fielding House, 13 Bruton Street, W1X 8JY. [*Died 26 April* 1980.

COURTNEY, Air Chief Marshal Sir Christopher (Lloyd), GBE 1945 (CBE 1919); KCB 1939 (CB 1932); DSO 1917; *b* 27 June 1890; *y* *s* of late W. L. Courtney, MA, LLD; *m* 1926, Constance Rayson (*d* 1974), *d* of G. E. Greensill. *Educ:* Bradfield Coll. Entered HMS Britannia as Naval Cadet, 1905; joined RN Air Service, 1912; served European War, 1914-18 (despatches, DSO, Legion of Honour); transferred to RAF, 1918; Directing Staff, RAF Staff Coll., Andover, 1925-28; served Southern Kurdistan, 1931 (CB); Chief Staff Officer, Iraq Command, 1931-33; Dir of Training, Air Ministry, 1933-34; Dir of Staff Duties, 1934-35; Dir of Operations and Intelligence and Dep. Chief of Air Staff, 1935-36; Air Officer Commanding British Forces in Iraq, 1937-38; commanding Reserve Command RAF, 1939-40; Air Mem. for Supply and Organisation on the Air Council, 1940-45 (Legion of Merit, US); retired, 1945. A Vice-Pres., Star and Garter Home, 1973 (Governor, 1952-73). Master of Vintners' Company, 1964-65 (Court, 1958). *Address:* 104 Bryanston Court, W1. *T:* 01-262 9030. *Club:* Royal Air Force.
[*Died 22 Oct.* 1976.

COURTNEY, Group Captain Ivon Terence, CBE 1919; RAF (retired); *b* 14 Oct. 1885; *y* *s* of late William McDougall Courtney, Stormonstown, Co. Dublin; *m* 1915, Emily Lilian (*d* 1964), *y* *d* of Alfred Campbell Courtney, Danesfield, Clontarf, Co. Dublin; one *s*. *Educ:* Tonbridge; Rossall. Commissioned Royal Marine Light Infantry, 1904; seconded to Naval Wing, RFC, 1912 for flying duty and to RNAS, 1914; permanently transferred to RAF, 1919; retired list, 1932. *Address:* National Westminster Bank, 26 Haymarket, SW1. [*Died 17 Oct.* 1978.

COURTNEY, Dame Kathleen (D'Olier), DBE 1952 (CBE 1946); Chairman and Joint President, United Nations Association, 1949-51; *b* 11 March 1878; *d* of Major D. C. Courtney, RE, Nullamore, Milltown, Co. Dublin, and Alice Margaret Mann. *Educ:* private schs; Lady Margaret Hall, Oxford. Hon. Sec. Nat. Union Women's Suffrage Socs, 1911-14; relief work in Europe during and after European War, 1914-18. Joined Exec. Cttee, League of Nations Union, 1928, Vice-Chm., 1939; Dep.-Chm. of UNA, 1945. During War of 1939-45 visited USA twice to lecture on behalf of MOI. *Recreations:* travelling, walking. *Address:* 3 Elm Tree Court, Elm Tree Road, NW8. *T:* 01-286 3691. *Club:* University Women's. [*Died 7 Dec.* 1974.

COURTOWN, 8th Earl of, *cr* 1762; **James Montagu Burgoyne Stopford,** OBE 1950 (MBE 1945); TD and clasp; DL; Viscount Stopford, 1762; Baron Courtown (Ireland), 1758; Baron Saltersford (Great Britain), 1796; *b* 24 Nov. 1908; *e* *s* of 7th Earl of Courtown and Cicely Mary Birch (*d* 1973), *S* father, 1957; *m* 1st, 1934, Christina Margaret (marriage dissolved, 1946), 3rd *d* of late Adm. J. Ewen Cameron, CB, MVO; two *d*; 2nd, 1951, Patricia, 3rd *d* of Harry S. Winthrop, Auckland, NZ; two *s* one *d*. *Educ:* Eton. Served War of 1939-45 (MBE). Lieut-Col commanding 1st Bn London Irish Rifles (Royal Ulster Rifles) (TA), 1947-51; Bt Col 1951. In various positions with Imperial Chemical Industries, 1928-70. Mem. Bd, Inveresk Research International, 1974-. Chm., Reg. Council, Sch. of Management Studies, Portsmouth Polytechnic (Hon. Fellow, 1971). DL Co.

of London, 1951. *Heir: s* Viscount Stopford. *Address:* Beech Shade, Cambridge Road, Beaconsfield, Bucks. *T:* Beaconsfield 3417; Marlfield, Gorey, Co. Wexford, Ireland. *T:* Gorey 21124. *Clubs:* Travellers'; Kildare Street (Dublin).

[Died 23 July 1975.

COUTANCHE, Baron, *cr* 1961, of St Brelade and of the City of Westminster (Life Peer); **Alexander Moncrieff Coutanche,** Kt 1945; Bailiff of Jersey, 1935-61; *b* Jersey, 9 May 1892; *yr s of* Adolphus Arnold Coutanche, notary, Jersey, and of Ina Finlayson, Glasgow; *m* 1924, Ruth Sophia Joan, CStJ (*d* 1973), *o c* of Leicester Gore; one *s. Educ:* Victoria Coll., Jersey; privately. Entered Middle Temple, 1912; called to Jersey Bar, 1913; English Bar, 1915; gazetted, general list, 1917; Claims Commission, France and Belgium, 1917-20; Staff Capt., 1919 (despatches, Chevalier de l'Ordre de la Couronne and Croix de Guerre, Belgium); Dep. of St Helier in States of Jersey, 1922-25; Solicitor-Gen. for Jersey, 1925-31; Attorney-Gen., 1931-35; Hon. Doctor, University of Caen (France), 1938; Hon. Bencher of the Middle Temple, 1961. Knight of Grace, Order of St John of Jerusalem, 1946; Silver Medal, RSPCA, 1939. *Publication:* (joint) Dictionary of Anglo-Belgian Law, 1920. *Address:* Clos des Tours, St Aubin, Jersey. *T:* Jersey, Central 41178. *Clubs:* Royal Commonwealth Society (Vice-Pres.), Royal Automobile (Hon.); Victoria (Jersey). *[Died 18 Dec. 1973.*

COUTTS DONALD, William, CA; Director, Urwick, Orr & Partners Ltd (Chairman, 1963-72); *b* Forfar, Scotland, 11 March 1906; *s of* James Donald and Betsy Milne Coutts; *m* 1936, Dora Eleanor Tiso; one *s. Educ:* Forfar Acad.; St Andrews Univ. Henderson & Loggie, CA, 1923-28; Chief Accountant, Forsters Glass Co. Ltd, 1928-30; Sec. and Chief Accountant, Scribbans & Co. Ltd, 1930-36; Urwick, Orr & Partners Ltd, 1936-: Dir 1940; Man. Dir, 1952-63. CA 1928, FCWA 1936, FBIM 1945. Pres., Inst. of Management Consultants, 1969-70; Chm., Management Consultants Assoc., 1960 and 1964; Member: NEDC, 1964-66; Council of British Inst. of Management, 1967-; formerly Mem., Council of Cost and Works Accountants. *Publications:* several pamphlets and articles on financial and cost accounting. *Recreations:* golf, cricket. *Address:* 16 The Downsway, Sutton, Surrey. *T:* 01-642 5683. *Clubs:* Devonshire; Effingham Golf, Harborne Golf (Birmingham). *[Died 15 April 1974.*

COVELL, Maj.-Gen. Sir Gordon, Kt 1946; CIE 1939; MD; IMS, retired; *b* 20 Oct. 1887; *s of* late Edwin Louis Covell; *m* Oona, *d* of late Col Kenneth Macleod, IMS; two *s* one *d. Educ:* King's Sch., Canterbury; Guy's Hosp. MB, BS 1913; DTM & H Eng 1922; DPH 1929; MD 1923. Maj.-Gen. 1944; late Dir Malaria Institute of India; retired, 1947; KHP, 1944-47. Walter Reed Medal for achievement in Tropical Medicine, 1960; Darling Medal for Malaria Research, 1961; Manson Medal of Royal Soc. of Tropical Medicine and Hygiene, for services to Tropical Medicine, 1971. *Address:* 13 Mount Street, Taunton, Somerset. *[Died 4 Oct. 1975.*

COVERDALE, Ralph; Founder and Chairman, The Coverdale Organisation, since 1965; *b* 13 Oct. 1918; *s of* Joseph Coverdale, Ingatestone, Essex, and Marie Bernadette Josephine Walmesley-Cotham; *m* 1944, Margaret Beatrice Elles; one *s* one *d. Educ:* Beaumont Coll.; Heythrop Coll.; St. Catherine's Coll., Oxford. DipPsych (Oxon) 1947, BLitt(Oxon) 1949. 10th King's Royal Rifle Corps (Captain), 1942-47. Motivation and Psychological Res., 1949-56; Exec. Develt Officer, Steel Co. of Wales, Steel Div., 1956-61; Head of Management Studies, Esso Petroleum Co. Ltd, 1961-65. *Address:* 32 Morpeth Mansions, Morpeth Terrace, SW1V 1BB. *Club:* Cavalry. *[Died 7 Feb. 1975.*

COWAN, Sir Christopher (George) Armstrong, Kt 1958; JP; *b* 6 April 1889; *s of* late William James Cowan and Frances Isabella Cowan, Wood Green, London; *m* 1912, Bertha Lydia Caroline (*d* 1978), *d of* late James and Emma Ross; one *s* (and one *s* decd). *Educ:* Merchant Taylors' Sch. Barrister-at-Law, Middle Temple, 1927; SE Circuit, Surrey and S London Sessions. Mem. Ruislip-Northwood Urban Dist Council, 1936-49. Mddx CC: Councillor, 1937, Alderman, 1951-58, Vice-Chm., 1955-56, Chm., 1956-57; Alderman, 1961-65; High Sheriff, Mddx, 1960; JP, 1942; Chm. Uxbridge Bench, 1947-64 (Dep.-Chm. 1944-47). Ex-Member: Standing Jt Cttee; Magistrates' Courts Cttee; Advisory Cttee; Agricultural Wages Cttee; NW Home Counties Regional Advisory Water Cttee, 1945-58, 1961-65; Northwood and Pinner Hosp. Bd, 1936-48 (Chm.). Member: Harefield and Northwood Group Hosp. Management Cttee, 1948-63; NW Metrop. Reg. Hosp. Bd, 1957-63; Chm. Nat. Assistance Tribunals, 1934-49; Chm. Cowan Brothers (Stratford) Ltd until 1968. *Address:* Kiln Farm, Northwood, Mddx. *T:* Northwood 21122. *[Died 16 March 1979.*

COWAN, Sir (Henry) Kenneth, Kt 1958; FRSE 1956; Chairman, Cruden Investments Ltd; Vice-Chairman, Crudens Ltd, Musselburgh, since 1969 (Chairman, 1967-69); Director: Cruden Foundation, since 1964; Eskside Securities Ltd; Trustee, Scottish Hospital Endowments Research Trust; Member, Industrial Injuries Advisory Council; *b* 17 June 1900; *e s of* Henry Cowan, Belfast; *m* 1st, 1933, Elinor Margaret Graham (*d* 1966), *er d* of George Craig, JP, Drumcovitt House, Feeny, Londonderry; no *c*; 2nd, 1970, Mrs J. C. McMillan, Edinburgh. *Educ:* Royal Belfast Academical Instn; Queen's Univ., Belfast. MB, BCh, BAO, 1921; DPH 1924; MD 1925. Asst Medical Officer of Health, Belfast, 1923, Leicester, 1928; Dep. County MO, Leics, 1933; County MOH, Glos, 1937, Essex, 1949-54; late Chief MO, Dept of Health for Scotland; Hon. Physician to the Queen, 1956-59. Mem., General Medical Council, 1955-63. Chm. Public Health Cttee, BMA, 1951-54; Mem. Standing Med. Advisory Cttee, Central Health Services Council, 1951-54. Smith Award, 1955. MRCPE 1956; FRCPE 1957; FRCPS(G) (Hon.), 1961. Hon. LLD Glasgow Univ., 1964. *Publications:* articles in various medical journals. *Recreation:* golf. *Address:* Claremont, Longniddry, East Lothian. *T:* Longniddry 3176. *[Died 16 June 1971.*

COWARD, Sir Noel, Kt 1970; *b* Teddington, 16 Dec. 1899; *s of* late Arthur Coward and Violet Veitch. *Educ:* Chapel Road Sch.; privately. Made first appearance on stage, 1910, and has made many other successful stage appearances in London and New York, also in cabaret in London and Las Vegas. Played King Magnus in The Apple Cart, Haymarket, 1953. FRSL. Hon. DLitt Sussex, 1972. *Plays:* I'll Leave It to You, 1920; The Young Idea, 1921; The Vortex, 1924; Easy Virtue, 1925; Fallen Angels, 1925; Hay Fever, 1925; On with the Dance (revue), 1925; The Queen was in the Parlour, 1926; This was a Man, 1926; The Marquise, 1927; Home Chat, 1927; Sirocco, 1927; This Year of Grace (revue), 1928; Bitter Sweet (operette), 1929; Private Lives, 1930; Cavalcade, 1931; Words and Music (revue), 1932; Design for Living, 1932; Conversation Piece, 1934; Point Valaine, 1945; To-Night at Eight-Thirty, 1936; Operette, 1938; Blithe Spirit, 1941; Present Laughter, 1942; This Happy Breed, 1943 (written 1939); Sigh No More (revue), 1945; Pacific 1860 (musical play), 1946; Peace In Our Time, 1947; Ace of Clubs (musical play), 1950; Relative Values (play), 1951; Quadrille, 1952; After the Ball (musical play), 1954; South Sea Bubble, 1956; Nude with Violin, 1956; Look After Lulu, 1959; London Morning (ballet), 1959; Waiting in the Wings, 1960; Sail Away (musical play), 1961 (USA), 1962 (Savoy Theatre); The Girl Who Came to Supper (USA), 1963; High Spirits, 1964; A Song at Twilight; Shadows of the Evening; Come into the Garden Maud, 1966; *Films:* In Which We Serve, 1942; This Happy Breed, 1944; Brief Encounter, 1945; Blithe Spirit, 1945; The Astonished Heart, 1950; Around The World in 80 Days, 1957; Our Man in Havana, 1959; Surprise Package, 1960; Bunny Lake is Missing, 1965; Boom, 1968; The Italian Job, 1968. *Publications:* Collected Sketches and Lyrics, 1931; Present Indicative (autobiography), 1937; To Step Aside, 1939; Middle East Diary, 1945; Star Quality (short stories), 1951; Noël Coward Song Book, 1953; Future Indefinite (autobiography), 1954; Pomp and Circumstance (novel), 1960; The Collected Short Stories of Noël Coward, 1962; Pretty Polly Barlow and other stories, 1964; Lyrics of Noël Coward, 1965; Bon Voyage (short stories), 1967; Not Yet the Dodo (verse), 1967. *Address:* Les Avants, sur Montreux, Switzerland. *Clubs:* Athenæum, Garrick.

[Died 26 March 1973.

COWDEROY, Most Rev. Mgr Cyril Conrad, DD; Archbishop and Metropolitan of Southwark, since 1965; *b* 5 May 1905; *s of* Frederick Cowderoy and Anne Marie (*née* Lawless). *Educ:* Dulwich Coll.; St John's Seminary, Wonersh. Priest, 1931; after further studies at L'Institut Catholique, Paris, appointed Professor, St Joseph's Coll., Mark Cross, Tunbridge Wells, 1932; Diocesan Secretary, 1937; Chancellor of Diocese of Southwark, 1946; Judge of Matrimonial Court, 1947; appointed Privy Chamberlain to HH the Pope, Dec. 1948. Bishop of Southwark, 1949-65. Grand Prior of Lieutenancy in England and Wales of Order of Knights of Holy Sepulchre of Jerusalem, 1954, Knight Grand Cross, 1961; Knight Grand Cross, Order of the Most Holy Saviour and St Bridget of Sweden, 1967. *Address:* Archbishop's House, St George's Road, Southwark, SE1. *T:* 01-928 5592. *[Died 10 Oct. 1976.*

COWELL, Maj.-Gen. Sir Ernest Marshall, KBE 1944 (CBE 1939); CB 1940; DSO 1918; TD; MD, BS London; FRCS; AMS(T); Legion of Merit, rank of Commander, 1944; Commander of the Grand Priory of the Hospital of St John of Jerusalem, 1945; Officier de la Légion d'Honneur, 1943; Croix de Guerre with palm; Hon. Member of Military Surgeons, USA; *b* 24 Feb. 1886; *s of* Jasper Cowell, Steyning, Sussex; *m* 1st, 1912, Dorothie (*d* 1962), *d* of Arthur Miller, ISO, late of India Office;

one *s* two *d*; 2nd, 1963, Mary K. Ebeling, *d* of Thomas Ebeling of Guernsey. *Educ:* Steyning Gram. Sch.; University Coll., London. MRCS, LRCP, MB, BS London, 1907; MD 1909; FRCS 1910. Surgical Specialist, BEF 1915-18 (DSO, despatches twice); Lieut-Col OC No. 1, CCS, BEF 1918-19; Commandant 1st Army Sch. of Instruction, RAMC; County Dir and County Controller, BRCS Surrey, 1927-38; ADMS 44th (Home Counties) Div. 1934-40; DDMS 3 Corps BEF, 1940; DDMS 2 Corps, 1940-42; DMS Allied Forces, North Africa, 1942, Maj.-Gen. (despatches); DDMS Northern Command, 1944. PMO Control Commn for Germany; Dir of Health Div., UNRRA Mission to Greece; late KHS Fellow of University Coll., London, 1918; Arris and Gale Lecturer, RCS, 1919; late Surg. Croydon Gen. Hosp., 1922; Hunterian Prof. Royal College of Surg., 1927; Freeman Borough of Croydon, 1945; Freeman of City of London, 1953; Mem: of Worshipful Company of Coopers. DL Surrey, 1927-68. *Publications:* Hernia, 1927; Pocket Book of First Aid in Accidents and Chemical Warfare, 1937; Field Service Notes for Regimental Officers, 1939; (with P. S. Mitchiner) Medical Organisation in Air Raids, 2nd edn 1941. *Recreations:* walking, gardening, fishing. *Address:* Stuart Lodge, Sausmarez Road, St Martin, Guernsey, CI.
[Died 26 Feb. 1971.

COWELL, Frank Richard, CMG 1952; BA, BSc (Econ), PhD London; retired Civil Servant; Secretary United Kingdom National Commission for UNESCO, 1946-58; *b* 16 Nov. 1897; *s* of William Frank Cowell and E. A. Pearce; *m* 1927, Lilian Margaret (*d* 1970), *d* of Rev. A. E. Palin; two *s*. *Educ:* Roan Sch., Greenwich: King's Coll., London; London Sch. of Economics. BA 1919, BSc (Econ) 1927. Rockefeller Foundation Fellow in the Social Sciences, 1929-31; PhD 1938. Served in HM Stationery Office, 1921-39; Foreign Office, 1939-46. Dep. Sec. Gen. British Council, May-Nov. 1940; served on British Mission to French National Cttee, 1940-43. *Publications:* Brief Guide to Government Publications, 1938; Cicero and the Roman Republic, 1948, 6th edn (Penguin), 1972; History, Civilization and Culture, 1952; Culture, 1959; Everyday Life in Ancient Rome, 1961, 9th edn 1976; Revolutions of Ancient Rome, 1962; Values in Human Society, 1970; The Dominance of Rome, 1970; The Athenæum: Club and Social Life 1824-1974, 1975; Gardens as Fine Art, 1978; Leibniz, 1978. *Address:* Crowdleham House, Kemsing, Kent. *T:* Sevenoaks 61192. *Club:* Athenæum.
[Died 13 Aug. 1978.

COWELL, Stuart Jasper, MA, MB, BCh Cantab; FRCP; Professor Emeritus in the University of London; *b* 9 Feb. 1891; *s* of Jasper Cowell, Steyning, Sussex; *m* 1925, May Penelope (*d* 1961), *d* of late Cecil Archibald Smith, CIE, MICE; one *s* two *d*. *Educ:* Steyning and Brighton Grammar Schs; Queens' Coll., Cambridge; University Coll. Hosp. Medical Sch., London. 1st Cl. Natural Science Tripos, 1912; Asst in Med. Unit, University College Hosp. Med. Sch., 1921; clinical asst to Sir Edward Mellanby (Medical Research Council) at Sheffield, 1923. Associate Ed. of Biochemical Journal, 1939-43; Editorial Board, Nutrition Abstracts and Reviews, 1954-56, and British Journal of Nutrition; Mem. of North-West Metropolitan Regional Hosp. Board, 1947-56; late Chm. Catering and Nutrition Cttee of King Edward Hosp. Fund for London. *Publications:* papers in scientific journals. *Recreations:* gardening, prawning, sailing. *Address:* The Flagstaff, Northam, N Devon. *T:* Bideford 2076.
[Died 1 Aug. 1971.

COWLEY, 6th Earl *cr* 1857; **Richard Francis Wellesley;** Baron Cowley, 1828; Viscount Dangan, 1857; a Conservative Whip, House of Lords, since 1974; *b* 12 June 1946; *s* of 5th Earl Cowley and Elizabeth Anne, *yr d* of Lieut-Col Pelham Rawstorn Papillon, DSO; *S* father, 1968; *m* 1971, Maria Delia, *yr d* of Enrique R. Buenaño; two *d*. *Educ:* Wellesley House, Broadstairs; Eton; Univ. of Birmingham. LLB 1969. Res. Officer in Cons. Res. Dept, 1971-74. A Lord in Waiting (Govt Whip), 1974. Dep. Sec., Cttee on Internat. Affairs and Migration, of General Synod, 1974-. *Heir: uncle* Hon. Garret Graham Wellesley [*b* 30 July 1934; *m* 1960, Elizabeth Suzanne Lennon; one *s* one *d*]. *Address:* 5 Stanhope Gardens, SW7. *Club:* Royal Bermuda Yacht.
[Died 13 Dec. 1975.

COWLING, Donald George, MBE 1945; JP; Chairman, City of Leeds Conservative Association, 1957-67 (Deputy Chairman 1956); *b* 27 Oct. 1904; *m* 1928, Muriel, *o c* of late Charles Richard Chambers; one *s* one *d*. Mem. Leeds City Council, 1930; Chm. Transport Cttee, 1938-41 and 1949-55; Mem. Local Price Regulation Cttee for NE Region, 1940-41; resigned from Council to join RAF 1941; released as Sqdn Ldr, 1945, and re-elected to City Council, 1946; Chm. Central Div. (Conservative Party), 1948-53, Chm. of SE Leeds Div., 1953-57; Dep. Lord Mayor, 1951-52; Lord Mayor of Leeds, 1953-54; Alderman of City of Leeds, 1949-55; resigned 1955; Hon. Alderman, 1967.

Mem. Court and Council University of Leeds, 1954-71; Mem. House Cttee Gen. Infirmary at Leeds, 1955-59; Mem. Cttee Leeds Triennial Music Festival, 1955-59; Mem. Company of Poulters; Pres. Nat. Fedn of Wholesale Poultry Merchants, 1955-61 (Chm., 1939-41 and 1949-55). Pres. Leeds Branch of Royal Society of St George, 1958-66. *Recreation:* golf. *Address:* Sandsend Court, Sandsend, N Yorks. *T:* Sandsend 328; The Thatched Cottage, Carlton Husthwaite, Thirsk, N Yorks. *T:* Hutton Sessay 318. *Clubs:* Leeds; Alwoodley Golf.
[Died 30 Jan. 1975.

COX, Arthur Henry, CMG 1938; *b* 8 Nov. 1888; *s* of Henry Thompson Cox, RN, Inspector-Gen. of Hospitals and Fleets; *m* 1929, Marjorie Thorpe Lewis; one *s*. *Educ:* Felsted (scholar); Corpus Christi Coll., Cambridge, MA (BA Mod. Langs). Asst District Commissioner, Uganda, 1911; Aide-de-Camp to Sir Robert Coryndon, Governor, Uganda, 1918-19; 1st Grade Administrative Officer, 1922; Dep. Provincial Commissioner, 1928; Acting Provincial Commissioner, July 1929 and June 1932; Asst Chief Sec., Uganda, 1930; Acting Dep. Chief Sec., March 1930-Oct. 1931; Provincial Commissioner, 1932; Resident of Buganda and Mem. of Executive Council, Uganda, 1932-44; retired, 1944; Civil Dispersals Officer, Uganda; discharged troops in Kenya, 1944-45; employed Colonial Office, 1947-49. *Address:* Rowlands, Old Hunstanton, Norfolk. *T:* Hunstanton 2375.
[Died 16 Jan. 1971.

COX, Euan Hillhouse Methven; *b* 19 June 1893; *o c* of Alfred W. Cox, Glendoick, Glencarse, Perthshire, and late Helen Salmon; *m* 1925, Norah Helen Cox; one *s* one *d*. *Educ:* Cargilfield; Rugby; Trinity Hall, Cambridge. Temp. Lieut Royal Marines, 1914-16; explored in Upper Burma, 1919, with Reginald Farrer; Gardening Editor, Country Life, 1922-27; Editor, The Garden, 1924-26; Founder and Editor, The New Flora and Silva, 1928-38. *Publications:* Rhododendrons for Amateurs, 1924; Farrer's Last Journey, 1926; The Evolution of a Garden, 1927; Primulas for Garden and Greenhouse (with G. C. Taylor), 1928; Wild Gardening, 1929; The Plant Introductions of Reginald Farrer, 1930; The Gardener's Chapbook, 1931; A History of Gardening in Scotland, 1935; A History of Plant Collecting in China, 1945; Modern Rhododendrons (with P. A. Cox), 1956; Modern Shrubs (with P. A. Cox), 1958; Modern Trees (with P. A. Cox), 1961. *Recreations:* gardening, botanical exploration, fishing, photography. *Address:* Glendoick, Perth. *T:* Glencarse 205.
[Died 26 March 1977.

COX, Sir Herbert Charles Fahie, Kt 1946; JP; Chief Justice of Basutoland, the Bechuanaland Protectorate, and Swaziland, 1956-61; *b* 1893; 2nd *s* of late Sir Charles T. Cox, KCMG, of British Guiana; *m* 1st, 1919, Dorothy, *o d* of late Sir Maurice Berkeley; one *s* one *d*; 2nd, 1933, Mabel, *o d* of late T. Wright, MD, Lee-on-the-Solent; one *s* one *d*. Barrister-at-Law, 1915; KC Nigeria, 1936; British Guiana Police, 1913-19; served European War, 1917-19; Asst Attorney-Gen., British Guiana, 1920-25; Attorney-Gen., Bahamas, 1925-29; MLC, 1926; Attorney-Gen., Gibraltar, 1929-33; Solicitor-Gen., Nigeria, 1933-35; Attorney-Gen., Nigeria, 1935-46; Chief Justice of N Rhodesia, 1946-52 (Chm. Northern Rhodesia Police Commission of Enquiry, 1946-47), Tanganyika, 1952-56. Chm., Commission of Enquiry into Provincial Disturbances, Sierra Leone, 1956. JP Wilts, 1963. CC, Dorset, 1963-69; Dep. Chm., Wilts QS, 1964-68. *Recreations:* tennis, golf, cricket. *Address:* Cloverlands, Farley, near Salisbury, Wilts. *Clubs:* Royal Commonwealth Society, East India, Sports and Public Schools.
[Died 21 Sept. 1973.

COX, Dame Marjorie (Sophie), DBE 1950 (CBE 1943; OBE 1937); *b* 13 Dec. 1893; Fellow of University College, London; retired; *d* of late Albert and Amelia Cox, Trowbridge, Wilts. *Educ:* University Coll., London. BA London. Entered Civil Service as temp. clerk in 1915 and became established through Lytton examination in 1921; Mem. Beveridge Cttee on Social Security; Dep. Sec. Min. of Pensions (later of Pensions and National Insurance), 1946-54. *Recreation:* reading. *Address:* 10 The Paragon, Wannock Lane, Willingdon, Eastbourne, East Sussex. *T:* Polegate 4159.
[Died 24 March 1979.

COX, Maj.-Gen. Maurice L.; see Lea-Cox.

COZENS-HARDY, 4th Baron, *cr* 1914, of Letheringsett; **Herbert Arthur Cozens-Hardy**, OBE 1966; JP, DL; Director of Pilkington Brothers Ltd, glass manufacturers, St Helens, 1938-71; *b* 8 June 1907; *o s* of 3rd Baron Cozens-Hardy and Gladys Lily (*d* 1975), *d* of Arthur Wrigley Cozens-Hardy; *S* father, 1956; unmarried. *Educ:* Winchester; Worcester Coll., Oxford. Pilkington Brothers Ltd, 1932-71. Chairman: St Helens Savings Cttee, 1950-60; Lancashire Magistrates Court Cttee, 1952-74; Prescot Magistrates, 1953-74; Knowsley Magistrates, 1974-75; Knowsley Magistrates Courts Cttee, 1974-75; Huyton Coll.,

Liverpool, 1956-75. Chm., St John Council for Lancashire, 1947-75; Bailiff of Egle, Order of St John, 1971-. Pres., Royal Lancs Agricultural Soc., 1959-63, Chm., 1965-. JP 1939, DL 1953, Lancs; DL Merseyside, 1974. GCStJ 1971. *Recreations:* usual. *Heir:* none. *Address:* Prior's Grove, Letheringsett Hill, Holt, Norfolk NR25 6RY; D5 Albany, Piccadilly, W1V 9RG. *T:* 01-734 4282. *Club:* Royal Automobile.
[*Died* 11 *Sept.* 1975 (*ext*).

COZZENS, James Gould; US author; *b* Chicago, USA, 19 Aug. 1903; *s* of Henry William Cozzens and Bertha Wood; *m* 1927, Bernice Baumgarten (*d* 1978). *Educ:* Kent Sch., Connecticut; Harvard University. *Publications:* Confusion, 1924; Michael Scarlett, 1925; Cockpit, 1928; The Son of Perdition, 1929; SS San Pedro, 1931; The Last Adam, 1933; Castaway, 1934; Men and Brethren, 1936; Ask Me Tomorrow, 1940; The Just and the Unjust, 1942; Guard of Honour, 1949; By Love Possessed, 1958; Children and Others, 1965; Morning, Noon and Night, 1968; A Flower in her Hair, 1974; A Rope for Dr Webster, 1976; Just Representations, 1978. *Recreation:* writing. *Address:* PO Box 2372, Stuart, Florida 33494, USA.   [*Died* 9 *Aug.* 1978.

CRABBE, Sir Cecil (Brooksby), Kt 1956; JP; *b* 24 June 1898; *s* of late Rev. Henry Brooksby Crabbe, Bradford, Yorks; *m* 1925, Margaret, *d* of late Rev. Herbert Henry Willmott, Rector of Rivenhall, Essex; one *s* one *d* (and one *s* decd). *Educ:* Trent Coll., Derbyshire; Royal Military Coll., Sandhurst. Served with Indian Army, NW Frontier and Iraq, 1918-22; admitted Solicitor, 1924; Legal Asst, Registry of Friendly Societies, 1925; Asst Registrar of Friendly Societies, 1940; Deputy Industrial Assurance Commissioner, 1947; Chief Registrar of Friendly Societies and Industrial Assurance Commissioner, 1954-63, retd. Hon. Fellow Building Societies Inst., 1955; Vice-Pres. Building Societies Assoc., 1963; Mem., Trustee Savings Banks Inspection Cttee, 1964-; Dir, Chelsea and South London Building Society, 1964-. Mem., Croydon and Warlingham Park Hosp. Management Cttee, 1963- (Chm., 1965-). JP Croydon, 1961-. *Address:* 54 Croham Park Avenue, South Croydon, Surrey CR2 7HL. *T:* 01-688 1705. *Club:* Athenæum.
[*Died* 20 *Dec.* 1971.

CRACROFT-AMCOTTS, Lt-Col Sir Weston, Kt 1954; MC 1917; DL, JP; Chairman Lindsey County Council, 1951-64; *b* 7 Nov. 1888; *er s* of Major F. A. Cracroft-Amcotts, late V Dragoon Guards, and Mrs F. A. Cracroft-Amcotts, *d* of Anthony Willson, Rauceby, Lincs; *m* 1927, Rhona, *d* of late E. C. Clifton-Brown, Burnham Grove, Burnham, Bucks; four *d*. *Educ:* Eton; RMA Woolwich. Commissioned RE, 1908; served European War, 1914-18; retired with rank of Major, 1920; commissioned as Major, 46th Bn Lincs Regt, (RE), TA, 1938; retired with rank of Lieut-Col, 1942; Lieut-Col, Home Guard, 1942-45. JP Lindsey, Lincs, 1924; DL Lincs, 1936; High Sheriff of Lincolnshire, 1954. *Address:* Hackthorn Hall, Lincoln. *T:* Welton 60212.   [*Died* 17 *Sept.* 1975.

CRADDOCK, Sir Beresford; *see* Craddock, Sir G. B.

CRADDOCK, George; *b* 26 Feb. 1897; *s* of late Amos George Craddock and of Athey Alpheaus Craddock, Northampton; *m* 1936, Doris Miriam Kimberley (*d* 1949); one *d*; *m* 1962, Margaret, *d* of late Mr and Mrs G. Morris, Bangor. *Educ:* Fircroft Coll.; Birmingham Univ. Joined Labour Party, 1918; Vice-Pres. Sparkbrook Divisional Labour Party; Pres. King's Norton Div. Labour Party. Contested Balsall Heath Ward, Birmingham City Council Elections, 1926, 1927, 1928. Labour Agent Thornbury Parly Div., 1929-36; Area Organiser Nat. Union Distributive and Allied Workers, 1936-49; MP (Lab) South Bradford, Dec. 1949-1970. Treas. Sheffield Trades and Labour Council, 1942-43; rep. Darnall Ward on Sheffield City Council, 1945-. *Recreations:* motoring, walking, reading; philatelist. *Address:* 25 High Trees, Dore, Sheffield. *T:* Sheffield 362842.   [*Died* 28 *April* 1974.

CRADDOCK, Sir (George) Beresford, Kt 1960; practising barrister; *b* 7 Oct. 1898; *m* 1936, Ethel Martin Bradford. *Educ:* St Andrews Univ. MA Economics and Philosophy; BSc Chemistry and Physics, with First Class Hons and special distinction in Chemistry; ARIC. Barrister-at-Law, Gray's Inn, 1947; chambers in Middle Temple. Held important executive posts in business at home, in India and in Africa, 1921-39. European War, 1914-18, Staff Lieut, RE Chemical Warfare Staff, having first served in RGA; War of 1939-45, Asst Dir, Ministry of Supply. Contested (Nat. Govt) Lichfield, Staffs, 1938 (by-election), and 1945; MP (C) Spelthorne Div. of Mddx, 1950-70; PPS to Rt Hon. Harold Watkinson, as Minister of Transport and Civil Aviation, 1956-59, and as Minister of Defence, 1959-62. Mem., Speaker's Panel of Chairmen, 1966-70. *Recreations:* golf and music. *Address:* Henley Down House,

Battle, Sussex. *T:* Crowhurst 203. *Club:* Carlton.
[*Died* 22 *Sept.* 1976.

CRADDOCK, Lt-Gen. Sir Richard Walter, KBE 1963 (CBE 1954; MBE 1940); CB 1959; DSO 1944; Lieutenant of HM Tower of London, 1966-69; *b* 3 Aug. 1910; *s* of late Sir Walter Craddock, DSO, MC, and Margaret Amy Craddock; *m* 1943, Josephine Pamela Ann (*née* Love); one *s* one *d*. *Educ:* Charterhouse; Royal Military Coll., Sandhurst. 2nd Lieut The Buffs, 1930; Col, 1951; Temp. Brig., 1951; Dir of Plans, War Office, 1951-53; Brigadier and Maj.-Gen., 1957; Maj.-Gen. i/c Administration, British Army of the Rhine, 1957-59; Director of Military Operations, War Office, 1959-62; Lieut-Gen. 1963; Comdr, British Forces, Hong-Kong, 1963-64; GOC-in-C, Western Comd, 1964-66. Mem. Cttee, Corps of Commissionaires, 1969-. Deputy Col The Queen's Own Buffs, 1965-66; Col The Queen's Regt, 1966-73. *Address:* Upcote, Chilbolton, Hants.   [*Died* 14 *Feb.* 1977.

CRADDOCK, Sir Walter Merry, Kt 1935; DSO 1919; MC; OStJ; *b* 1883; 2nd *s* of late Frederick Charles Craddock; *m* 1909, Margaret Amy (*d* 1948), *d* of late Anthony Henry Ten-Broeke; one *s*. Served European War, 1914-19, Lieut-Col 2/20th Bn London Regt (despatches thrice, MC, DSO). Commanded Calcutta Scottish IAF 1924-28; lately Sheriff of Calcutta. ADC to the King, 1925; Col, 1925; re-employed, 1940. High Sheriff of Glos, 1949. *Address:* Barns Close, Amberley, near Stroud, Glos. *T:* 2267. *Club:* Bengal (Calcutta).   [*Died* 23 *Dec.* 1972.

CRAGG, Ven. Herbert Wallace, MA; *b* 18 Nov. 1910; *s* of Albert and Emily Cragg; *m* 1938, Elsie Emery; three *d*. *Educ:* Tyndale Hall, Bristol; St John's Coll., Durham. LTh 1932, BA 1933, MA 1938. Curate: St Mary, Kirkdale, Liverpool, 1933-37; Cheadle Parish Church, Cheshire, 1937-38; Vicar: The Saviour, Blackburn, 1938-44; St James, Carlisle, 1944-57; Christ Church, Beckenham, 1957-78; Archdeacon of Bromley, 1969-78, Archdeacon Emeritus, 1978; Hon. Canon of Carlisle, 1956-57; of Rochester, 1963-78; Proctor in Convocation: for Carlisle, 1951-57; for Rochester, 1959-69. *Publications:* The Sole Sufficiency of Jesus Christ, 1961; The Holy Spirit and the Christian Life, 1962; The Encouragement of the Believer, 1964; Victory in the Christian Life, 1964. *Address:* Flat 10, 32 Albemarle Road, Beckenham, Kent BR3 2HJ.
[*Died* 27 *July* 1980.

CRAIG, Sir Arthur John Edward, Kt 1938; DL, JP; Custos Rotulorum of the Soke of Peterborough; *b* 9 June 1886; *s* of John Robert Craig; *m* 1908, Gertrude Ethel Rowe (*d* 1959); one *s* one *d*. *Educ:* St Peter's Coll. Mayor of City of Peterborough, 1928-29; five times Deputy Mayor; ex-Chm. Soke of Peterborough County Council; ex-Chm. County Finance and Gen. Purposes Cttee; ex-Chm. Governors Deacon's Sch., Peterborough; ex-Chm. ATC; Hon. Surveyor British Red Cross and Order of St John; Pres. Peterborough and North Northants Conservative Assoc.; Dir Woolwich Equitable Building Soc. Fellow Chartered Auctioneers and Estate Agents Inst. Chm. Arthur E. Craig & Co. Ltd, etc. Hon. Freeman of City of Peterborough. *Recreations:* billiards, golf. *Address:* Thorpefields, Peterborough. *Clubs:* Royal Automobile; City and Counties (Peterborough).   [*Died* 4 *May* 1972.

CRAIG, Elizabeth Josephine, MBE 1980; Cookery Expert, People's Friend; lecturer, broadcaster; *b* 16 Feb. 1883; *d* of late Rev. John Mitchell Craig, The Manse, Memus, Forfar, Angus, and Katherine Nichol; *m* 1919, A. E. Mann (*d* 1973), American War Correspondent and broadcaster; no *c*. *Educ:* George Watson's Ladies' Coll., Edinburgh. Editor of Woman's Life, 1915-18; Freelance from then onward, contrib. to daily, weekly, and monthly periodicals. Mem. Inst. Hygiene (MIH); Fellow of the Cookery and Food Association (FCFA); FRSA; Chevalière de Corteaux de Champagne; Dame de la Chaine des Rôtisseurs. *Publications:* Cooking with Elizabeth Craig, 1932, new edn 1961; (with A. Simon) Madeira, Wine, Cakes and Sauce, 1933; Entertaining with Elizabeth Craig, 1933; Standard Recipes, 1934; Economical Cookery, 1934; Wine in the Kitchen, 1934; Family Cookery, 1935; Woman, Wine and a Saucepan, 1936; Bubble and Squeak, 1936; Keeping House with Elizabeth Craig, 1936; Tested Recipes (boxed cards), 1936; The Housewife's Monthly Calendar, 1936; Cookery, 1937; Gardening, 1937; Housekeeping, 1937; Needlecraft, 1937; 1000 Household Hints, 1937; 1500 Everyday Menus, 1937; Simple Housekeeping, 1938; Simple Gardening, 1938; Enquire Within: the happy housewife's ABC, 1938; Cooking in Wartime, 1940; Practical Gardening, 1952; Court Favourites, 1953; Waterless Cookery, 1954; Beer and Vittels, 1955; The Scottish Cookery Book, 1956; Family Cookery, 1957, new edn 1971; Instructions to Young Cooks, 1957; Scandinavian Cooking, 1958; A Cook's Guide to Wine, 1959; Cottage Cheese and Yogurt, 1960; Banana Dishes, 1962;

Cooking Continental, 1965; What's Cooking in Scotland, 1965; The Art of Irish Cooking, 1969; The Business Woman's Cook Book, 1970; Hotch Potch, 1978; (ed) The Potluck Cookery Book by T. Campbell, 1962; (ed) Around the World on a Salad Bowl by V. Bennett and C. Kahman, 1963; (ed) Sunset: the Penguin salad book, 1965. *Recreations:* gardening, travelling, collecting antiques, attending wine tastings. *Address:* Withyfield, Green Lane, Farnham Common, Bucks. *Clubs:* Lyceum, Pen, Arts Theatre. [*Died 7 June* 1980.

CRAIG, Prof. John, MB, FRCPE; FSAScot; Professor of Child Health, University of Aberdeen, 1948-63, now Emeritus; *b* 4 Sept. 1898; *s* of John and Jane Craig; *m* 1929, Margaret, *y d* of late H. F. Morland Simpson, LLD; two *s. Educ:* Robert Gordon's Coll., Aberdeen; University of Aberdeen; Paris. Thompson Travelling Fellow of University of Aberdeen. Asst Physician, 1924, then Senior Physician, Royal Aberdeen Hosp. for Sick Children; Asst Physician, then Physician, Aberdeen Royal Infirmary, 1932-47. Paediatrician to Maternity Hosp. and City Hosp., Aberdeen; Pres., British Paediatric Assoc., 1956-57. Hon. Fellow, Amer. Acad. of Pediatrics. Hon. LLD. *Publications:* Pædiatrics in the North-Eastern Region of Scotland; A Short History of the Royal Aberdeen Hospital for Sick Children; articles in medical journals. *Recreations:* golf, archaeology. *Address:* 5 Albyn Terrace, Aberdeen. *T:* Aberdeen 26024. [*Died 19 April* 1977.

CRAIG, Sir John Herbert McCutcheon, KCVO 1949; Kt 1946; CB 1935; LLD; Deputy Master and Comptroller, Royal Mint, and ex-officio Engraver of the King's Seals, 1938-49, retired 1949; *b* 9 Feb. 1885; *s* of Robert James Craig, JP, and Anna Maria Millar; *m* 1920, Vera M. Worsfold (*d* 1974). *Educ:* Foyle Coll., Derry; Trinity Coll., Dublin (Classical Scholar). BA (Senior Moderator, University Student and Double Large Gold Medallist), 1907; LLD (jure dig.), 1946. Entered Treasury, 1908; Principal Asst Sec., Treasury, 1931. Freeman of City of London and Liveryman of Goldsmiths' Company, 1943. Chm. and Treasurer Sir John Cass's Foundation, 1950-57. *Publications:* Newton at the Mint, 1946; History of London Mint, 1953; A History of Red Tape, 1955; articles in Nature, Notes and Records of Royal Society, Proc. Royal Instn, etc. *Address:* Hydro Hotel, Eastbourne, East Sussex BN20 7HZ.
[*Died 8 April* 1977.

CRAIG, Prof. William Stuart McRae; Professor of Paediatrics and Child Health, University of Leeds, 1946-68, now Emeritus; *b* 19 July 1903; *s* of William Craig, MB, and Katherine Jane Stuart; *m* 1934, Beatrice Anne Hodgson. *Educ:* Bingley Grammar Sch.; Watson's Coll., Edinburgh; Universities of Edinburgh and Glasgow. BSc (Naval Architecture) Glasgow, 1924; Buchanan Scholarship, 1930; MB, ChB Edinburgh, 1930; MD Edinburgh, 1933; FRCPEd 1936; FRSE 1937; FRCP 1956. Formerly: Asst Paediatrician, Simpson Memorial Hosp., and Western Gen. Hosp., Edinburgh; Asst Pathologist, Royal Hosp. for Sick Children, Edinburgh; Children's Physician, Livingstone Dispensary, Edinburgh; Lectr and First Asst to Professor of Child Life and Health, University of Edinburgh; Hospital Officer and Medical Officer, Ministry of Health; EMS; Senior Paediatrician various Leeds hospitals; Consultant Adviser to City of Leeds Child Welfare and Sch. Health Cttees; Member: BMA; Yorks Council for Community Relations; Bd of Govs, Holly Bank Special Sch., Huddersfield; Chm., Leeds and District Spastic Soc. Honeyman Gillespie Lectr, 1952; first Charles McNeil Lectr, RCPE, 1969. Hon. Member: British Paediatric Assoc., 1969; Scottish Paediatric Soc., 1969. Corresponding Mem., Sociedade Portuguesa de Pediatria, 1952. Formerly Examiner in Child Health, Universities of Bristol, Aberdeen, Glasgow and Edinburgh, and RCPE. John Thomson Memorial Medal, 1931. *Publications:* Child and Adolescent Life in Health and Disease, 1946; Care of the Newborn, 4th Edn 1969; John Thomson, Pioneer and Father of Scottish Paediatrics, 1968; The Royal College of Physicians of Edinburgh, 1681-1973: its contribution to medicine, to the national history of Scotland, and to the civic history of Edinburgh, 1976; various reference books, medical and nursing periodicals. *Address:* Mellendean, Gifford, East Lothian. *Club:* Caledonian (Edinburgh). [*Died 21 June* 1975.

CRAIGAVON, 2nd Viscount (UK), *cr* 1927, of Stormont, County Down (NI); **James Craig,** Bt, *cr* 1918; *b* 2 March 1906; *s* of 1st Viscount and Dame Cecil Mary Nowell Dering, later Dowager Viscountess Craigavon, DBE (*d* 1960); *S* father, 1940; *m* 1939, Angela Fiona, *yr d* of Percy Tatchell, MRCS, LRCP; one *s* two *d. Educ:* Eton. Lieut-Comdr RNVR (retd). *Heir: s* Hon. Janric Fraser Craig, *b* 9 June 1944. *Address:* 27 Launceston Place, W8. *T:* 01-937 7615. [*Died 18 May* 1974.

CRAIGIE, James, OBE 1946; FRS 1947; MB, ChB, PhD, DPH; LLD St Andrews 1950; *b* 25 June 1899; *s* of James Craigie and Frances Stewart McHardy; *m* 1929, Margaret Kerr Scott Fotheringham; two *d. Educ:* Perth Acad.; University of St Andrews. Asst Medical Officer, Murray Royal, Perth, 1923; Asst in Bacteriology, University of St Andrews, 1927; Research Associate, Connaught Laboratories, Toronto, 1931, Research Mem., 1943; successively Lecturer in Epidemiology, 1932, Associate Prof. of Virus Infections, 1940, Prof. of Virus Infections, 1946, and Sec., 1935-45, at the Sch. of Hygiene, University of Toronto. Mem. of Scientific Staff, Imperial Cancer Research Fund, 1947-64; Mem., Joint United States-Canadian Commission (Rinderpest), 1942-46; Pres., Soc. of American Bacteriologists, 1946; FRS Canada, 1946; United States of America Typhus Commission Medal, 1946; Medal of Freedom, 1947; Stewart Prize (BMA), 1950. *Publications:* on bacteriology, virus diseases, typhoid phage-typing and experimental oncology. *Address:* 24 Inveralmond Drive, Edinburgh EH4 6JX.
[*Died 26 Aug.* 1978.

CRANBROOK, 4th Earl of, *cr* 1892; **John David Gathorne-Hardy,** CBE 1955; Viscount Cranbrook, 1878; Baron Medway, 1892; DL, JP Suffolk; Hon. MA Cantab; Member, East Suffolk County Council, 1934-74 (Chairman, 1950-57); *b* 15 April 1900; *e s* of 3rd Earl and Lady Dorothy Boyle, *y d* of 7th Earl of Glasgow; *S* father, 1915; *m* 1st, 1926, Bridget (who obtained a divorce 1930), *o d* of late Rupert D'Oyly Carte and later Dame Bridget D'Oyly Carte, DBE; 2nd, 1932, Fidelity, OBE 1972, JP Suffolk, *o d* of late Hugh E. Seebohm; two *s* three *d. Educ:* Eton; RMA, Woolwich. Gunner RFA, 1918-19; Lieut, RFA, 1921-32; Alderman LCC, 1928-30; Parliamentary Private Sec. to HM First Commissioner of Works (Earl Peel), 1927-28; Deputy Regional Commissioner for Eastern Civil Defence Region, 1940-45. Chm., East Anglian Regional Hosp. Bd, 1947-59. Hon. Air Cdre 3619 (Suffolk) Fighter Control Unit, RAuxAF, 1950-61. Trustee, British Museum (Natural History), 1963-73; Mem., Nature Conservancy Council, 1967-72. KStJ. *Heir: s* Lord Medway. *Address:* Red House Farm, Great Glemham, Saxmundham, Suffolk. *T:* Rendham 424. [*Died 22 Nov.* 1978.

CRANKO, John; Ballet Director, Wuerttembergische Staatsoper, Stuttgart, since 1961; Ballet Director, Munich, since 1968; *b* 15 Aug. 1927. *Educ:* Highlands North Sch., Johannesburgh. Started as dancer and choreographer, University of Cape Town Ballet and Cape Town Ballet Club; joined Sadler's Wells Ballet as a dancer, 1946; Resident Choreographer, 1951-57. Many ballets in repertoire of both Companies of the Royal Ballet; also for New York City Ballet, Ballet de l'Opéra de Paris, Ballet Rambert, and many opera ballets; produced Peter Grimes, Covent Garden, 1953. First revue, Cranks, written and produced Nov. 1952, at St Martin's Theatre, 1956. First British commissioned three-act ballet, The Prince of the Pagodas (score by Benjamin Britten), Royal Opera House, 1956, also La Scala, Milan and Metropolitan, New York, 1957; Ballets for Royal Opera House: Antigone, 1959; Brandenburg Concertos 2 and 4; Ballets for Stuttgart: Daphnis et Chloë, 1962; The Seasons, 1962; Romeo and Juliet, 1962; Leatro Armonico, 1963; Firebird, 1964; Jeu des Cartes, 1965; Onegin, 1965; Opus 1, 1965; Concerto for Flute and Harp, 1966; Nutcracker, 1966; Sonata for Cello Solo, 1967; Presence, 1968; Song of the Nightingale, 1968; Concerto, 1968; The Taming of the Shrew, 1969; Brouillard, 1970; Poème de l'extase, 1970; Orfeus, 1970; Carmen, 1971; Initials RBME (Brahms), 1971; Traces, 1973; Green, 1973. *Address:* 19 Alderney Street, SW1. *T:* 01-385 9974. [*Died 26 June* 1973.

CRANSWICK, Rt. Rev. Geoffrey Franceys, BA, ThD; *b* 10 April 1894; *s* of late Canon E. G. Cranswick, Sydney; *m* 1927, Rosamund Mary, 3rd *d* of late Blews Robotham, The Knoll, Littleover, Derby; one *s. Educ:* The King's Sch., Parramatta; Church of England Grammar Sch., N Sydney; University of Sydney (BA 1916); Ridley Hall, Cambridge. Tutor, Moore Theological Coll., Sydney, 1916; Travelling Sec., Australian Student Christian Movement, 1918; Curate, Parish Church, West Ham, 1920; Missionary CMS, Bengal, India, 1923-37, as Principal of King Edward's Sch., Chapra, Bengal; Organising Sec. CMS in Canterbury, Rochester and Chichester Dioceses, 1938; India Sec. at HQ CMS, 1938-43; Chm., India Cttee, Conference of British Missionary Socs, 1941; Bishop of Tasmania, 1944-63, retd. UNA Vice-Patron (Tasmania). *Recreations:* bowls, gardening. *Address:* 142 Davey Street, Hobart, Tasmania 7000, Australia. [*Died 19 July* 1978.

CRASKE, Rt. Rev. Frederick William Thomas; Assistant Bishop in diocese of London since 1961; Chairman of the Prison Chaplaincies Council of the Church Assembly, since 1961; *b* 11 May 1901; *s* of William James Craske; *m* Nellie, *d* of late Harold Wilson; two *s. Educ:* King's Coll. (City Exhibitioner), University of London (BA). Jelf Prize and AKC 1927; FKC

1954. Deacon, 1927; Priest, 1928; Curate of St Chrysostum, Victoria Park, Manchester, 1927-29; International Sec., 1929-30, London Sec., 1930-32, Student Christian Movement; Curate of All Hallows, Lombard Street, London, 1929-32; Lecturer, King's Coll., London, 1932; Vicar of: Read-in-Whalley, 1932-35; St John the Evangelist, Blackburn, 1935-39; Education Sec., Missionary Council of Church Assembly, 1939-50; Gen. Sec., Church of England Youth Council, 1942-44; Select Preacher, Cambridge Univ., 1943; Representative of British Council of Churches in Germany, 1950-53; Examining Chaplain to Bishop of Leicester, 1950-53; Bishop of Gibraltar, 1953-59; Moderator of the Central Advisory Council for the Ministry, 1960-65. Chaplain and Sub-Prelate, Order of St John of Jerusalem, 1956-. *Address:* 106 Grand Drive, Raynes Park, SW20.
[Died 10 *March* 1971.

CRASTER, Sir John Montagu, Kt 1955; *b* 5 June 1901; *s* of late Thos William Craster; *m* 1936, Vera Gwendolin, 5th *d* of late Robert Durward; no *c. Educ:* Clifton Coll.; Gonville and Caius Coll., Cambridge. High Sheriff of Northumberland, 1944. Chairman: Assoc. of Sea Fisheries Cttees for England and Wales, 1939-70; Northumberland Sea Fisheries Cttee, 1929-70; Alnwick Petty Sessions, 1957-72; Berwick-on-Tweed Conservative Assoc., 1946-49, 1953-56 (Pres., 1965-67); Alnwick RDC, 1945-48; CC Northumberland, 1947-57; CA, 1957-67; JP 1929-72. Alnwick NFU, 1932 and 1948; Northumberland Playing Fields Assoc., 1946-48; Member: Nat. Health Act Exec. Cttee, 1948-49; Northumberland Agric. Exec. Cttee, 1945-65; Exec. Cttee Northumberland County Landowners' Assoc., 1934-64; North Sunderland Harbour Commn, 1942-67; Vice-Chm., Farne Island Cttee of Nat. Trust, 1947-67; Mem. Home Office Advisory Cttee for Wild Birds' Protection Act, 1954-69; Pres. of Fisheries Organisation Soc., 1959-69, now Life Vice-Pres.; Member: Bledisloe Cttee Salmon and Freshwater Fisheries Acts, 1957-61; Humane Traps Panel, Dept of Agriculture for Scotland, 1965-71. Coronation Medal, 1953. *Publications:* Chapter XII, The Birds of Northumberland, in The Three Northern Counties of England, 1938; Naturalist in Northumberland, 1969; North-Country Squire, 1971; nature articles and notes to Cornhill Magazine, etc. *Recreations:* shooting, fishing, and ornithology. *Address:* Craster West House, Alnwick, Northumberland. *TA:* Craster, Craster. *T:* Embleton 225. *Club:* Farmers'.
[Died 8 *Dec.* 1975.

CRATHORNE, 1st Baron *cr* 1959, of Crathorne; **Thomas Lionel Dugdale,** 1st Bt, *cr* 1945; PC 1951; TD; Vice-Lieutenant, North Riding of Yorkshire, since 1957; R of O, Royal Scots Greys, 1928; Major Yorkshire Hussars Yeomanry, 1931; JP North Riding of Yorkshire; *b* 20 July 1897; *o s* of late J. Lionel Dugdale and late Maud Violet, *d* of G. W. P. Woodroffe, late Royal Horse Guards; *m* 1936, Nancy (*d* 1969), OBE 1961, *d* of Sir Charles Tennant, 1st Bt; two *s. Educ:* Eton; RMC Sandhurst. Joined Royal Scots Greys, 1916, and served European War, 1917-18; Capt. 1923; Adjt, Yorks Hussars (Yeomanry), 1927; War of 1939-45, on active service, 1939-41. MP (U) Richmond, Yorks, 1929-59; Parliamentary Private Sec. to Sir Philip Cunliffe Lister (when Pres. of Board of Trade, Aug.-Oct. 1931; Sec. of State for the Colonies, 1931-35 and Sec. of State for Air, 1935); Parliamentary Private Sec. to Mr Stanley Baldwin when Prime Minister, 1935-37; a Lord of the Treasury, 1937-40, and Dep. Chief Government Whip, 1941-42; Vice-Chm., Conservative Party Organisation, 1941-42, Chm., 1942-44. Pres. Nat. Union of Conservative and Unionist Assocs, 1951; Minister of Agriculture and Fisheries, 1951-54, resigned. UK Deleg., Council of Europe and W European Union, 1958-59, 1961-65; Delegate to NATO Parliamentarians Conf., 1958 (Pres., 1962-63) (Mem. Standing Cttee, 1958-65); Chairman UK National Cttee for Atlantic Congress, 1959; Mem. Adv. Commn on Central Africa, 1960; Chm. Deptl Cttee on the Law on Sunday Observance, 1961-64; Steward of Jockey Club, 1960-62 (Senior Steward, 1962); Mem., The Horserace Betting Levy Board, 1964-73; Chm. Political Honours Scrutiny Cttee, 1961-76; Chm. North of England Adv. Cttee for Civil Aviation, 1964-72. *Recreations:* shooting, fishing. *Heir:* s Hon. Charles James Dugdale [*b* 12 Sept. 1939; *m* 1970, Sylvia Mary, *yr d* of Arthur Montgomery, Wimbledon; one *d*]. *Address:* Crathorne Hall, Yarm, Cleveland. *T:* Eaglescliffe 780 235; House of Lords, SW1. *Clubs:* Carlton, White's, Buck's; Jockey (Newmarket).
[Died 26 *March* 1977.

CRAVEN, Prof. Avery O., LLD (Hon.), LittD (Hon.); Professor of History, The University of Chicago, 1927-54; now Emeritus Professor; *b* 1886; *s* of Oliver and Mary Pennington Craven; *m* 1936, Georgia Watson; one *d. Educ:* Simpson Coll (AB); University of Chicago (PhD); Harvard Univ. (MA). MA Cambridge, 1952. Instructor, Simpson Coll., 1908-11; Asst Prof., College of Emporia, 1920-23; Associate Professor; Michigan State Coll., 1924-25; University of Ill, 1925-27;

University of Chicago, 1927; Prof. of History, University of Sydney (Australia), 1948-49; Prof. of American History and Institutions, Cambridge, 1952-53. Hon. DHL: Wayne State Univ.; Purdue Univ. *Publications:* Soil Exhaustion as a factor in History of Virginia and Maryland, 1925; Edmond Ruffin, Southerner, 1931; The Repressible Conflict, 1936; Democracy in American Life, 1938; The Coming of the Civil War, 1942; The United States, Experiment in Democracy, 1947; Civil War in the Making, 1959; An Historian and the Civil War, 1964; Ending of the Civil War, 1968; Reconstruction, 1969; Rochel of Old Louisiana, 1975. *Address:* Dune Acres, RFD3, Chesterton, Indiana, USA. *T:* Chesterton 4722. *Club:* Quadrangle (Chicago, Ill).
[Died 21 *Jan.* 1980.

CRAWFORD, 28th Earl of, *cr* 1398, and **BALCARRES,** 11th Earl of, *cr* 1651; **David Robert Alexander Lindsay;** KT 1955; GBE 1951; DL; Baron Lindsay of Crawford before 1143; Baron Lindsay of Balcarres, 1633; Earl of Balcarres, Lord Lindsay and Balniel, 1651; Baron Wigan (UK), 1826; Premier Earl of Scotland; Head of House of Lindsay; Deputy Governor, Royal Bank of Scotland, since 1962; Trustee: British Museum, 1940-73; National Gallery, Oct. 1935-Dec. 1941, June 1945-June 1952, June 1953-July 1960 (Chairman, Jan. 1938-Dec. 1939 and May 1946-Dec. 1948); National Galleries of Scotland since 1947 (Chairman, 1952-); National Library of Scotland, since 1944 (Chairman, 1944-1974); The Pilgrim Trust since 1949; Chairman: Royal Fine Art Commission, 1943-57; National Trust, 1945-65; National Art-Collections Fund; *b* 20 Nov. 1900; *e s* of 27th Earl of Crawford and 10th of Balcarres and Constance (*d* 1947), *y d* of Sir Henry Pelly, 3rd Bt, MP, and the Lady Lilian Yorke; *S* father, 1940; *m* 1925, Mary, 3rd *d* of late Rt Hon. Lord Richard Cavendish, PC, CB, CMG; three *s. Educ:* Eton; Magdalen College, Oxford (Hon. Fellow, 1975). MP (C) Lonsdale Div. of Lancs, 1924-40. Tate Gallery, 1932-41; Mem. of Standing Commission on Museums and Galleries, 1937; Rector of St Andrews Univ., 1952-55. DL Fifeshire, 1953. Hon. LLD: St Andrews; Cambridge; Hon. LittD Manchester; Hon. DLit London; Hon. DLitt Exeter; Hon. DCL: Oxford; Warwick; Amherst Coll., Mass; Hon. DUniv York. RSA, FRIBA, FSA, FSAScot. *Heir:* s Baron Balniel, *qv. Address:* Balcarres, Colinsburgh, Fife. *Clubs:* Athenæum, Travellers'.
[Died 13 *Dec.* 1975.

CRAWFORD, Brig. Alastair Wardrop Euing; *b* 1896; *s* of Col E. R. Crawford, DL, of Auchentroig, Buchlyvie; *m* 1924, Helena Beatrice (*d* 1977), *d* of Adm. Sir Charles Dundas of Dundas, KCMG; one *s* two *d. Educ:* Glenalmond; RMC Sandhurst. Served European War, 1916-18; 2nd Lieut Royal Scots Greys, 1916; retired as Major, 1937. Recalled, 1939; Lt-Col Comdg 43rd Reconnaissance Regt, RAC, 1943-44; served in NW Europe, 1944-46, with HQ VIII Corps (despatches), Brig., 1945; retired, 1946. Mem. of Queen's Body Guard for Scotland (Royal Company of Archers), 1949. DL 1947-65, JP 1951-65. Vice-Lieut, 1964-65, Stirlingshire. *Recreations:* shooting, hunting. *Address:* La Fougeraie, Archirondel, Gorey, Jersey, CI. *T:* East 52504. *Clubs:* Cavalry and Guards, English-Speaking Union; New, Royal Caledonian Hunt (Edinburgh); Stirling and County.
[Died 3 *Oct.* 1978.

CRAWFORD, Sir Ferguson; *see* Crawford, Sir W. F.

CRAWFORD, Sir Frederick, GCMG 1961 (KCMG 1953; CMG 1951); OBE 1945; *b* 9 March 1906; *s* of James Mansfield Crawford, MD, Hull; *m* 1st, 1936, Maimie Alice (*d* 1960), *d* of John Harold Green, London and Cape Town; two *s*; 2nd, 1962, Clio, *widow* of Vasso Georgiadis, Uganda, and *d* of Jean Colocotronis, Athens. *Educ:* Hymers Coll., Hull; Balliol Coll., Oxford (BA). Colonial Civil Service; Cadet, Tanganyika, 1929; Asst District Officer, 1931; District Officer, 1941; seconded E African Governors' Conference, 1942-43 and 1945-46; Exec. Officer, Economic Control Board, Tanganyika, 1944-45. Economic Sec., N Rhodesia, 1947; Dir of Development, N Rhodesia, 1948-50. Governor and Comdr-in-Chief, Seychelles, 1951-53; Dep. Governor of Kenya, 1953-56; Governor of Uganda, 1956-Oct. 1961; Resident Director in Rhodesia: BSA Co., 1961-65; Anglo-American Corp. of SA Ltd, 1965-74. Retired. KStJ 1958. *Publication:* Review of the Northern Rhodesia Development Plan, 1948. *Recreations:* fishing, golf. *Address:* 89A Route de Florissant, Geneva, Switzerland. *Clubs:* Brooks's; Royal and Ancient Golf (St Andrews).
[Died 27 *May* 1978.

CRAWFORD, Joan; Actress; *b* 23 March; *d* of Thomas Le Sueur; *m* 1st, Douglas Fairbanks, jun. (divorced); 2nd, Franchot Tone (divorced); 3rd, 1942, Phillip Terry, actor (divorced, 1946); 4th 1955, Alfred N. Steele (*d* 1959); (one *s* three *d*, adopted). *Educ:* Kansas City. Won dancing contests; in chorus of Chicago revue; signed by J. J. Shubert for New York musical production; signed

by Metro-Goldwyn-Mayer Studios; later at Warner Brothers Studios; now free-lancing; appeared in Our Modern Daughters, Our Blushing Brides, Our Dancing Daughters, Possessed, Sadie McKee, Forsaking All Others, Gorgeous Hussy, Love on the Run, Last of Mrs Cheyney, The Bride Wore Red, Mannequin, The Women, No More Ladies, A Woman's Face, Reunion in France, Above Suspicion, Mildred Pierce, Humoresque, The Damned Don't Cry, Harriet Craig, This Woman is Dangerous, Torch Song, Johnny Guitar, Female on the Beach, Queen Bee, Autumn Leaves, The Story of Esther Costello; The Best of Everything; The Caretakers; Whatever Happened to Baby Jane?; Strait-Jacket; I Saw What You Did; Berserk!; Trog. *Publication:* (with Jane Kesner Ardmore) A Portrait of Joan, 1963; My Way of Life, 1972. *Recreations:* theatre, dancing. *Address:* 8008 W Norton Avenue, Los Angeles, Calif. 90046, USA.
[Died 10 May 1977.

CRAWFORD, Maj.-Gen. John Scott, CB 1945; CBE 1940; CEng, FIMechE; *b* 6 Feb. 1889; *s* of John Paton Crawford; *m* 1916, Amy Middleton-Andrews; two *s. Educ:* Liverpool Coll.; Campbell Coll., Belfast. RASC 1915-28; RAOC, 1928-39. Dir of Mechanization on formation of Ministry of Supply; Dep. Dir-Gen. of Tanks and Transport, and in 1943, Dep. Dir-Gen. of Armaments Production. Mem. of Council SMM & T (Vice-Pres., 1948-50; Hon. Treas. 1953-57). Mem. Inst. Engineering Inspection (Pres. 1953-54). Pres. Rubber Research Assoc., 1952-54. Vice-Pres. Liverpool Coll., Mem. Court of Worshipful Co. of Carmen, Master, 1957-58. Comdr, Order of Leopold II (Belgium), 1963. *Recreations:* golf, fishing. *Address:* 11 Glenmore House, Richmond Hill, Surrey. *T:* 01-940 1225. *Club:* Royal Automobile.
[Died 4 June 1978.

CRAWFORD, Sir (Walter) Ferguson, KBE 1958 (OBE 1921); CMG 1950; *b* 11 April 1894; *s* of H. F. Crawford, Melbourne, Vic., Australia; *m* 1927, Marjorie Vivienne Shirley; one *s* one *d. Educ:* Sydney Grammar Sch., Sydney, NSW; Sydney Univ.; New Coll., Oxford, NSW Rhodes Scholar, 1915. Served European War, 1914-18, in Argyll and Sutherland Highlanders, 1915-18 (despatches). Irak Political Service, 1919-21; Sudan Political Service, 1921-44; Governor Northern Province, Sudan, 1942-44; Palestine Govt Liaison Officer, 1944-46; Head of British Middle East Development Div. (Foreign Office), 1946-60. Dir-Gen., Middle East Assoc., 1960-64. *Recreation:* golf. *Address:* Baidland, Shant Lane, Churt, Surrey.
[Died 28 March 1978.

CRAWFORD, William Neil Kennedy Mellon, VRD 1955; Chairman, Amalgamated Quarries (Scotland) Ltd; Director, Robb Caledon Shipbuilders Ltd; *b* 8 Jan. 1910; *s* of Robert Crawford, MINA, MIES, and Flora Crawford (*née* Mellon); *m* 1939, Alison Gordon Lawrie, *d* of R. D. Lawrie, Edinburgh; two *d. Educ:* St Andrew's Coll., Dublin; George Watson's Coll., Edinburgh. Qual. Chartered Accountant, 1933; practiced in Edinburgh, 1933-77. Pres., Edinburgh Chamber of Commerce, 1975-77; Chm., Assoc. of Scottish Chambers of Commerce, 1976-77. Pres., Inst. Chartered Accountants of Scotland, 1973-74. Pres., Watsonian Club, 1977-78. MStJ 1972. *Address:* (home) Seaforth, Primrosebank Road, Edinburgh EH5 3JJ. *T:* 031-552 3806; (office) 18 Ainslie Place, Edinburgh EH3 6AX. *T:* 031-226 4161. *Clubs:* English-Speaking Union, Naval; New, Bruntsfield Links Golfing Society (Edinburgh).
[Died 4 Dec. 1978.

CRAXTON, (Thomas) Harold (Hunt), OBE 1960; Hon. RAM, Hon. RCM; Professor of Pianoforte, Royal Academy of Music, 1919-60; *b* 30 April 1885; *e s* of Thomas Robert Craxton, Devizes, Wilts; *m* 1914, Essie May Faulkner; five *s* one *d. Educ:* Latymer Upper Sch., Hammersmith. Accompanist to Madam Albani, Dame Clara Butt, Kennerley Rumford, Dame Nellie Melba and Elena Gerhardt, etc; has given many pianoforte recitals of early English music. *Publications:* pianoforte pieces and transcriptions of early writers. *Recreation:* golf. *Address:* 14 Kidderpore Avenue, NW3. *T:* 01-435 2965.
[Died 30 March 1971.

CREAMER, Amos Albert, DFC 1943; Public Trustee, since 1975; *b* 6 May 1917; *s* of late Amos and Anne Creamer; *m* 1946, Margaret Lloyd; one *s* one *d. Educ:* Owens Sch.; King's Coll., London. 1st class Hons LLB 1939. Entered Treasury, 1935, Inland Revenue, 1936. Served in RAF, Bomber and Training Comds (Sqdn Ldr), 1941-46. Entered Min. of Works, 1946; Asst Sec., 1956; Under-Sec., 1965; Under-Sec., Treasury, 1967, Civil Service Dept, 1968-75. *Address:* 5 Wildcroft Gardens, Edgware, Mddx.
[Died 22 Nov. 1978.

CREASEY, John, MBE 1946; author; *b* 17 Sept. 1908; *s* of Joseph Creasey and Ruth Creasey (*née* Creasey); *m* 1st, 1935, Margaret Elizabeth Cooke; 2nd, 1941, Evelyn Jean Fudge; 3rd, Jeanne

Williams; 4th, 1973, Mrs Diana Farrell. *Educ:* Fulham Elementary Sch.; Sloane Sch., Chelsea. Various clerical posts, 1923-35. Began writing, 1918, books, 1925; full time writing, 1935-; mostly crime novels; some travel. Liberal candidate, Bournemouth, 1950. Founder, All Party Alliance Movement, 1967; contested (APA) Nuneaton, 1967; Brierley Hill, April 1967; Gorton, Manchester, 1967; Oldham West, 1968. Founder Chm., Crime Writers' Assoc., 1953; Mem. Board of Mystery Writers of America, 1957-60 (Pres., 1966-67); Mem. Western Writers of America. Dir, Robert Sommerville Ltd (Literary Agents). *Publications:* 565 between 1932 and 1972; Toff series (55 titles); Dept Z series (30 titles); West of the Yard series (41 titles); Dr Palfrey series (33 titles); *pseudonyms:* as J. J. Marric, Gideon series (17 titles) (Gideon's Fire won 1961 "Edgar" for year's best crime novel, award of Mystery Writers of America); also books as Michael Halliday, Gordon Ashe, Anthony Morton (Baron series); as Norman Deane, and Jeremy York; *travel books:* Round the World in 465 Days, 1952; Let's Look at America, 1956; *philosophical:* Good, God and Man, 1968; *political:* Evolution to Democracy, 1969. *Recreation:* motoring. *Address:* New Hall, Bodenham, near Salisbury, Wilts. *T:* Bodenham 249; c/o Harold Ober, 40 East 49th Street, New York, NY 10017, USA. *Clubs:* National Liberal, Royal Automobile, Paternosters.
[Died 9 June 1973.

CREASY, Admiral of the Fleet Sir George Elvey, GCB 1953 (KCB 1949; CB 1944); CBE 1943; DSO 1940; MVO 1934; DL; *b* 13 Oct. 1895; *s* of late Leonard and late Ellen Maud Creasy; *m* 1924, Monica Frances Ullathorne; one *s. Educ:* RNC Osborne and Dartmouth. Joined HM Navy, 1908; Sub-Lt 1915; Lieut 1916; Comdr 1930; Capt. 1935; Rear-Adm. 1943; Vice-Adm. 1948; Adm. 1951; Adm. of the Fleet, 1955; Asst Dir of Plans, Naval Staff, 1936-38; comd 1st Destroyer Flotilla, 1938-40; Dir of Anti-Submarine Warfare, Naval Staff, 1940-42; commanded HMS Duke of York, 1942-43; Chief of Staff to the Allied Naval Commander-in-Chief, 1943-44; Admiral (Submarines), 1944-46; Flag Officer, Air, Far East, 1947; Fifth Sea Lord and Deputy Chief of Naval Staff (Air), 1948-49; Lord Commissioner of the Admiralty and Vice-Chief of Naval Staff, 1949-51; Commander-in-Chief, Home Fleet, 1952-54, and also Commander-in-Chief, Eastern Atlantic, under NATO, 1952-54; Commander-in-Chief, Portsmouth, 1954-57; also Commander-in-Chief, Home Station, Designate, 1954-57, and Allied C-in-C Channel Comd, under NATO, 1954-57. DL Essex, 1959. Comdr of the Order of Orange Nassau, 1942; Order of Polonia Restituta, 3rd class, 1942; Legion of Merit Degree of Comdr, 1946. *Address:* Old House, Great Horkesley, near Colchester, Essex. *T:* Great Horkesley 291. *Club:* United Service & Royal Aero.
[Died 31 Oct. 1972.

CREEDY, Sir Herbert (James), GCB 1933 (KCB 1919; CB 1915); KCVO 1923 (CVO 1917; MVO 1911); MA; Secretary and Registrar of the Distinguished Service Order since 1933; Member of Council, Union Jack Services Clubs; Member, Executive Committee, Lord Kitchener National Memorial Fund; *b* 3 May 1878; *m* 1904, Mabel Constance (*d* 1958), *d* of S. J. Lowry; one *d. Educ:* Merchant Taylors' Sch.; St John's Coll., Oxford (Scholar). 1st Class Classical Mods; 1st Class Lit. Hum.; Senior Scholar of St John's Coll., 1901-05; Hon. Fellow of St John's Coll., 1931; appointed to the War Office as Clerk of the Higher Division, 1901; seconded for special duty in S Africa, 1903; Resident Clerk, 1903-04; Private Sec. to Sir Edward Ward, Permanent Under-Sec. of State for War, 1903-08; Clerk to Comrs of Income Duty for Army Services, 1907-08; Asst Principal, War Office, 1908-20; Private Sec. to successive Secretaries of State for War (Col Seely, Mr Asquith, Earl Kitchener, Mr Lloyd George, Earl of Derby, Viscount Milner, and Mr Churchill), 1913-20; Asst to the Sec. of the War Office, 1916-20; Sec. of the War Office, 1920-24; Permanent Under-Sec. of State for War, 1924-39; Mem. and Sec. of the Army Council, 1920-39; retired from the Civil Service, 1939; re-employed with the Security Executive, 1940-45 (Chm., 1943-45). JP Co. of London, 1928-39; Governor of Wellington Coll., 1939-53, and Hon. Treas., 1941-50; a Comr Royal Hospital, Chelsea, 1945-57; a Trustee of Imperial War Museum, 1942-59; Member of various Cttees of the National Council, YMCA, 1939-64. OStJ 1931; Comdr Legion of Honour; Officer of the Belgian Order of the Crown; 2nd Class of the Russian Order of St Anne. *Address:* 93 Woodstock Road, Oxford. *T:* Oxford 55897. *Club:* United Service & Royal Aero.
[Died 3 April 1973.

CREIGHTON, Prof. Donald Grant, CC (Canada) 1967; University Professor, University of Toronto, 1967-71; Professor of History, 1945-71, and Chairman, Department of History, 1955-59, University of Toronto; *b* 1902; 2nd *s* of late Rev. William B. Creighton and of Laura Harvie; *m* 1926, Luella Sanders Browning Bruce; one *s* one *d. Educ:* Victoria Coll., University of Toronto; Balliol Coll., Oxford. Univ. Lectr, Dept of History, Univ. of Toronto, 1927; John Simon Guggenheim Memorial Fellowship, 1940-41; Rockefeller Fellowship, 1944-45; Nuffield Travelling Fellowship, 1951-52. Chm., Canadian Cttee, Encyclopedia Americana, 1956-63; Commonwealth Mem., Monckton Advisory Commn on Central Africa, 1959; Member: Ontario Adv. Cttee on Confedn, 1965-; Historic Sites and Monuments Bd of Canada, 1958-. Sir John A. Macdonald Prof., 1965. Fellow, Royal Soc. of Canada, 1946; Pres., Canadian Historical Assoc., 1956-57; Corresponding Member: Royal Historical Soc., 1966; British Acad., 1974. Tyrrell Medal, Royal Soc. Canada, 1951; Governor-General's Medal for Academic Non-Fiction, 1952 and 1955; Univ. of British Columbia's Medal for Biography, 1955; National Award in Letters, Univ. of Alberta, 1957. Molson Prize, awarded by Canada Council, 1964. Hon. LLD: Univs of New Brunswick, 1949; Queen's, Kingston, Ontario, 1956; Saskatchewan, 1957; British Columbia, 1959; St Francis Xavier, 1967; Victoria, BC, 1967; Dalhousie, 1970; Toronto, 1974; Hon. DLitt: Manitoba, 1957; McGill, 1959; Laurentian, 1970; Meml Univ., Newfoundland, 1974. *Publications:* The Commercial Empire of the St Lawrence, 1937; Dominion of the North: A History of Canada, 1944; John A. Macdonald: The Young Politician, 1952; John A. Macdonald: The Old Chieftain, 1955; The Story of Canada, 1959, 2nd edn, 1971; The Road to Confederation, 1964; Canada's First Century, 1970; Towards the Discovery of Canada, 1972; Canada: the heroic beginnings, 1974; The Forked Road: Canada, 1939-1957, 1976; Takeover (novel), 1978. *Address:* 15 Princess Street, PO Box 225, Brooklin, Ont, Canada. *Clubs:* Athenæum; Arts and Letters, University (Toronto).   *[Died 19 Dec. 1979.*

CRERAR, Hon. Thomas Alexander, PC (Canada); CC (Canada); LLD; *b* Molesworth, Ont, 17 June 1876; *s* of William S. Crerar, Scotch-Canadian, and Margaret McTavish, Scotch-Irish-Canadian; *m* 1906, Jessie, *d* of Alexander Hamilton, Solsgirth, Manitoba; one *d. Educ:* public schs and collegiate, Portage la Prairie, Manitoba. Teacher, farmer, grain elevator operator; invited to enter Union Government, 1917; PC Canada, 1917; Minister of Agriculture, 1917-19; MP Marquette, Manitoba, 1917-25; Leader of Progressive Party, 1921-22; appointed MP Brandon, 1929; Minister of Railways and Canals, 1929-30; defeated in election of 1930; Minister of Mines and Resources, Canada, 1935-45; Mem. Canadian Senate, 1945-66. Mem. of delegation representing Canadian Government at coronation of Their Majesties, 1937 and to Imperial Conference following; Representative of Canadian Government at Conference of Dominion Ministers to consider co-ordination of War effort, London, Nov. 1939. Former President: United Grain Growers Ltd; Grain Growers Export Co. Ltd; Public Press Ltd; and Country Guide Publishing Co. Ltd; Hon. Director, Algoma Steel Corp.; retd Director: Canada Steamships Ltd; Canada Permanent Trust; Modern Dairies of Winnipeg. Mem. United Church. Hon. LLD: Manitoba, 1954; Queen's, Kingston, 1967. *Address:* 2760 Lansdowne Road, Victoria, BC, Canada. *Clubs:* Manitoba, St Charles Country (Winnipeg); Rideau (Ottawa).   *[Died 11 April 1975.*

CRESSWELL, Rev. Cyril Leonard, KCVO 1959 (CVO 1946); MA, FSA, FRSA; Chaplain of The Queen's Chapel of the Savoy, 1933-61; Chaplain Emeritus of the Royal Victorian Order since 1961 (Chaplain, 1938-61); *b* 1890; *s* of late Rev. John Cresswell; *m* 1924, Madeleine Aglaé Blanche (*d* 1971), *d* of late Walter Southwell Jones. *Educ:* private; Emmanuel Coll., Cambridge; Ridley Hall, Cambridge. Curate of Holy Trinity, St Marylebone, 1919-23; Rector of St George's, Birmingham, 1923-26; Chaplain, St Mary's Hosp., Paddington, 1926-31; Mem. Governing Bd and Finance Cttee, 1931-48; Hon. Chaplain, 1931; Hon. Organising Sec., Anglican Evangelical Group Movement, 1941, Chm. 1942-43; Hon. Sec., Cromer Convention, 1927-34; Hon. Auditor, Clergy Orphan Corporation; Asst Grand Chaplain, Grand Lodge of England, 1946; Chaplain, Sancta Maria Lodge and Prince of Wales Lodge; Provincial Grand Chaplain, Middlesex, 1952; Mem. Executive, The Grenfell Assoc. of Great Britain and Ireland, 1930; Pres., Paddington and St Marylebone Rotary Club, 1934-35; Mem. Community Service Cttee of Rotary International Assoc. for Great Britain and Ireland, 1935; Burgess of the Manor and Liberty of the Savoy, 1934; Mem. Propaganda Cttee, King Edward's Hospital Fund for London, 1934; National Council of Social Service, 1935; Council of Bishop Wilson Theological Coll.; Court of the Corporation of the Sons of the Clergy; Trustee, Hyndman Bounty Trust, 1941-51; Council of Jerusalem and the East Mission, 1938-62; Gov., Cheltenham C of E Training Colls; Fellow, Royal Empire Soc.; Chaplain, The Saddlers' Co., 1942; Chaplain, Ven. Order of St John of Jerusalem, and Ecclesiastical Representative on Chapter Gen., 1962; Golden Lectr, 1944-45 and 1945-46; Worshipful Co. of Weavers, 1947; Chaplain to the Company and Limborough

Lectr, 1948-51; Freeman of City of London, 1948; Chaplain, Worshipful Co. of Farmers, 1949-67, and Mem. Court, 1949; Chaplain, Instn Electrical Engineers, 1951-61; Hon. Chaplain, Assoc. of Lancastrians in London, 1953-62 (Vice-Pres., 1962); Chaplain: Farmers' Club, 1951-67; Nat. Farmers' Union, 1955; Royal Agricultural Benevolent Instn, 1955; Royal Coll. of Veterinary Surgeons, 1956-62; Coun., The Fleming Memorial Fund for Medical Research, 1959; Vice-Pres., Univ. of London Assoc. of Lancastrians, 1960. *Recreations:* agriculture and farming, motoring, shooting, riding. *Address:* Three Barrows Place, Elstead, Surrey. *T:* Elstead 3286. *Clubs:* Athenæum, The Pilgrims, Royal Automobile.   *[Died 25 March 1974.*

CRESTON, Dormer (pen-name); *see* Colston-Baynes, D. J.

CRESWELL, Prof. Sir (Keppel) Archibald (Cameron), Kt 1970; CBE 1955 (MBE 1919); FBA 1947; FSA; Hon. DLitt Oxford; Hon. LitD Princeton; Hon. ARIBA; Professor of Muslim Architecture at the American University, Cairo, since 1956; Professor of Muslim Art and Archæology, at the Egyptian University, 1931-51; Rockefeller Foundation Fellowship, 1952-54; Order of Ismail (Comdr); Syrian Order of Merit, First Class; *b* 13 Sept. 1879; *o s* of Keppel Creswell, of Lloyd's, and Margaret, *d* of Thomas Henderson, Solicitor, Rugby. *Educ:* Westminster Sch. Studying Muslim art since 1910; served European war, 2/Lieut RFC, 1916; Staff Capt. RAF Middle East, 1918 (despatches thrice); Inspector of Monuments, Occupied Enemy Territory (Syria and Palestine), 1919-20; since then domiciled in Cairo; Cambridge Univ. Extension Lectr, 1924; on Cttee of Persian Exhibition, London, 1931; delivered Forlong Lectures (6), 1931; invited to Bicentennial of Princeton Univ. as Leader in Section of Near Eastern Art, 1947; awarded Sir Percy Sykes Memorial Medal by Royal Central Asian Society, 1948; Triennial Gold Medal of Royal Asiatic Society, 1959; Mem. Higher Council of Arabic Monuments and of Museum of Muslim Art; Mem. Council of Coptic Museum and of Coptic Archæological Soc.; Hon. Mem. Royal Central Asian Soc., American Oriental Soc. and Archäologisches Institut des Deutschen Reiches; Hon. Corresponding Mem. of Archæological Survey of India. Trustee Palestine Museum of Antiquities, 1949-54. Has travelled extensively in Syria, Palestine, Transjordan, Iraq, Eastern Turkey and Tunisia. *Publications:* Brief Chronology of the Muslim Monuments of Egypt, 1919; Origin of the Cruciform Plan of Cairene Madrasas, 1922; Archæological Researches at the Citadel of Cairo, 1924; The Works of Sultan Bibars, 1926; Early Muslim Architecture, vol. 1, 1932 (enl. edn in 2 vols, 1970), vol. 2, 1940; The Muslim Architecture of Egypt, Vol. 1, Fātimids, 1952, Vol. 2, Ayyūbids and Early Bahrite Mamlūks, 1959; A Short Account of Early Muslim Architecture (Pelican Book), 1958; A Bibliography of the Architecture, Arts and Crafts of Islam, 1961; also contributions to Burlington Magazine, The Indian Antiquary, Journal of RAS, Syria, Iraq, Ars Islamica, Byzantion, The Year-Book of Oriental Art, Archæologia, Ars Orientalis, the Encyclopaedia of Islam, new edn, The Ency. Brit., new edn, The Urdu Encyclopaedia of Islam, The Enciclopedia Universale dell' Arte, etc. *Address:* 2 rue Baehler, Qasr en-Nil, Cairo; School of Oriental Studies, The American University, Cairo. *T:* 40936. *Clubs:* Athenæum, Royal Automobile.   *[Died 8 April 1974.*

CRETNEY, Sir (William) Godfrey, Kt 1966; (first) Headmaster, The Regis School, Tettenhall, Wolverhampton, since 1955; *b* 24 Aug. 1912; *s* of Robert William and Amy E. Cretney; *m* 1940, Nancy Margaret, *d* of Lewis H. and Nancy Chesterton, Wallasey, Ches; two *s* one *d. Educ:* Douglas High Sch., IOM; Liverpool Univ. (BA Hons English, Dipl. Educn). War Service, Royal Corps of Signals, India Comd, 1940-46 (Major). Resident Master, Arnold Sch., Blackpool, 1934-38; Sen. English Master, Liverpool Inst. High Sch., 1939-48; (first) Headmaster, Castle Rushen High Sch., IOM, 1948-54. Member: Sec. of State's Consultative Cttee on Research into Comprehensive Educn, 1965-; Govt Cttee on Speech Therapy, 1969-; Educnl Res. Bd, SSRC, 1970-. Life Mem., Court of Governors of Birmingham, 1970. *Recreations:* walking, reading, sport. *Address:* 77 Yew Tree Lane, Tettenhall, Wolverhampton, Staffs. *T:* Wolverhampton 51012.   *[Died 17 May 1971.*

CREW, Francis Albert Eley, FRS 1939; TD; MD, DSc, PhD, DIH, FRCPE, FRSE; OStJ; Hon. DSc Benaras Hindu University; Hon. LLD Edinburgh University; Order of Polonia Restituta; Foreign Member Czecho-Slovakian Academy of Agriculture; Hon. Member National Veterinary Medical Association and Physiological Society of India; Member American Genetic Association; Hon. Member Polish Society of Arts and Sciences Abroad; Brigadier RAMC TA; late Commander, Edinburgh Special Constabulary; late Chairman Board of Governors, Royal (Dick) Veterinary College; *b* 1886; *m* 1913, Helen Campbell Dykes, MB, ChB (*d* 1971); one *s* one *d* ; *m*

1972, Margaret Ogilvie Withof-Keus, LRCS, LRCP. *Educ:* King Edward VI's High Sch., Birmingham; Univs of Birmingham and Edinburgh, MB, ChB 1912. Served European War, India and France, 1914-18; 6th Bn The Devonshire Regt and No 3 FA, RAMC Guards Div.; OC, Military Hosp., Edinburgh Castle, 1939-40; ADMS Edinburgh Area, 1940-42; Dir Medical Research, WO, 1942-46; Service Sub-Editor Official Medical History of the War. Asst in Natural History Dept, Univ. of Edinburgh, 1919-21; Buchanan Prof. of Animal Genetics, 1928-44 and Dir of Inst. of Animal Genetics, 1921-44, Univ. of Edinburgh; Prof. of Public Health and Social Medicine, Edinburgh Univ., 1944-55; Prof. of Preventive and Social Medicine, Ein Shams Univ., Cairo, Feb.-Nov. 1956; WHO Vis. Prof. of Prev. and Social Med., Univ. of Rangoon, 1957-58, Topiwala Nat. Med. Coll., Univ. of Bombay, 1959-60. Adviser in Genetics to Dir, Central Family Planning Inst., New Delhi, (for ODM), 1966-67. OC, Edinburgh Univ. OTC med. unit, 1920-29; Keith prizeman, RSE, 1937-39; Lt-Col Comdg 1st Edinburgh Bn Home Guard, 1954-56. Mem. Army Health Adv. Cttee, 1946-56; Chm. Board of Management, Edinburgh Central Group of Hospitals, 1946-56. 1st William Withering Lectr, Univ. of Birmingham, 1927; Milroy Lectr, RCP, 1928; Galton Memorial Lectr, Eugenics Soc., 1953; Charles Hastings Memorial Lectr, BMA, 1954; George Frederic Still Memorial Lectr, British Pædiatric Assoc., 1955; Nursing Mirror Lectr, Univ. of Edinburgh, 1962. Pres., 2nd Internat. Congress of Sex Research, 1930; Section D British Assoc., 1937; Assoc. of British Zoologists, 1937; Genetical Soc., 1938-39; VIIth Internat. Genetical Congress, 1939. Freeman, City of London, in Co. of Apothecaries. *Publications:* Official (Army) Medical History of the War; Health, its Nature and Conservation, 1965; The Foundations of Genetics, 1965; text-books on animal genetics, genetics of sexuality, organic inheritance in man, sex-determination, genetics of the budgerigar, genetics in relation to clinical medicine, essays in social medicine, hygiene; numerous papers dealing with these and related matters. *Recreations:* books, gardening, Mendelian experimentation with bantams and Australian finches. *Address:* Upton's Mill, Framfield, Sussex. *T:* Framfield 336. *Club:* Athenæum. *[Died 26 May 1973.*

CREWDSON, Bt-Col William Dillworth, CB 1947; TD; DL; JP; Member Westmorland County Council, 1924, Alderman, 1943, retired 1970; *b* 6 Nov. 1897; *e s* of late Canon Crewdson; *m* 1907, Cicely Maud (*d* 1966), *d* of John Bruce Nichols, Holmwood; three *d*. *Educ:* Marlborough Coll.; Trinity Coll., Cambridge. MA, LLB; Barrister-at-law; served European War, 1914-18, 4th Bn Border Regt; commanded 4th Bn The Border Regt 1919-25; commanded 11th Bn Westmorland Home Guard, 1940-45. *Address:* Helme Lodge, Kendal, Westmorland. *T:* Kendal 172. *[Died 19 Feb. 1972.*

CREWE, Bertie Gibson, CBE 1948 (OBE 1930; MBE 1926); *b* 15 Oct. 1884; *e s* of Frederick Crewe; *m* 1920, Ethel Emily Ireland (*d* 1960); two *d*. *Educ:* Bancroft's Sch., Woodford Wells. Secretary to British Empire Patents Conf., 1922, Patents Cttee of Imperial Economic Conf., 1923, Dating of Patents Cttee, 1926 and Copyright Royalty (Mechanical Musical Instruments) Enquiry, 1928; member of UK Delegation: to Conf. of Internat. Industrial Property Union at The Hague, 1925, Berne, 1926, London, 1934 and Neuchatel, 1947; to Confs of Internat. Copyright Union at Rome, 1928, Brussels, 1948; to Internat. Conf. on German-owned Patents at London, 1946; Asst Comptroller, HM Patent Office, 1938-50, UK Mem. Cttee of Copyright Experts of UNESCO, 1949. *Address:* Little Pentrelew Annexe, Restronguet Point, Feock, Truro, Cornwall. *T:* Devoran 862693. *[Died 15 June 1971.*

CRICHTON MAITLAND, Col Mark Edward Makgill; *see* Maitland.

CRICK, Rt. Rev. Douglas Henry, DD; Hon. Assistant Bishop, Diocese of Gloucester, 1957-67; Bishop of Chester, 1939-55; 2nd *s* of Rev. Philip Crick, MA, Waresley Vicarage, near Sandy; *m* 1st, 1914, Evelyn (*d* 1960), 2nd *d* of Rev. J. C. Vernon, Sherburn Vicarage, Malton, E Yorks; one *s* three *d*; 2nd 1961, Mary, 2nd *d* of Rev. B. Wright, Catbrook, Chipping Campden, Glos. *Educ:* Winchester Coll. (scholar); New Coll., Oxford (scholar). Ordained 1908; Chaplain, Mersey Mission to Seamen, 1908-12; Maltby Main Colliery Village, 1912-16; Asst Master Winchester Coll., 1916-17; Housemaster Bradfield Coll., 1917-18; Vicar of Wednesbury, Staffs, 1918-24; Rector of Stoke on Trent, 1924-35; Archdeacon of Stoke on Trent, 1932-35; Bishop Suffragan of Stafford, 1934-39; Rector of Edgmond, 1935-39; Prebendary of Lichfield Cathedral, 1929-39; Chaplain and Sub-Prelate Order of St John of Jerusalem; Chairman of Industrial Christian Fellowship, 1947-55. *Recreation:* reading. *Address:* The Haven, Chipping Campden, Glos. *T:* Evesham 840679.
[Died 5 Aug. 1973.

CRIPPS, Sir Cyril Thomas, Kt 1971; MBE 1944; Chairman, Pianoforte Supplies Ltd, Simplex Works, Roade, Northampton, since 1919; *b* 21 April 1892; *s* of Ernest Henry and Emmeline Harriet Cripps; *m* 1913, Amy Elizabeth Humphrey; one *s* two *d*. *Educ:* Archbishop Sumner's Memorial Sch., Kennington, London. Chairman, Northampton Rural District Council, 1961-74 (elected RDC, 1950; Vice-Chm., 1954); County Alderman, Northamptonshire County Council, 1963-74 (elected CC, 1954). Hon. LLD, Nottingham Univ., 1961; Treasurer, Nottingham Univ., 1964-73. *Address:* Three Ways, Roade, Northampton.
[Died 19 June 1979.

CRIPPS, Dame Isobel, GBE 1946; *b* 25 Jan. 1891; 2nd *d* of late Harold William Swithinbank, FRGS, DL, JP, RN, Denham Court, Bucks; *m* 1911, Rt Hon. Sir Stafford Cripps, PC, CH, FRS, QC (*d* 1952); one *s* three *d*. FRSA. Special Grand Cordon of Order of Brilliant Star, 1st class, China, 1946; Award of Nat. Cttee of India in celebration of Internat. Women's Year, 1976. *Address:* Greyholme, Minchinhampton, Stroud, Glos GL6 9HS. *T:* Brimscombe 3089. *[Died 11 April 1979.*

CRIPPS, William Parry, CBE 1964; *b* 23 June 1903; *o s* of late Captain Egerton Tymewell Cripps, MC, South Cerney Manor, Cirencester; *m* 1941, Catherine Isabel, 2nd *d* of late Rev. C. A. Sturges-Jones and *widow* of Major O. Oldridge de la Hey; one *s* decd. *Educ:* Wellington. Dir H. & G. Simonds Ltd, Reading, retired 1962; Chm. Cirencester Benefit Soc. CC Glos, 1961-; High Sheriff, Glos, 1963. *Address:* Stratton Cleeve, Cirencester, Glos. *T:* 3464. *[Died 18 Dec. 1972.*

CRISP, Col Rev. Alan Percy, DSO 1918; OBE 1944; VD; LLB; JP; Assistant Parish Priest, St George, Hobart, Tasmania, since 1970; *b* 23 Dec. 1889; *s* of late Samuel Percy and Myra Gertrude Crisp, Hobart; *m* Doris Lillian, 2nd *d* of late William Henry Ellis and Emily Selina Ellis, Dysart House, Kempton, Tasmania; one *s*. *Educ:* University of Tasmania. Enrolled a practitioner of the Supreme Court of Tasmania, 1912; Lieut in 3rd Field Artillery Brigade, Australian Imperial Forces, 1914; served on Gallipoli, 1915 (promoted Capt.); served in France and Belgium, 1916-18 (promoted Major, despatches thrice, DSO, Croix de Guerre); promoted Lieut-Col AMF; commanded 6th Field Artillery Bde, 1924-28 and 1939-40; ADC to Gov.-Gen. of Australia (Lord Gowrie), 1939-40; comd a Field Regt Royal Australian Artillery, 1940-42; Staff Officer with 2nd AIF, 1942-46 (Temp. Col, 1945); served Palestine, Egypt, New Guinea, Solomon Islands and Dutch East Indies; transferred to R of O, AMF, 1946, with rank of Hon. Col; Retired List, with rank of Hon. Col, 1948. Retired from active practice as Barrister and Solicitor, 1948. Police Magistrate, 1953-65; Chm. Licensing Court (Tasmania), 1954-65. Ordained Deacon of Church of England in Tasmania, 1969; Priest, 1970. *Recreation:* walking. *Address:* 4 Albuera Street, Hobart, Tasmania. *Clubs:* Royal Automobile of Tasmania, Naval and Military (Hobart.
[Died March 1972.

CRISPIN, Geoffrey Hollis, QC 1961; a Recorder (formerly Recorder of Rochester), since 1968; *b* 15 May 1905; *s* of Harry Crispin, Rochester; *m* 1931, Winifred, 4th *d* of A. J. Baldwin, Berkhamsted; two *s* one *d*. *Educ:* Rochester Mathematical Sch.; London Univ. Barrister-at-Law, 1937. Comr of Assize, 1963, 1965; Dep. Chm., Herts QS, 1965-71. *Address:* The Tile House, Chipperfield, Herts. *T:* Kings Langley 62264. *Club:* MCC.
[Died 16 April 1976.

CRITCHLEY, Alexander; accountant; *b* 17 Dec. 1893; *s* of William Edwin and Elizabeth Alice Critchley; *m* 1925, Lucy Lindasy; one *s* two *d*. *Educ:* Liverpool. FSAA 1924. Formerly Mem., Liverpool City Council; Hon. Alderman, City of Liverpool, 1964; MP (U) Edgehill Div. of Liverpool, 1935-45. Dep. Chm. Electricity Cttee, Liverpool City Council, 1922. *Recreations:* golf, tennis. *Address:* 3 Rydecroft, Vale Road, Woolton, Liverpool L25 7UT. *[Died 4 Sept. 1974.*

CROCKER, Sir William Charles, Kt 1955; MC; solicitor (retired); *b* 19 May 1886; *s* of T. E. Crocker; *m* 1st, Mary Madeline (*d* 1953), *d* of A. H. Tailby; one *s* five *d*; *m* 2nd, 1956, Ruth, *d* of Harry Chandler, Los Angeles, Calif., and *widow* of Col James G. Boswell. Served articles with father; admitted solicitor, 1912; Mem. of Disciplinary Cttee under Solicitors Act, 1949-60; Pres., Law Soc., 1953-54. Served European War, Artists Rifles; 2nd Lieut 4th Dorset Regt (MC). Hon. Mem. American Bar Assoc., 1958. *Publications:* Far from Humdrum, 1967; Tales From the Coffee House, 1973. *Recreations:* travel, reading. *Address:* Crockers', Seal Chart, Kent. *T:* Sevenoaks 61458; 1155 Oak Grove Avenue, San Marino, Calif., USA. *T:* Sycamore 32079. *Clubs:* Arts, Royal Automobile.
[Died 29 Sept. 1973.

CROFT, Sir John William Graham, 4th Bt cr 1818; Lieutenant late RHA; b 30 May 1910; s of late William Graham Croft, 4th s of 2nd Bt, and Marjorie, d of late Rev. T. G. S. Hall; S uncle, 1930. Educ: Stowe. Heir: cousin Major John Archibald Radcliffe Croft [b 27 March 1910; m 1953, Lucy Elizabeth Jupp; one s]. Address: Rayham Farm, Whitstable, Kent CT5 3DZ.
[Died 2 Feb. 1979.

CROFT-COOKE, Rupert, BEM (mil.); novelist, playwright, biographer, writer of books on travel, food and wine, circus, gypsies; b Edenbridge, Kent, 20 June 1903; s of late Hubert Bruce Cooke, London Stock Exchange, and late Lucy, d of Dr Alfred Taylor. Educ: Tonbridge Sch.; Wellington Coll., Salop (now Wrekin Coll.). Founded and edited weekly, La Estrella, Argentina, 1923-24; antiquarian bookseller, 1929-31; Lecturer in English Institute Montana, Zugerberg, Switzerland, 1931, etc. Joined Intelligence Corps, 1940; served Madagascar campaign (BEM (mil.)), 1942; commnd 3rd (Queen Alexandra's Own) Gurkha Rifles, 1943; Capt. (Field Security Officer) Poona Dist, 1944; Instr, Intell. Sch., Karachi, 1945; FSO, Delhi Dist, 1945-46. Book Critic, The Sketch, 1947-53. Publications: four early books of poems; Twenty Poems from the Spanish of Becquer, 1926; Some Poems, 1929; Troubadour, 1930; Banquo's Chair (play), 1930; Give him the Earth, 1930; Tap Three Times (play), 1931; Night Out, 1932; Cosmopolis, 1932; Release the Lions, 1933; Picaro, 1934; Shoulder the Sky, 1934; Deliberate Accident (play), 1934; Blind Gunner, 1935; Crusade, 1936; God in Ruins, 1936; Kingdom Come, 1937; The World is Young, 1937; Rule, Britannia, 1938; Darts, 1938; Pharaoh with his Wagons, 1938; How to get more out of Life, 1938; Same Way Home, 1939; Major Road Ahead (ed), 1939; Glorious, 1940; Octopus, 1946; Ladies Gay, 1946; The Circus Book (ed), 1947; Rudyard Kipling (English Novelists Series), 1948; Wilkie, 1948; Brass Farthing, 1950; Three Names for Nicholas, 1951; Cities, 1951; The Sawdust Ring, 1951; Nine Days with Edward, 1952; Harvest Moon, 1953; A Few Gypsies, 1955; Fall of Man, 1955; Sherry, 1955; Seven Thunders, 1956 (film, 1957); Port, 1957; Barbary Night, 1958; Smiling Damned Villain; Thief, 1960; English Cooking; Madeira, 1961; Wine and Other Drinks, 1962; Bosie, 1963; Clash by Night (film), 1963; Paper Albatross, 1965; The Gorgeous East, 1965; Feasting with Panthers, 1967; The Ghost of June, 1968; The Sound of Revelry, 1969; Wolf from the Door, 1969; Exotic Food, 1969; Exiles, 1970; Under the Rose Garden, 1971; While the Iron's Hot, 1971; The Unrecorded Life of Oscar Wilde, 1972; Nasty Piece of Work, 1973; autobiographical series, The Sensual World: The Man in Europe Street, 1939; The Circus has no Home, 1940; The Moon in My Pocket, 1948; The Life for Me, 1953; The Blood-Red Island, 1953; The Verdict of You All, 1955; The Tangerine House, 1956; The Gardens of Camelot, 1958; The Quest for Quixote, 1959; The Altar in the Loft, 1960; The Drums of Morning, 1961; The Glittering Pastures, 1962; The Numbers Came, 1963; The Last of Spring; The Wintry Sea, 1964; The Purple Streak, 1966; The Wild Hills, 1966; The Happy Highways, 1967; The Licentious Soldiery, 1971; The Dogs of Peace, 1973; The Caves of Hercules, 1974; The Long Way Home, 1975; The Green Green Grass, 1977. Address: c/o Grindlay's Bank Ltd, 13 St James's Square, SW1Y 4LF.
[Died 10 June 1979.

CROFT-MURRAY, Edward, CBE 1966; Keeper, Department of Prints and Drawings, British Museum, 1954-72; b Chichester, 1 Sept. 1907; s of Bernard Croft-Murray; m 1945, Giovanna, d of Count Aurelio Saffi; one d; m 1960, Rosemary Jill Whitford-Hawkey; one d. Educ: Lancing Coll.; Magdalen Coll., Oxford. Asst Keeper, Dept of Prints and Drawings, Brit. Museum, 1933; Dep. Keeper, 1953. Served War, 1939-46: Admiralty, 1939-40; Civilian Officer, Military Intelligence, War Office, 1940-43; Major, Allied Control Commission (Monuments and Fine Arts Section), Italy and Austria, 1943-46. Member: Bd, Cecil Higgins Art Gallery, Bedford; Council for Places of Worship; Whitworth Art Gall., Manchester; Benton Fletcher Collection, Fenton Hse (Nat. Trust); Advisor to Nat. Trust on musical instruments; Musicians' Union; Painter-Stainers' Co., 1971. FSA 1940. Publications: Venetian Drawings of the XVII and XVIII Centuries, at Windsor Castle (with Prof. Anthony Blunt), 1957; Catalogue of British Drawings in the British Museum, Vol. I (with Paul Hulton), 1960; Decorative Painting in England, 1537-1837, Vol. I, 1962, Vol. II, 1971; papers in Archaeologia, Apollo, Burlington Magazine, British Museum Year Book, Country Life and Walpole Society. Recreations: music (especially that of the XVIIIth and early XIXth century); study of wall-painting in England. Address: 4 Maids of Honour Row, Richmond Green, Surrey. T: 01-940 2548; Croft Castle, near Leominster, Herefordshire. Clubs: Athenæum, Beefsteak.
[Died 18 Sept. 1980.

CROFTON, 5th Baron cr 1797; Edward Blaise Crofton; Bt 1758; b 31 May 1926; o s of late Hon. Edward Charles Crofton and Cecilia Mabel, d of John T. Day and widow of Alexander Francis Macdonald; S grandfather, 1942; m 1st, 1948, Ann (marr. diss. 1963), e d of Group Capt. Charles Tighe, Ballina Park, Co. Wicklow; three s one d; 2nd, 1964, Mrs Mary Irvine Flach, er d of late J. I. H. Friend, OBE, MC, DL, JP, Northdown, Thanet. Heir: s Hon. Charles Edward Piers Crofton, b 27 April 1949. Address: Fowey Lodge, Fowey, Cornwall.
[Died 13 June 1974.

CROFTON, Brig. Roger, CIE 1942; MC; Indian Army (retired); b 13 March 1888; s of late Col Malby Edward Crofton; m 1914, Stella Clifton (d 1916), d of Judge T. G. Carver, KC; m 1921, Dorothy Frances (d 1953), d of Col H. M. Hatchell, DSO; one s; m 1954, Marjorie, widow of J. Johnston May. Educ: Rossall Sch.; RMA Woolwich. RA, 1907-32; served European War (MC, Bt Major, despatches twice); IA, 1932-42; Dir of Artillery (afterwards Armaments), 1938-42. Address: c/o Lloyds Bank Ltd, 6 Pall Mall, SW1.
[Died 4 May 1972.

CROFTS, John Ernest Victor; b 6 May 1887; e s of Rev. John Crofts, vicar of Dalton, near Southport; m 1915, Sibyl Ann, d of Rev. C. Hony, Woodborough, Wilts; two s. Educ: Magdalen Coll. Sch.; Queen's Coll., Oxford (Bible Clerk). First class hons in English Language and Literature, 1909; BLitt 1914; Senior Demy, Magdalen Coll., 1913-15; Asst Lecturer in English at University Coll., Reading, 1912-19; served with 101st Field Ambulance, 1915-18 (corporal); Winterstoke Prof. of English in the University of Bristol, 1919-41; Public Orator, University of Bristol, 1929-36; co-opted mem. of Bristol Education Cttee, 1938-41; mem. of John Lewis Partnership Ltd (Partners' Counsellor), 1941-52. Publications: Field Ambulance Sketches, by a Corporal, 1920; Gray, Poetry and Prose, 1926; Shakespeare and the Posthorses, 1927; Romeo and Juliet (The Warwick Shakespeare, 1938); Packhorse, Waggon and Post, 1967. Address: Stonethwaite, Borrowdale, Keswick, Cumberland.
[Died 8 May 1972.

CROKE, Air Commodore Lewis George Le Blount, CBE 1941; late Royal Air Force; b 28 July 1894; s of C. W. Le B. Croke, Solicitor; m 1925, Phyllis Mary, d of late George Churcher; two d. Educ: Merchant Taylors' Sch., London. Merchant Service, 1910-14; European War, Royal Naval Reserve, till 1917; RNAS and RAF Observer, 1917; took Wings, 1923; served in various Home Stations and abroad as Flight Comdr and Sqdn Comdr till 1939; Sqdn Leader, 1929; Wing Comdr, 1936; Group Capt., 1939; Air Commodore, 1941; retired list, 1945. Recreations: fencing and shooting. Address: White Cottage, Frampton, Dorchester, Dorset.
[Died 16 Feb. 1971.

CROMBIE, George Edmond, CMG 1950; HM Diplomatic Service, retired; b 14 June 1908; s of Dr James M. P. Crombie, Aberdeen. Educ: Fettes Coll., Edinburgh; Aberdeen Univ. Asst Principal, India Office, 1931; Principal, 1937. War of 1939-45. Lieut 1st Frontier Force Regt, Indian Army, 1942-45; served in Italy (despatches). Returned to India Office, 1945; Asst Sec., Burma Office, 1947; UK Dep. High Comr, Rangoon, 1947; Counsellor, HM Embassy, Rangoon, 1948-49; Dep. High Commissioner for UK, Madras, 1951-53; Counsellor, UK High Commission, Ottawa, 1955-58; Dep. High Commissioner for UK in Federation of Malaya, 1959-60; Counsellor, British Embassy, Dublin, 1961-65; British High Commissioner in The Gambia, 1965-67. Recreations: golf, swimming. Address: 212 Queen's Road, Aberdeen AB1 8DJ. Club: University (Aberdeen).
[Died 8 Dec. 1972.

CROMBIE, Rear-Adm. (Retd) John Harvey Forbes, CB 1952; DSO 1943; b 16 Feb. 1900; o s of late James Forbes Crombie, Woodside, Aberdeenshire; m 1934, Rosamond, e d of late Brig.-Gen. Rodney Style, Wierton Grange, Boughton Monchelsea, Kent; one s three d. Educ: St Aubyn's, Rottingdean; RN Colls Osborne and Dartmouth. Served European War, HMS Queen Elizabeth and HMS Oak, 1916-18. Qualified in Signals, 1924; later served on staffs of Adm. Sir Maurice Fitzmaurice, Adm. Sir Frederic Dreyer, Adm. Sir Howard Kelly, Adm. Sir William Fisher. Served War of 1939-45, HMS Repulse (despatches), 1939-41; Capt., 1941; Senior Officer Minesweepers, N Russia, 1941-43 (HMS Bramble); Dir of Minesweeping, 1943-46; HMS Vengeance, in command, 1946-48; HMS Mercury, in command, 1948-50; Rear-Adm. 1950; Flag Officer, Scotland, and Adm. Supt, Rosyth, 1951-53. ADC to King George VI, 1950; Mem. Queen's Body Guard for Scotland (The Royal Company of Archers). Order of Alexander Nevsky, 1943; Legion of Merit (USA), 1944; Order of Orange Nassau, 1945. Address: Gateside House, Gullane, East Lothian. T: Gullane 3139. Clubs: United Service and Royal Aero; New (Edinburgh).
[Died 31 Aug. 1972.

CRONE, Anne; author; Modern Languages Mistress, Princess Gardens School, Belfast, since 1948; *b* 16 Sept. 1915; *d* of William Crone, MBE, former Asst Sec., Ministry of Commerce for NI, and Mary Jane Plunkett. *Educ:* Methodist Coll., Belfast; Somerville Coll., Oxford (MA, BLitt). Three Prizes (Somerville); 1st Cl. Final Hon. Sch. Mod. Langs; Grad. Schol. Modern Languages Mistress, Victoria Coll., Belfast, 1938-45. *Publications:* novels: Bridie Steen, 1948 (New York), 1949 (London); This Pleasant Lea, 1951 (New York), 1952 (London); My Heart and I, 1955 (London). *Address:* 10 King's Road, Knock, Belfast 5. *T:* 653112.   *[Died 25 Oct. 1972.*

CRONE, Col Desmond Roe, CIE 1946; OBE 1941; MSc; *b* 24 Sept. 1900; 4th *s* of late John Smythe Crone, LRCPI, Willesden; *m* 1932, Margaret, 2nd *d* of late Rev. W. E. Wilkie Brown, MA, KIH, Edinburgh; three *s. Educ:* Kilburn Grammar Sch.; RMA Woolwich. Commissioned Royal Engineers, 1920; joined Survey of India, 1924; served with Indo-Afghan Boundary Commission, 1932; Operations NW Frontier, 1930 and 1933; Captain, 1931; Major 1938; Lt-Col 1945; retired 1948, Hon. Col. Senior Lectr in Surveying, University of the Witwatersrand, Johannesburg, 1947-49, and Queen's Univ., Belfast, 1954-62. FRSA 1934. *Publication:* Elementary Photogrammetry, 1963. *Recreations:* yachting, gardening. *Address:* 9 Levens Way, Silverdale, Carnforth LA5 0TG. *Club:* Royal Commonwealth Society.
                                                    [Died 23 Nov. 1974.

CRONIN, Henry Francis, CBE 1944; MC; BSc (Eng.); FCGI; FICE, FIWE; Chief Engineer, Metropolitan Water Board, London, 1939-59, retired; *b* 12 May 1894; *s* of Dominic and Annie Cronin; *m* 1926, Beatrice Warburton Stent; one *s. Educ:* Beaumont Coll.; Brighton Municipal Technical Coll.; City and Guilds Engineering Coll., South Kensington. Served European War, 1914-18, in Infantry and Royal Engineers (despatches, twice wounded, MC); entered service of Metropolitan Water Board in 1920; held various positions on Engineering Staff; Deputy Chief Engineer in 1933. President: Instn of Water Engineers, 1945-46; ICE, 1952-53. *Address:* Little Barnfield, Hawkhurst, Kent. *Club:* Athenæum.   *[Died 11 Jan. 1977.*

CRONYN, Captain St John, CBE 1951; DSO 1941; Royal Navy; *b* 20 May 1901; *yr s* of Dr J. G. Cronyn, Dublin; *m* 1937, Lilias Marion, *er d* of late P. W. Wake; no *c. Educ:* Royal Naval Colls, Osborne and Dartmouth; Gonville and Caius Coll., Cambridge. Midshipman, HMS Orion, 1917; served Yangtsze gunboat flotilla, Mediterranean station and Training Establishments; RN Staff Coll., 1934; Comdr, 1937; minesweeping, 1939-41 (DSO, despatches); Eastern Fleet, 1942-43; Capt., 1943; Tactical Division, Admiralty, 1944-45; Dir RN Tactical Sch., 1945-48; HMS Devonshire, 1948-50; Chief Staff Officer, Gibraltar, 1951-52 (CBE) (Ammunition Explosion); ADC to the Queen, 1952; retired list, 1953. *Recreations:* hockey, cricket, tennis. *Address:* 3 Mellieha Heights, Mellieha, Malta GC. *Club:* Naval and Military.   *[Died 16 March 1973.*

CROOKS, James, CVO 1958; FRCS; Hon. Consulting Ear, Nose and Throat Surgeon, The Hospital for Sick Children, Great Ormond Street; *b* 2 Oct. 1901; *s* of James amd Margaret Crooks, Loanhead, Midlothian; *m* 1st, 1931, Irene G. Heath (whom he divorced 1950); two *d*; 2nd, 1970, Caroline A. Woollcombe. *Educ:* University, Edinburgh; Royal Infirmary, Edinburgh; St Bartholomew's Hospital, London. MB, ChB, Edinburgh 1923; FRCS 1928. House Surgeon, Royal Infirmary, Edinburgh, 1924; House Physician, Casualty Officer, Resident Medical Supt, Surgical Registrar, The Hospital for Sick Children, 1924-31, Chm. Med. Cttee, 1950-53; Chm., Building Cttee, 1948-67. Kirk-Duncanson Research Scholar in USA, Vienna, Paris, Copenhagen, 1929-31; Fellow Royal Society of Medicine; Mem. Royal Medical Society Edinburgh; Hon. Mem. Brit. Paed. Assoc. *Publications:* The Ear, Nose and Throat in Garrod, Batten and Thursfield's Diseases of Children; Accessory Nasal Sinusitis in Childhood, 1936; Chronic Running Ear in Childhood, 1938; Tonsils and Adenoids: evaluation of removal in 50 Doctors' children; (with S. E. T. Cusdin) Suggestions and Demonstration Plans for Hospitals for Sick Children, 1947. *Recreations:* painting, sailing. *Address:* Meadow Farm, Ringshall, near Berkhamsted, Herts. *T:* Little Gaddesden 2295.
                                                    [Died 16 April 1980.

CROOKSHANK, Henry, CIE 1946; DSc (Dublin); BAI; BA, FNISc India, FGS, etc; *b* 13 Feb. 1893; *s* of Charles Henry Crookshank, Judge Commissioner, Land Commission, N Ireland; *m* 1921, Eileen Mary Somerville Lodge; three *d. Educ:* St Columba's, Rathfarnham; Trinity Coll., Dublin. Royal Dublin Fusiliers and Royal Engineers, 1914-18 (despatches); Geological Survey of India, 1920; recalled Royal Engineers, 1940-44; wounded Razmak, 1941; Offg Dir, Geological Survey of India, 1944-45; States Liaison Officer, Geological Survey of

India, Calcutta, 1946, retd. Dir, Geological Survey of Pakistan, 1948-56. *Publications:* The True Story of the Giant's Causeway, 1946; many papers to Geological Survey of India publications, etc. *Recreations:* golf, tennis, shooting. *Address:* c/o National and Grindlay's Bank Ltd, 13 St James's Square, SW1; Kilbogget Corner, Ballybrack, Co. Dublin.   *[Died 10 Aug. 1972.*

CROSBY, Harry Lillis, (Bing); singer; motion picture actor; *b* Tacoma, Washington, 2 May 1904; *s* of Harry L. and Catherine Crosby; *m* 1st, Wilma Wyatt (Dixie Lee) (*d* 1952); four *s*; 2nd, 1957, Kathryn Grant; two *s* one *d. Educ:* Gonzaga Univ., Spokane, Washington. 2 years vaudeville, 4 years vocal trio with Paul Whiteman band; over 20 years radio and records and motion pictures; over 300,000,000 record sales; with Paramount Production Incorporated, 1931-; *films include:* Here is My Heart; Pennies from Heaven; The Road to Singapore; Road to Zanzibar; Birth of the Blues; Holiday Inn; Road to Morocco; Star Spangled Rhythm; Going My Way; Bells of St Mary's; Welcome Stranger; Blue Skies; Road to Rio; The Emperor Waltz; Mr Music; Here Comes The Groom; Little Boy Lost; White Christmas; Country Girl; Anything Goes; Stage Coach; High Society. BBC Radio series, Bing, 1973. Best Actor Award (Oscar), 1944. Hon. DMus, Gonzaga Univ. *Publications:* Call Me Lucky, 1953; popular songs. *Relevant Publication:* Bing (by Ted and Larry Crosby). *Address:* 170 N Robertson Boulevard, Beverly Hills, Calif 90211, USA. *Clubs:* Lakeside Golf (Hollywood); Burlingame County; San Francisco Golf; Cypress Point; Royal and Ancient (St Andrews).   *[Died 14 Oct. 1977.*

CROSLAND, Rt. Hon. Anthony; *see* Crosland, Rt Hon. C. A. R.

CROSLAND, Rt. Hon. (Charles) Anthony (Raven), PC 1965; MP (Lab) Grimsby since Oct. 1959; Secretary of State for Foreign and Commonwealth Affairs, since 1976; *b* 29 Aug. 1918; *s* of late Joseph Beardsel Crosland, CB, and late Jessie Crosland; *m* 1st, 1952, Hilary Anne (marr. diss. 1957), *d* of Henry Sarson, Newbury, Berks; 2nd, 1964, Mrs Susan Barnes Catling, *d* of Mark Watson, Baltimore, Maryland; two step *d. Educ:* Highgate Sch.; Trinity Coll., Oxford (Scholar). First Class, Philosophy, Politics and Economics; Chm., Oxford Univ. Democratic Socialist Club; Pres., Oxford Union, 1946. Served War of 1939-45, fusilier, Royal Fusiliers, 1940; commissioned Royal Welch Fusiliers, 1941; joined Parachute Regt, 1942, and served N Africa, Italy, France, Austria; Capt., 1943-45. Fellow and lectr in Economics, Trinity Coll, Oxford, 1947-50; MP (Lab) South Glos, 1950-55; Minister of State for Economic Affairs, 1964-65; Sec. of State for Educn and Science, 1965-67; President of the Bd of Trade, 1967-69; Secretary of State: for Local Government and Regional Planning, 1969-70; for the Environment, 1974-76. President, Council of Ministers of EEC, Jan.-June 1977. Hon. Fellow, Trinity Coll., Oxford, 1966. Sec. of the Indept Commn of Inquiry into the Co-operative Movement, 1956-58, Chm. of Fabian Soc., 1961-62; Coun. Mem., Consumers' Assoc., 1958-63; Mem., Exec. Cttee, Town and Country Planning Assoc., 1971-72. *Publications:* (contributor) New Fabian Essays, 1952; Britain's Economic Problem, 1953; The Future of Socialism, 1956; The Conservative Enemy, 1962; (with Lord Boyle and Prof. Kogan) The Politics of Education, 1971; Socialism Now and Other Essays, 1974; var. Fabian pamphlets. *Address:* House of Commons, SW1. *Club:* Grimsby Labour.
                                                    [Died 19 Feb. 1977.

CROSLAND, Brig. Harold Powell, CB 1955; CBE 1943; MC 1918; TD; DL; late RA; Chairman: Zinc Development Assoc.; London Metal Exchange; President of the Board (late Chairman and Managing Director) of Metal Traders Ltd; Member Council (formerly Chairman), Lead Development Association; *b* 1893; *s* of Walter Crosland, JP, The Grange, Eaton Hastings, Faringdon, Berks; *m* 1916, Lilian Edith (*d* 1960), *d* of late Lieut-Col William Henry Hippisley, Scots Greys, Sparsholt Manor, Wantage, Berks; one *s* one *d. Educ:* Malvern. Joined Berkshire Yeomanry, 1912; served European War, 1914-18 in Gallipoli, Egypt, Palestine and Syria (wounded, despatches twice, MC); Capt., 1916; Major, 1920; Lieut-Col 99 Bucks and Berks Yeo. Field Brigade, RA, 1933-38; Bt Col, 1937; retired, 1938; re-employed, 1939. Chm. Berks T&AFA; DL Berks 1936. *Address:* Satwell Spinneys, Rotherfield Greys, near Henley-on-Thames, Oxon.   *[Died 9 July 1973.*

CROSS, Sir (Alfred) Rupert (Neale), Kt 1973; FBA 1967; Vinerian Professor in the University of Oxford, 1964-Sept. 1979; *b* 15 June 1912; *s* of Arthur George Cross and Mary Elizabeth (*née* Dalton); *m* 1937, Aline Heather Chadwick; no *c. Educ:* Worcester Coll. for the Blind; Worcester Coll., Oxford (Hon. Fellow, 1972). DCL 1958. Solicitor, 1939; Hon Master of the Bench, Middle Temple, 1972. Tutor, Law Soc., 1945-48; Fellow of Magdalen Coll., Oxford, 1948-64, Hon. Fellow 1975; Visiting Prof., Univ. of Adelaide, 1962, and Sydney, 1968. Hon. LLD:

Edinburgh, 1973; Leeds, 1975. *Publications:* Evidence, 5th edn, 1979; Precedent in English Law (3rd edn), 1977; (with P. Asterley Jones) Introduction to Criminal Law (7th edn), 1972; Cases in Criminal Law (5th edn), 1973; (with Nancy Wilkins) An Outline of the Law of Evidence (5th edn), 1980; The English Sentencing System, 1971, 2nd edn 1975; Punishment, Prison and the Public (Hamlyn Lectures), 1971; Statutory Interpretation, 1976; articles in Law Quarterly Review, Modern Law Review and Criminal Law Review. *Recreation:* chess. *Address:* Foxcombe Heath, Boars Hill, Oxford. *T:* Oxford 735142.
[*Died 12 Sept.* 1980.

CROSS, Rev. Leslie Basil, MA Oxon; Fellow, 1927-47, formerly Chaplain, Tutor and Junior Bursar of Jesus College, Oxford, Fellow Emeritus, 1960; *b* 18 April 1895; *s* of John James Cross, formerly Rector of Revesby, Lincs, and Mary Emma Aspden; *m* 1927, Gertrude (*d* 1971), 4th *d* of Walter Savill, Finches, Lindfield, Sussex. *Educ:* Trent Coll.; Keble Coll., Oxford; Wycliffe Hall, Oxford. Asst Master, Lake House Preparatory Sch., Bexhill-on-Sea, 1916-17; Housemaster, Stamford Grammar Sch., 1918-19; Headmaster, Trent Coll. Preparatory Sch., 1922-23; Chaplain and Lecturer in Theology, Jesus Coll., Oxford, 1923-26; Lecturer in Theology, to St Peters Hall, Oxford, 1928-33; Examining Chaplain to Archbishop of York, 1925-28; Examining Chaplain to Bishop of Manchester, 1929-39; and Truro, 1935-54; Vice-Principal, Ripon Hall, Oxford, 1933-54; Select Preacher, Oxford, 1935 and 1937; Proctor for University of Oxford in Convocation of Canterbury, 1936; Public Examiner in Final Honour Sch. of Theology, 1937-39; Estates Bursar, Jesus Coll., 1941-43, Senior Tutor, 1945-47; Junior Proctor, Oxford Univ., 1943-44. *Publications:* Essay in The Atonement in History and in Life; articles in The Modern Churchman, etc, and pamphlets. *Recreations:* fishing, shooting, gardening. *Address:* 27 Linton Road, Oxford.
[*Died 12 April* 1974.

CROSS, Sir Rupert; *see* Cross, Sir A. R. N.

CROSSE, Rev. Frank Parker; Rector of Upton Magna, Shrewsbury, 1960-67; *b* 24 Oct. 1897; *s* of Edmund Francis Crosse and Margaret Laidlaw Selby; *m* 1925, Isabel McIver McIntyre; two *d. Educ:* St Bees; RMC Sandhurst. Commissioned Regular Army, South Staffs Regt, 1916 (MC). Priest 1924; Vicar, Christ Church, Derry Hill, Wilts, 1926; Private Chaplain to Marquess of Lansdowne, 1927; Vicar, St Aldhelm's, Branksome, Bournemouth, 1931; Dean and Archdeacon of Grahamstown, 1934-44; Rector of Barlborough, 1944-51; Rector of Morton, Derby, 1951-60; Custos, Denstone Coll., 1955-71; Canon of Derby Cathedral, 1956-60. Vice-Provost and Senior Chaplain (Midland Div.) Woodard Schs, 1962-70. *Publication:* Intercessions in Time of War, 1939. *Address:* 24 Preston Trust Homes, Preston, Telford, Salop. *T:* Kinnersley 3669. [*Died 15 March* 1979.

CROSSFIELD, Robert Sands, OBE 1967; DL; JP; *b* 21 May 1904; *s* of Robert and Ellen Louise Crossfield, Ulverston; *m* 1929, Miriam, *d* of Rev. W. H. Wicks; no *c. Educ:* Earnseat Sch., Arnside; Millhill Sch., London. Director of a number of family private limited companies, now retired. Interested many years in local govt: Mem. Westmorland CC, 1940; CA, 1958-74; Chm. of Council, 1952-70. High Sheriff of Westmorland, 1970-71; JP 1945, DL 1971, Cumbria (formerly Westmorland). *Recreations:* golf, motoring. *Address:* Brantfell, Arnside, Cumbria. *T:* Arnside 761244. *Club:* Old Millhillians. [*Died 27 May* 1978.

CROSSLEY, Sir Julian (Stanley), Kt 1964; Director, Barclays Bank Ltd, Barclays Bank DCO (Chairman, 1947-64); Chairman, Dominion Students' Hall Trust; Governor (Vice-President, 1960-66); Wellington College; Governor, Queen Elizabeth House; Vice-President, Commonwealth Institute; Hon. Treasurer, The Pilgrims Society of Great Britain; *b* 3 Jan. 1899; *s* of Charles Wheatley Crossley, Longfield, Triangle, Halifax, and Caroline Smedley Marsden-Smedley; *m* 1928, Barbara Mary, *d* of Frederick Craufurd Goodenough; three *s* one *d. Educ:* Wellington Coll.; New Coll., Oxford. Midshipman RN, 1917-19. Entered service of Barclays Bank Ltd, 1921. *Address:* Severals, Alresford, Hants. *Clubs:* Brooks's; Royal Yacht Squadron. [*Died 26 Jan.* 1971.

CROSSMAN, Rt. Hon. Richard (Howard Stafford), PC 1964; OBE 1945; MA; *b* 15 Dec. 1907; *s* of late Mr Justice Crossman and late Helen Howard; *m* 1937, Inezita Hilda Baker (*d* 1952); *m* 1954, Anne Patricia, *d* of late A. P. McDougall; one *s* one *d. Educ:* Winchester (Schol.); New Coll., Oxford (Scholar, first in Mods and first in Greats). Fellow and Tutor of New Coll., Oxford, 1930-37; Asst Editor, New Statesman and Nation, 1938-55; Lecturer for Oxford Univ. Delegacy for Extra Mural Studies, and Workers' Educational Assoc., 1938-40; Leader of Labour group on Oxford City Council, 1934-40. Dep. Dir Psychological Warfare, AFHQ Algiers, 1943; Asst Chief Psychological Warfare Div. SHAEF, 1944-45; Mem. Anglo-American Palestine Commn, 1946; Mem. Malta Round Table Conf., 1955; Mem. Labour Party Exec., 1952-67; Chm. working party on Nat. Superannuation, 1956; on Science, 1963. MP (Lab) Coventry East, 1945-Feb. 1974; Minister of Housing and Local Government, 1964-66; Leader of the House, and Lord President of the Council, 1966-68; Secretary of State for Social Services, i/c Dept of Health and Social Security, 1968-70. Editor, New Statesman, 1970-72. *Publications:* Plato Today, 1937; Socrates, 1938; Government and the Governed, 1939; How we are Governed, 1939; Palestine Mission, 1947; (editor) The God that Failed, 1950; (editor and contributor) New Fabian Essays, 1952; The Charm of Politics, 1958; A Nation Reborn, 1960; Planning for Freedom, 1965; Inside View: three lectures on Prime Ministerial government, 1972; *posthumous publications:* The Diaries of a Cabinet Minister, vol. 1, 1964-66, 1975, vol. 2, 1966-68, 1976, vol. 3, 1968-70, 1977. *Address:* 9 Vincent Square, SW1. *T:* 01-834 6414; Prescote Manor, Banbury, Oxon. *Clubs:* Athenæum, Farmers', Garrick. [*Died 5 April* 1974.

CROSTHWAITE, Sir Bertram Maitland, Kt 1935; VD; *b* 9 Oct. 1880; *s* of late Rev. Samuel Maitland Crosthwaite and late Kate Bennett Colnett; *m* 1921, Nora Marsden, *d* of late Charles Earnest Higgin; one *s* one *d.* Joined Burma Railways Co. Ltd as Asst Traffic Supt, 1898; District Traffic Supt, 1905; Traffic Manager, 1924; commanded Burma Railways Bn (Indian Defence Force) with rank of Lt-Col; Hon. ADC to Viceroy; Mem. Railway Board (India), 1927; transferred to Indian State Railway Service, 1929; General Manager, Burma Railways, 1932; retired, 1935. *Address:* Kirkham Court, Denton Road, Eastbourne. *T:* Eastbourne 23363. [*Died 14 Jan.* 1974.

CROSTHWAITE, Cecil, MBE 1943; TD 1942 and 3 bars; JP; Lord-Lieutenant and Custos Rotolorum of Cleveland, since 1974; *b* 1909; *o s* of late Sir William Crosthwaite; *m* Norah Mahoney Bowden, twin *d* of late Frank W. Bowden; one *s* two *d* (and one *s* deced). *Educ:* Windermere; Uppingham. Served 50 Divl Sigs TA, 1929-39; 23 Divl Sigs TA, 1939-40; SO Northern Comd HQ, 1940-41; GSO WO, 1941-46; rep. Chamber of Commerce NR TA Assoc., 1947-65. Chm., Seahorse Securities Ltd, Tees Towing Co. Ltd, British Marine Mutual Insce Assoc. Ltd, British Tugowners' Assoc., 1957-61; Co-Founder, European Tugowners' Assoc., 1961 (Chm., 1975-); Dep. Chm., Lyon & Lyon Gp of Companies and Tees & Hartlepool Port Authority, 1969; Dir other shipping, transport and construction companies. French Vice-Consul, 1968; Mem. N of England Air Adv. Cttee, 1964; Pres., N of England TA&VRA, 1978 (Vice-Pres., 1975); Pres., St John Council, Cleveland. DL NR Yorks, 1963; JP Cleveland, 1974. KStJ 1974. *Recreations:* (some continuous, others as opportunity permits) hatha yoga, horticulture, sculpture, music. *Address:* Langbaurgh Hall, Great Ayton, North Yorkshire; Cleveland Buildings, Queen's Square, Middlesbrough, Cleveland TS2 1NX. *Clubs:* Carlton; Cleveland (Middlesbrough). [*Died 25 Dec.* 1978.

CROSTHWAITE-EYRE, Sir Oliver (Eyre), Kt 1961; Verderer of New Forest, 1948-74; Chairman: Eyre & Spottiswoode Ltd, 1961-73; Associated Book Publishers Ltd, 1963-73; 1900 Club, 1960-73; *b* 14 Oct. 1913; *e s* of Major J. S. Crosthwaite-Eyre and Dorothy Muriel Eyre; *m* 1939, Maria Alexandra Puthon; two *s* three *d. Educ:* Downside; Trinity Coll., Cambridge. Served War of 1939; enlisted private, 1940; commissioned, April 1940; served Norway, Middle East, and NW Europe (despatches). MP (C) New Forest Div. of Hants, 1950-68 (New Forest and Christchurch Div., 1945-50). DL Southampton, 1954. *Address:* Blenmans House, 12 Yellow Wood Lane, PO Chisipite, Salisbury, Rhodesia. *Club:* Salisbury (Rhodesia).
[*Died 3 Feb.* 1978.

CROUSAZ, Engineer Rear-Adm. Augustus George, CB 1937; *b* 13 April 1884; *s* of William de Prelaz Crousaz, Guernsey; *m* 1911, Dorothy Constance Skerry; one *d. Educ:* Elizabeth Coll., Guernsey. Royal Navy; Asst Engineer-in-Chief of the Fleet, 1932-36; retired list, 1939; Deputy Engineer-in-Chief of the Fleet, 1936-39. *Recreation:* tennis. *Address:* 33 Burgh Heath Road, Epsom, Surrey. [*Died 25 Aug.* 1977.

CROWE, Prof. Percy Robert, BSc Econ. (London); PhD (Glasgow); MA (Manchester); Professor in Geography, University of Manchester, 1953-71, Emeritus Professor, since 1972; a Pro-Vice-Chancellor, 1968-71; *b* 2 March 1904; *m* 1931, Margaret D. J. Robertson; two *s* one *d. Educ:* Henry Thornton Sch., Clapham, London; London Sch. of Economics and Political Science. Asst to Lecturer in Geography, Glasgow Univ., 1925-28; Commonwealth Fund Fellow, 1928-30; Lectr in Geography, Glasgow Univ., 1928-47; Technical Officer,

Meteorological Office, 1939-41; Commission in RAF 1944-45; Reader in Geography, University of London, and Head of Geography Dept, Queen Mary Coll., 1947-53. *Publications:* Concepts in Climatology, 1971; articles in geographical and meteorological jls. *Recreations:* hill walking, chess. *Address:* 239 Bramhall Lane South, Bramhall, Cheshire. *T:* 061-439 1134.
[*Died 8 Dec.* 1979.

CROWE, Hon. Philip Kingsland, Bronze Star (US Army) 1945; Ambassador of USA to Denmark, 1973-76; *b* 7 Jan. 1908; *s* of Earle Rosman Crowe and Kathleen McMullin Higgins Crowe; *m* 1937, Irene Pettus; three *d. Educ:* St Paul's Sch., Concord; Univ. of Virginia. Reporter and Editor, New York Evening Post, 1929-32; Broker, Milmine Bodman & Co., NY, 1932-35; Explorer, French Indo-China, 1935-36; Life and Fortune, 1936-40; with USAF HQ, England, 1940-42; Lt-Col; Chief, Secret Intell. Office of Strategic Services in India, Burma and China; Exec. Off., S China Comd of OSS; Special Rep. of Econ. Co-operation Mission to China, 1948-49; Rep. of USA to 10th Session of Econ. Commn (E Asia) of UN; US Deleg. to ECAFE Conf., 1954; Ambassador to Ceylon, 1953-57; Special Asst to Sec. of State, 1957-59; Ambassador to Union of S Africa, 1959-61; led expedns for wildlife conservation to 57 nations in Asia, Africa, S America, Australia, 1962-68; Ambassador to Norway, 1969-73. Director: World Wildlife Fund (Internat.); World Wildlife Fund (USA); African Wildlife Leadership Foundn; Amer. Cttee for Internat. Wildlife Protection; Trustee, Sch. of Advanced Internat. Studies of Johns Hopkins Univ.; Mem., Bd of Advrs, Fletcher Sch. of Law and Diplomacy, Tufts Univ. FRGS; Life Member: Royal Asiatic Soc.; Ceylon Wildlife Protection Soc.; Member: Council on Foreign Relations (NY); Soc. of Cincinatti; Soc. of Colonial Wars; Huguenot Soc.; St Nicholas Soc. Officer, Legion of Honour (France), 1959; Yun Hui of Cloud and Banner, 1st cl. (Rep. of China), 1961; Mil. Order of Christ, 1st cl. (Portugal), 1960; Grand Cross, Order of St Olav (Norway), 1973; Grand Cross, Order of Dannebrog (Denmark). *Publications:* Sport is Where You Find It, 1954; Diversions of a Diplomat in Ceylon, 1957; Sporting Journeys in Asia and Africa, 1966; The Empty Ark, 1968; World Wildlife: the last stand, 1970; Out of the Mainstream, 1970. *Recreations:* fishing, shooting, hunting. *Address:* Third Haven, Easton, Maryland 21601, USA. *Clubs:* Boodle's, White's, Flyfishers'; Brook, Century, Racquet and Tennis, Explorers, Anglers, Boone and Crocket (New York); Metropolitan, Dacor (Washington); Harvard Travellers (Boston); Chesapeake Bay Yacht (Easton, Md); Lakota, Round Table (Woodstock, Vt); Rand (Johannesburg); Hill (Ceylon); Norske Selskab, Royal Norwegian Yacht, Linge (Oslo); Royal Danish Yacht, Royal Shooting Brothers of Denmark (Copenhagen); 1001 (of World Wildlife Fund).   [*Died 16 Oct.* 1976.

CROWN, Mrs Leon; *see* Vyvyan, Jennifer B.

CROWTHER, Baron *cr* 1968 (Life Peer), of Headingley; **Geoffrey Crowther;** Kt 1957; Chairman, Commission on the Constitution, since 1969; Chancellor, The Open University, since 1969; Chairman, The Economist Newspaper Ltd; Director: Commercial Union Assurance Co. Ltd; Royal Bank of Canada; Member Governing Body, London School of Economics; *b* 13 May 1907; *s* of late Charles Crowther; *m* 1932, Margaret, *d* of E. H. Worth, Claymont, Delaware, USA; two *s* three *d* (and one *d* decd). *Educ:* Leeds Grammar Sch.; Oundle Sch.; Clare Coll., Cambridge (MA; Hon. Fellow, 1958); Yale Univ.; Columbia Univ. Pres. of Cambridge Union, 1928; Commonwealth Fund Fellow, 1929-31. Joined staff of The Economist, 1932; Asst Editor, 1935; Editor, 1938-March 1956. Wartime service in Min. of Supply, 1940-41, Min. of Information, 1941-42, and as Dep. Head of Joint War Production Staff, Min. of Production, 1942-43. Chm., Trust Houses Group Ltd, later Trust Houses Forte Ltd, 1960-71. Chairman: Central Advisory Council for Education (England), 1956-60; Cttee on Consumer Credit, 1968-71. Hon. LLD Nottingham, 1951; Hon. DSc (Econ.), London, 1954; Hon. LLD: Swarthmore, 1957; Dartmouth, 1957; Michigan, 1960; Liverpool, 1961; Hon. LittD Leeds, 1970. *Publications:* An Introduction to the Study of Prices (with Sir W. T. Layton), 1935; Ways and Means, 1936; Economics for Democrats, 1939; Ways and Means of War, 1940; An Outline of Money, 1941. *Recreations:* places, music, and history. *Address:* 51 Hyde Park Gate, SW7. *T:* 01-584 9497. *Clubs:* Brooks's; Links, Yale (New York).   [*Died 5 Feb.* 1972.

CROWTHER, Edward, CBE 1951; Chairman, Northern Gas Board, 1949-62, retired; *b* 7 Oct. 1897; *er s* of John Henry Crowther, Wallasey, Ches; *m* 1927, Gwyneth Ethel, *er d* of R. T. Lewis, Stoke-on-Trent; one *d. Educ:* Wallasey Grammar Sch.; Liverpool Univ. (Master of Engineering). Various appts in gas industry; Gen. Manager, Chief Engineer and Dir of Newcastle

upon Tyne and Gateshead Gas Co. immediately prior to nationalisation of gas industry; Pres., Instn of Gas Engineers, 1948-49. Hon. FICE. *Publications:* contribs to technical literature of gas industry. *Recreation:* golf. *Address:* c/o Mr R. Gallop, 40 Mayfield Gardens, Walton on Thames, Surrey KT12 5PP.   [*Died 13 Jan.* 1979.

CROYSDALE, Sir James, Kt 1953; *b* 15 June 1886; *s* of Charles Croysdale, worsted manufacturer, Leeds; *m* 1915, Jessie Gladys, *d* of Alfred Verity, Leeds; one *d. Educ:* Ilkley Grammar Sch. Admitted Solicitor, 1909; Pres. Leeds Law Soc., 1943. Leeds City Council, 1930-64; Leader, 1941-45 and 1951-53; Chm. Finance Cttee, 1941-45 and 1951-53; formerly Chm. of other cttees; Lord Mayor of Leeds, 1955-56; President: Leeds Conservative Assoc.; Northern Counties Chess Assoc., 1939-48; Mem. Bd of Management: Leeds Skyrac; Morley Trustees Savings Bank; Chm. Trustees, Leeds Children's Holiday Camp. *Address:* 39 Foxhill Court, Leeds LS16 5PN. *T:* Leeds 675101. *Club:* Leeds and County Conservative (President).
[*Died 17 Jan.* 1971.

CROZIER, Douglas James Smyth, CMG 1957; JP; Assistant Educational Adviser, Ministry of Overseas Development, 1963-68; Director of Education, Hong Kong, 1951-61; *b* 20 March 1908; *yr s* of late Thomas James Crozier, JP and Myra Elizabeth Crozier; *m* 1934, Ann Hobbs; one *s* one *d. Educ:* Portora Royal School; The Queen's Univ. of Belfast. Master, Education Dept, Hong Kong, 1931; POW in Japanese hands, 1941-45; Temp. Senior Inspector of Schools, 1949. MLC Hong Kong, 1951; MEC, 1956-61. Vice-Pres., Asia Christian Colls Assoc.; Mem., Gen. Synod, Church of Ireland. Mem., World Bank Economic Mission to Yemen Arab Republic, 1970. JP Co. Armagh, 1974. Hon. LLD: Hong Kong, 1961; Chinese Univ. of Hong Kong, 1969. *Recreations:* gardening, walking. *Address:* Rose Cottage, Tandragee, Co. Armagh, N Ireland BT62 2ER. *T:* Tandragee 840543. *Club:* Hong Kong (Hong Kong).
[*Died 17 Nov.* 1976.

CRUDDAS, Maj.-Gen. Ralph Cyril, CB 1953; DSO and Bar, 1943; retired; *b* 26 Aug. 1900; 2nd and *o* surv. *s* of late Rev. W. S. Cruddas and late Katharine, *d* of J. H. Peter-Hoblyn; *m* 1940, Edwina Marjorie Clare, 2nd *d* of Sir Charles Hanson, 2nd Bt; three *d. Educ:* Cheltenham Coll.; Royal Military College, Sandhurst. 2nd Lieut DCLI, 1919; Private Sec. to the Governor of Assam, 1933-35; served War of 1939-45, in Middle East, Italy and NW Europe; commanded 7th Battalion Oxford and Bucks Light Infantry, 1941-43; commanded: Cyrenaica District, 1947-48; Tactical Wing Sch. of Infantry, 1948-49; 133 Infantry Brigade, 1949-51; GOC Land Forces, Hong Kong, 1951-54; retired 1955. *Address:* Springfield House, Nunney, near Frome, Somerset. *T:* Nunney 309.   [*Died 29 April* 1979.

CRUICKSHANK, Prof. Robert, CBE 1966; MD (Aberdeen); FRCP; FRCPEd; DPH; FRSE; Retired; *b* Sept. 1899; *m* 1929, Margaret Petrie; one *s* one *d. Educ:* Univ. of Aberdeen. Anderson Travelling Fellowship, Univ. of Glasgow, 1922-24; Resident Med. Officer, Royal Hosp. for Sick Children, Glasgow, 1925, Belvidere Hosp. for Infectious Diseases, Glasgow, 1925-27; McRobert Lectr in Malignant Diseases, Univ. of Aberdeen, 1927-28; Lectr in Bacteriology, Univ. of Glasgow, and Bacteriologist to Glasgow Royal Infirmary, 1928-36; Pathologist in charge of LCC Group Laboratory, 1936-45; Dir, Central Public Health Laboratory of Public Health Laboratory Service, 1945-48; Prof. of Bacteriology in Univ. of London at St Mary's Hosp. Med. Sch., 1949-57, and Principal of Wright Fleming Inst. of Microbiology, 1955-57; Prof. of Bacteriology, Univ. of Edinburgh, 1958-66, now Emeritus; Prof. of Preventive Medicine, Univ. of West Indies, Kingston, Jamaica, 1966-68. Hon. LLD, Aberdeen, 1968. *Publications:* (ed) Modern Trends in Immunology, 1963, 2nd vol., 1968; (ed) Medical Microbiology, 12th edn, 1973; articles in med. jls embodying researches on the diagnosis and control of infectious diseases. *Recreation:* golf. *Address:* 17 Greenhill Gardens, Edinburgh 10.
[*Died 16 Aug.* 1974.

CRUM, Lt-Gen. Vernon Forbes E.; *see* Erskine Crum.

CRUSE, Rt. Rev. John Howard, MA; *b* 15 Feb. 1908; *s* of George Thomas Cruse; *m* 1942, Ethne (*d* 1977), *d* of Winslow Sterling-Berry, MB; no *c* ; *m* 1978, Violet, *d* of Charles Briscoe. *Educ:* Roborough Sch.; Jesus Coll., Cambridge; Wycliffe Hall, Oxford, 2nd Class Economics Tripos, 2nd Class Theological Tripos, MA, Jesus Coll. Curate of St John, Southall, 1932; Curate of Christ Church, Folkestone, 1934; Vicar of St Paul's, South Harrow, 1936; Vicar of Holy Trinity, Cambridge, 1942 (Chaplain to the Cambridge Pastorate); Exam. Chaplain to Bishop of Sodor and Man; Proctor in Convocation, 1948; Provost of Sheffield, 1949; Bishop Suffragan of Knaresborough,

1965-72. *Publication:* Marriage, Divorce and Repentance, 1949. *Recreations:* fishing and sailing. *Address:* Oakleigh, Lucks Green, Cranleigh, Surrey GU6 8DR. *T:* Cranleigh 3156.
[*Died* 11 *April* 1979.

CUBITT, Hon. (Charles) Guy, CBE 1973; DSO 1943; TD; DL; *b* 13 Feb. 1903; 3rd *surv. s* of 2nd Baron Ashcombe, CB; *m* 1927, Rosamond Mary Edith, *d* of Sir Montagu Cholmeley, 4th Bt; one *s* two *d. Educ:* Eton; RMC Sandhurst. Lt-Col Surrey Yeomanry (despatches, DSO); Hon. Col Surrey Yeomanry, 1951. Pres., Surrey Yeomanry Club. Life-Pres., The Pony Club, 1971; President: BHS, 1952; Royal Internat. Horse Show, 1979-. Vice Pres., Combined Training, 1979. Hon. Mem., BSJA, 1979. High Sheriff of Surrey, 1955; Surrey County Council, 1955 (Alderman, 1965-72); DL Surrey, 1956. *Address:* Dormers, Tetbury, Glos GL8 8HA. *T:* Tetbury 52423. *Club:* Cavalry and Guards.   [*Died* 23 *Aug.* 1979.

CUDMORE, Hon. Sir Collier Robert, Kt 1958; Leader of Liberal and Country Party, Legislative Council, South Australia, 1944-59; barrister; *b* 13 June 1885; *s* of Daniel H. Cudmore, Wentworth, NSW, and Victor Harbour, S Australia; *m* 1922, Phyllis, *d* of Dr A. E. Wigg; one *s* one *d. Educ:* St Peter's Coll., Adelaide; Adelaide Univ.; Magdalen Coll., Oxford (BA). Called to bar, Inner Temple, 1910; practised as barrister and solicitor, Adelaide, 1912-55. Served European War, 1915-18, RFA, France (wounded twice); Bn Comdr Volunteer Defence Corps, 1940. Dir, Elder Smith & Co. Ltd; Local Dir, North British and Mercantile Insurance Co.; Mem. Council, University of Adelaide; a Governor of St Peter's Coll., Adelaide. *Recreations:* rowing (rowed Oxford VIII, 1908-09; won Olympic Fours, 1908); bowls. *Address:* 5 Acacia Street, Medindie, South Australia. *Clubs:* Adelaide (Adelaide); Vincent's (Oxford); Leander.   [*Died* 16 *May* 1971.

CULLEN, Brian; *see* Cullen, J. B.

CULLEN, (James) Brian, CBE 1964; *b* 2 Nov. 1905; *s* of late J. Bertram Cullen and Emily (*née* Shaw); *m* 1936, Kathleen, *d* of late Thomas Jones; two *s* one *d. Educ:* King William Coll., Isle of Man. Entered Civil Service, 1940; Principal, Ministry of Supply, 1941; Asst Sec., Ministry of Supply, 1951; transferred to Board of Trade, 1954; seconded to Foreign Office, 1957 (HM Diplomatic Service, 1965); British Commercial Counsellor, Stockholm, 1957, Washington, DC, 1960; retired, 1966. *Publications:* numerous contribs to fishing jls, etc. *Recreations:* fishing, bird-watching, cooking. *Address:* Thie Vane, Malew, Isle of Man.   [*Died* 13 *Aug.* 1972.

CULLEY, Group Captain Stuart Douglas, DSO 1918; retired; Representative British and American Industries, Italy, since 1946; owner and sole director Messrs Stuart Culley, Milan; *b* 22 Aug. 1895; *s* of Walter J. Culley and Mabel A. Stather; *m* 1936, Marguerite Henriette Vulliamy, *d* of late Lieut-Col W. H. Battle, FRCS, RAMC (T). *Educ:* America, Canada, England. Joined RNAS, 1917; Grand Fleet and Sea Patrol, 1917-18 (DSO, despatches); Baltic Force, 1919; (despatches) Iraq, 1920-22 (GS medal with clasp, Iraq); Palestine, 1922-24; Staff Coll., 1930; India, 1931-35; Khajuri Plain, 1930-31 (Indian GS medal with clasp); Mohmand Operations, 1935 (despatches); Syrian Campaign, 1941 (despatches); Inspector, Royal Iraqi Air Force, British Military Mission to Iraq, 1937-40; OC Royal Air Force, Palestine and Transjordan, 1940-41; Air Min., 1941-42; N Africa, Italy, 1943-44; India, 1945; retired Dec. 1945. *Address:* Villa Stuart, Saló, Lago di Garda, Italy. *Clubs:* Royal Air Force, Naval and Military.   [*Died* 10 *June* 1975.

CULSHAW, John (Royds), OBE 1966; author and producer; *b* 28 May 1924; *s* of late Percy Ellis Culshaw and late Dorothy Royds Culshaw. *Educ:* King George V Sch., Southport, Lancs. RNAS (Fleet Air Arm), Lieut, 1942-46. The Decca Record Co. Ltd (Classical Recordings), 1946-54; Capitol Records Inc., Hollywood, USA, 1954-56; The Decca Record Co. Ltd (Manager, Classical Recordings), 1956-67; Head of Music Programmes, BBC TV, 1967-75. Mem. Arts Council and Chm., Music Panel, 1975-77. Senior Fellow in Creative Arts, Univ. of Western Australia, 1977. Vienna Philharmonic Orchestra: Nicolai Medal, 1959; Schalk Medal, 1967. *Publications:* Sergei Rachmaninov, 1949; The Sons of Brutus, 1950; A Century of Music, 1951; A Place of Stone, 1952; Ring Resounding, 1967; Reflections on Wagner's Ring, 1976; Wagner: the man and his music, 1979. Contributor: The Gramophone, Saturday Review (USA), High Fidelity (USA), etc. *Recreation:* flying. *Address:* 16 Arlington Avenue, N1. *T:* 01-359 2837.
[*Died* 27 *April* 1980.

CUMBER, William John, CBE 1943; farmer; *b* 21 Dec. 1878; *s* of William and Ellen Cumber; *m* 1904, Elizabeth (*d* 1965), *d* of Sir

Edward Brown; one *s* five *d. Educ:* Kendrick Sch., Reading. Farms 2000 acres in Berks and Wilts; Mem. of Berks War Agric. Cttee, 1916-19, and 1939-64; Chm. of Farmers' Club, 1939-46; Pres., Shire Horse Soc., 1939-46; Chm., Council of Agriculture for England, 1940; Mem. Luxmore Cttee on Agricultural Education, 1941-42; for many years Alderman Berks CC (Chm., 1954-57) and Chm. Agricultural Cttee of County Councils' Assoc. Pres., British Horse Soc., 1948, 1949; Pres., Smithfield Club, 1949-50; Pres., Shorthorn Soc., 1953-54. Hon. Fellow RASE; Master Worshipful Company of Farmers, 1956. *Address:* Conkers, Theale, Berks. *T:* Reading 302410. *Club:* Farmers'.   [*Died* 25 *Feb.* 1974.

CUMBERBATCH, Isaac William, CBE 1955 (OBE 1950); *b* Silverdale, Staffs, 11 Jan. 1888; *m*; one *s. Educ:* Church of England Sch., Silverdale; High Sch. and Sutherland Inst., Longton; North Staffs Technical Coll., Stoke-on-Trent. 1st class Hons in Principles of Mining (Bd of Educn). Formerly; Pres. N Staffs Br. Nat. Assoc. of Colliery Managers; Pres. N Staffs Inst. of Mining Engineers; Vice-Pres. Inst. of Mining Engineers; Pres. and Chm. N Staffs. Colliery Owners' Assoc. An Hon. Technical Mining Adviser on Manpower and Production, attached to Mines Dept, 1941; Production Dir, Cannock Chase Coalfield. Pioneer in research work carried out at Sneyd Colliery in N Staffs Coalfield on dust suppression. Chm. West Midlands Division National Coal Board, 1950-55. Member: Cttee to enquire into, and find a remedy for, dangers arising from Coal Dust in Mines; Cttee on Recruitment, Education and Training (responsible for Report published by Mining Assoc., 1945). JP Borough of Newcastle-under-Lyme 1945; MInstME. *Publications:* a number of papers before Nat. Assoc. of Colliery Managers and Inst. of Mining Engineers. *Address:* Highfields, Clayton Road, Newcastle, Staffs. *T:* Newcastle, Staffs, 67091.
[*Died* 11 *July* 1971.

CUMBERLEGE, Geoffrey Fenwick Jocelyn, DSO 1917; MC 1918; *b* 18 April 1891; 3rd *s* of late Henry Mordaunt and Blanche Cumberlege, Walsted Place, Lindfield, Sussex; *m* 1927, Vera Gladys, 3rd *d* of Major Sir A. D. Gibbons, 7th Bt; three *s* one *d. Educ:* Charterhouse; Worcester Coll., Oxford; MA. Hon. Fellow Worcester Coll., Oxford; Hon. DCL, Durham, 1953. Served France, 1915-18, Italy, 1918-19 (Croce di Guerra); substantive Capt. in Oxford and Bucks LI, Oct. 1917 (DSO, MC, despatches thrice); Manager of Oxford University Press in India, 1919-27, in USA, 1927-34. Publisher to the Univ. of Oxford, 1945-56. *Address:* Idlehurst, Birch Grove, Horsted Keynes, Sussex. *T:* Chelwood Gate 224. *Clubs:* United Oxford & Cambridge University; Royal Bombay Yacht (Bombay).
[*Died* 29 *July* 1979.

CUMINGS, Prof. John Nathaniel, MD, FRCP; Professor of Chemical Pathology, University of London, at the Institute of Neurology, National Hospital for Nervous Diseases, 1958-71, retired; *b* 4 Oct. 1905; *s* of Arthur N. Cumings; *m* 1940, Mary P. Parish; one *s* one *d. Educ:* King's Coll. and King's Coll. Hosp. Qualified King's Coll. Hosp., 1927; House Appts. and Asst Pathologist, King's Coll. Hosp.; MD 1931; Asst Pathologist, National Hosp., 1933; Clinical Pathologist, National Hospital, 1945; FRCP 1953. Hughlings Jackson Lecture, RSM, 1970. *Publications:* Cerebral Lipidosis, 1957; Heavy Metals and the Brain, 1959. *Address:* Manor Mead, Cross Road, East Preston, Sussex.   [*Died* 22 *Aug.* 1974.

CUMMING, Brig. Arthur Edward, VC 1942; OBE 1942; MC 1918; *b* 18 June 1896; *m* 1922, Elizabeth Doris Brown; (one *s* died of wounds in Italy, 1944). *Educ:* privately; Cadet Coll., Quetta. 2nd Lieut Indian Army, 1915; served in Mesopotamia and Palestine with 53rd Sikhs, Frontier Force, 1917-20 (MC); NW Frontier, India, with 3rd Royal Bn 12th Frontier Force Regt, 1921-22 and 1936-37; Comdt, 2nd Bn 12th Frontier Force Regt, 1940; served in Malaya, 1941-42 (wounded, VC); Bde Comdr, 1942 (OBE); Eastern Frontier, India, 1943; Comdr Dehra Dun Sub-Area, 1944-47; retired, 1947. Supt of Police, Kyrenia, Cyprus, Sept. 1956-59. *Recreation:* touring. *Address:* 2 Scotland Street, Edinburgh 3.   [*Died* 10 *April* 1971.

CUMMING, Sir Duncan (Cameron), KBE 1953 (CBE 1946); CB 1948; *b* 10 Aug. 1903; *s* of late Dr R. Cumming; *m* 1930, Nancy Acheson Houghton (*d* 1971); one *d. Educ:* Giggleswick; Caius Coll., Cambridge. Sudan Political Service, 1925; Chief Administrator, Cyrenaica (Brig.), 1942; Chief Civil Affairs Officer, Middle East (Maj.-Gen.), 1945-48. Governor, Kordofan Province, Sudan, 1949. Deputy Civil Sec., Sudan Government, 1950-51; Chief Administrator of Eritrea, 1951-52. Man. Dir, BOAC Associated Companies Ltd, 1955-59; BOAC Adviser on African Affairs, 1959-64. Pres., Soc. for Libyan Studies, 1969-74; Royal Geographical Society: Hon. Treasurer, 1971-74; Pres., 1974-77; Member: Mt Everest Foundn, 1971-77; British Inst., E

Africa. KStJ. *Address:* 22A Wimbledon Park Road, SW18 1LT. *Club:* Athenæum.   [*Died* 10 *Dec.* 1979.

CUNARD, Sir Henry (Palmes), 6th Bt *cr* 1859; *b* 12 Sept. 1909; *s* of late Capt. Alick May Cunard (*s* of William Samuel Cunard, a *g s* of 1st Bt) and Muriel Palmes; *S* kinsman, Sir Edward Cunard, 5th Bt, 1962. *Educ:* Eton; Trinity Coll., Cambridge. BA Hons 1931. *Heir: b* Major Guy Alick Cunard, *b* 2 Sept. 1911. *Address:* Place Newton, Wintringham, Malton, Yorks. *T:* Rillington 286. *Club:* Cambridge Union. [*Died* 16 *June* 1973.

CUNDALL, Charles, RA 1944 (ARA 1937); RWS 1941 (ARWS 1935); *b* 6 Sept. 1890; *s* of Charles Hellyar Cundall and Elizabeth Mary Fletcher; *m* 1923, Jacqueline Pietersen; one *d. Educ:* Ackworth Sch.; Royal Coll. of Art and Slade Sch.; Paris. Served in Royal Fusiliers, European War, 1914-17; Official War Artist to RN and RAF, 1940-45. Mem. of the New English Art Club, Royal Soc. of Portrait Painters, and Manchester and Bristol Academies of Fine Arts; pictures purchased by Tate Gallery, Contemporary Art Soc., Liverpool, Manchester, Bristol, and other galleries. *Recreations:* travelling, reading. *Address:* G4 Airlie House, 17 Airlie Gardens, W8 7AN. *T:* 01-229 7309; Barnyard Cottage, South Lane, Houghton, near Arundel, Sussex. *T:* Bury 529. *Clubs:* Arts, Garrick.
[*Died* 4 *Nov.* 1971.

CUNLIFFE, Hon. Geoffrey; *b* 26 Aug. 1903; 2nd *s* of 1st Baron Cunliffe and Edith Boothby (later Dowager Baroness Cunliffe, *d* 1965); *m* 1st, 1922, Patrick Sidney (*d* 1940), *o d* of late Robert B. Frend, Ardsallagh, Co. Tipperary; one *s* (and *er s* killed in action, 1945); 2nd, 1941, Gavrelle (marr. diss. 1947), *d* of William Arthur Thomas, and *widow* of Christopher Hobhouse; one *s* one *d*; 3rd, 1947, Barbara Waring, *d* of late Dr J. A. Gibb, Maidstone, Kent. *Educ:* Eton; Trinity Coll., Cambridge. Controller of Aluminium, Min. of Supply and Min. of Aircraft Production, 1939-41; Mem., Industrial and Export Council, Board of Trade, 1941; Dir of Office Machinery, BoT, 1941-42; Dep. Chm. and Man. Dir, British Aluminium Co. Ltd, 1947-59; Man. Dir of Norcros Ltd, 1959-63. A Dep. Pres., British Standards Instn, 1964-70 (Chm. Finance Cttee, 1959-61; Pres. of the Instn, 1961-63; Chm. Gen. Council, 1961-64). *Address:* Poyntzfield House, by Conon Bridge, Ross-shire.
[*Died* 25 *Nov.* 1978.

CUNNINGHAM, Ebenezer, MA; Fellow, St John's College, Cambridge, since 1911; *b* 7 May 1881; *m* 1908, Ada Collins (*d* 1969); one *s* one *d. Educ:* Owen's Sch., Islington; St John's Coll., Cambridge. Senior Wrangler, 1902; Smith's Prizeman, 1904; Fellow of St John's Coll., 1904; Lecturer in Mathematics, Liverpool University, 1904-07; University Coll., London, 1907-11; St John's Coll., Cambridge, 1911-46. Chm., Congregational Union of England and Wales, 1953-54. *Publications:* Principle of Relativity, 1914; Relativity and Electron Theory, 1915. *Address:* Sele House, Corbridge, Northumberland. [*Died* 12 *Feb.* 1977.

CUNNINGHAM, Sir Graham, KBE 1946; Kt 1943; LLB London; FSGT; *b* 19 May 1892; *s* of Daniel Cunningham and Charlotte Eliza Galetti; *m* 1st, 1924, Marjorie Minshaw Harris (decd); two *s* one *d*; 2nd, 1934, Olive St John Williams (*d* 1958); 3rd, 1958, Edith Ellen Smith. *Educ:* Bancrofts Sch., Woodford Wells, Essex. Chm., 1935-61 (Managing Dir, 1929-60) Triplex Safety Glass Company, Ltd; Chm. Shipbuilding Advisory Cttee, 1946-60; Mem. Economic Planning Bd, 1947-61; Dep. Chm. Royal Commission on the Press, 1961-62. Crown Governor, Dep. Chm. and Hon. Fellow, Imperial Coll. of Science and Technology; Past Pres. Soc. of British Gas Industries (1956); Past Pres., Soc. Glass Technology; Dep. Dir-Gen. Children's Overseas Reception Board, 1940; Dir of Claims, War Damage Commission, 1941; Chief Executive and Controller-Gen. Munitions Production, Ministry of Supply, 1941-46; Chm., Scrap Steel Investigation Cttee, 1946; US Medal of Freedom with Silver Bar, 1945; Chm. Dollar Exports Board, 1949. Liveryman of the Coach Makers and Harness Makers Company; Past Master, Curriers Company; Past Master, Glaziers Company. *Recreation:* gardening. *Address:* Woolmers, Mannings Heath, near Horsham, W Sussex. *T:* Horsham 3809. *Club:* Junior Carlton.   [*Died* 23 *Feb.* 1978.

CUNNINGHAM, Rt. Rev. Jack, OBE 1978; Curate-in-Charge of Mells with Vobster, Whatley, Chantry, Kilmersdon, Babington and Elm, since 1978; Assistant Bishop, Diocese of Bath and Wells, since 1978; *b* 1 Sept. 1926; *s* of James and Kathleen Eleanor Cunningham; *m* 1962, Marjorie Elizabeth Davies. *Educ:* Queen Elizabeth Gram. Sch., Wakefield, Yorks; Edinburgh Theological Coll. (GOE). RAF, 1945-48; Theological Coll., 1949-52; Curate, St Mark with St Barnabas, Coventry, 1952-58; Vicar: St Thomas, Longford, Coventry, 1958-62; St Alban, Coventry, 1962-67; Priest-in-Charge, St

Michael, Kitwe, Zambia, 1967-71; Bishop of Central Zambia, 1971-77. *Recreations:* golf, mountaineering. *Address:* The Rectory, Mells, near Frome, Somerset BA11 3PY. *T:* Mells 812320.   [*Died* 18 *Oct.* 1978.

CUNNINGHAM, Rt. Rev. James; *b* Manchester, 15 Aug. 1910; *s* of Patrick William Cunningham and Mary Elizabeth (*née* Meehan). *Educ:* Xaverian Coll., Manchester; St Joseph's Coll., Upholland, Lancs; Gregorian Univ., Rome. Ordained priest, Salford, 1937; Curate, Salford Cathedral, 1940-41; Bishop's Sec. and on staff of Salford Cathedral, 1941-53; Vicar Gen., Administrator and Canon of Salford Cathedral, 1953; Domestic Prelate, 1954-; Vicar Capitular, Salford Dio., 1955; Vicar Gen. of Salford Diocese, 1956-57; Auxiliary Bishop of Hexham and Newcastle, 1957-58, and Vicar Capitular, 1958-; Bishop of Hexham and Newcastle, 1958-74. *Address:* Bishop's House, East Denton Hall, 800 West Road, Newcastle upon Tyne, 5.
[*Died* 10 *July* 1974.

CUNNINGHAM, Sir Knox; see Cunningham, Sir S. K.

CUNNINGHAM, Sir (Samuel) Knox, 1st Bt, *cr* 1963; QC; *b* 3 April 1909; 4th *s* of late Rt Hon. Samuel Cunningham and late Janet McCosh; *m* 1935, Dorothy Enid, JP, *d* of late Edwin Riley. *Educ:* Royal Belfast Academical Institution; Fettes; Clare Coll., Cambridge. Business in Ulster, 1931-37; called to Bar, Middle Temple, 1939; Inn of Court of N Ireland, 1942. Served War of 1939-45, Scots Guards. Contested (U) West Belfast, 1943 and 1945; MP (UU) South Antrim, 1955-70; Parliamentary Private Secretary: to the Financial Sec. to the Treasury, 1958-59; to the Prime Minister, Rt Hon. Harold Macmillan, 1959-63. UK Deleg. to Council of Europe and WEU, 1956-59. Member: Ulster Unionist Council, 1943-; National Executive of Conservative Party, 1959-66; Life Member: RIIA, 1943; E-SU, 1943; National Trust, 1949. Provincial Grand Master, Masonic Prov. of Glos, 1970-. Pres., Old Fettesian Assoc., 1967-70; Chm., Nat. Council of YMCAs, 1949-67; Member: World Alliance of YMCAs, 1947-69; Orpington UDC, 1954-55; Freeman of the City of London, 1956-; Master, 1973-74 (Mem. Ct, 1965-), Worshipful Co. of Drapers; Governor, QMC, Univ. of London, 1967-74. Mem., Loyal Orange Institution, 1943-; Dep. Grand Master of Ireland, 1972-; Apprentice Boy of Derry, 1958-; Vice-President: Ulster Rifle Assoc., 1957-; Cambridge Univ. Boxing Club, 1974-. Author of One Man Dog, unpublished memoir of Harold Macmillan. *Recreations:* formerly boxing (Heavyweight Boxing Champion, Cambridge Univ., 1931), and travel. *Address:* Derhams House, Minchinhampton, Stroud, Glos GL6 9HA. *T:* Brimscombe 3278; 2 Essex Court, Temple, EC4. *Clubs:* Carlton; MCC; Hawks (Cambridge).   [*Died* 29 *July* 1976 (*ext*).

CUNNINGHAM-REID, Captain Alec Stratford, DFC; *s* of late Rev. A. M. Cunningham-Reid; *m* 1st, 1927, Ruth Mary Clarisse (from whom he obtained a divorce, 1940), *yr d* of 1st Baron Mount Temple, PC; two *s*; 2nd, 1944, Angela Williams (from whom he obtained a divorce, 1949); one *s* one *d*; 3rd, Hélène Taylor-Smith. *Educ:* University Coll., London; Clare Coll., Cambridge. Served European War, 1914-18; Royal Engineers and RFC (despatches, DFC); MP (U) Warrington, Lancs, 1922-23 and 1924-29; MP St Marylebone, 1932-45; (Independent, 1942-45); Parliamentary Private Sec. to Sir John Baird, Bt, First Commissioner of Works, 1922; promoted League of Youth and Liberty (LOYAL), 1923; Parliamentary Private Sec. to Rt Hon. Col Wilfrid Ashley, PC, MP, Minister of Transport, 1924. *Publications:* Planes and Personalities; Besides Churchill-Who?; Blame the Old Gang!; Will it be Peace?. *Address:* La Petite Ferme, 06560 Valbonne, France. *T:* Valbonne 67-00-41. *Club:* Bath.   [*Died* 26 *March* 1977.

CUNNISON, David Keith, CIE 1933; formerly Secretary, Bengal Chamber of Commerce, Calcutta; *b* 1881; *m* 1914, Helena, *d* of late George North, South Thoresby, Lincs; one *d. Educ:* George Watson's Coll. and Univ., Edinburgh, (MA, LLB). Delhi Durbar Medal, 1911. *Address:* Ravenscroft, Bulstrode Way, Gerrards Cross, Bucks.   [*Died* 25 *Jan.* 1972.

CUNYNGHAME, Sir (Henry) David St Leger Brooke Selwyn, 11th Bt (of Milncraig), *cr* 1702; *b* 7 Feb. 1905; *s* of Lieut-Col Sir Percy Francis Cunynghame, 10th Bt, OBE, DL, JP, and Maud Albinia Margaret (*d* 1948), *o d* of Major Selwyn-Payne, Badgeworth Court, Gloucester; *S* father, 1941; *m* 1941, Hon. Pamela Margaret Stanley, actress, *d* of 5th Baron Stanley of Alderley; three *s. Educ:* Eton. Formerly Mem., Board of Dirs of various British Motion Picture Producing and Distributing Companies. Served as Sqdn Ldr; RAFVR during War of 1939-45. *Heir: s* Andrew David Francis Cunynghame [*b* 25 Dec. 1942; *m* 1972, Harriet Ann, *d* of C. T. Dupont, Montreal]. *Address:* 15 Madeline Road, SE20. *T:* 01-778 7740. *Club:* Athenæum.
[*Died* 6 *Aug.* 1978.

CURRAN, Charles; MP (C) Uxbridge, 1959-66 and since 1970; *b* 1903; *m* Mona Regan; one *s. Educ:* Cardiff High Sch.; Stonyhurst. Called to Bar, Gray's Inn. Journalist. Fleet Street, 1928-55: London Evening News (Chief Sub-Editor, Asst Editor); Evening Standard (Features Editor, Asst Editor); Daily Mirror (Asst Editor); Contested (C): West Walthamstow, 1945; Uxbridge, 1951 and 1955. *Publication:* You Know You Can Trust Me (novel). *Address:* 9 Stone Buildings, Lincoln's Inn, WC2. *T:* 01-405 0975; 70 Park Mansions, Knightsbridge, SW1. *T:* 01-584 7845. *Clubs:* Press, Savage, Carlton.
[Died 16 Sept. 1972.

CURRAN, Sir Charles (John), Kt 1974; Director-General of the BBC, 1969-77; Consultant to BBC Board of Governors on international broadcasting matters, 1977-78; Managing Director and Chief Executive, Visnews, since 1978; *b* 13 Oct. 1921; *s* of Felix Curran and Alicia Isabella (*née* Bruce); *m* 1949, Silvia Meyer; one *d. Educ:* Wath-on-Dearne Gram. Sch., S Yorks; Magdalene Coll., Cambridge. Indian Army, 1941-45. Producer, Home Talks, BBC, 1947-50; Asst Editor, Fishing News, 1950-51; BBC, 1951-78, including appts as Canadian Rep., 1956-59 and Sec., 1963-66; Dir of External Broadcasting, 1967-69. Pres., European Broadcasting Union, 1973-78; Mem., Board, British Council, 1978- (Mem. Exec. Cttee, 1973-78); Mem., 'The Tablet' Trust, 1976-. Mem., UK Marriage Res. Centre. FBIM. Hon. DLitt City, 1977; DUniv Open, 1978. KCSS 1979. *Publication:* A Seamless Robe: broadcasting—philosophy and practice, 1979. *Recreation:* formerly refereeing coarse Rugby, now enjoying music. *Address:* Visnews Ltd, Cumberland Avenue, NW10 7EH. *T:* 01-965 7733. *Clubs:* United Oxford & Cambridge University, Garrick.
[Died 9 Jan. 1980.

CURRER BRIGGS, D. H.; *see* Briggs, D. H. C.

CURREY, Rear-Adm. Harry Philip, CB 1956; OBE 1941; *b* 18 Sept. 1902; *s* of Hon. H. L. Currey; *m* 1928, Rona Gwenllian Harkness; one *s* one *d. Educ:* RN Colls Osborne and Dartmouth. Served War of 1939-45: Western Approaches, GHQ, Cairo, E Indies Stn, Eastern Fleet, Mediterranean, British Pacific Fleet. Admty, 1945-47: Capt. of Dockyard, HM Dockyard, Devonport, 1948-50; HMS Bermuda, 1951-53; Flag Officer, Gibraltar and Adm. Supt, HM Dockyard, Gibraltar, 1953-56; retired, 1956. Mem. Cttee, RUKBA. *Recreations:* fishing, gardening. *Address:* Pond Cottage, Newton Valence, near Alton, Hants GU34 3RB. *T:* Tisted 281. *Club:* Naval and Military.
[Died 31 Oct. 1979.

CURRIE, George Boyle Hanna, MBE 1946; *b* 19 Dec. 1905; *s* of late Very Rev. William John Currie, BA, DD; *m* 1933, Stephanie Maud Evelyn Costello; two *s* two *d. Educ:* Campbell Coll., Belfast; Trinity Coll., Dublin (BA, MA, LLB). Called to Bar, Middle Temple, 1932; Northern Circuit, 1932; Councillor, Wirral UDC, 1934-50 (Chm. Council, 1938); contested (C) East Flintshire, 1950 and 1951; MP (UU) North Down, 1955-70. Served War, 1939-46 (MBE 1946); RAFVR (Sqdn Ldr). Mem., Council for Arab-British Understanding, 1970-71. *Recreations:* salmon fishing, golf. *Address:* (chambers) Queen Insurance Building D, Queen Avenue, 13 Castle Street, Liverpool L2 4UE. *T:* 051-236 5072; (residence) 1 Pump Court, Temple, EC4. *T:* 01-583 1594; Wyncote, Roscote Close, Lower Village, Heswall, Wirral, Merseyside. *T:* Heswall 1444. *Club:* County (Downpatrick).
[Died 20 Jan. 1978.

CURRIE, Lt-Col George Selkirk, CMG 1944; DSO 1918; MC 1916; Member, firm of Coopers and Lybrand; *b* 17 Oct. 1889; *m* 1927, Louisa Hope, *d* of George H. Napier, Montreal; two *s* two *d. Educ:* Perth, Ontario; McGill Univ. (BA). Served European War, 1914-18 (despatches twice, MC, DSO). Deputy Minister of National Defence (Army), Canada, 1942-44. *Address:* 695 Aberdeen Avenue, Westmount 217, Quebec, Canada. *Clubs:* University, Montreal Racquet, Royal Montreal Golf (Montreal); Forest and Stream (Dorval, PQ).
[Died 12 Aug. 1975.

CURRIE, Sir Walter Mordaunt Cyril, 5th Bt, *cr* 1846; Member of the Performing Right Society; *b* 3 June 1894; *s* of 4th Bt and Bertha (*d* 1951), *d* of T. A. Mitford Freeman; *S* father, 1941. *Educ:* Sherborne. Served European War, 1915-16, with RAOC. *Publications:* Some 25 lyrics and part songs, 2 cantatas; choral symphony, Odysseus; Nativity Play, The Three Kings, music by C. Armstrong Gibbs. *Address:* Chasefield Cottage, Wickham Bishops, Witham, Essex.
[Died 30 July 1978.

CURSITER, Stanley, CBE 1948 (OBE 1919); RSW; RSA 1937 (now Hon. retired Academician); FRSE; FEIS; FRIAS; DL; HM's painter and limner in Scotland since 1948; *b* Kirkwall, Orkney Isles, 1887; *s* of J. Scott Cursiter; *m* Phyllis Eda (*d* 1975), *d* of David Hourston of Greenfield; one *d.* Represented in

permanent collections of the Corporations of Liverpool, Oldham, Paisley, Cork; Scot. Mod. Arts; Director of National Galleries of Scotland, 1930-48. Served European War with Scottish Rifles and 4th Batt. Field Survey Royal Engineers (OBE, despatches twice). Freeman of City and Royal Burgh of Kirkwall, 1948. DL Orkney, 1971. Hon. LLD Aberdeen, 1959. *Address:* 70 Victoria Street, Stromness, Orkney.
[Died 22 April 1976.

CURSLEY, Norman Sharpe; *b* 13 April 1898; *s* of David and Mary Cursley; *m* 1922, Alice Nelly Hill (*d* 1972); one *s* one *d.* Formerly: Reporter, Leicester Daily Mercury, 1921; Special Writer, The Globe, 1922; Reporter, Daily Sketch, 1923; Reporter and News Editor, Westminster Gazette, 1924-28; News Editor, Daily News (Manchester), 1929-48; News Editor, News Chronicle (London), 1948; Asst Editor, News Chronicle, 1951, Editor and Director of the News Chronicle, 1958-60. *Address:* The Old Orchard, Puttenham, near Guildford, Surrey. *T:* Puttenham 298. *Club:* Press.
[Died 3 May 1972.

CURTEIS, Capt. Sir Gerald, KCVO 1954 (MVO 1927); RN, retired, Elder Brother of Trinity House from 1936, Deputy Master of the Corporation, 1948-61; Court of The London Assurance, 1953-63; *b* 16 Oct. 1892; *s* of late Robert Mascall Curteis, Piltdown, Uckfield; *m* 1st, Lettice (*d* 1918), *d* of late Canon Foster, Groombridge; no *c* ; 2nd, 1936, Dolla, *o d* of late Walter G. Darby, Markly, Sussex; one *s* two *d. Educ:* Parkside, Ewell; RN Colleges, Osborne and Dartmouth. Entered Navy, 1906; served European War in HM Ships Blonde, Warspite, Boadicea, Godetia; served in HMS Renown during tour of Duke and Duchess of York to New Zealand and Australia, 1927; Comdr, 1927; Captain, 1934; retired list, 1936; served War of 1939-45, in RN. Hon. Member Worshipful Company of Feltmakers. *Address:* Broomwood, Sevenoaks, Kent. *Clubs:* United Service and Royal Aero, MCC; (Hon. Member) Royal Corinthian Yacht.
[Died 24 Feb. 1972.

CURTHOYS, Roy Lancaster, CMG 1958; Chief Australian Correspondent, Times and New York Times, 1927-57, retired; *b* Ballarat, 4 Oct. 1892; *er s* of late Alfred George Curthoys, Perth, W. Australia; unmarried. *Educ:* privately; Hale Sch., Perth. Member, literary staff, Perth Daily News, 1910-16; West Australian, Perth, 1916-18; Melbourne Herald, 1919-20; joined Melbourne Argus Staff, 1920; on staff Australian Press Association, London, 1922-23; Asst Editor of Argus, 1925-28; Editor, 1929-35; Member of Federal Council of Australian Journalists Association, 1918-20. *Recreations:* music, walking. *Address:* PO Box 37, South Yarra, Victoria 3141, Australia.
[Died 24 Sept. 1971.

CURTIS, Maj.-Gen. Alfred Cyril, CB 1944; DSO 1942; MC; ADC to the King, 1944; *b* 2 Nov. 1894. Lieut, Indian Army, 1915; Captain, 1918; Major, 1932; Bt Lt-Col, 1936; Lt-Col, 1938; Col, 1940; temp. Maj.-Gen., 1944. Comdr Lucknow District, 1946; retired, 1948 as hon. Maj.-Gen.
[Died 13 Oct. 1971.

CURTIS, Sir George (Harold), Kt 1955; CB 1950; Chief Land Registrar, HM Land Registry, 1947-63; *b* 12 June 1902; *s* of Dr John Cyril Curtis and Mabel Curtis; *m* 1928, Susan Phyllis Elmer; no *c. Educ:* Swansea Grammar Sch.; Keble Coll., Oxford. BA (hons) 1923; Boxing Blue, 1924; BCL 1924. Bacon Scholar, Gray's Inn, 1924; called to the Bar, 1925; HM Land Registry, 1926; transferred to HM Treasury, 1940; Asst Secretary, 1945. President Caterham and Dist. Residents Assoc., 1957-61. Chairman, Cttee for secession of Nyasaland from Federation of Rhodesia and Nyasaland, March 1963, and of Cttee for dissolution of the Federation, Aug.-Dec. 1963; Member panel of Chairmen of Industrial Tribunals, 1965-67; President, Mumbles Chamber of Trade, 1966-. *Publication:* (with T. B. F. Ruoff) The Law and Practice of Registered Conveyancing, 1958. *Recreations:* golf in intervals from gardening. *Address:* Tyrnant, 14 West Cross Lane, West Cross, Swansea.
[Died 15 Jan. 1972.

CURTIS, Dame Myra, DBE, *cr* 1949 (CBE 1942); MA; Principal, Newnham College, Cambridge, 1942-Sept. 1954, retired; *b* 2 Oct. 1886. *Educ:* Winchester School for Girls (now St Swithun's); Newnham Coll., Cambridge. Civil Servant, 1915-41. Commissioner, War Damage Commission, 1943-59; Chairman of Interdepartmental Cttee on Children deprived of a normal home life, 1945-46; Member Central Land Board, 1947-59; Member General Medical Council, 1955-60. *Publication:* Modern Money (with Hugh Townshend), 1937. *Address:* 5a Northgate, Chichester, Sussex.
[Died 26 June 1971.

CURTIS, Sir Peter, 6th Bt, *cr* 1802; *b* 9 April 1907; *s* of late Edward Beaumont Cotton Curtis; *S* cousin, 1943; *m* 1934, Joan

Margaret Nicholson; one s two d. *Educ:* Winchester Coll. Lieut 16/5 Lancers, 1926-28 (SR); Lieut 16/5 Lancers, 1928-34. Served 1939-45 Shropshire Yeomanry, Div. HQ Armoured Div. and 38 (W) Infantry Div., and Pioneer Corps. *Recreations:* shooting, fishing, racing (horse). *Heir:* s William Peter Curtis, b 9 April 1935. *Address:* Little Manor, Bishop's Waltham, Hants.
[Died 28 Sept. 1976.

CURTIS, Air Vice-Marshal Walter John Brice, CB 1946; CBE 1941 (OBE 1919); b 9 Nov. 1888; m 1917, Kathleen Osman Mullery (d 1972); one s one d (and one s Flight-Lieut killed in action, Middle East, 1943). *Educ:* Lewisham House, Weston-super-Mare; Brighton Grammar Sch. RFC 1914; RAF 1918; Air Ministry, 1920-24; Iraq, 1924-27; Middle East, 1927-28; Coastal Command, 1930-32; India, 1933-38; Air Ministry, 1938-44; Dep. Director of Equipment, 1938-39; Director of Equipment, Air Commodore, 1940-44; AOC 55 (M) Wing, 1944-45; AOC 42 Group, July-Nov. 1945; AOC 40 Group, 1945-47; retired, 1947. Despatches 1941. *Recreations:* hockey, tennis, golf. *Address:* The Meads, Grange Road, Uckfield, Sussex. *T:* Uckfield 2000.
[Died 10 Nov. 1973.

CURTIS, Air Marshal Wilfred Austin, OC 1967; CB 1946; CBE 1943; DSC and bar 1917; ED 1945; Commander, US Legion of Merit; Chevalier, French Legion of Honour; Croix de Guerre with palm; LLD 1948; retired; b 21 Aug. 1893; s of Colin Mackenzie and Margaret Alice Sherwin; m 1924, Pearl Burford (decd); two s one d; m 1962, Mrs Maiola Englebright. *Educ:* Toronto Public and Technical Schools. Joined Canadian Army, 1915; transferred to Royal Naval Air Service, 1916; served as fighter pilot, France, 1917 and 1918; operated General Insurance business in own name at Toronto until outbreak of war, 1939; Director of Postings and Careers, 1940-41; Comd Uplands Air Training Station, 1941; Dep. C-in-C, RCAF overseas, Nov. 1941-44; Air Member Air Staff, Jan. 1944; Senior RCAF Member, Permanent Joint Board on Defence, Jan. 1944-Sept. 1947; Chief of Air Staff, Canada, 1947-53. Chancellor, York Univ., Toronto, 1960-68 (Hon. LLD 1968). Mem., Royal Canadian Military Inst. Hon. DMilSc RMC 1962. *Recreation:* golf. *Address:* Towers of Cable Beach, PO Box 4939, Nassau, Bahamas. *T:* 78-343. *Clubs:* Lyford Cay (Bahamas); York, Rosedale Golf (Toronto). *[Died* 7 Aug. 1977.

CURTIS BROWN, Spencer; b 1906; s of A. Curtis Brown and Caroline Lord; m 1928, Jean, d of Rev. W. Watson, DD; one d. *Educ:* Harrow; Magdalene Coll., Cambridge (History Exhibitioner). Personal Adviser to General Sikorski, Polish Prime Minister, 1941-43; Intelligence Corps (Special Services); assisted in reorganizing book trade in liberated countries, 1945; Chm., Curtis Brown Ltd, London, literary agents, 1945-1968; served on various Government Cttees concerned with book distribution. *Publications:* (jt author) The Dark Side of the Moon, 1946; biographical introduction to Elizabeth Bowen's Pictures and Conversations, 1975. *Recreation:* listening to other people. *Club:* Travellers'. *[Died* 16 Jan. 1980.

CURWEN, Dame (Anne) May, DBE 1949 (CBE 1943); MA Cantab; President, British Council for Aid to Refugees; Vice-President, UNA, UK Committee; b 7 May 1889; d of William Curwen and Emma Cook. *Educ:* Birkenhead High Sch.; Harrogate Coll.; Newnham Coll., Cambridge. Hons Historical Tripos, Parts I and II, MA 1920; History Mistress, Orme Girls' Sch., Newcastle, Staffs, 1914-16; Organising Secretary, Scottish Women's Hospitals, 1916-19; in Serbia in connection with inquiry into condition of women and children there, 1918-19; joined staff National YWCA in finance dept, 1919; Education Secretary, YWCA, 1920-30; National General Secretary, YWCA of Great Britain, 1930-49; Chairman, Women's Group on Public Welfare, 1948-60; Vice-Chm., Nat. Council of Social Service, 1956-70; HM Govt Delegate to the UN Refugee Fund, 1954-58 (Chairman, 1958); Vice-Chairman World Refugee Year, UK Cttee, June 1959-June 1960; UN Nansen Medal award, 1964. Jugo-Slav Order of St Sava (3rd Class), 1922; Order of Polonia Restituta, 1970. *Recreations:* reading, cooking. *Address:* 11 Marryats Court, Kennard Road, New Milton, Hants. *[Died* 13 Sept. 1973.

CUSACK, Hon. Sir Ralph Vincent, Kt 1966; **Hon. Mr Justice Cusack;** Judge of the High Court of Justice (Queen's Bench Division) since 1966; b 13 April 1916; s of late His Honour John Cusack, KC, and late Dora, d of R. Winder, Solicitor; unmarried. *Educ:* King's Coll. Sch.; University of London; and in Italy. LLB 1939; Barrister, Gray's Inn, 1940; Bencher, 1966. Served in Army, 1940-46; Staff Capt., HQ Eastern Command, 1943-44; Dep. Asst Military Secretary (Major), War Office, 1944-46. Freeman, City of London, 1949; Member General Council of the Bar, 1953-57, 1960-64; QC 1960; Recorder of Gloucester, 1961-64; of Wolverhampton, 1964-66; Comr of

Assize, South Eastern Circuit, July 1965; Leader of the Oxford Circuit, 1964-66. Deputy Chairman, Berkshire Quarter Sessions, 1962-68. Mem., 1974-76, Vice-Chm., 1975-76, Parole Bd. *Address:* 221 Ashley Gardens, Westminster, SW1P 1PA. *T:* 01-834 5610; Royal Courts of Justice, Strand, WC2. *Clubs:* Athenæum, Garrick. *[Died* 11 March 1978.

CUSDEN, Victor Vincent, OBE 1943; b 26 Jan. 1893; s of James Cusden and Elizabeth Susan Wakelyn; m 1927, Aimée Louise Charlotte Pauwels; one s (one d decd). *Educ:* Christ's Hospital. Interned during war at Ruhleben Camp, Germany, where studied for Consular Service; granted Civil Service Certificate as a Probationer Vice-Consul in the Consular Service, 1919; appointed to Salonica, 1919; transferred to Antwerp, 1920; acting Vice-Consul at Charleroi, 1920-21; given substantive rank of Vice-Consul, 1921; acting Consul-General at Antwerp, 1921-22-23; acting Vice-Consul at Ghent, 1921; transferred to Valparaiso, 1924; acting Consul-General at Valparaiso, 1924-25 and 1927; transferred to Barcelona, 1928; acting Consul-General at Barcelona in 1928, 1929 and 1930; acting Consul at Malaga, 1929; in charge of Consulate General at Dakar, 1930; Consul at Nantes, 1930 (did not proceed); Consul-General at Dakar, 1931; at Loanda, 1941; Izmir (Smyrna), Turkey, 1946-51; Retired, 1951. Coronation Medal, 1937. *Address:* Mayfield, Avisford Park Road, Walberton, Arundel, W Sussex BN18 0AP.
[Died 27 Aug. 1980.

CUSHION, Air Vice-Marshal Sir William Boston, KBE 1947 (CBE 1942; OBE 1927); CB 1944; RAF, retired; b 30 Jan. 1891; s of late William Cushion, Surlingham, Norwich; m 1917, Esther Jane Kenyon-Spooner; two d. *Educ:* Gresham's Sch., Holt; Faraday House, London, WC1. 2nd Lieut Manchester Regt, 1914; attached Royal Flying Corps, 1915; served France, 1915-18; permanent commission, Royal Air Force, 1919, as Flight Lieut; Sqdn Leader, 1921; served India, 1922-27; Wing Comdr, 1930; Iraq, 1933-35; Group Capt., 1937; Air Commodore, 1940; Temp. Air Vice-Marshal, 1942; late Director-General of Equipment, Air Ministry; British Overseas Airways Corp., retired, 1956. *Address:* 146 Rivermead Court, SW6. *T:* 01-736 4687. *Club:* Hurlingham. *[Died* 16 Jan. 1978.

CUSSEN, Edward James Patrick; His Honour Judge Cussen; a Circuit Judge (Additional Judge, Central Criminal Court), since 1971; b 21 Oct. 1904; e s of Patrick David Cussen and Mary (née Enright); m 1948, Veronica FitzSimon Hewett; one d. *Educ:* Beaumont Coll., Old Windsor; St John's Coll., Oxford. Called to the Bar, Inner Temple, 1931; Bencher of the Inner Temple, 1959. Civil Assistant, attached to the General Staff, War Office, 1940; Intelligence Corps, 1941-46 (Lieut-Colonel). Prosecuting Counsel to the Crown at North London Sessions, 1950; a Junior Prosecuting Counsel to the Crown at Central Criminal Court, 1953; Second Senior Prosecuting Counsel to the Crown, Central Criminal Court, 1959, Senior Prosecuting Counsel to the Crown, 1964-71. *Recreation:* tennis. *Address:* 1 Dr Johnson's Buildings, Temple, EC4. *T:* 01-353 1662. *[Died* 9 Nov. 1973.

CUTFORTH, Maj.-Gen. Sir Lancelot Eric, KBE 1958 (CBE 1949; OBE 1945); CB 1953; Chairman: London Area Transport Users' Consultative Committee, 1964-72; London Transport Passengers Committee, 1970-71; b 14 Aug. 1899; s of G. H. Cutforth; m 1925, Vera Reffell; two d. *Educ:* St Peter's Sch., York; Royal Military Academy, Woolwich. 2nd Lieut RA, 1918; AAG, War Office, 1941; DDOS 1942; DOS, HQ BAOR, 1946; DDOS, War Office, 1948; DOS, MELF, 1951; Maj.-Gen., 1951; Inspector, RAOC, War Office, 1953-55; Director of Ordnance Services, War Office, 1955-58, retired; Colonel Comdt RAOC, 1957-65; Director-General of Inspection, Ministry of Supply, 1958-60; Asst Master-Gen. of Ordnance (Inspection), WO, 1960-62. *Address:* Glade, Earleydene, Ascot, Berks SL5 9JY. *T:* Ascot 20923. *Club:* Army and Navy.
[Died 7 April 1980.

D

d'ABREU, Prof. Alphonso Liguori, CBE 1968 (OBE 1944); DL; Surgeon, United Birmingham Hospitals since 1946; Dean of Medical School 1959-63, Professor of Surgery, 1963-71 (of Cardiac Surgery, 1960-63), University of Birmingham, Emeritus Professor, 1971; Member, Central Health Services Council, 1964-71; Member, Medical Sub-Committee of University Grants Committee, since 1964; b 5 Aug. 1906; s of Dr John Francis d'Abreu and Teresa d'Abreu; m 1935, Elizabeth Throckmorton (d 1970); three d. Educ: Stonyhurst Coll.; Univ. of Birmingham. MB ChB Birmingham 1930; MRCS, LRCP 1930; FRCS 1932; ChM Birmingham 1936; FRCP 1968. House Surgeon and Surgical Registrar, Gen. Hospital, Birmingham; Jun. Asst, Surgical Unit, Cardiff Royal Infirmary, University of Wales, 1930-33, Asst Dir, 1933-39; Acting Prof. of Surgery, 1945-46. Lieut RAMC (Supp. Reserve), 1939; served War of 1939-45 (despatches), Major, RAMC 1939, Lt-Col, 1942-45; retd. Hon. Consultant in Thoracic Surgery to the Army, 1964-73. Vice-Pres., RCS, 1973- (Mem. Council, 1963-74; Hunterian Prof., RCS, 1939 and 1946, Mem. Court of Examiners, 1957-63). Vis. Lectr in Surgery, Med. Sch., Harvard Univ., USA, 1951; John Alexander Lectr, Univ. of Michigan, 1965; McLauchlin Gallie Vis. Prof., Canada, 1966; Vis. Prof., Boston City Hosp. (Harvard Unit), 1967. FRSocMed 1946-71 (Pres., Sect. of Surgery, 1966-67; President: Soc. of Thoracic and Cardiovascular Surgeons, 1969-70; Thoracic Soc., 1969-70. Hon. Col, RAMC (48 Div. TA, W Midland District, 1963-67). DL Warwicks, 1967. Publications: (with Prof. Lambert Rogers) Everyday Surgery, 1938; A Practice of Thoracic Surgery, 1st edn 1953, 3rd edn 1971; Intrathoracic Crises (with A. Brian Taylor and David B. Clarke), 1968; ed and contrib. Thoracic Surgery, (Butterworth's) Clinical Surgery, Contributions to med. journals. Recreations: fishing; Vice-Pres. Warwicks County Cricket Club. Address: Ford House, Coughton, near Alcester, Warwicks. Clubs: Athenæum, Forty Club. [Died 19 April 1976.

DAGGETT, William Ingledew; late Senior Ear, Nose and Throat Surgeon to King's College Hospital; Consulting Ear, Nose and Throat Surgeon to Leatherhead Hospital and St Luke's Hostel for Clergy; late Chairman King's College Hospital Group Medical Committee; late Brigadier RAMC; Consultant in Otolaryngology to Army; b 2 Oct. 1900; s of Dr H. Ingledew Daggett, Boroughbridge; m 1928, Eileen Hilda (marr. diss., 1947), d of Col T. W. Simpson; no c. Educ: Sedbergh (Exhibitioner); Caius Coll., Cambridge (Scholar, 1st Class Hons Nat. Sci. Tripos); King's Coll. Hosp. (Scholar), MA, MB, BChir Cantab; FRCS; recognised teacher University of London. Publications: in medical and surgical journals. Address: 15 Devonshire Close, W1. T: 01-580 5366. Club: Bath. [Died 26 Sept. 1980.

DAINTREE JOHNSON, Harold; see Johnson, H. D.

DAKERS, Mrs Andrew; see Lane, Jane.

DALE, Rt. Rev. Basil Montague, MA; b 12 April 1903; er s of late Rev. Canon Harold Montague Dale; m 1927, Kathleen, d of Lieut-Col C. A. E. O'Meara, CIE; one s. Educ: Dean Close Sch.; Queens' Coll., Cambridge; Westcott House Theological Coll. Historical and Theological Tripos, MA Cambridge. Ordained Diocese of Southwark, 1927; Curate, St Andrew's, Catford, 1927-29; in charge of All Saints, Putney, 1929-32; Vicar, St Andrew's, Handsworth, Birmingham, 1932-35; Vicar, Paignton, Devon, 1936-44; Chaplain to the King, 1948; Rector of Hatfield, Herts, 1945-49; Rural Dean of Hertford, 1948-49; Domestic Chaplain to the Marquess of Salisbury, 1946-49; Bishop of Jamaica, 1950-55; Rector of Haslemere, 1955-62; Asst Bishop of Guildford, 1955-67; Hon. Canon of Guildford Cathedral, 1961. Recreations: gardening, walking. Address: Little Waggoners, The Spinny, Grayshott, Hindhead, Haslemere, Surrey. [Died 1 Feb. 1976.

DALE, Francis Richard, CBE 1950; DSO 1919; MC; MA; Hon. MA London, 1948; b 7 March 1883; s of J. F. Dale, Coleshill, Warwicks; m 1909, Mary, d of E. J. M. Phillips, Liverpool; two s (and one s killed in action, 1943) two d. Educ: Oundle; Trinity Coll., Cambridge. Classical VI Form Master, Leeds Grammar Sch., 1906-19; The Royal Welch Fusiliers, 1916-19; demobilised, Feb. 1919; Headmaster, Plymouth Coll., 1920-29; Headmaster, City of London Sch., 1929-Aug. 1950; Pres., the Virgil Soc., 1952-54; Pres., Headmasters' Assoc., 1939-40. Temp. Lectr in Classics, King's Coll., London, 1953-55, 1959, Westfield Coll., 1960-62, 1964. Vice-Pres., Classical Association. Publications: On the Teaching of Latin; Paginæ Primæ; (with C. Craddock) Latin Elegy, Lyric and Epigram. Recreations: trans. of ancient verse into quantity in English; tape recordings of Latin and Greek. Address: Dingle Ridge, Arkley, Barnet, Herts. T: 01-449 6468. [Died 14 May 1976.

DALGETY, Arthur William Hugh; b Nov. 1899; 2nd s of late Major F. J. Dalgety and Hon. Mrs Dalgety of Lockerley Hall, Romsey; m; one s. Educ: Harrow; Sandhurst. Lieut 9th Queen's Royal Lancers, retired. Master: Dunston Harriers, 1923; Vine Hunt, 1924-29; own Stag-hounds, 1926; New Forest Buckhounds, 1936-38 and 1944-47; Southdown Foxhounds, 1929-52; Meynell Foxhounds, 1952-55; Isle of Wight Foxhounds, 1955-59; Hursley Foxhounds, 1959-64; Tedworth

Foxhounds, 1964-65; Ormond Foxhounds, 1965-; North Tipperary Foxhounds, 1965-68; own Beagles, 1950-63. Address: Balsdean, Brighton, Sussex. T: Brighton 33640; Lockerley Hall, Romsey, Hants; Emmel Castle, Cloughjordan, Co. Tipperary, Ireland. Club: Cavalry. [Died 20 Aug. 1972.

DALLAPICCOLA, Prof. Luigi; composer; piano teacher at Conservatorio Musicale, Florence, 1934-67; b 3 Feb. 1904; s of Pio Dallapiccola and Domitilla Alberti; m 1938, Laura Luzzatto; one d. Educ: Ginnasio-Liceo, Pisino d'Istria; Conservatorio Musicale, Florence. Became Italian Citizen, 1918. First visited London, 1938; again in 1946, and various European capitals during these years; USA: 1951, 1952, 1956, 1959, 1962, 1964, 1967, 1969. Member: Accad. Filarmonica Romana, 1947; also of various foreign academies, 1953-, incl. RAM. Dr hc Univ. of Michigan, Ann Arbor, 1967; Univ. of Durham, 1973; Univ. of Edinburgh, 1973. Grosser Kunstpreis des Landes Nordrhein-Westfalen für Musik, Düsseldorf, 1962; Musikpreis Ludwig Spohr, Braunschweig, 1964. Verdienstkreuz I Klasse des Verdienstordens der Bundesrepublik Deutschland, 1968, Arthur Honegger Prize, 1972; Premio Feltrinelli, Accad. Naz. dei Lincei, 1973. Has written since 1925; works include: Sei Cori di Michelangelo Buonarroti il Giovane, 1933-36; Divertimento in Quattro Esercizi, 1934; Musica per tre Pianoforti, 1935; Volo di Notte, 1937-39; Canti di Prigionia, 1938-41; Piccolo Concerto per Muriel Couvreux, 1939-41; Marsia, 1942-43; Liriche Greche, 1942-45; Il Prigioniero, 1944-48; Ciaccona Intermezzo e Adagio, 1945; Tre Poemi, 1949; Job, 1950; Tartiniana, 1951; Canti di Liberazione, 1951-55; Quaderno Musicale di Annalibera, 1952; Goethe-Lieder, 1953; Piccola Musica Notturna, 1954; Variazioni per Orchestra, 1954; An Mathilde, 1955; Cinque Canti, 1955; Tartiniana Seconda, 1956; Concerto per la Notte di Natale dell' Anno 1956, 1957; Requiescant, 1957-58; Dialoghi, 1960; Preghiere, 1962; Parole di San Paolo, 1964; Ulysses, opera, 1968; Sicut umbra, 1970; Tempus destruendi, Tempus aedificandi, 1970-71; Commiato, 1972. Many of his works have been recorded. Address: Via Romana 34, 50125 Firenze, Italy. T: 227698. [Died 18 Feb. 1975.

DALRYMPLE, Sir (Charles) Mark, 3rd Bt, cr 1887; RAuxAF; Market Gardener; b 13 May 1915; s of Sir David Charles Herbert Dalrymple, 2nd Bt, of Newhailes, and Margaret Anna (d 1962) (who obtained a divorce, 1919, and m 2nd, 1925, Sir Patrick Graham Blake, 5th Bt, who d 1930), y d of late Sir Mark Mactaggart Stewart, 1st Bt; S father, 1932; m 1946, Lady Antonia Marian Amy Isabel Stewart, o d of 12th Earl of Galloway. Educ: Canford Sch., Wimborne, Dorset. Lieut 4th/5th (Queen's Edinburgh) Royal Scots (TA), (52nd Searchlight Regt) The Royal Regt, 1937-40 (discharged due to insufficiently good eyesight). Aircraftman RAFVR, 1941-46 (1939-45 Star, France and Germany Star, Defence Medal, War Medal, 1939-45). Heir: none. Address: Newhailes, Musselburgh, Midlothian, Scotland. T: 031-665 2812; 12a Inver Court, Inverness Terrace, Bayswater, W2 6JB. T: 01-727 9993. Clubs: Lansdowne, Royal Over-Seas League; New (Edinburgh). [Died 29 June 1971 (ext).

DALRYMPLE, Sir Mark; see Dalrymple, Sir C. M.

DALRYMPLE-CHAMPNEYS, Captain Sir Weldon, 2nd Bt, cr 1910; CB 1957; MA, DM, BCh, DPH Oxon; Fellow and former Member of Council (Milroy Lecturer, 1950), Royal College of Physicians, London; Captain, Grenadier Guards (retired); Deputy Chief Medical Officer, Ministry of Health, 1940-56; President: Section of Epidemiology and Public Health, Royal Society of Medicine, 1943-45; Section of Comparative Medicine, 1954-55; Section of History of Medicine, 1957-59; Vice-President Emeritus, Royal Society of Health; Fellow and Ex-Chairman, Royal Veterinary College; Member of Council, Animal Health Trust; President, Federation of Civil Service Photographic Societies; President Hæmophilia Society; b 7 May 1892; o surv. s of Sir Francis Henry Champneys, 1st Bt, and Virginia Julian (d 1922), o d of late Sir John Warrender Dalrymple, 7th Bt, of North Berwick; S father, 1930; m 1st, 1924, Anne, OBE 1948 (d 1968), d of late Col A. Spencer Pratt, CB, CMG, Broom Hall, Kent; 2nd, 1974, Norma (Hon. Research Fellow, Somerville Coll., Oxford), widow of A. S. Russell and d of late Col R. Hull Lewis. Educ: Oriel Coll., Oxford (Hon. Fellow, 1967). Served European War, 1914-19 (wounded); Senior Asst MOH, Willesden UDC; Hon. Physician to the King, 1941-44; Lord of the Manor of Stanwick (Northants); assumed additional surname of Dalrymple by deed poll, 1924. Ex-Chm., Vegetable Drugs Cttee, Ministry of Supply. Past Pres., Joint Food and Agriculture Organisation/World Health Organisation Expert Cttee on Brucellosis. Corresp. Mem., Sociedad Peruana de Salud Publica. Hon. ARCVS. Hon. Diploma, Amer. Veterinary Epidemiological Soc. Publications: Reports to Ministry of Health on the Accommodation for the

Sick provided at certain Public Schools for Boys in England, 1928; Undulant Fever, 1929; Bovine Tuberculosis in Man, with special reference to infection by milk, 1931; The Supervision of Milk Pasteurising Plants, 1935; Undulant Fever, a Neglected Problem (Milroy Lectures, Royal College of Physicians), 1950; Brucella Infection and Undulant Fever in Man, 1960; also numerous articles in scientific journals. *Recreations:* yachting, swimming, travelling, photography, etc. *Heir:* none. *Address:* 39 Ritchie Court, 380 Banbury Road, Oxford. *T:* Oxford 58171.
[Died 14 Dec. 1980 (ext).]

DALRYMPLE-HAMILTON, Adm. Sir Frederick Hew George, KCB 1945 (CB 1941); JP; DL; *b* 27 March 1890; *s* of late Col Hon. North de Coigny Dalrymple-Hamilton, MVO, of Bargany, Girvan, Ayrshire; *m* 1918, Gwendolen (*d* 1974), *d* of Sir Cuthbert Peek, 2nd Bt; one *s* two *d*. *Educ:* HMS Britannia. Entered Royal Navy, 1905; served European War, 1914-18; Capt. 1931; Capt. Royal Naval Coll., Dartmouth, 1936-39; Capt. HMS Rodney, 1939-41, present at destruction of German battleship Bismarck (CB); Rear-Adm. 1941; Adm. Commanding Iceland, 1941-42; Naval Secretary to First Lord of Admiralty, 1942; Vice-Adm. 1944; Vice-Adm. Commanding 10th Cruiser Squadron and 2nd in Command, Home Fleet, 1944-45 (KCB); Vice-Adm. Malta and Flag Officer Central Mediterranean, 1945-46; Flag Officer Comdg Scotland and North Ireland, 1946-48; Adm., 1948; Adm., British Joint Services Mission, Washington, USA, 1948-50; retd list 1950. Mem., Queen's Body Guard for Scotland, Royal Company of Archers, 1947-73. JP and DL for Wigtownshire, 1952. *Address:* Bargany, Girvan, Ayrshire. *T:* Old Dailly 242. *Clubs:* United Service & Royal Aero; New (Edinburgh). [Died 26 Dec. 1974.

DALTON, Thomas Wilson Fox, CB 1946; *b* 28 Dec. 1886; *s* of late Rev. Edwin Dalton, DD, and Mary Eliza Dalton; *m* 1913, Mabel Louise (*d* 1974), *d* of late Rev. James Pickett; three *d*. *Educ:* Central High Sch., Leeds. Entered Board of Trade (Second Division Clerk), 1907; Ministry of Labour, 1916; Finance Officer to Commissioner for the Special Areas (England and Wales), Dec. 1934-Sept. 1939; Accountant-Gen., 1943-Dec. 1951, Min. of Labour and Nat. Service. *Address:* 2 Warren Close, Worthing, W Sussex. *T:* Worthing 65288. *Club:* National Liberal. [Died 9 Jan. 1977.

DALTON-MORRIS, Air Marshal Sir Leslie, KBE 1959 (CBE 1944); CB 1952; psa; retired as AOC-in-C, Royal Air Force Maintenance Command (1961-63); *b* 7 April 1906; *m* Marion, 2nd *d* of late A. G. Ellis, Bromley, Kent; one *d*. Entered Royal Air Force, 1924; experimental and test pilot, Martlesham Heath, 1926-28; Signals Course, Cranwell, 1929-30; RAF, Staff Coll., 1937; HQ No 2 Group, 1938-39; served War of 1939-45 (despatches, CBE); Deputy Chief Signals Officer, HQ Fighter Command, 1939-41. Bomber Command, 1941-43; SASO No 26 Group, 1943-44; Comd Signals Officer, HQ, Bomber Command, 1944-45; Dir of Radio and later Signals, Air Ministry, 1945-47; Commandant Central Signals Establishment, 1948-49; Comd Signals Officer, Middle East Air Force, 1949; Asst Chief of the Air Staff (Signals), 1952-56; AOC, No 90 Group, 1956-58; AOC-in-C, Signals Command, 1958-61. *Recreation:* golf. *Address:* 29 Chantry Close, Highcliffe-on-Sea, Christchurch, Dorset BH23 5NQ. *Club:* Royal Air Force.
[Died 28 Oct. 1976.

DALWOOD, Hubert, ARA 1976; Sculptor; Head of Sculpture Department, Central School of Art, since 1976; *b* 2 June 1924; *s* of Cyril Herbert Dalwood and Edith Mary (*née* Mitchell); *m* 1951, Mary Nicholson; two *d*; *m* 1963, Caroline Gaunt (marr. diss.); two *s*. *Educ:* Bath Acad. of Art. Gregory Fellow of Sculpture, Univ. of Leeds, 1955-58. First one-man exhibn, London, 1954; 1st Prize for Sculpture, John Moore's Exhibition, Liverpool, 1960; British Pavilion, Venice, 1962 (John Bright Prize-winner); Internat. Sculpture Symposium, Toronto, 1967; British Sculptors exhibn, RA, 1972; exhibitions at Cairo and Beirut, 1974. Chm., Arts Council Serpentine Gallery, 1973-75. Vis. Professor: Univ. of Wisconsin, 1967-68; Univ. of Florida, 1972; Churchill Memorial Fellow, 1972. Commissions for: Liverpool Univ.; Leeds Univ.; Nuffield Coll., Oxford; Wolverhampton Polytechnic; Birmingham Polytechnic; Landscape designs for: Govt of Saudi Arabia; State of Qatar, 1976. Work in collections: Tate Gallery; Museum of Modern Art and Guggenheim Museum, New York; Carnegie Inst., Pittsburgh; etc. *Address:* 71 Stepney Green, E1.
[Died 2 Nov. 1976.

DALY, Ashley Skeffington, FRCS; FFARCS; DA England; Consulting Anæsthetist London Hospital; late Anæsthetist to Royal Masonic Hospital; Brigadier, Consulting Anæsthetist to the Army; *b* 12 July 1882; *s* of late Frederick H. Daly, MD, JP, of Hackney; *m* Maude (*d* 1974), *d* of Arthur C. James of

Paignton; one *s* one *d*. *Educ:* Merchant Taylors' Sch.; London Hospital. MRCS, LRCP, 1905; DA England 1935; FRCS 1944; FFARCS 1948. Held various Resident Hospital appointments, 1903-09. *Publications:* articles on Anæsthetics, House-Surgeon's Vade Mecum and Manual of War Surgery. *Address:* Holcombe House, Moretonhampstead, Devon. *T:* Moretonhampstead 407. *Club:* MCC. [Died 15 Sept. 1977.

DALY, Ivan de Burgh, CBE 1959; FRS 1943; MA, MD Cambridge, MD Birmingham, FRCP; *b* 14 April 1893; *s* of late James Thomas Daly and Amy Pritchard; *m* Beatrice Mary, *e d* of Alfred Leetham, Ganton, Yorks; one *s* (and one *s* decd). *Educ:* Rossall; Gonville and Caius Coll., Cambridge; St Bartholomew's Hospital, 1st Class Natural Science Tripos Part I, 1914. Private RAMC, 1914; Flight Sub-Lieut RNAS, 1915-17; Capt. RAFMS; Mem. of Invaliding Medical Board, Hampstead and York, 1918; Asst in Department of Physiology, University Coll., London, 1919-23; Beit Memorial Research Fellow, junior 1920, 4th year 1923; Lecturer in Experimental Physiology in Univ. of Wales, Cardiff, 1923; Prof. of Physiology in the University of Birmingham, 1927-32; Prof. of Physiology, University of Edinburgh, 1933-47; Dir of Agricultural Research Council's Institute of Animal Physiology, Babraham, Cambridge, 1948-58; Dir Medical Research Council's Physiological Laboratory, Armoured Fighting Vehicle Training Sch., Lulworth, Dorset, 1942-45; Mem. Agricultural Research Council, 1945-47; Wellcome Trust Research Fellow, 1958-62; Vis. Research Worker, Laboratory of Physiology, Oxford Univ., 1958-70. Hon. Fellow Soc. Reg. Med., Budapest; Hon. Member: Thoracic Soc. (Pres., 1954-55); Physiological Soc., 1969. Harvey Lecturer, New York, 1936; Lyon Lecturer, Univ. of Minnesota, USA, 1951; Louis Abrahams Lecturer, RCP, 1956. Thruston Medal, Caius Coll., Cambridge, 1928; Baly Medal, RCP, 1959. Co-Editor of Quarterly Journal Experimental Physiology. *Publications:* (with Catherine Hebb) Bronchial and Pulmonary Vascular Systems, 1966; Physiological papers on the Cardiovascular System and Pulmonary Circulation in scientific jls. *Address:* 25 High Street, Long Crendon, Aylesbury, Bucks. *T:* Long Crendon 208298. *Club:* Athenæum.
[Died 8 Feb. 1974.

DALY LEWIS, Edward; *see* Lewis.

DAM, (Carl Peter) Henrik, DrSc; Professor of Biochemistry and Nutrition, Polytechnic Institute, Copenhagen (appointed while in the USA), 1941-65, and leader of biochemical division, Danish Fat Research Institute, 1956-63; *b* Copenhagen, Denmark, 21 Feb. 1895; *s* of Emil Dam and Emilie Peterson; *m* 1924, Inger Olsen; no *c*. *Educ:* Polytechnic Institute (MS Chemistry 1920) and University, Copenhagen (DrSc Biochemistry 1934). Instructor of Chemistry, Royal Agricultural Sch., Copenhagen, 1920; Instructor of Biochemistry, Univ. of Copenhagen, 1923; Asst Prof. of Biochemistry, 1928, Associate Prof., Biochemistry, 1931-41, Univ. of Copenhagen; Senior Research Associate, Univ. of Rochester, 1942-45; Associate Member, Rockefeller Institute, 1945-48. went to the US on a lecture tour, 1940, lectured in the US and in Canada, 1940-41; returned to Denmark, 1946; 2nd lecture tour in US and Canada, 1949. Worked with F. Pregl, Graz, Austria, 1925; with Rudolf Schoenheimer, Freiburg, Germany, 1932-33 (Rockefeller Fellow); with P. Karrer, Zürich, 1935 and later. Awarded share of 1943 Nobel Prize for Physiology and Medicine, 1944. Member: Danish Academy of Technical Sciences, 1947; Kgl. Danske Videnskabernes Selskab, 1948; Foreign Corresp. Member Royal Academy Medicine, Belgium, 1951; Gesellschaft für Ernährung, Germany, 1961. Fellow, American Institute of Nutrition, 1964. Hon. FRSE, 1953. Norman Medal, German Fat Research Society, 1960; Dr Sc (*hc*) University of St Louis, 1965. *Publications:* over 300 papers on biochemical subjects in British, other European, and American journals. Main subjects: Cholesterol Metabolism, The Discovery and further Investigation of Vitamin K, Studies on Vitamin E and Lipids, growth, gall stone formation, etc. *Recreations:* travels in Europe, the US and Canada. *Address:* Polytechnic Institute, Østervoldgade 10L, Copenhagen 1350, Denmark. [Died 24 April 1976.

d'AMBRUMENIL, Sir Philip, Kt 1945; *b* 28 Dec. 1886; 2nd *s* of Benerice Henry and Isabella d'Ambrumenil; *m* 1921, Gertrude Merriel, *e d* of C. H. Bailey, Newport, Mon.; one *s* one *d*. *Educ:* Rugby School. Entered Lloyd's, 1904; Gold Medal for services to Corporation of Lloyd's, 1943; Dep. Chairman War Risks Insurance Office (Ministry of War Transport, 1939-44; Dep Chairman of Lloyd's, 1945, 1946; Chairman, 1947; Dep Chairman Lloyd's Register of Shipping, 1948, 1949. Officier de l'Ordre de la Couronne, 1947; Officer of the Order of Orange Nassau, 1948; Knight of the 1st degree, Order of St Olav, 1948; Commander, Order of George 1st (Greece). *Address:* 1312

Minster House, St James's Court, SW1. *T:* 01-834 2360.
[Died 19 Sept. 1974.

DANCE, James, ERD 1954; MP (C) Bromsgrove, since 1955; *b* 5 May 1907; *s* of late Sir George Dance; *m* 1st, Charlotte (decd), *d* of George Herbert Strutt, Bridgehill, Belper; 2nd, 1934, Anne (CBE 1962), *d* of Colonel Arthur Travis Walker; one *s* three *d.* *Educ:* Eton Coll. Major, The Queen's Bays (2nd Dragoon Guards); served in France, Middle East and Italy, 1940-45. Chairman Rugby Division Conservative Assoc., 1946-48. Contested (C) Rugby, 1950 and 1951. PPS to Secretary of State for Air, 1957-60. *Recreations:* cricket, real tennis, golf. *Address:* Moreton House, Moreton Morrell, Warwickshire. *T:* Moreton Morrell 235; 8 York House, Turk's Row, SW3. *T:* 01-730 1343. *Clubs:* White's, MCC.   *[Died 16 March 1971.*

DANCKWERTS, Rt. Hon. Sir Harold Otto, PC 1961; Kt 1949; a Lord Justice of Appeal, 1961-69; *b* 23 Feb. 1888; *s* of William Otto Danckwerts, KC, and Mary Caroline Lowther; *m* 1st, 1918, Florence Mary Pride (*d* 1969); one *s* one *d.*; 2nd, 1969, Ella Hamilton Marshall, Glasgow. *Educ:* Winchester Coll.; Balliol Coll., Oxford (MA); Harvard Univ., USA. Called to Bar, Lincoln's Inn, 1913 (Certificate of Honour), Bencher, 1941, Treasurer, 1962. Mobilised as Lance Corp. and a farrier, Aug. 1914; during European War, 1914-19, served with E Riding of Yorkshire Yeomanry and Machine Gun Corps (Captain) (despatches); Tutor to Law Society, 1914-23; Reader to Law Society, 1923-41; Junior Counsel to Treasury and Board of Trade in Chancery matters and Junior Counsel to Attorney-General in Charity matters, 1941-49; Judge of the High Court of Justice (Chancery Division), 1949-61. *Address:* 4 Stone Buildings, Lincoln's Inn, WC2A 3XT. *T:* 01-242 4130. *Club:* Kennel.   *[Died 12 June 1978.*

DANDIE, James Naughton, CBE 1961; MC 1918; MA, LLB, SSC; *b* 2 June 1894; *s* of Alexander Dandie, Art Master, Edinburgh; *m* 1929, Anne Bonelly, *o d* of John Alexander Aitchison Calder; two *s. Educ:* George Watson's Coll., Edinburgh; Edinburgh University (1912-14 and 1919-22). On service with 1/1 Highland (Fife) RGA(T), 1914-19, retiring as Captain (France); despatches; 1917; MC 1918. President, Scottish Lawn Tennis Assoc., 1935. Hon. Sheriff Substitute, 1951; Council of Law Society of Scotland, 1950-66 (President, 1958-61); Legal Aid Central Cttee (Chairman, 1955-58); Law Reform (Scotland) Cttee, 1954-64. Hon. Member American Bar Assoc.; Hon. FRIAS, 1963. *Publications:* articles to legal journals. *Recreations:* photography; curling. *Address:* 16 Abercromby Place, Stirling. *T:* Stirling 2777. *Club:* Caledonian (Edinburgh).   *[Died 27 May 1976.*

DANDO, Kenneth Walter, RIBA; Director of Defence Services II (Under Secretary), Property Services Agency, Department of the Environment, since 1979; *b* 5 Jan. 1921; *s* of Walter Richard and Mabel Beatrice Mary Dando; *m* 1944, Hazel Burke Preston; two *s. Educ:* All Saints' Choir Sch., Bristol; RWA School of Architecture, Bristol. Articled pupil, W. S. Skinner & Sons, Bristol, 1936-39. War service, Royal Engineers, seconded RBS&M India (Captain), 1939-46. Assistant Architect, private practice and local authority, 1949-53; joined Min. of Works, Cardiff, 1953; Regional Architect, Min. of Public Bldg and Works, Aden, 1964-66; Suptg Architect, Directorate of Works (Navy), 1966-70; Director of Works (Army), 1970-79. *Recreations:* gardening, local affairs, walking, photography, French travel. *Address:* Hythe Cottage, Eastbourne Road, Godstone, Surrey RH9 8EH. *T:* Godstone 842381.
[Died 15 March 1980.

DANDY, James Edgar, MA Cantab; Keeper of Botany, British Museum (Natural History), 1956-66; *b* 24 Sept. 1903; *e s* of late John James Dandy, Preston, Lancs; *m* 1929, Joyce Isabelle Glaysher; one *s. Educ:* Preston Grammar Sch.; Downing Coll., Cambridge. Entered Herbarium, Royal Botanic Gardens, Kew, 1925; joined Dept of Botany, British Museum (Natural History), 1927. *Publications:* books and papers in scientific publications, chiefly on systematic botany. *Recreations:* angling, gardening. *Address:* Rowans, Grove Road, Tring, Herts. *T:* Tring 3122.
[Died 10 Nov. 1976.

DANE, William Surrey, CBE 1953; MC; Patron, The Association of Independent Hospitals (Chairman, 1960-63; President, 1963-69); Member Board of Governors, Hospital for Sick Children, Great Ormond Street, for 24 years (Vice-Chairman 1957-67); Member Committee of Management, Institute of Child Health, University of London, 1955-67; Member Council, Charing Cross Hospital Medical School, 1956-67; Life Vice-President Printers' Charitable Corporation; Hon. Vice-President Lloyd Memorial (Printers) Convalescent Home (President, 1950-61); a Vice-Chairman and Managerial Consultant of Odhams Press Ltd,

printers and publishers of Long Acre, WC2, 1959-March 1961 (Joint Managing Director, 1947-57, Managing Director, 1958); Chairman, Daily Herald, 1949-60; Member, General Advisory Council of the BBC, 1956-62; *b* 1892; *e s* of James Surrey Dane, Adelaide, SA; *m* 1919, Dorothy Mary, *d* of late Rev. W. A. Armstrong, MA, Funtington Vicarage, near Chichester; one *s* two *d.* Served European War, 1914-19, Captain and Adjt, Seaforth Highlanders (despatches, MC); during War of 1939-45 was a Director at Min. of Information, 1939, and Min. of Supply, 1941-45. *Address:* Apple Porch, Peaslake, near Guildford, Surrey. *T:* Dorking 730235.   *[Died 19 Jan. 1978.*

DANIEL, Henry Cave; *b* 16 Aug. 1896; *s* of late H. T. Daniel, Manor House, Stockland, Bridgwater; *m* 1931, Barbara, *d* of late Mrs Blain, King's Barrow, Wareham, Dorset; one *s* one *d. Educ:* Eton; RMC, Sandhurst. Joined 17th Lancers, 1914, and served European War, 1914-18, with that regiment, retiring in 1920. Rejoined Army, 1939, and served War of 1939-45, in France and England until invalided out in 1941. High Sheriff of Somerset, 1949. *Recreations:* hunting and shooting. *Address:* The Old Mill, Sparkford, Yeovil, Som. *T:* North Cadbury 427. *Clubs:* Cavalry and Guards; Somerset County (Taunton).
[Died 31 Jan. 1980.

DANIEL, (John) Stuart, QC 1961; *b* 17 Feb. 1912; *s* of Walter John Daniel and Nena Nithsdale Newall; *m* 1st, 1935, J. E. R. Thomson; one *s*; 2nd, 1944, Juliet Henley; one *d*; 3rd, Valerie. *Educ:* Haileybury; Merton Coll., Oxford. Called to Bar, Middle Temple, 1937. Member, Lands Tribunal, 1967-76. *Address:* Paradise Cottage, Great Wratting, Haverhill, Suffolk. *T:* Thurlow 328. *Club:* Garrick.   *[Died 24 Nov. 1977.*

DANIEL, Stuart; *see* Daniel, J. S.

DANNREUTHER, Rear-Adm. Hubert Edward, DSO 1916; *b* 12 Dec. 1880; *y s* of late Prof. Edward Dannreuther; *m* 1916, Janie, *y d* of late J. Hay Thorburn; three *s. Educ:* privately; HMS Britannia. Joined HMS Britannia, 1895; chief cadet Captain, 1896; Lieut, 1902; Gunnery Lieut of Exmouth, Flagship of Mediterranean Fleet, 1911-12; commanded Guard of Honour on official landing of the King at Malta, Jan. 1912; 1st and Gunnery Lieut of Invincible, in action of Heligoland Bight, 28 Aug. 1914; also of Invincible when Flagship of Vice-Adm. Sturdee at Battle of Falkland Islands, 8 Dec. 1914 (despatches, promoted to Commander); Senior of six survivors from HMS Invincible, 1916 (despatches, DSO); Order of St Anne, 3rd Class, with Swords; French Croix de Guerre with palms, 1917; Commander HMS Renown, 1916-19; HMS Excellent, 1919-20; Captain, 1920; Vice-President, Chemical Warfare Cttee, 1920-23; HMS Dauntless, 1924-26; Captain Superintendent of Training and in command of the Flinders Naval Depôt, Australia, 1927-29; HMS Eagle, 1929-31; Commodore of RN Barracks, Portsmouth, 1931-32; Rear-Adm. 1932; retired list, 1932. *Address:* Windycroft, Hastings, E Sussex. *T:* Hastings 420744.
[Died 12 Aug. 1977.

DANTER, Harold Walter Phillips; *b* 31 March 1886; *s* of late Lieut-Col F. W. Danter, VD, RE, JP, Gerrards Cross, Bucks; unmarried. *Educ:* Christ's Hospital, Hertford, London, and West Horsham. Clerk in the Bank of England, 1904-14. Held commission in 5th East Surrey Regt, 1908-10. Student at Lichfield Theological Coll., 1914-16; Deacon, 1916; Priest, 1917. Work with Church Army, BEF, France, 1918-19. Curate: St Paul's, Stafford, 1917-19; Holy Trinity, Woolwich, 1919-21; SS Mary and John, Oxford, 1921-28; Vicar of Pattishall, Northants, 1928-33; Rural Dean, Brackley III deanery, 1933-53; Vicar of Brackley, 1933-56; Non-residentiary Canon of Peterborough Cathedral, 1955-56; Canon Emeritus of Peterborough Cathedral, 1956-58. Received into the Roman Catholic Church, March 1958. *Publication:* The Hill of Daydreams (Poems), 1917. *Recreation:* general interest in art and literature. *Address:* 32 Thorncliffe Road, Oxford. *T:* Oxford 55598.
[Died 8 July 1976.

D'ARCY, Very Rev. Martin Cyril, SJ; MA; Hon. LLD Georgetown University, USA; Hon. DLitt, Fordham University, USA; Hon. LittD, Marquette University, USA; Hon. DLitt, National University of Ireland; FRSL; *b* Bath, 15 June 1888; *s* of Martin Valentine D'Arcy and Madoline Keegan and *gs* of Nicholas D'Arcy of Ballyforan, Co. Roscommon. *Educ:* Stonyhurst; Oxford (1st Class. Lit. Hum., Charles Oldham Prize, John Locke Scholarship, Greek Moral Philosophy Prize); Gregorian Univ., Rome. Priest, 1921; taught at Stonyhurst and worked at Farm Street Church, W1; The Master of Campion Hall, Oxford, 1932-45; Provincial of English Province of Soc. of Jesus, 1945-50. Conventual Chaplain to the Knights of Malta, 1956. Foreign Hon. Mem., Amer. Acad. of Arts and Sciences, 1960. *Publications:* The Mass and the

Redemption; Catholicism; Christ as Priest and Redeemer; The Spirit of Charity; Thomas Aquinas; The Nature of Belief; Death and Life; part author of God and the Supernatural, God and the Universe, A Monument to St Augustine, The Life of the Church; Mirage and Truth; The Problem of Evil; The Mind and Heart of Love; Communism and Christianity; The Meeting of Love and Knowledge; The Sense of History; No Absent God; Facing God; Of God and Man; Facing the Truth; Humanism and Christianity. *Address:* 114 Mount Street, W1. *Club:* Athenæum.
[Died 20 Nov. 1976.

DARKE, Harold Edwin, CBE 1966; Hon. MA Cantab; DMus Oxon; FRCM, FRCO; Hon. RAM; Professor, Royal College of Music, London, 1919-69; *b* 29 Oct. 1888; *s* of Samuel and Arundel Darke; *m* 1918, Dora Garland, the violinist who was first woman to lead Queen's Hall Orchestra; two *s. Educ:* Owen's Sch., Islington; Royal College of Music (Organ and Composition Scholar, Tagore Gold Medal). Pupil of Parratt and Stanford; Asst Organist, Temple Church, 1919; Organist, Stoke Newington Presbyterian Church, 1904; Organist, Emmanuel Church, West Hampstead, 1906; St James, Paddington, 1911; St Michael's Cornhill, 1916-66; Conductor, City of London Choral Union, 1925-31; Founder and Conductor of St Michael's Singers, 1919-66; Founder and Conductor of Wartime Choir, Drop in and sing, 1940; Pres., Royal Coll. of Organists, 1940-41; Pres., Cambridge Organist Assoc., 1941-45; Acting-Organist, King's Coll., Cambridge, 1941-45; Conductor, Cambridge Univ. Madrigal Soc., 1941-45. Fellow, King's Coll., Cambridge, 1945-49. Adjudicator of chief Musical Competitive Festivals; Toured US and Canada, 1938, 1949, Africa, 1955, W Indies, 1960, 1963, as Examiner for Royal Schools of Music and gave Organ Recitals. Fellow, Royal School of Church Music. Hon. Freeman Worshipful Company of Musicians, 1957; Freeman of the City of London. *Publications:* choral works: As the leaves fall, 1917; The Kingdom of God, 1921; Ring out ye crystal Spheres (St Michael's Festival), 1928; The Sower, 1929; O Lord, Thou art my God (Festival of Sons of Clergy), 1931; An Hymn of Heavenly Beauty (Worcester Festival), 1935; The Love which passeth Knowledge, 1939; Adventante Deo (St George's, Windsor), 1949; A Song of David (St Michael's and Worcester Festivals), 1956; Propers of the Communion (Coventry Consecration), 1961; Be strong and of a good Courage (Chelmsford Jubilee), 1964; Communion Service (Buffalo, USA), 1965; Festal Te Deum (Blackburn Cathedral), 1965; I will greatly rejoice (Winchester Choral Assoc.), 1966; Six Miniatures for Oboe and Piano, 1969; Rejoice, the Lord is King (Barnet Arts Festival), 1972. *Recreations:* photography, motoring. *Address:* Mackery End, Gazeley Road, Trumpington, Cambridge CB2 2HB. *T:* Cambridge 65137.
[Died 28 Nov. 1976.

DARLING, Rev. Charles Brian Auchinleck, CMG 1949; MA Cantab; *b* 5 March 1905; *s* of late Ven. James George Reginald Darling, sometime Archdeacon of Suffolk and Norah Lilian Loxdale Auchinleck; *m* 1939, Rachel Middleton Lankester, *d* of Capt. Cyril Lankester Paul, RA; one *s* one *d. Educ:* Framlingham Coll.; Jesus Coll., Cambridge. Colonial Admin. Service, 1928, Gold Coast Colony; seconded Colonial Office, 1939; Principal, Dominions Office, 1940-45; Asst Chief Secretary: East African Governors' Conference, 1945; East Africa High Commission, 1948; retd 1951; ordained, 1952; retd 1966. *Recreation:* fly-fishing. *Address:* Fallow Hill, Bromeswell, Woodbridge, Suffolk. *T:* Eyke 222. *[Died 26 Nov. 1978.*

DARLING, Maj.-Gen. Douglas Lyall, CB 1968; DSO 1943 and Bar, 1945; MC 1941 and Bar, 1942; GOC 53 (Welsh) Division (TA)/Wales District, Dec. 1963-May 1968, retired; *b* 3 Oct. 1914; *s* of late George Kenneth Darling, CIE; *m* 1953, Elizabeth Anne Forsyth; two *d. Educ:* Eton; Sandhurst. Commissioned into Rifle Bde, 1934. Served War of 1939-45 with Rifle Bde, and commanded 7th Bn The Rifle Bde, 1942-45. Comd Eaton Hall OCTU, 1945-48; GSO1, Plans, Min. of Defence, 1952-53; School of Infantry, 1954-55. GSO1, Staff Coll., 1956-58; Comd 133 Infantry Brigade, 1959-61; Imperial Defence Coll., 1962-63; Chief, British Commanders-in-Chief Mission to the Soviet Forces in Germany, 1963. *Recreations:* hunting, combined training and horse trials, sailing. *Address:* Darley House, Hullavington, Chippenham, Wilts. *T:* Hullavington 241. *Clubs:* Army and Navy; Royal Channel Islands Yacht.
[Died 28 Dec. 1978.

DARLING, Sir Frank F.; *see* Fraser Darling.

DARLINGTON, Reginald Ralph, PhD; FBA 1954; Professor of History in University of London (Birkbeck College), 1945-69, retired, Emeritus Professor 1969; Fellow of Birkbeck College, since 1970; *b* 6 Nov. 1903. *Educ:* University Coll., Reading. Lecturer in History, Bedford Coll. (University of London),

1927-36; Reader in Medieval History in University of London, 1936-39; Prof. of History, University Coll., Exeter, 1939-45. Creighton Lecturer, University of London, 1962. FRHistS; FSA. *Publications:* Vita Wulfstani, 1928; Darley Cartulary, 1945; VCH Wilts vol. ii, 1955; The Norman Conquest, 1963; Worcester Cartulary, 1968; papers in English Historical Review, History, etc. *Address:* Warrenhurst, 25 Wargrave Road, Twyford, Reading. *T:* Twyford (Berks) 345 109.
[Died 30 May 1977.

DARLINGTON, William Aubrey, CBE 1967; MA; author, journalist, and dramatist; dramatic critic of the Daily Telegraph, 1920-68; Member, Editorial Staff of the Daily Telegraph; *b* Taunton, 20 Feb. 1890; *o s* of late Thomas Darlington, HMIS Board of Education; *m* Marjorie (*d* 1973), *y d* of late Sydney Sheppard; one *d. Educ:* Shrewsbury; St John's Coll., Cambridge (Classical Scholar); Honours in Classics and in English Literature. Was a schoolmaster 1913-14; during war, held commission in 7th Northumberland Fusiliers (TF); began contributing to Punch and other periodicals in 1916; took up journalism as profession in 1919, being asst editor and afterwards editor of The World; joined staff of the Daily Telegraph as dramatic critic, 1920; for many years Mem. of Advisory Cttee for Diploma in Dramatic Art, London Univ.; Lecturer on Playwriting at East London Coll., London Univ., 1926-27; Pres., Critics' Circle, 1930; London Theatre Correspondent of New York Times, 1939-60. *Publications:* novels: Alf's Button; Wishes Limited; Egbert; Alf's Carpet; Mr Cronk's Cases; Alf's New Button; *theatre books:* Through the Fourth Wall; Literature in the Theatre; Sheridan; J. M. Barrie; The Actor and his Audience; The World of Gilbert and Sullivan; Six Thousand and One Nights; Laurence Olivier; *autobiography:* I Do What I Like; *plays:* Alf's Button; Carpet Slippers; Marcia Gets Her Own Back; The Key of the House; English version of A Knight Passed By, by Jan Fabricius; burlesque version of The Streets of London. *Recreation:* golf. *Address:* Monksdown, Bishopstone, Sussex. *T:* Seaford 892657. *Club:* Garrick. *[Died 24 May 1979.*

DARNLEY, 10th Earl of, *cr* 1725; **Peter Stuart Bligh;** Baron Clifton of Leighton Bromswold, 1608; Baron Clifton of Rathmore, 1721; Viscount Darnley, 1723; late Major, Dragoon Guards; *b* 1 Oct. 1915; *s* of 9th Earl and Daphne Rachel, *d* of late Hon. Alfred Mulholland; *S* father 1955. *Educ:* Eton; Royal Military College, Sandhurst. Served War of 1939-45 (prisoner). *Heir:* half-brother Hon. Adam Ivo Stuart Bligh [*b* 8 Nov. 1941; *m* 1965, Susan Elaine, *y d* of late Sir Donald Anderson; one *s* one *d*]. *Address:* Puckle Hill House, Shorne, Gravesend, Kent.
[Died 15 June 1980.

DART, Robert Thurston; King Edward Professor of Music, King's College, University of London, since 1964; Artistic Director of Philomusica of London (formerly Boyd Neel Orchestra), 1955-59; *b* 3 Sept. 1921; *s* of H. T. Dart. *Educ:* Hampton Grammar School; Chapel Royal, Hampton Court (chorister); Royal College of Music. ARCM 1942; BA London, 1942; Operational Research for RAF, 1942-45 (despatches). Cambridge University: Asst Lectr in Music, 1947-52; Lectr, 1952-62; Prof. of Music, 1962-64. Editor, Galpin Soc. Jl, 1947-55; Sec., Musica Britannica, 1950-64; Fellow, Jesus Coll., Cambridge, 1953-64. Visiting Lectr, Harvard Univ., 1954. Cobbett Medal, 1957. *Publications:* The Interpretation of Music, 1954; contributions to Grove's Dictionary (5th edn); Co-editor: Dowland's Ayres for Four Voices, 1953; Jacobean Consort Music, 1955; (ed) Bull's Keyboard Music, II, 1963; articles and reviews in Music and Letters, etc. *Recreation:* organology. *Address:* King's College, Strand, WC2. *Club:* Savile.
[Died 6 March 1971.

DARVILL, Harold Edgar; a Deputy Chairman of Barclays Bank Ltd, 1968-70 (Director and Vice-Chairman 1966-68, General Manager, 1959-66); Governor, Royal National Throat, Nose and Ear Hospital, 1967-70; *b* 1908; 2nd *s* of Edgar Darvill, Thames Ditton; *m* 1933, Constance Nellie, *d* of Joseph Clack, Bulawayo; one *s. Educ:* Dunstable Grammar Sch. Entered Barclays Bank 1932, after service with Barclays Bank DCO in Rhodesia. Served with RAF in N Africa, Sicily, France, and with RAAF until 1951. Fellow, Institute of Bankers; Dep. Chairman of Council, 1963-65. Chairman, Management Cttee, Institute of Laryngology and Otology, 1960-70. *Recreations:* travel, gardening. *Address:* Clac's Ley, Halstead, Kent. *T:* Knockholt 3247. *[Died 3 Feb. 1972.*

DARWIN, Sir Robin, (Robert Vere Darwin), Kt 1964; CBE 1954; RA 1972 (ARA 1966); Painter; President, Royal West of England Academy; Rector and Vice-Provost, Royal College of Art, 1967-71 (Principal, 1948-67); Member: Royal Mint Advisory Committee; Arts Advisory Council, Institute of

Directors; *b* 7 May 1910; *s* of late Bernard Darwin, CBE; *m* 1st, Yvonne, *d* of late H. J. Darby (marr. diss.); 2nd, Ginette, *d* of late F. W. Hewitt and Adriana Hugh-Smith. *Educ:* Eton Coll.; Slade Sch. Asst Master, Eton Coll., 1933-38; camouflage directorate, Ministry of Home Security, 1939-44; staff of Council of Industrial Design, 1945-46 (Member Council, 1947-55, and 1962-67); Professor of Fine Art, Univ. of Durham, 1946-47. Has held one-man shows at Redfern Galleries, 1933 and 1944; Messrs Agnews, 1935, 1938, 1940, 1951, 1952, 1955, 1961, 1964; Leicester Galleries, 1946. Pictures purchased by Contemporary Art Society and by Manchester, Leeds and other provincial Galleries. Member: Science Museum Adv. Council, 1951-59; Council, RSA, 1954-59; Nat. Adv. Council on Art Educn, 1959-69; Nat. Council for Diplomas in Art and Design, 1961-69; Governing Body Imp. Coll. of Science and Technology, 1966-71. Fellow UCL, 1962; Senior Fellow, RCA, 1971; Hon. Fellow, Soc. of Industrial Artists, 1950. Hon. DLitt: Newcastle 1964; Birmingham, 1966; Hon. Dr RCA 1971. Bicentenary Medal, RSA, 1962. *Address:* The Old Rectory, Ham, near Marlborough, Wilts. *T:* Inkpen 239. *Clubs:* Athenæum, Garrick.
[Died 30 Jan. 1974.

DARWIN, Ruth Frances, CBE 1938; *d* of late Sir Horace Darwin; *m* 1948, William Rees-Thomas, *qv.* Hon. Commissioner, 1921-31, Commissioner, 1931-32, a Senior Commissioner of Board of Control, 1932-49. *Address:* High Hackhurst, Abinger Hammer, Dorking, Surrey.
[Died 15 Oct. 1972.

DAS, Sudhi Ranjan; Chairman, Board of Directors of the Statesman Ltd, since 1968; *b* 1 Oct. 1894; *e s* of late Rakhal Chandra Das; *m* 1919, Swapana, 2nd *d* of late Rai Bahadur S. B. Majumdar; two *s* one *d. Educ:* Tagores Sch., Santiniketan; Bangabasi Coll., Calcutta; University Coll., London. Graduated Calcutta Univ., 1915; LLB London 1st class 1st, 1918; called to Bar, Gray's Inn, 1918; joined Calcutta Bar, 1919; Lecturer University Law College; Additional Judge, Calcutta High Court, 1942; Puisne Judge, Calcutta High Court, 1944; Chief Justice of East Punjab High Court, 1949; Judge, Federal Court of India, 1950; Judge, Supreme Court of India, 1950-56; Chief Justice of India, 1956-59. Vice-Pres., Indian Council for Cultural Relations, 1964-65. Mem., Univ. Grants Commn, 1962-. Vice-Chancellor, Visva-Bharati (University founded by Dr Rabindra Nath Tagore), 1959-65. Editor, Mulla's Transfer of Property Act. LLD *hc* : Calcutta Univ., 1957; Allahabad Univ., 1958; Dr *hc* Visva-Bharati, 1966. Fellow of University Coll., London, 1961. *Publications:* Amader Santiniketan; Amader Gurudeva; Jä Deklechi Jä Payechi; Smaraner Tulikäi. *Address:* Swapanpuri, Kalimpong, West Bengal, India.
[Died 16 Sept. 1977.

DASH, Sir Arthur (Jules), Kt 1952; CIE 1938; *b* York, 24 April 1887; *s* of Jules Janin Dash; *m* 1922, Greta Brancepeth Wardale (*d* 1974); one *d. Educ:* Worcester Cathedral King's Sch.; Christ Church, Oxford. Entered Indian Civil Service 1910 and posted to Bengal; joined Indian Army Reserve of Officers in 1915 and served on Frontier and in the Punjab; on return to Bengal served as District Magistrate, 1919-27 and sometime as Political Agent to the Tripura State; Secretary to Govt of Bengal in the Education Dept, 1928-31; in various Divisions as Commissioner from 1932; retired from ICS, 1942; Chairman, Bengal Public Service Commission, 1942-47 and of Eastern Pakistan Commission, Dacca, 1947-51. *Address:* Barton Lodge, Rolvenden, Cranbrook, Kent. *Club:* East India, Sports and Public Schools.
[Died 12 July 1974.

DASHWOOD, Sir Henry George Massy, 8th Bt, *cr* 1684; DL; *b* 11 May 1908; *s* of Sir Robert Henry Seymour Dashwood, 7th Bt, and late Margaret Helen, *e d* of late Lieut-Gen. G. Henry, CB; *S* father, 1947; *m* 1948, Susan Mary, *e d* of late Maj. Victor Montgomerie-Charrington, Grey Court, King's Sutton, Northamptonshire; one *s* one *d. Educ:* privately. DL Oxon, 1972. *Heir:* *s* Richard James Dashwood, *b* 14 Feb. 1950. *Address:* Ledwell House, Sandford St Martin, Oxford. *TA* and *T:* Great Tew 267.
[Died 5 Nov. 1972.

DATAR SINGH, Sardar Bahadur Sir, Kt 1939; Adviser, Animal Husbandry, Madhya Pradesh State, India; Member, Managing Board, Agriculture University, Jabalpur, MP; Adviser to CCG, Ministry of Food and Agriculture, India. *Educ:* India; went to England and took training in agriculture and dairy farming, 1919-21. Returned to India, 1921, and started career as agriculturist and dairy farmer in Montgomery District, Punjab, where he built up a big estate and pedigreed Sahiwal dairy herd; Vice-Chairman, Indian Council of Agric. Research, 1933-50; ex-Member Export Advisory Council; Food Advisory Council, and Selection Cttee for Armed Forces, War of 1939-45. Represented India at International Dairy Congress, Copenhagen, 1931, Berlin, 1937; Hon. Adviser for Cattle Develt to Mahatma

Gandhi from 1935 until his death in 1948 (in unique position, as both hon. adviser and govt official); Non-official Adviser to Govt of India for Trade Negotiations between British Govt and Govt of India and was sent to England in 1937 on this duty; led Indian Industrial Delegation to Australia and New Zealand, 1945; Indian delegate to International Wheat Agreement, 1948; Indian delegate at third FAO Conference, USA, 1948; Member FAO Council and Cttee, 1948-52. Pioneer in scientific breeding and dairy farming in India; Chairman Cattle Preservation and Development Cttee appointed by Govt of India, 1947; led Indian Delegation to FAO Livestock Conf., 1950 (Chm.); Chm. ISO Conf. on Shellac, New Delhi, 1950; Indian Deleg. to FAO Co-ordinating Cttee, and Council Meetings, 1952; Leader Indian Delegation to International Dairy Congress, Hague, 1953; to FAO Council, Rome, 1953. Formerly: Production Commissioner and Additional Secretary, in charge Production Division, Ministry of Food and Agriculture, Govt of India; Vice-President All India Cattle Show Society; Cattle Utilization Adviser to Govt of India and Vice-Chairman Indian Council of Agricultural Research; President: Indian Central Cotton, Jute, Sugarcane, Lac Cess Arecanut, Tobacco and Oilseeds Cttees; Development Adviser and Additional Sec. for Kashmir, Min. of Home Affairs, 1955. Sardar Bahadur, 1937. Awarded Medal by International Dairy Congress, 1949; FRSA; NDD. *Publications:* Reorganization of Goshalas and Pinjrapoles in India; several contributions on agricultural questions. *Address:* Bairagarh, Bhopal, MP, India. *Club:* Gymkhana (New Delhi).
[Died 17 May 1973.

DAUBENY, Sir Peter (Lauderdale), Kt 1973; CBE 1967 (OBE 1961); Artistic Director of the World Theatre Season, 1964-73 and 1975; *b* Wiesbaden, 16 April 1921; *s* of Col Cyril Daubeny and Margaret Duncan; *m* 1948, Mary Vyvyan Kempster; one *s* one *d. Educ:* Marlborough. Joined repertory company, at Liverpool Playhouse, under William Armstrong. Served War of 1939-45: Coldstream Guards (Lieut); invalided out, 1943. Formed play-producing company Peter Daubeny Ltd; productions included: Our Betters, But for the Grace of God, We Proudly Present, The Late Edwina Black, Fallen Angels, The Gay Invalid. In 1951 he began to present Ballet, Theatre and Opera Companies including: Rosario and Antonio; Antonio; Roland Petit; Pilar Lopez; Katherine Dunham; Sacha Guitry; Martha Graham; Moscow State Dance Cos: Beryozka and Moisseyev; Moscow State Puppet Theatre; Classical Theatre of China; Mozart Opera Company, Salzburg; Hungarian State Dance Company; Théâtre National Populaire; Bertolt Brecht's Berliner Ensemble; Edwige Feuillère Company; Maurice Chevalier; Jean Louis Barrault- Madeleine Renaud Company; recent productions and presentations: Moscow Art Theatre at Sadler's Wells; The Comédie-Française at Princes Theatre; Ibsen's Ghosts (Old Vic Prod.); Urfaust, at Princes Theatre (Ingmar Bergman's prod.); Jerome Robbins' Ballets: USA; Compagnie Marie Bell; Zizi-Jeanmaire; The House by the Lake (Duke of York's); The Aspern Papers (Queen's); Chin Chin (Wyndham's), 1961; The Connection (Duke of York's), 1961; Photo Finish (Saville), 1962; Micheál Mac Liammóir, Vittorio Gassman and his Teatro Popolare Italiano (Aldwych), 1963. World Theatre Seasons, produced for Royal Shakespeare Co., 1964-73 and 1975, including: Peppino De Filippo, Comédie-Française; Schiller, Greek Art, Abbey, Moscow Art and Polish Contemporary Theatres; Théâtre de France, Compagnia dei Giovani, Habimah, Actors' Studio and Czech National Theatres; National Theatre of Greece, Polish Popular Theatre, Leningrad, Gorki Theatre, National Theatre of Poland, Noh Theatre of Japan, Bremen Theatre, Cameri Theatre of Israel, Piccolo Theatre of Milan, Czech Theatre on the Balustrade, Rome Stabile Theatre, Royal Dramatic Theatre of Sweden, Bunraku National Theatre of Japan, Théâtre de la Cité, Lyons, Theatre Behind the Gate from Prague, New York Negro Ensemble Co., Anna Magnani, Cinoherní Klub of Prague, Catania Stabile Theatre of Sicily; Théâtre Michel of Paris, Genoa Stabile Theatre, Dormen Theatre of Istanbul, Nuria Espert Company of Spain, Natal Theatre Workshop Zulu Co. from S Africa, Eduardo De Filippo, Kathakali Drama Co. from India, Cracow Stary Theatre, Bochum Schauspielhaus from Germany, the Vienna Burgtheater, Rideau de Bruxelles, Gothenburg Stadtstheater, Tino Buazzelli Compagnia di Prosa, Robert Serumaga's Abafumi Co. from Uganda. Consultant Director, Royal Shakespeare Company, 1966-. Officer of the Legion of Honour, 1971 (Chevalier, 1957); Gold Cross of the Royal Order of King George I of Greece, 1965; Cavaliere, Order of Merit of the Republic of Italy, 1966; Gold Medal of Czechoslovakia, 1967; Order of Merit of German Federal Republic, 1971; Polonia Restituta, 1974; Comdr, Royal Order of Vasa, Sweden, 1974. *Publications:* Stage by Stage, 1952; My World of Theatre, 1971. *Recreations:* travelling, reading. *Address:* 26 Chester Square, SW1. *T:* 01-730 3939.
[Died 6 Aug. 1975.

DAUBNEY, Robert, CMG 1939; OBE 1937; MSc; MRCVS; formerly Veterinary Consultant to the FAO of the United Nations; *b* 1891; *s* of Robert Daubney, Southampton; *m* 1919, Jean Ethel Winifred, *d* of Thomas J. D. Ker, Hampstead. *Educ:* Manchester Grammar Sch.; Liverpool Univ.; George Washington Univ.; Cambridge Univ.; Royal Veterinary Coll., London. Served European War, 1914-19; Helminthologist Ministry of Agriculture, 1920; entered Colonial Service, 1925; Director of Veterinary Services, Kenya, 1937-47, of E African Central Veterinary Research Institute, 1939-47, retired; Veterinary Adviser to Egyptian Govt until 1951. *Publications:* Numerous on original research in Helminthology and Bacteriology (virus diseases). *Address: c/o* Williams & Glyn's Bank Ltd (Holt's Branch), Whitehall, SW1.
[*Died* 16 *April* 1977.

DAVEN-THOMAS, Rev. Canon Dennis; *see* Thomas, Rev. Canon Dennis D.

DAVENPORT, Dame Lilian (Emily Isabel Jane) B.; *see* Bromley-Davenport.

DAVEY, Prof. Thomas Herbert, OBE 1941; *b* 30 June 1899; *s* of Rev. Charles Davey, DD, Belfast, N Ireland; *m* 1935, Irene Margaret Cottom; one *s. Educ:* Royal Belfast Academical Institution; Queen's Univ., Belfast. War service, 1917-18; MB, BCh, BAO Belfast, 1925; MD 1934; Liverpool School of Tropical Medicine, 1929; Professor of Tropical Diseases of Africa, Liverpool School of Tropical Medicine, and Director of Sir Alfred Lewis Jones Research Laboratory, Freetown, Sierra Leone, 1938; Prof. of Tropical Hygiene, Liverpool School of Tropical Medicine, Liverpool Univ., 1945-61, now emeritus. *Publications:* (with Dr W. P. H. Lightbody) Control of Disease in the Tropics, 1956; Blacklock and Southwell's Guide to Human Parasitology, 1957. *Recreation:* gardening. *Address:* 87 Belmont Church Road, Belfast BT4 3FG. *T:* Belfast 658691.
[*Died* 29 *March* 1978.

DAVID, Herman Francis, CBE 1968; Chairman, Diamond Development Co. Ltd, since 1952; Chairman and/or Director of other Companies; Chairman, All England Lawn Tennis and Croquet Club and Chairman, Committee of Management of The Championships, Wimbledon, since 1959; *b* 26 June 1905; *er s* of late Herman David and Gertrude Florence David (*née* Feeny); *m* 1934, Mavis Jeanne, *er d* of late Lt-Col W. J. Evans, DSO, JP; one *s* two *d. Educ:* Stonyhurst Coll.; New Coll., Oxford (BA 1927). Oxford Half-Blue, Lawn Tennis, 1927. Rep. GB in Davis Cup, 1932, and in various international matches, 1930-39; Non-playing Captain, British Davis Cup, 1953-58. Served War, 1939-45, RAFVR; Fighter Comd Operations Controller; demobilised with rank of Wing Comdr. *Recreations:* lawn tennis, croquet, bridge. *Address:* 7 Parkside Gardens, Wimbledon Common, SW19 5EY. *T:* 01-946 4651. *Clubs:* Royal Air Force, All England Lawn Tennis and Croquet, Queen's; Edgbaston Priory Lawn Tennis, Tally-Ho Lawn Tennis (Birmingham); International Lawn Tennis Clubs of Great Britain, France, America, Australia, Belgium, Denmark, S Africa, Switzerland, Italy.
[*Died* 25 *Feb.* 1974.

DAVIDSON, Air Vice-Marshal (retired) Sir Alexander Paul, KBE, *cr* 1950 (CBE 1941); CB 1946; Director-General Organisation, Air Ministry, 1947-51, retired; *b* 26 July 1894; *s* of late Alexander Davidson, Walton-on-Thames; *m* 1933, Jane Elizabeth Dahlstrand, Malmö, Sweden; one *s. Educ:* City of London Sch.; RMC, Sandhurst. Commissioned Highland Light Infantry; Seconded RFC 1916; served throughout 1914-18 with RFC and RAF; transferred RAF 1923; HQ Iraq; ADC Governor-General Australia, Lord Stonehaven, 1925-28; psa 1930; Coastal Area RAF 1931-33; HQ Palestine and Transjordan, 1933-37; Staff Officer to Inspector-General, RAF, 1938; served War of 1939-45 (despatches four times, CBE, Polish Cross of Valour); Air Attaché Poland, Lithuania, Latvia and Estonia, 1939-40; Bomber Command, 1940-41; HQ Levant, 1942; HQ Middle East, 1942-43; AOA Malta, 1943; AOA Coastal Air Force, 1943-44; AOC Iraq and Persia, 1944; Air Ministry, Post-Hostilities Planning; Deputy Chief of Air Division, Control Commission, Germany, 1946; Chief of Combined Service Div., CCG, 1947. *Recreations:* squash and tennis. *Address:* Rock Cottage, Slapton, Kingsbridge, Devon. *T:* Torcross 386. *Club:* Royal Air Force.
[*Died* 24 *Jan.* 1971.

DAVIDSON, Very Rev. (Andrew) Nevile, DL; MA Edinburgh, Hon. DD Glasgow; Minister of Glasgow Cathedral, 1935-67; Moderator, General Assembly of the Church of Scotland, May 1962-May 1963; an Extra Chaplain to the Queen in Scotland since 1969 (Chaplain, 1952-69); Scottish Prelate, Order of St John of Jerusalem; Convener Church and Nation Committee of Church of Scotland General Assembly, 1954-60; *b* 13 Feb. 1899;

s of Rev. James Davidson, BD, and Constance, *d* of Sir Andrew Agnew of Lochnaw, 8th Bt, and Lady Louisa Noel; *m* 1944, Margaret Helen de Carteret, *er d* of late Colonel C. de C. Martin, MD, IMS. *Educ:* North Berwick; Edinburgh Univ. Vans Dunlop Scholarship in Philosophy; Asst Lecturer in Logic and Metaphysics, University of Edinburgh, for three years; studied divinity at New Coll., Edinburgh; Asst St George's, Edinburgh, 1924-25; Minister of St Mary's, Old Aberdeen, 1925-32; St Enoch's, Dundee, 1932-34; Joint-Founder in 1928 of the Dunkeld Fellowship and Founder in 1938, of the Friends of Glasgow Cathedral; served as Chaplain to the Forces with 52nd (Lowland) Div., 1940-42 (Hon. Mem., King's Own Scottish Borderers, 1944); Joint-Convenor of the Special Cttee which produced the Church of Scotland's Report on Evangelism, Into All the World, 1944-46; President: Scottish Church Society, 1945-47, and 1967-70; Church Service Society, 1948-50; a Chaplain to King George VI in Scotland, 1946-52; President New Coll. Union, 1953-55; Chairman BBC Scottish Religious Advisory Cttee, 1950-56; President Scottish Ecclesiological Society, 1956-57; Chairman Scottish Churches Ecumenical Cttee, 1950-63; Chaplain, Convention of Royal Burghs of Scotland, until 1975. Attended inauguration of United Church of S. India on 27 Sept. 1947, as official representative of Church of Scotland; at request of Foreign Mission Cttee, spent winter, 1947-48, visiting Mission Stations of Church of Scotland throughout India and Pakistan; Chairman: Commn on Spiritual Healing appointed by General Assembly, 1954-58; Multi-Lateral Church Conversation in Scotland, 1967-75. Winner of St Mungo Prize, 1958-61 (triennially awarded). Vice-President British Council of Churches, 1963-65; President, Society of Friends of Glasgow Cathedral, 1967; Convener, Inter-Church Relations Cttee of the Church of Scotland, 1964-69; Chm. of Council, Friends of St Mary's Church, Haddington. Macneil-Fraser Lectr, Trinity Coll., Glasgow. Hon. Chaplain, Forth Div. RNR. DL Glasgow, 1962. *Publications:* Reflections of a Scottish Churchman, 1965; book reviews and occasional contributions periodicals. *Recreations:* reading, motoring, travel. *Address:* Seafield House, West Barns, East Lothian. *T:* Dunbar 63236.
[*Died* 20 *Dec.* 1976.

DAVIDSON, Maj.-Gen. Francis Henry Norman, CB 1942; DSO 1919; MC (and Bar); *b* 1 April 1892; *s* of late Sir Leybourne Davidson; *m* Edna Mildred, *d* of J. G. Counsel, Bombay; two *s. Educ:* Marlborough; RMA. Entered Army 1911; served European War, 1914-19 (wounded, despatches four times, MC and bar, DSO); Bt Major, 1929; Major 1929; Bt Lt-Col, 1933; Colonel, 1938; Maj.-General 1941; GSO2, AHQ India, 1925-27; Brig. Major 12th Indian Inf. Bde, 1927-29; GSO2, War Office, 1930-34; Imperial Defence Coll. Course, 1935-36; GSO 2nd Grade Staff Coll., Camberley, 1937-38; GSO 1st Grade 2nd Division, Aldershot, 1938-39; CCRA 1st Corps BEF 1939-40; BGS X Corps, 1940; Director of Military Intelligence, War Office, 1940-44; MGGS British Army Staff, Washington, USA, 1944-46; retired pay, 1946. Colonel Comdt Intelligence Corps, 1952-60. *Address:* 82 Chelsea Park Gardens, SW3. *Clubs:* English-Speaking Union; Hurlingham.
[*Died* 15 *Jan.* 1973.

DAVIDSON, Prof. (James) Norman, CBE 1967; MD, DSc; FRS 1960; FRSE; FRCPE FRCPGlas; FRIC; Gardiner Professor of Biochemistry, Glasgow University, since 1947, and Director of the Biochemical Laboratories; *b* 5 March 1911; *s* of late James Davidson, FRSE, Edinburgh; *m* 1938, Morag McLeod, BSc, PhD, *d* of late Alexander Mathers McLeod, SSC, Edinburgh; two *d. Educ:* George Watson's Coll., Edinburgh; Edinburgh Univ. BSc (1st Class Hons Chemistry) 1934; MB, ChB (Hons) 1937; Vans Dunlop Entrance Scholar in Medicine, Robert Wilson Memorial Prizeman, Wellcome Gold Medallist; MD 1939; DSc (Edinburgh), 1945; Carnegie Research Fellow in Biochemistry at Kaiser Wilhelm Institut für Zellphysiologie, Berlin-Dahlem, 1937-38; Lecturer in Biochemistry, University of St Andrews, at University College, Dundee, 1938-40; Lecturer in Biochemistry, University of Aberdeen, 1940-45; Member Scientific Staff of Medical Research Council at National Institute for Medical Reasearch, Hampstead, NW3, 1945-46; Prof. of Biochemistry in University of London at St Thomas's Hospital Medical Sch., 1946-47; guest lecturer: Ghent, Brussels, Liège, 1954, Oslo and Uppsala, 1953, Paris, 1952, USA 1947, 1956, 1960, 1961, 1964, 1966, 1968, Warsaw, 1959, Moscow, 1961, Brazil, 1963, Malaysia, 1963. Formerly Examiner for Universities of St Andrews, Oxford, Cambridge, London, Leeds, Liverpool, Aberdeen, Birmingham, Singapore, Bristol, Dundee; Member: Editorial Board of British Journal of Nutrition; Biological Research Board, MRC, 1964-68; European Molecular Biology Organisation; Board of Management, Glasgow Royal Infirmary, 1948-72. President: Royal Society, Edinburgh, 1958-59, 1964-67 (Vice-Pres., 1955-58); Assoc. Clinical Biochemists, 1963-66; Mem. Council, Royal Soc., 1968-70. Vice-President, Saltire Society, 1959-62.

Chairman: Scottish Council Inst. Biology, 1959-60; Biochemical Society (Sec., 1946-52, Chm., 1961-63). Vice-Chairman, Advisory Cttee for Medical Research, Scotland, 1961-67. FRSM; FIBiol (Vice-Pres., 1961-63); FCS. Hon. Fellow, Soc. Ital. Biol. Sperimentale. Makdougall-Brisbane Prize, RSE, 1969. *Publications:* The Biochemistry of the Nucleic Acids, 7th edn, 1972; (with G. H. Bell and D. Emslie-Smith) Text-book of Physiology and Biochemistry, 8th edn, 1972; (with E, Chargaff) The Nucleic Acids: Chemistry and Biology, 1955; numerous biochemical papers in medical and scientific journals. *Recreations:* fishing, foreign travel, Scottish cultural activities. *Address:* Biochemistry Department, The University of Glasgow, Glasgow G12 8QQ; Penlee, Ledcameroch Road, Bearsden, G61 4AA. *T:* 041-942 4371. *Clubs:* Athenæum; New (Edinburgh).
[*Died* 11 *Sept.* 1972.

DAVIDSON, James Wightman, MA; PhD; Professor of Pacific History, Australian National University, since 1949; *b* 1 Oct. 1915; *s* of late George Wightman Davidson and late Edith Mabel Davidson (*née* Brown), both of Wellington, NZ; unmarried. *Educ:* Waitaki Sch., NZ; Victoria, University Coll., Wellington, NZ; St John's Coll., Cambridge; MA (NZ), 1st class hons in history, 1938; PhD Cantab, 1942. Research Assistant, Nuffield Coll., Oxford, 1941-42. Served in NZ Public Service, Internal Affairs Dept, 1938; External Affairs Dept, 1947; in UK Civil Service, Admiralty (Naval Intelligence Division), 1942-45; Colonial Office, 1945; Fellow of St John's Coll., Cambridge, 1944-51; University Lecturer in History, 1946-50; MLA, Western Samoa, 1949-50; Trusteeship Officer to Govt of Western Samoa, 1949-50. Assisted New Zealand Govt in working out proposals for constitutional reform in Western Samoa, 1947; Constitutional Adviser to Governments of: Western Samoa, 1959-61; the Cook Islands, 1963; Nauru, 1967-68; Consultant to Congress of Micronesia, 1969-72. *Publications:* The Northern Rhodesian Legislative Council, 1948; The Study of Pacific History, 1955; Samoa mo Samoa, 1967; (ed, with D. Scarr) Pacific Islands Portraits, 1970; articles in various historical and political journals. *Recreations:* tennis, swimming, sailing. *Address:* Australian National University, Canberra, ACT 2600, Australia. *T:* Canberra 959.323.
[*Died* 8 *April* 1973.

DAVIDSON, John Wallace Ord, CMG 1936; OBE 1926; member of London Stock Exchange, 1949-59; *b* 9 Nov. 1888; *s* of late George Greenshields Davidson; *m* 1935, Edith, *d* of late James Cory, Cory Manor, N. Devon. *Educ:* Christ's Hospital. HM Consular Service, China, 1909; served European War, Chinese Labour Corps, France, 1917-18; Acting Chinese Secretary, HM Legation, Peking, 1928-29; Acting Consul-General, Shanghai, 1933 and 1937; Consul-General, 1938; Counsellor, FO, 1945, Head of Prisoners of War Dept, 1945-46, and of Consular Dept, FO, 1946-48; retired on pension, 1948; a Governor of Christ's Hospital. *Address:* Cory Manor, near Holsworthy, N Devon. *T:* Bradworthy 318.
[*Died* 13 *Jan.* 1973.

DAVIDSON, Very Rev. Nevile; see Davidson, Very Rev. Andrew N.

DAVIDSON, Norman; see Davidson, J. N.

DAVIES, Alan B.; see Bowen-Davies.

DAVIES, Sir Alan Meredyth H.; see Hudson-Davies.

DAVIES, Rt. Hon. Sir Arthian; see Davies, Rt Hon. Sir (William) Arthian.

DAVIES, (Arthur Edward) Miles, CB 1956; *b* 26 Nov. 1903; *s* of Edward M. and Margaret Davies; *m* 1934, Elspeth Lang. *Educ:* University of Liverpool. Under Sec. Ministry of Education, 1950-58. *Address:* 6 Strathearn Place, W2. *Club:* Reform.
[*Died* 16 *Jan.* 1977.

DAVIES, Brian H.; see Humphreys-Davies.

DAVIES, Cuthbert Collin, PhD; Reader Emeritus in Indian History in the University of Oxford, since 1965; *b* 16 April 1896; *o s* of D. C. Davies, Narberth, Pembs; *m* 1918, Rachel Eleanor, *er d* of Rees Davies, JP, Carmarthen; one *s* one *d* (and one *d* decd). *Educ:* Narberth Grammar Sch.; University of Wales (Aberystwyth); Peterhouse, Cambridge. BA 1st Class Hons. Hist. Wales, 1923; PhD Cambridge, 1926. Temp. commn 15th W Yorks Regt, 1915; France, 1916-17 (twice wounded); Regular Commn 2/1st Gurkha Rifles, IA, 1918; Third Afghan War, 1919; ops in Waziristan, 1921-22; Comdg Dharamsala, 1922. Flt Lieut RAF, 1940. Lectr in Indian Hist., Sch. Oriental and African Studies, London Univ., and Supervisor of Indian Civil

Service Probationers, 1929; Visiting Prof. Boulder, Colorado, 1939; Visiting Prof. in South Asian History, University Wis., 1965. FRHistS, 1932; MA Balliol Coll., Oxford, 1936; Reader in Indian History, Oxford Univ., 1936-63; Corresponding Mem. Historical MSS. Commn, Government of India, 1953. Sir Jadunath Sarkar Gold Medal, Asiatic Soc. Bengal, 1959. *Publications:* The Problem of the North-West Frontier, 1932; Warren Hastings and Oudh, 1939; Benares Diary of Warren Hastings, 1948; Historical Atlas of the Indian Peninsula, 1949 (2nd edn 1959); Private Correspondence of Lord Macartney, 1950; Bharateeya Aitihasik Atlas, 1954. Contrib. to Cambridge History of India; New Cambridge Modern History; Army Quarterly; Eng. Historical Review; Journal E India Assoc.; Ency. Britannica; Ency. of Islam; Ency. Hebraica, History; Indian Archives; Annales Historiques de la Révolution Française; Handbuch der Weltgeschichte, etc. *Recreations:* fishing and walking. *Address:* The Garden House, Church Road, Knighton, Radnorshire LD7 1EB. *T:* Knighton 726.
[*Died* 5 *Nov.* 1974.

DAVIES, Rt. Rev. David Henry S.; see Saunders-Davies.

DAVIES, Derek G. G.; see Gill-Davies.

DAVIES, Rev. Ernest William; Rector of Piddlehinton, 1957-64; Rural Dean of Bere Regis, 1961-64; retired; *b* 23 May 1901; *s* of late Ernest James Davies; *m* 1928, Winifred Lancashire, Hythe, Kent; two *s* two *d. Educ:* Dulwich Coll.; St John's Coll., Oxford (Classical Scholar); 1st Class Hon. Mods 1922, 2nd Class Lit. Hum., 1924, BA 1924, MA 1927, Oxford Univ. Diploma in Education, 1934. Ordained priest, 1955. Headmaster, King's Sch., Rochester, 1935-57. *Address:* Weyside Cottage, Upwey, Weymouth, Dorset. *T:* Upwey 2011.
[*Died* 27 *March* 1978.

DAVIES, Evan Tom, DSc, PhD London; Dottore in Matematica Rome; MSc Wales; Professor of Mathematics, University of Waterloo, since 1971; *b* 24 Sept. 1904; *yr s* of Thomas and Elizabeth Davies, Pencader, Carmarthenshire; *m* 1st, 1941, Margaret Helen Picton (*d* 1944); no *c*; 2nd, 1955, Hilda Gladys Boyens; one *s. Educ:* Llandyssul County Sch.; University Coll., Aberystwyth; University Coll., Swansea; University of Rome; Sorbonne and Collège de France. Lecturer, King's Coll., London, 1930-46; Prof. of Mathematics, Univ. of Southampton (formerly University Coll., Southampton), 1946-69 (Emeritus, 1969); Dep. Vice-Chancellor, Southampton Univ., 1954-57; Prof. of Mathematics, Univ. of Calgary, 1969-71. *Publications:* papers in mathematical journals. *Recreations:* caravanning, foreign travel. *Address:* Mathematics Department, University of Waterloo, Waterloo, Ontario, Canada; 2 Uplands Way, Southampton. *T:* Southampton 56836.
[*Died* 8 *Oct.* 1973.

DAVIES, Haydn; *b* 8 May 1905; *o s* of late A. Davies, Abertysswg, Mon; *m* 1936, Mary, *e d* of late J. Dodd, Ealing; one *d. Educ:* Lewis Sch., Pengam, Glam.; University College of Wales, Aberystwyth; London School of Economics. BA (Hons) Wales. LCC Schoolmaster, 1926; President, London Schoolmasters Assoc.; Education Correspondent News Chronicle; Industrial Correspondent, The Star, 1935, and again 1952; MP (Lab.) SW St Pancras, 1945-50; contested York, 1950. Member National Union of Journalists. Worked during War of 1939-45 in Ministry of Economic Warfare and Board of Trade. *Address:* 32 Manor Road, Lillington, Leamington Spa, Warwicks.
[*Died* 18 *April* 1976.

DAVIES, Hector Leighton, CBE 1941; JP, DL; *b* Sebastopol, near Griffithstown, Mon, 18 April 1894; *e s* of late Sir John Cecil Davies, CBE, of the Mount, Gowerton, and later Stelvio, Newport, Mon; *m* 1924, Miss Ballantyne Poulton le Fylde; one *s* one *d. Educ:* Malvern Coll.; Technical Education, Swansea and Germany. Chm., Swansea Pilotage Authority; Past President of Council of Iron and Steel Institute; Past Chairman: Swansea Employment Cttee; Welsh Bd of Industry; Industrial Estates Management Corporation of Wales; S Wales Regional Industrial Advisory Cttee of National Savings Movement; Industrial Welfare Society. JP 1927; DL Glam 1956. *Address:* Cobwebs, Penmaen, Gower, Glam. *Clubs:* Royal Automobile; Bristol Channel Yacht (Swansea).
[*Died* 3 *Aug.* 1980.

DAVIES, Maj.-Gen. Henry Lowrie, CB 1945; CBE 1942 (OBE 1941); DSO 1934; MC; psc; *b* 25 Jan. 1898; *s* of Lieut-Colonel H. Davies, CMG; *m*; one *s* two *d*; *m* 1948, Margaret Jane Blomfield Plowden. *Educ:* Dover Coll.; RMC, Sandhurst. Joined 18th Royal Garhwal Rifles in India, 1916; served European War (Mesopotamia, Army of Black Sea); on NWF of India in Waziristan operations, 1922-23; in Mohmand operations NWF of India, 1933; passed Staff Coll., Quetta, 1928 and 1929; GSO3 Northern Command, 1931-32; Brigade Major Peshawar Brigade, 1933-35; GSO2 Military Dept, India Office,

1937; a Divisional Commander, Indian Army, 1942; served in Iceland (GSO1 Iceland Force), Burma (BGS Burma Army and Burcorps, 1942), Arakhan (Div. Comd), during War of 1939-45; Deputy CGS, GHQ, India; Comdt Staff Coll., Quetta; Deputy CGS, Pakistan Army, HQ; retired, 1948. Asst Director, Investigation Div., Ministry of Agriculture, Fisheries and Food, 1948-62; Historian, Cabinet Office (Historical Section), 1962-72, retd. *Recreation:* golf. *Address:* 28 Eaton Drive, Kingston on Thames, Surrey. *T:* 01-549 5372. *Clubs:* Naval and Military; Royal Mid Surrey Golf. *[Died 6 July 1975.*

DAVIES, Rt. Hon. John (Emerson Harding), PC 1970; MBE 1946; MP (C) Knutsford, 1970-Nov. 1978; Director, Hill Samuel Group, 1969-70 and since 1979; *b* 8 Jan. 1916; *s* of Arnold Thomas Davies, FCA, and Edith Minnie (*née* Harding); *m* 1943, Vera Georgina Bates; one *s* one *d. Educ:* St Edward's Sch., Oxford. Enlisted RASC, 1939; Commissioned 2nd Lieut, RASC, 1940; G2 (Tech.) Combined Ops Experimental Establishment (COXE), 1945-46. Joined Anglo-Iranian Oil Co., 1946; served in Stockholm, London and Paris, 1946-55; General Manager, Markets, 1956-60; Director BP Trading, 1960; Vice-Chairman and Managing Director, Shell Mex and BP, 1961-65; Director-General, CBI, 1965-69. Minister of Technology, July-Oct. 1970; Sec. of State for Trade and Industry and Pres., Bd of Trade, 1970-72; Chancellor of the Duchy of Lancaster, 1972-74; Opposition Front Bench Spokesman on Foreign and Commonwealth Affairs, 1976-78. Member: NEDC, 1964-72; Nat. Joint Advisory Council, Dept of Employment and Productivity (formerly Min. of Labour), 1965-69; British Productivity Council, 1965-69; British National Export Council, 1966-69; Council of Industrial Design, 1966-70; Public Schools Commission, 1966-68. Governor: St Edward's Sch., Oxford; Windlesham House School Trust; Pres., Incorporated Assoc. of Prep. Schools, 1974-. DUniv Essex, 1967; Hon. DTech Loughborough, 1972. FCA 1960 (ACA 1939); FRSA 1964; JDipMA 1965. *Recreations:* travel and music. *Address:* 79 Rivermead Court, SW6 3RZ. *Clubs:* Oriental, Hurlingham.
[Died 4 July 1979.

DAVIES, John L.; *see* Langdon-Davies.

DAVIES, Rev. (John) Trevor, MA, BD Edinburgh, PhD London; Minister of Religion; retired; Chairman: Wentworth Milton Mount School, Bournemouth; Congregational Union of England and Wales, 1960-61; *b* Mountain Ash, 2 May 1907; *s* of Thomas Davies, Neath, Glam.; *m* 1933, Alice Hitchen, Lancs; one *s. Educ:* County Sch., Neath; Yorkshire United Coll., Bradford; Edinburgh and London Universities. Formerly Minister of Congregational Churches: Heaton, Newcastle on Tyne; Clarendon Road, Watford; Cliff Town, Southend-on-Sea; Richmond Hill, Bournemouth. Lecturer in: Philosophy of Religion, New Coll., London, 1948-51; Psychology, King's Coll., London, 1950-51. Preaching tours in USA, 1954, 1958, 1964, and Canada, 1962. *Publications:* Sublimation, 1945; Lord of All, 1951; Corner Pieces, 1953; Richmond Hill Story, 1956; Is Anyone There?, 1960. Has written weekly column, in Christian World, since 1949. *Recreations:* golf, motoring. *Address:* 25 Widworth Drive, Broadstone, Dorset. *T:* Broadstone 6495. *Club:* Royal Over-Seas League. *[Died 5 May 1974.*

DAVIES, Lewis, OBE 1948; Chairman of Staffordshire County Council, 1949-53 (Vice Chairman, 1953-55), Member, 1925-58, retired; *b* 1 July 1886; *m* 1904, Bertha Griffiths; one *s* one *d* (also one adopted *s*). *Educ:* Brownhills Council Sch. Methodist: Sunday Teacher, 1904, Lay Preacher, 1908; all offices in Methodist Church, open to Laymen, to present time. CC 1925, CA, 1938; County Magistrate, 1934-. Chairman, County Magistrates, Lichfield and Brownhills Division, 1951-. Member CC Assoc., 1946-58; Chairman of a number of School Governing Bodies, member Labour Party, 1919-. Vice-President, North Staffs Univ. *Recreations:* bowls; formerly tennis, cricket, football. *Address:* Griffith House, Chasetown, near Walsall, Staffs. *T:* Brownhills 3121. *[Died 12 Jan. 1971.*

DAVIES, Sir Martin, Kt 1972; CBE 1965; FBA 1966; FSA; FMA; Director of the National Gallery, 1968-73; *b* 22 March 1908; *s* of Ernest Davies and Elizabeth Eleanor Taylor. *Educ:* Rugby; King's Coll., Cambridge. Became Assistant Keeper of the National Gallery, 1932; Deputy Keeper, 1947; Keeper, 1960. Hon. DLitt Exon, 1968. *Address:* 16 Rupert House, Nevern Square, SW5 9PL. *Club:* Reform. *[Died 7 March 1975.*

DAVIES, Miles; *see* Davies, A. E. M.

DAVIES, Reginald, CMG 1950; *b* 17 Nov. 1887; *y s* of late Rev. Owen Davies; *m* 1928, Gwenllyan Kathleen Butler Dew; one *s* one *d. Educ:* Hymers Coll., Hull; St Catharine's Coll., Cambridge (Scholar). BA (Hons Maths), 1909; rowed for Cambridge, 1910. Entered Sudan Political Service, 1911; Resident, Dar Masalit, 1920; Director of Intelligence, 1927; Asst Civil Secretary, 1929; Dep. Financial Secretary, 1930; Secretary for Economic Development, 1931; Chairman of the Board of Economics and Trade and Member of Governor-General's Council, 1934; retired 1935. Order of the Nile, 3rd Class, 1932. Dep. Director-General, Alexandria Municipality, 1935-39; Director Publicity Section of HM Embassy, Cairo, 1939-42. Finance Officer, The British Council, 1942-47. Asst Director-General, The British Council, 1947; retired 1953. *Publications:* The Camel's Back: Service in the Rural Sudan, 1957; various contributions to Sudan Notes and Records. *Recreation:* foreign travel. *Address:* 2 Stratton Audley Manor, near Bicester, Oxfordshire. *Club:* Leander. *[Died 18 Dec. 1971.*

DAVIES, Rhys, OBE 1968; novelist and short story writer; *b* 9 Nov. 1903; *s* of Thomas R. and Sarah A. Davies. *Educ:* Porth Co. Sch. *Publications:* The Withered Root, 1927; A Pig in a Poke, 1931; Count Your Blessings, 1932; The Red Hills, 1932; Love Provoked, 1933; Honey and Bread, 1935; The Things Men Do, 1936; A Time to Laugh, 1937; My Wales, 1937; Jubilee Blues, 1938; Under the Rose, 1940; Tomorrow to Fresh Woods, 1941; A Finger in Every Pie, 1942; The Story of Wales, 1943; The Black Venus, 1944; The Trip to London, 1946; The Dark Daughters, 1947; Boy With a Trumpet, 1949; Marianne, 1951; The Painted King, 1954; No Escape (play), 1954; Collected Stories, 1955; The Perishable Quality, 1957; The Darling of Her Heart, 1958; Girl Waiting in the Shade, 1960; The Chosen One, 1967; Print of a Hare's Foot, 1969; Nobody Answered the Bell, 1971; Honeysuckle Girl, 1975; contributions to numerous British and American periodicals; *posthumous publication:* The Best of Rhys Davies, 1979. *Recreations:* theatre; living in London; cultivating ruined characters. *Address:* c/o Curtis Brown Ltd, 1 Craven Hill, W2 3EW. *[Died 21 Aug. 1978.*

DAVIES, Stephen Owen; MP (Ind Lab) Merthyr Tydfil since 1970 (MP (Lab), 1934-70, for same constituency); lately chief Organiser to South Wales Miners' Federation; *b* Nov. 1886; *s* of late Thomas and late Esther Owen Davies; *m* 1934, Seph Davies, Gwauncaegurwen; two *s* three *d. Educ:* University College, Cardiff; Royal College of Science. Coalminer at 12 years of age; matriculated from coalface; graduated in Arts and returned to colliery as collier; check-weigher, 1913. Was trained as a Mining Engineer. Miners' Agent under S Wales Miners' Federation at Dowlais, 1918-34; Vice-President SWMF, 1924-33; represented Welsh Miners on MFGB 1924-34; Member Court of Governors of National Library of Wales, National Museum of Wales, University of Wales; presented evidence before several Government inquiries, etc. *Recreations:* walking, swimming. *Address:* Gwynfryn, Merthyr Tydfil, Glam. *T:* Merthyr 3410.
[Died 25 Feb. 1972.

DAVIES, Thomas A.; *see* Anwyl-Davies.

DAVIES, Rev. Trevor; *see* Davies, Rev. John Trevor.

DAVIES, Rt. Hon. Sir (William) Arthian, PC 1961; Kt 1952; DL; a Lord Justice of Appeal, 1961-74; *b* 10 May 1901; *s* of late Arthian Davies; *m* 1933, Mary Bailey, *d* of late Henry Liptrot; one *d. Educ:* Dulwich; Trinity Coll., Oxford (MA), 1st Cl. hons jurisprudence. Barrister, 1925; QC 1947; sometime Exr and Asst Reader to Council of Legal Education and Gresham Lecturer in Law; Junior Counsel to Ministry of Labour and National Service, 1934-47; Recorder of Merthyr Tydfil, 1946-49, Chester, 1949-52. JP (Bucks), 1948; DL 1967; Dep. Chairman Quarter Sessions: Co. Cardigan, 1949-52; Bucks, 1951-61, Chm. 1961-71. Bencher, Inner Temple, 1952; Judge of High Court of Justice, Probate, Divorce, and Admiralty Division, 1952-59; Judge of High Court of Justice, Queen's Bench Div., 1959-61. Dep. Chairman Parliamentary Boundary Commn for Wales, 1958-61; Chairman Home Office Cttee on Matrimonial Proceedings in Magistrates' Courts, 1958. Hon. Fellow, Trinity Coll., Oxford, 1969. *Address:* Ballinger Lodge, Great Missenden, Bucks.
[Died 19 Sept. 1979.

DAVIES, William John, CMG 1943; OBE 1929; *b* Carmarthen, 21 Feb. 1891; *s* of William and Sarah Davies; *m* 1921, Miriam Ellen Brown, Usk, Mon.; no *c. Educ:* Queen Elizabeth Grammar Sch., Carmarthen; University, Aberystwyth (BA 1912). Entered Japan Consular Service, 1913; Asst Japanese Secretary and Second Secretary to HM Embassy, Tokyo, 1918-34; Consul, Tokyo, 1934-37; Acting Counsellor of Embassy, 1936; Consul in Foreign Office, 1938; Consul-General at Harbin, 1939-41; Consul-General at Kobe, 1941; Foreign Office, 1943-45; Japanese Language Supervisor, BBC, 1946-50; external examiner in Japanese, University of London, 1948-51. *Address:* Tudor Cottage, 9 Westmeston Avenue, Rottingdean, Sussex. *T:* Brighton 32013. *[Died 19 June 1975.*

DAVIES, William Tudor, CBE 1963 (OBE 1960); FREconS; FBIM; JP; Barrister at Law and Economist; Independent Chairman and Adviser of Trade Associations; Adviser on industrial legislation and conciliation and international cartels; *b* Nantyglo, Gwent; *o s* of John Pritchard Davies; *m* 1937, Iva Mary, *yr d* of Philip Kyle, OBE. *Educ:* University of Wales, Aberystwyth; University of Bristol; University of Manchester. BA 1st Class Honours; 1st Class Diplomas in Theory and Practice of Education; Founder Member, Fellow and Hon. Life Member, British Institute of Management; Research Medallist, University of Bristol; Post-Graduate Research, University of Manchester; Post-Graduate Research, University of Cambridge; Lecturer in Economics; Editorial staff Manchester Guardian; Parliamentary candidate, 1922 and 1923; Editorial staff Financial News; Chairman of Joint Cttee of Building and Civil Engineering Industries set up under Control of Employment Act, 1939; Independent Chairman of Joint Industrial Council of Distributive Trades; Chairman of Wages Councils; Chairman, Reinstatement in Civil Employment Tribunals; Member: Further Education and Training Tribunal; London Conscientious Objectors' Tribunal, 1940-60; Chairman of National Insurance Tribunals; Independent Chairman of the National Conciliation Board for the Co-operative Service; Chairman of Boards of Inquiry under Ministry of Labour; Independent Chairman Local Appeal Boards; Independent Chairman Joint Cttee of North Wales Coal Industry; Chairman, Road Transport Inquiries under Road Traffic Acts, 1961, and Compulsory Purchase orders; Hearing Appeals from Licensing Authorities and Public Inquiries, Ministry of Transport; Member Isle of Man Traffic Tribunal; Commissioner of Inquiry in Nigeria for Secretary of State for the Colonies; Barrister and Solicitor of Supreme Court, Federation of Nigeria, etc. *Publications:* National Essay Prize on The Creation of an International Police Force (Welsh National Eisteddfod, Caernarvon, 1921); The Rationalisation of Industry, 1928; The Economic Task, 1931; The Economics of Plenty, 1934; Trade Associations and Industrial Co-ordination, 1938-39; Personnel Management and Essential Work Orders, 1944; National Insurance, Law of Tribunals, 1950. *Recreations:* golf, walking. *Address:* 2 Harcourt Buildings, Temple, EC4. *T:* 01-353 7202; Sunhaven, 35 Links Avenue, Gidea Park, Essex. *T:* Romford 41026. *Club:* National Liberal. *[Died 18 July 1978.*

DAVIES, William Watkin, MA, Barrister-at-law; retired as Lecturer in International Politics, Birmingham University; *b* 1895; *o s* of Rev. J. Gwynoro Davies, and Jane Mary, *d* of William Watkin, JP, Criccieth; *m* 1925, Cecily Dorothea, MB, BS, *e d* of Lieut-Col Cecil Crosskey, DL. *Educ:* Barmouth; Aberystwyth Coll.; St John's Coll., Oxford (Casberd Exhibitioner). Honour School of Modern History; Barrister-at-law, Gray's Inn, North Wales Circuit. History Master, Friends Sch., Saffron Walden, 1915-17; Barmouth County Sch., 1917-19; Lecturer in History and Economics for WEA, 1919-21; Lecturer in History, Bristol Univ., 1919-21; Lecturer for League of Nations Union; lectured at the International Summer School, Salzburg, 1921; Examiner in History for the Central Welsh Board, 1917-22; for the Northern Universities, 1922; Internal Examiner at Bristol Univ., 1921-22; Extension Lecturer for London Univ., 1925-27; member of various learned societies. *Publications:* Gladstone and the Unification of Italy; How to Read History (Japanese translation); Chapters in Outline of Literature and Art; Wales; A World Outlook; A Wayfarer in Wales; Lloyd George, 1863-1914; Articles in numerous journals; Editor of Welsh Outlook, 1925-27. *Recreations:* walking, foreign travel, music. *Address:* 77 Wentworth Road, Harborne, Birmingham 17. *[Died 25 Dec. 1973.*

DAVIES, Wyndham Matabele, QC 1946; BA, LLB; Stipendiary Magistrate of Pontypridd, 1949-66; Chairman Glamorgan QS, 1961-66 (Dep. Chairman, 1950-61); *b* 23 Dec. 1893; *s* of David John and Jane Davies; *m* 1936, Enid Maud (*d* 1971), *d* of James Jenkins, JP, and Catherine Jenkins; one *s.* Called to Bar, Lincoln's Inn, 1922. European War, 1914-18, served in France, Belgium, mainly with 1st S. Wales Borderers, 1915-19; War of 1939-45, Royal Corps of Signals, 1939-40. Special Divorce Commissioner, 1946-49. *Recreations:* fishing, golf. *Address:* The Long House, Lisvane, Glamorgan. *T:* Cardiff 756654. *Club:* Cardiff and County (Cardiff). *[Died 25 June 1972.*

DAVIES-COOKE, Col Philip Ralph, CB 1958; TD 1937; JP; DL; *b* 27 Nov. 1896; *s* of Major P. T. Davies-Cooke, OBE, DL, JP; *m* 1924, Kathleen Mabel Cooke (OBE 1964); two *s* one *d. Educ:* Eton; Royal Military Coll., Sandhurst. Served European War, 1915-18, with 1st The Royal Dragoons, also Ireland, 1920-23; with 5 RWF, 1924-29; QO Yorks Dragoons, 1930-45; and served War of 1939-45. Hon. Col 4 RWF, 1950-61; Chairman Denbigh/Flint T&AFA, 1950-61; Rep. Chairman for Wales on Council T&AFA, 1955-61. Chairman N. Wales Regional Advisory Cttee (Forestry), 1952-61. JP 1925, DL 1947, High Sheriff 1949, Vice-Lieutenant 1957-69, Flintshire; Chairman Petty Sessions Div. Magistrates, 1952-69. Landowner: N Wales and Yorks. *Publication:* Flintshire Shrievalty, 1949. *Recreations:* hunting, shooting. *Address:* Owston Hall, Doncaster, Yorks. *T:* Adwick-le-Street 2557. *Club:* Cavalry. *[Died 15 Nov. 1974.*

d'AVIGDOR-GOLDSMID, Major Sir Henry Joseph, 2nd Bt, *cr* 1934; DSO 1945; MC 1945; TD; DL, JP; Major RAC TA, late Royal West Kent Regiment; *b* 10 June 1909; *s* of Sir Osmond Elim d'Avigdor-Goldsmid, 1st Baronet; *S* father, 1940; *m* 1940, Rosemary Margaret Horlick, *d* of C. R. I. Nicholl; one *d* (and one *d* decd). *Educ:* Harrow; Balliol Coll., Oxford, MA, 1938. Served War of 1939-45 (despatches twice, MC, DSO). Alderman of Kent CC, 1951 (CC 1946); DL, JP Kent, 1949; High Sheriff of Kent, 1953. MP (C) Walsall S, 1955-Feb. 1974; PPS to Minister of Housing and Local Government, 1955-56; Chairman: Select Cttee on Nationalised Industries, 1970-72; Select Cttee on Corporation Tax, 1971; Select Cttee on Public Expenditure, 1972-74. Mem., Horse Race Totalisator Bd, 1973-76. Chairman: Bank Leumi (UK) Ltd, 1961-; Pergamon Press, 1969-71. Hon. Freeman, Borough of Walsall, 1974. *Heir: b* Maj.-Gen. James Arthur d'Avigdor-Goldsmid, CB, OBE, MC. *Address:* Somerhill, Tonbridge, Kent. *Clubs:* White's, Beefsteak. *[Died 11 Dec. 1976.*

DAVIS, Sir Alfred George Fletcher H.; *see* Hall-Davis.

DAVIS, Anthony Tilton, MA; JP; Head Master, Reading School, since 1966; *b* 14 Aug. 1931; *o s* of John and late Evelyn Davis; unmarried. *Educ:* St Bartholomew's Grammar Sch., Newbury; Reading Univ.; St John's Coll., Cambridge (Scholar). 1st class hons Class. Tripos Part I, 1954; 1st class hons (with distinction in Ancient History) Class. Tripos Part II, 1955. Sub-Lieut, RNVR, 1955-57. Asst Master and Classical Sixth Form Master, Harrow Sch., 1957-66 (Head of Latin, 1964-66). Pres., St John Ambulance Brigade (West Berks), 1972-; Member: Thames Valley Police Authority, 1972-; Court of Reading Univ., 1972-. JP Reading, 1971. *Publications:* Sallust, Catiline, 1967; articles and reviews in Greece and Rome and Didaskalos. *Recreations:* cricket (Captain, Berks CCC, 1960-70); music, water colours, ski-ing. *Address:* The Head Master's Lodge, Reading School, Reading, Berks. *T:* Reading 81886. *[Died 20 Nov. 1978.*

DAVIS, Archibald William; *b* 20 May 1900; *s* of late G. W. Davis, Crayford, Kent; *m* 1930, Eunice, *d* of late W. Pidd, Westwood, Coventry (*d* 1975); one *s. Educ:* Bablake Sch., Coventry; University College, London; Balliol Coll., Oxford; Emmanuel Coll., Cambridge. Entered HM Levant Consular Service, 1922; served at Consular posts in Iran, Turkey, Syria and Iraq; Political Officer, Aleppo (N Syria), 1941-42, with rank of Lt-Col; HM Consul-General, Basra, Iraq, 1946-49; Seville, Spain, 1950-53; retired 1953. *Address:* Rowanduz, Mendip Edge, Bleadon Hill, Weston-super-Mare, Avon. *T:* Bleadon 812830. *[Died 29 March 1979.*

DAVIS, Edward David Darelan, FRCS, LDS, RCS; retired as Consultant Surgeon and Lecturer, Nose, Throat, and Ear Department, Charing Cross Hospital; Surgeon EMS; Consultant Surgeon: Military Hospital, Millbank; Royal Dental Hospital; Metropolitan Ear, Nose, & Throat Hospital; Curator Ferens Institute, Middlesex Hospital; *b* 11 Aug. 1880; *s* of late Wm Davis; *m* 1911, Alice Mildred, *d* of H. C. Russell, JP; two *s* one *d. Educ:* Queen's Coll., Taunton; University Coll., Cardiff; Charing Cross Hospital. Graduated at Charing Cross Hospital, 1903, and held posts of House Physician, House Surgeon, Demonstrator of Anatomy and Clinical Asst to Nose, Throat, and Ear Dept; Senior Clinical Asst Throat Hospital, Golden Sq.; Clinical Asst to Surgical Out-patients and Ear Dept, Children's Hospital, Gt Ormond Street; Clinical Asst and Surgeon Laryngologist, Mt Vernon Hospital for Consumption; Mem. of the Council of the Otological Section (Pres.) and Laryngological Section (Pres.) of the Royal Society of Medicine; Semon Lecturer, 1947. Consulting Surgeon (nose, throat, and ear), Military Hospitals of London District; Surgeon Maxillo-Facial Red Cross Hospital and Officers' Hospitals; Surgeon 22 CCS, BEF. Late Treas. Medical Defence Union; FRSocMed, etc. *Publications:* various papers to Medical Journals and Transactions of Medical Societies. *Recreations:* golf, ski-ing, billiards. *Address:* 17 Priory Court, Granville Road, Eastbourne, Sussex. *T:* Eastbourne 29435. *Clubs:* Athenæum; Devonshire (Eastbourne). *[Died 20 Feb. 1976.*

DAVIS, Francis John, CMG 1970; OBE 1966; Chairman of Commission, Commonwealth Serum Laboratories, 1967-75; *b* 13 April 1900; *s* of Albert Henry Davis and Caroline Billing; *m* 1933, Thelma Doris Cox. *Educ:* State Schools, Victoria. Member of Parliament of Australia for Deakin, Vic, Dec. 1949-Nov. 1966 (Liberal). *Recreations:* travelling, walking, reading. *Address:* 5a/12 Marine Parade, St Kilda, Victoria 3182, Australia. *T:* 534.6164. *[Died 28 Feb. 1980.*

DAVIS, Sir Gilbert, 2nd Bt, *cr* 1946; Director: Atlas Stone Co. Ltd, SW1, 1922-72; Eastwoods Ltd, 1953-62; one of HM's Lieutenants, City of London, 1946-69; *b* 2 Aug. 1901; *er s* of Sir Charles Davis, 1st Bt, and Lady (Elsie) Davis (*née* Keeble) (*d* 1967), Barrington Hall, Cambridge; *S* father, 1950; *m* 1st, 1927, Kathleen Ford (marr. diss. 1944); one *s* one *d*; 2nd, 1944, Barbara Virginia Freydig (marr. diss. 1952); 3rd, 1952, Madeline Green (*née* Wellings). *Educ:* Clifton Coll.; Cambridge Univ. Liveryman, Grocers' Company, 1922; Mem. of Common Council, City of London (Broad Street Ward), 1946-69; Chm. City of London Police Cttee, 1952 and Labour Cttee, 1953-56. Dep. Governor of the Hon. The Irish Soc., 1960. Was until 1958 Mem. Council London Chamber of Commerce; Mem. of Lloyd's, 1934-. Vice-Pres., Inst. of Quarrying (Chm., London Branch, 1960-63); Chm. Admiralty Ferry Crew Assoc., 1960-63. Served War of 1939-45; Royal Navy. MIChemE, 1924-67. *Recreation:* sailing. *Heir: s* John Gilbert Davis [*b* 17 Aug. 1936; *m* 1960, Elizabeth, *d* of Robert Smith Turnbull, Falkirk; two *d*. *Educ:* Oundle; Royal Naval Coll., Dartmouth]. *Address:* 12 High Street, Fen Ditton, Cambridge. *Clubs:* East India, Sports and Public Schools, Royal Automobile. *[Died 14 March* 1973.

DAVIS, Sir Herbert, Kt 1943; CBE 1941; Vice-Chairman Unilever Ltd until 1956; *b* 12 March 1891; *m* 1912, Eva FitzGerald Radford (*d* 1971); one *d* (and one *d* decd). *Educ:* St John's Coll., Cambridge. *Recreation:* golf. *Address:* East Court, Effingham, Surrey. *T:* Bookham 111. *[Died 20 Feb.* 1972.

DAVIS, J. C. A.; *see* Ainsworth-Davis.

DAVIS, Leslie John, MD Ed.; FRCP London, Edinburgh and Glasgow; Professor Emeritus, University of Glasgow, 1961; Hon. Consulting Physician, Glasgow Royal Infirmary; *b* 1925; *s* of late John Davis; *m* 1938, Marjorie Adelaide, *yr d* of late Arthur Cleveland. *Educ:* University Coll. Sch.; Edinburgh Univ. Served at sea, 1918; MB, ChB, Edinburgh 1924; House Surgeon, Royal Infirmary, Edinburgh, 1925; Research Student, London Sch. of Tropical Medicine, 1926; Asst Bacteriologist, Wellcome Tropical Research Laboratories, 1927-30; Prof. of Pathology, Hong-Kong Univ., 1931-39; Dir, Medical Laboratory, Bulawayo, 1939-40; Asst and later Lecturer, Dept of Medicine, Edinburgh Univ.; Temp. Asst Physician, Royal Infirmary, Edinburgh, and later Physician, Municipal Hospitals, Edinburgh, 1940-45; Muirhead Prof. of Medicine, University of Glasgow, 1945-61; Consulting Physician to the Royal Navy, 1954-61. *Publications:* The Megaloblastic Anaemias (with A. Brown), 1953; numerous contribs to medical and scientific journals mainly on pathological and haematological subjects. *Recreations:* fishing, model engineering. *Address:* Norton Brook, Yarmouth, Isle of Wight. *T:* Yarmouth 474. *Club:* Royal Solent Yacht. *[Died 31 Oct.* 1980.

DAVIS, Dame Margaret; *see* Rutherford, Dame Margaret.

DAVIS, Prof. Ralph, FBA 1973; Professor of Economic History, University of Leicester, since 1964, Pro-Vice-Chancellor, since 1976; *b* 30 April 1915; *s* of Ernest Alfred and Emily Davis; *m* 1949, Dorothy Easthope; two *s* one *d*. *Educ:* London School of Economics (1946-50). Lectr and Reader in Economic History, Univ. of Hull, 1950-64. Trustee, Nat. Maritime Museum, 1968-75. *Publications:* Rise of the English Shipping Industry, 1962; Twenty-one-and-a-half Bishop Lane, 1962; Aleppo and Devonshire Square, 1967; Rise of the Atlantic Economies, 1973; many articles in jls, etc. *Address:* Department of Economic History, University of Leicester, Leicester LE1 7RH. *[Died 30 Sept.* 1978.

DAVIS, Maj.-Gen. Ronald A. B.; *see* Bramwell Davis.

DAVIS, Thomas Frederick; Metropolitan Magistrate, 1947-63, retired; *b* 9 Feb. 1891; *m* 1915, Rose Kipping (*d* 1966); one *s*; *m* 1967, Nora Gwendoline Roche. *Educ:* various; King's Coll., London. Served European War, 1914-18, France; Lieut East Surrey Regt, 1915-16 (wounded); Lieut Observer, RFC, 1916-17 (wounded); Capt. (Admin.) RAF, 1917-19. Barrister-at-Law, 1921-47. *Recreations:* golf, gardening and music. *Address:* Ardenwood, Copthorne, Crawley, Sussex. *T:* Copthorne 2320. *[Died 10 May* 1974.

DAVIS-GOFF, Sir Ernest (William); *see* Goff.

DAVISON, Rev. Leslie, BD (London); General Secretary, Home Mission Department of the Methodist Church, since 1965 (Secretary, 1957-65); *b* 8 June 1906; *s* of George Robert Davison and Naomi (*née* Beardsmore); *m* 1937, Irene Florence Lilley (*d* 1963). *Educ:* The Bede, Sunderland; Victoria Park United Methodist Coll., Manchester. Probationer at: Camelford and Wadebridge, 1927-28; Cheltenham, 1928-30; Waverley Park, London, 1930-37. Ordained, 1931; S London Mission, 1937-44. Alderman of Bermondsey, 1940-44; London County Councillor, 1942-44. Superintendent of Walsall Mission, 1944-50; Chm., Wolverhampton and Shrewsbury District, 1950-57; Sec. Home Mission Dept, Methodist Church, 1957-65. Pres., Methodist Conference, 1962-63. Hon. degrees: LHD, Kansas Wesleyan Univ.; DD, Dickinson Coll., Pa. *Publications:* Ballads of Bermondsey, 1942; The Cross in the Club, 1943; The Principles of Penal Reform, 1960. Ed, The Christian Replies, 1960; (jointly) The Pattern of Prayer, 1961; Preacher's Gold, 1962; Sender and Sent, 1969. *Recreation:* walking. *Address:* (home) 11 Hitherwood Court, SE19. *T:* 01-670 7940; (office) Methodist Church Home Mission Department, 1 Central Buildings, Westminster, SW1. *T:* 01-930 5911. *[Died 13 Jan.* 1972.

DAVISON, Ralph, OBE 1970; QPM 1962; DL; Chief Constable of Cleveland Constabulary (formerly Teesside Constabulary), 1968-76, retired; *b* 25 March 1914; *s* of Ralph Dixon Davison and Elizabeth (*née* Bulmer), Saltburn, Yorks; *m* 1939, Joyce, *d* of George Smith and Winifred (*née* Elstob), Spennymoor, Co. Durham; one *s* one *d*. *Educ:* Sir William Turner's Sch., Redcar. School Teacher, 1932; Liverpool City Police, 1934-56; Chief Constable, Middlesbrough, 1956-68. County Director, St John Ambulance Assoc., Cleveland, 1974. Coronation Medal, 1953; Police Long Service and Good Conduct Medal, 1956. DL Cleveland 1975. CStJ 1974 (SBStJ 1965). *Recreations:* photography, music, gardening, philately. *Address:* Esk Mill, Castleton, near Whitby, N Yorks. *T:* Castleton 626. *[Died 6 Dec.* 1977.

DAVY, Georges Ambroise, Hon. KBE 1955; Grand Officier, Légion d'Honneur; Commandeur des Palmes académiques; Commandeur d'Orange-Nassau, Commandeur de l'étoile de Sud; Grand Officier du Nichan-Iftikhar; DèsL; Member, Institut de France (Académie des Sciences Morales et Politiques) (Président, 1965); Hon. Dean of Faculty of Letters, University of Paris; Member, National Committee since 1960, Centre National de la Recherche Scientifique (Member Board, 1952); Director, Fondation Thiers, since 1955; Président de l'Institut Internationale de Philosophie politique, 1953-67; *b* 31 Dec. 1883; *s* of Jean-Marie Davy and Isabelle Piquois; *m* 1918, Marie-Rose Vial; two *s* two *d*. *Educ:* Ecole Normale Superieure; University of Paris. Agrégé de Philosophie, Docteur ès Lettres. Prof. of Literature, Dijon, 1919-30, Dean of the Faculty, 1922-30; Rector of Rennes Univ., 1931-38; Inspector-Gen. of Education, 1938-44. Prof. Fac. of Letters, University of Paris, 1944-55; Dean of Faculty of Letters, Paris, 1950-55. Président du haut comité sociologique de la France d'outremer. Prof. *hc* University of Brazil. Assoc. Mem. Belgian Royal Academy. Dr *hc* University of Brussels. *Publications:* La Foi jurée, 1922; Le Droit, l'idéalisme et l'expérience, 1923; Des clans aux empires, 1923; Sociologie politique, 1925; Sociologues d'hier et d'aujourd'hui, 1935; L'homme, le fait social et le fait politique; avec nombreuses lettres inédites de Durckheim et de Lévy-Bruhl, 1973, etc. *Address:* Fondation Thiers, 5 Rond Point Bugeaud, Paris 16e, France. *[Died 27 July* 1976.

DAWBARN, Graham Richards, CBE 1948; MA; FRIBA (retired); FRAeS; RIBA Distinction in Town Planning; *b* London, 8 Aug. 1893; *s* of late R. A. Dawbarn, MICE, MIEE; *m* 1923, Olive, *d* of late John Topham, Barrister-at-Law; two *d*. *Educ:* The King's Sch., Canterbury; Corpus Christi Coll., Cambridge. Served European War, 1914-17; Public Works Dept, Hong Kong, 1921-23; won in open competition Raffles Coll., Singapore (with Cyril Farey), 1924, and Constantine Technical Coll., Middlesbrough, 1925; awarded Henry Saxon Snell prize for hospital design, 1927, and Godwin and Wimperis Bursary for executed works, 1931; flew in light aeroplane with late Sir Nigel Norman 8000 miles through USA studying airports; founded with him firm of Norman & Dawbarn, 1933, and remained a senior partner in it until 1958; MOH Housing Medal, 1949; two architectural awards by Council of Festival of Britain, 1951; Bronze Medal, Paris Salon, 1957; President AA and member of RIBA Council, 1945-47; Hon. Corresponding member Danish Assoc. of Architects; member of professional and technical cttees including Business Buildings Cttee, London Airport Layout Panel and Terminal Buildings Cttee; Work (mainly in partnership) includes numerous Airport Buildings layouts and reports; Housing for three New Towns and various Boroughs; University and Medical Sch. for West Indies, the expansion scheme for the Imperial Coll., London, Adult Training Colleges and Schools; and with their Cons. Civil Engineer, the BBC Television Centre at Wood Lane. *Address:*

Ingram House, Whiteley Village, Walton-on-Thames, Surrey KT12 4EH. *Club:* Athenæum.   *[Died 30 Jan. 1976.*

DAWES, Edgar Rowland, CMG 1958; Vice-Chairman Australian Broadcasting Commission, 1945-67; Governor, Adelaide Festival of Arts, since 1965; Member of Board: Royal Adelaide Hospital; Queen Elizabeth Hospital; *b* 28 Nov. 1902; *s* of George and Gertrude Dawes, Norwood, SA; *m* 1926, Adeline Melba Hurcombe (decd); one *s* one *d*; *m* 1966, Patricia M., *d* of W. Henderson. *Educ:* Public and High Sch., Norwood; Adelaide Univ. Secretary, Australian Society of Engineers, 1926-39; MHA, SA, 1929-32; Director Industries Corp., 1935-39; Member Board, Inst. Medical and Veterinary Sciences, 1935-. Area Management Board (Govt Appt), Min. of Munitions, 1939-45; also Asst Controller, Gun Ammunition; Controller, Ordnance Production and Chief Technical Officer. Member first Council of National Univ., Canberra, 1953-57; Commonwealth Govt Delegate to UNSCAT Conference, Geneva, 1963. Director of private companies (Engineering), 1945-. Chm. and Comr, Charitable Funds, SA, 1967-; Dep. Chm., Inst. of Med. and Veterinary Science (IMVS), SA, 1967. *Recreations:* fishing and boating. *Address:* 18 St Georges Avenue, Glandore, SA 5037, Australia. *T:* 93.2673. *Club:* Naval and Military.
     [Died 4 Aug. 1973.

DAWKINS, Dr Charles John Massey; *b* 13 July 1905; *s* of C. W. Dawkins, CBE; *m* 1930, Dr Sylvia Mabel Ransford; one *s* two *d*. *Educ:* Mill Hill Sch.; Emmanuel Coll., Cambridge. MA, MD Cantab.; DA Eng. 1936; FFARCS Eng. 1948. Dental Anæsthetist, Middlesex Hospital, 1931-48; Senior Anæsthetist, UCH, 1946-70; Consulting Anæsthetist: Hampstead General Hospital; Paddington Green Children's Hospital; University College Hospital; Maidenhead Hospital; St Columba's Hospital; Manor House Hospital. Pres., Section of Anaesthetics, RSM. FRSocMed; Hon. Member; Assoc. of Anæsthetists; Finnish Society of Anæsthetists. *Publications:* Incidence of Anæsthetic Complications, 1937; contributor to Proc. Royal Society Med., etc. *Recreations:* sailing and gardening. *Address:* 27 Well Walk, NW3. *T:* 01-435 6633; River View, Bradwell-juxta-mare, Essex. *T:* Bradwell-on-Sea 243. *Club:* United Hospitals Sailing.
     [Died 8 Aug. 1975.

DAWNAY, Maj.-Gen. (retired) Sir David, KCVO 1968; CB 1952; DSO 1943 (Bar 1945); Secretary to the Ascot Authority and Clerk of the Course, Ascot, 1957-69; Commander 56th Armoured Division, 1954-57; *b* 10 July 1903; *s* of Maj. Hon. Hugh Dawnay, DSO, and Lady Susan Beresford; *m* 1926, Lady Katharine Nora Beresford; twin *s* one *d* (and one *d* decd). *Educ:* Eton Coll.; RMC, Sandhurst. Rifle Bgde, 1924; transferred 10th R. Hussars, 1924; Capt. 1930; War of 1939-45; Major, 1940; 2nd in Comd, North Irish Horse, 1940; CO 2nd Reconnaissance Regt, 1941; CO North Irish Horse, 1941; 2nd in Comd, 23rd and 26th Armoured Bdes, 1943; Comdr: 21 Tank Bde, 1943; 26 Armoured Bde, 1945; 86 Area, Venice, 1946; student, Staff Coll., Camberley, 1946; Comdr, 2nd Armoured Bde, 1947; Dep. Comdr, North Midland District, 1948; Comdr 8 Armoured Bde, 1948; Commandant, RMA, Sandhurst, 1951-54. Hon. Colonel, North Irish Horse, 1947-69, T&AVR, 1969-; Colonel: 10th Royal Hussars (Prince of Wales's Own), 1962-69; Royal Hussars, 1969-. Joint Master, Waterford Hounds, 1957-69. *Recreations:* hunting, cricket, lawn tennis, polo. *Address:* Whitfield Court, Waterford, Ireland. *T:* Waterford 84102. *Club:* Cavalry.   *[Died 3 Oct. 1971.*

DAWSON, Alistair Benedict, QC 1976; *b* 21 March 1922; 4th *s* of late Alexander Thomson Dawson and Isobel Margaret Dawson, Portelet House, Jersey. *Educ:* Stonyhurst Coll.; Balliol Coll., Oxford (MA 1947); Scots Coll. and Gregorian Univ., Rome. Served with 102 Medium Regt, RA, N Africa and Italy, 1943-45 (Lieut). Called to Bar, Middle Temple, 1951. Captain, HQRA 56 (London) Div., TA, 1952-57. Editor, Estates Gazette Digest, 1965-74. *Recreations:* gardening, cooking, music. *Address:* 2 Paper Buildings, Temple, EC4Y 7ET. *T:* 01-353 5835; 59 Westcroft Square, W6 0TA. *T:* 01-748 4914.
     [Died 19 Oct. 1978.

DAWSON, Frank Harold, CBE 1948; MC 1917; Director, The Cunard Steam-Ship Company Ltd, 1950-62, retired (General Manager, 1950-59); *b* 14 Feb. 1896; *m* 1924, Florence Kathleen, *d* of Captain James C. Barr, CB; two *d*. *Educ:* Liverpool Institute High Sch. Joined the Cunard Steam-Ship Co. Ltd, 1912. Served European War, 1914-20 (MC, despatches), Capt., The King's Regt (Liverpool). Chairman, Employers' Assoc. of the Port of Liverpool, 1954-57; Chairman, The Liverpool Steam-Ship Owners' Assoc., 1955-56. Hon. Captain RNR. *Address:* 4 Gunn Grove, Neston, Wirral L64 9PU. *T:* 051-336 2842.
     [Died 29 June 1972.

DAWSON, Comdr Sir Hugh Trevor, 2nd Bt, *cr* 1920; CBE 1950; Royal Navy, retired; *b* 17 Jan. 1893; *o* surv. *s* of Sir Trevor Dawson, 1st Bt, and Louise (*d* 1935), *d* of John Miller Grant; *S* father 1931; *m* 1918, Vera Anne Loch, *d* of late Sir F. L. Halliday; one *s* three *d*. *Educ:* Royal Naval Coll., Osborne and Dartmouth. *Heir:* *s* Hugh Halliday Trevor Dawson [*b* 6 June 1931; *m* 1955, Caroline Jane, *d* of Antony Acton; two *s*]. *Address:* Casina Lodge, 8 Park Village West, NW1. *T:* 01-387 2020.   *[Died 3 April 1976.*

DAWSON, (Sir) Lawrence Saville, 2nd Bt, *cr* 1929; does not use the title, and his name is not on the Official Roll of Baronets.
     [Died 14 Aug. 1974 (ext).

DAWSON, Maj.-Gen. Robert Boyd, CB 1969; CBE 1965; DSO 1941; *b* 21 July 1916; British, NZ Citizen (as also parents); *m* 1st, 1942, Valeska Christina Bess McIntosh (*d* 1961); one *s* (one *d* decd); 2nd, 1964, Doreen Margaret Gawden Bickford. *Educ:* Rotorua High Sch.; RMC, Duntroon, Aust. Commissioned into NZ Army, Dec. 1938. Served overseas with NZ Expedny Force, in Middle East, 1940-43 (despatches twice, DSO); commanded Infantry Bn in Occupation Forces, Japan, 1947-48; various staff appts, NZ Army HQ; JSSC, UK, 1953; NZ Chief Planner, SEATO Mil. Planning Office, Bangkok, 1957-59; QMG, NZ Army HQ, 1960-62; Comdr 28 Commonwealth Infty Bde Gp, Malaysia, 1963-64; IDC, London, 1965; Chief of the General Staff, NZ Army, 1967-70; Dir, Civil Defence, NZ Min. of Civil Defence, 1971-76, retired. *Recreations:* golf, gardening. *Address:* Allawah, 1 Waitui Crescent, Lower Hutt, New Zealand. *T:* Wellington 696-308. *Club:* United Services' Officers (Wellington, NZ).   *[Died 24 July 1977.*

DAWSON, Col Rupert George, CB 1945; TD; *b* 13 July 1887; *s* of late Peter Dawson, Drum Coille, Braco; *m* 1912, Juliette (*d* 1962), *er d* of late Senator J. M. Wilson, Montreal; two *s* two *d* (and one *s* and one *d* decd). *Educ:* Stonyhurst. Commissioned 2nd Lieut, 23 Oct. 1903, in 1st Vol. Bn, The East Lancashire Regt; resigned Aug. 1906; Served European War, 1914-19 (despatches twice); Lt-Col, 1920; Bt Colonel, 1924; Member Queen's Body Guard for Scotland (Royal Company of Archers) since 1938; Chairman TA Assoc., Perthshire, 1936-46. Served War of 1939-45, 1939-41. DL Perthshire, 1937-47; JP Perthshire, 1929-47. Privy Chamberlain of the Sword and Cape to the Pope, 1939, re-appointed (to HH Pope John XXIII) Dec. 1958 and (to HH Pope Paul VI) Sept. 1963. Seigneur de La Hague; Knight of Magistral Grace, Military Order of Malta; Knight Commander, Order of the Holy Sepulchre; Papal Medal, Bene Merenti, 1950. *Address:* La Hague Manor, St Peter, Jersey, Channel Islands. *Club:* Caledonian.   *[Died 1 Feb. 1975.*

DAWSON, William Siegfried; Professor of Psychiatry, University of Sydney, 1927-51; Hon. Consultant Psychiatrist, Royal Prince Alfred Hospital, Sydney, since 1951; *b* Skipton-in-Craven, 27 April 1891; *s* of late William Harbutt Dawson, and of late Anna (*née* Gruetz); *m* 1927, Gladys Lyle, *er d* of late W. G. Lauder Paton. *Educ:* Skipton Grammar Sch.; Sedbergh; Dulwich; Trinity Coll., Oxford; St Thomas's Hospital. MA and DM; FRCP; Foundation Fellow RACP; Gold Medallist, Royal Medico-Psychological Assoc. of Great Britain; Rockefeller Medical Fellow, 1925. Late Senior Assistant, Maudsley Hospital, London, and Teacher in Psychological Medicine, University of London; President Australasian Assoc. of Psychiatrists, 1946-47; Corresp. Member American Psychiat. Assoc.; Hon. Fellow Australian and New Zealand College of Psychiatrists. Lt-Col AAMC, retired. *Publications:* papers dealing with mental disorders. *Recreation:* travel. *Address:* 36 Salisbury Crescent, Oxford OX2 7TL. *[Died 13 March 1975.*

DAY, Sir Albert James Taylor, Kt 1954; CBE 1947 (OBE 1941); *b* 9 Feb. 1892; *s* of Albert Henry and Elizabeth Day; *m* 1919, Dorcas Gosling (*d* 1970); one *s* (and one *s* decd). *Educ:* Church and Secondary Schools. Civil Servant (PO), 1908-23; Asst Secretary Association of Executive Officers and other Civil Servants, 1923-29; General Secretary, 1929-30; General Secretary Society of Civil Servants, 1930-46; CS National Whitley Council: part-time Chairman Staff Side, 1939-46; Chairman, Staff Side, 1947-56. *Address:* Treemans, Lewes Road, Horsted Keynes, Sussex. *[Died 19 Oct. 1972.*

DAY, Edith; actress; *b* Minneapolis, USA, 10 April 1896; *d* of Oscar Day and Ella Mahla; *m* 1st, Carle E. Carlton (marr. dissolved); 2nd, Pat Somerset (marr. dissolved). First appearance on stage, Shubert Theatre, St Paul, Minn., Sept. 1915; Empire Theatre, London, 1920, as Irene O'Dare in Irene (which she had played at the Vanderbilt Theatre, New York); Jenny, in Jenny, Empire, 1922. Subsequently she played in New York and in London, etc. Later successes include: Nina Benedetto, in Wildflower, Casino, 1923; Rose Marie La

Flamme, in Rose Marie, Drury Lane, 1925 (for 2 years); Margot Bonvalet, in The Desert Song, Drury Lane, 1927-28 and Magnolia, in Show Boat, 1928-29; Rose Marie (revival), 1929-30. She appeared in Variety Theatres with Robert Naylor, in a repertory of songs, 1931-32. The Desert Song (revival), London Coliseum, 1936; Lolita, in Sunny River, Piccadilly, 1943. In Noel Coward's Waiting in the Wings, Duke of York's, 1960. First appeared in films, 1917. Has made numerous broadcasts.
[Died 1 May 1971.

DAY, Theodora, MA; *d* of late Stanley Day, FIA, Blackheath. *Educ:* Girton Coll., Cambridge. Principal, Brighton Diocesan Training Coll., 1927-38; Principal, Maria Grey Training Coll., NW6, 1938-49. *Address:* Nynehead Court, Wellington, Somerset. *[Died 5 March 1976.*

DAY-LEWIS, Cecil, CBE 1950; MA Oxon; CLit; FRSL; Author (C. Day Lewis); Poet Laureate, since 1968; Director, Chatto & Windus Ltd; *b* 27 April 1904; *s* of Rev. F. C. Day-Lewis and Kathleen Blake Squires; *m* 1st, 1928, Constance Mary King (marr. diss. 1951); two *s*; 2nd, 1951, Jill Angela Henriette Balcon; one *s* one *d*. *Educ:* Sherborne Sch. (scholar); Wadham Coll., Oxford (exhibitioner). Asst Master at Summerfields, Oxford, 1927-28; Larchfield, Helensburgh, 1928-30; Cheltenham Coll., 1930-35. Editor of books and pamphlets, Ministry of Information, 1941-46; Clark Lecturer, Trinity Coll., Cambridge, 1946; Professor of Poetry, Oxford Univ., 1951-56. Charles Eliot Norton Prof. of Poetry, Harvard Univ., 1964-65. Compton Lectr, Hull Univ., 1968. Vice-President: Royal Society of Literature, 1958-; London Library, 1968. Member: Arts Council, 1962-68; Irish Academy of Letters, 1968. Hon. Member, American Academy of Arts and Letters, 1966; Hon. Fellow, Wadham Coll., Oxford, 1968. Hon. DLitt: Exeter, 1965; Hull, 1970; Hon. LittD TCD, 1968. *Publications:* A Hope for Poetry, 1936; Poetry for You, 1946; Collected Poems, 1954; The Poetic Image, 1957; Pegasus and other Poems, 1957; The Buried Day, 1960; The Gate and other Poems, 1962; The Room and other Poems, 1965; The Whispering Roots, 1970, etc; translations: The Georgics of Virgil; The Aeneid of Virgil; The Eclogues of Virgil. Also detective novels under pseudonym of Nicholas Blake. *Relevant publication:* Cecil Day-Lewis, the Poet Laureate: a bibliography, 1968. *Address:* c/o Chatto & Windus, Ltd, 40 William IV Street, WC2. *[Died 22 May 1972.*

DEAN, Sir Arthur (William Henry), Kt 1946; CIE 1941; MC; ED; retired; *b* 7 Feb. 1892; *e s* of William James and Mary Elizabeth Dean, Brackley, Northants; *m* 1st, 1916, Ivie Stella (*d* 1950), 2nd *d* of late George Martin, Merton, Surrey; three *s* (one *d* decd); 2nd, 1951, Marjorie Ella, *o d* of late E. C. D. Robins, Southend. *Educ:* Rutlish Sch., Merton; Imperial Coll., London Univ. Bessemer Medallist, 1913; BSc (Eng.); Asst Engineer Troityzk Goldfields, Kotchkar, Russia, 1913-15; Military Service, 1915-19, temp. Commission RE, Tunnelling Companies (MC and Bar, despatches); Asst, Exec., Superintending, Additional Chief and Chief Engineer Govt of India, Public Works Dept, 1919-46; Chairman Delhi Improvement Trust, 1946-48; Chief Civil Engineer, Foreign Office Administration of African Territories, London, 1949-52; Gen Manager, Libyan Development Agency, Tripoli, 1952-62. CStJ 1946. Order of Istiklal (2nd Class), Libya, 1959. *Publications:* Proceedings Institution of Civil Engineers; 1934, Construction of a submersible road bridge over the Narbudda River (Cooper's Hill Medal and Telford Premium); 1939, Anti-Malarial Operations in the Delhi Urban Area; various papers to Indian Roads Congress. *Address:* 66 The Avenue, Worcester Park, Surrey. *T:* 01-337 4701. *[Died 24 Oct. 1976.*

DEAN, Basil, CBE 1947 (MBE 1918); Governing Director of B. D. Enterprises Ltd, since 1939, and of Basil Dean Productions, Ltd, 1926-64; *m* 1st, Esther van Gruisen (marr. diss. 1925); three *s*; 2nd, 1925, Lady Mercy Greville (marr. diss. 1933); one *d*; 3rd, 1934, Victoria Hopper (marr. diss. 1948). Organised and was First Controller of Liverpool Repertory Theatre (The Playhouse) until 1913; Cheshire Regt, 1914; Captain, 1916; Director Entertainment branch, Navy and Army Canteen Board, 1917; Joint Managing Director of Drury Lane Theatre, 1924-25; Managing Director of ReandeaN Co., St Martin's Theatre, London, 1919-25; founded and was first Chairman and Joint Managing Director Associated Talking Pictures, Ltd, ATP Studios, Ltd (re-named Ealing Studios), and their subsidiary companies, 1929-36; General European Representative of the Radio Keith Orpheum Corporation (USA); Chairman and Managing Director of Radio Keith Orpheum, Ltd, 1930-32; Shute Lecturer, Liverpool Univ., 1932-33; Director of National Service Entertainment, 1941; founder and director-general of Entertainments National Service Assoc. (ENSA), 1939; Director of Entertainments Navy, Army, and Air Force Institutes, 1939; produced Flecker's Hassan (musical score by

Delius), His Majesty's, 1923; A Midsummer Night's Dream, Drury Lane, 1924; other productions include The Skin Game, 1920; A Bill of Divorcement, 1921; Loyalties, 1922; The Constant Nymph, 1926; Young Woodley, 1928; The Circle of Chalk, 1929; Autumn Crocus, 1931; Call it a Day, 1935; When we are Married, 1938; Johnson over Jordan, 1939; The Diary of a Nobody, 1954; Who Cares?, 1956; Touch It Light, 1958; devised and presented Cathedral Steps before St Paul's Cathedral, and Coventry Cathedral, 1942, Salute to the Red Army, for Ministry of Information, Albert Hall, 1943; re-produced Hassan for South African National Theatre, 1950 and for Dublin Drama Festival, 1960. Mem. of Council, and Chm. Finance and Gen. Purposes Cttee, RADA, until 1972. *Publications:* various plays and pamphlets, including Marriages are made in Heaven (Manchester, 1908); Mother to be, Effie (Manchester, 1909); The Love Cheats (London, 1910); (with Barry Jackson) Fifinella (London, 1919); part author (with Margaret Kennedy) of Come with Me, 1928; (with George Munro), Murder Gang, 1933; The Actor and his Workshop, 1922; The Theatre in Emergency, 1939; The Theatre in Reconstruction, 1945; wrote official history of ENSA (The Theatre at War), 1956; *dramatisations:* The Constant Nymph (with Margaret Kennedy), 1926; Beau Geste (with P. C. Wren, 1928); Sleeveless Errand (with Norah James), 1933; The Heart of the Matter (with Graham Greene), 1949; The Diary of a Nobody (original book of George and Weedon Grossmith), 1954; *autobiography:* Vol. 1, Seven Ages, 1970; Vol. 2, Mind's Eye, 1973. *Address:* 102 Dorset House, Gloucester Place, NW1. *T:* 01-935 6154. *Club:* Garrick. *[Died 22 April 1978.*

DEAN, Commander Brian, DSO 1940; RN (retired); *b* 12 Feb. 1895; *e s* of late Captain F. W. Dean, RN (retired); *m* Hilda (*d* 1968), *yr d* of late John Saliba. *Educ:* Stratheden House, Blackheath; RN Colleges, Osborne and Dartmouth. Midshipman, 1912; Lieut, 1916; Comdr. (retired), 1940; wounded in Sept. 1915; spent most of European War in destroyers; Officer of Watch in HMS Lion at surrender of German Fleet, 1918; made a chart of River Orinoco, 1922; at defence of Hankow in Jan. 1927; qualified as Instructor in Chemical Warfare and as Interpreter in Spanish; Commanded HMS Sabre (destroyer), 1937-Dec. 1940; in her took part in evacuation of BEF from Dunkirk, making 10 trips and transporting 5,000 troops (DSO). Invalided on account of war injuries, 1947; served on Staff of Flag Officer, Scotland, as Deputy Command Mine-watching Service Officer, 1953-61. *Recreation:* small boat sailing. *Address:* PO Box 22, Otane, Hawke's Bay, New Zealand. *[Died 19 April 1976.*

DEAN, Henry Edwin, MBE 1943; JP; retired; *b* 29 Aug. 1881; *s* of George Dean and Eliza Blundell; *m* 1912, Olive Marie Bussey; one *s* one *d*. *Educ:* Village Sch., West Derby. Clerk, Judge Sir Alfred A. Tobin, 1896-1902; South African Constabulary, 1902-07; Fencing Dept, EAP, 1908; Transport Officer EAP, 1908-11; Office Superintendent Public Works Dept EAP, 1911-16; Accountant Public Works Dept EAP, 1916-21; Chief Accountant, Public Works Dept Tanganyika Territory, 1921-25; Gold Coast, 1925-32; Treasurer, Dominica, 1932-36; Mem. Council, Roseau, Dominica, 1932-36; Treasurer, St Lucia, 1940-44; late Member of Executive and Legislative Councils, Dominica and St Lucia; also formerly JP, Special JP, and Vis. JP, Dominica and St Lucia. *Recreations:* gardening, bowls and crosswords. *Address:* 206 The Gateway, Dover, Kent.
[Died 20 Sept. 1973.

DEAN, Sir Maurice (Joseph), KCB 1957 (CB 1946); KCMG 1949; *b* 16 Sept. 1906; *y s* of late W. J. Dean, Purley, Surrey; *m* 1943, Anne, *d* of W. F. Gibson, Cardiff; one *s* one *d*. *Educ:* St Olave's; Trinity Coll., Cambridge. Mathematical Tripos Part I, 1926; Part II, 1928; Mayhew Prize. Asst Principal, Air Ministry, 1929; Asst Under-Secretary of State, 1943; Deputy Secretary, Control Office for Germany and Austria, 1946; Deputy Under-Secretary of State, Foreign Office (German Section), 1947-48; Deputy Secretary, Ministry of Defence, 1948-52; Third Secretary, HM Treasury, 1952; Second Secretary, Board of Trade, 1952-55; Permanent Under-Secretary of State, Air Ministry, 1955-63; a Second Secretary, HM Treasury, Nov. 1963-64; Joint Permanent Under-Secretary of State, Dept of Education and Science, April-Oct. 1964; Permanent Secretary, Ministry of Technology, 1964-66. Dir, British Printing Corp., 1966-71. Co-opted, Member Cambridge Univ. Appointments Board, 1957-60; Member Cambridge Univ. Women's Appointments Board, 1963-76. Chairman, London Advisory Board, Salvation Army, 1968-76. Visiting Prof., Dept of Administration, Strathclyde Univ., 1966-76. Councillor, Bedford Coll., Univ. of London, 1972-76. Hon. LLD Strathclyde, 1970. *Posthumous publication:* The Royal Air Force and Two World Wars, 1979. *Address:* 27 Bathgate Road, SW19. *T:* 01-946 0290. *Clubs:* United Oxford & Cambridge University; Royal Wimbledon (Golf). *[Died 7 April 1978.*

DEAN, Prof. William Reginald, MA Cambridge; *b* 5 Nov. 1896; *er s* of late W. J. Dean, Purley, Surrey; *m* 1926, Dorothy, *er d* of late C. R. Terrett, Swansea; one *s* one *d. Educ:* Christ's Hospital; Trinity Coll., Cambridge. Mathematical Tripos, Part I, 1919; Part II, 1921; Rayleigh Prize, 1923; Adams Prize, 1951. Fellow of Trinity Coll., 1923-. Asst Prof., Imperial Coll. of Science, 1924-29; Lecturer, Trinity Coll., Cambridge, and University Lecturer in Mathematics, 1929-52; Goldsmid Prof. of Mathematics, University College, London, 1952-64. Visiting Prof., University of Arizona, USA, 1964-67. *Publications:* various papers on hydrodynamics and elasticity. *Address:* 43 Woodstock Road North, St Albans, Herts. *T:* St Albans 53834. *Club:* United Oxford & Cambridge University.
[Died 24 Jan. 1973.

DEANE, Major Donald Victor, CIE 1947; CBE 1959 (OBE 1941); RE (retired); Consultant to International Nickel Ltd, 1961-73; *b* 19 Oct. 1902; *s* of late V. M. Deane, Braiswick, Colchester, Essex; *m* 1929, Dorothy Doreen Cuerden; two *d. Educ:* Gresham's Sch., Holt; RMA, Woolwich. Commissioned into RE, 1922; proceeded to India, 1925; selected for special employment in Indian Mints, 1932; Mint Master, Calcutta, 1938. Retired from Army, 1947. Senior Master of the Indian Govt Mints, 1947-57, retired. 1939-45 Star; India General Service, Silver Jubilee, War, and India Service medals. *Recreation:* golf. *Address:* Tara, Fauvic, Jersey, CI. *T:* Jersey Central 53272. *Club:* Royal Jersey Golf. *[Died 25 Jan. 1978.*

DEANE, Nora Bryan, CBE 1957 (MBE 1947); Matron, Bristol Maternity Hospital, 1934-63, retired; *b* 1902; *d* of Stuart and Kathleen Deane, Rosscarbery, Co. Cork. *Educ:* privately. General Training, Prince of Wales's General Hospital, N15, 1924-28; Midwifery Training, Rotunda Hospital, Dublin, 1928-29. President: Royal College of Midwives, 1952-58; International Confederation of Midwives, 1954-57; National Council of Women of Great Britain, 1962-64; Vice-President, International Council of Women, 1966-. Coronation Medal, 1953. Hon. MA Bristol Univ., 1963. *Recreations:* travel, reading. *Address:* 1 Cotham Lawn Road, Bristol BS6 6DS. *Club:* Cowdray. *[Died 25 April 1973.*

DEANE, William, CBE 1952; *b* 4 Nov. 1894; 2nd *s* of W. H. Deane and Martha Deane (*née* Copeland), Hart, Co. Durham; unmarried. *Educ:* Grammar Sch., West Hartlepool. Post Office Savings Bank, GPO, 1910. Served European War, 1914-18, Royal Air Force; Air Ministry, 1919; Head, Parliamentary and Air Council Branch, 1940-45; Director of Administration and Finance, RAF Delegation, Washington, DC, 1945-46; Director of Accounts, Air Ministry, 1947-54, retired 1954. *Recreation:* œnology. *Address:* 54 Bishopric Court, Horsham, Sussex. *T:* Horsham 62921. *Club:* Reform. *[Died 17 Feb. 1972.*

DEANESLY, Margaret, MA; DLitt Lambeth; FSA; Professor of History, University of London, 1942-50, now Emeritus; *b* 5 March 1885; *d* of Samuel and Clara Maria Deanesly; unmarried. *Educ:* Godolphin Sch., Salisbury; Newnham Coll. Cambridge History Tripos, Part I, 1st Class, 1911; part II, 1st Class, 1912; Arthur Hugh Clough Scholarship, 1912; MA (Manchester), 1915; Marion Kennedy research studentship, 1916-17; Mary Bateson research fellowship, Newnham, 1917-20; lecturer in history, Armstrong Coll., Newcastle, 1920, Manchester, 1922-26; lecturer at R. Holloway Coll., University of London, 1936-39, at Bedford Coll., 1939-42. Birkbeck Lecturer, Cambridge, 1951. DLitt, Lambeth, 1962. *Publications:* The Incendium Amoris of Richard Rolle of Hampole, 1915; The Lollard Bible, 1920; History of the Medieval Church, 1925, 2nd edn 1929, 3rd edn 1934, 4th edn 1947, paperback 1969; preface to Burton Abbey, Staffs Record Society, 1936; A History of Europe from 476-911, 1956; The pre-Conquest Church in England, 1961; Sidelights on the Anglo-Saxon Church, 1962; Augustine of Canterbury, 1964; contributions to learned journals. *Recreations:* history of art, and archæology. *Address:* 196 Clarence Gate Gardens, NW1. *T:* 01-723 0912.
[Died 9 Oct. 1977.

DEARBERGH, Geoffrey Frederick; Registrar in Bankruptcy of High Court; Clerk of the Restrictive Practices Court; *b* 15 March 1924; *s* of Tom and Blanche Dearbergh; *m* 1954, Elizabeth Mary Bryant; two *d. Educ:* Winchester College. Served in Army (60th Rifles), 1942-47. Called to Bar, Inner Temple, 1948. *Address:* 10 Pembroke Road, W8 6NT. *T:* 01-602 5888. *[Died 3 July 1979.*

DE AZCARATE, Pablo; *see* Azcarate.

de BEER, Sir Gavin (Rylands), Kt 1954; FRS; FSA; MA, DSc Oxon; Hon. ScD Cantab; Hon. D.-ès-L. Lausanne; Hon. D. de l'Univ. Bordeaux; Chev. Lég. d'Hon.; Editorial Consultant, Thomas Nelson Ltd; *b* 1 Nov. 1899; *o s* of Herbert Chaplin de Beer and Mabel, *d* of John Rylands; *m* 1925, Cicely Glyn, *yr d* of Rev. Sir Hubert Medlycott, Bt. *Educ:* Ecole Pascal, Paris; Harrow Sch.; Magdalen Coll., Oxford. Lieut Grenadier Guards, 1918-19; Fellow of Merton Coll., 1923-38; Jenkinson Lecturer in Embryology, Oxford, 1926-38; served 1939-45, Lieut-Colonel Grenadier Guards, GSO1, Psychological Warfare at HQ 21 Army Group; Prof. of Embryology, University College, London, 1945-50; Director, British Museum (Natural History), 1950-60. President: Linnean Society, 1946-49; XV International Congress of Zoology, 1958. Trustee, National Portrait Gallery, 1961-67. Corres. Member: Académie des Sciences, Institut de France; Société d'histoire et d'archéologie de Genève; Société neuchâteloise d'histoire et d'archéologie; Societé vaudoise d'histoire et d'archéologie; Member: Institut International d'Embryol.; British Council; Hon. Member Society Zool. France, Société Royale Zool. Belgique, and Zool. Society, India. Geoffroy-St-Hilaire Gold Medal, 1954; Darwin medal, 1958; Linnean Gold Medal, 1958; Mendel Medal, 1965; Kalinga Prize, UNESCO, 1968. *Publications:* Growth, 1924; Introduction to the Study of Genetics, 1924; Comparative Anatomy, Histology and Development of the Pituitary Body, 1926; Introduction to Experimental Embryology, 1926 (Greek edn 1942); Vertebrate Zoology, 1928; Embryology and Evolution, 1930 (French edn 1933); Early Travellers in the Alps, 1930, new edn 1966; Alps and Men, 1932; The Elements of Experimental Embryology (with J. S. Huxley), 1933; A German Reader for Biology Students (with H. G. Fiedler), 1934; Le Voyage en Suisse de Mme Roland, 1937; Development of the Vertebrate Skull, 1937; On Shelley (with E. Blunden and S. Norman), 1938; Embryos and Ancestors, 1940 (3rd rev. edn 1962); Escape to Switzerland, 1945; Thomas Pennant's Tour on the Continent, 1948; Travellers in Switzerland, 1949; Beaujolois Campbell's Journey to Florence, 1951; Journal du voyage de Gibbon en Suisse, 1952; Speaking of Switzerland, 1952; Sir Hans Sloane and the British Museum, 1953; Archæopteryx, 1954; Alps and Elephants, 1955; The First ascent of Mont Blanc (with T. G. Brown), 1957 (Italian ed., 1961); The Sciences were never at War, 1960; Reflections of a Darwinian, 1962; Charles Darwin, 1963; Atlas of Evolution, 1964; Rede Lecture, Genetics and Prehistory, 1965; Hannibal's March, 1967; Voltaire's British Visitors, 1967; Gibbon and his World, 1968; Hannibal, 1969; Streams of Culture, 1969; Rousseau and His World, 1972. Editor and part author of Evolution: Essays presented to E. S. Goodrich, 1938; General Editor, British Men of Science; articles in Encyclopædia Britannica, Chambers's Encyclopædia, and papers in various scientific, military, literary, and alpine journals. *Recreation:* wandering about. *Address:* 3 West Close, Alfriston, Polegate, Sussex. *[Died 21 June 1972.*

DE BRIGARD, Camilo; Grand Officer, Order of Boyacá, Colombia; Ambassador of Colombia to the Court of St James's since 1970; *b* 24 Dec. 1906; *m* 1970, Imelda Restrepo de Brigard. *Educ:* Colegio Nacional de San Bartolome and Univ. Nacional, Bogotá, Colombia. MHR, 1930-36; Senator of the Republic, 1936-40; Mem. Adv. Commn of Min. for Foreign Affairs, 1936-40; Prof. of Internat. Public Law and Diplomatic History, Univ. Pontificia Javeriana, Bogotá, 1928-48; Sec.-Gen., IX Inter-American Conf., 1948; Colombian Lawyer to Internat. Court of Justice, The Hague, 1950; Colombian Ambassador to West Germany, 1952-57. Past Deleg. to Gen. Assemblies of the UN. Dir, (newspaper) El Siglo, Bogotá, up to 1969. Mem. Academia de la Lengua, Colombia. Holds foreign Orders of high degree. *Publications:* Los Límites entre Colombia y el Brasil, 1936; Estudios de Derecho Internacional Colombiano, 1940; El Contrato Colectivo de Trabajo, 1968; several articles in internat. and Colombian newspapers and magazines. *Address:* 73 Eaton Square, SW1; Calle 70 No 4-60, Bogotá, Colombia. *Clubs:* White's; Jockey, Country (Bogotá). *[Died 17 Jan. 1972.*

de BURGH, Captain Charles, DSO 1917; RN (retired); retired as Agent to Dean and Chapter of Durham Diocese, Lord Crewe Trustees, and Croxdale Estates (1933-52); *b* 17 July 1886; *s* of late Lieut-Colonel T. J. de Burgh of Oldtown, Naas, Co. Kildare; *m* 1910, Isabel Caroline Berkeley (*d* 1968), *d* of late Rev. Edward Fitzhardinge Campbell; two *d. Educ:* Tonbridge Castle; Stubbington. Entered Navy, 1902; joined the submarine service 1908; served submarines till 1914; HMS Antrim till 1915; rejoined submarine service, taking command of submarines, 1915; served subsequently in command of HM submarines during war (DSO) until 1923; Mobilisation Dept, Admiralty, 1923-25; commander HMS Valiant and Queen Elizabeth, 1925-26; in command, HMS Cyclops, 1926-27, 6th S/M Flotilla, 1928-29; CO Anti-submarine school (HMS Lucia), 1929-30; Officer Instructor to RNVR Tyne Div., 1930-32; retired, 1932; Naval Officer in Control of Shipping and Convoys, 1939-46. *Address:* Coolattin Lodge, Seaforde, Co. Down. *T:* Seaforde 24.
[Died 24 Jan. 1973.

de BURGH, General Sir Eric, KCB 1941 (CB 1932); DSO 1916; OBE; idc; psc; Indian Army, retired; *b* Oldtown, Naas, Ireland, 10 May 1881; *s* of late Lieut-Colonel Thomas John de Burgh, of Oldtown, Naas, Co. Kildare; *m* 1923, Mary (*d* 1934), *d* of late Lieut-Gen. Sir E. A. Fanshawe, KCB; two *d. Educ:* St Mark's Sch., Windsor; Marlborough Coll. 2nd Lieut, and Lieut, 3rd Royal Dublin Fusiliers (Militia); 2nd Lieut Manchester Regt 1903; Lieut, Captain, Major, 9th Hodson's Horse; Colonel Indian Army. 1923; Maj.-General, 1934; Lieut-General, 1938; General, 1940; served South Africa, 1902 (Queen's medal, 4 clasps); World War (1914 Star, GS and Victory Medals, despatches, DSO, Brevets of Major and Lieut-Colonel); Afghanistan and NWF, 1919 (despatches, medal and clasp); Waziristan, 1922 (despatches, OBE, clasp); Commanded, 1st Indian Div., Waziristan, 1937 (despatches, medal and clasp); GSO1, Staff Coll., Quetta, 1928-30; Brig., Gen. Staff, Eastern Command, India, 1930-31; Comm. 1st Risalpur Cavalry Brigade, India, 1931-34; Comdr, Lahore District, 1934-35; Deputy Chief of the Gen. Staff, Army Headquarters, India, 1935-36; Commander Rawalpindi District, 1936-38; Chief of Gen. Staff, India, 1939-41; retired, 1941. *Address:* Bargy Castle, Tomhaggard, Wexford, Ireland. *T:* Tomhaggard 3. *Clubs:* Special Forces; Kildare Street (Dublin). *[Died 6 Feb. 1973.*

DE BUTTS, Brig. Frederick Cromie, CB 1943; DSO 1917; MC; Indian Army, retired; *b* 6 Nov. 1888; *s* of Captain F. R. McC. De Butts, RA, and C.M., *d* of Captain Dalgairns Travers, 17th Foot; *m* 1st, K. P. M. (*d* 1916), *d* of O. O'Donnell, of Hintlesham, Suffolk; one *s*; 2nd, 1920, Sybil Katherine, *d* of late Canon H. W. Beauchamp of Copdock, Suffolk. *Educ:* Wellington Coll.; RMC, Sandhurst. Lt-Col, 1933; Colonel, 1938; Brigadier, 1940; retired, 1943. *Address:* The Old Vicarage, Great Gaddesden, Hemel Hempstead, Herts. *T:* Hemel Hempstead 62129. *[Died 7 Jan. 1977.*

de CANDOLE, Rt. Rev. Henry Handley Vully; *b* 25 May 1895; *s* of late Very Rev. H. L. C. V. de Candole, Dean of Bristol, and late Helen Edith, *d* of Sir Henry Thompson, 1st Bt; *m* 1937, Frances Sophia Cornwall, *d* of late Ven. A. W. Cornwall, Archdeacon of Cheltenham; no *c. Educ:* Marlborough Coll.; King's Coll. and Westcott House, Cambridge. Deacon, 1920; Priest, 1921; Asst Chaplain, Marlborough Coll., 1920-22; Resident Chaplain to Archbishop (Davidson) of Canterbury, 1923-26; Asst Curate of St John's, Newcastle on Tyne, 1926-31; Vicar, 1931-32; Chaplain of Peterhouse, Cambridge, 1932-34; Dean, 1933-34; Chaplain of Theological Coll., Chichester, 1934-37; Liturgical Missioner, diocese of Chichester, 1937-49; Priest-in-charge, Wiston with Buncton, Sussex, 1939-40; Vicar of Henfield, Sussex, 1940-49; Prebendary of Bracklesham in Chichester Cathedral, 1945-49; Bishop Suffragan of Knaresborough, 1949-65. *Publications:* The Church's Offering, 1935; The Sacraments and the Church, 1935; The Church's Prayers, 1939; The Story of Henfield, 1947; Lent with the Church, 1952; The Christian Use of the Psalms, 1955. *Address:* 21 Brunswick Drive, Harrogate, Yorks. *T:* Harrogate 3632. *[Died 16 June 1971.*

DEEDES, Percy Gordon, CMG 1962; OBE 1958; *b* 2 July 1899; twin *s* of late Gordon Frederic Deedes, Hythe, Kent, England; *m* 1927, Audrey Winifred (*d* 1968), *d* of late Alfred Riva Harvey, Salisbury, Rhodesia; one *d. Educ:* Repton. Served European War, 1917-19, RNAS and RAF as Flt Lieut. In business Kenya, 1920-23; Union of South Africa, 1923-28; farming in S Rhodesia 1928-51. Served War, 1940-42, RAF as Flt Lieut, in Greece and Middle East. Chm., Natural Resources Board of Rhodesia, 1951-65. *[Died 20 Aug. 1973.*

DEER, George, OBE 1944; *b* 29 March 1890; *m* 1916, Olive Stoakes; one *s* one *d. Educ:* Elementary. Trade Union Official for 30 years with Workers' Union, later Transport and General Workers' Union. Alderman and Councillor Lincoln City Council, 1922-38, 1945-50; Mayor of Lincoln, 1933-34; Sheriff of Lincoln, 1943-44. MP (Lab) Lincoln, 1945-50, Newark Div. of Notts, 1950-64. *Address:* 13 Hunsley Crescent, Grimsby. *T:* Cleethorpes 63624. *[Died 15 May 1974.*

DEEVES, Thomas William, CMG 1953; CBE 1949; MC and Bar, 1917; Civil Service, 1911-54; *b* 19 March 1893; *s* of S. Deeves, Kilcooly, Thurles, Co. Tipperary; *m* 1921 Lilian Mary Thornton (*d* 1969); one *s* one *d. Educ:* Lurgan Coll., N Ireland. Served European War, 1914-18. Formerly Asst Sec., Ministry of Food and Foreign Office. *Recreation:* fishing. *Address:* Crossways, Gerrards Cross, Bucks. *T:* Gerrards Cross 83279. *Club:* English-Speaking Union. *[Died 11 Sept. 1977.*

de FERRANTI, Sir Vincent Ziani, Kt 1948; MC; LLD (*hc*); DEng (*hc*); FIEE; Chairman, Ferranti Ltd, 1930-63; *b* 16 Feb. 1893; *s* of Dr Sebastian Ziani de Ferranti, FRS and Gertrude

Ruth Ince; *m* 1919, Dorothy H. C. Wilson; two *s* three *d. Educ:* Repton. Served European War, 1914-19, Royal Engineers, Capt. (MC); War of 1939-45, Major Comdg Field Coy. RE, France, 1939-40. Lieut-Col Comdg 63rd County of Lancs Bn Home Guard, 1940-44. Hon. Col 123 Field Engr Regt RE, TA, 1948-57. Chm., International Executive Council, and British National Cttee, World Power Conference, 1950-62; Brit. Electrical and Allied Mfctrs Assoc.: Chm. 1938-39, Vice-Pres. 1946-57, Pres. 1957-59; Pres. Instn of Electrical Engineers, 1946-47; Pres. British Electrical Power Convention, 1949-50; Pres. Television Soc., 1954-57. *Address:* Henbury Hall, Macclesfield, Cheshire. *T:* Macclesfield 22400. *Club:* Athenæum. *[Died 20 May 1980.*

de GUINGAND, Maj.-Gen. Sir Francis Wilfred, KBE 1944 (CBE 1943; OBE 1942); CB 1943; DSO 1942; Chairman: Rothmans of Pall Mall (UK); Carreras Ltd, 1967-68, and other Cos; Director and International Director of the Rothmans Group; *b* 28 Feb. 1900; *s* of late Francis J. de Guingand; *m* 1942, Arlie R., widow of Major H. D. Stewart, West Yorks Regt (marr. diss., 1957); one *d. Educ:* Ampleforth Coll.; RMC, Sandhurst. Joined W Yorks Regt, 1919; seconded to KAR, 1926-31; OC Troops Nyasaland, 1930-31; Adjt 1st Bn W Yorks Regt, 1932-34; Staff Coll., Camberley, 1935-36; Mil. Asst to Sec. of State for War (Mr Hore-Belisha), 1939-40; Dir Mil. Intell., Middle East, 1942; Chief of Staff: 8th Army, 1942-44; 21st Army Group, 1944-45; retd pay, 1947. DSM (USA); CL of M (USA); Legion of Honour (France); Croix de Guerre (France); Order of Kutuzov 1st Grade (Russia); Order of Orange Nassau (Dutch). *Publications:* Operation Victory, 1947; African Assignment, 1953; Generals at War, 1964; From Brass Hat to Bowler Hat, 1979. *Recreations:* shooting, fishing, golf, sailing. *Address:* Rothman's International Ltd, 15 Hill Street, W1; Residence Château Mont Joli, Boulevard Metropole, 06400 Cannes, France. *Clubs:* Army and Navy, Royal Automobile, White's; Rand, Country (Johannesburg). *[Died 29 June 1979.*

de HAAN, Edward Peter Nayler, CMG 1972; OBE 1945; HM Diplomatic Service; Counsellor, Foreign and Commonwealth Office, since 1977; *b* Wimbledon, 5 Dec. 1919; *s* of Peter de Haan and Gladys Norah de Haan (*née* Barrs); *m* 1st, 1945, Pauline Ratsey (marr. diss. 1958); one *s* two *d*; 2nd, 1960, Margaretha Wubbenhorst. *Educ:* Ellesmere Coll., Shropshire. Served War of 1939-45: joined Royal West Kent Regt, Dec. 1939; commissioned 2nd Lieut in The Queen's Royal Regt, 1940; transf. to Special Forces, Sept. 1941; served in N Africa and Italy; demob. as Major and joined Foreign Office, 1946. Has served in Middle East, Berne, Stockholm, Rome; FCO, 1969-75. *Recreations:* travel, fishing, music. *Address:* c/o Foreign and Commonwealth Office, SW1; 25 Milbourne Lane, Esher, Surrey. *T:* Esher 62539. *Clubs:* Junior Carlton, Special Forces. *[Died 26 July 1977.*

DEHLAVI, Samiulla Khan; Ambassador of Pakistan to Federal Republic of Germany, since 1975; *b* 14 Sept. 1913; *s* of late Sir Ali Mohomed Khan Dehlavi, JP, Barrister-at-Law; *m* 1938, Genevieve (*née* Chantrenne); two *s. Educ:* Rugby; University of Oxford (PPE). BA 1935; MA. Entered ICS, 1938; served as Dist and Secretariat officer in Undivided Bengal before Independence; entered Pakistan Foreign Service, 1949; Dep. Sec., Min. of Foreign Affairs, 1950; Chargé-Counsellor, Paris, until 1953; Jt Sec., Foreign Affairs, 1953-57; Ambassador to Rome (concurrently to Tunisia), 1957-61; Foreign Sec., Pakistan, 1961-63; Ambassador to Cairo (concurrently to Libya and Yemen), 1963-65; Ambassador to Switzerland, 1965-66; concurrently to Albania, 1966; High Comr in London, concurrently Ambassador to Ireland, 1966-68; Ambassador to France, 1968-72, concurrently Permanent Delegate to UNESCO, 1968-72; Ambassador to USSR, 1972-75. Mem., Pakistan Delegn to UN; Mem., UN Cttee for Elimination of all forms of Racial Discrimination, 1972-. Grand Cross of Merit of Italian Republic, 1961; Order of Sitara-e-Pakistan, 1967; Order of Hilal-é-Quaid-i Azam, 1971. *Recreations:* riding, tennis, big game hunting (India, Pakistan, Kenya, Sudan). *Address:* Pakistan Embassy, 24 Rheinallee, Bonn-Bad Godesberg, Federal Republic of Germany. *[Died Sept. 1976.*

DEHN, Paul (Edward); poet; author; *b* 5 Nov. 1912; *e s* of late Frederick and Helen Dehn. *Educ:* Shrewsbury Sch.; Brasenose Coll., Oxford. Served War, 1939-45, Special Forces, Major. Film Critic and columnist, Sunday Referee, 1936-39; Film Critic: Sunday Chronicle, 1945-53, News Chronicle, 1954-60; Daily Herald, 1960-63. *Screenplays:* (with J. Bernard) Seven Days to Noon, 1952 (Oscar, 1952); On Such a Night: the Glyndebourne film, 1955; Orders to Kill, 1958 (British Film Acad. Best British Screenplay Award); (with R. Maibaum) Goldfinger, 1964; The Spy Who Came In From The Cold, 1966; The Deadly Affair, 1965; The Taming of the Shrew (Zeffirelli film version), 1965; (with others) The Night of the Generals, 1966; Beneath the

Planet of the Apes, 1968; A Fragment of Fear, 1968 (also Assoc. Producer); Escape from the Planet of the Apes, 1970; Conquest of the Planet of the Apes, 1971; Battle for the Planet of the Apes, 1973; Murder on the Orient Express, 1974; *commentaries for documentaries:* Waters of Time, 1952 (Venice Award); A Place for Gold, 1960; *libretti* (one-act operas; all prod Aldeburgh and Sadler's Wells): Sir Lennox Berkeley: A Dinner Engagement, 1954; Castaway, 1967; Sir William Walton, The Bear, 1967; *lyrics:* Joie de Vivre, 1960; Moulin Rouge, 1961; I Am A Camera, 1961; The Innocents, 1961; *book and lyrics:* Virtue in Danger, 1963; many songs and sketches for West End revues. Pres., Critics' Circle, 1956. Former Councillor, RSPB. Cheltenham Festival Poetry Prize, 1957. *Publications: poetry:* The Day's Alarm, 1949; Romantic Landscape, 1952; Quake, Quake, Quake, 1960; The Fern on the Rock, 1965; adaptation of Oscar Wilde's A Woman of No Importance, 1954; For Love and Money, a Miscellany, 1956. *Recreation:* ornithology. *Address:* 18 Tite Street, Chelsea, SW3.   *[Died 30 Sept. 1976.*

de HOGHTON, Sir (Henry Philip) Anthony (Mary), 13th Bt *cr* 1611; *b* 19 April 1919; *e s* of Sir Cuthbert de Hoghton, 12th Bt, JP, and Helen (*d* 1943), *o d* of late Major Duncan Macdonald of Glencoe; *S* father 1958. *Educ:* Beaumont; Magdalen Coll., Oxford. *Heir:* half-*b* Richard Bernard Cuthbert de Hoghton [*b* 26 Jan. 1945. *Educ:* Ampleforth; McGill Univ.; Birmingham Univ.]. *Address:* Hoghton Tower, Hoghton, Lancs. *T:* Hoghton 452.   *[Died 20 Feb. 1978.*

de JERSEY, Rear-Adm. (retired) Gilbert Carey, CB 1959; *b* 5 Oct. 1905; British (Guernsey); *m* 1932, Patricia Wyndham Lee; two *s* three *d. Educ:* Elizabeth Coll., Guernsey; RNC's Osborne, Dartmouth and Keyham. Served as Cadet until 1923; successively Midshipman, Sub-Lieut and Lieut, 1923-34; Lieut-Comdr: Portsmouth Dockyard, 1936; HMS Malaya, 1938; Comdr: Admiralty, 1941; Singapore Dockyard, 1945; HMS Illustrious, 1948; Captain: Admiralty Overseeing, 1950; Admiralty, 1952; Singapore Dockyard, 1956; Admiralty, 1957; Rear-Adm. 1958; Director of Naval Ordnance, Admiralty, 1958-60, retired. Jurat of Royal Court, Guernsey, 1960. *Recreations:* walking, boat sailing. *Address:* Côte des Vardes, Montville Road, Guernsey, Channel Islands. *T:* Guernsey 20895.   *[Died 14 Dec. 1974.*

DEKOBRA, Maurice; Officer of the Legion of Honour; Grand Cross of St John the Baptist; Grand Officer of the Nicham Iftikar; Doctor of Letters, *hc*; novelist and playwright; *b* Paris, 1885; unmarried. *Educ:* College Rollin; Paris Univ. Corresp. for leading Paris newspapers in Europe, America, Africa; Lectr at Berlin Univ.; motored through Europe for the Figaro; mobilised during the war as liaison officer with the British, Indian and American Armies at the front; writes cosmopolitan novels which are translated in thirty languages, since 1924. Member: Internat. Acad., Washington, DC; Bolivian Acad. *Publications:* Messieurs les Tommies; Au Pays du Fox-Trot; Prince ou Pitre; Tu seras courtisane; Minuit... Place Pigalle: Mon Cœur au Ralenti; La Madone des Sleepings; La Gondole aux chimères; Flammes de Velours; Serenade au Bourreau; Le Sphinx a parié; L'Archange aux pieds fourchus; Phryné, 1931; Perfumed Tigers, 1931; La Volupté éclairant le Monde, 1932; Rue des Bouches Peintes, 1933; Confucius en pull over, 1934; Princess Brinda, 1934; His Chinese Concubine, 1935; A Frenchman in Japan, 1936; Blood and Caviare, 1937; The Widow with the Pink Gloves, 1938; Written with Lipstick, 1938; Death requests the pleasure..., 1939; Emigrants de Luxe, 1942; The Romance of a Coward, 1943; The Madonna in Hollywood, 1945; Shanghai Honeymoon, 1946; Hell is Sold Out, 1948; Operation Magali, 1952; Poison at Plessis, 1953; The Man Who Died Twice, 1954; Chinese Puzzle, 1955; The Lady is a Vamp, 1958; The 7th Wife of Prince Hassan, 1961. *Recreations:* riding, fencing, thought reading. *Address:* 12 rue Beaujon, Paris 8e, France.   *[Died 1 June 1973.*

de la BEDOYERE, Count Michael; Editor: Search Newsletter, 1962-68; Catholic Herald, 1934-62; *b* 16 May 1900; *s* of Comte Yvon de la Bedoyere, and Sybil Emily, *d* of Dr A. W. Thorold, sometime Bishop of Winchester; *m* 1st, 1930, Catherine (*d* 1959), *d* of Algar Labouchere Thorold; four *s* one *d*; 2nd, 1961, Charlotte Halbik; two *s. Educ:* Stonyhurst; Oxford Univ. (MA 1st Class Honours Modern Greats). Asst master at Beaumont Coll., 1928-29; Lecturer in Philosophy in University of Minnesota, USA, 1930-31; Asst Ed. of the Dublin Review, 1932-34. *Publications:* The Drift of Democracy, 1931; Lafayette, a Revolutionary Gentleman, 1933; George Washington, an English Judgment, 1935; Sociology: Vol. 5 of European Civilization: Its Origin and Development, 1936; Christian Crisis, 1940; Christianity in the Market Place, 1943; No Dreamers Weak, 1944; Catherine, Saint of Siena, 1946; The Life of Baron von Hügel, 1951; Living Christianity, 1954; The Layman in the Church, 1955; Cardinal Griffin, 1955; The Archbishop and the

Lady, 1956; The Meddlesome Friar, 1958; The Cardijn Story, 1958; François de Sales, 1959; Francis, Saint of Assisi, 1962; (ed) Objections to Roman Catholicism, 1964; (ed) The Future of Catholic Christianity, 1966. *Address:* Elylands, Edenbridge, Kent.   *[Died 13 July 1973.*

De la BÈRE, Sir Rupert, 1st Bt, *cr* 1953; KCVO 1953; Kt 1952; President, Proprietors of Hay's Wharf Ltd and other Companies; Alderman of City of London for Ward of Tower; *b* 16 June 1893; *s* of Lillian Margaret and Reginald De la Bère; *m* 1919, Marguerite (*d* 1969), *e d* of late Sir John Humphery; two *s* three *d. Educ:* Tonbridge Sch. Captain East Surrey Regt; served European War 1914-18, India, Mesopotamia, Egypt; seconded to RFC and RAF; graduated at Aboukir, Egypt. MP (C) Evesham Div. of Worcs, 1935-50, South Worcs, 1950-55; Sheriff of City of London, 1941-42; Lord Mayor of London, 1952-53. KStJ 1953. Knight Comdr, Order of the Dannebrog (Denmark), 1954; Knight Comdr Order of the North Star (Sweden), 1954. *Heir: s* Cameron De la Bère [*b* 12 Feb. 1933; *m* 1964, Clairemonde, *o d* of Casimir Kaufmann, Geneva; one *d*]. *Recreations:* aviation and squash racquets. *Address:* Crowborough Place, Crowborough, East Sussex. *T:* Crowborough 103. *Club:* Carlton.   *[Died 25 Feb. 1978.*

DELACOURT-SMITH, Baron *cr* 1967 (Life Peer) of New Windsor; **Charles George Percy Smith,** PC 1969; General Secretary, Post Office Engineering Union, since 1953; Adviser, Prison Officers' Association, 1956-69; *b* 25 April 1917; *o s* of Charles and Ethel Smith, Windsor, Berks; *m* 1939, Margaret Hando, Newport, Mon.; one *s* two *d. Educ:* County Boys' Sch., Windsor; Wadham Coll., Oxford (Scholar). Librarian, Oxford Union; Research Asst, New Fabian Research Bureau, 1938-39. Entered army (RE) in the ranks, July 1940; Commissioned Jan. 1943, RASC (despatches). MP (Lab) Colchester Div. of Essex, 1945-50; Mem., Executive, Labour Research Dept, 1947-51; Parliamentary Private Sec. to Sec. of State for Commonwealth Relations, 1947-49; Asst Sec. Civil Service Clerical Assoc., 1939-53. Chm., Civil Service Nat. Whitley Council (Staff Side), 1962-64. Mem. (part-time) British Airports Authority, 1965-69; Minister of State, Min. of Technology, 1969-70. Member: Shipbuilding Inquiry Cttee, 1965-66; Cttee on engagement and use of labour in construction, 1967-68. World Pres., Postal, Telegraph, and Telephone International, 1969. JP London, 1960-69. *Publications:* Britain's Food Supplies in Peace and War, 1940; (with John Parker, MP) Modern Turkey, 1940; edited (with M. I. Cole) Democratic Sweden, 1938. *Recreations:* reading, music, theatre. *Address:* 56 Aberdare Gardens, NW6.   *[Died 2 Aug. 1972.*

DELAFIELD, Max Everard, MC, MB, BCh, DPH; Professor Emeritus University of London; *b* 23 March 1886; *m* 1910; one *s; m* 1940, May, *d* of A. A. Purry, Hampstead. *Educ:* Merchant Taylors' Sch., London; Jesus Coll., Cambridge; St Thomas's Hosp. Late Prof. of Chemistry as applied to Hygiene at London Sch. of Hygiene and Tropical Medicine; formerly Head of Dept of Hygiene and Bacteriology, Queen Elizabeth Coll., Lecturer at University Coll. Hospital Medical Sch. and University Coll. *Recreations:* home and gardening. *Address:* 14 Lyttelton Court, N2. *T:* 01-455 2873.   *[Died 26 Dec. 1974.*

DELAMERE, 4th Baron *cr* 1821; **Thomas Pitt Hamilton Cholmondeley;** Captain Welsh Guards; Director, Proved Securities Ltd; *b* 19 Aug. 1900; *e s* of 3rd Baron and Lady Florence Cole (*d* 1914), 4th *d* of 4th Earl of Enniskillen; *S* father, 1931; *m* 1st, 1924, Phyllis Anne (marr. diss. 1944; she *d* 1978), *e d* of late Lord George Scott, OBE; one *s* two *d*; 2nd, 1944, Ruth Mary Clarisse (marr. diss. 1955), *yr d* of 1st Baron Mount Temple; 3rd, 1955, Diana Colvile, *yr d* of late Seymour Caldwell and of Mrs Caldwell, The Red House, Hove, Sussex. *Educ:* Eton. *Heir: s* Hon. Hugh George Cholmondeley [*b* 18 Jan. 1934; *m* 1964, Mrs Ann Willoughby Tinne, *o d* of late Sir Patrick Renison, GCMG; one *s*]. *Address:* Soysambu, Elementeita, Kenya. *Clubs:* White's, Turf.   *[Died 13 April 1979.*

DELAMOTHE, Hon. Sir Peter (Roylance), Kt 1973; OBE 1959; Agent-General for Queensland, in London, since 1971; *b* 29 June 1906; *s* of Charles Delamothe and Anna Mary Delamothe (*née* Oliver); *m* 1947, Joan Patricia Milner; one *s* two *d. Educ:* Mt Carmel Coll., Charters Towers, Queensland; Sydney Univ. (MB, BS). Medical practitioner, 1928-60. Served War, Wing Comdr, RAAF, 1940-44. Mayor of Bowen, Qld, 1946-58; MLA, Qld, 1960-71; Minister for Justice and Attorney-Gen., Qld, 1963-71. *Recreations:* sailing, golf. *Address:* 22 Westminster Gardens, Marsham Street, SW1. *T:* 01-828 2993. *Clubs:* Royal Automobile; Johnsonian (Brisbane, Qld). *[Died 26 Oct. 1973.*

DELARGEY, His Eminence Reginald John, Cardinal; Archbishop of Wellington (NZ), since 1974; *b* Timaru, NZ,

1914. *Educ:* Holy Cross College, Dunedin; Pontificio Collegio Urbano de Propaganda Fide, Rome. Titular Bishop of Hirina, 1957; Auxiliary Bishop of Auckland, 1958; Bishop of Auckland, 1970-74. Cardinal, 1976. *Address:* PO Box 198, Wellington, NZ; (residence) 21 Eccleston Hill, Wellington. *[Died 29 Jan. 1979.*

DELARGY, Captain Hugh James; MP (Lab) Platting Division of Manchester, 1945-50, Thurrock Division of Essex since 1950; *b* 1908; *s* of Bernard Delargy, Co. Antrim. *Educ:* France and Italy. Enlisted, 1941; five years' service in Royal Artillery; Captain 1944 (despatches). An Asst Govt Whip (unpaid), 1950-51; an Opposition Whip, 1951-52. A Vice-Chm., British Council, 1969-. *Address:* House of Commons, SW1. *[Died 4 May 1976.*

de LASZLO, Patrick David; Director: Harwin Engineers, Portsmouth; Trust Company of the West, Los Angeles; and several other companies; Chairman, Economic Research Council, since 1959; *b* 26 March 1909; *s* of Philip de Laszlo, MVO, and Lucy M. Guinness; *m* 1940, Hon. Deborah H. Greenwood (marr. diss.; she *m* 2nd, Roderick Walter); one *s* four *d*; *m* 1977, Baroness Sharples. *Educ:* Lancing; Balliol Coll., Oxford (Hons PPE and BLit Econs). Joined elder brother; worked with him on design of miniature radio valves which later became universal; Man. Dir, Celestion Ltd (Public Co. which had invented the loud speaker), 1937-49; company soon engaged on develt and prodn of mil. equipment for RAF, Admiralty and War Office; personally involved in design and develt of Proximity Fuse and other devices; started McMurdo Instrument Co. (Private Co.), which continued develt work on Proximity Fuse and other devices, inc. Escape Lights for Navy (later adopted by BOAC and most airlines of the world); Founder and Man. Dir, Halmatic Ltd, 1950-60 (which in that period developed technique for making large glass reinforced plastic hulls for boats up to 80', since universally adopted). Pres., Assoc. of Independent Businesses, 1976- (Chm., 1973-76). Westminster City Councillor, seven years; Chm., London Westminster Cons. Assoc., nine years. *Publications:* papers on economics (Economic Research Council). *Recreations:* tennis, water skiing. *Address:* Byron's Chambers, Albany, Piccadilly, W1V 9RD. *T:* 01-434 2621. *Clubs:* Boodle's, Carlton, Royal Automobile. *[Died 27 Oct. 1980.*

DE LA WARR, 9th Earl *cr* 1761; **Herbrand Edward Dundonald Brassey Sackville,** PC GBE 1956; DL; JP; Baron De La Warr, 1209 and 1572; Baron West, 1342; Viscount Cantelupe, 1761; Baron Buckhurst (UK), 1864; *b* 20 June 1900; *e s* of 8th Earl and Hon. Muriel Agnes Brassey (*d* 1930), 2nd *d* of 1st Earl Brassey; *S* father, 1915; *m* 1st, 1920, Diana (*d* 1966), *d* of late Gerard Leigh and of late Mrs Reginald Halsey; one *s* one *d* (and one *s* missing, presumed killed, War of 1939-45); 2nd, 1968, Sylvia, Countess of Kilmuir, DBE. *Educ:* Eton; Magdalen Coll., Oxford. Served as a sailor during the War; Parly Under-Sec., War Office, 1929-30; Parliamentary Sec., Ministry of Agriculture, and Dep. Minister of Fisheries, 1930-31 and 1931-35; Parliamentary Sec., Board of Education, 1935-36; Parliamentary Under-Sec. of State for the Colonies, 1936-37; Lord Privy Seal, 1937-38; Pres. of the Board of Education, 1938-40; First Commissioner Office of Works and Public Buildings, April-May, 1940; Chm. Estate Cttee, National Trust, 1950-51, and 1955-70; Postmaster-Gen., 1951-April 1955; Chm. Agricultural Research Council, 1944-49; Lord-in-Waiting to HM, 1924 and 1929-31; Chm. Joint East and Central Africa Board, 1955-58; Chm. Royal Commonwealth Society, 1960. Mayor of Bexhill, 1932-35; JP 1925-, DL 1956-, Sussex. FRSA 1962. *Heir:* s Lord Buckhurst, *qv. Address:* Fishers Gate, Withyham, Sussex. *T:* Hartfield 246; 1 Buckingham Mews, Stafford Place, SW1. *T:* 01-834 0477. *Clubs:* Turf, Pratt's, Farmers'; Sussex (Eastbourne). *[Died 28 Jan. 1976.*

DELBRIDGE, Rt. Rev. Graham Richard; Bishop of Gippsland, since 1974; *b* 22 May 1917; *s* of Richard and Evelyn Delbridge; *m* 1943, Audrey Doris Traversi; one *s* three *d*. *Educ:* Moore Theological College, NSW. Scholar in Theology, Australian College of Theology, 1955; Mem., Australian Coll. of Educn, 1970. Director of Youth Work, Sydney, 1943-52; Rector, Holy Trinity, Adelaide, 1952-57; Rector, St Matthew's, Manly, 1957-60; Archdeacon and Senior Chaplain to the Primate of Australia, 1963-68; Asst Bishop of Sydney and Bishop in Wollongong, 1969-74. *Recreation:* bush walking. *Address:* Bishopscourt, PO Box 383, Sale, Victoria 3850, Australia. *Clubs:* Royal Automobile, Sale Men's (Sale, Victoria); Savage (Melbourne). *[Died 8 June 1980.*

DELDERFIELD, Ronald Frederick, Dramatist and Author; *b* 12 Feb. 1912, *s* of William James Delderfield and Alice (*née* Jones), London; *m* 1936, May Evans; one *s* one *d*. *Educ:* West Buckland Sch. Newspaper reporter, sub-ed., and ed., Exmouth Chronicle, 1929-39; served in RAF, 1940-45; Air Min. Staff as Public

Relations Officer, 1944; Europe, 1944-45; resigned editorship Exmouth Chronicle, 1947. First play, Spark in Judaea, produced Ambassadors by New Plays and privately performed, 1937; Twilight Call (comedy), Birmingham Rep., 1939; Printer's Devil, Q and Embassy, London, 1939; This is my Life (with Basil Thomas), 1943; Spinster of South Street (York Drama Festival Play and tour), 1945; Worm's Eye View, Embassy and Whitehall, 1945 (filmed, 1950); Peace Comes to Peckham, Embassy and Prince's, 1947; All Over The Town, Playhouse, 1947; (filmed, 1948); The Queen Came By, Duke of York's, 1949; Wagonload o' Monkeys, Savoy, 1951; Where there's a Will, Garrick, 1951 (filmed 1953); Glad Tidings, 1952 (filmed); Golden Rain, 1952; All on a Summer's Day, 1953; The Orchard Walls, St Martin's, 1953; The Mayerling Affair (Pitlochry Festival), 1957; (with Michael Pertwee) Now and Forever (film), 1956; various broadcast sketches and short plays. *Publications:* All Over the Town (novel), 1947; Seven Men of Gascony (novel) (USA and Britain), 1949; Farewell the Tranquil Mind (novel) (USA and Britain), 1950; Nobody Shouted Author (reminiscences), 1951; Bird's Eye View (autobiography); The Adventures of Benn Gunn (novel and TV serial), 1956; The Dreaming Suburb (novel and radio serial), 1958; The Avenue Goes to War, 1958; There Was a Fair Maid Dwelling (published under title Diana, USA), 1960, The Unjust Skies (sequel); Napoleon in Love (novel and TV play), 1959, staged Pitlochry Festival, 1960; Stop at a Winner (filmed as On the Fiddle, 1961); The March of the Twenty-Six, 1962; My Dearest Angel (Pitlochry Festival); The Spring Madness of Mr Sermon (novel), 1963; The Golden Millstones (biography), 1964; Too Few For Drums (novel), 1964; Under an English Sky (travel), 1965 (USA 1967); A Horseman Riding By (novel), 1966; Cheap Day Return (novel), 1967; The Retreat from Moscow, 1967; The Green Gauntlet (novel), 1968; For My Own Amusement (essays), 1968; Imperial Sunset: the Fall of Napoleon, 1813-1814, (history), 1969 (USA 1968); Come Home Charlie and Face Them (novel), 1969; God is an Englishman (novel), 1970; Overture for Beginners (autobiography), 1970; Theirs was the Kingdom (novel), 1971; *posthumous publication:* Give Us This Day (novel), 1973. *Recreation:* swimming. *Address:* Sidmouth, E Devon. *[Died 24 June 1972.*

DELLER, Alfred, OBE 1970; singer; *b* Margate, Kent, 31 May 1912; *s* of Thomas William Deller and Mary Cave; *m* 1937, Kathleen Margaret Lowe; two *s* one *d*. *Educ:* secondary sch. Lay-Clerk, Canterbury Cathedral, 1941-47; Vicar-Choral, St Paul's Cathedral, 1947-61. Soloist in BBC Third Programme inaugural concert, 1946; sang role of Oberon in first perf. of A Midsummer Night's Dream (opera by Britten), 1960. Formed Deller vocal ensemble Consort, 1950; Deller Consort tours of Australia, NZ, and USA, 1964, 1967, 1969, 1972. Concert tours of America with Desmond Dupré, 1955, 1957, 1959, 1962, 1973. Founder and Artistic Dir, Stour Music Festival, 1963; Founder, Deller Académie de Musique Anglaise, Lacoste en Provence, 1971. Festivals: Edinburgh, Aldeburgh, Three Choirs, Royal Danish, Vienna, Stuttgart, Graz, Lucerne, Hitzacker, etc. Hon. Music Adviser, Univ. of Kent. Pres., Catch Club of America. Hon. RAM, 1976. Hon. DLitt Kent, 1977; Hon. DMus Leicester, 1978. *Relevant publication:* Hardwick: Alfred Deller, a Singularity of Voice, 1968. *Recreations:* conversation and country life. *Address:* Barton Cottage, The Street, Kennington, Ashford, Kent. *T:* Ashford 23838. *[Died 16 July 1979.*

DELLER, Capt. Harold Arthur; Commodore of Union Castle Mail SS Co. Ltd, 1960-62, retired; *b* 28 Aug. 1897; *s* of William John Deller, RN, and Edith Deller; *m* 1922, Mary Phyllis Elizabeth Deller (cousin); one adopted *d. Educ:* King Edward VII Sch., North Shields (Tynemouth), Northumberland. At sea as Cadet, SS Austrian Prince, from 1911. Served European War (Gen. Service and Merchant Service Medals) until captured at sea, July 1915. Joined Union Castle Mail SS Co., 1919, as Junior Officer. War of 1939-45 (Medal for Gen. Service, 1939-45 Star, Atlantic Star); first command, 1938. Capt. of various Mail Vessels from 1947, finally to Flagship, Pendennis Castle (RMS), 1960. Consultant, James A. Silver Ltd. Royal Order of Phoenix (Greece), 1941. *Publications:* contributor to South African Personality, and to English Digest. *Recreation:* painting. *Address:* 8 Reynolds Court, Romsey, Hants. *T:* Romsey 512779. *Clubs:* Southampton Master Mariners' (Southampton); Royal Motor Yacht (Poole). *[Died 26 Dec. 1976.*

DELMER, (Denis) Sefton, OBE 1946; writer on foreign affairs; *b* 24 May 1904; *s* of late Prof. F. S. Delmer, Hobart, Tasmania, English lecturer at Berlin Univ.; *m* 1935, Isabel (marr. diss., 1946), *d* of late Capt. P. O. Nicholas; *m* 1948, Zoë Ursula Black; one *s* one *d. Educ:* St Paul's Sch.; Lincoln Coll., Oxford. Joined Daily Express, 1927; Berlin Correspondent of Daily Express, 1928-33; Paris Correspondent, 1933-36; War Correspondent during Spanish Civil War, July 1936-Sept. 1938; Chief European

Reporter of the Daily Express from 1937; War Correspondent, Poland 1939, France, 1939-40, with French Army; Foreign Office, 1941-45; rejoined Daily Express, as Chief Foreign Affairs Reporter, 1945-59. Editorial adviser to Der Spiegel, Hamburg, 1963-64. *Publications:* Trail Sinister, 1961; Black Boomerang, 1962; Die Deutschen und ich, 1962; Weimar Germany, 1972; The Counterfeit Spy, 1973. *Address:* The Valley Farm, Lamarsh, near Bures, Suffolk. *T:* Twinstead 222. *Clubs:* Garrick, Press, Lansdowne.								[*Died* 4 Sept. 1979.

DELMER, Sefton; *see* Delmer, D. S.

del RE, Cavaliere Arundel; OBE 1920; MA London, MA Oxon, Balliol College; LittD, Tokyo University of Education, Japan; Professor Emeritus Nanzan Catholic University, Nagoya; Tutor and Lecturer, Victoria University, Wellington, New Zealand, 1958-67; *b* 29 Jan. 1892; *o s* of Capt. Pietro del Re (Royal Italian Army) and Bertha Fremoult Hill; *m* 1923; two *d. Educ:* Florence; University Coll., London. University Lecturer in Italian, Oxford, 1920-27; King's College, London University, 1922-27; Prof. of English Literature, Tokyo Imperial Univ. and Imperial Univ., Taihoku (Formosa), 1927-41; Adviser to the Civil Information and Educn Section, GHQ, SCAP, in Japan, 1945-51. Order of the Sacred Treasure, third class (Japan), 1963. *Publications:* John Florio's Firste Fruites, 1936; Commentary to Bridges' Testament of Beauty (Introduction), 1938; Creation Myths of the Formosan Savages, 1951, etc. *Address:* 17 Barnet Street, Highett, Melbourne, Vic. 3190, Australia.								[*Died* 20 July 1974.

DELYSIA, Alice; *b* March 1889; *d* of M. Lapize and Mme. Mathilde Douce; *m* 1944, Captain Kolb-Bernard, DSC, Agent Consulaire (for France). *Educ:* Convent des Sœurs de Nevers. Began under C. B. Cochran in Odds and Ends, 1914; More Pell Mell, Carminetta, As You Were, Afgar; went to America with Afgar, came back to London in Mayfair and Montmartre; went again to America in the Schubert revue Topics of 1924; came back to London in first straight play; successes: Her Past, Princess Charming, A Pair of Trousers, The Cat and The Fiddle, and Mother of Pearl, etc; first appearance in Australia, 1934; returned to London and made several subsequent tours; entered films, 1934, and appeared in Evensong. Enlisted with ENSA, May 1941, acting for troops in whole Middle East, then Normandy, Belgium, Holland, until end of war. King's Medal for Freedom; Africa Star, 8th Army; French Recognition Medal for War Services; Free French Medal; Order of Merit (Lebanon and Syria). *Recreations:* horse riding, walking, swimming.								[*Died* 10 Feb. 1979.

DE MEL, Most Rev. (Hiyanirindu) Lakdasa Jacob, DD; *b* 24 March 1902; *e s* of late Sir Henry De Mel, Colombo, Ceylon; *m* 1971, Mrs Joan Hamilton, widow of Lt-Col James Hamilton. *Educ:* The Royal Coll., Colombo; Keble Coll.; Cuddesdon Coll., Oxford (MA). Curate, St John the Divine, Kennington, 1926; Curate, St Paul's, Kandy, 1927; Incumbent, Christ Church, Baddegame, 1929; Vicar, St Paul's, Kandy, 1941; Officiating Chaplain, 34 Indian Div., 1942-45; Asst Bishop of Colombo, 1945; Bishop of Kurunagala, 1950; Bishop of Calcutta, 1962; Metropolitan of the Church of India, Pakistan, Burma and Ceylon, 1962; retired, 1970; now Metropolitan Emeritus. Hon. DD: Univ. of King's Coll., Halifax, 1956; Trinity Coll., Toronto, 1956; Wycliffe Coll., Toronto, 1963. *Publications:* contributor, Sinhalese Encyclopædia. *Recreations:* archaeology, art, music. *Address:* PO Box 68, Colombo, Sri Lanka.
								[*Died* 23 Oct. 1976.

de MENDIETA, Rev. Dr Emmanuel Alexandre A.; *see* Amand de Mendieta.

de MONTHERLANT, Henry; *see* Montherlant.

de MONTMORENCY, Sir Reginald (D'Alton Lodge), 18th Bt, *cr* 1631; *b* 13 March 1899; *y s* of John Kiddell de Montmorency and Ada Margaret Ligonier Balfour; *S* cousin, 1963; *m* 1928, Dorothy Victoria, 2nd *d* of Gilbert Walter Robinson. *Educ:* privately in England and Bruges for art. Served European War 1914-18: Hon. Artillery Co. and Royal Horse Artillery, 1917-19. P&O, 1915-17, shore service at home and abroad, 1919-25; Manager: (in Bombay) for Bell, Russ & Co. (East India merchants), 1925-33; A. Besse of Arabia and Manager of the Halal Shipping Co., 1933-35. Joined the staff of The Times, 1936 and retired 1967. Travelled widely in Commonwealth and other countries in connection with his work. *Recreations:* swimming, riding, walking and drawing. *Heir: cousin* Arnold Geoffroy de Montmorency, *b* 27 July 1908. *Address:* Bristol Cottage, Putney Heath, SW15. *T:* 01-788 2102. *Club:* Royal Commonwealth Society.								[*Died* 25 Nov. 1979.

DENING, Sir (Maberly) Esler, GCMG 1955 (KCMG 1950; CMG 1945); OBE 1939 (MBE 1919); HM Foreign Service, retired; *b* 21 April 1897; *o surv. s* of late Walter Dening, Ottery St Mary, Devon, and Lydia James. Enlisted in Australian Imperial Forces, 1915, and served in Egypt and France; demobilised 1919 with rank of Lieut; joined HM Consular Service, 1920, and served in Tokyo, Osaka and Kobe in Japan, Seoul (Korea), Manila (Philippines), Dairen and Harbin (Manchuria), 1920-38; appointed to Foreign Office, 1938; a First Sec. in HM Embassy, Washington, 1941. Served in the Home Guard (35th London), 1940-43; Chief Political Adviser to Supreme Allied Commander, South-East Asia, 1943-46; an Asst Under-Sec. of State, FO, 1946-50; special mission to Asia with rank of Ambassador, 1950-51; UK Political Representative in Japan, 1951-52; HM Ambassador to Japan, 1952-57. Head of UK Delegn to Antarctic Treaty Conference, Washington, 1959. Chairman, Royal Central Asian Soc., 1967-70. Order of the Rising Sun First Class (Japan), 1964. *Publication:* Japan, 1960. *Address:* Stanhope Court Hotel, 46 Stanhope Gardens, SW7. *Clubs:* Boodle's, Beefsteak, Royal Automobile.
								[*Died* 29 Jan. 1977.

DENING, Maj.-Gen. Roland, CB 1942; MVO 1935; MC 1918; DL; IA; psc; retired; *b* 13 Sept. 1888; *s* of late Lt-Gen. Sir Lewis Dening, KCB, DSO, and late Beatrice Catherine Scott; *m* 1917, Clare de Burgh (Kaisar-i-hind Gold Medal, 1942; DGStJ, 1963), *d* of J. H. Garratt, Greystones, Co. Wicklow; one *s* two *d. Educ:* Wellington Coll., Berks; RMA Woolwich. Entered Royal Field Artillery, 1907; Transferred to 18th Bengal Lancers, Indian Army, 1911; served European War 18th (KGO) Lancers, France 1914-18, Palestine and Syria 1918; DAAG 4th Cavalry Div. EEF 1918; DAAG Northforce EEF 1919; Instructor Cavalry Sch., Saugor, 1920-21; Attended Staff Coll., Quetta, 1922; Brigade Major, 1st Risalpur Cavalry Brigade, 1924-28; Brevet Lt-Col, 1930; Commandant, Equitation Sch., Saugor, 1931-34; Commandant, 19th KGO Lancers, 1934-36; Gen. Staff Officer 1st Grade, Peshawar District, 1936-38; Comm. Jullunder Brig. Area, India, 1938; Comdr 1st Abbotabad Inf. Bde, 1940; Maj.-Gen. 1940; Comdr Peshawar District, 1940-43; retired, 1944, Col 19th King George V's Own Lancers, 1945-49. Chm. Housing Cttee, Ottery St Mary UDC, 1948-51; Chm. British Legion Devon County, 1950-54; County Cadet Officer (Ambulance), St John Ambulance Brigade, Devon, 1951-61; Officer Brother, Order of St John of Jerusalem, 1958. Pres. Honiton and District Agricultural Assoc., 1957. Hon. Sec., Sidmouth and Ottery St Mary Div., SS&AFA, 1948-72. DL Devonshire, 1954. *Recreations:* polo, tennis, rackets. *Address:* Tipton Lodge, Tipton St John, near Sidmouth, East Devon EX10 0AW. *T:* Ottery St Mary 2027.								[*Died* 9 March 1978.

DENMAN, 4th Baron *cr* 1834, **Thomas Denman;** *b* 2 Aug. 1905; *o s* of 3rd Baron Denman, PC, GCMG, KCVO, and Hon. Gertrude Mary Pearson, GBE (*d* 1954), *o d* of 1st Viscount Cowdray; *S* father 1954. *Educ:* Eton; Trinity Coll., Cambridge. *Heir: cousin,* Capt. Sir Charles Spencer Denman, 2nd Bt.
								[*Died* 21 March 1971.

DENMAN, John Leopold, JP; FSA; FRIBA; Architect; practised in Brighton, Sussex; *b* 15 Nov. 1882; *s* of Samuel Denman and Elizabeth Harriet Morley; *m* 1912, Constance Winifred Bluett; one *s* two *d. Educ:* Brighton Grammar Sch.; Architectural Association Sch. Awarded 1st Premium in open competition for Women's Hospital, Brighton, and New Senior Sch. at Rickmansworth for Royal Masonic Institution for Girls; other architectural works include: Eridge Park, Sussex; renovation of Holy Trinity Church, Eridge Green; St Martin's Priory, Canterbury; Christ Church Cathedral Library and other destroyed property in precincts of Canterbury Cathedral; new Diocesan Offices, Canterbury; Harewood Court, flats for the aged at Hove for Royal Masonic Benevolent Institution; the new Sussex Eye Hospital, Brighton; Holiday Home and housing development, South Heighton, for Guinness Trust; rebuilding of tower at St Michael's Church, Southwick; Housing Scheme at Lindfield for Cuckfield UDC; Barclays Bank Ltd, Local Head Offices at Brighton; numerous church renovations incl. Brighton, Hove, and Arundel parish churches. Pres., Regency Soc. of Brighton and Hove; Vice-Pres., Sussex Archæological Soc.; Past-Pres. South-Eastern Society of Architects; Past Vice-Pres., RIBA. RIBA Distinction in Town Planning. Served with RE during European War, 1914-18. *Address:* Oldways, Hurstpierpoint, Sussex. *T:* Hurstpierpoint 832138.
								[*Died* 5 June 1975.

DENNING, Vice-Adm. Sir Norman (Egbert), KBE 1963 (OBE 1945); CB 1961; *b* 19 Nov. 1904; *y s* of late Charles and Clara Denning, Whitchurch, Hants; *m* 1933, Iris, *d* of late Captain R. and Mrs Curtis, Singapore; one *s* one *d* (and one *s* decd). *Educ:* Andover Grammar Sch., Hampshire. Joined RN, 1922; Naval

Intelligence Div., Operational Intelligence Centre, Admiralty, 1937-45; Comdr, 1941; Captain 1951; Dir of Administrative Planning, Admty, 1952; Dir, RN Coll., Greenwich, 1956; Rear-Admiral, 1958; Dep. Chief of Naval Personnel, 1958; Dir-Gen. of Manpower, 1959; DNI, 1960-64; Vice-Adm., 1961; Chief Naval Supply and Secretariat Officer, 1962-64; Deputy Chief of the Defence Staff (Intelligence), 1964-65; Sec., Defence Press and Broadcasting Cttee, 1967-72. *Address:* Rose Cottage, Micheldever, Hants. *T:* 268. *Club:* Royal Automobile.
[Died 27 Dec. 1979.

DENNISON, Adm. Robert Lee; DSM (US); Legion of Merit (Gold Star); US Navy; Commander in Chief, Atlantic and US Atlantic Fleet and Supreme Allied Commander Atlantic, 1960-63, retired; *b* 13 April 1901; *s* of Ludovici Waters and Laura Florence Lee Dennison; *m* 1937, Mildred Mooney; one *s* one *d.* *Educ:* US Naval Acad.; Pa State Coll. (MS); Johns Hopkins Univ. (EngD). Ensign, 1923; advanced through grades to Admiral, 1959. Served with Atlantic, Pacific and Asiatic Fleets; comd Ortolan, 1935-37, Cuttlefish, 1937-38; John D. Ford, 1940-41, Missouri, 1947-48; mem. jt war plans cttee of Jt Chiefs of Staff, 1944-45; Asst Chief of Naval Ops (polit-mil. affairs), 1945-47; naval aide to Pres. of USA, 1948-53; Cdr Cruiser Div. 4 Atlantic Fleet, 1953-54; Dir Strategic Plans Div., Asst Chief of Naval Ops (Plans and Policy), mem. jt strategic plans cttee of Jt Chiefs of Staff, 1954-56; Cdr First Fleet, Pacific Fleet, 1956-58; Dep. Chief Naval Ops (Plans and Policy), 1958-59; C-in-C, US Naval Forces, E Atlantic and Mediterranean, 1959-60. Hon. OBE 1946; Commander: Order of Naval Merit (Brazil); Order of the Crown (Belgium); Legion of Honour (France); Grand Cross, Order of Orange-Nassau (Netherlands), Grand Cross, Military Order of Aviz (Portugal). *Address:* c/o Trust Department Office, The Riggs National Bank, Washington, DC, USA. *Clubs:* Ends of the Earth, American (London); Metropolitan, Army-Navy, Chevy Chase (Washington, DC); New York Yacht.
[Died 14 March 1980.

DENNISON, Thomas Andrews; retired, 1957, as Puisne Judge of HM Supreme Court of Ghana; *b* 18 Sept. 1906; *s* of late Robert John Andrews Dennison; *m* 1937, Diana Mary Talbot; one *s.* *Educ:* Coleraine Academical Institution; Newcastle High Sch.. Staffs; Trinity Coll., Dublin (BA). Called to Irish Bar, 1931; joined Colonial Legal Service as Crown Counsel, Kenya Colony, 1935. Acted as Solicitor-Gen., Kenya, and nominated mem. of Legislative Council on various occasions. District Magistrate, Gold Coast, 1948. War of 1939-45, 1940-42, Lieut 4th Bn The King's African Rifles. *Recreations:* golf, swimming and photography. *Address:* PO Box 24867, Karen, Nairobi, Kenya. *Clubs:* University (Dublin); Muthaiga Country (Nairobi).
[Died 14 May 1972.

DENNY, James Runciman, MBE 1944; MA, MusB Cantab; West Riding Professor of Music, Leeds University, 1950-71; *b* 9 May 1908; *m* 1934, Agatha Nash; one *s* two *d.* *Educ:* Gresham's Sch., Holt; Royal College of Music; Christ's Coll., Cambridge. Music Dir, Bedford Sch., 1933-37; Music Asst, BBC, Belfast, 1937-39; Head of Midland Regional Music, BBC, and Conductor BBC Midland Chorus and Singers, 1946-50; Leeds Guild of Singers, 1952-55. Pres., Incorporated Soc. of Musicians, 1964. Hon. RAM. Served War of 1939-45, Royal Warwicks Regt; GSO1, India Command. *Publications:* The Oxford School Harmony Course, 1960; Hymn to Christ the King, 1963. *Address:* High Walls, West Winterslow, Salisbury, Wilts. *T:* Winterslow 862412.
[Died 29 May 1978.

DENNY, Adm. Sir Michael (Maynard), GCB 1954 (KCB 1950; CB 1940); CBE 1944; DSO 1945; Consultant, Cammell Laird (Chairman 1959-66); *b* Kempley, Glos, 3 Oct. 1896; *y s* of late Canon Edward Denny, MA; *m* 1923, Sara Annie Esmé (*d* 1971), *d* of late Col Loftus Welman, Royal Irish Rifles; no *c. Educ:* RN Colls, Osborne and Dartmouth. Naval Cadet, 1909; midshipman, 1914; Sub-Lieut 1916; Lieut 1917; Comdr 1930; Capt. 1936; Rear-Adm. 1945; Vice-Adm. 1948; Adm. 1952; served European War, 1914-19, in North Sea, HMS Neptune and Royal Sovereign; specialised in Gunnery, 1920, and awarded the Egerton Memorial prize; when not in sea appointment spent all service in gunnery experimental work, HMS Excellent; Fleet Gunnery Officer on staff of Adm. Sir W. W. Fisher, Mediterranean Fleet, 1932-34; Asst, and Dep. Dir of Naval Ordnance, Admiralty, 1937-40; commanded cruiser Kenya, 1940-42; Chief of Staff to C-in-C Home Fleet, 1942-43; commanded aircraft-carrier Victorious, 1944-45; Asst Chief of Naval Personnel and Dir of Personal Services, 1946-47; Flag Officer (Destroyers), Mediterranean Fleet, 1947-49; a Lord Commissioner of Admiralty, Third Sea Lord and Controller of the Navy, 1949-53; Commander-in-Chief Home Fleet, and Commander-in-Chief, Eastern Atlantic (NATO), 1954-55; Chm., British Joint Services Mission, Washington, DC, and UK

Representative on Standing Group of NATO Military Cttee, 1956-59; retired, 1959. *Recreations:* yachting, tennis. *Address:* Hampton Cottage, Down Ampney, Cirencester, Glos. *Club:* United Service & Royal Aero.
[Died 7 April 1972.

DENT, Alan Holmes, FRSA 1970; author, critic and journalist; *b* Ayrshire, Scotland, 7 Jan. 1905; *s* of John Dent, Westmorland, and Margaret Holmes, Yorks. *Educ:* Carrick Academy; Glasgow Univ. London dramatic critic of The Manchester Guardian, 1935-43; dramatic critic of Punch, 1942-43 and again in 1963. Served War of 1939-45, in RN Hosp., 1943-45. Dramatic Critic of News Chronicle, 1945-60; Film Critic of: the Sunday Telegraph, 1961-63; Illustrated London News, 1947-68. Frequent broadcaster since 1942. Shute Lecturer in the Art of the Theatre, Liverpool Univ., 1956. Pres. The Critics' Circle, 1962. Lectured on The Fine Art of Criticism at Toronto Univ., at Boston, at Vassar, at Princeton, and at Long Island and New York Universities, Nov. and Dec., 1966. Text-ed. of Sir Laurence Olivier's films of Henry V, Hamlet, and Richard III (text-adviser). Ed., Bernard Shaw and Mrs Patrick Campbell: their Correspondence, 1952. Will spend his old age planning a novel called The Milk of Paradise, and concluding his autobiography. *Publications:* Preludes and Studies, 1942; Nocturnes and Rhapsodies, 1950; My Dear America..., 1954; Mrs Patrick Campbell: a biography, 1961; Robert Burns in his Time, 1966; Vivien Leigh; a bouquet, 1969; World of Shakespeare: vol. 1, Plants, 1971; vol. 2, Animals and Monsters, 1972; vol. 3, Sports and Pastimes, 1973; My Covent Garden, 1973. *Address:* Chilterns Manor, Northern Heights, Bourne End, Bucks. *T:* Bourne End 28676.
[Died 19 Dec. 1978.

DENT, Prof. Charles Enrique, CBE 1976; FRS 1962; Professor of Human Metabolism, University College Hospital Medical School, since 1956; Hon. Consultant Physician, University College Hospital; *b* 25 Aug. 1911; *m* 1944, Margaret Ruth Coad; one *s* five *d. Educ:* Bedford Sch.; Wimbledon Coll.; Imperial Coll. of Science; University Coll., London. Research chemist, Imperial Chemical Industries (Dyestuffs Group), 1934-37. A/Capt. Intelligence Corps, BEF, 1939-40. Asst, Medical Unit, University Coll. Hosp. Medical Sch., 1944-51. Reader in Medicine, 1951-56. Humphry Davy Rolleston Lectr, RCP, 1962. MD: Louvain 1966; Uppsala 1974. Gairdner Foundn Award, 1965; Graham Gold Medal, Univ. of London, 1970. *Address:* 77 Eaton Rise, Ealing, W5. *T:* 01-997 3703.
[Died 19 Sept. 1976.

DENT, Dr Frederick (James), OBE 1958; FRS 1967; Director, Gas Council Midlands Research Station, 1952-67, retired; *b* 12 Oct. 1905; *s* of Frederick Dent and Sarah Liddell Dent; *m* 1942, Jean Marie Macvean; one *s* one *d. Educ:* Leeds Modern Sch.; Leeds Univ. BSc 1927; PhD 1929; DSc 1944. In charge of Gas Production Research, Jt Res. Cttee of Instn of Gas Engrs and Leeds Univ., 1929-41; Joint Asst Dir, Gas Research Bd, 1941-52. MacRobert Award, 1971. *Publications:* contribs to Trans Instn Gas Engineers. *Recreations:* sailing, photography. *Address:* 13 Valley View Court, Zaccheus Street, Msida, Malta.
[Died 5 Oct. 1973.

DENT, George Irving; Deputy Secretary, Department of Finance, Northern Ireland, since 1975; *b* 26 Oct. 1918; *s* of George Dent and Elizabeth (*née* Parkin); *m* 1945, Joyce Waterman; one *s* three *d. Educ:* High Storrs Grammar Sch., Sheffield; Oriel Coll., Oxford. MA Oxon, LLM, PhD London. Called to Bar, Gray's Inn. Army, RA, 1939-41; Intell. Corps, 1941-48; Min./Dept of Educn, NI, 1948-75. *Address:* 11 Hazelwood Park, Newtownabbey, Co. Antrim, N Ireland. *T:* Belfast 779923. *Club:* Civil Service.
[Died 22 Dec. 1976.

DENT, Rear-Adm. John, CB 1956; OBE 1941; *b* 5 Aug. 1899; *s* of late Thomas Dent, Yorks; *m* Nancy Alys Mary, *d* of late Mortimer Brutton Ford, Exmouth; one *s. Educ:* Sedbergh Sch. Joined RN, 1917; HMS Princess Royal, 1917-19; Naval Base, Constantinople, 1919-22; RN Coll., Dartmouth, 1924-29; Sec. to: Flag Officer (Submarines), 1929-31; C-in-C, East Indies, 1932-34; Second Sea Lord and Chief of Naval Personnel, 1935-38; C-in-C, Plymouth, 1938-39; C-in-C, Western Approaches, 1939-40; Vice-Controller of Navy, 1940-43 (OBE); HMS Devonshire, 1943-45; BSO, Singapore, 1945-46; HMS Ceres, 1946-47; idc 1948; Asst Dir of Plans, Admiralty, 1949-51; RN Barracks, Portsmouth, 1951-53; Staff of C-in-C Mediterranean, 1953-54; Chief Staff Officer (Administration), The Nore, 1954-58, retired. *Address:* Many Trees, Sway, Hants. *T:* Sway 2379.
[Died 16 Jan. 1973.

de PUTRON, Air Commodore Owen Washington, CB 1951; CBE 1946; RAF retired; *b* 4 July 1893; *s* of late Captain Beaumont de Putron, Guernsey, CI; *m* 1918, Phyllis Patricia, *d* of late Frederick Bestow, Kent; one *d. Educ:* private school. Dominion

Service, 1910; seconded to Army, 1914; commissioned Durham Light Infantry, 1914; permanent commn, RAF, 1919; served European War, 1914-18, in France, 1914-15 (very severely wounded; in hospital, 1915-17); attached to RFC, 1917; SO III, Ireland, 1918-20 (despatches); Sqdn Leader, 1930; Staff Officer, Iraq, 1930-33, ADGB, 1933-35; OC Army Co-op. Sqdn, 1935-36; Wing Comdr, 1937; Group Capt., 1940; Air Cdre, 1943; Air ADC, 1945-47, ADC, 1948-51, to King George VI. Provost Marshal and Chief of the Air Force Police, 1942-51; retired, 1951. As Provost Marshal visited many times all Theatres of War, 1943-45, and introduced RAF Police Dogs for guard duties in 1943; was reponsible for arranging for RAF Police to take over investigation into murder of fifty allied aircrew officers from breakout from Stalag Luft III. *Address:* Bluehayes, Beer, Devon. *Club:* Royal Air Force.   [*Died 17 Feb.* 1980.

DERBYSHIRE, Sir Harold, Kt 1934; MC; QC 1928; *b* 1886; *s* of James Derbyshire, Cherry Tree, Lancs; *m* 1915, Dorothea Alice, *d* of John Taylor, Crosshill, Blackburn; one *s* one *d. Educ:* Queen Elizabeth's Grammar Sch., Blackburn; Sidney Sussex Coll., Cambridge (Scholar); 1st Class Natural Science Tripos, MA, LLB. Barrister, Gray's Inn, 1911 (1st Cl. Bar Final and Certificate of Honour); practised Northern Circuit; Judge of Appeal, Isle of Man, 1933-34; Chief Justice, High Court, Calcutta, 1934-46; Jurisdiction: Bengal (now W Bengal and East Pakistan) and Assam, Population, 1946, seventy million, now divided among 3 High Courts at Calcutta, Dacca, and Gauhati. 1934-46: Fellow, Calcutta Univ.; Trustee, Victoria Memorial; Chm., Mayo Hosp. Bencher Gray's Inn 1931, Treasurer, 1948. Contested (L) Clitheroe, 1923, Royton, 1929. Served European War, 1914-19 (MC); served in France and Belgium, comdg first a Battery and later a Bde of Artillery; Liaison Officer between RA and RAF. Fruit Farmer since 1950. *Address:* Lindsey Lodge Farm, Hadleigh, Suffolk. *T:* Boxford 207.
                    [*Died 14 Sept.* 1972.

DE RENZY-MARTIN, Lt-Col Edward Cuthbert, CMG 1919; DSO 1917; MC 1916; Commander of Order of Skanderbeg; retired; *b* 1883; *s* of late Lt-Gen. Sir A. R. Martin, KCB; *m* 1st, 1912, Winifred Grace Alicia (*d* 1937), *d* of late E. C. P. Hull, of Park Gate House, Ham Common; one *s* three *d*; 2nd, 1942, Margaret Grant, MBE (*d* 1974), *e d* of late Dr A. C. Reid, 16 Pelham Road, Nottingham; one *s* one *d. Educ:* Wellington; RMC Sandhurst. Served European War, 1914-18 (despatches, CMG, DSO, MC, Bt Major; wounded, POW, 1918); Inspector of Albanian Gendarmerie, 1927-34; Hon. Attaché and Sec., British Embassy, Madrid, 1938-40. *Address:* 24 Elm Close, Mapperley Road, Nottingham.   [*Died 15 Dec.* 1974.

de RHÉ-PHILIPE, Maj.-Gen. Arthur Terence, CB 1944; OBE 1943; Chairman, GEC-Elliott Mechanical Handling Ltd; Managing Director, Spencer (Melksham) Ltd; *b* 2 Sept. 1905; *s* of late George William Vitalli de Rhé-Philipe, OBE; *m* Moira Evelyn, *d* of late Captain A. L. Cameron; two *d. Educ:* Cheltenham; RMA, Woolwich; Clare Coll., Cambridge. 2nd Lieut RE 1926; Capt. 1936; Temp. Major, 1939; Temp. Lieut-Col 1941; Temp. Col 1942; Temp. Brig.; Col 1948; Brig., 1953; temp. Maj.-Gen. 1953; Maj.-Gen. 1954. Dir of Movements, War Office, Sept. 1953-Dec. 1955, retired. Served War of 1939-45 in Great Britain, North Africa and Italy (OBE, CB). Col Comdt, RCT, 1965-70. Legion of Merit (US) 1943. *Recreations:* golf, cricket. *Address:* Keyford, Upton Scudamore, Warminster, Wilts.   [*Died 10 Oct.* 1971.

DERING, Lt-Col Sir Rupert (Anthony Yea), 12th Bt, *cr* 1626; *b* 17 Oct. 1915; *s* of late Capt. Rupert Chomeley Yea Dering, KOSB (killed in action, 1915); *S* cousin (Sir Anthony Myles Cholmeley Dering) 1958; *m* 1940, Betty Bridgett, *o d* of Lieut-Col V. P. Druce, Charminster, Dorset; one *d. Educ:* Downside; RMC, Sandhurst. 2nd Lieut, King's Own Scottish Borderers, 1935; retd through ill-health, 1947. *Heir:* none. *Address:* Bellings, Midhurst, Sussex. *T:* Midhurst 3404.
                    [*Died 16 March* 1975 (*ext*).

d'ERLANGER, Leo Frederic Alfred; Banker, retired; Director of public companies; *b* 2 July 1898; *s* of Baron François Rodolphe d'Erlanger and Elizabetta Barbiellini-Amidei; *m* 1930, Edwina Louise Pru; one *s* one *d. Educ:* Eton; Royal Military Coll., Sandhurst. War of 1914-18, Active Service First Bn Grenadier Guards. Officier de la Légion d'Honneur. *Address:* 10 Rue Robert de Traz, Geneva, Switzerland.   [*Died 25 Oct.* 1978.

DESBOROUGH, Vincent Robin d'Arba, FBA 1966; FSA 1956; Senior Research Fellow, New College, Oxford, since 1968; *b* 19 July 1914; *s* of Maximilian Julius Praetorius, PhD (killed on active service, European War, 1914-18), and of Violet Mary Francesca (*née* Parker; who changed the surname for herself and dependants from Praetorius to a family name of Desborough, by

deed-poll, after the death of her husband and the Russian Revolution); *m* 1950, Mary Hobson Appach; one *d* (one *s* decd). *Educ:* Downside Sch.; New Coll., Oxford. BA 1936; BLitt 1939; Charles Oldham Prize, 1939; MA 1949. Macmillan Student, British Sch. of Archæology at Athens, 1937-39. Served War of 1939-45, Royal Artillery (Temp. Captain, 1944). British Coun. (Sec. Registrar, Brit. Inst., Athens), 1946-47; Asst Dir, Brit. Sch. of Archæology at Athens, 1947-48; University of Manchester, 1948-68. Corresp. Mem., German Archæological Institute. Chm., Man. Cttee, British Sch. at Athens, 1968-72. *Publications:* Protogeometric Pottery, 1952; The Last Mycenaeans and their Successors, 1964; The Greek Dark Ages, 1972; contrib. to revised edn of Cambridge Ancient History; articles and reviews in archæological and classical jls. *Address:* 13 Field House Drive, Woodstock Road, Oxford OX2 7NT. *T:* Oxford 52285.
                    [*Died 24 July* 1978.

de SEGONZAC, A. D.; *see* Dunoyer de Segonzac.

des FORGES, Sir Charles Lee, Kt 1944; CBE 1941; *b* 20 July 1879; *s* of Walter Harry des Forges, Hull and Nottingham; *m* 1905, Alice Mary Stretton (*d* 1947); two *s*; *m* 1948, Doreen Clarke. *Educ:* privately at Hull and Nottingham. Asst Solicitor and Dep. Clerk of the Peace, Nottingham, 1902-12; Town Clerk and Clerk of the Peace, Rotherham County Borough, 1912-46; Secretary, Rotherham Region Joint Town Planning Cttee, 1922; Clerk to Rotherham Assessment Cttee, 1926; Clerk to South-West Yorks. Joint Board for the Mentally Defective, 1928-46. *Recreations:* fly-fishing, golf. *Address:* Bentwater, Churt, Surrey. *T:* Frensham 2604.   [*Died 11 Sept.* 1972.

DE SICA, Vittorio; Italian film director and actor; *b* 7 July 1901; *s* of Umberto and Teresa De Sica; *m* ; one *d*. Productions (in some of which he had acted) include: The Little Martyr; Tomorrow Is Too Late; Shoe Shine; Bicycle Thieves; Miracle in Milan; Umberto D; Bread, Love and Dreams; Bread, Love and Jealousy; The Sign of Venus; Scandal in Sorrento; Like Father, Like Son; Il Tetto; L'Oro di Napoli; Anna of Brooklyn; La Ciociara; The Last Judgement; Bocaccio 70; Yesterday, Today and Tomorrow; Un Mondo Nuovo; Marriage Italian Style; After the Fox; Woman Times Seven; Sunflower; The Garden of the Finzi-Continis (Golden Bear Award, Berlin Film Festival, 1971); A Brief Vacation.   [*Died 13 Nov.* 1974.

de SMITH, Prof. Stanley Alexander, MA, PhD; FBA 1971; Downing Professor of the Laws of England, and Fellow, Fitzwilliam College, University of Cambridge, since 1970; *b* 27 March 1922; *s* of Joseph de Smith and Jane Alexander; *m* 1946, Catherine Joan Natley (marr. diss. 1965); two *s* two *d*; *m* 1967, Barbara Lillywhite; two *d. Educ:* Southend High School; St Catharine's Coll., Cambridge. BA 1942, MA 1946; PhD London, 1959. Asst Lectr in Law London Sch. of Economics and Political Science, 1946; Lectr, 1948; Reader in Public Law, 1954. Military service, 1942-46; with 77th (DLOY) Medium Regt, RA, in NW European Campaign; subseq. on intelligence duties in Germany; despatches, 1945. Order of Leopold II, Croix de Guerre (1940) with palms, 1945; Captain 1946. Sec., Buganda Constitutional Cttee and Namirembe conf., 1954 Prof. of Public Law, Univ. of London, 1959-70; Constitutional Commissioner, Mauritius, 1961-68; Visiting Fellow, Research Sch. of Social Sciences, Australian National Univ., 1962; Visiting Prof., NY Univ. Sch. of Law, and Senior Fellow, NY Univ. Center for International Studies, 1967-68. Editor, Cambridge Law Jl. *Publications:* Joint editor, Commonwealth and Dependencies, Halsbury's Laws of England (3rd edition), 1953; The Vocabulary of Commonwealth Relations, 1954; Judicial Review of Administrative Action, 1959 (3rd edn 1973); The Lawyers and the Constitution, 1960; The New Commonwealth and its Constitutions, 1964; Microstates and Micronesia, 1970; Constitutional and Administrative Law, 1971 (2nd edn 1973); (jt editor) Administrative Law, Halsbury's Laws of England, 4th edn, 1973. *Address:* Fitzwilliam College, Cambridge; 2 Gog Magog Way, Stapleford, Cambridge CB2 5BQ. *T:* Shelford 3059.   [*Died 12 Feb.* 1974.

DESMOND, Astra, (Lady Neame), CBE 1949; BA London; Hon. RAM; Mezzo-soprano singer; Professor of Singing at Royal Academy of Music, 1947-63; President Incorporated Society of Musicians, 1950; President Society of Women Musicians, 1952-56; Member Arts Council Music Panel, 1953-59; Member of Carl Rosa Trust Council, 1956-58; *b* Torquay, 10 April 1893; *m* 1920, Sir Thomas Neame, *qv* ; two *s* (and one *s* deceased). *Educ:* Notting Hill High Sch. (Sch. Scholar); Westfield Coll., (Classical Scholarship); sang with Blanche Marchesi (Mary South Scholarship) and Louise Trenton; and Grenzebach and von Bos in Berlin. Has appeared at leading Festivals and Concerts since 1920; especially associated with Elgar's works, frequently under the composer's direction; sang in first broadcast of Stravinsky's

Oedipus Rex in 1928; has appeared in Opera with Carl Rosa Company; as guest artist at Sadler's Wells (Delilah and Carmen), Covent Garden (Ortrud and Fricka), and Glastonbury festivals; has toured in Scandinavia, Holland, France, the Balkans, Iberia, and New York both independently and for the British Council; sang in recitals and with the National Orchestra of Athens in April 1940 and again in 1946; in November 1941 was sent by the British Council on a tour of Portugal and Spain. Medal of S Olav (Norway), 1943. *Publications*: Grieg's Songs (Music and Letters, Oct. 1941); Dvořák's Songs, 1942; Sibelius' Songs, 1945; New English Version of Dvořák's Biblical Songs, 1949; Schumann Songs, 1972. *Recreation*: study of foreign languages. *Address*: Preston Lea, Faversham, Kent. *T*: Faversham 2012. *Club*: Cowdray. *[Died 16 Aug. 1973.*

de SOYSA, Rt. Rev. Charles Harold Wilfred; Bishop of Colombo, since 1964; *e s* of late Sir (Lambert) Wilfred (Alexander) de Soysa, and Evelyn Johanna Publina Fernando, OBE. *Educ*: Oriel Coll., Oxford; Cuddesdon Theol. College. BA 2nd class, Theology, 1932; MA 1945. Deacon, 1933; Priest, 1934. Church of St Jude, Hampstead Garden Suburb, 1933-36; Ceylon: St Paul, Kandy, 1936-40; Baddegama, 1940-41; Incumbent of Holy Emmanuel, Moratuwa, 1941-48; Sabbatical year, 1949-50; Principal of the Divinity Sch. of the Diocese of Colombo, 1950-64; Archdeacon of Colombo, 1955-64. Mem., Anglican-Roman Catholic Preparatory Commn, 1962-63. *Publication*: (Ed.) Church of Ceylon, her faith and mission, 1945. *Address*: Bishop's House, Steuart Place, Colombo, Ceylon. *Clubs*: United University; Havelock Golf (Colombo). *[Died 5 May 1971.*

de THIEUSIES, Vicomte A.; *see* Obert de Thieusies.

DETHRIDGE, Hon. George Leo, CMG 1972; Chairman, Victorian County Court, Australia, 1970-75; *b* 11 Dec. 1903; *s* of John Stewart Dethridge and Margaret Dethridge; *m* 1940, Ada Rosales Thomas; one *s* one *d*. *Educ*: Haileybury Coll.; Univ. of Melbourne. Appointed Judge of County Court, Victoria, Australia, 1946. *Recreations*: golf, swimming. *Address*: 61 South Road, Brighton, Victoria 3186, Australia. *T*: 925030.
[Died 8 Sept. 1978.

de TRAFFORD, Captain Sir Humphrey Edmund, 4th Bt, *cr* 1841; MC 1916; JP, DL late Coldstream Guards; *b* 30 Nov. 1891; *e s* of 3rd Bt and Violet (*d* 1925), *d* of late Capt. Franklin, 77th Regt; *S* father, 1929; *m* 1917, Hon. Cynthia Cadogan (*d* 1966), 3rd *d* of late Viscount Chelsea and Hon. Lady Meux; four *d*. *Educ*: Oratory Sch.; RMC Sandhurst. Served European War, 1914-18 (MC); a Steward of the Jockey Club, 1934, 1944 and 1951. JP 1944; DL 1946; High Sheriff 1945-46, Herts. *Heir*: *b* Rudolph de Trafford. *Address*: Newsells Park, Barkway, Royston, Herts.
[Died 6 Oct. 1971.

DEUTSCH, Dr John James, CC (Canada) 1969; Vanier Medal 1968; FRSC; Professor of Economics, Queen's University, Kingston, Ontario, since 1974; Member, Canada Council, since 1974; *b* 26 Feb. 1911; *s* of Carl and Elizabeth Deutsch; *m* 1940, Stephanie Frances Heaggerty; one *d*. *Educ*: Primary Sch., Quinton, Sask.; Campion Coll., Regina; Queen's Univ., Kingston (BCom). Research Asst, Bank of Canada, Ottawa, 1936; Dir of Research, Rowell-Sirois Commn, Ottawa, 1937; special wartime Asst to Under-Sec. of State for External Affairs, Dept of External Affairs, Ottawa, 1942; Mem. of Editorial Dept, Winnipeg Free Press, 1945; Dir, Internat. Economic Relations Div., Dept of Finance, Ottawa, 1946; Asst Dep. Minister of Finance, Ottawa, 1953; Sec. of Treasury Board, Govt of Canada, 1953; Head of Dept of Economics and Political Science, Univ. of British Columbia, 1956; Queen's Univ., Kingston: Vice-Princ. (Administration) and Prof. of Economics, 1959; Vice-Princ., 1962; Principal and Vice-Chancellor, 1968-74. Chm., Economic Council of Canada, 1963. Mem. Royal Commn on Newfoundland Finances, 1957; Chm., Royal Commn on Natural Gas Distribution of Greater Winnipeg, 1958; Industrial Inquiry Comr, Labour Dispute in the Forest Industry of BC, 1959; Econ. Adviser, Special Senate Cttee on Manpower and Employment, 1960; Chairman: Royal Commn on Higher Educn in New Brunswick, 1961; Adv. Cttee on Energy for Ontario, 1971; Cttee on impact and implications of fiscal constraints on hosp. employees; Trilevel Task Force on Public Finance, 1974; Univ. of New Brunswick at St John Review Cttee, 1974; Member: Special Commn of Inquiry into Unemployment Insce Act, 1961; Adv. Group on Executive Compensation in the Public Service, Ottawa, 1968; World Bank and IMF Cttee on Remuneration of Exec. Dirs; Royal Commn on Post-Secondary Educn, Ontario, 1962; J. W. Dafoe Foundn; Trustee Canada Studies Foundn; Special Adviser, Maritime Union Study, 1968; Member: Commn on Post-Secondary Educn in Ontario, 1969; Bd of Advisors, Energy Policy Project, Ford Foundn, 1972; Nat. Adv. Cttee on Northern Pipeline Financing, 1973; Ontario

Council on Univ. Affairs, 1974. Director: Canadian Imperial Bank of Commerce, 1967; International Nickel Co. of Canada Ltd, 1967; Alcan Aluminium Ltd, 1973; The Bell Foundation, 1973; F. P. Publications Ltd, 1973; Inst. for Res. on Public Policy, 1972; C. D. Howe Res. Inst.; Nat. Bd, Canadian Council of Christians and Jews; Associated Medical Services, 1974. Hon. Pres., Alma Mater Soc., Queen's Univ., 1974. Hon. LLD many Canadian univs. Vanier Medal, 1968; John Orr Award, Queen's Univ., 1969; Molson Prize, Canada Council, 1973; Montreal Medal, 1974. *Publications*: (jtly) The Canadian Economy: Selected Readings; (jtly) The American Economic Impact on Canada; (jtly) One Country or Two, 1971. *Address*: 223 Alwington Place, Kingston, Ontario, Canada. *Clubs*: Rideau (Ottawa); Cataraqui Golf and Country (Kingston).
[Died 18 March 1976.

de VALERA, Eamon; President of Ireland, 1959-73; Chancellor of National University of Ireland since 1921; *b* New York, USA, 14 Oct. 1882; *o c* of Vivion de Valéra (*b* Spain) and Catherine Coll (*b* Ireland); following his father's death was brought to Co. Limerick, as a child; *m* 1910, Sinéad Ni Fhlannagáin (*d* 1975); four *s* two *d* (and one *s* decd). *Educ*: Nat. Sch., Bruree; Christian Brothers' Sch., Rathluirc, Co. Cork; Blackrock Intermediate and University Colls, Dublin; grad. former RUI, postgrad. studies in that University in the NUI and in TCD. BA, BSc, HDip. in Ed. Secondary sch. teacher and Teachers' Training Coll. and Univ. lectr; for many years an active mem. of Gaelic League. Joined Irish Volunteers at foundn, 1913; OC 3rd Bn and Adj. Dublin Bde, Irish Volunteers, 1915-16, and Comdt in Irish National Uprising, Easter 1916; sentenced to death, commuted to penal servitude for life; released, Gen. Amnesty, June 1917; elected Sinn Féin MP, East Clare, 1917; President, Sinn Féin, 1917-26; Pres., Irish Volunteers, 1917-22; re-imprisoned, May 1918; escaped from Lincoln Gaol, Feb. 1919; Pres. of Irish Republic, 1919-22; visited the USA, seeking official recognition for Republic, 1919-20, and raised external loan of six million dollars for Irish Republican Government; rejected Anglo-Irish Treaty, Dec. 1921-Jan. 1922; founded Fianna Fáil, 1926; Pres. Fianna Fáil, 1926-59. Parly. rep for East Mayo 1918-21; MP for Down (N Ireland) 1921-29 and S Down (N Ireland), 1933-37; Leader of Opposition, IFS Parliament, 1927-32; Pres. Exec. Council IFS and Minister for External Affairs, 1932-37; introduced Constitution of Ireland Dáil Eireann, 1937; following enactment by the people, and coming into operation, of the new Constitution, became Taoiseach (Head of Government) and Minister for External Affairs in Government of Ireland, 1937-48, and Minister for Education, 1939-40; Leader of Opposition, Dáil Eireann, 1948-51 and 1954-57; Taoiseach again 1951-54 and 1957-59. Pres. of Council of League of Nations at its 68th and Special Sessions, Sept. and Oct. 1932; Pres. of Assembly of League of Nations, 1938. FRS 1968; Holds hon. degrees (LLD, PhD, ScD); MRIA; Hon. Bencher, Hon. Soc. of King's Inns; Hon. FRCSI. Decorations include: Grand Cross of: Order of Pius IX, 1933; Order of Charles, 1961; Supreme Order of Christ, 1962; Grand Cordon, Order of Leopold, 1968. *Address*: Talbot Lodge, Linden, Blackrock, Co. Dublin, Ireland. *[Died 29 Aug. 1975.*

de VAUX, Father Roland; Dominican; Dr Theol; Director of French-Biblical and Archæological School, Jerusalem, 1945-65; *b* 17 Dec. 1903. *Educ*: Paris. Prof., French Biblical and Archæological Sch., Jerusalem, 1933. Leader of Archæological Missions at Tell el Far'ah and Khirbet Qumrân; Co-dir of the Excavations in Jerusalem. Head of internat. team including Dead Sea Scrolls held in Jordan. Mem., Académie des Inscriptions et Belles Lettres, Paris; Hon. FSA; Corresp. FBA. Hon. DD: Dublin 1954; Louvain, 1964; Vienna, 1965; Hon. LLD, Aberdeen, 1964; Hon. DHL, Yale, 1965. *Publications*: La Genèse, 1951 (2nd edn 1962); Samuel, 1953 (2nd edn 1961); Rois, 2nd edn, 1959; Bible de Jérusalem; Les Institutions de l'Ancien Testament, I 1958, II 1960; Les Sacrifices de l'Ancien Testament, 1964; Studies in Old Testament Sacrifice, 1964; Bible et Orient, 1967; Histoire ancienne d'Israël, vol. I, 1971. *Address*: Ecole Biblique et Archéologique Française, POB 178, Jerusalem. *[Died 10 Sept. 1971.*

DEVENISH, Rev. Robert Cecil Silvester, MA; *b* 22 Nov. 1888; 3rd *s* of late Very Reverend R. J. S. Devenish, Dean of Cashel, Ireland; *m* 1923, Lily Darley, 2nd *d* of late Right Rev. W. R. Moore, Bishop of Kilmore, Elphin and Ardagh; two *d*. *Educ*: Midleton Coll.; Dublin University. Deacon, 1912; Priest, 1913; TCF, 1915-19; HCF, 1919; Chaplain Indian Ecclesiastical Establishment, 1919-43; Archdeacon of Lahore, 1934-40; Rector of St Paul's Naval and Garrison Church, Esquimalt, 1941-46; Chaplain of the Upper Chine Sch., Shanklin, I of W, 1946; Asst-Priest, St Mary Abbots Church, Kensington, W8, 1951-59; part-time help, Worplesdon, 1959-63. *Address*: Eastburn House, First Drive, Dawlish Road, Teignmouth, Devon. *[Died 23 Aug. 1973.*

DEVERS, Gen. Jacob Loucks; United States Army (retired); Chairman, American Battle Monuments Commission, 1959-69; *b* 8 Sept. 1887; *s* of Philip Kissinger Devers and Ella Kate Loucks; *m* 1st, 1911, George Hays Lyon (*decd*); one *d*; 2nd, 1975, Dorothy Cardwell Ham. *Educ:* York High Sch., York, Pa; US Military Academy, West Point, NY (BS 1909). Chief of Staff, Panama Canal Dept, 1939-40; Comdg Gen., 9th Infantry Division, 1940-41; Comdg Gen. of the Armored Force, 1941-43; Comdg Gen. European Theatre of Operations, US Army, 1943; Deputy Supreme Allied Comdr, Mediterranean Theatre, and Comdg Gen. North African Theatre of Operations, United States Army, 1944; commanded Sixth Army Group in France, 1944-45; Commanding General, Army Ground Forces, USA, 1945-48; Chief Army Field Forces, USA, 1948-49; retired from US Army, 1949. Managing Dir, AAA Foundation for Traffic Safety, Washington, DC, 1950; Technical Asst to Pres., Fairchild Engine and Airplane Corp., 1951-59. Chief Mil. Advr, UN Mission to India and Pakistan (concerning Kashmir), June-Dec. 1951. Dr *hc* Univ. of Nancy, 1945; Hon. LLD Williams Coll., 1946; Hon. DMS Norwich Univ., 1947; DHL York Coll., Pa, 1974. US Awards inc. Distinguished Service Medal with 2 Oak Leaf Clusters, Navy Distinguished Service Medal, and many campaign medals; George Catlett Marshall Medal, 1965; Benjamin F. Castle Meml Award, 1976; foreign awards inc. Hon. KCB, Grand Officer, Légion d'Honneur, etc. *Recreations:* polo, baseball, golf. *Address:* 1430 33rd Street, Northwest, Washington, DC 20007, USA. *Clubs:* Cosmos, Army-Navy (Washington, DC). 　　　　　　　　　　[*Died* 15 *Oct.* 1979.

DEVONPORT, 2nd Viscount, *cr* 1917, of Wittington, Bucks; **Gerald Chester Kearley;** Baron, *cr* 1910; 2nd Bt, *cr* 1908; *b* 16 Sept. 1890; *er s* of 1st Viscount and Selina (*d* 1931), *y d* of Edward Chester, Blisworth; *S* father, 1934; *m* 1938, Sheila Isabel, *e d* of Lieut-Col C. Hope Murray, Morishill, Beith, Ayrshire; one *s* one *d*. *Educ:* Eton; Exeter Coll., Oxford. War of 1914-18: RN Division; transf. to Scots Guards, 1916 (Lieut); seconded to Army Remount Services, France, 1917; War of 1939-45: Head Observer Royal Observer Corps; Bomb Reconnaissance Officer ARP Service. *Recreations:* travelling, shooting. *Heir: s* Hon. Terence Kearley [*b* 29 Aug. 1944; *m* 1968, Elizabeth Rosemary, *d* of J. G. Hopton]. *Address:* Peasmarsh Place, Sussex. *Clubs:* Carlton, Beefsteak, MCC; Sussex. 　　　　　　　　　　　　　　　[*Died* 29 *March* 1973.

De WAAL, Brig. Pieter, CB 1946; CBE 1944; *b* 31 Dec. 1899; *s* of Paul J. De Waal; *m* 1930, Isobel Peebles McLaggan; two *s*. *Educ:* Zeerust, Transvaal; Pretoria; Camberley Staff Coll. (psc); Imperial Defence Coll. (idc). BSc Transvaal University Coll. (University of South Africa), 1920. Commissioned in South African Permanent Force, 1922; OC SA Permanent Garrison Artillery, 1930-31; OC Cape Command, 1932; OC Roberts Heights Command, OC Special Service Battalion and Commandant Military Coll., 1933; Dir of Military Operations and Training, Defence Headquarters, 1934-39; UDF Liaison Officer on staff of GOC East Africa Command, 1940; Dep. Chief of Staff, Defence HQ, Pretoria, 1941-43; attached to SHAEF, 1944-45; Quartermaster-Gen. UDF, 1945-50; Naval and Marine Chief of Staff, UDF, 1951-52; Military and Naval Attaché to Union of South Africa Embassy, Washington, DC, USA, and Military, Air and Naval Adviser to High Commissioner for the Union of South Africa at Ottawa, Canada, 1953-54. Retd from R of O, S African Defence Forces, 1960. *Recreation:* woodwork. *Address:* Intaba, Wisteria Road, Claremont, Cape Province, South Africa. *Club:* Civil Service (Cape Town). 　　　　　　　　　　　　　　　[*Died* 23 *June* 1977.

DEWAR, Rev. Canon Lindsay, MA, BD; *b* 1891; *y s* of John Dewar, LRCP and S, Edinburgh; *m* 1926, Edith Marjorie (*d* 1968), *e d* of John William Hudson; one *s* one *d*. *Educ:* Westminster; King's Coll., London; Keble Coll., Oxford. Deacon, 1914; Priest, 1915; Asst Curate of Wimbledon, 1914-16; Temp. CF, 1916-18; lectr Bishops' Coll., Cheshunt, 1918-19; licensed preacher diocese of Oxford, 1919-21; Warden of St Anselm's Hall, Manchester, 1921-27; Vicar of St Marks, Witton, Blackburn, 1927-30; Canon of York Minster, 1930-35; Chancellor, 1933-35; Canon Missioner of Gloucester, 1935-37; Examining Chaplain to Archbishop of York, 1930-42; to Bishop of St Albans, 1954-55; Principal of Bishop's Coll., Cheshunt, 1937-55; Hon. Canon of St Albans, 1937-67; Canon Emeritus, 1967-; Rector of Much Hadham, 1955-67. *Publications:* Magic and Grace, 1929; (with C. E. Hudson) A Manual of Pastoral Psychology, 1932; Imagination and Religion, 1933; Man and God, 1935; Does God Care?, 1936; (with others) An Introduction to Pastoral Theology, 1937; (ed) Training in Prayer, 1937; What is the Purpose of Life?, 1938; Learning to Think, 1939; (with Phyllis Dent) Training in Worship, 1942; (with C. E. Hudson) Christian Morals, 1946; Psychology and the Parish Priest, 1949; Outline of New Testament Ethics, 1949;

The Moral Conduct of a Christian, 1951; The Holy Spirit and Modern Thought, 1959; Moral Theology in the Modern World, 1964; An Outline of Anglican Moral Theology, 1968. *Address:* c/o Mrs A. P. C. Pollard, Hazel Bank, 37 King's Road, Malvern Wells, Worcs WR14 4HL. *T:* Malvern 2261.
　　　　　　　　　　　　　　　[*Died* 29 *Oct.* 1976.

DEWAR, William McLachlan, CBE 1970 (OBE 1955); FRSE 1958; MA; Headmaster, George Heriot's School, Edinburgh, 1947-70; Director, Craigmyle (Scotland) Ltd, since 1971; *b* 19 April 1905; *s* of James McLachlan Dewar and Annie Kempie Cuthbert, Crieff; *m* 1935, Mary Sinclair, *d* of late John Anderson, Lerwick; two *s* one *d*. *Educ:* Morrison's Academy, Crieff; Edinburgh Univ.; Rome. MA 1928 (1st Cl. Classics), Vans Dunlop Scholar (Classics), 1927; John Edward Baxter Scholar, 1928. Asst Master, Aberdeen Grammar Sch., 1929-32; Senior Classics Master, Dumfries Academy, 1933-41; Rector, Greenock Academy, 1941-47. Commissioned RAF (VR), 1941; Mem. Scottish Air Cadet Council, 1948; Air Cadet Council, 1965-68. President: Scottish Schoolmasters' Assoc., 1944; Scottish Secondary Teachers' Assoc., 1947-49; Headmasters' Assoc. of Scotland, 1958-60; Member: Cttee on Grants to Students, 1958-60; Scottish Certificate of Education Examination Board, 1964-73; Scottish Council for Training of Teachers, 1959-67; Departmental Cttees on Secondary Sch. Curriculum, etc. Dir, Edinburgh Chamber of Commerce, 1964-67; Chm. Governors, Moray House Coll. of Education, 1958-71; Chm., City of Edinburgh Valuation Appeal Cttee, 1974-75; Dep. Chm., Lothian Valuation Appeal Panel, 1975-77. FRSA 1968. Hon. DLitt, Heriot-Watt, 1970. Chevalier des Palmes Académiques, 1961. *Publications:* The Law and The Teacher, 1955; numerous papers on classical and educational subjects. *Recreations:* study of puns; teacher politics; formerly hockey. *Address:* 35 Craiglockhart Grove, Edinburgh EH14 1ET. *T:* 031-443 3287. 　　　　　　　　　　　[*Died* 16 *Sept.* 1979.

de WATTEVILLE, John Edward, CBE 1946; JP; *b* 26 Jan. 1892; *s* of Walter de Watteville, MD, Kingussie; *m* 1922, Alexis Charlotte Margaret, *d* of Charles Bishop, London; two *d* (and one *s* killed in action 1945). *Educ:* Merchiston Castle; Edinburgh Univ. First Class Hons Classics, 1915. Served European War, 1914-18, Cameron Highlanders (Lieut), RFC and RAF (Flying Officer), 1915-19, wounded in France, 1917. Asst Principal, Scottish Office, 1919; Principal, 1921; Asst Sec., 1931; Under-Sec. (Scottish Home Dept), 1946; Dep. Sec., 1948; Sec. of Commissions for Scotland, 1953-66. JP City of Edinburgh, 1955. Croix de Guerre with Palm, 1917. *Address:* 12 Murrayfield Drive, Edinburgh EH12 6EB. *T:* 031-337 6674.
　　　　　　　　　　　　　　　[*Died* 4 *Jan.* 1976.

DEWEY, Cyril Marston; retired, 1969; Director and Deputy General Manager, Anchor Line Ltd, 1956-69; a Director, Walter Runciman & Co. Ltd, 1958-69; Shipping Adviser to Australian Commonwealth Government, 1949-51; *b* 28 Oct. 1907; *s* of late Marston Dewey and Lucie Cazaly; *m* 1935, Alicia P. Maldonado; two *d*. *Educ:* Streatham Grammar Sch. Asst Manager: Blue Star Line, Buenos Aires, 1935-45; Blue Star Line Ltd, London, 1946-49; Gen. Manager, Australian Shipping Board, 1951-55. *Recreation:* golf. *Address:* 1028 Preverenges, Switzerland. 　　　　　　　　　　　　[*Died* 9 *Sept.* 1973.

DEWEY, Thomas Edmund; Partner, Dewey, Ballantine, Bushby, Palmer and Wood, since 1955; *b* 24 March 1902; *s* of George Martin Dewey and Annie Thomas; *m* 1928, Frances E. Hutt (*d* 1970); two *s*. *Educ:* Univ. of Michigan (AB 1923); Columbia Univ., New York (LLB 1925). Admitted to New York Bar, 1926; Chief Asst US Attorney, Southern District of NY, 1931-33; US Attorney, 1933; private practice, 1934-35; Counsel Assoc. of Bar for removal of Municipal Court Judge, 1934; Special Asst Attorney-Gen. of US in special matters, 1934-45; Special Prosecutor Investigation of Organised Crime, New York, 1935-37; District Attorney, New York County, 1938-41; Governor of New York, 1942-54. Republican candidate for Presidency of US, 1944, 1948. Trustee of various charities. Holds numerous honorary degrees. *Publications:* Case Against the New Deal, 1940; Journey to the Far Pacific, 1952; Thomas E. Dewey on the Two Party System; contributor to magazines. *Address:* 141 East 72nd Street, New York, USA; Pawling, NY, USA. *Clubs:* Recess, Downtown, Links, Blindbrook, Indian Creek, City Mid Day, Augusta National, Quaker Hill (USA).
　　　　　　　　　　　　　　　[*Died* 16 *March* 1971.

DEWING, Maj.-Gen. Maurice Nelson, CB 1950; CBE 1944; DSO 1943; MC 1918; late Royal Artillery; *b* 11 Nov. 1896; *s* of late Rev. R. S. Dewing, Stowlangtoft, Bury St Edmunds, Suffolk; *m* 1921, Sheila, *d* of late E. R. Hawkins, JP, Squires Hill, Tilford, Surrey; two *s* (and one *s* decd). *Educ:* Malvern Coll.; RMA, Woolwich. Served European War, 1914-18, with

RA, 2nd Lieut, 1915; France and Belgium (MC, 1914-15 Star, two medals); War of 1939-45, in Middle East and Italy (despatches, DSO, CBE); Temp. Brigadier, 1942; Lt-Col, 1943; Col, 1946; Maj.-Gen., 1948; GOC 2nd AA Group, 1948-51; retired pay, 1951. *Address:* Tulse Hill, Zeals, Wiltshire.
[Died 3 Jan. 1976.

d'EYNCOURT, Sir (Eustace) Gervais T.; *see* Tennyson d'Eyncourt.

DE ZOYSA, Sir Cyril, Kt 1955; Proctor of the Supreme Court, Justice of the Peace and Unofficial Magistrate; *b* 26 Oct. 1897. *Educ:* Royal College, Ceylon. Chm. and Gov. Dir, Associated Motorways Group of Cos; Chairman: Sri Lanka Asbestos Products Ltd; Ceylon Synthetic Textiles Ltd; Usha Industries (Ceylon) Ltd; President: Young Men's Buddhist Assoc.; Ceylon Nat. Assoc. for the Prevention of Tuberculosis; Maha Bodhi Soc. of Ceylon; Managing Trustee, Kalutara Bodhi Trust; Vice-Pres., All Ceylon Buddhist Congress. Dep. Pres. of the Ceylon Senate, 1952-55, Pres., 1955-62. Pres., Incorporated Law Soc. of Ceylon, 1956-62; Mem., Council of Legal Educn, 1956-. *Recreation:* cricket (Royal College, Colombo, etc). *Address:* Park Flats, Park Street, Colombo 2, Sri Lanka. *T:* Colombo 22478. *Clubs:* Sinhalese Sports (Trustee and Vice-Pres.), Kalutara Town (Sri Lanka). *[Died 2 Jan. 1978.*

DIAMOND, Arthur Sigismund, MM 1918; Master of the Supreme Court, Queen's Bench Division, 1952-69; *b* 23 Dec. 1897; *s* of Rev. S. and Mrs Diamond, Leeds; *m* 1st, 1928, Gladys Elkah (*d* 1946), *d* of Edward Lumbrozo Mocatta: one *s* two *d*; 2nd, 1952, Sybil Grace, *d* of Edward Lumbrozo Mocatta. *Educ:* Leeds Grammar Sch.; Trinity Coll., Cambridge (MA, LLD). Called to the Bar, 1921. *Publications:* The Law of Master and Servant, 1st edn 1932; Primitive Law, 1st edn 1935; The Evolution of Law and Order, 1951; The History and Origin of Language, 1959; Primitive Law, Past and Present, 1971. FRAI. *Recreation:* gardening. *Address:* 9 Bracknell Gardens, NW3. *T:* 01-435 4201; Newhouse, Church Lane, Ripe, near Lewes. *T:* Ripe 449. *[Died 1 March 1978.*

DIBDEN, Commissioner Edgar; Chief of the Staff (Second-in-Command) of The Salvation Army, 1953-57; *b* 4 Dec. 1888; *s* of Henry and Frances Dibden; *m* 1914, Helena Bennett; one *s*. *Educ:* Grammar Sch.; The Salvation Army Training Coll., London. Salvation Army Officer, 1910. Formerly Vice-Chm. Salvation Army Trustee Co. Vice-President: Salvation Army Assurance Soc. Ltd; Reliance Bank Ltd; Salvation Army Fire Insurance Corp. Ltd; Salvationist Publishing & Supplies Ltd. Has held important administrative and financial positions in The Salvation Army; formerly: ADC to Gen. George Carpenter; Chancellor of the Exchequer of The Salvation Army. *Address:* 52 Village Way, Beckenham, Kent. *T:* Beckenham 3215.
[Died 10 Feb. 1971.

DIBLE, James Henry, LLD; MB, ChB (Glasgow); FRCP; FCPath; late Director, Department of Pathology, British Post-Graduate Medical School, 1937-57; Professor Emeritus, London University, 1955; *s* of Samuel Dible, Southampton, and Ellen Bell, Itchen; *m* Marjorie Yeo, *d* of S. J. Allen, Strines, Derbyshire; two *s* one *d*. *Educ:* King Edward VI School, Southampton; Glasgow Univ.; Hons graduate in medicine, 1912. Lieut RAMC, 1914 (1914-15 star); Capt. RAMC, 1915; Commanded No. 7 Mobile Laboratory, 1915-18, in French and Italian theatres of War (Czecho-Slovak Military Medal, 1st Class). George Holt Prof. of Pathology, Liverpool Univ., 1929-37; late Pres. Institute of Medical Laboratory Technology and Sims Woodhead Medallist; Humphrey Davy Rolleston Lecturer, RCP; Pres., Internat. Soc. of Geographical Pathology, 1961-63. Hon. Fellow: Royal Soc. of Medicine, 1962; Coll. of Pathology, 1967. Hon. LLD Glasgow, 1954. *Publications:* Recent Advances in Bacteriology, 3rd edn 1951 (with J. D. Maclennan); Pathology, 3rd edn 1950; Peripheral Vascular Disorders (with others), 1956; The Pathology of Limb Ischaemia, 1967; Napoleon's Surgeon, 1970; various papers in scientific and medical journals. *Address:* Nettleton House, Gerrard's Cross, Bucks. *T:* Gerrard's Cross 82692.
[Died 1 July 1971.

DIBLE, James Kenneth Victor; *b* 24 May 1890; *y s* of late William and Margaret Anne Dible, Bitterne Park, Southampton; *m* 1st, 1914, Muriel McQuade (decd); 2nd, Mabel Louise, *widow* of Rev. A. H. Hildesley, KIH (1st Class), MA. *Educ:* Haileybury Coll.; RMC Camberley. Entered Army 1909; retd, 1919, on appointment to HM Consular Service; Probationer Vice-Consul at Algiers, 1919; Vice-Consul, 1921; Acting Consul-Gen. there, 1921-22; transferred to Strasbourg, 1922; Acting Consul-Gen. there in 1922, and also in each year from 1924 to 1927; in charge of Vice-Consulate at Lima, 1927;

definitely transferred there, 1928; Acting Consul at Callao, 1928; Consul at Lima, 1928; acted as Chargé d'Affaires in 1929; transferred to Lille, 1930, and to Oporto, 1936; Consul-Gen. at Amsterdam, 1938; transferred to Bordeaux, 1939; seconded to Home Office, 1940-41; to Board of Trade, 1942-44; promoted Consul-Gen., attached Supreme Headquarters, Allied Expeditionary Force (with rank of Maj.-Gen.), 1944-45; Consul-Gen. at Valparaiso, 1945-50, retired 1950. *Address:* The Cottage, Buckden, Huntingdon PE18 9TF. *T:* Huntingdon 810347. *[Died 13 Dec. 1976.*

DIBLE, William Cuthbert, CIE 1938; late ICS; *b* 18 June 1886; *s* of William Dible, Southampton; *m* 1926, Florence H. B. Johnson (*d* 1948), Culpepper, Va, USA; *m* 1949, Dorothy Lings, Didsbury, Lancs. *Educ:* Charterhouse; Corpus Christi Coll., Oxford. Entered ICS 1910, as Asst Magistrate and Collector, United Provinces; served as Magistrate and Collector; Divisional Commissioner, 1934-42; Mem. Board of Revenue, United Provinces, India, 1942-45; Chm., Road-Lands Enquiry Cttee, War Transport Dept, Government of India; retired, 1946. *Address:* Cotton Wood, East Cliff, Bournemouth, Hants. *T:* Bournemouth 23352. *[Died 6 March 1971.*

DICKENS, Air Commodore Thomas Charles, CB 1955; CBE 1946; RAF retired; *b* 11 March 1906; *s* of T. J. Dickens; *m* 1936, Joyce Muriel Adamson; two *s*. *Educ:* Hymers Coll. Cadet Coll., Cranwell, 1925-26; Engineering Course, Henlow, 1931-33; Staff Coll., Andover, 1938. Served War of 1939-45 (despatches twice): Advanced Air Striking Force, 1939-40; Chief Engineer, RCAF Eastern Air Command, 1942-43; Bomber Command Stations, 1944-45; Staff of Officers' Advanced Training Sch., 1946-47. SASO N1 (B) Group, 1948-49; Air War Coll., USA, 1950; A/AOA, Fighter Command, 1951; idc 1952; Asst Chief of Staff, Logistics (Aircent), Fontainebleau, 1953-56; General Manager, Hong Kong Aircraft Engineering Co. Ltd, 1956-61; Rolls Royce Aero Engine Div., Derby, 1962-71. Congressional Silver Life Saving Medal (USA), 1950. *Address:* Kelso Cottage, Sion Road, Bath. *Clubs:* Royal Air Force; Hong Kong.
[Died 11 Jan. 1972.

DICKEY, Edward Montgomery O'Rorke, CBE 1952; MA; Hon. FRCA; *b* Belfast, 1894; *s* of Edward O'Rorke Dickey and Emily Monteith; *m* 1922, Eunice Howard (*d* 1976); one *s*. *Educ:* Wellington; Trinity Coll., Cambridge. Served War of 1914-18 in RGA. Art Master, Oundle, 1924-26; Prof. of Fine Art and Dir of the King Edward VII Sch. of Art, King's Coll., University of Durham, 1926-31; Staff Inspector for Art, Ministry of Education, 1931-57; first Curator of the Minories, Colchester (Victor Batte-Lay Trust), 1957-62. *Publications:* The Isle of Pheasants, 1926; A Picture Book of British Art, 1931; Industry and Art Education on the Continent (with W. M. Keesey), 1934. *Address:* Crossways Residential Home, 86 Hookham's Lane, Renhold, Bedford. *[Died 12 Aug. 1977.*

DICKINS, Bruce, MA Cantab; Hon. LittD Manchester; Hon. DLitt Edinburgh; FBA 1959; Elrington and Bosworth Professor of Anglo-Saxon, Cambridge University, Jan. 1946-Sept. 1957, since when Emeritus Professor; Fellow of Corpus Christi College, since 1946; *b* 26 Oct. 1889; *e s* of Henry Everard and Constance Dickins, Nottingham; *m* Mary Geraldine (*d* 1975), *e d* of late Sir Herbert J. C. Grierson; one *s* one *d*. *Educ:* Nottingham High Sch.; Magdalene College, Cambridge (Scholar). 2nd Class (Div. 1) History Tripos, Pt 1; 1st Class, Mediæval and Modern Languages Tripos; Allen Scholar. Acted for two years as Censor in War Office; served as 2nd Lieut, Hampshire Regt; Capt. on staff of Leeds Group and Sector, Home Guard, 1940-43; Lecturer, 1919-25, and Reader, 1925-31, in English Language, Edinburgh Univ.; Professor of English Language, Leeds Univ., 1931-45; sometime Donaldson Bye-Fellow for Research of Magdalene Coll., Cambridge; Pres. Yorks Soc. for Celtic Studies, 1936-38; Pres. Viking Soc., 1938-39; Pres. John Mason Neale Soc., 1952-57; Pres. Cambridge Antiquarian Soc., 1953-55. Sandars Reader in Bibliography, 1968-69. Sir Israel Gollancz Memorial Prize (British Academy), 1955. *Publications:* Runic and Heroic Poems of the Old Teutonic Peoples, 1916, 1968; Robert Henryson, The Testament of Cresseid, 1925; Scots Poems by Robert Fergusson, 1925; The Runic Inscriptions of Maeshowe, 1930; The Dream of the Rood (with Alan S. C. Ross), 1934; The Conflict of Wit and Will, 1937; John Mitchell Kemble and Old English Scholarship, 1940; (jointly) The Place-names of Cumberland, 1950-52; (with R. M. Wilson) Early Middle English Texts, 1951; Henry, First Duke of Lancaster, 1966; (with Alfred Fairbank) The Italic Hand in Tudor Cambridge, 1962; Two Kembles, 1974; contribs to various linguistic, literary, bibliographical, and archæological jls; Jt Editor, Leeds Studies in English and Kindred Languages, 1932-40; Editor, Yorkshire Celtic Studies, 1938-40; Dir and Gen. Editor, English Place-Name Soc., 1946-51; Pres.

Cambridge Bibliographical Soc., 1951-57, and Jt Editor of its Transactions, 1949-68. *Address:* c/o Hilton Hall, Hilton, Huntingdon, Cambs PE18 9NG. *T:* Papworth St Agnes 417.
[Died 4 Jan. 1978.

DICKINS, Brig. Frederick, CIE 1936; *b* 25 Nov. 1879; *s* of F. V. Dickins, CB; *m* 1st, 1906, Florence Mackay (*d* 1949); two *s*; 2nd, 1949, Audrey May Adam (*d* 1950). *Educ:* St Paul's Sch.; Scoones's. 2nd Lieut RA 1900; Indian Ordnance Dept, 1906; DADOS 2nd Indian Cavalry Div., France, 1914-16; Chief Ordnance Officer, Aden Field Force, 1918-19 (despatches); ADOS, AHQ, India, 1929; Dir of Ordnance Services, AHQ, India, 1935-36; retired 1936; Non-Intervention Board, Spain (Gibraltar), 1938; HM Consul at Cadiz, 1939; Censorship Dept, Sept. 1939; Min. of Economic Warfare, 1940-41; Schoolmaster, 1943-46. *Address:* c/o National & Grindlays Bank, 13 St James's Square, SW1.
[Died 11 Feb. 1975.

DICKINSON, Arthur Harold, CMG 1946; OBE 1938; KPM 1928; *b* 5 Oct. 1892; *s* of late Walter Dickinson, formerly of Leighton Hall, Caversham, and of Mary Mechan; *m* 1920, Ethel Constance Kitchen (*d* 1961); one *s* one *d. Educ:* Bromsgrove Sch. Cadet, Colonial Police Service, 1912; served in Straits Settlements; Inspector-Gen. of Police, Straits Settlements, 1939, and in addition Civil Security Officer, Malaya; Prisoner of War in Singapore, Feb. 1942-Aug. 1945; retired Nov. 1946. *Address:* The Old Kennels, Motcombe, near Shaftesbury, Dorset.
[Died 23 Nov. 1978.

DICKSON, Bonner William Arthur, CBE 1953; a Governor of the College of Aeronautics, since 1953; *b* 1887; *s* of Francis George Dickson; *m* 1915, Harriet Olive (*d* of Samuel Turney Johnson; (one *s* decd). Sometime Dir and Gen. Manager, Vickers-Armstrongs Ltd. (Aircraft Section); Acting Principal, Coll. of Aeronautics, Cranfield, July 1954-Sept. 1955. Hon. DSc Cranfield Inst. of Technology, 1973. *Address:* 70 Rivermead Court, Hurlingham, SW6. *Club:* Hurlingham.
[Died 6 April 1976.

DICKSON, Air Vice-Marshal Edward Dalziel, CB 1953; CBE 1946; RAF (Medical Branch), Retired; MD, FRCSE; Hon. Civilian Consultant in Oto-Laryngology to the Royal Air Force since 1955; *b* 10 Feb. 1895; *s* of late Dr E. D. Dickson, Physician, HBM Embassy, Constantinople; *m* 1st, Ethel Sinclair (*d* 1974), *d* of J. E. Grey, Pres. Royal College of Veterinary Surgeons, Edinburgh; one *s*; 2nd, 1975, Doris Muriel McGregor Millar, *d* of G. Millar, MC, FRCSE. *Educ:* privately; Edinburgh Univ.; London; Paris. MD (Edinburgh) 1951; MB, ChB (Edinburgh) 1918; FRCSE 1922; DLO RCPS Eng. 1925. Served European War, 1914-18, Capt. RAMC; ENT Specialist, 1918-22, Salonika, Serbia, Turkey. Hon. Aural Surg. British Hosp. (82nd Gen.), Constantinople, 1922; late Asst OP Dept, Central London Throat, Nose and Ear Hosp. Joined RAF 1923; Sqdn Ldr 1929; Wing Comdr 1935; Group Capt. 1940; Air Commodore, 1947; Air Vice-Marshal, 1951. KHS, 1948-52; QHS 1952-55. Senior Consultant, RAF, 1951-55. Consultant in Oto-Laryngology, RAF, 1938-55. FRSM (Pres. Section of Otology, 1952-53); Life Mem. Scottish Oto-Laryngological Soc.; Mem. Otological Sub-Cttee, Flying Personnel Research Cttee, and Life Member: British Assoc. of Oto-Laryngologists; British Soc. of Audiology; Pres., Royal Nat. Inst. for the Deaf, 1975- (Chm., 1960-71). Pres., IX Internat. Congress in Audiology, London, 1968. Sir William Dalby Prize in Otology, Royal Society of Medicine (jointly); Silver Medal for Distinguished Service (Serbia), 1920; Medal of Merit 1st Class (Czecho-Slovakia), 1946. *Publications:* contrib. to Aviation Oto-Laryngology (jointly), 1947; chapter on intense sound and ultrasound, in Industrial Medicine and Hygiene, Vol. II, 1954; numerous papers and reports on aviation otology and rhinology in learned journals. *Recreations:* gardening, music, conjuring. *Address:* 15 Frogston Road East, Liberton, Edinburgh EH17 8AB. *T:* 031-664 2573. *Clubs:* Royal Air Force, Savage; Magic Circle; University Union (Edinburgh).
[Died 14 April 1979.

DICKSON WRIGHT, Arthur; *see* Wright, A. D.

DIEDERICHS, Hon. Dr Nicolaas, DMS; State President of the Republic of South Africa, since 1975; *b* 17 Nov. 1903; *s* of Adriaan Petrus Johannes Diederichs; *m* 1932, Margaretha Jacoba Potgieter; one *s* two *d. Educ:* Boshof High Sch.; Grey Univ. Coll.; Univs of Munich, Cologne, Berlin and Leiden, MA, DLitt et DPhil. MP: Randfontein, 1948-58; Losberg, 1958-74; Overvaal, 1974-75. Minister of Econ. Affairs, 1958-67, of Mines, 1961-64, of Finance, 1967-75. Former Chm., Economic Inst.; Decimal Coinage Commn. Chancellor, Randse Afrikaanse Universiteit, 1968. Hon. DCom, Univ. of OFS, 1971; Hon. DComm: Stellenbosch, 1973; Randse Afrikaanse, 1976; Pretoria, 1976. Hon. Citizen, New Orleans; Freeman of several S

African cities and towns. Kt Grand Cross, Order of Merit, Italy; Grand Cross, Order of Merit, Paraguay. *Publications:* Vom Leiden und Dulden; Die Volkebond; Nasionalisme as Lewensbeskouing; Die Kommunisme; numerous articles and brochures. *Recreations:* reading, golf. *Address:* State President's Residence, Pretoria, Republic of South Africa.
[Died 21 Aug. 1978.

DIEFENBAKER, Rt. Hon. John (George), PC 1957; PC (Can.) 1957; CH 1976; QC; MP; LLD, DCL and LittD (Hon.); Doctor of Humanities (Hon.); Doctor of Sacred Letters (Hon.); FRSC; MP for Prince Albert, Sask., since Aug. 1953 (Lake Centre, 1940-53); lawyer; Leader of Canadian Progressive Conservative Party, Dec. 1956-Sept. 1967; Leader of HM Loyal Opposition, Parliament of Canada, during Spring 1957, and again April 1963-Sept. 1967; Prime Minister of Canada, June 1957-April 1963; *b* Grey County, Ont., 18 Sept. 1895; *s* of William Thomas Diefenbaker and Mary Florence (*née* Bannerman); *m* 1st, 1929, Edna Brower (*d* 1950); 2nd, 1953, Olive Evangeline, LLD, DCL (*d* 1976), *d* of Rev. Dr C. B. Freeman; one step *d. Educ:* Univ. of Saskatchewan, Saskatoon. BA 1915, MA 1916, in Political Science; served overseas with 196th Bn, as a Lieut, invalided 1917; LLB 1919, University of Saskatchewan. Called to the Bar of Saskatchewan, 1919; KC 1929; QC (Ont.) 1960. Admitted to Bars of Ontario, Alberta and BC; Hon. Bencher: Gray's Inn; Law Society of Upper Canada; Law Soc. of Saskatchewan; Hon. Mem., Illustre Nacional Colegio de Abogados (Mexico). Private practice or in partnerships (senior partner), Prince Albert, from 1919. Mem. of Council of Canadian Bar Association Saskatchewan (Vice-Pres., 1939-42; became Hon. Life Mem., 1957). Contested (Conservative) Prince Albert, 1925, 1926; elected MP Lake Centre, 1940. Chm. of first British Commonwealth Conf., at which Delegates from Congress of US attended, Ottawa, 1943; attended UN Assembly, as Adviser to Progressive Conservative Representative on Canadian Delegn, San Francisco, 1945; Mem. Canadian Delegn of Empire Parliamentary Assoc. in Bermuda and in Washington, DC, 1946; Mem. Canadian Delegn to Commonwealth Parl. Assoc. in New Zealand and Australia, 1950; Mem. Canadian Delegn to UN, 1952; Mem. Canadian Delegn to NATO Parliamentary Assoc., 1955. Minister in Attendance on the Queen, during her visit to N America, 1957; accompanied her on visit to Chicago, Royal Tour of 1959. Leader of Canadian Delegn to Conf. of Commonwealth Prime Ministers, London, 1957, 1960, 1961, 1962. Made World Tour of Commonwealth and NATO countries, 1958. Hon. Col. North Saskatchewan Regt, Royal Canadian Inf. Corps; Hon. Freeman, City of London, 1963. Hon. Chief: Cree Indians (Chief Great Eagle); Sioux (Chief Walking Buffalo); Kainai Chieftains (Chief Many Spotted Horses). 33°. Scottish Rite Mason. Chancellor, Univ. of Saskatchewan, 1968-. Holds 35 hon. degrees from universities and colleges both in Canada and abroad. Hon. FRSC; FRAIC. *Publications:* One Canada, vol. I, 1976, vol. II, 1977, vol. III, 1978. *Address:* House of Commons, Ottawa, Canada.
[Died 16 Aug. 1979.

DIGGLE, Rev. Reginald Fraser, CBE 1946; MC; MA; Hon. CF; *b* 18 June 1889; *s* of John William and Edith Diggle. *Educ:* Marlborough; Merton Coll., Oxford. Ordained, 1913; Domestic Chaplain to Bishop of Carlisle, 1913-14; Curate of St Martin's, Birmingham, 1914-15; Temp. Chaplain to Forces, 1918-19; Sec. and Domestic Chaplain to Bishop of Carlisle, 1915-20; Curate of St John's, Great Yarmouth, 1921-25; Rector of St Clement's, Worcester, 1925-37; Rural Dean of Worcester, 1932-37; Private Chaplain to Bishop of Worcester, 1934; Examining Chaplain to Bishop of Worcester, 1937; Hon. Canon of Worcester, 1936-69; Vicar of St Giles's, Oxford, 1937-60. Chaplain RAFVR, 1940-46; Asst Chaplain in Chief, RAF India, 1942-46. *Recreation:* gardening. *Address:* 55 Osler Road, Headington, Oxford. *T:* Oxford 61694.
[Died 21 Jan. 1975.

DILHORNE, 1st Viscount *cr* 1964, of Green's Norton; **Reginald Edward Manningham-Buller;** Baron, 1962; Bt, 1866; PC 1954; Kt 1951; DL; a Lord of Appeal in Ordinary, 1969-80; *b* 1 Aug. 1905; *o s* of Lt-Col Sir Mervyn Manningham-Buller, 3rd Bt; *S* to father's Baronetcy, 1956; *m* 1930, Lady Mary Lilian Lindsay, 4th *d* of 27th Earl of Crawford, KT, PC; one *s* three *d. Educ:* Eton; Magdalen Coll., Oxford. BA 1926. Called to Bar, Inner Temple, 1927. KC 1946. MP (C) Daventry Div. of Northamptonshire, 1943-50, and for South Northants, 1950-62. Parliamentary Sec. to Min. of Works, May-Aug. 1945; Mem., Rushcliffe Cttee on Legal Aid, 1944-45; Mem., Parliamentary Delegn to USSR, 1945, and Anglo-American Cttee on Palestine, 1946. Solicitor Gen., 1951-54; Attorney-Gen., Oct. 1954-July 1962; Lord High Chancellor of Great Britain, 1962-64. Recorder of Kingston-upon-Thames, Jan.-July 1962. Hon. DCL, South Methodist Univ., Dallas, Texas; Hon. LLD, McGill Univ., Canada. DL, Northants, 1967. *Heir: s* Hon. John Mervyn

Manningham-Buller, late Coldstream Guards [*b* 28 Feb. 1932; *m* 1955, Gillian Evelyn (marr. diss. 1973), *d* of Col George Stockwell; two *s* one *d*]. *Address:* 6 King's Bench Walk, Temple, EC4. *T:* 01-583 5836; Horninghold Manor, near Market Harborough, Leicestershire. *T:* Hallaton 641. *Clubs:* Pratt's, Buck's. *[Died 7 Sept.* 1980.

DILL-RUSSELL, Patrick Wimberley, CBE 1956; Chief Medical Adviser, Foreign and Commonwealth Office, Overseas Development Administration, 1971-73; retired; *b* 7 April 1910; *s* of John Dill-Russell, FRCS and Charlotte Evangeline Wimberley; *m* 1950, Vera Gorzeff; one *d. Educ:* Eltham Coll.; Manchester Grammar Sch.; Reading Univ.; London Univ.; St Thomas' Hospital. MRCS, LRCP 1935; FRSH. District Medical Officer, Cyprus, 1938-39; war service RAMC, Western Desert and Burma (despatches twice), 1939-44 (Major); Asst DMS Cyprus, 1947-50; DDMS Nyasaland, 1950-52; DMS Cyprus, 1952-56; DMS Fiji and Inspector-General S Pacific Health Service, 1956-62; Dep. Medical Adviser (title later changed to Medical Adviser) to Dept of Technical Co-operation, later Min. of Overseas Develt, now FCO (ODA), 1962-71. CStJ 1967. *Recreations:* reading, riding, fishing. *Address:* Flat 3, 42 Marryat Road, Wimbledon Common, SW19 5BD. *T:* 01-946 6935. *Club:* Naval and Military. *[Died 5 Aug.* 1977.

DILLON, 20th Viscount *cr* 1622; **Michael Eric Dillon;** Count in France, *cr* 1711; local Lt-Col retired, RHG; *b* 13 Aug. 1911; *o s* of 19th Viscount, and Juanita (*d* 1962), *d* of Brig.-Gen. Charles Edward Beckett, CB; *S* father, 1946; *m* 1939, Irène Marie France, *y d* of René Merandon du Plessis, Whitehall, Mauritius; four *s* three *d* (and one *d* decd). *Educ:* Eton; RMC Sandhurst. 2nd Lieut 15/19th Hussars, 1931; seconded to Transjordan Frontier Force, 1935; Lieut RHG, 1937; Capt., 1939; Major, 1946; retired, 1952. Knight of the Sovereign Order of Malta; Officer of Order of Orange-Nassau (Netherlands). *Heir: s* Hon. Charles Henry Robert Dillon [*b* 18 Jan. 1945; *m* 1972, Jane, *d* of John Young, Birtle, Lancs; one *s* one *d. Educ:* Downside; RMA Sandhurst; Royal College of Art, Kensington]. *Address:* Rath House, Termonfeckin, Drogheda, Co. Louth, Ireland. *Clubs:* Cavalry and Guards; Kildare Street and University (Dublin). *[Died 30 Nov.* 1979.

DILLON, Thomas; Professor of Chemistry, University College, Galway, 1919-54; *b* Inniscrone, Co. Sligo, 1884; *s* of late J. B. Dillon, Ballina, Co. Mayo, and Elizabeth Sullivan; *m* 1916, Geraldine, *d* of Count Plunkett; two *s* three *d. Educ:* Clongowes Wood Coll.; Queen's (now Univ.) Coll., Cork; RCS, Dublin. MA NUI, 1908; DSc 1910; ScD Dublin (*hc*) 1954; MRIA; Pres., Inst. of Chemistry of Ireland for 1954-56. Asst to Prof. of Chemistry, University Coll., Dublin, 1909-19. Mem. Executive Council, Sinn Fein, 1917-22 (Hon. Sec. 1917). *Publications:* papers on chemical subjects in Proc. Royal Dublin Soc. and RIA, and other scientific jls. *Address:* 13 Marlborough Road, Donnybrook, Dublin. *T:* Dublin 680365. *[Died 11 Dec.* 1971.

DILLWYN-VENABLES-LLEWELYN; *see* Venables-Llewelyn.

DILWORTH-HARRISON, Ven. Talbot; Archdeacon of Chesterfield Emeritus and Vicar of Edingley with Halam, Newark, since 1963; *b* 5 July 1886; *s* of James and Louisa Dilworth-Harrison; unmarried. *Educ:* Dean Close, Cheltenham; Keble Coll., Oxford; Cuddesdon. Lecturer S Boniface Coll., Warminster, 1907-08; Asst Curate S Mary's, Prestwich, 1909-17; Vicar of Ringley, Lancs, 1917-27; Vicar of S Bartholomew's, Brighton, 1927-34; Commissary to: Bishop of Trinidad, 1922-58; Archbishop of Brisbane, 1935-43; Bishop of Accra, 1936; Examining Chaplain to Bishop of Derby, 1934-63; Archdeacon, Vicar and Lecturer of Chesterfield, 1934-63. *Publications:* Three Centuries of a Village Sanctuary; A Scrapbook of Prayer; Everyman's Story of the Oxford Movement; The Catholic Faith and this Generation; Every Boy's/Girl's Confirmation Book; John Bull Considers his Church; Everyman's Confirmation Book. *Address:* Halam Vicarage, Newark, Notts.
[Died 16 May 1975.

DIMOLINE, Hon. Brig. Harry Kenneth, CBE 1943 (MBE 1938); DSO 1942; TD; CPM 1955; *b* 6 Sept. 1903; British; *s* of late C. A. F. Dimoline; *m* 1928, Amy Sybil Heap; one *s* one *d. Educ:* Sedbergh. Formed 68 Med. Regt, RA, 1939; campaigns: Eritrea, Western Desert, Alamein, Tripoli, Tunis, Italy, Burma (despatches four times, DSO, CBE); CRA 4 Indian Div., 1942-44 (Divisional Comdr, 1944); CRA 47 (London) Inf. Div., 1944; CRA 17 Indian Div. SEAC, Nov. 1944. Chief Commandant Malayan Police Volunteer Reserve, 1949-57. Colonial Police Medal, 1955. *Recreation:* riding. *Address:* High Compton, Donhead St Andrew, Shaftesbury, Dorset.
[Died 15 Nov. 1972.

DIMSDALE, Mrs Helen Easdale, FRCP; Neurologist, Royal Free Hospital, 1950-70, retired; Hon. Consultant Physician, Maida Vale Hospital (National Hospitals); *b* 2 July 1907; *m* 1930, Wilfrid Hampden Dimsdale; one *s. Educ:* Hayes Court, Kent; Girton Coll., Cambridge; UCH, London. MA Cl. I Nat. Sci. Tripos I, 1929; MD Cantab 1946; FRCP 1949. Resident appointments, University Coll. Hosp.; Medical Registrar, Elizabeth Garrett Anderson Hosp., 1938; Med. Registrar, 1940, and Neuropathologist, 1942, Maida Vale Hosp. for Nervous Diseases; First Asst, Dept of Neurology, London Hosp., 1942. Late Neurologist and Physician, Elizabeth Garrett Anderson Hosp., 1946; late Tutor in Medicine, Royal Free Hosp. Sch. of Med., 1952. Member: Assoc. of British Neurologists; Assoc. of Physicians. *Publications:* section on Diseases of the Nervous System, The Practice of Medicine (ed. J. S. Richardson Churchill), 1956; chapter (Acute Encephalomyelitis of Virus Origin) in Modern Trends in Neurology 2nd series (ed. D. Williams), 1957; contribs to medical periodicals. *Address:* Herons, 49 Firs Chase, West Mersea, Colchester CO5 8NN. *T:* West Mersea 2979. *[Died 20 April* 1977.

DIMSDALE, Sir John Holdsworth, 3rd Bt *cr* 1902; *b* 31 Dec. 1901; *s* of 2nd Bt and Edith Kate (*d* 1911), *d* of late John Connacher; *S* father, 1923; *m* 1949, Gisela Panova (*d* 1969); *m* 1975, Mrs A. E. G. Cleaton, Ryde, Isle of Wight. *Address:* 16 Willis Road, Swaythling, Southampton S02 2NT. *T:* Southampton 550151. *[Died 7 Feb.* 1978 (*ext*).

DINESEN, Thomas, VC 1918; French Croix de Guerre; Danish Knight of Danebrog; Civil Engineer; *b* 1892; *e s* of late Capt. W. Dinesen; *m* 1926, Jonna Lindhardt; two *s* two *d. Educ:* Rungsted Sch.; Polytechnical Sch., Copenhagen. Served European War, 1917-19, with Royal Highlanders of Canada; farmer in Kenya Colony, 1920-23. *Publications:* No Man's Land, 1929 (translated from Danish into English under the title Merry Hell); Twilight on the Betzy (Denmark, Norway, Sweden and Finland), 1951, (England and Holland), 1952; The Axe (Denmark), 1959; Boganis (Denmark), 1972; Anne Margrethe, my Great-Grandmother, 1974; Tanne, My Sister Karen Blixen (UK, as My Sister, Isak Dinesen), 1975. *Recreation:* travelling. *Address:* Leerbaek, Vejle, Denmark. *T:* 05 85 30 75.
[Died 11 March 1979.

DINGLE, Herbert, DSc, ARCS; Professor Emeritus of History and Philosophy of Science, University College, London, 1955 (Professor, 1946-55); formerly Professor of Natural Philosophy, Imperial College of Science and Technology, South Kensington; *b* 2 Aug. 1890; *s* of James Henry Dingle and Emily Jane Gorddard; *m* 1918, Alice (*d* 1947), *d* of late Frederick Westacott; (one *s* decd). *Educ:* Plymouth Science, Art, and Technical Schs; Imperial Coll. of Science and Technology. Mem. of British Government Eclipse Expeditions, 1927, 1932 and 1940 (cancelled owing to war); Mem. Internat. Astronomical Union, 1928-; Vice-Pres. Internat. Union for the History of Science, 1953-56; Pres. Brit. Soc. for History of Science, 1955-57; Pres., Royal Astronomical Society, 1951-53, Hon. Sec., 1929-32, Vice-Pres., 1938-39, 1942-44, 1948-50, 1953-54; Lowell Lecturer, Boston, USA, 1936; Corresp. Member: Inst. of Coimbra; Inst. of Advanced Studies, Cordoba, Argentina. *Publications:* Relativity for All, 1922; Modern Astrophysics, 1924; Science and Human Experience, 1931; Through Science to Philosophy, 1937; The Special Theory of Relativity, 1940; Mechanical Physics, 1941; Subatomic Physics, 1942; Science and Literary Criticism, 1949; Practical Applications of Spectrum Analysis, 1950; The Scientific Adventure, 1952; The Sources of Eddington's Philosophy, 1954; (with 1st Visc. Samuel) A Threefold Cord, 1961; Science at the Crossroads, 1972; The Mind of Emily Brontë, 1974; scientific papers in Proc. Royal Soc., Monthly Notices of Royal Astronomical Soc., Nature, Brit. Jl for the Philosophy of Science, Encyclopædia Britannica, etc; part author: Splendour of the Heavens, 1923; Life and Work of Sir Norman Lockyer, 1929; The New World Order, 1932; The New Learning, 1933; Science To-Day, 1934; (ed) A Century of Science, 1951; (ed jtly) Chemistry and Beyond: essays by F. A. Paneth, 1965. *Address:* 118 Marlborough Avenue, Hull, North Humberside HU5 3JX. *T:* Hull 443565. *Club:* Athenæum.
[Died 4 Sept. 1978.

DINGLE, Sir Philip (Burrington), Kt 1964; CBE 1954; Town Clerk of Manchester, 1944-66; *b* 19 Sept. 1906; *s* of Frederick Burrington Dingle and Jessie Roberta Elizabeth (*née* Needham); *m* 1938, Kathleen Mary, *d* of late Cecil Hurst, Sheffield; one *s* one *d. Educ:* Cheltenham Coll.; Sheffield Univ. LLM Sheffield, 1928. Articled to late Sir William Hart, Town Clerk of Sheffield, 1924-28; admitted Solicitor, 1928; Asst Solicitor to Sheffield Corporation, 1928-37; Dep. Town Clerk, Manchester, 1938-44; Member: Advisory Council on Child Care, 1948-52; Advisory Council on Clean Air, 1957-67; Council of Cheltenham Coll.,

1956-70 (Life Mem., 1965). Pres., Soc. of Town Clerks, 1961-62. Chm., City of Manchester Boy Scouts, 1946-66, Pres., 1968-72. Hon. LLD Manchester, 1960. *Address:* 93 Furniss Avenue, Dore, Sheffield S17 3QN.   *[Died 29 Aug.* 1978.

DINGLEY, Allen Roy, FRCS; formerly Consulting Surgeon, Royal National Throat, Nose and Ear Hospital, London; formerly Consulting Aural Surgeon, Sutton Hospital; *b* 28 Oct. 1892; *s* of Allen Dingley, FRCS. *Educ:* Leys Sch., Cambridge. Brackenbury Surgical Scholar, St Bart's Hospital, 1916. Mesopotamia Exped. Force, 1917-20, Surgical Specialist, 1919-20. Late Chief Asst, Throat Department, St Bart's Hospital. *Publications:* articles in medical journals on otolaryngology. *Recreation:* golf. *Address:* Cantley Cottage, Court Road, Banstead, Surrey. *T:* Burgh Heath 50378. *Club:* Walton Heath Golf.   *[Died 22 Dec.* 1978.

DINWIDDIE, Melville, CBE 1943 (OBE 1919); DSO 1917; MC 1915; DD; Controller, Scotland, British Broadcasting Corporation, 1933-57, retired; *b* 18 July 1892; 2nd *s* of late Rev. J. L. Dinwiddie, Ruthwell; *m* 1920, Arna, *e d* of late Alexander Guild, WS, Edinburgh; two *s* two *d*. Served European War, 1914-18 (despatches, DSO, OBE, MC); retd, 1924; was Asst at South Leith Parish Church; Minister of St Machar's Cathedral, Aberdeen, 1925-33. *Address:* 22 Polwarth Terrace, Edinburgh EH11 1NB.   *[Died 12 June* 1975.

DISNEY, Lieut-Col Henry Anthony Patrick; *b* 1893; *s* of Henry William Disney, Barrister-at-law, Metropolitan Police Magistrate, and Isabel Power; *m* 1915, Kathleen Maud Suffern; two *s* (and two *s* decd including one killed in War of 1939-45). *Educ:* Marlborough; Caius Coll., Cambridge (BA). Served European War, Cambridgeshire Regt; Pilot RFC, War Office Staff; DAQMG Italy; Wing Comdr RAF 1918. Dir Standard Telephones and Cables Ltd, Kolster Brandes Ltd, Creed and Co. Ltd, Standard Radio Relay Services Ltd, International Telephone and Telegraph Co. Ltd, 1919-32; joined Staff of E. K. Cole Ltd, 1932; Dir of Aeronautical Production, Air Min., 1936-38; Dir of Armament and Equipment Production, Air Min., 1938; left Min. of Aircraft Production, 1940, and rejoined RAF. Pilot Officer 1940; Wing Comdr 1941; Group Capt. 1944; released 1945; served in India, 1943-45. Dir of Brit. Export Trade Research Organisation, resigned, 1949; Staff Personnel Adviser, Rootes Group of Companies, 1950; Consultant Management Selection Ltd, 1957; John Tyzack & Partners Ltd, 1960; retired, 1962. Fellow Royal Commonwealth Society. Officer, Order of Crown of Italy. *Recreation:* philately. *Address:* Headbourne Worthy House, Headbourne Worthy, Winchester, Hants.   *[Died 20 Aug.* 1974.

DIVERS, Brig. Sydney Thomas, CB 1955; CBE 1944 (OBE 1940); DSO 1942; TD; company director; *b* 30 Jan. 1896; *s* of William and Alice Divers, Greenwich, Kent; *m* 1915, Rhoda Bertha Peck; two *s* two *d*. *Educ:* Greenwich Central Sch. Served Army, 1914-18, 1939-45 (USA Bronze Star, 1944; despatches 5 times); TA, 1914-19, 1924-51. Royal Observatory, Greenwich, 1910-14; HM Customs and Excise, 1919-34; Assistance Board, 1935-46; Ministry of Pensions and National Insurance, 1946-54 (Controller, Newcastle upon Tyne, 1951-54); Under-Sec.: Min. of Supply, 1956; Admiralty, 1957-59; UN Adviser, Administration: Burma, 1954-55; Nepal, 1959-62; Asia and Far East, 1962-64; UN Adviser, Social Security: Iraq, 1965-66; Trinidad 1967; Saudi Arabia 1971. Inst. of Public Administration; British Inst. of Management. *Recreations:* fishing, gardening, cattle breeding. *Address:* RD 2, Winton, Southland, New Zealand. *Club:* National Liberal.
                    [Died 23 Dec. 1979.

DIXEY, Marmaduke; *see* Howard, Geoffrey.

DIXIE, Sir (Alexander Archibald Douglas) Wolstan, 13th Bt *cr* 1660; *b* 8 Jan. 1910; *s* of Sir Douglas Dixie, 12th Bt, and Margaret Lindsay (*d* 1973), *d* of Sir A. Jardine, 8th Bt of Applegirth; *S* father, 1948; *m* 1st, 1940, Phyllis Pinnel (marr. diss. 1950), *d* of late Lt-Col Percy John Probyn, DSO; 2nd, 1950, Dorothy Penelope King-Kirkman; two *d*. *Educ:* St Joseph's Coll., Dumfries; Prior Park Coll., Bath. Hereditary Governor, Dixie Grammar Sch., 1948; Windsor Rural District Council, 1956-58. *Publication:* Is it True What They Say About Dixie?: the second battle of Bosworth (autobiog.), 1972. *Recreations:* cricket, tennis, squash. *Address:* Bosworth Park, Leics; Manor Park, Old Windsor, Berks.   *[Died 28 Dec.* 1975 (*ext*.)

DIXON, Maj.-Gen. Bernard Edward Cooke, CB 1947; CBE 1944; MC 1917; *b* 7 Sept. 1896; *s* of late George Frederick Dixon, MRCS, MRCP; *m* 1923, Elizabeth Norah Fitzpatrick (*née* Gibson); two *d*. *Educ:* Bedford Sch.; RMA Woolwich. Commissioned in RE, 1915; served in France, 1916-19

(despatches, MC); Lieut-Col 1939; Col 1942; Temp. Brig. 1940; Temp. Maj.-Gen. 1944; Brig. 1947; Middle East, 1940-43 (despatches twice); Italy, 1943-44 (CBE); E-in-C, GHQ Middle East, 1944-47 (CB); CE, HQ Western Command, 1947-48; retired, 1948, with hon. rank of Maj.-Gen. *Recreation:* yachting. *Address:* Tinkerborough Barn, Weston, Stafford.
                    [Died 9 Oct. 1973.

DIXON, Cecil Edith Mary, MBE 1939; formerly Professor of Piano and Accompaniment, RCM, retired; *b* 27 Nov. 1891; *d* of James Dickson and Margaret Emily Dixon. *Educ:* New Zealand and Australia. Was on the original staff of the BBC, remained there until Sept. 1943; toured for CEMA as a free-lance pianist till 1946; studied piano under Herbert Sharpe and the Royal College of Music and later with Tobias Matthay. *Recreations:* dogs and country walks. *Address:* 17 Milner Street, SW3 2QB. *T:* 01-589 0030.   *[Died 22 Feb.* 1979.

DIXON, Sir Charles William, KCMG 1945 (CMG 1932); KCVO 1961; OBE 1924; *b* 29 April 1888; *s* of John W. Dixon, Leeds, and Alice, *d* of Charles Hainsworth, Bramley, Yorks. *Educ:* Clifton; Balliol Coll., Oxford (Exhibitioner). 1st Class Classical Mods, 1909; 1st Class Lit. Hum., 1911. Entered Colonial Office, 1911; Private Sec. to the Permanent Under-Sec. of State (Sir George Fiddes), 1917-19; Asst Under-Sec. of State, Dominions Office (afterwards Commonwealth Relations Office), 1940-48; Adviser, Commonwealth Relations Office (now Commonwealth Office), 1948-67. *Address:* The Branksome Nursing Home, 35 Nelson Road, Poole, Dorset BH12 1ES. *T:* Bournemouth 763793.   *[Died 12 Sept.* 1976.

DIXON, Hubert John, MC, MA; retired as Headmaster of King's College School, Wimbledon (1934-60); *b* 5 June 1895; *s* of William Arthur and Caroline Dixon; *m* 1st, 1922, Mary Frances Arnold (*d* 1960); one *s* one *d*; 2nd, 1962, Yvonne Muriel Price. *Educ:* King Edward's Sch., Birmingham; Queen's Coll., Cambridge (Classical Exhibitioner). Sixth Form Master: Fettes Coll., Edinburgh, 1920-21; Dulwich Coll., 1921-34. Served with 1st Bn Royal Warwicks Regt in France, 1916-19 (MC, despatches). *Recreation:* reading. *Address:* 1 Lancaster Gardens, Wimbledon, SW19.   *[Died 15 March* 1971.

DIXON, Sir John, 2nd Bt *cr* 1919; *b* 13 June 1886; *s* of 1st Bt and Emily Katherine, 2nd *d* of G. Beacham Cole of Twickenham; *S* father, 1924; *m* 1910, Gwendolen Anne (*d* 1974); *d* of Sir J. L. E. Spearman, 2nd Bt; two *s* one *d*. Heir: *s* John George Dixon [*b* 17 Sept. 1911; *m* 1947, Caroline, *er d* of C. T. Hiltermann, 31 Melbury Court, London; one *d*]. *Recreations:* hunting, fishing and shooting. *Address:* Edgecombe Nursing Home, Hamstead Marshall, Newbury, Berks.   *[Died 7 Aug.* 1976.

DIXON, Most Rev. John Harkness; *b* 23 July 1888; *s* of Albert and Bertha Dixon, Iroquois, Ont; *m* 1917 Edith Millicent, *d* of Rev. T. Bailey; four *s* (one *d* decd). *Educ:* Univ. of Toronto (BA); Trinity Coll., Toronto (Scholar, BD). Deacon, 1912; Priest, 1913. Curate, Fenaghvale, Ont., 1912-13; Christ Church Cathedral, Ottawa, 1914-22; Minor Canon, Ottawa, 1913-22; Rector: S Bartholomew, Ottawa, 1922-32; Grace Church, Toronto, 1932-40; Dean and Rector, Christ Church Cathedral, Montreal, 1940-43; Bishop of Montreal, 1943-60; Archbishop of Montreal and Metropolitan of the Province of Canada, 1960-62; retired Sept. 1962. *Address:* Apt 304, 6201 Sherbrooke Street West, Montreal 261, PQ, Canada.   *[Died 1 April* 1972.

DIXON, John Reginald; Managing Director, 1923-66, Chairman, 1927-66, Cleveland Bridge & Engineering Co. Ltd; retired; *b* 19 Jan. 1886; *s* of Charles F. Dixon and Amy Beckett; *m* 1913, Elsie Margaret Gunion; two *s* (and *e s* killed AAF Dunkirk, 1940). *Educ:* Marlborough Coll. Joined Cleveland Bridge & Engineering Co., 1903; Works Manager, 1912. *Recreations:* gardening, shooting, travel; skiing in younger days. *Address:* Pitminster Lodge, Pitminster, Taunton, Som. *Clubs:* Junior Carlton, Ski Club of Great Britain, Alpine Ski.
                    [Died 5 March 1972.

DIXON, Rt. Hon. Sir Owen, PC 1951; OM 1963; GCMG 1954 (KCMG 1941); Chief Justice of Australia, 1952-64; *b* 28 April 1886; *s* of late Joseph William Dixon, Melbourne, Solicitor, and Edith Annie, *d* of late Edward Owen, Sydney; *m* 1920, Alice Crossland (*d* 1971), *d* of Rev. H. A. Brooksbank; two *s* two *d*. *Educ:* Hawthorn Coll., Melbourne; University of Melbourne. Called to Bar, Victoria 1910; KC 1922; Acting Judge of the Supreme Court of the State of Victoria, 1926; Justice, High Court of Australia, 1929-52; Chm. of Central Wool Cttee, 1940-42; Chm. of Shipping Control Board, 1941-42; Chm. of Commonwealth Marine War Risks Insurance Board, 1941-42; Chairman of: Marine Salvage Board, 1942; Allied Consultative Shipping Council in Australia, 1942; served as Envoy

Extraordinary and Minister Plenipotentiary of the Commonwealth of Australia at Washington, 1942-44; served as UN Mediator between India and Pakistan, Kashmir dispute, 1950. Howland Prize, Yale, 1955. Corres. Fellow, British Academy, 1970. Hon. DCL Oxford, 1958; Hon. LLD: Harvard, 1958; Melbourne, 1959; ANU 1964. *Address:* 4 Higham Road, Hawthorn, Victoria 3122, Australia. *Clubs:* Melbourne, Australian (Melbourne); Australian (Sydney).
[Died 8 July 1972.

DOAK, Sir James, Kt 1945; CA (Glasgow); *b* 1904; *m* 1931, Helen Gaylord; one *s* (and one *s* decd). Retired as Director: Legal & General Assurance Soc. Ltd (1951-72); J. H. Fenner & Co. (Holdings) (until 1973). *Address:* 8 Motcombe Court, Bedford Avenue, Bexhill-on-Sea, East Sussex.
[Died 9 July 1975.

DOBB, Maurice Herbert, MA Cantab; PhD London; FBA 1971; Emeritus Reader in Economics, University of Cambridge; Fellow of Trinity College, Cambridge; *b* 1900; *s* of Walter Herbert Dobb and Elsie Annie Moir, London; *m* Barbara Marian Nixon. *Educ:* Charterhouse; Pembroke Coll., Cambridge (Exhibitioner and Scholar). 1st Class Parts I and II, Econs Tripos. Research Student, LSE, 1922-24; Visiting Lectr in Russian Economic Studies, Univ. of London Sch. of Slavonic Studies, 1943-46; Visiting Prof. at Sch. of Economics, Univ. of Delhi, 1951; Marshall Lectr, Cambridge, 1972-73. Hon. DrEconSc Prague, 1964; Hon. DLitt Leicester, 1972. *Publications:* Capitalist Enterprise and Social Progress, 1925; Russian Economic Development since the Revolution, 1928; Wages, 1928 (revised edn 1956); Political Economy and Capitalism, 1937 (revised edn 1940); Studies in the Development of Capitalism, 1946; Development of Soviet Economy since 1917, 1948 (rev. edn 1966); collaborated in ed. Works and Correspondence of David Ricardo, 1951-55; On Economic Theory and Socialism, Collected Papers, 1955; An Essay on Economic Growth and Planning, 1960; Papers on Capitalism, Development and Planning, 1967; Welfare Economics and the Economics of Socialism, 1969; Theories of Value and Distribution since Adam Smith, 1973; Contributor to Chambers's Encyclopædia, International Encyclopædia of the Social Sciences; Enciclopedia Italiana; articles and reviews in the Economic Journal, Economica, Soviet Studies, etc. *Address:* Trinity College, Cambridge; College Farmhouse, Fulbourn, Cambs. *T:* Fulbourn 298.
[Died 17 Aug. 1976.

DOBBIE-BATEMAN, Rev. Arthur Fitzroy, CB 1948; *b* 1897; *s* of Richmond Bateman; *m* 1923, Margaret Laing Dobbie, MB, ChB, Edinburgh, DIH (*hc*), LSA. *Educ:* Bristol Grammar Sch.; Wadham Coll., Oxford; St George's, Windsor. Civil Service, 1923-52; Asst Curate, St John's, Frome, 1952-55, and 1969-73; Rector of Whatley with Chantry, Frome, 1955-69. *Publications:* St Seraphim of Sarov, 1936; The Return of St Seraphim, 1970. *Address:* The Hermitage, Gentle Street, Frome, Somerset. *T:* Frome 2502.
[Died 6 June 1974.

DOBBS, Richard Heyworth, MD, FRCP; retired; Consulting Pædiatrician: London Hospital, 1946-71; Queen Elizabeth Hospital for Children, 1939-71; Southend Hospital Group, 1946-71; Professor of Paediatrics, Ahmadu Bello University, Nigeria, 1972-77; *b* 10 May 1905; of British parentage; *m* 1930, Phyllis Leon; one *s* one *d*. *Educ:* Bedales Sch.; Downing Coll., Cambridge; London Hosp. MRCS, LRCP 1930; MB Cantab 1931; MD 1941; MRCP 1936; FRCP 1947. Pres., British Paediatric Assoc., 1970. Paediatrician, Internat. Grenfell Assoc., Newfoundland, Jan.-June 1972. Editor, Archives of Disease in Childhood, 1954-69. *Recreations:* gardening, music, cooking, travel. *Address:* 3 Oakhill Way, Hampstead, NW3. *T:* 01-435 4010.
[Died 21 Aug. 1980.

DOBIE, Marryat Ross, CBE 1953; BA; *b* Bellary, India, 1888; *s* of Surg. Lieut-Col Stanley Locker Dobie, IMS; *m* Grace Vera Patmore; two *d*. *Educ:* Fettes Coll., Edinburgh; Wadham Coll., Oxford. Asst in British Museum, 1912-14; Private in London Scottish, 1914-15; Officer in Intelligence Corps, 1915-19; Official of the Inter-Allied Rhineland High Commission, 1919-24; Official of the Inter-Allied Commission of Government and Plebiscite in Upper Silesia, 1921-22; Asst in National Library of Scotland, 1929-31; Keeper of Manuscripts, 1931-46; Librarian, 1946-53. Officer, Intelligence Corps, 1940-44. *Address:* 15 Church Road, Duffus, Elgin, Morayshire. *T:* Hopeman 674.
[Died 29 Oct. 1973.

DOBINSON, Prof. Charles Henry, CMG 1969; Professor of Education, University of Reading, 1951-68, now Emeritus; *b* 7 Oct. 1903; *s* of late Henry Mark Dobinson, and late Florence Gertrude (*née* Agate); *m* 1929, Dorothy Maude Shooter; one *s* one *d*. *Educ:* Brockley County Grammar Sch., London;

Wadham Coll., Oxford (MA). 2nd Cl. Hons Hon. Mods Maths; 1st Cl. Hons Oxford Hon. Sch. of Nat. Science (Geology); Diploma in Educn, Oxford; BSc London. Biology Master, Mill Hill Sch., 1927-33; Headmaster, King Edward VI Grammar Sch., Five Ways, Birmingham, 1933-45; Reader in Education, Oxford Univ., 1945-51. An adviser to UK first delegation to Unesco, 1946; Chm. Educn Cttee, Nat. Fedn of Community Assocs, 1949-62; a Governor of Unesco Internat. Inst. of Educn, Hamburg, 1950-65; Member: Banjo Commn on Education in Western Region of Nigeria, 1960-61; Advisory Commn on Higher Teacher Training in the Sudan, 1964. Visiting Prof., Summer Schs of Syracuse, New York, 1950, Arkansas, 1950, 1952, 1967, Syracuse, 1955, 1957, Cornell, 1959, Alberta, 1960, Missouri, 1961, 1963, 1964, 1966, 1968, 1970, 1973, Calgary, 1969. FGS. *Publications:* (ed) Education in a Changing World, 1950; Technical Education for Adolescents, 1951; Schooling 1963-1970, 1963; Jean-Jacques Rousseau, 1969; (ed) Comenius, 1970; various school text-books between 1929 and 1966; articles in UK press, 1970-, on technical educn in France and Germany; articles in educational press of UK, USA, France and Sweden. *Recreations:* gardening and reading. *Address:* The Old Barn, Sonning Common, near Reading, Berks. *T:* Kidmore End 2191.
[Died 26 Dec. 1980.

DOBRÉE, Lt-Col Bonamy, OBE 1929; late RA; Professor of English Literature, University of Leeds, 1936-55; *b* 1891; *s* of Bonamy Dobrée and Violet Chase; *m* 1913, Valentine (Gladys) (*d* 1974), *d* of Sir Alexander Brooke-Pechell, 7th Bt; one *d*. *Educ:* Haileybury; RMA Woolwich; Cambridge. Commissioned in RFA 1910; resigned 1913; rejoined Aug. 1914; served European War in France and Palestine (despatches); served also 1939-45. Cambridge 1920, Capt. of fencing team; BA 1921; MA 1926; resided abroad, 1921-25; Lecturer, London Univ., 1925-26; Prof. of English, Egyptian Univ., Cairo, 1926-29; Mem. Central Advisory Council for Education (England), 1944-53; Clark Lecturer, 1953; Gresham Prof. in Rhetoric, 1955-61; Lord Northcliffe Memorial Lecturer, 1963. Hon. Docteur de Dijon. Hon. DLitt, Kent at Canterbury, 1968. *Publications:* Restoration Comedy, 1924; Essays in Biography; Histriophone; Timotheus, 1925; Nonesuch Vanbrugh; Sarah Churchill, 1927; World's Classics Congreve, 1928; Restoration Tragedy, The Lamp and the Lute, 1929; (with Herbert Read) The London Book of English Prose, 1931; Variety of Ways; William Penn; St Martin's Summer: Letters of Lord Chesterfield, with Life, 1932; John Wesley, 1933; Giacomo Casanova, 1933; As Their Friends Saw Them, 1933; Modern Prose Style, 1934; (with G. E. Manwaring) The Floating Republic, 1935; (ed) The Letters of King George III, 1935; (ed) From Anne to Victoria, 1937; English Revolts, 1937; (with Edith Batho) The Victorians and After (Introduction to English Literature Series), 1938; The Unacknowledged Legislator, 1942; English Essayists (Britain in Pictures), 1947; (with Herbert Read) The London Book of English Verse, 1949; Alexander Pope, 1951; The Broken Cistern, 1954; The Early Eighteenth Century: Oxford History of English Literature, 1959; Three Eighteenth Century Figures, 1962; Rudyard Kipling, 1967; Milton to Ouida: a Collection of Essays, 1970. *Recreation:* gardening. *Address:* 15 Pond Road, Blackheath, SE3. *T:* 01-852 0679. *Ckub:* Athenæum.
[Died 3 Sept. 1974.

DOBSON, Cowan; RBA, FRSA; Hon. RP; portrait painter; *b* 1894; *s* of late H. J. Dobson, RCA; *m* 1931, Phyllis, *e d* of Lancelot Bowyer. Studied Edinburgh, Paris, London. Exhibited RA for over 50 years, and in leading galleries throughout the world. Commissioned by Govt to paint RAF VCs of War of 1914-18, now in Imperial War Museum. *Works include:* King Haakon; King Olaf; King George of Greece; Adm. Beatty; Amy Johnston; artist's wife Phyllis; Earl Atlee; King and Queen of Iraq; Duke of Argyll, and many civic dignitaries and industrialists. *Recreation:* magic. *Address:* Studio, 62 South Edwardes Square, W8. *T:* 01-602 6361. *Club:* Hurlingham.
[Died 11 May 1980.

DOBSON, Gordon Miller Bourne, CBE 1951; FRS 1927; DSc; formerly Reader in Meteorology, University of Oxford; *b* 25 Feb. 1889; *s* of late Thos Dobson, MD, Windermere; *m* 1st, 1914, Winifred Duncombe Rimer (*d* 1952); two *s* one *d*; 2nd, 1954, Olive M. Bacon. *Educ:* Sedbergh; Caius Coll., Cambridge. *Publications:* Photographic Photometry; Exploring the Atmosphere; papers on geophysical subjects. *Address:* Watch Hill, The Ridings, Shotover, Oxford OX3 8TB. *T:* Oxford 62511.
[Died 10 March 1976.

DOBSON, Raymond Francis Harvey; Director of Personnel, British Caledonian Airways, since 1970; *b* 26 April 1925; *s* of Tom Noel Dobson; *m* 1947, Vivienne Joyce Martin; three *s* one *d*. *Educ:* Purbrook Park Sch., Portsmouth. Radio Officer, Merchant Navy, 1940-47; Post Office, 1947-66. Trade Union

Official, Postal Workers' Union, 1950-66 (Mem. Nat. Exec., 1960-66). MP (Lab) Bristol North-East, 1966-70; PPS, Min. of Technology, 1967-69; Asst Govt Whip, 1969-70; Member: Select Cttee of Estimates, 1966-67; Select Cttee for Science and Technology, 1969. Member: British Caledonian Airways, 1970-; British Caledonian (Charter) Airways, 1970-; Board, Gambia Airways, 1974-77; Board, Sierra Leone Airways, 1974-80; Board, Air Liberia, 1976-80; Air Transport and Travel Ind. Trng Board, 1973-. *Address:* Tanquards, Reigate Hill, Reigate, Surrey. *T:* Reigate 43914.   *[Died 22 Sept. 1980.*

DOCKER, Sir Bernard (Dudley Frank), KBE 1939; *b* 9 Aug. 1896; *o s* of late Frank Dudley Docker, CB; *m* 1949, Norah, widow of Sir William Collins. *Educ:* Harrow. Former Chm., Birmingham Small Arms Co. Ltd and other companies. *Recreations:* golf, shooting, yachting. *Clubs:* Royal London Yacht; St Helier Yacht.   *[Died 22 May 1978.*

DODD, Charles Edward Shuter; *b* 2 May 1891; *s* of H. W. Dodd, FRCS, Harley Street, London; *m* 1921, Elizabeth Mabel (*d* 1973), *d* of Sir Henry Birchenough, 1st Bt, GCMG; one *s* one d. *Educ:* Harrow; Balliol Coll., Oxford. Exhibitioner and Hon. Scholar of Balliol; Hertford, Craven and Ireland Univ. Scholarships. Served European War, 1914-19, in Royal Welch Fusiliers (TF), Welsh Guards and Intelligence Corps; Third Sec., Diplomatic Service, 1919; 2nd Sec., 1920; 1st Sec., 1924; Counsellor, 1937; Envoy Extraordinary and Minister Plenipotentiary at Panama, 1939-43. Municipal Councillor (Progressive) for Lansdown Ward, Bath, 1952-61. *Address:* 7 The Circus, Bath, Avon.   *[Died 30 Aug. 1974.*

DODD, Rev. Charles Harold, CH 1961; MA (Oxford, Cambridge, Manchester); Hon. DD (Oxford, Cambridge, London, Manchester, Glasgow, Aberdeen and Wales); Hon. DLitt, Oxford; Hon. STD (Harvard); Hon. DTheol (Oslo); Docteur hc (Strasbourg); FBA 1946; Hon. Fellow, Jesus College, Cambridge, since 1949; Hon. Fellow, University College, Oxford, since 1951; *b* Wrexham, Denbighshire, 7 April 1884; *e s* of late Charles Dodd, FGS, and Sarah, *d* of Edward Parsonage, Wrexham; *m* 1925, Phyllis Mary, widow of John Elliott Terry, and *y d* of late George Stockings, Bournemouth; one *s* one d. *Educ:* Wrexham; University Coll., Oxford (Classical Scholar); Berlin; Senior Demy, Magdalen Coll., 1907-11; studied Theology meanwhile at Mansfield Coll., Oxford. Ordained, 1912; Minister of the Independent or Congregational Church at Warwick, 1912-15, 1918-19; Yates Lectr in New Testament Greek and Exegesis, Mansfield Coll., 1915-30; Univ. Lectr in New Testament Studies, Oxford, 1927-30; Grinfield Lectr on the Septuagint, Oxford, 1927-31; Rylands Prof. of Biblical Criticism and Exegesis, Manchester, 1930-35; Speaker's Lectr in Biblical Studies, Univ. of Oxford, 1933-37; Shaffer Lecturer, Yale Univ., 1935; Ingersoll Lecturer, Harvard Univ., 1935, 1950; Norris-Hulse Prof. of Divinity, Cambridge, 1935-49; Fellow of Jesus Coll., Cambridge, 1936-49; Hewett Lecturer, Episcopal Theological Seminary, Cambridge, USA, 1938; Olaus Petri Lecturer, University of Uppsala, 1949; Bampton Lecturer in America, Columbia Univ., 1950; Stone Lecturer, Princeton Theological Seminary, 1950; Visiting Prof. of Biblical Theology, Union Theological Seminary, New York, 1950; Gen. Dir, New Translation of the Bible, 1950-65; Joint Dir, 1966-70; Editor, Texts and Studies, 1953-62. Sarum Lectr, Oxford, 1954-55. Hon. Freeman, Wrexham, 1964. *Publications:* The Meaning of Paul for To-day, 1920; The Gospel in the New Testament, 1926; The Authority of the Bible, 1928; Ephesians, Colossians, and Philemon (Abingdon Commentary), 1929; The Bible and Its Background, 1931; The Epistle to The Romans (Moffatt Commentary), 1932; There and Back Again, 1932; The Bible and the Greeks, 1935; Parables of the Kingdom, 1935; The Apostolic Preaching and its Developments, 1936; The Present Task in New Testament Studies (Inaugural Lecture), 1936; History and the Gospel, 1937; The Johannine Epistles (Moffatt Commentary), 1946; The Bible To-day, 1946; Benefits of His Passion, 1947; About the Gospels, 1950; The Coming of Christ, 1951; Gospel and Law, 1951; Christianity and the Reconciliation of the Nations, 1952; According to the Scriptures, 1952; The Interpretation of the Fourth Gospel, 1953; New Testament Studies, 1953; Historical Tradition in the Fourth Gospel, 1963; More New Testament Studies, 1968; The Founder of Christianity, 1970 (Collins' Biennial Religious Book Award, 1971). *Address:* 1 Wellington Place, St Giles', Oxford.
                    [Died 21 Sept. 1973.

DODD, Sir John (Samuel), Kt 1947; TD; engineer; *b* 13 Oct. 1904; *s* of late William Dodd, JP, Keldwith, Windermere; *m* 1937, Margaret McDougall, *d* of late William Hamilton, Glasgow; four *s. Educ:* Uppingham; Rouen; Christ's Coll., Cambridge (MA). Contested Oldham (L) 1929 and (LNat) 1945; MP (LNat) Oldham, 1935-45. MIME; FRGS; Fellow, Royal

Philatelic Society, London; Past Pres., Assoc. of British Chambers of Commerce; Mem., Central National Service Cttee for Great Britain, 1939-40; Hon. Adviser on Tank Production and Chm. of Tank Production Groups, Ministry of Supply, 1940-41; Hon. Mem. Administrative Council, Cotton Research Corporation; Underwriting Mem. of Lloyd's; Late Major Royal Tank Regt TA. Chm. of Exec. Cttee of Nat. Liberal Council, 1947-49; Mem. of Lord Chancellor's Cttee on County Court Procedure, 1947-49. *Publications:* contribs to various periodicals and trade journals. *Recreations:* travel, yachting, mountaineering, philately. *Address:* Les Fraises, Rozel, Trinity, Jersey, Channel Islands. *T:* Jersey North 912. *Clubs:* Naval and Military; Royal Windermere Yacht; Royal Lytham and St Anne's Golf; Royal Channel Islands Yacht.
                    [Died 3 Sept. 1973.

DODDS, Sir Charles; *see* Dodds, Sir E. C.

DODDS, Sir (Edward) Charles, 1st Bt, *cr* 1964; Kt 1954; MVO 1929; DSc (London); FRS 1942; FRSE; FRCP, FRCPSG; FRIC; Emeritus Professor of Biochemistry, University of London (Courtauld Professor of Biochemistry and Director, Courtauld Institute of Biochemistry at Middlesex Hospital Medical School, 1927-65); *b* 1899; *o s* of late Ralph Edward and Jane Dodds, Darlington and London; *m* 1923, Constance Elizabeth (*d* 1969), *o d* of late J. T. and Katharine Jordan, Darlington; one *s. Educ:* Harrow Co. Sch.; Middx Hosp. Med. Sch. (MD, PhD). Pathologist, Royal Nat. Orthopædic Hosp. Lectures: Goulstonian, RCP, 1934; Harvey, New York Univ., 1935; Harben, Royal Inst. of Public Health, London, 1937; Cantor, RSA, 1939; Bertram Louis Abrahams, RCP, 1950; Purser, TCD, 1950; Sanderson-Wells, Middx Hosp., 1953; Dorothy Platt, King's Coll., 1953; Cavendish, W London Med. Chirurgical Soc., 1955; Guiteras, Amer. Urological Soc., Boston, 1956; Lane, Stanford Univ., 1956; Crookshank, RCS, 1959; Addison, Guy's Hosp., 1946, 1960; Linacre, St John's Coll., Cambridge, 1960; Comfort Crookshank, Middx Hosp., 1960. William Julius Mickle Fellowship, Univ. of London, 1943; Sims Travelling Prof., RCS, 1952. Harveian Librarian, RCP, 1949-62; President: RCP, 1962-66; BIBRA, 1972-; 4th Internat. Congress in Endocrinology, 1968; a Vice-Pres. and Mem. Council, Royal Soc., 1957-59; Vice-President: Eugenics Soc.; Arthritis and Rheumatism Council (Chm., Planning Sub-Cttee). Formerly Chairman: Scientific Adv. Cttee, British Empire Cancer Campaign; Governing Body, Lister Inst.; Science Cttee, British Heart Foundn. Formerly Chairman: Cttee of Management of Cancer Res. Inst., Royal Cancer Hosp.; Tropical Products Inst. Cttee, DSIR; Food Additives and Contaminants Sub-Cttee of Food Standards Cttee, and Adv. Cttee on Poisonous Substances used in Agriculture and Food Storage, Min. of Agriculture, Fisheries and Food; Scientific Adv. Cttee, Fleming Memorial Fund for Med. Res.; Adv. Council on Scientific Res. and Technical Develt. Mem., Heberden Soc.; formerly Mem., Nat. Res. Develt Corp. Hon. Member: Assoc. of Physicians; Pathological Soc. of Manchester; Amer. Soc. of Clinical Pathologists; Amer. Assoc. for Cancer Res.; New York Acad. of Sciences; Chilean Chem. Soc.; Chilean Med. Soc.; Biological Soc. of Chile; Radiological Soc. of Chile; Chilean League against Cancer; Soc. of Chemical Industry of France; Finnish Med. Soc. Duodecim; Royal Med. Acad. of Barcelona; Italian Chemical Soc.; Danish Soc. of Internal Medicine; Med. Soc. of Gothenburg. Foreign Corresp. Mem., Nat. Acad. of Medicine of France; Hon. Councillor, Consejo Superior de Investigaciones Cientificas of Spain. FInstBiol; Hon. FRCS, Hon. FRCOG, Hon. FRCPSG, Hon. FRACP, Hon. FRCPath; Hon. Fellow: Royal Coll. of Physicians and Surgeons (Canada); American Coll. of Physicians; Australian Postgraduate Fedn in Medicine. Hon. MD: Melbourne; Birmingham; Hon. ScD Cambridge; Hon. DSc Chicago; Hon. LLD Glasgow; Hon. Dr Bologna. Past Master, Worshipful Soc. of Apothecaries. KStJ. Gold Medal for Therapeutics, W London Med. Soc., 1938; Cameron Prizeman, Univ. of Edinburgh, 1940; Charles L. Meyer Prize and Walker Prize, RCS, 1946; Garton Prize and Medal, British Empire Cancer Campaign, 1948; Berzelius Medal, Swedish Med. Soc.; Medals of Univs of Ghent and Brussels; Pasteur Medal, Congress of Biological Chemistry of Société de Chimie Biologique Française; Gold Medal in Therapeutics, Soc. of Apothecaries, 1951; Gold Medal, Soc. of Chemical Industry, 1951; Harben Medal, Royal Inst. of Public Health, 1952. *Publications:* (with G. E. Beaumont) Recent Advances in Medicine; (with F. Dickens) Chemical and Physiological Properties of Internal Secretions; (with L. E. H. Whitby) The Laboratory in Surgical Practice; articles on biochemical subjects in various scientific jls. *Heir:* s Ralph Jordan Dodds [*b* 25 March 1928; *m* 1954, Marion, *e d* of late Sir Daniel Davies, KCVO; two *d*]. *Address:* 49 Sussex Square, W2. *T:* 01-723 0498. *Clubs:* Athenæum, Savage, Bath.
                    [Died 16 Dec. 1973.

DODDS, Eric Robertson, MA Oxon; Hon. DLitt (Manchester, Dublin, Edinburgh, Birmingham, and Belfast); FBA 1942; Corresponding Member of Academia Sinica, Bavarian Academy, American Academy of Arts and Sciences; Membre de l'Institut de France; Hon. Fellow, University College, Oxford; Hon. Student of Christ Church, Oxford; Regius Professor of Greek, University of Oxford, 1936-60; *b* 26 July 1893; *o s* of Robert Dodds, Headmaster of Banbridge Academy; *m* 1923, Annie (*d* 1973), *yr d* of late Rev. Canon A. D. Powell. *Educ:* Campbell Coll., Belfast; University Coll., Oxford. Lectr in Classics at University Coll., Reading, 1919-24; Prof. of Greek in the University of Birmingham, 1924-36. *Publications:* Select Passages Illustrative of Neoplatonism, 2 vols, 1923 and 1924; Thirty-two Poems, 1929; Proclus' Elements of Theology, 1933; Journal and Letters of Stephen MacKenna, 1936; Euripides' Bacchae, 1944; The Greeks and the Irrational, 1951 (Kenyon Medal, British Academy, 1971); Plato's Gorgias, 1959; Pagan and Christian in an Age of Anxiety, 1965; The Ancient Concept of Progress and other essays on Greek literature and belief, 1973; Missing Persons (autobiog.), 1977 (Duff Cooper Memorial Prize, 1977). *Recreation:* psychical research. *Address:* Cromwell's House, Old Marston, Oxford. [*Died 8 April 1979.*

DODDS, George Elliott, CBE 1973; former Editor and Director, Huddersfield Examiner; *b* 4 March 1889; *yr s* of George William and Elizabeth Anne Dodds, Sydenham, Kent; *m* 1918, Frances Zita MacDonald (*d* 1971), *yr d* of Rev. Joseph Johnson, Sale, Ches; two *d*. *Educ:* Mill Hill Sch.; New Coll., Oxford. Pres. Liberal Party Organisation, 1948-49; contested York City, 1922 and 1923, Halifax, 1929, Rochdale, 1931 and 1935. Pres., Unservile State Group. *Publications:* Is Liberalism Dead?, 1919; Liberalism in Action, 1922; The Social Gospel of Liberalism, 1926; Let's Try Liberalism, 1944; The Defence of Man, 1947; The Logic of Liberty (with Erna Reiss), 1966. *Recreation:* golf. *Address:* Belhaven, 230 Somerset Road, Huddersfield, West Yorks. *T:* Huddersfield 30597. *Clubs:* Reform, National Liberal; Old Millhillians. [*Died 20 Feb. 1977.*

DODDS, Harold Willis; President, Princeton University, 1933-June 1957; *b* Utica, Penna, 28 June 1889; *s* of Samuel Dodds and Alice Dunn; *m* 1917, Margaret Murray. *Educ:* AB Grove City (Pa) Coll., 1909; AM Princeton, 1914; PhD Pennsylvania, 1917. Instructor in Economics, Purdue Univ., 1914-16; Asst Prof. of Political Science, Western Reserve Univ., 1919-20; Sec., National Municipal League, 1920-28; Editor, National Municipal Review, 1920-33; Prof. of Politics, Princeton Univ., 1927-33; Executive Sec., US Food Administration, Pa, 1917-19; Electoral Adviser to Govt of Nicaragua, 1922-24; Technical Adviser to President, Tacna-Arica Plebiscitary Commn, 1925-26; Chief Adviser to President, National Board of Elections of Nicaragua, 1928; Consultant to Cuban Govt in Election Law Procedure, 1935; Chm., American Delegation, Anglo-American Conf. on the Refugee Problem, 1943, Bermuda; Chm., The President's Ctte on Integration of Medical Services in the Armed Forces, 1946; Mem., The President's Advisory Commn on Universal Training, 1947. Pres., Assoc. of American Univs, 1952-54; Chm., Personnel Task Force of Commn on Organization of Exec. Branch of the Govt, 1954-55; Chm., Joint Congressional Commn on James Madison Memorial. *Publications:* Out of This Nettle... Danger, 1943; The Academic President: Educator or Caretaker, 1962; various reports, pamphlets and articles on political and public administration. *Recreations:* golf and gardening. *Address:* Meadow Lakes 43-02, Hightstown, NJ 08520, USA. *Clubs:* Century, Princeton (New York); Nassau (Princeton). [*Died 25 Oct. 1980.*

DODDS, Sir James Leishman, KCMG 1950 (CMG 1938); *b* 1891; *s* of late Sir James Miller Dodds, KCB; *m* 1927, Etelka, *y d* of late Brig.-Gen. Sir Conyers Surtees, CB, CMG, and widow of Edward Bell, New York; one *d*. *Educ:* Marlborough; Wadham Coll., Oxford (Classical Exhib.). Served European War, 1915-19; entered Diplomatic Service, 1919; served Tokyo, 1919, Madrid 1923, Stockholm 1925, The Hague 1929, Berne 1933; Counsellor of Embassy, Japan, 1938-40; Envoy Ext. and Min. Plen. Bolivia, 1940-43; Cuba, 1944-49; Ambassador to Peru, 1949-51; retd, 1951. *Address:* Church House, Beckley, Sussex. *T:* Beckley 276. *Club:* Athenæum. [*Died 13 Aug. 1972.*

DODGE, Bayard, DD, LLD, MA, BD; Retired; *b* New York City, 5 Feb. 1888; *s* of late Cleveland Hoadley Dodge and Grace Parish; *m* 1914, Mary Williams Bliss; two *s* two *d*. *Educ:* Browning Sch., New York City; Princeton Univ.; Union Theological Seminary and Columbia Univ., New York City. Mem. of the Faculty of the American Univ. of Beirut, 1913-19; Acting Executive Secretary, 1919-20; Managing Dir of the Syria-Palestine Area of the Near East Relief, 1920-21; returned to American Univ., Beirut, 1921-22; Pres., American Univ. of Beirut, 1923-48. Mem. of the Trustee Board of the League of

Nations for Settlement of the Assyrians, 1936-42; Adviser, UN Relief for Palestine Refugees, Nov. 1948. Visiting Prof., Columbia Univ., 1949-54; Lecturer Princeton Univ., 1951-55; Cultural Affairs Officer, Cairo, 1955-56; Visiting Prof., American Univ. at Cairo, 1956-59. Corresp. Mem. Arab Acad., Syrian Republic, 1956. Hon. LLD: Occidental Coll., 1926; Yale Univ., 1949; Hon. DD, Princeton Univ., 1928; Hon. LittD, American Univ. of Beirut, 1966. Chevalier, Légion d'Honneur, 1927; Mérite Libanais, 1937; Mérite Syrien, 1937; Grand Officier de l'Ordre Royal du Phénix, 1937; Ordre de l'Instruction Publique, Lebanese Republic, 1942; Décoration de l'Instruction Publique de l'Iran, 1942; Hon. OBE, 1946; Commander, Pologna Restituta, 1947; Grand Officer, Order of Cedar (Lebanon), 1948; Commander, Order of Ismail (Egypt), 1948; Syrian Order of Umayya, 1948. *Publications:* The American University of Beirut, 1958; Al-Azhar, a Millennium of Muslim Learning, 1961; Muslim Education in Medieval Times, 1962; (ed and trans.) The Fihrist of Al-Nadim, 1971. *Address:* 19 Alexander Street, Princeton, New Jersey 08540, USA.
[*Died 30 May 1972.*

DODSON, John Michael; a Recorder of the Crown Court, since 1973; Chairman, Agricultural Land Tribunals, Yorkshire and Lancashire Area since 1971 (Northern Area, 1972-75); *b* 11 Aug. 1919; *s* of James Stuart and Norah Dodson. *Educ:* Leeds Grammar Sch.; Leeds Univ. LLB Hons 1939. Anti-aircraft cruisers, RNVR, 1940-42; RINVR, 1942-46: Base Gunnery Officer, Calcutta; Exec. Officer, Karachi. Called to Bar, Gray's Inn, 1949. *Recreations:* walking, travel, music. *Address:* 37 Park Square, Leeds LS1 2PD. *T:* Leeds 25890. [*Died 18 May 1977.*

DODWELL, David William, CIE 1946; BA (Hons) Oxon, MA, PhD, Columbia; Economic Adviser to Joseph Lucas Ltd, Birmingham, 1948-63, retd; *b* 13 Dec. 1898; *s* of Frederick William Dodwell and Martha Ann Williams Dodwell (*née* Carpenter), Banbury, Oxon; *m* 1924, Marcia Ada Bausor Bradley (later Rev. M. A. B. Dodwell, MA Oxon, of the Christian Community, Birmingham; she *d* 1964), *d* of late W. Harris Bradley, Wolverhampton; two *s* one *d* (and one adopted *d*). *Educ:* Grimsbury Council Sch., Banbury; Banbury Grammar Sch.; Balliol Coll., Oxford (the first pupil of a state secondary sch. to win a Balliol scholarship); Brackenbury Scholar of Balliol in Modern History, 1915. 2nd Lieut, Worcs Regt, served in Egypt, 1917-19. BA Oxon, 2nd class Hons Mod. Hist., 1921. Entered ICS and arrived Madras, 1922; served as Asst Collector, Sub-Collector and Collector in various districts of Madras Province, 1922-25, 1928-32, and 1934-35. Tutor to HH the Maharajah of Travancore, 1925-28. Beit Prize of Oxford Univ. for essay on British Nationality, 1929; granted special leave to hold a Commonwealth Fund Service Fellowship at Graduate Sch. of Economics, Columbia Univ., New York, 1932-34; MA 1933, PhD 1934, Columbia, in economics; attached to Finance Dept of Madras Govt, 1935; Finance Sec. to the Govt of Madras, 1942-48; retd, 1948. Mem. OEEC Mission to USA to study motor industry, 1952. *Publications:* Treasuries and Central Banks, 1934; Ways and Means Procedure, 1936. *Recreations:* gardening, music. *Address:* Ingle Nursing Home, 25 Abington Park Crescent, Northampton NN3 3AD.
[*Died 21 Dec. 1980.*

DOKE, Dr Clement Martyn, MA, DLitt; Professor Emeritus of Bantu Philology, University of the Witwatersrand; retired; *b* Bristol, 1893; *s* of late Rev. J. J. Doke, Baptist Minister; *m* 1919, Hilda F. Lehman (*d* 1948); one *s* four *d*. *Educ:* Transvaal Univ. Coll., Pretoria; London Univ. Came to S Africa, 1903; Staff of SA Baptist Mission Soc. in Lambaland, North Rhodesia, 1914-21; completed translation of New Testament into Lamba, 1918; appointed to staff of Univ. of the Witwatersrand, 1923; undertook research trip to NW Kalahari to study Phonetics of Qhung Bushman, 1925; research in NW Rhodesia in Phonetics among the Lamba, 1926; research in NW Rhodesia among the Ila, 1927; seconded by S Rhodesian Govt for linguistic survey of native languages of S Rhodesia, and awarded Carnegie travelling fellowship for the year 1929; Editor of the South African Baptist, 1922-47; Joint-editor of Bantu Studies, 1931-41; Joint-editor of African Studies, 1942-53. Chm. of the Central Orthography Cttee of the Union Government Advisory Cttee on African Studies, 1929; Chm. of the Inter-University Cttee on African Studies, 1935; Pres., Baptist Union of S Africa, 1949-50. Hon. DLitt Rhodes Univ., 1971; Hon. LLD Witwatersrand Univ., 1972. *Publications:* The Grammar of the Lamba Language; Hygiene Reader in Lamba, 1922; Dissertation on the Phonetics of the Zulu Language, 1923; Outline of Phonetics of the Language of the Qhung Bushmen, 1925; The Phonetics of the Zulu Language, Outline of Lamba Phonetics, 1926; Lamba Folklore and Proverbs (American Folklore Soc.), 1927; Text-Book of Zulu Grammar, 1927, 6th edn 1961; (ed) Grammar of the Sesuto Language (Jacottet); An Outline of Ila Phonetics,

1928; (with Rev. B. H. Barnes) The Pronunciation of the Bemba Language; The Problem of Word-division in Bantu, 1929; The Unification of the Shona Dialects (Govt Blue-Book); The Lambas of Northern Rhodesia; A Comparative Study in Shona Phonetics, 1931; (ed) Xhosa Baptist Hymnal, 1932; English-Lamba Vocabulary, 1933, 2nd rev. edn 1963; Bantu Linguistic Terminology, 1935; Text-Book of Lamba Grammar, 1938; Bantu: Modern Grammatical, Phonetical, and Lexicographical Studies since 1860, 1945; (ed) Longmans' Zulu Readers: Imvulamlomo, Ingqaqamazinyo, Ufundukhuphuke, 1946; Unokuhlekisa, Unozizwe, Usokuzula, 1947; Izinkamb'eAfrika, 1949; Ukuhlakaniph'eAfrika, 1950; (with late B. W. Vilakazi) Zulu-English Dictionary, 1948; The Southern Bantu Languages, 1954; Zulu Syntax and Idiom, 1955; (with late S. M. Mofokeng) Text-Book of Southern Sotho Grammar, 1957; (with D. McK. Malcolm and J. M. A. Sikakana) English and Zulu Dictionary, 1958; Lamba Bible Dictionary, 1959; trans. Bible into Lamba, 1959; Graded Lamba Grammar and Exercises, 1963; Trekking in South-Central Africa 1913-1919, 1975. *Address:* Flat 19, Marina Hills, Keam Road, Baysville, East London, 5201, South Africa. *T:* East London 20433.   [*Died* 23 *Feb.* 1980.

DOLL, William Alfred Millner, CMG 1943; *b* 19 Dec. 1885; *s* of Charles FitzRoy Doll, JP, and Emily Frances Doll, Hadham Towers, Much Hadham, Herts; *m* 1st, Walburga, *d* of Philip Ebe, Arbon, Switzerland; 2nd, Sybil, *d* of Richard Cunningham, Wadhurst, Sussex. *Educ:* Charterhouse (Scholar); Trinity Hall, Cambridge (Scholar); Bonn, Freiburg, Geneva, and Florence. BA 1907; MA 1912. N. M. Rothschild & Sons, 1912-24; served European War, 1914-19 (despatches, MSM; Orders of St Anne and St Stanislas, 3rd Cl); Inter-allied Commission in Bulgaria, 1925-30; British Delegate, 1926-30; Pres., 1926 and 1929; Financial Observer, State of Parana, Brazil, 1930-33; negotiated for Metropolitan Vickers financial agreement with Govt of Brazil for electrification of Central Railway, 1933-34; Financial Adviser, Ministry of Finance, Siam, 1936-42 (Order of Crown of Siam, 1st Cl.). Advisory Attaché, Bank of England, 1942-45; Financial Mem. of the De La Warr Mission to Ethiopia, 1944; Currency Adviser to Lord Louis Mountbatten's Command, South East Asia, 1945-46; Financial Adviser to Siamese Government, 1946-51. Légion d'Honneur, 1950. *Recreations:* music, natural history, philately, outdoor sports. *Address:* c/o National Westminster Bank Ltd, Aldersgate Branch, EC1. *Club:* MCC.   [*Died* 17 *June* 1977.

DOLPHIN, Albert Edward; *b* 8 Feb. 1895; *m* 1915, Emily Hazeltine, Todmorden, Yorks; two *s*. *Educ:* University of Saskatchewan. Went to Canada in 1913; after specialising in Finance and Economics, University of Saskatchewan, was associated in business with International Correspondence Schools; returned to England Dec. 1921 and joined Encyclopædia Britannica Co. Ltd; Dir, 1934. Administrateur of Encyclopædia Britannica SARL, France; Dir, Encyclopædia Britannica (South Africa) Pty. Ltd; Vice-Chm. and Managing Dir, Encyclopædia Britannica Ltd, 1947-53. Member: Chartered Institute of Secretaries; Association of Certified and Corporate Accountants. *Recreation:* philately. *Address:* Le Chalet, Mount Road, Thundersley, Essex.   [*Died* 27 *Aug.* 1972.

DOLPHIN, Rear-Adm. George Verner Motley, CB 1957; DSO 1944; retd; *b* 1902; *s* of late Capt. George Manaton Dolphin, Royal Navy, and late Anne Clare Savory; *m* 1926, Phyllis Margaret Dickinson; one *s*. *Educ:* RN Colls Osborne and Dartmouth. Entered RN, 1916; served in destroyers, 1924-32; Term Lieut, RNC Dartmouth. Served War of 1939-45: HMS Sheffield, on Northern Patrol, 1939; HMS Hermione, in Malta Convoys, 1940-41 (despatches); HMS Ramillies, E Africa, 1943; Capt. GG3 and Naval Officer in charge Gold Area for Normandy landings (DSO); Capt. of RNAS Rattray, 1945. Admiralty, Bath (DNE), 1946; Capt. of Dockyard, Portsmouth, 1948; Sen. Officer (Afloat), New Zealand Navy and Capt. of HMNZS Bellona and Black Prince, 1950; Cdre, Harwich, 1953; Admiral Superintendent, HM Dockyard, Chatham, 1954-58. *Recreations:* sailing, tennis, golf. *Address:* 6 Burford Lane, Ewell, Surrey KT17 3EY.   [*Died* 10 *July* 1979.

DOLPHIN, John Robert Vernon, CBE 1956; TD; part-time Consultant; *b* 1 Oct. 1905; *s* of H. E. Dolphin and Dorothy Dolphin, Christleton, Chester; *m* 1966, Mary Evelyn Fisher. *Educ:* Marlborough Coll.; Loughborough Engineering Coll. (DLC). Student Apprentice, Hydraulic Engineering Co., Chester, 1926-28; Inspector, Selection Trust Ltd, 1929-30; Man., Austin Hoy and Co. Ltd, 1930-34; Sales Manager and Engineer, Sheepbridge Coal and Iron Co. Ltd; John Dolphin Ltd, Consultants, 1938. Army, 1939, Lieut TA; Lieut-Col 1940; Commanding Officer Inter-Services Research Station, Welwyn. Managing Dir, Corgi Motor Cycle Co. Ltd, Dolphin Industrial Developments Ltd, and Hydraulic Developments Ltd, 1946-50;

Chief Engineer, Atomic Weapons Research Establishment, 1951-57; Engineer-in-Chief, Research Gp, UKAEA, 1957-59; Joint Managing Dir, Lansing Bagnall Ltd and J. E. Shay Ltd, 1959-64. Director, TI (Group Services) Ltd, 1964-68. FInstF 1939. *Inventions include:* Welman One-man Submarine; Welbike Parachutists' Motorcycle; Corgi Motorcycle; Harrier Folding Jeep; Hoy Double Box Coal Cutter Chain; Lina-Loda Freight Handling Machine; Turret (3-way reach) Truck. *Recreations:* swimming and yachting. *Address:* The Mill, Whitchurch-on-Thames, Oxon. *T:* Pangbourne 2480. *Club:* Royal Automobile.   [*Died* 2 *May* 1973.

DOMVILE, Adm. Sir Barry Edward, KBE 1934; CB 1922; CMG 1917; RN (retired); *b* 1878; *e s* of Adm. Sir Compton Domvile, GCB; *m* 1916, Alexandrina (*d* 1950), *d* of Mr von der Heydt; one *s* one *d* (and one *s* killed in action, 1941). *Educ:* HMS Britannia. Entered RN 1892; specially promoted Lieut, 1898; Beaufort Testimonial; Ryder Prize; Goodenough Gold Medal; Comdr. 1909; Capt. 1916; Rear-Adm. 1927; Gold Medallist, Royal United Service Institution, 1906; Asst Sec., Cttee of Imperial Defence, 1912-14; served European War in comd of HM Ships, 1914-19 (CMG); Dir of Plans Div., Admiralty, 1920-22; Chief of Staff, Mediterranean (Commodore, 2nd Class), 1922-25; Commanded HMS Royal Sovereign, 1925-26; Dir of Naval Intelligence Div., 1927-30; Rear-Adm. and Vice-Adm. commanding 3rd Cruiser Sqdn, Mediterranean, 1931-32; Pres., RNC Greenwich, and Vice-Adm. Commanding War Coll., 1932-34; Adm. and retired list, 1936. *Publications:* By and Large, 1936; Look to Your Moat, 1937; From Admiral to Cabin Boy, 1947. *Recreation:* outdoor sports. *Address:* Robin's Tree, Roehampton Vale, SW15. *T:* 01-788 3830. *Club:* Royal Yacht Squadron (Cowes).   [*Died* 13 *Aug.* 1971.

DONALD, Air Marshal Sir (David) G.; *see* Donald, Sir Grahame.

DONALD, Douglas Alexander; Sheriff of Inverness, Moray, Nairn, and Ross and Cromarty, at Inverness, since 1956. Sheriff Substitute of Inverness, Elgin and Nairn at Portree, 1940-45; of Argyll at Dunoon and of Bute at Rothesay. *Address:* Sheriff Court House, Inverness.   [*Died* 15 *Nov.* 1975.

DONALD, Air Marshal Sir Grahame, KCB 1944 (CB 1941); DFC; AFC; MA; *b* 1891; *s* of David Donald, MD; *m* 1916, Gwynneth Adrienne (*d* 1946), *d* of J. W. Martin, Filey; (one *s* killed in action, 1940; one *d* decd); *m* 1947, Ailsa Stevenson; one *d*. *Educ:* Dulwich Coll.; University Coll., Oxford. Served European War, 1914-18, with RNAS; joined RAF 1918. AOC-in-C Maintenance Command, 1942-47; retired, 1947. *Address:* The Manor Cottage, Tilford, Farnham, Surrey. *T:* Frensham 2135. *Club:* Royal Air Force.   [*Died* 23 *Dec.* 1976.

DONALD, Sir James Bell, Kt 1969; JP (Auckland, NZ); Managing Director, A. B. Donald Ltd, Auckland, NZ, and subsidiary Cos since 1900; *b* 13 Oct. 1879; 2nd *s* of late Alexander Bell Donald and Charlotte Donald; *m* 1968, Doris Sadie Olive Fair; no *c*. *Educ:* Queen's College, Auckland, NZ. Elected MP, 1929, and apptd Minister of the Crown, holding portfolios of Minister of Customs, Postmaster-Gen., Minister of Marine; Mem., Auckland Harbour Bd, 1935 (Chm., 1946-47); retd Oct. 1947. *Publication:* The Inheritance of the Lord, or the Israel of God, 1964. *Recreations:* bowls, Rugby football. *Address:* 34 Arney Road, Remuera, Auckland, NZ. *T:* Auckland 547726. *Clubs:* Auckland, Northern (Auckland).   [*Died* 4 *Dec.* 1971.

DONALD, Prof. Maxwell Bruce, SM (MIT); ARCSc; Hon. MIChemE; FRIC; Emeritus Professor of Chemical Engineering in the University of London; *b* 20 July 1897. *Educ:* Felsted Sch.; Royal Coll. of Science; Massachusetts Inst. of Technology. Served European War, Lieut and ADC, RA, 1915-19. Sir Alfred Yarrow Scholar, 1921; Demonstrator in Physical Chemistry, Royal College of Science, 1923; Chemical Engineer, Chilean Nitrate Producers Assoc., 1925; Adviser on bitumen emulsions, Royal Dutch-Shell Group, 1929; Lecturer in Chemical Engineering, University Coll., London, 1931; Reader, 1947; Ramsay Memorial Prof., 1951-65. Hon. Sec., Institution of Chemical Engineers, 1937-49, Moulton medallist, 1937, Osborne Reynolds medallist, 1940; Vice-Pres. 1950. DSIR Visitor to British Baking Research Assoc., 1949. *Publications:* (with H. P. Stevens) Rubber in Chemical Engineering, 1933 and 1949; Elizabethan Copper, 1955; Elizabethan Monopolies, 1961. *Address:* Rabbit Shaw, 6 Stagbury Avenue, Chipstead, Surrey CR3 3PA. *T:* Downland 53365.   [*Died* 6 *Jan.* 1978.

DONALD, William C.; *see* Coutts Donald.

DONALDSON, John Coote, CIE 1939; MC; Indian Civil Service, retired; *b* 24 May 1895; *s* of late John Donaldson, KC,

Dublin; *m* 1933, Barbara Maud, *d* of late Hon. Sir Charles Henry Bayley Kendall; one *s* one *d. Educ:* Felsted; Trinity Coll., Dublin (MA). Entered Indian Civil Service, 1920. *Address:* Medlars, Fairy Road, Seaview, IoW. *T:* Seaview 2379.
[Died 20 May 1980.

DONALDSON, Malcolm, MA Cantab; FRCS MB, BCh Cantab, FRCOG; FIHE; Consulting Physician Accoucheur, St Bartholomew's Hospital; Hon. Director Cancer Information Association, Oxford; Vice-President, British Cancer Campaign; late Vice-Chairman National Radium Commission; late Director of Cancer Department, St Bartholomew's Hospital; Consulting Gynæcologist, Mount Vernon Hospital, Northwood; Consulting Gynæcologist, Royal Northern Hospital; Cottage Hospital, Brentford; Potters Bar; etc; *b* 27 April 1884; *s* of John Donaldson, Chiswick; *m* 1st, 1919, Evelyn Helen Marguerite Gilroy; two *s* ; 2nd, 1940, Mia (*d* 1970), *widow* of Gregory J. M. Whyley, MA, LLB. *Educ:* Charterhouse; Trinity Coll., Cambridge; Natural Science Tripos. Served War of 1914-18, Major RAMC (despatches). Entered St Bartholomew's Hospital, 1906, and was appointed to the staff 1921; late examiner in Midwifery and Gynæcology, Cambridge Univ., London MB, and Central Midwives Board. *Publications:* Early Diagnosis and Treatment of Cancer, Institute of Public Health, 1929; Radiotherapy in Diseases of Women, 1933; Early Diagnosis of Malignant Disease (jointly), 1936; The Cancer Riddle, 1962; many articles dealing with Education of the Lay Public concerning Cancer and other medical papers. *Recreation:* rowing, won the University Sculls and rowed for the University against Oxford and later in the same year against Harvard University. *Address:* 337 Woodstock Road, Oxford. *Clubs:* Athenæum, Leander.
[Died 16 March 1973.

DONE, His Honour William Edward Pears, MC; FSA; retired County Court Judge; JP Middlesex, Hertford and West Sussex; *b* 10 March 1883; *s* of late William and M. E. Done, Groombridge, Sussex; *m* 1st, 1917, Beatrice Helen Sharpley (*d* 1952); one *d* ; 2nd, 1954, Gladys Bagley. *Educ:* Elizabeth Coll., Guernsey; Pembroke Coll., Oxford. Called to Bar, 1910; practised Common Law Bar and Western Circuit. Commission 5th Royal Sussex Regt, Sept. 1914; served in France, Belgium and Italy; Staff Capt. 145 Infantry Brigade, 1917 (despatches, MC, Croce di Guerra); returned to practice, 1919. Appointed County Court Judge, April 1945; circuits: Lambeth 1945, Edmonton 1945, Clerkenwell 1950; retired 1955. *Publications:* Looking back in Sussex, 1953; Chichester as the Romans called it, 1957; The Parish Church of St Peter and St Paul, West Wittering. *Recreations:* gardening, botany and local history. *Address:* Westringes, West Wittering, Chichester.
[Died 27 May 1976.

DONEGALL, 6th Marquis of (*cr* 1791), **Edward Arthur Donald St George Hamilton Chichester;** Hereditary Lord High Admiral of Lough Neagh; Viscount Chichester and Baron of Belfast, 1625; Earl of Donegall, 1647; Earl of Belfast, 1791; Baron Fisherwick (Gt Britain), 1790; *b* 7 Oct. 1903; *o c* of 5th Marquess and 2nd wife, Violet Gertrude, (*d* 1952), *o d* of Henry St George Twining, Halifax, NS; *S* father, 1904; *m* 1st, 1943, Gladys Jean (marr. diss. 1968), *yr d* of Captain Christian Combe; 2nd, 1968, Mrs Maureen McKenzie, *e d* of Major G. C. Scholfield, MC. *Educ:* Eton; Christ Church, Oxford. A Journalist; Lt-Col in the Army Cadet Force; British War Correspondent, 1939-45. *Heir:* 5th Baron Templemore. *Address:* Lord Donegall's Office, The Studio, 39 Clabon Mews, SW1. *T:* 01-589 6688. *Clubs:* Carlton, Press, MCC.
[Died 24 May 1975.

DONNELLY, Desmond Louis; Journalist; Chairman, ICPS Ltd, since 1972; Managing Director, Practical Europe Ltd, since 1973; Director of other companies; *b* 16 Oct. 1920; *o s* of late L. J. Donnelly, Assam, India, and Aimée Tucker; *m* 1947, Rosemary, *d* of late Dr John Taggart, Belfast; one *s* two *d* (of whom one *s* one *d* are twins). *Educ:* Brightlands Sch., Newnham, Glos; Bembridge Sch., Isle of Wight. Served War of 1939-45. RAF, 1940-46, Flight Lieut. Contested (Common Wealth), Evesham, 1945, (Lab), County Down, 1946; MP (Lab) Pembroke, 1950-68; resigned Labour Whip, 1968, on British withdrawals from East of Suez; MP (Ind) 1968-70; joined Cons. Party, 1971. Editor, Town and Country Planning, 1946-49; Dir of the Town and Country Planning Assoc., 1948-50, Mem. Council 1951-. Adviser to: David Brown Corp., 1954-71; Philips Industries, 1964-71; political columnist, Daily Herald, 1960-63; chief political corresp., News of the World, 1968-70. Pres., Brightlands Old Boys Assoc., 1968-; past Pres., Old Bembridgians Assoc. *Publications:* The March Wind, 1959; Trade With Communist Countries (with Alec Nove), 1960; David Brown's: The Story of a Family Business, 1960; No Gains without Pains, 1960; Years Ahead, 1964; Struggle for the World,

1965; The Nearing Storm, 1968; Gadarene '68, 1968; There is Another Britain, 1970. *Recreations:* swimming, walking and cricket (founder and organiser, British Empire Cricket XI, 1940). *Address:* 17 Morpeth Mansions, SW1. *T:* 01-834 5700. *Clubs:* Travellers', Royal Air Force, Chelsea Arts, MCC.
[Died 4 April 1974.

DONOVAN, Baron, *cr* 1964 (Life Peer); **Terence Norbert Donovan,** PC 1960; Kt 1950; a Lord of Appeal in Ordinary since 1963; *b* 13 June 1898; *m* 1925, Marjorie, *d* of Charles and Leah Murray, Winchester; two *s* one *d.* Called to Bar, Middle Temple, 1924; commenced to practise, 1932; QC 1945. Served in France, 1917-18, with Beds Regt, and later, with RAF. Called to Bar of Southern Rhodesia, 1937; entered Civil Service, 1920, leaving in 1932. Chm., Brit. Govt Legal Mission to Greece, 1945; Member: Denning Cttee on Divorce procedure, 1946; Lewis Cttee on Court Martial procedure, 1946-48; Chm.: Criminal Appeals Cttee, 1964; Royal Commission on Trade Unions and Employers' Assocs, 1965-68. MP (Lab) East Leicester, 1945-50; North East Leicester, Feb.-July 1950; Judge of King's Bench Div., High Court of Justice, 1950-60; a Lord Justice of Appeal, 1960-63. JP Hants. *Address:* House of Lords, SW1. *Club:* Athenæum.
[Died 12 Dec. 1971.

DONOVAN, Dame Florence (May); *see* Hancock, Dame Florence.

DONOVAN, John, CBE 1953; FCIT; retired; *b* 25 Dec. 1891; *s* of John Donovan, stevedore; *m* 1911, Annie Louise Burke; two *s* four *d* ; *m* 1964, Dame Florence May Hancock, *qv. Educ:* St Joseph's, Swansea, Dockworker, 1906-15. Served European War, 1914-18, Welsh Regt, 1915-19. Dockworker, 1919-25; Trade Union Sec., Cornwall, 1925-32; Trade Union Area Sec., 1932-40; National Docks Sec., Transport and Gen. Workers Union, 1940-47; Mem., Management Board, British Transport Docks, 1947-58. Mem. Falmouth Town Council, 1928-32; mem. Bristol City Council, 1937-40. *Recreations:* music, swimming, Rugby football. *Address:* 4 Melita Road, St Andrew's, Bristol BS6 5AZ. *T:* Bristol 43880.
[Died 13 Nov. 1971.

DONOVAN, John Thomas, CIE 1931; BA RUI; Barrister-at-law; *y s* of late William Donovan, Galway; *b* 12 Dec. 1885; *m* Sara (*d* 1972), *d* of C. Devane, Limerick; two *s* two *d. Educ:* Clongowes Wood Coll.; Queen's Coll., Galway; Trinity Coll., Dublin. Entered Indian Civil Service, 1910; Registrar of Co-operative Socs, Bengal, 1916-21; Dep. Commissioner of Darjeeling, 1921-22; Sec. to Govt of Bengal Agriculture and Industries Dept, and Mem. of the Bengal Legislative Council, 1922-24; Mem. of the Legislative Assembly of India, and District Magistrate, Hooghly, 1925-27; District Magistrate Bakarganj District, 1927-31; retired from Indian Civil Service, 1932; Organising Sec., Irish Bank Officials' Association, 1932-48; Hon. Fellow of Institute of Bankers of Ireland, 1935. *Address:* Fernhurst, Shrewsbury Road, Dublin. *T:* Dublin 692774.
[Died 2 March 1973.

DOREY, Edgar Aleck, CBE 1945; Jurat of Royal Court of Jersey, 1935-58; Juge d'Instruction (Magistrate) for Jersey, 1947-58; *b* 21 Oct. 1886; *s* of Thomas Dorey; *m* 1919, Olive Kathleen Giffard; one *s* one *d. Educ:* High Sch., Jersey. Capital and Counties Bank, 1902-18; retired to Jersey, 1931. *Address:* Stella Maris, Samares, Jersey. *T:* Central 22687. *Club:* United (Jersey).
[Died 6 April 1976.

DOREY, Stanley Fabes, CBE 1946; FRS 1948; DSc, CEng, FInstCE, Hon. FIMechE, FRINA, FIMarE, etc.; Chief Engineer Surveyor of Lloyd's Register of Shipping, 1932-56, retired; *b* 28 Nov. 1891; 2nd *s* of late Wm Dorey, London and Worthing; *m* 1st, 1920, Dorothy Ellen (*d* 1949), *o c* of late Richard Midworth, Bowes Park; one *s* two *d* ; *m* 2nd, 1956, Evelyn Josephine, *d* of late John Moffatt, Dublin. *Educ:* Owen's Sch., London; Durham Univ. Apprenticeship at Chatham Royal Dockyard, Whitworth Exhibitioner, 1912; Engineer-Lieut, Royal Navy, 1914-19; Engine and Ship Surveyor; Lloyd's Register of Shipping, 1919; Charles Parsons Memorial lecture and medal, 1942; Past President: Engineering Section, British Assoc.; Inst. of Marine Engineers; Institution of Mechanical Engineers; Inst. of Metals; Inst. of Refrigeration; Whitworth Soc. Hon. Vice-Pres. Royal Institution of Naval Architects; Hon. Fellow NE Coast Inst. of Engineers and Shipbuilders; Foreign Mem. Danish Academy of Technical Sciences. Liveryman of Company of Shipwrights, Freeman of City of London. *Publications:* papers to technical institutions and socs. *Recreation:* rural contemplation. *Address:* 3 Springwood Road, Heathfield, Sussex. *T:* Heathfield 3888. *[Died 30 Aug. 1972.*

DORLAND, Arthur Garratt, BA, MA, PhD; FRSC; Professor of History and Head of the History Department, University of

Western Ontario, London, Ontario, 1920-56 (appointed first J. B. Smallman Professor of History, 1955), retired 1956, Emeritus Professor, 1971; *b* Wellington, Prince Edward County, Ont, 1887; *s* of John T. Dorland, Jun., of Wellington, and Lavina Hubbs of Bloomfield, Ont; *m* 1912, Ellen Uprichard, *d* of Joseph H. Malone, Dublin; three *s* one *d*. *Educ:* Ashburton House, London, England; Bloomfield Public Sch.; Pickering Coll.; Queen's Univ.; Yale Univ.; Chicago Univ. Teacher of History and English, and Housemaster, Pickering Coll., 1911-14; Currier Fellow in History, Yale, 1914-15; Lecturer in History, Queen's Univ., Kingston, 1916-20; Clerk of Canada Yearly Meeting of the Religious Soc. of Friends, 1924. Pres. Coll. and Secondary Sch. Dept of Ontario Education Assoc., 1949; Pres. Section II Royal Society of Canada, 1949; Associate Ed., The Loyalist Gazette, 1966. Hon. LLD Univ. of Western Ontario, 1963. Canada Centennial Medal, 1967; Queen's Silver Jubilee Medal, 1978. *Publications:* The Royal Disallowance in Massachusetts, 1917; British North America since (1713), published in Expansion of the Anglo-Saxon Nations, 1920; A History of the Society of Friends (Quakers) in Canada, 1927; The Origins of the Holy Alliance, 1939; Our Canada, A History textbook, 1949; Former Days and Quaker Ways, 1965, 2nd illus. edn 1972; The Quakers in Canada, 1968. *Recreations:* gardening, boating. *Address:* Fair Acre, Wellington, Ont, Canada.   *[Died 26 June 1979.*

DORMAN-SMITH, Col Rt. Hon. Sir Reginald Hugh, PC 1939; GBE 1941; Kt 1937; JP; *b* 1899; *s* of Major E. P. Dorman-Smith, Bellamont Forest, County Cavan, Ireland; *m* 1921, Doreen Agnes Edith, *d* of Sir John Watson, 2nd Bt of Earnock; one *d* (and one *d* decd). *Educ:* Harrow; RMC Sandhurst. 15th Sikhs (IA) and 5th Batt. Queen's Royal Regt (TA); County Alderman, 1931-35, and JP for Surrey; MP (C) Petersfield Div. of Hants, 1935-41; Pres. National Farmers Union, 1936-37; Minister of Agriculture and Fisheries, 1939-40; Liaison Officer between Home Defence Forces and Govt Dept, 1940; Governor of Burma, 1941-46. High Sheriff, Hants, 1952; JP, Hants, 1960. KStJ. *Address:* Hunters Croft, Grayswood Road, Haslemere, Surrey GU27 2DL. *T:* Haslemere 3012. *[Died 20 March 1977.*

DORMER, 15th Baron (*cr* 1615); **Charles Walter James Dormer,** Bt 1615; Captain Life Guards; *b* 20 Dec. 1903; *s* of 14th Baron and Caroline May (*d* 1951), *y d* of late Col Sir Spencer Clifford; *S* father, 1922; *m* 1944, Lady Maureen Thérèse Josephine Noel, *o d* of 4th Earl of Gainsborough, Exton Park, Rutland; two *d*. *Educ:* Oratory Sch. and RMC, Sandhurst. ADC to Governor-Gen. of New Zealand, 1939-41. *Heir: b* Hon. Joseph Spencer Philip Dormer, Lieut Scots Guards, *b* 4 Sept 1914. *Address:* Grove Park, Warwick. *T:* Warwick 43633; 12 Campden House Court, 42 Gloucester Walk, W8.   *[Died 27 Aug. 1975.*

DORMER, Sir Cecil Francis Joseph, KCMG 1937; MVO; *b* 14 Feb. 1883; *y s* of late Hon. Hubert Dormer, and *g s* of 11th Baron Dormer; *m* 1915, Lady Mary A. C. Feilding (*d* 1973), *e d* of 9th Earl of Denbigh. *Educ:* St Augustine's Coll., Ramsgate. Clerk in Foreign Office, 1905; Acting 2nd Sec. in Diplomatic Service, 1911; Asst Private Sec. to Sec. of State for Foreign Affairs (Viscount Grey, KG, and Mr Balfour) 1915-19; Chargé d'Affaires, Caracas, 1919-21; Sec. of British Legation to the Holy See, Rome, 1921-25; Counsellor of Embassy at Tokio, 1926-29; Envoy Extraordinary and Minister Plenipotentiary Bangkok, 1929; Oslo, 1934; Ambassador to Polish Government in London, 1941-43. Grand Cross, Order of St Olav (Norway), 1940; Norwegian War Medal. *Address:* St Anne's Nursing Home, Wokingham, Berks.   *[Died 28 July 1979.*

D'ORMESSON, Count Wladimir Olivier Marie François de Paule Le Fèvre; Grand Croix de la Légion d'Honneur; Grand Croix de l'Ordre National du Mérite (Member Council of the Order); Croix de Guerre; French political essayist and journalist and former ambassador; Member of the French Academy since 1956; President Administration Council, Radiodiffusion-Télévision française, 1964-68; *b* St Petersburg, Russia, 2 Aug. 1888; *s* of Olivier, Comte d'Ormesson, and la Comtesse d'Ormesson (*née* Marguerite de la Guéronnière); *m* 1913, late Conchita de Malo; three *s* three *d*. *Educ:* Lycée Janson-de-Sailly; Ecole des Sciences Politiques, Paris. Leader writer for Figaro; foreign political ed. for Temps, Journal de Genève, etc. French Ambassador to: the Holy See, 1940; the Argentine Republic, 1945-48; the Holy See, 1948-56. Holds numerous foreign decorations. *Publications:* Les Jets d'Eau (poems), 1913; La Préface d'une Vie, 1919; Nos Illusions sur l'Europe Centrale, 1922; Dans la nuit européenne, 1923; Les Résultats de la politique de la Ruhr, 1924; La Première Mission de la France aux Etats-Unis, 1928; La Confiance en l'Allemagne?, 1928; La Paix religieuse, 1929; Notre Vieille Maison, 1931; Enfances diplomatiques, 1932; La Grande Crise mondiale de 1857, 1932; La Révolution allemande, 1934; Qu'est-ce qu'un Français?

(Clemenceau, Poincaré, Briand), 1935; Vue cavalière de l'Europe, 1936; Adieux, 1937; L'Eternel Problème allemand, 1945; La Ville éternelle, 1956; Mission à Rome, 1957; La Papauté, 1957; La Présence française dans la Rome des papes, 1958; La Ville et les Champs, 1960; Les Vraies Confidences, 1962; Auprès de Lyautey 1964; Le Clergé et l'Académie française, 1965; De Saint-Pétersbourg à Rome, 1969; Présence du Général de Gaulle, 1972; De vous à moi, 1973. *Address:* Château d'Ormesson, Ormesson-sur-Marne, Seine-et-Oise, France; 9 rue Salignac-Fénélon, 92 Neuilly sur Seine.
                                               [Died 15 Sept. 1973.

DORRELL, Bt Lieut-Col George Thomas, VC 1914; MBE 1925; *m* Lucy (*d* 1969); one *s* two *d*. Ranks, 1895-1914; served South African War, 1899-1902; Commissioned RHA, 1914; Capt. RFA, 1918; European War, 1914-18 (VC). Retired from Regular Army with rank of Major, 1921; granted commission as Capt. in Territorial RA, 1921; Major, 1924; Bt Lieut-Col 1929; Company Comdr, Home Guard, 1940-45. *Address:* 30 Bray Road, Cobham, Surrey.   *[Died 7 Jan. 1971.*

DOTT, Norman McOmish, CBE 1948; FRSE 1936; MB, ChB, FRCS (Ed.), 1923; retired 1962; Medical Officer, Regional Stoma Clinic, Astley Ainslie Hospital, Edinburgh, 1972; Professor Emeritus; Hon. Consulting Neurological Surgeon to: Royal Infirmary of Edinburgh; Western General Hospital, Edinburgh; Royal Edinburgh Hospital for Sick Children; *b* 26 Aug. 1897; *m* 1932, Margaret Robertson; one *d*. *Educ:* George Heriot's Sch., Edinburgh; University of Edinburgh. After leaving sch. was apprentice joiner, apprentice engineer; accidental injury to hip, 1913; Edinburgh Univ. Med. Sch., 1914; graduated (MB, ChB), 1919; Asst Surgeon, Deaconess and Chalmers Hosps, 1923; Jun. Assoc. in Neurological Surgery, Peter Bent Brigham Hosp., Boston, USA (with Dr Harvey Cushing), 1923-24; Surgeon in Ordinary, Royal Edinburgh Hosp. for Sick Children, 1925; Neurological surgery in private nursing homes in Edinburgh, 1924-31; Surgeon in Ordinary, Deaconess Hospital, 1929-31; Neurological Surgeon, Royal Infirmary, Edinburgh, 1931; resigned Deaconess and Chalmers Hospital posts, 1931, and Children's Hospital post, 1935, remaining attached as Neurological Surgeon. Lecturer in Neurological Surgery, University of Edinburgh, 1932; Dir of Neurology and Neurosurgery, Bangour EMS Hosp. (near Edinburgh), 1940. Formerly: Prof. of Neurological Surgery, University of Edinburgh, 1947-62; Neurological Surgeon to: Royal Infirmary, Edinburgh; Western Gen. Hosp., Edinburgh; Royal Edinburgh Hosp. for Sick Children. Mem. GMC, 1966-71; Chairman: Edinburgh Cttee, British Empire Campaign for Cancer Research, 1963-72; Epilepsy Soc., Edinburgh and SE Scotland, 1967-72; President: Scottish Assoc. for Occupational Therapy, 1960-72; Scottish Soc. for the History of Medicine, 1966-68; Hon. President: Scottish Paraplegia Assoc., 1963; Scottish Spina Bifida Assoc., 1965. Vice-Pres., RCS Edinburgh, 1957-67; Hon. FRSM, 1968; Hon. Mem. numerous European, North and South American, Middle Eastern, African and Asiatic Surgical and Neurosurgical Colls, Socs., etc. Freedom of the City of Edinburgh, 1962. Hon. MD Edinburgh, 1969. *Publications:* numerous surgical and neurosurgical. *Recreations:* fishing, travel, handicrafts. *Address:* 3 Chalmers Crescent, Edinburgh EH9 1TW. *T:* 031-667 2188.   *[Died 10 Dec. 1973.*

DOUBLEDAY, Frederic Nicklin; Consulting Dental Surgeon to Guy's Hospital; Vice-President Medical Defence Union; formerly Vice-President Royal Society of Medicine; Examiner in Dental Surgery to the Royal College of Surgeons of England; *b* 5 March 1885; *s* of F. W. Doubleday; *m* Esther Jane, 2nd *d* of Rev. J. A. Barrow-Clugh, BA, BD. *Educ:* Privately; Guy's Hosp. University of Berlin. Graduated from Guy's Hosp.; LDS, RCS 1908, LRCP, MRCS 1912; Fellow in Dental Surgery, RCS, 1947; Dental Societies Prizeman, 1907, and Dental Travelling Scholar in Berlin, 1909-10; formerly Ed. of the British Dental Journal; External Examiner to the University of Bristol; Extramural Lecturer to the University of Toronto; Dental Surgeon to King George Vth Hosp. for Treatment of Gunshot Injuries of the Face and Jaws; visiting Prof. of Dental Surgery, Fouad Univ., Cairo, 1948; Wallis Lecturer, Royal Society of Medicine, 1948; Hon. Member: Stomatological Soc. of Greece, 1948; Stomatological Soc. of Piedmont, Italy, 1951; Odontological Section, RSM, London, 1956. Hon. Life Mem. Brit. Dental Assoc., 1959. *Publications:* (part author) Guy's Hospital 1725-1948, 1951; many Papers on Medical and Dental Subjects, Lectures in United States, Canada, and other countries; Ed., The New Rambler, Jl of Johnson Society of London. *Recreations:* travel, walking, swimming. *Address:* Hartland, Moores Road, Dorking, Surrey. *T:* Dorking 3955.
                                               [Died 4 April 1971.

DOUBLEDAY, Sir Leslie, Kt 1957; JP; *b* 1887; *s* of Rev. John Doubleday, Sittingbourne, Kent; *m* 1912, Nora, *d* of William Foster, Tunbridge Wells; two *s* two *d. Educ:* Taunton; Wye Coll. Served European War, 1914-18, Kent Yeomanry (Capt.). Mem., Kent War Agricultural Executive Cttee, 1940-45. JP 1925 (Chm., Sittingbourne Petty Sessions, 1946-60); County Councillor, 1925-74, County Alderman, 1941-74, Kent; High Sheriff of Kent, 1942, 1951; Past Chm., Dartford Tunnel Joint Cttee. Past Master, Fruiterers' Company. Farmer. *Address:* Hempstead, Tonge, Sittingbourne, Kent. *T:* Sittingbourne 3981. *Club:* Farmers'. *[Died 6 Feb. 1975.*

DOUGHTY, Charles John Addison; QC 1954; a Recorder, and Honorary Recorder of Brighton, since 1972; *b* 21 Sept. 1902; *e s* of late Sir Charles Doughty, QC; *m* 1931, Adelaide Baillieu Shackell (*see* Dame Adelaide Doughty); one *s* one *d. Educ:* Eton; Magdalen Coll., Oxford. Called to Bar, Inner Temple, 1926. Served War of 1939-45, with Coldstream Guards, 1940-45. Contested Aston Div. of Birmingham, Gen. Election, 1950; MP (C) Eastern Division of Surrey, 1951-70. Recorder of Brighton, 1955-71. *Recreation:* fishing. *Address:* 2 Harcourt Buildings, Temple, EC4. *[Died 10 July 1973.*

DOUGLAS OF BARLOCH, 1st Baron, *cr* 1950, of Maxfield, Sussex; **Francis Campbell Ross Douglas,** KCMG 1947; MA; LLD (hc), Royal University of Malta; Partner in Douglas & Company, Solicitors; *b* Manitoba, 21 Oct. 1889; *s* of late Francis J. B. Douglas; *m* 1st, Minnie Findlay Smith, MA, JP, CStJ (*d* 1969); one *d*; 2nd, Adela Elizabeth, *widow* of Captain George La Croix Baudains, DSO, MC. *Educ:* Glasgow Univ. Journalist, Accountant, Solicitor; MP (Lab) for North Battersea, 1940-46; Parliamentary Private Sec. to Parliamentary Sec. of Board of Education, 1940-45; Parliamentary Private Sec. to Home Sec., 1945-46; Temp. Chm., House of Commons and Chm. of Standing Cttees, 1945-46; Chm. of Estimates Cttee, 1945-46; Mem. of Railway Assessment Authority, 1938-46; Mem. of Anglo-Scottish Railway Assessment Authority, 1941-46; Mem. of Public Works Loan Board, 1936-46; Chm. of Finance Cttee of LCC, 1940-46; Governor and Comdr-in-Chief of Malta, 1946-49; Vice-Chm. of Corby Development Corp., 1950-62; Deputy Speaker of House of Lords, 1962-; FRAS; KStJ. *Publications:* Land Value Rating, 1961; numerous pamphlets and articles on land tenure, taxation, soil fertility and nutrition. *Heir:* none. *Address:* 8 Cambridge Road, SW11. *T:* 01-228 2247; Maxfield Manor, Three Oaks, Sussex. *T:* Hastings 751074.
[Died 30 March 1980 (ext).

DOUGLAS, Lt-Col Archibald Vivian Campbell, MA; JP; DL; *b* 6 Nov. 1902; *s* of late Brig.-Gen. D. C. Douglas, CB, Mains, Milngavie, Dunbartonshire; *m* 1927, Elizabeth Cicely, 2nd *d* of late Sir Maurice de Bunsen, 1st Bt, PC, GCMG, GCVO, CB; two *d. Educ:* Eton; Christ Church, Oxford. 2nd Lieut Scots Guards, 1925; Captain 1931; Lt-Col 1943, DL 1953, Dunbartonshire; Mem. of Royal Company of Archers (Queen's Body Guard for Scotland). Vice-Lieutenant Co. Dunbarton, 1957-68. JP Perthshire, 1962. *Address:* Laraich, Aberfoyle, by Stirling. *T:* Aberfoyle 232. *Club:* New (Edinburgh).
[Died 28 Oct. 1977.

DOUGLAS, Very Rev. George James Cosmo; Dean of Argyll and The Isles since 1952; Provost of Cumbrae Cathedral and Rector of St Andrew, Millport, since 1949. *Educ:* University of Edinburgh (MA); Edinburgh Theological Coll. Curate, St Paul's Cathedral, Dundee, 1914-16. TCF, 1916-19; Vice-Principal, Dorchester Missionary Coll., 1919-22; Curate, Dundee Cathedral, 1922-29; Priest-in-charge, St Andrew and St George, Rosyth, 1929-36; St John Baptist, Dundee, 1936-50; Canon, St Paul's Cathedral, Dundee, 1942-50 (Hon. Canon, 1966); Exam. Chaplain to the Bishop of Brechin, 1949-; Exam. Chaplain to the Bishop of Argyll, 1952-. *Address:* The College, Millport, Isle of Cumbrae. *T:* Millport 353. *Club:* New (Edinburgh).
[Died 7 Jan. 1973.

DOUGLAS, Irvine; *see* Douglas, R. I.

DOUGLAS, James Archibald, MA, DSc; FGS; Professor Emeritus, Geology, in the University of Oxford since 1950; *b* 1 Dec. 1884; *s* of James Herbert Douglas, Ilkley, Yorks; *m* 1914, Hannah Call Weddell (*d* 1966); two *s* two *d. Educ:* Haileybury Coll.; Keble Coll., Oxford. Fellow University Coll., Oxford, 1937. Former Sec. and Vice-Pres. Geological Soc. of London. Served European War, Captain 1st Batt. Gordon Highlanders and 172 Tunnelling Co., RE; Lieut-Col, OC 6th Oxon (Oxford City) Bn HG, 1941. Bolitho Gold Medal, Royal Geol Society, Cornwall, 1939. Foreign Mem., Geol Soc. of Peru, 1952. *Recreation:* yachting. *Address:* Saxonbury, Yarmouth, Isle of Wight. *T:* Yarmouth 760380. *[Died 27 Feb. 1978.*

DOUGLAS, Maj.-Gen. John Primrose, CB 1968; OBE 1945 (MBE 1938); Deputy Director-General Army Medical Services, 1964-68; *b* 22 Feb. 1908; *m* 1934, Anne Fyfe. *Educ:* Perth Acad.; St Andrews Univ. MB, ChB 1930. Joined RAMC, 1933; served in Gibraltar, France, NW Europe, MELF, AFNORTH, BAOR, etc. DDMS, 21 Army Gp, 1944-46; GHQ, MELF, 1946-49; Med. Cons., NATO Coun., 1958-59; Inspector of Med. Services, 1961-63; DDMS, 1 (Br.) Corps, 1963-64. QHS, 1965-68. Col Comdt, RAMC, 1969-73. CStJ 1967 (OStJ 1945). Order of Merit, German Red Cross, 1938; Legion of Merit, US, 1945; Order of Orange Nassau, Netherlands, 1945; Order of White Lion, Czechoslovakia, 1946; Order of Leopold, Belgium, 1946. *Address:* c/o Williams & Glyn's Bank Ltd, Kirkland House, Whitehall, SW1. *[Died 4 Sept. 1975.*

DOUGLAS, Katharine Greenhill; Matron, St Mary's Hospital, Paddington, W2, 1949-63, retired; *b* 13 Jan. 1908; *yr d* of Rev. Daniel Greenhill Douglas and of Catherine Eudora Douglas. *Educ:* St Andrews Sch., Bexhill-on-Sea. Student Nurse, Nightingale Training Sch., St Thomas's Hospital, 1932-36; SRN 1936; Staff Nurse, St Thomas's Hospital, 1936-37; Pupil Midwife, Gen. Lying-In Hospital, SE1, 1937-38; SCM 1938; Ward Sister, St Thomas's Hospital, 1938-43; Administrative Sister, 1943-45; Dep. Matron, 1945-49. Chm., Standing Nursing Advisory Cttee, 1951-57; Mem. of Central Health Services Council, 1951-57. *Recreations:* music, needlework, tennis. *Address:* 7B Dorset Road South, Bexhill-on-Sea, Sussex TN40 1NH. *T:* Bexhill-on-Sea 215951. *[Died 26 Dec. 1979.*

DOUGLAS, Lewis Williams, GBE (Hon.), 1957; Hon. Chairman and Director, United California Bank International (President, 1967-73); Hon. Trustee, Mutual Life Insurance Co. of New York (Trustee, 1940-72, Chairman, Executive Committee, 1952-72); Hon. Chairman and Consultant, Southern Arizona Bank and Trust Company (Chairman and Director, 1949-66); *b* Bisbee, Arizona, USA, 2 July 1894; *e s* of late James Stuart Douglas and Josephine Williams; *m* 1921, Peggy, *d* of Fred G. Zinsser and Emma Sharman; two *s* one *d. Educ:* Montclair Acad.; Amherst Coll.; MIT. BA *cum laude* (Amherst); Woods Prize for scholarship, 1916. Served European War, 1917-18, 1st Lieut, FA, Cit. Gen. Pershing (Belgian Croix de Guerre); War of 1939-45, Dep. Administrator, War Shipping Admin., 1942-44; Mem., Combined Shipping Adjustment Bd; Special Advr, Gen. L. D. Clay, German Control Council, 1945. Instructor in hist., Amherst Coll., 1920; mining investment, banking, ranching and gen. business, Arizona, 1921-. Member: Arizona House of Reps, 1923-25; 70th-73rd Congresses, US, 1927-33; Congressman-at-large, Arizona; Dir of Budget, 1933-34; Vice-Pres. and Dir, American Cynamid Co., 1934-37; Principal and Vice-Chancellor, McGill Univ., 1938-40; Pres., Mutual Life Insce Co., NY, 1940-47, Chm., 1947-59; US Ambassador to the Court of St James's, 1947-50. Chairman: (also Dir) Western Bankcorporation Internat. Bank, 1962-67; Christiana Oil Corp., 1956-59 (Dir, 1956-64); (also Dir) Southwestern Research, 1961-64; Director: General Motors Corp., 1944-65 (Chm., Audit Cttee, 1945-47, 1951-65); Union Corp., 1951-73; Internat. Nickel Co. Inc. of Canada Ltd, 1951-71 (Mem., Exec. Cttee, 1955-59, Alternate Mem., 1960-61, Mem., Adv. Cttee, 1971-); (also Mem., Exec. Cttee) Western Bankcorporation; also Dir or former Dir of numerous other companies; Mem., Adv. Bd, Bank of New York, 1967-72. Director: Council on Foreign Relations, 1940-64 (now Emeritus); also rotating Mem., Exec. and Investment Policy Cttees, Empire Trust Co., 1956-66; Technical Studies Inc. and Rep. on Supervisory Bd, Channel Tunnel Study Gp; Admin. and Consulting Dir, Inst. of Atmospheric Physics, Univ. of Arizona; Member: US Investment Cttee, Employers' Liability Assce Corp. Ltd, 1951-52 (Chm., 1952-68); Pres.'s Task Force on Amer. Indians, 1966-67; Indian Econ. Develt Adv. Gp for Arizona; Finance and Internat. Cttees, US Chamber of Commerce; Nat. Emergency Cttee, Nat. Council on Crime and Delinquency; Mem. and former Mem., Adv. Bds, Cttees and Councils. Vice-Pres., Nat. Inst. of Social Scis; Member: Amer. Inst. of Mining, Metallurgical and Petroleum Engrs; Nat. Bd of Trustees, RSA (Benjamin Franklin Fellow); Hon. Pres., Nat. Soc. for Prevention of Blindness; Hon. Member Board: Acad. Political Sci. (Mem. Bd, 1937-62); Atlantic Council of US (Vice-Chm. and Dir Exec. Cttee, 1961-70). Adv. Mem. Bd of Managers, Meml Hosp. for Cancer and Allied Diseases (Chm., 1944-50); Mem., Bd of Trustees: Amherst Coll. (Emer.); Alfred P. Sloan Foundn; (also one of original mems) Sloan-Kettering Inst. for Cancer Res., 1945-47; Rockefeller Foundn and Gen. Educn Bd, 1935-60; Neurological Scis Foundn; Amer. Philosophical Assoc.; St Luke's Hosp., Phoenix; Hon. Trustee, Museum of Nat. Hist. Governor: Atlantic Inst., 1960-63 (Dir, 1963-73); Arctic Inst. of N America; Royal Shakespeare Theatre, Stratford-upon-Avon. Freeman, City of Edinburgh, 1950. Hon. Degrees: LLD: Amherst Coll., Harvard, 1933; Queen's Coll., Princeton, Brown, NY and Wesleyan

Univs, 1938; Arizona, 1940; Leeds, 1948; Bristol, London, St Andrews, 1949; Birmingham, Glasgow, Edinburgh, 1950; California, Columbia, Dalhousie, McGill, 1951; DCL Oxon, 1948. Grand Croix de la Légion d'Honneur (France), 1950; Grand Croix de l'Ordre de la Couronne (Belgium), 1951. *Recreations:* fishing, horse-back. *Address:* The Southern Arizona Bank Building, Tuscon, Arizona 85702, USA. *T:* (602) 792-5366; 1740 Broadway, New York, NY 10019. *T:* (212) 586-4000. *Clubs:* Athenæum, White's, Houghton, The Other, Thirty, Anglers' Co-operative Association; Links, Mining, Wyandanch, Angler's (New York); Old Pueblo, Mining of the South West (Arizona); National Press, Metropolitan (Washington); Union Interalliée (France); Balboa Club de Mazatlan (Mexico).
[Died 7 March 1974.

DOUGLAS, (Ronald) Irvine; Journalist; Press Adviser, Bank of NSW, since 1964; *b* Zeehan, Tasmania, 31 May 1899; *s* of Ronald C. G. and Jean Douglas; *m* 1935, Williamina, *d* of late Alexander and Williamina Murdoch. *Educ:* Selborne Coll., South Africa; Launceston High Sch., Tasmania. Ed. Sydney Sunday-Pictorial, 1927-28; Special representative of Sydney Morning Herald at UNO Conference, San Francisco, 1945; also had assignments to New Guinea, India, New Caledonia, New Zealand, SE Asia, etc.; Commonwealth Government Publicity Officer, 1934-38, also Private Sec. to Australian Prime Minister (Rt Hon. J. A. Lyons), 1936-38; Press Officer for Duke of Gloucester's Australian tour, 1934; Joint Press Officer for Imperial Conf., London, 1937; Manager and Ed., Australian Associated Press, London, 1940-44; London Manager and Ed., Sydney Morning Herald Overseas News Service, 1945-49. Political Correspondent, Sydney Morning Herald, 1949-52; Editorial staff, Mirror Newspapers, Ltd, Sydney, 1952-64; Federal Vice-Pres., Australian Journalists' Association, 1934; Hon. Sec. Overseas Empire Correspondents Association, London, 1940-43, Pres., 1944; Pres. London Association of British Empire Newspapers Overseas, 1947-48; Vice-Pres. Cen. Acclimatisation Soc., NSW, 1956-57. *Publications:* Opportunity in Australia, 1948; 2nd edn, 1958; 50 years with Bloxham and Chambers, 1971. *Recreations:* fly-fishing, shooting, golf, rowing. *Address:* 1 Stewart Street, Artarmon, NSW 2064, Australia. *Clubs:* Savage (London); NSW Sports, Journalists' (Sydney); Royal Sydney Golf. *[Died 9 Feb. 1973.*

DOUGLAS, William Orville; Associate Justice, Supreme Court of United States, Washington, DC, 1939-75, retired; *b* 16 Oct. 1898; *s* of William Douglas and Julia Bickford Fiske; *m* 1st, 1923, Mildred Riddle; one *s* one *d*; 2nd, 1954, Mercedes Hester; 3rd, 1963, Joan Martin; 4th, Cathleen Heffernan. *Educ:* Whitman Coll., Washington; Columbia Univ. Law Sch., New York City. Practised Law in New York City, 1925-27; Mem., Columbia Law Sch., Faculty 1925-28 and Yale Law Sch. Faculty, 1928-34; Dir, Protective Cttee Study, Securities and Exchange Comm., 1934-36; Mem., Securities and Exchange Comm., 1936-39, Chm., 1937-39. Fellow Royal Geographical Soc., London. *Publications:* Democracy and Finance, 1940; Being an American, 1948; Of Men and Mountains, 1950; Strange Lands and Friendly People, 1951; Beyond the High Himalayas, 1952; North From Malaya, 1953; Almanac of Liberty, 1954; Russian Journey, 1956; We The Judges, 1956; The Right of People, 1958; Exploring the Himalaya, 1958; West of the Indus, 1958; America Challenged, 1960; My Wilderness-The Pacific West, 1960; A Living Bill of Rights, 1961; Muir of the Mountains, 1961; My Wilderness-East to Katahdin, 1961; Democracy's Manifesto, 1962; Mr Lincoln and the Negroes, 1963; Freedom of the Mind, 1963; The Anatomy of Liberty, 1963; A Wilderness Bill of Rights, 1965; The Bible and the Schools, 1966; Farewell to Texas, 1967; Toward a Global Federalism, 1969; Points of Rebellion, 1970; International Dissent, 1971; Holocaust or Hemispheric Co-operation, 1972; The Three Hundred Year War, 1972; Go East Young Man, 1974; contrib. to various legal periodicals; *posthumous publication:* The Court Years, 1939-1975, 1980. *Recreations:* horseback riding, hiking. *Address:* Supreme Court of the US, Washington, DC 20543, USA; Goose Prairie, Washington 98929, USA. *Clubs:* University (Washington, DC); Yale, Circumnavigators', Explorers', Overseas Press Club (NY City); Himalayan (Delhi, India). *[Died 19 Jan. 1980.*

DOUGLASS OF CLEVELAND, Baron *cr* 1967 (Life Peer); **Harry Douglass,** Kt 1964; General Secretary, Iron and Steel Trades Confederation, 1953-67; *b* 1 Jan. 1902; *m* 1926, Edith Amer; one *d.* *Educ:* Elementary Sch. and WEA. Mem. Brit. Labour Party Exec. 1948-53; Pres., Internat. Metalworkers Federation, 1950-59; Member: Trades Union Congress, 1953-67 (Chm., 1966-67); Council, DSIR, 1954-59; Advisory Council, Export Credits Guarantee Dept, 1954-57, 1965-67; Iron and Steel Board, 1960-67; Export Council for Europe, 1961-67; NEDC, 1962-67; (part-time) Electricity Council, 1966-71;

Monopolies Commn, 1967-70; Chairman: TUC Economic Cttee, 1962-67; British Productivity Council, 1962-67. *Address:* 5 The Chase, Stanmore, Mddx. *T:* (home) 01-954 2101.
[Died 5 April 1978.

DOUTHWAITE, Arthur Henry, MD; FRCP; Consulting Physician Emeritus to Guy's Hospital, London; Director: Permanent Insurance Company; Medical Sickness Annuity and Life Assurance Society (Chairman); Medical Sickness Finance Corporation; *b* Chefu, China, 1896; *s* of late A. W. Douthwaite, MD, Sheffield, and Constance Groves, Redland, Bristol; *m* Gladys Olivia, *d* of late John Dannhorn; three *d.* *Educ:* Bristol Grammar Sch.; Bristol Univ.; University College, London; Guy's Hospital, London. Civilian Prisoner of War, Ruhleben, Germany, 1914-18; Beaney Prize for Pathology, 1921; Murchison Prize (Medicine) Royal College of Physicians, 1922; Science Scholarships, Middlesex Hospital and Guy's Hospital, 1919. Croonian Lecturer, Royal College of Physicians, 1956. Late Clinical Assistant, Assistant House Surgeon, House Physician, Medical Registrar and Tutor, Chief Assistant in Neurology, Guy's Hospital; Consulting Physician, Mitcham Cottage Hospital and Edenbridge Hospital; Cons. Physician, Horsham Hosp.; Examiner in Medicine and in Therapeutics, University of London, and Conjoint Board, and in Therapeutics, RCP; late Examiner in Medicine, University of Edinburgh; Physician in EMS; PP Medical Society of London and Harveian Soc.; Vice-Pres., Med. Defence Union; late Senior Censor, RCP; President British Gastroenterological Society; President, Section of Medicine, RSM. *Publications:* The Treatment of Rheumatoid Arthritis and Sciatica; The Treatment of Asthma; A Guide to General Practice; late Editor Hale-White's Materia Medica and French's Differential Diagnosis; various articles in Medical Journals. *Address:* Quarries, Itchingfield, Horsham, West Sussex. *T:* Slinfold 247. *[Died 24 Sept. 1974.*

DOVE-EDWIN, George Frederick, CMG 1969; Justice of Appeal, Sierra Leone, 1961-70; Judge, Gambia Court of Appeal, 1962-68, and President of the Court, 1968-70; Barrister-at-Law; *b* 18 May 1896; *s* of late James Nicol Edwin and Clarice Marion Edwin (*née* Dove); *m*; two *s* one *d*; *m* 1935, Ethel Elizabeth Jones; two *d* (and one *d* decd). *Educ:* CMS Grammar Sch., Freetown. Telegraphist, 1914-17; Fourah Bay Coll., 1917-18; Lincoln's Inn, 1920-23; called to Bar, 1923. Practised in Freetown, 1923-24; practised in Calabar, Nigeria, 1924-40; Magistrate, 1940-Jan. 1951; Acting Puisne Judge, Aba, Nigeria, Jan.-Feb. 1951; Puisne Judge, Nigeria, 1951-55; Judge of the High Court, Eastern Region of Nigeria, 1955-59; Member Victoria League. *Recreation:* tennis. *Address:* 11 Crescent Road, Wimbledon, SW20. *Club:* Royal Commonwealth Society.
[Died 24 Dec. 1973.

DOW, David Rutherford, MB, ChB (with distinction), MD (with commendation), DPH, FRCPE, FRSE; LLD University of St Andrews, 1959; Professor of Anatomy, University of St Andrews (Queen's College, Dundee), 1925-58, now Emeritus; Master of Queen's College, Dundee, 1954-58; *b* Crail, Fifeshire, 1887; *o s* of late Dr Dow, MA, MD, Crail; *m* 1942, Agnes W. Morton, MA, MB, ChB, Hon. LLD Dundee 1968. *Educ:* Waid Academy, Anstruther; University of St Andrews. Lecturer and Senior Demonstrator of Anatomy, University of St Andrews; Life Member of Anatomical Society of Great Britain and Ireland; Dundee Branch BMA (Pres., 1936-37). Hon. President, Crail Golfing Society. Commission RAMC 1st Southern General Hospital, Birmingham. *Publications:* papers in various journals. *Recreations:* golf, shooting, fishing. *Address:* 13 Marketgate, Crail, Fife KY10 3TH. *T:* Crail 302. *Club:* Royal and Ancient (St Andrews). *[Died 12 Nov. 1979.*

DOW, Sir Hugh, GCIE 1947 (CIE 1932); KCSI 1940 (CSI 1937); KStJ; *b* 8 May 1886; *s* of Alfred Dow; *m* 1913, Ann (CBE 1947, CStJ, K-i-H Gold Medal) (*d* 1956),*d* of J. Sheffield; one *s* one *d.* *Educ:* Aske's Hatcham Sch.; University Coll. London. Entered ICS, 1909; Secretary, Finance Dept, Bombay, 1923; Financial Adviser, Public Works in Sind, 1925; Financial Adviser, Public Works and Development, Bombay, 1926; Revenue Officer, Lloyd (Sukkur) Barrage, 1927; Member of the Sind Conference, 1932; Chairman of Sind Administrative Cttee, 1933-34; Joint Secretary, Commerce Dept, 1934; Secretary to the Govt of India, Commerce Dept, 1936-39; Director-General of Supply, and President of the War Supply Board, India, 1939-41; Governor of Sind, 1941-46; Governor of Bihar, 1946-47; Consul-General, Jerusalem, 1948-51; Chairman, Ordination Funds Commission, 1952; Chairman Royal Commission on East Africa, 1952-54; Chairman of Council, Royal Central Asian Society, 1957-58. *Address:* 16 Pall Mall, SW1. *Club:* Athenæum.
[Died 20 Nov. 1978.

DOW, Samuel; wine merchant; *b* 8 March 1908; *s* of John Archibald Dow and Jetta Findlay; *m* 1931, Margaret Stewart Cameron; two *d. Educ:* Glasgow High Sch.; Strathallan School. Chm., Scottish Wholesalers Wine Merchants Assoc., 1953-57; Pres., Wine and Spirit Assoc. of Great Britain (Inc.), 1964-65; Master, Worshipful Co. of Vintners, 1971. *Recreations:* golf, fishing. *Address:* 15 Mariscat Road, Glasgow G41 4NJ. *T:* 041-423 0357. *Clubs:* Caledonian; Royal Scottish Automobile (Glasgow); Troon Golf.   *[Died 2 Sept. 1976.*

DOWER, Col Alan Vincent Gandar, TD; DL; MFH; *b* 1898; *s* of late J. W. G. Dower and Mrs Dower, 17 Sussex Place, NW1; *m* 1928, Aymée Lavender, Jun. Com. (Temp. Sen. Com.) ATS, *d* of Capt. Sir George James Robert Clerk, 9th Bt, and Hon. Lady Clerk (*sister* of 6th Baron Sherborne, DSO); one *d. Educ:* RMC, Sandhurst; Oxford Univ. 2nd Lieut RW Surrey Regt, 1915; 2nd Lieut 2nd Dragoon Guards, 1916; served in France during European War, 1916-17; attached Royal Air Force, 1918; Capt. 2nd Dragoon Guards; Reserve of Officers, 1928; Major 35th AA Bn, RE, 1937; Lt-Col comdg 36th AA Bn, 1938-40; Comdg 39th (Lancs. Fus.) SL Regt, 1940; Comdg 84th SL Regt, 1951; Hon. Colonel 609 HAA Regt RA, 1947-55; Hon. Col, 4th Middx Bn Mobile Def. Corps, 1956-; Colonel, 1948, retired, 1954; Member Middx TA Association; MP (C), Stockport, 1931-35, Cumberland (Penrith and Cockermouth Div.), 1935-50; Member of Select Cttee on Estimates, 1938-39; Member Select Cttee of Public Accounts, 1945-50. Freeman of City of London; Liveryman, Barbers Company; FRGS; FZS. MFH South Oxfordshire Hunt, 1950-53; Joint Master Old Berkeley Hunt, 1953-; County Pres. for Oxfordshire, St John Ambulance Bde and Association, 1953- (Mem., Chapter General, 1971-). Member Executive and Council, Royal Society of St George; Patron, SSAFA Middlesex Appeals Cttee. DL, Middlesex, 1961-65; DL Greater London, 1965-. KStJ. *Recreations:* hunting, big game shooting, polo, tennis, golf. *Address:* 35 Lowndes Street, SW1. *T:* 01-235 1491; Newington House, Warborough, Oxfordshire. *T:* Warborough 205; High Head Castle, Cumbria. *Clubs:* Carlton, Naval and Military, Princes, Hurlingham, Queen's; Muthaiga (Nairobi).   *[Died 6 May 1980.*

DOWLING, Geoffrey Barrow, MD, FRCP; Hon. MD Universities of Utrecht and Pretoria; Consulting Physician to Department for Skin Diseases, St Thomas' Hospital; Consultant in Dermatology to RAF; Late Director, Institute of Dermatology; *b* Cape Town, 9 Aug. 1891; *s* of Thomas Barrow Dowling, Mus.Doc., and Minna Grant; *m* 1923, Mary Elizabeth Kelly (*d* 1965); two *s* two *d. Educ:* Dulwich Coll.; Guy's Hospital. Watson Smith Lecturer, RCP, 1955. Hon. Fellow Royal Society of Medicine (Ex-Pres. Section of Dermatology); Hon. Member (Pres. 1956) British Association of Dermatology. Hon. Member French and other foreign Dermatological Societies. *Publications:* papers on medical subjects. *Address:* 52 Ravenscourt Gardens, W6.   *[Died 1 June 1976.*

DOWN, Lt-Gen. Sir Ernest Edward, KBE 1953 (CBE 1943); CB 1949; late King's Shropshire Light Infantry; *b* 10 Feb. 1902. 2nd Lieut Dorset Regt, 1923; transferred to King's Shropshire Light Infantry, from Dorset Regt, 1935; Brigade Major, 1937-39; Colonel, 1944; temp. Maj.-Gen., 1944; Maj.-Gen., 1945; Lt-Gen., 1952; GOC British troops in Greece, 1947-48; Commander British Military Mission to Greece, 1948-49. Commander Mid-West District and 53rd (Welsh) Infantry Division (TA), 1950-52; Gen. Officer Commanding-in-Chief, Southern Command, 1952-55; retired, 1955. Colonel KSLI 1955-57. *Address:* Whistlers Mead, Appleshaw, near Andover, Hants SP11 9BH.   *[Died 15 Feb. 1980.*

DOWN, Air Commodore Harold Hunter, CBE 1945; AFC; late Royal Air Force; *b* 17 May 1895; *s* of Thomas Down, Jersey, Channel Islands; *m* 1931, Noëla Joyce Farrall; one *s.* Army and RFC 1915-18; RAF from 1918; Commandant, Central Flying School, 1940-42; commanded Bomber Operational Base, 1944-45; retired, 1945. *Address:* Stanley Wood, Lockeridge, Marlborough, Wilts. *T:* Lockeridge 247. *[Died 20 June 1974.*

DOWNING, Prof. Richard Ivan; Ritchie Professor of Research in Economics since 1954, Assistant Vice-Chancellor 1970-74, University of Melbourne; Chairman, Australian Broadcasting Commission, since 1973; *b* 13 March 1915; *s* of H. G. Downing and Pauline (*née* Domec-Carré); *m* 1965, Jean Olive, widow of Howard Norman and *d* of A. S. McGregor; one *d,* and four step *s* two step *d. Educ:* Scotch Coll., Melbourne; Univ. of Melbourne; King's Coll., Cambridge. BA Melbourne, DipEcons Cantab. Lectr, Univ. of Melbourne, 1940; Asst Econ. Consultant to Prime Minister, 1941-45; Econ. Div., ILO, 1945-47; Sen. Lectr, Univ. of Melbourne, 1947-49; Asst Econ. Adviser, ILO, 1950-53. Pres., Acad. of Social Scis in Australia, 1970-72; Chm., Ormond Coll. Council, 1970-; Chm., Australian Ballet Sch.,

1969-; Dir, Gas & Fuel Corp. of Vic, 1971-; Dir, Melbourne Theatre Co., 1962-; Trustee, National Gall. of Victoria, 1969-; Mem., Austr. Council for the Arts, 1973. *Publications:* National Income and Social Accounts, 1951; The Australian Economy, 1973; contrib. learned jls. *Address:* Yarra Braes Road, Eltham, Vic 3095, Australia. *T:* 439-9852. *Club:* Melbourne (Melbourne).   *[Died 10 Nov. 1975.*

DOWTY, Sir George (Herbert), Kt 1956; DL; Founder and Chairman of the Dowty Group of Companies; *b* 27 April 1901; *y s* of William Dowty and Laura (*née* Masters); *m* 1948, Marguerite Anne Gowans, *d* of late M. J. H. Lockie and Annie B. Lockie, Newmarket, Ont, Canada; one *s* one *d. Educ:* Worcester Royal Grammar Sch. Hon. Freeman of Borough of Cheltenham, 1955; Hon. Freeman of Borough of Tewkesbury, 1964. President of Royal Aeronautical Society, 1952-53; Hon. Fellow, 1967; RAeS Gold Medal for Advancement of Aeronautical Science, 1955. Treasurer, Society of British Aerospace Companies Ltd, 1961-68; President: The Society of British Aircraft Constructors, 1960-61; Gloucestershire and S. Worcestershire Productivity Association; Chairman: Industrial Development Board for Malta, 1960-63; North Gloucestershire Disablement Cttee, 1952-63. Hon. DSc: Bath Univ. of Technology, 1966; Cranfield Inst. of Technology, 1972. DL Glos, 1969. *Recreations:* blood-stock breeding, tennis, curling, golf. *Address:* Arle Court, Cheltenham, Glos. *T:* Cheltenham 21411. *Club:* United Service & Royal Aero.
                    [Died 7 Dec. 1975.

DOXIADIS, Constantinos Apostolos; Chairman, Doxiadis Associates International Co. Ltd, Consultants on Development and Ekistics, Athens; *b* 1913; *s* of Apostolos Doxiadis, Pediatrician, and Evanthia (*née* Mezeviri); *m* 1940, Emma Scheepers; one *s* three *d. Educ:* Technical Univ., Athens (Architect-Engineer); Berlin-Charlottenburg Univ. (DrIng). Chief Town Planning Officer, Greater Athens Area, 1937-38; Head, Dept of Regional and Town Planning, Ministry of Public Works, Greece, 1939-45; Lecturer and Acting Professor of Town Planning, Techn. Univ. of Athens, 1939-43; Minister and Permanent Secretary of Housing Reconstruction, Greece, 1945-48; Minister-Co-ordinator of Greek Recovery Program, 1948-51. Member of various delegations and cttees; Consultant to many organizations and governments of numerous countries; Researcher for National Assoc. of Housing and Redevelopment Officials (US) and various Athens Technol Organization projects. Has studied, planned and designed numerous human settlements and their development in many fields throughout the world. Visiting Lecturer at many US universities and colleges; Hon. LLD: Swarthmore Coll., 1962; Mills Coll., 1964; Univ. of Mich, 1967; Tulane Univ., 1968; Kalamazoo Coll., 1968; Hon. DH Wayne State Univ., 1964; Hon. LHD: N Mich Univ., 1965; Case Western Reserve Univ., 1969; Hon. DSc Detroit Inst. of Technology, 1966; Hon. DFA Univ. of RI; Hon. DSc: Univ. of Pittsburgh, 1967; Marietta Coll., 1969. Also various foreign awards including Aspen Award for Humanities, 1966. Greek Military Cross, 1941; Hon. OBE, 1945; Order of Cedar, Lebanon, 1958; Royal Order of the Phoenix, Greece, 1960; Yugoslav Flag Order with Golden Wreath, 1966. *Publications:* Raumordnung im griechischen Städtebau, 1937; A Simple Story, 1945 (in Greek); Ekistic Analysis, 1946; Destruction of Towns and Villages in Greece, 1946; (jointly) A Plan for the Survival of the Greek People (2 vols), 1947; Ekistic Policies for the Reconstruction of the Country with a 20-year Program, 1947; March of the People, 1948; Our Capital and its Future, 1960; Architecture in Transition, 1963; (with T. B. Douglass) The New World of Urban Man, 1965; Urban Renewal and the Future of the American City, 1966; Between Dystopia and Utopia, 1966; Emergence and Growth of an Urban Region, The Developing Urban Detroit Area: vol. I, 1966; vol. II, 1967; vol. III, 1970; Ekistics: An Introduction to the Science of Human Settlements, 1968; The Two-Headed Eagle, 1972; Architectural Space in Ancient Greece, 1972; Urban Crimes, 1973; Anthropopolis, 1974; The Great Ecumenopolis, 1974; Building Eutopia, 1975; several volumes on programs and projects for many areas and cities around the world. *Address:* Doxiadis Associates International, 24 Stratiotikou Syndesmou, Athens 136, Greece.   *[Died 28 June 1975*

DOYLE, Joseph, DSc, MRIA; Professor of Botany, University College, Dublin, 1924, Professor Emeritus, since 1961; Vice-President, Royal Dublin Society; *b* 1891; *Educ:* O'Connell Schs Dublin; University Coll. Dublin. Graduated in the Roya University of Ireland in Biology, 1910; studied in Germany *Publications:* various technical papers in the Proceedings of the Royal Dublin Society, The Royal Irish Academy and elsewher mainly on Conifers. *Address:* Carrigower, Mount Anville Road Dundrum, Dublin 14.   *[Died 11 April 1974*

DRAKE, Donald Henry Charles, CIE 1933; *b* 23 Aug. 1887; *m* 1915, Dorothy, *d* of Lt-Col Edmund Waller, OBE; one *s. Educ:* Blundell's Sch., Tiverton; Christ Church, Oxford. Entered Indian Civil Service 1911; retired, 1937. *Address: c/o* Lloyds Bank, Ltd, Cox & King's Branch, 6 Pall Mall, SW1.
[*Died* 11 *Aug.* 1974.

DRAKE, Sir Eugen M.; *see* Millington-Drake.

DRAKE, Harold William, CBE 1941; *b* 8 April 1889; *s* of William Henry Drake and Mary Ann Robinson; *m* 1st, 1918, Gertrude Alice Terry; 2nd, 1954, Sarah Louise Johnson (*d* 1964). *Educ:* City of London Sch. Colonial Service, 1914-46, Nigeria, Nyassaland and British Guiana; war service, Royal West African Frontier Force, Cameroons and East Africa, 1914-19. *Address: c/o* Barclay's Bank Ltd, 139/142 North Street, Brighton BN1 1RU. *Club:* East India, Sports and Public Schools. [*Died* 15 *Feb.* 1973.

DRAKE, John Collard Bernard, CSI 1933; CIE 1926; CBE 1930; Indian Civil Service, retired; *b* 7 March 1884; 3rd *s* of late Felix Drake of East Coker, Yeovil, Somerset. *Educ:* Blundell's Sch.; Balliol Coll., Oxford. Joined Indian Civil Service, 1908; Under-Sec. to Government of Bihar and Orissa, 1912-15; Private Sec. to Lieut-Governor of Bihar and Orissa, 1918; Indian Army Reserve of Officers, 1918-19; Under-Sec. to Government of India, 1919-20; Dep. Sec., 1921-24; Sec. to the High Commissioner for India in London, 1924-29; Joint Sec. to the Government of India, Dept of Commerce, 1929-32; Sec., 1932-33; Mem. Pensions Appeal Tribunals, 1944-66. *Address: c/o* Lloyds Bank Ltd, 6 Pall Mall, SW1. *Clubs:* East India, Sports and Public Schools; Bath and County. [*Died* 28 *Dec.* 1975.

DRAPER, William H., Jr, Hon. LLD; Investment Banker; Corporation Executive; Government Official; Director, US Leasing; *b* NY City, 10 Aug. 1894; *s* of William Henry Draper and Mary Emma (*née* Carey); *m* 1918, Katharine Louise Baum (decd); one *s* two *d* ; *m* 1949, Eunice Barzynski. *Educ:* New York Univ. (MA). Served European War, 1917-18, Major, Inf. US Army. With Nat. City Bank, NYC, 1919-21; Asst Treas. Bankers Trust Co., NYC, 1923-27; joined Dillon Read & Co. investment bankers, NYC, 1927, Vice-Pres., 1937-53; Exec. Officer, Chm. Bd, Mexican Light & Power Co., 1954-59; Partner, Draper, Gaither & Anderson, 1959-62; Chm., Combustion Engineering, Inc., 1962-65; Chm., Pension Corp. of America, 1965-67; Chief of Staff, 77th Div., org. Reserve Corps, 1936-40; War of 1939-45, on active duty as Col Inf. with Gen. Staff, US Army, Washington, 1940-41; comd 136th Inf. Regt, 33rd Inf. Div., 1942-44, incl. service in Pacific theater; in charge contract termination for War Dept, Washington, 1944; Brig.-Gen., 1945; Chief, Economic Div., Control Council for Germany, 1945-46; Economic Adviser to C-in-C, European theatre, 1947, with rank of Maj.-Gen.; Mil. Govt Advisor to Sec. of State at Moscow Conf. of Foreign Ministers, 1947; Under-Sec. of War (title after reorganization Under-Sec. of Army), 1947; resigned 1949. Legion of Merit (Army), 1943 and (Navy), 1945; Selective Service Medal, 1946; DSM (US), 1948; Order of Orange Nassau, Netherlands, 1949; Medal for Merit (US), 1953; Grand Cross, Order of Merit (Italy), 1954; Order of Sacred Treasure, Japan, 1973; Member: President's Advisory Cttee on Selective Service, Washington, 1940; Joint Army and Navy Cttee on Welfare and Recreation, 1941. Trustee The Kosciuszko Foundation; Mem. Council on Foreign Relations; Soc. of Amer. Magicians and Acad. of Political Science; Am. Legion (Westchester County Comdr, 1933-34); US Special Representative in Europe, with the rank of Ambassador, stationed in Paris, Jan. 1952-June 1953, representing US in the North Atlantic Council and OEEC, and supervising the Mutual Security Programme in Europe; Chm., President's Cttee on US Mil. Assistance, 1958-59; formerly Trustee Long Island Rail Road Co. and Chm., Long Island Transit Authority. Mem. Governing Body, Internat. Planned Parenthood Fedn; National Chm., Population Crisis Cttee, 1965-69, Hon. Chm. 1969-; US Mem., UN Population Commn, 1969-; Mem. Bd of Dirs, Atlantic Council of US, 1955-. Holds several hon. degrees. Republican. Presbyterian. *Address:* (Home) 2202 Foxboro Place NW, Washington, DC, USA; (Office) Population Crisis Committee, 1835 K St NW, Washington, DC. *Clubs:* Downtown Athletic, The Brook (New York); Army and Navy, Metropolitan (Washington); Port Royal Beach (Naples, Fla).
[*Died* 26 *Dec.* 1974.

DRAWBELL, James Wedgwood; Managing Editor, and Editorial Consultant, with Geo. Newnes Ltd (1946-64); previously Editor, Sunday Chronicle (1925-46); *b* 15 April 1899; *m* 1924, Marjorie Bull; one *s* one *d. Educ:* Edinburgh. Worked on newspapers in New York (The World); Montreal (Montreal Star); Edinburgh (Evening Dispatch); served with Royal Scots Fusiliers,

European War of 1914-18. *Publications:* Dorothy Thompson's English Journey, 1942; All Change Here, 1943; Night and Day, 1945; Drifts my Boat, 1946; The Long Year, 1958; The Sun Within Us, 1963; Time on My Hands, 1968; A Garden, 1970; Scotland: Bitter-Sweet, 1972. *Address: c/o* Midland Bank, 70 St Martin's Lane, WC2N 4JZ. *Clubs:* Scottish Liberal, Kilspindie Golf. [*Died* 6 *Feb.* 1979.

DRAYSON, Rear-Adm. Edwin Howard, CB 1945; CBE 1942 (OBE 1937); retired; *b* 1889; *m* 1914, Hilda Jeannie (*d* 1974), *d* of Isaac Harding; two *d* (one *s* killed in action, 1944); *m* 1974, Mrs Barbara Bennett. *Address:* Crail Cottage, Shute, Axminster, Devon. [*Died* 28 *Oct.* 1977.

DRENNAN, Basil St George; Clerk of Committees, House of Commons, 1958-60; *b* 22 Jan. 1903; *s* of Rev. William St George Drennan, MSc, and Kate, *d* of Josiah Lawrence Walker, Banbury; *m* 1960, Joan Madeline Norris, *d* of George Richards, FCH; one *s. Educ:* Leominster Grammar Sch.; Radley (scholar); Keble Coll., Oxford (exhibitioner, MA). Asst Clerk, House of Commons 1926; Sen. Clerk, 1940; attached Select Cttee on National Expenditure, 1940-45; Clerk to Select Cttee on Estimates, 1946; Clerk of Financial Cttees, 1948-52; Clerk of Private Bills and Taxing Officer, House of Commons, and Examiner of Petitions for Private Bills, both Houses of Parliament, 1953-58; (compiled, 1961-70, and ed) The Keble College Centenary Register 1870-1970, 1970. Centenary Fellow, Keble Coll., 1970; Pres., Keble Assoc., 1971. *Recreations:* gardening; going abroad; philately (FRPSL, 1962). *Address:* 16 Blandford Avenue, Oxford OX2 8DY. *T:* Oxford 58280.
[*Died* 12 *Nov.* 1976.

DRESDEL, Sonia; actress; *b* Hornsea, Yorkshire. *Educ:* High Sch. and University, Aberdeen. Repertory prior to 1940, then Old Vic, CEMA, and ENSA tours; Hedda Tesman in Hedda Gabler, Mrs Millamant in Way of the World, Mercury Theatre and tour, 1942; Clotilde in Parisienne, St James's, 1943; Olivia Russell in This Was a Woman, Comedy, 1944; name part in Laura, St Martin's, 1945; Nurse Wayland in The Sacred Flame, Comedy, 1946; Lend me Robin, 1949; The Power of Darkness, 1949; The Third Visitor, 1949; at Edinburgh Festival, 1950 (as Juno in The Queen's Comedy); Message for Margaret (Australia); Lady Starcross in After My Fashion, 1952. Edinburgh Festival, 1955, 1956; Dr Jo, 1955; at Aldwych, 1956; The Best Damn Lie, 1957; toured Africa, 1958; Dir of Productions, Harrogate Opera House, 1959; Christine in Mourning Becomes Electra, Old Vic, 1961; All's Well That Ends Well, Bristol Old Vic; The Possessed, Mermaid, 1963; Oedipus the King and Oedipus at Colonus, Mermaid, 1965; Dandy Dick, Mermaid, 1965; The Man in the Glass Booth, St Martin's, 1967; Brother and Sister, 1968, Hay Fever, 1970, Bristol Old Vic; tour of Lloyd George Knew My Father. *Films:* While I Live, This Was a Woman, The Fallen Idol, The Third Visitor, Clouded Yellow, Now and Forever, The Secret Tent, Oscar Wilde, The Break. *Television:* The Guardsman, Thérèse Raquin, Mrs Dot, Eternal Triangle, Way of the World, What's your Story, Sorry Wrong Number, Count Albany, Rebecca, Crime on my Hands, the Mayerling Tragedy, Twilight of a Warrior, Judge for Yourself, David Copperfield, The Publican's Story, Mystery of Edwin Drood, The Adventures of Alice, Solitaire (with Françoise Rosay), Saki, Maigret, Jane Eyre, Wives and Daughters, The Onedin Line, The Very Merry Widow, The Witch of Haddington, Bachelor Father, The Pallisers, Lizzie Dripping, Sutherland's Law. *Recreation:* gardening. *Address: c/o* Richard Stone, Rausley House, Mersham, Kent.
[*Died* 18 *Jan.* 1976.

DREW, Lt-Col Hon. George Alexander, PC Can. 1953; CC Canada 1967; CD; QC; LLD; Canadian barrister; former High Commissioner for Canada in the UK, and former Premier of Ontario and Minister of Education; Chairman Board, Lake Ontario Cement Ltd; Director of other companies; Governor, University of Toronto; Chancellor, University of Guelph; *b* Guelph, Ontario, 7 May 1894; *s* of late John J. Drew, KC, Guelph; *m* 1st, 1936, Florenza d'Arneiro (*d* 1965), *d* of Edward Johnson, CBE; one *s* one *d* ; 2nd, 1966, Phyllis C. McCullagh (*née* Laidlaw), widow of C. George McCullagh, Toronto. *Educ:* Guelph Collegiate Inst.; Upper Canada Coll.; University of Toronto. Called to Bar (Ontario), 1920; practised in Guelph, 1920-25; Asst Master Supreme Court, Ont., 1926; Master, 1929; KC 1933. Leader Cons. Party, Ont., 1938; Ontario Legislature, 1939-48; Leader, Opposition of Ontario, 1939-43; Prime Minister, Province of Ontario, 1943, until chosen Leader of Cons. Party of Canada, Oct. 1948; Leader of Opposition of Canada, 1949-56; High Comr for Canada in UK, 1957-64, retd Alderman, City of Guelph, 1921-24; Mayor, 1925. Served European War, 1914-18, 16th Battery, Canadian Expeditionary Force (wounded): comd 64th Battery; comd 11th Field Regt,

Royal Canadian Artillery, Guelph, Ont., 1929-36; Pres.
Canadian Artillery Assoc., 1932-33. Headed various Canadian
Delegations, 1958-62. Holds hon. doctorates. Is an Anglican.
Publications: Canada's Fighting Airmen; The Truth about the
War; Canada's Part in the Great War; Salesmen of Death; Tell
Britain; The Truth About War Debts; numerous articles.
Recreations: golf, fishing, photography. *Address:* Suite 2111, 44
Victoria Street, Toronto 1, Ont, Canada. *T:* 366-3452. *Clubs:*
York, Toronto, Toronto Golf, Albany, University (Toronto);
Rideau, Ottawa Country (Ottawa); Guelph Country; Caledon
Mountain Trout.   *[Died 4 Jan. 1973.*

DREWE, Basil, OBE 1943; MC; QC 1945; *b* 1894; *s* of late J. C.
Drewe, Castle Drogo, Drewsteignton, Devon; *m* 1919, Ruth (*d*
1945), *d* of F. C. Haselden, East Lymden, Ticehurst; two *s* one *d.*
Educ: Eton; Christ Church, Oxford. Called to Bar, 1920; Master
of Bench, Inner Temple, 1952. Devonshire Regt and RA, 1914-
18 (MC and Bar); RAF 1939-45 (OBE). *Address:* Castle Drogo,
Drewsteignton, Devon. *T:* Chagford 2206. *Club:* Athenæum.
                                                    [Died 9 June 1974.

DREWE, Sir Cedric, KCVO 1953; *b* 26 May 1896; 3rd *s* of late J.
C. Drewe, JP, of Castle Drogo, Drewsteignton. Devon; *m* 1918,
Beatrice Foster, *o d* of late Campbell Newington, JP of Oakover,
Ticehurst, Sussex; three *s* one *d. Educ:* Eton; Royal Military
Acad., Woolwich. Served with RFA, 1914-19. MP (C) South
Molton Division of Devon, 1924-29; Honiton Division, Devon,
1931-55; Parliamentary Private Sec. to Rt Hon. Sir R. Dorman-
Smith, 1939-40; to Rt Hon. R. S. Hudson (Ministry of
Agriculture), 1940-43; Asst Govt Whip, 1943; Lord
Commissioner of Treasury, 1944-45; a Conservative Whip,
1945-49. Deputy Chief Conservative Whip, 1949; Treasurer to
the Queen's Household, 1952-55 (to the Household of King
George VI, 1951-52). Governor Seale Hayne Agricultural Coll.,
1959. *Address:* Broadhembury House, near Honiton, Devon. *T:*
Broadhembury 205. *Club:* Carlton.   *[Died 21 Jan. 1971.*

DRIBERG, Thomas Edward Neil; *see* Bradwell, Baron.

DRIVER, Sir Godfrey (Rolles), Kt 1968; CBE 1958; MC; MA;
FBA 1939; Hon. DD: Aberdeen, 1946; Manchester 1956; Hon.
DLitt: Durham, 1948; Oxford, 1970; Hon. LittD, Cambridge,
1964; Professor of Semitic Philology, Oxford University, 1938-
62; Fellow, Magdalen College, 1919-62, Hon. Fellow since 1962;
Hon. Fellow, School of Oriental and African Studies, London,
1963; *b* 20 Aug. 1892; *s* of late Rev. S. R. Driver, DD, Regius
Prof. of Hebrew and Canon of Christ Church, Oxford, and
Mabel Burr; *m* 1924, Madeleine Mary, *d* of John Goulding,
Bridlington; three *d. Educ:* Winchester Coll. (Scholar); New
Coll., Oxford (Scholar). Junior Hall-Houghton Prize for
Septuagint, 1912; Pusey and Ellerton Hebrew Scholarship, 1912;
2nd class Classical Moderations, 1913; Gaisford Prizes for
Greek Prose, 1913 and Verse, 1916; BA, 1917, MA, 1919; Senior
Kennicott Hebrew Scholarship, 1921. Military service BEF
(wounded, despatches, MC), 1915-18; EEF, 1919; MEF, 1940-
42; Ministry of Information, 1943-44. Fellow, 1919, Classical
Tutor, 1919-28, Librarian, 1923-40, Vice-Pres., 1931-32 of
Magdalen Coll.; Lecturer, 1927-28 and Reader, 1928 in
Comparative Semitic Philology, Oxford Univ.; Pro-proctor,
1923, Hebrew Lecturer at St John's Coll., 1928-38; Dep. Prof. of
Hebrew, 1934, 1953-54, 1959-60; Grinfield Lecturer on the
Septuagint, Oxford, 1935-39; Joint Dir of New English Bible,
1965; Visiting Prof.: Chicago Univ., 1925; Louvain Univ., 1950;
Copenhagen Univ., 1953. Jt Editor, Jl of Theological Studies,
1933-40; Pres., Soc. for Study of Old Testament, 1937; Pres.,
International Organisation for the Study of the Old Testament,
1953-59; Leverhulme Fellow, 1939 (resigned owing to war);
Schweich Lecturer at British Academy, 1944; Cadbury
Lecturer, Birmingham, 1958; Walker Lecturer, Belfast, 1960,
Burkitt Medal for Biblical Studies, 1953. *Publications:* Report
on Kurdistan and the Kurds (for EEF), 1919; Letters of the First
Babylonian Dynasty, 1925; Grammar of the Colloquial Arabic
of Syria and Palestine, 1925; Nestorius, the Bazaar of
Heracleides (jointly with the Rev. L. Hodgson), 1925; Assyrian
Laws and Babylonian Laws (jointly with Sir J. C. Miles), 1935,
1952, 1955; Problems of the Hebrew Verbal System, 1936;
Semitic Writing, 1948, 1954, 1974; Aramaic Documents from
Egypt, 1953; Canaanite Myths and Legends, 1956; Aramaic
Documents of the Fifth Century BC (revised edn), 1955, 1965;
Aramaic Documents, 1957; The Judaean Scrolls, 1965. Articles
and reviews in English and foreign publications on Semitic
languages and Old Testament. *Recreation:* walking. *Address:* 41
Park Town, Oxford. *T:* Oxford 55165. *[Died 22 April 1975.*

DROUGHT, Charles W.; *see* Worster-Drought.

DROWER, Lady; (Ethel May Stefana); hon. DLitt Oxon; hon.
DD Uppsala; hon. Fellow, School of Oriental and African

Studies, University of London; writer and lecturer, student of
religions, languages and folklore of the Middle East, particularly
of the Mandæans; *b* 1 Dec. 1879; *d* of Rev. S. W. Stevens, MA,
LLM; *widow of* Sir E. M. Drower, KBE; two *s* one *d. Educ:* sch.,
travel, and long residence in Middle East. In earlier life wrote
novels and travel books under name of E. S. Stevens. Awarded
Lidzbarski Gold Medal by the Deutsche Morgenländische
Gesellschaft, 1964. *Publications:* novels: The Veil, 1909; The
Mountain of God, 1910; The Lure, 1911; The Long
Engagement, 1911; The Earthen Drum, 1912; Sarah Eden, 1914;
Allward, 1915; And What Happened? 1916; The Safety Candle,
1917; Magdalene, 1919; Sophy: a Tale of Baghdad, 1924; The
Losing Game, 1926; Ishtar, 1927; *travel books:* My Sudan Year,
1912; By Tigris and Euphrates, 1923; Cedars, Saints and Sinners
in Syria, 1926; *orientalia:* Folk Tales of Iraq, 1931 (under name
of Stevens); The Mandæans of Iraq and Iran: their Cults,
Customs, Magic, Legends, and Folklore, 1937 (reprinted
Leiden, 1962); Peacock Angel, 1941; Water into Wine: a study of
ritual idiom in the Middle and Near East, 1956; The Secret
Adam: a study of Nasoraean Gnosticism, 1960. Translations
from the Mandaic: The Book of the Zodiac, 1949; The Diwan
Abatur (Studi e Testi 151), 1950; Explanatory Commentary of
the Marriage Ceremony of the Great Shishlam (Biblica e
Orientalia No. 12), 1950; The Haran Gawaita and The Baptism
of Hibil-Ziwa (Studi e Testi 176), 176), 1953; The Canonical
Prayer Book of the Mandæans, 1959: A Thousand and Twelve
Questions (Deutsche Akademie der Wissenschaften), 1960; The
Coronation of the Great Sislam, 1962; A Pair of Nasoraean
Commentaries, 1963; A Mandaic Dictionary (with R. Macuch),
1963. *Address:* The Cottage, 8 Willenhall Avenue, New Barnet,
Herts. *T:* 01-449 4351.   *[Died 27 Jan. 1972.*

DRUCQUER, Sir Leonard, Kt 1968; CEng, FIEE; *b* 4 Feb. 1902,
s of late William Henry and Sophie Drucquer; *m* 1928, Inez
Hildegard Banham. *Educ:* Haberdashers' Aske's Sch.;
Polytechnic Coll. of Engineering, Regent Street, W1. Joined
British Thomson Houston Ltd, 1920; Manager, Switchgear
Sales, 1945; Manager, Home Sales (Plant and Apparatus), 1950;
Director, Home Sales, 1956; Dir and Gen. Manager, AEI Heavy
Plant Div., 1958; Consultant to Industrial Group, AEI, 1966-68
Pres. Instn of Electrical Engrs, 1965-66; Chm., Council of
Engineering Instns, 1967-69; Mem. Council, Loughborough
Univ. of Technology, 1967-; Governor, Lanchester Polytechnic
1969-72. *Recreation:* gardening. *Address:* Crick Manor, near
Northampton NN6 7TP. *T:* Crick 822353. *Club:* United Service
& Royal Aero.   *[Died 28 March 1975*

DRUITT, Sir (William Arthur) Harvey, KCB 1965 (CB 1951)
HM Procurator-General and Treasury Solicitor, 1964-71; *b* 19
April 1910; *s* of late Arthur Druitt, Gullane, East Lothian; *m*
1940, Joan Holdsworth, *d* of late L. D. P. Swift, Eastbourne; one
s (and one *d* decd). *Educ:* Edinburgh Acad.; Oriel Coll., Oxford
Entered Dept of HM Procurator-General and Treasury
Solicitor, 1937; Deputy Treasury Solicitor, 1956-63. *Address:* 76
Baron's Keep, Baron's Court, W14. *T:* 01-603 6433. *Clubs*
Athenæum, Hurlingham.   *[Died 6 Feb. 1973*

DRUMMOND, Sir William (Hugh Dudley) Williams-, 6th Bt cr
1828; retired; *b* 13 Feb. 1901; *s* of Sir Francis Dudley Williams
Drummond, KBE (4th *s* of 3rd Bt) (*d* 1935) and Marguerite
Violet Maud (*d* 1939), *d* of Sir Andrew Agnew, 8th Bt; *S* cousin
Sir James Hamlyn Williams Williams-Drummond, 5th Bt, 1970
unmarried. *Educ:* Eton. *Recreations:* hockey, tennis. *Heir:* none
Address: Guessens, Welwyn, Herts. *T:* Welwyn 4049.
                                            [Died 27 May 1976 (ext)

DRURY, Sir Alan (Nigel), Kt 1950; CBE 1944; FRS 1937; MA
MD Cantab; FRCP; MRCS; *b* 3 Nov. 1889; *s* of Henry George
and Elizabeth Rose Drury; *m* 1916, Daphne Marguerite
Brownsword (*d* 1975); one *s* one *d. Educ:* Merchant Taylors
Sch., London; Gonville and Caius Coll., Cambridge; St Thomas
Hospital, London. George Henry Lewes Student in Physiology
War service, Major RAMC, DADMS (Sanitary) 9th
Secunderabad Div., India; late Fellow of Trinity Hall
Cambridge; late Huddersfield Lecturer in Special Pathology
University of Cambridge; Mem. of Scientific Staff, Medical
Research Council, 1921-43; late Dir Lister Institute; Mem. of
Scientific Staff, Agricultural Research Council, 1952-60. Hon
Fellow Trinity Hall. *Publications:* in Heart, Journal of
Physiology, Quarterly Journal of Experimental Physiology, etc
Address: 36 Gretton Court, High Street, Girton, Cambridge
CB3 0QN. *T:* Cambridge 77181.   *[Died 2 Aug. 1980*

D'SILVA, Prof. John Leonard, JP; Halliburton Professor of
Physiology, King's College, London, since 1959; *b* 27 Oct. 1910
e c of Albert Robert and Kathleen Isabelle D'Silva; *m* 1936
Phyllis Maude Tyler; one *s* one *d. Educ:* South India. BS
(Special) Chemistry, King's Coll., London, 1929; PhD

Chemistry (Organic), 1931; Sir Halley Stewart Fellow, 1933; Demonstrator in Physiology at St Bartholomew's Medical Coll., 1936-39; DSc, 1940, MB, BS London, 1940-42, MRCP, 1942, FRCP 1969. House Physician, Medical Professorial Unit, St Bartholomew's Hosp., 1942; Chief Asst, St Bartholomew's Hosp., and Asst Physician, EMS, 1942-44; Lecturer in Physiology, 1944-46, Reader in Physiology, 1946-48, St Bartholomew's Hosp. Medical Coll., EC1; Prof. of Physiology, London Hosp. Med. Coll., E1, 1948-59. JP St Albans City Bench, 1964-71. *Publications:* papers in various medical journals. *Recreations:* gardening, photography. *Address:* Castle Cottage, 12 Farm Lane, Great Bedwyn, Marlborough, Wilts. *Club:* National Liberal. *[Died 20 Aug. 1973.*

D'SOUZA, Most Rev. Albert V.; *b* Mangalore, India, 5 April 1904. Priest, 1928; nominated Auxiliary Bishop of Mysore, 1959; consecrated Bishop, 1959; nominated Archbishop of Calcutta, Aug. 1962; took possession of Archdiocesan See of Calcutta, Dec. 1962; retired, 1969. *Address:* St Anthony's Institutes, Mangalore 2, Karnataka, India.
[Died 14 Aug. 1977.

DUCHESNE, Jacques; *see* Saint-Denis, Michel Jacques.

DUCKWORTH, Frederick Victor, CMG 1954; *b* 11 Aug. 1901; *s* of Arthur Robbins Duckworth and May Ellen Anderson; *m* 1939, Margaret Wade; one *d* (one *s* decd). *Educ:* North Point; Selwyn Coll., Cambridge. MCS, 1924; Magistrate, Singapore, 1925; Dist Officer, Balik Pulau, 1927; Asst Controller of Labour, Klang, 1928; Contr of Labour, Johore, 1933; Dep. Contr of Labour, FMS, 1938; Chief Press Censor, Malaya, 1940; Malayan Agent in South Africa, 1942; seconded to Kenya, 1943; ALFSEA, 1945; Col, Labour, Brit. Mil. Admin., Malaya, 1945; Comr for Labour, Fedn Malaya, 1950; Mem. for Industrial and Social Relations, 1953; British Adviser, Selangor, 1954-56; retired 1956. Selangor Meritorious Service Medal, 1956. *Recreations:* golf, tennis, trout-fishing. *Address:* Heathfield, Old Heath, Colchester, Essex. *T:* Colchester 5477.
[Died 18 May 1974.

DUCKWORTH-KING, Sir John (Richard), 7th Bt, *cr* 1792; *b* 11 June 1899; *o surv. s* of Col Sir Dudley Gordon Alan Duckworth-King, 5th Bt and Eva Mary, *d* of Maj.-Gen. Ralph Gore; *S* brother, 1952; *m* 1943, Alice Patricia, *d* of Thomas Rutledge, Fugar House, Ravensworth, Co. Durham. *Educ:* Wellington Coll.; RMC Sandhurst. Lieut Coldstream Guards, 1919-27; served War of 1939-45, Royal Air Force. *Recreations:* Joint Holder of Army Doubles Racquet Championship 1925, 1926 and 1927; Runner-up Army Racquet Singles, 1927. *Heir:* none. *Address:* c/o Commonwealth Trading Bank of Australia, Australia House, WC2. *Club:* Guards.
[Died 1 April 1972 (ext).

DU CROS, Sir (Harvey) Philip, 2nd Bt, *cr* 1916; *b* 19 June 1898; *s* of Sir Arthur Philip du Cros, 1st Bt and Maude (*d* 1938), *d* of late William Gooding, Coventry; *S* father 1955; *m* 1st, 1922, Dita Matilda (marr. diss., 1950), *d* of late Sir Claude Coventry Mallet, CMG and late Lady Mallet, CBE; one *s* two *d*; 2nd, 1950, Rosemary Theresa, MBE, *d* of Sir John Rees, 1st Bt, KCIE. *Educ:* Harrow. Served in European War with 3rd (King's Own) Hussars, 1916-19; War of 1939-45 (despatches), RA. Military Pioneer Corps, 1939-44. Dir of St Martin's Le Grand Property Co., etc. *Recreations:* fishing, golf, etc. *Heir:* *s* Claude Philip Arthur Mallet du Cros [*b* 22 Dec. 1922; *m* 1953, Mrs Christine Nancy Tordoff, *d* of late F. R. Bennett, Spilsby, Lincs; one *s*]. *Address:* Little Bocombe, Parkham, N Devon. *T:* Horns Cross 206. *Clubs:* Bath, Carlton. *[Died 11 Oct. 1975.*

DUDLEY, 13th Baron, *cr* 1439-1440 (called out of abeyance, 1916); **Ferdinando Dudley Henry Lea Smith;** late Lieut 8th Bn Worcs Regt; late Squadron Leader, RAF; *b* 18 June 1910; *s* of 12th Baron and Sybil Augusta (*d* 1958), *d* of Rev. H. W. Coventry, Rector of Severn Stoke, Worcester; *S* father 1936. *Heir:* sister, Hon. Barbara Amy Felicity Wallace [*b* 23 April 1907; *m* 1929, Guy Wallace (*d* 1967); three *s* one *d*]. *Address:* 12a Half Moon Street, W1. *Club:* Royal Air Force.
[Died 19 April 1972.

DUDLEY, Sir Alan Alves, KBE 1961; CMG 1948; Director, Electronic Components Board, since 1968; *b* 1907; *s* of Bertram and Ethel Dudley; *m* 1930, Isabel, *d* of David and Margaret Brunton; one *d*. *Educ:* St Christopher's Sch.; London Sch. of Economics; University Coll. of Wales, Aberystwyth. Asst Dir, British Library, New York, 1930-40; Dir, British Press Service and British Information Service, New York, 1940-42; Foreign Office, 1942-49 (Head of Information Policy Dept, 1946-49); Counsellor, UK Deleg. to OEEC, Paris, 1949-50; Head of UN Economic and Social Dept, FO, 1950-53; Dep. Commissioner-

Gen. for the UK in South-East Asia, 1953-56; HM Minister at Bucharest, 1956-59; HM Minister in UK Mission to UN, 1959-61; Under-Sec., Dept of Technical Co-operation, 1961-64; Dep. Sec., ODM, 1964-68. *Address:* 42 Rivermead Court, SW6. *T:* 01-736 1443; Plas Derwen, Llansantffraid, Mont. *T:* Llansantffraid 373. *Clubs:* Athenæum, English-Speaking Union.
[Died 13 Sept. 1971.

DUDLEY, Prof. Donald Reynolds; Professor of Latin, University of Birmingham, since 1955; Dean, Faculty of Arts, 1958-61; *b* 3 March 1910; *s* of J. J. Dudley; *m* 1938, Eryl Margaret, *d* of W. St Bodfan Griffith, Bangor, N Wales; two *d*. *Educ:* King Edward's Sch., Birmingham; St John's Coll., Cambridge. Henry Fund Fellow, Yale Univ., USA, 1932-33; Fellow, St John's Coll., Cambridge, 1935-37; Lecturer in Classics, Reading Univ., 1937-44; Fereday Fellow, St John's Coll., Oxford, 1938-41; Dir of Extra-Mural Studies, University of Birmingham, 1944-55. Visiting Lectr, Tulane Univ., New Orleans, USA, 1952. Member: Governing Body, King Edward's Foundation (Bailiff, 1963-64); Worcs Educ. Cttee. *Publications:* A History of Cynicism, 1937; Civilization of Rome, 1960; (with Graham Webster) The Rebellion of Boudicca, 1962, The Roman Conquest of Britain, AD 43-57, 1965; The Annals of Tacitus (trans.) 1966; Urbs Roma, 1967; The World of Tacitus, 1968; The Romans, 1970; (with T. A. Dorey) Rome Against Carthage, 1971; articles on Roman history; ed (with T. A. Dorey), Studies in Latin Literature and its Influence (9 vols publ. to date). *Recreations:* archæology and travel. *Address:* Blackhill, Malvern, Worcs. *T:* Colwall 202. *Club:* English-Speaking Union.
[Died 31 Aug. 1972.

DUDOK, Willem Marinus; architect, BNA; Officer of Order of Oranje-Nassau, Holland; Knight of Order of the Lion, Netherlands; *b* 6 July 1884; *s* of Johannes Cornelis Dudok and Cornelia Bertha Holst; *m* 1911, Marie Alette Smit; one *s* one *d*. *Educ:* Royal Military Academy, Breda. Was an officer of the corps of engineers, 1905-13; became an engineer of the city of Leiden, 1913; Dir Public Works in Hilversum, 1915; built many workmen's houses, schools, town hall 1928-31; also country houses, the Columbarium at Westerveld, 1925-26, extended, 1937-38; a quarter with middle class houses, Eindhoven, 1935-39; Stores, Beehive (de Bijenkorf) at Rotterdam, 1929-30 (destroyed during war); Cinema CA, Calcutta, 1936-38; Theatre, Utrecht, 1939-41; Offices for HAV Bank, Schiedam, 1934-35; "The Netherlands of 1845", Arnhem, 1938-39; office for crematorium at Westerveld, 1939-41; Dutch student-home in Cité Universitaire, Paris, 1927-38; Erasmus House, Rotterdam, 1937; town-planning, design for reconstruction of The Hague, Velsen-Ymuiden; Zwolle, Head Office for Royal Dutch Steelworks, Ymuiden, 1949-; Offices "The Netherlands of 1845", Rotterdam, 1952; Flats, Stores and housing in Hilversum, Amsterdam, Bussum, etc. since 1954; Aulas at new cemeteries in Velsen and Hilversum, 1962-64; Town Hall, Velsen, designed 1950, executed 1962-65; Harbour building at Amsterdam, 1960 (with R. M. H. Magnee), etc. Royal Gold Medal of RIBA, Gold Medal AIA, 1955, and other gold medals. Officer, Order of Crown of Belgium. *Publications:* articles on architecture and town planning. *Recreations:* music and drawing. *Address:* Utrechtscheweg 71, Hilversum, Holland. *TA:* Dudok, Hilversum. *T:* 7336. *[Died 6 April 1974.*

DUFF, Maj.-Gen. Alan Colquhoun, CB 1945; OBE 1941; MC 1916; Commander, Legion of Merit (USA), 1946; *b* 11 Nov. 1896; *e s* of J. D. Duff, Fellow of Trinity Coll., Cambridge, and Laura, *d* of Sir William Lenox-Conyngham, KCB; *m* 1935, Diana Francis, *d* of late Col R. P. Crawley, DSO, OBE, MVO; one *s* two *d*. *Educ:* Wellington Coll.; RMA, Woolwich. Commissioned Royal Engineers, 1915; Capt. 1918; Major, 1930; Lieut-Col 1938; Col 1941; Maj.-Gen. 1946. European War, 1915-18 (Gallipoli, Serbia, Macedonia, Palestine); Staff Coll., 1926-27; Nigeria Regt, 1930-35; Campaign in East Africa, 1941 (despatches twice); DQMG, War Office, 1943-44; DQMG, Allied Force HQ, Italy, 1945; Chief Admin. Officer to Field-Marshal Alexander and Actg Lieut-Gen., 1945; Maj.-Gen. i/c Administration Southern Command, 1946-47; retired pay, 1947. Gen. Manager, Stevenage Development Corporation, 1947-57. A Governor of Bryanston Sch. 1948-71. *Publications:* 65 RE, 1920; The Spine, 1929; On Helle's Wave, 1930; The House of the Apricots, 1933 (the three last under nom-de-plume Hugh Imber); Sword and Pen, 1950; Britain's New Towns, 1961. *Address:* Rider's Croft, Little Chesterford, Essex. *Club:* Naval and Military. *[Died 4 Nov. 1973.*

DUFF, Sir (Charles) Michael (Robert Vivian), 3rd Bt *cr* 1911; Lieutenant of Gwynedd, since 1974 (Lord Lieutenant of Caernarvonshire, 1960-74); *b* 3 May 1907; *s* of 2nd Bt and Lady (Gladys Mary) Juliet Lowther, *o d* of 4th Earl of Lonsdale (Lady Juliet Duff; *d* 1965); *S* father, 1914; *m* 1949, Lady Caroline Paget (*d* 1976), *e d* of 6th Marquess of Anglesey, GCVO; one adopted *s*. *Educ:* Sandhurst. Flying Officer late RAFVR. DL 1946, Vice-Lieutenant 1957-60, Caernarvonshire; High Sheriff of Anglesey, 1950-51. KStJ. *Recreations:* shooting and hunting. *Address:* Vaynol Park, Bangor, N Wales. *T:* Bangor 42. *Club:* White's. *[Died* 3 *March* 1980 (*ext*).

DUFF, Sir (Charles) Patrick, KCB 1932 (CB 1928); KCVO 1937 (CVO 1924); *b* 1889; *s* of late Harry Duff; *m* 1929, Margaret, *d* of late James Woodcock. *Educ:* Blundell's Sch., Tiverton; Balliol Coll., Oxford. Entered Bd of Trade by open competition (Cl. I), 1912; served European War, 1914-18, Gallipoli, France, Mesopotamia (wounded, despatches twice); Private Sec. to successive Presidents of the Board of Trade, 1919-23; Private Sec. to successive Prime Ministers (Rt Hon. Stanley Baldwin, Rt Hon. J. Ramsay Macdonald, Rt Hon. Stanley Baldwin, Rt Hon. J. Ramsay Macdonald), 1923-33; Sec., Ministry of Works and Public Buildings, 1933-41; Dep. High Comr, Canada, 1941-44; High Commissioner for the UK, New Zealand, 1945-49; a Church Commissioner for England, 1949-54. Chm. of the National Parks Commission, 1949-54; Mem. of Nature Conservancy, 1949-54. *Address:* Eight Bells House, Haddenham, Bucks. *Club:* United Oxford & Cambridge University. *[Died* 16 *Dec.* 1972.

DUFF, Sir Michael; *see* Duff, Sir C. M. R. V.

DUFF, Sir Patrick; *see* Duff, Sir C. P.

DUFFIELD, Anne; Writer of Fiction; *b* Orange, New Jersey; British Canadian; *m* 1921, Edgar Willoughby Duffield, OBE; no *c. Educ:* Westburne, Toronto; Mademoiselle Osselins, Paris. *Publications:* Some thirty-eight novels, first being The Lacquer Couch, 1928, and among others Grecian Rhapsody, The Dragon's Tail, The House on the Nile, Bubbling Springs, 1940, The Sweeping Tide, 1940; The Shadow of the Pines, 1940; A Bevy of Maids, 1941; The Inscrutable Nymph, 1942; Old Glory, 1943; Sunrise, 1943; Out of the Shadows, 1944; Tappy Came to Cairo, 1945; Repent at Leisure, 1945; Forever Tomorrow, 1946; Song of the Mocking Bird, 1947; Arkady, 1948; Dusty Dawn, 1949; Beloved Enemy, 1950; Sugar Island, 1951; Tomorrow is Theirs, 1952; Harbour Lights, 1952; The Grand Duchess, 1953; The Golden Summer, 1954; Come back Miranda, 1955; Fiametta, 1956; Castle in Spain, 1958; Violetta, 1960. *Recreations:* travel, ski-ing, Canadian canoe trips, reading, gardening. *Address:* 10 The Green, Aldbourne, Wilts. *TA:* Aldbourne, Wilts. *T:* Aldbourne 336. *[Died* 11 *Nov.* 1976.

DUGDALE, Amy K.; *see* Browning, A. K.

DUGUID, Maj.-Gen. David Robertson, CB 1945; MBE; FHWC; late REME; *b* 5 Dec. 1888; *s* of Jas. Duguid, Bo'ness, NB; *m* 1918, Mary Paris; three *s. Educ:* Bo'ness Academy; Heriot-Watt Coll., Edinburgh. Asst Engineer with Marshall & Duguid, Engineers, Bo'ness, 1912-15; with RAOC as Inspector of Ordnance Machinery, 1915-19; served throughout European War in France, Salonika and South Russia; with Inter-Allied Control Commission in Germany, 1919-24; Ordnance Mechanical Engineer, Western Command, UK, 1924-25; Asst Inspector of Guns and Carriages with CIA Dept, Woolwich Arsenal, 1925-29; OC RAOC Workshops, Woolwich Arsenal, 1929-32; OC Ordnance Workshops, Quetta Arsenal, India, 1932-37; OC RAOC Depot Workshops, Chilwell, 1937-39; OC Advanced Base Workshop, France, 1939-40; Deputy Dir of Mechanical Engineering, War Office, 1941-43; Dir of Mechanical Engineering, India, and Head of Corps of Indian Electrical and Mechanical Engineers, 1943-46; retired, 1946. Fellow, Heriot-Watt Coll., 1951. *Recreation:* golf. *Address:* 69 Dalkeith Road, Dundee. *[Died* 9 *Nov.* 1973.

DUGUID, Prof. John Bright, CBE 1966; MD (Aberdeen); Adviser in Histopathology, Institute for Medical Research, Kuala Lumpur, Malaya, Nov. 1960-69, retired; Emeritus Professor of Pathology, University of Durham, Professor, 1948-60; *b* 5 May 1895; *s* of John Duguid, Farmer, Black Dog, Belhelvie, Aberdeenshire; *m* 1925, Agnes Mildred Emslie Benzie, MB, ChB (*d* 1973); one *s* one *d. Educ:* Friends Sch., Wigton, Cumberland; Gordon's Coll., Aberdeen, MB, ChB (Aberdeen) 1920; MD (Aberdeen), 1925. Asst in dept of Pathology, Aberdeen Univ., 1922; Lecturer in Morbid Anatomy and Histology, Victoria Univ., Manchester, 1925; Lecturer in Pathology, Welsh Nat. Sch. of Medicine, Cardiff, 1926; Prof. of Pathology and Bacteriology, University of Wales, 1932. *Publications:* The Dynamics of Atherosclerosis, 1976; articles on arterial diseases and lung pathology. *Recreation:* angling. *Address:* 17 Cairn Road, Bieldside, Aberdeen. *[Died* 21 *Dec.* 1980.

DUKE, Sir Charles (Beresford), KCMG 1956 (CMG 1954); CIE 1947; OBE 1946; Director-General, Middle East Association, 1964-70; *b* 19 Dec. 1905; *o s* of late Arthur Herbert and Ann Victoria Duke, of Bangkok, Siam and Marlow, Bucks; *m* 1938, Morag Craigie, *o d* of Capt. Patrick Grant; two *d. Educ:* Charterhouse; Lincoln Coll., Oxford. Entered Indian Civil Service, 1928; appointed to United Provinces of Agra and Oudh, 1929; transferred to Indian Political Service, 1934; Asst Private Sec. to Viceroy, 1934-38; Sec. to Governor, NWFP, 1940-41; Political Agent, Waziristan, 1941-43; External Affairs Dept, Govt of India, New Delhi, 1943-47; transferred to HM Foreign Service, 1947; served in Pakistan, FO, Persia and Egypt, 1947-54; HM Ambassador to Jordan, 1954-56 and to Morocco, 1957-61; retired, 1961. *Recreation:* reading. *Address:* 15 Westgate Terrace, SW10; Cadenham Grange, Cadnam, near Southampton. *Club:* Athenæum. *[Died* 14 *Nov.* 1978

DUKE, Brig. Jesse Pevensey, DSO 1919; MC; *b* 10 June 1890; *s* of Lieut-Col Olliver Thomas Duke and Blanche Wheeler; *m* 1936, Marion (*d* 1973), *widow* of Major G. W. H. Massey. *Educ:* Wellington Coll.; Sandhurst. Gazetted to Royal Warwickshire Regt, 1910; served in international occupation of North Albania, 1914, subsequent to Balkan War; various Staff appointments in European War, 1914-18 (DSO, MC, Bt Majority); GSO 3 North Russia, 1920; Staff Coll., Camberley, 1921-22; GSO 3 and 2 Northern Command, 1923-27; Instructor, RMC Sandhurst 1929-32; Commanded 1st Bn Royal Warwickshire Regt, 1934-36; 1936-47: Col at War Office; AAG, HQ Eastern Command, 153 Inf. Bde; AAG Scottish Command; Army HQ India, Dir of Organisation, Selection of Personnel, India (temp. Brig.); retired, 1947. British Resident, CCG, 1947-50. *Recreations:* golf, painting. *Address:* c/o Lloyds Bank, 6 Pall Mall, SW1. *[Died* 11 *April* 1980

DUKE, Most Rev. William Mark; Titular Archbishop of Seleucia Isauria, since 1964; *b* St John, NB, 7 Oct. 1879. *Educ:* University of St Joseph, Memramcook, NB; Grand Seminary, Quebec Priest, 1905; ministered at Moncton, Shediac, Buctouche; Pastor, Cathedral Parish of St John, New Brunswick, 1912-28 Coadjutor with succession to Archbishop of Vancouver and Titular Archbishop of Fasi, 1928; Archbishop of Vancouver (RC), 1931-64. Asst at the Pontifical Throne, 1936. *Address.* 1114 Holy Rosary Residence, 1100 Burnaby Street, Vancouver 5, BC, Canada. *[Died* 31 *Aug.* 1971

DUKE-ELDER, Sir Stewart, GCVO 1958 (KCVO 1946); K 1933; GCStJ, FRS 1960; MA (first-class Hons.), BSc (Sp Distinction), DSc, PhD (London), MD (gold medal), ChB (S Andrews); FRCS, FRCP; Extra Surgeon-Oculist to the Queen 1965-73, Surgeon-Oculist, 1952-65 (formerly to King Edward VIII and to King George VI): Counsellor, Order of St John Hon. Ophthalmic Consultant to the Royal Air Force Ophthalmic Consultant, London Transport; Director of Research, Institute of Ophthalmology, University of London 1947-65; President, 1965; Hon. Consulting Ophthalmic Surgeon St George's Hospital, London and Moorfields Eye Hospital Fellow University College, London, and Institute of Ophthalmology; surgeon-oculist in London, 1929-76; *b* 22 April 1898; *m* 1928, Phyllis Mary, MB, BS, *d* of W. Edgar, London *Educ:* St Andrews and London Univs. St Andrews Univ., 1st Foundation Scholar, 1915; British Assocn medallist, 1915 Demr. of Physiology (St Andrews), 1918; University Coll Scholar, 1919; Demonstrator of Anatomy, 1920; Pres. Students Union and Representative Council, 1921; Royal Infirmary Edinburgh, 1922; St George's Hospital London, 1923; Henry George Plimmer Research Fellow, 1925; Sir Francis Lakin Research Scholar, 1926-29; Paul Philip Reitlinger Prizeman 1926; BMA Scholar, 1927; BMA Middlemore Prizeman, 1928 William Mackenzie Memorial Medallist (Glasgow), 1929 Research Associate, UC, London, 1930; Howe Lecturer in Ophthalmology, Harvard Univ., USA, 1930; Nettleship Meda for Research in Ophthalmology, 1933; Howe Medallist (USA) 1946; Research Medallist, American Medical Association, 1947 Donders Medallist (Holland), 1947; Doyne Medallist, Oxford 1948; Proctor Lect., USA, 1951; Gullstrand Medallist (Sweden) 1952; Craig Prizeman (Belfast), 1952; Medallist, Strasbourg Univ., 1952, Ghent Univ., 1953; Gonin Medallis (International), 1954; Lister Medal, 1956; Bowman Medal 1957; Ophthalmiatreion Medal, Athens, 1957; Charles Mickle Fellow, Toronto, 1959; Proctor Medal (USA) 1960 Fothergillian Medal, 1962; Lang Medal (Royal Society of Medicine), 1965. Served in Army during War of 1939-4 (Brigadier, RAMC), 1940-46; Consulting Ophthalmic Surgeon to the Army, 1946-61, now Emeritus; Examiner in Ophthalmology, RCS, 1947-51; Editor, Ophthalmic Literature Chm. Editorial Board, British Jl Ophthalmology, 1948-73. Hon Life Pres., International Council of Ophthalmology; Pas President: Faculty of Ophthalmologists; Ophthalmological Soc

UK; Hon. Member: American, Canadian, Australian, French, Belgian, Danish, German, Swedish, Dutch, Swiss, Italian, Lombardy, Greek, Pan-American, Mexican, Egyptian, All-Indian and Hyderabad Ophthalmic Socs; National Association for Research in Ophthalmology (USA); Ophthalmic Institute of Australia; Australian Coll. of Ophthalmology; Hon. Life Pres., Greek Ophthalmological Soc.; Hon. Mem. Royal Society Sciences, Uppsala; Fellow, Med. Soc. Sweden; Royal Netherlands Acad. of Sciences; Hon. Fellow, Internat. Soc. of Eye Surgeons; Hon. For. Mem., l'Académie royale de médecine de Belgique; Amer. Acad. Arts and Sciences; Member: Med. Acad., Rome; Royal Acad., Athens; Chm., Med. Advisory Cttee, Royal Commonwealth Soc. for the Blind; Consultant, National Soc., Prevention of Blindness, USA; Canadian Nat. Inst. Blindness; Hon. Fellow American Medical Assoc.; American Acad. Ophthalmology; Pan-American Med. Soc.; Pan-American Surg. Assoc.; Hon. DSc (Northwestern, McGill, Manchester), Hon. MD (Dublin), DM (Utrecht, Strasbourg, Ghent, Athens), LLD (St Andrews); Hon. FRCS Edinburgh; FACS; FRACS; Hon. FRSM; Fellow, UMIST; Hon. Col RAMC; Bronze Star Medal (USA); Star of Jordan (1st class). Kt Comdr, Royal Order of the Phoenix (Greece); Comdr of Orthodox Crusaders, Order of the Holy Sepulchre (Jerusalem). *Publications:* Text-Book of Ophthalmology, Vols I-VII, 1932-54; System of Ophthalmology, Vols I-XV, 1958-76; Century of International Ophthalmology, 1958; British Ophthalmological Monographs, III, 1927; IV 1930; Recent Advances in Ophthalmology, 1927, 4th edn 1951; Diseases of the Eye (16th edn), 1969; The Practice of Refraction, 8th edn, 1968; numerous scientific and clinical papers in the Proceedings of the Royal Society, Board of Research for Industrial Fatigue, and other British, European and American ophthalmic journals, etc. *Address:* 28 Elm Tree Road, NW8. *T:* 01-286 9491. *Club:* Athenæum.   [*Died 27 March 1978.*

DUKE-ELDER, Sir (William) Stewart; see Duke-Elder, Sir S.

DUKES, Cuthbert Esquire, OBE; MSc, MD, FRCS, DPH; FRCPath; Hon. Consultant Pathologist St Mark's Hospital; Hon. Consultant Pathologist, Institute of Urology, University of London; *b* Bridgwater, 24 July 1890; *s* of late Rev. E. J. Dukes and Edith Mary Dukes, BA; *m* Dr Ethel Dukes; one *s. Educ:* Caterham Sch.; Edinburgh Univ.; University Coll., London. Past President: Section of History of Medicine, Royal Society of Medicine, 1959; Section of Urology, Royal Society of Medicine, 1957; Medical Soc. of London, 1952; Assoc. of Clinical Pathologists, 1948-49; Section of Proctology, Royal Society of Medicine, 1944; Hunterian Medal and Triennial Prize, RCS of England, 1949-51; Hunterian Prof., RCS of England, 1952; Lettsomian Lecturer, Medical Soc. of London, 1948; Foundation Lecturer, Assoc. of Clinical Pathologists, 1958; Thomas Vicary Lecturer, RCS of England, 1960. Hon. Fellow: Royal Society of Medicine; Assoc. of Clinical Pathologists; Amer. Assoc. of Clinical Pathologists; Med. Soc. of London; Mem. of Pathological Soc. of Great Britain. *Publications:* Several contributions to medical and scientific journals. *Address:* 22 Albemarle, Wimbledon Park Side, SW19. *T:* 01-788 2699.   [*Died 3 Feb. 1977.*

DUMAS, Sir Lloyd, Kt 1946; FJI; FRGS; Chairman, 1942-67 (Managing Director, 1938-61, retired), Advertiser Newspapers Ltd, Adelaide; Managing Editor of The Advertiser and associated publications, 1929-53; Director: Advertiser Newspapers Ltd, 1931-67; Elder Smith & Co. 1941-67; Elder Smith-Goldsbrough Mort Ltd, 1962-67; Australian Newsprint Mills Ltd, 1938-66, Australian Associated Press, 1940-61 (Chairman, 1949-51, 1959-61); Herald and Weekly Times Ltd (Melbourne), 1946-67; Reuters, 1950-53; Television Broadcasters Ltd, 1959-67 (Chairman); *b* Mount Barker, S Australia, 15 July 1891; *y s* of C. M. R. Dumas; *m* Daisy (*d* 1962), *y d* of E. Smith Hall, S Australia; three *d. Educ:* Teachers' Training Coll., Adelaide. Joined The Advertiser Literary Staff as cadet, 1907; transferred to The Argus, Melbourne; subsequently accompanied Mr W. M. Hughes to Imperial Conference, London, 1918; re-joined The Argus on return, becoming Chief of Staff, 1921-24; Editor of the Sun News-Pictorial, 1924-27; Manager and Editor of Australian Newspapers Cable Service, London, 1927-29. Member Board: SA Nat. Gall., 1945-63 (Chm., 1956-63); Wyatt Benevolent Instn, 1962-70 (Chm., 1967-70). *Publication:* The Story of a Full Life (autobiog.), 1969. *Recreation:* golf. *Address:* Sunbury House, Dutton Terrace, Medindie, SA 5081, Australia. *Clubs:* Adelaide (Adelaide); Melbourne (Melbourne).   [*Died 24 June 1973.*

DUMAS, Sir Russell (John), KBE 1964; Kt 1959; CMG 1950; Director of a number of West Australian Companies; *b* 17 Jan. 1887; *s* of late C. M. R. and A. Dumas, Mount Barker, SA; *m* 1920, Muriel Elsie Rogers; one *s* one *d. Educ:* Prince Alfred

Coll., Adelaide, SA; Adelaide Univ., SA, ME (Adelaide), 1931. Carried out various engineering works in S and W Australia, including locks on River Murray, SA, irrigation works and dams in WA. Designed and supervised construction of Canning Dam (218 ft high) in WA and Stirling Dam, 150 ft high (highest earthen dam in Australia). Formerly Co-ordinator of Works and Industrial Development, State of Western Australia; Chm. State Electricity Commission of Western Australia, 1946-54, retired. MICE (London), 1925; MIEA, 1927. *Publications:* contributed papers to engineering journals. *Recreations:* golf and gardening. *Address:* Lawson Flats, 6 Esplanade, Perth, WA 6000, Australia.   [*Died 10 Aug. 1975.*

DUMINY, Jacobus Petrus; Principal and Vice-Chancellor, University of Cape Town, 1958-67; *b* 16 Dec. 1897; *s* of Johan Andreas Duminy and Maria Catherina Zeederberg; *m* 1930, Gwendoline Ellen Finnemore; two *s* one *d. Educ:* Cape Town Univ. (MA); Oxford Univ. (Rhodes Scholar) (MA, BSc); the Sorbonne. Lecturer in Mathematics and Astronomy, Transvaal Univ. Coll., 1923; Prof. in Mathematics, University of Pretoria, 1930. Principal, Pretoria Technical Coll., 1942. First Vice-Pres., Rotary International, 1969-70. Coronation Medal, 1953. Hon. LLD: Natal, 1962; Rhodes, 1967; Cape Town, 1973. *Publications:* Twilight over the Tygerberg, 1979; various papers on scientific and educational subjects. *Recreations:* tennis, reading, writing, music, drama. *Address:* 2 Winchcombe, The Cotswolds, Kenilworth, Cape, 7700, S Africa. *Clubs:* Vincent's (Oxford); City (Pretoria); Owl, WP Sports, WP Cricket (Cape Town).   [*Died 31 Jan. 1980.*

DUMMETT, Robert Bryan, CBE 1973; Chairman, London Board, Commercial Bank of Australia, since 1975 (Member, since 1972); Director, Midland and International Banks Ltd, since 1975; *b* 15 July 1912; 2nd *s* of G. H. Dummett; *m* 1936, Mary, *d* of R. A. Grieve; one *s* one *d. Educ:* Rugby Sch.; Göttingen Univ.; Trinity Coll., Cambridge. Joined Anglo-Iranian Oil Co., 1936. HM Legation, Berne, 1941-45. Managing Dir, BP Marketing Interests in Australia, 1953-57; a Man. Dir, BP Ltd, 1957-72; a Dep. Chm., BP Ltd, 1967-72. Grand Officer, Order of Merit (Italy), 1967, Cavaliere di Gran Croce, 1970. *Recreation:* gardening. *Address:* Gulson's, Boxted, Essex. *T:* Boxted 207; 4 Audley Square, W1. *T:* 01-499 2884. *Club:* Australian (Melbourne).   [*Died 14 Dec. 1977.*

DUNBABIN, Thomas, BA Oxon; MA (Tasmania); representative in Canada of Consolidated Press of Sydney, NSW, 1951-55; *b* Bream Creek, Tasmania, 6 July 1883; 4th *s* of late Thomas Dunbabin; *m* Beatrice Isabel Beedham, MA (Tasmania); one *d* (one *s* decd). *Educ:* University of Tasmania; Corpus Christi Coll., Oxford. Rhodes Scholar for Tasmania, 1906-9; scholar in geography, Oxford, 1908-9; on staff Mercury, Hobart, 1910-16; Argus, Melbourne, 1916-21; The Sun, Sydney, 1921; News Editor, The Sun, 1926-29; Editor and Manager, Australian Newspaper Cable Service, 1929-31; Editor of Daily Telegraph Sydney, 1931-34; Editor The Sun, 1934-36; Editor and Manager, Australian Newspaper Service, 1936-38; special writer, Daily Telegraph, Sydney, 1939-44; Commonwealth press attaché in Canada, 1944-45; Dir of Australian News Bureau, London, 1946-47; Dir of Australian News Bureau, New York, 1947-48; news editor of Commonwealth of Australia's short-wave world broadcasts, 1940; special correspondent for London Daily Chronicle on return of Amundsen from South Pole, 1912; Pres. Historical section, Australasian Association for Advancement of Science, Hobart meeting, 1928; mem. World's Geographical Conference, Amsterdam, 1938; representative of Australia and New Zealand Science Assoc. at British Assoc. Meeting, Cambridge 1938; Australian Press Attaché, Ottawa, Canada, 1948-50. *Publications:* The Making of Australasia, 1922; Sailing the World's Edge, 1931; Slavers of the South Seas, 1935; A Farm at the World's End, 1954. Tasmanian section of volume on Australasia in the Oxford Survey of the British Empire; contributions to Australian Encyclopædia, Encyclopædia Canadiana, Dictionary of Canadian Biography, and Oxford Junior Encyclopædia; historical and geographical essays and studies. *Address:* Medex Nursing Centre, 1865 Baseline Road, Ottawa, Ontario, Canada.   [*Died 2 Oct. 1973.*

DUNBAR of Mochrum, Sir Adrian Ivor, 12th Bt *cr* 1694; *b* 11 June 1893; *s* of Clement Adrian Dunbar (*d* 1940), and Emily Morgan; *S* kinsman, Sir Richard Sutherland Dunbar, 25 Jan. 1953; *m* 1st, 1917, Emma Marie, *d* of Jean Wittevrongel; one *s*; 2nd, 1930, Esther Naomi, *d* of William Henry Robinson; two *s*. Served European War 1914-19, in France, with Australian Imperial Force. Naturalized an American citizen, 1939. *Heir: s* Jean Ivor Dunbar, Younger of Mochrum [*b* 4 April 1918; *m* 1944, Rose Jeanne, *d* of Henry William Hertach; two *s* one *d*. Served as sergeant, Mountain Engineers, War of 1939-45]. *Address:* (seat) Mochrum Park, Kirkcowan, Wigtownshire.   [*Died 14 June 1977.*

DUNBAR, Alexander Robert, CBE 1964 (OBE 1956); FCIT; transport consultant; *b* 20 Oct. 1904; *s* of Robert MacKay Dunbar and Isabella Dunbar; *m* 1941, Margaret Wilby; one *s* one *d. Educ:* Whitehill Sch., Glasgow. Traffic Apprentice, LNER, 1924; various Rly Operating appts. Operating Supt (Eastern) BR, 1948; Asst Gen. Man., N Eastern Region, 1954; Manpower Adviser, British Transport Commission, 1958; Mem., British Railways Board, 1962. Chm., British Express Carriers Ltd, 1969-72. Chm., St Margaret's House Settlement; Member: Ind. Trng Service Bd; London University Appointments Board. Past Pres., Chartered Inst. of Transport; Past Pres. Rly Study Assoc.; Lieut-Col, Engineer and Rly Staff Corps, RE (TA). OStJ. *Publications:* various papers, Inst. of Transport. *Recreations:* walking and fishing. *Address:* 14 Hurley Court, Harmans Water, Bracknell, Berks RG12 3QH. *T:* Bracknell 56815. *[Died 3 Feb. 1980.*

DUNBAR, Maj.-Gen. Claude Ian Hurley, CB 1961; CBE 1950; DSO 1945; DL; late Foot Guards; *b* 1909; *s* of Col C. MacG. Dunbar, MC, of Pityoulish and Kincardine, Aviemore, NB; *m* 1940, Susan, *d* of Gerald Simonds, Farley Hill, near Reading; one *s* one *d. Educ:* RMC, Sandhurst, Commanded: 1st Bn Scots Guards, 1943; 3rd Armoured Bn Scots Guards, 1943-45; 1st Bn Scots Guards, 1945-47; AQMG, London District, 1948-49; Commanded: 2nd Guards Brigade, 1949-50; 4th Guards Brigade, 1950-52; Scots Guards Regt and Regimental District, 1952-54; Brig. A/Q, Eastern Command, 1954-57; Student, Imperial Defence Coll., 1958; Gen. Officer Commanding 42 (Lancs) Infantry Division TA, 1959-62, and North West District, 1960-62; GOC Berlin, British Sector, 1962; invalided, 1963. Croix de Guerre avec Palme (France), 1944; Silver Star (USA), 1947, DL Inverness-shire, 1965. *Recreations:* shooting and fishing. *Address:* Kincardine, Boat of Garten, Inverness-shire. *T:* Boat of Garten 216. *Club:* MCC. *[Died 18 May 1971.*

DUNBAR, Sir J(ohn) Greig, Kt 1962; DL; company director since 1931; *b* 19 Sept. 1906; *s* of John Gillison Dunbar and Anne Gardner Greig; *m* 1931, Elizabeth Hart Roy; two *s* one *d. Educ:* Royal High Sch., Edinburgh. Banking Apprenticeship, 1923-27; Company Sec., 1930; Bank Dir, 1963; Director: Royal Bank of Scotland, 1963-71; United Biscuits (Holdings) Ltd, 1965-71. Chm. Transport Users Consultative Cttee for Scotland, 1963-; Member: Council, Scottish Special Housing Assoc. Ltd, 1964-69; South of Scotland Electricity Bd, 1969-; Scottish Local Govt Staff Commn, 1973. Lord Provost, City of Edinburgh, 1960-63. DL, City of Edinburgh, 1963. Hon. LLD (Edinburgh), 1962. *Address:* 30 Midmar Gardens, Edinburgh EH10 6DZ. *Club:* New (Edinburgh). *[Died 4 Jan. 1978.*

DUNCAN, Alfred Charles; *b* 1886; *s* of Samuel Duncan and Mary (*née* McDowell); *m* 1st, 1913, Elizabeth Oakley; two *s*; 2nd 1930, Gwendoline Davies. *Educ:* Dublin and London Univs. Banking and business experience in Winnipeg, Canada, 1906-08; company and private secretarial experience in City of London, 1910-11; articled clerk to Messrs Franklin Wild & Co., Chartered Accountants, City of London, 1912-16. Served European War, 1914-18, with Artists Rifles, 1917-18. Qualified as Chartered Accountant, 1919. Odhams Press Ltd: Chief Accountant, 1920; Sec. and Chief Acct, 1921; Exec. Dir and Sec., 1942; Financial Dir, 1946; Financial and Joint Managing Dir, 1947; Chm., 1949-60. *Recreations:* golf, literature, preferably philosophical. *Address:* 7 Sherbrook Close, Budleigh Salterton, Devon. *T:* Budleigh Salterton 3416. *Club:* Golfers. *[Died 18 May 1979.*

DUNCAN, Colin; *see* Duncan, (P.) C.

DUNCAN, Surgeon Rear-Adm. David, CB 1957; OBE 1946; Retired as Medical Officer in Charge RN Hospital, Chatham and Staff Medical Officer to C-in-C, The Nore (1955-58), QHP 1955; *b* 21 Sept. 1900; *m* 1933, Vera McGeorge Payne (*d* 1973), Dumfries; one *s* one *d. Educ:* Aberdeen Univ. MB, ChB, 1924; joined RN, 1924; DPH 1929; MD 1934. Malariologist and hygienist, Singapore, 1930-38; Asst to Med. Dir Gen. of the Navy, 1939-46; staff of Flag Officer, Malaya, 1946-48; Asst to Med. Dir Gen., 1948-50; RN Hosp., Chatham; Senior Medical Officer in Charge of Medical and Hygiene Sections, and Naval MOH on staff of C-in-C, The Nore, 1950-53. Naval MOH to C-in-C, Portsmouth Command, 1953-55. OStJ 1947. *Publications:* various articles on the control of mosquitoes, and the prevention and treatment of malaria. *Recreations:* horticulture, golf. *Address:* Roundhill Farmhouse, Charlton Musgrove, Wincanton, Som. *[Died 5 Feb. 1974.*

DUNCAN, Sir James (Alexander Lawson), 1st Bt, *cr* 1957; *b* 1899; *m* Adrienne (*d* 1966), *d* of late William Brandon St Quintin; *m* 1966, Mrs B. M. M. Blair-Oliphant, *widow* of Major Philip Blair-Oliphant, Ardblair Castle. *Educ:* Marlborough.

Served European War, 1917-20, 2nd World War, 1940-45, Scots Guards. MP (U) North Kensington, 1931-45; (L-U) South Angus Div. of Angus and Kincardine, 1950-64. *Address:* Jordanstone, Alyth, Perthshire. *Clubs:* Carlton, Guards. *[Died 30 Sept. 1974 (ext).*

DUNCAN, Jane; Author since 1959; *b* 10 March 1910; *d* of Duncan Cameron and Janet Sandison. *Educ:* Lenzie Academy; Glasgow Univ. (MA). Various posts, mainly secretarial in nature, 1931-39. Served War of 1939-45, WAAF, mainly in Photographic Intelligence; demobilised with rank of Flight Officer. Commercial work, 1945-58. Spent years 1948-58 in Jamaica. *Publications:* My Friends the Miss Boyds, 1959; My Friend Muriel, 1959; My Friend Monica, 1960; My Friend Annie, 1961; My Friend Sandy, 1961; My Friend Martha's Aunt, 1962; My Friend Flora, 1963; My Friend Madame Zora, 1963; My Friend Rose, 1964; My Friend Cousin Emmie, 1964; My Friends the Mrs Millers, 1965; My Friends from Cairnton, 1966; My Friend My Father, 1966; My Friends the Macleans, 1967; My Friends the Hungry Generation, 1968; My Friend, the Swallow, 1970; My Friend Sashie, 1971; My Friends the Misses Kindness, 1974; as Janet Sandison: Jean in the Morning, 1969; Jean at Noon, 1970; Jean in the Twilight, 1972; Jean Towards Another Day, 1975; Letter from Reachfar, 1976; *for children:* Camerons on the Train, 1963; Camerons on the Hills, 1963; Camerons at the Castle, 1964; Camerons Calling, 1966; Camerons Ahoy!, 1968; Herself and Janet Reachfar, 1975. *Recreations:* reading, needlework, gardening. *Address:* The Old Store, Poyntzfield, By Conon Bridge, Ross IV7 8LU. *T:* Poyntzfield 249. *Club:* PEN International (Scottish Section). *[Died 20 Oct. 1976.*

DUNCAN, Sir John Norman Valette; *see* Duncan, Sir Val.

DUNCAN, (Peter) Colin, MC 1918; QC 1963; Barrister-at-Law; *b* 3 Oct. 1895; *s* of late Peter Thomas Duncan, MD and late Emma Gertrude, *er d* of late Rev. E. H. Genge. *Educ:* Rugby Sch.; Trinity Coll., Oxford. Barrister-at-Law, 1928; Master of the Bench, Inner Temple, 1960. Recorder of Bury St Edmunds, 1949-63; Recorder of Norwich 1963-68. Served European War, 1914-18, Queen's Royal Regiment, Capt. (despatches, MC), Gallipoli, Egypt, Palestine, France, Flanders; War of 1939-45, staff appointments, Lieut-Col. *Publications:* (with Anthony Hoolahan) Guide to Defamation Practice, 1953 (revised edn, 1958); (with B. T. Neill) Defamation, 1978. *Address:* 5 New Road, Ham Common, Richmond, Surrey. *T:* 01-940 5716; 1 Brick Court, Temple, EC4. *T:* 01-353 8845. *[Died 14 July 1979.*

DUNCAN, Sir Val, (John Norman Valette), Kt 1968; OBE 1944; Chairman and Chief Executive, The Rio Tinto-Zinc Corporation Ltd, since 1964; Chairman: Rio Algom Mines Ltd, Toronto; Director: Conzinc Riotinto of Australia Ltd; British Petroleum Co. Ltd, since 1974; a Director of the Bank of England, since 1969; *b* 18 July 1913; *s* of late Norman Duncan MC; *m* 1950, Lorna Frances (*d* 1963), *d* of late Robert Archer Houblon, Kelowna, BC, Canada. *Educ:* Harrow; Brasenose Coll., Oxford (MA, Law), Hon. Fellow, 1974. Called to English Bar, 1938. Served War of 1939-45: RE, mainly on staffs of Generals Montgomery, Eisenhower and Alexander; despatched (twice); Col. Asst Sec., Control Office for Germany and Austria 1946-47; Asst Dir Marketing, National Coal Board, 1947-48; joined The Rio Tinto Co. Ltd, 1948; Managing Dir, 1951 Chairman and Chief Executive, The Rio Tinto-Zinc Corp. Ltd 1964. Chm., Review Cttee on Overseas Representation, 1968-69 Chm., Council of Commonwealth Mining & Metallurgical Insts 1975-. Governor, Harrow Sch., 1971-. Awarded (twice) Legion of Merit (US); Comdr Order of Orange Nassau (Holland) *Address:* Edenbridge House, Edenbridge, Kent. *Clubs:* S James'; York (Toronto), Mount Royal (Montreal); Melbourn (Melbourne); Royal Yacht Squadron. *[Died 19 Dec. 1975.*

DUNCOMBE, Sir Everard (Philip Digby) Pauncefort-, 3rd Bt, *c* 1859; DSO 1918; DL, County of Bucks, 1934; JP, *b* 6 Dec. 1885; *s* of 2nd Bt and Flora, *d* of Sir Alexander Matheson, 1st Bt (sh *m* 2nd, Arthur Lucas); *S* father, 1895; *m* 1922, Evelyn Elvira, of Frederick Anthony Denny, Horwood House, Bucks; one one *d. Educ:* Eton; Trinity Coll., Cambridge (MA 1911). Hor Attaché at HM Embassy at Madrid, 1908-09; served Europea War, 1914-18 (DSO, Croix de Guerre). High Sheriff of Buckinghamshire, 1949-50. *Heir: s* Philip Digby Pauncefor Duncombe [*b* 18 May 1927; *m* 1951, Rachel Moyra, *yr d* Major H. G. Aylmer, 44 Eaton Place, SW1; one *s* two *d* *Address:* Lane End, Great Brickhill, Bletchley, Bucks. *[Died 8 Dec. 197*

DUNDAS, Sir Ambrose Dundas Flux, KCIE 1947 (CIE 1936 CSI 1946; ICS, retired; *b* 14 April 1899; *s* of late Rev. A. W. Flu

Dundas; *m* 1931, Mary Forrest, *d* of late Rev. Canon Bracewell; one *d. Educ:* Harrow; Royal Military Academy, Woolwich; Christ Church, Oxford. Indian Civil Service, 1922; Foreign and Political Dept, 1925; Political Agent, Tochi, 1928-31; Dep. Commissioner, Peshawar, 1934-36; Chief Sec. to Govt NWFP, 1937-41; Resident in Waziristan, 1941-43; Revenue Commr NW Frontier Province, 1943-45; Sec. Defence Dept, Govt of India, 1946-47; Agent to Governor-Gen., Baluchistan, 1947-48; Governor, North-West Frontier Province, 1948-49; retired, 1949. Lieut-Governor, Isle of Man, 1952-59. Chm. Bracknell Development Corporation, 1959-67 (Gen. Manager, 1950-52). KStJ 1953. *Address:* Southfield, Binfield, Berks. *Club:* Royal Automobile.   [Died 29 April 1973.

DUNLOP, Mrs Annie Isabella, OBE 1942; *b* 10 May 1897; er *d* of James Cameron and Mary Sinclair Cameron (née Cameron), Glasgow; *m* 1938, George Brown Dunlop (decd), publisher and newspaper proprietor. *Educ:* Glasgow High Sch. for Girls; Glasgow Univ.; Edinburgh Univ. MA Glasgow, 1919; PhD Edinburgh, 1922; Diplomée of the Vatican in Palaeography, 1930; DLitt St Andrews, 1934. Teaching of History, 1920-22; historical research and editing in Edinburgh, 1924-28; research at Vatican and other European Archives as Carnegie Fellow, 1928-31; Mem. staff of Scottish Record Office, 1934-38; part-time war teaching in History, Edinburgh Univ., 1942-48. Local Dir, Kilmarnock Standard and contributor to it. Mem. of Royal Commission on Ancient Monuments (Scotland); Mem., Advisory Council for Scottish Records. Hon. LLD St Andrews, 1950. *Publications:* King James's Secret (with R. S. Rait). 1927; Warrender Papers, 2 vols, 1931, 1932; Calendar of Scottish Supplications to Rome, 3 vols (first, with Rev. and Hon. E. R. Lindsay; third, with I. B. Cowan), 1934, 1956, 1970; The Apostolic Camera and Scottish Benefices, 1934; Life and Times of James Kennedy, Bishop of St Andrews, 1950; Acta Facultatis Artium Universitatis Sancti-andree (1413-1588), 1965. Contributions to Scottish Historical Review, miscellany vols of Scottish Hist. Soc. and other learned jls. *Address:* Torwood, London Road, Kilmarnock, Ayrshire. *T:* Kilmarnock 22239. *Clubs:* University Women's, Royal Over-Seas League; St Rule (St Andrews).   [Died 23 March 1973.

DUNLOP, Maj.-Gen. Dermott, CB 1949; CBE 1944; *b* 3 Nov. 1898; *s* of late Lieut-Col A. S. Dunlop, RA, Knowle, Lustleigh, S Devon; *m* 1935, Ethel Whitson Scott; two *s. Educ:* Sandroyd; Charterhouse; RMA, Woolwich. Commissioned RA 1916; served European War, 1916-19, France and Flanders, RHA (wounded); service at Home and Abroad in various Regtl Staff and Instructional appts, 1919-39; Bde Comdr UK, 1940-41; Middle East and 8th Army, 1942-45; UK, 1946-47; Comdr 2nd Army Group, RA, Tripolitania, 1947-48; GOC, Singapore District, 1948-51, and MEC, Colony of Singapore, 1948-51; Major, 1938; Temp. Lieut-Col 1939; Temp. Brig. 1941; Temp. Maj.-Gen., 1948; Maj.-Gen. 1949; retired, July 1951. Employed Colonial Office, 1951-66. *Address: c/o* Lloyds Bank Ltd, Cox's and King's Branch, 6 Pall Mall, SW1.   [Died 24 April 1980.

DUNLOP, Sir Derrick (Melville), Kt 1960; BA Oxon; MD; FRCP; Extra Physician to the Queen in Scotland since 1965 (Physician, 1961-65); Professor Emeritus of Therapeutics and Clinical Medicine, University of Edinburgh and Consulting Physician, Royal Infirmary, Edinburgh (Professor, 1936-62); *b* 1902; *s* of late George Harry Melville Dunlop, MD, FRCPE; *m* 1936, Marjorie, *d* of late H. E. Richardson, WS; one *s* one *d. Educ:* Oxford and Edinburgh Univs. Formerly: Chairman: Medicines Commn (1969-71); Ministry of Health's Cttee on Safety of Drugs (1964-69); British Pharmacopœia Commission; Vice-Chm. Regional Hosp. Board, SE of Scotland; Mem. Scottish Sec. of State's Adv. Cttee on Medical Research; Ministry of Health's Cttees on Drug Addiction and on Food Policy; Health Services Council's Cttee on Prescribing; Chm. Ministry of Agriculture's Cttee on Food Additives; Chm. Scottish Post-Graduate Medical Assoc. Non. Exec. Dir, Sterling-Wintle & Co. Sim's Commonwealth Travelling Prof.; Lumleian and Croonian Lectr, RCP; Gold Medal, RSoc Med., 1980. Ed. Quarterly Jl of Med. Hon. Fellow, Brasenose Coll., Oxford, 1968. Hon. FACP; Hon. FRCPE 1972. Hon. LLD Edinburgh, 1967; Hon. DSc Birmingham, 1967; Eire, 1968; Bradford, 1970. *Publications:* Clinical Chemistry in Practical Medicine; Textbook of Medical Treatment; numerous med. papers. *Recreation:* reading. *Address:* 28 Saxe-Coburg Place, Edinburgh EH3 5BP. *T:* 031-332 2170. [Died 19 June 1980.

DUNLOP, Sir John Kinninmont, KBE 1956 (CBE 1945; OBE 1937); CMG 1952; MC; TD; Military Historian; *b* 6 April 1892; *s* of late Andrew Dunlop, merchant; *m* 1922, Agnes Maitland Walker (*d* 1948); one *s. Educ:* Mill Hill Sch.; St John's Coll., Cambridge (History Scholar, MA, LLB); Queen Mary Coll., University of London (PhD). Served European War, 1914-18,

with 12th London Regt (Rangers) TF and Machine Gun Corps, France, Flanders and USA (wounded, despatches thrice, MC, Order of St Anne 4th class); rejoined Rangers after war and commanded the Battalion, 1935-37; explored and proved the Korba Coalfield, MP, India, 1924-27. From 1932 devoted energies to work on behalf of the Territorial Army, writing, lecturing, etc. In 1937 became AAG, TA at the War Office. Various A/Q appointments, 1939-43; joined Allied Commission Italy, 1943; Regional Commissioner (Brig.) Sardinia, 1943; Lazio and Umbria, 1944; Southern Italy, 1944; Venezia, 1945. Control Commission for Germany, 1946; Dep. Regional Commissioner, Hamburg, 1947; Land Niedersachsen, 1948; Land Commissioner, Hamburg, 1949; HM Consul-Gen., Hamburg, Sept. 1952-56; retired, 1957. Chm., Sevenoaks Urban District Council, 1964; Chm., Anglo-German Assoc., 1965-66; Pres. Kent Archæolog. Soc., 1967. Hon. Citizen of: Cagliari, Sardinia; Padua; Bolzano; Merano; Brezzanone; Brunico. *Publications:* several booklets on territorial matters, 1933-39; The Development of the British Army, 1899-1914, 1935; The Territorial Army of Today, 1939; Hamburg 800 AD-1945 AD, 1948: A Short History of Germany, 1957 (revised edn 1964); The Pleasant Town of Sevenoaks: A History, 1964. *Recreations:* opera, travel, local history. *Address:* Garden House, Solefields Road, Sevenoaks, Kent. *T:* Sevenoaks 52437. *Club:* Athenæum.
[Died 26 April 1974.

DUNLOP, Ronald Offory, RA 1950 (ARA 1939); RBA; London Group; artist; *b* Dublin 1894; *s* of D. N. Dunlop, Kilmarnock, and E. Fitzpatrick, Dublin. *Educ:* Friends' Sch., Saffron Walden. Studied at Manchester and Wimbledon Schs of Art; one of founders of the Emotionist Group of Painters and Writers; held first one-man-show at Redfern Galleries, 1928; held 1939 exhibition Reid and Lefèvre Galleries; exhibition, Upper Grosvenor Galleries, 1969; pictures purchased by the Chantrey Bequest for Tate Gallery, also purchased by Walker Art Gallery, Liverpool, Contemporary Art Soc., Leeds, Bradford, Hull, New South Wales, Australia, Preston, Southport, Glasgow, Aberdeen, Newcastle, Greenock, Bristol, Cheltenham and Rochdale Art Galleries for permanent collections. *Publications:* Modern Still Life Painting in Oils, 1947; Understanding Pictures, 1948; Painting for Pleasure, 1953; Sketching for Pleasure, 1960; Ancient Arundel; Landscape Painting; Struggling with Paint. *Address:* Old Mill Cottage, Barnham, Sussex. *T:* Eastergate 2084.   [Died 18 May 1973.

DUNMORE, 9th Earl of, *cr* 1686; **John Alexander Murray;** Viscount Fincastle, Lord Murray, 1686; Baron Dunmore (UK), 1831; Public Relations consultant; Director, Charles Barker Scotland Ltd; *b* 3 April 1939; *g s* of 8th Earl of Dunmore, VC, DSO, MVO; *o s* of Viscount Fincastle (killed in action, 1940) and Hon. Pamela Kate Hermon-Hodge (who *m* 2nd, 1944, Capt. Follett Watson Bell, RA, and *d* 1979), *e d* of 2nd Baron Wyfold, DSO, MVO; *S* grandfather, 1962; *m* 1967, Anne Augusta, *e d* of T. C. Wallace, Dounby, Orkney; two *d. Educ:* Eton. National Service, 1957-59, TA Service, 1959-65, The Queen's Own Cameron Highldrs. PRO, Schweppes (USA) Ltd, New York, 1964-67. Mem. Council, Nat. Trust for Scotland, 1974-79. MIPR 1968. *Recreation:* hill walking. *Heir: kinsman* Reginald Arthur Murray [*b* 17 July 1911; *m* 1948, Patricia Mary, *d* of Frank Coles; two *d*]. *Address:* 14 Regent Terrace, Edinburgh EH7 5BN. *Club:* Caledonian.   [Died 12 Aug. 1980.

DUNN, Sir John Henry, 2nd Bt, *cr* 1917; *b* 12 Dec. 1890; *s* of 1st Bt and Ellen, *d* of John Pawle; *S* father, 1926; *m* Mabel, *d* of Alfred Cook, Canterbury (formerly Mrs Harold Letton, Chicago). *Educ:* Downside. Was in South African Police; served European War, 1914-18 (wounded). *Heir: none.*
[[Died 3 Oct. 1971 (*ext*).

DUNN, Sir Philip (Gordon), 2nd Bt, *cr* 1921; *b* 26 Oct. 1905; *s* of Sir James Dunn, 1st Bt and Gertrude Patterson (*d* 1957), *d* of Herbert Molesworth Price, Montmorency, Quebec; *S* father 1956; *m* 1933, Lady Mary St Clair-Erskine (marr. diss., 1944; re-married, 1969), *d* of 5th Earl of Rosslyn; two *d. Educ:* Eton; Trinity Coll., Cambridge. Served War of 1939-45. *Heir: none. Address:* Stowell, Marlborough, Wilts. *T:* Pewsey 3439. *Club:* White's.   [Died 20 June 1976 (ext.).

DUNNING, John Ray, PhD, ScD; LLD; Lindsley Professor of Applied Science, Columbia University, New York; Dean Emeritus of the Faculty of Engineering and Applied Science, Columbia University, Scientific Director and Professor of Physics since 1946; *b* Shelby, Nebraska, USA, 24 Sept. 1907; *s* of Albert Chester Dunning and Josephine Thelen; *m* 1930, Esther Laura Blevins; one *s* one *d. Educ:* Nebraska Wesleyan Univ. (AB 1929, highest hons); Columbia Univ. (PhD 1934). Began as Physicist-radio engineer, 1927; with Columbia Univ. since 1929, as Asst in Physics, 1929-32; Univ. Fellow, 1932-33; Instructor in

Physics, 1933-35; Cutting Travelling Fellow, 1936; Asst Prof. of Physics, 1935-38; Associate Prof. of Physics, 1938; Official Investigator, Office of Scientific Research and Development, 1941-46; Dir of Research, Division 1, Research Laboratories, Columbia Univ., 1942-45; Dir, Division of War Research, Columbia Univ., 1945-46; Special Rep. Manhattan District, Operation "Cross-roads", Bikini, July 1946; Medal for Merit, 1946. Chairman: Mayor's Cttee on Atomic Energy, New York Golden Jubilee Anniversary, 1948; ASME National Research Council Cttee on Nuclear Energy Glossary, 1948; Basic Science Foundn; Nuclear Energy Policy Board; National Lecturer, Sigma Xi, 1948; Engineers Jt Council Cttee on Nuclear Engineering and Science; Vice-Pres., New York Academy of Sciences, 1951-; Trustee, Horace Mann Sch. for Boys, 1951-59; Bd of Visitors, US Military Academy, West Point, 1953- (Chm., 1954); Amer. Soc. for Engineering Educ. (Vice-Chm., Physics Div.), 1953-; Chm. NY Adv. Cttee on Scientific Manpower, 1956-; Mem. Scientific Adv. Panel, War Dept, 1956-. Fellow: Amer. Physical Soc.; NY Academy of Science; AAAS; Amer. Nuclear Soc.; Mem., Inst. of Radio Engineers, Optical Soc., Amer. Assoc. of Physics Teachers; Bd of Directors: The Oak Ridge Inst. of Nuclear Studies, 1950-; Fund for Peaceful Atomic Development, 1954-; Congressional Panel on Impact of Peaceful Uses of Atomic Energy, 1955-. Trustee Member: Engineering Index Inc., 1956-; Armstrong Memorial Research Foundn, 1957-; Science Service, 1958-; Mem. Adv. Committee: Nat. Urban League, Tech. Adv. Cttee, 1958-; Thomas A. Edison Foundn; Nat. Rivers and Harbors Congress, 1959-; Mem. Scientific Adv. Cttee, Dept of Defense, 1954-; Adv. Council for the Advancement of Industrial Research and Development in NY State, 1959-; Council for the Advancement of Science Writing, 1959-; NY State Science Advisory Council to the Legislature, 1963- (Chm.); Member: Nat. Acad. of Sciences, 1948; Amer. Inst. of Mining and Metallurgical Engineers; Amer. Soc. of Mechanical Engineers; Newcomen Soc. in N Amer., 1960-; Soc. for Hist. of Technology, 1962-; Nat. Sci. Foundn, Divisional Cttee for Mathematical, Physical and Engineering Sciences, 1958-; Empire State Atomic Development Associates. Chm., President's Cttee on Super Sonic Transport-Sonic Boom, Nat. Acad. of Sciences, 1964-; President: Hall of Science, City of NY, 1965; Inst. for Applied Science, 1969-; Chm., NYC Adv. Coun. on Science and Technology, 1965-. Phi Kappa Tau; Sigma Xi, Phi Kappa Phi; Sigma Pi Sigma; Tau Beta Pi; Theta Tau. Director City Investing Co. 1957; Oak Ridge Associated Univs, 1965-; Science Service, 1958. Stevens Award, 1958; Pupin Medal, 1959; Pegram Medal, 1964; Graduate Faculties Alumni Award, Columbia, 1967. Hon. ScD, Nebraska Wesleyan, 1945; Temple Univ., 1955; Whitman Coll., 1958; Trinity Coll., 1958; Hon. LLD: Adelphi, 1951; Phila Coll. of Osteopathy, 1961; Hon. DScEd, Coll. of Puget Sound, 1957; Hon. ScD: University of Jacksonville, 1965; Marquette Univ., 1967. *Publications:* Matter, Energy and Radiation (with H. C. Paxton), 1940; contrib. to Physics Review, Review of Scientific Instruments, American Journal of Physics, National Academy of Science; many monographs and papers on atoms, atomic transmutations, neutrons and nuclear physics and nuclear energy processes. *Recreations:* general interests: development of scientific teaching, researches in Atomic Transmutations, Nuclear Physics, Nuclear Energy, Atomic Power Systems. *Address:* Columbia University, School of Engineering, New York, NY 10027, USA. *T:* 280-2868; Spring Lake Road, Sherman, Connecticut. *Clubs:* Ambassador's, University, Columbia University, Engineers', Men's Faculty (New York); Cosmos (Washington). [*Died 25 Aug. 1975.*

DUNNING, Rev. Thomas George, MA, PhD; retired; General Secretary, Temperance Council of the Christian Churches, 1952-59; President, Baptist Union of Great Britain and Ireland, 1958-59; *b* 25 Dec. 1885; *s* of John Dunning; *m* 1923, Mary Bell Anderson (decd); *m* 1955, Doris Mabel Rose (*d* 1972), MBE; one *s* (of a former marriage). *Educ:* Glasgow Univ.; Scottish Baptist Theological Coll. Asst Minister, John Knox Street Baptist Church, Glasgow, 1915-17, Minister, 1917-23; Minister, Park Street Baptist Church, Luton, Beds, 1923-28; Dir of Education, Temperance and Social Service for Baptist Union of Great Britain and Ireland, 1928-52. Chairman: Bd of Governors of Stonar Sch., Wilts, 1948-58; British Lessons Council, 1947-59. *Publications:* author of various books on religion, citizenship, etc, 1926-. *Recreations:* golfing and gardening. *Address:* 4 Chichester Court, Pevensey Garden, Worthing, Sussex. *T:* Worthing 48475. [*Died 4 April 1975.*

DUNNINGTON-JEFFERSON, Lt-Col Sir John Alexander, 1st Bt, *cr* 1958; Kt 1944; DSO 1917; LLD (hon.) Leeds; DUniv. York; DL; JP; *b* 10 April 1884; *s* of late Capt. Mervyn Dunnington-Jefferson of Thicket Priory, York; *m* 1938, Isobel, *d* of Col H. A. Cape, DSO; one *s* one *d*. *Educ:* Eton; RMC, Sandhurst. Entered Army (Royal Fusiliers), 1904; retired 1919

with rank of Lieut-Col; served European War, 1914-18 (despatches six times, Bt Major, DSO); St Maurice and St Lazarus (Italy); Couronne and Croix de Guerre (Belgium); Legion of Honour (France). E Riding Yorks CC, 1922-74 (Chm., 1936-68). JP 1921, DL 1936, E Riding Yorks (later N Yorks). *Heir:* s Mervyn Stewart Dunnington-Jefferson [*b* 5 Aug. 1943; *m* 1971, Caroline Anna, *o d* of J. M. Bayley; two *d*]. *Address:* Deighton House, Escrick, York. *Clubs:* Travellers'; Yorkshire (York). [*Died 12 April 1979.*

DUNOYER DE SEGONZAC, André; artiste, peintre et graveur; *b* 6 Juillet 1884; *s* of Louis Dunoyer de Segonzac, officier de la Marine de Guerre; *m* 1964, Thérèse Longo Dorni. *Educ:* Lycée Henri IV, Paris. Servit Guerre Européenne, 1914-18 (Chevalier de la Légion d'Honneur, Croix de Guerre, 4 citations). First exhibition, Salon d'automne, 1908, since when has exhibited works in Europe and USA; Prix Carnegie, Pittsburgh, 1933; Prix de la Biennale de Venise, Médaille d'Or, 1934; Grande Médaille de la Ville de Paris, 1964. Membre de l'Académie Royale de Florence; Sociétaire du Salon d'Automne et des Peintres Graveurs Français. Hon. Member: Acad. Roy. de Belgique, 1948; Nat. Inst. of Arts and Letters of New York, 1955. Hon. RA, 1947. *Publications: illustrations:* Croix de Bois, de R. Dorgelès, Treille Muscate, de Colette, Georgiques, de Virgile, Le Lierre de P. Brisson, Sonnets de Ronsard, Sport de J. Giraudoux, etc. *Address:* 13 rue Bonaparte, Paris 6E, France. [*Died 17 Sept. 1974.*

DUNSHEATH, Percy, CBE 1946; MA Cantab, DSc (Eng) London; Hon. DEng Sheffield; Hon. LLD London; Member of Senate, University of London, 1946-67; *b* 16 Aug. 1886; *s* of late Hugh and Anna Dunsheath, Sheffield; *m* 1st, 1910, Elizabeth Alice, *d* of W. D. F. Vincent, Acton; one *d* decd and one *s* killed on active service; 2nd, 1938, Cissie Providence (*d* 1976), *d* of C. Houchen, Hempnall, Norwich. *Educ:* Sheffield Grammar Sch.; Universities of Sheffield, London and Cambridge (Mech. Sci. Tripos). GPO Engineer in Chief's office, 1908-19. Served European War, 1914-18; commissioned; France (despatches twice, OBE). Research Dir, W. T. Henley's, 1919; subs. Chief Engineer; retd, 1946. President, Instn of Electrical Engineers, 1945-46, Hon. mem., 1964-; Chm. of Convocation, University of London, 1949-61. Mem. Heyworth Cttee on Univ. appointments Boards, 1964. Pres. Internat. Electrotechnical Commn (1955-58); Pres. British Electrical Development Association (1952-53); Past Chm. Govs Woolwich Polytechnic; Pres. ASLIB (Assoc. Special Libraries Information Bureau), 1949, 1950; Chairman: London Reg. Academic Board Technical Educ., 1947-53; FBI Educ. Cttee, 1951-55; Cttee on Shortage of Science Teachers, 1954. Chm., Cambridge Instrument Co., 1956-63 (Dir 1950-64). Faraday lecturer, 1947; Royal Institution Christmas Lectures, 1949. Hon. Fellow, University Coll., London, 1967. *Publications:* The Graduate in Industry, 1947; (ed) A century of Technology, 1951; The Electric Current, 1951; Industrial Research, 1956; Convocation in the University of London, 1958; Electricity: How it works, 1960; A History of Electrical Engineering, 1961; Giants of Electricity, 1967; Dordogne Days, 1972; Nearly Ninety, 1975; many papers and articles on scientific, technical and educational subjects. *Recreation:* water colour painting. *Address:* c/o 130 Hookstone Drive, Harrogate, N Yorks HG2 8PF. [*Died 4 Oct. 1979.*

DUPREE, Sir Vernon, 3rd Bt, *cr* 1921; *b* 23 Dec. 1884; *s* of Sir William Thomas Dupree, 1st Bt, VD, TD, and 1st wife, Mary (*d* 1907), *d* of George Groves, Selsey, Sussex; *S* brother 1953; *m* 1st, 1912, Amy Marcella (*d* 1953), *d* of late John Price, Askeaton, Co. Limerick; one *d* (and one *s* killed in action, 1942); 2nd, 1955, Louise Jennie Hillyard. Formerly Capt. (Hon. Major) 7th Royal Fusiliers: served European War, 1914-18 (wounded). *Heir:* b Victor Dupree [*b* 19 Dec. 1887; *m* 1910, Gladys (*d* 1922), *d* of Charles Henry Lawson; 2nd, 1922, Margaret Cross; one *s*. Formerly Lieut 3rd Dragoon Guards and Royal Tank Corps (Capt. Reserve of Officers); served European War, 1914-18 (wounded, prisoner)]. *Address:* Downings, Prinsted, near Emsworth, Hampshire. [*Died 4 Sept. 1971.*

DUPREE, Sir Victor, 4th Bt *cr* 1921; *b* 19 Dec. 1887; *s* of Sir William Thomas Dupree, 1st Bt, VD, TD, and Mary (*d* 1907), *d* of George Groves, Selsey, Sussex; *S* brother, 1971; *m* 1st, 1910, Gladys (*d* 1922), *d* of Charles Henry Lawson; 2nd, 1922, Margaret Cross; one *s* one *d*. Formerly Lieutenant, 3rd Dragoon Guards and Royal Tank Corps (Captain, Reserve of Officers); served European War, 1914-18 (wounded, prisoner). *Heir: s* Peter Dupree [*b* 10 Feb. 1924; *m* 1947, Joan, *d* of late Captain James Desborough Hunt]. *Address:* 16A Montpelier Crescent, Brighton, East Sussex. [*Died 11 Aug. 1976.*

DURAND, Brigadier Sir Alan (Algernon Marion), 3rd Bt, *cr* 1892; MC 1919; Colonel (retired) and Hon. Brigadier RA; *b* 14

Oct. 1893; *s* of Lt-Col Sir Edward Law Durand, 1st Bt, CB, and Maude Ellen, 4th *d* of Algernon Charles Heber-Percy; *S* brother 1955; *m* 1st, 1924, Vivien Enid (from whom he obtained a divorce, 1936), *d* of late Herbert Chamberlain; one *d*; 2nd, 1944, Evelyn Sherbrooke, *d* of late C. Arnold Crane, Cheltenham, and *widow* of Sir Stanley Tubbs, 1st and last Bt. *Educ:* Cheltenham; RMA. 2nd Lieut RA 1913; served European War, 1914-18 (wounded twice, despatches twice): Captain 1917; served War, 1939-46; Belgium and France, 1939-40 (despatches); Egypt, 1944-46; Col 1942; retd 1946. DL Glos, 1950; High Sheriff, 1953; Vice-Lieutenant Glos, 1957-69. CC (Glos). *Heir: nephew* Rev. Henry Mortimer Dickon Marion Durand, *b* 19 June 1934. *Address:* Ellerncroft, Wotton-under-Edge, Glos. *Club:* Army and Navy. *[Died 16 Feb. 1971.*

DURWARD, James, CMG 1953; retired; *b* 3 Dec. 1892; *m* 1918; two *s*. *Educ:* Aberdeen Univ. Served European War, 1914-18, Captain, Royal Engineers. First Class Hons in Mathematics and Natural Philosophy, Aberdeen, 1918. Joined Meteorological Office, 1919; served at Sch. of Artillery, Larkhill, 1920-22; Asst-Supt and transf. to Calshot Flying Boat Base, 1922; Supt and transf. to RAF Middle East HQ, 1927; Dir of Iraqi Meteorological Service, 1937; Principal Technical Officer in home establishment, 1940; Asst Dir, 1946; Dep. Dir (Services), 1948. Order of Rafidain, Iraq, 1940. *Publications:* author of numerous Professional Notes in Meteorological Office series. *Recreations:* gardening, golfing and motoring. *Address:* 40 King's Road, Richmond, Surrey. *T:* 01-940 5201. *[Died 2 Dec. 1971.*

DUTHIE, Sir William (Smith), Kt 1959; OBE 1943; *b* 22 May 1892; *s* of Lewis Duthie, Portessie, Banffshire; *m* 1921, Elizabeth Tyson (*d* 1977); one *s* one *d*. *Educ:* Rathven and Buckie Schs. Bank of Scotland, 1908-11; Canadian Bank of Commerce, 1911-20; Canadian Army, 1915-16, Gordon Highlanders, 1916-18 (severely wounded); business in London, 1921 onwards; advised Food Defence Plans Dept Board of Trade on Bread Supplies from Oct. 1938; Chm. London Bread Supplies Cttee, 1939; Area Bread Officer London and SE England, 1940; Dir of Emergency Bread Supplies, Ministry of Food, 1941; Dep. Chief UNRRA Balkans Mission, Jan. 1945. MP (U) Banffshire, 1945-64. Resigned Party Whip, Oct. 1962-May 1964. Chairman: House of Commons Cons. and Unionist Mems. Fisheries Sub-Cttee, 1951-62; House of Commons Scottish Unionist Mems Cttee, 1958; Royal National Mission to Deep Sea Fishermen, 1954-71. FSAScot 1976. Freeman, Burgh of Buckie, Banffshire, 1960. *Publication:* ed with C. L. Foster: Letters from the Front, 1914-18, for Canadian Bank of Commerce, 1919. *Recreations:* golf, sailing, archæology. *Address:* Todearth Croft, Holmsburn Leslie, Insch, Aberdeenshire. *T:* Insch 436. *Club:* Caledonian. *[Died 17 Dec. 1980.*

du TOIT, Very Rev. Lionel Meiring Spafford, MA; Dean of Carlisle, 1960-73, Dean Emeritus, 1973; *b* 1903; 3rd *s* of late Justice A. P. N. du Toit, S Africa; *m* 1933, Gladys Evelyn (*d* 1978), 2nd *d* of late J. D. Hatt, Elsfield, Oxford; one *s* (decd). *Educ:* Manchester Grammar Sch.; Merton Coll., Oxford. Deacon 1928, Priest 1929; Asst Curate: Rochdale Parish Church, 1928-31; Swinton Parish Church, 1931-35; Rector, Christ Church, Moss Side, Manchester, 1935-43; Chaplain, Manchester Royal Infirmary, 1935-43; Lecturer, Egerton Hall Theological Coll., 1932-38; Vicar, St Mary's, Windermere, 1943-60. Proctor in Convocation, 1950-70; Dep. Prolocutor, York Convocation, 1967-70. *Recreation:* gardening. *Address:* The White House, Hospital Road, Bury St Edmunds, Suffolk. *T:* Bury St Edmunds 4125. *[Died 23 Jan. 1979.*

DUTT, (Rajani) Palme, BA Oxon; Editor of Labour Monthly since 1921; *b* Cambridge, 1896; *m* 1922, Salme (*d* 1964), *d* of Ernst Murrik, Walk, Estonia. *Educ:* Perse Sch., Cambridge; Balliol Coll., Oxford (First Classical scholar, first class hons). Imprisoned 1916, 1925; expelled from Oxford for propaganda of Marxism, 1917. Sec., International Section, Labour Research Dept, 1919-22; Chm., Communist Party Reorganisation Commission, 1922; Ed., Workers' Weekly, 1922-24; Ed., Daily Worker, 1936-38; Executive Cttee Mem. of the Communist Party, 1922-65. Contested (Communist) Sparkbrook Div. of Birmingham, 1945, Woolwich East, 1950. Hon. Dr of History, Moscow Univ., 1962. Lenin Centenary Medal, 1970. *Publications:* The Two Internationals, 1920; (ed) The Labour International Handbook, 1921; articles on Communism and The International in the Encyclopædia Britannica (12th edn); Modern India, 1926; Socialism and the Living Wage, 1927; Lenin, 1933; Fascism and Social Revolution, 1934; World Politics, 1918-36; (new edn with supplement, 1936-60, 1961). The Political and Social Doctrine of Communism, 1938; India To-day, 1940; Britain in The World Front, 1942; Road to Labour Unity, 1943; Britain's Crisis of Empire, 1949; India

Today and Tomorrow, 1956; Crisis of Britain and the British Empire, 1957; Problems of Contemporary History, 1963; Rise and Fall of the Daily Herald, 1964; The Internationale, 1964; Whither China?, 1967. *Address:* 8 Highfield Court, NW11. *[Died 20 Dec. 1974.*

DUTTON, Alan Hart, CMG 1958; MVO 1954; British Petroleum Co. Ltd; *b* 13 March 1913; *s* of late Thomas Dutton. Bolton Lancs; *m* 1940, Mollie Gledden, *d* of late Thomas Perry, Streetly End, Cambs; one *s* two *d*. *Educ:* Sedbergh Sch.; Brasenose Coll., Oxford. Colonial Service: Administrative Officer, Nigeria, 1936. RAF, 1940-45. Colonial Office, 1945-47; Senior Asst Sec. and Commissioner, Cyprus, 1947-52; Asst Chief Sec., Aden, 1952-56; Financial Sec., Aden, 1956-59. USA Silver Star, 1945. *Address:* Stubble Hill, Guildown Avenue, Guildford, Surrey. *T:* Guildford 67749. *Club:* East India, Sports and Public Schools. *[Died 24 Feb. 1974.*

DUTTON, Eric Aldhelm Torlogh, CMG 1946; CBE 1938 (OBE 1930); MA Oxon; Comdr Crown of Belgium; Order of Brilliant Star of Zanzibar; *b* 24 May 1895; 5th *s* of late Rev. Charles and Helen Dutton; *m* 1936, Myrtle Eleonore, *e d* of late Gen. Sir Hubert de la Poer Gough, GCB, GCMG, KCVO; two *s* one *d*. *Educ:* Hurstpierpoint; Keble Coll., Oxford. Joined West Yorks Regt Aug. 1914; Major, 1915; served in Gallipoli (wounded, despatches); passed ICS examination, 1920; Private Sec. to Sir Robert Coryndon, Governor of Uganda and subsequently of Kenya, 1920-25; Private Sec., to Lieut-Col Sir Edward Grigg, Governor of Kenya, 1925-30; Principal Asst Chief Sec., Northern Rhodesia, 1930; Chm. Northern Rhodesian Finance Commission, 1932; Chm., Town Planning Board, 1935; Administrative Sec., Northern Rhodesia, 1938; Colonial Sec., Bermuda, 1938-42; Chief Sec., Zanzibar, 1942-52; Chm., Town Planning Board, Zanzibar, 1943-52, and of Central Development Authority, 1946-52; Delegate to First African Conf., London, 1948; administered Govt in Bermuda and Zanzibar for various periods. *Publications:* The Basuto of Basutoland, 1923; Kenya Mountain, 1929; The Planting of Trees and Shrubs, 1937; Lillibullero, or The Golden Road, 1944. *Recreation:* architecture. *Address:* Villa Luiza, Rua do Pinheiro, Monte Estoril, Portugal. *[Died 27 Nov. 1973.*

DUVEEN, Claude Henry, MBE 1946; QC 1953; JP 1955; His Honour Judge Duveen; a Circuit Judge (formerly Judge of County Courts), since 1958; *b* 6 April 1903; *s* of Louis Duveen and Beatrice Salamon; *m* 1930, Eileen Schomberg; one *d*. *Educ:* Eton; New Coll., Oxford. Admitted Middle Temple, 1925; called to Bar, 1927; practised in London and on Midland Circuit, 1927-40, 1945-59. Served RAFVR, 1940-45. Dep. Chm., 1958-66, Chm., 1966-71, Berkshire QS. *Recreation:* roses. *Address:* Foxleigh Grange, Holyport, Berks. *T:* Maidenhead 27968. *Clubs:* United Oxford & Cambridge University, MCC. *[Died 6 Sept. 1976.*

DUVEEN, Sir Geoffrey, Kt 1948; VRD; *b* London, 4 July 1883; *s* of Henry J. and Dora Duveen; *m* 1907; one *s*; *m* 1942, Elise Adolph. *Educ:* Bath Coll.; Merton Coll., Oxford. Served European War, 1914-18, and War of 1939-45, in RNVR (retired as Comdr, RNVR). Barrister-at-Law (Inner Temple); MA (Oxon). Late Chm. of Royal Ear Hospital (moved Hosp. from Dean Street, Soho, to site adjacent to University Coll. Hosp., 1924); ex-mem. most Cttees of UCH and visitor for King Edward VII Hosp. Fund. Founded a post-grad. travelling lectureship in otology at University of London. Past Master, Worshipful Company of Plumbers. *Publications:* Postage Stamps of Gibraltar, 1932; The History of the Gold Sovereign, 1961 (with H. J. Stride). *Recreations:* salmon fishing, motoring, numismatics. *Address:* Flat 31, Grosvenor House, W1. *Club:* Royal Thames Yacht. *[Died 15 Nov. 1975.*

du VIGNEAUD, Prof. Vincent; Professor of Chemistry, Department of Chemistry, Cornell University, New York, 1967-75; Emeritus Professor of Biochemistry, Cornell University Medical College, New York, NY; *b* 18 May 1901; *s* of Alfred Joseph and Mary du Vigneaud; *m* 1924, Zella Zon Ford; one *s* one *d*. *Educ:* University of Illinois (BS 1923, MS 1924); University of Rochester, NY, USA (PhD 1927). Asst Biochemist, Philadelphia Gen. Hosp. and Graduate School of Medicine, University of Pa, 1924-25; Asst Biochemist, Graduate School of Medicine, University of Rochester, NY, USA, 1925-27; Nat. Research Council Fellow, Johns Hopkins Univ. Medical Sch., 1927-28; Kaiser Wilhelm Inst, Dresden, Germany; University of Edinburgh Medical Sch.; UCH Medical Sch., London, 1928-29; Assoc. Dept of Chemistry, Univ. of Illinois, 1929-30; Asst Prof., 1930-32; Prof. and Head of Dept of Biochemistry, George Washington Univ. Sch. of Medicine, 1932-38. Mem., Bd of Trustees, Rockefeller Univ. Numerous scientific awards, 1936-. Mem. Royal Society of Sciences of

Upsala (Sweden), 1950; Chandler Medal, Columbia Univ., 1955; Nobel Laureate in Chemistry, 1955; Willard Gibbs Medal, 1956. Hon. FRSE 1951; Hon. Fellow Chemical Soc. (London), 1955; Hon. FRIC 1959. Hon. ScD: New York Univ., 1955; Yale, 1955; Univ. of Illinois, 1960; Univ. of Rochester, 1965; St Louis Univ., 1965; George Washington Univ., 1968. *Publications:* A Trail of Research in Sulfur Chemistry and Metabolism and Related Fields, 1952; articles in: Jl of Biological Chemistry; Jl of Amer. Chemical Soc.; Jl of Medicinal Chemistry; Biochemistry. *Address:* 200 White Park Road, Ithaca, New York 14850, USA.
[Died 11 Dec. 1978.

DYER, Maj.-Gen. Godfrey Maxwell, CBE 1970 (OBE 1941); DSO 1945; psc, psa; Vice-President, "Not Forgotten Association", 1979; Managing Director, Old Palace Wine Co. Ltd, since 1962; *b* 10 Dec. 1898; *s* of A. R. Dyer, Winchester; *m* 1927, Evelyn Mary, *d* of George List, London and S Africa; two *s* (and one *s* decd). *Educ:* Bishops Stortford Coll.; Royal Military Coll., Sandhurst. 2nd Lt, IA, 1917. Served European War, 1914-19 (India and Middle East); War of 1939-45 (India, Middle East and Burma); GSO2, Air HQ India, 1940; GSO1, GHQ India, 1941 (OBE); Lt-Col and Comdt, 13th DCO Lancers, 1941; Iraq, Persia, N Africa; Brig. 1942; Bde Comdr, 1942-45; Burma (despatches twice, DSO); Dep. QMG, GHQ India, 1945; Maj.-Gen., 1945; retd, 1947. Pres., Indian Cavalry Officers' Assoc., 1978; Chm., British Assoc. for Cemeteries in S Asia, 1976. *Address:* 28 Bushwood Road, Kew, Richmond, Surrey. *T:* 01-948 2976. *Club:* Cavalry and Guards.   *[Died 1 Nov. 1979.*

DYER, Sir Leonard Schroeder Swinnerton, 15th Bt, *cr* 1678; Engineer; Chairman: Dyer Securities Ltd; Linford Estates Ltd; Milestone & Staniforth Ltd; Equipment Credit Ltd; Oxford & Cowley Ironworks Ltd; Estates & General Investments Ltd; *b* 30 March 1898; *s* of Sir Leonard Whitworth Swinnerton Dyer, 14th Bt, and Lucy (*d* 1948), *d* of late Hon. Francis Schroeder, New York; *S* father 1947; *m* 1925, Barbara, *d* of Hereward Brackenbury, CBE; one *s* one *d. Educ:* Repton. Served European War, 1914-18. RFA 1916-19. Pres. British Chess Federation, 1956-59 (Chm., 1951-56); Chm., Shropshire CC, 1969-72. *Recreation:* living peacefully. *Heir: s* Prof. Henry Peter Francis Swinnerton Dyer, FRS. *Address:* Westhope Cottage, Craven Arms, Salop. *T:* Seifton 219. *Club:* Bath. *[Died 10 June 1975.*

DYKE, Sidney Campbell, DM, FRCP, FRCPath; Hon. Senior Research Fellow, formerly Curator, Regional Histological Collection, University of Birmingham; Hon. Consultant Pathologist, The Royal Hospital, Wolverhampton and General Hospital, Walsall, Staffs; *b* 1886; *s* of John and Martha Dyke; *m* 1918, Janet Mary, *d* of W. D. Smith, Llanelly; one *s* one *d. Educ:* University of Toronto and Oxford (Coll. Exon). Journalism, Canada to 1910; Rhodes Scholar, British Columbia, 1910, 1st Class Natural Science, 1913; served European War, 1914-18, with King Edward's Horse and RAMC; Asst Bacteriologist Sch. of Medicine, University of Durham; Pathologist to Clinical Units, St Thomas' Hosp., London; Radcliffe Prize for Advancement of Medicine, 1929; late Chm. of Council, late Pres., late Hon. Sec. Assoc. of Clinical Pathologists; Hon. Member: American Soc. of Clinical Pathologists; Associacion Española de Biopatologica Clinica; Société Française de Biologie Médicale. Fellow, BMA. *Publications:* (ed) Recent Advances in Clinical Pathology, 1946, 1952, 1960, 1964, 1968, 1973; contribs to various med. jls. *Recreations:* fishing, walking. *Address:* Upper Green, Tettenhall, Wolverhampton. *T:* Wolverhampton 51394.   *[Died 3 March 1975.*

DYKSTRA, John; retired; Former Director of Ford Motor Company; Director of other Ford companies; Director, Tecumseh Products; Director and Consultant, Sheller-Globe Inc., Toledo, Ohio; *b* Netherlands, 16 April 1898; *s* of Theodore Dykstra and Nellie (*née* De Vries); came to America 1902; became American Citizen, 1919; *m* 1918, Marion S. Hyde; one *s* one *d. Educ:* Cass Technical High Sch., Detroit; (courses) La Salle Extension Univ. Started as apprentice die maker, 1914, while taking mechanical engineering courses. Served in Army, European War of 1914-18; returned to Detroit, 1919; associated with Oldsmobile Div. of Gen. Motors Corp. from 1934 (Manuf. Man., 1941-47); joined Ford Motor Company, 1947, as gen. production Asst to Vice-Pres. (manufacturing); Gen. Man. of former gen. manuf. div., 1948; a Ford Vice-Pres., 1950; Manufacturing Group Vice-Pres., 1957; Dir, 1958; Pres., 1961-63. Responsible for company's aircraft Engine Div., Oct. 1950-Sept. 1958; engaged in intensified quality control program for Ford products, as Vice-Pres. Manuf., 1958-61. Mem., Soc. of Automotive Engineers. *Recreations:* golf, fishing. *Address:* 1147 Glengarry Road, Birmingham, Michigan 48010, USA. *T:* Midwest 6-2111. *Clubs:* Athletic, Golf, Recess (all of Detroit).
[Died 2 March 1972.

DYMENT, Clifford Henry, FRSL 1951; author; *b* Alfreton, Derbyshire, 20 Jan. 1914; *e c* of late William Clifford Dyment and Elizabeth Riding, Caerleon, Mon; *m* 1947, Marcella (*d* 1968), *y d* of late Marcell and late Gisella Salzer, Vienna; no *c. Educ:* Grammar Sch., Loughborough. Freelance literary journalist and critic, 1934-40; writer of film commentaries and dir of documentary films for Min. of Information, British Council, War Office and other official bodies, 1942-48. Atlantic Award in Literature, 1950. Commentaries, BBC television series, The Face of Britain, 1951; Granada television series, Another World, 1964-65; Commentaries, BBC TV, 1968-70. *Publications:* First Day, 1935; Straight or Curly?, 1937; Selected Poems, 1943; The Axe in the Wood, 1944; Matthew Arnold: an introduction and a selection, 1948; Thomas Hood: a selection of his serious poems with an introduction, 1949; Poems 1935-48, 1949; Experiences and Places, 1955; C. Day Lewis (Writers and their Work), 1955; The Railway Game: an early autobiography, 1962; Fur, Feather and Fin (with Marcella Dyment, co-author, and Hafis Bertschinger, artist), 1968; Collected Poems, 1970. *Recreations:* sampling inexpensive wines, listening to 78 rpm gramophone records, collecting cigarette cards, playing the mouth organ. *Address:* c/o J. M. Dent & Sons Ltd, Aldine House, 10-13 Bedford Street, WC2.   *[Died 5 June 1971.*

DYSART, Countess of, *cr* 1643, 10th in line; **Wenefryde Agatha Greaves;** Baroness Huntingtower, 1643; *b* 13 Nov. 1889; *d* of Charles Norman Lindsay Scott and Lady Agnes Mary Tollemache, *d* of late Lord Huntingtower; *S* uncle 1935; *m* 1913, Major Owain Greaves, late Royal Horse Guards (served RHG, European War of 1914-18) (*d* 1941), two *d* (and one *d* decd). *Heir: d* Lady Rosamund Agnes Greaves, *b* 15 Feb. 1914. *Address:* 22 Marlborough Place, St Johns Wood, NW8.
[Died 2 June 1975.

DYSON, Sir Cyril (Douglas), Kt 1953; Managing Director of Dyson and Sons Ltd, 1948-72, retired; *b* 6 Dec. 1895; *s* of late Albert Harry Dyson and late Frances Emma Dyson (*née* White); *m* 1923, Sylvia Rix (*née* Lingwood); one *s* one *d. Educ:* Cliftonville Coll., Margate; Northampton Polytechnical Coll. (student of horology and of optics). Service in Berks Yeomanry and in the Tenth Hussars, 1914-19. Mem. of family business of jewellers, watchmakers and opticians since 1919. Mayor of the Royal Borough of New Windsor, 1952, 1953 (Councillor, 1943, Alderman, 1951). FSMC, FBHI. Pres., Nat. Assoc. of Goldsmiths of GB and Ireland, 1957-70. 1914 Star; Victory, Civil Defence, Gen. Service and Police medals; Coronation Medal, 1953. *Address:* 11 York Road, Windsor, Berks. *T:* 65572. *Clubs:* Rotary, and many local athletic.
[Died 28 June 1976.

E

EADES, Sir Thomas Arthur, Kt 1945; Hon. President, formerly Chairman, Automatic Telephone & Electric Co. Ltd, Liverpool; *b* 1888; *s* of William Joseph and Sarah Ellen Eades, Worcs; *m* 1914, Eleanor Rachel Jesper; one *s* one *d. Educ:* Wolverley; private. Chm. of Telephone Development Association, 1938, 1939, 1944, 1945, also Chm. of Telecommunication Engineering and Manufacturing Assoc., 1945, 1957. FCIS, FRSA, FBIM. *Publications:* articles to Technical Press. *Address:* Knightons, Keston, Kent.   *[Died 17 June 1971.*

EADIE, William Ewing; Director: The Burmah Oil Company Limited, 1950-67 (Chairman, 1957-64); Chartered Bank, 1957-72; Bank of Scotland (London), 1961-72; *b* 18 Oct. 1896; *s* of late John Ewing Eadie, *m* 1936, Dorothy Owen Jones. *Educ:* Harris Academy, Dundee. Served European War, 1914-19 (despatches 1918). Qualified Chartered Accountant, 1921; joined The Burmah Oil Co Ltd, Rangoon, 1921; seconded to Burmah-Shell, 1928-41; returned to The Burmah Oil Co. Ltd, London, 1941; Chief Accountant, 1948-50; appointed to Board of Directors, 1950; Asst Managing Dir, 1951; Managing Dir, 1955-61. *Recreations:* golf and motoring. *Address:* Duncrievie, Nairn. *T:* Nairn 52797. *Clubs:* Royal Commonwealth Society; Royal and Ancient Golf (St Andrews); Oriental, Bengal (Calcutta).
[Died 23 June 1976.

EARLE, Sir Hardman Alexander Mort, 5th Bt, *cr* 1869; TD; *b* 19 Aug. 1902; *s* of Lieut-Col Sir Algernon Earle, 4th Bt, and Edith, *d* of General Disney Leith, CB, of Glenkindie, Aberdeenshire, and *sister* of 7th Lord Burgh; *S* father, 1945; *m* 1931, Maie, *d* of John Drage, The Red House, Chapel Brampton; one *s* one *d.*

Educ: Eton. *Heir: s* Hardman George Algernon Earle [*b* 4 Feb. 1932; *m* 1967, Diana Gillian Bligh, *y d* of late Col F. F. B. St George, CVO; one *s* one *d*]. *Address:* 14 Kensington Gate, W8. *Club:* Cavalry and Guards.   [*Died* 17 Sept. 1979.

EASSIE, Maj.-Gen. William James Fitzpatrick, CB 1953; CBE 1943 (OBE 1941); DSO 1943; retired; *b* 28 Sept. 1899; *s* of late Brig.-Gen. F. Eassie, CB, CMG, DSO; *m* 1930, Margaret Joan, *d* of L. G. P. Thring, Cambridge; two *s* one *d. Educ:* St Columba's College, Dublin; RMC Sandhurst. 2nd Lieut Royal Dublin Fusiliers, 1919; transferred to RASC, 1923; Iraq (medal), 1930-31; Col, 1942; Brigadier, 1944; Maj.-Gen., 1952; served War of 1939-45: Middle East, Sicily, NW Europe (despatches four times, OBE, CBE, DSO); Dir of Supplies and Transport Far East Land Forces, 1949-51; Inspector RASC (Maj.-Gen.) 1951-54; ADC to King George VI, 1951; retired 1954. Commander Legion of Merit (US). *Address:* Orchard End, Wargrave, Berks. *T:* 2341. *Club:* Army and Navy.
[*Died* 13 *May* 1974.

EASTHAM, Leonard Ernest Sydney, MA Cantab, MSc Leeds; Emeritus Professor of Zoology, University of Sheffield (Professor, 1932-58); *b* 8 Feb. 1893; *s* of William Eastham, Penwortham, Preston; *m* K. M. Jackson, Bingley, Yorks; one *s* two *d. Educ:* Hutton Grammar Sch., Lancs; Harris Institute, Preston; Leeds Univ. War service Royal Engineers Special Brigade; National Diploma in Agriculture, 1914; graduated in Hons Zoology and in Agriculture, 1921; Lecturer in Zoology in the University of Birmingham, 1921-27; Lecturer in Advanced and Economic Entomology in the University of Cambridge, 1927-31. Pro-Vice-Chancellor, University of Sheffield, 1946-50. *Publications:* Scientific papers on Entomology. *Recreations:* gardening, music. *Address:* 12 New Road, Portesham, near Weymouth, Dorset.   [*Died* 19 *July* 1977.

EASTON, John Murray, FRIBA; Partner in Firm of Easton and Robertson Cusdin Preston and Smith, Architects (retired, 1963); *b* 30 Jan. 1889; *y s* of David Easton, Aberdeen; *m* 1927, Ruth Meryon, *d* of H. A. Tinker, Westover, Croyde, North Devon; two *s. Educ:* Aberdeen Grammar Sch. Architectural education Scotland and London; served with London Scottish, France and Belgium, 1914; Godwin Bursar, 1927; Pres. of Architectural Assoc., 1939-40; Vice-Pres. RIBA, 1945-47; RIBA Medals for best building of years 1928 and 1937 in London and 1938 in Cambridge; Royal Gold Medal for Architecture, 1955; Associé de l'Académie Royale de Belgique, 1958. Principal works: in London: Royal Horticultural Society's New Hall; Royal Bank of Canada; Metropolitan Water Board's Laboratories; No. 2-12 Gresham Street; Friend's & Century Insurance Co. (Dorking); in New York: British Pavilion, World's Fair, 1939; in Cambridge: reconstruction of Old Library, Pitt Press, Caius Coll. new buildings, and following Laboratories: Zoological, Anatomy, Engineering, Chemistry, Veterinary Anatomy and Chemical Engineering. Science and other buildings for Universities of London, Durham, Queen's Belfast, Reading and Malaya. Hospitals, including: Children's, Great Ormond Street; Queen Charlotte's Maternity; Children's, Dublin; Regional, Limerick; Royal Victoria, Belfast, Harlow; Hong Kong; Addenbrookes, Cambridge. *Address:* 7 St Hilda's Close, Christchurch Avenue, NW6. *Club:* Arts. [*Died* 19 *Aug.* 1975.

EASTWOOD, Frank Sandford, CBE 1951; FCIT; Major, late The 22nd (Cheshire) Regiment; Chairman of Traffic Commissioners and Licensing Authority, Yorkshire Traffic Area, 1939-65 (Ministry of Transport Appointment); Regional Transport Commissioner, 1939-65; *b* Broughton, Lancs, 1 Dec. 1895; *o s* of S. C. Eastwood, Broughton; *m* 1920, Constance, *o d* of A. Webb, Wrexham; one *s* one *d. Educ:* Manchester and Oxford. Served European War, 1915-18; Regimental and Staff Service, to Lieut-Col (wounded); The 22nd (Cheshire) Regt, 1919-21; seconded Criminal Investigation Dept, Royal Ulster Constabulary, 1922-23; Staff Capt., 49th (WR) Div. 1924-25; Staff Capt., 7th Inf. Bde, 1926; Staff Capt. Experimental Mechanised Force and Experimental Armoured Force, 1927-29; retired, 1930; Transport Adviser to large commercial companies, 1931-38; 1939-45 War appointment, Regional Transport Commissioner, North Eastern Region. *Recreations:* riding, tennis, and badminton. *Address:* Flat 1, 9 North Park Road, Roundhay, Leeds. *T:* Leeds 665649. *Club:* Constitutional.
[*Died* 18 *June* 1971.

EATON, Cyrus Stephen; industrialist and banker; Partner, Otis & Co., bankers; Organizer Republic Steel Corp. and United Light & Power Co.; Chairman Board of Directors: Chesapeake & Ohio Railway; Detroit Steel Corporation; Steep Rock Iron Mines Ltd; Director: Cleveland-Cliffs Iron Co.; Cleveland Electric Illuminating Co.; Kansas City Power & Light Co.; Sherwin-Williams Co.; Baltimore & Ohio Railroad Co.; *b* Nova Scotia, 27 Dec. 1883; *s* of Joseph Howe Eaton and Mary Adelle McPherson; *m* 1st, 1907, Margaret House; two *s* five *d*; 2nd, 1957, Anne Kinder Jones, *d* of Judge Walter Tupper Kinder; one step-*d. Educ:* McMaster Univ., Toronto (BA); Acadia Univ. (DCL). Trustee: University of Chicago, Denison Univ., Case Institute of Technology, Harry S. Truman Library, Metropolitan Park Board, Cleveland Museum of Natural History; Mem. of Coll. of Electors, Hall of Fame, Royal Norwegian Academy of Sciences, American Council of Learned Societies; American Historical Assoc., Amer. Philosophical Assoc. FAAS. Initiator Pugwash Intellectual Life Confs (Assoc. of Amer. Colls), 1956; Pugwash Internat. Confs of Nuclear Scientists, 1957; Member: Amer. Shorthorn Breeders' Assoc.; Amer. Acad. of Political and Social Science. Holds several hon. doctorates in Law from American, Canadian and European universities. Received Lenin Peace Prize, 1960. *Publications:* The Third Term "Tradition," 1940; Financial Democracy, 1941; The Professor Talks to Himself, 1942; Investment Banking-Competition or Decadence, 1944; A New Plan to re-open the US Capital Market, 1945; A Capitalist Looks At Labor, 1947; Is the Globe Big Enough for Capitalism and Communism?, 1958; Canada's Choice, 1959; The Engineer as Philosopher, 1961; and numerous articles and speeches on economics, politics and international affairs. *Recreations:* MFH Summit Hunt, tennis, yachting, ski-ing and skating. *Address:* Acadia Farms, Northfield, Ohio 44067, USA; Terminal Tower, Cleveland, Ohio 44101; Deep Cove Farms, Chester, Nova Scotia, Canada. *Clubs:* Union, Mayfield, Chagrin Valley Hunt, Summit Hunt (Cleveland); Metropolitan (New York); Glenelg Fishing; Royal Nova Scotia Yacht Squadron (NS).
[*Died* 9 *May* 1979.

EBBELS, Brig. Wilfred Austin, CBE 1943; late RA; *b* 1 April 1898; *s* of late W. P. Ebbels, Mauritius; *m* 1924, Phyllis (*née* Greenwood-Teale) (*d* 1973), *widow* of Capt. Arthur Toller, Welch Regt; two *d. Educ:* Yardley Court (Tonbridge); Marlborough Coll.; RMA, Woolwich. Commissioned, 1915; France and Flanders, 1916-18; Army of Occupation (Rhine), Jan.-June 1919; Acting Capt. Feb. 1918, Acting Major, Aug. 1918 (wounded, despatches, MC); appointed RHA July 1919; Capt., 1927; seconded Egyptian Army, 1928-34; Major, 1936; Instructor of Gunnery, 1937-40; Acting Lieut-Col Comd 11 (HAC) Regt RHA 1940; Western Desert MEF 1941-44; Brig. (CRA 10 Armoured Div.) 1942; retired pay, 1946. *Recreations:* shooting, fishing. *Address:* Walkern Hall, near Stevenage, Herts SG2 7JA.   [*Died* 12 *Oct.* 1976.

EBERT, Prof. Carl (Anton Charles), CBE 1960; Opera Director; naturalized American citizen; *b* Berlin, 20 Feb. 1887; *s* of Maria and Wilhelm Ebert; *m* 1st, 1912, Lucie Splisgarth (marr. diss., 1923); one *s* (and one *d* decd); 2nd, 1924, Gertrude Eck (*d* 1979); one *s* two *d. Educ:* Berlin, Friedrich Werder'sche Oberrealschule; Max Reinhardt's Sch. of Dramatic Art. Actor; Max Reinhardt's Deutsches Theater, Berlin, 1909-14; Schauspielhaus, Frankfurt, 1915-22; Staatstheater, Berlin, 1922-27; Founder and Dir of Schools of Dramatic Art: Frankfurt 1919, Berlin, Hochschule für Musik (Prof.), 1925; Gen.-Intendant (and Producer), Landestheater, Darmstadt, 1927-31; Intendant, Staedtische Oper, Berlin, 1931-33; A Director: Actors' Union, 1919-27; Deutscher Bühnenverein, 1927-33. Guest Producer since 1933 at Zürich, Basel, Maggio Musicale Florence, Verona, Salzburg Festival, Colon, Buenos Aires, Burgtheater and State Opera, Vienna, Cambridge Theatre, London (New London Opera Company), Scala, Milan, Royal Opera, Copenhagen, Metropolitan, New York; Artistic Dir and Producer, Glyndebourne Festival Opera, 1934-59; Producer Edinburgh Festival, 1947-55. Adviser on Theatrical Affairs to Turkish Min. of Educn, Ankara, 1936-47; Founder of Turkish State Sch. for Opera and Drama and of Turkish National Theatre. Prof. and Head of Opera Dept, University of S Calif, Los Angeles, 1948-54; Gen. Dir Guild Opera Co., Los Angeles, 1950-54, Artistic Dir since 1954; Intendant, Staedtische Oper, Berlin, 1954-61; Pres. German Section of International Theatre Institute, 1956-61. Guest Producer: Glyndebourne, 1962, 1963; Opera House, Zürich, 1963, 1965; Wexford Festival, 1965; Deutsche Oper, Berlin, 1967. Master Classes, BBC TV, 1965, 1967. Awarded Ernst Reuter Plakette, City of Berlin, 1957. Hon. MusDoc, Edinburgh, 1954, Hon Doc. of Fine Arts, University of S California, Los Angeles, 1955. Knight, Dannebrog Order, Denmark; Das Grosse Verdienstkreuz mit Stern, Germany; Das Grosse Ehrenzeichen for services to Mozart, Austria, 1959; Hon. Comdr of the Order of the British Empire, 1960; La Grande Médaille d'Argent de la Ville de Paris, 1961; Commendatore, Order of Merit (Italy), 1966; Hon. Member: Deutsche Oper, Berlin, 1961; Landestheater, Darmstadt, 1963; Hon. Life Mem., Bd of Dirs, Opera Guild of S Calif, LA, 1965. *Address:* 809 Enchanted Way, Pacific Palisades, Calif 90272, USA. *T:* 454-6705. *Club:* PEN (Internat.).   [*Died* 14 *May* 1980.

EBSWORTH, Brig. Wilfrid Algernon, CB 1950; CBE 1943; *b* 1 Feb. 1897; *s* of Rev. Algernon Frederic Ebsworth and Mary Frances Harcourt-Vernon; *m* 1st, 1925, Cynthia (*d* 1975), *d* of Edward Charles Bleck, CMG; one *s* one *d*; 2nd, 1976, Mrs Ethel Ridyard Dodd. *Educ:* Tonbridge Sch.; RMC Sandhurst. Served European War, 1914-18, 2nd Lieut The Sherwood Foresters (twice wounded). Regimental and Staff Service, Egypt, Turkey, and India, 1919-27; Staff Coll., 1928-29; Regimental and Staff Service in England, 1930-38; Instructor, Staff Coll., 1938-39; War of 1939-45, commanded 1st Bn The Sherwood Foresters, Palestine, 1939-40; GSO 1, Middle East, 1940-41 (despatches); Comd 22nd and 30th East African Brigades, Brig. Gen. Staff, East African Command and 15 Indian Corps, Burma, 1942-45; Comdr, British Army Staff, France, 1946-47; Dep. Fortress Comdr, Gibraltar, 1947-50; retd pay, 1950. Légion d'Honneur (Officier), Croix de Guerre avec palme, 1947 (France). *Address:* 32 Gretton Court, Girton, Cambridge. *[Died 10 Feb. 1978.*

ECCLES, Maj.-Gen. Ronald Whalley, CBE 1968; formed Dunwoody and Eccles, 1970; Associate T. Dunwoody and Partners, since 1970; *b* 25 Sept. 1912; *s* of W. J. Eccles, Wolverhampton; *m* 1938, Sadie Rodrigues; one *d*. *Educ:* Wolverhampton Sch. Alfred Herbert Ltd, 1931-36; Rolls Royce Ltd, 1936-39; RAOC, 1939-42; REME, 1942; Asst Dir of Inspection, IFVME, 1958-63, Dir, 1963-67; Asst Master Gen. of the Ordnance (Quality Assurance, formerly Inspection), MoD (Army), 1967-70. Col, 1960; Brig., 1964; Maj.-Gen., 1968; retired 1970. WhSch, CEng, FIMechE. *Recreations:* golf, bridge. *Address:* 9 The Spinney, Stanmore, Mddx. *T:* 01-958 7156. *[Died 2 Nov. 1975.*

ECKMAN, Samuel Jr, Hon. CBE 1947; Member, Advisory Committee of Royal Naval Film Corporation; *b* New York City; *m* 1919, Rae Harris. *Educ:* New York Public Schools; College of the City of New York. Entered Motion Picture industry in New York as exhibitor with his father; later elected Vice-Pres. of Goldwyn Distributing Corp.; subsequently on amalgamation with Metro, and formation of Metro-Goldwyn-Mayer, assumed charge of New England, New York, and New Jersey Districts; appointed Man. Dir of Metro-Goldwyn-Mayer Pictures Ltd, London, 1927, and continued as Chairman and Managing Director until 1954, Chm. until 1957. Former Capt. US Army Mil. Intelligence; during War of 1939-45 was Hon. Chm. USO, European Theatre of Operations. Member: the Pilgrims; Motion Picture Pioneers, New York; American Legion Post No. 1; Cinema Veterans, London (ex-Pres.); American Soc. in London (ex-Chm.); Cinematograph Films Council, 1941-44 and 1951-57; Pres., Kinematograph Renters Soc. (London), 1931-34. Mem. various Masonic bodies. *Address:* 945 Fifth Avenue, New York, NY 10021, USA. *Clubs:* American; Variety Clubs of Great Britain, New York and Israel; Army Athletic Association (US). *[Died 25 March 1976.*

EDDIS, Sir Basil Eden Garth, Kt 1929; *s* of late W. K. Eddis and Mrs Eddis, Penketh, Harrow; *m* 1930, Yolande, MBE 1944, JP (*d* 1965), *er d* of Michael Faraday, Aldeburgh, Suffolk. *Educ:* Charterhouse; University Coll., Oxford. Formerly partner in firm of Gillanders, Arbuthnot & Co., Calcutta. JP Suffolk, 1937. *Address:* Longcroft, Aldeburgh, Suffolk. *[Died 5 Nov. 1971.*

EDDY, John Percy, QC 1936; *b* Kidderminster, 19 May 1881; *yr s* of late Edward Eddy; *m* 1st, 1905, Alice Marion Evans (*d* 1968), *d* of late John Brymer; one *s* one *d*; 2nd, 1969, Charlotte Halford Armitstead, *widow* of Leslie Armitstead. Educ: King Charles I Sch., Kidderminster, and privately. Engaged for some years in journalism; was present at the Siege of Sidney Street, Jan. 3, 1911; called to the Bar, Middle Temple, 1911; joined the South Eastern Circuit; Judge, High Court of Judicature, Madras, 1929-30; Recorder of West Ham, 1936-49; Stipendiary Magistrate for East and West Ham, 1949-54. Served as Army Officer and with Min. of Nat. Service, 1917-18, and with Claims Commn, 1941-43; Mem. Gen. Council of the Bar, 1946-48; Divorce Comr, 1947; lectured at Yale, Duke, Northwestern (Chicago) and other American Univs, 1952; at McGill Univ., Montreal, and Univ. of Toronto, 1953; at Delhi, Madras and Bombay, 1963; at Karachi, Lahore, Delhi, Calcutta, Madras and Bombay, 1964; at Delhi, Madras, Bombay and Karachi, 1965. Pres., West Ham Hostel for Youths (an approved probation hostel), 1953-56; Chm., The Worcs Assoc., 1953-55. Round-the-World voyage with his wife, Charlotte, 1973. *Publications:* Guide to National Insurance, 1911; The Law of Distress for Rent, Rates and Tithe Rent-charge; (with F. H. Lawton) India's New Constitution, 1935; The Justices' Handbook, 1st edn 1947, 2nd edn 1951, 3rd edn 1953; Professional Negligence (five lectures), 1955; The Law of Copyright, 1957; Scarlet and Ermine: Famous trials as I saw them, 1960; (with L. L. Loewe) The New Law of Betting and Gaming, 1961, 2nd edn 1964; Justice of the Peace, 1963; I Know My Rights: The Citizen's Charter, 1967; (with L. L. Loewe) The New Gaming Act, 1968; India and the Privy Council: The Last Appeal, 1950; and other papers. *Address:* Francis Taylor Building, Temple, EC4. *T:* 01-353 2182; 7 Linkside Court, Richard Road, Blundellsands, Lancs L23 8TF. *T:* 051-924 5232. *Clubs:* MCC; Athenæum (Liverpool). *[Died 10 July 1975.*

EDELMAN, Maurice; MP (Lab) Coventry North West, since 1974 (Coventry West, 1945-50, Coventry North, 1950-74); author and journalist; *b* 2 March 1911; *s* of S. Edelman, Cardiff; *m* 1933; two *d*. *Educ:* Cardiff High Sch.; Trinity Coll., Cambridge. Exhibitioner in Mod. Langs, Trinity Coll., Cambridge, 1929; BA Cantab 1932; MA Cantab 1941. Engaged in industry and research in application of plastic materials to aircraft construction, 1932-41. Journalist and War Corresp. in N Africa and France. Vice-Pres., Anglo-French Parly Relations Cttee; Delegate to Consultative Assembly of Council of Europe, 1949-51, 1965-70, and Chm., Socialist Gp of WEU, 1968-70; Leader of Parly Delegn to Hungary, 1965; Special Rep. of Colonial Sec., to Cayman Islands and Turks and Caicos Islands, 1965. Vice-Chm., British Council, 1951-67; Mem., Adv. Council on Public Records, 1974-. Pres., Alliance Française (UK); Dir-Gen., Franco-British Council, 1974-. Chevalier de la Légion d'Honneur, 1954; Officier, 1960; Médaille de Paris, 1972. *Publications:* France: The Birth of the Fourth Republic (Penguin), 1945; David Ben-Gurion, 1964; The Mirror: A Political History, 1966; *novels:* A Trial of Love, 1951; Who Goes Home, 1953; A Dream of Treason, 1953; The Happy Ones, 1957; A Call on Kuprin, 1959; The Minister, 1961; The Fratricides, 1963; The Prime Minister's Daughter, 1964; Shark Island, 1967; All on a Summer's Night, 1969; Disraeli in Love, 1972; Disraeli Rising, 1975. TV plays include, The Trial of Admiral Byng (BBC 1958), and adaptations of novels. *Recreations:* tennis and painting. *Address:* House of Commons, SW1. *Clubs:* Garrick, Queen's, Hurlingham.
[Died 14 Dec. 1975.

EDGAR, Frederick Percy, OBE; late Midland Regional Controller, BBC; retired, 1948; *b* 3 March 1884; *s* of Edward and Sarah Lane Edgar; *m* 1914, Elsie Ann, *o d* of Edward and Jane Wright, Wolverhampton; one *s*. *Educ:* Stafford. Concert Platform, 1907-14; organising Camp and Military Hosp. Concerts, 1914-18; Concert Direction, 1919-21; Music Hall and Theatrical Stage, 1921-22; Broadcasting, 1922. *Recreations:* motor boating and sailing. *Address:* Bryony House, Bryony Road, Selly Oak, Birmingham 29. *[Died 21 April 1972.*

EDGAR, Gilbert Harold Samuel, CBE 1960; Chairman: H. Samuel Group of Companies, since 1935; Priory Gate Estates Ltd, since 1946; Underwriting Member of Lloyd's; *b* 1 Jan. 1898; *er s* of Edgar Samuel Edgar, Liverpool; *m* 1st, 1923, Eileen Victoria (*d* 1970), *yr d* of Sir Stuart Samuel, 1st Bt, MP for Tower Hamlets Div., 1900-18; one *d* (and one *d* decd); 2nd, 1971, Jessica Estelle Moritz. *Educ:* Charterhouse. Served European War, 1916, Lieut RHA (wounded); War of 1939-45, Sqdn Ldr, RAAF (Actg Wing Comdr). Mem. Coun., Royal Eye Hosp., 1934-60; assisted in foundn of Chair of Ophthalmology, RCS and Royal Eye Hosp., 1943; Governor, King's Coll. Hosp. Gp, 1951-61; on Bldg Cttee, RCOG, 1959-62; Founder, Edgar-Gentilli Memorial Schol. and Prize connected with Cancer Research. Contested (C) Smethwick, Gen. Elec. and By Elec., 1945; Chm. Wycombe Div. Conservative Assoc., 1955-60. CC, 1952-74, CA, 1964, Bucks. Lay Sheriff of City of London, 1963-64. Thames Conservancy, 1965-74. Trustee, Charterhouse Tercentenary Fund, 1948-63; Governor, Thomas Sutton's Hosp. in Charterhouse; Master, Worshipful Co. of Clockmakers, 1967-68. Hon. Fellow, RCOG, 1964. *Recreations:* farming, golf, shooting, fishing. *Address:* E 5, Albany, W1. *T:* 01-734 7836; Burrow Farm, Hambleden, Henley-on-Thames, Oxon RG9 6LT. *T:* Hambleden (Bucks) 256. *Clubs:* Bath, United and Cecil, City Livery; Huntercombe Golf (Oxon). *[Died 23 March 1978.*

EDGAR, Lieut-Gen. Hector Geoffrey, CB 1960; CBE 1955; General Officer Commanding Eastern Command, Australian Military Forces, 1960-63; *b* 31 Oct. 1903; *s* of Thomas George Edgar, Wedderburn, Vic., Australia; *m* 1929, Margaret A. (*d* 1972), *d* of Charles Cooper; two *s* one *d*. *Educ:* Albert Park Grammar Sch.; RMC Duntroon, Canberra; idc; psc; pac. Training in India, 1925-26; Military Coll. of Science, Woolwich, 1933-36. Served with Third Australian Div., New Guinea and Bougainville; Chief Instructor, Senior Wing, Australian Staff Coll., 1945; Inspector-Gen., Munitions, 1946-47; Dep. Dir, Staff Duties, Army HQ, 1948-49; IDC, 1950; Comdt, Australian Staff Coll., 1951-53; Dir of Staff Duties, 1954; Dep. Chief of Gen. Staff, and Mem., Military Board, Army Headquarters, 1954-58; GOC Southern Command, 1958-60. First Superintendent, Rocket Range, Woomera, South Australia, 1949. *Address:* Aitkenside, Cochranes Road, Ceres, Victoria 3221, Australia. *[Died 16 Dec. 1978.*

EDGCUMBE, (John) Aubrey Pearce, CMG 1929; CBE 1920; Deputy Comptroller General, Department of Overseas Trade, 1939-46, when he retired; *b* 21 Sept. 1886; 2nd *s* of late Sir Robert Edgcumbe; *m* 1932, Madeleine, *d* of Thomas Jones, Y Gaer, Brecon. *Educ:* Winchester Coll. (Senior Commoner); Magdalene Coll., Cambridge (Scholar); Classical Tripos, Class 1. Entered Board of Trade (Class 1 competitive examination), 1910; National Health Insurance Commission, 1912; War Trade Statistical Dept, 1916; Dir, 1918; attended Peace Conference, Paris, 1919; Dept of Overseas Trade, 1919; accompanied Special Service Sqdn during Empire Cruise, 1923-24, as Economic Adviser on Staff of Admiral in Command; Colonial Office, 1924; Private Sec. to Rt Hon. L. S. Amery, MP, 1924-29, and subs. to Lord Passfield, Sec. of State for Dominion Affairs and for Colonies. *Address:* Hunsett Mill, Stalham, Norfolk NOR 34Z. *T:* Stalham 449.   *[Died 26 Oct. 1974.*

EDGEWORTH, Lt-Col Kenneth Essex, DSO 1917; MC; FRAS; MIEE; Royal Corps of Signals (retired); *b* 26 Feb. 1880; *e s* of Thomas N. Edgeworth; *m* Isabel Mary, widow of Arthur F. Eves, Resident Engineer, Cawnpore, and *e d* of John Trench Pigott. *Educ:* Marlborough (House Schol. and Senior Mathematical Schol.); RMA Woolwich (Pollock Medal and Prizes for Maths and Chemistry). Entered RE, 1898; Captain 1908; Major 1915; Temp. Lt-Col 1916; Lt-Col 1920; served S Africa, 1900-02 (Queen's medal 2 clasps, King's medal 2 clasps); East Africa, 1903-04 (medal with clasp); Sudan, 1908 (Egyptian medal and clasp); European War (despatches thrice, DSO, MC, 3 medals); retired pay, 1926; Chief Engineer, Posts and Telegraphs Dept, Sudan, 1926-31. *Publications:* The Industrial Crisis; The Trade Balance; The Price Level; Unemployment Can be Cured; The Earth, the Planets and the Stars: their Birth and Evolution; papers on theoretical astronomy; biography. *Address:* Cherbury, Booterstown, Co. Dublin. *T:* Dublin 882241.   *[Died 10 Oct. 1972.*

EDMAN, Prof. Pehr Victor, FRS 1974; FAA 1968; Director at the Max-Planck-Institute for Biochemistry since 1972; *b* 14 April 1916. *Educ:* Karolinska Inst., Stockholm. MD 1946. Asst Prof., Karolinska Inst., 1946; Rockefeller Fellowship, Princeton, 1946-47; Assoc. Prof., Univ. of Lund, 1947-57; Dir of Research, St Vincent's Sch. of Medical Research, Melbourne, 1957-72. Britannica Award, 1968. *Publications:* contrib. scientific jls. *Address:* Max-Planck-Institut für Biochemie, 8033 Martinsried bei München, West Germany. *T:* München (089) 8585-475.   *[Died 19 March 1977.*

EDMONDS, Cecil John, CMG 1941; CBE 1930 (OBE 1925); *b* 26 Oct. 1889; *y s* of late Rev. Walter and Laura Edmonds; *m* 1935, Alison, *o c* of late George Hooper, Birmingham; one *s* two *d* ; *m* 1947, Phyllis, 2nd *d* of late F. L. Stephenson, Skegness; one *s*. *Educ:* Bedford Sch.; Christ's Hosp.; Pembroke Coll., Cambridge. Student Interpreter in HM Levant Consular Service, 1910; acting Vice-Consul, Bushire, 1913; Asst Political Officer, Mesopotamia, 1915 (Temp. Captain); SW Persia, 1917; Political Officer, British Forces, NW Persia, 1919 (Temp. Major, Special List); Special Duty in S Kurdistan, 1922; Divisional Adviser and Administrative Inspector in the Kirkuk and Sulaimani provinces under Iraq Govt, 1922; Political Officer with military columns in Kurdistan, 1924; Liaison Officer with League of Nations Commission of Inquiry into frontier between Iraq and Turkey, 1925; Asst Adviser, Min. of Interior, Iraq, 1926; Consul, 1928; British Assessor, League of Nations Commn of Inquiry into the frontier between Iraq and Syria, 1932; Mem. of Demarcation Commn of Iraqi-Syrian Frontier, 1933; Adviser, Min. for Foreign Affairs, Iraq, 1933; Mem. of Iraqi Delegation to League of Nations, annually 1932-38; Adviser to the Ministry of the Interior, Iraq, 1935-45; Consul-Gen., 1937. Order of the Rafidain (Cl. II), 1945; UK Perm. Deleg. to Internat. Refugee Organisation, 1947; Minister in HM Foreign Service, 1948; retired, 1950. Lecturer in Kurdish, Sch. of Oriental and African Studies, University of London, 1951-57. Burton Memorial Medal, 1963; Sykes Memorial Medal, 1966. *Publications:* Kurds, Turks and Arabs, 1957; (jt) A Kurdish-English Dictionary, 1966; A Pilgrimage to Lalish, 1967; contributions on Persian, Arabian and Kurdish subjects. *Recreation:* gardening. *Address:* 5 Longslip, Langton Green, near Tunbridge Wells, Kent TN3 0BT. *T:* Langton 2771. *Club:* Athenæum.   *[Died 11 June 1979.*

EDMONDS, Edward Alfred Jubal; Member, Panel of Chairmen of Medical Appeal Tribunals, since 1969; *b* Newcastle, Natal, 21 Aug. 1907; *s* of late Edward Jubal Edmonds, Solicitor, and of Hilda O'Rorke Edmonds (*née* Stanton); *m* 1937, Maria Pauline du Toit; one *s* two *d*. *Educ:* Hilton Coll., Natal; Houghton Coll., Johannesburg; Natal Univ. Coll. Admitted a Solicitor, 1932; Attorney of Supreme Court of South Africa, 1933; Advocate of High Court of Tanganyika, Nov. 1934; Advocate, Supreme Court of Natal, 1939; entered Colonial Legal Service as a Resident Magistrate, Tanganyika, 1946; Puisne Judge, Kenya, 1955-64; retired from Colonial Service, 1964; called to the Bar, Gray's Inn, 1965; Resident Judge, Sovereign Base Areas, Cyprus, 1965-69. *Address:* Ridgeway, Hogs Back, Seale, Surrey.   *[Died 15 April 1974.*

EDMONDS, Edward Reginald, CMG 1954; *b* 25 Nov. 1901; *y s* of late G. F. Edmonds; *m* 1928, Edna May Dennis (*d* 1955); one *s* one *d* ; *m* 1956, Dorothy Edith (*d* 1970) (she *m* 1st, 1923, Ewart G. Sheaves; he *d* 1925), *er d* of late Benjamin George Bishop, Woodford Green, Essex; *m* 1971, Dora Elizabeth, *yr d* of late Henry Bradstreet. *Educ:* King's Coll., London Univ. (BA). Entered Colonial Office, 1917; Asst Principal, 1938; Principal, 1941; Asst Sec., 1947; retired, 1961. Served in Uganda, 1926-28. *Address:* Prested Hall, Kelvedon, Essex. *T:* Kelvedon 70156.   *[Died 16 Nov. 1979.*

EDMONDSON, George D'Arcy, CMG 1953; CVO 1957; OBE 1946; HBM Consul-General at Boston, 1959-62, retired; *b* 18 July 1904; *s* of George D'Arcy Edmondson and Agnes Mary Whitell; *m* 1st, 1935, Gwynfa (marr. diss., 1955), *d* of Sir Robert Burton-Chadwick, 1st Bt; no *c* ; 2nd, 1955, Rosamond Burling, *d* of late Prof. Robert L. Taylor, Williamstown, Mass, USA; two step *s*. *Educ:* Wimbledon Coll.; University Coll., Oxford (Hons, Jurisprudence). Called to Bar, Inner Temple, 1928; Press Censorship Bureau, 1939; Ministry of Information, 1941; British Information Services, New York; Dir Reference Div., 1942; Actg Controller, 1944; Controller, 1945; Dir-Gen. of British Information Services in the US, and Counsellor, British Embassy, Washington, 1953. *Address:* Blow-Me-Down, Star Route 4, Windsor, Vt 05089, USA. *Clubs:* Achilles, Travellers'; St Botolph (Boston, USA).   *[Died 9 April 1976.*

EDWARDES-KER, Lt-Col Douglas Rous, OBE; Managing Director, Exe Shellfish Ltd; Principal, Seale Hayne Agricultural College, Newton Abbot, 1919-33; *b* 21 Jan. 1886; *s* of late Dr George Cordy Edwardes-Ker, Woodbridge, Suffolk; *m* 1912, Frances Edith Watts, Rampside, Lancs; two *s*. *Educ:* Woodbridge Sch.; Brasenose Coll., Oxford (Open Scholar). MA Oxon., 1st Class Hons; BSc London, 1st Class Hons. Coll. Warden and mem. of Staff of South-Eastern Agricultural Coll., Wye, 1909-14; enlisted in Buffs, Aug. 1914; Commission in Royal Engineers, rising to rank of Lt-Col; Asst Dir of Gas Services, BEF, France (OBE, despatches thrice; two French Croix de Guerre, one avec palme). *Recreations:* lawn tennis, for ten years Mem. of Devon County Team, and Vice-Chm. Devon County LTA; fly-fishing. *Address:* Green Hollow, Exmouth, Devon. *TA:* Exmouth. *T:* 2738. *Club:* Oxford University Alembic.   *[Died 16 Dec. 1979.*

EDWARDS, (Arthur) Trystan, MA Oxon; FRIBA; FRTPI; FRGS; *b* Merthyr Tydfil, 10 Nov. 1884; *s* of late William Edwards, MA (Oxon), LLD, formerly HMIS and Chief Inspector to the Central Welsh Bd; *m* 1947, Margaret Meredyth (*d* 1967), *d* of late Canon F. C. Smith, FRZS, FLS, Richmond (Surrey) and Hellingly. *Educ:* Clifton Coll.; Hertford Coll., Oxford (hons in maths and lit. hum.). Articled pupil to Sir Reginald Blomfield, RA, 1907-10; Dept of Civic Design, Liverpool Univ., 1911-12; served European War, 1915-18, Able Seaman Royal Navy, Fourth Destroyer Flotilla; Ministry of Health (Housing Dept), 1919-25. Founded Hundred New Towns Assoc., 1933, and subsequently submitted evidence on its behalf before various Govt commns. *Publications:* The Things Which Are Seen: a philosophy of beauty, 1921, rep. 1948, expanded to include a Prologue and an Aftermath, 1972; Good and Bad Manners in Architecture, 1924, rep. 1948, rev. title Primacy of the Street Formation, 1972; Architectural Style, 1925, rep. 1935, rev. title How to Observe Buildings, 1972; Sir William Chambers (Masters of Architecture series), 1926; Three Rows of Tape: a social study of the lower deck, 1929, rev. title Spoilt Child of the British Navy, World War I and after: experiences and reflections of an ex-able seaman RN, 1972; (with Cyril Farey, FRIBA) Architectural Drawing, Perspective and Rendering, 1931, rep. 1949; Modern Terrace Houses (publication sponsored by Chadwick Trust), 1946; A New Map of the World: the Trystan Edwards Projection, 1953, rev. edn The Science of Cartography: a new presentation, 1972; The Second Battle of Hastings 1939-45, 1970; Merthyr-Rhondda, The Prince and Wales of the Future, 1972; Multiple Stresses: some tributes and a plan for renovation, 1972; Fourth of the Visual Arts: architecture re-examined, 1972; Second-Best Boy: the autobiography of a non-speaker, 1972. *Address:* 7 Courtland Terrace, Merthyr Tydfil, Glam. *T:* Merthyr 2054. *Club:* Athenæum.   *[Died 30 Jan. 1973.*

EDWARDS, Lt-Col (Bt Col) Sir Bartle (Mordaunt Marsham), Kt 1956; CVO 1961; MC; Vice-Lieutenant of Norfolk since 1958;

served in HM Hon. Corps of Gentlemen-at-Arms, 1938-61; Standard Bearer, 1956-61; *b* 30 March 1891; *s* of Major Mordaunt Edwards, VC, and Alice, *d* of General Norton; *m* 1921, Daphne, MBE, *d* of late Sir Cyril Kendall Butler, KBE; two *s* (and *e s* killed in action, March 1943) one *d. Educ:* Eton; RMC Sandhurst. Joined the Rifle Brigade, 1910; served with that regt and on general staff during European War, 1914-18, in France, Salonika, and Palestine (MC, despatches twice); Commanded Suffolk and Norfolk Yeo. Artillery Brigade, 1931-35; High Sheriff of Norfolk, 1946-47; Mem., 1922-74, Chm., 1950-66, Norfolk CC; DL 1932, JP 1926, Norfolk. *Address:* Hardingham Hall, Norwich. *T:* Hingham 236. *Club:* Army and Navy. *[Died 28 May 1977.*

EDWARDS, Corwin D.; Professor of Economics, University of Oregon, 1963-71, now Professor Emeritus; Associate Editor, Antitrust Bulletin, since 1967; *b* 1 Nov. 1901; *s* of Granville D. Edwards and Ida May Moore; *m* 1st, 1924, Janet Ward; one *s* one *d* ; 2nd, 1948, Gertrud Greig. *Educ:* Univ. of Missouri (BA); Oxford Univ. (BLitt); Cornell Univ. (PhD). Asst Prof. of Economics, New York Univ., 1926-33; Economist and Tech. Dir, Consumers' Advisory Bd, National Recovery Administration, 1933-35; co-ordinator, trade practice studies, Nat. Recovery Admin., 1935; Economist, President's Cttee of Industrial Analysis, 1936; Asst Chief Economist, Federal Trade Commn, 1937-39; Chief of Staff, Amer. Tech. Mission to Brazil, 1942-43; Economist, Chm. Policy Bd, Anti-Trust Div., Dept of Justice, 1939-44; Consultant on Cartels, Dept of State, 1943-48; Prof. of Economics, Northwestern Univ., 1944-48; Head of Mission on Japanese Combines, 1946; Dir, Bureau of Economics, Federal Trade Commn, USA, 1948-53; US Rep., *ad hoc* Cttee on Restrictive Business Practices, 1952-53; Pitt Prof., Cambridge Univ., 1953-54; Prof. of Economics, Univ. of Virginia, 1954-55; Prof. of Business and Government, Graduate Sch. of Business, Univ. of Chicago, 1955-63. Member: Consumers Adv. Council, USA, 1967-69; Cttee on social effects of computer technology, Nat. Sci. Foundn, 1971-72. Chm., section on internat. enterprises, internat. mergers and internat. jt ventures, Conf. on Internat. Economy and Competition Policy, Tokyo, 1973. *Publications:* Maintaining Competition, 1949; Big Business and the Policy of Competition, 1956; The Price Discrimination Law: A Review of Experience, 1959; Trade Regulation Overseas, the National Laws, 1966; Control of Cartels and Monopolies, an International Comparison, 1967; Studies of Foreign Competition Policy and Practice (for Canadian govt), 1976; American Antitrust Policy toward Conduct by Powerful Enterprises, and, American and German Policy toward Conduct by Powerful Enterprises, in Jl of Reprints for Antitrust Law and Economics, 1978; Co-author: Economic Behavior, 1931; Economic Problems in a Changing World, 1939; A Cartel Policy for the United Nations, 1945; various govt reports and articles in professional jls. *Recreations:* swimming, sailing. *Address:* 11 New Jersey Avenue, Lewes, Delaware 19958, USA. *[Died 20 April 1979.*

EDWARDS, Gordon, CBE 1955; *b* 14 July 1899; *s* of Frank George and Emily Maude Edwards, Crouch End, N8; *m* 1929 Marjorie Agnes, *d* of A. J. Hobson, OBE, RCNC; one *s. Educ:* Southend High Sch. Served European War, Inns of Court OTC and Royal Tank Corps, 1917-20. Inland Revenue Dept, 1920-45; Asst Sec., Min. of National Insurance, 1946-57; Chief Insurance Officer under the National Insurance and Industrial Injuries and Family Allowances Acts, 1957-62; Under-Sec., Min. of Pensions and National Insurance, 1962-64. *Publications:* Roses for Enjoyment, 1962, rev. edn 1973; Mein Rosengarten, 1967; Wild and Old Garden Roses, 1975; numerous articles in horticultural press. *Recreations:* growing roses and painting. *Address:* Hobbits, Copyhold Lane, Cuckfield, West Sussex. *T:* Haywards Heath 54429. *Club:* St Stephen's. *[Died 25 March 1976.*

EDWARDS, Sir Goronwy; *see* Edwards, Sir J. G.

EDWARDS, Lt-Col Harold Walter, DSO 1918; MC; MA; DL; CC, W Riding Yorks, 1949-52; Director, Dewsbury and West Riding Building Society, 1953-62; City Councillor, Bradford, 1954-57; *b* 1887; *y s* of S. E. Edwards, CC; *m* 1913, Celia (*d* 1941), *d* of G. A. Smith, Handsworth; one *s* (and one *s* decd); *m* 1948, Mabel Reina Fox, Bradford. *Educ:* March Grammar Sch.; Christ's Coll., Cambridge. Five years Science Master at King Edward Grammar Sch., Camp Hill, Birmingham; Chief Sec., Birmingham Liberal Association; Private Sec., 1920-21; Principal and Dir of Technical Schs, Cheltenham; Headmaster, Heckmondwike Grammar Schs, 1924-48; retired, 1948. Four years' active service in France, Belgium, and Germany, with Royal Warwicks Regt and Signals (despatches twice, DSO, MC, Croix de Guerre (French); OC 41 Bn WR Home Guard, 1940-45. Prospective Parliamentary Candidate, Handsworth Div., Birmingham, 1918; Mem. Council IAHM, 1929, Joint

Hon. Sec. 1941, Pres. 1942, Hon. Treas. 1947; Mem. Joint Matric Board, 1945; Mem. Sulgrave Deputation to USA, 1920; Officier d'Académie, 1934. DL West Riding of Yorks, 1947. *Publications:* newspaper articles on the land question. *Recreations:* motoring, gardening. *Address:* 20 Beechwood Avenue, Wibsey, Bradford. *[Died 14 May 1973.*

EDWARDS, (Herbert Cecil) Ralph, CBE 1953; BA; FSA; Adviser on Works of Art to the Historic Buildings Councils of England and Wales, 1954-75; Keeper, Department of Woodwork, Victoria and Albert Museum, 1937-54, retired Oct. 1954; *b* 24 June 1894; *s* of late Rev. W. A. Edwards, formerly Rector of Tredington, Shipston-on-Stour, and of Edith Lilian, *e d* of late C. J. Collins Prichard, Pwyllywrach, near Cowbridge, Glamorgan; *m* 1926, Marjorie Ingham Brooke; three *s. Educ:* privately; Hertford Coll., Oxon. BA (War Degree). War of 1914-18, 2nd Lieut, twice invalided; Middle Temple, Final Bar Exam. 2nd Cl.; Mem. of Editorial staff of Country Life, 1921-26; Asst, Dept of Woodwork, Victoria and Albert Museum, 1926-28; Asst Keeper, 1st Class, 1928; Keeper, 2nd Class, 1937, 1st Class, 1945. Member: The Court of Govs, and Council, Nat. Museum of Wales and of Cttees of Art and Archæology (Chm., 1958-61); Cttee, Slade Sch. of Art. *Publications:* (with late Percy Macquoid) The Dictionary of English Furniture, 3 vols, 1924-27 (2nd edn, rev. and enl., 1953; one volume edn 1963); Georgian Cabinet-makers (with late Margaret Jourdain) (3rd edn 1955); Early Conversation Pictures, 1954; Introd. to Cat. for RA Exhibn "English Taste in the Eighteenth Century", 1955-56 and for exhibns for Arts Council and GLC; Co-Editor the Connoisseur Period Guides, 1956-58; various official publications and many articles on English pictures and decorative art in Apollo, Burlington Magazine and Connoisseur. *Address:* Suffolk House, Chiswick Mall, W4. *T:* 01-994 3381; Pontesgob Mill Cottage, Fforest, Abergavenny, Gwent. *Club:* Athenæum. *[Died 13 Dec. 1977.*

EDWARDS, Very Rev. Irven David; Dean of Wells, since 1963; *b* 19 Nov. 1907; *s* of Rev. J. Edwards, Prebendary of Lichfield Cathedral; *m* 1938, Diana Vernon Douglas, 2nd *d* of Rt Rev. D. H. Crick, *qv;* one *s* three *d. Educ:* Repton; Christ's Coll., Cambridge. Chaplain of Christ's Coll., Cambridge, 1935-40; Gen. Sec. of Central Advisory Council of Training for the Ministry, 1935-44; Rector of Milton, Hampshire, 1940-47; Vicar of Norton, Co. Durham, 1947-56; Archdeacon of Leicester and Vicar of All Saints', City and Diocese of Leicester, 1956-63. Examining Chaplain to Bishops of: Portsmouth, 1936-47; Manchester, 1938-40; Chester, 1940-50; Durham, 1949-52; Leicester, 1956-63. *Address:* The Dean's Lodging, 25 The Liberty, Wells, Somerset. *T:* Wells 72192. *[Died 14 Feb. 1973.*

EDWARDS, Sir (John) Goronwy, Kt 1960; MA; DLitt Oxon; Hon. DLitt Wales and Reading; Hon. LittD Leeds and Manchester; FBA 1943; FSA 1959; Director of the Institute of Historical Research and Professor of History, University of London, 1948-60, Professor Emeritus, 1960; Hon. Fellow of Jesus College, Oxford, 1949; Chairman, Royal Commission on Ancient Monuments in Wales and Monmouthshire, 1955-67; Member, Ancient Monuments Board for Wales, 1959-74; Member, Royal Commission on Historical Manuscripts, since 1953; *b* 14 May 1891; *s* of John William and Emma Edwards; *m* 1925, Gwladys, *e d* of Rev. William Williams. *Educ:* Holywell Grammar Sch.; Jesus Coll., Oxford (Scholar); Manchester Univ. (Research Scholar). 1st Class Modern History, 1913; 2nd Lieut Royal Welch Fusiliers, 1915: served in France; retired with rank of Capt., 1919; Fellow and Tutor of Jesus Coll., Oxford, 1919-48; Librarian, 1920-25; Junior Bursar, 1926-29; Senior Tutor, 1931-46; Vice-Principal, 1945-48; Examiner, Sch. of Modern History, Oxford, 1926-28, 1941-43; University Lecturer in Modern History, 1928-36, 1947-48; Proctor, 1932-33; Pres. of the Dafydd ap Gwilym Soc., 1919-48; Joint Editor of the English Historical Review, 1938-59. Member: Cttee on House of Commons Personnel and Politics 1264-1832, 1929-31; Grigg Cttee on Departmental Records, 1952-54; British Acad. Cttee on Research in Humanities and Social Sciences, 1958-60; UGC Cttee on Libraries, 1963-66. Rhys Memorial Lecturer, British Academy, 1944; David Murray Lecturer, University of Glasgow, 1955; Raleigh Lecturer, Brit. Acad., 1956; Creighton Lecturer, University of London, 1957; Ford's Lecturer, University of Oxford, 1960-61; President, Royal Historical Society, 1961-64. Cymmrodorion Medal, 1970. *Publications:* Flint Pleas, 1283-85, 1922; Calendar of Ancient Correspondence concerning Wales, 1935; Littere Wallie, 1940; articles in English Historical Review and other historical journals. *Address:* 35 Westmorland Road, SW13. *T:* 01-748 7197.

[Died 20 June 1976.

EDWARDS, Rev. Maldwyn Lloyd, PhD; Methodist Chairman in South Wales, 1957-71 (Cardiff and Swansea District of

Methodist Church); President, Methodist Conference, July 1961-62; *b* 18 May 1903; *s* of John Lloyd and F. B. Edwards, Liverpool; *m* 1931, Eleanor M. L. Broadbelt; two *d. Educ:* Liverpool Collegiate Sch.; Universities of Wales, Cambridge and London. MA Wales and Cambridge; BD Cantab; PhD London. Asst Tutor, Handsworth Coll., 1929-30; Methodist Minister in Central Halls in six industrial centres. Sec., Christian Citizenship Dept of Methodist Church, 1945-48. Hon. DD Wofford Coll., N Carolina, USA, 1956. *Publications:* many books including several on various phases of Methodism, and on sociology, including The Signs of Our Times (Cato Lecture); also some devotional books and a number of papers and pamphlets on social subjects. *Recreations:* Methodist history and sociology. *Address:* 60a Westover Road, Westbury-on-Trym, Bristol BS9 3LT.   *[Died 14 Oct. 1974.*

EDWARDS, Ralph; see Edwards, H. C. R.

EDWARDS, Sir Robert Meredydd W.; see Wynne-Edwards.

EDWARDS, Captain Roderick Latimer Mackenzie, CBE 1944; Royal Navy retired; *b* 1900; *s* of late Lt-Col C. and E. K. Mackenzie-Edwards; *m* 1929, Beryl Gertrude, *d* of late F. P. Clements, Maiden Newton, Dorset; one *d* (one *s* lost in sinking of HM Submarine Affray). *Educ:* Aldwick Preparatory Sch.; Osborne and Dartmouth. Served European War, 1916-18; specialised submarines, 1919; War of 1939-45; Capt.-in-Charge, Portland, 1947-49; retired list, 1950. Foreign decorations: Commander, Order of Orange Nassau, (Netherlands), 1945; Chevalier, Legion of Honour, 1945; Croix de Guerre with Palms (France), 1945. *Address:* Summerleaze, Maiden Newton, Dorchester, Dorset. *T:* Maiden Newton 244. *Club:* Royal Dorset Yacht.   *[Died 27 Nov. 1975.*

EDWARDS, Prof. Sir Ronald Stanley, KBE 1963; Chairman, British Leyland Ltd, since 1975; President, Beecham Group Ltd, since 1975 (Chairman, 1968-75); Director: ICI Ltd, since 1969; Hill Samuel Group, since 1974; Professor of Economics, with special reference to Industrial Organisation, in the University of London since 1949; Member, British Airways Board, since 1971; *b* 1 May 1910; *er s* of Charles and Alice Edwards; *m* 1936, Myrtle Violet Poplar; two *d. Educ:* Southgate County Sch. BCom (London), DSc (Econ.). Certified accountant. In professional accountancy, 1926-35; Asst Lectr and later Lectr in Business Administration with special reference to Accounting, London Sch. of Economics, 1935-40; Finance Mem. and Gen. Sec., Birmingham War Factories Jt Cttee, Dep. Dir of Labour and Asst Sec., Min. of Aircraft Production, 1940-45; Sir Ernest Cassel Reader in Commerce with special reference to Industrial Administration in University of London, 1946-49; Dep. Chm., Electricity Council, 1957-61, Chm., 1962-68. Member: Interdepartmental Cttee on Further Education and Training, 1944; Ministry of Fuel and Power Cttee on Electricity Peak Load, 1948; Advisory Council, Dept of Scientific and Industrial Research, 1949-54; Min. of Fuel and Power Cttee of Inquiry into the Organisation and Efficiency of Electricity Supply Industry, 1954-55; University Grants Cttee, 1955-64; NEDC 1964-68. Governor: Admin. Staff Coll., Henley, 1962-70; London Graduate Sch. of Business Studies, 1964-; LSE, 1968- (Hon. Fellow, 1975). Independent Chm., British Clock and Watch Manufacturers Assoc. (Watch Section), 1946-59, Hon. Pres., 1959-; Pres., Market Research Soc., 1965-69; Chairman: Govt Cttee of Inquiry into Civil Air Transport Industry, 1967-69; Govt Adv. Cttee on Appointment of Advertising Agents, 1970-73. Hon. LLD: Edinburgh, 1966; Strathclyde, 1973; Hon. DSc Bath, 1966; Hon. DLitt Warwick, 1973. *Publications:* Co-operative Industrial Research, 1950; Industrial Research in Switzerland, 1951; Business Enterprise, 1958; (with H. Townsend) Studies in Business Organisation, 1961; (with H. Townsend) Business Growth 1966; (with R. D. V. Roberts) Status, Productivity and Pay: a major experiment, 1971; contribs to Studies in Accounting (ed Baxter), Studies in Costing (ed Solomons), and to learned jls on economic, industrial and accounting questions. *Recreation:* sailing. *Address:* 49 Lowndes Square, SW1. *T:* 01-235 4253; Nothe House, Weymouth, Dorset. *T:* Weymouth 923.   *[Died 18 Jan. 1976.*

EDWARDS, Rev. Canon Rowland Alexander, MA; Canon Residentiary of Norwich, 1948-68, Canon Emeritus, 1968 (Vice-Dean, 1954-68); *b* 20 Aug. 1890; *s* of late Philip Harris Edwards, solicitor, and late Emily, *d* of Alexander Gribbon, Belfast; *m* 1923, Monica Winterburn (*d* 1972), Buckingham; two *s* two *d. Educ:* Campbell Coll., Belfast; St John's Coll., Oxford (Casberd Scholar). Graduated History, 2nd class. Ordained Dec. 1913; Chaplain, Christ's Hosp. Served European War, 1914-18; RAMC, Mesopotamia, 1916-19. Curate of Buckingham, 1920, of St Edmund's, Northampton, 1924; Vicar of St Faith's, Stepney, 1926, of Wisborough Green, Sussex, 1931; Rector of

Dartington, Devon, 1940; Rural Dean of Totnes, 1943; Senior Examining Chaplain to Bishop of Norwich, 1948. Editor, St Martin's Review, 1938-39. *Publications:* Plain Tales from the Slums, 1933; Jack, Jill and God, 1936; World Adrift, 1937; Is the Church Worth While?, 1938; City of God, 1939; The Upper Room, 1941; The Church and the Modern World, 1944; contributor to Am I My Brother's Keeper?, 1946; (play) The Fighting Bishop, 1950; Church and Chapel, 1952; The Gospel According to St John, 1954; contributor to journals, etc. *Recreation:* writing. *Address:* 60 The Close, Norwich. *T:* Norwich 24726.   *[Died 21 Sept. 1973.*

EDWARDS, Trystan; see Edwards, A. T.

EDWARDS, Lieut-Col Walter Manoel; *b* 17 Feb. 1885; *s* of late Major E. G. Edwards, RA; *m* 1947, Rosa Charlotte Pennick, *d* of Ireton and Ethel Jones; one *s* one *d. Educ:* Rugby; RMA Woolwich; Exeter Coll., Oxford. Commission in Royal Garrison Artillery, 1904; War Service, 1914-18 (despatches, MC); retired as Major, 1921; BA Oxon 1925, MA 1927; Fellow, Merton Coll., Oxford, 1925; Professor of Greek Language and Literature, University of Leeds, 1928-50; Lieut-Col (Reserve). *Publications:* contributions to: New Chapters in Greek Literature, 1930; Oxford Latin Dictionary, 1950-69; articles in classical and other periodicals. *Recreation:* reading. *Address:* 43 Cumnor Hill, Oxford.   *[Died 22 Jan. 1971.*

EDWIN, G. F. D.; see Dove-Edwin.

EGERTON, Lady Alice, CVO 1957; *b* 7 Aug. 1923; 6th *d* of 4th Earl of Ellesmere, MVO. *Educ:* privately. Lady-in-Waiting to Princess Elizabeth, Duchess of Edinburgh, 1949-52; Woman of the Bedchamber to The Queen, 1953-61. Served Red Cross Transport, 1941-45. *Address:* Stetchworth Park, Newmarket, Suffolk. *T:* Stetchworth 281; 26 Hans Crescent, SW1. *T:* 01-584 9432.   *[Died 7 Oct. 1977.*

EGERTON, Vice-Adm. (Henry) Jack, CB 1946; DL; *b* 29 March 1892; *s* of late Charles Augustus Egerton, Mountfield, Robertsbridge, and Lady Mabelle Egerton, *d* of 1st Earl Brassey, GCB; *m* 1919, Marion, *d* of Hon. Sir Gervase Beckett, 1st Bt; one *s* (*er s* killed in action, 1942). *Educ:* RNC Dartmouth, RN: Captain, 1934; Rear-Adm. 1944; Vice-Adm., 1948. Senior British Naval Officer, North Russia, 1944-45; Flag Officer, Malayan Area, 1946-47; retired list, 1948. DL North Riding, 1951-. *Recreations:* hunting and shooting. *Address:* Colville House, Coxwold, York. *Club:* United Service and Royal Aero.   *[Died 17 April 1972.*

EGGERS, Henry Howard, CMG 1950; OBE 1945; Director, Cable & Wireless Ltd, 1954-69 (Managing Director, 1955-69); *b* 13 Nov. 1903; *yr s* of late H. A. F. Eggers, London; *m* 1936, Sheila (marr. diss. 1949), *d* of late F. R. Addie, Dunblane; one *s* one *d. Educ:* Dulwich Coll.; Magdalen Coll., Oxford. Central and South American merchant, 1924-39; Ministry of Economic Warfare, 1940-45; HM Treasury, 1945-54. Order of Istiqlal (Jordan), 1965. *Address:* The Barn, Ockenden Lane, Cuckfield, Sussex. *T:* Haywards Heath 54363.   *[Died 18 July 1980.*

EGREMONT, 1st Baron *cr* 1963, and **LECONFIELD, 6th Baron** *cr* 1859; **John Edward Reginald Wyndham,** MBE 1945; JP; *b* 5 June 1920; *s* of 5th Baron Leconfield, DSO and Gladys Mary (*d* 1971), *o d* of F. J. W. Farquhar; *S* father 1967, as 6th Baron Leconfield, but prefers to be known as Lord Egremont; *m* 1947, Pamela, *d* of Captain the Hon. Valentine Wyndham-Quin; two *s* one *d. Educ:* Eton; Trinity College, Cambridge. Civil Servant, 1940-46; Conservative Research Dept, 1947-52. Private Secretary to the Prime Minister (Rt. Hon. Harold Macmillan), 1957-63 (when he was created 1st Baron Egremont). Trustee of the Wallace Collection, 1953-. JP West Sussex, 1953. High Sheriff of Sussex, 1960. *Publication:* Wyndham and Children First, 1968. *Heir: is* Hon. John Max Henry Scawen Wyndham, *b* 21 April 1948. *Address:* Petworth House, Sussex. *T:* Petworth 42447; Cockermouth Castle, Cumberland. *T:* Cockermouth 3118; 62 Chester Square, SW1. *T:* 01-730 2003. *Clubs:* Turf, White's, Beefsteak, Pratt's, Other, Sussex; Puffins (Edinburgh).   *[Died 6 June 1972.*

EHRENBERG, Victor Leopold, PhD; ancient historian; *b* 22 Nov. 1891; *s* of late Otto Maximilian Ehrenberg and Emilie Gabriele (*née* Fischel); *m* 1919, Eva Dorothea Sommer (*d* 1973); two *s. Educ:* Univs of Göttingen, Berlin and Tübingen. PhD 1920; Privatdozent, Univ. of Frankfurt, 1922; Prof. German Univ. at Prague, 1929; Prof. Emeritus, 1954. Emigration, 1939; naturalised in Great Britain, 1947. Classics Master, Carlisle Grammar Sch., 1941; Lectr, King's Coll., Newcastle on Tyne, 1941-45; Senior Classics Master, Bootham Sch., 1945-46; Lecturer, Bedford Coll., University of London, 1946; Reader in

Ancient History in the University of London, 1949-57. Visiting Prof., Brandeis Univ., USA, 1958; Martin Lecturer, Oberlin (Ohio), 1962; Hon. Res. Fellow, Bedford Coll., Univ. of London, 1966. Hon. LittD Cambridge, 1966. Jt Editor, Historia; Jt Founder of London Classical Soc., 1947; Sec. to Internat. Congress of Class. Studies, London, 1959. Corresponding Mem. Heidelberger and Osterreichischen Akademien der Wissenschaften. Gold Medal Pro Meritis of University of Graz, 1961. Great Cross of Merit of the German Federal Republic, 1966. *Publications:* Die Rechtsidee im frühen Griechentum, 1921; Neugründer des Staats, 1925; Alexander und Aegypten, 1926; Der griechische und der hellenistische Staat, 1932; Ost und West, 1935; Alexander and the Greeks, 1938; The People of Aristophanes, 1943, 3rd edn (paperback) 1962; L'Atene di Aristofane, 1957; Aristophanes und das Volk von Athen, 1968 (French edn prepared); Aspects of the Ancient World, 1946; (with Prof. A. H. M. Jones) Documents Illustrating the Reigns of Augustus and Tiberius, 1949, 2nd edn 1955; Sophocles and Pericles, 1954 (German edn 1956, Italian edn 1959); Der Staat der Griechen I, 1957, II, 1958, 2nd edn 1965 (The Greek State, 1961, Paperback, 1964, 2nd edn 1969, Lo Stato dei Greci, 1967, French trans. prepared); Von den Grundformen griechischer Staatsordnung, 1961; Society and Civilization in Greece and Rome, 1964 (Italian edn 1974); Polis und Imperium, 1965; The Hellenistic Age (Encyclop. Britannica), 1965; From Solon to Socrates, 1968 (2nd edn 1973, Spanish edn prepared); Man, State and Deity, 1974; many articles in English, American and German learned jls; appreciation and full bibliography: Historia X, 1961; Ancient Society and Institutions, Studies presented to VE, 1966. *Address:* 1/112 Fitzjohn's Avenue, NW3 6NT. *T:* 01-435 2456.   [Died 25 Jan. 1976.

EINZIG, Paul, DSc Pol. & Econ. (Paris); London Correspondent of the Commercial and Financial Chronicle, New York, since 1945; *b* Brasov (Transylvania), 25 Aug. 1897; *s* of late Bernard Einzig, Brasov, and late Giselle Weisz; *m* 1931, Eileen Ruth, *d* of late J. Telford Quick, St Mawes, Cornwall; one *s* one *d. Educ:* Brasov; Oriental Academy of Budapest; University of Paris. Paris Correspondent of the Financial News, 1921; Foreign Ed., 1923; Political Correspondent, 1939-45; Political Correspondent, Financial Times, 1945-56. British subject by naturalisation, 1929. *Publications:* Le Mouvement des Prix, 1923; International Gold Movements, 1929; The Bank for International Settlements, 1930; The Fight for Financial Supremacy, 1931; The World Economic Crisis, 1931; Behind the Scenes of International Finance, 1931; The Tragedy of the Pound, 1932; Finance and Politics, 1932; Montagu Norman, 1932; The Comedy of the Pound, 1933; The Economic Foundations of Fascism, 1933; The Sterling-Dollar-Franc Tangle, 1933; Germany's Default, 1934; The Economics of Rearmament, 1934; Exchange Control, 1934; France's Crisis, 1934; The Future of Gold, 1934; World Finance since 1914, 1935; Bankers, Statesmen and Economists, 1935; Exchange Clearing, 1935; Monetary Reform in Theory and Practice, 1936; The Theory of Forward Exchange, 1937; World Finance 1935-37, 1937; Will Gold Depreciate?, 1937; Foreign Balances, 1938; World Finance, 1937-38, 1938; Bloodless Invasion, 1938; Economic Problems of the Next War, 1939; World Finance, 1938-39, 1939; Economic Warfare, 1940; World Finance, 1939-40, 1940; Europe in Chains, 1940; Hitler's "New Order" in Europe, 1941; Economic Warfare, 1939-40, 1941; Appeasement Before, During, and After the War, 1941; Can We Win the Peace?, 1942; The Japanese "New Order" in Asia, 1943; Currency After the War, 1944; Freedom from Want, 1944; Primitive Money in its Ethnological, Historical and Economic Aspects, 1949; Inflation, 1952; How Money is Managed, 1954; The Economic Consequences of Automation, 1956; The Control of the Purse, 1959; In the Centre of Things: An Autobiography, 1960; A Dynamic Theory of Forward Exchange, 1961; The History of Foreign Exchange, 1962; The Euro-Dollar System, 1964; Monetary Policy: Ends and Means, 1964; Foreign Dollar Loans in Europe, 1965; A Textbook on Foreign Exchange, 1966; Foreign Exchange Crises, 1968; Leads and Lags, 1968; Decline and Fall? Britain's Crisis in the Sixties, 1969; The Euro-Bond Market, 1969; The Case against Floating Exchanges, 1970; The Case Against Joining the Common Market, 1971; Parallel Money Markets, vol. 1, 1971, vol. 2, 1972; The Destiny of the Dollar, 1972; The Destiny of Gold, 1972; A Textbook on Monetary Policy, 1973. *Recreations:* music, reading, walking. *Address:* 120 Clifford's Inn, EC4. *T:* 01-405 1444; Suffolks, Ashurst Wood, East Grinstead, Sussex. *T:* Forest Row 3386.
[Died 8 May 1973.

EISENBERG, Maurice; violoncellist; Concert-Artist, HMV Records; Director Founder, International 'Cello Centre in London, 1953-67 (Hon. Artistic Director, since 1967); Professor of Violoncello of Juilliard School of Music, NYC; US Representative, International Juries, Pablo Casals 'Cello

Competitions, Paris, Mexico, Israel, Budapest; *b* Königsberg, 24 Feb. 1902; *s* of Rev. Samuel Eisenberg and Fannie Eisenberg; *m* 1921, Paula Halpert; one *s* one *d. Educ:* Peabody Conservatory, Baltimore; studied with Klengel in Leipzig, Becker in Berlin, and at the Ecole Normale de Musique in Paris under Alexanian; under Casals in Spain for six years. Summer Master Classes, Internat. Summer Courses in Estoril, Portugal. *Publication:* Violoncello Playing of Today, 1956 (2nd edn). *Address:* 119 Cypress Street, Millburn, New Jersey 07041, USA.
[Died 13 Dec. 1972.

EKING, Maj.-Gen. Harold Cecil William, CB 1959; CBE 1954; DSO 1945; retired Jan. 1960; *b* 17 Nov. 1903; *s* of Harold Turney Eking; *m* 1st 1933, Eileen (*née* Brewer); one *s*; 2nd, 1943, Betty (*née* Stokes); one *d. Educ:* Rugby Sch.; RMA Woolwich. Commissioned Royal Engineers, 1924; Staff Coll., 1940; GSO1, 4 Div., 1941; 46 Div., 1942-43; CRE, 78 Div., 1943-44; CE, 13 Corps, 1944; Comd Engr Gp, Italy and Burma, 1945-46; CRE, Bde Comd and 2 i/c 10 Indian Div., 1946-47; Col GS, SME, 1948-50; Col AQ, Hong Kong, 1950; DDPS, War Office, 1951-54; Comdt, Sch. of Military Engineering, 1954-56; Chief Engineer, HQ Northern Army Group, 1956-60. *Address:* Pugg's Meadow, Kington Magna, Gillingham, Dorset. *Club:* Army and Navy.   [Died 12 March 1978.

ELDER, Sir (William) Stewart D.; see Duke-Elder.

ELDON, 4th Earl of, *cr* 1821; **John Scott,** GCVO 1963 (KCVO 1952); Baron Eldon, 1799; Viscount Encombe, 1821; Flight Lieutenant AAF; late Scots Guards; a Lord-in-Waiting to the Queen, 1934-68 (to King George VI, 1937-52); *b* 29 March 1899; *s* of late Viscount Encombe and Mary Laura Fraser (*d* 1946), *d* of 15th Baron Lovat; *S* Grandfather, 1926; *m* 1934, Hon. Magdalen Fraser, OBE 1953 (*d* 1969), *d* of 16th Baron Lovat; two *s. Educ:* Ampleforth Coll.; Magdalen Coll., Oxford. Served European War, 1918. Grand Officier, Légion d'Honneur. Owns about 10,000 acres. *Heir: s* Viscount Encombe. *Address:* Cardrona House, Innerleithen, Peeblesshire. *T:* Innerleithen 2426; 174 Cranmer Court, SW3. *T:* 01-589 0811. *Club:* White's.
[Died 20 Oct. 1976.

ELIBANK, 13th Lord *cr* 1643 (Scotland); **James Alastair Frederick Campbell Erskine-Murray;** Bt of Nova Scotia, 1628; *b* 23 June 1902; *s* of James Robert Erskine-Murray, DSc, Sqdn Ldr RAF, and Alleine F. F., *d* of Maj.-Gen. G. F. Gildea, CB; *S* to Barony and Btcy of kinsman, 3rd and last Viscount Elibank, 1962. *Educ:* Harrow; RMC Sandhurst. MA (2nd Class Hons in History), Glasgow, 1952. Commissioned 2nd Lieut, 1922; joined 2nd HLI, 1922; Lieut 1924; RARO, 1933; Capt. 1939; Major 1944. Served War of 1939-45. France, Dep. Asst Provost Marshal, Medical Base Sub-Area, Dieppe, Sept. 1939, and Le Havre, May 1940; OC Provost Co. 51 Div., June-Dec. 1940; Dep. Asst Provost Marshal, Port Said, 1941; attached Physical Trng, MEF, 1941-45; Asst Camp Comdt, GHQ, MEF, March-June 1945; UK 1945. Student Univ. of Glasgow, 1947. Scottish HQ Commissioner for Rover Scouts, 1951-62; Hon. Adviser in Recreational Training to Scottish HQ, Boy Scouts Assoc., 1963. Convener, Murray Clan Association. Mem. Soc. of Scottish Artists; FSAScot. *Recreations:* piping, sketching, mountaineering. *Heir: cousin* Alan D'Ardis Erskine-Murray [*b* 31 Dec. 1923; *m* 1962, Valerie Sylvia, *d* of Herbert William Dennis; two *s*]. *Address:* 3 Duncan Street, Edinburgh 9. *T:* 031-667 3983. *Club:* Royal Over-Seas League. [Died 2 June 1973.

ELIOTT LOCKHART, Sir Allan (Robert), Kt 1953; CIE 1943; *b* 3 Aug. 1905; *s* of late Col R. H. Eliott Lockhart, Royal Scots Greys, and M. C., *d* of William Eliott Lockhart, Cleghorn, Lanark; *m* 1939, Roslyn Maurice (marr. diss., 1947), *d* of Maurice Barton, Sydney, NSW; two *s*; *m* 1947, Sonia, widow of Major Hugh Lyons-Montgomery, *d* of B. C. J. Oldrini, Chilwell, Beeston, Notts; one *s. Educ:* Harrow. Lanarkshire Yeomanry, 1923-30. Gladstone Lyall & Co. Ltd, Calcutta, 1926-58, Managing Dir, 1948-58; Stewarts & Lloyds Ltd, 1958-67. Chairman: Lanark Race Course Ltd; Calcutta Branch of European Assoc., 1937-39; Mem. of All India Council, 1932-39; MLC Bengal, 1931-37; Dept of Supply, Govt of India, 1940-46; Dir-Gen. of Munitions Production, 1945-46; Pres. Associated Chambers of Commerce and Bengal Chamber of Commerce and Industry, 1951-52; Pres., UK Citizen's Assoc. of India, 1954-55. *Recreation:* shooting. *Address:* Cleghorn, Lanark. *T:* Lanark 2318. *Clubs:* Oriental; New (Edinburgh); Royal Calcutta Turf, Bengal, Tollygunge (Calcutta).   [Died 9 April 1977.

ELKINGTON, Reginald Lawrence, CBE 1957; retired as Controller of Export Licensing, Board of Trade (1947-58); *b* 25 May 1898; *s* of Edwin and Sarah Elkington; *m* 1925, Doris May Humphreys; one *s. Educ:* King Edward VI Grammar Sch., Totnes. Commissioned, 1917; served in France with West

Yorkshire Regt and Tank Corps. Entered Customs and Excise Dept, 1919. Board of Trade, 1939; Asst Sec. 1952. *Recreations:* bowls, travel, bridge, etc. *Address:* 30 Blenheim Road, SW20. *T:* 01-542 1912.   *[Died 22 July 1975.*

ELKINS, Sir Anthony (Joseph), Kt 1952; CBE 1944; Chairman: British Match Corporation Ltd, 1964-72; Gestetner Ltd, 1964-72; Vice-Chairman, Army & Navy Stores Ltd, 1965-71 (Director, 1954-72); *b* 30 May 1904; *s* of late Dr and Mrs F. A. Elkins, Herts; *m* 1930, Mabel Brenda Barker (decd); three *s* one *d*; *m* 1944, Ines Erna Miller (*née* Neele) (marr. diss.); *m* 1969, Nora Christianne Elliot (*née* Rowe). *Educ:* Haileybury Coll. With Gillanders Arbuthnot & Co. Ltd in India, 1924-54 (Chm., 1945-54); Chm., Darjeeling-Himalayan Railway Co. Ltd, 1945-48. Controller of Supplies (Bengal Circle), 1941-45; served on Cttees of India's First Five-Year Plan, 1949-51. President: Bengal Chamber of Commerce, 1949; Associated Chambers of Commerce of India, 1949; UK Citizens' Assoc. of India, 1953; Inst. of Export, 1967-70; Vice-Pres., Imperial Bank of India (Bengal Circle), 1949. Chm. of Bryant & May Ltd, 1955-64; Dir, Phoenix Assce Co., WA, 1973-74. Chairman: London and South-Eastern Resettlement Cttee, Regular Forces Resettlement Service, 1968-69 (Mem., 1961-69); Regional Industrial Cttee, Nat. Savings Movement, 1969-71. *Address:* 23 Clontarf Street, Sorrento, WA 6020, Australia. *Clubs:* Oriental; Western Australian Turf; Bengal, Royal Calcutta Turf (Calcutta); etc.
                                                    [Died 31 Oct. 1978.

ELLENBERGER, Lt-Col Jules, CMG 1925; ISO 1922; *b* 16 Jan. 1871; 5th *s* of late Rev. D. F. Ellenberger, Basutoland; *m* 1895, Fanny Sarah, *d* of late Eugene Casalís, MD, Paris; one *s*. *Educ:* Lovedale, South Africa; Lycée St Louis, Paris. Joined Bechuanaland Protectorate Service, 1890; Actg Asst Comr, Northern District, 1892, 1894; Interpreter: (English-Sechuana) to Bechuanaland Protectorate Concessions Commn, 1893; Sir Sidney Shippard's Boundary Commn (Bechuanaland Protectorate), 1894; Asst Resident Magistrate, 1898. Served South African War: Advanced Armoured Train from Rhodesia; with Plumer's Column to Relief of Mafeking. Comr for Oath of Allegiance, 1901; Asst Comr, Southern Protectorate, 1902; Mem., Sir Ralph Williams' special mission to Ngamiland, 1906; Special Comr, Ngamiland and Resident Magistrate, Northern Protectorate, 1908; Govt Sec., 1916; Actg Resident Comr, 1920, 1921, 1923; Special Duty, Ngamiland and Ghanzi Districts, 1920-21; Resident Comr, Bechuanaland Protectorate, 1923 (in command of Police with local rank of Lt-Col); retired, 1927. Represented: Bechuanaland Protectorate Govt at fixing of N-Eastern and N-Western beacons of Caprivi Zipfel; Northern Rhodesia, N-Western beacon, Angola-Caprivi Boundary, 1930; Chief Cordon Officer, Foot and Mouth Disease, Bechuanaland Protectorate, 1933; acted for Bechuanaland Govt, Commn to settle estate of Linchwe, late Chief of Bakgatla Tribe, 1935. JP Bechuanaland, 1891. *Address:* c/o PO Box 790, Salisbury, Rhodesia.   *[Died 20 Aug. 1973.*

ELLERMAN, Sir John Reeves, 2nd Bt *cr* 1905; Director of Ellerman Lines Ltd; *b* 21 Dec. 1909; *o s* of Sir John Ellerman, 1st Bt, CH, and Hannah (*d* 1939), *d* of George Glover; *S* father, 1933; *m* 1933, Esther, *d* of late Clarence De Sola, Montreal. *Heir:* none. *Address:* 19-21 Moorgate, EC2.
                                             [Died 17 July 1973 (ext).

ELLERTON, Air Commodore Alban Spenser, CBE 1944 (OBE 1919); RAF; Air ADC to the King, 1944 (ADC, 1949); *b* 3 Oct. 1894; 6th *s* of Alfred Ellerton, Hampstead; *m* 1919, Maureen Gilliland (*d* 1971), *o c* of T. F. Husband, ISO; two *s*. *Educ:* privately; Germany. Enlisted Coldstream Guards, Aug. 1914, on return from Germany; commission RFC 1916; Major HQ RFC 1917 (despatches twice); permanent commission RAF 1918; retd 1949. *Address:* 1 West Street, Rye, Sussex. *Club:* Royal Air Force.   *[Died 15 Dec. 1978.*

ELLICOTT, Langford Pannell, CBE 1959; Chief Housing and Planning Inspector, Ministry of Housing and Local Government, 1961-68; *b* 29 April 1903; *s* of Ernest Albert Ellicott, Wells, Som, and Mary Ellen Ellicott (*née* Hartnett); *m* 1935, Florence Louise, *d* of Charles Farraghan, Wadebridge, Cornwall; one *d*. *Educ:* Sedbergh Sch., Yorks; University Coll. London. ARIBA, RIBA Distinction in Town Planning, FRTPI. Housing and Planning Inspector, Ministry of Health, 1937; Sen. Planning Officer, London Region, Min. of Town and Country Planning, 1944-45; Regional Controller, W Midlands, 1946; Dep. Chief Planner, Min. of Town and Country Planning, later Min. of Housing and Local Govt, 1947-58; Chief Planner, 1959-60. *Recreations:* gardening, painting. *Address:* The Gate Cottage, Monken Hadley, Barnet, Herts. *T:* 01-449 3233.
                                                    [Died 20 Aug. 1972.

ELLINGTON, Hon. Edward Kennedy, (Duke); pianist, composer and band leader; *b* Washington, DC, 29 April 1899. *Educ:* Armstrong High Sch.; studied music with Henry Grant. First professional appearance, 1916; New York, 1922; engaged Cotton Club, NYC, 1927-32; tours include: Europe, 1933, 1938, 1948, 1950, 1958, 1963, 1964, 1965, 1966, 1967, 1969; for US State Dept: Near and Middle East, 1963; Japan, 1964; Dakar, 1966; S America and Mexico, 1968; Russia, 1971; S and Central America, 1971; Far East and Australasia, 1972; Scores for: Chocolate Kiddies, 1924; Jump for Joy, 1940; Beggar's Holiday, 1947; A Drum is a Woman, 1957; Anatomy of a Murder, 1959; Paris Blues, 1961; Turcaret, 1962; My People, 1963; Timon of Athens, 1963; Murder in the Cathedral, 1966; Assault on a Queen, 1966; Change of Mind, 1968. Major works include: Black Brown and Beige; Liberian Suite; Perfume Suite; Deep South Suite; Harlem; Shakespeare Suite (Such Sweet Thunder); Night Creature; Suite Thursday; Far East Suite; The Golden Broom and the Green Apple; First Sacred Concert, 1965; Second Sacred Concert, 1968; The River (ballet music), 1970; New Orleans Suite, 1970; Afro-Eurasian Suite, 1971; Goutelas Suite, 1971; Togo Brava Suite, 1971; Uwis Suite, 1972. Member: Nat. Council on the Arts, 1968; Nat. Institute of Arts and Letters, 1970; Royal Swedish Acad. of Music, 1971. Hon. degrees: Dr of Music: Wilberforce Univ., Ohio, 1949; Yale Univ., 1967; Morgan State Coll., 1967; Washington Univ., St Louis, 1967; Columbia Coll., Chicago, 1968; Brown Univ., 1969; Assumption Coll., Mass, 1970; Berklee Coll., Boston, 1971; Howard Univ., 1971; St John's Univ., Jamaica, NY, 1971; Wisconsin Univ., 1971; DHL, Christian Theological Seminary, 1970; Dr of Humanities: Milton Coll., Wis., 1964; Clark Coll., Atlanta, 1973; Dr of Fine Arts, California Coll. of Arts and Crafts, 1966. President's Gold Medal, 1966; The Medal of Freedom, 1969. *Publication:* Music is My Mistress (autobiog.), 1973. *Address:* 333 Riverside Drive, New York, NY 10025, USA.   *[Died 24 May 1974.*

ELLIOT, Lt-Col Henry Hawes, CIE 1941; MBE 1923; MC 1917; IMS, retd; *b* 22 May 1891; 6th *s* of late John Elliot, Binks, Roxburghshire. *Educ:* Monkton Combe Sch.; Durham; Edinburgh; Guy's Hospital. MB, BS Dunelm 1914; MRCS, LRCP 1915; FRCSE 1921; DMRE Cambridge 1926. Commissioned RAMC, 1915; attached 8th Welch Regt and 2nd Rifle Bde, Gallipoli and France, 1915-18 (twice wounded); entered IMS 1921; Waziristan Field Force, 1922-24; transferred Foreign and Political Dept 1929; Surgeon British Legation, Kabul, 1930-35; Surgeon to the Viceroy, 1936-43; Chief Medical Officer, Baluchistan, 1944; retired, 1946. *Address:* Springbank, Melrose, Roxburghshire. *Club:* East India and Sports.
                                                   [Died 5 March 1972.

ELLIOT, James Robert McDowell, CMG 1949; OBE 1945; *b* 1 Jan. 1896; *e s* of late Lieut-Col R. H. Elliot, IMS (and Ophthalmic Surgeon), and late Mrs E. C. I. Elliot; *m* 1922, Joan Helen Caudery, *d* of late Capt. A. S. Littlejohns, CMG, RN, and late Mrs Littlejohns; one *s* one *d*. *Educ:* Lancing Coll., Sussex. Served European War, 1914-19, in 2/4th Bn Wilts Regt, and Machine Gun Corps, Capt. (Actg Major). Cadet, Uganda, 1920; ADC 1922; District Officer, 1931; Senior District Officer, 1944; Provincial Commissioner, Uganda, 1945. Retired from Colonial Civil Service, Jan. 1950. Compiled labour enquiry reports, 1936 and 1937. *Address:* c/o Grindlay's Bank Ltd, 13 St James's Square, SW1; Flat A, 263 Goldhurst Terrace, NW6 3EP.
                                                    [Died 28 July 1980.

ELLIOT, Walter Travers S.; see Scott-Elliot.

ELLIOT, Air Chief Marshal Sir William, GCVO 1953; KCB 1951 (CB 1944); KBE 1946 (CBE 1942); DFC 1918; *b* 1896; *s* of late Gilbert John Elliot; *m* 1931, Rosemary (*d* 1971), *d* of Sir John Chancellor, GCMG, GCVO, GBE, DSO; one *s* one *d*. *Educ:* Switzerland; Tonbridge Sch. Served European War, 1914-18 (despatches, DFC and bar), South Russia, 1919; Asst Sec. to Cttee of Imperial Defence, 1937-39, and to War Cabinet, 1939-41; Fighter Command, 1941-42; Director of Plans, Air Ministry, 1942-44; AOC RAF, Gibraltar, Feb.-June 1944; AOC Balkan Air Force, 1944-45; Asst Chief Exec., Ministry of Aircraft Production, 1945-46; Asst Chief of Air Staff (Policy), 1946-47; C-in-C, Fighter Command, 1947-49; Chief Staff Officer to Minister of Defence and Dep. Sec. (Mil.) to Cabinet, 1949-51; Chm. of British Joint Services Mission, Washington, and UK Representative on the Standing Group of the Military Cttee of the North Atlantic Treaty Organisation, 1951-54. ADC to King George VI, 1950-52; ADC to the Queen, 1952-54. Chm. of Council, Royal Institute of International Affairs, Chatham House, 1954-58. *Address:* Stourpaine House, near Blandford, Dorset. *Clubs:* Brooks's, Buck's.   *[Died 27 June 1971.*

ELLIOTT, Albert George, CBE 1941; retired as Executive Vice-Chairman, 1955 (Joint Managing Director, 1951-55 and Chief Engineer, 1937-55), Rolls-Royce Ltd; *b* 3 Dec. 1889; *m* 1st, 1921, Cecilia, *d* of late Rennie Gray, Aberdeen; one *d* (decd); 2nd, 1962, Ann, *d* of late George Wrightson, Kirk Ireton, Derbs. *Educ:* Northampton Engineering Coll.; London Univ. Responsible for engine design with Napier Co.; joined Rolls-Royce Co. in 1912 to take charge of Engine Drawing Office, was attached to Sir H. Royce's personal staff and worked with him for 20 years; Chief Designer, 1929, responsible for both Car and Aero Engine Design; Chief Engineer of Aero Div., 1937; Chief Engineer and appointed to Board, 1945. Tech. Dir, Rotol Ltd, Cheltenham, 1946-55; Mem., Air Registration Bd, 1947-58; Gov., Loughborough Coll., 1950-62; Mem., Air Safety Bd, 1955-65; CEng; FRAeS; MIMechE; FRSA; Brit. Gold Medal, RAeS, 1954. *Recreations:* motoring, art, yachting. *Address:* Moray Lodge, 10 Willow Drive, Little Common, Bexhill-on-Sea, East Sussex TN39 4PX.   *[Died 13 Nov. 1975.*

ELLIOTT, Anthony; *see* Elliott, T. A. K.

ELLIOTT, Sir Claude (Aurelius), Kt 1958; OBE 1920; Hon. DCL (Durham); Fellow of Jesus College, Cambridge, since 1910; *b* 1888; *y s* of late Sir Charles Elliott, KCSI, Lieut-Governor of Bengal; *m* 1913, Gillian (*d* 1966), *d* of late F. T. Bloxam, Chief Chancery Registrar; one *s*. *Educ:* Eton; Trinity Coll., Cambridge. Tutor, Jesus Coll., 1914; Red Cross Unit in Flanders, 1915; then temporary work at Admiralty till 1919; sometime Univ. Lecturer in History, and Mem. of Univ. Financial Board, Gen. Board, and Council of Senate; Head Master of Eton Coll., 1933-49; Provost of Eton Coll., 1949-64; Pres. Alpine Club, 1950-52. *Address:* Lower Gatesgarth, Buttermere, Cockermouth, Cumberland. *Clubs:* Travellers', Alpine; Leander.   *[Died 21 Nov. 1973.*

ELLIOTT, Vice-Adm. Sir Maurice (Herbert), KCB 1956 (CB 1954); CBE 1952 (OBE 1938; MBE 1919); *b* 19 Feb. 1897; *s* of late Rev. Dr R. Elliott; *m* 1925, Margaret, *d* of late A. E. Ward, solicitor; no *c*. *Educ:* Dulwich Coll. Joined Navy, 1914; served throughout European War, 1914-18, in Grand Fleet; offices of Commanders-in-Chief, China and Portsmouth, 1919-26; Sec. to Vice-Adm. A. E. F. Bedford in various appts, 1926-37; served War of 1939-45, HMS Nelson, Admiralty, Newfoundland and Canada; Dep. Dir-Gen. Supply and Secretariat Branch, 1946-49; Command Supply Officer (Air), 1951-54; Dir-Gen. Supply and Secretariat Branch, 1954-57. *Recreation:* golf. *Address:* Pillar Box Cottage, Littleton, near Guildford, Surrey. *T:* Guildford 69103. *Club:* Army and Navy.   *[Died 26 March 1972.*

ELLIOTT, Rt. Rev. Robert Cyril Hamilton, DD; Hon. CF; *b* 18 Nov. 1890; *s* of Canon A. L. Elliott, MA, Rector of Killiney, County Dublin; unmarried. *Educ:* Trent College, Derbyshire; Trinity College, Dublin (MA). DD 1957. Deacon, 1914; priest, 1915; CF, 1917-19 (despatches twice). Rector of All Saints, Belfast, 1922-30; Vicar of Ballymacarrett, 1930-38; Dean of Down and Rector of Downpatrick, Co. Down, 1938-45; Incumbent of Belfast and Dean of St Anne's Cathedral, 1945-56; Bishop of Connor, 1956-69. Sub-Prelate, OStJ, 1969. *Recreation:* golf. *Address:* 9 Mount Aboo Park, Finaghy, Belfast 10.   *[Died 3 April 1977.*

ELLIOTT, (Thomas) Anthony (Keith), CMG 1968; HM Diplomatic Service; HM Ambassador, Tel Aviv, since 1975; *b* Burford, Oxon, 27 May 1921; *s* of Sir Ivo Elliott, 2nd Bt, ICS, Oxford, and of Margery (*née* Carey); *m* 1951, Alethea, *d* of late Major Alistair B. H. Richardson, King's Dragoon Guards, Richmond, Surrey; one *s* three *d*. *Educ:* Dragon Sch., Oxford; Eton (King's Schol.); Balliol Coll., Oxford. MA Oxon 1946. Served War of 1939-45: King's Shropshire LI, 1941-46; Capt.; served with East African Forces in Ethiopia and Somaliland. Joined HM Foreign Service, 1947; Third Sec., Belgrade, 1949-52; First Sec., Foreign Office, 1953; Head of Chancery, Peking, 1957-59; Athens, 1960-61; Foreign Office, 1961-65; Political Adviser, Govt of Hong Kong, 1965-68; Counsellor, Washington, 1968, Minister and Head of Chancery, Washington, 1970-72; Ambassador in Helsinki, 1972-75, and Head of British delegn, Conference on Security and Co-operation in Europe, Geneva, 1973-74. *Recreations:* exploring towns and buildings; music; labour and social history. *Address:* c/o Foreign and Commonwealth Office, SW1; Church Cottage, Taynton, Burford, Oxon. *T:* Burford 2197. *Clubs:* Brooks's, MCC; Hong Kong.   *[Died 28 Aug. 1976.*

ELLIS, Sir (Bertram) Clough W.; *see* Williams-Ellis.

ELLIS, Sir Charles Drummond, Kt 1946; FRS 1929; BA, PhD; Scientific Adviser to: British American Tobacco Co. Ltd; Gas Council; Battelle Memorial Institute; Tobacco Research

Council; Governor, Harrow; *b* 11 Aug. 1895; *s* of A. C. Ellis; *m* 1925, Paula Warzcewska. *Educ:* Harrow; RMA Woolwich; Trinity Coll., Cambridge. Fellow and Lectr of Trinity Coll., Cambridge; Lectr in Dept of Physics in Univ. of Cambridge; Wheatstone Prof. of Physics, King's Coll., London, 1936-46; Scientific Adviser to Army Council, 1943-46; Mem. Advisory Council on Scientific Research and Technical Development to Ministry of Supply, 1943-46; Scientific Mem. of National Coal Board, 1946-55; Pres. British Coal Utilisation Research Association, 1946-55; Mem. Advisory Council to Ministry of Fuel and Power, 1947-55; Mem. of Court of Governors, Administrative Staff Coll.; Senior Scientific Adviser Civil Defence London Region, 1947-65; Mem. Gas Council's Research Advisory Cttee, 1955-. *Publications:* (with Sir Ernest Rutherford and James Chadwick) Radiations from Radioactive Substances, 1930; various papers on radioactivity and connected problems. *Address:* 1 Arlington Close, Pinkneys Green, Maidenhead, Berks SL6 5JT. *Club:* Athenæum.
[Died 10 Jan. 1980.

ELLIS, Charles Howard, CMG 1953; CBE 1946 (OBE 1919); TD 1953; retired from Foreign Office; *b* 13 Feb. 1895; *s* of William Edward Ellis, Exeter, Devon, and Sydney, Australia, and Lillian Mary Hobday; *m* 1st, 1933, Barbara Mary Burgess-Smith (marr. diss., 1947); one *s* one *d*; 2nd, 1954, Alexandra Wood (*née* Surtees). *Educ:* Melbourne Univ; Oxford Univ.; Sorbonne. Served European War, 1914-18; Middlesex Regt; France, Egypt, India, Persia, S Russia; Afghan War, 1919; Caucasus and Black Sea, 1919-20; Foreign Office and Consular posts in Turkey, Berlin, Far East and USA, 1921-39; War of 1939-45; Col on staff of missions in USA and Egypt and Far East. Foreign Office and posts in Far East, 1946-53; retired, 1953. US Legion of Merit, 1946. *Publications:* The Transcaspian Episode, 1963; The Expansion of Russia, 1965; The New Left in Britain, 1968; Soviet Imperialism, 1970; Mission Accomplished, 1973. *Recreations:* music, drama, travel. *Address:* The Hollies, Hempnall, Norwich, Norfolk. *Clubs:* Travellers', Royal Automobile.   *[Died 5 July 1975.*

ELLIS, Sir Clough W.; *see* Williams-Ellis, Sir B. C.

ELLIS, Rt. Rev. Edward; *b* 1899; *s* of A. Ellis. *Educ:* Ratcliffe Coll.; Ven. English Coll., Rome; Gregorian Univ., DD and PhD. Formerly Administrator at St Barnabas's Cathedral, Nottingham; Bishop of Nottingham, (RC), 1944-74. *Address:* Nazareth House, Old Lenton, Nottingham. *[Died 6 July 1979.*

ELLIS, Rev. Canon Henry; Canon Residentiary and Precentor of Liverpool Cathedral since 1962; Rural Dean of Toxteth, since 1966; *b* 1909; *s* of William and Maud Ellis, Abbeywood, Breadsall, near Derby; *m* 1934, Marjorie Thelma (*née* Dobie); one *s* three *d* (and one *s* decd). *Educ:* St John's Coll., Durham. LRAM 1928; MA 1930. Deacon 1932; Priest 1933. Curate of Holy Trinity, St Helens, 1932-34; Curate of Prescot, 1934-38; Vicar of St Catharine's, Wigan, 1938-47; Rector of Wavertree, 1947-57; Vicar of Prescot, 1957-62. Hon. Chaplain and Divinity Lecturer, St Edmund's Coll., Liverpool, 1953-61; Canon Diocesan, 1960-62. *Address:* The Cathedral, Liverpool L1 7AZ. *T:* 051-709 6271; 8 Fawley Road, Liverpool L18 9TF. *T:* 051-724 1604.   *[Died 4 Aug. 1972.*

ELLIS, Hon. Sir Kevin, KBE 1969; MLA; Speaker, Parliament of New South Wales, 1965-73; *b* 15 May 1908; *s* of J. P. Ellis, Liverpool, England; *m* 1941, Bettie, *d* of C. Maunsell; one *s* one *d*. *Educ:* Fort Street Boys' High Sch.; Univ. of Sydney. LLB Sydney, 1931, 1st class Hons, Univ. medal, 2 schols; BEc Sydney, 1937. Served War of 1939-45: Middle East and Medit.; Flt Lt, RAAF on attachment to RAF. Supreme Court of NSW, Solicitor, 1932-. MLA (Coogee), 1948-53, 1956-62, 1965-73. Director: Nat. Heart Foundation of Australia (NSW Div.) (also Hon. Sec.), 1958-71; Prince of Wales Hosp., 1961-; Prince Henry Hosp., 1962-; Eastern Suburbs Hosp., 1968-; Nat. Heart Foundn of Australia, Canberra, 1965-71; Medical Foundn of Univ. of NSW, 1965-; Unisearch Ltd, 1970-. Mem. Council, Univ. of NSW, 1965-; Dep. Chancellor, 1970-; Past Fellow, Senate of Univ. of Sydney. *Recreations:* bowls, boating, and deep sea fishing. *Address:* 4 Wolseley Crescent, Point Piper, NSW 2027, Australia. *T:* 36.4076 (Sydney). *Clubs:* American National, Automobile (Sydney).   *[Died 22 Nov. 1975.*

ELLIS, Very Rev. Vorley Spencer; Dean of St Asaph, 1938-57; late Hon. Canon, Liverpool; *b* 1882; *s* of Rev. R. Ellis, LLD, Llangollen. *Educ:* Ruthin Grammar Sch.; Oxford. Asst Master at Worksop; Curate of Chesterfield; Vicar of Christ Church, Liverpool; of St Stephen's, Liverpool; of St Paul's, Stanley, 1937-38. *Recreation:* motoring. *Address:* Rectory Lane, Hawarden, Chester.   *[Died 2 Aug. 1977.*

ELLIS-REES, Sir Hugh, KCMG 1953 (CMG 1943); CB 1951; *b* 19 April 1900; *s* of Hugh Rees, Chelsea; *m* Eileen Frances Anne, *d* of Reginald Clench, Highgate; one *s*. *Educ:* Tollington Sch.; London Univ. Served with RAF, 1918-19; Inland Revenue, 1919-38; Asst Controller, Clearing Office, 1938-39; HM Treasury, 1940-48; Asst Sec., 1943; Under-Sec., 1948; Financial Adviser to British Embassy, Madrid, 1940-44; Mem. of UK Delegation to OEEC, with rank of Minister, 1948; Vice-Chm., Managing Bd of European Payments Union, 1950-51; Permanent Delegate, 1952, rank of Ambassador, 1954-60; Official Chm. of OEEC, 1952-60, retired. Head of World Bank Mission to Spain, 1961-62: Chm., Egyptian Grants Cttee and Egyptian Loans Advisory Bd, 1963-71; Administrator, Catholic Fund for Overseas Develt, 1963-69; Chm., Anglo-Spanish Soc., 1967-73. Dir, Tharsis Sulphur & Copper Co., 1963-. Grand Cross, Isabel la Catolica, 1967. *Address:* 14 St George's Court, Gloucester Road, SW7. *Clubs:* Carlton, Hurlingham.
[Died 17 July 1974.

ELLISON, Ven. Charles Ottley; Archdeacon of Leeds, 1950-69, Emeritus since 1969; Honorary Canon of Ripon Cathedral, 1953-62; *b* 8 Feb. 1898; *s* of late S. Ellison, Leeds; *m* 1926, Lavinia (*d* 1970), *d* of late J. E. MacGregor, Flers-Breucq, Nord, France; one *d*. *Educ:* Wrekin Coll.; University of Leeds (BSc); Ripon Hall, Oxford. Curate of St Chad, Far Headingley, Leeds, 1932-37; Vicar of Kippax, 1937-46; Surrogate, 1942-75; Rural Dean of Whitkirk, 1944-46; Vicar of Wetherby, 1946-55; Vicar of St John's, Briggate, Leeds, 1955-65. Pres., Yorks Assoc. of Change-Ringers, 1947-66; Chm., C of E Council for Social Aid, 1967-69; Mem., C of E Pensions Board, 1962-70. *Recreations:* numismatics, Sherlock Holmes. *Address:* 1 Burton Dene, Burton Crescent, Leeds LS6 4DN. *T:* Leeds 752191. *Club:* Leeds (Leeds).
[Died 12 Dec. 1978.

ELLISON, Prof. William, BSc, PhD (Dunelm); JP; Professor of Agriculture, University College of Wales, Aberystwyth, since 1946; Vice-Principal of the College, 1966-68; *b* 28 June 1911; *o s* of late William Ellison, Eden Hall, Horden, Co. Durham; *m* 1937, Florence Elizabeth, *yr d* of late J. W. Robinson; two *d*. *Educ:* St Cuthbert's Gram. Sch.; King's Coll., Newcastle upon Tyne, Durham Univ. Asst Lectr, Agricultural Botany, UCW Aberystwyth, 1934. Seconded as Chief Technical Adviser to Montgomeryshire WAEC, 1940-46. Hill Farming Research Organization, 1958-66. Member: UGC Agric. Cttee, 1965-75; NERC Land Use Research Cttee. Pres., Section M, Brit. Assoc. for Advancement of Science, 1966. JP County of Cardigan, 1957. *Publications:* Marginal Land in Britain, 1953; numerous contribs to scientific and agric. jls, on land reclamation, land use, grassland and crop production. *Recreations:* tennis, cricket. *Address:* Institute of Rural Science, Penglais, Dyfed. *T:* 3111. *Club:* Farmers'.
[Died 11 April 1978.

ELMHIRST, Leonard Knight, MA Cantab; BSc Cornell; Chairman, Dartington Hall Trust, since 1931; *b* 6 June 1893; 2nd *s* of Rev. William Heaton Elmhirst, BA Cantab and Mary Knight; *m* 1st, 1925, Dorothy Whitney Straight (*d* 1968); one *s* one *d*; 2nd, 1972, Dr Susanna Isaacs, FRCP, FRCPsych. *Educ:* Repton Sch.; Trinity Coll., Cambridge; New York State Coll. of Agriculture; Cornell Univ. Dir, Inst. of Rural Reconstruction Visva Bharati, Bolpur, Bengal, India, 1921-24; purchased Dartington Hall for the founding of experiment in Rural Industry, Research and Education, 1925; joint British-American agricultural mission to Middle East, 1942; Pres., Internat. Conf. of Agricultural Economists, 1930-61; Founder Pres., Internat. Assoc. of Agricultural Economists; Chm., Political and Economic Planning (PEP), 1939-53; Agricultural Adviser Govt of Bengal, 1944-45; Devon CC, 1937-52; Mem., Hobhouse Cttee on National Parks, 1945-47; Vice-Chm., Cttee on Footpaths and Access. Pres. Royal Forestry Soc. of England and Wales, 1946-48; Pres., Agricultural Economics Soc., 1949; a Development Comr, 1949-65; Council Mem., Festival of Britain, 1951; Mem., Indian Govt Cttee on Higher Education for Rural Areas, 1954-55; Mem. Council, Exeter Univ., 1955-71. Hon. Dr Pol Science, Freiburg Univ.; Hon. DLitt: Visva Bharati, 1960; Exeter, 1972; Hon. DCL: Durham, 1962; Oxford, 1970. *Publications:* Robbery of the Soil, 1922; Rural Reconstruction, 1923; The Application of Economic Research to a Village in Bengal, 1930; Trip to Russia, 1933; Social Trends in Rural Areas, 1938; Collected Notes on Agricultural Problems in Bengal, 1945; Rabindranath Tagore and Sriniketan, 1958; Rabindranath Tagore, Pioneer in Education, 1961. *Recreation:* care of trees. *Address:* Dartington Hall, Totnes, S Devon.
[Died 16 April 1974.

ELPHICK, Ronald, OBE 1970; Counsellor (Agriculture and Food), British High Commission, Canberra, since 1973; *b* 24 Sept. 1918; *s* of Harry Elphick and Margaret (*née* Hirst); *m* 1948, Lilian Evans; three *s*. *Educ:* Roundhay Sch., Leeds; London Sch. of Econs. Served War of 1939-46, Queen's Royal Regt and RA. Exchequer and Audit Dept, 1937; Festival of Britain, 1949; MAFF, 1952; 1st Sec. (Agric. and Food), British High Commn, Canberra, 1964. *Publications:* various articles on agriculture and trade. *Recreations:* cricket, book collecting, archaeology. *Address:* c/o Foreign and Commonwealth Office, SW1A 2AL. *Club:* Refugees (Canberra). *[Died 13 June 1977.*

ELPHINSTONE, 17th Lord *cr* 1509; **John Alexander Elphinstone,** DL; Baron Elphinstone (UK), 1885; *b* 22 March 1914; *e s* of 16th Baron Elphinstone, KT and Lady Mary Bowes Lyon, DCVO (*d* 1961), *d* of 14th Earl of Strathmore, KG, KT, GCVO; *S* father, 1955. *Educ:* Eton; Christ Church, Oxford. Served War of 1939-45, Black Watch. Captain Queen's Body Guard for Scotland (Royal Company of Archers). DL Angus, 1955. Former Dir, Bank of Scotland; Dir, Scottish Provident Institution. President: Scottish Assoc. Boys' Clubs; Royal Zoological Society, Scotland; Hon. Pres., Scottish Football Assoc. Chm. of Council, Scottish Branch, BRCS. *Heir:* nephew James Alexander Elphinstone [*b* 22 April 1953; *s* of late Rev. the Hon. Andrew Charles Victor Elphinstone and of Hon. Mrs Andrew Elphinstone, CVO]. *Address:* Drumklibo, Meigle, Perthshire. *T:* Meigle 216; Glenmazeran, Tomatin, Inverness-shire.
[Died 15 Nov. 1975.

ELPHINSTONE, Sir Howard (Graham), 4th Bt *cr* 1816; *b* 28 Dec. 1898; *o s* of Graham Warburton Elphinstone, ICS, 2nd *s* of 3rd Bt and Susan Sophy, *d* of late Henry C. R. Harley, Madanapalle, India (she *m* 2nd, George Middleton); *S* grandfather, 1917; *m* 1924, Alice Mary Emerton, *er d* of P. J. Emerton Brown; two *d*. *Educ:* Sedbergh Sch. Enlisted army, 1917-20; appointed Administrative Service, Kenya Colony, 1921. *Heir: cousin* Maurice Douglas Warburton Elphinstone, TD [*b* 13 April 1909; *s* of Rev. Maurice Curteis Elphinstone; *m* 1943, Helen Barbara, *d* of late George Ramsay Main; one *s* one *d*]. *Address:* Los Colones, La Jara, Sanlucar de Barrameda, Cadiz, Spain.
[Died 18 May 1975.

ELPHINSTONE, Rev. Kenneth John Tristram, QC 1979; Vicar-General of Province of York, since 1972; Dean of the Arches Court of Canterbury and Auditor of the Chancery Court of York, since 1977; Member of York Convocation and General Synod, since 1973; *b* 29 Nov. 1911; 3rd *s* of late Canon M. C. Elphinstone and Mrs C. G. Elphinstone; *m* 1938, Felicity, 4th *d* of late Sir Gerald Hurst, QC; one *d* (one *s* decd). *Educ:* Loretto; Jesus Coll., Cambridge (MA). Served War of 1939-45, Rifle Bde (Temp. Captain; POW). Called to Bar, Inner Temple, 1934; Mem., Lincoln's Inn, 1938, Bencher 1977; Mem. Gen. Council of the Bar, 1956-60. Chancellor: Diocese of Chester, 1950-77; Hereford, 1953-77; York, 1970-77. Ordained deacon and priest, 1964; Vicar of South Stoke, Somerset, 1966-74. Mem. Governing Body, SPCK, 1972-80. *Publications:* (with K. M. Macmorran) Handbook for Churchwardens and Parochial Church Councillors, new edn, 1979; Handbook of Parish Property, 1973. *Address:* 7 Egremont Street, Ely, Cambs. *T:* Ely 4476. *Club:* Athenæum.
[Died 16 May 1980.

ELTON, 1st Baron *cr* 1934, of Headington; **Godfrey Elton;** *b* 29 March 1892; *e s* of late Edward Fiennes Elton, Ovington Park, Hants, and Burleigh Court, Glos; *m* 1921, Dedi, *d* of Gustav Hartmann, Oslo, Norway; one *s* two *d*. *Educ:* Rugby Sch. (Head of Sch., 1910-11); Balliol Coll., Oxford. First Class Classical Mods, 1913. 2nd Lieut 4th Hants Regt, Sept. 1914; Captain 1918; served in Mesopotamia, Siege of Kut-el-Amara, 1915-16 (slightly wounded); Prisoner of war in Asiatic Turkey, 1916-18; Fellow of Queen's Coll., Oxford, and Lecturer in Modern History, 1919-39; Dean, 1921-23; Tutor, 1927-34; Supernumerary Fellow, 1939-. Contested (Lab) Thornbury Div. of Glos, 1924, 1929; resigned prospective candidature and was expelled from Labour Party as supporter of Mr MacDonald, Sept. 1931; Hon. Political Sec., National Labour Cttee, 1932; Hon. Ed. the News-Letter, 1932-38; Mem., Ullswater Cttee on the future of Broadcasting, 1935; Chm., Executive Cttee, Road Accidents Emergency Council, 1936-41; Chm., Commonwealth Youth Sunday Cttee, 1941-62; Pres., Metropolitan Assoc. of Building Socs, 1943-61; Mem., Archbishops' Commn on Evangelism, 1944; Gen. Sec., Rhodes Trust, 1939-59; Pres., Christian Service Union, 1941-63; Mem. of Royal Commission for Exhibition of 1851, 1943-64. Dir, Cape Asbestos Group, 1950-65; has done much broadcasting, "It occurs to me", etc. Is Independent in politics. *Publications:* Schoolboys and Exiles (verse), 1920; The Revolutionary Idea in France, 1789-1878, 1923; Years of Peace (verse), 1925; The Testament of Dominic Burleigh, 1926; Against the Sun, 1928; The Stranger, 1930; England Arise! a study of the pioneering days of the Labour Party, 1931; Towards the New Labour Party, 1932; Among Others, 1938; Life of James Ramsay MacDonald, Vol. I 1866-1919, 1939; It Occurs to Me, 1939; Notebook in Wartime, 1941; Saint George or the Dragon, 1942; Imperial Commonwealth,

1945; Such is the Kingdom, 1947; The Two Villages, 1949; General Gordon, 1954; Edward King and our times, 1958; General Gordon's Khartoum Journal (ed), 1961; Simon Peter, a study of discipleship, 1965; The Unarmed Invasion, 1965; contributor to DNB and many newspapers and journals. *Heir: s* Hon. Rodney Elton [*b* 2 March 1930; *m* 1958, Anne Frances, *d* of Brig. R. A. G. Tilney, CBE, DSO, TD; one *s* three *d. Educ:* Eton; New Coll., Oxford]. *Address:* The Dower House, Sutton Bonington, near Loughborough, Leics. *T:* Kegworth 2809. *Club:* Athenæum.   *[Died 18 April 1973.*

ELTON, Sir Arthur Hallam Rice, 10th Bt *cr* 1717; Chairman: Clevedon Printing Co. Ltd; Film Centre (International) Ltd; Radio Avonside Ltd, since 1972; Publisher, North Somerset Mercury; Director, Canadian Film Institute; *b* 10 Feb. 1906; *er s* of Sir Ambrose Elton, 9th Bt, and Dorothy Wynne (*d* 1957), *o d* of Arthur Wiggin, Oddington Estate, Ceylon; *S* father, 1951; *m* 1948, Margaret Ann Bjornson; one *s* two *d. Educ:* Marlborough Coll.; Jesus Coll., Cambridge. Joined script dept, Gainsborough Pictures Ltd, 1927, rep. company in Germany, 1929; joined Empire Marketing Bd Film Unit, 1931, and transferred to GPO Film Unit. With John Grierson and others helped to found theory and practice of documentary film and founded Film Centre Ltd, 1938; Supervisor of Films, MOI, 1941-45; Founder Pres., Scientific Film Assoc., 1943-46, 1953-56 (Chm., 1963-67); Film Adviser: Danish Govt, 1945-46; CCG, 1947-48. Governor, British Film Institute, 1949-50. Member: Council Nat. Film Archive, 1956; Assoc. of Cine and Television Technicians, 1928-; Experimental Production Cttee of British Film Inst., 1957-; joined Shell Internat. Petroleum Co. 1957, in charge of films, television, until 1960; Gen. Manager Publicity, Associated Electrical Industries Ltd, 1961-63; Film Adviser, Shell Internat. Petroleum Co., 1963-. Chairman: Film Centre (International) Ltd; Centre for Study of the History of Technology, Bath Univ.; British Industrial and Scientific Film Assoc., 1967-69; President: Friends of Nat. Film Archive, 1962-66; Brit. Nat. Film Catalogue, 1964-67; Internat. Scientific Film Assoc., 1968-71; Somerset Archaeological Soc., 1963; Brunel Soc., 1971-. Member: BBC Adv. Council, 1966-68; Working Party on Preservation of Technological Material, 1970. *Publications:* (with Robert Fairthorne) Why Aeroplanes Fly, 1936; How Motorcars Run, 1939; British Railways, 1946; (with Peter Brinson) The Film Industry in Six European Countries, UNESCO, 1950; The Film as Source Material for History, Aslib. Proc. Vol. VII No. 4, 1955; Gas for Light and Heat, A History of Technology Vol. IV, 1958; Editor, new enl. edn of Klingender, Art and the Industrial Revolution, 1968. *Recreation:* history of technology and industrial archæology. *Heir: s* Charles Abraham Grierson Elton, *b* 23 May 1953. *Address:* Clevedon Court, Som. *T:* Clevedon 2768. *Club:* Athenæum.   *[Died 1 Jan. 1973.*

ELTON-BARRATT, Major Stanley George Reeves; late 16/5th Lancers (R of O); Director of Barratt & Co., Ltd, London, 1923-67; *b* 10 Feb. 1900; *o surv. s* of late Sir Albert Barratt; granted Royal Licence and authority to use additional surname of Elton, 1970; *m* 1926, Mary Katherine Gloria, *e d* and *co-heir* of late Brig.-Gen. F. A. G. Y. Elton, RA; two *s* one *d. Educ:* Highgate. Served European War, 1918-19, Lieut 1st Res. Regt of Cavalry; attached Inns of Court Cav., 1924-25; Transfd 16/5 Lancers (R of O), 1935; re-employed, 1939, Remount Service, Capt.; served on Staff with Special Forces, 1940-44, Major 1942, retd 1945. Joint Master, Romney Marsh Hounds, 1929-30; Master or Jt-Master Old Berkeley Foxhounds, 1931-44; Master, Old Berkeley (East) Foxhounds, 1944-48; Jt Master, Coollattin Foxhounds, 1950-52. CC Herts, 1933-46; formerly Lord of the Manor of Loddington, Northants. OStJ 1931; Gold Staff Officer at Coronations, 1937 and 1953. *Recreation:* fox hunting. *Address:* Blackwell Hall, Chesham, Bucks. *T:* Little Chalfont 3483. *Clubs:* Special Forces, Royal Automobile. *[Died 28 July 1973.*

ELVEY, Lewis Edgar, CMG 1967; company director; *b* 18 Oct. 1908; *s* of Robert Montgomery Elvey and Kate (*née* Smith); *m* 1938, Mary, *d* of Thomas Regan and Mary (*née* Kilmartin); one *s* one *d. Educ:* Sch. of Mines, Western Australia. Mining Engineer. Chairman: Vickers Hadwa Pty Ltd (formerly Hadfields (WA) 1934 Ltd), 1966-; North Kalgurli Mines ltd, 1966-; Westralian Sands Ltd, 1967-; Director: Great Boulder Mines Ltd, 1965- (Gen. Man., 1951-66); The Griffin Coal Mining Co. Ltd, 1964-. President: Chamber of Mines WA, 1960-67; Australasian Inst. of Mining and Metallurgy, 1964. *Recreation:* golf. *Address:* 38 Pearse Street, Cottesloe, WA 6011, Australia. *T:* 3-1039. *Club:* Hannans (Kalgoorlie, WA).   *[Died 10 March 1974.*

ELWES, Simon (Edmund Vincent Paul), RA 1967 (ARA 1956); RP 1933; portrait painter and painter of flowers and landscapes; *b* 29 June 1902; *s* of late Gervase Elwes, DL, JP, Knight of Malta, Billing Hall, Northampton, and Roxby, Lincs and late Lady Winefride Feilding, 3rd *d* of Rudolph, 8th Earl of Denbigh and Desmond; *m* 1926, Hon. Gloria Rodd, 2nd *d* of 1st Lord Rennell of Rodd, PC, GCB, GCMG, GCVO; three *s. Educ:* The Oratory. Studied at the Slade Sch., 1919 and in Paris until 1926; Vice-Pres. Royal Society of Portrait Painters, 1953-. Created Knight of Malta, 1929. Served war of 1939-45, 10th Royal Hussars; Lt-Col 1944 (Public Relations). *Recreation:* painting landscape. *Address:* Old Place, Amberley, West Sussex. *Clubs:* White's, Chelsea Arts.   *[Died 6 Aug. 1975.*

ELY, Paul; Général d'Armée; Président du Comité d'Orientation et de Perfectionnement du Haut Enseignement de Défense; Grand Croix, Légion d'Honneur; Médaille Militaire; Croix de Guerre (1914-18, 3 citations), Croix de Guerre (1939-45, 2 citations), France; Croix de Guerre TOE (1 citation Indochine); *b* 17 Dec. 1897; *m* Graziella Ortoli. *Educ:* Lycée de Brest; Ecole Spéciale Militaire de Saint-Cyr; Ecole Supérieure de Guerre. Sous-Lt, 1918; CO 10th Bn de Chasseurs, 1941-42; Rep. of Allied High Command with Resistance, 1944; Gén. de Bde, 1945; Dir of Inf., 1945; Gén. de Div., 1946; Mil. Dir, Min. of Nat. Defence, 1946; Cmdr 7th Mil. Region, 1947; Chief of Staff to Inspector Gen. of Armed Forces, 1948; Général de Corps d'Armée, 1949; French Rep., to Western Union, 1948-49, and to Standing Group, NATO, 1950-53; Général d'Armée, 1953; Général Chef d'Etat Major Général des Forces Armées, 1953-54; C-in-C and Gen. Comr in Indo-China 1954-55; Chef d'Etat-Major Général des Forces Armées, 1956-58; Chef d'Etat-Major Général de la Défense Nationale, 1959-61. Hon. GBE (UK) and other foreign Grand Crosses etc., of Orders. *Publications:* L'Armée dans la Nation, 1961; L'Indochine dans la Tourmente, 1964; Suez: le 13 mai, 1969. *Address:* 4 rue Puvis de Chavannes, Paris.   *[Died 16 Jan. 1975.*

EMBERTON, John James, CMG 1944; MC 1918; *b* 26 Feb. 1893; *m* 1933, Sybil Challoner (*d* 1974), (author of Shrub Gardening for Flower Arrangement, 1965, Garden Foliage for Flower Arrangement, 1968, A Year in the Shrub Garden, 1972), *d* of late Dr David Ewart, OBE, Chichester; two *s. Educ:* Newcastle-under-Lyme. Hon. Artillery Co. and Royal Artillery, 1914-19 (MC); Nigeria Administrative Service, 1920-46 (retired); late Senior Resident, Plateau Province, Nigeria. Subsequently employed in CO and in CCG. *Recreations:* golf, gardening. *Address:* Little Close, Linkside East, Hindhead, Surrey. *T:* Hindhead 5701.   *[Died 10 Jan. 1976.*

EMBRY, Air Chief Marshal Sir Basil Edward, GCB 1956 (KCB 1953; CB 1945); KBE 1945; DSO 1938; DFC 1945; AFC 1926; retired as Commander, Allied Air Forces, Central Europe, North Atlantic Treaty Organisation, 1956; *b* 28 Feb. 1902; *s* of late James Embry, MA Cantab; *m* 1928, Hope, *d* of late Captain C. S. Elliot, RN; three *s* one *d. Educ:* Bromsgrove Sch. First Commission, 1921; served Iraq, 1922-27 (AFC) (ops in Kurdistan and Southern Desert); served Central Flying Sch. (A1 flying instructor), 1929-32; RAF Staff Coll.; psc 1933; India, 1934-39; Mohmand Operations, 1935 (despatches); Waziristan, 1937-38 (DSO); War of 1939-45 (despatches thrice, three Bars to DSO, CB, DFC, KBE); served in Bomber and Fighter Commands, Western Desert and 2nd TAF; Comd of No 2 Group Ops over Norway, NW Europe, Great Britain, 1939-41; Western Desert, 1941-42; NW Europe, 1943-45. ADC to the King, 1941-43; Asst Chief of Air Staff (Training), Air Ministry, 1945-48; Air Officer Commanding-in-Chief, Fighter Command, 1949-53. Chm., Rural Traders Co-operative of WA; Dep. Chm., Arabian/Australian Marketing Co. Chm., Cancer Res. Foundn of WA. Pres., RAF Escaping Soc. Knight Commander, 1st Class, Order of Dannebrog; Grand Officer Order of Orange Nassau, with swords; Comdr of Legion of Honour; Croix de Guerre. Hon. Freedom of Borough and Cinque Port of Dover; Freeman City of London; Hon. Liveryman, Worshipful Company of Glass-Sellers. Former Gen. Pres., Farmers Union of W Australia. *Publication:* Mission Completed, 1957. *Recreations:* farming, shooting, fishing. *Address:* Ardua, Cape Riche, via Albany, WA 6330, Australia. *T:* Mettler 473026.   *[Died 8 Dec. 1977.*

EMDEN, Alfred Brotherston, MA; Hon. DLitt; FBA 1959; FSA; Principal of St Edmund Hall, Oxford, 1929-51; Hon. Fellow of Lincoln College and St Edmund Hall; *b* 22 Oct. 1888; *e s* of His Honour Judge Alfred Emden. *Educ:* King's Sch., Canterbury; Lincoln Coll., Oxford (Scholar); Inner Temple. Head of Edghill House, Sydenham, 1913-15; AB (RNVR), 1915-19, serving in HMS Parker; Tutor and Bursar, St Edmund Hall, 1919; Vice-Principal, 1920; Member of the Hebdomadal Council, 1935-47; Lieut-Commander RNVR (Sp.), 1942-44. Corr. Fellow, Mediaeval Academy of America. Hon. LittD Cambridge. *Publications:* An Oxford Hall in Medieval Times, 1927; Joint Editor (with Prof. Sir F. M. Powicke) of Rashdall's Medieval

Universities, 1936; Biographical Register of the University of Oxford to AD 1500, in 3 vols, 1957-59; Biographical Register of the University of Cambridge to 1500, 1963; A Survey of Dominicans in England, 1967; Donors of Books to St Augustine's Abbey, Canterbury, 1968; Biographical Register of the University of Oxford 1501-1540, 1974; Medieval Decorated Tiles in Dorset, 1977. *Address:* Dunstan Cottage, Old Headington, Oxford.   *[Died 8 Jan.* 1979.

EMERY, Douglas, CB 1967; Under-Secretary, Ministry of Health, 1960-67, retired; *b* 4 Nov. 1915; *s* of late Frederick and Mary Emery; *m* 1945, Margaret Wickham Pennington; one *s* two *d. Educ:* Hull Grammar Sch.; Christ's Coll., Cambridge. 1st Class Hons History Tripos, 1936; 1st Class Hons Modern and Medieval Langs Tripos, 1937. Entered Ministry of Health as Asst Principal, 1938; Principal, 1946; Asst Secretary, 1953. *Recreation:* entering competitions. *Address:* La Conchée, Perelle, St Saviour's, Guernsey. *T:* Guernsey 64582.
[Died 24 Nov. 1974.

EMERY, Prof. Walter Bryan, CBE 1969 (MBE 1943); MA Liverpool 1939; DLitt London 1959; FBA 1959; FSA 1941; Edwards Professor of Egyptology, University of London (University College), 1951-70; Field Director of the Egypt Exploration Society since 1952; *b* 2 July 1903; *s* of Walter Thomas Emery and Beatrice Mary Benbow; *m* 1928, Mary Cowhey; no *c. Educ:* St Francis Xavier's Coll., Liverpool. Student Institute of Archæology, University of Liverpool, 1921-23; Asst on Egypt Exploration Society's expedition to Tell-el-Amarna, 1923-24; Director of Mond Excavations of University of Liverpool at Luxor and Armant, 1924-28; Egyptian Govt Service of Antiquities: Director Archæological Survey of Nubia, 1929-35; Director Excavation at North Sakkara, 1935-39. British Army service retiring with hon. rank of Lt-Col, 1939-46. HBM's Embassy, Cairo: Attaché, 1947-50; First Secretary, 1950-51. Norton Lecturer of Archæological Institute of America, 1954-55. Member: German Archæological Institute; L'Institut d'Egypte. *Publications:* Excavations and Survey between Wadi-es-Sebua and Adindan (with L. P. Kirwan), 1937; The Royal Tombs of Ballana and Qustol, 1938; The Tomb of Hemaka, 1939; Hor-Aha, 1940; Nubian Treasure, 1949; Great Tombs of the First Dynasty, Vol. I, 1949, Vol. II, 1954, Vol. III, 1958; Archaic Egypt, 1961; De Buck Memorial Lecture: A Funerary Repast in an Egyptian Tomb of the Archaic Period, 1962; Egypt in Nubia, 1965. *Address:* 1 Alleyn Road, West Dulwich, SE21; *T:* 01-670 4770. *Clubs:* Athenæum; Turf (Cairo).   *[Died 11 March* 1971.

EMLYN WILLIAMS, Arthur; *see* Williams.

EMMERSON, Mrs. C. L.; *see* Peto, G. E.

EMMET OF AMBERLEY, Baroness *cr* 1964 (Life Peer); **Evelyn Violet Elizabeth Emmet,** JP; DL; *b* Cairo, 18 March 1899; *er d* of 1st Baron Rennell of Rodd, PC, GCB, GCMG, GCVO (*d* 1941), and Lilias Guthrie (*d* 1951); *m* 1923, T. A. Emmet, late Royal Navy (*d* 1934), Amberley Castle, Sussex; two *s* two *d. Educ:* St Margaret's Sch., Bushey, and abroad; Lady Margaret Hall, Oxford (MA). JP Sussex, 1936. Member LCC, 1925-34 (Chairman several cttees); Member W Sussex CC, 1946-67; Alderman, 1952-66 (Chairman numerous cttees). Co. Organiser, WVS, 1938-45. Chairman: Conservative Women's National Advisory Cttee, 1951-54; Nat. Union of Conservatives, 1955-56; Lord Chancellor's Legal Aid Advisory Cttee, 1966-72. Full British Delegate to Assembly of United Nations in New York, 1952, and 1953. MP (C) East Grinstead Division East Sussex, 1955-64. A Dep. Speaker and a Dep. Chm. of Cttees, House of Lords, 1968-77; Mem., Select Cttee of the House of Lords EEC Cttee, 1974-77. DL West Sussex, 1977. *Recreation:* gardening. *Address:* Amberley Castle, Amberley, West Sussex. *T:* Bury (Sussex) 319; 3 Grosvenor Cottages, Eaton Terrace, SW1. *T:* 01-730 4627.   *[Died 10 Oct.* 1980.

EMMS, Mrs S. A. G.; *see* Charques, Dorothy.

EMSLIE, Prof. John William; Professor Emeritus of Veterinary Pathology, University of Glasgow; *b* 28 March 1901; *s* of John R. Emslie and Isabella Cassie; *m* 1932, Margaret Noble, MA, Aberdeen, *d* of Andrew Noble and Margaret Trail; one *s. Educ:* Robert Gordon's Coll., Aberdeen; University of Aberdeen; Royal Dick Veterinary Coll., Edinburgh. Assistant, Dept of Pathology, Royal Dick Veterinary Coll., Edinburgh, 1926-28; Head, Dept of Pathology, Glasgow Veterinary Coll., 1929-49; Prof. of Veterinary Pathology, Univ. of Glasgow, 1951-68. *Publications:* papers in professional journals. *Recreations:* gardening, wood-work. *Address:* 19 Lady Margaret Drive, Troon, Ayrshire. *T:* Troon 2346.   *[Died 1 June* 1973.

EMSLIE, Rosalie, RBA; artist (painter); *b* Jan. 1891; *d* of A. E. Emslie, RWS, and Rosalie M. Emslie, RMS; unmarried; (one adopted *s* decd). *Educ:* privately. Studied at Royal Academy Schools, London, Paris, Florence and Madrid. Exhibitor at RA, RBA, NEAC, London Group, etc.; also Paris Salon, Venice International, Carnegie Institute (Pittsburgh). Hon. Mention, Pittsburgh, 1925. Pictures at Buffalo Art Gallery, USA, Toronto Art Gallery, and in private collections. *Recreations:* reading and travel. *Address:* 2 Yorke Gardens, Reigate, Surrey.
[Died 28 Sept. 1977.

ENFIELD, Sir Ralph Roscoe, Kt 1947; CB 1944; MA; BSc; *b* 22 Dec. 1885; *s* of Ernest William Enfield, The Grove, Burton Joyce, Notts; *m* 1921, Doris Edith (*d* 1951), *d* of Edmund Hussey; one *s* one *d. Educ:* Bedales; High Sch., Nottingham; Christ Church, Oxford (scholar, exhibitioner, and Dixon Research Scholar). Entered Civil Service, 1913; Board of Trade, 1913-14; Ministry of Munitions, 1914-18; Ministry of Agriculture and Fisheries, 1919-52; Asst Secretary, 1936; UK Representative International Institute of Agriculture, 1934-38; Principal Asst Secretary, 1942; Chief Economic Adviser to Ministry of Agriculture and Fisheries, 1945-52; UK representative on Council of FAO of the UN, 1947-52. Pres., Agricultural Economic Soc., 1935-36. *Publications:* The Agricultural Crisis, 1920-23, 1924; various reports, articles, etc. *Address:* 12 Dunstan Road, NW11. *T:* 01-455 1805. *Club:* Reform.   *[Died 15 Feb.* 1973.

ENGELHARD, Charles William; Chairman: Engelhard Minerals & Chemicals Corporation; Engelhard Hanovia Incorporated; American-South African Investment Company Ltd; SA Forest Investment Ltd; Executive Committee, Eurofund Incorporated; Director of other companies; Commissioner, Port of New York Authority; *b* NY City, 15 Feb. 1917; *s* of late Charles Engelhard; *m* Jane Reis-Brian; five *d. Educ:* St Paul's Sch., NH; Princeton Univ. (BA). Served with US Army Air Corps, 1941-45; Pte; bomber pilot; Captain. Personal rep. of President at: Independence Day Ceremonies, Gabon, 1962; Coronation of Pope Paul VI and 1st Anniversary celebration of Algerian independence, 1963; Independence Day Ceremonies (and Head of US Delegation), Zambia, 1964; Member, Community Relations Service, 1964; Member, President's Cttee to study East West Trade, 1965. Trustee: American Heritage Foundation; American Museum of Immigration (Vice-Pres.); Bernardsville Library Assoc.; Cttee for Economic Development; Foxcroft Sch.; John F. Kennedy Memorial Library; Seton Hall Univ.; Atlantic Council of US Inc.; Foreign Policy Assoc.; NJ State Chamber of Commerce; NY Zoological Society; US Cttee for Refugees; World Wildlife Fund; Member: Citizens Cttee for Higher Education in NJ; Democratic State Cttee of NJ; Eleanor Roosevelt Mem. Foundation; Foundation for Advance of Graduate Study in Engineering, Newark; Newcomen Society in N America; Pres., Newark Mus.; Vice-Pres., Greater Newark Development Council; NJ Industrialist of Year, 1965; Brotherhood Award NJ Region, Nat. Conference of Christians and Jews, 1966. *Address:* (business) Engelhard Minerals & Chemicals Corporation, Engelhard Industries Div., 113 Astor Street, Newark, NJ 07114, USA; (home) Cragwood, Far Hills, NJ, USA. *Clubs:* Racquet and Tennis (NY); Ivy (Princeton); Monmouth Jockey (NJ); Rand (Johannesburg); Travellers' (Paris); Tarratine (Dark Harbor, Maine). *[Died 2 March* 1971.

ENGELMANN, Franklin; broadcaster (chairman and interviewer); *b* 4 March 1908; *s* of Friederich Engelmann and Ida Josephine Cox; *m* 1945, Erica Tyne; two *d. Educ:* Stationers' Company's Sch., Hornsey. Stock Exchange, 1925-36. Broadcasting Commentator for National Broadcasting Company of America, 1936-39; Staff Announcer, BBC, 1940-42. Served War: RE (Captain), 1942-46; service in Britain and NW Europe (American Bronze Star). Rejoined BBC, as Sen. Announcer and Asst Controller, Light Programme, 1946; resigned, 1954, to freelance. Programmes: Other Man's Farm; Ask Me Another; Down Your Way; Brain of Britain; Gardeners' Question Time. Variety Club Award of Radio Personality of the Year, 1961; Baird Silver Medal for Outstanding Contribution to TV, 1964. *Publications:* Other Man's Farm, 1962; British Scene, 1966. *Recreations:* travelling or sitting still. *Address:* 3 Elizabeth Court, 170 Hempstead Road, Watford WD1 3LR. *T:* Watford 43392.
[Died 2 March 1972.

ENGLAND, (Eric Cecil) Gordon; Business Consultant; Chairman, Lots Farm Ltd; *b* 5 April 1891; *s* of George England and Amy Attlee; *m* 1913, Doris Isabel Troughton; one *s* two *d. Educ:* New Coll., Eastbourne; Framlingham Coll., Suffolk. Trained as mechanical engineer Great Northern Railway works, Doncaster. Entered aviation in 1909. Holds pilot's certificate 68, became test pilot and aircraft designer. Manager of F. Sage &

Co., Aircraft Manufacturing Works, 1916-18; engaged in Automobile Industry, 1919-30. Became successful racing motorist. Designer of Gordon England motor-car body. Chairman and Managing Director, Gordon England, Ltd; President, Motor Agents Association, 1929; joined Vacuum Oil Co. Ltd, 1930-35, and became a Director; Managing Director, General Aircraft Ltd, 1935-42; Deputy Chairman, Aero Engines Ltd, 1936-43; Member of Gorell Cttee on Civil Aviation, 1932-33; Chairman, Engineering Industries Association, 1940-44; General Manager, Eugene Ltd, 1945-50. Life Member Council British Automobile Racing Club; Founder Member of Railway Conversion League. Member, Economic Research Council. FIMI, FRAeS, MIProdE. *Recreations:* motor racing, ecological research. *Address:* Flat 7, Lynwood, Rise Road, Sunninghill, Berks. *T:* Ascot 20655. *Club:* Royal Automobile.
[Died Feb. 1976.

ENGLAND, Rear-Adm. Hugh Turnour, CB 1947; DSO 1943 (Bar 1944); *b* 1884; *s* of late Captain W. G. England, RN; *m* Alice Marian (*d* 1968), *d* of late Rev. Claypon Bellingham, Dunany, Co. Louth, Ireland; one *s* two *d* (and one *s* killed on active service, Fleet Air Arm, War of 1939-45). *Educ:* Eastman's; HMS Britannia. Joined RN 1900. Served S African War; European War, 1914-19, Dardanelles and E Mediterranean (despatches, severely wounded); War of 1939-45, Commodore of Convoy, Principal Sea Transport Officer, Middle East, 1941-43; Commodore-in-Charge, Hamburg, and in command German Minesweeping Administration, 1945-47 (Croix de Guerre, France). ADC to the King, 1934; Rear-Adm. 1935; retired, 1935. *Address:* Dunany, Togher, Drogheda, Co. Louth, Eire. *T:* 041-52147. *[Died 25 Nov. 1978.*

ENGLAND, Peter Tiarks Ede, CB 1978; Deputy Under-Secretary of State (Army), Ministry of Defence, 1976-78, retired; *b* 4 April 1925; *s* of Benjamin and late Mabel Gwendoline Ranke England; *m* 1st, 1947; one *s* two *d*; 2nd, 1956, Veronica Ella Lydia Everett. *Educ:* Charterhouse; Magdalene Coll., Cambridge (Exhibr; MA). RNVR, 1943-46; Cambridge, 1946-49; joined War Office, 1949; Principal, 1953; Comd Sec., Western Comd, 1961-63; Asst Sec., 1963; Asst Under-Sec. of State, MoD, 1970; Under-Sec., CSD, 1973-74; Dep. Sec., NI Office, 1974-76. *Recreations:* hill walking, model railways. *Address:* 3 Engayne Gardens, Upminster, Essex RM14 1UY. *T:* Upminster 29096. *Club:* United Oxford & Cambridge University. *[Died 24 Aug. 1978.*

ENGLISH, Sir John; *see* English, Sir W. J.

ENGLISH, Joseph Sandys, BA, MD, BCh, BAO Dublin University; LM Rotunda; FRCOG; Hon. Consultant Obstetrician and Gynæcologist, North Down Group of Hospitals; *b* 3 Oct. 1890; *s* of Thomas James English, Lisburn, N Ireland; *m* 1925, Elizabeth Hamilton (*d* 1969), *d* of H. W. Mann, MD, Nairn; one *s* one *d*. *Educ:* Campbell Coll., Belfast; Trinity Coll., Dublin. Captain RAMC 1914 (1914-15 Star, Victory and General Service medals); External Maternity Assistant, Rotunda Hospital, Dublin, 1918; Assistant Master, Rotunda Hospital, Dublin, 1919-21; Professor of Midwifery and Gynæcology, King Edward VII College of Medicine, Singapore, 1922-48; formerly Gynæcologist to the General Hospital, Singapore; Obstetrician to the Maternity Hospital, Singapore; Consulting Gynæcologist to St Andrews Hospital, Singapore; Chairman Central Midwives Board, Straits Settlements; Representative of Malaya at 4th Conference of Child Welfare, 1925; President, Malaya Branch BMA, 1939-40. Interned Singapore, Feb. 1942-Aug. 1945. *Recreation:* golf. *Address:* Culmore, Park Close, Milford-on-Sea, Hants. *T:* Milford-on-Sea 2535. *[Died 19 Nov. 1971.*

ENGLISH, Commander Reginald Wastell, DSO 1940; Royal Navy; *b* 12 April 1894; *s* of late Marcus Valentine English, Orton Longueville, Peterborough, and Emmeline Fanny Whytehead, Acomb, York; *m* 1916, Olive Taylor (*d* 1964), Ermington, Devon; one *s* two *d*. *Educ:* Orleton Sch., Scarborough; Osborne and Dartmouth Colleges. Served RN, 1907-20, 1939-44. A/S Trawlers, home, USA, S Africa (DSO Dover). *Address:* Pemberton House, Pewsey, Wiltshire.
[Died 20 Aug. 1980.

ENGLISH, Sir (William) John, Kt 1972; MBE 1951; JP; Chairman, South Western Regional Hospital Board, since 1966; Part-time Member, South Western Electricity Board, since 1960; *b* 23 Nov. 1903; 4th *s* of William Mirl English, Aylburton, nr Lydney, Glos; *m* 1929, Edith May Moss, Collingbourne Ducis, Wilts; two *s* one *d*. *Educ:* Aylburton C. of E. Sch. Apprenticed Fairfield Shipbuilding Co., Boiler Maker, Chepstow, 1918-21; Engineer, West Gloucestershire Power Co., 1922-38; District Secretary, Transport and General Workers

Union, 1938-60. Mem., Bd of Governors, United Bristol Hosps, 1972-. Chairman, S. Western Federal Laundry, 1956-; Governor, various schools; Chairman, Yeovil Technical Coll. Mayor of Yeovil, 1957, 1958, 1959; JP Somerset, 1947 (Chairman of Bench, 1953-). *Recreations:* gardening, walking. *Address:* 91 Mudford Road, Yeovil, Somerset. *T:* Yeovil 4193.
[Died 28 Aug. 1973.

ENNOR, Sir Arnold Hughes, (Sir Hugh Ennor), Kt 1965; CBE 1963; Secretary, Commonwealth Department of Science, since 1973; *b* 10 Oct. 1912; *s* of Arnold Martin and Charlotte van de Leur Ennor; *m* 1939, Violet Phyllis Argall; one *s* one *d*. *Educ:* Melbourne Univ. DSc Melbourne, 1943. Research Biochemist, Baker Institute of Medical Research, Melbourne, 1938-42; Research with Ministry of Munitions and Armed Forces, 1942-46; Wellcome Research Fellow, Dept of Biochemistry, Oxford Univ., 1946-48; Professor of Biochemistry, Australian National University, Canberra, 1948-67; Dean of John Curtin School of Medical Research, 1953-67; Deputy Vice-Chancellor, Australian National Univ., 1964-67; Secretary: Commonwealth Dept of Educn and Science, 1967-73; Commonwealth Dept of Science, 1973-. Hon. DSc NSW, 1968; Hon. MD Monash, 1969. *Publications:* numerous contributions to Biochemical Journal, Journal of Biological Chemistry, etc. *Recreation:* tennis. *Address:* 3a Vancouver Street, Red Hill, Canberra, ACT 2603, Australia. *T:* 95 9426. *Clubs:* Commonwealth (Canberra); Athenæum (Melbourne). *[Died 14 Oct. 1977.*

ENSOR, Arthur Hinton; Director: Lloyds Bank Ltd, 1954-70 (Chief General Manager, 1946-54; Vice-Chairman, 1955-63); Legal & General Assurance Society Ltd, 1954-67; Bank of London & South America Ltd, 1950-66 (Deputy Chairman, 1955); National Bank of New Zealand Ltd, 1953 (Chairman 1955-65 and 1969); Regis Property Co. Ltd, 1955-71; *b* 14 Sept. 1891; *s* of John J. Ensor, Handsworth, Birmingham; *m* 1921, Sylvia Lockerbie (*d* 1975); one *s* two *d*. *Educ:* King Edward's High Sch., Birmingham. FRSA 1948. Pres., Institute of Bankers, 1952-53, 1953-54; Dir, National Cash Register Co. Ltd, 1954-64. Master of Worshipful Co. of Tallow-chandlers, 1958-59. *Recreations:* golf, gardening. *Address:* Slade House, 17 Pembroke Road, Moor Park, Northwood, Mddx HA6 2HP. *T:* Northwood 26343. *Club:* Boodle's. *[Died 5 Oct. 1977.*

ENTWISTLE, Major Sir Cyril Fullard, Kt 1937; MC 1918; QC 1931; LLB: Director, Decca Ltd; *b* 23 Sept. 1887; *s* of Joe Entwistle of St Annes; *m* 1940, Ethel M. Towlson, Skerryvore, Hale, Cheshire. *Educ:* Bolton Sch.; Victoria Univ., Manchester, 1st class hons LLB, Dauntsey Legal Scholar, Graduate Legal Scholar; Clement's Inn Prizeman, Daniel Reardon Prizeman, Travers Smith Scholar; called to Bar, 1919. Served European War (despatches, MC); commanded 235 Siege Battery, RGA; MP (L) South-West Hull, Dec. 1918-Nov. 1924; Dep. Chm. of Cttees, Feb.-Nov. 1924; MP (U) Bolton, 1931-45; formerly one of the two House of Commons assessors, appointed under the Parliament Act 1911; Chm. of Standing Cttees and Temp. Chm. of House of Commons; introduced as Private Member's Bill, Matrimonial Causes Act 1923. *Recreations:* golf, painting, fly-fishing, shooting. *Address:* 12 Durley Chine Court, West Cliff Road, Bournemouth, Hants. *T:* 26049. *[Died 9 July 1974.*

ERDELYI, Prof. Arthur, FRS 1975; FRSE; Professor of Mathematics, University of Edinburgh, since 1964; *b* 2 Oct. 1908; *s* of Ignac Diamant and Friderike (*née* Roth); *m* 1942, Eva Neuburg; no *c*. *Educ:* Madách Imre Fögimnázium, Budapest; Deutsche Technische Hochscule, Brno; Universities of Prague and Edinburgh. Cand. Ing. (Brno) 1928; Dr rer. nat. (Prague) 1938; DSc (Edinburgh) 1940. Asst Lectr, then Sen. Lectr, University of Edinburgh, 1941-49; Vis. Prof. of Maths, Calif Inst. of Technology, 1947-48; Prof. of Maths, Calif Inst. of Techn., 1949-64; Vis. Professor: Hebrew Univ., Jerusalem, 1956-57; Univ. of Melbourne, 1970. Scientific Cons. to Admty during War of 1939-45. FRSE 1945; For. Mem., Acad. of Sciences, Turin, 1953. Gunning Victoria Jubilee Prize, RSE, 1977. *Publications:* (jtly) Higher Transcendental Functions, 3 vols, 1953-55; (jtly) Tables of Integral Transforms, 2 vols, 1954; Asymptotic Expansions, 1956; Operational Calculus and Generalized Functions, 1962; past and present jt editor of several math. periodicals; contrib. research papers and reviews to encycls and math. jls. *Recreations:* music, walking. *Address:* Mathematics Department of the University, James Clerk Maxwell Building, The King's Buildings, Mayfield Road, Edinburgh EH9 3JZ. *T:* 031-667 1081. *[Died 12 Dec. 1977.*

ERHARD, Prof. Ludwig; *b* Fürth, Bavaria, W Germany, 4 Feb. 1897; *m* 1923, Luise Lotter; one *d*. *Educ:* Handelshochschule, Nuremberg (Dipl.-Kfm.); University of Frankfurt am Main (Dr rer. pol.). Asst and finally Deputy Head, Inst. für Wirtschaftsbeobachtung, Nuremberg, 1928-42; Head of Inst. für

Industrieforschung, Nuremberg, 1943-45; State Minister for Econ. Affairs, Bavaria, Oct. 1945-Dec. 1946; Hon. Prof., Ludwig-Maximilian-Univ., Munich, Nov. 1947; Chm. Sonderstelle Geld und Kredit (for currency reform), Bad Homburg, 1947; Dir, Dept of Economics, in United Economic Region, Frankfurt am Main, 1948; elected to 1st and subsequent Bundestage, 1949-; Minister of Economic Affairs, 1949-63; Vice-Chancellor, Federal Republic of Germany, 1957-63; Chancellor, 1963-66; Hon. Chm., CDU. Hon. Prof. (Rhineland) Friedrich-Wilhelm Univ., Bonn, 1950; German Governor, World Bank, 1952. Pres. Internat. Freedom Academy, 1969-. Holds foreign decorations, also numerous hon. doctorates from universities in Germany and abroad. Publications: Deutschlands Rückkehr zum Weltmarkt; Wohlstand für Alle; Deutsche Wirtschaftspolitik (all publ. Düsseldorf); The Economics of Success; numerous analyses, expertises, speeches, discourses, discussions, etc. Recreations: music (classical), discussions (serious themes, especially Economic Science). Address: 8 Johanniterstrasse, 53 Bonn, Germany. [Died 5 May 1977.

ERITH, Raymond Charles, RA, FRIBA; Architect in private practice (Raymond Erith & Quinlan Terry); b 7 Aug. 1904; e s of Henry Charles Erith; m 1934, Pamela, y d of Arthur Spencer Jackson; four d. ARIBA 1927; FRIBA 1946; ARA 1959; RA 1964. Works include: reconstruction of 10, 11 and 12 Downing Street; Library and Wolfson Buildings, Lady Margaret Hall, Oxford; Jack Straw's Castle, Hampstead; Common Room Building, Gray's Inn. Mem. Royal Fine Art Commn, 1960-. Address: Dedham House, Dedham, Essex. T: Dedham 3186. Club: Athenæum. [Died 30 Nov. 1973.

ERLANGER, L. F. A.; see d'Erlanger.

ERNST, Max; painter and sculptor; a founder of Dadaism and a pioneer Surrealist; b Brühl, Cologne, 2 April 1891; US citizen, 1948, French citizen, 1958; s of Philipp Ernst and Louise (née Kopp); m 1st, 1918, Louise Strauss (marr. diss.); one s; 2nd, 1927, Marie-Berthe Aurenche (marr. diss.); 3rd, 1941, Peggy Guggenheim (marr. diss.); 4th, 1946, Dorothea Tanning. Educ: Bonn Gymnasium (Baccalauréat) and University. Served European War of 1914-18 as Artillery Officer (wounded twice). Taught himself to paint. First exhibition, Bonn, 1912; subseq. exhibns in Paris, Berlin, New York, Chicago, New Orleans, London, etc. Retrospective exhibitions: Copley Galleries, Beverly Hills, 1948; La Hune bookstore, Paris, 1949; Galerie René Drouin, Paris, 1950; Brühl, 1951; Knocke-le-Zoute, Belgium, 1953; Kunsthalle, Berne, 1956; Musée d'Art Moderne, Paris, 1959; Museum of Modern Art, New York, 1961; Art Inst. of Chicago, 1961; Tate Gallery, London, 1962; Kunsthaus, Zurich, 1963; Walraff-Richartz Mus., Cologne, 1963; Orangerie, Paris, 1971. Represented at Dunn Internat. Exhibn, London, 1963. Grand Prize, Venice Biennale, 1954. Publications: La Femme 100 Têtes, 1929; Beyond Painting, and Other Writings by the Artist and His Friends, 1948, etc. Relevant publication: Max Ernst, by Patrick Waldberg, 1958. Address: 19 rue de Lille, 75007 Paris, France. [Died 1 April 1976.

ERNST, Morris Leopold; Lawyer; b Uniontown, Ala, 23 Aug. 1888; s of Carl Ernst and Sarah (née Bernheim); m 1923, Margaret Samuels; one s two d. Educ: Public Sch. and Horace Mann High Sch.; Williams Coll. (AB 1909); New York Law Sch. (LLB 1912). Manufacturer of shirts, 1909-11; retail furniture, 1911-15; Mem. law firm Greenbaum, Wolff & Ernst, New York, 1915-; served as Arbiter for Mayor La Guardia in taxicab strike, 1934; Mem., Mission to Virgin Islands, 1935; drafted Legislation for Governor Lehman on insurance and banking; Special Asst to Attorney-General on election fraud matters; Personal Representative to Pres. Roosevelt during Second World War on various missions to England; Mem., Governmental Mission to Germany, 1946. Special Counsel: Amer. Newspaper Guild; War Production Bd; Counsel: NY State Legislative Commn for Hard of Hearing; Dramatists' Guild; Authors' League of America; Mem., Chancellor's Council of Univ. of Texas, 1969. Representative of British and Amer. authors, particularly on censorship cases such as: The Well of Loneliness; Joyce's Ulysses; Marie Stopes' books; other volumes attacked in England and USA. Lectr, clubs and colls. Member: Pa Anthracite Coal Commn; NY State Banking Bd, 1933-45; Pres. Truman's Civil Rights Commn; Pres. Truman's Adv. Bd for PO; Bar Assoc., City of NY (Lawyer of the Year, 1960); NY County Lawyers' Assoc.; Phi Gamma Delta; Amer. Political Science Assoc.; Gargoyle Soc., Williams Coll. Hon. Member: Phi Beta Kappa; Nat. Hon. Fraternity of Alpha Kappa Delta; Gamma Chapter, NY Univ.; Williams Coll., 1961; Soc. of Anthropology, Sociology and Research, 1965. Hon. JD Nasson Coll., 1963; Hon. DHL Lincoln, 1964. French Legion of Honour. Publications: (with William Seagle) To the Pure, 1928; (with Pare Lorentz) Censored, 1930; America's Primer, 1931;

(with A. Lindey) Hold Your Tongue, 1932; (jtly) Sex Life of the Unmarried Adult, 1934; Ultimate Power, 1937; (with A. Lindey) The Censor Marches On, 1939; Too Big, 1940; The Best is Yet, 1945; The First Freedom, 1946; So Far So Good, 1948; (with David Loth) American Sexual Behavior and the Kinsey Report, 1948; For Better or Worse, 1952; Report on the American Communist, 1952; Utopia 1976, 1955; Touch Wood, 1960; (with Alan U. Schwartz) Privacy: The Right to be Let Alone, 1962; Untitled: The Diary of my 72nd Year, 1962; (with Alan U. Schwartz) Censorship: The Search for the Obscene, 1964; (with David Loth) How High is Up, 1964; (with Alan U. Schwartz) Lawyers and What They Do, 1964; (ed) The Teacher, 1967; (with Judith Posner) Comparative International Almanac, 1967; A Love Affair with the Law, 1968; (with Eleanora B. Black) Triple Crosstricks, 1968; (with Mary Batten) Discovery by Chance, 1968; (with David Loth) The Taming of Technology, 1972; The Great Reversals, 1973; Newsbreak, 1974; contribs to magazines and encyclopedias; weekly column in The Villager. Recreations: cruising, carpentry, boating. Address: (home) 2 Fifth Avenue, New York, NY 10011, USA; (office) 437 Madison Avenue, New York, NY 10022. Clubs: PEN, City (past Trustee), Williams, Players, NY University Faculty (New York). [Died 21 May 1976.

ERRINGTON, Sir Eric, 1st Bt cr 1963; Kt 1952; MA, JP; Barrister-at-law; b 17 March 1900; m 1924, Marjorie Grant Bennett; two s one d. Educ: Mill Hill Sch.; Liverpool Coll.; Trinity Coll., Oxford. 2nd Lieut Gordon Highlanders, 1918; called to Bar 1923 and practises on Northern Circuit; MP (U) Bootle Div. of Lancs, 1935-45; contested: Hanley Div. of Stoke-on-Trent 1929; Scotland Div. of Liverpool 1931; Bootle 1945; Edge Hill Div. of Liverpool, 1950; MP (C) Aldershot Div. of Hants, 1954-70. Chm. N-W Area of Conservative Assoc., 1946-51; Chm. National Executive Cttee of Conservative and Unionist Assoc., 1952-57; Pres. Wessex Area of Conservative Assocs, 1962-65; Vice-Pres. of Liverpool Constitutional Assoc.; Mem., UK Delegation to Council of Europe and Western European Union, 1962-66; Chm., Sub-Cttee of Estimates Cttee of House of Commons, 1963-70. Pres. National Federation of Property Owners, 1956-60; Pres. Hire Purchase Trade Assoc., 1965; Vice-Pres., Trustee Savings Bank Assoc., 1971. Member: Exec. Cttee Nat. Assoc. Boys Clubs, 1953; Liverpool City Council, 1934-35. JP City of Liverpool, 1948. Pres. of Liverpool Philomathic Soc., 1936-37; Chm. United Club, 1944-51. Pilot Officer AAF (Balloon Barrage), 1939; Wing Comdr, 1944. Recreations: golf, travelling. Heir: s Geoffrey Frederick Errington, Lt-Col, The King's Regt [b 15 Feb. 1926; m 1955, Diana, o d of E. Barry Davenport; three s]. Address: Lombard Chambers, Bixteth Street, Liverpool 3. T: 051-236 4328; Ynys Dwna, Trearddur Bay, near Holyhead. T: Trearddur Bay 408. Clubs: United Oxford & Cambridge University, United and Cecil; Liverpool Racquet (Liverpool). [Died 3 June 1973.

ERROLL, Countess of, 23rd in line, cr 1452; Diana Denyse Hay; Lady Hay, 1429; Baroness of Slains, 1452; 27th Hereditary Lord High Constable of Scotland, cr 1314; Celtic title, Mac Garaidh Mhor; 32nd Chief of the Hays since 1171; Senior Great Officer, Royal Household in Scotland; OStJ 1949; b 5 Jan. 1926; d of 22nd Earl and Lady Idina Sackville (d 1955), d of 8th Earl De La Warr; S father 1941; m 1st, 1946, Sir Ian Moncreiffe of that Ilk, 11th Bt (marr. diss. 1964), qv; two s one d; 2nd, 1964, Major R. A. Carnegie; one s. Heir: s Lord Hay. Address: Crimonmogate, Lonmay, Aberdeenshire. T: Lonmay 202. [Died 16 May 1978.

ERSKINE OF RERRICK, 1st Baron, cr 1964; John Maxwell Erskine, Bt 1961; GBE 1956 (CBE 1946); Kt 1949; LLD; FRSE; DL, JP; Governor of Northern Ireland, 1964-68; General Manager, 1932-53, and Director, 1951-69, The Commercial Bank of Scotland Ltd, subsequently National Commercial Bank of Scotland, now absorbed in Royal Bank of Scotland; Member Queen's Body Guard for Scotland (Royal Company of Archers), since 1935; formerly Chairman, Securicor (Scotland) Ltd; formerly Director, Caledonian Insurance Co., Guardian Assurance Co., and other companies; President, Scottish Savings Committee, 1958-72 (Chairman, 1945-58); Chairman Scottish Hospital Endowments Research Trust (Hospital Endowments Scotland Act), 1953-71; Vice-President, Trustee Savings Banks Association; Foundn Mem., The Thistle Foundation; b 7 Dec. 1893; s of late John Erskine, Kirkcudbright; m 1922, Henrietta, CStJ, d of late William Dunnett, East Canisbay, Caithness; one s one d. Educ: Kirkcudbright Acad.; Edinburgh Univ. Admitted Solicitor; Pres. Inst. of Bankers in Scotland, 1937-40; Pres. Edinburgh Chamber of Commerce and Manufacturers, 1941-44 (Hon. Life Mem., 1968); First Chm. Central Cttee of Scottish Chambers of Commerce (now the Scottish Chamber of Commerce), 1942-44; Mem. Hetherington Deptl Cttee on Hospital Policy in Scotland, 1942; Chm. King George and

Queen Elizabeth Officers' Club, Edinburgh, for Overseas Personnel under Empire Societies War Hosp. Cttee (War 1939-'45), latterly Chm. Scottish Cttee (CBE); Mem. Postmaster General's Adv. Coun., 1945-49; Mem. Scottish Cttee on Scottish Financial and Trade Statistics (Catto Cttee), 1950-52; Chm. Transp. Users' Consultative Cttee for Scotland, 1954-57; Mem. Central Transp. Consultative Cttee, 1954-57; Mem. Scottish Transp. Council, 1955-56; Pres. Scottish Council of Social Service, 1949-57 (Chm. 1945-49); Pres. Edinburgh Union of Boys' Clubs, 1945-56; Trustee and Mem. Exec. Cttee Carnegie Trust for Scottish Univs, 1944-57; Mem. Cttee of Management, Royal Victoria Hosp. Tuberculosis Trust, 1944-56; Mem. Nat. Ref. Tribunal for Coal Mining Industry, 1956-59; Member: War Works Commn, 1945-59; N of Scotland Hydro-Electric Bd, 1948-59 (Dep. Chm. 1960, 1961). Hon. Life Mem., N Ireland Chamber of Commerce and Industry, 1968; Hon. Mem., Company of Merchants of City of Edinburgh, 1970. Freeman, Royal Burgh of Kirkcudbright, 1967. JP 1932, DL 1940, Edinburgh. FRSE 1933; Hon. FRCPE 1972. Hon. LLD: Glasgow, 1962; Queen's Univ., Belfast, 1968. KStJ 1965. *Heir: s* Major Hon. Iain Maxwell Erskine. *Address:* The Croft-Westside, 8 Churchfields Avenue, Weybridge, Surrey KT13 9YA. *T:* Weybridge 54261. *Clubs:* New, Caledonian (Edinburgh) (Hon. Life Mem.). [*Died* 14 *Dec.* 1980.

ERSKINE, Sir Derek (Quicke), Kt 1964; *b* 12 Feb. 1905; *s* of late Sir James Monteith Erskine; *m* 1927, Elisabeth Mary, *d* of late Major R. S. Spurrier, King's Dragoon Guards; two *s* one *d. Educ:* Eton Coll.; RMC Sandhurst. King's Dragoon Guards, 1924-27, resigned. Settled in Kenya, Oct. 1927. DAQMG East Africa Command, 1942-45. MLC Kenya, 1948-51; MP and Chief Whip, Kenya African Nat. Union Parly Gp, 1961-64. Director: Securicor Ltd; Avery (Kenya) Ltd. *Recreations:* polo and racing. *Address:* Riverside, PO Box 40132, Nairobi, Kenya. *Clubs:* Cavalry and Guards; United Kenya, Muthaiga Country (Nairobi). [*Died* 6 *Sept.* 1977.

ERSKINE, Hon. Francis Walter; *b* 9 Jan. 1899; *y s* of the 12th Earl of Mar and 14th Earl of Kellie, KT; *m* 1925, Phyllis Burstall, Quebec; two *d. Educ:* Eton. Lieut, Scots Guards, 1917-25; Aide-de-Camp to Governor-Gen. of Canada (Lord Byng), 1921-25. Formerly Mem. of London Stock Exchange. Capt. Scots Guards, 1939-45. *Address:* 36 Hurlingham Court, SW6. *Clubs:* Guards, Pratt's. [*Died* 20 *Sept.* 1972.

ERSKINE, Maj.-Gen. (Hon.) Ian David, CB 1949; CBE 1947; DSO 1941; *b* 17 March 1898; *s* of late A. D. Erskine, OBE; *m* 1945, Mariora Hankey. *Educ:* Winchester; Sandhurst; Staff Coll., Camberley. Regtl Adjutant, Scots Guards, 1930-33; Staff Coll., Camberley, 1933-35; Brigade Major 1st Guards Brigade, 1935-39; Comdt Middle East Tactical Sch., 1939; Commanded 2nd Bn Scots Guards, 1940; Commanded 22nd Guards Brigade, 1941; Brig. Gen. Staff, Sudan, 1942; Brig. Comdr 148 Pre OCTU Training Establishments, 1943-45; Provost Marshal and Maj.-Gen., 1945-48; (Local Maj.-Gen.); retired 1949; hon. Maj.-Gen., 1951. *Recreations:* cricket, golf. *Address:* St Clement's House, Sandwich, Kent. *T:* Sandwich 2288. *Clubs:* Guards, Pratt's. [*Died* 27 *July* 1973.

ERSKINE, Keith David; Chairman, since 1973 and Managing Director, since 1960, Securicor Ltd; Chairman: Metal Closures Group Ltd, since 1959; Associated Hotels Ltd, since 1966 (Director, 1959-66); Director, London Advisory Board, Norwich Union Insurance Group, since 1967 (Chairman, 1964-67); Solicitor; Senior Partner, Hextall Erskine & Co., since 1946; *b* 11 June 1907; *m* 1944, Audrey Skinner, 2nd Officer in WRNS; one *s* five *d. Educ:* Westminster Sch. (Scholar). Qualified as Solicitor, 1933. War of 1939-45: Captain, RA, Middle East and Italy, 8th Army (despatches twice, 1944). Chm., Kensington Palace Hotel Ltd, 1959; Director: Norwich Union Life Insce Soc., 1965-66; Norwich Union Fire Insce Soc. Ltd, 1964-65; Scottish Union & Nat. Insce Co. (Scotland), 1962-65; Scottish Union & Insce Co. (London), 1956-64. Vice-Chm., British Security Industry Assoc. Ltd, 1973-. *Recreations:* ski-ing, fishing, gardening, swimming, working. *Address:* Beech Hurst, Waterhouse Lane, Kingswood, Surrey. *T:* Mogador 2738. *Club:* City of London. [*Died* 23 *April* 1974.

ERSKINE CRUM, Lt-Gen. Vernon Forbes, CIE 1947; MC 1944; appointed GOC Northern Ireland, February 1971; *b* 11 Dec. 1918; *yr s* of late Sir Walter Erskine Crum, OBE; *m* 1948, Rosemary Aimée Douglas, *d* of late Brig.-Gen. Sir Douglas Dawson, GCVO, KCB, CMG; one *s. Educ:* Eton; New Coll., Oxford. Commissioned Scots Guards, 1940. Served War of 1939-45, North-West Europe, 1944 (MC); Conference Sec. to Viceroy and Gov.-Gen. of India, 1947-48 (CIE); Regtl Adjt Scots Guards, 1948-51; Adjt RMA Sandhurst, 1951-54; Bde Major, Household Bde, 1954-57; Commandant Guards Depot,

1957-60; AAG London Dist, 1960-62; Sec. Jt Planning Staff, 1962-63; Comdr 4th Guards Bde, 1963-65; GOC 4th Div., BAOR, 1967-69; Chief Army Instructor, IDC, 1970. *Address:* Pear Tree Cottage, Windlesham, Surrey. *T:* Bagshot 3143. *Clubs:* Guards, Leander. [*Died* 17 *March* 1971.

ERSKINE-WYSE, Marjorie Anne, (Mrs Michael Erskine-Wyse); National Secretary, National Union of Townswomen's Guilds, 1965-76; *b* 14 Oct. 1914; *d* of late Robert Brooks Lester Thomas and Annie (*née* Moller), Melbourne, Australia; *m* 1943, Michael Erskine-Wyse. *Educ:* Box Hill Technical Coll., Melbourne (Dip. DSc). ABC Public Relations Officer, 1939. Programme and Presentation Officer, Far Eastern Bureau, Foreign Office, attached All-India Radio, New Delhi, 1944-45. Asst Editor, Home and Country, London, 1946; Sub-editor, Arab News Agency, Cairo, 1947-49; Freelance journalist SE Asia, 1950; Asst to Basil Dean in compilation of autobiography and Fest. of Brit. production of Flecker's Hassan, Cambridge Theatre, 1950-51; Admin. Officer, Nutrition Div. UN Food and Agric. Orgn, Rome, 1952-56; Conf. Sec. and Dep. Nat. Sec., NUTG, 1957-60; Features Editor, Beirut (Eng. Lang. daily), Lebanon, 1960-61; Editor, The Townswoman, and Public Relations Officer, NUTG, 1962-65. *Publication:* Understanding Music, 1971. *Recreations:* music, theatre, chess, swimming, riding. *Address:* 18 Gate Hill Court, W11 3QT. *T:* 01-727 9433. [*Died* 7 *Dec.* 1976.

ERVINE, St John Greer, FRSL; Dramatist and Novelist; Hon. LLD (St Andrews); Hon. DLitt Queen's University, Belfast; *b* Belfast, 28 Dec. 1883; *s* of late William Ervine, Belfast; *m* 1911, Leonora Mary (*d* 1965), *d* of late G. W. Davis, Birmingham. Trooper Household Battalion, Oct. 1916-April 1917; Lieut 1st Batt. Royal Dublin Fusiliers in France, Oct. 1917-May 1918, when wounded. Manager, Abbey Theatre, Dublin, 1915; Prof. of Dramatic Literature, Royal Society of Literature, 1933-36; Mem. of the Irish Academy; wrote The Magnanimous Lover (one-act play), 1907, produced at the Abbey Theatre, Dublin, 1913; Mixed Marriage (four-act play), 1910, Abbey Theatre, 1911; Jane Clegg (three-act play), 1911, Gaiety Theatre, Manchester, 1912; John Ferguson (four-act play), 1914, Abbey Theatre, 1916; The Ship (three-act play); Mary, Mary, Quite Contrary (four-act play); The Lady of Belmont (five-act play); Anthony and Anna (three-act play); The First Mrs Fraser, 1928 (three-act play); People of our Class, 1934 (three-act play); Boyd's Shop (four-act play), 1935; Robert's Wife (three-act play), 1937; The Christies (three-act play), 1939; Friends and Relations, 1940; Private Enterprise, 1947; My Brother Tom, 1952; Ballyfarland's Festival, 1953 and with H. G. Wells, The Wonderful Visit (five-act play); Esperanza, 1957. *Publications:* All the plays named above; Some Impressions of my Elders (essays), 1923; A Journey to Jerusalem, 1936; The Mountain, and other stories, 1928; and seven novels: Mrs Martin's Man; Alice and a Family; Changing Winds; The Foolish Lovers; The Wayward Man; the First Mrs Fraser; and Sophia; three political studies: Sir Edward Carson and the Ulster Movement, Parnell, If I Were Dictator; three books on Theatre Craft: The Organised Theatre, How to Write a Play, and the Theatre in my Time; God's Soldier (a life of Gen. Booth); Craigavon: Ulsterman; Oscar Wilde: a Present-Time Appraisal; Bernard Shaw: His Life, Work and Friends. *Address:* c/o Lloyds Bank, Seaton, Devon. *Club:* Garrick. [*Died* 24 *Jan.* 1971.

ESCOMBE, Captain William Malcolm Lingard, CBE 1960; DSO 1915; late 20th Battalion London Regiment (The Queen's Own) TA; *b* 1891; *m* 1st, 1915, Eileen M., 4th *d* of Dr W. Love, Hoddesdon, Herts; one *s*; 2nd, 1948, Elizabeth M., *d* of late Rev. W. D. Lindley and of Mrs Lindley, Wheathampstead, Herts. Entered army (TF), 1911; served European War, 1914-19 (despatches, DSO); Chm. and Managing Dir of Escombe McGrath, Co. Ltd, 1955-64. Master N Herts Beagles, 1929-32; Pres. Assoc. of Masters of Harriers and Beagles, 1938; Master of Merchant Taylors' Company, 1941-42 and 1957-58; late Supt Herts Spec. Constabulary. Chm. St Albans (Parliamentary) Div. Conservative and Unionist Assn, 1946-52, and Pres., 1951-58; Pres. Old Bradfieldian Soc., 1945-49. *Recreation:* following hounds. *Address:* Junipers, Wheathampstead, Herts. *Club:* City of London. [*Died* 21 *Nov.* 1973.

ESCRITT, Leonard Bushby, CEng; retired 1967; *b* 10 June 1902; *s* of William Escritt and Effie Florence Escritt (*née* Bushby); *m* 1932, Violet Phyllis Hallett. *Educ:* Strand Sch.; King's Coll., London Univ. Chartered Civil Engr and Incorporated Public Health Engr. John Taylor & Sons, 1923-29; Met. Borough Wandsworth, 1929-30; LCC, 1930-34 and 1948-63; Ranks Ltd, 1934-35; Howard Humphreys & Sons, 1935-39; part and whole-time private consulting practice, 1939-68; Regional Tech. Adviser, Min. of Home Security, 1939-44, Min. of Works, 1944-48; GLC, 1963-67. *Publications:* Sewerage Engineering, 1939;

Regional Planning, 1943; Surface Drainage, 1943; Sewerage Design and Specification, 1947; Sewage Treatment, 1950; A Code for Sewerage Practice, 1950; Surface-water Sewerage, 1950; Building Sanitation, 1953; Rifle and Gun, 1953; Rifleman and Pistolman, 1955; Sewerage and Sewage Disposal, 1956; The Work of the Public Health Engineer, 1959; The Small Cellar, 1960; Pumping Station Equipment and Design, 1962; Design of Surface-water Sewers, 1964; Escritt's Tables of Meter Hydraulic Flow, 1970; Sewers and Sewage Works, 1971; Public Health Engineering Practice, 1972; The Wine Cellar, 1972; contrib. Chambers's Encycl., Everyman's Encycl., Kempe's Engineers Year-book. *Recreations:* epée and sabre fencing, rifle and pistol shooting. *Address:* 68 Woodcrest Road, Purley, Surrey CR2 4JB. *T:* 01-660 1379. *[Died 7 Dec. 1973.*

'ESPINASSE, Prof. Paul Gilbert; Emeritus Professor of Zoology, The University, Hull; *b* 10 June 1900; *s* of late Rev. Richard Talbot 'Espinasse; *m* 1934, Margaret Patricia MacPherson Wattie; two *d. Educ:* privately; St Edmund Hall, Oxford. *Publications:* papers in learned journals. *Address:* 46 Marlborough Avenue, Hull HU5 3JS. *T:* Hull 43908.
[Died 10 May 1975.

ESPLEY, Arthur James, CBE 1951 (OBE 1918); JP; PhC; *b* 8 July 1888; *s* of late Thomas Espley, Audley, Staffs; *m* 1912, Elsie (*d* 1965), *d* of late William Thornber; four *s. Educ:* Accrington Technical Sch.; Birmingham Univ. Served European War, 1915-18 (OBE, despatches twice); Managing Dir and Vice-Chm., Timothy Whites & Taylors Ltd until 1944. Ministry of Aircraft Production; Dir-Gen. of Equipment, 1940-41; Member: Industrial Court of Arbitration; Railways Staff National Tribunal; Court of Inquiry, Dockyard, Malta, 1949; Court of Inquiry, Sugar Industry, Trinidad, 1955. Pres., Postgraduate Institute of Obstetrics and Gynæcology, London University; Ex-Chm. Queen Charlotte's and Chelsea Hospital for Women. *Address:* The Little Croft, Redwood Road, Sidmouth, Devon. *T:* Sidmouth 3711. *Club:* Constitutional. *[Died 23 July 1971.*

ESSAME, Maj.-Gen. Hubert, CBE 1945; DSO 1944; MC 1918; Military Lecturer, Broadcaster, Journalist and TV Advisor; *b* 24 Dec. 1896; *s* of late Ernest H. Essame, Wokingham, Berks; *m* 1st, 1926, Hilda Mary (decd), *d* of late T. J. Kennedy, ICS; two *s* one *d*; 2nd, 1964, Dorothy Mary, *er d* of late Sir Frank and Lady Fox, Sydney, Australia. *Educ:* Nottingham High Sch.; Staff Coll. Served BEF, 1916-18, with 2nd Northants Regt (wounded twice). Gen. Staff, WO, 1934-36; Major, 1938; CO 1st East Lancs Regt, 1941-42; Brig., 214 Independent Inf. Bde, 1942-43; 43rd Wessex Inf. Div., NW Europe, 1944-45; Maj.-Gen. 1947. Pres. Regular Commissions Board; retd 1949. Pres., W Wittering Horticulture and Produce Assoc. *Publications:* The 43rd Wessex Division at War, 1952; The North West Europe Campaign, 1944-45, 1962; (with E. M. G. Belfield) Battle for Normandy, 1965; The Battle for Germany, 1969; Normandy Bridgehead, 1970; Battle for Europe, 1918, 1972; Patton, 1974. *Recreations:* Military Historical Research; golf. *Address:* The Courtyard, West Wittering, near Chichester, West Sussex. *T:* West Wittering 2289. *[Died 2 March 1976.*

ESSENDON, 2nd Baron, *cr* 1932, of Essendon; Brian Edmund Lewis; 2nd Bt, *cr* 1918; *b* 7 Dec. 1903; *s* of 1st Baron and Eleanor (*d* 1967), *d* of R. H. Harrison of West Hartlepool; *S* father, 1944; *m* 1938, Mary, widow of Albert Duffil and *d* of late G. W. Booker, Los Angeles. *Educ:* Malvern; Pembroke Coll., Cambridge. *Recreation:* golf. *Address:* Avenue Eglantine 5, Lausanne 1006, Switzerland. *T:* 23.58.97. *Club:* Bath.
[Died 18 July 1978 (ext).

ETCHELLS, Frederick, FRIBA; (Retired) Architect and Artist; *s* of late John Charles Etchells; *m* 1932, Hester Margaret (*d* 1967), *d* of late Harrington Sainsbury, MD, OBE; one *d. Educ:* Classical and Architectural; Royal Coll. of Art; Paris. Has practised as an architect before and continuously since the war of 1914-18; works include: domestic and other buildings, and much church work, throughout the country. *Publications:* Translated Le Corbusier's Vers Une Architecture, and Urbanisme; various papers and articles on architectural subjects; (with Canon G. W. O. Addleshaw) The Architectural Setting of Anglican Worship, 1948. *Recreations:* rural. *Address:* c/o Mrs Wyatt, 7 Radnor Park Gardens, Folkestone, Kent.
[Died 16 Aug. 1973.

EUSTACE, Edward Arthur Rawlins, CIE 1947; OBE 1941; *b* 18 Nov. 1899; 2nd *s* of late Lieut-Col Edward Eustace and Mary, *d* of Maj.-Gen. Rawlins; unmarried. *Educ:* Wellington Coll.; RMC Sandhurst. 4th Gurkha Rifles, 1918-22; ICS, 1923-47. *Address:* Newstown, Tullow, Co. Carlow, S Ireland. *Club:* Athenæum. *[Died 28 Aug. 1972.*

EUSTACE, John Curtis Wernher, CIE 1945; MA; *b* 22 Nov. 1906; *o s* of late Maj.-Gen. A. H. Eustace, CB, CBE, DSO, 2nd Sikhs Punjab Frontier Force; *m* 1st, 1937, Pamela Mary (marriage dissolved, 1954), *o d* of late Sir Harold Glover; three *s*; 2nd, 1961, Alys, *o d* of late Donald S. Wedderburn Ogilvy, RNVR; four *d. Educ:* Wellington Coll.; Brentwood Coll., Vancouver Island; Exeter Coll., Oxford. BA 1928; Indian Civil Service, Punjab commn, 1929; Dep. Comr: Jhelum, 1933, Kangra, 1939, Lahore 1939 and 1947; Cooperative Dept, 1934-38. Prov. organiser National War Front and dep. Home Sec., 1942-46; retired 1947. With Guest, Keen & Nettlefolds (Midlands) Ltd, Birmingham, 1948-67. *Address:* Denton Lodge, Shute End, Wokingham, Berks. *[Died 21 Oct. 1972.*

EVAN-JONES, Cecil Artimus, CBE 1971 (MBE 1944); Secretary, Institute of Chartered Accountants in England and Wales, 1962-71, retired; *b* 1 March 1912; *m* 1941, Eileen Marjorie Yates; two *d. Educ:* St Edward's Sch., Oxford. Industry, 1931-39; served War of 1939-45, Gordon Highlanders; Dep. Sec., Soc. of Incorporated Accountants, 1946-57; with Inst. of Chartered Accountants, 1957-. *Recreations:* shooting, fishing. *Address:* Warehead House, Halnaker, Chichester, West Sussex. *T:* Halnaker 330. *Clubs:* MCC, East India, Devonshire, Sports and Public Schools; Royal London Yacht. *[Died 2 Jan. 1978.*

EVANS, Rev. Arthur Norman, MA Oxon; Perpetual Curate, St Andrew's, Waterloo Street, Hove, since 1961; *b* 18 Dec. 1900; *s* of Rev. Edward Foley Evans and Mary Walker; *m* 1925, Madge Cassienet Palmer; one *s* three *d. Educ:* St John's Sch., Leatherhead; Keble Coll., Oxford (Classical Exhibitioner). 2nd Class Hons Moderations, 3rd Class Literae Humaniores; Asst-master, St John's Sch., Leatherhead, 1923-24; Christ's Hosp., 1924-27; Headmaster of the Preparatory Dept. Christ's Hosp., 1927-34; Headmaster, Colet Court, Hammersmith, 1934-44. Headmaster of Bishop's Stortford Coll., 1944-57; ordained, Chichester Cathedral, 1958; Asst Curate, All Saints, Hove, 1958-61; MRST. *Address:* 50 Wilbury Road, Hove, Sussex BN3 3PA. *T:* Brighton 733106. *[Died 21 May 1975.*

EVANS, Charles Tunstall, CMG 1948; *b* 16 May 1903; *e s* of late Frank Alfred and Beatrice Evans, Birmingham; *m* 1938, Kathleen, *e d* of late Ernest Armstrong, Hankham Place, Pevensey; one *s* one *d* (and one *s* decd). *Educ:* King Edward's Sch., Birmingham; Christ's Coll., Cambridge. Colonial Administrative Service: Administrative Officer, Palestine, 1925; Deputy Dist Comr, 1939; Principal Asst Sec. 1942; Senior Dist Comr (Galilee), 1945; retired on termination of British Mandate, 1948. Seconded to Colonial Office, 1935-37; called to Bar (Middle Temple), 1941. Admitted solicitor, 1949. Asst Sec.-Gen., Order of St John of Jerusalem, 1950-51, Sec.-Gen., 1951-68, Registrar, 1968-75. Councillor, Cuckfield UDC, 1953-68, Chm., 1962-65. Gen. Comr of Income Tax, 1966-78, Chm., 1976-78. *Address:* Ash Lodge, 3 Calbourne, Muster Green, Haywards Heath, West Sussex RH16 4AQ. *T:* Haywards Heath 51435. *[Died 25 Sept. 1980.*

EVANS, David Morgan; Barrister, Wales and Chester Circuit; *b* 12 April 1892; *e s* of late Evan Price Evans and Sarah Anne Evans, Glasallt Isaf, Llangadoc, Carmns; *m* 1924, Mary Gwynedd, 2nd *d* of late Thomas Lloyd, Havenholme, Hadley Wood and Mrs J. T. Lewis, 9 Dawson Place, Bayswater, W2; two *s* one *d* (and one *s* decd). *Educ:* Llangadoc Sch.; Llandovery Coll.; Jesus Coll., Oxford (Classical Exhibn). MA Oxon. Barrister-at-law, Gray's Inn (Arden Prize). Legal Chm. Appellate Tribunal (Prescriptions) for South Wales under 1945 National Health Act; retd as Gen. Commissioner and Land Tax Commissioner; Deputy Chm. Cardiganshire Quarter Sessions, 1953-64. Formerly Legal Chm., Cardiff City's Rent Tribunal; Parish Councillor; Chm. Cardiff Mothercraft Clinic; Hon. Treasurer Oxford Soc., E Glam and Mon Br.; former Barr. Mem. Legal Aid Executive Cttee No 5 Area. Served 1915-19; Infantry; Artists' Rifles; Lieut 5th Bn (TF), The Welch Regt; 159 Bde Staff EEF Palestine, Egypt and Syria. *Recreations:* reading, gardening, fishing. *Address:* 33 Park Place, Cardiff; Brynderi, Hollybush Road, Cyncoed, Cardiff. *T:* Cardiff 33313; Cardiff 752148; Llanarth, Dyfed 383. *[Died 21 Nov. 1977.*

EVANS, Air Chief Marshal Sir Donald Randell, KBE 1964 (CBE 1944); CB 1955; DFC 1942; Commandant of the Imperial Defence College, 1968-69; retired, 1970; *b* 31 Jan. 1912; *o s* of late Col Percy Evans, CMG; *m* 1st, 1939, Pauline Mary Breach (marr. diss., 1950); one *s* (one *d* decd); 2nd, 1951, Eleanor Margaret (*née* Christie), widow of S/Ldr Philip Hunter, DSO; one *s. Educ:* Wellington Coll.; RAF Coll., Cranwell, 1930-32; Acting Group Capt., 1942; Group Capt., 1949; Actg Air Cdre, 1952; Air Cdre, 1956; Actg Air Vice-Marshal, 1957; Air Vice-Marshal, 1958; SASO, Fighter Command, 1957-58; Comdt, Sch. of Land/Air Warfare, 1959-61; Asst Chief of the Defence Staff,

1961-63; Chm., Chiefs of Staff working party on Defence Re-organisation, Ministry of Defence, 1963; Air Marshal, 1964; AOC-in-C, Technical Training Comd, 1964-66; Air Sec., MoD, 1966-67; Air Chief Marshal, 1967. Consultant on military aviation matters, Ferranti, Edinburgh, 1971-. Governor, Star and Garter Home. American Bronze Star, 1944. *Address:* c/o Lloyds Bank (Cox's and King's Branch), 6 Pall Mall, SW1. *Club:* Royal Air Force.   *[Died 9 April 1975.*

EVANS, Dame Edith, DBE, *cr* 1946; **(Dame Edith Mary Booth);** Actress; *b* London; *o d* of late Edward and Ellen Evans; *m* 1925, George Booth (*d* 1935). *Educ:* St Michael's Sch., Chester Square. Made first appearance at King's Hall, Covent Garden, Dec. 1912, as Cressida in Troylus and Cressida (Elizabethan Stage Soc., Dir William Poel); played in George Moore's Elizabeth Cooper, 1913; became mem. Vedrenne and Eadie Co., 1914, at Royalty; toured with Ellen Terry in Variety Theatres, 1918, as Mistress Ford (Basket Sc., Merry Wives of Windsor) also as Nerissa (Trial Sc., Merchant of Venice); part of Nerissa in its entirety, Court Theatre, 1919; Caroline in The Three Daughters of M Dupont, and Lady Utterwood in Heartbreak House (first prod.), etc., 1920; Mistress Page in Merry Wives of Windsor and Mrs Millamant in The Way of the World, Lyric, Hammersmith, 1922; The Serpent and The She-Ancient in Back to Methuselah: Birmingham Rep. Theatre (first prod.), 1923, Court Theatre, 1924; Helena in A Midsummer Night's Dream, Drury Lane, 1924; Joined Old Vic Co. for 1925-26 Season; returned to West End, 1926; Mrs Sullen in The Beaux Strategem, Lyric, Hammersmith, 1927; later went into jt management with Leon M. Lion at Wyndham's; again played in Back to Methuselah and as Josephine in Napoleon's Josephine, 1928; Florence Nightingale in The Lady With a Lamp (first prod.), Arts, then Garrick, 1929 (also in New York); Malvern Festival, 1929; Orinthia in The Apple Cart (first prod.), (also in London); Diana in The Humours of the Court. Went to Prince of Wales' under her own management, 1930. Later appearances include: Irela in Evensong, Queen's, 1932, and New York, 1933; Gwenny in The Late Christopher Bean, St James's, 1933; Duchess of Marlborough in Viceroy Sarah, Arts, 1934; Nurse in Romeo and Juliet, New York, 1934, and New, 1935; Agatha Payne in The Old Ladies, New, 1935; Arcadina in The Seagull, New, 1936; Country Wife, As You Like It, Witch of Edmonton, at Old Vic; As You Like It, Taming Of The Shrew, at New; Robert's Wife, Lady Bracknell in The Importance of Being Earnest, Cousin Muriel, at Globe; Kit Markham in Old Acquaintance, Apollo. Joined Company going to Gibraltar to entertain troops, 1942; Hesione Hushabye in Heartbreak House, Cambridge Theatre, 1943; tour of RAF camps, playing one night stands; Garrison Theatre, Salisbury, 1944; took Company to India for ENSA, 1945. Mrs Malaprop in The Rivals, Criterion, 1945-46; Katerina Ivanovna in Crime and Punishment, New, 1946; Cleopatra in Antony and Cleopatra, Piccadilly, 1946-47; Lady Wishfort in The Way of the World, and Madame Ranevsky in The Cherry Orchard, New, 1948; Lady Pitts in Daphne Laureola, Wyndham's, 1949, (also in New York); Helen Lancaster in Waters of the Moon, Haymarket, 1951-53; Countess Rosmarin Ostenburg in The Dark is Light Enough, Aldwych, 1954; Mrs St Maugham in The Chalk Garden, Haymarket, 1956; Queen Katherine in Henry VIII, Old Vic, 1958 (also in Paris). Stratford-upon-Avon: Countess of Rousillion in All's Well That Ends Well, Volumnia in Coriolanus, 1959; Margaret in Richard III, Nurse in Romeo and Juliet, 1961; Violet in Gentle Jack, Queen's, 1963; Judith Bliss in Hay Fever, National Theatre, 1964; Mrs Forrest in The Chinese Prime Minister, Globe, 1965; Narrator in The Black Girl in Search of God, Mermaid, 1968; Dear Antoine, Chichester Festival, 1971; Edith Evans... and Friends, Richmond, 1973, Haymarket, 1974. *Began film career in* The Queen of Spades, 1948; The Last Days of Dolwyn, 1948; The Importance of Being Earnest, 1951; Look Back in Anger, 1959; The Nun's Story, 1959; Tom Jones, 1963; The Chalk Garden, 1963; Young Cassidy, 1965; Fitzwilly Strikes Back, 1966; Prudence and the Pill, 1967; The Whisperers, 1967 (prize for best actress, Berlin Film Festival, 1967); Crooks and Coronets, 1969; The Madwoman of Chaillot, 1969; David Copperfield, 1970; Scrooge, 1970; A Doll's House, 1973; Craze, 1974; The Slipper and the Rose, 1976. Hon. DLit London, 1950; Hon. LittD Cambridge, 1951; Hon. DLitt: Oxford, 1954; Hull, 1968. Awards: Brit. Film Acad.; NY Film Critics; Hollywood Foreign Press; Variety Club of Great Britain. *Address:* c/o National Westminster Bank Ltd, 1 St James's Square, SW1.
     [Died 14 Oct. 1976.

EVANS, Ven. Eric Herbert; Archdeacon of Warrington, 1959-70, Emeritus since 1970; *b* 31 Jan 1902; *s* of late Captain E. B. Evans. *Educ:* Liverpool Institute; Bishop Wilson Theological Coll., Isle of Man. Rector of North Meols, Diocese of Liverpool, 1948-68. *Recreation:* travelling. *Address:* 36 Salford Road, Ainsdale, Southport, Merseyside. *T:* Southport 78715.
     [Died 25 Dec. 1977.

EVANS, Frankis Tilney, MB, BS; FRCS, Hon. FFARCS; Consulting Anæsthetist, since 1965; St Bartholomew's Hospital (Consultant Anæsthetist, 1924-65); St Mark's Hospital for Diseases of the Rectum (Consultant Anæsthetist, 1932-65); Royal Masonic Hospital (Consultant Anæsthetist, 1944-65); *b* 9 March 1900; *s* of Edwin Evans and Alice (*née* Motterway), both of London; *m* 1931, Viola Hamilton (*d* 1960), *o d* of Dr Robert Quennell, Brentwood, Essex; one *s* one *d. Educ:* Forest Sch., Snaresbrook, Essex; St Bartholomew's Hosp. MB, BS London, 1921. Surg. Sub-Lieut RNVR, 1918. Resident Anæsth., St Bart.'s, 1921; House Surg. St Bart.'s, 1922; Sen. Res. Anæsth., St Bart.'s, 1923-24. Formerly: Anæsthetist, Brompton Hosp.; Consulting Anæsthetist, King George Hosp., Ilford, Gerrard's Cross Hosp. Pres. Anæsth. Sect., Royal Society of Medicine, 1945; Examiner Fellow Fac. Anæsth., RCS; Examiner, Diploma Anæsth. Eng., 1952-56; Ext. Examr Diploma Anæsth., Ireland, 1954; Dean of Faculty of Anæsthetists, Royal College Surg. Eng., 1955-58; Mem. Council, RCS, 1955-58. *Publications:* (ed and contrib.) Modern Practice in Anæsthesia, 1949 and 1954; (co-ed) Modern Trends in Anæsthesia, 1958; (co-ed and contrib.) General Anæsthesia, 1959; (contrib.) Operative Surgery, (Rob and Smith, 1958); various articles in Lancet and BMJ. *Recreations:* music and sailing. *Address:* 3 St James's Close, Birdham, Chichester, West Sussex. *T:* Birdham 512714. *Club:* Savage.   *[Died 26 Aug. 1974.*

EVANS, Rear-Adm. George Hammond, CB 1968; Planning Inspector, Department of the Environment, since 1972; *b* 15 Jan. 1917; *er s* of late William and Edith Evans; *m* 1949, Margaret Ruth, *d* of late Captain C. C. Bell, DSO, RN, and Mrs Bell; one *s. Educ:* Bristol Grammar Sch. Commanded: HMS Eggesford, 1943-45; HMS Nepal, 1949-50; Naval Mem., Jt Intelligence Staff, Far East Station, 1951-52; Trng Comdr, RN Barracks, Chatham, 1952-54; Commanded: HMS Modeste, 1954-56; HMS Temeraire, 1957-58; Senior British Naval Officer, Ceylon, 1958-60; Deputy Asst Chief of Staff, SHAPE, 1960-62; Dir of Naval Recruiting, 1962-64; Capt. of Dockyard, Rosyth, 1964-66; Naval Deputy, Allied Forces, Northern Europe, 1966-69. Commander 1951; Capt. 1957; Rear-Adm. 1966; psc 1946; jssc 1957; retired, 1969. Royal Humane Society Medal for Lifesaving, 1942. *Recreations:* golf, sailing. *Address:* 8 Wyatt Court, Hinton St George, Somerset. *T:* Crewkerne 72904. *Club:* Army and Navy.   *[Died 5 Nov. 1980.*

EVANS, Professor Emeritus Griffith Conrad; Professor, Department of Mathematical Sciences, University of California, Berkeley, Calif, USA, 1934-55, retired; *b* Boston, Mass, 11 May 1887; *s* of George William Evans and Mary Taylor; *m* 1917, Isabel John; three *s. Educ:* Harvard Coll.; Harvard Univ.; University of Rome, Italy (Sheldon Fellow). BA Harvard Coll, 1907; PhD Harvard Univ., 1910; Instructor (part-time) Harvard, 1906, 1906-07, 1909-10; Asst Prof. and Prof., Rice Institute, 1912-34; Visiting Prof., summer, Calif, 1921, 1928, Chicago 1925, Minn 1931, Washington (Walker Ames Prof.) 1941, Rice Inst., Spring 1959; lectured in France and Belgium, 1929-30, and in Rome, Jan.-Feb., 1961. Capt., Signal Corps and Air Service, 1918-19; Technical Consultant and Scientific Expert, War Dept, Ordnance, 1943-47; Distinguished Assistance Award, 1946; Presidential Citation of Merit, 1948; National Research Council, 1927-30, 1940-43, and 1950-53; Member: American Acad. of Arts and Sciences, Boston; American Philosophical Soc., Philadelphia; Nat. Acad. of Sciences, Washington, DC; American Mathematical Soc. (Vice-Pres. 1924-26, Pres. 1938-40); Mathematical Assoc. of America (Vice-Pres. 1932); AAAS (Vice-Pres. for Economics, 1931, for Maths, 1936). LLD (hon.) University of Calif, 1956; new building for Mathematical Sciences at Univ. of California, Berkeley, named The Griffith C. Evans Hall and dedicated 14 Aug. 1971. *Publications:* Functionals and their Applications, 1918 (rev. 1964); Logarithmic Potential, 1927 (rev. 1969); Mathematical Introduction to Economics, 1930; Stabilité et Dynamique de la Production dans l'Economie Politique, 1932; technical and popular articles. *Recreation:* mostly writing. *Address:* PO Box 4728, Walnut Creek, Calif 94596, USA; (home) 319 North Gate Road, Walnut Creek, Calif. *Clubs:* Faculty, Arts (Berkeley); Sierra (Norden, Calif); University (San Francisco).   *[Died 8 Dec. 1973.*

EVANS, Lt-Col Harrie Smalley, CMG 1918; *b* 1887; *m* 1920, Marjorie Nightingale, *o d* of Millin Selby, of Lille, France, and Knocke, Belgium. Served European War, 1914-18, Australian Army Pay Corps (despatches, CMG). Chartered Accountant, Australia, to 1928; then 30 years with Austral Development Ltd, London, as Managing Director.   *[Died 1 Dec. 1971.*

EVANS, Herbert McLean, BS, MD, DMed *hc* Freiburg and Santiago, ScD San Marcos, Docteur *hc* (Paris); retired, 1953; Professor of Anatomy, University of California, 1915-52, Professor Emeritus, since 1952; Herzstein Professor of Biology and Director of the Institute of Experimental Biology, University of California, 1930-52. Professor Emeritus and Director Emeritus, since 1952; *b* 23 Sept. 1882; *s* of Dr C. W. Evans, Modesto, Calif; *m* 1st, 1905; one *d*; 2nd, 1932; one *d*; 3rd, 1945, Dorothy Frances Atkinson (*d* 1969). *Educ:* University of Calif; Johns Hopkins Univ., Baltimore, Md. Asst, Instructor, Associate and Assoc. Prof. of Anatomy, Johns Hopkins Univ., 1908-15; Research Associate Carnegie Institution of Washington, 1913-15. MD *hc*; Albert Ludwigs-Universität, Freiburg i. Br., 1930; Universidad Catholica of Chile, 1941; Docteur *hc*; Universidad Nacional of San Marcos de Lima, 1941; University of Paris, 1946; Universidad Central del Ecuador, 1954; ScD: University of Birmingham, 1950; Johns Hopkins Univ., 1957; LLD, University of California, 1955; Docteur ès Sciences, *hc* Université de Genève, 1956. John Scott Medal, 1928; gold medal (first award) for Scientific Exhibit, Am. Med. Assoc., San Francisco, 1946; Banting Medal, 1949; Squibb Award, Assoc. for Study of Internal Secretion, 1949; Charles Mickle Fellow, University of Toronto, 1949; Passano Award, Baltimore, 1952; F. H. A. Marshall Medal, 1967. Foreign Member of the Royal Society, 1951. Many lectureships in USA. Demonstrated origin of body vascular trunks from capillary plexes, 1909; explained physiological behaviour of vital stains of benzidine series, 1915; introduced use of certain azo dyes, especially Evans' Blue for estimation of blood volume, 1917; charted 48 chromosomes in man, 1918, 1929; (with J. A. Long) first description of oestrous cycle in rat, 1921, of essential value in isolation of female sex hormones; produced gigantism and other specific endocrine effects from anterior-hypophyseal hormones administered parenterally, 1922, and established separation of pituitary growth promoting substance of hormone, 1939, and finally purified this (with C. H. Li), 1944; production of permanent diabetes by chronic administration of anterior pituitary extracts, 1932; first detected criterion of vitamin A deficiency in continuous vaginal cornification, 1922; discovered vitamin E, essential for reproduction in higher animals, 1922, and (with O. H. and G. A. Emerson) first purified and determined empirical constitution of same, 1935; (with C. H. Li) was first to purify the anterior hypophyseal adrenocorticotropic hormone, 1942. Joint Editor of Am. Anatomical Memoirs, 1918-38, and Journal of Nutrition, 1928-33. Delegate to Third Internat. Conf. on Standardisation of Hormones, Geneva, 1938; delegate to Second Pan-American Congress of Endocrinology, Montevideo, 1941. *Publications:* over 600 scientific papers on anatomy, histology, embryology, cytology, physiology, biochemistry, nutrition, and endocrinology. *Recreations:* botany of Sierra Nevada arctic alpine zone, mountain climbing; book collecting (especially in field of history of medicine and science and of Western American exploration and pioneer life). *Address:* 511 Coventry Road, Berkeley, Calif, USA; University of California, Berkeley 4, Calif. *T:* (home) Landscape 5-9010; (university) 642-3535. *Clubs:* University of California Faculty (California); Roxburghe, Bohemian (San Francisco).
[*Died* 6 March 1971.

EVANS, Major James John Pugh, MBE; MC; *b* 13 May 1885; 3rd *s* of late Sir Griffith Evans, KCIE, DL, JP, and Lady Evans of Lovesgrove, Cardiganshire; *m* 1916, Viola Murielle, *e d* of late Lionel Robinson, DL, Old Buckenham Hall, Norfolk; one *s* (and one *s* decd). *Educ:* Eton; Sandhurst. Joined Royal Welch Fusiliers, 1905; Welsh Guards, 1915; served, France, 1915-19; Major, 1919; Brigade Major 1st Guards' Brigade, Aldershot, 1920-21. DL 1950, JP 1926-65, High Sheriff, 1927, Cardiganshire; DL Carmarthenshire, 1943-65; Mem. County Agric. Exec. Cttee, 1948. *Recreation:* painting. *Address:* c/o National Westminster Bank, Pont Street, SW1.
[*Died* 1 Feb. 1974.

EVANS, Dame Joan, DBE 1976; DLitt, DLit; Hon. LLD; Hon. LittD; FSA, FRHistS; Hon. FRIBA; Hon. Vice-President, Society of Antiquaries; Hon. Fellow of St Hugh's College, Oxford, 1936; Fellow of University College, London, 1950; *d* of late Sir John Evans, KCB, FRS. *Educ:* Berkhamsted Girls' Sch.; St Hugh's College, Oxford; University Coll., London. DLit London 1930; DLitt Oxford, 1932; Hon. LLD, Edinburgh, 1952; Hon. LittD, Cambridge, 1956; Librarian, St Hugh's Coll., 1917-22; Susette Taylor Fellow, Lady Margaret Hall, 1933-35; External Examiner in History of Art, London University, 1938-46; President, Royal Archæological Inst., 1948-51 (Treasurer, 1958-62); Pres. Soc. of Antiquaries, 1959-64 (Vice-Pres., 1948-52), Dir, 1954-59; Trustee: London Museum, 1951-69; British Museum, 1963-67; Mem. Adv. Coun. V. & A. Mus., 1953-67; Mem. Exec. Cttee, Friends of the National Libraries, 1955-67; Vice-Pres., Friends of the Ashmolean Museum, 1969.

Supernumerary Fellow, St Hugh's Coll., Oxford, 1951-58, Mem. of Council 1922-58. FRSL 1973. Hon. Mem., former Chm. Council and President, Bristol and Glos Archæological Soc.; Membre d'honneur Académie de Mâcon; Corresponding Fellow and Hon. Research Associate, Mediæval Academy of America; Hon. Fellow Huguenot Soc. of London; Membre honoraire, Société Nationale des Antiquaires de France, 1967; Membre de la Société de l'histoire de l'art français. Mem. Goldsmiths' Co., 1973. Gold Medal, Soc. of Antiquaries, 1973. Chevalier de la Légion d'Honneur. *Publications:* English Jewellery, 1921; Magical Jewels of the Middle Ages and the Renaissance, 1922; Anglo-Norman Lapidaries (with Prof. Studer), 1924; Life in Mediæval France, 1925 (reprinted 1957); St Joan of Orleans, 1926; The Unconquered Knight, a Chronicle of the deeds of Don Pero Niño, 1928; Pattern, a study of Ornament in Western Europe from 1180 to 1900, 1931; Monastic Life at Cluny, 1931; English Posies and Posy Rings, 1932; English Mediæval Lapidaries (with Dr Mary Serjeantson), 1933; Nature in Design, 1934; Index to Sir Arthur Evans' Palace of Minos, 1936; Joinville's History of St Louis, 1937; The Romanesque Architecture of the Order of Cluny, 1938; Taste and Temperament, 1939; Chateaubriand, 1939; Time and Chance, the story of Arthur Evans and his forebears, 1943; The Pursuit of Happiness, 1946; The Unselfish Egoist, 1947; Art in Mediæval France, 1948; English Art, 1307-1461 (Oxford History of English Art), 1949; Cluniac Art of the Romanesque Period, 1950; Style in Ornament, 1950; Dress in Mediæval France, 1952; A History of Jewellery, 1100-1870, 1953; John Ruskin, 1954; (ed) An Adventure, 1955; The Endless Web, Messrs John Dickinson & Co., 1804-1954, 1956; History of the Society of Antiquaries, 1956; The Diaries of John Ruskin, 1956, 1958, 1959; The Lamp of Beauty, 1959; Madame Royale, 1959; Monastic Architecture in France from the Renaissance to the Revolution, 1964; Prelude and Fugue (autobiography), 1965; The Victorians, 1966; (ed) Flowering of the Middle Ages, 1966; The Conways, 1966; articles in archæological periodicals. *Address:* Thousand Acres, Wotton-under-Edge, Glos. *T:* Wotton 3224. *Club:* University Women's. [*Died* 14 July 1977.

EVANS, Sir John (Harold), KBE 1958; CB 1948; *b* 16 Feb. 1904; *s* of William Evans, Lowestoft; *m* 1936, Phyllis (formerly Bathurst); one *s*. *Educ:* Lowestoft Secondary Sch.; University of London, King's Coll. Entered Civil Service, 1925. Dep. Chm., Bd of Inland Revenue, 1954-65. FKC 1959. *Address:* Whitehill Cottage, Meopham, Kent. *T:* Meopham 2284. *Club:* National Liberal.
[*Died* 27 May 1973.

EVANS, L(eonard) G(lyde) Lavington, CIE 1935; ICS; *b* 9 Nov. 1888; *s* of Frederick Lavington Evans; *m* 1925, Barbara Joan, *e d* of A. Durant Watson, Mill House, Mitcham Common; two *s*. *Educ:* Harrow; New Coll., Oxford. Entered ICS 1912; served in Bihar and Orissa until selected for Political Dept Govt of India; served as Political Officer in Mesopotamia 1918-20; thereafter in Indian States; officiating Agent to the Governor-Gen. Eastern States, 1935; officiated Resident, Mysore and Chief Commissioner, Coorg, 1935-36; retired, 1938. *Address:* Blake's House, Halse, Taunton, Somerset. *T:* Bishop's Lydeard 432235.
[*Died* 21 Sept. 1976.

EVANS, Merlyn Oliver; artist; *b* Cardiff, 1910; *s* of Pryce Oliver Evans and Minnie Veronica Evans (*née* Edwards); *m* 1950, Margerie Few; one *s* one *d*. *Educ:* Allan Glen's Sch., Glasgow; Glasgow Sch. of Art; Royal College of Art, London. Haldane travelling scholarship and Royal Exhibition prize. Began exhibiting, International Surrealist Exhibition, London, 1936; Salon de Mai, Paris, 1937. Lived in Natal, SA, 1938-41, and held 1st One-man Show in City Art Gall., Durban, 1939. War of 1939-45 (Italy Star, and war medals); served in N. Africa, Middle East (8th Army) and Italy, 1942-46 (demob, London). Since 1949 has held regular One-man Exhibns in London, also Philadelphia, 1964. Retrospective Exhibn of paintings, etchings and drawings: Whitechapel Art Gall., 1956; Chicago Art Inst., 1967; V & A, New Art Centre, 1972; Exhibition of paintings 1930-68, Marlborough New London Gall., 1968. Paintings and engravings have been included in many internat. exhibns, incl. São Paulo Biennials, 1953-54 and 1961; Brit. Pavilion, 30th Venice Biennale, 1960; Pittsburg International, 1964; Profile 3, Bochum, Germany, 1964; exhibns at Tate Gall. Work in public collections: Tate Gall.; Victoria and Albert Mus.; Nat. Mus. of Wales; Glasgow Mus. and Art Gall; State Galls of NSW and Victoria; Nat. collections in NZ and S Africa; Mus. of Modern Art, New York; Art Institute of Chicago, 1967; BM Dept of Prints and Drawings, 1972, etc. Work reprod in: Surrealism (by Herbert Read), British Painting (by Herbert Read); The Modern Movement in Art (by R. H. Wilenski). Gold Medal for Fine Art, National Eisteddfod of Wales, 1966. *Address:* 40a Downshire Hill, NW3. *Club:* Savile.
[*Died* 31 Oct. 1973.

EVANS, Trefor Ellis, CMG 1956; OBE 1948; Professor of International Politics, University of Wales, Aberystwyth, since 1969; *b* 4 March 1913; *s* of late John and Mary Evans; *m* Nest Margaret, *d* of late Trefor Williams, OBE and of Margaret Williams; two *d. Educ:* Cowbridge; Balliol Coll., Oxford; Hamburg. BA Oxon, 1934; DrPhil Hamburg, 1937. Appointed HM Consular Service, 1937; Vice-Consul, Beirut, 1937-39, Alexandria, 1939-41; Asst Oriental Sec. and Private Sec. to the Ambassador, with local rank of 3rd Sec. in Diplomatic Service, at HM Embassy, Cairo, 1941; local rank of 2nd Sec., 1942; Vice-Consul and Actg Consul, Damascus, 1945; Actg Consul, Aleppo, 1946; Actg 1st Sec., HM Legation, Beirut, 1946; 1st Sec. HM Foreign Service, 1946; Chargé d'Affaires, Beirut, 1947 and 1948; Head of Middle East Secretariat, FO, 1949-52; Oriental Couns., HM Embassy, Cairo, 1952-56; Counsellor Berne, 1957-59; Consul-Gen., Algiers, 1959-62; HM Ambassador to: Algeria, 1962-64; Syria, 1964-67; Iraq, 1968-69. Mem., Telecommunications Bd, Wales and Marches, 1970-. Coronation Medal, 1953. *Publications:* Mission to Egypt (1934-46) Lord Killearn, 1971; (ed and introd) The Killearn Diaries, 1934-1946, 1973. *Recreation:* tennis. *Address:* 20 New Street, Aberystwyth, Cardiganshire; Plas Maes-y-Groes, Talybont, Bangor. *Club:* Royal Automobile. *[Died 16 April 1974.*

EVANS, Ulick Richardson, CBE 1973; FRS 1949; ScD Cambridge 1932; ScD *hc* Dublin 1947; scientific writer and consultant; Emeritus Reader in Science of Metallic Corrosion, Cambridge University (Reader, 1945-54); Hon. Fellow, King's College, Cambridge; *b* 31 March 1889; unmarried. *Educ:* Marlborough Coll.; King's Coll., Cambridge. Served European War, 1914-14, Army (Signal Service), 1914-19. Engaged in research, writing and teaching at Cambridge Univ., 1921-55 (main subjects: Metallic Corrosion and the growth of thin Films on Metals). Hon. Dr of Metallurgy, Sheffield Univ., 1961. Palladium Medallist, Electrochemical Soc., 1955; Hothersall Medallist, 1957; Gold Medallist, Inst. of Metal Finishing, 1961; Cavallaro Medallist, 1971. Hon. Fellow UMIST, 1973. *Publications:* Metals and Metallic Compounds (4 vols), 1923; Corrosion of Metals, 1924 and 1926; Metallic Corrosion, Passivity and Protection, 1937 and 1946; Introduction to Metallic Corrosion, 1948 (and 1963); The Corrosion and Oxidation of Metals, 1960, supplementary vols, 1968 and 1976; papers in Proc. Royal Society, Trans. Faraday Soc., J. Chem. Soc., J. Iron Steel Inst., J. Inst. Met., etc. *Address:* 19 Manor Court, Grange Road, Cambridge. *T:* Cambridge 55005. *Club:* United Oxford & Cambridge University. *[Died 3 April 1980.*

EVANS, Sir William Shirley W. W.; *see* Worthington-Evans.

EVANS BEVAN, Sir David (Martyn), 1st Bt, *cr* 1958, of Cadoxton-Juxta-Neath; *b* 4 March 1902; *s* of Evan and Caroline Evans Bevan; *m* 1929, Eira Winifred Glanley; one *s* one *d. Educ:* Uppingham. Director of: Barclays Bank Ltd, 1938-72; Phœnix Assurance Co. Ltd, 1940-72. Governor of London House; Mem., Shipwrights Company. JP 1932-67; DL Glamorganshire; High Sheriff of Breconshire, 1929-30, of Glamorganshire, 1951-52; Freeman of Neath, 1949; Freeman of Port Talbot, 1952; KStJ; Sub-Prior, Order of St John for Wales. *Recreations:* shooting and fishing. *Heir: s* Martyn E. Evans Bevan [*b* 1 April 1932; *m* 1957, Jennifer Marion, *d* of Robert Hugh Stevens, Eardisley, Herefordshire; four *s*]. *Address:* Val au Bec, Les Routeurs, St Peter, Jersey, CI. *T:* West 389. *Club:* Carlton. *[Died 9 Sept. 1973.*

EVANS-LOMBE, Vice-Adm. Sir Edward (Malcolm), KCB 1954 (CB 1946); DL, JP; RN retired; *b* 15 Oct. 1901; *s* of Major A. Evans-Lombe, 40 Elm Park Gardens, SW10; *m* 1931, Diana Vivien Katharine Mackeson; one *s* one *d. Educ:* RN Coll., Dartmouth. Naval Asst to 3rd Sea Lord and Controller, Sept. 1939-April 1942; Commanding Officer HMS Glasgow, 1942-43; Director of Gunnery Div., Admiralty, 1943-44; Chief of Staff, Eastern Fleet, Aug.-Dec. 1944; Chief of Staff, British Pacific Fleet, 1944-46; Naval ADC to the King, 1948-49; Flag Officer, Training Sqdn, 1949-50; a Lord Commissioner of the Admiralty and Dep. Chief of Naval Staff, 1950-53; Comdr, Allied Naval Forces in Northern Europe, 1953-55; retired, 1955. JP Norfolk, 1960, DL 1961; High Sheriff, Norfolk, 1962. *Address:* The Grange, Little Melton, Norwich. *T:* Hethersett 260. *Club:* Naval and Military. *[Died 14 May 1974.*

EVANS-PRITCHARD, Sir Edward Evan, Kt 1971; MA Oxon; PhD London; FBA 1956; Professor of Social Anthropology, University of Oxford, 1946-70; Fellow of All Souls 1946-70 (Sub-Warden, 1963-65); *b* 1902; 2nd *s* of late Rev. Thomas John Evans-Pritchard; *m* 1939, Ioma (*d* 1959), *d* of late Rt Hon. G. Heaton Nicholls; three *s* two *d. Educ:* Winchester Coll. (Commoner); Exeter Coll., Oxford (Hon. Scholar). Six major and several minor anthropological expeditions to Central, East and North Africa, 1926-39; Prof. of Sociology, Egyptian Univ., Cairo, 1931-34; Leverhulme Fellow, 1935-36; Research Lecturer, Oxford, 1935-40; Hon. Research Asst University Coll., London; Active Service (despatches), 1940-45; Reader, Cambridge, 1945. Pres., Royal Anthropological Inst., 1949-51; Life Pres., Assoc. of Social Anthropologists. Mem., Amer. Philosophical Soc., 1968. Hon. Fellow, SOAS University of London, 1963. Mem. Hon., Inst. Française de Sociologie, 1950; For. Hon. Mem., Amer. Acad. of Arts and Sciences, 1958. Hon. DSc: University of Chicago, 1967; Bristol, 1969; Hon. DLitt Manchester, 1969. Chevalier, Legion of Honour (France), 1972. *Publications:* Witchcraft, Oracles and Magic among the Azande, 1937; The Nuer, 1940; The Sanusi of Cyrenaica, 1949; Kinship and Marriage among the Nuer, 1951; Social Anthropology, 1951; Nuer Religion, 1956; Essays in Social Anthropology, 1962; The Position of Women in Primitive Societies, 1965; Theories of Primitive Religion, 1965; The Zande Trickster, 1967; The Azande: history and political institutions, 1971; and numerous papers in scientific journals. *Recreations:* gardening, bird watching. *Address:* The Ark, Jack Straws Lane, Headington, Oxford. *[Died 11 Sept. 1973.*

EVERETT, Richard Marven Hale, QC 1952; JP; His Honour Judge Everett; a Circuit Judge (formerly Judge of County Courts), since 1971; *b* 26 June 1909; *s* of B. R. Everett, Solicitor; *m* 1935, Kathleen Lucy Eve; one *s. Educ:* Repton. Called to Bar, Gray's Inn, 1933; Master of the Bench, Gray's Inn, 1959, Treasurer, 1977. Recorder of: Deal, 1959-68; Maidstone, 1968-71; Leader, SE Circuit, 1968-71. Served War of 1939-45, in Army, 1941-43. JP Herts, 1953. *Publications:* Joint Ed. 4 edns of Willis' Workmen's Compensation Acts. *Recreation:* golf. *Address:* 54 Ashley Gardens, SW1. *T:* 01-828 3811. *Club:* Royal Automobile. *[Died 8 Aug. 1978.*

EVERS, H(enry) Harvey, MS, FRCS, FRCOG; Professor of Obstetrics and Gynæcology, University of Durham, 1950-58 (now Emeritus), also Obstetrician and Gynæcologist in charge of the Department at Royal Victoria Infirmary and Princess Mary Maternity Hospital, Newcastle upon Tyne, 1950-58 (now Hon. Obstetrician and Gynæcologist); Pastoral Visitor, Newcastle Regional Hospital Board; *b* 28 May 1893; 2nd *s* of Charles Henry Evers, Medical Practitioner; *m* 1923, Marian Isabel Graham; two *s. Educ:* Royal Grammar Sch., Newcastle upon Tyne; University of Durham. Co. of Northumberland, Sch. and Univ. Schol., 1911; Gibson, Outterson-Wood, etc. Schols, 1914; MB, BS (1st Cl. Hons), Durham, 1916; MS Durham (Hons), 1921; MRCS, LRCP, 1916; FRCS 1921. Surg. Prob. (RNVR), 1914-15; Capt., RAMC, 1916-20. Foundation Mem. Royal College of Obstetrics and Gynæcology, 1933; FRCOG 1937. Pastoral Visitor, Regional Adviser and Assessor, Newcastle upon Tyne, 1948; External Examiner, Univs of London, Liverpool, Manchester, Sheffield, Wales; Examiner Conjoint Bd, RCOG, Central Midwives Bd, etc.; Past Pres. North of England Obst. and Gyn. Soc. Formerly: House Surg. (General, Eye and Throat, Nose and Ear), Royal Victoria Infirmary, Newcastle upon Tyne, 1915; Hon. Asst Surg., Hosp. for Sick Children; Demonstrator in Anatomy and Operative Surgery, 1920; Lectr in Obstetrics and Gynæcology, 1930. *Publications:* various medical. *Recreations:* fishing, golf. *Address:* Oakwood Lodge, Clayton Road, Newcastle upon Tyne NE2 1TL. *T:* Newcastle upon Tyne 81-4441. *[Died 15 June 1979.*

EVILL, Air Chief Marshal Sir Douglas Claude Strathern, GBE 1946; KCB 1943 (CB 1940); DSC 1916; AFC 1919; *b* 1892; *m* 1920, Henrietta Hortense, *d* of Sir Alexander Drake Kleinwort, 1st Bt; one *s* two *d. Educ:* Royal Naval Colleges, Osborne and Dartmouth. Served European War, 1914-19 (DSC, AFC); War of 1939-45 (despatches twice, CB, KCB). Head of Royal Air Force Delegation in Washington, 1942; Vice-Chief of the Air Staff, and addtl Mem. of the Air Council, 1943-46; Air Chief Marshal, 1946; retired 1947. *Address:* South Lawn, Cheriton Close, Winchester, Hants. *Clubs:* United Service, Lansdowne. *[Died 22 March 1971.*

EVOE; *see* Knox, Edmund G. V.

EWART-BIGGS, Christopher Thomas Ewart, CMG 1969; OBE 1963; HM Diplomatic Service; Ambassador to the Republic of Ireland, since 1976; *b* 5 Aug. 1921; *s* of Lt-Col Henry Ewart-Biggs and Mollie Hilda Madelene Ewart-Biggs (*née* Brice); *m* 1st, 1952, Gavrelle Verschoyle (*d* 1959); 2nd, 1960, Felicity Jane Randall; one *s* two *d. Educ:* Wellington Coll.; University Coll. (History Scholar, 1939); BA Oxon 1945. Commissioned in Queen's Own Royal West Kent Regt, 1942; British Military Administration, Tripolitania, Civil Affairs Officer, Jefren, 1943; Arab Affairs Officer, 1945; Deputy Chief Sec. (Lt-Col), 1946; British Administration, Cyrenaica, 1947; Public Information

Officer, Cyrenaica, 1948. Appointed Second Sec., HM Foreign Service, 1949. Middle East Centre for Arab Studies, 1950; Political Officer, Qatar, 1951; Eastern Dept, FO, 1953; First Sec., HM Embassy, Manila, 1956; NATO Defence Coll., 1958; Asst, African Dept, FO, 1959; Algiers: Consul, 1961; Head of Chancery, 1962; Counsellor, 1963; Counsellor, FO, 1965-69, Brussels, 1969-71; Minister, Paris, 1971-76. *Address:* British Embassy, 33 Merrion Square, Dublin, Ireland; 31 Radnor Walk, Chelsea, SW3. *T:* 01-352 4275. *Clubs:* Brooks's, Hurlingham.
[Died 21 July 1976.

EWING, Sir Alexander (William Gordon), Kt 1959; MA (Edinburgh), PhD (Manchester); Professor of Audiology and Education of the Deaf and Director (1944-64) of Audiology and Education of the Deaf in the University of Manchester; *b* 6 Dec. 1896; *s* of late Rev. A. Gordon C. Ewing, MA, formerly Rector of St Vincent's Episcopal Church, Edinburgh; *m* 1st, 1922, Irene R. Goldsack (*d* 1959); no *c*; 2nd, 1961, Ethel Constance Goldsack. *Educ:* St Clare Preparatory Sch., Walmer, Kent; Dean Close Sch., Cheltenham; University of Edinburgh; University of Manchester. Service in HM Forces, 1918-19. Directed private clinic for deaf children and held hon. special lectureship in Dept of Educ. of the Deaf, University of Manchester, 1922-44. Norman Gamble Prize of the Royal Society of Medicine and Actonian Prize of Royal Institution, 1943 (with Dr Irene Ewing); Hon. Mem. Amer. Otological Soc., 1946-; Hon. Fellow Manchester Med. Soc., 1964-; (with Dr Irene Ewing) visited schs for the deaf in Canada, and in Australia and New Zealand at invitation of Govts concerned, to inspect and advise about their provision of education for the deaf, and conducted post-grad. courses during a summer session at North-Western Univ., Ill, 1949; later visits to USA incl. lectures and conf. papers. Mem. Med. Research Council's Cttee on the Physiology of Hearing and Cttee on the Educational Treatment of Deafness, 1932-52; Pres. Brit. Association of the Hard of Hearing, 1956-; Vice-Pres., National Coll. of Teachers of the Deaf, 1965-; Vice-Pres., Health Visitors' Assoc., 1966-. Hon. LittD, Ithaca, NY; Hon. LLD Manchester. *Publications:* Aphasia in Children, 1930; The Handicap of Deafness, 1938; (with I. R. Ewing) Opportunity and the Deaf Child, 1947; Speech and the Deaf Child, 1954 (with I. R. Ewing); Educational Guidance and the Deaf Child, 1957 (with others); New Opportunities for Deaf Children, 1961 (with I. R. Ewing); Teaching Deaf Children to Talk, 1964 (with E. C. Ewing); Hearing Aids, Lipreading and Clear Speech, 1967 (with E. C. Ewing); Hearing-Impaired Children under Five: a guide for parents and teachers, 1971 (with E. C. Ewing); articles and papers in the Journal of Laryngology and Otology, Lancet, Practitioner, Proc. Royal Society of Medicine, Teacher of the Deaf. *Recreations:* gardening, travel. *Address:* Horseshoe Cottage, Alderley Edge, Cheshire. *T:* Alderley Edge 583258.
[Died 29 April 1980.

EWING, Alfred Cyril, FBA 1941; LittD, MA; retired as Reader in Philosophy, University of Cambridge (1954-66); Fellow, Jesus College, Cambridge, 1962 (Hon. Fellow, 1966); *b* 1899; *s* of H. F. and E. M. Ewing; unmarried. *Educ:* Wyggeston Grammar Sch., Leicester; University Coll., Oxford (open exhibitioner). First class hons in Classical Moderations and Finals (Lit Hum); Bishop Fraser Scholar Oriel Coll., 1920; Senior Demy Magdalen Coll., 1921; John Locke Scholarship in Mental Philosophy, 1921; DPhil Oxon, 1923; Green Prize in Moral Philosophy, 1926; Temporary Lecturer at Michigan Univ., and Armstrong Coll., Newcastle; Asst Lecturer in Philosophy at University Coll., Swansea, 1927-31; Lectr in Moral Science, University of Cambridge, 1931-54. LittD Cantab, 1933; President of Aristotelian Soc., 1941-42. Visiting Professor: Princeton and Northwestern Univs, USA, 1949; South America and Univ. of South California, 1961; Univ. of Colorado, 1963; State Coll. of San Francisco, 1967; Univ. of Delaware, 1971. British delegate to Indian Silver Jubilee Congress of Philosophy in Calcutta, 1950; Hon. Treas. Internat. Fed. of Philosophical Socs, 1953-; Chairman: Faculty Board of Moral Science, Cambridge Univ., 1957-59 and 1964-66; Philosophy Section, British Academy, 1953-61. *Publications:* Kant's Treatment of Causality, 1924; The Morality of Punishment (with some suggestions for a General Theory of Ethics), 1929; Idealism, A Critical Survey, 1934; A Short Commentary on Kant's Critique of Pure Reason, 1938; Reason and Intuition (British Academy Lecture), 1941; The Individual, The State, and World Government, 1947; The Definition of Good, 1947; The Fundamental Questions of Philosophy, 1951; Ethics (Teach Yourself Series), 1953; The Idealist Tradition (sels) ed 1957; Second Thoughts in Moral Philosophy, 1959; Non-Linguistic Philosophy, 1968. Articles in Mind, Philosophy, Procs of Aristotelian Soc., Philosophy and Phenomenological Research, Review of Metaphysics, Theoria, Revue Internationale de Philosophie, Philosophical Studies, Hibbert Journal, Monist, Ethics, Analysis, Personalist,

Philosophical Quarterly, Religious Studies, Proc. Internat. Congresses of Philosophy, Indian Jl of Philosophy, Idealistic Studies, Internat. Logic Rev. *Recreations:* reading, walking. *Address:* 10 Lyndhurst Road, Manchester 20. *T:* 061-445 5121; Matterdale End, Penrith, Cumberland. *T:* Glenridding 282.
[Died 14 May 1973.

EWING, James, Comp. TI; FCIS; FBIM; Chairman, The Bradford Dyers' Association Ltd, 1947-62 (Joint Managing Director 1946-58); *b* 25 Aug. 1884; *s* of late Archibald and Jean Ewing, Edinburgh; *m* 1911, Margaret Nimmo; one *s* two *d*. *Educ:* Secondary Sch., Edinburgh; Heriot-Watt Coll., Edinburgh. With Bradford Dyers Assoc. Ltd, 1909, Mem. Bd, 1926-62. *Address:* Flat 41, Molyns House, Phyllis Court Drive, Henley-on-Thames, Oxon.
[Died 21 March 1975.

EXHAM, Maj.-Gen. Kenneth Godfrey, CB 1954; DSO 1945; retired as General Officer Comanding Nigerian Military Forces (1956-59); *b* 17 Sept. 1903; *er s* of late Col Frank Simeon Exham, DSO; *m* 1927, Joan Eleanor Stewart, *d* of Allan Ball Hamilton; no *c*. *Educ:* Radley Coll.; RMC Sandhurst. Commissioned, Duke of Wellington's Regt, 1923; served War of 1939-45; despatches 1946; Brit. Mil. Mission to USSR, 1941-43; Comd 56 Inf. Brigade, 1945; comd 151 Inf. Bde (TA), 1946-47; Dep. Dir Mil. Trg, 1948-51; idc, 1952; ADC to King George VI and to the Queen, 1950-53; Chief of Staff, HQ, Western Command, 1953-56; Comdt Queen's Own Nigeria Regt, 1956-59; Col The Duke of Wellington's Regt, 1958-65; Hon. Col 6/7 Bn The Royal Welch Fusiliers, TA, 1964-71. *Recreations:* shooting, fishing. *Address:* 5 Cotmore House, Bicester, Oxon. *Clubs:* Army and Navy; MCC.
[Died 28 Feb. 1974.

EYRE, Sir Oliver E. C.; *see* Crosthwaite-Eyre.

EYSTON, Capt. George Edward Thomas, OBE 1948; MC; MIMechE; MSAE; *b* 28 June 1897; *s* of E. R. J. Eyston; *m* 1924; two *d*. *Educ:* Stonyhurst; Trinity Coll., Cambridge. Served in European War, 1914-18, Lieut 3 Battalion Dorset Regt, and Staff Capt. Royal Artillery (despatches twice, wounded); served 2nd World War, a Regional Controller, Min. of Prodn. Holder of Land Speed Record three times in America and many other World's Records Motoring. Awarded Segrave Trophy, 1937, Gold Medal of AIACR; Chevalier of Legion of Honour. *Publications:* Flat Out; (with Barre Lyndon) Motor Racing and Record Breaking, 1935; (with W. F. Bradley) Speed on Salt, 1936; (ed) Fastest on Earth, 1939; Safety Last, 1976. *Address:* 524 Hillside Terrace, West Orange, New Jersey, USA. *Clubs:* Royal Automobile, Hawks, Leander; Royal Yacht Squadron; Seawanaka Corinthian (NY).
[Died 11 June 1979.

EZARD, Bernard John Bycroft, CBE 1957; *b* 13 Dec. 1900; *s* of late Edward Henry Ezard, MD, DSc Edinburgh, MA Cantab and late Jessie Hogg Ezard (*née* Glegg); *m* 1st, 1927, Mabel Elsie Burton (*d* 1970); one *s*; 2nd, 1971, Doreen Winifred Ward. *Educ:* Perse Sch.; Trinity Hall, Cambridge (MA, LLB). Called to the Bar (Middle Temple), 1922. Asst solicitor, Ministry of Labour and National Service, 1948-59; Solicitor to Ministry of Labour, 1959-62. *Recreations:* archæology, literature, walking. *Address:* Parkgate, 30 Upper South View, Farnham, Surrey. *T:* Farnham 6023.
[Died 24 Nov. 1976.

EZRA, Sir Alwyn, Kt 1936; FRGS, FRSA, FRES, FZS, JP, 1928; *b* 1900; *s* of Joseph Elias Ezra, Bombay. *Educ:* Bombay. Government Nominee on Bombay Municipal Corporation, 1929-32; Bombay Chamber of Commerce Representative on Corporation, 1932-35; represented Corporation on Board of Trustees of Prince of Wales Museum of Western India, and on Executive Cttee of Bombay Presidency Infant Welfare Soc.; Chairman: Central Cine Corp.; J. Curtis & Co. Ltd; MEMA Ltd; Patel (India) Ltd. Hon. Presidency Magistrate (Single Sitting) Bombay, 1931; Hon. Special Magistrate, Matheran, 1933; Mem., Executive Cttee St John Ambulance Association Indian Council, Advisory Cttee Jamsetji Jeejeebhoy and Allied Hospitals; and other cttees. Donor, Sir Alwyn Ezra Holiday Home for British Troops, Kashmir, and two Mobile Canteens for the Services. *Address:* Buckley Court, 25 Wodehouse Road, Bombay 1, India. *Clubs:* Willingdon, Orient, Turf (Bombay).
[Died July 1974.

F

FADDEN, Rt. Hon. Sir Arthur William, PC 1942; GCMG 1958 (KCMG 1951); Treasurer, Commonwealth of Australia, 1940-41 and 1949-58, also Deputy Prime Minister, 1949-58; Member Australian House of Representatives for Darling Downs, Qld, 1936-49 and for McPherson, Qld, 1949-58; *b* 13 April 1895; *s* of Richard Fadden, Ingham, North Qld; *m* 1916, Ilma Thornber; two *s* two *d*. Asst Treasurer and Asst Minister for Supply and Development, Australia, March 1940; Minister for Air and for Civil Aviation, Aug.-Oct. 1940; Prime Minister, Aug.-Oct. 1941; Leader of Opposition, 1941-43; of Country Party, 1941-58. Mem. of Advisory War Council, 1940-45. Acting Prime Minister 8 times, 1950-56. *Address:* Box 575J, GPO, Brisbane, Qld, Australia. [*Died 21 April 1973.*

FAGAN, Brian Walter, CBE 1949; MC 1918; *b* 13 Feb. 1893; *s* of late Sir Patrick Fagan, KCIE, CSI; *m* 1918, Mary Gwendoline Margaret, *er d* of late William Moir; two *s*. *Educ:* Rugby Sch. (Scholar); Queen's Coll., Oxford (Scholar). BA 1918. Served European War, 6th Batt. Oxford and Bucks Lt Inf., 1914-18; GSO3, 3rd Army, 1918 (despatches twice, wounded twice). Dir of Edward Arnold (Publishers) Ltd, retired 1960. Pres. of Publishers' Association, 1945-47. *Address:* The Wellington Hotel, Mount Ephraim, Tunbridge Wells, Kent. *T:* Tunbridge Wells 20286. [*Died 12 Jan. 1971.*

FAGE, Arthur, CBE 1953; FRS 1942; FRAeS, ARCS; formerly Superintendent of the Aerodynamics Division of National Physical Laboratory; *b* 4 March 1890; *s* of William John and Annie Fage; *m* 1920, Winifred Eliza Donnelly (*d* 1951); one *s* one *d*. *Educ:* Portsmouth Royal Dockyard Sch.; Royal College of Science (Royal Exhibitioner). *Publications:* numerous scientific papers, mostly on aero- and hydro-dynamics in Proc. Royal Society, etc. *Address:* 65 High Point, Richmond Hill Road, Edgbaston, Birmingham B15 3RS. [*Died 7 Nov. 1977.*

FAIRBAIRN, Thomas Charles; Hon. RCM; dramatist and producer of opera and pageants; *b* 26 March 1874; *s* of Charles Fairbairn and Emma Bastow; *m* 1904, Antonie Seiter, a singer of opera; two *s*. *Educ:* New Holland; Maxton, Scotland. Began as Engineer; later, Operatic vocalist and stage manager, Moody Manners Opera Co.; produced in Covent Garden and Drury Lane for Beecham Opera Cos; ran own opera cos in Surrey Theatre; produced opera in India and Burma; produced own dramatic version of Hiawatha, with the Royal Choral Society, Royal Albert Hall, 1924 (an annual event); founded Fairbairn Pageant Choir for Elijah in 1934; same year produced Hiawatha, Open Air Theatre, Scarborough, and other works, including Faust and Tannhäuser, all in Pageant form; Elijah, a Passion Pageant, and Faust with the Fairbairn Pageant Choir, Royal Albert Hall, 1936, 1937, 1938, and 1939. Produced Hiawatha in the Exhibition Building, Melbourne, Australia, 1939; in 1940 began to dramatise in music, drama and pageant form, The Holy Bible, from the fall of Lucifer/Satan, until the second coming of Christ, in 14 separate pageant performances, completed in 1972. *Publications:* Robert Burns, a folk song opera, produced by the Peoples Theatre, Dumbarton, 1939; The Bible Story, edn for schools, 1972. *Recreations:* writing, and endeavouring to restore the past glories of Glastonbury. *Address:* 41 Essex Park, W Finchley, N3. [*Died 6 Jan. 1978.*

FAIRBAIRN, Sir William Albert, 5th Bt of Ardwick, *cr* 1869; *b* 6 April 1902; *o surv. s* of 4th Bt and Jennie Cora, *d* of Albert Davis, Boston; *S* father, 1931; *m* 1925, Christine Renée Cotton, *y d* of late Rev. Canon Croft, Kelvedon Vicarage, Essex; two *s* one *d* (and one *d* decd). *Educ:* privately. *Heir: s* James Brooke Fairbairn [*b* 10 Dec. 1930; *m* 1960, Mary Russell Scott, *d* of Dr W. R. Scott, MB, ChB, FFARCS, Weymouth; two *s* one *d*]. *Address:* Loom House, Radlett, Herts. *T:* Radlett 6446. [*Died 18 Dec. 1972.*

FAIRBURN, Harold, CMG 1935; *b* 1884. Appointed Assistant Commissioner of Police, Federated Malay States, 1904; Deputy Commissioner, 1921; Inspector General of Police, Straits Settlements, 1925; retired, 1938. JP Hants, 1942. *Address:* 75 Sea Mills Lane, Bristol 9. *T:* 683952. [*Died 7 June 1973.*

FAIRFAX, James Griffyth; *b* 15 July 1886; *e s* of C. B. Fairfax, Sydney, NSW; *m* 1922, Rosetta Mary, *o d* of late Sir John Glover, GCMG, RN; one *d*. *Educ:* Winchester Coll.; New Coll., Oxford, 3rd Class Hon. Mods, 1st Class Hon. Sch. English Language. Called to Bar, Inner Temple, 1912; Bar of NSW, Australia, 1920; MP (C) Norwich, 1924-29; contested the Div., 1929; served European War, 1914-19 (Mesopotamia) (despatches four times); Capt. RASC attached 15th Indian Div.; mem. Exec. Council Assoc. Chambers of Commerce, 1928-45.

Publications: Poems, 1908; Troubled Pool, 1911; Horns of Taurus, 1912; Temple of Janus, 1917; Mesopotamia, Carmina Rapta, 1919; The Fifth Element, 1937; and numerous contributions to the Press. *Address:* Villa Sous la Madone, 06 Roquebrune, France. *TA:* Barclosea Monte Carlo. *T:* Roquebrune 829092. *Clubs:* Athenæum, Hurlingham. [*Died 27 Jan. 1976.*

FAIRFAX-LUCY, Major Sir Brian Fulke Cameron-Ramsay-, 5th Bt, *cr* 1836; *b* 18 Dec. 1898; *s* of Col Sir Henry William Cameron-Ramsay-Fairfax-Lucy, 3rd Bt, CB, and Ada Christina, *d* of Henry Spencer Lucy, Charlecote, Warwicks; *S* brother, 1944; *m* 1933, Hon. Alice Caroline Helen Buchan, *o d* of 1st Baron Tweedsmuir, PC, GCMG, GCVO, CH; one *s* one *d*. *Educ:* Eton; RMC. Queen's Own Cameron Highlanders: served European War, 1916-18 (wounded); NW Frontier, India, 1919-25 (ADC to GOC Madras District, 1922-25); Army of Occupation, Germany, 1926; Adjutant 2nd Cameron Highlanders, 1927-30; ADC to Lord High Commissioner to Gen. Assembly of Church of Scotland, 1931-34; retired, 1933; War of 1939-45 (Major). National Greyhound Racing Club: Steward, 1928-33; Stipendiary Steward, 1933-36. *Publications:* Author of a number of children's books, including: Horses in the Valley; The Horse from India; The Cat Did It; The Children of the House. *Recreations:* riding, breeding racehorses, shooting, fishing, gardening. *Heir: s* Edmund John William Hugh Cameron-Ramsay-Fairfax-Lucy, *b* 4 May 1945. *Address:* The Mill, Fossebridge, Glos. *T:* Fossebridge 261; Charlecote Park, Warwicks. *T:* Wellesbourne Park 675. *Club:* Lansdowne. [*Died 21 Jan. 1974.*

FAIRFIELD, (Josephine) Letitia Denny, CBE 1919; MD, ChB Edinburgh; DPH London; Barrister-at-Law of the Middle Temple; *b* 10 March 1885; *e d* of late C. Fairfield. *Educ:* Richmond High Sch.; Edinburgh Univ.; University Coll., London. Bathgate Memorial Prize of Royal College of Surgeons, Edinburgh, 1904; MB, ChB, Edinburgh, 1907; MD, 1911; Area Medical Controller QMAAC 1917; and transferred to the RAF Medical Service, 1918; RAMC, 1940-42; Lieut-Col (retired) RAMC; Senior Medical Officer, London County Council, 1911-48. Pres., Medico-Legal Soc., 1957 and 1958. Papal Medal, Pro Ecclesia et Pontifice, 1966. *Publications:* Trial of John Henry Straffen, 1954; Epilepsy, 1954. *Address:* 60 Beaufort Mansions, Beaufort Street, SW3. *T:* 01-352 3917. [*Died 1 Feb. 1978.*

FAIRFIELD, Sir Ronald (McLeod), Kt 1970; CBE 1966; BScEng, CEng, FIMechE, FIEE, FIEEE; Chairman: Chemring Ltd, since 1963; Automatic Light Controlling Co. Ltd, since 1963; Royal Worcester Ltd, since 1975 (Director, since 1971); Royal Worcester Spode Ltd, since 1976; Deputy Chairman, since 1974, Director, since 1972, Ransome, Hoffmann, Pollard Ltd; *b* Newcastle upon Tyne, 25 May 1911; *er s* of late Geoffrey Fairfield and Inez Helen Thorneycroft McLeod; *m* 1st, 1939, Mary Moore (marr diss. 1952); 2nd, 1971, Margaret Josephine Wiggans. *Educ:* Llandaff Cathedral Sch.; King Edward's Sch., Bath; Erith Tech. Coll.; London Univ. Trainee Apprentice, Callender's Cable & Con. Co. Ltd, 1929; Research Engr, 1932; Mullard Radio Valve Co., 1934; rejoined Callender Co., 1937 as Tech. Man. Leigh Works, and Erith Works, 1942; on amal. of Brit. Ins. Cables Ltd and Callender Co. in 1945 to form BICC, became Chief Engr (Designs and Processes) of new Co.; Director and General Manager: former St Helens Cable & Rubber Co. Ltd, 1948-51; W. T. Glover & Co. Ltd, 1952; BIC (Sub. Cables) Ltd, 1953 (later Dep. Chm.); apptd BICC Bd, 1954 as Dir (Prod. and Engrg); Dir (Home Ops), 1958; Asst Man. Dir, 1960; Jt Man. Dir, 1962; Dep. Chm. and Man. Dir 1963-70; Dep. Chm. 1970-72; Chm., BIC Con. Co. Ltd, 1964-68; Dep. Chm., Submarine Cables Ltd, 1961-66; Chm., European Cables Ltd, 1962-72. Mem., Cablemakers War Emergency Tech. Cttee; Mem. Cttee, Transmission Sect. (later Supply Sect.), IEE, 1943-45; IEE Premium for 1956-57; Mem., NEDC for Elec. Engrg Industry, 1964-71; Member Council, BEAMA (Pres., 1968-69). Gilbreth Gold Medal, Inst. of Work Study Practitioners, 1970. *Publications:* various Tech. papers. *Recreations:* game shooting, forestry. *Address:* Courts Farm, Haslemere, Surrey. *T:* Haslemere 3485. [*Died 25 Nov. 1978.*

FAIRHAVEN, 2nd Baron, *cr* 1929 (UK) and 1961 (UK) (new creation); **Henry Rogers Broughton;** Major, retired; *b* 1 Jan. 1900; 2nd *s* of late Urban Hanlon Broughton (who would have been granted a barony in 1929 had he lived) and *yr b* of 1st Baron Fairhaven (2nd *cr* 1961); *S* brother, 1966; *m* 1st, 1932, Hon. Diana Rosamond (*d* 1937), *o d* of late Capt. Hon. Coulson Fellowes; one *s*; 2nd, 1953, Joyce Irene, *widow* of Lieut G. H. C. Dickens, RN. *Educ:* Harrow; Royal Military College, Sandhurst. Joined Royal Horse Guards, 1919; Capt., 1926; retired, 1933; rejoined, 1939-45. *Heir: s* Hon. Ailwyn Henry George Broughton [*b* 16 Nov. 1936; *m* 1960, Patricia, *d* of Col J.

H. Magill; two s two d]. *Address:* 56 Eaton Place, SW1. *T:* 01-235 4174; South Walsham Hall, near Norwich, Norfolk. *T:* South Walsham 202. *Clubs:* Boodle's, Buck's.
[Died 6 April 1973.

FAISAL, King; see Saudi Arabia, HM the King of.

FALCON, Michael; b 1888; s of late Michael Falcon; m 1920, Kathleen, o d of late Captain Gascoigne, Seaforth Highlanders, and Mrs Gascoigne; one s three d. *Educ:* Harrow; Pembroke Coll., Cambridge. BA; LLB; Barrister-at-Law, Inner Temple; MP (U) East Norfolk, 1918-23; High Sheriff of Norfolk, 1943-44. *Address:* 10 Cathedral Close, Norwich NR1 4DH. *T:* Norwich 23984.   *[Died 27 Feb. 1976.*

FALCONER, Murray Alexander, MCh (NZ), FRCS, FRACS; FRCPsych; Director, Neuro-surgical Unit, Guy's, Maudsley, and King's College Hospitals, SE5, 1950-75; b 15 May 1910; s of Alexander R. Falconer, CBE, and Agnes J. Falconer; m 1939, Valda H. Falconer; two d. *Educ:* Otago University, Dunedin, NZ. Major RAMC, 1941-43. Assoc. Prof. of Neurosurgery, Otago Univ., 1943-50; Fellow, Mayo Foundation, Rochester, Minn., 1937-38; Nuffield Dominions Fellow in Surgery, University of Oxford, 1938-40; Hon. Consulting Neurological Surgeon, Johns Hopkins Hosp., Baltimore, Md, 1959-; Visiting Prof. of Surgery: Univ. of Calif., Los Angeles, 1960, 1966; Harvard Univ., 1971; St Louis Univ., 1972; Pittsburgh Univ., 1975. Comdr, Order of Cedars, Lebanon, 1959. *Publications:* several in medical journals. *Recreation:* golf. *Address:* 48 Durham Avenue, Bromley BR2 0QG. *T:* 01-460 5575. *Clubs:* Athenæum; Dunedin (NZ).   *[Died 11 Aug. 1977.*

FALK, Oswald Toynbee, CBE 1920; Partner in Falk and Partners; b 1879; s of late H. John Falk, West Kirby, Cheshire and Rachel, d of Joseph Toynbee. *Educ:* Rugby; Balliol Coll., Oxford. Treasury, 1917-19; Treasury Delegate, Paris Peace Conference, 1919. *Address:* Tall Trees, Boar's Hill, Oxford. *T:* Oxford 35649.   *[Died 11 Nov. 1972.*

FALLA, Sir Robert Alexander, KBE 1973; CMG 1959; FRSNZ; Chairman, Nature Conservation Council, New Zealand, 1962-74; b 21 July 1901; s of G. Falla; m 1928, Elayne M., d of A. Burton, Te Aroha; one s two d. *Educ:* Auckland Grammar Sch.; Auckland Univ. (MA, DSc). Lecturer, Auckland Teachers' Training Coll., 1925-30; Asst Zoologist, British, Australian and New Zealand Antarctic Research Expedition, 1929-31; Ornithologist, Auckland War Memorial Museum, 1931-35; Asst Dir, 1936-37; Dir, Canterbury Museum, 1937-47; Dir, Dominion Museum, Wellington, 1947-66. Served War of 1939-45. Delegate, First Gen. Conference, New Zealand Nat. Commission, UNESCO, 1946; Mem. Ross Sea Cttee, 1955. Polar Medal (bronze). *Publications:* (jtly) A Field Guide to the Birds of New Zealand, 1966, rev. edn, as The New Guide to the Birds of New Zealand, 1979; scientific papers and reports on Antarctic birds of Mawson expedition. *Address:* Kotari Road, Day's Bay, Wellington, New Zealand.   *[Died 23 Feb. 1979.*

FALLOWS, Rt. Rev. (William) Gordon; Bishop of Sheffield, since 1971; Clerk of the Closet to the Queen, since 1975; b 21 June 1913; s of William and Anne Joyce Fallows; m 1940, Edna Mary Blakeman; two s (one d decd). *Educ:* Barrow Grammar School; St Edmund Hall, Oxford; Ripon Hall. BA 1935, MA 1939. Deacon, 1936; Priest, 1937; Curate of Holy Trinity, Leamington Spa, 1936-39; Vicar of Styvechale, Coventry, 1939-45; OCF 1941-44. Rural Dean of Preston, 1946-55; Proctor in Convocation, 1950-55; Archdeacon of Lancaster, 1955-59; Vicar of Preston, 1945-59; Principal of Ripon Hall, Oxford, 1959-68; Bishop Suffragan of Pontefract, 1968-71; Canon of Blackburn, 1952; Examining Chaplain to Bishop of Wakefield, 1968-71; Chaplain to the Queen, 1953-68. Select Preacher, Univ. of Oxford, 1961. *Publication:* Mandell Creighton and the English Church, 1964. *Recreation:* fell walking. *Address:* Bishopscroft, Snaithing Lane, Sheffield S10 3LG. *T:* Sheffield 302170. *Clubs:* Authors; Sheffield.   *[Died 17 Aug. 1979.*

FALLS, Capt. Cyril Bentham, CBE 1967; b 1888; e s of late Sir Charles Fausset Falls; m 1915, Elizabeth Heath; two d. *Educ:* Bradfield Coll.; Portora Royal Sch., Enniskillen; London Univ.; abroad. Late Royal Inniskilling Fusiliers; served European War, with regiment, General Staff 36th and 62nd Divisions, Liaison Officer with French (despatches twice, French Croix de Guerre, two citations); employed, 1923-39, in Historical Section (Military Branch) Cttee of Imperial Defence. Military Correspondent of the Times, 1939-53; Chichele Prof. of the History of War, Oxford, and Fellow of All Souls Coll., 1946-53, Emeritus Prof., Oxford, since 1953. *Publications:* Official: the official military histories of the British Campaigns in Egypt and Palestine (first volume with Lieut-Gen. Sir George MacMunn),

WWW—10

Macedonia and France (1917, first volume); Unofficial: Rudyard Kipling, A Critical Study; The History of the 36th (Ulster) Division; The Critic's Armoury (essays); War Books, a Critical Guide; The Birth of Ulster; Marshal Foch (Order of Merit Series); The Nature of Modern Warfare, 1941; Ordeal by Battle, 1943; The Man for the Job (fiction); A Short History of the Second World War; Elizabeth's Irish Wars; A Hundred Years of War; Mountjoy-Elizabethan General; The Gordon Highlanders in the First World War; The First World War; The Art of War from the Age of Napoleon to the Present Day; Armageddon: 1918, 1964; Caporetto, 1917, 1966. *Recreations:* formerly yachting, shooting, and riding; now chiefly in recollection. *Address:* 16 Archery Close, W2. *T:* 01-262 1524. *Club:* Turf.   *[Died 23 April 1971.*

FANNER, John Lewis, MA; Headmaster of Alleyn's School, since 1967; b 7 Dec. 1921; s of H. L. Fanner, Croydon; m 1947, Jill Carne, o d of J. O. Corin, Illogan, Cornwall; two d. *Educ:* Whitgift Sch.; Brasenose Coll., Oxford (1st cl. Nat. Sci.). MA Oxon 1947. War service, RAF Technical Branch, 1942-45. Asst Master: Shrewsbury Sch., 1947-52; Harrow Sch., 1952-60; Headmaster, Lewes County Gram. Sch. for Boys, 1960-67. *Recreations:* reading, sailing. *Address:* 8 Dulwich Village, SE21. *T:* 01-693 2983; Gerrans, near Truro, Cornwall. *Club:* St Mawes, Percuil (Sailing).   *[Died 15 Dec. 1975.*

FANSHAWE, Maj.-Gen. Sir Evelyn Dalrymple, Kt 1961; CB 1946; CBE 1942; DL; b 25 May 1895; e s of late Gen. Sir Hew Dalrymple Fanshawe, KCB, KCMG; m 1920, Marie (d 1978) e d of late Sir Victor Harari, CMG; no c. *Educ:* King's Sch., Canterbury; Royal Military Coll., Sandhurst. 2nd Lieut The Queen's Bays. 1914; served European War, 1914-18, France, Egypt, Palestine, Mesopotamia, Persia, Russia, Syria (1914 star, Allied and Victory medals); ADC, GOC Cavalry Corps, 1915; seconded to RFC 1915-19; returned to Regt and made Adjutant, 1919; Lieut-Col The Queen's Bays, 1935; Col, 1938; Brig. to Comd. 20th Mech. Cav. Bde 1939; Comd. 20 Armd Bde 1940-41; Maj.-Gen. Armd Training and Comdr RAC Training Establishment, 1942-45; retired pay, 1945. UNRRA Dir in British Zone of Germany, 1945-48. Dir of the International Refugee Organisation in British Zone of Germany, 1948-52; Mission to Dominion Countries on behalf of UNO, 1952. Chm., Pre-Services Cttee, Northants TA Assoc., 1953-65; Pres., Northants Spastic Assoc.; Pres. Northants Outward Bound Cttee; Vice-President: Northants County Amateur Athletic Assoc.; Northants County Cricket Club. Hon. Treas. East Midlands Area, Conservative and Unionist Associations, 1952-67; Chm., Kettering Div., Conservative and Unionist Assoc., 1953-65 (Pres. 1965); Chm. of Stallion Cttee, Hunters Improvement Soc. (President 1965, 1975); President: Ponies of Britain Club, 1962; National Pony Soc., 1966, 1975; Pres., Anglo-Trakehner Horse Assoc., 1976. High Sheriff, Northants, 1960; DL Northants, 1961. King's Coronation Medal, 1937. *Recreations:* hunting, polo, yachting, shooting and fishing, racing, flying. *Address:* Guilsborough House, Northampton. *T:* Guilsborough 258. *Clubs:* Cavalry and Guards; Royal Armoured Corps Yacht; Travellers' (Paris).
[Died 14 March 1979.

FAREY-JONES, Frederick William; Chairman of Farey-Jones (Insurance) Ltd, Insurance Brokers; b 21 May 1904; s of Evan Francis and Gladys Gertrude Jones; m Lilian Ada (née Farey); one s one d. *Educ:* Queen Elizabeth's Grammar Sch., Carmarthen; Paris, Liége, Geneva. Founder of the Conference of International Air Traffic Operators; also founder of the revived Air Transport Association. Contested (C) Goole, 1950 and Pembroke, 1951; MP (C) Watford, 1955-64. Director: Australian Estates Ltd; Nelson Financial Trust Ltd; Charterland & General Ltd. Master, Worshipful Co. of Horners, 1970. FRSA. Knight Commander of Order of Civil Merit (Spain), 1958. *Address:* Ruffetts Wood, Chipstead, Surrey; 46 Chancery Lane, WC2. *Clubs:* United Service & Royal Aero, City Livery; Knights of the Round Table. *[Died 18 Feb. 1974.*

FARGHER, John Adrian, CMG 1957; The South Australian Railways Commissioner, 1953-66; b 13 Jan. 1901; s of Philip and Matilda Maud Fargher; m 1926, Elsie Pearl, d of Charles French; one s one d (and one d decd). *Educ:* Melbourne Univ (MCE). *Publications:* has contributed a number of Papers to Journal of The Institution of Engineers, Australia. *Recreation:* golf. *Address:* 8 Cambridge Terrace, Brighton, South Australia 5048, Australia.   *[Died 16 Nov. 1977.*

FARINGDON, 2nd Baron cr 1916; Alexander Gavin Henderson, Bt cr 1902; b 20 March 1902; e s of late Lt-Col Hon. H. G. Henderson, CVO, and Lady Violet Dalzell, sister of 15th Earl of Carnwath; S grandfather, 1934. *Educ:* Eton; McGill Univ., Montreal; Christ Church, Oxford (MA). Diploma of Internat.

Exhibn of Brussels, 1935. Auxiliary Fire Service, 1940; Column Officer, NFS, 1941; Staff 15 FF. Treasurer, Cttee of Inquiry into Non-Intervention in Spain, 1936; Pres., Swindon Branch, Labour League of Youth, 1936; Treasurer, Nat. Council for Civil Liberties, 1940-45; co-opted Mem. of Exec. Cttee, Inter-Parly Union (British Group), 1948; Mem., Colonial Economic and Develt Council, 1948-51; Mem., Parly Cttee of Labour Party, 1957-60. Fabian Society: elected and co-opted Mem. of Exec. Cttee, 1942-66; Vice-Chm., 1959-60; Chm., 1960-61. London County Council: co-opted Mem., Mental Hospitals Cttee, 1937-38; Mem. for W Woolwich, 1958-61; Alderman, 1961-65. Adv. Expert, GLC Historic Buildings Bd. President: Assoc. of Friends of City Churches, 1943; Theatres Adv. Council, 1964; British Fire Services Assoc., 1960-69. Chm., Cttee on Appearance of Local Authorities' Housing Estates. Member: Council, Nat. Buildings Record, 1942; Central Housing Adv. Cttee, 1946; No Conscription Council, 1946; Colonial Social Welfare Adv. Cttee, 1947-52; Central Adv. Water Cttee, 1949-52; Treatment, Offenders Cttee, CO, 1951; Historic Buildings Council, MPBW, 1964. Trustee, Wallace Collection, 1946-53, 1966-73. FRSA 1936. Master, Worshipful Co. of Plumbers, 1968-69. *Heir: n* Charles Michael Henderson [*b* 3 July 1937; *m* 1959, Sarah Caroline, *d* of Major J. M. E. Askew, CBE; three *s* one *d*]. *Address:* Buscot Park, Faringdon, Oxon. *Clubs:* Canning, Reform.   [*Died* 29 Jan. 1977.

FARMER, Norman William, CBE 1955; Director, S. W. Farmer & Son Ltd; *b* 11 Oct. 1901; *s* of Sydney William and Anna Emily Farmer; *m* 1925, Brenda Modwyn Briselden; one *s* one *d. Educ:* Hither Green Sch.; Addey and Stanhope Sch. Constructional Engineer in family business (established 1898). Deputy Chairman, London County Council, 1960-61; Chm., North Lewisham Conservative Assoc., 1946-64; Chm. London Conservative Union, 1959-60. Mem. of LCC for North Lewisham, 1945-65. Liveryman, Founders' Company; Life Deacon, Lewisham Congregational Church. *Address:* Avonhurst, Camden Park Road, Chislehurst, Kent. *Clubs:* Royal Automobile, City Livery, United Wards, Guild of Freemen.   [*Died* 22 Dec. 1971.

FARNCOMB, Rear-Adm. Harold Bruce, CB 1945; DSO 1943; MVO 1935; RAN retired; Solicitor; *b* Sydney, Australia, 28 Feb. 1899; *s* of Frank Farncomb and Helen Sampson; *m* 1927, Jean Ross Nott; no *c. Educ:* Royal Australian Naval Coll. Joined Royal Australian Navy, 1913; Grand Fleet, 1917-18; RN Staff Coll., 1923-24; Imperial Defence Coll., 1930; Comdr, 1932; HMAS Australia, 1933-35, return of Duke of Gloucester (MVO); Admiralty (NID), 1935-37; One of RAN representatives at the funeral of King George V; Attached to the Delegation from the Argentine Republic at the Coronation of King George VI; Capt., 1937; Commodore, 1st class, Dec. 1944. Commanded HMA Ships Perth, Canberra, Australia (1939-44), HMS Attacker (1944), HMA Squadron (1944-45), Commodore Superintendent of Training (1945-46), Commodore (later Rear-Adm.) Comdg Australian Squadron (DSO, CB, despatches thrice); Rear-Adm., 1947. Called to Bar, Supreme Court of NSW, 1958; transferred to Solicitor, 1963, Commander United States Legion of Merit; US Navy Cross. *Recreation:* lawn tennis. *Address:* 10 Wyldefel Gardens, Pott's Point, Sydney, Australia. *Clubs:* United Service; Australian (Sydney).
                                   [*Died* 12 Feb. 1971.

FARRELL, James Gordon; author; *b* 23 Jan. 1935; *s* of William Farrell and Josephine Farrell (*née* Russell). *Educ:* Rossall Sch.; Brasenose Coll., Oxford (BA). Harkness Fellowship, New York, 1966-68. *Publications:* The Lung, 1964; A Girl in the Head, 1967; Troubles, 1970 (Geoffrey Faber Memorial Prize); The Siege of Krishnapur, 1973 (Booker Prize); The Singapore Grip, 1978. *Address:* c/o Deborah Rogers Ltd, 29 Goodge Street, W1.
                                   [*Died* 12 Aug. 1979.

FARRELL, James Thomas; Novelist and Critic; *b* Chicago, Ill, 27 Feb. 1904; *m* Dorothy Butler (divorced); *m* Hortense Alden (divorced, 1955); one *s* ; re-married Dorothy Butler (separated). *Educ:* De Paul (now DePaul) Univ., Chicago; Univ. of Chicago; New York Univ., no degrees. Worked for express company, in gasoline filling station, as salesman, etc; received John Simon Guggenheim Memorial Foundation Fellowship in Creative Literature, 1926-37; Nat. Inst. Arts and Letters, NYC. Formerly Adjunct Prof., St Peter's Coll., Jersey City, NJ; in residence, Richmond Coll., Richmond, Va, Sept. 1969-Feb. 1970; Vis. Writer, English Dept, Glasboro Coll., NJ, 1973. Hon. Dr of Letters: Miami Univ., Oxford, Ohio, 1968; Columbia Coll., Chicago, 1974; Glassboro Coll., 1976; Illinois Univ., 1979; Bradley Univ., Illinois, 1979. Messing Award for Contributions to Literature, St Louis Univ. Library Associates, 1973; Nat. Foundn of Humanities Grant, 1978; Emerson-Thoreau Medal, Amer. Adad. of Arts and Sciences, 1979; Prof. Achievement

Award, Alumni Assoc., Univ. of Chicago. *Publications:* Young Lonigan—A Boyhood in Chicago Streets, 1932; Gas House McGinty, 1933; The Young Manhood of Studs Lonigan, 1934; Calico Shoes, 1934; Judgment Day, 1935; Guillotine Party and Other Stories, 1935; A Note on Literary Criticism, 1936; A World I Never Made, 1936; Can All This Grandeur Perish, 1937; The Collected Short Stories of James T. Farrell, 1937 (England, as Fellow Countrymen); No Star is Lost, 1938; Tommy Gallagher's Crusade, 1939; Father and Son, 1940 (in England, 1943); Ellen Rogers, 1941 (in England, 1942); $1000 a Week and Other Stories, 1942; My Days of Anger, 1943 (England 1945); To Whom it may Concern, 1944; The League of Frightened Philistines and other Papers; Bernard Clare, 1946 (England 1948); When Boyhood Dreams Come True, 1946; More Fellow-Countrymen, 1946; Literature and Morality, 1947; The Life Adventurous, 1947; A Misunderstanding, 1948; The Road Between, 1949; (under pseudonym of Jonathan Lituleson Fogarty) The Name is Fogarty; An American Dream Girl, 1950; This Man and This Woman, 1951; Yet Other Waters, 1952; The Face of Time (England), 1953; Reflections at Fifty (England), 1954; French Girls are Vicious, 1955; A Baseball Diary, also A Dangerous Woman and Other Stories, 1957; It Has Come to Pass, 1958; Boarding House Blues (novel), 1961; Side Street (stories), 1961; Sound of the City (stories), 1962; The Silence of History (novel), 1963; What Time Collects (novel), 1967; The Collected Poems of James T. Farrell, 1965; Lonely For the Future (novel), 1966; When Time Was Born (prose poem), 1966; New Year's Eve, 1929 (novel), 1967; A Brand New Life (novel), 1968; Childhood Is Not Forever and other Stories, 1969; Judith (novel), 1969; Invisible Swords (novel), 1970; Judith and other stories, 1973; The Dunne Family, 1976; Literary Essays 1954-1974; Olive and Mary Anne: five tales, 1977; The Death of Nora Ryan, 1978. *Address:* c/o Doubleday & Co., 277 Park Avenue, New York, NY 10017, USA.   [*Died* 22 Aug. 1979.

FARRELL, Michael James; Fellow, Gonville and Caius College, Cambridge, since 1958; Reader in Economics, Cambridge University, since 1970; *b* 9 May 1926; *s* of Richard James Farrell and Margaret Edith Deane; *m* 1952, Margaret Frances Bacon; five *s. Educ:* King Edward VII Sch., Sheffield; New Coll., Oxford (Scholar). MA Oxon 1953, MA Cantab 1953. Commonwealth Fund Fellow, 1951-53; Asst Lectr 1953-56, Lectr 1956-70, in Econs, Cambridge Univ.; Vis. Professor: Yale Univ., 1962; Univ. of California at Berkeley, 1966-67; Ford Distinguished Vis. Res. Prof., Carnegie-Mellon Univ., 1969. Fellow of Econometric Soc., 1962-; Editor, Jl of Industrial Econs, 1963-; Jt Man. Editor, Review of Econ. Studies, 1965-68. *Publications:* Fuller Employment?, 1965; (ed) Readings in Welfare Economics, 1973; articles in econ. and statistical jls. *Address:* Latham Close, Cambridge. *T:* Cambridge 56124.
                                   [*Died* 27 Oct. 1975.

FARRER, Hon. Dame Frances (Margaret), DBE 1950; MA; Director, Abinger Hall Estate Co., since 1942; *b* 17 March 1895; *d* of 2nd Baron Farrer. *Educ:* St Leonard's Sch., St Andrews; Newnham Coll., Cambridge. Hon. Sec. Leith Hill Musical Festival, 1919-39; Gen. Sec., National Federation of Women's Institutes, 1929-59; Member: Independent Television Authority, 1957-61; Post Office Advisory Council, 1957-64; Cttee on Rural Bus Services, 1959-61. *Address:* West Hackhurst, Abinger Hammer, Surrey.   [*Died* 27 Jan. 1977.

FARRINGTON, Benjamin; *b* 10 July 1891; *s* of Thomas Farrington and Mary Emily Foreman; *m* 1935, Ruth Hedwig Schechter (*d* 1942); *m* 1943, Cecily Barbara Sell; one *d. Educ:* University Coll., Cork; Trinity Coll., Dublin. Asst in Classics, Queen's Univ., Belfast, 1916-20; Lecturer in Greek, University of Capetown, 1920-22; Senior Lecturer in Classics, 1922-30; Prof. of Latin, 1930-35; Lecturer in Classics, University of Bristol, 1935-36; Prof. of Classics, University Coll., Swansea, 1936-56. *Publications:* Primum Graius Homo; Samuel Butler and the Odyssey; Science in Antiquity, rev. edn 1969; Science and Politics in the Ancient World, 1939; Greek Science: Its Meaning for Us, Vol. I. 1944, Vol. II, 1948, revised edn in one Vol., 1953; Head and Hand in Ancient Greece, 1947; Francis Bacon, Philosopher of Industrial Science (New York), 1949, new edn 1973; The Philosophy of Francis Bacon, 1962; Aristotle: The Founder of Scientific Philosophy, 1965; What Darwin Really Said, 1965; The Faith of Epicurus, 1967; etc. *Address:* 8 Daniell's Walk, Lymington, Hants. *T:* Lymington 2059.
                                   [*Died* 17 Nov. 1974.

FARROW, Leslie William, CBE 1947; FCA, FID, FRSA; chartered accountant; *b* 7 Oct. 1888; *s* of late Albert Lee Farrow and Elfleda Susan Taylor; *m* 1915, Elsie Beatrice Allman; three *d. Educ:* Alleyn's, Dulwich; London Sch. of Economics. Formerly: dir of public companies, mem. of the Bacon Development Board; Deputy Controller of Paper, 1939-40; Dir for Commercial Relations, 1940-42; Deputy Chm. Rubber Control Board, 1942; Deputy Dir-Gen. (raw materials), Ministry of Supply, 1942; Chm. National Brick Advisory Council, Ministry of Works and Planning, 1942; Chm. Paper Economy Cttee, Ministry of Production, 1942; Mem. of Board of Referees, 1948. Paper Trade Gold Medal Award, 1967. *Address:* Dengie Manor, near Southminster, Essex. *T:* Tillingham 216. *Club:* City of London. *[Died* 17 *March* 1978.

FAULKNER OF DOWNPATRICK, Baron *cr* 1977 (Life Peer), of Downpatrick; **Arthur Brian Deane Faulkner,** PC (Northern Ireland) 1959; *b* 18 Feb. 1921; *er s* of late James Alexander Faulkner, OBE, and of Nora Lilian Faulkner; *m* 1951, Lucy Barbara Ethel, *o d* of William Forsythe, JP, and Ethel Forsythe; two *s* one *d. Educ:* Elm Park, Co. Armagh, Northern Ireland; College of St Columba, Rathfarnham, Co. Dublin. Dir, Belfast Collar Co. Ltd, 1941-63. MP (U) East Down, Parlt of N Ireland, 1949-73; Mem. (U), S Down, NI Assembly, 1973-75; Mem. (UPNI), S Down, NI Constitutional Convention, 1975-76; Govt Chief Whip and Parly Sec., Min. of Finance, N Ire., 1956-59; Minister: Home Affairs, 1959-63; Commerce, 1963-69; Development, 1969-71; Prime Minister and Minister of Home Affairs, 1971-72; Chief Exec. Mem., NI Executive, 1974; Leader, UPNI, 1974-76. *Posthumous publication:* Memoirs of a Statesman, ed John Houston, 1978. *Recreations:* hunting (Master Iveagh Hunt); sailing. *Address:* Highlands, Seaforde, Co. Down, Northern Ireland. *T:* Seaforde 663. *Clubs:* Ulster, Ulster Reform (Belfast); Royal North of Ireland Yacht.
                                        [Died 3 *March* 1977.

FAULKNER, Harry, CMG 1949; Retired as Director Telecommunications Engineering and Manufacturing Association, 1954-62; *b* 17 April 1892; *s* of Harry Faulkner, Nottingham; *m* 1915, Elsie Emma Bray, Norwich; three *s. Educ:* High Pavement Secondary Sch. and University Coll., Nottingham. Laurence Scott & Co., Norwich, 1911-14; appointed Asst Engineer in GPO, 1914; served in Royal Engineers (Signals), 1916-19; Engineer-in-charge Rugby Radio Station, 1925; Suptdg Engineer, N Wales District, 1935; Dep. Regional Dir, Wales and Border Counties, 1939; Controller of Factories, 1941-44; Asst Engineer-in-Chief, GPO, 1944-47; Deputy Engineer-in-Chief, GPO, 1947-54. Mem. of Council, IEE, 1945-48; Chm. South Midland Section, IEE, 1938-39; Chm. London meeting of Internat. Consultative Radio Cttee, 1953; leader of UK delegn to several Internat. Radio Confs. *Publications:* papers read before IEE, Instn of PO Electrical Engrs, etc. *Recreation:* golf. *Address:* 36 Park Gate, Somerhill Road, Hove 2, Sussex. *T:* Hove 71871.   *[Died* 11 *Jan.* 1971.

FAULKNER, Vincent Clements; Editorial Consultant, The Foundry Trade Journal; *b* 27 Dec. 1888; *s* of Isaac and Hannah Faulkner; *m* 1929, Alice MacGregor; one *d. Educ:* Wesley Coll.; Sheffield Univ. Pioneer in making Steel by electricity; 1st metallurgist to make electric steel in Spain, 1916; Pres. Institute of British Foundrymen, 1926; Council of British Cast Iron Research Association, 1927; and of National Ironfounding Employers Federation, 1933; Oliver Stubbs Medallist, 1934; Vice-Pres. Institute of Vitreous Enamellers, and mem. of the University of Sheffield Advisory Cttee on Degree Course in Foundry Practice 1935; Hon. Mem. Czecho-Slovak Foundrymen's Association, 1946; Pres. International Cttee of Foundry Technical Associations, 1948; Hon. Mem. Institute of British Foundrymen, 1949; Livery of Founders' Company, 1949. Chm., Borough Polytechnic Foundry Advisory Cttee, 1953; Co-opted to Governing Bd Borough Polytechnic, 1956; Hon. Mem. German Foundrymen's Assoc. Prix d'Honneur, International Cttee of Foundry Technical Assocs, 1955; Hon. Mem. Nat. Soc. of Master Patternmakers. Hon. Mem. French Foundrymen's Assoc., 1959. Levy Medallist, 1961. *Publications:* Articles in Times, Sheffield Independent, Die Giesserei; Scientific Papers in Proceedings of Iron and Steel Inst., American Foundrymen's Soc., etc. *Address:* 15 Crescent Court, Surbiton, Surrey. *T:* 01-399 1496.   *[Died* 24 *May* 1975.

FAVILLE, Air Vice-Marshal Roy, CBE 1945; *b* Aug. 1908; *s* of late K. W. Faville, Hamilton, New Zealand; *m* 1936, Beatrice Marie Louise, *d* of late Major (retired) J. E. Orr; one *s* one *d. Educ:* Canterbury Coll., University of New Zealand (BEng.). Commissioned, RAF, 1932; OC 42 (TB) Sqdn, 1940-41; OC 140 Wing, 1946-47; Air Force Staff at British Joint Services Mission, USA, 1950-52; Imperial Defence Coll., 1953; OC, RAF, St Eval, 1954. RAF Staff Coll., Bracknell; Asst Comdt, 1955-56; Commandant Aug. 1956; Air Officer Commanding No. 22 Group, RAF, Buntingsdale Hall, Market Drayton, Shropshire, 1957-60, retired 1960. Gen. Manager, Libya, Richard Costain (Middle East) Ltd, 1960-64. Sec., Torch Trophy Trust, 1968-70. *Address:* A-4 Apartamentos Roma, Avenida de Roma, Estartit, Gerona, Spain. *Club:* Royal Air Force. *[Died* 18 *June* 1980.

FAWCUS, Louis Reginald, CSI 1946; CIE 1939; *b* 7 Nov. 1887; *m* 1914, Irene d'A. Lesser; one *s* one *d. Educ:* Uppingham; Trinity Coll., Cambridge; University Coll., London. Entered ICS 1911; Mem. Board of Revenue, Bengal, 1940; Adviser to Governor of Bengal, 1945-46. *Address:* c/o National and Grindlay's Bank, 13 St James's Square, SW1; Apartment 2, 830 Lake Street, San Francisco, Calif 94118, USA. *T:* Bayview 1.1823. *Club:* East India and Sports.   *[Died* 23 *May* 1971.

FAY, Rt. Rev. Mgr. Cyril Damian, CBE 1960 (OBE 1953); Parish priest of St John's, Alton, Staffs, since 1963; Domestic Prelate to the Pope, since 1957; Conventual Chaplain, Sovereign and Military Order of the Knights of Malta, since 1959; Principal Roman Catholic Chaplain, Royal Navy, and Vicar General to Archbishop David Mathew for the Royal Navy, 1956-63, retired; *b* St Helens, Lancs 1903; *s* of John Fay and Mary Elizabeth (*née* Flynn). *Educ:* Up Holland Coll., Lancs; Ecclesiastical Studies in Latin Patriarchal Seminary, Palestine. Ordained Jerusalem, 1927; served on Mission at Es-Salt and Amman, Transjordan; English Sec. to Latin Patriarch of Jerusalem, and Chaplain to English Speaking Community, 1929-33; short service commn in RAF as Chaplain, 1933; commissioned in RN, 1936; apptd to 1st Cruiser Squadron, Mediterranean Fleet, in HMS Devonshire, 1937; detached in HMS Shropshire to S Atlantic, Sept. 1939; HMS Assegai, Durban, S Africa, 1943-44; with Naval Forces, Germany, May 1945-48; RN Barracks, Portsmouth, 1948; Admiralty, 1956. Hon. Canon, Collegiate Church of St Lawrence, Vittoriosa, Malta, 1961. Kt, Equestrian Order of Holy Sepulchre of Jerusalem, 1968. *Address:* Aston Hall, Aston, Staffs. *T:* Aston 2001. *Club:* Army and Navy.   *[Died* 14 *Oct.* 1975.

FAYLE, Lindley Robert Edmundson, CBE 1957 (OBE 1946); DSO 1945; Brigadier, retired; Rating Secretary, Royal Ocean Racing Club, since 1957; Chief Measurer to Offshore Rating Council of International Yacht Racing Union, since 1969; *b* 31 July 1903; *s* of late Lieut-Col R. J. L. Fayle, DSO, RAMC and of Mrs Fayle; *m* 1928, Cicily Rosamonde Annette, *d* of late C. F. Bigge and late Mrs Bigge; one *s* one *d. Educ:* Avondale Sch., Clifton; Clifton Coll.; RMA, Woolwich. 2nd Lieut, RE, 1923; Lieut 1925; India (Royal Bombay Sappers and Miners), 1925-30; Asst Instr, SME, 1932-36; Capt. 1934; Ministry of Supply, 1938-40; Major 1940; Actg Lieut-Col 1941; Temp. Lieut-Col 1942; War Office, 1940-42; CRE Kent Corps Troops (later 15 (Kent) GHQ Troops), 1942-45, UK and NW Europe; CRE 5th Inf. Div., 1945-46; Temp. Col 1946. Min. of Supply, 1946-49; subs. Lieut-Col 1948; subs. Col 1949; Min. of Supply, 1949-53; Brig. 1953; Dir MEXE, 1953-57; Retired 1957. MIEE 1968 (AMIEE 1938); MIMechE 1968 (AMIMechE 1939); Associate, RINA, 1970. *Address:* Woodmansterne, 46 Foxholes Road, Southbourne, Bournemouth, Hants. *T:* Bournemouth 44694. *Club:* Royal Ocean Racing.   *[Died* 3 *Feb.* 1972.

FAYRER, Sir Joseph Herbert Spens, 3rd Bt, *cr* 1896; DSC 1941; Lieut-Comdr RNVR; *b* 20 Oct. 1899; *s* of Sir Joseph Fayrer, 2nd Bt, CBE, and Ella, *d* of late Col W. A. J. Mayhew, Bengal Army; *S* father, 1937; *m* 1st, 1926, Elizabeth (whom he divorced, 1936), *d* of late Capt. William Barker-Mill, Mottisfont Abbey; 2nd, 1939, Helen Diana Scott (*d* 1961), *o d* of late John and Jean Lang; one *s* one *d* ; 3rd, 1964, Noreen, *d* of late Rev. John Yuill Walker. *Educ:* Wellington Coll. *Heir: s* John Lang Macpherson Fayrer, *b* 18 Oct. 1944. *Address:* Overhailes, Haddington, E Lothian, Scotland. *T:* East Linton 258.   *[Died* 23 *July* 1976.

FAZAN, Sidney Herbert, CMG 1946; CBE 1934 (OBE 1930); *b* 27 June 1888; *s* of Dr C. H. Fazan, Wadhurst, Sussex; *m* 1924, Sylvia (marr. diss., 1946), *d* of Brian Hook, Churt, Surrey; one *s* four *d* ; *m* 1949, Phyllis, *d* of John Jeffery; one *s* one *d. Educ:* Epsom Coll.; Christ Church, Oxford. Provincial Commissioner, Kenya, and mem. of Legislative Council, 1936-42; Liaison Officer with East African Forces, 1943-46. *Address:* 110 Dorset Road, Bexhill-on-Sea, East Sussex.   *[Died* 14 *Feb.* 1979.

FEATHER, Baron *cr* 1974 (Life Peer), of the City of Bradford; **Victor Grayson Hardie Feather,** CBE 1961; General Secretary of Trades Union Congress, 1969-73 (Assistant General Secretary, 1960-69); Vice-Chairman, British Waterways Board, since 1974; *b* Bradford, 10 April 1908; *s* of Harry and Edith Feather; *m* 1930, Alice Helena Fernyhough Ellison; one *s* one *d. Educ:* Hanson, Bradford. Co-op. employee, 1923-37; joined TUC staff, 1937; Asst Sec., 1947-60. Sec. TUC delegn to USSR, 1943; assisted re-org. Greek trade unions, 1945, Berlin trade unions, 1949; India and Pakistan, 1959; settlement Japan rail strike, 1958; lectured on trade unions in USA, 1954, SE Asia, 1957. Member: Govt Cttee of Inquiry into Overseas Information Services, 1952; Internat. Confedn of Free Trade Unions (Vice-Chm.); Cttee on the Pay of Postmen, 1964; Kennedy National Memorial Cttee; Exec. Cttee Brit. Council; Royal Commn on

Local Govt in England, 1968-69; Advertising Standards Authority, 1962-70; Consumers Assoc. (Vice-Chm.); British Productivity Council; Design Council, 1971-; British N American Cttee; British/USA Bicentennial Liaison Cttee; Board of Trustees, Civic Trust; Outward Bound Trust; Exec. Cttee, Overseas Development Institute; NEDC, 1969-73; BNEC, 1968-71; Arts Council, 1974-76; Adv. Council, V&A; Chm., Standing Adv. Commn, Human Rights, NI, 1973; Dockyard Policy Adv. Bd; Inflation Accounting Cttee; Pres., Europ. Trade Union Confedn, 1973-74; Vice-President: Workers' Educational Assoc.; Inst. Manpower Studies; Greater London Arts Assoc.; a Vice-Chm., Nat. Savings Cttee, 1970-74; Governor; NIESR; BBC, 1973-; Trustee, Anglo-German Foundn for Study of Industrial Society; Member: Court of Univ. of Bradford (Sen. Vis. Fellow, 1974-77); Council of Open Univ., 1973-; Council of Toynbee Hall. Pres., Bradford City FC. FRSA. Hon. DTech Bradford, 1970; Hon. LLD Manchester, 1974; DUniv Open, 1974. *Publications:* Trade Unions, True or False, 1951; How Do the Communists Work?, 1953; Essence of Trade Unionism, 1963. *Recreations:* painting, reading, cricket. *Address:* 43 Shelley Crescent, Hounslow, Mddx. *T:* 01-570 6241. *Clubs:* Grillions; Lilycroft Working Men's. *[Died 28 July 1976.*

FEATHER, Norman, FRS 1945; FRSE 1946; PhD Cantab; Professor of Natural Philosophy, University of Edinburgh, 1945-75, now Emeritus; *b* Crimsworth, WR Yorks, 16 Nov. 1904; *s* of Samson and Lucy Feather; *m* 1932, Kathleen Grace Burke; one *s* twin *d*. *Educ:* Bridlington Sch., E Yorks; Trinity Coll., Cambridge (Scholar). BA Cantab, BSc London, 1926; PhD Cantab, 1930. Fellow of Trinity Coll., 1929-33; Associate in Physics, Johns Hopkins Univ., Baltimore, Md, 1929-30; University Demonstrator in Physics, Cambridge, 1933-35; Leverhulme Fellow and Lecturer, University of Liverpool, 1935-36; Fellow and Lecturer in Natural Sciences, Trinity Coll., Cambridge; University Lecturer in Physics, 1936-45. Mem. Ct, Heriot-Watt Univ., 1977-. Gen. Sec., 1956-66, and Pres., 1967-70, RSE. Mackdougall-Brisbane Prize, 1968-70. Hon. LLD Edinburgh, 1975. *Publications:* An Introduction to Nuclear Physics, 1936; Lord Rutherford, 1940; Nuclear Stability Rules, 1952; An Introduction to the Physics of Mass, Length and Time, 1959; An Introduction to the Physics of Vibrations and Waves, 1961; Electricity and Matter: an introductory survey, 1968; Matter and Motion, 1970; numerous papers on radioactivity and nuclear physics in Proc. Royal Society and other jls. *Address:* Department of Physics, James Clerk Maxwell Building, Mayfield Road, Edinburgh EH9 3JZ; 9 Priestfield Road, Edinburgh EH16 5HJ. *T:* 031-667 2631. *[Died 14 Aug. 1978.*

FEDDEN, Sir (Alfred Hubert) Roy, Kt 1942; MBE; Hon. DSc; Hon. FRAeS; Hon. FAIAA; Hon. FSE; FRSA; FIMechE; Member Lilienthal Society; Liveryman, Guild of Pilots; Fellow British Interplanetary Society; *b* 6 June 1885; *s* of Henry Fedden, JP; *m* 1948, Norah Lilian, 3rd *d* of Edgar Crew, Clifton. *Educ:* Clifton Coll.; Bristol Merchant Venturers Technical Coll. Drawing Office of Brazil Straker and Co., Fishponds, Bristol, 1906-08; Works Manager and Chief Engineer of Brazil Straker and Co., 1909-14; Technical Dir of Brazil Straker and Co., 1914; during European war remained Technical Dir and Chief Engineer of Fishponds Works which were employed in manufacture of Rolls-Royce and Renault aero engines and shells; founded Engine Dept, British Aeroplane Co., 1920; Chief Engineer, Bristol Aeroplane Co., Ltd, 1920-42; responsible for design and development of all Bristol Aero Engines until 1945; Special Technical Adviser to Minister of Aircraft Production, 1942-45; research work for Ministry of Supply, 1945-47; Aeronautical Adviser to NATO, 1952-53; Aircraft Consultant to Dowty Group, 1953-60. Hon. DSc: Bristol, 1934; Cranfield Coll. of Aeronautics, 1968; Cranfield Inst. of Technology, 1970. Belgian Bronze Medal, 1930; Royal Aeronautical Society Silver Medal, 1933; Manly Gold Medal, 1933; Simms Gold Medal, 1934, 1954; Guggenheim Trophy, 1938; Lilienthal Ring, 1938; Pres. Royal Aeronautical Society, 1938, 1939, 1945 (hon. fellow, Diploma, 1954); Board of Governors, College of Aeronautics, Cranfield 1946-69. *Publication:* Britain's Air Survival, 1957. *Recreations:* writing on aeronautical matters and fly-fishing. *Address:* Buckland Old Mill, Bwlch, Breconshire, S Wales. *T:* Bwlch 274. *Clubs:* Royal Thames Yacht; Bristol Yacht (Bristol). *[Died 21 Nov. 1973.*

FEDDEN, (Henry) Robin Romilly, CBE 1973; author; *b* 26 Nov. 1908; *s* of Arthur Romilly Fedden and Katharine Waldo Douglas, Chantemesle, Seine-et-Oise, France; *m* 1942, Renée Catzeflis; two *d*. *Educ:* Clifton; Magdalene Coll., Cambridge; and abroad. Lately Dep. Dir-Gen., 1968-74, and Historic Buildings Sec., 1951-74, Nat. Trust for Places of Historic Interest or Natural Beauty. Hon. Fellow, RIBA, 1974. *Publications:* As the Unicorn (novel), 1933; Suicide: a social and historical study, 1938; The Land of Egypt, 1939; Syria, 1946;

Crusader Castles, 1950; Alpine Ski Tour, 1956; Ski-ing in the Alps, 1958; The Enchanted Mountains, 1962; Chantemesle, 1964; The Continuing Purpose: A History of the National Trust, Its Aims and Work, 1968; The White Country (verse), 1968; Churchill at Chartwell, 1969; The National Trust Past and Present, 1974; (ed) Treasures of the National Trust, 1976; Egypt: Land of the Valley, 1977. Co-editor of Personal Landscape, 1941-44. *Recreations:* travel, mountaineering, ski-ing. *Address:* 20 Eldon Road, W8. *Clubs:* Brooks's, Beefsteak, Alpine. *[Died 20 March 1977.*

FEDDEN, Sir Roy; *see* Fedden, Sir A. H. R.

FEILDEN, Sir William Morton Buller, 5th Bt, *cr* 1846, of Feniscowles, Lancs; MC; *b* 20 May 1893; *o s* of Sir W. H. Feilden, 4th Bt; *S* father 1946; *m* 1st, 1922, Margery Hannah (*d* 1925), *o d* of Robert Knowles, JP, Ednaston, Derby; 2nd, 1927, Reva (*d* 1971), *d* of late Martin Morrison, Faceby, Yorks, and widow of Major Guy Winterbottom. Joined Derbyshire Yeomanry, 1912; served European War, 1914-18, Comd Derbyshire Yeomanry, Gallipoli Evacuation (despatches twice, MC, Italian Silver Medal, wounded 1916); District Remount Officer, Western Command, 1919-37; Commandant No. 6 Group Royal Observer Corps, 1938-45. *Heir: cousin,* Henry Wemyss Feilden, [*b* 1916; *e s* of late Colonel Wemyss Gawne Cunningham Feilden, CMG (3rd *s* of 3rd Bt); *m* 1943, Ethel Atkinson, Newcastle; one *s* two *d*]. *Address:* The Yelt Farm, Doveridge, Derby. *TA:* Doveridge, Derby. *T:* Uttoxeter 2074. *Club:* Boodle's. *[Died 22 June 1976.*

FEILING, Anthony, BA, MD, BCh Cambridge, FRCP; Consulting Physician to St George's Hospital, National Hospitals for Nervous Diseases, Royal National Orthopædic Hospital, and Epsom College; Emeritus Lecturer in Medicine, St George's Hospital; Fellow (late President and late Lettsomian Lecturer) of Medical Society of London; Fellow (late President, Section of Neurology, and late Member of Council) Royal Society of Medicine; President Association of British Neurologists, 1954; Member, Association of Physicians of Great Britain; Corresponding Member, Société de Neurologie de Paris; Vice-President International Congress of Neurologists, Paris, 1949; Member American Academy of Neurology; *b* Leatherhead, Surrey, 30 Sept. 1885; 2nd *s* of late Ernest Feiling and late Joan Barbara Hawkins; *m* 1919, Helga Isabel Hope, *d* of late Geoffrey Grahame Hawkins and late Inga Olsen; one *s*. *Educ:* Marlborough Coll.; Pembroke Coll., Cambridge. BA, Hons Nat. Sci. Tripos, 1906; MRCS, LRCP, 1909; MB, ChB Cambridge 1911; MD Cambridge 1914; FRCP 1921; late Casualty Physician and Temporary Asst Physician, St Bartholomew's Hospital; Physician to Metropolitan Hospital and to Western Ophthalmic Hospital; Dean of Medical School, St George's Hospital, 1926-36; Temp. Major RAMC (despatches); late Censor and Senior Censor, late Gouldstonian Lecturer, Royal Coll. of Physicians; Examiner in Medicine to Royal Coll. of Physicians, Universities of Cambridge, London, and Birmingham; Neurologist to Air Ministry; Gold Staff Officer at Coronation of King George VI; late Sector Hospital Officer, EMS, 1939-45. *Publications:* Modern Medical Treatment (jointly); Article, Multiple Neuritis, Oxford System of Medicine; numerous papers in medical journals. *Recreation:* travel. *Address:* Wychwood House, Good Easter, near Chelmsford, Essex. *[Died 20 May 1975.*

FEILING, Sir Keith (Grahame), Kt 1958; OBE 1918; DLitt, MA; Professor Emeritus in the University of Oxford since 1950; *b* 1884; *s* of late Ernest Feiling and late Joan Barbara Hawkins; *m* 1912, Caroline, *d* of late Dearman Janson and late Rachel Louisa Lloyd; one *s* two *d*. *Educ:* Marlborough; Balliol Coll., Oxford; Prize Fellow of All Souls Coll., 1906-11; Lecturer at University of Toronto, 1907-09; Lecturer at Christ Church, 1909; Student and Tutor, 1911-46; Chichele Prof. of Mod. Hist., Oxford, 1946-50; 2nd Lieut 3rd Black Watch, 1915; Sec. to Central Recruiting Bd, India, 1917-19; University Lecturer in Modern History, 1928-36; Ford's Lecturer in English History, 1931-32. Hon. Student of Christ Church, 1952. Hon. Mem. Mass Hist. Soc. *Publications:* History of the Tory Party (1640-1714), 1924; England under the Tudors and Stuarts (Home University Library), 1926; British Foreign Policy, 1660-1672, 1930; Sketches in Nineteenth Century Biography, 1930; The Second Tory Party, (1714-1832), 1938; The Life of Neville Chamberlain, 1946; A History of England, 1950; Warren Hastings, 1954 (James Tait Black Memorial Prize); In Christ Church Hall, 1960. *Address:* c/o Barclays Bank, Sloane Square, SW1. *[Died 16 Sept. 1977.*

FELGATE, Air Vice-Marshal Frank Westerman, CB 1958; CBE 1946; *b* 1901; *s* of John Wyncoll Felgate, South Africa; *m* 1931, May, *d* of Major J. W. Osborne, OBE, RAMC, retd. *Educ:*

Rondesbosch, South Africa. Served as Cadet with British India Steam Navigation Company, 1918, and later as navigation officer. Joined RAF, 1925; served War of 1939-45; Air Ministry; Rhodesian Air Training Group. Dir Equipment, HQ, MEAF, 1949-50; AOC 206 Group, MEAF, 1951; Dir of Movements, Air Ministry, 1952-55; Dir of Equipment (C), Air Ministry, 1956; Senior Air Staff Officer, Maintenance Command, Andover, 1956-59, retired. Wing Commander, 1942; Air Commodore, 1949; Air Vice-Marshal, 1956. *Address:* Heatherlea, 21 Downton Lane, Downton, Lymington, Hants. *T:* Milford-on-Sea 2947. *[Died 13 March 1974.*

FELL, Vice-Adm. Sir Michael (Frampton), KCB 1974 (CB 1969); DSO 1943; DSC 1944 (Bar, 1952); retired 1974; *b* 17 Jan. 1918; *yr s* of Herbert Leigh Fell and Winifred Adeline Fell; *m* 1948, Joan McLauchlan-Slater; no *c. Educ:* Harrow. Joined Royal Navy, 1938; Fleet Air Arm pilot, 1939-45: Norwegian campaign and Gibraltar, 1940; fighter squadron, Western Desert, 1941-42; Salerno landings, 1943; attack on battleship Tirpitz (DSO) and other Norwegian operations, 1943; Southern France landings and ops in Aegean Sea (DSC), 1944; various instructional flying appts, Gen. Service, and Naval Staff Course, 1945-50; Air Gp Comdr HMAS Sydney, 1950-52; served in Korea (bar to DSC); Comdr (Air) HMS Ark Royal, 1954-56; comd HMS Puma, 1957-58; Capt. 1958; comd RN Air Stn, Lossiemouth, 1958-61; Capt. (F), 3rd Frigate Sqdn Far East Fleet, comd HMS Loch Killisport, 1961-63; Chief of Staff to C-in-C Portsmouth, 1963-65; comd HMS Ark Royal, 1965-66; Flag Officer: Gibraltar, Nov. 1966-68; Carriers and Amphibious Ships (also NATO Cmdr, 2nd Carrier Striking Force), 1968-70; Flag Officer, Naval Air Comd, 1970-72; Chief of Staff to Comdr, Allied Naval Forces, Southern Europe, 1972-74. *Recreations:* fishing, boats, flying, gliding. *Address:* Jeremys, Stoughton, Chichester, West Sussex. *T:* Compton 351. *Clubs:* (Naval Mem.) Royal Yacht Squadron, Royal Naval Sailing Association.

[Died 3 Dec. 1976.

FELL, Sheila Mary, RA 1974 (ARA 1969); artist since 1950; *b* 20 July 1931; *d* of late John and of Anne Fell, Aspatria, Cumberland. *Educ:* Thomlinson Grammar Sch., Wigton, Cumberland; Carlisle Sch. of Art; St Martin's Sch. of Art, London. One Man Exhibitions: Beaux Arts Gallery, London, 1955, 1958, 1960, 1962, 1964; Derwent Centre, Cockermouth, Cumberland, 1961; Middlesbrough Art Gall., 1962; Maryport Educational Settlement, Cumberland, 1964; Abbot Hall Art Gall., Kendal, 1965; Queen Square Gall., Leeds, 1965; Stone Gall., Newcastle upon Tyne, 1967, 1969; Ashgate Gall., Farnham, 1974; other exhibitions: Jubilee fund-raising, Aspatria, Cumberland, 1977; British Painting 1952-77, Royal Acad., 1977; New Grafton Gall., London, 1979; Paintings in Public Collections: Arts Council; Contemporary Art Soc.; Tate Gallery; Municipal Galleries of Carlisle, Liverpool, Middlesbrough, Southport, Sunderland, Swindon and Newcastle upon Tyne; Abbot Hall Art Gall., Kendal; Eastbourne Art Gallery; City Art Galleries, Sheffield; works in many private Collections. FRSA 1973. 2nd prize, Junior Section, John Moore's Liverpool Competition, 1957; Boise Travelling Scholarship, 1958; awarded £500 (Arts Council purchase award scheme), 1967; Austin Abbey Award for Research into Mural Painting, 1970; Arts Council bursary award, 1976. *Publication:* chapter in Breakthrough, ed Ronald Goldmann, 1968. *Recreations:* travelling, reading, visiting friends. *Address:* 23 Champion Grove, SE5.

[Died 15 Dec. 1979.

FELTIN, His Eminence Cardinal Maurice; Archbishop of Paris, 1949-66; Grand' Croix de la Légion d'Honneur, Médaille Militaire, Croix de Guerre; *b* Delle, near Belfort, 15 May 1883. *Educ:* Collège St-Ignace, Dijon; Grand Séminaire St Sulpice, Paris. Bishop of Troyes, 1928; Archbishop of Sens, 1932; Archbishop of Bordeaux, 1935. Cardinal, 1953. Grande Médaille d'or des Arts, Sciences et Lettres, 1964; Médaille d'or de la ville de Paris, 1967. *Address:* 38 rue Maximilien Robespierre, 94320 Thiais, France. *[Died 27 Sept. 1975.*

FENBY, Charles; Editorial Director, Westminster Press Ltd, 1957-70; *b* 21 May 1905; *s* of Skelton Fenby; *m* 1941, June Head; one *s* one *d. Educ:* Royal Grammar School, Guildford; Wadham Coll., Oxford. Joined editorial staff of Westminster Gazette, 1926, transferred to Daily News, 1927; helped to launch Oxford Mail, 1928, Ed. until 1940. Joined Hulton Press, 1940, as Asst Ed., Picture Post; Ed., Leader Magazine, 1944-48. Returned to Westminster Press as Ed., Birmingham Gazette, 1949; Ed.-in-Chief and Dir, The Birmingham Gazette and Despatch Ltd, 1953-57; *Chairman:* British Cttee, Internat. Press Institute, 1960-72; Training and Educn of Journalists Cttee, Commonwealth Press Union. *Publications:* (with C. Day Lewis) Anatomy of Oxford, 1938; The Other Oxford, 1970. *Address:* 9

Holly Lodge Gardens, N6. *Club:* United Oxford & Cambridge University. *[Died 6 April 1974.*

FENN, Harold Robert Backwell; Professor Emeritus in the University of London since 1960, when retired from Guy's; Hon. Consultant, Guy's Hospital; late Locum Consultant to King's College Dental School and Royal Dental Hospital; *b* 14 Jan. 1894; *s* of S. Backwell Fenn, LRCP, MRCS, and Annie Smith; *m* 1926, Margaret Winter; two *d. Educ:* private sch.; Neuchatel, Switzerland. LDS Liverpool, 1919; DDS Pennsylvania, USA, 1920; FDS, RCS, 1948. Hon. Dental Surgeon, Liverpool Heart Hosp., 1926-29; Liverpool Dental Hosp., 1929-35; Lecturer in Dental Prosthetics and Mechanics, University of Liverpool, 1931-35; Examiner in Dental Prosthetics and Mechanics, University of Liverpool, 1931-35; Prof. of Prosthetic Dental Surgery, University of London, at Guy's Hosp., 1935-60; Internal Examiner, Dental Prosthetics, University of London; External Examiner, Dental Prosthetics, Universities of Manchester, Liverpool and Durham, 1944-. *Publication:* (part author) Clinical Dental Prosthetics. *Recreation:* gardening. *Address:* Madryn, Morley's Road, Weald, Sevenoaks, Kent. *T:* Weald 254. *[Died 12 Jan. 1974.*

FENNER, Tan Sri Sir Claude Harry, KBE 1965 (MBE 1946); CMG 1963; Special Representative in Malaysia of the Rubber Growers' Assoc.; *b* 16 Jan. 1916; *s* of late Major C. H. Fenner, MBE, Indian Army; *m* 1941, Joan Margaret, *d* of late J. Fenner, Brisbane, Queensland; one *d. Educ:* Highgate Sch. Probationary Asst Supt, Federated Malay States Police, 1936; Supt, 1950; Asst Commissioner, 1953; Senior Asst Commissioner (Head of Special Branch), 1954; Dep. Sec. (Security and Intelligence), Prime Minister's Dept, March 1958; Commissioner of Police, Sept. 1958; Dir of Police Affairs, 1962; Inspector Gen. of Police, Malaysia, 1963-66. War Service with Special Forces (Force 136), 1942-45, Lieut-Col. Colonial Police Medal, 1950; Queen's Police Medal, 1957. Panglima Mangku Negara, Fedn of Malaya, 1961; National Order of Vietnam, 3rd cl., 1965; Dato Paduka Makhota Brunei, 1966. *Recreations:* all forms of sport. *Address:* 1A Jalan Girdle, Kuala Lumpur, Malaysia. *T:* KL 27354. *Club:* Special Forces. *[Died 15 May 1978.*

FENTON, James Stevenson, CMG 1941; OBE 1935; *b* 9 Feb. 1891; *e s* of Rev. James Fenton, Dundee; *m* 1928, Margaret, *yr d* of Rev. Joseph E. Richers, BD, Blairgowrie; three *d. Educ:* Dundee High Sch.; Edinburgh Univ. (MA). Asst Dist Comr, Sierra Leone, 1915; Chief Comr, 1946; retd, 1947. Chief Electoral Comr, 1961-63. *Address:* 20 Moorgarth Avenue, York. *[Died 28 Sept. 1975.*

FENTON, Roy Pentelow, CMG 1961; Chief Executive, Keyser Ullmann (Holdings) Ltd, since 1975; *b* 1 July 1918; *s* of late Heber Fenton, Salford; *m* 1941, Daphne, *d* of late E. Cheason; one *s. Educ:* Salford Grammar Sch. Served, 1939-46; commissioned Lancs Fusiliers. United Kingdom Alternate Mem., Management Board of European Payments Union, 1954-57; Governor, Central Bank of Nigeria, 1958-63; Dep. Chief of Central Banking Information Dept, Bank of England, 1963-65; Chief, Overseas Dept, Bank of England, 1965-75. UK Mem., Man. Bd of European Monetary Agreement, 1967-72, Vice-Chm., 1968-72. *Address:* Flat K, 23 Warwick Square, SW1V 2AB. *T:* 01-821 0920; Burnham House, Burnham Market, King's Lynn, Norfolk. *T:* Burnham Market 291. *Clubs:* East India, Devonshire, Sports and Public Schools, Overseas Bankers. *[Died 5 April 1979.*

FENTON, Col Sir William (Charles), Kt 1954; MC; JP; Chairman of BBA Group Ltd, Cleckheaton, Yorks, 1954-69; *b* 29 Sept. 1891; *s* of John Fenton, Cleckheaton; *m* 1921, Margaret, *d* of Robert Hirst, Cleckheaton; three *s* one *d. Educ:* Heckmondwike Grammar Sch. Served European War, 1914-19; Major 4 Bn, Duke of Wellington's Regt (TF), 1918; Commanded Bradford Sector Home Guard, 1940-42 (Col). JP West Yorks, 1932. *Recreation:* fishing. *Address:* Fieldhead, Cleckheaton, West Yorks. *T:* Cleckheaton 2783.

[Died 24 Jan. 1976.

FERGUSON, Major Sir John (Frederick), Kt 1953; CBE 1948; QPM 1957; DL; Chief Constable of Kent, Aug. 1946-Oct. 1958, retd; *b* 23 Aug. 1891; *s* of Major J. Ferguson, IA; *m* 1929, Vera Millicent, *d* of late Brig.-Gen. F. C. Lloyd, CB; one *s. Educ:* Aberdeen Univ.; RMC Sandhurst. Joined Durham Light Infantry, 1912; served NW Frontier, India, 1912-16; served Palestine and Mesopotamia, 1916-18; Adjt 1st DLI, 1919-22; Staff Coll., 1926; Gen. Staff, Shanghai Defence Force, 1927; Brig. Major 2nd Rhine Bde and 14th Inf. Bde, 1928-31; Brevet Major, 1930; Subst. Major, 1931; Naval Staff Coll., 1932; retired, 1933. Chief Constable, Met. Police, 1933; Dep. Asst Commissioner, Met. Police, 1935-40; Commandant, Met. Police

Coll., 1938-39; rejoined Army Feb. 1940; GSO1, War Office; rejoined Met. Police Sept. 1940; Chief Constable Sussex Joint Police Force, 1943-45; Asst Commissioner of Police of the Metropolis, 1945-46. DL Kent, 1958. CStJ 1961. *Recreation:* golf. *Address:* 24 Watchbell Street, Rye, Sussex.
[Died 27 May 1975.

FERGUSON, Samuel Fergus, CBE 1952; Director, The Australian Association of British Manufacturers, 1927-62, now part-time consultant; *b* Melbourne, Australia, 27 Feb. 1897; *s* of Rev. Andrew Fergus Ferguson, late of Glasgow, and Catherine Oatt (*née* Brown); *m* 1st, 1929, Kathleen (*d* 1967), *d* of John and Annie Revell, late of Heathcote, Australia; 2nd, 1968, Elizabeth Isabel, *d* of late H. P. P. Daniel, and *widow* of Mr Justice Roper, NSW; no *c. Educ:* State Schs; privately; Melbourne Univ. National Bank of Australasia Ltd, 1913. Served European War, 1914-18, in AIF, 1916-19. British Phosphate Commission, Nauru, Central Pacific, 1922; AICA 1920; Licensed Company Auditor, 1926; practised as public accountant, 1926-27. *Publications:* Postwar World Trade, 1943; John Bull Gets Tough, 1944; contribs to daily press, England and Australia. *Recreations:* golf, swimming, reading. *Address:* 3/17 Wentworth Street, Point Piper, NSW 2027, Australia. *T:* 36.4863. *Club:* Athenæum (Melbourne). *[Died 29 April 1971.*

FERGUSON, Dr Thomas, CBE 1954; Emeritus Professor of Public Health, University of Glasgow; *b* 23 May 1900; *s* of Alexander Gray Ferguson and Agnes Ferguson; *m* 1927, A. Elizabeth Webster; no *c. Educ:* Edinburgh Univ. Late HM Medical Inspector of Factories; late Dept Chief Med. Officer, Dept Health, Scotland. Mem., MRC Cttee on Social Medicine and Chm. of Cttee on Carcinogenic Action of Mineral Oils; formerly Chm. Gen. Nursing Council, Scotland. Hon Consult. Physician: Glasgow Western Infirmary, Falkirk Royal Infirmary. *Publications:* The Dawn of Scottish Social Welfare, 1948; A Scottish Experiment in the Employment of Severely Disabled Men, 1948; The Young Wage Earner, 1951; The Young Delinquent in his Social Setting, 1952; Hospital and Community, 1954, 1962; Scottish Social Welfare, 1864-1914, 1958; Handicapped Youth, 1960; Children in Care and After, 1966; papers on public health and social medicine. *Recreations:* football, writing. *Address:* Chowrassie, Lezayre Road, Ramsey, IOM. *T:* Ramsey 3167. *[Died 1 May 1977.*

FERGUSON, William Alexander, OBE 1965; Secretary, British Museum (Natural History), 1959-65; *b* 13 Jan. 1902; *e s* of James Ferguson, boilermaker, Glasgow; *m* 1930, Jessie Miller Whitelaw: one *s. Educ:* Bellahouston Academy; Royal Technical Coll., Glasgow. Production Manager and Sec., Strand Films Ltd, 1937-41; Films Contracts Assessor, Min. of Information, then British Council, 1941-47; Studio Manager, Gainsborough Pictures, 1947-49; Principal Administrative Officer, Crown Film Unit, 1949-53; Finance Officer, British Museum, 1953-59. Founder and Pres., John Ferguson of Kirkhill Soc. *Address:* Holmes Cottages, Betchworth, Surrey. *T:* Betchworth 3106.
[Died 1 Dec. 1973.

FERGUSON JONES, Hugh; *see* Jones, H. F.

FERGUSSON, Bernard Edward; *see* Ballantrae, Baron.

FERGUSSON, Sir Ewen (MacGregor Field), Kt 1953; Director: Gopeng Consolidated; Kinta Tin Mines; Kinta Kellas Tin Dredging; Rooiberg Minerals Development; Tronoh Mines Ltd; Chairman and Managing Director, The Straits Trading Co. Ltd, 1946-65; *b* 16 Oct. 1897; *m* 1931, Winifred Evelyn Bagnall; two *s* one *d. Educ:* Coatbridge Sch., Lanarks. Capt. Royal Engineers, 1914-20. The Straits Trading Co. Ltd, 1920-65. Singapore: Chamber of Commerce, 1946-53; Adv. Council, 1946-47; Exec. Council, 1947-54; Mem. (for Chamber of Commerce) Legislative Council, 1947-54; MLA Singapore, 1959-60. Dir of Public Companies. Dept War Organisation of Industry, Aust., 1942-44. *Recreations:* golf, tennis. *Address:* c/o Chartered Bank, 38 Bishopsgate, EC2. *Clubs:* Singapore (Singapore); Royal Selangor Golf. *[Died 24 Oct. 1974.*

FERGUSSON of Kilkerran, Sir James, 8th Bt *cr* 1703; LLD (Glasgow); FRSE; JP; Lord Lieutenant of Ayrshire, since 1969; Member: Queen's Body Guard for Scotland (Royal Company of Archers); Royal Commission on Historical Manuscripts; Scottish Cttee on the History of Parliament; *b* 18 Sept. 1904; *e s* of 7th Bt and Lady Alice Boyle (*d* 1958), 2nd *d* of 7th Earl of Glasgow; *S* father, 1951; *m* 1930, Louise Frances Balfour, *o d* of Edgar Trevelyan Stratford Dugdale; two *s* one *d* (and one *d* decd). *Educ:* Eton; Balliol Coll., Oxford (BA 1925). Worked as bookseller and publisher, 1927-33; talks producer, BBC, Edinburgh, 1934-40; Overseas service, London, 1940-41; broadcast nightly as commentator on Nazi propaganda,

Overseas service, 1941-44; civilian lecturer with Middle East Forces, 1944-45; leader-writer, Glasgow Herald, 1945-49; Member, Board of Trustees: Nat. Galleries of Scotland, 1947-49; Nat. Library of Scotland, 1971-; Keeper of the Records of Scotland, 1949-69. Andrew Lang Lecturer, St Andrews, 1956-57. *Publications:* Letters of George Dempster to Sir Adam Fergusson, 1756-1813, 1934; Alexander the Third, 1937; William Wallace, 1938; The Green Garden (anthology), 1946; John Fergusson, 1727-1750, 1948; Lowland Lairds, 1949; Argyll in the Forty-Five, 1951; The Fergussons, 1956; The Kennedys, 1958; The Sixteen Peers of Scotland, 1960; The White Hind, 1963; The Curragh Incident, 1964; The Man behind Macbeth, 1969; The Declaration of Arbroath, 1970; Balloon Tytler, 1972; various articles on Scottish history and literature. *Heir: s* Charles Fergusson [*b* 10 May 1931; *m* 1961, Hon. Amanda Mary Noel-Paton, *e d* of Baron Ferrier, ED; two *s*]. *Address:* Kilkerran, by Maybole, Ayrshire KA19 7SJ. *T:* Crosshill 207. *Club:* New (Edinburgh). *[Died 25 Oct. 1973.*

FERGUSSON, John Douglas, FRCS; Honorary Consultant; Surgeon, St Peter's, St Paul's and St Philip's Hospitals; Surgeon and Urologist, Central Middlesex Hospital; *b* 5 Dec. 1909; *s* of John Newbery Fraser Fergusson and Mildred Gladys (*née* Mercer); *m* 1st, 1936, Alice Alyne (*d* 1968), *d* of Hon. Mr Justice Maartensz; two *s*; 2nd, 1969, Myrtle, *d* of Maj.-Gen. K. M. Body, CB, CMG, OBE. *Educ:* St Peter's, York; Cambridge Univ.; St Thomas' Hosp. 1st Class Hons Nat. Science Tripos, 1931; Coll. Prizeman and Scholar, St John's Coll., Cambridge; Open Univ. Scholar, St Thos Hosp.; Sutton Sams Prize, 1934, and Cheselden Medal for Surgery, 1936, St Thos Hosp.; MA 1945, MD 1946 Cantab; FRCS 1936; Hunterian Prof., RCS, 1945-46. Formerly Dir of Teaching and Res., Inst. of Urology, Univ. of London. Fellow and late Mem. of Council, Assoc. of Surgeons of Gt Britain and Ireland; Pres., British Assoc. of Urological Surgeons, 1970-72; Mem., Internat. Soc. of Urology; Former Mem., Bd of Governors, St Peter's, St Paul's and St Philip's Hospitals; FRSocMed (Pres. of Section of Urology, 1962-63). Hon. Editor, British Journal of Urology, 1966-72. Formerly Associate Examiner in Surgery, Univ. of London. *Publications:* various contribs to surgical and urological journals. *Recreation:* fishing. *Address:* 149 Harley Street, W1. *T:* 01-935 8273. *[Died 20 April 1979.*

FERNANDEL, (Fernand Joseph Désiré Contandin); French comedian; *b* Marseille, 8 May 1903; *s* of Denis Charles Contandin and Désirée (*née* Bedouin); *m* Henriette Manse; two *s* two *d*. On leaving school worked in a bank, soap factory, etc; first appeared as Fernandel, Nice, 1922; since 1930 has appeared in over 134 films, including The Little World of Don Camillo, 1953, and The Sheep has Five Legs, 1953; has also appeared in music hall, reviews, television, radio, and made records. Chevalier de la Légion d'Honneur, Officier des Palmes Académiques, Chevalier de l'Ordre des Arts et des Lettres. *Relevant Publication:* Fernandel, by Carlo Rim, 1952. *Address:* (business) 44 Avenue Foch, Paris 16e; (home) Villa Les Milleroses, Route des Trois-Lucs, Marseilles; l'Oustaü de la Mar, Carry-le-Rouet (BDR), France. *[Died 26 Feb. 1971.*

FERNANDO, Hugh Norman Gregory, OBE 1952; Chief Justice of Sri Lanka, 1966-74; *b* 17 Nov. 1910; *s* of late V. M. Fernando, Puisne Justice, Ceylon; *m* 1935, Doris Pieris; four *s. Educ:* St Joseph's Coll., Colombo; Balliol Coll., Oxford (BA, BCL). Called to Bar, Gray's Inn, 1933; Advocate, Ceylon, 1934; Asst Legal Draftsman, 1936; Legal Draftsman, Ceylon, 1949; Puisne Justice, 1955; Chief Justice and Chm., Judicial Service Commn, 1966. Officer Administering the Govt of Ceylon in Oct. 1967 and Feb. 1970. Master of the Bench, Gray's Inn, 1970; Hon. Master of the Bench, Middle Temple, 1970. Chm., UN Appeal for Children Cttee (Sri Lanka). Patron: Cheshire Homes Foundn; Eye Foundn of Sri Lanka. *Recreations:* bridge, billiards. *Address:* 129 Macarthy Road, Colombo 7, Sri Lanka. *Club:* Orient (Colombo). *[Died 24 March 1976.*

FERRAR, Lieut-Col Michael Lloyd, CSI 1927; CIE 1922; OBE 1919; JP Essex; *b* 16 April 1876; *s* of M. L. Ferrar, ICS; *m* 1st, 1903, Maud Evelyn (*d* 1906), *d* of W. B. Oldham, CIE, ICS; 2nd, 1912, Nancy (*d* 1962), *d* of John Grey Russell; two *s* two *d. Educ:* St Columba's Coll.; Rugby Sch.; Sandhurst. Served in Indian Army and Punjab Commission; Tirah Campaign, 1897-98 (medal 3 clasps); commanded Baluch Levy, D. G. Khan, 1902-06; Asst Colonisation Officer, Lyallpur, 1907-11; Postal Censor, Bombay, 1914-19 (OBE); Deputy Comr, Lahore, 1919-23 (CIE); Chief Comr, Andaman and Nicobar Islands, 1923-31 (CSI); retired, 1931. Examiner in Urdu, Cambridge Univ., 1932-62. Major, Home Guard, 1940-41. *Address:* 7 Newton Hall, Dunmow, Essex. *T:* Gt Dunmow 2434. *[Died 25 Feb. 1971.*

FERRARO, Prof. Vincenzo Consolato Antonino, PhD, DIC, FRAS; Professor of Mathematics, University of London (Queen Mary College), since 1952; *b* 10 April 1907; *s* of late Filippo Ferraro and Amalia Ferraro; *m* 1937, Maria Giovanna Giordano; one *s. Educ:* Holborn Estate Grammar Sch., London; Imperial Coll. of Science and Technology, London (scholar). Demonstrator in Mathematics, Imperial Coll., London, 1930-33; Asst Lecturer and Lecturer, King's Coll., London, 1933-47; Prof. of Applied Mathematics, University Coll. of the South West, Exeter, 1947-52. Member: Meteor Research Cttee, 1960-62; Sub-cttee for Geomagnetism and Aeronomy; Nat. Cttee for Geodesy and Geophysics; UGC Mathematical Sciences Sub-Cttee, 1967-72; Visiting Investigator, Dept of Terrestrial Magnetism, Carnegie Institution of Washington, USA, 1948: Visiting Prof., Yerkes Observatory, University of Chicago, USA, 1953; George A. Miller Visiting Prof. of Astronomy, University of Illinois, 1963. *Publications:* Electromagnetic Theory, 1954; Magneto-Fluid Mechanics (with C. Plumpton), 2nd edn 1966; papers on geomagnetism and astrophysics in scientific jls. *Recreations:* pictorial arts and music. *Address:* Queen Mary College, Mile End Road, E1; 266 Ballards Lane, N12.
[Died 4 Jan. 1974.

FERRIER, Sir (Harold) Grant, Kt 1969; CMG 1964; Vice Chairman, Weir Group (Australia) Pty Ltd; *b* 26 Aug. 1905; *m* 1949, Margaret James; one *d. Educ:* Sydney Grammar Sch. CEng, MIMarE. President: Metal Trades Employers' Assoc., 1949-51; Australian Metal Industries Assoc., 1951-52; Chamber of Manufactures of NSW, 1963-65; Associated Chambers of Manufactures of Aust., 1963-65; Chairman: The Commonwealth Portland Cement Co. Ltd and subsids, 1952-71; Associated Portland Cement Manufacturers (Australia) Ltd, 1952-71; State Develt Corp. of NSW, 1966-69; Heavy Engineering Industry Adv. Cttee to Commonwealth Govt, 1957-67; Nat. Employers Policy Cttee, 1962-64; Dep. Employer Mem., Gov. Body, ILO. Pres., Internat. Organisation of Employers, Geneva, 1966-67. *Recreations:* yachting and fly-fishing. *Address:* 9 Cliff View Road, Leura, NSW 2781, Australia. *Clubs:* Commonwealth (Canberra); Royal Sydney Yacht Squadron, Royal Sydney Golf, Rugby Union.
[Died 26 July 1976.

FERRYMAN, Col E. E. M.; *see* Mockler-Ferryman.

FESTING, Field Marshal Sir Francis Wogan, GCB 1957 (KCB 1956; CB 1946); KBE 1952 (CBE 1945); DSO 1942; DL; Chief of the Imperial General Staff, 1958-61; ADC General to the Queen, 1958-60; *b* 28 Aug. 1902; *o s* of late Brig.-Gen. F. L. Festing, CB, CMG; *m* 1937, Mary Cecilia, *er d* of late Cuthbert David Giffard Riddell, Swinburne Castle, Northumberland; four *s. Educ:* Winchester; RMC Sandhurst. 2nd Lieut Rifle Bde, 1921; psc 1934; Bt Major 1938; Lt-Col 1939; Instr Staff Coll., 1939; comd 2nd Bn East Lancs Regt, 1939; comd a Bde in Madagascar, 1941; comd 36th Div. in Burma, 1942-45; GOC Land Forces, Hong Kong, 1945-46; Maj.-Gen. 1942; Dir of Weapons and Development, War Office, 1947-49; Commander British Forces, Hong Kong, during 1949 (temp. Lieut-Gen.); Pres., Regular Commissions Board, 1950-51; Asst Chief of Staff (Organization and Training), Supreme Headquarters, Allied Powers in Europe, 1951-52; Lieut-Gen. 1952; GOC British Troops in Egypt, 1952-54; GOC-in-C, Eastern Comd, 1954-56; Gen. 1956; C-in-C FARELF, 1956-58; Col Comdt, The Rifle Bde, 1958; Field Marshal, 1960. Col Royal Northumberland Fusiliers, 1953-65. DL Co. Northumberland, 1962. Pres., Corps of Commissionaires, 1963-75. Comdr, Legion of Merit (USA); Comdr of the Cloud and Banner (China). DCL (*hc*) Newcastle upon Tyne, 1964. Kt of Malta, 1965. *Recreations:* hunting, yachting. *Address:* Birks, Tarset, Northumberland. *TA and T:* Greenhaugh 40221.
[Died 3 Aug. 1976.

FETHERS, Hon. Col (retired) Wilfrid Kent, DSO 1917; VD; FIIA; formerly Manager for Australia, Royal Insurance Co. Ltd, and Associated Companies; *b* Victoria, 26 Nov. 1885; *s* of William Fethers, *s* of James Fethers of Liverpool, England, who came out to Australia, 1852; *m* Phyllis Doyne, Sydney; one *s* two *d. Educ:* Caulfield Grammar Sch., Victoria. Commission in Victorian Volunteer Forces, 1905; served Gallipoli, Egypt, and France, 1914-18 (despatches). Took Australian contingent to New York to assist in Liberty Loan flotation in May 1918; Pres., Melbourne Metropolitan Fire Brigades Board, 1942; Pres., Council of Fire and Accident Underwriters of Australia, 1936 and 1944; Pres., Incorporated Australian Insurance Institute, 1941-42; Pres., Council of Marine Underwriters of the Commonwealth of Australia, 1941-42. Member: Board of Management, Alfred Hospital; Melba Trust for Limbless Soldiers. Trustee, Ed. Wilson Estate. *Address:* 41 The Ridge, Canterbury, Victoria 3126, Australia. *Clubs:* Australian, Naval and Military (Melbourne).
[Died 10 July 1976.

FETHERSTON-GODLEY, Brig. Sir Francis William Crewe, Kt 1937; OBE 1918; DL Glos; *b* 25 Jan. 1893; *s* of late Major H. C. Godley, DSO, 48th Regt; *m* 1919, Kathleen May Jenner Davies (marr. diss. 1940; she *d* 1955); one *s*; 2nd, 1941, Reine Cecilia Siddons Faulder (*d* 1958); 3rd, 1961, Alice Kathleen Llewhellin. *Educ:* Cheltenham; Royal Military Coll., Sandhurst. Served European War, 1914-19; Expedition NWF, 1920; War of 1939-45 (despatches, Croix de guerre). Assumed by royal licence additional name of Fetherston, 1923; National Vice-Chm., British Legion, 1932-34; National Chm., 1934-39; Provincial Comdt, Kenya Police Reserve, 1950-54; Queen's Colonial Police Medal; Commander of Légion d'Honneur and other foreign decorations. *Recreations:* yachting, shooting. *Address:* Les Varvots, St Lawrence, Jersey, Channel Islands. *Club:* Naval and Military.
[Died 12 July 1976.

FFRENCH-BLAKE, A. O'B.; *see* Blake.

FIDDAMENT, Air Vice-Marshal Arthur Leonard, CB 1948; CBE 1944; DFC; RAF (Retd); *b* 1 July 1896; *s* of late A. W. Fiddament, Norwich; *m* 1924, Doris Ward, Lincoln; two *d. Educ:* Norwich. Norfolk Regt, 1914-15; RE (Special Brigade), 1915-17; RFC 1917; India, 1920-24; RAF Staff Coll. (student), 1926; Air Ministry (intelligence), 1927-31; commanded 17 Squadron, 1931-32; RAF Staff Coll. (Directing Staff), 1932-35; commanded 30 Squadron, Iraq, 1935-36; idc 1937; Air Ministry (Plans), 1938-39; Air Ministry (Dominions Liaison), 1940; RAF Delegation, Washington, 1941; Dir of Personal Services, Air Ministry, 1942; Asst Comdt, RAF Staff Coll., 1943; AOC No 46 Group, 1944; Senior Air Staff Officer, Transport Command, 1944-46; AOC No 38 Group, RAF, 1946; retired, 1949. Officier de la Légion d'Honneur. *Address:* Greenlawn, 21 Rectory Road, Burnham on Sea, Som TA8 2BZ. *T:* Burnham on Sea 782415.
[Died 5 Aug. 1976.

FIELD, Edward, DSO 1918; Retired; Rag Merchant; President, Dewsbury Chamber of Commerce, 1954-57; *b* 22 May 1898; *s* of late Joseph Field and Louisa Wardell; *m* 1st, 1924, Florrie (*d* 1972), *d* of Alderman F. Greenwood, Dewsbury; one *d*; 2nd, 1973, Jennie Philipson, *widow* of Gordon Philipson, Scarborough. *Educ:* The Wheelwright Grammar Sch., Dewsbury. Artists' Rifles, 1916; 2nd Lieut, MG Corps, 1917 (DSO, despatches); Asst Officer in charge of Salvage Inspectorate, 1918; Managing Dir and Chm., Joseph Field, Ltd; Pres. British Woollen Rag Merchants Association, 1945-48; Technical Officer Wool Control (Salvage Section), 1940-45; Waste (MR) Wages Council; CO 2nd Cadet Battalion KOYLI (Major), 1942-46. Chm. Dewsbury and District Employment Cttee, 1956-68. FInstD, 1955-68. *Publications:* various articles on Social Credit 1930-46. *Recreations:* contract bridge (Yorks Individual Champion, 1960, Yorks Pairs Championship, 1961), motoring. *Address:* Greendale Court, Sea Cliff Crescent, Scarborough YO11 2XY. *T:* Scarborough 66446. *Club:* Dewsbury (Dewsbury).
[Died 5 Feb. 1978.

FIELD, Sir Ernest (Wensley Lapthorn), Kt 1953; CBE 1947; JP; The Director, Scottish Engineering Employers' Association, 1944-58, retired; *b* Alverstoke, 4 Feb. 1889; *s* of Frederick Ernest and Lily Mary Field; *m* 1916, Edith Maude Lillicrap, Plymouth (*d* 1969); no *c. Educ:* Froebel House Sch. Devonport; Queen Elizabeth Grammar Sch., Bideford; RN Engineering Coll., Keyham. Engineer Cadet, Royal Navy, 1905-09; various managerial positions in engineering works of John Brown & Co., Clydebank, 1909-34, and personal asst to Engineering-Dir, 1934-44. Was chm. of various Scottish cttees in connection with industry, etc.; an Office Bearer of various Scottish benevolent institutions. JP Co. of City of Glasgow. Has given several lectures on Industrial Relations, FIMechE, FRINA. *Recreation:* reading. *Address:* Green's Hotel, Woodlands Terrace, Glasgow G3 6DF.
[Died 15 Aug. 1974.

FIELD, George David, CBE 1944; MVO (4th class) 1936, (5th class) 1928; *b* 16 May 1887; *s* of Burns Field and Jane E. Rolfe, Horringer, Suffolk; *m* 1923, Edith (LRAM), *d* of late C. F. Howell; one *s* one *d. Educ:* Horringer Sch., Suffolk; Archbishop Tenison's Grammar Sch. Junior Clerk in Office of Paymaster of HM's Household, 1901-3; Clerk to Paymaster, 1903-20; Accountant (Pay Office) Buckingham Palace, 1920-32; Chief Accountant and Paymaster (HM's Household), 1932-49; Assessor and Collector of Income Tax (HM's Household), 1924-49; Sergeant at Arms to King George V, 1935; Sergeant at Arms to King George VI, 1937-49; retired, 1949. *Address:* Gossamer, 11 Hawley Road, Rustington, Sussex. *T:* Rustington 5982.
[Died 11 April 1975.

FIELD, Brig. Leonard Frank, CB 1953; CBE 1945; *b* 6 March 1898; *s* of Major Joseph Thomas Field and Amelia Phillips; *m* 1923, Genevieve Bowyer; one *s*; *m* 1958, Betty Sutcliffe; one *s* two *d. Educ:* Bedford; RMC, Sandhurst. Served European War: commissioned 2nd Lieut, 1916; War of 1939-45: DDMI (Far East), 1941; Dir of Intelligence, SW Pacific Command, 1942; Chief Chinese Liaison Officer, Burma, 1942; Military Attaché: China, 1945-49; Indo-China, 1951-52. Brig. 1952; retired Nov. 1952. Knight Comdr, Order of Orange Nassau (with Swords), 1945. *Address:* c/o Lloyds Bank Ltd (Cox's & King's), 6 Pall Mall, SW1.   *[Died 8 Nov. 1978.*

FIELD, Group Captain Roger Martin, CBE 1941; late RAF; *b* 27 Nov. 1890; *s* of Henry Field, Solicitor, The Quarry, Leamington Spa, and Margaret A. W. Bickmore; *m* 1932, Kathleen Mildred, *widow* of his Hon. Judge Dobb, and *e d* of late H. Caldwell Lipsett; no *c. Educ:* Rugby Sch.; Birmingham Univ. Enlisted RFA, 5 Aug. 1914; Flight Sub-Lt RNAS, Oct. 1914; Major RAF, 1918; seconded as Air Adviser to Govt of Finland 1925-28 (Order of White Rose); Air Attaché, Paris, Brussels, The Hague, Lisbon, Madrid, 1933-36; Inter-Services Mission to Portugal, 1937; France, 1939-40 (despatches); retired, 1943; holds Spanish Naval Order of Merit. *Recreations:* fishing, ski-ing, yachting. *Address:* Oakshott Hanger, Hawkley, Liss, Hants. *T:* Hawkley 297. *Club:* Sesame.   *[Died 18 Nov. 1974.*

FIELDEN, Lieut-Col Edward Anthony, MC; DL; JP; *b* 30 March 1886; *e s* of late E. B. Fielden, MP; *m* 1914, Phœbe, *d* of late Adm. Hon. T. S. Brand; three *s. Educ:* Eton; RMC, Sandhurst. 10th Hussars, 1906-21 (retired as Major); Brigade-Major, 6th and 8th Cavalry Brigades, BEF, 1917-18; re-employed 2nd in command OCTU, 1939-42; Lt-Col Home Guard, 1942; High Sheriff of Salop, 1954. Pres., Ludlow Div., Conservative Assoc., 1960-68. MFH, South Salop Hounds, 1925-29, and North Cotswold Hounds, 1929-32. JP 1946, DL 1952, Salop. *Recreations:* hunting, fishing. *Address:* Court of Hill, Ludlow, Salop. *T:* Cleehillstone 300. *Club:* Cavalry.
                          [Died 26 Aug. 1972.

FIELDEN, Air Vice-Marshal Sir Edward Hedley, GCVO 1968 (KCVO 1952; CVO 1943; MVO 1936); CB 1946; DFC 1943; AFC 1929; Senior Air Equerry to the Queen 1962-69, an Extra Equerry since 1970; Captain of Queen's Flight, 1952-62 (of King George VI's Flight, 1936-52); *b* 4 Dec. 1903; *e s* of Edward Fielden, MB, and Maud Fielden, Bracknell, Berks; *m* 1940, Mary Angela, *y d* of late Lieut-Col Henry Ramsden Jodrell, CMG; one *d* (and one *s* decd). *Educ:* Malvern. RAF 1924-29; Royal Air Force Reserve, 1929; Pilot to Prince of Wales, 1929; Extra Equerry, 1932: Equerry to King George VI, 1937; Extra Equerry to the King, 1946, to the Queen, 1952. *Recreations:* shooting, fishing. *Address:* Edenwater House, Ednam, Kelso, Roxburghshire. *T:* Kelso 2070. *Club:* Pratt's.
                          [Died 8 Nov. 1976.

FIELDEN, Lionel, CIE 1941; *b* 15 May 1896; *s* of late Joshua Fielden, Kineton, Warwickshire. *Educ:* Eton; Brasenose Coll., Oxford. Artists Rifles, 1914; RGA, 1915-19; Gallipoli, Palestine (capt.); League of Nations Secretariat, 1920-22; representative of High Commissioner for refugees in Greece and the Levant, 1922-23; sec. to Lord Pres. of Council, 1924; BBC 1927; Head of General Talks Dept, 1930-35; Controller of Broadcasting in India, 1935-40; Indian Editor, BBC, April-Nov. 1940; Ministry of Food; Ministry of Aircraft Production, 1941-42; editorial staff Observer, 1942; Major SOII CA Italy, 1943; Dir of Public Relations, Allied Control Commission, Italy, 1944-45. *Publications:* Beggar my Neighbour, 1943; The Natural Bent, 1960. *Recreation:* trying to avoid being organised. *Address:* Ca Dell' Osso, Carignano, Lucca, Italy. *T:* Lucca 59418.
                          [Died 1 June 1974.

FIELDEN, Thomas Perceval, MA; BMus Oxon, DMus Edinburgh; FRCM; Pianist and Composer; late Director of the Rhodesian Academy of Music, Bulawayo (1952-58); 2nd *s* of late John Fielden, Chichester, Sussex; *m* 1st, Edith, *d* of Richard Stapley, Wolverton; one *s* (one *d* decd); 2nd, Ethel, *d* of Major George Olden, OBE, MC, Braunton, Devon. *Educ:* Prebendal Sch., Chichester; Royal College of Music (Open Schol. Composition) 1902; Jesus Coll., Oxford (Organ Exhibner), 1905. Formerly: Dir of Music, Hurstpierpoint Coll., Sussex; Dir, of Music, Fettes Coll., Edinburgh; prof. and lecturer, Ladies' Coll., Cheltenham; Dir of Music, Charterhouse Sch., 1928-47; Prof. of Pianoforte, Royal College of Music, 1921-52. Has given pianoforte recitals in London, Berlin, Paris, Hanover, and in all the British Colonies. Lieut RFA, 1915; Lieut RNVR, 1943-45. *Publications:* The Science of Pianoforte Technique, 1927; Marks and Remarks, a study of examination problems, 1937; Part-songs (some Part-songs sung by Fleet Street Choir, etc); article on the Pianoforte, in Chambers's Encyclopædia; contrib. Proc. Royal Musical Assoc.; and to Music and Letters; editor (Associated Board) Chopin's Works. *Recreations:* tennis, sailing. *Address:* The Corner Cottage, Forest Green,

Nailsworth, Glos. *T:* Nailsworth 2952. *Clubs:* Naval, London.
                          [Died 15 Sept. 1974.

FIELDS, Dame Gracie, DBE 1979 (CBE 1938); MA; actress; *b* Rochdale, 9 Jan. 1898; *d* of Fred Stansfield and late Sarah Jane Bamford; *m* 1st, Archie Pitt (Selinger) from whom she obtained a divorce 1940 (he *d* 1940); 2nd, 1940, Monty Banks (Mario Bianchi) (*d* 1950), Film Director; 3rd, 1952, Boris Alperovici, Capri. *Educ:* Rochdale. Nine Command Performances, 1928, 1931, 1937, 1947, 1950, 1951, 1952, 1957, 1964. Silvania Television Award, 1956, for outstanding performance by an actress, in The Old Lady Shows Her Medals. Received hon. freedom of Rochdale, 1938. Order of St John of Jerusalem. MA (*hc*) Victoria Univ. Manchester, 1940. *Publication:* Sing as We Go, 1960. *Address:* Canzone del Mare, 80073, Capri, Italy.
                          [Died 27 Sept. 1979.

FIFOOT, Cecil Herbert Stuart, MA; FBA 1954; Fellow of Hertford College, Oxford, 1925-59, Hon. Fellow, 1963; *b* 1899; *s* of Sydney Fifoot and Maria Trevor; *m* 1924, Hjördis Baars, *yr d* of Dr Eriksen, Kongsberg, Norway; one *s. Educ:* Berkhamsted Sch.; Exeter Coll., Oxford (History Scholar). 2nd Lieut RFA 1917-18 (wounded, July 1918); 1st Class Law Sch., 1921; Barrister-at-law, Middle Temple, 1922; Bursar, Hertford Coll., 1926-34; Dean, 1940-44; Univ. Lecturer in Law, 1930-45; Senior Proctor, 1936; All Souls Reader in English Law, 1945-59; Reader in Common Law to the Inns of Court, 1954-67. *Publications:* English Law and its Background, 1932; Lord Mansfield, 1936; The Law of Contract (with Dr G. C. Cheshire), 1945, 8th edn, 1972; Cases on the Law of Contract (with Dr G. C Cheshire), 1945, 6th edn 1973; History and Sources of the Common Law, 1949; Judge and Jurist in the Reign of Victoria, 1959; Letters of F. W. Maitland (Selden Soc.), 1965; F. W. Maitland: a life, 1971. *Address:* 203 Braid Road, Edinburgh 10.
                          [Died 31 Jan. 1975.

FILDES, Sir Paul, Kt 1946; OBE 1919; ScD; FRS 1934; late Director of Chemical Bacteriology (Medical Research Council); *b* 10 Feb. 1882; *s* of late Sir Luke Fildes, KCVO, RA. *Educ:* Winchester; Trinity Coll., Cambridge; London Hospital. MA, MB, BCh, Cantab., 1909; Asst Bacteriologist, London Hospital, 1909-34; Pathologist, RN Hospital, Haslar, 1915-19; Surgeon Lt-Comdr RNVR, 1917; founder of British Journal of Experimental Pathology, 1920; Examiner in Pathology, University of Cambridge, 1933; Pres. of Pathological Section, Royal Society of Medicine, 1934; Mem. of the Scientific Staff, Medical Research Council, 1934-49; Examiner in Pathology, University of Oxford, 1937. Mem. Advisory Board, Bcit Memorial Research Fund, 1939-54; Mem. Governing Body, Lister Institute, 1942-56. Hon. ScD (Cantab.), 1948; Hon. ScD (Reading), 1959; Royal Medal, Royal Society, 1953; Copley Medal, Royal Society, 1963; Hon. Fellow Royal Society of Medicine, 1962. *Publications:* Haemophilia (with W. Bulloch) in Treasury of Human Inheritance, 1911; Syphilis from the Modern Standpoint (with J. McIntosh), 1911; various monographs and papers on pathological subjects. *Address:* 48 Melton Court, SW7. *Club:* Athenæum.   *[Died 5 Feb. 1971.*

FINBERG, Prof. Herbert Patrick Reginald, MA, DLitt (Oxon); FSA; FRHistS; general editor of the Agrarian History of England and Wales; *b* 21 March 1900; *e s* of A. J. Finberg; *m* 1933, Joscelyne Henrietta Prideaux Payne; two *s. Educ:* Merchant Taylors' School; St John's Coll., Oxford. Founded and directed The Alcuin Press, 1928-36; Dir of The Broadwater Press Ltd, 1936-44; Typographical Adviser to the Ministry of Works, 1944-48, and to HM Printers (Eyre and Spottiswoode Ltd), 1944-58. Designer of Twickenham edn of Alexander Pope, London Shakespeare, Latin-English Missal, Coronation Service. Editorial Dir of Burns Oates & Washbourne Ltd, 1944-49. Editor of the Agricultural History Review, 1953-64. Head of Dept of English Local History, University of Leicester, as Reader, 1952-63, Prof. 1963-65; Prof. Emeritus, 1966. Pres., British Agricultural Hist. Soc., 1965-68. Mem. Internat. Commn on English in the Liturgy. Prix Graphica Belgica, 1965. KSG 1971. *Publications:* Axel (from the French of Villiers de I'Isle-Adam), 1925; The Missal in Latin and English (with Rev. J. O'Connell), 1949; Tavistock Abbey, 1951; Devonshire Studies (with W. G. Hoskins), 1952; The Early Charters of Devon and Cornwall, 1953; Gloucestershire (in the "Making of the English Landscape" series), 1955; The Gostwicks of Willington, 1956; Gloucestershire Studies, 1957; The Early Charters of the West Midlands, 1961; The Early Charters of Wessex, 1964; Lucerna, 1964; Local History: Objective and Pursuit, 1967; West-Country Historical Studies, 1969; Anglo-Saxon England to 1042 (in Agrarian History of England, vol. 1), 1972; The Formation of England 550-1042, 1974. *Address:* 151 Park Road, Chiswick, W4. *T:* 01-994 8987.   *[Died 1 Nov. 1974.*

FINCH, Peter; actor; *b* London, 28 Sept. 1916 (Peter Ingle-Finch); *m* 1943, Tamara Tchinarova (marr. diss. 1959); one *d*; *m* 1959, Yolande Turner (marr. diss. 1966); one *s* one *d*; *m* 1973, Eletha Barrett; one *d*. *Educ:* North Sydney Inter High Sch., Australia. First appeared on stage, New South Wales and Qld, in While Parents Sleep, 1935; first part on London stage in Daphne Laureola, 1949. Chief stage appearances in: Captain Carvallo, St James's, 1950; Othello, (Iago), St James's, 1951; The Happy Time, St James's, 1952; Romeo and Juliet (Mercutio), Old Vic, 1952; An Italian Straw Hat, Old Vic, 1952; Two for the See-Saw, Haymarket, 1959; The Seagull, Queen's, 1964. Has appeared in numerous films since 1936, including the Battle of the River Plate, A Town Like Alice, The Shiralee, Robbery under Arms, Windom's Way, The Nun's Story, Kidnapped, The Sins of Rachel Cade, The Trials of Oscar Wilde, No Love for Johnnie, I Thank a Fool, In the Cool of the Day, Girl with Green Eyes, The Pumpkin Eater, Judith, Flight of the Phoenix, 10.30 One Summer Evening, Far From the Madding Crowd, Lylah Claire, The Red Tent, Sunday, Bloody Sunday, Lost Horizon, Bequest to the Nation, England Made Me, The Abdication, Network (posthumous awards: Hollywood Golden Globe 1976, Oscar, 1977). British Film Academy Award, 1956, 1961; Variety Club of GB Award, 1971; Soc. of Film and TV Arts award, 1971. *Address:* c/o BKM (Personal Management) Ltd, 27 Curzon Street, W1. *Club:* Garrick.   *[Died 14 Jan. 1977.*

FINDLAY, Alexander John, CMG 1937; *b* 1886; *s* of late James Smith Findlay, Aberdeen; *m* 1913, Primrose Alice, *d* of Arthur Aiken, Aberdeen. *Educ:* Aberdeen Grammar Sch.; Aberdeen Univ.; North of Scotland Coll of Agriculture; MA, BSc (Agric.), NDA, NDD. Entered Colonial Agricultural Service 1912; served in Dept of Agriculture, Nigeria, 1912-31; Dir of Agriculture, Zanzibar, 1931-37; retired 1937; Commissioner for the Colonial Exhibit, World's Fair, New York, 1939 and 1940; served Cameroons, 1915, with West African Frontier Force. *Address:* 24 Carden Place, Aberdeen.   *[Died 26 Dec. 1976.*

FINDLAY, Lt-Col Sir Roland Lewis, 3rd Bt *cr* 1925; Lieutenant-Colonel (retired) 2nd Dragoons (Royal Scots Greys); *b* 14 July 1903; 2nd *s* of Sir John Ritchie Findlay, 1st Bt, KBE, DL, JP; *S* brother, Sir (John) Edmund Ritchie Findlay, 1962; *m* 1st 1927, Barbara Joan, JP, Northants, *d* of late Major H. S. Garrard, Welton Place, Daventry, Northants; one *d*; 2nd, 1964, Mrs M. M. Cripps. *Educ:* Harrow; Royal Military Coll., Sandhurst. Lieut Royal Scots Greys, 1924, Capt., 1934. Served War of 1939-45, with Royal Scots Greys, 1939-43, Lieut-Col 21st Army Group, 1944; Col, ALFSEA, 1945-46. High Sheriff of Northants, 1956-57; DL Northants 1958-60. *Address:* Toll Bar House, Burley, Rutland, Leics. *Club:* Cavalry and Guards.
                                              [Died 28 July 1979 (ext).

FINER, Hon. Sir Morris, Kt 1973; **Hon. Mr Justice Finer;** a Judge of the High Court of Justice, Family Division, since 1973; *b* 12 Dec. 1917; *s* of Charles and Ray Finer; *m* 1943, Edith (*née* Rubner); two *s. Educ:* Kilburn Grammar Sch.; London Sch. of Economics and Political Science. Scholar, London Univ., 1936-39; LLB (Hons), 1939; called to the Bar, Gray's Inn, 1943; Master of the Bench, 1971. QC 1963. Governor, LSE, 1964- (Vice-Chm., 1970-). Board of Trade Inspector, Rolls Razor Ltd, 1964. Chairman: Cinematograph Films Council, 1966-73; Departmental Cttee on One-Parent Families, DHSS, 1969-74; Royal Commn on the Press, 1974-. *Publication:* Company Law, 1948. *Recreations:* reading, walking. *Address:* 10 Clorane Gardens, Hampstead, NW3. *T:* 01-435 7270. *Club:* Reform.
                                              [Died 14 Dec. 1974.

FINLAY, Thomas Victor William, CMG 1948; *b* 14 Nov. 1899; *e s* of Thomas Finlay, Armagh, N Ireland; *m* 1927, Eileen, *d* of John O'Connor, Crossmaglen, Co. Armagh; two *s. Educ:* King's Hospital, Dublin. Army (Inns of Court OTC), 1918-19; Royal Irish and Royal Ulster Special Constabulary, 1920-25; Nigeria Police, 1925; Commissioner of Police, Nigeria, 1946-50, retired. King's Police Medal, Colonial Police Medal, Coronation Medal, 1939-45 War Medal. *Recreations:* golf and bridge. *Address:* Arigideen, 6 Victoria Square, Rostrevor, Co. Down BT34 3EU. *T:* Rostrevor 451.   *[Died 19 June 1980.*

FINLETTER, Hon. Thomas Knight; *b* 11 Nov. 1893; *m* 1920, Margaret Blaine Damrosch (*d* 1966); two *d*; *m* 1949, Eileen Wechster Geist. *Educ:* Episcopal Academy, Philadelphia, Pa.; University of Pennsylvania, Philadelphia, Pa. Special Assistant to US Secretary of State, Washington, DC, 1941-44; Consultant to US Delegation to UNO Conference at San Francisco, 1945; Chairman President's Air Policy Commission, Washington, DC, 1947. Partner, Coudert Brothers (lawyers), New York, 1926-41, 1944-48; returned to firm, 1965; retired, 1970. Minister in charge of ECA Mission to the United Kingdom, 1948-49; Secretary of the Air Force, United States, 1950-53; Ambassador to NATO,

Paris, 1961-65. Hon. LLD: Univ. of Pennsylvania, 1950; Univ. of Rochester, 1950; Syracuse Univ., 1950; College of St Joseph, SJ, 1951; Rutgers Univ., 1959. *Publications:* Principles of Corporate Reorganization, 1937; Cases of Corporate Reorganization, 1938; Law of Bankruptcy Reorganization, 1939; Can Representative Government Do The Job?, 1945; Power and Policy, 1954; Foreign Policy: The Next Phase, 1958; Interim Report on the American Search for a Substitute for Isolation, 1968. *Recreations:* tennis and gardening. *Address:* 151 East 79 Street, New York, NY 10021, USA. *Clubs:* Athenæum (London); Knickerbocker, Century Association, (New York); Metropolitan (Washington).   *[Died 24 April 1980.*

FINLEY, David Edward; Director, National Gallery of Art, Washington, DC, 1938-56, retired; Chairman, White House Historical Association, since 1961; *b* 13 Sept. 1890; *s* of David Edward Finley and Elizabeth Lewis Gist; *m* 1931, Margaret Morton Eustis. *Educ:* University of South Carolina; George Washington Law Sch. AB (University of S. Carolina), 1910; LLB (George Washington Law Sch.), 1913; Doctor of Fine Arts (Yale), 1946; Doctor of Literature (S. Carolina), 1950; LLD George Washington Univ., 1960; Doctorate, Georgetown Univ., 1960; practised law, Philadelphia, 1915-17; European War, 1917-18, 2nd Lieut US Army; Asst Counsel War Finance Corp., 1921-22; Member War Loan Staff, US Treasury, 1922-27; special Asst to Secretary of Treasury, 1927-32; Adviser American delegation, London Financial Conference, 1931; Hon. Counselor American Embassy, London, 1932-33; practised law, Washington, 1933-37; President American Assoc. of Museums, 1945-49; Vice-President International Council of Museums, 1946-49; Chairman US National Cttee on International Co-operation among Museums, 1945-49; Chairman: National Trust for Historic Preservation, 1949-62; Commn of Fine Arts, 1950-63; White House Historical Assoc.; Vice-Chairman American Commission for Protection and Salvage of Artistic and Historic Monuments in War Areas, 1943-46; Trustee, Corcoran Gallery of Art, 1957, now Emeritus; Member: National Collection of Fine Arts Commission, Smithsonian Instn; Assoc. of Art Museum Directors. National Portrait Gallery Commission, 1963. Theodore Roosevelt Distinguished Service Medal for outstanding service by a private citizen, 1957; Joseph Henry Medal, Smithsonian Institution, 1967. *Address:* 3318 O Street, Washington, DC 20007, USA. *Clubs:* Metropolitan, Alibi, Chevy Chase (Washington, DC); Century (New York, NY).
                                              [Died 1 Feb. 1977.

FINNEMORE, Sir Donald Leslie, Kt 1947; Judge of High Court (Queen's Bench Division), 1948-64, retired (Probate, Divorce, and Admiralty, 1947-48); Chairman Warwickshire Quarter Sessions, 1950-71; JP Warwickshire; *b* 13 June 1889; *s* of late William and Kate Finnemore, and *g s* of late J. S. Wright, MP, Nottingham; unmarried. *Educ:* King Edward's Sch.; Pembroke Coll., Oxford (Scholar). First Class in Jurisprudence and Proxime Accessit for Vinerian Law Scholarship at Oxford; called by Inner Temple (Prize for Constitutional Law and Legal History) in 1914; Midland Circuit; served in France as BRCS Officer, 1916-19; Hon. Legal Adviser to Midland Regional Commissioner for Civil Defence, 1940-45; County Court Judge (North Staffs and Birmingham), 1940-44, (Wolverhampton, etc.), 1944-46; (Birmingham), 1946-47; Chairman Midland Conscientious Objectors Tribunal, 1940-47; Member of Matrimonial (Trial in Provinces) Cttee, 1942-43; Member, Criminal Law Revision Cttee, 1965-; contested (L) Sparkbrook, 1923, and Stourbridge, 1929, 1931, 1935; Life Governor of Birmingham Univ., 1945 (Hon. LLD 1966); Governor King Edward's Sch., 1946; Hon. Fellow Pembroke Coll., 1948; President Baptist Union of Great Britain, 1966-67. *Publication:* Boys!, 1925. *Recreations:* travel and The Boys' Brigade. *Address:* 2 Charles Road, Handsworth, Birmingham 20. *Club:* Reform.   *[Died 10 May 1974.*

FIREBRACE, Comdr Sir Aylmer Newton George, Kt 1945; CBE 1941; RN (retired); *b* 17 June 1886; *s* of Lt-Col George Firebrace, Royal Artillery; *m* 1912, Dorothy Vernon (*d* 1952), *d* of Douglas Grey; one *s* one *d. Educ:* HMS Britannia. Commander, 1917; Principal Officer, London Fire Brigade, 1919; Chief Officer of London Fire Brigade, 1938; Regional Fire Officer, London Region, 1939; Chief of the Fire Staff and Inspector-in-Chief of the Fire Services, 1941-47; retired 1947. King's Police and Fire Brigades Medal, 1936; Bronze Medal, Royal Humane Society, 1918; Commander of Order of St Olav (Norway), 1947. *Publications:* Fire Service Memories, 1948; If thou criest after Knowledge, 1952; Light on the Gospel of John, 1957; The Revelation to John, 1963. *Address:* 17 Lincoln House, Basil Street, SW3. *T:* 01-584 2826.   *[Died 8 June 1977.*

FISCHER, Harry Robert; Chairman of Fischer Fine Art Ltd, since 1971; *b* Vienna, 30 Aug. 1903; *s* of Dr Georg Fischer and

Clarisse (née Eisler); m Elfriede (née Lemmer); one s. Educ: Schottengymnasium, Vienna. Publisher and bookdealer, Vienna, 1918-38; emigrated to Great Britain, 1939; served with British Army, Pioneer Corps; Co-founder and Chm., Marlborough Fine Art, London, 1946-71. Grosses Bundesverdienstkreuz of Germany. Recreations: literature, music. Address: 30 King Street, SW1Y 4SQ. T: 01-839 3942. Clubs: Reform, Royal Automobile. [Died 12 April 1977.

FISCHER, John; Contributing Editor, Harper's Magazine, since 1967 (Editor-in-Chief, 1953-67); b 21 April 1910; s of John Simpson and Georgie Caperton Fischer; m 1936, Elizabeth Wilson; two d. Educ: Oklahoma Univ.; Oxford, England (Rhodes Scholar, 1933 and 1934-35). Reporter, Daily Oklahoman, 1932-33; US Dept of Agriculture, 1936; Washington Correspondent for Associated Press, 1937; Board of Economic Warfare, Intelligence Division, 1939; in India as Chief of Economic Intelligence, and Lend-lease, for Foreign Econ. Admin., 1943; Assoc. Editor, Harper's Magazine, 1944-47; Editor-in-Chief, General Book Dept of Harper & Row, Publishers, Inc.; leave of absence from Harper's to join Relief and Rehabilitation mission to the Ukraine, 1946. Member, National Advisory Commn on Rural Poverty. Trustee, Brookings Institution. Regents Prof., Univ. of Calif, 1969; Vis. Fellow, Yale Univ. Hon. Doctor: Kenyon Coll., 1953; Bucknell Univ., 1954; University of Massachusetts, 1956. Publications: Why They Behave Like Russians, 1947 (English title: Scared Men in the Kremlin); Master Plan USA, 1951; The Stupidity Problem, 1964; Vital Signs, 1975; The High Plains: an informal history, 1978; articles in Harper's, Life, New Yorker, Reader's Digest. Recreations: gardening, music, carpentry, travel. Address: Shell Beach Road, Guilford, Conn 06437, USA. Clubs: Century Association, American Association of Rhodes Scholars (New York City). [Died 18 Aug. 1978.

FISH, Sir (Eric) Wilfred, Kt 1954; CBE 1947; MD; DSc; FDSRCS; FRCS; Hon. Consulting Dental Surgeon to: St Mary's Hospital, Paddington; Royal Dental Hospital; late Hon. Director Department of Dental Science, Royal College of Surgeons; b 30 Jan. 1894; s of Rev. George M. C. Fish; m 1916, Hilda Gertrude, e d of Rev. S. J. Russell; one s one d; m 1950, Myfanwy Hazel Bruce Hodge (née Dunlop). Educ: Kingswood; Owen's Coll., Manchester; University College, London. LDS Manchester 1914; ChB 1916; Dumville Surgical Prizeman, 1916; MD 1924; DSc London 1933; FDSRCS 1947; FRCS 1961. Late Captain RAMC (SR); Temp. Surgical Specialist, Bombay Brigade; late Hon. Research Associate in Physiology, University College, London; Hon. Fellow Royal Society of Medicine, 1955; Hon. Member: British Dental Assoc., 1951; Dental Associations of: Vienna, 1931; Spain, 1932; Australia, 1938; Netherlands, 1939; Sweden, 1950; American Academy of Dentistry, 1957. Late Member Physiological Society. postgraduate lecturer, by invitation, to Dental Board of Victoria and South Australia, 1935. President XIth International Dental Congress, London, 1952; Chairman Dental Board, UK, 1944-56; Dean, Faculty of Dental Surgery, RCS, 1956-59; Hon. Consulting Dental Surgeon to the Army, 1959-64; President, GDC, 1956-64; Vice-Pres. d'Honneur, Internat. Dental Fedn. Hon. degrees: DDSc Melbourne, 1935; HDD Glasgow, 1955; DDSc Dunelm, 1959; ScD Trinity Coll., Dublin, 1960; FDSRCS Edinburgh, 1962; FFD, RCSI 1964; FDSRCP & S. Glasgow, 1967. John Tomes Prizeman, RCS, 1933; Howard Mummery Prizeman (1st award), 1933; Colyer Gold Medal, RCS, 1962; Wilfred Fish Research Fellowship, founded RCS, 1970; Sir Wilfred Fish Lecture, founded GDC, 1974. Publications: Principles of Full Denture Prosthesis; Experimental Investigation of the Enamel Dentine and Dental Pulp; Parodontal Disease; Surgical Pathology of the Mouth; papers in Proc. Royal Society, etc. Recreations: formerly stalking, now gardening. Address: Hurst Lodge, Sandgate Lane, Storrington, West Sussex. [Died 20 July 1974.

FISHENDEN, Margaret White, DSc, FInstP; formerly Reader in Applied Heat at Imperial College (University of London), (Mechanical Engineering Department); y d of late R. W. White; one s. Educ: University of Manchester, 1st class Honours in Physics, 1909; Higginbottom Scholar, 1907, Graduate Scholar, 1909; Beyer Fellow, 1910-11; Lecturer, University of Manchester, 1910-15; in charge of research work for Air Pollution Advisory Board of the Manchester Corporation, 1916-22; research work on Atmospheric Conditions, Humidity and Ventilation in Spinning Mills and Weaving Sheds, Domestic Heating, Heat Transfer, etc. Publications: House Heating, 1925; The Calculation of Heat Transmission, 1932; An Introduction to Heat Transfer, 1950; scientific and technical papers. Address: c/o 8 Severn Road, Chilton, Didcot, Oxon. [Died 21 Oct. 1977.

FISHER OF CAMDEN, Baron cr 1974 (Life Peer), of Camden in Greater London; Samuel Fisher, Kt 1967; FCIS; JP; Alderman, London Borough of Camden, 1971; Vice-President, London Diamond Bourse; President, Board of Deputies of British Jews, 1973-79 (Senior Vice-Pres., 1967-73); b 20 Jan. 1905; m 1930, Millie Gluckstein; one d (and one d decd). Educ: London. Mayor of Stoke Newington, 1953-54; first Mayor of London Borough of Camden, 1965-66. Last elected Chm., Metropolitan Water Bd, 1969-70. Chairman: London Labour Mayors' Assoc., 1953-; West Central Div. Justices. Chm., Governing Bd, World Jewish Congress, 1977-. Governor: University Coll. Hosp.; University Coll. Sch. JP Inner London, 1951. Recreations: reviewing historical and biographical books. Address: 48 Viceroy Court, Prince Albert Road, NW8 7PR. T: 01-586 2824. [Died 12 Oct. 1979.

FISHER OF LAMBETH, Baron cr 1961, of Lambeth (Life Peer); Most Rev. and Rt. Hon. Geoffrey Francis Fisher; PC 1939; GCVO 1953; Royal Victorian Chain, 1949; Hon. DD, LLD, and DCL; MA; b 5 May 1887; y s of late Rev. H. Fisher, Rector of Higham-on-the-Hill, Nuneaton; m 1917, Rosamond Chevallier, d of late Rev. A. F. E. Forman, and g d of Dr S. A. Pears, once Headmaster of Repton; six s. Educ: Marlborough Coll., Exeter Coll., Oxford (open scholar); First Class Honours in Moderations, 1908; Lit Hum 1910; Theology, 1911; Liddon Scholarship, 1911; Wells Theological Coll., 1911. Deacon, 1912; Priest, 1913. Hon. Fellow, Exeter Coll., Oxford, 1939; Asst Master, Marlborough Coll., 1911-14; Headmaster of Repton Sch., 1914-32; Bishop of Chester, 1932-39; Bishop of London, 1939-45; Archbishop of Canterbury, 1945-61. Dean of the Chapels Royal, 1939-45; Prelate of Order of British Empire, 1939-45; Prelate, 1946, and Bailiff Grand Cross, 1947, of Order of S John of Jerusalem; President of the World Council of Churches, 1946-54. Select Preacher, Oxford Univ., 1925-27, Cambridge Univ., 1937 and 1940; Freeman of Cities of London and Canterbury, 1952; of Croydon, 1961. Hon. Doctor of Laws (Universities of Pennsylvania and Columbia, 1946, Yale and British Columbia, 1954); Hon. DD: Oxford, 1933; Cambridge and Princeton, 1946, Edinburgh, 1953; Montreal, 1962; TCD 1963; Hon LLD: Pennsylvania and Columbia, 1946; London 1948; Manchester, 1950; Yale and BC, 1954; Rikkyo, Japan, 1959; Yonsel, Korea, 1959; Hon. DCL (Roman Catholic) University of the Assumption, Windsor, Canada; Hon. STD, Northwestern, Evanston, 1954; Doctor of Theology, General Theological Seminary, New York, 1957. Grand Cross of Greek Order of the Redeemer, 1947; Grand Cross of St Olav (Norway), 1947; Czechoslovak Order of the White Lion (II Class), 1948. Address: Trent Rectory, Sherborne, Dorset. T: Marston Magna 441. [Died 14 Sept. 1972.

FISHER, Allan George Barnard; b Christchurch, New Zealand, 1895; m Airini Pope; one s one d. Educ: University of Melbourne; London School of Economics. Prof. of Econs, University of Otago, Dunedin, 1924-35; Professor of Economics, University of Western Australia, 1936-37; Price Professor of International Economics, RIIA, 1938-46; (temporary appointment) Economist to Bank of New South Wales, Sydney, 1934; (temporary appointment) Counsellor, NZ Legation, Washington, 1944. Chief Editor, International Monetary Fund, retired 1960. Publications: Some Problems of Wages and their Regulation in Great Britain since 1918, 1926; Moscow Impressions, 1932; The Clash of Progress and Security, 1935; World Economic Affairs (in Survey of International Affairs, 1937, 1938); Economic Progress and Social Security, 1945; International Implications of Full Employment in Great Britain, 1946; (with H. J. Fisher) Slavery and Muslim Society in Africa, 1970; (with H. J. Fisher) trans. G. Nachtigal: Sahara and Sudan, vol. I, 1971, vol. II, 1980, vol. IV, 1974. Address: 76 Ormond Avenue, Hampton, Mddx. [Died 8 Jan. 1976.

FISHER, Brig. Arthur Francis, CBE 1945; DSO 1943; Farmer; b 11 July 1899; s of Major J. F. Fisher, RA, and Eleanor Mary (née Stanier); m 1926, Margaret Charlotte, d of General Sir George Kirkpatrick, KCB, KCSI; two s one d. Educ: Wellington Coll.; RMA Woolwich. Commissioned 2nd Lieut, RA, 1918; served European War, 1914-18 (despatches); transferred as Captain 12 R. Lancers, 1929; Staff Coll., 1935-36; Major, 1938; War Office, GSO2 1938; GSO1 1939; Comdg E. Riding Yeomanry, 1940-41; Brigadier 1941; Comdg various Brigades Home and Middle East; Acting Maj.-General. 1942; Brigadier RAC, 2nd Army, 1943-44; Dep. Director RAC, War Office, 1944-46; Ministry of Supply, 1946-52. Medal of Freedom with Bronze Palm (USA), 1945. Recreation: shooting. Address: Coopers Farm, Winterslow, Salisbury, Wilts. T: Winterslow 297. Club: Cavalry. [Died 28 Aug. 1972.

FISHER, Lieut-General Sir Bertie Drew, KCB, cr 1938 (CB 1929), CMG 1919; DSO 1915; Colonel 17th-21st Lancers, 1938-

47; *b* 13 July 1878; *m* 1918, Marjorie Frances, *d* of Lady Burdett, Foremarke Hall, Derbyshire; two *s*. *Educ:* Marlborough; New Coll., Oxford. Entered Army, 1900; Commissioned 17th Lancers, 1900; Captain, 1905; Major, 1914; Bt Lieut-Colonel 1916, Lieut-Colonel 1919; Colonel 1920; Maj.-General 1931; Lt-Gen. 1937; served South African War, 1900-02 (Queen's Medal 3 clasps, King's Medal 2 clasps); GSO3 (Military Aeronautics Dept), 1913-14. European War, 1914-18 (despatches four times, twice wounded, CMG, DSO and Bar, Bt Lieut-Colonel, Croix d'Officier Legion of Honour); ADC to the King, 1926-31; commanded 2nd Cavalry Brigade, 1923-27; Commandant Senior Officers' Sch., 1927-30; Brigadier, General Staff, Aldershot Command, 1930-31; Director of Recruiting and Organisation, War Office, 1932-34; Commadant RMC, Sandhurst, 1934-37; retired pay, 1938; GOC-in-Chief, Southern Command, Salisbury, 1939-40. *Address:* Hartley House, Turgis Green, Basingstoke, Hants. *T:* Turgis Green 277. *Club:* Cavalry.
[*Died 24 July 1972.*]

FISHER, Hon. Charles Douglas; Headmaster, Geelong Church of England Grammar School, since 1974; *b* 8 Oct. 1921; 3rd *s* of late Most Rev. and Rt Hon. Lord Fisher of Lambeth, GCVO, and of Lady Fisher of Lambeth; *m* 1952, Anne Gilmour (*née* Hammond); four *s* two *d*. *Educ:* Marlborough Coll.; Keble Coll., Oxford (MA). Mem. Australian Coll. of Educn. War Service, 1940-45; Oxford Univ., 1945-48; Asst Master, Harrow Sch., 1948-55; Sen. Master, Peterhouse Sch., Rhodesia, 1955-60; Headmaster: Scotch Coll., Adelaide, 1961-69; C of E Grammar Sch., Brisbane, 1970-73. *Address:* Geelong Church of England Grammar School, Corio, Victoria, Australia. *T:* Geelong 75-1452. *Club:* Melbourne (Melbourne). [*Died 5 Dec. 1978.*]

FISHER, John Lenox, CMG 1956; *b* 9 Oct. 1899; *s* of George Henry Fisher; *m* 1929, Kathleen Maysie Mackie; one *s* one *d*. *Educ:* Liverpool University. RFC/RAF, 1917-19 (Pilot, 2nd Lieut). Joined Bank of England, Oct. 1921; Asst Adviser, 1938; Dir of Operations, International Monetary Fund, Washington, DC, 1946-47; Dep. Chief Cashier, Bank of England, 1948-50; Adviser to Governors, Bank of England, 1950-59. Former Mem., E and W African Currency Bds. *Recreations:* gardening, golf, swimming. *Address:* The Little House, Tudor Close, Mare Hill, Pulborough, West Sussex. *T:* Pulborough 2163. *Clubs:* Oriental; West Sussex Golf (Pulborough). [*Died 27 Sept. 1976.*]

FISHER, Norman George; Chairman, Butterworth & Co. (Publishers) Ltd, since 1968; *b* 9 July 1910; *s* of late Thomas Daniel and Kate Fisher; *m* 1934, Jenny, *d* of late John and Barbara Cole; three *s* (one *d* decd). *Educ:* Cardiff High Sch.; St Edmund Hall, Oxford (MA). Asst to Education Sec., Cambs, 1938-46; Dep. Educ. Officer, Lancs, 1946-49; Chief Educ. Officer, Manchester, 1949-55; Principal, the Staff Coll. of the National Coal Board, 1955-61. War Service: RASC, RAEC, Commandant, Army Sch. of Education (ABCA); 1943; Command Educ. Officer, ALFSEA, 1945-46. Chairman: North Regional Advisory Council, BBC, 1953-55; The Fifty-One Soc., 1951-55; Seminar of the Caribbean Countries on Adult Education (at Jamaica), 1953; Gen. Advisory Council, BBC, 1955-62; OECD Project, Management Training; Printing and Publishing Industry Training Bd, 1968-; Council of Technical Examining Bodies. Reference Cttee, Dept of Educn and Science. Member: Cttee on Proceedings before Examining Magistrates, 1957; Cttee on Awards to University Students, 1958-60; Council BIM, 1962-66 (Fellow 1964-); Exec. Governor, Royal Shakespeare Theatre, 1963-; Drama Advisory Cttee, British Council. Chairman: Butterworth (Australia); Butterworth (New Zealand); Director: Triton Publishing Co. Ltd; Provident Clothing & Supply Co. Ltd. *Publications:* Walk at a Steady Pace, 1970; Rise at Dawn, 1971. *Recreations:* writing, reading, music, open-air pursuits. *Address:* 88 Kingsway, WC2. *Club:* Athenæum. [*Died 1 Feb. 1972.*]

FISHER, Sydney Humbert, CVO 1948; *b* 9 Feb. 1887; *s* of late Edward Fisher, Aspley Guise, Beds; *m* 1915, Doris Mary (*d* 1974), *d* of late Dr Adam Oakley; two *d* (one *s* missing presumed killed in action). *Educ:* Repton. Joined London North Western Railway, 1904; Chief Operating Manager: LMS Rly, 1944, London Midland Region, Br. Rlys, 1948; late Dep. Chief Regional Officer, London Midland Region, Railway Executive. Medal of Freedom with Bronze Palm (USA). *Address:* c/o Barclays Bank Ltd, Cirencester, Glos. [*Died 9 March 1980.*]

FISHER, Sir Woolf, Kt 1964; Chairman and Managing Director of Fisher & Paykel Ltd, since 1934; Chairman, New Zealand Steel Ltd, since 1965; *b* 1912; *s* of Michael Fisher; *m* 1935, Joyce, *d* of George Paykel. *Educ:* Mt Albert Grammar Sch., Auckland. Co-founder of Fisher & Paykel Ltd, 1934; Member: Council Auckland Chamber of Commerce, 1956-62; Council NZ Thoroughbred Breeders Assoc., 1948-; President: Auckland

Racing Club, 1973- (Mem., Cttee 1958-); Auckland Polo Club, 1957-62; Mem. Auckland Rotary, 1952-; Chairman: New Zealand Steel Investigating Co., 1960-65; New Zealand Steel Ltd., 1965-74. Pres. Outward Bound Trust of New Zealand, 1961-63; Trustee, New Zealand Inst. of Economic Research, 1958-62; Leader, New Zealand Trade Mission to Australia, 1959; Trade Promotion Council, 1962-63; Director: New Zealand Insurance Co. Ltd, 1963-; BNZ Finance Co. Ltd, 1966-. *Recreations:* shooting, fishing. *Address:* Ra Ora, Waiouru Road, Papatoetoe, Auckland, New Zealand. *T:* 598-935. *Clubs:* Northern, Professional (Auckland). [*Died 12 Jan. 1975.*]

FISKE, Baron *cr* 1967, of Brent (Life Peer); **William Geoffrey Fiske;** Kt 1965; CBE 1956; DL; Chairman, Decimal Currency Board, 1966-71; *b* 3 July 1905; *s* of William George Fiske and Clementina (*née* Gage); *m* 1st, 1930, Violet Amelia, *d* of Joseph Brookes; one *s* one *d*; 2nd, 1955, Josephine, *d* of Alan Coppin. *Educ:* Berkhamsted Sch. Bank of England, 1923-35; Civil Service, 1940-45. Parliamentary Candidate Hornsey, 1945. Mem. London County Council, 1946-65; Chm. Town Planning Cttee, LCC, 1949-55; Chm., Housing Cttee, LCC, 1955-60. Majority Party Chief Whip, LCC, 1960; Leader, Greater London Council, 1964-67. Pres., Nat. Fedn of Housing Assocs, 1971-; Chairman: Consultative Council for LEB, 1965-67; Housing Centre Trust, 1969-; Hanover Housing Assoc., 1970-. Mem. South Bank Theatre and Opera House Board, 1965-. Vice-Chairman: Sutton Dwellings Trust, 1957-67; The Centre for Environmental Studies, 1966-71. Pres., British Diabetic Assoc., 1970-. Hon. MRTPI. DL Greater London, 1967. *Recreations:* music, gardening, study of architecture. *Address:* House of Lords, SW1. [*Died 13 Jan. 1975.*]

FISON, Rt. Rev. Joseph Edward; Bishop of Salisbury, since 1963; *b* 18 March 1906; *s* of Frederick Flint Fison and Ethel Mary Fison; *m* 1944, Monica Irene Stober; two *s* two *d*. *Educ:* Orley Farm Prep. School; Shrewsbury School; The Queen's College, Oxford; Wycliffe Hall, Oxford. 2nd Cl. Hon. Mods, 2nd Cl. Lit Hum, 1st Cl.Theol.; BA Oxon 1929, MA 1934, BD 1950. Taught at English Mission Coll., Cairo, 1930-33; ordained Deacon and Priest, 1934; Tutor and Chaplain, Wycliffe Hall, Oxford, 1934-37; Curate, St Aldate's Church, Oxford, 1937-40; Chaplain to Forces, 1940-45; Senior Chaplain, Jerusalem, 1943-45; Canon Residentiary of Rochester Cathedral, 1945-52; Canon Residentiary and Sub-Dean of Truro Cathedral and Rector of St Mary's Truro, 1952-59; Vicar of St Mary the Great with St Michael and All Angels, Cambridge, 1959-63. Lectured in USA, 1956; Select Preacher, Cambridge Univ., 1957; Hon. Canon of Ely Cathedral, 1961-63. Chairman, Churches Council of Healing, 1964-68. Pres. Council, Marlborough Coll.; Governor: Sherborne Sch.; St Mary's, Calne; Bryanston Sch. Hon. DD Aberdeen Univ., 1958. *Publications:* The Blessing of the Holy Spirit, 1950; Understanding the Old Testament, 1952; The Christian Hope, 1954; The Faith of the Bible, 1957 (Penguin); Fire upon the Earth, 1958. Contributor to: The Gospel of Grace, 1936; The Triumph of God, 1948; Steps to Christian Understanding (ed R. J. W. Bevan), 1958; Lenten Counsellors, 1962. Editor of and Contributor to: On the Move to Unity, 1962. Article on Haggai in Encyclopædia Britannica (written for new edn). *Address:* South Canonry, 71 The Close, Salisbury, Wilts. *T:* Salisbury 4031. *Clubs:* Old Salopian, Oxford Society, Automobile Association; Cambridge Union Society.
[*Died 2 July 1972.*]

FITZ-GERALD, Sir Patrick (Herbert), Kt 1955; OBE 1944; retired; *b* 1899; *s* of Gerald and Florence Fitz-Gerald; *m* 1947, Dorothy Preece (marr. diss., 1957; she died 1960). *Educ:* Tonbridge Sch. Served European War, 1914-18 in Irish Guards, and War of 1939-45 as Lieut-Col Sherwood Foresters; despatches twice. *Recreations:* polo and cricket.
[*Died 8 Nov. 1978.*]

FITZGERALD, Walter, (Walter Fitzgerald Bond); Actor; *b* 18 May 1896; *s* of Rev. Richard James Bond, BD, and Julia Caroline Theresa (*née* Prynne); *m* 1st, Rosalie Constance Gray; one *s*; 2nd, Angela Dorothea Radford-Rowe (*d* 1970), *d* of Rev. Preb. P. T. R.-R. Kirk; three *s* one *d*. *Educ:* King's Coll., Taunton. Studied at Royal Academy of Dramatic Art. Toured with Mrs Patrick Campbell, 1923-24; first London appearance as Alf Cope in The Likes of 'Er, Century, 1924, with Lena Ashwell Players and remained with them until 1927; understudy to Sir Gerald du Maurier. St James's, 1928-29; toured in Canada with Sir John Martin-Harvey, 1929-30; London, 1930-31; toured Canada, 1932; Malvern Festival, July-Aug. 1932; went to America, 1933; London from 1933 (went to S Africa with Sir Seymour Hicks, 1936); toured 1938 and 1942; Mr Bolfrey in play of that name, Playhouse, 1943; Stephen Marlowe in Zero Hour, Lyric; Mr Darling and Capt. Hook in Peter Pan, Stoll; Charles in The Astonished Ostrich, St James's. At the Edinburgh

Festival, 1950, Jupiter in The Queen's Comedy. Recent London stage appearances; Sir Robert Rawley in The Paragon, Fortune; Relling in The Wild Duck, St Martin's; Charles Perrier in Marriage Story, Strand: Mr Owen in The Green Bay Tree, Playhouse; Captain Shotover in Heartbreak House, Arts; the King in Hamlet, New; toured India and Pakistan for British Council, 1950-51, playing Shylock, Brutus, Jacques, Iago; Henry Vining in The Day's Mischief, Duke of York's; Father Brown in The Living Room, Wyndham's (subseq. Henry Miller Theatre, New York); Ulysses in Tiger at the Gates, Apollo, and Plymouth Theatre, NY; The Best Damn Lie, Winter Garden; Gilt and Gingerbread, Duke of York's; Maj.-Gen. FitzAdam in The Amorous Prawn, Saville; Sir William Gascony in The Judge's Story, Ashcroft Theatre, Croydon; Twelve Angry Men, Queen's. *Films:* include: San Demetrio, London (Chief Engineer), 1942; Treasure Island (Squire Trelawney) (Walt Disney prod.), 1949; Mr Wardle in film of Pickwick Papers; Appointment in London; The Net; The Cruel Sea; Personal Affair (film of The Day's Mischief); Newspaper Story; Man in the Sky; Round the World in 80 days; Something of Value; Darby O'Gill and The Little People as Lord Fitzpatrick (Walt Disney prod.); Banner in the Sky (Walt Disney prod.). Has appeared on television frequently (Simon Peter in Paul of Tarsus, BBC Series), including programmes in New York and Hollywood. *Recreations:* work, family, home. *Address:* 6 Argyll Mansions, Hammersmith Road, W14. *T:* 01-602 2677. *Club:* Garrick.
[Died 20 Dec. 1976.

FITZGERALD, Most Rev. William Michael, OP; *b* 4 June 1906; *s* of John and Ellen Fitzgerald, Tralee, Co. Kerry. *Educ:* Christian Schools, Tralee; St Mary's, Tallaght, Co. Dublin; Pontificio Ateneo Angelicum, Rome. Served in several Trinidad parishes; Vicar General of Archdiocese of Port of Spain, 1948; retired from Archdiocese, 1968; Apostolic Administrator, 1966-68. *Address:* St Dominic's, Ennismore, Cork.
[Died 31 Oct. 1971.

FITZHERBERT, Maj.-Gen. Edward Herbert, CBE 1943; DSO 1918; MC; *b* 3 Dec. 1885; *s* of late Col E. H. Fitzherbert, King's Own Royal Lancaster Regt. *Educ:* Rossall Sch.; RMC Camberley. 2nd Lieut, ASC, 1905; Lieut, 1907; Capt., 1914; T/Major, 1914; a/Lieut-Col, 1917; Major, 1924; Lieut-Col, 1931; Col, 1935; Brigadier, 1939; Maj.-Gen., 1941; DAQMG, 1915-17; Asst Dir of Supplies and Transport, War Office, 1937-39; Asst Inspector, RASC, 1939; Inspector, RASC, 1940-43; retired pay, 1943; served European War, 1914-18 (despatches thrice, DSO, MC); served War of 1939-45, 1939-43. Col Commandant RASC, 1947-50. *Recreations:* golf and shooting. *Address:* c/o Lloyds Bank, Ltd, Cox & King's Branch, 6 Pall Mall, SW1. *Clubs:* Naval and Military, MCC.
[Died 1 Aug. 1979.

FITZSIMONS, Robert Allen, FRCS; Hon. Consulting Surgeon to Charing Cross Hospital and to The Metropolitan Hospital; *b* 16 March 1892; *s* of James Fitzsimons and Mary L. McDonald, Sligo; *m* 1927, Mary Patricia, *d* of Thomas McKelvey, Cardiff; one *s* one *d*. *Educ:* Summerhill Coll., Sligo; Birkbeck Coll., King's Coll., and Charing Cross Hospital Medical Sch., University of London. BSc London 1920; MB, BS London 1930; MRCS, LRCP, 1926; FRCS 1932. Formerly: Analyst to HM Govt Laboratory; House Surgeon and Surgical Registrar to Charing Cross Hosp.; Registrar to Royal National Orthopædic Hospital. Fellow of the Assoc. of Surgeons, Great Britain and Ireland. *Address:* 16 Lansdowne Road, W11. *T:* 01-727 5759.
[Died 2 May 1978.

FITZWILLIAM, 10th Earl *cr* 1716; **William Thomas George Wentworth-Fitzwilliam,** TD; JP; DL; Baron Fitzwilliam, 1620; Earl Fitzwilliam and Viscount Milton, 1716 (Irish honours); Baron Milton (Great Britain), 1742; Earl Fitzwilliam and Viscount Milton, 1746; Chairman, Milton (Peterborough) Estates Co.; Director: B.M.S.S. (Shrewsbury) Ltd; Neanco Holdings Ltd; Fitzwilliam (Peterborough) Properties Ltd; *b* 28 May 1904; *s* of late George Charles Wentworth-Fitzwilliam (*g g s* of 5th Earl) and Evelyn, *o d* of Charles Stephen Lyster; *S* cousin, 1952; *m* 1956, Joyce (who *m* 1922, Hon. Henry Fitzalan-Howard, later 2nd Visc. FitzAlan of Derwent (marr. diss., 1955; he *d* 1962); two *d*), *e d* of Col Philip Langdale, OBE, Houghton Hall, Yorks. *Educ:* Eton; Magdalene Coll., Cambridge. Joint Master Fitzwilliam Hunt, 1935-; Chm., Peterborough Royal Foxhound Show Soc., 1946-; Pres., Nat. Coursing Club, 1972-. Chm., Peterborough Divisional Cons. Assoc., 1947-75, Pres., 1975-. Patron, Fitzwilliam Coll., Cambridge. JP Peterborough, 1928; DL Huntingdon and Peterborough, 1965. Served War of 1939-45; American Bronze Star Medal. *Recreation:* shooting. *Heir:* none. *Address:* Milton, Peterborough. *T:* Castor 202; Wentworth Woodhouse, Rotherham. *Clubs:* Boodle's, Pratt's, White's.
[Died 21 Sept. 1979 (ext).

FLANDERS, Allan David, CBE 1971; MA Oxon; Reader in Industrial Relations, University of Warwick, since 1971; *b* 27 July 1910; *s* of Frederick William Flanders and Emily Louisa (*née* Shaw); *m* 1951, Annemarie Klara Laura (*née* Tracinski). *Educ:* Latymer Upper Sch.; Landerziehungsheim Walkemuhle, Germany. Research Asst, TUC, 1943-46; Head of Political Branch, Brit. CCG, 1946-47; Sen. Lectr in Industrial Relations, Univ. of Oxford, 1949-69; Faculty Fellow, Nuffield Coll., 1964-69. Vis. Prof. of Industrial Relations, Univ. of Manchester, 1969-71. Mem., Sec. of State's Colonial Adv. Cttee, 1954-62; Industrial Relations Adviser to Nat. Bd for Prices and Incomes, 1965-68; Full-time Mem., Commn on Industrial Relations, 1969-71. It Editor, Socialist Commentary, 1972-. *Publications:* Trade Unions, 1952 (7th rev. edn, 1968); The System of Industrial Relations in Great Britain (with H. A. Clegg), 1954; The Fawley Productivity Agreements, 1964; Industrial Relations: What is Wrong with the System?, 1965; Collective Bargaining: Prescription for Change, 1967; Experiment in Industrial Democracy (with R. Pomeranz and J. Woodward), 1968; (ed) Collective Bargaining (Modern Management Readings), 1969; Management and Unions, 1970. *Recreations:* television, music. *Address:* 36 Lindsey Crescent, Kenilworth, Warwicks. *T:* Kenilworth 55280.
[Died 29 Sept. 1973.

FLANDERS, Michael, OBE 1964; actor and writer; *b* London, 1 March 1922; *s* of Peter Henry Flanders and Rosa Laura (Laurie O'Beirne, violinist); *m* 1959, Claudia, *er d* of Prof. Robert Gorham Davis, Columbia Univ., USA; two *d*. *Educ:* Westminster Sch.; Christ Church, Oxford (MA). Acted with OUDS, ETC and professionally at Playhouse, 1941. AB on destroyer, 1942; Sub-Lieut RNVR, Coastal Forces; contracted poliomyelitis, 1943; discharged hospital but confined to wheel-chair, 1946. First broadcast, 1948; first televised, 1953; frequent appearances on all services since currently include: Scrapbook; Face The Music; Gala Performance; documentary commentary, incl. Royal Family, 1969, The Tribe that Hides from Man, 1970. From 1948 wrote for many revues. Main author Penny Plain, 1951; Airs on a Shoestring, 1953; Pay the Piper, 1954; Fresh Airs, 1956. Also wrote opera libretti, Three's Company, 1953, and A Christmas Story, 1954 (Antony Hopkins), both televised. Trans. The Soldier's Tale (Stravinsky) with Kitty Black, for Edinburgh Fest., 1954; trans. radiophonic opera Orestes (Henk Badings) for Radio-Unie (Hilversum), 1955, in which he took a leading role. With Donald Swann presented their two-man revue At the Drop of a Hat, New Lindsay Theatre, Dec. 1956; transferred to Fortune Theatre, Jan. 1957-May 1959; Edinburgh Fest., Aug. 1959; New York, Oct. 1959-May 1960; toured USA and Canada, Oct. 1960-March 1961; Geneva, May 1961; GB and Canada, Oct. 1962-March 1963. Joined Royal Shakespeare Co. in The Caucasian Chalk Circle, 1962; (with Donald Swann) At the Drop of Another Hat (Haymarket), Oct. 1963-March 1964; toured Australia and New Zealand, Aug.-Dec. 1964; Hong Kong, Jan. 1965; (Globe) Oct. 1965-Feb. 1966; toured USA and Canada, 1966; New York, 1966, 1967; 10 Years Hard (Revue), Mayfair, 1970. *Film:* The Raging Moon, 1970. *Publications:* Creatures Great and Small, 1964; Captain Noah and His Floating Zoo, 1971; Nasrudin The Wise, 1974. *Address:* 63 Esmond Road, Bedford Park, W4 1JE. *T:* 01-994 1962.
[Died 15 April 1975.

FLAVELLE, Sir (Joseph) Ellsworth, 2nd Bt, *cr* 1917; *b* 25 May 1892; *s* of Sir Joseph Wesley Flavelle, 1st Bt, and Clara, *d* of Rev. Oren Ellsworth; *S* father 1939; *m* 1917, Muriel McEachren; two *s* one *d*. *Educ:* St Andrew's Coll., University of Toronto. Trustee, Toronto General Hosp.; Mem. of Board, Community Welfare Council of Ontario; Mem. Advisory Council Knights of the Round Table. *Recreations:* yachting, photography. *Heir:* *s* Joseph David Ellsworth Flavelle [*b* 9 Nov. 1921; *m* 1942, Muriel Barbara, *d* of Reginald Morton; three *d*]. *Address:* Kingswold, RR2, King, Ontario, Canada; 780 Eglington Avenue, Toronto, Ont., Canada. *Clubs:* York, Royal Canadian Yacht (Toronto).
[Died 19 Dec. 1977.

FLAXMAN, Brigadier Sir Hubert (James Marlowe), Kt 1962; CMG 1954; retired as Chief Justice of Gibraltar (Dec. 1955-Sept. 1965); *b* 22 July 1893; *s* of James and Florence Flaxman; *m* 1st, 1920, Muriel Kathleen Bateman (*d* 1961); one *s*; 2nd, 1961, Vivien Aderna Barton. *Educ:* The Drapers' Sch., Purley. Political Officer, Mesopotamia, 1918; joined Sudan Civil Service, 1924, as District Commissioner; District Judge, 1926; Judge of the High Court, 1933. Called to the Bar, Middle Temple, 1934. Chief Justice of the Sudan, 1940; British Judge, Joint Court, New Hebrides, 1949; Resident Commissioner, New Hebrides, 1950-55; Acting Attorney-Gen., Gibraltar, Oct.-Dec. 1955. Served in the Army, 1914-21 and 1944-49 (despatches). Order of the Nile (4th Class), 1934. *Recreation:* gardening. *Address:* Ashton Cottage, Yaxley, near Eye, Suffolk. *Club:* East India, Sports and Public Schools.
[Died 23 June 1976.

FLEMING, Rev. James George Grant, DSO 1917; MC 1917; TD 1939; retired; *b* 2 April 1895; *s* of late James Fleming, Glenfarg, Craigleith, Edinburgh; *m* 1st, 1919, Daisy (*d* 1924), *s* of late Maj. W. J. Trotter, RAMC, Readstown, Co. Meath, Ireland; one *d*; 2nd, 1930, Saidie Caroline, *d* of late W. J. Stewart, MP, Crawfordsburn, Co. Down, Ireland; one *s*. *Educ:* Stewart's Coll., Edinburgh; Edinburgh Univ. (MA 1928). Army 1914-23. Served European War, 1914-18 (wounded; despatches; DSO; MC); Waziristan FF, 1919-21. Ordained 1930; Minister: Lasswade Old Parish Church, 1930-35; East Church of St Nicholas, Aberdeen, 1935-41; Banchory-St Ternan East Church. Banchory, Kincardineshire, 1952-65. Served 1939-47: SCF 9th (Highland) Div., 1939; SCF 51st (Highland) Div., 1940-42; DACG 1942; Senior Staff Chaplain, India, 1942-44; Asst Chaplain-Gen., L of C and Burma, 1944-46 (despatches twice); Hon. CF (1st class), 1947; C of S Chaplain, CCG and UK High Commission, Germany, 1948-52. Hon. Life Mem., Royal British Legion (Scotland), 1965. *Publications:* various. *Address:* Dunard, Banchory, Kincardineshire. *T:* Banchory 2828. *Club:* Royal Northern (Aberdeen). [*Died 19 Feb. 1978.*

FLEMING, John Marcus, CMG 1950; MA Edinburgh; Deputy Director, Research Department, International Monetary Fund, since 1964; *b* 13 March 1911; *s* of John and Helen Fleming, Bathgate, West Lothian; *m* 1936, Etta (marr. diss., 1958), *d* of Kapitän Leist, Vienna, Austria; two *d*; *m* 1959, Gloria, *d* of Wayne Hile, Detroit, Michigan, USA. *Educ:* Bathgate Academy; Edinburgh Univ. Mem. of Financial Section, League of Nations, 1935-37; Travelling Fellow of Rockefeller Foundation, 1937-39; Ministry of Economic Warfare, 1939-42; Cabinet Offices, Economic Section, 1942, Deputy Dir, 1947-51; Visiting Prof., Columbia Univ., New York, 1951-54; Chief, Special Studies Div., IMF, 1954; Adviser, IMF, 1959. Mem. of UK delegation to San Francisco Conference of 1945, and to meetings of Economic and Social Council, etc.; UK Rep. on Economic and Employment Commission of UN, 1950-51. *Publications:* Essays in International Economics, 1971; contrib. to learned journals in UK and USA on questions of economic theory and policy. *Recreations:* theatre, philosophy. *Address:* c/o International Monetary Fund, Washington, DC 20431, USA. [*Died 3 Feb. 1976.*

FLEMING, Peter; see Fleming, R. P.

FLEMING, Major Philip, DL, JP, N Bucks; *b* 15 Aug. 1889; *s* of Robert Fleming, LLD, JP; *m* 1924, Joan Cecil, *d* of late Sir Philip Hunloke, GCVO; one *s* two *d*. *Educ:* Eton; Magdalen Coll., Oxford. Stroked Leander VIII winners Olympic Games, 1912. Served European War, 1914-18, in Queen's Own Oxfordshire Hussars. Dir Robert Fleming & Co. Ltd, Merchant Bankers. High Sheriff of Oxon., 1948-49. *Recreations:* hunting, stalking, fishing. *Address:* Barton Abbey, Steeple Aston, Oxon. *T:* 227. *Club:* Carlton. [*Died 13 Oct. 1971.*

FLEMING, Richard Evelyn, MC; TD; merchant banker; a Director, Robert Fleming Holdings, Chairman 1966-74; Director, Barclays Bank Ltd and other companies; *b* 23 Feb. 1911; *s* of Major Valentine Fleming, DSO, MP, and Evelyn Ste Croix Fleming; *m* 1938, Hon. Dorothy Charmian Hermon Hodge, 3rd *d* of 2nd Baron Wyfold; five *s* three *d*. *Educ:* Eton; Magdalen Coll., Oxford. Served War of 1939-45, with Lovat Scouts and 5th (Sutherland) Bn, Seaforth Highlanders. Governor, The London Assurance, 1964-71; Chm., Sun Alliance & London Insurance, 1968-71. A Curator, Oxford Univ. Chest; Mem., Adv. Cttee of Saudi Arabian Monetary Authority. Trustee of Pilgrim Trust, 1948-75 (Chm., 1968-74). *Recreations:* most country pursuits. *Address:* Leygore Manor, Northleach, Glos. *T:* Northleach 234. *Club:* New (Edinburgh). [*Died 14 Aug. 1977.*

FLEMING, (Robert) Peter, OBE 1945; DL; *b* 31 May 1907; *e s* of late Major Valentine Fleming, DSO, MP, and Evelyn Beatrice Ste Croix Rose; *m* 1935, Celia (*see* Celia Johnson), *yr d* of Dr J. R. Johnson; one *s* two *d*. *Educ:* Eton; Christ Church, Oxford. 1st class English Literature, 1929; at one time travelled widely, generally as a Special Correspondent of The Times; Commissioned Grenadier Guards (Supp. R of O), 1930; served War of 1939-45, Norway, 1940 (mention); Greece, 1941 (wounded); SEAC 1942-45. Order of the Cloud and Banner (Chinese) for War Services. Commanded 4th Bn Oxford and Bucks Light Infantry (TA), 1951-54; promoted Bt Col and transferred to TARO, 1954. High Sheriff of Oxon., 1952. Pres. Oxfordshire Branch of Country Landowners Association, 1960-; DL Oxon, 1970. *Publications include:* Brazilian Adventure; One's Company; News from Tartary; Invasion, 1940; The Siege at Peking; Bayonets to Lhasa; The Fate of Admiral Kolchak; translated from French: Tibetan Marches by A. Migot. *Recreations:* shooting, riding. *Address:* Merrimoles House,

Nettlebed, Oxon. *T:* Nettlebed 304. *Club:* Garrick.
[*Died 18 Aug. 1971.*

FLETCHER, Prof. Frank Thomas Herbert, DLitt; retired as James Barrow Professor of French in the University of Liverpool (1946-65); *b* 6 Jan. 1898; *s* of George Fletcher and Kate Rhoda (*née* Gaunt); *m* 1933, Hilda Patricia, *d* of Henry and Martha Gibson-Jackson; three *d*. *Educ:* Birmingham and Nancy Univs. BA (Birmingham) 1922, MA 1923, Docteur de l'Université (Nancy) 1924, DLitt 1934, Officier d'Académie, 1948. Asst Lectr in French, University Coll. of Wales, Aberystwyth, 1924-25; Lectr, University of Birmingham, 1925-27; Assoc. Prof. of French, University of Toronto, 1927-32; Lectr, Goldsmith's Coll., University of London, 1932-36; Senior Lectr, University of Liverpool, 1936-46. Pres. Assoc. of Univ. Teachers, 1951-52; Sec.-Gen. Internat. Assoc. of Univ. Profs and Lectrs, 1952-61; Chm., Assoc. of Univ. Profs of French, 1963-65. *Publications:* La Langue des Vœux du Paon, 1924; Basic French Composition, 1934; Tour de France en auto, 1937; Montesquieu and English Politics, 1939; Pascal and the Christian Mystical Tradition, 1953. Numerous Textbooks; contribs to Modern Languages Review, French Studies, Modern Languages, Revue de Littérature Comparée, etc. *Recreation:* travel. *Address:* Torwood, Abbey Road, West Kirby, Merseyside. *T:* 051-625 8328. [*Died 29 May 1977.*

FLETCHER, Harold Roy, PhD, DSc, FRSE; Regius Keeper of the Royal Botanic Garden, Edinburgh, 1958-70; Her Majesty's Botanist in Scotland since 1967; Hon. Professor of Botany, University of Edinburgh, since 1968; *b* 14 April 1907; *s* of James Fletcher, Glossop, Derbs; *m* 1941, Evelyn Betty Veronica, *d* of Rev. Dr Andrew David Sloan, St Andrews; one *s* one *d*. *Educ:* Grammar Sch., Glossop; Victoria Univ., Manchester, Asst Lecturer in Botany, University of Aberdeen, 1929-34; Botanist, Royal Botanic Garden, Edinburgh, 1934-51; Dir, Royal Horticultural Society's Gardens, Wisley, Ripley. Woking, Surrey, 1951-54. Asst Regius Keeper, Royal Botanic Garden, Edinburgh, 1954-56. Sec., Internat. Commn for: Horticultural Nomenclature and Registration, 1956-66; Nomenclature of Cultivated Plants, 1956-66; Vice-Pres., Royal Society, Edinburgh, 1961-65; Pres., Botanical Soc., Edinburgh, 1959-60; Pres., Internat. Assoc. of Botanic Gardens, 1964-69; Gen. Sec., 10th Internat. Botanical Congress, 1964. Hon. DSc: Edinburgh 1971; St Andrews, 1972. VMH 1956, Veitch Gold Medal, RHS, 1964; Neill Prize and Medal for Nat. Hist., RSE, 1971-73. *Publications:* The Story of the Royal Horticultural Society, 1969; The Royal Botanic Garden, Edinburgh, 1670-1970, 1970; A Quest of Flowers, the Plant Explorations of Ludlow and Sherriff, 1975; numerous scientific papers chiefly on flora of Asia in Trans. Royal Society, Edinburgh, Trans. Botanical Soc., Edinburgh, Kew Bulletin; also numerous articles in horticultural and gardening journals. *Recreations:* music, art appreciation. *Address:* 29 Howard Place, Edinburgh EH3 5JY. [*Died 27 Aug. 1978.*

FLETCHER, Sir James, Kt 1946; Founder President, Fletcher Holdings Ltd; *b* 29 March 1886; *s* of John Shearer Fletcher; *m* Charlotte Muir Cameron; two *s* one *d*. *Educ:* Allan Glen's Coll., Glasgow. Arrived in New Zealand, 1908. Started in business in Dunedin, 1909, as a Building Contractor. Formed, with his brother William, Fletcher Bros Ltd in 1912 and The Fletcher Construction Company in 1919; the Company became Fletcher Holdings Ltd, 1940, and now owns and controls the following subsidiary companies: The Fletcher Construction Co. Ltd; The Fletcher Steel and Engineering Cos Ltd; The Fletcher Industries Ltd; The Fletcher Timber Co. Ltd; The Fletcher Merchants Ltd; The Fletcher Group Services Ltd; The Fletcher Trust and Investment Co. Ltd, all of New Zealand, and The Fletcher Construction Co. (Pty) Ltd, of Sydney. *Address:* 5 Omana Avenue, Auckland 3, New Zealand. *Club:* Northern (Auckland). [*Died 12 Aug. 1974.*

FLETCHER, (Leonard) Ralph, CB 1971; Secretary, University Grants Committee, since 1970; *b* 11 June 1917; *o s* of late L. R. and Mrs K. M. Fletcher, Atherton, Lancs; *m* 1948, Sheila Margaret Lerpinière; three *d*. *Educ:* Charterhouse; Balliol Coll., Oxford. 1st cl. Hon. Mods, 1st cl. Litt Hum. Temp. Asst Principal, Ministry of Agriculture and Fisheries, 1940-46; Asst Principal, Ministry of Education, 1946, Principal 1947, Asst Sec. 1956, Under-Sec. 1961; Asst Under-Sec. of State, Dept of Educn and Science, 1964-69. *Address:* Marlin Way, Cross Oak Road, Berkhamsted, Herts. *T:* Berkhamsted 3273.
[*Died 19 April 1974.*

FLEW, John Douglas Score, MRCS, LRCP, 1928; MB, BS (London) 1930; MD 1933; MRCOG 1933; FRCOG 1949; Obstetrical and Gynæcological Surgeon, University College Hospital, 1947-67, retired; Dean of the Medical School, 1954-60;

Fellow of University College, London, since 1958; *b* 8 Feb. 1902; *s* of J. P. Flew, JP, and P. E. Flew; *m* 1935, Annie Cantrell Taylor, MA, MB, BCh (Cantab.); three *s* one *d. Educ:* St Paul's; University Coll., and University Coll. Hosp., London. House appointments UCH and Queen Charlotte's Hosp., 1928-32; 1st Asst to Obst. and Gynæc. Unit, UCH, 1933-37; Ante-natal Phys., Queen Charlotte's, 1933-; Visiting Obst. Surg., Queen Mary's Maternity Hosp., Hampstead, 1933-47. Examiner Universities London and Oxford; Central Midwives' Board. *Publications:* articles in BMJ, Jl Obst. and Gynæc., etc. *Recreations:* gardening, fishing. *Address:* 19 Barham Road, Wimbledon, SW20. *T:* 01-946 1281.   *[Died 7 Feb. 1972.*

FLINN, Major William Henry, CMG 1941; OBE 1919; *b* 1895; *o s* of late S. J. Flinn; *m* Olive, *y d* of late G. E. T. P. Thompson, JP; one *s.* Royal Irish Regt and Staff, 1914-27; Colonial Sec., Barbados, 1938-42; Acting Governor, Barbados, 1939, 1940, and 1941; Colonial Sec., Jamaica, 1942-45; Acting Governor, Jamaica, 1943; Mem. Commission of Govt of Newfoundland, 1945-49. *Recreations:* salmon and trout fishing. *Address:* Kells Grange, Kells, Kilkenny.   *[Died 22 Sept. 1973.*

FLINT, Abraham John, DL; *His Honour Judge Flint;* Judge of Circuit No 18 (Nottingham) since 1957; Major, RA retired; *b* 1903; *s* of Abram Reginald Flint, solicitor, Derby; *m* 1930, Eleanor Mary; two *d. Educ:* Oundle. Called to the Bar, Inner Temple, 1929; MP (Nat Lab) Ilkeston Div. of Derbyshire, 1931-35. DL Notts, 1970. *Address:* The Cottage, Newton, Notts. *T:* East Bridgford 486.   *[Died 23 Jan. 1971.*

FLINT, Henry Thomas, PhD, DSc, MRCS, LRCP, DMRE (Cambridge); Hildred Carlile Professor of Physics, University of London, Bedford College, 1944-56; Professor Emeritus since 1956; *b* 4 Dec. 1890; *s* of Robert and Mary Jane Flint, Pillerton Hersey, Warwick; *m* 1933, Ruth Lieck; one *d. Educ:* Wyggeston Sch., Leicester; Universities of Birmingham and London. Asst Lecturer in Physics, Cardiff, 1919; Lecturer, Reading Univ. Coll., 1920; Lecturer, King's Coll., 1920-26; Reader in Physics, University of London, King's Coll., 1926-44. Clinical Asst in Radiology Dept., Westminster Hosp., 1930-33; Consultant Physicist to Westminster Hosp. and KCH Fellow of King's Coll., London, 1956. *Publications:* (with B. L. Worsnop) Advanced Practical Physics, 1923; Wave Mechanics, 1967; Geometrical Optics, 1936; The Quantum Equation and the Theory of Fields, 1966. *Recreations:* walking and riding. *Address:* Pillerton Hersey, Warwick. *T:* Ettington 262. *Club:* Athenæum.   *[Died 20 Nov. 1971.*

FLOWERDEW, Richard Edward, CIE 1937; MB, ChB Aberdeen; DTM&H London; Lieutenant-Colonel IMS (retired); *b* 26 Sept. 1886; 9th *s* of late Arthur J. B. Flowerdew, Billingford Hall, Scole, Norfolk; *m* 1912, Caroline Jane, (*d* 1957), *g d* of Col Sir Digby Mackworth, Bt; one *s. Educ:* Framlingham Coll., Suffolk; Aberdeen Univ. Indian Medical Service, 1909; served European War, 1914-21 (despatches twice); served Suez Canal Defences, Mesopotamia and North-West Frontier, India; Burma Jail Dept, 1922-30; Inspector-Gen. of Prisons, Bengal, 1931; retired, 1939. *Address:* PO Box 5948, Nairobi, Kenya, East Africa.   *[Died 9 Dec. 1971.*

FLOYD, Dr Alfred Ernest, OBE 1948; Organist of St Paul's Cathedral, Melbourne, Australia, 1915-47; *b* Birmingham, 5 Jan. 1877; *s* of Rev. C. H. and A. M. Floyd; *m* 1913, Frances Mary Griffiths, *d* of Dr W. Aylmer Lewis, Frankton Grange, Salop; two *s. Educ:* Bradford Grammar Sch.; the Leys Sch., Cambridge. Dep. Organist Winchester Cathedral; Organist Llangollen and Oswestry Parish Churches; Mus. Bac. Oxon., 1912; ARCM 1913; Mus. Doc. Cantuar, 1917; lecturer, writer, adjudicator, composer, broadcaster. Hon. DLitt Monash, 1971. *Publications:* Church music, part-songs, organ pieces, school songs. *Recreation:* walking. *Address:* 21 Selborne Road, Toorak, Victoria 3142, Australia.   *[Died 13 Jan. 1974.*

FLOYD, Charles Murray, OBE 1945; FRICS; FLAS; Member, Wiltshire County Council, since 1965; Chairman: Avon Rubber Co. Ltd, 1955-68; George Spencer Moulton & Co. Ltd, 1956-68; *b* 12 Sept. 1905; *s* of Sir Henry R. P. Floyd, 4th Bt (*d* 1915), RN, and late Dowager Lady Floyd; *m* 1948, Mary Elizabeth, *o d* of late Major R. F. Fuller, and *widow* of Lieut-Col P. J. S. Boyle, Royal Scots Fusiliers; three *s. Educ:* Eton; Trinity Coll., Cambridge (MA). Partner Powlett & Floyd, Chartered Surveyors and Land Agents, Bath, 1935-55. Served throughout War of 1939-45; BEF France, 1939-40, 21 Army Group, Normandy, Belgium and Germany, 1944-45; Lieut-Col RE (despatches, OBE). Mem. Cttee for England: HM Forestry Commn, 1954; Nature Conservancy, 1955; Mem., Nature Conservancy, 1958; Pres. Royal Forestry Society of England and Wales, 1954-56; Member: Royal Commission on Common Land, 1955-58; MPBW Cttee on Field Monuments, 1966-68. High Sheriff of Wilts, 1962-63. FLS. *Recreation:* natural history. *Address:* Great Chalfield, Melksham, Wilts. *T:* North Trowbridge 239. *Clubs:* Travellers'; University Estate Management (Cambridge) (Pres., 1956-57).
                    [Died 27 June 1971.

FLOYD, Sir John (Duckett), 6th Bt *cr* 1816; TD; Solicitor, retired 1968; *b* 1 Nov. 1903; 2nd *s* of Sir Henry Floyd, 4th Bt and Edith Ann (*d* 1955), *d* of late Major John Kincaid Smith, Polmont House, Stirlingshire; *S* brother, 1968; *m* 1929, Jocelin Evadne (JP Hants, 1947), *d* of late Sir Edmund Wyldbore Smith; two *s* (and one *s* decd). *Educ:* Eton; Trinity Coll., Cambridge (BA). Admitted a Solicitor, 1929; Senior Partner, Frere Cholmeley & Co., 28 Lincolns Inn Fields, WC2, 1952-68. Joined Hampshire Yeomanry, 1923; Adjutant, 1939; in comd same (as HAA), 1949-52. Served NW Europe, 1944. *Recreations:* hunting (formerly Chm., Hampshire Hunt Club); fishing. *Heir: er* surv. *s* Giles Henry Charles Floyd [*b* 27 Feb. 1932; *m* 1954, Lady Gillian Moira Katherine, 2nd *d* of 6th Marquess of Exeter, KCMG; two *s*]. *Address:* Lovington House, Alresford, Hants. *T:* Itchen Abbas 371.   *[Died 1 April 1975.*

FLOYER-ACLAND, Lt-Gen. Arthur Nugent, CBE 1940; DSO; MC; DL; *b* 1885; *s* of late Capt. J. E. Acland and N. L. N. Bankes, Wollaston House, Dorchester, Dorset; *m* 1913, Evelyn Stafford (*d* 1973), *d* of Stafford Still, Lincoln's Inn; one *s. Educ:* Blundell's Sch., Tiverton. Gazetted to the Duke of Cornwall's Light Infantry, 1907; served European War, France and Italy (DSO, MC, French Croix de Guerre (2 awards), Bt Major, 1917; despatches six times); graduated at Staff Coll., Camberley, 1921; Bt Lieut-Col 1927; Lieut-Col 1931; commanded 1st Bn The Duke of Cornwall's Light Infantry, 1931-34; Col 1934; AAG War Office, 1934-36; Comdr 3rd (Jhelum) Infantry Bde, India, 1936-38; served operations Waziristan NWFP, India, 1937-38 (despatches); Comdr 43rd (Wessex) Div. TA, 1938-39; Military Sec. to Sec. of State for War, 1940-42; Lt-Gen. 1941. High Sheriff, Dorset, 1953; DL Dorset, 1957. Assumed name of Floyer in addition to own name on succeeding to the estate of George Floyer of Stafford House, near Dorchester, 1927. *Address:* The Paddock, West Stafford, Dorchester, Dorset. *Club:* Army and Navy.   *[Died 18 Feb. 1980.*

FOAD, Roland Walter, CBE 1968; *b* 7 April 1908; *er s* of late Walter James Foad and late Frances Mary Foad (*née* Inge); *m* 1st, 1934, Isabel Sarah Stewart McKeen (*d* 1962); one *s* one *d*; 2nd, 1966, La Marquesa de Piedrabuena. *Educ:* Manwood's Sch., Sandwich. ACA 1929; FCA 1953 (Mem. Council, 1964-71). Dep. Controller, Raw Materials Accountancy, 1941-45; Chief Accountant, Industrial and Commercial Finance Corporation, 1946-48; Partner, McClelland Ker & Co., Chartered Accountants, 1949-53; Dir of Finance, Iron and Steel Board, 1954-62, Exec. Mem., 1962-67; UK Chm., Steel Cttee, Council of Assoc., ECSC, 1962-67. Liveryman, Co. of Wheelwrights. *Address:* 24 Clarendon Avenue, Leamington Spa, Warwicks.   *[Died 18 Jan. 1978.*

FOGARTY, Air Chief Marshal Sir Francis, GBE 1957 (KBE 1950); KCB 1953 (CB 1946); DFC; AFC; *b* 16 Jan. 1899; *s* of Michael Fogarty, Cork, Eire; *m* 1939, Fenella Evelyn, *d* of Capt. Forsyth Grant, Ecclesgreig, Kincardineshire; one *s* one *d. Educ:* Farran Ferris Coll., Cork. Served 98 Squadron, 1918; 84 Sqdn, 1920-23, 1923-30; Commanded 84 Squadron, 1935-37; Adjt County of Mddx Sqdn AAF, 1930-34; Comd 37 Bomber Sqdn, 1938-40; RAF Mission, Ottawa, 1943; SASO, No 4 Group, Bomber Comd, 1944; Air Officer i/c Administration Mediterranean Allied Air Forces, 1945; AOC, RAF, Italy, 1946; AOA, RAF, Mediterranean and Middle East, 1946-47; SASO, Flying Training Comd, RAF, 1947-49; C-in-C, Far East Air Force, 1949-52; Air Council Member for Personnel, 1952-56; Air ADC to the Queen, 1956-57; retired 1957. Pres., British Airport Construction and Equipment Association, 1970-; Dep. Pres., Air League. Dir, Racal Electronics. *Address:* Wey Cottage, Elstead, Surrey. *Club:* Royal Air Force.
                    [Died 12 Jan. 1973.

FOGH, Prof. Torkel W.; *see* Weis-Fogh.

FOLETTA, George Gotardo, CMG 1962; Governing Director, 1948-71, and Chairman, 1943-71, Prestige Ltd (Parent Co.) and all major subsidiaries in Australia and NZ; *b* 30 Jan. 1892; *s* of late H. G. Foletta, Ivanhoe, Vic., Australia; *m* 1915, A. Myra Cooper; four *s. Educ:* Prince's Hill State Sch.; South Melbourne Coll. Joined H. G. Foletta & Co., Merchants & Importers, 1909; Co-founder and Man., Atlas Knitting and Spinning Mills Pty Ltd, 1920 (which became Prestige Ltd, 1922); Man. Dir, Prestige Group of Cos, 1937-48, retd; Co-founder and first Pres., 1951-56, Aust. Industries Development Assoc. (AIDA); FAIM.

Member: Austr. Inst. Polit. Science; Economic Soc. of Aust. and NZ; Aust. and NZ Assoc. for Advancement of Science (ANZAAS). Trustee, Cttee for Econ. Develt of Australia (CEDA). *Publication:* (pr. pr.) The Foletta Family, 1969. *Recreations:* fly fishing, political science. *Address:* 6 Redesdale Road, Ivanhoe, Victoria 3079, Australia. *T:* 49.1320. *Club:* Athenæum (Melbourne). *[Died 25 April 1973.*

FOLL, Hon. Hattil Spencer; retired; *b* 31 May 1890; *s* of John Hattil and Kate Elizabeth Foll; *m* 1915; four *d* (one *s* decd). *Educ:* Clapham Collegiate Sch. Served AIF, European War, 1914-15; Home Forces, 1942-43; Minister for Repatriation and War Service Homes, Australia, 1937-39, and Minister for Health, 1938-39; Minister for the Interior, Commonwealth of Australia, 1939-41, and Minister of Information, 1940-41; Senator for Queensland, 1917-47; has served on numerous select cttees especially relating to returned soldier problems. Formerly pastoralist. *Recreations:* bowls, swimming. *Address:* 6 Arncliffe Avenue, Port Macquarie, NSW 2444, Australia. *T:* 83-1356. *Club:* Port Macquarie Bowling. *[Died 7 July 1977.*

FOOKS, Sir Raymond (Hatherell), Kt 1954; CBE 1949; KPM 1945; Chief Constable of Lincolnshire, 1934-54; *b* 23 June 1888; *s* of late W. H. Fooks, Cerne Abbas, Dorset, and Leigh-on-Sea, Essex; *m* 1st, 1922, Mary Gwendoline (*d* 1926), *d* of late Francis William Baily, Bishopstoke, Hants; one *s* one *d*; 2nd, 1935, Madeline Player (*d* 1953), *widow* of Lieut-Col R. D. Crosby, OBE, MC, The Royal Lincolnshire Regt; 3rd, 1954, Hon. Mrs Mary Josephine Bruce, *widow* of E. H. Bruce, Indian Police Service, and *e d* of 1st Baron Riverdale, GBE, LLD, JP. *Educ:* King Edward VI Sch., and University Coll., Southampton; Exeter Coll., Oxford. BA (London), 1908; MA (Oxford), 1933. Joined Indian Police Service, 1908; Supt, Punjab, 1919-31; served on NW Frontier of India in European War, 1914-19 (despatches); Deputy Inspector-Gen., 1931-33; retired, 1933. Barrister, Inner Temple, 1933. Deputy Pres. of the North Lincs Branch, British Red Cross Soc., 1959-60 (County Dir, 1954-58); DL County of Lincoln, 1956-59. *Recreations:* gardening and study. *Address:* Broom Hill Copse, Boar's Hill, Oxford. *T:* 35401. *[Died 22 Feb. 1978.*

FOORD-KELCEY, Air Vice-Marshal Alick, CBE 1956; AFC 1943; Executive Director, Federation of World Health Foundations, Geneva; *b* Viking, Alta, Canada, 6 April 1913; *s* of William Foord-Kelcey, MC (killed War of 1914-18); *m* 1st, 1944, Audrey Kathleen Richards (marr. diss.); two *s*; 2nd, 1951, Diane, *d* of Lloyd and Ethel Fenwick, Berkeley, Calif. *Educ:* King's Sch., Canterbury; Corpus Christi Coll., Cambridge. Mem., CUAS. commissioned RAF, Oct. 1935; 1935-39: fighter pilot and flying instructor, UK and Egypt; 1939-43: flying, flying instructor, and Air Staff posts, Egypt, Aden, Western Desert and UK; 1944-46: Jt Planning Staff, War Cabinet Offices; 1947-57: Flying, Stn Comdr, Air Staff, UK, Germany (Berlin airlift), BJSM Washington, AAFCE (Fontainebleau). RAF Staff Coll., 1943; Imperial Defence Coll., 1958. AOC No 11 Group, Fighter Comd, 1959-60; ACAS (Intell.), 1961-64, retd at own request. Dep. Dir Foreign Office Arms Control and Disarmament Research Unit, 1965-66. *Address:* 7 rue Robert-de-Traz, 1206 Geneva, Switzerland. *[Died 26 Oct. 1973.*

FOOT, Rt. Hon. Sir Dingle (Mackintosh), PC 1967; Kt 1964; QC 1954; *e s* of late Rt. Hon. Isaac Foot; *b* Plymouth, 1905; *m* 1933, Dorothy Mary, *er d* of late William Rowley Elliston, TD, LLB and Ethel Mary Walton, *niece* of Sir Frederick Wilson, Felixstowe (DL Suffolk, MP for Mid Norfolk, 1895). *Educ:* Bembridge Sch., Isle of Wight; Balliol Coll., Oxford. MA Oxon 1960. Pres., Oxford Univ. Liberal Club, 1927; Pres., Oxford Union Soc., 1928; contested Tiverton Div. of Devon, 1929; Dundee, 1945; North Cornwall, 1950 and 1951; MP (L) Dundee, 1931-45; Parliamentary Sec., Min. of Economic Warfare, 1940-45; joined the Labour Party, July 1956; MP (Lab) Ipswich, Oct. 1957-70; Solicitor-Gen., 1964-67. Led British Economic Warfare Delegn to Switzerland, 1945; Mem. of British Delegn to San Francisco Conf., 1945. Called to Bar, Gray's Inn, 1930; Bencher, 1952; Treasurer, 1968; Vice-Treasurer, 1969. Western Circuit. Admitted to Gold Coast Roll of Legal Practitioners, 1948; to Ceylon Roll of Advocates, 1951; to Nigerian Bar, 1955; to Northern Rhodesian Bar, 1956; to Sierra Leone Bar, 1959; to Supreme Court of India (as a Senior Advocate), 1960; to Bahrain Roll of Legal Practitioners, 1962; to Malaya Roll of Legal Practitioners, 1964; to S Rhodesia Roll of Legal Practitioners, 1964, to Northern Ireland Bar, 1970. Has also appeared in courts of Kenya, Uganda, Tanganyika, Nyasaland, Pakistan, Hong Kong, and before Commn of Human Rights at Strasbourg. Chm., Observer Trust, 1953-55. Chm., Soc. of Labour Lawyers, 1960-64. Commander, Order of the Cedars, Lebanon, 1969. Hon. LLD Dundee, 1974. *Publication:* British Political Crises, 1976. *Recreation:* football

fan. *Address:* 2 Paper Buildings, Temple, EC4. *T:* 01-353 9119. *Clubs:* Garrick, Beefsteak. *[Died 18 June 1978.*

FOOT, Robert William, OBE 1919; MC 1916; Member of Livery of Haberdashers' Company, since 1918, and Member of Court of Assistants, 1958-70; *b* 7 June 1889; *m*; two *s* one *d*. *Educ:* Winchester. Admitted a Solicitor, 1912; with Orr, Dignam & Co., Solicitors, in Calcutta, 1913-14. Served 1914-18, with RFA in Belgium and France, Staff Capt. 21st Divisional Artillery, Staff Capt. RA and DAQMG 1st Corps (despatches twice, OBE, MC); joined Gas Light and Coke Co., 1919; General Manager, 1928-41; acted at request of Govt, as Adviser to the BBC on War-Time Organisation; Joint Dir-Gen., BBC, 1942-43, Dir-Gen., 1943-44; Chm. of Mining Assoc. of Great Britain, 1944-47; President: British Coal Utilization Research Assoc., 1944-47. Coal Utilization Joint Council, 1945-47; Mining Assoc. of Great Britain, 1947-52; Dep.-Chm. and Man. Dir, Powell Duffryn Ltd, and Chm. Powell Duffryn Technical Services Ltd, 1947-52; Dir Barclays Bank Ltd, 1947-53; Dir Australia and New Zealand Bank Ltd, 1949-52; Chm. Wankie Colliery Co. Ltd, 1949-53. *Publication:* A Plan for Coal, 1945. *Address:* 18 Flag Court, Kingsway, Hove, Sussex. *T:* Brighton 70407. *[Died 2 April 1973.*

FOOT, Maj.-Gen. William, CB 1947; MC 1915; MB; *b* 2 Dec. 1889; *s* of A. R. Foot, DL, Dublin; *m* 1921, Aileen Katherina Curling, The Castle, Newcastle West, Co. Limerick; one *d*. *Educ:* Shrewsbury Sch.; Trinity Coll., Dublin. BA (Trinity Coll., Dublin), 1910; MB, BCh, BAO, LM (*Rot*), 1914; House Surg. Victoria Hospital, Blackpool; European War, 1914-18, joined RAMC 1914; served in France, 1914-18 (MC and bar); Afghan War, Indian Frontier, 1919; War of 1939-45, France, 1940; ADMS Division, DDMS, Persia and Iraq, 1943-45; DMS, MELF, 1946-47; Maj.-Gen.; late Deputy Dir of Medical Services, Eastern Command, UK; retired pay, 1949. KHP 1947. Hereditary Freeman of the City of Dublin; played hockey for Ireland, 1909, 1911, 1912. *Recreations:* sports and games; music. *Address:* Ashbourne, 49 Woodlands Park, Blackrock, Co. Dublin, Eire. *[Died 30 Oct. 1971.*

FORBES, Sir Douglas (Stuart), Kt 1964; Managing Director since 1940, Chairman of Directors since 1955, The Millaquin Sugar Co. Ltd; *b* 6 Feb. 1890; *s* of William Forbes, Brisbane, formerly of Aberdeen, Scotland; *m* 1916, Grace Isobel Fallon; one *d*. Banker and Company Director. Gen. Manager, Queensland National Bank Ltd, 1937-48; Dir, National Bank of Australasia Ltd, and Chm. of its Queensland Board of Advice, 1948-67; Dir, Castlemaine Perkins Ltd (Brewers), 1944- (Chm. of Dirs, 1958-): Chm. of Dirs, Queensland National Pastoral Co. Ltd, 1940-62; Dir, Qld Trustees Ltd, 1949-66; Dir, Brisbane Television Co. Ltd, 1958-71; Chairman of Directors: QOR Road Services Pty Ltd, 1966-; (Local) Boral Basic Industries Ltd, 1970-; Brisbane Gas Co. Ltd, 1971-. *Recreations:* golf and surfing. *Address:* 158 Lancaster Road, Ascot, Qld 4007, Australia. *Clubs:* Queensland, Tattersalls, Queensland Turf (Brisbane). *[Died 22 June 1973.*

FORBES, Air Chief Comdt Dame Katherine (Jane Trefusis); *see* Watson-Watt, Air Chief Comdt Dame Katherine.

FORBES-COCKELL, Seton; Chairman, Forbes Group of Companies, since 1953; *b* 14 Aug. 1927; *s* of Cedric Forbes-Cockell and Adelina Forbes-Cockell (*née* Reese); *m* 1951, Ann McVicker Forbes-Cockell (*née* Redfern); two *s* one *d*. *Educ:* Eton Coll. Mem. Stock Exchange, London, 1948-; Chm., Fulham Conservative Assoc., 1959-69 (Pres., 1969-); elected to GLC (Kensington and Chelsea), 1964 (re-elected, 1967, 1970); Leader of Opposition, Inner London Educn Authority, 1964-67; Chm., Thamesmead Cttee of GLC, 1967- (Mem. or Past Mem. various cttees of GLC). Alderman, Hammersmith Borough Council, 1968- (Dep. Leader, 1968-69, 1970-71); Chm., Borough Develt Group Cttee, 1968-69; Mayor of the London Borough of Hammersmith, 1969-70. Mem. Bd, PLA, 1969-; Mem., Lord Chancellor's Adv. Cttee on Justices of the Peace, Inner London Commn Area, 1970-. Mem. Court, Univ. of London, 1966-67; Chm., Nat. Educn Assoc., 1965-69. Freeman of City of London, 1955; Liveryman, Worshipful Co. of Carmen, 1955. *Publication:* The Conservation of Wealth, 1950. *Recreations:* shooting, riding, polo, reading. *Address:* 102 Rivermead Court, SW6. *T:* 01-736 4707; Lavender Farm, Ascot, Berkshire. *T:* Winkfield Row 4545. *Clubs:* City of London, City Livery, Junior Carlton, Hurlingham, Roehampton; Guards Polo (Windsor); Henley Royal Regatta (Henley); Surrey County Cricket. *[Died 19 Sept. 1971.*

FORBES-LEITH of Fyvie, Sir (Robert) Ian (Algernon), 2nd Bt *cr* 1923; KT 1972; MBE 1946; JP Co. of Aberdeen; Lord Lieutenant of the County of Aberdeen since 1959 (Vice-

Lieutenant, 1953); Member, Aberdeen CC, 1938 (Vice-Convener, 1950; Convener, 1955-58); Member of Queen's Body Guard for Scotland, The Royal Company of Archers; Major RA; Governor: North of Scotland College of Agriculture; Rowett Research Institute; *b* 27 Dec. 1902; *o surv. s* of Col Sir Charles R. Forbes-Leith, 1st Bt, and Hon. Ethel Louise Forbes-Leith, OBE (*d* 1930), *o d* of Baron Leith of Fyvie; *S* father, 1930; *m* 1927, Ruth Avis, *d* of Edward George Barnett, Halton, Corbridge, Northumberland; one *s* two *d* (and one *s* killed on active service). *Educ:* Eton. Served War of 1939-45 (despatches, MBE). Hon. LLD, Aberdeen, 1967. *Heir: s* Andrew George Forbes-Leith [*b* 20 Oct. 1929; *m* 1962, Jane Kate (*d* 1969), *o d* of late David McCall-McCowan and Mrs McCall-McCowan, Dalwhat, Moniaive, Dumfriesshire; two *s* two *d*]. *Address:* Kinharrachie, Ellon, Aberdeenshire. *Clubs:* White's; Royal Northern (Aberdeen); Leander.   [*Died 17 March* 1973.

FORD, Cdre Charles Musgrave, CBE 1946; RD; Commodore (retired) Royal Naval Reserve; Commodore of Cunard White Star Fleet, retired; *b* 1887; *m* 1959, Vera Gordon Evans. Joined Cunard Co. Ltd, 1912. Royal Naval Reserve ADC to the King, 1941-42. Served European War, 1914-18; War of 1939-45: Commodore of Ocean Convoys, 1940-42. Commanded several Cunard vessels, including SS Queen Mary and SS Queen Elizabeth. Order of St Anne, 3rd Class, 1915 (Russian); Commander Legion of Merit, 1949 (USA). *Address:* 3 Exeter Park Mansions, Bournemouth, Dorset. *T:* Bournemouth 292663.   [*Died 19 Dec.* 1974.

FORD, Ven. Frank Edward; Archdeacon of the East Riding, 1957-70, Archdeacon Emeritus since 1974; Rector of Cherry-Burton, 1965-70; *b* 9 July 1902; *s* of Frank Chubb Ford, MD, Wimbledon; *m* 1st, 1934, Mary Katherine Eve, *d* of Robert Hamilton Welchman, MA, Oxford; 2nd, 1953, Marjorie, *d* of Francis Benjamin Chatterton, Scarborough, and *widow* of John Stanley Snowball, Scarborough; one *s* one *d. Educ:* Lancing; Hertford Coll., Oxford; Westcott House, Cambridge. BA 1924, MA 1928. Rector of Bainton, 1957-65. *Recreations:* housework, gardening and crosswords. *Address:* Barnyard, Sinnington, York YO6 6RY. *T:* Kirkbymoorside 31797. *Club:* Royal Over-Seas League.   [*Died 26 Nov.* 1976.

FORD, John, (Sean O'Feeney); director of motion pictures, USA; *b* Cape Elizabeth, Me, 1 Feb. 1895; *s* of Sean O'Feeney and Barbara Curran; *m* 1920, Mary McBryde Smith; one *s* one *d.* Began as property man, Universal City, Calif., 1914; later became dir; has directed more than 80 pictures for Universal-Fox, Metro-Goldwyn Mayer, United Artists, Radio-RKO. Served as Lieut-Comdr, Comdr, Capt., US Navy, War of 1939-45; discharged as Rear-Adm. after service in Korea. NY Critics Award, 1935-39, 1940-41; Academy Motion Picture Arts and Sciences directorial Award, 1935, 1940, 1941, 1952. *Films include:* Arrowsmith, Stagecoach, Quiet Man, Long Voyage Home, Grapes of Wrath, How Green Was My Valley, The Informer, The Searchers, Gideon's Day, Donovan's Reef, The Man Who Shot Liberty Valance, Cheyenne Autumn, Seven Women. Received Academy Awards for two documentaries made for Government while in Navy: Midway, Dec. 7th. Amer. Film Inst. first annual award for life achievement; Brandeis Univ. Creative Arts award. Dr Fine Arts (Hon.) Univ. of Maine, 1939; MA (Hon.) Bowdoin Coll., Brunswick, Me, 1947; DHL, Brandeis Univ. Legion of Merit (Combat); Purple Heart; Air Medal; Commendation; Presidential Medal of Freedom; USN Distinguished Public Service Award; Chevalier Crown of Belgium; Knight Comdr, Italian Republic; Legion of Honour; Croix de Guerre; Knight of Malta, etc. Catholic. *Address:* (studio) 9601 Wilshire Boulevard, Suite 300, Beverly Hills, Calif 90210, USA.   [*Died 31 Aug.* 1973.

FORDE, Daryll, PhD London, FBA; Professor of Anthropology, University of London, 1945-69, and Fellow of University College since 1945; Director, International African Institute since 1944; *b* 16 March 1902; *o s* of Rev. J. P. D. Forde; *m* 1930, Joyce Marion (*née* Stock) (marr. diss., 1947); two *s* ; *m* 1948, Evelyn Harty, *y d* of late David Singer, former Chm. of Rowe Swann Ltd. *Educ:* Middlesex County Sch., Tottenham; University Coll., London. Lecturer, Dept of Geography, University Coll., 1923-28; Franks Student of the Soc. of Antiquaries, 1924; Commonwealth Fellow in Anthropology, University of Calif., USA, 1928-30; Gregynog Prof. of Geography and Anthropology, Univ. of Wales, 1930-45; Leverhulme Research Fellow, 1935; Anthropological Field Expeditions, Arizona and Northern Mexico, 1928-29; New Mexico, 1929; Nigeria, 1935 and 1939; Gambia, 1945; Dep. Head, US Sect., FO Res. Dept (formerly FRPS), 1941-43. Visiting Prof., Univ. of Calif, 1949 and 1956, Yale Univ., 1951, Harvard Univ., 1963. Wellcome and Rivers Medallist, Past Pres., and Vice-Pres., Royal Anthropological Institute. Past

Pres., Anthrop. Section, Brit. Assoc. Adv. Science. Frazer Lecturer, University of Liverpool, 1958; Munro Lecturer, University of Edinburgh, 1956; Lugard Memorial Lecturer, 1967; Huxley Meml Lecturer, 1970. Wellcome Medallist, Royal African Soc., 1970. *Publications:* Ancient Mariners, 1928; Early Cultures of Atlantic Europe, 1930; Ethnography of the Yuma Indians, 1931; Hopi Agriculture and Land Ownership, 1932; Habitat, Economy and Society, 1934, 12th edn 1967; Marriage and the Family in South-Eastern Nigeria, 1941; The Native Economies of Nigeria, 1946; African Worlds (ed and contrib.), 1953; Yakö Studies, 1964; West African Chiefs in the Nineteenth Century (ed), 1967, etc; editor of Ethnographic Survey of Africa, 1946-, of Africa, 1944-, and of African Abstracts, 1948-. *Address:* 8 The Boltons, SW10. *T:* 01-373 9805. *Club:* Athenæum.   [*Died 3 May* 1973.

FORDHAM, Lieut-Col (retd) Reginald Sydney Walter, ED; LLB; QC 1933; Formerly Chairman, Tax Appeal Board, Ottawa, 1969-72 (Assistant Chairman, 1962-69); retired 1972; Barrister-at-Law; *b* London, England, 9 May 1897; *m* 1925, Margaret Casson (*d* 1970), *d* of Dr E. T. Kellam, Niagara Falls, Canada; one *d. Educ:* privately; Univ. of Toronto; Osgoode Hall Law Sch. Called to Bar of Ont., 1921; served European War, France, with Canadian Infantry, as Lieut 1916; Capt. 1917 (wounded and prisoner, despatches); Alderman in Niagara Falls City Council four years; Mem., Court of Revision and Public Library Board; Bde Major, 5th Inf. Bde, 1934-36; Lieut-Col 1936; commanded Lincoln and Welland Regt, 1936-40; comd Welland Canal Force during last four months of 1939 until its dissolution; Comr of Refugee Camps, Dept of Sec. of State, Ottawa, and Home Office representative, 1941-43; Dir of Labour Projects (P of W), Dept of Labour, Canada, 1943. KStJ 1970 (CStJ 1964; OStJ 1941). *Publication:* Tax Appeal Board Practice, 1958. *Recreations:* riding, lawn-bowling, bridge, reading. *Address:* Apt 403, Strathcona Apartments, 404 Laurier Avenue E, Ottawa, Ontario K1N 6R2, Canada. *Clubs:* Rideau, Country, Le Cercle Universitaire (Ottawa); Ottawa Valley Hunt.   [*Died 17 Nov.* 1976.

FORDYCE, Christian James, MA; Dean of Faculties, University of Glasgow, since 1973; *b* Fraserburgh, 25 Sept. 1901; *s* of James Wilson Fordyce, MA, and Helen Wilson McAllan; *m* 1929, Catherine Mary Chilcott. *Educ:* University of Glasgow; Balliol Coll., Oxford (Scholar and Snell Exhibitioner). First Class Hons in Classics, Glasgow Univ., 1920; Gaisford Prize (Greek Prose), 1921; First Class, Classical Mods, 1922; Hertford Scholar, 1922; Craven Scholar, 1922; Chancellor's Prize (Latin Prose), 1923; First class, Literæ Humaniores, 1924; War Memorial Research Student in Classics, Balliol Coll., 1925; Lecturer in Greek in the University of St Andrews, 1925-26; Lecturer in Humanity in the University of Edinburgh, 1926; Fellow, Classical Tutor, and Librarian of Jesus Coll., Oxford, 1927-34; Prof. of Humanity, 1934-71, Clerk of Senate, 1940-71, Univ. of Glasgow. Hon. LLD St Andrews, 1962. Comdr, Order of St Olav, 1961. *Publications:* Commentary on Catullus, 1961; articles in classical journals; Editor of the Classical Review. *Address:* 1 Beaumont Gate, Glasgow W2. *T:* 041-334 4244.   [*Died 21 Sept.* 1974.

FOREMAN, Dr James Kenneth, CChem, FRSC; Deputy Director, National Physical Laboratory, since 1977; *b* 7 April 1928; *s* of late William James Foreman and of Grace Esther Foreman; *m* 1950, Celia Christine Joan Head (marr. diss. 1978); three *s* two *d. Educ:* Ashford Grammar Sch., Kent; Medway Technical Coll. (BSc 1949); DSc London 1976. CChem; FRIC 1964. Chemical Inspectorate, Min. of Supply, Woolwich Arsenal, 1949-51; UKAEA Windscale Works, Cumberland, 1952-66; Lab. of Govt Chemist, London: Supt of Research, 1966-70; Dep. Govt Chemist, 1970-77. *Publications:* Automatic Chemical Analysis, 1975; Topics in Automatic Analysis, 1979; papers in chem. jls on analytical and radio-chemistry. *Recreation:* music. *Address:* 18 Kendal Court, Augustus Street, Regents Park, NW1.   [*Died 14 Nov.* 1980.

FOREST SMITH, John, FRCP; Physician-in-charge, Children's Department, St Thomas's Hospital; Physician, Grosvenor Hospital for Women; *m* Marjory Bruce Murray; one *d. Educ:* St Thomas's Hosp. MRCS, LRCP 1916; FRCP 1931. Formerly Senior Censor, RCP, Physician and John and Temple Research Fellow, St Thomas' Hosp.; Examiner in Medicine, RCP, Univ. of Birmingham and Conjoint Board. Mem., Assoc. of Physicians. *Address:* 2K Portman Mansions, Chiltern Street, W1. *T:* 01-935 6452.   [*Died 3 Aug.* 1973.

FORESTER, 7th Baron (UK) *cr* 1821; **Col Cecil George Wilfrid Weld-Forester;** *b* 12 July 1899; *o s* of 6th Baron and Christine Isabel (*d* 1948), *d* of Duncan Davidson of Tulloch; *S* father, 1932; *m* 1931, Marie Louise Priscilla, CStJ, *d* of Col Sir Herbert Perrott, 6th Bt, CH, CB; one *s* four *d. Educ:* Durham Univ.

Joined Royal Horse Guards, 1918; served in France, 1918; Capt., 1921; ADC to Gov.-Gen. and Comdr-in-Chief, S Africa, 1924-27; Major, 1930; Bt Lieut-col 1934; Lieut-Col 1938; Lieut-Col commanding Royal Horse Guards, 1938-41; Acting Col CMF 1943 (despatches); served in BLA, 1944; retd pay with rank of Col, 1945. JP 1936; Mayor of the Borough of Wenlock, 1936-37 and 1961-62; Alderman, Borough of Wenlock, 1940; Alderman, Salop CC, 1960. Freeman, Borough of Wenlock, 1963. Owns about 10,000 acres. *Heir: s* Hon. (George Cecil) Brooke Weld-Forester [*b* 20 Feb. 1938; *m* 1967, Hon. Catherine Lyttelton, 2nd *d* of 10th Viscount Cobham, KG, PC, GCMG, GCVO, TD; one *s* three *d*]. *Address:* Old Hall, Willey, Broseley, Salop. *T:* Telford 882245; Bassett, Banket, S Rhodesia. *T:* Raffingord 2832. *Club:* Turf. [*Died* 4 Jan. 1977.

FORESTIER-WALKER, Major Sir George Ferdinand; *see* Walker.

FORGAN, Robert, MC; MA, MD, DPH; *b* 1891; *s* of late Rev. Robert Forgan, DD, Edinburgh; *m* 1st, Winifred Mary, *d* of Robert Cran, Ballater; one *d*; 2nd, Winifred Jan, *d* of Henry Rees, Kenton; one *s* two *d. Educ:* Aberdeen Grammar Sch.; Universities of Aberdeen and Cambridge. Served in RAMC, 1915-19 (MC); Specialist Medical Officer, Lanarks County Council, 1921-29; Mem. of Glasgow City Council, 1926-29; MP (Lab) West Renfrew Div., 1929-31. *Address:* Meadow Place, Hookend Lane, Doddinghurst, near Brentwood, Essex. *T:* Blackmore 821267. [*Died* 8 Jan. 1976.

FORGET, Sir Guy (Joseph), Kt 1971; CBE 1968; Ambassador of Mauritius, to France since 1968, and to Italy since 1970; Permanent Delegate to UNESCO since 1970; *b* 6 Aug. 1902; *s* of J. J. Léon Forget, Chief Officer Civil Status, and Yvonne (*née* Phélines); *m* 1925, M. L. Maud Reich; four *s* two *d. Educ:* Royal Coll., Curepipe, Mauritius. Higher Professional studies, Supreme Court, Mauritius; Solicitor's Diploma. Solicitor, High Court, 1927-57. Municipal Councillor, 1940; Dep. Mayor, 1958; Mayor of Port Louis, 1959; Mayor of Beau Bassin-Rose Hill, 1952. MLA, 1948-68; Dep. Prime Minister of Mauritius, 1965-68; Chm., Mauritius Labour Party, 1956-69; Minister: of Health, 1957-65; of Works, 1965-67; of State (Finance), 1967-68. *Recreations:* classical music, French literature. *Address:* (professional) 68 Boulevard de Courcelles, Paris 17ème, France. *T:* 227-30-19 and 227-34-33. *Clubs:* Cercle Littéraire de Port Louis, Cercle de Rose Hill, Stella Clavisque, Racing (all in Mauritius). [*Died* 2 Jan. 1972.

FORMAN, Rev. Adam, CBE 1919; *b* 25 Nov. 1876; *s* of J. T. Forman, Las Palmas; *m* 1908, Flora (*d* 1961), *d* of James Smith, Craigielands, Beattock; four *s* one *d* (and one *d* decd). *Educ:* Loretto; Pembroke Coll., Cambridge (MA). Cambridge Rugby XV, 1904-05 and 1905-06. Chaplain, Loretto Sch., Musselburgh, 1907-11; Curate of St Andrew's, Bishop Auckland, 1913-14; Sec. for Sphagnum Moss, Scotland, Red Cross, 1915-18. District Comr, Boy Scouts Assoc., 1936-. Silver Wolf Medal, 1961. Inspector Dumfriesshire Special Constabulary Moffat and Beattock District, 1939-45. *Recreations:* scouting, reading, music. *Address:* Dumcrieff, Moffat, Scotland DG10 9QW. *T:* Moffat 20060. *Club:* New (Edinburgh). [*Died* 19 Nov. 1977.

FORMAN, John (Calder), JP; Insurance Agent; *b* 1884; *m* ; one *s* one *d.* Member, Glasgow Town Council, 1928-45; Chairman, Glasgow Cooperative Conference Assoc.; Member, Amalgamated Engineering Union, 1906; MP (Lab-Coop) Springburn Div. of Glasgow, 1945-64. *Address:* 168 Knightswood Road, Glasgow G13 2XH. [*Died* 14 May 1975.

FORRES, 3rd Baron *cr* 1922, of Glenogil; **John Archibald Harford Williamson;** Bt, 1909; *b* 30 Oct. 1922; *s* of 2nd Baron and Jessie (*d* 1972), *er d* of late William Alfred Harford, JP, Petty France, Badminton, Glos; *S* father, 1954; *m* 1st, 1945, Gillian Ann Maclean (marr. diss. 1967), *d* of Major J. Maclean Grant, RA retd; one *s* two *d*; 2nd, 1969, Cecily Josephine (marr. diss. 1974), *e d* of Sir Alexander Gordon Cumming, 5th Bt, and of Countess Cawdor, and *widow* of 2nd Earl of Woolton. *Educ:* Eton; Trinity Coll., Cambridge. Served War of 1939-45: with Black Watch 51st (Highland) Div., North Africa, Sicily, Normandy (despatches) (Captain, Black Watch (RHR)), with 6th (British) Armoured Div., Italy, Austria, as ADC to Comdr, 1944-45. Director: Balfour Williamson & Co., 1954-67; Lobitos Oilfields Ltd, 1954-65; Bank of London and South America Ltd, 1961-68. UK Rep., Pacific Internat. Trade Fair in Peru, 1961. Pres., Royal Forest Agric. Assoc., Windsor, 1963-64. Founder Mem., British Charollais Cattle Soc., 1961. *Heir: s* Hon. Alastair Stephen Grant Williamson [*b* 16 May 1946; *m* 1969, Margaret, *d* of late G. J. Mallam, New South Wales; two *s*]. *Address:* Glenogil, By Forfar, Angus. *T:* Fern 226. *Clubs:* Brooks's, Pratt's. [*Died* 22 Sept. 1978.

FORREST, Gilbert Alexander; His Honour Judge Forrest; a Circuit Judge, since 1972 (a County Court Judge, 1970-72); *b* 27 July 1912; *s* of G. C. Forrest and Janet Forrest, Heaton Moor, Stockport; *m* 1937, Emily Maureen, *d* of Joseph Armstrong, Co. Fermanagh and Stockport; two *s* two *d. Educ:* Stockport Grammar Sch.; Manchester Univ.; St Edmund Hall, Oxford. Barrister, Gray's Inn, 1937; practised, Western Circuit, 1937-70. Lectr in Law, Bristol Univ., 1937-70. Dep. Chm., Somerset QS, 1966-71. Army, 1940, British Military Mission to N America, 1943-45; Captain, RAOC. *Publications:* articles in legal jls. *Recreations:* bird-watching, gardening. *Address:* 43 Canynge Road, Bristol BS8 3LH. *Club:* Bristol (Bristol). [*Died* 24 Sept. 1977.

FORREST, Richard Haddow, QC 1953; **His Honour Judge Haddow Forrest;** a Circuit Judge, since 1972; Lieutenant Bailiff of Jersey since 1970; *b* 13 Sept. 1908; *o s* of John Duggan and Marie Josephine Forrest; *m* 1936, Monica Constance Neville; two *s* two *d. Educ:* Merchant Taylors' Sch., Crosby; Pembroke Coll., Oxford (MA). Called to the Bar, Gray's Inn, 1932; Bencher, 1960. Recorder of Salford, 1956-64; Presiding Judge, Liverpool Court of Passage, 1964-71; Judge of Courts of Appeal, Jersey and Guernsey, 1965-71. Leader, Northern Circuit, 1968-71. King's Regiment, 1930-45 (SR, 1930-39). *Address:* High Wood, Firle Road, Seaford, Sussex. [*Died* 29 Oct. 1977.

FORRESTER, Charles, K-i-H 1944; BSc, FH-WC; FRSC, PhD (Edinburgh), MIChemE, SFInstF, FRSE; *b* 6 March 1895; *y s* of Wm Fordie Forrester, HM Sasines Office, Edinburgh; *m* 1932, Joyce Annie, *o d* of Horace Purver Gripton; one *s* one *d. Educ:* Heriot-Watt Coll. (later Univ.), Edinburgh. Prof. of Chemistry, Indian Sch. of Mines, Government of India, 1926, Vice-Principal, 1932, Principal, 1936-48; Chief Scientist's Div., Min. of Power, 1949-60, Dep. Chief Fuel Engr, later Senior Principal Scientific Officer; Brit. Coal Utilisation Res. Assoc., 1960-63; Royal Inst. of Chemistry, Council, 1948-52, 1960-63, Chm. Indian Sect., 1945-48; Institute of Fuel Council, 1932; Mem. of Mining, Geological and Metallurgical Inst. of India (Council, 1932-35 and 1942-48, Vice-Pres., 1938-39); Mem., Basic Chemicals Cttee (Supply Development Council, India), 1942-43; Mem., Fuel Research Cttee, CSIR, Govt of India. Founded, 1938, Blood Bank, Dhanbad, Bihar; social service at Leprosy Hospital, Sijua; advised CID Bihar on forensic laboratory, 1938; Kaisar-i-Hind Medal for public service in India, 1944. Editor, the Plant Engineer, 1953-55. Hon. Fellow, Heriot-Watt Coll. *Publications:* Trans Min. Geol. and Met. Inst. India (bronze, silver, and gold medals and twice Govt of India Prize, Rs 500); Journal of the Institute of Fuel, Proc. Indian Science Congr., Proc. Nat. Inst. Sciences, India; Fuel Research Report No. 1, CSIR (India); Editor and part-contributor, The Efficient Use of Fuel (HMSO), 1958. *Recreations:* gardening, Scottish country dancing, organ and classical music. *Address:* 1 Hampton Grove, Ewell, Epsom, Surrey KT17 1LA. *T:* 01-393 1004. [*Died* 5 Nov. 1980.

FORSDYKE, Sir (Edgar) John, KCB 1937; MA; Hon. ARIBA; Director and Principal Librarian of British Museum, 1936-50; *b* 12 Sept. 1883; 2nd *s* of F. P. Forsdyke, Hasketon, Suffolk; *m* 1942, Dea Gombrich, violinist, *e d* of Dr Karl Gombrich of Vienna; two *d. Educ:* Christ's Hospital; Keble Coll., Oxford (Scholar and Hon. Fellow). Entered British Museum, 1907; Keeper of Greek and Roman Antiquities in the British Museum, 1932-36. Military service, 1914-19, France, Macedonia, Egypt, Palestine; Capt., RFA. Editor Journal of Hellenic Studies, 1912-23; Hon. Sec. Hellenic Soc.; Hon. Member: Archæological Soc. of Athens; Archæological Inst. of America. *Publication:* Greece before Homer, 1956. *Address:* 13 Sandringham Road, NW11. [*Died* 3 Dec. 1979.

FORSEY, Prof. George Frank, MA; Professor of Classics in University of Southampton, 1926-54; *b* 15 May 1889; *s* of George and Sarah Colbert Forsey; *m* 1924, Caroline Alice Homeyer, *d* of Rev. George Homeyer; no *c. Educ:* University Coll., London. Lecturer in charge of Latin classes, Goldsmiths' Coll. (University of London), 1912-19. Served, 1915-19, in commissioned service in Mesopotamia with Machine Gun Corps, 1917-19. Lecturer in charge of Classics in University Coll., Southampton, 1919; subsequently Reader. Vice-Principal Southampton Univ., 1939-52, Deputy Vice-Chancellor, 1952-54. Has been at various times Member of Council of Classical Assoc. and Roman Soc., and co-opted mem. of Dorset Educn Cttee. For a number of years Examiner in Latin for Final and Higher Degrees in University of London. Fellow of University Coll., London 1953. *Publications:* occasional reviews or contributions in learned journals. *Address:* 12 Highfield Close, Southampton. *T:* Southampton 557002. [*Died* 19 Jan. 1974.

FORSHAW, John Henry, CB 1954; MC 1917; FRIBA; retired; Chief Architect and Housing Consultant, Ministry of Housing and Local Government, 1951-59, and of Ministry of Health, 1946-59; b 6 Sept. 1895; y s of late Henry Forshaw and Ellen, d of James Haselden; m 1923, Alice Holland, o d of H. W. Rigby-Jones, JP, Lathom; one s one d. Educ: Ormskirk Grammar Sch.; Liverpool Univ. (BArch, MA; Lever Prize, Dept of Civic Design). Formerly: Architect to the London County Council and Superintending Architect of Metropolitan Buildings, 1941-46, Deputy Architect, 1939-41; Dir, War Debris Survey, London Civil Defence Region, and Head of London (Heavy) Rescue Service, 1940-45; Chief Architect, Miners' Welfare Commn, 1926-39. Mem. Council, London Soc., Hon. Vice-Pres. Inst. of Landscape Architects; Mem., Min. of Housing Bailey Cttee Report, 1953. Served European War, 1915-19, Inns of Court Regt; Royal Engineers; Adjt 55th Divisional RE, Capt. (MC). County of London Plan, 1943, prepared with Sir Patrick Abercrombie; LCC reconstruction and housing schemes; pithead baths, welfare centres; experimental and demonstration housing. *Publications:* Lancaster Regional Planning Scheme, 1926; County of London Plan, 1943 (joint report). *Address:* Little Garth, Park Fell, Skelwith, near Ambleside, Westmorland. *T:* Ambleside 2354.   *[Died 16 Sept. 1973.*

FORSHAW, Thomas; President and Director, Burtonwood Brewery Co. (Forshaw's) Ltd (Chm. 1956-74); Chairman, Bangor Hotels Ltd; b 29 June 1888; e s of Richard Forshaw, County Councillor, Burtonwood, Lancs; m 1927, Margaret Jean, o d of Edgar Francis Snoad, Great Bookham, Surrey; two d. Educ: Sir Thomas Boteler Grammar Sch., Warrington. High Sheriff, Anglesey, 1944-45. *Address:* Penmorfa, Red Wharf Bay, Pentreath, Gwynedd LL75 8PZ. *T:* Pentreath 205.

[Died 4 Sept. 1976.

FORSSMANN, Werner (Theodor Otto), MD; surgeon and urologist; formerly Chief of the Surgical Department, Evangelisches Hospital, Düsseldorf; general practitioner from 1945; b 29 Aug. 1904; s of late Julius Forssmann and Emmy Forssmann (née Hindenberg); m 1933, Dr Elsbeth Forssmann (née Engel); six c. Educ: Askanisches Gymnasium; Univ. of Berlin (MD). First discovered technique of cardiac catheterisation when working at Eberswalde Surgical Clinic, near Berlin, 1929; worked with Dr Ferdinand Sauerbruch, 1931-32; subsequently Chief of Surgical Dept, City Hospital, Dresden. Served War of 1939-45 (POW); Honorarprofessor für Chirurgie und Urologie, Universitat Mainz, 1956; Honorarprofessor der Universität Düsseldorf, 1964. Prof. Hon. der Universidad Nacional de Córdoba/Argentinien, 1961. Mem., Perspektives in Biology and Medicine, 1968. For. Corres. Mem., BMA; Hon. Fellow Indian Acad. of Sciences, 1967. Leibniz-Medaille, der Deutschen Akademie der Wissenschaften, 1954; Gold Medal, Società Medico Chirurgica di Ferrara, 1968; Ordentliches Mitglied der Rheinisch-Westfälishcen Akad. der Wissenschaften des Landes Nordrhein Westfalen, 1968. Grosses Bundesverdienst Kreuz, 1958, mit Schulterband und Stern, 1964; Commandeur, Ordre des Palmes Académiques, 1971. Awarded (jointly) Nobel Prize for Medicine and Physiology, 1956. *Publications:* many articles in German medical journals. *Address:* 7861 Wies-Wambach, Schwarzwald, West Germany.
[Died 1 June 1979.

FORSTER OF HARRABY, 1st Baron cr 1959, of Beckenham; **John Forster,** KBE 1948; Kt 1939; QC 1946; Barrister-at-Law; Chairman of National Arbitration Tribunal since 1944; Judge, Administrative Tribunal, International Labour Organisation, 1957-60; b Carlisle, Cumberland, 15 Sept. 1888; yr s of John J. Forster; m 1917, Muriel, er d of late Samuel Vosper, Devonport; one d. Educ: Sedbergh. Called to Bar, Gray's Inn, 1919; served throughout European War (RA); presided over the Trinidad Labour Riots Commission, 1937, Court of Inquiry into London Bus Dispute, and other industrial inquiries. Deputy Umpire under Unemployment Insurance Act, 1935. Chairman, Railway Staff National Tribunal, 1940-60; Pres. of the Industrial Court, 1946-60. *Recreations:* fishing, gardening. *Address:* Broome, 84 Albemarle Rd, Beckenham, Kent. *T:* 01-460 2092; 1 Brick Court, Temple, EC4. *T:* 01-353 1687.

[Died 24 July 1972 (ext).

FORSTER, Rear-Adm. Herbert Acheson, MVO 1925; RN, retired; o surv. s of Paul Forster, Malverleys, Newbury; m Violet (d 1961), d of Major H. B. Dodgson, DSO; three d. Educ: HMS Britannia, Dartmouth. Served in HM Ships Agincourt and Resolution during 1914-18; Comdr HMS Southampton, Flagship, E Indies Station, 1921-23; HM Yacht Victoria and Albert, 1924-26; in comd RAN College, Jervis Bay, NSW, 1927-29; HMS Frobisher, 1929-30 and 1932-34; Naval Asst to Adm. Comdg Reserves, 1931-32; HMAS Australia, 1935-37; Rear-Adm., 1937; retired list, 1937. Served during 1939-45 as NOIC Isle of Man and in command of HMS St George, 1939-42 and as Naval Attaché, Buenos Aires, 1942-45. *Recreation:* shooting. *Address:* Barton Cottage, Barton Stacey, Winchester, Hants. *Club:* United Service & Royal Aero.   *[Died 12 Feb. 1975.*

FORSTER, Sir (Samuel Alexander) Sadler, Kt 1966; CBE 1956; Hon. DCL Durham; Chairman: English Industrial Estates Corporation, 1960-70; Malta Development Corporation, 1968-71; b 1900; o s of Fred J. Forster, JP, FCA, Middlesbrough; m 1st, 1928, Edna (d 1930), o d of Wm Henry Potts, Middlesbrough; one d; 2nd, 1932, Kathleen, d of Harold Bulmer, Great Ayton, North Yorks; one s. Educ: Middlesbrough High Sch. Chartered Accountant (not in practice since 1935); Industrial Man., Welwyn Garden City Ltd, 1936-41; Board of Trade (Dir for Industrial Estates in the Development Areas, 1945-48), 1941-48; Chm., North Eastern Trading Estates Ltd, 1948-60. Mem. Peterlee (New Town) Development Corp., 1950-59; Mem. Exec. Council, NE Industrial and Development Assoc., 1952-61, and Vice-Pres., 1957-61; Mem., Northern Economic Planning, 1965-69. Pres., National Assoc. for Advancement of Education for Commerce, 1954. Mem. Appointments Board, Universities of Newcastle and Durham, 1955-; Mem. Newcastle Regional Hospital Board, 1959-62; Chm. North of England Industrial Health Service, 1959-; Mem. Northern Adv. Cttee for Civil Aviation, 1964-71; Chm., Tyneside Productivity Assoc., 1966-. Pres., NE Div., YMCA, 1969-. Comdr Order of St Olav, 1962. *Publications:* Location of Industry Policy in Britain (for ECSC), 1965; numerous articles on industrial estates. *Recreations:* gardening, swimming, travel. *Address:* Welwyn Cottage, 29 Osbaldeston Gardens, Newcastle upon Tyne NE3 4JE. *T:* Gosforth 858485.
[Died 24 June 1973.

FORTESCUE, 6th Earl cr 1789; **Denzil George Fortescue,** MC 1918; TD; Viscount Ebrington, 1789; Baron Fortescue, 1751; b 13 June 1893; s of 4th Earl Fortescue, KCB, TD, and Hon. Emily Ormsby Gore, d of 2nd Baron Harlech; S brother 1958; m 1st, 1920, Marjorie (d 1964), OBE, d of late Col C. W. Trotter, CB, TD, and of Hon. Mrs Trotter, OBE; two s one d; 2nd, 1941, Sybil, d of 3rd Viscount Hardinge, CB; one s. Educ: Eton; New Coll., Oxford (MA). 2nd Lieut, Royal North Devon Hussars, 1913; Lieut-Col 96th Royal Devon Yeo. Regt, RA, 1935-41; Lieut-Col 1st Heavy Regt, RA, 1942-44. *Heir:* s Viscount Ebrington. *Address:* Ebrington Manor, Chipping Campden, Glos GL55 6NG. *T:* Paxford 230.   *[Died 1 June 1977.*

FORTUNE, Allan Stewart, CBE 1956; TD 1935; Chief Inspector, Department of Agriculture for Scotland, 1951-60; b 22 Sept. 1895; s of Allan Fortune, JP, Portsoy, Banffshire, Scotland, and Agnes Ballantyne Stewart, Meiklerig, East Lothian; m 1926, Margaret Donaldson, d of Thomas Smith, Blackpark, Stranraer; one d. Educ: Fordyce Academy, Banffshire; Edinburgh Univ. BSc (Agric.) Edinburgh, 1922. Dept of Agric. for Scotland: Inspector, 1922; Chief Inspector, 1951. Army Service: The Gordon Highlanders, 1914-36; commanded 6th Bn The Gordon Highlanders, 1931-36; retired with rank of Lt-Col-Bt-Col 1936; Reserve of Officers, TA, 1936-39. *Address:* 23 Hillpark Avenue, Edinburgh EH4 7AT. *T:* 031-336 4150. *[Died 19 March 1975.*

FOSKETT, Rt. Rev. Reginald, PhD, MA; Assistant Bishop of Carlisle, since 1971; b 1909; o s of A. E. and E. E. Foskett, Retford, Notts; m 1937, o d of Lt-Col J. W. C. and M. A. Kirk, Gedling, Notts; two d. Educ: Derby School; Keble College, Oxford; Cuddesdon College, Oxford. BA 2nd Class Hons Theol. 1931, MA 1935, Oxon; PhD Nottingham, 1957. Deacon, 1932; Priest, 1933; Curate of All Hallow's, Gedling, 1932-35; Curate of Mansfield, 1935-37; Curate in charge, Rainworth Conventional Dist, 1937-43; Rector of Ordsall, Notts, 1943-47; Surrogate, 1943-47 and 1948-57; Lecturer Notts County Training Coll. for Teachers, 1946-50; Vicar of Ilkeston, Derbys, 1948-57; Rural Dean of Ilkeston, 1950-57; Hon. Canon of Derby Cathedral, 1954-57; Exam. Chap. to Bp of Derby, 1954-57; Provost of St Mary's Cathedral, Edinburgh, 1957-67; Examining Chaplain to the Bishop of Edinburgh, 1959-67; Bishop Suffragan of Penrith, 1967-70. *Publications:* Some Scottish Links with the American Episcopal Church 1685-1785, 1962; (ed) The Zambesi Journal of Dr John Kirk, 1964; Zambesi Doctors (correspondence of Dr David Livingstone and Dr John Kirk), 1964. *Recreations:* reading and research. *Address:* Field Broughton Place, Field Broughton, Grange-over-Sands, Lancashire. *T:* Cartmel 414. *Club:* Overseas.
[Died 13 Nov. 1973.

FOSTER, Sir (Albert) Ridgeby, Kt 1964; b 12 June 1907; s of Albert John Foster; m 1937, Nancy Leigh; two s. Educ: Reading Sch.; Reading and Cambridge Univs; Imperial College of Tropical Agriculture, Trinidad. Imperial Chemical Industries (India) Ltd, 1933-64; Chairman, ICI (India), and associated companies, Alkali & Chemical Corp. of India, Indian

Explosives, Atic Industries, Chemicals & Fibres of India, 1961-64. Past Pres., Bengal Chamber of Commerce and Industry and of Associated Chambers of Commerce of India. Governor, India Institute of Technology, Delhi and Doon Sch. *Address:* Symnells, Aldington, Kent. *Clubs:* Oriental, Royal Commonwealth Society; Bengal, Royal Calcutta Turf, Tollygunge (Calcutta). *[Died 10 May 1973.*

FOSTER, Rev. Canon Charles, PhD, BSc (London), MA (Bristol); Hon. Chaplain, Winchester Cathedral, since 1970; Canon Emeritus, Portsmouth Cathedral, since 1968; *b* Willesden, 29 Sept. 1907; *o c* of Chas S. Foster, schoolmaster, and Gertrude Baker; *m* 1932, Marian Constance Mills, *y d* of Frederick Mills and Sarah Eleanor Marshall, Wednesfield, Staffs; one *s*. *Educ:* Latymer Upper Sch., Hammersmith; King's Coll., London; Bristol Univ.; St Augustine's Coll., Canterbury. First degree Physics and Maths, research degrees in Education. Asst Master, Midsomer Norton County Sch., 1931-35; Aylesbury Grammar Sch., 1936-41; Acting Headmaster, Royal Latin Sch., Buckingham, 1942-45; HM Inspector of Schs, 1946-54; Asst Curate, St Mary's, Alverstoke, 1955-59; Hon. Canon of Portsmouth, 1959-64; Canon Residentiary of Portsmouth Cathedral, 1964-68 and Diocesan Dir of Religious Education, 1959-68; Sen. Lectr in Divinity, King Alfred's Coll., Winchester, 1968-71. *Publications:* articles on science teaching, education and religion. *Recreations:* gardening, collecting porcelain douters. *Address:* Four Winds, Sleepers Hill, Winchester, Hants. *T:* Winchester 65381. *[Died 27 June 1972.*

FOSTER, F(ermian) Le Neve; *b* 3 Feb. 1888; *s* of late Herbert Le Neve Foster, Great Barr, Staffs; *m* 1915, Katie May Dorothy (*d* 1968), *d* of late C. W. Troughton, Blackheath, SE; three *s* (and two *s* decd). *Educ:* Shrewsbury. Admitted a Solicitor, 1910; Travers-Smith Law Scholar, 1910. Served European War, 1914-18, Capt. Inns of Court OTC (TA). Partner in Warren Murton & Co., Solicitors, 1919-53; Director: Industrial Public Companies, 1926-; Stanton Ironworks Co. Ltd, 1936-62; Crompton Parkinson Ltd, 1938-46; Stewarts & Lloyds Ltd, 1941-67; Chairman: British Van Heusen Co. Ltd, 1952-58; Smith's Potato Crisps Ltd, 1952-63; Smith's Potato Estates Ltd, 1952-66; Chm. (1926-61) and Man. Dir or Joint Man. Dir (1940-56), Davis & Timmins Ltd. A Governor of Shrewsbury Sch., 1952-65. *Recreations:* fishing and bridge. *Address:* Farlands, Chalfont St Giles, Bucks. *T:* Chalfont St Giles 2156.
[Died 25 Dec. 1972.

FOSTER, Francis; *see* Foster, Major R. F.

FOSTER, Geoffrey Norman; Director of Companies; *b* 16 Oct. 1884; *s* of Rev. Henry Foster and Sophia M. Harper; *m* 1915, Vera H. Prest; one *s* one *d*. *Educ:* Malvern Coll.; Worcester Coll., Oxford. Retired; represented Oxford *v* Cambridge at cricket, 1905-6-7-8, Association football, 1905-6-7-8, golf, 1906-7, raquets, 1906-7-8; has played representative football and cricket; Sec. of the Corinthians FC, 1919-24. *Publications:* contributor to papers on sporting matters. *Recreations:* all games and gardening. *Address:* 63 Chesterfield House, W1.
[Died 11 Aug. 1971.

FOSTER, Rev. Prof. John, DD; Professor of Ecclesiastical History, University of Glasgow, 1949, Emeritus, 1969; Dean, Faculty of Divinity, 1957-60; *b* 2 Oct. 1898; *s* of Bateman and Kate Foster, Bradford, Yorks; *m* 1926, Amy Dorothy Whittaker; two *s* one *d*. *Educ:* Bradford Grammar Sch.; Birmingham Univ.; Handsworth Theological Coll. RNVR, 1917-19: active service in armed trawlers in Home Waters. Ordained to ministry of Methodist Church, 1922, and to S China under Methodist Missionary Soc; Prof. of Church History: Union Theological Coll., Canton, 1926-37; Selly Oak Colleges, Birmingham, 1937-47. Delegate to Internat. Missionary Council, Madras, 1938, and Willingen, 1952; Consultant at First Assembly, World Council of Churches, Amsterdam, 1948. Examr to University of Wales, 1948-52, of Aberdeen, 1951-54, and of St Andrews, 1957-61; Visiting Prof., theol colls of India, 1954, and Nigeria, 1965. Frequent broadcaster, 1943-, and on TV, 1956-. Hon. DD Aberdeen, 1945. *Publications:* books on China, 1928-39; Then and Now, the Historic Church and the Younger Churches, 1942; After the Apostles, 1952; Beginning from Jerusalem, 1956; To All Nations, 1960; Five Minutes a Saint, 1964; They Converted our Ancestors, 1965; Men of Vision, 1965; God has no Favourites, 1968; Church History I: The First Advance, 1972; II: Setback and Recovery, 1973. *Recreation:* the countryside. *Address:* The Old Quarry, Kilcreggan, Dunbartonshire G84 0JA. *T:* Kilcreggan 2338.
[Died 3 Nov. 1973.

FOSTER, John Frederick, CMG 1964; Secretary-General, Association of Commonwealth Universities, London, 1964-70

(Secretary, Association of Universities of the British Commonwealth, 1947-64); *b* 28 March 1903; *s* of Frederick W. and Annie Foster, Melbourne, Vic.; *m* 1st, 1934, Winifred Betty Bedggood (*d* 1967); one *s* two *d*; 2nd, 1968, Margaret Sarah Bate, Vice-Principal, St Gabriel's Coll. of Educn, London. *Educ:* Wesley Coll., Melbourne; Queen's Coll., Univ. of Melbourne; London Sch. of Economics, MA, LLM (Melbourne) 1925; called to Victorian Bar, 1928; Vice-Master, Queen's Coll., Melbourne, 1928-34; Registrar, Univ. of Melbourne, 1937-47; Secretary: Australian Vice-Chancellor's Cttee, 1936-47; Cttee of Vice-Chancellors and Principals of Univs of UK, 1947-64. Exec. Sec., Marshall Aid Commemoration Commn, 1953-70; Sec., Commonwealth Scholarship Commn in the UK, 1959-70. Mem., Commonwealth Educn Confs, 1959 (Oxford), 1961 (New Delhi), 1968 (Lagos), and 1971 (Canberra); Sec., Kennedy Memorial Trust, 1966-70. Freeman, Drapers' Co. and of City of London; Trustee, Harlow Campus of Memorial Univ. of Newfoundland; Consultant, European Rectors' Conf. Hon. LLD: Laval Univ., Quebec, 1949; W Ontario, 1970; Glasgow, 1971; Melbourne, 1975; Hon. MA Oxford, 1953; Hon. DSc Salford, 1969; Hon. DUniv York, 1971. *Publications:* Editor, Commonwealth Universities Yearbook, 1947-62; Joint Editor, 1963-70. *Recreations:* gardening, photography. *Address:* Farthingale, Worlingworth, near Woodbridge, Suffolk IP13 7HW; 19 Mecklenburgh Square, WC1N 2AD. *Clubs:* Athenæum, Royal Commonwealth Society; Melbourne Cricket.
[Died 24 Sept. 1975.

FOSTER, Maj.-Gen. John Hulbert, CB 1978; Director Territorial Army and Cadets, Ministry of Defence, 1978-80; *b* 17 May 1925; *yr s* of late Lt-Col Thomas Hyland and Ethel Beatrice Foster; *m* 1947, Monica Davis; one *s* five *d*. *Educ:* Charterhouse. Commissioned RE, 1945; served: India, Burma, Nigeria, 1945-47; Kenya, 1948-50; Cyprus and Egypt, 1951-53. Instructor: RMA Sandhurst, 1953-56; Staff Coll., 1957; HQ Northern Command, 1958-60; OC, 23 Indep. Field Sqdn, 1961-63; JSSC, 1964; Min. of Defence, 1964-67; CO, 38 Engineer Regt, 1967-69, GSO1, CICC(West), 1969-70; CCRE, 1st British Corps, 1971-72; RCDS, 1973; Engineer-in-Chief (Army), 1975-77. *Recreations:* hunting, shooting, swimming. *Address:* Westow Lodge, Westow, York YO6 7LQ. *T:* Whitwell on the Hill 204. *Club:* Army and Navy. *[Died 24 May 1980.*

FOSTER, Leslie Thomas, CB 1966; *b* 24 Sept. 1905; *e s* of Thomas Henry and Elizabeth Foster; *m* 1933, Winifred Marie, *d* of Henry Stinchcombe. *Educ:* Reading Sch. Entered Office of Comr of Police of the Metropolis, 1930; Private Sec. to Comr (Air Vice-Marshal Sir Philip Game), 1940-41; transferred to Min. of Works, 1942; Principal, 1946; Asst Sec., 1952. Under-Sec., 1958; Dir of Establishments, Min. of Public Building and Works, 1964-67. *Address:* 11 Waldens Park Road, Horsell, Woking, Surrey. *T:* Woking 72777. *Club:* East India, Devonshire, Sports and Public Schools. *[Died 24 Feb. 1979.*

FOSTER, Major Reginald Francis; IA officer, retired; priest and author (pen name, Francis Foster); *b* 13 April 1896; *s* of late B. H. Foster, Buxted, Sussex; *m* 1951, Joan Elizabeth, *d* of Sir A. Harold Bibby, 1st Bt; one *d*; (three *s* two *d* by former *m*). *Educ:* Sloane Sch., Chelsea; privately; Community of the Resurrection, Mirfield. Served in Artists' Rifles, 1915, and (with rank of Lieut) in East Lancs Regt in France, 1915-17; transferred to Indian Army, 1918; served (with rank of Capt.) in 70th Burma Rifles and 38th Dogras in India, Palestine and Egypt, 1918-21; Adjutant of 91st Punjabis, and served (with rank of Major) in Waziristan Campaigns of 1919-21, 1921-24; retired from Indian Army, 1923; entered journalism and authorship, 1924; Chief Literary Adviser, Elkin Mathews and Marrot Ltd, 1925-27. Received into 3rd Order of Friars Minor, 1927. Ordained priest in Syro-Chaldean Church, 1933. Superior of the Order of the Divine Mission, 1934-40. Returned to Army during national crisis, 1940, and joined Queen's Royal Regt; seconded to Provost Service in Jan. 1941, and given command of 55th Divisional Provost Company, Corps of Military Police; re-posted, after sustaining an injury, to Queen's Royal Regt, Dec. 1941; formed and assumed command of No 1 Independent Company, Queen's Royal Regt, Oct. 1943; Commandant of invasion troops marshalling camps, Portsmouth and Winchester, 1944; invalided from service, 1945. *Publications:* The Missing Gates, 1925; The Lift Murder, 1925; Anthony Ravenhill, 1926; How to Write Short Stories, 1926; The Captive King, 1927; The Trail of the Thugs, 1927; Confession, 1928; The Music Gallery Murder, 1928; The Secret Places, 1929; The Moat House Mystery, 1929; Murder from Beyond, 1930; The Dark Night, 1930; Joyous Pilgrimage, 1930; Something Wrong at Chillery, 1931; The Wayside Book (part author), 1932; Famous Short Stories Analysed, 1932; Separate Star (autobiography), 1938; Longshanks and I, 1939; The Island, 1946; The Ancient Way, 1949; Modern Punctuation Handbook, 1947; Desert Journey,

1965; contrib. Promise of Greatness (a Great War Symposium), 1968; The Perennial Religion, 1969; The Unknown God, 1973; many short stories, essays, plays, etc. *Recreations:* philosophy, meteorology and drawing. *Address:* 39 Pembroke Court, Romiley, Cheshire.   [*Died* 28 *March* 1975.

FOSTER, Sir Ridgeby; *see* Foster, Sir A. R.

FOSTER, Air Chief Marshal Sir Robert Mordaunt, KCB 1950 (CB 1945); CBE 1944; DFC; DL; *b* 3 Sept. 1898; 3rd *s* of Col M. G. Foster; *m* 1940, Ruth Elliott, Broomswell, Suffolk; one *s* one *d. Educ:* Winchester. Joined Royal Flying Corps as pilot, June 1916; served in France, 1916-18 (despatches twice, DFC); India, 1919-23 (India Gen. Service Medal and 3 clasps); RAF Staff Coll., 1925-26; Iraq, 1926-32 (Gen. Service Medal and 2 clasps, Iraqi Campaign Medal). Served in Bomber Command, 1939-41; Near East, N Africa and Italy, 1941-45 (despatches, CBE, CB, Commander of Legion of Merit, USA); AOC Malta, 1944; AOC Desert Air Force, Italy, 1944-45; Chief of Air Div., Control Commn, Austria, 1945-46; AOC No 3 Group Bomber Comd, 1946-47; Asst Chief of Air Staff (Policy), 1947-49; AOC-in-C, Reserve Comd (now Home Command), 1949-51; C-in-C, 2nd (British) Tactical Air Force, 1951-53, 2nd Allied TAF, 1952-53; retired, 1954. DL Suffolk, 1968. *Recreations:* riding, shooting. *Address:* Stone Cottage, Great Glemham, Saxmundham, Suffolk. *Club:* Royal Air Force.   [*Died* 23 *Oct.* 1973.

FOSTER, Air Vice-Marshal William Foster MacNeece, CB 1933; CBE 1922; DSO 1917; DFC 1918; MA Oxon (hon.), 1941; Deputy Lord Mayor of Oxford, 1967 (Lord Mayor, 1966); *b* 21 Aug. 1889; *e s* of Col T. F. MacNeece, Castle Cary, Co. Donegal; *m* 1928, Jean, *d* of Ralph W. Bruce, Langtons, South Weald, Essex: two *d. Educ:* Cheltenham Coll.; Sandhurst. Served European War, 1914-18, promoted Lieut-Col RFC, Dec. 1916 (wounded, despatches, DSO, DFC); Chief Staff Officer Royal Air Force in Iraq, March 1921-Oct. 1922 (CBE, Gen. Service Medal and clasp); British Air Representative to Council of League of Nations, 1926-29; commanded No. 1 Air Defence Group Headquarters, 1929-34; retired list, 1937; British Commission for Exchange of Prisoners in Spain, 1938-39; Air Officer Commanding No. 6 Group RAF, 1939; Dep. Head of RAF Delegation, Washington, April 1942-Sept. 1943; Mem. of Combined Chiefs of Staff Cttee, Dec. 1942-May 1943; Head of Inter-Service Liaison Cttee, Washington, Oct. 1943-March 1944; Head of RAF Training Mission to China, Sept. 1944-April 1946; reverted to retired list Oct. 1946. Mem. Oxford City Council, 1950-. Sheriff of Oxford, 1963-64. Comdr of Legion of Merit (USA), Orders Cloud and Banner, and Loshu decoration (China). Assumed surname of Foster by Royal Licence, Aug. 1927. *Publications:* occasional verses in The Times, Spectator, etc, of which An Airman's Te Deum was printed in 1936 to music by Sir Walford Davies and in 1937 to music by Dr Martin Shaw. *Address:* 26 Northmoor Road, Oxford. *T:* 55588; The Corner House, Aldeburgh, Suffolk. *T:* 2568. *Clubs:* Army and Navy, Royal Air Force.   [*Died* 28 *March* 1978.

FOUCHÉ, Jacobus Johannes, DMS (South Africa) 1971; State President of the Republic of South Africa, 1968-75; *b* Wepener, OFS, 6 June 1898; *s* of late J. J. Fouché; *m* 1920, Letta Rhoda, *d* of late T. P. McDonald, Zastron, OFS; one *s. Educ:* Victoria Coll., Stellenbosch. MP for Smithfield, 1941-50 and for Bloemfontein West, 1960-68; Administrator of the OFS, 1951-59; Minister of Defence, 1959-66, of Agricultural Technical Services and of Water Affairs, 1966-68. DPhil (*hc*) Univ. of Stellenbosch, 1966. Hon. Col, Regt President Steyn, Bloemfontein. Freeman of several cities and towns in Republic of S Africa. Paraguayan Nat. Order of Merit, 1974. *Recreation:* farming. *Address:* 9 De Jongh Street, Strand, 7140, Republic of South Africa.   [*Died* 23 *Sept.* 1980.

FOWLE, Brig. John Le Clerc, CB 1946; CIE 1943; *b* 13 Sept. 1893; *e s* of late Col Sir (Henry) Walter Hamilton Fowle, KBE; *m* 1932, Kathleen Sylvestre Le Clerc Fowle, Kaisar-i-Hind Medal (Silver), 1946, ROI 1968, FRSA, Silver and Gold Medallist, Paris Salon, *d* of late Gerald Sichel, FRCS. *Educ:* RN Coll. Osborne, and Sandhurst. Indian Army, 1912-46; joined 15th Lancers (CM), 1913; last appt Comdr Jubbulpore Area, India. Served European War, 1914-19, Mesopotamia, S Persia (despatches); Waziristan, 1920-21 (despatches); War of 1939-45; Eastern Army and Fourteenth Army (despatches). *Recreations:* polo, racing, golf. *Address:* 65 Cheyne Court, Royal Hospital Road, SW3. *T:* 01-351 3878. *Club:* Cavalry and Guards.
                                          [*Died* 2 *March* 1978.

FOWLER, Rees John, CBE 1954; *b* 14 Oct. 1894; *s* of late Thomas and Sarah Ann Fowler; *m* 1924, Lillian Elizabeth Stockton; no *c. Educ:* Port Talbot Grammar Sch.; Aberystwyth Univ.; London Sch. of Economics. Vice-Consul, Mexico City,

1921; Caracas, 1923; Beira, 1925; Tunis, 1927; Acting Consul-Gen. at Tunis in 1927, 1928, 1929 and 1930; Vice-Consul, Frankfurt, 1930, Acting Consul-General there in 1931 and 1932; Vice-Consul, Hamburg, 1933, Acting Consul-Gen. there in 1933, 1934 and 1935; Acting Consul-Gen. at Danzig, 1935; Consul, Antofagasta, Chile, 1936; Chargé d'Affaires, La Paz in 1937 and 1938; Acting Commercial Sec. at Santiago, Chile, in 1938 and 1939; returned to Antofagasta, 1939; HBM Minister and Consul-Gen. to Republic of Honduras, 1945-50; Consul-Gen., Genoa, Italy, 1950-55, retired 1955. *Address:* Via Mameli 34/18, 16035 Rapallo, Italy.   [*Died* 17 *Feb.* 1974.

FOWLER, Robert MacLaren, OC 1967; BA, LLD; Hon. Chairman, BP Canada Ltd, since 1977 (Chairman, 1969-77); Director, C. D. Howe Research Institute; *b* 7 Dec. 1906; *s* of late Edward Bruce Fowler and Genevieve Amey Fowler, Peterborough, Ont.; *m* 1934, Sheila Gordon Ramsay, *d* of A. Gordon Ramsay, Toronto, Ont.; three *s* two *d. Educ:* University of Toronto; Osgoode Hall Law Sch., Toronto, Ont. Practised Law, Toronto, Ont., with McMaster, Montgomery, Fleury and Co., 1931-37; Legal Sec. to Chm., Rowell-Sirois Commn on Dominion-Provincial Relations, 1937-39; practised law, Toronto, Ont., with McCarthy and McCarthy, 1939-45; Sec. and Gen. Counsel, of War-time Prices and Trade Board, Ottawa, 1942-45; Pres., Canadian Pulp & Paper Assoc., 1945-72; associated in practice of law with Gowling, Mactavish, Osborne and Henderson, later Gowling and Henderson, 1945-72. Director: Canadian Enterprise Develt Corp.; Templeton World Fund Inc.; Templeton Growth Fund Ltd; Pres., Canadian Institute of International Affairs, 1945-50; Chm. Exec. Council, Canadian Chamber of Commerce, 1953-54; Mem., Economic Council of Canada, 1963-70; Chm.: Royal Commission on Broadcasting, 1956-57; Cttee on Broadcasting, 1964-65. Hon. LLD: Montreal, 1960; McGill, 1974. *Address:* 3470 Stanley Street, Apt M2, Montreal, Que, Canada H3A 1R9. *T:* 845-5000. *Club:* Mount Royal (Montreal).   [*Died* 13 *July* 1980.

FOWWEATHER, Frank Scott, MSc, MD (Liverpool) 1925; FRCP 1943; FRIC, DPH 1924; Professor of Chemical Pathology, Leeds University, 1946-56, Professor Emeritus, 1956; late Chemical Pathologist, Leeds General Infirmary; *b* 13 Aug. 1892; *e s* of W. T. Fowweather, engineer, late of Bolton, Lancs; *m* 1922, Nellie, *d* of A. N. Godwin Chester, and *g d* of late J. P. Birch, surgeon, Cotton Hall, Denbigh; no *c. Educ:* Municipal Secondary Sch., Bolton; Liverpool Univ. BSc, First Class Hons in Chemistry, and awarded Willox Exhibition and Isaac Roberts Scholarship, 1914, and MSc, 1915. Chemist with Evans, Sons, Lescher & Webb Ltd, Runcorn, 1915-16; chemist with British Dyes Ltd, Huddersfield, 1916-17; practised as analytical and consulting chemist at 62 Dale Street, Liverpool, 1917-22; MB, ChB, 1922; in general medical practice at Wallasey and at Ellesmere Port, 1922-24; Lecturer in Chemical Pathology, University of Leeds, 1924-30; Reader, 1930-46. *Publications:* A Handbook of Clinical Chemical Pathology; contributions to scientific journals. *Recreations:* gardening, bookbinding. *Address:* Cloverly Nursing Home, Brimstage Road, Wirral, Merseyside L63 6HF. *T:* 051-342 4661.
                                          [*Died* 25 *Feb.* 1980.

FOX, Rev. Canon Adam; Canon of Westminster, 1942-63; Canon Emeritus of Chichester; *b* 15 July 1883; *s* of late W. H. Fox; unmarried. *Educ:* Winchester Coll.; University Coll., Oxford (Exhibitioner). BA 1906; MA 1909; Hon. DD, St Andrews, 1947; Holy Orders, 1911; Asst Master at Lancing, 1906-18; Warden of Radley Coll., 1918-24; Asst Master Diocesan Coll., Rondebosch, 1925-29; Fellow of Magdalen Coll., Oxford, 1929-42; Prof. of Poetry, Oxford Univ., 1938-43; Select Preacher, Oxford, 1932-33, 1957-58; Cambridge, 1938 and 1949; Sacred Poem Prize, 1929; Exam. Chap. to Bishop of Southwark, 1933-47. Master of the Skinners' Company, 1947-48. *Publications:* Dominus Virtutum, 1936; Old King Coel, 1937; Plato for Pleasure, 1946; English Hymns and Hymn Writers (Britain in Pictures), 1947; Meet the Greek Testament, 1952; John Mill and Richard Bentley, 1954; Plato and the Christians, 1957; God Is an Artist, 1957; Dean Inge (James Tait Black Memorial Prize), 1960; English Well Used, an Anthology (with Sir Andrew Claye), 1968; (with G. and G. Keene) Sacred and Secular: a Companion, 1974. *Address:* 4 Little Cloister, Westminster Abbey, SW1P 3PL.   [*Died* 17 *Jan.* 1977.

FOX, Ven. (Benjamin) George (Burton), MC 1944; TD 1950; Archdeacon of Wisbech since 1965; Hon. Canon, Ely Cathedral, since 1968; *b* 28 July 1913; *s* of J. B. Fox, Manor Farm, Erpingham, Norfolk; *m* 1943, Hon. Margaret Joan Davidson, *d* of 1st Viscount Davidson, PC, GCVO, CH, CB; one *s* four *d. Educ:* Norwich Sch.; University of London. Curate: Emmanuel, Guildford, 1936-38; St Andrew's, Bath, 1938-39. Chaplain, HM Forces, 1939-45. Vicar, Potten End, 1945-46, St Andrew's,

Bedford, 1946-50, Dio. St Albans; Rector, Montego Bay, Jamaica, 1950-55; Archdeacon of Cornwall, Jamaica, 1950-55; Vicar, St Etheldreda's, Fulham, 1956-65; Vicar of Haddenham, Dio. Ely, 1965-. *Recreations:* cricket, boxing. *Address:* The Vicarage, Haddenham, Ely, Cambs. *T:* Ely 40309.
[*Died 6 Nov.* 1978.

FOX, Bernard Joshua, CBE 1964; QC 1939; Recorder of Belfast, 1944-60, retired; *b* 3 Feb. 1885; *s* of Herman and Dora Fox; *m* 1908, Elizabeth Myers; two *s. Educ:* Belfast Royal Academy; Royal University of Ireland. Called to Irish Bar, 1914. Auditor, Law Students Soc. of Ireland, 1913-14. Called to Inner Bar of Northern Ireland, 1939; Legal Adviser to Govt of Northern Ireland, 1939-44; Chairman: Price Regulation Cttee for Northern Ireland, 1940-44; Northern Ireland Teachers' Salaries Cttee, 1957; Northern Ireland Coal Inquiry Cttee, 1961. Hon. LLD Queen's Univ. of Belfast. *Recreations:* golf, bridge. *Address:* No 5 Flat, 693 Antrim Road, Belfast. *T:* Belfast 76058. *Club:* Ulster Reform (Belfast).
[*Died 25 Dec.* 1977.

FOX, Captain Charles, CBE 1943; Merchant Navy; Orient Steam Navigation Co., London, 1919-51, retired 1951; *b* 26 Sept. 1890; *s* of Frederick Fox, Withernwick, Holderness, E Yorks; *m* 1926, Irene Lillian (marr. diss.), *d* of J. Cadden, Colleray, Sydney, NSW; one *d*; *m* 1948, Marjory Elsie Inglis, Loughton, Essex. *Educ:* Trinity House Navigation Sch., Kingston-upon-Hull, Yorks. Went to sea, 1906, Merchant Navy; served European War, 1914-18, Lieut RNR; Lloyd's War Medal, 1944. Commodore of Orient Line Fleet, 1949-51. *Address:* 8 The Avenue, Betchworth, Surrey.
[*Died 15 Oct.* 1977.

FOX, Douglas Gerard Arthur, OBE 1958; MA, BMus Oxon; FRCO, FRCM; Hon. ARCM; Hon. RAM; MusD Edinburgh 1938; Organist Emeritus, Great St Mary's Church, Cambridge (Organist, 1957-63); *b* 12 July 1893; *s* of Gerard Elsey Fox and Edith Makinson Fox, Clifton, Bristol. *Educ:* Clifton Coll. (Music Scholar); Royal College of Music (Organ Scholar; Challen Gold Medal for pianoforte playing, 1912); Keble Coll., Oxford (Organ Scholar). FRCO 1911 (La Fontaine Prize); ARCM 1912. Lieut 4th Gloucester Regt; lost right arm, France, Aug. 1917; Pres., Oxford Univ. Musical Club, 1918; Dir of Music, Bradfield Coll., 1918-30; composed music for Bradfield Greek Play (Agamemnon), 1925, and Antigone, 1931; Conductor, Newbury Amateur Orchestral Union, 1923-30; Dir of Music, Clifton Coll., 1931-57. Has given several performances of Ravel Piano Concerto for the left hand, with BBC SO, LSO, LPO (some broadcast). Examnr, Associated Bd of Royal Schs of Music. Mem. Council, RCO, 1935-72; President: Incorporated Soc. of Musicians, 1958-59; Cambridge Philharmonic Soc., 1960-68; Co-Pres., Bristol Music Club, 1964. Governor, Clifton Coll., 1958-. Hon. DMus Bristol, 1966. *Publication:* Joseph Haydn: an introduction, 1929. *Address:* Cowlin House, 26 Pembroke Road, Clifton, Bristol BS8 3BB. *T:* Bristol 32848. *Club:* Savile.
[*Died 23 Sept.* 1978.

FOX, Ven. George; *see* Fox, Ven. B. G. B.

FOX, Uffa, CBE 1959; RDI; Owner and Managing Director of Uffa Fox Ltd, Cowes, designers and builders of small-class racers, including International 14-footer Avenger (52 firsts, 2 seconds, 3 thirds, in 57 starts 1928) and sliding-seat canoe East Anglian, winner of principal Canoe Cups in this country and in America and Canada in 1933; *b* Cowes, 15 Jan. 1898; *m* 1956, Mme Yvonne Bernard, Paris. Apprenticed with S. E. Saunders. Served European War, 1914-18, RNAS. In sliding-seat canoes, won Championship of America for paddling and sailing, and New York International Canoe Trophy, 1933. During War of 1939-45 designed and built craft for Admiralty, War Office and Air Ministry, amongst which was parachuted self-baling and self-righting Airborne Lifeboat, with engine and fuel for 1,000 miles, and food and clothing on board for a month, and capable of carrying 25 men over thousands of miles of stormy ocean. RDI (Royal Society of Arts), 1955. *Publications:* Sailing, Seamanship, and Yacht Construction; Uffa Fox's Second Book; Sail and Power; Racing, Cruising, and Design; Thoughts on Yachts and Yachting; Beauty of Sail; Crest of the Wave; Sailing Boats; Seamanlike Sense in Powercraft, 1968. *Address:* Uffa Fox Ltd, Cowes, Isle of Wight.
[*Died 26 Oct.* 1972.

FOX-ANDREWS, Norman Roy, QC; Recorder, retired; *b* 15 April 1894; *s* of Stephen and Emily Fox-Andrews; *m* 1st, 1921, Olive Dunn; one *d*; 2nd, 1931, Mary Butler (*d* 1970). *Educ:* Leys Sch.; Trinity Hall, Cambridge. Law Tripos Parts I and II. DCLI 1914-18. Called to Bar, Lincoln's Inn, 1921; Bencher Lincoln's Inn, 1951; KC 1945; QC 1952; Recorder of Bridgwater, 1945; Royal Commission on Capital Punishment, 1949; Recorder of Bournemouth, 1945-61, Bristol, 1961-64. RAF 1939-40. *Recreations:* gardening, philately. *Address:* 2 Bedford Road,

Moor Park, Northwood, Mddx. *T:* Northwood 21766.
[*Died 31 July* 1971.

FOY, Sir Thomas Arthur Wyness, Kt 1956; CSI 1947; CIE 1945; MICE; *b* 1895; *s* of late Dr Frederick Arthur Foy, London. *Educ:* Truro Coll.; Birmingham Univ. Chief Engineer and Sec., Punjab Public Works Dept (Irrigation Branch), 1945-47; Chief Engineer and Sec., Lower Sind Barrage, Govt of Sind, 1947-55. *Address:* c/o National and Grindlay's Bank Ltd, 13 St James's Square, SW1.
[*Died 11 Jan.* 1971.

FOYLAN, Rt. Rev. Michael; Bishop of Aberdeen, since 1965; *b* 29 June 1907; *s* of James Foylan and Anne Foylan (*née* Murphy). *Educ:* Blairs College, Aberdeen; St Sulpice, Paris. Curate, St Andrew's Cathedral, Dundee, 1931-36; Curate, St Joseph's, Dundee, 1936-46; Parish Priest, St Serf's, Highvalleyfield, Fife, 1946-49; Administrator of St Andrew's Cathedral, Dundee, 1949-65; Vicar General of Diocese of Dunkeld, 1952-65. Domestic Prelate of His Holiness the Pope, 1953. JP, County of City of Dundee, 1957. *Recreations:* walking, golf. *Address:* Bishop's House, 156 King's Gate, Aberdeen. *T:* Aberdeen 39154.
[*Died 28 May* 1976.

FOYLE, Gilbert Samuel; Founder Director, W. & G. Foyle Ltd (Booksellers); *b* 9 March 1886; *s* of William and Deborah Foyle; *m* 1911, Ethel Ellen Cook; two *s. Educ:* Owen's Sch., Islington; King's Coll., University of London. Served European War, 1914-18, France, 1916-17. With brother William, founded firm of W. & G. Foyle, Booksellers, 1903; Founder of Gilbert Foyle Educational Trust, administered by LCC. Freeman, City of London, 1935; Mem. of Eastbourne Town Council, 1952-62, resigned for health reasons. *Recreations:* reading, social work. *Address:* 4 Ashbourne Court, Eastbourne, Sussex. *T:* Eastbourne 3518.
[*Died 28 Oct.* 1971.

FRAMPTON, Algernon de Kewer, CMG 1952; *b* 30 Jan. 1904; *s* of Heathfield James and Elizabeth Frampton, Devon, England; *m* 1st, 1935, Marion May (*d* 1953), *d* of G. H. May, Inspector-Gen. of Police, Trinidad, BWI; 2nd, 1954, Emma Huggins (*née* Pereira) (*d* 1970); no *c. Educ:* Christ's Hosp.; Seale Hayne Agricultural Coll., Devon; School of Rural Economics, Oxford University; Wye Coll., Kent; Imperial Coll. of Tropical Agriculture, Trinidad, BWI. Joined Colonial Agricultural Service; Dept of Agriculture: Nigeria, 1927-29, British Guiana, 1929-35, Malaya, 1935-. Served War of 1939-45 (despatches); Capt., Volunteer Force (4th Malacca Bn), 1940; POW Singapore, 1942-45. Seconded from Malaya, 1946; Prof. of Agriculture, Imperial Coll. of Tropical Agriculture, Trinidad, BWI, 1946-49; Agricultural Adviser to Comptroller, Colonial Development and Welfare, BWI, 1949-58; Dir of Agriculture, Barbados, 1959-64; retd from Colonial Service, 1965. *Address:* San Amaro 18, Puerto de la Cruz, Tenerife, Canary Islands, Spain.
[*Died 15 April* 1974.

FRAMPTON, Henry James, CSI 1947; CIE 1941; MC; MA; *b* 14 Aug. 1897; *s* of Henry Manwell Frampton; *m* 1st, Alys Ann Mary, *d* of C. H. Holmes; 2nd, Hilda Mary, *d* of Rev. Alex. Brown; three *s* one *d. Educ:* Christ's Hospital; St John's Coll., Oxford. Joined Indian Civil Service, 1921; retired 1947. *Address:* Frenchay House, Beckspool Road, Frenchay Common, Bristol BS16 1NE.
[*Died 18 March* 1980.

FRANCIS, Sir (Cyril Gerard) Brooke, Kt 1938; QC (Tanganyika) 1934; Chief Justice of Bermuda and President Legislative Council, 1941, retired 1952; *b* 26 Nov. 1883; *m* 1909, Mavis Rodd, *y d* of late Richard Windeyer Robertson, NSW; no *c. Educ:* private tutor. Barrister-at-Law, Inner Temple, 1907; Fiji Civil Service in various administrative and legal appointments until transferred to British Honduras as Attorney-Gen. in 1921; Attorney-Gen., Zanzibar, 1924; Attorney-Gen., Tanganyika Territory, 1929; Chief Justice of Northern Rhodesia, 1934-39, and Member Rhodesian Court of Appeal, 1939; retired 1939; Major, second in command of Fiji Defence Force, 4 Aug. 1914 (mentioned by Army Council for services in connection defence Fiji); E Surrey Regt, 1915, and KAR, East Africa, 1916-19. *Address:* 6 Cadogan Gardens, SW3.
[*Died 16 Dec.* 1971.

FRANCIS, Lt-Col John Clement Wolstan, MBE; Vice-Lieutenant of Cambridgeshire, 1958-65; *b* 2 Aug. 1888; *s* of late Major Wolstan Francis, Cambridgeshire; *m* 1918, Evelyn Maud (*d* 1973); JP, *d* of Augustus William Benyon, Windsor; one *s. Educ:* Wellington; Pembroke Coll., Cambridge. Served European War, 1914-18. Major 1920, Lt-Col 1930; retired 1935. DL 1945, High Sheriff, 1954, Cambridgeshire. *Recreations:* horses and shooting. *Address:* Quy Hall, Cambridgeshire. *T:* Bottisham 205. *Clubs:* Cavalry and Guards; Royal Automobile.
[*Died 20 June* 1978.

FRANCIS, John Gordon Loveband, CBE 1964; *b* 4 Feb. 1907; *s* of late Dr J. E. Francis, Westward Ho!, N Devon; *m* 1935, Ann, *d* of late O. A. Sherrard, Lyme Regis, Dorset; four *d. Educ:* Blundell's Sch., Tiverton. Articled Clerk, E. C. Price, Son & Reid, 1926-32; Asst in Cost Office, Harris, Lebus & Co., Mass Production Furniture Manufacturers, 1933-34; Accountant, later Sec., Brickwood & Co., Brewers, Portsmouth, 1934-39. BBC: Asst Chief Accountant, 1939-43; Chief Accountant, 1943-59; Controller, Finance, 1959-69; Dir of Finance, BBC, 1969-71. FCA, ACMA. *Address:* Lingwood Grove, Blackheath, Guildford, Surrey. *T:* Bramley 2081.　　　*[Died 20 Aug. 1976.*

FRANCO BAHAMONDE, General Don Francisco; Head of Spanish State and Generalissimo of National Armies since 1936; *b* 4 Dec. 1892; *m* 1923, Doña Carmen Polo y Martinez-Valdés; one *d. Educ:* Infantry Academy. Took part in campaign, Morocco, 1912-17; with Oviedo garrison, 1917-20; Dep. Comdr, Foreign Legion, Morocco, 1920-23; Comdr, 1923-27; Dir.-Gen., Military Academy, Saragossa, 1927-31; Capt.-Gen., Balearic Islands, 1933; C-in-C Moroccan Army, 1935; Chief of Gen. Staff, 1935; C-in-C Canary Islands, 1936. Capt. 1914; Major 1916; Lieut-Col 1922; Col 1924; Maj.-Gen. 1934. Gran Cruz Laureada de San Fernando: Medalla Militar Individual; Gran Cruz de San Hermenegildo, etc. Also holds many foreign decorations. *Address:* Madrid, Spain.　　　*[Died 20 Nov. 1975.*

FRANÇOIS-PONCET, André, de l'Académie Française, 1952 et de l'Académie des Sciences morales et politiques; LLD; Grand Croix de la Légion d'Honneur; politician, diplomat and writer; Chancellor of the French Institute, 1961-64; *b* Provins, France, 13 June 1887; *m* 1920, Jacqueline Dillais; four *s* one *d.* Served European War, 1914-16, Lieut 304 Infantry Regt (Croix de Guerre). Mem. International Economic Mission, US, 1919; Govt delegate Conference of Genoa and in Ruhr. Founder and Dir, Bulletin de la Société d'Etudes et d'Informations économiques, 1920-24; Mem. Cttee Republican Party; Deputy, 1924-31; Under-Sec. of State, 1928-31; Ambassador to Germany, 1931-38; Ambassador to Italy, 1938-40; Mem. National Council, 1941; arrested by the Gestapo, 1943; liberated by the Allies, May 1945. President of the French Red Cross. Pres. Permanent Commission of International Red Cross, 1949-; French High Commissioner, Allied High Commission, Germany, 1949-55; French Ambassador to Western Germany, May-Sept. 1955. *Publications:* Les Affinités électives de Goethe, 1910; Ce que pense la jeunesse allemande, 1913; La France et le problème des réparations; Discours français; Réflexions d'un républicain moderne; Souvenir d'une Ambassade à Berlin, 1946; De Versailles à Potsdam, 1948; Carnets d'un Captif, 1952; Discours de Réception à l'Académie Française, Au Palais Farnese, 1961. *Address:* 92 rue du Ranelagh, Paris 16e.　　　*[Died 8 Jan. 1978.*

FRANGULIS, A. F.; Ambassador, Permanent Secretary-General of Académie Diplomatique Internationale; *b* the Piraeus, Greece, 8 Nov. 1888. *Educ:* Lycée in Athens and Constantinople; Universities of Athens, Geneva, Lausanne, Berlin and Paris. In 1920 and 1921, Mem. Greek Delegn to Supreme Council in London for negotiating terms of Peace with Turkey; rep. Greece in Council of League of Nations, with rank of Minister, with responsibility for negotiations respecting Northern Epirus, 1921; later was deleg. of Greece to Conf. of Ambassadors, with special ref. to settlement of territorial questions relating to delimitation of frontiers of that country; attended 1st, 2nd and 3rd Assembly of League of Nations as Delegate of Greece; in 1926 founded, in assoc. with MM Adatchi. Poullet, Guerrero, Franklin Roosevelt, Beneš, Titulesco, etc, the Académie Diplomatique Internationale; in 1933 and 1934, as deleg. to League of Nations at time of persecution of Jews in Germany, asked Assembly of Geneva to give internat. jurisdictional protection of human rights and individual liberties; that resolution was written into the Charter of United Nations at San Francisco in 1945. He spoke at Assemblies of League of Nations, 1933-39, on behalf of refugees and secured a resolution advocating the "chèque compensation" with a view to promoting exchanges between various nations. Delegate to League of Nations, 1920-44. *Publications:* Dictionnaire Diplomatique, vols I-VIII; La Conception Nouvelle de la Neutralité: Une ligue des Nations comme garantie d'une Paix durable; Wilson, sa vie et son œuvre; Les Précurseurs de la SDN; La Norvège et le droit des Gens; Le Principe des Nationalités et le droit de libre disposition; Les Sanctions contre les responsables de la Guerre; l'Albanie et l'Epire du Nord; La Question du Proche Orient; La Grèce et la Crise Mondiale (I-II vols); Le Pacte général de renonciation à la Guerre; La Garantie Juridictionnelle des Droits de l'Homme; Théorie et Pratique des Traités Internationaux; La Grèce, son Histoire Diplomatique, son Statut International (Vols I-II), etc. *Address:* 4 bis, Avenue Hoche, Paris.　　　*[Died 3 Dec. 1975.*

FRANKEL, Benjamin; composer; *b* 31 Jan. 1906; *s* of late Charles (Polish birth) and late Golda Dora (Austrian birth); *m* 1st, 1932, Joyce Stanmore Rayner (marr. diss. 1945); two *s* (one *d* decd); 2nd, 1945, Phyllis (Anna) Leat (*d* 1967); 3rd, 1972, Mrs Xenia Hamilton Kennaway. *Educ:* Latymer Sch., Hammersmith. Began as watchmaker's asst; studied piano, Cologne and Berlin with Victor Benham; earned living as jazz violinist in night clubs while continuing further studies at Guildhall Sch. of Music under Orlando Morgan; composition scholarship, Worshipful Co. of Musicians. Conducted in theatre for C. B. Cochran, Noel Coward and others; more than 100 original scores for films. Since 1958 resident in Switzerland. FGSM 1951. *Publications:* Quartets, Trios, other Chamber works, 8 Symphonies, Instrumental Mass, Songs, etc. (publ. England). *Recreations:* walking, claret. *Address:* Via ai Monti 11, Locarno, Switzerland. *T:* (093) 7.13.27.　　　*[Died 12 Feb. 1973.*

FRANKLIN, David; broadcaster and lecturer, sometime singer; *b* 17 May 1908; *s* of Henry James Franklin and Jane Maria Franklin (*née* Chapman); *m* 1931, Hilda Mary Bickell; two *d. Educ:* Alleyn's Sch., Dulwich; St Catharine's Coll., Cambridge. BA 1930. Asst Master, Sutton Valence Sch., 1930. Principal Bass, Glyndebourne Opera, 1936-39; after war service, Principal Bass, Royal Opera House, Covent Garden, and concerts, oratorio, and broadcasts, until 1951, when throat operation damaged top of voice. Since then, second career as broadcaster, in Round Britain Quiz, Any Questions?, various music programmes incl. Sunday Night at the London Coliseum, My Music, as Chm. of Twenty Questions, and in irregular series of feature programmes. Some appearances on TV, incl. Midland BBC series Franklin Afoot. Writers' Guild of Great Britain Award for best radio features script of the year, Cambridge Revisited, 1968. *Publication:* Basso Cantante, an autobiography, 1969. *Recreation:* work, which has been more fun than not working. *Address:* Cedry, Lenchwick, Evesham, Worcs. *T:* Harvington 497.　　　*[Died 22 Oct. 1973.*

FRANKLIN, John Lewis, MA, MD Cambridge; FRCP; Consulting Dermatologist: Westminster Hospital; Princess Beatrice Hospital; Edenbridge Cottage Hospital; *b* 13 Feb. 1904; *e s* of late Philip Franklin, FRCS; *m* 1937, Katharine Mary Raeburn Balmer (marr. diss. 1947); one *s* one *d*; *m* 1950, Sallie de Launay; *m* 1968, Dorothy Balderston. *Educ:* Epsom Coll.; Pembroke Coll., Cambridge; St George's Hosp. Medical Sch. Represented Cambridge Univ. versus Oxford at fencing with the épée, 1925. *Publications:* Diseases of the Skin (with Dr S. E. Dore), 1934; numerous papers on dermatological subjects. *Recreation:* fishing. *Address:* 100 Harley Street, W1. *T:* 01-935 6377.　　　*[Died 19 May 1972.*

FRASER OF LONSDALE, Baron *cr* 1958 (Life Peer); **William Jocelyn Ian Fraser,** CH 1953; Kt 1934; CBE 1922; Chairman of the Council of St Dunstan's since 1921; Life President, St Dunstan's, South Africa; Vice-President, Royal National Institute for the Blind; Trustee, South Africa Foundation; President and Director, Frasers Ltd, South Africa; President, Bass Charrington Vintners Ltd; Chairman, Sun Alliance Insurance Group (West End); Director, Canada Dry (UK) Ltd; *b* Eastbourne, 1897; *o s* of late William Percy Fraser and Ethel Maude, *d* of J. P. Cooke, Johannesburg; *m* Irene Gladys, CBE, *d* of George Mace, Chipping Norton; one *d. Educ:* Marlborough; RMC, Sandhurst. Served European War, 1915-16, 1st Batt. King's (Shropshire) Light Infantry, attached 1/4th Glosters; Mem. London County Council (North St Pancras Div.), 1922-25; MP (U) North St Pancras Div., 1924-29 and 1931-36, resigned; MP (U), Lonsdale Div. of Lancaster, 1940-50, Morecambe and Lonsdale Div. of Lancaster, 1950-58. Mem. Broadcasting Cttee of Inquiry, 1925-26; Governor, British Broadcasting Corporation, 1937-39 and 1941-46. Nat. Pres., British Legion, 1947-58. Pres., Internat. Congress of War Blinded, 1973. Barrister-at-Law, Inner Temple, 1932. Helen Keller Internat. Award, 1971. Comdr, Order of the Crown, Belgium, 1953; Officer of the Legion of Honour, French Republic, 1954; Cmdr, Order of Leopold, Belgium, 1972. *Publications:* Whereas I Was Blind, 1942; My Story of St Dunstan's, 1961. *Recreation:* fishing. *Address:* St John's Lodge, Inner Circle, Regent's Park, NW1. *T:* 01-935 8232; Low Wood House, Haverthwaite, Ulverston, Cumbria; Fraser House, Wepener, Orange Free State, South Africa. *Clubs:* Bath, Flyfishers'; Rand (Johannesburg).　　　*[Died 19 Dec. 1974.*

FRASER, Sir (Arthur) Ronald, KBE 1949 (MBE 1930); CMG 1934; *b* 3 Nov. 1888; *s* of late John and Louisa Fraser; *m* 1915, Sylvia Blanche Powell; two *s* two *d. Educ:* St Paul's. Served European War, Flanders and France, 1914-16 (wounded and disabled for further active service); civil servant; acted as Gen. Sec. during the Anglo-Argentine negotiations of 1933, and as Board of Trade Representative and adviser to HM Ambassador,

Buenos Aires, during the subsequent tariff negotiations, 1933; Minister (Commercial), HM Embassy, Paris, 1944-49, and Resident Government Dir, Suez Canal Co.; Pres. Caledonian Soc. of France, 1946-53. Companion Order of Orange Nassau. *Publications:* under the name of Ronald Fraser: The Flying Draper, 1924; Landscape with Figures, 1925 and 1952; Flower Phantoms, 1926; The Vista, 1928; Rose Anstey, 1930; Marriage in Heaven, 1932; Tropical Waters, 1933; The Ninth of July, 1934; Surprising Results, 1935; A House in the Park, 1937; Bird under Glass, 1938; Miss Lucifer, 1939; Financial Times, 1942; The Fiery Gate, 1943; Circular Tour, 1946; Maia, 1948; Sun in Scorpio, 1949; Beetle's Career, 1951; Glimpses of the Sun, 1952; Latin America: A Personal Survey, 1953; Bell From a Distant Temple, 1954; Flight of Wild Geese, 1955; Lord of the East, 1956; The Wine of Illusion, 1957; A Visit from Venus, 1958; Jupiter in the Chair, 1958; Trout's Testament, 1959; City of the Sun, 1961; Her-Bak Egyptian Initiate (trans. from the French), 1967; The Mysteries of Chartres Cathedral (trans. from the French of L. Charpentier), 1972; A Work of Imagination, 1974. *Address:* Swanlands, Hill Top Lane, Chinnor, Oxford OX9 4BH. *T:* Kingston Blount 51405. *[Died 12 Sept. 1974.*

FRASER, Colin Neil, QC Scotland 1958; Counsel to Secretary of State under Private Legislation (Scotland) Procedure 1958-71; *b* 21 Sept. 1905; *s* of late Robert Dick Fraser, CA; *m* 1937, Alix Leslie, *d* of late Alexander Stephen, shipbuilder, Glasgow; one *s* two *d.* *Educ:* Glenalmond; Glasgow Univ. (MA, LLB). Advocate, 1931; RA (Capt.), 1939-46; Pres., Pensions Appeal Tribunal (Scotland), 1946-58. *Recreations:* ski-ing, golf. *Address:* Woodend, Dirleton, East Lothian EH39 5ET. *T:* Dirleton 276. *Club:* New (Edinburgh). *[Died 7 Sept. 1979.*

FRASER, Very Rev. Dr Duncan; Moderator of the General Assembly of the Church of Scotland, May, 1964-65; Minister of the Church of Scotland, Invergordon, 1929-67 (Minister of the United Free Church of Scotland, Invergordon, 1927-29); *b* 7 Aug. 1903; *s* of Rev. Duncan Fraser, Bracadale, Isle of Skye; *m* 1935, Helen Louise, 2nd *d* of ex-Provost John Macdonald, Invergordon. *Educ:* Portree High Sch.; University of Edinburgh; New Coll., Edinburgh. MA Edinburgh, 1924; Hons Diploma in Theology, and Junior Cunningham Fellow, New Coll., Edinburgh, 1927; PhD Edinburgh, 1944; Hon DD, Edinburgh, 1958. Officiating Minister, RN, 1927-47; Officiating Chaplain, Army and RAF, 1939-45. Member: Ross-shire Educ. Cttee; 1946-49; Invergordon Town Council, 1954-55; Governor, Highlands and Islands Educ. Trust, 1961-70. JP, Ross and Cromarty, 1946-67. Freeman, Burgh of Invergordon, 1968. *Publications:* Life and Writings of James Fraser of Brea, 1944; Story of Invergordon Church, 1946; contribs to theological jls in UK and USA. *Recreations:* reading, motoring. *Address:* Seaview, Invergordon, Ross-shire. *T:* Invergordon 852207. *[Died 16 Sept. 1977.*

FRASER, Francis Charles, CBE 1962; FRS 1966; DSc; FIBiol; Deputy Chief Scientific Officer, British Museum (Natural History), 1960-65; re-employed, Principal Scientific Officer, 1965-69, retired 1969; *b* 16 June 1903; *y s* of James and Barbara Anne Fraser, Dingwall, Ross & Cromarty; *m* 1938, Anne Nuttall. *Educ:* Dingwall; Glasgow Univ. Demonstrator, Dept of Geology, University of Glasgow, 1924-25. "Discovery" investigations, 1925-33, with service in Discovery, William Scoresby, Discovery II and at shore station, S Georgia. Danish Atlantide Expedition, W Africa, 1945-46. British Museum (Natural History): Asst Keeper, Mammalian Osteology, 1933-48; Dep. Keeper of Zoology, 1948-57; Keeper of Zoology, 1957-64. Pres., Antarctic Club, 1973-74. Polar Medal, 1942. *Publications:* (with late J. R. Norman) Giant Fishes, Whales and Dolphins, 1937. Technical papers mainly on subjects relating to whales and dolphins. Reports on Cetaceans stranded on the British Coast, 1926-32, 1933-37, 1938-47, 1948-66. *Recreation:* gardening. *Address:* 78 Hayes Road, Bromley, Kent BR2 9AB. *T:* 01-460 3668. *Club:* Athenæum. *[Died 21 Oct. 1978.*

FRASER, Ian George Inglis, OBE 1975; Representative, British Council, Spain, since 1979; *b* 5 March 1923; *s* of late Rev. George Fraser and Mrs Mary Fraser (*née* Inglis); *m* 1949, Eve Uwins; three *s.* *Educ:* Bathgate Acad.; Edinburgh Acad.; Edinburgh Univ. (MA 1944). Temp. Asst Principal: Min. of Supply, 1944-46; BoT, 1946-48; British Council, 1948-: Asst, Visitors Dept, 1948-53; Asst Rep., Israel, 1953-56; Asst, Commonwealth Dept, 1956-60; Reg. Dir, Mbale, Uganda, 1960-62; Dep. Rep., Nigeria, 1962-67; Asst Controller, Books, Arts and Science Div., 1967-69; Dep. Controller, Overseas Div. A, 1969-72; Rep., Greece, 1972-76, Japan, 1977-79. *Recreations:* books, theatre, travel, talk. *Address:* c/o British Council, 10 Spring Gardens, SW1A 2BN. *T:* 01-930 8466; 16 Kensington Place, W8. *T:* 01-727 2940. *[Died 16 July 1980.*

FRASER, Rear-Adm. John Stewart Gordon, CBE 1946; DSO 1917; RN retired; *b* 1883; *m* 1915; one *s* two *d.* Served European War, 1914-18 (despatches, DSO); retired list, 1935. Called up and served in war of 1939-45 (despatches, CBE). *Address:* 41 Elizabeth Avenue, St Brelade, Jersey, Channel Islands. *Clubs:* United Service and Royal Aero; La Moye Golf (Jersey). *[Died 3 Nov. 1973.*

FRASER, Sir Keith Charles Adolphus, 6th Bt, *cr* 1806; *b* 14 Sept. 1911; *s* of Major Sir Keith Fraser, 5th Bt, and Lady Dorothy Coventry (*d* 1965), 2nd *d* of 9th Earl of Coventry; *S* father 1935; *m* 1934, Blanca de Undurraga y Sandiford (from whom he obtained a divorce, 1946), *d* of Julio de Undurraga; *m* 1947, Mrs Sybil Craven, *d* of George Savage. *Educ:* Eton; Cambridge. *Heir:* none. *Address:* c/o Brown Shipley & Co. Ltd, Founders Court, EC2. *[Died 13 May 1979 (ext).*

FRASER, Ronald; see Fraser, Sir A. R.

FRASER DARLING, Sir Frank, Kt 1970; DSc, PhD, LLD; FIBiol, FRSE; *b* 23 June 1903; *m* 1st, 1925, Marian Fraser; one *s*; 2nd, 1948, Averil Morley (*d* 1957); two *s* one *d*; 3rd, 1960, Christina Macinnes Brotchie. *Educ:* University of Edinburgh. On Agricultural Staff, Bucks County Council, 1924-27; Research Student, Inst. of Animal Genetics, Univ. of Edinburgh, 1928-30; Chief Officer, Imperial Bureau of Animal Genetics, 1930-34; Leverhulme Research Fellow, 1933-36; Carnegie Research Fellow, 1936-39; Dir, West Highland Survey, 1944-50; Rockefeller Special Research Fellow, 1950. Senior Lectr in Ecology and Conservation, Univ. of Edinburgh, 1953-58; Vice-Pres., Conservation Foundn, Washington, DC, 1959-72. Member: Royal Commn on Environmental Pollution, 1970-73; Nature Conservancy, 1969-73. Reith Lectr, 1969. Mungo Park Medallist, Royal Scottish Geographical Society, 1947; Centenary Medallist, US Nat. Park Service, 1972. Hon. LLD Glasgow; Hon. DSc: Heriot-Watt; New Univ. of Ulster; Williams Coll., Mass. Commandeur, Order of Golden Ark (Netherlands), 1973. *Publications:* Biology of the Fleece of the Scottish Mountain Blackface Breed of Sheep, 1932; Animal Breeding in the British Empire, 1934; Wild Life Conservation, 1934; A Herd of Red Deer, 1937; Bird Flocks and the Breeding Cycle, 1938; Wild Country, 1938; A Naturalist on Rona, 1939; The Seasons and the Farmer, 1939; Island Years, 1940; The Seasons and the Fisherman, 1941; The Story of Scotland, 1942; Wild Life of Britain, 1943; Island Farm, 1943; The Care of Farm Animals, 1943; Crofting Agriculture, 1945; Natural History in the Highlands and Islands, 1947; Report of the West Highland Survey, 1952; (with A. S. Leopold) Alaska: an Ecological Reconnaissance, 1953; West Highland Survey, 1955; Pelican in the Wilderness; Odyssey of a Naturalist, 1956; Wild Life in an African Territory, 1960; An Ecological Reconnaissance of the Mara Plains in Kenya Colony, 1960; The Unity of Ecology, 1963; The Nature of a National Park, 1968; Impacts of Man on the Biosphere, 1969; Wilderness and Plenty (Reith Lectures), 1970; scientific papers. *Recreations:* watching animals, English literature. *Address:* Lochyhill, Forres, Moray. *T:* Forres 2664. *Club:* Athenæum. *[Died 22 Oct. 1979.*

FREEDMAN, Prof. Maurice, MA, PhD; Professor of Social Anthropology, University of Oxford, since 1970; *b* 11 Dec. 1920; *s* of Harry Freedman and Minnie (*née* Glazer); *m* 1946, Judith Djamour; no *c.* *Educ:* Hackney Downs; King's Coll. London; London Sch. of Economics. RA (in ranks, subseq. commnd), 1941-45. Research Fellow, CSSRC, Singapore, 1949-50; Lectr, LSE, 1951-57; Reader, LSE, 1957-65. Consultant, WHO (in Indonesia), 1954. Vis. Assoc. Prof., Yale Univ., 1960-61; Vis. Prof., Cornell Univ., 1965. Prof. of Anthropology, LSE, 1965-70. Governor, LSE, 1966-70, and 1971-; Mem. Senate, Univ. of London, 1967-70. Pres., Royal Anthropological Inst., 1967-69. Mem., SSRC, 1972-73. Man. Editor, Jewish Jl of Sociology, 1959-71, Editor, 1971-. Malinowski Memorial Lectr, 1962; Hobhouse Memorial Lectr, 1975. *Publications:* (ed) A Minority in Britain, 1955; Chinese Family and Marriage in Singapore, 1957; Lineage Organization in Southeastern China, 1958; Chinese Lineage and Society, 1966; (ed) Social Organization, Essays Presented to Raymond Firth, 1967; (ed) Family and Kinship in Chinese Society, 1970; (ed and trans.) M. Granet, The Religion of the Chinese People, 1975; articles in Brit. Jl Sociology, Jl Asian Studies, Jl Royal Anthropological Inst., etc. *Address:* Institute of Social Anthropology, 51 Banbury Road, Oxford OX2 6PF. *T:* Oxford 55971; All Souls College, Oxford OX1 4AL. *T:* Oxford 22251. *[Died 14 July 1975.*

FREELAND, Lt.-Gen. Sir Ian (Henry), GBE 1971; KCB 1968 (CB 1964); DSO 1944; Vice Lord-Lieutenant, Norfolk, since 1978; *b* 14 Sept. 1912; *s* of late Maj.-Gen. Sir H. F. E. Freeland, KCIE, CB, DSO, MVO, RE; *m* 1940, Mary, *d* of late Gen. Sir C. C. Armitage, KCB, CMG, DSO; two *s* one *d.* *Educ:* Wellington

Coll.; RMC, Sandhurst. Commissioned into the Norfolk Regt, 1932; Adjt, 1940; Bde Major 7 Inf. Bde, 1942; GSO2 War Office (MT2), 1943; OC 7 Royal Norfolk, 1944; OC 1/5 Queen's, 1944-45; Col GS, HQ 8 Corps Dist, 1945-46; 2nd i/c 4th Armoured Brigade, 1946; GSO1 (SD), HQ BAOR, 1946-47; GSO1, BAOR Trg Centre, 1947-48; Comdt All Arms Training Centre, 1948-49; GSO1, War Office (Western Union), 1949-50; GSO1, Staff Coll., Camberley, 1951-53; OC 2 R Inniskilling Fusiliers, 1954-56; Comdr, 12 Inf. Bde, 1956-57; Imperial Defence Coll., 1958; Brigadier Q (Ops) War Office, 1959-61; GOC 54 (E Anglian) Div./Dist, 1961-63; GOC, E Africa Comd, 1963; British Land Forces, Kenya, and Kenya Army, 1963-64; Vice Adjt-Gen., MoD, 1965-68; Deputy CGS, 1968; GOC and Director of Operations, N Ireland, 1969-71; retired June 1971. Col, Royal Anglian Regt, 1971-76 (Dep. Col 1966-71). DL Norfolk, 1972. Croix de Guerre, 1940, with Palm (Belgium); Chevalier, Order of Crown, with Palm (Belgium). *Recreations:* shooting, cricket, golf, tennis. *Address:* Foxley Lodge, near Dereham, Norfolk. *Clubs:* Army and Navy; MCC; I Zingari; Free Foresters.
[Died 2 July 1979.

FREEMAN, Anthony Mallows; *see* Freeman, P. A. M.

FREEMAN, George Robert, CBE 1957; Nominal partner, formerly Senior partner, Gane, Jackson, Nelson & Freeman, Chartered Accountants, City-Gate House, Finsbury Square, EC2; *b* 31 July 1875; *yr s* of John Freeman, Winnipeg; *m* 1st, 1900, Lilian M. Rossiter (*d* 1920); one *s* two *d*; 2nd, 1923, Frieda E. de Buriatte; one *d*. *Educ:* Upper Canada Coll., Toronto; St John's Coll., Winnipeg. Articled to present firm, 1891; Chartered Accountant, 1897; Partner, 1903; FCA, 1909, elected to Council, 1915, Vice-Pres., 1924-25, Pres., 1925-26, Chm. Exam. Cttee, 1922-31, Chm. of Parliamentary and Law Cttee, 1936-44; nominated Rep. of Inst. on Trustees Savings Banks Inspection Cttee, 1921-60, Chm. 1938-60; resigned from most of his hon. appts 1957. Council of London Chamber of Commerce, 1922, Chm. of Journal Cttee, Mem. of Commercial Educn, Parliamentary and Commercial Law and Taxation Cttees; Royal Society of Arts Exams Cttee; Bd of Governors, City of London Coll. Pres. Chartered Accountants Benevolent Assoc. and a Vice-Pres. of London Chartered Accountant Students Soc.; Delegate from Inst. to Conf. Amer. Inst. of Accountants, St Louis, 1924, and to Dominion Assoc. of Chartered Accountants, Toronto, 1936, and Saskatoon, 1939. Officier d'Académie avec palmes (France), 1930. *Address:* Orillia, Greenhill Road, Otford, Kent. *T:* Otford 3200.
[Died 5 Oct. 1972.

FREEMAN, Patrick, MC 1943; QC 1970; *b* 8 June 1919; *s* of late Sir Ralph Freeman. *Educ:* Uppingham Sch.; Worcester Coll., Oxford (MA). Royal Artillery, 1939-45 (despatches 1944); Major. Called to Bar, Inner Temple, 1947; Bencher, 1978. *Address:* Gray's Inn Chambers, Gray's Inn, WC1.
[Died 5 Nov. 1978.

FREEMAN, (Philip) Anthony Mallows, MBE; FSA; MA; *b* 10 Nov. 1892; *o s* of Ann and late George Mallows Freeman, KC, JP, Grey Friars, Winchelsea; *m* 1928, Enid Campbell Adam (*d* 1949); no *c*. *Educ:* Eton; Oxford. Served European War, France, 1914-15, RA staff, 1917-18; Mayor of Winchelsea, 1930, 1931, 1944, 1945, 1946, 1952, 1953, 1957, 1962; High Sheriff of Sussex, 1939; Baron of the Cinque Ports, 1953. *Recreations:* fishing, shooting. *Address:* Wickham Manor, Winchelsea, Sussex. *T:* Winchelsea 216. *Clubs:* Bath, MCC.
[Died 9 Jan. 1971.

FREETH, Rt. Rev. Robert Evelyn, MA Cantab, ThD ACT; *b* 7 April 1886; *s* of Sir Evelyn Freeth and Florence Oakes; *m* 1913, Gladys Mary Snashall; two *s* one *d*. *Educ:* King's Coll. Sch., Wimbledon; Selwyn Coll., Cambridge (scholar), 1905; BA 2nd Cl. Classical Tripos, 1908. Ridley Hall, Cambridge, 1908; MA 1912; Derbyshire Prize, 1915. Deacon, 1909; Priest, 1910; Melanesian Mission, 1909-13; Curate, Christ Church, North Adelaide, South Australia, 1913-14; priest in charge, Angaston, 1914-15; Asst Chaplain, King's Sch., Parramatta, NSW, 1915-16; Precentor, St Andrews Cathedral, Sydney, and Principal of Choir Sch., 1916-18; Chaplain and House Master, King's Sch., Parramatta, 1918-20; Sydney Church of England Grammar Sch., 1920-27; Headmaster, Guildford Grammar Sch., Western Australia, 1928, resigned Dec. 1949. Canon of St George's Cathedral, Perth, WA, 1941-50. Archdeacon of Perth, WA, 1953-61; Asst Bishop of Perth, WA, 1957-62; retd, 1963. *Recreation:* gardening. *Address:* 142 Victoria Avenue, Dalkeith, Western Australia 6009, Australia. *[Died 16 Sept. 1979.*

FREKE, Cecil George, CIE 1937; MA Cantab, BSc London; Indian Civil Service (retired); *b* 8 Oct. 1887; *m* Judith Mary Marston; one *s* one *d*. *Educ:* Merchant Taylors' School, London; St John's Coll., Cambridge. Under-Sec., Government of India,

Commerce and Industries Dept, 1919; Dir-Gen. of Commercial Intelligence and Statistics, India, 1921-26; Financial Sec. to the Govt of Bombay, 1930-37. Vice-Pres., All-India Lawn Tennis Assoc., 1933-37. Sec., Iraq Currency Board, 1943-49; Dir, British National Cttee, International Chamber of Commerce, 1946-54. *Address:* c/o National and Grindlay's Bank, 23 Fenchurch Street, EC3. *Club:* United Service & Royal Aero.
[Died 3 June 1974.

FRENCH, Major Arthur Cecil, CBE 1952 (OBE 1947); Secretary, Council of Territorial and Auxiliary Forces Associations, 1947-61; *b* 11 Nov. 1896; *s* of Rev. W. A. French, Little Blakenham, Ipswich; *m* 1927, Audrey Frances, *d* of W. F. Paul, Ipswich; one *s* one *d*. *Educ:* Felsted; RMC, Sandhurst. Suffolk Regt, 1915. Brigade Major 6th Inf. Brigade, 1935-37; Brevet Major, 1937; retired, 1938. Sec. Cambs and Isle of Ely T&AFA, 1938-47; GSO2, 66 Div., 1939-40; psc 1931. *Recreations:* fishing and fruit growing. *Address:* Longacre, Stapleford, Cambs. *T:* Shelford 2135. *Club:* Army and Navy.
[Died 15 Oct. 1974.

FRENCH, Maj.-Gen. John, CB 1960; retired 1961; Chief of Industrial Section, Armament Control Agency, Western European Union, 1962-71; *b* 16 May 1906; *s* of Frederick Featherstonhaugh French and Edith l'Anson (*née* Watson); *m* 1935, Ursula Daphne (*née* Hutton); one *s* one *d* (and one *s* decd). *Educ:* Oundle; Corpus Christi, Cambridge (BA). Commissioned RTC, 1929; pac Military Coll. of Science, 1938; Instructor of Ballistics, Military Coll. of Science, 1939; Admiralty Research Laboratory, 1941; WTSFF 21 Army Gp, 1945; Dept of Artillery, Min. of Supply, 1946; Mem. of the Ordnance Board, 1949; British Joint Services Mission, Washington, 1952; Department of Artillery, Min. of Supply, 1955; Vice-Pres., Ordnance Board, 1958-60, Pres., 1960-61. *Recreation:* ocean racing. *Address:* c/o Banco Rural y Mediterraneo, Fuengirola (Malaga), Spain. *Clubs:* Royal Ocean Racing, RA Yacht (hon.); RAC Yacht.
[Died 7 Sept. 1978.

FRENCH, William Innes, DSO 1945; OBE 1950; TD; DL; CA; Partner of French & Cowan, Chartered Accountants, Glasgow, since 1934; *b* 4 Oct. 1910; *e s* of James Andrew French, CA, Glasgow, and Christina Helen Youl. *Educ:* Kelvinside Academy, Glasgow. Joined 9th (GH) Bn HLI, TA, 1928. Served War of 1939-45: 15th (Scottish), 76th (Norfolk) and 52nd (Lowland) Divs in regimental and staff appointments; psc (Camberley) 1942; GSO2, War Office, 1943. Commanded 1st Bn Glasgow Highlanders (52nd Division) in BLA, 1944-45 (DSO, despatches) and in TA, 1947-49 (OBE, Substantive Col 1949). Chartered Accountant, 1934. Mem. Council, Inst. of Chartered Accountants of Scotland, 1953-57. Pres., Glasgow Chamber of Commerce, 1958-60. Chairman: Sir William Arrol & Co. Ltd, Engineers, Glasgow, 1961-69; Scotcros Ltd; Dir, Scottish Life Assurance Co. Ltd, and other cos. Member: Scottish Industrial Estates Corp., 1960-; Council on Tribunals, 1962-. DL City of Glasgow, 1962. *Recreations:* reading, walking. *Address:* (home) 5 Whittingehame Drive, Glasgow W2. *T:* 041-339 3382; (office) 144 St Vincent Street, Glasgow C2. *T:* 041-221 2984. *Clubs:* Caledonian, East India and Sports; Western (Glasgow).
[Died 25 Dec. 1971.

FREND, Charles Herbert; Film Director since 1941; *b* 21 Nov. 1909; *s* of Edward Charles and Bertha Maud Frend; *m* 1940, Sonja Petra Baade Thornburn. *Educ:* King's Sch., Canterbury; Trinity Coll., Oxford. Entered cutting rooms at British Internat. Pictures, Elstree, 1931; became film editor, 1933; film editor for: Gaumont-British Picture Corp., 1934-37; Metro-Goldwyn-Mayer British Studios, 1937-39; Pascal Productions, 1940; became film dir for Ealing Studios, 1941; directed: The Big Blockade and The Foreman went to France, 1941; San Demetrio, London, 1943; The Return of the Vikings, Johnny Frenchman, 1944; The Loves of Joanna Godden, 1946; Scott of the Antarctic, 1947-48; A Run for your Money, 1949; The Magnet, 1950; The Cruel Sea, 1952; Lease of Life, 1954; The Long Arm, 1955; Barnacle Bill, 1957; Cone of Silence, 1960; Girl on Approval, 1961; While the Storm Lasts, 1962; The Sky-Bike, 1967. Mem. Order of Knighthood (First Class) of St Olav, 1953. *Recreation:* the cinema. *Address:* Flat 10, 111 Westbourne Terrace, W2. *T:* 01-723 0326. *[Died 8 Jan. 1977.*

FRERE, Brigadier Jasper Gray, DSO 1919; OBE 1946; MC; psc; BA; retired; *b* Kurow, New Zealand, 2 Jan. 1894; 5th *s* of late Ven. Hugh Corrie Frere and Florence, *d* of Robert Gray, first Bishop Metropolitan of Cape Town; *m* 1929, Cynthia Keble, *d* of late Rev. Arthur Keble White of Chevington, Suffolk; two *s*. *Educ:* Trinity Coll., Glenalmond; Keble Coll., Oxford; BA 1921. Served European War, 1914-18 (despatches four times, MC, DSO); operations in Waziristan, 1920-21; War of 1939-45 (OBE, Special Class Syrian Order of Merit); retired pay, 1946, Brig.

(hon.). General Sec., Catholic Marriage Advisory Council, 1948-50; Mem. Home Office Marriage Guidance Training Board, 1949-51; Chm., British Cttee and Mem. of Carnegie Council Internat. Union of Family Organisations, 1952-57, Vice-Pres., 1957-63. *Publications:* Frere of Suffolk and Norfolk, 1275-1965; sundry political and economic papers on the Middle East. *Address:* Redthorne, Yateley, Hants. *[Died 9 July 1974.*

FRESNAY, Pierre, (Pierre Laudenbach); French actor; *b* Paris, 4 April 1897. *Educ:* Lycée Henri-IV; Conservatoire de Paris. *Plays include:* Classiques, Marius, Vient de paraître, Léocadia, L'Hermine, Noë, Trois Valses, Du côté de chez Proust, Auprès de ma blonde, Les Œufs de l'autruche, Hyménée, Mon Faust, Le Neveu de Rameau, La Guerre civile, L'Idée fixe, Machiavel et Montesquieu, La Tour d'Einstein, On ne sait jamais, etc. *Films:* Marius, Fanny, La Dame aux Camélias, Koenigsmark, La Grande Illusion, Le Corbeau, Le Voyageur sans bagages, Monsieur Vincent, Barry, Dieu a besoin des hommes, Il est minuit, Docteur Schweitzer, Le Défroqué, The Aristocrats, Le Grand-patron, L'Homme aux clefs d'or, La Millième fenêtre, Les Vieux de la vieille, etc. Television: Le Neveu de Rameau, L'Idée fixe, Mon Faust, Tête d'horloge. Prize, Best Actor, Venice Biennale, 1947; Prix Féminin du Cinema, 1949. *Address:* 8 bis, Rue Saint-James, 92 Neuilly-sur-Seine (Seine), France. *[Died 9 Jan. 1975.*

FRESSANGES, Air Marshal Sir Francis Joseph, KBE 1955; CB 1945; idc, psa; RAF retired; *b* 27 Feb. 1902; *s* of Capt. G. Fressanges; *m* 1930, Joyce Helen Broadway; *m* Margaret Gordon Thomson. *Educ:* Royal Air Force Coll., Cranwell. Commissioned RAF 1923; Squadron Leader, 1936; Wing Commander, 1939; commanded Flying Boat Squadron in Battle of Atlantic, Jan. 1940-March 1941 (despatches); Group Capt. 1941; attached US Fleet, March-Sept. 1941 (US Legion of Merit); Dep. Dir of Overseas Operations, 1941-43; Air Commodore, 1943; Dir of Overseas Operations, 1943; AOC 47 Group, RAF, 1944-45; Dir of Operations, Air Ministry, 1946-48; idc 1949; Air Officer Commanding British Forces, Aden, 1950-52; Asst Chief of the Air Staff (Intelligence), 1952-54; Air Marshal, 1955; C-in-C FEAF and British Mil. Adviser to SEATO, 1954-57; retired; *Recreations:* tennis, golf, riding, fencing. *Address:* Blue Hayes, Bahati, Box 136, Nakuru, Kenya; c/o Coutts & Co., 1 Cadogan Place, SW1. *Clubs:* Royal Air Force; Jockey Club of Kenya. *[Died 17 Oct. 1975.*

FREUND, Sir Otto K.; *see* Kahn-Freund.

FREW, Air Vice-Marshal Sir Matthew Brown, KBE 1948; CB 1943; DSO 1918; MC; *b* 7 April 1895; *s* of Henry Lorimer Frew and Annie Brown; *m* 1921, Gertrude Fairley; one *s. Educ:* Hutcheson's Grammar Sch., Glasgow. Joined HLI, 1914; transferred RFC, 1916; Capt., 1917; Squadron Leader, 1927; Wing Comdr, 1934; Group Capt., 1938; Acting Air Vice-Marshal, 1942; Temp. Air Vice-Marshal, 1943; Air Commodore, 1943; Air Vice-Marshal, 1945; retired, 1948. Served European War, 1914-18 (DSO, MC and bar, Air Force Cross, Italian Silver Medal for Military Valour); Northern Kurdistan, 1931-32 (Bar to DSO). Comdr Royal Order of George I of Greece with swords, 1943; Belgian Military Cross, 1st Class, 1945. *Recreation:* Golf. *Address:* 7 Finsbury Court Arcade, Pretoria, South Africa. *Club:* Pretoria (Pretoria, SA). *[Died 28 May 1974.*

FREW, Engineer Rear-Adm. Sir Sydney (Oswell), KBE 1949; CB 1946. Joined Royal Navy, 1905; Engineer Captain, 1939; Engineer Rear-Admiral, 1945; retired list, 1950. Served European War, 1914-19. Grand Officer Order of Orange Nassau with Swords (Netherlands). *Address:* 3 Goldhurst Mansions, Goldhurst Terrace, NW6. *[Died 10 June 1972.*

FREWEN, Adm. Sir John Byng, GCB 1969 (KCB 1964; CB 1961); idc; Commander-in-Chief, Naval Home Command, 1969-70; *b* 28 March 1911; *s* of Capt. E. L. Frewen RN, Northiam, Sussex; *m* 1937, June Gwendolen Cazenove. Rear-Adm. 1959. Chief of Staff to the C-in-C, Home Fleet, Aug. 1959-April 1961; Flag Officer 2nd-in-Comd, Far East Station, 1961-62; Vice-Chief of the Naval Staff, 1963-65. C-in-C, Home Fleet and NATO C-in-C, Allied Forces, Eastern Atlantic, 1965-67; Nato C-in-C, Channel, 1966-67; C-in-C Portsmouth, 1967-69. Principal Naval ADC to the Queen, 1968-70. *Address:* Clench Green, Northiam, East Sussex. *T:* Northiam 2279. *[Died 30 Aug. 1975.*

FREWER, Rt. Rev. John, CBE 1957; *b* Fulletby Rectory, Horncastle, Lincs, 1 Nov. 1883; 3rd *s* of late Rev. Canon G. E. Frewer; unmarried. *Educ:* King's Sch., Canterbury; Lincoln Theological Coll. Deacon, 1908; Priest, 1909; Curate of St Nicholas, Skirbeck, 1908-11; Domestic Chaplain to Bishop of

Bunbury, West Australia, 1911-16; Priest-in-Charge, Yarloop, 1912-13; Rector of St David's, South Bunbury, 1913-16; Priest of Brotherhood of St Boniface, Williams, Diocese of Bunbury, 1916-29; Warden of the Brotherhood, 1919-29; Hon. Chaplain to Bishop of Bunbury, 1918-29; Canon of Bunbury, 1922-29; Bishop of North-West Australia, 1929-65. *Address:* Flat 4, Riley House, 20 Excelsior Street, Shenton Park, Western Australia 6008, Australia. *Club:* Royal Over-Seas League.
[Died 7 Dec. 1974.

FREYBERG, Lady, GBE 1953 (OBE 1943), (**Barbara Freyberg**); *d* of late Sir Herbert Jekyll, KCMG, and Lady Jekyll, DBE; *m* 1st, 1911, Hon. Francis McLaren, MP (killed in action, 1917); two *s*; 2nd, 1922, 1st Baron Freyberg, VC, GCMG, KCB, KBE, DSO (*d* 1963); one *s. Educ:* at home. Served during War of 1939-45 with Welfare Branch of New Zealand Div. in Egypt, Italy and London; Africa Star; 1939-45 Medal; Defence Medal; New Zealand War Medal; despatches, 1943. DGStJ. *Address:* 65 Chelsea Square, SW3. *T:* 01-352 5168. *Club:* Bath.
[Died 24 Sept. 1973.

FRIML, Rudolf; pianist and composer; *b* Prague, Czechoslovakia, 7 Dec. 1879. *Educ:* Prague Conservatoire of Music. Studied Piano with Prof. Jiranek, composition with Antonin Dvořák. Went to America 1904 for concert tour, playing his own piano concerto with New York Symphony Orchestra, Walter Damrosch, conducting. Composed and published several thousand piano, violin, 'cello, organ compositions. Among many musical comedies and operettas are: Firefly, High Jinks, Katinka, You're in Love, Gloriana, Tumble In, Sometimes, Blue Kitten, White Eagle, June Love, Little Whopper, Luanna, Peasant Girl, Annina, Bird of Paradise, Kitty Darling, Rose Marie, Vagabond King, Three Musketeers. His latest compositions are: Chinese Suite, Arabian Suite (Chinese operetta Sing Song Girl, two piano concertos and Round the World Symphony in manuscripts). When not travelling, resides in Hollywood. *Address:* American Society of Composers, Authors and Publishers, 575 Madison Avenue, New York.
[Died 12 Nov. 1972.

FRISCH, Otto Robert, OBE 1946; DSc; FRS 1948; Jacksonian Professor of Natural Philosophy, University of Cambridge, 1947-72, now Professor Emeritus; *b* Vienna, Austria, 1 Oct. 1904; *o s* of late Dr Justinian Frisch and Auguste Meitner; *m* 1951, Ursula, *o d* of Karl Blau; one *s* one *d. Educ:* Vienna Univ. (Dr phil 1926). Scientific research in Berlin, Hamburg, London, Copenhagen, Birmingham, Liverpool, Oxford, Los Alamos, Harwell, Cambridge. *Publications:* Meet the Atoms, 1947 (London); Atomic Physics Today, 1961 (New York); Working with Atoms, 1965 (Leicester); The Nature of Matter, 1972 (London); What Little I Remember, 1979 (Cambridge); numerous papers on various topics in atomic and nuclear physics, in scientific periodicals. *Recreations:* piano, table tennis. *Address:* Trinity College, Cambridge. *[Died 22 Sept. 1979.*

FRISCH, Prof. Ragnar Anton Kittil; Norwegian economist; formerly Director of Research, Economic Institute, Oslo University (Professor of Economics, 1931-71, now Emeritus); *b* 3 March 1895. *m* 1st, Marie Smedal (decd); one *d*; 2nd, 1953, Astrid Johannessen. *Educ:* Univ. of Oslo. Visiting Professor: Yale Univ., 1930; Sorbonne, 1933. Fellow and one of Founders of Econometric Soc., 1931. Chief Ed. of Econometrica, 1933-35. Chm., first session of Econ. and Employment Commn of UN. Member: Internat. Statistical Inst., 1937-; Norske Videnskapsakademi i Oslo; Kungl. Humanistiska Vetenskapssamfundet i Lund; Kungl. Svenska Vetenskapsakademien; Accademia Naz. dei Lincei, Rome (Antonio Feltrinelli Prize, 1961); Hon. Member: Amer. Acad. of Arts and Sciences; Amer. Economic Assoc.; Corresp. Mem., Royal Economic Soc.; Foreign Mem., American Philosophical Soc.; Advising Mem., Acad. of Human Rights, Rome; Fellow: Econometric Soc.; Inst. of Math. Statistics, USA; Corresp. Fellow, British Academy; Hon. Fellow, Royal Statistical Soc. Schumpeter Prize, Harvard, 1955; (jointly) Prize in Economics to the memory of Alfred Nobel, 1969. Hon. Doctorates: Handelshögskolan i Stockholm; Copenhagen; Stockholm Univ.; Hon. DSc: Cambridge, 1967; Birmingham, 1970. *Address:* Slemdalsveien 98, Vinderen, Oslo 3, Norway.
[Died 31 Jan. 1973.

FROOD, Hester; *b* 1882; *d* of James N. Frood, Topsham, Devon; *m* 1921, F. Gwynne Evans. *Educ:* Exeter High Sch. Studied Art at Exeter and Paris; exhibited at the RA, New English Art Club, International, etc; Etchings, Drypoints and Water Colour Drawings in: British Museum (presented additionally 12 drawings and one etching, 1966); South Kensington; Ashmolean Museum, Oxford; and various Municipal Galls. One-man shows at Colnaghi's: 1925, 1930, 1943, 1946, 1949; at Royal Memorial

Museum, Exeter, 1957; also (from 1925) in the USA, Scotland, provinces, etc. *Address:* Bradfield Place, Bradfield, near Manningtree, Essex.   [*Died* 10 *May* 1971.

FROST, Edward Granville Gordon, CBE 1953; JP; MA (Hon.); *b* 18 Feb. 1886; *s* of late Col H. Frost; *m* 1920, Dorothy Alice (*d* 1963), *d* of late Rev. J. A. Fletcher, Fransham, Norfolk; one *d. Educ:* Felsted Sch.; Pembroke Coll., Cambridge. 2nd Lieut 2 Volunteer Bn Cambs Regt, retired 1920; Commandant Red Cross to 1920. CC 1928, CA 1937-, Cambridge; Chm. Ely Dioc. Bd of Finance, 1937-63; JP Cambs, 1924-; Vice-Chm. Cambs Quarter Sessions, 1948-61; Chm. Cambridge County Council, 1949-May 1952; High Sheriff of Hunts and Cambs, 1957-58. Fellow, Corporation of SS Mary and Nicholas (Woodard Schs), 1969-. Defence Medal. *Recreations:* music, gardening. *Address:* 29 Barrow Road, Cambridge. *T:* 50543. *Clubs:* Cambridge County, University Union (Cambridge).   [*Died* 9 *Jan.* 1971.

FROWEN, Brig. John Harold, DSO 1941; OBE 1941; RA; retired; *b* 14 Sept. 1898; *s* of Fraser Frowen and Elizabeth Mary, *d* of late Sir John Heffernan, KCB, RN. *Educ:* privately; RMA Woolwich. 2nd Lieut RA, 1916; Capt. 1929; Major 1938; Temp. Lieut-Col 1940; Col, 1946; Brig., 1949; served in France and Flanders, 1917-19; India, 1919-26; Home, 1926-29; employed in mission to Egyptian Army, 1939-40; served Western Desert campaigns, Greece, Crete, etc (prisoner); repatriated UK 1943; BRA Southern Army, India Command, 1943-44; Comdt Artillery Sch., India, 1944-47; Comdr AA Bde, UK, 1947-51; loaned Pakistan Army, 1951-52; retd 1952. Sec. RA Institution, 1952-58; Sec. RA Printing Press, 1958-64. *Recreation:* played in Wimbledon lawn tennis tournament, 1929, 1930, 1931. *Address:* 29 Morden Road, SE3. *T:* 01-852 5308. *Club:* Army and Navy.
[*Died* 9 *Dec.* 1980.

FRY, Major Sir Leslie Alfred Charles, KCMG 1957 (CMG 1955); OBE 1947 (MBE 1944); *b* 17 April 1908; *o s* of late Capt. and Mrs A. A. Fry; *m* 1st, 1935; one *s* one *d*; 2nd, Marian Elizabeth Penelope Bentley, *o d* of late Norman Bentley, Pannal Hall, Pannal, Yorks. *Educ:* Royal Masonic Sch.; Royal Military College, Sandhurst. First commission, 1928; served with 4th PWO Gurkha Rifles; transferred Indian Political Service, 1933; Under-Sec., External Affairs Dept, Govt of India, 1941; Dep. Sec. 1946; retired from IPS and entered HM Foreign Service, 1947; 1st Sec., UK High Commission in India, 1947-48; Foreign Office, 1949-51; Counsellor, HM Embassy, Lisbon, 1951-53; Counsellor, Eastern Dept, FO, 1953-55; Minister to Hungary, 1955-59; Ambassador to Indonesia, 1959-63; Ambassador to Brazil, 1963-66. Grand Cross, Order of Southern Cross, Brazil, 1968. *Address:* Gorehill House, Gorehill, near Petworth, West Sussex. *T:* Petworth 42450. *Club:* Naval and Military.
[*Died* 21 *Oct.* 1976.

FRY, Sir (Theodore) Penrose, 3rd Bt *cr* 1894; *b* 6 April 1892; *e s* of Sir John Pease Fry, 2nd Bt and Margaret Theodora (*d* 1941), *d* of Francis Edward Fox, JP; *S* father, 1957; *m* 1924, Sheila Kaye-Smith (*d* 1956); no *c. Educ:* Winchester; King's Coll., Cambridge. Commission in 5th Durham LI (T), 1914-18; Anglican Clergyman, 1921-29; became RC, 1929. Served in National Fire Service, War of 1939-45. *Publications:* The Church Surprising, 1932; The Making of a Layman, 1938. *Heir:* *b* John Nicholas Pease Fry [*b* 23 Oct. 1897; *m* 1927, Helen Murray, *d* of late William Gibson Bott, MRCS, JP; one *d* (and one *d* decd)]. *Address:* c/o Barclay's Bank Ltd, High Street, Battle, Sussex.   [*Died* 6 *Aug.* 1971.

FRYE, Jack, CBE 1972; Chairman: B. Elliott Group of Companies, since 1955; Rotaflex (Gt Britain) Ltd and subsidiary cos, since 1962; Goldfields Industrial Corporation of South Africa and subsidiaries, since 1967; British Iron and Steel Consumers' Council, since 1967; *b* 2 Oct. 1914; 3rd *s* of late Hugo Frye and Beatrice Elliott; *m* 1937, Daphne Aron (marr. diss. 1956), *d* of late Eugene Aron; two *s* two *d*; *m* 1958, Lalita Rudra, *d* of late Prof. Rudra; *m* 1971, Marcella Scarafia. *Educ:* Badingham Coll., Leatherhead; Loughborough Univ. of Technology. Joined B. Elliott & Co. Ltd, 1932, Man. Dir, 1949. Governor: St Mary's Hospital, Paddington, 1972-73; Central Sch. of Art and Design, 1974-. Officer, Ordre du Mérite Français d'Outre Mer, 1965. *Recreations:* sailing, fishing, ski-ing. *Address:* 9 Swan Walk, SW3; Shelleys, Guestling, East Sussex. *Clubs:* Roehampton, Royal Automobile; Royal Corinthian Yacht, Royal Thames Yacht.   [*Died* 7 *Dec.* 1975.

FULLARD, George, ARA 1973; ARCA; Head of Department of Sculpture, Chelsea School of Art, since 1963; *b* 15 Sept. 1923; *s* of George Fullard and Henrietta Fullard (*née* Mathias); *m* 1946, Irena Corcoran. *Educ:* Sheffield Coll. of Art; Royal Coll. of Art. Served War, 17/21 Lancers, 1942-44. Commenced work as a practising artist, 1947; work in mixed exhibns incl. Arts Council

Contemporary Sculpture Exhibns, 1958-62; Battersea Park Open Air Sculpture Exhibns, 1963 and 1966; Painting and Sculpture of a Decade, Tate Gall., 1964; Pittsburgh Internat. Exhibn, 1964-67; British Sculpture in the Sixties, Tate Gall., 1965; Six Sheffield Artists, City of Sheffield Art Gall., 1966; British Sculptors, 1972, Royal Academy, 1972. *One man exhibitions:* Woodstock Gall., 1958; Gallery One, 1961; Marlborough New London Gall., 1964; Park Square Gall., Leeds, 1972; *Work in permanent collections:* Arts Council of Great Britain, Contemporary Arts Soc.; Nat. Gall. of S Australia; Lannan Foundn, Chicago; Chantrey Bequest; Ferens Gall., Hull, etc. *Recreations:* walking, shooting. *Address:* 11 Stanley Studios, Park Walk, SW10 0AE. *T:* 01-352 9996. *Club:* Chelsea Arts.   [*Died* 25 *Dec.* 1973.

FULLBROOK-LEGGATT, Maj.-Gen. Charles St Quentin Outen; *see* Leggatt.

FULLER, Leonard John, ROI 1932; RCA 1939; artist, portrait painter; Painter; Principal, St Ives School of Painting; Founder Member and First Chairman of Penwith Society of Arts in Cornwall; Hon. Vice-President, St Ives Society of Artists; Hon. Mem., Torbay Guild of Artists; *b* 11 Oct. 1891; *yr s* of late John Haire and Mary A. Fuller; *m* 1917, Marjorie Florence, 2nd *d* of late Tom Mostyn, ROI; one *s. Educ:* Dulwich Coll.; Royal Academy Schs (British Institution Scholar). Exhibited first picture Royal Academy, 1919; most prominent works include Silver and Blue, 1922, My Son John, 1923, Silver and Gold, 1929, Diana Fishwick, 1931, Jack Hobbs, 1934; Autumn Sunshine, 1933, purchased for permanent collection by city of Newport (Mon); We Want The King, RA 1938; Studio Haphazard (RA 1943), purchased by City of Newport; Moffat Lindner, RWS (RA 1944); Mr Gall (RA 1944); The Colourful Years (RA 1945), etc.; Very Rev. W. R. Matthews, 1957, purchased by the Dean and Chapter for the Chapter House, St Paul's; On the Verandah, 1960, by Plymouth Corporation Art Gallery; Sirens, by Education Cttee for Cornwall, 1963. Mrs Guthrie Smith for St Mary's Hosp., London; Col Sir Herbert Shiner, for Sussex CC; Lord Tredegar, Ald. Knight, for Newark Town Hall; F. G. Ormond, for Dean and Chapter, Truro Cathedral. Paris Salon, Artistes Français, Médaille d'argent 1927, Mention honorable 1931; Teacher of painting, St John's Wood Art Sch., 1922-32; Asst Art Master, Dulwich Coll., 1927-38; served European War, 1914-18, 10th Bn Royal Fusiliers, service in France, commissioned to East Surrey Regt 1915, transferring to Machine Gun Corps, rising to temporary rank of Captain; Home Guard, 1940-44. Rotarian. *Address:* 3 Seagull House, The Wharf, St Ives, Cornwall. *T:* St Ives 6826. *TA:* St Ives, Cornwall. *Club:* Chelsea Arts.   [*Died* 24 *July* 1973.

FULLERTON, Brigadier John Parke, DSO 1932; *b* Cawnpore, 8 Sept. 1894; *s* of late Major T. W. A. Fullerton, IMS; *g s* of Rev. Alexander Fullerton; *m* 1st, 1917, Georgina (*d* 1942), *d* of J. Hunter, Sligo; 2nd, 1945, Elizabeth, *d* of Lt-Col R. J. Marks, IMS; one *s* one *d. Educ:* Wellington Coll.; RMC, Sandhurst. KIC Commissioned 1914; entered 41st Dogras, now 3rd Bn The Dogra Regt; served Egypt and Mesopotamia, 1915-16 (wounded, despatches 1919, for services in India); Afghanistan, 1919; Mahsud, 1920; Waziristan, 1919-21; NWF, 1930-31 (DSO, despatches); NWF, 1938-39 (wounded, despatches); Area Commander Jullundur, 1941-44; Services Resettlement Liaison Officer, Punjab, etc., 1944-46; chief Civil Liaison Officer, Northern Area, 1946; Dir of Resettlement, GHQ, India, 1946-47; retired, 1947. *Address:* Bridge House, Hele, near Taunton, Somerset. *T:* Bradford-on-Tone 296.   [*Died* 19 *March* 1977.

FULTON, Alexander Strathern, CBE 1953; DLitt 1941; MA; Keeper, Department of Oriental Printed Books and Manuscripts, British Museum, 1940-53, retd; *b* Beith, Ayrshire, 18 Feb. 1888; *y s* of late James Graham Fulton, Craigellan, Beith, and Eleanor Strathern. *Educ:* Spier's Sch.; Glasgow Univ. MA (First Class Hons in Semitic Langs), 1910; Cleland and Rae-Wilson Gold Medallist; John Clark scholar; Asst Prof. of Semitic Langs, Edinburgh Univ., 1910-11; entered British Museum, 1911; Dep. Keeper, Dept of Oriental Printed Books and Manuscripts, 1936. At various times Examiner in Arabic and Hebrew for Glasgow and Edinburgh Univs, in Arabic for London and Manchester Univs, and Additional Lecturer in Arabic at the School of Oriental Studies, London Univ.; Fellow of Royal Asiatic Society. *Publications:* Supplementary Catalogue of Arabic Printed Books in the British Museum (with A. G. Ellis), 1926; Seond Supplementary Vol. (with Dr M. Lings), 1959; Vol. III of the Catalogue of Arabic Printed Books in the British Museum (Indexes), 1935; Facsimile of al-Kitab-al-Bari, edited with introduction, 1933; History of Hayy Ibn Yaqzan, Ockley's translation, revised and partly rewritten, with an introduction, 1929; articles in various periodicals. *Recreation:* walking. *Address:* 102 The Promenade, Peacehaven, East Sussex.   [*Died* 25 *June* 1976.

FULTON, Prof. Forrest; Professor of Virology in the University of London at The London School of Hygiene and Tropical Medicine since 1959; *b* 13 Aug. 1913; *o s* of late Leonard Jessopp Fulton, solicitor. *Educ:* Westminster; Pembroke Coll., Oxford. Read Law Oxford, 1931-33 then chose scientific career and studied Animal Physiology for remaining two years; BA 1935, MA 1939 (Oxon.); clinical work at London Hosp. BM, BCh, 1939, DM 1945 (Oxon.). Emergency Public Health Service, Oxford, 1939; worked for Med. Research Council on Typhus vaccines, London, 1942; after short period at Yale Univ., returned to London Univ. as Reader in Bacteriology and Immunology, 1949. FRCPath 1967. *Publications:* contrib. to Advances in Virus Research, Vol. V and many papers in journals concerned with microbiology and immunology. *Address:* London School of Hygiene and Tropical Medicine, Keppel Street, WC1.   *[Died* 27 Dec. 1971.

FURNESS, Sir Christopher, 2nd Bt, *cr* 1913; *s* of 1st Bt and Eleanor (*d* 1936), *d* of Matthew Forster, CE, of Mount Brown, South Australia; *b* 18 Oct. 1900; *S* father, 1914; *m* 1930, Flower (OBE 1970), *d* of late Col G. C. Roberts; three *s* one *d. Educ:* Charterhouse; Pembroke Coll., Cambridge. Vice-Pres. Royal Northumberland Yacht Club. Served RNVR European War, 1914-18, 1918-19, and War of 1939-45, 1940-45. *Heir: s* Stephen Roberts Furness [*b* 10 Oct. 1933; *m* 1961, Mary, *d* of Jack Fitzroy Cann, Cullompton, Devon; one *s* one *d.* Lieut, Royal Navy, retd]. *Recreation:* reading. *Address:* Netherbyres, Eyemouth, Berwickshire. *T:* 337; Glebe Cottage, Longformacus, Duns, Berwickshire. *T:* Longformacus 256. *Clubs:* Royal Over-Seas League; Caledonian (Edinburgh).   *[Died* 21 June 1974.

FURNESS, Stephen Noel, Barrister-at-Law; MA; *b* 18 Dec. 1902; 2nd *s* of late Sir Stephen W. Furness, Bt, and Eleanor Lady Furness. *Educ:* Charterhouse; Oriel Coll., Oxford. Called to Bar, Middle Temple, 1927; Contested Hartlepools (Liberal) 1929, Sunderland (L Nat) 1945; MP (L Nat) Sunderland, 1935-45; Parliamentary Private Sec. to Sir J. Simon, 1936-37; Asst Government Whip, 1937-38; Junior Lord of the Treasury, 1938-40; 1st Bn London Irish Rifles, Major; late Chairman, Furness Shipbuilding Co. Ltd. *Address:* Otterington Hall, Northallerton, Yorks. *Clubs:* Brooks's, Reform.   *[Died* 14 April 1974.

FURNESS-SMITH, Sir Cecil, Kt 1949; QC (Tanganyika Territory); JP; Chief Justice, Trinidad and Tobago, 1946-53; *b* 20 March 1890; *s* of Rev. George Furness-Smith, late of Riverdale Road, Twickenham Park, and Elizabeth Hayes, Edmondstown Park, Rathfarnham, Co. Dublin; *m* 1921, Mary Kathleen, *d* of John Price Hargreaves, The Moorlands, Oxton, Birkenhead; one *s. Educ:* Birkenhead Sch.; St John's Coll., Cambrdige. Colonial Administrative Service, Gold Coast 1914; called to Bar, Inner Temple, 1923; Colonial Legal Service, Crown Counsel, Gold Coast, 1925; Solicitor-Gen., Tanganyika Territory, 1932; Attorney-Gen., Zanzibar, 1936; Attorney-Gen., Tanganyika Territory, 1940. JP County of Devon, 1953. *Recreations:* golf and bridge. *Address:* Drummetts Lodge, Torrington, N Devon. *TA:* Torrington, Devon. *T:* Torrington 2165.   *[Died* 15 Aug. 1971.

FURSE, Rear-Adm. (John) Paul (Wellington), CB 1958; OBE 1946; CEng; FIMechE; FLS; retired; *b* 13 Oct. 1904; *s* of late Charles Furse, artist, and late Dame Katharine, GBE, RRC, Dir, WRNS; *m* 1929, Cicely Rathbone; one *s. Educ:* Osborne; Dartmouth; RN Engineering Coll., Keyham. Service in Submarines, etc, 1927-39; Asst Naval Attaché, Europe and the Americas, 1940-43; 5th and 4th Submarine Flotillas, 1943-46; Admiralty, 1947, Dir of Aircraft Maintenance and Repair, Admiralty, 1955-58; Dir-Gen. of the Aircraft Dept, Admiralty, 1958-59; retired, 1959. Botanical expeditions in Turkey and Iran, 1960, 1962; Afghanistan, 1964, 1966. VMH 1965. *Publications:* articles on flora of the Middle East in RHS Jl and Year Book, British Iris Soc. Year Book, Alpine Garden Soc. Bulletins. *Recreations:* mountains, ski-ing, botany, painting. *Address:* Hegg Hill, Smarden, Kent. *T:* Smarden 229. *Club:* Army and Navy.   *[Died* 8 Oct. 1978.

FURSE, Major Sir Ralph Dolignon, KCMG 1941 (CMG 1935); DSO 1918; Hon. DCL Oxford 1949; King Edward's Horse; *b* 1887; *s* of John Henry Monsell Furse; *m* 1914, Margaret Cecilia, *d* of late Sir Henry Newbolt, CH; two *s* one *d* (and one *d* decd). *Educ:* Eton; Balliol Coll., Oxford (MA). Asst Private Sec., Colonial Office, to Mr Harcourt, 1910-14; served European War, 1914-18 (despatches twice, DSO and bar); Asst Private Sec at the Colonial Office to Viscount Milner, 1919, Mr Churchill, 1921, the Duke of Devonshire, 1922; Private Sec. to Mr J. H. Thomas, 1924; to Mr Amery, 1924; to Lord Passfield, 1929. Dir of Recruitment, Colonial Service, 1931-48; Adviser to Sec. of State for Colonies on Training Courses for Colonial Service, 1948-50. *Publication:* Aucuparius: Recollections of a Recruiting

Officer, 1962. *Address:* Halsdon, Dolton, Winkleigh, N Devon. *T:* Dolton 214. *Club:* Savile.   *[Died* 1 Oct. 1973.

FURSE, Roger Kemble, RDI 1949; freelance theatre and film designer; painter; illustrator; *b* 11 Sept. 1903; *s* of late Lieut-Gen. Sir William Furse, KCB, KCMG; *m* 1936, Alice Margaret (*née* Watts) (marriage dissolved, 1951); no *c*; *m* 1952, Ines Sylvia Perg. *Educ:* St George's Choir Sch., Windsor Castle; Eton; Slade Sch. of Fine Arts. Worked in Paris, 1924-27, in USA, 1927-31 (commercial work, portraits, etc.); returned to London, 1931, since when has been designing for Theatre; and later, 1943, for films. *Films include:* Henry V, 1944; Odd Man Out, 1946; Hamlet, 1948; Ivanhoe, 1952; Knights of the Round Table, 1953; Helen of Troy, 1954; Richard III; The Prince and the Showgirl, 1956; St Joan; Bonjour Tristesse, 1957; Spartacus (in Hollywood), 1958-59; The Roman Spring of Mrs Stone, 1961; The Road to Hong Kong, 1961. *Plays* for which he has designed settings and costumes include: Victoria Regina, Gate, 1936; Othello, Old Vic, 1938; Spring Meeting, Ambassadors, 1938; Hamlet (mod. dress), Old Vic, 1938; Goodness How Sad!, Vaudeville, 1938; The Taming of the Shrew and Romeo and Juliet, Old Vic, 1939; Rebecca, Queen's, 1940; King Lear, Old Vic, 1940; Arsenic and Old Lace, Strand, 1942; Uncle Vanya, Westminster, 1943; The Duchess of Malfi, Haymarket, 1945; Henry IV (I and II), Old Vic Co., New, 1945; Portrait in Black, Piccadilly, 1946; (décor of) Venus Observed, St James's, 1949; Twelfth Night for Old Vic season, 1950-51; settings for Antony and Cleopatra, and Caesar and Cleopatra, St James's, 1951; Verdi's Don Carlos opera, Sadler's Wells, 1951; The Mortimer Touch, Duke of York's, 1952; settings for: Romeo and Juliet, for Old Vic, Edinburgh, 1952; The Italian Straw Hat, The Merchant of Venice, for Old Vic, 1952; The Mouse Trap, Ambassadors; Macbeth, Stratford Season, 1955; The Egg, Saville Theatre, 1957; Duel of Angels, 1958; Once More with Feeling, 1959; Look after Lulu, 1960; The Tumbler, New York, 1960; The Broken Heart, Chichester Festival Theatre, 1962; The Workhouse Donkey, Chichester Festival Theatre, 1963. Served War of 1939-45; joined Navy 1940; commnd in RNVR, 1941. *Recreation:* friends. *Address:* c/o National Westminster Bank Ltd, Tavistock Square, WC1.   *[Died* 19 Aug. 1972.

FUSSELL, Edward Coldham, CMG 1954; Governor, Reserve Bank of New Zealand, 1948-62; *b* Auckland, 16 July 1901; *s* of Rev. James Coldham Fussell; *m* 1935, Eileen, *d* of C. S. Plank; three *s* two *d. Educ:* King's Coll., Auckland; Victoria University Coll. (BA). With National Bank of NZ, 1919-34; Head Office, 1930. Rep. Associated Banks at Monetary Commn, 1934. With Reserve Bank of NZ, 1934-62; Asst to Governors, 1939; Dep.-Gov., 1941-48; rep. Reserve Bank on Royal Commn, 1955. Has attended financial confs in UK and USA, including Bretton Woods Conf., 1944. Served HG, War of 1939-45. Mem., Senate and Grants Cttee, University of NZ, 1951-60; Hon. Treas, University of NZ, 1954-60. *Recreation:* golf. *Address:* 5 Taumaru Avenue, Lowry Bay, Wellington, New Zealand. *T:* 684-686. *Clubs:* Wellington, Rotary International; Heretaunga Golf, Wellington Racing.   *[Died* 1 May 1978.

FYFFE, Lt-Gen. Sir Richard (Alan), KBE 1969 (OBE 1950); CB 1964; DSO 1945; MC 1943; *b* 12 Aug. 1912; *s* of Alan Herbert Fyffe and Veronica Fyffe; *m* 1937, Diana Gwyneth, *d* of Major and Mrs J. G. Moore-Gwyn, Clayton Court, Liss, Hants; three *d. Educ:* Winchester Coll.; RMC Sandhurst. 2nd Lieut The Rifle Bde, 1932, Lieut 1935; seconded for service with RAF, 1938-40; GSO3, War Office, 1940 (Captain); Student, Staff Coll., 1941; GSO2, HQ Army Co-op. Comd 1941 (Major); Regimental duty with The Rifle Bde in N Africa and Italy, 1942-45; GSO1 (DS), Staff Coll., 1945; Jt Services Staff Coll., 1947; GSO1 (Plans) FAR ELF, 1948; AAG War Office, 1950 (Bt Lieut-Col); Regtl Duty with The Rifle Bde, 1952, comdg 1st Bn, 1953 (Lieut-Col); Comdg 11 Inf. Bde (BAOR), 1955 (Brig.); Dep. Mil. Sec., War Office, 1957; IDC, 1959; Brig. Army Air Corps, 1960; DPR, War Office, 1961-62; GOC 54 (E Anglian) Div./Dist, 1963-65; Comdr Brit. Army Staff, Mil. Mem. Brit. Defence Staff, and Mil. Attaché, Washington, 1965-67; Dir, Service Intelligence, MoD, 1967-68. Dep. CDS (Intelligence), MoD, 1968-71; retired 1971. Colonel Commandant: 3rd Bn The Royal Green Jackets, 1968-71; Intelligence Corps, 1969-. *Address:* Green Hailey Farm House, Princes Risborough, Aylesbury, Bucks. *T:* Princes Risborough 3894. *Club:* United Service & Royal Aero.
                                     [Died 24 Dec. 1972.

FYLER, Maj.-Gen. Arthur Roderic, CB 1964; OBE 1954; *b* 28 June 1911; *s* of late Adm. H. A. S. Fyler, CB, DSO, and late Mrs H. A. S. Fyler; *m* 1940, Anthea Mary de Fontaine Stratton, *d* of late Lt-Col F. C. G. Stratton, TD, Nairobi, Kenya; two *s* two *d. Educ:* Charterhouse. 2/Lieut (Sup. Res.) The Buffs, 1931-34; 2/Lieut Queen's Own Royal West Kent Regt, 1934. Served War of 1939-45: E Africa, British Somaliland, Abyssinia (King's

African Rifles), NW Europe; despatches 1940 and 1954. AQMG, HQ Land Forces, Hong Kong, 1950-52; OC 1st Bn Queen's Own Royal West Kent Regt, 1953-55; Comd 130 (West Country) Infantry Bde (TA), 1955-58; Dep. Adjt Gen., GHQ, FARELF, 1958-61; Dir of Army Personnel Administration, 1961-64, War Office and MoD (A); retired 1964; reemployed as a Civil Servant by MoD(A), retired 1976. Vice-Chm., Soc. for Protection of Animals in N Africa, 1972, Chm. 1973-; Advisory Dir, Internat. Soc. for Protection of Animals, 1975-; Mem. Council, World Fedn for the Protection of Animals, 1976-. Pres., Squash Rackets Assoc., 1975-; Vice-Pres., Kent Squash Rackets Assoc., 1976-. *Recreations:* watching games and sports, appreciation of fine arts, the turf. *Address:* Starlings, Beechwood Road, Beaconsfield, Bucks. *T:* Beaconsfield 3321. *Clubs:* Naval and Military; Devon Dumplings Cricket; Escorts Squash Rackets. *[Died 15 Feb. 1980.*

FYNES-CLINTON, David Osbert; *b* 25 Jan. 1909; *s* of late Prof. O. H. Fynes-Clinton, University Coll. of North Wales, Bangor; *m* 1st, 1947, Betty Lawrence; one *s*; 2nd, 1958, Herta Sernetz. *Educ:* Clifton; St John's Coll., Oxford. Entered Consular Service, 1931; Genoa, 1931; Cairo, 1933; Colon, Panama, 1935; La Paz, Bolivia, 1938; Rio de Janeiro, 1940; Luanda, Angola, 1947; Basle, 1949; Consul-Gen. at Tananarive, Madagascar, 1952; Zagreb 1956; retired 1957. Joined Staff of UN, 1958, retired 1970. *Address:* c/o United Nations, Geneva, Switzerland. *[Died 22 Feb. 1978.*

FYSH, Sir (Wilmot) Hudson, KBE 1953; DFC 1917; FRAeS, MInstT, FRGSA; Chairman Qantas Empire Airways Ltd, 1947-66 (Chairman and Managing Director, 1947-55; Managing Director Qantas Ltd, 1922-34, and Qantas Empire Airways Ltd, 1934-47); Past Member Executive Committee, IATA (President, 1961); Fellow British Interplanetary Society; *b* 7 Jan. 1895; *s* of Frederic Wilmot Fysh and Mary Reed; *m* 1924, Eleanor Elizabeth Dove; one *s* one *d*. *Educ:* Geelong Church of England Grammar Sch. Served European War, 1914-18; Trooper in 3rd Aust. LH Regt; Lieut 1st Aust MG Section, Lieut No 1 Sqdn AFC (despatches, DFC). A founder of Qantas Ltd, 1920. Surveyed (jointly) original air route across Australia from Longreach to Darwin for Ross Smith Flight, 1919; Pilot 1st official air mail service in Eastern Australia; formerly: Dep. Chm., Australian National Travel Assoc.; Chm. Qantas Wentworth Holdings Ltd. Hon. DEng Tasmania, 1971. *Publications:* Taming the North, 1934; Qantas Rising, 1965; Qantas at War, 1966; Round the Bend in the Stream, 1968; Wings to the World, 1970; general writer on Air Transport. *Recreations:* dry fly fishing and country pursuits. *Address:* Lyndhurst Gardens, 3 Rosemount Avenue, Woollahra, Sydney, NSW 2025, Australia. *T:* FB1586. *Clubs:* Royal Air Force; Australian, Royal Sydney Golf, Rotary (Sydney); Queensland (Brisbane); Royal Aero (NSW). *[Died 6 April 1974.*

G

GABIN, Jean, (Alexis Jean Montgorge); Médaille Militaire; Croix de Guerre; French film actor; *b* 17 May 1904; *m* 1st, 1925, Marie Louise Basset (marr. diss.); 2nd, 1933, Jeanne Marchin (marr. diss.); 3rd, 1949, Dominique Fournier; one *s* two *d. Educ:* Paris. *Films include:* Pépé le Moko, Bandera, Belle Equipe, Bête humaine, Bas Fonds, Grande Illusion, French Can-Can, Quai des brumes, Jour se lève, Gueule d'amour, Remorques, Marie du port, Au Delà des grilles, Minute de Vérité, Touchez pas au Grisbi, La Nuit est mon royaume, Crime and Punishment, Chnouf, En cas de Malheur; The Case of Dr Laurent; Maigret Tend Un Piège; Le Clochard; Un Singe en Hiver; Les Grandes Familles; Le Président; The Big Snatch; The Sicilian Clan; La Horse; Le Chat (Best Actor Award, Berlin Film Festival, 1971); Le Drapeau noir flotte sur la marmite; Le Tueur. *Recreation:* stock-breeder. *Address:* La Pichonnière, 61 Bonnefoi, France. *[Died 15 Nov. 1976.*

GABOR, Prof. Dennis, CBE 1970; FRS 1956; DSc London 1964; DrIng Berlin, FInstP, FIEE; Professor Emeritus of Applied Electron Physics in the University of London, at Imperial College of Science and Technology (Reader in Electronics, 1949-58; Professor, 1958-67; Senior Research Fellow, 1967-76); Staff Scientist, CBS Laboratories, Stamford, Connecticut, USA, since 1967; *b* 5 June 1900; *s* of Bertalan Gabor and Ady (*née* Kálmán); *m* 1936, Marjorie Louise Butler, Rugby, *d* of J. T. Kennard Butler. *Educ:* Technical Univ., Budapest; Technische Hochschule, Berlin-Charlottenburg. Asst, TH, Berlin, 1924-26;

Research associate, German Res. Assoc. for High Voltage Plants, 1926-27; Research engineer, Siemens & Halske AG, Berlin-Siemensstadt, 1927-33; Research engineer, British Thomson-Houston Co., Rugby, 1934-48. Inventor of holography. Hon. Member Hungarian Academy of Sciences, 1964; Foreign Associate, Nat. Acad. of Sciences, USA, 1973. Thomas Young Medal and Prize, RPS, 1967; Cristoforo Colombo Prize, Genoa, 1967; Rumford Medal, Royal Soc., 1968; Michelson Medal, Franklin Inst., 1968; Medal of Honor, IEEE, 1970; Semmelweiss Medal, American Hungarian Med. Assoc., 1970; Holweck Prize, French Physical Soc., 1971; Nobel Prize for Physics, 1971; George Washington Award, Amer.-Hungarian Studies Foundn, 1973. Hon. FCGI, 1977. Hon. DSc: Southampton, 1970; Delft Univ. of Technology, 1971; Surrey, 1972; Engineering Coll., Bridgeport, 1972; City, 1972; Columbia, NY, 1975; Hon. LLD London, 1973. *Publications:* The Electron Microscope, 1946; Electronic Inventions and their Impact on Civilisation. 1959; Inventing the Future, 1963; Innovations, Scientific, Technological and Social, 1970; The Mature Society, 1972. About 100 scientific papers on electrical transients, gas discharges, electron dynamics, communication theory and physical optics. *Recreations:* swimming, writing on social problems. *Address:* (summer) La Margioretta, Viale dei Gigli 21, 00040 Lavinio Lido (Roma), Italy; (winter) Department of Electrical Engineering, Imperial College, SW7 2BT. *Club:* Athenæum. *[Died 9 Feb. 1979.*

GABRIEL, William Bashall, MS London; FRCS; Honorary Consultant Surgeon: Royal Northern Hospital; St Mark's Hospital. *Educ:* Epsom Coll.; Middlesex Hosp., London Univ., MRCS, LRCP, 1916; MB, BS, 1916; FRCS, 1918; MS London, 1919. Formerly House Surg., St Mark's Hosp.; (temp.) Surgeon-Lieut, RN. FRSocMed. *Publications:* Principles and Practice of Rectal Surgery (5th edn), 1963; articles in med. jls. *Address:* Fenside, Ludham, Great Yarmouth, Norfolk. *[Died 11 Nov. 1975.*

GAGGERO, Sir George, Kt 1941; OBE 1934; JP; *b* 5 April 1897; *e s* of late Joseph Gaggero and Mary Dassoy; *m* 1925, Mabel, *o d* of late James Andrews-Speed, CBE, JP, and Mrs Speed; two *s* two *d. Educ:* in Gibraltar, Germany and England. Chairman, M. H. Bland & Co. Ltd, 1914-70 (now Hon. President), and Bland Group of cos incl. Rock Hotel Ltd, Bland Cable Cars Ltd, Bland Line, Thomas Mosley & Co. Ltd, and M. H. Bland & Co. (UK) Ltd. Chairman: Gibraltar Stevedoring Co. Ltd, 1948-59; Stevedoring & Cargo Handling Co. Ltd, 1959-65; Gibraltar Shipping Assoc., 1956-60. President: Gibraltar Airways Ltd. (Chm. 1947-66); Gibraltar Employers Fedn, 1928-40. Director: Gibraltar Transporters Ltd, 1930-66; Mackintosh & Co. (Gibraltar) Ltd, 1943-67; Gibraltar Chamber of Comm., 1918-22; Rock Fire Assurance Co. Ltd, 1927-52. City Councillor, 1921-24; Unofficial Mem. Exec. Council, 1924-30 and 1936-43; Chief ARP Warden, Gibraltar, 1938-40; Chairman: Bench of Justices, 1949-59; Bd Dist Comrs, 1940-43; Merchant Navy Welfare Cttee, 1942-47; Member: Public Service Commn, 1956-58; Merchant Navy Club Cttee, 1922-70; served on many local cttees apptd by the Governor in connection with public matters. Swedish Consul, 1939, Swedish Consul-Gen., 1954-66. FRSA; Coronation Medals, 1937 and 1953; Chevalier (1st Class), Royal Swedish Order of Vasa, 1947. *Address:* 75 Prince Edward's Road, Gibraltar. *Clubs:* Royal Thames Yacht; Royal Gibraltar Yacht. *[Died 4 Sept. 1978.*

GAHAN, Frank, QC 1952; Lieutenant Bailiff and Magistrate, Guernsey, 1957-64; *b* 7 July 1890; *y s* of Henry Beresford Gahan and Mary Jane (*née* Burriss), London, Ontario; *m* 1st, 1919, Adelaide Hildegarde Grenside (*d* 1931); 2nd, 1934, Madge Sturgeon; no *c. Educ:* Trinity Coll., Toronto; Trinity Coll., Oxford. Served in Overseas Military Forces of Canada, 1916-19. LLB London 1919; BCL Oxon 1920; MA Oxon 1920. Yarborough-Anderson Scholar, Inner Temple, 1920-25; barrister-at-law, Inner Temple, 1921. Vice-Principal, Working Men's Coll., 1936-45; Hon. Fellow, 1957. *Publications:* Law of Damages, 1935; ed 10th edn Mayne on Damages, 1927; articles in 14th edn Encyc. Brit. *Address:* Sausmarez Place, Les Gravées, St Peter Port, Guernsey. *[Died 25 May 1971.*

GAINFORD, 2nd Baron of Headlam, *cr* 1917; **Joseph Pease;** TD; retired Major, Lovat Scouts; *b* 8 March 1889; *o s* of 1st Baron and Ethel (*d* 1941), *o d* of Sir Henry Havelock-Allan, 1st Bt; *S* father, 1943; *m* 1921, Veronica, *o c* of Sir George Noble, 2nd Bt; three *s. Educ:* Eton. *Heir:* s Hon. Joseph Edward Pease [*b* 25 Dec. 1921; *m* 1953, Margaret Theophila Radcliffe, *d* of late H. E. G. Tyndale, Winchester Coll. and of Mrs Tyndale, 60 Lansdowne Road, W11; two *d*]. *Address:* Duntaynish, Tayvallich, Argyll. *T:* Tayvallich 275. *[Died 23 Sept. 1971.*

GAINSBOROUGH, Hugh, MD, FRCP; Consulting Physician to St George's Hospital, since 1959; *b* 16 June 1893; *m* 1926, Maia Pilley (*d* 1939). *Educ:* Cambridge Univ.; St George's Hosp. Medical Sch. MA Cambridge 1919; MB, ChB, 1921, MD 1928; MRCS 1917; FRCP 1929. Late Examiner in Medicine, Conjoint Board and University of London. Formerly: Physician St George's Hosp., and London Jewish Hospital; Dir of Medical Unit, St George's Hosp. Medical Sch. Fellow Royal Soc. Med.; Member: Biochemical Soc.; Association of Physicians. *Publications:* Principles of Hospital Design (with John Gainsborough), 1964; articles in Quar. Jl Med., Lancet, BM Jl, Biochem. Jl, The Architects' Jl. *Address:* 22 Court Lane Gardens, SE21.   [*Died* 31 *Dec.* 1980.

GAISFORD, Lt-Col Sir Philip, Kt 1946; CIE 1942; *b* 28 Nov. 1891; *s* of Lt-Col Gilbert Gaisford, Indian Political Dept; *m* 1918, Sheila Mary, *d* of Lt-Col H. O'Reilly; three *s* one *d*. *Educ:* Wellington; RMC, Sandhurst. Royal Irish Fusiliers, 1911; entered Indian Army, 1912; served European War, Mesopotamia and Salonika, 1914-18; Resident for Kolhapur and the Deccan States, 1940-42; Resident for the States of Western India, 1942-44; Resident in Mysore, 1944-46; retired 1946. *Address:* Standard Bank of South Africa, Salisbury, Rhodesia.
                                                                  [*Died* 11 *Feb.* 1973.

GALBRAITH, Vivian Hunter, MA, FBA; Hon. DLit Belfast; Hon. LittD Manchester and Emory, Atlanta, USA; Hon. DLitt Edinburgh and Exeter; *b* 15 Dec. 1889; *s* of David Galbraith and Eliza Davidson McIntosh; *m* 1921, Georgina Rosalie Cole Baker; one *s* two *d*. *Educ:* Highgate Sch.; Manchester Univ.; Balliol Coll., Oxford (scholar). Lieut The Queen's (Royal West Surrey) Regt, 1915-18; Asst Lectr Manchester Univ., 1920-21; Asst Keeper of the Public Records, 1921-28; Fellow and Tutor in Modern History, Balliol Coll., Oxford and University Reader in Diplomatic, 1928-37; Prof. of History, Edinburgh Univ., 1937-44; Dir of Inst. of Historical Research in University of London, 1944-48; Regius Prof. of Modern History in University of Oxford, 1947-57; late Lecturer in Palaeography and Archives to the Sch. of Librarianship, London; Ford's Lecturer in English History, Oxford, 1940-41; David Murray Lectureship (Glasgow Univ.), 1943-44; James Bryce Memorial Lecturer, Somerville Coll., 1944; Creighton Lecturer (University of London), 1949; Purington Lectr Mount Holyoke Coll. (Mass), 1965; Penrose Lect (Amer. Phil. Soc.), 1966. Mem. American Philosophical Soc.; Hon. Fellow of Balliol Coll., Oxford, 1957; Hon. Fellow of Oriel Coll., Oxford, 1958. *Publications:* articles (Eng. Hist. Review); The Anonimalle Chronicle of St Mary's Abbey, York, 1927; An Introduction to the Use of the Public Records, 1934; The Literacy of the Medieval English Kings, 1935; The St Albans Chronicle, 1406-1420, 1937; Roger Wendover and Matthew Paris, 1944; Studies in the Public Records, 1949; Hereford Domesday (Pipe Roll Soc., 1950, with late James Tait); Historical Research in Medieval England, 1951; The Making of Domesday Book, 1961; The Historian at Work, 1962; An Introduction to the Study of History, 1964; Domesday Book: its place in administrative history, 1975. *Recreation:* golf. *Address:* 20a Bradmore Road, Oxford OX2 6QP.   [*Died* 25 *Nov* 1976.

GALE, Arthur James Victor, MA; *b* 10 Feb. 1895; *s* of James Webb and Emma Gale; *m* 1929, Gwendoline Veysey; one *s* one *d*. *Educ:* Latymer Upper Sch.; Selwyn Coll., Cambridge (Scholar). Special Brigade, RE, 1915-18; Asst Editor of Nature, 1920-38; Joint Editor, 1959-61. Pres., Selwyn Coll. Assoc., 1967-68. *Address:* 12 Hamilton House, Upperton Road, Eastbourne, East Sussex BN21 1LE. *T:* Eastbourne 28104.
                                                                    [*Died* 4 *Sept.* 1978.

GALE, Lt-Gen. Sir Humfrey Myddelton, KBE 1943 (CBE 1940); CB 1942; CVO 1943; MC; *b* 4 Oct. 1890; *e s* of Ernest Sewell Gale, Architect, Tile Cottage, Liphook; *m* 1917, Winifred (*d* 1936), 2nd *d* of William Cross; two *d*; *m* 1945, Minnie Grace (*d* 1970), widow of Charles Louis, Prince de Beauvau Craon (*d* 1942), and *d* of Count Gregorini-Bingham of Bologna. *Educ:* St Paul's Sch.; RMC, Sandhurst. Commissioned ASC 1911; served European War, 1914-18; GSO2, Staff Coll., Camberley, 1934-37; Col, 1937; Maj.-Gen., 1941; Temp. Lt-Gen. 1944; Dep. Chief of Staff and Chief Admin. Officer under Gen. Eisenhower, 1942-45; Personal Rep. in Europe of Dir.-Gen., UNRRA, 1945-47; retired pay, 1947. Chm., Basildon New Town Develt Corp., 1954-64. Col Comdt RASC, 1944-54; Col Comdt Army Catering Corps, 1946-58. Chief Commander Legion of Merit and DSM (USA); Officer, Legion of Honour. *Address:* 1 l'Avenue de Sully, La Tour de Peilz, Vaud, Switzerland. *Club:* United Service.   [*Died* 8 *April* 1971.

GALIPEAULT, Hon. Antonin, QC 1910; BA, LLL, LLD; resigned as Judge, Province of Quebec, 1961; now practising as counsel-lawyer; late head of the firm Galipeault, Lapointe &

Boisvert, advocates, 80 St Peter Street, Quebec; Batonnier of the Quebec Bar, 1921, 1922, 1923 and 1924, and Batonnier General of the Province of Quebec, 1923 and 1924; Dir, Quebec Technical Sch., of the Quebec Land Company, of the Limoilou Land Company, of the Sun Trust Company, of the Montmagny Electric Power Company; President of la Traverse de Levis Limitée; Dir Brasserie Champlain Limited; *b* Maskinongé, 7 Aug. 1879; *s* of Louis Edouard Galipeault, Notary, and Caroline Ratelle; *m* 1903, Ernestine, *d* of Elzéar Lamontagne, Montreal; three *s* one *d*. *Educ:* College of Joliette; Laval Univ. Called to Bar, Province of Quebec, 1900; began business as member of the firm of Lane & Galipeault; head of firm Galipeault, St-Laurent, Gagné, Métayer & Devlin, 1909-30; Contested (L) Legislative Assembly, County of Maskinongé, 1904; Alderman of Quebec, 1906 and 1908; MLA Bellechasse 1909-30; Deputy Speaker of the Legislative Assembly, 1914; Chm. of Cttees, 1914; Speaker of the Legislative Assembly, 1916; Minister of Public Works and Labour, 1919-30. Judge of Court of Appeals, Quebec, from 1930; Chief Justice of Queen's Bench, Province of Quebec, with title and quality of Chief Justice for Prov. Quebec, 1950-61; also apptd Administrator for Govt of Quebec. Roman Catholic. *Address:* 565 Grande Allée, East Quebec City, Quebec, Canada. *Clubs:* Garrison, Reform (Quebec); Reform, Canadian (Montreal); Laurentide Fish and Game.   [*Died* 12 *May* 1971.

GALLAGHER, John Andrew, FBA 1978; Vere Harmsworth Professor of Imperial and Naval History, Cambridge University, since 1971; Vice-Master, Trinity College, Cambridge; *b* 1 April 1919; *o c* of Joseph and Mary Adeline Gallagher; unmarried. *Educ:* Birkenhead Institute; Trinity Coll., Cambridge (MA). Major Schol., Trinity Coll., Cambridge, 1937. Royal Tank Regt, 1939-45. Fellow of Trinity Coll., Cambridge, 1948-63 (Dean of Coll., 1960-63, Sen. Research Fellow, 1971-72); University Lectr in History, Cambridge, 1953-63; Beit Prof. of History of British Commonwealth, Oxford, and Fellow of Balliol Coll., 1963-70; Rockefeller Foundn Fellow, 1967; Ford Lectr in English History, Oxford Univ., 1973-74; Wiles Lectr, QUB, 1973-74. *Publications:* Africa and the Victorians (with R. E. Robinson), 1961; Locality, Province and Nation (with G. Johnson and A. Seal); chapters in New Cambridge Modern History, volumes VII and XI; articles in learned jls. *Address:* Trinity College, Cambridge.   [*Died* 5 *March* 1980.

GALLEGHAN, Brig. Sir Frederick (Gallagher), Kt 1969; DSO 1942; OBE 1946; ISO 1959; ED 1937; Chairman NSW Services Canteens Trust Fund, since 1963; *b* 11 Jan. 1897; *s* of Alexander Galleghan; *m* 1st, 1922, Vera Florence Dawson (decd); 2nd, 1969, Persia Elspbeth Porter, *née* Blaiklock. *Educ:* Cooks Hill High Sch., Newcastle, NSW. Commissioned Aust. Cadet Corps, 1913. Served in AIF, 34th Bn, European War, 1914-18. Comd 2nd Bn, 1932-35, and 2/35 Bn, 1935-37, Newcastle, NSW; Comd 17 Bn, N Sydney, 1937-40. Served War of 1939-45: Comd 2/30 Bn 1940-42; first Aust. unit to engage Japanese, Malaya (DSO); POW, 1942-45: Comd AIF P's W, Malaya, and Dep. Comdr Allied P's W, Malaya, 1942-45; Comd Changi POW Camp, 1944-45 (OBE). Promoted Brig., 1945 (as from 1942), on return to Australia; Head, Aust. Mil. Mission to Germany, 1947-50 (Temp. Maj.-Gen.); retired 1959. Hon. Col 34 Bn, 1957-60; Hon. Col Aust. Cadet Corps, 1959-64. *Recreations:* reading, lawn bowls. *Address:* 68 Avenue Road, Mosman, NSW 2088, Australia. *T:* 969-6865. *Club:* Imperial Service (Sydney).
                                                                   [*Died* 20 *April* 1971.

GALLICO, Paul W(illiam); author and journalist; fiction writer, novelist, screen writer; *b* New York City, 26 July 1897; *s* of Paolo Gallico, Mantua, Lombardy, and Hortense Erlich, Vienna; *m* 1st, 1921, Alva Thoits Taylor (marr. diss., 1934); two *s* ; 2nd, 1935, Elaine St John (marr. diss., 1936); 3rd, 1939, Pauline Gariboldi (marr. diss., 1954); 4th, 1963, Baroness Virginia von Falz-Fein. *Educ:* Columbia Univ. (BS). Served European War, 1914-18; Gunner's Mate, USNR Force, 1918 (Victory Medal, 1918); served War of 1939-45: Amer. Expeditionary Force, European Theatre (Ribbon with battle star, 1945); War Correspondent, Cosmopolitan Magazine, 1944. Sports Editor, Columnist, Assistant Managing Editor, New York Daily News, New York, 1922-36. Film scripts include: Never Take No for an Answer (from the book The Small Miracle); Pride of the Yankees; The Clock; Lili; The Snow Goose. *Publications:* Adventures of Hiram Holliday, 1939; The Snow Goose, 1941; The Lonely, 1947; Jennie, 1950; Trial by Terror, 1952; The Small Miracle, 1952; Snowflake, 1952; The Foolish Immortals, 1953; Love of Seven Dolls, 1954; Ludmila, 1955; Thomasina, 1957; The Steadfast Man (a life of St Patrick), 1958; Flowers For Mrs Harris, 1958; The Hurricane Story, 1959; Mrs Harris Goes to New York, 1960; Too Many Ghosts, 1961; Confessions of a Story-Teller, 1961; Scruffy, 1962; Coronation, 1962; The Day the Guinea Pig Talked, 1963; Love, Let Me Not Hunger, 1963; The Hand of Mary Constable, 1964;

Mrs Harris, MP, 1965; The Day Jean-Pierre Went Round the World, 1965; The Man Who was Magic, 1966; The Story of Silent Night, 1967; Manxmouse, 1968; The Poseidon Adventure, 1969; The Day Jean-Pierre joined the Circus, 1969; Matilda, 1970; The Zoo Gang, 1971; Honourable Cat, 1972; The Boy Who Invented the Bubble Gun, 1974; Mrs Harris Goes to Moscow, 1974; Miracle in the Wilderness, 1975. *Recreation:* fencing. *Address:* 69 Great Russell Street, WC1. *Clubs:* Lansdowne, Epée, Buck's. *[Died 15 July 1976.*

GALLOWAY, 12th Earl of, *cr* 1623; **Randolph Algernon Ronald Stewart;** Lord Garlies, 1607; Bt 1627; Baron Stewart of Garlies (Great Britain), 1796; Lord Lieutenant of Kircudbrightshire, 1932-75; *b* 21 Nov. 1892; *s* of 11th Earl and Amy Mary Pauline (*d* 1942), *d* of Anthony John Cliffe of Bellevue, Co. Wexford; *S* father, 1920; *m* 1924, Philippa Fendall (*d* 1974), *d* of late J. Wendell, New York; one *s* one *d*. *Educ:* Harrow; RMC, Sandhurst. Gazetted Scots Guards, 1913; served European War, 1914-15 (prisoner); Hon. Attaché, HM Legation at Berne, 1918; ADC to Military Governor at Cologne, 1919; Lt-Col commanding 7th (Galloway) Bn KOSB, 1939-40, now Hon. Col; JP Kirkudbrightshire. Grand Master Mason of Scotland, 1945-49. *Heir: s* Lord Garlies. *Address:* Cumloden, Newton-Stewart, Kirkcudbrightshire. *Clubs:* Carlton; New (Edinburgh). *[Died 13 June 1978.*

GALLOWAY, Lt-Gen. Sir Alexander, KBE 1949 (CBE 1941); CB 1946; DSO 1941; MC 1918; retired; *b* 3 Nov. 1895; *yr s* of late Rev. A. and Mrs Galloway, Minto Manse, Hawick and Broadstone, Dunbar, Scotland; *m* 1920, Dorothy Hadden White; three *s*. *Educ:* King William's Coll. Served European War, 1914-18, Gallipoli, Egypt, Palestine, France, Belgium, 1914-19 (despatches, MC, 1914-15 Star, two medals); War of 1939-45, Middle East, Italy, North-West Europe (despatches twice, CBE, DSO, CB); GOC 30th Corps BAOR, 1946; GOC-in-C Malaya Command, 1946-47; High Commissioner and C-in-C, British Troops in Austria, 1947-50; retired, 1950. Chm., Jordan Development Bank, 1951-52; subsequently joined firm of Richard Costain Ltd, Building & Civil Engineering Contractors. 1st cl. Mil. Cross of Greece and of Czechoslovakia, Orders of Merit and White Lion of Czechoslovakia, Order of Orange-Nassau (Netherlands). *Address:* West Street, Norham, Northumberland. *[Died 28 Jan. 1977.*

GALLOWAY, Maj.-Gen. Rudolf William, CB 1944; CBE 1943; DSO 1919; MB, ChB; late RAMC; retired, 1950; *b* 22 July 1891; *s* of late Dr Alexander Rudolf Galloway, OBE, Aberdeen; *m* 1930, Lois Mary Kerr, *yr d* of Lt-Col A. Leaning, DSO; one *d* (one *s* decd). *Educ:* Aberdeen Grammar Sch.; Aberdeen Univ. Served European War, 1914-19 (despatches twice, DSO); Iraq, 1923; War of 1939-45 (despatches twice, CBE, CB). DDMS Western Command, 1946-50. Hon. Surg. to King George VI (KHS). *Publication:* Anatomy and Physiology of Physical Training, 1937. *Recreation:* writing. *Address:* Willow Bank, Church End, Great Dunmow, Essex. *T:* Dunmow 2468. *[Died 22 March 1976.*

GALWAY, 9th Viscount, *cr* 1727; **Simon George Robert Monckton-Arundell,** Baron Killard 1727; Baron Monckton (UK) 1887; DL; *b* 11 Nov. 1929; *o s* of 8th Viscount and Hon. Lucia White, *yr d* of 3rd Baron Annaly; *S* father, 1943; *m* 1953, Hon. Teresa Jane Fox-Strangways, *o d* of 7th Earl of Ilchester; one *d*. *Educ:* Eton. Commissioned in The Life Guards 1948; retd; Major 1960. DL Nottinghamshire, 1963. *Heir: kinsman* William Arundell Monckton, *b* 1894. *Address:* Bishopfield House, Bawtry, Doncaster, Yorks. *T:* Ranskill 224. *Clubs:* White's, Buck's. *[Died 1 Jan. 1971.*

GALWAY, 10th Viscount *cr* 1727; **William Arundell Monckton-Arundell;** Baron Killard, 1727; *b* 24 Sept. 1894; *s* of William Henry Monckton (*g s* of 5th Viscount) (*d* 1900), and Rose Ethel (*d* 1939), *d* of Henry Vatcher, Rosemount, Jersey; *S* kinsman, 1971; *m* 1939, Joan (*d* 1973), *o c* of late Major G. A. Williams, S Staffs Regt, Purbrook, Hants. *Educ:* Trinity College, Cambridge. *Heir: b* Edmund Savile Monckton [*b* 11 Sept. 1900; *m* 1927, Kathleen Joyce (*d* 1975), *yr d* of late James Musgrave; one *d*]. *[Died 15 Aug. 1977.*

GALWAY, 11th Viscount, *cr* 1727; **Edmund Savile Monckton-Arundell;** Baron Killard, 1727; *b* 11 Sept. 1900; *s* of William Henry Monckton (*g s* of 5th Viscount) (*d* 1900) and Rose Ethel (*d* 1939), *d* of Henry Vatcher, Rosemount, Jersey; *S* brother, 1977; *m* 1927, Kathleen Joyce (*d* 1975), *yr d* of late James Musgrave, MICE; one *d*. *Educ:* Charterhouse; Clare College, Cambridge (BA 1922, MA 1944). Solicitor, 1930-73. Civil Defence, 1937-58. *Heir: cousin* George Rupert Monckton, Lieut Comdr RCN retd [*b* 13 Oct. 1922; *m* 1944, Fiona Margaret, *d* of Captain W. de P. Taylor; one *s* three *d*]. *Address:* 5 Cranhill Road, Bath, Avon BA1 2YF. *[Died 30 Jan. 1980.*

GAMAGE, Sir Leslie, Kt 1959; MC; MA; FCIS; Chairman and Managing Director, General Electric Co. Ltd, 1957-60; *b* 5 May 1887; 2nd *s* of A. W. Gamage; *m* 1919, Hon. Muriel Elsie Hirst, DStJ (*d* 1969), *er d* of late Baron Hirst; no *c*. *Educ:* Marlborough; Exeter Coll., Oxford (Senior Scholar, Hons Degree). MA 1910; training for Law, 1910-14; Hons in Solicitors' Final Exam.; served in European War, 1914-18; Captain and Adjt 24th London Regt (MC, twice wounded and finally prisoner); with Gen. Electric Co. Ltd, 1919-60, first as Sec., then Dir, Gen. Manager, and Managing Dir; specialised in export and travelled widely in Empire; Pres.: Chartered Institute of Secretaries in its Jubilee Year, 1941; Institute of Export, 1942-58; Master Company of Glaziers, 1942; Royal Pinner Foundn (formerly Royal Commercial Travellers' Schs), 1950-72; Chief Business Adviser, Min. of Civil Aviation, 1947-60; Pres. of British Electrical and Allied Manufacturers' Association (BEAMA), 1959-60. CStJ. *Recreation:* golf. *Address:* Springmead, Ascot, Berks. *T:* Ascot 23619. *Club:* Buck's. *[Died 17 Oct. 1972.*

GAMBIER-PARRY, Maj.-Gen. Michael Denman, MC 1916; retired; *b* 21 Aug. 1891; *e s* of late Sidney Gambier-Parry and of Grace Gambier-Parry (*née* Denman), Duntisbourne Rous, Cirencester, Glos; *m* 1918, Barbara Evelyn, *e d* of late Captain H. M. Tufnell, Fairfields, Hatfield Peverell, Essex; one *s* two *d*. *Educ:* Eton; RMC, Sandhurst. Commissioned Royal Welch Fusiliers, 1911; Captain 1914; served European War, 1914-18, Gallipoli and Mesopotamia (6 mentions), Bt Major, 1917; temp. Lt-Col, 1917; psc, 1924; transferred Royal Tank Corps, 1924; Major, 1925; Bt Lt-Col, 1929; Lt-Col, 1935; War of 1939-45: Brig., Malaya Inf. Bde, 1938-40; ADC to King George VI, 1939-40; Maj.-Gen. 1940; Head of Military Mission to Greek Army (temp.), 1940; GOC, 2 Armoured Div., 1941; POW, Italy, 1941-43; retired 1944. DL Wilts, 1952-54; Mem. of Council Royal College of Music, 1951; FRCM 1961. *Address:* Forest Gate, Poundgate, Crowborough, East Sussex. *Club:* Naval and Military. *[Died 30 April 1976.*

GAMBLE, Rev. Arthur Mellor; Rector of Cley-next-the-Sea with Wiveton, since 1958, of Letheringsett with Glandford, since 1969; Head Master of Denstone College, 1941-57, retired; *b* 6 Feb. 1899; *s* of late P. A. Gamble, Morton; *m* 1924, Doris Mary, 2nd *d* of late Percy Evershed, The Plantation, Norwich; one *s* two *d*. *Educ:* Shrewsbury Sch. (Schol.); Oriel Coll., Oxford. Served European War in Royal Engineers in France and Belgium, 1917-19; Asst Master, Gresham's Sch., Holt, 1922; Housemaster, 1930. Ordained Deacon, March 1958, Priest, Sept. 1958. Mem. Diocesan Council for Education. *Recreations:* usual; OUAFC and Corinthians FC 1921. *Address:* Wiveton Rectory, Holt, Norfolk. *[Died 24 Oct. 1975.*

GAMBLE, Robert Edward, OBE 1969; FRSA; HM Diplomatic Service; on secondment to Department of Trade as Assistant Secretary, since Dec. 1974; *b* 22 Dec. 1922; *s* of William Harrison Gamble; *m* 1947, Mavis Alice Garland; one *s* two *d*. *Educ:* Alderman Newton's Sch., Leicester. Admiralty, UK and Levant, 1939-49; British Legation, Damascus, 1949-51; HM Vice-Consul: Bushire, Iran, 1951-52; Basra, Iraq, 1952-54; Second Sec., HM Embassy, Tel Aviv, 1954-58; First Sec., HM Embassy, Helsinki, 1958-61; Foreign Office, 1961-64; First Sec., HM Embassy, Vienna, 1964-70; Counsellor, Brit. High Commn, Sydney, NSW, 1970-73; Deputy Consul-Gen., Sydney, NSW, 1973-74. FRSA 1973. *Recreations:* painting, writing, drama, music, handicrafts. *Address:* c/o Foreign and Commonwealth Office, SW1; 20 Garrard Road, Banstead, Surrey. *T:* Burgh Heath 51522. *[Died 11 Oct. 1975.*

GAMMELL, Lt-Gen. Sir James (Andrew Harcourt), KCB 1944 (CB 1940); DSO 1917; MC; DL; *e s* of late Sir Sydney J. Gammell, Countesswells, Aberdeenshire; *b* 1892; *m* 1st, 1919, Gertrude (*d* 1960), *e d* of late Gilbert W. Don; two *s* two *d*; 2nd, 1964, Mrs Mary Kirkwood, widow of Comdr David Kirkwood, RN. *Educ:* Winchester; Pembroke Coll., Cambridge (BA, 2nd class Hons Hist. Trip.). Commission, Royal Field Artillery, Dec. 1912; served European War, 1914-18 (despatches 7 times, DSO, MC); promoted Major and transferred to QO Cameron Highlanders, 1927; Bt Lt-Col 1931; Instructor Staff Coll., Camberley, 1930-33; Lt-Col 1935; comd 1st Bn Queen's Own Cameron Highlanders, 1935-38; Col 1938; idc 1938; comd 4th Infantry Bde, 1938-40; Maj.-Gen. 1941; acting Lt-Gen., 1941; Temp. Lt-Gen., 1942; GOC-in-C Eastern Comd, 1942-43; Chief of Staff to Supreme Allied Comdr, Mediterranean Theatre, 1944; Lt-Gen. 1944; Representative of British Chiefs of Staff with USSR and Head of British Military Mission in Moscow, 1945; retd pay, 1946. DL Co. Angus, 1954. *Address:* Alrick, Glenisla, by Alyth, Perthshire. *T:* Glenisla 257; Westover, Abbots Leigh, Bristol. *T:* Pill 2357. *Club:* Naval and Military. *[Died 1 Aug. 1975.*

GAMMON, John Charles, OBE 1919; ACGI, MIStructE; President and Founder of Civil Engineering Companies; Gammon India Ltd, 1919; Gammon Malaya Ltd, 1924 (now Gammon South East Asia Berhad); Gammon Pakistan Ltd, 1947; Gammon East Pakistan Ltd, 1954; Gammon Gulf Ltd, 1958; *b* 2 June 1887; *m* 1954, Angela Duncan; two *s* one *d* (and one *s* two *d* by previous marr.). *Educ:* Felsted Sch.; Imperial Coll. of Technology, London Univ. (BSc 1st Class Hons). Advanced Workshop Student, Woolwich Arsenal, 1908-09; PWD India, 1910-14; Indian Army, 1914-19, serving 4 years in France with 3rd Sappers and Miners, with 1st Indian Field Sqdn, and on staff of Chief Engineer, 3rd Army in charge of Workshops, Stores and Bridging. *Publication:* Re-inforced Concrete Design Simplified, 1910. *Recreations;* directing and developing Trevose Golf Club; cricket, bridge. *Address:* 80 Eaton Square, SW1. *Clubs:* East India, Sports and Public Schools; Royal Yacht, Willingdon (Bombay); Sind (Karachi).
[*Died* 29 *April* 1973.

GANE, Sir Irving (Blanchard), KCVO 1954; Chamberlain of London, 1945-62; *b* 15 April 1892; *o c* of Douglas Montagu Gane and Florence Kate Blanchard; *m* 1916, Florence Montgomery (*d* 1951), *d* of Thomas Coulter, Bowmanville, Ontario; three *d*; *m* 1954, Mrs Valerie Woolland, *d* of Sir Donald Cory, 2nd Bt, and of Gertrude Lady Cory. *Educ:* Merchant Taylors' Sch. Admitted a Solicitor, 1914; Private First Bn, HAC, France, 1914-15; Gazetted to 2/22nd Bn London Regt (The Queens), France 1916, Salonika 1917, Palestine 1917-19; Adjt, Gen. Staff, GHQ, Palestine, 1918; Gen. Staff, War Office, 1940; retired, 1945, Major. A Vice-Pres., Royal Society of St George; a Vice-Pres., Ex-Services Mental Welfare Soc.; Chm., City of London Centre, St John Ambulance Assoc.; Hon. Sec., Tristan Da Cunha Fund; Mem. Court of Common Council for Ward of Farringdon Without, 1934-45; Mem. Court of Assts Merchant Taylors' Company, 1951, Master, 1959. KStJ. *Address:* Newmans, Pirbright, Woking, Surrey. *T:* Brookwood 2072. [*Died* 26 *March* 1972.

GANGULY, Most Rev. Theotonius A., CSC; DD, PhD; Archbishop (RC) of Dacca, since 1967; *b* Hashnabad, Dacca, Bengal, 18 Feb. 1920; *s* of Nicholas K. Ganguly. *Educ:* Little Flower Seminary, Dacca, Bengal; St Albert Seminary, Ranchi, India. PhD Notre Dame Univ., USA, 1951. Priest, 1946; Mem. of Congregation of Holy Cross, 1951; Prof., Notre Dame Coll., Dacca, 1952-60; Principal, Notre Dame Coll., 1960; Auxiliary Bishop of Dacca, 1960; Coadjutor Archbishop of Dacca, 1965. *Address:* Archbishop's House, PO Box 3, Dacca 2, Bangladesh. *T:* Dacca 242379. [*Died* 2 *Sept.* 1977.

GANNON, Brig. Jack Rose Compton, CBE 1945 (OBE 1942); MVO 1922; *b* 1882; *s* of John Gannon, St John's Coll., Cambridge; *m* 1910, Dorothy (*d* 1971) *d* of George Robertson, Melbourne; one *d*. *Educ:* Sutton Valence; RMC Sandhurst. South Staffords, 1902-06; 23rd and PAVO Cavalry, 1906-26; Commanded Sam Browne's Cavalry, 1927-32; ADC to Lord Willingdon when Governor of Bombay; Personal Military Sec. to Gen. Lord Rawlinson, C-in-C India, 1920-25; served European War, 1914-18; Afghan War, 1919; Mahsud and Waziristan Expeditions, 1919-20 (despatches twice); Asst Military Sec., GHQ Home Forces, 1939-43; Dep. Military Sec., 21 Army Group, 1943-45; Dep. Mil. Sec., BAOR, 1945-46 (despatches twice); retd, 1946. Manager, Hurlingham Club, 1934-39; Hon. Sec., Hurlingham Polo Assoc., 1934-; Pres., Arab Horse Soc., 1951; Pres., Nat. Pony Soc., 1954-. British Horse Society's Medal of Honour, 1970. Comdr of Legion of Merit (US), Knight Comdr of Order of Orange Nassau, Chevalier of Legion of Honour (France), Croix de Guerre (France). *Publication:* Before the Colours Fade, 1976. *Recreations:* formerly: polo, cricket, shooting. *Address:* King Edward VII Hospital, Midhurst, Sussex. *Clubs:* Cavalry and Guards, MCC.
[*Died* 25 *April* 1980.

GARBETT, Sir Colin (Campbell), KCIE 1941 (CIE 1917); CSI 1935; CMG 1922; FRGS; FRSA; OStJ 1938; *b* 22 May 1881; *s* of late Hubert Garbett, MICE, Castletown, Isle of Man; *m* 1st, 1911, Abra Faith Hughes-Garbett (*d* 1911); 2nd, 1919, Marjorie Josephine, *d* of late Lt-Col Maynard, IMS; one *d*. *Educ:* King William's Coll., Isle of Man (Sch. Capt. of Football; Victor Ludorum; Cricket XI); Jesus Coll., Cambridge (rowing, football and athletic colours, Victor Ludorum, Sen. Schol.). MA; BA (1st Class Hons Classics) 1903; LLB (2nd Class) 1904. ICS 1904; Asst-Censor, 1915; Revenue Comr, Mesopotamia, and also Administrator Agricultural Development Scheme (Military), 1917 (despatches twice); Secretariat Turkish Peace Treaty Delegn, 1919-20; Asst-Sec., India Office, 1919-20; Sec. High Comr, Iraq, 1920-22; returned to India, 1922; Dep. Comr, Attock; Campbellpur, 1925-29; Rawalpindi, 1929; Chief Sec. to Govt, Punjab, 1931; Comr, Multan Div., 1935; Financial Comr Punjab, 1937; Chm., Punjab Govt Forest Commn, 1937; Financial Comr, Punjab, 1939; Chm. Provincial Transport Authority and of Land Reclamation Board, Punjab; retired Dec. 1941 and became Chm. Interview Board Emergency Commissions (Defence Dept) till 1943; Senior Mem. Govt of India Commn on land schemes for demobilised soldiers; Regional Food Comr, Northern India; Minister for Agriculture, Bhopal, 1944-46; retired, 1946. Missions to Pakistan and India for Raw Cotton Commn, 1948 and 1949. Classics Master, Hilton Coll., Natal, SA, 1951-52. *Publications:* Friend of Friend, 1943; The Hundred Years, 1944; Sun of Tabriz, 1956; The Ringing Radiance, 1968. *Address: c/o* National and Grindlay's Bank Ltd, 13 St James's Square, SW1; 16 Bel Air. Whiteriver, Transvaal, S Africa. *Clubs:* Royal Commonwealth Society, East India, Sports and Public Schools, Royal Over-Seas League; Royal Bombay Yacht. [*Died* 10 *Aug.* 1972.

GARBETT, Captain Leonard Gillilan, CBE 1942; RN (retired); *b* 1 March 1879; *y s* of Rev. Charles Garbett, Vicar of Tongham, Surrey; *m* 1919, Millicent, *e d* of Canon Dunfield, St John's, Newfoundland; one *s* two *d*. *Educ:* HMS Worcester. Served afloat continuously and in European War, 1914-18, operations on Belgian Coast, 1914, and against German Cruiser Königsberg in Rufiji River, 1915; comd HMS Mersey, 1917-19, HM Surveying Ship, Merlin, 1920-21; Supt Naval Div., Meteorological Office, Air Min., 1921-37; Chief Supt Naval Met. Branch, Admty, 1937-39; Dir, Naval Meteorological Service, 1939-47. FRMetS; FRSA. Younger Brother of Trinity House. USA Legion of Merit, 1946. *Publications:* several professional papers. *Recreations:* fishing, riding. *Address:* The Cottage, Ashford Carbonell, Ludlow, Shropshire. *T:* Richard's Castle 250. *Club:* Army and Navy. [*Died* 5 *June* 1974.

GARDINER, Henry Rolf; Chairman of companies, and promoter of husbandry and of many international exchanges (camps, music, etc); author; *b* 5 Nov. 1902; *s* of Sir Alan Henderson Gardiner, DLitt, FBA, and Lady (Hedwig) Gardiner (*née* von Rosen); *m* 1932, Mariabella Honor Hodgkin; two *s* one *d*. *Educ:* West Downs, Winchester; Rugby Sch.; Bedales Sch.; St John's Coll., Cambridge (BA Hons). International work, 1924-32: Co-founder Musikheim (Coll.) Frankfurt/Oder, 1929; promoted voluntary work camps in Germany and Yorkshire, 1927-32; and Folk centre, Oosterbeeck, Holland, 1927-; British-German music exchanges, 1926-31; founded Travelling Morrice, 1924; British-German Baltic tour, 1932. Founded: the Springhead Estate, Dorset, 1933; Springhead Ring, 1933-62; Kinship in Husbandry, 1941-50; voluntary work-camps, summer schools, festivals, 1929-. Mem. Dorset CC, 1937-46; High Sheriff of Dorset, 1967-68. Pres., Dorset Fedn Young Farmers' Clubs, 1944-46; Pres., South Western Woodlands Assoc. Ltd, 1955-; Chairman: Dorset Br., CPRE, 1957-67 (Pres., 1970-72); Dorset Br., CLA, 1961-63; (Jt) Dorset and Somerset Rural Industries Cttee, 1951-69; European working party for landscape husbandry, 1963-71 (Lenné Gold Medal for landscape husbandry, awarded at Stassburg by Goethe Foundation, 1971); Chairman: Nchima Tea and Tung Estates Ltd, 1947-; Mchiru Co., 1950-; Dir, Bradbury, Greatorex and Co. Ltd, 1952-67. *Publications:* The Second Coming and other poems, 1921; Britain and Germany: symposium, 1928; World Without End, British politics and the younger generation, 1932; England Herself: ventures in rural restoration, 1943; Love and Memory: a garland of poems, 1960; Europe awaits British Ecological Leadership, 1972; also edited and largely wrote: North Sea and Baltic, 1932-42, and, Wessex Letters from Springhead, 1942-68. *Recreations:* folk dancing, choral singing, walking tours, forestry work. *Address:* Springhead, Fontmell Magna, Shaftesbury, Dorset. *T:* Fontmell Magna 206. *Club:* Farmers'.
[*Died* 26 *Nov.* 1971.

GARDNER, Arthur Duncan, MA, DM, FRCS, FRCP; Hon. Fellow of University College, Oxford, 1950; Professor Emeritus, Oxford, 1954; *b* 28 March 1884; *s* of late James William Gardner, The Stone House, Rugeley, Staffs; *m* Violet Mary, *d* of late John Fowler Newsam, The Hollies, Broxbourne, Herts; one *s* (and one *s* one *d* decd). *Educ:* Rugby; University Coll., Oxford. Member of Oxford hockey eleven, 1906; St Thomas's Hospital, 1908-15; Beaney Prize, House Surgeon, Casualty Officer, Lectr in Pathology, Research Asst. Radcliffe Travelling Fellowship, Oxford, 1914, Radcliffe Prize, 1923. Served in BEF as British Red Cross Surgeon, 1914; Dir of Standards Lab. (MRC) at Oxford, 1915-36; Reader in Bacteriology with title of Professor, 1936; Rede Lectr, Cambridge, 1953; Litchfield Lectr, Oxford, 1954; late Fellow of University Coll., Oxford; Regius Prof. of Medicine, Univ. of Oxford, 1948-54; Student of Christ Church, 1948-54; Hon. Consultant, Oxford United Hospitals, 1954. *Publications:* Microbes and Ultramicrobes, 1931; Bacteriology for Medical Students and Practitioners, 1933 (4th edn 1953); Penicillin as a chemotherapeutic agent (with Sir Ernst Chain,

Lord Florey and others), 1940; numerous contribs to medical scientific jls from 1914. *Address:* South Priory, Ipplepen, South Devon. *T:* Ipplepen 812619.   [*Died* 28 *Jan.* 1978.

GARDNER, Francis William; *b* 15 Jan. 1891; *s* of Frederick J. Gardner, Liverpool; *m* 1920, Gladys Robathan (*d* 1974). *Educ:* Queens' Coll., Cambridge. Joined C. A. Parsons & Co. Ltd, Newcastle upon Tyne, 1912. Served in RNAS (subsequently RAF), 1915-19. Returned to C. A. Parsons & Co. Ltd, holding office of Chief Engineer then General Manager; Director, 1939; retired from executive office, 1956; Chairman, 1959-60, now retired. *Address:* Birchy Hill Nursing Home, Sway, Lymington, Hants SO4 0BJ.   [*Died* 7 *Feb.* 1976.

GARDNER, Sir George William Hoggan, KBE 1959 (CBE 1951); CB 1955; consultant; *b* 4 May 1903; *m* 1st, 1932, Lorna Marian Boyd (*d* 1962); two *d*; 2nd, 1963, Helen Isabel Burgess. *Educ:* Campbell Coll., Belfast; Queen's Univ., Belfast. BSc, Queen's Univ., 1925. Dir of the Royal Aircraft Establishment, 1955-59; Controller of Aircraft, Min. of Aviation, 1959-63. Chm., John Brown Engineering (Clydebank) Ltd, 1966-70; Director: Constructors John Brown Ltd, 1967-71; John Brown & Co Ltd, 1963-72. FIMechE 1947; Hon. FRAeS 1962. Hon. DSc Queen's Univ., Belfast, 1957. *Address:* The Lawn, Pirbright Road, Farnborough, Hants. *T:* Farnborough, Hants, 42984.   [*Died* 22 *Aug.* 1975.

GARDNER, William Henry, CMG 1948; *b* 20 April 1895; *s* of William John Gardner, Walthamstow, Essex; *m* 1st, 1920, Dorothy Margaret (*d* 1950), *e d* of John William Freeman; one *s*; 2nd, 1964, Elsie Stephenson (*d* 1967), Edinburgh, *d* of Henry Stephenson, Co. Durham. *Educ:* Maynard Road Elementary Sch. and Sir George Monoux Grammar Sch., Walthamstow; King's Coll., London. Entered Civil Service as boy clerk, 1910; second div. clerk, 1913; Staff Clerk, 1929; Principal, WO, 1940; Asst Sec., WO, 1942; Asst Under-Sec. of State, 1952-55; retd from WO, 1955. Served European War, 1914-18, in Queen's Westminster Rifles, 1915-19; Lieut WO Home Guard, 1940-45. Lay Reader: dio. of Chelmsford 1922-; dio. of Edinburgh, 1965; Hon. Sec., Chelmsford Diocesan Union, CEMS, 1925-32, 1958-62; Vice-Chm., 1962-66, Vice-Pres., 1966-72. Dep. Leader, UK delegn to Geneva Conf. on Protection of War Victims, 1949. Hon. Mem., Florence Nightingale Internat. Nurses' Assoc., 1967. *Recreations:* walking, reading. *Address:* 3 Lonsdale Terrace, Edinburgh EH3 9HN. *T:* 031-229 7443. *Clubs:* Royal Commonwealth Society; Essex County Cricket.
                                    [*Died* 24 *Dec.* 1977.

GARDNER-BROWN, Anthony Geoffrey Hopwood, CMG 1958; *b* 1 Oct. 1913; *yr s* of late Rev. F. S. G. Gardner-Brown; *m* 1939, Margaret, *yr d* of H. Sparrow; three *d*. *Educ:* Marlborough; Pembroke Coll., Cambridge. Cadet, Colonial Administrative Service, Northern Rhodesia, 1936; District Officer, 1938; served 1st Bn Northern Rhodesia Regt, East Africa and Ceylon, 1940-43; Supervisor Colonial Service Courses, Cambridge Univ., 1949-51; Asst Sec. (Native Affairs), Northern Rhodesia, 1952; Colonial Sec., Bahamas, 1952-56; Federation of Nigeria: Dep. Chief Sec., 1956-58; Sec. for Defence and External Affairs, 1958-59; Dep. Governor-General, Nov. 1959-Oct. 1960; retired, 1961. Organiser, Community Council of Devon, 1961-63; Chm., Salaries Commn, Windward and Leeward Islands, 1965; Comr on Anomalies, Western Pacific High Commn, 1965; Salaries Comr, Barbados, Mauritius, 1966, Swaziland, 1967, Bermuda, 1969, Hong Kong, 1971. Chm., Somerset County Scout Council, 1967-70. *Recreation:* fishing. *Address:* The Old Rectory, Stawley, Wellington, Somerset. *T:* Greenham 672205.
                                    [*Died* 18 *Oct.* 1978.

GARNER, Sir Harry Mason, KBE 1951; CB 1948; FRAeS; Chief Scientist to Ministry of Supply, 1949-53; *b* 3 Nov. 1891; *s* of William Garner, Wymeswold, Loughborough; *m* 1921, Hilda Annie Green; one *s* one *d*. *Educ:* Market Bosworth Grammar Sch.; St John's Coll., Cambridge. Senior Scientific Officer, Royal Aircraft Establishment, 1927; Chief Technical Officer, Marine Aircraft Experimental Establishment, Felixstowe, 1929; Deputy Director Scientific Research, Ministry of Aircraft Production, 1943; Principal Director, Scientific Research (Air), Ministry of Supply, 1946-49. *Publications:* Oriental Blue and White, 1954; Chinese and Japanese Cloisonné Enamels, 1962; scientific on aerodynamics and on oriental art; *posthumous publication:* Chinese Lacquer, 1979. *Recreations:* music, oriental art. *Address:* Montford, 8 Grange Road, Camberley, Surrey. *T:* Camberley 22763. *Club:* Athenæum.   [*Died* 7 *Aug.* 1977.

GARNER, Robert Livingston; *b* Bolton, Mississippi, 7 Aug. 1894; *s* of late Robert Vincent Garner and Lillian Hardgrave Garner; *m* 1926, Ellen Wright Garner (decd); one *d*. *Educ:* Columbia Military Acad.; Vanderbilt Univ., Nashville, Tennessee (BS);

Columbia University School of Journalism, New York. Captain of Infantry, 77th Division, War, 1917-18. Guaranty Trust Company: Educational Department, 1919-20; Buying Department, 1920-25; Investment Department Continental Insurance Co., 1925-26; Guaranty Trust Co. as Asst Treasurer and subseq. Treasurer and Vice-President, 1926-43; Financial Vice-President and Director of General Foods Corp., 1943-47; Vice-President, International Bank for Reconstruction and Development, 1947-56; President, International Finance Corporation, 1956-61. Trustee, Vanderbilt Univ. Director, American Security & Trust Co., Washington. *Recreations:* golfing, fishing, shooting. *Address:* 730 15th Street, NW, Washington 5, DC, USA. *T:* 624-4597. *Clubs:* University, The Links (NY); Chevy Chase, Metropolitan (Washington).
                                    [*Died* 13 *Dec.* 1975.

GARNETT, Bernard John, CMG 1962; OBE 1950; HM Diplomatic Service, retired; *b* 20 June 1913; *o s* of late James Holden and Bertha Garnett; *m* 1950, Gwyneth May Jones; one *d*. *Educ:* Pembroke Dock County Sch.; The Leys; Emmanuel Coll., Cambridge. Entered HM Consular Service, 1936; has served at Bangkok, Lourenço Marques, Funchal, Algiers, Naples, and as a Foreign Service Inspector; Counsellor in British Military Government, Berlin, 1957-59; Counsellor (Commercial), Athens, 1960-63 (also Consul-General, 1960-62); Chief Inspector, HM Foreign Service, 1963-64, Diplomatic Service, 1965-66; Minister, UK Delegn to 18 Nation Disarmament Conf., Geneva, 1966-67; acting High Comr to Malaysia, 1967; retd 1968. *Address:* 38 Observatory Road, SW14 7QD.   [*Died* 4 *April* 1977.

GARNSWORTHY, Baron *cr* 1967 (Life Peer) of Reigate; **Charles James Garnsworthy,** OBE 1965; JP; DL; a Lord in Waiting (a Government Whip), since 1974; *b* 10 Dec. 1906; *s* of Charles Edward Garnsworthy and Helen Garnsworthy (*née* Edyvean); *m* 1st, 1943, Joyce Kingsley Morgan (marr. diss. 1972); 2nd, 1973, Sue Farley; one *s*. *Educ:* Wellington Sch., Som. Bldg Industry, 1925; Insce Agency, 1931; Royal Corps of Signals, 1940-45. Member: Banstead UDC, 1937-47; Surrey CC, 1952- (Alderman, 1966-74); Union of Shop Distributive and Allied Workers; (Coopted Mem.), LCC Children's Cttee, 1949-54; Chairman: De Burgh and Nork Park Schs, Banstead; Epsom Sch. of Art; Governors, Royal Alexandra and Albert Sch. Contested (Lab) Reigate, 1945, 1950, 1951, 1955, 1960 and 1964. JP 1959, DL 1973, Surrey. *Recreations:* walking, travel, theatre. *Address:* Little Dormers, Smith Lane, Lower Kingswood, Surrey. *T:* Mogador 2680.   [*Died* 5 *Sept.* 1974.

GARRETT, Lt-Gen. Sir (Alwyn) Ragnar, KBE 1959 (CBE 1944); CB 1957; formerly Chief of the General Staff, Australian Military Forces (1958-60); *b* 12 Feb. 1900; *o s* of Alwyn and Marie Garrett; *m* 1925, Shirley Lorraine Hunter; one *s* one *d*. *Educ:* Guildford Gram. Sch.; Royal Military Coll., Duntroon. Attached Queen's Bays, India, 1922-23; served with Austr. Mil. Forces, 1923-37; Staff Coll., Camberley, 1938-39; AIF, 1939-46; Comdt, Austr. Staff Coll., 1946; Principal Administrative Officer and Comdt Austr. Component, BCOF, Japan, 1947-49; Comdt Austr. Staff Coll., 1950-51; GOC, Western Command, 1951-52; DCGS Australia, 1953; Adjutant-Gen., 1954; GOC Southern Command, 1954-58; Principal of the Australian Administrative Staff Coll., 1960-65. Chm., Australian Shipping Service, 1966-70. *Recreations:* golf, tennis. *Address:* 16 Blake Court, Mount Eliza, Victoria, Australia. *Club:* Naval and Military (Melbourne).   [*Died* 4 *Nov.* 1977.

GARRETT, Sir (Joseph) Hugh, KCIE 1939; CSI 1931; ICS (retired); BA (Cantab); Captain, 10th Devon Bn Home Guard; *b* 22 June 1880; *s* of J. P. Garrett, Highgate; *m* Dilys M. Silvanus; one *d*; *m* 1967, Mrs F. M. Lipson-Ward. *Educ:* Highgate Sch.; Gonville and Caius Coll., Cambridge. Served in various districts of the Bombay Presidency as District Officer in later years chiefly in Gujarat; officiated on several occasions as Chief Sec. to Government of Bombay; Acting Governor of Sind, 1938. *Address:* South Devon Hotel, St Margaret's Road, St Mary Church, Torquay, Devon TQ1 4NP. *Club:* East India, Devonshire, Sports and Public Schools.   [*Died* 6 *Sept.* 1978.

GARRETT, Philip Leslie; Editor of The Ironmonger, 1934-53; *b* 11 Nov. 1888; *s* of late Joseph Payne Garrett, Highgate and Eleanor Adelaide Hope; *m* 1914, Phyllis Kathleen (*d* 1972), *d* of late Lewis Medland; two *s* one *d*. *Educ:* Highgate Sch. Admitted a solicitor, 1911; practised in partnership with father; joined editorial staff of The Ironmonger, 1914; Asst Ed., 1926; Mem. of Law Soc. and for many years of Board of Management of Royal Metal Trades Pension and Benevolent Soc.; Hon. Mem. Nat. Federation of Ironmongers and first Hon. Mem. and Governor, Nat. Inst. of Hardware. *Publications:* Literary contributions to various newspapers and periodicals. *Recreations:* ornithology,

reading. *Address:* Hilltop, Ballinger, Great Missenden, Bucks.
T: The Lee 253.   *[Died 8 Oct.* 1978.

GARRETT, Lieut-Gen. Sir Ragnar; *see* Garrett, Lieut-Gen. Sir
A. R.

GARRETT, Sir Ronald (Thornbury), Kt 1944; *b* 5 Nov. 1888; 3rd
s of late Samuel Garrett, Aldeburgh, Suffolk, late Pres. of Law
Soc.; *m* 1912, Catriona Marion Stewart Robertson (*d* 1961); one
s one *d. Educ:* Rugby Sch. Articled to his father, 1909; gave up
the law, 1912; entered employment of Anderson, Anderson &
Co., joint managers of Orient Steam Navigation Co. Ltd. Served
in the Army, Aug. 1914-Jan. 1919, retiring with rank of Capt.
Member of Council of Chamber of Shipping, retd 1958; first
Chm. of Nat. Dock Labour Corp; Chm. (1942-43) of London
Gen. Shipowners' Soc.; mem. Port of London Authority, 1934-
47; Underwriting Mem. of Lloyd's, 1952-; Chm., Lloyd's
Register of Shipping, 1946-57; Dir, Anderson Green & Co.
(Managers of Orient Line), 1924-58, retd. Pres. Inst. of Marine
Engineers, 1957; Chm. Central Transport Consultative Cttee for
Great Britain, 1958-62. Prime Warden, Worshipful Co. of
Shipwrights, 1956. *Recreations:* gardening, yachting, golf.
Address: Brockley Place, Bury St Edmunds, Suffolk. *T:* Hartest
278. *Club:* Royal Cruising.   *[Died 30 Jan.* 1972.

GARRETT, Sir William (Herbert), Kt 1958; MBE 1944; retired
as President, British Employers' Confederation, 1958-60; *b* 13
March 1900; *s* of William Henry Garrett and Mary Elizabeth
(*née* Odgers); *m* 1925, Marion Birchall (*d* 1967), *yr d* of Joseph
Henry Houghton; one *s* one *d. Educ:* Grove Park Sch.; Liverpool
Univ. Served RFC and RAF 1917-19. BSc Hons, 1921, PhD,
1923, Liverpool Univ. Mem. Civil Service Arbitration Tribunal,
1960-65; Chm., Association of British Chemical Manufacturers,
1959-61; Hon. Vice-Pres., Chemical Industries Assoc.
Publications: The Human Side of Industry, 1950; papers to
several technical journals, 1946-. *Recreations:* golf, music.
Address: 7c South Cliff Tower, Eastbourne, East Sussex BN20
7JN. *Club:* Junior Carlton.   *[Died 20 Aug.* 1977.

GARROD, (Herbert) Geoffrey, MA Oxon; Barrister-at-Law; *b* 31
Oct. 1886; *e s* of Herbert Baring Garrod, MA Oxon, Barrister-
at-Law, and Lucy Florence Colchester; *g s* of Sir Alfred Baring
Garrod, FRS, FRCP; *m* 1914, Margaret Langford (*d* 1953), *d* of
Benjamin Duke, MD; one *s* three *d. Educ:* Winchester Coll.
(Scholar); New Coll., Oxford (Scholar). Second Class in Class.
Mods, 1907, and in Final Hons, 1909; BA 1909; MA 1912;
literary and musical criticism in The Times, The Academy, The
Onlooker, Colour, etc; Called to Bar, Inner Temple, 1912;
Master St Paul's Preparatory Sch., 1914; City of London Sch.,
1915-19; Headmaster of Sevenoaks School, Kent, 1919-25;
Principal, Royal Academical Institution, Belfast, 1925-40; Lectr
in Classics, University Coll., Exeter, for three years; Dir of
Anglo-Brazilian Cultural Soc., Curitiba, Brazil, 1943-47; Senior
Classical Master, Fernden Sch., 1950-65. *Publications:* ed (with
mother), of Goethe, Dante's Faust and other Essays, by Herbert
Baring Garrod; various articles on literary and musical subjects.
Recreations: music (especially singing), stamp collecting,
yachting, walking, lawn tennis, boating, swimming. *Address:* 30
Rectory Gardens, Worthing, Sussex. *T:* Worthing 200380. *Club:*
Oxford and Cambridge Musical.   *[Died 22 May* 1974.

GARROD, Prof. Lawrence Paul, MD (Cambridge); FRCP; Vice-
President, British Medical Association; Emeritus Professor of
Bacteriology, University of London; *b* 7 Dec. 1895; *s* of late
Cubitt Garrod and Gertrude Dwelley Davey; *m* 1922, Marjorie,
d of late Bedford Pierce, MD, FRCP; three *s* one *d. Educ:* Sidcot
Sch.; King's Coll., Cambridge; St Bartholomew's Hosp. Surg.-
Sub-Lieut RNVR 1917-18; Brackenbury Scholar in Medicine, St
Bartholomew's Hosp., 1919; Gillson Scholar, Society of
Apothecaries, 1923-25; Studied clinical medicine for five years
after qualification; from 1925-61 held appointments on staff of
Dept of Pathology, St Bartholomew's Hosp.; late Bacteriologist
to St Bartholomew's Hosp. and to City of London; Editor,
British Jl of Experimental Pathology, 1951-57; late Consultant
in Antibiotics to the Army; late Hon. Consultant in
Chemotherapy, Royal Postgraduate Med. Sch.; late Examiner in
Pathology, Universities of London, Oxford and Cambridge;
formerly Pres. Institute of Medical Laboratory Technology.
FRSocMed (former Pres. Sect. Pathology). Hon. LLD
(Glasgow), 1965. Hon. FRCPath 1979. Hon. Alumnus Medical
Faculty, University of Louvain. *Publications:* Hospital
Infection, 1960-66; Antibiotic and Chemotherapy (jointly),
1963, 4th edn 1973; various papers, mainly on bacteriology and
chemotherapy. *Address:* Stradbroke, Gypsy Lane, Wokingham,
Berks.   *[Died 11 Sept.* 1979.

GARSTANG, Cecil, CBE 1969; Director, Thos Cook & Son Ltd,
Thos Cook & Son (Continental and Overseas) Ltd and Thos

Cook & Son SA Belge, 1964-73 (General Manager, 1960-69,
Managing Director, 1969-71); Director and Chairman, 1966-71
of Hernu, Peron & Stockwell Ltd, and England's & Perrott's
Ltd; Chairman, Sir Henry Lunn Ltd, and subsidiary companies,
1968-71; *b* 1 Dec. 1904; *s* of Arthur Harold Garstang and Lilian
Emma (*née* Meacock); *m* 1930, Winifred Eva Purkiss; two *s.
Educ:* Salisbury Cath. Sch.; Merchant Taylors' Sch. Joined Thos
Cook & Son Ltd, 1924. Served War of 1939-45, Econ. Adv. Br.
of FO and at Supreme HQ of AEF (Lt-Col). Vice-Chm. 1958-59,
Chm. 1960-62, Assoc. of British Travel Agents. MTAI.
Cavaliere Ufficiale, Order of Merit, Republic of Italy;
Commander, Order of the Falcon, Iceland, 1975; Hon. Citizen
of New Orleans. *Publications:* various papers on travel and
tourism. *Recreations:* travel, reading, gardening. *Address:* 66
Chiltern Avenue, Bushey, Herts. *T:* 01-950 2014. *Clubs:* Travel
Luncheon, Skal.   *[Died 16 Jan.* 1979.

GARSTIN, Lt-Col William Arthur MacDonell, CBE 1930 (OBE
1922); late Government of India Foreign and Political
Department; *b* 14 May 1882; *s* of John Henry Garstin, CSI; *m*
1915, Mary, *d* of James Ramsay-Smith, WS, Peebles; one *d.
Educ:* Sherborne Sch.; Sandhurst. Indian Army (7th Gurkha
Rifles). Transferred Political Dept, 1907. Dep. Comr Bannu, N-
WFP, 1920-23; Divisional and Sessions Judge, Peshawar Div.,
1925-28; Political Agent, Khyber Pass, 1928-30; Resident,
Gwalior, and Resident, Udaipur, 1932-35; Agent to the
Governor-Gen., Madras States (Travancore and Cochin), 1935-
37; retired, 1937. Frontier medals: Afghanistan, 1919;
Waziristan, 1921-24; NWFP, 1931-32. *Address:* 65 Campden
Hill Court, W8. *T:* 01-937 2074.   *[Died 31 May* 1975.

GARTHWAITE, Brig. Clive Charlton, CBE 1961; *b* 22 Oct.
1909; *er s* of late Major Alan Garthwaite, DSO, MC, The West
Garth, Guisborough, Yorks; *m* 1945, Hon. Elisabeth Clegg-Hill
(*née* Smyth-Osbourne) (*d* 1967); one *d. Educ:* Wellington Coll.,
Berks; Royal Military Academy, Woolwich. 2/Lieut Royal
Artillery, 1929; Hong Kong 1932-37; Major, 1939. Served in
Western Desert, 1941-42 (despatches); GSO1, 1949; Col 1955;
Brig. 1956; Comdr 5 Army Group RA, 1956-58; Comdt Sch. of
Artillery, Manorbier, 1958-60; Comdr Woolwich Garrison,
1960-63. Retired 1963. ADC 1960-63. *Recreations:* cricket, golf,
ski-ing, shooting. *Address:* Larkfield, Bacombe Lane,
Wendover, Bucks. *T:* Wendover 622206. *[Died 20 Jan.* 1979.

GARTLAN, Maj.-Gen. Gerald Ion, CBE 1940; DSO 1919; MC;
DL; JP; *b* 24 June 1889; *s* of late Alexander Gartlan of Cabra
House, Co. Down and Emily Hamill; *m* 1933, Dorothy Macafee;
two *d. Educ:* Downside Sch.; Sandhurst. 2nd Lieut Royal Irish
Rifles, 1909; Capt. 1915; Bt-Major, 1918; Major, 1924; Bt Lieut-
Col 1932; Lieut-Col 1933; Col 1937; served European War,
1914-18 (wounded twice, DSO, MC, Bt Majority, despatches);
served on Staff in France, Germany, Upper Silesia, Egypt, and at
War Office; commanded Depot, Royal Ulster Rifles, 1929-33;
commanded 2nd Bn The Royal Ulster Rifles, 1933-36; Brigadier
5th Infantry Brigade, 1938; War of 1939-45, France 1939-1940
(CBE, despatches); retired pay, 1944; idc; psc. DL 1952, High
Sheriff 1954, JP 1955, Co. Down. Hon Col 6th Bn Royal Ulster
Rifles, 1950-56. *Recreations:* polo, tennis, golf, hockey, fishing,
shooting. *Address:* Castle Park, Ardglass, Co. Down.
                                    [Died 15 July 1975.

GARTON, John William, JP; FCWA; Chairman: Brown Bayley
Ltd, 1957-69; Brown Bayley Steels Ltd, 1947-69; The Hoffmann
Manufacturing Company Ltd, 1952-69; *b* 29 Sept. 1895; *s* of late
William Garton and Mary Ann Garton, Sheffield; *m* 1922, Edris
Irene, *er d* of late Kennard Riley and Jane Riley, Llandudno;
one *s. Educ:* Sheffield. Served European War, 1914-19. Joined
steel industry as a boy being third successive generation in same
works. Served on Council of Institute of Costs and Works
Accountants, 1945-46; part-time mem. Iron and Steel
Corporation of Great Britain, 1951-53. JP Essex, 1954. Mem.
Advisory Cttee for Essex of Gen. Comrs of Income Tax, 1961-
68. *Recreations:* gardening, walking, fishing. *Address:*
Birchfield, Nethy Bridge, Inverness-shire. *Club:* Devonshire.
                                    [Died 20 Oct. 1971.

GARY, Romain, Officier de la Légion d'Honneur; Compagnon de
la Libération; Croix de Guerre; author; *b* Tiflis, Georgia, 8 May
1914; *s* of parents named Kacewgary (Kassevgari being the
spelling later used); *m* 1st, Lesley Blanch (marr. diss. 1963); 2nd,
1963, Jean Seberg (marr. diss.); one *s. Educ:* Lycée de Nice; Aix-
en-Provence; Universities of Paris and Warsaw. Served with
French Air Force, 1937-40; RAF and Free French Air Force in
Africa, Palestine and Russia, 1940-45. Joined French Foreign
Service, serving at embassies in UK, Bulgaria and Switzerland;
1st Sec., French delegation to United Nations; Consul-Gen. for
France at Los Angeles, USA, 1956-60. Directed films: Les
Oiseaux vont mourir au Pérou, 1968; Kill, 1971. *Publications:*

Education Européenne, 1943 (Eng. trans. Forest of Anger; revised as Nothing Important Ever Dies, 1961); Tulipe, 1946; Le Grand Vestiaire, 1949 (Eng. trans. The Company of Men, 1950); Les Couleurs du Jour, 1952 (Eng. trans. Colours of the Day, 1953); Les Racines du Ciel, 1956 (Prix Goncourt, Eng. trans. The Roots of Heaven, 1958); La Promesse de l'Aube, 1959 (Eng. trans. Promise at Dawn, 1962, filmed 1971); Lady L., 1959 (filmed 1965); Frère Océan, 1965; Pour Sganarelle, 1965; La Danse de Gengis Cohn, 1967; La Tête coupable, 1968; Le Mangeur d'étoiles, Adieu Gary Cooper, 1969; Chien Blanc, 1970 (Eng. trans. The White Dog, 1971); Europa, 1972; Les Enchanteurs, 1973; The Gasp, 1973; (as René Deville) Direct Flight to Allah, 1975; Au-delà de cette limite votre ticket n'est plus valable, 1976; The Way Out, 1977; Charge d'âme, 1978. *Address:* c/o Editions Gallimard, 5 rue Sebastien-Bottin, 75007 Paris, France. *[Died 2 Dec. 1980.*

GASCOYNE-CECIL, Victor Alexander; *b* 1891; *s* of Right Rev. Lord William Gascoyne-Cecil, late Bishop of Exeter, and Lady Florence Cecil; *m* 1915, Fairlie Estelle Caroline, *d* of Lieut-Col Arthur Watson, Suffolk Regt; two *s. Educ:* Westminster Sch.; Sandhurst. Hants Regt 1911; served European War, 1914-18, 1st Bn (wounded twice); Tank Corps, 1921-22; NW Frontier, India, 1922; retired, 1923 (Major); War of 1939-45, HM Forces, 1939-44. 1914 Star and War Medal, Indian Gen. Service, 1939-44, Defence and War Medal. JP Essex, 1936; High Sheriff, Essex, 1949; DL Essex, 1951-68. *Address:* Green Hanger, Rettendon Common, Chelmsford, Essex. *T:* Chelmsford 400311.
[Died 17 Jan. 1977.

GASKAIN, John Stuart Hinton, CBE 1968 (MBE 1950); Commandant of the Police College, Bramshill, Hants, 1966-68; HM Inspector of Constabulary, 1962-68, retired; *b* 11 May 1910; *s* of William Francis Gaskain and Gladys Therese Gaskain; *m* 1938, Nancy Evelyn Swan; one *s* one *d. Educ:* Haileybury Coll. Metropolitan Police, 1936-42; Hendon Police Coll., 1936-37. Barrister-at-Law, 1944. Asst Chief Constable of Norfolk, 1942-52; seconded as Commandant of Police Training Centre, Eynsham Hall, Witney, Oxfordshire, 1946-50; Chief Constable: Cumberland and Westmorland, 1952-59; Glos, 1959-62. Queen's Police Medal, 1960. OStJ 1962. *Recreation:* golf. *Address:* 10e Sussex Heights, St Margarets Place, Brighton, Sussex. *Club:* Royal Commonwealth Society. *[Died 16 Nov. 1971.*

GASSON, Sir Lionel Bell, Kt 1944; *b* 9 Aug. 1889; *s* of George Henry Gasson and Estelle Mary Bell; *m* 1916, Katherine Grace Moberly (*d* 1972); no *c. Educ:* Dulwich Coll. Joined Indian Police Service, 1910; King's Police Medal, 1928; Indian Police Medal, 1934; Dep. Inspector-Gen. of Police, 1936; Commissioner of Police, Madras City, 1939; Inspector-Gen. of Police, Madras Presidency, 1942; retired, 1944. *Recreations:* hunting, golf, fishing. *Address:* Rathwick, Gough Road, Fleet, Hants GU13 8LL. *T:* Fleet 7899. *Club:* East India, Devonshire, Sports and Public Schools. *[Died 16 March 1977.*

GATES, Sidney Barrington, OBE 1943; FRS 1950; Consultant, Ministry of Aviation, 1959-66; *b* 1893; *s* of Ernest Edwin Gates, Norwich; *m* 1915, Edith Annie Tofts, Cambridge; one *s* one *d* (and one *d* decd). *Educ:* City of Norwich Sch.; Corpus Christi Coll., Cambridge. Wrangler, 1914. Research work on stability and control of aircraft, Royal Aircraft Establishment, Farnborough, since 1915. Ed., of Scientific War Records of Min. of Supply (Air), 1944-46. Dep. Chief Scientific Officer, Min. of Supply (Air) 1950-52, Chief Scientific Officer, 1952-59. Hon. Fellow Royal Aeronautical Society, 1959 (FRAeS 1948). Literary Critic: The Nation, 1923; New Statesman, 1925; Times Literary Supplement, 1928-. *Publications:* Poems, 1925; The Mulligatawny Medallion, 1926; numerous papers on aeronautical theory in Reports and Memoranda of Aeronautical Research Council. *Recreations:* walking, gardening. *Address:* Apartment 6, Clare Park, Crondall, Surrey. *T:* Crondall 661.
[Died 12 June 1973.

GATES, Sylvester Govett, CBE 1944; Chairman: International Commercial Bank, since 1967; Tecalemit Ltd; Deputy Chairman: National Westminster Bank, since 1968; Standard Bank; Director, Standard & Chartered Banking Group Ltd; *b* 2 Sept. 1901; *s* of late Walter George Gates, CB, and Beatrice Helen Govett; *m* 1936, Pauline (*d* 1968), *d* of Algernon Newton, RA; one *s. Educ:* Winchester; New Coll., Oxford. First Class Hon. Mods, 1922; First Class Lit Hum, 1924; Commonwealth Fund Fellow (Private International Law), Harvard Univ., USA, 1925-27. Called to Bar, Inner Temple, 1928; practised London and Western Circuit, 1928-39; Controller of Home Publicity, Ministry of Information, 1941-44; attached to Office of Minister of Reconstruction, 1944; Mem. of Royal Commission on Taxation, 1951; Chm. Brit. Film Institute, 1956-64; Mem. Port of London Authority, 1958-64. *Address:* 29 Eaton Square, SW1; Manningford Abbas, Pewsey, Wilts. *[Died 1 Nov. 1972.*

GATHORNE-HARDY, Geoffrey Malcolm; *b* 28 Jan. 1878; *s* of late Hon. A. E. Gathorne-Hardy, Donnington Priory, Newbury; *m* 1914, Kathleen, *d* of late Henry Goschen; no *c. Educ:* Eton; New Coll., Oxford. Pres. Oxford Union, 1899. Called to Bar, Inner Temple, 1903; Served South African War, and European War, 1914-18 (MC, Belgian Croix de Guerre); Hon. Sec. Royal Institute of International Affairs, 1920-35; Asst Librarian, House of Lords, 1923-28. Hon. PhD (Oslo). Comdr Order of St Olav (Norwegian). *Publications:* The Norse Discoverers of America, 1921; Norway (Modern World series), 1925; A Short History of International Affairs, 1920-34, 1934; Final edn, 1949; War Poems of Nordahl Grieg, 1944; A Royal Impostor, 1956. *Recreations:* shooting and fishing. *Address:* Donnington Priory, Newbury, Berks. *T:* Newbury 241. *Club:* Junior Carlton.
[Died 7 Jan. 1972.

GATHORNE-HARDY, Hon. Robert; *b* 31 July 1902; *s* of 3rd Earl of Cranbrook and Lady Dorothy Boyle. *Educ:* Eton; Christ Church, Oxford. As a schoolboy, was an amateur geologist, collected flint implements and discovered a doubtfully palæolithic chalk carving in Suffolk; went to northern Labrador, thence to Oxford; studied for Medicine and took degree in Law; worked for a time on a monthly paper and afterwards at antiquarian bookselling, until the beginning of 1931; worked for many years in association with Logan Pearsall Smith. During War of 1939-45 was employed in Civil Defence, and finally as a builder's labourer on bomb damage in London. For many years shared in a private press. Mem. of Bradfield RDC, 1932-69 (Chm. 1953-61, Vice-Chm. 1961-62). Fellow of the Linnæan Soc., 1960. *Publications:* A Bibliography of the Works of Jeremy Taylor (in The Golden Grove by Logan Pearsall Smith), 1930; Lacebury Manor, 1930; Village Symphony, and other poems, 1931; The House by the Bay, 1932; Other Seas, 1933; Coronation Baby, 1935; The Wind and the Waterfall, 1938; Wild Flowers in Britain, 1938; Three Acres and a Mill, 1939; Garden Flowers, 1948; Recollections of Logan Pearsall Smith, 1949; The Tranquil Gardener, 1958; The Native Garden, 1962; Traveller's Trio, 1963; Amalfi: Aspects of the City and Her Ancient Territories, 1968; (with W. Proctor Williams) A Bibliography of the Writings of Jeremy Taylor to 1700, 1972. Editor: The Golden Shakespeare, selections chosen by Logan Pearsall Smith, 1949; A Religious Rebel, letters of Hannah Whitall Smith, 1949; Ottoline, memoirs of Lady Ottoline Morrell, 1963; *posthumous publication:* (ed) Ottoline at Garsington: memoirs of Lady Ottoline Morrell, 1974. *Recreations:* sight-seeing, bibliography, botany. *Address:* The Mill House, Stanford Dingley, near Reading, Berks. *T:* Bradfield 378. *[Died 11 Feb. 1973.*

GAULT, Brig. Sir James (Frederick), KCMG 1952; MVO 1943; OBE 1946 (MBE 1941); *b* 26 June 1902; *y s* of late Leslie Hamilton Gault; *m* 1st, 1936, Margaret Ella Campbell (marr. diss. 1960), *y d* of Brig.-Gen. Douglas Campbell Douglas, CB, Mains, Milngavie, Scotland, and Hon. Mrs Douglas; no *c* ; 2nd, 1960, Elizabeth Marchioness Townshend (who *m* first 7th Marquess Townshend, whom she divorced, 1960), *d* of Lieut-Col Thomas Luby, Indian Civil Service, Judicial Commissioner. *Educ:* Eton; Trinity Coll., Cambridge (BA). Joined Scots Guards, 1939; served War of 1939-45, in Middle East, North Africa, Sicily, Italy, N West Europe; Col 1944; RARO 1949; re-employed, 1950; Brigadier 1950; Military Asst, Supreme Commander Allied Powers in Europe, 1951-53. Order of Legion of Merit (USA). *Address:* Hemingstone Hall, near Ipswich, Suffolk. *T:* Coddenham 304; 51 Eaton Square, SW1. *T:* 01-235 7589. *Clubs:* White's, Turf. *[Died 14 Jan. 1977.*

GAUNT, William; Author and Painter; *b* Hull, 1900; *s* of William and Harriet Gaunt; *m* 1935, Mary Catherine O'Reilly (*née* Connolly) (*d* 1980). *Educ:* Hull Gram. Sch.; Worcester Coll., Oxford. BA Oxon 1922; MA 1926; AICA; Editor of numerous illustrated works, mainly on the Fine Arts. Exhibitions of paintings and drawings at Redfern Gallery, 1930; Leger Gallery, 1932; Reid and Lefevre Galls, 1936; Walker Galls., 1947; retrospective exhbn, Colchester, Hull and London, 1975. Art critic, Evening Standard, 1946; Special Correspondent to The Times on Art Subjects, 1957-. *Publications include:* Bandits in a Landscape, 1937; The Pre-Raphaelite Tragedy, 1942; (with F. G. Roe) Etty and the Nude, 1943; British Painting, 1945; (ed) Hogarth, 1947; (ed) William Morris: selections, 1948; The March of the Moderns, 1949; Victorian Olympus, 1952; (with J. Riddell) London in Colour, 1955; Renoir, 1952, 2nd edn, 1971; Chelsea, 1954; The Lady in the Castle (novel), 1956; Arrows of Desire, 1956; Teach Yourself to Study Sculpture, 1957; Kensington, 1958; The Observer's Book of Painting and Graphic Art, 1958; London, 1961; Everyman's Dictionary of Pictorial Art, 1962; ed, G. Vasari, Lives of the Painters, Sculptors and Architects, 1963; A Concise History of English Painting, 1964; The Observer's Book of Modern Art, 1964;

Oxford, 1965; The Observer's Book of Sculpture, 1966; A Companion to Painting, 1968; Flemish Cities, 1970; The Impressionists, 1970; The Great Century of British Painting, 1971; Turner, 1971; William de Morgan, 1971; The Restless Century, 1972; The Surrealists, 1972; Painters of Fantasy, 1974; Marine Painting, 1975; Court Painting in England: from Tudor to Victorian times, 1980. *Address:* 35b Lansdowne Road, W11. *T:* 01-727 6762. [*Died 24 May 1980.*]

GAUNTLETT, Major Eric Gerald, CBE 1919; DSO 1918; *b* 1 Nov. 1885; *s* of late T. L. Gauntlett, Putney, SW; *m* 1919, Hilda Mary Gerrard, RRC; one *s* (and two *s* decd). *Educ:* King's Coll. Sch.; King's Coll. Hospital. MB, BS (gold medal), London; FRCS; LRCP; Surgical Registrar and Tutor, King's Coll. Hospital; Asst Surgeon Paddington Green Children's Hospital; late Lieut-Col RAMC and Consulting Surgeon to the Salonica Forces (CBE, DSO, despatches four times); Major South Africa Medical Corps, 1942-46; retired, 1966. Hon. Associate of St John of Jerusalem, 1921. *Publications:* contributions to medical journals. *Address:* 3 Vint Crescent, Colchester, Essex. [*Died 26 Nov. 1972.*]

GAUSSEN, Maj.-Gen. Charles de Lisle, CB 1949; MC 1918; psc†; late RE; *b* 1 Aug. 1896; *m*; one *d.* 2nd Lieut, 1915; Lieut, 1916; Adjutant, 1916-18; Capt., 1918; Adj., 1926-28; Major, 1930; Lieut-Col, 1938; Temp. Col, 1940; Actg Brig., 1941; Brig., 1948; Hon. Maj.-Gen., 1950. Served European War, 1914-18, France and Belgium, 1915-18 (wounded, despatches twice, 1914-15 Star, British War Medal, Victory Medal, MC); GSO3, France, 1918-19; Staff Capt., France, 1919; Waziristan, 1921-24 (Medal and clasp); GSO3 India (temp.), 1921-23; Staff Capt., School of Military Engineering, 1931-32; GSO3, WO, 1932-35; Brig. Major, India, 1937-38; War of 1939-45 (despatches). Chief Eng. Northern Comd, India, 1946-47; E-in-C, India, 1947; Dep. E-in-C, WO, 1948-49; retired, 1950. *Address:* Tumble Top, Weedon, Aylesbury, Bucks. *Club:* Royal Over-Seas League. [*Died 18 July 1971.*]

GAUVAIN, (Catherine Joan) Suzette, (Mrs R. O. Murray); Consultant in Occupational Medicine; Hon. Senior Lecturer, London School of Hygiene and Tropical Medicine; *d* of late Sir Henry Gauvain, MD, MCh, FRCS, and Laura Louise (*née* Butler); *m* 1940, Ronald Ormiston Murray, MBE, MD; one *s* two *d. Educ:* St James', West Malvern; Grovely Manor, Boscombe; Somerville Coll., Oxford (MA); Radcliffe Infirmary, Oxford. MRCP, MFOM, FFCM, DPH. MO, Lord Mayor Treloar Orthop. Hosp., 1943-54; London Sch. of Hygiene and Trop. Med., 1958-73; Dept of Occupational Health, later TUC Centenary Inst. of Occupational Health: Research Asst, 1960-62; Lectr, 1962-69; Sen. Lectr, 1969-73; Employment Med. Adv. Service, Dept of Employment, 1973-: Dep. Chief Employment Med. Adviser, 1973-74; Actg Ch. Employment Med. Adviser, 1974-75; Dep. Dir of Med. Services, 1975-77; Consultant Advr on Medical Trng, Employment Medical Adv. Service, HSE, 1977-79. Mem. Permanent Commn, Internat. Assoc. of Occupational Health; Past Chm., London Assoc. of Soc. of Occupational Medicine; Past Pres., London Gp Med. Women's Fedn; Pres., Occupational Med. Sect., RSocMed, 1975-76. Chadwick Lectr, 1975. *Publications:* Occupational Health, a guide to sources of information, 1968, ed 2nd edn 1974; (chapters) Occupational Health Practice, ed Schilling, 1973; papers in BMJ, Lancet, Brit. Jl Occupational Med., Jl Soc. of Occupational Med., etc. *Recreations:* gardening, travelling. *Address:* 48 Witley Court, Woburn Place, WC1N 1HD. *T:* 01-837 7445; Little Court, The Bury, Odiham, Basingstoke, Hants. *T:* Odiham 2982. *Club:* Lansdowne. [*Died 23 Jan. 1980.*]

GAVITO, Vicente S.; *see* Sanchez-Gavito.

GAWNE, Ewan Moore, CSI 1945; CIE 1942; *b* 26 March 1889; *s* of Col J. M. Gawne; *m* 1st, 1913, Elizabeth, *d* of E. Oliver; one *d*; 2nd, 1946, Muriel Henderson (*d* 1947), Camberley. *Educ:* Wellington; Brasenose Coll., Oxford. Entered ICS, 1913; Mem., Board of Revenue, Madras, 1940; retd 1946. *Address:* Vine Cottage, South Warnborough, Basingstoke, Hants. [*Died 4 April 1978.*]

GAWTHORPE, Brig. John Bernard, CBE 1939; TD; Major (Hon. Brig.) (retired pay), late The West Yorkshire Regiment (Prince of Wales' Own); *b* Ossett, Yorks, 12 Nov. 1891; *e s* of late John H. Gawthorpe, Roundhay, Leeds; *m* 1915, Clarice Turner (*d* 1956), Roundhay; one *d. Educ:* Wakefield; Leeds. Territorial Army: 2nd Lieut 1911; Lieut 1913; Capt. 1915; Regular Army: Capt. (West Yorks Regt) 1917; Temp. Major (Machine Gun Corps), 1917-21; Bt Major, 1919; retd, 1931; Territorial Army: Lieut-Col Comdg 7th (Leeds Rifles) Bn West Yorks Regt 1934; Bt. Col 1938; Col 1938; served European War, France and Belgium, 1915, 1917, 1918 (wounded); North

Russia, 1919; Instructor: Machine Gun Sch., 1916 and 1919-21; Technical Officer, 1921-24; Infantry Brigade Commander (temp. Brig.), 1939-40; Active Service France and Belgium 1940, including evacuation of Dunkirk (despatches); Commander, Cambridge Sub-Dist, 1943-44; Hon. Col 12th (Yorks) Bn Parachute Regt (TA), 1949-56. Pres., 1940 Dunkirk Veterans' Assoc., 1975-76. *Recreation:* oil-painting. *Address:* 4 Bramhope Manor, Bramhope, Leeds LS16 9HI. *T:* Arthington 842384. [*Died 20 Aug. 1979.*]

GEARY, Major Benjamin Handley, VC 1915; MA Oxon; Sergeant-at-Arms, Ontario Legislature, 1947-71, retired; historian for the Legislature, retired; *b* 29 June 1891; *s* of late Rev. Henry Geary and Mrs Geary (*née* Alport); *m* 1st, 1922, Ruth Christiana (from whom he obtained a divorce, 1935; she *m* 2nd, 1935, James Courtenay Sherren), *d* of late C. E. Woakes; two *s*; 2nd, 1935, Constance Joan (*d* 1972), *d* of late Mr and Mrs F. H. Henderson-Cleland. *Educ:* Dulwich Coll. Preparatory School; St Edmund's Sch., Canterbury; Keble Coll., Oxford; Wycliffe Hall, Oxford. Master at Forest Sch., Essex, 1913. Served European War, 1914-18 (VC); retired Capt., East Surrey Regt; Curate of West Ham, 1921; Temp. CF, 1923; Chaplain to the Forces, 1926-27; resigned with rank of Capt. Travelling Sec. World Alliance for Internat. Friendship through the Churches, 1928; Continental Life Assurance Co., 1930; Toronto Better Business Bureau, 1935; Canadian Nat. Inst. for the Blind, 1937; Past-Pres. and Hon. Life Mem. Imperial Officers' Assoc. of Canada; Life Governor, Canadian Corps of Commissionaires; Dir, Kingsley Hall (Toronto) for Men. Hon. Member: University Club of Toronto, Empire Club, Civitan Club, Royal Canadian Military Institute, Royal Society of St George; Life-mem. St George's Soc.; Mem. Royal Commonwealth Soc., Royal Canadian Legion (ex-Pres. Woodbridge Branch; Hon. Pres., Gen. Nelles Branch), VC and GC Assoc., etc. Served War of 1939-45 with Canadian Army, 1940-46, Major. Canadian Centennial Medal, 1967. Hon. Life Mem., Niagara Peninsular Armed Forces Inst. *Recreations:* formerly: outdoor athletics, Rugby football (Surrey County cap), etc. *Address:* 329 Victoria Street, Niagara-on-the-Lake, Ontario, Canada. [*Died 28 May 1976.*]

GEDDES, 2nd Baron, *cr* 1942; **Ross Campbell Geddes,** KBE 1970 (CBE 1958); Chairman: Clerical, Medical and General Life Assurance Society; Monks Investment Trust Ltd; Deputy Chairman, Brixton Estate Ltd; *b* 20 July 1907; *s* of 1st Baron Geddes, PC, GCMG, KCB, and Isabella Gamble (*d* 1962), 3rd *d* of W. A. Ross, NY; *S* father 1954; *m* 1931, Enid Mary, *d* of late Clarance H. Butler, Tenterden, Kent and late of Shanghai; one *s* one *d* (and one *s* decd). *Educ:* Rugby; Caius Coll., Cambridge (MA). Shell Group of Oil Companies, 1931-46; British Merchant Shipping Mission, Washington, 1942-44; Deputy-Director Tanker Division, Ministry of War Transport, 1944-45. Dir, Limmer Holdings Ltd, 1957-71 (Chm., 1964-71); Dir, Peninsular and Oriental Steam Navigation Co., 1957-72 (Chief Exec., European and Air Transport Div., 1971-72); Chm., Trident Tankers Ltd, 1963-71; Director: Foseco Minsep Ltd; Minerals Separation Ltd; Technology Investments Trust Ltd; Cambridge Petroleum Royalties Ltd; Southern Pacific Properties Ltd; Chairman: Navy Dept Fuels and Lubricants Adv. Cttee, 1951-57; BTA, 1964-70; Min. of Transport Cttee of Enquiry into Carriers' Licensing, 1963-65. President: Inst. of Petroleum, 1956-57; Chamber of Shipping of the UK, 1968. Chm., Westminster Med. Sch. Council, 1968-, and Mem. Governing Body, Westminster Hosp., 1968-74. DL Midlothian, 1957-72. *Recreations:* gardening and yachting. *Heir:* s Hon. Euan Michael Ross Geddes [*b* 3 Sept. 1937; *m* 1966, Gillian, *yr d* of W. A. Butler; one *s* one *d*]. *Address:* Nagshead Field, Lymington, Hants. *T:* Lymington 3333. *Clubs:* White's, Brooks's; Royal Lymington Yacht. [*Died 2 Feb. 1975.*]

GEDDIS, Alderman Sir William (Duncan), Kt 1969; JP; clothing manufacturer; *b* 9 July 1896; *m* 1924, Ethel, *d* of Joseph Barron Wiley, Templepatrick; one *s. Educ:* Skerries Coll., Belfast. Served in RAOC, 1940-48, with rank of Major. Mem., Belfast Corporation, 1938-; Lord Mayor of Belfast, May 1966-69. *Recreation:* golf. *Address:* 7 Waterloo Park, Belfast 15. *T:* 76531. *Clubs:* Ulster Reform (Belfast); Fortwilliam Golf. [*Died 12 Dec. 1971.*]

GEFFEN, John Lionel Henry, MA; Chairman: Bonsoir Ltd; Taylor Law Ltd; Rosedale Industries Ltd; Stability Hosiery Ltd; Director, Keenan Spark Ltd; *b* 10 May 1925; *s* of Dennis Herbert and Marion Gwendoline Geffen; *m* 1956, Maureen Jane Stanley Mills; two *s. Educ:* Rugby; New College, Oxford (BA(Hons) 1949, MA 1950). Buyer/Director, Lawleys Ltd, 1954-59; Man. Dir, Hyde & Co., 1962-69; Man. Dir, BAC, 1969-70; Dir, Gardner Merchant (Trust House Subsidiary), 1969-70; Gp Man. Dir, Wharf Holdings Ltd, 1970-71; Dep. Chm. and

Chief Executive, Bensons Hosiery Holdings Ltd, 1972-73; Dir, Family Planning Assoc., 1974-75. *Recreations:* skiing, cricket, golf, squash, real tennis. *Address:* 103 Coleherne Court, SW5. *T:* 01-373 8378. *Clubs:* Army and Navy, MCC, Hurlingham; Middleton Sports, Bognor Regis Golf.   *[Died* 17 *Dec.* 1975.

GELLERT, Leon; journalist; *b* Adelaide, 17 May 1892; *s* of J. W. Gellert; *m* 1918, Kathleen Patricia (decd), *y d* of late William Saunders; (one *d* decd). *Educ:* Adelaide High Sch. and Adelaide Univ. (Bundey Prize for English Verse). Served with the original 10th Bn which landed on Gallipoli, 25 April 1915. Co-Editor (with late Sydney Ure Smith), Art in Australia Publications, 1921; later Dir, Art in Australia; Literary Editor and Feature Writer, Sydney Morning Herald, 1942-61. *Publications:* Songs of a Campaign, 1917, illus. by Norman Lindsay; Isle of San, illus. by Norman Lindsay, 1919; Desperate Measures, 1929; These Beastly Australians, illus. by Bernard Hesling, 1944; Week after Week, 1953; Year after Year, 1956. *Address:* 21 Lerwick Avenue, Hazelwood Park, SA 5066, Australia.
                                                                      [Died 22 *Aug.* 1977.

GENEVOIX, Maurice (Charles Louis); Grand Croix de la Légion d'Honneur; man of letters; Member of the French Academy since 1946 and Permanent Secretary, 1958-74; *b* 29 Nov. 1890; *m* Suzanne Neyrolles; two *d. Educ:* Lycées d'Orléans, Lakanal; Ecole normale supérieure. Served European War, 1914-18 (Croix de Guerre). Prix Goncourt, 1925. *Publications:* Sous Verdun, 1914; Nuits de guerre, 1917; Au seuil des guitounes, 1918; Jeanne Robelin, 1920; La Boue, 1921; Rémi des Rauches, 1922; Les Eparges, 1923; La Joie, 1924; Euthymos, vainqueur olympique, 1924; Raboliot, 1925; La Boite à pêche, 1926; Les Mains vides, 1928; Cyrille, 1928; L'Assassin, 1930; Rrou, 1931; HOE, 1931; Gai l'amour, 1932; Forêt voisine, 1933; Marcheloup, 1934; Tête baissée, 1935; Bernard, 1937; La Dernière Harde, 1938; Les Compagnons de l'Aubépin, 1938; L'Hirondelle qui fit le printemps, 1941; Laframboise et Bellehumeur, 1942; Eva Charlebois, 1944; Canada, 1945; Sanglar, 1946; L'Ecureuil du bois bourru, 1947; Afrique blanche, Afrique noire, 1949; Ceux de 14, 1950; L'Aventure est en nous, 1952; Fatou Cissé, 1954; Images pour un Jardin sans murs, 1955; Vlaminck, 1956; le Roman de Renard, 1958; Routes de l'Aventure, 1959; Au cadran de mon clocher, 1960; Vaincre à Olympie, 1960; Jeux de Glaces, 1961; La Loire, Agnès et les Garçons, 1962; Derrière les Collines, 1963; Christian Caillard, 1965; Beau-François, 1965. La Forêt perdue, 1967; Jardins sans murs, 1968; Tendre bestiaire, 1968; Bestiaire enchanté, 1969; Bestiaire sans oubli, 1971; La Grèce de Caramanlis, 1972; La Mort de Près, 1972; La Perpétuité, 1974; Un Jour, 1976; Lorelei, 1978; 30,000 Jours (autobiog.), 1980. *Address:* 17 rue Davioud, 75016 Paris, France. *T:* 520-78-17; Les Vernelles, 45550 St Denis de l'Hôtel, France.   *[Died* 8 *Sept.* 1980.

GENN, Leo John; Actor and Barrister-at-Law; *b* 9 Aug. 1905; *s* of William Genn and Rachel (*née* Asserson); *m* 1933, Marguerite, *d* of Edward van Praag and Catherine (*née* Bonnar); no *c. Educ:* City of London Sch.; St Catharine's Coll., Cambridge (MA). Called to Bar, Middle Temple, 1928. Actor as well as Barrister-at-Law since 1930. First appearance on professional stage, 1930, in A Marriage Has Been Disarranged, Nov., at Eastbourne, Dec. at Royalty, London; various parts at Royalty, 1931-32; Garrick, Gaiety, Wyndham's, 1932-33-34; joined Old Vic Company, appearing in numerous parts in Shakespeare, Shaw, Ibsen, Sheridan, Sept. 1934-March 1936; St Helena, Daly's, 1936; Old Vic: Feb.-April 1937 (in June, Horatio, at Elsinore); The Flashing Stream, The Lyric, 1938. First appearance in New York, April 1939, in same play. Joined Officers' Emergency Reserve, 1938; 2nd Lieut RA 1940; Capt. 1941; Maj. 1942; Lieut-Col 1943; comd No. 1 War Crimes Investigation Team, responsible for Belsen Concentration Camp Investigation; Asst Prosecutor Belsen Trial, 1945. Croix de Guerre, 1945. Resumed career in the theatre. Another Part of the Forest, New York, 1946; Jonathan, Aldwych, 1948; The Seventh Veil, Prince's, 1951; Henry VIII, Old Vic, 1953; The Bombshell, Westminster, 1954; Small War on Murray Hill, New York, 1957; The Hidden River, Cambridge, 1959; The Devil's Advocate, NY, 1961; Fair Game for Lovers, NY, 1964; 12 Angry Men, Queen's, 1964; The Sacred Flame, Duke of York's, 1967; The Only Game in Town, New York, 1968; Caesar and Cleopatra, US, 1968; Dr Faustus, US, 1969. First film, Jump for Glory, 1937. *Films include:* The Drum, Ten Days in Paris, Henry V, Desert Victory (Commentary), Theirs was the Glory (Commentary), Green for Danger, Mourning Becomes Electra, The Snake Pit, The Velvet Touch, The Wooden Horse, Quo Vadis, Plymouth Adventure, Red Beret, Personal Affair, The Green Scarf, Moby Dick, L'Amant de Lady Chatterley (in French), Beyond Mombasa, The Steel Bayonet, I Accuse, No Time To Die; Too Hot To Handle; It Was Night in Rome; The Longest Day; 55 Days at Peking; Ten Little Indians; Circus of Fear; Connecting Rooms;

The Bloody Judge; Rebound; Lizard in a Woman's Skin; Le Silencieux. TV since 1951; broadcasts since 1933; narrator: Coronation Programme, 1937, 1953. King George VI Memorial Programme, 1952; UN opening (from USA), 1947, etc. Distinguished Vis. Prof. of Theatre Arts, Pennsylvania State Univ., 1968, Univ. of Utah, 1969. Governor, Mermaid Theatre; Assessor, Yvonne Arnaud Theatre, Guildford; Councillor, Arts Educational Schools. *Publications:* magazine and newspaper articles. *Recreations:* ball games, books and The Bar. *Address:* Elmhurst Cottages, Itchingfield, Sussex. *T:* Slinfold 344. *Clubs:* Garrick; Stage Golfing; West Sussex Golf (Pulborough); Travellers' (Paris).   *[Died* 26 *Jan.* 1978.

GENTELE, (Claes-) Göran (Herman Arvid); General Manager, Metropolitan Opera, New York, since 1972; Director, Royal Opera, Stockholm, Sweden, 1963-71; *b* 17 Sept. 1917; *m* Marit Bergson; three *d. Educ:* Stockholm Univ. (MA); School of Royal Dramatic Theatre, 1941-44. Actor at Royal Dramatic Th., Stockholm, 1944, gradually began to direct plays (about a dozen until 1952); engaged as guest producer for Menotti's opera The Consul, Royal Opera House, Stockholm, 1952; Chief Producer, Royal Opera House, 1953-63, continuing to produce until leaving the Royal Opera in 1971. *Productions include:* Carmen, Madama Butterfly, Don Carlos, Salome (with Birgit Nilsson in her first Salome), Wozzeck, Der Rosenkavalier, The Turn of the Screw (Britten), Die Fledermaus, Don Giovanni, Otello, Tristan and Isolde, The Makropoulos Case (Janácek) etc; Verdi's The Masked Ball and Swedish "space opera" Aniara, 1958 and 1959, both given by Royal Swedish Opera in Edinburgh 1959, Covent Garden 1960, Expo 67 Montreal, Scandinavian capitals, and Munich, 1969; also some Swedish films, mostly comedies. *Address:* The Metropolitan Opera House, Lincoln Center, New York, NY 10023, USA.   *[Died* 18 *July* 1972.

GENTRY, Jack Sydney Bates, CIE 1946; CBE 1965 (OBE 1942); ERD 1964; JP; General Manager Tees Conservancy Commission, 1946-66; retired; *b* 4 Oct. 1899; *s* of Frederick and Emma Gentry; *m* 1931, Beatrice Colleen Cundy Wren. *Educ:* Christ's Hosp. Port of London Authority, 1916, Commercial Superintendent, 1945; commission, Hants Regt, 1918; RE, 1938; served War of 1939-45 (despatches twice); Major, 1939; Lieut-Col, Asst Dir of Docks, 1940; Col, Dep. Dir of Movements, 1942. Dep. Regional Port Dir, Calcutta, 1944-45. JP Co. Durham, 1949. MIT, 1947. *Recreations:* cricket (played for Hants, Surrey, Essex, 1919-26); golf, tennis. *Address:* Pancake Cottage, Loxwood, near Billingshurst, West Sussex RH14 0SJ. *T:* Loxwood 752289. *Clubs:* MCC; Christ's Hospital.
                                                                      [Died 16 *April* 1978

GEORGE, Ven. Christopher Owen; Rector of Sproughton and Archdeacon of Suffolk, 1947-62; Archdeacon Emeritus, St Edmundsbury and Ipswich, since 1962; *b* 30 Sept. 1891; *s* of late Thomas and Emily Marion George; *m* 1921, Kathleen Iris Maude (*d* 1970), *d* of late Walter Herbert Back; four *d. Educ:* Ipswich Sch.; Selwyn Coll., Cambridge. BA 1913, MA 1917. Deacon 1914, Priest 1915, Diocese of Norwich; Curate, Great Yarmouth, 1914-19; Associate Sec. Dr Barnardo's Homes, 1919 23: Asst Master, Ipswich Sch. 1923-27; Curate, St Mary-le Tower, 1923-25, St Clement, 1925-27, Vicar, St Augustine 1927-34 and Rector, St Mary Stoke, Ipswich, 1934-47 *Recreation:* reading. *Address:* The Old Rectory Flat, Harkstead Ipswich, Suffolk IP9 1DE.   *[Died* 8 *Sept.* 1977

GEORGE, Frank Bernard; retired as Managing Director, Conset Iron Company Ltd (1957-64); President, Iron and Stee Institute, 1963-64 (Vice-President 1962); *b* 20 July 1899; *s* of Si Edward George and Eleanor Dagnall; *m* 1927, Winifred Mary George; three *s. Educ:* Caldicott Sch., Hitchin; The Leys Sch Cambridge; Armstrong Coll., Durham Univ. Consett Iron Co Ltd, 1925-64. Pres. Cleveland Institution of Engineers, 1956-57 *Publications:* contrib. Iron and Steel Institute Journal. *Address* 2 Fir Tree Close, Bolton-le-Sands, Lancs. *T:* Hest Bank 3274
                                                                      [Died 6 *Oct.* 1974

GEORGE, Sir John (Clarke), KBE 1963 (CBE 1952); CEng Director: National Carbonising Co. Ltd; Chairman, Prestwic Precision Products Ltd; *b* 16 Oct. 1901; *s* of John Clarke George Gracemount, Aberdour, Fife; *m* 1929, Euphamia, *d* of Rober G. Donaldson, Priory, Ballingry, Fife. *Educ:* Ballingry Publi Sch., Fife. Entered coal mine at age of 14. Managing Directo New Cumnock Collieries, Ayrshire, 1938-46; Alloa Glass Work Co. Ltd, 1946-55; Chm., Joy Manufacturing Co. (UK) Ltd (no Scottish Mechanical Light Industries Ltd), to 1971. Mem. Allo Town Council, 1951-56; CC Clackmannanshire, 1949-5 Contested (C) S Div. of Ayrshire, 1950; MP (U) Pollok Div. Glasgow, 1955-64; Parly Sec., Min. of Power, 1959-62; Chm Unionist Party in Scotland, 1963-65. CStJ. *Address:* Seto Lodge, Ayr, Scotland. *T:* 62541. *Club:* Caledonian.
                                                                      [Died 14 *Oct.* 197

GEORGE, Mary Dorothy, OBE 1954; MA, LittD, FRHistSoc; Hon. Fellow of Girton College; *d* of late Alexander Gordon, barrister-at-law, and of late Harriet Emily, *d* of Rev. R. S. Tabor; *m* 1913, Eric Beardsworth George (*d* 1961), painter. *Educ:* St Leonards Sch., St Andrews; Girton Coll., Cambridge (1st Cl. Historical Tripos); London Sch. of Economics (research scholar). War Office, (MI5), 1915-19 (mentioned for valuable services). *Publications:* English Social Life in the Eighteenth Century, 1923; London Life in the XVIII Century, 1925, 1951, paperback 1966; England in Johnson's Day, 1928; England in Transition, 1931, 1952, 1964; British Museum Catalogue of Political and Personal Satires (caricatures), in continuation of that by F. G. Stephens, vols V-XI (1771-1832), 1935-54; English Political Caricature to 1792: a study of Opinion and Propaganda, 1960; English Political Caricature, 1793-1832, 1960; Hogarth to Cruikshank: Social Change in Graphic Satire, 1967. Contributions to Johnson's England, 1933, English Historical Review, Economic Journal, History, etc. *Address:* 51 Paulton's Square, SW3. *T:* 01-352 6228. *[Died 13 Sept. 1971.*

GEORGE, Thomas Neville, FRS 1963; FRSE, FGS, DSc Wales, PhD, ScD Cantab; Professor of Geology in the University of Glasgow, 1947-74, now Emeritus; *b* 13 May 1904; *s* of T. Rupert George, Swansea; *m* 1932, Dr Sarah Davies; no *c. Educ:* Dynevor Sch.; Swansea Grammar Sch.; Universities of Wales (Swansea Coll., Sen. Scholar, Univ. Res. Scholar), Cambridge (St John's Coll., Bonney Award) and London (British Coll.). Fellow of the University of Wales, 1926. Geologist on HM Geological Survey, 1930; Prof. of Geology and Head of the Dept of Geology and Geography, University Coll. of Swansea, 1933; Woodward Lectr, Yale Univ., 1956; Sen. Foreign Fellow (Nat. Sci. Foundation), Northwestern Univ., 1964; Vis. Prof., Universities of the Witwatersrand, Cape Town, and Natal, 1967; Distinguished Vis. Lectr, Univ. of Saskatchewan, 1974; Leverhulme Emeritus Fellow, 1977. Pres. Geology Section of British Assoc. (Liverpool), 1953. Chairman: Newbattle Abbey Coll. Exec. Cttee; Brit. Assoc. Glasgow Cttee; Mineral Resources Panel (Scottish Council); Geological Conservation Council; Vice-Pres., RSE, 1959-61. President: Geol. Soc. London, 1968-70; Assoc. University Teachers, 1959-60; Palæontological Assoc., 1962-64; Assoc. Teachers Geol., 1970-71 Scot. Field Studies Assoc., 1968-. Member: Nature Conservancy; Mineral Resources Consultative Cttee (Dept of Education and Science); Geology and Geophysics Cttee (NERC); Oceanography and Fisheries Cttee (NERC); Unit of Coastal Sedimentation (NERC); National Broadcasting Council (Scotland); Ct of Governors, Coleg Harlech. Corr. Mem., Geol. Soc. Belgium. Hon. LLD Wales 1970; Hon. D-ès-Sc (Rennes) 1956. Lyell Medal, Geological Soc. London, 1963; Clough Medal, Geol Soc. Edinburgh, 1973; Kelvin Prize, Roy. Philos. Soc., 1975; Neill Medal, RSE, 1978. Associate Editor, Royal Society. *Publications:* Evolution in Outline, 1951; British Regional Geology: North Wales, 1961; South Wales, 1969; Aspects of the Variscan Fold Belt (in part), 1962; The British Caledonides (in part), 1963; The Geology of Scotland (in part), 1964; University Instruction in Geology, 1965; (contrib.) The Upper Palaeozoic Rocks of Wales, 1974; contributions on geology and palæontology to technical journals. *Address:* c/o Department of Geology, University of Glasgow, Glasgow W2. *T:* 041-339 8855; 1 Princes Terrace, Glasgow G12 9JW. *[Died 18 June 1980.*

GEORGES, Sir (James) Olva, Kt 1971; OBE 1960 (MBE 1949); Senior Member, firm of J. E. W. Georges, General Merchants, since 1909; Chairman, Public Service Commission; Member, Judicial and Legal Commission, etc, the British Virgin Islands; *b* 14 July 1890; *m* 1916, Eunice Egberta O'Neal; no *c. Educ:* Road Town Methodist Sch. and Antigua Grammar Sch., BWI. Career as merchant, in BWI. Deputy Commissioner, 1946, 1954, 1956, and Administrator for one month in 1962. Rep. at WI Federation talks (Barbados: Jamaica). Member: Inter Virgin Islands Conf., 1951: Salaries Commn; Scholarship Cttee; etc. Methodist Circuit Steward, 1939-64. *Recreations:* cricket, tennis. *Address:* PO Box 31, Road Town, Tortola, Virgin Islands, BWI. *T:* 42418. *[Died 27 March 1976.*

GERAGHTY, Sir William, KCB 1976 (CB 1962); Second Permanent Under Secretary of State (Administration), Ministry of Defence, 1975-76; *b* 12 Feb. 1917; *e s* of Patrick and Elizabeth Geraghty; *m* 1946, Lilian Irene Travis; no *c. Educ:* Emanuel Sch.; Brasenose Coll., Oxford. 1st Cl. Hon. Mods 1937, 1st Cl. Lit Hum 1939. Appointed War Office, 1939. Served RA and RHA, 1940-45. Private Sec. to Secretaries of State for War, 1949-51. Imperial Defence Coll., 1955. Asst Under-Sec. of State, WO, 1958-60; Under-Sec., Cabinet Office, 1960-62; Dep. Under-Sec. of State: WO, 1962-64; (1) Army Dept, Min. of Defence, 1964-65; (Air), Min. of Defence, 1965; Administration, 1965-66; Dep. Sec., Min. of Aviation, 1966-67, Min. of Technology, 1967-

70, Min. of Aviation Supply, 1970-71; Controller (Personnel), MoD (PE), 1971-75. *Address:* 29 Park Lane, Cheam Village, Surrey. *T:* 01-643 3028. *Club:* United Oxford & Cambridge University. *[Died 7 May 1977.*

GERAHTY, Sir Charles Cyril, Kt 1939; QC, Trinidad, 1931; *b* 1888; *s* of Charles Echlin Gerahty; *m* 1st, 1915, Ethel Marian (*d* 1942), *d* of late Dr James Murray, MB, ChB; one *s* (younger killed in action April 1945); 2nd, 1948, Arminell Morshead (*d* 1966); 3rd, 1967, Mary Violet, *widow* of Gerald Watson, late of Pyrford, Woking. *Educ:* Trent Coll. Called to Bar, Middle Temple, 1909; Maj. (retd). 3rd Bn East Lancs Regt; Asst Resident, Nigeria, 1911; on active service, European War, 1914-18; Legal Asst, War Office, 1919; Pres., District Court, Cyprus, 1920; Attorney-Gen., Cyprus, 1926; Attorney-Gen., Trinidad, 1929; Puisne Judge, Straits Settlements (Singapore), 1932; Legal Adviser to Governor of Malta, 1935; Legal Sec. to Government of Malta, 1936; Chief Justice of Trinidad and Tobago and Pres. West Indian Court of Appeal, 1937-43; retired, 1943. Chm. of a Pensions Appeal Tribunal, England, April 1944. Dir-Gen. MGC Branch, Legal Div., CCG, Dec. 1944-July 1946; Acting Attorney-Gen. in Gibraltar, May-Aug. 1949; JP, 1951-55; Dep. Chm. Essex Court of Quarter Sessions, 1951-55. *Address:* Pendean Convalescent Home, Midhurst, Sussex. *[Died 6 June 1978.*

GERARD, Bt Col Charles (Robert Tolver Michael), DSO 1917; OBE 1944; late Grenadier Guards; late Commanding TA Battalion; JP Lancs; *b* 28 Feb. 1894; *s* of late Hon. R. J. Gerard-Dicconson; *heir-pres* to 4th Baron Gerard, *qv*; *m* 1st, 1915, Aimée (who obtained a divorce, 1930), *d* of Sir R. T. H. Clarke, 2nd Bt; two *s*; 2nd, 1930, Norma, *d* of Mrs Frankford Rogers. *Educ:* Eton; Sandhurst. Served European War (France), 1914-18 (despatches, DSO); Dep. Provost Marshal, London, 1939-45. *Address:* Doone, Sunningdale, Berks. *T:* Ascot 194. *Clubs:* Turf, White's. *[Died 14 Jan. 1971.*

GÉRAUD, Charles Joseph André; (Pertinax); Officer Legion of Honour, France, 1936; diplomatic correspondent, France-Soir, Paris, since 1944; contributor to: Daily Telegraph (London), since 1912, Foreign Affairs (New York), since 1937; *b* St Louis de Montferrand (Gironde), 18 Oct. 1882; *s* of Oscar Géraud and Marthe Faux; *m* 1914, Louise Banniard; no *c. Educ:* Bordeaux Univ. (Licencié-ès-lettres). London correspondent of L'Echo de Paris, 1908-14; Foreign Editor, L'Echo de Paris (Pertinax), 1917-38; Editor, L'Europe Nouvelle, 1938-40; contributor to: New York Times, Baltimore Sun and several other newspapers and reviews. *Publications:* Le Partage de Rome, a study of the Lateran Treaties, 1929; Les Fossoyeurs (Gamelin, Daladier, Reynaud, Pétain, Laval): French edn, 2 vols, NY, 1943; new edn, NY, 1945; English language edn, (The Gravediggers), NY, 1944, Paris edn, 1st vol., 1946. *Address:* 91 rue de l'Université, Paris 7e; Segur-le Château (Corrèze); 58 W 10th Street, New York City. *[Died 11 Dec. 1974.*

GERHARDIE, William Alexander, OBE 1920; MA, BLitt (Oxon); FRSL 1975; Author; *b* St Petersburg, 21 Nov. 1895; *y s* of late Charles Alfred Gerhardie, an English industrialist settled at St Petersburg, and Clara Wadsworth. *Educ:* The St Annen Schule, and Reformierte Schule, St Petersburg; Worcester Coll., Oxford. Served European War, 5th Reserve Cavalry (2nd Dragoons, Royal Scots Greys), 1915-16; with Military Attaché, British Embassy, Petrograd, 1916-18; attached 3rd Bn Scots Guards; British Military Mission to Siberia, 1918-20 (Order of St Stanislav, of Imperial Russia; Czecho-Slovak War Cross; despatches, OBE); demobilized, retaining rank of Capt., 1920; joined Officers' Emergency Reserve, 1940; BBC (European Div.), 1942-45. First Ed. of English by Radio. Knight of Mark Twain (in succession to Sir Max Beerbohm). *Publications:* Futility: A Novel on Russian Themes, 1922; Anton Chehov: A Critical Study, 1923; The Polyglots, a Novel, 1925; A Bad End, 1926; The Vanity-Bag; Donna Quixote: a Comedy in Three Acts; Pretty Creatures: Short Novels, 1927; Doom, a Novel, 1928; Pending Heaven, a Novel, 1930; Memoirs of a Polyglot, (autobiography), 1931, updated repr. 1973; The Memoirs of Satan (with Brian Lunn) 1932; The Casanova Fable (with Hugh Kingsmill), 1934; Resurrection, a Novel, 1934; Meet Yourself: character studies through self-analysis (with Prince Leopold Loewenstein), 1936; Of Mortal Love, a Novel, 1936; My Wife's the Least of It, a Novel, 1938; The Romanoffs: An Historical Biography, 1940, rev. edn 1971; My Literary Credo: an Introduction to the first Uniform Revised Edition of the Collected Works, 10 vols, 1947; I Was A King in Babylon-And You May Very Well Be Right, an implausible comedy, produced by Jerome Kilty, 1948 (Boston, USA); Highlights of Russian History, 1949; Analyze Yourself, an American adaptation of Meet Yourself, 1955; Rasputin, the ironical tragedy, prod. Vanburgh Theatre, London, 1960; The Fool of the Family (with

Lord Snow, a play), 1964; Donna Quixote, a lyrical comedy, prod. Little Theatre, London, 1968; Works, 2nd Collected Uniform Definitive Editions, 10 vols, 1970-74, containing 10 cumulative Critical and Biographical Prefaces by Michael Holroyd; The End of the World: Prognosis Dramatica chronicling a month in mid-next century, an ironical tragedy, 1976; essays; articles; broadcasts (inc. TV films); *posthumous publication:* God's Fifth Column, ed M. Holroyd and R. Skidelsky, 1981. *Address:* 19 Rossetti House, Hallam Street, Portland Place, W1. *T:* 01-580 4878. *[Died 15 July 1977.*

GERRARD, Major Frederick Wernham, CIE 1920; *b* 25 Nov. 1887; *s* of M. G. Gerrard; *m* 1928, Dorothy Ursula, *d* of G. H. Teague. Joined Indian Police Service, 1908. IARO: served with 116 Mahrattas, North West Frontier, India, 1915; with 114 Mahrattas, Mesopotamia, 1916-23 (despatches, 1918); with Civil Administration, Iraq, as Deputy Inspector-Gen. of Police, Baghdad, 1921-23; retired from Indian Police Service, 1933; Commissioner of Police Foreign Settlement of Shanghai; retired 1938. *Address:* 1601 Ross Street, Victoria, BC, Canada.
[Died 14 March 1974.

GERVERS, Brig. Francis Richard Soutter, CIE 1919; CBE 1929; late Royal Engineers; *b* Kimberley, 10 July 1873; *s* of late F. T. Gervers; *m* 1904, Beryl Firebrace; no *c*. *Educ:* United Services Coll., Westward Ho; RM Academy, Woolwich. Employed, 1901, Gold Coast Survey; served Mohmand, Malakand, and Tirah, 1897-98 (medal with two clasps); India, 1914-19 (medal); Afghanistan, 1919 (medal with clasp); European War (medal); retired, 1928; FRGS. *Recreations:* shooting, fishing. *Address:* Sloane House, Littleworth Avenue, Esher, Surrey. *Club:* United Service & Royal Aero. *[Died 13 July 1971.*

GERY, Henry Theodore W.; *see* Wade-Gery.

GETTY, J(ean) Paul; President: Getty Oil Co. since 1947; Mission Corporation since 1947; Trustee and Founder of the J. Paul Getty Museum, Malibu, Calif.; *b* Minneapolis, USA, 15 Dec. 1892; *s* of George Franklin Getty and Sarah Catherine McPherson Risher; *m* 1923 (marr. diss.); one *s* decd; *m* 1926 (marr. diss.); *m* 1928 (marr. diss.); one *s*; *m* 1932 (marr. diss.); two *s*; *m* 1939 (marr. diss.); one *s* decd. *Educ:* University of Southern California; University of California; Oxford Univ. (non-collegiate Diploma in Economics and Political Science). Pres. and Gen. Manager, George F. Getty Inc., 1930-33; Director: Petroleum Corporation, 1932-34; Tidewater Associated Oil Co., 1932-36; Pres. of other companies. Officier, Légion d'Honneur; Grande Médaille (silver), City of Paris. Hon. LLD, Ohio Northern Univ. *Publications:* A History of the Oil Business of George Franklin and J. Paul Getty, 1903-1939, 1940; Europe in the Eighteenth Century, 1949; (with Ethel Levane) Collector's Choice, 1955; My Life and Fortunes, 1963; How to be Rich, 1965; Joys of Collecting, 1965; The Golden Age, 1968; How to be a Successful Executive, 1971. *Recreation:* collecting art. *Address:* 17985 Pacific Coast Highway, Malibu, Calif., USA; Sutton Place, near Guildford, Surrey, England. *Clubs:* Explorers (New York); Beach (Santa Monica, Calif.); Los Angeles Athletic (Los Angeles); Nouveau Cercle (Paris).
[Died 6 June 1976.

GIBB, Andrew Dewar, QC (Scotland), 1947; Hon. LLD: Aberdeen and Glasgow; Regius Professor of Law in the University of Glasgow, 1934-58; *b* 1888; *s* of late Dr W. F. Gibb, Paisley; *m* 1923, Margaret Isabel, *d* of late Dr Walker Downie, Glasgow; one *s* two *d*. *Educ:* Glenalmond; Glasgow Univ., LLB (distinction), 1913; called to Scottish Bar, 1914; English Bar, 1917; served European War, 1914-19, Royal Scots Fusiliers and Staff; in practice English Bar since 1919; Lecturer on Law of England, University of Edinburgh, 1929; Lecturer on Law of Scotland, University of Cambridge, 1931; contested (U) Hamilton Div. of Lanarks, 1924; Greenock, 1929; (Scottish Nat.) Scottish Universities, 1935, 1936 and 1938; Chm. of Scottish National Party, 1936-40; Chm. of Saltire Soc., 1955-57; Pres., Scottish Covenant Assoc., 1957-. *Publications:* Law of Collisions on Land; Scottish Judicial Dictionary; A Preface to Scots Law; International Law of Jurisdiction; Select Cases in Law of Scotland; Scotland in Eclipse; With Winston Churchill at the Front; Scottish Empire; Scotland Resurgent; Law from over the Border. *Recreation:* sailing. *Address:* 15 Kirklee Road, Glasgow G12 ORQ. *[Died 24 Jan. 1974.*

GIBB, Sir Hamilton Alexander Rosskeen, Kt 1954; FBA 1944; MA; Hon. LLD Edinburgh; Hon. LittD Harvard; Hon. Dr Algiers; Commander of Order of Orange-Nassau; Chevalier of the Legion of Honour; Director, Center for Middle Eastern Studies, 1957-66; Hon. Fellow, St John's Coll., Oxford, 1955; Foundation Member, Fuad I Academy of Arabic Language, Cairo; Hon. Mem. Amer. Acad. of Arts and Sciences; Fellow

Danish Acad.; Mem. Amer. Philosophical Society; Associat Member Institut d'Egypte; Chairman, Permanent Committee o Geographical Names, 1947-55; *b* 2 Jan. 1895; *s* of A. C. Gibb Alexandria, Egypt; *m* Helen (*d* 1969), *d* of John Stark, DL, JF Edinburgh; one *s* one *d. Educ:* Royal High Sch., Edinburgh Edinburgh Univ.; London Univ. Served European War in RFA 1914-19; Lecturer, Sch. of Oriental Studies (University c London), 1921; Reader, 1929; Prof. of Arabic in The Universit of London, 1930; Laudian Prof. of Arabic, University of Oxford 1937; Haskell Lecturer, Chicago, 1945; University Prof. and J R. Jewett Prof. of Arabic, Harvard Univ., 1955-64. Triennia Gold Medal, Royal Asiatic Soc., 1969. *Publications:* The Ara Conquests in Central Asia; Arabic Literature (2nd edn enlarged 1963); Translation of Barthold's Turkestan; Travels of Ib Battuta; Studies in Contemporary Arabic Literature; Th Damascus Chronicle of the Crusades; Modern Trends in Islam Mohammedanism; (with Harold Bowen) Islamic Society and th West; (ed) Whither Islam. *Address:* The Olde House Cherington, Shipston on Stour, Warwicks. *T:* Little Cherringto 312. *[Died 22 Oct. 1971*

GIBB, Thomas George, CBE 1975; retired; *b* 21 Feb. 1915; 2nd of late Paul and Phyllis Gibb, Aldeburgh, Suffolk; *m* 194 Angela, *d* of late Canon and Mrs G. E. H. Theophilus; three one *d. Educ:* St Edward's Sch., Oxford. Joined LNER as Traffi Apprentice, 1933. Commissioned LNER Co. (Supp. Reserve RE, 1938; Capt. 1939; seconded Min. of Supply, 1941-45. Joine Currie and Co. (Newcastle) Ltd 1945, Dir and Gen. Man., 194 British Road Services, 1949, appointments including Divisiona Manager, NE Div., 1956; Chairman, British Road Services 1959; Vice-Chm. and Man. Dir, BRS Federation Ltd, 1963-6 Dir, Transport Holding Co., 1967-68; Man. Dir, Freightliner Ltd, 1969-72 (Chm. 1975); Exec. Dir, Nat. Freight Corp., 1972 75. Dir, M. S. Gibb Ltd. Sec., Smallpeice Trust Ltd, 1977- Mem., Road Transport Industry Training Board, 1966-69 Mem., Inst. of Transport (Vice-Pres., 1967-69). *Recreations* sailing, cricket, golf. *Address:* Savile Cottage, 26 Crag Pat Aldeburgh, Suffolk IP15 5BS. *T:* Aldeburgh 3273. *Club:* Clyd Cruising (Glasgow). *[Died 25 Jan. 198C*

GIBBERD, George Frederick, CBE 1962; Consulting Obstetri Surgeon Emeritus: Guy's Hospital; Queen Charlotte's Maternit Hospital; Honorary Consulting Gynæcologist, Samarita Hospital for Women; *s* of George William Gibberd and Jessi Waters; *m* 1930, Margaret Erica (*d* 1976), *y d* of Leslie Hug Taffs, Langley, Bucks; two *s* one *d. Educ:* Aske's Haberdashers Guy's Hosp. MB, MS London; FRCS; FRCOG; Sometim Examiner in Obstetrics and Gynæcology for Universities c Cambridge, London, Wales, Manchester and Leeds, fc Conjoint Examining Board of RCS and RCP, and for RCOG Vice-Pres. RCOG, 1958-61 (hon. Sec., 1938-47; Mem. Counci 1936-61); Sims-Black Travelling Prof., RCOG, 1952; Mem. c Gynæcological Visiting Society of Great Britain. Temp. Lieut Col, RAMC. Served War of 1939-45, in North Africa and Italy Consulting Gynæcological Surg., St John's Hosp., Lewishan Member: Medical Adv. Cttee, UGC, 1947-59; Maternit Services (Cranbrook) Cttee, 1956-59; Bd of Govs, Guy's Hosp Med. Sch., 1956-67, and Guy's Hosp., 1957-69. Hon. MI Melbourne, 1975. *Publications:* A Short Text-Book c Midwifery; (in collaboration) Queen Charlotte's Text-Book c Midwifery; contributions to medical literature. *Address:* Tollgate Drive, College Road, Dulwich, SE21. *Clu* Athenæum. *[Died 18 Sept. 197€*

GIBBONS, Col William Ernest, OBE 1944; TD; *b* 24 April 189 *s* of W. P. Gibbons, JP, Wombourne, Staffs; *m* 1922, Alm Pfister, OBE, JP (*d* 1955); one *d* ; *m* 1964, Verity Anne Parsor *Educ:* Bromsgrove Sch. CO 1/6 S Staffs Regt 1939-42; N Infantry Sch., 1942-44. Served European War, France and Italy 1917-18; War of 1939-45, France, 1940. MP (Nat. C) Bilstor Staffs, 1944-45. *Recreation:* fishing. *Address:* Old Farm House Bilbrook, near Wolverhampton, West Midlands. *T:* Copsa 3955. *[Died 15 Aug. 197€*

GIBBS, Dame Anstice (Rosa), DCVO 1967; CBE 1960; retired a Chief Commissioner and Chairman Girl Guides' Associatio (British Commonwealth) (1956-66); *b* 2 Jan. 1905; *d* of la Archdeacon The Hon. Kenneth Gibbs and late Mrs Gibb *Educ:* privately in England and France. Worked with Gi Guides from 1922; Dep. Chief Commissioner, 1954. Mem. Ctte of World Association of Girl Guides and Girl Scouts, 1952-6 Vice-Chm., 1954-60. *Address:* Blacknest Lodge, Brimpto Common, near Reading, Berks. *T:* Tadley 4365.
[Died 7 Feb. 197€

GIBBS, Hon. Sir Geoffrey Cokayne, KCMG 1955 (CMG 1945 Director, Australia and New Zealand Bank Ltd, 1936-7 (Chairman 1951-67), and of other companies; Chairmar

Imperial Relations Trust; National Corporation for the care of the Aged; *b* 20 July 1901; 2nd *s* of 1st Baron Hunsdon and Anna Maria, *d* of Richard Durant; *m* 1926, Helen Margaret, CBE 1961, *d* of C. F. H. Leslie; five *s* one *d*. *Educ:* Eton; Christ Church, Oxford. Min. of Economic Warfare, 1939-45. Past Chairman: Antony Gibbs & Sons Ltd, merchant bankers; Barclays Overseas Development Corporation; Adv. Council Export Credits Guarantee Dept. Trustee, Nuffield Foundn, 1943-73 (Chm. Managing Trustees, 1951-73). Mem. Court Grocers' Co. (Master, 1938-39). Hon. DCL, Oxford, 1966. *Address:* The Manor House, Clifton Hampden, Abingdon-on-Thames. *T:* Clifton Hampden 220. *Club:* Brooks's.
[Died 6 July 1975.

GIBSON, Sir Ackroyd (Herbert), 3rd Bt *cr* 1926; *b* 5 Aug. 1893; *s* of Sir Herbert Gibson, 1st Bt, and Lilian, *d* of Capt. Neilson Thomas, Sketty, Glam.; *S* brother, 1967; *m* 1918, Maud Lilian, *d* of E. C. Arnold, FRCS, and Fredrikke Wedel von Jarlsberg; one *s* two *d* (and one *s* decd). *Educ:* Stone House, Broadstairs; Malvern Coll. Woodworker and Designer. Served with RAF and 3rd Bn, Essex Regt, 1914-18. *Publications:* various articles. *Recreations:* gardening, literature, archæology, philosophy. *Heir: s* Rev. Father David Gibson, *b* 18 July 1922.
[Died 15 June 1975.

GIBSON, Alexander Boyce; Professor of Philosophy in the University of Melbourne, Australia, 1935-66, retired, 1966; *b* 10 March 1900; *s* of late William Ralph Boyce Gibson and Lucy Judge Peacock; *m* 1925, Kathleen Grace Derham, Melbourne; one *d*. *Educ:* Melbourne Grammar Sch; University of Melbourne; Balliol Coll., Oxford. Temporary Asst to the Professors of Moral Philosophy and Logic in the University of Glasgow, 1923-25; Staff Tutor to the Joint Tutorial Classes Cttee of the University of Oxford in North Staffs, 1925-27; Lecturer in Philosophy in the University of Birmingham, 1927-35. Hon. LittD, Cantab., 1948. *Publications:* The Philosophy of Descartes, 1932; Should Philosophers be Kings, 1939; (with A. A. Phillips) Thinkers at Work, 1946; Towards an Australian Philosophy of Education, 1962; Muse and Thinker, 1969; Theism and Empiricism, 1970; The Religion of Dostoevsky, 1973; articles in philosophical periodicals. *Recreations:* travel, listening to music. *Address:* 747 Canterbury Road, Mont Albert, Victoria 3127, Australia.
[Died 2 Oct. 1972.

GIBSON, Charles William, JP County of London; *b* Fulham, 1889; *m* 1915, Jessie Alice Davison; two *s* one *d*. *Educ:* Elementary Schools; WEA; Morley Working Men's Coll. Lambeth Borough Cllr, 1919-22; Mem. LCC for Kennington, 1928-49; Vice-Chm. LCC, 1941-42; Lambeth-Vauxhall, 1949-56; Chm. LCC Housing Cttee, 1943-50; Alderman, LCC, 1960; Mem. Central Housing Advisory Cttee, 1945-51. MP (Lab.) Kennington Div. of Lambeth, 1945-50, Clapham Div. of Wandsworth, 1950-Sept. 1959. On staff of Transport and General Workers Union. Retired. Hon. Fellow, Institute of Housing. *Address:* 25 Dalmore Road, West Dulwich, SE21. *T:* 01-670 1068.
[Died April 1977.

GIBSON, Rear-Adm. Cuthbert Walter Sumner, CB 1945; *b* 9 Dec. 1890; *s* of late Walter S. Gibson, MA, Oxford; *m* 1920, Grace Campbell (*d* 1968), *o d* of late Major L. H. Baldwin, 8th Gurkhas; one *s* one *d* (and *er s* killed in Kenya, 1953). *Educ:* RN Colls, Osborne and Dartmouth. Joined RNC Osborne as Naval Cadet, 1903; specialised in Engineering as Lieut 1913; Capt. (E) 1937. Served European War as Lieut (E) in Grand Fleet, Mediterranean and Submarines; War of 1939-45, Admiralty; Squadron Engineer Officer, Mediterranean; Staff Engineer Officer, Western Desert Ports; Fleet Engineer Officer, Levant; Rear-Adm. (E), 1943; Rear-Adm. (E) on Staff of C-in-C, Plymouth, 1944-47; retired list, 1947. *Address:* Tighnamara, Kilmelford, Argyll.
[Died 21 April 1971.

GIBSON, Sir Edmund Currey, KCIE 1941 (CIE 1933); *b* 6 July 1886; *s* of late Rev. Thomas William and Frances Georgina Gibson; unmarried. *Educ:* Merchant Taylors' Sch.; St John's Coll., Oxford. Joined Indian Civil Service in 1910; held various posts in the Central Provinces; Government of India Foreign and Political Dept, 1921; Commissioner, Ajmer-Merwara, 1924 and 1927; Political Agent, Eastern Rajputana States, 1925; Agent to the Governor-Gen., Eastern States, 1933-34; Resident at Gwalior, 1934-37; Resident, States of Western India, 1937-42; China Relations Officer, Calcutta, 1944-46. *Address:* Ramgarh, Clement Town, Dehra Dun, UP, India.
[Died 13 May 1974.

GIBSON, Very Rev. Matthew Sayer; Dean of the Diocese of Brechin since 1964; Canon of St Paul's Cathedral, Dundee, since 1956; Rector of St Mary Magdalene, Dundee, Diocese of Brechin since 1952. *Educ:* Edinburgh Theological Coll.; University of Durham (LTh 1940). Deacon, 1940; priest,

Brechin, 1941; Curate of St Mary Magdalene, Dundee, 1940-43; Curate-in-charge, St Ninian, Dundee, 1943-52. Chaplain to the Bishop of Brechin, 1952-59; Synod Clerk, Diocese of Brechin, 1957-64. *Address:* 14 Albany Terrace, Dundee, Angus. *T:* Dundee 23510.
[Died 10 Jan. 1971.

GIBSON, Sir William Waymouth, Kt 1939; BA, LLM Cantab; DCL Dunelm (*h c*); Past President of Law Society; Solicitor; *b* 30 Aug. 1873; *s* of William and Annie Gibson, Newcastle upon Tyne; *m* 1st, 1900, Anna Mary Penman; one *s*; 2nd, 1940, Alice (*d* 1958; she *m* 1st, George Sisson, Newcastle upon Tyne). *Educ:* Uppingham; Queens' College, Cambridge. *Address:* Kingmead, Riding Mill, Northumberland; 7 Grey Street, Newcastle upon Tyne. *T:* Riding Mill 286; Newcastle upon Tyne 20761. *Clubs:* Oxford and Cambridge University; Union (Newcastle upon Tyne).
[Died 21 April 1971.

GILBERT, Prof. Edmund William; BLitt, MA; Emeritus Professor of Geography in the University of Oxford, and Fellow Emeritus of Hertford College, Oxford, since 1967; *b* 16 Oct. 1900; *o c* of late Rev. R. H. Gilbert, Hemsworth, Yorks, and Mabel (*née* Billinton); *m* 1927, Barbara Maud, *y d* of late Rev. A. W. Flux Dundas; no *c*. *Educ:* St Peter's Sch., York; Hertford Coll., Oxford (Exhibitioner); Univ. of Basel. Herbertson Prizeman, 1924. Junior Lecturer in Geography, Bedford Coll. for Women (University of London), 1923-26; Lecturer in Historical Geography, University of Reading, 1926-29; Indep. Lecturer in Geography in Faculty of Letters, University of Reading, 1929-36; Research Lecturer in Human Geography, University of Oxford, 1936-43; Lecturer in Geography, Hertford Coll., Oxford, 1939-53; Prof. of Geography, Oxford Univ., and Fellow of Hertford Coll., Oxford, 1953-67. Served in Intelligence Div., Naval Staff, Admiralty, 1940-45; Reader in Human Geography in University of Oxford, 1943-53. Council of: RGS, 1948-51, 1954-56, 1959-62; Hakluyt Soc., 1936-41, 1946-50, 1952-56. Corresp. for Gt Brit. of Amer. Soc. for Professional Geographers, 1948-51; Trustee Oxford Preservation Trust, 1954-57. Hon. Mem., Gesellschaft für Erdkunde (Berlin), 1958. Herbertson Memorial Lecturer, 1960; Mackinder Centenary Lecturer (LSE), 1961; Murchison Grant (RGS), 1967; Tyneside Geographical Soc. Lecturer, 1967. *Publications:* The Exploration of Western America, 1800-50, 1933; An Historical Geography of England before AD 1800 (Contributor), 1936; A Survey of the Social Services in the Oxford District (Contributor), 1938; How the Map has Changed, 1938-40, 1941; Geography in the Twentieth Century (Contributor), 1951; Brighton: Old Ocean's Bauble, 1954; Geography as a Humane Study, 1955; The University Town in England and West Germany, 1961; University Towns (University of Sussex), 1962; British Pioneers in Geography, 1972; numerous papers on geographical subjects in Geographical Jl, Scottish Geographical Magazine, etc. *Recreations:* travel, photography, theatre, Staffordshire pottery. *Address:* Old Cottage, Appleton, Abingdon, Berks. *T:* Cumnor 2197.
[Died 2 Oct. 1973.

GILBERT, Sir Ian A. J.; see Johnson-Gilbert.

GILBERT, Sir (Joseph) Trounsell, Kt 1955; CBE 1949 (OBE 1933); QC (Bermuda) 1949; Chief Justice of Bermuda and Pres. of Legislative Council, Jan. 1952-July 1958, when retired; *b* 30 Aug. 1888; *s* of late Joseph Trounsell Gilbert and Grace Elizabeth Gilbert (*née* Gosling); *m* 1939, Frances Evelyn Steen; no *c*. *Educ:* Saltus Grammar Sch., Bermuda; Bedford Sch.; Brasenose Coll., Oxford. Barrister-at-Law, Lincoln's Inn, 1914. Asst-Collector, Zanzibar, 1912; 2nd Asst-Sec., 1915; 1st Asst-Sec., 1924; Asst-Chief Sec., 1928; invalided, 1933; private practice as barrister in Bermuda, 1935-38; Attorney-Gen. and Mem. of Executive Council, Bermuda, Jan. 1938-Jan. 1952. Brilliant Star of Zanzibar. *Recreations:* tennis, billiards. *Address:* Huntly, Paget, Bermuda. *T:* 3997. *Club:* United Oxford & Cambridge University.
[Died 23 Jan. 1975.

GILBERT, Keith Reginald, MA, DIC; Keeper of Mechanical and Civil Engineering, Science Museum, London, since 1962; *b* 19 Dec. 1914; *e s* of late Harry Reginald Gilbert, Edgbaston, Birmingham; *m* 1941, Lucie Marie (*d* 1971), *d* of late Dr jur. Oscar Auerbach, Vienna; *m* 1973, Electra Eleutheria, *d* of late John Michaelides, Athens. *Educ:* King Edward VI Sch., Birmingham; St John's Coll., Cambridge. Research Asst, Imperial Coll. of Science and Technology, 1937. Served War of 1939-45: Flg Officer, 1939, Flt Lieut, 1943, RAFVR. Asst Chief Res. Engr, CAV Ltd, 1945; entered Science Museum as an Asst Keeper, 1948, and took charge of collections of textile machinery, hand and machine tools, and fire fighting appliances; Dep. Keeper, 1955. Hon. Sec. of Newcomen Soc. (for study of Hist. of Engineering and Technology), 1957-66; Vice-Pres., 1963, Pres., 1971. Dickinson Meml Medal, 1972. *Publications:* Machine Tools in A History of Technology, Vol. IV, 1958;

Science Museum Monograph: The Portsmouth Block-making Machinery, 1965; Science Museum Catalogues: The Machine Tool Collection, 1966; The Fire Fighting Appliances Collection, 1969; Science Museum Illustrated Booklets: Fire Engines, 1966; Sewing Machines, 1970; Henry Maudslay, 1971; Textile Machinery, 1972; Early Machine Tools, 1973. *Address:* The Science Museum, South Kensington, SW7.
[Died 11 June 1973.

GILBERT, Sir Trounsell; *see* Gilbert, Sir J. T.

GILCHRIST, Captain Robert Allister, CBE 1972; RN; Naval Regional Officer for Scotland and Northern Ireland, since 1972; *b* 30 Aug. 1921; *s* of Alexander and Helen Gilchrist; *m* 1949, Heather Pamela Stuart Love; one *s* three *d. Educ:* McLaren High Sch., Callander. MBIM; psc, jssc. Captain 1962; MoD, 1963-65; Chief of Staff to Flag Officer Scotland and N Ireland, 1965-67; Chief of Allied Staff to NATO C-in-C Channel and Eastern Atlantic, 1967-69; Base Comdr Malta, Captain HMS St Angelo and Chief of Staff to Flag Officer Malta, 1969-71; ADC 1971; retd from active service, 1972. *Recreations:* shooting, fishing, country life, gardening. *Address:* 7 Chalmers Crescent, Edinburgh EH9 1TS. *Clubs:* Junior Army and Navy; Carrick (Glasgow).
[Died 21 July 1973.

GILCHRIST, Robert Niven, CIE 1934; Indian Educational Service (retired); *b* 1888; *m* 1917, Winifred Buyers, MA (Aberdeen) (*d* 1964). *Educ:* Aberdeen Grammar School; University of Aberdeen. MA Aberdeen; Triple Honours (Economic Science, History, Philosophy). Appointed to the Indian Educational Service, 1910; Prof., Presidency Coll., Calcutta, 1911-16; University Lecturer in Sociology, Acting Asst Dir of Public Instruction, 1914; Principal and Prof. of Political Economy and Political Philosophy, Krishnagar Coll., Bengal, 1916-21; Controller Labour Bureau, Government of India, 1921-22; Labour Intelligence Officer and Labour Commissioner, Bengal, 1922-34; Adviser to Government Delegations, Seventh, Eighth, and Ninth International Labour Conferences, Geneva, 1925 and 1926; Reforms Officer, Bengal, 1932; Reforms Commissioner and Joint-Sec. to the Government of Bengal, 1934-41; Mem. of the Bengal Legislative Council, 1927-37; retired, 1941. India Office (Principal), 1940-48. Mem. Board of Management, Aberdeen Gen. Hosps, 1951-57. Fellow of the Royal Economic and Royal Statistical Societies; late Fellow of Calcutta Univ. *Publications:* Indian Nationality, 1920; Principles of Political Science, 1921 (7th edn, 1952); Conciliation and Arbitration, 1922; The Executive and Judicial, 1923; The Payment of Wages and Profit Sharing, 1924; Report of the Reforms Office, Bengal, 1932-37; reviews and articles. *Address:* 4 Westholme Avenue, Aberdeen. *T:* Aberdeen 37039. *Clubs:* East India and Sports; University (Aberdeen).
[Died 21 Jan. 1972.

GILDING, Henry Percy, MA, BM, BCh Oxon, MD Birmingham; Emeritus Professor of Physiology, University of Birmingham, 1961; Bowman Professor of Physiology, University of Birmingham, 1933-60; Late Consulting Physiologist to Birmingham United Hospital; Hon. Treasurer Physiological Society, 1945-54; Hon. Treasurer British Abstracts of Medical Sciences, 1954-66; former Mem. Pneumoconiosis Med. Panel, Ministry of Pensions; *b* 4 March 1895; 3rd *s* of Arthur and Rose Gilding; *m* Violet Mary Frances, *yr d* of James and Mina Hazlitt-Brett; five *d. Educ:* St John's Coll., Oxford; St Bartholomew's Hosp. (Kirke's Scholar and Gold Medallist in Clinical Medicine). Demonstrator in Physiology, 1923-26; Senior Demonstrator, 1926-27, St Bartholomew's Hosp.; Asst in Pathology and Bacteriology and Fellow of the Rockefeller Institute, New York, 1927-29; Thomas Young Lecturer in Applied Physiology, St George's Hosp., London; Senior Lecturer in Physiology, University Coll., London, 1930-32; Reader in Experimental Physiology, 1932-33; late Examiner in Physiology for Universities of Durham, Oxford, Bristol, Leeds, London, St Andrews, Dublin and Wales, for Royal College of Surgeons, and Royal College of Surgeons, Dublin; Mem. of Council, British Assoc., 1950-55. Pres., Section I, British Assoc., 1951. Mem. Medical Reforms Commission, Government of Pakistan, 1960. Ranker in Northumberland Fusiliers (Tyneside Scottish), 1916-19. *Publications:* papers in Physiology and Pathology in the Journal of Experimental Medicine, and Proceedings of the Society of Experimental Biology, Journal of Physiology, etc. *Address:* Toll Gate House, 98 Priory Road, Birmingham B15 2RG. *T:* 021-440 2626.
[Died 15 Feb. 1973.

GILES, Rev. Alan Stanley, CB 1958; CBE 1953 (OBE 1946); MA; Dean of Jersey and Rector of St Helier, 1959-70; Hon. Canon of Winchester Cathedral, 1959-71, now Canon Emeritus; *b* 28 May 1902; *s* of late Rev. Alfred Albert Giles and late

Frances Giles; *m* 1934, Myrtle Catherine, *d* of late B. B. Osmaston, CIE; two *s* one *d. Educ:* Manchester Grammar Sch.; The Queen's Coll., Oxford (MA); Clifton Theological Coll. Ordained 1932; Curate, St Ebbes, Oxford, and Chaplain, Christ Church, Oxford, 1932-34; Chaplain, RAF: Cranwell, 1934-37; Singapore, 1937-42; Java, 1942-45; Home Estab., 1945-47; Asst Chaplain-in-Chief, 1947-53; Chaplain-in-Chief, 1953-59, retired. Canon and Prebendary of St Botolph in Lincoln Cathedral, 1953-59. Hon. Chaplain to King George VI, 1950-52, to the Queen, 1953-59. *Recreation:* painting. *Address:* 10 Hurst Hill, Lilliput, Poole, Dorset. *T:* Canford Cliffs 709403.
[Died 26 March 1975.

GILES, G. C. T.; Headmaster of the Acton County School for Boys, 1926-56, retired. *Educ:* Eton; King's Coll., Cambridge. Formerly Professor of English at the Public Commercial Sch., Athens; Brice Mackinnon Master at Geelong Grammar Sch., Victoria, Australia; and Senior Latin Master at the Latymer Upper Sch., Hammersmith; Executive Mem. of National Union of Teachers, 1937-49, Pres., 1944. *Address:* 29 Burlington Road, W4.
[Died 30 Oct. 1976.

GILKES, Antony Newcombe; High Master of St Paul's School, Jan. 1954-Sept. 1962; Director, Public Schools Appointments Bureau, 1962-68; *b* 2 Aug. 1900; *s* of Arthur Herman Gilkes (late Master of Dulwich Coll.) and Millicent Mary Gilkes; *m* 1930, Agatha Ruby, *d* of Bishop Shaw; four *s. Educ:* Dulwich Coll.; Christ Church, Oxford (Scholar). Asst Master St Paul's Sch., 1923-28; Uppingham Sch., 1928-46. Housemaster of Meadhurst, 1935-46; Master of Classical VIth, 1939-46; Headmaster of Dean Close Sch., 1946-53; OC Rutland Army Cadet Force, 1942-44. Mem. of Governing Body: King's Sch., Bruton, 1969-; Hazlegrove; Sunnyhill; Charlotte Mason Schs, 1944-69; Dulwich Coll. Preparatory Sch.; Highgate Sch., 1962-69; Reed's Sch., Cobham, 1962-69; Overstone Sch.; Burgess Hill Sch., 1944-69; Mem. Council, Atlantic Coll., 1960-70; Council, City Univ., 1966-70; Mem. Cttee, Clergy Orphan Corporation, 1962-70. *Publications:* Selections from the Old Testament, 1944; Selections from the New Testament, 1946; An anthology of Oratory, 1955; Independent Education, 1957; Faith for Modern Man, 1960; The Impact of the Dead Sea Scrolls, 1963; Einstein or Frankenstein, 1970; An Educational Hiatus, 1971. *Recreations:* music, cricket, travel. *Address:* Compton Cottage, Compton Pauncefoot, near Yeovil, Somerset BA22 7EN. *T:* North Cadbury 221.
[Died 14 Jan. 1977.

GILKS, John Langton, CMG 1933; MRCS, LRCP, FRCSE; Vice-President, British Medical Association; *b* 29 Aug. 1880; *s* of William John Gilks and Elizabeth Langton; *m* 1911, Margaret Annie (*d* 1957), *d* of Thomas Joseph Messom; one *s. Educ:* Merchant Taylors' Sch.; St Thomas's Hospital. Medical Officer, East Africa Protectorate, 1909; PMO, Kenya Colony and Protectorate, 1921; Dir of Medical and Sanitary Services, 1926-33; Mem. of Executive and Legislative Councils, Kenya, 1920-33; retired 1933; Governor of St Thomas's Hosp., 1926-48; Ed., East African Medical Journal, 1929-33; Capt. East Africa Medical Service, 1914; Major, 1915; Mem. of Council of British Medical Assoc., 1935-46. *Recreations:* fishing, shooting, golf. *Address:* 9 Grindleton Road, West Bradford, near Clitheroe, Lancs. *T:* Clitheroe 4234. *Club:* East India and Sports.
[Died 18 Aug. 1971.

GILL, Sir Archibald (Joseph), Kt 1949; BSc (Eng), CEng, FIEE, FIEEE; *b* 13 May 1889; *s* of William James Gill; *m* 1914, Irene Bassindale; one *s* one *d. Educ:* Regent Street Polytechnic; Paisley Technical Coll.; Glasgow Technical Coll.; London Univ. Pupil of Messrs Yarrow & Co. Ltd, engineers and shipbuilders; Draughtsman British Thomson Houston Co. Ltd, Rugby; entered PO Engineering Dept, 1913; Staff Engineer, radio branch, 1932; Asst Engineer-in-Chief, 1938; Dep. Engineer-in-Chief, 1944; Engineer-in-Chief, 1947-51; Chm. Radio Section Inst. of Electrical Engineers, 1938-39; Vice-Pres. IEE, 1945-50, Pres., 1950-51. *Address:* 24 Acacia Road, Hampton, Middlesex. *T:* 01-979 2689. *Club:* Athenæum.
[Died 10 April 1976.

GILL, Dr Stanley; Senior Consultant, PA International Management Consultants Ltd; *b* 26 March 1926; *s* of Walter Campbell Gill and Rhoda Harriett Gill (*née* Mitchell); *m* 1949, Audrey Eileen Lee; two *s* one *d. Educ:* Worthing High Sch.; St John's Coll., Cambridge (PhD). Fellow of St John's Coll., Cambridge, 1952-55; various positions, Computer Dept of Ferranti Ltd, 1955-63; Part-time Prof. of Automatic Data Processing, College of Science and Technology, University of Manchester, and ICT Ltd, 1963-64; Prof. of Computing Science, 1964-70, and Dir, Centre for Computing and Automation, 1966-70, Imperial Coll., Univ. of London. Pres., British Computer Soc., 1967-68. *Address:* 21 Speer Road, Thames Ditton, Surrey. *T:* 01-398 5507. *Club:* United Oxford & Cambridge University.
[Died 5 April 1975.

GILL-DAVIES, Derek George, DSO 1940; TD; TARO; *b* 30 June 1913; *s* of late Ernest George and Beatrice Jane Davies. *Educ:* Ardingly Coll. Brown-Firth Research Laboratories of Thos Firth & John Brown Ltd, 1932; in service of Firth-Vickers, 1934-62, Overseas Sales Manager, Firth-Vickers Stainless Steels Ltd; Director, Grängesberg-Nyby Stainless Steels (UK) Ltd, EC3 (Sales Co. in UK for Nyby Bruks AB, Sweden). Broadcast as a narrator for the BBC, 1938 and 1939. Commnd in 49th W Riding Div. RE, TA, 1934; Staff Coll., 1939, served abroad during War of 1939-45 (Lieut-Col) Norway, Iceland, SEAC (Burma and Malaya), China (despatches), 1st Bn Herts Regt TA, 1947-51, comdg 1949-51. Councillor Welwyn Rural District Council, 1948-51. *Recreations:* stalking, shooting and sailing. *Address:* 5 Park Close, Hatfield, Herts. *Clubs:* Naval and Military, Special Forces; Royal Engineer Yacht.
[Died 31 Oct. 1974.

GILLAN, Lt-Col Sir George van Baerle, KCIE 1944 (CIE 1934); late Indian Army, Indian Political Department; *b* 3 Sept. 1890; *o s* of Sir Robert Gillan, KCSI; *m* 1918, Sibell (Kaiser-i-Hind Medal), *y d* of late A. Bulloch Graham, Auldhouse, Crieff; no *c*. *Educ:* Fettes Coll., Edinburgh; Pembroke Coll., Cambridge. Entered Army, 1913; attached 1st Seaforth Highlanders, 1913-14; Lieut 9th Gurkha Rifles, 1914; Adjutant, 1915; Capt., 1916; served Mesopotamia Expeditionary Force (despatches, brevet of Major); Political Officer, Baghdad, 1918; Military Governor, Basrah, 1920-21; Iraq Administration, 1922-23; Under Sec. to the Govt of India, Foreign and Political Dept, 1924; HBM Consul-Gen. in Chinese Turkestan, 1925-27; First Asst Resident in Kashmir, 1928-31; Political Agent, Gilgit, 1931-34; Resident Jodhpur, 1937-39; Resident, Gwalior, 1940-42; Resident for Rajputana, 1942-46. CC Kirkcudbright, 1947-58. *Recreations:* shooting and fishing. *Address:* Blackford, Haugh of Urr, Castle Douglas, Kirkcudbrightshire. *T:* Haugh of Urr 256. *Club:* Navy and Navy.
[Died 19 Feb. 1974.

GILLANDERS, Jeannie Kathleen, CBE 1953; RRC 1st Cl. 1945; *b* 14 April 1896; *d* of late W. J. Gillanders and late A. J. Gillanders. General Training at Liverpool Royal Infirmary and Leeds Maternity Hospital. Joined Queen Alexandra's Royal Naval Nursing Service, 1924; Hon. Nursing Sister to King George VI, 1950-52; Matron-in-Chief Queen Alexandra's Royal Naval Nursing Service, 1950-53; Hon. Nursing Sister to the Queen, 1952-53. Officer Sister, Order of St John, 1952. *Recreations:* walking, interested in antique furniture. *Address:* 28 Manor Close, Henfield, Sussex. *T:* Henfield 2463. *Club:* Naval and Military.
[Died 27 Nov. 1971.

GILLEN, Stanley (James); Chairman and Chief Executive Officer, Ford of Europe Inc., 1969-71; Vice-President, Ford Motor Co. USA, 1967-71; Director, Ford of Britain, 1965-71; *b* 10 Aug. 1911; *s* of Bernard J. Gillen, Ohio, and Johanna P. Spillane, Wayne Co., USA; *m* 1935, Mary Elizabeth Marks; three *d. Educ:* St Frederick's High Sch., Pontiac, Mich.; University of Detroit. Fisher Body Div., Gen. Motors Corp., 1933-47; Ford Motor Co., USA: Contract Administrator, Defence Products, 1947-48; Controller, Steel Div., 1948-55; Controller, Tractor and Implement Div., 1955-56; Asst Gen. Man., Steel Div., 1956-60; Gen. Man., Steel Div., 1960-61; Gen. Man., Gen. Parts Div., 1961-65; Man. Dir and Chief Exec. Officer, Ford of Britain, 1965-67; Vice-Pres., Manufacturing Ford of Europe Inc., 1967-69. Chm., Autolite Motor Products Ltd, 1962-65; Director: Ford Credit Co. Ltd, 1965-67; Henry Ford & Son Ltd, Cork, 1965-67; Ford Werke, Germany, 1970-71; Sangamo Weston Ltd, 1972-; Sangamo Electric Co., 1973-75; AMBAC, USA, 1976-; FEMSA, Spain, 1976; Brown Bros Ltd, 1976; Casttenedolo Mfg Co. Spa, Brescia, Italy; Ambac BV Terheijdenseweg, Breda, Holland. Dir, Amer. Chamber of Commerce (UK), 1967; Member: British Manufacturers' Exec. Cttee, SMMT, 1965-67; National Advisory Council for Motor Manufacturing Industry (NACMMI), 1966-67. Design Council Awards Judge, 1976-77, 1977-78. Lord Wakefield Gold Medal, 1971. *Recreations:* golf, ski-ing, shooting, horology. *Address:* Flat 58, Campden Hill Court, Campden Hill Road, W8. *T:* 01-937 3479.
[Died 15 July 1978.

GILLESPIE, Brig. Dame Helen (Shiels), DBE 1954 (MBE 1945); RRC 1943; QARANC (retired); *b* 26 March 1898; *d* of John Gillespie and Isabella (*née* Dunlop), Edinburgh. *Educ:* George Watson's Ladies' Coll., Edinburgh. Professional Training, Western Infirmary, Glasgow, 1921-25. Joined Queen Alexandra's Imperial Military Nursing Service (QAIMNS), 1926. Service in: India, 1927-32, 1934-39; Middle East, 1939-42; South East Asia Command, 1944-46; War Office, 1946-49; BAOR, 1949-51; Commandant Depot and Training Establishment, QARANC, 1951-52; Matron-in-Chief and Dir of Army Nursing Services, War Office, 1952-56; QHNS 1952-56; retired pay, 1956. Col Comdt QARANC, 1956-61. *Recreations:*

music, drama, sports. *Address:* 6 Buckstone Gardens, Edinburgh 10.
[Died 25 Aug. 1974.

GILLETT, Sir Edward (Bailey), Kt 1948; Chartered Surveyor; *b* 2 Aug. 1888; 4th and *y s* of William Edward and Florence Gillett; *m* 1916, Bertha Helen (*d* 1957), *d* of William Henry Moss; two *d. Educ:* Marlborough Coll. Served European War, 1914-18, Capt. East Surrey Regt in Belgium, France and Italy. Pres. of Royal Institution of Chartered Surveyors, 1945-46. Crown Estate Commissioner, 1957-65. *Address:* Stables Cottage, Lydwicke, Slinfold, Horsham, West Sussex.
[Died 13 April 1978.

GILLETT, Eric Walkey, MA; FRSL; Hon. RCM; *b* Bowdon, 24 Aug. 1893; *s* of Samuel Walkey Gillett and Edith Suzette Barlow; *m* 1st, 1926, Joan Edwards (decd); one *s* (one *d* decd); 2nd, 1962, Nancy Miller (decd). *Educ:* Radley; Lincoln Coll., Oxford. Lectr to the Oxford Univ. Extension Delegacy, 1921; Lectr to the Extension Delegacies of the Universities of Cambridge and London, 1935; Warden of Chancellor's Hall and Lecturer in English Literature, University of Birmingham, 1922-27; Johore Prof. of English Language and Literature, Raffles Coll., Singapore, 1927-32; literary editing, publishing and broadcasting work, 1932-58; Gen. Editor, Royal National Institute for the Blind, 1958-61; RCM staff, 1961-71. London Dramatic Critic, Yorks Post, 1960-65. 2nd Lieut, 7th Batt. Lancs Fusiliers (TF); 1914; wounded 3rd battle of Ypres, Aug. 1917; invalided out with rank of Capt., 1919. *Publications:* Hush (in collaboration), 1920; Books and Writers, 1930; An Anthology of Verse for Children, 1930; Poets of Our Time, 1932; Maria Jane Jewsbury, 1932; Normal English Prose (with late T. Earle Welby), 1934; The Literature of England; AD 500 to 1942 (with W. J. Entwistle), 1943; revised edn, The Literature of England, AD 500 to 1946, 1947; The Literature of England, AD 500-1950, 1952; The Literature of England, AD 500 to 1960, 1961; Elizabeth Ham: By Herself (ed), 1945; J. B. Priestley's All About Ourselves (ed), 1956; Junior Film Annual, 1946-47 (ed), 1946; Eric Gillett's Film Book, 1947; Film Fairyland, 1948; Collins' Film Books, 1948, 1949, 1950, 1951; pamphlets, contributions to various periodicals. *Recreations:* reading, travelling, theatre and broadcasting. *Address:* Flat 4, 29 Brunswick Square, Hove, East Sussex BN3 1EJ. *T:* Brighton 731820. *Clubs:* United Oxford & Cambridge University, Royal Automobile, MCC; Vincent's (Oxford); Hove (Hove).
[Died 8 Dec. 1978.

GILLETT, Sir Harold; see Gillett, Sir S. H.

GILLETT, Sir Michael Cavenagh, KBE 1962; CMG 1951; retired from Foreign Service, 1963; *b* 12 July 1907; *s* of late Adm. Owen Francis Gillett, CB, and of Mabel Alice (*née* Cavenagh-Mainwaring); *m* 1952, Margaret Murray (*née* Hobbs); one *s* two *d. Educ:* Western Provinces Preparatory Sch.; Cheam; RN Colls, Osborne and Dartmouth; Manchester Univ. Student interpreter, HBM Consular Service in China, 1929; commissioned, 1931; served at Peking, Canton, Hankow, Nanking, Kashgar, Tengyueh, Chungking and Shanghai; Counsellor (Chinese Affairs), HBM Embassy, Peking, Dec. 1950-53; HM Consul-Gen. at Los Angeles, 1954-57; HM Ambassador to Afghanistan, 1957-63. *Publications:* Notes on Blue Turkish, and other contributions to Journal of Royal Asiatic Society (N China Branch). *Recreation:* Central Asia (FRGS, FRAS). *Address:* Beechmead, Alton Pancras, Dorchester, Dorset. *Club:* Junior Carlton. *[Died 20 Jan. 1971.*

GILLETT, Sir Stuart, Kt 1959; CMG 1952; *b* 1 June 1903; 2nd *s* of late T. G. Gillett, Faversham, Kent; *m* 1931, Irene Mary Holm; two *s. Educ:* Bedford Sch.; Wye Coll., Kent. Asst Agricultural Officer, Kenya, 1928; Agric. Officer and Experimentalist, Kenya, 1931; Senior Coffee Officer, Kenya, 1946; Commissioner of European Settlement, Kenya, 1947; Dir of Agriculture and Chm. European Settlement Board, Kenya, 1948; Chm. Overseas Food Corp., 1951-55; Chm., Tanganyika Agricultural Corporation, 1955-58; London Representative, Kenya Coffee Industry, 1958-66, retired. *Publications:* contributions to EA Agric. Journal and Kenya Coffee Board Bulletin. *Address:* Karibu, off Transfiguration Avenue, Lija, Malta. *Clubs:* Farmers'; Nairobi (Nairobi); Malta Union, United Services Sports, Marsa (Malta).
[Died 14 April 1971.

GILLETT, Sir (Sydney) Harold, 1st Bt, *cr* 1959; Kt 1953; MC 1916; Lord Mayor of London, 1958-59; *b* 27 Nov. 1890; *s* of William Henry Gillett, Highgate, Mx; *m* 1919, Audrey Isabel Penrose Wardlaw (*d* 1962); one *s. Educ:* Marlborough. Qualified as a Chartered Accountant, 1914; served European War, 1914-18. 1/7 Mx Regt (TA) (despatches, MC); War of 1939-45, 2nd i/c 17 Bn Essex HG, Certificate of Merit. Common Councilman, 1930, Alderman, 1948-69 (Ward of Bassishaw); Sheriff of City of

London, 1952-53; Chm. London Chamber of Commerce, 1956-58 (now a Vice-Pres.). Order of the Silver Wolf, Boy Scouts Assoc. Hon. Col 8th Essex (517 Light Anti-Aircraft) Cadet Regt; Past Prime Warden Worshipful Co. of Basketmakers; KStJ 1959 (CStJ 1951); Order of Homayoun (Iran), 1959; Gold Medal of Madrid, 1959. *Recreation:* riding. *Heir: s* Robin Danvers Penrose Gillett, RD. *Address:* Elm Cottage, Biddestone, near Chippenham, Wilts. *Club:* City of London.
[Died 21 Sept. 1976.

GILLIAT-SMITH, Bernard Joseph Leo; HBM Consul-General (retired); *b* 20 Oct. 1883; *s* of late Frederick Ernest Gilliat-Smith, The Oaks, Woodmansterne, Surrey, and of late Ellinor Marie Cockerell; *m* 1911, Ida Marie Szymonska-Lubicz; one *d* (and one *d* decd). *Educ:* private tuition in Belgium, Germany, and Spain; Gonville and Caius Coll., Cambridge. Levant Consular Service; served at Constantinople, Sofia, Beirut, Varna, Foreign Office (London), Tabriz, Copenhagen, Sarajevo, Leningrad, Bucharest, New Orleans, Smyrna; retired, 1943. *Publications:* linguistic articles in Journal of Gypsy Lore Society. *Recreations:* riding, swimming, walking, languages, botany. *Address:* Beech Tree House, Grayshott, Hindhead, Surrey.
[Died 28 April 1973.

GILLIES, Prof. Alexander; Professor of German Language and Literature, University of Leeds, 1945-72, Emeritus Professor, since 1972; *b* Sheffield, 26 May 1907; *s* of late A. Gillies and M. Gillies; *m* 1944, Camilla Hill Hay, MA, D de l'Univ. *Educ:* King Edward VII Sch., Sheffield; Universities of Sheffield and Göttingen. 1st cl. Hons Mod. Langs 1927, MA 1928 (Sheffield), DPhil 1933 (Göttingen). Asst Lecturer in German, University of Manchester, 1930-34; Head of Dept of German, University Coll., Hull, 1934-45; Visiting Lecturer on German Lit., Harvard Univ., USA, 1946-47, on leave of absence from Leeds; Dean of the Faculty of Arts, University of Leeds, 1951-53; Chm., Joint Matriculation Board, 1958-61 (Vice-Chm., 1955-58); Chm., Conference of University Teachers of German in Gt Britain and Ireland, 1966-67; Editor, Mod. Language Review, 1943-, and General Editor, 1956-60; co-editor, Year's Work in Modern Language Studies, 1937-40; Hon. Mem. Modern Humanities Research Assoc; Hon. Mem., Modern Language Assoc. of America; sometime External Examiner to the Univs of Belfast, Dublin, Glasgow, Hull, Liverpool, Nottingham, Oxford, St Andrews, Sheffield, Southampton, Reading. General Editor, Blackwell's German Texts. Medal of the Univ. of Tübingen, 1973. *Publications:* Herder and Ossian (Berlin), 1933; Herder, 1945; (ed) J. G. Herder, Journal meiner Reise im Jahre 1769, 1947, 2nd rev. edn 1969; (ed) Herzensergiessungen eines Kunstliebenden Klosterbruders, by W. H. Wackenroder and L. Tieck, 1948, 2nd rev. edn, 1966; Herder, der Mensch und sein Werk, (Hamburg) 1949; Goethe's Faust: an Interpretation, 1957; A Hebridean in Goethe's Weimar: The Reverend James Macdonald and the Cultural Relations between Scotland and Germany, 1969; (ed) J. G. Herder, Über die neuere deutsche Literatur, 1969; numerous contributions to Encyclopædia Britannica, etc; articles and reviews on German and comparative literature in various European and N American periodicals. *Recreations:* foreign travel, gardening, golf. *Address:* Gates House, Ripley Road, Knaresborough, North Yorks. *T:* Harrogate 862374.
[Died 25 Oct. 1977.

GILLIES, Hugh, CBE 1967; JP; PhD; Convener of County Council of Dunbarton, 1961; Chairman, Dunbarton County Licensing Board, 1967; *b* 16 Nov. 1903; *s* of Dugald Gillies and Hannah (*née* Greenhalgh); *m* 1933, Marion Rose (*née* Oswald); two *s* one *d. Educ:* Glasgow. Provost, Burgh of Kirkintilloch, 1952-58 (2 terms); Vice-Convener, Dunbarton CC, 1958-61. Mem., Cumbernauld New Town Develt Bd; Mem., Police Council for Gt Britain; Chm., Hosps Bd, Kirkintilloch and Council Hosps. Professional Linguist (knowledge 23 langs). JP 1952, Co. of Dunbarton. Freeman of City of London and Mem. Guild of Freemen. *Recreations:* local government, gardening; speaker on foreign affairs, Robert Burns, and literature in general. *Address:* Craighill, Elm Avenue, Lenzie, Co. of Dunbarton. *T:* 041-776 3293; (business) 041-221 0201. *Clubs:* Edinburgh Liberal; Glasgow Rotary.
[Died 3 Sept. 1978.

GILLIES, Dr John, CVO 1949; MC 1917; J. Y. Simpson Reader in Anæsthetics, University of Edinburgh, 1946-60, retd; *b* 6 Feb. 1895; *s* of late Archibald George Gillies and late Jessie Jane Shier; *m* 1924, Agnes McGilchrist Anderson; two *s* two *d. Educ:* Broughton Sch., Edinburgh; Edinburgh Univ. Served European War, 1914-18, with HLI, attaining rank of Capt. Graduated MB, ChB Edinburgh, 1923, DAEng, 1935, FRCSE, 1946, FFARCSEng, 1948, MRCPE 1950, FRCPE 1956, Hon. FFARACS 1956, Hon FFARCSI 1960, Hon. FRSM 1973. Pres., Assoc. of Anæsthetists of GB and Ireland, 1947, 1948, 1949. Vice-Dean, Faculty of Anæsthetists, RCS, 1956-58.

Publications: Textbook of Anæsthetics, 7th Edition, 1948; various papers to medical journals. *Recreation:* golf. *Address:* 18a Mortonhall Road, Edinburgh EH9 2HW. *T:* 031-667 4142.
[Died 18 July 1976.

GILLIES, Prof. Marshall Macdonald, MA Cantab; PhD (Edinburgh); retired as Professor of Classics, The University of Hull, now Professor Emeritus; Pro-Vice-Chancellor, 1962-68; *b* 27 April 1901; *s* of late Rev. J. Gillies, DD, Parish Minister of Lesmahagow. *Educ:* Eton; King's Coll., Cambridge; Edinburgh Univ.; New Coll., Oxford; Vienna University. Asst Lecturer in Greek, Liverpool Univ., 1924-28. Head of Dept of Classics on opening of University Coll., Hull, 1928; subsequently Prof. *Publications:* Apollonius Rhodius, Argonautica, Book III, 1928; sundry articles, etc., in classical journals. *Recreation:* Siamese cats. *Address:* 131 Westbourne Avenue, Hull, North Humberside. *T:* 42085.
[Died 21 March 1976.

GILLIES, Sir William George, Kt 1970; CBE 1957; RA 1971 (ARA 1964); RSA 1947 (ARSA 1940); PPRSW; Principal, College of Art, Edinburgh, 1961-66; *b* 1898; unmarried. FEIS 1966; Hon. DLitt (Edinburgh) 1966. *Address:* Temple Cottage, Temple, by Gorebridge, Midlothian.
[Died 15 April 1973.

GILLIGAN, Arthur Edward Robert; President of MCC, 1967-68; *b* 23 Dec. 1894; *s* of W. A. Gilligan, JP; *m* 1934, Katherine Margaret Fox. *Educ:* Dulwich Coll.; Pembroke Coll., Cambridge. Cambridge XI, 1919-20. Capt. of MCC: Australian Tour, 1924-25; India and Ceylon, 1926-27. Pres., Inst. of Groundsmanship. *Publications:* Collins Men, 1926; Sussex Cricket, 1932. *Recreation:* golf (Past President: English Golf Union, 1959; County Cricketers' Golfing Soc.; Pres., Sussex County Golf Union, 1972-, Captain 1952-72). *Address:* Cherry Trees, Mare Hill, Pulborough, West Sussex. *T:* Pulborough 2611. *Clubs:* MCC (Hon. Life Mem.); Royal Air Force; Sussex County Cricket (Patron, and Pres. 1974); Sussex Cricket Soc. (Patron); Storrington Cricket (Pres.); Forty (Pres. 1973, 1974); Surrey County Cricket (Hon. Life Mem.); Worplesdon Golf (Hon. Life Mem.), Seaford Golf (Hon. Life Mem.); Bognor Regis Golf (Pres.), W Sussex Golf (Pres.), Goodwood Golf (Hon. Life Mem.), Rye Golf, Ham Manor Golf (Hon. Life Mem.), Sussex Martlets Golfing Society (Captain), Seniors Golfing Society.
[Died 5 Sept. 1976.

GILMAN, Horace James, CBE 1944 (OBE 1942); DSO 1942; TD 1945; Deputy Chairman, Wm Cory & Son Ltd and Director, many subsidiary and associated companies until retirement, 1972; *b* 7 June 1907; *s* of late Owen H. Gilman, Liverpool; *m* 1937, Barbara, *d* of late W. H. Law, West Kirby, Wirral; no *c. Educ:* Liverpool Coll. Joined RASC (TA), 1930; Major, 1939; served in: France, 1940; Western Desert, 1941-43; Italy, 1944-45; Brig., 1944-45; Hon. Brig., TARO, 1946. Chief of Fuel and Power Division, CCG, 1946-48. Gen. Comr for Income Tax, City of London. Hon. Freeman of Company of Watermen and Lightermen of the River Thames (Master, 1970); Past Pres. and Hon. Vice-Pres., Assoc. of Master Lightermen and Barge Owners of Port of London. *Address:* 6 Zetland House, Marloes Road, W8. *T:* 01-937 6557.
[Died 14 June 1976.

GILMOUR, Sir John (Little), 2nd Bt, *cr* 1926, of Liberton and Craigmillar; a stockbroker; late Lieut-Col Grenadier Guards; RARO; *b* 5 June 1899; *e s* of Sir Robert Gilmour, 1st Bt, CB, CVO, DSO, and Lady Susan Lygon (*d* 1962, as Lady Susan Gilmour, DBE), 2nd *d* of 6th Earl Beauchamp; *S* father, 1939; *m* 1st, 1922, Hon. Victoria Cadogan (who obtained a divorce, 1929), *y d* of late Viscount Chelsea and Hon. Lady Meux; one *s* one *d*; 2nd, 1930, Lady Mary Kenyon Slaney, *d* of 3rd Duke of Abercorn, KG; one *s. Educ:* Eton. *Recreations:* shooting, fishing, golf. *Heir: s* Rt. Hon. Ian Hedworth John Gilmour, PC, MP. *Address:* Carolside, Earlston, Berwickshire. *T:* Earlston 272. *Clubs:* White's, Buck's; New (Edinburgh).
[Died 13 Feb. 1977.

GILRAY, Colin Macdonald, OBE 1951; MC; Principal, Scotch College, Melbourne, Australia, 1934-53; *b* 17 March 1885; 3rd *s* of Prof. Thomas Gilray, MA, LLD (Edinburgh) and Annie Macdonald; *m* 1917, Ethel Muriel, *d* of Arthur Standish, New Plymouth, NZ; one *d. Educ:* Otago Boys' High Sch. and Otago Univ. (BA), NZ Rhodes Scholar 1907, University Coll., Oxford, BA 1910, MA 1923 (2nd cl. Greats), Rugger Blue, Scottish and NZ International. Asst Master Mill Hill Sch., 1910-13; called to Bar, Middle Temple, 1913; 2nd Lieut XIIIth Rifle Brigade 1916; A/Capt. 1917 (MC); Capt. 21st OCB, 1918; engaged in legal practice, 1919-22, Otago, NZ; Headmaster John McGlashan Coll., Dunedin, NZ, 1922-34. Member: Otago Univ. Council, 1925-34; New Zealand Univ. Senate, 1927-34; NZ Rhodes Scholarship Selection Cttee, 1922-34; School Board (Melbourne), 1936-52; Council of University of Melbourne,

1939-63 (Dep.-Chancellor, 1954-57, 1959-61 and Mem. Council of Internat. House, 1959-70); Chm. Headmasters' Conference of Australia, 1949-51 (Sec., 1954-65); Mem. Prime Minister's Cttee on Tertiary Education, 1961-65. FACE 1960. Hon. MA 1936 and Hon. LLD 1956, Melbourne Univ. *Recreation:* reading. *Address:* Yarra Braes Road, Eltham, Victoria 3095, Australia. *Club:* Melbourne (Melbourne). *[Died 15 July 1974.*

GILROY, His Eminence Sir Norman (Thomas), Cardinal, KBE 1969; DD; *b* Sydney, NSW, 22 Jan. 1896; *s* of William James Gilroy and Catherine Slattery. *Educ:* Convent Schools of Sisters of the Good Samaritan and Sisters of Charity; Marist Brothers' School. Entered Postal Department, 1909; Wireless Operator on Commonwealth Transport Steamer Bulla carrying Australian troops to Egypt and Indian troops to the Dardanelles, 1915; present at landing of Troops on Gallipoli, 25 April 1915; entered St Columba's College, Springwood, 1917; Urban College of Propaganda, Rome, 1919; Priest for the Diocese of Lismore, NSW, 1923; Doctor of Theology, 1924; Secretary to the Apostolic Delegate, 1924-31; Secretary to Bishop and Chancellor of the Diocese of Lismore, 1931-34; Bishop of Port Augusta, South Australia, 1935-37; Titular Archbishop of Cypsela and Coadjutor to RC Archbishop of Sydney, 1937-40; Archbishop of Sydney, 1940-71; Cardinal, 1946. *Address:* St John Vianney Villa, Clovelly Road, Randwick, NSW, Australia. *[Died 21 Oct. 1977.*

GILSON, Etienne Henry, DLitt, PhD, LLD; Philosopher and Historian; *b* 13 June 1884; *m* 1908, Thérèse Ravisé; one *s* two *d*. *Educ:* Sorbonne. Prof. University of Lille, 1913; University of Strasbourg, 1919; Prof. of Medieval Philosophy, Sorbonne, 1921-32; Dir of Medieval Studies, University of Toronto, 1929; Prof. Coll. de France, 1932-51, retired, Hon. Prof., 1957. Corresp. Mem. British Acad.; Fellow French Acad., 1946. Holds numerous hon. degrees. Commandeur de la Légion d'Honneur; Croix de Guerre; Orden Pour le Mérite. *Publications:* Le Thomisme, 1922; La Philosophie de St Bonaventure, 1924; Introduction à l'étude de St Augustin, 1929; L'esprit de la philosophie médiévale, 1932; La théologie mystique de St Bernard, 1934 (Eng. trans. 1955); Le réalisme méthodique, 1935; Christianisme et philosophie, 1936; The Unity of Philosophical Experience, 1937; Héloïse et Abélard (Eng. trans. 1953); Reason and Revelation in the Middle Ages, 1938; Dante et la Philosophie, 1939; God and Philosophy, 1940; La philosophie au moyen âge, 1945; Being and Some Philosophers, 1949; L'école des muses, 1950 (Eng. trans., Choir of Muses, 1954); Jean Duns Scot, 1952; History of Christian Philosophy in the Middle Ages, 1954; Painting and Reality, 1957; Elements of Christian Philosophy, 1959; The Philosopher and Theology, 1962; Modern Philosophy, 1963; Introduction aux arts du beau, 1963; Matières et formes, 1964; The Spirit of Thomism, 1964; Recent Philosophy, 1966; D'Aristote à Darwin et retour, 1971; La Philosophie au Moyen Age, 2 vols, 1976. *Address:* 9 rue Saint-Romain, 75006 Paris, France. *[Died 19 Sept. 1978.*

GIMSON, Christopher, CIE 1943; BA; Indian Civil Service (retired); *b* 24 Dec. 1886; *s* of Josiah Mentor Gimson; unmarried. *Educ:* Oundle; Emmanuel Coll., Cambridge. Entered ICS 1911; late Political Agent in Manipur; retired, 1948. *Recreations:* walking, ball games, music. *Address:* Flat 18, The Albany, London Road, Leicester. *Clubs:* East India, Sports and Public Schools; Leicestershire Golf (Leicester). *[Died 8 Nov. 1975.*

GIMSON, Sir Franklin Charles, KCMG 1946 (CMG 1945); BA Oxon; *b* 10 Sept. 1890; *s* of late Rev. C. K. Gimson; *m* 1922, Margaret Dorothy, MBE, *d* of late Canon Ward; two *d*. *Educ:* Balliol Coll., Oxford. Cadet, Ceylon Civil Service, 1914; Controller of Labour, Ceylon, 1937; Colonial Sec., Hong Kong, 1941; Governor and C-in-C, Singapore, 1946-52. Freeman of City of Singapore, 1952; Hon. Doctor of Laws University of Singapore, 1952. KStJ. *Recreation:* walking. *Address:* Applegarth, Thornton-le-Dale, Pickering, Yorks. *Club:* Royal Commonwealth Society. *[Died 13 Feb. 1975.*

GIMSON, Col Thomas William; *b* 9 July 1904; 2nd *s* of late Thomas Wallis Gimson and Rosina Skerratt Forsyth; *m* 1958, Heather Mary, *d* of late Capt. P. D. C. Eliot, 14th Lancers, Indian Army, and of the Countess of Powis. *Educ:* Brighton Coll.; St John's Coll., Oxford. Commissioned North Staffs Regt; transferred Irish Guards, 1933; Internat. Force HQ, Saar Plebiscite, 1934; Palestine, 1938; Dunkirk, 1940; Combined Ops, 1943; NW Europe, 1944; Military Mission, Moscow, 1945; Military Attaché, Warsaw, 1946-48; Regtl Lt-Col comd Irish Guards, 1948-50; retd pay, 1950. *Address:* Les Pierrugues, 83240 Cavalaire, France. *Club:* Turf. *[Died 24 Dec. 1979.*

GIPSON, Lawrence Henry, PhD; Professor Emeritus, Lehigh University; *b* 7 Dec. 1880; *s* of Albert Eugene and Lina Maria Gipson (*née* West); *m* 1909, Jeannette Reed; no *c*. *Educ:* College of Idaho; University of Idaho; University of Oxford; Yale Univ. AB Idaho, 1903: Rhodes Schol., University of Oxford, 1904-07; BA 1907, MA 1951, PhD Yale, 1918. Prof. of History, College of Idaho, 1907-10; Farnham Fellow, Yale Univ. 1910-11; Prof. of History, Wabash Coll., 1911-17; Prof. of History and Political Science, Wabash Coll., 1917-24; Bulkley Fellow, Yale, 1917-18; Prof. of History and Govt and Head of Dept, 1924-46; Research Prof. of History, 1946-52, Professor Emeritus 1952-, Lehigh Univ.; Harold Vyvyan Harmsworth Prof. of Amer. History, University of Oxford, 1951-52; Fellow Queen's Coll., Oxford, 1951-52; Hon. Fellow, Lincoln Coll., 1965; Hon. Consultant in Amer. Hist. Library of Congress, 1965-67. Co-founder and past Pres. of Conference on British Studies; Mem., various hist. socs; past Pres. Pa Hist. Assoc.; past Mem. Bd of Eds, Amer. Historical Rev.; past Mem. Council of Inst. Early Amer. Hist. and Culture; holder of various grants in aid from: Amer. Council of Learned Societies, Amer. Soc. Sc., Res. Council, Lehigh Univ. Inst. of Res., and Rockefeller Foundation. Hon. Mem. Pa Hist. Junto, 1955; Phi Beta Kappa. Hon. DLitt, 1949; LHD 1951; LLD 1953; LHD 1955; LHD 1961; LLD 1962; LLD 1963; DLitt 1969. Porter Prize, Yale, 1918; Winsor Prize, Amer. Hist. Assoc., 1921; Loubat Prize, 1948; Bancroft Prize, 1950; Athenæum (Philadelphia) Award, 1953; Pulitzer Prize in History, 1962. *Publications:* Jared Ingersoll: A Study of American Loyalism in Relation to British Colonial Government, 1920; The Moravian White River Indian Mission, 1938; Lewis Evans, 1939; The British Empire before the American Revolution, vols I-XV, 1936-70 (rev. edns of vols I-III, 1958); Some Reflections upon the American Revolution and Other Essays in American Colonial History, 1942; The American Revolution as an Aftermath of the Great War for the Empire and Other Essays in American Colonial History, 1950; The British Empire in the Eighteenth Century, 1952; The Coming of the Revolution, 1763-1775, 1954; Jared Ingersoll: American loyalist, 1971; contrb. to various jls. *Address:* 825 Delaware Avenue, Bethlehem, Pa 18015, USA. *T:* 868-1649; (professional address) The Library, Lehigh University, Bethlehem, Pa 18015, USA. *Club:* Franklin Inn (Philadelphia). *[Died 26 Sept. 1971.*

GIRDLESTONE, Prof. Cuthbert Morton, Chevalier de la Légion d'Honneur; Professor of French, King's College, Newcastle upon Tyne (University of Durham), 1926-60, retired; *b* Bovey-Tracey, Devon, 17 Sept. 1895; *s* of James Hammond le Breton Girdlestone and Edith Margaret Coles; *m* 1923, Anne Marie Micheletti; two *d*. *Educ:* Southey Hall, Worthing; Immaculée Conception, Pau; Lycée de Pau; Sorbonne, Paris; Trinity Coll., Cambridge (Senior Scholar, 1920). Bachelier-ès-lettres, 1913; Licencié-ès-lettres, 1915; BA Cantab, 1921; MA Cantab, 1924. Lecturer in French, University of Cambridge, 1922. *Publications:* Dreamer and Striver: The Poetry of Frédéric Mistral, 1937; Mozart et ses concertos pour piano, 1939; Jean-Philippe Rameau: his life and work, 1957; Louis-François Ramond: sa vie et son œuvre littéraire, 1968; La tragédie en musique (1673-1750) considérée comme genre litteraire, 1973; articles on music, architecture, French literature. *Address:* 1 Parc de la Bérengère, 92210 Saint Cloud, France. *[Died 10 Dec. 1975.*

GIRI, Varahagiri Venkata; President of India, 1969-74; *b* Berhampore, 10 Aug. 1894. *Educ:* Nat. Univ. of Ireland. Barrister-at-law. Trade Union leader appointments include: Gen. Sec. and Pres., All India Railwaymen's Fedn; Pres., (twice) All India TUC; Indian workers' deleg. to Internat. Labour Conf., Geneva; workers' rep., Second Round Table Conf., London, 1931. Member, Central Legislative Assembly; Minister of Labour, Industries, Cooperation and Commerce, Madras Ministry, 1937-39; Minister in Madras Govt, 1946; High Commissioner for India in Ceylon, 1947-51; Minister of Labour, Govt of India, 1952-54. Governor: Uttar Pradesh, 1957-60; Kerala, 1960-65; Mysore, 1965-67. Vice-Pres. of India, 1967-69. *Publications:* Industrial Relations; Labour Problems in Indian Industry; Jobs for our Millions; The President Speaks: a compilation of speeches from May 1969-March 1970. *Address:* Girija, 1 Third Block, Jayanagar, Bangalore 11, India. *[Died 24 June 1980.*

GISHFORD, Anthony Joseph, CBE 1964; MA Oxon; Chairman of English Opera Group Ltd, since 1960; Director, Faber Music Ltd, since 1966; *b* 1908; *y s* of Edward Alexander Gishford and Florence Hawkes; unmarried. *Educ:* Westminster Sch.; Handelshochschule, St Gallen, Switzerland; Wadham Coll., Oxford. Served War of 1939-45, Intelligence Corps, 1939-42; Grenadier Guards, 1942-45. Editor of Tempo, 1947-58. Dir, Boosey & Hawkes Ltd, 1951-57; Chm., Boosey & Hawkes Inc.,

1957. Mem. executive cttee (Hon. Sec., 1952-64; Hon. Treasurer, 1971-) The Pilgrims of GB; a Vice-Pres., Youth and Music, 1963-. A Governor, Bridewell Royal Hospital and King Edward's School, Witley, 1946-; Chm., Quebec House Perm. Adv. Cttee, 1972-. *Publications:* The Correspondence of Richard Strauss and Hans von Bülow (trans.), 1953; (ed) Tribute to Benjamin Britten, 1963; (ed) Grand Opera, 1973. *Recreation:* gardening. *Address:* 4 The Grove, Highgate Village, N6 6JU. *T:* 01-340 2266. *Clubs:* Brooks's, Pratt's; Century (New York).
[*Died* 23 *Jan.* 1975.

GLADDING, Donald, CIE 1936; ICS (retired); *b* 22 Aug. 1888; *s* of Rev. Thomas Gladding; *m* 1915, Evelyn Avis McArthur (*d* 1951); no *c. Educ:* St Olave's, London; Brasenose Coll., Oxford. ICS 1913; Magistrate and Collector, Bengal, 1928; Deputy Sec. to Govt of India, Home Dept, 1931; Finance Sec., Govt of Bengal, 1933-39; Agent, Calcutta Electric Supply Corporation, Ltd, 1940-49. *Recreation:* golf. *Address:* Red Gables, Fleet, Hants. [*Died* 16 *July* 1971.

GLADSTONE, Adm. Sir Gerald Vaughan, GBE 1960; KCB 1957 (CB 1954); *b* 3 Oct. 1901; *yr s* of J. E. Gladstone, Llandaff and Braunton; *m* 1925, Marjorie (Justine), (*d* 1964), *e d* of J. Goring Johnston, NZ; two *s* one *d*; *m* 1966, Mrs Dora Brown (*née* Stewart), *widow* of Capt. (E) W. D. Brown, DSC, RN. *Educ:* RN Colls Osborne and Dartmouth. Midshipman, HMS Tiger, 1917; Rear-Adm. 1952; Vice-Controller of the Navy, 1952-53; Flag Officer Second in Command Far Eastern Station and Flag Officer Comdg 5th Cruiser Sqdn, 1953-55; Vice-Adm. 1955; Comdr, Allied Naval Forces, Northern Europe, 1955-57; Admiral, 1958; Comdr-in-Chief, Far East Station, 1957-60, retired 1960. *Address:* Forsters, Bradpole, Bridport, Dorset.
[*Died* 11 *July* 1978.

GLAISTER, John, JP; Emeritus Professor of Forensic Medicine, The University of Glasgow, 1931-62, retired; Medico-Legal Examiner to the Crown (retired except in special cases); Medical Referee under Cremation Act; *b* Glasgow, 1892; 2nd *s* of late Emeritus Prof. John Glaister, MD, LLD; *m* 1918, Isobel Rachel, *o d* of late Sir John Lindsay, KBE, DL, Town Clerk of Glasgow; two *d. Educ:* High Sch., and University, Glasgow. Bachelor of Medicine and Bachelor of Surgery, 1916; Doctor of Medicine with Hons, 1925; Dr of Science, 1927; FRSE; Fellow of Royal College of Physicians, Glasgow. Barrister-at-Law of Inner Temple, 1925. Asst in Forensic Medicine, Glasgow Univ., 1919-25, Lecturer Forensic Medicine, 1925-28; Lecturer on Forensic Medicine to the Police Force of the City of Glasgow, 1920-28; Medico-Legal Examiner and Adviser to the Corporation of Glasgow, 1920-28; Prof. of Forensic Medicine, the Faculty of Medicine, the University of Egypt, Cairo, and Medico-Legal Consultant to the Government of Egypt, 1928-32. Commissioned service with RAMC, 1916-19. Formerly External Examiner in Forensic Medicine, Universities of Edinburgh, Birmingham, Liverpool, Leeds, Aberdeen, St Andrews, and Sheffield. JP Co. of City of Glasgow. *Publications:* Text-Book of Medical Jurisprudence and Toxicology, 12th edn 1966; Recent Advances in Forensic Medicine, 1939; (joint) Hairs of Mammalia, with a special study of Human Hair, considered from the Medico-Legal Aspect; Medico-Legal Aspects of the Ruxton Case (joint); The Power of Poison, 1954; Final Diagnosis, 1964; numerous papers and monographs. *Address:* 3 Hatfield Drive, Glasgow W2.
[*Died* 4 *Oct.* 1971.

GLANVILLE, Sir William (Henry), Kt 1960; CB 1953; CBE 1944; DSc, PhD; FRS 1958; FICE, FIStructE; Consulting Engineer; Director of Road Research, Department of Scientific and Industrial Research, 1939-65; *b* 1900; *m* 1930, Millicent Patience, *d* of late E. John Carr; one *s* one *d.* Chairman: Advisory Cttee on Overseas (formerly Colonial) Road Research; Overseas Round Table Conf. on Highways; Internat. Cttee of Highway Research Bd, USA; Organising Cttee, Internat. Soc. of Soil Mechanics, 1957; Internat. Road Safety Research Conf., 1960; Co-Chm. First, Internat. Skid-Prevention Conf., 1958; Member: Informal Interdisciplinary Working Party of Engineering, Technology and Science Socs; Coun., Construction Industry Research and Information Assoc. (Chm., Information Cttee); Ministry of Transport Cttee on Road Safety, 1945-65; Royal Engineers Advisory Board, 1950-65; Cttee of Permanent International Assoc. of Road Congresses (Hon. Mem. Brit. Branch); Cttee of Internat. Assoc. of Bridge and Structural Engrg; Brit. Standards Codes of Practice Cttee, 1940-65; Bd, Brit. Nuclear Energy Conf., 1953-58; Colonial Research Council, 1954-59; Adv. Cttee, Transport and Road Res. Lab., 1972-; Past Pres. of Inst. of Civil Engineers (1950-51); Cantor Lecturer, Royal Society of Arts, 1950, 1954; Visiting Lecturer, Cape Town Univ., 1956; James Forrest Lecturer, Inst. of Civil Engineers, 1959. Fellow and Governor, Queen Mary Coll.,

London Univ.; Almoner and Governor, Christ's Hospital. Pres., Civil Service Motoring Assoc. Gold Medal (1961), Inst. of Struct. Engrs; Ewing Gold Medal (1962), Inst. of Civil Engrs. Viva Shield and Gold Medal, Worshipful Co. of Carmen, 1965. Hon. MIMunE, Hon. MInstHE, Hon. MACI; Hon. Mem. RE Inst.; Hon. Mem. Concrete Soc. *Publications:* various scientific and technical books and papers. *Address:* Langthwaite, 13 Kewferry Drive, Northwood, Mddx. *Club:* Royal Automobile.
[*Died* 30 *June* 1976.

GLASER, Mrs O. C.; *see* Wrinch, Dorothy.

GLASS, Prof. David Victor, FRS 1971; FBA 1964; Professor of Sociology, University of London, at London School of Economics, since 1948; *b* 2 Jan. 1911; *m* 1942, Ruth Durant; one *s* one *d. Educ:* Elementary Sch.; Raine's Grammar Sch.; London Sch. of Economics, London Univ. Chairman, Population Investigation Cttee; Past Pres., British Soc. for Population Studies; Hon. Pres., International Union for Scientific Study of Population; Mem., International Statistical Institute. For. Hon. Mem., Amer. Acad. Arts and Sciences, 1971; For. Associate, Nat. Acad. of Sciences (USA), 1973. Hon. DSc University of Michigan, 1967; Hon. DSocSci Edinburgh, 1973; Hon. DScEcon Queen's Univ. Belfast, 1974. *Publications:* The Town in a Changing World, 1935; The Struggle for Population, 1936; Population Policies and Movements in Europe, 1940; (ed) Introduction to Malthus, 1953; (ed) Social Mobility in Britain, 1954; (with E. Grebenik) The Trend and Pattern of Fertility in Great Britain, 1954; (ed) The University Teaching of Social Sciences: Demography, 1957; Latin American Seminar on Population: Report, 1958; Society: Approaches and Problems for Study, 1962 (co-ed); Differential Fertility, Ability and Educational Objectives, 1962; (ed jtly), Population in History, 1965; (ed jtly) Population and Social Change, 1972; Numbering the People, 1973; (with P. Taylor) Population and Emigration, 1976; papers in Population Studies (Jt Editor), British Journal of Sociology (Jt Editor), Proc. Royal Soc., Phil. Trans. Royal Soc. *Address:* 10 Palace Gardens Terrace, W8. [*Died* 23 *Sept.* 1978.

GLASSE, Alfred Onslow, CMG 1969; OBE 1952; MC 1917; CEng, FIEE, FNZIE; electrical engineer, New Zealand, retired; *b* 1889; *s* of William Stacey Glasse; *m* 1920, Ellen Emma Griffiths (*d* 1966); two *d. Educ:* Otago High Sch. Auckland Electric Power Bd, 1922-57 (Chief Engr, 1925-54, Cons. Engr 1954-57); Cons. Engr other Bds, etc, 1956-66. Member: Auckland City Council, 1956- (Dep. Mayor, 1962-70); Nat. Roads Bd, 1960-63; Auck. Harbour Bridge Authority, 1963-76; Auck. Metrop. Drainage Bd, 1957-64; Auck. Regional Planning Authority; Auck. War Memorial Mus. Council; Auck. Techn. Inst. Bd; St John Assoc. Past Pres., NZ Instn of Engrs. Also, as Pres. or on Council, numerous other Bds and Cttees. *Publications:* technical papers to various engineering jls. *Address:* 9 Eastbourne Road, Auckland 5, New Zealand. *Club:* Officers' (Auckland). [*Died* 13 *Dec.* 1977.

GLAZIER, Dr Edward Victor Denis, CB 1970; Director, Royal Radar Establishment, Malvern, since 1967; *b* 27 July 1912; *s* of Albert Glazier; *m* 1940, Marjorie May Burgess; one *s. Educ:* Northgate Sch.; London Univ. BSc 1935; PhD 1940. GPO Research Dept, 1934; Signals Research and Development Estab., 1942; Dir, Scientific Research (Electronics), Min. of Aviation, 1956; Royal Radar Estab., 1959. *Publications:* Services Textbook of Radio, Transmission and Propagation, 1958; Telecommunications (Vol. 1), 1962; papers on radio and radar. *Recreation:* sailing. *Address:* Royal Radar Establishment, Malvern, Worcs. *T:* Malvern 2733. [*Died* 6 *Jan.* 1972.

GLEGG, Alexander Lindsay, ACGI; AMIEE; Chairman of Hosa Research Laboratories, Sunbury-on-Thames; *b* London, 1882; *s* of late Sir Alexander Glegg, Aberdeen; *m* 1st, 1910, Lilian Grace Kilvington Olney (*d* 1951); twin *s*; 2nd, 1967, Janet Millar Manson. *Educ:* Dulwich Coll.; City and Guilds Central Technical Coll., S Kensington. Twice Pres. of the National Sunday Sch. Union and twice Pres. of the London Christian Endeavour; Pres. Christian Endeavour Union of Great Britain and Ireland; Past Pres. and Chm. Bible Testimony Fellowship; Pres., Chm. and Treas. of Advent Testimony and Preparation Movement; Pres., Movement for World Evangelisation; Pres. British Soc. for the Propagation of the Gospel among the Jews; Vice-Pres. of the Crusaders, and The Young Life Campaign; Hon. Trustee of Down Lodge Hall Mission, and Pres. of Landsowne Place Medical Mission, Bermondsey; Vice-Pres. of many other philanthropic bodies. *Publications:* Life with a Capital L; Youth with a Capital Why; Conquering the Capital I; How to run life at a profit; Four Score-and more; Walking on Two Feet. *Recreation:* golf (handicap 16). *Address:* Birchstone, Coombe Park, Kingston Hill, Surrey KT2 7JB. *T:* Kingston 5983. [*Died* 20 *June* 1975.

GLEN, Sir Alexander, KBE, cr 1956; CB 1950; MC 1918; Secretary, Department of Agriculture for Scotland, 1953-58; b 22 Nov. 1893; m 1924, Helen Gordon, d of late J. J. Kirk, St Andrews; one s one d. Educ: St Andrews and Oxford. Served in Army, 1915-19 (Black Watch). Entered Civil Service (Treasury), 1920; Dept of Agriculture for Scotland, 1935; Dep. Sec., 1945. Address: 17 Merchiston Gardens, Edinburgh 10. T: 031-337 5581.   [Died 16 Dec. 1972.

GLEN, John Mackenzie, CB 1945; b 12 April 1885; 2nd s of David James Glen, Edinburgh; m 1912, Jessie (d 1973), d of late Alexander McKercher, Edinburgh; one s. Educ: Daniel Stewart's Coll., Edinburgh; Edinburgh Univ. (MA 1st Class Hons). Entered first Div. of Civil Service, 1907. Served European War, 1914-18. Called to Bar, Lincoln's Inn, 1920. Principal Asst Sec., Ministry of Labour, 1937; Under-Sec., Ministry of Labour and National Service, 1945; retired. Address: c/o National Westminster Bank, Caxton House, Westminster, SW1.   [Died 29 Feb. 1976.

GLENARTHUR, 3rd Baron, cr 1918; **Matthew Arthur**, OBE 1945 (MBE 1943); Bt, cr 1903; DL; late Major (temporary Lieutenant-Colonel) Royal Scots Greys; b 12 May 1909; o s of 2nd Baron and Evelyn, e d of late Henry March-Phillipps, Tiverton; S father, 1942; m 1st, 1931, Audrey Lees-Milne (marr. diss. 1939); one d; 2nd, 1939, Margaret, o d of late Capt. H. J. J. Howie; two s one d. Educ: Winchester; Magdalen Coll., Oxford. DL (Ayrshire) 1948. Recreations: hunting and fishing. Heir: s Major Hon. Simon Mark Arthur [b 7 Oct. 1944; m 1969, Susan, yr d of Comdr Hubert Barry, Stockbridge, Hants; one s one d. Lieut, 10th Royal Hussars, 1966, Captain 1970]. Address: Stairaird, Mauchline, Ayrshire. T: Mauchline 211.
                                              [Died 19 May 1976.

GLENAVY, 3rd Baron, cr 1921; **Patrick Gordon Campbell**, Bt 1916; Author (as Patrick Campbell); Columnist, Sunday Times, since 1961; b 6 June 1913; s of 2nd Baron and Beatrice (née Elvery); S father, 1963; m 1st, 1941, Sylvia Willoughby Lee (marr. diss. 1947); 2nd, 1947, Cherry Lowson Monro (marr. diss. 1966); one d; 3rd, 1966, Mrs Vivienne Orme. Educ: Rossall; Pembroke, Oxford. Irish Marine Service, 1941-44. Columnist: Irish Times, 1944-47; Sunday Dispatch, 1947-59; Asst Editor, Lilliput Mag., 1947-53. Call My Bluff, TV programme, 1962-79. Publications: A Long Drink of Cold Water, 1950; A Short Trot with a Cultured Mind, 1952; Life in Thin Slices, 1954; Patrick Campbell's Omnibus, 1956; Come Here Till I Tell You, 1960; Constantly in Pursuit, 1962; How to become a Scratch Golfer, 1963; Brewing Up in the Basement, 1963; Rough Husbandry, 1965; My Life and Easy Times, 1967; A Bunch of New Roses, 1967; The Coarse of Events, 1968; The High Speed Gasworks, 1970; Fat Tuesday Tails, 1972; 35 Years on the Job, 1973; A Feast of True Fandangles, 1979. Recreations: golf and pleasure. Heir: b Hon. Michael Mussen Campbell, b 25 Oct. 1924. Address: La Tranche, 06650 Le Rouret, France.   [Died 9 Nov. 1980.

GLENDENNING, Raymond Carl; Sports Commentator, Journalist and Publicity Consultant; b 25 Sept. 1907; s of late Robert James and Mathilde Glendenning, Newport, Monmouthshire; m 1945, Sheilagh Dundee Millar. Educ: Newport High Sch.; London Univ. (BCom). Chartered Accountant, 1931. Joined BBC as Children's Hour Organiser (Cardiff 5WA), 1932; Outside Broadcasts Asst, Belfast, 1935; recalled to London Outside Broadcasts Staff, 1939; Asst Dir Outside Broadcasts, London, 1942; left permanent staff BBC, for full-time sports commentating and reporting, 1945; main BBC sports commentator on football, boxing, racing, tennis, etc., 1939-63. Television, film work, etc. Dir, Reading Standard Group Ltd, 1961-67; Editorial Dir, Golf News, 1963-67. Mem., Livery Co. of Carmen, 1952-. Publications: Just a Word in your Ear (autobiography), 1953; R. G.'s Boys' Book of Sport, 1950 to 1962. Recreations: water-colour painting, golf and snooker. Address: Flat 44, Green Hill Gate, Green Hill, High Wycombe, Bucks. T: High Wycombe 29932.   [Died 23 Feb. 1974.

GLENNIE, Brig. Edward Aubrey, CIE 1942; DSO 1917; FRAS, FRES, FRGS (Gold Medallist), FGS, FZS Scientific; Foundation FNI; Fellow, Conchological Society; late RE; b 18 July 1889; s of late Col E. Glennie; m 1923, Agnes Christina, d of W. Whigham, late Indian State Railways; (one s killed on active service, 1944). Educ: Haileybury. Entered Army, 1910; Capt. 1916; Major, 1926; Lieut Col, 1934; Col, 1937; late Dir Survey of India; retired 1948; served Mesopotamia, 1916-18 (despatches twice, DSO). Pres., British Cave Res. Assoc. Address: 15 Shrublands Road, Berkhamsted, Herts.   [Died 15 Feb. 1980.

GLENNIE, Adm. Sir Irvine Gordon, KCB 1945 (CB 1943); b 22 July 1892; o surv s of Capt. Gordon Glennie RN, and Edith, d of late Gen. J. Mitchell, RMLI; m 1928, Gwen, d of Edmund Evans; two s. Educ: RN Colls, Osborne and Dartmouth. Comdr 1928; Capt. 1933; Rear-Adm. 1941; Vice-Adm. 1944; served Home Fleet and China, 1910-14; in Destroyers, Grand Fleet, 1915-18; RNC, Dartmouth, 1922-24; commanding Destroyers, 1925-27 and 1932-34; Staff Coll., 1929; Admiralty, 1930-32; Imperial Defence Coll., 1935; commanding HMS Achilles, New Zealand Sqdn, 1936-39; commanding HMS Hood, 1939-41; Rear-Adm. Destroyers, Mediterranean, 1941-42; commanded Home Fleet Destroyers, 1943-44; Comdr-in-Chief, America and West Indies, 1945-46; retired list, 1947. Address: Wychwood, Fairfield Close, Lymington, Hants SO4 9NP. T: Lymington 72554.   [Died 8 Sept. 1980.

GLENTANAR, 2nd Baron, cr 1916; **Thomas Coats**; KBE, cr 1956; DL, JP, Aberdeenshire; Commander of the Order of St Olav; b 4 Dec. 1894; o s of 1st Baron and Margaret Lothian (d 1935), d of late James Tait Black of Underscar, Keswick; S father, 1918; m 1927, Grethe Dagbjört (d 1940), 2nd d of Thor Thoresen, of Oslo; one d. Educ: Eton; Christ Church, Oxford; abroad. Late Lieut 2/6 Black Watch and Signal Service, RE; served in France, European War (despatches); Chm. of British Legion (Scotland), 1923-29; Commissioner for Scotland, Boy Scouts Assoc., 1923-53; Chm. ATC Advisory Council for Scotland, 1941-45; Chm. ATC Scottish Welfare Council, 1942-45; Mem. Queen's Body Guard for Scotland (Royal Co. of Archers); Hon. Bencher, Middle Temple, 1950. Hon. LLD Aberdeen, 1966; Hon. FRCM, 1966. Heir: none. Address: Glen Tanar, Aboyne, Aberdeenshire. T: Aboyne 2450. Clubs: Carlton, Beefsteak; New (Edinburgh).
                                              [Died 28 June 1971 (ext).

GLOSSOP, Clifford William Hudson; agriculturist; Hon. (Life) Vice-President, South African Timber Growers Association; formerly Director of Yorks Electric Power Co., Electrical Distribution of Yorks Ltd, Thorne and District Water Co. (Chm.) and other companies; b 30 June 1901; s of late Major W. Glossop of Bramwith Hall, near Doncaster; unmarried. Educ: Harrow. Formerly Mem. of the Councils of the Royal Agricultural Society of England, The Yorkshire Agricultural Society, The Water Companies Association (Chm.), Yorks Institution for the Deaf; Pres. Elect British Friesian Cattle Soc., 1946 and 1947. MP (C) Penistone Division of Yorks, 1931-35; Mem. of Empire Parliamentary Association's delegation to Uganda and Tanganyika, 1934; Prospective Nat. C. candidate for Berwick-on-Tweed Division of Northumberland, 1936-38; prospective Nat. C. candidate for Howdenshire Division of Yorks, 1939-40 (resigned on appointment as Civil Servant; re-adopted candidate, 1944); Area Meat and Livestock Officer, Ministry of Food, for North-East England, 1940-44; MP (C) Howdenshire Division of Yorks, 1945-47; applied for Chiltern Hundreds, Oct. 1947. Formerly Divisional Comdr Doncaster Div. WR Special Constabulary; has travelled extensively throughout Europe, USA, Canada, West Indies, the Near East, New Zealand, Australia. Address: 5 Chaceley Place, Durban, South Africa. T: 347986/330080. Clubs: Carlton, Junior Carlton; Victoria (Pietermaritzburg).   [Died 4 July 1975.

GLOVER, Ronald Everett, CBE 1966; MA, DSc, FRCVS; retired as Principal and Dean of the Royal Veterinary College (University of London) (1955-65). Formerly Professor of Veterinary Pathology, University of Liverpool. Address: c/o Royal Veterinary College, Royal College Street, NW1 0TU. T: 01-387 2898.   [Died 12 Dec. 1975.

GLUCKMAN, Prof. (Herman) Max, BA Rand, MA, DPhil Oxon, MA Manchester; FBA 1968; Research Professor of Social Anthropology, University of Manchester, and holder of Special Fellowship from Nuffield Foundation, since 1971 (Professor of Social Anthropology, 1949-71); b Johannesburg, South Africa, 26 Jan. 1911; 2nd s of late Emmanuel Gluckman and of Kate Gluckman; m 1939, Mary Brignoli; three s. Educ: King Edward VII Sch., Johannesburg; Univ. of Witwatersrand; Exeter Coll., Oxford. Johannesburg Municipal Schol., 1928-30; Transvaal Rhodes Schol., 1934; Research for Nat. Bureau of Educnl and Social Research, S Africa, 1936-38; Asst Anthropologist, Rhodes-Livingstone Inst., Northern Rhodesia, 1939-41; Dir, 1941-47; Univ. Lectr in Social Anthropology, Oxford, 1947-49. Field Research: Zululand, 1936-38; Barotseland, 1939-47; Tonga of N Rhodesia, 1944; Lamba, 1946. Wellcome Medal, Royal Anthropological Inst., 1945; Rivers Memorial Medal, 1954; Lectures: Frazer Meml, Glasgow, 1952; Josiah Mason, Birmingham Univ., 1955-56; Munro Foundn, Edinburgh Univ., 1958 and 1960; Storrs, Yale Law Sch., 1963; Marett, Exeter Coll., Oxford, 1964, 1965; M. Cummings, McGill, 1971; J. B. Williams, Aberystwyth, 1972; Wilson Meml, Edinburgh, 1973. Vis. Fellow, ANU, 1960; Vis. Professor: Delhi Univ., 1960; MS Univ. of Baroda, 1960; Vis. Lectr, Yale Law Sch., 1966, 1968,

1974; Fellow, Center for Advanced Studies in the Behavioral Sciences, Palo Alto, 1967, 1971-72; Member: Human Sciences Cttee, DSIR, 1958-63; Exec. Council, Internat. African Inst., 1959- (and Consultative Dir, 1968-); Social Anthropology Sub-cttee, Social Science Research Council, 1966-69; Social Studies Sub-cttee, University Grants Cttee, 1966-70. Served N Rhodesia Defence Force, 1940-45. Chm. Assoc. of Social Anthropologists of the British Commonwealth, 1962-66. Foreign Hon. Mem., Amer. Acad. of Arts and Sciences, 1970. Dr *hc* Soc. Sc., Univ. de Bruxelles, 1965. *Publications:* Economy of the Central and Barotse Plain, 1941; Essays on Lozi Land and Royal Property, 1943; The Barotse Native Authorities, 1943; (with others) Land holding and Land-usage among the Tonga of Mazabuka District, 1945; The Judicial Process among the Barotse of Northern Rhodesia, 1955 (rev. edn 1967); Rituals of Rebellion in South-East Africa, 1954; Custom and Conflict in Africa, 1955; (ed jtly and contrib.) Seven Tribes of British Central Africa, 1951; Order and Rebellion in Tribal Africa, 1963; Politics, Law and Ritual in Tribal Society, 1965; The Ideas in Barotse Jurisprudence, 1965; (ed and contrib.) Essays on the Ritual of Social Relations, 1962, Closed Systems and Open Minds, 1964; Ideas and Procedures in African Customary Law, 1969; The Allocation of Responsibility, 1972; various papers in symposia, and in anthropological journals. *Recreations:* golf, sailing, cricket, watching Association football, reading. *Address:* Sheen, Ladybrook Road, Bramhall, Cheshire. *Club:* Royal Commonwealth Society.   [*Died* 13 *April* 1975.

GLUCKMANN, Grigory; Artist-painter; *b* Russia, 25 Oct. 1898; *m*; American citizen. *Educ:* Ecole des Beaux Arts, Moscow. In Paris from 1924, left for US, 1941. Exhibited at the Salon des Tuileries, Salon d'Automne (Sociétaire), Salon National des Beaux-Arts (Sociétaire), from 1925; retrospective exhbn, Desert Mus., Palm Springs, 1972; numerous one-man shows in Paris, London, New York, Los Angeles, Chicago, etc; from 1924, represented in Musée du Luxembourg, Paris (2 paintings), Petit Palais, Paris (2), Art Institute of Chicago, Phoenix Mus. of Art, Charles and Emma Frye Mus., Seattle, Los Angeles County Mus., La Jolla Mus. of Art, San Diego Mus. of Art and various other galleries and collections. Watson F. Blair Prize at the International Water Colour Exhibn, 1938, and at 56th Annual Exhibn, 1945, the Art Inst. of Chicago. FRSA 1948, Benjamin Franklin Fellow, 1968; FIAL 1965. Illustrated: Nuits Florentines by Heinrich Heine; Salvator Rosa by Hoffmann; Manon Lescaut by l'Abbé Prévost. *Relevant publication:* Grigory Gluckmann, by Arthur Millier. *Address:* 155 North Hamel Drive, Beverly Hills, Calif 90211, USA. *T:* 652-0482.   [*Died* 23 *July* 1973.

GLUCKSTEIN, Isidore Montague; President, J. Lyons & Co. Ltd, 1961-68, retired (Chairman, 1956-60); *b* 2 Nov. 1890; *s* of Montague and Matilda Gluckstein; *m* 1920, Rosalind Sophie (*d* 1973), *d* of Rev. Michael Adler, DSO, CF, BA, and Sophie Adler; one *s* died of wounds, one *d* decd. *Educ:* St Paul's Sch.; Sidney Sussex Coll., Cambridge (MA). Served European War, 1914-18; Capt., London Regt (wounded, despatches). Called to the Bar, Inner Temple, 1919. Vice-Pres., Anglers' Co-Operative Association. *Recreation:* fishing. *Address:* 35 Cumberland Terrace, Regent's Park, NW1. *Clubs:* Flyfishers', Buck's.   [*Died* 16 *Jan.* 1975.

GLUCKSTEIN, Sir Louis Halle, GBE 1969 (CBE 1964); Kt 1953; TD 1950; QC 1945; Colonel 5th Suffolk Regiment TA; Director, British Transport Hotels Ltd, 1963-78; *b* London, 23 Feb. 1897; *s* of late Joseph Gluckstein, OBE, and Francesca (*née* Halle), MBE, JP; *m* 1925, Doreen, *d* of Alexander Klean, London; two *s* one *d. Educ:* St Paul's Sch. (Schol.); Lincoln Coll., Oxford (Schol., MA; Hon. Fellow, 1968). Served European War, 1915-18, Lieut Suffolk Regt (wounded, despatches); served War of 1939-45: France, 1940 (despatches); Italy, 1944. Called to Bar, Lincoln's Inn, 1922, Bencher, 1952, Treasurer, 1970. MP (U) East Nottingham, 1931-45; contested East Nottingham, 1929, 1945 and 1950; contested Holborn and St Pancras South, 1951; DL County of London, 1952-77, retired; Mem., LCC for St Marylebone, 1955-64; Mem., GLC for City of Westminster, 1964-67; Alderman, 1967-73; Chm., Finance and Supplies Commn, 1967-68; Chm., GLC, 1968-69. Chairman: Board of Army Kinema Corp., 1956-68; Services Kinema Corp., 1969-79. Pres., Royal Albert Hall, 1965 (Vice-Pres., 1961-65); Vice-Pres., Old Pauline Club, 1958, Pres., 1966-69. Pres., St Marylebone Conservative Assoc., 1967-. A Governor of St Paul's Schools, London, 1968. Mem., Bd of Trustees, London Festival Ballet, 1969-; Pres., St John's Wood Protection Soc., 1973-; Mem. Council, Imp. Soc. of Knights Bachelor, 1973-; Chm. Council, Queen Alexandra's House, 1974-. Commendatore, Italian Order of Merit, 1969. *Recreations:* golf, shooting. *Address:* 39 Elm Tree Road, NW8 9JR. *T:* 01-286 7169. *Clubs:* Carlton, Savage; Leander.   [*Died* 27 *Oct.* 1979.

GLYN, Col Sir Richard Hamilton, 5th Bt *cr* 1800, and 9th Bt *cr* 1759; OBE 1955; TD 1941; DL; *b* 12 Oct. 1907; *e s* of Sir Richard Fitzgerald Glyn, 4th and 8th Bt, DSO; *S* father, 1960; *m* 1st, 1939, Lyndsay Mary Baker (marr. diss. 1969; she *d* 1971); two *s* one *d*; 2nd, 1970, Mrs Barbara Henwood. *Educ:* Worcester Coll., Oxford. 2nd Lieut QO Dorset Yeo. Fd Regt, RA, TA, 1930; comd 141 Dorset Yeo. Fd Regt, RA, TA, 1944-45; comd 294 QO Dorset Yeo. Fd Regt, RA, TA, 1952-55; Hon. Col 1959; ADC, 1958-62. Called to Bar, Lincoln's Inn, 1935. Dep. Chm., Dorset QS, 1952-57. MP (C) North Dorset, 1957-70. Mem., Chelsea Borough Council, 1948-50 (Vice-Chm., Housing Cttee); Mem., Shaftesbury RDC, 1957. PPS to Sir D. Eccles (Pres. Board of Trade), June-Oct. 1958. Vice-Chm., Cons. Agric. Cttee, 1959-65, Chm., Cons. Army Cttee, Vice-Chm., Cons. Defence Cttee, 1961-68; Mem., Select Cttee on Estimates (Defence and Overseas), 1964-70; Comr, Commonwealth War Graves Commn, 1965-70. Chairman: Kennel Club, 1973-76; Canine Consultative Council, 1974-79; United and Cecil Club, 1960-64; President: Soc. of Dorset Men, 1963-70; Cruft's Dog Show, 1976- (Chm., 1963-73). DL Dorset 1960. *Publications:* Bull Terriers and How to Breed Them, 1937 (6th edn 1953); A Short Account of the Queen's Own Dorset Yeomanry, 1943; Champion Dogs of the World, 1967; (ed) The World's Finest Horses and Ponies, 1971. *Recreations:* sport, travel and pedigree livestock. *Heir:* *s* Richard Lindsay Glyn [*b* 3 Aug. 1943; *m*; one *s* one *d. Educ:* Eton]. *Address:* 53 Belgravia Court, Ebury Street, SW1W 0NY. *Clubs:* Pratt's, Kennel.
                                                          [*Died* 24 *Oct.* 1980.

GLYN HUGHES, Hugh Llewelyn; *see* Hughes, H. L. G.

GLYN-JONES, Sir Hildreth, Kt 1953; TD 1950; FPS 1975; Judge of the High Court of Justice, Queen's Bench Division, 1953-68; *b* 19 March 1895; *s* of late Sir William Samuel Glyn-Jones and Mary Evans; *m* 1921, Kathleen, *d* of Thomas Melville; two *d* (and one *d* decd). *Educ:* City of London Sch. Military service, 1914-19 and 1939-44 (Middx Regt, Machine Gun Corps and Judge Advocate-General's Office). Qualified pharmacist, 1920; called to Bar, Middle Temple, 1921, Bencher, 1951; QC 1943; Wales and Chester circuit; Recorder of Merthyr Tydfil, 1944-45; Recorder of Cardiff, 1945-53. Deputy Chm., Berks Quarter Sessions, 1951-62. JP Berks, 1951. *Address:* 33 The Strand, Topsham, Exeter EX3 0AY. *T:* Topsham 5483.
                                                          [*Died* 30 *April* 1980.

GODBER, 1st Baron *cr* 1956, of Mayfield; **Frederick Godber,** Kt 1942; Grand Officer in Order of Orange Nassau, 1947; Chairman, Commonwealth Development Finance Co. Ltd, 1953-68; *b* 6 Nov. 1888; *s* of Edward and Marion Louise Godber; *m* 1914, Violet Ethel Beatrice Lovesy; two *d.* Spent 10 years in the United States, 1919-29; Pres., Rhoxana Corp., 1922-28; Dir, Shell Union Oil Corp., 1922-46; Chm., Shell Union Oil Corp., 1937-46; one of Managing Dirs of Royal Dutch/Shell Group, 1929-46; Chm. and Man. Dir, Shell Transport & Trading Co. Ltd, 1946-61; Chm., Shell Petroleum Co. Ltd, 1946-61. During war of 1939-45, Chm. of Overseas Supplies Cttee of Petroleum Board and served on number of Govt Missions. Hon. Bencher, Middle Temple, 1954. Hon. Liveryman, Leathersellers' Co., 1962. Hon. FInstPet, 1965. Cadman Medal, 1957. A Trustee of Churchill Coll. Trust Fund, Cambridge, 1958-. *Recreations:* gardening and farming. *Address:* Cranesden, Mayfield, East Sussex. *T:* Mayfield 3271.
                                                          [*Died* 10 *April* 1976 (*ext*.)

GODBER OF WILLINGTON, Baron *cr* 1979 (Life Peer), of Willington in the County of Bedfordshire; **Joseph Bradshaw Godber;** PC 1963; DL; *b* 17 March 1914; 5th *s* of late Isaac Godber and B. M. Godber (*née* Chapman), Willington Manor; *m* 1936, Miriam Sanders; two *s. Educ:* Bedford Sch. Entered family business, 1932. County Councillor, Beds, 1946-52. MP (C) Grantham, Lincs, 1951-79; Asst Govt Whip, 1955-57; Joint Parliamentary Sec., Min. of Agriculture, Fisheries and Food, 1957-60; Parliamentary Under-Sec. of State, Foreign Office, 1960-61; Minister of State, 1961-63; Sec. of State for War, June-Oct. 1963; Minister of Labour, 1963-64; Leader, British Delegn to: United Nations General Assembly, 1961-62; 18-Power Disarmament Conference, 1962-63; Commonwealth Parly Assoc., 1970; Chief Opposition Spokesman on Agriculture, 1965-70; Minister of State, FCO, 1970-72; Minister of Agriculture, Fisheries and Food, 1972-74. Chairman: Sidney Banks Ltd, 1974-; Tricentrol Ltd, 1976-79; Retail Consortium, 1976-79; Director: Booker McConnell Ltd, 1974-; British Home Stores Ltd, 1977-; Consultant, Beecham's Foods, 1974-. DL Bedfordshire, 1979. *Recreations:* gardening, shooting. *Address:* Willington Manor, near Bedford. *T:* Cardington 284. *Club:* Farmers'.   [*Died* 25 *Aug.* 1980.

GODDARD, Baron (Life Peer), *cr* 1944, of Aldbourne; **Rayner Goddard**; PC 1938; GCB 1958; Kt 1932; Lord Chief Justice of England, 1946-58, retired; *b* 1877; *m* 1906, Mary Linda (*d* 1928), *d* of Sir Felix Schuster, 1st Bt; three *d. Educ:* Marlborough; Trinity Coll., Oxford. BA 1898; MA 1931. Hon. Fellow, Trinity Coll., Oxford, 1940; Hon. DCL, Oxford, Montreal and New York Univs; Hon. LLD, Cambridge and Sheffield Univs. kc 1923. Recorder of Poole, 1917-25, of Bath, 1925-28, of Plymouth, 1928-32; Judge of High Court, King's Bench Division, 1932-38; Lord Justice of Appeal, 1938-44; a Lord of Appeal in Ordinary, 1944-46. *Address:* Queen Elizabeth Building, Temple, EC4. *T:* 01-353 5480. *[Died 29 May 1971.*

GÖDEL, Prof. **Kurt**; Professor, School of Mathematics, Institute for Advanced Study, Princeton, NJ, since 1953; *b* 28 April 1906; *s* of Rudolf and Marianne Gödel; *m* 1938, Adele Porkert; no *c. Educ:* Univ. of Vienna, Austria. Dozent, Univ. of Vienna, 1933-38; Mem., Inst. for Advanced Study, 1933, 1935, 1938-52. Einstein Award (jt), 1951; Nat. Medal of Science, 1974; holds hon. doctorates from Univs in USA, 1951-. Member: Nat. Acad. Sci. (USA); Amer. Phil. Soc.; Amer. Acad. Arts and Sci.; Hon. Mem., London Math. Soc., 1967; For. Mem., Royal Soc., London, 1968; Corresp. Mem., Inst. de France, 1972; Corresp. Fellow, British Academy, 1972. *Publications:* The Consistency of the Continuum Hypothesis, 1940; Contribs to: Monatsh. für Math. und Phys.; Proc. Nat. Acad. Sci.; Reviews of Mod. Phys.; Internat. Cong. Math., 1950; Dialectica, etc. *Address:* Institute for Advanced Study, Princeton, NJ, USA. *T:* WA4-4400. *[Died 14 Jan. 1978.*

GODFREY, Sir **John** (**Albert**), Kt 1950; *b* 17 Feb. 1889; *s* of Robert Arthur Godfrey; *m* 1924, Teresa Christine Kilgallin. *Educ:* Tollington Central Sch.; Civil Service Dept of King's Coll., London. Entered Customs and Excise Dept, 1911; Superintending Inspector, 1944; Deputy Chief Inspector, 1946; Chief Inspector, 1947-54. *Recreation:* motoring. *Address:* 258 Fir Tree Road, Epsom Downs, Surrey. *T:* Burgh Heath 51839. *[Died 12 Nov. 1973.*

GODFREY, Adm. **John Henry**, CB 1939; *b* 10 July 1888; *s* of Godfrey Henry Godfrey; *m* 1921, Bertha Margaret, *d* of Donald Hope; three *d. Educ:* King Edward's Sch., Birmingham; Bradfield Coll.; HMS Britannia. Capt. 1928; Rear-Adm. 1939; Vice-Adm. 1942; Adm. (retd) 1945; specialised in navigation. Served in HMS Euryalus, Dardanelles, 1915: present at re-occupation of Sollum, bombardment of Smyrna and Red Sea ops in support of Arab forces; on staff of C-in-C Mediterranean, 1916-19; Dep. Dir, Royal Naval Staff Coll., 1929-31; comd HM Ships Kent and Suffolk, 1931-33; Deputy Dir, Plans Division, Admiralty, 1933-35; commanded HMS Repulse, 1936-39. Dir of Naval Intelligence, 1939-42; Flag Officer Commanding Royal Indian Navy, 1943-46 Chm., Chelsea Hosp. Management Cttee, 1949-60; formerly Mem. Bd of Governors: Queen Charlotte's Hosp., Chelsea Hosp. for Women; Mem. Council: Roedean Sch.; King Edward's Hosp. Fund for London. Founder, Centre for Spastic Children, Chelsea. Order of the Nile; Chevalier, Legion of Honour. *Address:* White Stacks, Wilmington, near Polegate, Sussex. *T:* Alfriston 313. *Clubs:* Athenæum, Garrick, United Service and Royal Aero, Chelsea Arts. *[Died 29 Aug. 1971.*

GODFREY, Air **Commodore Kenneth Walter**, CB 1955; CBE 1954; retired; *b* 23 Jan. 1907; *s* of late Walter Godfrey; *m* 1932, Norah Josephine, *d* of J. Fleeman; one *s.* Granted commission in RAFVR, 1939; Gen. Duties Br., 1940; 22 (Torpedo) Bomber Sqdn; joined RAF Regt on formation, 1942. Served War, 1939-45 (Croix de Guerre with Palm; despatches twice). Comd RAF Regt Wing, Germany, 1945; Directorate of Comd and Staff Training, Air Min., 1946-48; comd RAF Station, Dumfries, 1951; apptd Senior Ground Defence Staff Officer, Technical Training Comd, 1952; Group Capt. 1952; comd Aden Protectorate Levies, 1953-55; Dep. Dir of Ground Defence, Air Ministry, 1955-59; ADC to the Queen, 1958-61; Air Cdre 1959; Dir of Ground Defence, Air Ministry, 1959-62; Actg Air Vice-Marshal, June 1962; Comdt-Gen. RAF Regt, and Inspector of Ground Defence, Air Min., 1962-63. *Recreations:* gardening, golf. *Club:* Royal Air Force. *[Died 10 Sept. 1979.*

GODFREY, Sir **Walter**, KBE 1964 (CBE 1952); BA; *b* 14 Dec. 1907; *s* of late Frank Godfrey; *m* 1943, Elizabeth Houston; three *s. Educ:* Battersea Grammar Sch.; Jesus Coll., Cambridge. BA Hons, 1929. Joined Dept of Overseas Trade, 1929; Trade Comr Service in India, Calcutta, 1930-38; Commercial Sec., British Embassy, Paris, 1938-40; Secretariat of Willingdon Mission to S America, Nov. 1940-Feb. 1941; Commercial Sec., British Embassy, Washington, 1941; Private Sec. to Sec. for Overseas Trade, 1942-43; Commercial Sec., Office of British Reptn to French Cttee for National Liberation, Algiers, 1944; Commercial Sec., British Embassy, Paris, 1944-46; UK Trade

Comr, Calcutta, 1946; Actg Senior UK Trade Comr, Delhi, 1947; UK Senior Trade Comr in Pakistan, Karachi, 1947-50; Minister (Commercial), British Embassy, Rio de Janeiro, 1952; Minister (Commercial), British Embassy, Cairo, 1954-56; Senior Inspector of Foreign Service Establishments, 1957-60; Ambassador to Korea, 1961-66. Hon. Chm., Anglo-Korean Soc., 1971-. *Address:* 109 Albemarle Road, Beckenham, Kent. *T:* 01-460 3958. *[Died 18 Oct. 1976.*

GODFREY, Sir **William Maurice**, 7th Bt *cr* 1785, of Bushfield, Co. Kerry; *b* 8 March 1909; *s* of 6th Bt and Eileen Mary (*d* 1971), *d* of late J. E. Currey, MD, Lismore; *S* father, 1935; *m* 1933, Caroline Iris, *d* of late Alban George Robins, Tunbridge Wells; three *d. Educ:* Clifton. Dir W. M. Godfrey & Partners Ltd. *Recreations:* fishing and gardening. *Address:* Ballinagroun, Annascaul, Tralee, Co. Kerry, Ireland.
[Died 25 Nov. 1971 (ext).

GODLEY, Brig. Sir **Francis W. C. F.**; see Fetherston-Godley.

GODMAN, Col **John**, CBE 1957; DL; *b* 9 May 1886; *s* of E. T. Godman, DL; unmarried. *Educ:* Eton. 15/19 Hussars, 1905-30; commanded, 1926-30. Glos County Council, 1931 (Chm., 1946-56). Mem., Severn River Board (Chm., 1950-67). JP 1938, DL 1946, High Sheriff 1942, Gloucestershire. *Recreations:* shooting and fishing. *Address:* Banks Fee, Moreton-in-Marsh, Glos. *T:* Stow-on-the-Wold 5. *Club:* Cavalry and Guards.
[Died 1 Oct. 1978.

GOENKA, Rai Bahadur Sir **Badridas**, Kt 1934; CIE 1928; *b* Calcutta, 29 July 1883; *s* of late Ramchander Goenka; *m* 1899, Manorama, 2nd *d* of late Durga Prasad Rais, Farrukhabad. *Educ:* Presidency Coll., Calcutta; Calcutta Univ. (BA). Director: Reserve Bank of India, 1935-41; State Bank of India, 1955-57; Rallis India Ltd, 1940-65; Imperial Bank of India, 1932-35, 1941-55; President: Federation of Indian Chambers of Commerce and Industry, 1945-46; Marwari Assoc., 1928-30; Indian Chamber of Commerce, 1941-42; Trustee: Calcutta Improvement Trust, 1928-40; Victoria Memorial Hall, Calcutta; Chairman: Famine Relief Cttee, Bengal, 1942; Bengal Textile Assoc., 1945; Member: Bengal Legislative Council, 1923-35; Bengal Banking Enquiry Commn, 1929; Sheriff of Calcutta, 1932-33. Made Rai Bahadur, 1925. *Address:* Goenka Nivas, 19 Belvedere Road, Calcutta 27, India. *T:* 45-1202.
[Died 26 Feb. 1973.

GOEPPERT MAYER, Prof. **Maria**; see Mayer.

GOFF, Sir **Ernest** (**William**) **Davis-**, 3rd Bt *cr* 1905; *b* 11 June 1904; *s* of 2nd Bt and Margaret Aimée, *d* of late Rt Hon. Sir C. S. Scott, GCB; *S* father, 1923; *m* 1941, Alice Cynthia Sainthill Woodhouse (marr. diss. 1960); one *s* three *d. Heir: s* Robert William Davis-Goff [*b* 12 Sept. 1955; *m* 1978, Sheelagh Chadwick, *d* of Mr and Mrs Terence Chadwick, Lissen Hall, Swords]. *Address:* Ardbrack Cottage, Kinsale, Co. Cork, Eire. *Club:* Kildare Street and University (Dublin).
[Died 26 March 1980.

GOFF, Rt. Hon. Sir **Reginald** (**William**), PC 1975; Kt 1966; **Rt. Hon. Lord Justice Goff**; a Lord Justice of Appeal, since 1975; *b* 22 March 1907; *s* of late William Kingsley Goff, East India and China Tea Merchant, and late Louisa Goff; *m* 1944, Marjorie Morwenna Curnow, *d* of late Rev. A. Garfield Curnow, Wallington; two *d. Educ:* Sutton County Grammar Sch.; King's Coll. and University Coll., London. LLB (London) First Class Hons, 1928, and Certificate of Honour in the Bar examination, 1928. Called to the Bar, Lincoln's Inn, 1929; Bencher, 1959, Treasurer, 1974. War of 1939-45: Auxiliary Fire Service, 1939-42; RAF, 1942-46 (AJAG, 1945-46). Elected to Gen. Council of Bar, 1958. A Judge of the High Court of Justice, Chancery Div., 1965-75. Fellow, UCL, 1968-; FKC, 1970. *Address:* Kingsley Croft, Downs Way, Tadworth, Surrey. *T:* Tadworth 3636.
[Died 17 Jan. 1980.

GOITEIN, **Hugh Hirsch**, LLD; Barrister-at-Law; *b* 7 June 1896; *s* of late Kalman Goitein and Elizabeth Barnett; *m* 1938, Freda, *o d* of late Col Albert William Goodman, MP, Old Dean Hall, Camberley, Surrey; one *s* one *d. Educ:* City of London Sch.; University Coll., London. Barstow Law Scholar; called to Bar, 1923; joined the South Eastern Circuit; Mem. of the International Law Assoc. and the Grotius Soc.; Prof. of Commercial Law in the Univ. of Birmingham, 1930-62. *Publications:* The Law as to CIF Contracts, 2nd edn, 1926; Official edn in Polish Umowy CIF, 1929; contribs to the 14th edn of the Encyclopædia Britannica; Company Law, 1960; other works include Primitive Ordeal and Modern Law and More's Utopia (ed. for Broadway Translations). *Recreations:* travel, walking. *Address:* Top Farm, Broadway, Worcs.
[Died 20 Dec. 1976.

GOLD, Ernest, CB 1942; DSO 1916; OBE; FRS 1918; MA; *b* 1881; *s* of late John Gold, and Ellen (*née* Peckett), Rowington, Warwicks; *m* 1907, Catherine L. (*d* 1973), *d* of late John Harlow, and Mary (*née* Bowie), Edinburgh; one *d. Educ:* Coleshill Grammar Sch.; Mason's Coll., Birmingham; St John's Coll., Cambridge. Third Wrangler, 1903; Nat. Sci. Tripos, Part II, 1904; Fellow of St John's Coll., Cambridge, 1906; Schuster Reader in Dynamical Meteorology, 1907-10; discovered in 1908 a rational physical explanation of the Isothermal Condition of the Upper Atmosphere or Stratosphere; Pres., Royal Meteorological Society, 1934-36 (Symons Medallist, 1926), Hon. Mem., 1958; Hon. Mem. Amer. Meteorological Soc., 1959; Pres. International Commission for Synoptic Weather Information, 1919-47, and of Meteorological Sub-Commn of International Commn for Aerial Navigation, 1922-46; served European War, 1915-19 (despatches, DSO); in Meteorological Office, 1910-47; US Medal of Freedom with Silver Palms, 1946; Internat. Meteorological Organisation (IMO) Prize and Medal, 1958. *Publications:* Physical and Meteorological Papers and Reports in Proc. Royal Soc., Jl of Royal Meteorological Soc., Reports of British Assoc., Proc. Vienna Academy, and in Memoirs of Meteorological Office, London. *Recreation:* gardening. *Address:* 8 Hurst Close, Hampstead Garden Suburb, NW11 7BE. *T:* 01-455 1209. *[Died 30 Jan.* 1976.

GOLD, James Herbert; *b* 21 Jan. 1885; *s* of Joseph and Aphra Gold of Birmingham; *m* 1909, Kathleen (*d* 1955), *d* of A. E. Cutter of Knutsford, Cheshire; two *s* one *d. Educ:* King Edward's Sch., Birmingham; University Coll., London. Solicitor; Bachelor of Laws and University Law Scholar of Univ. of London, 1904; Scott Scholar of the Law Soc., 1907. Joint MFH Ludlow, 1928-30; County Councillor for Cheshire (Northwich Div.), 1928-30; Principal (temp.) Ministry of Works and Ministry of Fuel and Power (Open Cast Coal Production), 1941-45; formerly a Dir of Brunner Mond & Co. Ltd, and other companies. *Recreations:* hunting, shooting, golf. *Address:* Brookfield Farm, Warfield, Berks. *T:* Winkfield Row 2281. *[Died 28 July* 1974.

GOLDEN, Lt-Col Harold Arthur, CBE 1960; QPM 1954; *b* 1896; *s* of Arthur Golden, Norwich; *m* 1929, Freda Mary, *d* of Ernest W. Lightfoot, Carlisle; one *d. Educ:* Norwich Sch.; St John's Coll., Cambridge. Barrister, Gray's Inn, 1935. Served European War, with RE, 1915-19. Major 1935; retd 1935; re-empld, 1943-45. Chief Constable, Salop, 1935-46; Chief Constable of Wilts, 1946-63. County Dir, Wilts Branch, British Red Cross Society, 1964-66. *Recreations:* fishing, gardening. *Address:* 8 Newfound Drive, Cringleford, Norwich, Norfolk. *T:* Norwich 52250. *[Died 19 April* 1976.

GOLDIE, Rt. Rev. Frederick, MA, BD; Bishop of Glasgow and Galloway, since 1974; *b* 1 Sept. 1914; *s* of John and Maria Goldie, Glasgow; *m* 1940, Margaret Baker McCrae, MA; one *s* one *d. Educ:* Strathbungo Academy, Glasgow; Hatfield Coll., Durham; New Coll. and Coates Hall, Edinburgh. Open Exhibnr, Hatfield Schol., LTh, BA 1938, Durham; BD Edinburgh, 1939; MA Durham, 1946. Curate at Govan, 1938; Rector at Hillington, Glasgow, 1939-49; Lecturer at Theological Coll., Edinburgh, 1940-63; Rector at Dumbarton, 1949-63; Canon of St Mary's Cathedral, Glasgow, 1956; Dean of Glasgow and Galloway, 1963-74; Rector of St Margaret's, Glasgow, 1963-74. *Publication:* A History of the Episcopal Church in Scotland, 1950, rev. edn 1976. *Recreations:* reading, walking. *Address:* Bishop's House, 14 Clevedon Crescent, Glasgow G12 0PB. *T:* 041-339 0554. *Club:* Western (Glasgow). *[Died 23 Oct.* 1980.

GOLDIE, Robert George, CBE 1949; *b* 4 Oct. 1893; *e s* of Charles Goldie and Lilian (*née* Steggall); *m* 1st, 1924, Ann Mary Laptew (*d* 1930); 2nd, 1933, Helen MacLean Homan; one *s* three *d. Educ:* Victoria Coll., Jersey, CI. Served European War, 1914-18, in 28th London Regt (Artists' Rifles) and Loyal North Lancs Regt (despatches 1918). Entered Consular Service, 1919; Vice-Consul: at Hamburg, 1920-21 and 1924-27; at Naples, 1921-24; at Colon (Panama), 1927-39; at Boston (USA), 1929-30; Chargé d'Affaires and Consul at Santo Domingo, 1930-32 and at San Salvador, 1932-35; Consul at Gothenburg (Sweden), 1935-39, and at Málaga (Spain), 1939-45; Consul-Gen. at Milan, 1945-50, at Antwerp, 1950-53; retired Oct. 1953. *Recreation:* gardening. *Address:* 2 Friar's Road, Winchelsea, Sussex. *[Died 6 March* 1971.

GOLDNEY, Maj.-Gen. Claude Le Bas, CB 1943; CBE 1940; MC; *b* 4 Dec. 1887; *s* of late Col W. H. Goldney, RE; *m* 1938, Nora (*d* 1968), *yr d* of late Surg. Maj.-Gen. Sir Gerald Bomford, KCIE; no *c. Educ:* Dover Coll.; Portsmouth Grammar Sch.; RMA Woolwich. Commnd in Glos Regt 1906; Transf. ASC 1910; served European War, France, 1914-18 (despatches, MC); Col 1937; ADS & T, Egypt, 1938; ADS & T, Aldershot, 1939; served

War of 1939-45; DDS & T, 1st Corps, with BEF, to France, 1939; DDS & T, 3rd Corps, until evacuation Dunkirk, 1940 (CBE, CB, despatches thrice); Acting Maj.-Gen. 1941; Dir of Supplies and Transport, GHQ, Middle East Force, 1941-44; ADC to HM the King, 1942-44, retired 1944. *Recreation:* fishing. *Address:* 38 Mount Hermon Road, Woking, Surrey. *[Died 2 Jan.* 1978.

GOLDNEY, Sir Henry Hastings, 4th Bt, *cr* 1880; MC; JP; *b* 3 July 1886; *s* of Sir Frederick Hastings Goldney, 3rd Bt; S father, 1940; *m* Violetta (*d* 1965), *o d* of W. C. Barnes. *Educ:* Harrow; Trinity Coll., Cambridge. Served European War as Lieut, Royal Engineers, 1914-17 (despatches, MC). *Club:* Carlton. *[Died 26 Feb.* 1974 (*ext*).

GOLDSMID, Major Sir Henry Joseph d'A.; *see* d'Avigdor-Goldsmid.

GOLDSMITH, Sir Allen (John Bridson), KCVO 1970 (CVO 1962); FRCS; Surgeon-Oculist to the Queen, 1965-74; Surgeon-Oculist to HM Household, 1952-65; Hon. Consultant Surgeon, Moorfields Eye Hospital since 1958; Ophthalmic Surgeon: Middlesex Hospital, 1946-74, now Emeritus; Royal National Orthopædic Hospital, 1946-74, now Emeritus; King Edward VII Hospital for Officers since 1954; *b* 27 Nov. 1909; *s* of Bridson K. Goldsmith, MD; *m* 1936, Mabel Rosemary Elise, *d* of Herdman Porter, MD; one *s* two *d. Educ:* King William's Coll., Isle of Man; Middlesex Hosp. MRCS, LRCP 1931; FRCS 1934; MB, BS London (Distinctions Medicine and Pathology), 1931. Demonstrator in Physiology, Senior Broderip Scholar, Lyell Gold Medallist, House Physician, House Surg., Asst Pathologist, Middlesex Hosp., 1931-35; House Surg., Resident Surgical Officer, 1935-37, Pathologist, 1937-40, Moorfields Eye Hosp.; Surgeon and Pathologist, Central London Eye Hosp., 1937-48; Ophthalmic Surgeon, Paddington Green Children's Hosp., 1937-46; Surg., Moorfields Eye Hosp., 1948-58. Lectr in Ophthalmol., Univ. of London, 1938. Examnr in Ophthalmol., RCP and RCS, 1948. FRSM 1934 (Hon. Sec. Ophthalmological Section, 1941-43; Vice-Pres., 1968-71); Member: Ophthalmological Soc. UK (Hon. Sec., 1950-52; Vice-Pres., 1969-72); Royal Institution, 1943-68; French Ophthalmological Soc., 1946; Governor, Middlesex Hosp., 1957-73. *Publications:* (jointly) Recent Advances in Ophthalmology, 5th edn; various papers in ophthalmic and medical jls. *Recreations:* gardening, fishing, reading. *Address:* Matthew Farm, Shottenden, Canterbury, Kent. *T:* Canterbury 76332. *[Died 13 Dec.* 1976.

GOLDSMITH, Dr William Noel; Consulting Dermatologist: University College Hospital, London; St John's Hospital, Lewisham; West Herts Hospital, Hemel Hempstead; Italian Hospital; Consulting Physician, St John's Hospital for Diseases of the Skin; Emeritus Consultant Dermatologist, West End Hospital for Neurology; *b* 26 Dec. 1893; *s* of Ernest Goldschmidt and Bertha Feist; *m* 1969, Irene Sharp. *Educ:* Rugby Sch.; Pembroke Coll., Cambridge; UCH Medical Sch., London. Qualified MRCS, LRCP 1918; RAMC, 1918-20; MRCP 1922; Radcliffe Crocker Travelling Scholarship, 1924 (Vienna and Breslau); MD Cambridge 1927; Physician Skin Dept, University Coll. Hosp., 1932-59; FRCP 1937; Chief Ed., British Jl of Dermatology, 1939-48. Pres., St John's Hosp. Dermatological Soc., 1936-38; Pres., Dermatological Section of RSocMed, 1949-51; Pres., British Assoc. of Dermatology, 1957. Mem. Panel on External Radiotherapy, of Cttee on Radiological Hazards to Patients (Adrian Cttee), 1957-60. Hon. Member: British Assoc. of Dermatology; Dermatological Section, RSM; Austrian, German, Danish and Berlin Dermatological Socs; Amer. Dermatological Assoc.; Corresp. Member: Hungarian, Swedish and French Dermatological Socs. *Publications:* Recent Advances in Dermatology, 1936, 2nd edn (with Dr F. F. Hellier), 1954; articles chiefly in British Jl of Dermatology. *Recreations:* music, photography. *Address:* Flat 18, 2 Mansfield Street, W1M 9FE. *T:* 01-580 1606. *[Died 4 April* 1975.

GOLDWYN, Samuel; motion picture producer; General Partner, Samuel Goldwyn Productions; *b* Warsaw, Poland, 27 Aug. 1882; *s* of Abraham and Hannah Goldfish; *m* 1st, 1910, Blanche Lasky (divorced 1915); one *d*; 2nd, 1925, Frances Howard; one *s. Educ:* night schs, New York. Emigrated to United States, 1896; naturalised US, 1902; organised Jesse Lasky Feature Photoplay Co., 1913; organised Goldwyn Pictures Corp. (later Metro-Goldwyn-Mayer), 1916; has produced own films independently since 1923. Presidential Medal for Freedom, 1971. *Address:* Samuel Goldwyn Productions, 1041 N Formosa Avenue, Los Angeles, Calif 90046, USA. *[Died 31 Jan.* 1974.

GONARD, Prof. Samuel Alexandre; President, International Committee of the Red Cross, since 1964 (Member 1961-); *b* 8 June 1896; *m* 1944, Manon Bosshardt; one *s* one *d. Educ:* Univ.

of Neuchâtel (Bachelor of Law). Chief of personal Staff to C-in-C Swiss Army, 1939; Brig. 1943; Vice-Chief, Gen. Staff of Swiss Army, 1943; Comdr, 14th Div.; Comdr, 9th Div., 1944; Prof., Mil. Sect., Fed. Polytech. High Sch., Zürich, 1946-53; Comdr 3rd Army Corps, 1951; Comdr, 1st Army Corps, 1954; Expert on Fed. Commn for the study of UN Charter; Mem. Fed. Commn for Nat. Defence, 1951-61; Prof. Grad. Inst. of Internat. Studies, University of Geneva, 1961. *Publications:* La Recherche operationnelle et la Décision. Has contrib. to numerous mil. and internat. affairs reviews. *Recreations:* literature, the arts, travelling. *Address:* Les Gonelles, Corseaux sur Vevey, Vaud, Switzerland. *T:* (021) 51.33.33. *[Died 3 May 1975.*

GOOCH, Brig. Richard Frank Sherlock, DSO 1945; MC 1940; Gentleman Usher to the Queen, 1964-69, Extra Gentleman Usher, 1962-64, and since 1969; *b* 8 Nov. 1906; 3rd *s* of Sir Thomas V. S. Gooch, 10th Bt; *m* 1939, Barbara Susan Hoare; two *s. Educ:* Harrow; Caius Coll., Cambridge (MA). Joined Coldstream Guards, 1927; Adjutant, 1934-37; ADC to the Viceroy of India, 1937-39; psc 1942; Bde Major, 5th Guards Armoured Bde, 1942-43. Comd 1st Coldstream, 1944-45; AA and QMG, Guards Div., 1945-46; Comd 2nd Coldstream, 1946-49; AAG, HQ London Dist, 1949-51; Comd 32 Guards Bde, 1951. City Marshal to the City of London, July-Dec. 1957; Private Sec. to the Lord Mayor of London, 1957-62. Grand Sword Bearer, Grand Lodge of England, 1954; Dep. Prov. Grand Master for Suffolk, 1970. Croix de Guerre (with Palm), France, 1944; Chevalier of Order of Crown, Belgium, 1945; Croix de Guerre (with Palm), Belgium, 1945. *Recreation:* shooting. *Address:* Oakhill Farm, Earl Soham, Woodbridge, Suffolk. *T:* Earl Soham 251. *Clubs:* Boodle's, Pratt's. *[Died 6 June 1973.*

GOOCH, Col Sir Robert Eric Sherlock, 11th Bt, *cr* 1746; KCVO 1973; DSO 1941; DL, JP; Member of HM Body Guard of the Honourable Corps of Gentlemen-at-Arms, 1950-73, Lieutenant, 1968-73 (Clerk of the Cheque and Adjutant, 1963-67, Standard Bearer, 1967-68); *b* 6 May 1903; *e s* of Sir T. V. S. Gooch, 10th Bt, and Florence Meta (*d* 1932), *y d* of late James Draper, St Heliers; *S* father, 1946; *m* 1926, Katharine C. (*d* 1974), *er d* of late Maj.-Gen. Sir E. W. C. Chaytor, KCMG, KCVO, CB; two *s* one *d. Educ:* Eton. Served War of 1939-45 (despatches twice, DSO); OC The Life Guards, 1943-46; commanded 1st Household Cavalry Regt, 1942-44. Col commanding The Household Cavalry, 1944-46; retd pay, 1946. Mem. of East Suffolk County Council, 1946-74 (Chm., 1957-67); County Alderman, 1951; High Sheriff of Suffolk, 1950. Mem. of House of Laity of Church Assembly, 1948-55. Mem. Council, Royal Agricultural Soc. of England, 1950 (Dep. Pres., 1960; Pres., 1961; Vice-Pres., 1961; Chm., 1963-67; Trustee, 1964); Liaison Officer to the Minister of Agriculture, 1952-62. Chm. Suffolk Agricultural Exec. Cttee, 1954-62; Pres., The Royal Smithfield Club, 1966. Hon. Col 4th Bn The Suffolk Regt (TA), 1953-61; Hon. Col Suffolk and Cambs Regt (TA), 1961-67. *Heir: s* Richard John Sherlock Gooch, *b* 22 March 1930. *Address:* Benacre Hall, Wrentham, Beccles, Suffolk. *Club:* Turf. *[Died 13 Nov. 1978.*

GOODDEN, Abington, CBE 1956; retired, as a Consul-General, from HM Diplomatic Service, 1960; *b* 7 Dec. 1901; *s* of late Dr Wyndham C. Goodden and Clara Joan (*née* Smith); *m* 1930, Johanna Arnolda Jordaan (*d* 1962), South Africa; one *s. Educ:* Eton (King's Scholar, 1915); King's Coll., Cambridge. Vice-Consul: Hamburg, 1926-27; Lourenço Marques, 1928-30; Naples, 1931-33; Vice-Consul and Third Sec. of Embassy, Santiago (Chile), 1933-37; attached to Special Representative of Cuba at Coronation of HM King George VI, 1937; Vice-Consul, New York, 1937-38; Consul: Valencia, 1939; Madrid, 1939-41; Chargé d'Affaires *ad interim,* Managua (Nicaragua), 1941-42; Consul, Ponta Delgada (Azores), 1943-45; rep. of CCG (British Element) at Frankfurt, 1945-46; Consul and First Sec. of Embassy, Madrid, 1946-47; Dep. Consul-Gen., Batavia (now Djakarta), 1947-49; Commercial Counsellor, HM Embassy, Oslo, 1950-53; Consul-Gen., Seville, 1953-60. Coronation Medal, 1937; Portuguese Life-Saving Society's Medal, 1946. *Address:* 62 Westbourne Terrace, W2. *[Died 25 Jan. 1978.*

GOODERHAM, Very Rev. Hector Bransby, MA; retired; Hon. Canon, St Mary's Cathedral, Edinburgh, 1971; *b* 11 Oct. 1901; *o s* of Edward Bransby Gooderham and Louisa Elizabeth Gooderham, Richmond, Surrey; *m* 1928, Esther Beatrice, *d* of William Orr, JP, Edinburgh; one *s* one *d. Educ:* George Heriot's Sch.; Edinburgh Univ.; Westcott House, Cambridge. MA 1st Cl. Hons, Edinburgh, 1923 (Vans Dunlop Scholar in Logic and Metaphysics). Curate: St Mary's Cathedral, Glasgow, 1924; St John's, Edinburgh, 1925; Rector: St John's, Selkirk, 1929-37; St Baldred's, North Berwick, 1937-49; Provost of the Cathedral Church of St Mary, Edinburgh, 1949-56; Vicar of St Peter's,

Cranley Gardens, South Kensington, London, 1957-63. Formerly also: Lecturer, Edinburgh Theological Coll., 1934-43; Canon of St Mary's Cathedral, Edinburgh, 1948. *Recreations:* walking, motoring. *[Died 30 Dec. 1977.*

GOODEVE, Sir Charles Frederick, Kt 1946; OBE 1941; FRS 1940; FRIC; FIM; FCIT; MSc Manitoba; DSc London; Comdr RNVR (retired); Consultant, British Steel Corporation, since 1969; Director, London & Scandinavian Metallurgical Co. Ltd, since 1971; *b* 21 Feb. 1904; *s* of Canon F. W. Goodeve, Winnipeg, Canada; *m* 1932, Janet I. Wallace, PhD; two *s. Educ:* Univ. of Manitoba; University Coll., London. Asst Lectr, Univ. of Manitoba; 1851 Exhibition Scholar, 1927; Lectr and later Reader in Physical Chemistry, University Coll., London, Fellow, UCL, 1946; Dep. Dir, Dept of Miscellaneous Weapon Development, Admiralty, 1940-42; Asst and later Dep. Controller for R&D, Admiralty, 1942-45; Dir, BISRA, The Inter-Group Laboratories of the British Steel Corp., formerly British Iron and Steel Research Assoc., 1945-69. Director: ICFC, 1965-74; Technical Develt Capital Ltd, 1966-74; Nat. Indust. Fuel Efficiency Service, 1968-72. Pres., Faraday Soc., 1950-52; Chm., Operational Research Club, 1947-51; Vice-Pres., Parliamentary and Scientific Cttee, 1950-62; Mem., Lord President's Advisory Council on Scientific Policy, 1953-56; Pres. Chemical Section, British Assoc., 1956; Master, Worshipful Co. of Salters, 1958-59; Pres., Iron and Steel Inst., 1961-62; a Vice-Pres., Royal Soc., 1968-70. Scientific Adviser, British Transport Commn, 1948-58. Governor, Imperial Coll., London, 1961-73; Fellow, 1967-. Mem., Council of Tavistock Inst. of Human Relations; Vice-Chm., Orgn for Promoting the Understanding of Society, 1975-. Fellow, Metallurgical Soc. AIME, 1967. Hon. DSc: Manitoba, 1946; Sheffield, 1956; Birmingham, 1962; Newcastle-upon-Tyne, 1970; Salford, 1974. US Medal of Freedom with Silver Palm; Bessemer Gold Medallist, 1962; Carl Lueg Gold Medallist, 1962; Silver Medal, Operational Research Soc., 1964. *Publications:* (part author) Iron and Steel Productivity Report; numerous in scientific journals. *Address:* 38 Middleway, NW11 6SG. *T:* 01-455 7308. *Club:* Athenæum. *[Died 7 April 1980.*

GOODFELLOW, Keith Frank, QC 1967; a Recorder of the Crown Court, since 1972; Practising Member of the Bar since 1952; *b* 26 March 1926; *s* of late L. T. Goodfellow and E. M. Goodfellow (*née* Dendy); *m* 1949, Rosalind Erica (*née* Griffith-Jones); two *s* one *d. Educ:* St Dunstan's Coll., Catford, SE6; Sidney Sussex Coll., Cambridge (Open Schol. in Hist. 1944; BA, Law, 1st cl. 1949; LLB 1st cl. 1950; MA 1952). Harmsworth Scholar, Middle Temple, 1950, called to Bar, Middle Temple, 1951, Bencher 1972. *Publication:* Outline of the Law of Rating (with W. Scrivens), 1955. *Recreation:* exercising children and dogs. *Address:* Harlyn, Sandy Way, Cobham, Surrey. *T:* Oxshott 3142. *[Died 4 Sept. 1977.*

GOODFELLOW, Sir William, Kt 1955; Director: Amalgamated Dairies Ltd; Refrigeration Engineering Co. Ltd; Sulphur & Chemical Importing Co. Ltd; Avalon Investment Trust Ltd; Challenge Investment Co. Ltd; *b* 26 May 1880; *s* of Thomas and Jane G. Goodfellow; *m* 1913, Irene C. Chamberlin; four *s* one *d* (and one *s* killed on active service as Fleet Air Arm Pilot). *Educ:* Mt Eden Primary Sch.; Auckland Grammar Sch. Freeman of City of London, 1951. Hon. LLD, Auckland, 1963. *Recreations:* fishing, gardening. *Address:* 30 Devore Street, St Heliers Bay, Auckland, New Zealand. *Club:* Northern (Auckland, NZ). *[Died 5 Nov. 1974.*

GOODHART, Arthur Lehman, (Hon.) KBE 1948; QC 1943; FBA 1952; MA, LLM, LLD, DCL; Master of University College, Oxford, 1951-63, retired; Professor of Jurisprudence, Oxford, 1931-51; Professor Emeritus since 1951; Editor, Law Quarterly Review; *b* NY City, 1 March 1891; *s* of late Philip J. Goodhart and Harriet Lehman; *m* 1924, Cecily, *d* of Eric M. Carter, Beaulieu, Hants; three *s. Educ:* Hotchkiss Sch.; Yale Univ.; Trinity Coll., Cambridge. Asst Corp. Council for NY City, 1915-17; Capt., Ord. USA, 1917-19. University Lectr in Law, Cambridge, 1919-31; Counsel to Amer. Mission to Poland, 1919; Officier d'Académie de France, 1920; Sec. to Vice-Chancellor of Cambridge Univ., 1921-23; Ed., Cambridge Law Journal, 1921-25. Hon. Bencher, Lincoln's Inn, 1938; Hon. Fellow of Trinity Coll., Corpus Christi Coll., Trinity Hall, Cambridge; Hon. Fellow of Nuffield Coll., University Coll., Oxford; Associate Fellow of Jonathan Edwards Coll., Yale Univ.; Chm. Southern Price Regulation Cttee, 1940-51; Member: Royal Commission on the Police; Monopolies Commission; Law Revision Cttee; Supreme Court Procedure Cttee; Company Law Revision Cttee; Alternative Remedies Cttee; Law Reports Cttee; Amer. Law Inst.; Chm. Internat. Law Assoc.; Curator, Bodleian Library; Deleg., OUP; Pres., Selden Soc., 1964; Pres., Public Teachers of Law, 1950; Vice-Pres.,

British Academy, 1962; Vice-Pres., Pilgrims, 1963; Pres., American Soc., 1951; Pres., International Assoc. of University Professors, 1948; Pres., Pedestrians' Assoc. for Road Safety, 1951-63; Vice-Président de l'Institut International de Philosophie du Droit; Hon. Mem. American Academy of Arts and Sciences; Visiting Professor: Yale Univ., 1928-29; Harvard Law Sch., 1964; University of Virginia Law School, 1965; McGill Univ. Law Sch., 1966; Tulane Univ. of Louisiana, 1967; Univ. of Arizona, 1967; Scholar-in-Residence, NYC Bar Assoc., 1966. Hon. LLD: Edinburgh; Queen's Univ., Belfast; Yale; Wesleyan Univ.; California; Columbia; London; New York; Williams Coll.; Princeton; Harvard; Dartmouth Coll.; Pennsylvania; Dalhousie; Melbourne; Tulane Univ. of Louisiana; Cincinnati; Hon. DLitt, Cambridge. *Publications:* Poland and the Minority Races, 1920; Essays in Jurisprudence and the Common Law, 1931; Precedent in English and Continental Law, 1934; The Government of Great Britain, 1946; English Contributions to the Philosophy of Law, 1949; Five Jewish Lawyers of the Common Law, 1950; Ed. Pollock's Jurisprudence and Essays, 1961; English Law and the Moral Law, 1953; Law of the Land, 1966; and legal articles and essays. *Address:* University College, Oxford; Whitebarn, Boars Hill, Oxford. *T:* Oxford 35294. *Clubs:* Athenæum, Oxford and Cambridge University, Savile, Pilgrims'; Century, Yale, Alpha Delta Phi, University. *[Died* 10 Nov. 1978.

GOODHART, Sir John (Gordon), 3rd Bt *cr* 1911; MA, MB, BChir; General Practitioner since 1947; *b* 14 Dec. 1916; *s* of Gordon Wilkinson Goodhart, MD, FRCP; *S* uncle, 1961; *m* 1944, Margaret Mary Eileen, *d* of late Morgan Morgan, Cray, Brecon; one *s* one *d. Educ:* Rugby; Trinity Hall, Cambridge; Guy's Hospital Med. Sch. MRCS, LRCP, 1941. Served as Surg-Lieut, RNVR, 1942-46. *Recreation:* golf. *Heir: s* Robert Anthony Gordon Goodhart [*b* 15 Dec. 1948; *m* 1972, Kathleen Ellen, *er d* of Rev. A. D. MacRae, Inverness; one *s* one *d*]. *Address:* Holtye, 17 Mavelstone Close, Bromley, Kent. *T:* 01-460 6700. *[Died* 13 Jan. 1979.

GOODMAN, Bruce Wilfred, CBE 1971; Director: Marks & Spencer Ltd, since 1952; The Prudential Assurance Co. Ltd, since 1970; *b* Birmingham, 26 March 1906; *er s* of Lionel and Tressie Goodman; *m* 1932, Cecil May, *o d* of Harry and Amy Bailey, Handsworth; one *s* three *d. Educ:* Oundle School. FCA. Asst Sec., Montague L. Meyer Ltd, 1930-32; joined Marks & Spencer, 1932; Sec. 1940; Dir 1952; Asst Man. Dir 1963; Vice-Chm. 1965-71; Jt Man. Dir 1967-71. Member: Decimal Currency Board, 1966-71 (Chm., Coinage Cttee); Sir Robert Bellinger's CS Manpower Panel, 1968-71; Court of Patrons, RCS, 1970; Council, British Heart Foundn; Council, British Postgrad. Med. Fedn. *Address:* Moray House, Gerrards Cross, Bucks. *T:* Gerrards Cross 82521; 65 Portman Towers, W1. *T:* 01-486 2556. *Club:* MCC. *[Died* 2 April 1974.

GOODMAN, Neville Marriott, CB 1961; MA, MD Cantab; PhD London; DPH London; FRCP; retired as Deputy Chief MO, Ministry of Health (1960-April 1963); *b* 22 April 1898; *o c* of Roger Neville Goodman, MD, and Louisa Harvey Marriott; *m* 1st, 1928, Beatrix Warr Edwards (*d* 1970); 2nd, 1971, Phyllis Mary Bucknell. *Educ:* Mill Hill Sch.; RMC Sandhurst; Pembroke Coll., Cambridge; London Hospital. House physician, surgeon, Receiving Room Officer, Ear, Nose and Throat Dept, London Hosp. Served European War, 1914-18, with 4th Bn The Worcs Regt, 1917-19; retd with rank of Capt. General practice, Lymington, Hants, 1925-32; Asst County MOH, Surrey CC, 1933-34; Min. of Health, 1934-63. Mem., Health Cttee, League of Nations, 1938-45; Br. Delegate Office Internat. d'Hygiène publique, Paris, 1938-45; Dir of Health, European Regional Office, UNRRA, 1945-47; Dir of Field Services, WHO, 1946-49. Hon. Fellow, Lady Margaret Hall, Oxford, 1978. OStJ 1936; Méd. de la Reconnaissance française. *Publications:* International Health Organisations and their Work, 1952, new edn 1971; Wilson Jameson: Architect of National Health, 1970; articles on medicine and public health. *Recreation:* gardening. *Address:* Mill Wall House, Sandwich, Kent CT13 9BQ. *T:* Sandwich 2344. *Club:* Athenæum. *[Died* 30 April 1980.

GOODMAN, Maj.-Gen. Walter Rutherfoord, CB 1954; DSO 1945; MC 1918; retired; *b* 7 Feb. 1899; *s* of Walter James Goodman, JP, Trim, Co. Meath; *m* 1932, Mary, *d* of Lt-Col C. C. Barnes; two *d. Educ:* Ellesmere Coll., Salop. 2nd Lieut, Special Reserve, Jan. 1917, Regular, Feb. 1918, Royal Artillery; served European War, 1914-18, and War of 1939-45. Retired, 1955. Col Comdt, RA, 1955-64. *Address:* Bealings Holt, Little Bealings, Suffolk. *Club:* Army and Navy. *[Died* 7 Oct. 1976.

GOODRICH, Carter; Andrew Mellon Professor of History, University of Pittsburgh, USA, 1963-71; *b* 10 May 1897; *s* of

Charles Lyman Goodrich and Jeannette (Margaret) Carter; *m* 1921, Florence (Perry) Nielsen; one *s* two *d. Educ:* Amherst Coll., AB 1918; University of Chicago, PhD, 1921. Scholar and Fellow of Amherst Coll., 1919 (research on British Labour problems), 1921-22, 1923-24 (research on Amer. coal industry); Instructor in Economics, Amherst Coll., 1922-23; Economics Dept, University of Michigan, 1924-27 (Asst Prof.), 1927-29 (Assoc. Prof.), 1929-31 (Prof.); Prof. of Economics, Columbia Univ., 1931-63; Prof. Emeritus, 1963-. Fellow of Social Science Research Council, 1927 (research on Australian and New Zealand labour movements); Dir, Study of Population Redistribution (Wharton Sch., Univ. of Pennsylvania), 1934-36; United States Labour Comr, Geneva, Switzerland, 1936-37 and 1938-40; Special Asst, American Ambassador to Great Britain, 1941; US Government Member of Governing Body, International Labour Office, 1936-46, Chm. 1939-45; Executive Officer, Economics Dept, Columbia Univ., 1946-49; Chm., Preparatory Cttee, UN Resources Conference, 1948-49; Consultant, United Nations, 1947-51; UN special Rep. to Bolivia, 1952-53; Chief, UN Economic Survey Mission to Viet Nam, 1955-56. Rep. Columbia Univ. Sch. of Business to University of Buenos Aires, 1961-62. President, Economic History Association, 1954-56. Mem. Amer. Philosophical Soc., Century (New York); Fellow, American Acad. of Arts and Sciences. Hon. LHD Amherst Coll., 1958. Order of the Condor of the Andes, Bolivia, 1953. *Publications:* The Frontier of Control, 1921; The Miner's Freedom, 1925; Government Promotion of American Canals and Railroads, 1960; as senior author, Migration and Economic Opportunity, 1936; Canals and American Economic Development, 1961; as editor, The Government and the Economy, 1783-1861, 1967. *Address:* 4601 Bayard Street, Pittsburgh, Pa 15213, USA.

[Died 8 April 1971.

GOODRICH, Dame Matilda, DBE 1947; RRC; retired; *d* of Henry Portry Goodrich, Methwold, Norfolk. Matron-in-Chief, Queen Alexandra's Royal Naval Nursing Service, 1944-47. Retired, 1947. *Address:* Bow-Wood Gardens, Bow-Wood Road, Claremont, Cape Town, South Africa. *[Died* 13 Aug. 1972.

GOODSON, Arthur; *b* 23 April 1913; *e s* of late John William Goodson and Emma Georgina Goodson (*née* Hodges); *m* 1938, Ethel Joan Simmons; two *d. Educ:* Maidenhead County Boys' Sch.; London Sch. of Economics (BSc (Econ) Hons). Officer of Customs and Excise, 1934; seconded to Min. of Supply, 1940; Principal, 1949; NATO Defence Coll., 1956; 1st Sec., UK Delegn to NATO, 1957; Principal, Min. of Aviation, 1960; Asst Sec., 1961; Dir-Gen. of Financial and Economic Affairs, European Launcher Develt Organisation, 1967; Under-Sec., Min. of Aviation Supply, 1970, DTI, 1971-73, retired. *Recreations:* gardening, golf, philately. *Address:* 14 Broomfield Park, Westcott, Dorking, Surrey. *T:* Dorking 5310.

[Died 14 *March* 1975.

GOONETILLEKE, Sir Oliver Ernest, GCMG 1954 (KCMG 1948; CMG 1941); KCVO 1954; KBE 1944; BA London; LLD Ceylon; FRSA; FRES; Underwriting Member of Lloyd's, London, since 1964; *b* 1892; *s* of A. E. Goonetilleke; *m* 1920, Esther Jayawardena (*d* 1931); one *s* two *d*; *m* 1968, Phyllis Millar. Asst Auditor for Railways, Ceylon, 1921; Asst Colonial Auditor, 1924; Colonial Auditor June 1931; Auditor-Gen., July 1931; Civil Defence and Food Commissioner, Ceylon, 1942; Mem., Ceylon War Council, 1942; Financial Sec., 1945-47; Min. of Home Affairs and Rural Development, Ceylon, 1947-48; Ceylon High Comr in London, 1948-51; Min. of Home Affairs and Rural Development, Ceylon, 1951-52; of Agriculture and Food, 1952-53, also Leader of the Senate; Min. of Finance, Ceylon, Oct. 1953-54; Governor-Gen. of Ceylon, 1954-62. Ceylon Government Deleg. to Internat. Railway Congress, Cairo, 1933; Chm. Retrenchment Commn, 1945. Director: Plantation & Mining Agencies Ltd; Veeraswamy's Restaurant. *Address:* 14 Albion Gate, Hyde Park Place, W2. *T:* 01-723 5814. *Club:* National Liberal. *[Died* 17 *Dec.* 1978.

GORDON, Sir Archibald McDonald, Kt 1952; CMG 1946; LLB; Barrister-at-Law; formerly Counsellor and Labour Attaché, British Embassy, Washington, DC, USA; *b* 29 Oct. 1892; *s* of Archibald McDonald Gordon, OBE, JP, and Miriam M. Gordon, Seaton Lodge, N16; *m* 1924, Dorothy Katharine (*d* 1959), *d* of late Charles Silvester Horne, MP and Hon. Mrs Silvester Horne, *g d* of 1st Baron Cozens Hardy, PC, former Master of the Rolls; two *s* one *d. Educ:* King's Coll., London, WC1; London Sch. of Economics. Entered Civil Service 1912. Regional Industrial Commissioner London and South Eastern Region, 1942; Asst Sec., Ministry of Labour and National Service, 1944; First Sec. and Labour Attaché, British Embassy, Washington, 1942; Counsellor, 1943-54. Mem. UN Delegations to: UN (San Francisco, New York), ILO (New York, London,

Paris, Geneva, Montreal, San Francisco), 1945-51; Chm. Arbitration Tribunal for Jamaican Sugar Industry, 1951; Pres., United Nations League of Lawyers; Mem. Industrial Disputes Tribunal, 1956; Mem. of Panel of Independent Chairmen of National Conciliation Board for the Co-operative Service; National Conciliation Board for the Co-operative Insurance Society's service; and Scottish Co-operative Wholesale Society's Conciliation Board. Dir-Gen., UK Council of European Movement, 1957-61; Chairman: Royal Mutual Benefit Building Society; British-American Associates; Bd of Govs, St George's Sch., Harpenden, 1956-64; Mem. Exec. Council, Hospital Saving Association, 1963, Chm., 1967; Pres., Brit. Hosps Contributary Schemes Assoc. (1948), 1967. Trustee, Liverpool Victoria Friendly Soc. Barrister-at-Law, Gray's Inn. *Address:* Bridge House, Gerrards Cross, Bucks. *T:* Gerrards Cross 82131; 5 King's Bench Walk, Temple, EC4. *T:* 01-353 2882. *Clubs:* Brooks's, Reform, MCC.   *[Died 23 Nov. 1974.*

GORDON, Brig. Barbara (Masson), CB 1971; RRC 1964; Matron-in-Chief and Director Army Nursing Service, 1968-73; *b* 28 Jan. 1913 (Scottish); *d* of Major R. G. Gordon, DSO, MC, MB, ChB, RGA (killed on active service, 1918) and late Mrs B. M. Gordon. *Educ:* St Leonards Sch., St Andrews, Scotland. Trained Edinburgh Royal Infirmary, 1933-37, Oxford Radcliffe Infirmary, 1937. Joined QAIMNS, 1939. Served BEF, MELF and in Germany, 1939-45; in UK, Malta, Egypt and Far East, 1945-68. QHNS 1968-73. CStJ 1971. *Recreations:* golf, walking. *Address:* Lettoch, St Andrews, Fife. *T:* St Andrews 3214. *Club:* St Rule (St Andrews).   *[Died 15 Feb. 1980.*

GORDON, Dr Christie Wilson, TD 1952; Regional Medical Officer, West Midlands Regional Health Authority, 1973-76; *b* 13 Dec. 1911; *s* of John Gordon and Mary Gordon; *m* 1942, Robina Alice Munro; one *s*. *Educ:* Academy, Buckie; Univs of Aberdeen, London and Johns Hopkins. MB, ChB 1938; DPH 1946; DrPH Johns Hopkins 1947. FRCP 1971; FFCM 1972; MIBS 1932. House Phys. and House Surg., Aberdeen Royal Infirmary, 1938-39; served War of 1939-45, RAMC; Hon. Lt-Col RAMC (TARO) (Hon. Mem. RAMC Mess 1961); Rockefeller Scholar, 1946-48; part-time Lectr, Hosp. Admin, London Sch. of Hygiene and Trop. Med., 1949-52; part-time Sen. Clinical Lectr, Dept of Social Medicine, Univ. of Birmingham, 1952-76. Birmingham Regional Hosp. Board: Admin. MO, Asst, subseq. Dep. Admin. MO, 1948-57; Sen. Admin. MO, 1957-73. QHP, 1974-77. Member: Central Midwives Bd, 1967-73; DHSS Management Study Steering Cttee on Management arrangements for the reorganised NHS, 1971-72; Council, Univ. of Birmingham, 1976-. Sec., Midland Medical Benevolent Soc., 1976-; Mem. Council, British Inst. of Mental Handicap, 1978. Fellow, WHO, 1965. Hon LLD Birmingham, 1975. *Publications:* papers on public health and hospital services in Lancet, BMJ, etc. *Recreation:* golf. *Address:* 9 Fountain Road, Edgbaston, Birmingham B17 8NJ. *T:* 021-429 2710. *Clubs:* (Chm.) Aberdeen University (Midlands); Edgbaston Golf.   *[Died 9 Aug. 1979.*

GORDON, Christopher Martin P.; *see* Pirie-Gordon.

GORDON, Prof. Donald James, MA Edinburgh, PhD Cantab; FRHistSoc; Professor of English in the University of Reading, 1949-76, now Emeritus; *b* 19 July 1915; *s* of Thomas and Sarah Gordon. *Educ:* Dumfries Academy; University of Edinburgh; Trinity Coll., Cambridge. Lecturer in English: Univ. of Liverpool, 1942-46; Univ. of Reading, 1946-49. Corresp. Mem., Accademia Olimpico of Vicenza, Italy. *Publications:* (with Jean Robertson) A Calendar of Dramatic Records in the Books of the Livery Companies of London, 1485-1640, 1955; (ed) Fritz Saxl: Memorial Essays, 1957; Images of a Poet: W. B. Yeats, 1961; Renaissance Imagination, 1975; papers on problems connected with Renaissance Imagery, and on connexions between literature and visual arts in late nineteenth century. *Address:* 8 Alexandra Road, Reading.   *[Died 22 Dec. 1977.*

GORDON, Sir Eyre, Kt 1939; CSI 1935; CIE 1931; ICS, retired; *b* 28 Feb. 1884; *s* of Alexander H. Gordon, D.L., Delamont, Killyleagh, Co. Down; *m* 1912, Lilias Edith (*d* 1933), *d* of Capt. A. Lenox Napier, OBE, Merchiston, Manor Road, Sidcup; one *d* (one *s* died on active service). *Educ:* Rossall; Queen's Coll., Oxford, BA. Entered Indian Civil Service, 1908, Chief Sec. to CP Government, 1931; Mem. of Executive Council Central Provinces, 1933-36; Chm. Indian Public Service Commission, 1936-42; Divisional Food Officer for SE Division, 1942; for Midland Division, 1944-46; Chm. NI Joint Electricity Cttee, 1948-55. *Address:* Clonsheen, Tullybrannigan Road, Newcastle, Co. Down, Northern Ireland.   *[Died 28 July 1972.*

GORDON, Sir Garnet (Hamilton), Kt 1962; CBE 1951 (OBE 1945); QC 1957; Chairman, Geest Industries (WI), since 1962; *b*

16 Sept. 1904; 2nd *s* of George Stevenson Emmanuel Gordon and Nancy Gordon (*née* Hepburn); *m* 1937, Sheila Perot Christiani (*d* 1969), *e d* of Henry P. Christiani, MBE, and Lilian (*née* Newsum); two *s*. *Educ:* St Mary's Coll., St Lucia; The Middle Temple. Practised at the Bar, 1927-54, resumed practice, 1962. Mem. Castries Town Board, 1940-47 (Chm. 1947); MLC, St Lucia, 1935-51, MEC, 1942-51. Mem. British Section, Caribbean Commission, 1946-50; Mem. Standing Closer Assoc. Cttee, 1948-49; Man. Dir, The Voice Publishing Co. Ltd, and Ed., The Voice of St Lucia, 1940-54; Mem. Council, University Coll. of the West Indies, 1947-54; Trade Comr in the UK for the BWI, Brit. Guiana and Brit. Honduras, 1954-58; Comr in the UK for the West Indies, Brit. Guiana and Brit. Honduras, 1958-62. MHA St Lucia, 1964-69. Pres., St Lucia Bar Assoc., 1964-; Chm, Caribbean Cttee of Fedn of Commonwealth and British Chambers of Commerce; formerly Pres., Caribbean Assoc. of Industry and Commerce; Pres., Fedn. of Commonwealth Chambers of Commerce. *Address:* La Rosière, Castries, St Lucia, West Indies. *Clubs:* Athenæum, Royal Commonwealth Society.   *[Died 8 Aug. 1975.*

GORDON, Brig. John Evison, CIE 1947; OBE 1943; psc† retired; *b* 21 June 1901; *s* of Webster Boyle Gordon, CIE, Monkstown, Co. Cork, Eire; *m* 1936, Frances Elizabeth, *d* of Lt-Gen. Sir Joseph Talbot Hobbs, KCB, KCMG; one *d*. *Educ:* Wellington Coll.; RMC, Sandhurst. Commissioned 1920; joined Probyn's Horse (5th King Edward VII's Own Lancers), 1922. Staff Coll., 1935-36. Served NWF of India, 1930-31 and 1937-39; War of 1939-45: DAQMG, 4 Ind. Div., 1940; GSO 1. Staff Coll., Quetta, 1942; AQMG 4 Corps, 1943; temp. Col 1944; temp. Brig. 1945; retired, 1948. *Address:* Manor Farm, Wootton, Boars Hill, Oxford OX1 5JL. *T:* Oxford 735186. *Club:* Army and Navy.   *[Died 19 Dec. 1977.*

GORDON, Brig. John Keily, DSO 1919; *b* 31 March 1883; *m* 1921, Beatrice Mary Grove, *d* of Comdr Hans Fell White and *widow* of Capt. G. E. S. Cotter; one *s*. *Educ:* Wellington; RMA, Woolwich. Served Mesopotamia, 1917-18 (despatches, DSO). Comdr, RA 50th (Northumbrian) Div., TA, 1935-39; retired 1939; re-employed as Comdr Catterick Area, 1939-41. *Address:* Fir Holt, Crowthorne, Berks.   *[Died 19 Nov. 1976.*

GORDON, John Rutherford; Editor-in-Chief, Sunday Express; Trustee of Beaverbrook Foundation; *b* 8 Dec. 1890; *m* 1st, 1915, Evelyn Hinton (*d* 1967); 2nd, 1972, Mrs Margaret Blundell-Ince. *Educ:* Morgan Academy, Dundee. Chief Sub-Editor, London Evening News, 1922; Chief Sub-Editor, Daily Express, 1924; Editor, Sunday Express, 1928; Dir Beaverbrook Newspapers Ltd, 1931-69; Dir, Sunday Express, 1946. Life Vice-President: Institute of Journalists, (Pres., 1948-49); Newspaper Press Fund; Press Club. Hon. LLD University of New Brunswick, 1966. *Address:* 78 Addiscombe Road, Croydon, Surrey. *Clubs:* Garrick, Press.   *[Died 9 Dec. 1974.*

GORDON, Sir Lionel Eldred Pottinger S.; *see* Smith-Gordon.

GORDON, Captain Oliver Loudon, CB 1946; MVO 1934; *b* 26 Jan. 1896; *s* of late W. M. Gordon, Brechin, Angus, Scotland; *m* 1923, Aileen Mabel Marguerite Baker (*d* 1969); two *s*. *Educ:* Aldenham; RN Colls Osborne and Dartmouth. Entered Navy as Cadet, 1909; Comdr 1931; Capt. 1939. Served in HM Yacht Victoria and Albert, 1932-34 (MVO). In Command of HMS Exeter from March, 1941, till sunk by Japanese Forces in the Java Sea on 1st March 1942. POW in Japan till Sept. 1945; HMS Cleopatra, in command, 1946-48; Retired List, 1948. *Publication:* Fight It Out (autobiography), 1958. *Address:* 22 Marshal's Drive, St Albans, Herts. *T:* St Albans 53261.
                              [Died 30 Jan. 1973.

GORDON, Percival Hector, OC 1968; CBE 1943; retired as Judge of Court of Appeal for Saskatchewan, Canada, 1935-61, now associate counsel in firm of Embury, Molisky, Gritzfeld & Embury, Regina; *b* 27 Jan. 1884; *s* of Leslie Gordon, Craigmyle, Scotland, and Clara Elizabeth Hector, Toronto; *m* Harriet S. (*d* 1959), *d* of John and Mary Kennedy, Dixie, Ont.; one *d*. *Educ:* Trinity Coll. Sch., Port Hope, Ont.; Trinity Coll., Toronto Univ. (BA 1905, MA 1906, BCL 1909). Athletic champion of sch. and coll.; admitted Saskatchewan Bar 1908, Ont. Bar 1933; KC 1928; practised in Saskatchewan, 1908-33, Ont. 1933-35; represented Saskatchewan in Natural Resources Royal Commission, 1933-34; Life Mem., Law Soc. of Sask., 1965. Chancellor Anglican Diocese of Qu'Appelle, 1921-42; Chm. of Executive Cttee Canadian Red Cross Soc. 1941-44 (Hon. Counsellor, Canadian Red Cross, 1934). LLD (hon.) Manitoba Univ. 1943. Jubilee Medal, 1935; Coronation medal, 1937; Order of Polonia Restituta, 1946; Greek Red Cross Medal, 1949. First Citation by Nat. Red Cross Soc., 1970. *Publication:* Fifty Years in the Canadian Red Cross, 1969. *Recreations:* shooting, gardening. *Address:* 2424 College Avenue, Regina, Sask., Canada. *Club:* Assiniboia (Regina). [*Died* 6 *April* 1975.

GORDON, Capt. Roderick Cosmo, DSO 1941; RN, retired; *b* 17 Feb. 1902; *s* of Alexander S. Gordon; *m* 1932, Estelle Boulton; one *d*. *Educ:* RN Colls, Osborne and Dartmouth. Midshipman from 1918 in HMS New Zealand till end of European War, 1914-18; commanded destroyers HMS Verity, 1934-36, HMS Hereward, 1936-38; Comdr, 1938; commanded destroyers, HMS Intrepid, 1939-41, HMS Savage, 1943; Actg Capt., 1944-48; reverted to Comdr, 1948; Admiralty, 1948-51; retired, with rank of Capt., 1952. *Address:* Stream Cottage, Wrecclesham, Farnham, Surrey. *T:* Farnham 5715. [*Died* 25 *Sept.* 1975.

GORDON, Seton, CBE 1939; BA Oxon; FZS; author and nature photographer; *b* 11 April 1886; *o s* of late William Gordon, LLD, OBE, Advocate, and late Mrs Ella Mary Gordon, FRSL; *m* 1st, 1915, Evelyn Audrey (*d* 1959), *d* of late Howard Pease of Otterburn, Northumberland; one *s* two *d*; 2nd, 1960, Betty, *d* of Mr and the Hon. Mrs G. Murray Smith, and widow of Col R. Badger, Biddlesden Park, Brackley. *Educ:* privately; Oxford Univ.; BA (hons) in Natural Science and Diploma in Rural Economy. Studied Forestry in Russia, Germany, and France; Admiralty Patrol Officer in Argyllshire and Inner Hebrides, 1914-16; afterwards served as Naval Centre Officer (Lieut RNVR); has lectured on Bird Life before the Royal Institution, Royal Scottish Geographical Society, Eton, Winchester, Harrow, etc.; Photographer with the Oxford Univ. Spitsbergen Expedition, 1921. JP Inverness-shire. *Publications:* Birds of the Loch and Mountain; The Charm of the Hills; Hill Birds of Scotland; The Land of the Hills and Glens; Wanderings of a Naturalist; Amid Snowy Wastes; Hebridean Memories; The Cairngorm Hills of Scotland; The Immortal Isles; Days with the Golden Eagle; The Charm of Skye; In the Highlands; Islands of the West; Highways and Byways in the Western Highlands; Thirty Years of Nature Photography; Afoot in Wild Places; Edward Grey of Fallodon and his Birds; Wild Birds in Britain; In Search of Northern Birds; A Highland Year; Highways and Byways in the Central Highlands (illustrated by Sir D. Y. Cameron, RA); Afoot in the Hebrides, 1950; The Highlands of Scotland, 1952; The Golden Eagle, 1955; Highland Days, 1963; Highland Summer, 1971; and many contributions to periodicals and the Press. *Recreations:* golf, represented Oxford, 1911; mountain climbing; fishing; Highland pipe-playing (member of the Scottish Pipers' Soc.). *Address:* Upper Duntulm, Isle of Skye. *TA:* Portree. *T:* Duntulm 206. *Clubs:* Bath; Vincent's (Oxford). [*Died* 19 *March* 1977.

GORDON-WALKER, Baron *cr* 1974 (Life Peer), of Leyton; **Patrick Chrestien Gordon Walker,** PC 1950; CH 1968; Member, European Parliament, 1975-76; *b* 7 April 1907; *s* of Alan Lachlan Gordon Walker and Dora Marguerite Chrestien; *m* 1934, Audrey Muriel Rudolf; twin *s* three *d*. *Educ:* Wellington Coll; Christ Church, Oxford, MA, BLitt. Student and History Tutor, Christ Church, 1931-40; BBC European Service (German workers), 1940-44; Asst German Service Dir, BBC, 1945. Chm. British Film Institute, 1946; Vice-Chm. British Council, 1947. MP (Lab) Smethwick, 1945-64; contested (Lab) Leyton, Jan. 1965; MP (Lab) Leyton, 1966-Feb. 1974. PPS to Mr Herbert Morrison, MP, 1946; Parliamentary Under-Sec. of State, Commonwealth Relations Office, 1947-50; Sec. of State for Commonwealth Relations, 1950-51; Sec. of State for Foreign Affairs, Oct. 1964-Jan. 1965; Leader, UK Delegn to Council of Europe, 1966; Chm., Book Development Council, 1965-67; Minister without Portfolio during 1967; Sec. of State for Educn and Science, 1967-68. *Publications:* The Sixteenth and Seventeenth Centuries, 1935; Outline of Man's History, 1939; The Lid Lifts, 1945; Restatement of Liberty, 1951; The Commonwealth, 1962; The Cabinet, 1970. *Recreations:* reading and writing. *Address:* 105 Frobisher House, Dolphin Square, SW1V 3LL. [*Died* 2 *Dec.* 1980.

GORE, John Kearns; a Recorder of the Crown Court, since 1974; *b* 3 Aug. 1924; *s* of late John Gore, Lathom, Lancs and Mary Evelyn Gore; *m* 1961, June Stananought Pritchard, JP; one *s* one *d*. *Educ:* Worcester Coll., Oxford. BA Hons Jurisprudence 1948. Served with RAFVR, 1943-45, wounded NW Europe 1944. Called to Bar, Gray's Inn, 1949, practised Northern Circuit from 1950. Chm., Nat. Insce Tribunal, 1972-78; Chm., Brockhall Hosp. Enquiry, 1973. Mem. No 7 (NW) Legal Area Cttee, Law Soc., 1970-. *Recreations:* music-making, model railways. *Address:* Fruit Exchange Building, Victoria Street, Liverpool; 2 Pump Court, Temple, EC4; (home) 4 Harrod Drive, Birkdale, Southport, Merseyside. *Club:* Athenæum (Liverpool). [*Died* 18 *Feb.* 1980.

GORE, Lieut-Col Sir Ralph St George Brian, 11th Bt, *cr* 1621; *b* 31 May 1908; *s* of Sir Ralph St George Claude Gore, 10th Bt,

and Elsie Vaughan Grigg; *S* father, 1961; *m* 1st, 1947, Phyllis Gabrielle Brooke-Hitching (marr. diss. 1965), *d* of M. Von der Porten, New York; one *d*; 2nd, 1965, Mavis Pamela Gray (marr. diss. 1970); 3rd, 1971, Irene Lamont, *d* of A. J. Marshall, Stranraer. *Educ:* Eton; RMC. Formerly Royal Dragoons. *Recreation:* yachting. *Heir: kinsman* St George Ralph Gore [*b* 14 Dec. 1914; *m* 1950, Shirley, *d* of Clement Tabor; one *s* three *d*]. *Address:* c/o Royal Bank of Scotland, Burlington Gardens, W1. *Club:* Royal Yacht Squadron. [*Died* 28 *June* 1973.

GORE, Sir (St George) Ralph, 12th Bt *cr* 1621; grazier since 1937; *b* 14 Dec. 1914; *s* of St George Richard Gore (*d* 1952); *S* kinsman, Sir Ralph St George Brian Gore, 11th Bt, 1973; *m* 1950, Shirley, *d* of Clement Tabor; one *s* three *d*. *Educ:* The King's School, Parramatta. 11th Light Horse Regiment until 1950; elected to Shire Council of Waggamba, 1946-52. *Heir: s* Richard Ralph St George Gore [*b* 19 Nov. 1954. *Educ:* The King's Sch., Parramatta; Univ. of New England]. *Address:* Wycanna, Talwood, Queensland 4322, Australia. *T:* Talwood 2S. *Club:* Queensland. [*Died* 13 *Nov.* 1973.

GORHAM, Maurice Anthony Coneys; Author and Journalist; *b* London 1902; *o s* of late J. J. Gorham, MD, Clifden, Connemara. *Educ:* Stonyhurst; Balliol Coll., Oxford. Entered journalism, 1923; on editorial staffs of Weekly Westminster, Westminster Gazette; joined Radio Times, 1926; Art Ed., 1928; Ed., 1933-41; North American Service Dir, BBC, 1941-44; Dir of Allied Expeditionary Forces Programme, 1944-45; Head of Light Programme, 1945; Head of Television Service, 1946-47; Dir of Radio Eireann (Irish broadcasting service), 1953-60. *Publications:* The Local, 1939; Sound and Fury (Twenty-One Years in the BBC), 1948; Back to the Local; Television, Medium of the Future, 1949; Professional Training for Radio (enquiry for Unesco); Inside the Pub, 1950; Showmen and Suckers; Londoners, 1951: Broadcasting and Television since 1900, 1952; Forty Years of Irish Broadcasting, 1967; Ireland from old Photographs, 1971; Dublin from Old Photographs, 1972; Dublin Old and New, 1975. *Address:* 33 Sydney Parade Avenue, Dublin. *T:* Dublin 692587. *Club:* University (Dublin). [*Died* 9 *Aug.* 1975.

GORMAN, Sir Eugene, KBE 1966 (CBE 1960); MC 1917; QC (Melbourne); *b* Goornong, Victoria, 10 April 1891; *s* of Patrick and Mary Gorman; *m* 1920, Marthe Vallée (*d* 1966); one *s*. *Educ:* St Joseph's Coll. (Sydney, NSW). Barrister, 1914; KC 1929; AIF, 1914-19 and 1940-44 (despatches 1942); Capt., 1st AIF; Brig. 1944. Chief Comr, Aust. Comforts Fund, 1941-42; Chief Inspector, Aust. Army Admin, 1942; Consul-Gen., NEI, 1942 until Japanese occupation. Consul for Greece, retd 1955; Chm., Aust. Dried Fruits Bd, 1956-68; President: Opportunity Youth Clubs, 1953-72; Australian Branch, Internat. Social Services, retd 1969. Gold Cross of Greek Red Cross; Kt Comr, Royal Order of Phoenix (Greece), 1953. *Publication:* With the 22nd Battalion, 1919. *Recreation:* racing. *Address:* Equity Chambers, 472 Bourke Street, Melbourne, Victoria 3000, Australia. *T:* 67-3164. *Clubs:* Portland (London); Athenæum (Melbourne); Victoria Racing (Committeeman 27 years). [*Died* 19 *July* 1973.

GORST, Elliot Marcet, QC 1953; *b* 18 Nov. 1885; *o s* of Herbert Charles Gorst, Liverpool, and Jessie Elliot-Blake; *m* 1914, Hester Gaskell, 3rd *d* of Walter Holland, Carnatic Hall, Mossley Hill, Liverpool; one *d*. *Educ:* Temple Grove; Harrow; Jena; Sorbonne; Florence. Barrister, Inner Temple, 1912. Served European War, 1915-19. Contested (MR) Bow and Bromley, 1926, S Poplar, 1928; contested (C) Poplar (South), 1929. Mem. of Bar Coun., 1932 and 1948-52; Deputy Judge, Bloomsbury County Court, 1940-42. Mem. of Legal Deleg. to USSR, 1954. Chm., Kent and Sussex Poetry Soc., 1953-; Chm. Bournemouth Swanage Motor Road and Ferry Co., 1925-61; Dir Carbon Electric Holdings Ltd, 1961-72 (Chm. 1962-64). Farms in Kent (pedigree herd of Sussex cattle and flock of Hampshire Down sheep; toured S Africa and Rhodesia, 1964, as mem. Sussex Cattle Soc.). *Publications:* Guide to Railway Rates Tribunal and Title on Railways and Canals in Halsbury's Statutes. *Recreations:* fishing, riding. *Address:* 6 Pump Court, Temple, EC4. *T:* 01-353 7242; 16 Abingdon Villas, W8. *T:* 01-937 7494; Catt's Place, Paddock Wood, Kent. *T:* Paddock Wood 2232. [*Died* 28 *Nov.* 1973.

GORT, 7th Viscount (Ireland) *cr* 1816; **Standish Robert Gage Prendergast Vereker;** MC; Baron Kiltarton, 1810; *b* 12 Feb. 1888; *s* of 5th Viscount and Eleanor (*d* 1933), *d* and co-heiress of R. S. Surtees of Hamsterley Hall, Co. Durham [she *m* 2nd, 1908, Col S. M. Benson]; *S* brother 1946; *m* 1921, Bessy (*d* 1972), CStJ 1969, *d* of late Aubone Surtees, Dinsdale Manor, Co. Durham. *Educ:* Harrow; Trinity Coll., Cambridge. Served European War, 1914-19 (MC, despatches, thrice wounded); Sheriff of Durham,

1934. KStJ. *Heir: kinsman,* Colin Leopold Prendergast Vereker, Lt-Comdr RNVR [*b* 21 June 1916; *s* of late Comdr Leopold George Prendergast Vereker, RD, RNR; *m* 1946, Bettine Green; two *s* one *d*]. *Address:* Hamsterley Hall, Rowlands Gill, Newcastle upon Tyne; Bunratty Castle, Co. Clare. *Clubs:* Carlton; Manitoba (Winnipeg); Kildare Street (Dublin).
[*Died* 21 *May* 1975.

GOSCHEN, 3rd Viscount *cr* 1900, of Hawkhurst; **John Alexander Goschen,** KBE 1972 (OBE (mil.) 1944); Colonel, formerly Grenadier Guards; a Deputy Speaker, and Deputy Chairman of Committees, House of Lords; *b* 7 July 1906; *e* surv. *s* of late Hon. Sir William Henry Goschen, KBE (2nd *s* of 1st Viscount) and late Geraldine Elizabeth, *d* of Rt Hon. J. W. Mellor, PC, KC; *S* uncle, 1952; *m* 1st, 1934, Hilda Violet Ursula (from whom he obtained a divorce, 1950), *d* of late Lieut-Col Hon. St Leger Henry Jervis, DSO; no *c*; 2nd, 1955, Alvin, *yr d* of late H. England, Durban, S Africa; one *s* one *d. Educ:* Eton; RMC Sandhurst. 2nd Lieut Grenadier Guards, 1926; served War of 1939-45, in Grenadier Guards (appointments on the staff), N Africa (OBE), Italy, France and Greece; Lt-Col 1941. Captain of the Yeomen of the Guard (Asst Govt Chief Whip in the Lords), 1962-64 and 1970-71; Chief Opposition Whip, House of Lords, 1964-70. *Recreations:* hunting, shooting and fishing. *Heir: s* Hon. Giles John Harry Goschen, *b* 16 Nov. 1965. *Address:* Hilton House, Crowthorne, Berks. *Club:* Cavalry and Guards. [*Died* 22 *March* 1977.

GOSCHEN, Maj.-Gen. Arthur Alec, CB 1935; DSO 1900; DL Glos 1953; *b* 6 Jan. 1880; 3rd *s* of H. Goschen, Heathfield, Surrey; *m* 1908, Marjorie Mary, *d* of late Major W. Blacker, Castle Martin, Newbridge, Co. Kildare; one *s* three *d. Educ:* Eton. Entered RA 1899; served S Africa, 1899-1901 (despatches, Queen's medal, 2 clasps, DSO); European War, 1914-18 (wounded, Bt Lieut-Col, 2 bars, DSO, Croix de Guerre); Instructor, Staff Coll., Quetta, 1925-29; Garrison Commander and Commandant, RA Depot, Woolwich, 1929-31; Brigadier, RA, Aldershot Command, 1931-34; ADC to the King, 1932-34; Comdt, Royal Military Academy, Woolwich, 1934-38; retired pay, 1938; Area Commander, 1939-41; Col Comdt RHA, 1942-48; Col-Comdt RA 1941-48. *Address:* King's Hay, Eastleach, Cirencester, Glos. [*Died* 28 *June* 1975.

GOTHARD, Sir Clifford (Frederic), Kt 1959; OBE 1956; JP; Chartered Accountant in practice, Coxon, Bannister & Gothard, Burton-on-Trent, since 1925; Director: Marston, Thompson & Evershed, Ltd; Burton Daily Mail Ltd; has estate at Drakelowe, Derbyshire; *b* 9 June 1893; *s* of Frederic Gothard and Mary Gothard (*née* Startin); *m* 1961, Margaret Vera Hall. *Educ:* Burton-on-Trent Grammar Sch.; Birmingham Univ. BScEng 1915. Served European War, 1914-18, Royal Artillery (Captain). Institute of Chartered Accountants: Associate, 1924; Fellow 1929. His interests include religious, educational, agricultural bodies. District Staff Officer, Midland Command, with rank of Squadron-Leader; supervised Air Training Corps Units, 1939/45. Mem. of certain special cttees of Assoc. of British Chambers of Commerce, etc; Pres., Burton Div. Conservative Assoc., 1973- (Chm., 1945-73); Vice-Pres., West Midlands Union of Conservative and Unionist Assocs; Mem., Conservative Commonwealth and Overseas Council. JP for County Borough, Burton-on-Trent, 1940-. Life Member: Royal Agricultural Society of England, 1921-; Canadian Chamber of Commerce in Great Britain (Inc.). Court of Governors: Birmingham Univ. (Life Gov.); Keele Univ. *Recreations:* travel, shooting, fishing, sailing, gardening, reading. *Address:* Bearwood House, Burton-on-Trent, Staffs. *T:* 63112, (office) 64866. *Club:* Abbey (Burton-on-Trent). [*Died* 31 *May* 1979.

GOUGH, Sir (Arthur) Ernest, Kt 1966; *b* 7 Jan. 1878; *s* of Richard and Elizabeth Gough; *m* 1913, Florence Tomkins; one *s* (decd). Railway Official. Mem., Cardiff City Council, 1919-52; Lord Mayor of Cardiff, 1933-34. Mem., S Wales Electricity Board, 1948-52. JP Cardiff, 1932-52. *Address:* 2 Tydraw Road, Cardiff. *T:* 499159. [*Died* Oct. 1974.

GOUGH, Col (Charles) Frederick (Howard), MC 1943; TD 1948, 1st clasp 1973; *b* 16 Sept. 1901; *yr s* of late Lt-Col Charles Hugh Henry Gough, IA; *m* 1929, Barbara May Pegler; one *s* one *d. Educ:* RN Colls., Osborne (Honourable Mention 1915) and Dartmouth. Midshipman in HMS Ramillies and HMS Witherington, 1917-20; left Navy, 1920. Took up farming and horse-breeding in India; returned to UK, 1922, and joined a firm of Lloyd's insurance brokers; Dir of a number of companies. Joined London Rifle Bde (TA), 1924, served until 1929 when he went on to TARO; rejoined London Rifle Bde, 1939, and served War of 1939-45; comd 1st Airborne Reconnaissance Squadron, Italy; qualified parachutist (Holder, Royal Aero Club Parachutist Certificate no 1); demobilised 1945 (despatches

1940; MC 1943; prisoner at Arnhem, 1944, escaped 1945); commanded 11th Bn Parachute Regt TA 1946-48. Hon. Colonel: Sussex Yeomanry, 1959-63; 16 Ind. Coy, Parachute Regt (VR), 1971-74. MP (C) Horsham Division of West Sussex, 1951-64. Vice-Pres. of Lloyd's Branch of British Legion, and Trustee of Airborne Forces Security Fund; Pres. South Lewisham Conservative Assoc., 1951-71; Chm. Horsham Div. Cons. Assoc., 1964-70 (Pres., 1970); Pres. City of London Young Conservatives, 1964-70. Pres., Fedn of Sussex Industries, 1972-73. Governor Cutty Sark Soc.; Trustee, Maritime Trust; Chm., Royal Aero Club, 1958-68. Prime Warden, Fishmongers Co., 1971-72. *Address:* Weavers, Lodsworth, near Petworth, West Sussex. *Club:* Buck's. [*Died* 19 *Sept.* 1977.

GOUGH, Harold Robert; President British-American Tobacco Co. Ltd, SW1, 1950-60, retired; *b* 15 Dec. 1889; *s* of late Robert and late Annie Gough, Bower Ashton, Som; *m* 1st, 1921, Elizabeth Gilchrist McIntyre (*decd*); 2nd, 1941, Barbara Hall Watson; no *c. Educ:* Merchant Venturers Sch. Joined British-American Tobacco Co. Ltd 1905; Dir 1926; Dep. Chm. 1932; Chm. 1947. *Recreations:* shooting, fishing. *Address:* Pilcot Farm, Dogmersfield, Basingstoke, Hants. *Club:* Oriental.
[*Died* 27 *Dec.* 1975.

GOULBURN, Maj.-Gen. Edward Henry, DSO and Bar 1944; DL; *b* 27 May 1903; *s* of late Brig.-Gen. C. E. Goulburn, DSO, and of Grace Ethel, *d* of late W. H. Foster, Apley Park, Bridgnorth, Salop. *Educ:* Eton and Sandhurst. Grenadier Guards, 1924; Adjutant, 1st Bn, 1931-34; Adjutant, RMC, Sandhurst, 1938-40; OC 1st Bn Gren. Guards in France, Belgium and Holland, 1942-44; Brigadier Cmdg 8th British Infantry Bde Holland and Germany, 1944-45; 1st Guards Bde, Palestine, 1945-46; Maj.-Gen. Cmdg Allied Military Mission to Italian Army, 1946-47; Lt-Col Comdg Gren. Guards, 1948-50. DL Surrey, 1962. Comdr Order of Orange Nassau. *Recreations:* farming, sport, travel. *Address:* Betchworth House, Betchworth, Surrey. *T:* Betchworth 3315. *Clubs:* Turf, Pratt's.
[*Died* 15 *Feb.* 1980.

GOULD, Frederick, OBE 1941; JP, Alderman CC Somerset, retired; *b* 28 June 1879; *s* of Joshua and Eliza Gould; *m* 1903; two *s* one *d. Educ:* Church of England Elementary Sch. Kitchen and stable boy, 3 years; boot operative, 24 years; political agent, 3 years; MP (Lab.) Frome Division Som, 1923-24, and 1929-31; Contested East Leicester 1935. *Recreations:* fishing, bowls. *Address:* Midsomer Norton, near Bath, Som. *T:* Midsomer Norton 2362. [*Died* 23 *Feb.* 1971.

GOULD, Sir Robert Macdonald, KBE 1953; Kt 1948; CB 1946; War of 1914-18: Artists Rifles, 1914; Middlesex Regt, 1916, severely wounded; invalided 1919. Late Chief Industrial Commissioner, Ministry of Labour and National Service. Retired, 1952. Dir of cos, 1952-62. *Address:* Littleden, Tilford, near Farnham, Surrey. *Club:* United Service and Royal Aero.
[*Died* 10 *Nov.* 1971.

GOULDEN, Mark; Chairman, W. H. Allen & Co. Ltd, Publishers, 1939-76; Director, Howard and Wyndham Ltd, 1971-76; *b* Clifton, Bristol; 2nd *s* of late Morris and Eve Goulden; *m*; two *s* one *d.* Began journalism with Cambridge Daily News; served Royal Engineers, Managing Editor and Dir, Eastern Morning News and Hull Evening News, 1923-30; Managing Editor, Yorkshire Evening News, Leeds, 1930-32; Managing Editor Sunday Referee, 1932-36; Editor-in-Chief, Argus Press Ltd; Managing Editor, Cavalcade and other publications: Director: Illustrated Publications Ltd, Bicycle Publishing Co. Ltd; Macfadden's Magazines Ltd, 1937-40; seconded to Head Office, Doubleday & Co., NY, 1961-63; written and lectured extensively on newspapers, advertising and publishing. British Delegate World Advertising Convention, Philadelphia, 1927; former member Nat. Council Advertising Clubs: Council Newspaper Proprietors Assoc., etc.; inventor, Gouldris Matrix Machine; a pioneer of civil aviation in England. *Publication:* Mark My Words! (autobiog.), 1978. *Recreations:* flying, motoring, golf. *Address:* 10 Lowndes Square, SW1. *Clubs:* Press, Paternosters, Savage; Players' (New York).
[*Died* 3 *May* 1980.

GOW, Andrew Sydenham Farrar, MA; FBA 1943; Hon. DLitt (Durham); Hon LLD (Edinburgh); Fellow of Trinity College, Cambridge; on committee of National Art-Collections Fund; *b* 27 Aug. 1886; *e s* of Rev. James Gow, LittD, sometime Headmaster of Westminster, and Gertrude Sydenham, *d* of G. P. Everett-Green. *Educ:* Rugby Sch.; Trinity Coll., Cambridge. Porson Prizeman, 1906, 1907; Browne Medallist, 1907, 1908; Charles Oldham Scholar, 1909, 1910; Fellow of Trinity Coll., 1911; Asst Master at Eton Coll., 1914-25; Trinity Coll., Cambridge: Lectr, 1925-46; Tutor, 1929-42; Praelector, 1946-51;

University Lectr, 1925-51; Brereton Reader in Classics, 1947-51; a Trustee of the National Gallery, 1947-53. Kenyon Medal, British Acad., 1972. *Publications:* A. E. Housman: A Sketch and List of his Writings, 1936; Letters from Cambridge (1939-1944), 1945; Theocritus (text, translation, and commentary), 2 vols, 1950, 2nd edn 1953, repr. 1965, 1974; Bucolici Graeci (Oxford Classical Texts), 1952, 2nd impression 1958; The Greek Bucolic Poets (introd. and trans.), 1953, repr. (USA), 1972; The Greek Anthology: sources and ascriptions, 1958; Machon (introd., text, and commentary), 1965; (with A. F. Scholfield) Nicander (text, trans., and notes), 1953; (with Prof. D. L. Page) The Greek Anthology: Hellenistic Epigrams (text and commentary), 2 vols, 1965; The *Garland* of Philip (text, translation and commentary) 2 vols, 1968; contribs to Jl of Hellenic Studies, Jl of Philology, Classical Quarterly, Classical Review, etc; editor of A. E. Housman's Manilius (edn 2), 1937, and with Prof. D. S. Robertson, of W. Ridgeway's The Early Age of Greece, vol. II, 1931. *Address:* Trinity College, Cambridge. *T:* Cambridge 58201.   *[Died* 2 *Feb.* 1978.

GRACE, John; *s* of Thomas Wilkinson Grace, Whitby Old Hall, Chester; *b* 16 Nov. 1886; *m* 1929, Ione Rideal (marr. diss., 1932). Solicitor, 1911; partner, Bate, Edgar, Grace & Rylands, of Manchester; MP (C) Wirral Div., 1924-31; 2nd Lieut Duke of Lancaster's Yeo., in France, 1914-17; called to Bar, Middle Temple, 1923; practice in Chester and N Wales Circuit.
[Died 8 *Dec.* 1972.

GRACE, Sir Raymond Eustace, 6th Bt *cr* 1795; Major Royal Inniskilling Fusiliers; *b* 6 Jan. 1903; *s* of Sir Valentine Raymond Grace, 5th Bt; *S* father, 1945; *m* 1st, 1930, Anita Elizabeth Othwell Ash (marr. diss. 1935), *d* of P. D. W. C. Gaussen, KC; 2nd, 1940, Molly Rosamond Evelyn (*d* 1942), *d* of Maj.-Gen. Robert St Clair Lecky, CB, CMG; 3rd, 1946, Evelyn, *d* of late William Schomberg Henchie. *Educ:* Downside Sch.; Trinity Coll., Dublin Univ. *Recreations:* golf, tennis. *Heir:* none. *Address:* 13 Leeson Park, Dublin, Eire.
[Died 16 *April* 1977 (*ext*).

GRACIAS, His Eminence Cardinal Valerian; Archbishop of Bombay since Dec. 1950; Cardinal since Jan. 1953; *b* 23 Oct. 1900; *s* of José Antonio and Charlotte. *Educ:* St Patrick's High Sch., Karachi; St Joseph's Seminary, Mangalore; Papal Seminary, Kandy; Gregorian Univ., Rome. Secretary to Archbishop of Bombay, 1929-36; Chancellor of Archdiocese, 1929; Rector of Pro-Cathedral, Dec. 1941; Titular Bishop of Tannis and Auxiliary to Archbishop of Bombay, 1946-50; Consultor to Sacred Congregation for the Oriental Churches, Sacred Congregation of the Sacraments and Sacred Congregation for the Propagation of the Faith; Member: Council for the Implementation of the Constitution on the Sacred Liturgy; Commission for the Revision of the Code of Canon Law; Pontifical Commission for the Study of Family and Population Problems. Awarded Padma Vibhushan (India), 1966. *Publications:* Features of Christian Life; Heaven and Home; The Vatican and International Policy; The Decline of Public Morals; The Chief Duties of Christians as Citizens. *Address:* Archbishop's House, Bombay 400039, India. *T:* 231 093 and 231 193.   *[Died* 11 *Sept.* 1978.

GRACIE, Alan James, CMG 1957; *b* 23 March 1904; *s* of late David Smart Gracie and late Margaret MacArthur (*née* Campbell), Duddingston, Edinburgh; *m* 1933, Isobel, *d* of late James Dick Gracie, Lanark; two *s* one *d*. *Educ:* Royal High Sch., Edinburgh; Edinburgh Univ. Entered Malayan Civil Service, 1928; Asst Adviser, Trengganu, 1929-32; Sec. to Resident, Pahang, 1933-34; Asst Sec., Federal Secretariat, 1935-37; Asst Adviser, Segamat, Johore, 1937-39. Prisoner of War, Singapore, 1942-45. Malayan Establishment Officer, 1949-53; Federation Establishment Officer, 1954-57; retired, 1958. *Address:* 24 Regent Terrace, Edinburgh EH7 5BS. *T:* 031-556 7463.
[Died 26 *May* 1973.

GRACIE, Instructor Capt. Henry Stewart, CB 1956; MA; FSA; RN retired; *b* 6 Aug. 1901; *s* of late Capt. G. S. Gracie, Leonard Stanley, Glos; *m* 1932, Dorothy Constance (*d* 1960), *d* of Rev. Edward Senior, Sheffield. *Educ:* Pocklington Sch.; St John's Coll., Cambridge (BA). Joined RN as Instr Lt, 1923; Instr Comdr 1937; Instr Capt. 1949. Command Instructor Officer Portsmouth (actg Capt.), 1946-49; Fleet Instructor Officer, Mediterranean, 1949-52; Dir of Studies, RN Coll., Greenwich, 1953-56. Naval ADC to the Queen, 1955-56. Retired 1956. Hon. Editor, Trans Bristol and Glos Archæological Soc., 1956-73. *Publications:* papers in various archæological jls. *Recreations:* prehistoric archæology. *Address:* Thrupp House, Stroud, Glos GL5 2DD. *T:* Stroud 4572.   *[Died* 7 *Feb.* 1979.

GRAHAM, Captain Lord Alastair Mungo; late Royal Navy; *b* 1886; *y s* of 5th Duke of Montrose; *m* 1st, 1916, Lady Meriel Olivia Bathurst (*d* 1936), *d* of 7th Earl Bathurst; two *s* two *d* ; 2nd, 1944, Sheelah Violet Edgeworth, *d* of late Essex Edgeworth Reade and of Sheelah, Lady Ruggles-Brise. Served Dardanelles, 1915 and War of 1939-45. Mem., Church Assembly, 1948-60; a Church Comr, 1957-60. Mem., E Suffolk CC, 1947-60 (Alderman, 1957-60). *Recreations:* shooting, fishing, golf. *Address:* Chantry Farm, Campsea Ashe, Woodbridge, Suffolk.
[Died 26 *Nov.* 1976.

GRAHAM, Angus, MA, FSA; Member of Royal Commission on Ancient Monuments (Scotland), 1960-74; *b* 1892; *yr s* of late R. C. Graham, Skipness, Argyll. *Educ:* Winchester Coll.; New Coll., Oxford. Served European War, 4th Highland LI, 1914-19. British Forestry Commission, 1920-22 (district officer); Price Bros and Co. Ltd, Quebec, 1922-25 (forester); Quebec Forest Industries Association, Ltd, 1925-33 (sec.-treasurer); Royal Commission on Ancient Monuments (Scotland), 1935-57 (sec.). *Publications:* Forests in the National Development, 1923; Quebec Limit-Holders' Manual, 1932; The Golden Grindstone, 1935; Napoleon Tremblay, 1939; papers in Proc. Society of Antiquaries of Scotland, Jl Royal Society Antiquaries of Ireland, Jl of Forestry. *Address:* 1 Nelson Street, Edinburgh EH3 6LF. *T:* 031-556 1534. *Club:* New (Edinburgh). *[Died* 25 *Nov.* 1979.

GRAHAM, Maj.-Gen. Douglas Alexander Henry, CB 1944; CBE 1942; DSO 1943; MC; *b* 26 March 1893. Capt. 1916; Major, 1930; Lt-Col 1937; Col 1940; Maj.-Gen. 1944. Served European War, 1914-18 (wounded, despatches, MC, French Croix de Guerre); Palestine, 1936-39; War of 1939-45 (despatches, CBE, DSO and Bar, CB; Legion of Merit, Comdr; French Legion of Honour, Officier; Croix de Guerre, Order of St Olaf). Retired pay, 1947. *Address:* 43 Airlie Street, Brechin, Angus. *T:* Brechin 2629. *Club:* Army and Navy.   *[Died* 28 *Sept.* 1971.

GRAHAM, Brig. Lord (Douglas) Malise, CB 1936; DSO 1917; MC; RA; *b* 14 Oct 1883; 2nd *s* of 5th Duke of Montrose; *m* 1919, Hon. Rachael Mary Holland, *y d* of 2nd Viscount Knutsford; two *s*. *Educ:* Cheltenham; Woolwich. ADC to Gen. Sir Charles Fergusson, 1914; Brigade-Major, 1916; served European War, 1914-18 (despatches, MC, DSO); Asst Dir of Artillery, War Office, 1931-34; Comdt, Sch. of Artillery, Larkhill, 1934-36; retired, 1936; Military Attaché, Paris, 1940; reverted to retired pay, 1945. *Address:* Througham Place, Beaulieu, Brockenhurst, Hants. *T:* East End 685. *Club:* Cavalry. *[Died* 20 *Nov.* 1974.

GRAHAM, Sir (Frederick) Fergus, 5th Bt *cr* 1783; KBE 1956; HM Lieutenant, Cumberland, 1958-68; formerly Captain Irish Guards; *b* 10 March 1893; *er s* of Sir Richard Graham, 4th Bt, and Lady Cynthia Duncombe (*d* 1926), 3rd *d* of 1st Earl of Feversham; *S* father, 1932; *m* 1918, Mary Spencer Revell, CBE, *o c* of late Maj.-Gen. Raymond Reade, CB, CMG; one *s*. *Educ:* Eton; Christ Church, Oxford. BA 1914; MA 1920; is Lieut-Col late 6th Bn Border Regt (TA); formerly Hon. Col 4th Battalion Border Regt TA; TD; JP for Cumberland; Patron of 2 Livings. Served European War, Irish Guards SR, 1914-19 (wounded, despatches); MP (U) North Cumberland, 1926-35, (C) Darlington, 1951-Sept. 1959. *Heir:* *s* Major Charles Spencer Richard Graham. *Recreation:* shooting. *Address:* Netherby, Longtown, Carlisle, Cumbria. *T:* Longtown 206. *Club:* Farmers'.   *[Died* 1 *Aug.* 1978.

GRAHAM, George, MD Cambridge, FRCP; Retired Consultant Physician St Bartholomew's Hospital; *b* 27 Feb. 1882; *s* of late William Edgar Graham and late Jane, *d* of Thomas Newton. *Educ:* St Paul's Sch.; Trinity Coll., Cambridge (Exhibitioner); Natural Science Tripos, Class I, 1903, Part II, Class II, 1904; Senior Entrance Scholarship, St Bartholomew's Hosp.; München; Otto Beit memorial Fellow, 1912-14; late Physician Royal Northern Hosp., and East London Hosp. for Children; late Mem. of North-East Regional Metropolitan Hospital Board, 1948-57; late Chm. Hosp. Management Cttee (Central Group), 1949-59; Governor St Bartholomew's Hospital. Senior Censor, 1947-48; Goulstonian Lecturer, 1921, Croonian Lecturer, 1940 Harveian Orator, 1953, of Royal Coll. of Physicians. Lettsomian Lectures, Medical Soc. of London, 1938; Harben Lectr, Royal Inst. of Public Health and Hygiene, 1949. Master, Worshipful Company of Barbers, 1963-64. Temp. Capt., RAMC, 1916-19 (despatches). *Publications:* various contributions to scientific and medical publications. *Recreations:* golf and walking. *Address:* 49a Acacia Road, NW8. *T:* 01-722 8930. *Clubs:* Savile, Athenæum; Denham Golf (Denham); St Enodoc Golf (Wadebridge). *[Died* 12 *Nov.* 1971.

GRAHAM, Sir George (Goldie), Kt 1952; OBE 1947; JP; DL; retired as Secretary of The Scottish Football Association (1928-57); formerly Director (Scottish Board) Legal and General

Assurance Society; *b* 10 Feb. 1892; *s* of William John Graham, contractor, Glasgow; *m* 1916, Mary France Watson, Glasgow; two *s*. *Educ:* Allan Glen's Sch., Glasgow. JP 1940, DL 1955, Glasgow. CStJ 1964. *Address:* Norden, Douglas Place, Largs, Ayrshire. *T:* Largs 2767.   [*Died* 16 Jan. 1974.

GRAHAM, (Godfrey) Michael, CMG 1954; OBE 1946; Director of Fishery Research, 1948-58; Lecturer in Biology Department, University of Salford, since 1966; *b* 22 Feb. 1898; *s* of J. W. Graham, Principal of Dalton Hall, Manchester; *m* 1925, Edith Mary, *d* of Prof. Alex. Meek Durham; two *s* one *d*. *Educ:* Bootham, York; King's Coll., Cambridge. Served European War: Telegraphist, RNVR, 1917; Sub-Lt, 1918; Naturalist, Fisheries Dept, from 1920; served War, 1942-45 (despatches), Hon. Wing Comdr (Op. Res.), RAFVR. *Publications:* The Victoria Nyanza and its Fisheries, 1929; Soil and Sense, 1941; The Fish Gate, 1943; Rational Fishing of the North Sea Cod, 1948; Human Needs, 1951, illustr. 1955; Sea Fisheries, 1956; A Naturalist's Ecology, 1972; articles on crowds in Human Relations, 1964. *Recreation:* farming. *Address:* Rivington, near Bolton, Lancs.   [*Died* 1 Jan. 1972.

GRAHAM, Hugh, DSc; 2nd *s* of late John Graham, Belfast, N Ireland; *m* 1933, Patricia Millar. *Educ:* Queen's Univ., Belfast (Research Scholar of HM Commissioners of the Exhibition of 1851); Durham Univ. Sometime Lecturer in Chemistry, University of London (King's Coll.); and Reader in Organic Chemistry, Queen's Univ., Belfast. Formerly Chief Alkali Inspector for Northern Ireland, retired 1953. Mem. of Soc. of Chemical Industry; ARIC. *Publications:* (with A. W. Stewart) Recent Advances in Organic Chemistry (7th edn), 1948-49; numerous publications in scientific jls. *Address:* Fairway Cottage, 46 Circular Road, Castlerock, Co. Derry BT51 4XA.   [*Died* 31 May 1975.

GRAHAM, Sir (John) Reginald (Noble), 3rd Bt of Larbert, *cr* 1906; VC 1917; OBE 1946; Major, Argyll and Sutherland Highlanders, TF and MGC; *b* 17 Sept. 1892; *e s* of Sir J. F. N. Graham, 2nd Bt; *S* father, 1936; *m* 1920, Rachel Septima, *d* of Col Sir Alexander Sprot, 1st and last Bt; one *s* one *d*. *Educ:* Cheam; Eton; Cambridge. Served European War (Mesopotamia and Palestine), 1914-18 (VC); Emergency Commission Sept. 1939 (Staff Capt.); Served on Staff at War Office, Essex Div. and Scottish Comd, temp. Lt-Col 1944-46 (OBE). Gentleman Usher of the Green Rod to the Most Noble Order of the Thistle, 1959-79. *Heir: s* Sir John Alexander Noble Graham, KCMG. *Address:* The Mailens, Gullane, East Lothian EH31 2BB.   [*Died* 6 Dec. 1980.

GRAHAM, Lord Malise; *see* Graham, Brig. Lord Douglas Malise.

GRAHAM, Michael; *see* Graham, Godfrey Michael.

GRAHAM, Maj.-Gen. Sir Miles (William Arthur Peel), KBE 1945 (CBE 1943; OBE 1942); CB MC; DL; Hon. President: GRA Trust Ltd and subsidiaries; GRA and White City (Manchester) Associated and subsidiaries; Chairman: A. C. Cossor Ltd, 1947-68; Totalisators Ltd and subsidiaries, 1947-73; Deputy Chairman, Franco Signs Ltd and subsidiaries; Director, Times Publishing Co., 1946-62; *b* 11 Aug. 1895; *s* of late Major Henry Graham and late Ellen, CBE (*née* Peel; she *m* 2nd, 1908, the first and last Baron Askwith); *m* 1st, 1918, Lady Evelyn King, *e d* of 3rd Earl of Lovelace; (one *s* killed in action, 1944) one *d*; 2nd, 1943, Irene Lavender, widow of Lieut-Col William Seely and *d* of Richard Francklin. *Educ:* Eton (scholar); Trinity Coll., Cambridge. Joined 2nd Life Guards, 1914; served European War, 1914-18 (twice wounded, despatches twice, MC); Capt. and Adjutant, 1916; rejoined Life Guards from Reserve, Sept. 1939, as Capt.; Maj.-Gen. 1944; served War of 1939-45, Chief Administrative Officer to FM The Viscount Montgomery, 1942-46 (OBE, CBE, CB, KBE, despatches, Comdr of Legion of Merit, US, Officier Légion d'Honneur, Croix de Guerre avec Palmes, Knight Grand Officer of Orange-Nassau). Formerly CC Notts. DL Notts, 1973. Has travelled extensively. *Recreations:* shooting and fishing. *Address:* Wiverton Hall, Bingham, Notts. *T:* Bingham 37372; 3 West Eaton Place, SW1. *T:* 01-235 3646. *Club:* Turf.
[*Died* 8 Feb. 1976.

GRAHAM, Sir Montrose Stuart, 12th Bt *cr* 1629; *b* 4 Aug. 1904; *s* of Sir Montrose Stuart Graham, 11th Bt and Helen Ursula, *d* of John Henderson, Lerwick; *S* father, 1939; *m* 1932, Elizabeth Ann, *d* of John Gerken; two *s*. *Heir: cousin* Ralph Wolfe Graham [*b* 14 July 1908; *m* 1949, Geraldine, *d* of Austin Velour, Brooklyn, New York; two *s*]. *Address:* 45 Aster Avenue, North Merrick, Long Island, New York 11566, USA.   [*Died* 1975.

GRAHAM, Sir Reginald; *see* Graham, Sir J. R. N.

GRAHAM, Colonel Robert M.; *see* Mould-Graham.

GRAHAM, Stanley Galbraith, MD, LLD (Hon.), FRCPGlas, FRCPE; retired; *b* 2 Oct. 1895; *s* of Dr Peter Graham and Mary Reid; *m* 1925, Grace Anderson; two *s*. *Educ:* Toronto, Vienna, Glasgow. MB 1916, MD (Hons) 1924, Toronto. Served European War, 1914-18, Mesopotamia (RAMC). Fellow in Pathological Chemistry, 1919-20, University of Toronto; Assistant to Professor of Medical Paediatrics, University of Glasgow, 1924-30; Leonard Gow Lecturer, University of Glasgow, 1930-47; Professor of Child Health, University of Glasgow, 1947-61. Hon. Member American Acad. of Pediatrics and of Canadian Paediatric Society; Member: Association of Physicians of Great Britain and Ireland; British Paediatric Association (Pres. 1954-55). President Royal Faculty of Physicians and Surgeons, Glasgow, 1954-56. Hon. LLD, Toronto, 1955. *Publications:* (co-author) Acidosis and Alkalosis; Notes on Infant Feeding; numerous papers in medical journals. *Address:* Westerton, Callander, Perthshire. *T:* Callander 30006. *Club:* Royal Scottish Automobile.   [*Died* 14 Feb. 1975.

GRAHAM, Stephen; author; *b* 1884; *s* of P. Anderson Graham; *m* 1909, Rosa Savory (*d* 1956); *m* 1956, Vera Mitrinovic. Attracted to Russia by the spirit in Russian literature, gave up life in London and took his chances with Russian peasants and students, with whom he lived in Little Russia and Moscow; has tramped in the Caucasus and the Crimea, in the Ural Mountains, in the Far North of Russia, has accompanied the Russian peasant pilgrims to Jerusalem, and has also followed up the tide of emigration to America, tramping to the farms of the West; travelled in Central Asia, 1914; Egypt, Bulgaria, and Roumania, 1915; Northern Norway and Murmansk, 1916; served European War in 2nd Bt Scots Guards as private, 1917-18; walked across Georgia, 1919; tramping with Vachel Lindsay In Far West, 1921; Tour in Mexico with friend Wilfrid Ewart, in which the latter was accidentally shot on Old Year's Night, 1922-23; explored Soviet frontier from Lake Ladoga to the Black Sea, 1924; Dalmatia and the Balkans, 1925; Carpathian Russia, 1926; Bosnia, 1929-30; Macedonia, 1935; Swaziland and Transvaal, 1936; FRSL 1950; BBC Foreign Service, 1941-65; Tour of Southern States of America, 1967-68; Councillor of The Poetry Society, 1949; contributed series of signed articles to The Times, 1914-15, 1916, 1924, 1926; Order of St Sava, Jugoslavia, 1936. *Publications:* A Vagabond in the Caucasus; Undiscovered Russia; A Tramp's Sketches; Changing Russia; With the Russian Pilgrims to Jerusalem, 1913; With Poor Emigrants to America, 1914; Russia and the World, 1915; The Way of Martha and the Way of Mary, 1915; Through Russian Central Asia, 1916; Russia in 1916, 1917; Priest of the Ideal, 1917; Quest of the Face, 1918; Private in the Guards, 1919; Children of the Slaves, 1920; The Challenge of the Dead, 1921; Europe-whither bound?, 1921; Tramping with a Poet in the Rockies, 1922; Under-London, 1923; In Quest of El Dorado, 1924; Life and Last Words of Wilfrid Ewart, 1924; Russia in Division, 1925; London Nights, 1925; Midsummer Music, 1926; Gentle Art of Tramping, 1927; New York Nights, 1928; The Lay Confessor, 1928; (editor) The Tramp's Anthology, 1928; Life of Peter the Great, 1929; The Death of Yesterday, 1930; St Vitus' Day, 1930; A Modern Vanity Fair, 1931; (editor) Great Russian Short Stories, 1929; Great American Short Stories, 1931; Stalin: an Imperial Study, 1931; Life of Ivan the Terrible, 1932; One of the Ten Thousand, 1933; Twice Round the London Clock, 1933; Boris Godunof, 1933; The Padre of St Jacobs, 1934; Lost Battle, 1934; Balkan Monastery, 1935; A Life of Alexander II, Tsar of Russia, 1935; African Tragedy, 1937; Alexander of Yugoslavia, 1938; The Moving Tent, 1939; From War to War, 1940; Thinking of Living, 1949; Summing-Up on Russia, 1951; 100 Best Poems in the Language, 1953; Pay as You Run, 1955; Part of the Wonderful Scene-an Autobiography, 1964. *Address:* 60 Frith Street, Soho, W1. *T:* 01-437 3771. [*Died* 15 March 1975.

GRAHAM, Col William James, MC 1917; Vice-Lieutenant of Kincardineshire, 1959-64; *b* 14 March 1890; *e s* of D. W. Graham, Hilston Park, Monmouth, and late Emmilene, *d* of late Major Carnegy, Royal Scots Fusiliers; *m* 1st, 1915, Yvette (marr. diss., 1930), *d* of late Baron Jules d'Anethan, Brussels; one *s*; 2nd, 1933, Alexandra Mary, 3rd *d* of late James Finlayson, Johnstone, Renfrewshire. *Educ:* Cheltenham Coll.; Pembroke Coll., Cambridge. 2nd Lt, 3rd (SR) Bn Gordon Highlanders, 1910-12; 2nd Lt Gordon Highlanders, 1912; served in European War, 1914-18, France and Belgium (wounded, despatches); commanded 3rd King's African Rifles, Kenya, 1929-33; Lieut-Colonel, 1938; served War of 1939-45, Malaya; Colonel, 1941; retired, 1946. Colonel The Gordon Highlanders, 1948-58. Member of Royal Company of Archers, Queen's Body Guard for Scotland, 1940. DL Kincardineshire, 1953. Chevalier,

Order of the Crown of Belgium. *Address:* Hill House, Donhead St Andrew, Shaftesbury, Dorset. *T:* Donhead 388. *Clubs:* Army and Navy, MCC. *[Died* 14 *May* 1971.

GRAHAM-CAMPBELL, Rt. Rev. Archibald Rollo, CBE 1965; Assistant Bishop, Diocese of Peterborough, since 1965; *b* 18 Feb. 1903; *s* of late Sir Rollo Frederick Graham-Campbell. *Educ:* Eton; King's Coll., Cambridge; Cuddesdon Theological Coll., 1st class Classical Tripos, Pt I, 1923; 1st class Classical Tripos Pt II, 1924; 2nd class Theological Tripos, Pt II, 1925; BA 1924; MA 1929; Deacon, 1926; Priest, 1927; Curate of St John, Middlesbrough, 1926-30; Assistant Master, Eton Coll., 1930-37; Vicar of St Paul, King Cross, 1937-42; Fellow, Dean and Chaplain of King's Coll., Cambridge, 1942-48; Examining Chaplain to Bishop of St Albans and to Bishop of Lincoln, 1946-48; Bishop of Colombo, 1948-64; Rector of Kislingbury with Rothersthorpe, 1965-68. Hon. Canon of Peterborough, 1967-. *Address:* 4 Penfold Drive, Great Billing, Northampton. *T:* Northampton 890498. *Clubs:* MCC, United Oxford & Cambridge University. *[Died* 11 *April* 1978.

GRAHAM-VIVIAN, (Richard) Preston, MVO 1961; MC; Norroy and Ulster King of Arms, 1966-71, retired; *b* 10 Aug. 1896; 2nd *s* of late Sir Richard James Graham, Bt, and Lady Cynthia Duncombe; assumed additional surname of Vivian by Royal Licence, 1929; *m* 1921, Audrey Emily, *o c* of late Major Henry Wyndham Vivian and late Lady Maude Clements (who *m* 2nd, Christopher Foulis Roundell, CBE; he *d* 1958); one *s* one *d. Educ:* Eton; Trinity Coll., Cambridge (BA). Served European War, 1915-19, as Lieut in 21st and 7th Bns KRRC (twice wounded, prisoner, MC). Bluemantle Pursuivant of Arms, 1933-47; Windsor Herald of Arms, 1947-66; Earl Marshal's Secretary, 1954-61. FZS (Life). Hon. FSG; Vice-Pres., Irish Genealogical Res. Soc., 1968-. OStJ, 1949. *Address:* Wealden House, Warninglid, Haywards Heath, West Sussex. *T:* Warninglid 272. *Club:* Travellers'. *[Died* 30 *Sept.* 1979.

GRAHAME-THOMSON, Leslie; *see* MacDougall, Leslie Grahame.

GRAINGER-STEWART, Brig. Thomas, CB 1952; MC 1917; TD 1934 (3 bars); DL; retired as Deputy Secretary, Scottish Education Department; *b* 12 Jan. 1896; *s* of late Alexander Arthur Grainger-Stewart and of late Emily Francis Adam; *m* 1931, Pansy Gertrude Kemp (*d* 1976), *d* of late J. T. Salvesen, shipowner, Leith; no *c. Educ:* Edinburgh Academy; Edinburgh Univ. Called to Scottish Bar, 1921; Secretary, Educational Endowments (Scotland) Commn, 1929-36; Asst Sec., Scottish Education Dept, 1937-46; Under-Secretary, 1947-48; Deputy Secretary, 1949-59. Served European War, 1914-18, with 16th and 17th (Service) Battalions, The Royal Scots, 1914-19; France and Flanders, 1916-19, 2 Lt to Captain. Joined 7th/9th (Highlanders) Bn, The Royal Scots, TA, 1920; comd the Bn, 1932-38; Colonel 1936; Brigadier 1939; War of 1939-45, comd 155th (East Scottish) Infantry Bde, TA, 1939-42 (France, 1940); ADC to King George VI, 1943, and to Queen Elizabeth II, 1952-53. Hon. Colonel, 7th/9th (Highlanders) Bn, The Royal Scots, TA, 1955-60. Joined HM's Body Guard for Scotland, the Royal Company of Archers, 1931; Brigadier, 1940; Ensign, 1950; Lieutenant, 1953; Captain, 1965. DL County of City of Edinburgh, 1960. Member Scottish Cttee of Arts Council of Great Britain, 1961-66; Member Restrictive Practices Court, 1961-64. *Recreations:* archery, swimming, gardening. *Address:* Easter Belmont, 1 Easter Belmont Road, Edinburgh EH12 6EX. *T:* 031-337 6920. *[Died* 14 *Feb.* 1979.

GRAND, Maj.-Gen. Laurence Douglas, CB 1950; CIE 1946; CBE 1943 (MBE 1923); FICE; Director of Fortifications and Works, War Office, 1949-52; *b* 10 Aug. 1898; *s* of late D. H. Grand; *m* 1930, Irene Lola Hilda Mathew (*d* 1971); one *s* one *d. Educ:* Rugby; Woolwich; Cambridge. *Recreation:* sailing. *Address:* Delaford Manor, Iver, Bucks. *[Died* 22 *Nov.* 1975.

GRANGE-BENNETT, Rev. Canon Ronald du Pré, TD; LTh; HCF; Assistant Chaplain, Elmhurst Ballet School, Camberley; *b* Bolton, Lancashire, 18 Feb. 1901; *s* of Rev. John Grange-Bennett, of Bewsey Old Hall, Warrington, Lancs., and Matilda Agnes du Pré, of Cape House, Samares, Jersey; *m* 1925, Violet Edith Bryant, Clifton; two *s. Educ:* Kingswood Sch.; RMC Sandhurst; Lichfield Theological Coll.; LTh Serampore Univ., India. Commission East Lancashire Regt on Passing out of Sandhurst, 1920; served in Jamaica, 1920-22; retired 1922 and studied for Holy Orders; Deacon 1924; Curate, Holy Trinity, Birchfield, Birmingham; Priest, 1925; Royal Army Chaplain's Dept, 1925-27; Principal, S Paul's Theological Coll., Mauritius, 1927-31. Bishop's Domestic Chaplain, Mauritius, 1928-31. Short service Commn in RAF Chaplain's Dept, 1931-34; Vicar of S Augustine-the-Less, Bristol, 1934-38; Campaign Director,

Bishop of Lichfield's Campaign Appeal, 1938-39. Rejoined Royal Army Chaplains Dept (TA), 1939; served in UK, France, and Middle East (8th Army); demobilised, 1945. Religious Editor of English Service of French Radio, Paris, and Hon. Assistant Chaplain, St George's Paris, 1945-46; Vicar of Minehead, 1946-52; Vicar of Ruislip, Middlesex, 1952-62; Rector of Ascot, Berks., Oct. 1962-67; Hon. Canon of Mauritius, 1961. Golden Lecturer to the Haberdashers' Company, 1951-52. *Address:* Kingshurst, Heathway, Camberley, Surrey. *T:* Camberley 65734. *[Died* 12 *June* 1972.

GRANSDEN, Sir Robert, Kt 1946; CBE 1942; *b* 10 Dec. 1893; *m* 1925, Dorothy Irene McCord; three *s. Educ:* Foyle Coll., Londonderry. British Civil Service, 1914; 2nd Lieut Royal Air Force, 1919; HM Treasury, 1920-22; transferred to NI Civil Service, 1922; Private Secretary to Minister of Finance, 1923-25; Principal Officer, Ministry of Home Affairs, 1925-33; Cabinet Secretariat, Deputy Clerk Privy Council, 1933; Asst Secretary to Cabinet, 1937; Secretary to Cabinet, Clerk of Privy Council and Private Secretary to Prime Minister, 1939-57; Agent for the Government of N Ireland in Great Britain, 1957-62. Past Pres., Foyle Coll. Old Boys' Assoc., Londonderry. American Medal of Freedom (Bronze Palm). *Address:* Flat 3, 44 Wilbury Road, Hove, Sussex. *Clubs:* Constitutional (Hon.); London and Hove (Hove). *[Died* 10 *April* 1972.

GRANT, Rt. Hon. Lord; Rt. Hon. Lord Justice-Clerk; William Grant, PC 1958; TD; Lord Justice-Clerk of Scotland, since 1962; *b* 19 June 1909; *s* of late Edward Grant and Margaret Jane Kennedy; *m* 1936, Margaret Katharine, *d* of J. W. Milne, CA, London; two *s* one *d. Educ:* Fettes Coll.; Oriel Coll., Oxford (BA); Edinburgh Univ. (LLB). Admitted to Faculty of Advocates, 1934. Served War of 1939-45, 2nd Lieut RA (TA), 1939, DAAG, War Office, 1944. Resumed practice as Advocate, 1945; QC (Scot.) 1951; Chairman, National Health Service (Scotland) Tribunal, 1949-54; Solicitor-General for Scotland, 1955-60; MP (C) Woodside Division of Glasgow, 1955-62; Lord Advocate, 1960-62. Chm., Cttee on the Sheriff Court, 1963-67; Mem., Cttee on Law of Contempt of Court, 1971. Governor, Fettes, 1952 (Chairman 1965); Director, Scottish Opera Ltd, 1965. Member Royal Company of Archers (Queen's Body Guard for Scotland); Hon. LLD Manitoba, 1961; Hon. Mem. Canadian Bar Assoc., Hon. Fellow, Oriel Coll., Oxford, 1963. Hon. Colonel 357 (Lowland) Light Regt RA (TA), 1956-61. *Recreations:* golf, shooting. *Address:* 30 Moray Place, Edinburgh. *T:* 031-225 4406; Sputieburn, The Doll, Brora. *T:* Brora 461. *Clubs:* Caledonian, United Service & Royal Aero; Scottish Arts, New (Edinburgh). *[Died* 19 *Nov.* 1972.

GRANT, Dr Duncan James Corrowr, RDI; Painter; *b* Rothiemurchus, Inverness, 1885; *s* of Major Bartle Grant and Ethel Grant; unmarried. *Educ:* St Paul's Sch. Studied at Westminster School of Art, Slade School, in Italy and in Paris, under Jacques Emile Blanche. Original Member London Artists' Association, Member of Camden Town Group and of London Group. Retrospective exhibitions, Tate Gallery, D'Offay Gallery, and Scottish Nat. Gall. of Modern Art, 1975. Made RDI, 1941, for printed textiles. Dr, Univ. of the Arts, 1921. *Address:* Charleston, Firle, East Sussex. *[Died* 8 *May* 1978.

GRANT, Gordon, CB 1956; Secretary, Trade Marks, Patents and Designs Federation, 1970-73; *b* 13 Oct. 1907; *o s* of Harry Wykeham and Blanche Grant; *m* 1932, Lilian, *d* of William Gunner, two *d. Educ:* Christ's Hosp. Asst Traffic Supt, GPO, 1926; Principal Min. of Supply, 1939; Min. of Labour, 1940; Prin. Private Sec. to Rt Hon. Ernest Bevin, 1942-44; Asst Sec., 1944; Sec. Catering Wages Commission, 1944-45; idc 1949; Under Sec., Min. of Materials, 1951-54; Under Sec., Board of Trade, 1954-58; Comptroller-Gen., Patents, Designs and Trade Marks, 1958-69. *Address:* 4 Camborne House, Camborne Road, Sutton, Surrey. *T:* 01-643 2582. *[Died* 7 *Nov.* 1979.

GRANT, John Leslie, CIE 1942; *b* 12 Oct. 1890; *m* 1927, Joy Edith Horn; one *s* one *d. Educ:* Felsted Sch. Entered Indian Service of Engineers in 1913 and served in Sind and Iraq on Irrigation work and also on roads and building works, 1918-20; Chief Engineer in Sind and Sec. to Govt Public Works Dept, Sind, 1941-46; retired, 1948. Officer in RE in War of 1914-18. *Recreations:* collection of antiques, archæology, travel. *Address:* The House on the Bend, Sea Lane, East Preston, West Sussex. *T:* Rustington 3408. *[Died* 24 *Feb.* 1975.

GRANT, John Sharp, MD, FRCSE, FRCPE, FACP; Medical Consultant, British Transport Docks Board; Hon. Medical Consultant, Bowden House Clinic, Harrow-on-the-Hill; *b* 2 April 1909; *s* of late Andrew MacKenzie Grant, JP, and Elsie Ann Sharp; *m* 1st, 1938, Sheena Marjory (marr. diss. 1972), *d* of late Rev. D. M. Cameron; one *d* ; 2nd, 1974, Daphne Ruth, *y d* of late W. H. White. *Educ:* Kingussie Sch., Inverness-shire; Edinburgh Univ. MB, ChB 1934; FRCSE 1937; MD 1949; MRCPE 1969. Med. Adviser, British Railways Bd, 1963-65; Chief Medical Officer, British Rlys Bd, 1965-71. Visiting Lectr in Industrial Medicine: Queen's Coll., Dundee (now Dundee Univ.), 1962-; Examr for DIH Exam. Bd in England, 1966-; Chm. of Commn of Enquiry to Examine and Report on Transport Med. Services in Fedn of Central Africa, 1960; Vice-Pres., Union Internat. des Services Médicaux des Chemins de Fer, 1954-; Mem. Council, Royal Inst. Public Health and Hygiene, 1961-; Mem., Soc. of Occupational Med., 1965-; Occupational Health Sect., RSM (Pres. 1971); Member: Industrial Injuries Adv. Council, 1966-; Med. Adv. Council, Migraine Trust, 1970. KStJ. *Publications:* contrib. Occupational Health, Medical Annual; (Jt Editor) Medical Services in Transport, 1966; various papers in med. jls. *Recreations:* golf, fishing. *Address:* 9 Devonshire Place, W1. *T:* 01-935 8801; 2 Vernon Mansions, Queens Club Gardens, W14. *Club:* Caledonian.   [*Died* 14 *Dec.* 1974.

GRANT, Leonard Bishopp, CIE 1936; TD 1923; ED 1943; Secretary United Service Club, Simla, 1922-47; Colonel Commanding The Simla Rifles Auxiliary Force, India, 1923-47; *b* 16 Nov. 1882; *s* of W. Leonard Grant, Sittingbourne, Kent; *m* 1922, Eileen Staveley, *d* of late E. Neild Shackle, Botwell House, Hayes, Middlesex; three *d. Educ:* Felsted Sch. 4th Bn The Buffs, 1909-23; served European War, active service, 1915-16-18-19 (Brevet Major, despatches twice); General Staff Officer, Aden, 1919-20; DAAG Army HQ, India, 1920-22. *Address:* Burnt House, Benenden, Kent.   [*Died* 2 *March* 1974.

GRANT, Peter Forbes, CBE 1961 (MBE 1953); Assistant Under-Secretary of State, Home Office, since 1972; *b* 15 July 1921; *s* of late C. W. Grant, ICS; *m* 1942, Elizabeth Ann, *d* of late A. G. Shirreff, ICS; one *s* one *d. Educ:* Canford Sch.; Hertford Coll., Oxford (MA). Royal Artillery. Colonial Admin. Service, Nigeria, 1942-61 (Perm. Sec., Min. of Educn, Eastern Region, 1958-61); Principal, Min. of Housing and Local Govt, 1961; Asst Sec., 1966. *Recreations:* walking, reading. *Address:* 35 Ovington Street, SW3 2JA. *T:* 01-589 0809; Built Farm, Hambleden, Henley-on-Thames. *T:* Hambleden 481. *Club:* Royal Commonwealth Society.   [*Died* 1 *Feb.* 1974.

GRANT, Rt. Hon. William; *see* Grant, Rt Hon. Lord.

GRANT LAWSON, Sir P.; *see* Lawson.

GRANT-SUTTIE, Col Hubert Francis; *see* Suttie.

GRANT WATSON, Herbert Adolphus, CMG 1933; *b* 4 Jan. 1881; *s* of Robert Grant Watson, Diplomatic Service; *m* 1st, 1905, Anna (*d* 1953), *d* of William G. Low, New York; one *s* (and one *s* killed on active service); 2nd, 1953, Katherine, *d* of John J. Whelan, Frant, Sussex. *Educ:* Eton; Trinity Coll., Cambridge. Attaché in Diplomatic Service, 1905; attaché at HM Embassy, Washington, 1906; 3rd Sec., 1907; transferred to Rio, 1908; to Brussels, 1910; 2nd Sec., 1912; transferred to Foreign Office, Feb. 1915; to Copenhagen, Aug. 1915; 1st Sec., 1919; employed on special service in the Baltic Provinces, 1919; transferred to Lisbon, 1920; Counsellor of Embassy, 1925; Envoy Extraordinary and Minister Plenipotentiary to Central American Republics, 1928-33; to Cuba, 1933-35; to Finland, 1935-37; to Cuba, 1937-40. *Publication:* Mission to the Baltic in 1919. *Address:* Woodberry, West Overcliff Drive, Bournemouth. *Clubs:* St James', Vikings. [*Died* 21 *Nov.* 1971.

GRANTCHESTER, 1st Baron, *cr* 1953, of Knightsbridge in the City of Westminster; **Alfred Jesse Suenson-Taylor,** Kt, *cr* 1935; OBE, MA Cantab; FRGS; FCII; FRSA; Barrister-at-Law; *b* 14 Aug. 1893; *s* of late Alfred George and Mary Taylor; *m* 1920, Mara Henriette (Mamie) (*d* 1976), *d* of late Albert Suenson, Copenhagen; one *s* one *d. Educ:* Epsom Coll.; King's Coll., Cambridge. Served Gallipoli and France 1914-18 (despatches twice, OBE, two French decorations, rank of Major); Contested Isle of Thanet Div. of Kent, 1922 and 1929; Member: Royal Institute of International Affairs; Mont Pelerin Soc. (international economic); Gov. Brit. Soc. for Internat. Understanding; Delegate to Assemblies Council of Europe and WEU, 1957-66; Mem. Delegns to Washington, Iran, Turkey, and Greece; visits to SE Asia, 1966, 1968; originator of unofficial meetings at Strasbourg of delegates from EFTA countries; Pres. Emeritus, London Liberal Party; Pres. Insurance Inst. of Kent, 1933-34; Vice-Pres. Insurance Institute of London; Vice-Pres. United Nations Assoc.; Director: County Fire Office Ltd, 1934-68; London and Manchester Assurance Co. Ltd, 1934-67 (Chm. 1953-61); Onyx Country Estates Ltd; Canal Randolph Corp. (USA); United Stockyards Corporation (USA). Dato Seri Laila Jasa, Brunei; DHBS, DSNS, Brunei. *Publications:* Industrial

Assurance Law; Editor, the Owl, a quarterly jl of internat. thought. *Heir: s* Hon. Kenneth Suenson-Taylor, QC. *Address:* 38 Orchard Court, Portman Square, W1. *T:* 01-486 7021; 52 Westminster Mansions, 1 Little Smith Street, SW1. *T:* 01-799 3782. *Club:* English-Speaking Union.   [*Died* 2 *July* 1976.

GRANTHAM, Sir Alexander (William George Herder), GCMG 1951 (KCMG 1945; CMG 1941); *b* 15 March 1899; *s* of F. W. Grantham and A. von Herder; *m* 1st, 1925, Maurine Samson (*d* 1970), San Francisco; no *c* ; 2nd, 1972, Mrs. M. E. Lumley. *Educ:* Wellington; RMC, Sandhurst; Pembroke Coll., Cambridge, MA. Gazetted 18th Hussars, 1917; Colonial Administrative Service, Hong Kong, 1922; called to Bar, Inner Temple, 1934; attended Imperial Defence Coll., 1934; Colonial Sec., Bermuda, 1935-38; Colonial Sec., Jamaica, 1938-41; Chief Sec., Nigeria, 1941-44; Governor, Fiji, and High Commissioner for Western Pacific, 1945-47; Governor Hong Kong, 1947-57. Hon. Fellow, Pembroke Coll., Cambridge. Hon. LLD Hong Kong Univ. *Address:* 90 Piccadilly, W1. *Club:* Cavalry and Guards.   [*Died* 4 *Oct.* 1978.

GRANVILLE-SMITH, His Honour Stuart Hayne, OBE 1946; a Circuit Judge (formerly Judge of County Courts), 1947-75; *b* 7 May 1901; *s* of Granville Smith, Master of the Supreme Court of Justice, 1900-25, and Nellie Claire Mead; *m* 1935, Elisabeth Mary Woodcock (*d* 1976); one *s* one *d. Educ:* Marlborough Coll.; Oriel Coll., Oxford. Called to Bar, Inner Temple, 1925; Midland Circuit; North London Sessions. Prosecuting Counsel for Post Office, Midland Circuit, 1932. Served War of 1939-45, on active service with RAF 1940-46 (Wing Comdr); Control Office and Control Commission for Germany, 1946-47.
                                                    [*Died* 29 *Nov.* 1977.

GRASETT, Lt-Gen. Sir (Arthur) Edward, KBE 1945; CB 1940; DSO 1919; MC 1915; Colonel Commandant Royal Engineers, 1945-55; *b* 1888, *e s* of late A. W. Grasett, Toronto; *m* 1935, Joan Mary, 2nd *d* of late J. K. Foster, Egton Manor, Yorks; one *d. Educ:* Upper Canada Coll., Toronto; Royal Military Coll., Kingston. Entered RE 1909; served European War (despatches five times, DSO, MC); Operations on NW Frontier of India, 1921-23; Staff Coll., Camberley, 1920; Imperial Defence Coll., 1931; GSO1 Staff Coll., Camberley, 1935-37; Brig., Gen. Staff, Northern Command, 1937-38; GOC China, 1938-41; Divisional Comdr, 1941; Corps Comdr, 1941-43; War Office, 1944; SHAEF 1944-45; Lt-Governor and C-in-C of Jersey, 1945-53; retired pay, 1947. KStJ. Chief Comdr Legion of Merit (USA); Grand Cross of the Crown (Belgium); Comdr of the Legion of Honour, Croix de Guerre (France); Order of the Red Banner (USSR). *Address:* St Amands, Adderbury, Oxon. *Clubs:* Army and Navy, Leander.   [*Died* 4 *Dec.* 1971.

GRATIAEN, (Edward Frederick) Noel, CMG 1952; QC 1962; *b* 30 Dec. 1904; *s* of late W. E. Gratiaen, Ceylon; *m* 1936, Zillah Weinman; one *d. Educ:* St Thomas' Coll., Ceylon; Exeter Coll., Oxford; QC (Ceylon) 1946; formerly Attorney Gen. and Puisne Justice, Ceylon. Past Pres., Blackheath Football Club. *Address:* 1 Radnor House, Manor Way, Blackheath, SE3. *Clubs:* Athenæum; Army and Navy.   [*Died* 20 *Feb.* 1973.

GRATTIDGE, Captain Harry, OBE 1940; retired 31 Dec. 1953, as Commodore, Cunard Line; *b* 30 Dec. 1890; *s* of George Grattidge and Nellie Tildesley; *m* 1917, Dorothy K. Sale (marriage dissolved), Plymouth; one *s. Educ:* Stafford Grammar Sch. Joined Cunard Line as Junior Officer, 1914; in command SS Ascania, 1943-44. After comdg various other ships became Capt. of Queen Mary, 1949-52; Queen Elizabeth, 1952-53. Lecture tour in USA, 1957. *Publication:* Captain of the Queens. *Address:* 33 High Worple, Rayners Lane, Harrow, Middlesex HA2 9SX. *Club:* County Conservative (Stafford).
                                                    [*Died* 29 *Oct.* 1979.

GRAVELY, Sir Walter B.; *see* Booth-Gravely.

GRAVES, Charles Patrick Ranke, MA; Writer; *b* 1 Dec. 1899; *s* of late Alfred Perceval Graves and late Amalie von Ranke; *m* 1929, Margaret Ethel (Peggy) (*d* 1962), *o d* of late Hon. Rowland Leigh; *m* 1966, Vivien Winch (*née* St George). *Educ:* Charterhouse; St John's Coll., Oxford. Edited Isis; later columnist, Sunday Express, Daily Express, Sunday Chronicle, Sunday Graphic, Bystander, Sunday Dispatch, Daily Mail, News of the World. *Publications:* And the Greeks; Gone abroad; Panorama; Gone abroad again; The Price of Pleasure; Triptyque to Spain; Deauville Taxi; Other People's Money; Swiss Summer; You're Welcome; War over Peace; The Pope Speaks; The Thin Blue Line; Life Line; Off the Record; The Avengers; Londoner's Life; Seven Pilots; The Home Guard of Britain; The Black Beret; Great Days; Five Survive; Pride of the Morning; Dusk to Dawn; Atlantic Queens at War; Switzerland Revisited; The Riviera

Revisited; Women in Green; the Story of St Thomas's; Ireland Revisited; Italy Revisited; The Big Gamble; The 3rd vol. of Regimental history of The Royal Ulster Rifles; The Cochran Story; The Bad Old Days; Royal Riviera; Champagne and Chandeliers; The Art of Egmontese; None But the Rich; Palace Extraordinary; Leather Armchairs; Fourteen Islands in the Sun; The Rich Man's Guide to Europe; The Legend of Linda Martel; Invasion by Virus; Enjoy Life Longer. *Recreations:* golf, and gin rummy. *Address:* Les Rocques Barrées, Guernsey, CI. *Clubs:* Curzon House; Cercle des Capucines (Paris); Royal Channel Islands Yacht, Royal Guernsey Golf.   *[Died* 21 *Feb.* 1971.

GRAVES, Sir Hubert (Ashton), KCMG 1953 (CMG 1947); MC; *b* 10 Aug. 1894; *m* 1st, 1921, Madeleine Constance Marie Michelle Bourdillon *(deceased*); one *s* ; 2nd, 1929, Albertine Louise Macon; one *d.* European War, 1914-18, Served with Leics Regt and Machine Gun Corps; entered Consular Service, 1926; served in various posts in Japan and Far East until 1941; seconded to Naval Board and Dept of External Affairs, Australia, for special duties, 1942-45; Controller, Far Eastern Div., Political Intelligence Dept, 1945; Counsellor British Embassy, Washington, DC, USA, 1946-51; Minister to Associate States of Vietnam, Cambodia and Laos, 1951-Oct. 1954, when became Ambassador to Vietnam (on the raising of status of the post to an Embassy); retired, 1955. *Address:* East Dean, St Mary's Road, Leatherhead, Surrey. *T:* Leatherhead 2541.   *[Died* 5 *April* 1972.

GRAY, Air Vice-Marshal Alexander, CB 1944; MC; RAF retired; *b* 8 Sept. 1896; *m* 1922, Leonora Mary; two *d* and one step-*d.* Deputy Air Commander, RAF Component, Eastern Air Command, South-East Asia Command, 1944; Dir of Flying Training, Air Ministry, 1945; Air Officer Commanding, Air Headquarters, Iraq, 1947; retired, 1949. *Address:* 8 Greenwood Avenue, Ferndown, Dorset.   *[Died* 16 *May* 1980.

GRAY, David, OBE 1968; *b* 2 April 1906; *er s* of W. S. Gray; *m* 1938, Betty R. Humphry, Southsea; one *s. Educ:* The Grammar School, Carlisle; Merton Coll., Oxford; London Sch. of Economics. Cadet, Malayan Civil Service, 1930; Chinese Secretariat, Singapore, 1934; interned, Singapore, 1942-45; Dept of Labour, Federation of Malaya, 1947; Sec. for Chinese Affairs, Fedn of Malaya, 1951; Actg Chief Sec., Fedn of Malaya, 1952; Resident Councillor, Penang, 1954; Actg Chief Sec., Fedn of Malaya, and Officer Administering the govt of Fedn, 1955-56. Secretary-General, Engineering Industries Assoc., 1956; Sec., The Industrial Soc., 1958-68. *Recreation:* golf. *Address:* 17 Vicarage Hill, Farnham, Surrey. *Club:* Royal Over-Seas League.
[Died 1 *Nov.* 1976.

GRAY, Sir George (Mervyn), Kt 1972; CVO 1963; CBE 1958; Under-Secretary and Permanent Head, New South Wales Premier's Department, Secretary to the Cabinet, and Secretary, Crown Employees Appeal Board, since 1956; *b* 30 Sept. 1910; *s* of George Gray, London; *m* 1938, Marjorie (*d* 1963), *d* of S. E. Stobo; two *s. Educ:* University of Sydney, NSW (BA). Joined NSW Public Service 1925; Sec., NSW Reconstruction Adv. Cttee, 1941-43; Sec., Reconstr and Develt Div., 1943-46; Attaché, Australian Embassy, Washington, USA, 1946-47; Asst Under-Sec., Premier's Dept, 1948-56; Dir, Royal Visits to NSW: 1958, 1959, 1963, 1964, 1965, 1970. *Address:* 12 Rosebery Road, Killara, NSW 2071, Australia. *T:* 46-2649.
[Died 25 *Aug.* 1973.

GRAY, Sir James, Kt 1954; CBE 1946; MC; FRS 1929; ScD; Fellow of King's College, Cambridge, since 1914; Professor of Zoology, Cambridge Univ., 1937-59, now Emeritus Professor; Member Development Commission, 1951-59 (formerly Chairman of the Fishery Advisory Committee); Trustee of British Museum, 1948-60; *b* 14 Oct. 1891; *s* of James Gray; *m* 1921, Norah C. King; one *s* one *d. Educ:* Merchant Taylors' Sch., London; King's Coll., Cambridge (Scholar). Capt. The Queen's Royal West Surrey Regt, 1914-18; Balfour Student, 1919-23; Reader in Experimental Zoology, Cambridge Univ. Fullerian Prof. of Physiology, Royal Institution, 1943-47; Mem. Agricultural Research Council, 1942-47; President: Marine Biological Assoc., 1945-55; Brit. Assoc. for the Advancement of Science, 1959; Eugenics Soc., 1962.- Hon. LLD (Edinburgh, Aberdeen); Hon. DSc (Durham, Manchester, Wales). *Publications:* Scientific papers; Ciliary Movement; Experimental Cytology; How Animals Move; Animal Locomotion. *Recreations:* golf, angling. *Address:* King's Field, West Road, Cambridge. *T:* 50439.   *[Died* 14 *Dec.* 1975.

GRAY, Vernon Foxwell, CIE 1936; *b* Singapore, 1 Sept. 1882; *s* of Alfred Thomas Gray and Jane Ann Foxwell; *m* 1st, 1919, Bertha Marie (*d* 1928), *d* of late James Walter Champion Stevens; one *d* ; 2nd, 1929, Marian Agnes Conley (*d* 1931), *d* of late Col Peter

Burke; 3rd, 1937, Frances Buckland (*d* 1957), *d* of late Arthur Newman. *Educ:* Solihull Sch. Chm. and Pres., Punjab Chamber of Commerce, 1920-27 and 1938-39; Mem. of Punjab Legislative Council, 1923-29; Sole Representative Associated Chambers of Commerce of India-Ceylon at 10th Congress Assoc. Chambers of Commerce of Empire, in London, 1924; late Dir R. J. Wood and Co., Ltd, India; late Dir of John Bolton and Co., Ltd, Manchester; Jubilee Medal, 1935; Coronation Medal, *Recreations:* formerly: riding, fishing, tennis, golf. *Address:* Kilpeacon House, Grey Road, Altrincham, Cheshire.
[Died 27 *Oct.* 1978.

GRAY, Sir William, 2nd Bt, *cr* 1917; DL; late Yorkshire Regiment; *b* 18 Aug. 1895; *o s* of 1st Bt and Kate, *d* of late C. T. Casebourne, CE; *S* father, 1924; *m* 1st, 1929, Josephine (*d* 1943), *d* of William Henry Eveleigh; one *s* (and *er s* decd); 2nd, 1947, Mrs Beryl Henshaw, *d* of Alfred Stott, Liverpool. *Educ:* Loretto Sch., Edinburgh. Served European War, 1914-18, as Capt. Yorks Regt (despatches; wounded, prisoner); High Sheriff of Co. Durham, 1938-39. *Recreations:* shooting, fishing. *Heir: g s* William Hume Gray, *b* 26 July 1955. *Address:* Orchard Cottage, Egglestone, Barnard Castle, Durham. *T:* Cotherstone 228.
[Died 28 *Jan.* 1978.

GRAY HORTON, Lt-Col W.; *see* Horton, W. G.

GREAVES, Sir John (Bewley), Kt 1953; CMG 1948; OBE 1944; *b* 6 June 1890; 2nd *s* of late John and Mary Greaves; *m* 1918, Grace Anne (*d* 1976), *d* of late W. T. Lock. *Educ:* Cardiff High Sch.; University Coll., Cardiff. Served European War, 1914-19, 21st Royal Fusiliers and 12th South Wales Borderers. Joined Dept of Overseas Trade, 1919; Asst Trade Commissioner, Vancouver, 1931; Trade Commissioner, Winnipeg, 1937-39; Trade Commissioner, Toronto, 1939-45. Acting Senior Trade Commissioner in Canada for periods during 1938, 1943 and 1944; Commercial Counsellor, British Embassy, Washington, 1945-47; United Kingdom Senior Trade Commissioner in Australia and Economic Adviser to United Kingdom High Commissioner, 1948-54, retired 1954. *Address:* Wanganui, New Zealand.   *[Died* 28 *June* 1977.

GREAVES, Prof. Robert William; Professor of History, University of Kansas, 1968-79, now Emeritus; *b* 27 May 1909; *s* of William Atkins Greaves and Olive Greaves (*née* Whatnall), Leicester; *m* 1955, Rose Louise Coughlin, Kansas City, Kansas, USA. *Educ:* Alderman Newton's Sch., Leicester; Merton Coll., Oxford (Exhibr, Harmsworth Schol.). BA, 1st cl. Mod. History, 1930; 2nd cl. PPE, 1931; MA 1934; DPhil 1936. Temp. Lectr, Queen's University of Belfast, 1935; Asst in History, Bedford Coll., London, 1935-39. Temp. Admin Officer, HM Treasury, 1940-42, Min. of Production, 1942-45; Asst Private Sec. to Chancellor of Exchequer, 1942, to Minister of Production, 1942-43. Bedford Coll., University of London: Lectr in History, 1945-50; Reader in History, 1950-62; Prof. of Modern History, 1962-68; Head of Dept of History, 1962-68; Vice-Princ., 1964-65. Birkbeck Lectr in Eccles. History, Trinity Coll., Cambridge, 1963-64. Vis. Professor: University of Kansas, 1965-66; University of Toronto, 1967-68. Hon. Sec., Royal Historical Society, 1955-58. *Publications:* The Corporation of Leicester 1689-1836, 1939, 2nd edn 1970; The First Ledger Book of High Wycombe, 1957; Autobiography and Court Papers of Archbishop Secker (in preparation); contrib. to Victoria County History of Leicestershire and to New Cambridge Modern History; articles and reviews in English Historical Review, Jl Eccles. History, History, etc. *Address:* 1920 Hillview Road, Lawrence, Kansas 66044, USA. *T:* 913-842-9161. *Clubs:* Reform, Royal Commonwealth Society. *[Died* 11 *Aug.* 1979.

GREEN, Prof. Cecil Alfred, MD, PhD, DPH Edinburgh; FRCPath; Professor of Bacteriology, University of Newcastle upon Tyne, 1963-74; Director of Department of Microbiology, Royal Victoria Infirmary, Newcastle upon Tyne, 1947-74; Consultant Microbiologist, Sunderland Royal Infirmary, since 1974; *b* 5 Nov. 1908; *s* of George Alfred Green and Anne Bell; *m* 1940, Jemina Stewart Scott; one *s* one *d. Educ:* Dunfermline High Sch.; Edinburgh Univ. MB, ChB Edinburgh, 1932, and Vans Dunlop Scholar; Crichton Research Fellow, Edinburgh Univ., 1933-35; Lecturer in Bacteriology, Dept of Bacteriology, Edinburgh Univ., 1935-38; Bacteriologist to Edinburgh Royal Infirmary; Empire Rheumatism Council Research Scholar, 1938-39. Professor of Bacteriology, University of Durham, 1960-63; MD Gold Medal (Edinburgh) 1941. Surg. Comdr, RNVR, 1939-45. *Publications:* articles in med. jls on researches into and control of infectious diseases. *Address:* The Red House, Jesmond Park East, Newcastle upon Tyne.
[Died 20 *Feb.* 1980.

GREEN, Ernest, CBE 1950; JP; LLD, MA; *b* 28 Jan. 1885; *s* of Horatio E. Green, Engineer; *m* 1911, Emma, 3rd *d* of John T. Wilde, cutlery manufacturer, Sheffield; no *c. Educ:* elementary sch. Organising Sec. (Yorks) Clerical Workers Union, 1916-23; Yorks District Sec., Workers' Educational Association, 1923-29; National Organising Sec., 1929-34; General Sec., 1934-50; Hon. Treasurer, 1951-62. Member: Civil Service Arbitration Tribunal, 1949-63; Management Cttee of Workers' Travel Assoc., 1934-64. JP Surrey, 1933; Hon. MA, Manchester, 1937; Hon. LLD Leeds, 1952. *Publications:* Education for a New Society; Adult Education-why this apathy?, 1954; contributor to Year Book of Education, and leading educational journals. *Recreation:* gardening. *Address:* Guardian Court, Flat 7, Wells Promenade, Ilkley, Yorks. *[Died 12 Nov. 1977.*

GREEN, Francis Henry Knethell, CBE 1949; MD, FRCP; Retired; *b* 27 August 1900; *e s* of late Knethell Wade Green; *m* 1933, Elsie Joyce, *o d* of late Karl Hinde; no *c. Educ:* Highgate Sch.; St Bartholomew's Hosp., London. Joined administrative staff of Medical Research Council, 1929; asst Sec., 1946-49, formerly Publications Officer; Principal Medical Officer on headquarters staff, 1949-55; Sec., War Wounds Cttee, 1940-45. Member of: Grand Council, British Empire Cancer Campaign, 1951-55; National Radium Commission, 1941-46; Sec., Scientific Advisory Cttee, Lady Tata Memorial Trust, 1934-55; Scientific Sec., Wellcome Trust, 1955-63; Scientific Adviser, British Heart Foundation, 1963-67. Bradshaw Lecturer, Royal College of Physicians, 1954. *Publications:* various papers in scientific jls, dealing chiefly with the organisation of medical research and clinical trials in Great Britain; jt editor, Medical Research volume of Official Medical History of the Second World War. *Address:* 129 Nether Street, N12 8AB. *T:* 01-445 4195. *Club:* Athenæum. *[Died 30 April 1977.*

GREEN, Geoffrey; His Honour Judge Green; a Circuit Judge (formerly a Judge of County Courts), since 1969; *b* 10 Sept. 1918; *s* of Arthur Green, Ombersley, Worcs; *m* 1955, Olive Mary Elizabeth Batchelor; two *s* one *d. Educ:* Worcester Royal Grammar Sch.; Hertford Coll., Oxford. Served in RA and Indian Mountain Artillery, 1939-46 (despatches); Major. Barrister, Lincoln's Inn, 1947. Dep. Chm., Herefordshire QS, 1966-71. Chm., Agricultural Land Tribunal, West Midlands Area, 1965-69; Chm., Industrial Tribunals, 1965-68; Mem., Parole Bd, 1976-78. *Recreation:* golf. *Address:* 239 Wells Road, Malvern Wells, Worcs WR14 4HF. *T:* Malvern 4020.
[Died 2 Sept. 1978.

GREEN, George Conrad, CMG 1948; MBE 1926; *b* 5 April 1897; 3rd *s* of late J. F. Green, Lancs and British Guiana; *m* 1932, Dorothy Elizabeth, *d* of late Mrs E. Hill, Enfield, Middx; one *s* one *d. Educ:* British Guiana. Entered Colonial Service, British Guiana (Colonial Sec.'s Office), 1912; Principal Asst Colonial Sec., 1932; Administrator of Grenada, 1942; retired from Colonial Service, 1951; attached to Colonial Office, 1951-59. Sec., Br Guiana section, Wembley Exhib., 1924; Sec., Br. Guiana delegn, West Indies Conf., London, 1926; Sec. to various Cttees and Commissions, including Br. Guiana Constitution Commission, 1927. Organised Civil Defence in Br. Guiana, 1941-42; Actg Governor, Windward Islands, various periods, 1947 and 1949; Governor's Deputy on many occasions. *Address:* Lamaha, Marina Park, Brixham, Devon. *[Died 29 May 1976.*

GREEN, Henry, (Henry Vincent Yorke); Managing Director of Engineering Co., Birmingham; *b* 29 Oct. 1905; *s* of V. W. Yorke; *m* 1929, Hon. Adelaide Mary Biddulph; one *s. Educ:* Eton; Magdalen Coll., Oxford. Engineer in Food and Drink Trade; War of 1939-45, full time NFS (in the ranks), 1939-43. *Publications:* Blindness, 1926; Living, 1929; Party Going, 1939; Pack My Bag (autobiog.), 1940; Caught, 1943; Loving, 1945; Back, 1946; Concluding, 1948; Nothing, 1950; Doting, 1952. *Relevant publication:* The Novels of Henry Green by Edward Stokes, 1959. *Recreation:* romancing over the bottle, to a good band. *Address:* c/o The Hogarth Press, 40-42 King William IV Street, WC2. *[Died 13 Dec. 1973.*

GREEN, Brig. Michael Arthur, CBE 1945 (OBE 1939); MC 1918; *b* 3 Oct. 1891; *s* of William Wheeler Green and Georgina (née Day); *m* 1931, Winifred Shotter. *Educ:* Wimbledon Coll., Surrey. Commissioned Glos Regt, 1914; served European War, 1914-18, France, Belgium; Adjt 1st Bn Glos Regt; GSO3 19 Army; Bde Major 14th Inf. Bde, 30th Inf. Bde; GSO2 EEF; Bde Major Cairo, 1919-22; accelerated, Northampton Regt, 1922; served India. Instructor, RMC Sandhurst, 1924-28. GSO2 PT Eastern Command, 1934-36; Gold Coast Regt, Comdg Sierra Leone Bn, 1930-32; Bt Major 1932; Sec., Army Boxing, 1934-36; Comdg Gold Coast Regt, 1936-39; Comdt, Army Physical Training Sch., 1939-40; Officer Commanding Brigade, France, 1940; Commanding Sierra Leone, 1940-41; East Africa, 1942;

Commanding RAF Regt 2nd TAF, 1943-46 (France and Germany); retired, 1946. Sec. Worcs County Cricket Club, 1946-51; Sec., Royal Selangor Golf Club, Kuala Lumpur, Malaya, 1953-63. Chm. Army Cricket and Army Association Football; Manager, MCC Touring Team, South Africa, 1948-49. MCC Touring Team Australia, 1950-51. OStJ 1935. *Recreations:* formerly: cricket (Glos CCC, Army, MCC); Rugby football (Army, Surrey, Harlequins); Association football (Army, Corinthians, Casuals, Surrey). *Publication:* Sporting Campaigner, 1956. *Clubs:* Naval and Military, MCC (Hon. Life Mem.). *[Died 28 Dec. 1971.*

GREEN, Roland, FZS; MBOU; *b* Rainham, Kent, 9 Jan. 1895; *s* of Roland Green, Naturalist; unmarried. *Educ:* Sir Joseph Williamson's Sch., Rochester. Artist; Specialises in Bird and Animal life; annual one man show of paintings and etchings in Nov. at Ackermann Galleries; painted large frescoes in oil of Bird Life for Lord Desborough KG, at White Slea Lodge, Hickling Bird Sanctuary; Lecturer on Bird Watching and How to draw Birds: Hon. Fellow, Royal Society Protection of Birds; Associate Mem. of American Ornithologists' Union. *Publications:* Birds in Flight (Pycraft); Birds and their Young (Coward); Illustrations to Avicultural Magazine; Etchings published, Snipe, Canada Geese, Mallard, Over the Sand Hills, Kingfishers, How I Draw Birds, etc. *Recreations:* music, golf, nature study. *Address:* The Studio, Hickling Broad, Norfolk.
[Died 18 Dec. 1972.

GREEN, Prof. Ronald Bramble, CBE 1961; MA Dunelm; MB, BS London; FRCS; Hon. DCL Dunelm; late Dean of Medicine and Professor of Anatomy, King's College, University of Durham, now Professor Emeritus; *b* 1 Aug. 1895; *s* of Frank E. Green and Christina Swanson; *m* 1925, Doris Kathleen Conway; one *s. Educ:* University Coll. and University Coll. Hospital, London. Demonstrator of Anatomy, University Coll.; Demonstrator and Lecturer in Anatomy, University of Durham; late Lieut-Col RAMC, TA (Durham Univ. Senior Training Corps). *Recreation:* fishing. *Address:* 30 Brandling Park, Newcastle upon Tyne NE2 4RR. *[Died 27 April 1973.*

GREEN, Ronald Frank, CB 1958; Permanent Secretary, Ministry of Health and Social Services, Northern Ireland, 1964-70 (Ministry of Health and Local Government, Northern Ireland, 1958); *b* 20 Sept. 1905; *s* of Ernest and Ethel Cranstone Green; *m* 1932, Margaret Mitchell McBride; two *s. Educ:* Friends Sch., Lisburn; Bootham Sch., York. Civil Service, NI 1923; Private Sec. to Minister of Labour, NI, 1934; Asst Sec., Ministry of Public Security, 1940; Asst Sec., Ministry of Health and Local Govt, 1944; Second Sec., Ministry of Finance, 1955. *Recreation:* yachting. *Address:* Plymouth Hoe, Stoney Road, Dundonald, Belfast. *T:* Belfast 63175. *Clubs:* Irish Cruising (Dublin); Strangford Lough Yacht (Co. Down). *[Died 3 June 1971.*

GREEN, William Allan McInnes, CMG 1964; Consultant; retired as Town Clerk and Chief Executive Officer, City of Perth, WA, (1944-66); *b* 27 Jan. 1896; *s* of Thompson and Margaret Green, Adelaide, South Australia; *m* 1932, Edyth Irene, *d* of E. J. Thomas, Adelaide; two *d. Educ:* Adelaide High Sch.; South Australian Sch. of Mines; University of Adelaide (BE). Served European War, 1914-18, with AIF, Second Tunnelling Company. Design Engineer, Adelaide City Council, 1928-34; Asst Engineer and Architect, Launceston, 1934-37; City Building Surveyor and City Architect, Perth City, 1937-44. FSASM 1928; Life Fellow, RAIA, 1971 (FRAIA 1944, ARAIA 1932); AMIEA 1932. *Recreations:* golf, bowls. *Address:* Apartment 18, 42 Victoria Avenue, Claremont, WA 6010, Australia. *T:* 31-2572. *Club:* Weld (Perth, WA).
[Died 5 Sept. 1972.

GREEN, Lt-Gen. Sir (William) Wyndham, KBE 1945; CB 1942; DSO 1918; MC 1916 and bar 1917; *b* 1887; *s* of Captain Percy Green, The Buffs; *m* 1st, 1916, Madge Bellairs (decd); one *d*; 2nd, 1924, Primrose, *d* of A. Townshend Cobbold, OBE; one *d* (one *s* decd). Served European War, 1914-18 (despatches, MC with bar, DSO, Croix de Guerre); NW Frontier, 1930 (despatches); Bt Lieut-Col, 1929; Lieut-Col 1935; Col 1937; Maj.-Gen. 1941; Acting Lieut-Gen. 1945. Chief Instructor (Equipments), School of Artillery, 1937-38; Commandant, Military Coll. of Science, Woolwich, 1938; 2nd in Comd Gibraltar, 1941-42; GOC AA Div. and Gps, 1942-45; GOC-in-C, AA Command, 1945-46; retired, 1946, as Lt-Gen. Vice-Chm., Kent T & AFA, 1948-52, Chm., 1952-54; Vice-Pres., 1954-56; Hon. Col 410 Coast Regt RA (Kent) TA, 1949-56; Chm. Canterbury Diocesan Bd of Finance, 1953-61. Col Commandant RA, 1947-52, DL Kent, 1949. A Governor Dover Coll., 1959-72. Polonia Restituta 3rd Class, 1943. *Address:* Little Gables, New Romney, Kent. *T:* New Romney 2137. *Club:* Band of Brothers. *[Died 12 Nov. 1979.*

GREENACRE, Brigadier Walter Douglas Campbell, CB 1952; DSO 1945; MVO 1927; late Welsh Guards; Extra Equerry to the Queen since 1952 (to King George VI, 1936-52); *b* Durban, S Africa, 20 March 1900; *er s* of late Walter Greenacre, OBE, Durban; *m* 1928, Gwendolen Edith, *d* of late Lieut-Col L. R. Fisher-Rowe; three *s* two *d. Educ:* Leys Sch., Cambridge. Equerry to Prince of Wales, 1924-26; Extra Equerry to Prince of Wales, 1926-36; Welsh Guards, 1918-47; raised 3rd Bn Welsh Guards, 1941; commanded: 2nd Armoured Bn Welsh Guards, 1941-43; Col 5th Guards Armoured Bde, 1943-44; Brig. (temp.), 1944; 6th Guards Armoured Bde, NW Europe, 1944-45; 6th Guards Brigade, 1945-47, BAOR; Schleswig-Holstein Sub Area, 1947-48; 128 Inf. Bde TA, 1948-49; 17th Infantry Bde & Dist, MELF, 1950-52; Col, Gen. Staff, 1947; Brigadier, 1951; retired pay, 1952. *Recreations:* shooting, golf. *Address:* Rendham Barnes, Saxmundham, Suffolk. *T:* Rendham 467. *Clubs:* White's, Pratt's.   *[Died 15 Aug. 1978.*

GREENFIELD, Sir Cornelius (Ewen MacLean), KBE 1965 (MBE 1944); CMG 1956; Chairman, Rhodesian Banking Corporation Ltd; *b* 2 May 1906; *s* of Rev. C. E. Greenfield; *m* 1934, Brenda, *d* of E. M. Diaper; one *s* two *d.* Formerly Sec. to the Treasury, Rhodesia. Trustee, Automobile Assoc. of Rhodesia. *Recreation:* bowls. *Address:* 26 Greenhithe Lane, Borrowdale, Salisbury, Zimbabwe. *Club:* Salisbury (Salisbury).   *[Died 21 May 1980.*

GREENFIELD, Brig. Hector Robert Hume, CBE 1945; retired; *b* 21 June 1893; *o s* of late Col Hume Greenfield, JP, Fascadale, Ardrishaig, Argyll, and Edna Constance, *d* of Robert Leake, MP; *m* 1st, 1918, Ivy Maud (*d* 1947), *e d* of Sir Henry Dering, 10th Bt, of Surrenden Dering, Kent, and *widow* of Capt. R. A. C. Murray, Seaforth Highlanders; one *d*; 2nd, 1948, Mary Patricia, *d* of Major H. E. O'B. Traill, DSO, Dundooan, Coleraine, Co. Londonderry; one *s. Educ:* Eton; RMC, Sandhurst. Served for a year in Merchant Navy, as an apprentice in a sailing ship to Australia and round Cape Horn. 2nd Lieut Argyll and Sutherland Highlanders, 1912; European War, 1914-19 (severely wounded, Serbian Order of the White Eagle). Specially employed War Office for 3 years; Asst to Military Attaché, Paris, 1918-19; Asst Military Sec., Gibraltar, 1921-22; psc†, 1926-27; Staff Capt., DAAG and GSO2; Sec., War Block Cttee, AHQ, India, 1934-35; commanded 2nd Bn Argyll and Sutherland Highlanders, 1938-40. War of 1939-45: Col (AA and QMG) 1940; Brig. 1940; Commander 15th Infantry Brigade, 1940-43; Commandant, Middle East Staff Coll., Haifa, 1943-44; Commander, Eritrea District, MEF, 1944-46 (despatches, CBE). Retired 1946. Dep. Sec., Govt Hospitality Fund, 1946-49; Ceremonial Officer, Festival of Britain, 1950-51. Dep. Chm. and Chm., Lochgilphead Hospitals Board, 1960-70. Mem. Queen's Body Guard for Scotland (Royal Company of Archers). Commander Order of Dannebrog (Denmark), 1951. *Address:* Scallastle, Kilmartin, Argyll. *T:* Kilmartin 230. *Clubs:* Naval and Military; New (Edinburgh).   *[Died 19 Feb. 1975.*

GREENHAM, Robert Duckworth, RBA; ROI; professional artist and writer; *b* Streatham, 6 Sept. 1906; *s* of George F. Greenham, MBE, MIEE, and Isobel Greenham; *m* 1937, Kay Gilbert Fahey (divorced, 1942); *m* 1943, Joan Anne Benbow (*d* 1962); two *d*; *m* 1964, Janet Phyllis Williams. *Educ:* Dulwich Coll. Studied art at Byam Shaw, and later at the Royal Academy Schs; silver medals, Landseer Scholarship, and British Institute Scholarship. Exhibits at Royal Academy, Royal Portrait Society, etc., and the New English Art Club, Provincial exhibitions, and Internat. Exhibitions at Carnegie Institute, Pittsburgh, USA; paints many portraits of film stars, including Anna Sten, exhibited at RA 1935, Elisabeth Bergner, exhibited RA 1936, Greta Garbo, exhibited RA 1937, and Ann Todd, exhibited RBA 1943; one-man show in New York, 1937; Poster work for London and N Eastern Railway, 1938-39. Conscripted into Inns of Court Regt, 1941; 2nd Lieut 1941, Corps Camouflage Officer; Lieut 1942; invalided from Army, 1943; exhibited again Royal Academy and other shows. Picture bought by Australian Govt from Royal Academy, 1945; Council of Imperial Arts League, 1946-48; Council of Royal Society of British Artists, 1946-49. Did a series of figure paintings for Lintas International Advertising Ltd. RBA Bronze Medal for painting, 1946. Since 1949 has turned almost entirely to landscapes and seashore paintings; temporary Art Critic for The Scotsman, 1959 and 1960; resumed portrait and figure work, 1964. Teacher (part-time) of Advanced Art, Camberley Adult Further Educn Centre, 1968-73; Teacher (part-time) of Art Therapy, Coldingley Prison, Bisley, 1969. Senior Member: RBA, 1963; ROI, 1963. *Publications:* many technical articles on Art. *Recreations:* wine-making, gardening and Modern English Competitive-style Ballroom Dancing (International Award and Gold Medals). *Address:* Cheriton Manor, Bay, Gillingham, Dorset. *T:* Gillingham 2667; 14B Langham Mansions, SW5. *T:* 01-373 0814. *Club:* Chelsea Arts.   *[Died 13 March 1976.*

GREENIDGE, Charles Wilton Wood; Vice-President, Anti-Slavery Society, 1968 (Secretary 1941-56, Director 1957-68); *b* 1889; *y s* of late Charles Joseph Greenidge, member of the Colonial Parliament of Barbados West Indies; unmarried. *Educ:* Harrison Coll., Barbados; Downing Coll., Cambridge. Magistrate, St Kitts, LI 1919; Magistrate Barbados, 1923; Judge of Court of Appeal, Barbados, 1925; Magistrate, Port of Spain, Trinidad, 1927; acted Solicitor-Gen. and Attorney-Gen. of Trinidad; mem. of the Legislative Council of Trinidad; Chief Justice of British Honduras, 1932-36; Solicitor-Gen., Nigeria, 1936-41; Member: Commission on Development of British Guiana and British Honduras, 1947; UN's Cttee of Experts on Slavery, 1950-51. MLC Barbados, 1958-62. *Publication:* Slavery, 1958. *Recreations:* music and walking. *Address:* Fontabelle, New Street, Santa Venera, Malta. *Club:* National Liberal.   *[Died 28 April 1972.*

GREENLEAVES, Herbert Leslie, CBE 1958; retired, Foreign Service, 1960; *b* 10 May 1897; *s* of late Herbert Greenleaves and Jane Elizabeth Ford; *m* 1938, Cecilia Joyce, *d* of late Commander F. W. Parker; one *d* (one *s* decd). *Educ:* Liverpool Coll. 2nd Lieut (Territorials), 1915; active service Egypt, France, Belgium, 1916-19. British Vice-Consul, Florence, 1939; Acting Consul there, 1939-40; British Vice-Consul, Tangier, 1940-43, and Casablanca, 1943. Hon. Commission Lieut-Comdr RNVR (Special Branch), 1943. Service French North Africa and Italy. Consul, Florence, 1945-52; Consul, Lille, 1952-55; Consul-Gen., Lyons, 1955-60. *Recreations:* chess, bridge. *Address:* Peel House, North Perrott, Crewkerne, Somerset.   *[Died 1 Sept. 1975.*

GREENSLADE, David Rex William, CBE 1977; Vice-Chairman of Press Council since 1975 (Member since 1960); Joint Managing and Editorial Director, Mansfield and North Nottinghamshire Chronicle Advertiser, and Worksop Guardian; *b* 15 Dec. 1916; *s* of Rev. R. R. Greenslade; *m* 1st, 1939, Mary E. Bull (marr. diss.); two *d*; 2nd, 1964, L. Anne Waterfield; one *d. Educ:* Ashville Coll., Harrogate. Pres., Guild of British Newspaper Editors, 1967-68; Pres., The Newspaper Soc., 1975-76. Chairman: Weekly Newspaper Advertising Bureau, 1969-71; North Midlands Assoc. of Newspaper Owners, 1957-58 and 1970-71; Member: Nat. Council for Training of Journalists, 1966-69; Inst. of Journalists; Internat. Press Inst.; Internat. Conf. of Weekly Newspaper Editors; BBC Midlands Adv. Council, 1962-65; Councillor, Local Radio Assoc., 1968-72; Mem., Nottingham Circuit Adv. Cttee for Crown Courts, 1972-74; Mem., Nottinghamshire Animal Shelter, RSPCA (Chm., 1970-); Fellow, Wildfowl Trust. Freeman, City of London; Clerk, William Singleton Almshouses; Trustee, N. M. Hardy Foundn. Freeman, Guild of Air Pilots and Air Navigators; Pres., Royal Air Forces Assoc (Mansfield); Vice-Pres., Royal British Legion (Mansfield). *Recreations:* flying (Chm. Sherwood Flying Club, 1967-70, Pres., 1974-), breeding wildfowl. *Address:* The Homestead, Halloughton, Notts. *Clubs:* Press; (Pres. 1964-) Sherwood Forest Motor; (Past Pres.) Mansfield Rotary; British Light Aviation Centre.   *[Died 16 Jan. 1977.*

GREENSLADE, Rev. Stanley Lawrence, DD; FBA 1960; Canon of Christ Church and Regius Professor of Ecclesiastical History, Oxford University, 1960-72; Emeritus Student of Christ Church, Oxford, 1972; *b* 14 May 1905; *s* of late William Greenslade and Alice Sear; *m* 1929, Phyllis Dora Towell; one *s* one *d. Educ:* Christ's Hosp.; Hertford Coll., Oxford (Open Classical Scholar, Class I, Hon. Classical Mods, Lit. Hum. II, Theology I); Wycliffe Hall, Oxford. Curate of St Mary's, Beeston, Leeds, 1929-30; Fellow, Chaplain, and Tutor in Theology, St John's Coll., Oxford, 1930-43; Lightfoot Prof. of Divinity, Univ. of Durham, 1943-50; Van Mildert Prof. of Divinity, Univ. of Durham, 1950-58; Ely Prof. of Divinity, Cambridge Univ., 1958-59; Fellow of Selwyn Coll., Cambridge, 1958-59. Senior Denyer-Johnson Scholar (Oxford Univ.), 1933. Canon of Durham, 1943-58; Examining Chaplain to Bishop of Durham, 1943-58; to Bishop of Bradford, 1956-61; to Bishop of Chelmsford, 1933-43; to Bishop of Leicester, 1932-47. Ecumenical activities incl. Mem. of Faith and Order Cttee of WCC and of Anglican-Methodist, Anglican-Presbyterian, Anglican-Lutheran and Anglican-Orthodox Conversations. Hon. DD Edinburgh. *Publications:* The Work of William Tindale, 1938; The Christian Church and the Social Order, 1948; Schism in the Early Church, 1953; Church and State from Constantine to Theodosius, 1954; Early Latin Theology, 1956; ed The Cambridge History of the Bible: The West from the Reformation to the Present Day, 1963; Shepherding the Flock, 1967; introd. to facsimile The Coverdale Bible 1535, 1975. *Recreations:* music, bibliography. *Address:* Homestall, Church Lane, South Moreton, Didcot, Oxon OX11 9AF. *T:* Didcot 812088.   *[Died 8 Dec. 1977.*

GREENWAY, 3rd Baron *cr* 1927; **(Charles) Paul Greenway;** Bt 1919; Insurance Broker and Underwriter, Lloyd's, London; *b* 31 Jan. 1917; *s* of 2nd Baron Greenway and Eileen (*d* 1963), *d* of late Maj.-Gen. Sir Harry Triscott Brooking, KCB, KCSI, KCMG; *S* father, 1963; *m* 1939, Cordelia Mary, *d* of late Major H. C. Stephen, late Northumberland Fusiliers; three *s. Educ:* Winchester; Cambridge (MA). Private, Royal Hampshire Regt; Commissioned The Buffs, 1940; Major, 6 Airborne Div., 3rd Parachute Bde, 1942-46, France, India, Palestine. Citizen and Vintner Freeman of the City of London, 1938. Bailli délégué, Confrérie de la Chaîne des Rôtisseurs de la Grande Bretagne. *Recreations:* sailing, ocean cruising. *Heir: s* Hon. Ambrose Charles Drexel Greenway, *b* 21 May 1941. *Address:* 703 Collingwood House, Dolphin Square, SW1. *Clubs:* City Livery; Royal London Yacht, Royal Fowey Yacht, Island Sailing, House of Lords Yacht, Lloyd's Yacht, Mylor Sailing.
[Died 14 Sept. 1975.

GREENWELL, Captain Sir Peter (McClintock), 3rd Bt, *cr* 1906; TD; DL; formerly 98th (Surrey and Sussex Yeomanry) Field Regiment (TA); *b* 23 May 1914; *s* of 2nd Bt and Anna Elizabeth (*d* 1957), *e d* of late Adm. Sir Francis Leopold McClintock, KCB; *S* father, 1939; *m* 1940, Henrietta, 2nd *d* of late Peter and Lady Alexandra Haig-Thomas; two *s* one *d. Educ:* Winchester; Trinity Coll., Cambridge (BA). Served War of 1939-45 (despatches, 1946, prisoner). Chm., Ransomes, Sims and Jefferies Ltd, 1969-78. Trustee, Royal Agric. Soc. (Dep. Pres., 1971). JP Suffolk, resigned, 1958; High Sheriff of Suffolk, 1966; DL Suffolk, 1973. *Heir: s* Edward Bernard Greenwell [*b* 10 June 1948; *m* 1974, Sarah Louise, *yr d* of late Lt-Col P. M. G. Anley; one *d*]. *Address:* Butley Abbey Farm, Woodbridge, Suffolk. *T:* Orford 233.
[Died 2 Dec. 1978.

GREENWOOD, Brig. Harold Gustave Francis, CBE 1942; MC; retired; *b* 15 Nov. 1894; *s* of late Lieut-Col H. S. Greenwood, VD, Kingston, Canada, and Matilda, *d* of Sir Henri Joly de Lotbinière, KCMG; *m* 1928, Gwyneth Francis, *d* of late E. B. Lemon, Winnipeg and late Mrs Ogilvie, Victoria, Canada; one *d. Educ:* Bishops Coll. Sch., Lennoxville, Canada; RMC, Canada. Served European War, 1914-18 (despatches twice, MC); NW Frontier Province, India, 1923-24 (despatches twice, Bt Major); lately Brigadier Engineer Staff, GHQ, India; and Chief Engineer 11th Army Group, SE Asia Command; retired pay, 1947. *Address:* c/o Lloyds Bank Ltd, Pall Mall, SW1; 3 Highlands Road, Buckingham, Bucks MK18 1PN.   *[Died 8 July 1978.*

GREENWOOD, John Eric; Director Boots Pure Drug Co. Ltd, 1920-53 (Joint Vice-Chairman, 1951); *b* 23 July 1891; 4th *s* of late Thomas Greenwood; *m* 1921, Doris Mary Radford (*d* 1973); one *s* two *d. Educ:* Dulwich; King's Coll., Cambridge. Served European War 1914-18, E Surrey Regt and Grenadier Guards (wounded, despatches); retd with rank of Capt. MA, LLB Cantab; FCA 1960; JP Nottingham 1947-53. Civil Service Arbitration Tribunal, Chancellor of Exchequer's Panel, 1936-49. Member of: Board of Trade Retail Trade Cttee, 1941; Catering Wages Commn, 1943-46; Royal Commn on Taxation of Profits and Income, 1950-55; Court of Inquiry into Omnibus Industry Dispute, 1946; Court of Inquiry into Road Haulage Dispute, 1947. President Rugby Football Union, 1935-6-7. *Recreations:* fishing, gardening; played Rugby football for Cambridge Univ. 1910-11-12-13-19 (Capt. 1912-19), for England 13 times (Capt. 1920). *Address:* The Priory of Lady St Mary, Wareham, Dorset. *T:* Wareham 2772. *Club:* White's.   *[Died 23 July 1975.*

GREENWOOD, Ranolf Nelson, MC 1917; JP; *b* 10 May 1889; *m* 1st, 1916, Beatrice Marion (*d* 1947), *d* of late Rev. Llewellyn L. Montford Bebb, DD, Principal of Lampeter Coll., S Wales; four *s* two *d*; 2nd, 1953, Kathleen Winifred Whiteside. *Educ:* Uppingham. Admitted a Solicitor, 1913; partner, firm Travers, Smith Braithwaite & Co., 1919-67. Served European War, 1914-19; 3rd Bn (Res.), Cheshire Regt, Adjt, 1st Bn, 1916; Major, DAAG 16th Div. 1918 (despatches twice); returned to City, 1919. Comdg Home Guard Bn, 1942-45. JP Herts 1932. *Address:* The Headlands, 2 Oakham Road, Braunston, Rutland.
[Died 15 April 1977.

GREENWOOD, Rt. Rev. Tom, DD; *b* 1 Jan. 1903; *s* of Mitchell and Ellen Greenwood; *m* 1934, Isabel Dunham Gilbert; one *s* three *d* (and one *s* decd). *Educ:* Trinity Coll., Toronto (LTh). DD (*Jure Dignitatis*) Trinity Coll., 1952. Deacon, 1933; Priest, 1934. Arctic Mission at Fort McPherson, 1934-36; in American Ch., 1936-37; Diocese of London: Permission to Officiate (Colonial Clergy Act) at St John the Baptist, Greenhill, 1937-38; Curate, 1938-40; Vicar of St Peter's, Hale, 1940-46; Curate-in-charge of St Elizabeth's, Ashley, 1944-46; Proctor in Convocation, Chester, 1945-46; Rector of Fort McMurray, 1946-49; Rector of Yellowknife, 1949-52; Bishop of Yukon, 1952-61; Vicar of Whitegate, Asst Bishop, Dio. Chester and

Hon. Canon of Chester Cathedral, 1962-65, Canon Emeritus, 1965; Asst Bishop of Cariboo, 1965-69, retired. *Address:* 2 Farnham Crescent, Ottawa, Ontario K1K OE8, Canada.
[Died 1 Feb. 1974.

GREENWOOD, Walter; novelist and dramatist; *b* Salford, Lancs, 17 Dec. 1903; *e s* of late Tom and Elizabeth M. Greenwood. *Educ:* Langworthy Road Council Sch., Salford; by self. Began part-time work as milk-roundsman's boy and pawnbroker's clerk at twelve years of age; left school at thirteen; worked as office boy, and as stable boy at millionaire's private stable, then at racing stable; clerk, packing-case maker, sign-writer, car-driver, warehouseman, salesman; never earned more than 35/- a week until employed for few months in automobile factory; on "dole" three or four times. Hon. DLitt, Salford, 1971. *Publications:* Lancashire (County Books), 1949; *novels:* Love on the Dole, 1933 (play (jointly), 1934; film, 1941); His Worship the Mayor, 1934; Standing Room Only, 1936; The Cleft Stick (short stories), 1937; The Secret Kingdom, 1938; Only Mugs Work, 1938 (play, 1938); How the Other Man Lives, 1939; Something in My Heart, 1944; So Brief the Spring, 1950; What Everybody Wants, 1953; Down by the Sea, 1956; *plays:* My Son's My Son (jointly), 1935; Give Us This Day, 1936; The Practised Hand (one act play), 1936; The Cure for Love, 1945 (film, 1949); So Brief the Spring, 1945; Too Clever for Love, 1951; Saturday Night at the Crown, 1953 (novel, 1959); Happy Birthday (one act play), 1954; Happy Days, 1959; Fun and Games, 1961; This is your Wife, 1964; *autobiography:* There Was a Time, 1967 (play, 1968; prod. as Hanky Park, Mermaid, 1971); *films:* No Limit (George Formby film), 1935; Sidney Howard Film, 1936; Merchant Navy Film, 1942; Six Men of Dorset, 1944; Eureka Stockade, 1947; Chance of a Lifetime, 1949. The Secret Kingdom (BBC TV serial), 1960. *Recreations:* riding, rowing, fishing. *Address:* c/o The Midland Bank Ltd, 10 Victoria Street, Douglas, Isle of Man; 7 Osborne Terrace, Douglas, Isle of Man.   *[Died 13 Sept. 1974.*

GREER, Rt. Rev. William Derrick Lindsay; *b* 28 Feb. 1902; *s* of Rev. Richard Ussher Greer and Elizabeth Lindsay Greer; *m* 1946, Marigold, *d* of late Rev. E. Stogdon; one *s* two *d. Educ:* St Columba's Coll., Co. Dublin; Trinity Coll., Dublin. Assistant Principal, Ministry of Home Affairs, N Ireland, 1925-29; Curate, 1929-32, and Vicar, 1932-35, of St Luke's Church, Newcastle upon Tyne; General Sec. Student Christian Movement of Gt Britain and Ireland, 1935-44; Principal of Westcott House, Cambridge, 1944-47; Bishop of Manchester, 1947-70, retired. DD (jure dig.), TCD, 1947; Hon. DD Univ. of Edinburgh, 1951; Hon. LLD Manchester, 1971. *Recreations:* walking, gardening. *Address:* The Old Rectory, Woodland, Broughton in Furness, N Lancs. *T:* Broughton in Furness 442.
[Died 30 Oct. 1972.

GREESON, Surgeon Vice-Adm. Sir (Clarence) Edward, KBE 1950; CB 1945; retired; *b* 29 Nov. 1888; *s* of Rev. John Greeson; *m* 1st, 1911, Katharine Whyte (*d* 1959); one *d*; 2nd, 1959, Mrs Marion Meredith Edgecombe (*d* 1968); 3rd, 1969, Hon. Mrs Michael Scott. *Educ:* Aberdeen Grammar Sch.; Aberdeen Univ. (MB, ChB 1910; MD 1913). Surgeon, Royal Navy, 1914; Surgeon Capt., 1939; Surgeon Rear-Adm., 1945; Surgeon Vice-Adm., 1948. Served European War, 1914-19: battles of Heligoland Bight, Falkland Islands, Gallipoli; Shanghai Defence Force with 12th RM Bn, 1927; War of 1939-45: Fleet MO, Mediterranean Fleet, 1939-42; Battle of Matapan; Medical Dir-Gen. of the Navy, 1949-52; KHP 1946-52; QHP 1952; retd list, 1952. CStJ, 1948. *Address:* The Dell House, Alderney, CI.
[Died 10 June 1979.

GREGG, Humphrey P.; *see* Procter-Gregg.

GREGG, James Reali; *b* 16 Nov. 1899; *e s* of late James Gregg, OBE, JP, Carnmoney, Co. Antrim, N Ireland; *m* 1930, Nina Hamilton Smith, *d* of late William H. Smith, Upton Park, Templepatrick, N Ireland; no *c. Educ:* Royal Belfast Academical Institution; Lathrop Sch., Mo, USA; Hampden-Sidney Coll., Va; Harvard Coll., Harvard Univ.; St Catharine's Coll, Cambridge Univ. (MA). Called to Bar, King's Inn, Dublin, 1923; Gray's Inn, London, 1939; KC (Uganda) 1944. Chm., Court of Referees, NI, 1928; Nyasaland: Acting Attorney General, 1937-38; Uganda: Solicitor General, 1939, Attorney General, 1943; Puisne Judge, Nyasaland, 1948; Judge of the Supreme Court, Hong Kong, 1953; Sen. Judge of Supreme Court of Hong Kong, 1959-61 (Acting Chief Justice, Hong Kong, Feb.-Nov. 1960); retired. *Recreation:* golf. *Address:* PO Box 91, Hermanus, Cape Province, South Africa. *Club:* Hong Kong (Hong Kong).   *[Died 16 Dec. 1978.*

GREGG, Milton Fowler, VC 1918; OC 1967; CBE 1946; MC 1917, and Bar 1918; Canadian High Commissioner to Guyana,

1964-67, retired; *b* Mountain Dale, NB, Canada, 10 April 1892; *m* 1919, Amy Dorothy Alward, of Havelock, NB; one *d*; *m* 1964, Erica, *widow* of Kjeld Deichmann, Sussex, NB. *Educ:* Public Sch., New Brunswick; Provincial Normal Sch., Fredericton NB; Acadia Univ., Wolfville, NS (hon. MA). As a boy lived on a farm; enlisted as a private while at coll., 1914; went to France with 13th Batt. Royal Highlanders of Canada 1915 (wounded, Festubert); later obtained Commission in KORLR; transferred to Royal Canadian Regt; in France, 1917 (wounded, MC) (bar to MC, wounded, Cambrai, 1918, VC); Adjt; returned Canada, 1919; Major in Governor-General's Foot Guards; Dominion Treasurer Canadian Legion, BESL 1934-39; On outbreak of war, 1939 was posted 2nd in command Royal Canadian Regt and proceeded to England with it 1939; Lieut-Col commanding West Nova Scotia Regt 1940; Commandant, Canadian OCTU, England, 1941; Col Commandant Officers' Training Centre, Canada, 1942; Brig. Commandant Canadian Sch. of Infantry, 1943. Minister of Fisheries, Canada, 1947-48; Minister of Veterans' Affairs, 1948-50; Minister of Labour, 1950, till defeated in General Election, 10 June 1957. United Nations Technical Assistance in Iraq, 1958-59; United Nations Children's Fund in Indonesia, 1960-63. Now with voluntary agencies related to internat. affairs, conservation, rural renewal, military and veterans' affairs. *Address:* Thorn Cottage, RR3, Fredericton, New Brunswick, Canada. *[Died 13 March 1978.*

GREGORY, Arnold; industrial consultant; *b* Salford, Lancs, 14 Nov. 1924; *s* of Samuel Gregory and Ethel (*née* Aspinall-Stockwell); *m* 1945, Elizabeth Spooner; one *d. Educ:* Manchester and Salford Municipal Schs; Manchester Coll. of Technology. Parly Agent, Manchester (Wythenshawe), 1955; contested (Lab) Stafford and Stone, 1959. Lectr and Tutor, Nat. Council of Labour Colls, 1956-64. MP (Lab) Stockport North, 1964-70. Contracts Manager and Consultant (Textiles), 1958-. Mem., Parly Select Cttee on Science and Technology, 1965-70. Sec., 1972 Industry Gp. Co-opted Mem., Labour Party NEC sub-cttees on Industry, Consumer Affairs etc, 1973-. *Publications:* Science and Technology in Europe, 1970; British Computers and Industrial Innovation, 1971; contribs to Labour periodicals and newspapers. *Recreations:* reading, gardening, theatre. *Address:* 138 Eskdale Avenue, Chesham, Bucks. *T:* Chesham 5661. *Club:* Reform. *[Died 30 July 1976.*

GREGORY, Vice-Adm. Sir David; *see* Gregory, Vice-Adm. Sir G. D. A.

GREGORY, Vice-Adm. Sir (George) David (Archibald), KBE 1964; CB 1962; DSO 1939; retired, 1966; *b* 8 Oct. 1909; *s* of late Lt-Col G. M. A. Gregory, RA (retired), Tayfletts House, Perth; *m* 1933, Florence Eve Patricia, *yr d* of late James Hill, Lambourne House, Bagshot; two *s. Educ:* RN Coll., Dartmouth. Joined Submarine Service, 1931, and served in it at home and on China station; served War of 1939-45, in comd of HM Submarines and on Staff of C-in-C Home Fleet (DSO and Bar, despatches); Capt. (S/M) 2nd and 5th Submarine Squadrons, 1954-57; Commodore, Hong Kong, 1957-60; Admiral Superintendent HM Dockyard, Devonport, 1960-64; Flag Officer, Scotland and Northern Ireland, 1964-66. Mem., Queen's Body Guard for Scotland (Royal Company of Archers). *Recreations:* shooting, fishing. *Address:* Greymount, Alyth, Perthshire. *T:* Alyth 548. *Club:* United Service & Royal Aero. *[Died 21 March 1975.*

GREGORY, Theophilus Stephen, MC; Author and Journalist; *b* 23 Nov. 1897; *s* of Stephen Herbert and Mabel Gregory; *m* 1925, Hilda Harper Road; one *d. Educ:* Kingswood Sch.; New Coll., Oxford. Served European War, 1914-18, HAC and 13th KRR (MC), 1916-18. Methodist Minister, 1921-35; received into Catholic Church, 1935. Editor of The Dublin Review, 1945-47. Pres. Aquinas Soc., 1945. *Publication:* The Unfinished Universe, 1935. *Address:* The Cottage, Badby House, Daventry, Northants NN11 4NH. *T:* Daventry 2035. *[Died 11 Aug. 1975.*

GREIG, Maysie, (Mrs Jan Sopoushek); author; pen-names: Maysie Greig and Jennifer Ames; *d* of Dr Robert Greig-Smith, bacteriologist, NSW; *m* 1937, Maxwell Murray (*d* 1956), author; one *s*; *m* 1959, Jan Sopoushek. *Educ:* Presbyterian Ladies' Coll., Pymble, NSW. Started as journalist on Sydney Sun and came to London to write a London column. Started writing short stories for Westminster Gazette and serials for Daily Sketch and Mirror. Went to New York and Boston where her first novel was published and later filmed; has had several novels filmed in Hollywood. Most novels serialised in leading women's jls in Eng. and Amer. Life Mem. Romantic Novelists' Assoc., London. *Publications:* 200 novels in England and America. *Address:* 15 Craven Hill, W2. *Clubs:* (Vice-Pres. NSW, Sydney European Rep.) PEN; Women Writers (Sydney). *[Died 10 June 1971.*

GREIG, Rear-Adm. Morice Gordon, CB 1963; DSC 1944; Chairman, Public Service Commission, Bermuda, since 1968; *b* 20 March 1914; *s* of late Gordon Eastley Greig, Malayan Civil Service, and late Elsie Challoner Greig (*née* Lake); *m* 1st; two *s* three *d*; 2nd, 1960, Stephanie Margaret; one step *d. Educ:* RNC, Dartmouth. Joined Royal Navy as Cadet, 1927. War of 1939-45: Western Approaches, Mediterranean (HMS Orion) and Combined Ops. Comdr, 1947-52, Admiralty, Staff Course, HMS Vigo, in command; Captain, 1952-61, Admiralty, course at IDC and HMS Girdle Ness, in command; Rear-Adm 1962-65, Chief of Staff and Dep. to Chm., Brit. Defence Staffs, Washington. Dir-Gen., Winston Churchill Memorial Trust, 1965-67. *Recreations:* painting, music, sailing. *Address:* Somerset, 19-20 Bermuda. *Club:* Army and Navy. *[Died 13 Jan. 1980.*

GREIG DUNBAR, Sir John; *see* Dunbar, Sir J. G.

GRENFELL, 2nd Baron *cr* 1902, of Kilvey; **Pascoe Christian Victor Francis Grenfell,** CBE 1974; TD 1946; late Colonel KRRC; *b* 12 Dec. 1905; *s* of 1st Baron and Hon. Aline (*d* 1911), *o d* of late Lewis A. Majendie of Hedingham Castle, Essex; *S* father, 1925; *m* 1st, 1932, Elizabeth Sarah Polk (Betty) (whom he divorced, 1946; she *m* 1946, Berkeley Stafford), *o d* of late Capt. Hon. Alfred Shaughnessy and of Hon. Lady Legh; one *s* one *d*; 2nd, 1946, Irene Lilian, *er d* of H. A. G. Cartwright, Buenos Aires; one *d.* Former Chm. of Cttees, House of Lords. Hon. Treasurer: ICAA; Grenfell Assoc. of GB and Ireland. *Heir: s* Hon. Julian Pascoe Francis St Leger Grenfell, *qv. Address:* 13 Liphook Crescent, Forest Hill, SE23. *T:* 01-699 8528. *[Died 24 Sept. 1976.*

GRENFELL, Joyce Irene, OBE 1946; Actress and Writer (all own material, talks, articles, etc.); *b* 10 Feb. 1910; *d* of late Paul Phipps, FRIBA, and late Nora Langhorne; *m* 1929, Reginald Pascoe Grenfell. *Educ:* Claremont, Esher, Surrey. Radio critic on the Observer 1936-39; Farjeon's Little Revue, 1939-40; Farjeon's Diversion, 1940-41; Farjeon's Light and Shade, 1942. Entertained troops, N Ireland, 1942; Welfare Officer, Can. Red Cross, 1941-43; entertained troops in hosps, Algiers, Malta, Sicily, Italy, Egypt, Trans-Jordania, Palestine, Syria, the Lebanon, Irak, Iran, India in 2 tours, 1944 and 1945. Noel Coward's Sigh No More, 1945-46; Tuppence Coloured, 1947-48; Penny Plain, revue, 1951-52. Films from 1949: Poets Pub, Stage Fright, Run for Your Money, The Happiest Days of Your Life, The Galloping Major, Laughter in Paradise, Pickwick Papers, Genevieve, The Million Pound Note, Forbidden Cargo, Belles of St Trinian's, The Good Companions, Here Comes the Bride, Blue Murder at St Trinian's, The Pure Hell of St Trinian's, The Americanization of Emily; Radio: We Beg to Differ, from Sept. 1949. Toured Canal Zone, entertaining troops, 1953. Joyce Grenfell Requests the Pleasure, Fortune Theatre, 1954, also Bijou Theatre, New York, 1955. Appeared on TV, New York, 1955. During 1956: concert tour, N Rhodesia; TV Series, BBC; TV and 20 concerts, USA; during 1957: tour of solo show; 4-week season, London; during 1958: Recital tour, Canada and USA; 3-week season, New York; during 1959: played 13 weeks solo engagement, Sydney, Australia; during 1960: toured USA, Canada, etc.; Seven Good Reasons, Scala Theatre, London; 6-week concert tour Great Britain; during 1962: solo show, Theatre Royal, Haymarket; 4-week concert tour, Great Britain; during 1963: Festival Performing Arts, TV, New York; concert tour (July-Oct.), Hong Kong, Singapore, Australia, New Zealand; during 1964: Two "Joyce Grenfell" (45 min.) shows for BBC2; concert tours of Switzerland and Canada; played in film The Yellow Rolls-Royce; during 1965: four-week season, Queen's Theatre, London; concert tour, England; two more (50 min.) solo programmes for BBC; during 1966: concert tour of Great Britain (7 weeks); tour of Australia, New Zealand; during 1967: concert tour of Great Britain (7 weeks); tour of Colls and Univs, USA; during 1968: concert tour GB; Solo BBC TV show; during 1969: Concert tour Hong Kong, Australia; solo BBC TV show; during 1970: Spring tour of England (8 weeks); concert tour, USA; Concert tour, GB, 1971; Face the Music, quiz, BBC2, 1971-; four TV solo shows, BBC, 1972. President: Soc. of Women Writers and Journalists, 1957-; Time and Talents Settlement; Mem. Pilkington Cttee on Broadcasting, 1960-62. Council Mem., Winston Churchill Meml Trust, 1972-. Hon. Fellow: Lucy Cavendish Coll., Cambridge; Manchester Polytechnic. *Publications:* (with Sir Hugh Casson) Nanny Says, 1972; Joyce Grenfell Requests the Pleasure (autobiog.), 1976; George don't do that, 1977; Stately as a Galleon, 1977; In Pleasant Places (autobiog.), 1979; contributions of light verse to Punch, of poetry to Observer, etc.; further contributions, light articles for various women's magazines. *Recreations:* listening to music; watching birds; finding wild flowers. *Address:* Flat 8, 34 Elm Park Gardens, SW10. *[Died 30 Nov. 1979.*

GRENFELL PRICE, Sir Archibald; *see* Price, Sir A. G.

GRESLEY, Sir Nigel, 12th Bt, *cr* 1611; *b* 22 April 1894; *s* of Sir Robert Gresley, 11th Bt, and Lady Frances Louisa Spencer Churchill (*d* 1954), *e d* of 8th Duke of Marlborough; *S* father, 1936. *Heir: kinsman* William Francis Gresley [*b* 10 Oct 1897; *m* 1923, Ada May, *d* of late George Miller]. *[Died* 13 *Jan.* 1974.

GRESLEY, Sir William (Francis), 13th Bt *cr* 1611; *b* 10 Oct. 1897; *s* of William Stukeley Gresley (*d* 1923) and Maria Elizabeth (*d* 1916), *d* of late James Archer; *S* kinsman, Sir Nigel Gresley, 12th Bt, 1974; *m* 1923, Ada May, *d* of late George Miller. *Heir:* none. *Address:* 59A Grand Avenue, Southbourne, Bournemouth.   *[Died* 11 *July* 1976 (*ext*)

GRESSON, Rt. Hon. Sir Kenneth (Macfarlane), PC 1963; KBE 1958; Judge of Supreme Court of New Zealand 1947-57; President of New Zealand Court of Appeal, 1957-63; Member Judicial Committee of the Privy Council, since 1963; President, Indecent Publications Tribunal (NZ); *b* 18 July 1891; *s* of John Beatty Gresson; *m* 1917, Athole Bruce (*d* 1971); one *s* one *d.* *Educ:* Wanganui Coll. Sch.; Univ. of NZ. LLB 1914. Served European War, 1914-18, with 1st NZ Expeditionary Force (Major). In practice as Barrister and Solicitor, Christchurch, NZ, 1918-47. Chancellor, Diocese of Christchurch (C of E); Dean of Faculty of Law, Canterbury Univ. Coll., 1936-47. Hon. LLD Canterbury, NZ, 1972. *Address:* 20A Idris Road, Fendalton, Christchurch, New Zealand.   *[Died* 7 *Oct.* 1974.

GRESWELL, Richard Egerton, CMG 1963; MBE 1946; with Department of Transport, Taunton, Somerset; *b* 6 May 1916; *s* of late Ernest Arthur Greswell, Wayvile House, Bicknoller, Taunton, Som., and Grace Lillian (*née* Egerton); *m* 1948, Jean Patricia, *d* of Lieut-Col J. R. Hutchison, DSO; two *s* one *d.* *Educ:* Repton Sch.; Hertford Coll., Oxford (MA). HM's Overseas Civil Service in Northern Nigeria, 1938-63. War Service Royal West African Frontier Force (Artillery), East Africa and Burma Campaigns. Lt-Col, 1939-46. Sir John Hodsoll Award, 1966-67. *Publication:* Civil Defence and the County Council, 1967. *Recreations:* shooting, golf. *Address:* Wayvile House, Bicknoller, Taunton, Somerset. *T:* Stogumber 335. *Clubs:* Royal Commonwealth Society; Somerset County (Taunton).   *[Died* 5 *April* 1979.

GREW, Major Benjamin Dixon, OBE 1954; Governor HM Prison, Wormwood Scrubs, 1945-56; *b* 25 June 1892; *s* of Benjamin Grew and Minnie Jane Moore; *m* 1921, Eleanor Flora Enid, *d* of Burton Swift, JP, High Sheriff, Montgomeryshire, 1913; one *d. Educ:* Wordsworth Sch. Joined Scots Guards, 1910; an Old Contemptible; wounded first battle of Ypres, 1914, and battle of Loos, 1915; Northumberland Fusiliers, 1915-23; Egyptian Army, 1917, 1919; Palestine Administration, 1919-22; Dep. Mil. Governor, Nazareth, and Senior Inspector, Nablus, Palestine, 1919-22; Governor HM Prisons: Maidstone, 1930-37; Durham 1937-40; Wandsworth, 1940-45. Bar Student, Mem. Gray's Inn, 1932. New Forest RDC, 1958-64. Chm. of Governors, Priestlands Sch., Lymington, 1963-67. *Publication:* Prison Governor, 1958. *Address:* Latchmoor Farm, Tile Barn Lane, Brockenhurst, Hants.   *[Died* 23 *June* 1977.

GREY, Sir Robin (Edward Dysart), 6th Bt, *cr* 1814; retired banking executive; *b* 12 Nov. 1886; *s* of Edward George Grey; *S* Kinsman, Sir (Harry) Martin Grey, 5th Bt, 1960; *m* 1918, Maude Wilson; one *s* (decd). *Educ:* Rockhampton Grammar Sch., Qld, Australia. Joined The Union Bank of Australia Ltd, as a junior, and retired as Inspector for Queensland. *Heir: g s* Anthony Dysart Grey [*b* 19 Oct. 1949; *m* 1970, Donna Daniels (decd)]. *Address:* 35 Abbott Street, Ascot, Qld 4007, Australia. *Club:* Brisbane (Brisbane).   *[Died* 2 *June* 1974.

GREY-SMITH, Sir Ross, Kt 1966; *b* 22 July 1901; *s* of Francis Grey-Smith and Sybella Anne (*née* Ross); *m* 1932, Betty, *d* of Charles Fairbairn; no *c. Educ:* Melbourne C of E Grammar Sch.; Univ. of Melbourne. Admitted to Victorian Bar, 1926; commenced practice as Solicitor, 1926. Served with RAAF in New Guinea, NEI, and commanded advance Echelon at Labuan landing (Borneo), 1945. Pres., Old Colonists' Assoc., 1948-49. Mem. Race-courses Licensing Bd, 1968-69; Member Committee: Royal Victorian Aero Club, 1931-32; Oaklands Hunt Club, 1932-38 (Vice-Pres., 1955-); Victoria Racing Club, 1938- (Chm., 1962-69); Moonee Valley Racing Club, 1935-38. Notary Public (Pres. Soc. of Notaries, 1962-63). Chm., Wm Drummond Ltd (Jewellers). *Recreations:* racing, shooting. *Address:* 7 Fairlie Court, South Yarra, Victoria 3141, Australia. *T:* 26-2718; 374 Little Collins Street, Melbourne, Victoria 3000. *T:* 67-8481. *Clubs:* Melbourne, VRC, VATC, MVRC, MCC, RACV (all in Melbourne).   *[Died* 14 *July* 1973.

GREY WALTER, William; *see* Walter, W. G.

GRIERSON, John, CBE 1961; British Film Producer; *b* Kilmadock, Scotland, 26 April 1898; *s* of Robert Morrison and Jane (Anthony) Grierson; *m* 1930, Margaret Taylor. *Educ:* Glasgow and Chicago Univs. MA, LLD, Glasgow. RNVR, 1915-19. Associated in formation of Empire Marketing Board and GPO Film Units, Central Film Library, Film Centre, Films of Scotland Cttee, National Film Board of Canada and Group 3. Gen. Man. Canadian Wartime Information Board, 1942-43; Dir Mass Communications, Unesco, 1946-48; Controller Films Central Office of Information, 1948-50. Productions include: Drifters, 1929; Song of Ceylon, 1934; Night Mail, 1936; World in Action Series, 1942-43; The Brave Don't Cry, 1952; Man of Africa, 1953; This Wonderful World, TV, 1961. Hon. DLitt, Heriot-Watt, 1969. Golden Thistle Award, 1968. *Publications:* articles collected in Grierson on Documentary, 1946. *Address:* Tog Hill, Calstone, Calne, Wilts.   *[Died* 19 *Feb.* 1972.

GRIEVE, Christopher Murray, JP, Angus; (writes under pseudonym of Hugh McDiarmid); author and journalist; *b* Langholm, Dumfriesshire, 11 Aug. 1892; *m* 1st, Margaret Skinner; one *s* one *d*; 2nd, Valda Trevlyn; one *s. Educ:* Langholm Academy; Edinburgh Univ. One of the Founders of the Scottish Nationalist Party; Founder of Scottish Centre of PEN Club; regular contributor to many British and foreign newspapers and periodicals. Pres., Poetry Soc., 1976. Hon. Fellow, Modern Language Assoc. of America; Prof. of Literature to Royal Scottish Academy, 1974. Hon. LLD Edinburgh, 1957; Hon. RSA. *Publications:* Prose: Annals of the Five Senses, 1923; Contemporary Scottish Studies, 1926; Albyn, or the Future of Scotland, 1927; The Present Condition of Scottish Arts and Affairs, 1927; The Handmaid of the Lord (a novel, from the Spanish of Ramón Maria de Tenreiro), 1930; Scottish Scene, 1934; At the Sign of the Thistle, 1934; Scottish Eccentrics, 1936; The Scottish Islands, 1939; Lucky Poet (autobiography), 1943, repr. 1972; Poetry: Sangschaw, 1925; Penny Wheep, 1926; A Drunk Man looks at the Thistle, 1926; To Circumjack Cencrastus, 1930; Stony Limits and other poems, 1932; First Hymn to Lenin and other Poems, 1931; Second Hymn to Lenin and other Poems, 1935; The Birlinn of Clanranald (from the Scots Gaelic of Alexander MacDonald), 1935; Direadh, 1939; Golden Treasury of Scottish Poetry, 1940; Cornish Heroic Song for Valda Trevlyn, 1943; Speaking for Scotland (pub. USA only), 1946; A Kist of Whistles, 1952; R. B. Cunninghame Graham, a Centenary Study, 1955; In Memoriam James Joyce, 1957; The Battle Continues; Three Hymns to Lenin, 1957; Burns today and tomorrow, 1959; The Kind of Poetry I Want, 1961; Collected Poems (1920-61), 1962; The Company I've Kept; A Lap of Honour; Celtic Nationalism; The Uncanny Scot; A Clyack Sheaf; More Collected Poems, etc. Trans. The Threepenny Opera, Prince of Wales, 1972; Direadh, 1, 2, 3, 1974; Hugh MacDiarmid Anthology, 1974. *Recreation:* Anglophobia. *Address:* The Cottage, Brownsbank, by Biggar, Lanarkshire.
                                                  [Died 9 *Sept.* 1978.

GRIEVES, Joseph Arthur, QC 1958; **His Honour Judge Grieves;** a Circuit Judge (formerly Chairman of SE Area, Greater London Quarter Sessions), since 1967; *b* 15 July 1907; *s* of Arthur Grieves, Leicester; *m* 1935, Anna Lloyd Amphlett; two *s* two *d. Educ:* Wyggeston Sch., Leicester; Exeter Coll., Oxford. Called to Bar, Inner Temple, 1933; joined Midland Circuit, 1933. Recorder: of Lincoln, Jan.-Aug. 1960; of Birmingham, 1960-64; Deputy Chairman: Middlesex QS, 1965-67; Peterborough QS, 1960-64; Co. London QS, 1964-65. RAFVR, 1941-45. *Address:* 5 Pump Court, Temple, EC4. *T:* 01-353 2628; 53 Central Hill, Upper Norwood, SE19. *T:* 01-670 0455. *Club:* Reform.   *[Died* 25 *Aug.* 1976.

GRIFFIN, Air Vice-Marshal Charles Robert, CB 1978; FRCS; Senior Consultant to the RAF, since 1978 (Consultant Adviser in Orthopaedic Surgery, Royal Air Force, since 1971); *b* 15 May 1919; *s* of Charles Morgan Griffin and Sidney Weir Griffin; *m* 1961, Agnes Ray Turnbull; two *s. Educ:* Morgan's Sch., Castleknock, Co. Dublin; Trinity Coll., Dublin (BA, MB, BCh 1941). FRCS 1957. House Phys./Surg., Adelaide Hosp., Dublin, 1941-42; RAF Medical Br., 1942; served War: RAF stations Abingdon and Biggin Hill; N Africa, Malta and Italy with 72 Fighter (Spitfire) Sqdn and Desert Air Force Trng Wing; Comd and Air Min. appts, RAF Hosp., Wroughton, 1949; Surg. Registrar, Royal Postgrad. Hosp., Hammersmith, 1951; Canal Zone Egypt, Cyprus and Aden, 1952-56; RAF Hosp., Wroughton, 1957-58; Orthopaedic Registrar, Robert Jones and Agnes Hunt Orthopaed. Hosp., Oswestry, 1959-60; RAF Hosp., Wegberg, Germany, 1961-64; PM RAF Hosp., Halton, 1965-67; PA RAF Hosp., Wroughton, 1967-71; Central Med. Estabt, RAF, London, 1971-; Dean of Air Force Medicine, 1976-78.

QHS 1976-. CStJ 1972. *Publications:* contrib. ME section, The Medical History of the Second World War, Vol. III, 1955; contrib. Proc. RSM. *Recreations:* Rugger (from touch-line), fishing, gardening. *Address:* St Julian's Farm, South Marston, Wilts SN3 6RY. *T:* Stratton St Margaret 2367. *Club:* Royal Air Force. *[Died 8 June 1979.*

GRIFFIN, Sir Elton Reginald, Kt 1970; CBE 1967; Vice-Chairman and Chief Executive, Boral Ltd, Sydney, Australia, since 1972 (General Manager, 1947-72); *b* 1906; *s* of late Frank Carlton Griffin, Gordon, New South Wales; *m* 1st, Betty Maud (decd), *d* of late Arthur Vickery, Bellevue Hill, NSW; 2nd, Valerie Catherine, *d* of George Tripp, Qld. *Educ:* Sydney Grammar Sch. Served War of 1939-45: Captain AIF. FCA (Aust.). *Address:* c/o Boral Ltd, 221 Miller Street, North Sydney, NSW 2060, Australia; (private) 17 Ilya Avenue, Bayview, NSW. *Club:* Royal Yacht Squadron.
[Died 16 June 1975.

GRIFFIN, Maj.-Gen. John Arnold Atkinson, DSO 1918; *b* 1891; *s* of late Comdr John Griffin, RN; *m* 1915, Marjorie Annie (*d* 1968), *d* of Rev. Alan Williams; one *s* one *d*; *m* 1970, Astri, *widow* of I. R. L. Stanton. *Educ:* Sherborne; RMC Sandhurst. Served European War, 1914-18 (despatches thrice, DSO); commanded 1st Bn, Lincs Regt, 1935-39; retired pay, 1945; Col Royal Lincs Regt, 1948-58. *Recreations:* yacht racing, shooting. *Address:* Harepath, East Boldre, Brockenhurst, Hants. *T:* East End 267. *Club:* Royal Lymington Yacht.
[Died 25 March 1972.

GRIFFIN, Mrs R. L.; *see* Chapman, Mrs H. W.

GRIFFITH, Cyril Cobham, OBE 1962; MC 1917; President, Engineering Components Ltd, since 1968 (Chairman, 1948-68); *b* 2 Jan. 1891; *s* of Patrick Gill and Josephine Ellen Griffith; *m* 1920, Louisa Ellen Mathews; two *s* (and two *s* decd). *Educ:* Highgate Sch., Highgate, London. Joined Edwin Cooper & Co., 1909. Served European War, 1914-18, with Royal Hants Regt, in Gallipoli and Macedonia (MC, despatches). Rejoined Edwin Cooper, 1919, and subsequently Coopers Mechanical Joints Ltd, 1920. Mem. of Council of Soc. of Motor Manufacturers and Traders Ltd, 1935-39; Dep. Regional Controller, Eastern Region, MAP, 1940-42; Pres., Slough Social Fund, 1951; Chm., Southern Regional Board for Industry, 1949-52. Mem. of the Livery of the Worshipful Co. of Coachmakers and Coach Harness Makers, London. High Sheriff of Bucks, 1959. Greek Military Cross, 1918. *Recreations:* golf, fishing. *Address:* Stoke Lodge Corner, Stoke Poges, Bucks. *T:* Fulmer 2067. *Club:* Royal Automobile. *[Died 31 July 1972.*

GRIFFITH, Hugh Emrys; Actor since 1938; *b* 30 May 1912; *s* of William and Mary Griffith, Marian Glas, Anglesey; *m* 1947, Adelgunde Margaret Beatrice von Dechend; no *c. Educ:* Llangefni Gram. Sch., Anglesey. Banking, 1929-37; Leverhulme Schol., RADA, 1938-39; Bancroft Gold Medallist, RADA, 1939; various West End Productions, 1939-40; 1st Bn Royal Welch Fusiliers, with service in the Far East, 1940-46. Stratford-upon-Avon Festival Season, 1946; Trinculo, Touchstone, Holofernes, First Witch, King of France, and Mephistophiles in Dr Faustus, Cardinal Montichelso in The White Devil, Duchess, 1947; The Playboy of the Western World and Machiavelli's Mandragola, Mercury, 1947 and 1948. The Comedy of Good and Evil, Arts, 1948; Swansea Festival, 1949, King Lear; also King Lear in Welsh, BBC 1949; Lyric and Duke of York's, 1950-51: Point of Departure (Anouilh's Eurydice), The Father, also the same part in New York. Stratford-upon-Avon Festival of Britain, 1951: John of Gaunt, Glendower, and Caliban. Andrew Deeson in Escapade, St James's and Strand, 1952-53; Bellman, in The Dark is Light Enough, Aldwych, 1954; General St Pé, in The Waltz of the Toreadors, Arts and Criterion, 1956-57; W. O. Gant in Look Homeward, Angel, Barrymore Theatre, New York, 1957-58; Count Cenci, in The Cenci, Old Vic, 1959; Azdak, in The Caucasian Chalk Circle, Aldwych, 1962; the Teacher in Andorra, Biltmore Theatre, New York, 1963; Falstaff, in Henry IV, Parts I and II, Stratford-upon-Avon Festival Season, 1964; Prospero in The Tempest, Nottingham Playhouse and European Tour for British Council. *Films include:* A Run for Your Money, The Galloping Major, The Titfield Thunderbolt, The Beggar's Opera, The Sleeping Tiger, Gone to Earth, Passage Home, The Good Companions, Lucky Jim, Ben Hur (American Oscar, 1959), Exodus, The Counterfeit Traitor, Mutiny on the Bounty, The Inspector, Term of Trial, Tom Jones, The Bargee, Hide and Seek, Oh Dad! Poor Dad! Mama's hung you in the Closet, and we're all feeling so sad, How to steal a Million, Danger Grows Wild, A Sailor from Gibraltar, Brown Eye-Evil Eye, Dare I Weep, Dare I Mourn, The Chastity Belt, The Fixer, Oliver!, Start the Revolution Without Me, Wuthering Heights, Cry of the Banshee, Dr

Phibes, The Gingerbread House, Dr Phibes Rises Again, Canterbury Tales, What!, Lead Us not into Temptation, Luther, Final Programme, Craze, Take me High, The Cousin, Legend of the Werewolf, The Passover Plot, Casanova and Co., Joseph Andrews, The Last Remake of Beau Geste, The Hound of the Baskervilles. Various broadcasts and TV incl. series Walrus and the Carpenter, 1965, Tchekov's The Proposal, Uncle Rollo, Clochemerle series, Owen MD, The Joke, A Legacy series, Grand Slam. Hon. DLitt, Univ. of Wales, 1965. *Recreation:* writing. *Address:* c/o International Creative Management, 22 Grafton Street, W1. *Club:* Garrick. *[Died 14 May 1980.*

GRIFFITH, (Llewelyn) Wyn, CBE 1961 (OBE (mil.) 1918); Hon. DLitt University of Wales; Chairman of Council of Honourable Society of Cymmrodorion, 1952-73; Vice-Chairman, Arts Council, 1952-61; *b* 30 Aug. 1890; *e s* of John Griffith, BSc, Dolgellau; *m* 1915, Winifred Elizabeth Frimston; one *s* (and one *s* killed in action, 1942). *Educ:* Grammar Sch., Dolgellau. Asst Surveyor of Taxes, 1909; Asst Sec., Inland Revenue, 1945-52. Served European War, Capt. RWF and General Staff, 1914-19. Chm. Welsh Cttee of Arts Council, 1949-56; Chm., National Book League, 1957-58; Vice-Pres. of London Centre of PEN; Mem., Departmental Cttee on Foot and Mouth Disease, 1952-54. Cymmrodorion Medal, 1970. Croix de Guerre (French), 1918. *Publications:* Up to Mametz, 1931; Branwen, 1934; Spring of Youth, 1935; The Wooden Spoon, 1937; Can Wales Unite?, 1940; Word from Wales, 1941; The Barren Tree and other Poems, 1945; The Way Lies West, 1945; The Voice of Wales, 1946; The Welsh and Their Country, 1947; The Welsh, 1950; Thomas Edwards (Twm o'r Nant), 1953; The British Civil Service, 1854-1954, 1954; Libretto of Menna, opera, by Arwel Hughes, 1954; Wales in Colour, 1958; T. E. Ellis, MP, 1959; The Saga of Pryderi, 1962; (trans.) Tea in the Heather, 1968; (trans.) The Living Sleep, 1976; short stories in Welsh. *Address:* 4 Park View Road, Berkhamsted, Herts. *T:* Berkhamsted 5042.
[Died 27 Sept. 1977.

GRIFFITH, Patrick Waldron Cobham; Chairman, Turner & Newall Ltd, 1976-79; *b* 26 April 1925; *s* of late Cyril Cobham Griffith and Louisa Ellen (*née* Mathews); *m* 1955, Sonia Pamela Clark; one *s* two *d. Educ:* Bryanston Sch. Fleet Air Arm, 1943-46. Engineering Components Ltd, 1946-51; Mem., Aston Martin works team, 1951-54; Engineering Components Ltd: Sales Dir, 1955-58; Vice-Chm., 1959-68; Chm. and Man. Dir, 1968. Turner & Newall Ltd: Dir, 1968; Jt Man. Dir, 1972-74; Dep. Chm., 1974-76. Soc. of Motor Manufacturers & Traders: Chm. of Accessory & Components Cttee, 1974-76; Vice-Pres., 1976-79; Mem. Council, 1974-79. Vice-Chm., Slough Community Centre, 1966-72; Mem., Slough Social Fund, 1966-72; Chm., Slough Duke of Edinburgh Award Cttee, 1967-72. Renter Warden, Coachmakers and Coach Harness Makers' Co., 1979. Won (with Peter Collins): Goodwood 9-hour race, 1952; RAC Tourist Trophy, 1953. *Recreations:* golf, gardening, swimming. *Address:* c/o Turner & Newall Ltd, 20 St Mary's Parsonage, Manchester M3 2NL. *T:* 061-833 9272. *Clubs:* Bath, Royal Automobile, Naval; St James's (Manchester). *[Died 28 Jan. 1980.*

GRIFFITH, Wyn; *see* Griffith, (L.) W.

GRIFFITH-JONES, Sir Eric (Newton), KBE 1962; CMG 1957; QC (Kenya) 1954; Chairman, Commonwealth Development Corporation, since 1972 (Deputy Chairman, 1971-72); Chairman: The Guthrie Corporation Ltd and associated companies; Property Holdings (Pennine) Ltd; Director: Provident Mutual Life Assurance Association; Sutcliffe Mitchell (Insurances) Ltd; *b* 1 Nov. 1913; *s* of late Oswald Phillips Griffith-Jones and late Edith Sydney (*née* Newton); *m* 1946, Mary Patricia, *widow* of F. E. Rowland, and *d* of late Major W. T. Heagerty and of Mrs T. H. Holyoak; one *s* two *d* (and one *s* decd). *Educ:* Cheltenham Coll. Barrister-at-law, Gray's Inn, 1934; Advocate and Solicitor, Straits Settlements, and Johore, 1935; Crown Counsel, SS (Singapore), 1939; Mil. service, 1941-46. Capt., SS Volunteer Force (Efficiency Medal; POW 1942-45). Crown Counsel, Malayan Union, 1946; Federation of Malaya: Sen. Federal Counsel, 1948; Legal Adviser: Selangor, 1948-49, Perak, 1949-51. Actg Sol.-Gen. and Actg Attorney-Gen., 1951. Solicitor-Gen., Kenya, 1952-55. Dep. Speaker, Kenya Legislative Council, 1954-55; Attorney-Gen. and Minister for Legal Affairs, Kenya, 1955-61; Acting Chief Sec. Kenya, 1955-61 (occasions); Dep. Governor, 1961-63; Actg Governor (on occasions), 1959, 1961, 1962, 1963. Chm., Rubber Growers' Assoc. Ltd, 1970-71. Vice-Chm., Perak River Hydro-Electric Power Co. Ltd, 1973-76. Pres., Liverpool Sch. of Tropical Med., 1978- (Vice-Pres., 1975-78). FBIM. *Recreations:* tennis, golf, shooting and water ski-ing. *Address:* 33 Hill Street, W1A 3AR. *T:* 01-629 8484; 120 Fenchurch Street, EC3M 5AA; The Combe, Rogate, near Petersfield, Hants. *T:* Milland 466. *Clubs:* Sussex County Cricket, Royal & Ancient Golf, Liphook

Golf; Nairobi and Karen Country (Kenya); Port Dickson (Malaysia). [Died 13 Feb. 1979.

GRIFFITH-JONES, (John) Mervyn (Guthrie), CBE 1977; MC 1943; His Honour Judge Griffith-Jones; Common Serjeant in the City of London, since Oct. 1964; b 1 July 1909; e s of late John Stanley Griffith-Jones, JP; m 1947, Joan Clare Baker; two s one d. Educ: Eton; Trinity Hall, Cambridge. Called to the Bar, Middle Temple, 1932; Master of the Bench of the Middle Temple, 1958. Served War of 1939-45. Coldstream Guards in Western Desert, North Africa and Italy (despatches). One of the British Prosecuting Counsel at the trial of Major War criminals at Nuremberg, 1945-46; Counsel to the Crown at North London Sessions, 1946-50; one of the Counsel to the Crown at the Central Criminal Court, 1950-59, and First Senior, 1959-64. Recorder of Grantham, 1957; Recorder of Coventry, 1959; Chm., Norfolk QS, 1965-71; a Dep. Chm., City of London QS, 1969-71. Mem. Standing Cttee on Criminal Law Revision, 1958; Councillor, Westminster City Council, 1944-54. Liveryman, Glazier's Company; Lieutenancy, City of London. Mem. of the Pilgrims of Great Britain. One-man exhibitions of paintings, London, 1969, 1971, 1973, 1975, 1976. Recreations: painting, shooting, sailing. Address: 5 Blithfield Street, W8. T: 01-937 1105; Water Hall, Wighton, Wells, Norfolk. T: Walsingham 300. Clubs: MCC, White's, Pratt's. [Died 13 July 1979.

GRIFFITHS, David; Miner; b 22 March 1896; m; one s one d. Educ: Goldthorpe Elementary Sch. Member of the Dearne UDC, 1924-46 (Chairman three times); MP (Lab) Rother Valley Div., West Riding of Yorkshire, 1945-70. Member, Commonwealth War Graves Commission, 1961-70. Formerly Member Don Valley Board of Guardians, and of Swinton and District Isolation Hospital Committee. [Died 13 Jan. 1977.

GRIFFITHS, Gilbert, BA, LLB; Barrister-at-Law; a Deputy Circuit Judge, 1974-77, retired; b 21 July 1901; s of Harry Griffiths, Bilston, Staffs; m 1927, Bertha Verena, d of late Dan Gill, JP, Old Hill, Staffs; no c. Educ: King Edward's Sch., Birmingham; Trinity Hall, Cambridge. BA and LLB 1924; called to Bar, Inner Temple, 1925; joined Oxford Circuit. Recorder of Dudley, 1944-71; Asst Recorder of Birmingham, 1968-71; a Recorder of the Crown Court, 1972-74. Recreation: gardening. Address: 2 Fountain Court, Birmingham B4 6DR. T: 021-236 3882. [Died 5 Feb. 1979.

GRIFFITHS, Rt. Hon. James, PC 1945; CH 1966; b Ammanford, Sept. 1890; m 1918, Winnie Rutley, Overton, Hants; two s two d. Educ: Bettws Council Sch., Ammanford; Labour Coll., London. Hon. LLD University of Wales, 1946. Sec. Ammanford Trade Council, 1916-19; Agent Llanelly Labour Party, 1922-25; Miners' Agent Anthracite Mines Association, 1925-36; Pres., South Wales Miners' Federation, 1934-36; Mem. Executive Cttee of Miners' Federation of Great Britain, 1934-36. MP (Lab) Llanelly, 1936-70; Minister of National Insurance, 1945-50; Sec. of State for the Colonies, 1950-51. Mem. National Executive Labour Party, 1939-59 (Chm., 1948-49); Deputy Leader and Vice-Chm., Parliamentary Labour Party, 1956-59; Sec. of State for Wales, 1964-66. Mem. BBC Gen. Advisory Council, 1952. JP Brecon 1930. Publication: Pages from Memory, 1969. Address: 72 Elmfield Ave, Teddington, Mddx. [Died 7 Aug. 1975.

GRIFFITHS, William; MP (Lab) Moss Side Division of Manchester, 1945-50, Exchange Division of Manchester since 1950; b Moss Side, Manchester, 7 April 1912; m 1949, Decia, o d of Noel and Jean Robinson, Blackpool, Lancs; one s one d. Educ: Manchester Elementary Sch.; private tutor. Profession, consulting ophthalmic optician; Fellow of British Optical Assoc. Joined Labour Party, 1932. Adopted as prospective Parliamentary Candidate, 1937; Parly Private Sec. to Min. of Health, 1950-51, to Min. of Labour, Jan.-April 1951. Served War of 1939-45, in Army, 1940-46; was with 8th Army at Alamein; commissioned in Middle East, 1944. Address: 11 Crossgate Avenue, Manchester M22 7AN. T: 061-998 3165; 24 Onslow Avenue, Richmond, Surrey. T: 01-940 4887. [Died 14 April 1973.

GRIGG-SMITH, Rev. Canon Thomas, MA; Canon Emeritus. Educ: Gonville and Caius Coll., Cambridge (Choral Exhib.); Egerton Hall, Manchester, BA 1912; MA 1916; deacon, 1913; priest, 1914; Curate, Burnley Parish Church, 1913-15; Christ Church, Harwood, 1916; Dir of Religious Educ., Diocese of Manchester, 1916-29; Lecturer in Voice Production and Elocution (1913-29) and Education (1921-29) at Egerton Hall; Vicar of Warley, Yorks, 1929-37; Rector of Chipstead, Surrey, 1939-45; Churches' Cttee Representative, S-E Command, 1942-45; Dir of Education, Diocese of Portsmouth, 1948-52; Portsmouth Cathedral: Canon Residentiary, 1945-55, and

Canon-Chancellor, 1949-55; now Canon Emeritus; Vicar of Yelverton, Devon, 1954-58. OCF. Publications: The Use of the Voice, 1917; The Child's Knowledge of God, 1929; Macmillan Syllabuses of Religious Instruction, 1921-22; For Youth and the Years, 1935; Intinction and the Administration of the Chalice, 1950; Church Teaching for Confirmation and After, 1954; Editor: Prayers for Day and Sunday School, 1921; Training in Faith, Worship and Service, 1922-24; Hosanna, 1930; revised Handbook of Christian Teaching, 1938; Prayers for School, Church and Home, 1951. Recreations: tennis, walking, fishing, riding, music. Address: 2 Place House Close, Catisfield, near Fareham, Hants. T: Titchfield 3003. [Died 18 Oct. 1971.

GRIMES, Ven. (Cecil) John; Archdeacon of Northampton and Canon Residentiary of Peterborough, 1941-59; Treasurer, 1946-59; Examining Chaplain to Bishop of Peterborough, 1939-59; Archdeacon and Canon Emeritus, 1959; b Stratford-on-Avon, 1881; y s of Joseph Grimes, Stratford-on-Avon; m 1st, 1905, Sophie (d 1923), y d of late Charles Alfred Perkin; 2nd, 1925, Caroline Blanche, 3rd d of late Sir G. B. Bowen, KBE, DL; three s. Educ: Stratford-on-Avon; London Univ.; Cuddesdon Coll., Oxford. Trained as Civil Engineer; MIEE; DD 1945; FSA 1959; Resident Engineer at HM Dockyard, Devonport, 1903-7, Asst Engineer, Calcutta Port Comrs, 1907-10; Deacon, 1912; Priest, 1913; St Giles', Reading, 1912-15; Chap., Indian Ecclesiastical Establishment (Bengal), 1915-24; served with Mesopotamia Expeditionary Force in RE as Dep.-Asst and Asst Dir of Military Works, 1917-19; Vicar of St Matthew's, Westminster, 1924-25; Archdeacon of Calcutta and Examining Chaplain to the Bishop of Calcutta, 1926-33; Commissary to Bishop of Calcutta, 1934-51; Vicar of St John the Baptist, Peterborough, 1933-38; Proctor in Convocation for Diocese of Peterborough, 1937-41; Canon of Peterborough, (non. res.), 1937-41; Rector of Thorpe Malsor, Kettering, 1938-41; Rural Dean of Peterborough First Deanery, 1934-38; Surrogate, 1934; Rural Dean of Rothwell Second Deanery 1938-41; Mem. Canon Law Commission, 1939-47; Fellow of Woodard Corporation, 1943-52, 1969-; Select Preacher Cambridge, 1946; Oxford, 1947. Mem. Bd and Admin. Cttee of Church Comrs, 1948-63; Pro-Prolocutor Canterbury Convocation, 1950-59. Publication: Towards an Indian Church, 1946; (ed) Spencer Leeson, 1958. Address: The Vineyard, Minster Precincts, Peterborough PE1 1XU. T: Peterborough 62406. [Died 19 Nov. 1976.

GRIMSDITCH, Herbert Borthwick; Executive editor, The Book of Knowledge, 1951-63; a biographical correspondent of Dictionary of National Biography since 1934, and of The Times since 1938; b 28 Feb. 1898; o s of Frederick J. D. Grimsditch, Liverpool; m 1928, Marie Sophie Gibson; one s. Educ: private sch., Liverpool; University of Liverpool, BA 1st class hons English and University Schol., 1923; MA (by Thesis) 1925. Asst., University Library, Liverpool, 1914-20 (broken by 15 months in RAF Naval kite balloon section); undergraduate, 1920-23; Asst Editor, The Studio, 1923-29; Prof. of English, University of Neuchâtel, Switzerland, 1930-33; freelance writer, chiefly for Cambridge Bibliogr. of Eng. Lit., 1934-36; Asst Editor, The Artist, 1936-38; freelance, chiefly for The Times, 1938-41; Cipher Officer, War Office, 1942; BBC monitoring editorial, 1942-45; on Illustrated, 1945-47; Chambers's Encyclopædia (in charge of make-up), 1947-50; freelance, 1950-51. Publications: Character and Environment in the Novels of Thomas Hardy, 1925; William Hogarth, 1926; Wm Beckford's Vathek (a new trans.), 1929, 1953, 1958; Pitfalls in Everyday French, 1933; Kunitz and Haycraft, British Authors of the Nineteenth Century (part-author), 1937; This is England, 1941; Kunitz and Haycraft, Twentieth Century Authors (part-author), 1942; The Paintings of H. H. Newton, 1952; sundry translations. Contributions to Works of Reference: The Artist's Year-Book, 1937-38; Cambridge Bibliography of English Literature, 1940; Dictionary of National Biography, 3 decennial supplements, 1937, 1949, 1959 (and a 4th in press); Chambers's Encyclopædia, 1950, and rev. edn; Cassell's Encyclopædia of Literature, 1953; The Book of Knowledge, 1954, 1959 (London); The World of Music, 1954; New Universal Encyclopedia, 1959; Children's Encyclopedia, 1961, 1963; The Book of Knowledge, 1963 (New York); Junior Year Book, 1964. Contributions to: The Times; Current Biography (New York); London Mercury; Bookman; Studio; Architects' Journal; Artist; Art Review; Observer; Spectator; Illustrated; John Bull; Everybody's; Liverpool Daily Post, etc. Recreations: intelligent conversation, listening to classical music. Address: 84 West Heath Road, Hampstead, NW3. T: 01-455 9422. [Died 9 Oct. 1971.

GRIMSTON OF WESTBURY, 1st Baron, cr 1964; Robert Villiers Grimston, Bt cr 1952; BSc, ACGI; b 8 June 1897; e s of late Hon. Robert Grimston, Canon of St Albans; m 1923, Sybil (d 1977), e d of late Sir Sigismund Neumann, Bt; three s two d. Educ: Repton; City and Guilds Engineering Coll., London Univ.

Commissioned RGA (6″ Howitzers), 1916; served in Salonika and Palestine, 1916-19. MP (C) Westbury Div. Wilts, 1931-64; Junior Lord of the Treasury, 1937; Asst Whip (Unpaid), 1937; Vice-Chamberlain of HM's Household, 1938-39, Treasurer, 1939-42; Asst Postmaster-Gen., 1942-45; Parliamentary Sec., Ministry of Supply, 1945; Dep. Chm. of Ways and Means, 1962-64. Mem., UK Delegn to Gen. Assembly of UN, 1960. Pres. Urban District Councils Association, 1949-70. Comdr Parly Home Guard, 1941-42. *Heir: s* Hon. Robert Walter Sigismund Grimston [*b* 14 June 1925; *m* 1949, Hon. June Mary Ponsonby, *d* of 5th Baron de Mauley; two *s* one *d*]. *Address:* The Old Rectory, Westwell, Burford, Oxon. *Club:* Carlton.
[Died 8 Dec. 1979.

GRIPENBERG, Georg Achates, MA, LLB; Finnish Diplomat; Finnish Ambassador to Uunited Nations, 1954-56; Permanent Finnish Delegate to UN, 1956-59; *b* 18 May 1890; *s* of Claes Alexis Constantin Gripenberg, Conseiller d'Etat Actuel and Finnish Minister to Stockholm, and Agnes Maria, *d* of Victor von Haartman, Conseiller Intime and Marshal of House of Nobles; *m* 1927, Margaret (DStJ; Knight, Order of Leopold II, Queen Elisabeth medal (Belgium); Croix de Guerre with Silver Star; Chevalier, Legion of Honour (France); FANY service medal; American Red Cross Service medal; Cross of Liberty 1st cl. (Finland)), *d* of Edward Moseley-Williams; one *d*. *Educ:* Helsingfors and Upsala Univs; London Sch. of Economics and Political Science. Entered Finnish Foreign Service, 1918; Chargé d'Affaires, Brussels, 1921, The Hague, 1922, Madrid, 1923; Minister, 1925; Minister in Rio de Janeiro, Buenos Aires, Santiago de Chile, 1929-32; to Court of St James's, 1933-41; to the Holy See, 1942-43; Minister in Stockholm, 1943-54. D *hc*, University of Helsinki, Finland. Cross of Liberty 1st cl. with sword and 3rd cl., Grand Cross White Rose and Finnish Lion, Commemoration Medal Finnish War of Independence, Commemoration Medal 1939-40, 1941-45, Red Cross Medal (Silver) (Finland); KStJ; KCSS Grand Cross; Grand Cross of Northern Star with chain (Sweden); Grand Officer Ismail Order (Egypt); Knight, Order of the Crown (Belgium); Knight, Order of Carlos III, Order of Isabel la Catolica 1st cl. (Spain); Knight of Dannebrog; Officer, Order of the Crown (Italy); George V Silver Jubilee medal; Gustaf V Jubilee medal. *Publications:* Life of Major-General Hans Henrik Gripenberg, 1937; Reminiscences of a Chief of Mission, 1959; London-the Vatican-Stockholm, 1960; Finland and the Great Powers, 1965. *Recreations:* reading, tennis, riding, ski-ing. *Address:* 11 Ostra Brunnsparken, Helsingfors, Finland; PO Box 1365, Southern Pines, North Carolina 28387, USA. *[Died 31 May* 1975.

GRISEWOOD, Frederick Henry, OBE 1959; free-lance broadcaster and lecturer, since retirement, 1948; Outside Broadcasts Department, and headquarters staff, BBC, 1929-48; Announcer, BBC, 1929-37; *b* 11 April 1888; *e s* of A. G. Grisewood, Rector of Daylesford, Worcs; *m* 1st, 1915, Gladys Elizabeth (marriage dissolved), *e d* of W. T. Roffey, Writtle, Chelmsford, Essex; one *d* ; 2nd, 1941, Aileen Croft, *er d* of E. C. Scriven, Leeds, Yorks. *Educ:* Radley; Magdalen Coll., Oxford. Studied singing; opera and concert work in London, Paris, and Munich under Victor Beigel, R. von zur Mühlen and George Henschel; sang bass solo part in first performance in England of Henschel's Requiem at Queen's Hall with Carrie Tubb, Muriel Foster, Gervase Elwes, 1913; served European War, 1914-18, 1/4th Oxon. and Bucks Light Infantry, France, 1915, Adjutant, 1915; invalided out of Army, 1918; Agent for Daylesford Estate, 1918-29. *Publications:* Our Bill, 1934; The World Goes By (Autobiography), 1952; My Story of the BBC, 1959; many articles in magazines and periodicals. *Recreations:* played cricket and tennis for Worcs, hockey for Oxon and Southern Trials; collecting antiques and old glass; fishing and gardening. *Address:* Hewshotts, Liphook, Hants. *T:* Liphook 3229.
[Died 15 Nov. 1972.

GROHMAN, Vice-Adm. H. T. B.; *see* Baillie-Grohman.

GRONCHI, Giovanni; Member of Senate of the Italian Republic; President of Italy, 1955-62; *b* Pontedera, 10 Sept. 1887; *s* of Sperandio Gronchi and Maria (*née* Giacomelli); *m* ; two *c.* *Educ:* Pisa Univ. Served European War of 1914-18 as a Volunteer. A founder of Italian Popular Party (Popolare), 1919; Head of Confederation of Christian Workers, 1919. Elected MP, 1919, and became Under-Sec. for Commerce and Industry, 1922; retired (parliamentary mandate), 1923-42; Minister for Industry, Commerce and Labour, 1944-45; Minister of Commerce, 1945. Elected to Constituent Assembly of Republic of Italy, 1946; Pres. Christian Democrat Parliamentary Group, 1946-48; Speaker, Chamber of Deputies, 1948-55. *Address:* Senato della Repubblica, Rome, Italy; Via Carlo Fea 7, Rome, Italy. *[Died 17 Oct.* 1978.

GROPPER, William; artist; *b* 3 Dec. 1897; *s* of Harry Gropper and Jenny Nidel; *m* 1924, Sophie Frankle; two *s. Educ:* Ferrer Sch. of Art; National Academy of Design; New York Sch. of Fine and Applied Art. Began as artist New York Tribune, 1919; later illustrator of many books; Murals: US Post Office, Freeport, LI; New Interior Bldg, Washington, DC; Northwestern PO, Detroit, Mich.; Schenley Corp., NY; five stain-glass windows for Temple Har-Zion, at River Forest, Ill, 1966. *Represented in:* Metropolitan Museum of Art, Museum of Modern Art, Whitney Museum of Am. Art (all New York); St Louis Museum, Mo.; Museum of Western Art, Moscow, USSR, Hartford Museum, Conn.; Art Institute of Chicago, Ill.; Gimbel Pa Art Coll.; Phillips Memorial Museum, Washington; Newark Museum, NJ; Pa Acad. of Art Museum, Philadelphia, Pa; Walker Museum of Minneapolis, Minn.; Fogg Art Museum, Cambridge, Mass; Los Angeles County Museum, Calif.; Encyclopædia Britannica Collection; National Gallery, Prague; City Museum, Sofia; Brooklyn Museum, New York; Museum of City of New York; Syracuse Univ.; Boston Museum of Fine Art; Brandeis Univ.; IBM Collection; Hirshhorn Collection. Collier prize for Illustration, 1920; Harmon prize, 1930; John Simon Guggenheim Fellowship, 1937; First prizes in lithography, John Herron Art Inst., Ind.; Artist for Victory, Metropolitan Museum of Art; Patron's purchase prize, Los Angeles County Museum, Calif., purchase award, first biennial exhibition drawings, USA (St Paul, Minnesota). Ford Foundation Award, 1965; Tamarind Fellowship Award, 1966-67. Mem., Nat. Inst. of Arts and Letters, 1968. *Publications:* The Golden Land (Political Cartoons), 1927; 56 Drawings of USSR (Paris), 1928; Alay-Oop (Story in Pictures), 1930; Gropper (Collection of Art), 1938; Lidice (Portfolio drawings), 1943; Your Brother's Blood Cries Out (War sketches), 1945; Never to Forget (Warsaw Ghetto), 1947; Portfolio Caucasian Studies, 1950; Portfolio American Folklore Lithographs, 1953; Hound Dog Moses and the Promised Land (with Walter D. Edmonds), 1954; The Little Tailor, 1955; Capricios (Portfolio of lithographs), 1957; Twelve Etchings (Portfolio), 1965; The Shtetl, 1970; illustrated thirty books. *Address:* 33 Hickory Drive, Great Neck Estate, Long Island, NY 11021, USA. *T:* 485-7038. *Club:* Artists Equity.
[Died 6 Jan. 1977.

GROVE, George Alexander, QC 1969; Professor of Equity since 1952, Dean of Faculty of Law, 1968-70, University of Birmingham; *b* 14 Oct. 1908; *s* of Alexander Oliver George Mantle Grove; *m* 1934, Marion Jessie Greaves; one *s. Educ:* King Edward's Sch., Birmingham; University of Birmingham. Solicitor, 1930-46. RAF (Squadron Leader), 1940-46 (despatches). Barrister-at-Law, 1946-; Reader in Equity, University of Birmingham, 1946-52. *Address:* 1 Stone Buildings, Lincoln's Inn, WC2; *T:* 01-242 3118; The Mill House, Naunton, Glos. *T:* Guiting Power 215. *Club:* Garrick.
[Died 25 April 1971.

GROVE, Sir Walter Felipe (Philip), 4th Bt *cr* 1874, of Ferne, Wilts; *b* 18 March 1927; *s* of late Walter Peel Grove (3rd *s* of Sir Walter John Grove, 2nd Bt) and Elena Rebecca, *d* of late Felipe Crosthwaite, Santa Rosa, Lower California, Mexico; *S* uncle, Sir Gerald Grove, 3rd Bt, 1962. Resides abroad. *Heir: b* Charles Gerald Grove, *b* 10 Dec. 1929.
[But his name did not appear on the Official Roll of Baronets.
[Died 22 May 1974.

GROVER, Maj.-Gen. John Malcolm Lawrence, CB 1945; MC; *b* 6 Feb. 1897; *s* of late General Sir M. H. S. Grover, KCB, KCIE; *m* 1930, Betty Chune, *d* of late Maj.-Gen. L. Humphry, CB, CMG, Army Medical Service; one *s. Educ:* Winchester; RMC, Sandhurst. Commissioned King's Shropshire LI, 1914; served European War, 1914-18, France and Belgium (wounded thrice, MC and Bar); Operations NW Frontier, India, 1930-31; War of 1939-45, France and Belgium, 1939-40 (despatches); India and Assam, (Kohima-Imphal operations), 1942-44. Commanded 1st KSLI, 1938-39; GSO1 5th Div., 1940; 11th Inf. Brigade, 1940; 29th Independent Brigade Gp, 1941; 2nd Division, 1941-44; Dir of Army Welfare Services, War Office, 1944-48; retired, 1948. General Sec., Officers' Association, 1948-61. Col KSLI, 1947-55. Commissioner, Royal Hospital, Chelsea, 1957-66. OStJ 1961. *Address:* Bowmans, Crowborough, East Sussex. *Club:* Army and Navy. *[Died 11 June* 1979.

GRUBB, Sir Kenneth (George), KCMG 1970 (CMG 1942); Kt 1953; Chairman, House of Laity, Church Assembly, 1959-70; *b* 9 Sept. 1900; *s* of Rev. H. P. Grubb and M. A. Crichton-Stuart; *m* 1st, 1926, Eileen Sylvia Knight (*d* 1932); 2nd, 1935, Nancy Mary Arundel; three *s* one *d. Educ:* Marlborough Coll. President: CMS, 1944-69; Cheltenham Training Colls, 1948-79; Grubb Inst. of Behavioural Studies; Asia Christian Colls Assoc; Argentina Diocesan Assoc.; Chairman: Commission of Churches on Internat. Affairs, 1946-68; Missionary and

Ecumenical Council, Church Assembly, 1964-67; Royal Foundation of St Katharine, 1957-77; Vice-President: Inst. of Race Relations, 1965-73; British Council of Churches, 1965-68. Vice-Pres. or Trustee of many other institutions including Inst. of Strategic Studies; a Church Commissioner, 1948-73; Hon. Fellow and Trustee, St Peter's Coll., Oxford. Missionary, 1923-28; Survey Application Trust, 1928-39, 1953-; Controller in Ministry of Information, 1941-46; Sec.-Gen., Hispanic Council, 1946-53; Publicity Consultant, Rank Organisation, 1955-59. Director: Argentine Club Ltd; Craigmyle & Co. Ltd, and subsidiaries. United Kingdom Delegate: Unesco, 1954; Atlantic Congress, 1959. Hon. LLD Muhlenberg, Pa, 1951. *Publications:* numerous works on Latin America; World Christian Handbook, 1949, 1953, 1957, 1962, 1968; A Layman Looks at the Church, 1964; Crypts of Power (autobiography), 1971. *Address:* The Moot Farm Cottage, Downton, Salisbury, Wilts SP5 3JP. *T:* Downton 20433. *Clubs:* Canning, Naval and Military; Nikaean.
[*Died 3 June 1980.*]

GRUMMITT, John Halliday; Principal, Royal Academical Institution, Belfast, 1940-59; *b* 29 Jan. 1901; *s* of Charles C. Grummitt and Annie E. Halliday; *m* 1931, Mary Christine Bennett; two *s* two *d. Educ:* Cheltenham; Caius Coll., Cambridge. Schs Sec., Student Christian Movement, 1923-28; Senior Classical Master, Ipswich Sch., 1929-30; Head of Classical Dept, Epsom Coll., 1930-33; Headmaster, Victoria Coll., Jersey, 1933-40. *Publication:* The Sacrament of Life, 1931. *Recreations:* music, bridge. *Address:* Clovelly, Holywood, Co. Down. *T:* H.2434. [*Died 29 Jan. 1979.*]

GRYLLS, Rear-Adm. Henry John Bedford, CB 1956; *b* 24 Aug. 1903; *s* of late C. B. Grylls, CB, CBE, and late Mrs Grylls; *m* 1938, Ruth Ellison, *d* of late S. E. Minnis, CBE; one *s* one *d. Educ:* RN Colleges Osborne and Dartmouth. Midshipman, HMS Durban, 1921; Sub-Lieut 1924; Engineering Courses and Advanced Engineering Course, 1924-28; Lieut (E), HMS London, 1928-31; HM Dockyard, Chatham, 1931-34; Lieut-Comdr (E), HMS Rodney, 1934-37; Comdr (E) 1937; Engineer-in-Chief's Dept, Admiralty, 1938-41; Engineer Officer, HMS Duke of York, 1941-44; HM Dockyard, Devonport, 1944-45; Dockyard Dept, Admiralty, 1945-47; Capt. (E) 1946; Chief Engineer, HM Dockyard, Singapore, 1948-51; Asst Engineer-in-Chief, 1951-54; Rear-Adm. (E) 1954; Engineer Manager, HM Dockyard, Devonport, 1954-58, retired. *Address:* Penshurst, 6 Mornington Park, Wellington, Som. *T:* Wellington 2931.
[*Died 1 July 1978.*]

GUBBINS, Sir Colin McVean, (Maj.-Gen., retired), KCMG 1946 (CMG 1944); DSO 1940; MC; DL; *b* 2 July 1896; *s* of late J. H. Gubbins, CMG, Diplomatic Service, and late Helen Brodie, *d* of late C. A. McVean, JP; *m* 1919, Norah Creina Somerville (marriage dissolved, 1944), *d* of late Surgeon-Comdr Philip Somerville Warren, RN; one *s* (*er s* killed in action, Italy, 1944); *m* 1950, Anna Elise, *widow* of Lieut R. T. Tradin, Royal Norwegian Air Force, Oslo. *Educ:* Cheltenham Coll.; Royal Military Academy. 2nd Lieut RFA 1914; served European War, 1914-19, France, Belgium, North Russia (wounded, MC, 1914 Star with clasp, Order of St Stanislas 3rd Class); Acting Capt., 1915; Acting Major, 1917; Brigade Major, RA, 1921-22, Ireland; GSO3, AHQ, India, 1925-28; Staff Coll., 1928-29; GSO3, War Office, 1931-32; Brigade Major, RA, 1933-34; Brevet Major, 1934; GSO2, War Office, 1935-39; Brevet Lieut-Col, 1939; Acting Col, 1940; Acting Brigadier, 1940; Lieut-Col 1941; Col 1942; temp. Maj.-Gen. 1943; served War of 1939-45 (DSO, CMG, KCMG, Polish Croix de Vaillance) in Poland. (Chief of Staff to Brit. Mil. Mission), France, Norway (raised and commanded Independent Companies, later Commandos), N Africa, Italy, Far East. Raised and commanded Auxiliary Units, June 1940, for special duties under GHQ, Home Forces; Special Operations Exec. (SOE), Nov. 1940-Jan. 1946. Retd pay, 1946. DL Islands Area of the Western Isles, 1975. Officier Légion d'Honneur; Grand Officier Order of Leopold; Belgian Croix de Guerre; Order of Dannebrog, 1st cl.; Royal Order of St Olaf; Grand Officer Order of Orange Nassau and Polonia Restituta; Commander Legion of Merit, USA. Comdr Order of White Lion. *Publication:* (jt author) The Fourth Dimension of Warfare, 1968. *Recreations:* shooting, fishing. *Address:* Obbe, Isle of Harris, Scotland PA83 3TU. *Clubs:* Army and Navy, Special Forces. [*Died 11 Feb. 1976.*]

GUBBINS, Major William John Mounsey, TD 1946; DL; *b* 23 Aug. 1907; *s* of late Col R. R. Gubbins, DSO, JP, The Old Hall, Rockcliffe, Carlisle; *m* 1932, Marjorie Mary, *d* of late T. O. Carter, The Place, Armathwaite, Cumberland; two *s. Educ:* Sherborne Sch. High Sheriff of Cumberland, 1959-60; DL of Cumberland, 1961-. *Recreations:* shooting, fishing, gardening. *Address:* Eden Lacy, Lazonby, Cumbria. *T:* Lazonby 337. *Club:* County (Carlisle). [*Died 30 July 1979.*]

GUEST; *see* Haden-Guest.

GUEST, Air Marshal Sir Charles Edward Neville, KBE 1954 (CBE 1945; OBE 1936); CB 1946; Advisor on Flight Safety, BOAC, since 1961; *b* 1900; *s* of Rev. H. J. Guest; *m* 1945, Moira, *d* of late K. Cameron, Motherwell; two *s. Educ:* King Edward's Sch., Birmingham. AOC No 229 Group, India, 1943-45; AOC Transport Command Group in India, 1945; Senior Air Staff Officer, HQ Air Command, Singapore, 1946-47; AOC No 1 Group, Bomber Command, 1947-48; Asst Chief of the Air Staff (Ops), 1948-52; AOC-in-C, Transport Command, 1952-54; Inspector-Gen. of the RAF, 1954-56, retired. *Recreations:* golf, tennis, philately. *Address:* Knodishall Lodge, Saxmundham, Suffolk. [*Died 23 June 1977.*]

GUEST, Col Hon. Sir Ernest Lucas, KBE, *cr* 1944 (OBE 1938); CMG 1949; CVO 1947; JP; Hon. LLD; Minister of Air, 1939, of Internal Affairs, 1944, of Finance, Defence, and Air, 1946, Southern Rhodesia; *b* 20 Aug. 1882; *s* of H. M. Guest, JP, Kerksdorp, Transvaal; *m* 1911, Edith May Jones, Singapore; (two *s* killed in War) two *d. Educ:* St Andrew's Coll. Sch., Grahamstown; South African Coll., Cape Town. Solicitor; Mem. of firm of Coghlan, Welsh & Guest, Salisbury. Elected to Parliament, 1928 (Charter); Minister of Mines and Works, 1938. Served Anglo-Boer War (King's and Queen's Medal, 5 clasps); European War, German South-West Africa and Western Front (1915 Star, Gen. Service and Victory medals) Lecture tour, 1919, in USA on behalf Dept Public Information. Knight, Order of the Phœnix (Greece); Companion, Order of the White Eagle (Serbia). *Recreations:* shooting, golf. *Address:* PO Box 53, Salisbury, Rhodesia. *Clubs:* Salisbury (Salisbury, Rhodesia); Bulawayo (Bulawayo); Umtali (Umtali). [*Died 20 Sept. 1972.*]

GUI, Vittorio; Commander of the Crown of Italy, 1923; Gold Medal for Culture (Italy) 1957; orchestral conductor; Artistic Counsellor at Glyndebourne, Sussex, 1960-65; *b* 14 Sept. 1885; *m* 1st, 1911, Mary Bourbon del Monte S Maria; three *s*; 2nd, 1936, Elda Salaroli-Enriques; two step *s. Educ:* Rome. Debut as conductor of orchestra, Dec. 1907; has conducted orchestras all over Europe. Founder of Teatro di Torino, 1925; Founder of Orch. Stabile, Florence, and of Maggio Musicale, 1933. Hon. citizen of Pesaro. Order of St Iago y Espada, Portugal, 1921; Comdr of Order of Gustavus Vasa, Sweden, 1941, etc. *Publications:* several musical compositions including songs and an opera for children (Fairy-tale), 1927; also a book of musical essays, articles in magazines, and a study of Boito's Nerone. *Address:* Villa San Maurizio, Fiesole (Florence), Italy. *T:* 59232. [*Died 16 Oct. 1975.*]

GUILLEBAUD, Claude William, CBE 1948; Fellow in 1915, Tutor, 1926-52, Senior Tutor, 1952-56, St John's College, Cambridge; Emeritus University Reader in Economics, Cambridge; *b* 2 July 1890; *s* of Rev. Ernest Delabere Guillebaud and Mabel Louisa Marshall; *m* 1918, Marie-Thérèse Prunner; two *d. Educ:* Repton Sch.; Manchester Univ.; St John's Coll., Cambridge. Adam Smith Prize, 1914; with Supreme Economic Council in Paris, 1919-20; Sec. of Cttee on Prices under Profiteering Acts, 1920-21; Senior Proctor of Cambridge Univ., 1933-34; Chm. of Baking Wages Council, 1940; unlicensed Place of Refreshment Wages Board, 1945, Road Haulage Wages Council, 1947, National Joint Wages Council for the Biscuit Industry, 1942; Independent Mem. of Agricultural Wages Boards for England and Wales, and Scotland, 1956; Member: Council Royal Economic Society; Industrial Disputes Tribunal, 1952; Royal Commission on Scottish Affairs, 1952; East Anglian Regional Hosp. Board, 1958; Bd of Govs, United Cambridge Hosps, 1963; Chm. Cttee of Investigation into Cost of the Nat. Health Service, 1953; Chm. Railway Pay Cttee of Enquiry, 1959; Lay Mem., Gen. Medical Council, 1959. *Publications:* The Works Council: A German Experiment in Industrial Democracy, 1928; The Economic Recovery of Germany, 1933-38; Contributor to second vol. Cambridge History of the British Empire; The Wages Council System in Great Britain, 2nd edn 1962; Economic Survey of the Sisal Industry of Tanganyika, 1959 (3rd edn 1966); Wage Determination and Wages Policy, 2nd edn 1967; Variorum edn of Marshall's Principles of Economics, 1961; The Role of the Arbitrator in Industrial Wage Disputes, 1970. *Recreation:* golf. *Address:* St John's College, Cambridge; 36 Wilberforce Road, Cambridge. *T:* Cambridge 50829. [*Died 23 Aug. 1971.*]

GUILLEBAUD, Walter Henry, CBE 1951; *b* 2 July 1890; *s* of Ernest Delabere Guillebaud and Mabel Louisa (*née* Marshall); *m* 1st, 1916, Alice Betty Stocks (*d* 1919); 2nd, 1921, Dorothy Joyce Young; two *d. Educ:* Monkton Combe Junior Sch.; Repton Sch.; Victoria Coll., Manchester Univ.; St John's Coll., Cambridge Univ. BA Nat. Sci. Tripos; Diploma of Agriculture and Diploma of Forestry, Cambridge. Asst Inspector in Forestry

Branch of Board of Agriculture and Fisheries, 1914; Forestry Commission: Research Officer, 1919; Divisional Officer in charge of Div. 5, 1925; Chief Research Officer, 1928; Actg Dep. Surveyor, Forest of Dean, 1939; Dir of Research and Education, 1945; Dep. Dir-Gen., 1948-53; Mem. of Standing Cttee of International Union of Forest Research Organizations, 1949. Sec., Retired Men's Club, Gerrards Cross, 1962. *Publications:* numerous contributions to technical journals. *Recreations:* gardening, reading. *Address:* Yatesbury, Oval Way, Gerrards Cross, Bucks. *T:* Gerrards Cross 83608.   *[Died 1 Nov. 1973.*

GUINNESS, Henry Samuel Howard; formerly Director, Guinness & Mahon Ltd, Dublin, and Senior Partner in Guinness Mahon & Co., London; *b* 1888; *e s* of late Howard Guinness and Mary Alice (*née* Guinness), Dublin; *m* 1913, Alfhild Holter, Oslo; three *d. Educ:* Winchester; Balliol Coll., Oxford. Banking education in USA and Germany; Hon. Financial Adviser at Foreign Office, 1919-20; joined family banking firm of Guinness Mahon & Co. as a Partner, 1923, Senior Partner, 1937-65; created, simultaneously with his wife, Chevalier Order of St Olav, Norway, 1947. Has travelled extensively in USA, Canada and Scandinavia. *Recreations:* salmon fishing and travelling in Norway. *Address:* 17 College Green, Dublin; 66 Monkstown Road, Monkstown, Co. Dublin; 3 Gracechurch Street, EC3. *Clubs:* Kildare Street (Dublin); Royal St George Yacht (Co. Dublin).   *[Died 10 April 1975.*

GULBENKIAN, Nubar Sarkis; Hon. Counsellor at the Turkish Embassy since 1966; *b* 2 June 1896; *o s* of C. S. Gulbenkian and Nevarte (*née* Essayan); *m* 1st, 1922, Herminia Elena Josefa Rodriguez Feijóo; 2nd, 1928, Dore Freeland; 3rd, 1948, Marie Berthe Edmée, *o d* of Louis de Ayala, Château d'Ay, Marne, France, and of Annette (*née* Gunning). *Educ:* Orley Farm; Harrow; Bonn Univ.; Trinity Coll., Cambridge (MA, LLB); Middle Temple. Attached French Ministry of Supply (Petroleum Section), 1917-21; with Royal Dutch Shell Group, 1922-25; worked with his father in oil and finance, 1925-55; engaged in Middle East Oil negotiations, 1926-28 and 1948-54; Dir, Iraq Petroleum Co., 1917-25 and 1928-38. Commercial Attaché to Iranian Embassy, 1926-51 and again 1956-65. Hon. Pres., Armenian Church Trustees, 1955-, and of Assoc. of Economic Representatives, 1956-. Vice-Pres. Royal Central Asian Soc., 1967-. FRGS. Legion of Honour, Chevalier, 1919, Comdr 1928; Order of St Gregory the Illuminator (with diamonds), 1957; Order of Taj, 1962. *Publication:* (autobiography) Pantaraxia, 1965. *Recreation:* pantaraxia. *Address:* Domaine des Colles, 06 Valbonne, France. *T:* 93.67.63.56; The Old House, Hoggeston, near Bletchley, Bucks; 8/55 Park Lane, W1Y 3DH. *T:* 01-493 1316. *Clubs:* St James'; Travellers' (Paris).   *[Died 10 Jan. 1972.*

GUMBLEY, Douglas William, CBE 1932; ISO; Rafidain, 1934; *b* 14 Aug. 1880; *s* of William Gumbley, AMICE; unmarried. Formerly Indo-European Telegraph Department (Government of India). Served European War, 1914-18, Major Royal Engineers (despatches, OBE), Inspector-Gen. of Posts and Telegraphs, and Dir of Civil Aviation, Iraq, 1919-34; Dir of Civil Aviation, Palestine, 1934-47; Iraq Petroleum Co. Ltd, 1947-52. *Address:* Green Patch, Yew Tree Shute, Sandford, Wroxall, Isle of Wight. *Club:* East India, Sports and Public Schools.
                                                      [Died 5 Feb. 1973.

GUNN, Air Marshal Sir George (Roy), KBE 1967 (OBE 1946); CB 1965; Medical Officer, Margaret Pyke Centre for Study and Training in Family Planning, since 1971; *b* 23 Dec. 1910; *s* of late Donald Gunn, Edinburgh; *m* 1937, Violet Eleanor Munro, Evanton, Ross-shire; one *s* one *d. Educ:* Royal High School and Edinburgh Univ. MB ChB (Edinburgh) 1934; MRCP (Edinburgh); DPH London 1952; FRCP (Edinburgh), 1971. Served War of 1939-45, RAF: Lossiemouth, 1939-43; India and Burma, 1943-45; OC RAF, Hosp., Changi, Singapore, 1952-54; Dep. Dir Med. Org. AM, 1958-61; PMO, RAF Germany, 1961-63; Dir Health and Research, Min. of Defence Air Dept, 1963-65; PMO, RAF Bomber Command, 1965-67; DGMS (RAF), 1967-71; retired 1971. QHP 1965. *Recreations:* golf, gardening, etc. *Address:* 27 Moor Lane, Rickmansworth, Herts. *T:* Rickmansworth 74897. *Clubs:* Royal Air Force; Royal and Ancient (St Andrews).   *[Died 27 Feb. 1974.*

GUNN, Neil M., LLD; writer; *b* 8 Nov. 1891; *m* 1921, Jessie D. Frew. *Educ:* Highland Sch.; privately. Resigned from Civil Service, 1937. *Publications: novels:* Grey Coast, 1926; Morning Tide, 1931; The Lost Glen, 1932; Sun Circle, 1933; Butchers Broom, 1934; Highland River, 1937 (Tait Black Prize); Wild Geese Overhead, 1939; Second Sight, 1940; The Silver Darlings, 1941; Young Art and Old Hector, 1942; The Serpent, 1943; The Green Isle of the Great Deep, 1944; The Key of the Chest, 1946; The Drinking Well, 1947; The Shadow, 1948; The Silver Bough,

1948; The Lost Chart, 1949; The Well at the World's End, 1951; Bloodhunt, 1952; The Other Landscape, 1954; *short stories:* Hidden Doors, 1929; The White Hour, 1950; *essay:* Whisky and Scotland, 1935; *travel:* Off in a Boat, 1938; Highland Pack, 1950; *autobiography:* The Atom of Delight, 1956; various one-act plays. *Address:* Dalcraig, Kessock, Inverness.
                                                      [Died 15 Jan. 1973.

GUNNARSSON, Gunnar; StkF (Grand Cross, Order of Icelandic Falcon); RD (Kt of Dannebrog); FIAL; author; Hon. Professor; Dr.litt.ísl. hc; Dr hc; Hon. President, Bandalag Islenzkra Listamanna, Congress of Cultural Freedom, Icelandic Centre; Hon. Member Mark Twain International Society; *b* Valbjós-stað in Fljótsdal in Norður-Múlasysla. Island (Iceland). 18 May 1889; *s* of Gunnar H. Gunnarsson and Katrin Þórarinsdóttir; *m* 1912, Franzisca Jörgensen; two *s. Publications:* Borgarættin. 1912-14 (Guest the One-Eyed, 1920); Ströndin, 1915; Vargur i véum, 1916; Drengurinn, 1917; Föstbræður, 1918 (The Sworn Brothers, 1920); Sælir eru einfaldir, 1920 (Seven Days' Darkness, 1930); Fjallkirkjan I-V, 1923-28 (Ships in the Sky, 1937; The Night and the Dream, 1938; Icelandic edition in 1 volume with illus by G. G. jr 1951); Svartfugl, 1929 (The Black Cliffs, 1967); Jón Arason, 1930; Vikivaki, 1932; Blindhús, 1933; Jörð, 1933; Hvitikristur, 1934; Grámann. 1936; Aðventa, 1937 (Eng. Advent, Amer. The Good Shepherd, 1940); Heiðaharmur, 1940; Sálumessa, 1952; Brimhenda, 1954; 6 vols short stories; 4 plays. *Address:* Dyngjuvegi 8, Reykjavik, Ísland (Iceland). *Club:* PEN (hon.).   *[Died 21 Nov. 1975.*

GUNTER, Rt. Hon. Raymond Jones; PC 1964; *b* 30 Aug. 1909; *s* of Miles Gunter, Llanhilleth, Mon; *m* 1934, Elsie (*d* 1971), *d* of James Elkins, Nantyglo, Mon; one *s. Educ:* Abertillery and Newbridge Secondary Schs. Railway Clerks Assoc. branch officer, 1929-41; joined Royal Engineers, 1941, as Sapper; commissioned, 1943; Staff Captain 1944-45. MP (Lab) South Eastern Div. of Essex, 1945-50, Doncaster, 1950-51, Southwark, 1959-72; Mem, National Executive of the Labour Party, 1955-66; Minister of Labour, 1964-68; Minister of Power, April-June 1968. Pres. Transport Salaried Staff Association, 1956-64. Chm., Labour Party, 1965. Director: Securicor Ltd, 1969-; Industrial Communications Ltd, 1970-. *Address:* 12 Westminster Palace Gardens, SW1. *T:* 01-222 4424. *Club:* Reform.
                                                      [Died 12 April 1977.

GUNTER, Sir Ronald Vernon, 3rd Bt, *cr* 1901; Temporary Lieutenant RNVR; *b* 8 March 1904; *s* of Sir Nevill Gunter, 2nd Bt, and Clara Lydia, widow of John Pritchard-Barrett of Sydenham; *S* father, 1917; *m* 1st, 1925, Anne (who obtained a divorce, 1932, and *m* 2nd, 1939, William Johnston Dyson), *d* of C. Lovell Simmonds, St John's Coll. Park; two *d;* 2nd, 1932, Dorothy Eleanor Johnston (marr. diss. 1950), *d* of H. E. Capes; 3rd, 1950, Mrs Vera Irene Wynn Parry (marr. diss. 1955), *d* of Sir Henry Philip Price, Bt; 4th, 1955, Phyllis Lesley Wallace, *d* of William St Clair Johnston. *Heir:* none. *Address:* Mill Hamlet Cottage, Sidlesham, Chichester, West Sussex PO20 7NB.
                                                      [Died 27 Jan. 1980 (ext.)

GUPPY, Ronald James, CB 1967; Receiver, Metropolitan Police District, 1974-76; *b* 7 July 1916; *s* of late James Guppy; *m* 1943, Elsie Fuller; one *s* one *d. Educ:* Victoria Coll., Jersey; St John's Coll. Cambridge. Home Office, 1939-67. Served War of 1939-45, in RE and RA. Principal Private Sec. to Home Sec., 1953-55; Asst Sec., 1955; Asst Under-Sec. of State: Home Office, 1961-67, and 1974; Dept of Educn and Science, 1967-69; Sec. Commn on the Constitution, 1969-73. *Address:* Rozel House, Broad Lane, Hampton-on-Thames, Mddx. *T:* 01-979 2409. *Club:* United Oxford & Cambridge University.   *[Died 27 Jan. 1977.*

GURION, David B.; see Ben-Gurion.

GURNEY, Norman William, CBE 1959; JP; retired land agent; *b* 4 May 1880; *s* of James and Elizabeth Gurney; *m* 1910, Millicent Surman (*d* 1960), two *s. Educ:* St George's Sch., Harpenden. County Council, 1922, CA 1934-70, JP 1938, Bucks; High Sheriff, Bucks, 1952. Member: Amersham RDC, 1922-49 (Chm., 1927-41); Beaconsfield UDC, 1922-47 (Chm. 1938); Chairman: Bucks Agricultural Wages Bd, 1948-69; Bucks Local Valuation Panel, 1952-67; Chalfont & District Permanent Building Soc., 1940-; Pres. Bucks Parish Councils Assoc., 1947-65; Chm. Bucks County Council, 1947-62. Horner and Freeman of City of London. Served City of London Rough Riders, S Africa, 1902; Worcs Regt European War, 1914-18, Capt. *Address:* Woodlands, Beaconsfield, Bucks. *T:* 3184.
                                                      [Died 10 Oct. 1973.

GUTHRIE, Douglas James, MD, DLitt, FRCSE, FRCPE, FRSE; formerly Lecturer on History of Medicine, Edinburgh University; Cons. Aural Surgeon, Edinburgh Royal Hospital for

Sick Children; *b* 8 Sept. 1885; *s* of late Rev. William Guthrie, Dysart, Fife; *m* 1st, 1909, Helen (*d* 1950), *d* of James Stark, Glasgow and Rangoon; 2nd, 1953, Margaret Jean, *d* of James Guthrie, Dunblane.*Educ:* Edinburgh, Jena and Paris. MB, ChB (with Hons), 1907; DLitt Edinburgh, 1967. awarded McCosh Travelling Scholarship post graduate study in Hamburg, Jena, Berlin and Vienna; engaged in general practice for six years; MD, 1909; FRCS, 1913; FRCP, 1961; served RAMC for 2 years and later with RAF as Commandant, RAF Officers Hospitals; specialised in Otology and Laryngology, 1919-; retired from practice, 1946; Ear and Throat Surgeon, Royal Hospital for Sick Children and Surgeon to Ear and Throat Infirmary, 1919; Lecturer on Diseases of Ear, Nose and Throat, School of Medicine of Royal Colleges, Edinburgh, 1920; Lecturer on History of Medicine, University of Edinburgh, 1945-56; FRSM 1920, and since then Member of Council, Sections of Otology and Laryngology, 1956-57; President, Section of Otology, 1936-37, Section History of Medicine, 1956-57; Assistant Editor, Journal of Laryngology, 1921-29; President: Edinburgh Branch, BMA, 1935-36; Founder and Hon. President Scottish Society of History of Medicine, 1948; Royal Physical Society; FSA; Hon. FRSGS, 1958; Vice-President, Royal Society of Edinburgh, 1960; President, British Society for History of Medicine, 1965. Hon. FRSM 1967. *Publications:* A History of Medicine, 1945; Lord Lister, His Life and Doctrine, 1949; From Witchcraft to Antisepsis (Clendening Lectures, University Kansas), 1954; Janus in the Doorway, 1963; and many papers on otolaryngology and on the history of medicine. *Recreations:* travel, photography, writing. *Address:* 21 Clarendon Crescent, Edinburgh EH4 1PU. *T:* 031-332 1820. *Club:* New (Edinburgh).
[*Died* 8 June 1975.

GUTHRIE, Sir Giles (Connop McEacharn), 2nd Bt, *cr* 1936; OBE 1946; DSC 1941; JP; Merchant Banker; *b* 21 March 1916; *s* of Sir Connop Guthrie, 1st Bt, KBE, and late Eila, *d* of Sir Malcolm McEacharn of Galloway House, Wigtownshire; *S* father, 1945; *m* 1939, Rhona, *d* of late Frederic Stileman and Mrs Stileman, Jersey, CI; two *s* (and one *s* decd). *Educ:* Eton; Magdalene Coll., Cambridge. Winner with late C. W. A. Scott, of Portsmouth-Johannesburg Air Race, 1936; Served War of 1939-46 in Fleet Air Arm, Lieutenant Commander, 1943. Chairman and Chief Executive, BOAC, 1964-68; Mem. Bd, BEA, 1959-68; Chm., Air Transport Insurance Ltd, Bermuda, 1969-71; formerly: a Man. Dir, Brown Shipley & Co. Ltd; Dep. Chm., North Central Finance Ltd; Director: Prudential Assurance Co; Radio Rentals Ltd, and other cos. Governor, The London Hospital, 1965-68; a Vice-Chairman, 1968. JP West Sussex, 1955. *Recreations:* Conservation and Dendrology. *Heir:* *s* Malcolm Connop Guthrie [*b* 16 Dec. 1942; *m* 1967, Victoria, *o* *d* of late Brian Willcock and of Mrs Willcock, Belbroughton, Worcs; one *s* one *d*]. *Address:* Rozel, Jersey, Channel Islands. *Clubs:* MCC; Royal Yacht Squadron (Cowes).
[*Died* 31 Dec. 1979.

GUTHRIE, Prof. Malcolm, PhD, BSc; FBA 1968; Professor of Bantu Languages, University of London, 1951-70, Professor Emeritus 1970; Head of Department of African Languages and Cultures, School of Oriental and African Studies, 1950-68; *b* 10 Feb. 1903; *s* of Malcolm Guthrie and Maude Louise Lindeboom; *m* 1931, Margaret Helen Near (*d* 1968). *Educ:* Northgate, Ipswich; University of London. Missionary, Belgian Congo, 1932-41; Lecturer in Bantu Languages, London, 1942-47; Reader in Bantu Languages, 1947-51. *Publications:* Grammaire et Dictionnaire de Lingala, 1939; The Classification of the Bantu Languages, 1948; Bantu Word Division, 1948; The Bantu Languages of Western Equatorial Africa, 1953; Comparative Bantu, Vol. 1, 1967, vols 3 and 4, 1970, vol 2, 1971; Collected Papers in Bantu Linguistics, 1970; articles in Bulletin of School of Oriental and African Studies, Africa, African Language Studies. *Address:* Brambletye, Cowden, Kent.
[*Died* 22 Nov. 1972.

GUTHRIE, Robin Craig; RP 1961; portrait, genre and landscape painter and draughtsman; Member of: Royal Society of Portrait Painters; Society of Mural Painters; Past Member of NEAC; *b* Harting, Hampshire, 15 June 1902; *s* of late James Joshua Guthrie and of Marion Stuart Craig; *m* Cathleen Maltby; one *s*; *m* Deborah Dering; one *d* (one *s* decd). *Educ:* Home; Slade Sch.; University College, London. Exhibited first at Goupil Gallery, also at New English Art Club, Royal Academy, etc., and abroad; One-man exhibitions: Goupil Gallery, 1926, Fine Art Society, 1939, Colnaghi's Gallery, 1946; paintings and drawings have been acquired by or presented to the Tate Gallery, Victoria and Albert Museum, National Portrait Gallery, British Museum, Contemporary Art Society, the Duveen Fund, Manchester Art Gallery, Manchester Whitworth Institute, Stoke-on-Trent Art Gallery, National Gallery of Canada, Fogg Art Museum, Cambridge, Mass., USA, and National Gallery of New South

Wales; National War Records Collection; Director of Boston Museum School of Fine Art, USA, 1931-33; Instructor in drawing at the Royal College of Art, 1950-52; Instructor: St Martin's School of Art; City and Guilds of London Art School. Has painted Royal and commemorative occasions for Royal Marines, Royal Scots Greys and Royal Tank Regiments. *Publications:* illustrated editions from the Pear Tree Press, the Morland Press, etc. *Recreation:* fishing. *Address:* 1 Sydney Close, 76 Fulham Road, SW3. *T:* 01-584 1726. *Club:* Chelsea Arts.
[*Died* 27 Jan. 1971.

GUTHRIE, Sir (William) Tyrone, Kt 1961; Chancellor, Queen's University, Belfast, 1963-70; *b* 2 July 1900; *s* of Thomas Clement Guthrie, surgeon; *m* 1931, Judith, *d* of E. G. Bretherton; no *c*. *Educ:* Wellington Coll.; St John's Coll., Oxford. Administrator Old Vic and Sadler's Wells, 1939-45; Director of the Old Vic. 1951-52; founded Tyrone Guthrie Theatre, Minneapolis, 1963. Many productions in London, New York, also Australia, Finland, Israel; Repertory and Tour, including musical comedy, farce, opera, but mostly of classical nature. Hon. Fellow, St John's Coll., Oxford, 1964. Hon. DLitt: Trinity Coll., Dublin, 1964; Queen's Univ., Belfast; St Andrews Univ.; Franklyn and Marshall Univ., Penn., USA; University of Western Ontario; Ripon Coll., Wisconsin, USA; Citadel Military Coll., Charleston, SC. *Publications:* Squirrel's Cage, The Flowers Are Not For You To Pick, and Matrimonial News (microphone plays), 1931; Theatre Prospect, 1932; Top of the Ladder, 1950; A Life in the Theatre, 1960; A New Theatre, 1964; In Several Directions, 1965; (ed) Three Plays of Armand Salacrou, 1968. *Address:* Annagh-ma-Kerrig, Doohat, Newbliss, Co. Monaghan, Eire.
[*Died* 15 May 1971.

GUTT, Camille; Belgian Minister of State; became one of partners in Banque Lambert, 1951; *b* Brussels, 14 Nov. 1884; *s* of Max Gutt and Pauline Schweizer; *m* 1906, Claire Frick; one *s* (and two *s* killed on active service). *Educ:* Brussels University (graduated in Political and Social Sciences, 1904; Doctor of Law, 1906). Barrister and journalist, 1906; Volunteer in Belgian Army, 1914-18; Secretary-General of Belgian War Material Purchasing Commission, London, 1916; Secretary-General of Belgian Delegation to Reparations Commission, Aug. 1919; Chief Secretary (Chef de Cabinet) to Belgian Minister of Finance, 1920. Assistant Delegate for Belgium to Reparations Commission, 1924; Assistant to M. Francqui, Chancellor of the Exchequer, 1926; Belgian Member of the Young Cttee, Jan. 1929; Plenipotentiary for Belgium in discussions which led to an agreement with Germany about reimbursement of the Marks of Occupation in June 1929; Plenipotentiary for Belgium in negotiations connected with the Hoover Moratorium, 1931; sent on official mission to USA, May 1934; Minister of Finance in the Theunis Cabinet, Nov. 1934; Minister of Finance in the Pierlot Cabinet, Feb. 1939; arrived in London, Aug. 1940; Minister of Finance, 1939-45, National Defence, 1940-42, Communications, 1940-42, and Economic Affairs, 1940-45; Man. Dir International Monetary Fund, 1946-51; President International Chamber of Commerce, 1955. Grand Cordon de l'Ordre de Léopold; Grand Cross of the Order of the British Empire (GBE); Grand Cordon de l'Ordre d'Orange Nassau; Grand Cordon de l'Ordre de la Couronne de Chêne; Grand Cordon de l'Ordre pour le Mérite; Grand Officier de l'Ordre de la Légion d'Honneur; and various other distinctions including war medals, 1914-18. *Publications:* Pourquoi le franc belge est tombé, 1935; numerous articles in daily newspapers and magazines. *Recreation:* racing. *Address:* 70 avenue Bel Air, Brussels.
[*Died* 7 June 1971.

GUTTMANN, Sir Ludwig, Kt 1966; CBE 1960 (OBE 1950); MD, FRCP, FRCS; FRS 1976; FRSA; Emeritus Consultant, Stoke Mandeville Hospital; Director: National Spinal Injuries Centre, Stoke Mandeville Hospital, Aylesbury, 1944-66; Stoke Mandeville Sports Stadium for the Paralysed and other Disabled, since 1969; Consultant to: Duchess of Gloucester House (Ministry of Labour) 1950; Star and Garter Home for Ex-Servicemen, Richmond (Vice-President, 1976); Chasely Home for Ex-Servicemen, Eastbourne; *b* 3 July 1899; *s* of Bernhard and Dorothea Guttmann; *m* 1927, Else (*née* Samuel) (*d* 1973); one *s* one *d*. *Educ:* Breslau and Freiburg Universities (Germany). MD Freiburg, 1924; MRCP, 1947; FRCS, 1961; FRCP, 1962. Lecturer in Neurology, University of Breslau, 1930; Director, Dept of Neurology and Neuro-Surgery, Jewish Hospital, Breslau, 1933-39; Research Fellow, Dept of Surgery, Oxford Univ. (Senior Common Room, Balliol Coll.) 1939-43; Founder of Stoke Mandeville Games, 1948. First Albee Memorial Lecturer (Kessler Institute, New Jersey, USA), 1952; Ord. Professor (now Emeritus), Univ. of Cologne, Germany, 1954. FRSocMed; Member: British Assoc. of Neurologists, 1947; British Physiological Assoc., 1947; Hon. Member of Medical Societies. President: Med. International Society of Paraplegia,

1961-69; British Sports Association for the Disabled. 1962; International Sports Association for the Disabled, 1966. OStJ 1957. Hon. Freeman, Borough of Aylesbury, Bucks, 1962. Hon. DChir Durham, 1961; Hon. LLD Dublin, 1969; Hon. DSc Liverpool, 1971; Hon. FRCP(C). Commander de l'Ordre Oeuvre Humanitaire, France, 1952; First Recipient of Rehabilitation Prize, World Veterans Federation, 1954; Rehabilitation Prize, Reichsbund, Germany, 1977; Gold Medal for Verdiensten, Holland, 1958; Commendature dell' ordine Al Merito, Italy, 1961; Officer, Order Oranje-Nassau, Holland, 1962; Grand Cross of Merit, Germany, 1962; Commandeur de l'Ordre de Léopold II, Belgium, 1963; Ordre du Mérite Combattant, France, 1963; Order of the Rising Sun, Japan, 1964; Order of Merit, Bavaria, 1971; Golden Star, Order of Merit, Germany, 1972; Olympic Gold Medal of Labour, Belgium Govt, 1972; Gold Medal, Dept. of Culture, Finland, 1975; Medaille d'Or du Sport et Jeunesse, France. Institutions and streets named for him: Dr Guttmann Laane, Doorn, Holland, 1953; Instituto Guttmann for Spinal Cord Injuries, Barcelona, 1965; Ludwig Guttmann Strasse, Heidelberg, 1973; Sir Ludwig Guttmann Institute for Spinal Cord Injuries and Neurological Rehabilitation, Tel Hayomer Hosp., Israel, 1978. *Publications:* Vol. VII Handbuch der Neurologie (Germany), 1936; Surgical Practice Vols 2 and 6, 1948 and 1949; Vol. Surgery, Official British Medical History of Second World War, 1953; Modern Trends in Diseases of the Vertebral Column, 1959; (ed) Neuro-Traumatology, vol. II, 1971; Spinal Cord Injuries: Comprehensive Management and Research, 1973. Editor International Journal, Paraplegia, 1963-. *Recreations:* sport, photography, travelling. *Address:* Menorah, 26 Northumberland Avenue, Aylesbury, Bucks. *T:* Aylesbury 24901. *Club:* Athenæum.   [*Died* 18 *March* 1980.

GUY, Rt. Rev. Basil Tudor, MA; Bishop of Gloucester since 1962; *b* 9 March 1910; *s* of late Basil Guy and Edith Walrond Guy; *m* 1939, Mary Lilian Joan Ritson; two *s* one *d. Educ:* Forest Sch.; Keble Coll., Oxford; Wells Theological Coll. Ordained, 1934; Asst Curate, Wanstead, 1934-41; Vicar of Bradninch, Devon, 1941-46; Vicar of Tavistock, Devon, 1946-56; Prebendary of Exeter Cathedral, 1952-56; Archdeacon of Bedford, 1956-58; Examining Chaplain: to Bp of Exeter, 1952-56; to Bp of St Albans, 1956, Bishop Suffragan of Bedford, 1957-62. *Recreations:* cricket, golf, fishing, drama. *Address:* Palace House, Pitt Street, Gloucester GL1 2BQ. *T:* Gloucester 24598. *Club:* United Oxford & Cambridge University.
                                                        [*Died* 2 *March* 1975.

GUY, Hon. James Allan, CBE 1968; JP; Senator, Australian Parliament, 1949 and 1951, retired 1956; *b* Launceston, Tas, 30 Nov. 1890; *s* of James Guy, Senator in Commonwealth Parliament, and Margaret McElwee; *m* 1st, 1916, Amy Louisa Adams (*d* 1951); one *s*; 2nd, 1952, Madge Kernohan. *Educ:* Tasmanian State Education. Member for Bass in Tasmania State Parliament, 1916-29; Chief Secretary and Minister for Mines, 1923-24; Chief Secretary and Minister for Railways, 1924-28; Deputy Premier, 1925-28; acting Premier, July 1926-Dec. 1926; Deputy Leader of the Opposition, June 1928-Sept. 1929. Member for Bass in Commonwealth Parliament, 1929-34; Asst Minister of State for Trade and Customs, 1932-34; Member for Wilmot, 1940-46; Government Whip, 1941-42; Opposition Whip, 1942-46. Represented Tasmanian Government at the opening of the Commonwealth Parliament at Canberra, May 1927; Member: Commonwealth Parliamentary Joint Cttee of Public Accounts, 1929-31; Commonwealth Parliamentary Standing Cttee on Broadcasting; Senate Standing Cttee on Regulations and Ordinances, 1950-55; Empire Parliamentary Delegation visiting Great Britain, Canada, and America, 1943; Temp. Chairman of Cttees, 1940. Life Title of "Honourable" conferred by King George VI, 1936. Alderman Launceston City Council, 1928-31. *Recreations:* motoring, bowling. *Address:* 2 Hastings Place, Sylvania Waters, NSW 2224, Australia. *T:* Sydney 522.7289.   [*Died* 16 *Dec.* 1979.

GUY, Oswald Vernon, CBE 1947; DSO 1918; MA; *b* 15 Dec. 1890; *s* of late Rev. Canon D. S. Guy; *m* 1920, Ethel Frances (*d* 1964), *d* of late Colonel R. K. Teversham, DSO, OBE. *Educ:* Marlborough; Jesus Coll., Cambridge. 9th PWO West Yorkshire Regt, Sept. 1914; Tank Corps, 1917-19 (Major, DSO, MC and bar, Legion of Honour). Secretary, Cambridge Univ. Appointments Board, 1932-52; Temp. Assistant Secretary Ministry of Labour, 1940-44. *Address:* Teversham, Orchard Close, Ferndown, Dorset.   [*Died* 16 *Feb.* 1973.

GUY, Sydney Slater, FIMechE, MIEE, MSAE; Founder of Guy Motors Ltd (1913), Chairman and Managing Director of the Company, retired 1957 (organizations acquired by Jaguar Co. in 1961, subsequently by Leyland Motor Group); *b* 31 Oct. 1884; *m* Leila Brooks, Hale Barns; two *s* one *d.* Pupil, Bellis & Morcom;

Repairs Manager, Humber Ltd, 1905-08; Works Manager, Sunbeam Motor Car Co. Ltd, 1908-13. Council Member, Society Motor Manufacturers, for 33 years; Vice-President 1928-29; Hon. Member, 1957. Responsible for first British V8 cylinder car in 1919 and first rear engined 4 wheel driven armoured car in 1937. Past President: Flatcoated Retriever Association; Leintwardine Fishing Club. Liveryman Worshipful Company of Carmen. FRSA. *Publications:* various. *Recreations:* fly fishing, shooting, photography. *Address:* Sauchieleigh, Albrighton, Salop. *T:* Albrighton 2288. *Clubs:* Royal Automobile; Royal Anglesey Yacht.   [*Died* 21 *Sept.* 1971.

GWATKIN, Frank T. A. A.; see Ashton-Gwatkin.

GWATKIN, Brig. Sir Norman (Wilmshurst), GCVO 1963 (CVO 1946; MVO 1937); KCMG 1964; DSO 1944; Comptroller, Lord Chamberlain's Office, 1960-64; Secretary and Registrar of the Order of Merit since 1963; Extra Equerry to King George VI, 1950-52, to the Queen since 1952; *b* 2 Aug. 1899; *s* of H. F. W. Gwatkin; *m* 1957, June Wilson; one adopted *d. Educ:* Clifton; Royal Military Coll. Coldstream Guards, 1918; Adjt 1st Bn Coldstream Guards; Adjt RMC, Sandhurst, 1930; Bt Major, 1935; Lieut-Colonel, 1940; retired pay, 1946. *Recreations:* shooting, fishing. *Address:* Bedwells, Knodishall, Saxmundham, Suffolk. *T:* Leiston 830647. *Club:* United Service and Royal Aero.   [*Died* 31 *July* 1971.

GWILLIM, Calvert Merton, MD, FRCS, FRCP; Obstetric Surgeon, St George's Hospital; Consulting Physician, Lying-in Hospital, York Road; Surgeon, Samaritan Hospital for Women; retired. *Educ:* St Bartholomew's Hospital; St George's Hospital. DPH 1923; MD London (Obst. and Gyn.), 1924; MD (Med.), 1924; MRCS, LRCP 1921; MRCP, 1925; FRCS, 1927; FRCP, 1940; FRCOG, 1942. Formerly: Gynæcological Registrar and Obst. Tutor and Asst Medical Registrar, St George's Hospital; Registrar-General, Lying-in Hospital, York Road. FRSocMed; Member BMA. *Address:* 26 Alexandra Road, Reading, Berks RG1 5PD.   [*Died* 2 *Sept.* 1972.

GWILT, Richard Lloyd, CBE 1953; FFA, FIA, FRSE; formerly General Manager and Actuary, Scottish Widows Fund and Life Assurance Society (retired 1961); Director, Scottish Widows' Fund; *b* 25 July 1901; *m* 1926, Marjory, 2nd *d* of late David Beveridge Mair; three *s* one *d. Educ:* George Watson's Coll., Edinburgh. FFA 1922; FIA 1923; President: Insurance Society of Edinburgh, 1951-52; Faculty of Actuaries, 1952-54. Chairman: Associated Scottish Life Offices, 1956-58; Scottish Hospital Endowments Research Trust, 1954-66; Dir, Scottish-American Investment Co. Ltd, 1939-69. *Publications:* contributions to actuarial journals. *Recreation:* fishing. *Address:* 23a Dick Place, Edinburgh. *T:* 031-667 6263. *Club:* Scottish Mountaineering.   [*Died* 21 *Aug.* 1972.

GWYER, Barbara Elizabeth, MA; Hon. Fellow, St Hugh's College, Oxford, since 1946; *o d* of late John Edward Gwyer. *Educ:* The Grove Sch., Highgate; Lady Margaret Hall, Oxford. Educational Organiser, WRCC Educational Dept, 1906-08; Vice-Warden, Ashburne Hall, Manchester Univ., 1910-13; Warden, University Hall, Leeds, 1917-24; Principal, St Hugh's Coll., Oxford, 1924-46. *Address:* New Patch, Stokenchurch, High Wycombe, Bucks. *T:* Radnage 3368.
                                                        [[*Died* 16 *Feb.* 1974.

GWYNN, Denis Rolleston, DLitt, MRIA, FRHistS; Member of the Irish Academy of Letters; Research Professor of Modern Irish History, University College, Cork, 1946-63; Editor Cork University Press, 1954-63; *b* 1893; *s* of late Stephen Gwynn; *m* 1963, Alice, widow of John A. McEnery and *d* of late Dr Edward Trudeau and Lady Lavery. *Educ:* Clongowes Wood Coll.; London University; National University of Ireland. Served in France as Lieut, Royal Munster Fusiliers; attached Ministry of Information; Assistant Editor Everyman and Review of Reviews, and Editor National Press Agency, 1918-20; spent three years as a journalist in France; London Editor, The Freeman's Journal, 1924; editorial staff, Westminster Gazette, 1925; literary adviser and a Director of Burns, Oates and Washbourne and Editor of the Dublin Review, 1933-39; contributor to leading reviews and to Encyclopædia Britannica and other encyclopædias. *Publications:* The Catholic Reaction in France; The Action Française Condemnation; The Irish Free State, 1922-27; The Struggle for Catholic Emancipation; A Hundred Years of Catholic Emancipation; Daniel O'Connell; Cardinal Wiseman; Edward Martyn and the Irish Revival; The Life and Death of Roger Casement; The Life of John Redmond; Pius XI; De Valera; The O'Gorman Mahon; The Vatican and War in Europe; The Second Spring; Lord Shrewsbury, Pugin and the Catholic Revival; Father Dominic Barberi; Bishop Challoner; Young Ireland and 1848; O'Connell, Davis and the

Colleges Bill; The History of Partition, 1950; Father Luigi Gentili, 1951; Thomas Francis Meagher, 1962; (ed) Dr Walter McDonald's Reminiscences of a Maynooth Professor, 1967. *Address:* Rosenallis, Seamount Road, Malahide, Co. Dublin.
[Died 10 *April* 1971.

GWYNNE, Lieut-Colonel Sir Roland Vaughan, Kt 1957; DSO 1917; DL; JP; *s* of late James Eglinton Gwynne and Mary Earle Gwynne of Folkington Manor, Polegate, Sussex, and 97 Harley Street, W1; unmarried. *Educ:* privately; Trinity Hall, Cambridge. Called to Bar, Inner Temple, 1910; practised Probate and Divorce Courts; served in the Sussex Yeomanry since 1904; European War, commanded the 10th Queen's Royal West Surrey Regt (twice wounded, despatches, DSO); High Sheriff of Sussex, 1926-27; Mayor of Eastbourne, 1928-29, 1929-30, and 1930-31; Chairman, Hailsham Rural District Council, 1924-47; Alderman and Chairman of the East Sussex Co. Council, 1937-40; JP Sussex and Eastbourne; Chairman Hailsham Justices, 1932-, and Chairman Eastbourne Justices. *Address:* Wootton Manor, Folkington, Polegate, Sussex. *TA:* Gwynne, Polegate. *T:* Polegate 2036.   *[Died* 15 *Nov.* 1971.

GYEE, Sir Maung, Kt 1942; *b* 1886; *s* of U San U of Shwegyin; *m* Ma Aye Yee; two *s* three *d. Educ:* Rangoon, Calcutta, London and Oxford. MA Calcutta, 1909; called to English Bar (Middle Temple), 1911. Minister of Education, Burma Government, 1923-25; Delegate to Round Table Conference, 1931; to Coronation, 1937; President of the Senate, 1937-40; Counsellor to Governor of Burma, 1940-42; Judge of Supreme Court, 1943-44; Minister for Public Works and Rehabilitation, Executive Council, 1946-47; High Commissioner for Burma in the UK, 1947; Ambassador of Republic of Burma in UK, Jan.-Oct. 1948. President Burma branch Empire Parliamentary Association. *Address:* 313 Prome Road, Rangoon, Burma.
[Died 16 *July* 1971.

H

HAARHOFF, T. J., BA (Cape), BLitt (Oxon), LittD (Amsterdam); FRSA (London); FIAL (Switzerland); Hon. DLitt: Natal; Cape Town; Emeritus Professor of Classics, University of the Witwatersrand, Johannesburg, South Africa; formerly South African Representative on UNESCO; a Governor of SA Broadcasting Corporation; *b* 30 April 1892; *s* of Rev. Dr B. J. Haarhoff, Inspector of Schools, Cape Province, and Magdalena Johanna Marais, Paarl, CP; *m* Jessie Kilburn Davis, MA (Oxon); two *s. Educ:* S. A. College Sch. and College, Cape Town; Porter Scholarship (Hon.) and Rhodes Scholarship, 1913; Worcester Coll., Oxford. Lecturer in English Literature, University, Cape Town, 1916; Lecturer in Classics, University, Cape Town, 1919. *Publications:* Schools of Gaul, 1920; Primi Gradus, 1922; Studies in Roman Imperialism (with Jan H. Hofmeyr), 1921; Die Romeinse Boer, 1925; Die Klassieke in S. Afrika, 1930; Tria Corda (Afrikaans Verse), 1930; Vergil in the Experience of S. Africa, 1931; Coming of Age: Essays in S. African Citizenship and Politics (with J. H. Hofmeyr and others), 1930; The Holistic Attitude in Education, 1932; Die liefde van Catullus (narrative poem), 1933; The Achievement of Afrikaans (with C. M. van den Heever), 1934; The Short Story in the Classics (Afrikaans), 2 vols, 1934; Afrikaans, its origin and development, 1936; Briewe aan Reinhard (Travels in the Aegean); The Stranger at the Gate: a study in racial co-operation, 1938; Life and Thought in the Greek and Roman World (with M. Cary), 1940; SA and the Crisis of Civilisation, 1940; Spiritual Evolution in S. Africa, 1945; Vergil the Universal, 1949; Why not be Friends?, 1957; The ABC of Afrikaans; Die Antieke Drama, I; Smuts the Humanist, 1970. *Recreation:* walking. *Address:* Almondbury, Stanford Road, Rondebosch, CP, S Africa.   *[Died* 30 *Aug.* 1971.

HACKETT, Sir Maurice (Frederick), Kt 1970; OBE 1958; Chairman, NW Metropolitan Regional Hospital Board, 1965-74 (Member, 1949-74); *b* Wood Green, N22, 11 Nov. 1905; British; *m* 1924, Deborah Levene (*d* 1969); one *s. Educ:* Glendale Secondary Sch., Wood Green. Press Dept, Labour Party Headquarters, 1935-40. With Min. of Information, then Central Office of Information, 1940-65 (Head of Speakers' Sect.; Chief Reg. Officer, London SE Region; Head of Tours Divn); Chm., SE Region Economic Planning Council, 1966-71; Mem., Land Commn, 1969-71. 1st Nat. Chm., Labour Party League of Youth; Chm., Southgate, Sth Kensington, Barnet and Herts Federation Labour Parties. Mem., East Barnet UDC, 1942-46.

Chairman: Barnet Group Hosp. Management Cttee, 1948-60; St Bernards Hosp. Management Cttee, 1960-62; SW Middx Hosp. Management Cttee, 1962-65; Mem., Gen. Nursing Council for England and Wales, 1969-73. *Recreations:* cinema, travel. *Address:* 2 Chesterfield House, South Grove, Highgate, N6. *T:* 01-348 2667.   *[Died* 16 *Feb.* 1980.

HACKING, 2nd Baron, *cr* 1945, of Chorley; **Douglas Eric Hacking,** 2nd Bt, *cr* 1938; Major RA; BA (Cantab); *b* 7 Dec. 1910; *s* of 1st Baron, PC, OBE, DL, JP, and Margery Allen, OBE 1956, *e d* of late H. H. Bolton, JP, Newchurch-in-Rossendale; *S* father 1950; *m* 1936, Daphne Violet, *e d* of late Robert Leslie Finnis, Kensington, W; two *s* two *d. Educ:* Charterhouse; Clare Coll., Cambridge. Admitted Solicitor, 1935; Partner, Baileys, Shaw & Gillett, 1945-64. President: National Deaf Children's Soc.; British Amateur Dancers' Assoc.; Governor: Middlesex Hospital, 1953-56; Star and Garter Home for Disabled Sailors, Soldiers and Airmen, 1955-65; Member: Council of Trust Houses Forte Ltd (Chm.); Nat. Council for Care of Old People; Council, Distressed Gentlefolks Aid Assoc.; Chm. of Trustees of Whiteley Homes. Directorships include: Gen. Accident Fire & Life Assurance Corp. Ltd; Royal Academy of Music, 1960-65. Consultant, Wedlake Letts & Birds. Court of Worshipful Co. of Makers of Playing Cards. Served War of 1939-45, Royal Artillery. *Heir: s* Hon. Douglas David Hacking [*b* 17 April 1938; *m* 1965, Rosemary Anne, *e d* of F. P. Forrest; one *s* one *d*]. *Address:* c/o Messrs Wedlake Letts & Birds, 6 Stone Buildings, Lincolns Inn, WC2; 46 Phillimore Gardens, W8. *T:* 01-937 6070. *Clubs:* MCC, Pilgrims.   *[Died* 7 *Nov.* 1971.

HADDOCK, Maurice Robert, CBE 1963 (OBE 1945); ERD; General Manager and Secretary, National Dock Labour Board, 1955-70; *b* 26 July 1909; *s* of late Percy G. Haddock; *m* 1938, Rita Claridge; one *d. Educ:* St Paul's Sch.; Magdalene Coll., Cambridge. Served War, 1939-46, Royal Engineers (Transportation). Hon. Col 81 Port Regt, RE (AER) (incorporated in RCT, 1965), 1955-67; ADC to the Queen, 1959-64. Port Controller, Hamburg, 1945-49. Asst Sec., Docks & Inland Waterways Executive, 1949-52; Asst Gen. Manager and Sec., National Dock Labour Board, Sept. 1952-Oct. 1955. Officer Order of Leopold, 1945. *Address:* 14 Copse Edge Avenue, Epsom, Surrey. *T:* Epsom 21479. *[Died* 21 *Nov.* 1974.

HADDOW, Prof. Sir Alexander, Kt 1966; MD, DSc, PhD; FRS 1958; FRSE; Professor of Experimental Pathology, University of London, 1946-72, now Professor Emeritus; Director, Chester Beatty Research Institute, Institute of Cancer Research, Royal Cancer Hospital, Fulham Road, SW3, 1946-69; *b* 18 Jan. 1907; *s* of William and Margaret Haddow, Broxburn, West Lothian, Scotland; *m* 1st, 1932, Lucia Lindsay Crosbie Black (*d* 1968); one *s*; 2nd, 1969, Feo Standing. *Educ:* Broxburn High Sch.; University of Edinburgh (MB, ChB 1929; PhD 1937; MD (Gold Medal) 1937; DSc 1938). Wellcome Gold Medal, History of Medicine. Carnegie Research Student and House Physician, Royal Infirmary of Edinburgh; Davidson Research Fellow and Lecturer in Bacteriology, University of Edinburgh; Laura de Saliceto Student, University of London; Life Mem., Royal Medical Society of Edinburgh; Foreign Hon. Member, Amer. Acad. Arts and Sciences, 1961; Pres., British Assoc. for Cancer Research, 1968, Vice-Pres., 1971-; Vice-Pres., British Cancer Council. Fellow: Inst. of Biology; Acad. Royale de Méd. de Belgique; RSA; FRSocMed; Pres., Section of Oncology, RSM, 1970-71; late Mem., Press Council; Mem., British Assoc. for World Govt and Parly Group for World Govt; late Chm., BBC Science Consultative Group; Pres. International Union Against Cancer, 1962-66; Member: Society for Study of Growth and Development (US); New York Acad. of Sciences; American Association for Cancer Research. Lectures: Dohme, Baltimore, 1955; Harben, 1969; Karnofsky Meml, Houston, 1970; Kennaway Meml, 1972. Hon. FRCP 1968; Hon. FRSocMed 1975; Hon. Member: Czechoslovak Med. Soc., 1966; Hungarian Acad. of Sciences, 1967. MD *hc* Univ. of Perugia, 1957; Dr *hc* Univ. of Helsinki, 1965; Hon. DSc Edinburgh, 1967; DUniv Liège, 1967. Katherine Berkan Judd Award (Memorial Hosp., NY), 1948; Walker Prize (RCS of England), 1951; Robert Roesler de Villiers Award (Leukemia Soc., NY), 1960; Claude Perchot Prize (Fac. de Méd., Paris, 1960); Gold Medal in Therapeutics (Soc. of Apothecaries of London, 1963); Sidney Farber Med. Res. Award, Boston, 1970; Internat. Union against Cancer Award, 1970; Italian Soc. of Toxicology Diploma and Medal, 1971. Officer, Order of Don Carlos Finlay, Cuba, 1957; Officier de l'Ordre de la Santé Publique, France; Croix de Chevalier de la Légion d'Honneur, 1965. *Publications:* papers in various scientific and medical journals. *Recreations:* bibliography, painting, music. *Address:* The Lodge, Pollards Wood, Nightingales Lane, Chalfont St Giles, Bucks. *T:* Little Chalfont 2474. *Clubs:* Chelsea Arts, Hanstown.
[Died 21 *Jan.* 1976.

HADDOW, Prof. Alexander John, CMG 1959; DSc, MD, FRCPGlas, DTM&H; FRS 1972, FRSE; Administrative Dean, Faculty of Medicine, 1970-78, and Professor of Administrative Medicine, University of Glasgow, 1971-78; *b* 27 Dec. 1912; *s* of Alexander and Margaret Blackburn Haddow; *m* 1946, Margaret Ronald Scott Orr; two *s*. *Educ:* Hillhead High Sch., Glasgow; Glasgow Univ. Strang-Steel Research Scholar (zoology), Glasgow Univ., 1934-35; Medical Research Council Junior Research Fellow in Tropical Medicine, 1938-41. Entomologist, Yellow Fever Research Institute, Entebbe, 1942-45; Staff Mem., International Health Div., Rockefeller Foundation, 1945-49; Overseas Research Service, 1950-65; Epidemiologist, East African Virus Research Institute, 1950-52; Acting Dir, 1952-53; Dir, 1953-65; Sen. Lectr in Epidemiology, Univ. of Glasgow, 1965-70, also Dir, Cancer Registration Bureau, W of Scotland Hosp. Region, 1966-70; Titular Prof. of Tropical Medicine, Glasgow Univ., 1970-71. Hon. Prof. of Medical Entomology, Makerere Coll., The University Coll. of East Africa, 1962-65. Mem. WHO expert panel on virus diseases, 1953. Trustee, Uganda National Parks, 1955-65; Life Honorary Park Warden, 1965-. Chalmers Gold Medal, Royal Soc. Tropical Medicine and Hygiene, 1957. Stewart Prize, BMA, 1962; Keith Prize, RSE, 1968. *Publications:* contributions to learned journals. *Address:* 16 Hamilton Drive, Glasgow G12 8DR. *T:* 041-339 7187.
[Died 26 Dec. 1978.

HADEN-GUEST, 2nd Baron, *cr* 1950, of Saling, Essex; **Stephen Haden Haden-Guest;** translator and editor of scientific works; *b* 7 June 1902; *er s* of Leslie Haden Haden-Guest, 1st Baron, MC, and Edith (*d* 1944), *d* of Max Low, London; *S* father 1960; *m* 1948, Barbara Ann (marr. diss., 1954), *d* of late James Harvey Pinson, of West Virginia, USA; one *d*. *Educ:* St John's House Sch.; Institut St Cyr, Nevers, France; University Coll., London; London Sch. of Economics. BA (Hons), London, 1922. Served War of 1939-45: with British Information Services, New York, 1941-45 (Ed. and Translator). With United Nations Information Office, 1943-46; Editorial Adviser to the American Geographical Soc., 1948-54. *Heir: b* Hon. Richard Haden Haden-Guest [*b* 1904; *m* 1st, 1926, Hilda (marr. diss., 1934), *d* of late Thomas Russell-Cruise; one *d*; 2nd, 1934, Olive Maria, *d* of late Anders Gotfrid Nilsson; one *s* decd; 3rd, 1949, Marjorie, *d* of late Dr Douglas F. Kennard, of Clacton-on-Sea. *Educ:* Bembridge, IOW]. *Club:* English-Speaking Union (New York).
[Died 21 Dec. 1974.

HADLEY, Patrick Arthur Sheldon, MA, MusD Cantab; FRCM; composer; Emeritus Professor of Music in the University of Cambridge (Professor of Music and Precentor of Caius, 1946-62); *b* 5 March 1899; 2nd and *o* surv. *s* of late Dr W. S. Hadley, Master of Pembroke Coll., Cambridge, 1912-27, and of late Edith Jane, *d* of Rev. Robert Foster, one-time Vicar of St Peter's, Athlone; unmarried. *Educ:* Winchester Coll.; Pembroke Coll., Cambridge; Royal Coll. of Music (where studied composition under Vaughan Williams and conducting under Boult and Sargent). Served War of 1914-18 in RFA, 1917-18 (wounded in France). Mem. of Teaching Staff of RCM, 1925-62. Fellow of Gonville and Caius Coll., Cambridge, 1938, and Lecturer in University Faculty of Music; deputised during most of War of 1939-45 for Mr Boris Ord as conductor of Cambridge Univ. Musical Soc., introducing to Cambridge two major works by Delius, Appalachia and The Song of the High Hills. *Publications:* various songs and choral pieces; a few large-scale concert works for chorus and orchestra with soli, such as Fen and Flood (words by C. L. Cudworth), performed King's Lynn Festival, 1956; Norwich Festival, 1958. Music for the Greek Play, Antigone (Sophocles), at Cambridge, 1939; Agamemnon (Aeschylus), 1953; A Latin Coronation Ode for chorus and orchestra perf. at Cambridge, June 1953. Many compositions remain in manuscript, including a Cantata for Lent perf. at the St Bees Festival, 1963, and subsequently by the Cambridge Univ. Musical Soc. *Address:* Shallcross, Heacham, near King's Lynn, Norfolk. *T:* Heacham 220.
[Died 17 Dec. 1973.

HAGESTADT, Leonard, CMG 1966; OBE 1955; Counsellor (Labour), British Embassy, Paris, 1960-68, retired; *b* 12 June 1907; *s* of William Samuel Hagestadt and Emma (*née* Fish); *m* 1934, Constance Margaret Louise Valentine, Edinburgh; one *s* one *d*. *Educ:* Boulevard Sch., Kingston-upon-Hull; BCom (London). Various posts in Min. of Labour, 1930-60. *Address:* 58 Park Hall Road, SE21. *T:* 01-670 8011.
[Died 19 June 1974.

HAGGERSTON of Haggerston, Captain Sir (Hugh) Carnaby de Marie, 11th Bt, *cr* 1642; Captain late 5th Fusiliers; JP Northumberland; *b* March 1906; *s* of 10th Bt and Florence (*d* 1955), 3rd *d* of W. H. Perrin; *S* father, 1925; *m* 1933, Mary Ridgway, *e d* of late Mrs L. P. Macy, Beauly, Charlottesville, Va, USA; three *d* (and one *s* and one *d* decd). *Educ:* The Oratory Sch. Owns about 3,500 acres in Northumberland. *Heir: b* Ralph Stanley de Marie Haggerston [*b* 6 Aug. 1912; *m* 1956, Joan Adelene Blythe-Perrett]. *Address:* Harelaw House, Chathill, Northumberland. *T:* Chathill 24.
[Died 11 Sept. 1971.

HAGGERSTON, Sir Ralph, (Raphael Stanley de Marie), 12th Bt *cr* 1642; Accountant; *b* 6 Aug. 1912; *s* of Sir Edward Charlton de Marie Haggerston, 10th Bt and Florence (*d* 1955), *d* of W. H. Perrin; *S* brother, 1971; *m* 1956, Joan Adelene, *d* of late William Blythe-Perrett. *Educ:* Ampleforth College, York. *Heir: kinsman* Michael Fergus Maxwell Scott [*b* 23 July 1921; *m* 1963, Deirdre Moira, *d* of late Alexander McKechnie; two *s* one *d*]. *Address:* 106 Ormonde Court, Upper Richmond Road, SW15. *T:* 01-789 4356.
[Died 3 Jan. 1972.

HAGUE, Sir (Charles) Kenneth (Felix), Kt 1953; CEng, FIMechE; *b* 17 Sept. 1901; *s* of late Albert Hague and Florence Muriel Flux; *m* 1926, Marjorie, *d* of Samuel Thornton; one *s* one *d*; *m* 1960, Mrs Helen Wallace Sutherland. *Educ:* New College Sch., Oxford; Leeds University. Joined Babcock & Wilcox Ltd, 1924; Chairman, 1960-68. Deputy Chairman, Royal Ordnance Factories Board, 1951-58; Member, Iron and Steel Board, 1959-64. Member UK Management/Labour Delegation to USA, 1941; British Representative on Public Utilities Cttee of Combined Production and Resources Board, Washington, 1944; Member Engineering Advisory Council, 1947-52; Past-President (1948-50), British Engineers' Association; Past President, Institute of Mech. Engineers, 1961-62, Hon. Fellow, 1967; Past President, Engineering Employers' Federation, 1958-60. Founder-Chairman, Council of Engineering Institutions, 1962-64. Hon. LLD Glasgow. *Recreation:* golf. *Address:* Poland Mill, Odiham, Hants. *T:* Odiham 2251. *Clubs:* Junior Carlton; Rand (Johannesburg).
[Died 4 Feb. 1974.

HAGUE, Sir Kenneth; *see* Hague, Sir C. K. F.

HAHN, Kurt (Matthias Robert Martin), CBE 1964; Hon. LLD; *b* Berlin, Germany, 5 June 1886; *s* of Oskar Hahn and Charlotte (*née* Landau); became British citizen, 1938. *Educ:* Wilhelmgymnasium, Berlin; Christ Church, Oxford; Universities of Berlin, Heidelberg, Freiburg, Göttingen. Returned to Germany, Aug. 1914; during war: Lector of English newspapers (first for German Foreign Office, then for Supreme Command); Private Secretary: to Prince Max von Baden, the last Imperial Chancellor, Jan. 1919; to Dr Melchior, a delegate in Versailles, April-June 1919; returned to Prince Max and helped him to found Salem Co-educational School at Salem Castle, 1920; arrested by Nazis, March 1933; released and protected through intervention of Ramsay MacDonald; emigrated to Britain, July 1933; founded Gordonstoun Sch., 1933-34; retired, 1953; Co-Founder with Lawrence Holt of Outward Bound Sea Sch., Aberdovey, 1941; announced at Bruges, Atlantic Colleges project, 1957; Co-Founder with Sir Lawrence Darvall of United World Coll. of the Atlantic, Wales, 1962. Hon. LLD, Edinburgh, 1953; Hon. Dr phil: Göttingen, 1956; Tübingen, 1961; Berlin, 1966. Grosses Verdienstkreuz des Verdienstordens der Bundesrepublik Deutschland, 1961; Freiherr-vom-Stein Prize, 1962; Foneme Prize, Milan, 1968. *Recreations:* lawn tennis, walking, applied history. *Address:* 7777 Salem, Baden, Federal Republic of Germany; Brown's Hotel, London, W1.
[Died 14 Dec. 1974.

HAILE SELLASSIE, KG 1954; GCB (Hon.); GCMG (Hon.); Royal Victorian Chain; Field Marshal (Hon.) of the British Army; Emperor of Ethiopia, 1930, deposed 1974; *b* 23 July 1892; 2nd *s* of HH Ras Makonnen, a great-grandson of Sahle Sellassie, King of Shoa; his mother belonged to the nobility of the Wollo; *m* 1911, Woyzero Menen (*d* 1962), a *g d* of King Mikael of Wollo; one *s* one *d* (and two *s* and two *d* decd). On the accession of the Empress Zauditu, 1916, proclaimed heir-apparent and Prince Regent, and invested with the Grand Cordon of the Order of Solomon; took Ethiopia to the League of Nations, 1923; proclaimed abolition of slavery, 1924; visited the principal European Capitals 1924; crowned King of Ethiopia, 7 Oct. 1928; succeeded to the Imperial Throne 2 April and crowned Emperor 2 Nov. 1930; proclaimed, by his own free will, constitution with two legislative chambers, 1931. As a result of Italian aggression in 1935 and unsupported by the League of Nations he was forced to quit his capital on 2 May 1936; took refuge in Great Britain during his period of exile; re-entered his capital after victorious campaign and the eventual driving out of the enemy, 5 May 1941. Amongst reforms initiated since his return were the abolition of serfdom on 2 Nov. 1941, and of the legal status of slavery on 26 Aug. 1942; created history by giving Revised Constitution, 1955, granting free democratic elections based on adult franchise for both men and women, without any popular demand at all; first elections successfully concluded, Sept. 1957. Entered into diplomatic relations with most of the important

nations of the world and visited them officially; secured reintegration of Eritrea, 1952. Is a devoted student; has founded several educational, medical and other institutions in Addis Ababa and other cities of Ethiopia; has also, in pursuit of the same objects, despatched young Ethiopians to study in America, Europe, India, Japan and Egypt; gave own ancestral Palace, in Addis Ababa, as seat of University, Dec. 1961. LLD (Hon.): Cambridge, 1924; Columbia, Howard, McGill, Montreal, Michigan, Athens, Laval, 1954; Banaras, Moscow, Charles; DCL (Hon.) Oxford, 1954; Doc. Ag. (Hon.) Bonn, 1954. Grand Cross of the Order of the Légion d'Honneur; of the Annunsiata; of Leopold, Belgium; of the Lion d'or de la Maison de Nassau, Luxemburg; of the Lion of the Netherlands; of Mohammed Ali, Egypt; of the Saviour, Greece; of the Seraphines, Sweden; Grand Collar of Carlos III, Spain, etc. *Publications:* heywatenna ya-Ityopya, ermejja (My Life and Ethiopia's Progress) (autobiog.), Part I, 1973. *Recreations:* gardening, tennis, ancient and modern history, comparative religion, riding, and walking.
[Died 27 Aug. 1975.

HAILES, 1st Baron, *cr* 1957, of Prestonkirk; **Patrick George Thomas Buchan-Hepburn,** PC 1951; GBE 1957; CH 1962; *b* 2 April 1901; *y s* of late Sir Archibald Buchan-Hepburn, 4th Bt of Smeaton-Hepburn, East Lothian; *uncle* and *heir-pres.* to Sir Ninian Buchan-Hepburn, 6th Bt; *m* 1945, Diana, *d* of late Brig.-Gen. Hon. Charles Lambton, DSO, and *widow* of Major W. Hedworth Williamson. *Educ:* Harrow; Trinity Coll., Cambridge. Hon. Attaché HM Embassy, Constantinople, 1926-27; contested (C) Wolverhampton East, 1929; Member of the LCC (North Kensington), 1930-31. MP (C) E Toxteth Division of Liverpool, Feb. 1931-Feb. 1950, Beckenham Division, 1950-57; PPS to Rt Hon. Oliver Stanley, 1931; Junior Lord of the Treasury, 1939, and again 1944; Conservative Deputy Chief Whip, July 1945, and Chief Whip, 1948; Parly Sec. to the Treasury and Government Chief Whip, 1951-55; Minister of Works, 1955-57; Governor-General and C-in-C of the West Indies, 1958-62. Served in the War, 1940-43, with RA and on staff. Chm., Historic Buildings Council for England, 1963-73. KStJ. *Address:* 1 Pelham Place, SW7. *T:* 01-589 1870. *Clubs:* Carlton, Travellers'. *[Died 5 Nov. 1974 (ext).*

HAIN, Henry William Theodore, CBE 1943; retired; *b* 17 Aug. 1899; *e s* of late H. M. Hain, Leamington Spa, Warwicks; *m* 1928, Dorothy Eileen, 2nd *d* of Mrs E. Wysard; one *s* one *d.* *Educ:* Warwick Sch.; Birmingham Univ. BSc (Hons) in Civil Engineering, 1923; commissioned Royal Artillery, 1918-19. Joined Braithwaite & Co., Engineers, Ltd of Westminster, 1923; Managing Dir, 1961-64, retired 1965. Chm., Indian Engineering Assoc., 1939-43; Managing Dir, Braithwaite & Co. (India), Ltd, 1935-50; former Dir, Braithwaite & Co., Engineers Ltd, retired 1972. *Recreation:* gardening. *Address:* Heather Cottage, The Barton, Cobham, Surrey. *T:* Cobham 2727.
[Died 24 Nov. 1972.

HAINES, Maj.-Gen. James Laurence Piggott, CB 1952; CBE 1950; *b* 27 Nov. 1896; *s* of W. J. Haines, Witney; *m* 1st, 1930, Edith Nancy Freeman (*d* 1956); no *c*; 2nd, 1957, Jane Elizabeth, *d* of G. Drury, PC, Cootehill, County Cavan. *Educ:* Brighton Coll., Royal Military Academy, Woolwich. Served European War, 1916-19; Iraq Levies, 1925-27; Military Coll. of Science, pac, 1927-30; Technical Staff Appointments, UK, Canada and USA, 1930-49; Vice-Pres. Ordnance Board, 1949; Pres. Ordnance Board, 1951-52; retired pay, 1952. Managing Dir, Aron Meters Ltd, 1952-59. *Address:* 29 Park Gate, Somerhill Road, Hove BN3 1RL. *Club:* United Service & Royal Aero.
[Died 15 July 1974.

HAKE, Herbert Denys, OBE 1961; MA; retired as Headmaster, The King's School, Parramatta, NSW, Australia (1939-64); *b* 8 Nov. 1894; *s* of late E. D. Hake; *m* 1938, Elizabeth Barton; three *d.* *Educ:* Haileybury Coll.; Queens' Coll., Cambridge. Served European War, Hants Regt, 1914-19, India and Mesopotamia (Capt., despatches); Asst Master, Haileybury Coll., 1921-38; Temporary Asst Master, St John's Coll., Johannesburg, 1927-28; Chm., Headmasters' Conference of Australia, 1951-54. FACE 1962. *Address:* Hailey, Mills Road, Glenhaven, NSW 2154, Australia. *Clubs:* MCC (London); Australian (Sydney).
[Died 12 April 1975.

HALE, Sir Edward, KBE 1952; CB 1942; Hon. LLD Leeds, 1959, Belfast, 1959, London, 1961; *b* 1895; *er s* of late Dr G. E. Hale, Eton; *m* 1930, Joan Latham (*d* 1971), *er d* of late Sir Alexander (Hon. Mr Justice) Bateson; two *d.* *Educ:* Tonbridge Sch.; Corpus Christi Coll., Oxford. MA; entered Treasury, 1921; Secretary to University Grants Cttee, 1951-57; Administrative Head, Historical Branch, Cabinet Office, 1958-60. *Address:* The Grange, Goring, Reading, Berks RG8 9EN.
[Died 6 Nov. 1978.

HALE, Herbert Edward John, OBE 1970; HM Diplomatic Service; *b* 1 Jan. 1927; *s* of Herbert Frederick John Hale and Nora (*née* Smith); *m* 1951, Audrey Evelyn Barden; one *s* one *d.* *Educ:* Bec School. Admty, 1943-45; Fleet Air Arm, 1945-48; FO, 1948; UK Delegn to UN, NY, 1949; Consulate-General, NY, 1950 (Vice-Consul, 1951); Vice-Consul: Kansas City, 1953; Bremen, 1954; FO, 1957; UK Delegn to OECD, Paris, 1962 (1st Sec., 1963); Consul (Commercial), São Paulo, 1965-69; FCO, 1969, Head of Commodities Dept, 1971-72, Inspector, 1972-73; Consul-Gen.: Stuttgart, 1973-77; São Paulo, 1977-78. Officer Cruzeiro do Sul (Brazil), 1968. *Recreations:* music, reading, golf. *Address:* c/o Foreign and Commonwealth Office, SW1; 6 Beresford Avenue, Tolworth, Surrey KT5 9LJ. *T:* 01-399 5649.
[Died 22 June 1978.

HALE, Lionel Ramsay; journalist and dramatist; *b* 26 Oct. 1909; 2nd *s* of James and Lylie Hale; *m* 1939, Betty Tayler (*d* 1952); one *s* one *d*; *m* 1955, Crystal Pudney, *e d* of late Sir Alan Herbert; one *d.* *Educ:* Charterhouse; Balliol Coll., Oxford. Asst Lit. Ed., News Chronicle, 1933-37; Dramatic Critic, News Chronicle, 1937-40; Govt service, 1940-46; Dramatic Critic, Daily Mail, 1946-48. General Editor, Evans Plays, 1949. Organiser, Nat. Library Week, 1969; Festival Organiser, Islington '70. Sec.-Gen., British Homœopathic Assoc., 1971-73. Dramatic and literary criticism for various newspapers and magazines, including Observer, and over 150 contribs to Punch; frequent broadcasting for BBC; many dramatic adaptations for BBC radio and for TV (BBC and ITV), and original TV play, Afternoon in River Walk, 1961. *Plays:* Beargarden, 1931; She Passed Through Lorraine, 1931; These Two, 1933; The Mocking Bird, 1933; Festival Time, 1937; Gilt and Gingerbread, 1959; Bring Up The Rainbow, 1965; prepared a complete version of Macbeth which the Old Vic toured in 1940-41, with Sybil Thorndike and Lewis Casson, nine supporting players and two narrators. *Publications:* The Old Vic, 1949-50; A Fleece of Lambs, 1961. *Address:* 76 Noel Road, N1. *T:* 01-226 4597.
[Died 14 May 1977.

HALIFAX, 2nd Earl of, *cr* 1944; **Charles Ingram Courtenay Wood,** Bt 1784; Baron Irwin, 1925; Viscount Halifax, 1866; Lord-Lieutenant of Humberside, since 1974 (for East Riding of Yorks, 1968-74); *b* 3 Oct. 1912; *e s* of 1st Earl of Halifax, KG, PC, OM, GCSI, GCMG, GCIE, TD, and Lady Dorothy Evelyn Augusta Onslow, CI, DCVO (*d* 1976); *S* father 1959; *m* 1936, Ruth (JP 1956 ER Yorks), *d* of late Captain Rt Hon. Neil James Archibald Primrose, MC, sometime MP; one *s* two *d.* *Educ:* Eton; Christ Ch., Oxford. 2nd Lieut Royal Horse Guards, 1934-37; War of 1939-45, Middle East, Captain. MP (U) York, 1937-45. Pro-Chancellor, Hull Univ., 1974-. High Steward of York Minster, 1970-. Mem. of Jockey Club; Senior Steward, 1950, 1959; owner of Shirley Heights, 199th Derby Winner, 1978. Mem. of National Hunt Cttee; Joint Master, Middleton Foxhounds, 1946-; DL, E Riding of Yorks and Kingston upon Hull, 1955-68; JP, E Riding of Yorks, 1963-68; Chm., E Riding of Yorks CC, 1968-74. KStJ 1970. *Recreations:* hunting, shooting. *Heir: s* Lord Irwin. *Address:* Garrowby, York YO4 1QD. *T:* Bishop Wilton 236; Alston Lodge, Bury Road, Newmarket. *T:* Newmarket 4342. *Clubs:* Turf, White's.
[Died 19 March 1980.

HALIFAX, Dowager Countess of; Dorothy Evelyn Augusta Wood, CI 1926; DCVO 1953; JP; an Extra Lady of the Bedchamber to Queen Elizabeth the Queen Mother since 1946; *b* 7 Feb. 1885; *yr d* of 4th Earl of Onslow, PC, GCMG; *m* 1909, Hon. Edward Frederick Lindley Wood (later 1st Earl of Halifax, KG, PC, OM, GCSI, GCMG, GCIE; he died 1959); two *s* (and one *s* killed in action, 1942) twin *d* (one decd). *Educ:* privately. Vicereine of India, 1926-31. A Lady of the Bedchamber to Queen Elizabeth the Queen Mother, when Queen, 1937-46. JP East and West Ridings of Yorks, 1935. Hon. LLD Leeds, 1939. DGStJ. *Recreations:* gardening, travel, reading. *Address:* Bugthorpe, York. *T:* Bishop Wilton 442. *[Died 2 Feb. 1976.*

HALL, Daniel George Edward, MA, DLit, FRHistS, FRAS; Professor Emeritus in the University of London since 1959; *b* 1891; *e s* of Daniel Hall of Offley, Hitchin, Herts, and Elinor Ann Field; *m* 1919, Helen Eugenie (*d* 1962), *o d* of late John Banks, Wynberg, SA; two *s* (and *e s* killed in action Nov. 1943) two *d.* *Educ:* Hitchin Grammar Sch.; King's Coll., Univ. of London. BA 1st Class Hons in Hist., Univ. of London, 1916; Gladstone Meml Prize and Inglis Studentship, KCL, 1915; Asst Lectr in History, KCL, 1916-17; MA 1918; DLit 1930; with the Lena Ashwell Concert Parties on the Western Front in 1916 and early 1917; Inns of Court OTC at Berkhampstead, 1917-19; Senior History Master: Royal Grammar Sch., Worcester, Jan.-July 1919; Bedales Sch., 1919-21; Prof. of History, Univ. of Rangoon, 1921-34; Headmaster of Caterham Sch., 1934-49; Prof. of Hist. of SE Asia, Univ. of London, 1949-59. Temp.

Mem. Legislative Council of Burma, 1923-24; Corr. Mem. Indian Historical Records Commn, 1925; Mem. Panel of Additional Lectrs, SOAS, Univ. of London, 1940-49. Vis. Lectr, Johns Hopkins Univ. Sch. of Advanced Internat. Studies Summer Sch., Washington, DC, 1955. Visiting Professor: Cornell Univ. Dept of Far Eastern Studies, 1959-60 and 1963; Univ. of Syracuse Summer Sch., 1963; Univ. of BC, 1964-65; Monash Univ., Vic, Aust., 1965; Univ. of BC, 1965-66; Cornell Univ., 1966, 1967-69, 1970-71, 1972; Univ. of Michigan, 1966; Univ. of BC, 1967. Royal Society of Arts Silver Medal, 1944. Hon. Fellow, SOAS, 1959. *Publications:* Imperialism in Modern History, 1923; A Brief Survey of English Constitutional History, 1925, rev. and enl., 1939; Early English Intercourse with Burma, 1587-1743, 1927, 2nd edn 1968; The Dalhousie-Phayre Correspondence, 1852-56, 1929; The Tragedy of Negrais, 1752-59, 1931; Studies in Dutch Relations, with Arakan, 1936; Dutch Trade with Burma in the 17th Century, 1939; Europe and Burma, 1945; Burma, 1950, rev. and enl., 1956, 1960; A History of South-East Asia, 1955, rev. and enl., 1964, 4th edn 1979; Michael Symes: Journal of his second mission to Ava in 1802, 1955. Joint-author: a Handbook to the League of Nations for India, Burma and Ceylon, 1926; A High School British History, 1714-1930, 1935, rev. and enl., 1946; A Handbook of Oriental History, 1951; (ed) Historians of South-East Asia, 1961; Henry Burney: a political biography, 1974; articles in historical journals. *Recreation:* music. *Address:* 4 Chiltern Road, Hitchin, Herts. *T:* Hitchin 51662.   [Died 12 Oct. 1979.

HALL, Lady, (Edna); see Clarke Hall.

HALL, Edwin G. S.; see Sarsfield-Hall.

HALL, Geoffrey William, CEng, FRAeS; retired as Director of The Fairey Co. Ltd and as Chairman of Roger Laurent SA Belgium and of Fairey SA Belgium (both subsidiaries of Fairey Co.); *b* 18 Oct. 1906; *s* of Henry Clayton Hall and Frances Rebecca Jackson; *m* 1946, Eileen Florence Tripp; two *s*. *Educ:* City and Guilds Engineering Coll.; Royal College of Science. Apprenticed to Fairey Aviation Co. Ltd; learned to fly, London Aeroplane Club, 1927; Experimental Engineer, Aero Engine Test and Development, Rolls-Royce Ltd, 1928-32. Re-joined Fairey Aviation Co. Ltd; engaged on Aircraft and Engine Development; appointed Asst Chief Engineer, Chief Development Engineer and then Chief Research Engineer; Dir, 1949, becoming Engineering Dir, 1950, Asst Managing Dir, 1955 and Managing Dir, 1956; Chm. and Managing Dir, 1957-59; Chm., The Fairey Company Ltd, 1960-61. Mem., Radio Soc. of Gt Britain (RSGB). Licensed Radio Amateur with Call Sign G3UBQ. First Fairey Memorial Lecture, RAeS, 1959. Liveryman, Worshipful Co. of Coachmakers and Coach Harness Makers. *Recreations:* flying, sailing, radio. *Address:* Dellwood, 11 Pinewood Close, Iver Heath, Bucks. *T:* Iver 828. *Club:* United Service & Royal Aero.   [Died 27 May 1974.

HALL, George Derek Gordon, FBA 1975; President of Corpus Christi College, Oxford, since 1969; *b* 8 Nov. 1924; *e s* of late Albert Avondale Hall and of Elizabeth Winifred Hall; *m* 1952, Susan Penelope, *d* of Vice-Adm. J. W. Carrington. *Educ:* South Shields High Sch.; Appleby Grammar Sch.; The Queen's Coll., Oxford (MA). Served in RAF, 1943-46. Lectr in Law, University Coll. of Wales, Aberystwyth, 1948-49; Fellow and Tutor in Law, Exeter Coll., Oxford, 1949-69; Junior Proctor, 1962-63; Hebdomadal Council, 1963-73; Gen. Bd of the Faculties, 1963-73 (Vice-Chm., 1967-69); Asst Lit. Dir, Selden Soc. Hon. Fellow, St Cross Coll., Oxford, 1974. *Publications:* Glanvill (Nelson's Medieval Texts), 1965; (with E. de Haas) Early Registers of Writs, 1970; articles in historical and legal periodicals. *Recreations:* fishing, bee-keeping. *Address:* Corpus Christi College, Oxford. *T:* Oxford 49431. [Died 15 Sept. 1975.

HALL, George Edmund, CMG 1978; HM Diplomatic Service; Ambassador to Brazil, since 1979; *b* 29 Sept. 1925; *s* of late George Albert Hall and Phyllis Louise Hall (*née* Papps); *m* 1948, Margaret Patricia Smith; two *s*. *Educ:* Highbury County Sch.; Trinity Hall, Cambridge (BA). Joined RAFVR 1943; served RAF Blind Landing Experimental Unit; demobilised as Flying Officer, 1947. Joined Foreign (subseq. Diplomatic) Service, 1950; Third Sec., Foreign Office, 1950-53; Third, Second and First Sec. (Commercial), Mexico City, 1953-58, FO, 1958-61; First Sec., Head of Chancery and First Sec. (Information), Lima, 1961-64; FO, 1964-69; Counsellor, Sept. 1968; Counsellor, Lisbon, 1969-72; Consul-General, São Paulo, 1973-77; Asst Under-Sec. of State, FCO, 1977-79. Member: British-Mexican Soc. and Anglo-Peruvian Soc. (Exec. Cttee, 1965-69); Bd of Management, Inst. of Latin American Studies, London Univ., 1966-69. *Recreations:* reading, listening to music, swimming. *Address:* c/o Foreign and Commonwealth Office, SW1. *Club:* Buck's.   [Died 1 Nov. 1980.

HALL, Grahame; see Muncaster, Claude.

HALL, Sir John, Kt 1973; OBE 1945; TD 1946; MP (C) Wycombe Division of Bucks, since Nov. 1952; chairman and director of companies in chemical and brewing industries; *b* 21 Sept. 1911; *m* 1935, Nancy, *er d* of late W. Hearn Blake; one *s* one *d*. Served War of 1939-45, RA, TA; Commissioned RAOC, 1940; Staff Coll., Camberley, 1941-42; various Staff appts, 1942-45; Lt-Col 1943. Mem. Grimsby Borough Council, 1946-48; contested (C) Grimsby, 1950, (C) East Fulham, 1951; PPS to Minister of Fuel and Power, 1956 and to Minister of Supply, 1957-59. Mem., Select Cttee on Public Acts, 1958-64; Vice-Chairman: Cons. Parly Trade and Industry Cttee, 1964-65; Finance Cttee, 1965-68, 1969-72, 1974- (Chm., 1973-74); Cons. Parly 1922 Cttee, 1970-; Mem., Select Cttee on Expenditure, 1970-72 (Chm. Sub-Cttee for DoE and Home Office); Chm., Select Cttee on Nationalised Industries, 1972-74. Treasurer, 1967, Vice-Chm., 1968-70, Chm., 1970-73, Inter-Parly Union (British Br.), and Vice-Chm., Internat. Executive. Mem. Order of Diplomatic Merit (Korea), 1975. *Address:* 41 Carlisle Mansions, Carlisle Place, SW1; Marsh, Great Kimble, Bucks. *Club:* Naval and Military.   [Died 19 Jan. 1978.

HALL, Sir John Hathorn, GCMG 1950 (KCMG 1941; CMG 1935); DSO 1919; OBE 1931; MC; *b* 19 June 1894; *m* 1927, Torfrida Trevenen Mills; two *d*. *Educ:* St Paul's Sch.; Lincoln Coll., Oxford. Served European War, 1914-19 (despatches, MC, DSO, Croix de Guerre (Belgium)); Egyptian Civil Service, Ministry of Finance, 1919-21; Asst Principal, Colonial Office, 1921; Principal, 1927; seconded to Foreign Office, 1932; Chief Sec. to Govt of Palestine, 1933-37; British Resident, Zanzibar, 1937-40; Governor and C-in-C, Aden, 1940-44; Governor and C-in-C of Uganda, 1944-51; retd, 1951. Past Chm., Clerical, Medical & General Life Assurance Soc.; formerly Dir, Midland Bank Ltd and other cos. 1st Cl. Order of the Brilliant Star of Zanzibar; KStJ. *Address:* 128 Rivermead Court, Hurlingham, SW6 3SD. *Clubs:* Athenæum, Hurlingham.
                    [Died 17 June 1979.

HALL, Sir Julian Henry, 11th Bt, *cr* 1687; *b* 22 Feb. 1907; *s* of Sir Martin Julian Hall, OBE, 10th Bt; *S* father 1958. *Educ:* Eton; Balliol Coll., Oxford (BA). Editor of Colour, 1931. Served with Intelligence Corps and in Special Forces, 1939-45. Home Talks Dept, BBC, 1948-51; contrib. articles on the contemporary theatre. *Publications:* Laura Seaborne, 1932; The Senior Commoner, 1934; Two Exiles, 1936. *Heir:* cousin Col Lionel Reid Hall, MC [*b* 1 Feb. 1898; *m* 1921, Mary Marjoribanks Moore, *d* of late Maj.-Gen. Sir Gerard Moore Heath, KCMG, CB, DSO, and *widow* of Capt. J. D. G. MacNeece, MC, RFA; three *d*]. *Address:* Flat G, 33 Eaton Square, SW1. *Club:* Garrick.   [Died 28 Jan. 1974.

HALL, Kenneth Lambert, CMG 1938; *b* 14 May 1887; *s* of late Thomas Lambert Hall, MRCS and *g g s* of William Hall of Arlington Manor, Bibury, Glos; *m* 1915, Mabel (*d* 1976), *d* of Towry Piper of Barnard Castle, Durham; one *s* decd. *Educ:* Hereford Sch.; Brasenose Coll., Oxford (Somerset Scholar). Entered Northern Nigerian Political Service as Asst Resident, 1912; Principal Asst Sec., Nigerian Secretariat, 1927; acting Dep. Chief Sec., 1927-30; Mem., Legislative Council, Nigeria; acting Sec., Southern Provinces, Nigeria, 1930; Chief Sec., Nyasaland, 1931-41; acting Governor and Comdr-in-Chief, Nyasaland on various occasions; Sec. Nyasaland Northern and Southern Rhodesia Inter-territorial Conference, 1941; retired, 1945. *Address:* St Luke's, 20 Linton Road, Oxford.
                    [Died 13 March 1979.

HALL, Sir Lionel (Reid), 12th Bt *cr* 1687; MC 1918; retired Army Officer (Colonel); *b* 1 Feb. 1898; *s* of Captain Lionel Erskine Hall (*d* 1948), late 4th Bn, S Staffordshire Regt; *S* cousin, 1974; *m* 1921, Mary Marjoribanks Moore MacNeece, *d* of late Maj.-Gen. Sir Gerard Moore Heath, KCMG, CB, DSO; three *d*. *Educ:* Wyggeston Grammar Sch.; RMC, Sandhurst; Staff Coll., Camberley (psc). Commissioned 1916, The Royal Scots; served European War, 1916-19 (despatches, wounded, MC); transferred Royal Signals, 1926; NW Frontier of India, 1935 (medal) and War of 1939-45 (despatches, medal); retired from Army, 1947. County Councillor (North Riding), 1964-74. *Recreations:* gardening, photography. *Heir:* b Neville Reynolds Hall [*b* 16 Feb. 1900; *m* 1957, Dorothy Maud, *d* of late William Lawrence Jones]. *Address:* The Lodge, Scorton, Richmond, N Yorks. *T:* Old Catterick 607.   [Died 22 April 1975.

HALL, Magdalen K.; see King-Hall.

HALL, Sir Neville (Reynolds), 13th Bt *cr* 1687; retired; *b* 16 Feb. 1900; *s* of Captain Lionel Erskine Hall (*d* 1948) and Jane Augusta Hall (*d* 1949), *d* of late Thomas Leethem Reynolds; *S*

brother, 1975; *m* 1957, Dorothy Maud, *d* of late William
Lawrence Jones. *Educ:* Oundle; Royal Coll. of Science (ARCS);
Keble Coll., Oxford (BSc). Demonstrator, Royal Naval
Engineering Coll., Keyham, 1924-28; research at Oxford, 1928-
31; Lecturer, Royal Naval Coll., Dartmouth, 1931-63.
Publications: various scientific articles of no great importance.
Recreation: designing and making clocks. *Heir: b* Sir Douglas
Hall, KCMG. *Address:* Ash Cottage, Ash, Dartmouth, S
Devon. *T:* Blackawton 288.   *[Died 5 July 1978.*

HALL, Percival Stanhope, CMG 1952; CBE 1921 (OBE 1920;
MBE 1919); late Chairman John Loudon & Co. Ltd, London
Bridge, SE1; *b* 1879; *s* of William Henry Hall, JP, Aldeburgh; *m*
1926, Edith (*d* 1964), widow of T. P. Tebbutt, Northampton.
Educ: Ipswich Sch. Dir of Meat Contracts, Min. of Food, in
European War, 1914-18, Temp. Lieut RASC; Dir of Bacon
Imports, Ministry of Food, War of 1939-45; also Dir of bacon
and ham, 1946-52. Orders of Crown of Italy and Crown of
Belgium, and Medal Agricole, France; Coronation Medal, 1953.
Address: Kingsworthy, 26 Tangiers Road, Guildford, Surrey.
                                                          [Died 16 May 1972.

HALL, Col (Hon.) Philip de Havilland, DSO 1919; MC; TD;
Consulting Engineer; *b* 28 Aug. 1885; *s* of late Dr F. de
Havilland Hall; *m* 1925, Eleanor Louise Kirby; one *s* one *d.*
Educ: Tonbridge Sch. (Foundation Scholar); Glasgow Univ.;
BSc(Eng). MInstCE; Col RE, TA; OC 323rd Anti-Aircraft Co.
RE, 1934; CRE Somerset 1941-42; Dep. Chief Engineer S
Midlands Dist, 1942-43; retired, 1945, with Hon. rank of Col.
Served European War, CRE 50th Div., 1914-19 (despatches
thrice, MC, DSO). *Address:* 19 Hartington Mansions,
Eastbourne, Sussex. *T:* Eastbourne 26934. *Clubs:* East India,
Sports and Public Schools; Devonshire (Eastbourne).
                                                          [Died 28 May 1972.

HALL, Roger Wilby, MVO 1944; DL; JP; *b* 6 Oct. 1907; *s* of late
A. W. Hall, London and Southwick, Sussex; *m* 1937, Audrey
Mary Stuart, *d* of late Sir Henry Wheeler, KCSI, KCIE; two *s*
two *d.* *Educ:* Charterhouse; Jesus Coll., Cambridge. Mem. of
London Stock Exchange, 1932. Joined 72nd (Middx) S/L Regt,
TA, May 1939; commissioned Dec. 1939; transferred to Life
Guards, Jan. 1943; Temp. Major, 1943. Served 1939-45, with
RA (TA) AA Home Service, and 2nd Household Cavalry Regt
(BLA and BAOR). DL Sussex, 1956; High Sheriff of Sussex,
1957-58; JP W Sussex, 1961. *Recreation:* shooting. *Address:*
Glebe House, West Grinstead, Horsham, Sussex. *T:* Partridge
Green 341. *Clubs:* Buck's, Turf.   *[Died 8 July 1973.*

HALL, Ronald; Librarian, John Rylands Library, Manchester,
retired 1970; *b* 8 Feb. 1900; *s* of Alfred and Elizabeth Hall; *m*
1925, Jessie Isobel Coggan (*d* 1966); two *s.* *Educ:* Manchester
Grammar Sch.; London Univ. (Ext.). BA 1930; Hon. MA
Manchester, 1966. Asst Librarian, John Rylands Library, 1915;
Keeper of Printed Books, 1950; Acting Librarian, 1960. Served
with RAF, 1938-45. *Publications:* contribs to journals; co-editor,
Bulletin of the John Rylands Library. *Recreations:* walking,
gardening, amateur theatre. *Address:* Trafford House, 442 Bury
Old Road, Prestwich, Manchester M25 5PQ. *T:* 061-773 4774.
                                                          [Died 10 Feb. 1975.

HALL, Rt. Rev. Ronald Owen, CMG 1966; MC; *s* of Rev. Cecil
Gallopine Hall, MA, and Constance Gertrude, *d* of Rev. Henry
Berners Upcher; *m* 1923, Nora Kathleen Suckling-Baron; one *s*
one *d* (and *er s* decd). *Educ:* Royal Grammar School, Newcastle
upon Tyne; Bromsgrove Sch.; Brasenose Coll., Oxford (Schol.).
MA Oxford, 1965. Served European War, 1914-19 (despatches,
MC and Bar); Distinction in Literæ Humaniores and BA, 1920
(shortened course after war service); ordained to Newcastle
Cathedral for work with Student Christian Movement;
Missionary Sec., Student Christian Movement up to 1925; Sec.
YMCA, China till 1926; Vicar, St Luke, Newcastle upon Tyne,
1926-32; Bishop of Victoria, Hong Kong, 1932; Bishop of Hong
Kong and S China until 1951; then of smaller see of Hong Kong,
1951-66. Chm., Council of the Church of South-East Asia, 1955-
62. Hon. DD: Hong Kong Univ., 1965; Church Divinity Sch. of
Pacific, 1966. *Publications:* A Family in the Making, 1925;
China and Britain, 1927; The Art of the Missionary, 1942.
Address: The Home Farm, Lewknor, Oxford. *T:* Kingston
Blount 51275.   *[Died 22 April 1975.*

HALL, Lieut-Col Walter D'Arcy, MC; *b* Australia, 10 Aug. 1891;
s of late Thomas Skarratt Hall, of Weeting Hall, Brandon,
Norfolk; *m* 1920, Ann Madelaine Brook (marr. diss.); two *s* one
d ; *m* 1957, Ruth Penelope Owen. *Educ:* Eton; Sandhurst. Joined
20th Hussars, 1911; served European War, 1914-19 (MC and
Bar, Croix de Guerre avec Palme et Etoile); served War 1939-45.
MP (U) Brecon and Radnor, 1924-29 and 1931-35. *Address:*
Magnolia Cottage, Lower Woodford, Salisbury, Wilts SP4 6NQ.
Club: Cavalry and Guards.   *[Died 22 Jan. 1980.*

HALL-DAVIS, Sir Alfred (George Fletcher), Kt 1979; Director,
Bass Ltd; *b* 21 June 1924; *s* of late George Hall-Davis, BA, MB;
m 1956, Margaret Carr, *d* of George Rushworth, JP, Colne,
Lancs; one *d.* *Educ:* Clifton Coll., Bristol. MP (C) Morecambe
and Lonsdale, Lancs, 1964-79; PPS, DES, 1970-73; an Asst
Govt Whip, 1973-74. *Recreation:* walking. *Address:* Whinberry
Harbour, Salterforth, Colne, Lancs BB8 5SN. *T:* Barnoldswick
812173.   *[Died 20 Nov. 1979.*

HALL-PATCH, Sir Edmund Leo, GCMG 1951 (KCMG 1947;
CMG 1938); formerly Director: Standard Bank (Chairman,
1957-62); Commercial Union Assurance Company and other
public companies; *b* 1896; *s* of W. F. McD. Hall-Patch. Asst
Sec., Treasury, 1935-44; HBM Financial Commissioner in the
Far East, 1940; Asst Under-Sec. of State, Foreign Office, 1944; a
Dep. Under-Sec. of State, Foreign Office, 1946-48; Chm. of
Executive Cttee of Organization for European Economic Co-
operation, with rank of Ambassador, 1948; late Permanent UK
Representative on Organization for European Economic Co-
operation, at Paris; UK Executive Dir of International
Monetary Fund and of the International Bank for
Reconstruction and Development, 1952-54, with the personal
rank of Ambassador. Retired 1954. *Club:* Brooks's.
                                                          [Died 1 June 1975.

HALLETT, Vice-Adm. John H.; *see* Hughes-Hallett.

HALLIFAX, Mrs Joanne Mary, JP; Central President of
Mothers' Union, 1962-70; *b* 28 Nov. 1900; *d* of Sir Robert
Hughes, 12th Bt (*d* 1951) and Edith Lady Hughes; *m* 1923, Vice-
Adm. R. H. Hallifax, CB, CBE (killed on active service, 1943);
one *s* two *d.* *Educ:* privately. JP, Hants, 1948. *Recreations:*
travelling, gardening, music. *Address:* Longcroft, Shedfield,
near Southampton. *T:* Wickham 3145.   *[Died 1 May 1972.*

HALLOWES, Basil John Knight, CIE 1941; ICS (retired); *b* 27
Aug. 1884; *s* of Rev. J. F. T. Hallowes, MA Cantab; *m* 1st, Mary
Catherine Lascelles Ward; 2nd, Joyce Mortimer. *Educ:* Mill
Hill; Caius Coll., Cambridge. Entered Indian Civil Service,
1909; retired, 1944. *Recreations:* shooting; played hockey for
Cambridge Univ., South of England and Mddx. *Address:* The
Beauthorns, Hatherley Road, Cheltenham. *T:* Cheltenham
22508.   *[Died 4 April 1973.*

HALLPIKE, Charles Skinner, CBE 1958; FRS 1956; FRCP,
FRCS; *b* 19 July 1900; *s* of Frank Robert Hallpike and
Rosamund Helen Skinner; *m* 1935, Barbara Lee Anderson; two
s one *d.* *Educ:* St Paul's Sch., W14; Guy's Hospital, SE1
(Entrance Schol. in Arts and Beaney Prizeman in Pathology);
MB, BS London 1926; FRCS 1931; FRCP 1945. William J.
Mickle Fellow, London Univ., 1941; Dalby Prizeman, 1943,
Gamble Prizeman, 1934 and 1947, Hughlings Jackson Memorial
Lecturer and Medallist, 1967, Royal Society of Medicine;
Bárány Medallist, Univ. of Uppsala, 1958; Guyot Medallist,
Univ. of Groningen, 1959. House Surg., Aural Depts Guy's
Hosp. and Cheltenham Gen. Hosp., 1924-27; Bernhard Baron
Research Fellow, Ferens Inst. of Otology, Middx Hosp., 1929;
Duveen Travelling Student, Univ. of London, 1930; Rockefeller
Travelling Fellow, 1931; Foulerton Research Fellow, Royal
Society, 1934; Mem. Scientific Staff, Med. Research Council,
1940; Aural Physician and Dir of Otological Research Unit, of
Medical Research Council, National Hosp. for Nervous
Diseases, Queen Square, WC1, 1944-65, now Hon. Aural
Physician; Dir of Research, Ferens Inst. of Otolaryngology,
Middlesex Hosp., 1965-68. Mem. Collegium
Otorhinolaryngologicum Amicitiae Sacrum (Shambaugh
Prizeman, 1955); Hon. Fellow Royal Academy of Medicine,
Ireland; FRSocMed (Hon. Sec. 1938, and Editorial Rep., 1946-
52, Pres., 1965, Hon. Mem., 1970, Sect. Otol.); Mem. Flying
Personnel Research Cttee, 1938-55. *Publications:* papers on
otology, physiology, and pathology of the ear in Proc. Royal
Society, Jl Physiology, Jl Pathology, Jl Laryngology and
Otology, etc. *Address:* Fern Lodge, Ashurst Road, West Moors,
Wimborne, Dorset BH22 0LS. *T:* Ferndown 874418.
                                                          [Died 26 Sept. 1979.

HALLSWORTH, Sir Joseph, Kt 1946; Hon. MA Manchester,
1942; Hon. LLD Manchester, 1954; *b* Audenshaw, near
Manchester, 2 Dec. 1884; *s* of Samuel and Elizabeth Hallsworth;
m 1908, Jessie Schofield (*d* 1946), Fairfield, Manchester; one *d*
(and one *s* decd). *Educ:* elementary, commercial, and tech.
schools in Manchester district. Entered service of Co-operative
Employees' Union, later the NUDAW, as confidential clerk to
then Sec., 1902; Asst Sec.; contested (Lab) Stretford, Lancs,
Parliamentary Division, 1918; Sec. of Trade Unions' Side of
National Conciliation Boards for the Co-operative Service,
1927-47; Mem. of Trade Boards Administration Cttee, 1921;
Mem. of General Council of TUC, 1926-47, Pres., 1938-39;

visited India for the Congress in 1927-28; was mem. British representation International Labour Conference, Geneva, 1927-37; Workers' Delegate in 1938 and 1939 and again (at New York and Washington) 1941, (Philadelphia and Washington) 1944, (Paris) 1945, (Montreal) 1946, (Geneva) 1947. Pres. of Internat. Federation of Commercial, Clerical, and Technical Employees until 1947; travelled much in connection therewith since 1920; Mem. Governing Body of ILO, Geneva until 1948; Sec.-Gen., Nat. Union of Distributive and Allied Workers (now Union of Shop, Distributive and Allied Workers), 1916-49. Mem. Home Office Cttee on Hours of Work of Young Persons in Unregulated Occupations, 1936; Mem. Ministry of Labour Cost of Living Advisory Cttee, 1936 and 1946-47; Mem. Holidays with Pay Cttee, 1937; Mem. Central Price Regulation Cttee under Prices of Goods Act, 1939, and Goods and Services (Price Control) Act, 1941-47; also of Joint Consultative Cttee and Nat. Joint Advisory Council to Ministry of Labour until 1947; Mem. of Ministry of Labour Factory and Welfare Board until 1947 and of other Govt Cttees including the War Damage Commission; Mem. of National Coal Board and Chm. of Miners' Welfare Commission, 1947-49; Chm. North Western Electricity Board, 1949-55, retired. *Publications:* Protective Legislation for Shop and Office Employees; The Legal Minimum; Commercial Employees and Protective Legislation; Road Transport Workers' Wages; Co-operative Shop Managers' Wages; Trade Board Rates and Standard Rates of Wages; Union by Industry; Labour after the War, and others; (jointly) Working Life of Shop Assistants; Labour Conditions in India. *Address:* 9 Alan Road, Withington, Manchester M20 9NQ. *T:* 061-445 1764.
[Died 19 July 1974.

HALMOS, Prof. Paul; Professor of Sociology, The Open University, since 1974; *b* 19 Dec. 1911; *s* of Maurice Halmos and Ethel Soós; *m* 1st, 1937, Edith Halmos (*née* Molnár); one *s*; 2nd, 1972, Ena Edwards. *Educ:* Budapest, Hungary (Dr Jur 1935); London (BA 1945, PhD 1950). Lectr in Social Psychology, SW Essex Technical Coll., 1947-56; Lectr, Sen. Lectr, Tutor in Charge of Social Studies, Univ. of Keele, 1956-65; Prof. of Sociology, University Coll., Cardiff, Univ. of Wales, 1965-74. Distinguished Vis. Prof., Wayne State Univ., USA, 1972. *Publications:* Solitude and Privacy, 1952; Towards a Measure of Man, 1957; The Faith of the Counsellors, 1965; The Personal Service Society, 1970; The Personal and the Political, 1978; (ed) Sociological Review Monographs, 1958-74; (ed) Sociology and Social Welfare Series, 1966-. *Recreations:* philately, painting, mosaics. *Address:* The Open University, Walton Hall, Milton Keynes MK7 6AA.   *[Died 18 Oct. 1977.*

HALSTED, Maj.-Gen. John Gregson, CB 1940; OBE; MC; *b* 16 Aug. 1890; 2nd Lieut Loyal Regt, 1910; Capt., 1915; Bt Major, 1919; Major, 1928; Bt Lieut-Col, 1931; Lieut-Col, 1935; Col, 1937; Maj.-Gen., 1941; served European War, 1914-18 (wounded twice, despatches twice, Bt Major, MC); Palestine, 1936-39 (despatches, OBE); War of 1939-45 (CB), France 1939-40; MGA 1941; Vice-QMG, War Office, 1945; retired pay, 1946. *Address:* c/o Lloyds Bank, Woodbridge, Suffolk. *Club:* Naval and Military.   *[Died 8 May 1980.*

HAMER, Jean; *see* Rhys, Jean.

HAMILTON, 14th Duke of, *cr* 1643, Scotland, and **BRANDON,** 11th Duke of, *cr* 1711, Great Britain; **Douglas Douglas-Hamilton;** PC 1940; KT 1951; GCVO 1946; AFC 1935; Royal Victorian Chain, 1964; LLD, Universities of St Andrews and Edinburgh; FRCSE; FRGS; DL; Hereditary Keeper of Palace of Holyroodhouse; Lord High Commissioner to the General Assembly of the Church of Scotland, 1953, 1954, 1955 and 1958; Lord Steward of HM Household, 1940-64; Chancellor St Andrews University since 1948; President, Air League of the British Empire; *b* 3 Feb. 1903; *e s* of 13th Duke; *S* father 1940; *m* 1937, Lady Elizabeth Percy, *er d* of 8th Duke of Northumberland, KG; five *s*. *Educ:* Eton; Balliol Coll., Oxford. Mem. of Royal Company of Archers. Hon. Pres. of Boys' Brigade, 1963 (Treas., 1938-62); Director: Scottish Aviation Ltd, Prestwick; Securicor (Scotland) (Pres.); Chm. Scottish Bd, Nationwide Building Soc.; Pres. Building Societies Assoc., 1961-65 (now Vice-Pres.). Served in 602 City of Glasgow RAAF Squadron which he commanded, 1927-36; served Royal Air Force, 1939-45 (despatches), Hon. Air Cdre. MP (U) East Renfrewshire, 1930-40; Chief Pilot Mount Everest Flight Expedition, 1933. Pres. British Air Line Pilots' Assoc., 1937-, and Chm. Cttee on Pilot Training. Liveryman, Guild of Air Pilots and Air Navigators, 1963. Pres. of Air League, 1959-68. *Publication:* (with Gp Capt. D. F. McIntyre) The Pilot's Book of Everest, 1936. *Recreations:* boxing, gliding, ski-ing, swimming. *Heir:* *s* Marquess of Clydesdale. *Address:* Lennoxlove, East Lothian. *T:* Haddington 2156. *Clubs:* Royal Air Force, United Service & Royal Aero; Western (Glasgow); New (Edinburgh).
[Died 30 March 1973.

HAMILTON, His Honour Allister McNicoll; Judge of County Courts Circuit No 23 (Coventry, Northampton), 1947-66; *b* 23 Jan. 1895; *s* of Donald Hamilton; *m* 1944, Mary Glen Rankin; one *s* one *d*. *Educ:* Liverpool Univ. (LLB Hons). Served throughout European War, 1914-18, as officer with Infantry and Trench Mortar Battery (wounded); called to Bar, Gray's Inn, 1919; in business, 1919-22; Northern Circuit, 1922-47. *Address:* Mayriggs, Brechin Road, Kirriemuir, Angus. *T:* Kirriemuir 2576.   *[Died 8 Feb. 1973.*

HAMILTON, Archibald; *b* 28 June 1895; 2nd *s* of late Archibald Hamilton and Mrs Hannah Hamilton, Motherwell; *m* 1930, Janet Gibson McBride, MA, *d* of late John McBride, Motherwell; no *c*. *Educ:* Dalziel High Sch., Motherwell; Glasgow University. Graduated BL, and passed as Solicitor, 1920; partner Maclay Murray and Spens, Solicitors, Glasgow, 1929-44; Sheriff Substitute of Fife and Kinross, 1944-52; Sheriff Substitute of Aberdeen, Kincardine and Banff, 1952-71; retired. *Address:* 73 Fountainhall Road, Aberdeen. *T:* 23587.
[Died 25 Sept. 1974.

HAMILTON, (Arthur Douglas) Bruce, CMG 1964; *b* 3 July 1900; *s* of Walter Bernard Hamilton, Author and Barrister-at-Law, and Ellen Adèle Hamilton (*née* Hockley); *m* 1934, (Marie) Aileen (Lorna) Laurie. *Educ:* Westminster Sch.; University College, London. BA London 1926; PhD London 1947. Asst Master, Harrison Coll., Barbados, 1926-29. Senior History Master, 1938-50; Principal, Barbados Evening Institute and Technical Institute, 1950-55; Chm., Barbados Public Service Commission, 1957-64; Pres., Barbados Arts Council, 1959-60. *Publications:* novels include: To be Hanged, 1930; Middle Class Murder, 1935; Pro, 1946; Let Him have Judgment, 1947 (US and play title, Hanging Judge); So Sad, So Fresh, 1952; Too Much of Water, 1958, Etc.; *biography:* The Light Went Out: the life of Patrick Hamilton, 1972; *play:* (with Diana Hamilton) The Home Front, 1930; *historical:* Barbados and the Confederation Question, 1957. *Recreations:* music, literary studies, cricket. *Address:* 26 West Hill Street, Brighton, Sussex.
[Died 24 March 1974.

HAMILTON, Arthur Plumptre Faunce, CIE 1947; OBE 1938; MC 1918; Inspector-General of Forests, Indian Forest Service, 1945-49; *b* 7 Oct. 1895; *s* of Francis Robert Abingdon Hamilton and Alice Emilia Plumptre; *m* 1925, Olivia Urmston Seth-Smith; one *s* one *d*. *Educ:* Trent Coll., Derbyshire; Lincoln Coll., Oxford. Served European War, 1914-19, in British Army, 8th Bn Sherwood Foresters and 2nd Bn Royal Tank Corps (temp. Major). Joined Indian Forest Service, 1921; served in Punjab. Forestry Commissioner, 1953-60. *Recreations:* shooting, fishing. *Address:* c/o Barclays Bank Ltd, Saxmundham, Suffolk.
[Died 17 Jan. 1977.

HAMILTON, Bruce; *see* Hamilton, A. D. B.

HAMILTON, Charles Keith Johnstone, MC; BA, BM Oxford; FRCP; Consulting Physician, Children's Department, Charing Cross Hospital; *b* 1890; *s* of late C. W. Hamilton, MD; *m* Christine Mary (*d* 1959), *y d* of late Ernest Durrant. *Educ:* privately; Lincoln Coll., Oxford; St Thomas' Hospital. Served European War 1914 in King Edward's Horse and Royal Field Artillery (wounded, MC); late Hon. Medical Dir Violet Melchett Infant Welfare Centre; late Consulting Paediatrician to LCC, and to Taunton and Somerset Hospital. John Temple Research Fellow, St Thomas' Hosp.; Mem., British Pædiatric Assoc. *Publications:* The Principles of Infant Nutrition (with K. Tallerman); Heart Disease in Childhood (with H. B. Russell); contributions to medical journals. *Recreations:* hunting, fishing, gardening. *Address:* Castle Farm, Exford, Som. *Club:* United Oxford & Cambridge University.   *[Died 5 July 1978.*

HAMILTON, Sir (Charles) William (Feilden), Kt 1974; OBE; inventor; Founder and Director, C. W. F. Hamilton & Co. Ltd and C. W. F. Hamilton Marine Ltd, Christchurch, New Zealand; *b* Ashwick Station, Fairlie, NZ, 26 July 1899; *s* of W. F. Hamilton; *m* 1923, Margery L., *d* of G. T. Wills, London; one *s* one *d*. *Educ:* Christ's Coll., New Zealand. Has owned Irishman Creek Station, Fairlie, 1921-; developing engineering, there, 1936; opened engrg works at Middleton, Christchurch, 1945. Inventor, in sphere of marine jet propulsion. Knighted for engineering services. *Recreations:* motor racing, jet boating, climbing. *Address:* c/o C. W. F. Hamilton & Co. Ltd, Box 709, Christchurch, New Zealand; Irishman Creek Station, Fairlie, New Zealand.   *[Died 30 March 1978.*

HAMILTON, Captain Lord Claud (Nigel), GCVO 1949 (KCVO 1937; CVO 1933; MVO 1916); CMG 1920; DSO 1914; late Grenadier Guards; *b* 10 Nov. 1889; 7th *s* of 2nd Duke of Abercorn; *m* 1933, Mrs Violet Newall. *Educ:* Wellington.

Entered Army, 1911; served European War, 1914-19 (despatches twice, DSO); Equerry to Prince of Wales, 1919-22; Deputy-Master of HM's Household, 1922-24; Equerry to King George V, 1924-36; Comptroller and Treasurer in Queen Mary's Household, 1936-53; Extra Equerry to the Queen, 1953-. *Address:* Jannaways, Bagnor, Newbury, Berks. *T:* Newbury 553; 8 Russell Court, Cleveland Row, St James's, SW1. *T:* 01-930 1152.   *[Died 22 Aug. 1975.*

HAMILTON, Emily Moore, MBE; *d* of late Rev. J. S. Hamilton, MA, Abbey Church, Dublin; *m* 1925, Prof. J. H. Richardson, CMG (*d* 1970); twin *d. Educ:* Victoria Coll., Belfast. Associate of the Royal College of Music, London. During European War, 1914-18, organised Girl Messenger System for West End Government Offices, 1915-18; Asst Commandant Women's Royal Air Force, 1918-19. First Staff officer, International Labour Office, League of Nations, Geneva, 1920-23; Save the Children Fund refugee work in Greece, 1923-24; War of 1939-45: supervision of women in explosives factory, Toronto, 1940. Red Cross work in Bermuda and Bahamas, 1941-43. *Address:* 8 Douro Court, Mont Pihel, Jersey, CI. *T:* Central 34717.
[Died 8 Aug. 1972.

HAMILTON, Adm. Sir Frederick Hew George D.; *see* Dalrymple-Hamilton.

HAMILTON, Rev. Herbert Alfred; *b* 16 June 1897; *s* of Alfred and Ada Elizabeth Hamilton; *m* 1st, 1929, Winifred Alice Johnson (*d* 1936); two adopted *s*; 2nd, 1937, Phyllis Noella Pye (*d* 1944); one *d*; 3rd, 1944, Ellen Crossman Allen; one *s* one *d. Educ:* Merchant Taylors', Crosby; Manchester Univ.; Lancs Independent Coll. Ordained, 1924; Pastorates: Bolton, 1924-29; Birmingham, 1929-33; Sec. for Education and Youth Service, Congregational Union of England and Wales, 1933-45; Principal, Westhill Training Coll., Birmingham, 1945-54; Minister, Union Church, Brighton, 1954-63. Chm., Congregational Union of England and Wales, May 1961-62; Associate Gen. Sec., World Council of Christian Education, 1963-65; Asst Gen. Sec., World Council of Churches, 1965-66. Retired as consultant to the World Council of Christian Education, 1966. *Publications:* How to Say your Prayers, 1933; The Family Church, 1940; Church Youth Training, 1944; Conversation with God, 1955; contrib. to Expository Times, Times Educl Supplement, etc. *Recreations:* music, painting, conversation. *Address:* 22 Damian Way, Keymer, Hassocks, West Sussex.   *[Died 13 Nov. 1977.*

HAMILTON, Sir Horace (Perkins), GCB 1942 (KCB 1921; CB 1918); UK Member, Commonwealth Economic Committee, 1947-61 (Chairman, 1947-49); *b* 20 Nov. 1880; *o s* of Horace Hamilton, Ashford, Kent; *m* 1915, Amy (*d* 1970), *d* of Sydney Turner Klein; one *s* two *d. Educ:* Tonbridge Sch.; Hertford Coll., Oxford. Entered Inland Revenue Dept, 1904; transferred to Treasury, 1912; Private Sec. to Chancellor of the Exchequer, 1912-18; Dep. Chm. Board of Inland Revenue, 1918-19; Chm. Board of Customs and Excise, 1919-27; Permanent Sec., Board of Trade, 1927-37; Permanent Under-Sec. of State for Scotland, 1937-46. Advised Control Office for Germany and Austria on application of Whitley system to British civilian staffs in Control Service, 1946; advised Syrian Govt on taxation system of Syria, 1946-47; Mem., Interdepartmental Cttees on remuneration of specialists and of dentists, 1947-48; Vice-Chm. Advisory Cttee on Awards for Consultants and Specialists, 1948-60; Chm., OEEC Cttee on Internal Financial Stability, Paris, 1949; Mem., Deptl Cttee on Scottish Financial and Trade Statistics, 1950-52; Chm. Cttee on Regional Bds for Industry, 1953; Pres., Old Tonbridgian Soc., 1950-60; Pres., Tonbridge Sch. Clubs, St Pancras, 1934-64. *Address:* Leigham Grange, Leigham Court Road, SW16. *Club:* Athenæum.   *[Died 15 Sept. 1971.*

HAMILTON, James Gilbert Murdoch, FRCPEd; Consultant Physician, Royal Infirmary, Edinburgh, since 1939; Principal Medical Officer, Scottish Widows Fund and Life Assurance Society, since 1954; *b* 14 July 1907; *s* of William Henry Hamilton, SSC, and Margaret Paterson Mackenzie; *m* 1937, Elizabeth Frary King, Boston, Mass, USA; two *s* one *d* (and one *d* decd). *Educ:* George Watson's Coll., Edinburgh; Edinburgh Univ. MB, ChB, Edinburgh, 1931; MRCP, 1934, FRCPEd, 1939. Commonwealth Fund Fellow, Boston, Mass, 1935-37. Mem., Gen. Medical Council, 1958-. Vice-Pres., BMA, 1966-. *Publications:* contrib. to Brit. Medical Jl, Lancet, Brit. Heart Jl, Amer. Heart Jl; chapter on Life Assurance in Encyclopaedia of General practice. *Recreations:* formerly golf, now committee work. *Address:* 24 Mortonhall Road, Edinburgh 9. *T:* 031-667 5439. *Club:* University Staff (Edinburgh). *[Died 6 July 1972.*

HAMILTON, Brig. James Melvill, DSO 1916; retired; *b* 4 Nov. 1886; *o s* of late Lewis Hamilton; *m* 1st, 1913, Violet Anne

Colquhoun (*d* 1950); 2nd, 1950, Amelia Grenfell. *Educ:* Winchester; Sandhurst. Joined The Gordon Highlanders, 1907; Lt-Col 1934; Col 1938; Brig. 1938-41; Comd 144 Inf. Bde, Sub-Area Comd 1941-43; Col CA/Military Government, 1943-46; Served European War, 1914-19 (despatches five times, DSO, Legion of Honour); War of 1939-45 (despatches). *Address:* 6 Orchard Rise, Richmond, Surrey. *Club:* Royal Automobile.
[Died April 1972.

HAMILTON, John Almeric de Courcy, CMG 1946; MC; Sudan Political Service (retired); *b* 7 Oct. 1896; *s* of late Henry de Courcy Hamilton; *m* 1960, Noreen, 2nd *d* of late Lieut-Col and Mrs H. K. Hamilton-Wedderburn. *Educ:* Cheltenham; King's Coll., Cambridge. BA 1920; MA 1933; served with 4th Bn Royal Hampshire Regiment, 1914-19 (wounded, MC); Sudan Political Service, 1920; District Commissioner, 1920-32; Sudan Agent, Cairo, 1932-34; seconded to Egyptian Govt, 1935-37 and to British Embassy, Cairo, 1937-41. Counsellor at the Legation, Beirut, 1941-42; Minister of State's Office, Bagdad and Cairo, 1942-46; Counsellor, British Embassy, Cairo, 1947-56; retired 1957. *Address:* 15 Collingham Road, SW5. *Club:* Athenæum.
[Died 24 Nov. 1973.

HAMILTON, Sir William; *see* Hamilton, Sir C. W. F.

HAMILTON, Prof. William James, MD, BCh (Belfast), DSc (Glasgow); FRCS; FRCOG; FRSE; Professor of Anatomy, University of London, 1947-70, Professor Emeritus, 1971; Professor of Anatomy at the Royal Academy of Arts; *b* 1903; *s* of late Andrew and late Emmeline G. Hamilton, Roselle, Whitehead, Co. Antrim, N Ireland; *m* 1933, Maimie, *o d* of late Samuel Young, Ingleside, Myrtlefield Park, Belfast; four *s* one *d. Educ:* Queen's Univ. Belfast, BSc, 1926, First Class Hons; MB, BCh, BAO, 1929, First Class Hons and First Place; MSc 1931; MD 1936, High Commendation, Queen's Univ., Belfast; DSc, 1934, Glasgow Univ.; various Scholarships and Exhibitions at Queen's Univ. and Royal Victoria Hosp., Belfast, 1925-29; Struthers Anatomical Prize and Gold Medal, University of Glasgow, 1932; Neill Prize, Royal Society of Edinburgh, 1938; formerly Lecturer in Anatomy in University of Glasgow and Dep. Dir of Anatomy at St Thomas's Hosp. Medical Sch.; Prof. of Anatomy in Univ. of London at St Bartholomew's Hosp. Medical Coll.; Regius Prof. of Anatomy at Glasgow Univ., 1945-47. Pres. Anatomical Soc. of Great Britain and Ireland, 1953-55, Sec., 1964-67. Chm. Special Adv. Bd of Vet. Med. in Univ. of London. Member: Senate, University of London, 1962-64; Sch. Council, Royal Vet. Coll.; Bd of Governors, Queen Charlotte's and Chelsea Hosps, 1966-69; SW Metropolitan Regional Hosp. Bd, 1959-68. Sometime External Examr in Univs of: Aberdeen, Belfast, Bristol, Cambridge, Cardiff, Liverpool and Manchester; also in Primary FRCS, RCS of England. FRCS 1968. Hon. DSc Queen's Univ., Belfast, 1968. John Hunter Medal and Triennial Prize, RCS, 1973. *Publications:* Memoirs on Embryology and related subjects in Transactions of Royal Society of Edinburgh and Journal of Anatomy; Text Book on Surface and Radiological Anatomy (with Appleton and Tchaperoff), 1938, 5th edn 1971; Textbook on Human Embryology (with Boyd and Mossman), 1945, 4th edn 1971; Editor Textbook of Human Anatomy, 1956; The Human Placenta (with Boyd), 1970; contributions to: Vol. 2 of Marshall's Physiology of Reproduction (ed Parkes), 3rd edn, 1952; Queen Charlotte's Textbook of Obstetrics (ed Tomkinson), 11th edn, 1956, 12th edn, 1970; British Obstetric and Gynaecological Practice (ed Claye and Bourne), 2nd edn, 1953, 3rd edn, 1963; Modern Trends in Obstetrics (ed Bowes), 1st series, 1950, 2nd series, 1955; Diseases of the Ear, Nose and Throat (ed Scott-Brown, Ballantyne and Groves) 2nd edn, 1965, 3rd edn, 1971; Scientific Foundations of Obstetrics and Gynaecology (ed Philipp, Barnes and Newton), 1970. *Address:* Tara, 45 Wolsey Road, Moor Park, Northwood, Middlesex. *T:* Northwood 22258.
[Died 3 May 1975.

HAMILTON-KING, Mrs Grace M.; Principal, Royal School of Needlework, 1950-66; *d* of late Canon Arthur West and of Mrs Louisa Oliver; *m* 1932, Edward Hamilton-King (decd). *Educ:* St Clair, Tunbridge Wells; Effingham House, Bexhill; Lytton House, London. London Academy of Music, 1922-23; Miss Kerr-Sander's Secretarial Coll., 1930-31; Temp. Administrative Officer, Home Office, 1941-45. Coronation Medal, 1953. *Address:* c/o Lloyds Bank, Pantiles Branch, 1 London Road, Tunbridge Wells, Kent.   *[Died 7 Nov. 1980.*

HAMLING, William, JP; MP (Lab) Greenwich, Woolwich West, since 1974 (Woolwich West, 1964-74); *b* 10 Aug. 1912; *s* of William and Charlotte Hamling, Liverpool; *m* 1940, Olive Victoria, *d* of William and Henrietta Sophia Fraser, Liverpool; two *d. Educ:* Liverpool Inst. High Sch. for Boys; University of Liverpool. Schoolmaster and Lecturer. Commissioned in Royal

Marines, 1941; served until 1946. An Asst Govt Whip, 1969-70; an Opposition Whip, 1970-72. Trustee, Nat. Maritime Museum, 1967-; Governor, The Foudroyant Trust; Chm., Defence of Literature and the Arts Soc. JP Liverpool, 1948-51; JP Blackheath, 1963. *Address:* 4 Commonwealth Way, SE2. *T:* 01-854 6778. *[Died 19 March 1975.*

HAMMILL, Captain Charles Ford, CIE 1944; *b* 27 Nov. 1891; *s* of Capt. Tynte Ford Hammill, CB, RN; *m* 1933, Cynthia, *d* of late Adm. Sir Howard Kelly, GBE, KCB. Entered RNC, Osborne, 1904. Served in HMS Colossus, European War, 1914-18. Commanded HMS Enterprise, 1938, HMS Cornwall, 1939-41; Naval Attaché, Paris, 1934-37; Commodore, Senior Naval Officer Persian Gulf, 1942-44; Commodore in Charge Royal Naval Establishments, Durban, 1944-46; retired, 1943. *Address:* Bleak House, Slindon, Arundel, West Sussex. *T:* Slindon 281. *Club:* Naval and Military. *[Died 30 Aug. 1980.*

HAMMOND, John Colman, OBE 1959; MA; Retired as Headmaster, Harrison College, Barbados, WI (1949-65); *b* 24 Nov. 1906; *s* of late Ven. T. C. Hammond; *m* 1943, Marjorie (*née* Cruse); one *s* one *d*. *Educ:* Rossall Sch.; Pembroke Coll., Cambridge (MA). Senior History Master, St John's Sch., Leatherhead, Surrey, 1929-46; House Master, 1934-46; Headmaster, Sompting Abbotts Sch., Sussex. 1947-49. Coronation Medal, 1953. *Recreation:* bridge. *Address:* 23 Riggindale Road, Streatham, SW16. *T:* 01-769 4541. *[Died 15 Dec. 1979.*

HAMMOND, Kay, (Dorothy Katharine); actress; *b* 18 Feb. 1909; *d* of late Sir Guy Standing, KBE, and late Dorothy Plaskitt (professionally known as Dorothy Hammond); *m* 1st, 1932, Sir Ronald George Leon, 3rd Bt (marriage dissolved); two *s*; 2nd, 1946, Sir John Selby Clements, CBE. *Educ:* The Lodge, Banstead, Surrey. Studied at Royal Academy of Dramatic Art. Among London appearances are: Beatrice in Nine Till Six, Arts and Apollo, 1930; Evergreen, Adelphi, 1930; Daphne Hibberd in Can the Leopard...?, Haymarket, 1931; Emmie in My Hat, New, 1932; Elsa Frost in Woman Kind, Phoenix, 1933; Elizabeth Rimplegar in Three-Cornered Moon, Westminster, 1934; Dorothy Wilson in Youth at the Helm, Globe, 1935; Hon. Ursula Maddings in Bees on the Boatdeck, Lyric, 1936; Diana Lake in French Without Tears, Criterion, 1936-38; Adeline Rawlinson in Sugar Plum, Criterion, 1939; Elvira in Blithe Spirit, Piccadilly, St James's and Duchess, 1941-44; Amanda in Private Lives (revival), Apollo, 1944-45; Lady Elizabeth Grey in The Kingmaker; Melantha in Marriage à la Mode, by John Dryden, St James's, 1946; Mrs Sullen in The Beaux' Stratagem, by George Farquhar, Phoenix and Lyric, 1949; Ann in Man and Superman, New, 1951; The Happy Marriage, Duke of York's, 1952; Eliza in Pygmalion, St James's, 1953-54; The Little Glass Clock, Aldwych, 1954-55; Lydia Languish in The Rivals, Saville, 1956; Millamant in The Way of the World, Saville, 1956; The Rape of the Belt, Piccadilly, 1957; Gilt and Gingerbread, Duke of York's, 1959; The Marriage-Go-Round, 1959. In numerous films, 1931-. *Address:* 4 Rufford Court, 109 Marine Parade, Brighton, East Sussex BN2 1AT. *T:* Brighton 63026. *[Died 4 May 1980.*

HAMNETT, Baron *cr* 1970 (Life Peer), of Warrington; **Cyril Hamnett;** DL; Director, Hugin Cash Register Ltd; *b* 20 May 1906; *e s* of James Henry Hamnett and Gertrude Hilton; *m* 1929, Elsie Cox (*d* 1970); one *d*. *Educ:* elementary and Manchester Technical School. Engineering Journalism, Editor and Publicity Officer to Union of Shop, Distributive & Allied Workers until 1952; Admin. Officer, 1953-66. Chairman: Reynolds News and Sunday Citizen, 1953-67; Co-operative Press Ltd, 1953-77 (Director, 1947); Mem., Newspaper Proprietors' Assoc., 1953-67; Mem., British Press Council, 1956-65. Dir, Nor-West Cooperative Soc. Ltd, 1946-73; Mem., Central Exec., Co-operative Union, 1953-74 (Chm. Parly Cttee, 1969-74). Chm., Warrington New Town Develt Corp., 1969-77. Manchester City Magistrate, 1950-76 (Chm. of Licensing Bench, 1962-65, 1968-76); Mem., Licensing Planning Cttee, 1960-77; Mem. of Tribunals. DL Greater Manchester, 1979. Hon. Fellow, Manchester Polytechnic. *Publications:* pamphlets and articles to magazines, newspapers, on industrial, trade union and co-operative subjects. *Recreation:* the pursuit of the unattainable. *Address:* 11 Bolton Avenue, Manchester M19 1RP. *T:* 061-432 4801. *Club:* Sloane. *[Died 17 March 1980.*

HAMPDEN, 5th Viscount, *cr* 1884; **David Francis Brand;** *b* 14 June 1902; 2nd *s* of 3rd Viscount Hampden, GCVO, KCB, CMG; *S* brother, 4th Viscount, 1965; *m* 1936, Imogen Alice Rhys, *d* of 7th Baron Dynevor; one *s* two *d*. *Educ:* Eton; Trinity Coll., Cambridge. Herts Regt, 1938; served with 29th Independent Brigade Group; DAA&QMG, Madagascar, 1942; Bde Major, Burma, 1944 (despatches); Lt-Col 1944. *Heir: s* Hon.

Anthony David Brand [*b* 7 May 1937; *m* 1969, Cara Fiona, *e d* of Claud Proby; two *s* one *d*]. *Address:* Trevor House, Glynde, East Sussex. *T:* Glynde 295. *Club:* White's. *[Died 4 Sept. 1975.*

HAMPDEN, John, MA Oxon; author and publishers' editor; *b* 6 Feb. 1898; *e s* of Francis John Hampden; *m* 1st, Doreen Springall; one *s* one *d*; 2nd, Rosalind Vallance, author and playwright; one *d*. *Educ:* St Martin's, Dover; privately; Exeter Coll., Oxford. Skeat Prize, 1921. English Master, Royal Grammar Sch., Guildford, 1922-29; Lectr in and later Prof. of English Literature, Queen's Coll., London, 1929-32; Gen. Editor, Thomas Nelson & Sons Ltd, 1932-37; Nat. Book Council, 1938-39; Min. of Information, 1940-41. British Council, 1941-63: Books and Periodicals Adviser, 1959-63; Head of Literature Group of Depts, 1947-59; Dep. Controller, Arts and Science Div., 1950-59; etc. Editor, British Book News, 1942-46; Mem. Council and Exec., Nat. Book League, 1946-63; a Dir, British Nat. Bibliography, 1950-63; Hon. Life Mem., Soc. of Bookmen and PEN. *Publications:* Critical editions of many 16th, 17th and 18th century English plays; Havelok and Sir Orfeo; Drake's Raid on the Treasure Trains (with Janet Hampden); An Eighteenth Century Journal; edns of Lamb's Essays, Hazlitt's Essays, Johnson's Lives of the Poets (with Rosalind Vallance); The Book World Today; Books, from Papyrus to Paperback (with Esther S. Harley); A Picture History of India; New Worlds Ahead; Francis Drake, Privateer; The Spanish Armada; The Tudor Ventures; five vols of folk tales; anthologies, textbooks, contribs to literary jls and BBC programmes. Much pseudonymous work. *Recreations:* walking, talking. *Address:* Robin House, 55 St Mary's Terrace, Hastings, East Sussex. *T:* Hastings 436565. *[Died 7 Aug. 1974.*

HAMPSON, Arthur Cecil, MC; MA, MD, FRCP; Consulting Physician to Guy's Hospital; Hon. Consulting Physician to Queen Mary's Hospital for the East End, and to Bromley, Beckenham and Purley Hospitals; *b* 1894; *s* of late Robert Hampson, Southport; *m* 1926, Anne Ramsbottom. *Educ:* Southport; Cambridge; Guy's Medical School. Served European War, 1915-19, Major, RA (SR). Hilda and Ronald Poulton Research Fellow, Guy's Hosp., 1926-30; Asst Physician Children's Dept, Guy's Hosp., 1930-35. Mem. Assoc. of British Physicians and other societies; Hon. Mem., British Paediatric Assoc. Hon. Visiting Physician to Johns Hopkins Hosp., USA, 1952. *Publications:* contributions to medical journals. *Recreations:* gardening, golf. *Address:* Little Hurnford, Snowshill, Broadway, Worcs. *T:* Broadway 3204. *Club:* Athenæum. *[Died 26 Sept. 1972.*

HAMPTON, 5th Baron, *cr* 1874; **Humphrey Arthur Pakington,** Bt 1846; OBE 1942; DL; *b* 8 Sept. 1888; 4th *s* of 3rd Baron (*d* 1906); *S* brother, 1962; *m* 1913, Grace Dykes (*d* 1959), 3rd *d* of Rt Hon. Sir A. Spicer, 1st Bt, PC; one *s* three *d*. Entered Navy, 1903; retired 1920 as Lieut-Comdr; Comdr, retired, 1928. Trained at Architectural Association; Holloway Scholarship, 1922; Architectural Association Diploma and FRIBA (retired); Pres. of Architectural Assoc., 1934-36; partner in Pakington & Enthoven, Architects, 10 Bayley Street, Bedford Square, WC1; rejoined Navy, 1939; Staff of C-in-C, Western Approaches, 1939-45. DL, Worcs. 1953. *Publications:* various novels including: Four in Family; Aston Kings; The Washbournes of Otterley; Catherine Chailey; John Brandon; How the World Builds, an Introduction to Architecture; English Villages and Hamlets; Bid Time Return, an autobiography. *Heir: s* Hon. Richard Humphrey Russell Pakington [*b* 25 May 1925; *m* 1958, Jane Elizabeth Farquharson, *d* of T. F. Arnott, OBE, TD, MB, ChB; one *s* two *d*]. *Address:* The Old Rectory, Holt, near Worcester. *T:* Ombersley 243. *Club:* Athenæum. *[Died 17 Feb. 1974.*

HAMSON, Vincent Everard; *b* 2 Nov. 1888; 2nd *s* of late John Hamson, Bedford; *m* 1912, Florence Reynolds, St Albans; one *s* one *d*. *Educ:* Bedford. Reporter Bedfordshire Times and various provincial papers; Exchange Telegraph Co., 1920; Official Report (Hansard), 1927, Asst Editor, 1947; Editor, Official Report of Debates, House of Commons (Hansard), 1951-54, retired Nov. 1954. Librarian and Archivist, Parliamentary Press Gallery, 1931-37. Pres., Incorporated Phonographic Soc., 1952. *Recreation:* alpine gardening. *Address:* 60 Cheston Avenue, Shirley, Croydon CR0 8DB. *T:* 01-777 1331. *[Died 27 Oct. 1975.*

HANBURY, Brig. Richard Nigel, CBE 1954; TD 1943; DL; JP; retired; *b* 7 Oct. 1911; *s* of Nigel Hanbury, Green End House, Ware, Herts; *m* 1936, Anne Mildred, *d* of E. Perceval Alers Hankey, Stourton, Wilts; two *d*. *Educ:* Eton; Magdalene Coll., Cambridge. Served War of 1939-45, with RA (France, N Africa, Italy and Austria); Lieut-Col 1943; Brig. 1950. Hon. Col: Herts Yeo. (479 HAA), 1954; Herts Yeo. (286 Fd), 1957; Hon. Brig.

TA retired. ADC (TA) to the Queen, 1958-63, retd. Chm. and Managing Dir, Gripper and Wrightman Ltd, malsters, 1946-59. DL, 1951, JP 1962, Herts; High Sheriff of Herts, 1960. Hon. Colonel: 286 The Hertfordshire and Bedfordshire Yeomanry, 1963-67; The Bedfordshire and Hertfordshire (T), 1967-69. *Recreations:* hunting, sailing. *Address:* Hay Lodge, Braughing, Ware, Herts. *T:* Puckeridge 372. *Club:* Leander (Henley).
[Died 22 March 1971.

HANCOCK, Dame Florence (May), DBE *cr* 1951 (CBE 1947; OBE 1942); Chief Woman Officer, Transport and General Workers' Union, 1942-58; Director of Remploy Ltd, 1958-66; *b* 25 Feb. 1893; *d* of Jacob and Mary Hancock; *m* 1964, John Donovan, CBE (*d* 1971). *Educ:* Chippenham Elementary Sch. Full-time official of Workers' Union, 1917; Mem. of General Council of the TUC, 1935-58; Pres. of British TUC 1947-48; Dir Daily Herald, July 1955-March 1957. A Governor of the BBC, 1956-62. *Recreations:* reading and needlework. *Address:* 4 Melita Road, Bristol 6. *T:* Bristol 43880. *Club:* English-Speaking Union.
[Died 14 April 1974.

HANCOCK, Sir Patrick (Francis), GCMG 1974 (KCMG 1969; CMG 1956); HM Diplomatic Service, retired; Secretary, The Pilgrim Trust, since 1975; *b* 25 June 1914; *s* of late R. E. Hancock, DSO; *m* 1947, Beatrice Mangeot; one *s* one *d*. *Educ:* Winchester Coll.; Trinity Coll., Cambridge. Entered HM Foreign Service, 1937. Appointed Principal Private Sec, to Foreign Sec., 1955; Head of Western Dept, Foreign Office, 1956; Ambassador to Israel, 1959-62; Ambassador to Norway, 1963-65; Asst Under-Sec. of State, FO, 1965-68. Dep. Under-Sec. of State, FCO, 1968-69; Ambassador in Rome, 1969-74. Commander, Order of North Star, 1956. *Recreation:* salmon fishing. *Address:* 5 Shelley Court, Tite Street, SW3; The Old Vicarage, Affpuddle, Dorset. *T:* Puddletown 315.
[Died 1 Feb. 1980.

HANCOX, Leslie Pascoe, CIE 1946; OBE 1939; *b* 18 May 1906; *s* of Thomas and Maria Pascoe Hancox; *m* 1936, Heather Alexandra Thomson; one *s* one *d*. *Educ:* St Olave's Sch.; Christ's Coll., Cambridge. Entered Indian Civil Service, 1929; Asst Magistrate, United Provinces, 1929-30; Joint Magistrate, United Provinces, 1931-35; District Magistrate, United Provinces, 1935-42; Sec. to Govt United Provinces, Civil Supplies Dept, 1942-44; Finance Sec., Government of the United Provinces, Lucknow, UP, India, 1945-47, retired from ICS, 1947. The British Oxygen Co. Ltd, 1949-. *Recreations:* cricket, tennis, squash rackets. *Address:* 1 Rutland Lodge, 1 Clifton Road, SW19.
[Died 13 March 1975.

HANDFIELD-JONES, Ranald Montagu, MC; Consulting Surgeon, St Mary's Hospital; Consulting General Surgeon, the Hospital for Women, Soho Square; Member Court of Examiners, RCS; Examiner in Surgery to Universities of London, Cambridge, Liverpool, Leeds and Manchester; *b* 12 May 1892; *s* of late C. R. Handfield-Jones, MD, and Alice Jervis; *m* 1920; three *s* one *d*. *Educ:* Epsom Coll.; St Mary's Hospital Medical Sch.; London Univ.; Epsom Scholarship to St Mary's Hosp.; Master of Surgery (University of London), MB, BS (Hons in Surgery and Midwifery, University Gold Medallist); FRCS; Hunterian Prof., RCS. Served European War in France, Oct. 1914-May 1918; prisoner of war, May-Nov. 1918. *Publications:* The Essentials of Modern Surgery (with A. E. Porritt), 5th edn, 1955; Surgery of the Hand, 2nd edn 1946; papers to medical journals. *Recreations:* entomology, cricket, golf, photography. *Address:* 9 Hurlingham Gardens, SW6. *T:* 01-736 5671.
[Died 21 April 1978.

HANDFORD, Stanley Alexander, MA Oxon; *b* Manchester, 1898; *s* of late Thomas Edward Handford, Harrogate; *m* 1923, Doris (*d* 1975), *d* of late James Henry Ollerhead, Oswestry. *Educ:* Bradford Grammar Sch.; Balliol Coll., Oxford (Classical Schol.); 1st class Hon. Classical Moderations and Craven Scholarship, 1920; Ireland Scholarship, 1921; 1st Class Literae Humaniores and Charles Oldham Prize, 1922; Asst Lecturer in Classics, University Coll. of Swansea, 1922-23; Asst Lectr and Lectr, King's Coll., London, 1923-46; Reader, 1946-66. *Publications:* Revision of L. W. Hunter's Aeneas on Siegecraft, 1927; Xenophon's Anabasis, Books III and IV, 1928; The Latin Subjunctive, 1947; Caesar's Conquest of Gaul (Penguin Classics), 1951; Caesar's Gallic War, Books II and III, 1952; Fables of Aesop (Penguin Classics), 1954; Pocket Latin-English Dictionary, 1955; Sallust's Jugurthine War and Conspiracy of Catiline (Penguin Classics), 1963; Tacitus's Agricola and Germania (Penguin Classics), 1970. *Recreation:* music. *Address:* Hurstleigh, Elm Park Road, Pinner, Mddx HA5 3LE.
[Died 7 Oct. 1978.

HANGER, Hon. Sir Mostyn, KBE 1973; Chief Justice of Supreme Court of State of Queensland, 1971-77; *b* 3 Jan. 1908; *s* of Thomas Hanger; *m* 1936, Greta Lumley Robertson; three *s* one *d*. *Educ:* Gympie State High Sch.; Queensland Univ. BA 1929; LLM 1941. Admitted to Bar, 1930; QC 1950; Supreme Court Judge, 1953; Pres., Industrial Court, 1962-71; Actg Chief Justice, 1970-71. Served with RAAF in New Guinea, 1942-45 (Flt-Lt). *Recreations:* golf, orchids. *Address:* 73 Seventh Avenue, St Lucia, Brisbane, Qld 4067, Australia. *T:* 3713393. *Clubs:* Queensland, United Services (Brisbane).
[Died 11 Aug. 1980.

HANHAM, Sir Henry (Phelips), 11th Bt, *cr* 1667; *b* 6 April 1901; *s* of Sir John Alexander Hanham, 9th Bt and Hon. Cordelia Lucy (*d* 1945), 2nd *d* of 1st Lord Ludlow; *S* brother 1955. *Educ:* Winchester; Magdalen Coll., Oxford. Served War of 1939-45, RA. *Heir: kinsman* Michael William Hanham, DFC [*b* 31 Oct. 1922; *m* 1954, Margaret Jane, *o d* of Wing-Comdr Harold Thomas, RAF; one *s* one *d*]. *Address:* Dean's Court, Wimborne, Dorset.
[Died 23 Nov. 1973.

HANKEY, Very Rev. Cyril Patrick; Dean of Ely, 1951-69, Emeritus since 1969; *b* 1886; *s* of Rev. Claude Hankey; *m* 1925, Frances Mary Harris (*d* 1966); one *s* one *d*. *Educ:* Haileybury; Pembroke Coll., Cambridge; Ely Theological Coll. Principal, Dorchester Missionary Coll., 1916-22; Vicar of St Matthew's, Westminster, 1922-24; Vicar of St Mary's the Less, Cambridge, 1925-38; Chaplain of St John, Menton, France, 1938-41; Vicar of Aldenham and Rural Dean of Watford, 1941-46; Vicar of St Paul's, Bedford, and Rural Dean of Bedford, 1946-51. *Publications:* Lives of the Serbian Saints, 1921; The Young Priest, 1933; A Confession of My Faith, 1940; Signposts on the Christian Way, 1962 (USA). *Address:* Lychgate Cottage, Dorchester-on-Thames, Oxford. *T:* Warborough 476.
[Died 9 Dec. 1973.

HANKIN, Arthur Maxwell, CMG 1955; Sudan Political Service, retired; Comptroller, Forces Help Society and Lord Roberts Workshops, 1963-70; *b* 27 Nov. 1905; *e s* of Seymer and Ethel Hankin; *m* 1938, Helen Elizabeth English; one *s* two *d*. *Educ:* Bromsgrove Sch.; Worcester Coll., Oxford. Joined Sudan Political Service, 1928; Private Sec. to Governor General of Sudan, 1938; Dir of Establishments, Sudan Govt, 1953; retired from Sudan 1955. Order of the Nile (4th class), 1940. *Recreations:* tennis and gardening. *Address:* Ivor Lodge, Milton Lilbourne, Pewsey, Wilts. *T:* Pewsey 3207. *Club:* United University.
[Died 19 March 1972.

HANLEY, Denis Augustine; *b* 1903; *s* of late Edmund Hanley, Kintbury, Berks; *m* 1935, Kathleen Mary, *d* of J. P. Eyre, 56 York Terrace, Regent's Park; three *d*. *Educ:* Downside; Trinity Coll., Cambridge. MP (C) Deptford, 1931-35. Royal Naval Scientific Service, 1938-54. *Address:* Woodcombe, Oxbridge, Bridport, Dorset. *T:* Netherbury 343. *[Died 10 June* 1980.

HANLON, Air Vice-Marshal Thomas James, CB 1969; CBE 1959; Staff Controller, Clerical, Medical and General Life Assurance Society, SW1, since 1971; *b* 15 July 1916; *s* of late James Francis Hanlon, Dublin; *m* 1965, Susan Janet Elizabeth (*née* Williams); one *s*. *Educ:* Belvedere Coll. Dublin; RAF Coll., Cranwell. Sqdn Service, Bomber Comd, 1937-39; No. 8 Sqdn, Aden, 1939-42; Air Min., 1943-46; Bomber Comd, 1946-47; OC, RAF White Waltham, 1948; HQ No. 65 (London) Gp, 1949; HQ Allied Forces Central Europe (NATO), 1950-53; Air Sec.'s Dept, Air Min., 1953-58; HQ Transport Comd, 1958-60; OC, RAF Stn Steamer Point, Aden, 1961-62; SASO, RAF Record Office, Glos, 1964-65; AOC, RAF Record and Pay Office, Glos, 1965-68; AO i/c Admin., HQ Maintenance Comd, RAF Andover, 1968-71, retired from RAF, 1971. psc 1943; jssc 1947; idc 1963; MBIM 1967; FIPM 1974. *Address:* c/o National Westminster Bank Ltd, 36 St James's Street, SW1. *Club:* Royal Air Force.
[Died 6 Jan. 1977.

HANMER, Lt-Col Sir (Griffin Wyndham) Edward, 7th Bt, *cr* 1620, *re-cr* 1774; late Shropshire Yeomanry and Royal Air Force; JP Flintshire; High Sheriff, 1932; Master of Sir W. W. Wynn's Hounds, 1946-53; *b* 30 Aug. 1893; *s* of 6th Bt, and Essex (*d* 1952), *d* of W. Selby Lowndes, Whaddon Hall, Bucks; *S* father, 1922; *m* 1st, 1921, Aileen Mary (*d* 1967), *er d* of Capt. J. E. Rogerson; one *s* three *d*; 2nd, 1968, Mrs Angela Mary Bromley, *widow* of Richard Nightingale Bromley. *Educ:* Wellington Coll. Owns about 7000 acres; Mem. of Jockey Club (Sen. Steward, 1944) and National Hunt Cttee. *Recreations:* hunting, shooting, racing, stud farm, and farming (Red Polls). *Heir: s* John Wyndham Edward Hanmer, Capt. The Royal Dragoons [*b* 27 Sept. 1928; *m* 1954, Audrey Melissa, *d* of Major A. C. J. Congreve, Cockspur Hall, Tenbury Wells, Worcs; two *s*]. *Address:* Bettisfield Park, Whitchurch, Salop. *TA* and *T:*

Bettisfield 280. *Clubs:* Cavalry and Guards, Jockey.
[*Died* 1 Jan. 1977.

HANMER, Marguerite Frances; *b* 1895; 2nd *d* of late Sir Wyndham Hanmer, 6th Bart, and Essex, Lady Hanmer (*d* 1952). *Educ:* Private. High Sheriff, Montgomeryshire, 1946. *Address:* Bryn Conroy, Llanbrynmair, Powys. *T:* Llanbrynmair 219. [*Died* 16 Dec. 1975.

HANNAFORD, Charles Arthur, RBA; *b* Aug. 1887; *er s* of C. E. Hannaford; *m* 1920, Phyllis, *yr d* of late Frederick A. Allchin, JP, Fowey, Cornwall. *Publication:* The Charm of the Norfolk Broads, 1949. *Recreation:* yachting. *Address:* The Boat House, Wroxham, Norfolk. *T:* Wroxham 2716. *Club:* Norfolk Broad Yacht (Wroxham). [*Died* 8 Aug. 1972.

HANNAFORD, Guy George, CMG 1957; OBE 1951; representative of Morgan Grenfell International, in Rome, until 1975; *b* 31 Aug. 1901; *s* of late Charles Archibald Hannaford and Marguérite Fillhard. *Educ:* privately; Sorbonne, Paris. Served, 1939-47, with gen. staff (France, Gibraltar, N Africa, Italy) (despatches twice); Lieut-Col 1942. Entered Foreign Office, 1947; Counsellor and Legal Adviser, Rome, 1947-61; Dir, Radio Maritime Co., Rome; British Rep. on Anglo-Italian Conciliation Commn, 1949-60; resigned from Foreign Office, 1961. Founder-Mem., Anglo-Italian Inst. for a European Market, 1966. Cross, Order of Merit of Knights of Malta; Medal of Freedom with Silver Palm, USA; Hon. Comdr Order St Maurice and Lazarus, Italy; Lateran Cross (1st class), Holy See. *Publications:* articles in legal and political reviews. *Recreation:* collecting early Chinese and Persian ceramics and drawings. *Address:* via Porta Pinclana 6, Rome, Italy. *T:* 483838. [*Died* 1 June 1976.

HANNAH, Air Marshal Sir Colin Thomas, KCMG 1972; KCVO 1977; KBE 1971 (CBE 1954; OBE 1951); CB 1959; Governor of Queensland, 1972-77; *b* 22 Dec. 1914; *s* of late Thomas Howard Hannah; *m* 1939, Patricia, *d* of Harold Gordon; one *d*. *Educ:* Hale Sch., Perth; RAAF Coll. Served War of 1939-45; Dep. Dir, Armament, 1941-43; OC 6 Squadron, New Guinea, 1943-44; OC W Area, 1945-46; OC RAAF Amberley, 1949-51; DPS and DGP, 1951-54; IDC, 1955; Sen. ASO, RAF HQ FEAF, Singapore, 1956-59; Dir-Gen., Plans and Policy, 1959-61; DCAS, 1961-65; Operational Comd, RAAF, 1965-67; AOC, Support Comd, 1967-70; Chief of Air Staff, RAAF, 1970-72. ADC to HM The Queen, 1952-56. DGU 1975. KStJ 1972. *Recreations:* golf, fishing. *Address:* c/o National Bank of Australasia Ltd, 308/322 Queen Street, Brisbane, Queensland 4000, Australia. *Clubs:* Australian (Sydney); Queensland (Brisbane). [*Died* 22 *May* 1978.

HANNEN, Nicholas James, OBE; actor; *b* London, 1 May 1881; *s* of Sir Nicholas John Hannen and Jessie Maria Harriette Woodhouse; *m* 1st, 1907, Muriel Melbourne Victoria Morland (*d* 1960); two *d* (one *s* decd); 2nd, Athene Seyler, *qv*. *Educ:* Radley; Heidelberg; Rouen. Spent sixteen years of his early life in China and Japan; after leaving sch. studied for the Foreign Office before becoming apprenticed as an architect under Sir Edwin Lutyens; finally went on the Stage in 1910 under the management of late George Edwardes; remained in Musical Comedy for four years during which he studied under the late Rosina Filippi; joined the Glasgow Repertory Company early in 1914; at St James Theatre under George Alexander when war broke out, and made his first London success subsequently as Nelson in Thomas Hardy's The Dynasts under Harley Granville Barker; played in New York in Granville Barker's repertory season of Shakespeare and Shaw early in 1915; returned to England May 1915 and joined the RASC serving throughout in France in the 40th Div., SO 120th Brigade; SO Div'l Troops; SSO Div. (despatches, OBE); has played many parts from Greek Tragedy to Modern Comedy; his special successes in the latter being the Conquering Hero, Escape, The Fanatics, Many Waters, To see Ourselves, Sour Grapes, Accent on Youth, Winter Sunshine, and Waste; has toured with Athene Seyler (Mrs Athene Hannen) in South Africa, Egypt and Australia, and played in representative British Companies in Finland, France and USA; mem., Old Vic Company, 1944-47; has since appeared in Shakespeare, Shaw and Tchekov in Old Vic and John Clements's companies; film appearances include Who killed John Savage?, Fear, King Henry V, Quo Vadis, and Richard III; is uncompromisingly opposed to the opening of Theatres on Sundays. *Recreation:* trying to play games. *Address:* Lamb's Cottage, Ludham, Norfolk. *Clubs:* Garrick, Beefsteak, Green Room; Leander (Henley). [*Died* 25 *June* 1972.

HANNON, Ven. Arthur Gordon, MA, TCD; retired, with General Licence from the Bishop of Down and Dromore, 1960; *b* 16 April 1891; *s* of John Alexander Hannon and Martha

Matilda, *d* of Rev. James Rice, BD, TCD; *m* 1923, Hilda Catherine Stewart-Moore Denny, *g d* of late Provost Traill of TCD; five *s* one *d. Educ:* Corrig Sch., Kingstown; Trinity Coll., Dublin; Honoursman Literature, Logic and Ethics, and Modern History (1st Class), Exhibitioner. Auditor of Coll. Theological Soc. TCD, represented Dublin Univ. in Athletics. Flour Milling Industry, 1911-13; Curate of Drumcondra and North Strand, Dublin, 1915-17; Head of Trinity Coll. Mission in Belfast, 1917-20; Rector of Ballymoney, 1920-24; Rector of Shankill Parish, Lurgan, 1924-40; Precentor of Dromore, 1924-32; Archdeacon of Dromore, 1933-40; Examining Chaplain to Bishop of Down, 1935-40; General Licence from Bishop of Down, 1940-54; Head of Community Relations Training Centre, 1940-54; Vicar of Kilbroney, Co. Down, 1954-60. Irish Representative, Congress of Europe, 1948. Chm., Churches' Industrial Council, 1959-61. *Publications:* The War and Foreign Missions, 1915; The Kingdom of God in Ireland, 1936. *Address:* Iderone, Mosside, Ballymoney, Co. Antrim, N Ireland. [*Died* 2 Jan. 1978.

HANSEN, Alvin H(arvey), PhD, LLD; Lucius N. Littauer Professor of Political Economy, Harvard University; *b* 23 Aug. 1887; *s* of Niels Hansen and Bergita Marie Nielnen; *m* 1916, Mabel Lewis; two *d. Educ:* Yankton Coll. (BA 1910, LLD 1936); University of Wisconsin (MA 1915, PhD 1918). John Simon Guggenheim Fellowship, 1928-29; Dir of Research and Sec. of Commission of Inquiry on National Policy in International Economic Relations, 1933-34; Chief Economic Analyst, State Dept, Washington, DC, 1934-35; Economic Adviser to Prairie Provinces on Canadian Dominion-Provincial Relations, 1937-38; Mem. Advisory Council on Social Security, 1937-38; Chm., US-Canadian Joint Economic Cttee, 1941-43; Special Economic Adviser, Federal Reserve Board, 1940-45; Pres., American Economic Assoc., 1938. *Publications:* Cycles of Prosperity and Depression, 1921; Business Cycle Theory, 1927; Principles of Economics (with F. B. Garver), 1928, revised edition 1937, 1947; Economic Stabilization in an Unbalanced World, 1932; Full Recovery or Stagnation, 1938; Fiscal Policy and Business Cycles, 1941; State and Local Finance in the National Economy (with H. S. Perloff), 1944; America's Role in the World Economy, 1945; Economic Policy and Full Employment, 1946. Monetary Theory and Fiscal Policy, 1949; Business Cycles and National Income, 1951; A Guide to Keynes, 1953; The American Economy, 1957; Economic Issues of the 1960's, 1960; The Dollar and the International Monetary System, 1965. *Address:* 56 Juniper Road, Belmont, Mass, USA. *T:* Belmont 484-4721. [*Died* 6 June 1975.

HANSEN, David Ernest, CMG 1949; Principal, Christchurch Technical College, Christchurch, NZ, 1919-50, retired 1950; *b* Auckland, New Zealand, 9 May 1884; *s* of Lars and Mary Anne Hansen; *m* 1916, Margaret Emma Hampson; one *s* one *d* (and one *s* decd). *Educ:* Thames High Sch.; Auckland Grammar Sch.; Auckland Univ.; Canterbury Univ., NZ. Was a Post-graduate research student, Berlin Univ., Karlsruhe Technische Hochschule, 1909-11. MSc 1st Hons, MA, Dr Ingenieur. Science Master, Christchurch Technical Coll., 1908, 1909; Research Student Berlin and Karlsruhe (Electro-Chemistry), 1909, 1910, 1911; Principal Southland Technical Coll., 1912-19; Pres. Southland WEA, 1918-19; Christchurch District Cttee, WEA: Mem. 1952, Hon. Life Mem. 1961; Member: Canterbury Univ. Council, 1952-61; Regional Council of Adult Education, 1952-60; Risingholme Community Centre, Exec., 1944, Life Mem. and Patron, 1961; Life Mem., New Zealand Disabled Servicemen's Rehabilitation Board; Chm. Te Waipounamu Coll. (Maori Girls') Coun., 1956-64; Mem., Cttee of Crippled Children's Soc., 1950-61; Mem. Canterbury and Westland Auxil. Brit. and Foreign Bible Soc., 1950 (Chm. 1956-64, Mem. of Dominion Council, 1956-64). *Recreation:* gardening. *Address:* 30 Locarno Street, Christchurch, New Zealand. *T:* 101964. [*Died* 30 Dec. 1972.

HANSEN, Harry; Vice-President, Hastings House, Publishers, Inc., since 1965; *b* Davenport, Iowa, 26 Dec. 1884; *s* of Hans Hansen and Christine Jochims; *m* 1914, Ruth McLernon; two *d. Educ:* University of Chicago (PhB 1909). Ed. University of Chicago Magazine and Alumni Secretary, 1909-11; war corr. Chicago Daily News, 1914-16; corr. at Paris Peace Conference, 1919; literary ed. Chicago Daily News, 1920-26, New York World, 1926-31; New York World-Telegram, 1931-48; Editor, World Almanac, 1948-65; Chm., editorial board, East and West Association; mem. editorial board, Armed Services Editions; judge, Metro-Goldwyn-Mayer novel award; Lectr Columbia Univ., University of Colorado, Miami Univ., etc. *Publications:* The Adventures of the Fourteen Points, 1919; Midwest Portraits, 1923; Carl Sandburg the Man and his Poetry, 1924; Your Life Lies Before You (novel), 1935; The Chicago (Rivers of America), 1942; North of Manhattan, 1950; Scarsdale; Colonial Manor to Modern Community, 1954; Old Ironsides, 1955; The

Story of Illinois, 1956; History of the American Civil War, 1961; The Boston Massacre, 1970; Longfellow's New England, 1972. Co-author, Writing Up the News, 1940; Journalism in Wartime, 1943; The Aspirin Age, 1949; contr. Encyc. Britann., Universal Jewish Encyc. Editor O. Henry Prize Stories, 1933-40; American Guide Series, 1966-; New England Legends and Folklore, 1967. Translations from German, inc. Wasserman. *Address:* 10 E 40th Street, New York, NY 10016, USA. *Clubs:* Coffee House, Overseas Press (New York); Tavern (Chicago).
[Died 2 Jan. 1977.

HANSFORD, S(idney) Howard, MA, DLit; Professor Emeritus of Chinese Art and Archæology in the University of London and Hon. Fellow, School of Oriental and African Studies, 1966; *b* London, 22 June 1899; *s* of late Sidney Robert Hansford; *m* 1929, Doris Irene, *er d* of late Capt. Herbert Mansfield Pinkham; two *s* one *d. Educ:* Mill Hill Sch.; University of London. Served in France, 1918, 2nd Lieut, RFA. Partner in firm of Wright & Hansford, China and Japan Merchants, 1923-35; Universities' China Cttee. Student in China, 1938-39; Special Intelligence Officer, Foreign Office, 1940-45; Chinese Government Scholar, University of London, 1945-47; Lectr in Chinese Art and Archæology, Courtauld Inst. of Art, 1947-55; Prof. of Chinese Art and Archæol. in University of London (Sch. of Oriental and African Studies) and Head of the Percival David Foundation of Chinese Art, 1955-66. Vis. Lectr in the Fine Arts, Harvard Univ., 1960. Vice-Chm., China Soc.; Member: Univs' China Cttee in London; Exec. Coun. of Oriental Ceramic Soc.; MRAS. *Publications:* Chinese Jade Carving, 1950; A Glossary of Chinese Art and Archæology, 1954; The Seligman Collection of Chinese and Central Asian Bronzes and Chinese Jades and Sculptures, 1957; Great Buildings of China, 1965; Chinese Carved Jades, 1968; Jade, Essence of Hills and Streams, the von Oertzen Collection, 1969; articles in Jl of Royal Asiatic Soc., Trans of Oriental Ceramic Soc., Oriental Art, etc. *Address:* Cherrywood, Granville Road, Limpsfield, Oxted, Surrey. *T:* Oxted 2714.
[Died 1 April 1973.

HANSON, Prof. Albert Henry; Professor of Politics, University of Leeds, since 1963; *b* 20 April 1913; *s* of Henry Herbert Hanson and Rosa Anne Hanson (*née* Duck); *m* 1937, Joan Madge Cansick; one *s* one *d. Educ:* Jesus Coll., Oxford; London Univ. Inst. of Education. Served as Major, RA, 1941-46. History Master: Grammar Sch. for Boys, Preston, 1935-39; City Boys' Sch., Leicester, 1939-41; Sen. Lectr in History, Cooper's Hill (Emergency) Trng Coll., 1946-48; Lectr in Public Administration, University of Leeds, 1948-56; Dir of Research, Public Administration Inst., Ankara, 1953-54; Reader in Public Admin., University of Leeds, 1956-63; Res. Fellow, Nuffield Coll., Oxford, 1960-61. *Publications:* Public Enterprise and Economic Development, 1959 (2nd edn, 1965); Parliament and Public Ownership, 1961; Nationalisation, 1963; (with Prof. H. V. Wiseman) Parliament at Work, 1963; The Process of Planning: A Study of India's Five Year Plans, 1966; Planning and the Politicians, 1969; (with Dr Malcolm Wallis) Governing Britain, 1970; articles and reviews for Times Lit. Supp., Public Administration, Parly Affairs, etc. *Recreations:* music, travel. *Address:* 15 Park View Crescent, Roundhay, Leeds 8. *T:* Leeds 662092.
[Died 27 April 1971.

HANSON, Prof. (Emmeline) Jean, FRS 1967; Director, Muscle Biophysics Unit, Medical Research Council, 1970; Professor of Biology, School of Biological Sciences, King's College, University of London, since 1966; *b* Newhall, Derbyshire, 1919; *d* of late Thomas Hanson and of Emma Jane Badger. *Educ:* High Sch. for Girls, Burton-on-Trent; Bedford Coll., University of London. BSc (Zoology) 1941, PhD 1951, London. Cancer Research, Strangeways Research Lab., Cambridge, 1942-44; Demonstrator in Zoology, Bedford Coll., London, 1944-48; Mem. Scientific staff of MRC Biophysics Research Unit, King's Coll., London, 1948-70. Rockefeller Foundn Res. Fellow, Dept of Biol., MIT, 1953-54; Hon. Lectr in Biophysics, King's Coll., London, 1964. *Publications:* articles in scientific periodicals. *Recreations:* music, fell-walking, travel, cooking. *Address:* 50 Southwood Park, Southwood Lawn Road, N6.
[Died 10 Aug. 1973.

HANSON, Frederick Horowhenua Melrose, CMG 1961; DSO 1943, and Bar 1945; OBE 1942; MM 1918; ED 1954; New Zealand Commissioner of Works, 1955-62, retired; Member of NZ Council for Technical Education; Chairman, NZ Defence Survey Committee, 1962; *b* Levin, New Zealand, 9 July 1896; *s* of Frederick Hanson; *m* 1924, Constance M., *d* of Edward Grindley. *Educ:* Wellington Coll.; Victoria Univ. Coll. Served European War, 1914-18 (MM), 1st NZEF, Wellington Regt. Educated and trained as civil engineer. With Public Works Dept, 1921-39. Served War of 1939-45 (despatches, DSO, bar, wounded thrice): 2 NZEF, CRE 2 NZ Div., CE 2 NZEF; Brig.

NZ Chief Highways Engineer, 1946-49; Dep. Commissioner of Works, 1949-55. Territorial Mem. Army Bd, 1948-55. First Chm., NZ Nat. Roads Bd, 1954-55; Past Pres., NZ Instn of Engineers. FICE; FNZIE; MSINZ. *Publications:* on soil mechanics, foundations and road engineering. *Recreations:* shooting and fishing. *Address:* 17 Portland Crescent, Thorndon, Wellington 1, NZ. *Club:* United Services Officers' (Wellington, NZ).
[Died 15 July 1979.

HANSON, Prof. Jean; *see* Hanson, Prof. E. J.

HAPPELL, Sir Arthur Comyn, Kt 1947; ICS (retired); *b* 20 Oct. 1891; *s* of late W. A. Happell, Indian Civil Service, and Mrs Happell, Tunbridge Wells, Kent; unmarried. *Educ:* Tonbridge; King's Coll., Cambridge. Served in Suffolk Regt during European War, 1914-18; demobilised with rank of Capt. 1919; Indian Civil Service, 1921; served in Madras Presidency, Asst and Sub-Collector and Joint Magistrate, 1921-25; Under and Dep. Sec. to Govt, 1925-26; Registrar, High Court, 1926-29; District and Sessions Judge, 1930-41; Judge, High Court, Madras, 1941-48. *Recreations:* golf and reading. *Clubs:* East India, Sports and Public Schools, Roehampton.
[Died 29 July 1975.

HAPPELL, Brig. William Horatio, CIE 1943; Indian Army, retired; *b* 15 April 1890; *s* of W. A. Happell, ICS; *m* 1925, Ivy Ellen Grimley. *Educ:* Tonbridge; RMC, Sandhurst. Commissioned, 1909; despatches, 1918; Judge Advocate-Gen. in India, 1938-44; retired, 1944. *Address:* Pond Mead, 37 Village Way, Dulwich, SE21.
[Died 4 Feb. 1971.

HAPPOLD, Frederick Crossfield, DSO 1916; *b* 15 Feb. 1893; *s* of A. C. Happold, Lancaster; *m* 1933, Dorothy Vectis Halbach; one *s. Educ:* Rydal Sch.; Peterhouse, Cambridge, MA; Hon. LLD Melbourne. Served European War, 1914-18 (despatches, DSO); Asst Master, The Perse Sch., Cambridge, 1920-28; Lecturer in History at Cambridge Univ., 1922-28; Headmaster, Bishop Wordsworth's Sch., Salisbury, Wilts, 1928-60. *Publications:* The Adventure of Man; The Finding of the King; The Approach to History; Citizens in the Making; This Modern Age; Towards a New Aristocracy; Everyone's Book about the English Church; Adventure in Search of a Creed; Mysticism; Religious Faith and Twentieth Century Man; The Journey Inwards; Prayer and Meditation, and other books and articles on religious, educational and historical subjects. *Address:* High Elms, Sandy Lane, Redlynch, Salisbury, Wiltshire. *T:* Downton 280.
[Died 15 July 1971.

HARBERTON, 9th Viscount, *cr* 1791; **Henry Ralph Martyn Pomeroy;** Baron Harberton, 1783; *b* 12 Oct. 1908; *s* of 8th Viscount and late Mary Katherine, *o d* of A. W. Leatham, JP; *S* father 1956. *Educ:* Eton. *Heir:* *b* Lieut-Col Hon. Thomas de Vautort Pomeroy [*b* 19 Oct. 1910; *m* 1st, 1939, Nancy Ellen (marriage dissolved, 1946), *d* of late C. A. Penoyer; 2nd, 1950, Pauline Stafford (*d* 1971), *d* of late Wilfred Sidney Baker, Stoke, Plymouth; 3rd, 1978, Wilhelmine (Wilma), *d* of Heinrich Wahl and *widow* of Sir Alfred Butt, 1st Bt]. *Address:* 38 Thurloe Square, SW7. *T:* 01-589 6767.
[Died 25 May 1980.

HARBOUR, Brian Hugo, CBE 1964; Director, Transport Holding Company, 1963-73; *b* 5 Oct. 1899; *s* of late Samuel and Georgina Harbour; *m* 1928, Joan Kirsten, *er d* of Rev. Charles and Mrs Emily Sykes, Halifax; two *s. Educ:* elementary sch.; Brockley County Sch., London, SE; London Sch. of Economics. Joined Underground group of companies as a junior clerk, 1913; transferred to London Passenger Transport Bd, 1933; Personal Asst to Chm. of Bd and Sec. of Standing Jt Cttee of LPTB and main line railway companies, 1937-43; Commercial Manager, 1943-46; Operating Manager (country buses and coaches), 1946-54; Member: London Transport Executive, 1954-62; London Transport Board, Nov. 1962-Nov. 1963; London and Home Counties Traffic Advisory Cttee, 1956-62; London Travel Cttee, 1958-62. FCIT. *Recreations:* reading, walking. *Address:* 7 Selwyn House, Selwyn Road, Eastbourne, Sussex BN21 2LF. *T:* Eastbourne 27284.
[Died 21 Dec. 1974.

HARCOURT, 2nd Viscount, *cr* 1917; **William Edward Harcourt,** KCMG 1957; OBE 1945 (MBE 1943); Baron Nuneham, *cr* 1917; Chairman, Legal and General Assurance Society Limited, 1958-77; Chairman of Trustees: Rhodes Trust, since 1975; Oxford Preservation Trust, since 1958; Chairman, Board of Governors of Museum of London, since 1965; Vice Lord-Lieutenant of Oxfordshire since 1963; Hon. Fellow, St Antony's College, Oxford; *b* 5 Oct. 1908; *o s* of 1st Viscount and Mary Ethel (*d* 1960), GBE, *o d* of late Walter H. Burns of New York and North Mymms Park, Hatfield; *S* father, 1922; *heir-pres.* to 10th Baron Vernon; *m* 1st, 1931, Hon. Maud Elizabeth Grosvenor (marr. diss., 1942), *o d* of 4th Baron Ebury, DSO,

MC; two *d* (and one *d* decd); 2nd, 1946, Elizabeth Sonia (*d* 1959), *widow* of Capt. Lionel Gibbs, and *d* of late Sir Harold Snagge, KBE. *Educ:* Eton; Christ Church, Oxford, MA. Served War of 1939-45, with 63rd (Oxford Yeomanry) AT Regt RA and on staff. Man. Dir, Morgan Grenfell & Co. Ltd, 1931-68, Chm., 1968-73; Minister (Economic) HM Embassy, Washington, and Head of UK Treasury Delegation in USA, 1954-57; UK Exec. Dir of International Bank for Reconstruction and Development and of International Monetary Fund, 1954-57; Mem., Departmental (Radcliffe) Cttee on Working of Monetary and Credit Policy of United Kingdom, 1957-59 and of Departmental (Plowden) Cttee on Overseas Representational Services, 1962-64. Hon. DCL Oxon, 1978; Hon. DLitt City, 1978. *Address:* 23 Culross Street, W1. *T:* 01-629 6061; Stanton Harcourt, Oxon. *T:* Standlake 296.
[Died 3 Jan. 1979 (ext).

HARDAKER, Alan, OBE 1971; Director-General, Football League, since 1979; *b* 29 July 1912; *s* of John Hardaker and Emma Hardaker; *m* 1937, Irene Mundy; four *d. Educ:* Constable Street Elementary; Riley High Sch., Hull. Entered Town Clerk's Dept, Hull, 1929; Lord Mayor's Sec., Hull, 1936-39; war service in RNVR, 1939-46 (Lt-Comdr); Lord Mayor's Sec., Portsmouth, 1946-51; joined Football League staff, 1951; Gen. Sec., 1957-79. *Publication:* (with Bryon Butler) Hardaker of the League, 1977. *Recreation:* fishing. *Address:* 317 Clifton Drive South, St Annes-on-Sea, Lancs FY8 1HN. *T:* St Annes 723014. *Clubs:* Variety; Shark Angling Club of Great Britain.
[Died 4 March 1980.

HARDIE, Archibald William, CBE 1974; Managing Director, Mitchell for Oils Ltd, since 1965; *b* 27 Feb. 1911; *s* of William Hardie and Janet Tait McCrae; *m* 1939, Helen Wightman Robertson; five *s. Educ:* Queen's Park Sch., Glasgow. FCCA. Man. Dir, Shell/BP Scotland, 1957-65. Chairman: Scottish Tourist Bd, 1967-71; Irvine Develt Corp., 1967-74. *Recreation:* golf. *Address:* 33 Cleveden Road, Glasgow G12 0PH. *T:* 041-339 5974; Steele Road Cottage, Newcastleton, Roxburghshire TD9 0SQ. *Club:* Royal and Ancient (St Andrews).
[Died 22 March 1980.

HARDIE, Captain Maurice Linton, CBE 1961; DSC 1944; RN retired; *b* 29 July 1909; *s* of late Martin Hardie and Agnes Madeline Pattisson; *m* 1942, Patricia Josephine, *d* of G. St Noble, Barcelona; one *s* one *d. Educ:* RN Coll., Dartmouth. Specialised in navigation, 1933. War Service included Inglefield, 1939-42; Minelaying Sqdn, 1942-43; invasion of Normandy, 1944; Fleet Navigating Officer, Mediterranean, 1944-47. Comd Starling, 1947-48; Staff of C-in-C, East Indies, 1948-50; Capt. (D) Portsmouth, in Boxer, 1951-52; Naval Officer-in-Charge, Auckland, NZ, 1952-54; comd Defender, 1955-56; Dir of Naval Equipment, Admlty, 1957-59; Capt. of Coll., at Greenwich, 1959-60; retired, 1961. Bursar and Clerk to the Governors, Portsmouth Grammar Sch., 1962-70. *Address:* Kentons, 16 Havant Road, Emsworth, Hants PO10 7JE. *T:* Emsworth 2586. *Clubs:* United Service & Royal Aero, MCC; Royal Naval and Royal Albert Yacht (Portsmouth). *[Died 9 Dec. 1972.*

HARDIE, Rt. Rev. William Auchterlonie, MA, BD; *b* 14 Oct. 1904; *s* of P. Hardie, Melbourne; *m* 1932, Katherine Weeks (*d* 1973); two *s* one *d. Educ:* Univ. of Queensland. BA 1928, MA 1936, Univ. of Queensland; BD Melbourne Coll. of Divinity, 1931. Deacon, 1930; priest, 1931; Curate of Holy Trinity, Fortitude Valley, Brisbane, 1930-33; Chaplain Southport Sch., 1933-37; Rector of Holy Trinity, Woolloongabba, Brisbane, 1937-46; Warden of St John's Coll., Brisbane, 1946-50; Canon of St John's Cathedral and Examining Chaplain to the Archbishop of Brisbane, 1947-50; Archdeacon of Moreton, 1948-50; Dean of Newcastle, NSW, 1950-61; Bishop of Ballarat, 1961-75. Served War of 1939-45 as Chaplain, Royal Australian Air Force, 1941-44. *Address:* Lis Escop, South Street, Creswick, Vic. 3363, Australia. *[Died 31 Jan. 1980.*

HARDING, George Richardson, DSO 1918; MBE 1944; Member, Post Office Advisory Council, 1946-66; *b* 15 Sept. 1884; *s* of George S. and Margaret Harding; *m* 1921, Grace Henley, *d* of late Thomas H. Darby; two *s. Educ:* Brighton. Civil Engineer, Railway and gen. construction work, England and Canada, 1901-14; Royal Engineers, 1914-19 (despatches 4 times, DSO); Home Guard, Hampstead Rocket AA Battery, 1942-45 (MBE). Vice-Chm. Aplin & Barrett, Ltd, 1949-56; Chm., 1956-60; Chm. Maconochie Bros, Ltd, 1926-42; Mem. of Exec. Cttee The Canners' (War Time) Assoc., 1942-43; Member: National Advisory Council for Fire Prevention, 1941-45; Food Prices Control Cttee, 1940-; Chm. of Council London Chamber of Commerce, 1941-44, Vice-Pres. 1944-; Pres., Food Manufacturers Federation Inc., 1937-44; Chairman: Council, British Food Manufacturers Research Assoc., 1942-50, Vice-

Pres., 1950-; Food Manufacturers Export Group, 1940-; Vice-Pres. Assoc. of British Chambers of Commerce, 1948-55; Member Council of Foreign Bondholders, 1944-56. *Recreation:* gardening. *Address:* Wildwood, Abbots Drive, Virginia Water, Surrey. *T:* Wentworth 2137. *[Died 28 Oct. 1976.*

HARDING, Gerald William Lankester, CBE 1957; Fellow of University College, London; Director, Department of Antiquities, Hashemite Kingdom of Jordan, 1936-56; *b* 8 Dec. 1901; *s* of William Arthur Harding and Florence Maud Lankester. Excavating with Sir Flinders Petrie near Gaza, Palestine, 1926-32; Asst Dir, Wellcome Archæological Research Expedition to Near East at Tell Duweir (Lachish), Palestine, 1932-36. Star of Jordan, Second Class, 1952. *Publications:* (with E. Mackay) Bahrein and Hamamieh, 1928; (with E. Macdonald and J. L. Starkey) Beth Pelet II, 1930; (with others) Lachish I; (with O. Tufnell and C. H. Inge) Lachish II; Some Thamudic Inscriptions from Jordan, 1952; Four Tomb Groups from Jordan, 1953; The Antiquities of Jordan, 1959; Archæology in the Aden Protectorate, 1964; An Index and Concordance of Pre-Islamic Arabian Names and Inscriptions, 1971. Articles in Quarterly of the Dept of Antiquities of Palestine Annual of the Jordan Dept of Antiquities, Palestine Exploration Quarterly, etc. *Address:* POB 9788, Amman, Jordan. *[Died 11 Feb. 1979.*

HARDING, Mrs J. P.; *see* Manton, Sidnie M.

HARDINGE, 4th Viscount *cr* 1846, of Lahore, and of King's Newton, Derbyshire; **Caryl Nicholas Charles Hardinge,** MBE 1946; Greenshields Incorporated (investment dealers) and Greenshields Ltd; Chairman: Ritz-Carlton Hotel Co. of Montreal Ltd; Dale-Ross Holdings Ltd; Member: Montreal Stock Exchange; Canadian Stock Exchange; Toronto Stock Exchange; Director: The Jockey Club Ltd; Mt Royal Jockey Club Inc.; Electra Investments (Canada), Ltd; Holt, Renfrew & Co. Ltd; Phœnix Assurance Company; Markborough Properties Ltd; Trizec Corporation Ltd; International Atlantic Salmon Association; Acadia Life Insurance Co; *b* London, England, 25 Dec. 1905; *s* of 3rd Viscount Hardinge of Lahore, and Mary, Marchioness of Abergavenny (*d* 1954); *S* father 1924; *m* 1928, Margaret Elizabeth Arnott, *d* of Hugh Fleming, Ottawa; one *s* two *d. Educ:* Harrow, Served with 7th Queen's Own Hussars as Lieut and as ADC to Governor-Gen. of Canada, 1926-28. Partner, Kitcat & Aitken, London, 1931-51, and mem., London Stock Exchange. Served as Military Asst, with rank of Major, to Adjt-Gen. to the Forces, 1941-45. *Heir: s* Hon. (Henry) Nicholas (Paul) Hardinge [*b* 15 Aug. 1929; *m* 1955, Zoë Molson, Canada; three *s*]. *Address:* 1523 Summerhill Avenue, Montreal, Canada. *Clubs:* Turf; Toronto (Toronto); Mount Royal, Mount Bruno Country, Montreal Racket, St James's (Montreal); Lyford Cay (Nassau). *[Died 13 June 1979.*

HARDINGE, Sir Robert, 6th Bt *cr* 1801; *b* 3 Dec. 1887; *s* of Edmond Cecil Hardinge (*d* 1890) (*g s* of 2nd Bt) and Harriet, *d* of James Fontaine; *S* kinsman, Sir Charles Edmund Hardinge, 5th Bt, 1968; *m* 1st, 1911, Emma Vera (marr. diss., 1938), *d* of Charles Arnold; one *s* one *d* ; 2nd 1947, Mrs. Nellie May Houser (decd). *Heir: s* Robert Arnold Hardinge, *b* 19 Dec. 1914. *Address:* Cherrelyn Manor Nursing Home, 5555 S Elati Street, Engelwood, Colorado, USA. *[Died 20 July 1973.*

HARDISTY, Charles William, CB 1950; *b* 18 Jan. 1893; *s* of late Charles Henry Hardisty, Manchester; *m* 1922, Dorothy Mayhew Girling. *Educ:* Manchester Grammar Sch.; St John's Coll., Cambridge. Served in Army, 1916-18, and Naval Intelligence Service, 1918-19. Joined HM Customs and Excise, 1919; Commissioner of Customs and Excise, and Dir of Establishments and Organisation, 1946-54, retired. *Address:* Fjaerland, 10 Pine Trees Close, Worlingham, Beccles, Suffolk.
[Died 29 Dec. 1973.

HARDWICK, Donald Ross, CIE 1947; KPM; *b* 26 Feb. 1895; *s* of Arthur Hardwick, MD; *m* 1st, 1918, Lilian Rosa (*d* 1956), *d* of George Thomas Rees; (one *s* decd); 2nd, 1957, Madeleine Bosworth (*d* 1964); 3rd, 1965, Doris Maud Noakes (*d* 1972). *Educ:* Blundells Sch., Tiverton, Devon. Joined Indian Police, 1914; Deputy Inspector-General, Intelligence Branch, Bengal, 1943; Commissioner of Police, Calcutta, 1946-47. King's Police Medal, 1944, Indian Police Medal, 1939; Jubilee Medal, 1935, Coronation Medal, 1937. *Recreation:* bridge. *Address:* 1 Wykeham Lodge, Woodend Road, Torquay, Devon. *T:* Torquay 23353. *Club:* Royal Torbay Yacht (Torquay).
[Died 6 Jan. 1977.

HARDWICKE, 9th Earl of *cr* 1754; **Philip Grantham Yorke;** Baron Hardwicke, 1733; Viscount Royston, 1754; Major SAS; company director; *b* 9 April 1906; *s* of late Hon. Alfred Yorke, 2nd *s* of 7th Earl and Gladys Dunlop (*d* 1933), *d* of Andrew

Vans Dunlop Best (she *m* 2nd, Hon. Percy Thellusson); *S* uncle, 1936; *m* 1st, 1934, Sarah (*d* 1965), *d* of late Rt Hon. Sir Francis Lindley, PC, GCMG; (one *s* decd) three *d*; 2nd, 1970, Mrs Enid Boulting. *Educ:* Eton; RMC. *Recreations:* yachting, shooting, fishing, hunting. *Heir: g s* Viscount Royston. *Address:* 10 Egerton Place, SW3. *T:* 01-589 1716. *Clubs:* White's; Royal Yacht Squadron (Cowes); Household Brigade Yacht; Travellers' (Paris); Brook, Racquet and Tennis (New York).
[Died 31 Dec. 1974.

HARDY; *see* Gathorne-Hardy.

HARDY, Rev. Canon Basil Augustus; Canon Residentiary of Chester Cathedral since 1946 and Precentor since 1943; *b* 1901; *s* of Rev. Henry Hardy, MA; *m* 1935, Helena Edgar English. *Educ:* Trinity Coll., Glenalmond; Keble Coll., Oxford; Westcott House, Cambridge. Asst Curate St Matthew's, Thorpe Hamlet, Norwich, 1924-27; Chaplain and Asst Master, Elstree Sch., 1927-38; Headmaster of the Choir Sch. and Chaplain Choral, Chester Cathedral, 1938-46. MA 1927, MRST 1944, FTCL 1954; Hon. Sec. Choir Schools Assoc., 1946-57; Chaplain to High Sheriff of Cheshire, 1947; Proctor in Convocation and Mem. of Church Assembly, 1955-64; Chaplain to Mayor of Chester, 1956; Headmaster of the Choir Sch., Chester Cathedral, 1955-63. *Recreations:* woodwork and clocks. *Address:* 13 Abbey Street, Chester. *T:* Chester 20157.
[Died 15 Oct. 1973.

HARDY, Sir Edward, Kt 1945; *b* 1 Aug. 1887; *s* of Col Charles Stewart Hardy, Chilham Castle, Canterbury, and Fanny Alice, *d* of Matthew Bell, Bourne Park, Canterbury. *Educ:* Eastbourne Coll.; Wye Coll. Positions held at various times and now relinquished: Member of Kent County Council for 33 years (Alderman, 1935-58, Chm., 1936-49); Governor of Wye Coll. for 26 years (Chm. 16 years; Chm. Finance and General Purposes Cttee 25 years); Chm. and/or President Ashford Division of Kent Conservative Assoc. for 30 years; Deputy Chm. Kent War Agricultural Executive Cttee, 1939-46. Formerly: JP for Kent; Mem. LPTB; Mem. London Transport Executive; Vice-Chm. Kent Standing Joint Cttee; Supervisor of Special Constables, Ashford Div.; responsible for organising the first Royal Observer Corps Posts in Kent; Canterbury Diocesan Conf.; Canterbury Diocesan Board of Finance; Pres. Kent or Romney Marsh Sheepbreeders' Assoc.; Kent River Authority; Vice-Pres. County Councils Assoc.; Chm., Kent Br. of CLA; Chm., Kent Jt Adv. Water Cttee; Vice-Pres., Nat. Fedn of Young Farmers' Clubs; Dep. Chm., Sponsors of the University of Kent at Canterbury. Is a Life Vice-Pres. (Past Pres.), Kent Fedn of Young Farmers' Clubs. Hon. Fellow, Wye Coll., University of London. Hon. DCL University of Kent at Canterbury. Farms 1497 acres in Kent. *Recreations:* shooting, fishing, producing dramatic performances. *Address:* Boughton Court, Ashford, Kent. *T:* Wye 812413. *Club:* Junior Carlton.
[Died 3 July 1975.

HARDY, Francis, MA, LLD; *b* 26 March 1879; *m* 1907, E. M. Oerton (*d* 1948); one *s. Educ:* Trinity Coll., Dublin. Headmaster, Elizabeth Coll., Guernsey, 1924-39; called to Bar, Gray's Inn, 1945. *Publication:* A Headmaster Remembers, 1969. *Address:* King Edward VII Hospital, Guernsey, CI.
[Died 29 April 1977.

HARE, Rt. Rev. John Tyrrell Holmes; Bishop Suffragan of Bedford, since 1968; *b* 24 Nov. 1912; *s* of Henry and Beatrice Hare, Tamworth, Staffs; *m* 1944, Mary Eirene Sumner Wetherall, *d* of late Rev. A. S. Wetherall; two *s. Educ:* Brighton Coll.; Corpus Christi Coll., Oxford (MA); Cuddesdon Theological Coll. Ordained, 1937; Curate: St Francis of Assisi, West Bromwich, 1937-39; Epping, 1939-40; St Mary, Hendon, 1940-46; Vicar: St Matthias, Colindale, 1946-51; St Andrew, Bedford, 1951-62; Rural Dean of Bedford, 1958-62; Hon. Canon of St Albans, 1961-62; Archdeacon of Bedford, 1962-73. Proctor in Convocation of Canterbury, 1960-70. Chm., Bedford Marriage Guidance Council, 1972-; Pres., Bedfordshire Rural Community Council, 1974-; Mem., S Bedfordshire Community Health Council, 1974-. *Recreations:* doing it yourself, gardening, bird-watching. *Address:* 168 Kimbolton Road, Bedford MK41 8DN. *T:* Bedford 57551.
[Died 25 Oct. 1976.

HARE, Major Sir Ralph Leigh, 4th Bt *cr* 1818; late Coldstream Guards; *b* 19 Jan. 1903; *s* of 3rd Bt and Lady Florence Mary Constance Marsham, *d* of 4th Earl of Romney; *S* father, 1933; *m* 1st, 1928, Doreen (marr. diss. 1944), *e d* of late Sir Richard Bagge, DSO; one *s* one *d*; 2nd, 1945, Natalie (marr. diss. 1958), *o c* of Mrs E. Vincent Irwin and of late Capt. Baron de Langué; two *d*; 3rd, 1960, Barbara, *y d* of late Joseph Walton; one *d. Educ:* Eton. *Heir: s* Thomas Hare [*b* 27 July 1930; *m* 1961, Lady Rose Amanda Bligh, *d* of 9th Earl of Darnley, and of Mrs Nancy

Cotterell; two *d*]. *Address:* Stow Bardolph, King's Lynn, Norfolk. *Club:* Cavalry and Guards.
[Died 30 Oct. 1976.

HARE, Robertson, OBE 1979; actor; *b* 17 Dec. 1891; *s* of Frank Homer Hare and Louisa Mary Robertson; *m* 1915, Irene Mewton (*d* 1969); one *d. Educ:* Margate Coll. Trained under Cairns James; first walked on as torch bearer in Sir John Martin Harvey's production of Oedipus Rex, Covent Garden, 1912; first big part Grumpy in the play of that name, 1914-16; joined the Army and served in France, 1917-18; opened with Tom Walls Leslie Henson management at Shaftesbury Theatre, 1922, in farce Tons of Money; continued association with this management when they transferred to Aldwych Theatre and remained there with the Ben Travers farces for eleven years; film work in parts created in the farces; teamed up with Alfred Drayton, 1936, in Vernon Sylvaine's Aren't Men Beasts, Strand Theatre, followed by Spot of Bother by same author, Ben Travers' two farces Banana Ridge and Spotted Dick, Sylvaine's Women Aren't Angels, Ben Travers' play She Follows Me About; with Alfred Drayton in Sylvaine's farce, Madame Louise, Garrick; with Ralph Lynn in Ben Travers' Outrageous Fortune, Winter Garden; with Alfred Drayton, then Arthur Riscoe, in Sylvaine's farce, One Wild Oat, Garrick, 1948 (filmed, 1951); with Arthur Riscoe in Sylvaine's farce, Will Any Gentleman?, Strand, 1950; with Ralph Lynn in Ben Travers' Wild Horses, Aldwych, 1952; The Party Spirit, 1954; Man Alive, Aldwych, 1956; The Bride and the Bachelor, Duchess, 1956; Fine Fettle, Palace, 1959; The Bride Comes Back, Vaudeville, 1960-61; A funny thing happened on the way to the Forum, Strand, 1963; Oh Clarence!, Lyric, 1968. Has appeared in many films, from 1929. Author of Our Dear Relations (prod 1925), and (with Sydney Lynn) The Dark Room (prod 1927). BBC TV Series, All Gas and Gaiters, 1968-70. *Publication:* Yours Indubitably, 1957. *Recreations:* writing, swimming, golf. *Club:* Savage.
[Died 25 Jan. 1979.

HARGREAVES, His Honour Sir Gerald de la Pryme, Kt 1944; County Court Judge Circuit No 18, 1922-23; Circuit No 46, 1923-28; Circuit No 48, 1928; Circuit No 37, 1928-55; *s* of Thomas and Constance Hargreaves, Oakhurst, Birkdale, Lancs; *m* 1955, Mrs Winifred Elsie Johnson. *Educ:* Eton; Magdalen Coll., Oxford. Called to Bar, 1905; Mem. of Northern Circuit; Unionist candidate for Osgoldcross Div. of Yorks, Jan. 1910; Monmouth Boroughs, Dec. 1910; prospective Unionist candidate for Bedford, 1911-18; served with Bedfordshire Yeomanry, 1914-17; attached as Court-Martial Officer Xth Army Corps, 1917-19 (despatches, Belgian Croix de Guerre). Served with Home Guard, 1942-45. Chm. of London Tribunal for Conscientious Objectors, from 1939. *Publications:* Deeds of Arrangement; Operettas. *Recreations:* lawn tennis, golf, music, painting. *Address:* Mount Rise, Gorey, Jersey, CI. *T:* East 71. *Clubs:* 1900, United and Cecil, Queen's, All England Lawn Tennis and Croquet, International Lawn Tennis, Bar Lawn Tennis Society.
[Died 29 April 1972.

HARINGTON, Sir Charles (Robert), KBE 1962; Kt 1948; FRS 1931; MA, PhD; Hon. ScD Cambridge; Dr (*hc*), Paris; Hon. DSc London; Consultant Adviser to Medical Research Council, 1966-67; *b* 1 Aug. 1897; *er s* of Rev. Charles Harington; *m* 1923, Jessie, 2nd *d* of Rev. James Craig; one *s* two *d. Educ:* Malvern Coll.; Magdalene Coll., Cambridge; University of Edinburgh. Research Asst in Department of Therapeutics, University of Edinburgh, 1920; Lecturer in Pathological Chemistry, University Coll. Hospital Medical Sch., London, 1922; Reader in Pathological Chemistry, Univ. of London, 1928; Prof. of Chemical Pathology in the Univ. of London, 1931-42; Dir of Graham Medical Research Laboratories, UCH Medical Sch., 1937-42; Dir of National Institute for Medical Research, 1942-62; Consultant Adviser to the Secretary, Medical Research Council, 1962-64; Second Sec. (Acting), Medical Research Council, 1965-66. Editor of the Biochemical Journal, 1930-42; Mem. of Med. Research Council, 1938-42; Mem. of Agricultural Research Council, 1941-45; Croonian Lectr of Royal Society, 1944; Hon. Fellow of Magdalene Coll., Cambridge, 1944; Hon. Freeman, Soc. of Apothecaries, 1949; Hon. FRSM 1959; Hon. FRCP 1963. Royal Medal, Royal Society, 1944; Gold Medal, Soc. of Apothecaries, 1953; Nuffield Lectr and Medallist, RSM, 1963. *Publications:* The Thyroid Gland: its Chemistry and Physiology, 1933; papers on chemical and biochemical subjects, mainly in the Biochemical Journal. *Recreation:* fishing. *Address:* 33 Sylvan Avenue, Mill Hill, NW7. *T:* 01-959 4278. *Club:* Athenæum.
[Died 4 Feb. 1972.

HARINGTON, His Honour John Charles Dundas, QC 1957; a Judge of County Courts, later a Circuit Judge, 1958-73; *b* 27 June 1903; *yr s* of Sir Richard Harington, 12th Bt and Selina Louisa Grace (*d* 1945), *d* of 6th Viscount Melville; *m* 1941, Lavender Cecilia, *d* of late Major E. W. Denny, Garboldisham

Manor, Diss, Norfolk; two s one d. *Educ:* RN Colleges, Osborne and Dartmouth; Christ Church, Oxford. Called to Bar, 1928. Served War of 1939-45, RNVR, 1939-44. Recorder of Banbury, 1951-55; Recorder of New Windsor, 1955-58; Judge of County Courts (Hants Circuit), 1958-61. Herefordshire QS: Dep. Chm., 1953-57, Chm., 1957-71. *Recreations:* various. *Address:* Whitbourne Court, Worcester.   *[Died 5 Sept. 1980.*

HARKNESS, Sir Douglas (Alexander Earsman), KBE 1956 (CBE 1946); retired Civil Servant; Councillor, Clifton Ward, Belfast Corporation, 1967-73; *b* 12 Sept. 1902; *o c* of late George Wightman Harkness and Jane Earsman Harkness; *m* 1936, Annie, *o d* of late J. C. M. Blow and of Jane Sibbald Blow; one s one d. *Educ:* Newport (Mon.) High Sch.; University of Glasgow. 2nd Class Hons in History, 1922; 1st Class Hons in Economic Science, 1923; Reid Stewart Fellow, 1923-24. Min. of Agriculture, Northern Ireland, 1924; Lecturer in Agricultural Economics, Queen's Univ., Belfast, 1926; Asst Sec., Min. of Agriculture, 1936; Perm. Sec., 1948; Second Sec., Min. of Finance, 1952; Perm. Sec. to Min. of Finance, Northern Ireland, and Head of Northern Ireland Civil Service, 1953-61; Economic Adviser to the Government of Northern Ireland, 1961-63. LLD (*hc*) Queen's Univ. of Belfast, 1962. *Publications:* War and British Agriculture, 1941; A Tract on Agricultural Policy, 1945; Bolingbroke, 1957; various articles on economic and agricultural subjects. *Recreation:* golf. *Address:* 33 Knockdene Park, Belfast 5. *T:* 654051.   *[Died 28 Dec. 1980.*

HARLAN, John Marshall; US Legion of Merit; Associate Justice, Supreme Court of the United States, 1955-71; *b* Chicago, Ill, 20 May 1899; *s* of John Maynard Harlan and Elizabeth Palmer (*née* Flagg); *m* 1928, Ethel Andrews, New Haven, Conn; one d. *Educ:* Chicago Latin Sch.; Appleby Sch.; Lake Placid Sch.; Princeton Univ.; Balliol Coll., Oxford; New York Law Sch. AB Princeton, 1920; Rhodes Scholar, Oxford Univ., 1921-23; BA Jurisprudence, MA; Hon. Fellow, Balliol Coll., 1955; LLB New York Law Sch., 1924. Admitted to New York Bar, 1925; joined firm of Root, Clark, Buckner & Howland (subsequently Root, Ballantine, Harlan, Bushby & Palmer), 31 Nassau Street, New York City, as an associate, 1923; mem. of firm, 1931-54; specialised in litigation throughout. Asst US Attorney, Southern District of New York, 1925-27; Chief Counsel to NY State Crime Commission, 1951. US Court of Appeals, Second Circuit, 1954. Member: American Bar Assoc.; NY State Bar Assoc.; Assoc. of the Bar of City of NY; NY County Lawyers Assoc. (Dir 1938-42); American Law Institute; Dir of National Legal Aid Assoc. Hon. Master of the Bench, Inner Temple, 1969. Hon. LLD: Brandeis Univ., Evansville Coll., New York Law Sch., Princeton Univ., 1955; Columbia Univ., Oberlin Coll., 1956. Served War as Col, US Army Air Force; stationed in England, 1943-45 as Chief of Operations Analysis Section Eighth Air Force, and subsequently mem. of Planning Section for Occupation of Germany, US Strategic Air Forces in Europe. Croix de Guerre (France); Croix de Guerre (Belgium). *Address:* 1677 31st Street, NW, Washington, DC, USA; Weston, Conn. *Clubs:* Century Association, University (NYC); Country (Fairfield, Conn.); Ivy (Princeton, NJ).   *[Died 29 Dec. 1971.*

HARLAND, Ven. Lawrence Winston, MBE 1952; Archdeacon of Rochester and Residentiary Canon of Rochester Cathedral, 1951-69, now Emeritus; *b* 10 Nov. 1905; *s* of Harry Harland, Bradford, Yorks; *m* 1933, Rita Doreen Harrison; two s one d. *Educ:* Sidney Sussex Coll., Cambridge; Chichester Theological Coll. BA (Cantab) 1931; MA 1934. Curate of: Holy Trinity, Bingley, 1933; Christ Church, Skipton, 1936; Priest in Charge, St Martin's, Bradford, 1937; Vicar of Menston in Wharfedale, 1939. War of 1939-45: CF, RARO, 1939; Dunkirk, 1940; HCF 1942. Priest-Vicar of Lichfield Cathedral, 1946; Gen. Sec., Christian Reconstruction of Europe, 1947; Gen. Sec. Advisory Cttee of Christian Churches for the Festival of Britain, 1951. Chaplain to the Queen, 1966-75. *Address:* St David's, 11 Broadmark Lane, Rustington, W Sussex BN16 2NW. *T:* Rustington 3864.   *[Died 10 March 1977.*

HARLECH, Dowager Lady, DCVO 1947; **Beatrice Mildred Edith;** Extra Lady of the Bedchamber to the Queen Mother, since 1953; *b* 10 Aug. 1891; *d* of 4th Marquess of Salisbury, KG, GCVO; *m* 1913, 4th Baron Harlech, KG, PC, GCMG (*d* 1964); two s three d (and one s decd). *Address:* 14 Ladbroke Road, W11. *T:* 01-229 6679.   *[Died 3 Dec. 1980.*

HARLEY, Sir Stanley (Jaffa), Kt 1958; DL; President, Coventry Gauge & Tool Co. Ltd, since 1971 (Chairman and Managing Director, 1963-70); *b* 12 Nov. 1905; *s* of late Sir Harry Harley, CBE and Mrs Lydia Harley; *m* 1931, Rhona Townsend; two s one d. *Educ:* Wrekin Coll., Wellington, Salop; Birmingham Univ. Apprenticed to Coventry Gauge & Tool Co. Ltd, 1926; completed training at Coventry, on Continent, and in USA;

Joint Man. Dir, Coventry Gauge & Tool Co. Ltd, 1935; Man. Dir, 1946, 1951; Dep. Chm. 1946; Chm. 1951; Dir, Tube Investments Ltd, 1969-71. Hon. Controller of Jigs, Tools and Gauges, Machine Tool Control, Min. of Supply and Min. of Production, 1940-46. Pro-Chancellor, Warwick Univ., 1973-. Hon. DSc Warwick, 1978. DL Co. Warwick, 1967. *Recreations:* golf, travel. *Address:* No 1 Sunrise Cottage, Leek Wootten, Warwick. *Clubs:* Royal Automobile; Drapers (Coventry).
                    [Died 2 Sept. 1979.

HARLOW, Christopher Millward, CIE 1942; BSc; *b* 5 Jan. 1889; *s* of late John Starcke Harlow; *m* 1921, Doris Gertrude Chittenden; two s one d. Joined Indian Forest Service, 1911; Chief Conservator of Forests, Central Provinces and Berar; retired, 1946. *Address:* The Glebe House, Occold, near Eye, Suffolk. *T:* Occold 239.   *[Died 19 Feb. 1972.*

HARMAN, Sir (Clement) James, GBE 1964; JP; one of HM Lieutenants for City of London, 1952-69; Chairman: Provincial Flats Ltd; Harman Properties Ltd; Managing Director, Bryanston Property Co. Ltd, and other companies; *b* 15 May 1894; *e s* of late Clement Valentine Harman, Frinton Hall, Essex; *m* 1917, Mary Abigail (*d* 1967), *d* of Arthur John Childe-Freeman, Gaines, Worcs; one s (one d decd). *Educ:* London Univ.; Zürich and Paris. Freeman, City of London, 1936; Liveryman, Worshipful Cos of Painter-Stainers, Clockmakers (Mem. Court of Assts; Master, 1961, 1963), Plumbers (Mem. Court of Assts; Master, 1958). Mem. Court of Common Council for Ward of Bread Street, 1949; Governor: Christ's Hosp., 1952-69; Royal Bridewell Hosp. (King Edward Sch., Witley); Chm., City of London Licensing Planning Cttee, 1955-63; Life Gov., Sheriffs' Fund Soc.; Sheriff of City of London, 1951-52; Alderman, City of London, 1952-69 (Ward of Candlewick); Lord Mayor of London, 1963-64. A Church Comr for England, 1966-69. Served European War, 1914-18: Royal Welch Fusiliers; subseq. Gen. Staff (Intelligence) 31st Divl HQ, 7th Corps HQ, 2nd Army HQ; BEF France and Flanders; MEF campaigns, Gallipoli and Salonika. Capt., 7th Surrey Home Guard, 1940-45. Hon. Col, TA, 1963. KStJ; Order of the Falcon with Star (Iceland), 1963; Order of Two Niles (Sudan), 2nd Class, 1964. *Address:* 12 South Audley Street, W1. *T:* 01-499 1601, 01-499 2180; Croft House, Buxton Road, Eastbourne, East Sussex. *T:* Eastbourne 34256. *Clubs:* Athenæum, Garrick, City Livery (Pres. 1961-62), United Wards.   *[Died 15 Sept. 1975.*

HARMAN, Sir James; see Harman, Sir C. J.

HARMAN, Robert Douglas K.; see King-Harman.

HARMER, Lewis Charles, MA, PhD Cantab; Licencié ès Lettres Bordeaux; Drapers' Professor of French, University of Cambridge, 1951-67; Fellow of Trinity College, Cambridge, 1944-67; *b* 22 June 1902; *s* of Charles Collins Harmer and Kate Lewis; *m* 1940, Nina, *o d* of Eugène Le Prévost; two s two d. *Educ:* Universities of London, Bordeaux and Cambridge. Modern and Medieval Languages Tripos, Cambridge, 1930-33; Lecturer in French, University of Cambridge, 1936-51. *Publications:* The French Language Today, 1954; Vocabulary in French and English, A Facsimile of Caxton's edition *c* 1480 (Textual Introduction), 1964; Introd. Montaigne's Essays, trans. by J. Florio, 1965; (with F. J. Norton) A Manual of Modern Spanish; contribs to Encyclopædias and learned Jls. *Address:* Trinity College, Cambridge.   *[Died 28 March 1975.*

HARMSWORTH, Sir (Arthur) Geoffrey (Annesley), 3rd Bt *cr* 1918; FSA; President: Harmsworth Press Ltd; West Country Publications Ltd; Director: Western Morning News Co. Ltd; Western Times Co. Ltd; Daily Mail & General Trust Ltd; F. Hewitt & Son (1927) Ltd; News Holdings Ltd; *b* 29 March 1904; *y s* of Sir Leicester Harmsworth, 1st Bt and late Annie Louisa Scott; *S* brother, 1962. *Educ:* Harrow. War Correspondent, 1939-40. Sqdn Leader RAFVR. *Publications:* The Maid of the Mountains, Her Story (with Miss José Collins), 1932; Abyssinian Adventure, 1935; I Like America, 1939; Northcliffe (with Reginald Pound), 1959. *Address:* White Cottage, Tealby, Lincoln.   *[Died 23 Oct. 1980 (ext).*

HARMSWORTH, Sir Hildebrand Alfred Beresford, 2nd Bt, *cr* 1922; *b* 27 May 1901; *s* of 1st Bt and Kathleen Mary (*d* 1966), *d* of E. D. Berton, MB; *S* father, 1929; *m*; one s one d. *Educ:* Harrow. *Heir: s* Hildebrand Harold Harmsworth [*b* 5 June 1931; *m* 1960, Gillian Andrea, *o d* of William John Lewis; one s two d]. *Address:* Deepdene, Haslemere, Surrey. *T:* Haslemere 2092.
                    [Died 15 Nov. 1977.

HAROLD, Eileen, MA Oxon; Headmistress, Haberdashers' Aske's School for Girls, West Acton, 1944-68; *b* 7 Dec. 1909; *d* of Charles and Margaret Harold. *Educ:* Herts and Essex High

Sch., Bishop's Stortford; Lady Margaret Hall, Oxford. On Classical Staff of Sherborne Sch. for Girls, Dorset, 1931-34; on Classical Staff of Haberdashers' Aske's Sch. for Girls, West Acton, 1934-40; Headmistress of North London Collegiate Sch., 1940-44. *Address:* Sigwells House, near Sherborne, Dorset.
[*Died* 11 *June* 1974.

HARPER, George MacGowan; *b* 18 March 1899; 3rd *s* of James Harper, MD; *m* 1st, 1930, Ruth Musgrave, 2nd *d* of late Sir Ernest Musgrave Harvey, KBE (marr. diss., 1947); one *d* (one *s* dedc); 2nd, 1973, Daphne Patricia, *d* of late Lt-Gen. Sir William Thomson, KCMG, CB, MC. *Educ:* Tonbridge; Royal Military Academy, Woolwich. Served with RHA, France, 1918. Entered Lloyd's, 1921; first served on Cttee of Lloyd's, 1945; Dep. Chm. of Lloyd's, 1953. *Recreation:* golf. *Address:* Greenacres, Kelsale, Saxmundham, Suffolk IP17 2RD. *T:* Saxmundham 2201. *Clubs:* Brooks's, Naval and Military; Honourable Company of Edinburgh Golfers; Aldeburgh Golf.   [*Died* 4 *March* 1976.

HARPER, Joseph, JP; MP (Lab) Pontefract and Castleford, since 1974 (Pontefract, March 1962-1974); Comptroller of HM Household, since 1974; *b* 17 March 1914; *m* 1939, Gwendoline Hughes; two *s* two *d. Educ:* Featherstone Elementary Sch. Started work at Snydale Colliery, Yorks, 1928. Deleg. for Local Branch of NUM, 1943-62; served on Yorks area NUM Exec. Cttee, 1947-48 and 1950-52. Mem. Featherstone UDC, 1949-63 (Chm., 1955-56 and 1961-62); Chm. Featherstone Managers of Primary Schs and Governors of Secondary Sch., 1955-62; Vice-Chm. Divl Educn Executive, 1955-62; Mem. Osgoldcross Cremation Board, 1957-62; Mem. Pontefract and Castleford HMC, 1958-; an Asst Government Whip, 1964-66; a Lord Comr of the Treasury, 1966-70; an Opposition Whip, 1970-74. JP, WR Yorks, 1959. *Recreations:* music, watching Rugby League football. *Address:* House of Commons, SW1; 11 Bedford Close, Purston, Featherstone, near Pontefract, W Yorks.
[*Died* 24 *June* 1978.

HARPER, Sir Richard Stephenson, Kt 1958; JP; *b* 30 Dec. 1902; *o s* of late Alderman Richard S. Harper, JP and Mrs Edith C. Harper, JP, Harnham House, Slade Lane, Manchester 19; *m* 1942, Lily, *o d* of late Nathaniel and Elizabeth Walker, Manchester; one *s. Educ:* Manchester Grammar Sch.; Chorlton-cum-Hardy Grammar Sch.; Bonar Law Coll., Ashridge, Herts. Electrical and Gen. Engineering, 1920-25; Priv. Sec. to Ald. R. S. Harper Sen., 1925-32; City Councillor, Manchester, 1932-51; Alderman, City of Manchester, 1951-; Lord Mayor of Manchester, 1954-55. Chm. of several Corporation Cttees at various times; Dir (apptd by Manchester Corp.), Manchester Ship Canal Co. Ltd, 1945-71; contested (C) Exchange Div. Gen. Election, 1950. Religion: Church of England; special interest housing. Divl Warden Civil Defence, Manchester, 1937-46 (CD Medal, 1946). JP Manchester 1949. Hon. Freeman, City of Manchester, 1973. *Publications:* political pamphlets. *Address:* 1 Baslow Drive, Hazel Grove, Stockport, Cheshire. *T:* Poynton 5062. *Clubs:* local political.   [*Died* 16 *Nov.* 1973.

HARREY, C. O. W.; *see* Wakefield-Harrey.

HARRIES, Rear-Adm. David Hugh, CB 1961; CBE 1952; RAN (retired); *b* 27 June 1903; *s* of David Henry Harries, Melbourne, Australia; *m* 1933, Margaret, *d* of Edric H. Street, Camden, New South Wales; two *s. Educ:* Melbourne Church of England Gram. Sch.; Royal Australian Naval College, Jervis Bay, NSW; 2nd Naval Mem., Aust. Naval Bd, 1952-53; Rear-Adm. 1954; Head of Australian Joint Service Staff, Washington, DC, USA, 1953-55; Flag Officer comdg HM Australian Fleet, 1956-58; retired 1960. US Legion of Merit, 1955. *Recreations:* golf, foreign languages. *Address:* 3 Graylind Place, Vaucluse, NSW 2030, Australia. *Clubs:* Union, Royal Sydney Golf (Sydney); Naval and Military (Melbourne).   [*Died* 6 *July* 1980.

HARRIES, Air Vice-Marshal Sir Douglas, KCB, *cr* 1947 (CB 1943); AFC 1918; retired; *b* 31 March 1893; 2nd *s* of W. J. Harries, Sidcup, Kent; *m* 1924. *Educ:* Royal Naval Colleges, Osborne and Dartmouth. Retired list, 1946. *Address:* Mill Lane Cottage, Crondall, near Farnham, Surrey. [*Died* 6 *Dec.* 1972.

HARRIES, Victor Percy, CB 1953; solicitor; *b* 27 Oct. 1907; *s* of late Henry Percy Harries; *m* 1932, Etheldreda (Audrey), *d* of late Joseph Lorkin; one *s* two *d. Educ:* Ealing Priory Sch.; St Benedict's; University of London (LLB Hons). Admitted Solicitor (Hons), 1930; Partner in firm of Reynolds, Sons & Gorst, London, until 1939; Principal, Min. of Supply (later Aviation), 1939; Asst Sec., 1940; Principal Asst Sec., 1944; Under Sec., 1949. Sec. and Solicitor, British Airports Authority, 1965-71. Mem., Hon. Soc. of Cymmrodorion. *Address:* Stannards View, Frith End, Bordon, Hants.
[*Died* 17 *Feb.* 1977.

HARRIMAN, Sir George (William), Kt 1965; CBE 1951 (OBE 1943); President, British Leyland Motor Corporation, since 1968 (Chairman, 1968); *b* 3 March 1908; married. Joined Austin Motor Company, 1940; appointed to Board, 1945; Works Director; Deputy Chairman, Austin Motor Co., 1952-61; appointed to Board of British Motor Corporation on its formation, 1952; Deputy Managing Director, 1952-56; Deputy Chairman and Joint Managing Director, 1956-58; Deputy Chairman and Sole Managing Director, 1958-61; Chairman and Managing Director, 1961; Executive Chairman, 1967-68. Chairman, British Motor Holdings, 1967-68; Chairman and Managing Director, Austin Motor Co., 1961-68. Pres., Soc. of Motor Manufacturers and Traders, 1967-69. *Recreations:* golf, fishing. *Address:* British Leyland Motor Corporation Ltd, Longbridge Works, Birmingham. *T:* 021-475 2101.
[*Died* 29 *May* 1973.

HARRIS, Sir Archibald, Kt, *cr* 1944; *b* 10 Dec. 1883; *s* of Rev. Isidore Harris, MA, London; *m* 1919, Phoebe (*d* 1962), *d* of Ernest Meyer, Ladbroke Grove, London, and West Street House, Eastry, Kent. *Educ:* University Coll. Sch. Entered firm of Louis Bamberger & Sons, London (Timber Importers), in 1901, Partner, 1919; Dir Bambergers Ltd until 1963 (a former Vice-Chm.). Temporary 2nd Lieut RASC (T) Aug. 1914 and Temporary Capt. Oct. 1914; served France and Macedonia, 1915-18 (despatches twice, Bt Major). Pres. Timber Trade Federation of UK 1937-39; Mem. Timber Trade Federation's delegation to Imperial Conference, Ottawa, 1932; Timber Controller, Ministry of Supply, 1939-47. Officier de l'ordre de la Mérite Agricole, 1937; American Medal of Freedom, 1947. *Recreations:* travel, bridge. *Address:* 32 London House, Avenue Road, NW8. *T:* 01-586 0995. *Clubs:* Bath, Hardingham, East India and Sports; Royal Thames Yacht. [*Died* 21 *June* 1971.

HARRIS, Sir Charles (Felix), Kt 1968; MD, FRCP; Hon. FRCS; Officier Orde van Oranje-Nassau; Consulting Physician for Diseases of Children, late Physician i/c the Children's Department St Bartholomew's Hospital; Physician, The Westminster Children's Hospital, Vincent Square; Consultant Pædiatrist to London County Council; Member of Senate since 1950, of Court since 1951, University of London (Vice-Chancellor of the University, 1958-61); *b* 30 March 1900; *s* of G. Felix Harris and Ellen Charles; *m* 1929, Edith Nadejda Goldsmith; no *c. Educ:* Epsom Coll.; St Bart.'s Hosp. Medical Coll. House Physician, and Chief Asst St Bartholomew's Hospital (Kirkes Scholarship, 1922, Lawrence Research Scholarship, 1925), House Physician Hospital for Sick Children, Great Ormond Street; Asst, with Rockefeller Fellowship, Pediatrics Dept Johns Hopkins Hospital, Baltimore, USA; Med. Off. i/c (EMS) St Bartholomew's Hospital, London, 1939-46; sometime Examiner in Children's Diseases, Leeds, Birmingham and Aberdeen; Dean, Faculty of Medicine, University of London, 1952-56; Dean, St Bartholomew's Hosp. Med. Coll., 1945-52, Warden, 1936-45, Vice-Pres., 1960-65. Chm. Convocation, Univ. of London, 1961-73. Hon. Sec., Royal Society Medicine, 1941-46; Pres. British Pædiatric Assoc., 1962-63. Hon. Fellow, Sch. of Pharmacy. Editor Archives of Disease in Childhood, 1934-38. Hon. LLD London, 1972. *Publications:* various in medical and scientific journals. *Recreations:* shooting, gardening. *Address:* Combe Wood Cottage, Ewshott, Hants. *T:* Crondall 203. *Clubs:* Oriental; North Hampshire Golf.
[*Died* 10 *March* 1974.

HARRIS, Charles Reginald Schiller, MA, DPhil Oxon, PhD Princeton and Adelaide; FCIT; *b* 10 April 1896; *e s* of late Sir Charles Harris, GBE, KCB; *m* 1931, Lucia Marie Ghislaine, *o d* of late Dom José de Figueiredo de Pitinga and of late Mrs C. T. Terry; one *d. Educ:* Clifton Coll.; Corpus Christi Coll., Oxford (Scholar). 1st Class Lit. Hum., 1920; Senior Demy, Magdalen Coll., Oxon, 1920-21; Jane Eliza Procter Visiting Fellow, Princeton Univ., New Jersey, 1922-23; Fellow of All Souls Coll., Oxford, 1921-36; Editor of The Nineteenth Century and After, 1930-35; Leader Writer on the Staff of the Times, 1925-35, and the Economist, 1932-35; Dir-Gen., Buenos Aires Gt Southern and Western Railways, 1935-59; Dir, Entre Rios, Argentine North Eastern and Central Uruguay Railways, 1939-47. Commercial Counsellor HM Legation, Reykjavik, Iceland, 1940-42; Lieut-Col General List; Dir Property Control, AMGOT, Sicily, 1943, Allied Control Commission, Italy, 1944; Sec. to Adv. Gp of Experts on admin. personnel and budgetary matters, Preparatory Commn of UN, 1945; Historical Sect., Cabinet Office, 1945-58; Reader in Studies in the Humanities of Medical Students and Tutor of St Mark's Coll., Adelaide Univ., 1958-65. Vis Lectr, Lake Erie Coll., Ohio, 1973. Hon. Fellow, St Mark's Coll., Adelaide. Hon. DLitt Lake Erie Coll., 1973. *Publications:* Duns Scotus, 1927; Germany's Foreign Indebtedness, published under auspices of RIIA, 1935; vol. on Allied Administration of Italy, 1943-45, in the Official History

of the Second World War, 1958; The Heart and the Vascular System in Ancient Greek Medicine, 1973. *Recreation:* fishing. *Address:* Rock House, Wheatley, Oxon. *Club:* Athenæum.
[Died 17 Aug. 1979.

HARRIS, (Emanuel) Vincent, OBE; Hon. DLitt, Exeter; RA 1942 (ARA 1936); FRIBA; Treasurer of the Royal Academy, retired, 1954; *s* of Major Emanuel Harris and Mary Vincent; *m* Edith (*d* 1965), *d* of William Maule, MD. *Educ:* Kingsbridge Gram. Sch. Architect for Manchester Central Library and Town Hall Extension, Sheffield City Hall, Leeds Civic Hall, University Coll. of SW, Exeter, Glamorgan County Hall, Surrey County Hall, Somerset County Hall, Bristol Council House; Science Buildings taunton Sch.; Nottinghamshire County Hall; selected Architect in competition for HM New Government Buildings, Whitehall, and many other public buildings. Royal Gold Medal for Architecture, 1951. *Address:* Chard School, Chard, Somerset. *Clubs:* Athenæum; Savage, Reform; Nottinghamshire (Nottingham).   [Died 1 Aug. 1971.

HARRIS, Frederic Walter, CBE 1972; Chairman, Marshall's Investments Ltd; *b* 6 March 1915; *s* of Alice and Walter Harris; *m* 1st, 1939, Betty Eileen Benson (*d* 1955); one *s* two *d* ; 2nd, 1957, Joan Hope, *d* of David N. K. Bagnall, Overmist, Tadworth, Surrey. *Educ:* Belmont Coll. Streatham. Founded food-producing company as Dir, 1934; Joint Man. Dir of same company known as Marshall's Universal Ltd, 1939, Man. Dir, 1945-63; Chm. and Man. Dir, 1964-75, Pres., 1975- (company's capital now £1,357,571). MP (C), North Croydon, 1948-55, North West Croydon, 1955-70. Freeman of City of London; granted Freedom of Croydon, 1970; Liveryman of Basketmakers. *Address:* Wood Rising, The Ridge, Woldingham, Surrey. *T:* Woldingham 2365.   [Died 4 Jan. 1979.

HARRIS, Lt-Gen. Sir Frederick, KBE 1953 (CBE 1944); CB 1949; *b* 21 June 1891; *s* of J. Porter Harris; *m* 1918, Sheila Isabel (*d* 1967), *d* of W. Boyd; one *s* one *d*. *Educ:* Coleraine Sch.; Trinity Coll., Dublin. Lieut RAMC 1915; Capt. 1916; Major 1927; Lieut-Col 1940; Temp. Col 1941; Temp. Brig. 1944; Col 1945; Actg Maj.-Gen. 1947; Temp. Maj.-Gen. 1947; Maj.-Gen. 1948. European War, 1914-19, Gallipoli Egypt, France, Italy (MC, 1915 star, Allied and Victory medals, despatches, twice wounded); NW Frontier of India, 1936-37 (medal and clasp); War of 1939-45 on staff of Northern Command, India, 1939-41; on staff of GHQ India Command, 1941-45; Deputy Dir Medical Services 12 Army, Sept.-Dec. 1945 (Burma Star, Defence Medal, 1939-45 War medal); DDMS, Burma Command, Jan.-July 1946; Asst Dir Med. Services, Aldershot and Hants District, 1946-47; DMS, MELF, 1947-48; Dep. Dir.-Gen., Army Med. Services, Dec. 1948-Apr. 1952; Dir-Gen., Army Medical Services, WO, April 1952-56; QHS, 1946-56; retired May 1956. *Address:* 609 Nelson House, Dolphin Square, SW1V 3NZ.
[Died 1 Oct. 1976.

HARRIS, Prof. Geoffrey Wingfield, CBE 1965; FRS 1953; MA, MD, ScD Cantab; DM Oxford, 1962; Dr Lee's Professor of Anatomy, University of Oxford, since Oct. 1962; Hon. Director of MRC Neuroendocrinology Research Unit, since 1962; Hon. Consultant in Psychiatry, Oxford United Hospitals and Oxford Regional Hospital Board; *b* 4 June 1913; *s* of late Tom Harris, Ballistics Research Dept, Woolwich Arsenal; *m* 1st, 1936 (marr. diss. 1951); one *s*; 2nd, 1951, Margaret, *d* of late Dr M. J. O'Kane, Cushendall; two *d*. *Educ:* Dulwich Coll.; University Coll., London Univ.; Emmanuel Coll., Cambridge; St Mary's Hospital, London. Scholar (Emmanuel); Colin Mackenzie Prize, 1935; Marmaduke Shield Student in Anatomy, Cambridge, 1935; Harmsworth Scholar, St Mary's Hosp., 1936; Agnes Cope Prize and Wallace Memorial Prize, 1939. Res. MO, Hillingdon County Hosp., 1939-40. Univ. of Cambridge: Demr in Anat., 1940-47; Lectr in Anat. 1947-48; Lectr in Physiology, 1948-52. Senior Lecturer in Physiology, Univ. of London, 1952; Fitzmary Prof. of Physiology, Institute of Psychiatry, London Univ., 1952-62. Claude Bernard Visiting Prof. Univ. of Montreal, 1950; Visiting Prof.: Univ. of Calif., Los Angeles, 1953; Univ. of Calif. San Francisco, 1954-55; Rockefeller Univ., NY, 1967. Lectures: Herter, Johns Hopkins Hosp., 1955; Sharpey-Schafer, Edinburgh Univ., 1957; Richardson, Massachusetts Gen. Hospital, 1958; Upjohn, San Francisco, 1964; Feldberg, Cologne, 1964; Keith Harrison Memorial, Melbourne, 1965; Charnock Bradley, Edinburgh, 1966; Rehfuss, Philadelphia, 1967; Harry Burr Ferris, Yale, 1967; Member: Society for Endocrinology; Society for Study of Fertility; Anatomical Soc.; Physiol. Soc. Hon. Member: Swiss Soc. for Endocrinology; Amer. Acad. of Arts and Sciences; Royal Acad. of Denmark; Amer. Assoc. Anatomy, 1970; Corresp. Mem., Sociedad Argentina de Biologia, 1970. Fred Lyman Adair Award, Amer. Gynaec. Soc., 1969; Baly Medal, RCP, 1969; Amory Prize, Amer. Acad. Arts and Sciences, 1970; Dale Medal, 1971. DSc

(Detroit), 1965; Hon. DUniv, Strasbourg, 1969. *Publications:* Neural Control of the Pituitary Gland, 1955; scientific papers dealing with Neuroendocrinology, Jl Physiol, etc. *Recreations:* reading, forestry, and travel. *Address:* Department of Human Anatomy, South Parks Road, Oxford. *T:* 58686; Campsfield Wood, Woodstock, Oxon.   [Died 29 Nov. 1971.

HARRIS, Rev. Preb. Herbert, MVO 1962; MA; retired; *b* 2 Sept. 1884; *s* of Alfred and Mary Harris; unmarried. *Educ:* Merchant Taylors' Sch., London; St Catharine's Coll. and Westcott House, Cambridge. BA 1906, MA 1911, Cambridge. Ordained, 1907; Curate of Gt Torrington, 1907-11; of S. Saviour, Alexandra Park, N22, 1911-24; Vicar of S Saviour, Alexandra Park, N22, 1924-47; Rural Dean of Tottenham, 1934-46; Chaplain at Hampton Court Palace, 1947-61; Rural Dean of Hampton, 1948-56. Prebendary of St Paul's Cathedral, 1944-61, Emeritus, 1961. *Recreation:* cricket. *Address:* 38 St Cross Road, Winchester, Hants. *T:* Winchester 2923. [Died 19 Aug. 1971.

HARRIS, Dr Leslie Julius, ScD Cantab, DSc Manchester, PhD Cantab; FRIC; FRSM; first Director of Dunn Nutritional Laboratory (Medical Research Council and University of Cambridge), 1927-63, retired; *b* Liverpool, 1898; *s* of late John and Edith Harris; *m* 1927, Rose (*d* 1971), *d* of late Dr and Mrs J. Snowman; two *s*. *Educ:* Liverpool Coll.; Dalton Hall, University of Manchester; Emmanuel Coll., Cambridge. Leblanc Medal, 1921; Meldola Medallist of Royal Institute of Chemistry, 1925; Coronation Medal, 1953; Emeritus Mem. Biochem. Soc.; Hon. Member: Physiolog. Soc.; Chem. Soc., Royal Institute of Chemistry, etc; Mem. Regent House, University of Cambridge; ex-Assessor, Food Investigation Board; joint founder, first Hon. Sec. (1941-47) and Pres. (1953-56), The Nutrition Soc.; Founder, and Sec.-Gen. (1946-60), Internat. Union of Nutritional Sciences; ex-Mem. Accessory-Food-Factors Cttee (Med. Res. Council); Past-Pres. Biological Methods Gp, Soc. for Analytical Chemistry; Past member: Cttee of Biochemical Soc.; Survey Gp on Animal Nutrition (Agric. Res. Council); various Govt Cttees (on Welfare Foods; Chemical Additives; Scientific Promotions, etc.); Biological Council; Joint Editor: Internationale Zeitschrift für Vitaminforschung; World Review of Nutrition and Dietetics, and formerly of Br. Journ. of Nutrition, of Proceedings of the Nutrition Soc. and of Br. Journ. of Social Medicine; past Trustee, Assoc. of Scientific Workers; ex-Mem. of Cambridge Univ. Educational Film Council; a Vice-Pres., Annual Meeting, BMA, 1948; Hon. Sec. Section I, 1st International Congress of Biochemistry, 1949; Vice-Pres., Ann. Congress of Royal Sanitary Institute, 1951; an Hon. Chm., 12th Internat. Congress of Pure and Applied Chemistry, NY, 1951; Pres. of Honour, Internat. Vitamin Congress, Milan, 1953; Contrib. of articles, on Vitamins in British Encylopædia of Medical Practice, in Annual Reviews of Biochemistry, 1932-35, in Chemical Society's Annual Reports, 1939-42, in Thorpe's Dictionary of Pure and Applied Chemistry, in Chambers's Encyclopædia, 1950, in The Medical Annual, 1957-62, etc.; Royal Instn. Lectr on Vitamins, 1934; Boyle Lectr, Univ. of Oxford, 1942; De Lamar Lecturer, Johns Hopkins University, 1951; Visiting Lecturer: Harvard, Yale, Berkeley, Cornell, and Columbia Univs, 1951; India, Israel, 1958; Prague, 1959, etc. *Publications:* Vitamins in Theory and Practice (1st edn, 1935; 4th edn, 1955; Dutch, Polish, American and Italian edns, 1936, etc); Vitamins and Vitamin Deficiencies, Vol. I, 1939; (with J. Needham and others) Hopkins and Biochemistry, 1949; Vitamins, a Digest of Current Knowledge, 1951; (with A. S. MacNalty and others) The British Medical Dictionary, 1961; (with J. Needham and others) The Chemistry of Life, 1970 (for. edns 1972); papers in Proc. Royal Society, Biochem. Jl, Lancet, Brit. Jl of Nutrit, etc. *Recreations:* studying (particularly linguistics), painting, sculpture, etc; Past Hon. Treas., Cambridge Drawing Soc. *Address:* 16 Winchester Drive, Pinner, Mddx HA5 1DB. *T:* 01-866 2831.   [Died 21 June 1973.

HARRIS, Brigadier (Hon.) Sir Lionel Herbert, KBE 1957 (CBE 1945; OBE 1943); TD 1942; Engineer-in-Chief, GPO, 1954-60, retired; *b* 15 April 1897; *s* of Thomas Harris, London; *m* 1920, Daisy Edith Barkel, London; one *s*. *Educ:* Sir Walter St John's, London; Imperial Coll. of Science. FCGI, BScEng, MScEng, MIEE. Served European War, 1914-18, Australian Signals, 1915-19; Engineering Dept, GPO, 1922-39; 44th Home Counties Division Signals, TA, 1926, Hon. Col, 1950-55; War of 1939-45, commanded GHQ, Signals, 1941-42; CSO, Lines of Communication, 1942-43; Chief, Telecommunications, SHAEF, 1943-45; Regional Dir, GPO Scotland, 1945-49; Controller of Research, GPO. 1949-54. Legion of Merit, US, 1945; Legion of Honour, Croix de Guerre, France, 1945. *Publication:* Signal Venture, 1951. *Address:* 21 Dove Park, Hatch End, Middx. *T:* 01-428 5013.   [Died 18 March 1971.

HARRIS, Sir Percy W.; see Wyn-Harris.

HARRIS, Dr Robert John Cecil; consultant microbiologist; Director, Microbiological Research Establishment, Porton, 1971-79; *b* 14 March 1922; *er s* of John Henry and Suzannah Harris; *m* 1946, Annette Constance Daphne Brading; one *s* one *d. Educ:* Maidstone Grammar Sch.; Imperial Coll of Science and Technology, London. PhD London; FRIC, FIBiol, FRCPath. Laura de Saliceto Student, London Univ., 1947-51; Research Fellow, British Empire Cancer Campaign (Inst. of Cancer Research), 1951-58; Head, Div. of Experimental Biology and Virology, Imperial Cancer Research Fund, 1958-68; Head, Dept of Environmental Carcinogenesis, Imperial Cancer Research Fund, 1968-71. Pres., Inst. of Biol., 1978-80. Hon. DTech Brunel, 1973. *Publications:* Cancer: the nature of the problem, 1962, 3rd edn 1976; scientific papers in cancer jls. *Address:* 24 Harnwood Road, Salisbury, Wilts SP2 8DB. *T:* Salisbury 29570.
[*Died 20 Oct. 1980.*

HARRIS, Sidney; Member, British Steel Corporation, 1968-70 (Member Organising Committee, 1967); Director, Iron & Steel Corporation, 1967; *b* 28 July 1903; *m* 1929, Elsie May South; one *s* one *d. Educ:* Harden, Yorks. Started work in textile industry as a half-timer, 1915; started work in iron and steel industry at Rotherham, with Steel Peech & Tozer (now United Steel Cos), 1922. Mem., Rotherham Co. Borough Coun., 1943-67 (Mayor and Alderman, 1958). Nat. Pres., British Iron & Steel Workers' Union, 1956; Exec. Mem., BISAKTA, 1948-66 (a Founder, 1930, and Sec., 1935-66, Temple 2 Br.). Hon. Freeman of Rotherham, 1971. *Recreations:* (now watching) football; fishing. *Address:* 242 Badsley Moor Lane, Rotherham, Yorks. *T:* Rotherham 78096.   [*Died 7 March 1976.*

HARRIS, Vincent; see Harris, E. V.

HARRIS, Sir William (Henry), KCVO, *cr* 1954 (CVO 1942); MA, DMus Oxon; FRCO, FRCM, Hon. RAM; Organist of St George's Chapel, Windsor, 1933-61; Professor of Organ and Harmony, Royal College of Music, 1921-53; *b* 1883; *m* Kathleen Doris (*d* 1968), *y d* of late J. P. Carter, Redland, Bristol; two *d.* Organ Scholar RCM 1899; Organist of New Coll., Oxford, 1919-28; of Christ Church Cathedral, Oxford, 1928-33; Conductor of Oxford Bach Choir, 1926-33; President Oxford University Musical Soc., 1921; Dir Balliol Concerts, 1925-33; Conductor St George's Chapel Special Choir, 1933; Conductor Slough Philharmonic Soc., 1941-44. Windsor and Eton Choral Soc., 1944-49. Pres. Royal Coll. of Organists, 1946-48; Dir, Musical Studies, Royal School of Church Music, 1956-61. *Publications:* including a Carnegie award, a setting of The Hound of Heaven for Baritone Solo, Chorus, and Orchestra; Michael Angelo's Confession of Faith, for Solo, Chorus, and Orchestra; Psalm 103 for double Choir, etc. *Address:* 64a Heath Road, Petersfield, Hants. *T:* 2168.   [*Died 6 Sept. 1973.*

HARRISON, Sir Archibald Frederick, Kt 1955; CBE 1947; Secretary, Trade Marks, Patents and Designs Federation, 1959-69, retired; Solicitor to the Ministry of Labour and National Service, 1949-59; Government Delegate to the ILO Conferences, 1956-58; *b* 1894; *s* of F. W. Harrison, journalist; *m* 1st, 1923, Mabel Glendinning (*d* 1970); two *d*; 2nd, 1974, Estella Macraith, *widow* of H. A. Macraith. *Educ:* Appleby, Westmorland; Queen's Coll., Oxford. Served War, 1914-18; Border Regt, NW Frontier, India. Called to Bar, 1919, Inner Temple. *Address:* 58 Nightingale Road, Rickmansworth, Herts. *T:* Rickmansworth 73849.   [*Died 18 Nov. 1976.*

HARRISON, Arthur Neville John, CIE 1936; *b* 15 Sept. 1881; *s* of late John Henry Harrison, ICS; *m* 1st, 1914, Helen Zoë Foote (*d* 1934); 2nd, 1934, Frances Mary De Havilland (*d* 1962); no *c. Educ:* Cheltenham Coll.; Lincoln Coll., Oxford (scholar). Government of India PWD, Accounts, 1904; Madras, 1905-9; Eastern Bengal Railway (Calcutta), 1909-14; Auditor Jodhpur-Bikanir Railway (Rajputana), 1914-24; Chief Auditor Bombay, Baroda and Central India Railway (Bombay), 1924-36; officiated Agent BB & CI Railway, Bombay, 1933, 1934, and 1935; retired, 1936; Treasurer of the International Zone of Tangier (Morocco), 1940; Petrol Rationing Authority, Delhi, 1941-42; Deputy Military Accountant Gen. Administration, Delhi, India, 1942-43; Admiralty Courier, 1945; Finances Officer, East Asia, Rice Commn, Bangkok, 1945-47. *Recreation:* bridge. *Address:* c/o National Westminster Bank, High Street, St Peter's Port, Guernsey, CI.   [*Died 31 March 1973.*

HARRISON, Sir (Bernard) Guy, Kt 1951; late Chairman, Harrison & Sons, Ltd; *b* 2 July 1885; *s* of Bernard Bowles Harrison; *m* 1st, 1907, Cicely Ann (*d* 1957), *d* of late H. N. Vicat; one *s* one *d*; 2nd, 1958, Iris, *y d* of late E. R. C. Hall. *Educ:* Sevenoaks Sch. Pres. London Master Printers' Assoc.,

1931-32; Pres. British Federation of Master Printers, 1933-34; Pres. Printing & Allied Trades Research Assoc., 1952-56; Chm., Joint Industrial Council (Printing & Allied Trades), 1939-45; Master of Stationers' Company, 1948-49. Governor, North Western Polytechnic, 1947-57. Pres., Printers' Pension Corporation, 1959-60. *Publications:* occasional contribs to Astronomical and Ornithological Jls. *Recreations:* astronomy, ornithology, botany and entomology. *Address:* Beenleigh Manor, Habertonford, Totnes, Devon. *T:* Habertonford 234. *Club:* Athenæum.   [*Died 21 April 1978.*

HARRISON, Sir Cyril (Ernest), Kt 1963; Chairman, English Sewing Cotton Co. Ltd, 1963-68 (Director 1942; Managing Director, 1948; Vice-Chairman 1952); a Deputy Chairman, Williams & Glyn's Bank, 1969-72 (Joint Deputy Chairman, Williams Deacon's Bank Ltd, 1961); former Director, The Royal Bank of Scotland; *b* 14 Dec. 1901; *s* of Alfred John Harrison, MIGasE, and Edith Harrison, Great Harwood, Lancs; *m* 1927, Edward Wood, FCA, JP, Burnley; two *s. Educ:* Burnley Grammar Sch. President: Manchester Chamber of Commerce, 1958-60; Cotton, Silk and Man-made Fibres Res. Assoc. Member: NW Electricity Bd, 1963-72; S Manchester Hosp. Management Cttee; Council, Manchester Business Sch.; Grand Council, CBI; Court of Govs, University of Manchester. Chm., Christie Hospital and Holt Radium Inst., 1959-61; Chm., NW Regional Council of FBI, 1957-59; Pres., FBI, 1961-63. Mem. National Economic Development Council, 1962-64. Chm., Bd of Governors, United Manchester Hospitals, 1967-74. Hon. MA, Victoria Univ. of Manchester, 1960. Comp. Textile Inst.; FBIM; FCIS. *Recreation:* golf. *Address:* 8 Harefield Drive, Holly Road South, Wilmslow, Cheshire. *T:* Wilmslow 522186.
[*Died 14 March 1980.*

HARRISON, Very Rev. Douglas Ernest William; Dean of Bristol, 1957-72; *b* 30 March 1903; *s* of late Ernest and Beatrice Harrison, Downend, Bristol; *m* 1933, Monica Aileen, *d* of Rev. A. L. F. Baker; one *s* two *d. Educ:* Bristol Grammar Sch.; St John's Coll., Oxford (Scholar) Wycliffe Hall, Oxford. 1st class Hons. Sch. of Nat. Sci. 1925; MA 1928. Curate St John, Waterloo, Liverpool, 1926-30; Chaplain St Peter's Hall, Oxford, and Curate of St Peter-le-Bailey, 1930-31; Chaplain Wycliffe Hall, Oxford, 1931-33, Vice-Principal, 1933-42; Acting Chaplain, Wadham Coll., Oxford, 1939-42, Examining Chaplain to the Bishop of Rochester, 1940-45; Canon Residentiary of Sheffield Cathedral, Examining Chaplain to Bishop of Sheffield and Director of Ordinands, 1942-57; Archdeacon of Sheffield, 1943-57; Examining Chaplain to the Bishop of Blackburn, 1966-72. Select Preacher at Oxford, 1947-48, Cambridge, 1960. Mem. of C of E Bd of Educn 1957-72; Vice-Chm., Council of Church Colls of Education, 1957-71; Mem., Liturgical Commission, 1955-72 (Vice-Chm., 1962-72); Chm., The Churches' Joint Liturgical Group, 1963-72; Mem. Council of Religious Communities, until 1972. OStJ. Hon. DLitt Bristol, 1969. *Publications:* Common Prayer in the Church of England, 1946; The Ethics of the Gospel, 1949. *Recreations:* carpentry, church architecture. *Address:* 95A Pembroke Road, Bristol 8. *T:* Bristol 35865.   [*Died 22 Feb. 1974.*

HARRISON, Rt. Hon. Sir Eric John, PC 1952; KCMG 1962; KCVO 1954; Freeman of City of London, 1957; company director; *b* 7 Sept. 1892; *s* of Arthur Harrison, Birmingham, England, and Sydney, Australia; *m* 1st, 1920, Mary McCall (decd); three *d*; 2nd, 1944, Linda R., *d* of John Fullerton, Sydney. *Educ:* Crown Street Sch., Sydney. Served European War, 1914-18, with AIF (France) and 1939-45 as Capt. and Liaison Officer to US Forces; MHR, Australia, (L) Wentworth, NSW, 1931-56; Minister for Interior, 1934; Mem. Jt Cttee, Public Works, 1937 and 1943-46; Minister without portfolio, 1938-39; PMG and Repatriation Minister, 1939-40; Minister for Trade and Customs, 1940-41; Mem. Economic Cabinet, 1939-41; Dep. Leader, Liberal Party, 1944; Dep. Leader, Opposition, 1944-49 (actg Leader Oppn, latter half 1948); Minister for Defence, 1949-50; Resident Minister for Commonwealth of Australia in London and Minister for Interior, Australia, 1950-51. Vice-Pres. of Executive Council, Leader of the House of Representatives, and Minister for Defence Production, Australia, 1951-56. Minister in charge of Royal Visit, 1952 (cancelled); Minister in charge, Royal Tour, 1954; Acting Prime Minister, June 1954; Acting Treasurer, June 1954; Minister for the Army and Minister for the Navy, 1955-56; High Commissioner for the Commonwealth of Australia in London, 1956-64. *Recreations:* rowing (Mem. Australian team, Henley-on-Thames, 1919), sailing, golf, reading. *Address:* Stoke Lodge, 111 Neerim Road, Castle Cove, Sydney, NSW 2069, Australia. *Clubs:* Union; Elanora Country (Sydney). [*Died 26 Sept. 1974.*

HARRISON, Gabriel Harold; Chairman: Amalgamated Investment & Property Co. Ltd, since 1960; Saint Anne's on the Sea Land and Building Co. Ltd, since 1961; Grand Junction Co. Ltd, since 1971; Midhurst White Holdings Ltd, since 1973; *b* 17 June 1921; *s* of late Samuel Harrison and Esta Harrison (*née* Romain); *m* 1st, 1946, Helena Rose (marr. diss. 1967); one *s* one *d*; 2nd, 1967, Joy Gale. *Educ:* Kilburn Grammar Sch., London. Served War, First Div. AA Signals (Territorial), 1939-43; served W Africa, 1942-43. Mem. (C) for E Willesden, Mddx CC, 1962-65. Vice-Chm., Advisory Council, Student Co-operative Dwellings Ltd, 1970-; Since 1972: Chm., World of Property Housing Trust; Mem. Cttee of Management, Royal Nat. Life-Boat Instn; Trustee, Southwark Playgrounds Trust; Pres., S Fylde Scout Assoc.; Barclaybonds Adv. Cttee (Barclays Bank Trust Co. Ltd); Adv. Cttee, Barclaytrust International Property Fund. Chm., Contemporary Dance Trust Ltd, 1974-; Trustee, Architectural Heritage Fund, 1974-. Freeman of City of London, 1973; Mem. Carmen's Company. *Publication:* Rage of Sand (social history of St Anne's on Sea), 1971. *Recreations:* social history, the arts, swimming, travel. *Address:* 40 Clarence Terrace, Regent's Park, NW1 4RD. *T:* 01-262 4275. *Clubs:* Carlton, City Livery, Royal Automobile. *[Died 4 Dec. 1974.*

HARRISON, Sir Guy; *see* Harrison, Sir B. G.

HARRISON, Sir Harwood; *see* Harrison, Sir James Harwood.

HARRISON, His Honour James Fraser; Judge of County Courts, 1940-62; retired; Commissioner of Divorce; JP Lancs, 1938, Cheshire, 1942; *b* 7 May 1890; *s* of late James Fraser Harrison, Caerwys, Flintshire; *m* 1915, Betty (*d* 1960), *er d* of late Alfred Broadhurst, Bramhall, Cheshire; one *s*. *Educ:* Liverpool Coll.; Sedbergh; Liverpool Univ. LLM (Hon.) Liverpool Univ., 1942. Called to Bar, Inner Temple, 1912; practised Liverpool and Northern Circuit; Army, 1914-18; Asst Recorder of Liverpool, 1929-40; Dep. Chm. Preston, Manchester and Liverpool County Quarter Sessions, 1938-40; Aliens Tribunal, 1939; a Dep. Chm. of Appeal Cttees for County of Lancaster, 1943-60 and Chester, 1943-46; Hon. Independent Referee Lancs and Cheshire Coal Mining Conciliation Board, 1945-62; HM Commissioner of Assize, Northern Circuit, 1946. *Address:* Alexandra Court Hotel, Liverpool 17. *T:* 051-727 2551. *Club:* Lyceum (Liverpool). *[Died 16 Jan. 1971.*

HARRISON, Sir (James) Harwood, 1st Bt *cr* 1961, of Bugbrooke; TD (2 bars) 1947; MA; *b* 6 June 1907; *e s* of late Rev. E. W. Harrison, MA, Bugbrooke, Northampton; *m* 1932, Peggy Alberta Mary, *d* of late Lieut-Col V. D. Stenhouse, TD, JP, Minehead; one *s* one *d*. *Educ:* Northampton Grammar Sch.; Trinity Coll., Oxford. Hons degree (jurisprudence), 1928; MA 1946. Mem. Ipswich County Borough Council, 1935-46; Chm. Mental Hosp., 1938. Commissioned 4th Bn The Suffolk Regt, TA, 1935; Capt. 1939; Major 1940; captured (Singapore), 1942; on Burma Railway, 1943; Lieut-Col comdg 4th Suffolks, 1947; Bt-Col 1951; TARO 1951-65. Mil. Mem. Suffolk T & AFA, 1951-. Contested Eye Div. of Suffolk, 1950; MP (C) Eye, 1951-79; PPS to Mr Harold Macmillan, Minister of Housing and Local Govt, 1953-54; Asst Whip, 1954-56; a Lord Commissioner of the Treasury, 1956-59; Comptroller of HM Household, 1959-61. Presented and sponsored Private Mem.'s Bills: Road Transport Lighting (Rear Lights) Act, 1953; Road Traffic Act, 1964. Pres., Nat. Union of Conservative and Unionist Assocs Eastern Area, 1963-66 (Chm. 1956-59, Vice-Chm. 1953-56); Chairman: Unionist Club, 1966-; Defence and External Affairs Sub-Cttee of Expenditure Cttee, 1971-79; Brit. Br., IPU, 1973-74 (Vice-Chm., 1970; Treas., 1968). Pres. Ipswich and District Far East POW Fellowship, 1953. Chm., Cap Estate (St Lucia) Ltd; Dir of Chalwyns Ltd and other companies. Has lectured extensively in America, Europe and Africa. Patron, Lord of Manor and Land-Owner at Bugbrooke. *Recreation:* sailing. *Heir:* s Michael James Harwood Harrison [*b* 28 March, 1936; *m* 1967, Rosamund Louise, *d* of Edward Clive, Bishops Waltham; two *d*]. *Address:* Little Manor, Hasketon, Woodbridge, Suffolk. *T:* Woodbridge 3542. *Clubs:* Carlton, Crockford's, Pratt's. *[Died 11 Sept. 1980.*

HARRISON, Maj.-Gen. Sir James (William), KCMG 1968; CB 1968; CBE 1958; idc; Governor of South Australia, since 1968; *b* 25 May 1912; *s* of James Samuel Harrison, Camperdown, Vic.; *m* 1940, Patricia Hellen, *d* of Col. F. W. Lennox; two *s*. *Educ:* Geelong Coll.; RMC Duntroon. Commnd RAA, 1932; regimental appts until 1939; served 1939-45 in Middle East (despatches), SW Pacific Area, NW Europe. Aust. Staff UK, 1954-56; GOC, W Comd, 1957-59; Chm., Jt Planning Cttee, Dept of Defence, 1960-61; QMG Australian Army, 1962-63; Adjt Gen., 1963-66. GOC Eastern Comd, Australia, 1966-68. KStJ 1969. *Recreations:* golf, books. *Address:* Government House, Adelaide, South Australia. *Club:* Naval and Military (Melbourne). *[Died 15 Sept. 1971.*

HARRISON, John Vernon, MA, DSc; FRSE; geologist; formerly Reader in Structural Geology, Oxford University; *b* 16 March 1892; *s* of late J. Frederick Harrison, MInstCE; *m* 1939, Janet Mithcell (*d* 1971), *d* of D. M. Dingwall, Flisk, Newburgh, Fife. *Educ:* George Watson's Coll., Edinburgh; Allan Glen's Sch., Glasgow; Glasgow Univ. Explored in Persia, Central and South America, West Indies, and Borneo. Grand Officer, Order for Distinguished Services to Peru. *Publications:* papers on geology and geography. *Recreation:* hill-climbing. *Address:* 59 Bagley Wood Road, Kennington, Oxford. *Club:* Athenæum. *[Died 31 July 1972.*

HARRISON, Air Vice-Marshal Richard, CB 1944; CBE 1943; DFC; AFC; late RAF; *b* 29 June 1893; *s* of late Mansfield Harrison, Pocklington, Yorks; unmarried. *Educ:* Highgate; Scarborough Coll.; Sheffield Univ. European War, 1914-19 (despatches); Palestine; Iraq (despatches twice); Egypt; War of 1939-45 (despatches thrice); retired, 1946. Officier Légion d'Honneur; Croix de Guerre (France). *Club:* Royal Air Force. *[Died 18 May 1974.*

HARRISON, Ven. Talbot D.; *see* Dilworth-Harrison.

HARRISON, Prof. Wilfrid; Professor of Politics, University of Warwick, 1964-75, now Emeritus; *b* 30 May 1909; *s* of W. T. and Amy Harrison, Glasgow; *m* 1943, Elizabeth Sara, *d* of Rev. P. J. and Linda Sweeny, Ardagh, Co. Limerick; two *d*. *Educ:* Hyndland Sch., Glasgow; University of Glasgow (MA 1931); Queen's Coll., Oxford (BA 1933, MA 1937). Senior Demy of Magdalen Coll., Oxford, 1933; Lecturer in Politics, Queen's Coll., Oxford, 1935; Fellow of Queen's Coll., 1939-57, Dean, 1940; Prof. of Political Theory and Institutions, University of Liverpool, 1957-64; Pro-Vice-Chancellor, Univ. of Warwick, 1964-70. Temporary Civil Servant, Ministry of Supply, 1940-45. Editor of Political Studies, 1952-63. Hon. DLitt Warwick, 1979. *Publications:* The Government of Britain, 1948; Conflict and Compromise, 1965; (ed) Bentham's Fragment on Government and Introduction to the Principles of Morals and Legislation, 1948; articles in Chambers's Encyclopædia and various journals. *Recreations:* piano; cooking. *Address:* 73 Coten End, Warwick. *[Died 15 Oct. 1980.*

HARRISON, William Herbert; Chairman of Power Plant Gears Limited; Director: Hawson Ltd; AAH Ltd; *b* 1909; *s* of late Lt-Col William Edward Harrison, OBE, Wychnor Park; *m* 1934, Elcha Cecelia (marr. diss.), *d* of late Charles Hore-Ruthven, Norwich; four *d*. *Educ:* Harrow. High Sheriff of Staffordshire, 1964. *Recreations:* racing, shooting and fishing. *Address:* Wychnor Park, near Burton-on-Trent, Staffs. *T:* Burton-on-Trent 790209. *Club:* Boodle's. *[Died 16 May 1975.*

HARRISON, Tom, DSO 1946; OBE 1959; Senior Research Associate in Anthropology and South-east Asia Program, Cornell University; Emeritus Curator, Sarawak Museum; Visiting Professor and Director of Mass-Observation Archive, University of Sussex; *b* 26 Sept. 1911; *s* of late Gen. G. H. Harrison, DSO, and Mrs Betha Clayton (marr. diss., 1954; she *d* 1961), *d* of late T. Pellatt, Durnford Sch., Dorset; one *s*; 2nd, 1956, Dr Barbara (marr. diss. 1970), *d* of Dr Gerhart Güttler, Berlin, Nikolassee and Bad Tolz, Germany; 3rd, 1971, Baronne Christine Forani (Sculptor, Croix de Guerre, 1945), widow, *d* of Prof. N. Bonncompagnie, Brussels. *Educ:* Harrow; Pembroke Coll., Cambridge. Biological upbringing and training; left Harrow (where wrote standard book on the birds of the district) to go on Oxford Univ. Expedn to Arctic Lapland; spent time on uninhabited British islands; in Central Borneo where led large Oxford Expedition, and then for two years in New Hebrides, Western Pacific; one year living among cannibal mountain tribes of Malekula (Cuthbert Peak award, RGS). On return to England, 1936, determined, instead of studying primitive people, to study the cannibals of Britain, so started with Charles Madge new type of social research organisation, called Mass-Observation. Radio critic Sunday Observer, 1941-44; served in KRRC, Green Howards and Reconnaissance Corps, 1942-44; Paratroop Major with Special Operations Executive, 1944-45 (DSO); first white man to be dropped in Borneo, to organise guerillas in Sarawak and Dutch Borneo prior to Allied landings; Officer Administrating Interior Borneo for Mil. Admin., 1946; Govt Ethnologist and Curator of Museum, Sarawak, 1947-66; Vis. Prof., Cornell, 1967-68. Chm., Marine Turtle Specialist Gp, IUCN, 1974. Reviews Editor, IUCN bulletin, Morges, Switzerland; Ethnological Expedns for Sarawak Govt to Kelabit Plateau Central Borneo, 1947-64. Speleological Soc. Award, USA, 1960; José Rizal Centennial Medal, Philippines, 1961; Founder's Medal of Royal Geographical Soc., 1962; RSA Medallist, 1964. Dato Seri Lela Jasa (Brunei), 1972. *Publications:* Birds of NW Middlesex, 1930; The Great Crested Grebe Census, 1931; Letter to Oxford, 1933;

numerous papers in scientific journals on biological studies and exploratory work, 1932-36; Savage Civilisation, 1937; Borneo Jungle, 1938; Mass-Observation, 1937; Britain, by Mass-Observation, 1939; War begins at Home, 1940; Home Propaganda, 1941; People in Production, 1942; Living Among Cannibals, 1942; The Pub and the People, 1943; People's Homes, 1943; World Within: a Borneo Story, 1959; Britain Revisited, 1961; The Peoples of Sarawak, 1961; Brunei: Background to a Revolt, 1963; The Malays of Sarawak, 1969; papers on ethnology of South East Asia in Jls of Asiatic Soc., Polynesian Soc., South Seas Soc., Man, etc., 1948-74; (with Prof. S. J. O'Connor) The Prehistoric Iron Age Workings of Sarawak, 1969; Gold and the Megalithic in Borneo, 1970; (with Barbara Harrisson) The Prehistory of Sabah, 1971; (jt) Primitive Erotic Art, 1973; Prehistoric Wood, 1974; *posthumous publication:* Living Through the Blitz, 1976. *Recreations:* living among strange people and listening to them talk about themselves; collecting strange objects; television (with Hugh Gibb, won Eurovision Grand Prix, Cannes Film Festival for TV film, Birds' Nest Soup, one of a series of 6, in The Borneo Story). *Address:* 45 Avenue Lancaster, 1180 Brussels, Belgium. *T:* 3740385; c/o Vice-Chancellor's Office, University of Sussex, Brighton, Sussex. *Clubs:* Travellers', Special Forces; Brunei Yacht; International House of Japan; Cercle des Nations (Brussels).
[*Died* 18 Jan. 1976.

HARROD, Sir Roy (Forbes), Kt 1959; FBA 1947; Hon. Dr (Law), Poitiers; Hon. LLD Aberdeen; Hon. Dr (Laws) University of Pennsylvania; Hon. DLitt: Glasgow; Warwick; Stockholm; Hon. Student of Christ Church, since 1967; Hon. Fellow of Nuffield College; *b* 13 Feb. 1900; *s* of Henry Dawes Harrod and Frances Marie Desirée Harrod; *m* 1938, Wilhelmine, *e d* of late Capt. F. J. Cresswell, The Norfolk Regt, and Lady Strickland, DBE; two *s. Educ:* Westminster Sch. (Scholar); New Coll., Oxford (Scholar), Hon. Fellow 1975; 1st class in Lit. Hum., 1921; 1st class in Modern History, 1922. Enlisted, Sept. 1918; Lecturer at Christ Church, 1922-24; Student, 1924-67; Junior Censor, 1927-29; Senior Censor, 1930-31; Mem. of the Hebdomadal Council of Oxford University, 1929-35; Bodleian Library Commission, 1930-31; University Lecturer in Economics, 1929-37 and 1946-52; Nuffield Reader in Economics, 1952-67. Visiting Professor for one term: Univ. of Pennsylvania, 1964, 1967, 1969, 1970; Univ. of Maryland, 1971; Claremont Grad. Sch., 1972. Pres. of Sect. F of Brit. Assoc., 1938; served under Lord Cherwell on Mr Churchill's private statistical staff in Admiralty, 1940, and in Prime Minister's office, at full time, 1940-42, and subsequently in advisory capacity; also statistical adviser to Admiralty, 1943-45; Vice-Pres., the Royal Economic Society (Mem., Council since 1933); Jt Editor, Economic Journal, 1945-61; Mem. of UN Sub-Commission on Employment and Economic Stability, 1947-50; Fellow of Nuffield Coll., 1938-47, and 1954-58; Hon. Fellow, 1958. Economic Adviser, International Monetary Fund, 1952-53; Sir George Watson Lecturer in American History, 1953; Bernard Harms Prize (Keil), 1966. Mem. Migration Board, Commonwealth Relations Office, 1953-66. Curator of Christ Church Pictures, 1956-64. Exec. Cttee of sponsors of East Anglia Univ., 1959-64; Pres. Royal Economic Soc., 1962-64; Mem., Royal Swedish Acad. of Science. *Publications:* International Economics, 1933 (revised edn, 1957, much revised 5th edn 1975); The Trade Cycle, an Essay, 1936; Britain's Future Population, 1943; A Page of British Folly, 1946; Are These Hardships Necessary? 1947; Towards a Dynamic Economics, 1948; The Life of John Maynard Keynes, 1951; And So It Goes On, 1951; Economic Essays, 1952, rev. edn 1972; The Dollar, 1953; The Foundations of Inductive Logic, 1956, 2nd edn 1974; Policy Against Inflation, 1958; The Prof. (A Personal Memoir of Lord Cherwell), 1959; Topical Comment, 1961; The British Economy, 1963; Reforming the World's Money, 1965; Towards a New Economic Policy, 1967; Dollar-Sterling Collaboration, 1968; Money, 1969; Sociology, Morals and Mystery, 1971; Economic Dynamics, 1973; papers in the Economic Journal, the Quarterly Journal of Economics, Economica, Mind, etc. *Address:* The Old Rectory, Holt, Norfolk. *T:* Holt 2204; 51 Campden Hill Square, W8. *T:* 01-727 8485.
[*Died* 8 March 1978.

HARROP, Maj.-Gen. William Harrington H.; see Hulton-Harrop.

HARSANT, Maj.-Gen. Arnold Guy, CB 1952; OBE 1935; FRCS; MD; MS; Limb-fitting Surgeon, Queen Mary's Hospital, Roehampton; *b* 16 Nov. 1893; *s* of F. A. Harsant, LDS, and Rosetta Harsant; *m* 1934, Mabel Sarah Bailey; one *d. Educ:* St Paul's Sch., West Kensington; The London Hosp. MRCS, LRCP, 1916; DTM and H 1922; MB, BS 1930; FRCS 1930; MD 1931; MS London 1933. Commissioned in Regular Army RAMC; served in Salonica Campaign, 1916-18 (despatches);

subsequently served in Mesopotamia, India, China, Egypt; Maj.-Gen., 1951; Cons. Surgeon, Egypt and Palestine Forces, Sept.-Dec. 1936; Prof. of Surgery, Egyptian University, 1937-45; Cons. Surgeon, BAOR, 1945-49; Dir of Surgery and Consulting Surgeon to the Army, 1949-53. KHS 1949. Order of St Sava, 1916; Order of the Nile, 1937. *Address:* 16 Roehampton Gate, SW15. *T:* 01-876 8924.
[*Died* 8 April 1977.

HARSTON, Major Sir Ernest (Sirdefield), Kt 1958; CBE 1953 (OBE 1947); Hon. Recorder, British Commonwealth Ex-Services League, since 1962 (Hon. Secretary, 1942-62. Executive Chairman 1961-62); Solicitor, New Zealand, since 1918, England since 1935; *b* 21 Aug. 1891; *s* of Harry Loversedge Harston; *m* 1919, Ruth Barbara, *d* of Sir George Shirtcliffe, Wellington, NZ; one *d* (one *s* killed in action). *Educ:* Napier High Sch.; St John's Coll., New Zealand Univ. Served European War, 1914-18 (despatches), with New Zealand Forces; Egypt, Dardanelles, France; Defence Headquarters, Wellington; Major, 1917. Secretariat, League of Nations, 1926-30; Mem. Marylebone Borough Council, 1944-50. War of 1939-45, Home Guard and Admiralty Ferry Crews. Mem., Arts Educational Trust Ltd, 1966-73. OStJ 1960. *Recreation:* sailing. *Address:* The Hard, Swanwick Shore, near Southampton. *T:* Locksheath 2107. *Clubs:* Carlton, Royal Thames Yacht (Rear Cdre, 1954, 1955); Royal Cruising; Law Society Yacht (Cdre, 1960-62).
[*Died* 27 June 1975.

HART, Sir William (Ogden), Kt 1961; CMG 1946; Chairman, Northampton New Town Development Corporation, 1968-76; *b* 25 May 1903; *s* of late Sir William Edward Hart, OBE; *m* 1927, Dorothy Eileen, *d* of late Col D. W. Churcher, Royal Irish Fusiliers; three *s* one *d. Educ:* Rugby Sch.; New Coll., Oxford. Called to Bar (Lincoln's Inn), 1928; Fellow of Wadham Coll., Oxford, 1926-47; Tutor, 1934-47; Bursar, 1928-40; Hon. Fellow, 1962; Min. of Shipping, 1940-41; joined British Merchant Shipping Mission, Washington, 1941, and Head of the Mission, 1944-46. Gen. Man., Hemel Hempstead Development Corp., 1947-55; Dir-Gen. and Clerk to the Greater London Council, 1964-68 (Clerk of London County Council from 1956). Chm., Commn on Broadcasting of the General Synod of the Church of England, 1971-73. Member: SSRC, 1965-70; Bd, Nat. Bus Company, 1968-71. Hon. FRIBA; Hon. MRTPI. *Publication:* (with Sir William E. Hart) Introduction to the Law of Local Government and Administration, 1934. *Address:* Turweston Lodge, near Brackley, Northants. *Club:* United Oxford & Cambridge University.
[*Died* 29 April 1977.

HART-SYNNOT, Ronald Victor Okes, DSO 1900; OBE 1919; late Lieutenant East Surrey Regiment; Emeritus Fellow of St John's College, Oxford, 1949; *b* 24 July 1879; *s* of late Maj.-Gen. FitzRoy Hart-Synnot, CB, CMG; *m* 1912, Violet (*d* 1973), *e d* of late Rev. Lord Theobald Butler; one *s. Educ:* King William's Coll.; Sandhurst; South-East Agricultural Coll., Wye; MA Oxon, BSc London. Joined Regiment, 1899; served South Africa, 1899-1902, including Colenso, and as ADC to Maj.-Gen. FitzRoy Hart, including Spion Kop, Potgieter's Drift, Pieters Relief of Ladysmith, etc (despatches twice); in Orange River and Cape Colonies, 1901-02 (Queen's Medal with 5 clasps, King's medal with 2 clasps); resigned commission, 1904; Private Sec. to Sir Horace Plunkett, 1909; Dean, Faculty of Agriculture and Horticulture, University Coll., Reading, 1909-14 and 1919-20; ADC to HE Gen. Sir Reginald Hart in Guernsey, 1915; Headquarters Staff, Southern Command, Salisbury, Feb. 1916; Dep. Asst Dir of Labour, 1918; temp. Capt., 1915; temp. Major, 1918. Bursar, 1920-49, Fellow, 1922-49, of St John's Coll., Oxford. *Publications:* articles on agricultural subjects in Quarterly Review, XIX Century, Banker, and other periodicals. *Address:* 21 Belsyre Court, Oxford.
[*Died* 20 April 1976.

HARTE, Wilma Pansy; Under-Secretary, Department of Education and Science, since 1968; *b* 19 Nov. 1916; *d* of late William and Mary Harte. *Educ:* St Christopher Sch., Letchworth, Herts; University Coll., London. Min. of Labour, Third Class Officer, later Asst Principal, 1939-47; Asst Sec., Royal Commn on Equal Pay, 1944-46; Min. of Education: Asst Principal, 1947-48; Principal, 1948-60; Asst Sec., 1960-68; Dept of Educn and Science: Asst Under-Sec. of State and Head of Schools Branch, 1968-73; Head of External Relations Br., 1973-75; Head of Schs Br. III, 1975-. *Recreation:* listening. *Address:* 9 Kent Terrace, Park Road, NW1. *T:* 01-723 4961.
[*Died* 30 Jan. 1976.

HARTLAND, Alderman William John, CBE 1965; JP; Executive Officer and Council Member, Tenovus Cancer Information Centre; *b* 19 Feb. 1909; *s* of William Edward Hartland and Minnie Evelyn (née Herbert); *m* 1934, Phyllis, *y d* of Annie and Late John Lewis Morris, Cardiff; one *s. Educ:* Llandovery Coll. Partner in Meat Manufacturing Firm, 1930-59. Member: Cardiff

CC, 1946- (Whip to Conservative Gp, 1948-57; Leader, Conservative Gp, 1957-70); Bd of Govs, Cardiff Royal Infirmary, 1939-48; Bd of Govs, Nat. Library of Wales, 1949-56; Govs, Nat. Museum of Wales, 1949-56; Cardiff North HMC, 1948-69; Health Educn Council, 1968-; Welsh Hosp. Bd; Chm., Cardiff SE Conservative Assoc.; Vice-Pres., Internat. Union of Local Authorities; Lord Mayor of Cardiff, 1964-65; Deputy Lord Mayor, 1967-68. JP Cardiff, 1950. OStJ 1966. MRSH 1965. *Recreations:* football, cricket, reading. *Address:* 27 Princes' Avenue, Roath Court, Cardiff. *T:* Cardiff 42851 (business), 25333 (private). *Club:* (Hon. Life Mem.) Splott Conservative (Cardiff). *[Died 28 June 1972.*

HARTLEY, Brig.-Gen. Sir Harold (Brewer), GCVO 1957 (KCVO 1944); CH 1967; Kt 1928; CBE 1919; MC; FRS 1926; MA, Oxford; Hon. DCL Oxford; Hon. LLD Edinburgh; Hon. DSc Sheffield, Birmingham, Princeton, Southampton; Hon. Associate, Manchester College of Technology; Hon. Fellow Balliol College, Oxford, 1941; Director, Readex Microprint Corporation (UK), Ltd; *b* London, 3 Sept. 1878; *o s* of late Harold T. Hartley; *m* Gertrude (*d* 1971), *e d* of late A. L. Smith, Master of Balliol; one *s* one *d*. *Educ:* Dulwich Coll.; Balliol Coll. Oxford (1st Class Nat. Science). Natural Science Tutor and Bedford Lectr in Physical Chemistry, Balliol Coll., Oxford, 1901-31; Jowett Fellow, 1928-31; Research Fellow, 1931-41. Capt. 7th Leics Regt, 1914-15; Chemical Adviser to the 3rd Army, 1915-17; Asst Dir Gas Services, GHQ, France, 1917-18; Controller Chemical Warfare Dept, Ministry of Munitions, 1918-19 (MC, despatches thrice). A Dir, Gas Light and Coke Co., 1922-45 (a Dep. Governor, 1942-45). Chm. of Fuel Research Board, 1932-47; Dir of Times Publishing Co., 1936-60; Hon. Adviser on development of home-produced fuels, Ministry of Fuel and Power, 1939-47; Vice-Pres, and Dir of Research, LMS Railway, 1930-45; Chm., Railway Air Services, 1934-45; Prime Warden of Goldsmiths' Company, 1941-42; Chairman: British European Airways Corporation, 1946-47; British Overseas Airways Corporation, 1947-49; Electricity Supply Research Council of British Electricity Authority, 1949-52; Pres. Institute of Chemical Engineers, 1951-52, and 1954-55. Pres. British Assoc. for the Advancement of Science for 1950; Chairman: British National Cttee and International Executive Council, World Power Conference, 1935-50; Fourth World Power Conference, 1950; Pres. World Power Conference, 1950-56; Chairman: Energy Commission, OEEC, 1955-56; Council, Duke of Edinburgh's Study Conference on Human Problems of Industrial Communities, 1954-56; Pres., Soc. of Instrument Technology, 1957-61; Scientific Adviser to Constructors John Brown Ltd, 1954-61. Lubbock, Citrine and Romanes Lectureships, 1964. Rly Engrg Medal Inst. of Transport, 1932; Wilhelm Exner Medal, 1937; Osborne-Reynolds Medal of Instn of Chem. Engrs, 1954; Birmingham Medal of Instn of Gas Engrs, 1958; Kelvin Gold Medal, 1965; Herbert Hoover Medal, 1968; Berzelius Medal, Royal Swedish Acad., 1971. *Publications:* Balliol Men, 1963; ed, The Royal Society: its origins and founders, 1960; Man and Nature (Romanes Lecture), 1964; Humphry Davy, 1966; Studies in the History of Chemistry, 1971. *Address:* c/o 20 Fitzjames Avenue, W14. *T:* 01-603 3078. *Clubs:* Athenæum (Hon. Mem.), Travellers'. *[Died 9 Sept. 1972.*

HARTLEY, Leslie Poles, CBE 1956; CLit 1972; author and critic; *b* 30 Dec. 1895; *s* of H. B. Hartley, JP, Fletton Tower, Peterborough; unmarried. *Educ:* Harrow; Balliol Coll., Oxford. Has written literary criticism for the weekly reviews (Spectator, Week-end Review, Sketch, Time and Tide, etc.) since 1923. Clark Lecturer, Trinity Coll., Cambridge, 1964. *Publications:* Night Fears (short stories), 1924; Simonetta Perkins (novel), 1925; The Killing Bottle (short stories), 1932; The Shrimp and the Anemone (novel), 1944; The Sixth Heaven (novel), 1946; Eustace and Hilda (novel, James Tait Black Memorial Prize), 1947; The Boat (novel), 1950; The Travelling Grave and other Stories, 1951; My Fellow Devils (novel), 1951; The Go-Between, 1953 (W. H. Heinemann Foundation award) (filmed 1971); The White Wand (short stories), 1954; A Perfect Woman (novel), 1955; The Hireling (novel), 1957; Facial Justice (novel), 1960; Two for the River (short stories), 1961; The Brickfield (novel), 1964; The Betrayal, 1966; The Novelists' Responsibility (lectures and essays), 1967; Poor Clare, 1968; The Collected Stories of L. P. Hartley, 1968; The Love-Adept (novel), 1969; My Sisters' Keeper, 1970; The Harness Room, 1971; The Collections, 1972; *posthumous publications:* Mrs Carteret Receives, 1973; The Will and the Way, 1973. *Recreations:* rowing, swimming, walking. *Address:* Avondale, Bathford, Somerset. *T:* Bath 88117; Flat 10, 53 Rutland Gate, SW7. *Clubs:* Athenæum, Beefsteak; Bath and County (Bath). *[Died 13 Dec. 1972.*

HARTLEY, Percival Hubert Graham Horton-Smith, OBE 1945; on the staff of Richard Arnold & Son, Average Adjusters, since 1971; *b* 27 Sept. 1896; *s* of late Sir Percival Horton-Smith Hartley, CVO, MD; *m* 1923, Mary Grizel, *d* of late Sir George Seaton Buchanan, CB, MD. *Educ:* Eton; St John's Coll., Cambridge (Entrance Scholar). Asst Master at Eton Coll., 1922-56 (House Master, 1933-51). With O. Gross & Sons (Shipowners), 1957-71. Served European War 1915-18, Coldstream Guards (Special Reserve) and again 1940-45 in Staff appointments, and in Allied Military Government, Italy (Freedom of City of Bologna, 1945); released with rank of Col, 1946. Master of the Worshipful Company of Ironmongers, 1953-54. *Recreations:* rowing (Eton VIII 1915, Cambridge crew 1920-21-22), climbing, sailing. *Address:* Dorney House, Dorney, near Windsor, Berks. *T:* Burnham 4983. *Clubs:* Athenæum; Leander. *[Died 3 Jan. 1977.*

HARTNELL, Sir Norman (Bishop), KCVO 1977 (MVO 1953); Dressmaker by appointment to HM the Queen, and to HM Queen Elizabeth the Queen Mother; Member Incorporated Society of London Fashion Designers (Chairman 1947-56); Ex-Vice-President Clothing Institute; *b* 12 June 1901. *Educ:* Magdalene Coll., Cambridge. Awarded Officier d'Académie by French Government, 1939; Royal Warrant, 1940; Neiman-Marcus Award, USA, for world influence on fashion, 1947. *Publications:* Silver and Gold (autobiography), 1955; Royal Courts of Fashion, 1971. *Recreations:* painting, riding, swimming. *Address:* 26 Bruton Street, Mayfair, W1. *[Died 8 June 1979.*

HARTRIDGE, Hamilton, FRS 1926; MA, MD, ScD (Cambridge); MRCP; Emeritus Professor of Physiology, University of London, since 1949; *b* 7 May 1886; *e s* of Henry Hill Hartridge, Oakwood Hill, Surrey; *m* 1916, Kathleen, *d* of Hugo Wilson, Kegworth, Leicestershire; one *s* three *d*. *Educ:* St Vincent's, Eastbourne; Harrow Sch.; King's Coll., Cambridge (Exhibitioner 1907, Fellow 1912-26). Horton-Smith Prize, 1918; Experimental Officer, Kingsnorth Airship Station (RAF), 1915-19; Lecturer in Special Senses and Senior Demonstrator in Physiology at Cambridge Univ., 1919-27; Prof. of Physiology at St Bartholomew's Hosp. Med. Coll., 1927-47; Dir, Vision Research Unit, MRC, 1947-51. Many inventions, from intrinsic electric light and scale for mirror galvanometer, 1904, to a projection microscope for large audiences, 1932. Hon. Fellow of Royal Photographic Society, 1957; FInstP 1962; Hon. Mem., Physiol Soc., 1968. *Publications:* Colours and how we see them, 1949; Recent advances in the Physiology of Vision, 1950; Editor (with Prof. J. di Silva) of Bainbridge and Menzies Essentials of Physiology, 1929; papers and research on the optics of the eye, on the visual perception of fine detail, on the optics of the microscope, on the resonance theory of hearing, on carbon monoxide gas in tobacco smoke and in the blood of a cigarette smoker, and on bats' radar. *Recreations:* motoring, metal working, and sketching. *Address:* Benridge, Frithwood Avenue, Northwood, Mddx. *T:* Northwood 21844. *[Died 13 Jan. 1976.*

HARTUNG, Ernst Johannes, DSc; Professor of Chemistry, University of Melbourne, 1928-53; Emeritus Professor since 1953; *b* Victoria, 23 April 1893; 2nd *s* of Carl August Ernst Hartung, Leipzig, and Ida Emilie, *d* of F. A. Hagenauer, Vic.; *m* 1922, Gladys, *d* of F. W. Gray, Glos; two *d*. *Educ:* Wesley Coll., Melbourne; University of Melbourne. BSc, 1913; DSc, 1919; Tutor in Chemistry, Trinity Coll., Melbourne, 1914; Lecturer and Demonstrator in Chemistry, University of Melbourne, 1919; Associate Prof., 1924; Winner of David Syme Scientific Research Prize, Australia, 1926; President of the Australian Chemical Institute, 1928. *Publications:* The Screen Projection of Chemical Experiments, 1953; Astronomical Objects for Southern Telescopes, 1968. Various scientific papers, including a series on Studies with the Micro-balance, and Studies in Membrane Permeability in Journal of Chemical Society, London, Transactions of Faraday Society, London. *Recreation:* astronomy. *Address:* Lavender Farm, Woodend, Vic 3442, Australia. *[Died 30 Jan. 1979.*

HARTY, Maj.-Gen. Arthur Henry, CIE 1942; MB, BS, MRCS, LRCP, 1914; IMS, retired; *b* 13 Aug. 1890; *s* of T. Harty and M. E. Fowles; *m* 1919, Gladys Maud Davies; one *s* one *d* (and one *s* decd). *Educ:* Jamaica Coll., Jamaica; Queen's Univ., Kingston, Canada (MB, BS 1912). Joined Royal Navy as Surgeon, Aug. 1914; served in Grand Fleet and Mediterranean Fleet in European War; joined Indian Medical Service, 1919; Burma, 1920-23; Bombay Presidency and Sind 1923-42; Inspector-Gen., Civil Hospitals, Central Provinces, 1942-45; Maj.-Gen. 1946; Surgeon-Gen., Bombay, 1945-48. KHP, 1945-48. *Address:* c/o Grindlay's Bank Ltd, 13 St James's Square, SW1; 5 Gladstone Drive, Kingston 10, Jamaica, West Indies. *[Died 19 Oct. 1977.*

HARVEY, Laurence, (born **Larushka Mischa Skikne**); actor; *b* Yonishkis, Lithuania, 1 Oct. 1929; *s* of Ber and Ella Skikne; *m* 1957, Margaret Leighton (marr. diss., 1961); *m* 1968, Joan Cohn (marr. diss., 1971); *m* 1973, Paulene Stone; one *d* one step *d*. *Educ:* Meyerton Coll., Meyerton; Earl of Athlone High Sch., Johannesburg, South Africa. Johannesburg Repertory, 1943. Served South African Army, 1943-46; arrived England, 1946; studied at RADA for 3 months. Manchester Library Theatre, 1946-47. Appeared in Hassan, London, 1951. Stratford-on-Avon: 1952: Tullus Aufidius in Coriolanus; Orlando in As You Like It; Malcolm in Macbeth; also appeared in Volpone; 1954: Romeo in Romeo and Juliet; Troilus in Troilus and Cressida. Further parts, taken in London, New York, etc.: Angelo in Island of Goats, New York, 1955; Captain Absolute in The Rivals, and Horner in The Country Wife, London, 1955-56; The Country Wife, London and New York, 1957-58. Directed Simply Heavenly (Coloured Musical), London, 1958. Played title role in Henry V, Old Vic tour of America, 1958-59, and at Old Vic, London, 1959-60; Time of the Barracudas, USA, 1963; The Outrage, USA, 1963; Arthur, in Camelot, Drury Lane, 1964; The Winter's Tale: (Edinburgh, Cambridge), 1966; subseq. (Edinburgh, London); Arms and the Man and The Alchemist, Chichester, 1970; Child's Play, Queen's, 1971. First film, House of Darkness, 1947. *Films include:* Man From Yesterday; Man on the Run; Cairo Road; Black Rose; The Scarlet Thread; The Wall of Death; Gathering Storm; I Believe in You; Women of Twilight; Innocents in Paris; Romeo and Juliet; The Good Die Young; King Richard and the Crusaders (in Hollywood); I Am A Camera; Storm Over The Nile; Three Men In A Boat; After the Ball; Truth About Women; The Silent Enemy; Room At The Top; Expresso Bongo; The Alamo (Texas) USA; Butterfield 8 (New York); The Long and the Short and the Tall; Summer and Smoke; The Manchurian Candidate; Two Loves, Walk on the Wild Side, Brothers Grimm, Tamiko (all in Hollywood); The Running Man; The Ceremony (prod, dir and acted); Of Human Bondage; Darling; Life at the Top; The Spy with the Cold Nose; The Winter's Tale; Dial M for Murder (film TV); Dandy in Aspic; Cherry with Creme de Cacao; Struggle for Rome; The Magic Christian; She and He; Hall of Mirrors; WUSA; Night Watch. TV appearances in London, including Arms and the Man, 1970, and in America. *Recreations:* swimming, tennis, Rugby football, physical culture. *Address:* c/o Romulus Films Ltd, Brook House, Park Lane, W1. *T:* 01-493 7741. *Club:* Royal Automobile   [*Died 25 Nov.* 1973.

HARVEY, Air Marshal Sir Leslie Gordon, KBE 1955; CB 1946; retired; *b* 11 April 1896; *s* of Thomas Gordon Harvey, Cowden, Kent; *m* 1926, Mary Sophia Clowser; one *d*. *Educ:* Commercial Sch., Maidstone, Kent. Served in Royal Warwicks Regt, 1914-17; Active Service with 7th Bn 48th Div. in France; seconded as 2nd Lieut Royal Warwick Regt to RFC, 1917; with 20 Squadron in India on North-West Frontier, 1919-24; specialised in Aeronautical Engineering at RAF Engineering Coll., 1925-27; Wing Commander in Dept of Dir of Research and Development, 1938-39; Group Capt. Commanding Airborne Forces Experimental Establishment, Ringway, Manchester, and later at Sherbourn-in-Ilmet, 1939-42; Group Capt. Commanding No. 8 Sch. of Technical Training, Weeton, Technical Training Command, 1942-43; Chief Engineer No. 45 (Atlantic) Group, Transport Command, Dorval, 1943-44; Temp. Air Commodore, HQ Transport Command as Chief Maintenance Officer and latterly as Senior Technical Staff Officer; Air Commodore, 1946; Air Officer Commanding No. 47 Group Transport Command, Milton Ernest, Bedford, 1946-48; Air Vice-Marshal, 1948; Air Officer Commanding No. 24 Group, Technical Training Command, 1948-50; SASO Technical Trg Comd, 1950-52; AOC-in-C Maintenance Comd, 1952-55 (Air Marshal). Retired, 1955. *Recreations:* cricket, Adastrian and RAF. *Address:* Stanfield, Begbroke, Oxford.   [*Died 14 Oct.* 1972.

HARVEY, Sir Richard Musgrave, 2nd Bt, *cr* 1933; Lieutenant-Commander, RN retired; *b* 1 Dec. 1898; *s* of Sir Ernest Musgrave Harvey, 1st Bt, KBE and Sophia (*d* 1952), *y d* of late Capt. Catesby Paget; *S* father 1955; *m* 1930, Frances Estelle, *er d* of late Lindsay Crompton Lawford, Montreal; one *s* one *d*. *Educ:* Royal Naval Colls, Osborne and Dartmouth. *Heir: s* Charles Richard Musgrave Harvey [*b* 7 April 1937; *m* 1967, Celia Vivien, *d* of G. H. Hodson; one *s* one *d*]. *Address:* Chisenbury Priory, Pewsey, Wilts.   [*Died 1 Sept.* 1978.

HARVEY, Wilfred John; Governor, HM Prison, Pentonville, 1954-57, retired; *b* 21 June 1895; *m* 1921, Susan Sansom; one *s* one *d*. *Educ:* Temple Cowley Sch., Cowley, Oxford. Served European War, 1914-18, regular soldier, RA. Prison Officer, Wandsworth Prison, 1926; Housemaster, Feltham Borstal Instn, 1933; Dep.-Governor, 1942; Governor i/c: Boys' Prison, Wormwood Scrubs Prison, 1942; Borstal at Sherwood, Nottingham, 1945; Borstal Instn, Feltham, 1948. *Recreations:*

cricket, soccer, boxing. *Address:* Pasadena, 38 Preston Road, Weymouth, Dorset.   [*Died 9 Oct.* 1971.

HARVEY EVERS, H.; see Evers, H. H.

HARVIE ANDERSON; see Skrimshire.

HASELL, Edward William; *b* 16 Jan. 1888; *m* 1920, Gertrude, OBE 1958, *d* of John Stroyan, Lanrick Castle, Perthshire and Kirkchrist, Wigtownshire; two *d*. *Educ:* Rossall; Queen's Coll., Oxford. Served European War, 1914-18, with Westmorland and Cumberland Yeomanry, Major 1919. JP 1922, DL, 1927, and High Sheriff, 1927, Westmorland; Vice-Lieut of Westmorland, 1958-65. *Recreations:* shooting, farming, forestry. *Address:* Dalemain, Penrith, Cumberland. *T:* Pooley Bridge 223.
                                    [*Died 13 July* 1972.

HASKELL, Arnold Lionel, CBE 1954; FRSL 1977; Chevalier de la Légion d'Honneur, 1950; writer, lecturer, and journalist; Director, Royal Ballet School, 1946-65, Governor, 1966-77; a Governor, The Royal Ballet, 1957-80; *b* 1903; *s* of late J. S. Haskell and Emmy Mesritz; *m* 1st, 1927, Vera Saitzoff (*d* 1968); two *s* one *d*; 2nd, 1970, Vivienne Marks. *Educ:* Westminster; Trinity Hall, Cambridge (MA). Mem., editorial staff, William Heinemann Ltd, 1927-32; joint founder of Camargo Soc., 1930; visited America with Russian Ballet, 1933-34; dance critic, Daily Telegraph, 1935-38; Founder the Vic-Wells Ballet Benevolent Fund, 1936, Patron 1980; visited Australia, guest critic for Melbourne Herald and Sydney Daily Telegraph, 1936-37; Australia, 1938-39; toured Spain, Portugal and Germany for British Council, 1950-51, Italy, Yugoslavia and Greece, 1953, Germany and Italy, 1954, Italy 1955; visited USSR to study ballet and to lecture, 1960 and 1962, and as guest of Youth Organisation, 1967. Visited Cuba as guest of National Council of Culture, 1967, and lectured there for three months, 1968. Advised Dutch Government Commission on formation of a National ballet, 1954; Vice-Pres. jury, Varna dance competition, 1964, 1965, 1966 and 1970; Mem. jury, Internat. Ballet contest, Moscow, 1969 and 1973; Vice-Pres. Royal Academy of Dancing; Vice-Pres., Catholic Stage Guild; Governor, Trent Park Training Coll., 1953-58 and 1961; Council, Royal West of England Academy, 1961; Trustee, Holburne Menstrie Museum, 1970-80; Vice-Pres. and Trustee, Bath Preservation Trust. Hon. Member: Bath Inst. of Medical Engrg, 1971; Council, Bath Univ., 1971-76. Hon. DLitt Bath, 1974. Queen Elizabeth II Award, Royal Acad. of Dancing, 1980. *Publications:* Some Studies in Ballet, 1928; The Sculptor Speaks, 1932; Black on White, 1933; Balletomania, 1934; Diaghileff, 1935; Prelude to Ballet, Balletomane's Scrapbook, 1936; Dancing Round the World, 1937; Ballet Panorama, 1938; Ballet, a complete guide to appreciation, 1938; Balletomane's Album, 1939; Waltzing Matilda: a background to Australia, 1940; Australia, 1941; The Australians, 1943; The National Ballet, 1943; The Dominions-Partnership or Rift?, 1943; British Ballet, 1939-45; The Making of a Dancer, 1946; Ballet Vignettes, 1949; In His True Centre (autobiography), 1951; edited Ballet-to Poland in aid of Polish Relief Funds, 1940, and Ballet Annual, 1947-62; Saints Alive, 1953; co-edited Gala Performance, 1956; The Russian Genius in Ballet, 1962; Ballet Retrospect, 1964; What is Ballet, 1965; Heroes and Roses, 1966; Ballet Russe: the Age of Diaghilev, 1968; Infantilia, 1971; Balletomane at Large (autobiog.), 1972; Balletomania, Then and Now, 1976, rev. edn 1979; contrib. Encyclopædia Britannica, British Journal of Aesthetics, Chambers's Encyclopædia and Annual Register. *Recreations:* travelling, opera-going, collecting sculpture, juvenilia. *Address:* 6A Cavendish Crescent, Bath, Avon BA1 2UG. *T:* Bath 22472. *Club:* Garrick.   [*Died 15 Nov.* 1980.

HASLEGRAVE, John Ramsden, CBE 1975 (OBE (mil.) 1945); TD 1949; DL; *b* 15 April 1913; *s* of Col H. J. Haslegrave, CMG, TD, JP, and Mrs H. J. Haslegrave, OBE, MA; *m* 1957, Mary Kingswell; two *d*. *Educ:* Queen Elizabeth Grammar Sch., Wakefield; Peterhouse, Cambridge (MA, LLB). Solicitor 1938. Served War of 1939-45: 1/4 Bn KOYLI (TA); UK, Norway and Iceland; psc 1944; GSO2 WO; GSO1 GHQ Middle East; subseq. served with 4th Bn KOYLI TA, 1947-54, comdg, 1951-54; Col 150 Inf. Bde TA, 1958-60. Articled to Town Clerk, Chester, 1934-37; Dep. Town Clerk, Nuneaton, 1938-39, 1946-47; Asst Solicitor, Nottingham, 1947-49; Asst Town Clerk, Birmingham, 1949-52; Dep. Town Clerk, Leeds, 1952-60; Town Clerk and Chief Executive Officer, Portsmouth, 1960-74; Chief Exec., City of Portsmouth, 1974-77. Dir, Portsmouth Building Soc. Former Lay Canon, Portsmouth Cathedral; Governor, Portsmouth Grammar Sch. Hon. Fellow, Portsmouth Polytechnic. DL Hampshire 1975. *Recreations:* tennis, ski-ing, rugby football, golf, walking. *Address:* 27 Eastern Parade, Southsea, Portsmouth PO4 9RD. *T:* Portsmouth 732996; Blakehills Cottage, Mungrisdale, Penrith, Cumbria. *Club:* Royal Automobile.   [*Died 26 May* 1980.

HASTED, Maj.-Gen. William Freke, CB 1946; CIE 1943; CBE 1941; DSO 1937; MC; late Royal Engineers; *b* 28 Sept. 1897; *s* of late W. A. Hasted, Lindfield, Sussex; *m* 1920, Hella Elizabeth Mary (*d* 1961), *d* of Lieut-Col A. E. Cuming, Doneraile, Co. Cork; no *c. Educ:* Cheltenham Coll.; Cambridge Univ.; Royal Military Academy, Woolwich. First Commission, 1915; European war (2nd Division) 1916-18 (despatches, MC); Instructor RM Academy Woolwich, 1924-26; Instructor RMC of Canada, Kingston, Ont. 1926-30; OCRE South Irish Coast Defence, 1932-36; Bengal Sappers-Miners (Peshawar), 1936-37; Headquarters Northern Command, India, 1937; Waziristan Operations, 1937 (despatches twice, DSO); CRE Waziristan District, 1938-41; Waziristan Admadzai Operations, 1940 (despatches CBE); Deputy Chief Engineer, HQ Xth Army, 1941-42; Deputy Engineer-in-Chief (Air), GHQ, New Delhi, 1942-43; Chief Engineer 14 Army, 1944-45 (CB); Chief Engineer, Allied Land Forces SEAC, 1945-46; Engineer-in-Chief in India, 1946-47; late Controller of Aerodromes; retired pay, 1948. Pres., Loughborough Coll., Leics, 1951. Controller of Development, Kuwait, Persian Gulf, 1952; retired from Persian Gulf, 1954. *Recreations:* shooting, fishing, tennis; International Hockey, England, 1923; Hockey, Army and Combined Services, 1922-25. *Address:* c/o Lloyds Bank, Pall Mall, SW1.
[Died 29 Oct. 1977.

HASTILOW, Cyril Alexander Frederick, CBE 1955 (OBE 1947); Chairman, Smith & Nephew Associated Companies Ltd, 1962-68 (Director, 1958); *b* Birmingham, 31 May 1895; *s* of Frederick Hastilow; *m* 1922, Doreen Madge, MA, *d* of J. H. Hateley; two *s* one *d. Educ:* Central Grammar Sch., Birmingham; Birmingham Univ. MSc 1919; BCom. 1920; FRIC 1926. Chief Chemist, Docker Bros., 1920-32; Sales Manager, 1932-39; General Manager, 1939-46; Chairman, 1946-60. Asst Controller, Miscellaneous Chemicals Control, Ministry of Supply, 1942-44; Dir, Paint Materials, Min. of Supply, 1944-45. Pres. Paint Materials Trade Association, 1945-47; Dir Pinchin Johnson & Associates Ltd, 1946-62; Mem. Industrial Estates Management Corporation for England, 1960-65. Pres. Birmingham Chamber of Commerce, 1953-54, Hon. Treasurer, 1970-71; Vice-Pres. Soc. of Brit. Paint Manufacturers, 1958-60. Mem. Court of Governors, Birmingham Univ., 1946-; Mem. Bd of Governors, United Birmingham Hosps, 1949-57; Mem. House Cttee, Queen Elizabeth Hosp., 1947-60. Chm., Hamlin Churchill Childbirth Injuries Fund, 1968-. Chm. and Hon. Sec. Warwicks County Cricket Club, 1948-62, Vice-Pres., 1966-74, Pres., 1974-; Pres. Warwicks Youth Cricket Council, 1961- (Chm. 1951-61); Member: MCC Cttee, 1964-67; MCC Youth Cricket Assoc., 1952-70. *Recreations:* interested in all outdoor sports, particularly cricket. *Address:* 43 Moor Green Lane, Moseley, Birmingham B13 8NE. *T:* 021-449 0883. *[Died 30 Sept. 1975.*

HASTINGS, Anne Wilson; formerly HM Superintending Inspector of Factories; *b* Kinneff, Kincardineshire; *d* of Rev. James Hastings, DD, Editor of the Dictionary of the Bible, etc, and Wilson Hastings; *m* Leonard J. Page, CEng, FRINA (*d* 1972). *Educ:* Leeds Girls' High Sch.; Aberdeen Univ. MA (1st class Hons Mental Philosophy); Bain Gold Medallist, 1916; Fullerton Scholar, 1916-17. Joint-Editor of Expository Times, 1922-65. *Address:* 105 Argyle Road, W13. *T:* 01-997 1959.
[Died 23 March 1975.

HASTINGS, Rev. Edward, MA, DD; *b* Kinneff, Kincardineshire, March 1890; *s* of late Rev. James Hastings, DD. *Educ:* Aberdeen Univ.; New Coll., Edinburgh. Ordained minister at Errol, Perthshire in 1921; resigned charge 1923 to undertake editorial work. *Publications:* The Speaker's Bible; The Local Colour of the Bible (with Dr Charles W. Budden); Joint-Editor of The Expository Times, 1922-65. *Address:* 11 King's Gate, Aberdeen AB2 6BL. *T:* Aberdeen 26048.
[Died 1 Aug. 1980.

HASTON, Dougal; Director, International School of Mountaineering, Leysin, Switzerland, since 1966; *b* 19 April 1940; *s* of Robert and Margaret Haston. *Educ:* Edinburgh Univ. Mountaineering, Principal Ascents: Eiger N Face, 1963; Eiger Direct, 1st winter ascent, 1966; Matterhorn N Face, winter ascent, 1967; Annapurna S Face (26,545 ft), 1st ascent, 1970; Changabang (22,800 ft), 1st ascent, 1974; Monch N Face, 1st ascent, 1974; Triolet Direct N Face, 1st winter ascent, 1975; Everest SW Face, 1st ascent, Sept. 1975; Mt McKinley S Face Direct, 1st ascent, 1976. *Publications:* Eiger Direct (with P. Gillman), 1966; In High Places, 1972; The Eiger, 1974. *Recreation:* skiing. *Address:* International School of Mountaineering, 1854 Leysin, Switzerland. *T:* 025 6 23 21. *Clubs:* Alpine; Groupe de Haute Montagne (France); Swiss Alpine. *[Died 17 Jan. 1977.*

HATHAWAY, Dame Sibyl Mary, DBE 1965 (OBE 1949); Dame de Serk; *d* of late W. F. Collings, Seigneur of Serk; widow of Dudley Beaumont, *s* of Capt. Spencer Beaumont; two *s* (and *e s* killed in 1941) one *d* (and two *d* decd); *m* 1929, Robert Woodward Hathaway (*d* 1954), *s* of Charles Hathaway, New York. *Publications:* Maid of Sark, 1939; Dame of Sark, 1961. Heir to title: *g s* Michael Beaumont. *Address:* La Seigneurie, Island of Sark. *Club:* Junior Carlton. *[Died 14 July 1974.*

HATHERTON, 6th Baron, *cr* 1835; **John Walter Stuart Littleton;** *b* 9 Aug. 1906; *s* of 4th Baron Hatherton and Hester Edithe (*d* 1947), *d* of Thomas Tarrant Hoskins, MD, Tasmania; *S* brother, 1969; *m* 1st, 1932, Nora Evelyn (*d* 1955), *d* of R. C. Smith, Edgbaston; one *d*; 2nd, 1955, Mary Alice, *d* of John Roberts, Ruthin. *Educ:* Cranleigh. Heir: *b* Hon. Thomas Charles Tasman Littleton, TD [*b* 6 Oct. 1907; *m* 1933, Ann Scott, *o d* of late Lt-Comdr Thomas McLeod, RN; one *d*]. *Address:* Madeira House, Church Stretton, Salop.
[Died 27 June 1973.

HATTERSLEY, Alan Frederick, MA, DLitt; Professor Emeritus of History, University of Natal; Member Union Archives Commission, 1948-64; *b* 6 April 1893; *o s* of F. Kilvington Hattersley, Fairlawn, Harrogate. *Educ:* Leeds Grammar Sch.; Downing Coll., Cambridge. Professor of History and Political Science, University of Natal, 1923-53. Hon. DLitt (Natal), 1957. Fellow, Natal Soc., 1970. Civic honours conferred by Pietermaritzburg, 1972. *Publications:* A Short History of Western Civilisation 1927; A History of Democracy, 1930; South Africa (Home University Library), 1933; History Teaching in Schools, 1935; More Annals of Natal, 1936; Pietermaritzburg Panorama, 1938; Later Annals of Natal, 1938; Portrait of a Colony, 1940; The Natalians, 1940; Hilton Portrait, 1945; Journal of J. S. Dobie, 1945; The British Settlement of Natal, 1950; Carbineer, 1950; A Victorian Lady At the Cape, 1951; A Hospital Century, 1955; Oliver the Spy and Others, 1959; The First South African Detectives, 1960; The Convict Crisis and Growth of Unity, 1965; An Illustrated Social History of S Africa, 1969. *Recreation:* Emeritus Commissioner, Boy Scouts Association, South Africa. *Address:* Inglemoor House, 1 Sanders Road, Pietermaritzburg, S Africa. *TA:* Univcoll.
[Died 10 July 1976.

HATTON, Frank; MP (Lab) Manchester, Moss Side, since 1974 (Manchester Exchange, June 1973-1974); *b* 25 Sept. 1921; *s* of James Hatton and Edith Latham; *m* 1949, Olive Kelly; two *s. Educ:* Manchester Central High School for Boys. Railway Clerk, 1939-51; Personnel Officer, Central Electricity Generating Board, 1951-73. Member: Manchester City Council, 1954-74 (Alderman, 1971-74); Manchester District Council, 1973-74; Chairman: Manchester Educn Cttee, 1962-67, 1971-74; Educn Cttee, Assoc. of Municipal Corporations, 1972-74; Local Authorities Higher Educn Cttee, 1972-74; Vice-Pres., Assoc. of Educn Cttees, 1973-74; Member: Cttee on Supply and Training of Teachers; Burnham Cttee. Chm., Manchester Polytechnic, 1972-74; Member of Council: Univ. of Manchester; Univ. of Manchester Inst. of Science and Technology; former Mem. Council, Open University; Governor, Cheadle Hulme Sch.; former Governor: Manchester Grammar Sch.; Chetham's Hosp. Sch. of Music. Mem. TGWU. Former Sec. and Agent, Manchester Exchange Constituency Labour Party; contested (Lab) Manchester (Moss Side), 1970. JP Manchester, 1965. *Address:* 50 Merston Drive, East Didsbury, Manchester M20 0WT; House of Commons, SW1. *[Died 16 May 1978.*

HATTON, Maj.-Gen. George Seton, CB 1950; DSO 1942; OBE 1941; psc 1935; *b* 13 Feb. 1899; *s* of late Edwin Fullarton Hatton and late Marion Isobella (*née* Seton-Browne); *m* 1949, Hilda Mary Arthur (*widow*), OBE 1955; no *c. Educ:* Upper Canada Coll.; Royal Military Coll. of Canada; Cambridge Univ. Commnd as 2nd Lieut, Royal Engineers, 1917; served European War, 1914-18, with RE in France and Belgium, and on Staff in Turkey, 1920-23; regimental duty with RE in Egypt and at home, 1924-34; on Staff India, 1936-39 and accompanied 11th Ind. Inf. Bde to Middle East as Brigade Major, 1939; served War of 1939-45; Staff services in Middle East, 1939-44, including appointments in Western Desert as AA and QMG 7th Armoured Div., and BGS 30 Corps; also senior administrative appointments with Ninth Army and GHQ (despatches). Served in North West Europe, 1945, on Staff SHAEF and 21 Army Group and in comd as Brig. (despatches). Dep. Comdr L of C, 1946, and later Comdr of Br troops Low Countries. Returned to UK, 1947, as Brig. A/Q; Chief of Staff HQ Southern Command, Salisbury, 1949-51; Maj.-Gen., Administration, BAOR, 1951-54; Maj.-Gen. 1950; retired 1955. Deputy Federal Civil Defence Co-ordinator for Canada, 1955-59. *Recreation:* photography. *Address:* Seton, Hillbrow Road, Liss, Hants. *T:* Liss 2639. *Club:* Royal Commonwealth Society. *[Died 24 March 1974.*

HAUFF, Mrs Janet Alderson; Under-Secretary, Department of Health and Social Security (formerly Ministry of Health), since 1966; *b* 24 Sept. 1913; *d* of William Fitzjohn Crisp and Ethel May Crisp; *m* 1940, Charles Kenneth Hauff (*d* 1967). *Educ:* Mexborough Grammar Sch.; Girton Coll., Cambridge (BA). Entered Civil Service, 1941. FRGS. *Recreations:* Antarctic travel, photography, flying. *Address:* 31 Campden Grove, Kensington, W8 4JQ. *T:* 01-937 3852.   *[Died 18 Sept.* 1973.

HAULFRYN WILLIAMS, John; *see* Williams.

HAVELOCK, Eric Henry Edwardes, CB 1950; CBE 1943 (OBE 1936); Secretary, Development Commission, 1934-55; *b* 9 July 1891; *s* of late George Eric Havelock and Elizabeth Maria Caroline, *d* of late Lewis Nanney, Horne Hall, Co. Durham; *m* 1st, 1919, Christina Ramsay Scott (*d* 1958), *d* of late Alexander Moodie, Edinburgh; one *d*; 2nd, 1962, Eileen (*d* 1971), *widow* of Maj.-Gen. W. R. Paul, CBE. *Educ:* Norfolk House Sch., Beaconsfield; Rugby; Highgate Sch.; Merton Coll., Oxford. BA 1918. War Refugees Cttee, 1914-15; Underground Rlys, 1915-16; Cabinet Reconstruction Cttee and Min. of Reconstruction, 1916-19 (private sec. to Sec.); Asst Sec., Develt Commn, 1919-34; Asst Sec., Agric. Research Council, 1931-34, Admin. Sec., 1934-50. Hon. Mem. Marine Biological Assoc.; Freshwater Biological Assoc.; Challenger Soc. for Promotion of Oceanography. Trustee, Rural Industries Bureau, retired 1968. FRSE 1945. Gold Palms of Order of Crown of Belgium, 1916. *Address:* c/o Barclays Bank Ltd, 27 Regent Street, SW1.
      [Died 24 Dec. 1974.

HAVELOCK-ALLAN, Sir Henry Ralph Moreton, 3rd Bt, *cr* 1858; *b* 31 Aug. 1899; *s* of Allan Havelock-Allan (*d* 1949), (2nd *s* of 1st Bt) and of late Annie Julia, *d* of Sir William Chaytor, 3rd Bt; *S* uncle 1953. *Educ:* Sandroyd Sch.; Charterhouse. Formerly Lieut Scots Guards. *Heir: b* Anthony James Allan Havelock-Allan. *Address:* c/o The National Westminster Bank, 320 Euston Road, NW1.   *[Died 4 Nov.* 1975.

HAVERS, Sir Cecil (Robert), Kt 1951; QC 1939; Deputy Dean of the Arches, 1970; retired as Judge of the High Court of Justice, 1967 (Probate, Divorce and Admiralty Division, 1951-52; Queen's Bench Division, 1952-67); *b* 12 Nov. 1889; *s* of Daniel Havers and Agnes Buckingham; *m* 1916, Enid F. O. Snelling (*d* 1956); three *s* one *d*. *Educ:* Norwich Grammar Sch.; Corpus Christi Coll., Cambridge. Classical Scholar, Corpus Christi Coll., 1909, BA (Hons) Classics, 1912, LLB (Hons), 1913; MA; Hon. Fellow, 1975. Served European War, 1914-19, Capt. 5th Hants RTF and Tank Corps (despatches); Recorder of Chichester, 1939-51; Commissioner in Gold Coast, 1944-45; HM Commissioner of Assize, Oxford and Midland Circuits, 1949; called to Bar, Inner Temple, 1920, Certificate of Honour; Bencher, Inner Temple, 1946; Treasurer, 1971. *Publication:* Landlord and Tenant Act, 1927, 1928. *Recreations:* lawn tennis, golf. *Address:* 8 Lichfield Road, Kew Gardens, Surrey. *T:* 01-940 2658. *Clubs:* United Oxford & Cambridge University, Garrick.   *[Died 5 May* 1977.

HAVERS, Air Vice-Marshal Sir (Ephraim) William, KBE 1946 (CBE 1941); CB 1944; *b* 15 Oct. 1887; *m* 1st, 1920, Blanche Mary Somerville Macey (*d* 1968); one *s* one *d*; 2nd, 1970, Mary Elizabeth Ritchie (*d* 1978). Served European War, RFC, 1915-19, France (despatches); Air Ministry, Industrial Whitley Council, 1921-23; Iraq, 1923-25; Coastal Command, 1926-28; RAF Staff Coll., 1929; Senior Equipment Staff Officer Air Defences, Great Britain, 1930-32; HQ Middle East, Egypt, 1932-34; Dir-Gen. of Equipment, Air Ministry, 1940-42; AOC No. 40 Group, RAF, 1943-46; retired 1946; Govt Missions in Middle East, HQ Cairo, 1946-48; Consultant to Ministry of Supply, 1952-53. District Comr S Wight Scouts, 1950-55. *Address:* Tenter Lodge, Waterside, Knaresborough, North Yorks. *T:* Harrogate 862312.   *[Died 28 Feb.* 1979.

HAVINDEN, Ashley Eldrid, OBE 1951; RDI 1947; FSIA; Hon. DA Manchester, 1961; Designer, Typographer, Painter, signs work Ashley; Master of Faculty of Royal Designers for Industry, 1967-69; Director, W. S. Crawford Ltd, Advertising Agents, 1929-67 (joined 1922); Director, Design International Ltd, Industrial Research and Design, 1949-67; *b* 13 April 1903; *s* of G. E. Havinden and Nellie, *d* of J. Latter; *m* 1928, Margaret Kirk, *d* of John Sangster; one *s* one *d*. *Educ:* Christ's Hospital. Held retrospective exhibition of posters and advertisement designs at Lund, Humphries Gallery, 1937; work included in Exhibitions in Paris (Union des Artistes Moderne, 1933; French Pavillon de Publicité, Paris Exposition, 1937) and USA; Mem. Display Cttee for British Pavilion, Paris Exhibition, 1937; Fellow of Soc. of Industrial Artists, 1946 (Mem. of Council, 1946-47; Pres. 1953); NRD; Fellow of Central Institute of Art and Design, FRSA, Fellow of Institute of Practitioners in

Advertising; President: Advertising Creative Circle, 1955 (Hon. Mem., 1966); The Double Crown Club, 1956; Président D'Honneur (Prés., 1957-59), Alliance Graphique Internationale; Gov. London Coll. of Printing, 1950-67 (Chm., 1955-56, 1958-59); Visitor Graphic Sch. of Royal College of Art, 1955-57. Gov. The Central Sch. of Arts and Crafts, 1959-67; Mem. Advisory Cttee, the new Sch. of Art at Chelsea, 1958-65. Governor, 1965-67. First one-man exhibition of paintings at The London Gallery, 1937; paintings also represented in Exhibitions at Reid and Lefevre Gallery, 1939, and Leicester Galleries, 1939, Marlborough Fine Arts, 1965; one-man exhibition of Rugs and Fabrics at Duncan Miller Gallery, 1937; Designer of Men's Wear Section for Council of Industrial Design Exhibition, Britain Can Make It, Victoria and Albert Museum, 1946. Textiles and Rugs represented in Exhibitions in London, Paris, and San Francisco. Exhibited posters and advertising designs in National Museum, Stockholm, 1952; AGI Exhibitions, Louvre, Paris, 1955; RBA Gallery, London, 1956; Lausanne, 1957; Milan, 1961; Amsterdam, 1962; Hamburg, 1964; New York 1966. Served in War of 1939-45 Capt., Staff Officer, Camouflage. *Publications:* Line Drawing for Reproduction, 1933, revised edn, 1941; Advertising and the Artist, 1956; numerous articles on Industrial Art and allied subjects. *Address:* Roxford, Hertingfordbury, Herts. *T:* Hertford 2151. *Clubs:* Arts, Garrick.   *[Died 31 May* 1973.

HAWGOOD, John Arkas; Professor of American History, University of Birmingham, 1964-72 (of Modern History, 1945-64, and of Government, 1945-58); *b* Brighton, Sussex, 20 Nov. 1905; *m* 1927, Alison, *d* of late Rev. J. H. Bowker; four *s* one *d*. *Educ:* Leyton Sch.; University Coll., London (Andrews Scholar, Pollard Prizeman; Fellow, 1971); Universities of Heidelberg, Vienna, Yale, Wisconsin, etc. BA (London) 1st class hons in history, 1926; MA 1928; DLit 1944; PhD (Heidelberg) in Political Science and Sociology, 1928; MCom (Birmingham) *ex officio,* 1946; Anglo-German Exchange Scholar, Heidelberg, 1926-27; Hon. Hilfslektor, Univ. of Vienna, 1927-28; Research Fellow in the Social Sciences of Rockefeller Foundation, in Austria and Germany, 1927-28, and in the USA, 1928-29 and 1934-35. Asst Lectr in History, University Coll., London, 1929-31; Reader in Modern History, University of Birmingham, 1931-45. Seconded for service under Foreign Office, 1939-45 (Head of German Section, Foreign Research and Press Service, 1939-40; with Political Intelligence Dept, 1940-43; with Political Warfare Executive, 1943-45); Dir, Europa Publications, Ltd, 1945-68. Research Associate, Hoover Inst., Stanford Univ., 1950; Consultant, Library of Congress, 1952 and 1960; Mem. Council European Assoc. for American Studies, 1954-, Council International Political Science Assoc., 1955-58; Resident Fellow, Newberry Library, Chicago, 1956; Vis. Prof., Univ. of Kansas, 1969. First Alfred A. Knopf Western History Prize, 1966; Western Heritage and Western Writers of America Non-Fiction Awards, 1967. *Publications:* Political and Economic Relations between the USA and the German Provisional Central Government at Frankfurt-am-Main in 1848-49, 1928; Modern Constitutions since 1787, 1939; The Tragedy of German-America, 1940, repr. 1970; The Citizen and Government, 1947; The Evolution of Germany, 1955; First and Last Consul (T. O. Larkin and the Americanization of California), 1962, 2nd edn 1970; The American West (US title America's Western Frontiers), 1967, etc.; contrib. to Chambers's, Collier's and other Encyclopædias. *Address:* Court Place, Old Marston, Oxford OX3 0PQ. *T:* Oxford 41198.   *[Died 16 Sept.* 1971.

HAWKES, Frederic Clare, CBE 1957; *b* 25 Sept. 1892; *er s* of late F. J. Hawkes, London; *m* 1st, 1921, Erica Heinrich (*d* 1932); no *c*; 2nd, 1938, Phyllis Elizabeth Watson; two *s* one *d*. *Educ:* St Paul's Sch.; Merton Coll., Oxford (MA); Clare Coll., Cambridge (MA by incorporation). Served European War, 1915-19. Min. of Agriculture and Fisheries, 1919-21. Sec., 1920-33, and Asst Dir, 1925-33, of National Inst. of Agricultural Botany, Cambridge. Sec. of Wheat Commission, 1933-37; Sec. of Chartered Auctioneers' and Estate Agents' Institute, 1938-57, Hon. Fellow, 1957-70. Pres. of the College of Estate Management, 1957-58. Master, Worshipful Company of Farmers, 1959-60. Hon. Mem. RICS, 1970-. *Address:* 17 Eastheath Gardens, Wokingham, Berks. *T:* Wokingham 786599. *Club:* United Oxford & Cambridge University.   *[Died 13 Nov.* 1974.

HAWKEY, Sir Roger (Pryce), 2nd Bt, *cr* 1945 of Woodford; company director; *b* 25 June 1905; *o s* of Sir James Hawkey, 1st Bt, and Vera Kathleen (*d* 1949), *d* of late F. E. Price; *S* father 1952; *m* 1st, 1931, Julia Elizabeth Austin; one *d*; 2nd, 1947, Mabel Dorothy, *d* of Sir Thomas McConnell, CBE, MP, of Belfast. *Educ:* Chigwell Sch. Served War of 1939-45, with RN; Lieut-Comdr, RNVR. *Heir:* none. *Address:* Great Coopers, Takeley, Essex. *T:* Takeley 362. *Club:* MCC.
      [Died 11 Nov. 1975 (*ext*).

HAWKINS, Adm. Sir Geoffrey Alan Brooke, KBE *cr* 1952; CB 1949; MVO 1925; DSC 1917; *b* 13 July 1895; *e* s of late Capt. Hawkins, St Fentons, Baldoyle, Co. Dublin; *m* 1926, Lady Margaret Scott (*d* 1976), *d* of 7th Duke of Buccleuch; one s two d. *Educ:* Royal Naval Colls, Osborne and Dartmouth. Served European War, 1914-18 (DSC); War of 1939-45 (despatches). ADC to Governor-Gen. of South Africa, 1924-27; attached to staff of Prince of Wales, S African tour, 1925. Flag Officer, Malta, 1950-52; retired list, 1952. Attached to staff of Princess Royal, WI tour, 1960 and 1962. *Address:* Grafton Underwood, Kettering. *T:* Cranford 245. *Club:* Naval and Military.
[*Died 5 Oct.* 1980.

HAWKINS, Maj.-Gen. George Ledsam Seymour, CB 1943; MC; Indian Army, retired; *b* 13 May 1898; s of G. E. Hawkins, Apton Hall, Rochford, Essex; *m* 1921, Katharine Marian (*d* 1957), *d* of George Hancock, Templecombe, Somerset; one d (one s decd). Commd S Staffs Regt, Aug. 1914; trans. to RFA, 1915; served European War (MC), France and Belgium; trans. to Indian Army, 1925; served NWF (Waziristan), 1936-37 (despatches); Ordnance Consulting Offr, India Office, 1937-41; served World War II (CB), Dir of Ordnance Services, India; retd 1945. Col Comdt, IAOC, 1945-56; Reg. Dir, Southern Reg. Min. of Works, 1945-57. *Address:* The Cottage, Elsing Mill, Dereham, Norfolk.
[*Died Oct.* 1978.

HAWKINS, Jack, CBE 1958; actor and producer; *b* 14 Sept. 1910; s of Thomas George Hawkins and Phoebe Goodman; *m* 1st, 1932, Jessica Tandy; one d; 2nd, 1947, Doreen Lawrence; two s one d. *Educ:* Trinity County Sch., Mddx. Studied with Italia Conti; first appearance on stage, Dec. 1923; subsequently appeared regularly in the Theatre and Films in London and New York until War of 1939-45. Joined Royal Welch Fusiliers, 1940; served with 2nd Div. in India and Burma; demobilised, 1946, with Hon. rank of Col; reappeared in the Theatre and Films, 1947. Mem. Bd of Governors, London Independent Television Producers Ltd, 1963. *Films include:* The Cruel Sea, Man in the Sky, The Long Arm, Bridge on the River Kwai, Ben Hur, League of Gentlemen, Lawrence of Arabia, Lord Jim, Guns at Batasi, La Fayette, Masquerade, Great Catherine, Shalako, Battle of Waterloo, When Eight Bells Toll, Jane Eyre, Nicholas and Alexandra; co producer The Ruling Class. *Publication:* Anything for a Quiet Life (autobiog.), 1973. *Recreations:* music, riding and fishing. *Address:* The Penthouse, 34 Ennismore Gardens, SW7. *Clubs:* Garrick, Royal Automobile.
[*Died 18 July* 1973.

HAWKINS, Leonard Cecil, CBE 1962; *b* 23 April 1897; 2nd s of late Fred and Martha Hawkins, Churchill, Somerset; *m* 1926, Janet Grace Seager; one s. After service with BEF in France (31/10th Royal Fusiliers) joined staff of City firm of chartered accountants, 1918-29; admitted Incorporated Accountant (hons), 1925; Fellow, 1944; Mem. Coun., 1947; CA and Mem. Coun. Inst. of Chartered Accts in England and Wales, 1957-62; joined Underground Railways and London Gen. Omnibus Co., 1929; Asst Comptroller, London Passenger Transport Bd, 1933; Comptroller, 1940-47; concurrently Joint Gen. Man., London Aircraft Production, 1943-45; full time Mem., London Transport Exec., 1947-62; Mem., National Incomes Commn, 1962-65. Chm. Transport Commission of Inquiry, Singapore, 1955; Leader, UK Advisory Mission under Colombo Plan to advise Ceylon Govt on reorganisation of Ceylon's omnibus services, 1957; an Hon. Adviser, Admin. Staff Coll., 1949-59. OStJ 1962. *Publications:* Accountancy in a Large-Scale Industrial Undertaking, 1947; Financial Control in Industry, 1950; Measurements of Efficiency, 1950; Mass Transportation in the Future, 1961, etc. *Address:* 29 Clarence Road North, Weston-super-Mare, Somerset. *T:* 983. *Clubs:* Weston-super-Mare; Royal Mid-Surrey Golf.
[*Died 7 Oct.* 1974.

HAWKINS, Sir Michael Babington Charles, KCVO 1968 (CVO 1960); MVO 1951); MBE 1944; Private Secretary to the Duke of Gloucester, 1958-74 (Assistant Private Secretary and Equerry, 1948-57); Secretary: King George's Jubilee Trust, since 1971; Queen's Silver Jubilee Appeal, since 1977; *b* 27 July 1914; s of L. G. Hawkins, West Bilney Hall, Norfolk; *m* 1947, Virginia Anne, *d* of Gp Capt. Noel Heath, Sydney, Aust.; one d. *Educ:* Cheltenham Coll. Solicitor, Supreme Court, 1935. Served 10th Royal Hussars; Western Desert, 1940-42 (despatches twice); Hqrs Allied Armies, Sicily and Italy, 1942-44. ADC to Governor-Gen. of Australia, 1945-47. A Vice-Chm., British Boys Movement for Australia. Governor, Royal Nat. Orthopaedic Hosp. KStJ 1973. Order of Dannebrog, 1948. *Recreation:* gardening. *Address:* Weston Patrick House, near Basingstoke, Hants. *T:* Long Sutton 396; 13 Courtenay Square, SE11. *T:* 01-735 4205. *Clubs:* Cavalry and Guards, Pratt's.
[*Died 26 May* 1977.

HAWKINS, Reginald Thomas, CBE 1949; *b* 13 May 1888; s of Robert William Hawkins; *m* 1914, Margaret T. (*d* 1972), *e d* of James Rennie Addison; one d (one s killed in action, RAF, 1944). *Educ:* Owen's Sch., Islington; Edinburgh Univ. (MA). Entered Civil Service, 1904; Scottish Education Dept, 1910. Served European War, 1914-18, with London-Scottish Regt in France, Salonika and Egypt. Asst Sec., Scottish Education Dept, 1939; Under-Sec., Scottish Education Dept, 1949-52; retired, 1952. Sec. to Advisory Council on Education in Scotland, 1935-38. *Publications:* articles on educational finance. *Address:* c/o Mrs Cameron, 65 Elwyn Road, March, Cambridgeshire. *T:* March 3258.
[*Died 6 June* 1978.

HAWKINS, William Francis Spencer, CBE 1968; a Master of the Supreme Court (Chancery Division), 1933-Jan. 1969, Chief Master, 1959-Jan. 1969; *b* Richmond, Surrey, 13 Feb. 1896; s of Francis William Hawkins; *m* 1933, Eva Lilian, *d* of William Graham; one s one d. *Educ:* Rugby. Served European War, 1914-18: on active service, 1915-19, Salonika and British Army of the Black Sea, Signal Officer with 27th Div. Artillery and 80th Inf. Bde (despatches twice). Admitted a solicitor, 1921; Partner with Bird and Bird, Gray's Inn, 1928. Post Invasion Warden, War of 1939-45. Trustee United Law Clerks Soc., 1940-76. Pres. of Wimbledon Hockey Club, 1952-60, and of Old Rugbeian Soc., 1957-59. Sometime Mem. Coulsdon and Purley, UDC and Council of the Magistrates Assoc. JP Surrey, 1947; Chm. Wallington Petty Sessions Div. Bench, Oct. 1958-60. *Address:* Rossley, Snowhill, Copthorne, Sussex RH10 3HA. *T:* Copthorne 712013.
[*Died 14 May* 1979.

HAWKS, Ellison, FRAS, FZS; Captain RFA, TF; Managing Director Poland's Packing Cases Ltd; Real Photographs Ltd; Direct Trading Organisation Ltd; Ellison Hawks Ltd; New Mornington Hotels Ltd; Broadstairs Photo. Works Ltd; *b* Hull, 13 March 1889; *o* s of Matthew H. Hawks, Derwenthaugh, Gateshead-on-Tyne, and Rowena Reynard Hull; *m* 1921, Edna, *e d* of J. Dawson Fawcett, Leeds and Harrogate; one s two d. *Educ:* Bebington Coll., Rock Ferry, Wirral; William Hulme Grammar Sch., Manchester. Chief Clerk, Accident Dept, Commercial Union Assurance Co. Ltd, Leeds, 1913-15. Active Service, 1915-19, Asst Provost Marshal, D Area, Northern Command, 1916-19; Advertising Manager, Meccano Ltd, Liverpool, 1921-35; Gen. Editor Amalgamated Press, Ltd, London, 1936-40; Lecturer in Astronomy (Lecture League, London). *Publications:* Scientific publications of general interest, covering Astronomy, Geology, Microscopy, Nature Wonders, Radio, etc. include: Stars Shown to the Children; The Starry Heavens; Engineering for Boys; Pioneers of Wireless; Pioneers of Plant Study; Remarkable Machinery; Electrical Wonders; Nature Wonders; Water Wonders; Marvels and Mysteries of Science; How it Works; The Triumph of Man in Science and Invention; How it is Made, etc; Scientific papers; articles in encyclopædias and in general science works, magazines, periodicals, and newspapers; Editor: Romance of Reality Series; Meccano Magazine, 1921-35; The Dog Owner. Author of most of the current volumes in Cassell's Motoring Series (popular cars). *Recreations:* dogs (English Setters), photography, philately. *Address:* 20 Delamere Road, Ainsdale, Southport, Lancs. *T:* Southport 77549. *Clubs:* Author's, Royal Aero.
[*Died 5 April* 1971.

HAWKSLEY, Richard Walter Benson, TD 1948; *b* Birkenhead, 14 March 1915; s of late Dr Walter Linney Hawksley; *m* 1939, Jean, *d* of Harold Lilley; three s one d. *Educ:* Stamford Sch. Mann Egerton & Co. Ltd: joined as pupil, 1934; Chm./Man. Dir, 1957-74; Consultant, 1974-. Joined TA, 9th Bn Royal Fusiliers, 1937. Served with Royal Fusiliers throughout War of 1939-45, in UK and Middle East. Attended Staff Coll., Camberley; demobilised, rank Major, 1946. Pres., Motor Agents Assoc., 1968-69; Mem. Council, MAA, 1966-. *Recreations:* cruising and sailing on Norfolk Broads; travel. *Address:* 67 The Close, Norwich NR1 4DD. *T:* Norwich 22780. *Clubs:* Naval and Military; Norfolk (Norwich); Norfolk Broads Yacht (Wroxham).
[*Died 27 Jan.* 1976.

HAWKSWORTH, Frederick William, FIMechE; *b* 10 Feb. 1884; *m. Educ:* Swindon. Apprenticeship GWR, Swindon; Chief Draughtsman, 1925-31; Asst to Chief Mechanical Engineer, 1932-41; Chief Mechanical Engineer, Great Western Railway, 1941-48; British Railways Western Region, 1948-49; retired Dec. 1949. Mem. Council, IMechE, 1939-49; Chm. Swindon Borough Magistrates, 1951-59; formerly Mem. Regional Council for Further Education (for the South West). JP Borough of Swindon, 1933-59, Freeman, 1960. *Recreation:* music. *Address:* 30 Tithe Barn Crescent, Swindon, Wilts. *T:* Swindon 22287.
[*Died 13 July* 1976.

HAWORTH, James; Member, London Midland Railway Board, 1956-67; *b* 10 Nov. 1896; *m* 1919, Cassie Pughe, *d* of T. R. Thomas, Towyn; *m* 1973, Louisa Belcher. Councillor, Bootle, 1923-30, Alderman, JP, 1930-42. Contested (Lab) West Derby (Liverpool), 1935; MP (Lab) Walton Div. of Liverpool, 1945-50. Mem., National Executive, The Labour Party, 1953-55; Hon. Treasurer, National Federation of Professional Workers, 1949-56; Life Mem., Industrial Soc.; Pres., Transport Salaried Staffs Assoc., 1953-56. *Recreation:* making socialists. *Address:* 4 Archery Court, Archery Road, St Leonards-on-Sea, E Sussex.
[Died 16 Dec. 1976.

HAWTHORN, Maj.-Gen. Douglas Cyril, CB 1946; DSO 1945; *b* 1897; *s* of late Edgar Hawthorn; *m* 1919, Maude Marie, *d* of late John Henry Price. 2nd Lieut KOYLI, 1917; transferred to Indian Army 1918, 1st Punjab Regt; served European War, 1914-18; France, NW Frontier of India, Palestine; Mahsud and Waziristan operations, NW Frontier of India, 1920-23; passed Staff Coll., Quetta, 1930-31; asst Commandant and Chief Instructor Tactical Sch., India, 1941-42; served War of 1939-45; commanded 62 Indian Inf. Bde, Chief of Staff 15 Indian Corps, Arakan (DSO); commanded 23rd Indian Div., Malaya (CB), and Java (despatches), Comdr of Java in Netherland East Indies, 1945-46, took the surrender of the Japanese Comdr in Java; Dir of Military Trng, India, 1946-47; Dep. Chief of Gen. Staff to Supreme Comdr India and Pakistan, 1947; retired, 1948. Chm. Burma Star Assoc., 1949-55. *Address:* 647 Nell Gwynn House, Sloane Avenue, SW3 3BE. *Club:* United Service & Royal Aeor.
[Died 19 Aug. 1974.

HAWTREY, Sir Ralph (George), Kt 1956; CB 1941; FBA 1935; Hon. DSc (Econ) London; *b* 1879; *s* of George Procter Hawtrey; *m* 1915, Hortense Emilia d'Aranyi (*d* 1953). *Educ:* Eton; Trinity Coll., Cambridge (19th Wrangler). Entered Admiralty, 1903; Treasury, 1904-45; Dir of Financial Enquiries, 1919-45; special leave from the Treasury to lecture on Economics at Harvard Univ., 1928-29; Pres. Royal Econ. Society, 1946-48; Price Prof. of International Economics, Chatham House (RIIA), 1947-52. Hon. Fellow Trinity Coll. Cambridge, 1959. *Publications:* Good and Bad Trade, 1913; Currency and Credit, 1919 (4th edn 1950); The Exchequer and the Control of Expenditure, 1921; Monetary Reconstruction, 1923, 2nd edn 1926; The Economic Problem, 1926; The Gold Standard in Theory and Practice, 1927, 5th edn 1947; Trade and Credit, 1929; Economic Aspects of Sovereignty, 1930 (2nd edn 1952); Trade Depression and the Way Out, 1931 (2nd edn 1933); The Art of Central Banking, 1932; Revision of G. Armitage Smith's Principles and Methods of Taxation, 1935; Capital and Employment, 1937 (2nd edn 1952); A Century of Bank Rate, 1938; Economic Destiny, 1944; Economic Rebirth, 1946; Bretton Woods for Better or Worse, 1946; Western European Union (for a Chatham House Study Group), 1949; The Balance of Payments and the Standard of Living, 1950; Towards the Rescue of Sterling, 1954; Cross Purposes in Wage Policy, 1955; The Pound at Home and Abroad, 1961; Incomes and Money, 1967. *Address:* 29 Argyll Road, W8. *T:* 01-937 3805. *Club:* United Oxford & Cambridge University.
[Died 21 March 1975.

HAY, Col James Charles Edward, CBE 1937; MC; TD; DL; Sheriff-Substitute of Lanarkshire at Glasgow, 1946-59, at Hamilton, 1959-61; solicitor; *b* 6 June 1889; *s* of late William Thomas Hay, solicitor, Hamilton; *m* 1929, Mary Buchanan Thomson; two *s. Educ:* Academy, Hamilton; Glasgow Univ. Hon. Col (late CO) 6th Battalion The Cameronians; late Comdr 156 (West Scottish) Infantry Bde; late Hon. Col 3rd (Lanarkshire) Army Cadet Bn; served European War, 1914-18; War of 1939-45 (despatches). Late Vice-Chm., Secretary, and Military Mem., Lanarkshire T&AFA. DL Co. of Lanark, 1933. *Recreations:* bowls, motoring, fishing. *Address:* 18 Lethame Road, Strathaven, Lanarkshire.
[Died 24 July 1975.

HAY, Sir James (Lawrence), Kt 1961; OBE 1918 (MBE 1918); President, Hay's-Wright Stephenson Ltd, Christchurch, New Zealand, since 1967 (Managing Director, 1929-61; Chairman, 1955-67); *b* 17 May 1888; *s* of William Hay, Lawrence, NZ; *m* 1st, 1918, Davidina Mertel (*d* 1969), *d* of William Gunn, Christchurch, NZ; two *s* two *d*; 2nd, 1970, Olive Musgrove, Christchurch. *Educ:* Lawrence District High Sch. Sen. YMCA Sec., 1st NZEF in France and Egypt, 1915-19 (MBE, OBE). Gen. Sec. New Zealand YMCA, Wellington, 1921-25. Founded Hay's Ltd, Department Store, 1929. Christchurch City Council, 1944-53. Chm. Canterbury Nat. Savings Cttee, 1939-45. Chm. Christchurch Civic Music Council, 1944-63; Chm. Canterbury Museum Trust Bd, 1946-53. President: NZ Retailers Fedn, 1940; NZ Council of YMCA; NZ Inst. of Management (Canterbury); Royal Christchurch Musical Society; Mem. NZ Savings Cttee, 1962-65. Hon. Fellow, NZ Institute of Management; Hon. FTCL 1968. Jubilee Medal, 1935;

Coronation Medal, 1953; Canterbury Soc. of Arts Medal for services to the Arts. *Recreations:* bowls, music. *Address:* Braemore, 111 Puriri Street, Christchurch, NZ. *T:* 46-680.
[Died 26 March 1971.

HAY, Lady Margaret (Katharine), DCVO 1971 (CVO 1953); Woman of the Bedchamber to the Queen since 1953; *b* 9 May 1918; *o d* of late Brig.-Gen. Lord Henry Seymour, DSO, and of Lady Helen Seymour; *m* 1948, Sir Alan Philip Hay, KCVO, TD; three *s*. Lady-in-Waiting to Princess Elizabeth, 1947-52, to the Queen, 1952. *Address:* 10 Kensington Palace, W8. *T:* 01-937 5514; Eaton Boat, Eccleston, Chester. *T:* Chester 374643.
[Died 24 May 1975.

HAY, Noel Grant, QC (Nigeria) 1955; Attorney-General, Western Region, Nigeria, 1954-58, retired; *b* 21 Dec. 1910; *s* of William Grant Hay, Barrister, NZ, and Jessie Margaret Talboys; *m* 1937, Clare Morton. *Educ:* Otago Univ., Dunedin, New Zealand (BA; LLM Hons); Oxford Univ. Asst District Officer, Nigeria, 1937; Magistrate, Nigeria, 1939-42; Legal Dept, Nigeria, 1943-53; Senior Crown Counsel, 1949. Legal Sec., 1950. *Recreations:* golf, tennis, fishing. *Address:* 39B Kotare Street, Christchurch, New Zealand. *Club:* South Canterbury (Timaru).
[Died 7 Dec. 1974.

HAY, Lt-Gen. Sir Robert, KCIE 1947 (CIE 1942); MB, ChB Edinburgh 1912; DPH Glasgow 1928; DTM&H Liverpool, 1927; *b* 8 March 1889; *s* of late Robert Erskine Hay, The Kilt, Castlecary; *m* 1928, Mary Carnegie McAusland; two *d* (one *s* decd). *Educ:* George Watson's; Edinburgh Univ. RAMC SR, 1914; IMS 1917; late Dir-Gen. IMS; KHP, 1944-48; retired, 1948, KStJ 1948. Hon. FRCPE, 1969. *Address:* Little Rulwood, Denholm, Hawick, Roxburghshire. *T:* Denholm 302.
[Died 18 May 1980.

HAY, Rt. Rev. Robert Milton, MA, BD; Suffragan Bishop of Buckingham, 1944-60; Hon. Canon of Christ Church, Oxford, since 1937; Hon. Assistant Bishop, Diocese of Oxford, 1960-70; *b* 30 Aug. 1884; *er s* of Robert Hay, Lauder, Scotland, and London; *m* 1909, Esmay Alice (*d* 1959), 2nd *d* of Joseph Foster, Hon. MA Oxon; one *s* one *d*; *m* 1960, Agnes Mary, *e d* of late Bishop and Mrs E. D. Shaw. *Educ:* Merchant Taylors' Sch., London; St John's Coll., Oxford (scholar); Wells Theological Coll. BA (2nd class Lit. Hum.) 1907; MA 1910; BD 1924; Curate of St Pancras, London, 1909-15; Vicar of Summertown, Oxford, 1915-23; of SS Philip and James, Oxford, 1923-39; Rector of Taplow, Bucks, 1939-53. Proctor in Convocation, 1929-57. Hon. Clerical Sec. Oxford Diocesan Conference, 1934-44; Rural Dean of Oxford, 1937-39; Archdeacon of Buckingham, 1944-57. *Address:* Greenhills, 26 Wooburn Green, High Wycombe, Bucks. *T:* Bourne End 20944.
[Died 23 Oct. 1973.

HAYDON-LEWIS, Jack; *see* Lewis.

HAYES, Michael, MA, BL; Professor of Modern Irish, University College, Dublin, retired Oct. 1960; *b* 1 Dec. 1889; *s* of John and Jane Hayes; *m* 1917, Margaret Kavanagh; one *s* one *d* (and *er s* decd). *Educ:* Christian Schs, Synge Street, and University Coll., Dublin. Asst Prof. of French in University Coll., Dublin, until 1922; Minister for Education, Dail Eireann, 1922; Speaker, Dail Eireann, and Chm. of the Civil Service Commission, Saorstat Eireann, 1922-32; Leader of Fine Gael Party in Senate, Republic of Ireland, 1938-65; retired 1965. *Recreation:* golf. *Address:* 143 Templeogue Road, Dublin.
[Died 11 July 1976.

HAYGARTH JACKSON, Harold; *see* Jackson, H. H.

HAYMAN, Perceval Mills Cobham; *b* 31 Oct. 1883; 2nd *s* of Canon Henry Telford Hayman, TD, MA, and Mrs Hayman, JP; *m* 1st, 1914, Susan Moon (*d* 1924), *d* of late W. H. Hartley, Hoarstones and Fence Gate, Lancs; one *s* (and one *s* killed in action, 1943); 2nd, 1928, Agnes Vera, *d* of late Gerald Hall Kennedy; one *d. Educ:* Eastbourne; abroad. Called to Bar, Inner Temple, 1913. Served European War, 1914-19, with E Lancs Regt (wounded, 1918), and as District Courts Martial Officer; retired from active list, 1919, with rank of Capt. Admitted Solicitor, 1919; Group Registrar of County Courts, 1932-56; District Registrar, High Court, 1939-56 and Hon. Mem. Registrars Assoc.; re-admitted to the Bar, Inner Temple; Hon. Mem. Oxford Circuit. Member: Glos Diocesan Board of Finance, 1942-67; Standing Joint Cttee, 1942-58; a Founder, Lilian Faithfull Homes for Old People (Chm. 1952-59); Chm. Council Friends of Tewkesbury Abbey, 1958-66. Home Guard, 1940-44; Corp. Mem. Cheltenham Ladies' Coll., 1944. Deputy Chm. Glos QS, 1947-58. JP Co. Glos, 1942. FRGS, Hon. FZS. District and Asst County Comr, NE Lancs Scouts, 1922-39;

Scout Medal of Merit and Hon. Comr, 1939. Coronation Medal, 1953. Masonry: Deputy Provincial Grand Master, Glos, 1950. *Publications:* Some Elementary Notes on Military Law and Procedure (4 Editions, 1941); Foreword to Brewer's Dictionary of Phrase and Fable (centenary edn), 1970; numerous contributions on military law to legal publications, etc. *Recreations:* formerly cricket, hockey; now watching cricket. *Address:* Dolphin House, Charlton Park Gate, Cheltenham, Glos. *T:* Cheltenham 24725. *Clubs:* Junior Carlton, MCC; Farmers'; New (Cheltenham).   *[Died 9 Jan. 1974.*

HAYNES, Robert, CB 1973; Deputy Under-Secretary of State (Personnel and Logistics), Ministry of Defence, since 1972; *b* 16 June 1920; *s* of A. J. and A. M. Haynes; *m* 1945, Joan Isabel Harris; one *s* (one *d* decd). *Educ:* Manchester Grammar Sch.; (scholar) Trinity Coll., Cambridge (MA). Served War: Ordinary Seaman and Temp. Lieut, RNVR, 1940-45. Asst Principal, Air Ministry, 1946; Private Sec. to Chief of Air Staff, 1948-51; Asst Sec., 1955; Asst Under-Sec. of State, and Principal Establishment Officer, Air Min., 1961; Asst Under-Sec. (Air Staff), 1968. *Recreations:* gardening, railway modelling. *Address:* 7 Malmains Way, Beckenham, Kent BR3 2SA. *T:* 01-650 0325.   *[Died 27 Sept. 1976.*

HAYWARD, Alfred Robert, RP; ARWS 1960; NEAC; artist; portrait, water colours and landscape painter; mural decorator; *b* London, 1875; *m*; one *d. Educ:* privately; S Kensington; The Slade Sch. Freeman of City of London. Examples of his paintings are included in the following permanent collections: Brighton Museum; Municipal Gallery, Johannesburg; National Museum of Wales, Cardiff; Public Art Gallery, Christchurch, New Zealand; Imperial War Museum; International Gallery of Modern Art, Venice; Tate Gallery, Millbank; Whitworth Institute, Manchester; Municipal Gallery, Southampton; Emmanuel Coll., Cambridge; an Exhibition of Water Colours and Paintings of Venice held at the Leicester Galleries, Jan. 1924; Exhibition of Paintings held at Wildenstein Galleries, 1936; exhibited pictures in London since 1896, principally at The New English Art Club, The Royal Society of Portrait Painters, The Royal Academy, and at Paris, Rome, Venice, and Pittsburgh. Retrospective Exhibition: Federation of British Artists, 1964; FBA Gallery, 1967; Harvane Gallery, 1970. Joined Artists Rifles beginning of European War, 1914-18; 2nd Lieut RGA (SR) 1916 (Anti-Aircraft); Lieut 1917; Official War Artist during last few months of the War; awarded Mention Honorable Paris Salon, 1921; a Decoration representing the First Governor and presented by the Bank of England placed in Royal Exchange, 1923; the decoration of the Safety Curtain, De La Warr Pavilion, Bexhill-on-Sea, 1939; awarded a Civil List Pension, 1943; lately teaching painting and drawing from life, City and Guilds School of Art. *Address:* 14 Manor Gardens, Hampton-on-Thames, Middx. *T:* 01-979 4223. *Clubs:* Chelsea Arts, National Book League.   *[Died 2 Jan. 1971.*

HAYWARD, Rev. Edward, MA; retired as Rector of Maresfield (1956-59); *b* 15 June 1884; *s* of Joseph and Annie Hayward, Stanbridge House, Holt, Wiltshire; *m* 1st, 1908, Constance Alethe Perry (*d* 1930); one *s* one *d*; 2nd, 1933, Eileen, *o d* of Charles A. Swan, Lisbon; two *s. Educ:* Monkton Combe School; Sidney Sussex College (Senior Classical Scholar, 1903, Stewart of Rannoch Scholarship, 1904), and Ridley Hall, Cambridge. 2nd Class Honours, Theo. Tripos, 1906; 3rd Class Honours, Theo. Trip., Part ii, 1907. Curate of S Silas Lozells, Birmingham, 1907-11; CMS Missionary at Panyam, N Nigeria, 1911-19; Organising Secretary, CMS, 1920-23; Secretary for Far East Missions, CMS, 1923-26; Headmaster, Monkton Combe School, 1926-46; Rector of Eastrop, Basingstoke, 1949-55. *Address:* 3 Rotherfield Road, Boscombe, Bournemouth, Hants. *T:* Bournemouth 44995.   *[Died 30 Jan. 1974.*

HAYWARD, Graham William, MD London; FRCP; Senior Physician: St Bartholomew's Hospital, London; National Heart Hospital, London, since 1947; Cardiologist, King Edward VII Hospital for Officers, since 1964; *b* 7 June 1911; *s* of William George Hayward, OBE; *m* 1946, Mary Anna Harding, Philadelphia, USA; two *s* one *d* (and one *s* decd). *Educ:* Cardiff High School; St Bartholomew's Hosp. and University of London. MD London, 1937, MB, BS (Hons Med., Path., Surgery, Midwifery and Forensic Med. and Univ. Gold Medal), 1935; FRCP 1946. Kirkes Schol. and Gold Medal, Clin. Med., 1933; Brackenbury Schol. in Med., 1933; Willett Medal, Op. Surg., 1934 (St Bartholomew's Hosp.). Fellowships: Rockefeller Foundation, USA, 1937-38; Research in Med., Penna Hosp., Philadelphia, 1937-38; Mackenzie Mackinnon Research, Royal Coll. Physicians, 1939. Lieut-Col. NZ Med. Corps; served in Middle East and Italy as OC Med. Div., 3rd NZ Hosp., 1940-45. Asst Dir Med. Professorial Unit, St Bartholomew's, and Reader in Med., Univ. of London, 1945-47; Asst Physician, St

Bartholomew's, 1944-55. Dean, Inst. of Cardiology, Univ. of London, 1948-61. Examiner in Medicine: Univ. of London, 1952-58; Univ. of Khartoum, 1956; Univ. of Cambridge, 1958; University Coll. of The West Indies, 1959-60. Croonian Lectr, RCP, 1972. Member: Association Physicians Great Britain; Cardiac Soc. *Publications:* articles in medical and scientific journals on cardio-vascular subjects. *Recreation:* gardening. *Address:* 149 Harley Street, W1. *T:* 01-935 4444; Colyton, 103 Totteridge Lane, N20. *T:* 01-445 1761.   *[Died 26 Nov. 1976.*

HAYWARD, Sir Isaac (James), Kt 1959; LLD; JP; *b* Blaenavon, Monmouthshire, 17 Nov. 1884; *m* 1st, 1913, Alice Mayers (decd); three *s* (and one *s* killed 1944); 2nd, 1951, Violet Cleveland. *Educ:* non-provided elementary school. Trade Union Office for 28 years, National Union of Enginemen, Firemen, Mechanics, and Elec. Workers; from 1938, until retirement in 1946, Gen. Sec. to Union. London County Council: Member, 1928-65; Chairman of General Purposes Committee, 1937-38; Public Assistance Committee, 1934-37; Education Committee, 1945-47; Welfare of the Blind Committee, 1938-39; Chief Whip, 1932-47; Leader of the Council, 1947-65. Chairman, London Electricity Consultative Council, 1948-60. Member of London and Home Counties Jt Electricity Authority from inception, 1925, until nationalisation, 1949; late Member of No 9 and 10 Areas (London) of District Jt Industrial Council for Electrical Supply Industry; Member: BEA Board, 1946-48; London Electricity Bd, 1948-60; Court of University of London; South Bank Theatre and Opera House Board, 1962-. Hon. FRIBA 1970. JP London 1938. *Recreations:* bowls, chess. *Address:* 140 Chudleigh Road, SE4. *T:* 01-690 0323.   *[Died 3 Jan. 1976.*

HAYWARD, Tom Christopher, CBE 1946; DL; Clerk of the Peace and County Council for West Sussex, 1938-66 and Clerk to Lieutenancy for Sussex, 1938-68, retired; *b* 25 Nov. 1904; *s* of Major P. C. G. Hayward, Needham Market, Suffolk; *m* 1930, Sybil Lisette Grainger-Brunt; one *s* one *d. Educ:* Cheltenham Coll.; Corpus Christi Coll., Cambridge (BA). Solicitor, 1929; Assistant Solicitor, Bath City Council, 1929, Oxfordshire County Council, 1929; Senior Asst Solicitor, E Sussex County Council, 1930; Deputy Clerk of the Peace and of County Council for Staffs, 1934. Controller for Civil Defence for W Sussex. Lord of the Manor, Thorndon-cum-Hestley Hall, Suffolk. DL Sussex, 1968. *Recreations:* hunting, shooting, golf, cricket. *Address:* Threeways, Canon's Close, Aldwick, Sussex. *Clubs:* Royal Automobile, MCC; Sussex. *[Died 4 June 1975.*

HEADLAM, Air Vice-Marshal Frank, CB 1965; CBE 1958 (OBE 1954); Head, Australian Joint Services Staff, London, 1968-71; *b* 15 July 1914; *s* of Malcolm Headlam, Oatlands, Tasmania; *m* 1940, Katherine Beatrice (marr. diss. 1956), *d* of P. S. Bridge, Victoria; one *s* one *d. Educ:* Clemes Coll., Hobart. Pilot Officer RAAF 1934. Served War of 1939-45 (SE Asia, Northern Australia). Gp Capt. 1942; Air Cdre 1953; Dir-Gen. of Plans, 1958; Mem. for Personnel Dept of Air, 1957 and 1959; Air Vice-Marshal 1961; Air Officer Commanding Operational Command, RAAF Penrith, NSW, 1961-62; Air Officer Commanding 224 Gp, Far East Air Force, 1962-64; Dep. Chief of Air Staff, RAAF, 1965-66; AOC Support Comd, RAAF, Melbourne, 1966-67. ADC to the Queen, 1954; Extra Gentleman Usher to the Queen, 1970-71. *Recreations:* tennis, golf, fishing, shooting. *Address:* 5 Thornton Street, Kew, Victoria, Australia. *Clubs:* Melbourne; Melbourne Cricket; Lawn Tennis Association of Victoria.   *[Died 27 Dec. 1976.*

HEAF, Prof. Frederick Roland George, CMG 1957; MA; MD 1923; FRCP 1946; MRCS 1918; Emeritus Professor University of Wales, since 1961; Consultant to Ministry of Health, 1947-63, to Scottish Health Department, and to Colonial Office, 1948-68; *b* 21 June 1894; *o s* of late Julius R. Heaf, Cambridge; *m* 1920, Madeleine (*d* 1966), *y d* of John Denison, Ilkley, Yorks; two *s* one *d. Educ:* Oundle; Sidney Sussex Coll., Cambridge; St Thomas' Hosp., London. Medical Superintendent: Warwick Sanatorium, 1922-30; Colindale Hosp., 1930-36; Sen. Medical Officer, LCC, 1936-49; David Davies Prof., University of Wales, 1949-60. Hon. Consulting Physician: Welsh Hosp. Board and SE Metrop. Hosp. Bd, 1949-; British Legion, 1944. Hon. Member: Brit. Tuberc. Assoc.; (Sen. Mem.) Thor. Soc., 1961; Med. Soc. of Sweden; Salonika Med. Assoc.; Tuberculosis Assoc. of Turkey. FRGS 1961. *Publications:* Rehabilitation of the Tuberculous (jointly), 1938; Recent Advances in Respiratory Tuberculosis (6th Edn) (jointly), 1968; Symposium of Tuberculosis (ed), 1957. *Recreations:* archæology, geology, photography. *Address:* Broadgate, Witney Road, Freeland, Oxon. *T:* Freeland 881311. *Club:* National Liberal.   *[Died 4 Feb. 1973.*

HEALD, Charles Brehmer, CBE 1919; MD Cantab; FRCP; Consulting Physician Royal Free Hospital; Consulting Physician for Rheumatic Diseases, Middlesex Hospital; late

Medical Consultant, RAF; Medical Adviser, Department of Civil Aviation, Air Ministry; late Chairman and Medical Director, Rural Rheumatism Centre (Cotswolds); *b* 3 Dec. 1882; *s* of Walter Heald and Emily Krabbé; *m* Edith Hildegarde, *d* of Arthur Mason, Walton-on-Thames; three *d. Educ:* Tonbridge; Caius Coll., Cambridge; St Bartholomew's Hosp. Temp. Surg., Royal Navy; Lieut-Col (temp.) RAMC; Principal Medical Officer, RAF, Middle East; FRSM. *Publications:* Injuries and Sport; The Genesis of Aviation Medicine (Historical Section, Cabinet Office) (restricted edn), 1966; on Rheumatism and Physical Health to medical journals. *Recreations:* woodwork, gardening. *Address:* Tally-Ho Cottage, Chipping Campden, Glos. *T:* Campden 401. *Club:* United Oxford & Cambridge University.   [*Died* 9 Feb. 1974.

HEALD, Edith Shackleton; journalist; *yr d* of late J. T. Heald and Mary Shackleton. Formerly dramatic critic and leader writer on the Evening Standard; book reviewer. *Address:* The Chantry House, Steyning, West Sussex BN4 3YB. *T:* Steyning 813163.
[*Died* 5 Nov. 1976.

HEALD, Henry Townley; Chairman, Heald Hobson and Associates, Inc., 1966-71; President of the Ford Foundation, 1956-65; *b* 8 Nov. 1904; *s* of Frederick De Forest and Nellie Townley Heald; *m* 1928, Muriel Starcher; no *c. Educ:* State Coll. of Washington, Pullman, Washington; University of Ill, Urbana, Ill. BS (State Coll. of Washington), 1923; MS (University of Ill), 1925. Successively Asst Prof., Associate Prof., Prof. of Civil Engineering, Dean of Freshmen, Dean of Engineering, and Pres., Illinois Inst. of Technology, Chicago, Ill, 1927-52; Pres., New York Univ., Feb. 1952-Sept. 1956. Hon. degrees: DEng, Rose Polytechnic Inst, 1942, Clarkson Coll. of Technology, 1948; LLD, Northwestern Univ., 1942, Rutgers Univ., 1952, Hofstra Coll., 1955, Fairleigh Dickinson Coll., 1956, Princeton Univ., 1956, University of Pittsburgh, 1956, Columbia Univ., 1954, University of State of New York, 1962; University of Ill, 1963, Case Western Reserve Univ., 1968; LHD, Rollins Coll., 1953, Pacific Lutheran Univ., 1966, Northern Illinois Univ., 1966, Brandeis Univ., 1966, College of Wooster, 1966; DSc, Newark Coll. of Engineering, 1954, Union Coll., 1956, Pratt Inst., 1954; DCL New York Univ., 1956; DH, Cornell Coll., 1967. *Publications:* articles and addresses. *Address:* 106 South Interlacken Avenue, Winter Park, Florida 32789, USA. *Clubs:* University; Winter Park.   [*Died* 23 Nov. 1975.

HEALD, William; Member, Press Council, 1967-77; News Editor, "Lancaster Guardian", Newspaper Series, 1955-75; *b* 16 March 1910; *s* of William Heald, OBE, and Elizabeth Ann Heald; *m* 1938, Elizabeth Elsie Mount; two *d. Educ:* Lancaster Royal Grammar Sch. Lancashire Evening Post, 1933-55. Mem. Exec. Council, Nat. Union of Journalists, 1955-; Nat. Pres., NUJ, 1963-64. Governor, London Coll. of Printing. *Address:* 74 Wyresdale Road, Lancaster LA1 3DY. *T:* Lancaster 63787. *Club:* Press.   [*Died* 19 June 1979.

HEALEY, Sir Edward Randal C.; see Chadwyck-Healey.

HEALY, Rt. Rev. John Farmer, CBE 1971; DD, DCL; Bishop of Gibraltar, since 1956; *b* 3 Dec. 1900; *s* of Edward Lee Healy and Louisa A. Healy (*née* Edwards). *Educ:* Wimbledon Choir Sch.; St John's Seminary, Wonersh; English Coll., Valladolid. Ordained, 1927; DD 1928; DCL 1930. Secretary to the Catholic Bishop of Southwark, 1930-37; Sec. and Treas., Southwark Catholic Rescue Soc., 1937-48; Parish Priest of Sacred Heart, Camberwell, 1948-56. *Address:* Bishop's House, Gibraltar. *T:* 3120.   [*Died* 17 Feb. 1973.

HEAPE, William Leslie, CMG 1942; Colonial Service, retired; *b* 1896; 2nd *s* of late H. Heape, Forde, Ashford Carbonel, Ludlow; *m* Anice, *d* of Capt. Chandler, Army Medical Service; one *s* one *d. Educ:* Rugby; RMC, Sandhurst. Commissioned East Lancs Regt, 1914; BEF France, 1915 (severely wounded); served ground staff, RAF 1917; War Office, 1918-19; entered Colonial Civil Service, 1919, Asst Sec., Somaliland Protectorate; attached for duty, Colonial Office, 1926; Secretariat Tanganyika Territory, 1929; Private Sec. to Governor of Barbados, 1933-35; Colonial Sec., Grenada, 1935-40; Bahamas, 1940-43; Colonial Sec., British Guiana, 1944-50; Officer Administering the Government, 1944, 1946, 1947, 1948 and 1949; retired from Colonial Service 1949; re-employed, Colonial Office, 1950-58. *Address:* St George's, Whitchurch Canonicorum, Bridport, Dorset.   [*Died* 29 Dec. 1972.

HEARD, Gerald; see Heard, H. F. G.

HEARD, Henry Fitz Gerald; author; *b* 6 Oct. 1889; *y s* of late Prebendary H. J. Heard; unmarried. *Educ:* Sherbourne; Gonville and Caius Coll., Cambridge. Literary Editor of The

Realist, 1929; Fortnightly Broadcast on This Surprising World, 1930-34; Broadcast Series; Science in the Making, 1934; Ayer Lecturer, Colgate Rochester Seminary, 1946; visiting consultant (dept of Philosophy), Washington Univ., St Louis, USA, 1951 and 1952, 1955-56; two-year Bollinger Foundation Grant, 1955-56; Haskell Foundation Lecturer at Oberlin Coll., Oberlin, Ohio, 1958. *Publications:* Narcissus (To-day and To-morrow Series); The Ascent of Humanity (awarded by British Academy grant from Henrietta Hertz Fund); The Social Substance of Religion; The Emergence of Man; This Surprising World; These Hurrying Years; Science in the Making; The Source of Civilisation; Exploring the Stratosphere: The Third Morality; Pain, Sex and Time; The Creed of Christ; The Code of Christ; Man the Master; Taste for Honey; Reply Paid; Desert Dialogue; Preface to Prayer; Gamaliel's Gospel; The Eternal Gospel; Dopplegangers; Is God Evident?; The Lost Cavern; The Black Fox; The Book of Wishes; The Riddle of the Flying Saucers (Is Another World Watching?), publ. GB (and US); The Human Venture; The Perennial Praxis; The Five Ages of Man; Five Cloven Men; The Four Classes of Men. *Address:* 322 East Rustic Road, Santa Monica, Calif 90402, USA.   [*Died* 14 Aug. 1971.

HEARD, Brig. Leonard Ferguson, CBE 1943; JP; *b* 30 Oct. 1903; *er s* of late Lieut-Col Samuel Ferguson Heard, and late Florence Roberta Heard (*née* Allan), Magilligan, Co. Londonderry; unmarried. *Educ:* Shrewsbury Sch.; RMA, Woolwich. Entered RE 1923; Capt. 1934; Major, 1940; Col 1947; Brig. 1949; ADC to the Queen, 1954-57; retired, 1957; French Croix de Guerre (with palm) 1945. High Sheriff, Co. Londonderry, 1964. *Address:* Magilligan, Co. Londonderry, N Ireland. *T:* Bellarena 208. *Club:* Naval and Military.   [*Died* 8 April 1976.

HEARD, His Eminence Cardinal William Theodore, BA (Oxon); DPh, DD, DCL; Auditor of the Sacred Roman Rota, 1927-62 (Dean, 1958); Cardinal Protector of the English College, Rome, from 1962; Prelate of the Sacred Congregation of the Rites, 1944; *b* Edinburgh, 24 Feb. 1884; *s* of Rev. W. A. Heard, LLD. *Educ:* Fettes Coll., Edinburgh; Balliol Coll., Oxford, Hon. Fellow, 1964; English Coll., Rome. Rowed in Oxford Eight, 1907; admitted Solicitor, 1910; received into Catholic Church, 1910; ordained Priest, 1918; stationed at Dockhead, Bermondsey, 1921-27; Mem. Pontifical Commn for the interpretation of the Codex, 1959. Cardinal, Dec. 1959. Archbishop, 1962. Hon. LLD Edinburgh, 1968. *Address:* Via di Monserrato 45, 00186 Roma, Italy.   [*Died* 16 Sept. 1973.

HEARN, Col George William Richard, CBE 1959; KPM; DL; Chief Constable of Staffordshire, 1950-61; *b* 11 Aug. 1893; *es* of Sir Walter Risley Hearn, KBE, Buckingham; *m* 1st, 1921, Mabel Jean Winifred (*d* 1963), *e d* of late John T. C. Eadie, JP, Aldershawe, Lichfield; (one *s* decd); 2nd, 1964, Pamela Frances Mary, *widow* of John Francis Phillips, Brocton Leys, near Stafford. *Educ:* Uppingham. Served European War, 1914-18, joined DLI, 1914. South Staffs Regt 1915; Dep. Asst Provost-Marshal, 59th Div. Capt. 1921; retd 1935; Bt Major 1940; Hon. Col 5th Bn The South Staffs Regt (TA), 1946-58. Asst Chief Constable of Staffs, 1935-50; actg Inspector of Constabulary, NE Civil Defence Region, 1940-43. DL Staffs, 1947. King's Police Medal, 1947; OStJ 1951. *Address:* Farley Hill Court, near Reading, Berks. *T:* Eversley 3386.   [*Died* 11 Nov. 1973.

HEATH, Maj.-Gen. Gerard William Egerton, CB 1949; CBE 1945; DSO 1945; MC 1916; retired; *b* 17 March 1897; *s* of late Maj.-Gen. Sir G. M. Heath, KCMG, CB, and Mary (*née* Egerton); *m* 1923, Hilda Mary, (*née* Houldsworth) (from whom he obtained a divorce, 1931); two *d* ; *m* 1933, Gwendda Curtis (*née* Evans). *Educ:* Wellington Coll.; RMA Woolwich. Commissioned RA, 1915; served European War, 1915-18 (wounded); War of 1939-45 (despatches, 1940); CRA 43rd Div., 1942-44; CCRA 12 Corps, 1944-45; CCRA 1st Airborne Corps, 1945; Commandant Sch. of Artillery, Larkhill, 1945-47; GOC 1st Anti-Aircraft Group, 1947-49; GOC Troops, Malta, 1949-51. Pres. Regular Commissions Board, 1951-54, retired Nov. 1954. Col Comdt RA and Royal Malta Artillery, 1955, RHA 1957. *Recreations:* shooting and all forms of mounted sport. *Address:* Westbrook Farm, Avebury, Wilts. *T:* Avebury 248. *Club:* Naval and Military.   [*Died* 13 July 1980.

HEATH, Harry Cecil; General Manager, United Kingdom Temperance Alliance Ltd, 1963-72, retired; *b* 1898; *e s* of Harry Heath, Wellington, Shropshire; *m* 1st, 1924, Margaret (*d* 1928), *e d* of George Harvey, JP, Wellington; two *d* ; 2nd, 1930, Muriel Grace, *e d* of Joseph B. Adams, Ambergate. *Educ:* Newport Grammar Sch.; Pembroke Coll., Oxford, BA (Hons English). Commissioned in the Cheshire Regt, 1917; Mem. Inner Temple; called to Bar, 1938; General Sec. of the United Kingdom Alliance, 1926-62; Editor of The Licensing Magistrate; Joint Hon. Sec. National Temperance Federation; Pres. Nat. Assoc. of

Temperance Officials, 1935-37; Hon. Sec. British Section Internat. Temperance Union; Extension Lecturer, University of London, 1946; Vice-Chm., Churches' Council on Gambling; Chairman, Good Templar Children's Home; Chm., Friends' Temperance Union; Collegiate Assoc.; Chm. Internat. Cttee on Alcohol and Road Traffic, 1950-60; Pres., National United Temperance Council; Pres., National Brotherhood Movement, 1960-61; Pres., United Kingdom Alliance, 1963-70; Chm., Ansvar Insurance Co. Ltd. *Publications:* Drink and Sport; Temperance Exhibitions; The Case against the Public Ownership of the Drink Trade; Alcohol and Democracy; Drink and Motoring; a Survey of Magisterial Practice in relation to Occasional Licences; Alcohol and World Traffic Safety; The Drink Problem in War Time; A Citizen Addresses the Licensing Justices; A Post-War Plan for the Temperance Movement; It's Your Money They Want; End This Colossal Waste of Food; The Control of a Dangerous Trade; Social Economics in Relation to the Alcohol Problem; Some Fallacies concerning the Nationalisation of the Drink Trade; A Summary of the Licensing Act, 1949; Drink and the Press; The Citizen's Guide to Licensing Procedure; The Licensing Act, 1961; Academic Apathy, and other pamphlets; Contrib. to Everyman's Encyclopædia and Encyclopædia Britannica. *Recreations:* Member of the Magic Circle; motoring. *Address:* 62 Becmead Avenue, Streatham, SW16. *T:* 01-769 6649.
[Died 3 Aug. 1972.

HEATHCOAT-AMORY, Major Sir John, Bt; *see* Amory.

HEATON, Mrs Gwenllian Margaret, CBE 1946; TD; *b* 12 March 1897; *o c* of late Lieut-Col B. E. Philips, DL, JP, Rhual, Mold, Flintshire; *m* 1921, Commander H. E. Heaton, DL, JP, RN (retd); two *s. Educ:* privately. Local service as VAD European War, 1914-18. Enrolled in Auxiliary Territorial Service Sept. 1938; embodied Aug. 1939 with rank of Senior Commander. Served on Staff at HQ Western Command, 1940-44 and HQ Eastern Command, 1944-45; Chief Commander 1941; Controller, 1942, with appointment as DDATS. Released with Age and Service Group July 1945. *Address:* Garregwen, Pantymwyn, Mold, Clwyd. *T:* Pantymwyn 234.
[Died 30 Jan. 1979.

HEATON, Herbert, MA (Leeds), MCom (Birmingham), DLitt (Leeds); Professor Emeritus Economic History, University of Minnesota (Professor 1927-58; Chairman History Department, 1954-58); *b* Silsden, Yorks, 6 June 1890; *s* of Fred and Eva Heaton; *m* 1914, Ellen Jane (*d* 1956), *d* of W. J. and A. Houghton, Cheltenham; one *s* two *d*; *m* 1959, Marjorie Edith Ronson, Cheltenham. *Educ:* Batley Gram. Sch. Morley Secondary Sch.; Leeds Univ.; London Sch. of Economics. 1st Class History Hons BA (Leeds 1911); Rutson Research Scholar, 1911; Fellow Leeds Univ., 1912; Asst Lecturer in Economics, Birmingham Univ., 1912-14; Lecturer in History and Economics, University of Tasmania, 1914-17; Lecturer in Economics and Dir of Tutorial Classes, University of Adelaide, 1917-25; Sir John A. Macdonald Prof. of Economic and Political Science, Queen's Univ., Kingston, Canada, 1925-27; Pres. WEA of Australia, 1919, 1922-25; Special lecturer on Australian problems in London, Cambridge, Toronto, Edmonton, 1924; Guggenheim Fellow, 1931-32; Visiting professor: Princeton Univ., 1939-40; Johns Hopkins Univ., 1961; University of Utah, 1962, 1969; University of British Colombia, 1962-63; University of Texas, 1964; University of California at Davis, 1965; University of California at Riverside, 1966; Michigan State University, 1968; Disting. Vis. Prof. Pennsylv. State Univ., 1958-60. Sec. of Social Science Research Council's Cttee on research in Econ. Hist., 1941-54; Pres. Econ. History Assoc., 1948-50. Corres. FBA 1967. *Publications:* History of Yorkshire Woollen and Worsted Industries, 1920, 1965; Mod. Econ. Hist., with Special Reference to Aust., 1920; Welfare Work, 1919; History of Trade and Commerce, with Special Reference to Canada, 1928 (rewritten 1953); The British Way of Recovery, 1934; An Economic History of Europe, 1936 (rewritten 1948); Edwin F. Gay: American Scholar in action, 1952; Articles in econ. jls, etc. *Recreations:* golf, motoring and music. *Address:* 5148 Luverne Avenue, Minneapolis, Minn 55419, USA. *Club:* Campus (Minn).
[Died 27 Jan. 1973.

HEATON, Sir (John Victor) Peregrine Henniker-, 3rd Bt, *cr* 1912; RAF retired; *b* 15 Jan. 1903; *e s* of Sir John Henniker Heaton, 2nd Bt; *S* father, 1963; *m* 1st, 1927, Gladys (marr. diss., 1937), 2nd *d* of Peter E. Tyson, Alnwick, Northumberland; two *d*; 2nd, 1948, Margaret Patricia, *d* of late Lieut Percy Wright, Canadian Mounted Rifles (killed in action); one *s* one *d. Educ:* HMS Conway. Served War of 1939-45 (despatches), Pilot Officer RAF, 1940; Sqdn-Ldr, 1944; Asst Provost Marshal, Austria, 1945; Deputy Provost Marshal, Levant, 1945-48; Wing-Commander, 1948; retired, 1958; Mem. Council, Anglo-Arab

Assoc. *Recreation:* yachting. *Heir:* s Yvo Robert Henniker-Heaton, *b* 24 April 1954. *Address:* 14 Woodville Road, Ealing, W5. *T:* 01-997 2097. *Club:* Royal Thames Yacht.
[Died Oct. 1971.

HEATON, Rose Henniker (Mrs Adrian Porter); *b* London, 1884; *d* of late Sir John Henniker-Heaton, Bt, Postal Reformer, and Rose Bennett; *m* 1914, Lieut-Col Adrian Porter (*d* 1954), King's Messenger; one *d. Publications:* The Perfect Hostess; The Perfect Schoolgirl; The Perfect Christmas; The Perfect Cruise; Mr Manners; Dinner with James; Chez James (with Sir Duncan Swann); Contract with James; Cruising with James; Life of Sir John Henniker-Heaton; Roseleaves (verses); The Perfect Address Book; Running a House without Help. *Recreations:* travelling and listening-in. *Address:* c/o Mrs L. Buckley, Sheepcote, Bartestree, Hereford.
[Died 8 Oct. 1975.

HEATON, Trevor Braby, OBE 1919; DM, MA Oxon; MRCP; Student Emeritus of Christ Church, Oxford; *b* Oslo, Norway, 9 Aug. 1886; 2nd *s* of late Rev. A. F. Heaton, Rector of Covington, Hunts; *m* 1920 Constance Irene, *d* of late J. W. Wheeler-Bennett, JP; one *s* two *d. Educ:* Charterhouse; Christ Church, Oxford; Guy's Hospital. 1st class Natural Science, Oxford, 1909; Medical Registrar, Guy's Hospital, 1913; Capt. RAMC (SR), 1915-19. Dr Lee's Reader in Anatomy, Christ Church, Oxford, 1920-54. *Publication:* The Human Body, 1927. *Address:* 3 St Martin's Square, Chichester, Sussex. *T:* Chichester 83941.
[Died 18 Jan. 1972.

HECKSTALL-SMITH, Hugh William, MA; author; *b* 24 July 1896; *s* of late Malden and of Ada Victoria Heckstall-Smith; *m* Eileen Violet Mary (*d* 1971), *d* of Surgn Rear-Adm. I. H. Anderson, Twyford, Hants; one *s. Educ:* Tonbridge Sch.; Sidney Sussex Coll., Cambridge. Served European War, 1915-19 (wounded). Stowe Sch. (Science Tutor), 1923-33; Headmaster, Grammar Sch., Ludlow, 1933-35; Headmaster, Chippenham Grammar Sch., Wilts, 1935-39; farming in Radnorshire, 1939-47; Chm., Knighton Branch NFU, 1946; Mem., Min. of Agric. Machinery Working Party, 1946-51; Mem. Management Cttee, Moorhaven (Mental) Hospital, Devon, 1951-69. Mem. Soc. of Friends (Quakers), 1935-. *Publications:* First Electrical Theory, 1930, revised 1950; Intermediate Electrical Theory, 1932, revised 1958; The Bases of Atomic Physics, 1956; Atomic Radiation Dangers, 1958; Doubtful Schoolmaster (an autobiography), 1962. *Recreation:* trying to understand, not only with the mind. *Address:* Brooking House, Tigley Cross, Totnes, Devon TQ9 6DW.
[Died 17 Sept. 1973.

HEDGES, Sidney George; author and journalist; *b* Bicester, Oxon, 25 March 1897; *s* of G. W. and M. A. Hedges; *m* 1930, Mary, *y d* of G. H. Dixon, Retford; one *s. Educ:* Town Elementary Sch. and evening classes. War service in Malta, 1915-19; tried carpentering, drapery trade, music teaching, orchestral playing, lecturing-freelance and for Empire Marketing Board, before settling as writer. Has been National Pres. of Methodist Assoc. of Youth Clubs; Mem. of Bd, Nat. Sunday Sch. Union; Chm., Nat. Harmonica League; Pres. of British Temperance Youth; Founder-leader, Red Rhythmics pioneer harmonica band, 1935-56; European adjudicator, Fédération Internationale de l'Harmonica. *Publications:* more than one hundred books-a dozen novels; twenty works on swimming (originator of modern surface-diving and seal stroke); as many more on indoor and outdoor games, and on youth club and Sunday School work; others autobiographical and on music, skating, hobbies. (Some trans. into French, Dutch, Norwegian, Italian, Hindi). Editor of: Christian Youth Handbook; Things to Do books; Universal Book of Hobbies. Chief works: The Complete Swimmer, Indoor and Community Games, Youth Club Programmes, The Youth Sing Book, Pendlecliffe School stories; recent anthologies of prayers and scriptural excerpts from the world's Living Religions. Contributor to Chambers's Encyclopædia; to magazines on both sides of the Atlantic, and broadcaster on many subjects. *Recreations:* youth work, swimming, violin playing, travel, skating. *Address:* Banbury Road, Bicester, Oxon. *T:* Bicester 2239. *Club:* Royal Commonwealth Society.
[Died 18 July 1974.

HEDLEY, Maj.-Gen. Robert Cecil Osborne, CB 1951; CBE 1947; DSO 1944; retired; *b* 31 Oct. 1900; *s* of late Major R. C. Hedley, Corbridge, Northumberland; *m* 1945, Lucy, *d* of late J. D. N. Strang and Mrs Strang, Oakwood, Hexham, Northumberland. *Educ:* St Bees Sch.; RMC, Sandhurst, 2nd Lieut IA, 1920; Lieut 5th Royal Gurkha Rifles (Frontier Force) 1923; Capt. 1928; Coy. Officer, RMC, Sandhurst, 1935-38; Major, 1938; Dep. Asst Military Sec., GHQ, MEF, 1941-42; Lieut-Col Comdt 2nd Bn 5th Royal Gurkha Rifles (Frontier Force), 1942-44; Brig. Comdg 48 Ind. Inf., Bde, 1944-45; HQ ALFSEA, 1945-46; Maj.-Gen. Comdg 26 Indian Division, 1946-

47; Brig. Comdt School of Infantry, Mhow, 1947; Brig. Comdg Br. Gurkha Troops in India, 1948; Brig. Comdg Johore Sub-Dist, Malaya, 1948-49; Brig. Comdg 48th Gurkha Inf. Bde, 1949-50; Maj.-Gen. Bde of Gurkhas, and GOC South Malaya District, 1950-51; retired, 1952. Schools Liaison Officer, Western Command, 1952-61. IGS Medal with clasp, Waziristan, 1923-24; NW Frontier Clasp to IGS Medal, 1930. Served War of 1939-45, Middle East, 1941 (despatches): Burma, 1942-45 (despatches, DSO and 2 bars); Sumatra, 1946 (CBE, Gen. Service Medal and Clasp); Malaya (CB despatches twice and clasp), 1948-51. *Address:* The Dene, Haydon Bridge, Northumberland; c/o National and Grindlay's Bank, Ltd, 13 St James's Square, SW1. *[Died 19 Nov. 1973.*

HEDLEY-WHYTE, Angus, DSO 1940; TD; MB, MS, FRCS; FRCSE; LRCP; Honorary Consultant Surgeon: Royal Victoria Infirmary, Newcastle upon Tyne; Tynemouth Victoria Jubilee Infirmary and Preston Hospital, North Shields; lately Consulting Surgeon: Richard Murray Hospital; South Moor Hospital; *b* 23 Aug. 1897; *o s* of Dr John Whyte, JP, Gosforth, Newcastle upon Tyne; *m* 1930, Nancy Nettleton; two *s* one *d.* *Educ:* Ackworth Sch., Yorks; University of Durham, MB, MS (Hons) 1924; BS 1919, with 1st class Hons in Surgery; St Bartholomew's and London Hospitals. Successively House Surgeon in Special Depts, House Surgeon, House Physician, Hon. Registrar, Asst Hon. Surgeon, Royal Victoria Infirmary, Newcastle upon Tyne and Hon. Surgeon Hospital for Sick Children, Newcastle upon Tyne; lately Consulting Surgeon, AMS; Pres., Proctological Section, Royal Society of Medicine; Member: RCS, 1943-49; Court of Examiners Council, RCS, 1950-58; Medical Officer, Northumb Hussars Yeomanry, 1927-32; MO 149 (Northumbrian) Field Ambulance, 1932-40 (OC 1937-40); served War of 1939-45 (despatches, DSO). Hon. Col 50th (N) Div., RAMC units. *Publications:* various medical. *Address:* Ruthven, 10 Adderstone Crescent, Jesmond, Newcastle upon Tyne 2. *T:* 811660. *Clubs:* Thatched House, Junior Carlton. *[Died 12 Aug. 1971.*

HEENAN, His Eminence Cardinal John Carmel, DD, PhD; Archbishop of Westminster since 1963; Cardinal since 1965; *b* 26 January 1905; *s* of James Carmel and Anne Heenan (*née* Pilkington). *Educ:* Ushaw; English Coll., Rome. Ordained, 1930; work in East End of London, 1931-47; Superior of the Catholic Missionary Society, 1947-51; Bishop of Leeds, 1951-57; Archbishop of Liverpool and Metropolitan of Northern Province, 1957-63. *Publications:* Priest and Penitent, 1936; Cardinal Hinsley, 1945; Letters from Rush Green, 1948; The People's Priest, 1951; Our Faith, 1957; My Lord and My God, 1958; (co-author) Dialogue: The State of the Church Today, 1968; Not the Whole Truth (autobiog.), 1971; A Crown of Thorns: an autobiography, 1951-1963, 1974. *Address:* Archbishop's House, Westminster, SW1. *[Died 7 Nov. 1975.*

IEGER, Prof. Robert; formerly First Conductor of State-Opera, Munich; *b* Strassbourgh, 19 Aug. 1886. *Educ:* Strassbourgh, Zürich, Lyon, Munich. Conductor at the Operas in Strassbourgh, Barmen; First Conductor at the Volks-opera in Vienna, 1911; Dir of the Opera in Nuremburg, 1912-19; First Conductor at the Munich Opera, 1919-25; First Conductor of the State Opera Vienna, 1925-33; Dir of the Concerts of the Soc. of Friends of Music, Vienna; Conductor at the State Opera, Berlin, 1933-45; Conductor at the Royal Opera in London, 1926-36. Formerly Pres., Hochschule für Musik, Munich. *Publications:* Trio for Piano; Ein Fest zu Haderslev, Opera; Concert for Violin, First Symphony; A Song of Peace, Chorus work; Second Symphony; Nine Songs; Verdi-Variations; Der Bettler Namenlos, Opera; Der Verlorene Sohn (the prodigal son), Opera: A Serious Prelude and a Gay Fugue for Orchestra, op. 26; Lady Hamilton, Opera; Dramatic Overture, op. 28; Henry the Lion, Opera; A serious Symphonie (the third one) op. 30; Variations and Fugue on a Baroque theme for Orchestra, op. 32a; Chaconne and Fugue on a twelve-tone series, op. 35; 4 alte Marienlieder for a high soprano and orchestra, op. 42; Concerto for Violoncello and Orchestra, op. 43; Don Carlos-Variations, op. 44; Te Deum for 2 soli, choir and orchestra, op. 45. *Address:* Widenmayerstrasse 46 I, Munich, Germany. *[Died 14 Feb. 1978.*

IEGGS, G. B. M.; *see* Mitchell-Heggs.

IEIDEGGER, Martin; retired; *b* Messkirch, Baden, 26 Sept. 1889; *m* 1917, Elfride Petri; two *s* one *d.* *Educ:* Gymnasium and University, Freiburg i. Br., Privatdozent Freiburg i. Br., 1915; ordentlich Professor, University Marburg, 1923; Professor of Philosophy, University of Freiburg-i.-Br., 1928, Professor Emeritus, 1951. *Publications:* Die Kategorien und Bedeutungslehre des Duns Scotus, 1916; Sein und Zeit, 1927; Was ist Metaphysik?, 1929; Vom Wesen des Grundes, 1929;

Kant und das Problem der Metaphysik, 1929; Die Selbstbehauptung der deutschen Universität, 1933; Hölderlin und das Wesen der Dichtung, 1936; Vom Wesen der Wahrheit, 1943; Erlänterungen zu Hölderlins Dichtung, 1944; Platos Lehre von der Wahrheit, mit einem Brief über den Humanismus, 1947; Holzwege, 1950; Einführung in die Metaphysik, 1953; Der Feldweg, 1953; Aus der Erfahrung des Denkens, 1954; Was heisst Denken?, 1954; Vorträge und Aufsätze, 1954; Was ist das-die Philosophie?, 1956; Zur Seinsfrage, 1956; Der Satz vom Grund, 1957; J. P. Hebel, 1957; Identität und Differenz, 1957; Unterwegs zur Sprache, 1959; Gelassenheit, 1959; Nietzsche, 1961; Die Frage nach dem Ding, 1962; Kants These über das Sein, 1963; Die Technik und die Kehre, 1963; Wegmarken, 1967; Zur Sache des Denkens, 1969; Phainomenologie und Theologie, 1970; Schelling, 1971; Fruhe Schriften, 1972. *Address:* Freiburg i. Br., Fillibach 25, Germany.
[Died 26 May 1976.

HEILBRONN, Prof. Hans Arnold, FRS 1951; FRSC; PhD, MA; Professor of Mathematics, University of Toronto, since 1964; *b* 8 Oct. 1908; *m* 1964, Mrs Dorothy Greaves. Bevan Fellow of Trinity Coll., Cambridge, 1935-40; Henry Overton Wills Professor of Mathematics, University of Bristol, 1949-64. *Publications:* scientific papers in several periodicals. *Address:* 538 Kensington Towers, 21 Dale Avenue, Toronto 5, Canada. *T:* 416-962 0720. *[Died 28 April 1975.*

HEILPERN, Godfrey, QC 1962; a Recorder, since 1972 (Recorder of Salford, 1964-71); *b* 29 Oct. 1911; *s* of Marcus and Rose Heilpern; *m* 1944, Anne Sheila Cohen; one *d.* *Educ:* Manchester Grammar Sch.; Hertford Coll., Oxford. Open classical exhibn to Hertford Coll., Oxford, 1930; First Class Hons in Final Sch. of Jurisprudence, 1934; Harmsworth Schol., Middle Temple, 1935, Bencher, 1968. Called to Bar, 1938; has practised on Northern Circuit, 1938. *Recreations:* golf, bridge, reading, travel. *Address:* 16 Ballbrook Avenue, Didsbury, Manchester 20. *T:* Didsbury 1326. *Clubs:* Royal Automobile; Dunham Forest Golf (Dunham). *[Died 3 May 1973.*

HEISENBERG, Dr Werner; Director Emeritus of the Max-Planck-Institute for Physics and Astrophysics, Munich; Professor at University of Munich; President, Alexander von Humboldt-foundation; *b* 5 Dec. 1901; *s* of August Heisenberg and Annie Wecklein; *m* 1937, Elisabeth Schumacher; three *s* four *d.* *Educ:* Universities Munich and Göttingen. Dr phil. Munich, 1923; Privatdozent, Göttingen, 1924; Lectr at Univ. of Copenhagen, 1926; Prof., University of Leipzig, 1927-41; Prof., University of Berlin and Dir of the Kaiser-Wilhelm-Institute for Physics in Berlin, 1941-45; Prof. University of Göttingen and Dir of the Max-Planck-Institute for Physics in Göttingen, 1946-58; Dir, Max-Planck-Institute for Physics and Astrophysics, Munich, 1958-70. Gifford Lecturer, St Andrews Univ., 1955-56. Foreign Member, Royal Society, 1955. Nobel Prize for Physics, 1932; Pour le Mérite für Wissenschaften und Künste, 1957. *Publications:* papers about atomic physics, quantum theory etc., in different periodicals; Die physikalischen Prinzipien der Quantentheorie, Leipzig, 1930, 4th edn, 1944 (Engl. edn Chicago, 1930); Wandlungen in den Grundlagen der Naturwissenschaft, Leipzig, 1935, 9th edn, 1959; Vorträge über kosmische Strahlung, Berlin, 1943, 2nd edn, 1953; Die Physik der Atomkerne, Braunschweig, 1943; Das Naturbild der heutigen Physik, 1955; (trans. various langs); Physics and Philosophy, 1958 (New York) (trans. various langs); Introduction to the Unified Field Theory of Elementary Particles, 1966; Einführung in die einheitliche Feldtheorie der Elementarteilchen, 1967; Das Naturgesetz und die Struktur der Materie: Natural Law and the Structure of Matter (in German and English), 1967; Der Teil und das Ganze, 1969 (trans. as Physics and Beyond, 1971); Schritte über Grenzen, 1971. *Address:* München 40, Rheinlandstrasse 1, West Germany. *T:* 327001. *[Died 1 Feb. 1976.*

HEISER, Victor George, MD; Consultant, Industrial Health; Consultant, Leonard Wood Memorial for Eradication of Leprosy, since 1970; *b* 5 Feb. 1873; *s* of George and Mathilde Lorentz; *m* 1940, Marion Phinny (*d* 1965). *Educ:* private tutors; Jefferson Medical Coll., Pennsylvania. Entered US Marine Hosp. Service, 1898; special detail to Europe to study plague, 1899; to Canada with regard to emigration, 1901; deleg. Internat. Congress on Medicine, Egypt, 1902; Chief Quarantine Officer, Philippine Islands, 1903-15, Dir of Health, 1905-15; with Prof. Gilman Thomas, organised rehabilitation nationwide under the name of Clinic for the Functional Rehabilitation of Soldiers, Sailors and Civilians; Dir for East, Internat. Health Bd, Rockefeller Foundation, 1914-27; Assoc. Dir, Internat. Health Div., Rockefeller Foundation, 1927-34 (retd); Consultant to Cttee on Healthful Working Conditions, Nat. Assoc. of Manufacturers, 1938-; Pres. Internat. Leprosy Assoc., 1931-38;

Chm., Advisory Cttee on Medicine and Public Health, NY World's Fair, 1939; Member: Amer. Red Cross Commission to Italy, 1917; Cttee on Health and Medical Relief, US Railroad Admin, 1918-20; Advisory Council, Nat. Health Admin., China; Director: Amer. Museum of Health 1940-; NY Post-Grad. Hosp., 1932-49; connected with work of stamping out plague, cholera, smallpox, etc., in various countries, also with building of Philippine Gen. Hosp., Coll. of Medicine and Surgery (served as Prof. of Hygiene), and many hosps throughout the Philippines; Pres. NY Soc. of Tropical Medicine, 1948. *Publications:* Sanitary Code for the City of Manila; Manual for the Bureau of Health, Manila; An American Doctor's Odyssey, 1936; You're the Doctor, 1939; Toughen Up, America!, 1941; (co-author): Handbook of Medical Treatment, 1918; Oxford System of Medicine, 1921; Practice of Medicine in the Tropics, 1922; A System of Pediatrics, 1924; A Textbook of Medicine by American Authors, 1926; Cyclopedia of Medicine, 1932; articles in medical journals, magazines and Encyclopedia Americana. *Address:* Manhattan House, 200 East 66th Street, New York, NY 10021, USA. *Clubs:* Army and Navy (Manila and Washington, DC); Century, New York Athletic (New York); The Sanctum (Litchfield).   *[Died 27 Feb. 1972.*

HELLER, Hans, MD (Cambridge), PhD, FRCP; FIBiol; Research Fellow, Department of Anatomy, University of Bristol, since 1972; Editor, Journal of Endocrinology, since 1963; *b* Brno, Czechoslovakia, 25 Sept. 1905; *s* of Dr Joseph Heller, Brno; *m* 1933, Josephine Gertrude, *d* of Dr E. Libich; two *d. Educ:* Emmanuel Coll., Cambridge; University Coll. Hosp., London. University Lecturer in Pharmacology, Vienna, 1931-34; Research Grantee, University Coll. Hosp. London, 1935-39; Beit Memorial Fellow for Medical Research, 1939-41; University of Bristol: Lecturer in Pharmacology, 1942-44, Reader, 1944-49, Prof., 1949-71 (Emeritus 1971), Dean of Faculty of Medicine, 1966-69. Visiting Professor: NY University Medical Coll., 1949; Univ. of WA, 1971-72; Visiting Scientist, US Dept of Health, Washington, DC, 1958. Pres. European Soc. for Comparative Endocrinology, 1965-69; Chm., Soc. for Endocrinology. *Publications:* papers on endocrinological subjects in Journal of Physiology, British Journal of Pharmacology, Jl of Endocrinology, etc.; Ed., The Neurohypophysis, 1957; Oxytocin, 1961; Neurosecretion, 1962; Comparative Endocrinology, 1963; Internat. Encyclopedia of Pharmacology and Therapeutics, Sect. 41, 1970. *Recreations:* travelling, numismatics. *Address:* 29 Druid Road, Bristol 9. *T:* 684152.   *[Died 29 Dec. 1974.*

HELLER, J. H. S.; *see* Heller, Hans.

HELMORE, Sir James (Reginald Carroll), KCB 1954; KCMG 1948 (CMG 1946); *b* 1 July 1906; *s* of R. M. Helmore; *m* 1930, Margaret Eleanor, *er d* of Rev. H. J. Green; no *c. Educ:* St Paul's Sch. (Scholar); New Coll. (Scholar). Entered Bd of Trade, 1929; Private Sec. to the Pres., 1934-37; Under-Sec., 1946; Second Sec. Board of Trade, 1946-52; Mem. Economic Planning Board, 1952; Permanent Sec., Min. of Materials, 1952; Permanent Sec., Min. of Supply, 1953-56; retired July 1956. Chm. of UN Interim Co-ordinating Cttee, for Internat. Commodity Arrangements, 1947-53. *Club:* Travellers'.
                                           [Died 5 March 1972.

HELSBY, Baron *cr* 1968 (Life Peer); **Laurence Norman Helsby,** GCB 1963 (CB 1950); KBE 1955; a Director: Rank Organisation, since 1968; Imperial Group, since 1968; Industrial and Commercial Finance Corporation, 1972-78; Midland Bank, since 1968; Chairman, Midland Bank Trust Co., 1970-78; *b* 27 April 1908; *s* of late Wilfred Helsby; *m* 1938, Wilmett Mary, *yr d* of late W. G. Maddison, Durham; one *s* one *d. Educ:* Sedbergh; Keble Coll., Oxford. Lecturer in Economics, University Coll. of the South West, 1930-31; Lecturer in Economics, Durham Colls in the University of Durham, 1931-45; Asst Sec., HM Treasury, 1946; Principal Private Sec. to the Prime Minister, 1947-50; Dep. Sec., Min. of Food, 1950-54; First Civil Service Commissioner, 1954-59; Permanent Sec., Min. of Labour, 1959-62; Joint Permanent Sec. to the Treasury and Head of the Home Civil Service, 1963-68; Sec., Order of the British Empire, 1963-68. Hon. Fellow, Keble Coll., Oxford, 1959; Hon. LLD Exeter, 1963; Hon. DCL Durham, 1963. *Address:* Logmore Farm, Dorking, Surrey. *Club:* United Oxford & Cambridge University.
                                           [Died 5 Dec. 1978.

HEMMING, Lt-Col Henry Harold, OBE 1948; MC 1916; Chairman, Municipal Group of Companies, 1950-76; former Chairman, Brintex Ltd; Director, Glass's Guide Service Ltd (formerly Chairman); *b* Toronto, Canada, 5 April 1893; *o s* of late H. K. S. Hemming and late Louisa Hemming (*née* McFee); *m* 1931, Alice Louisa Weaver, OBE; one *s* one *d. Educ:* Aldenham Sch., England; McGill Univ., Montreal (BA); Ecole

des Sciences Politiques, Paris. Served European War, 1914-19, in France (Major; despatches 3 times); on Sir Douglas Haig's staff at GHQ, 1918. Banking in New York, 1920-24; Vice-Pres. Harris Forbes & Co. Ltd, London Investment Bankers, 1924-31; Mem. London Stock Exchange, 1933-50. War of 1939-45: Sch. of Artillery, Larkhill, Senior Instructor at Survey Wing, Lieut-Col. Vice-Pres. Frobisher Ltd, Canada, International Mining Finance, 1950-57. Hon. Pres., Field Survey Assoc.; Member: Royal Institution; Royal Geographical Soc. Pres., McGill Soc. of GB; Liveryman of Worshipful Company of Stationers and Newspaper Makers. Freeman of City of London. *Publication:* translated the works of André Siegfried (the French economist), 1925-39. *Address:* 35 Elsworthy Road, NW3. *T:* 01-722 6619. *Clubs:* Athenæum, Little Ship, Geographical, Canada, Pilgrims, Ends of the Earth.   *[Died 1 Nov. 1976.*

HENDERSON, Ann, RSA 1973 (ARSA 1969); sculptor; Lecturer, Edinburgh College of Art; *b* Caithness, 11 Oct. 1921; *d* of George and Jessie Ann Henderson, farmers; unmarried. *Educ:* Edinburgh College of Art (DA); Ecole des Beaux Arts, Paris. *Recreations:* poetry and crofting. *Address:* 5 Learmonth Gardens Mews, Edinburgh. *T:* 031-332 4842; Balinoe Croft, Ardgay, Ross-shire. *T:* Ardgay 362.   *[Died 14 April 1976.*

HENDERSON, Sir Charles James, KBE, *cr* 1946; Hon. President British Chamber of Commerce, France, and President, 1930-31, 1934-35, 1942-45; a former Trustee and Chairman of British Charitable Fund; Member and former Chairman, Cttee of Management of the Hertford British Hospital, Paris; President, Board of Governors, British American Hospital, Nice; Director of various companies operating in France; *b* London, 9 Nov. 1882; *s* of Henry Henderson and Marie Tharp; *m* 1st, 1909, Freda Marguerite Dorothy Seerancke Archer, MBE (*d* 1964); one *s* one *d*; 2nd, 1964, Emma Lilian Nikis (Chevalier, Légion d'Honneur; Médaille Militaire), *née* Tattersall, *widow* of Mario Nikis. *Educ:* privately; City of London Sch. Mem. of London Stock Exchange, 1904-19. Served European War, France, 1914-18; Chm. British Chamber of Commerce Delegation to France, Sept. 1944; former Chm., British Legion, Paris. Freeman, City of London, 1919. Chevalier, Légion d'Honneur. *Address:* Parc Springland, Avenue de Vallauris, Cannes, AM, France. *Club:* Junior Carlton.   *[Died 31 May 1974.*

HENDERSON, Sir Ian (Leslie), KBE 1958; CMG 1952; *b* 6 July 1901; *o s* of late Lieutenant-Colonel Hugh Leslie Henderson, 1st Bn (Princess Louise's) Argyll and Sutherland Highlanders) and of Martha Saumarez (*née* Grosvenor); *m* 1927, Phyllis Mary, *o d* of late James Thornton, JP. *Educ:* Rugby Sch. (Head of Sch.); Trinity Coll., Oxford (MA). Sen. Schol., Lit. Hum. Entered HM Consular Service, 1924; served at Genoa, 1926 and 1929, Zürich, 1928, Lourenço Marques, 1930, Antwerp, 1932, being Actg Consul-Gen. at all posts. Consul, Innsbruck, 1933; Civil Observer in Sudeten-German districts of Czechoslovakia, 1938, attached to Viscount Runciman's Mission to Prague, 1938; Consul, Rosario, 1939; Chargé d'Affaires, San Salvador, 1940; Foreign Office, 1942; Counsellor (Commercial), Prague, 1946; Ambassador at Asuncion, Paraguay, 1952-53 (Minister, 1949-52); Consul-Gen., Rotterdam, 1953-54; HM Ambassador to Panama, 1954-60, retired. Coronation Medal, 1953. *Recreations:* reading, gardening. *Address:* 2 Wellswood Park, Torquay, Devon. *T:* 23777. *Club:* Travellers'.
                                           [Died 11 May 1971.

HENDERSON, James Bell, CBE 1942; retired; *b* 29 June 1883; *s* of David Henderson and Flora Falconer Bell; *m* 1917, D. N. Graham; two *s. Educ:* Dumbarton Academy; Royal Technical College, Glasgow. Joined British India Steam Navigation Co. 1904; Merchant Navy as Marine Engineer officer; joined BISN Co.'s engineers shore staff, Calcutta, 1916; Gen. Manager, 1939-42. *Recreations:* golf, billiards, fishing. *Address:* 28 Seafield Street, Cullen, Banffshire, Scotland. *Club:* St Nicholas Golf (Prestwick).   *[Died 11 Aug. 1975*

HENDERSON, Sir John, Kt 1964; DL; JP Glasgow; former Chairman, J. Henderson, Ltd, Produce Importers, Glasgow; *b* 12 July 1888; *s* of John Henderson and Ellen Shiels; *m* 1st, 1918, Nessie Brander (*d* 1971), Crosshill, Glasgow; one *s* one *d*; 2nd, 1972, Margaret Whitely, widow. *Educ:* Martyrs Sch., Glasgow Mem., Glasgow Corporation, 1926-46. Mem., Inter-Parliamentary Delegation to Finland, Israel, Austria, Western Germany, Belgium and Czechoslovakia. Magistrate and Police Judge, City of Glasgow; Chm. Scottish Unionist and Nat. Liberals' Cttee; Chm. Scottish Fact and Faith Films Soc.; House of Parliament Christian Fellowship; Pres. Internat. Council for Christian Leadership; Deacon, Incorporation of Bonnet-makers and Dyers. MP (C) Cathcart Div. of Glasgow, Feb. 1946-Sept. 1964. Distinguished Service Cross of Salvation

Army, 1969 (Founder Chm., Glasgow Adv. Bd). *Publications:* contribs to various religious periodicals. *Recreations:* President Glasgow Corporation Bowling Club; Hon. President Queen's Park Bowling and Tennis Club. *Address:* Dundrennan, 658 Clarkston Road, Netherlee, Glasgow. *T:* 041-637 4321; Strand Palace Hotel, WC2. *Club:* Conservative (Glasgow).

[Died 28 May 1975.

HENDERSON, Sir John Craik, Kt 1953; *b* 21 Dec. 1890; *s* of late Robert Jenkinson Henderson, JP, and Agnes Craik; *m* Ivie Hestor Mary, *d* of late Harry Lester Hertslet, MVO of Lord Chamberlain's Office; one *d*. *Educ:* George Watson's Coll., Edinburgh; University of Glasgow. Joined Royal Scots, 1914; commissioned, 1914, and served until 1919; Prof. of Mercantile Law at University of Glasgow, 1929-40; MP (C) for North-East Leeds, 1940-45; Mem. of Conscientious Objectors' Tribunal for South-West Scotland, 1939-40; formerly Pres. Scottish Unionist Assoc. Hon. President: Glasgow YMCA; Franco-Scottish Soc. (Glasgow and West of Scotland); Glasgow Old People's Welfare Cttee. Chm. Group considering British Parly System (Gp responsible for "Parliament-A Survey"). Legion of Honour. *Recreations:* shooting, golf. *Address:* Bridge House, Loxwood, Sussex. *T:* Loxwood 328; 190 St Vincent Street, Glasgow. *T:* 041-221 9005. *[Died 3 Oct. 1971.*

HENDERSON, Air Vice-Marshal Malcolm, CB 1942; CIE 1938; CBE 1953; DSO 1916; RAF, retired; Director General, Over-Seas League, 1946-56; *b* 1 June 1891; 2nd *s* of late Lessels Henderson and *g s* of late George Malcolm, Dundee; *m* 1918, Elizabeth, *d* of late Frederick Craig, St Columb, North Cornwall; two *s* one *d* (and one *s* killed in action over France (Dunkerque), RAF, 1940). Served War of 1914-18 with Seaforth Highlanders, RFC and RAF; seriously wounded with 18 Sqdn RFC, losing leg by direct hit from AA. Comd 47 Sqdn, 1922-25; RAF Staff Coll., 1926; IDC 1933; AOC: 14(F) Gp, 1940; 13 (F) Gp, 1942; 12 (F) Gp, 1945; retd 1946. Croix de Guerre with Palmes (France). *Address:* Beach House, Pevensey Bay, East Sussex. *[Died 7 March 1978.*

HENDERSON, Philip Prichard; author; *b* 1906; *m* 1st, 1938, Millicent Rose (marr. diss. 1947); 2nd, 1948, Belinda, *e d* of Sir Horace Hamilton, GCB; two *s*. *Educ:* Bradfield. Asst Editor, Everyman's Library, 1929-32; Fireman, National Fire Service, 1939-43; Co-Editor, British Book News, 1943-46; Editor, Feature Articles, British Council, 1958-63; Publications and Recorded Sound Dept, 1963-64. *Publications:* First Poems, 1930; A Wind in the Sand, 1932; Events in the Early Life of Anthony Price, a Novel, 1935; Literature and a Changing Civilization, 1935; The Novel Today, 1936; And Morning in His Eyes, A Book about Christopher Marlowe, 1937; The Poet and Society, 1939; Editor of: The Complete Poems of John Skelton, 1931 (4th edn 1966); Edmund Spenser's Shepherd's Calendar, and other poems, 1932; Shorter Novels: 16th-18th Century, 3 vols; George Crabbe: Poems, 1946; Emily Brontë: Poems, 1947; The Letters of William Morris, 1950; The Complete Poems of Emily Brontë, 1951; Christopher Marlowe, 1952 (new edn 1974); William Morris (Writers and Their Work: No 32), 1952 (revised edn 1969); Samuel Butler, 1953 (new edn 1967); The Life of Laurence Oliphant, 1956; Christopher Marlowe (Writers and Their Work: No 81), 1956 (revised edn 1971); Richard Cœur de Lion, 1958, new edn 1976; William Morris, His Life, Work and Friends, 1967, new edn 1973; Swinburne: the portrait of a poet, 1974; Tennyson: poet and prophet, 1978. *Address:* c/o A. M. Heath & Co. Ltd, 40-42 William IV Street, WC2N 4DD. *[Died 13 Sept. 1977.*

HENDERSON, Ralph, CB 1959; OBE 1946; Director of Stores, Admiralty, 1955-60, retired; *b* 15 Aug. 1897; *s* of James Ralph Henderson, Perth, Scotland (author, pen-name Sandy McNab); *m* 1923, Gladys Dunnett; two *s*. *Educ:* Perth Academy. Entered Civil Service, 1913. Served in Army, 1915-19, Lieut, Royal Field Artillery. Naval Store Officer, Naval Base, Singapore, 1939-42; Deputy Dir of Stores, Admiralty, 1944. French Croix de Guerre (with palm), 1918. *Recreation:* golf. *Address:* 18 Wykeham Court, Wykeham Road, Worthing, West Sussex. *T:* Worthing 203187. *[Died 10 July 1979.*

HENDERSON, Richard McNeil, CBE 1939; FInstCE; FIMechE; *b* Glasgow, 14 Jan. 1886; *s* of George Henderson and Margaret McNeil; *m* 1920, Mary Esme Woodcock, London; two *s* one *d*. *Educ:* Allan Glen's Institution; Royal Technical College, Glasgow. Entered Colonial Govt Service as Engineer, 1912; Dir of Public Works, Hong Kong, 1932; retired 1939. *Recreations:* golf, tennis, swimming, etc. *Address:* 1 Winton Drive, Edinburgh 10. *[Died 16 March 1972.*

HENDREY, Eiluned, (Mrs Graeme Hendrey); *see* Lewis, Eiluned.

HENDRY, (Alexander) Forbes, OBE 1957; MC 1940; TD 1947; DL; JP; Consultant, Russell & Aitken, WS, Edinburgh, Falkirk

and Denny; *b* 24 Oct. 1908; *s* of late Alexander Hendry, Solicitor, Denny, and Catherine Ann Forbes; *m* 1939, Margaret Whitehead; one *s* two *d*. *Educ:* Stirling High Sch.; Univ. of Glasgow (MA, LLB). Admitted Solicitor, 1932; Town Clerk of Denny and Dunipace, 1934-59. Commissioned 7th Bn The Argyll and Sutherland Highlanders (TA), 1935. Served War of 1939-45 in France, Middle East, North Africa, Sicily and North West Europe; Lt-Col 1953; TARO 1956. Chairman and Managing Dir, Cannerton Brick Co. Ltd; Chm., Cruikshank & Co. Ltd, and Dir other companies. Contested (C) Lanarkshire North, 1955. MP (C) West Aberdeenshire, 1959-66. Mem., Parliamentary Delegn to Tunisia, 1961; Vice-Chm., Anglo-Tunisian Parliamentary Group, 1965; Mem., Executive Cttee, British Branch, Inter-Parly Union, 1963-65; Chairman: W Stirlingshire Cons. Assoc., 1968; Central and Southern Area, Scottish Cons. and Unionist Assoc., 1971; Local Govt Adv. Cttee, Scottish Cons. Party, 1971; Vice-Pres., Scottish Cons. and Unionist Assoc., 1972, Pres., 1974-75. Chm., Aberlour Child Care Trust. Town Councillor, Burgh of Denny and Dunipace, 1969, Provost, 1971-74; DL Stirlingshire 1965, JP Stirlingshire 1971; Hon. Sheriff, Tayside Central and Fife, 1976. *Recreations:* trees, solving crosswords. *Address:* Braes, Dunipace, Denny, Stirlingshire. *T:* Denny 822345. *Clubs:* Caledonian (Edinburgh); County (Stirling). *[Died 18 Nov. 1980.*

HENDRY, Forbes; *see* Hendry, A. F.

HENDY, Sir Philip, Kt 1950; *b* 27 Sept. 1900; *s* of Frederick James Roberts Hendy and Caroline Isobel Potts; *m* 1st, Kythé Ogilvy; one *s* one *d*; 2nd, Cicely, *widow* of Christopher Martin. *Educ:* Westminster School; Christ Church, Oxford. Lecturer and Asst to the Keeper, The Wallace Collection, London, 1923-27; lived in Florence, Italy, 1927-30; Curator of Paintings, Museum of Fine Arts, Boston, Mass, USA, 1930-33; Dir, City Art Gallery and Temple Newsam, Leeds, 1934-45; Slade Prof. of Fine Art, Oxford Univ., 1936-46; Director, National Gallery, London, 1946-67; Adviser, Israel Museum, Jerusalem, 1968-71. President: Internat. Council of Museums, 1959-65; ICOM Foundation, 1965-70. *Publications:* Hours in the Wallace Collection, 1926; The Isabella Stewart Gardner Museum, Catalogue of Paintings and Drawings, Boston, 1931, 2nd edn 1974; Matthew Smith (Penguin Modern Painters), 1944; Giovanni Bellini, 1945; Spanish Painting, 1946; The National Gallery, London, 1955; Masaccio (Unesco), 1957; Piero della Francesca and the Early Renaissance, 1968. *Address:* Whistlers Barn, Great Haseley, Oxford. *Club:* Athenæum.

[Died 6 Sept. 1980.

HENEAGE, Lt-Col Sir Arthur Pelham, Kt 1945; DSO 1917; DL; Member, Central Advisory Water Committee, Ministry of Health; Alderman Lindsey CC; *b* 11 July 1881; *s* of late Capt F. W. Heneage, RE (*s* of late E. F. Heneage, MP for Grimsby), and Ann, *d* of late Maj.-Gen. E. C. A. Gordon, RE; *m* Anne, *d* of late Brig.-Gen. N. D. Findlay, CB, RA; two *s* two *d* (and one *s* decd). *Educ:* Eton; RM Academy, Woolwich. Joined the RFA 1900; served European War, 1914-18, on the French and Balkan Fronts as Staff Capt., Staff Officer, RA, and commanding a Field Artillery Brigade (despatches thrice); retired pay, 1924; JP parts of Lindsey; late a mem. of the Inter-allied Commission of Control in Berlin; Chm. Central and Associated Chambers of Agriculture, 1927; MP (C) Louth, 1924-45; Parliamentary Private Sec. to Minister of Transport, 1931-33, to Asst Postmaster-Gen., 1936-38; to Minister of Pensions, 1939-45; Mem. of Central Advisory Cttee to Min. of Pensions, 1939-45; Pres. Catchment and Rivers Boards Association; Chm. Cttee relating to Public Water Supply, 1939-; Gathering Grounds Sub-Cttee, 1948-; Land Drainage Sub-Cttee, 1951-; Mem. Lincolnshire River Board, 1951-. Mem. Central Advisory Water Cttee, Min. of Housing and Local Govt; late Hon. Col 529 Light AA Regt; late Hon. Col 53rd (City of London) AA Brigade (TA); late Mem. Central National Service Cttee for Great Britain; Vice-Pres. Urban District Council Association, 1925-45; Vice-Pres., Rural District Council Assoc., 1931-45; Chm. Lincs Branch CLA. DL Lincs 1936; High Sheriff of Lincs, 1947. *Recreation:* shooting. *Address:* Walesby Hall, Market Rasen, Lincs. *T:* Tealby 277. *Club:* Cavalry. *[Died 22 Nov. 1971.*

HENIG, Sir Mark, Kt 1965; Chairman: English Tourist Board, since 1969; East Midlands Gas Consumers' Council (formerly Gas Consultative Council), since 1968; Deputy Chairman, National Gas Consumers' Council, since 1973; *b* 11 Feb. 1911; *e s* of Harry and Gertrude Henig; *m* 1937, Grace (*née* Cohen); one *s* one *d*. *Educ:* Wyggeston Grammar Sch., Leicester. Mem. Leicester City Council, 1945-70, Alderman, 1958-70; High Bailiff, City of Leicester, 1965, Lord Mayor, 1967-68. Chm., Assoc. of Municipal Corporations, 1966-67. Member: Commn on the Constitution, 1969-73; Prime Minister's Cttee on Local

Govt Rules of Conduct, 1973-74; Water Space Amenity Commn, 1973-. Chm., East Midlands Economic Planning Council, 1968-71. Vice-Chm., Leicester Theatre Trust, 1973-; Governor and Exec. Mem. Council, Royal Shakespeare Theatre. Dir, ATV Network Ltd, 1975-. Hon. LLD Leicester, 1977. *Address:* 35 Stanley Road, Leicester LE2 1RF. *T:* 708425. *Club:* Reform. *[Died 30 Jan. 1979.*

HENLEY, 7th Baron (Ire.), *cr* 1799; **Michael Francis Eden; Baron Northington (UK)** *cr* 1885; *b* 13 Aug. 1914; *er s* of 6th Baron Henley and Lady Dorothy Howard (*d* 1968), 3rd *d* of 9th Earl of Carlisle; *S* father, 1962; *m* 1st, 1943, Elizabeth, *d* of Sir A. L. Hobhouse (marriage dissolved by divorce, 1947); one *d*; 2nd, 1949, Nancy (marr. diss. 1975), *d* of Stanley Walton; two *s* three *d*. *Educ:* Eton; Balliol Coll., Oxford. Served War of 1939-45: Coldstream Guards, 1940-41; Household Cavalry, 1941-46. Pres., Liberal Party, 1966-67. Chm., CPRE, 1972-. *Heir: s* Hon. Oliver Michael Robert Eden, *b* 22 Nov. 1953. *Address:* Scaleby Castle, Carlisle. *Clubs:* Brooks's, Pratt's. *[Died 20 Dec. 1977.*

HENN, Thomas Rice, CBE 1945; MA; Hon. DLitt (Dublin); Hon. LLD (Victoria); Emeritus Fellow of St Catharine's College, Cambridge; Emeritus Reader in Anglo-Irish Literature; *b* 10 Nov. 1901; 2nd *s* of Francis Blackburn Henn, Barrister-at-Law, Paradise, Ennis, Co. Clare, Ireland; *m* 1926, May Enid, *d* of E. A. Roberts, MD; one *d* (one *s* decd). *Educ:* Aldenham Sch.; St Catharine's Coll., Cambridge. Mod. Lang. Scholar of St Catharine's Coll.; Class I English Tripos, 1922; Charles Oldham Shakespeare Scholar, Members' English Prizeman, 1923. Asst, Burmah Oil Co., 1923-25; Fellow of St Catharine's Coll., 1926-69; Prælector, 1927; Tutor, 1934; Special Pro-Proctor, 1934-39; Senior Tutor, 1945-57; Pres., 1957-61, 1968-69. Gov. of Aldenham Sch. Donnellan Lecturer, TCD, 1965; Warton Lecturer, British Academy, 1965. Served War of 1939-45, The Welch Regt; 2nd Lieut 1940; Brigadier, General Staff, 1945; France and Italian Campaigns (despatches twice); Staff Coll. (War Course); US Legion of Merit. Hon. Fellow of Trumbull Coll., Yale; FRSL. Seatonian Prizeman, 1957, 1966, 1973. *Publications:* Longinus and English Criticism, 1934; The Lonely Tower, 1950; Practical Fly-Tying, 1950; The Apple and the Spectroscope, 1951; The Harvest of Tragedy, 1956; Prose for Science, 1960; Passages for Divine Reading, 1963; Synge's Plays and Poems, 1963; Poems, 1964; Rudyard Kipling, 1967; The Bible as Literature, 1970; The Living Image, 1972; The Weazel's Tooth, 1974; articles and reviews. *Recreations:* shooting, fishing, sailing. *Address:* 32 Millington Road, Cambridge. *T:* Cambridge 50176; St Catharine's College, Cambridge. *T:* Cambridge 59445. *[Died 10 Dec. 1974.*

HENNESSY, James P.; see Pope-Hennessy.

HENNIKER, 7th Baron, *cr* 1800; **John Ernest De Grey Henniker-Major; Bt** 1765; **Baron Hartismere (UK)** 1866; sits in House of Lords as Baron Hartismere; formerly Land Agent for: Lord Mostyn (N Wales); W. D. Mackenzie (Henley-on-Thames); Sir Percy Loraine, Bt and Lord Henniker (Suffolk); *b* 18 Jan. 1883; *y s* of 5th Baron Henniker and Alice Mary (*d* 1893), *o d* of 3rd Earl of Desart; *S* brother 1956; *m* 1914, Molly (*d* 1953), *d* of late Sir Robert Burnet, KCVO; two *s*. *Educ:* Radley; Royal Agricultural College, Cirencester (Hons Diploma). Page of Honour to Queen Victoria, 1895-99; served in Army and RAF, 1914-19 (French Croix de Guerre). FLAS. *Heir: s* Hon. Sir John Patrick Edward Chandos Henniker-Major. *Address:* Thornham Hall, Eye, Suffolk. *T:* Mellis 207 and 314. *[Died 9 Feb. 1980.*

HENNIKER-GOTLEY, George Rainald, CIE 1944; DSO 1918; *b* 5 Sept. 1893; *s* of Rev. George Henniker-Gotley; *m* Lorna Earle, *y d* of Stanley Dorling; one *s* one *d*. *Educ:* Sherborne Sch.; Brasenose Coll., Oxford. Served European War (DSO, despatches thrice). Indian Forest Service, 1921-47; Conservator of Forests, NW Frontier, 1939-45; Chief Conservator of Forests, Punjab, India, 1945-47. *Recreations:* fishing, gardening. *Address:* Twynax, Ford Lane, Farnham, Surrey. *T:* Farnham 3504. *Club:* United Oxford & Cambridge University. *[Died 4 Jan. 1974.*

HENNIKER-HEATON; see Heaton.

HENRIQUES, Prof. (Louis) Fernando, MA, DPhil Oxon; Professorial Fellow and Director of Centre for Multi-Racial Studies (formerly Research Unit for Study of Multi-racial Societies), University of Sussex, since 1964; *b* Kingston, Jamaica, 1916; *y s* of Cyril Charles Henriques and of Mrs Edith Emily Henriques; *m* 1948, Rosamund Ann, *e d* of late Dr F. R. Seymour, Ministry of Health, London; three *s*. *Educ:* St Aloysius Coll., London, N6; London School of Economics; Brasenose Coll., Oxford. National Fire Service, London, 1939-

42. Senior History Scholar, Brasenose Coll., 1942-45; President, Oxford Union Society, Trin. Term, 1944; Carnegie Research Fellow, 1946-47. Grad. Asst, Institute of Social Anthropology, University of Oxford, 1947-48; Lecturer in Social Anthropology, University of Leeds, 1948-64; Director of sociological research projects, sponsored by Nuffield Foundation, 1952-54; Coal Industry Social Welfare Organisation, 1954-58; DSIR, 1955-56; Sociol. Member UN Tech. Assist. Admin. Rural Electrification Survey, Ghana, 1957; Dean, Faculty of Economics and Social Studies, University of Leeds, 1960-62; Wyndham Deedes Scholar, 1963; Member Council, Institute of Race Relations, London, 1965-; Member SE Economic Planning Council, 1966-68. Ford Prof. in Comparative History, MIT, 1971. Broadcaster in Overseas Services of BBC, 1939-. *Publications:* Family and Colour in Jamaica, 1953, rev. edn, 1968; Jamaica, Land of Wood and Water, 1957; Coal is Our Life (with N. Dennis and C. Slaughter), 1956, rev. edn, 1969; Love in Action, 1959; Prostitution and Society, Vol. I, 1962, Vol. II, 1963, Vol. III, 1967; Children of Caliban, 1974. Contributions to: Handbook of Latin American Studies, 1966; Ciba Foundation Report on Immigration, 1966; Encyclopædia Britannica, 1966; English Language Editor, Library of Sexual Behaviour, 1970; Gen. Editor, Library of Race Relations, Conway Maritime Press, 1971-; various papers in sociological journals. *Recreations:* bibliomania, camping sauvage, people. *Address:* The Coach House, Beechland, Newick, Sussex. *T:* Newick 2367. *Clubs:* Athenæum, Royal Commonwealth Society, Savile, Centro Español de Londres. *[Died 26 May 1976.*

HENTY, Hon. Sir (Norman Henry) Denham, KBE 1968; Leader of the Government in the Senate, Australia, 1966-67; Minister for Supply, 1966-68; Senator for Tasmania 1950-68; Commissioner, Overseas Telecommunications, 1968-74; *b* 13 Oct. 1903; *s* of Thomas Norman and Lily Henty; *m* 1930, Faith Gordon Spotswood; two *s* one *d*. *Educ:* Launceston Church Grammar Sch. Managing Director, T. Norman Henty Pty Ltd, 1937-50. Chm., Public Works Cttee, 1955-56; Minister for Customs and Excise, 1956-64; Minister for Civil Aviation, 1964-66. Alderman, Launceston City Coun., 1943-50; Mayor, City of Launceston, 1948-49. *Recreations:* golf, billiards. *Address:* 11 Beulah Gardens, Launceston, Tasmania 7250, Australia. *T:* Launceston 2-3031. *Clubs:* Tasmanian (Hobart); Launceston, Northern (Launceston); Commercial Travellers Association (Australia). *[Died 9 May 1978.*

HEPPELL, Ralph Gordon; Administrator and Secretary, The Royal Free Hospital Group, 1947-70, retired; *b* 24 Nov. 1910; *s* of Ralph Nicol Heppell and Annie Gordon; *m* 1940, Yvonne Jean Grant; one *s* two *d*. *Educ:* Durham Sch. Dep. Clerk to Governors, Guy's Hosp., SE1, 1940-44; Superintendent-Sec., Christie Hospital, Manchester, 1944-47; Mem. of Cttee of Management of the Institute of Dental Surgery, Eastman Dental Hospital. *Publications:* various articles in hospital journals. *Recreations:* gardening, reading. *Address:* 1 Double Cottages, Loxhill-Hascombe, Surrey. *T:* Hascombe 347. *[Died 16 Sept. 1976.*

HEPWORTH, Dame Barbara, DBE 1965 (CBE 1958); Sculptor; *b* Wakefield, Yorks, 10 Jan. 1903; *d* of late H. R. Hepworth, CBE, and Gertrude A. Johnson; *m* 1st, John Skeaping, RA (marr. diss., 1933); one *s* (killed in action, RAF, 1953); 2nd, Ben Nicholson, OM (marr. diss., 1951); triplets: one *s* two *d*. *Educ:* Wakefield High Sch.; Leeds Sch. of Art; Royal Coll. of Art; Florence; Rome. A Trustee of the Tate Gallery, 1965-72. Grand Prix, 5th São Paulo Biennial, 1959. Foreign Minister's Award, Mainichi Exhibition 7th Biennial, Tokyo, 1963. Hon. ARCA 1964; Senior Fellow, RCA, 1970; Hon. Fellow, St Annes Coll., Oxford, 1968. Honorary Member: Amer. Acad. of Arts and Letters; Amer. Nat. Inst. of Arts and Letters. Hon. DLitt: Birmingham, 1960; Leeds, 1961; Exeter, 1966; Oxford, 1968; London, 1970; Manchester, 1971. Bard of Cornwall, 1968. Hon. Freeman, St Ives, 1968. International de L'Art Féminin Award, 1970. *Works:* one-man exhibition at 25th Biennale in Venice, Brit. Pavilion, 1950; *retrospective exhibitions:* Whitechapel Art Gall., 1954 and 1962; also in Paris, Amsterdam, Brussels, New York, Philadelphia, Chicago, (touring) Scandinavia, 1964-65, Rijksmuseum, Kröller-Müller, Holland, 1965, etc; Battersea Park Sculpture Exhibns, 1949, 1951, 1960, 1963, 1966 and in Holland Park, 1954, 1957; (2 sculptures) Festival of Britain 1951; Tate Gallery, 1968; Hakone, Kyoto and Osaka, 1970; also *out-door* Sculpture exhibitions in Europe and USA. Permanent London Gallery, Marlborough Fine Art Ltd. *Works in permanent collections:* in London: Tate Gallery; Arts Council of Gt Britain; British Council; LCC; Victoria and Albert Museum; in USA; United Nations, New York; Museums of Modern Art, New York, Albright Gallery, Buffalo; Smith Coll. Museum; Yale Univ., Museum, and Steinberg Hall at Washington Univ.; in Scottish National Gallery of Modern Art, Edinburgh;

National Galleries of Canada, Australia and New Zealand; Museum of Modern Art, São Paulo, Brazil; Mus. of Fine Art, Valparaiso, Chile; Museo de Bellas Artes, Caracas; Middelheimpark, Antwerp, Belgium; Gemeentemuseum, The Hague, and Rijksmuseum, Kröller-Müller, Holland; Dag Hammarskjöld Museum, Backakra, Sweden; Carlsberg Foundation, Denmark; The Marie-Louise and Gunnar Didrichsen Art Foundation, Helsinki, Finland; The Israel Museum, Jerusalem; The Ulster Museum, Belfast; Ferens Art Gallery, Hull; Glynn Vivian Art Gall., Swansea; Leeds, Manchester, Wakefield, Bristol, Birmingham and Aberdeen City Art Galleries; Hakone and Kyoto, Japan; also Herts CC and Harlow and St Ives (Cornwall) Borough Councils. *Films:* film on her sculpture produced by British Film Institute, 1953; (BBC TV) 'Barbara Hepworth' (commentary by Barbara Hepworth and Bernard Miles), 1961; Westward Television Colour Film, 1967. *Publications:* 'Barbara Hepworth' Ariel Series, foreword William Gibson, 1946; 'Barbara Hepworth' Carvings and Drawings, foreword Herbert Read, 1952; Monograph 'Barbara Hepworth' Europäische Bildhauer, Allert de Lange, Amsterdam, 1958; 'Barbara Hepworth', foreword J. P. Hodin, 1961 (Edn Griffon, Neuchâtel); 'Barbara Hepworth' (monograph) Art in Progress Series, text by Michael Shepherd, 1962; 'Barbara Hepworth-Drawings from a Sculptor's Landscape', by Alan Bowness, 1966; Barbara Hepworth (Monograph), World of Art Series, text by Prof. A. M. Hammacher, 1968; The Pictorial Autobiography of Barbara Hepworth, 1970; The Complete Sculpture of Barbara Hepworth 1960-69, ed by Alan Bowness, 1971. *Recreations:* music, reading, gardening. *Address:* Trewyn Studio, St Ives, Cornwall. *T:* St Ives 6226.   [*Died 20 May 1975.*

HERBAGE, Julian Livingston-; musicologist, writer, broadcaster; *b* Woking, 10 Sept. 1904; *yr s* of late Walter Herbage and late Ruth Ann Livingston; *m* 1944, Anna (OBE 1966; Hon. ARAM 1967), *d* of late Sir Samuel Instone. *Educ:* Royal Naval Coll., Osborne and Dartmouth; St John's Coll., Cambridge (Choral Student). Arranged and conducted Love in a Village, Everyman Theatre, 1923; Conductor and Composer of incidental music, Savoy Theatre, 1924; Liverpool Repertory Theatre, 1925; joined BBC 1927; edited and conducted revivals of Operas, Cantatas, and Masques by Purcell, Arne, Handel, etc; organised Foundations of Music programmes, including From Plainsong to Purcell with Sir Richard Terry, Bach Celebration with Dr Sanford Terry, Handel and Scarlatti Celebrations with Prof. E. J. Dent; edited Purcell's King Arthur for performance at Queen's Hall, 1935; Asst Dir of Music, British Broadcasting Corporation, 1940-44; resigned from BBC, 1946; edited Handel's Messiah for special bicentenary broadcast, 1942; Chm. Henry Wood Concert Society, 1959-61. Editor, with Anna Instone, BBC radio programme, Music Magazine since inception, 1944-73. *Publications:* Arne's "Comus" (Musica britannica); Perseus and Andromeda (Operatic Masque after Handel); Suite from Purcell's King Arthur; Arne's Overture in B flat; The Humours of Bath (Suite); songs and instrumental pieces. *Books:* Messiah; Arnold Bax (Penguin British Music of our Time); Sibelius (Penguin Symphony series); Handel's Oratorios (Handel Symposium); The Baroque Era; contributions on musical subjects to various journals. *Address:* 8 Treborough House, Nottingham Place, W1.   [*Died 15 Jan. 1976.*

HERBERT, Sir Alan Patrick, CH 1970; Kt 1945; author and barrister-at-law; Staff of Punch (A.P.H.); *b* 24 Sept. 1890; *e s* of P. H. Herbert, India Office, and Beatrice Selwyn; *m* 1914, Gwendolen, 2nd *d* of late Harry Quilter; one *s* three *d*. *Educ:* Winchester (Exhibitioner); New Coll., Oxford (Exhibitioner); 1st Class, Jurisprudence, 1914. Served with Royal Naval Division (Hawke Batt.), 1914-17; Gallipoli Peninsula (despatches); France (wounded); called to Bar, Inner Temple, 1918, but never practised; for two years Private Sec. to Sir Leslie Scott, KC, MP; began writing for Punch, 1910, joined Staff, 1924; represented Punch at Third Imperial Press Conference, Melbourne, Australia, 1925; MP (Ind.) Oxford Univ., 1935-50, when Univ. seats abolished; introduced in House of Commons in 1937 a Marriage Bill, passed into law as the Matrimonial Causes Act, 1937. Served with River Emergency Service, Thames, London, from 3 Sept. 1939, and joined Naval Auxiliary Patrol, June 1940, Petty Officer-two good conduct badges; a Thames Conservator, 1940; Trustee National Maritime Museum, 1947-53. President: London Corinthian Sailing Club; Black Lion Skittles Club; Inland Waterways Assoc.; Soc. of Authors; Chm., British Copyright Council. Freeman of Hammersmith, 1969. Hon. Doctor of Laws, Queen's Univ., Kingston, Ont, 1957; DCL Oxford, 1958. *Publications:* The Bomber Gipsy; The Secret Battle; The House-by-the-River, Light Articles Only; The Wherefore and the Why; Tinker, Tailor...; The Man About Town; The Old Flame; Laughing Ann; She Shanties; Riverside Nights; Plain Jane; Misleading Cases; The Trials of Topsy;

Topsy, MP; Honeybubble & Co.; La Vie Parisienne (adaptation); The Water Gipsies; More Misleading Cases; Ballads for Broadbrows; No Boats on the River, 1932; Still More Misleading Cases, 1933; Holy Deadlock, 1934; What a Word, 1935; Uncommon Law, 1935; Mild and Bitter, 1936; The Ayes Have It, 1937; Sip!, Swallow!, 1937; General Cargo, 1939; Siren Song, 1940; Let us be Glum, 1941; Well, Anyhow..., 1942; Bring Back The Bells, 1943; A Better Sky, Less Nonsense, 1944; Light the Lights, The Battle of the Thames, 1945; The Point of Parliament, 1946; Topsy Turvy, 1947; Mr Gay's London, 1948; A Book of Ballads; Topsy Omnibus, 1949; Independent Member, 1950; Number Nine, Come to the Ball (with Reginald Arkell), 1951; Full Enjoyment, Codd's Last Case, Why Waterloo?, 1952; Pools Pilot, 1953; The Right to Marry, 1954; No Fine on Fun, 1957; Made for Man, 1958; Look Back and Laugh (selection), 1960; Silver Stream, 1962; Bardot MP? And Other Modern Misleading Cases, 1964; Watch This Space, 1964; The Thames, 1966; Wigs at Work, 1966; Sundials or Fun with the Sun, 1967; The Singing Swan, 1968; In the Dark, 1969; A.P.H.: his life and times, 1970. *stage:* Two Gentlemen of Soho; *musical plays:* King of the Castle (with William Armstrong), Fat King Melon (for children), Riverside Nights (with Nigel Playfair); Plain Jane, the Blue Peter, Perseverance, Policeman's Serenade (one act); La Vie Parisienne, Tantivy Towers, Helen, Derby Day, Mother of Pearl, Paganini (with Reginald Arkell), Big Ben, Bless The Bride, Tough at the Top, The Water Gipsies; Streamline (with Ronald Jeans), Home and Beauty (Cochran revues). *Recreations:* sailing, lawn tennis, the piano, skittles, etc. *Address:* 12 Hammersmith Terrace, Hammersmith, W6. *T:* 01-748 1627. *Clubs:* Savage, Beefsteak, Grillions.
[*Died 11 Nov. 1971.*

HERBERT, Desmond Andrew, CMG 1966; DSc; Emeritus Professor of Botany, University of Queensland; *b* 17 June 1898; *s* of Andrew Herbert; *m* 1922, Vera McNeilance Prowse; two *s* two *d*. *Educ:* Melbourne C of E Grammar Sch.; University of Melbourne. BSc 1918; MSc 1920; DSc 1931. Govt Botanist, W Australia, 1919-21; Prof. of Plant Physiology, University of Philippines, 1921-24; University of Queensland: Lectr in Botany, 1924-40; Associate Prof. of Botany, 1941-50; Dean, Faculty of Science, 1950-63; Prof. of Botany, 1950-65; Emer. Prof., 1966. Pres. of various learned societies. *Publications:* Gardening in Warm Climates, 1952; numerous papers in scientific jls. *Recreation:* horticulture. *Address:* 47 Adamson Street, Wooloowin, Qld 4030, Australia. *T:* Brisbane 62-3975.
[*Died 8 Sept. 1976.*

HERBERT, Edwin Savory; *see* Tangley, Baron.

HERBERT, His Honour Jesse Basil, MC 1918; QC 1949; a Judge of the County Courts, Circuit 44, Westminster, 1959-71 (34, Brentford etc, 1958-59, 58 and 41, Southend etc., 1957-58); *b* 17 March 1899; *s* of late Sir Jesse Herbert; *m* 1922, Hon. Isabella Russell Rea, *er d* of 1st Baron Rea; two *d*. *Educ:* Westminster; Christ Church, Oxford. Served in Flanders, 1918; Private Sec. to Rt Hon. H. H. Asquith, 1923-25; called to Bar, 1922; Master of the Bench of the Inner Temple, 1957. *Address:* 2 Crown Office Row, Temple, EC4. *T:* 01-583 5144. *Club:* Garrick.
[*Died 19 Sept. 1972.*

HERBERT, Roscoe, CB 1952; CMG 1944; *b* 1895; *s* of late James Herbert; *m* Lillie May, *er d* of late Elisha Steward, Wolverhampton; one *s* one *d*. *Educ:* Wolverhampton Sch. Called to Bar, Middle Temple, 1930; entered Civil Service, 1913; Chief British Economic Adviser, North African Economic Board, French North Africa, 1942-43; Asst Dep. Dir-Gen. UNRRA, 1944-46; Under-Sec., Ministry of Food, 1947-54; Dep. Sec., Ministry of Food, 1954-55; Gen. Manager, Potato Marketing Bd, 1955-60. Mem., Agricultural Market Develt Cttee, 1962-73. *Address:* Downside, Tennyson's Lane, Haslemere, Surrey. *T:* Haslemere 2663.
[*Died 6 Nov. 1975.*

HERBERT, Walter Elmes, FDS, RCS 1948; FRSM; Professor of Dental Surgery, University of London, 1938-67, now Emeritus; Director of Department of Conservative Dental Surgery, Guy's Hospital Dental School, 1931-67; Lecturer in Operative Dental Surgery, 1933-67; *b* Sept. 1902; *s* of H. W. Herbert, Egham, Surrey; *m* 1933, Joyce Mary Griffith Clogg, MB, BS; one *s* one *d*. *Educ:* Queen' Coll., Taunton; Guy's Hospital Medical and Dental Schools (travelling Dental Scholar, 1928); North Western Univ., Chicago. LDS RCS 1925; MRCS, LRCP 1928. Demonstrator in Operative Dental Surgery, Guy's Hospital, 1929-31; Univ. Reader in Conservative Dental Surgery, 1933-38. Vis. Prof. of Dentistry, Sch. of Dentistry, Nat. Univ. of Iran, Tehran, 1969-70. *Publications:* Operative Dental Surgery (with J. B. Parfitt), 4th edn 1939—7th edn 1955, (with W. A. Vale), 8th edn, 1962; Cancer of Stomach, in London, in Stockholm and in Amsterdam (jointly) Guy's Hospital Reports, 1939; The

Training of the Dental Surgeon, 1962; and various contributions to British Dental Journal. *Recreations:* mountaineering, gardening. *Address:* Half Acre, 58 Kingswood Firs, Grayshott, Hindhead, Surrey GU26 6ER. *T:* Hindhead 4563. *Club:* Alpine.
[Died 19 Oct. 1980.

HERBERTSON, James John William, MVO 4th class 1943; OBE 1918; Officer of Order of Orange Nassau, 1949; MA Oxon; *b* 29 Dec. 1883; *s* of James Grozier Herbertson, Glasgow; *m* 1919, Lilian, *d* of A. Rawlinson Wood, Denstone Coll.; two *d.* *Educ:* St Albans Sch.; Jesus Coll., Oxford. European War, HAC 1st Bn, 1914; Capt. 1918, GSO3 IV Army; Political Officer Inter-allied Rhineland High Commission, 1919-29; Acting British High Commissioner, 1929-30. Air Ministry and Ministry of Civil Aviation, 1937-50; retired, 1950. *Address:* 7 Westbourne Mansions, Sandgate Road, Folkestone, Kent. *T:* 53054.
[Died 23 Aug. 1974.

HERCUS, Sir Charles Ernest, Kt 1947; DSO 1918; OBE 1919; FRCP; FRACP; fRACS; retired 1958, as Dean of the Medical Faculty, University of Otago, New Zealand; Professor of Bacteriology and Public Health, 1922-58, Emeritus Professor since 1959; *b* 13 June 1888; *s* of Peter and Jane Hercus; *m* 1923; two *s* one *d. Educ:* Christchurch Boys' High Sch.; Otago Univ. Qualified in Dentistry and Medicine. Served European War, 1914-18, in the Field throughout, and overseas, War of 1939-45, in NZ TA, as OC Otago Univ. Medical Corps. *Publications:* The Otago Medical School under the First three Deans, 1963; numerous in medical journals. *Recreation:* tennis. *Address:* 19 Wallace Street, Dunedin, NZ. *T:* 20451. *Clubs:* University, Otago (Dunedin).
[Died 26 March 1971.

HERD, Harold; author and journalist; *b* 1893; *m* 1923, Kate (*d* 1973), *y d* of late John Lancaster, Skipton; one *d.* Began journalistic career as a reporter on the West Yorkshire Pioneer; was successively Editor of the Flintshire News, Editor and Manager of the Flintshire Observer. Asst Editor of Mayfair, Editor of the Magazine of To-day, and Editor of To-day and To-morrow. Founded The Regent Institute (Principal, 1919-67); edited the Fleet Street Annual, 1930-59; contributed extensively to daily and weekly Press. Served in the Cheshire Regt, etc., 1915-18. *Publications:* The Making of Modern Journalism, 1927; The Newspaper of Tomorrow, 1930; Press Days, 1936; Panorama 1900-1942, 1942; Roman Road (play), 1945; The March of Journalism (a history of the British Press), 1952; Seven Editors, 1955; A Press Gallery, 1958, etc. Edited, the English Collection, the Writer's Library, the Outline Series, and various anthologies. *Address:* 79 Westbourne Terrace, W2 6QS. *T:* 01-262 9375.
[Died 26 May 1976.

HERITAGE, Stanley James; Under Secretary, Chairman, Yorkshire and Humberside Economic Planning Board, and Regional Director for Yorkshire and Humberside, Departments of the Environment and Transport, since 1977; *s* of late Albert Charles Heritage and Lizzie Victoria Heritage. *Educ:* Wallington High Sch. Ministry of Public Building and Works: Middle East Reg., 1965; HQ, 1967; Reg. Dir, Far East Reg., 1971; Reg. Planning Controller, NW Reg., DoE, 1972; Dir, NW Reg., PSA, 1974. *Recreation:* music. *Address:* 17 Woodville Court, Old Park Road, Roundhay, Leeds LS8 1JA. *T:* Leeds 662730. *Clubs:* Civil Service; Leeds (Leeds).
[Died 20 April 1980.

HERKLOTS, Rev. Hugh Gerard Gibson, MA, DD; Moderator of the Church Colleges of Education, 1959-67; Residentiary Canon of Peterborough, since 1959; *b* Sikandra, India, 5 Sept. 1903; *s* of late Rev. Bernard Herklots, MA, and late Emily Frances Bazeley; *m* 1930, Helen Beveridge, *d* of late Professor Murgoci, Bucarest; two *s* two *d. Educ:* Trent Coll., Derbyshire; Ordination Test Sch., Knutsford; Trinity Hall and Ridley Hall, Cambridge. MA (Cantab) 1929. Editor of the Granta, 1925-26; President Cambridge Union Society, 1926; Curate of Holy Trinity, St Marylebone, 1927-30; Canon of St John's Cathedral, Winnipeg; Professor of Exegetical Theology in St John's Coll., 1930-36; Member of the Council of the University of Manitoba, 1933-36; Member of the General Synod of the Church of England in Canada, 1934; Rector of Flixton near Manchester, 1936-41; Commissary to Archbishop of Rupert's Land, 1936; Youth Secretary, British Council of Churches, 1942-45; Director of Religious Education, Diocese of Sheffield, 1945-51; Vicar of Doncaster, 1951-59; Hon. Canon of Sheffield, 1945-59; Examining Chaplain to the Bishop of Manchester, 1938-41; Select Preacher, Cambridge University, 1943, 1955; Member, Youth Advisory Council (Board of Education), 1942-45; Archbishops' Evangelistic Commission, 1944; Associate of the Sheffield Society of Artists, 1951; Delegate to Second Assembly of World Council of Churches, 1954; Member Commission for Revision of Catechism, 1958. Hon. DD, St John's Coll.,

Manitoba, 1967. *Publications:* Jack of All Trades, 1926; The New Universities, 1928; Hospital Sketches (edited), 1929; Paper Aeroplanes, 1931; Not as the Scribes, 1934; The First Winter, 1935; The Yoke of Christ, 1938; Hear our Prayer, 1940; For Such a Time as This, 1945; Philippians (Devotional Commentary), 1946; These Denominations, Grant us Thy Salvation, 1946; Pilgrimage to Amsterdam, 1947; Nathan Söderblom, 1948; Amsterdam 1948, 1948; A Fresh Approach to the New Testament, 1950; Magnificent Heritage, 1950; The Hope of our Calling, 1954; How Our Bible Came to Us, 1954; Publicans and Sinners, 1956; Operation Firm Faith, 1957; The Ten Commandments and Modern Man, 1958; The Gospel in a World of Conflict, 1960; Frontiers of the Church, 1961; The Call of God, 1962; Behind the New Testament, 1962; The Church of England and the American Episcopal Church, 1966; The People of God, 1968; An Old Testament Dozen, 1970. *Recreations:* reading, writing, painting. *Address:* Canonry House, 14 Minster Precincts, Peterborough. *T:* 62125. *Club:* Athenæum.
[Died 17 May 1971.

HERON, (Cuthbert) George; His Honour Judge Heron; a Circuit Judge, since 1974; *b* 8 April 1911; *s* of late Lieut-Commander George Heron, RN, and late Kate Heron; *m* 1937, Maud Mary Josephine Hogan; one *s* one *d. Educ:* St Bede's Coll., Manchester; Manchester Univ. (LLB). Solicitor, 1934; called to Bar, Middle Temple, 1944; Oxford Circuit; Recorder of Lichfield, 1968-71; Hon. Recorder, 1972-; a Recorder of Crown Court, 1972-74. Served RAF, 1939-45 (Flt-Lieutenant). *Recreations:* reading, motoring, foreign travel. *Address:* 160 Wake Green Road, Moseley, Birmingham B13 9QD. *T:* 021-777 1960; Lamb Building, Temple, EC4. *Clubs:* Union, Worcestershire (Worcester).
[Died 27 Nov. 1979.

HERRING, Robert; *b* London, 13 May 1903; *y s* of Arthur Herring and Clara Helena Williams. *Educ:* Clifton Coll.; King's Coll., Cambridge. MA (Cantab), 1928, History and 2nd Class Hons English; Asst Editor, The London Mercury, 1925-34; film critic on The Manchester Guardian, 1928-38; incorporated The London Mercury in Life and Letters, 1938; Editor, Life and Letters, 1935-50. *Publications:* The President's Hat (travel), 1926; Films of the Year, 1928; Adam and Evelyn at Kew (novel), 1930; Cactus Coast; The Impecunious Captain (play), 1944; Westward Look (poems), 1946; The Life and Death of St George; edited Plays of Sheridan and of Goldsmith in English Literature Series, 1927-34; (Jt) Leaves in the Storm, 1948; Happy Days and Holidays, 1949. *Recreation:* old age. *Address:* 7(W), Chelsea Embankment, SW3.
[Died 4 Nov. 1975.

HERRINGTON, Hugh Geoffrey, CBE 1954; *b* 28 Sept. 1900; *s* of Hugh William Herrington; *m* 1926, Olive, *d* of James Procter. *Educ:* Bablake Sch., Coventry, Warwickshire. Man. Dir, 1950-66, Dep. Chm., 1966-70, High Duty Alloys; Dir, Aluminium Wire & Cable Co., 1948-70; Dir, Hawker Siddeley, 1957-70. FRAES. *Address:* Two Wells, Skittle Green, Bledlow, Bucks. *T:* Princes Risborough 4534.
[Died 22 July 1980.

HERRON, Hon. Sir Leslie James, KBE 1966; CMG 1964; Lieutenant-Governor of New South Wales and its dependencies, since 1972; *b* 22 May 1902; *s* of Henry Herron; *m* 1930, Andree L., *d* of late F. Leverrier, KC; one *d. Educ:* Sydney Grammar Sch.; University of Sydney. Admitted Bar, 1925; KC 1939. Acting Judge, 1939; Judge of Supreme Court, 1941; Acting Chief Justice, March-Oct. 1962; Chief Justice of the Supreme Court of NSW, 1962-72. Trustee: Australian Museum; Sydney Cricket Ground. President: NSW Div., St John Ambulance Assoc.; Australian Golf Club. KStJ 1964. *Recreation:* golf. *Address:* Mevagissey, 6 Mannerin Place, Castle Cove, NSW 2069, Australia. *T:* 403286. *Clubs:* Australian, Australian Jockey (Sydney); Royal Automobile of Australia.
[Died 3 May 1973.

HESKETH, Air Vice-Marshal Allan, CB 1946; CBE 1944; (OBE 1941); DFC; Royal Air Force, retired; AOC No 3 Group, Bomber Command, 1949; AOC No 23 Group, Flying Training Command, 1951-52; Air Vice-Marshal, 1949; AOA Flying Training Command, 1952-54; retired, 1954. *Address:* c/o Lloyds Bank Ltd, Cox's and King's Branch, 6 Pall Mall, SW1.
[Died 9 March 1973.

HESLOP, Air Vice-Marshal Herbert William, CB 1946; OBE; CEng; MFRAeS, MIEI; RAF, retired; *b* 29 Oct. 1898; *m* 1937, Phyllis Bletsoe, *d* of H. Brown, Sywell House, Sywell; two *s. Educ:* Durham School. Cadet RFC 1917; commissioned RFC 1917; 20 Squadron, France, 1918; 28 Squadron, India, 1919; instructor on engineering duties, Halton, 1923; Long engineering course, Henlow, 1924; chief engineer officer, Armament and Gunnery School, Eastchurch, 1925; Royal Canadian Air Force, Canada, on exchange engineering duties,

1927-29; 24 Communication Sqdn, Northolt, 1929; Squadron Leader 1933; chief engineer officer, Cranwell, 1933; chief RAF engineer officer, HMS Glorious, 1935; Wing Commander 1937; employed Directorate of Research and Development, 1937; head of RDA4 branch AMRD, Air Ministry; British Purchasing Commission, New York and Washington, 1940; Group Captain 1940; Flying Training Command HQ for engineer duties, 1943; Command Engineer Officer, 1943; Air Commodore 1943; Director Aeronautical Inspection Service, Air Ministry, 1947-51; Senior Technical Staff Officer, Bomber Command, 1951-52; Senior Technical Staff Officer, Middle East Air Force, 1952-54; Air Vice-Marshal, 1953; retired 1955. *Address:* High Barn, Pound Lane, Sonning, Berks. *T:* Reading 693150. *Club:* Royal Air Force.   *[Died 27 Dec. 1976.*

HESS, Prof. Walter Rudolf; Emeritus Professor (Professor of Physiology and Director of the Physiological Department, University of Zürich, 1917-51); *b* 17 March 1881; *s* of Prof. Dr Clemenz Hess, Switzerland, and Gertrud (*née* Fischer Saxon); *m* 1909, Luise Sandmeyer; one *s* one *d. Educ:* Gymnasium at Frauenfeld (Thurgau), Switzerland. Medical studies, 1900-05, at the Universities of Lausanne, Berne, Berlin, Kiel, Zürich. Postgraduate: Asst at Dept of Surgery and of Ophthalmology, 1905-08; MD Zürich 1906. Practitioner: oculist, 1908-12; Asst and lecturer in Physiol. at Zürich and Bonn, 1913-17. Retired, 1951. Dr hc: Philosophy, Berne, 1933; Medicine, Geneva, 1944; Science, McGill Univ., Montreal, 1953; Medicine, Freiburg (Br). Hon. member of different societies of Physiol., Ophthalm. and Neurol. Hon. and corresponding Member of different Academies. Ludwigmedaille der deutschen Gesellschaft für Kreislaufforschung, 1938; Marcel Benoist Prize, 1933; Nobel Prize, 1949; Johannes Müller Medal, 1971. *Publications:* Monographs: Die Regulierung d. Blutkreislaufes, 1930; Die Regulierung d. Atmung, 1931; Die Methodik d. lokalisierten Reizung subkortikaler Hirnabschnitte, 1932; Das Zwischenhirn u. d. Regulation v. Kreislauf u. Atmung, 1938; Vegetative Funktionen u. Zwischenhirn, 1949; Die funktionelle Organisation d. vegetat. Nervensystems, 1948; Das Zwischenhirn, 1949; Diencephalon, 1954; Hypothalamus and Thalamus, 1956, 2nd edn 1968; The functional organisation of the Diencephalon, 1957; Psychologie in biologischer Sicht, 1962, 2nd edn, 1968. *Recreations:* taking care of the garden, fruit trees and vineyards. *Address:* Via Gabbio 6, 6612 Ascona, Switzerland. *T:* 093/25406.   *[Died 12 Aug. 1973.*

HEWAT, Aubrey Middleton, MD, ChB (Edinburgh), DPH, RCP and SE; late Principal Medical Officer, Public Health Department, LCC; *b* 17 Sept. 1884; *er s* of late Richard G. Hewat, Edinburgh, and late Harriet Aitken Middleton; *m* 1912, Mary Victoria (*d* 1969), *e d* of late E. H. Claye, Derby; five *s. Educ:* Fettes Coll., Edinburgh; Edinburgh Univ. Research Scholar, Royal Victoria Hospital for Consumption, Edinburgh; Resident Medical Officer, Edinburgh Maternity Hospital; Asst Medical Officer of Health, Derby and East Suffolk; Tuberculosis Officer, Preston, Lancs; Medical Officer of Health, Borough of Nuneaton and Metropolitan Borough of Fulham; Fellow of Society of Medical Officers of Health and of Royal Institute of Public Health and Hygiene; Capt. RAMC (retired). *Publications:* Annual Reports on State of Health of Nuneaton (1919-21) and Fulham (1922-25); numerous papers on public health subjects. *Recreation:* gardening. *Address:* Botfield Nursing Home, Glyne Ascent, Bexhill, East Sussex. *T:* Bexhill 212857. *Club:* Cooden Beach Golf.   *[Died 6 Nov. 1976.*

HEWER, Prof. Humphrey Robert, CBE 1971 (OBE 1959); Professor of Zoology, Imperial College, University of London, 1964-70, now Emeritus Professor; *b* 16 Aug. 1903; *s* of Basil Hewer and Annie Elizabeth (Hargroves); *m* 1927, Olive Mary La Trobe Stooke; two *d. Educ:* Fulneck Sch.; Imperial Coll. Lectr in Zoology, Imperial Coll., 1926-37; Asst Prof. and Reader in Zoology, Imperial Coll., 1937-64. Chief Rodent Officer, Min. of Food, 1941-45. Chairman: Adv. Cttee, Infestation Control Laboratory, Min. of Agric. Fish. and Food, 1965-; Farm animal Welfare Adv. Cttee, Min. of Agric. Fish and Food, 1967-. *Publications:* British Seals, 1973; various scientific publications in Proc. and Trans Royal Society London, J. Zool. Linn. Soc. London; Proc. Zool Soc. London, etc. *Recreations:* reading, natural history. *Address:* 6 Armstrong Close, Brockenhurst, Hants. *T:* Brockenhurst 2375.   *[Died 23 Feb. 1974.*

HEWITSON, Captain Mark; retired as National Industrial Officer of General and Municipal Workers' Union, Oct. 1964; *b* 1897; *m* Gwynneth, *d* of James Wicks, Sunningwell. Served Northumberland Fus and West Yorks 1916-20, and in Pioneer Corps, 1940-42. Member Durham CC, 1930-40; Pres., Public and Civil Service International, 1937-40; Pres., General Factory Workers International, 1945-50. MP (Lab) Hull Central, 1945-55, Hull West, 1955-64. Past Member Nat. Exec. Cttee, Labour

Party, *Address:* 57 Sunningwell Village, near Abingdon, Berks.
                                                    [Died 27 Feb. 1973.

HEWITT, Lieut-Col Dudley Riddiford, CIE 1919; retired Indian Army; *b* 1877; 2nd *s* of late Capt. James Dudley Ryder Hewitt, RN; *m* 1913, Marjorie Middlemas (*d* 1954), 2nd *d* of late William Fleming Inglis, Shanghai; two *d. Educ:* Wanganui, New Zealand. Served with 4th New Zealand Regt, South African War, 1900; E Lancs. Regt 1900-02; Indian Army, 1902-28 (17th Cavalry, 1902-05; Remount Depart, 1905-28). *Address:* The Old Rectory, West Stow, Bury St Edmunds, Suffolk.
                                                    [Died 19 Nov. 1971.

HEWITT, Sir Edgar R. L.; see Ludlow-Hewitt.

HEWITT, Admiral Henry Kent, Hon. KCB; retired; *b* Hackensack, New Jersey, 11 Feb. 1887; *s* of Robert Anderson Hewitt and Mary Kent; *m* 1913, Floride Louise Hunt; two *d. Educ:* US Naval Academy (graduated 1906); Naval War Coll., 1928-29; Served European war, 1917-18; Capt. 1932; Rear-Adm. 1940; Vice-Adm. 1942; Adm. 1945. Commanded: Amphibious Force, Atlantic Fleet, 1942; landings in Morocco, 1942; US Naval Forces in North-West African Waters (US Eighth Fleet), Feb. 1943; American half of the invasion of Sicily, July 1943; Allied Forces which effected landing at Salerno, 1943; Allied Forces, which on 15 Aug. 1944, established the Seventh Army on shore in Southern France; US Twelfth Fleet (Naval Forces in Europe), 1945-46; US Naval Rep., UN Military Staff Cttee, 1946-49. Navy Cross with gold star, Navy DSM with gold star, Army DSM and Oak Leaf Cluster, Grand Officer Legion of Honour, France, Order of Leopold, Belgium, Order of Orange-Nassau, Holland, and many other decorations. *Recreations:* walking, riding. *Address:* Foretop, Orwell, Vermont 05760, USA. *Clubs:* Army Navy (Washington, DC); University, Century (NY City).   *[Died 15 Sept. 1972.*

HEWITT, Sir John (Francis), KCVO 1971; CBE 1964; Trustee: Chevening Estate (Deputy Chairman); Dorneywood Trust; Attlee Memorial Foundation; Member, London Advisory Board, Norwich Union Insurance Group; *b* 12 Nov. 1910; *o s* of late Rev. John Francis Hewitt, MA and of late Frances Hilda Hewitt, BLitt; *m* 1938, Betty Mida Pantin Dale-Glossop, *o d* of late Lieut-Col H. Dale-Glossop, MBE, and of Mrs T. E. Carew-Hunt; one *s* one *d. Educ:* St Lawrence Coll., Ramsgate and privately. London Stock Exchange, 1928; joined Board of Trade, 1941; Imperial Defence Coll., 1947; Board of Trade, 1948-57; HM Customs and Excise (International Div.), 1957-61; Secretary for Appointments to the Prime Minister, 1961-73, and Ecclesiastical Secretary to the Lord Chancellor, 1965-73. Chm., Ellison House (Probation Hostel) Camberwell, 1961-73. Vice-Pres., Age Action Year, 1976; Governor, St Michael's Sch., Limpsfield. *Address:* Wellow House, Wellow, Bath, Avon. *T:* Combe Down 832314. *Club:* Travellers'. *[Died 19 Nov. 1979.*

HEWITT, Sir Joseph, 2nd Bt, *cr* 1921; Major RA; *b* 8 Sept. 1907; *s* of 1st Bt and Margaret Eliza (*d* 1950), *d* of George Guest of Barnsley; *S* father, 1923; *m* 1940, Marguerite, *yr d* of Charles Burgess; two *s* one *d. Educ:* Uppingham Sch. *Recreation:* gardening. *Heir: s* Nicholas Charles Joseph Hewitt [*b* 12 Nov. 1947; *m* 1969, Pamela Margaret, *o d* of Geoffrey Hunt, Scalby; one *s*]. *Address:* Lebberston Hall, near Scarborough, Yorks. *T:* Cayton 271.   *[Died 1 Oct. 1973.*

HEWLETT, Baron *cr* 1972 (Life Peer), of Swettenham; **Thomas Clyde Hewlett,** Kt 1964; CBE 1959; MA; MIEx; Chairman since 1971, Managing Director since 1965, Anchor Chemical Co. Ltd (Export Director, 1950-61; Joint Managing Director, 1961-65; Deputy Chairman, 1968-71), and Chairman of subsidiary Cos; Chairman: Borg Warner Chemicals UK Ltd, since 1970; Burco Dean Ltd, since 1975; Chairman, North West Industrialists' Council, since 1971; *b* 4 Aug. 1923; *s* of late Thomas Henry Hewlett, JP (MP, Manchester Exchange, 1940-45); *m* 1949, Millicent, *d* of Sir John (William) Taylor, KBE, CMG; two *s. Educ:* Clifton; Magdalene Coll., Cambridge. Served War of 1939-45, Royal Marines (Lieut). BA 1948 (2nd Cl. Hons, Econs and Polit. Tripos); MA 1952. Pres., Cambridge Union, 1948; Chm., Cambridge Univ. Conservatives, 1948. Chm., NW Br. of Inst. of Export, 1961-66. Mem. Manchester City Council, 1949-56; President: Manchester and Salford Street Children's (Wood Street) Mission Management Cttee, 1972- (Chm., 1968-72); 2/230th Boy Scouts, 1957-70, Life Hon. Mem., 1970; 1st Wythenshawe Boy Scouts, 1958-67; Vice-Pres., City of Manchester County Scout Council, 1972; Mem. Youth Cttee, Manchester City Council, 1959-65; Vice-Pres. Manchester Br. Cripples Aid Soc., 1963-; Mem. Manchester Cttee RNLI, 1964-; Vice-Chm., Manchester Naval Officers, 1974-; President: NW Br. Economic League, 1976-; Australian British Trade Assoc., 1978-. President: Manchester Br. BIM, 1972-; PRI, 1975- (Pres.

IRI, 1972-74). Pres., Altrincham and Sale Div. Young Conservs Assoc., 1961-69; Chairman: Altrincham and Sale Div. Cons. Assoc., 1954-61 (Vice-Pres. 1961); NW Area Young Conservs, 1951-53; Dep. Chm., Wythenshawe Div. Cons. Assoc., 1953-54; Vice-Chm. Nat. Young Conservs, 1953; Chm. Exec. Cttee, Nat. Union Cons. and Unionist Assocs, 1965-71 (Pres. NW Area, 1966-69, Chm. 1961-66); President: Cons. Political Centre, 1974-76; Nat. Union of Cons. Party, 1976-; Churchill Club of Manchester, 1978-. Pres., Northern Lawn Tennis Club, 1973; Mem. Council, Nat. Rifle Assoc., 1973. Trustee, Royal Exchange Theatre, 1974- (Jt Chm. Trust Appeal Cttee, 1974-). Manchester University: Mem. Cttee of Governors, 1966-; Mem. Court, 1976-; Governor, Clifton Coll., 1972- (Mem. Council, 1973-); Pres., Blackburn Coll. of Technol. and Design, 1978-. JP Manchester, 1965-72. FPRI 1966; FBIM 1969. *Recreations:* gardening, photography. *Address:* Dane Edge, Swettenham, Congleton, Cheshire CW12 2LQ. *T:* Lower Withington 363; Anchor Chemical Co. Ltd, Clayton, Manchester M11 4SR. *T:* 061-223 2461-6. *Clubs:* Carlton, Cambridge Union.
[Died 2 July 1979.

HEWSON, Sir Bushby; *see* Hewson, Sir J. B.

HEWSON, George Henry Phillips, MA, MusD (Dublin); FRCO (hc); Professor of Music, Dublin University, 1937-62, now Emeritus; *b* 19 Nov. 1881; *s* of Edmund and Caroline Hewson; *m* 1929; three *d. Educ:* St Patrick's Cathedral Grammar Sch.; Trinity Coll., Dublin. Organist and Choirmaster. Chapel Royal, Dublin Castle; Armagh Cathedral. Hon. Fellow, Trinity Coll., Dublin, 1962. *Publications:* Anthems, Services, Part-songs. *Recreations:* motoring, tennis. *Address:* 18 Gilford Road, Sandymount, Dublin. *T:* Dublin 683614. *Clubs:* Hibernian Catch, University (Dublin).   *[Died 21 Nov. 1972.*

HEWSON, Sir (Joseph) Bushby, Kt 1958; RD 1941; Judge of High Court of Justice, Probate, Divorce and Admiralty Division, 1958-66; *b* 1 June 1902; 2nd *s* of Wilfred Bushby Hewson; *m* 1933, Helen Mary Ropner; one *d. Educ:* HMS Conway, Rock Ferry, Ches. Midshipman, Royal Naval Reserve, 1920; Extra Master, 1928; called to Bar, Inner Temple, 1936; Bencher, 1958. Comdr Royal Naval Reserve, 1942. Served War of 1939-45, in Royal Navy. Junior Counsel to Admiralty (Admiralty Court), 1952-58; QC 1958. FRInstNav; FRGS; Founder Mem., Nautical Inst. *Publication:* A History of the Practice of Navigation, 1951. *Recreation:* marine sketching. *Address:* 77 Eyre Court, St John's Wood, NW8 9TX. *T:* 01-722 4041. *Club:* MCC.   *[Died 22 May 1976.*

HEYDON, Sir Peter (Richard), Kt 1970; CBE 1959; Secretary, Department of Immigration, Australia, since 1961; *b* 9 Sept. 1913; *s* of Vigar and Emily Heydon; *m* 1942, Naomi Slater, Ottawa; one *s* two *d. Educ:* Fort Street High Sch., Sydney; Univ. of Sydney (BA, LLB). Admitted NSW Bar, 1936; Dept of External Affairs, 1936; Private Sec. to Minister, 1936-37 and to Attorney-General, 1938; 2nd Sec, Australian Legation, Washington, 1940-42 and Moscow, 1942-44; Counsellor, London, 1947-50 and the Hague, 1950; Minister to Brazil, 1951-53; High Comr to New Zealand, 1953-55 and to India, 1955-58; Asst Sec. 1959-60 and 1st Asst Sec. 1960-61, Dept of External Affairs. *Publications:* Quiet Decision (a study of G. F. Pearce), 1965; contrib. to Australian Dictionary of Biography. *Recreation:* golf. *Address:* 18 Tennyson Crescent, Forrest, ACT 2603, Australia. *T:* 73-2266. *Clubs:* Reform; University (Sydney); Commonwealth (Canberra).   *[Died 15 May 1971.*

HEYER, Georgette; novelist; *b* 16 Aug. 1902; *d* of George Heyer, MA, MBE; *m* 1925, George Ronald Rougier, CBE, QC; one *s. Educ:* various schools. *Publications:* The Black Moth, These Old Shades, Devil's Cub, The Conqueror, Regency Buck, An Infamous Army, Death in the Stocks, Behold, Here's Poison, A Blunt Instrument, Royal Escape, No Wind of Blame, The Spanish Bride, The Corinthian, Faro's Daughter, Penhallow, Friday's Child, The Reluctant Widow, The Foundling, Arabella, The Grand Sophy, Duplicate Death, The Quiet Gentleman, Cotillion, Detection Unlimited, The Toll-Gate, Bath Tangle, Sprig Muslin, April Lady, Sylvester, The Unknown Ajax, A Civil Contract, The Nonesuch, False Colours, Frederica, Black Sheep, Cousin Kate, Charity Girl, Lady of Quality; *posthumous publication:* My Lord John, 1975. *Address:* c/o Mrs Owen, 78 Narrow Street, E14.   *[Died 5 July 1974.*

HEYGATE, Sir John (Edward Nourse), 4th Bt, *cr* 1831; writer (retired); *b* 19 April 1903; *s* of Arthur Conolly Gage and Frances Evelyn Rowley Heygate; *S* uncle, 1940; *m* 1st, 1930, Hon. Evelyn Florence Margaret Winifred Waugh (marr. diss. 1936), 2nd *d* of 1st Lord Burghclere; 2nd, 1936, Gwyneth Eliot (marr. diss. 1947), 2nd *d* of J. E. H. Lloyd; two *s*; 3rd, 1951, Dora Luz (*d* 1968), *d* of John Harvey. *Educ:* Eton; Balliol Coll., Oxford

(BA). Served War of 1939-45 as Bombardier, RA. *Heir: s* George Lloyd Heygate, *b* 28 Oct. 1936. *Address:* Bellarena, Limavady, Co. Londonderry, N Ireland. *T:* Bellarena 207.
[Died 18 March 1976.

HEYTESBURY, 5th Baron *cr* 1828; **William Leonard Frank Holmes à Court;** Bart 1795; *b* 17 April 1906; *o s* of 4th Baron and Sybil Mary (*d* 1937), *d* of late Capt. F. B. Morris; *S* father, 1949; *m* 1926, Beryl (*d* 1968), *y d* of A. E. B. Crawford, DCL, of Aston Clinton House, Bucks; one *s. Educ:* Pembroke Coll., Cambridge (BA). *Heir: s* Hon. Francis William Holmes à Court [*b* 8 Nov. 1931; *m* 1962, Alison, *e d* of Michael Graham Balfour; one *s* one *d*]. *Address:* Westover, Heytesbury, Wilts. *T:* Sutton Veny 324.   *[Died 27 Nov. 1971.*

HEYWOOD, Wilfred Lanceley, CBE 1958 (OBE 1951); Member, Restrictive Practices Court, 1958-68, and 1970-71; *b* 11 Sept. 1900; *s* of Edward James and Ellen Ann Heywood, Wooldale, Yorks; *m* Vera, *d* of Allen and Edith Boothroyd, Honley, Yorks; one *s. Educ:* Wooldale Council Sch.; evening classes, WEA. Formerly Gen. Sec., Nat. Union of Dyers, Bleachers and Textile Workers; Member: Gen. Council TUC, 1948-57; Brit. Wool Marketing Bd, 1950-57; Monopolies Commn, 1953-56; NCB, 1955-57; PIB, 1968-70; Royal Commission on the Working of the Tribunals of Inquiry (Evidence) Act, 1921, 1966-. *Address:* 41 Holland Avenue, SW20. *T:* 01-946 8176.   *[Died 8 Oct. 1977.*

HEYWOOD-LONSDALE, Lt-Col Arthur, CBE 1968; MC 1943; JP; *b* 13 May 1900; *m* 1931, Jean Katharine, *o d* of Hon. Claud Eustace Hamilton Russell; one *s* (and one *s* decd). *Educ:* Eton; Royal Military Coll. Sandhurst. Joined Grenadier Guards, 1919; retired 1931; re-employed 1940-45 (Major 1943). Capt. Shrops Yeomanry, 1931, Major 1938. Lieut-Col comdg Shrops Yeo., 1947-50. JP 1933, CC 1934, CA 1950, Chairman, CC, 1966-69, DL, 1951-70, Lord-Lieutenant, 1970-75, High Sheriff, 1957-58, Salop. KStJ 1970. *Address:* Shavington Grange, Market Drayton, Salop. *T:* Calverhall 652. *Clubs:* Guards, Turf, Pratt's.
[Died 14 March 1976.

HEYWORTH, 1st Baron, *cr* 1955, of Oxton; **Geoffrey Heyworth,** Kt 1948; Hon. LLD: St Andrews, 1950; Manchester, 1950; London, 1962; Bristol and Sussex, 1966, Southampton, 1970; Hon. DCL Oxon, 1957; Hon. DLitt Warwick, 1967; Hon. Fellow Nuffield College, Oxford; *b* 18 Oct. 1894; *s* of Thomas Blackwell Heyworth, Oxton, Birkenhead, and Florence Myers, Bradford, Yorks; *m* 1924, Lois Dunlop, Woodstock, Ontario, Canada; no *c. Educ:* Dollar Acad. Joined Lever Brothers Ltd at Liverpool, 1912; various positions in Canada and England until 1931; Canadian Army, 1915-18; Dir parent company, Lever Bros Ltd (now Unilever Ltd), from 1931; Chm. Unilever Ltd, 1942-60. Chm. Gas Industry Cttee, 1945; Mem. Company Law Amendment Cttee, Bd of Trade, 1943; formerly part-time mem., London Transport and NCB. Mem. Royal Commission on Taxation of Profits and Income, 1951. Chairman: Council on Productivity, Prices and Incomes, 1960-62; Cttee on Research in Social Sciences, 1963-65; Court of Governors, London Sch. of Hygiene and Tropical Medicine, 1964-70; Pres., Nat. Council of Social Service, 1961-70. Grand Officer, Order of Orange Nassau, 1947. *Address:* 29 Sussex Square, W2. *Club:* Athenæum.
[Died 15 June 1974 (ext).

HIBBERT, Denys Heseltine, CBE 1954; Director of Education and Member of Legislative Council, British Solomon Islands Protectorate, 1966-70, retired; *b* 17 Oct. 1905; *s* of late Rev. and Mrs E. H. Hibbert; *m* 1931, Siblie Langmuir Napier; three *d. Educ:* Radley Coll.; Worcester Coll., Oxford. Sudan Political Service, 1928; Warden, Gordon Coll., Khartoum, 1943-45; Asst Dir of Education, 1945-50; Dir of Education, Sudan, 1950-54. Headmaster, Portsmouth Grammar Sch., 1954-65. Adviser in Education, Abu Dhabi, Trucial States, Jan.-July, 1965. Life Governor, CMS, 1963. *Recreation:* bridge. *Address:* Little Acre, Godshill, Fordingbridge, Hants. *T:* Fordingbridge 53316.
[Died 15 May 1977.

HIBBERT, Francis Dennis, CMG 1958; ED 1946; *b* 18 Aug. 1906; *s* of Preb. F. A. Hibbert, MA, Headmaster of Worksop Coll. and of Denstone Coll., and Prebendary of Lichfield Cathedral; *m* 1939, Annie Doreen Coomber; one *d. Educ:* Denstone Coll.; Bloxham Sch.; St John's Coll., Cambridge (MA). Joined Educ. Dept, Nigeria, as Supt of Education, 1929; served Bauchi, Katsina and Plateau Provinces, and Northern Provinces HQ Office, Kaduna, 1929-40. Commnd Supplementary Reserve, The Nigeria Regt, RWAFF, 1930; served 6th Bn The Nigeria Regt, HQ 3rd W African Infantry Bde, and The West African Trg and Reinforcement Camp, Nigeria and India, 1940-45 (Major). Rejoined Educ. Dept., Nigeria, 1946; served Bornu and Plateau Provinces, and HQ

Offices, Lagos and Kaduna; Chief Educ. Officer, Northern Region, 1951; Dep. Dir of Education, Northern Region, 1952; Chm., Public Service Commn, Northern Region, Nov. 1954-Oct. 1958, retired. Min. of Overseas Develt, 1962-69. *Recreations:* watching cricket and gardening. *Address:* Hemphayes, Charlton Mackrell, Somerton, Somerset. *T:* Charlton Mackrell 386. [Died 18 Nov. 1975.]

HICKFORD, Lawrence David, CMG 1972; OBE 1957; JP; Member, New Zealand Dairy Board, since 1961; Chairman, Okato Dairy Co., New Zealand, since 1955 (Director, 1929-); Chairman or Director of Dairy Industries: Barbados, Trinidad and Jamaica, also Trinidad Processing Co.; farmer; *b* Taihape, NZ, 4 Nov. 1904; *s* of David and Emma Hickford; *m* 1927, Keitha May Wooldridge. Commissioned in TF, 1926; served in NZ Home Forces during War of 1939-45; Staff Captain in Mounted Rifles Bde; 2nd in Comd, Armoured Regt, rank Major. Farming at Okato, Taranaki, in partnership with C. G. Cocksedge, 1925-; 1,200 acres developed (dairying, sheep, beef and pigs). Chm. or Sec. numerous organisations in district, 1922-; still serving as Chm. Domain and Cemetery Bds, etc. Frequent overseas travel on business of Dairy Industry. Serves on many cttees of NZ Dairy Board; Dir, NZ Rennet Co., 1950-; Past Dir, Egmont Box Co. (liquidated); Dir, Nat. Dairy Assoc. of NZ for 23 yrs and Chm. for 10 yrs; on Exec. of Fedn of Taranaki Dairy Factories for over 30 yrs and Pres. for 14 years; Chm., Nat. Dairy Fedn of NZ for 10 years; Chm., Okato Veterinary Gp, embracing a number of Dairy Cos, 1945-; Mem., NZ Veterinary Services Council and NZ Animal Health Adv. Cttee; Mem. Taranaki CC, 1936- (Chm., 1951); Member: Airport Adv. Cttee, Hydatids Cttee, Pest Destruction, Fire Bd, Dist. Roads Council; Egmont Nat. Park Bd for 15 years, etc. Farmers' Union and Federated Farmers: Branch Chm. and Mem. Provincial Exec., 1925-61 (excl. some War yrs); Mem. Dominion Council for many years and Dominion Vice-Pres. for 2 yrs; elected Dominion Life Mem. 1961. Member and Patron of a number of Provincial Organisations. JP 1948-. *Address:* Dover Road, Okato, Taranaki, New Zealand. [Died 23 April 1978.]

HICKIE, Brig. George William Clement, CBE 1943 (OBE 1920); RIASC (retired); *b* 2 March 1897; *s* of late Major W. B. Hickie, IA; *m* 1924, Nora Margaret Peel Corbin; no *c*. *Educ:* Cheltenham; Imperial Services Coll.; RMC Sandhurst. Served European War, 1914-18; BEF France, EEF Egypt and Palestine (despatches twice); DADST, British Mil. Mission, South Russia, 1919-20 (despatches, OBE, 2nd class Order of St Stanislaus); Northern Command, India, ADS 1938-39. ADST Peshawar Dist 1939-40; Dep. Dir of Transport, Army HQ, India, 1940-41; DDS and T Tenth Army, British Forces in Iraq and Paiforce, 1941-43 (CBE); Brig. NW Army, India Command, 1943; DDST, GHQ, India, 1944-45; offg DST, GHQ, India, 1945 (Actg Maj.-Gen.); Brig. RIASC, Northern Command, India, 1945-47; retired, 1947. *Recreations:* tennis, cricket, golf. *Address:* c/o Lloyds Bank Ltd, 6 Pall Mall, SW1; 25 Southfields Road, Eastbourne, Sussex. *T:* Eastbourne 22602. [Died 3 Jan. 1972.]

HICKLING, Charles Frederick, CMG 1951; MA, ScD Cantab; Fisheries Adviser, Department of Technical Co-operation, 1961, retired 1962; *b* 15 Aug. 1902; *s* of late R. A. Hickling, Chik Ballapura, S India; *m* 1930, Marjorie Ellerington, *d* of late Henry Blamey, Dovercourt; two *s*. *Educ:* Taunton Sch.; St Catharine's Coll., Cambridge (Scholar); Dept of Oceanography, Univ. of Liverpool, 1925-26; Ministry of Agriculture and Fisheries, 1927-45; Port Fishery Capt., Milford Haven, 1939-45; Buckland Prof., 1934; Acting Dir, Tropical Fish Culture Research Institute, Malacca, 1957-59; Fisheries Adviser to Sec. of State for the Colonies, 1945-61. In Malaya with Nuffield Foundn res. grant, 1963-65, NERC res. grant, 1967-69. In 1956 the Jamaican freshwater species *Cichlaurus hicklingi* was dedicated to him by H. W. Fowler. *Publications:* The Hake, 1934; Tropical Inland Fisheries, 1961; Fish Culture, 1962 (new edn, 1970); The Farming of Fish, 1968; Estuarine Fish Farming, 1970; (contrib.) Exploring the Ocean World (new edn, 1972); (with P. Lancaster Brown) The Seas and Oceans in Colour, 1973; Water as a Productive Environment, 1975; numerous publications and monographs on fisheries, fisheries biology and zoology. *Address:* 95 Greenway, N20 8EL. [Died 14 June 1977.]

HICKMAN, Sir (Alfred) Howard (Whitby), 3rd Bt, *cr* 1903; *b* 29 Jan. 1920; *s* of Major Sir Alfred Hickman, 2nd Bt, and Lilian Brenda, *o d* of late B. Howard Mander and Mrs Mander, of Trysull Manor, Wolverhampton; *S* father, 1947; *m* 1948, Mrs Margaret D. Thatcher, *o d* of Leonard Kempson; one *s*. *Educ:* Eton. *Heir:* *s* Richard Glenn Hickman, *b* 12 April 1949. *Address:* Twin Cottage, Batlers Green, Radlett, Herts. *T:* Radlett 6605. [Died 10 April 1979.]

HICKS, Brig. Sir (Cedric) Stanton, Kt 1936; CStJ; MSc (1st Class Hons), MB, ChB NZ; MD Adelaide; PhD Cantab; FRIC (London), FCS (London); FRSA; Emeritus Professor of Human Physiology and Pharmacology in University of Adelaide (Professor 1926-58); *b* Mosgiel, NZ, 2 June 1892; *s* of George Henry Hicks and Sarah, *d* of Stanton Evans; *m* 1st, Florence (marr. diss. 1948), *e d* of John Haggitt, Dunedin, NZ; two *s* (and one *s* decd); 2nd, 1948, Valerie, *d* of Lt-Col S. H. Hubbard, Peppermint Grove, WA. *Educ:* Otago Boys High Sch.; Otago Univ. (Selwyn Coll.); Trinity Coll., Cambridge; Universities of Zürich and Vienna. Junior National Scholar, 1906; erected and operated first wireless telegraph in NZ 1908; BSc 1913; MSc 1914; NZ National Research Scholar; produced report on Preservation of Structural Timber, 1915; Synthesis of Chloramine with J. K. H. Inglis for War Purposes and Enlistment, 1916 NZMC Expeditionary Force: AIF, 1939-45; Government Analyst, Otago and Southland, New Zealand, 1918-23; established Clinical Pathology Laboratory, Otago Medical Sch., 1922; Clinical Pathologist, Otago Hosp. and Medical Sch.; with A. M. Drennan initiated research into Endemic Goitre in New Zealand, 1920-23; Beit Memorial Research Fellow and Research Studentship, Trinity Coll., Cambridge, 1923; Mem. of Cttee on Endocrine Research, Medical Research Council, 1925-26; PhD Cantab 1925; Sheridan Research Fellow, Univ. of Adelaide, 1926-31; Mem. Commonwealth National Research Council, 1930; Commonwealth Nutrition Advisory Cttee, 1936-38; Nutrition Cttee Council National Health and Medical Research, 1939-59; Vice-Pres. Nat. Old People's Welfare Council. Dir Army Catering, Allied Land Forces, and AMF, 1942-52. Mem. Med. Advisory Cttee, Army, Navy and Air Force, 1940; Scientific Advisory Cttee, (Food Stuffs), 1941; Personnel Research Cttee, 1941. Founded Australian Army Catering Corps, 1942. Scientific Mission, US and UK, 1944; Pres. Council Social Services, SA, 1946-48; Chm. Defence Food Stuffs Res. Cttee, 1949-59. Scientific Food Consultant, Army, Australia, 1952-73. Lectures: Sanderson Wells, Univ. of London, 1950; CIBA, 1950. Man. Editor, Australian Jl of Exptl Biol. and Med. Sci.; Member Editorial Board: Excerpta Medica, Amsterdam; Internat. Jl of Vitamin Research, Bern. *Publications:* Molecular Structure and Physiological Action; Physiological Observations on the Aboriginals of Central Australia on Expeditions in 1931-32-33, 1934, 1936 and 1937, and Chemistry and Pharmacology of Native Poisons; Food and Folly, 1952; Life from the Soil, 1953; Physiology of Nutrition, 1957; Terrestrial Animals in the Cold: Studies of Primitive Man, 1964; Land Reform in Southern Italy, 1969; Nutritional Requirements of Living Things, 1972; Prospectives on the Environment, 1973; Man and Natural Resources, 1976; scientific papers. *Recreations:* travel, gardening, mechanical tinkering. *Address:* Woodley, Glen Osmond, SA 5064, Australia. *Club:* Naval and Military (Adelaide). [Died 7 Feb. 1976.]

HICKS, John Donald; A. F. and May T. Morrison Professor of History, University of California (Berkeley), 1942-57, Emeritus since 1957; *b* Pickering, Missouri, 25 Jan. 1890; *s* of Rev. John Kossuth Hicks and Harriett Gertrude Wing; *m* 1921, Lucile Harriet Curtis, St James, Minn.; three *d*. *Educ:* Northwestern Univ.; Univ. of Wisconsin. BA, 1913, MA 1914, Northwestern University: PhD 1916, Wisconsin Univ. Asst Prof. and Prof. of History, Hamline Univ., 1916-22; Prof. of Hist., North Carolina Coll. for Women, 1922-23; Prof. of Amer. Hist., University of Nebraska, 1923-32; Prof. of Hist., University of Wisconsin, 1932-42. Teacher, summers, numerous Amer. Univs. Visiting Lecturer, Harvard Univ., 1st half year, 1931-32; Visiting Professor of American History and Institutions, Univ. of Cambridge. 1950-51 (Hon. MA). Professorial Fellow, Trinity Hall. Phi Beta Kappa Visiting Scholar, 1958-59. Hon. LLD: Northwestern Univ., 1956; Univ. of San Francisco, 1957; Univ. of California, 1960; Hon. LittD Univ. of Nebraska, 1971. *Publications:* The Populist Revolt, 1931; The Federal Union, 1937; The American Nation, 1941; A Short History of American Democracy, 1943; (co-author with Theodore Saloutos) Agricultural Discontent in the Middle West, 1900-39, 1950; The American Tradition, 1955; Republican Ascendency, 1921-1933, 1960; Rehearsal for Disaster: The Boom and Collapse of 1919-1920, 1961; My Life With History: an autobiography, 1968; numerous articles in historical publications and encyclopædias. *Address:* 66 Southampton Avenue, Berkeley, Calif 94707, USA. [Died 5 Feb. 1972.]

HICKS, Reginald Jack; HM Diplomatic Service; Deputy High Commissioner, Bridgetown, Barbados, 1978-79; *b* 22 Jan. 1922; 3rd *s* of late Victor Hicks and Emily Hicks, Enfield; *m* 1946, Jean Sims; one *d*. *Educ:* Enfield Grammar Sch. HM Office of Works and Public Buildings, 1938. RAF (VR), 1941-46: Flying Instructor, US Army Air Corps, 1941-42, with subseq. service in Middle East and Burma (No 28 Sqdn); Flt-Lt. Min. of Works,

1946; Chief Clerk, New Delhi, 1951; seconded to Public Services Commn, Fedn of Rhodesia and Nyasaland, 1957; transf. to CRO, 1961; 1st Sec., Enugu, 1964-66; 1st Sec., Bathurst, 1966; 1st Sec. (Consular), New Delhi, 1966-69; Head of Parly Comr and Cttees Unit, FCO, 1969-73; Consul-Gen., Auckland, 1973-78. *Recreations:* golf, travel. *Address:* c/o Foreign and Commonwealth Office, SW1A 2AL; 67 Hayes Lane, Kenley, Surrey.   [*Died 26 May* 1980.

HICKS, Brig. Sir Stanton; *see* Hicks, Brig. Sir C. S.

HICKS BEACH, Major William Whitehead, TD; DL; solicitor; *b* 23 March 1907; *s* of late Ellis Hicks Beach, Witcombe Park, Glos; *m* 1939, Diana, *d* of C. G. Hoare, Yateley Hall, Elmham, Dereham, Norfolk; one *s* two *d. Educ:* Eton; Magdalene Coll., Cambridge. A solicitor since 1932 and a partner in Payne, Hicks Beach & Co., 10 New Square, Lincoln's Inn, WC2, since 1933. Served throughout War of 1939-45 with Royal Gloucestershire Hussars and retired as Major. Contested (C) Cheltenham, 1945; MP (C) Cheltenham, 1950-64. DL, Glos, 1963. *Recreations:* hunting, shooting and fishing. *Address:* Witcombe Park, near Gloucester. *Clubs:* Turf Bath; New (Cheltenham).
                    [*Died 1 Jan.* 1975.

HICKSON, Geoffrey Fletcher, CBE 1973; MA; Secretary of Board of Extra-Mural Studies, University of Cambridge, 1928-67; Fellow of Fitzwilliam College, 1963-67; *b* 4 July 1900; *s* of late Professor S. J. Hickson, FRS; *m* 1934, Jane Margaret Amy, *er d* of late Dr W. R. Cazenove; two *s* one *d. Educ:* Uppingham Sch. (Scholar); Clare Coll., Cambridge (Archdeacon Johnson Exhib.). Historical Tripos, 1921 and 1922; Gladstone Prize, 1924. Asst Master, Highgate Sch., 1924. Asst Sec., Board of Extra-Mural Studies, Univ. of Cambridge, 1925. Mem. Council of Senate, 1947-62; Mem. Cambridge City Council, 1943-74; Chm. Cttee for Education, 1946-64; Mayor, 1947-49 and 1962-63; Alderman, 1952-74; Mem. Gen. Purposes Cttee, Assoc. of Municipal Corporations, 1956-74 (Dep. Chm., 1969-73); Chm., Non-County Boroughs Cttee for England and Wales, 1969-74. Chm. Central Cttee for Adult Education in HM Forces, 1957-60. Trustee of Uppingham Sch., 1957-77. Hon. Freeman, City of Cambridge, 1974. *Recreations:* music and golf. *Address:* 16 Rathmore Road, Cambridge CB1 4AD. *T:* Cambridge 44472. *Club:* United Oxford & Cambridge University.
                    [*Died 31 Oct.* 1978.

HIGGIN, Walter Wynnefield; DL County of Chester; Partner in Smith, Coney and Barrett, Liverpool, retired; *b* 18 Dec. 1889; *s* of W. S. Higgin and J., *d* of J. Saunders, Annan, Dumfries; *m* 1918, Olive, *d* of A. B. Earle, Old Hall, Puddington, Ches; three *s. Educ:* Gresham's Sch., Norfolk. Partner, W. S. Higgin and Co., Cotton Merchants, 1918; retired, 1924; joined Smith, Coney and Barrett, 1931; Pres. Liverpool Cotton Association Ltd, 1943-45; 2nd Lieut 6th Bn The King's Liverpool Regt 1910; joined RFC 1915; Capt., 1916; Major, 1918; High Sheriff of Ches., 1938. *Recreations:* shooting, fishing. *Address:* Puddington Hall, Wirral, Cheshire. *TA:* Neston, Wirral. *T:* 051-336 2120. *Club:* Travellers'.   [*Died 9 Aug.* 1971.

HIGGS, Captain Michael Arnold, CB 1977; RN; *b* 16 Feb. 1927; *s* of Dr J. S. Higgs and Mrs Higgs; *m* 1950, Willie Doreen Stirling; three *s* two *d. Educ:* RNC, Dartmouth. Midshipman 1944; CO HMS Dundas, 1959; Exec. Officer, HMS Hampshire, 1961; Captain 1967; PSO to Royal Malaysian Navy, 1967-69; idc 1970; Captain (D1), Far East, 1971; Captain (F2), 1972; staff, Nat. Defence Coll., 1972-74; Captain, BRNC Dartmouth, 1974-76; apptd Flag Officer, Gibraltar, 1976; invalided 1976. *Recreations:* gardening, shooting. *Address:* Waltham House, Stroud, Petersfield, Hants. *T:* Petersfield 3991. *Club:* Army and Navy.
                    [*Died 14 Dec.* 1978.

HIGGS, Sydney Limbrey, FRCS; Consulting Orthopædic Surgeon, St Bartholomew's Hospital; Hon. Consulting Surgeon, Royal National Orthopædic Hospital; Hon. Consulting Orthopædic Surgeon, North-East Metropolitan Regional Hospital Board; *b* 12 Sept. 1892; widower; one *d. Educ:* St John's Coll., Cambridge; St Bartholomew's Hospital. MB, BCh, MA, Cambridge, 1919; MRCS, LRCP 1917; FRCS 1922. Formerly: Regional Orthopædic Consultant, EMS; Surgeon, Queen Mary's Hospital, Roehampton; Hon. Consulting Orthopædic Surgeon to the Army, Eastern Command. Fellow British Orthopædic Association; Fellow Royal Society of Medicine. *Publications:* contributions to medical journals. *Address:* Phœnix, West Wittering, near Chichester, West Sussex. *Club:* Royal Yacht Squadron.   [*Died 21 Nov.* 1977.

HIGGS-WALKER, James Arthur, MA Oxon; Headmaster of Sevenoaks School, 1925-54; *b* 31 July 1892; *s* of W. H. Higgs-Walker, Wychbury House, Hagley, Worcestershire; *m* 1917,

Muriel Jessie, *e d* of Rev. Harold Earnshaw Smith, Himley Rectory, Staffs, and *g d* of Hon. Henley Eden; one *d. Educ:* Repton; St John's Coll., Oxford (Scholar). Served European War, Capt. in the Worcs Regt, in Egypt, Mesopotamia, Italy, 1914-19; House-Master and Chief History Master at Oundle Sch., 1919-25. *Publications:* European History, 1789-1815; Introduction to Eighteenth Century French Society; contributor to History and other periodicals. *Recreation:* member of Oxford University Authentics Cricket Club, and has played cricket for Worcs. *Address:* Long Barn, Chelwood Gate, Sussex.
                    [*Died 3 Sept.* 1979.

HIGHAM, Anthony Richard Charles, TD 1945; Senior Surgeon, St Peter's Hospital Group, 1968-72; Surgeon, St Paul's Hospital, 1939-72; Surgeon i/c Genito-Urinary Department, Queen Mary's Hospital, Stratford, E15, 1948-72; *b* 11 June 1907; *e s* of late Lieut-Col B. Higham, CIE; *m* 1931, Mary (*d* 1970), *er d* of late J. W. W. Shepley, Highfield House, Glossop; two *s. Educ:* Epsom Coll.; St George's Hospital; FRCS 1932. Mem., Board of Governors St Peter's, St Paul's and St Philip's Hospitals, 1948-72; Dean, St Paul's Hospital, 1948-51; Dean, Institute of Urology, University of London, 1951-67; Everidge Prize in Urology, 1952. FRSM; Foundation Mem. British Assoc. of Urological Surgeons. Mem., International Society of Urology. Commissioned RA (TA), 1927; transferred to RAMC (TA), 1930; served throughout War of 1939-45, in UK (with Commandos), Africa, Iraq, Sicily and Italy (Actg Col, OC 22 Gen. Hosp., 1945). Polish Golden Cross of Merit with Swords, 1948. *Publications:* occasional contrib. to medical literature. *Recreation:* motoring. *Address:* 3 Nightingale Close, Storrington, Sussex. *Club:* Royal Automobile.
                    [*Died 13 June* 1975.

HIGHAM, Thomas Farrant; Official Fellow, 1914-58, Dean, 1919-33, Senior Tutor, 1938-39 and 1945-48, and Emeritus Fellow, since 1958, Trinity College, Oxford; Public Orator, Oxford University, 1939-58 and sometime University Lecturer in Greek and Latin Literature; *b* 20 Sept. 1890; *y s* of late Sir Thomas Higham, KCIE; *m* 1915, Mary Elisabeth *e d* of late Dr B. M. H. Rogers; one *s* one *d. Educ:* Clifton Coll.; Trinity Coll., Oxford. 1st class, Class. Hon. Mods, 1911; Gaisford Prize, Greek Verse, 1912; 2nd Lieut 9th (Ser.) Bn OBLI, Dec. 1914; attached GSI, British Salonika Force and Constantinople, 1916-19; Capt., 1917 (despatches, Greek medal for Military Merit); Proproctor, Oxford Univ., 1921-22, 1927-28; Senior Proctor, 1932-33; Attached to Foreign Office, 1940-45. Member: Council St Hilda's Coll., Oxford, 1934-42; Governing Body, St Paul's Schs, 1934-64; Council, Clifton Coll., 1953-66; Council, The Oxford Soc., 1952-69. Vis. Prof. in Classics, Stanford Univ., Calif, 1962-63. *Publications:* Orationes Oxonienses Selectae, 1960; Dr Blakiston Recalled, 1968; co-editor: The Mind of Rome, 1926; The Oxford Book of Greek Verse, 1930, and the same in translation, 1938; From the Greek, 1943; Some Oxford Compositions, 1949; Ovidiana, Recherches sur Ovide, 1958; More Oxford Compositions, 1964; Ancient Literary Criticism, 1972; articles in Greek Poetry and Life, 1936, Classical journals, etc. *Recreation:* conchology. *Address:* 2 William Orchard Close, Old Headington, Oxford OX3 9DR. *T:* Oxford 65113.
                    [*Died 29 Jan.* 1975.

HIGHET, Gilbert (Arthur); Anthon Professor of the Latin Language and Literature, Columbia University, New York, 1950-72, now Professor Emeritus; *b* 22 June 1906; *o s* of Gilbert Highet, Superintendent, Postal Telegraphs, Glasgow, and Elizabeth Gertrude Boyle; *m* 1932, Helen Clark, novelist, *o d* of Donald McInnes, Glasgow; one *s. Educ:* Hillhead High Sch., Glasgow; Glasgow Univ. (DLitt 1951); Balliol Coll., Oxford. Snell Exhibitioner and Hon. Schol., Balliol, DLitt 1956. Fellow of St John's Coll., Oxford, 1932; Prof. of Greek and Latin, Columbia Univ., 1938-50; on leave for war service, 1941-46; with British mission in US and later in Mil. Govt, Germany (British Zone); commissioned, 1943; Lt-Col 1946. Became US citizen, 1951. Guggenheim Meml Fellow, 1951. Hon. Degrees: DLitt: Syracuse, 1960; Columbia, 1977; LHD: Case Inst. of Technology, 1962; Adelphi, 1964; Massachusetts, 1973. FRSL 1959. Mem. Bd of Judges, Book-of-the-Month Club, 1954-; Chm. Editorial Adv. Bd, Horizon, 1958-77. Wallace Award, Amer.-Scottish Foundn, 1973. *Publications:* The Classical Tradition: Greek and Roman Influences on Western Literature, 1949; The Art of Teaching, 1950; People, Places and Books, 1953; Juvenal the Satirist, 1954; The Mind of Man, 1954; A Clerk of Oxenford, 1954; Poets in a Landscape, 1957; Talents and Geniuses, 1957; The Powers of Poetry, 1960; The Anatomy of Satire, 1962 (Award of Merit, American Philological Association, 1963); Explorations, 1971; The Speeches in Vergil's Aeneid, 1972; The Immortal Profession, 1976; Translator of Werner Jaeger's Paideia: the Ideals of Greek Culture, 1939-44. Contributor: The Classical Review, The American Journal of

Philology, etc. *Recreations:* two-piano duets, photography. *Address:* 15 Jeffreys Lane, East Hampton, New York 11937, USA. *Clubs:* Century (New York); Maidstone (East Hampton).
[Died 20 Jan. 1978.

HILBORNE, Rev. Frederick Wilfred, CBE 1957; *b* 5 March 1901; *yr s* of Frank and Eleanor Hilborne; *m* 1929, Irene May Wheatland (*d* 1978); one *s* one *d*. *Educ:* Eastbourne Coll.; Handsworth Theological Coll. Ordained into Ministry of Methodist Church, 1929. Commissioned in Royal Army Chaplains' Dept, 1929; served in Malta, 1932-35. War Service: BEF, 1939-40; MELF 1942; CMF, 1943-45. CF 3rd Class, 1939; CF 2nd Class, 1943; CF 1st Class, 1950. Appointed Dep. Chaplain-Gen. to the Forces and Hon. Chaplain to the Queen, 1953; relinquished both appointments and placed on retired pay, Dec. 1956. *Address:* Spinnakers, 78 Old Fort Road, Shoreham-by-Sea BN4 5HA. *T:* Shoreham-by-Sea 2088.
[Died 26 Nov. 1980.

HILDITCH, Clarence Clifford; General Secretary, Co-operative Union Ltd, since 1972; *b* 23 Dec. 1912; *s* of Clifford and Elizabeth Hilditch; *m* 1938, Nellie Megan Russell; two *s*. *Educ:* Rivington and Blackrod Grammar Sch.; Manchester Univ. (BA Com). Pilot, RAF, 1941-46, Flt Lieut 1943. Asst to Principal, Co-operative Coll., 1937; Sec., Co-operative Bakery Trade Assoc., 1946; Sec., Co-operative Laundry Trade Assoc., 1946; Asst Gen. Sec., Co-operative Union Ltd, 1951. *Recreations:* football, cricket, motoring. *Address:* Co-operative Union Ltd, Holyoake House, Hanover Street, Manchester M60 0AS. *T:* 061-834 0975.
[Died 10 Aug. 1974.

HILL, 7th Viscount, *cr* 1842; **Gerald Rowland Clegg-Hill;** Bt 1726-27; Baron Hill of Almarez and of Hawkstone, Salop, 1814; formerly Major, Royal Welch Fusiliers; *b* 31 March 1904; *s* of 6th Viscount Hill, DSO, and Mildred (*d* 1934), *d* of Thomas Bulteel, Radford, S Devon; *S* father 1957; *m* 1st, 1930, Betty (marriage dissolved, 1942), *yr d* of late Brig.-Gen. George Nowell Thomas Smyth-Osbourne, CB, CMG, DSO; one *s* (and one *s* decd); 2nd, 1942, Catherine Mary (Molly), *o d* of late Dr Rowland Venables Lloyd-Williams, Maiford, Denbigh. *Educ:* Shrewsbury; RMC, Sandhurst. *Heir: s* Hon. Antony Rowland Clegg-Hill, Lieut, Royal Artillery [*b* 19 March 1931; *m* 1963, Juanita Phyllis, *d* of John W. Pertwee, Salfords, Surrey]. *Address:* Coton Hall, Whitchurch, Salop. *T:* Whixall 353.
[Died 11 May 1974.

HILL, Adrian Keith Graham, PPROI (PROI 1968-72, ROI 1929); RBA 1926; RI 1928-36; Society of Graphic Arts, 1931; Painter in Water Colours and Oils; Member Society for Education in Art, 1947; Governor, Federation of British Artists, 1968; President: Chichester Art Society, 1969; Midhurst Art Society, 1972; Vice-President: St James's Art Society, 1947; National League of Hospital Friends, 1950; Vice-President, British Society of Aesthetics (founder member), 1960; British Association of Art Therapists, 1966; Broadcaster on Sound and TV; *b* Charlton, Kent, 24 March 1895; *s* of Graham Hill; *m* Dorothy Margaret Whitley; one *s*. *Educ:* Dulwich; St John's Wood Art Sch.; Royal College of Art. Joined HAC 1914; overseas, 1916-19; Lieut 1917; Official War Artist, Collection of 190 War Pictures at Imperial War Museum, London; Life Master and Lectr on Anatomy, Westminster Sch. of Art, 1935-38; External Examr for Teachers' Cert., Durham Univ., 1938-39; apptd under Pilgrim Trust Grant to depict The Changing Face of Britain, 1940; Art Lectr to HM Forces, 1943-44; Founder, Red Cross Soc. Hosp. Picture Library, 1944; Governor: Chichester Sch. of Art, 1951-62; Midhurst Grammar Sch., 1957-67; Vice-Pres., Ancient Monuments Soc., 1960 (FAMS 1958). Work exhibited at Royal Acad. Salon, New English Art Club, London Gp, USA, Canada, S Africa, etc.; De Laszlo Silver and Bronze Medals, Royal Society of British Artists; awarded Prix Catherine-Hadot, Académie Nationale de Médecine, Paris, 1947. Works represented in: Victoria and Albert Museum, Bradford Corp. Art Gall., Municipal Galls of Cork, Derby, Brighton, Northampton, Lane, Oldham, Hinckley, Letchworth, and Lever Art Galls; Collection of War Pictures at Headquarters of Hon. Artillery Company; One-man Exhibitions: 1938, 1940, 1961, 1964, 1966, 1968, 1971, 1972. *Publications:* On Drawing and Painting Trees, 1936; On the Mastery of Water Colour Painting, 1938; Art versus Illness, 1945; Trees Have Names, 1949; Painting Out Illness, 1951; A Book of Trees, 1951; The Pleasures of Painting, 1952; Adventures in Line and Tone, 1954; What Shall We Draw?, 1956; Oil Painting for Beginners, 1957; Art as a Hobby, 1958; The Beginner's Book of Watercolour Painting, 1959; Knowing and Painting Trees, 1960; Sketching and Painting Out of Doors, 1961; Drawing the Countryside, 1961; Sketching and Painting Indoors, 1962; Basic Anatomy, 1962; Faces and Figures, 1962; Adventures in Painting, 1962; How to Draw, 1963; Seascapes

and Landscapes, 1964; Flower Drawing and Painting, 1965; Architecture in Landscape, 1966; How to Paint in Water Colour, 1967; Further Steps in Oil Painting, 1969; Introduction to Drawing and Sketching, 1971; Trees in Landscape, 1976. *Address:* Old Laundry Cottage, Midhurst, West Sussex. *T:* Midhurst 2018. *Clubs:* Alleyn, HAC, National Book League.
[Died 22 June 1977.

HILL, Archibald Vivian, CH 1946; OBE (mil.) 1918; FRS 1918; MA, ScD; Hon. LLD Edinburgh, Belfast; Hon. MD, Louvain, Brussels, Toulouse; Hon. DSc, Pennsylvania, Bristol, Manchester, Oxford, Algiers, Liège, Johns Hopkins, Brazil, Columbia, Rochester, Rockefeller, Exeter; Foulerton Research Professor, Royal Society, 1926-51; *b* 26 Sept. 1886; *m* 1913, Margaret Neville (*d* 1970), *d* of late Dr J. N. Keynes; one *s* two *d* (and one *s* decd). *Educ:* Blundell's Sch., Tiverton; Trinity Coll., Cambridge (Scholar). 3rd Wrangler, 1907; Class I. Natural Sciences Tripos Part II. (Physiology), 1909; Fellow of Trinity Coll., Cambridge, 1910-16; Hon Fellow, 1941; Fellow of King's Coll., Cambridge, 1916-25; Hon. Fellow, 1927; Brackenbury Prof. of Physiology, Manchester Univ., 1920-23; Nobel Prize, Physiology and Medicine, 1922; Jodrell Prof. of Physiology, University Coll., London, 1923-25; Hon. Prof., 1926-51; Hon. Fellow, 1948; Mem. Cttee of Award, Commonwealth Fund Fellowships, 1934-39; Sec. of Royal Society, 1935-45, For. Sec., 1945-46, Royal Medal, 1926, Copley Medal, 1948; Mem. Univ. Grants Cttee, 1937-44; Chm. Executive Cttee National Physical Laboratory, 1939-45; Attaché, British Embassy, Washington, 1940; MP (Ind. C), Cambridge Univ., 1940-45; Member: War Cabinet Scientific Advisory Cttee, 1940-46, Inter-departmental Cttee on Medical Schs, 1942-44; Colonial Research Cttee, 1942; Science Cttee, British Council, 1946-56; Scientific Adviser, Govt of India, 1943-44; Trustee, British Museum, 1947-63; Trustee, Natural History Museum, 1963-65; Chairman: Research Defence Soc., 1940-51; Soc. for the Protection of Science and Learning, 1946-63 (Pres., 1963-); President: Soc. for Visiting Scientists, 1952-66; British Assoc. for the Advancement of Science for 1952; Marine Biological Assoc., 1955-60; Old Blundellian Club, 1964-; Mem. Commission on Higher Education for Africans in Central Africa, 1952; Sec. General, Internat. Council of Scientific Unions, 1952-56; Foreign, Hon. or Assoc. Mem. of various foreign acads and socs. Served 1914-19, Captain and Brev. Major Cambs Regt and Dir of Anti-Aircraft Experimental Section, Munitions Inventions Dept; since then mem. of various cttees on air defence, etc (incl. Tizard Cttee, 1935-40). Medal of Freedom with Silver Palm, USA, 1947; Chevalier of the Legion of Honour, 1950. *Publications:* Living Machinery, 1927; The Ethical Dilemma of Science, 1960; Trails and Trials in Physiology, 1965; First and Last Experiments in Muscle Mechanics, 1970; monographs and papers in scientific jls, chiefly on physiological subjects. *Address:* 11a Chaucer Road, Cambridge CB2 2EB. *T:* Cambridge 54551.
[Died 3 June 1977.

HILL, Charles Loraine; Chairman: Bristol City Line of Steamships Ltd; Charles Hill of Bristol Ltd; also Chairman or Director of several other companies; *b* 1891; *s* of late Chas Gathorne Hill, MA, JP; *m* 1st, 1916, Mary A. (marr. diss. 1944), *d* of Major J. C. Harford; two *s* one *d* (and two *d* decd); 2nd, 1944, Mrs John Taylor (*née* Grant-Richards). *Educ:* Eton; Cambridge (BA). JP Som, 1923. *Address:* Grove House, Alveston, Bristol, Avon. *T:* Thornbury 412273. *Club:* Brooks's.
[Died 14 Dec. 1976.

HILL, Clifford Francis; HM Diplomatic Service; Consul-General, Durban, since 1977; *b* 27 Jan. 1930; *s* of William Bucknell Hill, Teignmouth, Devon; *m* 1953, Cicely Margaret Taylor; two *s* one *d. Educ:* Falmouth Grammar Sch.; Jesus Coll., Cambridge. RNVR, 1949-50. Entered Foreign (subseq. Diplomatic) Service, 1953; 3rd Sec. and Private Sec. to HM Ambassador, Tokyo, 1953-58; FO, 1959-60; 1st Sec., Office of Comr-Gen. for SE Asia, Singapore (later Office of Political Adviser, C-in-C Far East), 1960-64; seconded to CRO, 1964-66; 1st Sec., Information, Washington, 1966-69; FO, 1969-71; seconded to Home Office and subseq. NI Office for service in Belfast, 1971-73; Head of Cultural Exchange Dept, FCO, 1974-77. *Address:* c/o Foreign and Commonwealth Office, SW1.
[Died 7 March 1979.

HILL, Sir Cyril Rowley; *see* Hill, Sir (George) Cyril Rowley.

HILL, Rev. Canon Douglas George; Canon Emeritus of Ely, since 1979; Examining Chaplain to the Bishop of Ely and Director of Studies in Ely Diocese, since 1965; *b* 1912; *s* of George and Edith Hill, Grimsby, Lincs; *m* 1944, Margaret Esther, *d* of late Judge Sir Gerald Hurst, QC; no *c. Educ:* St James' Choir Sch., Grimsby; Gonville and Caius Coll., Cambridge; Lincoln Theological Coll. Schol. Gonville and Caius Coll., 1931-35; MA

1938. Deacon, 1936, Priest 1937, Lincoln; Curate of: Louth with Welton-le-Wold, 1936-40; Crosby, Dio. of Lincoln, 1940-42; St Nicholas, Chislehurst, 1943-45; Vicar of Eynsford, Kent, Dio. of Rochester, 1945-56; Rector of Papworth Everard, Cambridge, Dio. of Ely, and Chaplain to Papworth Village Settlement and Hosp., 1956-60; Residentiary Canon of Ely Cathedral, 1960-65; Principal, Ely Theological Coll., 1960-64; Hon. Canon of Ely, 1965-79; Rector of: Leverington, 1965-74; Teversham, 1974-79. *Recreations:* travel and walking. *Address:* 20 Malcolm Place, Cambridge CB1 1LS. *T:* Cambridge 51575.
[Died 27 April 1980.

HILL, Captain Duncan C., DSO; Royal Navy retired; *b* 10 April 1900; 2nd *s* of late Alick S. Hill, Elmfield, Coventry; *m* 1944, Chief Officer Roseanne Maureen Uprichard, WRNS, Elmfield, Portadown, Northern Ireland; one *s* one *d. Educ:* Oundle; Royal Naval Colls, Osborne and Dartmouth. In various ships from 1917; at Royal Naval Staff Coll., 1936-37; Admiralty, 1937-39; HMS Vindictive, July-Aug. 1939; HMS Royal Arthur, 1939-40; HMS Nelson, 1940-42; HMS President, 1942-44; Naval Force Commander, Burma, 1944-45; Naval Attaché, Moscow, 1945-48; CO, HMS Sirius, 1948-49, HMS Cleopatra, 1949-50, HMS Ganges, Shotley, 1950-51; retd 1951. Gen. Manager, Massey Ferguson Training Centre (UK), 1951-69. *Recreations:* tennis, squash, golf, cricket; ex-football; RN and RM squash champion, 1935. *Address:* Bockendon Grange, Westwood Heath, Coventry, West Midlands. *T:* Coventry 461624. *Clubs:* Incogniti; Jesters.   *[Died 2 May* 1977.

HILL, Eveline, (Mrs J. S. Hill), JP; *b* 16 April 1898; *d* of Richard and Mary A. Ridyard; *m* 1922, John Stanley Hill (*d* 1947); one *s* two *d. Educ:* Manchester Education Cttee Schs. On leaving sch. entered parents' catering business and continued until marriage; assumed joint control, with brother, of the business on Father's death. Manchester City Council, Didsbury Ward, as Conservative rep., 1936-66; CA 1957; County Borough organizer, WVS, Manchester, 1943-50; MP (C) Wythenshawe Division of Manchester, 1950-64. JP Manchester, 1945; Hon. Alderman, 1966.   *[Died 22 Sept.* 1973.

HILL, Sir Francis; see Hill, Sir J. W. F.

HILL, Sir (George) Cyril Rowley, 8th Bt *cr* 1779 of Brook Hall, Londonderry; journalist; *b* 18 Dec. 1890; *o s* of Sir George Rowley Hill, 7th Bt, and Alice Estelle Harley (*d* 1940), *d* of Edward Bacon, Eywood, Kington, Herefordshire; *S* father, 1954; *m* 1919, Edith Muriel, *d* of W. O. Thomas, Oakhurst, Liverpool, and Bryn Glas, Mold, North Wales. *Educ:* St Cyprian's, Eastbourne; Wellington Coll., and abroad. *Heir:* cousin George Alfred Rowley Hill [*b* 11 Oct. 1899; *m* 1st, 1924 (marr. diss. 1938); one *s* ; 2nd, 1938; one *s* one *d*]. *Address:* 59 Imperial Avenue, Westcliff-on-Sea, Essex. *T:* Southend-on-Sea 75891.   *[Died 6 July* 1980.

HILL, Graham, OBE 1968; company director; Grand Prix racing driver, 1958-75; *b* 15 Feb. 1929; *s* of Norman H. D. Hill and Constance M. Hill; *m* 1955, Bette P. Hill; one *s* two *d. Educ:* Hendon Technical Coll. Served RN, 1950-52. Racing Driver: Team Lotus, 1958-59, 1967, 1968, 1969; BRM, 1960-66; Porsche, 1960; R. R. C. Walker, 1970; Brabham Racing team, 1971, 1972; Embassy Racing Team, 1973. World Champion Racing Driver, 1962, 1968; Runner-up (or 2nd) World Champion Racing Driver, 1963, 1964, 1965; 1st, Dutch Grand Prix, May 1962; 1st, German Grand Prix, Aug. 1962; 1st, Italian Grand Prix, Sept. 1962; 1st, South African Grand Prix, Dec. 1962; 1st, Monaco Grand Prix, 1963, 1964, 1965, 1968, 1969; 1st, Tourist Trophy, Aug. 1963 and 1964; 1st, American Grand Prix, 1963, 1964, 1965; 1st, Spanish Grand Prix, 1968; 1st, Reims 12 hr, July 1964; 1st, Indianapolis, 1966; 1st, Mexican Grand Prix, 1968; 1st (co-driver), Le Mans 24 hour race, 1972. Mem. Council, Inst. for Advanced Motorists, 1972-; Pres., Grand Prix Drivers' Assoc. *Recreations:* flying, shooting, golf. *Address:* Lyndhurst, Shenley, Herts. *Clubs:* London Rowing, British Racing Drivers, Leander.   *[Died 29 Nov.* 1975.

HILL, Sir James, 3rd Bt *cr* 1917; Chairman of Directors of Sir James Hill & Sons Ltd, Bradford; *b* 29 May 1905; *s* of Sir Albert Hill, 2nd Bt; *S* father 1946; *m* 1930, Marjory, *d* of late Frank Croft, Brocka, Lindale, Grange-over-Sands; one *s* four *d. Educ:* Wrekin Coll., Salop. *Heir: s* James Frederick Hill [*b* 5 Dec. 1943; *m* 1966, Sandra Elizabeth, *o d* of J. C. Ingram; two *d*]. *Address:* Brea House, Trebetherick, near Wadebridge, Cornwall. *T:* Trebetherick 2483. *Club:* Bradford.   *[Died 19 March* 1976.

HILL, Sir (James William) Francis, Kt 1958; CBE 1954; DL; solicitor; company director; *b* 15 Sept. 1899; *s* of James Hill and Millicent (*née* Blinkhorn). *Educ:* City Sch., Lincoln; Trinity Coll., Cambridge. MA 1925, LLM 1926, LittD 1950

(Cambridge). 2nd Lieut KRRC, 1918. Admitted Solicitor, 1926. Senior partner Andrew and Co., Lincoln, Solicitors. Mem. Lincoln City Council, 1932-74 (Mayor, 1945-46); Hon. Freeman, Lincoln, 1961; Mem. Nottingham University Coll. Council, 1938-48; Pres. Nottingham Univ. Council, 1948-68; Pro-Chancellor, 1959-72; Chancellor, 1972-78. Mem., Royal Commn on Local Govt in England, 1966-69. Chairman: Assoc. of Municipal Corporations, 1957-66; Municipal Mutual Insurance Ltd, 1972-78; formerly Governor, Administrative Staff Coll.; President: European Conf. of Local Authorities, Strasbourg, 1966-68; International Union of Local Authorities, The Hague, 1967-71; Member: Historic Buildings Council, 1968-71; Adv. Board for Redundant Churches, 1969-75. Chm. of Governors: Lincoln Christ's Hosp. Foundation, Girls' High Sch., and Lincoln Sch., 1935-66. Hon. LLD Nottingham and Birmingham; Hon. DLitt Leicester. FSA, FRHistS (Hon. Vice Pres.). Contested (L) Peterborough, 1929, (C) Lincoln, 1950. DL Lincoln, 1974. *Publications:* Medieval Lincoln, 1948; Tudor and Stuart Lincoln, 1956; Georgian Lincoln, 1966; Victorian Lincoln, 1974; (ed) Banks Family Papers, 1952; contribs to historical and local govt jls. *Recreation:* local history. *Address:* The Priory, Lincoln. *T:* Lincoln 25759. *Club:* United Oxford & Cambridge University.   *[Died 6 Jan.* 1980.

HILL, John Gibson, CB 1973; *b* 3 March 1910; *s* of Thomas Hill, Master Mariner, Islandmagee, Co. Antrim, and Anna Bella (*née* McMurtry); *m* 1944, Marian Fyffe Wilson, Belfast; one *s* one *d. Educ:* Royal Belfast Academical Instn; QUB (BA). Solicitor, 1934. Entered Civil Service, NI, 1935, Legal Asst, Min. of Finance; Dep. Principal, Assistance Bd, 1942; Min. of Home Affairs, NI: Dep. Principal, 1944; Principal, 1953; Asst Sec., 1960; Permanent Sec., 1970-73. *Recreations:* watching Rugby, yachting. *Address:* 7 York Avenue, Whitehead, Co. Antrim, Northern Ireland. *T:* Whitehead 3250. *Clubs:* Instonians Rugby; County Antrim Yacht.   *[Died 18 Jan.* 1975.

HILL, Mrs John Stanley; see Hill, Eveline.

HILL, Prof. Kenneth Robson; Vice-Chancellor, University of Benin, Nigeria, since 1972; OF Pathology, Royal Free Hospital School of Medicine, University of London; *b* 20 April 1911; *s* of Frederick and Lydia Hill; *m* 1938, Elsie Wade; one *s* one *d. Educ:* Washington Secondary Sch.; King's Coll. and Westminster Hosp., Univ. of London. BSc 1932; AKC 1932; MB, BS 1943; MD 1946; MRCP 1957; FRIC 1962; FRCPath 1964; FRCP 1970. Served RAMC, OC Med. Res. Unit, West Africa, 1939-45. Rockefeller Fellowship at Johns Hopkins Hosp., Baltimore, USA, 1947-48. Prof. of Pathology, University Coll. of the West Indies, 1949-56; WHO Consultant to Govt of Indonesia, 1950; WHO Consultant to India, Med. Educn, 1967; WHO Consultant for Treponematosis, 1950-72; Vis. Prof., Univ. of Alexandria, 1962; External Examr in Pathology: Univ. of Baghdad, 1961, 1962; Univ. of Khartoum, 1962, 1972; Malta, Singapore, 1963; Ibadan, 1966; Ghana, 1968-70; Ahmadu Bello Univ., Nigeria, 1972; RCS&P Ireland, 1972. Chairman: Group Adv. Med. Cttee, Royal Free Hosp.; Path. Adv. Cttee, NW Regional Med. Bd; Soc. Health Education; Pres., British Soc. of Clinical Cytology; Member: Medical Advisory Cttee, Min. Overseas Development; British Voluntary Programme. Chm., Bd of Governors, Watford Tech. Coll.; Governor, Boreham Wood Grammar Sch. *Publication:* Atlas of Framboesia (WHO), 1951; The Medical Auxiliary, 1971. *Recreations:* service overseas; medical education. *Address:* 12 Aldenham Avenue, Radlett, Herts. *T:* Radlett 6847. *Clubs:* Athenæum, MCC, Anglo-American Sporting.   *[Died 19 Feb.* 1973.

HILL, Maj.-Gen. Leslie Rowley, OBE 1919; *b* Musselburgh, 28 Dec. 1884; 5th *s* of late Lieut-Col R. R. C. Hill; *m* 1916, Eileen Dorothy Hutchinson (*d* 1962); one *s* three *d. Educ:* Wellington Coll.; RMA Woolwich. Commissioned RA, 1904; Army student, Japan, 1910-14; served European War, 1914-16 (wounded), also War of 1939-45, 1939-40. Gen. Staff, 1917-21; Military Attaché, Tokyo, 1925-30; Lieut-Col, 1933; Col, 1933; Brig., 1936; Maj.-Gen., 1938; retired, 1940. *Recreation:* gardening. *Address:* Halketts, Kings Hill, Beech, Alton, Hants. *T:* Alton 62258.   *[Died 17 Dec.* 1975.

HILL, Martin; see Hill, W. M.

HILL, Osman; see Hill, W. C. O.

HILL, Reginald Dykers Richardson; Judge of the Federal Court of Appeal, Malaysia, 1959-63; *b* 11 July 1902; *s* of Michael Dykers and Eliza Sophia Dasent, Brit. Guiana; *m* 1926, Gwendolen Emily Mary (*d* 1969), *e d* of Frank Sale, Birmingham; one *s. Educ:* Cranleigh Sch., Surrey. Called to the Bar, Gray's Inn, 1924. Private practice, Brit. Guiana, 1924; Stipendiary Magistrate, Brit. Guiana, 1930; Resident

Magistrate, Jamaica, 1937; Chief Magistrate, Palestine, 1944; Puisne Judge, Malayan Union, 1947. Badlishah Decn of Loyalty, Kedah, 1958. *Recreations:* social. *Address:* 12 Wilbury Grange, Wilbury Road, Hove BN3 3GN. *Clubs:* West Indian; Hove (Hove).   [*Died* 21 *Jan.* 1973.

HILL, Reginald Harrison, MA (Oxon); FLA 1928; Librarian and Secretary to the Trustees of the National Central Library, 1945-58, retired; *b* 24 Nov. 1894; *s* of William and Edith Margaret Hill, Oxford; *m* 1922, Winifred I. Langford (*d* 1956); two *s* decd. *Educ:* City of Oxford Sch.; St Catherine's Coll., Oxford. Bodleian Library, Oxford: Under-Asst, 1908-11; Senior Asst, 1911-33; Sec. to Bodley's Librarian, 1931-33; Sec. of the Library, 1933-44. Sec., Friends of the Bodleian, 1929-33. First Hon. Sec. of University and Research Section of Library Assoc., 1928-30. Rockefeller Research Fellow, visiting United States Libraries, 1934; Adviser (Libraries) to UK Delegn, UNESCO, Paris Conf., 1946; Chm., UK Libraries Advisory Cttee, UNESCO, 1948-66; Chm., Educn and Library Cttee of Polish Research Centre, 1958-67. Sec., British Academy Cttee on Provision for Research, 1958-61. Edited Bodleian Quarterly Record, 1914-17, 1919-31. Hon. Member: Osler Club; Polish Inst. *Publications:* The Shelley Correspondence in the Bodleian Library, 1926; Bibliotheca Osleriana, 1929 (with Dr W. W. Francis and Dr T. A. Malloch); reports and papers in Library Assoc. Record, etc. *Recreations:* bibliography, gardening. *Address:* Visitation Convent, Pymore Road, Bridport, Dorset DT6 3AP. *T:* Bridport 24316, 24328.   [*Died* 15 *Oct.* 1976.

HILL, Sir Reginald (Herbert), KBE 1942; CB 1933; *b* 27 Nov. 1888; *s* of Herbert Charles Hill and Caroline Brown; *m* 1918, Mary Catherine (*d* 1964), *d* of T. H. McGinn; one *s* one *d. Educ:* Merchant Taylors' Sch.; St John's Coll., Oxford. Entered Board of Trade, 1912; Dep. Sec., Min. of Transport, 1940; Min. of War Transport, 1941-54; Dep. Dir-Gen. (Inland Transport), Min. of War Transport, 1941-47; Chm. Docks and Inland Waterways Board of Management, British Transport Commission, 1948-54. Medal of Freedom with silver palm, US, 1947; Ordre du Mérite Maritime, France, 1950. *Address:* Lammermoor Nursing Home, Shenfield Common, Brentwood, Essex.   [*Died* 26 *Dec.* 1971.

HILL, Reginald John James, CIE 1947; MA; Principal, Ministry of Overseas Development, 1964; retired, 1965; *b* 1 July 1905; *s* of James Hill and Winifred Alexander; *m* 1932, Margaret St Barbe McNeil-Smith; one *s* one *d. Educ:* Dunfermline High Sch., Fife, Scotland; Universities of Edinburgh, Göttingen (Germany); Lyon (France); Emmanuel Coll., Cambridge. Joined ICS, 1928; Asst Comr, 1928; Dep. Comr, 1935; Financial Sec. to Govt, Central Provinces and Berar, 1944; entered HM Treasury, 1947; Colonial Office, 1949; Dept of Technical Co-operation, 1961. *Recreations:* fishing, gardening, cricket, field sports. *Address:* The Pound Cottage, Bisley, Surrey. *T:* Brookwood 3054.
                                          [*Died* 24 *Jan.* 1977.

HILL, William Charles Osman, MD; *b* 13 July 1901; *s* of late James Osman Hill and of Fanny Martin; *m* 1947, Yvonne, *o d* of late Harold Stranger, KC, MP. *Educ:* King Edward VI Sch., Birmingham; Birmingham Univ. University of Birmingham: MB, ChB 1924, MD (Hons) 1925; Richards Memorial Prize; Junior Medical Prize; Ingleby Schol. in Midwifery; Asst Lecturer in Zoology, 1924-25; Lecturer in Anatomy, 1925-30; Prof. of Anatomy, Ceylon Medical Coll. (later University of Ceylon), 1930-44 (Registrar, 1938-40); Reader in Physical Anthropology, University of Edinburgh, 1945-50; Prosector to the Zoological Soc. of London, 1950-62; Associate Dir, Yerkes Primate Research Center, 1962-69. Editor-in-Chief, Ceylon Jl of Science, 1932-44; Gen. Editor, Zoo Penguins, 1957. Visiting Prof. of Anatomy, Emory Univ., Georgia, 1957-58. External Examiner in Univ. Coll., Colombo (Zoology), and in Universities of Cambridge, Edinburgh and Reading; Part-time Lecturer in Morphology, Charing Cross Hospital Medical Sch., 1954-62; Mem., Board of Studies in Anatomy, University of London; Hunterian Trustee, Royal College of Surgeons of England, 1962-. FRSE (Gold Medal, Makdougal-Brisbane Prize, 1955); FLS; FRAI; FZS; Anatomical Soc. of Great Britain and Ireland (Hon. Mem. and late Vice-Pres.). Asst Comr St John's Ambulance Assoc. (Ceylon Branch), 1938-43. *Publications:* Comparative Anatomy and Taxonomy of the Primates (8 vols), 1953, 1955, 1957, 1960, 1962, 1966, 1967, 1970, 1974; Man's Ancestry, 1954; Man as an Animal, 1957; Evolutionary Biology of the Primates, 1972; numerous papers on primate morphology, anthropology and human anatomy. *Recreations:* field ornithology, botany, photography and travel. *Address:* Oakhurst, Dixwell Road, Folkestone, Kent; University of Turin, Via Accademia Albertina 17, Turin, Italy.
                                          [*Died* 25 *Jan.* 1975.

HILL, (William) Martin, CMG 1973; Special Fellow, United Nations Institute for Training and Research, since 1972; *b* Cork, Ireland, 8 April 1905; *s* of William Henry Hill, FRIAI, and Stella A. Hill; *m* 1932, Diana Grove Annesley; one *s. Educ:* Malvern Coll.; Oriel Coll., Oxford (MA); London Sch. of Economics; Univ. of Vienna (Rockefeller Fellowship). Official of League of Nations, 1927-46: serving part of this period with Econ. and Financial Section, part with Polit. Section; Sec., Bruce Cttee, 1939, and Economic and Financial Cttees, 1942-45; Special Adviser, San Francisco Conf., and Chief of Admin. and Budgetary Section, Preparatory Commn of UN, 1945. Joined permanent staff of UN as Special Adviser to Sec.-Gen., 1946; Dep. Exec. Asst to Sec.-Gen. and Dir of Co-ordination for Specialized Agencies and economic and social matters, 1948-55; Dep. Under-Sec. for Economic and Social Affairs, 1955-66; Asst Sec.-Gen. for Inter-agency Affairs, 1967-70. After retirement, Special Consultant to Sec.-Gen., 1971-72. *Publications:* Commercial Policy in the Inter-War Period, 1942; Quantitative Trade Controls (with Prof. G. Haberler), 1943; The Economic and Financial Organization of the League of Nations, 1945; Immunities and Privileges of International Officials, 1947; The Administrative Committee on Co-ordination, in The Evolution of International Organizations (ed E. Luard), 1966. *Recreation:* music. *Address:* 260 Snowden Lane, Princeton, New Jersey, USA. *T:* (609) 921-7967. *Club:* Athenæum.
                                          [*Died* 18 *May* 1976.

HILL, William Wills, MA (Hon.) Birmingham 1936; BSc London; Member of Convocation, and former Member of the Senate, University of London; first Hon. Member of National Campaign for Nursery Education; Editor of Schoolmaster and Woman Teacher's Chronicle, 1933-46; *b* 9 Sept. 1881; *m* 1905, May Frances (*d* 1960), *d* of William and Elizabeth Dixon, Kingston-upon-Thames; two *s. Educ:* Page Green Sch., Tottenham; East London Technical Coll.; Westminster Training Coll. Headmaster of Secondary Schs in Leics, 1907-33; Pres. of National Union of Teachers, 1928; Mem. of Executive, 1921-33; Pres. of Barwell Co-operative Soc., 1917-21. Gold Medal for Ball Room Dancing, Imp. Soc. of Teachers of Dancing, 1967. *Recreations:* swimming, dancing, bowls, gramophone, theatre. *Address:* 45 Queen's Avenue, Muswell Hill, N10. *T:* 01-883 2885. *Club:* Arts Theatre.   [*Died* 30 *Oct.* 1974.

HILL-WOOD, Sir Wilfred (William Hill), KCVO 1976; CBE 1946; Adviser, Morgan Grenfell Holdings Ltd, since 1980; *b* 8 Sept. 1901; 2nd *s* of Sir Samuel Hill Hill-Wood, 1st Bt; *m* 1947, Diana Marian, *widow* of Wing Comdr Harry Manners Mellor, MVO, RAF, and *d* of Major Hugh Wyld. *Educ:* Eton; Trinity Coll., Cambridge. Managing Director, Morgan, Grenfell & Co. Ltd, 1939-67, Mem., Directors' Adv. Cttee, 1967-80. Director: Anglo-American Securities Corp. Ltd; North Atlantic Securities Corp. Ltd. *Address:* Flat 4, Cornwall Mansions, 33 Kensington Court, W8. *Club:* White's.   [*Died* 10 *Oct.* 1980.

HILLARD, Ronald Johnstone, CMG 1950; *b* 6 May 1903; *yr s* of late Rev. A. E. and late Mrs Hillard; *m* 1st, 1933 (marr. diss. 1950); one *s*; 2nd, 1950, Anne Josephine (*d* 1952), *yr d* of late B. J. F. Picton, Sherborne; one *d*; 3rd, 1954, Joan, *o c* of late Conyers Boldron Toller, Coldstream Guards. *Educ:* St Paul's Sch., London; Christ Church, Oxford. Scholar of Christ Church, Oxford, 1922-25; Rugby Blue, 1923-24, 1924-25; International (England) Rugby Cap, 1925. Sudan Political Service, Dec. 1925-46; Sec. to Governor-Gen.'s Council, 1932-34; Dir, Dept of Economics and Trade, Sudan Govt, 1946-49; Mem. of Governor-Gen.'s Council, 1946-48; Councillor without Portfolio on Executive Council and MLA, Sudan, 1949-52; Gen. Manager, Sudan Railways, 1949-52; Dir, Tunnel Portland Cement Co. Ltd, 1953-54; Chm. and Man. Dir, E African Portland Cement Co. Ltd, 1955-68. Pres., Nairobi Chamber of Commerce, 1961-62. Order of the Nile, 4th Class, 1936. *Recreations:* reading, writing. *Address:* 6 Egdon Glen, Crossways, near Dorchester, Dorset. *T:* Warmwell 342. *Club:* English-Speaking Union.   [*Died* 23 *March* 1971.

HILLARY, Michael, DSO 1917; OBE 1918; FASA; retired; *b* 20 Feb. 1886; *s* of Thomas Hillary, Adelaide, S Australia; *m* 1916, Edwyna Mary (*d* 1966), *d* of Dr J. W. Hope, Perth, WA; (one *s* killed on active service, 1943). *Educ:* private school; Adelaide Univ. Officer of the Commonwealth Treasury Dept, 1909-24; Sec., War Gratuities Board, 1920; War Pensions Branch, Repatriation Dept, 1921; Private Sec. to Prime Minister, 1922; Special Duty Australia House, London, including reporting to Royal Commission in Australia on Nat. Insurance in the UK, the Continent and USA, 1923-24; transferred to Sudan Govt, 1924: Asst Dir of Accounts, 1924-29; Dir of Accounts, 1929-33; Auditor-Gen., 1933-38. Served European War, 1914-18, in Mesopotamia (DSO, OBE, despatches twice). *Recreations:* sailing and golf. *Address:* 61 Clarewood Court, Seymour Place, W1. *T:* 01-723 0615. *Club:* Athenæum. [*Died* 23 *Oct.* 1976.

HILLER, George François, CMG 1962; DSO 1945; Commercial Counsellor, British Embassy, Brussels, since 1968; *b* 15 Dec. 1916; *s* of late George Spicer Hiller and Alice Prud'hon; *m* 1963, Judith, *e d* of John J. Buchanan, 67 Chester Square, SW1, and late Mrs Buchanan; one *s* two *d. Educ:* Lycée Janson de Sailly, Paris; Exeter Coll., Oxford. Served War of 1939-45 (DSO). Asst Principal, Dept of Overseas Trade, 1945; 2nd Sec. (Commercial), Madrid, 1946; 1st Sec. (Commercial), 1948, transferred to Lima, 1949; transferred to Foreign Office and attached to Joint Services Staff Coll., Nov. 1951-May 1952; 1st Sec. (Commercial), Tehran, 1954; Head of Chancery, Tehran, 1957; Counsellor, 1959; Head of Eastern Dept, Foreign Office, 1959-63; Counsellor: Political Advisers Office, Singapore, 1963-65; UK Delegation to NATO, 1965-68. *Recreations:* travelling, photography. *Address: c/o* Foreign and Commonwealth Office, SW1. *Club:* Travellers'.   *[Died 22 Nov. 1972.*

HILLGARTH, Capt. Alan Hugh, CMG 1943; OBE 1937; RN, retired; *b* 7 June 1899; *s* of late Willmott Henderson Hillgarth Evans, MD, FRCS and Anne Frances Piercy; assumed surname of Hillgarth by deed poll, 1928; *m* 1st, 1929, Hon. Mary Sidney Katherine Almina Hope-Morley (marr. diss. 1946), 3rd *d* of 1st Baron Burghclere; one *s*; 2nd, 1947, Jean Mary (*d* 1975), *e d* of Frank Cobb; two *s* one *d. Educ:* Royal Naval Colls, Osborne and Dartmouth; King's Coll., Cambridge. Entered Royal Navy, 1912; Vice-Consul at Palma, 1932-37; Consul, 1937-39; Naval Attaché at Madrid, 1939-43; Chief of Intelligence Staff, Eastern Fleet, 1943-44; Chief of British Naval Intelligence, Eastern Theatre, 1944-46. *Publications:* various novels. *Recreation:* forestry. *Address:* Illannanagh House, Ballinderry, Co. Tipperary. *T:* Ballinderry 3. *Clubs:* Army and Navy, Garrick.
[Died 28 Feb. 1978.

HILLINGDON, 4th Baron *cr* 1886; **Charles Hedworth Mills;** Bt 1868; Captain, Life Guards; *b* 12 Jan. 1922; *er* and *o* surv. *s* of 3rd Baron and of Hon. Edith Mary Winifred, Cadogan (Edith, Lady Hillingdon, DBE), *e d* of Henry Arthur, Viscount Chelsea; *S* father 1952; *m* 1947, Lady Sarah Grey Stuart, 2nd *d* of 18th Earl of Moray; three *d* (one *s* decd). *Educ:* Eton; Magdalen Coll., Oxford. 2nd Lieut Coldstream Guards, 1941; transferred Life Guards, 1942; Captain, 1943. *Heir: cousin* Patrick Charles Mills, MC, TD. *Address:* Messing Park, Kelvedon, Essex. *T:* Tiptree 364. *Club:* White's.   *[Died 6 May 1978.*

HILLS, Lt-Col John David, MC; MA; Head Master of Bradfield College, 1939-55; *b* 1895; *s* of late Rev. Henry Gardner Hills and Isabel, *d* of Frederick Cattley, St Petersburg; *m* 1932, Lady Rosemary Baring, *er d* of 2nd Earl of Cromer, GCIE, GCVO; one *s* two *d. Educ:* Merchant Taylors' Sch.; Lincoln Coll., Oxford (Classical Exhibitioner). Served European War in 5th Bn Leics Regt (despatches twice, MC with bar, Croix de Guerre); Asst Master, Eton Coll., 1921, Housemaster, 1932, Sen. History Master, 1935-39; Comdg OTC, 1930-32; Lt-Col TA Reserve, 1932-50. Dir Schs Empire Tour, Canada, 1932; Lectr HM Forces, Middle East, 1945; Lectr for The Times, 1955-66. *Recreations:* genealogy and heraldry. *Address:* House by the Dyke, Chirk, Wrexham, N Wales. *T:* Chirk 3207.
[Died 14 July 1975.

HILTON OF UPTON, Baron *cr* 1965 (Life Peer); **Albert Victor Hilton;** JP; *b* 14 Feb. 1908; *s* of Thomas and Anne Hilton; *m* 1944, Nelly Simmons (*d* 1976); (two *s* decd). *Educ:* Norfolk Elementary Schs. Labour Party Agent, E Norfolk, 1936-45. TU Officer, National Union of Agricultural Workers, 1946-59; MP (Lab) SW Norfolk, March 1959-Sept. 1964; a Lord in Waiting, 1966-70. Vice-Pres., 1963-64, Pres., 1964-66, NUAW; Member: Labour Party National Executive Cttee, 1963-; East Anglia Economic Planning Council, 1966-; Chm., National Brotherhood Movement, 1967. A Methodist Lay Preacher, 1932-. JP 1949, CC 1951-70, Norfolk. *Recreation:* Association football (County colours, Norfolk, 1932). *Address:* 9 Spinners Lane, Swaffham, Norfolk. *T:* Swaffham 21341.
[Died 3 May 1977.

HILTON, Conrad (Nicholson); Chairman: Hilton Hotels Corporation, since (formation of company) 1946; Hilton International Company since 1968; *b* 25 Dec. 1887; *s* of August Holver Hilton and Mary Laufersweiler; *m* 1925, Mary Barron; two *s* (and one *s* decd). *Educ:* St Michael's Coll., Santa Fé; New Mexico Mil. Inst.; New Mexico Sch. of Mines. MHR, New Mexico, 1912-13; Partner, A. H. Hilton & Sons, 1915. 2nd Lieut, US Army, 1917-19. Bought first hotel, Cisco, Texas, 1919; bought, sold and operated hotels, 1919-46; organized Hilton Hotels Corp., 1946; founded Hilton Internat. Co., 1948 (of which he is now Chm.); bought Waldorf-Astoria, 1949; bought Statler Hotel chain, 1954. Chm. of 2 companies, operating 155 hotels around the world. Holds several hon. doctorates; also knighthoods, etc in foreign Orders. *Publications:* Be My Guest,

1957; Inspirations of an Innkeeper, 1963. *Recreation:* golf. *Address:* 9990 Santa Monica Boulevard, Beverly Hills, Calif, USA. *T:* 277-6203. *Clubs:* Metropolitan (New York City); Chicago Athletic; Los Angeles Country; Bel Air Country.
[Died 3 Jan. 1979.

HILTON, Gwen, CBE 1959; FRCS; Hon. Radiotherapist, University College Hospital, London; *b* 22 Sept. 1898; *d* of M. J. M. Hill, Professor of Pure Mathematics, University Coll., London; *m* 1925, Reginald Hilton (*d* 1969); one *d. Educ:* Roedean Sch.; University Coll. and Hosp. Hons BSc in Physiology, 1921; MB, BS London 1924; DMR&E 1932; FFR 1940; FRCS 1955. Fellow of University Coll. *Publications:* papers on radiotherapy treatment in cancer. *Recreations:* gardening, study of languages. *Address:* 8 Elm Tree Road, St John's Wood, NW8.   *[Died 8 July 1971.*

HILTON, Maj.-Gen. Richard, DSO 1944; MC 1915; DFC and Bar, 1918; retired; *b* 18 Jan. 1894; 2nd *s* of John Edward Hilton, JP, Lambourn, Berks; *m* 1917, Phyllis Martha, *e d* of late Rev. S. H. Woodin, MA, Rector of Yarmouth, IoW; two *s. Educ:* Malvern; RMA Woolwich. Served European War, 1914-18, Western Front, in RA, RFC and RAF (wounded); commissioned 2nd Lieut, RGA, 1913; seconded to RFC, 1915; Lieut, 1915; Capt., 1917; Sqdn Comdr, 1918. Seconded to Tank Corps, 1922-23; Indian Mountain Artillery, 1924-30, 1934-38; Staff Capt., War Office, 1930-33; Major 1934; Bt Lt-Col 1937; Lt-Col 1939. War of 1939-45, BEF, 1939-40; Chief Instructor (Air), Sch. of Artillery, 1940; CRA 15th (Scottish) Div., 1941-44 (wounded); BGS to Allied Liberation Forces, Norway, 1945; Dep. Chief of British Mission to Soviet Zone of Germany, 1946-47; Military Attaché in Moscow, 1947-48; retd, 1948. Comdr, Order of St Olav, Norway, 1945. *Publications:* Military Attaché in Moscow, 1949; Nine Lives, 1955; The Indian Mutiny, 1957; The North-West Frontier, 1957; The Thirteenth Power, 1958; Imperial Obituary, 1968; contrib. to Blackwoods, Nineteenth Century and After, Service and other Journals. *Recreations:* languages, chess, world affairs, travel. *Address:* Buckingham Hotel, Buxton, Derbyshire SK17 9AS.   *[Died 26 July 1978.*

HILTON, Roger, CBE 1968; Artist; *b* 23 March 1911; *s* of O. Hilton, MD, and Louisa Holdsworth (*née* Sampson); *m* 1st, 1957, Ruth Catherine David; one *s* one *d*; 2nd, 1965, Rosemary Julia Phipps; two *s. Educ:* Bishop's Stortford Coll.; Slade Sch., London. Served in HM Forces, 1939-45 (POW 1942-45). One Man Exhibitions: Gimpel Fils, 1952, 1954, 1956; Waddington Galls, 1960, 1962, 1964, 1966. 1st prize, John Moores Exhibition, Liverpool, 1963. Retrospective Exhibitions: Serpentine Gall., 1974; Edinburgh, 1974. Represented Great Britain at Venice Biennale, 1964 (UNESCO Prize). *Address: c/o* Waddington Galleries, 2 Cork Street, W1. *[Died 23 Feb. 1975.*

HILTON-SERGEANT, Maj.-Gen. Frederick Cavendish, CB 1956; CBE 1955; retired 1957; Medical Adviser, British Red Cross, 1957-70; *b* 25 Feb. 1898; *s* of F. M. C. Sergeant, Liverpool; *m* 1929, Kathleen Margaret Howard, 2nd *d* of Howard J. Walker, Dalton Grange, Parbold; two *d. Educ:* Calday Sch.; Liverpool Univ. MB, ChB (Liverpool) 1921; DPH (Eng.) 1938; MFCM 1973; Leishman Prize, RAM Coll., 1932. 2nd Lieut, RFA, 1917-18; entered RAMC, 1923; served India, NW Frontier; China, Shanghai; and ME countries; Capt. 1926; Major 1934; Lieut-Col 1946; Brig. 1951; Maj.-Gen. 1953. Dep. Dir Hygiene, British Troops in Egypt and Ext. Examr in Preventive Medicine, Kasr-el-Aini Univ., Cairo, 1943-46; Dep. Dir Hygiene, W Comd, 1947-48; Prof. of Hygiene, RAM Coll., 1949; Comdt Army Sch. of Health, 1949-50; DDMS, Brit. troops in Egypt, 1951-52; DDMS, N Comd, 1953; Comdt and Dir of Medical Studies, Royal Army Medical Coll., 1953-57. QHP 1953-57. FRSM; FSocMOH. OStJ. *Publications:* contribs to Jl of RAMC. *Recreations:* ski-ing, sailing, tennis, golf. *Address:* Home Cottage, Quality Street, Merstham, Surrey. *T:* Merstham 3988.   *[Died 17 Feb. 1978.*

HINCHCLIFFE, Sir (George) Raymond, Kt 1957; Judge of High Court of Justice, Queen's Bench Division, 1957-73; Presiding Judge, North Eastern Circuit, 1970-73; *b* 2 March 1900; *s* of late A. E. T. Hinchcliffe, Woodside, Huddersfield; *m* 1st, Hilda Sydenham (*d* 1938); 2nd, Hannah Sophia Eadie. *Educ:* Leys Sch.; Trinity Hall, Cambridge. 2nd Lieut RAF, 1918; called to Bar, Middle Temple, 1924; KC 1947; Bencher Middle Temple, 1953; went North Eastern Circuit; Deputy Div. Food Officer, North Eastern Division, 1939-42; Dir of Services for North Eastern Region of Ministry of Fuel and Power, 1942-45; Recorder of Berwick-upon-Tweed, 1939-47, of Middlesbrough, 1947-50, of Leeds, 1950-57; Deputy Chm., Quarter Sessions, WR Yorks, 1947, Chm. 1954-57; Attorney-Gen., Co. Palatine of Durham, 1950-57 (Solicitor-Gen., 1947); Chancellor of Diocese of Bradford, 1950-57. Hon. Fellow, Trinity Hall, Cambridge,

1959. Hon. LLD Leeds, 1959. *Address:* Queen Elizabeth Building, Temple, EC4. *T:* 01-583 4040. *Club:* Bath.
[Died 6 Sept. 1973.

HINCHCLIFFE, Brig. John William, DSO 1940; *b* 24 June 1893; *s* of late Rev. J. H. Hinchcliffe; *m* 1946, Millicent Damaris Reader Harris, *d* of late Sir Skinner Turner. *Educ:* Lancing Coll.; Caius Coll., Cambridge; RMC, Sandhurst. Joined Northamptonshire Regt, 1915; served European War, 1914-18; served India, 1919-25; China, 1927-29; Adjt, Shanghai Volunteer Corps, 1929-32; India, 1932-36; Northern Ireland, 1936-39; France, outbreak of war, 1939-40; Commanded 2nd Battalion The Northants Regt, 1940-42; Comdr Tehran Sub-Area, 1942-43; Commanded South Iraq Area, Paiforce, 1945; retired pay, 1946; Deputy Commissioner London (Prince of Wales's) District St John Ambulance Bde, 1952-66; KStJ 1964. *Address:* Grey Walls, Lymington Road, Milford-on-Sea, Hants SO4 0QN. *T:* Milford-on-Sea 2356. *Clubs:* Naval and Military, MCC. *[Died 21 Oct.* 1975.

HINCHCLIFFE, Sir Raymond; *see* Hinchcliffe, Sir G. R.

HINCHLIFFE, Sir (Albert) Henry (Stanley), Kt 1953; JP; DL; BA Oxon; Chairman Glazebrook Steel & Co. Ltd, Manchester, retired, 1971; Director, Barclays Bank, 1952-69, also Local Director, Manchester Board, 1943-70; *b* 10 May 1893; *s* of Edward Stanley Hinchliffe, Mucklestone, Market Drayton; *m* 1921, Vera, JP (*d* 1979), *d* of Frederick Liddell Steel, Ranton Abbey, Staffs; three *d. Educ:* Cheltenham; Keble Coll., Oxford. Enlisted North Staffs Regt 1914; commissioned, 1915; wounded at Loos, 1915; invalided on account of wounds, 1916; Finance Dept, India, 1916-19; India Office, 1919-20. County Councillor Staffs, 1942-55. Dir Manchester Chamber of Commerce, 1938-72, Emeritus 1972-; Pres., 1944-46; Pres., Assoc. of British Chambers of Commerce, 1950-52; Chm. UK Cttee, Federation of Commonwealth Chambers of Commerce, 1961-63; Leader of British side in UK, Canada Trade Conference, 1949, 1951, 1954, 1955. Dir LNER, 1944 until nationalisation; Mem., Manchester Joint Research Council (Chm., 1944-48). Governor of Manchester Grammar Sch., 1940-76. Member: Central Transport Consultative Cttee, 1948-51; Advisory Council, DSIR, 1949-54; Dollar Exports Advisory Council, 1951-52; National Research Development Corp., 1955-58; Management Cttee, St Mary's Hospitals, Manchester, 1926-59; Chm., Min. of Health Cttee on Cost of Prescribing, 1957-59; Member: (original) ITA, 1954-59; Court of Governors, Manchester Univ.; Finance Cttee, Keele Univ.; Trustee, John Rylands Library, 1952-72. JP Manchester 1942; High Sheriff 1944, DL 1946, Staffs. *Publications:* The Bar Sinister, 1935; contributor to Fortnightly Review and other periodicals. *Recreations:* ancient churches, country pursuits. *Address:* Mucklestone Old Rectory, Market Drayton, Salop. *TA* and *T:* Ashley 2188. *Clubs:* Lansdowne, MCC; St James's (Manchester).
[Died 16 April 1980.

HINCHLIFFE, (Frank) Philip (Rideal), QC 1968; **His Honour Judge Hinchliffe;** a Circuit Judge (formerly a Judge of County Courts), since 1971; *b* 13 Jan. 1923; *er s* of George Hinchliffe and Margaret Hinchliffe, JP, BSc; *m* 1954, Ann Rosamund Featherby; three *s. Educ:* Worksop Coll.; New Coll., Oxford. Pres., Oxford Union Soc., Trinity Term, 1942; 2nd cl. hons Jurisprudence Oxon, 1942; MA 1943. War Service, RA, 1942-46 (despatches, 1945); Capt. Called to Bar, Inner Temple, 1947 (Entrance Schol.). Dep. Chm., Westmorland QS, 1969-71. Pres., SW Pennines Magistrates' Assoc., 1974-. *Recreations:* bridge, golf. *Address:* Westmains, 251 Hale Road, Hale, Cheshire WA15 8RE. *T:* 061-980 6391; 5 Essex Court, Temple, EC4. *T:* 01-353 4365. *[Died 18 Oct.* 1976.

HINCHLIFFE, Sir Henry; *see* Hinchliffe, Sir (A.) H. (S.).

HINCHLIFFE, Philip; *see* Hinchliffe, F. P. R.

HIND, Maj.-Gen. Neville Godfray, CSI 1943; MC; *b* 8 Jan. 1892; *s* of A. E. Hind, FRCS, Portland House, Jersey; *m* 1921, Marguerite Kay (*d* 1953), *d* of late Capt. A. R. K. Hall, Royal Irish Rifles; one *s* decd; *m* 1958, Mrs Noël Mansfield, *widow* of Humphrey Mansfield, and *d* of late Thomas Harvey Browne, Sydney, NSW. *Educ:* Winchester; Royal Military Academy, Woolwich. 2nd Lieut 1911; 2nd Gurkhas (The Sirmoor Rifles), 1912; served in France, Egypt, and Baluchistan, 1914-18 (despatches); Waziristan, 1919-20 (despatches, MC); Staff Coll., 1923; Bde Major, Zhob, 1924; GSO2, Northern Command, India, 1926; Asst Sec. Cttee Imperial Defence, 1930; Comdt 2/2nd Gurkhas, 1935; Deputy Sec. Defence Dept, India, 1938; Comdr Jubblepur Area, 1940; Comdr Sind District, India, 1942; Maj.-Gen. 1943; retired, 1945. Order of Polonia Restituta, 1943. KStJ 1966. *Address:* Le Pré de Becasse, Longueville, Jersey. *T:*

Central 20164. *Club:* United Service & Royal Aero.
[Died 11 Jan. 1973.

HINDE, Lt-Col Reginald Graham; Indian Political Service, retired; FLAS; *b* 19 May 1887; *o s* of late Arthur Percival Hinde, Beaumont Hall, Lancaster; *m* 1928, Eileen, *er d* of late Sir Henry Sutcliffe Smith, Ingerthorpe Grange, Markington, Yorks; two *s. Educ:* Eastbourne Coll.; Sandhurst. Commissioned in Indian Army, 1907; attached 89th (Princess Victoria's) Royal Irish Fusiliers; appointed to 124th (Duchess of Connaught's Own) Baluchistan Infantry, 1908; served in Baluchistan and China; proceeded to Persia with Sir Percy Sykes' Mission and DAA and QMG to Force, July 1916; recruiting duty in Kalat State, 1918; Comdt Sarhad Levy Corps, East Persia, 1919; transferred to Political Dept, 1920; Asst Political Agent, Makran, and Comdt Makran Levy Corps, 1920-21; Asst Commissioner Dera Ismail Khan and Sub-Divisional Officer, Tank, North-West Frontier Province, 1922; HBM's Vice-Consul Dizful Arabistan, Persia, 1923; HBM's Consul and Political Agent, Muscat, Oman, Arabia, 1923-24; Asst Resident in Kashmir and British Joint Commissioner, Ladakh, 1925-26; Sec. to the Agent to the Governor-Gen. Punjab States, 1927; Political Agent Southern States of Rajputana, 1929; Sec. to the Agent to the Governor-Gen. in Central India, 1929-30; Boundary Settlement Officer in Central India, 1930-31; Political Agent in Bundelkhand, 1931; in Bhopal, 1931-33; in Loraiai, 1933-36; in Raipur, 1936-38; Resident Agent, Castle Howard Estate, Yorks, 1940-51; Forestry Consultant, 1952-57. *Recreations:* fishing and racing. *Address:* Otterden Place, Eastling, Faversham, Kent. *T:* Eastling 342. *[Died 31 Jan.* 1971.

HINDLE, Edward, FRS 1942; MA, ScD Cambridge, PhD California; Hon. FIBiol; Hon. Fellow of the Imperial College of Science and Technology, London University; Scientific Director of Zoological Society of London, 1944-51; *b* Sheffield, 21 March 1886; *s* of late Edward James Hindle and Sarah Elizabeth (*née* Dewar); *m* 1919, Irene Margaret (*d* 1933), *d* of late John Twist, Prescot, Lancs. *Educ:* Magdalene Coll., Cambridge; Royal Coll. of Science and King's Coll., London; Institut Pasteur, Paris; California Univ., Berkeley; Rhodesian Gold Medallist, 1912; Charles Kingsley Lectr and Bye Fellow of Magdalene Coll., Cambridge, 1913; Prof. of Biology, Sch. of Medicine, Cairo, 1919-24; Milner Research Fellow, London Sch. of Hygiene and Tropical Medicine, 1924-27; Kala Azar Commission of the Royal Society to Northern China, 1925-27; Beit Memorial Research Fellow in Tropical Medicine, 1927-33; William Withering Lectr, Birmingham Univ., 1935; Regius Prof. of Zoology, Univ. of Glasgow, 1935-43; Joint Editor Parasitology and sectional Editor, Tropical Diseases Bulletin; Mem. Scientific Advisory Cttee, Laboratory Practice; Gen. Sec., British Assoc. for the Advancement of Science, 1946-51; Hon. Sec., RGS, 1951-61, Hon. Vice-Pres., 1962-; Founder-Pres., Inst. of Biology; Past Pres., Zoology Section of International Union of Biological Sciences; Pres., Universities Fedn of Animal Welfare; Founder Pres. and Hon. Vice-Pres., Zoological Soc. of Glasgow; Past Pres. Royal Phil. Soc. of Glasgow; Founder Dir Int. Wildfowl Research Bureau; Membre Correspondant: Soc. de Pathologie Exotique; Soc. Belge de Médecine Tropicale; Soc. Royale Entomologique d'Egypte. Médaille Geoffroy Saint-Hilaire (en or) de la Soc. d'Acclimatation de France, 1951; served European War, 1914-19, with Signal Service in France and Palestine, Lt-Col comdg Glasgow Univ. OTC, 1936-43; Belgian Croix Civique (1st class), 1931. *Publications:* Flies and Disease-Blood-sucking Flies, 1914; numerous papers relating chiefly to original work in protozoology and parasitology, especially insect-transmitted infections. *Recreations:* music, motoring, and travelling. *Address:* 5 Eton Avenue, NW3 3EL. *T:* 01-794 2243. *Club:* Athenæum. *[Died 22 Jan.* 1973.

HINDLEY, Brig. Geoffrey Bernard Sylvester, CBE 1955 (OBE 1943); *b* 25 Oct. 1902; 2nd *s* of late Sir Clement D. M. Hindley, KCIE, and of Lady Hindley; *m* 1934, Ruth, *d* of late T. H. and Mrs Corfield; one *s* one *d. Educ:* Oundle Sch.; RMA Woolwich. Commissioned, 1923; NW Frontier (Ind. Gen. Service Medal and clasp), 1930; Staff Coll., 1937-38; Temp. Lt-Col 1941, subst. 1947; Temp. Col 1943, subst. 1947; Temp. Brig. 1943, Brig. 1952. Served War of 1939-45, Middle East, Sicily, Italy. Dep. Dir Staff Duties, WO, 1945-47; Comdr Gold Coast District and Comdt Gold Coast Regt, RWAFF, 1947-49; Comdr 15th AA Bde, 1949-52; Dep. QMG, HQ Northern Army Group and BAOR, 1953-56; retd 1956. General Manager: Hemel Hempstead Development Corp., 1956-62; (Hemel Hempstead) Commission for the New Towns, April-Nov. 1962; Welwyn Garden City and Hatfield Development Corps, 1962-66; (Welwyn Garden City and Hatfield), for the Commission for the New Towns, 1966-67. *Address:* 24 Eastport Lane, Lewes, East Sussex BN7 1TL. *T:* Lewes 3432. *[Died 19 Dec.* 1980.

HINDLEY-SMITH, James Dury, MA Cantab, MRCS, LRCP; Consultant Physician, retired; late Clinical Assistant Actino-therapy Department, St George's Hospital; Fellow of Royal Society of Medicine; Member of Senate, University of Cambridge; Member Royal Institution of Great Britain; *b* 6 Jan. 1894; *e s* of late W. Hindley-Smith, Wigan and Southport, Lancs and Mrs C. E. Hindley-Smith, JP; *m* 1st, Josephine (*d* 1953), *d* of E. McMaster, BA, LLB, Afton, Freshwater, Isle of Wight; two *s*; 2nd, 1956, Penelope King-King (*d* 1962), *d* of late H. D. Lynes; 3rd, Ruth, *d* of late A. J. Brough. *Educ:* Uppingham; Magdalene Coll., Cambridge; St George's Hosp. Served European War with Field Artillery and General Staff, 1914-19. *Publications:* Chronic Rheumatism and the Pre-Rheumatic State; Chronic Streptococcal Toxaemia; various contribs to contemporary medical literature. *Recreations:* golf and music. *Address:* Foxe's Bay, PO Box 31, Montserrat, West Indies. *Club:* Carlton.   *[Died 8 May 1974.*

HINDMARSH, Prof. W(illiam) Russell, MA, DPhil; Professor of Atomic Physics, University of Newcastle upon Tyne, since 1961, and Dean of the Faculty of Science, since 1972; *b* 7 Nov. 1929; *er s* of Clifford and Ruth Hindmarsh; *m* 1954, Margaret Mary Harrison; one *s* two *d. Educ:* Gosforth County Grammar Sch.; Wadham Coll. Oxford. Open minor schol., Wadham Coll., 1948, first class hons in Physics, 1951, MA and DPhil Oxford, 1954. Scientific Officer, 1954-55, and Sen. Scientific Officer, 1955-56, at AERE, Harwell; Demonstrator, 1956-59, and Sen. Research Officer, 1959-61, at University Observatory, Oxford. Vice-Pres., Methodist Conf. of Great Britain, 1970-71. *Publications:* Atomic Spectra, 1967; Science and Faith, 1968; papers in scientific journals. *Recreation:* music. *Address:* School of Physics, The University, Newcastle upon Tyne NE1 7RU. *T:* 28511.   *[Died 29 Dec. 1973.*

HINTON, Geoffrey Thomas Searle, CBE 1967; HM Diplomatic Service, retired; *b* 18 June 1918; *s* of Francis John Hinton and late Mabel Frances Hinton (*née* Minns); *m* 1942, Averin Dora Macalister; one *s* two *d. Educ:* Christ Coll., Brecon; Worcester Coll., Oxford (MA). Min. of Information, 1941; HM Forces, 1943-46; entered Foreign (subseq. Diplomatic) Service, 1946; served in: Cairo, 1947; Bangkok, 1957; Paris, 1966; Counsellor, FCO, 1970-76. *Recreations:* languages, place-names, narrow-gauge railways, cricket. *Address:* The Steps, Withington, Cheltenham, Glos. *T:* Withington 228. *Clubs:* Royal Commonwealth Society; Talyllyn Railway Preservation Society.
                                [Died 27 March 1980.

HINTON, Prof. Howard Everest, FRS 1961; Professor of Zoology (formerly Professor of Entomology), University of Bristol, since 1964, and Head of Department of Zoology, since 1970; *b* Mexico, 24 Aug. 1912; *s* of George Boole Hinton; *m* 1937, Margaret Rose Clark; two *s* two *d. Educ:* schools in Mexico and California; Univ. of California (BSc); King's Coll., Cambridge (PhD, ScD). Biological expeditions to Mexico, 1933, 1934, and to Peru, Bolivia, Brazil, 1937. Asst Keeper, British Museum (Natural History), 1939-49; Reader in Entomology, Univ. of Bristol, 1950-64. Hon. Consulting Entomologist, Infestation Div., Min. of Agric., 1947-49. President: Soc. for British Entomology, 1954-55; Royal Entomological Soc. of London, 1969-70 (Hon. Fellow, 1977); British Entomological and Nat. Hist. Soc., 1972. Senior Fellowship, Australian Acad. of Sciences, 1963. Hon. Investigator, Inst. of Ecology of Mexico, 1977-. Associate Editor, Royal Society, 1968-70; Editor: Jl of Insect Physiology; Insect Biochemistry; Jl of Entomology, Series A. *Publications:* a monograph of the beetles associated with stored products, Vol. 1, 1945; (with A. M. S. Dunn) Mongooses; their natural history and behaviour, 1967; papers in learned journals. *Recreations:* entomology, shooting. *Address:* 16 Victoria Walk, Bristol BS6 5SR. *T:* Bristol 41433; Department of Zoology, University of Bristol BS8 1UG.
                                [Died 2 Aug. 1977.

HINTON-COOPER, Harold, CIE 1945; ED 1943; retired; *b* 20 May 1891; *s* of Bernard Hinton-Cooper; *m* 1916, Winifred, *d* of late W. H. Lawson, JP, Swindon; one *s. Educ:* Deal Coll.; Swindon Technical Coll. Training on GWR, 1907-12; appointed Asst Loco. Supt, Indian State Rlys, 1914; Dep. Chief Mechanical Engr, India, 1936-39; Chief Mechanical Engr, 1939-46; retd 1946. Afghan Medal, 1919; Coronation Medal, 1937. *Recreations:* golf, photography. *Address:* 49 Kenton Lane, Harrow, Mddx.   *[Died 22 Nov. 1980.*

HIRSCH, Maj.-Gen. Charles Ernest Rickards, CB 1956; CBE 1945; Chairman, Ex-Services Mental Welfare Society, 1969-73; *b* 11 Jan. 1903; *s* of late Henry Hirsch, Armagh, N Ireland; *m* 1933, Margaret Agnes Mary (*d* 1974), *d* of late Comdr L. E. Traherne, Coedarhydglyn, near Cardiff; two *s. Educ:* Armagh Royal Sch.; Royal Military College, Sandhurst. Commissioned

2nd Lieut Welch Regt, 1923; served in Norway, 1940; Italy, as BGS (Intelligence), 15 Army Group, 1944-45. Dep. Dir, Military Intelligence, War Office, 1945-48; Senior Army Liaison Officer in S Africa, 1948-51; BGS to C-in-C (Designate), UK Land Forces, 1951-54; Dep. Chief of Staff, HQ, UN Command, Tokyo (Maj.-Gen.), 1954-56; Deputy Chief of Staff, HQ Allied Land Forces Central Europe, 1956-58, retd. Hon. Col, 5th Bn, The Welch Regt, 1959-65. Comdr Legion of Merit (USA), 1945. *Recreations:* golf, gardening. *Address:* Moorlands, Aldershot Road, Fleet, Hants. *T:* Fleet 6008.   *[Died 20 March 1975.*

HIRST, Sir Edmund (Langley), Kt 1964; CBE 1957; FRS 1934; MA, PhD (St Andrews); DSc (Birmingham); MSc (Manchester); FRIC; FRSE; FH-WC (*hc*); Forbes Professor of Organic Chemistry, Edinburgh University, 1947-68, now Professor Emeritus; *b* 1898; *s* of Rev. Sim Hirst, BD; *m* 1st, 1925, Beda Winifred Phoebe Ramsay; 2nd, 1949, Kathleen Jennie Harrison, HMI. *Educ:* Northgate Sch., Ipswich; Madras Coll., St Andrews; St Andrews University. Asst in Chemistry, United Coll. of St Leonard and St Salvator, St Andrews Univ., 1920-23; Asst Lectr, Victoria University of Manchester, 1923-24; Lecturer in Chemistry, Armstrong Coll., University of Durham, 1924-26; Lecturer in Organic Chemistry, University of Birmingham, 1927-35; Reader in Chemistry, University of Birmingham, 1935-36; Alfred Capper Pass Prof. of Chemistry, Univ. of Bristol, 1936-44; Sir Samuel Hall Prof. of Chemistry and Dir of Chemical Lab., Univ. of Manchester, 1944-47. Vis. Lectr, Norwegian Univs, 1953, and Univs in W Germany, 1955. Davy Medal of Royal Soc., 1948; Longstaff Medal of Chem. Soc., 1957. Lectures: Tilden, Chem. Soc., 1939; Hugo Muller, Chem. Soc., 1948; Bruce Preller, RSE, 1951; Pedler, Chem. Soc., 1955; Bakerian, Royal Soc., 1959. Pres. Chem. Sect., British Association, 1950; Vice-Pres., Chem. Soc., 1952-55, Pres., 1956-58; Pres., RSE, 1959-64. Gunning Victoria Jubilee Prize, RSE, 1965. Hon. Mem., Polish Chemical Soc., 1959. Chm. Chemistry Research Bd, DSIR, 1950-55; Chm. Scientific Advisory Cttee, Inst. of Seaweed Research, 1952-63. Hon. Mem. RIA. Hon. LLD: St Andrews; Aberdeen; Birmingham; Strathclyde; Hon. ScD Trinity Coll., Dublin; Hon. DSc Heriot-Watt. *Publications:* in Jl Chem. Soc., Trans Faraday Soc., Biochemical Jl, mainly connected with chemistry of carbohydrates and Vitamin C. *Address:* 27 Mortonhall Road, Edinburgh EH9 2HS. *T:* 031-667 4701.   *[Died 29 Oct. 1975.*

HIRST, Sir (Frank) Wyndham, KBE, *cr* 1953 (CBE 1947; OBE 1933); Public Trustee, 1949-56, retired. Formerly Assistant Public Trustee. Admitted Solicitor, 1912. *Address:* 61 Magdalen Road, Wandsworth Common, SW18; c/o Public Trustee Office, Kingsway, WC2.   *[Died 27 Jan. 1972.*

HIRST, Sir Wyndham; *see* Hirst, Sir F. W.

HISCOCKS, Edward Stanley, CBE 1963; MSc; FRIC; *b* 2 Oct. 1903; *s* of late Edward and Annie Hiscocks, Bristol; *m* 1930, Joy M. L. Turner; one *s. Educ:* The Bishop Gore Sch., Swansea; University of Wales. Dept of Government Chemist, 1926-39; Head of Technical Branch, Raw Materials Dept, Ministry of Supply, 1939-44; Sec., National Physical Laboratory, DSIR, 1944-57; Dir, UK Scientific Mission (North America); Scientific Attaché, Washington, DC, 1957-60; Scientific Adviser to UK High Commissioner, Ottawa, 1957-60; Dir, Tropical Products Institute, 1960-66. *Publications:* Laboratory Administration, 1956; papers on physical chemistry and latterly articles and papers on organization and administration of scientific research. *Recreations:* travel, writing. *Address:* 1 Parsons Mead, East Molesey, Surrey. *T:* 01-979 8988.   *[Died 26 Sept. 1973.*

HISLOP, Prof. Joseph, FGSM 1953; Professor of Singing, Guildhall School of Music and Drama, 1952-64; Adviser on Singing to Royal Opera, Covent Garden and Sadler's Wells Theatre, 1948-54; formerly Principal Professor of Singing at Royal Academy of Music and of Royal School of Opera, Stockholm (title of Professor conferred by King of Sweden, 1949); *b* Edinburgh, 5 April 1884; *m* Karin Asklund, Gothenburg, Sweden; one *s* two *d; m* 1940, Agnes Fraser, *d* of Walter Passmore, London. *Educ:* St Mary's Cathedral Sch., Edinburgh; Royal Sch. of Opera, Stockholm (vocal teacher, Dr Gillis Bratt), and Milan. Made debut Royal Opera House, Stockholm, 1914; has sung in most of the leading opera houses in Europe and of North and South America; has toured in Australia and South Africa. Film, The Loves of Robert Burns, 1930. Gold Medal, Literis et Artibus, Sweden, 1922; Order of Dannebrog, Denmark, 1926; Order of the Vasa, Sweden, 1929. *Recreation:* painting. *Address:* Berryside Farm, By Leven, Fifeshire. *T:* Peat Inn 339.   *[Died 6 May 1977.*

HISLOP, Margaret Ross, RSA 1964 (ARSA 1950); *b* 27 June 1894; *d* of Thomas and Mary Grant; *m* 1921, Andrew Healey

Hislop; one d. *Educ:* W. Calder (Midlothian) High Sch. Trained Edinburgh Coll. of Art (Diploma, Drawing and Painting, 1917). Works (oil) in collections at Edinburgh, Greenock, Dundee, Glasgow and in Australia. *Recreations:* gardening, etc. *Address:* 10 Inverleith Row, Edinburgh EH3 5LS. *T:* 031-556 4291.
[Died 8 May 2972.

HITCHCOCK, Sir Alfred (Joseph), KBE 1980; film producer-director; *b* 13 Aug. 1899; *s* of William and Emma Hitchcock; *m* 1926, Alma Reville; one d. *Educ:* St Ignatius Coll., London. Junior technician at Famous Players Lasky British Studios, 1920; Scenario writer, art dir, production manager, Gainsborough Pictures, 1923; Motion Picture Dir, 1925. Films include: The Lodger, Farmer's Wife, The Ring, Blackmail, Juno and the Paycock, Murder, Skin Game, Man Who Knew Too Much, Thirty-Nine Steps, Secret Agent, Sabotage, Young and Innocent, The Lady Vanishes, Jamaica Inn, Rebecca, Foreign Correspondent, Mr and Mrs Smith, Suspicion, Saboteur, Shadow of a Doubt, Lifeboat, Spellbound, Notorious, Paradine Case, Rope, Under Capricorn, Stage Fright, Strangers on a Train, I Confess, Dial M for Murder, Rear Window, To catch a Thief, The Trouble with Harry, The Wrong Man, Vertigo, North by Northwest, Psycho, The Birds, Marnie, Torn Curtain, Topaz, Frenzy, Family Plot. Television: Alfred Hitchcock Presents (1959-62), Alfred Hitchcock Hour (1963-65). Hon. DHumL, Columbia, 1972. Irving G. Thalberg Meml Award; Milestone Award, Producers' Guild, 1965; D. W. Griffith Award, Directors' Award, 1968; C. B. de Mille Award, 1972; Life Achievement Award, Amer. Film Inst., 1978. Chevalier, Légion d'Honneur. *Relevant publication:* Hitch, by John Russell Taylor, 1978. *Address:* 10957 Bellagio Road, Bel Air, Los Angeles, California 90024, USA. *[Died 29 April 1980.*

HITCHENS, Ivon; see Hitchens, S. I.

HITCHENS, (Sydney) Ivon, CBE 1958; painter; *b* London, 3 March 1893; *o s* of Alfred Hitchens, painter and Ethel Margaret Seth-Smith; *m* 1935, Mary Cranford, *o d* of Rev. M. F. Coates, Hove; one *s. Educ:* Bedales; St John's Wood Art Schs; Royal Academy Schs. Member: 7 & 5 Soc.; London Group. One-man Exhibitions: Mayor Gallery, 1925; Arthur Tooth & Son, 1928; London Artists Assoc., 1929; Mansard Gallery, 1930; Lefevre Galleries, 1932, 1935, 1937; Leicester Galleries, 1940, 1942, 1944, 1947, 1949, 1950, 1952, 1954, 1957, 1959; Waddington Galleries, 1960, 1962, 1964, 1966, 1968, 1969, 1971, 1973, 1976; Poindexter, New York, 1966. Works purchased by Arts Council, and British Council; Stuyvesant Foundation; Ministry of Public Building and Works. Has also exhibited in New York World's Fair, 1939; UNESCO, Paris, 1946; British Painting since Whistler, National Gallery; Recent Tate Gallery Acquisitions, National Gallery, 1942; Tate Gallery Continental Exhibition, 1946-47; British Council Exhibitions; European Capitals, 1947, and Australia, 1949; Whitechapel Art Gallery, 1950; Contemporary Art Soc., The Private Collector, Tate Gallery, 1950, 1952. Purchase Prize, Arts Council Exhibition "50 painters for 1951"; British Council Hitchens and Nicholson Exhibition to Japan, 1953; Mural painting for Cecil Sharp House, London, 1954, Venezuela, 1955; twenty paintings in British Pavilion, XXVIII Biennale, Venice, 1956 (subseq. exhibited in Vienna and Munich, 1956, Paris and Amsterdam, 1957); Masters of British Painting, 1800-1950, Museum of Modern Art, New York, 1956; International Exhibition Brussels, 1958. Large landscape for Nuffield College, 1959; XI Premio, Lissone, Italy, 1959; 12th Exhibition International Assoc. art critics Exhibn, 1960; Exhibn British Paintings, 1720-1960, USSR, 1960. 3 Masters of Mod. Brit. Ptg; Arts Council 1961; 20th Cent. Brit. Ptg: Brit. Council, Portugal, 1961; Kompas Sledelijk Museum, Eindhoven, Holland, 1962; Brit. Art Today, San Francisco, Dallas, Santa Barbara, 1962-63; Coll. E. LeBas, RA, 1963; Mural for Sussex Univ., 1963; Brit. Ptg in the "Sixties", Tate Gallery, 1963; Three British Painters, NZ, 1964; Ptg and Sculpture of a Decade, Gulbenkian Exhibn, 1964; The Bliss Travelling Collection. *Retrospective Exhibitions:* Temple Newsam, Leeds, 1945; Graves Art Gall., Sheffield, 1948; Tate Gallery, London, 1963; Southampton, 1964; Worthing Art Gall., 1966; Rutland Gall., London, 1972; Burlington House, 1979. *Represented in Public Collections of:* Leeds, Liverpool, Aberdeen, Wakefield, Shrewsbury, Salford, Hull, Manchester, Glasgow, Leicester, Bath, Birmingham, Bristol, Barnsley, Nottingham, Norwich, Southampton, Eastbourne, Newcastle upon Tyne, Huddersfield, Rochdale; also in Oxford and Cambridge Colls; Nat. Museum of Wales, Cardiff; Glynn Vivian Gall., Swansea; Victoria and Albert Museum, 1942; Cambridge, Fitzwilliam Museum; Tate Gall., 1938, 1941, 1942, 1959, 1965; Musée Nat. d'Art Moderne, Paris, 1957; Australian Nat. Galleries of Adelaide, Melbourne, Sydney; USA: Toledo Museum of Art and Albright Gall., Buffalo; Art Gall. of Seattle; Gothenberg Art Museum, Sweden; Nat. Gall., Oslo; Nat. Gall.

of Canada, Ottawa; Art Gall. of Toronto; Nat. Gall. of New Zealand; Ashmolean Museum, Oxford; the Queen's private collection of pictures; tapestry mural 10 ft × 20 ft, Chase Manhattan Bank, London. *Relevant Publications:* Penguin Modern Painters, by Patrick Heron, 1955; Ivon Hitchens, ed Alan Bowness, 1973. *Recreation:* streams. *Address:* Greenleaves, Petworth, Sussex. *[Died 29 Aug. 1979.*

HITCHINGS, Group Capt. John Phelp, CBE 1944; DL; Director, J. Cox & Co.'s Succrs Ltd, Bedminster, Bristol; *b* 2 Aug. 1899; *m* 1928, Gwendolyn Joyce Mary Newth; one *s* one d. *Educ:* Queen's Coll., Taunton. Served in RFC and RAF, 1917-18 and 1939-45; in business as Sole Leather Tanner, 1919-67. DL Avon 1974. *Recreation:* golf. *Address:* 19a The Avenue, Clifton, Bristol BS8 3HG. *T:* Bristol 36276. *[Died 11 Jan. 1979.*

HITCHMAN, Sir (Edwin) Alan, KCB 1952 (CB 1948); Deputy Chairman, United Kingdom Atomic Energy Authority, 1964-66 (full-time Member, 1959); *b* 16 Nov. 1903; *s* of E. B. Hitchman, Newbury; *m* 1937, Katharine Mumford, *d* of Frank Hendrick, New York City; two *s. Educ:* St Bartholomew's Grammar Sch., Newbury; Downing Coll., Cambridge. Asst Principal, Ministry of Labour, 1926; Principal Private Sec. to Mr E. Brown, 1939, and to Mr E. Bevin, 1940, when Ministers of Labour; Principal Asst Sec., 1941; Under-Sec., 1946; transferred to HM Treasury, 1947; Dep. to Chief Planning Officer, 1948-49; Third Sec., HM Treasury, 1949-51; Perm. Sec. to Min. of Materials, 1951-52; Mem. Economic Planning Board, 1951-52; Chm. Agric. Improvement Council for England and Wales, 1952; Permanent Sec. to Min. of Agriculture and Fisheries, 1952-55, to Min. of Agriculture, Fisheries and Food, 1955-59. *Address:* 13 Wellington Square, Chelsea, SW3. *T:* 01-730 9359. *Club:* United Oxford & Cambridge University. *[Died 2 July 1980.*

HIVES, Rt. Rev. Harry Ernest, BA, DD; *b* 20 Sept. 1901; *s* of Richard Charles Hives and Rose Annie Watson; *m* 1927, Erla Ruth Wait; two d. *Educ:* Univ. of Saskatchewan (BA); Emmanuel Coll., Saskatoon (LTh Hons). Deacon, 1926; Priest, 1927. Curate-in-Charge, Cumberland House, 1926-27; Incumbent, 1927-29; Lac la Ronge, 1929-38; Paynton with Bresaylor, 1938-40; Lashburn, 1940-42; Rector of Battleford, 1943-50; Hon. Canon, St John's Cathedral, Saskatoon, 1943; Bishop's Commissary for Indian Affairs, 1945; Domestic Chaplain to Bishop of Saskatoon, 1949; Archdeacon of Indian Affairs, 1953; Bishop of Keewatin, 1953-69, retired 1969. DD (Emmanuel Coll., Saskatoon), 1954. *Publication:* Cree Grammar, 1948. *Address:* 108-2333 Beach Drive, Victoria, BC, Canada. *[Died 27 Jan. 1974.*

HOAR, Arthur Stanley George, CMG 1969; retired; *b* 17 July 1903; *s* of Arthur George Hoar and Emma Alice Hoar (née de Beaucamp); *m* 1930, Florence May Leigh; two *s* one d. *Educ:* Owen's Sch.; London Univ. Various positions, Bank of England, 1923-46; Dir-Gen. of Banking Branch, CCG (BE), 1945-46; Internat. Bank for Reconstruction and Development: Asst Loan Dir, 1946-51; Loan Dir, 1951-52; Dir of Operations for Europe, Africa and Australasia, 1952-55; Commonwealth Development Finance Co. Ltd: Gen. Manager, 1955-56; Managing Dir, 1956-68; Director: CDFC (Australia) Ltd, 1963-68; CDFC Holdings Ltd (Toronto), 1964-68; CDFC (Malaysia) Ltd, 1965-68. *Recreations:* archæology, history, gardening. *Address:* Chevy Chase, 26a Stratton Road, Beaconsfield, Bucks. *T:* Beaconsfield 3446. *[Died 8 March 1972.*

HOAR, Hon. Ernest Knight, JP; *b* 20 Oct. 1898; *s* of Henry Knight Hoar and Sarah Ann Hoar, Luton, England; *m* 1924, Dorothy Helen Tomlin, Leicester, England; one *s. Educ:* Luton, England. Served European War, 1914-18, for 4½ years. Emigrated to Western Australia, 1922; entered Western Australian Parliament, 1943; Minister for Lands, Agriculture and Immigration, in the State Government, 1953-57; Agent-Gen. for Western Australia in London, 1957-65. Retired, 1965. *Recreation:* golf. *Address:* 61 Moreing Road, Attadale, WA 6156, Australia. *[Died 1 May 1979.*

HOARE, Sir Archer, Kt 1955; CBE 1939; *b* 6 March 1876; *m* 1908, Agnes Falconer Harby (d 1969), *d* of Charles E. Harby, Southgate; one *s* one d. *Educ:* Richmond, Surrey. Entered Customs and Excise Dept, 1896; Dep. Chief Inspector, 1936; Collector, Port of London, 1938-40; Middlesex County Council: Councillor, 1940; Alderman, 1949-65; Chm. Establishment Cttee, 1949; Education Cttee, 1949-52, 1960-65; Vice-Chm. of Council, 1951-52, Chm., 1953-54. Court of Univ. of London, 1952-67; Court of Mill Hill Sch., 1949-58; Hendon-Harrow War Pensions Cttee, 1940, Chm., 1941-63. LLD London, 1964. *Address:* 42 Love Lane, Pinner, Mddx HA5 3EX. *T:* 01-866 3449. *[Died 22 Sept. 1973.*

HOARE, Christopher Gurney, MC 1918; Stockbroker in Hoare & Co.; *b* 29 June 1882; *s* of R. G. Hoare, Jesmond Park, Newcastle on Tyne; *m* 1907, Eveline Hamilton Lucas (*d* 1960); one *s* one *d*. *Educ:* Harrow; King's Coll., Cambridge (MA). At Cambridge Master of Trinity Foot Beagles; joined 2nd Line Essex Yeomanry, 1914; transferred to Royal Horse Guards. *Recreations:* hunting, shooting. *Address:* Gateley Hall, Elmham, Dereham, Norfolk. *Clubs:* Buck's, Bath.
[*Died* 22 *Nov.* 1973.

HOARE, Rear-Adm. Dennis John, CB 1945; FIMechE; *b* 16 April 1891; *s* of late Herbert K. Hoare, Portsmouth; *m* 1919, Madeline (*d* 1975), *d* of T. Morris Prosser, JP, Newport, Mon.; two *s*. *Educ:* RNEC Keyham; RNC, Greenwich. HMS Collingwood, 1913-15, followed by service in HMS's Birkenhead, Goshawk and Glorious. Lecturer in Applied Mechanics at RNC Greenwich, 1919-24; then served in HM Ships Malaya and Shakespeare. Admiralty, 1926; HMS Exeter, 1930; later appointments included Fleet Engineer Officer, Mediterranean, Fleet Engineer Officer, Submarines, Asst Engineer-in-Chief, Superintendent Admiralty Engineering Laboratory; retired July 1945. Dir of Research, British Internal Combustion Engine Research Assoc., 1945-58. Chevalier Order of Aviz (Portugal), 1921; Grand Officer, Order of Orange-Nassau (Netherlands), 1947. *Address:* Hall Cottage, Old Road, Ruddington, Nottingham NG11 6NF. *T:* Nottingham 216542.
[*Died* 15 *Feb.* 1979.

HOARE, Maj.-Gen. Lionel Lennard, DSO 1916; *b* Staplehurst, 24 July 1881; *s* of William Hoare of Staplehurst and Laura, 2nd *d* of Sir John Lennard, 1st Bt of Wickham Court, West Wickham, Kent; *m* 1912, Audrey (*d* 1963), *e d* of Lieut-Col G. H. Woodard; three *d*. *Educ:* Lambrook; Eton; RMA Woolwich. Joined Royal Field Artillery, 1899; served S Africa, 1901-02 (Queen's medal 5 clasps); transferred to Army Ordnance Dept, 1906; Capt. 1908; Major 1914; Temp. Lt-Col 1916-25; Lieut-Col 1925; Col 1932; Brig., 1935; Maj.-Gen. 1938; served European War, 1914-19 (despatches twice, DSO); Instructor RAOC Sch. of Instruction, 1926-31; Asst Dir of Ordnance Services, War Office, 1931-35; Dep. Dir of Ordnance Services, Royal Arsenal, Woolwich, 1935-38; Principal Ordnance Officer, War Office, 1938-39; retired pay, 1939; Dir of Progress and Inspection, and Military Adviser, Min. of Supply, 1939-45; Pres., Council of Big Ben Silent Minute Observance, 1941-62; Vice-Chm., Rochester Diocesan Board of Finance, 1949-67; Mem. of Church Assembly, 1950-65. *Recreations:* various. *Address:* South Lodge, Wrotham, Kent. *T:* Fairseat 2382. *Club:* MCC.
[*Died* 26 *Jan.* 1975.

HOARE, Sir Peter (William), 7th Bt *cr* 1786, of Luscombe, Devon; Managing Partner of C. Hoare & Co., Bankers, of Fleet Street and Park Lane, London; Director: Messrs Hoare Trustees; Eagle Star Insurance Co. Ltd; *b* 22 July 1898; *o s* of late P. A. M. Hoare; *S* cousin 1947; *m* 1929, Laura Ray, *o d* of Sir John Esplen, 1st Bt, KBE; two *s*. *Educ:* Harrow. Served European War, 1917-19, France and Germany, Lieut RGA (TF), wounded 1918. Metropolitan Special Constable, 1926. Aviator's Cert., Royal Aero Club, 1927; Owner of first Gypsy Moth GEB2Y, 1928; Mem., RYS Syndicate taking yacht Sceptre to USA to challenge for America's Cup, 1958. Mem. IAM, 1963. High Sheriff of Devon, 1955. *Recreations:* fishing and shooting. *Heir:* *s* Peter Richard Hoare, *b* 22 March 1932. *Address:* Luscombe Castle, Dawlish, Devon. *Clubs:* Travellers', Garrick, MCC; Royal Yacht Squadron. [*Died* 29 *May* 1973.

HOARE, Col Robert Rawdon, DSO 1940; MC 1918; Director-General, Economic League, 1945-59; *b* 16 May 1897; *s* of late Gerald Eugene Hoare, Cromer, Norfolk, and Rosabelle Mary, *d* of late Rawdon Hunter-Muskett, DL, JP, Hingham Hall, Norfolk. *Educ:* Beaumont Coll., Windsor. Entered Army, Aug. 1914, RA; apptd Royal Horse Artillery, 1916 (wounded, MC); Regular Army Reserve of Officers, Major, 1922; recalled to command "K" (Hondeghem) Bty RHA, 1939; served War of 1939-45 (wounded twice, despatches twice, Africa Star, 8th Army Clasp, Italian Star); Temp. Lieut-Col RHA 1940; commanded 5 RHA, Aug. 1940-43; Head of RA Training Team, Free French and Polish Forces, 1943; Col 1943; Chief Artillery Adviser, Brit. Mil. Mission to the Egyptian Army, 1944. Croix de Guerre with gold star, 1947. Mem. Bd of Govs, Royal Nat. Orthopædic Hospital, 1947-59; Trustee of Albany, 1955-67. *Publications:* two books on travel, 1936 and 1937; numerous articles on travel, 1928-37. *Recreations:* walking, reading, travel.
[*Died* 11 *Aug.* 1977.

HOARE, Sir Samuel, KBE 1970; Kt 1957; CB 1949; *b* 1896; *s* of Barnard George Hoare, Inverness. *Educ:* Inverness Royal Academy; Aberdeen Univ. Served Cameron Highlanders, in Salonica, 1916-18. Appointed Home Office, 1920; Asst Under-

Sec. of State, 1948-61; Head of Internat. Div., 1950-61. Has represented UK on various international bodies, including Gen. Assembly and Economic and Social Council of UN; Member: Human Rights Commn of UN, 1952-69; Council of Europe Cttee of Experts on Human Rights, 1961-73. Hon. LLD Aberdeen, 1971. *Address:* 11 Mulberry Close, Beaufort Street, SW3. *T:* 01-352 5697. [*Died* 31 *March* 1976.

HOBBS, Harold William, CB 1965; CBE 1955; Chartered Mechanical Engineer; formerly Professional Adviser to the Royal Mint; *b* 1903; *s* of Thomas Harold Hobbs, London; *m* 1941, Greta Kathleen, *d* of Michael Boyne. *Educ:* Woolwich Polytechnic. Dep. Controller, Royal Ordnance Factories, MoD (Army), 1962-66. FIMechE. *Address:* 17 Riefield Road, Eltham, SE9. *T:* 01-850 5861; 41 Links Crescent, St Mary's Bay, Romney Marsh, Kent. [*Died* 6 *May* 1976.

HOBBS, Maj.-Gen. Reginald Geoffrey Stirling, CB 1956; DSO 1942; OBE 1944; *b* 8 Aug. 1908; *e s* of late Brig.-Gen. Reginald Francis Arthur Hobbs, CB, CMG, DSO, Sutton Veny, Warminster, Wilts; *m* 1935, Mary Jameson, *d* of late Maj.-Gen. Hugo De Pree, CB, CMG, DSO, Beckley, Rye, Sussex; one *d*. *Educ:* Wellington; RMA Woolwich. 2nd Lieut RA, 1928; Staff Coll., 1940; BEF, 1940; RHA Eighth Army, Western Desert, 1942-43; Staff, 21 Army Group NW Europe, 1944-45; Lieut-Col 1942; temp. Brig. 1947; Chief of Staff, Combined Ops, 1948; idc, 1949; CRA 1st Inf. Div., 1950-51; Comd 2 Inf. Bde, 1952; Maj.-Gen. 1955; Comdt, RMA Sandhurst, 1954-56; Near East, 1956; Dir of Royal Artillery, War Office, 1957-59; GOC 1 Div., 1959-60; Col Comdt, Royal Regt Artillery, 1963-68; Hon. Col, Essex Yeomanry, 1961-66; Pres., Regular Commissions Bd, 1961-62; Lieut-Governor and Sec., Royal Hospital, Chelsea, 1962-67. Order of White Lion 3rd Class, and Military Cross (Czechoslovakia), 1945; Officer of Legion of Honour and Croix de Guerre with Palm (France), 1958. *Recreation:* English Rugby International, 1932; Pres. of the Rugby Football Union, 1961-62. *Address:* Lerags House, Oban, Argyll. *T:* Oban 2450. *Club:* Army and Navy. [*Died* 7 *Nov.* 1977.

HOBHOUSE, Edmund W. Neill, MA, MD Oxon, FRCP; Consulting Physician, Victoria Hospital for Children and West End Hospital for Nervous Diseases; Hon. Consulting Neurologist, Royal Free Hospital; *b* 1888; *e s* of late Rev. W. Hobhouse, DD, and Violet, *y d* of Edmund McNeill, DL, Craigdunn; *m* 1920, Phyllis, *d* of late Sir William J. Smyly; two *d*. *Educ:* Winchester; New Coll., Oxford. House Physician, etc, St Thomas's Hosp.; RMO City of London Hosp. for Diseases of Chest; served in RAMC; Physician to Out-patients, Hampstead Gen. Hosp.; Neurologist, Ministry of Pensions. *Publications:* Nervous Disorder in Infancy and Childhood, 1932; contributions to Lancet and other medical journals. *Address:* May Cottage, Mortimer Common, Berks. [*Died* 12 *Feb.* 1973.

HOBSON, Alfred Dennis, MA; FRSE; FZS; FIBiol; retired as Professor of Zoology, University of Newcastle upon Tyne (formerly King's College, University of Durham) and Hon. Director of Dove Marine Laboratory, Cullercoats (1932-66); now Emeritus Professor; *b* 25 July 1901; *o s* of late Alfred Edward Hobson and Anna Maria Magdalen Kershaw; *m* 1924, Mary Gladys Petra Paula (*d* 1972), *o d* of late John Woods, Walton-le-Dale; no *c*. *Educ:* Highgate Sch.; Christ's Coll., Cambridge. Natural Sciences Tripos, Part I Class II and Part II Class II, Frank Smart Prizeman, 1923. Asst in Dept of Zoology, University Coll., London, 1923-25; Lecturer in Experimental Zoology, University of Edinburgh, 1925-32; Ray Lankester Investigator at the Marine Laboratory, Plymouth, 1928-29. A Vice-Pres. of Natural History Soc. of Northumberland, Durham and Newcastle upon Tyne. *Publications:* scientific papers, chiefly on experimental cytology and parasitology, in Proc. RSE, Jl of Experimental Biology, etc. *Recreations:* reading, philately. *Address:* 13 Kingsland, Newcastle upon Tyne NE2 3AL. *T:* Newcastle 81.1689. [*Died* 11 *July* 1974.

HOBSON, Harold; consulting engineer, retired; *b* 1 June 1891; *s* of John Atkinson and Florence Edgar Hobson; *m* 1914, Coralie Jeyes von Werner (*d* 1946); one *s* one *d*; *m* 1948, Margaret Hand (*née* Busvine). *Educ:* private schs in England and USA; King's Coll., London. Cons. Engineer with Merz and McLellan of 32 Victoria Street, 1914-25; Joint Manager, County of London Electric Supply Co. Ltd, 1925-28; Commercial Manager, Central Electricity Bd, 1928-35, Gen. Manager, 1935-44, Chm., 1944-47. *Recreation:* gardening. *Address:* The Pastures, Hilton, Hunts. *T:* Papworth St Agnes 285. *Clubs:* Reform, Oriental.
[*Died* 12 *June* 1973.

HOBSON, Neville, MC; JP; solicitor, Beverley; Director, Municipal Mutual Insurance Ltd; *b* 13 April 1886; *s* of Charles William Hobson, solicitor, and Louisa Elizabeth Hobson; *m*

1919, Sarah Kathleen Darneley (d 1965); two s one d. Educ: Beverley Grammar Sch.; Bridlington Sch. Hons, Law Soc., 1908. Served European War, 1914-18, enlisted Yorks Regt, 1914; Lieut West Riding Regt, 1915; Capt. and Adjutant, 19th London Regt, 1916; HQ Staff, 60th Div., in France, Balkans and Palestine, 1917 (despatches, MC). Chm., Rural District Councils Assoc. of England and Wales, 1947-52; Mem. of Rly Assessment Authority, 1936-48. Founded CLB and Boys' Club, Beverley, 1908; original mem. of National Fitness Council; York Diocesan Lay Reader. Hon. Freedom, Borough of Beverley, 1958; Mayor of Beverley, 1966; Pres., Yorks Parish Councils Assoc., 1967. Publications: ABC of Rating and Valuation, 1925; The Bridge Players' Note Book, 1926; Bankruptcy and Deeds of Arrangement, 1931; A Treasury of Inspiration, 1934; Unity, Peace and Concord, 1940; The Borough, Urban and Rural Councillor, 1947; Law of Town and Country Planning, 1948; (Supervising Ed.), Hobson's Local Government, 1951; Reflections, 1964. Recreation: Youth Club activities. Address: Ellerker Road, Beverley, North Humberside. TA: Beverley. T: Beverley 881618. [Died 2 July 1975.

HODD, Ven. Henry Norman, TD 1949; MA; Archdeacon of Blackburn since 1962; b 8 May 1905; s of Rev. Francis Arnold and Elizabeth Hodd; m 1930, Violet Murray Kennedy MacIntyre; two s. Educ: St Peter's Sch., York; Keble Coll., Oxford; Westcott House, Cantab. Curate, Leeds Parish Church, 1929-32; Senior Curate, Christ Church, Harrogate, 1932-35; Vicar, University Church, Leeds, 1935-42; Chaplain to the Forces, TA, 1937; Active Service, 1939-45; Staff Chaplain HQ Northern Command, 1942-45; Vicar and Rural Dean: Retford, 1945-51; Mansfield, 1951-59; Hon. Canon, Southwell, 1953; Adviser on Christian Stewardship to the Church of England, 1959-62. Publications: Prayers for Stewardship Campaigns, 1960; Before His Face, 1960. Recreations: occasional golf, and sea fishing. Address: Balderstone Vicarage, near Blackburn, Lancs. T: Mellor 2232. Club: Royal Commonwealth Society. [Died 25 April 1973.

HODGE, Alan; Joint Editor of History Today since 1951; b 16 Oct. 1915; s of late Capt. T. S. Hodge, RD, RNR; m 1948, Jane, d of late Conrad Potter Aiken; two d. Educ: Liverpool Collegiate Sch.; Oriel Coll., Oxford. Asst Private Sec. to Minister of Information, 1941-45. Editor of The Novel Library (Hamish Hamilton), 1946-52. Publications: (with Robert Graves) The Long Week-End, 1940; The Reader Over Your Shoulder, 1943; (with Peter Quennell) The Past We Share, 1960. Address: 6 Lancaster Road, SW19. T: 01-946 4101. [Died 25 May 1979.

HODGE, John Douglass Vere, CIE 1929; b 17 Oct. 1887; 4th s of late Rev. Edward Vere Hodge and Helen, d of late John Bacchus, JP; m 1920, Elspeth Stuart, 2nd d of late Robert Henderson; one d. Educ: Durham Sch.; Pembroke Coll., Cambridge. Entered Indian Civil Service, 1912; held various posts under Government of Bengal and Government of India; Deputy Sec. to Government of India, 1926-29; Commissioner, Chittagong Division, Bengal, 1936-38; retired, 1939; Ministry of Home Security, 1939-45; Allied Commn for Austria, 1945-46. Address: Anchor Cottage, Portloe, near Truro, Cornwall. T: Veryan 359. [Died 3 April 1973.

HODGE, Stephen Oswald Vere, CMG 1942; b 14 July 1891; s of late Rev. C. F. D. Hodge; m 1919, Margaret Mary Vere Neilson, d of W. Fitzroy Neilson; three s. Educ: Durham Sch.; Christ Church, Oxford. Served European War 1914-18, Lieut unattached list 1915-18 (despatches). Asst Dist Commissioner, Kenya, 1913; Sen. Dist Commissioner, 1935; MLC, Kenya, 1937-45; Provincial Comr, Kenya, 1939-46; retd, 1946. Provincial Comdt, Kenya Police Reserve, Rift Valley Prov., Kenya, 1952-53; Staff Officer to Prov. Comr, Rift Valley Prov., Kenya, 1953-54. Address: Sidai, PO Box 183, Nakuru, Kenya. T: Subukia 4Y10 (Kenya). Clubs: Royal Commonwealth Society; Muthaiga Country (Nairobi); Rift Valley Sports (Nakuru). [Died 17 Feb. 1979.

HODGE, Sir William (Vallance Douglas), Kt 1959; FRS 1938; MA, ScD; FRSE; Lowndean Professor of Astronomy and Geometry, Cambridge University, 1936-70, now Professor Emeritus; Master of Pembroke College, 1958-70 (Fellow, 1935-58, Hon. Fellow since 1970); b 17 June 1903; s of Archibald James Hodge and Janet Vallance; m 1929, Kathleen Anne Cameron; one s one d. Educ: George Watson's Coll. and University, Edinburgh; St John's Coll., Cambridge. Smith's Prizeman, 1927; Lecturer, Bristol Univ., 1926-31; Fellow of St John's Coll., 1930-33; 1851 Exhibition, Senior Studentship, 1931; University Lecturer, Cambridge, 1933-36; Visiting Lectr Harvard Univ., 1950; Pres. London Math. Soc., 1947-49; Pres. Cambridge Phil. Soc., 1947-49; Pres. Math. Assoc., 1955; Vice-Pres. Internat. Math. Union, 1954-58; Physical Sec. of Royal

Society, 1957-65 (Vice-Pres. 1958-65); Pres. Internat. Congress of Mathematicians, 1958. Hon. Fellow, St John's Coll., Cambridge, 1964. For. Hon. Mem., Amer. Acad. of Arts and Sciences, 1958; For. Member: Amer. Phil. Soc.; Royal Danish Acad., 1966; For. Associate, Amer. Nat. Acad. Sci., 1959. Adams Prize, 1937; Berwick Prize, London Math. Soc. 1952; Royal Medal, 1957, Copley Medal, 1974, Royal Soc.; De Morgan Medal, London Math. Soc., 1959; Gunning Victoria Jubilee Prize, Royal Society of Edinburgh, 1969. Hon. LLD Edinburgh, 1958; Hon. DSc: Bristol, 1957; Leicester, 1959; Sheffield, 1960; Exeter, 1961; Wales, 1961; Liverpool, 1961. Publications: Theory and Applications of Harmonic Integrals, 1941 (2nd edn, 1952); (with D. Pedoe) Methods of Algebraic Geometry, vol. i, 1947, vol. ii, 1952, vol. iii, 1954; numerous papers in British and foreign mathematical jls. Address: 16 Amhurst Court, Grange Road, Cambridge. [Died 7 July 1975.

HODGES, Rt. Rev. Evelyn Charles, DD; b Towlerton House, Co. Carlow, 8 Aug. 1887; s of Rev. W. H. Hodges; m 1927, Violet Blanche, d of George Hill Crawford, Dublin; one s one d. Educ: Rathmines; Mountjoy; Trinity Coll., Dublin (BA, Moderator, Large Gold Medal, 1910, MA 1913, BD 1923, 2nd Class Divinity Testimonium 1911, Higher Diploma on Education 1920). Curate Asst of Drumcondra and North Strand, Dublin, 1911-14; of Rathmines, Dublin, 1914-17; Diocesan Inspector of Schs (Dublin, Glendalough and Kildare), 1917-24; Incumbent of Rathmines, 1924-28; Principal of Church of Ireland Training Coll (for Teachers), 1928-43; Canon of St Patrick's Cathedral, Dublin, 1934-43; Bishop of Limerick, Ardfert, and Aghadoe, 1943-60, retired. Address: 14 Shandon Street, Edinburgh EH11 1QH. [Died 18 March 1980.

HODGES, Herbert Arthur; Professor of Philosophy in the University of Reading, 1934-69; Emeritus since 1969; b 4 Jan. 1905; s of Willis Hodges and Lily Malaingre Dyson; m 1939, Vera Joan, y d of late Rev. John Willis; two s one d. Educ: King Edward VII Sch., Sheffield; Balliol Coll., Oxford (Classical Scholar). Craven Scholar, 1923; First Class in Honour Moderations, 1924; First class in Literae Humaniores, and BA, 1926; John Locke Scholar, War Memorial Student of Balliol Coll., and Senior Demy of Magdalen Coll., 1926; Lecturer in Philosophy at New Coll., 1927; Lecturer in Philosophy in the University of Reading, 1928; MA, DPhil, 1932. Mem. of Royal Commission on Betting, Lotteries and Gaming, 1949-51; Master, Guild of St George, 1954-73. Publications: Wilhelm Dilthey: an Introduction, 1944; Christianity and the Modern World View, 1949; The Philosophy of Wilhelm Dilthey, 1952; Languages, Standpoints and Attitudes, 1953; Anglicanism and Orthodoxy, 1955; The Pattern of Atonement, 1955; Death and Life have Contended, 1964; (with A. M. Allchin) A Rapture of Praise, 1966; articles in philosophical and theological journals. Recreation: listening to music. Address: 3 Grahame Avenue, Pangbourne, Berks RG8 7LF. T: Pangbourne 3112. [Died 2 July 1976.

HODGES, Captain Michael, CB 1968; OBE 1946; Royal Navy (retired); b 8 Sept. 1904; s of Admiral Sir Michael Hodges, KCB, CMG, MVO; m 1946, Heather Hayes; one s. Educ: RN Colleges Osborne and Dartmouth. Entered Royal Navy, 1918; Fleet Signal Officer, Mediterranean, 1936-38; Chief Signal Officer, Combined Ops, 1942-44; Signal Officer-in-Chief, SE Asia, 1944-45; HMS Duke of York, 1945-46; Dep. Dir of Signals, Admiralty, 1948-50. Invalided from RN and joined Civil Service, 1950; Under-Sec., Ministry of Defence, 1962-63; Cabinet Office, 1963-68, retired. Address: 4 Cygnet House, SW3. T: 01-584 2972. [Died 19 June 1977.

HODGES, Sir Reginald (John), Kt 1951; JP; b 21 March 1889; s of late William Abraham Hodges, East Bridgford, Notts; m 1st, 1918, Doris Rhona Buchanan; one d; 2nd, 1930, Gwendoline Jeanie Buchanan (d 1961); 3rd, 1963, Mrs Claudia Roberts (née Lucas). Educ: Sedbergh Sch.; Trinity Coll., Oxford (MA); Grootfontein Sch. of Agriculture, Middelburg, Cape Province. Served European War in Egypt, Palestine, France, in Denbigh (Hussars) Yeomanry, 1914-18; Cunard Steam Ship Co., Ltd, 1919-30; Manager and, later, Dir of Anchor Line (Henderson Bros) Ltd, 1930-35; Asst General Manager, Mersey Docks and Harbour Board, 1935-39; Deputy General Manager, 1939-41; General Manager and Secretary, Mersey Docks and Harbour Board, 1941-54. Past Dir, British Insulated Callender's Cables Ltd; Dir, Humphreys Ltd. OStJ 1954. Address: Waverley House, Edgeworth, near Stroud, Glos. T: Miserden 340. Club: Royal Liverpool Golf (Hoylake). [Died 13 Jan. 1973.

HODGSON, His Honour Arthur John; Judge of County Courts (Kingston and Wandsworth), 1950-60, retired; b 23 Aug. 1887; y s of Joseph and Emma Hodgson, Higher Bebington, Cheshire; m 1918, Ruth Irene Bateman (d 1969), MB ChB, Kendal,

Westmorland; one *d. Educ:* Birkenhead Sch.; Clare Coll., Cambridge (exhibitioner and scholar; Nat. Sci. Tripos; MA); Liverpool Univ. (LLB). Called to Bar, Inner Temple, 1913. Served European War in The King's (Liverpool) Regt and attached staff, 1914-19. Practised on Northern Circuit and in London, 1919-50. *Publications:* Shipping Documents, 1929; Carriage of Goods by Sea Act, 1932; (with G. R. Rudolf) Lowndes and Rudolf on General Average and the York-Antwerp Rules, 1948. *Recreations:* reading, crosswords. *Address:* The End House, 7 Stonehill Close, East Sheen SW14 8RP.   *[Died* 31 *Dec.* 1971.

HODGSON, Ernest Atkinson, PhD; *b* 15 Oct. 1886; *e s* of Henry Dent Hodgson, Penrith, and Ellen E. Young; *m* 1st, 1912, Elizabeth Humphrey; two *s*; 2nd, 1923, Gladys Prittie; 3rd, 1948, Eva Jarrett Astley. *Educ:* Hamilton Collegiate; University of Toronto; University of Chicago; Saint Louis Univ. Asst Seismologist, Dominion Observatory, Ottawa, 1914-17; Seismologist, 1917-19; Head Mathematical Master, Galt Collegiate, Galt, Ontario, 1919-20; Chief, Division of Seismology, Dominion Observatory, Ottawa, Canada, 1920-47; Asst Dir Dominion Observatory, Ottawa, Canada, and Chief, Division of Seismology, 1948-51; retired, 1951. After retirement tutor in maths and astronomy to school and degree students. Past Pres. Seis. Soc. Am. and Dir, 1920-50; Editor, Bibliography of Seismology, 1926-48; FRSC 1936; Soc. of the Sigma Xi, 1945. Sir Casimir Gzowski Medal; Royal Astronom. Soc. Canada Gold Medal, 1960; Merit Award for scientific research in seismology, St Louis Univ. *Publications:* technical papers on seismology and on rockbursts in mines, in scientific journals and in the Publications of the Dominion Observatory, Ottawa; maths textbooks. *Recreation:* bowling. *Address:* Box 520, Port Perry, Ont., Canada. *T:* 985-2166.   *[Died* 3 *May* 1975.

HODGSON, Sir Gerald Hassall, Kt 1943; *b* Scawby, Lincs, 20 July 1891; *s* of Rev. F. D. Hodgson, late of St Peters, Broadstairs; *m* 1st, 1924, Margaret Emma Hogge (*d* 1925), Ferndown, Dorset; 2nd, 1929, Sylvia Joan Lawrence; one *s* one *d. Educ:* Westminster Sch. National Provincial Bank, 1908-11; Parry & Co. Ltd, Madras, 1911; Capt. 6th Bn Royal West Kent Regt (France), 1916-19; Director: Parry & Co. Ltd, Madras, 1928-44; The Royal Blackheath Golf Club. *Publication:* Thomas Parry, Freemerchant, Madras, 1788-1824, 1938. *Address:* 3 Darwin Court, North Park, Eltham, SE9 5BD. *T:* 01-850 7331.
                                                     [Died 1 *July* 1971.

HODSOLL, Wing Comdr Sir (Eric) John, Kt 1944; CB 1934; *b* 1894; *s* of late Commander J. F. Hodsoll, RNR, and late Wilhelmina Ann White; *m* 1st, 1919, Winifred Joyce (*d* 1935), *d* of Col Morton Tomlin, OBE, TD, DL; one *d*; 2nd, 1937, Elisabeth Morton, *y d* of late Col Morton Tomlin; twin *d. Educ:* Christ's Hosp. Trained in engineering, Great Western Railway Works, Swindon, 1911-14; joined RNAS, 1914; served Calshot, 1915-17; Commanded Seaplane Base, Alexandria, 1918 (despatches thrice); Air Ministry, 1919-22; Staff Coll., Camberley, 1923-24; HQ RAF, India, 1925-29; Asst Sec., Cttee of Imperial Defence, 1929-35; retired list, RAF, 1935; Asst Under-Sec. of State, Home Office, in charge of Air Raid Precautions Department, 1935-37, Inspector-General, 1938-48; Dir-Gen., Civil Defence Training, 1948-54. Chief Civil Defence Adviser, and i/c Civil Emergency Planning Section, to North Atlantic Treaty Organization, 1954-61, retired. Pres., Nat. Voluntary Civil Aid Service, 1970-. Hon. Mem., Indian Inst. of Civil Defence. First Gold Medal of Inst. of Civil Defence, 1959. Gold Medal of Danish Civil Defence Assoc. Distinguished Service Award, Office of Civil and Defense Mobilization (US). OStJ. Hon. Chief of Scancee Tribe, Alberta, Canada. *Address:* Merlewood Cottage, Tarrant Rushton, Blandford Forum, Dorset. *T:* Blandford 2237.   *[Died* 14 *March* 1971.

HODSON, Major Sir Edmond Adair, 5th Bt, *cr* 1789; DSO 1917; late Rifle Brigade; *b* 22 March 1893; *e s* of late R. E. Hodson and Margaret, *d* of Rev. Stanley Pemberton; *m* 1928, Anne Elizabeth Adderley, *yr d* of Lt-Col H. Adderley Cradock, Hill House, Sherborne St John; *S* uncle, 1921; two *s. Educ:* Marlborough; Trinity Coll., Cambridge. Served European War, 1914-18 (DSO); retired pay, 1929. *Heir: s* Michael Robin Adderley Hodson [*b* 5 March 1932; *m* 1963, Katrin Alexa, *d* of Edwin Bernstiel, Dinas Powis, Glamorgan; two *d*]. *Address:* The White House, Awbridge, Romsey, Hants. *[Died* 7 *Sept.* 1972.

HODSON, Air Vice-Marshal George Stacey, CB 1946; CBE 1942; AFC 1919; retired; *b* 2 May 1899; *s* of Percy George Hodson, London; *m* 1923, Eileen Marlon, *d* of Charles Sandell, Amesbury, Wilts; two *s. Educ:* Dulwich. Air Officer in charge of Training, Bomber Command, 1945; AOA Coastal Command, 1946; AOC No 205 Group, RAF, Mediterranean and Middle East, 1947; SASO, Home Command, 1949-51; retired, 1951.

Address: Richmond, Rudwich Close, Felpham, Bognor Regis, West Sussex PO22 7NG.   *[Died* 1 *Oct.* 1976.

HOEHNE, Most Rev. John, MSc, DD; Archbishop, since 1966, and Metropolitan of Rabaul; *b* Herbern, Germany, 12 Aug. 1910; *s* of M. Hoehne, Herbern. *Educ:* Germany. Dir, Native Seminary, 1939-45; Parish Priest, Namatanai, New Ireland, 1945-49; Dir, St Mary's, Vuvu, 1949-50; Dir, Kininigunan, 1951-56; Manager General of Catholic Mission, Vunapope, 1956-63; Vicar Apostolic from 1963. Grosses Verdienstkreuz, Federal Republic of Germany. *Publications:* contribs to Zeitschrift für Neue Missionswissenschaft. *Recreation:* native psychology. *Address:* Archbishop's House, PO Box 414, Rabaul, Papua and New Guinea.   *[Died* 27 *May* 1978.

HOFFMAN, Paul Gray; Administrator, United Nations Development Programme, 1966-72; Managing Director, United Nations Special Fund, 1959-65; *b* Chicago, Ill, 26 April 1891; *s* of George Delos Hoffman and Eleanor Lott; *m* 1915, Dorothy Brown (*d* 1961); five *s* two *d*; *m* 1962, Anna Rosenberg Hoffman. *Educ:* La Grange (Ill) High Sch.; University of Chicago. Started in automobile business as porter for Chicago distributor of Halladay car; joined Studebaker, 1911; 1st Lieut, US Army, 1917-19. Vice-Pres. of Studebaker Corporation, 1925-33; Pres., 1935-48; Chm., 1953-56; Federal Reserve Bank (Chicago), 1942-49; Administrator of ECA (Marshall Plan), 1948-50; Pres. and Dir of the Ford Foundation, 1951-53. Mem. of US Delegation to United Nations, 1956-57. Director: NY Life Insurance Co.; Encyclopædia Britannica; Encyclopædia Britannica Films, Inc.; Adviser/Director, Time, Inc.; Director Emeritus, United Airlines. Chm., Public Policy Cttee, The Advertising Council, Inc.; Hon. Chm., UN Assoc. of USA; Member: Automotive Safety Foundn (Pres., 1937-41, Pres. and Chm. 1941-42, Chm. 1942-48); Business Advisory Council, Dept of Commerce, 1941-61; Hon. Mem., The Business Council, 1962-. Trustee: Cttee for Economic Develt (Chm., 1942-48); Kenyon Coll., 1940-60; University of Chicago, 1937-50. Republican; Mason. Delta Tau Delta (Nat. Pres., 1940-42). Has numerous hon. degrees; many awards and medals. *Publications:* Seven Roads to Safety, 1939; Peace Can Be Won, 1951; 100 Countries: one and a half billion people, 1960; World Without Want, 1962; various articles. *Address:* (offices) United Nations, New York, NY 10017, USA; 444 Madison Avenue, New York, NY 10022, USA; (home) 2 East 88th Street, New York, NY 10028. *Clubs:* Metropolitan (Washington, DC); Century Association (New York); California, Thunderbird Country (California).   *[Died* 8 *Oct.* 1974.

HOG, Major Roger Thomas Alexander, MC; *b* 19 June 1893; *s* of late Steuart Bayley Hog, of Newliston; *m* 1937, Marjorie St Clair, *d* of Charles F. Wood. *Educ:* Winchester Coll.; RMA Woolwich. Served European War, 1914-19 and War of 1939-45, Royal Artillery, retired as Major. Formerly Vice-Lieutenant of West Lothian. *Address:* Logie West, Crossford, Dunfermline, Fife. *T:* Dunfermline 23054. *Club:* New (Edinburgh).
                                                     [Died 9 *Aug.* 1979.

HOGARTH, Dr Margaret Cameron; formerly Chairman: Executive Committee, Central Council for District Nursing in London; Medical Advisory Committee Nursery School Association of Great Britain and Northern Ireland; Governor, Gipsy Hill Training College, Surrey County Council; Member Executive Committee, Children's Aid Society; a Vice-President of the Health Visitors Association; *b* 10 March 1885; *d* of Farquhar Macdonald, MA, Rector of Dingwall Academy, Ross-shire; *m* 1914, late Archibald Henry Hogarth, CBE, DCM, MA, MD Oxon, DPH; one *s. Educ:* Dingwall Acad.; Aberdeen Univ. Various Resident Hosp. appts, 1907-11, in London and Provinces, specialising in Obstetrics, Gynæcology, Eye and Ear and Child Diseases; Med. Supt, Eastby Sanatorium, Yorks; gen. practice, Colchester and London; Asst MOH and Dep. MOH, Bucks, 1911-12; Medical service under LCC, 1912-24; again with LCC, 1928-50 (Div. Med. Off., Principal Asst and Sen. MO); Ophthalmologist to two LCC eye clinics and, for a period, to LCC Schs for blind and blind and deaf children. Ext. Examr, Hygiene, to Goldsmiths' Trg Coll.; MO to certain Voluntary Maternity and Child Welfare centres and Ante-Natal Clinics. MO, Min. of Health, 1924-28; apptd Govt Rep. League of Nations Nutrition Cttee, 1936; Institute of Education, University of London: Ext. Examr Health Educ.; Mem. Health Educ. Panel, 1953-59; Lectr on Anatomy and Physiology to School of Dramatic Art and Speech Trg. *Publications:* various reports on specific subjects to LCC and Min. of Health; Public Health Reviews for Lancet; Survey of District Nursing in the Administrative County of London (publ. LCC); Medicine as a Career for Women (publ. Brit. Fedn University Women); Health in the Nursery School. *Recreations:* reading, picture galleries. *Address:* Ashley Lodge Nursing Home, Carlton Road, Ealing, W5.   *[Died* 5 *July* 1980.

HOGBEN, Lancelot, FRS 1936; MA Cantab; DSc London; *b* Southsea, 9 Dec. 1895; *e s* of Thomas Hogben; *m* Enid (marr. diss., 1957), *d* of Rev. James Charles, Denbigh; two *s* two *d* ; *m* Sarah Jane, *e d* of John Evans. *Educ:* Trinity Coll., Cambridge (Senr Scholar); Frank Smart Prizeman, Cambridge; Mackinnon Student of the Royal Society, 1923. Lecturer in Zoology, Imperial Coll. of Science, 1919-22; Asst Dir Animal Breeding Research Dept, 1923; Lecturer in Experimental Physiology, Edinburgh, 1923-25; Asst Prof. of Zoology, McGill, 1925-27; Prof. of Zoology, University of Cape Town, 1927-30; Prof. of Social Biology, University of London, 1930-37; Regius Prof. of Natural History, University of Aberdeen, 1937-41; Mason Prof. of Zoology, Birmingham Univ., 1941-47, Prof. of Medical Statistics, 1947-61; Vice-Chancellor, University of Guyana, 1963-65, now Emeritus. Hon. Sen. Fellow in Linguistics, Birmingham Univ., 1961-64. Keith Prize and Gold Medal, Royal Society of Edinburgh, 1936; Croonian Lecture, 1942. Hon. LLD Birmingham; Hon. DSc Wales. *Publications:* The Comparative Physiology of Internal Secretion; The Nature of Living Matter; Nature and Nurture; Mathematics for the Million, 1936; Science for the Citizen, 1938; Dangerous Thoughts, 1939; Chance and Choice, Vol. I, 1950; Vol. II, 1955; Statistical Theory, 1957; Mathematics in the Making, 1960; Essential World English, 1963; The Mother Tongue, 1964; The Vocabulary of Science, 1970. Scientific memoirs on genetics, ductless glands, the physiology of colour change and medical statistics in Proc. Royal Society, B Journal Exper. Biology, Quarterly Journal Exper. Physiology, Biochem. Journal, Journal of Genetics, British Journal Soc. Medicine, etc; articles in the Encyclopædia Britannica. *Address:* Lloches y Fwyalchen, Glynceiriog, near Llangollen, N Wales. *[Died 22 Aug. 1975.*

HOGG, Sir Cecil; *see* Hogg, Sir J. C.

HOGG, Cuthbert Stuart, CMG 1965; Chartered Accountant since 1935; *b* 1 April 1911; *s* of J. S. Hogg; *m* 1939, Eileen Griffiths; three *s. Educ:* Whangarei High Sch. Director: Alliance Textiles Ltd; Bryant & May Ltd, NZ; Kirkcaldie & Stains Ltd; Leopard Brewery Ltd; Lombard NZ Ltd, and others. Chm., NZ RFU, 1953-62. *Address:* PO Box 10340, Wellington, NZ. *T:* 51-949. *Clubs:* Wellington, Wellesley, Commercial Travellers' (all in Wellington). *[Died 20 April 1973.*

HOGG, Edward Gascoigne, CMG 1932; *b* 22 Jan. 1882; *s* of late Edward Hogg, Average Adjuster; *m* 1st, 1910, Beatrice, *d* of F. Filleul Hensley; two *s* one *d* ; 2nd, 1928, Olivia Valentine, *d* of William Holmes; two *s* one *d. Educ:* Charterhouse; New Coll., Oxford. Egyptian Civil Service, 1906-31; Adviser to Ministry of Finance, Iraq, 1931. *Address:* Yattendon, Newbury, Berks. *[Died 7 Feb. 1971.*

HOGG, George Robert Disraeli, CB 1955; CBE 1946; *b* 23 June 1894; *s* of John Hogg; *m* 1919, Daisy Winifred Martin (*d* 1976); two *d. Educ:* Westminster City Sch.; St John's Coll., Oxford. First Cl. Hons in Mathematics, 1916; BA 1919; Lecturer in Mathematics, Sir John Cass Technical Institute, 1919-20; entered Administrative Class, Home Civil Service and joined Dept of Scientific and Industrial Research, 1920; Under-Sec., 1950-57. Served European War, 1914-18, Army and Royal Air Force (meteorological officer, Lieut), 1916-19. *Recreations:* mathematical problems; chess. *Address:* 189 Sheen Lane, East Sheen, SW14 8LE. *T:* 01-876 3275. *[Died 20 Dec. 1977.*

HOGG, Sir (James) Cecil, KCVO 1972 (CVO 1961); FRCS; Aurist to the Queen, since 1961; Dean of the Institute of Laryngology and Otology, University of London, 1961-65; late Examiner in Surgery, University of Bristol; Hon. Consulting Surgeon, Ear, Nose and Throat Department, St Bartholomew's Hospital, Royal National Throat, Nose and Ear Hospital; Consulting Laryngologist, King Edward VII Hospital, Midhurst, since 1960; *b* 25 Aug. 1900; *s* of late James Ewell Hogg; *m* 1936, Pollie Victoria Dalby; one *s* one *d. Educ:* Haileybury Coll.; Gonville & Caius Coll., Cambridge; St Bartholomew's Hosp. BA Cambridge 1922; MRCS, LRCP 1925; MA, BChir Cambridge 1926; FRCS 1930; House Surg. and House Surg., Ear, Nose and Throat Dept, St Bartholomew's Hosp., 1926-27; Chief Asst, Throat and Nose Dept, St Bartholomew's Hosp., 1931-35; Asst Surg., Throat and Ear Dept, Brompton Hosp. for Diseases of the Chest, London, 1936-46. FRSocMed (Pres.; Section of Laryngology; Vice-Pres. Section of Otology; formerly Hon. Sec. Section of Laryngology and Section of Otology); formerly Hon. Treasurer British Assoc. of Otolaryngology; Mem. BMA. *Publications:* various papers in medical jls and chapters in medical textbooks. *Recreations:* tennis, ski-ing. *Address:* 2 Upper Harley Street, NW1. *T:* 01-935 3884. *Clubs:* Bath, Ski Club of Great Britain.
[Died 5 Aug. 1973.

HOGG, Margaret, CBE 1917; SRN; Member, Trained Nurses Committee, and Regional Matron, Southern Area British Red Cross and Order of St John of Jerusalem, 1939-46; *b* 1877; 3rd *d* of late Thomas T. Hogg, Gravesend, Kent. *Educ:* home and private sch. Was Civil Matron, Queen Alexandra's Imperial Army Nursing Board. Principal Matron, Mem. of Cttee and Acting Matron-in-Chief Territorial Army Nursing Service; Hosp. Visitor and Mem. of Gen. Nursing Council for England and Wales; Mem. Voluntary Advisory Nursing Board HM Prisons. Trained at Guys Hosp., SE; Night Superintendent, Ward Sister, Asst Matron and Matron of same Hosp.; retired, 1927. *Recreation:* music. *[Died 25 Oct. 1975.*

HOGG, Norman, CBE 1969; JP; DL; Member, North of Scotland Hydro-Electric Board, since 1961; *b* 22 Nov. 1907; *s* of Hugh Hogg and Susan Gallow; *m* 1936, Mary Wilson; one *s. Educ:* Causewayend Sch., Aberdeen. Trade Union Officer, 1947-. Member: Aberdeen Town Council, 1943-48, 1951-72; Guest Cttee on Scottish Licensing Law, 1959; Aberdeen Milk Marketing Board; Scottish After Care Council; former Chm., NE Consultative Group; Zone Comr, N Zone Scotland Civil Defence, 1970-74. Trustee, Aberdeen Savings Bank, 1970-. JP Aberdeen, 1948; Lord Provost of Aberdeen and Lord Lieutenant of the County of the City of Aberdeen, 1964-67; DL Aberdeen, 1970. Hon. LLD Aberdeen, 1967. *Address:* 14 Sanday Road, Aberdeen. *T:* Aberdeen 34860. *[Died 25 June 1975.*

HOGG, Brig. Oliver Frederick Gillilan, CBE 1943; pac; *b* 22 Dec. 1887; *s* of late Col Arthur Melvill Hogg, 6th Bombay Cavalry; *m* 1919, Ella Harold (*d* 1968), *d* of Arthur Harold Hallam, Shanghai; one *s. Educ:* Bedford Sch.; RMA, Woolwich. 2nd Lieut, RA 1907; Capt. 1914, Major, 1926; Lieut-Col 1934; Col 1935; Brig. 1939; retired, 1946; served European War (France) 1914-18 (1914 Star, British War and Victory Medals); Inspector of Danger Buildings, RGPF, 1915-16; Asst Supt RSAF, 1916-19; Asst Inspector Armaments Inspection Dept, 1921-25; Inspector AID, 1927-30; Mil. Asst to CSOF, 1933-36; War of 1939-45 (Defence and War Medals); Sec., Ordnance Board, 1936-39; Asst Master Gen. of the Ordnance, War Office, 1939; Dep. Dir of Military Administration, Ministry of Supply, 1939-41; Dir of Military Administration, Ministry of Supply, 1941-46; Leverhulme Research Fellow, 1950-51; FSA (Mem. Council, 1953-55); FRSA; FRGS; FRHistS; FAMS; Fellow, Soc. of Genealogists (Mem. Exec. Cttee, 1959-62); Mem., Soc. for Army Historical Research; Vice-Pres. Greenwich Conservative Assoc., 1957- (Hon. Treasurer, 1956-57); a Vice-Pres., Rescue. Order of Polonia Restituta, 3rd class. *Publications:* The History of the 3rd Durham Volunteer Artillery, 1860-1960, 1960; English Artillery 1326-1716, 1963; The Royal Arsenal: Its Background, Origin and Subsequent History, 2 vols, 1963; Further Light on the Ancestry of William Penn, 1965; Clubs to Cannon, 1968; Artillery: its origin, heyday and decline, 1970; The Woolwich Mess (2nd edn), 1971; historical and technical articles dealing with artillery and small arm subjects in Army Jls, etc.; Contrib. on artillery, engines of war and The Board of Ordnance, to Chambers's Encycl. *Recreations:* walking and boating. *Address:* 1 Hardy Road, Blackheath, SE3 7NS. *T:* 01-858 3306. *Club:* Naval and Military. *[Died 19 Feb. 1979.*

HOGG, Percy Herbertson, CBE 1965; retired; *b* 22 Dec. 1898; *s* of Andrew Herbertson Hogg, SCC, Edinburgh, and Mary Burrell Hogg; *m* 1925, Jean Kemp Selkirk; one *s* one *d. Educ:* Daniel Stewart's Coll., Edinburgh. Solicitor, Edinburgh, 1923-47; Dir, The Distillers Co. Ltd, 1952-65; Managing Dir, 1949-60, Chm., 1961-65, John Haig & Co. Ltd, Distillers. *Address:* 1 Northdown Road, Belmont, Surrey SM2 6DY. *T:* 01-642 4962. *[Died 20 Dec. 1978.*

HOLBROOK, Col Sir Claude Vivian, Kt 1938; CBE 1919; Officier, Légion d'Honneur; Royal Army Service Corps (retired); *b* 1886; 3rd *s* of late Col Sir Arthur R. Holbrook, KBE; *m* 1st, 1913, Katharine (*d* 1966), *d* of late C. F. Elston; two *s* ; 2nd, 1967, Joan, *d* of late Theodore Petersen and *widow* of Capt. J. L. Elston, The Northants Regt. Served European War, 1914-19; also 1939-43. DL 1931-67, Warwicks. *Address:* Upper Durford, near Petersfield, Hants. *Club:* Royal Thames Yacht. *[Died 15 Oct. 1979.*

HOLBROOK, Rear-Adm. Leonard Stanley, MVO 1901; RN, retired; 2nd *s* of late Col Sir Arthur R. Holbrook, KBE; *b* 1882; *m* 1920, Gladys Nina (*d* 1968), *d* of J. C. Grove of Stonehouse, Penn, Bucks, and *widow* of Major R. Spencer Britten; one *s. Educ:* privately. Entered HMS Britannia, 1896; Sub-Lt 1901; Lieut 1902; Lt-Comdr 1910; Comdr, 1914; Captain 1920; Rear-Adm. 1932; served with Naval Guard of Honour at Windsor at Queen Victoria's funeral; European War, 1914-17 (prom. Commander); lent to Australian Navy, 1929; commanded Australian Squadron, 1931-32; ADC to the King, 1932; retired

list, 1932; War of 1939-45. *Address:* White Webbs, Bury, Pulborough, Sussex. *T:* Bury 412. *Club:* Savage.
[*Died* 29 *Aug.* 1974.

HOLBROOK, Cmdr Norman Douglas, VC 1914; RN retired; *b* 9 July 1888; 4th *s* of late Col Sir Arthur R. Holbrook, KBE; *m* 1919, Viva (*d* 1952), *d* of late Frederick Woodin and *widow* of F. E. Dixon (one *s* killed in action, 1945); *m* 1953, Gundula, *d* of Dr A. Feldner, Innsbruck. When in command of submarine B11 in European War, 1914-17, dived under five rows of mines in the Dardanelles, 13 Dec. 1914, and torpedoed Turkish battleship Messudieh (VC, subsequently slightly wounded while on patrolling duties). *Address:* Stedham Mill, Stedham, near Midhurst, W Sussex. *T:* Midhurst 3391. *Club:* Savage.
[*Died* 3 *July* 1976.

HOLCROFT, Sir Reginald Culcheth, 2nd Bt (2nd *cr*); *cr* 1921; TD; JP; *b* 6 April 1899; *s* of 1st Bt and Annie Gertrude (*d* 1929), *d* of late Rev. J. Coombes; *S* father, 1951; *m* 1st, 1928, Mary Frances (*d* 1963), *yr d* of late William Swire, CBE; two *s* two *d*; 2nd, 1965, Elizabeth, Countess of Bandon. *Educ:* Radley Coll.; RMC Sandhurst; Exeter Coll., Oxford. JP Salop 1934, High Sheriff, 1950. *Heir:* *s* Peter George Culcheth Holcroft [*b* 29 April 1931; *m* 1956, Rosemary Rachel, *yr d* of late G. N. Deas; three *s* one *d*]. *Address:* Wrentnall House, Pulverbatch, Shrewsbury, Salop. *Club:* Cavalry and Guards.
[*Died* 6 *June* 1978.

HOLDEN, Sir George, 3rd Bt, *cr* 1919; *b* 6 Dec. 1914; *s* of Sir George Holden, 2nd Bt, and Margaret, *d* of Thomas Smith, JP, of Astley, near Manchester; *S* father, 1937; *m* 1937, Betty, *d* of late W. Shaw, 70 Portland Place, W1; one *s* two *d* (and two *s* decd). *Educ:* Oundle. *Heir:* *g s* John David Holden, *b* 16 Dec. 1967. *Address:* Lynville, Portland Road, Dorking, Surrey. *T:* Dorking 3697.
[*Died* 2 *Dec.* 1976.

HOLDEN, Harold Henry, ARCA, AMC, RWS; *b* 1885. *Educ:* Settle; Skipton; Leeds School of Art; Royal College of Art, London. Head of the Art Dept, Leeds Modern Sch., 1910; Principal of the Sch. of Arts and Crafts, Cheltenham, 1914; Principal Leeds Coll. of Art, 1922; Dir of Art Education and Principal of The College of Arts and Crafts, Birmingham, 1928-46; retired, 1946. *Address:* 3 Southwood Drive, Westbury-on-Trym, Bristol.
[*Died* 19 *April* 1977.

HOLDEN, Sir James (Robert), Kt 1963; farmer; *b* 1 Feb. 1903; *s* of late Hubert William Holden, Turramurra, NSW, and Annie Maria, *d* of Robert Turner, Victoria; *m* 1934, Prudence Elsie Staughton; four *d. Educ:* Sydney C. of E. Grammar Sch., NSW. Resident Dir, General Motors-Holden's Pty Ltd, Woodville, SA, 1952-71, retired. *Recreation:* fishing. *Address:* PMB 193, Rocky River Service, Kangaroo Island, SA 5223, Australia. *Club:* Adelaide.
[*Died* 21 *Sept.* 1977.

HOLDER, Prof. Douglas William, MA, PhD, DSc; DIC; FRS 1962; FCGI; CEng; FICE; FRAeS; AFAIAA; Professor of Engineering Science and Head of Department of Engineering Science, Oxford University, since 1961; Fellow of Brasenose College, Oxford, since 1961; *b* 14 April 1923; *s* of late W. A. Holder and Ann Daniel; *m* 1946, Barbara Woods; two *d. Educ:* Imperial Coll. of Science and Technology. Aircraft and Armament Experimental Establishment, 1943; Nat. Physical Laboratory, 1944-61; Head of High Speed Laboratory, 1950-61 (dep. Chief SO (Personal Merit), 1957). Chairman: Enquiry into Precision Approach Radar, BoT, 1969; Royal Society ad hoc Cttee on Technology, 1963-65; Aerodynamic Cttee, RAeS, 1964-68. Member: ARC, 1964-68 (Chm. Aerodynamics Cttee, Hypersonics Sub-Cttee; Mem. Fluid-motion Cttee, Guidance and Control Cttee); Adv. Council on Scientific Research and Tech. Development, MoD, 1964-68; Defence Scientific Adv. Council, 1971-; Adv. Council for Applied R&D, 1976-; Adviser to HM Govt on future of Rolls Royce RB-211 engine, 1971; Mem. or Chm., various cttees and working parties of MoD, 1964-; Member: Standing Adv. Cttee on Artificial Limbs, Dept Health and Social Security (formerly Min. of Health), 1966-70; Hydraulic Research Bd, 1963-65; Vis. Bd, Nat. Physical Laboratory, 1967-69; Schools Council Science and Technology Cttee, 1964-70; Academic Adv. Cttee, Coll. of Aeronautics, 1964-65; Adv. Council, RMCS, 1964- (Chm., 1976-); RMA, 1969-; Council, Royal Society, 1969- (Mem. Educn Cttee, 1969-, Ind. Activities Cttee, 1969-); Court and Council, Cranfield Inst. Technology, 1970-. CEI Educn and Training Cttee, 1970-; SRC Mechanical and Production Engrng Cttee, 1971-, Aeronautical and Mechanical Engrg Cttee, 1973-; UGC Technology Sub Cttee, 1974-; Chairman: Royal Society/CEI Educn Cttee, 1974-; Royal Society Working Party on Medical Engrg, Applications of Science and Technology to assist British Industry, 1975-. Visitor, Central Electricity Research Laboratory, 1962-70; Chm.

of Governors, Oxford Polytechnic, 1970-. Visiting Prof., University of Michigan, 1964. Fellow, Imperial Coll. London, 1972. *Publications:* books, monographs and papers mainly on fluid mechanics and related topics. *Recreations:* tennis, golf. *Address:* Department of Engineering Science, Parks Road, Oxford OX1 3PJ. *T:* Oxford 56120; Woods End, Hamels Lane, Boar's Hill, Oxford. *T:* Oxford 735171. [*Died* 18 *April* 1977.

HOLDSWORTH, David, CBE 1976; QPM 1968; Chief Constable, Thames Valley Police, 1970-78; *b* 10 May 1918; *s* of late Captain F. J. C. Holdsworth, DL, JP, The Mount, Totnes, Devon. *Educ:* Sherborne; Metropolitan Police Coll., Hendon. Commnd Devonshire Regt, 1943; landed D Day, 1944; served in France, Belgium and Holland (wounded, despatches). Rejoined Metropolitan Police, 1945; Stn Inspector, Chelsea, 1945-52; Staff Officer, Police Coll., 1953-56; Asst Chief Constable, Wilts, 1956-64; Chief Constable, Oxon, 1964-68; Dep. Chief Constable, Thames Valley Police, 1968-70. District Comr, Boy Scouts' Assoc., Mid-Wilts, 1957-64; Chm., Exec. Cttee, Oxfordshire Scouts Assoc. Pres., Chief Constables' Club, 1976-77. Scouts Medal of Merit, 1975. Comdr, Order of Orange Nassau, 1972; Grosses Verdienstkreuz des Verdienstordens der Bundesrepublik Deutschland, 1972; Comdr, Order of Aztec Eagle, Mexico, 1973; Comdr, Order of Dannebrog, 1974; Médaille de Bayeux, 1974. *Publication:* The New Society: Development of Pop and Free Festivals in the Thames Valley Police Area, 1972-1975, 1975. *Recreation:* oil painting. *Address:* c/o Chief Constable's Office, Police Headquarters, Kidlington, Oxford OX5 2NX. *T:* Kidlington 4343. [*Died* 28 *Sept.* 1978.

HOLDSWORTH, Mrs Mary, MA; Principal, St Mary's College, Durham University, 1962-74, Second Pro-Vice-Chancellor, 1973-74; *b* Voronezh, Russia, 24 Oct. 1908; *d* of late Col A. Zvegintzov, Chev. Gardes, Member of Duma, and Catherine Sverbeev; *m* 1940, Richard William Gilbert Holdsworth, Fellow, University College, Oxford, Flt-Lt RAFVR (killed on active service, 1942); one *d. Educ:* Cheltenham Ladies' Coll.; St Hugh's Coll., Oxford. Worked in banking and industry, 1931-37; College Sec., University College, Oxford, 1937-40; Air Ministry, 1942-43; Tutor for Education in the Forces, N Ireland, 1943-45; Secretary and Senior Research Officer, OU Institute of Commonwealth Studies, 1948-62. Member Royal Institute of International Affairs, 1961-. *Publications:* Turkestan in the 19th Century, 1959; Soviet African Studies, 1918-59 (annotated bibliography for RIIA), 1961; articles, reviews. *Recreations:* gardening, walking. [*Died* 30 *Dec.* 1978.

HOLE, Edwyn Cecil, CBE 1946; *s* of late George Walter Hole and Emma, *d* of George Jolly Grace; *m* 1919, Laura Hélène Marianne, *d* of late John Richard de Fonton; one *s* one *d. Educ:* St Olave's; Heidelberg; Paris; Pembroke Coll., Cambridge. Student Interpreter in the Levant, 1911; special service in Turkey, Bulgaria and Greece, 1914-16; served at Janina and Mitylene till 1919; on staff of British High Commissioner at Constantinople, 1919, Smyrna, 1919-22; acting Consul-Gen. Salonica, 1922-24; served with League of Nations Commission of Enquiry into the murder of Gen. Tellini, Janina, 1923; Corfu, 1925; Consul Damascus, 1926-32, Athens, 1932-36, Marrakesh, 1936; Dept of Overseas Trade, 1936; Consul-Gen. at Salonica, 1938-41; at Smyrna, 1941-45; at Nice 1945-50; retired 1950; Hon. Consul at Málaga, 1952-57. *Publications:* Syrian Harvest, 1955; Andalus: the Muslims in Spain, 1958; Also Ran, reminiscences, 1966. *Recreations:* historical research, music. *Address:* 31 Fairburn Court, Putney, SW15. *T:* 01-789 2827. [*Died* 5 *June* 1976.

HOLE, Francis George, CBE 1963; FCA; *b* 29 Nov. 1904; *e s* of late Francis Hole; *m* 1934, Jean Mary, *d* of late Judge L. C. Thomas; one *s* one *d. Educ:* King's Coll. Sch. ACA 1929; senior asst, Thomson McLintock & Co., 1930; accountant, LMS Hotel Services, 1934; succeeded Arthur Towle, Controller, LMS Hotel Services, 1945; Mem. of Hotels Executive, British Transport, 1948-53; on discontinuance of Executive, Chief of British Transport Hotels and Catering Services, 1954-55; Gen. Manager, 1955-58; Chm. and Gen. Manager, 1959-62; Dir and Gen. Manager, British Transport Hotels Ltd, 1963-68, Man. Dir, 1969. Member: Council of Management, Executive Cttee and Scottish Cttee of British Hotels and Restaurants Assoc., 1944-71; Nat. Council, Bd of Management (Chm.), and Scottish Cttee, British Hotels, Restaurants and Caterers Assoc., 1972-; British Tourist and Holidays Board and Chm. of Hotels Cttee, 1947-48; Licensed Residential Establishment and Licensed Restaurant Wages Board, 1946-51; Board, BTA, 1964-70; Hotel and Catering Ind. Training Bd, 1969-. Chm. of the Governing Body of King's Coll. Sch.; Mem. of Coun., Radley Coll. *Address:* Little Rex, St Andrews Square, Surbiton, Surrey. *T:* 01-399 1958. [*Died* 22 *Sept.* 1973.

HOLFORD, Baron cr 1965, of Kemp Town (Life Peer); **William Graham Holford,** Kt 1953; RA 1968 (ARA 1961); FRIBA, FRTPI; architect and planning consultant; Professor of Town Planning, University College, London, 1948-70, now Emeritus Professor; Director, Leverhulme Trust Fund, since 1972; *b* 22 March 1907; *s* of William George Holford and Katherine Palmer; *m* 1933, Marjorie, *d* of John and Caroline Brooks. *Educ:* Diocesan Coll., Capetown, S Africa; Liverpool Sch. of Architecture. American Scholar of the Soc. of Arts and Sciences, New York, USA, 1929; Degree of BArch (1st Class Hons), University of Liverpool; Rome Scholar in Architecture, 1930; Florence Bursar of RIBA, 1935; Pres., RIBA, 1960-62. Architect of houses, factories, university and public buildings; planning consultant to City of London, County of Cambridge, etc; Romanes Lectr, Oxford, 1969; Member: Royal Fine Art Commission, 1943-69; Historic Buildings Council for England, 1953-; Hon. Mem., ICE, 1968. A Trustee, British Museum, 1969-; Treasurer, Royal Acad. of Arts, 1970-; Governor, Wye Coll., Univ. of London, 1968-. Prime Warden, Goldsmiths' Co., 1962-. Hon. Fellow, UCL, 1973. Hon. DCL Dunelm 1960; Hon. LLD Liverpool, 1961; Hon. DLitt: Oxon, 1964; Exon, 1968. Gold Medal of Town Planning Institute, 1961; Royal Gold Medal for Architecture, 1963. *Publications:* The Great Baroque Masquerade, 1932; Town and City, 1942; Reconstruction in the City of London, 1947; Cambridge Planning Proposals, 1950; Corby New Town, 1952; Design in Town and Village, 1953; Report... on the Precincts of St Paul's, 1956; Durban 1985, a plan for central Durban in its regional setting, 1968. *Address:* 20 Eccleston Square, SW1; 133 Marine Parade, Brighton, East Sussex. *Clubs:* Savile, Athenæum.   *[Died 17 Oct. 1975.*

HOLLAND, Edgar William, CIE 1944; *b* 28 April 1899; *s* of Rev. Edgar Rogers Holland, MA, and Ellen Angela (née Jellicorse); *m* 1928, Doris Marjorie (*d* 1973), 2nd *d* of George Waverling Schoneman, late Postmaster-Gen., Bengal and Assam, and Hilda Edith (née Hope Ross). *Educ:* Rossall Sch.; Brasenose Coll., Oxford. Served in European War, 1914-18, in Royal Artillery, France, 1918. Entered Indian Civil Service, 1923, posted to Bengal Province; Commissioner of Commercial Taxes, 1941; Sec. to Government in Public Health Dept, 1943; Commissioner of Dacca Div., 1945; Chairman, Calcutta Improvement Trust, 1947; retired from ICS, 1948; Asst Governor HM Prison Service, 1951-56. *Recreations:* rowing, tennis, walking.   *[Died 30 Dec. 1973.*

HOLLAND, Frank, CBE 1964; retired as official of LCC, 1964; *b* 21 Sept. 1899; *s* of H. J. E. Holland; *m* 1931, Elsie Freda Smith; one *s. Educ:* King Edward VI Sch., Lichfield. Entered service of LCC, 1915; Dep. Comptroller, 1949, Comptroller, 1956-64. Incorporated Accountant, 1930. Mem. Coun., London Hostels Corp. and Chm. of Finance and Gen. Purposes Cttee. *Recreations:* walking, motoring, gardening, archaeology, geology. *Address:* Cherrywood, 6 Weedon Lane, Amersham, Bucks. *T:* Amersham 5577.   *[Died 2 Aug. 1972.*

HOLLAND, Major John Vincent, VC 1916; Indian Army, retired; *b* Athy, Co. Kildare, July 1889; *e s* of John Holland, MRCVS, Model Farm, Athy, Co. Kildare; *m* 1917, Frances (decd), *y d* of Joseph Grogan, JP, Manor House, Queenstown and Rossleague; one *s* (and one *s* decd). *Educ:* Clongowes Wood Coll.; Liverpool Univ. Travelled extensively in South America (Brazil, Argentine, Chili and Bolivia), where engaged in ranching, railway engineering, and hunting; returned to England on outbreak of war; enlisted in 2nd Life Guards, 2 Sept. 1914; gazetted to Leinster Regt Feb. 1915; attached to 2nd Royal Dublin Fusiliers in France (wounded in 2nd battle of Ypres); returned to France; attached to 7th Leinster Regt as Batt. Bombing Officer; saw service at Loos, Hulloch, and Somme, 1916 (despatches and awarded Parchment of 16th Irish Div.; VC for conspicuous bravery in leading an attack at the capture of Guillemont, 3 Sept. 1916); retired, 1922. *Recreations:* hunted a great deal with Kildare, Queen's County, and Co. Carlow foxhounds; big game abroad; tennis, cricket. *Address:* Model Farm, Athy, Co. Kildare. *TA:* Athy.   *[Died 27 Feb. 1975.*

HOLLAND, Robert Henry Code, CBE 1969; retired publisher; Chairman, Book Centre Ltd; formerly Deputy Chairman, Sir Isaac Pitman & Sons Ltd; *b* Manchester, 22 Feb. 1904; *e s* of late Robert W. Holland, OBE, LLD, and Annie Glover Code; *m* 1st, 1927, Eveline Mary (*d* 1965), *d* of late W. J. Bonnett; one *s* two *d*; *m* 2nd, 1970, Dorothy, *d* of late Alfred Stockdale, Flixton. *Educ:* Newport (Mon.) High Sch.; University Coll., London. BA Hons Mod. Hist., 1924; Barrister-at-Law, Middle Temple, 1929. Editor, Butterworth & Co. (Publishers) Ltd, 1925-30; Legal Editor, Sir Isaac Pitman & Sons Ltd, 1931-37; Sales Manager, 1938-40; Publishing Director, 1940-65; Managing Director, 1966-68. President, Publishers' Association, 1949-51; Pres., Soc. of Commercial Teachers, 1959-62. Liveryman, Stationers'

Company; Freeman of City of London. *Publications:* (Joint Ed.) Slater's Mercantile Law, 7th-12th edns, 1931-50; Editor: Law and Practice of the Stock Exchange, 5th edn, 1932; Pitman's Commercial Law 12th edn, 1939; (Jt Ed) Law, Justice and Equity, 1967. *Recreation:* books. *Address:* Caunton House, 28 Watchbell Street, Rye, Sussex. *T:* Rye 2269. *Clubs:* Reform; Dormy (Rye).   *[Died 17 March 1974.*

HOLLAND-MARTIN, Adm. Sir Deric (Douglas Eric), GCB 1964 (KCB 1960; CB 1958); DSO 1943; DSC 1939, and Bar, 1943; Lord-Lieutenant of Hereford and Worcester, since 1976 (Lieutenant, 1974-76); *b* 10 April 1906; 4th *s* of late R. M. Holland-Martin, CB, and late Mrs Holland-Martin, Overbury Court, Tewkesbury; *m* 1951, Rosamund Mary Hornby, OBE; one *s* one *d. Educ:* Royal Naval Coll., Osborne and Dartmouth. Midshipman HMS Iron Duke, 1924-27; Sub-Lieut HMY Victoria and Albert, 1928; HMS Effingham, 1929-31; Royal Naval Coll. Dartmouth, 1931-33; in comd of HM Ships, Tartar, Holderness, Nubian, Faulknor, during War of 1939-45; Comdr 1940; Capt. 1946; Naval Attaché to Argentine, Paraguay and Uruguay, 1947-49; in command of HMS Agincourt, 1949-50; idc 1951; Director of Plans, Admiralty, 1952-53; in command HMS Eagle, 1954; Flag Officer Flotillas, Mediterranean, 1955-57; Dep. Chief of Naval Personnel, 1957; Second Sea Lord and Chief of Naval Personnel, 1957-59; Flag Officer Air (Home), 1960-61; Comdr-in-Chief, Mediterranean, and C-in-C Allied Forces, Mediterranean, 1961-64; Commandant, Imperial Defence Coll., 1964-66. Rear-Adm., 1955; Vice-Adm., 1958; Admiral, 1961. Retired, 1966. Vice-Adm. of the UK and Lieut of the Admiralty, 1973-76. A Trustee, Imperial War Museum, 1966, Vice-Pres. and Chm. 1967-; Chm., Cttee of Inquiry into Trawler Safety, 1968; Mem., White Fish Authority and Herring Ind. Bd, 1969. DL 1968, Vice-Lieutenant, 1973, Worcester. *Recreations:* shooting, fishing. *Address:* Bell's Castle, Kemerton, Tewkesbury, Glos. *T:* Overbury 333. *Clubs:* White's, MCC.   *[Died 6 Jan. 1977.*

HOLLENDEN, 2nd Baron, cr 1912; **Geoffrey Hope Hope-Morley;** Past President of the Wholesale Textile Association; High Sheriff County of London, 1917; JP Kent; *b* 28 Jan. 1885; *e s* of 1st Baron and Laura M. (*d* 1945), *d* of Rev. G. Royds Birch; *S* father, 1929; *m* 1st, 1914, Hon. Mary Gardner (from whom he obtained a divorce, 1928), 3rd *d* of 1st Baron Burghclere; two *d*; 2nd, 1929, Muriel Ivy (*d* 1962), 3rd *d* of Sir John E. Gladstone, 4th Bt; 3rd, 1963, Mrs Violet Norris Howitt, *widow* of Frank Howitt, Harley Street, W1. *Educ:* Eton; Trinity Coll., Cambridge. Pres., Salmon and Trout Association. *Heir:* nephew Gordon Hope Hope-Morley. *Address:* Ravensbourne, Stoke Fleming, near Dartmouth, Devon. *T:* Stoke Fleming 349.   *[Died 19 Oct. 1977.*

HOLLIDAY, Gilbert Leonard Gibson, CMG 1954; HM Ambassador to Morocco, 1965-69, retired; *b* 10 April 1910; *s* of late Rev. Andrew Barnes Holliday and late Violet Holliday (née White), Wigton, Cumberland; *m* 1st, 1934, Ana María (*d* 1952), *d* of late SeñorDon Juan R. López, Honduras; two *s*; 2nd, 1954, Margaret Mitford, *d* of late Brig. James Stewart, IA; 3rd, 1958, Jane Mary Wilkinson; one *s* two *d. Educ:* Rydal Sch.; Queen's Coll., Oxford. Laming Travelling Fellow, Queen's Coll., Oxford, 1931-32; served in Consular and Diplomatic Services at Buenos Aires, Valparaiso, Santiago, Katowice, Los Angeles, Foreign Office, New York, Warsaw, Paris, Berne and Stockholm; Ambassador to Laos, 1956-58; Foreign Office, 1958-60; Ambassador to Bolivia, 1960-64. *Recreation:* gardening. *Address:* (home) Notton Lodge, Lacock, Chippenham, Wilts SN15 2NF. *T:* Lacock 282.   *[Died 15 Dec. 1980.*

HOLLINGHURST, Air Chief Marshal Sir Leslie (Norman), GBE 1952 (KBE 1945; CBE 1944; OBE 1932); KCB 1948 (CB 1942); DFC 1918; retired; *b* 2 Jan. 1895; *yr s* of late C. H. Hollinghurst, Brentwood, Essex. Served European War, 1914-19, Gallipoli, Salonika, France (DFC); transferred RFC from Middlesex Regt, 1916; Afghanistan and NW Frontier, 1919; graduated Royal Air Force Staff Coll., 1925; Shanghai Defence Force, 1927; NW Frontier, 1920-34 (despatches, OBE); commanded No. 20 Squadron, 1933-34; Instructor, RAF Staff Coll., 1935-37; graduated Imperial Defence Coll., 1928; Air Ministry, 1939; Group Catain 1939; Director of Organisation, 1940; Air Commodore, 1941; Air Vice-Marshal, 1942; Commendation, 1941; Director-General of Organisation, RAF, 1941-43; AOC No. 38 Group, 1943-44; Air Marshal Commanding Base Air Forces, South-East Asia, 1944-45; Temp. Air Marshal, 1946; Air Marshal, 1947; Air Member for Supply and Organisation on the Air Council, 1944-48; Inspector-General of the RAF, 1948-49; Air Council Member for Personnel, 1949-52. Retired 1952. *Address:* 12 Newnham House, Manor Fields, Putney Hill, SW15. *T:* 01-788 1065. *Clubs:* United Service, Royal Air Force, East India and Sports.   *[Died 8 June 1971.*

HOLLINGWORTH, John; *b* 3 June 1885; *s* of Francis, *s* of Archdeacon Hollingworth, and Cecilia, *d* of Rev. W. Tomkins; unmarried. *Educ:* Bradfield Coll.; Peterhouse, Cambridge (Scholar). Wrangler, 1907; ACGI, 1909; BScEng London; 1st class hons, 1910; DSc London, 1928; MScTech Manchester, 1936; FIEE; FCGI 1937; Demonstrator, City and Guilds (Eng) Coll., 1911-13; Lecturer, College of Technology, Manchester, 1913-21; Lieut RNVR and later Captain RAF at Wireless Experimental Establishment, Biggin Hill, 1917-19; scientific assistant, National Physical Laboratory, 1921-26; Radio Research Station, Slough, 1926-31; Professor of Electrical Engineering in the University of Manchester and the College of Technology, 1932-52; retired 1952. *Publications:* various papers on Radio-Telegraphic subjects in Proceedings of Royal Society and Journal of Institution of Electrical Engineers. *Address:* The Manor House, Rowde, Devizes, Wilts.			*[Died* 6 *Feb.* 1976.

HOLLIS, Christopher; *see* Hollis, M. C.

HOLLIS, (Maurice) Christopher; Chairman, Hollis and Carter; Member of Editorial Board of the Tablet; Member of Board of Punch; *b* 29 March 1902; 2nd *s* of late Rt Rev. George Arthur Hollis, Bishop of Taunton; *m* 1929, Margaret Madeline King; three *s* one *d. Educ:* Eton; Balliol Coll., Oxford. Toured USA, New Zealand, and Australia, as member of Oxford Union Debating Society, 1924-25; Asst Master Stonyhurst Coll., 1925-35; engaged in economic research at Notre Dame University, Indiana, USA, 1935-39; served War of 1939-45, with RAF. MP (C) Devizes Division of Wilts, 1945-55. *Publications:* American Heresy; Dr Johnson; Monstrous Regiment; Erasmus; Dryden; St Ignatius; Thomas More; Breakdown of Money; Two Nations; Foreigners Aren't Fools; We Aren't So Dumb; Lenin; Foreigners Aren't Knaves; Our Case; Italy in Africa, 1941; Noble Castle, 1941; Death of a Gentleman, 1943; Fossett's Memory, 1944; Rise and Fall of the ex-Socialist Government, Letters to a Sister, 1947; Can Parliament Survive?, 1949; A Study of George Orwell, 1956; The Ayes and the Noes, 1957; Along the Road to Frome, 1958; Eton, 1960; The Homicide Act, 1964; The Papacy, 1964; The Oxford Union, 1965; Newman and the Modern World, 1968; A History of the Jesuits, 1968; The Mind of Chesterton, 1969; Parliament and its Sovereignty, 1973; The Seven Ages (autobiog.), 1974; Oxford in the Twenties, 1976; general journalism. *Recreations:* tennis, watching cricket, squash rackets. *Address:* Little Claveys, Mells, near Frome. *T:* Mells 327.				*[Died* 5 *May* 1977.

HOLLIS, Sir Roger (Henry), KBE 1966 (OBE 1946); Kt 1960; CB 1956; Attached Ministry of Defence; retired; *b* 2 Dec. 1905; *s* of late Rt Rev. George Arthur Hollis, Bishop of Taunton; *m* 1st, 1937, Evelyn Esmé (*née* Swayne) (marr. diss., 1968); one *s* ; 2nd, 1968, Edith Valentine (*née* Hammond). *Educ:* Clifton Coll.; Worcester Coll., Oxford. *Address:* Crossways Cottage, Catcott, near Bridgwater, Somerset.			*[Died* 26 *Oct.* 1973.

HOLLOND, Prof. Henry Arthur, DSO 1918; OBE 1919; Fellow of Trinity College, Cambridge, since 1909; Hon. Bencher Lincoln's Inn, since 1935; *b* 14 Oct. 1884; *o surv. s* of late Arthur Edward Hollond of Great Ashfield House, Bury St Edmunds; *g s* of Rev. Edmund Hollond, Benhall Lodge, Saxmundham, Suffolk; *m* 1929, Marjorie, PhD Columbia Univ., Fellow of Girton Coll., Lecturer in Economics in the University of Cambridge, *er d* of Herman Tappan, Gloucester, Mass. *Educ:* Rugby Sch. (Classical Scholar, Head of the School); Trinity Coll., Cambridge (Classical Scholar); Classical Tripos Part I 1905, Law Tripos (both Parts) 1906, 1907; President of the Union Society, 1906; called to the Bar, Lincoln's Inn, 1911; attended the Law School of Harvard Univ., 1913-14; held a commission in Wessex (Hants) RGA (TF) 1914-20, retiring with rank of Major (DSO, OBE for services as DAAG on General Headquarters Staff, France); Reader in English Law, Cambridge Univ., 1919-43; Dean of Trinity Coll., 1922-50; Secretary, University of Cambridge Commissioners, 1923-27; Rouse Ball Professor of English Law, 1943-50; President Society of Public Teachers of Law, 1937-38; Chairman of Department of Criminal Science, Cambridge, 1949-55; Vice-Master of Trinity Coll., 1951-55; Reader in Legal History to the Inns of Court, 1945-68. *Address:* 3 Madingley Road, Cambridge. *T:* Cambridge 62811.
[Died 20 *Oct.* 1974.

HOLLOWAY, John Edward, DSc; Hon. LLD, Hon. DCom; Director of Companies; *b* 4 July 1890; *s* of George John Holloway and Hester Maria Holloway (*née* Enslin); *m* 1913, Christina Maria Purchase (*d* 1967); one *s* three *d* (and one *d* decd). *Educ:* Stellenbosch Univ. (BA); London School of Economics. DSc (Econ) London, 1917, Hutchinson Research Medallist. Lecturer Grey University College, 1917-19; Lecturer and Professor Transvaal University College, 1919-25; Director Census and Statistics, 1925-33; Econ. Adviser to Treasury, 1934-

37; Secretary for Finance, 1937-50; Chairman: Native Economic Commn, 1930-32; Customs Tariff Commn, 1934-35; Gold Mining Taxation Cttee, 1945; SW Africa Financial Commn, 1951; Univ. Finances Commn, 1951-53; Commn on Univ. Facilities for Non-Europeans, 1953; Member, SW Africa Commn, 1934-35; Transkeian Commn of Enquiry, 1962-63; Adviser Ottawa Conference, 1932, and Montreal Conference, 1958. World Economic Conference, 1933; Imperial Conference, 1937; Conferences of Finance Ministers, 1949, 1950, 1954; Delegate, Bretton Woods Conference, 1944; Leader S African Delegation: Conferences on Trade and Employment, Geneva, 1947, and Havana, 1948; formerly Alternate Governor IMF. Director: African Batignolles Construction Ltd; Anglo-Alpha Cement; Consultant to Barclays National Bank; formerly Director: South African Marine Corporation; South African Iron and Steel Corporation, and other cos; Member Atomic Energy Board. Resigned from these boards when appointed Ambassador in Washington, July 1954; High Commissioner for The Union of South Africa in London, 1956-58. Founder Mem. and Former Vice-President, S African Foundation; former Mem. Council, University of Pretoria. Successfully advocated one ounce gold coin (Krugerrand). *Publications:* Apartheid: a challenge, 1964; various articles, chiefly about gold in the monetary system and race relations in South Africa. *Recreations:* bowls, fly-fishing. *Address:* 63 Fourth Street, Linden, Johannesburg, 2195, South Africa. *Clubs:* Pretoria and Pretoria Country (Pretoria, SA).			*[Died Oct.* 1979.

HOLMAN, Sir Adrian, KBE 1954; CMG 1936; MC; *b* 22 Dec. 1895; *s* of late Richard Haswell Holman; *m* 2nd, 1940, Betty, *o d* of Sir Gilbert Fox, 1st Bt. *Educ:* Copthorne Sch., Crawley, Sussex; Harrow; New Coll., Oxford. Served European War, 1915-18 (MC, despatches); entered Diplomatic Service as 3rd Secretary, 1920; HM Embassy, Brussels, 1921-24; 2nd Secretary, 1922; HM Embassy, Rome, 1924-26; Paris, 1926-31; First Secretary, 1931; First Secretary, HM Legation, Peking, 1931-35; Foreign Office, 1935-38; HM Embassy, Berlin, 1938-39; The Hague, 1939; Bagdad, 1940; Counsellor, 1940; Teheran, 1942; British Mission, Algiers; Minister at HM Embassy, Paris, 1944; British Political Representative in Rumania, 1946-47, Minister, 1947-49; Minister, Cuba, 1949-50, Ambassador to Cuba, 1950-54; retired from HM Foreign Service, May 1954. Coronation Medals, 1937, 1953; Chevalier of the Order of Leopold. *Recreations:* fishing and gardening. *Address:* Bohunt Manor, Liphook, Hampshire GU30 7DL. *T:* Liphook 722208. *Club:* Bath.				*[Died* 6 *Sept.* 1974.

HOLMAN, James Frederick, CBE 1967; Chairman, Compair Ltd, since 1968; *b* 11 March 1916; *s* of late John Leonard and Gladys Frederica Holman; *m* 1948, Linden Travers; one *d. Educ:* Rugby; Trinity Hall, Cambridge. MA; CEng, FIMechE, FIProdE, FBIM. Holman Bros Ltd: London Dir, 1945-50; Sales Dir, 1950-58; Jt Man. Dir, 1958-67; Chm., 1962-68; Dir, Baker Perkins Holdings Ltd, 1973-. Chm., SW Economic Planning Council, 1971-; President: Falmouth and Camborne Conservative and Unionist Assoc., 1950-65; Surf Life Saving Assoc. of Gt Britain, 1958-; Vice-Pres., British Mechanical Engrg Confedn, 1969-; Governor: Cornwall Techn. Coll., 1952-71; Camborne Sch. of Mines, 1959-; Member: Africa Cttee, British Nat. Export Council, 1965-71; CBI Overseas Cttee, 1968-72. Bard, Cornish Gorsedd, 1972. *Recreations:* sailing, surfing, gardening. *Address:* 6 Stavordale Lodge, Melbury Road, W14. *T:* 01-602 3710; Loraine, St Ives, Cornwall. *T:* St Ives 5822. *Clubs:* Bath; Royal Yacht Squadron, Royal Ocean Racing, Royal Cornwall Yacht.			*[Died* 8 *Dec.* 1974.

HOLMAN, Percy, BSc; Paper Merchant; *b* 5 April 1891; *s* of S. H. Holman; *m* 1918, Dorothy Anderson (*d* 1976); one *s* two *d. Educ:* Mill Hill Sch.; London School of Economics (London Univ.). Entered business 1913. Service in France with BRCS, 1915-18. Member Middlesex CC, 1928-31; Member Teddington UDC, 1928-34. Contested (Lab) Twickenham, 1931, 1932, 1934 and 1935; MP (Lab-Co-op) Bethnal Green, 1950-66, (Lab-Co-op) Bethnal Green South-West, 1945-50). *Recreation:* walking. *Address:* 3 Arundel Court, Wimbledon, SW19 4AF. *T:* 01-946 3497.				*[Died* 9 *June* 1978.

HOLMES, Eric Gordon, MA, MD Cantab; MRCP London; retired; *b* 16 Aug. 1897; *s* of Rev. Richard Holmes and Catherine Emily Compton-Rickett; *m* 1st, 1924, Barbara Elizabeth (marr. diss., 1946), *d* of late Sir Frederick Gowland Hopkins, OM; one *s* one *d* ; 2nd, 1946, Helen Merle, *d* of W. E. Stephen, Melbourne, Australia; three *s. Educ:* Rugby Sch.; Christ's Coll., Cambridge (Scholar); St Bartholomew's Hospital. 2nd Lieut RGA, 1917; served in France, 1917-18; Prisoner of War; Christ's Coll., Cambridge, 1919-21; 1st Class, Part II Nat. Science Tripos (Physiology), 1921; Demonstrator in Physiology, St Bartholomew's Hospital, 1923-24; Grocer's Company Research

Scholar, 1924-26; Assistant to the Downing Professor of Medicine, Cambridge, 1926-31; University Lecturer in Pharmacology, 1931-33; Rockefeller Fellowship, held at University of Harvard, 1938; Fellow, 1930-46, and Tutor, 1931-46, of Downing College; University lecturer in Biochemistry, Cambridge, 1933-46; deputy for the professor of Biochemistry, 1940; Professor of Physiology and Director of Research Unit, Makerere Coll., Kampala, Uganda, 1946-55; Director, East African Institute for Medical Research, Mwanza, Tanganyika, 1955-60; Senior Research Fellow, CSIRO, University of Adelaide, 1960-66; Senior Research Officer, Inst. of Medical and Veterinary Science, Adelaide, 1966-69. Served War of 1939-45 in RAMC, Middle East and Burma, Lt-Col. *Publications:* The Metabolism of Living Tissues; Papers in The Biochemical Journal, British Journal of Experimental Pathology and elsewhere on the Metabolism of the Central Nervous System, the effects of Toxæmia upon Metabolism, Malnutrition and other subjects; contributor to the Annual Review of Biochemistry. *Recreations:* shooting, fencing, mountaineering. *Address:* 196 King William Road, Hyde Park, South Australia 5061, Australia.
[Died 20 May 1972.

HOLMES, Ven. George Hedley, BA, LTh; Archdeacon of Prince Albert, 1933-41, now Hon. Archdeacon of British Columbia; *b* 24 May 1883; *s* of John Hedley Holmes, Liverpool, and Christina Shimmin; *m* 1915, Elsie Kathleen Lawley, Uttoxeter, Staffs; one *s* two *d*. *Educ:* Liverpool Coll.; Emmanuel Coll., Saskatoon; University of Saskatchewan. Deacon, 1913; Priest, 1914; Incumbent of Hardisty, Alta, 1914-19; Rector of St George's, Saskatoon, 1919-29; Rural Dean of Saskatoon, 1923-29; Canon Residentiary of St Alban's Cathedral, Prince Albert, 1929-33; Secretary-Treasurer and Registrar of Diocese of Saskatchewan, 1933-41; Rector of Salt Spring Island, BC, 1941-62, retired. Hon. DD, 1966. *Recreations:* gardening and motoring. *Address:* Box 17, Ganges, BC, Canada.
[Died 5 Sept. 1972.

HOLMES, Sir Horace (Edwin), Kt 1966; NCLC Lecturer; *b* 30 March 1888; *s* of William and Martha Holmes; *m* 1912, Nellie Florence Marshall. *Educ:* elementary and technical schools; WEA classes. Miner and trade union official. Member of South Yorks Wages Board, Joint Board, Conciliation Board, advisory committees on mining, Recruitment, Safety, Welfare, etc. Member of Royston Urban District Council (Yorkshire) for 24 years; WR CC 12 years. Sergt, W. Yorks, 1915-18 (DCM). JP West Riding of Yorkshire, 1938-59. MP (Lab) Hemsworth Division of West Riding of Yorks, 1946-Sept. 1959. Parliamentary Private Secretary to Minister of Fuel and Power, 1947-51; one of the Opposition Whips, 1951-59. *Recreations:* music, books, gardening, walking. *Address:* 16 Park Avenue, Lakeside Estate, Hartsholme, Lincoln. *T:* Lincoln 21953.
[Died 9 Sept. 1971.

HOLMES, Air Vice-Marshal Peter Hamilton, CB 1965; OBE 1945; CEng 1966; FRAeS 1965; *b* 4 Oct. 1912; *s* of late E. Hamilton Holmes, CMG, late Foreign Service; *m* 1940, Barbara Joan, *d* of late A. R. F. Bosman, Windlesham, Surrey; two *s*. *Educ:* Wellington Coll. Joined RAF on Short Service Commission, 1932; permanent commission, 1937; specialised in Signals, 1937; on Signals duties in UK and NW Europe, throughout War; Group Captain, 1945; Staff Coll., Bracknell, 1946; Directing Staff, JSSC, 1947-49; various Signals appointments at home and overseas as Group Capt., 1950-59; Air Commodore, Deputy Chief of Staff, HQ 2 ATAF Germany, 1959-61; Imperial Defence Coll., 1962; Air Vice-Marshal, 1963. Air Officer i/c Administration, Maintenance Command, 1963-65; retired 1965. *Recreations:* fishing, gardening. *Address:* Old Basing House, Basingstoke, Hants. *T:* Basingstoke 3555. *Club:* Royal Air Force.
[Died 27 April 1977.

HOLMES, Sir Stephen (Lewis), KCMG 1950 (CMG 1942); MC 1918; MA; *b* 5 July 1896; *s* of late Basil Holmes and Isabella, *d* of Dr J. H. Gladstone, FRS; *m* 1922, Noreen, *o d* of late E. F. C. Trench, CBE, TD; one *s* one *d* (and one *s* decd). *Educ:* Westminster; Christ Church, Oxford. 2nd Lieut RGA (SR) 1915; served European War, France and Belgium, 1916-19 (MC, despatches twice, acting Major); entered Colonial Office, 1921; Principal, Dominions Office, 1928; Imperial Defence Coll. 1934; Senior Secretary, Office of High Commissioner for United Kingdom in Canada, 1936-39; Asst Sec., Dominions Office, 1939-43; Dominions Office representative, Washington, 1943-44; Deputy High Commissioner for the United Kingdom, Canada, 1944-46; Under Secretary, Board of Trade, 1946; Second Secretary, Board of Trade, 1947-51; Deputy Under-Secretary of State, Commonwealth Relations Office, 1951-52; High Commissioner for the UK in Australia, 1952-56. Master of the Leathersellers' Company, 1967-68. *Address:* Pinyons, Sandhurst, Hawkhurst, Kent. *Club:* Athenæum.
[Died 20 April 1980.

HOLROYD, Sir Ronald, Kt 1963; FRS 1960; MSc; PhD; a Deputy Chairman of Imperial Chemical Industries Ltd, 1957-67; *b* 26 April 1904; *s* of Sykes Holroyd and Florence Holroyd (*née* Whitlam); *m* 1931, Kathleen Mary Addey (*d* 1966); one *s*. *Educ:* Holgate Grammar Sch., Barnsley; Sheffield Univ. Scientific Officer, Safety in Mines Research Board, 1926-28; Various appointments in ICI, 1928-52. Director: ICI, 1952-67; Canadian Industries Ltd, 1956-60; British Nylon Spinners, 1958-67 (Chm, 1964-67); African Explosives and Chemical Industries, 1960-67; Member: Board of Governors, Westminster Hospital, 1957-69; Trustees, Uppingham Sch., 1957-70; Academic Planning Cttee, University College of Sussex, 1958-67; Council, Sussex Univ., 1967-69; Ministry of Power Advisory Cttee on Research and Development, 1963-65; President, Soc. Chemical Industry, 1965; Chairman, Fire Service Inquiry, 1967; Hon. Fellow, Manchester Inst. of Science and Technology, 1968. DSc (*hc*): Oxford, 1958; Sheffield, 1959; Hull, 1960; TCD, 1966; Hon. DTech Bradford, 1967. Coal Science Medal (BCURA), 1953; Castner Medal of Society Chemical Industry, 1958. FRSA 1963. *Recreations:* golf, motoring. *Address:* Rose Cottage, Buckden, near Skipton, Yorks. *T:* Kettlewell 218.
[Died 29 Sept. 1973.

HOLT, Ernest James Henry, CMG 1957; CBE 1953; Bank Manager, Lloyds Bank, Belgravia, 1926-45, retired; Hon. Secretary Amateur Athletic Association, 1937-46; Hon. Secretary and Treasurer, International Amateur Athletic Federation, 1946-52; Director of Organisation, Olympic Games, 1948; Advisor, Olympic Games, 1956; *b* 2 Sept. 1883; *s* of Frank Ernest Holt and Florence Ann Holt (*née* Short); *m* 1914, Winifred Gladys, *d* of William D'Acier Baxter and Selina Baxter; two *s* one *d*. *Educ:* Rosemont House, Newport, Shropshire. Joined Lloyds Bank Ltd, 1900; Manager Belgravia Branch, London, 1927; retired, 1945. Director of Organisation, Olympic Games, London, 1946-48; Advisor and Technical Director, Olympic Games, Melbourne, 1953-56. *Recreations:* Athletics and Association Football. *Address:* Oakholme, 22 Fordbridge Road, Sunbury-on-Thames, Surrey. *T:* Sunbury 82309.
[Died 21 Nov. 1972.

HOLT, Herbert, RP; portrait painter; *b* 7 Aug. 1894; *s* of Henry A. Holt, stained-glass artist, and Alice Seddon, schoolmistress; *m* Nora Norbury; one *s*. *Educ:* Cowley Sch., St Helens; St Helens, Liverpool and Slade Art Schools. *Publication:* Portrait Painting in Oils, 1958. *Address:* 3 Bathurst Street, Blackburn, Lancs. *T:* Blackburn 61461. *Clubs:* Chelsea Arts; Artists', Liverpool, Liver Sketching (Liverpool).
[Died 4 June 1978.

HOLT, Major Herbert Paton, MC; *b* Montreal, 10 Dec. 1890; *e s* of Sir Herbert Holt; *m* 1st, Aileen Elizabeth (*d* 1945), *d* of G. L. Cains, Montreal; (one *s* killed in action 1944); two *d*; *m* 2nd, 1946, Opal Eree M'Ilhenny, *d* of C. A. McCaulay, Meadville, USA. *Educ:* St Alban's Sch.; Royal Military Coll. of Canada. Joined 3rd Dragoon Guards, 1910; served European War, 1914-18 (wounded, MC); retired as Captain, 1920; MP (C) Upton Division of West Ham, 1924-29; High Sheriff of Wilts., 1935-36; served France Sept. 1939-Feb. 1940, Major attached Pioneer Corps; invalided out Sept. 1940. *Publication:* History of 3rd (P. of W.) Dragoon Guards, 1914-18. *Recreation:* racing. *Address:* Ballycrystal House, Nassau, Bahamas; Send Grove, Woking, Surrey. *Clubs:* Cavalry, Royal Automobile, Buck's, White's; Mount Royal (Montreal).
[Died 1 June 1971.

HOLT, Sir Stanley (Silverwood), Kt 1964; Hon. President: Stanley Holt & Son Ltd; Chairman, Victoria Buildings (Wigan) Ltd; *b* 5 June 1892; *s* of William Henry Holt, Manchester; *m* 1st, 1916, Dorothy Silverwood Clough (*d* 1943); one *s* three *d*; 2nd, 1955, Joan Freda Howarth Appleton. *Educ:* High Lane, Manchester. Formerly Director: Benmore Distilleries Ltd; Palace Theatre, Manchester; Severn & Co. Ltd; James Smith & Co. ltd; R. M. Bird & Co. President: Moss Side Conservative Association, 1945-; Wine and Spirit Trades Benevolent Society, 1957; Lancashire County Cricket Club, 1961-62; Chairman, City of Manchester Conservative Association, 1961-66, President, 1967. *Recreations:* political, charitable and cricket activities. *Address:* Mere Dene, Mere, Cheshire. *T:* Bucklow Hill 830006. *Clubs:* Constitutional, MCC.
[Died 26 Oct. 1973.

HONE, Sir Brian (William), Kt 1970; OBE 1969; Chairman, Commonwealth Secondary Schools Libraries Committee, 1971-75; *b* 1 July 1907; *s* of Dr F. S. Hone, CMG, Adelaide; *m* 1933, A. E. Boyce; three *s* one *d*. *Educ:* Prince Alfred Coll., Adelaide; Univs of Adelaide and Oxford. Asst Master, Marlborough Coll., Wilts, 1933-40; Headmaster, Cranbrook Sch., Sydney, 1940-50; Headmaster, Melbourne Church of England Grammar Sch., 1950-70. Chm., HMC of Independent Schools of Australia, 1954-57; Mem. Council: Monash Univ., 1959- (Dep. Chancellor, 1973-74); Australian Nat. Univ., 1960-75, etc. *Publications:*

Cricket Practice and Tactics, 1937; (ed jtly) The Independent School, 1967. *Recreations:* tennis, walking. *Address:* 97 Sackville Street, Kew, Victoria 3101, Australia. *Club:* Melbourne (Melbourne). *[Died 28 May 1978.*

HONE, Sir Evelyn (Dennison), GCMG 1965 (KCMG 1959; CMG 1953); CVO 1954; OBE 1946; *b* 13 Dec. 1911; 2nd *s* of late Arthur Rickman Hone, MBE, Salisbury, S Rhodesia, and late Olive Gertrude Fairbridge (*née* Scanlen); *m* 1946, Helen Joy Mellor; one *s* two *d. Educ:* Wellington Coll.; Rhodes Univ., S Africa; New College, Oxford Univ. Rhodes Scholar (Rhodesia), 1931; entered Colonial Service as Administrative Officer (cadet), Tanganyika Territory, 1935; Secretary to Government, Seychelles, 1944; Asst Secretary, Palestine, 1946; Colonial Secretary, British Honduras, 1948-53. Chief Secretary: Aden, 1953-57, N Rhodesia, 1957-59; Governor of Northern Rhodesia, 1959-64 (when the territory became the Republic of Zambia). Adviser, West Africa Cttee, 1967-75. Member: Central Council, Royal Over-Seas League, 1969-74; Council, Royal African Soc., 1971-; Pres., Zambia Soc., 1969. Hon. LLD, Rhodes Univ., 1964. *Address:* The Mill House, North Marston, Buckingham MK18 3PD. *[Died 18 Sept. 1979.*

HONEYMAN, Sir George (Gordon), Kt 1961; CBE 1953; QC 1955; JP; *b* 10 March 1898; *y s* of Andrew Stark Honeyman, Glasgow, and Jemima Margaret, *d* of James Maclaren, Dundee; *m* 1933, Evelyn Goldsworth, Southport; two *d. Educ:* Glasgow High Sch.; Glasgow Univ. MA 1921, LLB 1923, LLD (Hon.), 1964. Served European War, 1914-18, Lieut Royal Sussex Regt, 1917-19. Called to Bar, Inner Temple, 1924; North East Circuit. Surrey QS: Dep. Chm., 1962-69; Chm., 1969-71. Chairman: Retail Distributive Trades' Commissions of Inquiry, 1946; Commission of Inquiry, Copper Mining Industry, Nothern Rhodesia, 1957; Board of Inquiry, Sugar Milling Industry, Fiji, 1959; Commission of Inquiry, Sugar Industry, Trinidad, 1962-63; Civil Service Arbitration Tribunal, 1952-68; Agricultural Wages Board, 1953-68; a Chm., Industrial Court, 1949-67; Member: Nat. Arbitration Tribunal, 1951-59. Master of the Bench, Inner Temple, 1961. Chm., Approved Coal Merchants' Scheme, 1962. *Recreation:* gardening. *Address:* 5 Paper Buildings, Temple, EC4. *T:* 01-353 8494; Elm Bank, Godstone, Surrey. *T:* Godstone 2295. *[Died 26 May 1972.*

HONEYMAN, Tom John, JP; LLD; *b* 10 June 1891; 4th *s* of Tom Honeyman, Fife, and Elspeth Smith, Morayshire; *m* 1920, Victoria Catherine Burnett, Friockheim; two *s* one *d. Educ:* Queen's Park Sch. and University, Glasgow. Graduate in medicine, Glasgow, 1916. Served European War, 1914-18, Salonika and India, RAMC. FRCPGlas 1925; FMA 1951; FEIS 1955. Univ. Asst, Depts of Physiology and Medicine; practised until 1929. Dir, Lefevre Gallery, until 1939. Dir, Glasgow Art Gallery, 1939-54. Rector of Glasgow Univ., 1953-56. Awarded St Mungo Prize for Citizenship, 1943. Past Chairman: Scottish Tourist Cttee; Citizens' Theatre. Hon. Pres., The Provand's Lordship Soc.; Pres., Glasgow Tree Lovers' Soc. *Publications:* Monograph on Leslie Hunter, 1937; Three Scottish Colourists, 1950; The Clear Horizon, 1954; Patronage and Prejudice in Art, 1967; Art and Audacity, 1971; articles on art and tourism in various periodicals, weekly and daily newspapers, art catalogues, etc. *Recreations:* talking, travel, theatre. *Address:* 20 Queen's Gate, Glasgow. *T:* 041-339 2179. *Club:* Glasgow Art. *[Died 5 July 1971.*

HOOD, Lt-Gen. Sir Alexander, GBE 1946 (CBE 1939); KCB 1943 (CB 1942); KCVO 1953; *b* 25 Sept. 1888; *s* of Alexander Hood, Trinity, Edinburgh; *m* 1st, Evelyn Dulcia, CStJ, *d* of George Ellwood, Kensington, W; 2nd, Mrs Helen Winifred Wilkinson, Hamilton, Bermuda. *Educ:* George Watson's Coll.; Edinburgh Univ. MB, ChB, 1910; MD 1931. House Surgeon Royal Infirmary, Edinburgh, 1910-11; Lieut RAMC, 1912. Served European War, 1914-18, in France and Belgium. Capt. 1915; Major 1924; Lieut-Col 1934; Col (Brevet) 1938, (Subst.) 1939; (despatches Palestine, 1939); Brig. 1940; Maj.-Gen. 1941; Lt-Gen. 1941. Sometime DDMS, British Forces in Palestine and Trans-Jordan; Dir-Gen., Army Medical Services, 1941-48; Chm. of Governors of Star and Garter Home for Disabled Sailors, Soldiers and Airmen, 1948; Governor and C-in-C, Bermuda, 1949-55. KHP 1941. Hon. degrees: FRCSE, 1942; FRCP, 1944; LLD Edinburgh, 1945; DCL Durham, 1946; FRFPSG, 1946. Hon. Freeman of Barbers' Company. Knight of Order of White Lion of Czechoslovakia, 1944; Knight of Order of Orange Nassau, 1945; Commander of Order of Crown of Belgium, 1945; Commander of American Legion of Merit, 1945. *Address:* Montalto, Baileys Bay, Bermuda. *Club:* Royal and Ancient Golf. *[Died 11 Sept. 1980.*

HOOD, Rev. Canon (Archibald) Frederic, CBE 1967; Canon Residentiary, Chancellor and Chapter Treasurer of St Paul's Cathedral, 1961-Jan. 1970; Canon of Monmouth, 1940-69; Freeman of City of London, 1957; *b* 12 Dec. 1895; *s* of late Archibald Hood, MB, and Mrs Stanley Clay, *d* of late Ven. F. W. Edmondes, sometime Archdeacon of Llandaff; unmarried. *Educ:* St Andrew's, Eastbourne; privately; University Coll., Oxford. BA (1st Class Theology), 1916; Liddon Student, 1916; MA 1920; DD Nashotah, 1949; Senior Denyer and Johnson Scholar, 1921; FRGS 1920. Served in Volunteer Force, 1914-16; Asst Master at Lockers Park, Hemel Hempstead, 1916-18; Bishops Coll., Cheshunt, 1918-19; travelled round the world, 1919-20; Deacon, 1920; Priest, 1921; Vice-Principal of St Stephen's House, Oxford, 1920-22; studied at Bonn, 1922; Asst Chaplain, Exeter Coll., Oxford, 1922-23; Librarian, Pusey House, Oxford, 1922-34; Principal, 1934-52; Governor, 1957; Guild Church Vicar of St Mary Aldermary, EC4, 1954-61. Exam. Chaplain to Bishop of Monmouth, 1921-45; Mem. Governing Body of Church in Wales, 1933-71; Ecclesiastical Judge of Provincial Court of Church in Wales, 1967; Chm. of Exec. Cttee of Church Union, 1935-36 (Vice-Pres.). Select Preacher, Oxford, 1946-48; August Preacher, 1946, Lent Preacher, 1949, New York Cathedral; University Preacher, Chicago, 1949, Yale, 1951, Harvard, 1951, Columbia, 1955 and 1957; Gore Lectr, Westminster Abbey, 1959; a Governor of St Stephen's House, Oxford, and St Michael's Coll., Llandaff, Liddon House; Commissary to Bishop of St John's, CP, 1951; Chm., Church Moral Aid Assoc., 1952-58; Pres., Assoc. for Promoting Retreats, 1955-58; Past Pres., Sion Coll.; Pres., St Paul's Cathedral Lecture Soc., 1961-Jan. 1970; Sub Dean of Order of British Empire, 1962-71. ChStJ. Hon. Canon, St John's Cathedral, Umtata, S Africa, 1970-. *Publications:* The Christ of St Mark, 1928; God's Plan, 1955 (new edn 1961); The Chapel of the Most Excellent Order of the British Empire, 1967; contributor to Church Times; former contributor to: Catholic Sermons, 1932; Union of Christendom, 1938; Darwell Stone, 1943; Cowley Sermons, 1947; Chambers's Encyclopedia, 1950; Oxford Dictionary of the Christian Church, 1957; DNB, 1941-50; Anglo-Catholic Congress Report, 1930, 1948; The Church Quarterly Review, Time and Tide, Expository Times, etc. *Recreation:* swimming. *Address:* 606 Rodney House, Dolphin Square, SW1V 3LU. *T:* 01-834 3800 Rodney 606. *Clubs:* Athenæum, Brooks's, Travellers'. *[Died 26 Jan. 1975.*

HOOD, Clifford Firoved; Director Emeritus, Trans World Airlines; *b* Monmouth, Ill., 8 Feb. 1894; *s* of Edward Everett Hood; *m* 1917, Emilie R. Tener (decd); two adopted *s* decd; *m* 1943, Mary Ellen Tolerton. *Educ:* Univ. of Illinois (BS). Technical apprentice Packard Electric Co., Ohio, 1915, Sales Engineer, 1915-17; with American Steel and Wire Co., 1917-49; operating clerk, 1917; war service, 1st Lieut, US Army, 1917-19; foreman, Amer. Steel and Wire Co., 1919-25; asst superintendent, South Works, Worcester, Mass, 1925-27; superintendent, 1927-28; asst manager, subseq. manager, Worcester district, 1928-35; Vice-Pres. in charge of operations, 1935-37; Exec. Vice-Pres., 1937; Pres., 1938-49; Pres., Carnegie-Illinois Steel Corp., 1950; Exec. Vice-Pres. in charge operations, US Steel Co., 1951-52; Pres. US Steel Corporation, 1953; retired May 1959. Mem. Amer. Iron and Steel Inst. Protestant. Holds several hon. degrees in law and engineering, from 1952. *Address:* One Royal Palm Way, Palm Beach, Florida 33480, USA. *Clubs:* Bath and Tennis, Seminole, Everglades, Beach (Palm Beach); Duquesne (Life member) (Pittsburgh). *[Died 9 Nov. 1978.*

HOOD, Prof. Francis Campbell, MA (Edinburgh, Oxon and Dunelm); Professor Emeritus since 1955; Professor of Political Theory and Institutions, University of Durham, 1946-55; *b* 30 March 1895; *y s* of late Alexander Hood, Edinburgh; *m* 1st, 1921, Mary (marr. diss. 1939), *d* of Matthew Horsley, Hartlepool; one *s* killed on active service, 1945; 2nd, 1940, Muriel, *o d* of late Joseph Dodds, Kyleglas, Limerick; one *d. Educ:* Melville Coll.; University of Edinburgh (1st Cl. Hons in History, and Kirkpatrick Scholar, 1916); Balliol Coll., Oxford (Hon. Exhibitioner 1916, 1st Cl. Hons in Modern History, 1918). Board of Trade (temp.), 1918; Min. of Labour (temp.), 1919; Lectr in History, Univ. of Birmingham, 1919-20; National Federation of Iron and Steel Manufacturers, 1920-22; Lecturer in Economics and History, 1922-31; Lecturer in History, 1931-40; Reader in History, 1940-45, Univ. of Durham. *Publication:* The Divine Politics of Thomas Hobbes, 1964. *Address:* Kingsgate, Bow Lane, Durham. *T:* Durham 3651. *[Died 22 Nov. 1971.*

HOOD, Rev. Canon Frederic; *see* Hood, Rev. Canon (A.) F.

HOOD, William Francis, LLB (Lond); Master of the Supreme Court (Taxing Office), 1946-71; *b* 27 Sept. 1902; *s* of Wm Charles Reginald Hood, solicitor, and Margaret Frances, *d* of John McKissock, Glaick, Leswalt, Stranraer; *m* 1928, Gwendolen Lloyd, *d* of Rex Lloyd Turner, Croydon; two *d.*

Educ: Haileybury (Schol.). Asiatic Petroleum Co. Ltd, 1921-23; solicitor (Hons), 1929; Partner, Barnett Tuson & Co., EC2, 1936-46; RNVR 1941-45; Lieut-Comdr, 1945; Board of Management, Metropolitan Ear, Nose and Throat Hospital, 1945-47. Life Governor, Haileybury, 1972-; Editor Haileybury Register, 1962, 1974; Pres., Haileybury Soc., 1976-77. Pres., Brighton and Hove Musical Club, 1966-67, 1971-72. Prison visitor for many years. *Recreations:* travel, music, drama. *Address:* Poyningshurst, Slaugham, Sussex RH17 6AD. *T:* Handcross 400336. *[Died 12 April 1980.*

HOOK, Very Rev. Norman; Dean of Norwich, 1953-69, Dean Emeritus since 1969; *b* 1898; *e s* of late S. A. Hook and late Mrs Hook, Brough, Westmorland; *m* 1927, M. I. Sugden, *d* of Rev. E. H. Sugden; one *d* (and one *d* decd). *Educ:* Appleby Sch.; Univ. of Durham. Rector of Enborne, Berks, 1927-31; Vicar of West Norwood, SE27, 1931-37; Vicar of Knutsford, 1937-45; Vicar of Wimbledon, Rural Dean and Canon of Southwark, 1945-53. *Publications:* Holy is His Name: Studies in the Problem of Evil, 1957; The Eucharist in the New Testament, 1965; Christ in the Twentieth Century, 1968; contrib. Theology, Expository Times. *Recreations:* motoring and gardening. *Address:* 2 East Pallant, Chichester, West Sussex. *[Died 20 May 1976.*

HOOKE, Sir Lionel (George Alfred), Kt 1957; Chairman since 1962 and Managing Director, 1945-68, Amalgamated Wireless (Australasia) Ltd; *b* 31 Dec. 1895; *s* of Frank William and Ethel Margaret Hooke; *m* 1930, Eilleen Clarice Sparks; one *s. Educ:* Brighton Grammar Sch., Vic., Australia. Joined Amalgamated Wireless (A/asia) Ltd, 1913; Shackleton Polar Expedition, 1913-14; Pilot, Royal Naval Air Service, War of 1914-18. Executive, Amalgamated Wireless (A/asia) Ltd, 1919-. Mem., Senate, Univ. of Sydney, 1961-69. Chm., Electronics & Telecommunications Industry Adv. Cttee, 1965-. *Address:* Sidmouth, 26 Buckingham Road, Killara, NSW 2071, Australia. *T:* 49.3093. *Clubs:* Antarctic; Australian, Union (Sydney); Naval and Military (Melbourne). *[Died 17 Feb. 1974.*

HOOKER, Sir Leslie (Joseph), Kt 1973; Founder Chairman, Hooker Corporation Ltd; *b* 18 Aug. 1903; Australian; *m* 1934, Madeline Adella Price; two *s* one *d. Educ:* Public Sch. Career in Real Estate Investments and Finance. *Recreation:* swimming. *Address:* 14a Hopetoun Avenue, Mosman, NSW 2088, Australia. *T:* 9694165; Hooker Corporation Ltd, Hooker House, 175 Pitt Street, Sydney, NSW 2000, Australia. *T:* 20367. *Clubs:* American National, Tattersalls, Sydney, Commonwealth, Australian Golf (all Sydney). *[Died 29 April 1976.*

HOOPER, Howard Owen, CB 1964; CMG 1952; Assistant Under Secretary of State, Ministry of Defence, 1964-71, retired; *b* 17 Oct. 1911; *s* of late R. H. Hooper and Mrs E. A. Hooper, St Stephen in Brannel, Cornwall; *m* 1937, Margaret Oliff, *d* of late S. H. and C. L. Marshall, Newbury. *Educ:* St Austell Grammar Sch.; Merton Coll., Oxford (Exhibitioner), BA 1933, MA 1963; DipEd Oxon 1934. Entered Civil Service, 1935; Asst Sec., British Supply Bd, N America, 1939-41; Sec. (UK), Combined Raw Materials Bd, Washington, 1946; Asst Sec., BoT, 1946; Mem., Trade Missions to Argentina and Brazil, 1947-49; Counsellor, Washington, 1951 (Dep. to UK Mem., Internat. Materials Conf.); Principal Estabt and Finance Officer, Min. of Materials 1952-54; Under-Secretary: BoT, 1954-55; Cabinet Office, 1955-58; Min. of Supply, 1958-59; WO, 1960-64. Comr, Queen Victoria Sch., Dunblane, 1965-71. Coronation Medal, 1953. *Publications:* contribs to Dictionary of National Biography. *Recreation:* history. *Address:* Englefield, Bridge Road, Cranleigh, Surrey. *T:* Cranleigh 3407.
[Died 2 Nov. 1980.

HOOPER, John Robert Thomas, TD, JP; Metropolitan Magistrate since 1961; *b* 7 Nov. 1914; *s* of late F. C. Hooper, Eastington, Glos, and Liverpool, and H. L. Hooper *(née* Beale), Hyde, Glos; *m* 1948, Dorinda Marian, *d* of Lieut-Col G. B. de Courcy Ireland, MVO, MC; three *d. Educ:* Repton; Sidney Sussex Coll., Cambridge. BA (Hons) Cantab 1936, MA 1961. Served War of 1939-45: Middlesex Yeomanry, 2nd Lieut 1939, Major 1942; Greek, Iraq and Syrian Campaigns, 1941; Western Desert and N Africa, 1942-43 (wounded, despatches); passed Parachute Course, 1944; OC Beach Bde Signals, 1945. Barrister, Inner Temple, 1939 (Yarborough Anderson Scholar, 1950); London and Midland Circuit; an Asst Recorder of Birmingham, 1960-61; Dep. Chm., Bucks QS, 1961-71. Chm., Central Council of Probation and After Care Cttees, 1972. JP Bucks, 1961. *Recreations:* swimming, reading. *Address:* Beech Lawn, Chalfont Heights, Chalfont St Peter, Bucks. *T:* Gerrards Cross 82283. *Clubs:* Cavalry, Lansdown. *[Died 26 Feb. 1975.*

HOOTON, John Charles, CMG 1963; MBE 1945; QC (Bermuda) 1959; Under-Secretary (Legal), Advisory Division,

HM Procurator-General and Treasury Solicitor's Department, 1974-77 (Assistant Solicitor, 1970-74); *b* 1912; *m* 1938, Jessica Patricia, *d* of R. J. Manning; two *s.* Served War of 1939-45; Lt-Col General List (despatches, Croix de Guerre, MBE). Palestine Police, 1932; Police, Gold Coast, 1937-49. Called to the Bar, Gray's Inn, 1949. Crown Counsel, Gold Coast, 1951-53 (Senior Asst Legal Sec., East African Common Services Organisation, 1953); Attorney-Gen., Bermuda, 1958-61; Legal Sec. to East African Common Services Organisation, 1961, retd from Org., 1962, re-apptd on contract, 1962-63; temp. Senior Asst, CO, 1963-64. *Address:* Dingleden House, Benenden, Kent. *Club:* Oriental. *[Died 22 July 1980.*

HOOVER, Prof. Calvin Bryce, PhD; Professor of Economics since 1927, and Dean of the Graduate School, 1938-48, Duke University; *b* Berwick, Illinois, 14 April 1897; *s* of John Calvin and Margaret Roadcap Hoover; *m* 1919, Faith Miriam Sprole; two *d. Educ:* Monmouth Coll. (AB); Univ. of Wisconsin (PhD). Phi Beta Kappa. 123rd Field Artillery, US Army, 1917-19, AEF, battles of St Mihiel and Meuse-Argonne. Instructor, Univ. of Minnesota, 1923-25; Asst Prof., Duke Univ., 1925-27; Social Science Research Fellow in Russia, 1929-30; Associate Editor, South Atlantic Quarterly; Economic Adviser, Dept of Agriculture, 1934; Consumers' Counsel, Agricultural Adjustment Administration, 1935; Consultant: National Resources Planning Board, 1937; Advisory Commn to Council of National Defense, 1940; Office of Price Administration and Civilian Supply, 1941; Pres., Southern Economic Assoc., 1936-37; Vice-Pres., Amer. Econ. Assoc., 1940; Pres., 1953; Econ. Adviser US Group Control Commn in Germany, 1945; President's Cttee on Foreign Aid, 1947; Economic Adviser US Special Representative in Europe, 1948. Distinguished Fellow, Amer. Econ. Assoc., 1966. Hon. Litt D: Columbia, 1934; Monmouth Coll., 1935; Hon. LLD, Case Western Reserve, 1968. Medal of Freedom, US, 1946. *Publications:* Economic Life of Soviet Russia, 1931; Germany Enters the Third Reich, 1933; Dictators and Democracies, 1937; International Trade and Domestic Employment, 1945; The Impact of Federal Policies on the Economy of The South, 1949; (jointly) Economic Resources and Policies of the South, 1951; The Economy, Liberty and The State, 1959; Economic Systems of the Commonwealth, 1962; Memoirs of Capitalism, Communism and Nazism, 1965. *Address:* Duke University, Durham, N Carolina 27701, USA. *Club:* Cosmos (Washington, DC). *[Died 23 June 1974.*

HOOVER, John Edgar, Hon. KBE, *cr* 1947; Director, Federal Bureau of Investigation, United States Department of Justice, since 1924; *b* 1 Jan. 1895; *s* of Dickerson Naylor Hoover and Annie Marie Scheitlin; unmarried. *Educ:* George Washington Univ. Law Sch. (LLB 1916, LLM 1917). Started Government service with Library of Congress, Washington, DC, as clerk while attending law sch. at night. Upon obtaining legal degree and admission to the Bar in Washington, DC, entered US Dept of Justice in 1917; Special Asst to the Attorney Gen., 1919; Asst Dir of the then Bureau of Investigation, 1921. Trustee, George Washington Univ.; Mem. Bd of Dirs of Boys' Clubs of America. Holds numerous hon. degrees. Is a Mason, 33°; Grand Cross of Honour, Supreme Council, Scottish Rite, 33°, 1965. Medal of Merit (US), 1946; etc. *Publications:* Persons in Hiding, 1938; Masters of Deceit, 1958; A Study of Communism, 1962; J. Edgar Hoover on Communism, 1969; numerous articles on scientific crime detection, causation and prevention of crime. *Recreations:* baseball, tennis, football. *Address:* Federal Bureau of Investigation, 9th Street and Pennsylvania Avenue, Washington, DC 20535, USA. *Clubs:* Columbia Country (Washington, DC); Chevy Chase (Md). *[Died 2 May 1972.*

HOPE, Sir James, 2nd Bt *cr* 1932; MM 1918; JP; farmer; *b* 2 May 1898; *s* of Sir Harry Hope, 1st Bt and Margaret Binnie Holms-Kerr; *S* father 1959. *Educ:* Fettes Coll. Served European War, 1916-19, with Black Watch (MM). District Chm., East Lothian Agricultural Executive Cttee, 1938-45. JP for East Lothian. *Heir: b* Robert Holms-Kerr Hope [*b* 12 April 1900; *m* 1928, Eleanor (*d* 1967), *d* of late Very Rev. Marshall Lang, DD, Whittingehame, East Lothian]. *Address:* Eastbarns, Dunbar, East Lothian. *T:* Innerwick 212. *Club:* New (Edinburgh).
[Died 8 Oct. 1979.

HOPE, Capt. Laurence Nugent, DL; JP; Landowner; Welsh Guards (SR); *b* 14 Oct. 1890; *s* of James L. A. Hope and Eliza, *d* of Sir Peter Coats, Auchendrane, Ayr; *m* 1st, Hilda Mary (*d* 1938) *d* of late M. J. Hunter, JP, Stoke Hall, Derbs; one *s* one *d*; 2nd, 1941, Constance Elizabeth, *d* of late E. A. Shell. *Educ:* Clifton Coll.; Trinity Hall, Cambridge (BA). Commission Royal North Devon Hussars (Yeo.), 1913-19, (Substantive Capt.), Gallipoli, Egypt, and Palestine; transferred as Capt. (SR) to the Welsh Guards, 1920. DL 1953, JP 1920, High Sheriff, 1923, Herefordshire. *Recreations:* hunting, shooting, fishing, photography. *Address:* Whitney Court, Whitney, Hereford. *Clubs:* Guards, Army and Navy. *[Died* 27 Sept. 1973.

HOPE, Lt-Col Sir Percy (Mirehouse), Kt 1954; OBE 1918; JP; DL; Chairman and Managing Director, Lake District Hotels and Pape's Garages, Coaches and Motors, and other cos; *b* Keswick, 17 July 1886; *s* of Joseph Fearon Hope; *m* 1919, Constance Maud Mark (*d* 1970); no *c. Educ:* Keswick Sch.; King's Coll., London. Articled J. J. Bell, MICE, County Surveyor and Bridge Master, Cumberland; Lieut The Border Regt, 1911; attached GS, Burma Div., 1916; Staff Coll., Mhow, India, 1917; RE Officer i/c Water Supplies, Mesopotamia, 1917; Deputy Dir of Works, Baghdad, 1917; Asst Dir of Works, GHQ, MEF, 1918-19 (OBE, Bt Major, despatches twice); LRIBA; CEng; Fellow, Inst. Municipal and County Engineers; Chairman of Governors: Keswick Sch.; Lairthwaite School; Trustee Fitz Park; Trustee Hewitson Cottage Hosp.; Alderman, Cumberland County Council; Mem., Lake District Planning Board; Chm., National Council of British Hotels and Restaurants Association. Master Blencathra Foxhounds. DL Cumberland, 1961. *Recreations:* cricket, Rugby football (county cap), tennis, golf. *Address:* 39 Brundholme Terrace, Keswick, Cumberland. *T:* 162. *Clubs:* Royal Automobile; Border County (Carlisle). *[Died* 6 Dec. 1972.

HOPE-WALLACE, Philip Adrian, CBE 1975; freelance journalist; *b* 6 Nov. 1911; *o s* of Charles Nugent Hope-Wallace and Mabel Chaplin. *Educ:* Charterhouse; Balliol Coll., Oxford; abroad. International Broadcasting Co., France, 1934; Public Relations, Gas Light & Coke Co., 1935-36; Correspondent, The Times, 1935-39; Press Officer, Air Ministry, 1939-45. Critic of music and drama to: various journals; Time and Tide, 1945-49; The Listener; The Manchester Guardian (now The Guardian), 1946-76. Broadcasting, journalism. Lectured at home and abroad. *Publications:* A Key to Opera, 1939; pamphlets on the drama, music, etc; *posthumous publication:* Words and Music, 1981. *[Died* 3 Sept. 1979.

HOPPÉ, E. O., FRPS; author and photographer; *b* Munich, 1878. *Educ:* Paris and Vienna. Has devoted much of his time in theory and practice to the recognition of Photography as an Art Medium; is represented with works in National and Municipal Art Galleries and Museums; Japan, in 1924, acquired a collection of 400 of his prints for a permanent exhibition; travelled extensively throughout the world. Editor, Pictorial Geography. *Publications:* The Russian Ballet; Lovable London; In Gipsy Camp and Royal Palace; Picturesque Great Britain; This Romantic America; Cities Time has Passed By; Man and His Work; Achievement; In Passing; Bali; The Fifth Continent; London, 1932; Round the World with a Camera, 1935; A Camera on Unknown London; The Image of London; The London of George VI, 1937; Taken from Life (with J. D. Beresford); The Book of Fair Women (with Richard King); Gods of Modern Grub Street (with A. St John Adcock); More Gods (with A. St John Adcock); London Types (with Pett Ridge); Career with Camera; Hundred Thousand Exposures; Rural London; Jamaica-Island of many Waters; Pirates, Privateers and Gentlemen Adventurers; and numerous articles on art and travel. *Recreations:* fly-fishing, motoring, travelling off the beaten track. *Address:* Wildhern, near Andover, Hants. *Club:* Savage. *[Died* 9 Dec. 1972.

HOPPS, Air Vice-Marshal Frank Linden, CB 1945; CBE 1943; AFC; CIAgrE; retired, 1950. Directing Staff, RAF Staff Coll., 1938-39; AOC No 16 Gp, Chatham, 1943-45 (despatches); Air Officer i/c Administration British Air Forces of Occupation (Germany), 1945-47; AOC No 19 Group, Coastal Command, 1947. Chief Executive, Agricultural Engineers Assoc. Ltd, 1953-68. Order of Kutusov (USSR). *Address:* c/o Lloyds Bank, Palmeira Branch, Hove, East Sussex. *[Died* 10 Oct. 1976.

HOPSON, Sir Donald (Charles), KCMG 1968 (CMG 1961); DSO 1945; MC 1944; TD 1948; HM Diplomatic Service; Ambassador to Argentina, since 1973; *b* 31 Aug. 1915; *s* of late Charles Edward Hopson and Ida Snowdown; *m* 1st, 1945, Denise Dreux (marr. diss. 1971); one *d*; 2nd, 1971, Annelise Risbjerg Nielsen, Copenhagen, Denmark. *Educ:* Christ's Hospital, Horsham; University Coll., Oxford (MA). Kelsall & Kemp Ltd, Rochdale, 1938-39. 2nd Lieut 5th (Territorial) Bn Lancs Fusiliers, April 1939; served France and Belgium, 1940; Capt. and Adjt 5 Lancs Fus., 1940; No 3 Commando, 1943, Sicily and Italy (despatches); Normandy, 1944, Major 2 i/c 3 Commando; Bde Major First Commando Bde, 1945, Belgium, Holland, Germany. HM Foreign (subseq. Diplomatic) Service, 1945; 2nd Sec., Copenhagen, 1946-48; Consul, Saigon, 1948-50; 1st Sec., Budapest, 1950-52; FO, 1952-55; Counsellor, Head of Chancery, Buenos Aires, 1955-57; Head of Information Research Dept, FO, 1958-62; Ambassador to Laos, 1962-65;

Ambassador to Mongolia, 1965-66, and Chargé d'Affaires, Peking, 1965-68; Ambassador to Venezuela, 1969-72. *Recreations:* walking, bird-watching. *Address:* British Embassy, Buenos Aires, Argentina. *Club:* United Oxford & Cambridge University. *[Died* 26 Aug. 1974.

HORENSTEIN, Jascha; Conductor; *b* Kiev, 6 May 1899; American citizen; *s* of Abraham Horenstein and Marie (*née* Jekels); *m* Ernestina Diaz; one *s. Educ:* Vienna Univ.; Vienna Academy. Conductor: Vienna Symphony Orchestra, 1923; Berlin Symphony Orchestra, 1925-28; Musical Dir, Düsseldorf Opera, 1929-33. Has conducted with the principal orchestras throughout the world, including the Berlin Philharmonic, Royal Philharmonic, New York Philharmonic, Amsterdam Concertgebauw, BBC Symphony, London Symphony, Brussels Philharmonic, Warsaw Philharmonic, Moscow Philharmonic, Leningrad Philharmonic, French National, and Israel Philharmonic Orchestras; also at La Scala and The Royal Opera House, Covent Garden. He has appeared at the Festivals of Vienna and Edinburgh, and the Maggio Fiorentino of Florence, among other festivals. Grand Prix du Disque (three times). *Recreations:* reading, collecting collages and abstract paintings. *Address:* 12 Chemin du Coteau, Lausanne-Pully, Switzerland. *T:* 28.62.05. *[Died* 2 April 1973.

HORLICK, Lt-Col Sir James Nockells, 4th Bt *cr* 1914; OBE 1919; MC; 2nd *s* of Sir James Horlick, 1st Bt; *S* nephew (Sir Peter Horlick, 3rd Bt), 1958; *m* 1911, Flora Macdonald Martin (*d* 1955); one *s* one *d* (and one *d* decd); *m* 1956, Joan MacGill. *Educ:* Eton; Christ Church, Oxford. Coldstream Guards; served European War, 1914-18 (OBE, MC); MP (U) Gloucester, 1923-29; retired, 1929; Sheriff of Berks, 1938; late Hon. Col 1st Surrey Rifles. Victorian Medal of Honour and Gold Medal, Royal Horticultural Society, 1964. *Recreation:* gardening. *Heir: s* John James Macdonald Horlick [*b* 9 April 1922; *m* 1948, June, *d* of Douglas Cory-Wright; one *s* two *d*]. *Address:* Timbers, Nuffield, near Henley-on-Thames, Oxon; Isle of Gigha, Argyll, Scotland. *Clubs:* Bath, Beefsteak, Buck's. *[Died* 31 Dec. 1972.

HORNBY, Sir (Henry) Russell, 2nd Bt, *cr* 1899; *b* 12 Sept. 1888; *s* of 1st Bt and Letitia (*d* 1937), *d* of Capt. W. R. Browne; *S* father 1928; *m* 1913, Dorothy Elma, *o d* of late Maj.-Gen. Sir W. Fry, KCVO, CB; one *d*. Was on active service in France. *Heir:* none. *Address:* Barraclough, Clitheroe, Lancs. *Club:* Junior Carlton. *[Died* 3 Jan. 1971 (*ext*).

HORNE, Frank Robert, CBE 1958; MA, NDA, NDD (Hons); FRAgSs, FIBiol; Vice-President, National Institute of Agricultural Botany, since 1970, Director, 1945-70; Scientific Adviser to Home Grown Cereals Authority, since 1970; *b* 9 June 1904; *m* 1929, Marjorie Bannister; one *s* three *d. Educ:* Hele's Sch., Exeter; Seale-Hayne Coll.; Christ's Coll., Cambridge; West of Scotland Agric. Coll. (Steven Memorial Prizeman); Gresham's Sch., Holt. Head of Botanical Dept, Seale-Hayne Agric. Coll., 1928-44 (Research Grant for Plant Breeding, 1931-44); Chief Tech. Officer and Dep. Exec. Officer, Devon War Agricultural Exec. Cttee, 1940-44; Chm., Min. of Agric. Cttee on Seeds (Horne Report), 1950; Chm. Pest Infestation Research Board, DSIR, 1952-57; Pres., British Grassland Soc., 1957-58. Chairman: European Productivity Agency (OECD) Cttees on Herbage Varieties and Internat. Seed Certification, 1954-59; Pres., World Seed Year Meeting, FAO (UNO), Rome, 1962; Nat. Certification Authority for Herb Seeds, 1967-. Mem. Council, British Assoc., 1967-72 (Pres. Section M); Member: Internat. Commn, Nomenclature Cultivated Plants, 1956-; European Barley Cttee, 1950-73; Nat. Fedn Young Farmers' Clubs (Dep. Chm.). Mem., Regent House, Cambridge Univ., 1949-. Foreign Mem. (Academician), Royal Swedish Acad. of Forestry and Agriculture, 1968-; Hon. Life Mem., Swedish Seed Research Assoc., 1961. Commodore, Cambridge Univ. Cruising Club, 1961-63. *Address:* Angle Cottage, Longmeadow Lane, Lode, Cambridge CB5 9ES. *T:* Cambridge 811503. *Club:* Farmers'. *[Died* 27 June 1975.

HORNE, Maj.-Gen. Gerald Tom Warlters, CB 1949; CBE 1945 (OBE 1944); *b* 4 March 1898; *s* of late Thomas Warlters Horne and late Cornelia Horne (*née* Ellis); *m* 1921, Janetta Marie Graham; one *d* (and one *s* killed in action, 1944). *Educ:* Repton; RMA Woolwich. Commissioned 2nd Lieut Royal Regt of Artillery, 1917; served European War, 1914-18, transferred to Royal Army Ordnance Corps, 1925; Capt., 1925; Major, 1936; Staff Coll., 1938-39; War of 1939-45, BEF France, 1939-40; War Office, 1940-44; Italy, 1944-45; War Office, Dep. Dir Ordnance Services (Brig.), 1945-48; Maj.-Gen., 1948; Dir of Ordnance Services (War Office), 1948-51; retired, 1951. Bronze Medal for Valour (Italian), 1918. *Recreations:* golf and gardening. *Address:* 28 Smarts Heath Road, Mayford, Woking, Surrey. *[Died* 10 Jan. 1978.

HORNE, Major William Guy; b 19 Sept. 1889; yr s of Sir W. Edgar Horne, 1st Bt; m 1921, Louisa Carey (d 1962), y d of Herbert Carey Hardy, JP, Chilworth Manor, Surrey. Educ: Eton. Joined 19th Royal Hussars, 1912. Served European War in France, 1914-18; Cavalry Liaison Officer to Gen. Denikine in South Russia, 1919-20; transferred to 10th Royal Hussars, 1922; served in Europe, Egypt and Sudan; retired with rank of Major, 1931. AAF, 1938-43, retired with rank of Group Capt. Dir, Prudential Assurance Co. Ltd, 1931-42. Master, Clothworkers' Co., 1957-58. Recreation: golf. Address: Villa l'Olivade, 06 Roquefort-les-Pins, France. Clubs: Cavalry, MCC.
[Died 3 Aug. 1974.

HORNER, Mrs Sibyl Gertrude, CBE 1957; MB, BS; DPH Oxon; DIH; HM Senior Medical Inspector of Factories, 1957-61; b 18 Oct. 1895; 5th d of late Arthur Overton and Mary Overton, Forest Row, Sussex; m 1931, Bernard Stuart Horner, OBE; no c. Educ: London Sch. of Medicine and St Mary's Hosp., Paddington. MB, BS London 1919. HM Medical Inspector of Factories (Home Office), 1924; HM Dep. Senior Medical Inspector of Factories (Min. of Labour), 1948. Mem. Order of St John of Jerusalem. Recreations: horticulture, travel, walking. Address: Eaton Cottage, Esher, Surrey. T: Esher 63574.
[Died 14 Feb. 1978.

HORNSBY, Harker William; Principal Assistant Solicitor, Department of Health and Social Security, since 1970; b 8 Feb. 1912; s of William Hornsby, BA; m 1937, Agnes Nora, d of William T. Phillips; one s. Educ: Coatham Sch.; Jesus Coll., Oxford (MA). Admitted a solicitor, 1937. Served with Sydney Morse & Co., 1937-40. Served war in Army, 1940-46, Captain Pack Transport, RASC. Entered Solicitor's Dept, Min. of Nat. Insurance, 1946; Asst Solicitor, 1955. Publication: Poems, 1930. Recreations: literature, cricket. Address: The Corner Cottage, 46 High Street, Wimbledon, SW19. T: 01-946 2918.
[Died 8 Sept. 1971.

HORNSBY, Captain James Arthur; b 14 May 1891; s of James William Hornsby, late of Laxton Park, Stamford; m 1917, Cecily Mary Elizabeth, d of late Col S. W. Lane, CBE; one s two d. Educ: Eton; Magdalene Coll., Cambridge. Capt. late 5th Lancers; Sheriff of Rutland, 1940; Joint Master Meath Hounds, 1928-32; Master Duhallow Hounds, 1932-33; Joint Master Woodland Pytchley, 1933-35; Master Duhallow Hounds, 1946-62. Address: Ballygiblin, Cecilstown, Mallow, Co. Cork.
[Died 2 Sept. 1972.

HORNUNG, Lt-Col Sir John (Derek), KCVO 1976; OBE 1944; MC 1940; Lieutenant of the Queen's Bodyguard of the Yeomen of the Guard since 1971; Chairman, Sena Sugar Estates Ltd, since 1964; b 3 Jan. 1915; er s of late Lt-Col Charles Bernard Raphael Hornung. Educ: Eton. 2nd Lieut Irish Guards, 1936; served War of 1939-45, France and NW Europe; Lt-Col 1944; retd 1948. High Sheriff for Sussex, 1962; Exon Queen's Bodyguard of the Yeomen of the Guard, 1954-67, Clerk of the Cheque and Adjt, 1967-71. Steward of the Jockey Club, 1968-70. Recreations: breeding and racing thoroughbreds; shooting. Address: Ivorys, Cowfold, Horsham, West Sussex. T: Cowfold 240. Clubs: Jockey, White's.
[Died 26 Aug. 1978.

HORNYOLD-STRICKLAND, Henry, JP; FSA; Lord Lieutenant of Westmorland, 1957-65; b 1890; s of Alfred Hornyold, Blackmore Park, Worcs and Alice, d of Julien de La Chere and niece of 1st and last Viscount Llandaff; assumed by Royal Licence, 1932, additional name and arms of Strickland; m 1920, Mary Christina (d 1970), d of 1st and last Baron Strickland; one s one d. Educ: Beaumont; Magdalen Coll., Oxford. Elec. Engineer (retd); High Sheriff Co. Westmorland, 1937. Publications: Stricklands of Sizergh; Lancashire MPs, 1290-1550; various articles. Address: Sizergh Castle, near Kendal, Cumbria. T: Sedgwick 203. Clubs: Lansdowne; Union (Malta).
[Died 24 Sept. 1975.

HOROBIN, Sir Ian (Macdonald), Kt 1955; b 1899; e s of late Principal J. C. Horobin, Homerton Coll., Cambs, and of late Mrs M. A. Cloudesley Brereton. Educ: Highgate; Sidney Sussex Coll., Cambridge (MA). RAF, 1918-19 and 1939-46. Warden of Mansfield House Univ. Settlement, refounded and endowed, 1923-61. MP (Nat) Central Div. of Southwark, 1931-35; contested (C) Oldham (West), 1950; MP (C) Oldham East, 1951-Sept. 1959; Parl. Sec., Min. of Power, 1958-59. Gazetted a Life Peer, March 1962, but withdrew acceptance, April 1962. Publications: Pleasures of Planning, 1935; Poems, 1935; More Poems, 1939; Collected Poems, 1972. Address: c/o The Standard Chartered Bank, 38 Bishopsgate, EC2.
[Died 5 June 1976.

HOROBIN, Norah Maud, BSc (London); Head Mistress, Roedean School, Brighton, 1947-61, retired; b 7 Feb. 1898; d of late J. C. Horobin, MA Cantab, Principal of Homerton Coll., Cambridge, and late Mrs M. A. Cloudesley Brereton. Educ: North London Collegiate Sch.; King's Coll., London. Head Mistress: Dulwich High Sch., 1935-38; Sunderland High Sch., 1938-47. Address: 1 Evelyn Terrace, Brighton BN2 2EP.
[Died 3 Feb. 1976.

HORROX, Lewis; Professor of English Language and Literature, University of Exeter, 1924-61; b 27 April 1898; s of William Horrox, architect, and Annie Lewis; m 1920, Gladys Maud Cawston; one d. Educ: Caius Coll., Cambridge (scholar); Christopher James Research Studentship, 1920-23. Supervisor in English Studies at Caius Coll., and Lecturer for the English Tripos at Cambridge, 1920-24. Publication: Edition of Milton's Comus, etc, 1927. Recreation: walking. Address: 5 St James' Terrace, Winchester, Hants.
[Died 20 Feb. 1975.

HORSFALL, Sir (John) Donald, 2nd Bt, cr 1909; JP; b 1 June 1891; s of Sir John Cousin Horsfall, 1st Bt of Hayfield, Crosshills, near Keighley; S father, 1920; m 1914, Henrietta (d 1936), d of W. Musgrave of Otley; three s; m 1953, Gladys, widow of Percy Taylor, Knowle Spring House, Keighley. Educ: Uppingham. Dir, John C. Horsfall & Sons Ltd, Worsted Spinners, Glusburn, near Keighley (formerly Chm.); Underwriter at Lloyd's; Dir, Halifax Building Soc., 1945-71; Chm. Skipton Conservative Assoc., 1924-37; High Sheriff, Yorks, 1927-28; JP WR Yorks, 1928. Recreations: shooting, golf, racing. Heir: s Major John Musgrave Horsfall, MC, TD, JP, 6th Bn Duke of Wellington's Regt [b 26 Aug. 1915; m 1940, Cassandra Nora Bernardine, d of late George Wright, Brinkworth Hall, Elvington, York; two s one d]. Address: Studley Hotel, Harrogate, North Yorks. Club: Portland.
[Died 25 March 1975.

HORTON, Lt-Col W(illiam) Gray, MC 1917; Scots Guards, retired; Director, SA Coppee Rust MV, Brussels; Sole Owner, Gray Horton Products; b 24 Aug. 1897; s of William S. and Lottie Gray Horton, New York; m 1st, 1930, Gwendolen Anna Le Bas (d 1944); one s one d; 2nd, 1949, Baroness Tornaco (d 1972), Brussels. Educ: Harrow; RMC, Sandhurst (joined, 1916, when still an American citizen). Served European War, 1st Bn Scots Guards, 1917 (wounded, MC). Adjutant 1st Bn, 1926. Joined Le Bas Group of businesses, 1932; re-joined regt, July 1939. Served War of 1939-45: Eastern Comd, 1939; special service, France, 1940; comdg 70th Bn E Surrey Regt, 1941; formed and commanded Fighter Comd Battle Sch., 1943; commanded RAF Regt 85 gp, 1944, in England, Normandy, Belgium and Germany; GSO1, Berlin Air Comd, 1945 (despatches, 1946). One of Comdrs of Gold Staff Officers at Coronation; Coronation Medal, 1953. Inventor of Graphdex and Project Activating Signal Systems which are initiating a new science of Business Control; Co-inventor of lever type of tubular scaffold coupler. Mem. of Lloyd's; Mem., Worshipful Co. of Ironmongers. Publication: Data Display Systems, 1969 (Spanish trans. Sistemas De Información Gráfica). Recreations: hunting, winter sports (rep. Gt Britain, bobsleigh driver, Olympic games, Chamonix, 1924), cricket. Address: 72 Roebuck House, Stag Place, Palace Street, SW1. T: 01-834 5476; 16 Roebuck House, SW1. T: 01-828 9216. Clubs: White's, Guards, MCC, All England Lawn Tennis.
[Died 13 July 1974.

HORTON-SMITH-HARTLEY, P. H. G.; see Hartley, P. H. G. H. S.

HORWILL, Sir Lionel Clifford, Kt 1947; b 19 Sept. 1890; s of Frank James Horwill, Stoke, Devonport; m 1934, Dr Vera Merrick Walker, Edinburgh; one s one d. Educ: Royal Dockyard Sch.; Devonport; Plymouth Technical Sch., Plymouth; Royal College of Science, London; Wadham Coll., Oxford. Entered Indian Civil Service, 1914; Indian Army Reserve of Officers, 1916-19, serving in India and Mesopotamia. Administrative posts of ICS, 1920-25; District and Sessions Judge in various parts of Southern India, 1925-36; Acting Judge, High Court, Madras, 1936; Judge, High Court, Madras, 1940-50, retired, 1950. Recreation: walking. Address: 220 Middleborough Road, Blackburn South, Victoria 3130, Australia. T: 890381. Club: Madras.
[Died 30 May 1972.

HOSKINS, Sir Cecil (Harold), Kt 1960; retired; b 11 Nov. 1899; m 1913, Dorothy Gwynn Loveridge; four s two d. Educ: Newington Coll., Sydney. Formerly: Ironmaster; Chm. Australian Mutual Provident Soc., Sydney. Recreations: motoring, gardening. Address: Cardrona, Moss Vale, NSW, Australia. T: Moss Vale 42. Clubs: Union, Elanora, Kensington (Sydney); Australian (Melbourne).
[Died 8 March 1971.

HOSKYNS-ABRAHALL, Sir (Theo) Chandos, Kt 1950; CMG 1942; *b* 17 Dec. 1896; *o s* of Chandos William Hoskyns-Abrahall, MRCS, LRCP; *m* 1925, Clare Constance Drury; two *s* one *d*; *m* 1944, Lois Jennet Ogle. *Educ:* Epsom Coll. Served European War, 1915-20, Capt., London Regt in France, Salonika, and Palestine; Administrative Officer, Nigeria, 1921; Senior District Officer, 1936; Resident, 1937; Deputy Chief Sec., 1939; Acting Chief Sec., Nigeria, and Governor's deputy, various occasions, 1939 onwards; Chief Commissioner, Western Provinces, Nigeria, 1946-51; Lieut Governor, Western Region, 1951-52. Officer Legion of Honour, 1950. *Recreation:* painting (various one-man exhibitions London and elsewhere). *Address:* 6 The Green, Colne Engaine, Colchester, Essex. *T:* Earls Colne 2770.   *[Died 24 Jan. 1975.*

HOTBLACK, Maj.-Gen. Frederick Elliot, DSO 1917, MC; late Royal Tank Corps; *b* 1887; *s* of F. M. Hotblack, Norwich. Served European War, 1914-18 (DSO and bar, MC and bar, Legion of Honour, Order of St Anne, five times wounded); Brigade Major, 1st Rhine Brigade, 1921; General Staff Officer, War Office, 1927; Instructor Staff Coll., Camberley, 1932-35; Military Attaché, British Embassy, Berlin, 1935-37; General Staff, War Office, 1937-39; General Staff BEF Sept. 1939; Commander Division, 1939-40; ADC to the King, 1939; retired pay, 1941. Mem. Royal Tank Regimental Assoc. *Address:* 24 Emerson Court, Wimbledon Hill Road, Wimbledon SW19 7PQ.   *[Died 9 Jan. 1979.*

HOTCHIN, Sir Claude, Kt 1967; OBE 1952; JP; Company Director and Grazier, Western Australia; Art Patron and Philanthropist since 1916; *b* 7 March 1898; *s* of John Robert Hotchin and Bertha Mary Hotchin (*née* Brown); *m* 1925, Doris May Clarkson; one *d*. *Educ:* Quorn and Broken Hill Public Schs; Hayward's Coll., Adelaide. District Comr, Boy Scouts, 1931-35; Foundation Mem., WA Soc. for Crippled Children, 1938 (Hon. Mem., 1954-); Member: Bd of Trustees, Public Library, Museum and Art, Gallery, of WA, 1948-60; Board of Western Australian Art Gallery, 1960-65 (also first Chm.); Senate, University of WA, 1951-69. Chm., Commonwealth Australia Jubilee Art Cttee for Western Australia, 1951. Chm., Friends of Royal Perth Hosp., 1969-75. Hon. LLD Univ. of WA, 1974. *Recreations:* golf, swimming, motoring, gardening. *Address:* Melville House, 5 Hotchin Avenue, Albany, Western Australia 6330. *T:* 95-1076. *Clubs:* Albany, Perth Rotary (Hon. Sec., 1931-34; Pres., 1935-36) (Perth, WA).   *[Died 3 June 1977.*

HOUBLON, Mrs Doreen A.; *see* Archer Houblon.

HOUGH, Rev. Lynn Harold, AB, BD, DD; LHD Vermont, 1932; ThD; LittD; LLD Pittsburgh; JUD, Boston; Dean of Drew Theological Seminary, 1934-47, and Professor of Homiletics and the Christian Criticism of Life, 1930-47; *b* 10 Sept. 1877; *s* of Franklin M. Hough and Eunice R. Giles; *m* 1936, Blanche, *widow* of Stephen Van R. Trowbridge, *d* of late Byron Horton. *Educ:* Scio Coll.; Drew Theological Seminary. For 16 years was the Pastor of Methodist Churches in New Jersey, New York, and Maryland; Prof. of Historical Theology in Garrett Biblical Institute, 1914-19; sent to Great Britain by Lindgren Foundation of Northwestern Univ. to interpret America and the moral and spiritual aims of the War, 1918; preaching and speaking in Gt Britain at invitation of Ministry of Information, 1942; Merrick Lecturer, Ohio Wesleyan Univ., 1923; Cole Lecturer at Vanderbilt Univ., 1919; Pres. Northwestern Univ., USA, 1919-20; Pastor, Central Methodist Episcopal Church, Detroit, 1920-28; Pres., Detroit Council of Churches, 1926-28; Minister, American Presbyterian Church, United Church of Canada, 1928-30; Pres. of the Religious Education Council of Canada, 1929-30; Samuel Harris Lecturer, Bangor Theological Seminary, 1930; Ayer Lecturer, Colgate-Rochester Divinity Sch., 1930; Sam P. Jones Lecturer at Emory Univ., 1935; Fred J. Cato Lecturer, General Conference of Methodist Church of Australasia, Brisbane, 1941; Easter Lecturer, Bexley Hall, Kenyon Coll., 1945; Southwestern Lecturer, Southwestern Univ., 1945; Chancellor's Lecturer at Queen's Univ., Kingston, Ont., Christian Humanism and the Modern World; Pres. of the Assoc. of Methodist Theological Schs, USA, 1942; Mem. Exec. Cttee Federal Council of Churches of Christ in America, 1936-48. *Publications:* Athanasius the Hero; The Lure of Books; The Theology of a Preacher; The Men of the Gospels; The Quest for Wonder; The Man of Power; The Clean Sword; The Productive Beliefs; Flying over London; The Eyes of Faith; The Opinions of John Clearfield, 1921; Life and History; A Little Book of Sermons, 1922; Synthetic Christianity (Merrick Lectures); The Imperial Voice, 1924; The Lion in his Den; Evangelical Humanism (Fernley Lecture), 1925; Adventures in the Minds of Men, 1927; Imperishable Dreams, 1929; (ed and contrib.) Whither Christianity, 1929; The Artist and the Critic (Samuel Harris

Lectures), 1930; Personality and Science (Ayer Lectures), 1930; The University of Experience, 1932; Vital Control (Forest Essays, First Series), 1934; The Church and Civilization, 1934; The Great Evangel, 1936; The Civilized Mind (Forest Essays, Second Series), 1937; Free Men (Forest Essays, Third Series), 1939; The Christian Criticism of Life, 1941; Adventures in Understanding, 1941; Patterns of the Mind, 1942; Living Democracy, 1943; The Meaning of Human Experience, 1945; Christian Humanism and the Modern World (Chancellor Lectures), 1948; The Dignity of Man, 1950; Great Humanists, 1952; The Great Argument, 1953; The Living Church, 1959. *Address:* c/o Crary, Underhill Road, Scarsdale, NY 10583, USA. *Clubs:* National Liberal, Authors'; University, Century, The Pilgrims (New York).   *[Died 14 July 1971.*

HOUGHTON, Charles Thomas, CB 1951; CBE 1941; Under-Secretary, Ministry of Agriculture and Fisheries, 1946-56; *b* 12 Aug. 1892; *m* 1921, Anne, *d* of Thos Hunt, Ince, Lancs; one *s* one *d*. *Educ:* Hindley and Abram Grammar Sch.; London Sch. of Economics. Entered Board of Agriculture and Fisheries, 1912; Private Sec. to Permanent Sec., Ministry of Agriculture and Fisheries, 1920-21; Private Sec. to five successive Ministers of Agriculture 1921-29; an Asst Sec. to United Kingdom Delegation to Imperial Economic Conference, Ottawa, 1932; Asst Sec., Ministry of Agriculture and Fisheries, 1934; First Sec. to Cattle Cttee (under Cattle Subsidy Scheme), 1934-35; Agricultural Representative on UK Delegation to Conference of British Commonwealth Statisticians, Ottawa, 1935; Principal Finance Officer, Ministry of Agriculture, 1937-39; Asst Sec., Ministry of Food, 1939-42; Principal Asst Sec., Ministry of Agriculture, 1944; Under-Sec., 1946; Principal Establishment Officer, 1944-55. *Publication:* Paper on A New Index Number of Agricultural Prices, before Royal Statistical Society, Jan. 1938. *Address:* 2 The Bower Garden, London Road, Maldon, Essex. *T:* Maldon (Essex) 53963. *Club:* Royal Commonwealth Society.   *[Died 5 April 1975.*

HOUGHTON, Rt. Rev. Frank; *b* Stafford; *s* of Thomas and Elizabeth Houghton; *m* Dorothy Cassels, *d* of first Bishop in Western China. *Educ:* Clarence Sch., Weston-super-Mare; St John's Hall, Highbury; BA London Univ., 1913. Ordained 1917 to Curacy of St Benedict, Everton; Curate of All Saints, Preston, 1919-20; Missionary in China, China Inland Mission, 1920-26; Editorial Sec., China Inland Mission, London, 1928-36; Bishop of Eastern Szechwan, 1937-40; Gen. Dir, China Inland Mission, 1940-51; Vicar of St Marks, New Milverton, Leamington, 1953-60; Rector of St Peter's, Drayton, Banbury, 1960-63; retired, 1963. *Publications:* The Two Hundred, 1932; China Calling, 1936; If We Believe 1952; Amy Carmichael of Dohnavur, 1953; The Fire Burns on, 1964; Living your Life, 1966. *Address:* 4 Wellington Road, Parkstone, Poole, Dorset.
                                                     [Died 25 Jan. 1972.

HOUGHTON, Sir William (Frederick), Kt 1967; Education Officer of the Inner London Education Authority, 1965-71 (of LCC, 1956-65); *b* 30 Nov. 1909; *m* 1936, Mary Newton; one *s* (and one *s* decd). *Educ:* Christ's Coll., Cambridge Univ. BA 1931; MA 1936. Teaching, Methodist Coll., Belfast, and Wirral Grammar Sch., Cheshire, 1932-36; Asst to Sec., E Suffolk Educ. Cttee, 1936-38; Dep. Dir of Education, W Sussex, 1938-41; Chief Education Officer, Darlington, 1941-47; Dep. Education Officer, Birmingham, 1947-52; Dep. Education Officer, London, 1952-56. Hon. FCP 1965. Hon. DUniv Surrey, 1968. *Publication:* Greeks and Romans, 1935. *Recreations:* reading, theatre, sport, travel. *Address:* 42 Brookfield, Highgate West Hill, N6.   *[Died 16 Nov. 1971.*

HOULDEN, George Houldsworth, CBE 1955 (MBE 1942); CEng; MRINA; Chairman of Vickers Ltd Shipbuilding Group, 1965-67; *b* 10 Sept. 1902; *s* of late George Houldsworth Houlden, Knutsford, Cheshire; *m* 1924, Winifred Crawford (*d* 1971), *d* of David Lindsay Largie of Montrose; three *s* one *d*. *Educ:* Robert Gordon's Technical Coll., Aberdeen. Apprenticed with Hall, Russell & Co. Ltd, Aberdeen. Joined Vickers Ltd, Barrow-in-Furness, 1924; joined Management Staff at Barrow, 1933; transferred to Walker Yard as Personal Asst to Gen. Manager, 1943; Dep. Gen. Manager of Walker Yard and a Special Dir, Vickers-Armstrongs Ltd, 1946; Gen. Manager of Walker Yard, 1950; Dir, 1953, Managing Dir, 1954, Chm. and Man. Dir, 1962-64, Chm., 1964-65, of Vickers-Armstrongs (Shipbuilders) Ltd. Member: Board of Cockatoo Docks and Engineering Co. (Pty) Ltd, Sydney, 1954-65; Board of Vickers Ltd, 1957-67. *Recreation:* fishing. *Address:* Beda Lodge, Hookergate, Rowlands Gill, Co. Durham. *T:* Rowlands Gill 2236.   *[Died 16 Oct. 1972.*

HOULTON, Sir John (Wardle), Kt 1947; CSI 1945; CIE 1939; President of the Senate of Swaziland, since 1968; *b* 28 Jan. 1892;

m 1927, Gwynneth Clause, *d* of Dr Muspratt Comley (marr. diss. 1958); one *d*; *m* 1960, Lily, *widow* of Frederic Kingsley. *Educ:* Perse Sch.; Christ's Coll., Cambridge. 2nd Lieut Suffolk Regt, Spec. Res. of Officers, Sept. 1914. Served European War (wounded); acting Lieut-Col 1918. Entered ICS, Bihar Prov., 1920; Dist Magistrate, 1924; Dir of Land Records, 1928; Revenue and Commerce Sec., 1933; Chief Sec., 1943; Adviser to the Governor, 1944; retd, 1948. *Publication:* Bihar, the Heart of India, 1950. *Recreations:* writing, golf, shooting. *Address:* South Wind, Malkerns, Swaziland.   *[Died 9 Nov.* 1973.

HOURIGAN, Thomas, CBE 1973; JP; DL; Vice-Chairman: Wigan Area Health Authority, since 1974; North Western Regional Water Authority, since 1973; *b* 1 Dec. 1904; *m* 1929, Agnes Cassidy; one *s* two *d*. *Educ:* St Joseph's Primary Sch., Leigh. NUPE Trade Union Organising Officer, 1938-57; Sec. Manager, Leigh Rugby League Football Club, 1957-69; Member: Leigh Borough Council, 1934-74; Lancs CC, 1946-; Manchester Regional Hosp. Bd, 1948-; Past Member: Lancs Exec. Council; United Manchester Hosps; Mayor of Leigh Borough, 1949-50; Former Chairman: Lancs County Fire Bde Cttee; Lancs Co. Health Cttee; Chm., Manchester Reg. Hosp. Bd, 1966-74; Vice-Chairman: former Mersey River Bd; Mersey and Weaver River Authority (since inception). Contested (Lab) Preston North, 1951. JP Leigh Borough, 1949-; Lancs CC, 1946-74; County Alderman, Lancs, 1957-74; Borough Alderman, Leigh, 1953-74; Leader, Wigan Metrop. Dist Council, 1973-. DL Lancs, 1974. Hon. Freeman, Borough of Leigh, 1972. Hon. MA (Manchester), 1963. *Recreations:* sports, gardening, reading. *Address:* 10 Wenlock Road, Leigh, Lancs. *T:* Leigh 73858.
                                                  [Died 22 Nov. 1975.

HOUSSAY, Prof. Doctor Bernardo Alberto; President, National Scientific Research Council, Buenos Aires; Director, Instituto de Biologia y Medicina Experimental, Obligado 2490, Buenos Aires; *b* Buenos Aires, 10 April 1887; *s* of Alberto Houssay and Clara Laffont; *m* 1920, Maria Angélica Catán; three *s*. *Educ:* Buenos Aires. Pharmacist, 1904; Med. Doctor, Buenos Aires, 1911. Prof. of Physiology: Veterinary Sch., Buenos Aires, 1910-19; Medical Sch., Buenos Aires, 1919-43, 1945-46, 1955-57; Research Prof. of the University of Buenos Aires, 1957-69. Hitchcock Prof., University of California, 1948. Mem. Advisory Cttee of Medical Research: WHO; Pan-American Health Organization. Mem. numerous societies and academies, both Argentinian and Foreign; Foreign Mem. Royal Society. Former President: Nat. Acad. of Medicine (Buenos Aires); Argentine Assoc. for Advancement of Sciences (Hon Pres.); Internat. Union of Physiological Sciences; President: Argentine Soc. of Biology; Argentine Soc. of Physiology. Holds numerous hon. presidencies, hon. professorships, and hon. doctorates (including Dr *hc* Oxford, Cambridge and Glasgow), etc. Winner of: National Prize Sciences, Buenos Aires, 1923; Charles Mickle Fellowship, Toronto, Canada, 1945; Banting Medal, American Diabetes Assoc., 1946; Research Award, American Pharmaceutical Manufacturers' Assoc., 1947; Baly Medal, Royal Coll. of Physicians, London, 1947; Nobel Prize for Physiology and Medicine, 1947; James Cook Medal, Sydney, 1948; Dale Medal, Soc. for Endocrinology, London, 1960; Weizmann Prize in Sciences and Humanities, 1967. Has several foreign orders. *Publications:* Textbook on Human Physiology (Spanish, English, French, Portuguese, Italian, Greek edns); many scientific papers on Hypophysis, Diabetes, Hypertension of Renal Origin, Pancreas, Adrenals, Thyroid, Endocrinology, Alloxan, Thymus, Venoms, Pharmacodynamics, Medical Education, etc. *Address:* (private) Viamonte 2790, Buenos Aires, Argentina. *T:* 87-8748.   *[Died 21 Sept.* 1971.

HOUSTOUN, Robert Alexander, MA, PhD, DSc, FRSE, FInstP; Hon. Research Fellow, University of Glasgow; *b* 1883; unmarried. *Educ:* Hillhead High Sch.; Universities of Glasgow (was Metcalfe Fellow and 1851 Research Fellow), Göttingen, and Cambridge (Scholar of Emmanuel Coll.). On the Staff of the Natural Philosophy Dept of the University of Glasgow, 1906-74. *Publications:* Studies in Light Production, 1912; An Introduction to Mathematical Physics, 1912; A Treatise on Light, 1915; Elements of Physics, 1919; Light and Colour, 1922; Intermediate Light, 1925; Intermediate Electricity and Magnetism, 1928; Intermediate Heat, 1929; Intermediate Physics, 1930; Vision and Colour Vision, 1932; Physical Optics, 1957; numerous scientific papers in the Proceedings of the Royal Society, The Proceedings of the Royal Society of Edinburgh, the Philosophical Magazine, etc. *Address:* The University, Glasgow.
                                                  [Died 4 May 1975.

HOUTHUESEN, Albert Antony John; artist, since 1928; *b* 3 Oct. 1903; *s* of Jean Charles Pierre Houthuesen and Elizabeth Emma Petronella Wedemeyer; *m* 1931, Catherine Mary Dean, painter. *Educ:* St Martin's Sch. of Art (evening classes); Royal Coll. of Art (scholarship, 1924; Dip. ARCA 1927). Exhibitions: Reid Gall., 1961 (first exhibn at age of 58), 1962, 1963; Victor Waddington Gall., 1964-66; Mercury Gall., 1967, 1969, 1972; exhibns arranged by Richard Nathanson, 1974, 1975, 1976, also 1977 exhibn at Barling's, arranged to coincide with BBC Omnibus film, Houthuesen—a Private Life. Pictures in public collections: Tate, Leeds, Sheffield, Carlisle and Nottingham Galls; BM and V&A Museum. *Publications:* Houthuesen (an appreciation introd. by Sir John Rothenstein), 1969 (signed and limited edn of 250 copies, nos 1-120 incl. lithograph drawn and signed by artist); Folio of Five Lithographs, 1972 (limited edn of 50) (both Mercury Graphics). *Recreations:* painting, drawing, graphics. *Address:* 5 Love Walk, SE5 8AD. *T:* 01-703 6122.
                                                  [Died 20 Oct. 1979.

HOWARD OF GLOSSOP, 3rd Baron *cr* 1869; **Bernard Edward Fitzalan-Howard**, MBE 1920; *b* 10 May 1885; *s* of 2nd Baron and Clara, *d* of J. Greenwood of Swarcliffe, Ripley, Yorks; *c* and *heir-pres.* of 16th Duke of Norfolk, *qv*; *S* father, 1922; *m* 1914, 11th Baroness Beaumont, OBE (*d* 1971); four *s* four *d*. *Educ:* Oratory Sch., Edgbaston; Trinity Coll., Cambridge. *Heir: s* 12th Baron Beaumont. *Address:* 23 Lennox Gardens, SW1. *T:* 01-589 2824.   *[Died 24 Aug.* 1972.

HOWARD, Capt. Alan Frederic William, DSO 1940; RN, retired; *b* 11 April 1883; *s* of late William Howard *m* 1921, Kathleen Jocelyn, *d* of Charles Campbell Riley; two *s*. *Educ:* late Mr C. Luton, Farnborough Park, Hants; HMS Britannia. Served European War and War of 1939-45 (despatches twice, Croix de Guerre with palm, DSO). *Address:* Hazelgrove, Slindon, Sussex. *T:* Slindon 255.   *[Died 19 Nov.* 1971.

HOWARD, Hon. Sir Arthur Jared Palmer, KBE 1953; CVO 1937; Treasurer, St Thomas' Hospital, 1943-64; Chairman of Delegacy, King's College, University of London since 1951; Chairman City Parochial Foundation; late Captain Scots Guards; *b* 1896; *s* of 3rd Baron Strathcona; *m* 1922, Lorna Stanley, *d* of 1st Earl Baldwin, KG, PC, FRS; two *s* two *d*. Served European War, 1914-17 (wounded, Croix de Guerre); Principal Warden London Civil Defence Region, 1939-42. MP (C) S George's Division of Westminster, 1945-50. Mem. (part-time), S Eastern Electricity Bd, 1953-64. JP West Sussex, 1939. *Address:* Wappingthorn, Steyning, Sussex; 6 Chesterfield Street, W1. *Club:* Guards.   *[Died 25 April* 1971.

HOWARD, Edwin Johnston, MA, PhD; Professor of English, Miami University, Oxford, Ohio, 1942-68; *b* 10 July 1901; *s* of William Bakewell Howard and Elizabeth Johnston; *m* 1934, Miriam Elizabeth White; one *d*. *Educ:* Cornell Univ. Instructor of English at the University of Rochester, 1925-26; Asst Prof. of English at Beloit Coll., 1929-30; Associate Prof. of English, Miami Univ., 1930-42; Exchange Prof., 1941 summer term, University of Washington (Seattle). Editor, The Fisherman magazine, 1957-58. *Publications:* articles on Old English, Elizabethan literature, angling and fishing tackle, and photography in journals; (ed) Ten Elizabethan Plays, 1931; (ed) Sir Thomas Elyot's The Defence of Good Women, 1940; (ed) Pleasant Quippes for Upstart Newfangled Gentle-women, 1942; (co-editor) The Canterbury Tales, 1946; (ed) Of the Knowledge Which Maketh a Wise Man, 1946; Geoffrey Chaucer, 1964; English Around the World, 1969. *Recreations:* photography and fishing. *Address:* 5035 Bonham Road, Oxford, Ohio 45056, USA. *T:* Oxford 35044. *Club:* Torch.   *[Died 2 May* 1971.

HOWARD, Frederick Richard, CB 1956; CMG 1950; lately Assistant Secretary, Air Ministry; *b* 7 June 1894; *m* 1920, Nellie Lewis. *Educ:* Strand Sch.; King's Coll., London; privately. Entered HM Civil Service, 1913, National Insurance Audit Dept. Served European War, 1914-18, in Civil Service Rifles, Aug. 1914-Jan. 1919; transferred to Air Ministry on release from Army, 1919; Private Sec. to successive Parliamentary Under-Secs of State for Air, 1937-39; Sec. to Riverdale Mission to Canada to plan Empire Air Training Scheme for Aircrew, 1939-40. *Recreations:* motoring, gardening, photography. *Address:* 22 Hadley Road, Enfield, Mddx.   *[Died 20 Oct.* 1977.

HOWARD, His Honour Geoffrey; former Judge of County Courts (1952-63); Master of the Bench, Inner Temple, 1951-68; *b* Nov. 1889; *y s* of late E. Howard; widower; one *d*; *m* 1969, Mrs Ingwelda von Heitmann-Gorkë. *Educ:* Haileybury Coll.; Christ Church, Oxford (BA 1912; MA 1967). "Temporary Gentleman", Royal Fusiliers, 1914-18. Called to Bar, 1919; practised London and Western Circuit. *Publications:* (as Marmaduke Dixey) Hell's Bells (novel), 1936; Words, Beasts and Fishes (verse), 1937; Tight Little Island (novel), 1938; The Beauties of Bridge (verse), 1939. *Address:* 1 King's Bench Walk, Temple, EC4; 3 Belvedere, Mellieha Heights, Malta. *T:* Mellieha 73-815.   *[Died 30 May* 1973.

HOWARD, Sir Gerald; see Howard, Sir Stephen Gerald.

HOWARD, Maj.-Gen. Gordon Byron, CBE 1945; b 8 May 1895; s of Samuel William and Maud Margaret Howard; m 1919, Ada Becket Woods, Montreal; one d. Educ: Toronto Public Schs; Upper Canada Coll.; Royal Military College, Kingston. Joined Royal Canadian Ordnance Corps, 1914; Ordnance Coll., Woolwich, 1919; Military Coll. of Science, 1928-31; Chief Inspector Armaments, Canada, 1934-40; Deputy Inspector-Gen., Inspection Board, 1940-43; Controller-Gen. and Chairman Inspection Board of UK and Canada, 1943-47; retired 1947. Recreation: badminton. Address: 57 Drake Street, Sault Ste Marie, Ontario, Canada.   [Died 26 Dec. 1976.

HOWARD, Lieut-Col Hon. Henry Anthony Camillo, CMG 1960; b 3 March 1913; s of 1st Baron Howard of Penrith, PC, GCB, GCMG, CVO, and Lady Isabella Giustiniani-Bandini (d of Prince Giustiniani-Bandini, 8th Earl of Newburgh); m 1937, Adele Le Bourgeois, d of late Reese Denny Alsop, New York City, USA; four d (and one d decd). Educ: Newman Sch., NJ, USA; Downside; RMC Sandhurst. Commissioned, Coldstream Guards, 1932; seconded Somaliland Camel Corps, 1935-36; resigned commission, 1937; Asst Sec., Council of Foreign Bondholders, 1937-39. Served War of 1939-45 (despatches). Entered Colonial Service, 1946; Administrative Officer, Kenya, 1947; Private Sec. to Governor, 1952-53; seconded as Commissioner, Virgin Islands, 1954; Administrator, 1956; Administrator of St Kitts, Nevis and Anguilla, 1956-65. Recreation: shooting. Address: Bushby House, Greystoke, Penrith, Cumbria CA11 0TF.   [Died 19 Oct. 1977.

HOWARD, Leon Alexander L.; see Lee Howard.

HOWARD, Hon. Mabel Bowden; Member for Sydenham, Labour Party, Parliament of New Zealand, since 1943; b Adelaide, S Australia, 18 April 1894; 2nd d of Edwin John Howard, Deputy Speaker in first Labour Government in New Zealand; came to NZ on death of mother, Harriet Howard, in 1903. Educ: New Brighton Sch. and Technical Coll. Was sec. for many years of one of largest industrial unions in NZ, only woman ever to hold such a position; mem. City Council, Drainage Board, Hosp. Bd, Tramway Bd, for many years. Elected to Parliament (NZ) in 1943; in 1946 elections secured highest individual vote and majority ever recorded in NZ; first woman to be elected to Cabinet in NZ; Minister for Health in the Government of New Zealand, 1947-49; Ministry of Social Security, Minister for Welfare of Women and Children, and Minister in Charge of Child Welfare Dept, NZ, 1957-60. During war years was Chm. of Women's War Service Auxiliary in home town of Christchurch. Pres. Soc. Prevention Cruelty to Animals (SPCA); responsible for Act for protection of animals, passed in NZ, 1960. Recreations: reading, needlework, gardening; caring for old folk. Address: 147 Pages Road, Christchurch, New Zealand; Parliament House, Wellington, New Zealand.
                                                    [Died 23 June 1972.

HOWARD, Sir (Stephen) Gerald, Kt 1961; JP; Judge of the High Court of Justice (Queen's Bench Division), 1961-71; Barrister-at-law; b 7 June 1896; o s of late Major S. G. Howard, CBE, DL, and Mary M. Howard, The Moat, Upend, Newmarket; m 1934, Claudia Primrose, d of late Graves Stoker, MD, FRCS, Dublin and London, and Mrs Stoker, Gaddesden Hall, Gaddesden, Herts; two s. Educ: Harrow; Balliol Coll., Oxford. Flight Lieut RFC and RAF, 1916-18; Balliol Coll., Oxford, 1918-21; called to Bar, Lincoln's Inn, 1924; Bencher, 1942; QC 1950. Recorder of Bury St Edmunds, 1943-45; a senior Prosecuting Counsel, 1945-50; Recorder of Ipswich, 1947-58; Recorder of Southend, 1958-61. Chm. of Quarter Sessions: for Cambridgeshire, 1947-52; for East and West Suffolk, 1952-61. MP (C) Cambridgeshire, 1950-61. JP Cambridgeshire, 1942; High Sheriff of Cambs and Hunts, 1945-46. Recreation: shooting. Address: The Moat, Upend, Newmarket, Cambs. T: Newmarket 730234.
                                                    [Died 25 June 1973.

HOWARTH, Herbert Lomax; b 3 March 1900; er s of Herbert and Emma Margaret Howarth; m 1926, Mildred, e d of James and Janet Dodd; no c. Educ: Darlington Grammar Sch.; Preston Grammar Sch.; Magdalen Coll., Oxford. Joined Westminster Gazette, 1922. Council of the Newspaper Soc., 1939-64 (Chm. Labour Cttee, 1948-50; Chm. Technical Cttee, 1952-55). Dir Press Association Ltd, 1954-61 (Chm. 1958-59); Dir Birmingham Post & Mail Ltd, 1957-66; Dir Reuters Ltd, 1958-61, Trustee, 1963-73. Managing Dir, Westminster Press Provincial Newspapers Limited, 1953-64, retired. Address: Top End, Storth, Milnthorpe, Westmorland. T: Milnthorpe 3195. Club: United Oxford & Cambridge University.
                                                    [Died 19 March 1974.

HOWE, Sir Ronald (Martin), Kt 1955; CVO 1950; MC 1916; President, Group 4 Total Security; director of other cos; b 5 Sept. 1896; s of Frank Gull Howe, journalist, and Clara Harriet Mackenzie; m 1974, Mrs Patrick St G. Perrott. Educ: Westminster Sch. (King's scholar); Christ Church, Oxford (scholar). Served Royal Sussex Regt, 1915-19 (MC, wounded), Capt., 1917. Called to Bar, Inner Temple, 1924; Legal Officer, Dir of Public Prosecutions Dept, 1924-31; Chief Constable CID, New Scotland Yard, 1932; Asst Commissioner in charge of CID, 1945-53; Dep. Commissioner, 1953-57. Studied police methods in USA, Canada and all principal European countries; British Representative on Internat. Criminal Police Commission, 1945-57. Officer French Legion of Honour; Commander Royal Danish Order of Dannebrog; Officer Royal Netherlands Order of Orange-Nassau. Publications: The Pursuit of Crime, 1961; The Story of Scotland Yard, 1965. Address: Queens Laws, Kingsway, Craigwell, near Bognor Regis, Sussex. Clubs: Naval and Military, Buck's.   [Died 30 Aug. 1977.

HOWELL, Charles Alfred, OBE 1965; retired Clerical Officer, National Carriers Ltd (formerly British Railways); b 22 Oct. 1905; s of Charles and May Louise Howell; m 1927, Ivy Jeanette Silvester; one d. Educ: Winshill Secondary Sch., Burton-on-Trent. A railway guard; Branch Sec., Derby No 1 Branch, NUR, 1939-55; Mem. of LM Region Sectional Council No 3 (Traffic Grades), 1943-55; Mem. of National Executive Cttee, NUR, 1951-53; Voluntary Tutor, National Council of Labour Colls; Mem. of Derby County Borough Council, 1943-53; Sec. of Derby Trades Council, 1945-56, 1966-; Chm. of Derby Borough Labour Party, 1950-51; Mem. Derby and S Derbyshire Assessment Tribunal, 1948-59; Member: Derby No 2 HMC, 1948-66; Derby No 1 HMC, 1966-74; Derby and S Derbyshire Valuation Panel, 1973-; Chairman: Derwent Hosp. (Derby), 1948-74; Draycot Hosp., 1967-74. MP (Lab) Perry Barr Div. of Birmingham, 1955-64; an Opposition Whip, 1959-64. Secretary: Derby Area Trades Union Council, 1966-; N Midlands Fedn of Trades Councils, 1973-74; Derbyshire Assoc. of Trade Councils, 1974-; Mem., Trades Councils Jt Consultative Commn, 1974. Address: 36 Cardigan Street, Cowsley Estate, Derby DE2 6DW. T: Derby 43878.   [Died 17 Oct. 1974.

HOWELL, Sir Evelyn Berkeley, KCIE 1932 (CIE 1916); CSI 1919; b Calcutta, 1877; s of A. P. Howell, ICS; m 1912, Laetitia Cecilia, d of Brig.-Gen. G. P. Campbell, RE; two s one d. Educ: Charterhouse; Emmanuel Coll., Cambridge. Entered ICS 1900; Political Asst, NWF Province, 1906; Dep. Commissioner, 1907; District Judge, 1907; served Zakha Khel Expedition, 1908 (medal and clasp); Dep. Commissioner, Kohat, 1910; Censor of Indian Mails, Indian Expeditionary Force, France, 1914-16 (CIE); HM's Consul, Muscat, 1916; Dep. Civil Commissioner, Basrah Wilayat, Mesopotamia, 1917-18 (CSI); Military Governor, Baghdad, 1918; Revenue Sec., Mesopotamia, 1918-20; Dep. Foreign Sec., India, 1922; Officiating Foreign Sec., 1923-24 and 1926-27; Resident in Waziristan, 1924-26, in Kashmir, 1927-29; Foreign Sec. to Government of India 1930-32; retired 1933; Pres. of the Frontier Defence Cttee under the Government of India, 1931. Publications: Poems of Khushhal Khan (with Sir Olaf Caroe), 1963; contrib. NWFP Gazetteer and various articles. Address: 18 Manor Court, Pinehurst, Cambridge. T: 50702.   [Died 23 Oct. 1971.

HOWELL, Prof. William Gough, DFC 1943; ARA 1974; Professor of Architecture, Cambridge University, since 1973; Partner, Howell, Killick, Partridge & Amis, Chartered Architects; b 5 Feb. 1922; s of Charles Gough Howell (Attorney-Gen., Straits Settlements) (died in internment, Formosa, 1942) and late Sidney Gretchen Howell (née Innes-Noad); m 1951, Gillian Margaret Sarson; three s one d. Educ: Marlborough Coll.; Gonville and Caius Coll., Cambridge; Architectural Assoc., London. MA (Cantab); AA Dipl. (Hons); RIBA. Served War: commissioned RAFVR, 1940; Fighter Command, 1940-41; night-fighter Sqdns in UK, Middle East and Malta, 1941-43; Central Fighter Estabt, 1944-45. Architectural trng, 1945-50; LCC Architects Dept, Housing Div., 1950-56; on staff of Regent St Polytechnic Sch. of Architecture, 1956-58. Formed practice of Howell, Killick, Partridge & Amis, 1958. Has served on: Council of Architectural Assoc., Architects' Registration Council; (currently) RIBA Council; Chm., Bldg Res. Estabt Adv. Cttee. Chm., RIBA Drawings Collection. Professorial Fellow, Gonville and Caius Coll., 1973. Designed Buildings at: Univs of Oxford, Cambridge, Birmingham, Warwick and Reading; also Young Vic Theatre, London; Christ's Hosp. Sch. Arts Centre. Publication: Popular Arts of the First World War (with Barbara Jones), 1972. Recreations: riding, shooting, skiing; watching Rugby football; listening to Wagner. Address: Fen Ditton Hall, Cambridge; The Chapel, Great Bedwyn, Wilts. T: Great Bedwyn 556. Club: Reform.   [Died 29 Nov. 1974.

HOWES, Bobby; actor; *b* Chelsea; *s* of Robert William Howes and Rose Marie Butler; *m* Patricia Malone (*d* 1971); one *s* one *d*. *Educ:* privately. Started on stage with Sable Fern, stayed 1 year; then with dancing team for 1 year; Royal Gotham Quartette followed for 3 years; served European War, 1914-18: in 12th London Rangers for 3 years; took part in most big battles, but was unharmed; joined Jack Hulbert's Pot Luck, after war, then Little Revue, Six-Cylinder Love, We, Blue Kitten, Vaudeville Varieties, Blue Train, The Yellow Mask, Mr Cinders, Sons O'Guns; signed contract for Drury Lane Song of The Drum. *Films include:* Guns of Loos, Third Time Lucky, Lord Babs, For the Love of Mike, Over the Garden Wall, Please Teacher, Sweet Devil, Yes, Madam, Happy Go Lovely, Good Companions, Watch it Sailor. *Theatre:* as Dir Saville Theatre, appeared in For the Love of Mike, followed by Tell her The Truth and He Wanted Adventure, based on Ambrose Applejohn's Adventure; left Saville Theatre to play at London Hippodrome in Yes, Madam; followed by Please Teacher, Big Business and Hide and Seek; Bobby, Get Your Gun, Adelphi; All Clear, Queen's; Shephard's Pie, Princes; Lady Behave, His Majesty's; Let's Face It, Hippodrome; Halfway to Heaven, Princes; Cinderella, Winter Garden; Here Come the Boys, Saville; Roundabout, Saville; Paint Your Wagon, Her Majesty's, The Geese are Getting Fat, Phœnix, etc. Went to New York, to play Finian in Finian's Rainbow, 1960 (also name-part in Liverpool prod., 1958; Melbourne, 1963-64). Tours: Harvey, The Entertainer, Finian's Rainbow, Gazelle in Park Lane. Has appeared on television both in Britain and in USA. *Recreations:* golf, motoring, swimming, cricket. *Address:* 62 Holland Park, W11. *T:* 01-727 6201.   [Died 27 April 1972.

HOWES, Ernest James; *b* 27 Aug. 1895; 2nd *s* of William Quinton Howes and Eleanor Brett; *m* 1922 (marriage dissolved); one *d*; *m* 1944, Sheila Burke; one *s*. *Educ:* privately. Served European War, 1914-18. Comdt of Police, Jerusalem. 1920; Comdt, Arab Legion Training Sch., 1921; ADC to HH Amir (later King) Abdulla, 1921-25; Air Liaison Officer, RAF, in Iraq, 1926-35; Asst Political Sec., Aden, 1936-42. In charge of British Information Services, Middle East, 1945. First Sec. (Information) British Legation, Beirut, 1946; Political Adviser to British Resident, Benghazi, 1951; Consul, Kermanshah, 1951-52; Consul, Aleppo, 1952. HM Consul-Gen., Asmara 1954. Retired from the Foreign Service, 1957. *Publication:* Aleppo and the Turkey Merchants, 1956. *Recreations:* gardening, cooking. *Address:* 84 Eastbourne Road, Lower Willingdon, Sussex.   [Died 22 April 1974.

HOWES, Frank Stewart, CBE 1954; MA; FRCM; Hon. RAM; Lecturer at the Royal College of Music, 1938-71; *b* 2 April 1891; *s* of George Howes, Oxford; *m* 1929, Barbara Tidd Pratt; one *s* three *d*. *Educ:* Oxford High Sch.; St John's Coll., Oxford; Royal College of Music. Joined staff of The Times, 1925, and of the Royal College of Music, 1938; Editor, Folk Song Journal (later Journal of the English Folk Dance and Song Society), 1927-46; Chm. Musicians' Benevolent Fund, 1938-56; Music Critic of The Times, 1943-60: Pres. Royal Musical Association, 1948-58; Chm. BBC Central Music Advisory Council, 1950-55. *Publications:* Borderland of Music and Psychology, 1926; Byrd, 1928; Key to the Art of Music, 1935; (with Philip Hope-Wallace) Key to Opera, 1939; Full Orchestra, 1942; Man, Mind and Music, 1948; The Music of Vaughan Williams, 1954; Music and its Meanings, 1958; The Music of William Walton, 1965; The English Musical Renaissance, 1966; Folk Music of Britain and Beyond, 1970. *Recreations:* aquatics and motoring. *Address:* Newbridge Mill, near Witney, Oxon. *T:* Standlake 245. *Club:* Athenæum.   [Died 28 Sept. 1974.

HOWES, Henry William, CMG 1951; OBE 1948; MA, MSc, PhD London; lecturer, author; *b* 1896; *e s* of late William and Laura Howes, Norwich; *m* 1923, Clarisse Vera, *y d* of late James Charles Bond, Rattlesden, Suffolk; one *d*. *Educ:* Bracondale and Grammar Schs, Norwich; Univs of London and Wales. Served European War, 1914-18, Royal Marines, 1915-17. Teaching in grammar schools, in Polytechnics and Institutes, 1921-36; Principal, Norwich City Coll. and Sch. of Art, 1936-44; Mem. of Exec. of Eastern Counties Cttee for Adult Educn. In HM Forces, 1940-44; first Dir of Educn, Gibraltar, 1944-49, City Councillor, 1945-49; Dir-Gen. of Education, Ceylon, 1949-54; Hon. Educn Adviser, Ceylon Army, 1951-; Mem. Court and Council, University of Ceylon, 1949-54. Educational Adviser, Caribbean, for Unesco, 1954; Educational Adviser, Odhams, 1956-57; Dir of Education, British Honduras, 1958-60; Mem. Council, University Coll. of West Indies, 1958-60; Adviser on Secondary Education, British Honduras, 1960; Unesco Adviser on Adult and Youth Education, Dominica, West Indies, 1962. Overseas Educational Adviser, Harrap's, 1963-67; Hon. Historical Adviser to Govt of Gibraltar, 1964-72. Hon. Life Mem., Ceylon Nat. Assoc. for Prevention of Tuberculosis.

Chevalier of Order of Crown (Belgium), 1937; Officer of Order of Leopold II (Belgium), 1970; Kt Comdr, Order of Alfonso X, el Sabio (Spain), 1966; Kt of Order of St Gregory the Great, 1957; Officer of Order of Palmes Académiques (France), 1976. *Publications:* Bruges, 1935; Santiago de Compostela and its Prehistoric Origin, 1936; The Story of Gibraltar, 1948; The Gibraltarian:-The Origin and Development of Population in Gibraltar since 1704, 1951; Presenting Modern Britain, 1965; We Go to Spain, 1967; Anglo-Flemish Relations (in Flemish), 1979. *Recreation:* Spanish and Flemish studies. *Address:* 11 Franklins Road, Stevenage, Herts. *T:* Stevenage 2512.
                                  [Died 28 Sept. 1978.

HOWGILL, Richard John Frederick, CBE 1949; Music Controller, BBC, 1952-59; *b* 21 April 1895; *s* of late Richard Frederick Howgill by first wife; *m* 1925, Hilda Mary, *d* of late Edwin Alexander; one *s* one *d*. *Educ:* Emanuel Sch.; studied piano, violin and composition, privately. Served European War, 1914-18, in France and Mesopotamia; Mesopotamian Railways, 1919-21; Performing Right Soc., 1922-23; joined BBC, 1923, to take charge of its copyright dept; was subsequently Asst Dir of Programme Administration; Dir of Programme Administration; Asst Controller, Administration; Asst Controller, Programmes; Controller, Entertainment. *Address:* Branscombe, Sullington Warren, Storrington, Sussex. *T:* Storrington 2471.
                                  [Died 24 May 1975.

HOWICK OF GLENDALE, 1st Baron, *cr* 1960; **Evelyn Baring,** KG 1972; GCMG 1955 (KCMG, 1942); KCVO 1947; DL; late Indian Civil Service; a Director of the Swan Hunter Group Limited; Chairman, Nature Conservancy, since 1962 (Member, 1961-); *b* 29 Sept. 1903; *s* of 1st Earl of Cromer and (*o c* by 2nd wife) Lady Katharine Thynne (*d* 1933), 2nd *d* of 4th Marquess of Bath; *m* 1935, Lady Mary Cecil Grey, *er d* of 5th Earl Grey; one *s* two *d*. *Educ:* Winchester; New Coll., Oxford. First Cl. Hons History, 1924. Entered ICS, 1926; Sec. to Agent of Govt of India in S Africa, 1929; retired, 1934; Governor of S Rhodesia, 1942-44; High Commr for UK in Union of SA, and High Commr for Basutoland, the Bechuanaland Protectorate and Swaziland, 1944-51; Governor and C-in-C, Kenya, also Chm. of the East Africa High Commn, 1952-59; Chm., Commonwealth Develt Corp., 1963-72 (Dep. Chm., 1960, Chm., 1960-63, Colonial Develt Corp.). Mem., The Times Trust, 1967-; Vice-Pres., Liverpool Sch. of Tropical Medicine, 1967-. Chm. British N American Cttee, 1970-. Hon. Fellow, New Coll., Oxford, 1960. Hon. DCL Newcastle, 1968; Hon. DSc Reading, 1970. DL Northumberland, 1968. Queen's Commendation for Brave Conduct, 1959. KStJ. *Recreation:* mountaineering. *Heir: s* Hon. Charles Evelyn Baring [*b* 30 Dec. 1937; *m* 1964, Clare, *d* of Col Cyril Darby; three *d*. *Educ:* Eton; New Coll., Oxford]. *Address:* Howick, Alnwick, Northumberland. *Club:* Brooks's.
                                  [Died 10 March 1973.

HOWMAN, Brig. Ross Cosens, CIE 1945; OBE 1939; retired; *b* 11 July 1899; *s* of late Martin Langston Howman, OBE; *m* 1930, Cecil, *d* of late Edmond Hardie Elles, OBE; two *s*. *Educ:* Edinburgh Academy; Cadet Coll., Wellington, S India; Commissioned IA, 1918; served European War, 1914-18; Third Afghan War, 1919 (7th Gurkha Rifles); OC Escort Naga Hills Expedn, 1926-27; psc Camberley 1933; Wa Operations, Burma Frontier, 1933 (Burma Rifles); GSOIII, 1934; DAAG, 1935, Waziristan District; DAAG, Waziristan Div.; DAA and QMG, Waziristan Force, 1936-39 (despatches thrice) (8th Punjab Regt); GSO II, GHQ (India), 1940. Raised and commanded 1st Bn, The Assam Regt, 1941; GSO I, 1942; DDMI, 1943; Dir of Security, India Comd, 1944-45; Gen. Staff, War Office, 1946-47; retired, 1948. *Publications:* contributor to journals and magazines. *Recreations:* gardening, fishing, writing. *Address:* Balmacneil House, Dunkeld, Perthshire. *T:* Ballinluig 254. *Club:* Naval and Military.   [Died 9 Oct. 1976.

HOY, Baron *cr* 1970 (Life Peer), of Leith, Edinburgh; **James Hutchison Hoy,** PC 1969; DL; *b* 21 Jan. 1909; 3rd *s* of William and Sarah Hoy, Edinburgh; *m* 1942, Nancy Hamlyn Rae McArthur; one *s*. *Educ:* Causewayside and Sciennes Public Schs, Edinburgh. Interior Decorator. MP (Lab) Leith, 1945-50, Leith Div. of Edinburgh, 1950-70; PPS to Sec. of State for Scotland, 1947-50; Joint Parly Sec., Min. of Agriculture, Fisheries and Food, 1964-70. Vice-Pres. Trustee Savings Bank Assoc., 1957; joint Pres., Nat. Assoc. of Inshore Fishermen, 1963. DL Edinburgh, 1958. *Address:* 77 Orchard Road, Edinburgh EH4 8EX. *Clubs:* Beefsteak; Royal Scots (Edinburgh).
                                  [Died 7 Aug. 1976.

HOYLE, George, CMG 1954; retired; *b* 8 May 1900; 3rd *s* of George Harry and Mary Elizabeth Hoyle, Leeds; *m* 1936, Margaret Stewart, *d* of Ernest and Beatrice Reed, Bridlington; two adopted *s*. *Educ:* Leeds Grammar Sch.; The Queen's Coll.,

Oxford. Colliery Undermanager, 1930-33; Junior Inspector of Mines, 1933-41; Senior Inspector, 1941-50; Divisional Inspector, 1950-58; Dep. Chief Inspector, 1958-66. *Recreations:* collecting old glass, gardening. *Address:* 14 Arnold's Close, Hutton, Brentwood, Essex CM13 1EZ. *T:* Brentwood 226176.
[Died 9 Feb. 1979.

HOYLE, (John) Clifford; retired; lately Physician and Director, Department of Medicine, King's College Hospital; Emeritus Physician, King Edward VII Hospital; Consulting Physician, Brompton Hospital; *b* 4 July 1901; *s* of John and Esther Hoyle; *m* 1931, Mary Irene Rosewarne; two *s. Educ:* Rydal; Manchester Univ. MB, BS (London), 1925; MD (London) 1929 (Gold Medal in Medicine); Res. Asst, Dept of Pharmacology, Cambridge Univ., 1927-30; MRCP 1931; FRCP 1938; Ernest Hart Scholar, British Medical Assoc., 1928-30; Gillson Scholar, Society of Apothecaries, 1932-34; Medical First Asst and Lectr in Pharmacology, London Hosp., 1930-33; Paterson Research Scholar, Cardiac Dept, London Hosp., 1933-35; Sen. Mem., Assoc. Physicians; Hon. Mem., and former Pres., Thoracic Soc.; FRSM. *Publications:* (with M. Vaizey) Chronic Miliary Tuberculosis, 1937; various contributions to medical journals on physiology, pharmacology and diseases of lungs and cardiovascular system. *Recreations:* writing, literature. *Address:* 3 Boscawen, Cliff Road, Falmouth, Cornwall. *T:* Falmouth 311702.
[Died 10 Feb. 1976.

HSU CHEN-PING, Rt. Rev. Francis; Bishop of Hong Kong (RC), 1969-73; *b* 20 Feb. 1920. Ordained, 1959; consecrated Auxiliary Bishop of Hong Kong, 1967; nominated Apostolic Administrator of Hong Kong, 1968. *Address:* Bishop's House, 16 Caine Road, Hong Kong. *T:* H-232487/221009/220486.
[Died 23 May 1974.

HUBBARD, Charles Edward, CBE 1965 (OBE 1954); *b* 23 May 1900; *s* of Charles Edward Hubbard and Catherine Billing; *m* 1st, 1927, Madeleine Grace Witham (*d* 1961); one *s*; 2nd, 1963, Florence Kate Hubbard. *Educ:* King Edward VII Grammar Sch., King's Lynn. Royal Gardens, Sandringham, Norfolk, 1916-20; Royal Gardens, Oslo, Norway, 1919. RAF, 1918-19. Royal Botanic Gardens, Kew, 1920-65: Student Gardener, 1920-22; Tech. Asst, 1922-27; Asst Botanist, 1927-30; Botanist, 1930-46; Prin. Sci. Officer, 1946-56; Sen. Prin. Sci. Officer 1956-59; Dep. CSO, 1959-65; Dep. Dir of Royal Botanic Gardens, Kew, 1959-65, and Keeper of Herbarium and Library there, 1957-65. Linnean Gold Medal, 1967; Veitch Gold Meml Medal, 1970. Hon. DSc Reading, 1960. *Publications:* Grasses, 1954, 1968; numerous pubns on the Gramineae (Grasses) in various botanical books and jls. *Recreations:* walking; natural history. *Address:* 51 Ormond Crescent, Hampton, Mddx TW12 2TJ. *T:* 01-979 6923.
[Died 8 May 1980.

HUBBARD, Commodore (Robert) Lancelot F(ortescue), CBE 1957; RD, RNR retired; Elder Brother, Trinity House; *b* 16 March 1887; *s* of Commander R. R. F. Hubbard, RNR, and Lizzie Hubbard (*née* Sydenham); *m* 1st, 1914, Jessie Baldwin (*d* 1952), *d* of late Harry Staniland; three *s* two *d*; 2nd, Patience Eva, *d* of late Arthur Shipton. *Educ:* Dulwich Coll. Merchant Navy; served Loch Garry, 1902-9, leaving as First Mate; Orient Steam Navigation Co., 1909, and later commanded several of their liners till elected an Elder Brother, Trinity House, in 1937, retired as active Elder Brother, 1957. Passed Extra Master, 1910; Royal Navy: Midshipman, RNR, 1908; served in many of HM Ships; attached HMS Fox, during Persian Gulf operations, 1910; served European War, 1914-18 (despatches thrice) on Belgian coast and against Königsberg in E Africa; commanded Destroyers 1916-18; served War of 1939-45, Commodore of convoys. Rep. Trinity House on Internat. Conference, Safety of Life at Sea, 1946. Reserve Decoration, 1920; Bronze Medal, Royal Humane Society, 1910. *Recreations:* golf, gardening. *Address:* Orontes, Shute Road, Kilmington, near Axminster, Devon; Trinity House, Tower Hill, EC3. *T:* 01-480 6601. *Club:* National Liberal.
[Died 24 April 1972.

HUBRECHT, Jan Bastiaan, PhD Ultraj; MA Cantab; FRAS; *b* 13 April 1883; 2nd *s* of late Professor A. A. W. Hubrecht, Utrecht, Holland; *m* 1907, Jonkvrouwe Leonore van Alphen; two *s* three *d. Educ:* High Sch., Utrecht; University, Utrecht; Christ's Coll., Cambridge. Isaac Newton student, 1907; did research in Astrophysics at Solar Physics Observatory, Cambridge, 1907-12; lectured on Astrophysics, University of Manchester, 1913; entered Dutch Diplomatic Service, 1915; Attaché, London, 1915; Tokio, 1917; Foreign Office, The Hague, 1919; Second Sec., 1919; Washington, 1919; First Sec., 1923; Madrid, 1924; Counsellor, 1926; London 1927; Netherland Minister: Rio de Janeiro, 1930; Bucharest, 1934; Rome, 1937; handed his passports by Italian Govt upon Italy's entry into War, 1940; proceeded to Indonesia and was interned

there for over two years by Japanese, 1941. *Publication:* The Solar Rotation by Spectroscopic Observations, 1915. *Recreations:* books, puzzles. *Address:* Hoofdstraat 185, Driebergen, Holland.
[Died 13 Dec. 1978.

HUDSON, Sir Edmund (Peder), Kt 1963; FRSE 1948; Vice-President, Association of Agriculture; *b* 1 May 1903; *e s* of late Harold Hudson and Helen Ingeborg Olsen; *m* 1934, Bodil Catharina Böschen, Bergen, Norway; three *s. Educ:* Marlborough Coll.; King's Coll., Cambridge. Open Schol., 1922; Harold Fry Research Student, 1925; MA; Imperial Chemical Industries Ltd, Billingham, 1929-34; Scottish Agricultural Industries Ltd: Dir 1934, Asst Man. Dir, 1947, Managing Dir, 1957-62; Dir, Scottish Widows' Trust & Life Assurance Soc., 1961-76, Chm., 1967-69. Pres. Fertiliser Manufacturers' Assoc., 1948-49; Chairman: Assoc. of Chemical & Allied Employers, 1953-55; Scottish Technical Educn Consultative Council, 1959-71. Member: Pilkington Cttee on Broadcasting, 1960-62; Chancellor of Exchequer's Panel, Civil Service Arbitration Tribunal, 1963-68. Rector's Assessor, University Court, University of Edinburgh, 1961-63. Chairman: Napier Coll. of Science and Technology, Edinburgh, 1965-68; Academic Adv. Cttee, Heriot-Watt Univ., 1966-71. FBIM, 1960-72. Mem. Council, Outward Bound Trust, 1964-73. Hon. DSc Heriot-Watt Univ., 1966. *Address:* 35 Ravelston Dykes, Edinburgh EH12 6HG. *T:* 031-337 3457. *Clubs:* New, Royal Forth Yacht (Edinburgh).
[Died 15 Aug. 1978.

HUDSON, Rowland Skeffington, CMG 1946; *b* 1 April 1900; *s* of late Commander William Joseph Villiers Hudson, Royal Navy; *m* 1928, Jean Mallagh Fegan; two *s. Educ:* St Edward's Sch., Oxford. 2nd Lieut Royal Air Force, April 1918; Probationer, BSA Co., N Rhodesia, 1919; Asst Native Commissioner, N Rhodesia, 1922; Native Commissioner, 1925; Asst Chief Sec., 1936; Labour Commissioner, 1940; Provincial Commissioner, 1944; Sec. for Native Affairs, 1945; Mem. Royal Commission on land and population in East Africa, 1953; Commissioner, Provincial Devolution, N Region, Nigeria, 1956; Head of African Studies Branch, Colonial Office, 1949-61; Special Administrative Adviser, Barotseland, 1963-64; Head of Administrative Services Branch, Ministry of Overseas Development, 1964-65; retired, 1966. *Recreation:* gardening. *Address:* 4 New Church Road, Hove, Sussex BN3 4FH.
[Died 17 Dec. 1980.

HUDSON, Sir William, KBE 1955; FRS 1964; MICE; Commissioner, Snowy Mountains Hydro-Electric Authority, Australia, 1949-67; *b* 27 April 1896; *s* of Dr James Hudson, Nelson, NZ; *m* 1927, Eileen, OBE 1959, *d* of John Trotter, Fairlie, NZ; two *d. Educ:* Nelson Coll., NZ; University of London; Post-graduate course in Hydro-Electric Engineering, Grenoble, France. BSc (1st Cl. Hons), Univ. of London; Diploma (with distinction) in Civil Engineering, University Coll., London; Head Medal for Civil Engineering, University Coll., London. Served European War, France, 1916-17. Civil Engineering and Contracting Dept, Armstrong-Whitworth & Co. Ltd, London, 1920-21; Public Works Dept, New Zealand, 1923-24; Armstrong-Whitworth & Co. Ltd, Arapuni Hydro-Electric Scheme, NZ, 1924-27; Public Works Dept, NSW, 1928; First Asst to Resident Engineer, Metropolitan Water, Sewerage and Drainage Board, Sydney, NSW, 1928-30; Sir Alexander Gibb & Partners, London, Engineer-in-charge of construction work, Galloway (Scotland) Hydro-Electric Scheme, 1931-36; Metropolitan Water, Sewerage and Drainage Board, Sydney: Resident Engineer in charge of construction, Woronora Dam, 1937; Inspecting Engineer and Chief Construction Engineer, 1938-43; Engineer-in-Chief, 1948-49. Coronation Medal, 1953. Australasian Engineer Award for 1957 and Kernot Memorial Medal for Distinguished Engineering Achievement in Australia, 1959. Fellow University Coll., London, 1961-; Hon. Fellow, Royal Inst. of Architects, Australia, 1968. Hon. Member: Australasian Inst. of Mining and Metallurgy, 1961; Instn of Engrs, Australia, 1962; Instn of Royal Engineers, 1968. Dr of Laws (*hc*) Australian National University, 1962; Hon. Dr of Engineering, Monash Univ., Melbourne, 1968. James Cook Medal (Royal Society NSW), 1966. *Recreation:* yachting. *Address:* 39 Flanagan Street, Garran, ACT 2605, Australia.
[Died 12 Sept. 1978.

HUDSON-DAVIES, Sir Alan (Meredyth), Kt 1975; CBE 1966 (OBE 1946); retired; *b* 23 Jan. 1901; *s* of John and Alice Hudson-Davies; *m* 1st, 1928, Andrea (marr. diss. 1956), *d* of Consul Bernt Reinhardt, Kristiansand, Norway; two *s* one *d*; 2nd, 1956, Marfa, *d* of Fyodor Chaliapin, Paris; two step *d. Educ:* Bancroft's Sch.; King's Coll., Cambridge (Minor Schol.). 1st cl. hons Nat. Sci. Tripos Pt I, BA Cantab 1923. Nat. Inst. of Industrial Psychology, 1924-27; Asst Commercial Man., ICI Billingham, 1927-33; Dir and Works Man., H. P. Bulmer & Co.

Ltd, 1933-41; Chm. Birmingham Man-Power Bd, Min. of Lab. and Nat. Service, 1941-46; Man. Dir 1946, Chm. 1964, Fibreglass Ltd; Dir, Pilkington Bros Ltd, 1951-71. Mem. Reconstruction Cttee, Birmingham CC, W Midland Gp for Post War Planning, 1943-46; Chm., Instn of Works Managers, 1961; Chm., NHS Adv. Cttee on Management Efficiency, 1962-66; Chm. Bd of Governors, United Liverpool Hosps, 1967-74; Mem. Univ of Liverpool Court and Council, 1951-73. Hon. LLD Liverpool, 1974. FIWM, FIBM. *Recreations:* arts, books, building. *Address:* 8 Grosvenor Road, Liverpool L19 0PL. *T:* 051-427 1236. *Club:* Athenæum. [*Died 14 Sept. 1975.*

HUDSPETH, Major Henry Moore, DSO 1918; MC; MSc; FInstD; *b* 10 May 1886; *s* of J. W. Hudspeth, Willington, Durham; *m* 1919, *o d* of T. S. Gill, Doncaster; one *s* two *d. Educ:* King James Grammar Sch., Bishop Auckland; Armstrong Coll., Newcastle. Mining Apprenticeship with R. L. Weeks, Durham; County Council Senior Exhibitioner at Armstrong Coll.; Daglish Fellow abroad in France and Germany; Colliery Under-manager; Asst Agent; HM Inspector of Mines, Leeds and Doncaster; Officer RE, 3+ years in Belgium (despatches); HM Senior Inspector of Mines in West Scotland; HM Divisional Inspector of Mines, Yorks; Witness before Subsidence Commission; Assessor, Royal Commission Coal Industry, 1925; Chief Mining Engineer and Mem. of the Safety in Mines Research Board; HM Deputy Chief Inspector of Mines; Joint Managing Dir Airedale Collieries Ltd; T. & R. W. Bower Limited; Dir Glass Houghton and Castleford Collieries, Ltd; Pontefract Collieries Ltd; Yorkshire Coking and Chemical Co. Ltd; Deputy Dir of Production, North Eastern Division, National Coal Board; Deputy Chm. South Wales District Valuation Board; Past Pres. Midland Institute of Mining Engineers. Retired Mining Engineer. *Publications:* Electricity at Shamrock Colliery, Germany; Electric Winding; joint author Magnitude and Variation of Haulage Loads; Forces induced by the Extraction of Coal, and some of their effects on Coal Measure Strata, The Léon-Montluçon Firedamp Detector, Trans. Inst. Min. E. *Recreation:* golf. *Address:* Meads Way, Chesterfield Road, Eastbourne. [*Died 19 Sept. 1971.*

HUFTON, Philip Arthur, CB 1969; Deputy Director, Royal Aircraft Establishment, 1966-73; *b* 13 Oct. 1911; *s* of Mr and Mrs J. W. Hufton, Widnes, Lancs. *Educ:* Wade Deacon Grammar Sch., Widnes; Manchester Univ. MSc 1934. Joined Royal Aircraft Establishment, 1934; Superintendent of Performance, Aircraft and Armament Establishment, Boscombe Down, 1947; Head of Aerodynamics Dept, RAE, 1959-66. British Gold Medal for Aeronautics, 1970. *Publications:* Reports and Memoranda of the Aeronautical Research Council. *Address:* The Old Coach House, The Old Manor, Hartley Wintney, Hants. *T:* Hartley Wintney 2120.
[*Died 11 Nov. 1974.*

HUGESSEN; see Knatchbull-Hugessen.

HUGGINS, Sir John, GCMG, *cr* 1949 (KCMG, *cr* 1943; CMG 1939); MC; *b* 17 Sept. 1891; *s* of late William Huggins; *m* 1st, 1929, Molly (marriage dissolved, 1958), *d* of Charles Francis Joseph Green; three *d*; 2nd, 1958, Mrs Margaret Hitchcock. *Educ:* Bridlington Sch.; Leeds Univ. Served European War, 1914-19; Capt., Yorks Regt; active service, Gallipoli, Egypt, France (despatches, MC); Malayan CS, 1920-38; held various appointments in that Service, including Private Sec. to Governor of Straits Settlements and High Commissioner for Malay States, 1926-27; Acting Malayan Establishment Officer, 1934-38; Colonial Sec., Trinidad, 1938-42; Governor's Deputy, Sept.-Nov. 1938; Acting Governor, 1938-39, 1941, and 1942; Head of British Colonies Supply Mission, Washington, 1942-43; Captain-General and Governor-in-Chief of Jamaica, 1943-51. KStJ 1945. *Recreations:* cricket, tennis, golf. *Address:* Fieldway, West Strand, West Wittering, Sussex. [*Died 2 June 1971.*

HUGH-JONES, Evan Bonnor, CB 1953; MC 1915; *b* 1890; *s* of Ll. Hugh-Jones, CBE, Wrexham; *m* 1st, 1918, Elsie M. Iggulden (*d* 1950); one *s* one *d*; 2nd, 1952, Maud, *widow* of Thomas Lundon, MP. *Educ:* Oundle; McGill Univ., Montreal. Major in Royal Engineers, European War (despatches twice, MC); Chief Engineer (Roads), Ministry of Transport 1949-54, retired. *Address:* 1 Clavering Walk, Cooden, Sussex. *T:* Cooden 4210.
[*Died 8 Nov. 1978.*

HUGHES, Arthur Montague D'Urban, MA; Emeritus Professor, University of Birmingham, since 1940; *b* Worthing, Sussex, 3 Nov. 1873; *s* of Rev. Edwin M. M. Hughes, Curate of St Thomas, Exeter, and Margaret Ann Richmond; *m* 1906, Wilhelmina Langenheim, Kiel, Germany; one *d. Educ:* St Edmund's Sch., Canterbury; St John's Coll., Oxford (Classical Scholar, Second Class Moderations, First Class Lit. Hum.).

Lecturer for Oxford Univ. Extension Delegacy; English Lektor, Univ. of Kiel, 1905-14; Mem. of Staff, Oxford Univ. Press, 1915-21; Lecturer in English Literature, Birmingham Univ., 1921-31; Lectr St John's Coll., Oxford, 1923-29; Reader in English, Birmingham Univ., 1931-35; Prof. of English Language and Literature, University of Birmingham, 1935-39. *Publications:* The Nascent Mind of Shelley, 1947, repr. 1970; Editions: Carlyle's Past and Present, Shelley's Poems, 1820, Tennyson's Poems, 1842, and several volumes in Clarendon English Series. *Recreation:* walking. *Address:* 42 Weoley Hill, Selly Oak, Birmingham. *T:* 021-472 0371. [*Died 11 Jan. 1974.*

HUGHES, G(eorge) Bernard, FRSA; author; formerly Editor-in-Chief of The Queen; *o s* of late Charles Bernard Hughes, Heath Town, and Lydia, *o d* of William Shepherd, Lane Head, Staffs; *m* Therle Marguerite Conway, *o d* of C. Conway Plumbe, BSc; two *s. Educ:* Wolverhampton Sch. Volunteered for active service; served with 1st Royal Marine Batt. at Arras, Paschendaele and Cambrai, 1916-19; HM Inspector of Factories, 1940-45. *Publications:* The Story of the Locomotive; The Circus; Dry Batteries, 1940; Modern Industrial Lighting, 1941; Collecting Antiques, 1949; More About Collecting Antiques, 1952; Living Crafts, 1953; Old English, Scottish and Irish Table Glass, 1956; Horse Brasses and Other Curios, 1956; Small Antique Silverware, 1957; English Glass for the Collector, 1958; Victorian Pottery and Porcelain, 1959; English and Scottish Earthenware, 1960; English Pottery and Porcelain Figures, 1964; Country Life Collector's Pocket Book of China, 1965; Antique Sheffield Plate, 1970; Old English Snuff-Boxes, 1971. (With Therle Hughes): English Painted Enamels, 1950; Three Centuries of English Domestic Silver, 1952 and After the Regency, 1952; Old English Porcelain and Bone China, 1955; The Collector's Encyclopædia of English Ceramics, 1956; Small Antique Furniture, 1958; Country Life Collector's Pocket Book, 1963; Collecting Miniature Antiques, 1973. Contributions to: Encyclopædia Britannica; The Connoisseur Concise Encyclopædia of Antiques, vols 1 to 5; The Connoisseur Period Guides, 1956, 1957; Country Life; The Connoisseur; Apollo. *Address:* Fairlight House, Hythe, Kent. *T:* Hythe 67512.
[*Died 2 Aug. 1975.*

HUGHES, Guy Erskine, CMG 1949; *b* 7 March 1904; *s* of late Major C. G. E. Hughes, the Cheshire Regt, and Florence, *d* of late S. A. Waters, sometime of Royal Irish Constabulary; *m* 1930, June, *d* of Donald Spicer, Ghent; three *s* one *d. Educ:* Harrow Sch.; Trinity Coll., Cambridge. Messrs Mather & Platt, Ltd; apprentice engineer, 1925-28; ICI Ltd, 1928-35; Messrs Ed. Sharp & Sons, Ltd; Dir, 1935-39. Served War of 1939-45, in RNVR; demobilised as Temp. Comdr RNVR (Sp.), 1945. Chief, Food, Agriculture and Forestry, CCG, 1946; Overseas Food Corp., Urambo, 1950. Managing Dir, Imperial Chemical Industries (South Africa) Ltd, 1952-58; Managing Dir, African Explosives and Chemical Industries Ltd, 1958-66. *Recreation:* fly-fishing. *Address:* Waterbank, Norham, Berwick upon Tweed. *Clubs:* Boodle's; Rand, Country (Johannesburg).
[*Died 8 Jan. 1980.*

HUGHES, H(ugh) L(lewelyn) Glyn, CBE 1945; DSO 1916; MC; MRCS, LRCP; FRCGP; Director, South East London General Practitioner Centre, 1958-68; Senior Administrative Medical Officer, South-East Metropolitan Regional Hospital Board, 1947-57; President Harveian Society, 1947; President, Casualties Union, since 1953; Secretary and Secretary, Research Committee, Medical Council on Alcoholism, 1969-71; Foundation Member, Hon. Treasurer, 1952-65, and Hon. Fellow, Royal College of General Practitioners; Vice-President (Hon. Secretary 1940-41) Medical Society of London; *b* 25 July 1892; *s* of Dr H. G. Hughes, formerly of Ventersburg, ORC; *m* 1920, Armorel Anselma Swynford-, *o d* of late T. Rought Jones, East Grinstead; one *s* two *d*; *m* 1949, Thelma Marion, *d* of Edward Pembroke, Eltham, Kent. *Educ:* Epsom Coll.; University Coll. Hosp., London (Scholar); Carr Exhibition, matric. 1st Class; Fellowes Medal for Clinical Medicine, 1914. Asst Physician Child Welfare Dept, University Coll. Hosp.; House Physician and House Surg. University Coll. Hosp., Asst Surg. Cheltenham Eye, Ear and Throat Hosp.; Obstetric Asst University Coll. Hosp. Served European War, 1914-18 (DSO and bar, MC, despatches, Croix de Guerre avec palme). Attached 1st Wilts, 1915-18; Grenadier Guards, 1918-19; War of 1939-45 (despatches, CBE, 2nd bar to DSO), Comdr Legion of Merit, US, OStJ. ADMS Guards Armoured Div.; Brig. DDMS VIII Corps; Brig. DDMS 2nd Army; Vice-Dir Medical Services BAOR, 1945; Comdt Depot RAMC, 1945-47; Inspector of Training, 1946-47; Hon. Col RAMC. Pres. The Bridge in Britain, 1967. Pres. Barbarian Football Club; Pres. Blackheath Football Club, 1930-55, 1970-71. Treasurer, Epsom Coll. *Publications:* Peace at the Last, 1960; Death (contrib. to Encyclopedia of General Practice), 1964. *Recreations:* Rugby

Football, golf, rifle-shooting. *Address:* 17 Cadogan Square, SW1. *T:* 01-235 5161. *Clubs:* Army and Navy, Pratt's; Royal and Ancient (St Andrews); Royal St George's; Pine Valley (USA). *[Died 24 Nov. 1973.*

HUGHES, John Turnbull, OBE 1959; Information Adviser, Civil Service Department, since 1970; *b* 8 June 1919; *s* of Maurice and Helen Hughes. *Educ:* City Grammar Sch., Chester; Liverpool Univ., Officer, 2nd King Edward VII's Own Gurkha Rifles, 1940-46. Private Sec. to Governor of Bengal, 1945-46; Commonwealth Office, 1947-67; Chief Information Officer, Civil Service Comnn, 1967. *Recreations:* theatre, walking, painting. *Address:* 15 Sackville Gardens, Hove, East Sussex BN3 4GJ. *T:* Brighton 777800. *Club:* Garrick.
[Died 25 April 1977.

HUGHES, Joseph John; Hon. Mr Justice Hughes; Judge of the Supreme Court of Zambia (formerly the Court of Appeal for Zambia), since 1971; *b* Dublin, 29 April 1928; *s* of Michael Joseph Hughes and Norah Mary Hughes (*née* Breen); *m* 1955, Maeve Swords; three *d*. *Educ:* O'Connell Sch., Dublin; Incorporated Law Soc. of Ireland Law Sch.; University Coll., Dublin. Solicitor of the Supreme Court, Ireland, 1950; Solicitor and Barrister, High Court for Zambia, 1966; Solicitor of the Supreme Court in England, 1969. Northern Rhodesia: Resident Magistrate, 1958; Dep. Registrar of the High Court, 1962; Sen. Resident Magistrate, 1964. Zambia: Registrar of the High Court, 1968; Actg Puisne Judge, High Court, 1969, Puisne Judge, 1970. *Recreations:* travel, golf. *Address:* Judge's Chambers, The Supreme Court, PO Box RW 67, Ridgeway, Lusaka, Zambia. *T:* (chambers) 51577; (residence) 51447. *Clubs:* Challoner, Irish (London); Jockey Club Zambia; Wild Geese Society of Zambia. *[Died 4 June 1976.*

HUGHES, Richard (Arthur Warren), OBE 1946; DLitt (*honoris causa*) University of Wales, 1956; FRSL; Hon. Member, American Academy of Arts and Letters and National Institute of Arts and Letters (Blashfield Foundation Address, 1969); author; *b* 1900; *s* of Arthur Hughes and Louisa Warren; *m* 1932, Frances, 2nd *d* of late Gardner S. Bazley and Mrs Francis Cadogan, Hatherop Castle, Fairford, Glos; two *s* three *d*. *Educ:* Charterhouse; Oriel Coll., Oxford (Hon. Fellow 1975). First play, The Sisters' Tragedy, produced London, 1922; contributor to London and American literary journals; co-founder of the Portmadoc Players; A Comedy of Good and Evil, produced London, 1925; also first author in the world of wireless plays; Vice-Chm. (till 1936) of the Welsh National Theatre; Petty-Constable of Laugharne, 1936. Served in Admiralty, 1940-45 (OBE). *Publications:* Gipsy-Night, and other Poems, 1922; The Sisters' Tragedy, 1922; The Sisters' Tragedy, and other Plays (The Sisters' Tragedy, The Man Born to be Hanged, A Comedy of Good and Evil, Danger), 1924; Poems by John Skelton (edited), 1924; A Moment of Time (Collected Stories), 1926; Confessio Juvenis (Collected Poems), 1926; Plays, 1928; A High Wind in Jamaica (The Innocent Voyage), 1929 (filmed 1965); The Spider's Palace (children's stories), 1931; In Hazard, 1938; Don't Blame Me (children's stories), 1940; Volume in Official History of the War (Civil Series); The Administration of War Production (with J. D. Scott), 1956; The Fox in the Attic (Vol. I of the Human Predicament), 1961; Gertrude's Child (children's story), 1966; Gertrude and the Mermaid (children's story), 1971; The Wooden Shepherdess (Vol. II of The Human Predicament), 1973; *posthumous publication:* In the Lap of Atlas: stories of Morocco, 1979. *Recreations:* sailing, travel. *Address:* c/o Chatto & Windus, 40-42 William IV Street, WC2. *Clubs:* Pratt's, United Oxford & Cambridge University, Garrick, Beefsteak; Royal Welsh Yacht (Caernarvon). *[Died 28 April 1976.*

HUGHES, Thomas Lewis, CBE 1943; *b* 27 July 1897; *s* of late R. D. Hughes; *m* 1927, Helen Mary Beynon; three *s*. *Educ:* Birkenhead Sch. Served European War, 1915-18 (France); Indian Army, 1918-22; Indian Civil Service, Burma, 1923-39; Political Sec. to Burma Chamber of Commerce, 1939-42; despatches; Sec. to Governor of Burma, 1942-46; Treasury, 1948-50. Mem. for Stoke Poges, Eton RDC, 1958-74. Hon. Sec. Stoke Poges Golf Club, 1955-62. *Address:* Redwood Cottage, Stoke Poges, Bucks. *T:* Farnham Common 2383. *Club:* East India, Devonshire, Sports and Public Schools.
[Died 13 Oct. 1980.

HUGHES, Rt. Rev. William James, DD; Rector of Port Burwell, Ontario, Canada, 1970-76; *m* 1958, Ada Maud Baker. *Educ:* College of Resurrection, Mirfield, University of Leeds (BA 1919). Hon. DD Leeds, 1947; DD Lambeth 1958. Deacon, 1921; Priest, 1922; Vicar of St Benedict, Bordesley, 1927-30; Rector of St George's Cathedral, Georgetown, Guiana, 1930-44; Sub-Dean, 1930-37; Dean, 1937-44; Bishop of British Honduras, 1944-45; Bishop of Barbados, 1945-51; resigned, 1951; Vicar of

St George, Edgbaston, and Assistant Bishop of Birmingham, 1951-53; Hon. Canon, Birmingham Cathedral, 1952-53; Bishop of Matabeleland, 1953-61; Archbishop of Central Africa, 1957-61; Bishop of Trinidad and Tobago, 1961-70. Formerly MLC Barbados. Sub-Prelate, Order of St John of Jerusalem, 1958. *Publication:* Think Again, 1947. *Address:* RR2, Vienna, Ont NOJ 1Z0, Canada. *[Died 5 Dec. 1979.*

HUGHES-HALLETT, Vice-Adm. John, CB 1945; DSO 1942; Royal Navy, retired; *b* 1 Dec. 1901; *s* of late Col Wyndham Hughes-Hallett; unmarried. *Educ:* Bedford Sch.; Osborne and Dartmouth; Gonville and Caius Coll., Cambridge. Midshipman in HMS Lion, May 1918; Norwegian campaign, 1940, in HMS Devonshire (despatches); Naval Comdr at Dieppe Raid (DSO); Commodore Commanding Channel Assault Force and Naval Chief of Staff (X), 1942 and 1943; Capt. of HMS Jamaica, Dec. 1943; in command of HMS Vernon, 1946-48 and of HMS Illustrious, 1948-49; Vice-Controller of the Navy, 1950-52; Flag Officer, Heavy Sqdn, Home Fleet, 1952-53; retired in Sept. 1954 on adoption as Conservative candidate. MP (C) East Croydon, 1954-55, North-East (constituency altered), 1955-64; British Representative at the Council of Europe, 1958-60; Parliamentary Sec. to the Ministry of Transport for Shipping and Shipbuilding, 1961-64. Gov. Westminster Hosp., 1957-60. Consultant Dir, British Shippers' Council, 1964-69. W Sussex CC, 1969-70. *Address:* New House, Slindon, Arundel, Sussex. *T:* Slindon 274. *[Died 5 April 1972.*

HUGHES-ONSLOW, Sir Geoffrey Henry, KBE 1959; DSC 1918; Lord Lieutenant of Ayrshire, 1950-69; *b* 28 Oct. 1893; *s* of Major Arthur Hughes-Onslow, 10th Hussars, and Anne Kathleen Whitehead; *m* 1918, Hon. Eileen Mabel Lowther Crofton, *d* of 4th Baron Crofton; four *d*. *Educ:* Cheam; RN Colls, Osborne and Dartmouth. Served in RN until 1920, retiring with rank of Lieut; War of 1939-45, in RN, as Lieut-Comdr and Comdr. Mem. Ayrshire CC 1922-55; Convener, 1949-55. Succeeded to estate of Alton Albany on death of father in 1914, now farms a large part of the estate. *Recreations:* shooting, fishing, ornithology. *Address:* Alton Albany, Barr, Ayrshire. *T:* Barr 228. *Clubs:* Naval and Military; New (Edinburgh). *[Died 27 Nov. 1971.*

HUGHES PARRY, Sir David; *see* Parry.

HULBERT, Dame Cicely; *see* Courtneidge, Dame Cicely.

HULBERT, Jack; actor, dramatic author, manager, producer; *b* Ely, 24 April 1892; *s* of Dr H. H. Hulbert; *m* Cicely Courtneidge (Dame Cicely Courtneidge, DBE); one *d*. *Educ:* Westminster; Gonville and Caius Coll., Cambridge. First appearance on professional stage, in The Pearl Girl, Shaftesbury Theatre, 1913; played in: Bubbly and Hullo Paris in Paris, 1919; Bran Pie; Little Dutch Girl; Pot Luck. Produced: The Blue Train; prod. and played in: By the Way, London and New York; Lido Lady; Clowns in Clover; The House that Jack Built; Follow a Star; prod. Folly to be Wise. Spent 10 years in *films:* Ghost Train; Sunshine Susie; Jack's the Boy; Jack Ahoy; Bulldog Jack; Jack of all Trades; Falling for You, etc.; Produced and played in: Under your Hat; Something in the Air; Full Swing (Palace Theatre); prod. Under the Counter; prod. and played in Here come the Boys; prod. and played for TV: Here come the Boys; Cinderella; Dick Whittington; The Golden Year; played in Hulbert Follies; Housemaster; Smith; The Squeaker; The White Sheep of the Family; prod. Gay's the Word; played in: The Reluctant Debutante; The Bride Comes Back; The Spider's Web; Let's Be Frank; The Amorous Prawn; Dear Octopus, etc. Served European War, 1917-19. Commandant in Special Constabulary, 1940-57. *Publication:* The Little Woman's Always Right (autobiog.), 1975. *Address:* c/o Herbert de Leon Ltd, Fielding House, 13 Bruton Street, W1X 8JY. *[Died 25 March 1978.*

HULBERT, Wing Comdr Sir Norman (John), Kt 1955; DL; *b* 1903; *s* of late Norman Hulbert; *m* 1938, Eileen Pearl, MB, BChir, JP (marr. diss., 1960), *d* of late Dr Gretton-Watson, London; two *d*; *m* 1966, Eliette, *d* of Baron F. G. von Tschirschky und Boegendorff, CVO, Salzburg. *Educ:* Cranbrook; Tonbridge. Served RN Transport, 1918; served in an operational cmd of RAF, 1939-43; British Liaison officer with Polish Forces in Gt Britain, 1943-45. Mem. LCC, East Islington, 1934-37; MP (C) Stockport, 1935-50, North Div. of Stockport, 1950-64; PPS to Pres. of Board of Trade and Minister of Production, 1944-45; Mem. of House of Commons Select Cttee on Estimates, 1945-50; Temp. Chm. of House of Commons and Chm. of Standing Cttees, 1950-64; Freeman of City of London; Liveryman: Shipwright's Co.; Guild of Air Pilots and Navigators. Hon. Col 461 HAA Regt RA (TA), 1952-55; DL Middlesex, 1952-65; DL London, 1965. Order of Polonia Restituta, 1945. *Address:* The Priory, Dorchester-on-Thames,

Oxon. *T:* Warborough 249. *Clubs:* Carlton, Press, Royal Automobile, United Service & Royal Aero. *[Died* 1 *June* 1972.

HULL, Sir Hubert, Kt 1959; CBE 1945; *b* 10 Sept. 1887; 2nd *s* of Robert Hull, Preston, Lancs; *m* 1915, Judith, *e d* of P. F. S. Stokes, Barrister-at-Law; two *s* four *d. Educ:* Stonyhurst. Called to Bar, Inner Temple, 1910; Bencher 1945. Temp. Civil Servant, 1914-19, Junior Counsel to Ministry of Agriculture and Fisheries and Commissioners of Crown Lands; temp. Civil Servant, 1939-48, Asst Procurator-Gen.; an Official Referee of Supreme Court, 1949-50; Mem. Royal Commission on Press, 1947. Pres. of Transport Tribunal, 1951-62. Officer Order of Oranje Nassau, 1949. *Publications:* legal only. *Recreations:* walking and housework. *Address:* 59 Campden Hill Road, Kensington, W8. *T:* 01-937 5503. *Club:* Reform.
[Died 24 *March* 1976.

HULLAH-BROWN, J., MusBac (Dunelm), LRAM, ARCM, ARCO, AMusTCL; Professor of Music; *b* 8 Oct. 1875; *s* of James Conway Brown; *m* 1923, Hilda May Chatfield; one *d. Educ:* Farnham; privately; self-taught in music and art. Organist and choir-master, Cobham (Surrey) Parish Church, 1899-1906; Music and Art Master, Sandroyd Preparatory Sch., Cobham; Active Service, 1914-19; private teacher, lecturer (Music and Art). *Publications:* Water-Colour Guidance; Sketching Without a Master, and other works on Art; Technique of the Fiddle Bow; Children's Violin Books; Violin Glissando; Peter Pan Class Violin Tutor; Bow-craft Series, Concertinos, and other musical works. Author of the Violinda method and books. *Address:* Matatoki Road, RD1 Thames, New Zealand.
[Died 17 *Feb.* 1973.

HULME-MOIR, Rt. Rev. Francis Oag, AO 1976; ED 1949; Bishop to the Australian Armed Forces, since 1965, and Chaplain-General (CE), Australian Army, since 1974; *b* 30 Jan. 1910; 2nd *s* of Alexander Hugh and Violet Beryl Hulme-Moir; *m* 1937, Ena Dorothy Smee; two *s* one *d. Educ:* Moore Theological Coll.; Sydney Univ. ThL, ACT, 1935. Deacon, 1936; Priest, 1937. Chaplain to Forces, 1936; Chaplain, AIF, 1939-45 (despatches, 1944); Dep. Asst Chaplain-Gen., 1942; Asst Chaplain-Gen., 1945; Senior Chaplain, NSW, 1946; Archdeacon of Ryde, 1947; Archdeacon of Cumberland, 1950; Bishop of Nelson, New Zealand, 1954-65; Coadjutor Bishop and Dean of Sydney, 1965-67; Coadjutor Bishop, Northern Region, 1968; Sen. Asst Bishop of Sydney, 1967-75. Senior Anglican Chaplain to all NZ Services, 1959-64; Chaplain to NSW Police Force, 1965. ChStJ 1975. *Recreations:* golf, gardening, fishing. *Address:* 15 Acacia Street, Collaroy Plateau, NSW 2098, Australia. *Clubs:* Union, Tattersall's, Australasian Pioneers (all Sydney); Royal Sydney Motor Yacht. *[Died* 10 *March* 1979.

HULTON-HARROP, Maj.-Gen. William Harrington, CB 1959; DSO 1944; General Officer Commanding Catterick Area, 1959, retired; *b* 7 May 1906; *s* of Hugh de Lacy Hulton-Harrop and Delitia Mary (*née* Hulton); *m* 1937, Pamela Scholefield; one *d. Educ:* Charterhouse; RMA Sandhurst. 2nd Lieut KSLI, 1926; served War of 1939-45, N Africa, Sicily, Italy and Palestine. Lieut-Col 1942; Brig. 1949; Maj.-Gen. 1957; Commander 50th Division (TA) and Northumbrian District, 1956. *Address:* The Old Forge, Vernham Dean, Andover, Hants; c/o Lloyds Bank, 6 Pall Mall, SW1. *[Died* 29 *June* 1979.

HUMBLE, Prof. Joseph Graeme, CVO 1955; Hon. Consulting Haematologist, Westminster Hospital, since 1978; *b* 10 July 1913; 2nd *s* of late Wensley Taylor Humble and late Louisa Ann (*née* Witham), Mansfield, Notts; *m* 1942, Elsie May (Anne), *d* of late A. Hunt, Mendlesham, Suffolk; three *s* (and two *s* decd). *Educ:* Bedford Modern Sch.; Westminster Hosp. Med. Sch., University of London. MRCS, LRCP 1937, MRCP 1959, FRCPath 1955, FRCP 1970. Westminster Hospital: House Physician Children's Dept, 1937-38; Junior Asst Pathologist, 1938-39; Acting Asst Pathologist and Temp. Lecturer in Pathology and Bacteriology, 1939-46; Haematologist, 1946-49; Hon. Consultant Haematologist, 1949-78; Reader, 1965-72, Professor of Haematology, 1972-78, Westminster Med. Sch., Univ. of London, Professor Emeritus, 1978-. Member: Royal Society of Medicine; London Med. Soc. *Publications:* Westminster Hospital 1716-1966: a history, 1966, 2nd edn, Westminster Hospital, 1716-1974, 1974; various articles in Med. Jls. *Recreations:* cricket, golf, history. *Address:* Tree Shadows, Roman Road, Dorking, Surrey. *T:* Dorking 5296.
[Died 10 *June* 1980.

HUME, Basil; *see* Hume, John Basil.

HUME, John Basil, MS, FRCS; Consulting Surgeon, St Bartholomew's Hospital; Surgeon St Andrew's Hospital, Dollis Hill; Member of Senate, University of London, Deputy Vice-Chancellor, 1965; Member of Board of Governors of St Bartholomew's Hospital; *b* 1893; *s* of David Hume, Whitby, Yorks; *m* 1925, Marjorie Poole; four *d. Educ:* Bootham Sch., York; St Bartholomew's Hospital (Brackenbury Scholar, Kirkes Gold Medal and Luther Holden Scholar). Captain RAMC (SR) during European War, served in German East Africa; subsequently Hunterian Professor: Examiner for Royal College of Surgeons; Lecturer in Anatomy and Surgery at St Bartholomew's Hospital. *Publications:* many articles in medical journals. *Recreation:* fly-fishing. *Address:* 73 Southway, NW11 6SB. *T:* 01-455 5041. *[Died* 2 *March* 1974.

HUME-WILLIAMS, Sir Roy Ellis, 2nd Bt, *cr* 1922; *b* 31 July 1887; *s* of Rt Hon. Sir Ellis Hume-Williams, 1st Bt, PC, KBE, KC; *S* father, 1947; *m* 1st, 1915, Norah (marr. diss., 1949, she *d* 1964), *y d* of late David Anderson, Sydney, NSW; 2nd, 1949, Frances Mary (Molly), *er d* of Major Arthur Groom, OBE, Warham Wells, Norfolk. *Educ:* Eton; Trinity Hall, Cambridge. Cons. Engineer, 1910-14. Served in European War, 1914-19; retired with rank of Captain, RASC. Schoolmaster, 1920-48. *Recreations:* cricket, hockey, tennis, golf, skating. *Heir:* none. *Address:* Ardlui, The Highlands, East Horsley, Surrey. *Clubs:* Royal Automobile, MCC. *[Died* 30 *Aug.* 1980 (*ext*).

HUMPHREY, Marshal of the Royal Air Force Sir Andrew (Henry), GCB 1974 (KCB 1968; CB 1959); OBE 1951; DFC 1941; AFC 1943 (and two bars, 1945, 1955); Chief of the Defence Staff, since 1976; *b* 10 Jan. 1921; *m* 1952, Agnes Stevenson, *yr d* of late James Wright and of Mrs Marjorie Wright. *Educ:* Bradfield Coll.; RAF Coll. Cranwell. RAF service since 1940, both at home and overseas. Made record flight, Cape Town to London, 1953; first RAF jet flight to N Pole, 1954. Station Commander, Royal Air Force, Akrotiri, Cyprus, 1959-61; Imperial Defence Coll., 1962; Dir of Defence Plans, Air, at Ministry of Defence, 1962-65; AOC Air Forces Middle East, 1965-68 (despatches); Air Member for Personnel, 1968-70; AOC-in-C, RAF Strike Comd, 1971-74; Comdr UK Air Defence Region (NATO), 1971-74; Chief of the Air Staff, 1974-76. Air ADC to the Queen, 1974-76. *Address:* The Old School House, Evenlode, Moreton-in-Marsh, Glos. *Clubs:* Athenæum, Royal Air Force. *[Died* 24 *Jan.* 1977.

HUMPHREY, Senator Hubert Horatio, Jr; United States Senator from Minnesota (Democrat), 1949-64 and since 1970; Deputy President of the Senate, since 1977; Member Board, Encyclopædia Britannica, Inc., since 1959; *b* Wallace, South Dakota, USA, 27 May 1911; *s* of Hubert Horatio Humphrey; *m* 1936, Muriel Fay Buck; three *s* one *d. Educ:* Denver Coll. of Pharmacy; University of Minnesota (AB) and Louisiana State Univ. (AM). State Dir, War Production Training and Re-employment Div., 1941-42; Asst Regional Dir, War Manpower Commn, 1943; Professor of Political Science, Macalester Coll., Minnesota, 1943-44; Radio News Commentator, 1944-45; Mayor, City of Minneapolis, 1945-48; US Senate Asst Majority Leader, 1961-64; Vice-President of the US, 1965-69. Jt Prof., Macalester Coll. at St Paul and Univ. of Minnesota at Minneapolis, 1969-70. American delegate to UN, 1956-57. Member: Phi Beta Kappa; Delta Sigma Rho; Amer. Polit. Sci. Assoc. Holds many honorary degrees. Democrat. *Publications:* The Cause is Mankind, 1964; The War On Poverty, 1964; School Desegregation: Documents and Commentaries, 1964; The Political Philosophy of the New Deal, 1970; The Education of a Public Man, 1977. *Address:* Waverley, Minnesota 55390, USA; 350 North Street SW, Washington, DC 20024, USA.
[Died 13 *Jan.* 1978.

HUMPHREYS, Humphrey Francis, CBE 1957 (OBE 1928); MC; TD; LLD (Birmingham and Glasgow), MB, ChB; MDS; FDS England; Hon. FDS RCSE, Hon. FRSM 1971; FSA; Hon. Colonel RAMC (TA); DL, Co. Warwickshire; *b* 19 June 1885; *s* of John Humphreys, MA, PhD, FSA, and Frances Lisseter; *m* 1920, Constance Evelyn Hudson; two *s. Educ:* Bromsgrove School; Birmingham University (Scholar); Harvard University, USA. In RAMC TA, 1914-49; served European War, 1914-18, staff (despatches 3 times, MC); raised 1939 and commanded 1939-45, 14th General Hospital RAMC TA, UK, France, India, SE Asia; Hon. Phys. to the King, 1934-49; Professor of Dental Surgery, 1935-52; Vice-Principal, University of Birmingham, 1949-52; Vice-Chancellor, Univ. of Birmingham, 1952-53; President: Birmingham Archæological Society, 1953-58; Midland Medical Soc., 1954-55; Birmingham Nat. Hist. Soc., 1953-55; Section of Odontology RSM 1947-48; late Examiner to RCS and Univs Bristol and Sheffield; late member: Birmingham Regional Hospital Board; advisory committees to University Grants Committee, Medical Research Council, Nuffield Hospitals Trust, Ministry of Health. *Publications:* Text Book of Surgery for Dental Students; numerous articles in medical, dental, and archæological periodicals. *Recreations:* gardening, archæology. *Address:* Church Farm, Hampton in Arden, Warwickshire. *T:* Hampton in Arden 2607. *Club:* Union (Birmingham). *[Died* 21 *March* 1977.

HUMPHREYS-DAVIES, Brian, CB 1964; Assistant Under-Secretary of State, Ministry of Defence, since 1964 (Air Ministry, 1956-64); *b* 18 Feb. 1917; *y s* of late J. W. S. Humphreys-Davies, Southfields, Eastbourne; *m* 1948, Gillian *d* of late Major Colin Cooper, Barnwell Castle, Northants; one *s* one *d. Educ:* Sherborne; Balliol Coll., Oxford. Asst Principal, Air Ministry, 1938; served War of 1939-45, RA: BEF, 1939-40; British North Africa Force, 1943; Haifa Staff Coll., 1943; 40th Indian Inf. Bde, 1944; Control Commission for Germany, 1944-45, Lieut-Col 1945. Rejoined Air Ministry, 1945; Private Sec. to Chief of Air Staff, 1946-48; Imperial Defence Coll., 1955. Trustee, Imperial War Museum, 1968-. *Address:* c/o National Westminster Bank, Eastbourne, Sussex. *Club:* Reform.
[Died 14 *March* 1971.

HUMPHRYS, Lt-Col Sir Francis Henry, GCMG 1932 (KCMG 1929); GCVO 1928; KBE 1924; CIE [)]'; formerly of Charlton Park, Canterbury; *b* 24 April 1879; *e s* of late Rev. Walter Humphrys, MA, Oxford, and Helen Agnes, *d* of Rev. A. F. Boucher; *m* 1907, Gertrude Mary, DBE 1929, *e d* of Col Sir Harold Arthur Deane, KCSI, First Chief Commissioner, North-West Frontier Province, India; one *s* two *d. Educ:* Shrewsbury; Christ Church, Oxford. Gazetted 2nd Lieut, 2nd Worcestershire Regt 1900; served S African War, 1900-01 (Queen's medal, 3 clasps); held various political appointments on NW Frontier, India, 1904-17; Political Officer with troops, 1917 (despatches); served European War in Europe as pilot, RAF, 1918; Political Agent, Khyber, 1919; Deputy Foreign Sec. to the Government of India, 1921; HBM Envoy Extraordinary and Minister Plenipotentiary at Kabul, 1922-29; High Commissioner and Commander-in-Chief in Iraq, 1929-32; British Ambassador in Baghdad, 1932-35; Chm. British Sugar Corp., 1939-45; Chm. Iraq Petroleum Co., 1941-50; Vice-Chm. Associated Portland Cement Manufacturers, 1936-53; Chairman: Clerical Medical and General Life Assurance Society, 1948-59; Brixton Estates Ltd, 1950-57. Jubilee medal, 1935; Coronation medal, 1937; Order of Sardar-i-ala of Afghanistan, 1928; Grand Cordon Order of Two Rivers, Iraq, 1933. *Recreations:* cricket, shooting, fishing, aviation. *Address:* 4 Whitehall Court, SW1. *Clubs:* MCC, United Service and Royal Aero; Grillions.
[Died 28 *Aug.* 1971.

HUNLOKE, Henry Philip, TD 1946; Lt-Col, Royal Wiltshire Yeomanry; *b* 1906; *o s* of late Major Sir Philip Hunloke, GCVO; *m* 1929, Lady Anne Cavendish (who obtained a divorce, 1945), *d* of 9th Duke of Devonshire, KG; two *s* one *d*; *m* 1945, Virginia Clive (who obtained a divorce, 1972); one *d* (and one *d* decd); *m* 1972, Ruth Holdsworth. MP (U) Western Div. of Derbyshire, 1938-44. Served War of 1939-45 in Middle East (despatches). *Address:* 267 The Green, East Grafton, near Marlborough, Wilts. *[Died* 13 *Jan.* 1978.

HUNT, Surgeon Rear-Adm. Frederick George, CB 1952; CBE 1948; OStJ 1947; Royal Navy; *b* July 1894; *s* of Dr A. M. Hunt, Coolaney, Co. Sligo, Ireland; *m* 1926, Christina Leonard (*d* 1961); no *c. Educ:* Mount St Joseph's, Roscrea, Ireland; National Univ. of Ireland. Qualified MB, BCh, 1917; joined Royal Naval Medical Service: Surgeon Rear-Adm., 1949; KHP 1949; QHP 1952; retired list, 1952. *Recreations:* fishing, bridge. *Address:* The Old Cottage, Burgwallis, near Doncaster, South Yorkshire. *Club:* Royal Automobile. *[Died* 13 *Oct.* 1975.

HUNT, Rear-Adm. Geoffrey Harry C.; *see* Carew Hunt.

HUNT, Col (George) Vivian, OBE 1943; TD 1943; MA 1926; LLB 1928; Senior Partner in Wake Smith and Company, solicitors, Sheffield, retired; *b* 30 July 1905; *er s* of John Edwin Hunt, Crabtree Meadow House, Hope, Derbyshire; *m* 1935, Sylvia Anne, *d* of John Stanley Tyzack, Oakholme House, Sheffield; three *s. Educ:* Malvern Coll.; King's Coll., Cambridge (MA, LLB Hons). Commissioned RA (TA) 1926. Lt-Col 1940; invented Hunt Trainer, 1940; took part in North African, Sicilian and Italian campaigns with 78th Infantry Diviision, 1942-44; reconnoitred and laid out original defences North-East of Beja, Tunisia, which subseq. became known as 'Hunt's Gap'; Col 1944; Hon Col 513 LAA Regt RA (TA), 1947-55; retired from TA, 1956. JP for City of Sheffield, 1956-70. *Recreations:* golf, gardening. *Address:* The Lodge, Woodvale Road, Sheffield S10 3EX. *T:* Sheffield 660017. *Club:* Sheffield (Sheffield).
[Died 11 *Aug.* 1979.

HUNT, Herbert James; Senior Fellow in French, University of Warwick, since 1966; Professor of French Language and Literature, Royal Holloway College, University of London, 1944-66; *b* 2 Aug. 1899; *s* of James Henry and Mary Anne Hunt, Lichfield; *m* 1925, Sheila Jessamine Spielman (*d* 1961); two *s* three *d*; *m* 1963, Queenie Winifred Sundaram. *Educ:* King Edward VI Grammar Sch., Lichfield; Magdalen Coll., Oxford. Asst Master: Imperial Service Coll., Windsor, 1923-25; Durham School, 1925-27. Lectr, Fellow, Tutor, St Edmund Hall, Oxford, 1927-44; Fellow Emeritus 1953. Lecturer: Exeter Coll., Oxford, 1927-44; Jesus Coll., Oxford, 1930-44. *Publications:* Le Socialisme et le romantisme en France, 1935; The Epic in Nineteenth Century France, 1941; Victor Hugo: Légende des siècles (Selection and Annotations), 1944; Honoré de Balzac, a Biography, 1957; Balzac's Comédie Humaine, 1964; (ed) Eugénie Grandet, 1967; trans.: Cousin Pons, 1968; Lost Illusions, 1971; A Murky Business, 1972; The Thirteen, 1973; articles in Mercure de France, Revue d'Histoire Littéraire de la France, Modern Language Review, French Studies, etc. *Address:* Mill Close, Tredington, Shipston-on-Stour, Warwicks. *T:* Shipston 581. *[Died* 2 *Nov.* 1973.

HUNT, John Francis, CBE 1964; Under-Secretary and Controller of Supply, Ministry of Health, 1965-68, retired, 1968; *b* 10 Sept. 1906; *s* of late John William Hunt and late Beatrice (*née* Cass); *m* 1933, Vera Mary (*née* Jenkins) (*d* 1976); three *s. Educ:* Sir John Talbot Grammar Sch., Whitchurch, Shropshire; Liverpool Univ.; London Univ. (External). BSc Liverpool, 1st cl. hons Mathematics, 1928; Derby Scholar, 1928-29; LLB London, 2nd cl. hons (External), 1946. Entered Civil Service (District Audit), 1929; Asst District Auditor, 1929; Sen. Asst 1938; Deputy, 1947; transf. to Accountant-General's Dept, Min. of Health, 1947; Asst Acct-Gen., 1947; Deputy, 1951; Asst Secretary, 1958; Transf. to Supply Div., 1960. Mem. Surrey CC, Dorking North, 1970-77. *Recreations:* reading, walking. *Address:* 13 Glebe Road, Dorking, Surrey. *T:* Dorking 4493. *Club:* Royal Automobile. *[Died* 22 *May* 1979.

HUNT, Richard William, DPhil; FBA 1961; Sub-Librarian and Keeper of Western Manuscripts, Bodleian Library, and Fellow of Balliol College, Oxford, 1945-75; *b* 11 April 1908; *m* 1942, Katharine Eva Rowland (*d* 1977); three *s. Educ:* Haileybury Coll.; Balliol Coll., Oxford. Lecturer in Palaeography, Univ. of Liverpool, 1934; Lectr in Palaeography and Transmission of Classical Latin Texts, Univ. of Oxford, 1948-75; Sandars Reader in Bibliography, Cambridge Univ., 1959-60. *Publications:* articles in learned journals. *Address:* 45 Walton Street, Oxford. *T:* Oxford 57632. *[Died* 13 *Nov.* 1979.

HUNT, Thomas Cecil, CBE 1964; DM Oxford, FRCP, MRCS; Consulting Physician: St Mary's Hospital, Paddington; Royal Masonic Hospital; King Edward VII Hospital for Officers; Examiner in Medicine, Royal College of Physicians and London University; Chairman, The Medical Sickness, Annuity & Life Assurance Society, since 1974; *b* 5 June 1901; *s* of Rev. A. T. G. Hunt; *m* 1930, Barbara, *d* of Egerton Todd, London; one *s* two *d. Educ:* St Paul's Sch.; Magdalen Coll., Oxford (Demy); 1st class hons final Physiology; Theodore Williams Scholarships Anatomy, 1922; Pathology, 1924; Demonstrator and Tutor Physiology, Oxford, 1924-25; Radcliffe Prize Pharmacology, 1924; University Scholar St Mary's Hosp., 1924; BM, BCh Oxford, 1926; Radcliffe Travelling Fellowship, 1927; Asst Medical Unit St Mary's, 1927-28; MRCP, 1928; Medical Registrar St Mary's Hosp., 1928-30; Mackenzie Mackinnon Res. Fellow, 1930-31; Mem. Assoc. of Physicians, Great Britain and Ireland, 1931; Fellow, Royal Soc. Medicine (Past Pres. Clinical Sect.); Senior Censor, RCP, 1956; 2nd Vice-Pres., RCP, 1967. Past President: British Soc. Gastro-enterology; Med. Soc. London: World Organisation Gastro-Enterology; Oxford Graduate Medical Club; Chm., British Digestive Foundn; Hon. Mem. Societies of Gastro-enterology, France, Belgium, Mexico, Nigeria, Switzerland and Sweden. Lt-Col 1940-44, Service West Africa, North Africa; Brig. RAMC, 1944-45; Consultant Persia Iraq Command. *Publications:* Peptic Ulcer, Brit. Ency. Med. Pract., 1938; Harveian Oration, RCP, 1972; various contribs to medical jls on digestive diseases. *Recreations:* books, gardening. *Address:* 53 Townshend Road, NW8 6LJ. *T:* 01-722 5324 (home); 01-935 4766 (professional). *Clubs:* MCC; Vincent's (Oxford). *[Died* 22 *Dec.* 1980.

HUNT, Col Vivian; *see* Hunt, Col G. V.

HUNTER, Donald, CBE 1957; MD, FRCP; Consulting Physician to the London Hospital, 1927-63; Curator of Museum, London Hospital Medical College, 1933-63; Director, Department for Research in Industrial Medicine, MRC, London Hospital, 1943-63; Member World Health Organisation Expert Advisory Panel on Social and Occupational Health, Geneva; Member, Commission Permanente et Association Internationale pour la Médecine du Travail, Geneva; Founder Editor, British

Journal of Industrial Medicine, 1944; *b* 11 Feb. 1898; *s* of late George Hunter; *m* Mathilde, *d* of late Rev. Gustave Bugnion, Lausanne; two *s* two *d*. *Educ:* London Hospital. Medical Registrar, London Hosp., 1923-25; Res. Fellow, Harvard Medical Sch. and Massachusetts General Hospital, Boston, 1926. Lectures: Goulstonian, RCP, 1930; Arris and Gale, RCS, 1931; Croonian, RCP, 1942; Cutter, Harvard, 1945; George Haliburton Hume, Newcastle, 1946; Frederick Price, QUB, 1949, and Trinity Coll., Dublin, 1956; Ernestine Henry, RCP, 1950; Maitland Oration, Sydney Hosp., 1950; McIlrath Guest Prof. in Medicine, Royal Prince Alfred Hospital, Sydney, Australia, 1950; Vis. Lectr, in Medicine, Univ. of Cape Town, 1953; Sir Arthur Sims Commonwealth Travelling Prof., 1955; Prosser White Orator, 1956; Schorstein Lectr, 1956; Harveian Orator, RCP, 1957; Sir Charles Hastings Lectr, 1958; Cai Holten Lectr, Aarhus, Denmark, 1966; John Ash Lectr, Birmingham, 1972. Hon. DSc Durham; Hon. DIH Soc. Apoth., London; Hon. FRCPI; Hon. Foreign Mem. American Acad. of Arts and Sciences. Lately Cons. in Occupational and Environmental Medicine, The Middlesex Hosp., WI; Res. Fellow in Occupational Health, Guy's Hosp., SE1. Ex-member: Pharmacopœia Commission; Industrial Health Research Board; Poisons Board; ex-Senior Censor, Royal College of Physicians; ex-President, Association Physicians Great Britain and Ireland. *Publications:* (with Dr R. R. Bomford) Hutchison's Clinical Methods, 15th edn, 1968; The Diseases of Occupations, 6th edn, 1978; Health in Industry, 1959; various contributions to medical and scientific journals. *Address:* 13 Hitherwood Drive, SE19 1XA. *[Died* 11 *Dec.* 1978.

HUNTER, Ian Basil; stage and screen actor; *b* Cape Town, S Africa, 13 June 1900; *s* of Robert and Isabella Hunter; *m* 1926, Casha (*née* Pringle); two *s*. *Educ:* St Andrew's Coll., Grahamstown, South Africa; Aldenham, Radlett, Herts; Bradfield Coll., Berks. Served European War, 1917-18, King Edward's Horse. First appearance New Theatre, 1919; subsequently London and New York; Hollywood, 1934-42. Served RNVR, 1942-45. Latterly stage screen and television, Hollywood, New York and London. *Recreations:* sailing, golf, ornithology. *Club:* Garrick. *[Died* 22 *Sept.* 1975.

HUNTER, Norman Charles; playwright and novelist; *b* 18 Sept. 1908; *s* of late Lieut-Col C. F. Hunter, DSO, late of 4th Dragoon Guards, and of Mrs N. W. Hunter (*née* Cobbett); *m* 1933, Germaine Dachsbeck, Brussels; no *c*. *Educ:* Repton; Royal Military College, Sandhurst. Commissioned 4/7 Dragoon Guards, 1930; relinquished commission, 1933; Mem. BBC staff, 1938-39; served War of 1939-45, in RA England and Italy. *Publications:* novels include: The Ascension of Mr Judson, 1949; The Losing Hazard, 1950; plays include: All Rights Reserved, 1935; Ladies and Gentlemen, 1937; Grouse in June, 1939; Waters of the Moon, 1951; A Day by the Sea, 1953; A Touch of the Sun, 1958; A Piece of Silver, 1960; The Tulip Tree, 1962; The Excursion, 1964; The Adventures of Tom Random, 1967. *Recreations:* fishing, travelling. *Address:* Pantlludw, Machynlleth, Montgomeryshire. *T:* Machynlleth 2218. *Clubs:* PEN, Dramatists. *[Died* 19 *April* 1971.

HUNTING, Sir Percy (Llewellyn), Kt 1960; Director, Hunting Group of Companies (Chairman, 1927-60); *b* 6 March 1885; *e s* of late Charles S. and Agnes Mona Hunting; *m* 1910, Dorothy Edith (*d* 1958), *e d* of late Daniel Maule Birkett, JP; one *s* (and one *s* lost on active service, HMS Repulse, 1941); *m* 1960, Evelyn Marion Birkett, Cranleigh. *Educ:* Loretto; Paris; Armstrong Coll., Newcastle on Tyne (marine engineering); North Eastern Marine Engineering Co. Served European War: 4th (Terr.) Bn Northumberland Fusiliers, 1914-16; seconded 30 Sqdn RFC and 3rd Wing, GHQ Mesopotamia, 1916-18 (despatches twice). International Tanker Owners' Assoc. Ltd (Dep. Chm.) 1934-50; British Chamber of Shipping Oil Tanker Cttee (Vice-Chm.), 1933-35, (Chm.), 1935-40; Tramp Tanker Cttee (Chm.), 1940-43. FICS; MInst Petroleum Technologists; Companion Royal Aeronautical Society; Mem. Photogrammetric Soc. of Gt Brit.; Mem. Soc. of Naval Architects and Marine Engineers (USA); Assoc. Mem. Indep. Petroleum Assoc. of America. *Publication:* The Group and I (private circulation). *Recreations:* arboriculture, travel. *Address:* Old Whyly, East Hoathly, near Lewes, Sussex. *T:* Halland 216. *Clubs:* Travellers', Royal Air Force.
[Died 2 *Jan.* 1973.

HUNTINGTON-WHITELEY, Captain Sir (Herbert) Maurice, 2nd Bt, *cr* 1918; CEng, MIEE, RN (retired); *b* 25 July 1896; *s* of Sir Herbert James Huntington-Whiteley, 1st Bt and Florence Kate (*d* 1948), *e d* of W. B. Huntington, JP, DL; *S* father, 1936; *m* 1919, Lady (Pamela) Margaret, 3rd *d* of 1st Earl Baldwin of Bewdley, KG, PC, FRS; two *s*. *Educ:* Eton. High Sheriff of County of Worcester, 1968. *Heir:* *s* Hugo Baldwin Huntington-

Whiteley. *Address:* The Old Hill, Astley, Stourport-on-Severn, Worcs. *T:* Stourport 2895. *Club:* United Service & Royal Aero.
[Died 18 *May* 1975.

HURCOMB, 1st Baron, *cr* 1950, of Campden Hill; **Cyril William Hurcomb,** GCB, 1946 (KCB 1938; CB 1922); KBE 1929 (CBE 1918); President, Society for the Promotion of Nature Reserves, 1951-61; Member, Nature Conservancy, 1953-62 (Chairman, 1961-62) and now Member of its Committee for England; Vice-President, International Union for the Protection of Nature, 1954-60; President, Royal Society for Protection of Birds, 1962-66; Chairman, Advisory Committee on Meteorological Office, 1958-70; Founder-President, Council for Nature, 1958; Trustee: British Museum, 1960-63; The World Wildlife Fund, 1961-71, Vice-President, 1974; *b* 1883; *m* 1911, Dorothy Brooke (*d* 1947); two *d*. *Educ:* Oxford High Sch.; St John's Coll., Oxford (Scholar, 1901, Hon. Fellow, 1938). Entered Secretary's Office, the Post Office, 1906; Private Sec. to Post-master General, 1911; Dep. Dir, and later, Dir of Commercial Services, Ministry of Shipping, 1915-18; Permanent Sec., Ministry of Transport, 1927-37; President, Institute of Transport, 1935-36; Chm., Electricity Commission, 1938-47; Dir-Gen., Ministry of Shipping, 1939-41; Dir-Gen., Ministry of War Transport, 1941-47; Chm. of British Transport Commission, 1947-53. Silver Medal, Zoological Soc. of London, 1965. Chevalier of the Legion of Honour; Grand Officer Order of Orange-Nassau; Knight Grand Cross Order of St Olav; Grand Officer Order of the Crown of Belgium; Grand Cross of Order of George I, King of the Hellenes. *Recreations:* fishing and birds. *Address:* 47 Campden Hill Court, W8. *Club:* Athenæum.
[Died 7 *Aug.* 1975 (*ext*).

HUROK, Sol, US Impresario; *b* Pogar, Russia, 9 April 1888; *s* of Israel and Naomi Hurok; *m*; one *d*; *m* 1939, Emma Runitch. *Educ:* Russia. Became US citizen, 1914. Manager of weekly concerts at Hippodrome, NYC, 1915. Since then has been impresario for many famous dancers and musicians, including: Anna Pavlova, Isadora Duncan, Feodor Chaliapin, and numerous living artistes of various countries. Has presented many ballet companies in America, including: Sadler's Wells (now the Royal Ballet); Ballets Russes de Monte Carlo; Bolshoi, Kirov, Royal Danish, and Stuttgart Ballets; Moiseyev Dance Co. Has also presented in America: Emlyn Williams as Charles Dickens, Jean Louis-Barrault in French plays, French theatre companies, the Old Vic Company, Moscow Art Theatre; also Bands of British Regiments. Holds: Hon. doctorates; Legion of Honour (France); Hon. CBE 1960. *Address:* 1370 Avenue of the Americas, New York, NY 10019, USA. *[Died* 5 *March* 1974.

HURRY, Leslie; artist; *b* 10 Feb. 1909; *s* of Alfred George Hurry and Edith Louise Perry Butcher. *Educ:* St John's Wood Art Schs; Royal Academy Schools. Theatrical productions, settings and costumes: Hamlet Ballet, Sadler's Wells Co., 1942; Le Lac des Cygnes, Sadler's Wells Co., 1943 and 1952; La Scherzi della Sortie, Mercury Ballet, 1951; Hamlet, Old Vic, 1944; Turandot, Covent Garden Opera, 1947; Medea, Edinburgh Festival, 1948; Cymbeline, 1949, King Lear, 1950, Stratford Memorial Theatre; La Forza del Destino, Edinburgh Festival (Glyndebourne Opera), 1951; Tamburlaine, Old Vic, 1951; Living Room, Wyndhams, 1953; Venice Preserv'd, Lyric, Hammersmith; Der Ring des Nibelungen, Covent Garden Opera; The Tempest, Old Vic; Richard II, Old Vic; Measure for Measure, Old Vic (Australian Tour); Tamburlaine (Toronto and New York); Timon of Athens (Old Vic Theatre); The Gates of Summer (Provinces); The Moon and Sixpence, Sadler's Wells Opera Co.; Richard II, Old Vic Co. (Amer. and Canadian Tour); Richard III, Old Vic; The Hidden King, Edinburgh Festival; Henry VI, Parts I, II, III, Old Vic; Cat on a Hot Tin Roof, Comedy Theatre; King Lear, Old Vic; Hamlet Ballet (revival); Tristan and Isolde, Covent Garden Opera; costumes and setting for Mary Stuart (Edinburgh Fest., Old Vic), 1958; The Cenci, Old Vic; Andrea Chénier, Sadler's Wells Opera; St Joan, Old Vic; Troilus and Cressida, Royal Stratford Theatre; The Duchess of Malfi, Aldwych; Hamlet, Stratford upon Avon; Becket, Aldwych; Mourning Becomes Electra, Old Vic; St Joan, American Tour and Old Vic; A Village Romeo and Juliet (Delius Festival) Sadler's Wells Opera Co.; The Tempest, Old Vic; Beggar's Opera, Royal Shakespeare Co., Aldwych; (costumes) Maggie May, King Lear, Julius Cæsar, Stratford, Ont.; Swan Lake, Royal Ballet Touring Co.; Nicholas Romanov, Manitoba Theatre Centre, Canada; Stratford Festival, Canada: Last of the Tsars; The Government Inspector; Albert Herring; A Midsummer Night's Dream; La Cenerentola; School for Scandal; Sadler's Wells Opera Co.: Fidelio; Queen of Spades; Hamlet (opera, Humphrey Searle), Royal Opera, Covent Garden; Scénes d'Amour, Royal Ballet; Pericles, Stratford, Ont; Caesar and Cleopatra, Shaw Festival Theatre, Niagara on the Lake, Canada, etc. *Exhibitions:* Wertheim, 1937; Redfern, 1941,

1942, 1945; Rowland Browse Delblanco, 1946-50; Paintings and Theatre Designs (auspices Nat. Gall., Canada); Theatre Designs, Arts Council, 1964; paintings, Mercury Gall. (one-man shows, 1969, 1972, 1975, 1979). *Works in galleries:* Victoria and Albert Museum; Birmingham City Art Gallery; Whitworth Art Gallery, Manchester; Brighton Art Gallery; Melbourne Art Gallery, Australia; among Recent Acquisitions, BM Dept of Prints and Drawings, 1967-72. *Publications:* (Theatre Design) Leslie Hurry, 1946; (Paintings and Drawings) Leslie Hurry, 1952. *Address:* The Bunting's, Hundon, near Clare, Suffolk. *T:* Hundon 269.   [*Died* 20 *Nov.* 1978.

HURST, Sir Alfred (William), KBE 1929; CB 1926; *b* 1 Aug. 1884; *s* of G. E. Hurst; *m* 1909, Gertrude Alice, *e d* of W. H. Hurst; one *s* one *d. Educ:* Market Bosworth; Emmanuel Coll., Cambridge (Senior Scholar and Dixie Scholar); First Class Natural Sciences Tripos, 1905; Senior Optime Mathematical Tripos, 1906. Entered HM Treasury (first place in Civil Service (Class I) Exam.), 1907; Under-Sec. Treasury, 1932; seconded for Service with Import Duties Advisory Cttee as Adviser and Personal Asst to Chm., 1932; Under-Sec. for Mines, 1940-42; in charge of Reconstruction. Secretariat of the War Cabinet, 1942-44. Independent Chm. of London Builders' Conference, 1936-40 and 1944-57. *Address:* Burke's Grove, Burke's Road, Beaconsfield, Bucks.   [*Died* 24 *March* 1975.

HURST, Sir Donald; *see* Hurst, Sir J. H. D.

HURST, Edward Weston, MD, DSc (Birmingham); FRCP; retired 1969; formerly Consultant Pathologist to Industrial Hygiene Research Laboratories, Imperial Chemical Industries Ltd, Macclesfield; *b* Birmingham, 1900; *s* of Edward William Hurst and Clarinda, *d* of Thomas Wem; *m* 1926, Phyllis Edith, *d* of J. G. Picknett, MA, Leicester; three *d*; *m* 1942, Barbara Ternent, *d* of W. T. Cooke, DSc, Adelaide; one *s* one *d. Educ:* King Edward's Sch., Birmingham; Birmingham Univ. BSc 1920; MB, ChB, 1922; Hons in Obstetrics and Gynæcology, Queen's and Ingleby Scholarships; Walter Myers Travelling Student, Univ. of Birmingham, 1923-24; MD, 1924; Postgraduate study and research work at National Hospital, Queen Square, London, 1923-25; Pathologist to Miller General Hospital for South-East London, 1926-28; Pathologist to Milbank Fund for Research on Poliomyelitis, 1928-32; DSc, 1932; MRCP, 1932; FRCP, 1940; Associate at Rockefeller Institute, Princeton, NJ, 1932-34; Mem. of Research Staff, Lister Institute of Preventive Medicine, London, 1932-36; Reader in Experimental Pathology, University of London, 1932-36; Dir of the Institute of Medical and Veterinary Science, Adelaide, 1936-43; Keith Sheridan Professor of Experimental Medicine, University of Adelaide, 1938-43; William Withering Lecturer, University of Birmingham, 1935; Sir Joseph Bancroft Orator, Qld Branch BMA, 1940; G. E. Rennie Memorial Lecturer, RACP, 1941. *Publications:* Numerous contributions to pathology and allied subjects in English and foreign journals. *Recreation:* photography. *Address:* 46 Vermont Close, Winchester Road, Bassett, Southampton SO1 7LT.   [*Died* 16 *Dec.* 1980.

HURST, Harold Edwin, CMG 1932; MA, DSc Oxon; FInstP; Professional Associate, Institution of Water Engineers; Hydrological Adviser, Ministry of Irrigation, Egypt, retired; *b* 1 Jan. 1880; *s* of Charles Hurst, Wigston Magna, Leics; *m* 1st, Winifred, *d* of late Capt. A. B. Hawes; 2nd, Marguerite, *d* of late Dr G. C. B. Hawes, Pangbourne; two *s. Educ:* Alderman Newton's Sch., Leicester; Hertford Coll., Oxford. Lectr and demonstrator Oxford Univ. Electrical Laboratory, 1903-6; Joined Survey of Egypt, 1906; Dir-Gen., Physical Dept, Min. of Public Works, Egypt, 1919-46. Thrice awarded Telford Premium, and Telford Gold Medal, 1957, by Instn of Civil Engrs for work on the utilization of Nile waters; Order of the Nile 2nd Class; Order of Ismail 3rd Class; travelled extensively in the Nile Basin for purposes of hydrological reconnaissance. *Publications:* papers on physics, the measurement of water, the magnetic survey of Egypt, and the Nile Basin, 1931 onwards; The Nile, 1952, 1957; (with Black and Simaika) Long Term Storage, 1965. *Recreations:* mechanical work, fishing, shooting. *Address:* Guildway, 48 Church Road, Sandford-on-Thames, Oxford OX4 4XZ. *T:* Oxford 777293. *Club:* Gezira Sporting (Cairo).   [*Died* 7 *Dec.* 1978.

HURST, His Honour Sir (James Henry) Donald, Kt 1954; retired as Judge of County Courts; *b* 1895; *er s* of late J. G. Hurst, KC, Recorder of Birmingham; *m* 1924, Laura Olive, *d* of late James Bannister, Leicester; two *d. Educ:* King Edward VI Sch., Birmingham; Wadham Coll., Oxford. Served European War, 1914-18, Argyll and Sutherland Highlanders (wounded). Judge of County Courts Circuit 23 (Coventry, Northampton, etc), 1937-41; Circuit 36 (Oxford, Reading, etc), 1941-62, and of Circuit 53 (Cheltenham, Tewkesbury, Northleach, etc), 1943-62;

retd Oct. 1962. Chm. Oxfordshire QS, 1947-62, Dep. Chm., 1962-67. *Address:* Clare Park, Farnham, Surrey. *T:* Aldershot 850681. *Club:* National Liberal.   [*Died* 21 *June* 1980.

HURSTFIELD, Joel, DLit (London); Astor Professor of English History, University College, London, 1962-79, now Emeritus Professor; Senior Research Associate, Huntington Library, California, since 1979; *b* 4 Nov. 1911; *m* Elizabeth Valmai Walters, Hirwaun, Glam; one *s* one *d. Educ:* Owen's Sch.; University Coll., London. BA; Pollard and Gladstone Prizes. Mem. Brit. Univs Debating Team (USA Tour), 1934. University of London Postgrad. Studentship, 1935-36; Asst Lectr (later Lectr) University Coll., Southampton, 1937-40; Asst Comr, Nat. Savings Cttee, 1940-42; Official Historian, Offices of War Cabinet, 1942-46. Lecturer: QMC, London, 1946-51; UCL, 1951-53; Reader in Mod. Hist., 1953-59, Prof. of Mod. Hist., 1959-62, Fellow, 1963-79, Hon. Res. Fellow, 1979-, University College London. Vis. Prof., USA, 1967; Public Orator, Univ. of London, 1967-71; Shakespeare Birthday Lectr, Washington, 1969; James Ford Special Lectr in History, Oxford, 1972; Sen. Res. Fellow, Folger Shakespeare Library, Washington, 1973; John Coffin Meml Lectr, Univ. of London, 1974; Andrew Mellon Senior Res. Fellow, Huntington Library, USA, 1977-78; A. H. Dodd Meml Lectr, University Coll., Bangor, 1978; Creighton Lectr, Univ. of London, 1978. Hon. DLitt Southampton. *Publications:* Control of Raw Materials, 1953; The Queen's Wards, 1958; Elizabeth I and the Unity of England, 1960; The Elizabethan Nation, 1964; Freedom, Corruption and Government in Elizabethan England, 1973; (ed jtly) Elizabethan Government and Society, 1961; (ed) Tudor Times (English History in Pictures), 1964; (ed jtly) Shakespeare's World, 1964; (ed) The Reformation Crisis, 1965; (ed jtly) Elizabethan People: state and society, 1972: (ed) Historical Association Book of the Tudors, 1973; The Historian as Moralist: reflections on the study of Tudor England, 1975; The Illusion of Power in Tudor Politics, 1980; Man as a Prisoner of his Past: the Elizabethan experience, 1980; articles and reviews in History, Eng. Hist. Rev., Econ. Hist. Rev., The Times, Guardian, Daily Telegraph, etc. *Recreations:* walking in cities, the theatre. *Address:* 7 Glenilla Road, Hampstead, NW3. *T:* 01-794 0160. *Club:* Athenæum.   [*Died* 29 *Nov.* 1980.

HUSSEY, Dyneley, MA (Oxon); Music Critic to The Listener, 1946-60; *b* 27 Feb. 1893; *s* of Col Charles Edward Hussey, Salisbury; *m* 1st, 1926, Irene Letitia Melville Duncan (*d* 1941); one *s* two *d*; 2nd, 1946, Dr Florence Kathleen Costello. *Educ:* King's Sch., Canterbury; CCC, Oxford. Served European War, 1914-18, Lieut, Lancs Fusiliers, 1914-17; Asst to Asst Sec., Finance, Admiralty, 1917-22. Music Critic: on the Times, 1923-46; Saturday Review, Week-End Review, Spectator, successively, 1924-46. War of 1939-45: Administrative post at Admiralty. *Publications:* Wolfgang Amadeus Mozart, 1928; Verdi, 1940 (revised, 1968); Some Composers of Opera, 1952. *Recreations:* gardening, photography and foreign travel. *Address:* 26 Albert Road, Cheltenham. *Club:* United Oxford & Cambridge University.   [*Died* 6 *Sept.* 1972.

HUTBER, Patrick; Associate Editor, Now Magazine, since 1979; Director, Cavenham Communications Ltd, since 1979; *b* 18 May 1928; *s* of Hubert Anderson Mackintosh Hutber, OBE and Edith Mary (*née* Bull); *m* 1959, Josephine Mary Robbie; one *s* three *d. Educ:* Ealing County Grammar Sch.; New Coll., Oxford (Galsworthy Scholar; MA). Sec. and Librarian, Oxford Union Soc., 1951. Special trainee, J. Lyons, 1952; Inst. of Bankers 1954; Financial Times, 1957-63 (Commercial Editor, 1959; "Lex", 1961); founded, as free-lance contrib., "Questor" column, Daily Telegraph, 1964; Financial Dir, Link Information Services, 1965; City Editor, Sunday Telegraph, 1966-79; Chm. of Trustees, Soc. of Clinical Psychiatrists Res. Fund, 1975-; Mem. Council of Management, University Coll. at Buckingham, 1976-. Financial Journalist of the Year Award, 1972. *Publications:* The Decline and Fall of the Middle Class, 1976; (ed) What is Wrong with Britain?, 1978. *Recreations:* gardening, riding, music (esp. opera). *Address:* The Old Rectory, Drayton Parslow, Milton Keynes, Bucks. *T:* Mursley 241. *Club:* Garrick.
                                                        [*Died* 3 *Jan.* 1980.

HUTCHINGS, Sir Robert Howell, KCIE 1946 (CIE 1935); CMG 1943; *b* 11 March 1897; *s* of late Charles Robert Hutchings, MA; *m* 1st, 1925, Irene Millicent (*d* 1953), *d* of Rev. A. Willifer Young; three *s*; 2nd, Lydia Gladys, *d* of J. H. Lightburn. *Educ:* St Paul's Sch., London; Trinity Coll., Oxford. Served European War, France, 1916-18; joined ICS 1920; Sec. to Government of India Food Dept, 1943; Mem. for Food and Agriculture, Governor General's Executive Council, India, July-Aug. 1946. Dir, Glaxo Laboratories Ltd, later Glaxo Group Ltd, 1947-67. Chairman: Joint UK Australian Mission on Rice Production in Ceylon, 1954; Cttee on National Security, Ghana,

1958; British and Foreign Bible Society, 1962-64. *Address:* Labadi, Pennington Cross, Lymington, Hants. *Club:* Oriental.
[*Died* 8 *Jan.* 1976.

HUTCHINS, Ven. George Francis; Archdeacon of Cheltenham, 1965-76, now Archdeacon Emeritus; *b* 8 Oct. 1909; *s* of late Frank and Lucy Hutchins; *m* 1935, Margaret Annie Powell; two *s* one *d. Educ:* Plymouth Coll.; University of Bristol (MA). Curate, St Matthew Moorfields, Bristol, 1934-35; Vicar: St Clement and St Swithin, Barbados, BWI, 1935-38; Holy Innocents, Barbados, 1938-43; St Matthias and St Lawrence, Barbados, 1943-48; All Saints, Gloucester, 1948-55; Rector, Dursley, Glos, 1955-61; Canon Missioner, Dio. Gloucester, 1961-65. Hon. Canon, Gloucester Cathedral, 1968. *Recreations:* walking, reading, railways. *Address:* 15 Hollis Gardens, Hatherley, Cheltenham, Glos.   [*Died* 3 *Feb.* 1977.

HUTCHINS, Robert Maynard; President, The Fund for the Republic, USA, and Center for Study of Democratic Institutions; President University of Chicago, 1929; Chancellor University of Chicago, 1945-51; *b* 17 Jan. 1899; *s* of William James Hutchins and Anna Laura Murch; *m* 1921, Maude Phelps McVeigh (marr. diss. 1948); three *d*; *m* 1949, Vesta Sutton Orlick. *Educ:* Oberlin Coll.; Yale Univ. AB, Yale, 1921, Hon. AM 1922; LLB, 1925; LLD, WVaU, Lafayette Coll., and Oberlin Coll., 1929, Williams Coll., 1930, Berea Coll., 1931, Harvard Univ. 1936; Tulane Univ. 1936; Universities of Copenhagen, 1946; of Illinois (LittD), 1947; of Frankfurt, 1948; of Stockholm, 1949; Rollins Coll., 1950; Chicago, 1951; of Rochester, 1958. Master in English and Hist., Lake Placid Sch., 1921-23; Sec., Yale Univ., 1923-27; admitted to practice, Connecticut Bar, 1927; Lecturer, Yale Law Sch., 1925-27; acting Dean, 1927-28; Dean, 1928-29; Prof. of Law, 1927-29; Dir of Encyc. Britannica, Inc., Encyc. Brit., Ltd, and Encyc. Brit. Educnl Corp. (formerly EB Films Inc), 1943-74; in ambulance service, USA, 1917-19; with Italian Army, 1918-19. Chairman: Commn on Internat. Economic Relations, 1933-34; Commn on Freedom of Press, 1945-47; Pres. Cttee to Frame a World Constitution, 1945-46; Chairman: Goethe Bicentennial Foundation, 1949; The Great Books Foundation, 1947-51; Bd of Editors, Measure, 1949-51; Bd of Editors, Encyc. Brit., 1946-74. Associate Dir, Ford Foundation, 1951-54; Sir George Watson Prof. of American History, 1954; lectures given at Universities of Manchester, Birmingham, Edinburgh, Oxford, and University Coll. of North Staffs. Order of the Coif; Hon. Mem. Chicago Bar Assoc.; Officer of Legion of Honor; Croce di Guerra; Goethe plaque, City of Frankfurt, 1949; Grand Cross of Order of Merit (Germany), 1954. Aspen Founders Award, 1969. *Publications:* No Friendly Voice, 1936; The Higher Learning in America, 1936; Education for Freedom, 1943; St Thomas and the World State, 1949; Morals, Religion, and Higher Education, 1950; The Conflict in Education, 1953; The University of Utopia, 1953; Freedom, Education, and the Fund, 1956; Some Observations on American Education, 1956; The Learning Society, 1968. *Address:* c/o The Fund for the Republic, Inc., PO Box 4068, Santa Barbara, Calif 93103, USA. *Clubs:* (Hon.) Tavern, (Hon.) Law.   [*Died* 14 *May* 1977.

HUTCHINSON, Arthur Stuart Menteth; novelist; *b* 2 June 1879; *s* of late Lieut-Gen. H. D. Hutchinson, CSI; *m* 1926, Una Rosamond, *d* of late John Henry Bristow-Gapper; two *s.* Editor Daily Graphic, 1912-16. *Publications:* Once Aboard the Lugger, 1908; The Happy Warrior, 1912; The Clean Heart, 1914; If Winter Comes, 1921; This Freedom, 1922; The Eighth Wonder, 1923; One Increasing Purpose, 1925; The Uncertain Trumpet, 1929; The Golden Pound, 1930; The Book of Simon, 1930; Big Business, 1932; The Soft Spot, 1933; A Year That The Locust, 1935; As Once You Were, 1938; He Looked for a City, 1940; It Happened Like This, 1942; Bring Back The Days, 1958. *Address:* c/o Society of Authors, 84 Drayton Gardens, SW10.
[*Died* 13 *March* 1971.

HUTCHINSON, Rev. Canon Deryck Reeves; Canon Residentiary and Precentor of Chichester Cathedral since 1961; *b* 26 Aug. 1911; *s* of Charles Reeves Hutchinson and Alice Elizabeth (*née* Oldman); *m* 1942, Beatrice Maud Hammond. *Educ:* Merchant Taylors' Sch.; Oriel Coll., Oxford. BA (2nd cl. Mod. Hist.) 1933 (2nd cl. Theol., 1934), MA 1937; Deacon, 1935; Priest, 1936; Curate of Cranbrook, 1935-38; Chaplain, Salisbury Theological Coll., 1938-41, Vice-Principal, 1941-43; Lectr, St Boniface Coll., Warminster, 1939-41; Curate of Ripon, 1943-44; Vicar of Holy Trinity, Yeovil, 1944-49; Vice-Principal, Wells Theological Coll., 1949-58; Exam. Chaplain: to Bp of St Edmundsbury and Ipswich, 1941-54; to Bp of Bath and Wells, 1951-58; Editor, Bath and Wells Diocesan Gazette, 1952-56; Prebendary of Wells Cathedral, 1957-58; Lectr, Brasted Training Centre for Theological Students, 1958-61; Anglican Chaplain to Students, University of Reading, 1961. *Recreations:*

motoring, gardening. *Address:* The Residentiary, Chichester, Sussex. *T:* Chichester 82961.   [*Died* 15 *April* 1971.

HUTCHINSON, Frederick Heap, CIE 1947; *b* 16 Oct. 1892; *s* of late William Henry Heap Hutchinson, Hull; *m* 1st, 1924, Dorothea Mary (*d* 1967), *d* of late Rev. G. F. Feild, Hampstead; three *s* one *d*; 2nd, 1968, Violet Mary, *d* of Major L. H. Robertson, RA, Romford, and *widow* of Major H. E. P. Yorke, MC, RAMC, Jersey. *Educ:* Rugby; Oundle; City and Guilds Coll., London. Served as Capt. i/c 120th Labour Corps, Persia, 1918-19. Indian Service of Engineers, 1914, posted to United Provinces; on deputation to Govt of Mauritius, 1938 and 1939; Chief Engineer, UP India, 1943-47; retired from ISE, 1947. Mem. of West Africa Rice Mission, 1948; Consulting Engineer for Drainage and Irrigation to the Government of British Guiana, 1949-52. *Recreations:* shooting, golf, yachting, reading. *Address:* 4 Victoria Crescent, Dover, Kent. *T:* Dover 1946.
[*Died* 7 *Jan.* 1975.

HUTCHINSON, Geoffrey Clegg; *see* Ilford, Baron.

HUTCHINSON, Sir Herbert John, KBE 1948 (CBE 1939); CB 1943; BSc (Econ.); *b* 22 Oct. 1889; *s* of late George Hutchinson, Lee; *m* 1926, Kathleen Eleanor (*d* 1969), *d* of late J. J. Byrne. *Educ:* St Dunstan's Coll.; University Coll. Sch.; London Univ. Entered Board of Trade, 1908; Asst Sec., Import Duties Advisory Cttee, 1932; Sec., 1939; Under-Sec., Ministry of Supply, 1941-46; Second Sec. Board of Trade, 1946-47; Sec. of NCB, 1947-51; Director-General, British Paper & Board Makers' Association, 1951-60. *Address:* Dean Cottage, Withdean Road, Brighton. *T:* Brighton 505444. *Club:* United Service and Royal Aero.   [*Died* 6 *Dec.* 1971.

HUTCHINSON, John, OBE 1972; FRS 1947; LLD (St Andrews); VMH, FLS; Corresponding Member of Philadelphia Academy of Science and the Botanical Society of America; Hon. Fellow and Herbert Medallist, American Amaryllis Society; Loder Cup for work on Rhododendrons, 1941; Hon. Fellow Botanical Society, Edinburgh, 1945; *b* 7 April 1884; *s* of Michael Hutchinson, Blindburn, Wark-on-Tyne, Northumberland; *m* 1910, Lilian Florence Cook, Richmond; two *s* three *d. Educ:* Wark; Rutherford Coll., Newcastle; privately. Asst for India, Royal Botanic Gardens, Kew, 1907-9, 1916-19; Asst for Africa, 1909-16; Asst in charge of African Section, 1919-36; Keeper of Museums of Botany, 1936-48; Botanical Tour in S Africa, 1928-29; in Rhodesia, 1930; Cameroons Mtn, 1937. Veitch Memorial Gold Medal, 1946; Darwin-Wallace Centenary Medal, 1958; Linnean Gold Medal, 1965. *Publications:* The Families of Flowering Plants, 1926 and 1934 (vol. ii), 3rd edn 1972; contributions towards a Phylogenetic Classification of Flowering Plants (Kew Bulletin); Floras of Tropical and South Africa (in part); Flora of West Africa; Common Wild Flowers, More Common Wild Flowers, and Uncommon Wild Flowers I (Penguin Books); British Wild Flowers, 2 vols, new edn 1972; A Botanist in Southern Africa; Evolution and Classification of British Flowering Plants; (with R. Melville) The Story of Plants; (with H. Hahnewald) Wild Flowers in Colour (Penguin Books); (with C. Abbott) Bouquet of Wild Flowers; The Genera of Flowering Plants; Evolution and Phylogeny of Flowering Plants, 1969; numerous papers on the botany of Africa, Canary Islands, etc. *Recreations:* black and white drawing, botanical exploration. *Address:* 12 Kenmore Close, Kent Road, Kew, Richmond, Surrey. *T:* 01-940 6811.   [*Died* 2 *Sept.* 1972.

HUTCHINSON, Sir Lewis (Bede), KBE 1952; CB 1947; Deputy Secretary, Ministry of Supply, 1949-59, retired; *b* 3 Jan. 1899; *o s* of late Lewis John Hutchinson, Leytonstone, Essex; *m* 1926, Eileen, *d* of late Arthur Eaton, Norwood, SE; one *d. Educ:* Leyton County High Sch. Barrister-at-law, Middle Temple, Cert. of Honour, 1928; served European War, 1914-18, with London Regt, 1917-19; served overseas (wounded); Inland Revenue Dept, 1916; Air Ministry, 1937; Ministry of Aircraft Production, 1940; Ministry of Supply, 1941. Chm. Woolwich Review Cttee, 1959-60. Dir, Projectile & Engineering Co. Ltd, 1959-65. *Address:* 16 Woodland Way, West Wickham, Kent. *T:* 01-777 1034. *Clubs:* United Service & Royal Aero, Royal Automobile.   [*Died* 24 *May* 1975.

HUTCHINSON, Ormond, CMG 1974; Chairman of Directors, Hutchinson Motors Ltd, Ford Dealers, Christchurch, New Zealand (retd as Managing Director, 1973); Director, The Colonial Motor Co. Ltd, Wellington, NZ; *b* 12 April 1896; *s* of Alexander Gilbert and Katherine Hutchinson; *m* 1945, Joan Margery Hutchinson; one *s. Educ:* Wellington, NZ. Served European War, 1914-18, with NZ Artillery (Messines, 1917, Passchendaele, 1917; two service medals). Joined Colonial Motor Co. (sole rights importing and distributing all Ford products in NZ); he became the Company's regular caller of motor dealers in South Island, using the model T; subseq. Manager, Timaru plant, and came to Christchurch as Manager of a dealership, 1934. Colonial Motor Company controls over 20 motor dealers throughout New Zealand. Vice-President: New Zealand Trotting Conf. (Past Pres. and Life Mem., New Brighton Trotting Club); Sumner Lifeboat Inst.; Mount Pleasant Yacht Club; New Brighton Power Boat Club. *Address:* 44 Cannon Hill Crescent, Christchurch 8, New Zealand. *T:* Christchurch, NZ 843-423. *Clubs:* Canterbury, Midland (Past Pres. and Life Mem.) (Christchurch, NZ). *[Died 16 June 1978.*

HUTCHINSON, Ray Coryton, FRSL; novelist; *b* London, 23 Jan. 1907; *yr s* of late Harry Hutchinson, Watford; *m* 1929, Margaret, *er d* of late Capt. Owen Jones, CBE; two *s* two *d.* *Educ:* Monkton Combe; Oriel Coll., Oxford. In the Army, 1940-45. *Publications:* Thou Hast A Devil, 1930; The Answering Glory, 1932; The Unforgotten Prisoner, 1933; One Light Burning, 1935; Shining Scabbard, 1936; Testament, 1938 (Sunday Times Gold Medal for Fiction, 1938); Last Train South, play, 1938; The Fire and the Wood, 1940; Interim, 1945; Elephant and Castle, 1949; Recollection of a Journey, 1952; The Stepmother, 1955; March the Ninth, 1957; Image of my Father, 1961; A Child Possessed, 1964 (W. H. Smith and Son Literary Award, 1966); Johanna at Daybreak, 1969; Origins of Cathleen, 1971. *Address:* c/o Curtis Brown Ltd, 1 Craven Hill, W2 3EW.
[Died 3 July 1975.

HUTCHISON, Brig. Sir Eric Alexander Ogilvy, 2nd Bt, *cr* 1923; RA; MB, ChB Edinburgh; *s* of 1st Bt and Jane Moir Ogilvy (*d* 1935), *d* of late Alexander Ogilvy Spence, banker; *b* 28 Feb. 1897; *S* father, 1925; *m* 1st, 1924, Bethia Maud (from whom he obtained a decree of divorce, 1943; she *d* 1971), *d* of Lieut-Col F. D. S. Fayrer, IMS; three *d*; 2nd, 1944, Olive, *d* of late Frederick Kerss, Newcastle; one *d.* *Educ:* Edinburgh Acad.; Royal Military Academy, Woolwich; Edinburgh Univ. Served in RA 1915-25 and RA (TA), 1925-47. Mem. of Royal Company of Archers (Queen's Body Guard for Scotland). *Heir:* none. *Recreations:* golf, motoring, metal working. *Address:* 9a, Palmerston Road, Edinburgh 9. *T:* 031-667 1341. *Clubs:* Caledonian United Service, Royal Forth Yacht (Edinburgh).
[Died 7 Feb. 1972 (ext).

HUTCHISON, Sir James Riley Holt, 1st Bt, *cr* 1956; DSO 1945; TD; JP; *b* 10 April 1893; *s* of late Thomas Holt Hutchison, Shipowner, and Florence Riley; *m* 1928, Winefryde Eleanor Mary, *d* of late Rev. R. H. Craft; one *s* (one *d* decd). *Educ:* Harrow; France. Shipowner, 1912. Served with Lanark Yeomanry and 17th Cavalry, Indian Army, throughout war, 1914-18; Hon. Col Lanarkshire Yeomanry, 1948-58. Dir of companies (Ailsa Shipbuilding Co. Ltd and others); President: Westminster Chamber of Commerce, 1963; Associated British Chambers of Commerce, 1960-62 (Dep.-Pres. 1958); UK Council of European Movement, 1955; Mem. Export Council for Europe, 1960; Nat. Pres. Incorporated Sales Managers' Assoc., 1949-51; Parl. Chm. Dock and Harbour Authorities Assoc. Served France, N Africa and on Staff, 1939-45. MP (U) Glasgow Central, 1945-50, Scotstoun Div. of Glasgow, Oct. 1950-Sept. 1959. Pres. Assembly of WEU, 1957-59. Parl. Under-Sec. of State and Financial Sec., War Office, 1951-54, and Vice-Chm. HM Army Council. JP Perthshire. Hon. LLD Glasgow, 1973. Chevalier Legion of Honour, 1945; Croix de Guerre; OStJ 1972. *Publication:* That Drug Danger, 1977. *Recreations:* writing, music, shooting, games. *Heir:* s Peter Craft Hutchison [*b* 5 June 1935; *m* 1966, Virginia, *d* of John M. Colville, Gribloch, Kippen, Stirlingshire; one *s*]. *Address:* Rossie, Forgandenny, Perthshire. *T:* Bridge of Earn 265; 32 Moore Street, SW3 2QW. *Clubs:* Cavalry and Guards; Western (Glasgow).
[Died 24 Feb. 1979.

HUTCHISON, William; Under-Secretary, Scottish Education Department, since 1972; *b* 4 April 1926; *s* of late James Hutchison and Thomasina Hutchison; *m* 1952, Ruth Ormiston Dabb, MA; one *s* one *d.* *Educ:* Hawick High Sch.; Edinburgh Univ. (MA (Hons)). Joined Inland Revenue, 1952; Principal, Ministry of Health, 1960; Asst Sec., Scottish Home and Health Dept, 1966. *Recreations:* music, walking. *Address:* 29 Liberton Brae, Edinburgh 16. *T:* 031-664 3765.   *[Died 5 May 1976.*

HUTCHISON, William Gordon Douglas; *b* London, 26 Sept. 1904; *y s* of late Col K. D. Hutchison, RGA, and late Mrs Rivers-Moore, Remenham House, near Henley-on-Thames. *Educ:* King William's Coll., Isle of Man. Old Vic, 1921; toured in several plays, 1924; Liverpool Repertory Theatre, 1925; The Right Age to Marry, Playhouse; toured with Arthur Bourchier in The Halo; The Old Adam, Kingsway, 1926; toured in The Street Singer, 1927; toured with Violet Vanbrugh in The Duchess Decides and Robert Atkins' Shakespearian Company to Egypt, 1928; The Trial of Mary Dugan, Queen's Theatre;

Passing Brompton Road, with Dame Marie Tempest, Criterion, 1929; The Autocrat, Kingsway; toured in Magic Slippers; These Pretty Things, with Marie Löhr, Garrick; left the stage to study politics; MP (C) Romford Division of Essex, 1931-35; returned to the stage, 1936, to act in Lady Precious Stream, USA, 1937; The Dictator in Judgement Day, Embassy Theatre; a Kiss for Cinderella, Phœnix Theatre, 1938; Road to Gandahar, Garrick; The First Television Serial, Ann and Harold, 1939; Judgement Day, Phœnix, 1940; In Good King Charles Golden Days, Tour and New Theatre; Their Finest Hour, Comedy; Nineteen Naughty One, Prince of Wales, 1941; joined Royal Navy as ordinary seaman, Aug. 1941; Asst Instructor, Nov.; Able Seaman, May 1942; Sub-Lieut RNVR Sept. 1942; Acting Lieut Feb. 1943; Lieut March 1943; Liaison Officer with French Navy, 1942-43-44. Started firm, Sloane Decoration, Sept. 1946. Returned to Theatre, June 1947; Lady Precious Stream, Midsummer Night's Dream, Open Air Theatre, Regent's Park.
[Died 18 July 1975.

HUTT, Sir (Alexander McDonald) Bruce, KBE 1956 (OBE 1943); CMG 1949; Administrator, East Africa High Commission, 1954-59; *b* 9 Feb. 1904; *s* of late John Hutt; *m* 1929, Margaret Helen, *er d* of late George Murray, Hill Crest, Natal, SA; two *s.* *Educ:* St Andrew's Coll., Grahamstown, S Africa; University Coll., Oxford (BA). Entered Tanganyika Administrative Service as Cadet, 1926; Asst Dist Officer, 1928; Private Sec. and ADC, 1933; Asst Sec., Secretariat, 1935-37; Dist Officer, 1938; Dep. Provincial Commissioner, 1944; Provincial Commissioner, 1946; Dep. Chm., Development Commission, 1946; Acting Chief Sec. and Governor's Deputy, 1948-49; Mem. for Development and Works, Tanganyika, 1949-50; Deputy Chief Sec., 1950-51; Chief Sec., Tanganyika, 1951-54. Acting Governor, Tanganyika, 1953. *Publications:* (jointly) Anthropology in Action, 1935; first editor, Tanganyika Notes and Records. *Recreations:* golf, swimming, fishing, and shooting. *Address:* PO Box 33, Hill Crest, Natal, South Africa. *Clubs:* Royal Commonwealth Society; Vincent's (Oxford).
[Died 24 March 1978.

HUTTON, Air Vice-Marshal Arthur Francis, CB 1955; CBE 1948; DFC 1935; FRAeS; FIMechE; *b* 9 Dec. 1900; *s* of Rev. A. W. Hutton; *m* 1927, Florence Strickland Oxley; one *s* two *d.* *Educ:* Queen Elizabeth's Gram. Sch., Darlington; Armstrong Coll., Newcastle; St Catharine's Coll., Cambridge (BA). Commissioned RAF 1924; DIC 1931; Officer Comdg No 28 Squadron, 1936; Officer Comdg No 52 Wing, 1939; Sen. Tech. Staff Officer, Far East, 1946; Dir of Engineering, Air Ministry, 1949; Sen. Tech. Staff Officer, Coastal Command, 1951; AOC No 43 Group, 1952; SASO Technical Training Command, 1953; Dir-Gen. of Engineering, Air Ministry, 1955-58, retd. Technical Consultant, Negretti & Zambra Ltd, 1959-61. MIMechE 1952. *Recreations:* shooting, golf. *Address:* Lower Berrick Farm, Berrick Salome, Oxford. *T:* Stadhampton 891065.
[Died 16 Feb. 1979.

HUTTON, Rear-Adm. FitzRoy Evelyn Patrick, CB 1945; *b* 16 Jan. 1894; *s* of William Coats Hutton and Ethel FitzRoy Merriman; unmarried. *Educ:* RN Colleges, Osborne and Dartmouth. Lieut RN 1915; qualified as Gunnery Officer, 1917; Comdr 1927; Captain 1933. Commanded HM Ships Penelope (1936-39), Hermes (1939-40), Warspite (1942-43); Chief of Staff to C-in-C China, 1940-41; Commodore, Algeria, 1943-44; Commodore and Flag Officer, Belgium, 1944-45; Flag Officer, Western Germany, 1945-46; retired list, 1946; Grand Cross of Leopold II (Belgian), Commander Legion of Merit (American), Officier Légion d'Honneur (French). *Recreation:* shooting. *Address:* Talcotts, Colchester CO3 3SR. *T:* Colchester 74693.
[Died 15 Aug. 1975.

HUTTON, John Campbell; artist; *b* New Zealand, 8 Aug. 1906; *s* of Colin Campbell Hutton and Penrhyn Florence Olive Hutton (*née* Fleming); *m* 1934, Helen Sara Blair; three *s.* *Educ:* Wanganui Collegiate School, NZ. Studied law until age of 25 and then abandoned it for art, in which he is self-taught; came to England as an artist in 1935 and worked extensively as a mural painter. Mural paintings for Festival of Britain, 1951, orient liners Orcades and Orsova, Buckingham Palace, Southampton liner terminal, etc. In engraved glass, Dunkirk War Memorial window in France; Guildford Cathedral. Has developed a special technique for large-scale engraving of his designs on glass which has been used for the Great Glass Screen which forms the West Front of new Coventry Cathedral; large screen in engraved glass, Plymouth Civic Centre; engraved glass panels; Shakespeare Centre, Stratford upon Avon; new Nat. Lib. and Archives, Ottawa; Civic Centre, Newcastle upon Tyne; Nat. Art Gall. of NZ, Wellington; glass engraving represented in: Victoria and Albert Museum, London; National Museum of Scotland, Edinburgh; Thanksgiving Chapel, Dallas, Texas; First Christian

Church, Tyler, Texas; Corning Museum of Glass, New York. One man exhibn, Commonwealth Inst. Art Gallery, 1969; touring retrospective exhibn, NZ, 1972-73. Designs also in stained glass and mosaic. *Recreation:* playing the Spanish guitar. *Address:* The Studio Barn, Oxford Road, Clifton Hampden, Abingdon, Oxon OX14 3EW. *T:* Clifton Hampden 7490.
[*Died* 28 *July* 1978.

HUTTON, Rear-Adm. Reginald Maurice James, CB 1951; CBE 1945; DSO 1942 (Bars, 1942, 1943); Clerk to the Governors, Christ's Hospital, Sherburn, 1953-64; *b* 28 Sept. 1899; *s* of Reginald Hutton, Wootton Bridge, I of W; *m* 1930, Lois, *d* of M. P. Griffith-Jones, CBE; four *s. Educ:* Osborne and Dartmouth. Went to sea, 1915; served in battle cruisers and destroyers. Staff Coll., 1930. Commander, 1932; Captain, 1941; Rear-Admiral, 1950. Commanded HMS Laforey, 1941-43, in Mediterranean, as Captain D 19 Flotilla; commanded HMS Tyne, 1943-44; Commodore "D", Home Fleet, 1944-45; Chief of Staff to Naval C-in-C, Germany, 1945-46; Dir, Royal Naval Staff Coll., 1947-48; commanded HMS Triumph, 1949; Senior Naval Member on Staff of Imperial Defence Coll., 1950-52; retired list, 1953. *Recreation:* fishing. *Address:* Oaklawn, Wootton Bridge, Isle of Wight.
[*Died* 18 *Jan.* 1973.

HUTTON, Robert Crompton; Recorder of Reading 1951-70 (of Oswestry, 1937-51); Chairman of Gloucestershire Quarter Sessions, 1943-70 (Deputy Chairman, 1941-43); Chairman, Agricultural Land Tribunal, South Eastern Area, 1959-70; *b* 8 Aug. 1897; *s* of late Stamford Hutton, OBE; *m* 1927, Elfreda Bruce; three *s* one *d. Educ:* Winchester; Trinity Coll., Cambridge. Served European War, 1914-19, with 2/1 Royal Gloucestershire Hussars and Signals. Called to Bar, Inner Temple, 1923. TA, Royal Corps of Signals, 56th (1st London) Divl Signals, 1926-30. *Address:* 2 Harcourt Buildings, Temple, EC4; Harescombe Grange, Glos. *T:* Painswick 813260.
[*Died* 16 *Nov.* 1978.

HUTTON, Thomas Winter; *b* Kiukiang, China, 14 Oct. 1887; *s* of Thomas Hutton; *m* 1913, Katie Marguerite Thornbery; one *s* one *d. Educ:* King Edward's Sch., Birmingham; Merton Coll., Oxford (Postmaster). Asst Editor, Birmingham Gazette, 1910; Leader writer, Daily Dispatch, Manchester, 1911; Asst Editor, Liverpool Courier, 1911-13; Asst Editor, Birmingham Post, 1913; Editor, The Birmingham Post, 1945-49; retired, 1949. Served with Royal Warwickshire Regt, 1915-19. Chm. Sch. Cttee, King Edward's Sch., Birmingham; Bailiff of the Governors, 1953-54. Mem. Cttee Assoc. of Governing Bodies of Public Schs, 1954-67, Dep.-Chm. 1960-66; Mem. Council, Public Schs Appointments Bureau, 1953-66. *Publication:* King Edward's School, Birmingham, 1552-1952, 1952. *Address:* 27 Woodbourne, Augustus Road, Edgbaston, Birmingham. *T:* 021-454 2713.
[*Died* 18 *Feb.* 1973.

HUTTY, Sir Fred (Harvey), Kt 1971; JP; *b* 9 Dec. 1903; *s* of Clarence Harvey Hutty and Mary Hutty, Kingston-upon-Hull; *m* 1931, Nora, *d* of Alfred Moreton Manning, Wallasey; three *d* (and one *d* deced). *Educ:* Hymers Coll., Kingston-upon-Hull; London Univ. (BCom). Entered Wallasey County Borough Council, 1950; Alderman, 1966-74; Mayor, 1969-70. Chm, Wallasey Educn Cttee, 1955-65, and 1967-72; Pres., Assoc. of Educn Cttees, 1966-67; Leader, Management Panel, Burnham Cttee, 1970-; Chairman: Nat. Cttee for Audio-Visual Aids in Educn, 1968-; Nat. Safety Educn Cttee, RoSPA, 1968-; Educn Fedn for Visual Aids, 1970-; Chm. of Dirs, Council and Educn Press, 1969-; Mem., Public Schs Commn. 1968-70. Man. Dir, Northern Industrial Chemicals, 1947-. JP Wallasey. 1952. *Recreations:* reading, writing. *Address:* 114 The Cliff, Wallasey L45 2NW. *T:* 051-639 2847.
[*Died* 14 *Dec.* 1974.

HUXLEY, Gervas, CMG 1954; MC; *b* 6 April 1894; *e s* of Henry Huxley and Sophy Wylde Stobart; *gs* of Rt Hon. Thomas Henry Huxley, PC, etc; *m* 1931, Elspeth Josceline Grant; one *s. Educ:* Rugby; Balliol Coll., Oxford. European War, 1914-18 (MC, despatches twice); Sec. Publicity Cttee Empire Marketing Board, 1926-32; Adviser to Minister of Information on publicity to and about the Empire and on relations with American Forces in UK until 1945; Organizing Dir and Vice-Chm., International Tea Market Expansion Board, 1935-67; Hon. Adviser on public relations matters to Sec. of State for the Colonies, 1947-63; Exec. Cttee, British Council, 1953-64; Commissioner, Nat. Parks Commn, 1954-66. *Publications:* Talking of Tea, 1956; Endymion Porter, 1959; Lady Denman, 1961; Lady Elizabeth and the Grosvenors, 1965; Victorian Duke, 1967; Both Hands, 1970. *Recreation:* gardening. *Address:* Woodfolds, Oaksey, Malmesbury, Wilts. *T:* Crudwell 252. *Clubs:* Athenæum, Oriental.
[*Died* 2 *April* 1971.

HUXLEY, Sir Julian (Sorell), Kt 1958; FRS 1938; MA; DSc; biologist and writer; *b* 22 June 1887; *e s* of late Leonard Huxley; *m* 1919, Marie Juliette Baillot of Neuchâtel, Switzerland; two *s. Educ:* Eton (King's Scholar); Balliol Coll., Oxford (Brackenbury Scholar). Newdigate Prizeman, 1908; 1st in Nat. Sci. (Zoology), 1909; Naples Scholar, 1909-10; Lecturer in Zoology, Balliol Coll., 1910-12; Research Associate, 1912-13, and Asst Professor, 1913-16, The Rice Institute, Houston, Texas, USA; Staff Lieut GHQ, Italy, 1918; Fellow of New Coll. and Senior Demonstrator in Zoology, Oxford Univ., 1919-25; Oxford Univ. Expedition to Spitsbergen, 1921; Professor of Zoology, King's Coll., London, 1925-27; Hon. Lecturer, King's Coll., London, 1927-35; Pres. National Union of Scientific Workers, 1926-29; Fullerian Professor of Physiology in the Royal Institution, 1926-29; Sec., Zoological Soc. of London, 1935-42; Biological Editor, Ency. Brit., 14th edn; general supervisor of biological films for GB Instructional Ltd, 1933-36, and for Zoological Film Productions, Ltd, 1937; visited East Africa to advise on Native Education, 1929; Mem. of General Cttee for Lord Hailey's African Survey, 1933-38; Romanes Lectr, Oxford, 1943; mem. of Commission Higher Educn in W Africa, 1944; member: Editorial Board, New Naturalist, 1944-; Cttee on National Parks, 1946; Dir-Gen. of Unesco, 1946-48. Galton Lecturer, 1937 and 1962; William Alanson White Lecturer, Washington, DC, 1951; first Alfred P. Sloan Lecturer, Sloan-Kettering Inst. for Cancer Research, 1955; Vis. Prof., Chichago Univ., 1959. Coto Doñana Expedition, 1957; Adviser to Unesco on Wild Life Conservation in eastern Africa, 1960; Leader, Unesco Mission on Wild Life Conservation to Ethiopia, 1963; Jordan Expedition, 1963; Organizer, Royal Society Symposium on Ritualization in Animals and Man, 1965; Past Pres. Inst. of Animal Behaviour; Pres., Eugenics Soc.; Past Chm. Assoc. for the Study of Systematics. Dr *hc* Universities of: Caracas, 1947, San Carlos de Guatemala, 1947, San Marcos de Lima, 1947, Athens, 1949, Columbia, 1954, Birmingham, 1958; Hon. Mem. Fac. of Biology and Medicine, University of Santiago de Chile, 1947; Hon. Mem. Soc. of Biology, University of Montevideo, 1947; Corr. Mem. Acad. des Sciences (Paris), 1948; For. Mem. Hungarian Acad. of Science, 1948. Kt, Order of the Golden Ark, 1973. Kalinga Prize, UNESCO, 1953; Darwin Medal, Royal Society, 1957; Darwin-Wallace Commemorative Medal, Linnean Soc., 1958; first British Zoologists' Gold Medal, Zool Soc. of London, 1974. *Publications:* The Individual in the Animal Kingdom, 1911; Essays of a Biologist, 1923; The Stream of Life, 1926; Essays in Popular Science, 1926; Religion without Revelation, 1927; Animal Biology (with J. B. S. Haldane), 1927, revised edn 1957; The Science of Life (with H. G. and G. P. Wells), 1929; Ants, 1929; Bird-watching and Bird Behaviour, 1930; Africa View, 1931; What Dare I Think?, 1931; An Introduction to Science (with E. N. Da C. Andrade), vols 1-4 (Simple Science), 1931-35; Problems of Relative Growth, 1932; The Captive Shrew and other poems, 1932; The Elements of Experimental Embryology (with G. R. de Beer), 1934; Scientific Research and Social Needs, 1934; If I were Dictator, 1934; The Private Life of the Gannets (a film, with R. M. Lockley; Oscar Award), 1934; T. H. Huxley's Diary on the Rattlesnake (ed), 1935; We Europeans (with A. C. Haddon), 1935; At the Zoo, 1936; The Living Thoughts of Darwin, 1939; The New Systematics (ed), 1940; The Uniqueness of Man, 1941; Democracy Marches, 1941; Evolution, The Modern Synthesis, 1942, 3rd revised edn, 1974; TVA: Adventure in Planning, 1943; Evolutionary Ethics, 1943; On Living in a Revolution, 1944; Evolution and Ethics: 1893-1943 (part author), 1947; Man in the Modern World, 1947; Soviet Genetics and World Science, 1949; Evolution in action, 1952; Evolution as a Process (ed), 1953; From an Antique Land, 1954 (rev. edn 1966); Kingdom of the Beasts (with W. Suschitzky), 1956; Biological Aspects of Cancer, 1957; New Bottles for New Wine, 1957; (ed.) The Humanist Frame, 1961; Conservation of Wild Life in Central and East Africa, 1961; Essays of a Humanist, 1963; The Human Crisis, 1964; Darwin and his World (with H. B. D. Kettlewell), 1965; The Wonderful World of Evolution, 1969; Memories, vol. I., 1970, Vol 11, 1972. Scientific papers, wireless talks and discussions, lectures, film commentaries, television programmes, miscellaneous articles. *Recreations:* travel, bird-watching. *Address:* 31 Pond Street, Hampstead, NW3. *Club:* Athenæum.
[*Died* 14 *Feb.* 1975.

HUXLEY, Michael Heathorn; *b* 9 Aug. 1899; *s* of Henry Huxley and Sophy Stobart; *m* 1926, Ottilie de Lotbinière Mills; one *s* one *d* (and one *s* deced). *Educ:* Rugby. Entered Diplomatic Service, 1922; served in Tehran and Washington and in the Foreign Office; Second Secretary, 1925; First Sec., 1934; resigned in order to launch and edit The Geographical Magazine, 1934; recalled for war service by Foreign Office, Sept, 1939; resumed editorial work, 1945; resigned editorship, 1959. *Address:* Buckhold, Lodsworth, near Petworth, West Sussex. *Club:* National Liberal.
[*Died* 7 *Jan.* 1979.

HYAMS, Edward; author; free-lance journalist; *b* 30 Sept. 1910; *s* of late Arthur Hyams and Dolly Hart, London; *m* 1933, Hilda Mary Aylett (marr. diss.); *m* 1973, Mary Patricia Bacon. *Educ:* University College Sch., London; Lycée Jaccard and Univ., Lausanne (MèsL). Advertising and various jobs, both office and manual, 1930-40. Served War, RAF, 1940-41; RN, 1941-42; commissioned RNVR, 1942-47. Thereafter novelist and free-lance journalist writing for New Statesman, Punch, Financial Times, Illustrated London News, etc. Atlantic Award in Literature, 1948; Scott-Moncrieff Prize, 1964. *Publications: novels and other fiction:* Wings of the Morning, 1938; A Time to Cast Away, 1940; To Sea in a Bowl, 1941; William Medium, 1947; Blood Money, 1948; Not in Our Stars, 1949; The Astrologer, 1950; Sylvester, 1951; Gentian Violet, 1953; Stories and Cream, 1954; The Slaughterhouse Informer, 1955; Into the Dream, 1957; Taking it Easy, 1958; All We Possess, 1961; A Perfect Stranger, 1964; The Last Poor Man, 1966; The Mischief Makers, 1968; Cross Purposes, 1970; The Death Lottery, 1971; The Final Agenda, 1973; Prince Habib's Iceberg, 1974; Morrow's Ants, 1975; *conservation:* From the Waste Land, 1950; Soil and Civilization, 1952; A Prophecy of Famine (with H. J. Massingham), 1953; *social history:* Vin, 1959; The New Statesman: a history of the first 50 years, 1963; New Statesman (an Anthology), 1963; Dionysius, 1964; Killing No Murder, 1969; Animals in the Service of Man, 1971; Plants in the Service of Man, 1971; A Dictionary of Modern Revolution, 1973; The Millenium Postponed, 1974; The Changing Face of England, 1974; Terrorists and Terrorism, 1974; *gardening:* The Grape Vine in England, 1950; (ed) Vineyard in England, 1954; The Orchard and Fruit Garden (with A. A. Jackson), 1961; Strawberry Growing Complete, 1962; The English Garden, 1964; An Englishman's Garden, 1965; Irish Gardens, 1967; Great Botanical Gardens of the World, 1969; The English Cottage Garden, 1970; A History of Gardens and Gardening, 1971; *biography:* The Gardener's Bedside Book, 1968; The Traveller's Bedside Book (with Mary Bacon), 1970; Capability Brown and Humphry Repton, 1971; contributor to horticultural press; *posthumous publication:* The Story of England's Flora, 1978. *Recreations:* travel, gardening, garden designing, talking. *Address:* The Old School House, Brampton, Beccles, Suffolk. *T:* Brampton 658. *[Died 25 Nov. 1975.*

HYAMSON, Derek Joseph; Master of the Supreme Court, Queen's Bench Division, since 1969; *b* 12 Feb. 1914; *o s* of Lionel and Jane Hyamson; *m* 1952, Cynthia Mary O'Shea; one *d. Educ:* Brighton Coll.; St Catharine's Coll., Cambridge. Served War in R Artillery, 1939-46 (Lt-Col, 1944). Admitted as a Solicitor, 1939; called to the bar, Middle Temple, 1946; practised London and South Eastern Circuit, 1946-69. *Address:* 9 Ashmere Avenue, Beckenham, Kent BR3 2PQ. *T:* 01-650 3512. *[Died 24 Nov. 1971.*

HYDE, Francis Edwin; Chaddock Professor of Economic History, University of Liverpool, 1970-75, now Emeritus (Chaddock Professor of Economics, 1948-70); *b* 18 July 1908; *s* of Walter Henry Hassall Hyde and Charlotte Ann Sharp; *m* 1st, 1935, Marian Rosa (*d* 1967), *d* of Thomas Abercromby Welton and Rosa Sheppard; one *d*; 2nd, 1970, Anne Elizabeth Evans. *Educ:* Wolverton Grammar Sch.; University of Liverpool; University of London; Harvard Coll., USA. BA, First Cl. Hons in History (Liverpool), 1929; MA (Liverpool), 1931; PhD (Econ.) London Sch. of Economics, 1931. Commonwealth Fund Fellow, 1931-33; Gladstone Memorial Fellow and University Fellow, 1929-31; Houblon-Norman Fellow, 1948; FRHistS. Lecturer in Economics and Economic History, 1934-48; Dean, Faculty of Arts, 1949-53, Pro-Vice-Chancellor, 1960-64, Univ. of Liverpool. Board of Trade, 1941-45; Pres., Liverpool Economic and Statistical Soc.; Chm., University Press of Liverpool; Hon. Treasurer Joint Matriculation Board, 1955-66; Mem. University Council, 1957-75. Editor of Business History. *Publications:* Mr Gladstone at the Board of Trade, 1934; The Import Trade of the Port of Liverpool, 1946; Economic History of Buckinghamshire, 1948; Stony Stratford, 1948; Blue Funnel: A History of Alfred Holt & Co., 1956; (with others) A New Prospect of Economics, 1958; Harrisons of Liverpool, 1830-1939, 1966; Shipping Enterprise and Management, 1967; (with Dr Sheila Marriner) The Senior: John Samuel Swire 1825-98, 1967; Liverpool and the Mersey, 1971; Far Eastern Trade, 1973; Cunard and the North Atlantic, 1975; reviews and articles in Economic Journals. *Recreations:* walking and rock climbing. *Address:* Heather Cottage, Village Road, West Kirby, Merseyside. *T:* 051-625 7632. *[Died 27 Dec. 1978.*

HYDE, Henry Armroid, CIE 1936; MC; retired; *b* 17 Jan. 1885; *s* of Henry Thomas Hyde, late Administrator General of Bengal, and Amy Dougal; *m* 1921, G. H. A. Thompson; one *s. Educ:* Rugby; Coopers Hill. Joined Public Works Dept, India, 1906; commission in the Reserve of Officers, 1915; went to France,

RFA, 1916 (MC); demobilised, 1919; rejoined PWD; Major AIRO, 1927-32; Chief Engineer and Sec. to Govt of Central Provinces, India, 1932-37; retired 1940; joined RAF as Pilot Officer, 1940, for station defence; discharged on medical grounds, 1943. *Recreations:* all forms of sport. *Address:* c/o National Westminster Bank Ltd, Trafalgar Square, WC2.
[Died 4 April 1976.

HYDE-CLARKE, (Ernest) Meredyth, CBE 1962 (MBE 1942); Director of Organisation of Employers' Federations, etc (formerly Overseas Employers' Federation), 1957-71 (Secretary, 1953-57); *b* London, 3 May 1905; *ys* of Percy Clarke, LLB and Alice Mary Young; *m* 1st, 1930, Edith Margaret, *e d* of late Albert and Florence Stevenson, Alderley Edge; two *d*; 2nd, 1970, Barbara Joan (*d* 1972), *y d* of late Clare and of Florence Gilmour, London, Ont. *Educ:* St George's Sch., Harpenden; University of London; Wadham Coll., Oxford. Administrative Service, Kenya, 1927-50; Resident Magistrate, 1934; Dir of Manpower and Labour Commissioner, MLC Kenya, 1945-50; Permanent Sec., Ministry of Local Govt, Ghana, 1950-52; Establishment Sec., Ghana, 1952-53. Member: Honeyman Commn of Enquiry, N Rhodesia, 1957; Kenya Constitutional Commn (Boundaries), 1962; Council for Technical Education and Training for Overseas Countries (Management Gp), 1962-; Assoc. Mem. Commonwealth Parliamentary Assoc., 1953-. British Employers Technical Adviser/Delegate to various ILO conferences, 1953-60; Mem., Programme Adv. Cttee, Turin Training Centre, 1970-. *Publications:* various reports on industrial relations. *Address:* Cromer Hyde, Lemsford, Welwyn, Herts. *T:* Welwyn Garden 27114; 13 Chiesanuova Levanto, La Spezia, Italy. *Clubs:* Royal Commonwealth Society; Nairobi (Kenya). *[Died 10 Oct. 1972.*

HYND, John Burns; *b* 4 April 1902; *s* of Henry Hynd, Perth, Scotland, and Ann Hynd, JP, Perth; *m* 1927, Elsie Margaret Doran; one *d. Educ:* St Ninian's Episcopal Sch., Perth; Caledonian Road Sch., Perth. Railway Clerk, District Office, LMSR, Perth, 1916-25; Trade Union Clerk (NUR), 1925-44; MP (Lab) Attercliffe Div. of Sheffield, 1944-70; Chancellor of the Duchy of Lancaster, and Minister for Germany and Austria, 1945-47; Minister of Pensions during 1947; Mem. of General Medical Council, 1950-55. Chm., Anglo-German and Anglo-Latin American Parly Groups. Grand Cross of Merit with Star (West German Republic), 1958; Chevalier of the Legion of Honour; Great Golden Cross of Honour with Star (Austria). *Publication:* Willy Brandt: A Pictorial Biography, 1966. *Recreations:* chess, golf, photography, etc. *Address:* 18 Lakeside, Enfield, Middx. *T:* 01-363 2920. *[Died 8 Nov. 1971.*

HYNES, Sir Lincoln (Carruthers), Kt 1971; OBE 1967; Consultant, Commonwealth Broadcasting Network, Australia; *b* Balmain, NSW, Australia, 14 April 1912; *s* of Rev. Francis William Hynes and Mabel Evelyn Hynes; *m* 1939, Enid May Brunskill; three *d. Educ:* Sydney High Sch., NSW. General Manager: 4BC, Brisbane, 1951; Queensland Network, 1951-56; Chief General Manager, Commonwealth Broadcasting Network (2UW, 4BC, 4RO, 4GR, 4MB), 1956-74; also Alternate Director of this Network; Dir, Australian Television Facilities, 1960-75. Chairman: Royal North Shore Hosp. of Sydney, 1968- (Dir, 1960-68); Darling Downs TV Ltd, Toowoomba, 1970- (Dir, 1959-70); CBN Sales Pty Ltd, 1970-74; Thos. Cook Pty Ltd, 1973-. Pres., Fedn of Australian Commercial Broadcasters, 1958-59, 1971-72 (Federal Council Mem., 1956; Sen. Vice-Pres., 1969-71); Pres., NSW Br. of Australian Hosp. Assoc., 1969-71; Sen. Vice-Pres., Australian Hosp. Assoc., 1971-73, Pres., 1973-74. Hon. Vice-Pres., NSW Paraplegic and Quadriplegic Assoc., 1969-; Chairman: Community Systems Foundn (Australia), 1974-76 (Dir, 1972-74); 2UW-Lions Blind Appeal Cttee, 1956-74. *Recreations:* cattle breeding, bowls. *Address:* Ilkley, 35 Powell Street, Killara, NSW 2071, Australia. *T:* 498-3917. *Clubs:* Royal Commonwealth Society; Rotary, American National, Imperial Service (all in Sydney). *[Died 7 Aug. 1977.*

HYTTEN, Torleiv, CMG 1953; Vice-Chancellor, University of Tasmania, 1949-57, retired; *b* Drammen, Norway, 17 Feb. 1890; *s* of late E. O. Hytten, Tönsberg, Norway; *m* 1922, Margaret Frances (*née* Compton); one *s* (and one *s* decd). *Educ:* Tönsberg; University of Tasmania. MA, 1st Cl. Hons Economics. Went to Australia, 1910; Journalist, 1920-26; University of Tasmania: Lecturer in Economics, 1926; Professor of Economics, 1929-35; Dir of Tutorial Classes, 1928-32. Economic Adviser: Tasmanian Govt 1929-35; Bank of NSW, 1935-49. Conducted case for Tasmanian Govt before Commonwealth Public Accts Cttee, 1930-31, before Commonwealth Grants Commn, 1933-34. Chm. Tasmanian State Employment Council, 1932; Delegate 16th Assembly, League of Nations, 1935; Chm. Aust. Nat. Cttee, Internat. Chamber of Commerce, 1949; Mem., Commonwealth Bank Bd, 1954-59. Conducted enquiry into Transport Problems in Qld, 1958. Knight 1st Class, Order of St Olav (Norway), 1951; Chevalier, Order of the Crown (Belgium), 1957. *Publications:* articles to Economic Record and similar periodicals, principally on economics of transport, and banking. *Address:* Forestgait, 22 King's Gate, Aberdeen AB9 2YL. *T:* Aberdeen 28473.

[Died 2 Jan. 1980.

I

IFE, HH Aderemi I, The Oni of Ife since 1930; **Sir Titus Martins Adesoji Tadeniawo Aderemi;** PC (Western Nigeria) 1954; KCMG 1962 (CMG 1943); KBE 1950; Governor, Western Region, Nigeria, 1960-63; President House of Chiefs, Western Nigeria, 1954-60; Chairman, Council of Obas and Chiefs, Western Nigeria, since 1966; Member, Western House of Chiefs, since 1951; *b* Ife, 1889; Akui House of Ife Royal family; *m* 1910 (polygamous marriage); several *c. Educ:* CMS Sch., Ife. Joined staff of govt railway construction, 1909; Civil Service, 1910; resigned, and started trading and motor transport business, 1921. Founded Oduduwa Coll. (first secondary sch. for boys in Ife Division), 1932. Mem. House of Assembly, Western Nigeria, 1946. MLC, Nigeria, 1947; Mem., Nigerian House of Representatives, 1951-54; Central Minister without Portfolio, 1951-55. Mem. Nigeria Cocoa Marketing Board, 1947; Dir Nigerian Produce Marketing Company Ltd, 1947. Visited England, July-Oct. 1948; delegate to African Conference, London, 1948; led Nigerian Delegation to Coronation, 1953; delegate to Conference for revision of Nigerian Constitution, in London, July-Aug. 1953, and at Lagos, Jan. 1954; delegate to Nigerian Constitutional Confs, London, May-June 1957, Sept.-Oct. 1958. Hon. LLD University of Ife, 1967. *Recreations:* cricket and tennis; hunting game (before accession to the throne). *Address:* The Afin (Palace), Ife, Nigeria, West Africa. *[Died July 1980.*

IGGULDEN, Sir Douglas (Percy), Kt 1969; CBE 1954; DSO 1945; TD 1942; DL; President, Kent Rent Assessment Panel, since 1972; Chief Valuer, Valuation Office, Board of Inland Revenue, 1966-71 (Deputy Chief Valuer, 1950-66); *b* 4 May 1907; *s* of late Percy Edwin Iggulden, JP, and Agnes Iggulden, Herne Bay; *m* 1932, Mollie Gertrude Margaret, *d* of late Sydney Root, Herne Bay; one *d. Educ:* Kent Coll., Canterbury. FRICS. Articles and private practice as a surveyor, 1924-37; joined Valuation Office, Board of Inland Revenue, 1937. TA service: commissioned in 4th Bn The Buffs, 1924; mobilized, 1939; France (despatches), 1939-40; Malta, 1940-43, comd 4th Buffs, 1942; POW Leros, 1943; demobilized, 1945 (Major; Hon. Lt-Col). DL Kent, 1972. Commander Royal Order of the Dannebrog, Denmark. *Address:* 19 Marlborough Court, Earls Avenue, Folkestone, Kent CT20 2PN. *T:* Folkestone 53036.

[Died 30 May 1977.

ILES, Air Vice-Marshal Leslie Millington, CBE 1942; AFC 1918; *b* 4 Oct. 1894; *s* of Henry and Mary Elizabeth Iles, The Orchard, Fairford, Glos; *m* 1st, 1924, Beatrice May Till (*decd*); one *s;* 2nd, 1936, Thelma Celia Newman; one *s. Educ:* Bancroft's Sch., Woodford Green, Essex; St Catharine's Coll., Cambridge (BA Hons, Mech. Sci. Tripos); Imperial Coll. Science and Technology (DIC). Territorial Gunners, Hants RHA, 1913; transferred to RFC 1917, continuous service with RFC and RAF since then; served European War, 1914-18 (despatches, AFC); War of 1939-45 (despatches, CBE). Commanded RAF Officers' Sch. of Aeronautical Engineering; 102 Sqn; 226 Gp, India; Controller of Technical Services, British Air Commn at Washington, 1945; Dep. Dir Military Aircraft R and D, 1947; retired from RAF, 1948. DIC; AFRAeS. *Recreations:* golf, shooting. *Address:* 6 Heathside, Hanger Hill, Weybridge, Surrey. *T:* 48350. *Club:* Burhill Golf (Walton-on-Thames). *[Died 13 Dec. 1974.*

ILFORD, Baron *cr* 1962, of Bury (Life Peer); **Geoffrey Clegg Hutchinson,** Kt 1952; MC 1916; TD; QC 1939; Hon. Freeman of Borough of Ilford, 1954, and of London Borough of Camden; Chairman, National Assistance Board, 1954-64; Governor and Almoner of Christ's Hospital; Chairman, Commission appointed by Church Assembly on pastoral legislation, 1955; *b* 14 Oct. 1893; *y s* of late Henry Ormerod Hutchinson, VD, JP; *m* Janet Bidlake, *y d* of late Henry Frederick Keep. *Educ:* Cheltenham Coll.; Clare Coll., Cambridge (Scholar). MA, 1919; joined The Lancs Fusiliers, 1914; served Brit. Exped. Force, 1915-16, 1918-19 (wounded, MC); Brit. Exped. Force, France, 1940; Deputy-Asst Military Sec., War Office, 1941-42; Hon. Col

5th Bn The Lancs Fusiliers, 1948-54; called to Bar, Inner Temple, 1920; Bencher, 1946; Northern Circuit; MP (C) Ilford, 1937-45; Ilford North, 1950-54. Mem. of Select Cttee on National Expenditure, 1942-45, of Speaker's Conf., 1944, of Consolidation Cttee, 1951-53. Pres., British Waterworks Assoc., 1947; Pres., Water Companies Assoc., 1951-54; Chm., E Surrey Water Co., 1952-54; Dir, Colne Valley Water Co., 1944-54; Pres., Non-County Boroughs Assoc., 1937-44; Hon. Mem., National and Local Govt Officers' Assoc.; Mem. Hampstead Borough Council, 1931-37 (Chm., Finance Cttee, 1936-37); Alderman, LCC, 1944-49; represented Hampstead on Council, 1949-52. Chm. Home Counties North Provincial Area Council, Conservative Party, 1946. Pres., Assoc. of Municipal Corporations, 1964-68; Life Vice-Pres., Assoc. of Municipal Corporations, 1968; Comr (Appeals) London Govt Staff Commn, 1964; Gov. Nat. Corp. for Care of Old People, 1965-69; Master, Needlemakers' Company, 1967. *Address:* 2 Paper Buildings, Temple, EC4. *TA:* 57 Temple. *T:* 01-353 5835; 12 Church Row, NW3. *Club:* Carlton (Trustee).

[Died 20 Aug. 1974.

ILIFF, Neil Atkinson, CBE 1970; Consultant on Environmental Conservation to Shell Group, since 1972; Member, Royal Commission on Environmental Pollution, since 1970; *b* 23 May 1916; *s* of late Charles Wilkinson Iliff and Dorothy Atkinson; *m* 1950, Ann, *d* of Rt Hon. Sir Kenneth Pickthorn, 1st Bt; one *s* four *d. Educ:* Oundle; King's Coll., Cambridge (Major Scholar). Served with HM Forces, 1940-46 (despatches); Lt-Col, Royal Engineers. Fellow and Lectr, King's Coll., Cambridge, 1946-47. Joined Shell, 1948; USA, 1950-51; Germany, 1955-58; Dep. Chm., Shell Chemicals UK Ltd (previously Shell Chemical Co Ltd), 1968-71 (Man. Dir, 1960-68). President: British Plastics Federation, 1965-67; Soc. of Chemical Industry, 1967-69 (Chm. Council, 1969-70); Chemical Industries Assoc., 1968-70. Chm., Economic Development Cttee for the Newspaper, Printing, and Publishing Industry, 1968-71; Member: Adv. Council of Technology; Economic Development Cttee for the Chemical Industry; Council BIM, 1971-; Governing Body, Imperial Coll., 1968; Governor, Sedbergh Sch., 1969. Hon. Fellow, Univ. of Manchester Inst. of Science and Technology, 1969. FRSA 1968. Hon. DSc Heriot-Watt, 1968; Hon. DTech Loughborough, 1971. *Publications:* papers in Chemistry and Industry. *Recreation:* sailing. *Address:* 17 Hale House, 34 De Vere Gardens, W8. *T:* 01-937 6223; Rosehill, Orford, Suffolk; *T:* Orford 344; Shell Centre, SE1. *T:* 01-934 3700. *Clubs:* Carlton; Aldeburgh Yacht. *[Died 5 Jan. 1973.*

ILIFF, Sir William (Angus Boyd), Kt 1961; CMG 1944; MBE 1924; *b* 2 Oct. 1898; *s* of late John Boyd Iliff, Kircubbin, Co. Down; *m*; two *d*; *m* 1947, Jacqueline Lois Christine Reepmaker-d'Orville; one *s. Educ:* Mountjoy School, Dublin; Cadet Coll., Wellington, India, Commissioned to IA, 1916. Served on NW Frontier, Mesopotamia, N Persia and S Russia. Entered N Ireland Civil Service, 1922. Private Sec. to Rt Hon. J. M. Andrews, DL, MP; Assist Sec., Ministry of Labour, 1935; Major Supp. Res. RA 1938; served in France, Dunkirk, 1940; Permanent Sec., Ministry of Public Security (Northern Ireland), 1940-41; Financial Counsellor at British Legation, Tehran, 1941-44; Financial Adviser to Governor of Burma, 1944; Representative of HM Treasury in Middle East, 1944-48; Loan Dir, International Bank, 1948, Asst to Pres., 1951, Vice-Pres., 1956-62. Acted as IBRD Rep., in negotiations between Govt of UAR and Cie Financière de Suez leading to Agreement of 1958, settling compensation issue arising out of nationalisation of former Suez Canal Co.; acted 1954-60 as IBRD Rep., in negotiations between India and Pakistan leading to Indus Waters Treaty of 1960. *Address:* Gasper, near Stourton, Wilts. *T:* Bourton 370. *Club:* Travellers'. *[Died 29 Dec. 1972.*

ILLINGWORTH, Leslie Gilbert; Political Cartoonist, Punch and Daily Mail; *b* Barry, Glam, 2 Sept. 1902; 2nd *s* of Richard Frederick Illingworth and Helen, *d* of Alexander MacGregor; unmarried. *Educ:* Barry County School; Royal College of Art; Slade School, London Univ. Political Cartoonist, Western Mail, Cardiff, 1921; first contributed to Punch, 1927; Free-lance Artist, 1926-39; joined Daily Mail, 1939; joined Punch as Junior Cartoonist, 1945. *Recreation:* gardening. *Address:* Silverdale, Robertsbridge, East Sussex. *T:* Robertsbridge 154. *Clubs:* Chelsea Arts, Royal Automobile. *[Died 20 Dec. 1979.*

ILOTT, Sir John (Moody Albert), Kt 1954; JP; President: J. Ilott Ltd; Golden Bay Cement Co. Ltd; *b* 12 Aug. 1884; *s* of John and Elizabeth Ilott (*née* Baldwin); *m* 1912, Hazel E. M. Hall; one *s* one *d* (and one *d* decd). *Educ:* Terrace Sch.; Wellington Coll.; Victoria Univ. Employed J. Ilott Ltd, 1903-. President Emeritus, NZ Crippled Children Soc. (Inc); Mem., J. R. McKenzie Trust; Past Vice-Pres., Rotary Internat. Jubilee Medal, 1935; Coronation Medal, 1953. Hon. LLD Victoria Univ., 1964.

Recreation: bowls. *Address:* Apartment 5, Broadwater, 214 Oriental Parade, Wellington, New Zealand. *Clubs:* Wellesley (Wellington); Wellington Golf (Life Mem.), Miramar Golf (Life Mem.), both Wellington. *[Died 15 June 1973.*

ILYUSHIN, Sergei Vladimirovich; Order of Lenin (5 times); Soviet aircraft designer; Professor, N. E. Zhukovsky Air Force Engineering Academy; Lieutenant-General, Engineering Technical Service; *b* 31 March 1894. *Educ:* Air Force Engineering Academy. *Principal designs:* TsKB-30 twin-engine plane, 1936; IL-2 armoured attacker, 1939; IL-12 twin-engine passenger plane, 1946; IL-18 (Moscow) turbo-prop passenger plane, 1957; IL-62 passenger airliner, 1962. Corresp. Mem., 1943-68, Mem., 1968-, USSR Acad. of Sciences. Lenin Prize 1960. *Address:* Ministry of Defence, 34 Sophia Embankment, Moscow, USSR.   *[Died 9 Feb. 1977.*

IMBERT-TERRY, Major Sir Edward (Henry Bouhier), 3rd Bt, *cr* 1917; MC 1944; *b* 28 Jan. 1920; *s* of Col Sir Henry B. Imbert-Terry, 2nd Bt, DSO, MC, DL, and Dorothy Lady Imbert-Terry (*d* 1975); *S* father, 1962; *m* 1944, Jean (*JP* 1973), 2nd *d* of late A. Stanley Garton; two *s* two *d.* *Educ:* Eton Coll.; New Coll., Oxford. Coldstream Guards, 1940-51; retired as Major, 1951. *Recreation:* golf. *Heir: er s* Andrew Henry Bouhier Imbert-Terry [*b* 5 Oct. 1945; *m* 1972, Sarah Margaret Evans (marr. diss. 1974)]. *Address:* Mead Meadow House, near Chobham, Surrey. *T:* Chobham 8500. *Clubs:* Army and Navy, MCC.
[Died 27 Nov. 1978.

INAYAT MASIH, Rt. Rev.; *see* Masih.

INCE, Captain Edward Watkins W.; *see* Whittington-Ince.

INDORE, Ex-Maharaja of, GCIE 1918; HH Tukoji Rao Holkar; *b* 26 Nov. 1890; *S* as Maharaja of Indore, 1903, and as Premier Ruling Prince of Central India; *m* 1928, Nancy Miller (Maharanee Sharmishthabai Holkar); one *d* ; abdicated in favour of his son (by a former marriage), 1926 (*s* Maharaja Sir Yeshwant Rao Holkar, GCIE, *d* 1961). *Educ:* Mayo Chiefs' Coll., Ajmere; Imperial Cadet Corps. Visited Europe, 1910; attended Coronation, 1911; again visited Europe, 1913 and 1921. *Recreations:* riding, shooting, lawn tennis. *Address:* Lal Bagh Palace, Indore, MP, India.   *[Died 21 May 1978.*

ING, Harry Raymond, FRS 1951; *b* 31 July 1899; *s* of Arthur Frank William Ing and Anne (*née* Garrard); *m* 1941, Catherine Mills Francis, *d* of Bertie Mills and Sarah Francis. *Educ:* Oxford High Sch.; New Coll., Oxford. Sen. Scholar. New Coll., Oxford, 1921-23. Univ. Demonstrator in Chemistry, Oxford, 1921-26; Ramsay Memorial Fellow, 1926-27; Lectr, 1929, and Reader, 1935, in Pharmacological Chemistry, Univ. of London, University Coll.; Rockefeller Fellow, 1938-39; Univ. Reader in Chemical Pharmacology, Oxford, 1945-66, now Emeritus. *Publications:* Chapters in Heterocyclic Compounds (ed Elderfield, New York); and in Advanced Organic Chemistry, Vol. III (Ed Gilman, New York); numerous papers in chemical, pharmacological and physiological journals, etc. *Recreation:* walking. *Address:* 6 Linton Road, Oxford OX2 6UG. *T:* Oxford 56968. *Club:* Athenæum.   *[Died 23 Sept. 1974.*

INGILBY, Sir Joslan William Vivian, 5th Bt, *cr* 1866; late Scots Guards; DL; JP; *b* 1 Sept. 1907; *o s* of Sir William Henry Ingilby, 4th Bt, and Hon. Alberta Diana Vivian (*d* 1968), 3rd *d* of 1st Baron Swansea; *S* father 1950; *m* 1948, Diana, *o d* of late Sir George Colvin, CB, CMG, DSO; one *s* two *d.* *Educ:* Eton. Served War of 1939-45; Major, Scots Guards, retired. DL 1952, JP 1952, West Riding, Co. of York. *Heir: s* Thomas Colvin William Ingilby, *b* 17 July 1955. *Address:* Ripley Castle, Harrogate, West Riding, Yorks. *T:* Harrogate 770186. *Club:* Guards.   *[Died 7 June 1974.*

INGLE-FINCH, Peter; *see* Finch, Peter.

INGLIS, Sir Claude Cavendish, Kt 1945; CIE 1936; FRS 1953; BA, BAI, MAI (*hc*); FICE; FAMSocCE; Chartered Civil Engineer; Consultant; *b* 3 March 1883; *s* of Sir Malcolm Inglis, DL, and Caroline Johnston; *m* 1912, Vera St John Blood (*d* 1972); one *s.* *Educ:* Shrewsbury; Trinity Coll., Dublin. Irrigation branch Bombay PWD, 1906-38; Initiated and directed Irrigation Research and Development, Bombay Presidency and Sind, 1916-38; Dir Indian Waterways Experiment Stn, Poona, 1938-45; Initiated and directed Hydraulics Research Stn, Dept of Scientific and Industrial Research, Howbery Park, Wallingford., Berks, 1947-58. Ewing Medal, Inst. of Civil Engineers. *Publications:* The Behaviour and Control of Rivers and Canals; various Technical Papers dealing with training and control of rivers and estuaries, coast protection, irrigation and model investigation. *Address:* 7 Holmgarth, Furners Mead, Henfield,

Sussex. *T:* Henfield 3266. *Club:* English-Speaking Union.
[Died 29 Aug. 1974.

INGLIS, Maj.-Gen. George Henry, CB 1952; CBE 1950; JP; Vice-Lieutenant of Cumberland, 1969-74; *b* 22 Aug. 1902; *s* of late Col Henry Alves Inglis, CMG, Dalston, Cumberland; *m* 1940, Margaret Edith, *d* of C. H. Shaw, Ullswater. *Educ:* Ardvreck, Crieff; Wellington Coll.; RMA Woolwich. 2nd Lt RA 1922. Served War of 1939-45, France, SEAC, MELF (despatches Burma, 1946, Palestine, 1949), temp. Brig., 1944. Comdg 18 Trng Bde, Oswestry, 1948; Comdr 52 Lowland Div. TA and Lowland Dist, 1950-52; Maj.-Gen. 1951; Gen. Officer Commanding Nigeria District, 1953-56; retired, 1956. Chairman: Carlisle Diocesan Board of Finance, 1961-70; Cumbrian (formerly Carlisle & NW Counties) Trustee Savings Bank, 1967-73. Vice-Pres., Royal British Legion, 1978- (Pres. NW Area, 1973-). JP Cumberland, 1958; High Sheriff of Cumberland, 1961; DL Cumberland, 1962. Col Comdt RA, 1960-67. *Address:* Crosby House, Crosby-on-Eden, Carlisle CA6 4QZ. *T:* Crosby-on-Eden 239. *Club:* Army and Navy.
[Died 2 March 1979.

INGLIS, Vice-Adm. (retd) Sir John Gilchrist Thesiger, KBE 1959 (OBE 1943); CB 1957; Director of Naval Intelligence, 1954-60; *b* 8 June 1906; *s* of Rupert Edward Inglis and Helen Mary Inglis, *d* of W. O. Gilchrist; *m* 1945, Maud Dorrien Frankland; one *d.* *Educ:* RNC, Osborne and Dartmouth, Lt RN, 1929; qualified as Signal Officer, 1932; Comdr 1940; Captain, 1944; Rear-Adm., 1954; Vice-Adm., 1958. *Recreations:* shooting and farming. *Address:* Wield Manor, Alresford, Hants. *T:* Medstead 3188. *Club:* Naval and Military.
[Died 29 Oct. 1972.

INGLIS of Glencorse, Sir Maxwell (Ian Hector), 9th Bt (formerly Mackenzie of Gairloch, *cr* 1703); JP; Lord-Lieutenant of Midlothian, 1964-72; *b* 18 Oct. 1903; *o s* of Hector Ian Maxwell Mackenzie-Inglis of Glencorse, and Dora, *d* of Robert Mole, Beoley Hall, Worcs; *S* kinsman (Sir Hector David Mackenzie, of Gairloch, Bt), 1958; *m* 1932, Dorothy Evelyn (*d* 1970), MD, JP, *d* of Dr John Stewart, Tasmania; one *s.* *Educ:* Winchester; Trinity Coll., Cambridge. Gold Coast Political Service, 1928-37: Midlothian County Council, 1938-67; Convener of Co. 1946-47; Wing Comdr, RAFVR(T), retired. Mem. of Queen's Body Guard for Scotland, Royal Company of Archers. DL 1957, JP 1946, Midlothian. *Recreation:* travel. *Heir: s* Roderick John Inglis of Glencorse, Yr, MB, ChB [*b* 25 Jan. 1936; *m* 1960, Rachel, *d* of Lt-Col N. M. Morris, Dowdstown, Ardee, Co. Louth; three *s* (incl. twin *s*) one *d*]. *Address:* Loganbank, Milton Bridge, Penicuik, Midlothian. *T:* Penicuik 72686. *Club:* New (Edinburgh). *[Died 22 July 1974.*

INGRAM, Sir Herbert, 3rd Bt *cr* 1893; Partner, Cazenove & Co., 1947-70, retired; *b* 18 April 1912; *s* of Sir Herbert Ingram, 2nd Bt and Hilda Vivian Lake (*d* 1968); *S* father, 1958; *m* 1935, Jane Lindsay, *d* of J. E. Palmer Tomkinson; three *d* (one *s* decd). *Educ:* Winchester; Balliol Coll., Oxford. Served War of 1939-45 (despatches): Grenadier Guards and REME, Major. *Recreations:* golf, ski-ing. *Heir: g s* James Herbert Charles Ingram, *b* 6 May 1966. *Address:* Hurst Lodge, near Reading, Berks. *T:* Twyford (Berks) 341088. *Club:* White's.
[Died 3 July 1980.

INGRAM, Prof. John Thornton; Professor of Dermatology, University of Durham, 1958-63, University of Newcastle upon Tyne, 1963-64, retired, now Emeritus; *b* 4 March 1899; *s* of Albert James and Florence Annie Ingram; *m* 1st, 1927, Lucy Graham; one *d* ; 2nd, 1959, Kathleen Annie Raven (*see* Dame Kathleen Annie Raven). *Educ:* Hele's Sch.; University Coll., Exeter; London Univ., MB, BS London 1923; MD 1926; MRCS, LRCP 1923; MRCP 1926; FRCP 1936. Lectr in Dermatology, Univ. of Leeds, 1927-58; Physician i/c Dermatological Dept, Gen. Infirmary, Leeds, 1927-58; Physician, Royal Victoria Infirmary, Newcastle upon Tyne, 1958. Councillor Royal Coll. of Physicians, 1952-54; Mem., GMC, 1952-54; Lectures: Watson Smith, RCP, 1954; Paul O'Leary, Chicago, 1956; Litchfield, Oxford, 1960; Scott-Heron, Belfast, 1963; Pres. British Assoc. of Dermatology, 1947; Pres. Dermatology Section, RSM, 1957-59. Hon. Mem. Dermatological Socs of New York, America, France, Scandinavia, Denmark, Germany, Austria, Australia. *Publications:* (with R. T. Brain) Sequeira's Diseases of the Skin; Industrial Dermatoses and the Industrial Injuries Act, 1968; Clinical Dermatology: an individual Approach, 1969; Nursing Care of the Patient with Skin Diseases, 1970; contribs to numerous medical text books and numerous articles in British, American, Scandinavian, Pakistan and Australian medical journals. *Recreations:* painting and literature. *Address:* Jesmond, Burcott, Wing, near Leighton Buzzard, Beds LU7 0JU. *T:* Wing 244. *Club:* Athenæum.   *[Died 23 June 1972.*

INGRAMS, William Harold, CMG 1939; OBE 1933; b 3 Feb. 1897; s of Rev. W. S. Ingrams, The Schools, Shrewsbury; m 1930, Doreen, y d of Rt Hon. Edward Shortt, KC; two d. Educ: Shrewsbury. Served European War, KSLI, 1914-18 (wounded); 2nd Lieut Sept. 1914; Lt, Nov. 1914; Asst District Commissioner, Zanzibar, 1919; 2nd Asst Sec., 1925; Asst Col Sec. Mauritius 1927; Acting Colonial Sec., Jan.-May, and Aug. 1932-April 1933; Political Officer, Aden, 1934; British Resident Adviser at Mukalla, S Arabia, 1937-40; Acting Governor of Aden, 1940; Chief Sec. to Govt, Aden, 1940-42; Resident Adviser Hadhramaut States and British Agent Eastern Aden Protectorate, 1942-45; seconded as Asst Sec. Allied Control Commission for Germany (British Element) 1945-47; Chief Comr, Northern Territories, Gold Coast, 1947-48; Mission to Gibraltar, 1949, to Hong Kong, 1950, to Uganda, 1956; Adviser on Overseas Information, CO, 1950-54; Editor, Commonwealth Challenge, and if you ask me, 1952-66; Joint Research Dept, Foreign and Commonwealth Offices, 1966, retd 1968. Class IV Order of Brilliant Star, Zanzibar, 1927; awarded conjointly with wife, Lawrence Memorial Medal, 1939, and founder's Medal of RGS, 1940; Burton Memorial Medal, 1943. Publications: Dialects of Zanzibar Sultanate, 1924; Chronology and Genealogies of Zanzibar Rulers, 1926; Guide to Swahili Examinations, 1927; Zanzibar, Its History and People, 1931; School History of Mauritius, 1931; School Geography of Mauritius, 1932; Report on Social, Economic and Political Condition of the Hadhramaut, 1935; Arabia and the Isles, 1942 (3rd Edn, 1966); Seven Across the Sahara, 1949; Hong Kong, 1953; Uganda: a crisis of Nationhood, 1960; The Yemen: Imams, Rulers and Revolutions, 1963; numerous pamphlets, articles and broadcasts. Address: Uphousden, near Ash-next-Sandwich, Canterbury, Kent. [Died 9 Dec. 1973.

INIGO-JONES, Captain Henry Richmund, CIE 1947; b 26 Aug. 1899; s of Rev. Ralph William Inigo-Jones, Kelston Park, Bath. Somerset; m 1st, 1925, Hester Rhoda (d 1948), d of late Herbert Smith, Great Ryburgh, Norfolk; one s one d; 2nd, 1951, Maidie Cubitt (from whom he obtained a divorce, 1961), London, SW. Educ: Elstow Sch., Bedford; Thames Nautical Training Coll.; HMS Worcester. Joined Royal Indian Marine (which later became Royal Indian Navy), 1920; transferred to Royal Navy on Indian Independence, and loaned to Indian Navy; Commodore-in-charge, Bombay, until 1951, when retired. Address: c/o Grindlay's Bank Ltd, 13 St James's Square, SW1Y 4LF. Club: Naval. [Died 7 May 1978.

INMAN, 1st Baron, cr 1946, of Knaresborough; Philip Albert Inman, PC 1947; JP County of London; President, former Chairman, Charing Cross Hospital; President, Charing Cross Hospital Medical School; Member of Council, King Edward's Hospital Fund; Patron, Independent Hospitals Association; director of publishing, hotel and industrial companies; an underwriting member of Lloyd's; b 12 June 1892; s of Philip Inman; m 1919, May Amélie, o d of Edward Dew, Harrow; one d (and one s decd). Educ: Harrogate; Leeds Univ. Former Chm. of BBC and of Central Bd of Finance of Church Assembly; Lord Privy Seal during 1947; Chm. Hotels Executive, British Transport, 1948-51; a Church Commissioner, 1946-57. Mem. of Court, Worshipful Co. of Needlemakers; Hon. FRSH. Publications: The Human Touch; The Silent Loom; The Golden Cup; Oil and Wine; Straight Runs Harley Street (Novel); No Going Back (Autobiography). Recreations: walking, reading, golf. Address: Knaresborough House, Warninglid, Haywards Heath, West Sussex RH17 5SN. T: Warninglid 225. Club: Athenæum. [Died 26 Aug. 1979 (ext).

INNES of Learney, Sir Thomas, GCVO 1967 (KCVO 1946); Lord Lyon King of Arms, and Secretary to the Order of the Thistle, 1945-69; Marchmont Herald, since 1969; Heraldic and Peerage Lawyer; Hon. LLD St Andrews, 1956; FSA Scotland; Member of the Royal Company of Archers (Queen's Body Guard for Scotland); Baron of Aberkerder, Kinnairdy and Yeuchrie; Genealogist to Priory of Scotland in the Order of St John, 1947-70, Preceptor of Torphichen since 1970, KJStJ, 1947; Chairman of Postmaster General's Stamps Committee (Scotland), 1956-57; Commissioner of Supply for Aberdeenshire, 1926-29; Member of National Building Records Scottish Council since 1941; Member of Council of Scottish History Society, Scottish Record Society, Scottish Ecclesiological Society (President 1957-60), Scottish Ancestry Research Society; Vice-President Scottish Genealogy Society; Vice-President Society of Genealogists; Trustee of Sir William Fraser's Foundation; b 26 Aug. 1893; o s of late Lt-Col Francis N. Innes of Learney, DL, and Margaret Anne, d of Archer Irvine-Fortescue of Kingcausie, Kincardineshire, and gs of late Col Thomas Innes of Learney, CVO, LLD, DL; m 1928, Lady Lucy Buchan, 3rd d of 18th Earl of Caithness, CBE; three s one d. Educ: Neuchatel; Edinburgh Academy and Univ. Carrick

Pursuivant of Arms, 1926-35; Advocate, Scots Bar, 1922; Albany Herald, 1935-45; was interim Lyon Clerk and Keeper of the Records in Court of Lord Lyon, May-Sept. 1929 and 1939-40. Herald-en-liaison with Armed Forces (Scotland), 1940-45. Hon. Sec. Scot. (Literary) Text Soc., 1932-54. Publications: many articles on Scots Heraldry, History, and Peerage Law; contributor to Green's Encyclopædia of the Laws of Scotland, Encyclopædia of Scot. Legal Styles and Encyclopædia Britannica; (ed) 4th and 5th edn Clans, Septs and Regiments of Scottish Highlands, 1952, 1955; Scots Heraldry, 1934, 1956; (ed) 25th edn Scottish Clans and Their Tartans, 1939; The Scottish Parliament, its Symbolism and its Ceremonial, 1933 (in Jur. Rev.) The Old Mansion House of Edinight, 1937; Observations on Armorial Conveyancing, 1940; Law of Succession in Ensigns Armorial, 1941; Tartans of the Clans and Families of Scotland, 1948; Robes of the Scots Feudal Baronage (in Soc. of Antiquaries of Scotland); Margaret Fair Tercentenary Book, 1950. Recreations: art, architecture, and literature (Scots and mediæval), visiting places of historic interest. Heir: e s Thomas Innes of Learney, yr [b 22 Jan. 1930 (Baron of Learney, Superior of Torphins); m 1958, Rosemary Elizabeth, yr d of late Brig. C. V. S. Jackson, CIE, CBE; one d]. Address: Laigh Riggs, Torphins, Aberdeenshire; Kinnairdy Castle, Bridge of Marnoch, Banffshire; 35 Inverleith Row, Edinburgh. T: 031-552 4924. Club: New (Edinburgh). [Died 16 Oct. 1971.

INNES, Sir Walter James, 15th Bt, cr 1628; b 8 Aug. 1903; s of late Hector Innes (6th s of 11th Bt) and Annie Jane, d of W. Fraser; S cousin 1950. Heir: kinsman Ronald Gordon Berowald Innes, OBE 1943 [b 24 July 1907; m 1st, 1933, Elizabeth Haughton (d 1958), e d of late A. Fayle, Merlin, Clonmel, Co. Tipperary; two s one d; 2nd, 1961, Elizabeth Christian, e d of late Lt-Col C. H. Watson, DSO. Educ: Harrow]. Address: Carlos Pellegrini 485, 4 piso, Dep. B, Buenos Aires, Argentina. [Died 2 Sept. 1978.

INNES, William Arnold; Commercial Consultant; Hon. President and Consultant to Cerebos Ltd and Associated Companies, 1962-69 (Chairman 1951-62); b 13 Nov. 1902; 3rd s of late Charles Robertson Innes, Edinburgh and Kingston upon Hull, and late Ann Florence Innes (née Buckley); m 1927, Dorothea Lois, o d of late William Douglas, WS, Edinburgh, and Jane Mary (née MacDonald); two d (and one d decd). Educ: Hymers Coll. Founder and Chm., The Alliance of Produce Importers and National Wholesale Distributors, and Chm. of Produce Importers (Alliance) Ltd, 1932-38; Dir Cerebos Ltd, 1939; formed and managed cttee set up in 1940 by agreement with Min. of Food to organise and maintain national distribution of salt; acted in advisory capacity to various sections of Bd of Trade and Min. of Supply, 1939-45; Formerly Chairman (retd 1962): Brand & Co. Ltd, Saxa Salt Co. Ltd, Bisto Ltd, The Middlewich Salt Co. Ltd, Henry Seddon & Sons Ltd, Scott (Midlothian) Ltd, John Crampton & Co. Ltd, Stamina Foods Ltd, Cerebos (Ireland) Ltd, Cerebos (Australia) Pty Ltd, Cerebos (Canada) Ltd, Cerebos (South Africa) Ltd. Mem., Court of Patrons RCS. Life Governor: Imperial Cancer Research Fund (Vice-Pres.); Royal Caledonian Schools; Heart Foundation. Recreations: travelling, gardening, golf, fishing. Address: Chapel Green House, Earlsferry, Elie, Fife. T: Elie 422. Clubs: Caledonian; Elie Golf House (Elie); Denham Golf (Denham). [Died 2 Sept. 1973.

INNES-WILSON, Col Campbell Aubrey Kenneth, CBE 1954 (OBE 1946, MBE 1943); b 20 June 1905; s of late Captain R. A. K. Wilson, KSLI; m 1939, Lorna Isabel, d of late Major G. G. P. Humphreys, Donaghmore House, Castlefinn, Co. Donegal; one s. Educ: Fettes; Royal Military Academy, Woolwich; St John's Coll., Cambridge. 2nd Lt, RE 1925. Joined Survey of India, 1929; Dir, Eastern Circle, Survey of India, 1946; Dep. Surveyor-Gen. of India, 1947; Surveyor Gen. of Pakistan, 1950-54. Served War of 1939-45; Iraq and Persia, 1941-43 (MBE); Burma, 1943-45 (OBE, despatches twice). FRICS; FRGS. Address: 41 Horsecastles Lane, Sherborne, Dorset DT9 6BU. T: Sherborne 2486. [Died 12 Sept. 1978.

INONU, Gen. Ismet; Leader of the Republican People's Party, Turkey, 1938-72; b Izmir, Asia Minor, 24 Sept. 1884; s of Reshid, judge and legal adviser to Governmental Depts, and Djevriye; m 1916, Mevhibe; two s one d. Educ: Military Artillery Coll. and Military Academy, Istanbul. Capt. Gen. Staff, 2nd Army, Edirne, 1906; Major, chief Gen. Staff, Army of Yemen, 1912; Lt-Col 1914; Col 1915; Comdr 4th Army Corps, 1916; Comdr 20th Army Corps, later 3rd Army Corps, 1917; Under-Sec., Ministry of War, Istanbul, 1918; left Istanbul, joined Mustafa Kemal (Atatürk) and National Struggle movement in Ankara; became dep. of Edirne and Chief of Great Gen. Staff, 1920; Comdr Western Front; victorious, 1st and 2nd Battles of Inönü, Brig.-Gen. 1921; Lt-Gen. 1922; appointed

Minister of Foreign Affairs, while he kept his rank in army in accordance Constitution, 1922; signed Treaty of Lausanne, 1923; Prime Minister, Oct. 1923-Nov. 1924 and March 1925-Oct. 1937; Pres. of the Republic of Turkey, 1938-50; Leader of the Opposition, Turkish Parliament, 1950-60; Prime Minister of Turkey, 1961-65; again Leader of the Opposition, 1965-72. Gen., 1926; retired from army, 1927. *Recreations:* fond of books; equitation, chess, bridge, billiards. *Address:* Cankaya, Ankara, Turkey. *[Died 25 Dec. 1973.*

INSALL, Group Captain Gilbert Stuart Martin, VC 1915; MC; RAF retired; *b* 1894; *e s* of G. J. Insall, Sevington, Kent; *m* 1926, Olwen Scott, *o d* of J. A. Yates; two *s. Educ:* Anglo-Saxon Sch., Paris. Was studying as a dentist in Paris on outbreak of war; enlisted as private in UPS Royal Fusiliers (18th Service Batt.); went to Brooklands on transfer to RFC 1915; flew to France in summer as pilot; on 7 Nov. he forced to earth an Aviatik and descended to less than 500 feet under heavy fire to allow his gunner to destroy the enemy machine within the German lines, was shot down in trenches on the way back at 200 feet, repaired machine during night under concentrated shell-fire, and flew back to his aerodrome at dawn (despatches, VC); pursued German machine on 14 Dec. across the lines; when well inside lines engaged the hostile machine and got hit by machine-gun bullet in petrol tank; while trying to plane back an anti-aircraft shell burst under the machine wounding him and his observer, Corpl Donald; unable to reach lines, he landed, and was taken prisoner, after trying to destroy his machine; underwent two operations whilst in captivity, one of which was the extraction of a large piece of anti-aircraft shell from his back; escaped from Heidelberg Camp, 1916; recaptured after five days; escaped from Crefeld, recaptured same day; sent to Ströhen, near Hanover; managed finally to reach Dutch Frontier, Aug. 1917 (MC); permanent Commission RAF Aug. 1919; retired from RAF, 1945. *Recreations:* hockey, shooting, fishing, archæology, *Address:* Monks Mill, Scrooby, near Doncaster, Yorks. *[Died 17 Feb. 1972.*

INSKIP, Maj.-Gen. Roland Debenham, CB 1939; CIE 1938; DSO 1916; MC; IA; retired; *b* 1885; *s* of late Rev. O. D. Inskip, Rector of Harleston, Norfolk; *m* 1918, Evelyn (marriage dissolved, 1928), *d* of John Rickard, Tudor House, Fairford, Glos.; one *s* (and one killed in France Jan. 1944); *m* 1929, Mabel Louisa, *d* of Mackay John Scobie, Bournemouth. *Educ:* Framlingham Coll.; RMC, Sandhurst. Served NW Frontier of India, 1908 (medal and clasp); European War (France, Mesopotamia, Palestine), 1914-18 (despatches five times, DSO, MC); Bt Major, 1918; Bt Lt-Col, 1928, NW Frontier of India, 1930 (clasp); Waziristan, 1937-38-39 (CIE, despatches twice, medal and 2 clasps); Commandant 6th Royal Batt. 13th Frontier Force Rifles, 1932-34; Gen. Staff Officer First Grade, AHQ, India, 1934-35; Col 1935; Imperial Defence Coll., 1936; Comdr, 1st (Abbottabad) Infantry Brigade, India, 1937-39; Maj.-Gen. 1939; a District Comdr, India, 1941; GOC Ceylon, 1941-42; retired, Sept. 1942; re-employed Oct. 1942-Feb. 1946; Chief of Staff Bhopal State Forces, Feb. 1946-April 1947; Col 6th Royal Bn (Scinde) The FF Rifles, 1943-56; Hon. Col 1st Bn (Scinde) The FF Rifles, 1963- (Pakistan Army). *Address:* c/o Lloyd's Bank, 6 Pall Mall, SW1. *[Died 23 Nov. 1971.*

INVERFORTH, 2nd Baron, *cr* 1919, of Southgate; **Andrew Alexander Morton Weir;** Chairman and Governing Director of Andrew Weir & Company Ltd, 1955-70, President since 1971; *b* 12 Sept. 1897; *o s* of 1st Baron Inverforth, PC, and Anne (*d* 1941), *y d* of Thomas Kay Dowie; 4th father 1955; *m* 1929, Iris Beryl, *d* of late Charles Vincent, 4th Bn The Buffs; two *s. Educ:* St Paul's Sch. Comdr, Order of Dannebrog (Danish), 1947. *Recreation:* yachting. *Heir: s* Hon. (Andrew Charles) Roy Weir. *Address:* 24 Clarence Terrace, NW1. *Clubs:* Royal Automobile, Royal Yacht Squadron. *[Died 17 Nov. 1975.*

IRVINE, Rt. Hon. Sir Arthur (James), PC 1970; Kt 1967; QC 1958; MP (Lab) Edge Hill Division of Liverpool, since 1947; *b* 14 July 1909; *s* of late J. M. Irvine, KC, Sheriff of Renfrew and Bute; *m* 1937, Eleanor, *d* of late E. E. T. Morris, Petersfield, Hants; four *s. Educ:* Angusfield Sch., Aberdeen; Edinburgh Academy; Edinburgh Univ. (MA 1929), Oriel Coll., Oxford (BA 1931, MA 1957). Pres., Oxford Union, 1932; called to Bar, Middle Temple, 1935; also Mem. of Inner Temple; Sec. to Lord Chief Justice of England, 1935-40; UK delegate to Council of Europe, 1961-62; Master of the Bench, Middle Temple, 1965; Chm. House of Commons Select Cttee on Procedure, 1965; Solicitor-General, 1967-70. Recorder of Colchester, 1965-67. Hon. Fellow, Oriel Coll., 1969. Contested Kincardine and West Aberdeenshire (L), 1935 and 1939 (by-election). DAAG HQ Eastern Command, 1944; DAMS HQ Land Forces, Greece, 1944-45 (despatches). Contested (Lab) Twickenham, 1945 and South Aberdeen (by-election), 1946. *Address:* 20 Wellington

Square, SW3. *T:* 01-730 3117; 4 Paper Buildings, Temple, EC4. *T:* 01-353 8408. *[Died 15 Dec. 1978.*

IRVINE, Prof. William Tait; Consultant Surgeon to the Libyan Government, since 1973; *b* 19 March 1925; *s* of George Irvine; *m* 1950, May Warburton; two *d. Educ:* by his father and at Univs of Glasgow, McGill and Minnesota, USA. BSc 1944, MB, ChB, 1947, FRCSE 1950, FRCS 1952, ChM (Hons) 1956, MD (Hons) 1957. Archibald Fellow in Surgery, McGill Univ., 1954; Mayo Foundation Fellow, Mayo Clinic, USA, 1955; Lectr in Surgery, Univ. of Glasgow, 1956; Asst Surg., The London Hospital, E1, 1957-60; Prof. of Surgery, Univ. of London, at St Mary's Hosp., 1960-72. *Publications:* various papers on surgical subjects. Editor: Modern Trends in Surgery; Scientific Basis of Surgery. *Recreations:* walking, reading. *Address:* 12 Kildare Terrace, W2. *T:* 01-229 6069. *[Died 11 May 1980.*

IRVINE-JONES, Douglas Vivian; Sheriff-Substitute of Inverness, Moray, Nairn and Ross and Cromarty, 1952-71; *b* 20 March 1904; *s* of late Henry Irvine-Jones, MD, and of Mrs Irvine-Jones, Edinburgh; *m* 1937, Angela Mary, *d* of late Sir John Couper MVO, OBE, and Lady Couper, North Berwick; no *c. Educ:* Daniel Stewart's Coll., Edinburgh; Edinburgh Univ. (MA, LLB). Solicitor, 1930; Advocate of the High Court of Judicature at Rangoon, 1930; Mem., Faculty of Advocates, 1945; Sheriff-Substitute of Dumfries, 1950-52. *Recreations:* fishing, shooting. *Address:* Crannach, Lamington, Kildary, Rossshire. *[Died 21 Nov. 1974.*

IRVING, David J. M.; see Mill Irving.

IRWIN, Lt-Gen. Noel Mackintosh Stuart, CB 1940; DSO 1918 and two bars 1918, 1919; MC; Croix de Guerre (France); *b* India, 24 Dec. 1892; *e s* of William Stuart Irwin of Motihari, Bihar and Orissa, India; *m* 1918, Margaret Maud (*d* 1963), *d* of late B. Bavin; one *s*; *m* 1966, Mrs Elizabeth Collier (*née* Fröhlich). *Educ:* Marlborough Coll.; RMC, Sandhurst; joined The Essex Regt, 1912; promoted Major, The Border Regt, 1927; Brevet Lt-Col 1931; Colonel, 1934; Major-Gen. 1940; temp. Lt-Gen. 1942; Lt-Gen. 1944; served France with Battalion Aug. 1914-17; commanded 2nd Batt. Lincs Regt 1917-18; 8th Batt. Leicester Regt 1918; 1st Batt. Lincs Regt 1918-19; Temp. Colonel, France 1919; (DSO and 2 bars; MC and Croix de Guerre; 1914 star; despatches 5 times); Staff Coll., 1924-25; General Staff, Rhine, 1926-27; India, 1929-33; Chief Instructor RMC, Sandhurst, 1933-35; Imperial Defence Coll., 1936; GSO 1st Grade, the British troops in China, 1937-38; Commander 6th Infantry Brigade, 1939; France, India and Burma, 1939-43; Commanded 2 Inf. Div., 38 (Welsh) Div., 11th Corps, 4th Indian Corps, Eastern Army, India, West Africa Command, 1946-48; retired, 1948. *Recreations:* Captain Marlborough College Shooting VIII; hockey, Regt and Army. *Address:* Alfoxton Cottage, Holford, Somerset. *[Died 21 Dec. 1972.*

IRWIN, Prof. Raymond, MA Oxon; FLA; Professor of Library Studies, University of London, 1957-69, now Emeritus Professor; Director of the School of Librarianship and Archives, University College, London, 1944-69; *b* 14 March 1902; *s* of late John T. Irwin, Maryport, Cumberland, and Elizabeth (*née* Pollard), Eccles, Manchester; *m* 1st, 1929, Ivy Summerville Viggers (*d* 1973); 2nd, 1974, Mary Elsie Allen. *Educ:* King's Coll., Taunton; St John's Coll., Oxford. County Librarian, Northamptonshire, 1924; County Librarian, Lancs, 1944. Hon. Treas. of Library Assoc., 1947-54, Vice-Pres., 1954, President, 1958, Hon. Fellow, 1963. *Publications:* The National Library Service, 1947; Librarianship: Essays on Applied Bibliography, 1949; (ed) The Libraries of London, 1949 (rev. edn 1961); British Bird Books: an Index to British Ornithology, 1951; British Birds and their Books: catalogue of exhibn for Nat. Book League, 1952; The Origins of the English Library, 1958; The Heritage of the English Library, 1964; The English Library: sources and history, 1966; many articles in periodicals. *Recreations:* wild flowers, birds, gardening, reading, music. *Address:* 24 Central Drive, Lytham St Anne's, Lancs. *T:* Lytham 736702. *[Died 13 Dec. 1976.*

IRWIN, William Henry; Resident Judge, HM's Court of Sovereign Base Areas of Akrotiri and Dhekelia, Cyprus, 1961-65, retired; *b* 13 Sept. 1907; *o s* of William Irwin, JP, Aughnacloy, Co. Tyrone, and of Florence, *d* of Rev. J. A. Allison; *m* 1935, Olive, *d* of C. Jones Henry, Ardtarmon, Sligo; one *s* one *d. Educ:* Royal Belfast Academical Institution; Trinity Coll., Dublin (BA 1930). Called to Bar, Inn of Court of Northern Ireland, 1932; Northern Ireland Circuit; District Magistrate, Gold Coast, 1936; Acting Solicitor-Gen., Gold Coast, 1941-42 and 1947; Judge of the Supreme Court of Trinidad and Tobago, 1947; Mem. of West Indian Court of Appeal, 1951; Senior Puisne Judge, Trinidad and Tobago, 1952-

54; Puisne Judge, Nigeria, 1954; Judge of High Court, Western Region, Nigeria, 1955-61; Acting Chief Justice, Western Region, Nigeria, 1958 and 1960. Mem. of HBM's Full Court for the Persian Gulf, 1962. *Address:* c/o Lloyds Bank Ltd, 6 Pall Mall, SW1. *[Died 23 July 1974.*

IRWIN, William Knox, MD; FRCSE; Consulting Surgeon, St Peter's and St Paul's Hospitals for Genito-Urinary Diseases, London; *b* 1883; *s* of late William Irwin, Drumquin, Co. Tyrone; *m* 1930, Edith Isabel Mary, *d* of late Rev. J. T. Collins, MA; one *s*. *Educ:* Royal School, Dungannon; Aberdeen Univ.; Edinburgh; Berlin. MB, ChB 1908; MD (Hons), 1913; late Senior Resident Surgical Officer, W London Hospital; Hon. Consulting Genito-Urinary Surgeon, Eltham and Mottingham Hospital; Senior Surgeon, Hendon Emergency Hosp.; Lecturer, Post-Graduate Institute of Urology, University of London; etc. Hon. Corres. Mem. Italian Society of Urology; Membre de la Société Internationale d'Urologie; Fellow Royal Society of Medicine. *Publications:* Urinary Surgery, 2nd edn 1927; contributions to Surgery of Urinary Organs in British Journal of Surgery, Lancet, British Journal of Urology, British Medical Journal, Medical Press and Circular, Urologic and Cutaneous Review, etc. *Recreations:* riding, gardening, reading. *Address:* c/o National Westminster Bank Ltd, 1 Cavendish Square, W1. *Club:* Athenæum. *[Died 18 July 1973.*

ISAACS, Rt. Hon. George Alfred, PC 1945; DL, JP; Chairman Kingston County Bench 1943-45; *b* London, 1883. Past Alderman, Borough of Southwark; Mayor of Southwark, 1919-21; contested North Southwark, 1918; Gravesend, 1922; MP (Lab) Gravesend, 1923-24, North Southwark, 1929-31 and 1939-50, Southwark, 1950-Sept. 1959. Parl. Priv. Sec. to Sec. of State for Colonies, 1924, to Sec. of State for Dominions, 1929-31, to First Lord of the Admiralty, 1942-45; Minister of Labour and Nat. Service, 1945-Jan. 1951; Minister of Pensions, Jan.-Oct. 1951. Served on Govt's Departmental Cttee on Coroners and Departmental Cttee on Workmen's Compensation; also Mem. of Royal Commission on Workmen's Compensation. Sec. of Nat. Soc. of Operative Printers and Assistants, 1909-49; Past Pres., Printing and Kindred Trades Federation; Chm., Trades Union Congress General Council, 1945; Pres., World Trade Union Conference, London, 1945; Liveryman of the Worshipful Company of Stationers. Hon. Freeman of Borough of Southwark, 1957. JP 1929, DL 1947, Surrey. *Publication:* The Story of the Newspaper Printing Press. *Address:* Mole Cottage, 166 Portsmouth Road, Cobham, Surrey. *[Died 26 April 1979.*

ISAACS, Jacob, MA Oxon; Professor Emeritus, University of London, since 1964; Professor of English Language and Literature at Queen Mary College, University of London, 1952-64; *b* 1896; *s* of Rev. M. D. Isaacs and Jessie, *d* of Rev. Moses Bregman; *m* 1933, Enid Austin Dickie; two *d*. *Educ:* Exeter Coll., Oxford (1st Cl. Hons English). Civil Service, 1912-16; Lieut Royal Garrison Artillery (T), served in France; Asst Lecturer, University Coll. of N Wales, Bangor, 1921-24; Asst Lecturer, King's Coll., London, 1924-28; Lecturer, 1928-42; Professor of English Language and Literature, Univ. of Jerusalem, 1942-45; Mem. of Council, Stage Society and Film Society. *Publications:* Shakespeare as Man of the Theatre, 1927; Production and Stage Management at the Blackfriars Theatre, 1933; Shakespeare Scholarship, and Later Shakespeare Criticism, in Companion to Shakespeare Studies, 1933; Coleridge's Critical Terminology, 1936; Sixteenth Century Bible Versions, and The Authorised Version and after, 1940; An assessment of Twentieth Century Literature, 1951; The Background of Modern Poetry, 1951; Shakespeare's Earliest Years in the Theatre, 1953; William Poel's Prompt Book of Fratricide Punished, 1956; general editor, English Library Reprints; joint editor (with Dr W. Rose) of Contemporary Movements in European Literature; article on Dramatic Criticism, Encyclopædia Britannica (14th Edition); contributed to Times, Times Literary Supp., Art News and Review, Observer, Listener, Spectator, etc. *Recreations:* art history, theatrical history, book collecting, travelling, and reading dictionaries. *Address:* Little Court, Court Yard, Eltham, SE9. *T:* 01-850 7866. *[Died 12 May 1973.*

ISAACSON, Sir Robert (Spencer), KBE 1966; CMG 1955; *b* 11 Nov. 1907; *s* of late Arthur Spencer Isaacson and Dorothy Isaacson (*née* Lance); *m* 1938, Margaret Viola Lage, *e d* of Sir Rowland F. W. Hodge, 1st Bt. *Educ:* Radley. British Embassy, Rio de Janeiro, 1940-47; British Legation, Bucharest, 1948; British Embassy: Athens, 1948-52; Washington, 1952-55; Paris, 1955-59; Rio de Janeiro, 1959-63; Ambassador to Guatemala, 1963-64; Ambassador to Switzerland, 1964-67. *Recreations:* fishing, shooting, bridge. *Address:* The Old Manse, Broughton, Stockbridge, Hants. *[Died 17 June 1972.*

ISHAM, Sir Gyles, 12th Bt, *cr* 1627; MA; FSA; DL; *b* 31 Oct. 1903; *o* surv. *s* of Sir Vere Isham, 11th Bt, and Millicent (*d* 1961), *d* of late Henry Halford Vaughan; *S* father 1941. *Educ:* Rugby; Magdalen Coll., Oxford (Demy). MA 1930; Pres. of the OUDS, 1925; Pres. of the Oxford Union, 1926; adopted stage as a profession on coming down from Oxford, 1926, making his first appearance professionally under the management of the late J. B. Fagan; toured the English Provinces and the USA; appeared in New York and London, and later in films in both England and America; has played leading Shakespearean parts at the Old Vic, Memorial Theatre, Stratford-on-Avon, in the USA, and at the Open-Air Theatre, Regent's Park; has toured Canada and South Africa. Joined London Irish Rifles (TA) April 1939, Sergeant Aug. 1939; 2nd Lieut King's Royal Rifle Corps, Feb. 1940; served with 1st Bn Western Desert Campaign, Egypt, from 1 May 1940; on staff of Eighth Army when formed Sept. 1941; left for staff appt at GHQ ME (Major), July 1942; GSO1 (Intelligence) HQ Ninth Army, April 1943-Dec. 1944; on return to England, filled GSO1 appt War Office, March-Aug. 1945; Defence Security Officer HQ Palestine, Sept. 1945-Sept. 1946; demobilised (deferred) Lieut-Col, Dec. 1946. Contested (C) Kettering (Northants), 1950. Farms 500 acres of his own land. DL 1952, CC 1955-64, High Sheriff 1958-59, Northants. A Trustee of the Nat. Portrait Gall., 1964-71. Pres., Assoc. of Independent Hosps. 1969-; Chm. Cttee, St Andrew's Hosp., Northampton, 1956-73. *Publications:* All Saints, Lamport, 1950; The Duppa-Isham Correspondence, 1650-60 (Northants Record Soc. Vol. XVII), 1955; The Story of Clipston Grammar School, 1956; Easton Mauduit, 1968; The Diary of Thomas Isham of Lamport, 1971; All Saints, Rushton, 1973. Editor, Northamptonshire Past and Present, 1960-73. *Heir:* cousin, Ian Vere Gyles Isham, *b* 1923. *Address:* Lamport Hall, Northampton. *Club:* Beefsteak. *[Died 29 Jan. 1976.*

ISITT, Air Vice-Marshal Sir Leonard (Monk), KBE 1946 (CBE 1939); retired as Chairman, Standard-Triumph (NZ) Ltd, and Chairman of Directors, NZ National Airways Corporation, and Tasman Empire Airways, Ltd; *b* 27 July 1891; *m* 1920; two *d*. *Educ:* Mostyn House, Parkgate, Cheshire, England; Christchurch Boys' High School, Christchurch, New Zealand. Farming early years; NZ Rifle Brigade, 1915-16; Royal Flying Corps/Royal Air Force, 1917-19; transferred Royal New Zealand Air Force, 1919; Air Force Mem. for Personnel, 1937; RNZAF Representative, Ottawa and Washington, 1940-41; Air Officer Commanding RNZAF, United Kingdom, 1942-43; Chief of the Air Staff, RNZAF, 1943-45. *Recreation:* fishing. *Address:* Golf Road, Paraparau Beach, NZ. *TA:* Wellington, New Zealand. *[Died 21 Jan. 1976.*

ISLE, William Herbert Mosley, CBE 1969; Chairman, Economic Development Committee for Wool Textile Industry, 1964-70; director of various companies; *b* 11 Oct. 1896; *s* of late William Mawson Isle and late Ellen Isle (*née* Ingham); *m* 1925, Victoria Constance Irene Feather (*d* 1963); one *s*. *Educ:* privately; Pembroke Coll., Cambridge. Qualified ACA, 1924; Partner in: Thoseby, Son & Co., Bradford, 1930; Peat, Marwick, Mitchell & Co., 1953; retired, 1964. *Recreation:* golf. *Address:* Badgergate, Burley Woodhead, near Ilkley, Yorkshire. *T:* Burley-in-Wharfedale 3044. *Clubs:* United Oxford & Cambridge University; Union (Bradford), Bradford (Bradford). *[[Died 2 Sept. 1973.*

ISLES, Prof. Keith Sydney, CMG 1967; retired; *b* 4 Aug. 1902; 2nd *s* of Sydney Henry Isles and Margaret Ellen Knight, Tasmania; *m* 1926, Irene Frances Clayton; one *s* two *d*. *Educ:* Universities of Tasmania, Adelaide and Cambridge. BCom, Tasmania; MA, MSc, Cambridge. Fellow of Laura Spelman Rockefeller Memorial at Univ. of Cambridge, 1929-31; Wrenbury Schol. and Adam Smith Prize of Univ. of Cambridge; Lecturer in Political Economy, University of Edinburgh, 1931-37; Prof. of Economics: University College of Swansea, 1937-39; University of Adelaide, 1939-45; Queen's Univ. of Belfast, 1945-57. Vice-Chancellor of the University of Tasmania, 1957-67; Vis. Prof. of Economics, New Univ. of Ulster, 1968-69. Economic Adviser to Commonwealth Rationing Commn, 1942. Served Commonwealth Mil. Forces (rank of temporary Lieut-Col) 1944-45. Jt Local Sec., meeting of British Assoc. for the Advancement of Science, in Belfast, 1952. Hon. LLD: St Andrews, 1963; Queen's Univ., Belfast, 1969; Hon. DLitt Tasmania, 1968. *Publications:* Wages Policy and the Price Level, 1934; Money and Trade, 1935; with N. Cuthbert: chapters in Ulster Home Rule (ed Wilson), 1955, and An Economic Survey of Northern Ireland (HMSO), 1957; articles in various journals. *Recreations:* reading, gardening, photography, motoring. *Address:* 91 Esplanade, Rose Bay, Hobart, Tasmania 7015, Australia. *Club:* Tasmanian. *[Died 18 June 1977.*

ISSERSTEDT, Hans S.; see Schmidt-Isserstedt.

ITURBI, José; Grand Cross of Alphonso X the Wise, 1947; Grand Cross of Isabel the Catholic, 1975; Gold Medal of Labor, Spain, 1968; Commandeur, Légion d'Honneur, 1976; Companion, Order of St Michael (Greece); Order of St George (Greece); Concert Pianist, Conductor, Composer; *b* Valencia, Spain, 28 Nov. 1895; *s* of Ricardo and Theresa Iturbi; *m* 1915, Maria Giner (*d* 1927); (one *d* decd). *Educ:* College and Academies at Valencia. Began to play piano at age of three; at seven, recognised as a child prodigy, was teaching pupils three and four times his age; graduated from Conservatory in Valencia and later was sent to Barcelona to study with Joaquin Malats. After graduating from Paris Conservatoire at age of 17½ with the highest Grand Prix, he became head of Piano Faculty at Geneva Conservatoire, a post once held by Liszt; American début, 1929. Regular conductor of Rochester Philharmonic, 1936-44; Guest Conductor New York Philharmonic, Philadelphia Orchestra, Detroit Symphony, Chicago, Dallas, Los Angeles, Atlanta, and all leading symphony orchestras of United States; also all leading symphony orchestras of England, France, Spain, Mexico, S America, S Africa, Holland, Belgium, Israel, Italy, Argentina, Uruguay, Venezuela, Peru, etc. He averaged 200 concerts a year. In several films. Member: Royal Acad. of Fine Arts San Fernando, Madrid; Royal Acad. of Fine Arts San Carlos, Valencia. Pre-eminent Son of Valencia, 1971; Quevado Gold Medal for the Arts, Spain, 1972; Gold Medal, Circle of Bellas Artes, Madrid; Colossal of Rhodes Award, Valencia, 1975; FFF Award of Spanish Press, 1976. *Recreation:* flying. *Address:* 915 North Bedford Drive, Beverly Hills, Calif 90210, USA.   [*Died 28 June 1980.*

IVATT, Henry George, CEng, FIMechE, MILocoE; Retired; Director of Brush Traction Ltd as Consultant, 1957; Director and General Manager, Brush Traction Ltd, 1955; Director of Brush Bagnall Traction Ltd, as Consultant for diesel electric locomotives, 1951; Director, Remploy Ltd, 25 Buckingham Gate, SW1, 1952; *b* 4 May 1886; *s* of late H. A. Ivatt, Locomotive Engineer of former Great Northern Rly; *m* 1913, Dorothy Sarah Harrison (*d* 1962); no *c. Educ:* Uppingham. Mechanical and technical training at Locomotive Works, Crewe, of former London and North-Western Railway. Served European War, 1914-18, in France on staff of QMG, Mechanical Transport, with rank of Major. Dep. Locomotive Supt of former North Stafford Rly, 1919; Works Supt, Derby Locomotive Works, LMS Rly Co., 1928; Divisional Mechanical Engineer, Scottish Div., LMS Rly Co., 1932; Principal Asst for Locomotives to Chief Mechanical Engineer, LMS Rly Co., 1937; Chief Mechanical and Electrical Engineer, London Midland Region, British Railways, 1948-51; LMS Rly, 1946-48, retd 1951. Consultant for diesel traction, Brush Electrical Engineering Co. Ltd, 1958-64. *Address:* Chantry House, Melbourne, Derbyshire. *T:* Melbourne 2615.
[*Died 4 Oct. 1972.*

IVELAW-CHAPMAN, Air Chief Marshal Sir Ronald, GCB 1957 (KCB 1953; CB 1949); KBE 1951 (CBE 1943); DFC 1918; AFC 1930; *b* 17 Jan. 1899; *s* of late Joseph Ivelaw-Chapman, Cheltenham; *m* 1930, Margaret, *d* of late C. W. Shortt, Beckenham; one *s* one *d. Educ:* Cheltenham Coll. 2nd Lieut Royal Flying Corps, 1917; European War, 1917-18; at home, India, and Iraq, 1919-20; Kabul evacuations (awarded AFC); served War of 1939-45: in various executive and staff appointments, 1939-43; prisoner of war, 1944-45. AOC No. 38 Group, 1945-46; Directing Staff, Imperial Defence Coll., 1947-49; C-in-C Indian Air Force, 1950-51; AOC-in-C Home Command, 1952; Deputy Chief of the Air Staff, 1952-53; Vice Chief of the Air Staff, 1953-57; retired, 1957. Pres. Cheltonian Society, 1956-57; Dir of Resettlement, Ministry of Labour, 1957-61. Mem. of Observer Trust, 1957-66. Pres. of Council, Cheltenham Coll., 1968-72; Vice-Pres., RAF Escaping Society. *Publication:* (with Anne Baker) Wings over Kabul, 1976. *Recreation:* fishing. *Address:* Knockwood, Nether Wallop, Hants. *Club:* Royal Air Force.   [*Died 28 April 1978.*

IVERSEN, Johannes, DrPhil; Senior Geologist at the Geological survey of Denmark since 1942; Lecturer at the University of Copenhagen, 1955-69; *b* 1904; *s* of Hans Iversen and Anna Iversen (*née* Asmussen); *m* 1939, Aase Thorlacius-Ussing; one *d. Educ:* Copenhagen. DrPhil 1936. FilDr *hc* Uppsala 1957; DSc *hc* Cambridge 1966. *Publications:* Land Occupation in Denmark's Stone Age, 1941 (2nd edn 1964); Textbook of Pollen Analysis (with Knut Faegri) 1950 (2nd rev. edn 1964). *Address:* Rörskaersvej 10, 2820 Gentofte, Denmark. [*Died 17 Oct. 1971.*

J

JACK, Hon. Sir Roy (Emile), Kt 1970; MP (Nat) for Rangitikei, New Zealand; Speaker of the House of Representatives, since 1976; barrister and solicitor, Jack, Riddet, Young & Partners; *b* New Plymouth, 12 Jan. 1914; *s* of John Bain Jack; *m* 1946, Frances Anne, *d* of Dr G. W. Harty; one *d. Educ:* Wanganui Collegiate Sch.; Victoria University of Wellington, NZ (LLB). Served War 1939-45, RNZAF. Judge's Associate, barrister and solicitor, 1935-38; entered practice as barrister and solicitor, Wanganui, 1946. Mem., Wanganui City Council, 1946-55; Dep. Mayor, 1947-55. MP: for Patea, 1954-63; for Waimarino, subseq. Rangitikei, 1963-; Deputy Speaker, House of Representatives, 1961-66, Speaker, 1967-72; Attorney General and Minister of Justice, Feb.-Nov. 1972. *Recreations:* music (especially violin), reading, skiing, flying, gliding. *Address:* Parliament House, Wellington, New Zealand. *T:* Wellington 738288; (private) 49 College Street, Wanganui, New Zealand. *T:* Wanganui 57640. *Club:* Wanganui.   [*Died 24 Dec. 1977.*

JACKS, Graham Vernon, MA, BSc; Director, Commonwealth Bureau of Soils, 1946-66; *b* 30 March 1901; *s* of late Dr L. P. Jacks; *m* 1933, Violet Elizabeth, *d* of late Henry Tompkins; one *s* one *d. Educ:* Dragon Sch., Oxford; Magdalen Coll. Sch., Oxford; Christ Church, Oxford (scholar). Min. of Agriculture Research Scholar, 1926-29; Lectr in Soil Science, Imperial Forestry Institute, 1929-31; Dep. Dir, Imperial Bureau of Soil Science, 1931-46; Editor, Journal of Soil Science, 1949-61; Mem. of Nature Conservancy, 1959-65. *Publications:* Soil, Vegetation and Climate, 1933; Tropical Soils in Relation to Tropical Crops, 1936; (with R. O. Whyte) Erosion and Soil Conservation, 1937; (with R. O. Whyte) The Rape of the Earth, 1938; (with H. Scherbatoff) The Minor Elements of the Soil, 1940; Land Classification, 1946; Soil, 1954. *Address:* 5 Kirkdale Road, Harpenden, Herts AL5 2PT. *T:* Harpenden 3353.
[*Died 10 Aug. 1977.*

JACKSON, Alexander Young, CC (Canada) 1967; CMG 1946; RCA 1919; Landscape Painter; *b* Montreal, 3 Oct. 1882; *s* of Henry Jackson and Georgina Young; unmarried. *Educ:* Public Schools, Montreal. Worked in the lithographic business; studied art in Montreal, Chicago, and at the Académie Julian, Paris; has painted landscape all over Canada, as far north as Ellesmere Island; during European War served in France with the Canadian infantry; represented by paintings in McMichael Canadian Collection, Kleinburg, Ontario, National Gallery of British Art, National Gallery of Canada, Art Galleries of Montreal, Toronto, Vancouver, etc. Hon. degrees from: Queen's Univ., Kingston, Ont (LLD); McMaster Univ., 1953; Carleton Univ., 1957; Univ. of British Columbia, 1964; McGill Univ., 1967. *Recreations:* canoeing, fishing. *Address:* c/o R. McMichael Esq, Kleinburg, Ont, Canada. *Club:* Arts and Letters (Toronto).   [*Died 5 April 1974.*

JACKSON, Col Arnold N. S. S.; see Strode-Jackson.

JACKSON, Charles d'Orville Pilkington, ARSA, FRBS, FRSA; sculptor; *b* Garlenick, Cornwall, 1887; *s* of late Louis Pilkington Jackson, MRCS, LRCP; *m* 1st, 1916, Eve Cornish Dening (*d* 1951); one *s* one *d*; 2nd, 1958, Audrey Ethelwyn O'Brien, *yr d* of late E. W. Clark, Oxford. *Educ:* Loretto Sch.; Coll. of Art, Edinburgh (Diploma of Sculpture and Travelling Scholarship, Edinburgh, 1910); British Sch. at Rome, 1910-11; served European War, 1914-19, RFA (despatches); War of 1939-45, AA, RA; Pres., SSA, 1942-45; Mem. Royal Fine Art Commission for Scotland, 1944-63; Principal Works: Sculpture on Scottish National War Memorial, Stowe Sch. Chapel, Paisley Abbey, David Livingstone Memorial, Blantyre, Lanarks, and Royal Scots Monument, Edinburgh, Regimental Monument Royal Scots Fusiliers, Ayr; Equestrian Monument of King Robert the Bruce at Bannockburn, replica at Calgary, Alberta; Durham LI meml panels, Durham Cathedral. Portraiture: including David Livingstone at Newstead Abbey; James Clark Maxwell, Univ. of Aberdeen; Lord Lugard, University of Hong Kong, replica in Nat. Portrait Gall.; portrait medals include E. Sharpey Schaffer, physiologist. John Bruce Award of Merit (gold medal) for RCSE; Mungo Park Award RGSS. Military Statuettes, 1633-1918, Scottish United Services Museum, and Imperial War Museum; Equestrian Statuettes: Robert the Bruce; Edward the Black Prince; Statuettes of Prince Charles Stuart and Calgary Highlanders, at Calgary, Alberta. Maces of: Sch. of Medicine, University of St Andrews; City of Singapore; Coll. of Physicians, Surgeons and Gynæcologists of South Africa; Gillan Trophy ATC; (with David Linton, DSc) the Orographical Globe in Geological Survey and Museum, South Kensington, Eton Coll., Cranwell RAF Coll., Inst. of Tech., Mass, USA. *Address:* 4 Polwarth Terrace, Edinburgh EH11 1NE. *T:* 031-229 4805. *Club:* Caledonian (London).   [*Died 20 Sept. 1973.*

JACKSON, Sir Christopher M. M.; *see* Mather-Jackson, Sir G. C. M.

JACKSON, Egbert Joseph William, CB 1950; MC 1918. *Educ:* Sheffield University (MA, Gladstone Memorial Prizeman, 1912). Assistant Lecturer, Sheffield University, 1913-14; Lecturer in Economics, Birmingham University, 1914-19. Served European War, 1916-18. Entered Ministry of Education, 1919; Staff Inspector of Commerce, 1936; Asst Secretary, Ministry of War Transport, 1940-45; Chief Inspector, Ministry of Education, 1945-51; retired, 1951. *Address:* Marana Tha, Whisper Wood, Loudwater, Rickmansworth, Herts WD3 4JU. *T:* Rickmansworth 72363.   [*Died 29 Sept. 1975.*

JACKSON, Rt. Rev. Fabian Menteath Elliot; Assistant Bishop of Bath and Wells, 1950-67; Prebendary of Wells Cathedral since 1954; *b* 22 Nov. 1902; *s* of William Henry Congreve and Maud Helen Jackson; unmarried. *Educ:* Westminster Sch.; University of London; Ely Theological Coll. BA Hons Classics, London, 1925; Deacon, 1926; Priest, 1927; S Augustine's, Kilburn, 1926-38; Priest-in-Charge of S Barnabas, Northolt Park, 1938-43; Vicar of All Saints, Clifton, 1943-46; Bishop of Trinidad, 1946-49, resigned, 1949; Rector of Batcombe with Upton Noble, Somerset, 1950-67. *Address:* St Monica's Home, Westbury on Trym, Bristol BS9 3UN.   [*Died 16 July 1978.*

JACKSON, Col Sir Francis (James) Gidlow, Kt 1955; MC 1917; TD 1930; *b* 16 Sept. 1889; 2nd *s* of late Charles Gidlow Jackson, JP, CA; unmarried. *Educ:* Bilton Grange; Rugby. Admitted Solicitor, 1912; Served European War, 1914-19; Egypt, Gallipoli, France and Belgium. Served France, 1940. *Recreation:* fishing. *Address:* Domus, Enville Road, Bowdon, Cheshire. *Club:* The Manchester (Manchester).   [*Died 12 Jan. 1979.*

JACKSON, Col Frank Lawson John, OBE 1959; TD; *b* 12 June 1919; *s* of S. V. Jackson. *Educ:* Oundle. Commissioned 6th Bn North Staffs Regt, TA, 1938. Served War of 1939-45 in Ireland, and as Chief Instructor. Commanded Bn, 1954-58; Lt-Col, 1954; Hon. Col, 1959; Col 1963. Mem. Burton-on-Trent County Borough Council, 1948-54. MP (C) South-Eastern Div. of Derbyshire, Oct. 1959-Sept. 1964. Barley merchant; Mem. Inst. of Brewing. *Address:* 1 Hamilton Road, Burton-on-Trent, Staffs. *T:* 64615. *Clubs:* East India, Sports and Public Schools, 1900; Burton.   [*Died 29 March 1976.*

JACKSON, H(arold) Haygarth, MC; Director and Member, Management Board, Bleachers' Association Ltd, 1948-62; Chairman, North West Regional Board for Industry, 1958-64; Chairman, The Midland Leather Co. Ltd; Director, Manchester Chamber of Commerce, to 1968; Member of Grand Council, Federation of British Industries, to 1965; Vice-Chairman, National Library for the Blind (Northern Branch) to 1964; Member, National Production Advisory Council on Industry to 1964; Member, General Council, British Standards Institute, to 1962; *b* 6 June 1896; *m* 1923, Frieda, *d* of Alderman and Mrs J. A. Barraclough, Rochdale; one *s* one *d*. Served European War, 1914-18: with 6th Bn Manchester Regt, Egypt, Gallipoli, France and Belgium; Mem. of British Military Mission to USA, 1918 (MC 1917; despatches 1918). Managing Dir, James F. Hutton & Co. Ltd, 1933-40; Executive Mem. of The Cotton Board, 1940-48; Adviser, Control Commission in Germany, 1946; Mem. of Cotton Board Missions to USA, India, Pakistan, Japan, Central African Federation and European countries, 1948-57; Finishing Trades Employer Mem. of Cotton Board, 1949-58; Industrial Mem., Economic Commission for Asia and the Far East, Manila, Philippines, 1953; Chm., United Tanners' Federation, 1958-61; Pres., British Leather Federation, 1963-64. Officer Order of Orange Nassau (Netherlands), 1947; Officer Order of the Crown (Belgium), 1948; Chevalier of the Legion of Honour (France), 1950. *Address:* Highwayside, Talbot Road, Bowdon, Cheshire; Whitecroft Ltd, Blackfriars' House, Parsonage, Manchester 3.   [*Died 1 Sept. 1972.*

JACKSON, Sir Harold (Warters), Kt, *cr* 1952; Solicitor; *b* 5 April 1883; *e s* of late Rev. J. Harding Jackson; *m* 1911, Margaret, (*d* 1959), *y d* of late Thomas Jubb; one *s*. *Educ:* Wesley Coll., Sheffield. LLB (London); LLD (Sheffield). Admitted solicitor, 1905; mem. of Sheffield City Council, 1911-67, Alderman, 1928, Lord Mayor, 1930-31, Freeman, 1945; Sheffield Town Trustee. Formerly: Pres. Assoc. of Education Cttees; Mem. Court of Sheffield Univ. *Address:* 19 Slayleigh Lane, Sheffield. *T:* 33883.   [*Died 4 Dec. 1972.*

JACKSON, Harry; *b* 5 July 1892; *s* of John Henry Jackson and Ada Catherine Jackson (*née* Beavan); *m* 1919, Mabel Alice Parkinson; one *s* one *d*; *m* 1957, Nora Richardson Fage. *Educ:* Holt Sch., Liverpool. Midland Bank Ltd, 1908-19; Asst Sec.

Guaranty Trust Co. of New York, Liverpool, 1919-24; Barclays Bank Ltd, Liverpool, 1924-52; Pres. Liverpool and District Inst. of Bankers, 1948; served European War, 1914-19 with 9th Bn King's Liverpool Regt and Royal Dublin Fusiliers; Local Govt Service in Wirral, Cheshire, 1925-33 and 1936-53. Vice-Chm. 1953-54, Chm. April 1954, Liquidator Sept. 1954-June 1956, Raw Cotton Commission. *Recreation:* gardening, fishing. *Address:* 3 Thornton House, Thornton Hough, Wirral, Merseyside. *T:* 051-336 3413. *Club:* Cheshire County Cricket.   [*Died 30 Nov. 1976.*

JACKSON, Gen. Sir Henry Cholmondeley, KCB 1936 (CB 1919); CMG 1920; DSO 1916; Colonel of Bedfordshire and Hertfordshire Regiment, 1935-47; *b* Cambridge, 12 Aug. 1879; *e s* of late Henry Jackson, OM; *m* 1919, Dorothy Nina, RRC (*d* 1953), 3rd *d* of late Gen. Lord William Seymour. *Educ:* Haileybury; Trinity Coll., Cambridge. Joined 1st Beds Regt 1899; Capt., 1906; Adjutant, 1903-06; Major, 1915; Maj.-Gen. 1930; Lt-Gen. 1935; Gen. 1939; Adjutant Mounted Infantry Sch., Longmoor, 1908-12; PSC; served European War, 1914-18 (despatches eight times, CB, DSO, Bt Col, twice wounded); Commandant Machine Gun Sch., Netheravon, 1924-26; Small Arms Sch. and Machine Gun Sch., 1926; Dir of Military Training, AHQ, India, 1926-30; ADC to HM, 1928-30; Commander 2nd Div., 1931-35; General Officer Commanding-in-Chief, Western Command, 1936-39 and 1940; retired pay, 1939. *Recreation:* hunting. *Address:* West House, Piddletrenthide, Dorchester, Dorset. *Club:* United Service & Royal Aero.   [*Died 19 Oct. 1972.*

JACKSON, Sir Hugh (Nicholas), 2nd Bt, *cr* 1913; late Lt R W Fusiliers; *b* 21 Jan. 1881; *s* of 1st Bt and Alice Mary (*d* 1900), *y d* of William Lambarde, JP, DL, of Beechmont, Sevenoaks, Kent; *S father,* 1924; *m* 1931, Violet Marguerite Loftus, *y d* of Loftus St George; one *s* one *d*. *Heir: s* Nicholas Fane St George Jackson. *Address:* 38 Oakley Street, SW3.   [*Died 1 Nov. 1979.*

JACKSON, Sir John Montrésor, 6th Bt, *cr* 1815; elected Member of London Stock Exchange, 1948; formerly engaged on development work for Ministry of Aircraft Production; formerly with BBC; *b* Buenos Aires, Argentina, 14 Oct. 1914; *o surv s* of Sir Robert Montrésor Jackson, 5th Bt, and Katherine, *y d* of late John Abrey, The Glen and Barden Park, Tonbridge; *S father,* 1940; *m* 1953, Mrs E. Beatty. *Educ:* Tonbridge Sch.; Clare Coll., Cambridge. BA, 1936; London Stock Exchange, 1937-39; at outbreak of war, 1939, embodied with Territorial Army, RA (AA); released on medical grounds, May 1940. *Recreations:* golf, swimming and rowing. *Heir: kinsman* Robert Jackson [*b* 16 March 1910; *m* 1943, Maria E. Casamayou; two *d*]. *Address:* Rose Cottage, Charing, Kent.   [*Died 31 May 1980.*

JACKSON, Sir Richard (Leofric), Kt 1963; CBE 1958; Director, Security Services Ltd, and Securicor Ltd (Joint Vice-Chairman), since 1963; *b* 12 July 1902; 3rd *s* of late William Jackson, Barrister-at-Law, of Calcutta; *m* 1930, Mary Elizabeth, *o d* of late Charles Blois Pooley, CIE; one *d*. *Educ:* Cheam Sch.; Eton; Trinity Coll., Cambridge. Called to the Bar, Middle Temple, 1927; Appointed to Staff of Dir of Public Prosecutions, 1933; appointed Sec. of Metropolitan Police Office, 1946; Asst Commissioner, Criminal Investigation Dept, New Scotland Yard, 1953-63; Pres., International Criminal Police Organisation (Interpol), 1960-63 (British Representative, 1957, Mem. Exec. Cttee, 1958). A Mem. of Police Mission to Federation of Malaya, 1949. FRSA 1964. *Publications:* (ed) Criminal Investigation (Hans Gross), 5th edn, 1962; Occupied with Crime, 1967. *Address:* 10 Persfield Mews, Ewell, Surrey. *T:* 01-393 1251. *Club:* Royal Automobile.   [*Died 17 Feb. 1975.*

JACKSON, Rt. Rev. Robert Wyse, DD; *b* 12 July 1908; *o s* of Richard Jackson and Belinda Hester Sherlock; *m* 1st, 1933, Margaretta Nolan Macdonald; one *s* one *d*; 2nd, 1952, Lois Margery Phair: four *s* one *d*. *Educ:* Abbey Sch., Tipperary; Bishop Foy Sch., Waterford; Trinity Coll., Dublin; Middle Temple; Egerton Hall, Manchester. BA (Hons Law), LLB; MA; LLD; LittD; DD 1961. Barrister, 1932; Curate of St James, Broughton (Dio. Manchester); 1934; Curate-in-charge, Corbally, Diocese of Killaloe, 1937; Rector of St Michael's, Limerick, 1939; Dean of the Cathedral Church of St John the Baptist and St Patrick's Rock, Cashel, 1946-60; Prebendary of Swords in St Patrick's Cathedral, Dublin, 1949-60; Bishop of Limerick, Ardfert and Aghadoe, 1961-70. Mem. Soc. of Antiquaries of Ireland; Water Colour Soc. of Ireland. Exhibitor, RHA, 1971. Godfrey Day Memorial Lectr, Dublin Univ.; MRIA. Freeman of Limerick, 1970. *Publications:* Pleadings in Tort, 1933; Scenes from Irish Clerical Life in the Seventeenth and Eighteenth Centuries, 1938; Jonathan Swift, Dean and Pastor, 1939, repr. 1970; Swift and his Circle, 1945, repr. 1970; King of the Friday, 1949; Oliver Goldsmith, Essays Towards an

Interpretation, 1951; Church of Ireland History, 1600-1932, 1953; The Celtic Cross, an Anthology of Devotion, 1954; An Introduction to Irish Silver, 1964; Voices at the Cross, 1965; The Relationship of Swift and Stella, 1967; The Best of Swift, 1967; Cathedrals of the Church of Ireland, 1971; Irish Silver, 1972; The Story of Limerick, 1973; The Story of Kilkenny, 1974; The Scoundrel of Cashel, Miler Magrath, 1974; contrib. to Hermathena, JRSAI; collaborator in: The Legacy of Swift, 1948; Music in Ireland, 1952; (in Irish) Bedell's Apocrypha, 1973; *novels:* Spanish Man Hunt; The Journal of Corinna Brown. *Recreations:* painting, Swiftiana, exploring church silver. *Address:* Vellore, Whitshed Road, Greystones, Co. Wicklow. *T:* 874901; Bishopscove, Camp SO, Co. Kerry.
[*Died* 21 *Oct.* 1976.

JACKSON, Sir Wilfrid Edward Francis, GCMG 1943 (KCMG 1931; CMG 1919); Governor and Commander-in-Chief, Tanganyika Territory, 1941 to April 1945; *b* 1883; *e s* of late Sir Henry Moore Jackson, GCMG; *m* 1921, Isobel, *d* of late Humphrey Morgan, Donegal, Ireland, and *widow* of Capt. H. H. d'Estamps Vallancey, RFA. *Educ:* Stonyhurst Coll., Blackburn; Lincoln Coll., Oxford; BA. Personal Sec. to Governor of Trinidad, 1905-6; Private Sec. to Governor and Clerk Executive Council, Bahamas, 1906-7; Asst Collector, Uganda, 1907; Acting District Commissioner, 1911; Acting Asst Chief Sec., 1912; First Asst Sec., 1912; Colonial Sec. and Registrar-General, Bermuda, 1916; Colonial Sec., Barbados, 1921; Mem. Legislative Council; Acting Governor Barbados, May-Oct. 1922, June-Sept. 1924, Aug. 1925-Jan. 1926; Colonial Sec., Trinidad, 1926-29; Acting Governor, Trinidad, April-Nov. 1927, and May-Aug. 1929; Colonial Sec., Gold Coast, 1929-30; Governor and Commander-in-Chief, Mauritius, 1930-37; British Guiana, 1937-41. *Address:* c/o Barclays Bank (DC & O), Capetown, South Africa. *Clubs:* Junior Carlton, East India and Sports.
[*Died* 28 *March* 1971.

JACOB, Ernest Fraser, FBA 1946; FSA; FRHistS; MA; DPhil; Fellow and Librarian of All Souls College; *b* 12 Sept. 1894; *s* of late Professor Ernest Henry Jacob and Emma, *d* of late James Fraser, Leeds. *Educ:* Winchester; New College, Oxford. Stanhope Prize, 1920; Gladstone Prize, 1920; Lecturer in Medieval History, King's Coll., London, 1922-24; Lecturer in History and Student of Christ Church, Oxford, 1924-29; Prof. of Medieval History in the University of Manchester, 1929-44; Chichele Prof. of Modern History, Oxford, 1950-61. Prof. Emeritus, 1961. Membre Assesseur, Comité Internat. des Sciences historiques, 1960-; Creighton Lectr, 1951; Mem. of the Church Assembly, 1945-65; Church Comr, 1948-68; served on Archbishops' Commissions: Relations of Church and State, 1932-35; Canon Law, 1944-46; Church Courts, 1952-54; Crown Appointments, 1962-65; Birkbeck Lecturer in Ecclesiastical History, Trinity Coll., Cambridge, 1936-37; Mem. of Royal Commission on Historical Manuscripts; during 1914-18 served with 1st Battalion Hants Regt; Capt. 1917 (wounded twice, despatches). Senior Operations Officer, North West Region (Civil Defence), 1939-41. Hon. LittD Manchester, 1957. *Publications:* Illustrations to the Life of St Alban, 1924; Studies in the Period of Baronial Reform and Rebellion, 1925; (with C. G. Crump) The Legacy of the Middle Ages, 1926; Innocent III and Henry III of England, Cambridge Medieval History; trans of Bémont, Simon de Montfort, 1929; The Register of Archbishop Henry Chichele, 4 vols, 1938-47; Essays in the Conciliar Epoch, 1953; Henry V and the Invasion of France, 1947; (ed and contrib.), Italian Renaissance Studies, 1960; The Fifteenth Century, 1961; Archbishop Henry Chichele, 1967; Essays in Later Medieval History, 1968. *Address:* 205 Woodstock Road, Oxford. *Club:* Athenæum.
[*Died* 7 *Oct.* 1971.

JACOB, Rhoda Hannah, MA Cantab; FRSA; *b* 5 June 1900; *y d* of late Ernest S. and late Lydia J. Brooksby Jacob. *Educ:* Dulwich High School; Sydenham High School, GPDST; Girton Coll., Cambridge (Classical Tripos). Teacher: Queenswood, Clapham Park, 1922-25; Richmond County Sch. for Girls, 1926; Kensington High School, 1926-35; Headmistress: Harrogate Coll., Yorks, 1935-52; Falmouth County High Sch., Cornwall, 1957-65. Archaeological Research Sec. to Sir Charles Walston, 1925; Triple Blue (hockey, netball, tennis); Hockey, County and Territorial (Surrey and South of England). *Recreations:* motoring, reading, archaeology. *Address:* Tregarth, 16 Spernen Wyn Road, Falmouth, Cornwall TR11 4EH. *T:* Falmouth 313067.
[*Died* 25 *Jan.* 1979.

JACOBSEN, Prof. Arne; Architect; *b* 11 Feb. 1902; *s* of Johan Jacobsen, Merchant, and Pauline (*née* Salmonsen); *m* 1943, Jonna Jacobsen (*née* Møller); two *c*. *Educ:* The Royal Danish Academy. Has been responsible for many private and public buildings; villas, halls, banks, commercial structures, Royal

Hotel, Copenhagen, St Catherine's Coll., Oxford. Central Bank of Denmark, project of Parliament Building Islamabad, Pakistan, etc. Exhibitions: RIBA, London, 1959; Stedelijk Museum, Amsterdam, 1959; Paris, 1961; Zürich, 1962; Hanover, 1962; Vienna, 1963; Dortmund, 1963; Glasgow, 1968. FAIA 1962. Member: Academie Serbe des Sciences et des Arts, Beograd; Akademie der Bildende Künste, Berlin. Hon. Corresp. Mem., RIBA, 1963, etc. Hon. DLitt Oxford, 1966; Hon. LLD Strathclyde, 1968. Awards: Gold Medal of Royal Danish Acad., 1928; Eckersberg Medal, 1936; Prize of Honour, Biennale, São Paulo, Brazil, 1954; C. F. Hansen Medal, 1956; Grand Prix, Architecture d'aujourd'hui, 1960; Akademisk Arkitektforening's Medal of Honour, 1962; The Prince Eugen Medal, Sweden, 1962; RIBA Bronze Medal, 1965. *Publications:* (*relevant*): Bogen om Arne Jacobsen, 1954, 1957 (by Johan Pedersen); Arne Jacobsen (by Tobias Faber), 1964; numerous contributions by writers to Arkitektens and to other learned jls, since 1928, both in Denmark and abroad. *Address:* Strandvej 413, Klampenborg, Denmark. *T:* OR 7010.
[*Died* 24 *March* 1971.

JAEGER, Prof. John Conrad, FRS 1970; MA Cantab, DSc Sydney; Emeritus Professor of Geophysics, 1973 (Professor of Geophysics, 1952-72, and Head of Department of Geophysics and Geochemistry, 1965-71), Australian National University, Canberra; *b* Sydney, 30 July 1907; *s* of Carl Jaeger, Stockton-on-Tees; *m* 1st, Sylvia Percival Rees (marr. diss.); 2nd, Martha Elizabeth, (Patty), *d* of George Clarke, Hobart. *Educ:* C of E Grammar Sch., Sydney; Universities of Sydney and Cambridge. Lectr in Mathematics, later Prof. of Applied Maths, Univ. of Tasmania, 1935-51. Hon. DSc Tasmania. *Publications:* (with H. S. Carslaw) Operational Methods in Applied Mathematics, 1941, 2nd edn 1948; (with H. S. Carslaw) Conduction of Heat in Solids, 1947, 2nd edn 1959; An Introduction to the Laplace Transformation, 1949, 3rd edn (with G. H. Newstead) 1969; Elasticity, Fracture and Flow with Engineering and Geological Applications, 1956, 3rd edn 1969; An Introduction to Applied Mathematics, 1951, 2nd edn (with A. M. Starfield), 1974; (with N. G. W. Cook) Fundamentals of Rock Mechanics, 1969, 2nd edn 1976. *Recreations:* farming, conservation of Australian antiquities. *Address:* Private Bag 5, Post Office, Sorell, Tasmania 7172, Australia.
[*Died* 13 *May* 1979.

JAHN, Gunnar; Norwegian economist and statistician; Chairman Nobel Peace Prize Committee since 1942; *b* 10 Jan. 1883; *s* of Christian Fredrik Jahn and Elisabeth Wexelsen; *m* 1911, Martha Larsen; no *c*. *Educ:* University of Oslo (graduate in Law and in Political Economy); Universities of Berlin, Heidelberg and Paris. Sec. Central Bureau of Statistics, Oslo, 1910-17; Dir, Central Rationing Board, 1918-20; Dir Central Bureau of Statistics, 1920-45; Lectr in statistics, University of Oslo, 1913-20; Minister of Finance, Norway, 1934-35 and 1945; Gov., Bank of Norway, 1946-54. Chairman: Norwegian Jt Cttee of the Research Councils, 1954-60; Economic Assoc. of Norway, 1954-59; Norwegian Whaling Council, 1954-60; Cttee for International Whaling statistics; Member: Acad. of Science in Oslo, 1927-; Econometric Soc.; Statistical Cttee, League of Nations, 1928-30; Statistical Expert Cttee, ILO, 1936-40; UN Statistical Commn, 1946-50. Governor for Norway of Internat. Bank and Fund, 1946-54. Hon. Mem. Internat. Statistical Institute (Vice-Pres. 1947-51); Fellow Royal Statistical Soc., London, 1955-. *Publications:* Types of Houses in Rural Norway, 1920; Statistical Methods, 1937; How to make Trout Flies, 1938; The Longbow, 1938; Miscellany (articles and speeches), 1949; Bank of Norway during 150 years, Part I: 1816-1940. *Recreations:* trout fishing; archery, etc. *Address:* Husebyvegen 12, Smestad, pr Oslo, Norway. *T:* 55 83 30.
[*Died* 1 *Feb.* 1971.

JAHN, Prof. Hermann Arthur, PhD; Professor of Applied Mathematics, University of Southampton, 1949-72; *b* 31 May 1907; *s* of Friedrich Wilhelm Hermann Jahn and Marion May Curtiss; *m* 1943, Karoline Schuler; one *s* one *d*. *Educ:* City Sch., Lincoln; University Coll., London; University of Leipzig. BSc (London) 1928, MSc (London) 1935, PhD (Leipzig) 1935. Davy Faraday Research Laboratory, Royal Instn, London, 1935-41. RAE, Farnborough, 1941-46; University of Birmingham, 1946-48. *Publications:* scientific papers relating mainly to Group Theory and Quantum Mechanics. *Address:* 93 Highfield Lane, Southampton. *T:* Southampton 555039. [*Died* 24 *Oct.* 1979.

JALLAND, Rev. Trevor Gervase, DD Oxon, 1941; MA; Head of the Department of Theology, University of Exeter, 1957-62, retired; Lecturer in Theology since 1945, Senior Lecturer, 1956; Member of the Faculty of Theology, University of Oxford, 1944; *b* 14 Oct. 1896; *s* of George Herbert and Mary Mahalah Jalland; *m* 1944, Beatrice Mary (*d* 1972), *er d* of late Prof. Alexander Hamilton Thompson, CBE, MA; one *s*. *Educ:* Oundle. Served

European War, 1915-19; 2nd Lieut Leicester Yeo., 1916; Capt. acting, 1918; Magdalen Coll., Oxford (Squire Scholar, Exhibitioner), 1919, 1st Class Theology. Deacon, 1922; Vice-Principal St Stephen's House, Oxford, 1922; Ellerton Prize Essay, 1922; Priest, 1923; Joint Junior Denyer Johnson Scholar, 1925; Asst Chaplain Exeter Coll., 1924; Prox. Acc. Senior Denyer Johnson Schol., 1925; Priest in charge St Luke's, Swindon, 1925-33; Surrogate, 1933; Vicar of St Thomas the Martyr, Oxford, 1933-45; Warden of the Society of Sacred Study, Diocese of Oxford, 1934-45. Bampton Lecturer for 1942; Proctor in Convocation, Dioc. Oxford, 1944-50; Fellow of the Corporation of SS Mary and Nicolas, 1948-50; Proctor in Convocation, Dio. Exeter, 1950-70. *Publications:* This our Sacrifice, 1933; The Life and Times of St Leo the Great, 1941; The Church and the Papacy (Bampton Lectures), 1944; The Bible, the Church and South India, 1944; Origin and Evolution of the Christian Church, 1950. Various articles and reviews in Church publications; contributor, Catholic Sermons, 1931, The Office and Work of a Priest, 1937, The Priest as Student, 1939, and Thy Household the Church, 1943; The Apostolic Ministry, 1946. *Recreations:* French bulldogs, foreign bird keeping, motor boating. *Address:* 6a Cranford Avenue, Exmouth, Devon. *T:* Exmouth 5414.   *[Died 14 May 1975.*

JAMER, Herman Watson; Agent-General for Atlantic Provinces of Nova Scotia, New Brunswick, Prince Edward Island and Newfoundland, 1958-68; *b* 18 May 1904; of Scottish-English parentage; *m* 1937, Marian Jeannette Dinwoodie; one *s. Educ:* Fredericton, New Brunswick, Canada. Ford Motor Company of Canada, 1934-58. Loaned to Ministry of Supply (Technical), 1943-45. District Manager Atlantic Provinces, Ford of Canada, 1948-58. Hon. LLD Mount Allison Univ., NB, 1958. *Recreations:* field and stream; metal and wood working. *Address:* St John West, New Brunswick, Canada. *T:* 1-506 672 2558.   *[Died 21 April 1972.*

JAMES, Wing Comdr Sir Archibald (William Henry), KBE 1945; MC; *b* 1893; *s* of late H. A. James, of Hurstmonceux Place, Sussex; *m* 1st, 1919, Bridget, *d* of late Murray Guthrie, MP, of Torosay Castle, Isle of Mull; one *s* one *d*; 2nd, 1940, Eugenia, *widow* of Patrick Stirling, younger, of Kippendavie; two *s. Educ:* Eton; Trinity Coll., Cambridge. 3rd Hussars, RFC and RAF, 1914-26. MP (U) Wellingborough Division of Northants, 1931-45. Parliamentary Private Sec. to R. A. Butler, India Office and Ministry of Labour, 1936-38; Board of Education, 1942; Hon. First Sec. British Embassy, Madrid, 1940-41. *Address:* Champions Farm, Thakeham, Pulborough, West Sussex. *T:* West Chiltington 3250. *Clubs:* Boodle's, Pratt's; Salisbury (Rhodesia).   *[Died 5 May 1980.*

JAMES, Rev. Canon Arthur Dyfrig, MA; Vicar of Tilstone Fearnall, Cheshire, since 1956, and of Wettenhall, since 1969; Headmaster of Christ College, Brecon, 1931-56; Member of Governing Body of the Church in Wales, 1933-56; Hon. Chaplain to the Bishop of Swansea and Brecon, 1947-53; Canon of Hay in Brecon Cathedral, 1953-59, Hon. Canon, since 1959; *b* 24 May 1902; *s* of late Very Rev. H. L. James, DD; *m* 1936, Ann Pamela Mary, *d* of late J. S. Pincham; four *s. Educ:* Rossall; Jesus Coll., Oxford (Scholar), 1st Class Classical Moderations, 2nd Class Lit. Hum. Sixth Form Master, St Edward's Sch., Oxford, 1925-31; Select Preacher, Oxford, 1925-34; Chaplain to High Sheriff of Breconshire, 1944-45, 1946-47, 1949-51, 1955-57; Asst Inspector of Schools, Diocese of Chester, 1957; Exam. Chaplain to Bishop of Chester, 1958-68; Priest-in-charge of Wettenhall, 1958; part-time Lecturer in Classics, St David's Coll., Lampeter, 1961-62, 1966-68. *Address:* The Vicarage, Tilstone Fearnall, near Tarporley, Cheshire. *T:* Tarporley 2449.   *[Died 17 June 1980.*

JAMES, Rt. Hon. Sir Arthur (Evan), PC 1973; Kt 1965; DL; **Rt. Hon. Lord Justice James;** a Lord Justice of Appeal, since 1973; *b* 18 May 1916; *s* of John William and Ethel Mary James; *m* 1939, Eileen Brenda (*née* Mills); one *s* three *d. Educ:* Caterham Sch.; Jesus Coll., Oxford (Hon. Fellow, 1972). BCL (Oxon.) 1939. Harmsworth Scholar, Middle Temple, 1939; Barstow Scholar, Council of Legal Education, 1939. Joined Midland Circuit, 1939. QC 1960; Recorder of Great Grimsby, 1961-63; Recorder of Derby, 1963-65; Dep. Chm., Warwicks Quarter Sessions, 1962-71; a Judge of the High Court, Queen's Bench Div., 1965-72. Mem., Parole Bd, 1967-70 (Vice-Chm., 1970). Chairman: V&G Tribunal of Inquiry, 1971; Cttee on Distribution of Criminal Business, 1973-. Trustee, Barber Inst. of Fine Arts, 1974-. DL Co. Warwick, 1967. *Recreation:* gardening. *Address:* Royal Courts of Justice, Strand, WC2.   *[Died 13 May 1976.*

JAMES, Edward, JP Glamorgan; Barrister and Parliamentary Journalist; *b* 20 June 1885; *yr s* of late Thomas James, JP, of

Porthcawl, Glam, and Rhoda, *d* of Thomas Evans, of Neath. *Educ:* Porthcawl; Bridgend County Sch. Called to the Bar at Lincoln's Inn, 1922. Began career as a journalist on the Glamorgan Gazette, Bridgend, and afterwards served on editorial staff of Cardiff Western Mail; London Editor of that paper 1914-59, and Chief of Parliamentary Staff 1914-59 (retired); Chm. of the Lobby Journalists of Parliament, 1924-25; Vice-Chm., 1922-23; Chm. of Press Gallery and Cttee Member for twelve years; Chm. Newspaper Conference, 1947 and 1948, Vice-Chm. 1940-47; Vice-Pres. and Council Mem. of the Honourable Society of Cymmrodorion and other Welsh societies; Executive Cttee of Welsh National Eisteddfod for many years; initiated as Bard of Gorsedd of Wales with the title of Ap Baglan, 1935. Jt Organiser, POW Service, Westminster Abbey, 1918; jt sec., Regtl Cttee of London Welsh Anti-Aircraft Regt formed 1939; Mem. of Holborn Borough Council, 1935-65; Alderman, 1945-65; Chm. of Libraries Cttee, 1939-41; again (Vice-Chm.), 1961-62; Member: Law and Parliamentary Cttee, 1943-45; Vice-Chm. 1959, Chm., 1963, Finance Cttee, 1953-65; Chm. Rating and Valuation Cttee, 1949-65; Rating and other Local Govt. Cttees of Assoc. of Municipal Corporations, 1963-. JP Glamorgan, 1936-; FJI; Holborn Soc.; Executive, Holborn Conservative Assoc.; Clwb y Cymry; Liveryman, Stationers' and Newspaper Makers' Soc., Freeman of City of London; Mem. (and London Rep.), Lloyd George Statue Cttee; Empire Games Reception Cttee, 1958. British Legal Party to Canada and USA, 1930; Bronze Medallist of Royal Humane Society. Past Master Kentish Lodge 3021; Past Assistant Grand Dir of Ceremonies. *Publications:* Stirring Deeds in France and Flanders; political essays. *Recreations:* motoring and play-going. *Address:* Heathlands, Porthcawl, Glamorgan. *T:* Porthcawl 2034; 34 Harlyn Drive, Pinner, Mddx. *T:* 01-866 4614.
          [Died 7 July 1971.

JAMES, Rev. Edwin Oliver, MA, DLitt (Oxon), PhD (London); Hon. DD St Andrews; FSA; Chaplain, All Souls College, Oxford, since 1960; University Professor of the History and Philosophy of Religion, University of London, 1948-55 (Professor of the Philosophy of Religion in the University of London (King's College), 1945-48); Professor Emeritus, 1955; Fellow of University College, London, 1946; Fellow of King's College, London, 1950; Wilde Lecturer in Natural and Comparative Religion, Oxford University, 1939-42; Examining Chaplain to the Bishop of Wakefield, 1938; Editor of Folklore since 1932; Forwood Lecturer in Philosophy of Religion, University of Liverpool, 1949-50; Visiting Lecturer, University of Amsterdam, 1949; Marburg, 1960; Jordan Bequest Lecturer, 1961; *b* 30 March 1888; *s* of late William and Sophia Mary James; *m* 1911, Clarese Augusta Copeland, LLD; one *s. Educ:* University College Sch.; Exeter Coll., Oxford; University College, London. Diploma in Anthropology, University of Oxford; Curate, St Mark's, Low Moor, 1911-13; Curate-in-charge, St Peter's, Hucknall Torkard, 1913-14; Rector of Alvescot and Vicar of Shilton, Oxon, 1914-17; Vicar of St Peter's, Limehouse, 1917-21; Holy Trinity, Reading, 1921-23; St Thomas's, Oxford, 1923-33; Lecturer and Tutor in Anthropology in University of Cambridge, 1928-33; Professor of History and Philosophy of Religion, University of Leeds, 1933-45; Visiting Lecturer in History of Religion, University College of North Wales, 1942, 1943; Examiner in Comparative Religion, University of Durham, 1931-37; Universities of Manchester, London and Sheffield, 1935, Oxford, 1936, 1938, 1939, 1944, 1949, 1952, 1955, 1957, 1958, 1959, 1962, 1963, 1965-67; London (Theol.) 1942-45, 1952 (MTh), since 1947; Wales, 1949-52; TCD, 1960; Manchester, 1953, 1962-64, 1969; Bristol, 1961-63; President: Folklore Society, 1930-32 (Research Medal, 1962); Yorkshire Society for Celtic Studies, 1943-44; Anthropoloical Sect., British Assoc. for the Advancement of Science,, 1952, Member of Council, 1957-62. *Publications:* Primitive Ritual and Belief, 1917; Introduction to Anthropology, 1919; The Stone Age, 1927; The Beginnings of Man, 1928; The Christian Faith in the Modern World, 1930; Origins of Sacrifice, 1933; Christian Myth and Ritual, 1933 (2nd edn 1965); Old Testament in light of Anthropology, 1935; In the Fulness of Time, 1935; Origins of Religion, 1937; Introduction to comparative study of Religion, 1938 (new edn, 1961); The Social Function of Religion, 1940, 2nd edn, 1948 (French translation, 1950); Christianity in England, 1948; The Beginnings of Religion, 1948, 1958 (Spanish translation, 1955; Italian translation, 1968); The Concept of Deity, 1950; Marriage and Society, 1952 (2nd edn 1965); The Nature and Function of Priesthood, 1955 (German translation, 1956); The History of Religions, 1956 (2nd edn 1965); Prehistoric Religion, 1957 (trans. various languages); Myth and Ritual in the Ancient Near East, 1958 (German translation, 1959); French and Italian translations, 1960); The Cult of the Mother goddess, 1959 (French translation, 1959, German translation, 1962); The Ancient Gods, 1959 (French, Italian, German, Polish Spanish,

Portuguese translations); Seasonal Feasts and Festivals, 1961 (French translation); Sacrifice and Sacrament, 1962; The Worship of the Sky-god, 1963; Sanctuaries, Shrines and Temples, 1964 (Spanish translation); The Tree of Life, 1966; Christianity and Other Religions, 1967; Creation and Cosmology, 1969. Contributions to Encyclopædia of Religion and Ethics, Dictionary of National Biography, Chambers's Encyclopædia, Encyclopædia Britannica, and scientific and theological journals. *Recreations:* foreign travel, golf. *Address:* Hidsfield House, Cumnor Hill, Oxford. *T:* Cumnor 2040; All Souls College, Oxford. *Club:* Athenæum. *[Died 6 July 1972.*

JAMES, F(rank) Cyril; Chevalier de la Légion d'Honneur, 1948; Principal and Vice-Chancellor, McGill University, Canada, 1939-62, Principal Emeritus since 1962; President of the International Association of Universities, 1960-65 (Hon. President since 1965) (Member Executive Board, 1955-); *b* 8 Oct. 1903; *s* of Frank James and Mary Lucy Brown; *m* 1926, Irene L. V. Leeper; (one *d* decd). *Educ:* Oldfield Road Sch.; Hackney Downs Sch., London; LSE, Univ. of London (BCom, 1923); Univ. of Pennsylvania (AM, 1924, PhD, 1926). Has been awarded Hon. Degrees by Universities and Colleges in Europe, Asia, USA and Canada. FRSC 1948. Guggenheim Honour Cup, University of Pennsylvania, 1941. B'nai Brith Humanitarian Award, 1952. Hon. Fellow, London Sch. of Economics, 1960. Clerk in Barclays Bank, London, 1921-23; Instructor in Finance and Transportation, University of Pennsylvania, 1924-27; Asst Professor of Finance, 1927-33, Associate Professor, 1933-35, Professor, 1935-39; Chairman, Grad. Faculty in Social Science, 1936-37; Professor of Finance and Economic History, 1938-39; Professor of Political Economy, McGill Univ., 1939-62; Economist, First Nat. Bank, Chicago, 1937-38; Member: of Council of Education of Province of Quebec, 1940-63; of Exec. Cttee of National Conference of Canadian Universities, 1940-52 (Vice-Pres. 1946-48, Pres. 1948-50); of Executive Council of Assoc. of Universities of British Commonwealth, 1948-51, 1959-62 (Chairman, 1949); of Board of Directors of Canadian University Foundation (Vice-Chairman) 1959-62; Commonwealth Consultant, Inter-University Council, London, 1961-64; of Sub-Cttee on Demobilisation and Rehabilitation, Ottawa, 1940-42; Chairman, Advisory Cttee on Reconstruction, Dominion of Canada, 1941-44; Member University Advisory Board Dept of Veterans Affairs, Ottawa, 1945-50; Vice-Chairman Counseil d'Orientation Economique, Quebec, 1961-; Chairman of Advisory Board, Lady Davis Foundation, 1947-50; Member Fellowship Cttee, Beaver Club Trust, 1948-50; Trustee, Mackenzie-King Scholarships Foundation, since 1950; Chairman, Joint Hospital Cttee, Montreal, 1942-52; Governor Royal Victoria Hospital, 1940-62; Montreal General Hospital, 1942-62; Montreal Children's Hospital, 1946-60; Hon. President Polish Institute of Arts and Sciences (Canada), 1942-63; Director American Academy of Political and Social Science since 1937, Vice-Pres. since 1952; Pres. World University Service of Canada, 1957-59; Member Board of Directors, The Pulp and Paper Research Inst. of Canada, 1948-62; Montreal City and District Savings Bank, 1953-; Bellairs Research Institute and Bellairs Investment Trust, Barbados, 1955-. Member Exec. Cttee, Oxfam, 1965- (Chm., 1971-); Pres., Internat. Assoc. for Federal Union, 1972-. Member: Bd of Govs, Birkbeck Coll., 1967-; Standing Conf. of British Organisations for Aid to Refugees, 1968-; Victor Gollancz Memorial Trust, 1968. Member Canadian Inst. International Affairs; and many economical and historical societies; Phi Beta Kappa. *Publications:* Cyclical Fluctuations in the Shipping and Shipbuilding Industries, 1927; The Economics of Money, Credit and Banking, 1930, 3rd ed., 1940; England Today, A Survey of Her Economic Situation, 1931; The Road to Revival, 1932; The Meaning of Money (with others), 1935; The Economic Doctrines of J. M. Keynes (with others), 1938; The Growth of Chicago Banks, 2 vols, 1938, 2nd edn 1970; Economic Problems in a Changing World (with others), 1939; On Understanding Russia, 1959; Formal Programmes of International Co-operation between Universities (with others), 1960; University Autonomy, its Meaning To-day (with others), 1965. *Recreations:* motoring, reading, photography. *Address:* McGill University, Montreal, 2. *TA:* McGill University, Montreal; Univasoc, Paris; Pipers Croft, Devonshire Avenue, Amersham, Bucks. *Clubs:* Athenæum; University, McGill Faculty, Grenadier Guards (Montreal). *[Died 3 May 1973.*

JAMES, Sir Frederick Ernest, Kt 1941; OBE 1919; Chevalier de l'ordre de Léopold I, 1919; Director, Tata Ltd, London; *b* 1891; *s* of late Rev. G. H. James, Letchworth; *m* 1919, Eleanor May Thackrah, CBE 1949; no *c.* Served European War, 1915-19: General Secretary YMCA, Calcutta, 1920-28; Member Bengal Legislative Council, 1924-28; Political Adviser to United Planters Association and British Commercial Interests in South India, 1929-41; Member Madras Legislative Council and

Madras Corporation, 1929-32; Member Indian Central Legislature, 1932-45; Director Board International Rotary, 1934-35; Chairman Commission Rotary International Administration, 1936-37; Representative in New Delhi of Tata Industrial Group, 1941-46; Member Indian Health Survey and Development Cttee, 1944-46; Deputy Chairman and Managing Director, Tata Ltd, London, 1947-62. Member, University College Cttee, 1948- (Treasurer, 1952-62, Vice-Chairman, 1955-62, Hon. Fellow, 1957); President, Westminster Chamber of Commerce, 1959-62 (Chairman, 1953-59); Director Commonwealth Trust; Chairman Finance Cttee Chelsea and Kensington Hospital Group. Contested (L) Sudbury and Woodbridge Parliamentary Division, 1950. *Address:* Yafford, Shorwell, Isle of Wight. *[Died 18 Jan. 1971.*

JAMES, Sir Jack; see James, Sir John H.

JAMES, Sir John Hastings, (Sir Jack), KCVO 1970; CB 1953; Deputy Master and Comptroller of the Royal Mint, and *ex officio* Engraver of HM's Seals, 1957-70; *b* 4 June 1906; *s* of late C. F. James; *m* 1st, 1935, Lady Ann Florence Cole (marr. diss., 1950), *e d* of 5th Earl of Enniskillen; one *s*; 2nd, 1963, Lady Maryoth (marr. diss., 1971), *d* of late Lord Edward Hay, and *widow* of Sir Gifford Fox; 3rd, 1971, Heather, *d* of late Brig. C. A. Lyon, and *widow* of Stephen Potter. *Educ:* Gresham's Sch., Holt; Merton Coll., Oxford. Entered Admiralty, 1929; Imperial Defence Coll., 1938; Under Sec., Admiralty 1948-57; CStJ. *Recreations:* reading, fishing. *Address:* Flat 4, 84 Elm Park Gardens, SW10. *T:* 01-351 0394. *Club:* Turf.

[Died 27 May 1980.

JAMES, John Richings, CB 1966; OBE 1956; Professor of Town and Regional Planning, University of Sheffield, 1967-78, now Emeritus; Pro Vice-Chancellor, 1970-75; *b* 27 Oct. 1912; 2nd *s* of late Henry James, Crook, County Durham, and Florence James; *m* 1946, Elizabeth Emily Frances, 2nd *d* of late Dr A. E. Morgan; five *d. Educ:* Wolsingham Grammar Sch.; King's Coll., London (BA); Inst. of Education. Schoolmaster, 1937-40; Naval Intelligence, 1940-45. Research Officer (Newcastle Regional Office), Min. of Town and Country Planning, 1946-49; Sen. Research Officer (London), Min. of Housing and Local Govt, 1949-58; Dep. Chief Planner, MHLG, 1958-61; Chief Planner, 1961-67. UK Rep. on UN Cttee for Housing, Building and Planning, 1967-77; Mem., Peterborough Develt Corp., 1970-. FRTPI (MTPI 1962); Hon. FRIBA 1969. *Publications:* Greece (3 vols), 1943-45. Contrib. to Chambers's Encyclopædia (Greece and Greek Towns and Islands). Articles on Land Use: Royal Society of Arts Jl, Royal Geog. Society Jl, etc. *Address:* 347 Fulwood Road, Sheffield S10 3BQ. *[Died 22 Sept. 1980.*

JAMES, Dr John (William), CB 1970; retired; Deputy Chief Medical Adviser, Department of Health and Social Security, 1968-71; *b* 23 March 1907; *s* of Thomas and Sarah James (née Sherman); *m* 1st, Dr Margaret Helen Morton (*d* 1953); 2nd, 1955, Jean Bruce Morton, 5th *d* of Dr John Leyden Morton. *Educ:* University Coll. and University Coll. Hosp. Med. School. MRCS, LRCP 1933. Hosp. appts, 1933-40, at: University Coll. Hosp.; Bolingbroke Hosp.; Queen Mary's Hosp., Roehampton; Chapel Allerton Hosp., Leeds; Comr of Med. Services, Min. of Pensions, Northern Region, 1941-53; Sen. Med. Off., Min. of Pensions and Nat. Insce, 1953-62; Princ. Med. Off., 1962-65; Dep. CMO, Min. of Social Security, 1965-68. *Publications:* articles on aspects of medical evidence. *Recreations:* gardening, music, theatre. *Address:* Hobarts, Blickling, Norwich NR11 6NF. *Club:* United Oxford & Cambridge University.

[Died 8 Dec. 1975.

JAMES, Brig. Manley Angell, VC 1918; DSO 1943; MBE 1958; MC; DL; late Gloucestershire Regiment and Royal Sussex Regiment; *b* Odiham, Hants, 12 July 1896; *s* of Dr John Angell and Emily Cornell James; *m* 1928, Noreen Cooper, Bristol; one *s. Educ:* Bristol Grammar Sch. Temp. 2nd Lieut Glos. Regt 1914; served in France and Belgium with 8th Glos. Regt, 1915-18 (wounded three times, prisoner of war, despatches, MC, VC, 1915 Star, British War Medal, Victory Medal); Col, 1941; War of 1939-45 (wounded, Africa Star, 1939-45 Star, Italy Star, Defence Medal, 1939-45 war medal); GSO1 54 Div. March-July 1940; BGS 8 Corps, 1940-41; Comd 128 Inf. Bde, 1941-43; Brig. Inf. Middle East, 1943-44; BGS (Trg) Home Forces, 1944-45; Cmd 140 Inf. Bde, July-Oct. 1945; CRO Air HQ BAFO (Germany), 1945-48; Dir of Ground Defence, Air Ministry, 1948-51; retired from army, 1951. Works Defence Officer, Bristol Aeroplane Co. Ltd, 1951-61. rsc. DL, Glos, 1957, Avon, 1974. AFICD. *Recreations:* golf, fishing, cricket, shooting, gardening. *Address:* Strathmore, Passage Road, Westbury-on-Trym, Bristol. *T:* Bristol 501481. *Club:* Royal Over-Seas League.

[Died 23 Sept. 1975.

JAMES, Norah C.; *b* 22 Sept. 1901; *d* of late John H. Cordner-James. *Educ:* Francis Holland Sch., Baker Street, London; Slade Sch. of Art, where she studied sculpture. Was an organising sec. to the Civil Service Clerical Assoc., Advertising and Publicity Manager to Jonathan Cape, publishers; wrote first novel in 1929; joined ATS as private; invalided out of the ATS, Nov. 1943. *Publications:* Sleeveless Errand, 1929 (published USA); Hail! All Hail! (limited edn), 1929; Shatter the Dream, 1930; To Be Valiant, 1930 (published USA); Wanton Ways, 1931; Tinkle the Cat, 1932; Hospital (USA as Nurse Ariadne), 1933; Jake the Dog, 1933; Jealousy, 1933; Mrs Piffy, 1934; Strap-hangers (USA as Sacrifice), 1934; Cottage Angles, 1935; The Lion Beat the Unicorn, 1935; Return (USA as Two Divided by One), 1935; By a Side Wind, 1936; Sea View, 1936; Women Are Born to Listen, 1937; Stars Are Fire, 1937; The House by the Tree, 1938; As High as the Sky, 1938; Mighty City, 1939; I Lived in a Democracy (autobiography), 1939; Gentlewoman, 1940; The Long Journey, 1941; The Hunted Heart, 1942; Two Selfish People, 1942; Enduring Adventure, 1944; One Bright Day, 1945; There Is Always Tomorrow, 1946; Father, 1946; Penny Trumpet, 1947; Brittle Glory, 1948; (with B. Beauchamp) Green Fingers and the Gourmet, 1949; Swift to Sever, 1949; Pay the Piper, 1950; Pedigree of Honey, 1951; Cooking with Cider, 1952; So Runs the River, 1952; A Summer Storm, 1953; Silent Corridors, 1953; Over the Windmill, 1954; Wed to Earth, 1955; Mercy in Your Hands, 1956; The Flower and the Fruit, 1957; The True and the Tender, 1958; Portrait of a Patient, 1959 (repr. as Tangled Destiny, 1961); The Shadow Between, 1959; The Uneasy Summer, 1960; Wind of Change, 1961; A Sense of Loss, 1962; Sister Veronica Greene, 1963; Bright Day Renewed, 1964; Small Hotel, 1965; Hospital Angles, 1966; Double Take, 1967; Point of Return, 1969; There is No Why, 1970; Ward of Darkness, 1971; The Doctor's Marriage, 1972; If Only, 1972; The Bewildered Heart, 1973; Love, 1975. *[Died 19 Nov. 1979.*

JAMES, Philip (Brutton), CBE 1951; Hon. FMA; Librarian of the Royal Academy of Arts, since 1969; *b* 31 Oct. 1901; *e s* of late Rev. John C. and of Margaretta James; *m* 1926, Bertha, *d* of late Canon Victor L. Whitechurch; one *s* one *d. Educ:* Sherborne Sch.; University Coll., London (Fellow). Sub-Librarian Middle Temple, 1923; Victoria and Albert Museum (Library), 1925; Keeper of the Library, 1936; lent to the Ministry of Home Security, 1939-41; Deputy Sec. of CEMA, 1941; Dir of Art, CEMA and The Arts Council of Great Britain, 1942-58; Dir of Waddesdon Manor, Bucks (National Trust, James de Rothschild Bequest), 1958-59; Sec. and Editor of the Museums Association, 1960-64. Knight Comdr, Order of the Aztec Eagle, Mexico; Chevalier de l'Ordre de la Couronne, Comdr, Order of Leopold II, Belgium; Comdr, Order of the Lion, Finland; Comdr, Order of Merit, Germany. *Publications:* Early Keyboard Instruments, 1930; Children's Books of Yesterday, 1933; (Editor) A Butler's Recipe Book (1719), 1935; English Book Illustration, 1800-1900, 1947; Van Gogh, 1948; Henry Moore on Sculpture, 1966. *Recreation:* music. *Address:* Starveacre, Chalfont Road, Seer Green, Bucks. *T:* Beaconsfield 6665.   *[Died 29 April 1974.*

JAMES, Philip Gaved, CBE 1969; *b* 24 Sept. 1904; *s* of Samuel T. G. James and Frances L. R. James (*née* Richards); unmarried. *Educ:* Amersham Gram. Sch.; London Sch. of Economics. Chartered Accountant. With professional accountancy firms, 1921-34; various posts, London Passenger Transport Bd (later London Transport Exec.), 1934-60; Chief Financial Officer, 1948-60; Chief Accountant, BTC, 1960-62; Financial Controller, Brit. Rlys Bd, 1962-65; Mem. Brit. Rlys Bd, 1965-69; part-time Mem. BR London Midland Bd, 1969-73. *Publications:* contribs to various professional accountancy jls. *Recreation:* gardening. *Address:* 48 Southampton Road, Lymington, Hants SO4 9GQ. *T:* Lymington 73942. *Club:* Reform.   *[Died 12 April 1978.*

JAMES, Richard Lewis Malcolm, CMG 1949; *b* 15 June 1897; *s* of R. E. James, solicitor, Cardiff; *m* 1921, Eva Hayes Bates; one *s* one *d. Educ:* Cardiff High Sch.; Merthyr Intermediate Sch.; London Univ. Civil Service: War Office, 1914-19; Exchequer and Audit Dept, 1920-42; Treasury, 1942-46; Commissioner for Finance, Newfoundland, 1946-49; Asst Sec., Ministry of Power, 1950-59. *Recreations:* gardening, motoring. *Address:* 14 Cosdach Avenue, Wallington, Surrey. *T:* 01-647 5793.
                                        [Died 15 Oct. 1972.

JAMES, Thurstan Trewartha; Consultant, Air Affairs; Editor, The Aeroplane, 1945-65, retired; *b* 7 May 1903; *s* of Alfred James, Mining Engr, and Jeanne Hammond Cloutte; *m* 1929, Doris, *o d* of J. Kennedy Allerton, Worthing; one *s* one *d. Educ:* Rugby; Royal School of Mines. After mining in Portugal, 1921, and studying general engineering, worked as fitter in shops at Beardmore's Dalmuir, on first multi-engined all-metal aircraft

in this country; joined Short Brothers to work on all-metal flying-boats, 1926. Joined Technical Staff of The Aeroplane, 1929; founded first gliding weekly, The Sailplane and Glider, 1930. Served at Air Ministry and Ministry of Aircraft Production, 1939-45, becoming a Dir of Aircraft Production. Liveryman, Coach Makers' and Coach Harness Makers' Co. Hon. Companion Royal Aeronautical Society, 1965. *Address:* 23 Arundel Road, Kingston-upon-Thames, Surrey. *T:* 01-942 8657. *Clubs:* United Service & Royal Aero, Royal Air Force Reserves.
                                        [Died 11 April 1975.

JAMES, William Garnet, OBE 1960; composer and solo pianist; retired as Federal Controller of Music, of the Australian Broadcasting Commission; *b* Ballarat, Vic., Australia, 28 Aug. 1895; *s* of Louisa Chapman, pianist, and Andrew James, publisher; *m* Saffo Arnav, operatic singer. *Educ:* Melbourne Univ. (Scholar); 1st Class Hons in each year for composition and pianoforte playing; came to London in 1914 and studied under Arthur de Greef; played several important concertos with Orchestra at Queen's Hall; from 1915 has performed at Queen's Hall Promenade Concerts, Ballad Concerts, Royal Albert Hall Special Concerts, International Celebrity Concerts, and Provincial Concerts. Compositions: a Ballet produced at the Savoy Theatre, London, 1916, and an Orchestral Suite at the Queen's Hall, etc; Sea Sketches (for piano); Album of 5 pianoforte pieces; The Golden Girl (operetta in one act). Songs: The Sun-God, The Flutes of Arcady, In the Gardens of England, A Warwickshire Wooing, The Sweetest Song, Six Australian Bush Songs, Summer Rain, The Radiant Morn, Madelina, The Showman, Come, gather Roses, I was carried by a Fairy, Moonlit Lake, The First Cuckoo, Sometimes just at Twilight, Cupid's Arrows, Spanish Dances for Piano, When Cupid comes Calling, Six Maori Love Songs, Vol. I Sea Shanties, Skies of Home, Covent Garden, Bush Song at Dawn, Vols I, II, III of Australian Christmas Carols, etc. *Recreations:* tennis, cricket. *Address:* Macleay Regis, Macleay Street, Potts Point, Sydney, NSW 2011, Australia.   *[Died 10 March 1977.*

JAMES, Admiral Sir William Milbourne, GCB 1944 (KCB 1936; CB 1919); *b* 22 Dec. 1881; *s* of Major W. C. James, 16th Lancers, *o s* of Lord Justice Sir W. M. James and Effie, *d* of Sir J. E. Millais, 1st Bt, PRA; *m* 1915, Dorothy (*d* 1971), OBE 1943, *y d* of late Adm. Sir Alexander Duff, GCB, GBE; one *s* decd, one *d* decd. *Educ:* Trinity Coll., Glenalmond; HMS Britannia. Sub-Lieut 1901; Lieut 1902; Commander, 1913; Capt., 1918; Rear-Adm., 1929; Vice-Adm., 1933; Admiral, 1938; Deputy Dir, Royal Naval Staff Coll., Greenwich, 1923-25, Dive 1925-26; Naval Asst 1st Sea Lord, 1928; Chief of Staff, Atlantic Fleet, 1929-30, Mediterranean Fleet, 1930; Commanding Battle Cruiser Squadron, 1932-34; Lord Commissioner of Admiralty and Deputy Chief of Naval Staff, 1935-38; Commander-in-Chief, Portsmouth, 1939-42; Chief of Naval Information, 1943-44; MP (U) for North Portsmouth, 1943-45. DL Surrey, 1958-65. President Union Jack Services Clubs, 1955-64. *Publications:* The British Navy in Adversity, 1926; Blue Water and Green Fields, 1939; Admiral Sir William Fisher, 1943; Portsmouth Letters, 1946; The British Navies in the Second World War, 1946; The Order of Release, 1947; The Durable Monument, 1948; Old Oak, 1950; The Sky Was Always Blue, 1951; The Eyes of the Navy, 1955; A Great Seaman, 1956. *Address:* Wynd House, Elie, Fife. *Club:* United Service & Royal Aero.
                                        [Died 17 Aug. 1973.

JAMES, Prof. William Owen, MA, DPhil; FRS 1952; Fellow, Imperial College, 1969 (Senior Research Fellow, 1967-70); London University Professor of Botany, and Head of Department at Imperial College of Science and Technology, 1959-67, now Emeritus Professor; *b* 21 May 1900; *s* of William Benjamin James and Agnes Ursula (*née* Collins); *m* 1928, Gladys Macphail Redfern; two *d. Educ:* Tottenham Grammar Sch.; Universities of Reading and Cambridge. BSc (London); PhD (Cambridge); MA, DPhil Oxon. Research Institute of Plant Physiology, Imperial Coll., 1926-27. Demonstrator in Plant Physiology, Oxford, 1928-55; Reader in Botany, Oxford, 1946-58. Part owner and co-editor of the New Phytologist, 1931-61; Director of Oxford Medicinal Plants Scheme, 1940-52. Member: Vegetable Drugs Cttee of Ministries of Health and Supply, 1940-45; Central Garden Produce Cttee (Ministry of Agriculture). Chairman, Teaching of Biology Cttee, 1962-67. Hon. ARCS 1964. Foreign Member: Swedish Royal Academy of Science; Amer. Society of Plant Physiologists; Deutsche botanische Gesellschaft, and Leopoldina. *Publications:* Elements of Plant Biology, 1949; Introduction to Plant Physiology, 7th edn 1973 (German edn 1965, Spanish edn 1967, Hungarian edn 1969); Plant Respiration, 1953 (Russian edn 1956); Background to Gardening, 1957; Cell Respiration, 1971; (jt) Biology of Flowers, 1935; papers on plant respiration, nutrition, alkaloid synthesis, etc, in botanical and allied journals.

Recreations: gardening, boating, Hi Fi and reading. *Address:* 13A Lyndfield Lane, Newlands, Wellington 4, New Zealand. *T:* Wellington 784 339.   [*Died* 15 *Sept.* 1978.

JAMESON, Noel Rutherford, CBE 1952; Sheepfarmer, New Zealand, since 1919; *b* 24 Dec. 1892; *s* of late James Samuel Jameson; *m* 1927, Olive Catherine Wilson; one *s*. *Educ:* Wellington Coll.; King's Coll., Auckland. Served European War with NZ Mounted Rifles. Chm., NZ Wool Board, 1945-53; Chm., NZ Wool Commission, 1963-65 (Dep. Chm., 1951-53). *Recreation:* golf. *Address:* 50 Iona Road, Havelock North, Hawkes Bay, New Zealand.   [*Died* 17 *April* 1971.

JAMISON, Evelyn Mary, MA Oxon; Hon. Fellow, Lady Margaret Hall, Oxford; FSA; Fellow Royal Historical Society; Corresponding Fellow, Accademia Pontaniana, Naples; *b* 24 Feb. 1877; *d* of Arthur Andrew Jamison, MD, MRCP, and Isabella Green. *Educ:* Francis Holland Sch., Graham Terrace; Lady Margaret Hall, Oxford. Research Fellow Somerville Coll., 1903-06; Bursar and Librarian Lady Margaret Hall, 1907; Asst Tutor, 1917; Vice-Principal and Tutor, Lady Margaret Hall, 1921-37; University Lecturer in History, Oxford, 1928-35. *Publications:* The Norman Administration of Apulia and Capua, 1127-1166, in Papers of the British School at Rome, vol. vi, 1913; Italy before 1250, in Italy Medieval and Modern, 1917; papers on Medieval History of South Italy and reviews in English Historical Review and in Italian and English Journals, 1929-68; S Maria della Strada at Matrice, its History and Sculpture, in Papers of the British Sch. at Rome, vol. xiii, 1938; The Sicilian Norman Kingdom in the Mind of Anglo-Norman Contemporaries, Annual Italian Lecture, 1938, British Academy; Admiral Eugenius of Sicily, 1957 The Catalogus Baronum, a new edn, Pt II in the press with Istituto storico Italiano per il Medio evo (Fonti per la storia d'Italia), Rome. *Recreations:* study of architecture, formerly travel, climbing and walking. *Address:* 11 Priory Mansions, Drayton Gardens, SW10. *T:* 01-373 8699.   [*Died* 9 *May* 1972.

JANES, Sir Herbert (Charles), Kt 1954; Founder and Chairman of H. C. Janes Ltd, Builders and Civil Engineers, retired from Chairmanship, July 1962; *b* 10 Oct. 1884; *s* of Charles Walter Janes; *m* 1st, 1911, Edith Brown, Luton; one *s* three *d* (and *er s* killed, RAF, 1943); 2nd, 1944, Hilda Horsfall, Bradford. *Educ:* Luton. Mem. Luton Borough Council, 1942-58; Mayor, 1953-54. Pres. Baptist Men's Movement, 1943; Pres. Mid-Herts Sunday Sch. Union, 1939-45; Pres. Luton and Dunstable Master Builders Assoc., 1945-46; Pres. Beds Union of Baptist and Congregational Churches, 1947-48; Chm. Baptist Missionary Soc., 1949-50; Treas. Baptist Commonwealth Soc., 1946-62. Pres., Baptist Union of Great Britain and Ireland, 1956; Founded: The Janes Trust (from which many charitable bequests have been made); Sir Herbert Janes Village for Old People at Luton, 1958; Green Hills Youth Rendezvous, Worthing, 1962; Green Hills Club for Old People, Luton, 1963. Has travelled considerably. *Recreations:* golf, bridge, travel, cinephotography. *Address:* 74 Seabright, West Parade, Worthing.   [*Died* 21 *June* 1977.

JANES, Norman Thomas, RWS, RE, RSMA; Painter, Etcher and Wood Engraver; *b* Egham, Surrey 1892; *s* of Arthur T. Janes and Ada Louise Croxson; *m* 1925, Barbara Greg; one *s* two *d*. *Educ:* Slade Sch. (drawing and painting); Central Sch. of Arts and Crafts (etching); Royal Coll. of Art. Served in the London Irish Rifles and the Royal Irish Regt, 1914-19; France, 1915-17; RAF 1941-45; served in Middle East for three years (despatches). Exhibited from 1921 at Internat. Soc., Royal Academy, New English Art Club, Goupil Gallery, Society of Wood Engravers and principal provincial galleries; abroad at Florence, Venice, Prague, Chicago, Stockholm, Johannesburg, New York; works purchased for permanent collections of British Museum, Victoria and Albert Museum, Imperial War Museum, London Museum, City of London, Manchester City Gallery, Whitworth Gallery (Manchester), Bradford, Brighton, National Gallery of New Zealand, New York Public Library, Brooklyn Museum, Cincinnati, Pasadena, Brisbane and others. One-man exhibitions: Beaux Arts Gallery, London, 1932 and 1945; Middlesbrough, 1962; Clifton, 1975. *Recreations:* books, garden. *Address:* 70 Canonbury Park South, N1. *T:* 01-226 1925.
                                            [*Died* 23 *Sept.* 1980.

JANSON, Stanley Eric, MA, PhD, BSc; Keeper, Department of Astronomy and Geophysics, Science Museum, London, 1967-69, retired; *b* 22 Nov. 1908; *s* of late O. E. Janson and late May Janson (*née* Drucquer); *m* 1939, Irene G. M. Wentworth; two *d*. *Educ:* Highgate Sch.; Gonville and Caius Coll., Cambridge. BSc 1930, MA 1933, PhD 1934. Assistant to Prof. of Chemistry, University of Cambridge, 1930-35; Asst Keeper, Science Museum Library, 1935; Seconded to Ministry of Supply, 1939-

45; Dep. Keeper, Science Museum Library, 1947; Keeper, Dept of Chemistry, 1959-67. *Publications:* various papers on organic chemistry in scientific journals. *Recreations:* gardening, music. *Address:* 68 Tosswill Road, Tahunanui, Nelson, New Zealand.
                                            [*Died* 25 *Oct.* 1974.

JANSZ, Sir (Herbert) Eric, Kt 1953; CMG 1946; Chairman, Public Service Commission, Ceylon, 1950-60; *b* 1890; Cadet Ceylon Civil Service, 1914; District Judge, Ratnapura, 1925; Asst Settlement Officer, 1928; Settlement Officer, 1938; subsequently Commissioner of Lands, Ceylon, retd 1945. Parly Sec. to Min. of Educn, 1947-48, and to Min. of Finance, 1948-50, Ceylon. *Address:* Fortis House, Hammers Lane, Mill Hill, NW7 4DJ.   [*Died* 5 *Jan.* 1976.

JARDINE, John, CB 1948; OBE 1919; MD; FRCSE; DPH; FRSE; Chairman General Board of Control for Scotland, 1947-62; *b* 13 Dec. 1881; *s* of John Jardine, Penicuik; *m* 1917, Mary Alexander Hay; one *s* one *d*. *Educ:* George Heriot's Sch.; Edinburgh Univ. Medical Officer for Schools, Midlothian, 1909-24; Medical Officer to Scottish Education Dept, 1924-30; Asst Sec., 1930-43; Principal Asst Sec., 1943-45. *Publications:* numerous. *Recreations:* golf, curling. *Address:* 14 Cobden Crescent, Edinburgh 9. *T:* 031-667 1450. [*Died* 13 *Sept.* 1974.

JARDINE, Lionel Westropp, CIE 1939; late ICS; *b* 15 Feb. 1895; *s* of late Sir John Jardine, 1st Bt, KCIE, LLD, Godalming; *m* 1922, Marjorie Mildred Woods, Englefield Green, Surrey, one *s* two *d*. *Educ:* Charterhouse (Scholar); Wadham Coll., Oxford (Exhibitioner). Served European War, 1914-18 (despatches, wounded); Political Service, Mesopotamia, 1919-21 (general service medal and bar, Iraq); entered ICS, 1921; NW Frontier, 1924-31 (general service medal, 1931) and 1936-39; Finance Minister, Kashmir State, 1932; Dep. Commissioner, Peshawar, 1936; Revenue and Divisional Commissioner, N-WFP, India, 1938-43 and 1944; Resident for Baroda and the Gujerat States, India, 1943-44; left India, 1947, to join Dr F. N. D. Buchman in the work of Moral Re-armament. FRGS. *Publication:* They called me an Impeccable Imperialist, 1979. *Address:* 6 Victoria Road, W8 5RD. *T:* 01-937 7074. *Club:* Naval and Military.
                                            [*Died* 9 *May* 1980.

JARDINE-BROWN, Prof. Robert; Principal of College of Estate Mangement, 1955-72, now Emeritus, and Dean of Faculty of Urban and Regional Studies, Reading University, since 1967 (on integration of College with University); *b* 16 March 1905; *s* of Walter Falconer Brown, MB, CM, DPH, and Catherine Edith (*née* McGhie); *m* 1938, Ormonde Joan (*née* Butler); two *s*. *Educ:* Ayr Academy; Univs of Glasgow and Edinburgh. MA 1926, LLB 1928, Glasgow; DLitt 1947, Edinburgh. Called to Bar, Middle Temple, 1931; Advocate of Scots Bar, 1945. Has held various posts, incl.: Legal Adviser and Business Man., BBC, 1936-45; Sec., Univ. of Edinburgh, 1945-47. Mem., English Agricultural Wages Board, 1959-72; Mem., Scottish Agricultural Wages Board, 1963-72. Officer, Order of Orange Nassau. *Publications:* mainly legal and educational in English and American jls. *Recreations:* walking, reading, appreciation of visual art. *Address:* High Point, Riverview Road, Pangbourne, Berks. *T:* Pangbourne 2849. *Clubs:* Chelsea Arts; Royal Cornwall Yacht.   [*Died* 3 *Sept.* 1972.

JARMAN, Rev. Canon Cyril Edgar; Canon Residentiary, Chester Cathedral, 1943-73, Vice-Dean, 1965-73; *b* 2 Dec. 1892; *s* of William and Annie Jarman, Cliftonville, Margate; *m* 1928, Alice Josephine, *d* of Canon Stockley, Wolverhampton, Chancellor of Lichfield Cathedral; two *d*. *Educ:* Holy Trinity Sch., Margate; The Theological Coll., Lichfield. Deacon, 1916, Lichfield, Priest, 1918; Curate, St James', Wednesbury, 1916-22; Curate St Peter's, Wolverhampton, 1922-25; Vicar, St Mary's, Shrewsbury, 1925-37; Vicar, Penkridge, 1937-43; Prebendary of Lichfield Cathedral, 1941-43. Proctor in Convocation, Lichfield, 1935-43; Examining Chaplain to Bishop of Chester, 1939-73; Chaplain to High Sheriff of Cheshire, 1955. *Recreations:* reading, walking. *Address:* The Flat, Croft House, Hazler Crescent, Church Stretton, Salop. *T:* Church Stretton 2506.
                                            [*Died* 30 *Aug.* 1978.

JARROLD, (Herbert) John, CBE 1969; MA; JP; Chairman, Jarrold & Sons Ltd, since 1937; *b* 16 Feb. 1906; *s* of late T. H. C. Jarrold, and *g g g s* of John Jarrold, founder of Jarrold & Sons Ltd (1770); *m* 1st, 1932, Catherine Grace Elliott (*d* 1973); three *s*; 2nd, 1974, Joan, *widow* of Michael Pank. *Educ:* Norwich Sch.; Queens' Coll., Cambridge. Studied printing and bookbinding in Leipzig; joined Jarrold & Sons Ltd, 1927. Councillor, Norwich City Council, 1936-47; Sheriff of Norwich, 1947-49, Alderman, 1949-56. Pres., British Fedn of Master Printers, 1961-62; Chm., Printing, Packaging and Allied Trades Research Assoc., 1964; Pres., Norwich Incorporated Chamber

of Commerce, 1965-67. JP Norwich 1949; Lord Mayor of Norwich, 1970-71. *Publications:* many articles on colour reproduction and printing. *Address:* 1A Church Avenue, Norwich NR2 2AQ. *T:* Norwich 54612. *Club:* National Liberal.
[*Died 19 July 1979.*]

JARVIS, Alan Hepburn; Chairman, Society of Art Publications, Ottawa, since 1959; *b* 26 July 1915; *s* of Charles Arthur Jarvis and Janet Mackay, Brantford; *m* 1955, Elizabeth Devlin Kingsmill; one *s* two *d. Educ:* University of Toronto; University Coll., Oxford; Graduate Sch. of Fine Art, New York Univ. Ministry of Aircraft Production, 1941-45; Priv. Sec. to Sir Stafford Cripps, 1945; Dir of Public Relations, Council of Industrial Design, 1945-47; Dir, Pilgrim Pictures Ltd, 1947-50; Head of Oxford House, Bethnal Green, 1950-55; Dir, National Gallery of Canada, 1955-59. Hon. LLD, Waterloo Univ., 1966. *Publications:* (ed.) Democracy Alive, The Collected Speeches of Sir Stafford Cripps, 1946; The Things We See-Indoors and Out, 1946; (with Sir Gordon Russell) How to Buy Furniture, 1953; (ed) Canadian Painters Series: David Milne, 1965. *Recreation:* sculpting. *Address:* Apartment 201, 16 Clarence Square, Toronto 135, Ont, Canada. *Club:* Carlton (Toronto).
[*Died 3 Dec. 1972.*]

JAYETILEKE, Sir Edward (George Perera), Kt 1951; QC (Ceylon) 1938; *b* 11 Oct. 1888; *s* of John Gratiaen Perera Jayetileke and Maria Perera; *m* 1915, Grace Victoria Abeyesundere; one *s* three *d. Educ:* Royal College, Colombo. Called to the Ceylon Bar, 1910; Solicitor-Gen., 1941; Attorney-Gen., 1941; Puisne Justice, 1942; Senior Puisne Justice, 1949; Chm. Judicial Service Commission, 1950-51; Chief Justice, Ceylon, 1950-51. *Recreations:* racing, bridge, horticulture. *Address:* Tilakasthan, Gregory's Road, Colombo 7, Sri Lanka. *T:* 9440. *Clubs:* Ceylon Turf, Orient (Colombo); Galle Gymkhana (Galle).
[*Died 2 Aug. 1975.*]

JEANS, Sir Alick, (Alexander Grigor), Kt 1967; TD; JP; Chairman and Managing Director, The Liverpool Daily Post and Echo Ltd; *b* 29 July 1912; *s* of late Allan Jeans; *m* 1939, Jean Mary Plummer; three *s. Educ:* Rugby; University Coll., Oxford. Chm., Press Association, 1953-54; Pres., Newspaper Soc., 1959-60. *Address:* Inchbroom, Farr Hall Road, Heswall, Cheshire. *T:* 051-342 2561. *Clubs:* Royal Thames Yacht, Army and Navy; Old Hall, Exchange and Palatine, Racquet, Press (Liverpool).
[*Died 1 April 1972.*]

JEANS, Ronald; *s* of late Sir Alexander Jeans; *m* 1916, Margaret Evelyn Wise; one *s* one *d. Educ:* Loretto. Studied art at the Slade Sch. for a while; then entered business in Liverpool; after some years gave this up for writing; was one of the founders of the Liverpool Playhouse, the second Repertory Theatre in England, in 1911; for this theatre in its early days wrote several plays, and later devoted his whole attention to intimate revues which were produced by André Charlot, C. B. Cochran, Jack Hulbert, etc.; later reverted to plays with Lean Harvest, Can the Leopard?, The Composite Man, Ghost for Sale, and Young Wives' Tale (1949); Count Your Blessings (1951); Grace and Favour, 1954; Double Take, 1958. Founded (with J. B. Priestley) the London Mask Theatre Company, 1938 and revived this company, 1947. *Publications:* Vignettes from Vaudeville; Odd Numbers; The Stage is Waiting; one Dam Sketch After Another; Charlot Revue Sketches, Review of Revues, Sundry Sketches, After Dark, Lean Harvest, Blackout Sketches, Bright Intervals; Writing for the Theatre, 1949. *Address:* 85 Marine Parade, Brighton, Sussex. *Clubs:* Royal Automobile, Dramatists'.
[*Died 16 May 1973.*]

JEANS, Ursula; Actress; *b* India; *d* of Major Charles McMinn; *m* 1st, Robin Irvine (*decd*); 2nd, Roger Livesey, no *c. Educ:* Sacred Heart Convent, Cavendish Square, London. Made first appearance Theatre Royal, Nottingham, 1925, as Sophie Binner in Cobra, after training Royal Academy Dramatic Art, London; first appearance on London stage as Angela in The Firebrand, Wyndham's, 1926, followed by numerous stage successes including Elsie Fraser in The First Mrs Fraser, Haymarket, 1929, Flaemmchen in Grand Hotel, Adelphi, 1931, Sarah Traille in Lovers' Leap, Vaudeville, 1934, Penelope Marsh in Short Story, Queen's, 1935; Alithea in The Country Wife, Old Vic, 1936, etc.; also a season of classical plays at the Old Vic Theatre, 1933-34, Viola in Twelfth Night, Anya in The Cherry Orchard, Anne Bullen in Henry VIII, Mariana in Measure for Measure, Cecily Cardew in The Importance of Being Earnest, Angelica in Love for Love, Miranda in The Tempest; and a further season, 1939, as Kate Hardcastle in She Stoops to Conquer, Petra in The Enemy of the People, Katherine in The Taming of the Shrew; toured as Mary of Magdala in Family Portrait, 1940; Joanna in Dear Brutus, Globe, 1941; toured as Elvira in Blithe Spirit, 1942, as Sara Müller in Watch on the Rhine, 1943 (also at Aldwych,

1943); on tour with ENSA in Dear Brutus, Watch on the Rhine, Springtime for Henry, It Depends What You Mean; Frances in The Banbury Nose, Wyndham's, 1944; with ENSA in Middle and Far East, 1945-46, playing Lady Teazle in School for Scandal and Elizabeth Barrett in The Barretts of Wimpole Street; played Helen in Ever Since Paradise (by J. B. Priestley), New, 1947; Lavinia in The Cocktail Party, Edinburgh Festival, 1949; Mary Bernard in Man of the World, Lyric (Hammersmith), 1950; toured Italy with Old Vic Co., as Olivia in Twelfth Night, June 1950; Dame Overdo in Bartholomew Fair, Edinburgh Festival, 1950; Old Vic, 1950-51; Olivia in Twelfth Night, Dame Overdo in Bartholomew Fair, Lady Cicely Waynflete in Captain Brassbound's Conversion, Mistress Ford in The Merry Wives of Windsor; Jean Moreland in Third Person, Arts, 1951, and Criterion, 1952; Lady Pounce-Pellott in the Baikie Charivari, Glasgow Citizen's Theatre, 1952; Margaret Bell in The Teddy Bear, St Martin's, 1953; Barbary Leigh in Uncertain Joy, Court Theatre, 1955; Mrs Tarleton in Misalliance, Lyric Theatre (Hammersmith), 1956; Lady Touchwood in The Double Dealer, Edinburgh Festival and Old Vic, 1959; Ivette in the Twelfth Hour, 1964; Lady Markby in An Ideal Husband, Strand, 1965. First appearance on NY stage, 1938, as Pauline Murray in Late One Evening. First film part was in The Gipsy Cavalier. *Films include:* Quinneys, The Flying Fool, Cavalcade, I Lived with You, Woman In The Hall, The Weaker Sex, North West Frontier. *Recreations:* riding, swimming and golf. *Address:* c/o International Famous Agency, 11-12 Hanover Street, W1.
[*Died 21 April 1973.*]

JEBB, Eglantyne Mary, CBE 1950; MA Oxon; Principal of the Froebel Educational Institute, Roehampton, Roehampton Lane, SW15, 1932-55; retired 1955; *b* 22 Dec. 1889; *d* of Rev. Heneage Horsley Jebb and Geraldine Croker Russell. *Educ:* Streatham Coll. for Girls; Lady Margaret Hall, Oxford; Class I, in Hons Sch. of English Language and Literature; trained at S Mary's Coll., Lancaster Gate, W, for London University Teachers' Diploma, 1912-13; Asst English Tutor, Somerville Coll., Oxford, 1913-19; English Lecturer, Education Dept, University of Birmingham, 1919-31; Visiting Lecturer Wellesley Coll., Mass, USA 1928-29. *Address:* Tansey, Wintergreen Lane, Winterbrook, Wallingford, Oxfordshire. [*Died 6 May 1978.*]

JEFFERSON, Lt-Col Sir John Alexander D.; *see* Dunnington-Jefferson.

JEFFORD, Vice-Adm. (Retd), James Wilfred, CB 1953; CBE 1951 (OBE 1941); *b* 22 March 1901; *o s* of James Harris Jefford; *m* 1926, Dorothy Kate Caswell; one *d. Educ:* HMS Worcester. Sub-Lieut, RIN, 1922; Commander, RIN, 1941; Captain RIN, 1946; Rear-Adm., 1947. Transferred to special list of Royal Navy and appointed Flag Officer commanding Royal Pakistan Navy, on inception of Pakistan, 1947; appointment upgraded to C-in-C, 1950; Vice-Admiral Royal Pakistan Navy, 1953; appointment terminated, 1953; Chm. Penang Harbour Board, 1955-57; Chm. Penang Port Commission, 1956-57; retired 1957. Served European War, 1914-18, as midshipman; War of 1939-45, commanding HMI Ships Indus and Godavari; various staff and shore appointments. *Address:* Pennyroyal, Willey Lane, Sticklepath, near Okehampton, Devon EX20 2NG.
[*Died 1 Jan. 1980.*]

JEFFREY, Maj.-Gen. Hugh Crozier, CBE 1974; MD, FRCPEd, FRCPath, DTM&H; National Medical Director, Scottish National Blood Transfusion Service, since 1974; *b* 9 April 1914; *s* of Rev. William George Jeffrey and Sarah Jane Crozier; *m* 1952, Anna Halpenny; one *d. Educ:* Dalkeith High Sch.; Univ. of Edinburgh. MD Edinburgh 1973. Commissioned RAMC, 1938; Consultant Pathologist, 1955; Prof. of Pathology, Royal Army Medical Coll., 1960; Dep. Dir of Pathology, FARELF, 1964; Dir of Army Path. and Cons. Pathologist to the Army, 1967-74. QHS 1969-74. *Publications:* Atlas of Medical Helminthology and Protozoology (jtly), 1966; articles in med. jls. *Recreations:* golf, fishing, philately. *Address:* 44 Lygon Road, Edinburgh EH16 5QA. *Club:* Caledonian (Edinburgh).
[*Died 27 Nov. 1976.*]

JEFFRIES, Sir Charles Joseph, KCMG 1943 (CMG 1937); OBE 1928; *b* 1896; *e s* of late C. D. Jeffries, Beckenham, Kent; *m* 1921, Myrtle, *d* of late Dr J. H. Bennett; three *d. Educ:* Malvern Coll.; Magdalen Coll., Oxford (Classical Demy). 2nd Lieut Wilts Regt 1915; Lieut 1917; Invalided from Army, 1917; 2nd Class Clerk, Colonial Office, 1917; Principal, 1920; Asst Sec. and Establishment Officer Colonial Office, 1930-39; Asst Under-Sec. of State, 1939-47; Joint Dep. Under-Sec. of State, Colonial Office, 1947-56; retd 1956. Hon. Sec. Corona Club, 1921-49; Mem. of House of Laity, Church Assembly, 1950-55; a Vice-Pres. of USPG; Sec., Ranfurly Library Service. A Governor of Malvern Coll. *Publications:* The Colonial Empire and its Civil

Service, 1938; Creed or Common Sense, 1943; Nebuchadnezzar's Image, 1947; Partners for Progress, 1949; The Colonial Police, 1952; The Colonial Office (new Whitehall Series), 1956; Joseph in Transit, 1958; Towards the Centre, 1959; Transfer of Power, 1960; Signpost in the Fog, 1961; Proud Record, 1962; Ceylon: The Path to Independence, 1962; Illiteracy: a World Problem, 1967; O.E.G.: a biography of Sir Oliver Ernest Goonetilleke, 1969; Whitehall and the Colonial Service, 1972; (ed) Review of Colonial Research, 1940-60, 1964. *Address:* 1 Brograve Gardens, Beckenham, Kent. *T:* 01-650 1629. *Club:* Royal Commonwealth Society.
[Died 11 Dec. 1972.

JEFFS, Ernest Harry; Editor, The Christian World, 1936-61; *b* 1885; *s* of late Harry Jeffs; *m* 1909, Mary Grantham; two *d.* *Publications:* Princes of the Modern Pulpit, 1931; The Doctor Abroad, 1933. *Recreations:* reading and walking. *Address:* Gresty Lodge, Station Road, Alsager, Stoke-on-Trent.
[Died 4 Nov. 1973.

JEGER, George; JP; MP (Lab) Winchester Division of Hampshire, 1945-50, Goole Division of the West Riding of Yorkshire since 1950; *b* 19 March 1903; *m* 1950, Sybil, *d* of late Abraham Prinsky; one *d.* Mayor of Shoreditch, 1937-38; Mem. Shoreditch Boro' Council 1926-40; JP County of London. Sec. Spanish Medical Aid Cttee, 1936-40; Army, 1940-45. Chm., Anglo-Austrian Soc., 1963-. Kt Comdr, Order of Liberation of Honour in Gold (Commander 1st Class) Austria, 1967. *Recreations:* walking, motoring, music, the theatre. *Address:* 2 Parkfields, Putney, SW15. *T:* 01-788 9555. *[Died 6 Jan. 1971.*

JELLETT, John Holmes, OBE 1944; DSc, MA, FICE, FIMechE, FRSA; Consulting Engineer in private practice; Director, Anglo-Dutch Dredging Co. Ltd, since 1970; Consultant to E. W. H. Gifford & Partners since 1966; *b* 20 April 1905; *s* of Henry Holmes Jellett and Beatrice Inez (*née* Smythies); *m* 1937, Frances Sybil Graham; two *s.* *Educ:* Shrewsbury Sch.; Gonville and Caius Coll., Cambridge. BA 1927, MA 1945; DSc Southampton 1968. Rendel Palmer & Tritton: civil engrg pupil, 1927-30; Asst Engr, 1930-32; Asst Engr, Sir Robert Elliott Cooper, 1932-33; Asst Civil Engr, Civil Engr and Suptg Civil Engr, Dept of CE-in-C, Admty, 1933-46; Temp. Capt., RNVR (Special), 1944-45; Dep. Docks Engr, Docks Engr and Chief Docks Engr, Southampton, 1946-66. Consultant to E. W. H. Gifford & Partners, 1966-70. Member Council: ICE, 1952, Vice-Pres. 1963, Pres. 1968; Engineers' Guild, 1950, Pres., 1962-64. *Publications:* contribs to Proc. ICE. *Address:* 30 Bassett Wood Drive, Southampton SO2 3PS. *Club:* United Service & Royal Aero. *[Died 17 June 1971.*

JELLICOE, Rear-Adm. Christopher Theodore, CB 1955; DSO 1942; DSC 1939, and Bar, 1943; *b* 20 June 1903; *s* of Rev. T. H. L. Jellicoe and Theodora (*née* Boyd); *m* 1937, Marion Christina Lacy; one *d.* *Educ:* RN Coll., Osborne and Dartmouth. Joined RN 1917; Qualified as Lieut (T), 1930-31; Commander 1939; Commanded destroyers Winchelsea, Southwold and Jackal and served as Staff Officer (Ops) to C-in-C Home Fleet, 1939-43; Captain Dec. 1943; Comd HMS Colombo, 1944; Dep. Dir, Ops Div., Admiralty, 1945-47; Captain in Charge, Sheerness, 1947-48; Naval Asst to First Sea Lord, 1948-50; Comd HM Ships Triumph and Illustrious, 1951-52; idc 1953; Naval ADC to the Queen, 1953; Rear-Adm. 1953; Flag Officer, Admiralty Interview Board, 1955-56; retired 1956. *Address:* Orchard Cottage, Storrington, Sussex. *[Died 15 April 1977.*

JELLINEK, His Honour Lionel, MC 1918; Judge of County Courts, Surrey, 1958-71; *b* 30 Nov. 1898; *s* of Robert Jellinek, Company Director, London, and Alice Jellinek (*née* Kennedy); *m* 1923, Lydia, *d* of Ernst Moller, merchant, Oslo; one *d.* *Educ:* Repton; Lincoln Coll., Oxford. Lieut RFA, 1917-19. Called to Bar, Middle Temple, 1923. Art Critic, Sunday Referee, 1926-27. Major RA, 1941-45. Deputy Chm., Essex Quarter Sessions, 1956-58; Chm. Agricultural Land Tribunal, South Eastern Region, 1956-58. Vice-Pres. and Chm. Guildford Symphony Orchestra, 1963. JP Essex 1956. King Haakon VII's Frihets Medal, 1945. *Recreation:* music, especially chamber music (viola). *Address:* Wolfeton Manor, Charminster, Dorchester, Dorset DT2 9QN. *T:* Dorchester 4356. *[Died 8 Oct. 1979.*

JENKIN, Mary Elizabeth, MBE 1945; *b* 8 Jan. 1892; *d* of Professor C. F. Jenkin and Mrs C. F. Jenkin. *Educ:* Norland Place Sch.; St Paul's Girls Sch.; Oxford High Sch.; Oxford University. Worked in the Intelligence Division, Admiralty, 1916-20. MA Oxon, 1921; held various secretarial posts and travelled in Egypt and India, 1921-27; joined BBC, 1927; Head of the BBC Children's Hour, 1950-53; retd 1953. *Recreations:* acting, painting, reading. *Address:* Southfield House, Painswick, Glos. *Club:* University Women's. *[Died 17 May 1979.*

JENKIN-JONES, Charles Mark, CBE 1947; MInstT; CStJ; *b* 2 Nov. 1885; *s* of late Charles and Mable Jenkin-Jones, London; *m* 1913, Violet Olive, *yr d* of late John George and Clara Wood, Hull; one *s* one *d.* *Educ:* Brighton Coll.; Queen's Coll., Oxford (Open Classical Scholar). Entered Service NE Railway Coy 1908; Superintendent, NE Area, L and NE Rly, 1924; Divisional Gen. Manager, York, 1936-47; Railway Operating Gold Medal, Inst. of Transport, 1934; Visited Palestine to Report on Palestine Railways at request of Government, 1935; Represented British Dock Owners at International Labour Conferences, Geneva, 1928, 1929, 1932; Employers' Delegate at Tripartite Conference on Railway Hours, Geneva, 1939; Major, Engineer and Railway Staff Corps, 1925-36; Vice-Chm. Yorks (E Riding) Agricultural Wages Board, 1932-36; Member of: Tyne Improvement Commission, 1936-47; Governing Body Brighton Coll., 1934-49; Church Schools Coy, London, 1943-54; Mem. of Oxford Univ. Appointments Cttee, 1934-52; Vice-Pres. Oxford Soc., and Pres. of York and District Branch; Mem. York A Group Hospital Management Cttee, 1948-51; Mem. of Leeds Univ. Appointments Board, 1948-52; a Governor of St Peter's Sch., York, 1948-62; Chm., York Coll. for Girls, 1963- (Vice-Chm., 1960-63). Chm., Purey Cust Nursing Home, York, 1953-69. *Address:* Dringcote, Tadcaster Road, York. *T:* York 66348.
[Died 8 Jan. 1971.

JENKIN PUGH, Rev. Canon Thomas; see Pugh.

JENKINS, Leslie Augustus Westover, CBE 1971; Chairman, Forestry Commission, 1965-70; Chairman, National Industrial Fuel Efficiency Service, 1968-72; Director since 1954; *b* 27 May 1910; *s* of L. C. W. Jenkins; *m* 1936, Ann Barker (*née* Bruce), *d* of R. Hugh Bruce, St John, NB, Canada; no *c.* *Educ:* Lancing Coll. Chm. and Managing Dir, John Wright & Sons (Veneers) Ltd, 1956-59; Man. Dir, I. & R. Morley Ltd, 1959-63; Director: Restall Brown & Clennell Ltd, 1963; G. N. Haden & Sons Ltd, 1967; Haden-Carrier Ltd, 1971-77; Airscrew-Weyroc, 1971. Member: Industrial Coal Consumers Council, 1947- (Dep. Chm., 1971-73); BNEC, 1964-73 (a Dep. Chm. 1966-73); Consultative Cttee, ECSC, 1973-; Vice-Pres., CBI, 1965-68, Mem. Council, 1968-74; Pres., Nat. Assoc. Brit. Manufacturers, 1963-65. FRSA 1972; MInstF 1959; FBIM 1966 (Mem. Bd, 1968-). *Publication:* Woodlands of Britain (RSA Cantor Lectures), 1971. *Recreations:* yachting, golf. *Address:* Lyneham Lodge, Hook Park, Warsash, Hants. *T:* Locks Heath 3366. *Clubs:* Royal Ocean Racing, Royal Southern Yacht.
[Died 10 June 1978.

JENKINS, Robert Christmas Dewar, JP; *b* 29 Sept. 1900; *s* of late J. Hamilton Jenkins; *m* 1927, Marjorie, *d* of late Andrew George Houstoun; three *d.* *Educ:* Latymer Upper Sch. Mem. Kensington Borough Council, 1927-68, Leader of Conservative Party of Royal Borough of Kensington, 1945-53; Mem. LCC for Kensington (S), 1934-49; Mayor of Kensington, 1939-45. MP (C) Dulwich Div. of Camberwell, 1951-64. JP County of London, 1946; Alderman of Kensington, 1947. Chairman, Royal Borough of Kensington and Chelsea, 1964. Hon. Freeman, Royal Borough of Kensington, 1964-. Served in Inns of Court OTC and KRRC, 1918-19. *Recreation:* phrenology. *Address:* 24 Albemarle, Wimbledon Parkside, SW19. *T:* 01-788 4722. *[Died 25 June 1978.*

JENKINS, William Frank, CB 1949; CBE 1943; ARCO; *b* 14 May 1889; *m* 1923, Marjorie Newton-Jones. Called to Bar, Gray's Inn, 1922, Dir-Gen. Disposals, Ministry of Supply, 1946; Under-Sec. (Contracts) Ministry of Supply, 1947-53; Principal Finance Officer, UK Atomic Energy Authority, 1954-57, retired. *Address:* The Gateway, Forest Moor Road, Knaresborough HG5 8JY. *[Died 11 Aug. 1980.*

JENKS, Clarence Wilfred; Director-General of the International Labour Office, since 1970; Chairman of Board, International Institute of Labour Studies, Geneva, and International Centre for Advanced Technical and Vocational Training, Turin; *b* 7 March 1909; *e s* of late Richard and Alice Sophia Jenks; *m* 1949, Jane Louise, *d* of Frederick S. Broverman, NY City; two *s.* *Educ:* Bootle Secondary Sch.; Liverpool Collegiate Sch.; Gonville and Caius Coll., Cambridge, Hon. Fellow 1971; Geneva Sch. of International Studies. BA 1931; MA 1936; LLD 1953; Cecil Peace Prize, 1928; Pres. of Cambridge Union Soc., 1930; called to the Bar by Gray's Inn, 1936. Mem. of Legal Section of Internat. Labour Office, 1931; Legal Adviser, 1940; Asst Dir-Gen., 1948-64; Dep. Dir-Gen., 1964-67; Principal Dep. Dir-Gen., 1967-70; Adviser to Venezuelan Government on labour legislation, 1938; Mem. ILO Delegns: at UN Monetary and Financial Conference, Bretton Woods, 1944; UN Conf. on International Organisation, San Francisco, 1945. Intergovernmental Copyright Conf., 1952; International Confs on the Peaceful Uses of Atomic Energy, 1955 and 1958; United

Nations Conferences on Law of the Sea, 1958 and 1960, Diplomatic Intercourse and Immunities, 1961, Law of Treaties, 1968; at Gen. Assembly and Economic and Social Council of United Nations and other international conferences and cttees; Prof., The Hague Acad. of International Law, 1939, 1950, 1955, and 1966; Hon. Prof., Universidad Nacional Mayor de San Marcos de Lima, and Univ. of Lima, 1972. Member: Institute of International Law; International Academy or Comparative Law; Corresponding Mem., International Academy of Astronautics. Hon. LLD: Edinburgh, 1967; Delhi, 1971; Seoul National, 1971; La Plata, 1972. *Publications:* The Headquarters of International Institutions, 1945; The International Protection of Trade Union Freedom, 1957; The Common Law of Mankind, 1958; Human Rights and International Labour Standards, 1960; International Immunities, 1961; The Proper Law of International Organisations, 1962; Law, Freedom and Welfare, 1963; The Prospects of International Adjudication, 1964; Space Law, 1965; Law in the World Community, 1967; The World Beyond the Charter, 1968; A New World of Law?, 1969; Social Justice in the Law of Nations, 1970; (ed) The International Labour Code, 1939 and 1952; Constitutional Provisions concerning Social and Economic Policy, 1944; contribs to British Year Book of International Law and other Legal jls. *Recreations:* rowing, swimming, mountain-walking, ski-ing, skating. *Address:* International Labour Office, Geneva, Switzerland. *T:* Geneva 326200; 3 rue de Contamines, Geneva, Switzerland. *T:* Geneva 354235. *Clubs:* Athenæum, Reform; Cosmos (Washington). *[Died 9 Oct. 1973.*

JENSEN, Dr Johannes Daniel; Professor of Physics, Heidelberg University, since 1949; *b* 28 June 1906. *Educ:* Hamburg University. Professor of Physics, Hannover Inst. of Technology, 1941. Professor *hc* Hamburg Univ., 1947; Member: Heidelberg Academy of Sciences, 1949; Max Planck Gesellschaft, 1961; Deutsche Akademie der Naturforscher, Leopoldina, Halle, 1964; Nobel Prize for Physics (jtly), 1963. *Publications:* (with Maria Goeppert-Mayer) Elementary Theory of Nuclear Shell Structure, New York, 1955; Editor (with Otto Haxel) Zeitschrift für Physik, 1956-. *Recreation:* physics. *Address:* Ruprecht-Karl-Universität, Grabengasse 1, 6900 Heidelberg, Germany. *[Died 11 Feb. 1973.*

JEPHCOTT, Sir Harry, 1st Bt *cr* 1962; Kt 1946; MSc (London); FRIC; FPS; Hon. President, late Chairman, Glaxo Group Ltd; Director Metal Box Co. Ltd, 1950-64; *b* 15 Jan. 1891; *s* of late John Josiah Jephcott, Redditch; *m* 1919, Doris Gregory, FPS; two *s*. *Educ:* King Edward's Grammar Sch., Camp Hill, Birmingham; West Ham Technical Coll., London. Called to Bar (Middle Temple), 1925. Chm. Council, Dept Scientific and Industrial Research, 1956-61; Pres. Royal Inst. of Chemistry, 1953-55; Chm. Assoc. of British Chemical Manufacturers, 1947-52, Pres. 1952-55. Mem. Advisory Council Scientific Policy, 1953-56; Chm. Cttee Detergents, 1953-55. Chm. School of Pharmacy, University of London, 1948-69. Hon. Fellow, School of Pharmacy, 1966. Governor London Sch. of Economics, 1952-68; Governor North London Collegiate Sch., 1957-. Hon. DSc (Birmingham), 1956. Hon. FRCGP 1960; Hon. FRSocMed 1961. *Heir:* *s* John Anthony Jephcott, BCom [*b* 21 May 1924; *m* 1949, Sylvia Mary, *d* of Thorsten Frederick Relling, Wellington, NZ; two *d*]. *Address:* Weetwood, 1 Cheney Street, Pinner, Mddx HA5 2TF. *T:* 01-866 0305. *Club:* Athenæum.
[Died 29 May 1978.

JEPSON, Richard Pomfret, FRCS, FRACS; Professor of Surgery, Adelaide University, Australia, 1958-68; now in private practice; *b* 15 Feb. 1918; *s* of W. N. and L. E. Jepson, Whalley, Lancs; *m* 1951, Mary Patricia Herbert Oliver; five *d*. *Educ:* St Mary's Grammar Sch., Clitheroe, Lancs; Manchester Univ., BSc, MB, ChB. House Surgeon, Manchester Royal Infirmary, 1941-42; Neurosurgical specialist, Major, RAMC, 1942-46; Asst Lecturer, Lecturer and Reader in Surgery, University of Manchester, 1946-54; Prof. of Surgery, University of Sheffield, 1954-58. Hunterian Prof., RCS, 1951; Commonwealth Fund Fellowship, 1951; Research Fellow, Western Reserve Univ., Cleveland, Ohio, 1951-52. Hon. Surgeon: Queen Elizabeth Hosp., 1958-68; Royal Adelaide Hosp., 1958-68 (Hon. Vascular Surgeon, 1968-78). *Publications:* articles in physiological and surgical journals. *Recreations:* varied. *Address:* 112 Barnard Street, N Adelaide, S Australia 5006, Australia. *Club:* Adelaide.
[Died 19 Oct. 1980.

JEPSON, Stanley; *b* 1894; *s* of Samuel Jepson, Spalding; *m* Elizabeth, *d* of late Major G. Casswell, Gosberton, Spalding; one *d*. *Educ:* Moulton. Served (Captain) Indian Army, European War, and 3rd Afghan War, 1919; retired 1921; The Yorkshire Post, 1925-27; Editor of the Illustrated Weekly of India, 1928-47. *Publications:* Motor Runs from Bombay, 1934; Big Game Encounters, 1936; The Overland Route from India, 1938; Indian

Lenslight, 1947. *Address:* Bentcliffe, St Aubin, Jersey, CI.
[Died 16 June 1976.

JERRAM, Sir (Cecil) Bertrand, KCMG, *cr* 1947 (CMG 1938); *b* 22 Oct. 1891; *y s* of late C. S. Jerram, Talland, Cornwall. *Educ:* Hillside, Godalming; King's Sch., Canterbury; Pembroke Coll., Cambridge. Entered Levant Consular Service in 1913; employed at Odessa, Kiev, Moscow; arrested and imprisoned by Bolshevik forces at Moscow in 1918; Vice-Consul, Novorossisk, 1919-20; Asst Agent, Moscow and Leningrad, 1923-27; Acting Consul, Bergen, 1927-28; Consul and Chargé d'Affaires ad interim, Tallinn, 1928-30; Commercial Sec., Helsingfors, 1930-33; Commercial Counsellor. Warsaw, 1933-37; Commercial Counsellor to HM Embassy in Spain (at Hendaye), 1937; Asst Agent, Salamanca and Burgos, 1938; Acting Agent at Burgos and HM Chargé d'Affaires in Spain, 1939; Commercial Counsellor to HM Embassy at Buenos Aires, 1939; Minister (Commercial), 1944-45; Minister in Stockholm, 1945-47; Ambassador 1947-48; Minister to Austria, 1948-49; Special Ambassador for Great Britain, Austr. and NZ at inauguration of Gen. Odria as Pres. of Perú, 1950; Ambassador to Chile, 1949-51; retired from the Foreign Service, 1951. Leader of UK Delegation: at Ecosoc Conf., Santiago, 1951; to Plenipotentiary Conf. of Internat. Telecommunications Union, Buenos Aires, 1952. Silver Jubilee Medal, 1935; Coronation Medal, 1937. *Recreation:* travel. *Club:* Athenæum. *[Died 28 Jan. 1971.*

JERRAM, Brig. Roy Martyn, DSO 1940; MC 1918; Legion of Merit (USA); Royal Tank Regiment; retired, 1947; *b* 10 Nov. 1895; *e s* of late Admiral Sir Martyn Jerram, GCMG, KCB; *m* 1926, Monica Gillies; two *s* one *d*. *Educ:* Marlborough. Served European War, Hants Regt, 1914-17; Tank Corps, 1917 (MC); Tank Engineer and GSO 2, Army HQ, India, 1931-35; DAD Mechanisation, War Office, 1937-40; AQMG, GHQ, France, 1940 (DSO); commanded 7th (Army) Bn R Tank Regt 1st Libyan Campaign, 1940-41 (despatches twice, bar to DSO); Comdr 33 Army Tank Bde, 1941-42; DDG Petroleum Warfare Dept, 1943-44; Comdr Assault Training and Development Centre, 1944-45; Control Commission, Germany, 1945-52; Red Cross, Japan, Korea, 1952, 1953. *Address:* Trehane, Trevanson, Wadebridge, Cornwall. *T:* Wadebridge 2523. *Club:* Royal Commonwealth Society. *[Died 6 April 1974.*

JERRARD, Brig. Charles Ian, CB 1954; CBE 1945; retired 1953; *b* 13 June 1900; *s* of Harry Jerrard, Uplyme, Dorset; *m* 1st, 1931; one *s*; 2nd, 1949, Joan Ma Mathein Mya; one *s* one *d*. *Educ:* Bishop Veseys, Sutton Coldfield; Cadet Coll., Wellington. Commissioned, Indian Army, 1920; Regimental Officer, 1 Bn 12 FF Regt, 1920-25; Adjt Depot,. 12 FF Regt, 1926-28; Staff Coll., Quetta, 1935-36; Brigade Major, Wana Brigade, 1937-38; Company Comdr, RMC Sandhurst, 1938-39; Chief Instructor, 169 OCTU, 1939-40; GSO 2 Ops, 12 Corps 1940-41; GSO 2 14 Indian Div., 1941; GSO 1 Ops 4 Corps, Assam, 1941-42; Commandant 8/12 FF Regt, 1943; Comd 98 Indian Inf. Bde, 1944-47; Operations Waziristan, 1924-37; Assam, Burma, 1942-43; Burma, 1944-45 (CBE, despatches thrice); Burma Anti Dacoit, 1946-47; Acting Maj.-Gen. 1945; Dir Military Training and Education, Pakistan Army, 1948-53; Hon. Brig. 1954. *Recreation:* gardening. *Address:* Solway Cottage, Uplyme, Dorset. *T:* Lyme Regis 2333. *[Died 18 Jan. 1977.*

JESSEL, Sir George, 2nd Bt, *cr* 1883; MC; JP; late Capt. 5th Buffs; Life President, Imperial Continental Gas Association (late Chairman and Director); *b* 28 May 1891; *er s* of 1st Bt and Edith (*d* 1956), 2nd *d* of Rt Hon. Sir Julian Goldsmid, 3rd Bt, MP, *S* father, 1928; *m* 1923, Muriel (*d* 1948), *d* of Col J. W. Chaplin, VC, and *widow* of Major F. Swetenham; one *s*; *m* 1948, Elizabeth, Lady Russell of Liverpool, *d* of late Dr David Ewart, OBE, MD, FRCS, Chichester. *Educ:* Eton; Balliol Coll., Oxford (MA). Served European War, 1914-18 (severely wounded, despatches, MC). JP Kent, 1940; High Sheriff of Kent, 1958. *Heir:* *s* Charles John Jessel [*b* 29 Dec. 1924; *m* 1956, Shirley Cornelia, *o d* of John Waters, Northampton; two *s* one *d*]. *Address:* Ladham House, Goudhurst, Kent. *T:* Goudhurst 203. *Clubs:* Garrick, Brooks's, Army and Navy, MCC.
[Died 18 Aug. 1977.

JESSEL, Sir Richard (Hugh), Kt 1960; Chairman and Managing Director, Jessel Toynbee & Co. Ltd, Discount Brokers, 1943-60, retired; *b* 21 Feb. 1896; 2nd *s* of late Sir Charles James Jessel, 1st Bt; *m* 1st, 1923, Margaret Ella (*d* 1953), *d* of late Sir George Lewis, 2nd Bt; two *s* one *d*; 2nd, 1954, Daphne (*d* 1971), *widow* of Major T. G. Philipson, MC, the Life Guards, and *d* of late W. B. Gladstone; 3rd, 1972, Diana, *widow* of Lt-Col George Trotter, late Royal Scots Greys. *Educ:* Eton. Founded Jessel Toynbee & Co., 1922; Limited Co. (private), Chm., 1943; Public Co., 1946; Public Works Commissioner, 1949-60; Exports Credits Guarantee Dept Advisory Council, 1951-60 (Dep.

Chm., 1959). Served European War, 1914-18, Lt 2/7 Bn Hants Regt; served War of 1939-45, with Ministry of Economic Warfare, 1939-41; Priority Officer, Air Ministry, 1941-44. *Recreations:* racing, gardening. *Address:* The White House, Steeple Morden, Royston, Herts SG8 0PE. *Clubs:* Brooks's, MCC.   [*Died 15 July* 1979.

JESSOP, Joseph Chasser, MA, PhD (St Andrews); FRHistS 1930; retired as Headmaster, Lossiemouth School (1933-58); *b* 13 Jan. 1892; *s* of Thomas Jessop and Helen Baird Alexander; *m* 1922, Ida Hallsey Bates, Stourbridge; twin *d. Educ:* Montrose Academy; St Andrews Univ., MA (Hons) 1915. Captain of St Andrews Univ. Golf Club; served in India, Egypt, and France as Lt in Black Watch for 3+ years (European War); wounded and gassed in France; after convalescence appointed Chief Education Officer to 4th (Res.) Black Watch. Taught in: Selkirk High Sch.; Hutchesons' Boys' Grammar Sch., Glasgow; Brechin High Sch. *Publications:* Education in Angus: an Historical Survey of Education up to the Act of 1872 from Original and Contemporary Sources, 1931, published under the auspices of the Scottish Council for Research in Education; Teach Yourself Golf, 1950. *Recreation:* golf; three times golf champion of Forfarshire; former amateur record-holder of Eden, St Andrews, Montrose, Edzell, and Moray Golf Courses; three times winner of Montrose, four times winner of Moray, Open Amateur Golf Tournaments. SGU Northern District champion. *Address:* 5 Old Mill Road, Inverness. *T:* Inverness 30480. *Clubs:* Scottish Universities Golfing Society; Moray Golf (Hon. Life Mem.).
                                                 [*Died 22 Nov.* 1972.

JESSOP, Thomas Edmund, OBE 1945; MC 1918; MA, BLitt; Hon. LittD (Dublin); Hon. DLitt (Hull); Fellow of the British Psychological Society, Foreign Fellow, Accademia Nazionale dei Lincei (Rome); Médaille d'honneur, Brussels University; Ferens Professor of Philosophy in the University of Hull, 1928-61, Professor Emeritus since 1961; *b* Huddersfield, 10 Sept. 1896; *s* of Newton Jessop; *m* 1930, Dora Anne Nugent Stewart (*d* 1965), MA (Glasgow). *Educ:* Heckmondwike Sch., Leeds Univ.; Oriel Coll., Oxford. Served with Duke of Wellington's West Riding Regt on the Western Front, 1916-18 (twice wounded); Asst Lecturer in Logic and Metaphysics, University of Glasgow, 1925-28; Chm. of E and N Yorks and North Lindsey Adult Education Cttee, 1936-37; Donnellan Lectr, Dublin, 1944; Dunning Trust Lectr, Kingston, Ontario 1948; Visiting Professor: Brussels Univ., 1953; Los Angeles State Coll., 1963; San Francisco State Coll., 1970. Vice-Pres. Methodist Conf., 1955; Member: of World Methodist Council Exec. (1956-66); of Editorial Bd of SCM Press; of Editorial Bd of Archives Internationales d'Histoire des Idées, of Council of Royal Institute of Philosophy, of Institut International de Philosophie, and of Yorks Executive of Royal Society of St George; Chm. of Adult Religious Education Sub-Cttee of Brit. Council of Churches, 1948-61. *Publications:* Lugano and its Environs, 1924; Montreux and Lake of Geneva, 1925; Locarno and its Valleys, 1927; Bibliography of George Berkeley, Bishop of Cloyne, 1934, rev. and enl. edn 1974; The Philosophical Background, in France, Companion to French Studies, 1937; Berkeley's Principles of Human Knowledge, 1937; The Scientific Account of Man, in The Christian Understanding of Man, 1938; Bibliography of Hume and of Scottish Philosophy, 1938; part-translator of A Hundred Years of British Philosophy by R. Metz, 1938; Law and Love, a study of the Christian Ethic, 1940; Science and the Spiritual, 1942; The Treaty of Versailles, 1942; Effective Religion, 1944; Education and Evangelism, 1947; The Works of George Berkeley (joint ed.), 1948-57; The Freedom of the Individual in Society, 1948; Reasonable Living, 1948; Berkeley, Philosophical Writings selected and edited, 1952; Social Ethics, 1952; On Reading the English Bible, Peake Lecture, 1958; "Writers and their Work" (British Council): contrib. Berkeley, 1959, Hobbes, 1960; Introduction to Christian Doctrine, 1960; The Christian Morality (Cambridge Open Divinity Lectures), 1960; The Enduring Passion, 1961; Spinoza on Freedom of Thought, 1962; Berkeley, Antologia degli Scritti Filosofici, 1967; George Berkeley in Italia: il viaggio di un erudito, 1979; contribs to encyclopædias and philosophical periodicals. *Recreation:* gardening. *Address:* 73 Park Avenue, Hull. *T:* 442606.   [*Died 10 Sept.* 1980.

JEWELL, Maurice Frederick Stewart, CBE 1954; JP; DL; *b* 15 Sept. 1885; *s* of Maurice Jewell and Ada Brown; *m* 1911, Elsie May Taylor (*d* 1974); one *s* five *d. Educ:* Marlborough Coll. Served European War, 1914-19, with Royal Field Artillery; Major 1916. JP 1926, DL 1947, Worcs. *Recreations:* formerly cricket (President of Worcs County Cricket Club, 1950-54). *Address:* Bramble End, Birdham, Chichester, West Sussex PO20 7QN. *T:* Chichester 512478. *Club:* Worcestershire (Worcester).
                                                 [*Died 28 May* 1978.

JEWESBURY, Reginald Charles, MA; DM Oxon; FRCP London; Consulting Physician in Paediatrics: St Thomas Hospital; Victoria Hospital for Children, Chelsea; St Luke's Hospital, Guildford; *b* Ceylon, 1878; *s* of late Charles F. Jewesbury, MRCS, LRCP; *m* Anne C. Oliphant Williamson; two *s. Educ:* Westminster Sch.; Christ Church, Oxford; St Thomas's Hospital, Bristowe medal, 1906; Late Physician in charge of Children's Dept, St Thomas's Hospital; Fellow, and Ex-Pres., section for study of Diseases in Children, Royal Society Medicine. Retired. *Address:* 73 Albion Gate, W2. *T:* 01-262 5821. *Club:* United Service and Royal Aero.
                                                 [*Died 28 Nov.* 1971.

JOELSON, F(erdjnand) Stephen; writer on African affairs since 1917; editor, author, broadcaster and publisher; *b* 3 Jan. 1893; *e s* of late George and Sarah Jane Joelson; *m* 1921, Florence Emily, *er d* of late William and Elizabeth Buchanan; one *d. Educ:* Cardiff High Sch.; privately, on Continent and in prisoner-of-war camps. Asst manager of rubber estate, E Africa, 1914; POW German E Africa, (Aug.) 1914-17; then Intelligence Officer, GHQ, Dar es Salaam; official interpreter in French, German and Swahili at mil. courts, and liaison officer with Belg. Mil. Mission, GHQ; invalided home; demobilised, 1920. Sec. to internat. businessman; resigned 1924 to found London weekly newspaper East Africa, renamed East Africa and Rhodesia, 1936, and Rhodesia and Eastern Africa, 1966, to mark sympathy with Rhodesian claim for independence. Actively edited journal throughout 43 years until Brit. Govt's imposition of sanctions compelled cessation of publication, 1967. Was Chm. East Africa, Ltd, and Africana, Ltd, which published the newspaper and many vols on Af. affairs. Also Chm., Gold Areas of East Africa, Ltd. Formerly: Gov., Commonwealth Inst.; Vice-Pres., Royal African Society (hon. life Mem. and medallist, 'for dedicated service to Africa'); Mem. Coun., Royal Commonwealth Soc.; Mem. Grand Council, Royal Over-Seas League, Chm. E African Gp; Mem. Cttee, Royal Commonwealth Soc. for the Blind; Mem. Overseas Cttee, Inst. of Journalists. Co-founder, with late L. S. Amery, Colonial League, formed to oppose German colonial claims. Rep. Govt of Tanganyika Territory on adv. cttee to E African Office in London, 1925-39; mem. London Cttee of Voice of Kenya throughout its existence. Twice Chm. E African Dinner Club, and mem. cttee 50 years. FJI; Founder Mem., Commonwealth Writers of Britain. Mem. Council, Anglo-Rhodesian Soc. *Publications:* Tanganyika Territory, 1920; Germany's Claims to Colonies, 1939; compiled Settlement in East Africa, 1927, Eastern Africa Today, 1928, Eastern Africa Today and Tomorrow, 1934, Rhodesia and Eastern Africa, 1958, etc. *Recreations:* reading, writing, book-collecting, travel, watching cricket, gardening, reflecting in a hot bath. *Address:* Westwood, Cotlands, Sidmouth, Devon. *T:* Sidmouth 4753. *Club:* Royal Commonwealth Society.   [*Died 10 April* 1979.

JOHN, Robert Michael; HM Diplomatic Service; Consul-General, Bordeaux, since 1978; *b* 7 May 1924; *s* of E. A. H. John; *m* 1952, Anne Phebe Clifford Smith; two *d. Educ:* Merchant Taylors' Sch., Sandy Lodge. Served Indian Army (9th Jat Regt), 1942-47. Entered HM Foreign (subseq. Diplomatic) Service, 1950; 2nd Sec., Comr-General's Office, Singapore, 1952-56; 1st Sec. (Commercial), British Embassy, Rio de Janeiro, 1956-60; FO, 1960-64; 1st Sec. (Commercial), subseq. Counsellor (Commercial), British Embassy, Warsaw, 1964-67; British Consul-General, Osaka, Japan, 1967-71; Rio de Janeiro: Minister (Commercial), 1971-72; Consul General and Dir of Trade Promotion, Brazil, 1972-74; Ambassador to Panama, 1974-78. *Recreations:* reading, gardening. *Address:* c/o Foreign and Commonwealth Office, SW1. *Club:* Travellers'.
                                                 [*Died 20 May* 1980.

JOHN PAUL I, His Holiness Pope, (Albino Luciani); *b* Forno di Canale, 17 Oct. 1912; *s* of Giovanni Luciani. *Educ:* Gregorian Univ., Rome. STD (Hons). Ordained Priest, 1935; Curate and teacher, Belluno; Prof. of Dogmatic and Moral Theology, Belluno Seminary, 1937-47; Pro-Vicar-General, dio. of Belluno, 1948; Bishop of Vittorio Veneto, 1958-69; Patriarch of Venice, 1969-78; created Cardinal, 1973; elected Pope 26 Aug. 1978. *Address:* Apostolic Vatican Palace, Vatican City, Italy.
                                                 [*Died 28 Sept.* 1978.

JOHNSON, Alvin Saunders, PhD; President Emeritus of the New School for Social Research, New York City, since 1946; *b* Homer, Nebraska, 18 Dec. 1874; *s* of John Johnson and Edel Marie Bille Johnson; *m* 1904, Margaret Edith Henry; two *s* five *d. Educ:* University of Nebraska, AB 1897, AM 1898; Columbia Univ., 1898-1901; PhD 1902. Fellow in Greek, University of Nebraska, 1898; Tutor in Economics, Bryn Mawr, 1901-02; Tutor, Instructor, Asst Professor, Columbia, 1902-6; Professor of Economics, University of Nebraska, 1906-08; of Texas, 1908-10; Associate Professor of Economics, University of Chicago,

1910-11; Professor of Economics, Stanford University, 1911-12; Cornell Univ., 1912-16; Prof. of Political Science, Stanford Univ., 1916-17; Associate Editor, New Republic (NY), 1917-23; Associate Editor, Encyclopædia of the Social Sciences, 1928-34; Dir, New School for Social Research, 1922-46. *Publications:* Rent in Modern Economic Theory, 1902; Introduction to Economics, 1909; The Professor and the Petticoat (a novel), 1914; John Stuyvesant Ancestor and Other Sketches, 1917; Spring Storm (novel), 1936; Pioneer's Progress (autobiography), 1952; The Battle of the Wild Turkey and Other Tales, 1961; A Touch of Color and other Tales, 1963. *Address:* 200 North Broadway, Nyack, NY; 395 Riverside Drive, New York City. *T:* Elmwood 8-0892.   [*Died 7 June* 1971.

JOHNSON, B. S., (Bryan Stanley William Johnson); poet, novelist, film director; *b* 5 Feb. 1933; *s* of Stanley Wilfred and late Emily Jane Johnson; *m* 1964, Virginia Ann (*née* Kimpton); one *s* one *d. Educ:* King's Coll., Univ. of London. First Gregynog Arts Fellow, Univ. of Wales, 1970. Chm., Gtr London Arts Assoc. Literature Panel, 1973. Poetry Editor, Transatlantic Review, 1965-. *Films:* (cinema, as dir and writer) You're Human Like the Rest of Them, 1967 (Grand Prix, Tours, 1968; Grand Prix, Melbourne, 1968); Up Yours Too, Guillaume Apollinaire!, 1968; Paradigm, 1969; *Films:* (television, as dir and writer) nine documentaries for BBC2, LWT, HTV, etc. *Plays:* (as dir) Backwards, and, The Ramp, Mermaid, 1970; (as writer) Entry (radio), 1965; BSJ v God, Basement Theatre, Soho, 1971; Not Counting the Savages, BBC TV, 1971. *Publications: poetry:* Poems, 1964 (Gregory Award of 1962); Poems Two, 1972; Penguin Modern Poets 25, 1973; *novels:* Travelling People, 1963 (Gregory Award of 1962); Albert Angelo, 1964; Trawl, 1966 (Somerset Maugham Award of 1967); The Unfortunates, 1969; House Mother Normal, 1971; Christie Malry's Own Double-Entry, 1973; *short stories:* Aren't You Rather Young To Be Writing Your Memoirs?, 1973; (jointly with Zulfikar Ghose) Statement Against Corpses, 1964; Penguin Modern Stories Seven, 1971; *text* (for photographs by Julia Trevelyan Oman): Street Children, 1964; (ed) The Evacuees, 1968; (ed with Margaret Drabble) London Consequences, 1972; (ed) All Bull: the National Servicemen, 1973; *play:* You're Human Like the Rest of Them (Penguin New English Dramatists 14), 1970. *Recreation:* Chelsea FC. *Address:* 9 Dagmar Terrace, N1 2BN. *T:* 01-226 9033. *Clubs:* Institute of Contemporary Arts, Kismet.
                                    [*Died 13 Nov.* 1973.

JOHNSON, Christopher Hollis, CBE 1958; DSc; PhD; Director, Explosives Research and Development Establishment, Waltham Abbey (Ministry of Aviation), 1959-64, retired; *b* Reading, Berks, 18 March 1904; *s* of Ernest G. and Agnes M. Johnson; *m* 1st, 1930, Irene Kathleen (*née* Gilbert) (*d* 1963), Farnham, Surrey; no *c*; 2nd, 1966, Mrs Vera G. Lester (*widow*); five step *c. Educ:* Reading Sch.; University Coll., London. BSc 1st Cl. Hons (Chemistry), 1925; PhD London, 1927; Ramsay Gold Medal, 1927; DSc London, 1940. Teaching Fellow, Univ. of California, Berkeley, 1927-29; Lectr in Physical Chemistry, Univ. of Bristol, 1930-37; Senior Lectr in Inorganic Chemistry, Univ. of Birmingham, 1937-41; Research Manager, Shell Petroleum Co., 1942-48. Min. of Supply, 1948-59: various posts, the last being: Director, Materials and Explosives Research, Shell-Mex House. *Publications:* contribs to Phil. Mag., Chemical Society, Faraday Society. *Address:* Foxwold, Silford Cross, Bideford, N Devon. *T:* Bideford 4232.
                                    [*Died 9 April* 1978.

JOHNSON, Dr Donald McIntosh, MA, MB, BCh Cambridge; MRCS, LRCP; Chairman and Managing Director of Johnson Publications Ltd; *b* 17 Feb. 1903; *s* of late Isaac Wellwood Johnson, Bury, Lancs, and Bertha Louise Hall; *m* 1st, 1928, Christiane Marthe Coussaert, Brussels; one *s*; 2nd, 1947, Betty Muriel Plaisted, Oxford; one *s* one *d. Educ:* Cheltenham Coll.; Gonville and Caius Coll., Cambridge; St Bartholomew's Hospital (Entrance Schol.). Qualified as doctor, 1926; barrister-at-law, 1930. Medical Officer, Cambridge University East Greenland Expedn, 1926; Casualty Officer, Metropolitan Hospital, 1926; House Physician, East London Hospital for Children, Shadwell, 1927; Medical Officer to Harrington Harbour Hosp., Internat. Grenfell Assoc., Labrador, 1928-29; General Practitioner, Thornton Heath, Croydon, 1930-37; a Demonstrator of Anatomy, Oxford Univ., 1937-39. Served War in RAMC (Capt. TA), 1939-45. Mem. Croydon Medical Board, Ministry of Labour and National Service, 1951-55; MP (C) Carlisle, 1955-63, (Independent C) 1963-64; first MP to raise parly debate on the Ombudsman. *Publications:* The End of Socialism, 1945; A Doctor Regrets, 1948; Bars and Barricades, 1952; Indian Hemp, a Social Menace, 1952; A Doctor Returns, 1956; A Doctor in Parliament, 1958; Welcome to Harmony, 1962; The British National Health Service: Friend or Frankenstein?, 1962; A Cassandra at Westminster, 1967; A

Doctor Reflects, 1975. *Recreations:* golf, photography. *Address:* 55 Langley Park Road, Sutton, Surrey. *T:* 01-642 6530.
                                    [*Died 5 Nov.* 1978.

JOHNSON, Dorothy, CBE 1955; BA; HM Deputy Chief Inspector of Factories, Ministry of Labour, 1947-55, retired; *b* 20 Dec. 1890; *e d* of late Thomas and Emily Johnson. *Educ:* Leeds Univ. Health and Welfare Branch, Min. of Munitions, 1917-21; HM Inspector of Factories, Home Office, 1922; HM Superintending Inspector of Factories, 1942. Called to the Bar, Middle Temple, 1955. *Address:* Hylands Hotel, Filey, North Yorks.   [*Died 22 Nov.* 1977.

JOHNSON, Maj.-Gen. Dudley Graham, VC 1919; CB 1939; DSO 1914; MC 1918; *s* of late Capt. William Johnson, Inniskilling Dragoons, and Mrs Rosina Johnson, Oddington, Moreton-in-Marsh, Glos; *b* 13 Feb. 1884; *m* Marjorie (*d* 1950), *o d* of Rev. Arthur George Grisewood, Rector of Daylesford, Chipping Norton; one *s* two *d.* Served Tsingtau, 1914 (despatches, DSO), European War, Gallipoli, 1915, France, 1916-18, Germany, 1919 (VC, bar to DSO, MC); Chief Instructor Small Arms Sch., Hythe, 1919-23; Bt Lt-Col 1924; Chief Instructor, Machine Gun Sch., Netheravon, 1926-28; Lt-Col 1928; Comd 2nd Bn North Staffordshire Regt, 1928-32; Col 1932; Comdr 12th (Secunderabad) Inf. Bde, 1933-36; Comdt, Small Arms Sch., Netheravon, and Officer in charge of Records, Small Arms School Corps, 1936-38; Maj.-Gen., 1938; Comdr of the 4th Division, 1938-40; GOC Aldershot Command, 1940; Inspector of Infantry, 1941; retired, 1944. Col of South Wales Borderers, 1944-49. *Address:* 2 Heathfield Court, Fleet, Hants. *Club:* Army and Navy.   [*Died 21 Dec.* 1975.

JOHNSON, Eric Seymour Thewlis, MC 1918; *b* 8 Sept. 1897; *e s* of Ernest Johnson, TD, MA, JP. *Educ:* Winchester; Royal Military College, Sandhurst. 2nd Lieut, 16th Lancers, 1916; Lieut 1918-20. Cattle ranching, British Columbia, 1923-30; trained race-horses under National Hunt Rules, in England, 1931-40. War of 1939-45: served with 51st Training Regiment, RAC, and RAC Depot; retired 1945, with rank of Major. MP (C) Blackley Division of Manchester, 1951-64. *T:* (club) 01-499 1261. *Club:* Cavalry and Guards.   [*Died 22 July* 1978.

JOHNSON, Eyvind; Swedish novelist; *b* 29 July 1900. Worked in a quarry, lumber trade and a brickyard, 1914-19, until settling in Stockholm and starting to write. Mem., Swedish Acad., 1957-. Hon. PhD Gothenburg, 1953. Nordic Council Prize for Literature, 1962; (jtly) Nobel Prize for Literature, 1974. *Publications:* over 30 novels and stories including: Romanen om Olof, 4 vols (autobiographical), 1934-37; Grupp Krilon, 1941, Krilons resa, 1942; Krilon sjalv, 1943; Sju liv (short stories), 1944; Strändernas svall, 1946; Drömmar om Rosor och eld, 1949; Molnen över Metapontion, 1957; Hans nades tid, 1961; Livsdagen lang, 1964; Stunder, vagor, 1965. *Address:* Vitsippsvägen 8, Saltsjöbaden 2, Sweden. [*Died 25 Aug.* 1976.

JOHNSON, Sir Frederic (Charles), Kt, *cr* 1952; CB 1946; Receiver for the Metropolitan Police District and Courts, 1945-52; *b* 13 Dec. 1890; *s* of Benjamin Johnson, Leeds; *m* 1916, Constance Annie Ridley; three *s. Educ:* Leeds Grammar Sch.; Sidney Sussex Coll., Cambridge. Wrangler, 1912; Natural Sciences Tripos, 1913; entered Home Office, 1913; Asst Under-Sec. of State 1938. *Address:* Hembury Fort House, Honiton, Devon. *T:* Broadhembury 334.   [*Died 31 May* 1972.

JOHNSON, George Arthur; *b* 31 Oct. 1903; *s* of late Arthur Johnson; *m* 1931, Marie Constance Ross-Hurst; no *c. Educ:* Christ's Hospital; St Edmund Hall, Oxford. BA Oxon 1st Cl. Modern History, 1925. Asst Editor, The Mail, Madras, 1926-42; Asst Editor, The Statesman, 1942-51; Editor of The Statesman, Calcutta and Delhi, 1951-62, retired. *Address:* 12a Albert Hall Mansions, SW7. *Clubs:* Oriental; Bengal (Calcutta).
                                    [*Died 3 June* 1972.

JOHNSON, Maj.-Gen. Sir George Frederick, KCVO 1957; CB 1951; CBE 1949; DSO 1944; DL; *b* 28 Nov. 1903; *s* of F. P. and F. M. Johnson; *m* 1938, Lady Ida Ramsay, *d* of 14th Earl of Dalhousie; two *s* one *d. Educ:* Eton; King's Coll., Cambridge. Commissioned Scots Guards, 1925; psc 1935; GSO1 London District, 1939; served War of 1939-45; Comdr 3rd Bn Scots Guards, 1940; Comdr 201 Guards Brigade, Western Desert, 1942; Comdr 32 Guards Brigade, NW Europe, 1944-45; Lieut-Col commanding Scots Guards, 1945-47; Comdr 1st Guards Brigade, Palestine, 1947-48; Tripoli, 1948-49; Chief of Staff, Scottish Command, 1949-53; GOC, London District, 1953-57, retired. DL Cumberland, 1959; High Sheriff of Cumberland, 1966. *Recreations:* shooting, fishing, ornithology, entomology. *Address:* Castlesteads, Brampton, Cumbria. *T:* Brampton 2272. *Club:* Turf.   [*Died 23 July* 1980.

JOHNSON, Air Marshal George Owen, CB 1943; MC; retired 1947; *b* 24 Jan. 1896; *s* of late George Edward Johnson, Woodstock, Ontario, and late Mrs Johnson, Toronto 5, Ontario; *m* 1st, 1924, Jean Eleanor McKay (*d* 1968), Pembroke, Ont; two *d*; 2nd, 1968, Sarah Jane Roberts, RRC (*d* 1977). *Educ:* Woodstock, Ontario; RAF Staff Coll., Andover (1927); Imperial Defence Coll. (1937). Lieut, CSCI, Canada, 1913-16; RFC, and RAF 1917-19; Royal Canadian Air Force, 1920-47; AOC, Western Air Command, RCAF, Vancouver, BC, 1938-39; Deputy Chief of Air Staff, Ottawa, 1939-42; AOC, No 1 Training Command, RCAF, Toronto, 1942; AOC-in-C, Eastern Air Command, RCAF, Halifax, NS, 1943-45; AOC-in-C RCAF, Overseas, 1945-46. *Address:* 6688 Ash Street, Vancouver, BC V6P 3K4, Canada.   *[Died 28 March* 1980.

JOHNSON, Harold Cottam, CB 1970; CBE 1961 (OBE 1954); Keeper of Public Records 1966-69; *b* 24 July 1903; *e s* of Burley Johnson, Wakefield, and Louisa Cottam; *m* 1929, Esmé Lane; one *s* one *d. Educ:* Wakefield Grammar Sch.; University Coll., Oxford (MA). Asst Keeper, Public Record Office, 1927-54; Principal Asst Keeper, 1954-59; Deputy Keeper, 1959-66. Sec., Cttee appointed by British Academy for the preparation of a Dictionary of Medieval Latin, 1935-70. Treasurer, Pipe Roll Soc., 1950-69. Mem. Council, Bedford Coll., London, 1969-71. FRHistS. *Publications:* Surrey Taxation Returns, Part II, 1931; Register of Henry Chichele, Archbishop of Canterbury, Vol. II (with E. F. Jacob), 1938; Warwickshire Quarter Sessions Records, Vols I to VII (with S. C. Ratcliff), 1935-46; Vol. VIII, 1953; Vol. IX (with N. J. Williams), 1964; Minutes of Proceedings in Wiltshire Quarter Sessions (1563-72), 1949. *Recreations:* music, gardening. *Address:* Hawthorn, 39 Algarth Rise, Pocklington, York. *T:* Pocklington 3103.
     [Died 19 *Dec.* 1973.

JOHNSON, H(arold) Daintree, MA, MD; MChir Cantab; FRCS; retired; Hon. Surgeon, Royal Free Hospital, 1947; Senior Lecturer in Surgery, Royal Postgraduate Medical School; lately Member of Court of Examiners, Royal College of Surgeons; Late Examiner in Surgery, University of London; *b* 26 May 1910; *s* of Sir Stanley Johnson, sometime MP, and Lady Johnson (*née* Edith Heather); *m* 1944, Margaret Dixon; one *s* (and one *s* decd). *Educ:* Westminster; Christ's Coll., Cambridge; St Thomas's Hospital. Leverhulme Scholarship in Surgical Research, RCS, 1948. Surgical Registrar, St Thomas's Hosp., 1941; Surg. First Asst, London Hosp., 1942; Surg. Specialist, 224 and 225 Parachute Field Ambs, 6th Airborne Div., RAMC, 1943-46; FRSM; Fellow, Assoc. of Surgeons of Gt Britain and Ireland; Mem., Brit. Soc. of Gastro-enterology; Corr. Mem., Surgical Research Soc. *Publications:* (ed) Surgical Aspects of Medicine, 1959; The Cardia and Hiatus Hernia, 1968; The Swollen Leg, 1975; chapters in: Techniques in British Surgery, 1950; Management of Abdominal Operations, 1953 and 1957; Operative Surgery, 1967; Surgery of the Stomach and Duodenum, 1969 (USA); papers on various surgical subjects in Brit. Med. J., Lancet, Brit. J. Surg., Gut, Gastroenterol. (USA), Surgery Gynæcology and Obstetrics (USA), Surgery (USA), American J. Surg. (USA), Annals of Surgery (USA), J. thorac. cardiovasc. Surg. (USA), etc; letters in Nature, Times and Guardian. *Recreations:* farming, research. *Address:* 5 Holly Terrace, Highgate Village, N6. *T:* 01-340 3050; Red House Farm, Sible Hedingham, Essex. *T:* Hedingham 201. *Club:* Elizabethan.   *[Died* 2 *April* 1980.

JOHNSON, Prof. Harry Gordon, FRSC 1976; FBA 1969; Professor of Economics: University of Chicago, since 1959; University of Geneva, since 1976; *b* 26 May 1923; *s* of Harry H. and Frances L. Johnson; *m* 1948, Elizabeth Scott Serson; one *s* one *d. Educ:* University of Toronto Schs; University of Toronto; Cambridge Univ.; Harvard Univ. Various univ. teaching posts, 1943-49; Lectr in Economics, Cambridge Univ., 1950-56; Fellow of King's Coll., Cambridge, 1950-56; Prof. of Economic Theory, Manchester Univ., 1956-59; Prof. of Economics, LSE, 1966-74. Vis. Prof., Univ. of Toronto, 1952, 1967; Vis. Prof., Northwestern Univ., 1955; Pres. Canadian Political Science Assoc., 1965-66; Chm., Assoc. of Univ. Teachers of Econs, 1968-71. Fellow, Econometric Soc., 1972. Pres., Eastern Econ. Assoc., 1976-77. Hon. LLD: St Francis Xavier Univ., 1965; Univ. of Windsor, Ont, 1966; Queen's Univ., Ont, 1967; Carleton Univ., 1970; Univ. of W Ontario, 1973; Hon. DLitt Sheffield, 1969; Hon. DSc Manchester, 1972. *Publications:* The Overloaded Economy, 1952; International Trade and Economic Growth, 1958; Money, Trade and Economic Growth, 1962; Canada in a Changing World Economy, 1962; The Canadian Quandary, 1963; The World Economy at the Crossroads, 1965; Economic Policies Toward The Less Developed Countries, 1967; Essays in Monetary Economics, 1967; Aspects of the Theory of Tariffs, 1971; The Two-Sector Model of General Equilibrium, 1971; Macroeconomics and Monetary Theory, 1972; Inflation and the Monetarist Controversy, 1972; Further Essays in Monetary Economics, 1973; The Theory of Income Distribution, 1973; On Economics and Society, 1975; Technology and Economic Interdependence, 1975; (ed) Money in Britain, 1959-1969, 1970; (ed with others) Readings in British Monetary Economics, 1972; (ed) The New Mercantilism, 1975; (ed with J. Frenkel) The Monetary Approach to the Balance of Payments, 1976; articles on monetary theory, international trade, banking, in various economic jls. *Address:* University of Chicago, 1126 East 59th Street, Chicago, Ill 60637, USA.
     [Died 8 *May* 1977.

JOHNSON, Col Harry Hall, CIE 1934; MM 1916; IA retired; *b* 18 Aug. 1892; *m* 1930, Marjorie Phyllis Cooke; two *s*. Served European War, 1914-18, France and Belgium (despatches twice, military medal); Third Afghan War, 1919; Operations NW Frontier of India, 1924, 1930 and 1937-38 (despatches). Served in Indian Political Dept, 1930-41: Resident in Waziristan, 1937-38, and HBM's Consul-General, Kashgar, 1938-40. War of 1939-45, service in Burma, China, Ceylon and India including 204 Military Mission to China, 1941-42; Hon. Col 1947. *Address:* Sunny Hill House, Bruton, Som. *[Died* 11 *Aug.* 1973.

JOHNSON, Sir John Paley, 6th Bt, *cr* 1755; MBE 1945; Lt-Col, RA (retired); *b* 12 June 1907; *s* of Captain Robert Warren Johnson, RN (killed in action, Sept. 1914); *S* cousin, Sir Edward Gordon Johnson, 5th Bt, 1957; *m* 1st, 1929, Carol, *d* of late Edmund Haas, New York, USA; one *s* one *d*; 2nd, 1940, Jasmine, *d* of Hon. Noel Bligh; one *d*; 3rd, 1949, Rosemary, *d* of late Arthur Cohen. *Educ:* Wellington Coll., Berks; Royal Military Academy, Woolwich. Commissioned RA, 1927; resigned, 1930; Mem. of London Stock Exchange, 1930-33; rejoined RA, 1938. Served War of 1939-45 (MBE): Far East, Middle East, Italy. Chief Instructor (Col), Turkish Staff Coll., 1945-49. MFH West Kent Foxhounds, 1958-61. Mem., Kent CC, 1965-74. *Publication:* The North American Johnsons, 1963. *Recreations:* show-jumping, hunting, cricket, lawn tennis, royal tennis, squash rackets. *Heir:* *s* Peter Colpoys Paley Johnson, Capt., RA [*b* 26 March 1930; *m* 1956, Clare, *d* of Nigel Patrick Bruce, BM, BCh; one *s* two *d*; *m* 1973, Caroline Elisabeth, twin *d* of late Wing Cdr Sir (Eric) John Hodsoll, CB, and of Lady (Elisabeth) Hodsoll]. *Address:* Warrigal Farm, Dartford, Kent. *Clubs:* Carlton, MCC, Royal Automobile. *[Died* 14 *Dec.* 1975.

JOHNSON, Lyndon Baines; President of the United States, 1963-69; *b* Stonewall, Texas, 27 Aug. 1908; *s* of Sam Ealy and Rebekah Baines Johnson; *m* 1934, Claudia Alta (Lady Bird) Taylor; two *d. Educ:* Southwest Texas State Teachers Coll. (BS 1930); Georgetown Law Sch., DC. Comdr, USNR, Active Duty, 1941-42 (Silver Star, 1942); resigned Navy commn, 1964. Teacher, Cotulla and Houston, Texas, public schs, 1930-31; Sec. to Congressman Richard Kleberg, 1931-35; Texas Dir of Nat. Youth Administration, 1935-37; elected to 75th Congress, 1937-38 (succ. James B. Buchanan), 10th District of Texas; re-elected 76th-80th Congresses, 1938-48; US Senator, 1949-61; Democratic Minority Leader, 83rd Congress; Democratic Majority Leader, 84th-86th Congresses. Elected Vice-President, 8 Nov. 1960, took office, 20 Jan. 1961; acceded to Presidency, 22 Nov. 1963, on death of President Kennedy; elected President, 3 Nov. 1964; took office 20 Jan. 1965. During Vice-Presidency, Chairman: National Aeronautics and Space Council; President's Cttee on Equal Employment Opportunity; Peace Corps Advisory Council. Hon. LLD: Southwestern Univ., Texas, 1943; Howard Payne Univ., Texas, 1957; Brown Univ., RI, 1959; Bethany Coll., W Va, 1959; Univ. of Hawaii, 1961; Univ. of Philippines, 1961; Gallaudet Coll., DC, 1961; East Kentucky State Coll., 1961; William Jewell Coll., Missouri, 1961; Elon Coll., NC, 1962; Southwest Texas State Teachers Coll., 1962; Wayne State Univ., Mich., 1963; Jacksonville Univ., Fla, 1963; McMurray Coll., Ill., 1963; Univ. of Maryland, 1963; Tufts Univ., Mass, 1963; Univ. of California, 1964; Univ. of Texas, 1964; Swarthmore Coll., Pa, 1964; Syracuse Univ., New York, 1964; Georgetown Univ., DC, 1964; Univ. of Kentucky, 1965; Baylor Univ., Texas, 1965; Howard Univ., DC, 1965; Catholic Univ., DC, 1965; Princeton Univ., 1966; Univ. of Denver, 1966; Texas Technol Coll., 1967; Thomas More Coll., Kentucky, 1968; St Francis Coll., NY, 1968; Texas Christian Univ., 1968; Hon. DCL: Holy Cross Coll., Mass, 1964; Univ. of Michigan, 1964; Univ. of Rhode Island, 1966; Hon. Doctor of Humane Letters: Oklahoma City Univ., 1960; Yeshiva Univ., NY, 1961; Hon. Doctor of Letters: Glassboro Coll., NJ, 1968; Hon. Doctor of Lit.: St Mary's Coll., Calif., 1962; Hon. Doctor of Political Science: Chulalongkorn Univ., Thailand, 1966. *Publications:* My Hope for America, 1964; A Time for Action, 1964; This America, 1966; No Retreat from Tomorrow, 1967; To Heal and to Build, 1968; The Choices We Face, 1968; The Vantage Point: perspectives of the Presidency, 1963-69, 1971. *Address:* LBJ Ranch, Stonewall, Texas 78671.   *[Died* 22 *Jan.* 1973.

JOHNSON, Most Rev. Martin (Michael), DD; *b* Toronto, 18 March 1899; *s* of Oliver Johnson and Julia (*née* Radey). *Educ:* St Francis Sch.; St Augustine's Seminary, Toronto (DD). Priest, 1924; Assistant in Churches in Toronto, 1924-28; Chancellor, Archdiocese, Toronto, 1935-54; Rector, St Michael's Cathedral, Toronto, 1935-36; Bishop of Nelson, 1936; Coadjutor Archibishop of Vancouver, 1954, Archbishop, 1964-69. *Address:* 4670 Piccadilly South, West Vancouver, BC, Canada. [*Died 29 Jan. 1975.*

JOHNSON, Thomas Frank, OBE 1919; author; Member, Académie Diplomatique Internationale, Paris, and Institut d'Histoire de l'Emigration politique contemporaine; *s* of Alexander Howard Johnson, East Grinstead; *m* 1921, Evelyn (Rona), *e d* of Charles Welch Lee; one *s*. *Educ:* Polytechnic; privately France and Germany. Inland Revenue up to 1910; Education Dept, London County Council, 1910-11; Special Inspector, Public Control Dept, London County Council, 1912-14; volunteer Officer European War, 1914-18, Belgian, French, Roumanian, Russian, Italian, and Bulgarian Fronts; Military Missions to Bulgaria, Roumania, Ukraine, and Poland, 1918-19; Personal Sec. to Dr Nansen, 1921-22; League of Nations Asst High Commissioner for Refugees, 1923-31; Sec. Gen., Nansen International Office for Refugees under League of Nations, 1931-37; Officer RAFVR, Oct. 1939 (France); SE European Manager, BBC, 1942; European Publicity Officer, BBC, 1943. Sec. Gen. of several International Conferences on Refugee Questions, 1922-36; Refugee Settlement Missions to Central Europe and Balkans, 1922-26; Armenian Refugee Settlement Mission, Syria, 1926; Mem. of League Refugee Settlement Commission to Brazil, 1934. Founder, Internat. (Relations) Clubs, 1944, and of Internat. Residential Clubs, 1947 (in suspension pending improved relations with Russia); Comdr Order of St Stanislaus; Officer Order of St Vladimir, and of Star of Roumania. *Publications:* International Tramps; From Chaos to Permanent World Peace, 1938; numerous articles on international affairs. *Recreations:* golf, lawn tennis, cricket. *Address:* Byeways, Frith Hill, Godalming, Surrey. *T:* Godalming 6065. *Club:* Allied Circle. [*Died 5 Feb. 1972.*

JOHNSON, William Evelyn Patrick, AFC 1931; CPA; CEng, FRAeS; Partner, Cleveland and Johnson, Chartered Patent Agents; *b* 7 April 1902; *s* of A. A. Johnson, Sunderland, and Amelia Johnson; *m* 1933, Patricia Margaret Anne Watkins; one *s* one *d*. *Educ:* Gresham's Sch., Holt. Qualified Patent Agent, 1925; commnd RAF, 1926; formed and commanded first Instrument Flight, Central Flying Sch.; made first solo blind flight in world, 1931 (AFC); resumed patent practice, 1932 (Flt Lt, RAFO); became Patent Adviser to Power Jets Ltd, when it was formed by Sir Frank Whittle, 1936; returned RAF on flying duties, 1939, and in Jan. 1940 seconded to Power Jets and continued responsibility for Whittle and kindred gas turbine patents. *Publications:* articles, broadcasts, etc, covering aviation, invention and gas turbines, in UK and abroad. *Recreations:* sailing, flying, controversy. *Address:* 32 Well Walk, Hampstead, NW3. *T:* 01-435 1664. [*Died 28 May 1976.*

JOHNSON, William Joseph, CMG 1936; OBE 1927; *b* 1892; *e s* of late Arthur Benjamin and Barbara Johnson; *m* 1st, 1921, Maud (*d* 1955), 2nd *d* of late Benjamin Woodward, CC, JP; 2nd, 1957, Olga Bryne, 2nd *d* of late John Roch George. Served during European War in E Africa, India, Egypt and Palestine, 1914-20 (despatches); Colonial and Foreign Services, 1914-49; Treas. Palestine Govt and Mem. of Exec. and Advisory Legislative Councils, 1932-40; Chm. of several cttees, in Palestine, on taxation, banking, commerce and industry, agriculture, and transport. Financial Adviser to HM Ambassador at Cairo, 1940-49; HM Govt's representative on British Govt Cotton Buying Commission, 1940, and on Joint Anglo-Egyptian Cotton Commission, 1941. Dir of United Dominions Trust Ltd and certain associated companies, 1949-61. *Address:* Westfield, 91 Bromham Road, Bedford. [*Died 7 April 1971.*

JOHNSON-GILBERT, Sir Ian (Anderson), Kt 1959; CBE 1952; LLD; *b* 23 Oct. 1891; *s* of late Thomas Johnson-Gilbert, Coldoch, Perthshire; *m* 1922, Rosalind Sybil, *d* of Major O. J. Bell, Royal Welch Fusiliers, London; two *s*. *Educ:* Edinburgh Academy. Served European War, 1914-18, Highland Light Infantry, and Pilot Royal Flying Corps. Mem. Town Council, Edinburgh, 1936-60 (Chm. Public Assistance Cttee, 1944-47; Chm. Welfare Cttee, 1949-52). Chm. West Edinburgh Unionist Assoc., 1942-57; Mem. Edinburgh ATC Cttee; Chm. SE Fire Area Jt Cttee (Scotland), 1948-57. Member: Licensing Authority for Public Service Vehicles, Scottish Traffic Area, 1951-58; Nat. Broadcasting Council for Scotland. DL 1944, JP 1944, Edinburgh; Lord Provost of Edinburgh, and Lord Lieutenant of Edinburgh, 1957-60. Hon. LLD Edinburgh Univ.,

1959. *Recreation:* golf. *Address:* 3 Ravelston Dykes, Edinburgh 4. *T:* 031-332 1022. *Clubs:* Scottish Conservative, Royal Scots (Edinburgh). [*Died 6 Dec. 1974.*

JOHNSTON, Alice Crawford, CBE 1958 (OBE 1942); MA; *b* 1902; *d* of late Lord Sands, DD, LLD, Senator of Coll. of Justice, Scotland. *Educ:* Queen Margaret's Sch., Scarborough; Lady Margaret Hall, Oxford. Tutor, Bonar Law Coll., Ashridge, 1933-38; Head of WVS Evacuation Dept, 1939-43; Temp. Principal, Ministry of Labour, 1943-44; other WVS appointments; Social Services Administrator, WRVS, 1954-74. Dep. Chm., Nat. Assistance Bd, 1961-64 (Mem. 1948-64); Mem., Royal Commn on Local Govt in Greater London Area, 1957-60. *Address:* 18 Lennox Gardens, SW1. *T:* 01-589 9771. *Club:* University Women's. [*Died 8 Oct. 1976.*

JOHNSTON, A(nthony) G(ordon) Knox, CMG 1954; Bahamas Government Liaison Officer, Freeport, Grand Bahama, 1961-67, retired; *b* 21 April 1909; *e s* of late Andrew and Jessie Knox Johnston; *m* 1934, Jean Corstorphine, *o c* of late James Fergusson, Allestree, near Derby; one *s*. *Educ:* Derby Sch.; Edinburgh Univ. (MA); Oriel Coll., Oxford. Cadet, Colonial Administrative Service, Northern Rhodesia, 1931; seconded Colonial Office, 1940-41; Clerk of Executive and Legislative Councils, NR, 1943-46; Asst Chief Sec. and Sec. Devel. Authority, 1946-50; Asst Chief Sec. EA High Commission, Nairobi, 1950; acted as Administrator on a number of occasions, 1950-55; Chief Administrative Sec. E Africa High Commn, 1954-58, retd 1958; Dep. Colonial Sec., Bahamas (temp.), 1958; Colonial Sec. (Supernumerary), March 1960-Jan. 1961; Acting Gov., Bahamas, June and July 1960. *Address:* Barclays Bank Ltd, St James's Street, Derby. [*Died 28 Dec. 1972.*

JOHNSTON, Frederick Mair; Founder member of Press Council, since 1953; Chairman: F. Johnston & Co. Ltd, Newspaper Proprietors, Falkirk, since 1935; Johnston Group of Scottish Weekly Newspapers; *b* 20 Oct. 1903; *y s* of Patrick Mair Johnston, Falkirk and Leith; *m* 1934, Muriel Kathleen Macbeth, *y d* of James Currie Macbeth, Solicitor, Dunfermline, Fife; three *s* one *d*. *Educ:* Stewart's Coll., Edinburgh. Journalist, Dumfries & Galloway Courier, 1922; Evesham Standard (Editor), 1927; The Scotsman, 1931. President, Scottish Newspaper Proprietors' Association, 1950-52, Hon. Treasurer 1967-. *Recreations:* reading, gardening. *Address:* Arnot Grange, Falkirk, Stirlingshire. *T:* Falkirk 21870. [*Died 22 Nov. 1973.*

JOHNSTON, George Douglas; Barrister-at-Law; *b* 16 Jan. 1886; *s* of John M. C. and Sophia Johnston; *m* 1922, Elfreda Josephine Wallis (*d* 1966); no *c*. *Educ:* Westminster; Christ Ch., Oxford (MA, BCL 1st Class). Vinerian Scholar, 1909; Inner Temple: called to the Bar, 1910; Bencher, 1939; Treasurer for 1963. Practised in Chancery Div., 1910-62. Mem. Council of Legal Educn, 1946-63. Sussex Archaeological Soc., 1909 (Council, 1941-71); former Vice-Pres., Selden Soc.; FSA 1957. *Publications:* numerous articles in Sussex Notes and Queries (Editor, 1952-71). *Recreations:* walking, English topography. *Address:* Stones, Wisborough Green, Billingshurst, Sussex. *T:* Wisborough Green 227. [*Died 20 June 1971.*

JOHNSTON, James Osborne; Director of Social Work, Corporation of Glasgow, 1969-75; *b* 18 June 1921; British; *m* 1971, Rosemary Guiton; two *d* by a former *m*. *Educ:* Allan Glen's Sch., Glasgow. Post Office, 1938-40; RAF, 1940-46; Scottish Educn Dept, 1946-65; Scottish Home and Health Dept, 1965-67; Social Work Services Group, 1967-69. *Recreations:* walking, talking. *Address:* Sandybrae, Twynholm, Kirkcudbrightshire. [*Died 23 March 1978.*

JOHNSTON, Joseph, MA Dublin, MA Oxon; Fellow since 1913 and Senior Fellow since 1943 of Trinity College, Dublin; Professor of Applied Economics since 1939; *b* 20 Aug. 1890; *s* of John Johnston, Tomagh, Castle Caulfield, Co. Tyrone; *m* 1914, Clara Jane, *d* of late Robert Wilson, Keenagh, Co. Longford; one *s* one *d*. *Educ:* Royal Sch., Dungannon; Trinity Coll., Dublin; Lincoln Coll., Oxford. BA Dublin (First Class Classics and Ancient History), 1910; BA Oxon. First Class Lit Hum 1912; Albert Kahn Travelling Fellow, 1914-15; Lectr in Ancient History, 1916-32; Barrington Lectr in Economics (extern), 1920-35; Mem. of Agricultural Commn, 1923-24; Mem. of Prices Tribunal, 1926-27; Rockefeller Fellow for Economic Research (in Europe), 1926-27; Mem. of Cttee of Inquiry on Post-Emergency Agricultural Policy, 1942-45; Mem. Industrial Taxation Cttee, 1953-56; Lectr in Economics, Sch. of Commerce, 1925-32; Lectr in Applied Economics, 1932-39; Representative of Dublin Univ. in Senate of Eire, 1938-43 and 1944-48; nominated Senator, 1951-54. Pres. Statistical and Social Inquiry Soc. of Ireland, 1950-51, 1951-52 and 1952-53. *Publications:* Civil War in Ulster (pamphlet), 1914; A. K.

Travelling Fellow Report, 1919; A Groundwork of Economics, 1925; The Nemesis of Economic Nationalism, 1934; Irish Agriculture in Transition, 1951; The Sickness of the Irish Economy (pamphlet), 1957; Why Ireland needs the Common Market, 1962; Irish Economic Headaches: a Diagnosis, 1966; Berkeley's Querist in Historical Perspective, 1970; articles in Economic Jl, also numerous contribs to Hermathena, 1938-53, in interpretation of Bishop Berkeley's Querist, etc. *Recreation:* motoring. *Address:* at 53 Thornhill Road, Mt Merrion, Co. Dublin. *T:* 882348; 39 Trinity College, Dublin. *T:* 72941, ext. 430.   *[Died 26 Aug. 1972.*

JOHNSTON, William, CMG 1950; retired; *b* 7 Dec. 1890; *s* of James Johnston and Jessie Spence Anderson; *m* 1923, Freda, *d* of late George Nelson, JP, Liverpool; no *c. Educ:* Burntisland; Glasgow; privately. Savings Bank, London, 1910; Officer HM Customs and Excise, UK, 1911; Deputy Comptroller Customs, Mauritius, 1920; acted Comptroller Customs and Harbour Master, also MLC on numerous occasions, 1923-31; Collector-Gen., Jamaica, 1932; Colonial Sec. and Financial Sec., British Honduras, 1934-40; administered Government, British Honduras, 1937, 1939, and 1939-40; Comptroller of Customs, Sierra Leone, 1940-42; Dir of Supplies, Sierra Leone, 1942-44; Comptroller of Customs, Tanganyika, 1944-46; Comr of Customs, Kenya and Uganda, 1946-48; Comr, East African Customs and Excise, 1949-51. *Recreations:* golf, etc. *Address:* 77 Alinora Avenue, Goring-by-Sea, Worthing, West Sussex. *T:* Worthing 45165.   *[Died 3 July 1976.*

JOHNSTON-SAINT, Captain Peter Johnston, MA Cantab; FRSE; FZS; FSAScot; CStJ; Officier Légion d'Honneur; Officer Order of the Spanish Republic; Roumanian Order Meritul Sanitar, 1st Class; late IA; *e s* of late James Saint and Blanche, *d* of late Charles Harcourt Moffatt; *m* Clare (*d* 1967), *e d* of William Mansell MacCulloch, MD, Seigneur of Les Touillets, Guernsey, and Jurat of the Royal Court; two *d. Educ:* Rossall; St John's Coll., Cambridge. Served on NW Frontier, India, Egypt, 1908-14, and in France with 1st Indian Cavalry Division, 1914-15 (wounded); Adjt, No 40 Sqdn and 5th Wing, RFC, 1916; Bde-Maj., Cadet Bde, RAF, 1917-18; retd 1920. Assistant Wellcome Research Instn, 1921; Asst Dir, Museum of Medical History, 1934-47. FRSM, 1936-45. Birdwood Medal, RSA, 1927. *Publications:* Jessamine Flowers and Green Leaves, a collection of Poems translated from the Persian, 1925; Outline of a History of Medicine in India, 1927; Green Hills and Golden Sands, on travel in Normandy and Brittany, 1944; Castanets and Carnations, on travel in Spain, 1946; articles in French and English scientific journals. *Recreations:* travelling, writing, sailing. *Address:* c/o Viscountess Sandon, 5 Tregunter Road, SW10. *Clubs:* United Service & Royal Aero, Pilgrims; Cercle Interallié (Paris).   *[Died 1 July 1974.*

JOHNSTONE, Gerald Ewart, CB 1959; Principal Assistant Solicitor to the Treasury, 1956-67; *b* 26 June 1906; *o s* of late Rev. David Ewart Johnstone and late Alice Mary, *e d* of Rt Rev. J. M. Speechly, sometime Bishop of Travancore and Cochin; *m* 1935, Dorothy Betty, *y d* of late Thomas Stone, Exeter. *Educ:* Westminster Sch.; Christ Church, Oxford (BCL). Barrister-at-law, Gray's Inn, 1930; Solicitor's Dept, Min. of Agriculture and Fisheries, 1935-36; Treasury, Solicitor's Dept, 1936-39; Legal Adviser Min. of Economic Warfare, Mem. of Contraband, Enemy Exports and Blockade Cttees and of Cttee on Censorship, 1939-46; Chm. of Bermuda Contraband and Enemy Exports Cttee, 1941; Asst Solicitor to the Treasury, 1946-55; Legal Adviser to Min. of Food, 1954-55; Asst Solicitor to Min. of Agriculture, Fisheries and Food, 1955-56. *Publications:* articles in the Field, Countryman, etc on nature topics. *Recreations:* wild life preservation and watching cricket. *Address:* Nywood, Dunnings Road, East Grinstead, Sussex. *T:* East Grinstead 22194. *Club:* United Oxford & Cambridge University.   *[Died 23 March 1973.*

JOHNSTONE, Kenneth Roy, CB 1962; CMG 1949; Deputy Director-General of the British Council, 1953-62, retired; Chairman, International Department, British Council of Churches, 1963-71; *b* 25 Sept. 1902; 2nd *s* of late Edward Henderson Johnstone and late Stella Fraser; *m* 1944, Mary Pauline, *d* of R. C. Raine. *Educ:* Eton; Balliol Coll., Oxford. Entered HM Diplomatic Service, 1926; served in Warsaw, 1928, Oslo, 1930, Sofia, 1931, and London; seconded to British Council, 1936; resigned to join Welsh Guards, 1939; served War of 1939-45: France, 1940; North Africa, 1942; Staff in Middle East and Greece, 1943-45 (Col). Readmitted to Foreign Service, 1945, and rejoined British Council. Chm. Council, SSEES, London Univ., 1965-76. Gold Cultural Medal (Italy); Gold Cross of Order of King George I (Greece). *Publications:* translated: Ivo Andric, Bosnian Story, 1959; Devil's Yard, 1962; Djilas, Montenegro, 1963; Amandos, Introduction to Byzantine History, 1969; Zakythinos, The Making of Modern Greece, 1976; Prevelakis, The Tale of a Town, 1976. *Address:* 4 Priory Crescent, Lewes, East Sussex. *T:* Lewes 3738. *Club:* United Oxford & Cambridge University.   *[Died 10 Nov. 1978.*

JOHNSTONE, Morris Mackintosh O.; *see* Ord Johnstone.

JOHNSTONE, Maj.-Gen. Reginald Forster, CB 1958; CBE 1950; *b* 14 May 1904; 3rd *s* of Edwin James Johnstone, Rougham Hall, Suffolk; *m* 1935, Madeline Thornhill, *er d* of E. T. B. Simpson, Walton Hall, Wakefield, Yorks; one *s. Educ:* Charterhouse; Pembroke Coll., Cambridge (BA). Comd 2nd Bn The Royal Scots, 1943-44; Comd 22nd East African Bde, 1944-46 (Burma); Comd 24th Independent Infantry Bde, 1947-50; Dep. Dir Military Intelligence, War Office, 1950-53; Dep. Adjt-Gen., BAOR, 1953-56; Dir of Personal Services, War Office, Sept. 1956-Nov. 1959. *Recreations:* photography, natural history. *Address:* The Cedar House, Gough's Lane, Bracknell, Berks. *T:* Bracknell 23204.   *[Died 10 May 1976.*

JOHNSTONE-BURT, Charles Kingsley, CBE 1950; FICE; *b* 14 March 1891; *m* 1917, Mary Younger (*d* 1964); one *s* one *d. Educ:* Highgate Sch., London; Durham Univ. BSc in Mechanical Engineering, 1911; BSc in Civil Engineering, 1912. Designer: Grand Trunk Pacific Railway, Winnipeg, Canada, 1913; Sir Wm Arrol & Co. Ltd, Glasgow, 1914-18. Served under Civil Engineer-in-Chief, Admiralty, at Rosyth, Devonport, Portland, Portsmouth, Gibraltar, Ceylon, Singapore Naval Base (in charge of development construction), and Admiralty Headquarters, 1918-39; Asst Civil Engineer-in-Chief, 1939; Deputy Civil Engineer-in-Chief, 1940; Principal Deputy Civil Engineer-in-Chief, 1943, until retirement in 1951. AMICE 1916; MICE 1933. *Address:* West Winds, Kingsway, Craigweil, Bognor Regis, Sussex. *T:* Pagham 3450.   *[Died 4 July 1973.*

JOLLY, General Sir Alan, GCB 1968 (KCB 1964; CB 1962); CBE 1955 (OBE 1946); DSO 1944; idc; jssc; psc; Quarter-Master-General, 1966-69; *b* Melbourne, 12 Nov. 1910; *s* of J. M. Jolly; *m* 1939, Margaret Russell. *Educ:* King's Coll. Sch.; RMC Sandhurst. Served NW Frontier of India, 1936-37 (medal with clasp). Served War of 1939-45 (DSO, OBE). Commnd 144 RAC and 4th Royal Tank Regt in NW Europe, 1944-45; DQMG, BAOR, Oct. 1957-59; GOC 5 Div., 1959-60; GOC 1 Div., 1960-61; Chief of Staff, HQ Southern Comd, 1961-62; VQMG, War Office, 1962-64; Comdr, Far East Land Forces, 1964-66. Colonel Commandant: RAC (RTR Wing), 1964-68; Royal Tank Regt, 1964-69; ADC (General) to The Queen, 1968-69. *Club:* Army and Navy.   *[Died 15 Sept. 1977.*

JOLLY, James Hornby; Director, Midland Bank Ltd, 1947-67; *b* 26 Feb. 1887; *e s* of William and Ellen Jolly, Preston, Lancashire; *m* 1912, Elizabeth Parkinson; one *d* (one *s* Flying Officer, RAF, missing 1944). *Educ:* Baines's Grammar Sch., Poulton Le Fylde. Chartered Accountant, 1909; Blaenavon Co. Ltd, 1911; Sec., Guest, Keen & Nettlefolds Ltd, 1918; Chm., Guest, Keen & Nettlefolds Ltd, 1947-53; Chm., Guest, Keen Iron & Steel Co. Ltd, 1946-57. *Recreations:* fell-walking, psychic research. *Address:* Langdale, Barnt Green, near Birmingham.
                                            [Died 25 July 1972.

JOLLY, Rev. Canon Reginald Bradley, MA; OCF; Canon Emeritus of Worcester Cathedral since 1965 and of Winchester Cathedral since 1947; *b* 1 Oct. 1885; *s* of Rev. John Jolly, Vicar of Thornton, Bradford, and Mary Elizabeth Harding, Leicester; *m* Muriel Ada Crawshaw, Ilkley; three *s* two *d. Educ:* Bradford Gram. Sch.; Emmanuel Coll., Cambridge (Sizar). Deacon, 1909; Priest, 1910; Proctor-in-Convocation for Diocese of Winchester; formerly: Curate of Aston, Birmingham; Vice-Principal of Bishop Wilson Theological Coll., and Vicar of Kirk Michael; Diocesan Chaplain and Hon. Chaplain to the Bishop of Sodor and Man; Diocesan Inspector of Schs; Vicar of St Thomas, Douglas, IOM; Chaplain to the Forces; Metropolitan Sec., CMS; Chaplain to the High Sheriff of Surrey; Vicar of Christ Church, Woking, with St Paul's; Chaplain to the Southern Railway Orphanage; Sec., Guildford Diocesan Bd of Missions; Rector of St Mary's (Mother Church of) Southampton, 1928-45; Rural Dean of Southampton, 1930-45; Vicar, 1945-58, and Rural Dean, 1949-58, of Kidderminster; Hon. Canon of Worcester, 1951-65; Vicar of Overbury with Teddington, with Alstone and Little Washbourne, 1958-64, also Rural Dean of Bredon, 1962-64, retired. Public Preacher, Diocese of Exeter, 1968-. Formerly: Chaplain to Blakebrook County Hosp. Kidderminster; Chaplain to Kidderminster and District Gen. Hosp.; Commissary to Bishop of Armidale and to Archbishop of British Columbia; Proctor-in-Convocation for Diocese of Worcester, 1951 and 1955-61. Joyce of Exmoor Lectr, Dio. of Exeter, 1969. *Recreation:* golf. *Address:* Bessemer Thatch, Berrynarbor, N Devon.   *[Died 9 Sept. 1972.*

JONES; see Griffith-Jones.

JONES; see Wynne-Jones.

JONES, Brig. Alan Harvey, CBE 1955; TD 1947; DL; Secretary, Haydock Park Racecourse, since 1965; Brigadier late RA (TA); b 17 April 1910; s of late William and Agnes Jones; m 1938, Mary Scholfield; one d. Educ: King William's Coll., Isle of Man. Commissioned Manchester Regt, 1933; commanded 65th AA Regt, 1942-46 and 96th Army Group, RA, 1951-55. ADC (TA) to the Queen, 1958-63. DL, County Palatine of Lancaster, 1961-. Pres., SSAFA NW, Mem. Council, SSAFA. Recreation: sailing. Address: Haydock Park, Newton-le-Willows, Merseyside. T: Ashton-in-Makerfield 77124; Ty Plant, Rhosneigr, Anglesey. T: Rhosneigr 493. Clubs: Naval and Military; St James's (Manchester).   [Died 21 Aug. 1975.

JONES, A(lan) Trevor, MD; FRCP; DPH; Provost of The Welsh National School of Medicine, University of Wales, 1955-Sept. 1969, retired; b 24 Feb. 1901; y s of Roger W. Jones, MA, JP, Pengam, Glam.; m 1931, Gwyneth, y d of Edward Evans, Hammersmith; one s one d. Educ: Lewis' Sch., Pengam; University Coll., Cardiff; University Coll., London; University Coll. Hosp., London. MD London 1927; DPH 1929; FRCP 1953. Resident appts, University Coll. Hosp., 1925-28; Dep. Supt, Marylebone Hosp., London, 1928-30; Gen. practice and Hon. Mem. Hosp. Staff, Carmarthen, 1930-34; MOH Carmarthen; MO, Welsh Bd of Health, 1934; Hosp. Officer for Wales, 1937-47; Sen. Admin. MO, Welsh Regional Hosp. Bd, 1947-55; Univ. of Wales Rep., Gen. Med. Council, 1956-69; Vice-Chm., Bd of Govs, United Cardiff Hosps. Commonwealth Fund Travelling Fellow, 1963. Hon. LLD Wales, 1970. Publications: Maternal Mortality in Wales, 1937; Survey of Hospital Services of South Wales, 1945; New Medical Teaching Centre, Cardiff, 1966, new edn 1971; articles in medical and public health jls. Recreations: photography, gardening. Address: Siljan, White's Hill, Stock, Essex CM4 9QD.
                                        [Died 10 June 1979.

JONES, Sir Andrew; see Jones, Sir W. J. A.

JONES, Arthur Davies; b 1897; s of late Evan Jones, JP, Trimsaran; m 1942, Rosemary, 2nd d of late Rev. Frank Long-Price, Clearbrook, Llanarthney. Educ: Mill Hill; Emmanuel Coll., Cambridge. High Sheriff Carmarthenshire, 1941-42. Address: Clearbrook Hall, Llanarthney, Dyfed.
                                        [Died 7 March 1980.

JONES, Arthur R.; see Rocyn-Jones.

JONES, Brig. Arthur Thomas C.; see Cornwall-Jones.

JONES, Benjamin Rowland R.; see Rice-Jones.

JONES, Sir (Bennett) Melvill, Kt 1942; CBE 1938; AFC 1918; FRS 1939; Hon. FRAeS; Hon. FAIAA; Hon. Fellow, Canadian Aeronautics and Space Institute, 1965; Francis Mond Professor of Aeronautical Engineering, Cambridge University, 1919-52; Fellow of Emmanuel College; Chairman Aeronautical Research Council, 1943-47; b 28 Jan. 1887; s of Benedict Jones, Barrister-at-law, Liverpool, and Henrietta Melvill; m Dorothy Laxton Jotham (d 1955), Kidderminster; one s one d (and one s killed in action, War of 1939-45). Educ: Birkenhead Sch.; Emmanuel Coll., Cambridge. Mechanical Science Tripos, 1909. Aeronautical research at the National Physical Laboratory, 1910-13; Sir W. Armstrong, Whitworth & Co., 1913; Royal Aircraft Establishment, 1914; Armament Experimental Station, Orfordness, 1916; qualified as a pilot and served as observer with No. 48 Sqdn RAF, 1918; Technical Dept Air Ministry, 1918; attached Ministry of Aircraft Production, 1939-45. Publications: Aerial Surveying by Rapid Methods, 1925 (jointly with the late Major J. C. Griffiths); Aerodynamic Theory, Vol. 5, Div. N, 1935; various reports of the Aeronautical Research Cttee. Address: Lower Watertown, Umberleigh, N Devon. Club: Athenæum.   [Died 31 Oct. 1975.

JONES, Bobby; see Jones, Robert Tyre.

JONES, Cecil Artimus E.; see Evan-Jones.

JONES, Charles Mark J.; see Jenkin-Jones.

JONES, David, CH 1974; CBE 1955; b Brockley, Kent, 1 Nov. 1895; s of James Jones, Holywell, Flintshire, and Alice Ann Bradshaw, Rotherhithe, Surrey; unmarried. Camberwell Sch. of Art, 1910-14; served on West Front with 15th Bn Royal Welch Fusiliers, 1915-18; Westminster Art Sch., 1919-21; became a Roman Catholic, 1921; engravings for the Chester play of The Deluge, The Ancient Mariner, etc., 1924-28; paintings largely in water-colour from 1927 onwards; represented at the Chicago Exhibition, the Venice Biennial Exhibition, the World's Fair, New York, British Art since Whistler, National Gallery, 1940, Six Watercolour Painters of To-day, National Gallery, 1941, the Tate Gallery's Wartime Acquisitions, National Gallery, 1942, one-man exhibition shown by CEMA at various centres in England and Wales, 1944; represented in the two exhibitions: Nine British Contemporaries and Modern British Paintings from the Tate Gallery, shown under the auspices of the British Council in Paris and other capitals, 1945-46; represented at various Festival exhibitions, 1951, and at Biennial International Water-colour Exhibition, Brooklyn, USA, 1952-53; a comprehensive retrospective exhibition shown, under the auspices of the Arts Council, in Wales, in Edinburgh and at the Tate Gallery, 1954-55; Word & Image IV, exhibition at NBL of paintings, engravings, drawings etc, 1972, shown with additions at Nat. Museum, Cardiff, Nat. Library of Wales, Aberystwyth, Bangor, and other Welsh centres, 1973. Works acquired by Contemporary Art Soc., Tate Gallery, Victoria and Albert and British Museums, National Museum of Wales, Sydney Art Gallery, Toronto Art Gallery, Arts Council, British Council, and by private collectors; Member: Hon. Society of Cymmrodorion; Soc. for Nautical Research. DLitt (hc), University of Wales, 1960; FRSL. Hon. Mem. RWS 1961. Gold Medal for Fine Arts, Royal National Eisteddfod of Wales, 1964; Midsummer Prize, Corporation of London, 1968. Publications: In Parenthesis, 1937 (New York 1962) (Hawthornden Prize for 1938); The Anathemata, 1952 (New York 1963) (Russell Loines Memorial Award for Poetry, Nat. Inst. of Arts and Letters, New York, 1954); The Wall, 1955 (Harriet Munroe Memorial Prize, 1956); Epoch and Artist: Selected Writings (edited by Harman Grisewood), 1959, New York 1964; The Tribune's Visitation, 1969; The Sleeping Lord and other fragments, 1974; relevant publications: Agenda, special issue, June 1967, containing six written pieces, 18 drawings etc, a translation, and critical articles by 12 contributors; David Jones, Artist and Writer, by David Blamires; a second special issue of Agenda, 1974. Address: at Monksdene, 2 Northwick Park Road, Harrow, Mddx.
                                        [Died 28 Oct. 1974.

JONES, Sir (David) Fletcher, Kt 1974; OBE 1959; Founder, Fletcher Jones & Staff Pty Ltd and associated companies; b 14 Aug. 1895; s of Samuel Henry and Mahala Jones; m 1st, 1922, Rena Ellen Jones (decd); two s one d; 2nd, 1971, Aida Margaret Rhoda Wells. Educ: Golden Square State Sch.; adult industrial management courses. Served European War, 1914-18, 57 Bn AIF, Egypt and France. Clothing manufacturer and retailer. Mem. Victoria Promotion Cttee, Melbourne, 1962-75; Chm. of Dirs, Warrnambool Woollen Mill Co. Ltd, 1943-59, and Hanro (Australia) Knitting Mills Ltd, 1959-63; Dir, Leviathan Ltd, Melbourne, 1948-53. Publication: Co-op Pie, 1937. Recreations: travel, swimming, reading. Address: Floral Place, PO Box 100, Warrnambool, Vic. 3280, Australia. T: 62-8011. Clubs: Royal Automobile of Victoria, Toc H (Melbourne); (Past Pres. and Sec.) Rotary (Warrnambool).   [Died 22 Feb. 1977.

JONES, Douglas V. I.; see Irvine-Jones.

JONES, Eli Stanley, DD; b Clarksville, Maryland, 3 Jan. 1884; m 1911, Mabel Lossing; one d. Educ: City Coll., Baltimore; Asbury Coll. A Missionary of Methodist Episcopal Church in India, 1907; Pastor of English Church in Lucknow; Superintendent of Lucknow District and Principal of Sitapur Boarding Sch.; Evangelical work for North India Conference, 1917; Evangelist to the educated classes throughout India and the East; spent some months in the sch. of Dr Rabindranath Tagore, Bengal, 1926; elected to Episcopacy, Methodist Episcopal Church, 1928, resigned. Publications: The Christ of the Indian Road; Christ at the Round Table; The Christ of Every Road; The Christ of the Mount; Christ and Human Suffering, 1938; Christ and Communism, 1935; Victorious Living, 1936; Christ and Present World Issues, 1937; Along the Indian Road, 1939; Is the Kingdom of God Realism?, 1941; Abundant Living, 1942; The Christ of the American Road, 1944; The Way, 1947; Mahatma Gandhi-an Interpretation, 1948; The Way to Power and Poise, 1949; How to be a Transformed Person, 1951; Growing Spiritually, 1953; Mastery, 1955; Christian Maturity, 1957; Conversion, 1959; In Christ, 1961; The Word Became Flesh, 1963; Victory through Surrender, 1966; A Song of Ascents, a spiritual autobiography, 1969; The Reconstruction of the Church: On What Pattern?, 1970. Address: c/o Methodist Division, World Missions, 475 Riverside Drive, New York, NY 10027, USA.   [Died 25 Jan. 1973.

JONES, Eric Kyffin, CBE 1962 (MBE 1948); Chairman, Welsh Board of Health, 1961-Aug. 1962; b 4 Dec. 1896; s of Hugh Kyffin Jones and Catherine Jane (née Williams); m 1920, Helen

Roberta Patricia (*née* Montgomery); one *d. Educ:* St Margaret's, Liverpool. Home Office, Boy Clerk, 1912; Welsh Board of Health: Principal, 1948; Asst Sec., 1955; Chm. (Under-Sec.), 1961. OStJ 1964. *Address:* 10 Penydre, Rhiwbina, Cardiff. *T:* Cardiff 62421.   [*Died* 3 *Nov.* 1977.

JONES, Ernest; *see* Jones, William Ernest.

JONES, Evan Bonnor H.; *see* Hugh-Jones.

JONES, Sir Fletcher; *see* Jones, Sir D. F.

JONES, Frank Ernest, MBE 1947; BSc; CEng, MIEE; Senior Director (Customer Services), Post Office, since 1972. Electrical Industry, 1933-39. Served War of 1939-45, RAFVR. GPO, 1947-; Administrative Staff Coll., 1953; Imperial Defence Coll., 1962; Senior Dir, Postal Services, PO Corp., 1971. *Address:* Telecommunications Headquarters, 2-12 Gresham Street, EC2V 7AG. *T:* 01-432 1234.   [*Died* 1 *Oct.* 1974.

JONES, Frederick Herbert P.; *see* Page-Jones.

JONES, Frederick William F.; *see* Farey-Jones.

JONES, Sir George B. T.; *see* Todd-Jones.

JONES, George Lewis; Coordinator, Senior Seminar in Foreign Policy, US Department of State, since 1964; *b* 18 Jan. 1907; *s* of George Lewis Jones and Emma Little, both of Maryland USA; *m* 1935, Mary Warner Cooke; two *s* one *d. Educ:* Univ. of Virginia; Harvard Univ.; Christ's Coll., Cambridge. Clerk to Commercial Attaché, London, 1930-32, Cairo, 1932-34; Asst Trade Comr, Cairo, 1934, Athens, 1935-38; Asst Commercial Attaché, Athens, 1938-41; Third Sec., Cairo, 1941-42; Asst Chief, Div. of Near East Affairs, Dept of State, 1942-46; Second Sec., London, 1946-49; National War Coll., 1949; Policy Planning Staff, Dept of State, 1950; Dir, Office of Near Eastern Affairs, 1950-52; Principal Officer, Tunis, 1952; Counselor, Cairo, 1953; Minister-Counselor, Tehran, 1955; Ambassador to Tunisia, 1956; Asst Sec. of State for Near Eastern and South Asian Affairs, 1959; Minister, American Embassy in London, 1961-64. FZS. *Address:* 1644 Avon Place NW, Washington 20007, USA. *Clubs:* Metropolitan, Chevy Chase (Washington, DC).   [*Died* 13 *Nov.* 1971.

JONES, Gwilym Peredur, MA, LittD (Liverpool); Professor of Economics in the University of Sheffield, 1948-57; Emeritus Professor, 1957; *b* 24 April 1892; *s* of J. H. and Elizabeth Jones, Birkenhead; *m* 1920, Winifred Agnes Riley, Ulverston, Lancs; two *d. Educ:* University of Liverpool. Lord Howard de Walden Fellow in Welsh History, Liverpool Univ., 1920-23; tutor in History, Economic History and Political Theory for Liverpool Extramural Board, 1920-26; Lecturer in Economic History in University of Sheffield, 1926, Reader, 1946; Sec. to Sheffield Regional Cttee for Adult Education in HM Forces, 1940-46. Vice-Pres., Cumberland and Westmorland Antiq. and Arch. Soc., 1962. *Publications:* The Political Reform Movement in Sheffield (Hunter Arch. Soc. Trans. 1929-30); The Extent of Chirkland, 1391-93, 1933; Workers Abroad, 1939; contrib. to Cambridge Economic History of Europe, Vol. II, 1952; (with Dr A. G. Pool) A Hundred Years of Economic Development, 1940; (with Prof. D. Knoop) The Mediaeval Mason, 1933; also with Prof. D. Knoop, articles in Economic History, Economic History Review, RIBA Journal, etc., on history of building and works on freemasonry, 1932-47; (with Rev. C. M. L. Bouch) The Lake Counties, 1500-1830, 1961; Short History of Witherslack, 1971. *Recreations:* Welsh studies. *Address:* 16 Priory Lane, Grange-over-Sands, Cumbria. *T:* Grange-over-Sands 2285.
                                           [*Died* 12 *Feb.* 1975.

JONES, Harry; *see* Orton-Jones, Harry.

JONES, Sir Henry M.; *see* Morris-Jones.

JONES, Captain Henry Richmund I.; *see* Inigo-Jones.

JONES, Air Cdre Herbert George, CBE 1942; ACIS 1906; *b* 26 Nov. 1884; *s* of George Reuben Jones; *m* 1913, Clarisse Lisney West; one *s* one *d. Educ:* privately. Joined Royal Army Pay Corps, 1914; Royal Air Force, 1918. Served European War, 1914-18 (despatches twice); War of 1939-45 (despatches twice); retired Nov. 1944. Chartered Sec. *Address:* 5 Cotman Gardens, Edgware, Middlesex.   [*Died* 24 *Oct.* 1979.

JONES, Sir Hildreth G.; *see* Glyn-Jones.

JONES, Hugh Ferguson, OBE 1971; JP; Regional Manager, Lombard North Central Ltd, Bankers; *b* 14 June 1913; *s* of Isaac

Jones and Isabella Jones (*née* Stewart); *m* 1942; one *s. Educ:* Alun Grammar Sch., Mold; City of Liverpool Technical Coll; Master Mariner (Foreign going), with Ellerman Hall Line Liverpool, 1929-47. Elected to Cardiff City Council, 1952 Alderman 1967-74, Lord Mayor, 1971-72; Co. Councillor, New S Glamorganshire CC, 1973-. Dir. of Welsh National Theatre Mem. Court of Governors, Univ. of Wales. Liveryman of Hon Co. of Master Mariners and Freeman of City of London, 1968 JP Cardiff, 1957. *Recreations:* nautical education and marine studies, music and the arts, outdoor sports in general. *Address* 160 Pencisely Road, Llandaff, Cardiff. *T:* Cardiff 561744 *Knighthood gazetted, 25 June 1979.*   [*Died* 15 *June* 1979

JONES, James; author; *b* Robinson, Illinois, 6 Nov. 1921; *s* o Ramon Jones and Ada (*née* Blessing); *m* 1957, Gloria Mosolino one *s* one *d. Educ:* Universities of Hawaii and New York. Served with US Army, 1939-44 (bronze star and purple heart) *Publications:* From Here to Eternity, 1951 (National Bool Award, US); Some Came Running, 1957; The Pistol, 1959; The Thin Red Line, 1962; Go to the Widow-Maker, 1967; The Ice Cream Headache, 1968; The Merry Month of May, 1971; A Touch of Danger, 1973; Viet Journal, 1974; *posthumou publication:* Whistle, 1978. *Recreations:* shooting, skindiving *Address:* Dell, 1 Dag Hammarskjold Plaza, New York, N\ 10017, USA; 10 Quai d'Orléans, Ile Saint-Louis, Paris 4e France.   [*Died* 9 *May* 1977

JONES, James Ilston, CBE 1974 (OBE 1963); Chief Electora Officer for Northern Ireland, since 1972; *b* 7 March 1911; *s* o Ilston Jones and Elspet Fearnside; *m* 1936, Maisie Agnes Beer two *s* one *d. Educ:* Taunton's Sch., Southampton; University Coll., Southampton. HMSO, 1938-71 (Dir, N Ireland Office Belfast, 1955-71). War service, Royal Corps of Signals, 1940-46 *Recreations:* yachting, angling. *Address:* 21 Ward Avenue Bangor, Co. Down, N Ireland. *T:* Bangor (NI) 65747.
                                          [*Died* 12 *March* 1976

JONES, Ven. James William Percy; Archdeacon of Huntingdon 1947-55, Canon Emeritus since 1955; *b* 22 April 1881; *s* of lat Canon D. Jones; *m* 1917, Judith Efa Bonnor-Maurice (*d* 1959) one *s* one *d* (and one *s* killed in action). *Educ:* Oswestry Pembroke Coll., Oxford, Queen's Coll., Birmingham, 1904; MA 1907. Hon. CF 1921. Curate: Perry Barr, 1905-08; Nassington with Yarwell, 1908-13 and 1914-15; Llanfechain, 1913-14 Market Harborough, 1915-16. Asst Dir of Religious Educatior 1922-32; Rural Dean of Leightonstone, 1930-47; Exam Chaplain to Bishop of Ely, 1941; Hon. Canon Ely Cathedral 1941-47, Canon Emeritus, 1954; Vicar of Great Gidding and Little Gidding, 1916-57, with Steeple Gidding, 1926-57 *Recreation:* formerly golf. *Address:* Cae Hywel, Llansantffraid Powys.   [*Died* 4 *Dec.* 1980

JONES, John Harry; Emeritus Professor, University of Leeds; *l* Wales, 27 July 1881; *m* 1914, Eva (*d* 1955), *d* of late Henr Cuthbertson, Journalist, Newcastle and Oxford; one *d. Educ* Swansea Grammar Sch.; University Coll., Cardiff; Universitie of Leipzig and Berlin. BA first-class Hons in Economics an Political Science, 1903; MA, 1904; Fellow University of Wales 1904-7; LLD *Hon. Causa,* University of Wales, 1946. Ass Lecturer in Economics, University of Liverpool, 1907-9 Lecturer in Social Economics, University of Glasgow, 1909-19 Prof. of Economics and head of Economics Dept, University o Leeds, 1919-46; OTC, 1915; War Trade Dept, 1915; Ministry o Munitions, 1916-18; of Labour, 1918; Appointed Mem. of Trad Boards, 1919-22; Impartial Mem. West Riding Agricultura Wages Cttee, 1925-46; formerly Mem. of Board of Educatio Consultative Cttee on Adult Education; Mem. Economi Advisory Council Cttee on the Slaughtering of Livestock, 193C 32 and Cttee on Cattle Diseases, 1932-34; Pres. Section F. o British Association, 1933; Chairman, Nova Scotia Roya Commission of Economic Enquiry, 1934; Mem., Roya Commission on the Geographical Distribution of the Industria Population, 1937; Mem. Road Research Board; Impartial Men Surrey Agricultural Wages Cttee, 1947. Guy Silver Meda Royal Statistical Society, 1934; Hon. Treas. Royal Statistica Society, 1947-50. *Publications:* The Tinplate Industry, 1914; Th Economics of War and Conquest, 1915; Social Economics, 191 Economics of Private Enterprise, 1926; The Federal Reserv System, 1926; The Economics of Saving, 1934; Editor, Th Economics Educator, 1928-29; Report on Road Accident published for Ministry of Transport by HM Stationery Office 1946; The Structure of Industry, 1948; Josiah Stamp: Publi Servant, 1964, etc. *Club:* National Liberal. [*Died* 6 *April* 197

JONES, Sir (John) Henry M.; *see* Morris-Jones.

JONES, Prof. John Kenyon Netherton, FRS 1957; FRSC 196(FCIC 1961; Chown Research Professor, Queen's University

Kingston, Ontario, since 1953; *b* 28 Jan. 1912; *m* 1937, Marjorie Ingles Noon; two *s* one *d*. *Educ:* Waverley Grammar Sch., Birmingham; Birmingham Univ. BSc (Hons) 1933; PhD 1936; DSc 1948. Lecturer, Bristol University, 1936-44; Senior Lecturer, Manchester Univ., 1945-48; Reader, Bristol Univ., 1948-53. *Publications:* in Jl of Chem. Soc., Biochem. Jl, Canadian Jl of Chem. *Recreations:* photography, gardening. *Address:* Box 31, Treasure Island, RRI, Kingston, Ontario, Canada. *T:* 613-548-4340. *[Died 13 April 1977.*

JONES, John Walter; Provost of The Queen's College, Oxford, 1948-62, retired; Hon. Fellow of Emmanuel College, Cambridge, 1949; Hon. Fellow of Queen's College, Oxford, 1962; *b* 21 July 1892; *s* of late William and Hannah Jane Jones, Merthyr Tydfil. *Educ:* Merthyr County Sch.; University Coll. of Wales, Aberystwyth; Emmanuel Coll., Cambridge (Scholar and Research Student). First Class in Law Tripos, Parts I and II; George Long Prize and Yorke Prize, Cambridge; Constitutional Law Prize, Barstow Scholarship and Certificate of Honour of the Inns of Court; Barrister-at-Law of the Inner Temple; Lecturer and Tutor in Law, University of Liverpool, 1920-26; Fellow, Tutor, and Praelector in Law, Queen's Coll., Oxford, 1927-48; University Lecturer in Law, 1937-48; Junior Proctor, 1942-43. *Publications:* Bona Fide Purchase of Goods (Yorke Prize Essay, 1918); Historical Introduction to the Theory of Law, 1940, repr. 1956, 1969; The Law and Legal Theory of the Greeks, 1956; contributions to various legal periodicals. *Recreation:* walking. *Address:* 68 Staunton Road, Headington, Oxford. *T:* Oxford 61315. *Club:* National Liberal.
[Died 18 Dec. 1973.

JONES, Joseph, CBE 1941; *b* 10 Jan. 1890; *s* of late David E. Jones, Llangollen, Denbighshire; *m* 1919, Gwladys M. (*d* 1961), *d* of Owen Davies, Llanmaes, St Fagans, near Cardiff; (one *d* decd). *Educ:* Llangollen; Cardiff. Joined Glamorgan Constabulary, 1911; Superintendent, 1932; Deputy Chief Constable, 1936; Chief Constable of Glamorgan, 1937-51. Officer Brother Order of St John; King's Police Medal for Distinguished Service, 1947. *Recreations:* bowls, shooting, etc. *Address:* Fron Esgyn, Fron Cysyllte, Llangollen, Clwyd.
[Died 20 May 1979.

JONES, Keith M.; *see* Miller Jones.

JONES, Lewis; *see* Jones, George Lewis.

JONES, Maj.-Gen. Llewelyn W.; *see* Wansbrough-Jones.

JONES, Martin, FRAgS; Professor Emeritus of Agricultural Botany, University of Newcastle upon Tyne (formerly King's College), since 1962; *b* 19 May 1897; *s* of J. G. Jones, Ruel Issa, Bow-street, Cardiganshire; *m* 1927, Olwen Elizabeth Watkin; two *s*. *Educ:* University Coll. of Wales, Aberystwyth. Welsh Plant Breeding Station, Aberystwyth, 1920-28; Jealott's Hill Agric. Research Stn, Berks, 1928-37; North of Scotland Coll. of Agriculture, Aberdeen, 1937-47; Prof. of Agricultural Botany, King's Coll., Newcastle upon Tyne, 1947-62. Pres., Brit. Grassland Soc., 1951-52; Pres., Agric. Section of Brit. Assoc., Aberdeen, 1963. Chm. Scientific Advisory Cttee, Sports Turf Research Inst., Bingley, 1948-60. *Address:* Y Winllan, Antaron Avenue, Southgate, Aberystwyth. *T:* Aberystwyth 7781. *Club:* Farmers'.
[Died 30 Dec. 1979.

JONES, Judge Marvin; Senior Judge, United States Court of Claims, since 1964, serving under assignment of Chief Justice of Supreme Court on US Courts of Appeal throughout the United States; *b* near Gainsville, Texas; *s* of Horace K. and Dosia Jones. *Educ:* Southwestern Univ. (AB); University of Texas (LLB). Chm. Board Legal Examiners, West Texas, 1912-16; served in Congress, 1917-40; Chm. House Cttee on Agriculture, 1931-40; Judge, US Court of Claims, 1940-64. During War of 1939-45, Asst to James F. Byrnes, Dir of Economic Stabilization. Pres. of First Internat. Conf. of 44 nations on Food and Agriculture, Hot Springs, Va, 1943; War Food Administrator (US), 1943-45; Chief Judge US Court of Claims, 1947-64. *Publications:* How War Food Saved American Lives, 1945; Should Uncle Sam Pay—When and Why?, 1963; Marvin Jones Memoirs, 1973. *Recreation:* fishing. *Address:* (Business) Senior Judge, US Court of Claims, 717 Madison Place, NW, Washington, DC 20005; (Home) 2807 Hughes Street, Amarillo, Tex 79109. *TA:* Business 382-2768-Washington. *Clubs:* University, National Press, Lawyers (Washington, DC); Amarillo (Amarillo, Texas).
[Died 4 March 1976.

JONES, Sir Melvill; *see* Jones, Sir B. M.

JONES, Norman Edward, CMG 1969; company director; *b* 2 Aug. 1904; *s* of Edward J. Jones; *m* 1928, Mabel Elizabeth

Swainson; one *s*. *Educ:* Hamilton and Cooks Hill High Schs, Newcastle, Australia; Newcastle Technical Coll. (Dip.Chem. Hons). Managing Dir, The Broken Hill Proprietary Co. Ltd, 1952-66. Director: The Broken Hill Proprietary Co. Ltd; Australian Paper Manufacturers Ltd; The National Bank of Australasia Ltd; Colonial Mutual Life Assce Soc. Ltd. Pres., The Iron and Steel Institute, 1967-68. Hon. DSc: Univ. of New South Wales; Univ. of Newcastle, NSW. *Recreation:* gardening. *Address:* 136 Kooyong Road, Toorak, Victoria 3142, Australia. *T:* 20 3365. *Clubs:* Melbourne, Australian, Adelaide, Union, Athenæum (Melbourne); Weld (Perth); Newcastle (Newcastle).
[Died 10 Aug. 1972.

JONES, Captain Oscar Philip, CVO 1952; OBE 1945; FRGS; FRAeS; *b* 15 Oct. 1898; *s* of Oscar Jones, Beckenham; *m* 1st, 1920, Olive Elizabeth Turner (decd); one *s* decd; 2nd, 1963, Kathleen Jacobs, ARAM, JP, Liverpool. *Educ:* Beckenham, Kent. Served European War, Royal Engineers, 1916-17; Royal Flying Corps and RAF, 1917-19. Berkshire Aviation Tours, 1920-22; Instone Airline, 1922-24; Imperial Airways, 1924-40; Brit. Overseas Airways Corporation, 1940-65; Senior Captain North Atlantic, 1946-55; Special Liaison Officer, BOAC, Worldwide Goodwill and Lecture tours, 1955-65. RAFO and RAFVR, 1924-54. Founder Mem. and Warden, Guild of Air Pilots, 1929 (Deputy Master 1934); Warden, 1954-58; Cumberbach Trophy, 1931; Master Pilot's Certificate, 1935; FAI Gliding Certificate "C", 1939; OC No. 2 ATA Pool, 1940; Flight Capt., Atlantic, 1941; Flight Capt., Landplanes, 1942-45; Air Efficiency Award, 1943; Wing Cmdr, RAFO, 1945. Mem. BOAC "25" Club (Pres. 1952), also Speedbird Club. Flew the Queen, when Princess Elizabeth, to Canada, 1951; Britannia Trophy Award, 1951. Guild Master Pilot's Certificate, 1954. Past Pres., Bull-Terrier Club. *Recreations:* swimming, dog judging (International), light aeroplane flying, riding. *Address:* Squirrels, Spinney Lane, Pulborough, West Sussex RH20 2NX. *T:* West Chiltington 3140. *Clubs:* Royal Air Force Reserves; Southern Aero (Shoreham); Scottish Flying; Tiger.
[Died 21 June 1980.

JONES, Maj.-Gen. Percy George C.; *see* Calvert-Jones.

JONES, Sir Peter (Fawcett) Benton, 3rd Bt *cr* 1919; OBE 1945; *b* 9 Jan. 1911; *s* of Sir Walter Benton Jones, 2nd Bt and Lily Marguerite (*d* 1938), *d* of late James Dixon Fawcett; *S* father, 1967; *m* 1936, Nancy, *o c* of late Warley Pickering; one *s* one *d*. *Educ:* Charterhouse; Trinity Coll., Cambridge (MA). FCA; Chartered Accountant, 1932-39. Served with Army, 1939-45 (despatches); Lieut-Col 1943. United Steel Cos, 1945-70. *Recreations:* shooting, fishing, stalking. *Heir:* *s* Simon Warley Frederick Benton Jones [*b* 11 Sept. 1941; *m* 1966, Margaret Fiona, *d* of David Rutherford Dickson, Ipswich]. *Address:* Irnham, near Grantham, Lincs. *T:* Corby Glen 336.
[Died 11 Nov. 1972.

JONES, Peter Howard, CB 1968; Assistant Under-Secretary of State, Ministry of Defence, 1964-68; *b* 3 March 1911; *s* of William Howard Jones, MB, BS London, and Mabelle Rose Jones; *m* 1939, Ann Hall; two *d*. *Educ:* St Paul's Sch.; Balliol Coll., Oxford. 1st Cl., Class. Mods and Litt. Hum. Entered Admiralty, 1934; Under-Sec., 1957. *Address:* 32 Merrow Chase, Levylsdene, Merrow, Guildford, Surrey. *T:* Guildford 62646.
[Died 13 June 1975.

JONES, Philip Asterley, LLB London; retired Solicitor; *b* 21 June 1914; *s* of Leonard Asterley Jones, St Albans; *m* 1941, Ruth Florence Davis; two *s* (and one *s* decd). *Educ:* Tonbridge Sch.; Law Society's Sch. of Law. Admitted as Solicitor, 1937. Mem. St Albans City Council, 1938. MP (Lab) Hitchin, 1945-50. Served War of 1939-45; Driver RASC Sept. 1939, DAQMG 1943 (despatches). Lecturer in Law at Law Soc., 1945-51; Consultant to Guildford Coll. of Law, on practical training, 1969-72; Dir, vocational trng courses, Birmingham, 1972-75; Hd of Dept of Law, City of Birmingham Polytechnic, 1975-77. Editor, Solicitors' Journal, 1956-68; Editor, Local Govt Chronicle, 1950-63, Legal Editor, 1963-69. *Publications:* (with Sir Rupert Cross) An Introduction to Criminal Law, 1948, 8th edn (with R. I. E. Card), 1976; Cases on Criminal Law, 1949, 6th edn by R. I. E. Card, 1977. *Address:* 17 Fugelmere Close, Harborne, Birmingham B17 8SE. *T:* 021-429 3235. *[Died 23 Oct. 1978.*

JONES, Philip R. B.; *see* Bence-Jones.

JONES, Ranald Montagu H.; *see* Handfield-Jones.

JONES, Reginald Trevor, CIE 1943; MC 1918; FInstCE; *b* 19 Dec. 1888; *s* of late Trevor Jones, Midland Bank, Carlisle; *m* 1922, Edith Aileen (*d* 1970), *d* of late W. Theodore Carr, CBE, MP, Carlisle; one *d*. *Educ:* Malvern Coll. Articled E. Purnell

Hooley, MInstCE, 1906-10; joined Indian Service of Engineers, 1912; Chief Engineer and Sec. to Govt, Panjab PWD, 1939; retired Dec. 1943. Capt. 5th Royal Leicestershire Regt, 1914; seconded IA, 1915, attached RE (1st KGO Bengal Sappers and Miners); NWFP, Mesopotamia, Palestine, 1915-19 (despatches, MC). *Address:* Appletrees, Love Lane, Petersfield, Hants. *T:* Petersfield 3573. *[Died 2 May 1974.*

JONES, Sir Reginald Watson; see Watson-Jones.

JONES, Richard Francis L.; see Lloyd Jones.

JONES, Air Marshal Sir R(obert) Owen, KBE, *cr* 1953; CB 1944; AFC; retired; *b* 19 April 1901; *s* of late F. M. and late Mrs Jones; *m* 1928, Betty Hambleton Hood; one *s* one *d. Educ:* Epworth College, Rhyl; Caius Coll., Cambridge. Joined RAF 1924; comd 11 Squadron, 1935-38; British Air Commission, Washington, 1941-43; Ministry of Aircraft Production, 1943-46; Technical Services (Plans) Air Ministry, 1946-47; AOC No. 24 Group, Technical Training Command, 1947; Senior Air Staff Officer, RAF Reserve Command, 1949; AOC No. 24 Group, Technical Training Command, 1949-52; Controller of Engineering and Equipment, Air Ministry, 1952-56. Pres. Instn Mechanical Engineers, 1958-59; Pres., Royal Aeronautical Society, 1961. Commander Legion of Merit (American), 1946. *Recreation:* fishing. *Address:* The Paddock, Westerton, Chichester, Sussex. *[Died 13 Oct. 1972.*

JONES, Robert Tyre, (Bobby); Attorney-at-Law; Partner in the firm of Jones, Bird, & Howell, Atlanta, USA; *b* Atlanta, Georgia, 17 March 1902; *s* of Robert P. Jones and Clara Thomas; *m* 1924, Mary Malone, Atlanta; one *s* two *d. Educ:* Technical High Sch., and Georgia Inst. of Technology, Atlanta; Harvard; Emory University. Admitted to Georgia Bar, 1928; National Amateur Golf Champion, 1924, 1925, 1927, 1928, 1930; National Open Champion, 1923, 1926, 1929, 1930; awarded Sullivan Memorial Prize, 1930; Open Championship of Great Britain, 1926, 1927, 1930; Amateur Champion Great Britain, 1930. Vice-Pres. Spalding Sales Corp.; Director: The Southern Co.; Canton Textile Mills, Inc.; Jones Mercantile Co. Relieved from active duty as Lieut-Col USAAF at end of War of 1939-45. *Publications:* Down the Fairway, 1927; Golf is My Game, 1960; Bobby Jones on Golf, 1966; Bobby Jones on the Basic Golf Swing, 1969. *Address:* Haas-Howell Building (4th floor), Atlanta, Ga 30303, USA. *[Died 18 Dec. 1971.*

JONES, Prof. Royston Oscar; Professor of Spanish, Cambridge University, since 1973; Fellow of Downing College, Cambridge, since 1973; *b* 28 Oct. 1925; *s* of David Jones and Gwladys Mary Williams; *m* 1948, Elvira Ranz y Díez de Artázcoz; three *d. Educ:* Neath Grammar Sch.; King's Coll., London. BA Hons First Class, 1946, MA (London) 1949, FKC 1972. Asst Lecturer, University of Aberdeen, 1948; Lecturer: University of St Andrews, 1949; King's Coll., London, 1950; Reader and Head of Dept, Queen Mary Coll., London, 1956; Cervantes Prof. of Spanish, Univ. of London at King's Coll., 1963-73. *Publications:* Critical edition of Lazarillo de Tormes, 1963; Poems of Góngora, with introduction, 1966; A Literary History of Spain, vol. 2, The Golden Age: Prose and Poetry, 1971 (General Editor of whole work, 1971-72); articles in Mod. Lang. Review, Bulletin of Hispanic Studies, Boletin de la Real Academia, etc. *Recreations:* music, solitude, photography. *Address:* Faculty of Modern Languages, Sidgwick Avenue, Cambridge. *[Died 17 July 1974.*

JONES, Rt. Rev. Thomas Edward, MBE 1956; ThD; *b* 7 March 1903; *s* of Thomas and Charlotte Jones; *m* 1929, Lucy Vincent; one *s* two *d. Educ:* Ridley Coll., Melbourne; Australian College of Theology. Deacon, 1927; Priest, 1928; ThL 1928; ThD 1961. Curate of Moreland, 1927-28; Priest-in-Charge of Boggabilla, 1929-32; Victorian Secretary, Bush Church Aid Society, 1932-34; Licentiate to Officiate, Diocese of Sydney, 1934-58; Organising Secretary, Bush Church Aid Society of Australia and Tasmania, 1934-58; Hon. Canon of Sydney, 1956-58; Bishop of Willochra, 1958-69. Coronation Medal, 1953. *Publication:* These Twenty Years: A History of Bush Church Aid Society to 1940. *Address:* 109 Glengyle Terrace, Plympton, SA 5038, Australia. *T:* 972642. *[Died 16 May 1972.*

JONES, Rt. Rev. Thomas Sherwood, DD; *b* 4 March 1872; one *s* two *d* (and two *s* one *d* decd). *Educ:* London Coll. of Divinity; University of Durham (MA). Hon. DD 1931. Deacon, 1897; Priest, 1898; perpetual curate of St Martin-in-the-Fields, Liverpool, 1903-11; Vicar of: St Cleopas, Toxteth Park, 1911-16; St Mary, Birkenhead, 1916-20; Rector of Middleton, 1920-45; Rural Dean of Middleton, 1920-30; Hon. Canon of Manchester, 1927-30; Canon Emeritus, 1946; Bishop of Hulme, 1930-45. *Address:* Cranford, Aviary Road, Pyrford, near Woking, Surrey. *T:* Byfleet 45158. *[Died 16 Oct. 1972.*

JONES, W(alter) Idris, CBE 1954; BSc Wales, Hon. DSc 1957; PhD Cantab; CEng, MIChemE, FRIC, FIMinE, FInstF; Member (part-time): Government Water Resources Board, 1964-65; Wales Gas Board, since 1964; Director-General of Research National Coal Board, 1946-62; Director General of Research and Development (Coal Processing and Combustion), National Coal Board, 1962-63, retired 1963; *b* Llanelli, Carmarthenshire, 18 Jan. 1900; *s* of Frederick and Elizabeth Jones; unmarried. *Educ:* University Coll. of Wales, Aberystwyth; Gonville and Caius Coll., Cambridge. BSc Hons Chemistry, 1921; Rhondda and Frank Smart Studentships at Gonville and Caius Coll., 1922-26; PhD Cantab 1925; Cambridge Univ. Rugby XV, 1923-25; Wales Rugby XV 1924-25, v. England, France, Ireland and Scotland. ICI (F & SP) Ltd, Billingham, 1926-33; research on methanol and ammonia synthesis, gasification, hydrogenation of coal, etc; Group Manager in Oil Div.: Research Manager, Powell Duffryn Ltd, 1933-46; Vice-Pres., Inst. Chemical Engrs, 1955; Mem. of Council, Inst. Fuel (Pres., 1953-54-55; Treas., 1964); Pres. and Chm. of Council, British Coal Utilisation Research Assoc., 1955-63. Member and Vice-Pres., Hon. Soc. of Cymmrodorion; Member: National Council for Technol. Awards, 1955-62; Court, Univ. of Wales; Court and Council, Univ. of Wales Inst. of Science and Technology; Court and Council, University Coll. of Wales, Aberystwyth, 1957-70 (Vice-Pres., 1963-71); Chm. University of Wales Appointments Board, 1957-68. Mem. Court and Industrial Cttee, Nat. Museum of Wales, 1968-. Mem. Water Advisory Cttee (Wales), 1958-59. Chm., BSI (Solid Fuel Industry Standards Cttee), 1948-63; Chm., London Secretariat, Commonwealth Conf. for Fuel Research, 1961-63; Mem., Parly and Sci. Cttee, 1955-64. RA Cadet Bn, 1918; Major (GI) E Glamorgan Sector, HG. *Publications:* papers in Scientific and Technical jls. *Recreations:* walking, music. *Address:* 9b The Cathedral Green, Llandaff, Cardiff. *T:* Cardiff 563995. *[Died 5 July 1971.*

JONES, Rev. William David; Clerk of the General Assembly, The Presbyterian Church of Wales, 1968-73; Moderator of the General Assembly, The Presbyterian Church of Wales, 1974-75; *b* 8 July 1909; British (Welsh); *m* 1939, Gwen Evans, Bala, Merionethshire; two *s* one *d. Educ:* UC of N Wales, Bangor (BA); United Theol Coll., Aberystwyth. Ordained, 1936. Minister at: Chwilog, Caern, 1936-45; Bontnewydd, Caern, 1945-50; Edge Lane, Liverpool, 1950-74. Sec., Calvinistic Methodist Orphanage, Bontnewydd, 1945-50. Asst Sec., Gen. Assembly (PCW), 1957-58; Statistician, Gen. Assembly (PCW), 1960-64. Liverpool Presbytery (PCW): Sec., 1951-53; Moderator, 1954. Governor/Manager, Newsham County Schools, Liverpool, 1960-74 (Chm., 1969). Part-time Chaplain, Walton Hosp., Liverpool, 1958-68. *Recreation:* fishing. *Address:* 177 Penrhos Road, Bangor, North Wales LL57 2BX. *T:* Bangor 4089. *[Died 7 Jan. 1976.*

JONES, Very Rev. William Edward; Vicar of Penally, 1964-69, retired; *b* 1897; *s* of Captain David Hughes Jones and Elizabeth Jones, Aberystwyth; *m* 1935, Rachel Marianne Powell; one *s* three *d. Educ:* St David's Sch., Lampeter; Jesus Coll., Oxford (Mathematical Exhibition). BA 1922; MA 1924. Minor Canon of Brecon Cathedral, 1922-28; Priest-in-Charge, Kondinin, WA, 1928-33; Diocesan Missioner, Swansea and Brecon, 1934-35; Rector St Luke's, Cottesloe, WA, and Rural Dean, 1936-43; Chaplain AMF, 1941-45; Rector St Mary's, West Perth, 1943-49; Canon of St George's, Perth, 1944-49; Dean of Brecon, 1950-64, and Vicar of St Mary's, Brecon, 1950-64; Hon. Canon of Brecon Cathedral, 1964-69. *Recreations:* Rugby football, music, cabinet-making. *Address:* Caldey View, Penally, Tenby, Dyfed. *T:* Tenby 3112. *[Died 11 June 1974.*

JONES, (William) Ernest, CBE 1961 (OBE 1945); retired as: Chairman, Southern Regional Board for Industry, 1961-65; Member British Egg Marketing Board, 1961-66; Member (Part-time) Transport Holding Company, 1963-65; *b* 14 April 1895; *s* of Arthur and Constance Jones; *m* 1918, Annie Helen Fall (*d* 1960); one *d*; *m* 1962, Catherine L. Taylor. *Educ:* Renishaw Council Sch. Commenced work at 13 years of age in a boot repairing shop; entered coalmining underground at 14 years of age; employed at Southgate and Cresswell Collieries, Derbyshire, 1910-18; employed at Rossington Colliery, South Yorks, 1918; appointed Branch Official of Mineworkers' Union, 1921; Colliery Checkweighman, 1926; Mem. Doncaster RDC, 1924-39; Mem. West Riding County Council, 1928-42; West Riding Magistrate, 1936; Mem. Executive Cttee of MFGB 1938 Gen. Sec. of Yorks Miners' Assoc., 1939; seconded to act as Regional Labour Dir, Ministry of Fuel and Power, 1942-44; Vice-Pres. of National Union of Mineworkers, 1950; Pres National Union of Mineworkers, 1954-60, retd; Mem. Gen Council, TUC, 1950-60; Sec., Miners' International Federation 1957-60. Member: Radcliffe Cttee on working of the Monetary

System; Monopolies Commission, 1959-69; National Savings Cttee, 1961-. Hon. LLD Leeds, 1961. *Recreation:* gardening. *Address:* Diggers, Moat Lane, Pulborough, Sussex. *T:* Pulborough 2718.   *[Died 19 July 1973.*

JONES, Sir (William John) Andrew, Kt 1943; CMG 1937; *b* 5 Nov. 1889; 2nd *s* of late Rev. J. Jones, formerly Rector of Itton, Chepstow; *m* 1916, Catherine Muriel, 2nd *d* of A. S. Evans, Cowbridge; one *s* one *d. Educ:* Cowbridge Grammar Sch.; Jesus Coll., Oxford. Joined Colonial Administrative Service, 1913; Provincial Commissioner, 1927; Sec. for Native Affairs, 1931; Dep. Governor, 1931, 1932; Chief Commissioner, Northern Territories, Gold Coast; Accredited Representitive on three occasions at Sessions of Permanent Mandates Commission; Dep. Chm. West African Governors Conference, 1941; Chief Sec. to resident Minister W Africa, 1942-45; Head of British Food Mission to Canada, 1946-53. *Address:* The Knap House, Ramsbury, Marlborough, Wilts.   *[Died 20 June 1971.*

JONES, William Neilson, MA; Professor Emeritus, University of London since 1948; *b* 1883; *s* of William Beale Jones, London, and Jessie Gilchrist Neilson, Glasgow; *m* 1st, 1912, Mabel Cheveley Rayner (*d* 1948); *m* 2nd, 1957, Margaret, *widow of* Dr J. W. Trevan, FRS, and *d* of late Sir H. Llewellyn Smith, GCB. *Educ:* King's Coll. Sch., London; Emmanuel Coll. (Foundation Scholar), Cambridge. First Class Part I, Natural Science Tripos, Second Class Part II; Lecturer in Botany at University Coll. Reading, 1908; Asst Lecturer in Botany at Bedford Coll., 1913; head of the dept, 1916; Prof. of Botany, Bedford Coll., London, 1920-48; during European War, 1914-18, conducted investigations for the Health of the Munition Workers' Cttee of the Ministry of Munitions, and held commission as Capt. RAF. *Publications:* original scientific investigations in various branches of botany; A Text-book of Plant Biology (with M. C. Rayner, DSc); Plant Chimaras; Problems in Tree Nutrition (with M. C. Rayner) new enl. edn 1969; The Growing Plant. *Address:* 169 Woodside Green, SE25. *T:* 01-654 5798.
[Died 8 Oct. 1974.

JONES-ROBERTS, Kate Winifred, OBE; *b* 29 Nov. 1889; *d* of Catherine and Rees Roberts, Llys Dorvil, Blaenau Ffestiniog, N Wales; *m* J. Jones-Roberts (*d* 1962), Barrister-at-Law. *Educ:* University Coll. of N Wales, Bangor; Newnham Coll., Cambridge. BA (Wales). JP (Merioneth); Merioneth CC 1939-53; Dep. Chm., Merioneth QS, 1955-64; Chairman: Ffestiniog Bench of Magistrates, 1959-64; Merioneth Magistrates Court Cttee, 1962-64; Merioneth Probation Cttee, 1955-64; Merioneth Appeal Tribunal (Nat. Assistance), 1951-62; N Wales Mental Hosp. Management Cttee, 1948-51; Merioneth Children's Homes, 1948-63; Welsh Tourist Board, 1950-52; Vice-President: University Coll. of N Wales, Bangor, 1956-61; Coleg Harlech, 1949-; Merioneth Historical Soc., 1947-67. Member: University Coun. (Wales), 1949-68; Merioneth Education Cttee, 1939-70; Children and Welfare Cttees of Merioneth CC, 1953-67 (Chm., Children Cttee, 1948-53); Welsh Regional Hosp. Board, 1947-54; Board of British Travel and Holidays Assoc., 1947-53; Advisory Cttee on Child Care, 1948-50; Welsh Jt Education Cttee, 1948-52; Nathan Cttee on Charitable Trusts, 1950-53; Royal Commission on Marriage and Divorce, 1951-55. Tutor, Coleg Harlech, 1960-66. *Address:* Penrhiw, Ffestiniog, N Wales.
[Died 3 June 1971.

JORDAN, Prof. Wilbur Kitchener; Professor of History, Harvard University, 1946-72; Williams Professor of History and Political Science, Harvard University, 1965-72; now Emeritus Professor; *b* 15 Jan. 1902; *s* of William and Emma Shepard Jordan; *m* 1929, Frances Ruml. *Educ:* Oakland City Coll. (AB 1923); Harvard (AM 1928, PhD 1931). Instructor in History, Harvard Univ., 1931-37; Prof. of History, Scripps Coll., 1937-40; Prof. of History and Gen. Editor, University Press, University of Chicago, 1940-43; Pres., Radcliffe Coll., 1943-60. Sterling Fellow, Harvard Univ., 1930-31; Guggenheim Fellow, 1943. Corres. Fellow, British Acad., 1969. Hon. LHD, Bates Coll., 1944; Hon. DLitt: Oakland City Coll., 1960; Reed Coll., 1967; Hon. LLD: University of Vermont, 1962; Dartmouth Coll., 1966; Hon. LittD, Oxford Univ., 1964. *Publications:* The Development of Religious Toleration in England (4 vols), 1932-40, London; Men of Substance, 1942, Chicago; Philanthropy in England, 1480-1660, 1959, London; The Charities of London, 1480-1660, 1960, London; The Charities of Rural England, 1480-1660, 1961, London; The Social Institutions of Lancashire, 1962, Manchester; The Chronicle and Political Papers of King Edward VI, 1966 (Ithaca, NY and London); Edward VI: The Young King, 1968 (London); Edward VI: The threshold of power, 1970 (London) (Press faculty award, Harvard, 1971; Schuyler Prize, Amer. Hist. Assoc., 1972). *Address:* 3 Concord Avenue, Cambridge, Mass 02138, USA.   *[Died 3 June 1980.*

JORDAN MALKIN, Harold; *see* Malkin, H. J.

JORY, Philip John, DSO 1919; retired as Senior Ear, Nose and Throat Surgeon, St George's Hospital, 1958; *b* 1 March 1892; *s* of Rev. J. D. Jory; *m* 1925, Yvonne Moullé; four *s* one *d. Educ:* Nelson Coll., NZ; Otago Univ., NZ. NZ Univ. Sen. Schol., 1910; MB, ChB (NZ) 1919; FRCS Eng. 1924. ENT Surgeon: St George's, Mt Vernon, Barnet General, Woodford Jubilee and Harpenden Memorial Hosps. FRSocMed (Former Pres. Otology Section). Served European War, 1914-18 and War of 1939-45 (Col RAMC). *Address:* c/o Williams & Glyn's Bank Ltd, Kirkland House, Whitehall, SW1; Monksmead, Old Felixstowe, Suffolk. *T:* Felixstowe 4675.   *[Died 6 April 1973.*

JOSEPH, Sir (Samuel) Norman, KCVO 1969; Kt 1963; CBE 1953; Director, J. Lyons Co. Ltd, 1948-73; Hon. Catering Adviser, Home Office, since 1953; Catering Consultant, British Transport Hotels Ltd, since 1972; *b* 12 Dec. 1908; *s* of John and Dora Joseph; *m* 1932, Mina Stern; one *d. Educ:* Bedales. Started with J. Lyons and Co. Ltd, 1926. Served War of 1939-45 (despatches twice). Bronze Medal (USA), 1945. Former Dir, Strand Hotels Ltd (Dep. Chm.) and Cumberland Hotels Ltd; Chm., Town and Country Catering Co., 1962-72. *Recreations:* tennis, snooker, bridge. *Address:* Wolsey Spring, George Road, Kingston Hill, Kingston-on-Thames, Surrey.
[Died 17 Nov. 1974.

JOULES, Horace, MD, FRCP; Physician and Medical Director, Central Middlesex Hospital, 1935-65; *b* 21 March 1902; *s* of Richard Edgar and Emily Ann Joules; *m* 1930, Mary Sparrow; two *s* one *d* (and one *s* decd). *Educ:* Cardiff and London Univs. Qualified Middlesex Hosp.; MRCS, LRCP, 1924; MB, BS, 1925; MD (Gold Medal), 1928; MRCP 1928; FRCP 1943; Junior Appointments, Middlesex Hosp., Brompton Hosp., Ancoats Hosp.; Physician, Selly Oak Hosp., Birmingham, 1929; Examiner in Medicine, University of Cambridge and Royal College of Physicians. *Publications:* (ed) Doctors View of War, 1938; articles in medical journals. *Recreations:* gardening, ornithology. *Address:* 20 Templewood Road, Parson's Heath, Colchester, Essex.   *[Died 25 Jan. 1977.*

JOY, Sir George Andrew, KBE 1949; CMG 1945; *b* 20 Feb. 1896; 3rd *s* of late George Edward Joy, Ashford, Kent, and Elizabeth Ellen Breakwell, Dublin; *m* 1925, Hettie Claire Wallace (*d* 1966), Sydney, Aust.; one *s* ; *m* 1968, Pauline Rhoda Ossorn (*née* Whishaw). *Educ:* Xaverian Coll., Bruges, Belgium. Military Service, 1914-23; entered Colonial Service, 1924; Resident Commissioner, Anglo-French Condominium, New Hebrides, 1928, and Deputy Commissioner, Western Pacific; also Consul for the Hoorn and Wallace Islands. Resident Adviser to Sultans in the Hadhramaut States of Southern Arabia, 1940; Civil Sec. to Govt of Aden, and Comr of Civil Defence, 1942-46; Governor and C-in-C, St Helena and Dependencies, 1946-53; retd 1954. Vice-Pres., Soc. for Psychical Research. *Address:* Bay Tree Cottage, Beckley, Rye, Sussex. *T:* Northiam 3204.
[Died 25 April 1974.

JUBB, Edwin Charles, CB 1942; OBE 1925; *b* 1883; *s* of Edwin Charles Jubb, Hull; *m* 1912, Emily Herbert (*d* 1964), *d* of late Charles Powell, Co. Limerick, one *s* one *d* (and one *s* decd). *Educ:* Rossall; Pembroke Coll., Cambridge. 14th Wrangler 1906; Second Class Hons Science Tripos, 1907; entered Civil Service, 1908; Dir of Navy Contracts Admiralty from 1936; retired 1947. *Recreations:* cricket and singing. *Address:* Warren House, Farnham Common, Bucks. *T:* Farnham Common 3952. *Club:* Royal Commonwealth Society.   *[Died 14 Dec. 1978.*

JUDA, Hans Peter, CBE 1970 (OBE 1955); Chairman: Limited Editions Ltd; Headlines Ltd; I. T. Publications Ltd; *b* 25 Sept. 1904; *s* of Leopold and Hedwig Juda; *m* 1931, Elsbeth Ruth, *d* of Prof. J. Goldstein. *Educ:* Munich, Freiburg, Berlin, Frankfurt (MA) and Paris Univs. Financial Editor, Berliner Tageblatt, 1928-33; Founder, Publisher and Editor of The Ambassador (British Export Magazine), 1935-70. Director: Thomson Publications Ltd, 1964-74; Burlington Magazine Publications Ltd, 1964-74; Kraus-Thomson Organization Ltd, 1967-74; PEISA (Barcelona), 1965-74. Chm. of Governors, Central Sch. of Art and Design. Hon. DesRCA, 1959 (Senior Fellow, 1969); Hon. FSIA, 1956. Bi-Centenary Medal, RSA, 1965. Order of Southern Cross, Brazil, 1968. *Publications:* regular features on art, applied art, industrial design and export promotions, in The Ambassador, 1935-70; also contribs to other jls. *Recreation:* publishing. *Address:* The Penthouse, 10 Palace Gate, W8. *T:* 01-584 8907; 38 Church Lane, Fawley, Bucks. *T:* Henley-on-Thames 3980.   *[Died 3 Feb. 1975.*

JUDD, Charles Wilfred, CBE 1954; Joint President, United Nations Association (Director-General, 1945-64); *b* 27 Oct.

1896; *o s* of Charles Henry and Isobel Judd; *m* 1927, Helen Osborn Ashcroft, *d* of Rev. Dr Frank Ashcroft, Edinburgh; two *s* one *d. Educ:* Farnham Gram. Sch.; University Coll., London. Served European War, 1914-18: RAMC, Western Front and Italy. Hon. Sec., Nat. Union of Students, 1922-23. League of Nations Union: Sec. British Univs. League of Nations Soc. from formation, 1924-29; Chief Educn Officer, 1929-39; Asst Sec., 1939-43; Sec. and Dir-Gen, 1943-65. Hon. Sec. Geneva Inst. of Internat. Relations, 1929-39; London Internat. Assembly, 1940-45. Part founder and Sec., Coun. for Educn in World Citizenship, 1939-45. World Fedn of United Nations Associations: Mem. Exec. Cttee, 1946-66; Chm., 1955-57; missions to USA, China, India, SE Asia and West Africa. *Publications:* Assault at Arms (with Sir Ronald Adam), 1960; pamphlets and articles on UN affairs. *Recreations:* walking and travelling. *Address:* 42 The Crescent, Belmont, Sutton, Surrey. *T:* 01-642 5017. *Club:* English-Speaking Union.
[*Died* 19 *Feb.* 1974.

JUDE, Sir Norman (Lane), Kt 1965; JP; Member of Legislative Council, Southern District, South Australia, 1944-71; *b* 7 April 1905; *o s* of Alexander and Susan Jude, Moseley, Birmingham, Eng.; *m* 1935, Nancy M., *d* of Keith Bowman, Poltalloch, S Aust.; one *s* three *d. Educ:* Stamford Sch., Lincs; Roseworthy Agricultural Coll., SA. Dipl. of Roseworthy Agric. Coll. (RDA). Took up land at Carolside, Naracoorte, SA, as fat lamb and baby beef producer, 1936; mem. Council of SA Stockowners Association, 1938-40. Founded and became first Pres. of SE Fire-Fighting Assoc. Minister of Railways, Minister of Roads and Minister of Local Government, 1953-65; Mem. Aust. Transport Advisory Council, 1953-65; former mem. Subordinate Legislation Cttee. Company Dir. Pres., Aust. Road Fedn, SA Branch. *Recreations:* field shooting, interstate hockey and Rugby football (Pres. SA Rugby Union). *Address:* Robin Hill, 109 North-East Road, Collinswood, S Australia 5081, Australia. *T:* Adelaide 44-6000. *Clubs:* Adelaide, Royal Adelaide Golf, Amateur Sports of SA (Patron), Stock Exchange, Tattersall's (Adelaide).
[*Died* 18 *Feb.* 1975.

JUDGES, Arthur Valentine, DSc (London); Emeritus Professor, University of London; Fellow of King's College, University of London, since 1957; *b* 14 Feb. 1898; 2nd *s* of late Rev. William Worthington Judges, and late Caroline Susan Judges (*née* Lang); *m* 1927, Kathleen Mitchell, *e d* of late Francis Voltaire Mitchell; two *d. Educ:* St Felix Sch., Felixstowe; Southend-on-Sea High Sch.; King's Coll., London; London Sch. of Economics and Political Science. Served European War, with London Rifle Brigade, Machine-Gun Corps and Tank Corps, 1915-18; Lecturer, London Sch. of Economics and Political Science, 1927-38; Hon. Sec., Council for Preservation of Business Archives, 1934-38; Leverhulme Research Fellow in USA and Canada, 1938-39; Reader in Economic History, University of London, 1938-48; Joint Dir of Royal Historical Society, 1938-45; Ministry of Labour and National Service, 1940-44; Labour Adviser and Asst Sec., Ministry of Production, 1944-45; pt-time mem. of Cabinet Office staff, 1945-53; Professor of the History of Education, King's Coll., London, 1949-65; mem. of Central Advisory Council for Educn in England, 1951-60. Chairman: Editorial Bd, Brit. Jl of Educational Studies, 1952-61; Standing Conference on Studies in Education, 1955-61; Conference of Heads of University Depts of Education, 1959-64; Royal Commission on Education in S Rhodesia, 1962-63. Lecturer, Goldsmiths' Coll., 1965-71. *Publications:* books and articles on historical and educational subjects. *Address:* Oliver House, Strand-on-the-Green, W4. *T:* 01-994 1122. *Club:* Athenæum.
[*Died* 13 *Feb.* 1973.

JULIAN, Sir (Kenneth) Ivor, Kt 1958; CBE 1950; Chairman, South-East Metropolitan Regional Hospital Board, 1946-68, retired; *b* 3 Dec. 1895; *s* of late Henry Matthew Julian, Basingstoke, Hants, and late Elizabeth Isabella McKay, Aberdeenshire; *m* 1936, Rosemary Staunton (*d* 1971), *d* of late Charles Edgar Terry and late Virginia Constance Terry, Hove; no *c. Educ:* St Anne's Sch., Redhill. Served War of 1914-18 (Army). Chm., Royal Sussex County Hospital, Brighton, 1946-48; Dir of several Companies. Mem. of Bd of Governors of Guy's Hosp. *Recreations:* golf, tennis. *Address:* 4 Ash Close, Dyke Road Avenue, Hove, Sussex. *T:* Brighton 52852. *Club:* Brooks's.
[*Died* 29 *March* 1971.

JULYAN, Lt-Col (retd) William Leopold, TD; MA Oxon; JP; *b* 7 Dec. 1888; *e s* of Benjamin and Emma Jane Julyan, St Austell, Cornwall; *m* Marie Eileen Phyllis Bennett, LRAM. *Educ:* School of Rural Economy, Oxford; University Coll. Oxford. Distinction in Final Schools of Agriculture and Rural Economy. Served in France and Flanders during European War 1914-18, as Subaltern and Capt. on regimental duties, and as Major and Lt-Col on the Administrative Staff (despatches twice); Lt-Col,

Duke of Cornwall's Light Infantry, Territorial Army (retired); employed on staff duties during the war to 1945; commanding 8 Devon/Cornwall HG, 1953-57. Mem. of Gray's Inn, Inns of Court; travelled East African Dependencies and South Africa, 1931, to study agricultural and educational conditions. Warden of the Lord Wandsworth Agricultural Coll., 1922-45; Lecturer for Central Office of Information and for Imperial Institute. Leverhulme Research award, 1952-53. *Publications:* contributions to Educational and Agricultural Journals from time to time. *Recreations:* seeing rural England, interest in bygones of the farm and countryside and rural crafts. *Address:* Cotehele House, St Dominic, Cornwall. *Club:* Royal Commonwealth Society (Life Member). [*Died* 19 *Feb.* 1972.

JUSTICE, James Robertson; *see* Robertson-Justice.

K

KAHN-FREUND, Sir Otto, Kt 1976; FBA 1965; QC 1972; Professor of Comparative Law, University of Oxford, 1964-71; Emeritus Fellow, Brasenose College, 1971; *b* 17 Nov. 1900; *s* of Richard and Carrie Kahn-Freund; *m* 1931, Elisabeth (*née* Klaiss); one *d. Educ:* Goethe-Gymnasium, Frankfurt-am-Main; Universities of Frankfurt, Heidelberg, Leipzig, London. Doctor of Laws (Frankfurt) 1925, Master of Laws (London) 1935. Judge in German Courts, 1928-33. Barrister-at-Law (Middle Temple), 1936-; Hon. Bencher, Middle Temple, 1969. Asst Lecturer, Lecturer, and Reader in Law, 1935-61, Professor of Law, 1951-64, LSE. Arthur Goodhart Prof. of Legal Sci., and Professorial Fellow, Cambridge University, 1975-76; Hon. Fellow, Trinity Hall, Cambridge, 1977. Co-editor, Modern Law Review; Hon. Pres., Internat. Soc. for Labour Law and Social Legislation; Mem., Royal Commission on Trade Unions and Employers' Assocs, 1965-68. Doctor of Laws (*hc*): Bonn, 1968; Stockholm, 1969; Brussels, 1969; Paris, 1972; Leicester, 1973; Leuven, 1974; York (Canada), 1975; Cambridge, 1977. *Publications:* Law of Carriage by Inland Transport, 4th edn, 1965; (Co-editor) Dicey and Morris, Conflict of Laws, 9th edn 1973; English edn of Renner, Institutions of Private Law and their Social Functions, 1949; Co-author, The System of Industrial Relations in Great Britain, 1954; Co-author, Matrimonial Property Law, 1955; Co-author, Law and Opinion in England in the 20th Century, 1959; The Growth of Internationalism in English Private International Law, 1960; Labor Law and Social Security in: American Enterprise in the Common Market, 1960; Delictual Liability and the Conflict of Laws, 1968; Labour and the Law (Hamlyn Lectures), 1972, 2nd edn 1977; (jtly) A Source-Book on French Law, 1973, 2nd edn 1979; General Problems of Private International Law, 1975; Selected Writings, 1978; Labour Relations: Heritage and Adjustment (Thank-Offering to British Fund Lectures 1978), 1979; numerous articles and notes in legal periodicals. *Recreations:* reading and walking. *Address:* Roundabouts, Shottermill, Haslemere, Surrey GU27 3PP. *T:* Haslemere 3774. *Club:* Athenæum. [*Died* 16 *Aug.* 1979.

KALERGI, R. N.; *see* Coudenhove-Kalergi.

KAPP, Edmond Xavier; artist; *b* London, 5 Nov. 1890; *s* of late E. B. Kapp, London and Bella Wolff, New York; *m* 1st, 1922, Yvonne Cloud, writer; one *d* ; 2nd, 1932, Polia Chentoff, artist (*d* 1933); 3rd, 1950, Patricia Greene, writer. *Educ:* Owen's Sch., London; Paris; Berlin University; Christ's Coll., Cambridge (Scholar). BA. Served European War, 1914-19, BEF France; Lieut Royal Sussex Regt; Staff Capt. Spec. Appt Intelligence GHQ (M in D); first one-man shows of drawings and caricatures, Cambridge, 1912, London, 1919; Chief Master in painting, Maurice Sterne, Rome 1922-23; subseq. Exhibitions of paintings, drawings, lithographs at the Leicester Galleries and Wildenstein Gall., London; Brighton; Bath; Birmingham; Manchester; Bradford; Newcastle; Buffalo, USA; Toronto, Canada; UNESCO, Paris; Geneva; Monte Carlo, Milan, etc; Picasso sits for portrait and lithograph, 1938; represented in National Gallery Exhibition (British Art since Whistler), 1945; invited to exhibit *hors concours* 1st French Biennale Internat., Menton, 1951; Wakefield, York, Harrogate, 1957; invited by Whitechapel Art Gallery, London, to hold 50-year Retrospective Exhibition of paintings and drawings, 1961; Bear Lane Gallery (abstract paintings only), Oxford, 1962; Royal Festival Hall, 1968. Music into Art Programme, BBC TV, 1968. Works acquired by: British Museum; Victoria and Albert Museum; National Portrait Gallery; Imperial War Museum;

London Museum; S London Art Gallery, Camberwell; Contemporary Art Soc., London; Perth Museum and Art Gallery, WA; Yale Law Sch. Library, USA (legal portraits as stained-glass windows); Bibliothèque Nationale, Paris; Tel-Aviv Gallery, Israel; Palais de la Paix, Geneva; Fitzwilliam Museum, Cambridge; Ashmolean, Oxford; Manchester; Whitworth (Manchester); Leeds; Birmingham; Bradford; Wakefield; Kettle's Yard Museum of Modern Art, Cambridge; and other provincial galleries; 240 drawings acquired by Barber Inst. of Fine Arts, Birmingham, 1969; also in private collections made by Samuel Courtauld, Lord Clark, Sacha Guitry, Sir Hugh Walpole, Daniel de Pass, Jim Ede, Lord Goodman, etc.; 70 drawings, commnd by the London Philharmonic Orchestra, 1943, and exhibited London and provincial city Art Galleries. The Nations at Geneva, 1934-35, series of twenty-five portraits on the stone, commissioned by British Museum and Nat. Portrait Gallery and acquired for other collections; complete set of Original Lithographs acquired by Buffalo City (Albright) Art Gallery (USA), 1939. Commissioned as Official War Artist, 1940; as Official Artist to UNESCO, Paris, 1946-47 (20 portrait-drawings). Commissioned to make 8 portraits for Gonville and Caius and Christ's Colls., Cambridge and Merton Coll., Oxford, 1965-66, and Provost Lord Caccia for Eton College, 1975. Since 1960, apart from occasional portraits his painting has been exclusively abstract. *Publications:* Personalities, Twenty-four Drawings (Secker, 1919); Reflections, Twenty-four Drawings (Cape, 1922); Ten Great Lawyers (plates in colour), (Butterworth, 1924); Minims. Twenty-eight Abstract Drawings; with Yvonne Cloud, Pastiche: A Music-Room Book (Faber, 1925 and 1926); his work is reproduced in: Modern Drawings (by Campbell Dodgson); History of Caricature (by Bohun Lynch); Encycl. Britannica (XIII edn); From Sickert to 1948 (by John Russell); Things New and Old (by Max Beerbohm); Modern Caricaturists (by H. R. Westwood), etc. *Recreations:* music and nonsense. *Address:* 2 Steele's Studios, Haverstock Hill, NW3 4RN. *T:* 01-722 3174.   [*Died 29 Oct. 1978.*

KAPP, Helen; Director, Abbot Hall, Kendal, 1961-67, retired; *b* London, 17 Dec. 1901; *d* of late E. B. Kapp, London, and Bella Wolff, New York. *Educ:* Maria Grey Sch.; Slade Sch. of Art; University Coll., London; Paris. Painter and illustrator; one-man shows; London, 1939; Haifa, 1946; Wakefield, 1954; Guide-Lecturer for Arts Council (CEMA) 1940-45; Lecturer for War Office, 1946-48; Lecturer, Extra Mural Dept, London Univ., 1948-51; Dir City Art Gallery and Museum, Wakefield, 1951-61. *Publications:* Illustrated: (with Gerald Bullett) Seed of Israel, 1929; (with John Collier) The Scandal and Credulities of John Aubrey, 1931; (with E. S. Rohde): Vegetable Cultivation and Cookery, 1938; Rose Recipes, 1939; (with Basil Collier): Take 40 Eggs, 1938; Catalan France, 1939; (with Harold Morland) Satires and Fables, 1945; Toying with a Fancy, 1950; Wrote: Enjoying Pictures, 1975. *Recreations:* music, conversation and idleness. *Address:* 17 Carr Avenue, Leiston, Suffolk IP16 4JA. *T:* Leiston 830010.   [*Died 13 Oct. 1978.*

KARMINSKI, Rt. Hon. Sir Seymour Edward, PC 1967; Kt 1951; a Lord Justice of Appeal, 1969-73; *b* 28 Sept. 1902; *s* of Eugène and Rita Karminski, 82 Portland Place, W1, and Frinton-on-Sea, Essex; *m* 1927, Susan Elizabeth Burney; two *d*. *Educ:* Rugby; Christ Church, Oxford. BA 1923 (1st Class Modern History); MA. Called to Bar, Inner Temple, 1925; Master of the Bench, 1951; Reader, 1971; Treas., 1973. KC 1945; Judge of the High Court of Justice (Probate, Divorce and Admiralty Div.), 1951-69. Joined RNVR 1940; Lieut-Cdr 1943. *Recreations:* golf, fishing. *Address:* 32 Abingdon Court, Abingdon Villas, W8 6BT. *T:* 01-937 7613; Lyncewood, Easton, Woodbridge, Suffolk. *T:* Wickham Market 402. *Club:* Garrick.   [*Died 29 Oct. 1974.*

KARRER, Paul; DrPhil; Professor of Chemistry, University of Zürich, since 1918; Director of Chemical Institute, Zürich, since 1919; *b* Moscow, 21 April 1889; *s* of Paul Karrer and Julie Lerch; *m* 1914, Helena Froelich; two *s*. *Educ:* Wildegg; Lenzburg, Aarau; University of Zürich (DrPhil). Asst, Chemical Institute, University of Zürich, 1911-12; Chemist, Georg-Speyer-Haus, Frankfurt-am-Main, 1912-18. Member, numerous socs and academies, etc. Marcel Benoist Prize (Switzerland); Cannizzaro Prize (Rome); Nobel Prize for Chemistry, 1937. DrMed *hc*; DrPharm *hc*; DrPhil *hc*; Dr rer nat *hc*. *Publications:* Zahlreiche wissenschaftliche Abhandlungen über Kohle hydrate, Alkaloide, Lecithine, Anthocyanidine und insbesondere über Carotinoide, Vitamine (Vit. A, B2, E, K, B1), über Cofermente (Codehydrasen, gelbes Coferment, Codecarboxylase), und Alkaloide (curare); Lehrbuch der organischen Chemie (erschienen in deutscher, englischer, italienischer, französischer, spanischer und japanischer Sprache, 15 Auflagen); Monographie über Carotinoide, 1948. *Address:* Spyristeig 30, Zurich, Switzerland. *T:* Zürich 28.11.20.
          [*Died 18 June 1971.*

KARSAVINA, Tamara, (Mrs H. J. Bruce); President of the Licentiate Club of the Royal Academy of Dancing, since 1954; *b* 10 March 1885; *d* of Platon Karsavin and Anna (*née* Khomiakova); *m* 1915, H. J. Bruce; one *s*. *Educ:* Imperial Theatre Sch., St Petersburgh, Russia. Artist of the Marinsky Theatre, St Petersburgh, 1902-19, Prima Ballerina: Leading Dancer of Ballets Russes of Serge Diaghilev, 1909-22; guest artist, 1923-29. First London appearance (under name of Tamara Karsavina), in Divertissement, Coliseum, 1909; Armide, in Le Pavillon d'Armide, at first appearance of Imperial Russian Ballet at Covent Garden, 1911; in subsequent years danced frequently in England. Is resident in London. Fellow, Royal Acad. of Dancing. Gold Medal of Order of St Vladimir; Order of the Red Cross; Palmes Académiques; Order of the Emir of Bokhara. Holder of Royal Academy of Dancing Coronation Award for 1954. *Publications:* Theatre Street, 1930; Ballet Technique, 1956; Flow of Movement, 1962. *Recreations:* gardening, interior decoration.   [*Died 26 May 1978.*

KÄSTNER, Erich, Dr phil; *b* Dresden, 23 Feb. 1899. *Educ:* Universities of Leipzig, Rostock, Berlin. *Publications:* novels: Fabian, 1931 (Eng. trans. Fabian); Drei Männer im Schnee, 1934 (Eng. trans., Three Men in the Snow); Die verschwundene Miniatur, 1935 (Eng. trans. The Missing Miniature); Der kleine Grenzverkehr, 1938 (Eng. trans. A Salzburg Comedy); Notabene 45, 1961; *juvenile novels:* Emil und die Detektive, 1928 (Eng. trans. Emil and the Detectives); Pünktchen und Anton, 1931 (Eng. trans. Anneluise and Anton); Der 35. Mai, 1931 (Eng. trans. The 35th May); Das fliegende Klassenzimmer, 1933 (Eng. trans. The Flying Classroom); Emil und die drei Zwillinge, 1934 (Eng. trans. Emil and the Three Twins); Konferenz der Tiere, 1949 (Eng. trans. The Animals' Conference); Das doppelte Lottchen, 1949 (Eng. trans. Lottie and Lisa); Das Schwein beim Friseur, 1962; Der Kleine Mann, 1963 (English trans. The Little Man); Der Kleine Mann und die kleine Miss, 1967; *he retold:* Till Eulenspiegel, 1938 (Eng. trans. Till the Jester); Der gestiefelte Kater, 1950 (Eng. trans. Puss in Boots); Münchhausen, 1951 (Eng. trans. Baron Münchhausen); Die Schildbürger, 1954 (Eng. trans. The Simpleton); Don Quichotte, 1956 (Eng. trans. Don Quixote); Gullivers Reisen, 1961; *volumes of poems:* Herz auf Taille, 1928; Lärm im Spiegel, 1929; Ein Mann gibt Auskunft, 1930; Gesang zwischen den Stühlen, 1932; Dr Erich Kästners lyrische Hausapotheke, 1936; Kurz und bündig, Epigramme, 1948; Bei Durchsicht meiner Bücher, 1946; Die dreizehn Monate, 1955; Eine Auswahl, 1956; Probepackung, 1957; (selection, Eng. trans.) Let's Face It, 1963; *juvenile poetry:* Arthur mit dem langen Arm, 1932; Das verhexte Telefon, 1932; *essays:* Der tägliche Kram, 1948; Die kleine Freiheit, 1952; Kästner für Erwachsene, 1966; *plays:* Emil und die Detektive, 1930; Pünktchen und Anton 1932; Zu treuen Händen, 1948; Die Schule der Diktatoren, 1956; *biography:* Als ich ein kleiner Junge war, 1957 (Eng. trans. When I was a Little Boy); *other works:* Gesammelte Schriften, 1959; Gesammelte Schriften für Erwachsene, 1969; Friedrich der Grosse und die deutsche Literatur, 1972. *Address:* Flemingstr. 52, Munich 81, Germany.   [*Died 29 July 1974.*

KATENGA, Bridger Winston; Malaŵi Independence Medal, 1964; Malaŵi Republic Medal, 1966; High Commissioner for Malaŵi in Kenya, since 1972; *b* 20 June 1926; *m* 1956, Nomsa Seraphine; four *s* three *d*. *Educ:* Jan Hofmeyr Sch. of Social Work, Johannesburg (Dip. in Social Welfare); La Salle Extension Univ. (LLB); Chicago. Social Worker, 1951-64; Ambassador in Addis Ababa, New York and Bonn (W Germany), 1964-69; High Comr in London, 1970-72; Ambassador to Belgium, The Netherlands, Portugal and the Holy See, 1970-72; Minister of Community Development and Social Welfare, Malaŵi, 1972. *Recreations:* reading, draughts, billiards. *Address:* Malaŵi High Commission, PO Box 30453, Nairobi, Kenya.   [*Died 11 April 1975.*

KATER, Sir Gregory (Blaxland), Kt 1974; CEng; Chairman, The Commercial Banking Company of Sydney Ltd, Australia; *b* 15 May 1912; *s* of late Hon. Sir Norman William Kater; *m* 1937, Catherine Mary Ferris-Scott; two *s* one *d*. *Educ:* The King's Sch., Sydney, Aust.; Cambridge Univ., Eng. (MA). Chartered Electrical Engineer; Grazier. Chairman: Electrical Equipment of Australia Ltd, 1939; Mercantile & General Reinsurance Co. of Aust. Ltd and Mercantile & General Life Reassurance Co. of Aust. Ltd, both 1957; Oil Search Ltd (Dir 1950, Chm. 1957); Permanent Trustee Co. Ltd (Dir 1951, Chm. 1956); Metal Manufactures Ltd (Dir, 1963, Chm. 1976); CSR Ltd (Dir 1949). Director: H. E. Kater & Son Pty Ltd, Merino Stud, 1948; Vickers Australia Ltd, 1965; Vickers Cockatoo Docks Pty Ltd, 1972; W. R. Carpenter Holdings Ltd, 1970. Vice-Pres., NSW Soc. for Crippled Children, 1950. Liveryman, Worshipful Co. of Broderers, London. *Recreation:* golf. *Address:* 106 Victoria Road, Bellevue Hill, NSW 2023, Australia. *T:* 36 7295. *Clubs:*

Carlton; Australian, Royal Sydney Golf, Union (all of Sydney, Aust.). *[Died 9 July 1978.*

KATZ, Mindru; concert pianist; *b* 3 June 1925; *s* of Bernard Katz and Olga Avramescu; single. *Educ:* Bucharest Royal Academy of Music (under Florica Musicescu). Gave first public recital, 1931; first concert with Bucharest Philharmonic Orchestra, 1947. Subsequently, concert tours in all the continents. Has made numerous recordings. Prizewinner, International Piano Competitions, Berlin, Prague, 1951 and Bucharest, 1953. Emeritus Artist, Rumania, 1953; First Class State Prize, Rumanian People's Republic, 1954. *Recreations:* mountaineering, chess, films, drawing. *Address:* c/o Ibbs & Tillett, 124 Wigmore Street, W1H OAX; 45 Hanassi Street, Nof-Yam, Israel. *T:* 932415. *[Died 30 Jan. 1978.*

KAY, Herbert Davenport, CBE 1946 (OBE (mil.) 1919); DSc Manchester, PhD Cantab; FRS 1945; Professor Emeritus, University of Reading; *b* Heaton Chapel, Lancs, 1893; *s* of John Kay and Ellen (*née* Davenport); *m* 1925, Beatrice, *e d* of William Lee, York; four *s. Educ:* Manchester Gram. Sch.; Universities of Manchester (University Scholar, 1914), London, Cambridge, Freiburg i/B. Served European War, 1914-18 (wounded, despatches, OBE). Beit Memorial Fellow, 1922; Senior Beit Fellow, 1925; Biochemist, London Hosp., 1925; Prof. of Biochemistry, University of Toronto, 1931; Research Prof. of Biochemistry, University of Reading and Dir National Institute for Research in Dairying, 1933-58; Dir, Twyford Laboratories Ltd, 1959-62. Pres., Section M, British Assoc., 1950; Pres., Studies Commission, Internat. Dairy Fedn, 1950-57. Gold Medallist, Society of Dairy Technology, 1957. Hon. Sec., Biochemical Soc., 1927-29; Vice-Pres., Soc. of Chem. Industry, 1957-60; Hon. Member: Soc. of Applied Bacteriology; Soc. of Dairy Technology (Founder Pres., 1943-44); Royal Agricultural Society; Hon. Fellow, Inst. of Food Science and Technology. Consultant, FAO. *Publications:* papers in scientific and technical journals. *Recreations:* walking, gardening. *Address:* 39 St Peter's Avenue, Caversham, Reading RG4 7DH. *T:* Reading 474502. *Club:* Athenæum. *[Died 24 Nov. 1976.*

KAY, Sydney Entwisle, CBE 1948 (MBE 1918); *b* 18 July 1888. *Educ:* Sutton Valence Sch.; Emmanuel Coll., Cambridge (First Class Hons Mediæval and Modern Languages Tripos). Vice-Consul in Consular Service, 1911; Consul at Stockholm, 1920; Consul-General: Lourenço Marques, 1933-39; Milan, 1939-40; Commercial Counsellor, Lisbon, 1940; Consul-Gen. at Marseilles, 1944; retired, 1948. *Address:* Résidence Leclos de Cimiez, Bloc D2, 31 avenue Cap de Croix, 06 Nice, France. *[Died 31 Sept. 1978.*

KAY, Very Rev. William, DSO 1919; MC, MA; Provost of Blackburn Cathedral, 1936-61; *b* 1894; *e s* of William Henry Kay, Withnell, Chorley, Lancs; *m* Helen Nora (*d* 1974), *d* of late Edgar Brierley, Sandfield, Rochdale; four *d. Educ:* Hatfield Coll.; Durham Univ. Late 1st Batt. The Grenadier Guards, and 2nd Batt. The Manchester Regt. (MC and two bars, DSO); Vicar of Cresswell, Derbyshire, 1922-28; Rural Dean of Bolsover, 1928; Rector of Whitwell with Steetley, 1928-29; Vicar of Newark, 1929-36; Hon. Canon of Southwell, 1932-36; Rural Dean of Newark, 1933-36. *Address:* Woodruffe, Brockenhurst, Hants. *T:* 2196. *[Died 6 Jan. 1980.*

KAYE, Ven. Martin; Archdeacon of Craven since 1972; *b* 15 May 1919; *s* of late Dr Henry Wynyard Kaye and late Amy Kaye; unmarried. *Educ:* Winchester; Christ Church, Oxford (BA 1941, MA 1944); Cuddesdon Theological College. Deacon 1948; priest 1949. Served in RASC (Major), 1940-46 (despatches). Curate of St Aidan's, Grangetown, Sunderland, 1948-50; Tutor and Chaplain of Cuddesdon College, 1950-55; Domestic Chaplain to Archbishop of York, 1956-60; Asst Secretary of Central Advisory Council for the Ministry, 1961-67; Canon Residentiary of Norwich Cathedral, and Examining Chaplain to Bishop of Norwich, 1967-72. *Recreations:* gardening, sailing. *Address:* Rathmell Vicarage, Settle, N Yorks BD24 0LA. *T:* Long Preston 385. *Club:* Royal Commonwealth Society. *[Died 16 June 1977.*

KAZANJIAN, Varaztad Hovhannes, CMG 1918; oral and plastic surgeon; retired; Professor Emeritus of Plastic Surgery, Harvard, USA, 1947; Senior Consulting Surgeon: Massachusetts Eye and Ear Infirmary; Massachusetts General Hospital; Boston City Hospital; New England Deaconess Hospital; Mount Auburn Hospital; Beth Israel Hospital and others; *b* Armenia, 18 March 1879; *s* of Hovhannes and Anna Kazanjian; *m* 1923, Marion V. Hanford; one *s* two *d. Educ:* Harvard Univ. (DMD 1905; MD 1921). Member, Harvard Unit Brit. Expeditionary Force, 1915-19; served as Major and surg. specialist for wounds of jaws and face (despatches thrice). Member: State and

National Medical and Dental Soc.; Amer. Assoc. Plastic Surgeons (Past Pres.); Amer. Assoc. Plastic and Reconstructive Surgery; American Assoc. of Maxillofacial Surgery (Past Pres.); Amer. Acad. of Ophthalmology and Otolaryngology; Amer. Soc. Oral Surgeons (Past Pres.); Fellow, Amer. Coll. of Surgeons; Internat. Soc. of Surgeons; Boston Surgical Soc. Diplomate, Board of Plastic Surgery. DSc (Hon.) Bowdoin, 1952; Hon. Member: Hellenic Soc. of Oral Surgery, Athens, Greece, 1959; British Assoc. of Plastic Surgeons, 1966; Hon. Fellow in Dental Surgery, RCPGlas, 1967. New York University Presidential Citation, 1962. *Publications:* The Surgical Treatment of Facial Injuries (with J. M. Converse, MD); numerous articles on plastic and reconstructive surgery and prosthetic restoration of the face and jaws. *Address:* 191 Clifton Street, Belmont, Mass 02178, USA. *Clubs:* Harvard, Boston (Mass); Faculty (Cambridge, Mass).
[Died 19 Oct. 1974.

KEARTON, Prof. William Johnston, DEng, FIMechE, FRINA; Emeritus Professor, Liverpool University, since 1958; *b* 26 March 1893; *s* of Christopher and Dinah Kearton; *m* 1917, Janet Miller; one *d* decd. *Educ:* University of Liverpool. Commenced practical training with Vickers, Sons, and Maxim, at the Naval Construction Works, Barrow-in-Furness, 1909; Vickers Scholar, 1913. Lecturer in Engineering, Liverpool Univ., 1919-37; Senior Lecturer in Mechanical Engineering, Liverpool Univ., 1937-47; Dean of the Faculty of Engineering, Liverpool Univ., 1948-53; Harrison Prof. of Mechanical Engineering, Liverpool University, 1947-58, retd. *Publications:* Steam Turbine Theory and Practice, 1922; (Jt) Alignment Charts, 1924; Turbo-Blowers and Compressors, 1926; (Joint) Turbo-Gebläse und Kompressoren, 1929; Steam Turbine Operation, 1931; papers in Proc. Inst. of Mech. Engineers. *Recreations:* various. *Address:* 32 Popples Drive, Illingworth, Halifax, W Yorks. *T:* Halifax 246273. *[Died 29 May 1978.*

KEATING, John, (Seän Céitinn); RHA; Hon. RA; Hon. RSA; Painter; *b* Limerick, 29 Sept. 1889; *s* of Joseph Keating and Anne Hannan; *m* 1919, May, *d* of John Walsh, Eadstown, County Kildare; two *s. Educ:* St Munchin's Coll., Limerick. At twenty went to Dublin, having won a Scholarship in Art at the Dublin Metropolitan Sch. of Art; spent four years in Aran, off the west coast of Ireland; came back to Dublin and won the Taylor Scholarship in Painting; worked with Sir William Orpen in London until 1916; returned to Ireland in that year. *Recreations:* reading and idling. *Address:* Ait an Cuain, Ballyboden Road, Rathfarnham, Co. Dublin. *T:* 904957.
[Died 21 Dec. 1977.

KEATING, Paul John Geoffrey; Permanent Representative of Ireland to the United Nations, since 1978; *b* 13 Aug. 1924; *s* of Joseph Hannan Keating and Mary Mercedes Joyce; *m* 1952, Teresa McGowan; one *s* one *d. Educ:* Presentation Coll., Glasthule; Trinity Coll., Dublin; Sorbonne, Paris. Entered Irish Foreign Service as Third Sec., 1949; Vice-Consul, New York, 1951; Sec., Irish Mission to UN, 1956; First Secretary: Dublin, 1960; London, 1962; Counsellor, London, 1964; Chief of Protocol, Dublin, 1967; Ambassador: Lagos, 1968; Bonn, 1970; Asst Sec. and Political Dir, Dept of Foreign Affairs, Dublin, 1972; Dep. Sec., 1973; Sec., 1974; Ambassador, Court of St James's, 1977-78. Grand Officer, Order of Leopold II, Belgium, 1968. *Address:* Permanent Mission of Ireland to the UN, I Dag Hammarskjold Plaza, 885 Second Avenue, 19th Floor, New York, NY 10017, USA. *Clubs:* Garrick; Kildare Street and University (Dublin). *[Died 13 March 1980.*

KEAY, Sir Lancelot Herman, KBE 1947 (OBE 1934); MArch Liverpool; City Architect and Director of Housing, Liverpool, 1925-48; *b* 3 Aug. 1883; 2nd *s* of late Henry William Keay, JP, Elms-Meade, Eastbourne; *m* 1920, Iris, *er d* of late E. G. Stone, Clifton, Guernsey; two *d. Educ:* Eastbourne Coll.; Brighton Sch. of Art. Held architectural appointments at Norwich and under Corporations of Birmingham and Liverpool; served in Royal Engineers during European War with 34th Div. in France and as CRE Kantara Area, Egypt; in Liverpool responsible for erection of over 35,000 houses and flats, and for effecting rebuilding of slum areas and for four re-development schemes comprising 850 acres in centre of City; Consultant, Sir Lancelot Keay and Partners; First Chairman: Bracknell New Town Development Corporation; Basildon New Town Development Corporation; Member: Housing Advisory Cttee, 1936-57; Advisory Council on Building and Civil Engineering Research and Development, 1947-57. Past Pres. RIBA, 1946-48. *Publications:* Frequent contributor to Technical Journals. *Address:* 22 Hyde Park Gardens, W2 2LY. *Clubs:* Athenæum, Arts.
[Died 2 Nov. 1974.

KEEL, Jonathan Edgar, CB 1956; retired; *b* 21 Feb. 1895; *s* of Wm Keel, JP and Elizabeth Keel; *m* 1927, Olga Constance Pointing (*d* 1975); one *s*. *Educ:* Middlesbrough High Sch. Inland Revenue as second division clerk, 1912; transferred to Tax Dept as Surveyor of Taxes, 1916; transferred to Air Ministry with rank of Principal, 1938; went to USA as Dir of Finance and Administration of British Air Commission, 1940; Asst Sec., 1941; Ministry of Aircraft Production, 1944; Min. of Civil Aviation, 1946; Under Sec., 1948; in charge of Safety and General Dept, 1948-53; UK Rep. on Coun. of Internat. Civil Aviation Org., Montreal, 1953-57; retd from Public Service, 1957. *Recreations:* horse racing by television, reading, cooking. *Address:* 5 Redcroft Walk, Cranleigh, Surrey. *T:* Cranleigh 3282. *[Died 11 April 1979.*

KEELING, (Cyril) Desmond (Evans), CB 1977; Secretary to the Price Commission, 1975-78; *b* 13 April 1921; *s* of late Cyril F. J. Keeling, MC, and Susan Evans Keeling; *m* 1947, Megan Miles; one *d*. *Educ:* Southend High Sch., Peterhouse, Cambridge. Parts I and II, Economics, Cambridge, 1939-41 and 1945-46. Served 1941-45 in Infantry (wounded, despatches): Adjutant 5th Bn Wilts Regt, 1944-45. Research, LSE, 1946; Ministry of Works, 1947; Asst Sec., 1960; Dir, Treasury Centre for Administrative Studies, 1963-65; Under-Sec., Treasury, and Dir of Training, 1965-68; Under-Sec., Civil Service Dept, 1968-69, MAFF, 1970-74; Dep. Sec., 1975. Fellow-Commoner, Emmanuel Coll., Cambridge, Michaelmas 1969; Study at London Graduate Business Sch., 1970. Chm. Council, RIPA, 1977-. *Publications:* Management in Government, 1972; articles in public administration journals. *Recreation:* gardening. *Address:* Headlong Hill, Stokesheath Road, Oxshott, Surrey. *T:* Oxshott 2616. *Club:* United Oxford & Cambridge University. *[Died 6 June 1979.*

KEELING, Edward Allis; *b* 1885; *m* 1920, Countess Magda Gaetani d'Aragona (*d* 1945), Rome. *Educ:* Eton; Christ Church, Oxford; Third Sec., Diplomatic Service, 1913-19; Second Sec., 1919-20; First Sec., 1920; Counsellor of Embassy, Brazil, 1931; Minister to Venezuela, 1932-36; British Consul-Gen. with rank of Minister at Tangier, 1936-39. *Address:* via Cadamosto 13, 00154 Rome, Italy. *Clubs:* Beefsteak, Pratt's; Circolo della Caccia (Rome). *[Died 17 Sept. 1975.*

KEELING, Sir John (Henry), Kt 1952; Director, Safeguard Industrial Investments Ltd, 1953-69 (Chairman, 1953-66); Vice-Chairman, Bowater Paper Corp. Ltd, 1945-67; Chairman, West Riding Worsted and Woollen Mills Ltd, 1944-62 (Director, 1962-68); *b* 18 Aug. 1895; *s* of John Henry Keeling and Mary, *d* of Edward P. Allis, Milwaukee, Wisconsin; *m* Dorothy *d* of Dr Morgan I. Finucane and Jane Sheridan; three *s* one *d*. *Educ:* Summerfields, St Leonards, and Oxford; Eton. Queen's Royal West Surrey Regt Territorials, 1914-18, when transferred to Coldstream Guards. In 1923 founded London and Yorkshire Trust Ltd (with Reginald E. Cornwall), past Dir and Chm., retd 1972. Min. of Aircraft Prod., 1940-45; Dep. Aircraft Distrib., 1943-45; Dep. Chm., BEA, 1947-65. *Address:* Hurst House, Sedlescombe, Sussex. *T:* 340; Grosvenor House, Park Lane, W1. *T:* 01-499 2987. *Club:* White's. *[Died 22 Nov. 1978.*

KEENE, Sir Charles (Robert), Kt 1969; CBE 1950; JP; Chairman, Kingstone Ltd; *b* 21 Sept. 1891; *s* of late Charles Edward Keene; *m* 1st, 1921, Ruth Stocks (*d* 1949); two *s* (one *s* decd); 2nd, 1952, Hetty Swann. Dep. Regional Comr (N Midland Region), 1941-44. Member, Leicester City Council, 1926-70: Alderman, 1945-70; Lord Mayor, 1953-54; Chairman: Town-Planning Cttee, 1942-53; Slum Clearance Cttee, 1952-62; Educn Cttee, 1953-62; High Bailiff, Leicester, 1935-36. Pro-Chancellor, Univ. of Leicester; Chairman: Governors of Leicester Colls of Art and Technology, 1927-69; City of Leicester Polytechnic, 1969-71 (Hon. Fellow 1970); Charles Keene Coll. of Further Education, 1961-70; Council of University of Leicester, 1928-72; Governors, Gateway Sch., 1928-68. JP Leicester 1940. Hon. Freeman, City of Leicester, 1962. Hon. LLD Leicester Univ., 1963. *Address:* Gaulby, Leicestershire. *T:* Billesdon 215. *[Died 26 July 1977.*

KEENE, Mary Frances Lucas, DSc, MB, BS (London); FRCS; Professor Emeritus in Anatomy, University of London; former Lecturer and Past President, Royal Free Hospital School of Medicine; Past President of the Medical Women's Federation; Past President of the Anatomical Society of Great Britain and Ireland; Vice-President, The Medical Protection Society; late Examiner in Anatomy, Universities of London and Bristol: Conjoint Board, England; University of South Wales, and to Royal College of Surgeons, England; *d* of late G. J. Lucas of Milton Court, near Gravesend; *m* 1916, Richard F. (*decd*), *s* of late Henry Keene. *Educ:* Eversley, Folkestone; London (RFH) School of Medicine for Women. Took Degree, London Univ.,

Bachelor of Medicine and Bachelor of Surgery, 1911; Lecturer in Embryology and Senior Demonstrator in Anatomy at above Medical School, 1914; Lecturer and Head of Department (same school), 1919. *Publications:* various papers in scientific journals. *Recreations:* gardening, reading, beginning painting. *Address:* Newhaven, The Droveway, St Margaret's Bay, Dover, Kent. *T:* Dover 852138. *[Died 9 May 1977.*

KEENE, Vice-Adm. Philip R.; *see* Ruck Keene.

KEEVIL, Colonel Sir Ambrose, KBE 1962 (CBE 1944; MBE 1918); Kt 1952; MC 1917 (Bar 1918); DL; President (formerly Chairman), Fitch Lovell Ltd and Chairman various other companies; *b* 1893; *s* of late Clement Keevil; *m* 1918, Dorothy Pearsall, *d* of Arthur Andrews, JP, Southfields, Ryde, I of W; one *s* one *d*. *Educ:* University College Sch.; France. Served European War, 1914-19, with Royal Munster Fusiliers; retired 1921. Chm. Wholesale Produce Merchants Assoc.; Pres. Metropolitan Market Clerks Benevolent Institution, 1934-36; Chm. London Provision Exchange, 1938-39; Chm. Albert & Victoria Hospital Aid Soc., 1938-40; Master Worshipful Co. of Poulters, 1938-39, 1958-59. Chm. Co-ord Cttee of Produce and Provision Exchanges of UK, 1938-41; Chm. London Area Cttee, Ministry of Food, 1939-42 and Chm. Co-ord. Cttee London, Southern, Eastern and South Eastern Areas, Min. of Food, 1941-42. Mil. Mem. Surrey T & AFA, 1940-50 and 1952-. Comdr Home Guard Sector of London Dist, 1942-45 and Surrey E Sector, 1952-55; Chm. E Surrey Conservative Assoc., 1945-51 (Pres. 1951-); Hon. Treas, Union of Cons. Assocs for Kent, Surrey and Sussex, 1947-60, Vice-Pres., 1960-; Vice-Chm. Cons. Central Board of Finance, 1953-61; Chm. Surrey Playing Fields Association, 1952-; Chairman of Governors: Reedham School, Purley, 1963-72, Pres. 1972; Moor Park Coll., 1964-72. President: East Surrey Horse Society and Hunter Trials, 1955-; Surrey Small Bore Rifle Association, 1965-68. Chairman: Surrey Rifle Association, 1967-69; Swinton Coll. Education Cttee, 1960-69; Springfield Group Hospital Management Cttee, 1964-68. Life Vice-Pres., Greater London Area Conservative Assoc. DL Surrey, 1944; High Sheriff, Surrey, 1956-57. Chevalier Ordre de Mérite Agricole (France), 1939; Chevalier Legion of Honour, 1956. *Publications:* John Bell-a man!; The Story of Fitch Lovell. *Recreations:* people, horses, and dogs. *Address:* Bayards, Warlingham, Surrey. *T:* Upper Warlingham 4256. *Clubs:* Bath, MCC, City Livery. *[Died 9 Feb. 1973.*

KEIGHTLEY, Gen. Sir Charles (Frederic), GCB 1953 (KCB 1950; CB 1943); GBE 1957 (KBE 1945; OBE 1941); DSO 1944; DL; President: British Legion South West Area and Dorset County; Vice-President, Royal Victoria Patriotic Fund Corporation; *b* 24 June 1901; *s* of late Rev. C. A. Keightley; *m* 1932, Joan Lydia, *d* of late Brig.-Gen. G. N. T. Smyth Osborne, CB, CMG, DSO, Ash, Iddesleigh, N Devon; two *s*. *Educ:* Marlborough Coll.; RMC, Sandhurst. 5th Dragoon Guards, 1921; served in Palestine, Egypt and India; Adjutant 5th Royal Inniskilling Dragoon Guards, 1930-33; Staff Coll., 1934-35; Staff Officer to Dir Gen., TA, 1936; Bde Major, Cairo Cav. Bde, 1937-38; Instructor Staff Coll., Camberley, 1938-40; Served War of 1939-45 (despatches thrice); AAQMG 1st Armoured Div. in France, 1940; Comd 30th Armd Bde, 1941-42; Comd 6th Armoured Div. in Tunisia, 1942-43; Comd 78th Div. in Italy, 1943-44; Comdg V Corps in Italy and Austria, 1944-45; DMT, War Office, 1946-47; Milit. Sec. to Sec. of State for War, 1948; C-in-C, BAOR, 1948-51; C-in-C Far East Land Forces, 1951-53; C-in-C, Middle East Land Forces, 1953-57; ADC Gen. to the Queen, 1953-56; Governor and C-in-C of Gibraltar, 1958-62. Kermit Roosevelt Lecturer to the USA, 1957. Col 5th Royal Inniskilling Dragoon Guards, 1947-57; Col Comdt, RAC (Cavalry Wing), 1958-68. DL Dorset, 1970. American Legion of Merit, 1942; Grand Officer, Legion of Honour, 1958. KStJ. *Recreations:* gardening, fishing, shooting. *Address:* White Kennels, Tarrant Gunville, Dorset. *Clubs:* Cavalry, Lansdowne. *[Died 17 June 1974.*

KEIGWIN, Richard Prescott, MA Cantab; *b* Colchester, 8 April 1883; 4th *s* of Charles David and Louisa Keigwin. *Educ:* Colet Court; Temple Grove; Clifton; Peterhouse, Cambridge (Classical Exhibitioner); France and Germany. Mod. Lang. master, Royal Naval Coll., Osborne; served European War, 1914-18, as Lieut RNVR (Belgian Order of Leopold); Editor, The Granta, 1919; housemaster at Clifton, 1920-35; Warden of Wills Hall, University of Bristol, 1935-45; President, Old Cliftonian Society, 1957-59. Danish Order of the Dannebrog; King Christian X's Frihedsmedaille; Hans Christian Andersen Prize, Copenhagen, 1964. *Publications:* Lanyard Lyrics; Lyrics for Sport; The Jutland Wind; Kaj Munk (some examples of his work); In Denmark I was born; new translations of Hans Andersen; Five Plays by Kaj Munk; English libretto of Carl Nielsen's Opera Saul and David; numerous other verse and prose translations from the Danish; contributions to periodicals in England, Denmark and America. *Recreations:* cricket, etc.; (represented Cambridge Univ. at cricket, rackets, hockey, Association football). *Address:* The Old Forge, Polstead, Suffolk. [*Died* 25 *Nov.* 1972.

KEILLER, Brian Edwin, CMG 1961; Farmer (dairy and pig), 1930-59; now retired; *b* Bulls, NZ, 18 July 1901; *s* of E. Keiller, Bulls, NZ, and Muriel Kathrine Waitt; *m* 1932, Helena Maude Harcourt; two *s* one *d. Educ:* Wanganui Collegiate Sch., Wanganui, NZ. Dep. Chm. from its inception of Nat. Pig Industry Council, also Chm. Wellington Dist Pig Council (15 yrs), retd, 1953; original Mem. NZ Horse Soc., 1951; Mem. Council, Royal Agric. Society, 1942- (Chm. 1945-52); represented NZ Meat Bd, 1949; Hon. Life Mem. Royal Agric. Society of England; Treas., Manawatu Agric. and Pastoral Assoc., 1951- (Mem., 1933, Chm., 1942-51). Mem. Wellington Harbour Bd, 1947- (Chm. 1957-61); Pres. Harbours Assoc. of NZ, 1957-61. Chairman: Watson Bros Ltd; Everyday Products Pty Co., 1966; Dir, Barnard and Abraham Ltd. Pres. Wanganui Old Boys' Assoc., 1951-55 (centenary, 1954); Governor: Massey Agric. Coll., 1954-63; Mem, Exec. Cttee, Nga Taura Girls' Sch., 1959- (former Chm.); Chm., Carnot Sch. for Girls, 1951-. Held various offices in Manawatu. War of 1939-45: Home Guard and Chm. Manawatu Primary Production Council. Coronation Medal, 1953. *Recreations:* golf (Chm. Greens Research Cttee of NZ Golf Council, retd 1956), ski-ing, fishing. *Address:* Atawhaiiti, 88 Te Awe Awe Street, Palmerston North, New Zealand. *T:* 80655. *Clubs:* Wellington, Wellington Racing (Life Mem.), Manawatu Racing (Life Mem.), Palmerston North. [*Died* 17 *Dec.* 1977.

KEIR, Sir David Lindsay, Kt 1946; MA Oxon; Hon. DCL Oxon; Hon. LLD Glasgow, Dublin, New Brunswick, Queen's, Kingston and Queen's, Belfast; Hon. DLitt Sussex; Hon. Fellow of University College, Balliol and New College, Oxford; Hon. FRIBA; *b* 22 May 1895; *er s* of Rev. William Keir; *m* 1930, Anna Clunie, *yr d* of R. J. Dale, Montreal; one *s* one *d. Educ:* Glasgow Univ.; New Coll., Oxford. Served in King's Own Scottish Borderers, 1915-19. Fellow, 1921-39, Dean, Estates Bursar, University Coll., Oxford; University Lecturer in English Constitutional History, 1931-39; Pres. and Vice-Chancellor, The Queen's Univ., Belfast, 1939-49; Master of Balliol Coll., Oxford, 1949-65. Exchange tutor, Harvard Univ., 1923-24; Donnellan Lecturer, Trinity Coll., Dublin, 1942; Vice-Pres., Ulster Soc. for Irish Historical Studies, 1942; Vice-Pres., NI Council for Orthopædic Development, 1949-; Pres. Scottish History Soc., 1958-62; Hon. Member: Royal Society of Ulster Architects; Oxfordshire Soc. of Architects. Trustee, R. V. Stanley's Match. *Publications:* Cases in Constitutional Law (with F. H. Lawson), 1928 (5th edn 1967); The Constitutional History of Modern Britain, 1938 (9th edn 1968). *Recreations:* sailing, walking, gardening. *Address:* Hillsborough, Boars Hill, Oxford. *T:* Oxford 35219. [*Died* 2 *Oct.* 1973.

KEIRSTEAD, Burton Seely; Professor of Economics, University of Toronto, 1954-72, retired; *b* 17 Nov. 1907; *s* of late Wilfred Currier Keirstead; *m* 1933, Marjorie Stella Brewer; one *s* one *d. Educ:* Fredericton Grammar Sch.; University of New Brunswick; Exeter Coll., Oxford (Rhodes Scholar, 1928). LLD hc University of NB, 1949. Prof. of Economics and Political Science, Univ. of New Brunswick, 1931-42; Visiting Professor at University of Arizona, 1937-38; McGill University: Bronfman Professor of Economics and Political Science, 1942-46; Dow Professor of Economics, 1946-54; Chairman, Dept. of Economics and Politics, 1947-50; Chairman, Social Sciences Group, 1951-54; represented Oxford v. Cambridge at ice-hockey, 1930. Fell. Roy. Soc. Canada; sometime mem., Bd of Editors, Canadian Journal of Economics and Political Science; Mem. Roy. Economic Soc., Canadian Economics Assoc.; sometime member Conseil Supérieur du Travail, Quebec; political commentator, Canadian Broadcasting Corporation. Hon. LLD, Mount Allison Univ., 1969. *Publications:* The Essentials of Price Theory, 1942; The Economic Effects of the War on the Maritime Provinces of Canada, 1944; The Theory of Economic Change, 1948 (Japanese edn 1955); An Essay on the Theory of Profits and Income Distribution, 1953; Canada in World Affairs, Vol. VII (1951-53), 1955; Capital, Interest and Profits, 1959 (Japanese edn 1972); The Canadian Economy: Selected Readings (ed with Deutsch, Levitt and Will), 1961 (2nd edn 1966); The Federal Shipping Service, 1962; contributions to Canada After the War (ed Brady and Scott), 1943; The British Commonwealth at War (ed Elliott and Hall), 1943; Expectations and Uncertainty in Economics (ed Carter and Ford), 1972; Encyclopédie Française, Tome IX, 1963; International Encyclopedia of the Social Sciences, 1967; Encyclopædia Britannica, 1971 edn; various articles on economic and political subjects, and some detective fiction and short stories.

Recreations: fishing, swimming. *Address:* Apt 1, 376 Connaught Street, Fredericton, NB, Canada; (winter) c/o Development Bank, Bridgetown, Barbados, West Indies. *Clubs:* Faculty (Montreal); Faculty (Toronto). [*Died* 5 *May* 1973.

KEKWICK, Alan, MA, MB, BCh, FRCP; Professor of Medicine, now Emeritus, University of London; Physician, Middlesex Hospital, W1; *b* 12 April 1909; 2nd *s* of John Kekwick and Catherine Lesslie Curror-Prain; *m* 1939; one *s*; *m* 1949, Elizabeth Dorothy Forster Shackleton; one *s* one *d. Educ:* Charterhouse Sch.; Emmanuel Coll., Cambridge; Middlesex Hosp. Medical Sch. Qualified medical practitioner, 1933; RMO Middlesex Hosp., 1936-39; Leverhulme Research Scholar, 1939-41; Lt-Col (Temp.) RAMC, 1943-45; ex-Censor and Senior Censor RCP; Examiner in Medicine and Physiology, Makerere Coll., Uganda, University Coll. of West Indies, University Coll. Ibadan, Baghdad Univ., London and other English Univs. Hon. Librarian and Mem. of Council, Royal Society Medicine, 1951; Chm., Pharmacological Sub-cttee, Min. of Health; Member: Med. Research Soc. and Physiological Soc., New York Acad. of Sciences and Internat. Soc. of Internal Medicine; Hosp. Cttee King Edward VII Hosp. Fund; Bd of Management, Medical Insurance Agency (Chm.). Mem. Senate and Academic Council, University of London. FACC. *Publications:* papers on dehydration, blood transfusion, including continuous drip blood transfusion, on wound shock, on nutritional problems including those in Bantu natives and obesity. *Address:* Pitts Folly, Hadlow, Kent. *Clubs:* Athenæum; Maidstone. [*Died* 5 *April* 1974.

KELCEY, Air Vice-Marshal Alick F.; see Foord-Kelcey.

KELLAR, Prof. Robert James, CBE 1968 (MBE 1943); MB, ChB, FRCSEd, FRCPEd, FRCOG; Professor of Obstetrics and Gynæcology, University of Edinburgh, 1946-74; *yr s* of James Dodds Ballantyne Kellar and Florence Maud Kellar (née Coveney); *m* Gertrude Aitken; two *s* one *d. Educ:* Univ. of Edinburgh; MB, ChB, 1931; MRCPEd, 1934, FRCSEd, 1935; FRCOG, 1945; FRCPEd, 1946. Univ. of Edinburgh: Annandale Gold Medal for Clinical Surgery, Wightman Prize for Clinical Medicine, Murchison Prize for Medicine (halved), Buchanan Prize for Midwifery and Diseases of Women, 1931, Simpson Prize for Obstetrics, 1932; Lister Prize for Surgery, 1934; Freeland Barbour Fellowship in Obstetrics; Leckie Mactier Research Fellow, 1934-35; Beit Memorial Research Fellow, 1935-37. Formerly: Reader in Obstetrics and Gynæcology, University of London, British Post-Graduate Medical Sch.; Asst. Obstetrical Unit, University Coll. Hosp.; Tutor in Clinical Gynæcology, House Surgeon Out-patients Department and to Prof. of Midwifery, Royal Infirmary, Edinburgh. Lt-Col, Royal Army Medical Corps; Officer in charge of a Surgical Div. (despatches, MBE). Mem. Council, RCOG, 1963. Hon. Fellow Amer. Assoc. of Obst. and Gynæcol. *Address:* 27 Hope Terrace, Edinburgh EH9 2AP. [*Died* 9 *Oct.* 1980.

KELLETT, Maj.-Gen. Gerald, CB 1959; CBE 1957; *b* 24 Oct. 1905; *s* of Surgeon Rear-Adm. L. H. Kellett, RN; *m* 1941, Elizabeth Bridges; one *s* one *d. Educ:* Bedford Sch.; RMA Woolwich. Commissioned 2nd Lt Royal Artillery, 1925, Capt. 1937, Major 1942, Lt-Col 1948, Col 1951, Brig. 1955, Maj.-Gen. 1957. Dir of Inspectorate of Armaments, 1954-56; Dir-Gen. of Artillery, War Office, 1957-60; retired from Army, Jan. 1961. *Address:* Rendham Road, Saxmundham, Suffolk. *T:* Saxmundham 2194. [*Died* 6 *July* 1973.

KELLOCK, Hon. Roy Lindsay, CC (Canada) 1971; QC (Canada); Counsel, Messrs Waterous, Holden, Kellock and Kent, Ontario; *b* Perth, Ontario, 12 Nov. 1893; *s* of James F. and Annie M. Kellock; *m* 1932, Elinor Harris; one *s* one *d. Educ:* Harbord Collegiate; McMaster Univ.; Osgoode Hall. Called to Bar of Ontario, 1920; KC (Canada) 1934. Joined Mason, Foulds, Davidson & Kellock, 1920; Justice, Court of Appeal for Ontario, 1942; Judge, Supreme Court of Canada, 1944-58, retd. Chancellor, McMaster University, Hamilton, Canada, 1955-60. Hon. LLD, McMaster, 1950. Hon. DCL, Acadia, 1952. *Address:* 20 Wellington Street, Brantford, Ontario, Canada. *Clubs:* National (Toronto); Brantford. [*Died* 12 *Dec.* 1975.

KELLY, Brig. George Alexander, CB 1946; *b* 24 Aug. 1888; *s* of John J. Kelly, Roscommon; *m* 1923, Sydney Russell Stanley (*d* 1971); one *d. Educ:* Castleknock Coll., Dublin; Royal Veterinary Coll. of Ireland. Commissioned RAVC 1911; Bt Lieut-Col 1935; ADVS India, 1936-39; DDV and RS MEF. Served France, 1914-16, Waziristan, 1919 (despatches); Middle East Force, 1940-42 (despatches); WO, Dir Army Vet. and Remount Services, 1943-47; retd, 1947; formerly Col Comdt Royal Army Veterinary Corps. *Address:* c/o Williams & Glyn's Bank Ltd, Whitehall, SW1. [*Died* 16 *April* 1973.

KELLY, Sir Gerald (Festus), KCVO, *cr* 1955; Kt, *cr* 1945; PPRA 1954 (PRA 1949; RA 1930; ARA 1922); RHA 1914; Hon. RSA; Hon. FRIBA; Hon. LLD (Cambridge and TCD); Mem. Royal Fine Art Commission, 1938-43; *b* 1879; *o s* of Rev. F. F. Kelly; *m* 1920, Lilian, 5th *d* of S. Ryan. *Educ:* Eton; Trinity Hall, Cambridge. The State Portraits of the King and the Queen, 1945. Pictures in many public collections. Membre correspondant de la section de peinture de l'Académie des Beaux Arts de l'Institut de France, 1953; Académico Correspondiente de la Réal Academia de Bellas Artes de San Fernando, Madrid, 1953. Commander of Legion of Honour, 1950; Commander of Order of Oranje Nassau, 1953. *Address:* 117 Gloucester Place, Portman Square, W1. *T:* 01-935 0148. *Club:* The Club.
[*Died 5 Jan.* 1972.

KELLY, Dr Mervin J.; Consultant to Chairman of the Board, International Business Machines, 1961-65 and 1968-70 (Consultant to the President, 1959-61); Consultant to president of Bausch & Lomb Inc., 1959-62; *b* 14 Feb. 1894; *s* of Joseph Fenemore Kelly and Mary Etta Kelly (*née* Evans); *m* 1917, Katharine Milsted; one *s* one *d. Educ:* University of Missouri (BS); University of Kentucky (MS); University of Chicago (PhD). Western Elec. Co. Research Physicist, 1918-25. Bell Telephone Labs: Research Physicist, 1925-34; Development Dir of Transmission Instruments and Electronics, 1934-36; Dir of Research, 1936-44; Exec. Vice-Pres., 1944-51; Pres., 1951-59. Mem. Nat. Acad. of Sciences, 1945; Mem. Amer. Philosophical Soc. 1952; For. Mem. Swedish Royal Acad. of Sciences, 1956. Hon. Degrees: DEng University of Missouri, 1936; DSc University of Kentucky, 1946; LLD University of Pa, 1954; DEng New York Univ., 1955; DEng Polytechnic Inst. of Brooklyn, 1955; DSc University of Pittsburgh, 1957; Dr University of Lyons, 1957; Dr Eng. Wayne State Univ., 1958; DSc Case Inst. of Tech., 1959; Dr Eng. Princeton Univ., 1959. Presidential Certificate of Merit, 1947; US Air Force Assoc. Trophy, 1953; Industrial Research Institute Medal, 1954; Christopher Columbus Internat. Communication Prize, 1955; Air Force Exceptional Service Award, 1957; James Forrestal Medal, Nat. Security Industrial Assoc., 1958; John Fritz Medal Award, 1959; Stevens Honor Award, Stevens Inst. of Technology, 1959; Golden Omega Award, 1960; Hoover Medal Award, 1961. Chicago Alumni Medal, 1959; Mervin J. Kelly Award in Telecommunications (by Amer. Inst. Elec. Engrs) for 1960. *Publications:* numerous in scientific and tech. jls of USA. *Recreations:* golf and gardening. *Address:* (office) International Business Machines, 590 Madison Avenue, New York, NY 10022, USA. *T:* (212) 753-1900; (home) 2 Windemere Terrace, Short Hills, New Jersey 07078, USA. *T:* (201) 3793319. *Club:* University (New York).   [*Died 18 March* 1971.

KELLY, Richard Barrett Talbot, MBE; MC; RI 1924; late RA; retired as Art Master, Rugby School, 1966; *b* 20 Aug. 1896; *s* of late R. Talbot Kelly, RI, RBC and Lilias Fisher Lindsay; *m* 1924, Dorothy, *d* of late Edgar Bundy, ARA, RI; one *s* one *d. Educ:* Rugby; Royal Military Academy, Woolwich. Served in Royal Artillery, 1915-29; European War, France, 1915-18, (MC, despatches), India, 1919-22; retired from Army, 1929; War of 1939-45 (MBE): Chief Instructor at War Office Sch. of Military Camouflage. Exhibitor at Royal Academy, RI, Paris Salon, and all important Municipal Galleries, as well as in Canada; various display designs for museums and exhibitions; Design Consultant, Pavilion of the Natural Scene, Festival of Britain, 1951; designed displays in new Museum of Natural History, Kampala, Uganda, 1964. Lectured on Art and taught in USA by invitation, 1968. *Publication:* The Way of Birds, 1937; Paper Birds, Birds of Mountain & Moor (Puffin Books); Illustrations for Sea Birds (King Penguin); Bird Life and the Painter. *Recreation:* study of bird life. *Address:* 22 St Philip's Road, Stoneygate, Leicester. *T:* 37143.   [*Died 30 March* 1971.

KELLY, Sir Robert (McErlean), Kt 1969; JP; President, Celtic FA Co. Ltd, since 1947 (Director, 1932, Chairman, 1947-71); *b* 17 Oct. 1902; *s* of James Kelly, JP; *m* 1933, Marie Josephine Reilly; no *c. Educ:* St Aloysius Coll., Glasgow; St Joseph's Coll., Dumfries. President: Scottish Football League for six years; Scottish Football Assoc. for four years (Vice-Pres. for four years). *Publication:* Celtic, 1971. *Recreations:* reading, gardening. *Address:* Marisdale, East Kilbride Road, Burnside, Rutherglen, Scotland. *T:* 041-634 4078.   [*Died 21 Sept.* 1971.

KELSO, Maj.-Gen. J. E. U.; *see* Utterson-Kelso.

KEMP, Maj.-Gen. Geoffrey Chicheley, CB 1942; MC; *b* 28 Dec. 1890; *s* of Brig.-Gen. G. C. Kemp, CB, CMG; *m* 1927, Isabel Rosemary Gore Graham (*d* 1960); three *d. Educ:* private and RMA, Woolwich. Joined RFA, 1910; Capt., 1916; Major, 1929; Bt Lieut-Col, 1934; Lieut-Col, 1937; Col, 1938; Maj.-Gen., 1941; served European War, France and Belgium (wounded twice,

despatches, MC); Major Inst. in Gunnery (Art.) School of Artillery, 1929-32; Brig.-Comdr (temp. Brig.), 1938-40; Comdr Orkney and Shetland Defences, 1939-42; Pres. War Office Selection Boards in this country and in Middle East, 1943; retired 1946; Col Commandant, RA, 1948. *Recreations:* all forms of sport, *Address:* Thurston Lodge, North Berwick, East Lothian. *T:* North Berwick 2204.   [*Died 5 Feb.* 1976.

KEMPE, Rudolf; Principal Conductor for life, 1970, Royal Philharmonic Orchestra; Generalmusikdirektor, Münchner Philharmoniker, München, since 1967; Principal Conductor, BBC Symphony Orchestra, since 1975; also long contracts with Royal Opera, Covent Garden; *b* 14 June 1910; *m* ; three *d. Educ:* State Orchestra Sch., Dresden. Principal Oboist and Repetitor, Gewandhaus, Leipzig, 1929-36; started conducting in Leipzig, 1936; Dir of Music, State Orchestra, Dresden, 1949; General Musikdirektor, München Staatsoper, 1952-54; Artistic Dir, Tonhalle Orchestra, Zürich, 1965-72; Chief Conductor, 1961-63, Artistic Dir, 1964-75, Royal Philharmonic Orchestra. Subseq. Conductor Salzburg Festival, 1955, 1959, 1962, Edinburgh Festival, 1956, 1959, 1961, and Bayreuth, 1960, 1961, 1962, 1963, 1967; also conducted for many great orchestras of the world and in famous opera houses. Gold Medal, München Leudtet—Den Freunden Münchens, 1975. Broadcasts and recordings. Bayrischer Verdienstorden, 1971; Nägeli Medal Zürich. *Address:* 8 München 2, Rindermarkt 3-4, Germany.
[*Died 11 May* 1976.

KEMSLEY, Sir Colin Norman T.; *see* Thornton-Kemsley.

KENDALL, Arthur Wallis, VRD; MS, FRCS; formerly Surgeon to King's College Hospital and to Queen Elizabeth Hospital for Children; *b* 3 Dec. 1904; *s* of Dr John Arthur Kendall; *m* 1930, Verna, *d* of late Sir John Winthrop Hackett, KCMG; two *s* two *d. Educ:* Barnard Castle Sch.; King's Coll., London. Lecturer in Surgery and Surgical Pathology, King's Coll. Hospital; Examiner in Surgery, University of London and Soc. of Apothecaries. Mem. of Court of Examiners, RCS. Served during war of 1939-45 as Surgeon Capt. RNVR (VRD). *Publications:* various medical. *Recreation:* golf. *Address:* 23 Margin Drive, Wimbledon, SW19. *Club:* Savile.   [*Died 26 Feb.* 1975.

KENDALL, Edward Calvin, PhD; Visiting Professor in Chemistry, James Forrestal Research Center, Princeton University, since 1951; Emeritus Professor of Physiologic Chemistry, University of Minnesota (Mayo Foundation), since 1951; *b* 8 March 1886; *s* of George Stanley Kendall and Eva Frances (*née* Abbott); *m* 1915, Rebecca Kennedy; one *s* one *d* (and two *s* decd). *Educ:* Columbia Univ., USA. BS 1908, MS 1909, PhD 1910, Alexander Hamilton Award (Columbia Univ.), 1961. Research chemist (thyroid gland), Parke Davis and Co., Detroit, 1910-11; St Luke's Hosp., New York City, 1911-14; Mayo Clinic: Head of Section on Biochemistry, 1914, Prof. of Physiologic Chemistry, 1921. Isolated active constituent of thyroid gland, 1914; investigations on glutathione resulting in its preparation in crystalline form and determination of its structure, 1926-30; undertook investigation of adrenal cortex, 1930; (with Dr L. H. Sarett) cortisone was prepared, 1948. Hon. doctor of science: University of Cincinnati, Yale Univ., Western Reserve Univ., Williams Coll., National Univ. of Ireland, Columbia Univ. Mem. many societies, both American and foreign. Holds various American awards for research, from 1921; (jointly) Nobel Prize for Physiology and Medicine, 1950. Gold Medal for Scientific Achievement, American Med. Assoc., 1965. *Publications:* Thyroxine, 1929; Autobiography to 1951, 1971. Numerous articles in scientific journals. *Recreations:* chess, outdoor activities. *Address:* 3 Queenston Place, Princeton, New Jersey, USA. *Club:* Nassau (Princeton).
[*Died 4 May* 1972.

KENDALL, James; MA; DSc (Edinburgh); LLD (Glasgow); FRS 1927; Professor of Chemistry, University of Edinburgh, 1928-59, now Emeritus (Dean of the Faculty of Science, 1953-54 and 1957-59); Vice-President, British Association for the Advancement of Science, 1951; *b* Chobham, Surrey, 30 July 1889; *s* of William Henry Kendall and Rebecca Pickering; *m* 1st, 1915, Alice (*d* 1955), *d* of Thomas Tyldesley, Victoria, BC; one *s* two *d*; 2nd, 1955, Jane Bain, *d* of late Malcolm Steven, Auckingill, Caithness. *Educ:* Farnham Grammar Sch.; University of Edinburgh; Nobel Institute, Stockholm. Prof. of Chem., Columbia University New York City, 1913-26; Professor of Chem., Washington Square Coll., New York Univ., 1926-28; Dean of the Graduate Sch., New York Univ., 1927-28; Visiting Professor, Stanford Univ., 1919 and 1923; University of Calif, 1923; Pennsylvania State Coll., 1927; Chm., New York Section, American Chemical Soc., 1925; Hon. Member, American Institute of Chemists. Lieut, US Naval Reserve, 1917-19; Lieut-Comdr, 1924-26. Pres. Royal Society of Edinburgh, 1949-54

(General Sec., 1936-46). *Publications:* At Home among the Atoms, 1929; Breathe Freely!, 1938; Young Chemists and Great Discoveries, 1939; Great Discoveries by Young Chemists, 1953; Humphry Davy, Pilot of Penzance, 1954; Michael Faraday, Man of Simplicity, 1955; contributions to scientific journals in the field of inorganic and physical chemistry; revisions of chemistry textbooks of Alexander Smith. *Address:* 26 Lasswade Road, Eskbank, Midlothian EH22 3EE. *T:* 031-663 2146. *Clubs:* Chemists' (New York); New (Edinburgh). *[Died* 14 *June* 1978.

KENDRICK, Sir Thomas Downing, KCB 1951; FBA 1941; FSA; Hon. DLitt (Durham and Oxford); Hon. LittD (Dublin); Hon. FRIBA; Director and Principal Librarian of British Museum, 1950-59, retired; *b* 1895; *m* 1st, 1922, Helen Kiek (*d* 1955); *m* 2nd, 1957, Katharine Elizabeth Wrigley. Keeper of Brit. Antiquities, Brit. Museum, 1938-50. Hon. Fellow Oriel Coll., Oxford. Mem. Royal Commn of 1851; Foreign Mem. Royal Swedish Acad. of Letters, History and Antiquities; Mem. German Archæological Inst. *Publications:* The Druids, 1927, repr. 1966; Archæology of the Channel Isles, vol I, 1928; A History of the Vikings, 1930, repr. 1968; Anglo-Saxon Art to AD 900, 1938, repr. 1972; Late Saxon and Viking Art, 1949, repr. 1974; British Antiquity, 1950, repr. 1970; The Lisbon Earthquake, 1956; Saint James in Spain, 1960; Great Love for Icarus, 1962; Mary of Agreda, 1967. *Address:* Old Farm House, Organford, Poole, Dorset. *Club:* Athenæum.
[Died 2 *Nov.* 1979.

KENILWORTH, 2nd Baron, *cr* 1937, of Kenilworth; **Cyril Davenport Siddeley,** CBE 1951; TD 1942; Lord of the Manor of Kenilworth; *b* 27 Aug. 1894; *e s* of 1st Baron and Sara Mabel Goodier (*d* 1953); *S* father 1953; *m* 1919, Marjorie Tennant, *d* of late Harry Firth; one *s* one *d. Educ:* St Lawrence Coll., Ramsgate. Formerly Lieut-Col and Hon. Col 7th Bn Royal Warwickshire Regt (TA); served European War, 1914-19, France and Belgium (despatches twice, 1914-15 Star); War of 1939-45, France, 1940 (despatches). Vice-Chm. and Chm. Coventry and Warwicks Hosp., 1925-29; DL Warwicks, 1942-67; Sheriff of Warwicks, 1944-45; Master Coachmakers and Coach harness makers of London, 1956-57; a Manager Coventry Trustee Savings Bank; formerly Chm. Coventry Diocesan Bd of Finance. Pres. Queen Victoria Memorial Hosp., Nice, 1961-64. *Recreation:* motoring. *Heir: s* Hon. John Davenport Siddeley. *Address:* Hotel L'Horizon, St Brelade's Bay, Jersey, Channel Islands. *[Died* 11 *Aug.* 1971.

KENNEDY, Sir Derrick (Edward de Vere), 6th Bt *cr* 1783; farming since 1974; *b* 5 June 1904; *s* of George Edward de Vere Kennedy (*d* 1922) (2nd *s* of 2nd Bt) and Julia Ellen Beatrice (*d* 1933), 4th *d* of Sir John Craven Carden, 4th Bt; *S* cousin, 1974; *m* 1st, 1926, Phyllis Victoria Levine (marr. diss. 1945), *d* of late Gordon Fowler; two *s* one *d*; 2nd, 1945, Barbara Mary Worthington (*d* 1959). *Educ:* Clifton Coll.; Dublin Univ. Tea Planter, Ceylon, 1923-39 and 1945-46. Served War of 1939-45, Major Royal Ulster Rifles. Hotelier in Ireland, 1947-66; retired, 1966. *Recreations:* philately, shooting. *Heir: s* George Ronald Derrick Kennedy, OBE, Lt-Col RA [*b* 19 Nov. 1927; *m* 1949, Noelle Mona Green; one *s* one *d*]. *Address:* Johnstown Kennedy, Rathcoole, Co. Dublin. *T:* 589203.
[Died 27 *June* 1976.

KENNEDY, Frank Robert, CMG 1947; OBE 1937; *b* 9 Nov. 1895; *s* of late Rev. R. J. Kennedy; *m* 1917, Ethel Florence Jennett (*d* 1970); one *s* two *d. Educ:* Weymouth Coll.; Queens' Coll., Cambridge (BA). Served European War, 1914-18, 16th Middlesex Regt, 1914-16; Machine Gun Corps, 1916-19; Colonial Administrative Service, Uganda, 1920; District Officer, 1932; Deputy Provincial Commissioner, 1939; Development and Welfare Sec. and Adviser on Native Affairs, 1944; Sec. for African Affairs, 1946; retd 1948; Trusteeship Dept, United Nations, 1949-52. *Address:* Long Corner, Menin Way, Farnham, Surrey. *T:* Farnham 6357. *[Died* 6 *Jan.* 1971.

KENNEDY, Sir James (Edward), 5th Bt *cr* 1836; farmer; *b* 18 Jan. 1898; *s* of Sir John Charles Kennedy, 3rd Bt (*d* 1923) and Maude (*d* 1939), *d* of Sir James Macaulay Higginson; *S* brother, 1968. *Educ:* Malvern Coll. *Recreation:* shooting. *Heir: cousin* Captain Derrick Edward de Vere Kennedy [*b* 5 June 1904; *m* 1st, 1926, Phyllis Victoria (marr. diss. 1945), *d* of late Gordon Fowler; two *s* one *d*; 2nd, 1945, Barbara Mary (*d* 1959), *d* of late William Shepherd]. *Address:* Johnstown Kennedy, Rathcoole, Co. Dublin. *T:* Celbridge 289203. *[Died* 24 *June* 1974.

KENNEDY, Hon. Sir Robert, Kt 1949; MA, LLM, FRIH(NZ); Judge of Supreme Court of New Zealand, 1929-50; Royal Commissioner Orakei Native Reserves; Chairman Royal Commission on Waterfront Industry; Commission on Police Conduct; *b* Southland, NZ, 18 May 1887; *o s* of John James

Kennedy and Agnes Dow; *m* Alice Denniston Troup. *Educ:* Southland Boys' High Sch. (dux); Victoria Coll., New Zealand Univ. (Junior and Senior Univ. Scholar, First Class Hons). Jacob Joseph Research Scholar in Arts and Law; First Junior and First, with distinction, Senior Civil Service, 1906; admitted as Barrister and Solicitor, 1909. *Recreations:* fishing and gardening. *Address:* Whitelee, Waikanae, NZ.
[Died 19 *April* 1974.

KENNEDY, William Quarrier, FRS 1949; retired as Professor of Geology, University of Leeds (1945-67), now Emeritus; Founder and first Director of Research Institute of African Geology in the University of Leeds, 1955-67; *b* 30 Nov. 1903; *s* of John Gordon Kennedy and Peterina Webster; *m* 1st, 1933, Elizabeth Jane Lawson McCubbin; one *s* two *d*; 2nd, 1962, Sylvia Margaret Greeves; one *s* one *d. Educ:* Glasgow High Sch.; Glasgow Univ.; University of Zürich. Geologist and senior geologist in the geological survey of Great Britain, 1928-45. Leader of the British Ruwenzori Expedition, 1951-52; Scientific Dir, Royal Society's expedition to Tristan da Cunha, 1962. Hon. Oppenheimer Research Fellow, Univ. of Leeds; Hon. Regent, St Salvator's Coll., Univ. of St Andrews. Clough Medal, 1966; Lyell Medal, 1967. *Publications:* various in scientific journals. *Address:* 2 Stone Rings Lane, Harrogate, N Yorks.
[Died 13 *March* 1979.

KENNEDY SHAW, W. B.; see Shaw.

KENNER, George Wallace, FRS 1964; PhD, ScD Cantab; MSc Manchester; Royal Society Research Professor, University of Liverpool, since 1977; *b* Sheffield, 16 Nov. 1922; *s* of Professor James Kenner, FRS; *m* 1951, Jillian Gervis, *d* of Angus K. Bird, Cambridge; two *d. Educ:* Manchester Grammar Sch.; Manchester Univ. Holder of DSIR Senior Award at Christ's Coll., Cambridge, 1944-46; Research Fellow of Trinity Hall, Cambridge, 1946-49; University Demonstrator, Cambridge, 1946-53; Rockefeller Foundation Fellow, Eidgenössische Technische Hochschule, Zürich, 1948-49; Staff Fellow of Trinity Hall, 1949-57; University Lecturer, 1953-57; Heath Harrison Prof. of Organic Chemistry, Liverpool Univ., 1957-76. President: British Assoc., Section B, 1974; Chem. Soc. Perkin Div., 1974-76. Lectures: Tilden, Chem. Soc., 1955; Simonsen, 1972; Bakerian, Royal Society, 1976; Pedler, 1977. Meldola Medal, RIC, 1951; Corday-Morgan Medal, Chem. Soc., 1957. *Publications:* papers in Jl Chem. Soc. and Tetrahedron. *Recreations:* sailing, motorcycling, modern art. *Address:* The Robert Robinson Laboratories, Oxford Street, Liverpool L69 3BX. *T:* 051-709 6022. *[Died* 25 *June* 1978.

KENNER, James, FRS 1925; DSc (London); PhD (Heidelberg); Fellow of Queen Mary College, London; Emeritus Professor of Technological Chemistry in the University of Manchester; formerly Professor of Organic Chemistry, Pure and Applied, University of Sydney, Australia; *b* Morpeth, 1885; *m* 1918, Annie Moore, *d* of Dr S. Mathews; one *s. Educ:* Universities of London and Heidelberg. On Staff Sheffield Univ., 1909; Military and Munition Service, 1914-19. *Publications:* papers in Proc. and Trans Chem. Society; Berichte der deutschen chemischen Gesellschaft; Tetrahedron, Nature, Chemistry and Industry; Annual Reports of the Chemical Society; Society of Chemical Industry. *Address:* 32 Rathmore Road, Oxton, Birkenhead L43 2HF. *[Died* 30 *June* 1974.

KENNY, Sean; Designer; *b* 23 Dec. 1932; *s* of Thomas J. Kenny and Nora Gleeson; *m* Jan Walker (marr. diss.); *m* 1967, Judy Huxtable (marr. diss.). *Educ:* St Flannan's Coll., Ireland; School of Architecture, Dublin. Designer of sets for stage productions: Shadow of a Gunman, 1957; Bloomsday, Hamlet, 1958; Coriolanus, Sugar-in-the-Morning, Lock up your Daughters, The Hostage, Cock-a-Doodle-Dandy, Glimpse of the Sea, 1959; Julius Caesar, Treasure Island, The Lily White Boys, Henry V, Great Expectations, Oliver!, Laughing Academy, Here is the News, Tchin-Tchin, 1960; Why the Chicken, The Devils, Altona, The Miracle Worker, Arms and the Man, Stop the World…, Romeo and Juliet, 1961; Blitz, King Priam, Uncle Vanya, 1962; Pickwick, Beggar's Opera, Hamlet, Uncle Vanya, 1963; Maggie May, 1964; Flying Dutchman, Roar of the Greasepaint…, 1965; Four Musketeers! 1967; Gulliver's Travels (also adapter and director), 1968; Les Noces (Royal Swedish Ballet Co. Stockholm), Uncle Vanya (Haifa), Lock Up Your Daughters, 1969; Peer Gynt (Chichester), 1970; King Pinam, 1972; Here are Ladies, 1972. Sets for TV and films: Windmill near a Frontier, 1960; The Plough and the Stars, 1961; I Thank a Fool, 1962. Architecture and interior design: Quinn House, Londonderry, 1953; Theatre, Casino de Liban, 1965; University of Sussex Fine Arts Centre Theatre, 1969; Canadian World Exhibition, Montreal, 1967; Gyrotron Spectacular Ride; Section 1, British Pavilion; New Wintergarden Theatre, Drury Lane,

1969-70; Mobile Theatre for Welsh Theatre Co., 1967; Casino de Paris, Dunes Hotel, Las Vegas, 1967; Irish Pavilion, 57th Street, New York City, 1968. Tony Award for sets for Oliver!, 1963. *Address:* c/o PLR Ltd, 33 Sloane Street, SW1.
                                                                    [Died 11 June 1973.

KENRICK, Brig. Harry Selwyn, CB 1945; CBE 1941; ED 1941; Superintendent-in-Chief, Auckland Hospitals, 1946-61; retired; *b* 7 Aug. 1898; *s* of late W. G. K. Kenrick, Stipendiary Magistrate, Auckland, NZ, and Beatrice Thom; *m* 1926, Lorna Winifred Dick; two *d. Educ:* Waitaki; Oamaru, NZ; Otago Univ., NZ; Edinburgh Univ. MB, ChB (NZ), 1924; FRCS (Edinburgh), 1926; practised as consulting Obstetrician and Gynæcologist in Auckland, NZ, 1928-39. Served as infantry officer with NZ Division in France, 1916-18 (wounded); maintained interest in Territorial work and on outbreak of war, 1939, appointed ADMS Northern Command; went overseas, 1940, in command of a NZ Field Ambulance; ADMS, NZ Division, 1940 (despatches for services in Greece and CBE for Service as Senior Medical Officer in Battle for Crete, also Greek Military Cross for this); formerly Col Commandant, RNZAMC and Hon. Surgeon to the Governor-General of NZ; DMS, NZEF (CB). *Address:* 37 Victoria Avenue, Remuera, Auckland, New Zealand. *Clubs:* Northern, Officers (Auckland, NZ).
                                                                    [Died 20 June 1979.

KENT, Rockwell; *b* Tarrytown, New York, 21 June 1882; *s* of Rockwell and Sara Holgate Kent; *m* 1st, Kathleen Whiting; two *s* three *d;* 2nd, Frances Lee; 3rd, Sally Johnstone. *Educ:* Columbia Univ. Architect, painter, wood-engraver, lithographer, writer, traveller, editor, illustrator, carpenter, fisherman, dairy farmer. Hon. Member: Acad. of Fine Arts of USSR; Soc. of Typographic Arts; Internat. Longshoremen's and Warehousemen's Union; Mem., Nat. Inst. of Arts and Letters. Lenin Peace Prize, 1967. *Publications:* Wilderness, 1919; Voyaging, 1924; N by E, 1930; Rockwellkentiana, 1933; Salamina, 1935; This is My Own, 1940; It's Me O Lord (Autobiography); Of Men and Mountains, 1959; Rockwell Kent's Greenland Journal, 1963; miscellaneous reviews, essays, etc. *Address:* Au Sable Forks, New York, USA.
                                                                    [Died 13 March 1971.

KENYATTA, HE Hon. Mzee Jomo, CGH; MP; (First) President of the Republic of Kenya since Dec. 1964; Prime Minister, also Minister for Internal Security and Defence, and Foreign Affairs, Kenya, since 1963; *b* (approximately) 1889; *m*; four *s* four *d. Educ:* Church of Scotland Mission, Kikuyu, Kenya; London School of Economics, Great Britain. General Sec., Kikuyu Central Assoc., 1922. Founded first African-owned journal, Mwigwithania, 1928; sent by Kenya Africans to Britain to press case for Independence; travelled extensively in Europe: represented Ethiopia at the League of Nations, briefly, during war; Pres., first Pan-African Congress, Manchester, Gt Britain, 1945; Pres., Kenya African Union, 1947-52; imprisoned and detained by British, 1952-61; elected *in absentia,* while in restriction at Lodwar, Pres., Kenya African National Union, 1960; MLC 1962; Minister of State for Constitutional Affairs and Economic Planning, 1962. Hon. LLD: University of E Africa, 1965; Manchester Univ., 1966. KStJ 1972. *Publications:* Facing Mt Kenya; Kenya, The Land of Conflict; My People of Kikuyu; Harambee. *Address:* PO Box 30510, Nairobi, Kenya. *T:* Nairobi 27411; Ichaweri, Gatundu, Kenya.
                                                                    [Died 22 Aug. 1978.

KENYON, Sir Bernard, Kt 1962; Clerk of the Peace and County Council of West Riding of Yorkshire, 1943-69, retired; *b* 28 June 1904; *s* of late Harry Kenyon, Penzance, Cornwall; *m* 1936, Doreen Mary, *d* of late Lawrence Richmond, CBE; one *s* two *d. Educ:* Taunton Sch., Taunton; Sidney Sussex Coll., Cambridge. Dep. Clerk of the West Riding County Council, 1941-43. *Address:* Newholm, Field Side, Linden Lane, Whitby, N Yorks.
                                                                    [Died 26 Aug. 1977.

KENYON, Dame Kathleen (Mary), DBE 1973 (CBE 1954); MA; DLitt, DLit, LHD, FBA; FSA; Principal of St Hugh's College, Oxford 1962-73; *b* 5 Jan. 1906; *e d* of late Sir Frederic G. Kenyon, GBE, KCB. *Educ:* St Paul's Girls' Sch.; Somerville Coll., Oxford. Asst at excavations, British Assoc's expedition to Zimbabwe, S Rhodesia, 1929, Verulamium, 1930-35, Joint Expedition to Samaria, Palestine, 1931-34; Dir, excavations at Jewry Wall site, Leicester, 1936-39, Viroconium, Salop, 1936-37, the Wrekin, Salop, 1939; Southwark, 1945-48; Breedon-on-the-Hill, Leics, 1946; Sutton Walls, Herefords, 1948-51; Sabratha, Tripolitania, 1948-49, 1951; Jericho, Jordan, 1952-58; Jerusalem, Jordan, 1961-67. Sec., University of London Inst. of Archæology, 1935-48; acting Dir, 1942-46; Sec., Council for British Archæology, 1944-49; Lecturer in Palestinian Archæology, University of London, Institute of Archæology,

1948-62; Dir, British Sch. of Archæology in Jerusalem, 1951-66. Divisional Comdt and Sec., Hammersmith Div., British Red Cross Soc., 1939-42; Dir, Youth Dept British Red Cross Soc., 1942-45. Norton Lecturer, Archæological Institute of America, 1959; Schweich Lecturer, British Academy, 1963; Haskell Lecturer, Oberlin Coll., Ohio, 1976. Hon. Fellow: Somerville Coll., 1960; St Hugh's Coll., Oxford, 1973. Trustee, British Museum, 1965-78. Hon. DLitt Exon; Hon. Dr Theol Tübingen. Grand Officer, Order of Istiqlal (Jordan), 1977. *Publications:* Verulamium Theatre Excavations, 1935; Excavations at Viroconium, 1940; Excavations on the Wrekin, 1943; Excavations at the Jewry Wall Site, Leicester, 1948; Excavations at Breedon-on-the-Hill, Leicester, 1950; Beginning in Archæology, 1952; Excavations at Sutton Walls, Herefordshire, 1954; Digging Up Jericho, 1957; contributor to Samaria-Sebaste, 1, 1942 and 3, 1958; Excavations at Jericho I, 1960 and II, 1965; Archæology in the Holy Land, 1960, rev. edn 1978; Amorites and Canaanites, 1967; Jerusalem: excavating 3,000 years of History, 1968; Royal Cities of the Old Testament, 1971; Palestine in the Time of the Eighteenth Dynasty, 1971; Digging up Jerusalem, 1974; The Bible and Recent Archaeology, 1978. *Recreation:* gardening. *Address:* Rose Hill, Erbistock, Wrexham, Clwyd. *T:* Overton-on-Dee 355. *Clubs:* University Women's, VAD Ladies.
                                                                    [Died 24 Aug. 1978.

KER, Douglas R. E.; *see* Edwardes-Ker.

KER, Frederick Innes, CBE 1943; MEIC; PEng; *b* 29 Oct. 1885; *s* of late Ven. John Ker, DD, LLD, and Mary Thomson Cousins, Montreal; *m* 1919, Amy (*decd*), *d* of late F. N. Southam, OBE, Montreal; two *s* two *d* (and one *s* decd). *Educ:* Montreal High Sch.; McGill Univ. Civil Engineer, 1909-21; entered Journalism, 1921. Pres. Canadian Daily Newspapers Assoc., 1930; Editor and Publisher, The Hamilton Spectator, Hamilton, Ont, 1930-51; Pres. Canadian Press, 1946-48. Delegate to various Imperial Press Conferences, 1930-50; Hon. Life Mem., Commonwealth Press Union. Chm. National Press Cttee on War Finance, 1940-46. An Hon. Governor of McMaster Univ., Hamilton, Ont. *Publications:* Canada and Intra-Empire co-operation, 1938; Press Promotion of War Finance, 1946. *Recreations:* yachting, golf, curling. *Address:* Malahide House, Port Talbot, RR1 Fingal, Ont, Canada. *Clubs:* University, Montreal (Montreal); Hamilton, Hamilton Golf (Hamilton).
                                                                    [Died 24 Sept. 1977.

KERBY, Captain Henry Briton, MP (C) for West Sussex (Arundel and Shoreham Division) since March 1954; *b* 11 Dec. 1914; *m* 1947, Enid, *d* of late Judge M. F. P. Herchenroder, CMG, CBE; two *d. Educ:* on Continent, and Highgate Sch. Regular Army, 1933-37; Hon. Attaché, Diplomatic Service, Brit. Legation, Riga, 1939-40; Actg Brit. Consul, Malmö, Sweden, 1940; specially employed under War Office, 1941-45. Contested Spelthorne (L), 1945, and Swansea (West) (C), 1951. Mem. of Parliamentary Delegation to Denmark, 1955, Israel, 1957, USSR, 1957, 1959, Nationalist China (Formosa), 1958, Federation of Rhodesia and Nyasaland, 1961. Member: Southampton Univ. Court, 1959-63; University of Sussex Court, 1961-68. FRGS 1962. Commander's Cross of Order of Polonia Restituta (Poland); Haakon VII Cross (Norway); Christian X pro Dania Medal (Denmark); Knight's Cross, 1st Cl. of Order of White Rose (Finland); Comdr, Royal Yugoslav Order of St Sava. *Address:* Hobbs Farm House, Yapton, Arundel, Sussex. *T:* Middleton-on-Sea 2012.
                                                                    [Died 4 Jan. 1971.

KERLEY, Sir Peter (James), KCVO 1972 (CVO 1952); CBE 1951; MD, FRCP, FRCR, DMRE; Emeritus Consultant, X-Ray Department, Westminster Hospital; Emeritus Consultant Adviser to Ministry of Health on radiology; Emeritus Consultant Radiologist to: King Edward VII Sanatorium, Midhurst; The National Heart Hospital; Ministry of Aviation; late Hon. Editor of the Journal of Faculty of Radiologists (now Clinical Radiology); Examiner in radiology: RCP; University of Leeds; Faculty of Radiologists, University of Liverpool; *b* Dundalk, Ireland, 27 Oct. 1900; *s* of Michael and Matilda Kerley; *m* 1929, Olivia MacNamee (*d* 1973), Enniskillen; two *d. Educ:* University Coll., Dublin (MB 1923 and MD 1932); University of Vienna (Diploma, 1924); Cambridge Univ. (DMRE 1925). Major RAMC 1939-44. President: Radiology Section, RSM, 1939-40; Faculty of Radiologists, 1952-55. FRSM; Hon. Fellow: Amer. Coll. of Radiology; Australasian Coll. of Radiology; Faculty of Radiologists of Ireland; Radiological Soc. of Chicago; Radiological Soc. of Toronto. Röntgen Award, 1944; Gold Medal, RCR, 1976. OStJ 1958. *Publications:* Recent Advances in Radiology, 4th edn; (with Shanks) A Text-Book of Radiology in 6 vols; also various articles on diseases of the Chest and Digestive Tract. *Recreation:* fishing. *Address:* 11 Wimpole Street, W1M 7AB. *T:* 01-580 1660; 9 Heath Rise, SW15. *Clubs:* White's, Travellers'; Royal Wimbledon Golf.
                                                                    [Died 15 March 1979.

KERMODE, Air Vice-Marshal Alfred Cotterill, CBE 1956 (OBE 1944); MA; CEng; FRAeS; Royal Air Force; retired; Aeronautical adviser to Sir Isaac Pitman & Sons Ltd, 1961; *b* 30 Jan. 1897; *s* of late Rev. S. A. P. Kermode, Isle of Man, and late Lucy Emma (*née* Lynam); *m* 1946, Rose Price Nowell (*née* Roberts); three *s*. *Educ:* Dragon Sch., Oxford; Oundle Sch. (Scholar); Clare Coll., Cambridge (Scholar). Served European War as Pilot in RNAS and RAF, 1916-19. Experimental flying (as technical observer), RAE, Farnborough, 1921-23; entered RAF Educl Service, 1923; served at schs of tech. trng, Cranwell and Halton, 1923-36; Sch. of Aeronautical Engineering, Henlow, 1936-38; RAF Coll., Cranwell, 1938-39; served War of 1939-45, as Chief Ground Instructor: Central Flying Sch., Upavon, 1940-41; No. 3 BFTS, Oklahoma, USA, 1941-42; ECFS, Hullavington, 1942-46; Sen. Tutor (Aeronautical Science and Engineering), RAF Coll., Cranwell, 1946-48; Comd Educn Officer: Far East Air Force, 1948-51; Maintenance Comd, 1951-52; Technical Training Command, 1952-55; Dir of Educational Services, Air Ministry 1955-60; retired, 1960. ADC to the Queen, 1953-56. *Publications:* Mechanics of Flight, 1930; Flight without Formulae, 1938; The Aeroplane Structure, 1938; (co-author) Hydrofoils, 1966. *Recreations:* Cine-photography, writing, dramatic production, travel, gardening. *Address:* Staplewood, Nether Wallop, Hants. *T:* Wallop 333.
[Died 23 Feb. 1973.

KERNOFF, Harry, RHA 1935; Professional Artist, Portrait, Landscape and Mural; *b* London, 9 Jan. 1900; *s* of Isaac Kernoff (Russian Jewish) and Katherine A'Barbanelle (Old Spanish Jewish Stock), family migrated to Dublin, May 1914. *Educ:* Elementary Sch., London; Metropolitan Sch. of Art, Dublin. All Ireland Taylor Art Scholarship, 1923; Exhibits yearly RHA, from 1926; 16 One-man Exhibitions in Dublin Yearly, 1926-58; 1 Ex. Gieves Gallery, London, 1931; One-man Show, White Gallery, 1938; 1 Ex. Castlebar, Co. Mayo, 1947; Exhibited Mural at Royal Academy, 1931, and in Paris, Chicago, New York, Amsterdam, Cork, Glasgow and Wales 1953, etc.; 80 small oils, Toronto, 1965. *Work in public collections:* 3 Pictures in Belfast Art Gallery (1 water colour, 2 woodcuts); 3 pictures in Nat. Art Gallery of Ireland; 2 Oil Paintings Municipal Gallery, Dublin (Street Scene, Brazen Head); 2 Oil Paintings Limerick Art Gallery; 2 Oil Paintings in Waterford Art Gall.; Oil Painting in Castlebar Gallery, 1947; 3 Oils in Killarney Art Gallery; 1 Oil in Monaco. Pictures in World's Fair, Glasgow, 1938; and World's Fair, New York, 1939; Oil, Killarney Landscape, in Irish Legation, Washington, 1959-63; Oil, Irish Volunteer, purchased by Irish Government, 1946; Oil, Turf-Girl, Tel-Aviv, 1950; Oil, Thomas Ashe, Teacher's Club, 1953; Oil, Berkeley Univ., Calif, USA, 1966; 3 Portraits, National Gall. of Ireland, 1968. 10 works, Arts Festival in Nova Scotia, 1957; Exhibitions: Ritchie Gall., (NS) Dublin, 1958 (oils, pastels, water colours); Lugano, 1964; Robertstown, Kildare, 1968 (40 portraits from James Joyce to Brendan Behan); Dublin, 1973; one-man exhbn, Dublin, 1974. Paintings in many private collections. Sold Portraits (in 1965) of: James Joyce (USA); W. B. Yeats (England); James Stephen; Brendan Behan; Oliver St John Gogarty (USA); Sean O'Casey, etc. Interested in Modern Movements in Art. Mem. Royal Dublin Society, 1947-. *Publications:* 1 Colour Reprod. in Twelve Irish Artists, 1940; Ltd Edn Book of Woodcuts (220 signed and numbered copies), 1942; Book of New Woodcuts (Ltd Edn 300 signed), 1944, (Ltd Edn 400 signed and numbered), 1951; Calendar for Egan's Tullamore, 1952; Calendar for Cherry-Tree, Dublin, 1955; Woodcuts in Ireland of the Welcomes, 1955; 12 Woodcuts in New Irish Poets, USA, 1948; Woodcuts in Bi-Cen. Guinness Harp, 1959; 6 Oils, Dublin Scenes, in Irish Tatler, 1959; (new 4 colour print, 16 ins × 16 ins) A Bird Never Flew on One Wing, 1961; New Colour Prints, Old Claddagh, Galway, 1962. Illustrated: Centenary Books, 1946-; Storyteller's Childhood, 1947; Tinker Boy, 1955. *Recreations:* swimming, verse. *Address:* 13 Stamer Street, Dublin 8, Ireland. *T:* Dublin 751675. *Clubs:* United Arts, Royal Dublin Society (Dublin).
[Died 25 Dec. 1974.

KERR, Mrs Anne Patricia, (Mrs R. W. Kerr); *b* 24 March 1925; *d* of late Arnold Bersey and Kathleen (*née* Mitchell); *m* 1st, 1944, James Doran Clark; one *s*; 2nd, 1960, Russell Whiston Kerr, MP. *Educ:* St Paul's Girls' Sch. Served with WRNS, 1943-45. Worked in theatre, films, TV and radio as an actress, interviewer and broadcaster. Mem. of London CC, 1958-61 and 1961-65. MP (Lab) Rochester and Chatham, 1964-70. Chm., Women Against The Common Market, 1970-. *Recreations:* travel, theatre, camping. *Address:* 37 Popes Avenue, Twickenham, Middx. *T:* 01-894 4343.
[Died 29 July 1973.

KERR, Captain Frank Robison, DSO 1915; MB ChB (Melbourne); DPH (Melbourne); MD (Melbourne); RAMC, SR; late Dep. Dir of Health for Victoria, Commonwealth Dept of Health, retired; Registrar, Anti-Cancer Council of Victoria; *b* Melbourne, Australia, 5 April 1889; *s* of John H. Kerr, Paymaster, Treasury, Melbourne; *m* 1916, Myrtle, *d* of John M'Meekin, Mortlake, Victoria; two *s* one *d*. *Educ:* Camberwell Grammar Sch. and Wesley Coll., Melbourne; Queen's Coll., University of Melbourne. Rhodes Scholar, Victoria, 1913; proceeded to Oxford (University Coll.), 1913-14, there studied physiology; served European War, 1914-19 (despatches, DSO, for splendid devotion to duty in peril of his own life at Cuinchy, Sept. 1915); Mem. of Royal Society of Australia. Congregational. *Publications:* Inquiry into Morbidity Statistics of Victorian State School Teachers, 1923; Inquiry into the Health of Workers in Gasmaking Plants, 1927; Foundations: The Building of a Man, 1939; Days after To-morrow, 1944; articles in scientific journals. *Recreations:* triple blue, Melbourne, in cricket, football, athletics; 5 miles cross-country champion, Victoria, 1910, etc; formerly hiking, mountaineering. *Address:* 48 Wentworth Avenue, Canterbury, Melbourne, Vic. 3126, Australia. *T:* 839094. *Club:* Melbourne Cricket (Melbourne).
[Died 3 May 1977.

KERR, Sir Hamilton (William), 1st Bt, *cr* 1957; MA; *b* 1 Aug. 1903; *s* of Henry S. Kerr, Long Island, New York, and Olive Grace (who *m* 2nd, 1909, 3rd Baron Greville, OBE), *d* of J. Grace of Leybourne Grange, Kent. *Educ:* Eton; Balliol Coll., Oxford; MA Oxon and Cantab. Oxford Running Blue, half mile; worked on Daily Mail and Daily Telegraph. Flying Officer No 909 (County of Essex) balloon Sqdn AAF, 1939; Flt Lt, 1941. MP (C), Oldham, 1931-45. Parliamentary Private Sec. to Mr Duff Cooper when First Lord of the Admiralty; Parliamentary Private Sec. to Captain H. H. Balfour, Under-Sec. of State for Air, 1942-45; Parliamentary Sec. Ministry of Health, 1945; Parliamentary Private Sec. to Mr Harold Macmillan when Minister of Defence, 1954, when Sec. of State for Foreign Affairs, 1955 and when Chancellor of Exchequer, 1955-56; MP (C) Cambridge, 1950-66. Delegate to Consultative Assembly of Council of Europe, Strasbourg, 1952. Chancellor, Primrose League, 1961-63. Master, Worshipful Company of Pattenmakers, 1966-67. Mem. St John's Coll., Cambridge. Hon. LLD Cantab, 1972. Chevalier de la Légion d'Honneur, 1960. *Recreations:* tennis, painting. *Address:* 71 Westminster Gardens, Marsham Street, SW1; The Mill House, Whittlesford, Cambridge. *Clubs:* Carlton, Brooks's.
[Died 26 Dec. 1974 (ext).

KERR, Maj.-Gen. Sir (Harold) Reginald, KBE 1946; CB 1945; MC 1918; FCIT; psc; *b* 22 April 1897; *s* of H. F. Kerr; *m* 1921, Helen Margaret (*d* 1974), *d* of B. M. Tuckett; two *s*. *Educ:* Bedford Sch.; Royal Military College, Sandhurst. Commissioned 1914 in ASC and served as a Regimental Officer and on the staff in France and Flanders, 1914-19, and subsequently on the Staff with the army of occupation in Germany until 1920. Was Instructor at Royal Military College, 1924-28; Adjutant, RASC Training Coll., 1929-30; Student Staff Coll., 1931-32; Staff Officer, Sudan, 1934; Staff Officer, 3rd Div., 1935-36; Chief Instructor at Royal Army Service Corps Training Centre, 1937-39; Instructor in the Senior Wing Staff Coll., 1939-40; Dep. Quartermaster-Gen., British Army Staff, Washington, June 1941-Nov. 1942; Maj.-Gen. i/c Administration, Eastern Command, Dec. 1942-May 1943; Dir of Supplies and Transport, War Office, 1943-46; Maj.-Gen. i/c Administration, Far East Land Forces, 1946-48; retd 1949. Divisional Manager, British Road Services, Midland Div., 1949-54; Chm. and Gen. Manager, British Waterways, 1955-62; Consultant, British Waterways Board, 1963. Col Comdt, RASC, 1949-59. *Recreation:* four-in-hand driving. *Address:* Timber Lodge, Lyme Regis, Dorset. *T:* Lyme Regis 2772. *Club:* Army and Navy.
[Died 1 Nov. 1974.

KERR, Lt-Col Sir Howard, KCVO 1948 (CVO 1942; MVO 1929); CMG 1935; OBE 1922; Equerry to Duke of Gloucester, 1924-46, Comptroller, 1946-50, Extra Equerry, 1950-74; *b* 25 Nov. 1894; *s* of late Capt. Walter Raleigh Kerr, *g s* of Lord Robert Kerr, and of Annabel, *d* of Hon. James Jackson Jarves, Boston, Mass.; *m* Christina, *d* of late Arthur Ram, of Ramsfort, County Wexford; three *s*. *Educ:* Lower Canada Coll., Montreal; Trinity Coll., Cambridge. Joined 11th Hussars (now Royal Hussars), 1914; served European War, 1914-19; ADC to Viscount Fitzalan of Derwent, Lord Lieutenant of Ireland, 1921-22; Private Chamberlain to the Pope, 1928. Accompanied Duke of Gloucester on Garter Mission to Japan, 1929, and on visit to Australasia, 1934-35; was Personal Asst to HRH with BEF in France, 1939-40, and accompanied HRH on visits to Gibraltar, 1941 and 1942; Chief of Staff to HRH on tour of Middle East Forces and India and Ceylon, 1942. Temporarily attached to US Army in France, Belgium and Holland in 1944. Retired pay, 1950. Life Governor Queen Mary's Hospital; Mem. Board of Govs, Royal Nat. Orthopædic Hosp. (Dep. Chm.,

1957-60). A Fellow in Perpetuity of the Metropolitan Museum of New York, 1954; Associate of Yale Univ., USA. Councillor Shardlow Rural District Council, Derbs, 1954-57. Royal Humane Society of Canada's Medal for Life Saving; Chevalier of the Order of Belgium; Order of the Sacred Treasure of Japan. *Recreations:* hunting and boxing; played for England, The United Services, Lower Canada Coll. and St John's Sch., Montreal, at Ice Hockey. *Address:* The Dower House, Melbourne, near Derby. *T:* Melbourne (Derbs) 2696. *Club:* Bath.   *[Died 11 July 1977.*

KERR, Lt-Col Sir L. W. H.; see Kerr, Lt-Col Sir Howard.

KERR, Sir Reginald; see Kerr, Sir (H.) R.

KERR, Mrs Russell Whiston; see Kerr, Mrs A. P.

KERR-MUIR, Ronald John, OBE 1945; TD 1945; Deputy Chairman, Meat and Livestock Commission, since 1973; *b* 20 Dec. 1910; *s* of Harold Frank Muir and Annie Margaret Kerr; *m* 1936, Margaret, *d* of Harold Rodier; two *s* two *d. Educ:* King Edward VI Sch., Southampton; The Queen's Coll., Oxford (MA, BSc). Asst Master: Hymer's Coll., Hull, 1933-35; Oundle Sch., 1935-39. Served War, Lt-Col, Royal Engineers, 1939-46 (US Bronze Star, 1943). With Courtauld's Ltd, 1946-71 (Dir, 1958-71); Pres., Lustre Fibres Inc., New York, 1946-50; Exec. Vice-Pres., Courtauld's (Canada) Ltd, 1954-58; Leader, FBI Research Delegn to USSR, 1963. Mem., Industrial Tribunals, Dept of Employment, 1971-. Pres., The Textile Inst., 1967-69; Pres., Coventry Chamber of Commerce, 1964-66; Council, Coventry Cathedral, 1958-; Councillor, Wilmslow UDC, 1953-54; Mem. Council: Univ. of Warwick, 1961- (Treas., 1965-); CBI, 1965-; Chm., Social Security Cttee, 1967-; Chm., Nat. Sulphuric Acid Assoc., 1967-69; Mem., Man Made Fibres, ITB, 1966-71; Cotton and Allied Textiles, ITB, 1969-71; Hon. Treas., Nat. Council of Social Service, 1972-; Dep. Chm., Charities Aid Fund, 1973-; Mem., Animals Bd of Jt Consultative Org. for Research and Develt in Agriculture and Food, 1973-; Mem., Royal Commn on Civil Liability, 1973-. Governor: King Edward VI Sch., Southampton; King Henry VIII Sch., Coventry; The Ladies' Coll., Cheltenham (Chm. of Council, 1973-); Bedford Coll., London. CompTI, 1969. *Recreations:* cricket, fishing, gardening. *Address:* Prior's Field, Fieldgate Lane, Kenilworth, Warwicks. *T:* Kenilworth 53231. *Clubs:* Marylebone Cricket, XL, The Pilgrims; St James's (Manchester).   *[Died 29 Jan. 1974.*

KERRIDGE, Sir Robert (James), Kt 1962; Managing Director, Kerridge Odeon; Director of over 50 companies; *b* 29 Oct. 1901; British; *m* 1922, Phyllis Elizabeth Roland; three *s* two *d. Educ:* Christchurch, NZ. Qualified in Accountancy, 1920; Principal, Kerridge Commercial Coll., 1920-29. Engaged in transport and newspaper business for a number of years. Acquired first theatre, 1920; subseq. numerous theatres, and controlling interest of NZ Theatres Ltd (W. R. Kemball); also took over: Fullers Theatre Corp. Ltd, John Fuller & Sons Ltd; J. C. Williamson Picture Corp. Ltd; company now directs well over 100 theatres and some merchandising companies. FRSA. CStJ. Cavaliere Dell'Ordine Al Merito Della Repubblica (Italy), 1958; International Order of the Lion. *Recreations:* farming, golf, fishing. *Address:* 1 Judge Street, Parnell 1, Auckland N2, NZ. *T:* 44091. *Club:* Auckland (New Zealand). *[Died 26 April 1979.*

KERRIGAN, Daniel Patrick, QC 1966; *b* 14 Jan. 1909; *s* of Patrick and Margaret Kerrigan; *m* 1936, Margaret (*née* Thomson); two *s. Educ:* Perth Academy; Edinburgh Univ. Called to the Bar, Middle Temple, 1933. War Service, RNVR, 1939-46. *Publications:* (jtly) Hill and Kerrigan Law of Housing; (jtly) Hill and Kerrigan Town and Country Planning Act, 1947; (jtly) Kerrigan and James Town and Country Planning Act, 1954; (jtly) Kerrigan and McDonald Land Commission Act, 1967; titles in Halsbury's Statutes and Halsbury's Laws. *Address:* 5 Pump Court, Temple, EC4; Homestead, Postling, Hythe, Kent.   *[Died 31 Oct. 1971.*

KERTESZ, Istvan; General Music Director, Opernhaus Köln, Germany, since 1964, Opera Director since 1969; *b* Budapest, Hungary, 28 Aug. 1929; *s* of Miklos Kertesz and Margit Kertesz (*née* Muresian); *m* 1951, Edith Kertesz (*née* Gabry); two *s* one *d. Educ:* Acad. Franz Liszt, Budapest; Accad. Santa Cecilia, Rome. Prin. Conductor, Philharmonic Orch., Györ, 1953-55; Conductor, State Opera House, Budapest, 1955-57; Gen. Mus. Dir, Augsburg Opera House, 1958-63; Conductor, Salzburg Festival, 1961-64; Principal Conductor, London Symphony Orchestra, 1965-68. Festivals: Salzburg, Edinburgh, Lucerne, Vienna, Bath, Spoleto, Gulbenkian, Lisbon, Montreux, Israel, Adelaide, German-Mozart, Osaka, Vienna, Ravinia Park. Tours: USA, with Hamburg Radio-Orch., 1963; Switzerland,

and World Tour with LSO, 1964, 1966. Has conducted with over eighty leading orchestras all over the world, including LSO, RPO, Vienna Philharmonic Berlin Philharmonic, Concertgebouw of Amsterdam, Orchestre de la Suisse Romande, and Israel Philharmonic. Operas: Covent Garden, Teatro Colon, La Scala. Prof., Salzburg, Summer-Acad. for conducting, 1964. Hon. Master degrees for conducting: Budapest, 1953; Rome, 1958 (*cum laude*); Premio D'Atri, Rome, 1958. Has made many prize-winning recordings. *Recreations:* cars, boats, skiing, reading. *Address:* Köln, Germany.   *[Died 16 April 1973.*

KESWICK, David Johnston, CMG 1946; JP; *b* 6 July 1901; *s* of Henry Keswick and Ida Wynifred Johnston; *m* 1928, Nony Barbara Pease (*d* 1969); three *d. Educ:* Eton Coll.; Trinity Coll., Cambridge. Asst Private Sec. to Governor-Gen. of New Zealand, 1924-27; Private Sec. to Sir Thomas Inskip, KC, MP, Attorney-Gen. 1927-29; Samuel Montagu & Co., Bankers, 1930-39 and from demobilisation. Commissioned KOSB Sept. 1939; employed on staff duties; demobilised, 1946. Mem., Royal Company of Archers (Queen's Body Guard for Scotland). JP Dumfriesshire 1958. *Recreations:* all country pursuits, painting. *Address:* Cowhill, Dumfries. *T:* Newbridge 304. *Clubs:* Boodle's; New (Edinburgh).   *[Died 12 April 1976.*

KETTLEWELL, Dr (Henry) Bernard (Davis); retired; Senior Research Officer, Genetics Unit, Department of Zoology, University of Oxford, 1954-74; Emeritus Fellow of Wolfson College, Oxford; *b* 24 Feb. 1907; *s* of late Henry Kettlewell and late Kate Davis; *m* 1936, Hazel Margaret, *d* of Sir Frank Wiltshire, MC; one *s* one *d. Educ:* Charterhouse; Paris; Caius Coll., Cambridge. MA, MB, BChir Cantab; DSc Oxon, 1975; MRCS, LRCP. Hosp. appts, St Bartholomew's, Miller and Hackney Hosps; subseq. GP, Cranleigh; Anaesthetist, St Luke's Hosp., Guildford; served War of 1939-45, EMS Woking War Hosp.; emigrated to S Africa, 1949-52; research Internat. Locust Control, Cape Town Univ.; undertook several expedns to Kalahari, Belgian Congo, Mozambique, and Knysna Forest; Nuffield Research Fellowship, Dept Genetics, Dept Zoology, Oxford, 1952; lecture tours in USA and Canada; visited Brazil, 1958 on occasion of Darwin Centenary for Life Magazine, and Czechoslovakia, 1965 as Govt guest; co-founder, Rothschild-Cockayne-Kettlewell Collection of British Lepidoptera (now Nat. Collection RCK) in British Museum of Natural History, London; on several cttees for Nature Conservancy. Producer of several films showing basic evolutionary principles. Darwin Medal, USSR, 1959; Mendel Medal, 1965. *Publications:* Butterflies and Moths, 1963; (with Julian Huxley) Darwin and his World, 1965; (contrib.) Ecological Genetics and Evolution, 1971; The Evolution of Melanism, 1973; (contrib.) Evolution: The Modern Synthesis, ed Julian Huxley, 3rd edn, 1974; (contrib.) Encyclopedia Italiana, 1974; numerous papers in Nature, Heredity, Science, Scientific American, and other sci. jls on genetics and ecological subjects, esp. industrial melanism. *Recreations:* shooting, salmon fishing, devising lobster traps, gardening (growing hybrid beans and azaleas). *Address:* Steeple Barton Vicarage, Oxford OX5 3QP. *T:* Steeple Aston 40357, Oxford 25789.   *[Died 11 May 1979.*

KEY, Sir Charles (Edward), KBE 1956 (CBE 1946); CB 1952; *b* 22 March 1900; *s* of late E. T. and late F. M. Key, Tunbridge Wells; *m* 1st, 1935, Doris May Watkins (decd); no *c*; 2nd, 1953, Annie Elizabeth Reap. *Educ:* St John's, Tunbridge Wells. War Office, 1915-60: Assistant Secretary, 1942; Director of Finance, 1949-54; Deputy Under-Secretary of State, War Office, 1954-60, retired. Medal of Freedom with bronze palm (USA), 1946; Officer Order of Orange-Nassau (Netherlands), 1947. *Address:* The Cottage, Highfield Road, East Grinstead, West Sussex RH19 2DX. *T:* East Grinstead 25321. *Club:* Reform. *[Died 3 June 1978.*

KEY, Edward Emmerson, MVO 1969; HM Consul-General, Jerusalem, since 1974; *b* 28 Feb. 1917; *s* of late Rev. William T. Key, Chipping Norton, Oxfordshire, and Annie Mary Key; *m* 1948, Louise Ada Doodson (*née* Bryan); two *d* and one step *s. Educ:* Bromsgrove; Brasenose Coll., Oxford. Served War, 1939-45, in Army. Foreign (later Diplomatic) Service, 1946: Second Sec., Bucharest, 1946-47; Vice-Consul, Bordeaux, 1947-49; Vice-Consul, Lille, 1949-52; Beirut, 1952; Foreign Office, 1954; NATO, Paris, 1957; FO, 1961; First Sec., British Mil. Govt, Berlin, 1963-67; Consul, Jerusalem, 1967-69; HM Embassy, Vienna, 1967-71; Acting Consul, Beira; Acting High Commissioner, Gaborone; Chargé d'Affaires, Lomé, 1971; Consul-General, Tangier, 1972-74. *Recreations:* golf, gardening, listening to music, scrabble. *Address:* 19A The Avenue, Beckenham, Kent. *Club:* Reform.   *[Died 13 May 1976.*

KHACHATURYAN, Aram Ilych; Order of Lenin, 1939; Russian composer and conductor; *b* Tiflis, Georgia, 6 June 1903; 3rd *s* of an Armenian bookbinder; *m* 1936, Nina Makarova, composer; one *s* one *d. Educ:* Moscow Univ. Studied biology, but soon accepted for Genesin Music Sch. ('cello, composition; grad. 1929); Moscow Conservatoire, 1929-34 (pupil of Miaskovsky). His First Symphony performed at the Conservatoire, 1934, Leningrad, 1936, and elsewhere in Russia and abroad during this period. The Piano Concerto in D flat, 1936, introd. at Queen's Hall, London, 1940, later in America and Europe. Teacher, Genesin Musical-Pedagog. Inst., 1950, also Prof. in composition at Moscow Conservatoire, 1950; first trip abroad, Dec. 1950, meeting other composers in Rome; first visit to Britain, 1955, conducting his music in London and Manchester; tour of Latin America, 1957, and elsewhere later; conducted programme of own works with London Symphony Orch., Jan. 1977. Other distinctions and awards include: Merited Artist; Member Supreme Soviet of Armenian Soviet Socialist Republic; People's Artist of USSR, 1954; Lenin Prize, 1959. Particularly interested in folk and national music; widely popular works inc. Spartacus suites (used as incidental music for The Onedin Line, BBC TV), and Sabre Dance. *Works: chamber music:* Dance in B flat for violin and piano, 1926; Song-Poem for violin and piano, 1929; Sonata in D minor for violin and piano, 1932; String Quartet in C major, 1932; Double Fugue for string quartet, 1932; Trio in G minor for clarinet, violin and piano, 1932; *piano music:* First Album of Children's Pieces, 1926-47; Poem in C sharp minor, 1927; Dance, 1927; 7 Recitatives and Fugues, 1928-36; Suite, 1932; Toccato, 1932; 3 Marches, 1939-44; 3 Pieces for two pianos, 1945; 5 Pieces from the music to Othello, 1955; 4 Pieces from the music to Macbeth, 1955; Sonatina in C major, 1958; Sonata, 1961; Second Album of Children's Pieces, 1965; *orchestral:* Dance Suite, 1932-33; Symphony No 1, 1934; The Valencian Widow, Suite, 1939-40; Symphony No 2, 1943-44; Gayaneh, Suites Nos 1-3, 1943; Masquerade, Suite, 1944; Solemn Overture, To the End of War, 1945; Russian Fantasy, 1946; Symphony No 3 (Symphony-Poem), 1947; Symphonic Dithyramb in Memory of Lenin, 1948; The Battle of Stalingrad, Suite, 1949-50; Solemn Poem, 1950-52; Concert Waltz, 1955; Spartacus, Suites Nos 1-3, 1955; Poema Festivo, 1956; Greetings Overture, 1958-59; Lermontov Suite, 1959; Spartacus, Suite No 4, 1966; *concertos, etc:* Piano Concerto in D flat, 1936; Violin Concerto in D minor, 1940 (also for flute and orch.); Cello Concerto in E major, 1946; Concerto-Rhapsody for piano, 1955, rev.; Concerto-Rhapsody for violin, 1961; Concerto-Rhapsody for cello, 1963; *voice and orchestra:* Three Concert Arias (Armenian texts), 1944-46; Ode of Joy, for mezzo-soprano, choir, ten harps, unison violin, band and orch., 1956; Ballade about the Fatherland, for bass and orch., 1961; *ballets:* Happiness, 3 acts, 6 sc., 1939; Gayaneh, 1st version, 4 acts, 5 sc., 1940-42, rev. 1952; 2nd version, 3 acts, 7 sc., 1957; Spartacus, 4 acts, 9 sc., 1950-56, rev. 1957-58; *incidental music:* Macbeth, 1933, 1955; The Valencian Widow, 1940; Masquerade, 1940; The Kremlin Chimes, 1942; Deep Prospecting, 1943; Ilya Golovin, 1949; King Lear, 1955; also music for plays by various Armenian playwrights, etc; *film music:* Pepo, 1934; Zangezur, 1938; The Garden, 1938; Salavat Yulayev, 1939; Prisoner No 217, 1945; The Russian Question, 1948; Vladimir Ilyich Lenin, 1948-49; They Have a Native Country, 1949; The Battle of Stalingrad (two series), 1949; The Secret Mission, 1950; Admiral Ushakov, 1953; Ships storming the Bastions, 1953; Othello, 1955; Saltanat, 1955; The Duel, 1957; *songs, etc; band music:* songs for voice and piano, for mixed choir and piano, marching and working songs, folk song arrangements, etc; music for military and brass bands, and for balalaika; National Anthem of Soviet Armenia, 1944 (adopted 1945). *Address:* c/o Laudan International Promotions, 20 Edith Road, West Kensington, W14 9BA. *T:* 01-603 4736. *[Died 1 May 1978.*

KHAMA, Sir Seretse M., KBE 1966 (OBE 1963); first President, Republic of Botswana, since 1966; Prime Minister of Bechuanaland, 1965-66; *b* 1 July 1921; *s* of Sekgoma and Tebogo Khama; *m* 1948, Ruth Williams; three *s* one *d. Educ:* Fort Hare, University of South Africa (BA); Balliol Coll., Oxford; Inner Temple. Bechuanaland: MEC, 1961; Pres., Democratic Party, 1962; MLA, 1965. Chancellor, University of Botswana, Lesotho and Swaziland, 1967-70. Hon. PhD, Fordham, NY, 1967; Hon. LLD: Univ. of Botswana, Lesotho and Swaziland, 1965; Princeton, 1976; Harvard, 1978; Hon. DLitt City Univ., 1978. Grand Comdr, Order of the Lion of Malaŵi, 1967; Royal Order of Sobhuza II Grand Counsellor, Swaziland, 1978. Hon. Fellow, Balliol Coll., Oxford, 1969. Nansen Medal, 1978. *Address:* State House, Gaborone, Botswana. *[Died 13 July 1980.*

KHAN, Brig. Fazalur Rahman; Ambassador of Pakistan to the Court of St James's, since 1979; *b* 1914. *Educ:* Punjab Univ.; Staff Coll., Quetta. Commissioned Army, 1940. Served War of 1939-45, Middle East and Italy (despatches). Appts on Gen. Staff; Comd Infty Bn and a Brigade; Dir of Mil. Ops and Brig., Gen. Staff. Dir, Bureau of Nat. Reconstruction, and Sec., Min. of Information and Broadcasting, 1958-60; Managing Dir, Fauji Foundation, 1963-70. *Address:* Embassy of Pakistan, 35 Lowndes Square, SW1X 9JN. *T:* 01-235 2044. *[Died 12 July 1980.*

KHAN, Field-Marshal Mohammad Ayub, (Hon.) GCMG 1960; NPk; HJ; President of Pakistan, 1958-69; *b* Rehana, 14 May 1907; *m* Zubeida Khatoon; four *s* three *d. Educ:* Aligarh Moslem Univ.; Royal Military Coll., Sandhurst. Commissioned, 1928. Served War of 1939-45. Col, 1947; Maj.-Gen. and first Commander, East Pakistan Division, 1948; Adjutant-Gen., 1950; General and first Pakistani Commander-in-Chief of Pakistan Army, 1951; Minister of Defence, Pakistan, 1954-55; Chief Martial Law Administrator and Supreme Commander of all Armed Forces, 1958; Field-Marshal, 1959. *Publication:* Friends Not Masters, a Political Autobiography, 1967. *Recreations:* riding, shooting, reading, golf and horticulture. *Address:* Rawalpindi, Pakistan. *[Died 20 April 1974.*

KHAN, Gen. Yahya; *see* Yahya Khan, Gen. Agha Muhammad.

KHRUSHCHEV, Nikita Sergeyevich; Hero of the Soviet Union; Hero of Socialist Labour (3); Order of Lenin (6); Order of Red Banner of Labour; Order of Suvorov (1st and 2nd cl.); Order of Kutuzov (1st cl.); Order of Great Patriotic War (1st cl.); *b* Kalinovka, near Kursk, 17 April 1894. *Educ:* Industrial Institute, Donetsk; Moscow Industrial Acad. Joined Communist Party, 1918; fought in Civil War, 1918-20; Sec., Moscow City Party Cttee, 1932-34; elected to Central Cttee of Communist Party, 1934-; Sec., Moscow Regional and Moscow City Cttees, 1935-38; responsible for industrialisation programme and construction of Moscow subway; designated Mem. of Supreme Soviet by Krasnaya Presnya district of Moscow, 1937; First Sec., Communist Party of the Ukraine, 1938-49; full mem. of the political bureau, 1938-49, and Mem. of the Presidium of CPSU Central Cttee, 1949-. Organised guerrilla defence of the Ukraine, 1941, given rank of Lieut-Gen. During War of 1941-45, Mem. of the military councils of the Kiev Special Military District, the South-Western direction, the Stalingrad, Southern and first Ukrainian fronts. Chm. Ukraine Council of Ministers, 1947; transf. back to Moscow Regional Cttee, 1949, Sec. of the Central Cttee, 1949-53; First Sec. of Central Cttee of Communist Party, 1953-64; Chm. of Council of Ministers of USSR, 1958-64; Serp i Molot (Sickle and Hammer) gold medal (3); Laureate of Internat. Lenin Peace Prize. *Publications:* For Durable Peace and Peaceful Co-existence, 1958; Let us Live in Peace and Friendship, 1959; For Victory in Peaceful Competition with Capitalism, 1959; A World Without Arms-A World Without War (speeches and interviews), 1960; Peace and Happiness for the Peoples, 1960; For Peace, for Disarmament, for Freedom of the Peoples, 1960; The Foreign Policy of the Soviet Union, 1961; Communism-Peace and Happiness for Peoples, 1962; Construction of Communism in the USSR and the Development of Agriculture (7 vols) 1962-63; The Noble Mission of Literature and Art, 1963; To Prevent War and to Safeguard Peace, 1963. Several vols of speeches (Eng. trans), 1959-61 (London). *Relevant publication:* Khrushchev Remembers, 1970. *Address:* Moscow, USSR. *[Died 11 Sept. 1971.*

KIDD, Franklin, CBE 1950; FRS 1944; MInstR; FRSA; MA Cantab, DSc London; Director of Food Investigation, Department of Scientific and Industrial Research, 1947-57, retired; *b* 1890, *e s* of late Benjamin Kidd, author of Social Evolution, The Science of Power, etc; *m* 1920, Mary Nest, *d* of late John Owen, Rt Rev. the Lord Bishop of St Davids. *Educ:* Tonbridge Sch.; St John's Coll., Cambridge; Fellow of St John's Coll., 1913-19, 1950-58. 12 months in Australia and NZ reporting to Govts on organisation of food research, 1927; Chm. Royal Commission (South Africa) to enquire into precooling of Deciduous Fruit, 1936; Chm. of Food Group of Soc. of Chemical Industry, 1936-38; Supt, Low Temperature Research Station, Cambridge, 1934-47. Mem. Board of Governors, Nat. Coll. of Food Technology, 1950; Mem. Nat. Council for Technological Awards, Board of Studies in Technologies other than Engineering, 1955; Kamerlingh Onnes Gold Medallist, 1963. *Publications:* Papers in various scientific journals and Food Investigation Special Reports; also Almond in Peterhouse and other Poems, 1950; The Peopled Earth in Five Movements, 1964. *Recreations:* fishing, bee-keeping. *Address:* Appleby Cottage, 24 Woodlands Road, Great Shelford, Cambs CB2 5LW. *T:* Shelford 2138. *[Died 7 May 1974.*

KIDD, Frederic William, CIE 1943; KPM 1931; Indian Police (retired); *b* 1 Sept. 1890; *s* of late F. W. Kidd, MD, 17 Lower Fitzwilliam Street, Dublin, Ireland; *m* 1924, Margaret Blake Loveday; one *s* one *d ; m* 1956, Helen Beatrice Woods (née

Blake). *Educ:* Tipperary Grammar Sch.; Trinity Coll., Dublin. Indian Police, 1911; various posts in Bengal Province; Deputy Commissioner Calcutta Police, 1919-28; Supt of Police, Midnapore, 1929-31; Darjeeling, 1932-33; Dacca, 1935-37; Central Intelligence Officer, Calcutta, 1938-39; Deputy Director, Intelligence Bureau, Home Dept, Govt of India, 1940-44. *Address:* Lower Coach House, Westwell, Tenterden, Kent. *T:* Tenterden 3110.   *[Died 3 July 1971.*

KIDSON, Harold Percy, MA, BSc (NZ); late Rector, Otago Boys' High School, Dunedin, New Zealand; retired 1948; *b* 11 June 1887; *s* of Charles and Christiana Kidson; *m* 1914, Dorothy Owen; two *d*. *Educ:* Nelson Coll., NZ; Canterbury University Coll., NZ; Sorbonne, Paris. Asst Master at Nelson Coll., Christchurch Boys' High School, NZ, Mathematical Sch., Rochester, England; Inspector of Secondary Schs, Department of Education, New Zealand; Principal Hutt Valley High Sch.; Formerly Pres. New Zealand Secondary Schs Association, and Mem. Otago Univ. Council. *Recreations:* fly-fishing, silviculture. *Address:* Wanaka, Otago, NZ.
                                             [Died 26 April 1971.

KILHAM ROBERTS, Denys, OBE 1946; MA; Barrister-at-Law; Consultant, Society of Authors (previously Secretary-General); *b* 2 April 1903; *m* 1st, Elizabeth Hume Bone; one *d*; 2nd, Mary, *o d* of late Dr T. K. Maclachlan. *Educ:* St Paul's Sch.; Magdalene Coll., Cambridge. Called to Bar, Inner Temple, 1928. Took active part in creation of League of Dramatists, Composers' Guild, Screenwriters' Assoc. and Radiowriters' Assoc. Has edited numerous periodicals and miscellanies. *Publications:* Titles to Fame, 1937; Straw in the Hair, 1938; The Centuries' Poetry 5 vols 1938-54; Stories of W. W. Jacobs, 1959; contribs on legal and literary subjects, wine and racing, to British and foreign books and periodicals. *Recreations:* growing vegetables, looking up old friends, and writing frivolous verse. *Address:* Magpie Cottage, Hall Street, Long Melford, Suffolk; 84 Drayton Gardens, SW10.   *[Died 15 March 1976.*

KILLBY, Leonard Gibbs, CMG 1946; BA, BSc (Oxon); *b* 1883; *y s* of late James and Anne Killby; *m* 1926, Marjorie Mayson, *e d* of late Sir Mayson Beeton, KBE; no *c*. *Educ:* Brentwood Sch., Essex; New Coll., Oxford (Scholar). BA 1904, 1st Class Hons, School of Natural Science (Chemistry); Demonstrator in Chemistry, Christ Church, 1904-6; BSc (Oxon) 1907; on staff of City and Guilds of London Institute Department of Technology, 1906-20; succeeded Sir Philip Magnus as Superintendent of the Dept, 1914; served European War, 1915-18, first in France and subsequently attached Ministry of Munitions Chemical Warfare Dept, Capt. General List (despatches); Sec., Empire Cotton Growing Corporation, 1920-44, Dir, 1944-47. *Recreations:* gardening, photography. *Address:* Little Orchard, Charlbury, Oxford.   *[Died 9 Aug. 1975.*

KILLEY, Prof. Homer Charles; Professor of Oral Surgery, University of London, since 1959; Hon. Consultant in Oral Surgery, and Head of Department of Oral Surgery, Eastman Dental Hospital, since 1959; Hon. Consultant, Westminster Hospital Teaching Group; *b* 5 May 1915; *s* of Thomas H. Killey and Marguerite Killey (née Parker); *m* 1940, Phoebe (née James); one *s*. *Educ:* King William's Coll., Isle of Man. KCH, LDSRCS, 1937; HDD Edinburgh, 1939; FDSRCS, 1948; Guy's Hospital, MRCS, LRCP, 1950; FDSRCS (Edinburgh) 1961. Consultant in oral and maxillo-facial surgery, Maxillo-facial Unit, Rooksdown House, Basingstoke, also Consultant in Oral Surgery, Holy Cross Hosp., Haslemere, Queen Mary's Hosp., Roehampton, and Aldershot Gen. Hosp., 1950-59. Hon. Civilian Lecturer in Maxillo-facial Injuries, Royal Army Dental Corps Depot, Aldershot, 1950-; Legg Memorial Lecturer, 1967. Member: Board of Dental Studies, University of London; Dental Adv. Bd, Med. Protection Soc.; British Assoc. of Head and Neck Oncologists; Associate Mem. British Assoc. of Plastic Surgeons; Fellow, Internat. Assoc. of Oral Surgeons; FZS; FICS; FRSM; Foundn Fellow Brit. Assoc. of Oral Surgeons; Fellow, RSH. *Publications:* Fractures of the Facial Skeleton (with N. L. Rowe), 1955, 2nd edn 1968; Fractures of the Middle Third of the Facial Skeleton, 1965, 2nd edn 1971; (with L. W. Kay) The Impacted Wisdom Tooth, 1965; Benign Cystic Lesions of the Jaws, 1966, 2nd edn 1972; Fractures of the Mandible, 1967, 2nd edn 1971; (with L. W. Kay) The Prevention of Complications in Dental Surgery, 1969; (with G. Seward and L. W. Kay) An Outline of Oral Surgery, Parts I and II, 1971; The Maxillary Sinus and its Dental Implications, 1975; *chapters in:* Holdsworth's Cleft Lip and Palate, 3rd edn 1963, 4th edn, 1970; Morrant's Modern Trends in Dental Surgery, 1963; Hamilton Bailey's Emergency Surgery, 8th edn, 1967; Thomas' Oral Pathology, 6th edn, 1970; contrib. to learned jls. *Recreations:* reading and music. *Address:* Institute of Dental Surgery, Eastman Dental Hospital, Gray's Inn Road, WC1. *T:* 01-837 7251.   *[Died 8 May 1976.*

KILLICK, Brig. Sir Alexander Herbert, Kt 1956; CBE 1944; DSO 1919; MC; *b* 10 Feb. 1894; *m* 1920, Mary Catherine, *d* of Ira Wentzel, Bellwood, Penn, USA; one *d* (one *s* decd). *Educ:* Dulwich Coll.; Exeter Coll., Oxford (MA); Staff Coll., Camberley (psc). Served European War 1914-19 (despatches, DSO, MC, Order of Nile of Egypt); retired (RARO) 1932. Sec., Royal Institution of Chartered Surveyors, 1932-59; Hon. Mem., 1959-; Sec.-Gen., Internat. Fedn of Surveyors, 1934-38. War of 1939-45: recalled to Colours (RARO); Gen. Staff, War Office, 1939-40; Joint Sec. (Mil.), Army Council Secretariat, WO, 1941-45, retd 1945; Hon. Brig. 1945. Mem., Mining Qualifications Bd, Min. of Power, 1959-62; Pres. Coll. of Estate Management, 1960-61; Director: London Merchant Securities and associated companies; Carlton Industries; Trustee, The Rayne Foundation; Mem., Professional Classes Aid Council; Freeman, Worshipful Company of Farmers. *Address:* 100 George Street, W1H 6DJ. *Clubs:* Army and Navy, St Stephen's.   *[Died 4 Feb. 1975.*

KILMAINE, 6th Baron, *cr* 1789; **John Francis Archibald Browne,** Bt 1636; CBE 1956; a Trustee: the Historic Churches Preservation Trust; the Dulverton Trust (Secretary, 1953-66); High Steward of Harwich, 1966-76; a Governor of the Thomas Wall Trust; *b* 22 Sept. 1902; *e s* of 5th Baron and Lady Aline Kennedy (*d* 1957), *d* of 3rd Marquess of Ailsa; *S* father 1946; *m* 1930, Wilhelmina Phyllis, *o d* of Scott Arnott, Tanners, Brasted, Kent; one *s* two *d*. *Educ:* Winchester; Magdalen Coll., Oxford, MA. On staff of British Xylonite Co. Ltd, 1925-29; Administrative Sec. to University Coll., Southampton, 1930-33; Sec. of the Oxford Society, 1933-40, Chm., 1949-73; Sec., Pilgrim Trust, 1945-67; Chairman: Charities Investment Managers Ltd, 1965-74; Rochester Diocesan Adv. Cttee for care of Churches, 1970-75. Served War of 1939-45 as Lt-Col RASC and on Staff, 1940-45 (despatches twice). Hon. DCL Oxford, 1973. *Heir: s* Hon. John David Henry Browne [*b* 2 April 1948. *Educ:* Eton. Dir, Fusion (Bickenhill) Ltd]. *Address:* The Mount House, Brasted, Kent. *Club:* Travellers'. *[Died 26 July 1978.*

KILMARNOCK, 6th Baron, *cr* 1831; **Gilbert Allan Rowland Boyd,** MBE (mil.) 1945; TD 1972; Hon. Lt-Col RA (TA), (retired); late Hertfordshire Yeomanry; Chief of the Clan Boyd; *b* 15 Jan. 1903; *yr s* of 21st Earl of Erroll; *S* to Barony of brother, 22nd Earl of Erroll, 1941; assumed surname of Boyd instead of Hay, 1941; *m* 1st, 1926, Hon. Rosemary Guest (marr. diss. 1955; she *m* 2nd, 1955, John Berger, and *d* 1971), *er d* of 1st Viscount Wimborne; two *s* two *d*; 2nd, 1955, Denise, *o c* of late Major Lewis Coker and of Mrs T. E. Fenlon; two *s*. *Educ:* Cheltenham Coll. Served War of 1939-45, N Africa and Italy with 1st Div. as DAAG, 1943-44 (despatches, MBE). Asst Military Sec. to Supreme Allied C-in-C Mediterranean Theatre, 1945. Deputized for Lord High Constable of Scotland at Coronation of HM the Queen, 1953. Vice-Chm., 1963-65, Chm., 1965-67, Baltic Mercantile & Shipping Exchange; Chm., Harris and Dixon Ltd, 1967-72. Pres. Inst. of Chartered Shipbrokers, 1959-62; Pres. London Chamber of Commerce, 1961-63. Chief of the Scottish Clans Assoc. of London, 1962. A Freeman of the City of London; A Liveryman of the Worshipful Company of Shipwrights. President: Sino-British Trade Council, 1961-63; Royal Caledonian Schools, Bushey, Herts, 1964-. *Recreations:* shooting, gardening. *Heir: s* Hon. Alastair Ivor Gilbert Boyd, Lieutenant Irish Guards, retired [*b* 11 May 1927; *m* 1954, Diana Mary (marr. diss. 1970), *o d* of D. Grant Gibson. Served Palestine, 1947-48]. *Address:* 28 Eaton Terrace, SW1. *T:* 01-730 8393. *Clubs:* White's; Puffins (Edinburgh).
                                             [Died 15 May 1975.

KILMOREY, 5th Earl of, *cr* 1822; **Francis Jack Richard Patrick Needham;** Viscount Kilmorey, 1625; Viscount Newry and Mourne, 1822; *b* 4 Oct. 1915; *er s* of Major Hon. Francis Edward Needham, MVO, Gren. Guards (*d* 1955) and of Blanche Esther Combe; *S* uncle, 1961; *m* 1941, Helen Bridget, *y d* of Sir Lionel Faudel-Phillips, 3rd and last Bt; three *s*. *Educ:* Stowe; RMC, Sandhurst. 2nd Lt Gren. Gds, 1935. Served War of 1939-45 (wounded): Europe and N Africa; Major 1943. *Recreations:* shooting, fishing. *Heir: s* Viscount Newry and Morne (Needham, Richard Francis). *Address:* Via San Leonardo 32, Florence, Italy. *T:* Florence 220284. *Club:* Turf.
                                             [Died 12 April 1977.

KILPATRICK, Dr George Gordon Dinwiddie, DSO 1919; ED 1950; BA, DD; LLD; DCL; Principal, United Theological College, Montreal, 1938-43 and again, 1945-55, retired; Assistant Minister of St Andrews United Church, Toronto, since Sept. 1955; *b* 12 April 1888; *s* of Thomas Buchanan Kilpatrick and Anna Orr; *m* 1920, Ruth McGillivray Fotheringham; three *s* one *d*. *Educ:* Grammar Sch., Aberdeen, Scotland; The Collegiate, Winnipeg; Toronto Univ.; Knox Theological Coll., Toronto; New Coll., Edinburgh. Travelling Scholarship to Germany, 1913-14; Asst Minister Westminster Presbyterian

Church, Toronto; Canadian Expeditionary Force (42nd Bn Royal Highlanders) 1915-19, (DSO, despatches, two medals); Minister St Andrew's Presbyterian Church, Ottawa, 1919-25; Minister Chalmers United Church, Ottawa, 1925-29; Minister Melrose Church, The United Church of Canada, 1929-38. Dir of Education, Canadian Army (rank-Col), 1943-Dec. 1945. The DD has been conferred by 4 Colleges. *Publication:* A Quiver of Arrows. *Address:* 9 Deer Park Crescent, Apartment 403, Toronto, Ontario M4V 2C4, Canada. *Clubs:* Royal Montreal Curling, McGill University Faculty (Montreal).
[*Died* 11 *Oct.* 1975.

KIMALEL, Shadrack Kiptenai; High Commissioner for Kenya in London, since 1979; *b* 7 Dec. 1930; *s* of Chief Joel Malel; *m* 1959, Jebitok Rop; two *s* two *d. Educ:* University College of Makerere, Uganda. BA London, DipEd East Africa. Teacher, 1957-61; Education Officer (Administration), 1962-63; Provincial Education Officer, 1964-66; Asst Director of Education, 1966-67; Dep. Director of Education, 1967-70; High Commissioner for Kenya: to India, 1970-77; to Nigeria, 1977-79. Hon. Charter Fellow, College of Preceptors, 1980. *Recreations:* reading, table tennis, hockey. *Address:* 78 Winnington Road, Hampstead, N2 0TU. *T:* 01-455 5419. *Club:* Mount Kenya Safari.
[*Died* 28 *Dec.* 1980.

KIMBALL, Major Lawrence; *b* 1900; *s* of Marcus Morton Kimball; *m* 1st, 1927, Kathleen Joan (marr. diss., 1946), *o surv d* of late H. R. Ratcliff of Stanford Hall, Loughborough; one *s* one *d*; 2nd, Gillian, *d* of late W. S. Tresawna, Leven House, Abergavenny, and widow of Capt. John Waterman. *Educ:* abroad; Caius Coll., Cambridge. Barrister-at-Law, Gray's Inn, 1926; MP (U) Loughborough Div. of Leics, 1931-45; High Sheriff of Rutland 1931. Lt PAO Leics Yeo., 1929; Capt. 67th LAA Regt, RA, 1939; Major 1940. *Address:* Down House, Redlynch, Salisbury, Wilts. *T:* Downton 347. *Clubs:* St James', Army and Navy.
[*Died* 30 *Dec.* 1971.

KIMBER, Gurth, CMG 1952; *b* 19 Jan. 1906; *s* of late R. J. Kimber; *m* 1943, Joan, *d* of late Roy Gibson; two *d. Educ:* Perse; Clare Coll., Cambridge. Appointed Dominions Office, 1928; Asst UK Government Representative, Canberra, 1934-35; Official Sec., United Kingdom High Commissioner's Office, Canberra, 1946-50; Dep. High Commissioner for the UK, Bombay, 1952-54; Counsellor, British Embassy, Dublin, 1956-60; British Dep. High Commissioner, Canberra, 1962-65; retired, 1966. *Recreation:* sailing. *Address:* 32 Bear Street, Nayland, Suffolk.
[*Died* 7 *Dec.* 1978.

KIMMINS, Lt-Gen. Sir Brian Charles Hannam, KBE 1956 (CBE 1944); CB 1946; DL; retired; *b* 30 July 1899; *s* of late Dr Charles William Kimmins and Dame Grace Kimmins, DBE; *m* 1929, Marjory, *d* of late Lt-Col W. J. Johnston, CBE, Lesmurdie, Elgin, Scotland; one *s* two *d. Educ:* Harrow; RMA, Woolwich. Commissioned RA 1917; served France and Flanders, 1918; in RHA in India, 1920-26; RHA in Egypt, 1926-28; ADC to Lord Lloyd, High Commissioner for Egypt and the Sudan, 1928-29; Adjutant RMA, Woolwich, 1930-33; Bde Major 147 Inf. Bde (TA), 1935-37; Staff Coll., Minley Manor, 1938-39; GSO 2 HQ, BEF, France, 1939-40: Instructor Staff Coll., 1940-41; GSO 1 ops GHQ Home Forces, 1941; DDMT War Office, 1941-42; BGS Southern Command, 1942; CRA Guards Armoured Div., 1943; Director of Plans, SEAC, 1944; Asst Chief of Staff, HQ, SACSEA, 1945; Chief of Staff HQ Combined Operations, 1946; Dir of Quartering, War Office, 1947-50; GOC, Home Counties District and 44th Div. TA, 1950-52; Dir, Territorial Army and Cadets, 1952-55; GOC Northern Ireland District, 1955-58. Col Comdt, Royal Artillery, 1955-64. DL, Somerset, 1968. Legion of Merit degree of Comdr (USA), 1946. Legion of Honour degree of Officer, Croix de Guerre (France), 1949. OStJ 1959. *Recreations:* fishing, golf. *Address:* Lamb Cottage, South Petherton, Somerset. *Club:* Army and Navy.
[*Died* 15 *Nov.* 1979.

KIMPTON, Lawrence Alpheus; Director, Standard Oil (Indiana), 1958, Executive, 1960, Vice-President, 1963, Assistant to Chairman of the Board, 1969-71, retired; *b* 7 Oct. 1910; *s* of Carl Edward Kimpton and Lynn (née Kennedy); *m* 1st, 1943, Marcia Drennon (*d* 1963); 2nd, 1975, Mary Townsend Kimpton. *Educ:* Stanford Univ., Stanford, Calif. (AB, MA); Cornell Univ., Ithaca, NY (PhD). Hon. DSc, Beloit Coll., 1952; Hon. LLD of several univs; 24th Hon. Stanford Fellow, 1959. Deep Springs Coll., Calif: Instructor, 1935-36; Dean and Dir, 1936-41; Dean, College of Liberal Arts, Prof. of Mathematics and Philosophy, University of Kansas City, 1942-43; University of Chicago: Chief Admin. Officer, Atomic Bomb Project, 1943-44; Prof. of Philosophy and Education, 1944-46; Academic Vice-Pres., Prof. of Philosophy and Education, 1946-47; Vice-Pres. in Charge of Development, 1950-51; Chancellor and Prof. of

Philosophy, 1951-60; Dean of Students, Prof. of Philosophy, Stanford Univ., 1947-50; Hon. Trustee: Museum of Science and Industry, 1961; Univ. of Chicago; Newberry Library, 1962-. Director: Chessie System; C&O Railroad; B&O Railroad. *Recreations:* boating, reading. *Address:* Box 211, Lakeside, Michigan 49116, USA. *Clubs:* Chicago, Commercial, Tavern, Wayfarers' Chicago Yacht (Chicago); Bohemian (San Francisco).
[*Died* 31 *Oct.* 1977.

KINAHAN, Adm. Sir Harold (Richard George), KBE 1949 (CBE 1942); CB 1945; retired; *b* 4 June 1893; *s* of Vice-Adm. R. G. Kinahan, Belfast; *m* 1919, Mary Kathleen Downes (*d* 1970); two *d. Educ:* RN Colls, Osborne and Dartmouth. Entered RNC, Osborne, 1906; Lt 1914; Comdr 1927; Capt. 1934; Rear-Adm. 1943; Vice-Adm. 1947; Adm. 1950. DPS, Admiralty, 1944-46; Flag Officer Comdg 1st Cruiser Sqdn, Mediterranean Fleet, 1946-47; Vice-Pres., 1947-49, Pres., 1949-50, Ordnance Board; Pres., RNC, Greenwich, 1950-52; retired list, 1952. *Address:* Severnridge, Almondsbury, Bristol.
[*Died* 22 *March* 1980.

KINDERSLEY, 2nd Baron, *cr* 1941, of West Hoathly; **Hugh Kenyon Molesworth Kindersley,** CBE 1945 (MBE 1941); MC 1918; Director, Lazard Brothers & Co. Ltd, 1965-71 (Chairman, 1953-64; Managing Director, 1927-64); *b* 1899; *s* of 1st Baron Kindersley, GBE, and Gladys Margaret Beadle; *S* father 1954; *m* 1921, Nancy Farnsworth, *d* of Dr Geoffrey Boyd, Toronto; one *s* two *d. Educ:* Eton. Served European War, Scots Guards, 1917-19 (MC). War of 1939-45, Scots Guards, 6th Airborne Div., temporary Brig. (MBE, CBE). Chairman: Rolls Royce Ltd, 1956-68; Guardian Royal Exchange Assurance Ltd, 1968-69; Governor, Royal Exchange Assurance, 1955-69; Dir, Bank of England, 1947-67. Chm., Review Body on Doctors' and Dentists' Remuneration, 1962-70. Pres. and Past Chm., Arthritis and Rheumatism Council. Hon. FRCS, 1959; Mem., Court of Patrons, RCS, 1960; Hon. Gold Medal, RCS, 1975. High Sheriff of the County of London, 1951. Comdr, Royal Order of St Olav of Norway, 1958. *Heir: s* Hon. Robert Hugh Molesworth Kindersley, Lt, Scots Guards [*b* 18 Aug. 1929; *m* 1954, Venice Marigold (Rosie), *d* of late Capt. Lord (Arthur) Francis Henry Hill; three *s* one *d. Educ:* Eton; Trinity Coll., Oxford; Harvard Business Sch., USA. Served in Malaya, 1949]. *Address:* Ramhurst Manor, near Tonbridge, Kent. *T:* Hildenborough 832174. *Clubs:* White's, Cavalry and Guards.
[*Died* 6 *Oct.* 1976.

KING, Sir Alexander Boyne, Kt 1944; CBE 1937; DL 1947; LLD 1957; JP; director of cinema companies, *b* Glasgow, 1888; *s* of late James L. King and late Mrs King (*d* 1965), *d* of late John Craig, Glasgow; two *d. Educ:* Rutland Crescent Sch., Glasgow. Entered Theatrical Profession, 1900, and Cinematograph Industry, 1913; Past President, Cinematograph Exhibitors' Assoc. (1949-50). Chairman: Films of Scotland Cttee; Grants Sub-Cttee Scottish Advisory Cttee to Army Benevolent Fund. KStJ 1964. Officier de la Légion d'Honneur, 1961. *Recreations:* golf, fishing. *Address:* Tigh-na-Righ, The Grove, Whitecraigs, Giffnock, Glasgow G46 6RW; 309 Sauchiehall Street, Glasgow G2 3HN. *TA:* Kenafilm Glasgow. *T:* (office) 041-332 8668; (home) 041-638 1000. *Clubs:* Royal Scottish Automobile (Glasgow); Royal and Ancient (St Andrews); Western Gailes, Nairn, Old Troon Golf.
[*Died* 12 *Feb.* 1973.

KING, Sir Anthony (Highmore), Kt 1962; CBE 1953; Senior Master and Queen's Remembrancer, 1960-62; Queen's Coroner and Attorney, Master of the Crown Office and Registrar of the Court of Criminal Appeal, 1946-62; *b* 22 April 1890; 2nd *s* of Sir George Anthony King; *m* 1934, Winifride Botterell McConnell; no *c. Educ:* Winchester Coll.; Corpus Christi Coll., Oxford. Barrister-at-Law, Inner Temple, 1913. Served European War, 1914-18: France; Lt East Surrey Regt (wounded); Min. of Nat. Service, 1916-18. Asst Registrar, Court of Criminal Appeal, 1933. Master, Scriveners' Company, 1933 and 1947. Hon. Liveryman, Glass-Sellers' Company, 1966. *Address:* Linden Lea, Leigh Place, Cobham, Surrey. *T:* Cobham (Surrey) 2256.
[*Died* 28 *March* 1977.

KING, Sir (Clifford) Robertson, KBE 1960 (CBE 1954); Director, Pirelli-General Cable Works Ltd, since 1963 (Chairman, 1963-66); Chairman, Electricity Council, 1959-61, retired; *b* 6 Feb. 1895; *s* of William and Edith L. King, Ilkeston, Derbs; *m* 1926, Dorothy V. N. Latimore, Ilkeston; one *s* one *d. Educ:* Ilkeston Secondary Sch.; Heanor Technical Sch. Served European War, 1914-18, with Sherwood Foresters and as a commissioned Officer with Northumberland Fusiliers. Joined Derbs and Notts Electric Power Co., 1919; Dep. Gen. Man. of Derbs and Notts, Leicester and Warwick, and associated Companies within the Midland Counties Group, 1936, General Manager, 1940-48; Chm., The East Midlands Electricity Board,

1948-57; Mem. of the British Electricity Authority, 1950-51, and of Central Electricity Authority, 1956-57; Chm. Nat. Inspection Council for Electrical Installation Contracting, 1956-58; Dep. Chm. Central Electricity Generating Board, 1957-59; Chm. Electrical Development Assoc., 1955-56. *Recreations:* cricket, football, hockey. *Address:* (private) Riverside House, Borrowash, near Derby.   [*Died 16 Aug.* 1976.

KING, Colin Henry Harmsworth; Chairman and Chief Executive since 1975, Managing Director since 1972, Wall Paper Manufacturers Ltd; *b* 20 June 1931; *s* of Cecil Harmsworth King and Agnes Margaret King; *m* 1956, Alison Marguerite Husbands; one *s* one *d. Educ:* Eton. Coldstream Guards, 1949-51; Anglo Canadian Pulp & Paper Mills, 1951-61; joined Reed Paper Group in Commercial Depts, 1961: Personal Asst to Sir Don Ryder, 1963-66; managerial and directorial positions in Reed Paper & Board (UK) Ltd, 1970; Dir, Reed International, 1972. Mem., Design Council, 1974. *Recreations:* gardening, reading. *Address:* Brooms Down, Wateringbury, Kent ME18 5PE. *T:* Maidstone 812671.   [*Died 18 Jan.* 1977.

KING, Cyril Lander, QC; *b* 1883; *e s* of George Lander King, London; *m* 1913, Eirene Laetitia, *d* of James Fergusson; two *d.* Called to the Bar, Middle Temple, 1919; KC 1937; Bencher, 1943. *Address:* New Court, Temple, EC4. [*Died 24 June* 1972.

KING, E(dward) J(ohn) Boswell, CBE 1942; MC; *s* of late Edward Charles King; *m* 1935, Edith (*d* 1949), *e d* of late Arthur Milan Beckwith, Belleville, Illinois, USA. *Educ:* Christ's Hospital. Entered service of London County Council, 1930; Chief Asst Public Assistance Dept 1932; Dir of London County Council Rest Centres, 1941-42; Chief Officer of Supplies, London County Council, 1943-51; Mem. Board of Trade Furniture Production Cttee, 1944-48; appointed by Uganda Government to report on administration of supplies and stores, 1954-55. First Fellow and First Pres., Inst. of Public Supplies. *Publications:* Public Supplies, 1954; The Blue Pheasant, 1958; Lost Girl, 1959. *Recreations:* photography, painting for pleasure. *Address:* c/o Midland Bank Ltd, Devonshire Road, Bexhill-on-Sea, Sussex. *Club:* Athenæum.   [*Died 1 Jan.* 1975.

KING, Adm. Edward Leigh Stuart, CB 1940; MVO 1925; *b* 1889; *e s* of C. J. S. King of Chardstock; *m* 1917, Lilian Alice (*d* 1944), *d* of Edward Strickland, Clifton; no *c.* Served in HMS Repulse during Prince of Wales' African and S American Tour, 1925; Dir of Plans, Admiralty, 1933-35; Chief of Staff to Commander-in-Chief, Home Fleet, 1938; ADC to the King, 1938; commanded a Cruiser Sqdn, 1940-41; a Lord Commissioner of the Admiralty and an Asst-Chief of Naval Staff, 1941-42; Principal Naval Liaison Officer to Allied Navies, 1943; retired, 1944. DL Cornwall, 1953. *Address:* Ruan Minor, Helston, Cornwall. *Club:* United Service.   [*Died 8 May* 1971.

KING, Mrs Grace M. H.; *see* Hamilton-King.

KING, Maj.-Gen. Harold Francis Sylvester, CB 1952; CBE 1949 (MBE 1940); retired; *b* 16 Oct. 1895; *m* 1919, Bertha Eveleen Alldred one *d. Educ:* Forest Sch., Walthamstow, E17. Served European War, 1914-18 (France). RFA 1915; RAOC, 1926; served War of 1939-45 (Middle East and Persia); Lt-Col 1942; Col 1948; Brig. 1950; Maj.-Gen. 1950; Inspector, Royal Army Ordnance Corps, 1950-53, retired 1953. Hon. Col, RAOC Supplementary Reserve, 1954-55. *Address:* 45 Woodland Way, Petts Wood, Kent. *T:* Orpington 5575.   [*Died 19 Feb.* 1974.

KING, Sir John Richard D.; *see* Duckworth-King.

KING, Sir Louis, Kt 1969; CMG 1962; CVO 1963; Under-Secretary, Secretary to Minister of Health and Clerk of Executive Council, South Australian Government, 1961-69, retired; *b* 15 April 1904; *s* of late Ernest and Mary C. King; *m* 1938, Audrey Cleve Sutton; no *c. Educ:* Adelaide High Sch. Entered Public Service of South Australia, 1920; Sec., Agent General for South Australia in London, 1938-46; Sec., Minister of Agriculture, 1947-54; Sec. to Premier and Sec. to Minister of Immigration, 1954-61. *Recreations:* bowls and gardening. *Address:* 12 Fortrose Street, Glenelg, SA 5045, Australia. *T:* 95-3519.   [*Died 22 Sept.* 1972.

KING, Sir Peter (Alexander), 7th Bt *cr* 1815; Company Director; *b* 13 Nov. 1928; *s* of Sir Alexander William King, 6th Bt and Dorothy Alice (*d* 1961), *d* of H. W. Champion; *s* father, 1969; *m* 1957, Jean Margaret, *d* of Christopher Thomas Cavell, Deal; one *s* one *d. Educ:* Cliftonville Coll.; Cranbrook School. *Recreations:* fishing and all sports. *Heir: s* Wayne Alexander King, *b* 2 Feb. 1962. *Address:* Charlestown, 365 London Road, Upper Deal, Deal, Kent. *T:* Deal 4855. *Clubs:* Royal Marine Association, Headquarters (Portsmouth).   [*Died 10 July* 1973.

KING, Philip; playwright and actor; *b* 1904. First play produced, 1940. *Plays include:* Without the Prince, 1940; Come to the Fair, 1940; See How They Run, 1944; (with Falkland L. Cary) Crystal Clear, 1945; On Monday Next..., 1949; (with Anthony Armstrong) Here We Come Gathering, 1951; As Black as She's Painted, 1952; Serious Charge, 1953; (with Falkland L. Cary), Sailor Beware, 1955; Watch It Sailor, 1961; Pools Paradise, 1961; (with Falkland L. Cary), Rock-A-Bye, Sailor, 1962; How Are You, Johnnie, 1963; (with Falkland L. Cary), Big Bad Mouse, 1966; I'll Get My Man, 1966; (with Parnell Bradbury) Dark Lucy, 1970; (with John Boland) Murder in Company, 1972; (with John Boland) Elementary My Dear, 1974; (with John Boland) Who Says Murder?, 1975. *Address:* 3 Woodland Way, Withdean, Brighton BN1 8BA. *T:* Brighton 505675. *Clubs:* Constitutional, Savage.   [*Died 9 Feb.* 1979.

KING, Sir Robertson; *see* King, Sir C. R.

KING, William Charles Holland, FRBS; *b* 5 Oct. 1884; *s* of Charles Holland and Martha King, Cheltenham; *m* Constance, *e d* of A. J. Bagley; two *d. Educ:* Cheltenham Grammar Sch.; Royal Academy Schs, London (Landseer Schol.). Exhibitor at Royal Academy and other exhibitions, 1910-. *Works:* Busts of Louise, Dowager Duchess of Beaufort; 10th Duke of Beaufort; 8th Earl of Bessborough; 9th Earl of Bessborough; Viscount Peel; Hon. Windham Baring; Lady Ulrica Baring; Sir Max Waechter; Lady Max Waechter; Hon. Desmond Ponsonby; F-M Sir Henry Wilson; P. A. Laszlo de Lombos; Mrs H. A. Rose; Mrs Lynch; Evelyn d'Alroy; Dr Paula Machado of Rio de Janeiro; Mrs E. Barrett; the late Sir Robert Mond; Garden Statuary at Bessborough, Ireland, and Canford Manor, Dorset; Figure-heads for yachts for Lord Tredegar and Mr Lionel de Rothschild; Memorials to late King Edward at Bagshot, Baron Carlo de Tuyll at Horton, Glos, Gen. Sir F. Maude, Sir Peile Thompson, Bt, Capt. Gordon Duff at Drummuir, Col E. Barrett at Farnham, Silvester Horne at Whitfields (London), Rev. Kirkpatrick at St Augustine's, Kilburn, Earl of Carnarvon at Campo Santo, Genoa, E. Grace at Westcliffe; Panel and Statues of co-Founders All Souls Coll., Oxford; War Memorials: Men of SE & C Railway at Dover, Wolverhampton, Latimer, etc. Formerly Pres. Royal Society of British Sculptors. RBS Gold Medal for Distinguished Services to Sculpture. *Address:* The House of St Francis, Whitwell, Ventnor, IOW.

[*Died 12 May* 1973.

KING-HALL, Magdalen, (Mrs Patrick Perceval-Maxwell); *b* 22 July 1904; *yr d* of late Admiral Sir George King-Hall and Lady King-Hall; *m* 1929, Patrick Perceval-Maxwell; two *s* one *d. Educ:* Downe House; St Leonard's Sch. *Publications:* The Diary of a Young Lady of Fashion, 1925; I think I remember, 1927; The Well-meaning Young Man (with L. King-Hall), 1930; Gay Crusaders, 1934; Maid of Honour, 1936; Jehan of the Ready Fists, 1936; Lady Sarah, 1939; Sturdy Rogue, 1941; Somehow Overdone, 1942; Lord Edward, 1943; Life and Death of the Wicked Lady Skelton, 1944; How Small a Part of Time, 1946 (published in USA as The Lovely Lynchs, 1947); Lady Shane's Daughter, 1947; Tea at Crumbo Castle, 1948; The Fox Sisters, 1950; The Edifying Bishop, 1951; The Venetian Bride, 1954; Hag Khalida, 1954; 18th Century Story, 1956; The Story of the Nursery, 1958; The Noble Savages, 1962. *Address:* c/o Mrs Walker, St Columb's Moville, Co. Donegal, Eire. *T:* Moville 32.

[*Died 26 Feb.* 1971.

KING-HARMAN, Captain (Robert) Douglas, DSO 1941; DSC and Bar; Royal Navy; *b* Barbadoes, BWI, 18 Aug. 1891; 2nd *s* of Sir C. A. King-Harman, KCMG (*d* 1939), and Lady (Constance) King-Harman (*d* 1961), Ouse Manor, Sharnbrook, Bedfordshire; *m* 1st, 1916, Lily Moffatt (marr. diss., 1926; she *d* 1966); one *s* ; 2nd, 1927, Elizabeth Lilian Bull (*d* 1974); 3rd, 1975, Eve Mary Palmer. *Educ:* Royal Naval Coll., Dartmouth. Entered Navy, 1904; served in destroyers, Grand Fleet and Dover Patrol, 1914-18; at Jutland; DSC given for his part in HMS Swift in action between destroyers Swift and Broke and German destroyers, 1917; the bar to DSC was for minesweeping after the Armistice of 1918; retired 1928 and entered Singapore Pilotage; returned to Navy, Sept. 1939 and served until 1946; retired from Singapore Pilotage, 1948. *Address:* Jakins, Great Gransden, Cambs. *T:* Great Gransden 346.

[*Died 30 May* 1978.

KINGSFORD, Reginald John Lethbridge, CBE 1963; MA; Fellow of Clare College, Cambridge, since 1949; *b* 10 Sept. 1900; *o s* of late Rev. R. L. Kingsford and late Gertrude Rodgers; *m* 1927, Ruth (*d* 1971), *o d* of late W. F. A. Fletcher, Biggleswade; one *s. Educ:* Sherborne Sch. (scholar); Clare Coll., Cambridge (scholar). General Manager, Cambridge Univ. Press, London, 1936-48; Sec. to the Syndics of the Cambridge University Press, 1948-63. Mem. of Council, Publishers' Association, 1940-53;

Pres. of Publishers' Association, 1943-45; Mem. Governing Body of Sherborne Sch., 1945-71. *Publication:* The Publishers' Association, 1896-1946, 1970. *Recreation:* books. *Address:* 2 Barrow Close, Cambridge. *T:* 52963.   *[Died 12 Dec. 1978.*

KINGSLEY, J(ohn) Donald; Special Representative for Middle East Affairs, The Ford Foundation, since 1968; *b* 25 March 1908; *s* of John H. and Carolyn Donaldson Kingsley; *m* 1st, 1930, Alice W. Boyd (marr. diss.); one *d*; 2nd, 1946, Ruth Caplan; one *s* one *d. Educ:* Syracuse Univ. (MA, PhD); London Sch. of Economics; University of Louisville (LLD). Prof. of Politics, Antioch Coll., 1933-42; Asst Regional Dir, US War Manpower Commn, 1943-44; Dep. Exec. Dir, US War Manpower Commn, 1945; Dep. Dir, Office of War Mobilization and Reconversion, 1946; Programme Co-ordinator, The White House, 1947; Asst Federal Security Administrator, 1948; Dir-Gen., International Refugee Organization, 1949-52; Agent-Gen., United Nations Korean Reconstruction Agency, 1951-53; Administrator, Paris Refugee Reparations Fund, 1949-58; The Ford Foundation: Resident Rep. (W Africa), 1959-63; Dir for ME and Africa, 1963-68. *Publications:* Public Personnel Administration (with W. E. Mosher), 1936, 1940; Representative Bureaucracy, 1944. *Recreations:* painting, sailing. *Address:* PO Box 2379, Beirut, Lebanon. *Clubs:* Overseas Press (New York); Ikoyi (Lagos); Capitol Democratic (Washington).   *[Died 1 June 1972.*

KINGSMILL, Lieut-Col William Henry, DSO 1943; MC 1940; Grenadier Guards, Retired; *b* 1 Dec. 1905; *s* of late Lieut-Col Andrew de Portal Kingsmill, DSO, OBE, MC, DL; *m* 1st, 1929, Aileen Kyrle Smith (from whom he obtained a divorce); 2nd, 1939, Diana Ivy, *widow* of Lieut-Col Guy Kingston Olliver; no *c. Educ:* Eton; RMC, Sandhurst. Joined Grenadier Guards 1925; transferred to RARO 1929; Dir of Cos., 1932-39; rejoined Grenadier Guards, Aug. 1939. Served France and Belgium, 1939-40 (MC); North Africa 8th Army, 1942-43; Italy, 1943-44 (DSO); commanded 6th Bn Grenadier Guards, 1943-44. MP (C) Yeovil Div. of Somerset, 1945-51. Chm. of companies; company dir, 1946-. *Recreations:* golf, tennis, shooting, yachting. *Address:* Sydmonton Court, Burghclere, near Newbury, Berks. *T:* Burghclere 332; 7 Cheyne Gardens, SW3. *T:* 01-352 5419. *Clubs:* Guards, White's.   *[Died 3 June 1971.*

KINGSTON-McCLOUGHRY, Air Vice-Marshal Edgar James, CB 1950; CBE 1943; DSO 1918; DFC 1918; AFRAeS; retired; *b* 10 Sept. 1896; *s* of late James Kingston-McCloughry, N Adelaide, SA; *m* 1924, Freda, 2nd *d* of late Sir Alfred Lewis, KBE; two *d. Educ:* Trinity Coll., Cambridge (MA); Adelaide Univ. Fellow of South Australian Sch. of Mines and Industries, 1914; entered Army, 1914; Lieut Engineer, 1915; Capt. Flying Corps, 1917; served European War, 1914-18; Egypt, 1916 (DSO, DFC and bar); psa 1928; qualified RAF Staff Coll., 1929; qualified Camberley Staff Coll., 1935; Asst Comdt, RAF Coll., Cranwell, 1938; AOC No 44 Group, 1942; Head Planner, Air Operations, AEAF, 1943-44 (Overlord); Air Mem. Govt of India Frontier Defence Cttee, 1945; Air Mem. C-in-C India Reorganisation Cttee of Armed Forces, 1945-46; Senior Air Staff Officer, RAF, India Command, April 1946; AOC No 18 Group and Senior Air Officer Scotland, Jan. 1947; SASO, HQ, Fighter Comd 1948-50; AOC No 38 Group, 1950; Chief Air Defence Officer, Ministry of Defence, 1951-53, retired 1953. Member: RIIA; Inst. for Strategic Studies. *Publications:* Winged Warfare, 1937; War in Three Dimensions, 1949; The Direction of War, 1955; Global Strategy, 1957; Defence, 1959; The Spectrum of Strategy, 1963. *Address:* Fordel Croft, Glenfarg, Perthshire. *T:* Glenfarg 308. *Club:* United Oxford & Cambridge University.   *[Died 13 Nov. 1972.*

KINNAIRD, 12th Baron *cr* 1682; **Kenneth FitzGerald Kinnaird,** KT 1957; KBE 1946; Baron Kinnaird of Inchture, 1682; Baron Kinnaird of Rossie (UK), 1860; LLD (Hon.) St Andrews; late Captain Scottish Horse; Lord Lieutenant of County of Perth, 1942-60; Lord High Commissioner to General Assembly of Church of Scotland, 1936-38; Member Royal Company of Archers, Queen's Body Guard for Scotland; *b* 31 July 1880; *s* of 11th Baron and Mary Alma (*d* 1923), *d* of Sir Andrew Agnew, 8th Bart; *S* father, 1923; *m* 1903, Frances Victoria (*d* 1960), *y d* of late T. H. Clifton, Lytham Hall, Lancs; two *s* one *d* (and two *d* decd). *Educ:* Eton; Trinity Coll., Cambridge. Served with Scottish Horse, European War, 1914-18. Chm. Scottish Branch Brit. Red Cross Soc., 1935-56; Chm. Perth (East) Agricultural Cttee, 1939-47. Mem. Jt County Council of Perth and Kinross, 1925-61. *Heir: s* Master of Kinnaird, *qv. Address:* Rossie Priory, Inchture, Perthshire. *T:* Inchture 246. *Clubs:* Travellers'; New (Edinburgh).   *[Died 5 July 1972.*

KINNELL, Rev. Gordon, BD, FKC; Rector of Westmill, 1955-63, retired; Provost of St Andrew's Cathedral, Aberdeen, 1932-

55; *b* 2 May 1891; *s* of Samuel and Elizabeth Kinnell; *m* 1928, Annie, 2nd *d* of Harry Dunford; one *s* one *d. Educ:* Ipswich Middle Sch.; King's Coll., London. Curate of: St Andrew's, Battersea, 1915-20; Christ Church, Clapton, 1920-23; Asst Diocesan Supernumerary in Diocese of Glasgow and Galloway, 1923; Rector of All Saints, Bearsden, 1923-31; Rector of S James, Cupar, Fife, 1931-32; Warden of Scottish Society of Reparation, 1937-39; Examining Chaplain to Bishop of Aberdeen, 1940; Hon. Canon of Christ Church Cathedral, Hartford, Conn, 1951; Hon. Canon of St Andrew's Cathedral, Aberdeen, 1956. *Recreation:* golf. *Address:* 5 Southview Road, Danbury, Essex.   *[Died 18 Nov. 1971.*

KINROSS, 3rd Baron *cr* 1902, of Glasclune; **John Patrick Douglas Balfour;** author and journalist; *b* 25 June 1904; *er s* of 2nd Baron and Caroline Elsie (*d* 1969), *d* of Arthur H. Johnstone-Douglas, DL; *S* father 1939; *m* 1938, Angela Mary (from whom he obtained a divorce, 1942), *o d* of late Capt. George Culme-Seymour. *Educ:* Winchester; Balliol Coll., Oxford (BA 1925). Worked on editorial staffs of various newspapers; travelled extensively in Middle East, Africa and elsewhere. Served RAFVR MEF, 1940-44 (despatches); Press Counsellor and Dir Publicity Section, British Embassy, Cairo, Egypt, 1944-47. *Publications:* (as Patrick Balfour): Society Racket, 1933; Grand Tour, 1934; Lords of the Equator, 1937; The Ruthless Innocent, 1950; The Orphaned Realm, 1951; (as Lord Kinross) Within the Taurus, 1954; The Century of the Common Peer, 1954; Europa Minor, 1956; Portrait of Greece, 1956; The Candid Eye, 1958; The Kindred Spirit, 1959; The Innocents at Home, 1959; Atatürk: The Rebirth of a Nation, 1964; Portrait of Egypt, 1966; The Windsor Years, 1967; Between Two Seas, 1968; (with D. H. Gary) Morocco, 1971; Hagia Sophia, 1972. *Recreation:* cooking. *Heir: b* Lt-Col Hon. David Andrew Balfour, OBE, TD [*b* 29 March 1906; *m* 1st, 1936, Araminta (from whom he obtained a decree of divorce, 1941), *d* of Lt-Col W. E. Peel, DSO; one *d*; 2nd, 1948, Helen (*d* 1969), *d* of late Alan Hog, Edinburgh; one *s* (*b* 1 Oct. 1949); 3rd, 1972, Mrs Ruth Middleton]. *Address:* 4 Warwick Avenue, W2. *Clubs:* Travellers', Beefsteak.   *[Died 4 June 1976.*

KINTORE, Countess of (11th in line), *cr* 1677; **(Ethel) Sydney Keith;** Lady Keith of Inverurie, 1677 (Scotland); *b* 20 Sept. 1874; *e d* of 9th Earl of Kintore, KT, PC, GCMG (*d* 1930); *S* brother, 10th Earl of Kintore, 1966; officially recognised by the name of Keith and Chief of the name of Keith by warrant of Lord Lyon King of Arms, 1966; *m* 1905, John Baird (*e s* of Sir Alexander Baird of Urie), Visc. Stonehaven (*cr* 1938), PC, GCMG, DSO (*d* 1941); one *s* (and one *s* killed, Bomber Command, War of 1939-45) two *d* (and one *d* decd). *Heir: s* 2nd Viscount Stonehaven. *Address:* Rickerton House, Stonehaven, Kincardineshire. *T:* Stonehaven 2756. *Club:* English-Speaking Union.
              [Died 21 Sept. 1974.

KIPPING, Sir Norman (Victor), GCMG 1966; KBE 1962; Kt 1946; JP; *b* 11 May 1901; *y s* of P. P. and Rose E. Kipping, London; *m* 1928, Eileen Rose; two *s* one *d. Educ:* University Coll. Sch.; Birkbeck Coll., London. Research Dept, GPO, 1920-21, as jun. engineer; Internat. Western Electric Co., 1921-26; Standard Telephones & Cables Ltd, 1926-42, finally as works manager; Head of Regional Div., Min. of Production, 1942-45; Under-Sec. Bd of Trade, 1945; Dir-Gen., FBI, 1946-65; retired 1965 on formation of Confedn of British Industry. Dir, Brit. Overseas Fairs Ltd from foundation, 1953 (Chm. 1958-66). FIEE, FIPE (Chm. Council, 1940-41). Chm. Coun. University Coll. Sch., 1960-71; President: Consultative Council of Professional Management Orgs, 1966-76; Anglo-Finnish Soc., 1966-74; Past Sec., Anglo-Amer. Coun. on Productivity; past Member: Br. Productivity Coun.; Dollar Exports Coun.; Export Coun. for Europe; Brit. Nat. Export Coun.; Nat. Prod. Advisory Council; BBC Adv. Council; Fulton Cttee on Civil Service. Led missions for FBI to India, Japan, Nigeria and for HM Govt to Zambia. Hon. Fellow, BIM (Elbourne Lectr, 1965). Hon. DSc Loughborough, 1966. Commander: Order of Dannebrog (Denmark), 1948; Order of the Lion (Finland), 1959; Order of Merit of the Italian Republic, 1962; Order of Vasa (Sweden), 1962. *Publication:* The Suez Contractors, 1969; Summing Up (memoirs), 1972. *Recreations:* shooting, gardening. *Address:* 36 Barrydene, Oakleigh Road North, Whetstone, N20 9HG. *T:* 01-445 4054. *Club:* East India, Devonshire, Sports and Public Schools.   *[Died 29 June 1979.*

KIRBY, Sir James (Norman), Kt 1962; CBE 1956; MIProdE; Chairman: James N. Kirby group of companies since 1924; International Products Ltd and subsidiaries; Champion Spark Plug Co. (Australia) Pty Ltd; Wales Unit Investment Pty Ltd (subsid. of Bank of NSW); Reinsurance Co. of Australasia Ltd; Director: Dow Chemical (Australia) Ltd; Mutual Life & Citizens' Ltd; Australian General Electric Pty Ltd; Australian

General Electric (Appliances) Pty Ltd; Australia & New Guinea Corp. Ltd; *b* 15 June 1899; *s* of Louis Kirby, Melbourne; *m* 1926, Agnes Anne Wessler; two *s*. *Educ:* Sydney. Pres., Electrical & Radio Development Assoc. of NSW; Dir, National Heart Foundation of Aust.; Governor, Science Foundation for Physics within University of Sydney; Life Governor, Australian Inst. of Management. *Recreations:* golf, fishing. *Address:* 205 Salisbury Road, Camperdown, NSW 2050, Australia. *T:* LA 0455. *Clubs:* Royal Sydney Yacht Squadron, Australian Golf, NSW, American National (all in Australia). [*Died 30 July* 1971.

KIRBY, Air Cdre John Lawrance, CB 1946; CBE 1943; JP; DL; RAF; *b* 1899; *s* of Wilson Kirby, York; *m* 1941, Rachel Margaret Cunningham, *y d* of R. G. Smith; two *s* three *d*. *Educ:* Archbishop Holgate's Sch., York. JP Grimsby, 1951; DL Lincs, 1952. *Address:* Utterby Close, Louth, Lincs. *T:* North Thoresby 240. [*Died 20 Feb.* 1980.

KIRK, Adam Kennedy; retired; *b* 24 March 1893; *s* of John and Mary Kirk, Melbourne; *m* 1921, Freda Minnie Matthews; one *d* (one *s* killed, RAF). *Educ:* public schs, Melbourne. Served with Australian Forces, 1914-18 (Anzac Decoration; 1914-18 medals): landing at Gallipoli, 1915. Founder, Kirk & Co. (Tubes) Ltd (now part of American combine). Past Mem., local Coun. (Chm., 1946-47); Past Mem., Surrey CC; Sheriff of London, 1960-61; Master, Poulters' Co.; Past Master, Joiners' and Ceilors' Co.; Freeman and Liveryman, Founders' Co. MIM; MInst British Foundrymen; MInstBE. OStJ; Grand Officer, Republic of Tunisia; Lion of Finland; Nepal Decoration. *Recreations:* racehorse owner, cricket, Rugby football, golf. *Address:* Oakdene, Ladyegate Road, Dorking, Surrey. *Clubs:* Devonshire, Eccentric, City Livery, United Wards; Ascot, Goodwood, Epsom, Fontwell. [*Died 10 March* 1975.

KIRK, Alexander Comstock; US Ambassador (retired); *b* 26 Nov. 1888; *s* of James Alexander Kirk and Clara Comstock. *Educ:* Yale; Harvard; Ecole Libre des Sciences Politiques. American Embassy, Berlin, 1915; American Legation, The Hague, 1917. Amer. Commission to negotiate peace, Paris, 1918-19; Asst to Sec. of State, 1919; Amer. Embassy, Tokyo, 1920; Amer. Legation, Peking, 1922; Amer. Embassy, Mexico City, 1924; Dept of State, Washington, DC, 1925; Amer. Embassy, Rome, 1928-38; Chargé d'Affaires, Moscow, 1938, Berlin, 1939; Minister-Counsellor, Rome, 1940; Envoy Extraordinary and Minister Plenipotentiary to Egypt and Saudi Arabia, 1941; Ambassador to Govt of King of Hellenes, 1943; US Rep., Advisory Council for Italy, 1944; US Adviser to Supreme Allied Comdr-in-Chief Mediterranean Theatre; Ambassador to Italy, 1944; retired, 1946. *Address:* 4630 Calle Altivo, Tucson, Arizona 85718, USA. [*Died 23 March* 1979.

KIRK, Geoffrey William, CMG 1959; Ambassador to El Salvador, 1960-67; *b* 9 Aug. 1907; *o s* of Percy R. Kirk and Alice H. York; *m* 1935, Maria Annunziata Montrezza; no *c*. *Educ:* Mill Hill Sch.; London Univ. Mem. of HM Foreign Service. First Sec., Panama, 1948-50; Prague, 1950-53; Commercial Counsellor, HM Embassy, The Hague, 1953-60. Hon. Comdr, Order of Orange-Nassau (Netherlands), 1958. *Club:* Reform. [*Died 30 July* 1975.

KIRK, Rt. Hon. Norman Eric, PC 1972; MP (Lab) for Lyttelton, New Zealand, since 1957; Prime Minister and Minister of Foreign Affairs, since Dec. 1972; *b* Waimate, Canterbury, NZ, 6 Jan. 1923; *s* of Norman and Vera Kirk; *m* 1941, Ruth Miller; three *s* two *d*. *Educ:* Linwood Avenue Sch., NZ. Formerly stationary engine driver. Mayor of Kaiapoi, 1953-57. Vice-Pres., NZ Labour Party, 1963-64, Pres., 1964-66; Leader, Parly Labour Party, 1965-; Leader of the Opposition, 1965-72. Pres., Summer Lifeboat Inst., 1961-. *Address:* The Residence, 30 Forres Street, Seatoun, Wellington, New Zealand.
[*Died 31 Aug.* 1974.

KIRK, Sir Peter (Michael), Kt 1976; MP (C) Saffron Walden since March 1965; Leader, Conservative Delegation to European Parliament, Strasbourg, since 1973; *b* 18 May 1928; *er s* of Rt Rev. Kenneth Escott Kirk, sometime Bishop of Oxford; *m* 1950, Elizabeth Mary, *d* of late R. B. Graham; three *s*. *Educ:* Marlborough; Trinity Coll., Oxford; Zürich Univ. Pres., Oxford Union, 1949. Journalist in Glasgow, London, USA, and Foreign Correspondent world-wide. MP (C) Gravesend Div. of Kent, 1955-64; Parliamentary Under-Sec. of State, War Office, 1963-64; Parliamentary Under-Sec. of State for Defence: for the Army, MoD, April-Oct. 1964; for the Navy, MoD, 1970-72. UK Delegn to Council of Europe, 1956-63, 1966-70; Chairman: Non-Represented Nations Cttee, Council of Europe, 1959-61; Gen. Affairs Cttee, WEU, 1960-63; Budgetary and Administrative Cttee, WEU, 1968-69; Political Affairs Cttee, Council of Europe, 1969-70. Mem. Carshalton UDC, 1952-55.

Publications: One Army Strong?, 1958; various newspaper articles. *Recreations:* walking, listening to music. *Address:* Coote's Farm, Steeple Bumpstead, near Haverhill, Suffolk. *T:* Steeple Bumpstead 388. *Club:* Brooks's. [*Died 17 April* 1977.

KIRKALDY, Prof. Harold Stewart, CBE 1958; MA, LLB; Fellow since 1944, Vice-President and Bursar, 1965-70, of Queens' College, Cambridge; *b* 27 Dec. 1902; *s* of late David and Anne Kirkaldy; unmarried. *Educ:* Grove Academy, Broughty Ferry; University of Edinburgh. Called to Bar, Middle Temple, 1928; Asst Sec. British Employers' Confederation, 1929-39; Gen. Sec. Iron and Steel Trades Employers' Assoc., 1939-45; Prof. of Industrial Relations, Cambridge Univ., 1944-63, Emeritus Prof. since 1967. Mem. of British Delegation at International Labour Conference, 1929-44; Mem., Cttee of Experts on Application of Internat. Labour Conventions, 1946-; Mem., 1946-76 (Chm., 1956-76) Administrative Bd of Staff Pensions Fund of Internat. Labour Office; Chm. of UN Joint Staff Pensions Board, 1960-62; Chm. of various Wages Councils under Wages Councils Act, 1946-62; Chm. for Eastern Region of Minister of Labour's Compensation Appeal Tribunal, 1949-59; Chm., Cambridge and District Employment Cttee, 1957-69; Mem. of Industrial Disputes Tribunal, 1952-59; Chm. of Courts of Arbitration under Industrial Courts Act, 1958-62; Chm. of Commissions of Inquiry under Wages Councils Act, 1949-62; Chm. of Bd of Inquiry into Trinidad Oil Industry, 1955; Chm. of BBC Arbitration Tribunal, 1958; Pres. of Mauritius Trade Disputes Arbitration Tribunal, 1959; Chm. of Industrial Disputes Tribunal, Isle of Man, 1960; Mem. Cttee on Remuneration of Ministers and Members of Parliament, 1963-64; Dep. Chm., Nat. Incomes Commn, 1962-65. Perin Memorial Lecturer, Jamshedpur, India, 1946. *Address:* 31a The Strand, Walmer, Deal, Kent. *Club:* United Oxford & Cambridge University. [*Died 20 Sept.* 1976.

KIRKBRIDE, Sir Alec Seath, KCMG 1949 (CMG 1942); Kt 1946; CVO 1954; OBE 1932; MC; Ambassador in Libya, 1954, retired (Minister, 1951-54); Director of the British Bank of the Middle East, 1956-72; *b* 19 Aug. 1897; *m* 1st, 1921, Edith Florence James (*d* 1966); three *s*; 2nd, 1967, Ethel Mary James. Military Service, 1916-21; British Rep., Es Salt, Transjordan, 1921; Junior Asst Sec., Palestine Govt, 1922, Asst Sec., 1926; Asst British Resident, Transjordan, 1927; District Commissioner, Galilee and Acre, 1937; British Resident, in Transjordan, 1939; Minister to the Hashemite Kingdom of the Jordan, 1946; representative of HM Government to Permanent Mandates Commission, Geneva, 1936, 1938, and 1939. *Publications:* A Crackle of Thorns, 1956; An Awakening, 1972; From the Wings, 1976. *Address:* 33 Fernhurst Drive, Goring by Sea, Worthing, West Sussex. [*Died 22 Nov.* 1978.

KIRKCONNELL, Watson, OC (Canada) 1969; MA; PhD; DLitt; DPEc; LLD; LHD; DesL; DCL; President Emeritus, Acadia University, Wolfville, Nova Scotia, Canada; *b* Port Hope, Ontario, Canada, 1895; 2nd *s* of T. A. Kirkconnell, BA, LLD, and Bertha Watson; *m* 1st, 1924, Isabel (*d* 1925), *e d* of James Peel; twin *s*; 2nd, 1930, Hope, *d* of Andrew Kitchener; three *d*. *Educ:* Queen's Univ., Kingston (University medallist in classics); Lincoln Coll., Oxford. FRSC (Lorne Pierce Medal, 1942). Mem., Sch. of Slavonic and E European Studies, Univ. of London. President: Canadian Authors' Assoc., 1942; Baptist Fedn of Canada, 1953; Chm., Humanities Research Council of Canada, 1944. Mem. several foreign learned societies; Knight (Officers' Cross), Order of Polonia Restituta; Knight Comdr, Order of the Falcon (Iceland); Medal of Honour, PEN Club of Hungary; Gold Medal of Freedom, Hungarians in Exile, 1964. Granted Scottish coat of arms by Lord Lyon, 1974. *Publications:* Victoria County Centennial History, 1921; International Aspects of Unemployment, 1923; European Elegies, 1928; The European Heritage, 1930; The North American Book of Icelandic Verse, 1930; The Tide of Life and other Poems, 1930; The Magyar Muse, 1933; The Eternal Quest, 1934; A Canadian Headmaster, 1935; Canadian Overtones, 1935; A Golden Treasury of Polish Lyrics, 1936; The Death of Buda (from the Magyar of Arany), 1936; Primer of Hungarian, 1938; Titus, the Toad, 1939; Canada, Europe, and Hitler, 1939; The Ukrainian Canadians and the War, 1940; The Flying Bull, and other Tales, 1940; Canadians All, 1941; Twilight of Liberty, 1941; Seven Pillars of Freedom, 1944; National Minorities in the USSR, 1946; Red Foe of Faith, 1946; (with S Marion) The Quebec Tradition, 1946; (with A. S. P. Woodhouse) The Humanities in Canada, 1947; The Celestial Cycle, 1952; The Mod at Grand Pré, 1955; Pan Tadeusz (from the Polish of Mickiewicz), 1961; (with C. H. Andrusyshen) The Ukrainian Poets, 1963; (with C. H. Andrusyshen) Complete Poetical Works of Taras Shevchenko, 1964; The Theme of Samson Agonistes in World Literature, 1964; Centennial Tales, and Other Poems, 1965; A Slice of Canada, Memoirs, 1966; The Fifth Quarter-Century,

1968; Awake the Courteous Echo, 1972; Rest, Perturbed Spirit, 1974; Climbing a Green Tree, 1974. *Address:* 101 Main Street, Wolfville, Nova Scotia, Canada. [*Died* 26 *Feb.* 1977.

KIRKLAND, Edward Chase; Professor Emeritus of American History, Bowdoin College; *b* 24 May 1894; *s* of Edward and Mary Chase Kirkland; *m* 1924, Ruth Stevens Babson; one *s. Educ:* Dartmouth Coll. (AB); Harvard Univ. (MA, PhD). Private 1st Cl., US Ambulance Corps with the French Army, 1917-19 (Croix de Guerre, 1918). Instructor: Dartmouth Coll., 1920-21; Mass Inst. of Technology, 1922-24; Professor: Brown Univ., 1924-30; Bowdoin Coll., 1930-55. Visiting Prof., University of Wisconsin, 1951; Commonwealth Lecturer, University Coll., London, 1952; Pitt Prof. of Amer. History and Instns, Cambridge Univ., 1956-57 (MA Cambridge 1956). Hon. LittD: Dartmouth Coll., 1948; Princeton Univ., 1957; Bowdoin Coll., 1961. *Publications:* The Peacemakers of 1864, 1926; History of American Economic Life, 1st edn 1932, 4th edn 1969; Men, Cities and Transportation: A Study in New England History (2 vols), 1948; Business in the Gilded Age, The Conservatives' Balance Sheet, 1952; Dream and Thought in the Business Community, 1860-1900, 1956; Industry Comes of Age; Business, Labor, and Public Policy, 1860-1897, 1961; Charles Francis Adams, Jun., 1835-1915: The Patrician at Bay, 1965; A Goldentree Bibliography: American Economic History since 1860, 1971. *Recreations:* gardening, walking. *Address:* Thetford Center, Vermont 05075, USA; c/o Pembroke College, Cambridge. [*Died* 24 *May* 1975.

KIRKPATRICK, Rev. Canon Herbert Francis; Hon. Canon of Ely Cathedral, since 1964; Archdeacon of Ely, 1947-61; Examining Chaplain to Bishop of Bath and Wells, 1944-60, to Bishop of Ely since 1947; retired; *b* 31 July 1888; *s* of late Very Rev. A. F. Kirkpatrick, DD. *Educ:* Marlborough Coll.; Jesus Coll., Cambridge (Rustat Scholar). BA; Lady Kay Scholar; 2nd Cl. Classical Tripos: 2nd Cl. Theological Tripos; MA; Cuddesdon Theological Coll., 1912-13. Deacon, 1913; Priest, 1914; Curate S John Evangelist, Middlesbrough, 1913-16; Cockington, Torquay, 1916-19; Vicar of All Saints', Cambridge, 1919-22; Principal of the Missionary Coll. of S Peter and S Paul, Dorchester, Oxon, 1922-47; Commissary to the Bishop of Labuan and Sarawak, 1938-48; Officiating Curate in charge of Launton, 1940-44; Rector of Bathwick with Woolley, Bath, 1944-47; Lecturer at Cuddesdon Coll., Oxford, 1941-43; Prebendary of Combe II in Wells Cathedral, 1945-47. *Address:* 44 Tunwell's Lane, Great Shelford, Cambridge CB2 5LJ. *T:* Shelford 3181. [*Died* 21 *July* 1971.

KIRKPATRICK, Air Vice-Marshal Herbert James, CB 1957; CBE 1945; DFC 1941; RAF (retired); *b* 30 Oct. 1910; *s* of late Maj.-Gen. Charles Kirkpatrick, CB, CBE, IA, Larchwood, Pitlochry, Perthshire, and Elsie Isobel, *d* of H. J. H. Fasson, ICS; *m* 1937, Pamela Evelyn Darvill, *d* of Lt-Col H. D. Watson, IA, retired, Colchester; three *s* two d. *Educ:* Cheltenham Coll.; Trinity Coll., Oxford (MA). Mem. Oxford Univ. Air Sqdn, 1929-32; entered RAF, 1933; served in India, 1933-35; Instructor and Adjutant OU Air Sqdn, 1936-39; served War of 1939-45 (despatches twice, DFC, CBE): Air Staff Fighter Comd, 1939-40; served in Bomber Comd, 1941-45, and in Transport Comd, 1946-48; Instructor at RAF Staff Coll., 1949-51; Chief Instructor, RAF Flying Coll., 1951-53; Imperial Defence Coll., 1954; Dir of Operational Requirements (A), 1955-57; ACAS (Op. Req.), 1957; Chief of Staff, 2nd Allied Tactical Air Force, 1957-60; Air Officer Commanding No 25 Group, 1961-63. *Address:* c/o Lloyds Bank (Cox's and King's Branch), 6 Pall Mall, SW1; Rectory Hill Cottage, East Bergholt, Colchester, Essex CO7 6TH. *T:* East Bergholt 536. *Club:* Royal Air Force. [*Died* 28 *Aug.* 1977.

KITCHEN, Sir Geoffrey, Kt 1963; TD; Chairman: United British Securities Trust Ltd, since 1965; *b* 20 Dec. 1906; *m* 1946, Joan Aistrope. *Educ:* Bradford Grammar Sch.; St John's Coll., Oxford (MA). Served War of 1939-45, RA, with 8th Army in Middle East and Italy (despatches); Lt-Col. Pearl Assurance Co. Ltd, 1934-76: Dir, 1948; Dep. Chm., 1952; Chm., 1956-71; Pres., 1972-76. Director: Estates & General Investments Ltd; Kellock Holdings Ltd; Michael Hooker and Associates Ltd; Schlesinger Ltd; Trident Gen. Insurance Co. Ltd; Trident Life Assurance Co. Ltd; United Kingdom Property Co. Ltd. Chm., London and Holyrood Trust Ltd, 1964-71. Chm., Industrial Life Offices' Assoc., 1958-60. Governor, St Mary's Hosp., 1960-63. Pres. of Appeals, NPFA, 1965-66. Life Associate, British Red Cross Soc. Freeman, City of London; Liveryman and Mem. Court, Worshipful Co. of Gunmakers (Master, 1969). *Recreations:* shooting, golf, tennis. *Address:* Holmbushes, Wisborough Green, West Sussex. *T:* Loxwood 752243. *Club:* Carlton. [*Died* 7 *Dec.* 1978.

KITCHING, Wilfred, CBE 1964; retired as General of The Salvation Army (1954-63) and from Chairmanship of various Salvation Army Companies, etc; *b* 22 Aug. 1893; *s* of late Commissioner Theodore Kitching, CBE; *m* 1929, Kathleen Bristow. *Educ:* Friern Barnet Grammar Sch. Corps and Divisional Officer, 1915-25, 1929-39; National Sec. for Salvation Army Bands 1925-29, National Young People's Sec. 1939-45; Field Sec., 1945-46; Chief Sec. for Australia, 1946-48. Territorial Leader for Sweden, 1948-51. British Commissioner, Officer responsible for Evangelical and Red Shield Services in Great Britain and Ireland, 1951-54. *Publications:* A Goodly Heritage (autobiography); numerous instrumental and vocal compositions published by The Salvation Army. *Recreation:* music. *Address:* 19 Montserrat, West Parade, Bexhill on Sea, East Sussex. [*Died* 15 *Dec.* 1977.

KITSON, Geoffrey Herbert, OBE 1948; TD; DL; company director; *b* 22 June 1896; *s* of Henry Herbert Kitson, Leeds; *m* 1923, Kathleen Mary Alexandra, *d* of James Paul, Bramhope; three *s* one d. *Educ:* Charterhouse. Mem. Leeds City Council, 1930-38; as Chm. Leeds Corp. Gas Cttee, was Pres. Brit. Commercial Gas Assoc., 1931; Dir, Leeds Permanent Building Soc., 1934-74; Pres. Leeds Chamber of Commerce, 1935-36. DL W Riding of Yorks, 1963. Hon. LLD Leeds Univ., 1963. Hon. Col 249 (W Riding Artillery) Regt RA, 1957-63. *Recreations:* shooting, gardening. *Address:* West Lawn, Linton, Wetherby, West Yorks. *T:* Wetherby 2950. *Club:* Leeds (Leeds). [*Died* 7 *Nov.* 1974.

KITSON, Sir George (Vernon), KBE 1957 (CBE 1946); *b* 10 Feb. 1899; *s* of late George Kitson, Wakefield; *m* 1935, Phoebe, *yr d* of late John Owen George, Hirwaun, Glamorganshire; no *c. Educ:* Queen Elizabeth Grammar Sch., Wakefield; Clare Coll., Cambridge (MA). Served RFC and RAF, 1917-19; apptd Student Interpreter in China Consular Service, Dec. 1922; served as Vice-Consul in Peking, 1924, Shanghai, 1925, Canton, 1926-28, Mukden, Newchwang, and Harbin, 1929, Chungking, 1929-31 (Actg Consul-Gen., Feb.-April 1930), Shanghai, 1931-34 (Actg Consul, 1932); FO, 1935; served as Consul, Hankow, 1936, Swatow, 1936-37, Chefoo, 1937-38; Actg Chinese Sec., Peking, 1938; Consul, Shanghai, 1939-40, Nanking, 1941-42; Consul, and Chinese Sec. at HM Embassy, Chungking, 1942-45; Counsellor, FO, 1945-47; Deputy High Commissioner for the UK at Bombay, 1947-50; Counsellor, Office of Commissioner General for SE Asia, Singapore, 1951-52; HM Consul-General at Milan, 1952-58; retd 1959. High Sheriff of Breconshire, 1968-69. *Recreations:* gardening, fishing. *Address:* Llais-yr-Afon, Crickhowell, Powys. *T:* Crickhowell 810298. [*Died* 29 *May* 1980.

KITSON, Captain James Buller, DSO 1916; Royal Navy, retired; *b* Dec. 1883; *s* of Rev. J. Buller Kitson, Rector of Lanreath; *m* 1913, Hon. Frances Margaret Palmer Howard (*d* 1958), *e d* of late R. J. B. Howard and late Baroness Strathcona and Mount Royal; two *s* two d. Joined RN 1898; Lieut 1905; Commander, 1917; served European War, including Jutland Bank (despatches, DSO); retired list, 1925; Captain, retired, 1928. *Address:* Lower Farm, Madehurst, near Arundel, West Sussex; Fursecroft, George Street, W1. *Club:* Royal Yacht Squadron. [*Died* 7 *Dec.* 1976.

KITSON CLARK, George Sidney Roberts, MA; LittD (Cambridge); Reader in Constitutional History, Cambridge, 1954-67, retired, 1967; Fellow of Trinity College, Cambridge, since 1922; University Lecturer, Cambridge University, since 1929; Praelector, Trinity College, since 1953; *b* 14 June 1900; 2nd *s* of Lieut-Col Edwin Kitson Clark and Georgina, *d* of late George Parker Bidder, QC. *Educ:* Shrewsbury, Trinity Coll., Cambridge. Lecturer, Trinity Coll., Cambridge, 1928; Tutor, 1933-45; founded Cambridge University Educational Films Council, 1947, and helped to found British University Film Council, 1948 (first Chm., 1948-51); Visiting Lecturer University of Pennsylvania, Pa, 1953-54; Chm., Faculty Bd of History, Cambridge Univ., 1956-58; Ford's Lecturer, Oxford Univ., 1959-60; Maurice Lecturer, King's Coll., London, 1960; George Scott Visiting Fellow, Ormond Coll., University of Melbourne, 1964; Birkbeck Lecturer, Cambridge, 1967. Hon. DLitt: Durham, 1960; E Anglia, 1970; Glasgow, 1971, Leeds, 1973. Foreign Hon. Mem., American Acad. of Arts and Sciences, 1975. *Publications:* Peel and the Conservative Party, 1929 (new edn 1965); Sir Robert Peel (Great Lives Series), 1936; The English Inheritance, 1950; Ainslie Memorial Lecture, 1953; The Romantic Element 1830-1850 (in Studies in Social History, ed J. H. Plumb), 1955; The Kingdom of Free Men, 1957; Guide for Research Students working on Historical subjects, 1958; The Making of Victorian England, 1962; An Expanding Society: Britain 1830-1900, 1967; The Critical Historian, 1967; Churchmen and the Condition of England, 1832-1855, 1973;

articles in Trans Royal Historical Soc., Economic History Review, Journal of Modern History (Chicago), The Historical Journal (Cambridge), etc. *Address:* Trinity College, Cambridge CB2 1TQ. *T:* Cambridge 58201. *Club:* Athenæum.
[Died 8 Dec. 1975.

KITTERMASTER, F. Ronald, BA; Headmaster, The King's School, Worcester, 1942-59; *b* 26 Oct. 1899; *s* of F. J. Kittermaster, Rugby School; *m* 1930, Meriel Greenstock; one *d.* *Educ:* Rugby Sch.; RMA Woolwich. BA London, 1941. Royal Field Artillery, 1918-21; Prince of Wales's College, Dehra Dun, India, 1921-27; Duke of York's Sch., Dover, 1927-28; Canford Sch., 1928-42. *Publication:* The Victory March, 1921. *Recreations:* ski-ing, gardening, lobster catching. *Address:* c/o Old Farmhouse, Compton Abbas, Shaftesbury, Dorset. *Clubs:* Free Foresters, Butterflies, Harlequins. [Died 7 March 1972.

KITTS, Sir Francis (Joseph), Kt 1966; Mayor of Wellington, New Zealand, 1956-74; *b* 1914. Elected to: Wellington City Council, 1950; Wellington Harbour Board, 1950; Wellington Hospital Board, 1950. MP for Wellington Central, 1954-60. *Address:* 25a Shannon Street, Mount Victoria, Wellington 1, New Zealand.
[Died 16 March 1979.

KLEINWORT, Sir Cyril (Hugh), Kt 1971; Director, Kleinwort, Benson, Lonsdale Ltd (Chairman, 1968-77); Chairman, Kleinwort, Benson Ltd, 1966-71; Joint Vice-Chairman, Commercial Union Assurance Co., 1959-75; Chairman, Committee on Invisible Exports, 1968-75; *b* 17 Aug. 1905; *s* of Sir Alexander D. Kleinwort, 1st Bt; *m* 1933, Elisabeth Kathleen Forde; three *d.* *Educ:* privately. Served as Lieut-Commander, RNVR, 1939-45. Member: British Overseas Trade Bd, 1972-75; Adv. Cttee, Queen's Award to Industry, 1971-75. One of HM Lieutenants, City of London, 1976-. Hon. DLitt City, 1973. *Recreations:* hunting, yachting. *Address:* 64 Sussex Square, W2; Eyford House, Upper Slaughter, near Cheltenham. *T:* Stow on the Wold 30380. [Died 8 Sept. 1980.

KLEINWORT, Ernest Greverus; Director, Kleinwort, Benson, Lonsdale Ltd, 1961-74 (Chairman, 1961-68); *b* 13 Sept. 1901; *s* of late Sir Alexander Drake Kleinwort, 1st Bt, and late Etienette, Lady Kleinwort (*née* Girard); *heir-pres.* to Sir Alexander S. Kleinwort, 2nd Bt; *m* 1932, Joan Nightingale, MBE, JP, *d* of late Prof. Arthur William Crossley, CMG, CBE, FRS, LLD, DSc; one *s* one *d.* *Educ:* Jesus Coll., Cambridge. Partner Kleinwort Sons & Company, 1927-47. RAFVR, 1942-45. Actg Chm. of Kleinwort, Sons & Co. Ltd, 1947-61; Chm. Kleinwort Benson Ltd, 1961-66; Member: Accepting Houses Cttee, 1945-66; Internat. Board of Trustees, World Wildlife Fund, 1967-76 (Mem. of Honour, 1976). Council, Wildfowl Trust, 1971- (Vice-Pres., 1970-). Comdr of Order of Golden Ark, Netherlands, 1974. *Recreations:* landscaping and development of his garden, charitable work, swimming. *Address:* Heaselands, Haywards Heath, West Sussex; 50 South Audley Street, W1. [Died 3 Nov. 1977.

KLEMPERER, Otto; musical conductor; *b* Breslau, Germany, 14 May 1885; *s* of Nathan and Ida Klemperer; *m* 1919, Johanna Geissler; one *s* one *d.* *Educ:* Conservatory, Frankfurt and Berlin. Conductor: German National Theatre, Prague, 1907-10; Hamburg Opera House, 1910-13; Barmen Opera, 1913-15; Strasbourg Opera, 1915-17; Cologne, 1917-24, Gen. Music Dir, 1923-24; Wiesbaden, 1924-27; First Conductor, Berlin State Opera and Philharmonic Choir, 1927-33; Dir Los Angeles Philharmonic, 1933-39; since then Guest-Conductor in US, Canada, South America, Australia, Europe, Israel, Soviet Union; conducted concerts in the Festival Hall, 1954, 1955, 1956, 1957, 1958, and annually 1960-71; retired from concert platform, 1972, but continues recording. Covent Garden, 1961, 1962, 1963, 1969. Appointed (for life) Principal Conductor of Philharmonia Orchestra of England, 1959, but when Philharmonia Orchestra disbanded, became Hon. Pres. and Principal Conductor for Life of New Philharmonia Orch. Nikisch Prize, Leipzig, 1966. LLD, Occidental Coll., Calif, and University of California, Los Angeles, 1937. Hon. RAM, 1971. Goethe Medal, Berlin, 1933; Grand Medal of Merit with Star, Federal Republic of Germany, 1958, Order of Merit, 1967. *Publications:* Songs, 1915 (publ. Mainz, Germany); Missa Sacra, 1919 (publ. Mainz, Germany); Minor Recollections, 1964 (publ. London); Symphony in Two Movements, 1962 (publ. London); Symphony No 2, 1970 (publ. London); *relevant publication:* Conversations with Klemperer, ed and trans. P. L. F. Heyworth, 1973 (German edn 1974). *Address:* Dufourstrasse 104, 8008 Zürich, Switzerland. [Died 6 July 1973.

KLETZKI, Paul, (Paul Klecki); conductor since 1929; composer; Musical Director and Conductor of Dallas Symphony Orchestra, 1954-58; *b* Lodz, Poland, 21 March 1900; *m* 1928,

Celine H. Woodtli. *Educ:* Warsaw Univ.; Conservatorium; Berlin Academy of Music. Professor, Conservatoire de Musique, Lausanne, 1940-45 (now Hon. Prof.). Has been conducting all over Europe, 1945-; Conductor, Suisse Romande Orchestra, 1958-70; also made tours to Australia and Latin America. *Publications:* symphonies, orchestral works and chamber music. *Address:* c/o Hurok Concerts Ltd, 1370 Avenue of the Americas, New York, NY 10019, USA. [Died 5 March 1973.

KLIJNSTRA, Gerrit Dirk Ale, Knight, Order of Netherlands Lion, 1972; Commander of Order of Oranje Nassau, 1975 (Officer 1963); Hon. KBE 1973; Advisory Director, Unilever NV, since 1975; Director: Imperial Chemical Industries, since 1974; Commercial Union Assurance Company, since 1976; Supervisory Director, Amro Bank, Amsterdam, since 1973; *b* 5 Jan. 1912; *m* 1939, Elizabeth van Sijn; three *d.* *Educ:* Gymnasium, Amersfoort; Delft Univ. (degree Chem. Engrg). Joined Unilever, 1938; Technical Dir, Unilever Indonesia, 1946-50; Technical Head, Unilever Germany, 1950-54; Dir, Unilever Ltd, 1955-75, Chm., 1971-75. *Recreations:* sailing, golf, music. *Address:* Pinetrees, Sands, Farnham, Surrey. *T:* Runfold 2520. [Died 18 Dec. 1976.

KLYNE, Prof. William; MA Oxon, DSc London, PhD Edinburgh; Professor of Chemistry, Westfield College, University of London, 1960-77; *b* 23 March 1913; *s* of late Carl Adolphe Klein and Ivy Adkin, Enfield, Middx; *m* 1949, Dr Barbara Evelyn Clayton; one *s* one *d.* *Educ:* Highgate Sch.; New Coll., Oxford. Asst in Medical Chemistry, University of Edinburgh, 1936-39, Lecturer, 1939-47; Lecturer in Biochemistry, Postgrad. Med. Sch. of London, 1947-52; Reader in Biochemistry, London, 1952-60; Dean, Fac. of Science, Westfield Coll., 1971-73, Vice-Principal, 1973-76. Mem. Editorial Board, Biochemical Journal, 1949-55. Hon. Sec., Chemical Soc., 1966-72; Vice-Pres., Perkin Div., Chemical Soc., 1972-75. Mem. Jt Commn on Biochemical Nomenclature, IUPAC-IUB, 1977. *Publications:* Practical Chemistry for Medical Students, 1946; Chemistry of Steroids, 1957; (with Dr J. Buckingham) Atlas of Stereochemical Correlations, 1974; (ed 3 vols with Prof. P. B. D. de la Mare) Progress in Stereochemistry, 1954-62; contrib. to chemical and biochemical journals. *Address:* 19 Malcolm Road, SW19. *T:* 01-946 4194; Bay View, Studland, Swanage, Dorset BH19 3AS. *T:* Studland 325. *Club:* Athenæum. [Died 13 Nov. 1977.

KNATCHBULL-HUGESSEN, Hon. Adrian Norton, QC (Canada) 1932; LLD; Barrister, Bar of Province of Quebec; Member of Senate, Canada, 1937-67; *b* 5 July 1891; *y s* of 1st Baron Brabourne, PC; *m* 1922, Margaret, *o d* of G. H. Duggan, Montreal; four *s* one *d.* *Educ:* Eton; McGill Univ., Montreal. Admitted to Quebec Bar, and joined the present firm of Laing, Weldon and Courtois, 1914; served in Canadian Heavy Artillery, 1916-19, spending one year at the front; contested St Lawrence St George div. of Montreal, 1935; Dir, International Paints (Canada) Ltd; Chancellor of Anglican Diocese of Montreal, 1946-66; Bâtonnier of Bar of Prov. of Quebec, 1960-61. *Recreations:* golf, ski-ing. *Address:* 4306 Montrose Avenue, Westmount, Montreal, Canada. *TA:* Fleural, Montreal. *Clubs:* University, Royal Montreal Golf, Royal St Lawrence Yacht (Montreal); Rideau (Ottawa). [Died 30 March 1976.

KNATCHBULL-HUGESSEN, Sir Hughe Montgomery, KCMG, 1936 (CMG 1920); *b* 26 March 1886; *s* of late Rev. R. B. Knatchbull-Hugessen and Rachel Mary, *d* of late Sir Alexander Montgomery, Bt; *m* Mary, *d* of late Brig.-Gen. Sir R. G. Gordon-Gilmour, Bt, CB, CVO, DSO; one *d* (and one *d* decd). *Educ:* Eton; Balliol, Oxford. Foreign Office, 1908; attached to British Delegation at Peace Conference, Jan. 1919; First Sec. in HM Diplomatic Service, 1919; Counsellor, 1926; Counsellor HM Embassy, Brussels, 1926-30; British Minister to the Baltic States, 1930-34; British Minister in Teheran, 1934-36; Ambassador in China, 1936-37; Ambassador to Turkey, 1939-44; Ambassador in Brussels and Minister to Luxembourg, 1944-47. *Publications:* Diplomat in Peace and War, 1949; Kentish Family, 1960. *Address:* The Red House, Barham, near Canterbury, Kent. *Club:* Anglo-Belgian. [Died 21 March 1971.

KNEALE, Sydney James, CBE 1963 (OBE 1944); HM's First Deemster and Clerk of the Rolls, 1958-69; Deputy Governor of the Isle of Man; *b* 3 July 1895; *s* of William Henry Kneale, Douglas, Isle of Man; *m* 1928, Margaret Alexandra Burnett; two *s* (and one *d* decd). *Educ:* Douglas Higher Grade and Eastern District Secondary Schs. Served European War in ranks and as commissioned officer, 6th Kings Liverpool Rifles, 1914-19. Admitted to Manx Bar, 1921; Asst Island Comr of Sea Scouts, 1929-45; Lt-Col First Battalion Manx Home Guard, 1940-44; Chm. Isle of Man Sea Cadet Corps, 1944-69; HM's Attorney-General, 1944-57; HM's Second Deemster, 1957-58. Coronation

Medal, 1953. *Publications:* Notes for Isle of Man Justices of the Peace, 1956; Manx Coroners, 1958. *Recreations:* golf, Association football, rugby, cricket. *Address:* Vicarage Road, Braddan, Isle of Man. *T:* Douglas 5637. *Club:* Manx Automobile (Douglas). [*Died* 17 *Dec.* 1975.

KNIGHT, Most Rev. Alan John, CMG 1954; DD; Archbishop of West Indies, since 1950, and Bishop of Guyana, since 1937; Sub-Prelate of The Venerable Order of St John of Jerusalem; *s* of John William Knight and Henrietta E. A. Shillito. *Educ:* Owen's School; Cambridge (MA, LLB). DD (Lambeth) 1950. Asst Master University College School (Junior School), 1923; Bishop's College, Cheshunt, 1924; Deacon, 1925; Priest, 1926; Curate at St James', Enfield Highway, 1925-28; Headmaster of Adisadel College, Gold Coast, 1928-37. FCP 1966. *Address:* Austin House, Georgetown, Guyana. *T:* Georgetown 02-64239; c/o National Westminster Bank Ltd, Felixstowe, Suffolk.
[*Died* 29 *Nov.* 1979.

KNIGHT, Gerald Hocken, CBE 1971; MA, MusB Cantab; DMus Lambeth; FRCM; FRCO (Choirmaster's Diploma); FRSCM; ADCM; Director of the Royal School of Church Music, 1952-72 (Associate-Director, 1947-52); Overseas Commissioner of the Royal School of Church Music, 1973-78; Hon. Organist to Archbishop of Canterbury, since 1953; *b* 27 July 1908; *o s* of Alwyne and Edith Knight, Wyngarvey, Par, Cornwall. *Educ:* Truro Cathedral Sch.; Peterhouse, Cambridge (Choral Exhibitioner); College of St Nicolas, Chislehurst; Royal College of Music. Asst Organist, Truro Cathedral, 1922-26; Peterhouse, Cambridge, 1926-29; John Stewart of Rannoch Scholar in Sacred Music, Cambridge Univ.; Organist and Choirmaster, St Augustine's, Queen's Gate, South Kensington, 1931-37; Tutor, College of St Nicolas, Chislehurst, 1932-38; Organist and Master of the Choristers, Canterbury Cathedral, 1937-52; Warden and Fellow of College of St Nicolas, Canterbury, 1945-52; External Examiner, Yorks Trg Colls Exam. Bd, 1937-41; Airman, RAF, 1942-43; Education Officer, Royal Air Force, 1943-45. Mem., House of Laity, Church Assembly, 1945-55; Mem., Archbishops' Psalter Revision Commission, 1958-63. Hon. Fellow: St Michael's Coll., Tenbury, 1953; Westminster Choir Coll., Princeton, New Jersey, USA, 1965. Hon. RAM; Hon. FTCL. *Publications:* Accompaniments (with J. Eric Hunt) to Merbecke's Communion Service, 1933; Music for Dorothy L. Sayers' plays, The Zeal of Thy House, 1937, and The Devil to Pay, 1939. Jt Musical Editor, Hymns Ancient and Modern, revised 1950; Jt Editor (with Dr William L. Reed), The Treasury of English Church Music, 1965; (ed) The Revised Parish Psalter, 1967; A Manual of Plainsong (Revised Psalter), 1969; Accompaniments for Unison Hymn-Singing, 1971. *Address:* 18 Warrington Crescent, Maida Vale, W9 1EL. *T:* 01-286 2410. *Club:* Athenæum. [*Died* 16 *Sept.* 1979.

KNIGHT, Gilfred Norman; President of the Society of Indexers since 1969; *b* 12 Sept. 1891; *y s* of William Frederick Knight, Solicitor; unmarried. *Educ:* Bradfield Coll.; Balliol Coll., Oxford (MA). Tancred Scholar, Lincoln's Inn, 1914; called to Bar, Lincoln's Inn, 1918. Served European War, 1914-18: commnd in E Surrey Regt, 1914; severely wounded at Battle of Loos, 1915; Captain and Adjt, No 16 Officer Cadet Bn, 1917; Staff of Judge Advocate-General, 1918-19. Sec. to West Indian and Atlantic Gp, British Empire Exhibn, 1923, 1924. Asst Sec. to West India Cttee, 1919-26, and 1938-39. Sec. to Co. of London TA&AFA, 1927. Guardian to Heir Apparent of Rampur State, India, 1931-32. Civil Service: Censorship, 1940-42; War Office, 1942-56. Founded Soc. of Indexers, 1957 and first Hon. Sec.; Chm., 1962. Wheatley Gold Medal for outstanding index, 1967; Carey Award, Soc. of Indexers, 1977. Is a Freemason (LGR). *Publications:* Chess Pieces: An Anthology, 1949; (with F. L Pick) The Pocket History of Freemasonry, 1953; The Freemason's Pocket Reference Book, 1955; (ed) Training in Indexing, 1969; (with W. F. Guy) King, Queen and Knight: A Chess Anthology, 1975; (with R. J. Stevens) Indexing, The Art of, 1978; (with Frederick Smyth) The Pocket Cyclopædia of Freemasonry, 1978; numerous contribs to West Indies Chronicle, Chess, Masonic Record, and The Indexer. *Recreations:* chess, book reviewing. *Address:* Scio House, Roehampton, SW15 3TD. *T:* 01-789 1649. *Clubs:* Civil Service; Hastings Chess; Barnet Chess (Hon. Life Pres., 1972).
[*Died* 17 *Aug.* 1978.

KNIGHT, Jasper Frederick, FCA; Director, Unilever Ltd and Unilever NV, 1958-70; Chairman, Warwick Securities, 1970-71; *b* 3 Oct. 1909; *er s* of late Jasper Webb Knight and Esther Austin Knight (*née* Low); *m* 1935, Elizabeth Margaret, *o d* of late Dr Andrew Wilson and Margaret Wilson (*née* Kintrea); two *s* one *d*. *Educ:* Eton; Exeter Coll., Oxford. BA 1930. Articled Peat Marwick Mitchell & Co., London, 1931. ACA 1934; FCA 1960. Finance Dir, then Principal Asst Sec., Ministry of Food, 1939-

45. Asst Chief Accountant, Unilever Ltd, 1945-48; Chief Accountant, 1948-52; various positions in Unilever in Germany and England, 1952-57; Chm. Van den Berghs & Jurgens Ltd, 1957-58. Part-time Member: Iron and Steel Board, 1964-65; National Board for Prices and Incomes, 1965-67; Council, Inst. of Chartered Accountants, 1966-70. Hon. Treasurer, Wycombe Div. Cons. Assoc., 1970-. Jt Master, Old Berkeley Beagles, 1967-. Medal of Freedom (Silver Palm) (US), 1945. JDipMA, 1965. *Recreations:* beagling, boating and gardening. *Address:* Little Colstrope, Hambleden, Henley-on-Thames, Oxon. *T:* Hambleden 306. *Clubs:* Lansdowne, Leander, London Rowing.
[*Died* 27 *Jan.* 1972.

KNIGHTS, Maj.-Gen. Robert William, CB 1969; CBE 1960; GOC Southern Command, Australia, 1966-69, retired; *b* 24 June 1912; *s* of late William James Knights, Canberra, Australia; *m* 1937, Betty Adrienne, *d* of late George Leonard Davis, Sale, Victoria, Australia; one *s* two *d*. *Educ:* Telopea Park High Sch., Canberra; Royal Military College, Duntroon, Canberra. Lt, Australian Staff Corps, 1932; Adj., CMF, 1933-39. Served War of 1939-45: Middle East and Australia, Lt-Col, 1943. Staff, RMC, Duntroon, 1945-47; AHQ, 1947-49; Joint Services Staff Coll., UK, 1949; seconded Dept of Defence, 1950-51; Dir of Personnel Administration, AHQ, Melbourne, 1951-54; Brig., 1954; idc, 1957; Maj.-Gen., 1958; Head of Australian Joint Services Staff, London, 1958-59; Extra Gentleman Usher to the Queen, 1958-60; GOC, W Comd, Aust., 1960; Comdt, RMC, Duntroon, 1960-61; Chm., Joint Planning Cttee, Dept of Defence, Australia, 1962-63. QMG, AHQ, Australia, 1964-66. *Address:* 128 Empire Circuit, Yarralumla, ACT 2600, Australia. *Clubs:* Naval and Military (Melbourne); Commonwealth (Canberra). [*Died* 4 *Aug.* 1975.

KNILL, Sir Ian S.; see Stuart-Knill.

KNOTT, Lt-Gen. Sir Harold (Edwin), KCB 1963 (CB 1961); OBE 1945; MA; MD; DPH; *b* 15 May 1903; *s* of Arthur Knott; *m* 1929, Dora Georgina, *d* of Dr J. Bradley; four *s* one *d*. *Educ:* King's Hosp., Dublin; Trinity Coll., Dublin. MA, MD Dublin, 1935; DPH (London) 1936. Comnd, 1929; served in India, 1930-35; Egypt, BLA, India, 1938-47; Col, and Comdt Army Sch. of Health, 1949-53; Brigadier: Dep. Dir Army Health, Northern Army Group, 1953-55; DDMS, West Africa, and ADMS, Ghana, 1955-57; ADMS, Aldershot Dist, 1957-58; Maj.-Gen., DDMS, Eastern Command, 1958-61; Lt-Gen. 1961; DGAMS, 1961-65, retired, 1965. QHP 1960-65. Hon. LLD (Dublin) 1961. CStJ 1962. *Recreation:* golf. *Address:* La Belle Hougue, Fauvic, Grouville, Jersey, Channel Islands. *T:* Jersey East 185. *Clubs:* Army and Navy; Dublin University (Dublin); Victoria, Royal Jersey Golf (Jersey). [*Died* 28 *Aug.* 1974.

KNOWLAND, William Fife; Newspaper Publisher; *b* 26 June 1908; *s* of Joseph Russell and Ellie (Fife) Knowland; *m* 1st, 1926, Helen Davis Herrick; one *s* two *d*; 2nd, 1972, Ann Dickson. *Educ:* University of California, Berkeley, Calif (AB 1929). Pres., Publisher and Editor, Oakland, Calif, Tribune, 1933-; Member: California State Assembly, 1933-35; California State Senate, 1935-39; Republican National Cttee, 1938; Chm. Republican Nat. Exec. Cttee, 1941-42. Served War with US Army, from private to Major, 1942-45 (serving in Europe). On service overseas when apptd US Senator to fill unexpired term; elected for six-year term, 1946; re-elected, 1952; Chm. Republican Policy Cttee (Senate), 1953; Senate Republican Leader, 1953-59. Hon. LLD (holds several hon. degrees in the USA). *Address:* Oakland Tribune, 401 13th Street, Oakland, California 94604, USA. *T:* 273-2200. *Clubs:* Mason (Scottish 33°), Native Sons of the Golden West, Elks, Eagles, Moose, Athenien-Nile; Bohemian (San Francisco). [*Died* 23 *Feb.* 1974.

KNOWLES, Rev. David; see Knowles, Rev. Michael Clive.

KNOWLES, Rt. Rev. Donald Rowland, OBE 1951; Assistant Bishop of Nassau and the Bahamas; *b* 14 July 1898; *s* of Frederick F. and Addie A. Knowles, Long Island, Bahamas; *m* 1933, Carolyn Elizabeth Knowles; two *s*. *Educ:* Boys' Central School, Nassau; St Paul's College, Burgh, Lincs; Hatfield College, Durham. BA (Hons Theol.) First Class. Government Service, Nassau, 1915-19. Deacon, 1923; Priest, 1924. Curate, Andros Is., Diocese of Nassau, 1923-25; Priest-in-Charge: Long Cay, Acklins, Crooked Islands, and Inagua, 1925-35; Eleuthera, 1935-38; Rector, St Matthew's Nassau, 1938-53; Canon, 1944; Archdeacon of Bahamas, 1951; Bishop of Antigua, 1953-69; Rector, St Margaret's, Nassau, 1970-75. *Address:* PO Box ES 5375, Nassau, NP, Bahamas. [*Died* 26 *Sept.* 1977.

KNOWLES, Air Vice-Marshal Edgar, CB 1965; CBE 1959 (MBE 1944); BSc; FRAeS; Director of Educational Services, RAF, 1960-67, retired; *b* 11 Sept. 1907; *o s* of Ernest Knowles

and Annie Collins, Bradford; *m* 1935, Jane, *er d* of William Griffiths and Annie Evans, Coedely; two *d. Educ:* Colne Grammar; University Coll. and King's Coll., London. Sen. Science Master, Harrogate Grammar Sch., 1929-35; entered RAF Educl Service, 1935; served at Sch. of Tech. Trg, Halton, 1935-40; Air Ministry, 1940-43; Senior Education Officer, Middle East, 1943-47; Air Ministry, 1947-48; HQ, 23 Group, 1948-50; Command Educn Officer, Transport Comd, 1950-51; Dir of Studies, RPAF Cadet College, Risalpur, Pakistan, 1951-52; Dep. Dir of Educnl Services, Air Ministry, 1952-53; Principal Education Officer, Halton, 1953-55; Command Educn Officer, Tech. Trg Comd, 1955-60; ADC to the Queen, 1956-60. Group Capt. 1952; Air Cdre, 1959; Air Vice-Marshal, 1960. Chairman: Bucks County Branch, SS&AFA; County War Pensions Cttee. *Address:* 5 Dobbins Lane, Wendover, Bucks. *T:* Wendover 622216. *Clubs:* Royal Air Force; Ashridge Golf.
[Died 8 Feb. 1977.

KNOWLES, Sir Francis (Gerald William), 6th Bt, *cr* 1765; FRS 1966; Professor of Anatomy, King's College, London, since Oct. 1967; *b* 9 March 1915; *s* of Sir Francis Howe Seymour Knowles, 5th Bt, and Kathleen Constance Averina, *d* of William Lennon; *S* father 1953; *m* 1948, Ruth Jessie, *widow* of Pilot Officer R. G. Hulse, RAF, and *d* of late Rev. Arthur Brooke-Smith; one *s* three *d* (of these one *s* one *d* are twins). *Educ:* Radley; Oriel Coll., Oxford. BA 1936; MA and DPhil 1939; DSc 1963. Oxford Univ. Naples Schol., 1937; Royal Society Browne Fund Bermuda Schol., 1949; Nuffield Foundation Schol., 1953. Head of Biology Dept, Marlborough Coll., 1938-58; Lectr in the Dept of Anatomy, Birmingham Univ., 1958-63; Prof. of Comparative Endocrinology, Birmingham Univ., 1967 (Reader, 1963-67). *Publications:* Man and Other Living Things, 1945 (2nd edn, 1960); The Living Organism, 1948; Biology and Man, 1950; Diagrams of Human Biology, 1950; Freshwater and Saltwater Aquaria, 1953; (co-author) Endocrine Control in Crustaceans, 1959; (co-author) Animal Hormones, 1966. Research publications on neuroendocrinology. *Recreation:* travel. *Heir: s* Charles Francis Knowles, *b* 20 Dec. 1951. *Address:* Avebury Manor, Avebury, Wilts. *T:* Avebury 203. *Club:* Athenæum.
[Died 13 July 1974.

KNOWLES, John; Solicitor; Assistant Public Trustee, 1956-60, retired 1960; *b* 8 March 1898. *Educ:* Abingdon Sch.; Pembroke Coll., Oxford (BA). Served with Lancs Fusiliers in European War, 1917-19. Qualified as Solicitor, 1925. A Chief Administrative Officer, Public Trustee Office, 1955. *Address:* c/o The Public Trustee Office, Kingsway, WC2.
[Died March 1977.

KNOWLES, Joshua Kenneth, CBE 1953; General Secretary, National Farmers' Union, 1945-70; *b* 4 Dec. 1903; *s* of Robert Dixon Knowles and Annie Rawcliffe, Greenmount, Lancs; *m* 1928; one *s*. *Educ:* The Old College, Windermere; Midland Agricultural Coll., Sutton Bonnington, Loughborough (now Nottingham Univ.). Farming, 1922-45, at Morley, Derbyshire. Derbyshire Council Deleg., NFU, 1933-43; Vice-Pres., NFU, 1943; Pres., NFU, 1944. Liveryman, Co. of Farmers. *Recreation:* fishing. *Address:* 3 Manor Way, Holyport, Maidenhead, Berks. *T:* Maidenhead 21729. *Clubs:* City Livery, Farmers', Royal Automobile.
[Died 4 July 1974.

KNOWLES, Rev. Michael Clive (in religion **David**), OSB, MA, LittD, FBA, FSA; *b* 1896; *o s* of late Harry Herbert and Carrie Knowles, Studley, Warwicks. *Educ:* Downside; Christ's Coll., Cambridge; Collegio Sant' Anselmo, Rome. Entered novitiate at Downside, 1914; Priest, 1922; Editor of Downside Review, 1930-34; Fellow of Peterhouse, Cambridge, 1944-63; University Lecturer in History, 1946; Prof. of Medieval History, 1947-54; Regius Prof. of Modern History, 1954-63. President: Royal Hist. Soc., 1956-60; Classical Assoc., 1974-75. Ford's Lecturer in English History, Oxford, 1948-49; British Academy Raleigh Lecturer, 1949; Creighton Lecturer, London, 1956; Sarum Lecturer, Oxford, 1964-65; Hon. Mem. Royal Irish Academy, 1955; Mem. Pontifical Hist. Institute, Rome; Corresp. Mem. Monumenta Germaniæ Historica, 1965; Associate, Acad. Royale de Belgique, 1973; Hon. Fellow: Christ's Coll., Cambridge, 1958; Peterhouse, Cambridge, 1963. Hon. DD Cambridge, 1969; Hon. DLitt: Oxford, 1952; Bristol, 1956; Leicester, 1962; Kent, 1969; Birmingham, 1972; DLit London, 1963; DUniv York, 1969. *Publications:* The Monastic Order in England, 1940 (revised 1963); The Religious Houses of Medieval England, 1940 (enlarged edn with R. N. Hadcock, 1953, rev. edn 1971); The Religious Orders in England: vol I, 1948; vol. II, 1955; vol. III, 1959; The Monastic Constitutions of Lanfranc, 1951; The Episcopal Colleagues of Archbishop Thomas Becket, 1951; Monastic Sites from the air (with J. K. St Joseph), 1952; Charterhouse (with W. F. Grimes), 1954; The English Mystical Tradition, 1961; Saints and Scholars, 1962; The Evolution of

Medieval Thought, 1962; The Historian and Character, 1963; Great Historical Enterprises, 1963; From Pachomius to Ignatius, 1966; What is Mysticism?, 1967; Christian Monasticism, 1969; The Christian Centuries, 1969; Thomas Becket, 1970; Heads of Religious Houses, 940-1216 (with C. N. L. Brooke and V. London), 1972; articles in Downside Review, English Historical Review, Cambridge Historical Review and Journal of Ecclesiastical History. *Address:* 9 Old House Close, Church Road, Wimbledon, SW19. *T:* 01-946 0010; The Old Cottage, Linch, Liphook, Hants. *T:* Milland 227. *Club:* Athenæum.
[Died 21 Nov. 1974.

KNOX, Collie; author and journalist; *s* of late Edmund Francis Vesey Knox, KC, MP, Shimnah, Newcastle, Co. Down; *m* 1944, Gwendoline Frances Mary (marriage dissolved, 1948), *yr d* of late I. Davidson Mitchell. *Educ:* Rugby; RMC, Sandhurst. Regular Commission in Queen's Royal Regiment. Seconded to RFC. Served European War, 1914-18 (wounded, 1916, when pilot); Captain on staff at War Office and in India, Uganda, Anglo-Egyptian Sudan. Served with Regt during Irish Rebellion at Londonderry and Co. Cork; on staff of GOC London Air Defences, 1917, at Horse Guards; on staff of late Lord Lloyd when Gov. of Bombay; on staff of late Sir Geoffrey Archer during his whole terms of office when Gov. of Uganda and Gov.-Gen. of the Sudan; Bimbashi (Lt-Col) in Sudan Defence Force, 1925. Entered Fleet Street, in 1928 on Daily Express; joined Daily Mail as Special Columnist, 1933, until War broke out; rejoined Daily Mail as Columnist, March 1945; resigned from Daily Mail, Oct. 1955; Feature writer for Newnes & Pearson Publications and Daily Mirror Group, till 1963; Special London Columnist and drama critic of Morning Telegraph, New York, 1955-; was first radio columnist-critic. Has written 14 books, 30 songs (lyrics). Contributed during War of 1939-45 to Ministry of Information, and to Service Publications; on Special Duties; Dir of Public Relations, ENSA, Drury Lane Theatre, WC2, 1943-45. *Publications:* It Might Have Been You (autobiography), 1938; Collie Knox Calling, 1937; Draw Up Your Chair, 1938; Collie Knox Again, 1938; Collie Knox Re-Calls, 1940; Heroes All, 1941; Atlantic Battle, 1941; For Ever England, 1943; The Un-Beaten Track, 1944; People of Quality, 1947; It Had To Be Me, 1947; We Live and Learn, 1951; Steel at Brierley Hill (A Centenary History of Round Oak Steelworks), 1957. *Recreations:* lyric-writing, golf, lawn tennis, motoring. *Address:* 10e Sussex Heights, St Margarets Place, Brighton, E Sussex BN1 2FQ. *T:* Brighton 24753. *Club:* Garrick. *[Died 3 May 1977.*

KNOX, Edmund George Valpy; *b* 1881; *e s* of late Rt Rev. E. A. Knox, DD, and Ellen Penelope, *d* of Dr Valpy French, Bishop of Lahore; *m* 1st, 1912, Christina Frances (*d* 1935), *y d* of Dr E. L. Hicks, Bishop of Lincoln; one *s* one *d* ; 2nd, 1937, Mary Eleanor Jessy, *d* of Ernest Howard Shepard, *qv*. *Educ:* Rugby; Corpus Christi Coll., Oxford. Hon. MA, Oxford; Fellow Institute of Journalists. Staff of Punch, 1921; Editor, 1932-49. Leslie Stephen Lecture, 1951. Pen-name Evoe. Served in Lincs Regt, 1914-19 (wounded at Passchendaele). *Publications:* The Brazen Lyre; A Little Loot; Parodies Regained; These Liberties; Fiction As She Is Wrote; An Hour from Victoria; Fancy Now; It Occurs to Me; Gorgeous Times; Quaint Specimens; Awful Occasions; Poems of Impudence; I'll Tell the World; Wonderful Outings; Here's Misery; Blue Feathers; This Other Eden; Things That Annoy Me; Slight Irritations; Folly Calling; (ed) Anthology of Humorous Verse; Adventures of a School. Articles in several encyclopaedias. *Recreations:* reading and writing. *Address:* 110 Frognal, Hampstead, NW3. *Club:* Athenæum.
[Died 2 Jan. 1971.

KNOX, Sir Edward (Ritchie), Kt 1956; MC 1918; Partner, Harrison, Knox and Leslie, 1922-59, retired; Director: CSR Co. Ltd, 1923-64 (Chairman, 1933-59); Commercial Banking Co. of Sydney Ltd, 1928-64 (Chairman, 1939-59); United Insurance Co. Ltd, 1930-64 (Chairman, 1942-53); Perpetual Trustee Co. Ltd, 1935-64; CSR Chemicals, 1948-64 (Chairman, 1948-61); *b* 27 Nov. 1889; *er s* of Thomas Forster and Amy Hope Knox, Sydney; *m* 1923, Barbara Mary, 2nd *d* of H. P. Owen, Sydney; one *s* one *d*. *Educ:* Sydney Church of England Grammar Sch.; Sydney Grammar Sch. Clerk, Dalgety & Co. Ltd, Sydney, 1908-12; pastoral pursuits, 1913-14, and 1919-21. Served with RFA, 1915-18. Accountancy, 1922-56; FCA Aust. 1936. *Recreations:* golf and fly-fishing. *Address:* 22 Victoria Road, Bellevue Hill, NSW 2023, Australia. *Clubs:* Union, Royal Sydney Golf (Sydney).
[Died 26 March 1973.

KNOX, Gen. Sir Harry (Hugh Sidney), KCB 1935 (CB 1919); DSO 1917; *b* 5 Nov. 1873; 4th *s* of late Vesey Ed. Knox, Shimnah, Newcastle, Co. Down; *m* 1904, Grace Una (*d* 1954), *d* of Rev. R. A. Storrs, Rector, Shanklin, Isle of Wight; one *d*. *Educ:* St Columba's Coll., Rathfarnham, Dublin. 5th RI Rifles, 1890-93; Northants Regt, 1893-1919: served Samana, Tirah, and

NW Frontier, India, 1897-98 (medal, 3 clasps); Uganda Protectorate with Uganda Rifles, 1900-01; Adj. 1st Batt. Northants Regt, 1902-05; Staff Coll., Quetta, 1908-09; Gen. Staff AHQ, India, 1911-14; BEF, France, 1915-19; Gen. Staff HQ V Army Corps, 1915; GSO I 15th Scottish Div., 1915-17; Brig.-Gen. Staff XV Army Corps, 1917-19, commanding 29th Div. (temp.) Aug. 1918 (wounded, despatches seven times; Brevet Lt-Col, Brevet Col, DSO, CB, Croix de Guerre, Officier Legion of Honour, Officier, Couronne Belge); acting Maj.-Gen., Gen. Staff, First Army, 6 Feb.-7 March 1919; Maj.-Gen. 1926; Commanded 3rd Infantry Brigade, Bordon, 1923-26; Dir of Military Training, War Office, 1926-30; commanded 3rd Div., 1930-32; ADC to the King, 1925-26; Lt-Gen. 1932; Lt of Tower of London, 1933-35; Gen., 1936; Adj. Gen. to the Forces, 1935-37; retired pay, 1938; Governor of Royal Hospital, Chelsea, 1938-43; Col Northants Regt, 1931-43. *Recreations:* gardening, shooting, fishing. *Address:* Hillborough Cottage, Highcliffe, Hants. *T:* Highcliffe 3465. *Club:* United Service.
[Died 10 June 1971.

KNOX, Sir Malcolm; *see* Knox, Sir T. M.

KNOX, Sir Robert Wilson, Kt 1934; company director; *b* 17 May 1890; *s* of late Hon. William Knox; *m* 1914, Ivy Victoria Clarke; one *s* one *d.* *Educ:* Melbourne Church of England Grammar Sch. Pres. Melbourne Chamber of Commerce, 1928-31, and Associated Chamber of Commerce of Australia, 1934-36; Chm., Australian National Cttee, Internat. Chamber of Commerce, 1933-36; consultant to Australian Delegation Ottawa Conference, 1932; First Federal Pres. Australian Assoc. British Manufacturers, 1929; Dir, Dunlop Rubber Co. Ltd, and other industrial companies; Commissioner Australian Red Cross Soc., Egypt, France. *Recreation:* golf. *Address:* Greenknowe Court, Toorak, Victoria 3142, Australia. *TA:* Knox, Melbourne. *Clubs:* Melbourne, Australian (Melbourne).
[Died 21 April 1973.

KNOX, Sir (Thomas) Malcolm, Kt 1961; Principal, University of St Andrews, 1953-66; Hon. Fellow, Pembroke College, Oxford, 1950; Hon. LLD Edinburgh, Pennsylvania and Dundee; Hon. DLitt Glasgow; *b* Birkenhead, Cheshire, 28 Nov. 1900; *e s* of James Knox, MA, and Isabella Russell Marshall, Tillicoultry, Clackmannan; *m* 1st, Margaret Normana McLeod Smith (*d* 1930), Tarbert, Harris; 2nd, Dorothy Ellen Jolly (*d* 1974), Thornton-le-Fylde, Lancs; 3rd, Joan Mary Winifred Sumner, MA, Marlow. *Educ:* Mostyn House, Parkgate, Cheshire; Bury Grammar Sch.; Liverpool Institute; Pembroke Coll., Oxford. Entered business of Lever Brothers Ltd as Sec. to 1st Lord Leverhulme, 1923; various executive and secretarial positions in firms managing Lever Brothers' West African interests, 1925-31; Lecturer in Philosophy, Jesus Coll., Oxford, 1931-33; Fellow and Tutor, 1933-36; Lecturer in Greek Philosophy, Queen's Coll., Oxford, 1934-36; Prof. of Moral Philosophy, University of St Andrews, 1936-53, Dep. Principal, 1951-52. Acting Principal, 1952-53. Gifford Lecturer, University of Aberdeen, 1965-66 and 1967-68. Chm. Govs of Morrison's Acad., Crieff, 1946-62; Chm. Advisory Council on Education in Scotland, 1957-61; Mem. Catering Wages Commission, 1943-46; Mem. Nat. Reference Tribunal for the Coal Industry of Great Britain, 1943-56; Mem. Review Body on Doctors' and Dentists' Remuneration, 1962-65. *Publications:* Translation, with commentary, of Hegel's Philosophy of Right, 1942; Hegel's Early Theological Writings, 1948; Hegel's Political Writings, 1964; Hegel's Aesthetics, 1975; Hegel's Natural Law, 1975; Action, 1968; A Layman's Quest, 1969; A Heretic's Religion, 1976; articles and reviews in periodicals. *Address:* 19 Victoria Terrace, Crieff, Perthshire. *T:* 2808.
[Died 6 April 1980.

KNOX JOHNSTON, A. G.; *see* Johnston.

KNOX-SHAW, Thomas, CBE 1954; MC; MA; Hon. ARIBA; Fellow of Sidney Sussex College (Master, June 1945-57); 2nd *s* of late C. T. Knox-Shaw; *b* 27 Nov. 1886. *Educ:* Blundell's Sch., Tiverton; Sidney Sussex Coll., Cambridge (Mathematical Scholar); 4th Wrangler, 1908; Class I Div. II in Part II Mathematical Tripos, 1909; Fellow, 1909; Coll. Lectr, 1914; Tutor, 1919-29; University Lectr in Mathematics, 1926-29; Mem. of the Council of the Senate, 1920-24, 1925-30, 1945-50; Treasurer of the University of Cambridge, 1929-45; Cambridge City Councillor, 1944-52; Chm., United Cambridge Hosps, 1948-55. During European War, 1914-18, served as Adjutant 1st Battalion York and Lancaster Regt, and on Infantry Brigade Staffs in France and Salonica (MC, Belgian Croix de Guerre, despatches thrice). *Recreation:* golf. *Address:* Sidney Sussex College, Cambridge. *Clubs:* Oxford and Cambridge University; Hawks, University Pitt (Cambridge).
[Died 24 July 1972.

KNUTSFORD, 4th Viscount *cr* 1895; **Thurstan Holland-Hibbert,** Bt 1853; Baron, 1888; Barrister; *b* 19 June 1888; *e s* of 3rd Viscount and Ellen (*d* 1949), *e d* of Sir Wilfrid Lawson, 2nd Bt of Brayton, Cumberland; *S* father, 1935; *m* 1912, Viola Mary (*d* 1964), *d* of Thomas Meadows Clutterbuck, Putteridge Bury, Herts; one *s* one *d.* *Educ:* Eton; Cambridge Univ., BA. Called to Bar, Inner Temple, 1914; late Royal Scots Greys; Master of Avon Vale Foxhounds, 1924-33; Joint Master VWH (Cirencester) 1935. *Heir:* *s* Hon. Julian Thurstan Holland-Hibbert, CBE. *Address:* Munden, Watford, Herts.
[Died 17 Feb. 1976.

KOCH, Ludwig, MBE 1960; Author and Lecturer; *b* 13 Nov. 1881; *m* 1912, Nellie Sylvia Herz; one *s* one *d.* *Educ:* Frankfurt A. M.; Paris; Milan. Violinist, pupil of Prof. Hugo Heermann, 1890-1902; Lieder and Oratorio Singer, pupil of Clara Sohn, Johannes Meschaert and Jean de Reszke, 1905-14; responsible for repatriation of Allied Prisoners of War, 1918-19; Delegate for the occupied zone in Germany, 1919-25; Syndic of the City of Frankfurt A. M. for Publicity, Propaganda and Exhibition, 1926-28; Creator and Organiser of International Music Exhibition, Music in the Life of Nations, 1927; Dir of the Culture Dept of German Gramophone, Odeon and Parlophone Company, 1928-35; first out-door recording of Songs of Wild Birds; Originator of Sound-Books; since 1936 in this country as Naturalist, Author of Sound-Books, Lectr, Broadcasts and Synchroniser of Nature Films, 1948-51; joined BBC with his famous collection of bird and animal sounds for purpose of completing the library and making it available to the public. Grosse Verdienstkreuz des Verdienstorden der Bundesrepublik Deutschland, 1962. *Publications:* Songs of Wild Birds (with E. M. Nicholson), 1936; More Songs of Wild Birds (with E. M. Nicholson), 1937; Hunting by Ear (with Michael Berry and D. W. E. Brock), 1937; Animal Language (with Julian Huxley), 1938; Memoirs of a Birdman, 1955; Bird Song (text and recording by Ludwig Koch), 1960. (ed) Encyclopedia of British Birds, 1955. *Address:* Bird Cottage, 39 Walton Avenue, South Harrow, Mddx.
[Died 4 May 1974.

KOELLE, Vice-Adm. Sir Harry (Philpot), KCB 1959 (CB 1957); *b* 16 Aug. 1901; *s* of late Rev. C. Philpot Koelle, Rector of Wickford, Essex, and Durley, Hampshire; *m* 1st, 1930, Enid (*d* 1942), *d* of C. F. Corbould Ellis, JP, Reading; one *d*; 2nd, 1948, Elizabeth Anne, *d* of late Sir Philip Devitt, 1st and last Bt; two *d.* *Educ:* Rossall; RN Colleges, Osborne and Dartmouth. Joined RN 1915. Served HMS Bellerophon and Renown, 1917-18. Served War of 1939-45: HMS Royal Sovereign and Duke of York; Deputy Dir of Manning, Admiralty, 1945-48. Dir of Welfare and Service Conditions, Admiralty, 1953-55; Command Supply Officer, Plymouth, 1955-57; Dir-General Supply and Secretariat Branch, Admiralty, 1957-60. Comdr 1938; Capt. 1948; Rear-Adm. 1955; retired 1960. *Recreation:* racing. *Address:* Mill House, Thornford, near Sherborne, Dorset. *Club:* Army and Navy.
[Died 19 May 1980.

KOENIGSBERGER, Prof. Franz, DSc; FIMechE; Professor of Machine Tool Engineering, University of Manchester Institute of Science and Technology, 1961-75, now Emeritus; *b* 9 Nov. 1907; *s* of Hans and Margaret Koenigsberger; *m* 1934, Lilli Gertrude Kate (*née* Schlesinger); one *s* one *d.* *Educ:* Goethe-Schule, Berlin; Technische Hochschule, Berlin-Charlottenburg. Research Asst for Machine Tools, Technische Hochschule, Berlin-Charlottenburg, 1931-32; Draughtsman and Designer of machine tools, 1932-35; Chief Designer and Chief Engr, Machine Tool Dept, Ansaldo SA, Genoa, 1936-38; Chief Mech. Engr, Cooke & Ferguson Ltd, Manchester, 1939-47; Lectr in Mech. Engrg, 1947-54; Sen. Lectr in Prod. Engrg, 1954-57; Reader in Machine Tools and Prod. Processes, The Manchester Coll. of Science and Technology, 1957-61. Managing Editor, Industrial and Production Engineering International (Munich); Jt Editor, Fertigung (Bern, Switzerland). President: Manchester Assoc. of Engineers, 1965-66; Internat. Inst. of Prod. Engrg Research (CIRP), 1965-66; Manchester Technology Assoc., 1971-72. Thomas Lowe Gray Prize, 1944, and Water Arbitration Prize, 1951, of Instn of Mech. Engrs; Constantine Medal, 1956, and Butterworth Medal, 1961, of Manchester Assoc. of Engineers; Inst. Prod. Engrs Medal, 1966. Medaille de Vermeil, Soc. d'Encouragement de la Récherche et l'Invention, 1972. DrIngEh Berlin, 1969; Hon. Dr Ghent, 1970; Hon. DTech Bradford, 1974; Hon. Fellow, Manchester Polytechnic, 1975. *Publications:* Design for Welding, 1948; Welding Technology, 1949 (1953, 1961); Spanende Werkzeugmaschinen, 1961; Design Principles of Metal Cutting Machine Tools, 1964; (with J. Tlusty) Machine Tool Structures, 1970; (with C. Ruiz) Design for Strength and Production, 1970; papers in Proceedings Institution Mechanical Engineers, The Production Engineer, Welding Jl, British Welding Jl. *Recreations:* music, photography. *Address:* 7 Singleton Road, Heaton Moor, Stockport SK4 4PW. *T:* 061-432 4677.
[Died 22 Jan. 1979.

KOEPPLER, Prof. Sir Henry, (Sir Heinz), Kt 1977; CBE 1967 (OBE 1957); FRHistS; Provost of the Institute for the Study of Interaction between Foreign and Domestic Policies, and Distinguished Visiting Professor, Baylor University, Waco, Texas, since 1978; Managerial Consultant, Shell International Petroleum Company, since 1977; *b* 30 June 1912; *o s* of late Friedrich and Gertrude Koeppler. *Educ:* Univs of Berlin, Heidelberg, Kiel (Christian Albrecht Haus), Magdalen Coll., Oxford. MA, DPhil(Oxon). Sen. Demy, Magdalen Coll., 1937-39; Lectr, Bd of Faculty of Modern History, Oxford, 1937-39. Political Intelligence Dept, FO, 1940-42; Asst Regional Dir, Political Warfare Exec., 1943-45; Warden: Wilton Park, 1946-77; European Discussion Centre, 1972-77; Asst Under-Sec. of State, FCO, 1975-77. Visiting Prof. Univ. of Heidelberg, 1960-61; Consultant, Ford Foundation, 1961; Visiting Distinguished Prof., Ohio State Univ., 1966; Vis. Prof. of West-European Studies and Government, Indiana Univ., Bloomington, USA, 1970. President's Medallion for service to internat. educn, Wisconsin Univ., 1974; first Joseph Bech Meml Gold Medal, 1977. *Publications:* A Lasting Peace (with M. Garnett), 1940; articles in: Jl of Theological Studies, English Historical Review, The Round Table; *relevant publication:* A Unique Contribution to International Relations: the story of Wilton Park, by D. M. Keezer, 1973. *Recreation:* diminishing jargon. *Address:* 111 Ashley Gardens, SW1P 1HJ. *T:* 01-828 2828; Department of Political Science, Baylor University, Waco, Texas 76704, USA. *Clubs:* Athenæum; Chanctonbury Ring (Wiston); Cornwallis Post (San Francisco).   *[Died 31 March 1979.*

KOHAN, Major Charles Mendel, OBE, MA; Barrister-at-Law, retired; *b* 15 Nov. 1884; *y s* of M. Kohan and *g s* of G. J. Bloomfield, Chapel-en-le-Frith, Derbyshire; *m* 1932, Ethel May Ashford. *Educ:* Manchester Grammar Sch.; Trinity Coll., Cambridge (Open Scholarship for History; Hons, Parts I and II, Historical Tripos; Chancellor's Medal for English Verse). Asst Sec. to the Royal Statistical Society, 1909-14. Served in Royal Artillery, 1914-19 (Western Front), and on the General Staff, Headquarters, Fourth Army, BEF, 1918-19 (OBE); called to Bar, Inner Temple, 1919; late Hon. Sec. Mansion House Council on Health and Housing; Commission in Army Emergency Reserve, Sept., 1939; transferred to Offices of the War Cabinet, 1942; an Official Historian in the Cabinet Secretariat, 1944-52; Dir, New Health Trust, 1952. *Publications:* History of the Second World War (Civil Series): Works and Buildings, 1952. Miscellaneous contributions to the Press. *Recreations:* fishing, motoring, amateur drama. *Address:* 2 Penn Mead, Penn, Bucks. *T:* Penn 2719. *Clubs:* Royal Automobile, United and Cecil.
                    [Died 13 Dec. 1974.

KOKOSCHKA, Oskar, CBE 1959; artist and writer; *b* Pöchlarn, Austria, 1 March 1886; *m* Olda (*née* Palkovsky); British subject since 1947. *Educ:* Vienna Sch. of Industrial Art. Worked in Vienna from 1905; in Berlin, 1910, joined group of expressionist painters; first one-man exhibn, Paul Cassirer's Gall., 1910; contrib. to Der Sturm. Served as Cavalry Officer, Russian and Italian fronts, 1915-17 (wounded). Prof. Acad. of Art, Dresden, 1919-24; travelled throughout Europe, North Africa and Near East, painting landscapes and panoramic views of cities, 1924-31; returned to Vienna, 1931; to Prague, 1934, became a Czech citizen; works included in Nazi exhibn of "Degenerate Art", Munich, 1937; to England, 1938; Founder, Internat. Summer Acad. of Fine Arts, Salzburg, and taught there, 1953-63. Has held one-man exhibns in Austria, Germany, Italy, Holland, France, Switzerland, USA, etc; in Great Britain: Tate Gallery, 1962; Marlborough Fine Art Galleries, 1967, 1969, 1976. Order of Merit of Federal Republic of Germany, 1956. Winner of the Rome Prize, 1960; Erasmus Prize (jt), 1960; Hon. Academician, Royal Academy, 1970; Hon. DLitt Oxon, 1963. Freedom of Vienna, Salzburg and Pöchlarn. *Works include:* portraits, landscapes, illustrations, compositions (politically symbolic works, etc). *Publications:* A Sea ringed with Visions (short stories), 1962; Mein Leben (autobiography), 1971 (My Life, 1974); London Views, British Landscapes, 1972; Saul and David (lithographs), 1973; Das Schriftliche Werk (ed H. Spielmann), 4 vols, 1973-76; *plays:* Mörder, Hoffnung der Frauen, 1907; Der brennende Dornbusch, Hiob, 1911; Orpheus and Eurydice, 1916, etc; *relevant publications:* Kokoschka: The Work of the Painter, by H. M. Wingler, 1958; Oskar Kokoschka: The Artist and his Time, by J. P. Hodin, 1966; Oskar Kokoschka: das Druckgraphische Werk, by H. M. Wingler and Friedrich Welz, 1976. *Address:* 1844 Villeneuve, Vaud, Switzerland.
                    [Died 22 Feb. 1980.

KOLLER, Prof. Pius Charles, PhD, DSc; Professor Emeritus, University of London, since 1969 (Professor of Cytogenetics, Institute of Cancer Research, University of London, 1944-69, retired); *b* 3 April 1904; *m* 1946, Anna Edith Olsen, Denmark; three *d*. *Educ:* Universities of Budapest, Cambridge and

Edinburgh. PhD Budapest, 1926; DSc Edinburgh, 1934. Rockefeller Fellow, Pasadena, Calif, 1936-37; Lecturer, University of Edinburgh, 1938-44; Research Cytologist, Royal Cancer Hospital, 1944-46, and Chester Beatty Research Inst., 1946-69. Vis. Prof., Harvard Med. Sch., 1970. Consultant, Internat. Atomic Energy Agency, Bandung, Indonesia, 1970. *Publications:* Chromosomes and Genes, 1968; Chromosome Breakage: a chapter in Progress in Biophysics, 1969; The Role of Chromosomes in Cancer Biology, 1972; numerous scientific papers in Jl of Genetics, Heredity, Brit. Jl of Cancer etc, 1936-68. *Recreations:* philosophy, gardening, reading. *Address:* Brushwood, 37 Gaviots Way, Gerrard's Cross, Bucks. *T:* Gerrard's Cross 82057.   *[Died 29 June 1979.*

KOSTELANETZ, André; orchestra conductor; *b* Leningrad, Russia; *s* of Nachman Kostelanetz and Rosalie Dimscha; *m* 1st, 1938, Lily Pons, soprano (marr. diss. 1958; she *d* 1976); 2nd, 1960, Sara Gene Orcutt (marr. diss., 1969). *Educ:* St Peter's Sch.; St Petersburg Conservatory of Music. Hon. MusD: Albion Coll., Albion, Mich, 1939; Cincinnati Conservatory of Music, 1945. Came to United States 1922, naturalised 1928. For many years conducted own shows over Columbia Broadcasting System; directed music for several motion pictures; selected by radio editors of US and Canada for Fame Award as leading conductor for several years running. Made overseas tours conducting soldier orchestras organized and trained by him, N Africa, Persian Gulf, Italian Theatre, summer 1944; China, Burma, India and European theatres, winter 1944-45. Regular guest conductor with all leading orchestras in US (New York Philharmonic, Boston Symphony, Philadelphia Orchestra, San Francisco Symphony, etc), Canada, S America and Europe. Inaugurated Special Non-Subscription Concerts of New York Philharmonic Orchestra, 1953; Principal Conductor and Artistic Dir, NY Philharmonic Promenades. Records with his own orchestra for Columbia Records. Awarded Asiatic-Pacific ribbon by Army for overseas services. *Address:* 1995 Broadway, New York, NY 10023, USA.   *[Died 13 Jan. 1980.*

KOSYGIN, Alexei Nikolaevich; Hero of Socialist Labour (twice); Order of Lenin (six times); Order of the Red Banner; Chairman, Council of Ministers of the Union of Soviet Socialist Republics, 1964-80; Member, Politburo of the Central Committee of the Communist Party since 1966 (also Member, 1948-52); *b* Petersburg (Leningrad), 21 Feb. 1904. *Educ:* Leningrad Co-operative Technical Sch.; Leningrad Textile Inst. Worked in consumer co-op. system in Siberian Territory, 1924-30; Foreman, Shop Superintendent, Zhelyabov Textile Mill, Leningrad, 1935-37; Dir, October Spinning and Weaving Mill, Leningrad, 1937-38; Head of Dept, Leningrad Regional Cttee of CPSU(B), 1938; Chm. Leningrad City Council, 1938-39; People's Commissar for Textile Industry, 1939-40; Dep. Chm. Council of People's Commissars of the USSR, 1940-46; Chm. Council of People's Commissars of RSFSR, 1943-46; Deputy of Supreme Soviet, 1946-; Dep. Chm., Council of Ministers of the USSR, 1946-March 1953, Dec. 1953-1956, 1957-60; Minister: of Finance, 1948; of Light Industry, 1949-53; of Light and Food Industry, 1953; of Consumer Goods Industry, 1953-54; First Dep. Chm. USSR Council of Ministers' State Economic Commn in charge of current economic planning, and Minister of the USSR, 1956-57; Chm., State Planning Cttee, 1959-60 (First Dep. Chm., 1957); First Dep. Chm., 1960-64, Council of Ministers of USSR. Mem. of Communist Party of Soviet Union, 1927-; Mem. Central Cttee, CPSU, 1939-; Alternate Mem., Politburo, CPSU(B), 1946-48; Mem. Politburo, CPSU(B) Central Cttee, 1948-52; Alternate Mem., Presidium, CPSU Central Cttee, 1952-53, 1957-60; Mem. Presidium, CPSU Central Cttee, 1960-66; Mem. Politburo, CPSU Central Cttee, 1966-. *Address:* The Kremlin, Moscow, USSR.
                    [Died 18 Dec. 1980.

KOTELAWALA, Col Rt. Hon. Sir John (Lionel), PC 1954; CH 1956; KBE 1948; *b* 1897; *m*; one *d*. *Educ:* Christ's Coll., Cambridge; Royal College, Colombo. Mem. State Council, 1931; Minister for Communications and Works, 1935; Minister for Transport and Works, 1947; Prime Minister and Minister of Defence and External Affairs, Ceylon, 1953-56. LLD University of Ceylon. Grand Cross, Legion of Honour (France), 1954; Grand Cross, Order of Merit (Italy), 1954; Grand Cross, Order of Rising Sun (Japan), 1954; Grand Cross, Order of Merit (Germany), 1955; Grand Cross, Order of White Elephant (Thailand), 1955. *Publication:* An Asian Prime Minister's Story, 1956. *Recreations:* polo, tennis, riding. *Address:* Brogues Wood, Biddenden, Kent; Ratmalana, Sri Lanka. *Clubs:* Orient, No 10 (Institute of Directors); Sinhalese Sports; Eighty.
                    [Died 2 Oct. 1980.

KOTHAVALA, Tehmasp Tehmul, CIE 1943; retired; *b* 6 Feb. 1893; *s* of Tehmul R. Kothavala; *m* 1918, Shernaz

Munchershaw Disana; two s one d. Educ: Baroda and St Xavier's Colls. Graduated, 1915; MA 1916; BSc 1916; joined Bombay Civil Service, 1919; Sec. to Government Bombay Revenue Dept, 1936; Collector, Bijapur, 1938; Revenue Officer, Loyd Barrage, Sind, 1939; Collector, Sukkur, 1940; Sec., Provincial Transport Authority and Motor Transport Controller for the Province of Bombay, from 1941; Settlement Commissioner, Dir Land Records and Inspector-Gen. of Registration for the Province of Bombay, 1948-50. Adviser to HH the Maharaja of Kolahpur, 1954; Public Relations Adviser, Wandleside National Conductors, 1964. Recreations: riding, shooting, natural history. Address: 7 Ahmednagar Road, Yerarda, Poona-6, India. Clubs: Willingdon Sports (Bombay); Western India Turf, Poona (Poona).   [Died 20 Aug. 1977.

KOZYGIN; see Kosygin.

KRATOVIL, Bohuslav G., PhD; author; formerly politician and ambassador; b 21 Oct. 1901; s of V. A. Kratovil; m 1946, Helene Gut-Schenk (d 1956); one s. Educ: Universities of Prague, Brno and Paris. Official of Czechoslovak Ministry of Education, 1930-39; War Cross, 1939; in prison in Germany, 1939-45; Mem. of Parliament, Czechoslovakia, 1945-46; Czechoslovak Ambassador in London, 1947-49; Czechoslovak Ambassador to India, 1949-51 (resigned his appointment because of political disagreements with the Czechoslovak Government; granted asylum in Great Britain and subsequently British citizenship). Name inscribed in Golden Book of Jerusalem. Publications: Translations into Czech from different languages of various works on Psychology and Pedagogy and original publications on Pedagogy, 1925-35; The Position of the Intelligentsia in the Post-War Period, 1946; Czechoslovak Cultural Traditions, 1946; Czechoslovak-British Relations, 1947; articles on internat. policy in British, Continental and Indian papers (Observer, Central European Observer, Indian News Chronicle, Daily Mail, Manchester Guardian, the Spectator, Jornal do Brasil), 1951-71. Recreation: Tennis. Address: 41 Broadhurst Gardens, NW6.   [Died 28 Aug. 1972.

KRAUS, Otakar, OBE 1973; operatic singer; b Prague, 1909; m Maria Graf; one s. Educ: privately; in Prague and in Milan. Engaged as Principal Baritone, National Opera House, Bratislava; subsequently at: Opera House, Brno; State Opera House, Prague; Royal Opera House, Covent Garden. Has also appeared with Carl Rosa Opera, English Opera Group, at Glyndebourne, Bayreuth, Aldeburgh, Vienna State Opera, Munich, Venice, (Scala) Milan, Nederlandsche Opera, Amsterdam. Address: 223 Hamlet Gardens, W6. T: 01-748 7366.   [Died 28 July 1980.

KRAUSE, Madame Otto; see Lehmann, Lotte.

KRIPS, Josef; Conductor Emeritus, San Francisco Symphony Orchestra; Permanent Guest Conductor, Vienna State Opera, since 1931; b Vienna, 8 April 1902; s of Dr Josef Krips and Luise Seitz; m 1947, Mitzi Wilheim; m 1969, Harrietta Freün von Prochazka. Educ: Acad. of Music, Vienna. Studied under Eusebius Mandyczewsky and Felix von Weingartner. Made début as conductor, Vienna, 1921; with Vienna Volksoper under Weingartner, 1921-24; Chief of Opera Dept: Stadttheater, Aussig ad Elbe, 1924-25; Stadttheater, Dortmund, 1925-26; Dir-Gen. of Music, Staatstheater, Karlsruhe, 1926-33; Permanent Conductor, Vienna State Opera, 1933-38; Prof. at Vienna Acad. of Music, 1935-38; Conductor, Opera, Belgrade and Philharmonic, 1938-39; under Hitler, no permission to conduct, 1939-45; reorganised musical life in Vienna in Opera, concerts and Hofkapelle, 1945; opened Salzburg Festival, 1946 and appeared there, 1946-50 and 1969; Conductor-in-chief: Vienna State Opera, 1945-50; London Symphony Orchestra, 1950-54; Buffalo Philharmonic Orchestra, 1954-63; San Francisco Symphony Orchestra, 1963-70. Toured: Mexico, 1953, 1954; Switzerland, 1955; Australia, 1955, 1959; NZ, 1959; Japan, 1968; also USA, Canada, Israel, etc. Guest Conductor at Rome, Paris, Grand Opéra de Paris, Copenhagen, Moscow, Leningrad, Budapest, Edinburgh, Bregenz, Amsterdam, Lucerne, Athens, Bayreuth, Berlin, Munich, Strasbourg, Bordeaux, Nice, Basle, Zürich, USA (Metropolitan Opera, 1966-), Israel, Aix-en-Provence Festival, Stockholm, etc, and frequently in Great Britain (Covent Garden Opera, 1963-, London Symphony, London Philharmonic, Royal Philharmonic, Hallé, Liverpool Philharmonic Orchestras). Vice-Pres., Anglo-Austrian Soc., 1962-. Bd Mem., Soc. of Music Friends, Vienna, 1962- (Hon. Mem. 1973); Hon. Member: Gustav Mahler Soc., 1962-; Vienna State Opera, 1968; Vienna Beethoven Soc., 1972. Hon. Citizen, City and County of San Francisco, 1970. Has made numerous recordings. Ring of UN, 1947; Nicolai Medal, Vienna Philharmonic Orchestra, 1947; Medal of Vienna Hofmusikkapelle (to the Founder of Vienna

Mozartrenaissance), 1948; Bruckner Medal (European), 1953; Bruckner Medal, Amer. Bruckner Soc., 1956; Chancellor's Medal, Univ. of Buffalo, 1961; Vienna Ring of Honour, 1962; Mozart Ring, Austria, 1965; Grosses silbernes Ehrenzeichen, Austria, 1967; Franz Schalk Gold Medal, Vienna Philharmonic Orchestra, 1972; Grosses goldenes Ehrenzeichen for merits to Vienna, 1972; Decca Grand Prix du disque for recordings of Haydn Symphonies. Grand Officier, Ordre de Leopold II (Belgium), 1971. Address: 6 Riant-Château, 1842 Territet, Vaud, Switzerland.   [Died 13 Oct. 1974.

KRISHNA MENON, Vengalil Krishnan; Indian Statesman and Lawyer; Member, Lok Sabha, for Trivandrum City, Kerala, since 1971 (for Midnapore, West Bengal, 1969-71); Senior Counsel, Supreme Court of India, at New Delhi; Chairman, Indian Academy of International Law and Diplomacy; Hon. Professor, Jawaharlal Nehru University; Visiting Professor, University of Delhi; b 3 May 1896; s of late K. Krishna Kurup and late Lakshmi Kutty Amma, Malabar, India; unmarried. Educ: Municipal Sch., Brennen Coll., Tellicherry; Ganpat High Sch., Calicut; Zamoris Coll., Calicut; Presidency Coll. and Law Coll., Madras; London Sch. of Economics; London Day Training Coll.; University Coll., London; Middle Temple, London; King's Inns, Dublin. Lecturer, National Univ., Adyar, Madras, 1919-23. Degrees in Arts, Science and Law, and Diploma in Education, London Univ. Practised at the Bar. Home Rule League, 1911-23. Joined Indian National Congress, from which he resigned 1966. Has been teacher, journalist and publicist. President: India League, 1947- (Sec., 1927-47); Indian Soc. of Internat. Law; All India Peace Council: Hon. Pres., World Peace Council. Borough Councillor, St Pancras, 1934-47; parliamentary candidate (Lab.), Dundee, 1938-41. High Commissioner for India, 1947-52, and formerly Indian Ambassador to the Republic of Ireland. Rep. India at UN General Assembly, Lake Success, 1946; visited various European capitals as Pandit Nehru's personal envoy, 1947. Called to Irish Bar, 1952. Rep. India at UN Gen. Assembly annually, 1952-62. Mem. of Indian Parliament (Council of States), 1953-57; Lok Sabha, 1957-67, 1969-. Cabinet Minister without Portfolio, 1956-57; Minister for Defence, 1957-62; Minister of Defence Production (for a short period), 1962. Freeman, Borough of St Pancras. Hon. LLD: Glasgow; Saugor; Osmania; Utkal; Brunswick; DLitt, Mysore; Hon. Fellow, LSE, 1960. First Award of Padma Vibushan, 1954. Publications: (with Ellen Wilkinson) Condition of India; first editor Pelican Books; editor Twentieth Century Library; several pamphlets and articles. Address: c/o Lawyers' Chambers, Supreme Court of India, New Delhi, India. Clubs: India (London); Gymkhana (New Delhi).   [Died 5 Oct. 1974.

KRISHNA SHUMSHERE, Jung Bahadur Rana, General, KCSI (Hon.) 1945; KBE (Hon.) 1937; 1st Class Orders of Star of Nepal, om Rama Patta, Trishakti Patta and Gorkha Dakshina Bahu; Nepal Pratap Bardhak, Assam-Burma, Special Earthquake and Nepalese Gallantry Medals; Grand Cross Order of Leopold II (Belgium); Grand Cordon Order of the Cloud and Banner (China); b 8 Feb. 1900; s of late Maharaja Chandra Shumshere Jung Bahadur Rana, GCB, GCSI, GCMG, GCVO, DCL, Prime Minister and Supreme Commander-in-Chief of Nepal, 1901-1929, and Bada Maharani Loka Bhakta Lakshmi Devi; m Princess Tara Rajya Lakshmi, d of late Maharajadhiraja Prithvi Bir Bikrum Shaha, King of Nepal. Educ: Singha Durbar, Kathmandu, Represented his country at funeral of King George V; Nepalese Envoy Extraordinary and Minister Plenipotentiary at Court of St James's, 1935-1939. GOC-in-C Nepalese Contingent in India, 1943-45 (despatches, 1939-45 Star and Burma Star, Defence Medal and War Medal); retired, 1949. Recreations: reading and music. Address: (temp.) Jaya-Bhavan, Bangalore, 1, South India.   [Died 19 May 1977.

KÜCHEMANN, Dietrich, CBE 1964; Dr rer nat; FRS 1963; FRAeS, FIMA; FAIAA; Consultant, Aerodynamics Department, Royal Aircraft Establishment, Farnborough, since 1946; b Göttingen, Germany, 11 Sept. 1911; s of Rudolf Küchemann and Martha Egener; m 1936, Helga Janet Praefcke; one s two d. Educ: Oberrealschule, Göttingen; Göttingen and München Univs. Aerodynamic research at: Aerodynamische Versuchsanstalt, Göttingen, 1936-46; Royal Aircraft Establishment, Farnborough, Hants, 1946- (Head of Aerodynamics Dept, 1966-71). Vis. Prof., Imperial Coll., London, 1972-. Hon. Mem., Aeronaut. Soc. of India. Hon. DSc Cranfield Inst. Technology, 1973; DrIng E.h. Technische Universität Berlin, 1975; Hon. DSc Engrg Bristol, 1975. Publications: Aerodynamics of Propulsion, 1953; (ed) Progress in Aeronautical Sciences, vols 1-10, 1961-70; (ed) Progress in Aerospace Sciences, vols 11-14, 1970-; contrib. to Incompressible Aerodynamics, 1960; Prandtl's Strömungslehre, 6th edn, 1965. Articles chiefly in: Jl Fluid Mechs, ZAMM, Jl

RAeS, Jl Aeron. Sci., Aeron. Quart., Luftfahrtforschg., Zeitschr. Flugw., Progress in Aeron. Sci., Repts and Mem. of ARC. *Recreation:* music. *Address:* Steding, 32 Echo Barn Lane, Farnham, Surrey. *T:* Farnham, Surrey, 4947.
[Died 23 Feb. 1976.

KUIPER, Gerard Peter; Director of Lunar and Planetary Laboratory, University of Arizona, since 1961; Team Member on Mercury-Venus 1973 Mission; *b* 7 Dec. 1905; *s* of G. Kuiper and Anna de Vries-Kuiper; *m* 1936, Sarah Parker Fuller; one *s* one *d. Educ:* University of Leyden, Netherlands. PhD Leyden 1933. Post-doctoral Fellow, University of California, 1933-35; Lecturer, Harvard Univ., 1935-36; Prof. of Astronomy, University of Chicago, 1936-; Dir Yerkes observatory, University of Chicago, and McDonald obs., University of Texas, 1947-49 and 1957-60. Civilian war service, 1943-45. Principal Investigator on NASA's Ranger Program, 1963-66. Janssen Medal of French Astronomical Soc. (for discovery of satellites of Uranus and Neptune); Rittenhouse Medal (for his theory of origin of solar system); Dryden Res. Lecture and Award, Amer. Inst. of Aeronautics and Astronautics (for outstanding contribs in research), 1969; Kepler Gold Medal, Amer. Assoc. for Advancement of Sci., 1971. Member: Nat. Acad. of Sciences, Amer. Acad. of Arts and Sciences; Internat. Astronomical Union; Amer. Astronomical Soc.; Astronomical Soc. of the Pacific; Royal Astronomical Society of London (Associate); Netherlands Soc. of the Sciences (For. Mem.), Royal Netherlands Academy of Sciences (For. Mem.). Comdr, Order of Orange Nassau (Netherlands). *Publications:* (ed) The Atmospheres of the Earth and Planets, 1949, 2nd edn, 1952; (ed) The Solar System, 4 vols, 1953-60; (ed) Stars and Stellar Systems, 8 vols, 1960-73; Atlases of the Moon issued by him and his staff: Photographic Lunar Atlas, 1960 (Chicago); Orthographic Lunar Atlas, and Rectified Lunar Atlas, 1961-63 (Arizona); Consolidated Lunar Atlas, 1967; contributions to Astrophysical Journal, etc; Editor, LPL Communications, vols 1-9, nos 1-183. *Recreations:* photography, travel. *Address:* Lunar and Planetary Laboratory, University of Arizona, Tucson, Arizona 85721, USA.
[Died 23 Dec. 1973.

KURZ, Prof. Otto, FBA 1962; *b* 26 May 1908; *s* of Dr Maximilian Kurz and Anna Kurz; *m* 1937, Hilde (*née* Schuller); one *d. Educ:* University of Vienna. Librarian, Warburg Institute, 1944-65; Prof. of History of Classical Tradition with special ref. to Near East, Univ. of London, 1965-75. Visiting Lecturer, Hebrew Univ., Jerusalem, 1964, and 1973; Slade Prof. of Fine Arts, Oxford, 1970-71. Hon. Fellow: Associazione Francesco Francia, Bologna; Raccolta Vinciana, Milan; Accademia Clementina, Bologna. *Publications:* contributions to learned journals. *Address:* PO Box 4130, Jerusalem, Israel.
[Died 3 Sept. 1975.

KWAN, Sir Cho-Yiu, Kt 1969; CBE 1965 (OBE 1959); Member of Executive Council, Government of Hong Kong, since 1961; Solicitor, Senior Partner of C. Y. Kwan & Co., Hong Kong; *b* 10 July 1907; *s* of Kwan Yick Chow and Yue Kam; *m* 1934, Chow Wai Fun; two *s* two *d. Educ:* Diocesan Boys' Sch.; University College, London University. Vice-Pres., Standing Mil. Court, Hong Kong, 1946. Pres., Law Society, Hong Kong, 1950-51; Dep. Comr of Civil Aid Services, 1951-66; Mem., Urban Council, 1956-61; MLC, 1959-66. Chm. Council, Chinese Univ. of Hong Kong, 1963-71; Mem. Court, Univ. of Hong Kong; Vice-Chm. and a Founder, Hong Kong Housing Soc.; Chm. or Mem. of Cttee of a number of social, charitable and educational institutions. Hon. Dr of Laws (Chinese Univ. of Hong Kong), 1964. *Address:* 8 Shouson Hill Road, Hong Kong. *T:* 92537. *Clubs:* Chinese Country, Royal Jockey (Hong Kong).
[Died 7 Dec. 1971.

KYDD, Ronald Robertson, BA; LLB; Advocate; Sheriff of Fife and Kinross at Cupar and Kinross since 1960; *b* 21 Feb. 1920; *yr s* of Arthur Robertson Kydd, manufacturer, Dundee, and of Elizabeth Munro Stevenson; *m* 1951, Margaret Virginia, *e d* of Andrew St Clair Jameson, WS, Edinburgh; two *d. Educ:* Dundee High Sch.; Dalhousie Castle Sch.; Fettes Coll.; Trinity Hall, Cambridge (Open Scholar; BA); Edinburgh Univ. (Thow Scholar in Scots Law; LLB with Dist.). Passed Advocate (admitted to Faculty of Advocates in Scotland), 1945; in practice at Scottish Bar, 1945-56; Sheriff-Substitute of Fife and Kinross at Dunfermline and Kinross, 1956-60. *Recreations:* golf, gardening. *Address:* Middle Balado House, Kinross. *T:* Kinross 2236. *Clubs:* New (Edinburgh); Royal and Ancient (St Andrews); Honourable Company of Edinburgh Golfers.
[Died 10 Oct. 1972.

L

LACEY, Gerald, CIE 1942; BSc; FCGI; FICE; FRSA; Chartered Civil Engineer; Consultant, Sir M. Macdonald and Partners, 1950-75, retired; *b* 26 July 1887; 3rd *s* of late Thomas Stephen Lacey, MInstCE; *m* 1918, Elsie Ann, *d* of Charles Willford, ISO, PWD; two *s. Educ:* Westminster City Sch.; City and Guilds Central Tech. Coll., London. Course in civil and mechanical engineering, Central Tech. Coll., 1904-07; Bramwell medallist; BSc Engineering, 1st Class Hons, London Univ.; early training with G. H. Hill and Sons, Consulting Engineers, Westminster, Thames Conservancy and Chiswick Urban District Council; Assistant Engineer, Indian Service of Engineers, 1910; Military Service attached 1st KGO Sappers and Miners, 1917-19; 3rd Afghan War, 1919; Under-Secretary to Government, PWD, 1924-27; Irrigation Research Officer and Prof. Civil Engineering, Roorkee Coll., 1928-32; Superintending Engineer, 1934; Member of Council Inst. of Civil Engineers, 1940; Chief Engineer Eastern Canals. Irrigation Branch PWD, UP, 1941; retired 1942; Lieut-Colonel Corps of Indian Engineers, 1942-44; Prof. Civil Engineering, Roorkee Coll., March 1945; Principal Roorkee Coll., Dec. 1945; retired, Dec. 1946; Member: Colonial Office East Africa Rice Mission, 1948; British Honduras Rice Mission, 1949; Abyan Mission (Aden Protectorate), 1951; British Guiana Mission, 1953; Co-Director FAO, UN Training Centre and Study Tour on Irrigation and Drainage, held in USSR 1956; Aden Protectorate, 1957. Drainage and Irrigation Adviser, part-time, CO, 1950-58. Kennedy Gold Medal of Punjab Engineer Congress, 1930; Awarded Telford Gold Medal of InstCE, 1958. *Publications:* Papers in Procs ICE, 1930, 1934, 1946, 1958, 1972 and 1973. *Address:* Cottage on the Links, Steepways, Hindhead, Surrey GU26 6PG. *T:* Hindhead 5742. *Club:* East India, Devonshire, Sports and Public Schools.
[Died 26 April 1979.

LACEY, Walter Graham, CSI 1947; CIE 1939; *b* 17 July 1894; *s* of late Rev. R. L. Lacey, Exmouth; *m* 1920, Helen Frances Joan Pell-Smith; two *s. Educ:* Bedford Sch.; Balliol Coll., Oxford. Served in European War, Bedfordshire Regt and Machine Gun Corps, 1914-19; Indian Civil Service, 1919-47. *Publication:* The Census of Bihar and Orissa, 1931. *Address:* Compton Beeches, Compton, Winchester. *T:* Twyford (Hants) 713218. *Club:* Oxford Union.
[Died 17 March 1974.

LACHMAN, Harry; impressionist painter; film director; *b* La Salle, Illinois, 29 June 1886; *m* 1927 (in France), Quon Tai, Chinese concert singer. *Educ:* La Salle High Sch.; High School at Ann Arbor. Orphan at age of ten. Made his own way by selling newspapers, waiting on table at college; Cover Artist, Saturday Evening Post, Colliers, McCall's Cosmopolitan Magazines; went to France with his savings, 1912, and painted for the first time in his life; three months later had two pictures accepted and hung in the Salon Nationale, Paris; since then has shown in various American Exhibitions, England, Spain, and Paris Salons; four paintings bought by the French Government for the Musée du Luxembourg, the National Museum of France; decorated with the cross of the Legion of Honor for services rendered 1914-20 and for artistic achievements; managed the Metro-Goldwyn Studio in Nice, 1927; directed pictures in England for Paramount, 1929: Under the Greenwood Tree, The Outsider, Aren't We All, Down Our Street; directed pictures in France for Paramount, 1930: La Belle Marinière, La Couturière de Luneville, Mistigri; went to Hollywood to direct for Fox, 1932: Face in the Sky, Paddy the Next Best Thing, Charlie Chan at the Circus, Baby Take a Bow (first Shirley Temple starring picture), The Man Who Lived Twice, The Devil is Driving, It Happened in Hollywood, Our Relations, No Time to Marry, George White Scandals, Charlie Chan in Rio, Murder Over New York, Dead Men Tell; went to England to direct for Fox, 1939: They Came By Night, 1942. Discovered: Rita Hayworth, Merle Oberon, Margot Graham, Binnie Barnes, Phyllis Calvert, Jean Gabin; directed: Spencer Tracy, Gertrude Lawrence, Sir John Gielgud, Cary Grant, Madeline Renaud, Grace Moore, Noël, Pierre Blanchard. After 30 years returned to painting and exhib. in Hammer Galls, New York; exhib. Los Angeles, 1959. Has been painting in Spain, Morocco, Italy and France. Represented in: Chicago Art Inst.; Luxembourg Museum, Paris; Min. of Beaux Arts, Paris; Museum of Modern Art, Rome, etc. Chevalier de l'Ordre des Arts et des Lettres France,1967; Most Honoured Citizen of Los Angeles; Knight of Mark Twain.

Recreation: fishing. *Address:* 718 N Beverly Drive, Beverly Hills, Calif 90210, USA.   [*Died* 20 *March* 1975.

LACK, David, FRS 1951; MA, ScD; Director, Edward Grey Institute of Field Ornithology, Oxford, since 1945; Fellow of Trinity College, Oxford, since 1963; *b* 16 July 1910; *s* of H. Lambert Lack, MD, FRCS; *m* 1949, Elizabeth Silva; three *s* one *d. Educ:* Gresham's Sch., Holt; Magdalene Coll., Cambridge. Zoology master, Dartington Hall Sch., 1933-40. Army Operational Research Group, 1940-45. *Publications:* The Life of the Robin, 1943; Darwin's Finches, 1947; Robin Redbreast, 1950; The Natural Regulation of Animal Numbers, 1954; Swifts in a Tower, 1956; Evolutionary Theory and Christian Belief, 1957; Enjoying Ornithology, 1965; Population Studies of Birds, 1966; Ecological Adaptations for Breeding in Birds, 1968; Ecological Isolation in Birds, 1971. *Recreation:* home help. *Address:* Edward Grey Institute of Field Ornithology, Oxford.
[*Died* 12 *March* 1973.

LACK, Henry Martyn, RE 1948 (ARE 1934); ARCA 1933; Artist; *b* 5 Dec. 1909; *s* of Arthur Henry Lack, Bozeat, Northants, and Laura Sophia Keyston; *m* 1941, Phyllis Mary Hafford, Leicester; no *c. Educ:* Wellingborough Sch.; Leicester College of Art (Royal Exhibition); Royal College of Art. Member of Sakkarah Expedition (Egypt), 1934-36. Master: Christ's Hospital, Horsham, 1937-46; Northampton School of Art, 1947; Tutor, Engraving School, RCA, South Kensington, 1947-53; Senior Master, Hastings School of Art, 1953-68, Acting Principal part 1968; Mem. Epigraphic Survey, Oriental Inst., Univ. of Chicago, at Luxor, Egypt, 1968-76. Served War of 1939-45 (Captain), in North Africa, Sicily, Italy and Middle East, 1942-46. Represented by prints in BM and V&A; Works purchased by Contemporary Art Soc., British Council, Univ. of Reading, S London Art Gallery. Has exhibited widely abroad through the British Council and at home at Royal Academy and Royal Society of Painter-Etchers and Engravers, etc. *Recreations:* travel, gardening. *Address:* 17 White Rock, Hastings, Sussex TN34 1JY.   [*Died* 16 *Feb.* 1979.

LACON, Sir George Vere Francis, 7th Bt, *cr* 1818; *b* 25 Feb. 1909; *s* of Sir George Haworth Ussher Lacon, 6th Bt and Vere Valerie Florence Eleanore (*d* 1916), *o d* of late H. S. H. Lacon, Ormesby Hall, Norfolk; *S* father 1950; *m* 1935, Hilary Blanche (marriage dissolved, 1956) *yr d* of C. J. Scott, Adyar, Walberswick; two *s*; *m* 1957, Kathlyn, *d* of late E. Pilbrow, London. *Educ:* Eton. *Heir:* *s* Edmund Vere Lacon [*b* 3 May 1936; *m* 1963, Gillian, *o d* of J. H. Middleditch, Wrentham, Suffolk; one *s* one *d*]. *Address:* Cliff House, Southwold, Suffolk.
[*Died* 26 *Oct.* 1980.

LAFERTÉ, Hon. Hector, QC 1919; BA; LLL; LLD; *b* St Germain de Grantham, Drummond Co., 8 Nov. 1885; *s* of Joseph Laferté and Georgiana Jeanne Tessier; *m* 1911, Irène Senécal, St Césaire, PQ. *Educ:* Seminary, Nicolet; Laval Univ. Called to Bar, 1909; Mem. of the Council of the Bar; was lawyer for the bootmakers at the time of the strike 1913; is legal adviser for many corporations, and also of several Labour Unions; elected to Legislative Assembly for Drummond 1916, 1919, 1923, 1927 and 1931; Dep. Speaker of the Legislative Assembly and Chm. of Cttees, 1923; first Pres. of the Liberal Federals Club, Quebec; attended convocation of Canadian and American Barristers in London and Paris, 1924; Speaker of the Legislature of Quebec, 1928; Minister of Col., Game and Fisheries, 1929; Life mem. of Société Zoologique of Quebec since 1933; Legislative Council of Quebec, and Pres. of the Council, 1934; Leader of Opposition of Legislative Council, 1936, and again 1945; Pres. of Council, 1940 and 1960-66; Liberal Catholic. *Address:* 41 St Louis Street, Quebec, Canada.
[*Died* 13 *Sept.* 1971.

LAFFAN, Robert George Dalrymple; Fellow of Queens' College, Cambridge; *b* 21 Oct. 1887; *s* of Edward Sidney Laffan, ICS, *s* of Lt-Gen. Sir Robert Laffan, KCMG, and Gertrude, *d* of Gen. Hew Prendergast, late RE; *m* 1st, 1923, Katharine (*d* 1937), *d* of George Frederick Bindloss; no *c*; 2nd, 1939, Hon. Mabel (*d* 1968), *d* of 1st Baron Chalmers and widow of Sir M. Stevenson, KCMG. *Educ:* Eton; Balliol Coll., Oxford (Scholar). Pres. of the Oxford Union Soc., 1909; 1st Class, Modern History, 1910; Fellow of Queens' Coll., Cambridge, 1912; Asst Curate of St Olave's, York, 1912-13; Temporary Chaplain to the Forces, 1914-18; attached to Serbian Army, 1916-18; Order of St Sava (Yugoslavia) 3rd class, 1919; Select Preacher, Cambridge, 1922, Oxford, 1930-31; Examining Chaplain to the Bishop of Wakefield, 1928-33; University Lecturer, Cambridge, 1927-53; Tutor of Queens', 1931-35; Bursar, 1935-39; received into Catholic Church, 1933; served in R. Institute of International Affairs (wartime organisation), 1939-43; Research Dept Foreign Office, 1943-46; Italo-Yugoslav Boundary Commission, 1946.

Publications: The Serbs, Guardians of the Gate, 1918; Select Documents of European History, 1930; Translation of Pasquet's Origins of the House of Commons; The Crisis over Czechoslovakia, 1951; contributor to Cambridge Medieval History and to the History of the Peace Conference of Paris. *Address:* White Shutters, Exlade Street, near Woodcote, Reading, Berks. *T:* Checkendon 316. *Clubs:* Royal Over-Seas League, MCC.   [*Died* 27 *April* 1972.

LAGERKVIST, Pär (Fabian); PhD; Swedish Dramatist, Poet, Novelist; *b* 23 May 1891; *s* of Anders Johan Lagerquist and Johanna (*née* Blad); *m* 1st, 1918, K. D. J. Sorensen (marriage dissolved, 1925); 2nd, 1925, E. L. Hallberg, widow of Gösta Sandels. *Educ:* University of Uppsala. First book, and some poems, published 1912; visited Paris and was influenced by movements in modern painting, 1913; first play, 1917; theatre critic for Stockholm newspaper Svenska Dagbladet, 1919; subs. visited France and Italy frequently; dramatisation of Bödeln (The Hangman) given in London, 1935. Mem. Swedish Acad. of Lit., 1940; Hon. PhD Gothenburg, 1941; Nobel Prize for Literature, 1951. *Publications:* between 30 and 40 books; several plays and poetry. (Trans.); Guest of Reality (vol. incl. also The Eternal Smile and The Hangman). Eng. 1936; The Dwarf (novel), (US) 1945, (Eng.) 1954; Barabbas (novel), (US) 1951, (Eng.) 1952 (trans. many langs., dramatized and filmed, 1952); The Eternal Smile and other Stories, (US) 1954; The Marriage Feast and other Stories, (Eng.) 1955; The Sibyl (novel), (US and Eng.), 1958; The Death of Ahasuerus (US and Eng.), 1962; Two of his plays, The Man Without a Soul, and Let Man Live, have been included in Scandinavian Plays of the Twentieth Century, 1944, 1951; Midsummer Dream in the Workhouse (play), London, 1953; Pilgrim at Sea (novel), (US and Eng.), 1963; The Holy Land (novel), (US and Eng.), 1966; Mariamne (novel (US and Eng.), 1968. *Address:* 18151 Lidingö, Sweden; c/o Random House Inc., 201 East 50th Street, New York, NY 10022, USA; c/o Albert Bonniers Förlag, 605 Madison Avenue, New York, NY 10022, USA.   [*Died* 11 *July* 1974.

LAILEY, John Raymond N.; *see* Nicholson-Lailey.

LAING, Sir John (William), Kt 1959; CBE 1951; FIOB; Life President John Laing and Son Ltd, since 1957; *b* 24 Sept. 1879; *s* of John Laing, Sebergham, Cumberland; *m* 1910, Beatrice (*d* 1972), *y d* of William Harland, Chartered Accountant, Stockton on Tees; two *s. Educ:* Carlisle Grammar Sch. Past Member: Building Research Cttee (Chm. 1945); Nat. House Builders' (Past Vice-Chm.); Registration Council (Past Chm. Specification Cttee); Inst. of Builders (Past Mem. Council); Fedn of Civil Engrg Contractors (Past Mem. Cttee); British Standards Instn (Past Mem. Standing Cttee). Pres. London Bible Coll. Vice-President: British and Foreign Bible Soc.; Crusaders' Union; Mem. Council, Scripture Gift Mission; Trustee, Inter-Varsity Fellowship Trust Ltd; Vice-Pres. Fact and Faith Films. *Address:* Fair Holme, Marsh Lane, Mill Hill, NW7.   [*Died* 11 *Jan.* 1978.

LAING, Malcolm Buchanan, CMG 1945; OBE 1939; Commissioner for Local Government, British Guiana, 1938-51; retired; *b* 17 April 1890; *y s* of late John Bridges Laing, Wickham, Hants; *m* 1916, Marjory (*d* 1953), widow of John Bourke and *er d* of Dr F. A. Neal; one *s*; *m* 1954, Mary Treadwell. *Educ:* Forest Sch., Essex. Entered Colonial Civil Service 1914, British Guiana; Protector of Immigrants, 1920; Liaison Officer to Parliamentary Commission, 1926; Private Sec. to Governor of British Guiana, 1929; Liaison Officer to West Indian Sugar Commission, 1929; District Commissioner, 1932; MLC 1935; Liaison Officer to West India Royal Commission, 1939; acted as Colonial Sec., British Guiana, 1943, 1944, 1945. *Recreations:* tennis, golf and fishing. *Address:* 19 Arundel Road, Worthing, Sussex.   [*Died* 13 *July* 1974.

LAING, Percy Lyndon, CMG 1970; retired as Commissioner of Works, NZ; Director, New Zealand Forest Products Ltd; *b* 12 July 1909; *s* of Percy William and Jessie Laing, Dunedin, NZ; *m* 1937, Mabel Collis Wood; one *s. Educ:* Otago Boys' High Sch.; Univ. of Canterbury, NZ. Chief Designing Engineer, NZ Min. of Works, 1951-55; Dir. of Roading (Highways), 1959-62; Comr of Works, 1965-69, retd. Pres. NZ Inst of Engineers, 1962. *Publications:* contribs to engineering jls, etc. *Recreations:* golf, fishing. *Address:* 53 Chesham Avenue, Taupo, New Zealand. *T:* 2115K. *Club:* Wellington (Wellington, NZ).
[*Died* 27 *Nov.* 1979.

LAKE, Captain Sir Atwell Henry, 9th Bt, *cr* 1711; CB 1945; OBE 1919; US Legion of Merit degree of Commander, 1945; RN retired; *b* 13 Feb. 1891; *s* of late Admiral Atwell Peregrine Macleod Lake; *S* cousin, 1924; *m* 1922, Kathleen Marion, *d* of late Alfred Morrison Turner, Broughton, West Derby,

Liverpool; three s. Served European War, 1914-18, in HMS Lion; present at Battle of Jutland; War of 1939-45, Chief of Staff to Commander-in-Chief, Portsmouth, with rank of Commodore, 1939-42; Chief of Naval Staff, New Zealand, and First Member of Naval Board with rank of Commodore, 1942-45. Formerly ADC to King George VI. *Heir: s* Atwell Graham Lake, *b* 1923. *Address:* Hedgerow Cottage, Barnsfold Lane, Rudgwick, Sussex. *T:* Rudgwick 534.   *[Died 27 Nov.* 1972.

LAKIN, Charles Ernest, MD London; FRCP, FRCS; Consulting Physician Middlesex Hospital; Advisory Physician Golden Square Throat Hospital; late Physician London Fever Hospital; late Medical Referee to HM Treasury; Hon. Librarian Medical Society of London; ex-President Section of Medicine, Royal Society of Medicine; late Examiner in Medicine in Universities of Cambridge, London and Birmingham; Lumleian Lecturer, Royal College of Physicians; Lettsomian Lecturer Medical Society of London; Lecturer in Medical Pathology, Middlesex Hospital Medical School; *b* 1878. *Educ:* Middlesex Hospital. Fellow Royal Society of Medicine; late Senior Censor Royal College of Physicians; President Medical Society of London; Pathologist Middlesex Hospital and Addington Park War Hospital; Clinical Assistant Hospital for Children, Great Ormond Street; Demonstrator in Anatomy, Middlesex Hospital, and Clinical Assistant in Dermatological Department; First Entrance Scholarship, Broderip and Freeman Scholarships, Middlesex Hospital. *Publications:* contributions on Medicine and Pathology to medical journals. *Address:* West Stow Hall, Bury St Edmunds, Suffolk. *T:* Culford 288. *[Died 3 May* 1972.

LAKIN, Sir Henry, 3rd Bt, *cr* 1909; *b* 8 Oct. 1904; *s* of Sir Richard Lakin, 2nd Bt, and Mildred Alice (*d* 1960), *d* of G. J. Shakerley; *S* father, 1955; *m* 1927, Bessie (*d* 1965), *d* of J. D. Anderson, Durban; one *s* (one *d* decd); 2nd, 1965, Grace, *d* of John Kyme, Manchester. *Educ:* Eton; Jesus Coll., Cambridge. BA 1926. *Heir: s* Michael Lakin [*b* 28 Oct. 1934; *m* 1st, 1956, Margaret (marr. diss., 1963), *d* of Robert Wallace, Co. Armagh; 2nd, 1965, Felicity-Ann, *d* of A. D. Murphy, Kenya; one *s* one *d*]. *Address:* Torwood, PO Rosetta, Natal, S Africa.
                                                              [Died 24 July 1979.

LAKIN, John Edmund Douglas; Director, Pye Group, since 1973; *b* 18 Oct. 1920; *s* of Maj.-Gen. J. H. F. Lakin, CB, CSI and Mrs H. D. Lakin (*née* Baird); *m* 1943, Nancy Valjean (*née* Wilson); one *s* (and one *s* decd). *Educ:* Eton College. Royal Artillery, 1939-41; Intell. Corps, 1941-45; Project Manager, Pye Ltd, 1945-50; HM Diplomatic Service, 1950; British Middle East Office, 1952-55; Bonn, 1957-60; Diplomatic Wireless Service, 1960-66; Asst Sec., FCO, 1966-69; Under-Sec., Cabinet Office, 1969-73. *Recreations:* automobile engineering, music, golf. *Address:* The Farm House, Lye Green, Chesham, Bucks. *T:* Chesham 2034. *Club:* Naval and Military. *[Died 13 Oct.* 1977.

LAMARQUE, Walter Geoffrey, MBE 1947; *b* 12 Feb. 1913; *s* of late Charles and Elma Lamarque, West Byfleet, Surrey; *m* 1945, Patricia Aikman; two *s* one *d. Educ:* Marlborough Coll.; Oriel Coll., Oxford (Scholar). 1st Class Classical Mods, 1934; 2nd Class Lit.Hum., 1936. Indian Civil Service, 1936-47; served in Madras Presidency, and in Government of India at New Delhi and Calcutta. Joined Board of Trade, 1947; UK Trade Commissioner, Melbourne, Australia, 1947-50; Karachi, 1951-55. Joined Commonwealth Relations Office, 1957; First Secretary (Finance), UK High Commission Office, Ottawa, 1957-60; British Deputy Commissioner, Enugu, Nigeria, 1960-63; Africa Economic Department, CRO, 1963-65; Head of E Africa Dept, ODM, 1965-71; Permanent UK Deleg. to FAO, 1971-73. *Recreations:* fox-hunting, golf. *Address:* Elphin House, Coxwold, York YO6 4AD. *T:* Coxwold 452. *Club:* Yorkshire (York). *[Died 15 March* 1979.

LAMB, Rev. John, CVO 1952 (MVO 1947); Parish Minister of Crathie, Aberdeenshire, 1937-63; Domestic Chaplain to the Queen, in Scotland, 1952-64, Extra Chaplain since 1964; *b* 31 Jan. 1886; *s* of Rev. John Lamb, West Kilbride, Ayrshire; *m* 1912, Catharine Smith Hendrie, *d* of Rev. George S. Hendrie, Dalmellington, Ayrshire; one *s* one *d. Educ:* Hutchesons' Grammar Sch. and High Sch., Glasgow; Glasgow Univ. (MA), Edinburgh Univ. (BD, DD 1953, Glover Scholar). Parish Minister of Fyvie, Aberdeenshire, 1912; of Hyndland, Glasgow, 1923. Domestic Chaplain to King George VI, in Scotland, 1937-52, to the Queen, 1952-64; Chaplain attached 51st Division (6th and 7th Black Watch), European War, 1914-18. *Recreations:* angling, gardening, hill walking. *Address:* Kincairney, Auchterarder, Perthshire. *Club:* Caledonian (Edinburgh).
                                                              [Died 23 July 1974.

LAMB, Lynton Harold; RDI 1974; FRSA 1953; FSIA 1948; Painter, Book Illustrator, Designer; *b* 15 April 1907; *s* of Rev.

W W W — 16

Frederick Lamb and C. A. Brown; *m* 1933, Barbara Grace Morgan, *d* of Rev. J. H. Morgan and G. H. May; two *s. Educ:* Kingswood Sch., Bath; LCC Central School of Arts and Crafts. Served as Camouflage Staff Officer, 1940-45. Mem., Staff, Slade Sch. of Fine Art, 1950-71; Lectr on Methods and Materials, Painting Sch., RCA, 1956-70. Member, London Group; President Society of Industrial Artists, 1951-53. Decorations in various mediums for Orient Liners, 1935-50; first exhibition of paintings, Storran Gallery, 1936; designed Commemorative Binding for lectern Bible, St Giles Cathedral, 1948, and for Coronation Bible, 1953. Adjudicator, National Book League's Exhibition of Book Design, 1950; participant in Arts Council's Exhibition of Painting for 1951 Festival of Britain. Designed the £1 (International Philatelic Art Society award, 1960), 10/-, 5/- and 2/6 postage stamps for new reign, 1955, and air mail stamp, 1957; designed Purcell Memorial, Royal Festival Hall, London, 1959; Member: Art Panel, The Arts Council, 1951-54; Council of Industrial Design, 1952-55; National Advisory Committee on Art Examinations, 1953-58; Graphic Panel, National Council for Diplomas in Art and Design, 1962; External Examiner (Fine Art), University of Reading, for Diplomas of Scottish Central Art Institutions, 1962, 1963, and Liverpool College of Art, 1965-68. Co-editor with Prof. Quentin Bell of Oxford Paperbacks, Handbooks for Artists; Contributor to Oxford Illustrated Old Testament, 1968. *Publications:* The Purpose of Painting, 1936; County Town, 1950; Preparation for Painting, 1954 (Penguin edition, 1960); Cat's Tales, 1959; Drawing for Illustration, 1962; Death of a Dissenter, 1969; Materials and Methods of Painting, 1970; Worse than Death, 1971; Picture Frame, 1972; Man in A Mist, 1974; contrib. to Chambers's Journal, Signature, Motif, etc. *Recreation:* village cricket. *Address:* Sandon, near Chelmsford, Essex. *T:* Chelmsford 71141. *[Died 4 Sept.* 1977.

LAMB, His Honour Percy, QC; MA; an Official Referee of the Supreme Court of Judicature, 1959-69; Chancellor of the Diocese of Rochester, 1954-71; *b* 26 Sept. 1896; *s* of Thomas Lamb and Bertha (*née* Poole); *m* 1923, Constance White; one *s* two *d. Educ:* Mill Hill School. Served European War, 1914-18, HAC (Lieut); Queen Victoria's Own Corps of Guides, Frontier Force (Captain), 1918-22, Afghanistan, 1919 (Medal and Clasp). Called to the Bar by Gray's Inn, 1923, Bencher, 1947; KC 1949; Treasurer, Gray's Inn, 1962. Recorder of Faversham, 1948-50, of Rochester, 1950-59; First and only Chairman, Inns of Court Executive Council, 1962-67. Commissioner of Assize, Oxford Circuit, 1965, Midland Circuit, 1966. *Publications:* (jointly: Lamb and Evans) Law and Practice of Town and Country Planning, 1950; A Guide to Rating Practice and Procedure, 1951 (2nd edition, 1956) (3rd edition, 1963); Lamb's Encyclopædia of Housing, 1957. *Recreations:* lawns and painting. *Address:* Roughwood, Chislehurst, Kent. *T:* 01-467 1527.   *[Died 28 Oct.* 1973.

LAMBERT, Charles Ernest, CMG 1953; Assistant Secretary Colonial Office, 1947-61; *b* 28 Aug. 1900; *s* of late John and late Mary Eleanor Lambert; *m* 1929, Constance (*d* 1971); one *s. Educ:* Aske's Haberdashers' Hampstead Sch. On Military Service, 1918-19. Appointed Colonial Office, 1923; Registrar, UK High Commission in Canada, 1928-32 (on secondment); Assistant Principal, 1937; Principal, 1941; Assistant Secretary, 1947. Visited W Africa as Sec. Civil Service Salaries Commn, 1945-46, similarly for E Africa, 1947. Accompanied the then Secretary of State for the Colonies on a visit to Central Africa, 1950. *Address:* Holmwood, Ballinger Road, South Heath, Great Missenden, Bucks. *T:* Great Missenden 2696.
                                                              [Died 8 May 1974.

LAMBERT, Frank, CBE 1948; MA; *b* London, 4 June 1884; *m* 1929, Dorothy Elizabeth, *d* of Major E. H. Beeton, OBE, RAMC. *Educ:* St Olave's Grammar Sch.; Christ's Coll., Cambridge. Assistant Curator, Guildhall Museum, London, 1908-24; served with Essex and Suffolk Regiments, 1916-19; Curator, Stoke-on-Trent Art Gallery and Museums, 1924-27; Director, Leeds City Art Gallery, 1927-31; Extension Lecturer, London Univ., 1920-24; Extension Lecturer, Leeds Univ., 1927-31; Director, Walker Art Gallery, Liverpool, 1932-52; Sydney Jones Lecturer in Art, Liverpool Univ., 1937-38; President, North-Western Federation of Museums, 1941; President, Museums Association, 1946-48. *Publications:* papers in Archæologia, The Studio and other journals. *Address:* 49 Bath Street, Southport, Lancs. *[Died 13 Jan.* 1973.

LAMBERT, Maj.-Gen. Harold Roger, CBE 1941; DSC 1916; RM, retired; *b* 26 Jan. 1896; *y s* of late G. B. Lambert, PWD, Madras, India; *m* 1918, Ruth Noel St Clair (*d* 1955), *d* of late Rev. Dr W. St Clair Tisdall, DD; (one *s,* Lieut RN, DSC and bar, missing, presumed killed, 1943); *m* 1955, Elizabeth Lois King-Church. *Educ:* Dulwich Coll. 2nd Lieut RM, 1913; served in European War, 1914-19; Royal Naval Staff Coll., Greenwich,

1924-25; Staff Coll., Camberley, 1927-28; Plans Division of Naval Staff, Admiralty, 1929-32 and 1933-36; Senior Officer RM, on Staff of C-in-C, Portsmouth, 1936-38; commanded RM Field Formations in Orkneys, Norway, Iceland, Middle East and Sicily, 1939-44; Maj.-Gen. 1942; ADC to the King, 1943; Comdt Portsmouth Div. RM, 1944; 1939-43 Star, Africa Star, Italy Star; retired 1944. Chm., St Birinus Gp Hosps Management Cttee, 1951-61; Member: Oxon CC, 1955-61; Rural Dist Council, Henley, 1958-61. *Address:* 27 Victoria Hill, Eye, Suffolk. *T:* Eye 313. [*Died 28 Jan.* 1980.

LAMBERT, His Honour Robert, JP; County Court Judge, Circuit No 3 (Cumberland), 1968-70; retired; *b* 28 May 1908; *e s* of late R. F. W. Lambert, Preston; *m* 1936, Doris Mary, *d* of late Robert Casson, Preston; two *s* two *d. Educ:* Preston Grammar Sch.; London Univ. (LLB). Called to Bar, Lincoln's Inn, 1931; Tancred Student, 1929, George V Coronation Scholar and Buchanan Prizeman, 1931 (all of Lincoln's Inn). Practised Manchester and Northern Circuit. War of 1939-45: Sqdn-Leader, RAF (VR); served UK, Iceland and NW Europe, Coastal Command and JAG's Staff. Dep. Chairman, Lancashire County QS, 1961-62; Chairman, Agric. Land Tribunal, Lancs-Yorks area, 1962; Dep. Chairman, Mental Health Review Tribunal, Manchester region, 1960-62; Chairman, Preston (South) Conservative Association, 1954-62. JP, Co. Lancaster and Preston Borough, 1960, Co. Westmorland, 1969. *Publication:* Ebb Tide (play), 1930. *Recreations:* amateur play production, small-boat cruising. *Address:* Wavertree Lodge, Bowness-on-Windermere, Westmorland. *T:* Windermere 2345.
[*Died 21 Nov.* 1971.

LAMBERT, Victor Albert George, CB 1957; CBE 1951 (OBE 1944); Chairman: Modern Materials Management Ltd; J. E. Shay Ltd; *b* 24 May 1897; *m* 1929, Kathleen Florence Browne, Colchester; one *s* (decd). *Educ:* Colchester Technical Coll. Served Royal Horse Artillery, Near East, 1914-19. Royal Ordnance Factories: Assistant Director, 1939; Deputy Director (Engineering), 1941; Director (Guns), 1942. Deputy Director-General Housing Supplies, 1945, Director-General, 1946; Director-General of Armaments Production, Ministry of Supply, 1947-57. FIMechE. *Recreations:* gardening and golf. *Address:* Bayford, St Paul's Road, Dorking, Surrey. *T:* Dorking 2588. *Clubs:* National Liberal, City Livery.
[*Died 26 July* 1971.

LAMBERT, Maj.-Gen. William Harold, CB 1954; CBE 1944; *b* 29 May 1905; *s* of late Brig.-General T. S. Lambert, CB, CMG, and late Geraldine Rachel (*née* Foster); *m* 1933, Rachel Nina Maxwell; two *d. Educ:* The New Beacon, Sevenoaks; Charterhouse; RMC Sandhurst. Commissioned 1924; Lieut, 1926; ADC to GOC-in-C Western Command, India, 1929-31; Adjut 1st E. Lancs Regt, 1932-35; Adjut Depot, E. Lancs Regt, 1936-37; Captain, 1937; psc 1938; GSO3 War Office, 1939-40; GSO2, 44 Div. 1940-41; GSO1 44 Div. 1941-42; OC4 Royal West Kent Regt, 1942-43; GSO1 Instructor, Staff Coll., Haifa, 1943-44; BGS 13 Corps, Feb.-Nov. 1944; Comdt 13 Inf. Bde, 1944-45; BGS 30 Corps Dist., 1945-46; Assistant Comdt Staff Coll., Camberley, 1946-47; idc 1948; DDSD(A) War Office, 1948-52; Comdt 18 Inf. Bde March-Sept. 1952 and Jan.-Aug. 1953; Comdt 1 Malay Inf. Bde, 1952-53; Comdt 1st Federal Div., Malaya, 1953-55; Director, Personnel Administration, War Office, 1955-58, retired. *Recreation:* sailing. *Address:* Little Redlap, near Dartmouth, Devon. *T:* Dartmouth 2679.
[*Died 4 May* 1978.

LAMBOOY, Maj.-Gen. Albert Percy, CB 1950; OBE 1946; *b* 30 Nov. 1899; *s* of Theodore Lambooy; *m* 1926, Doris (decd); two *d. Educ:* Queen Elizabeth's Sch., Crediton; RMA Woolwich. Commissioned 2nd Lieut from RMA Woolwich, 1919; Captain, 1932; Major, 1938; Temp. Colonel, 1943; Lieut-Colonel, 1946; Colonel, 1946; Temp. Brigadier, 1946; Maj.-General, 1949. Dep. Director of Artillery, Ministry of Supply, 1942-45; Dep. Chief Engineer, Armaments Design, 1945-48; Director General of Artillery, Ministry of Supply, 1948-53; retired 1953. *Recreations:* golf and theatre. *Address:* Scio House, Portsmouth Road, SW15. [*Died 2 Oct.* 1976.

LAMOND, Sir William, Kt 1936; *b* 21 July 1887; *s* of late Thomas Lamond and Jane MacDonald; *m* 1914, Ethel Speechly (*d* 1939); one *s* ; *m* 1946, Norah Aitken. *Educ:* Harris Academy, Dundee. Joined Royal Bank of Scotland, Meigle, 1902; Bank of Bombay, 1907; Managing Governor, Imperial Bank of India, 1934; Managing Director, Imperial Bank of India, 1935-45; Member Indian Central Banking Enquiry Cttee, 1943-45; President, Indian Institute of Bankers, 1943-45. Dir, Calcutta Electric Supply Corp. Ltd, 1949-69. JP Bombay 1924-45. *Address:* 23 Rivermead Court, Hurlingham, SW6. *Clubs:* Oriental; Bengal (Calcutta). [*Died 6 Feb.* 1974.

LAMPE, Rev. Prof. Geoffrey William Hugo, MC 1945; DD; FBA 1963; Regius Professor of Divinity, Cambridge University, 1971-79; Fellow of Gonville and Caius College, since 1960; Hon. Canon of Ely Cathedral, since 1971 (Canon, 1960-71); *b* 13 Aug. 1912; *s* of late B. M. Lampe and Laura M. Lampe; *m* 1938, Elizabeth Enid Roberts; one *s* one *d. Educ:* Blundell's Sch.; Exeter Coll., Oxford (scholar, MA), DD 1953; Queen's Coll., Birmingham. Ordained, 1937; Curate of Okehampton, 1937-38; Assistant Master, King's Sch., Canterbury, 1938-41; Chaplain to the Forces, 1941-45; Fellow and Chaplain of St John's Coll., Oxford, 1943-53, Hon. Fellow, 1976; Professor of Theology, Birmingham Univ., 1953-59; Dean of the Faculty of Arts, 1955-59; Vice-Principal, 1957-60; Ely Prof. of Divinity, Cambridge Univ., 1959-71; Bampton Lectr, Oxford Univ., 1976. Hon. DD, Edinburgh, 1959; Teol. Dr (*hc*) Lund, 1965. Hon. Canon of Birmingham Cathedral, 1957-59. Comdr, Order of North Star (Sweden), 1978. *Publications:* Aspects of the New Testament Ministry, 1948; The Seal of the Spirit, 1951; Reconciliation in Christ, 1956; (ed) Justification by Faith, 1954; I Believe, 1960; (ed) A Patristic Greek Lexicon, vol. 1, 1961-vol. 5, 1969; (ed) The West from the Fathers to the Reformation (Cambridge History of the Bible), 1969; God as Spirit, 1977; various essays in symposia and articles in theological journals. *Address:* Gonville and Caius College, Cambridge; Prospect Cottage, 43 Warkworth Street, Cambridge CB1 1EG. [*Died 5 Aug.* 1980.

LAMPLUGH, Rt. Rev. Kenneth Edward Norman; Residentiary Canon, 1951-62, Hon. Canon, 1962, Hon. Chaplain, 1972, Winchester Cathedral; Chaplain and Sub-Prelate of the Venerable Order of St John of Jerusalem, since 1962; *b* 9 Nov. 1901; *m* 1928, Naomi Ford (*d* 1973); three *s* one *d. Educ:* King's Coll., Cambridge; Cuddesdon Coll., Oxford. Deacon 1925; Priest 1926; Curate of Lambeth, 1925-28; Curate of Pietermaritzburg Cathedral, Natal, 1928-31; Vicar of St Mary's, Durban, 1931-33; Vicar of Hartley Wintney, 1934; Commiss. to Bishop of Natal, 1937; Vicar of Lymington, 1941; Rural Dean of Lyndhurst, 1942; officiating CF, 1940-46; Archdeacon and Canon Residentiary of Lincoln, 1947-51; Warden of Lincoln Diocesan Association of Lay Readers, 1947; Suffragan Bishop of Southampton, 1951-71. Examining Chaplain to Bishop of Winchester, 1951-71. Chaplain, QEII Premier World Cruise, 1975. Chairman: Wessex Council on Alcoholism, 1969; Atherley School, Southampton, 1952-71; Talbot Heath School, Bournemouth, 1962-71; Council of Southampton University, 1951-71. Fellow, Soc. of St Mary and St Nicholas, Lancing, 1952. Pres., Hants Assoc. for the Blind, 1951-72; Chm., Hants and IoW Assoc. for the Deaf, 1951-72. Stowaway, Master Mariners' Club, Southampton, 1978. *Recreation:* travelling. *Address:* Butts Close Cottage, Winchester, Hants. *T:* Winchester 68533. [*Died 2 Oct.* 1979.

LAMPSON, Sir Curtis George, 3rd Bt, *cr* 1866, FRGS, FZS; Member of British Institute of Plastics; *b* 23 Jan. 1890; *s* of 2nd Bt and Sophia, *d* of Manuel Van Gelderen; *S* father, 1899; *m* 1921, Maud Lawton (*d* 1960), *d* of Alfred Wrigley, Bolton, Lancs; one *d. Educ:* Charterhouse. Explored French Central W. Africa and Libyan Desert; visited Poland, Lithuania, Latvia and Estonia, under auspices of respective Governments to study Agrarian Reform and Vilna Question; lectured on both subjects throughout Great Britain and USA; 1st Lieut Somerset LI, 1914-16; Captain, Motor Transport in Egypt, 1916-18; Lecturer on Travel; broadcaster on art and travel, Great Britain and USA; author of The Life of Edward Jenner, adapted for television; contributed to Sunday Times, New York Times, Cape Times, XIX Century and After, Daily Express, Accountancy, etc.; various articles syndicated in USA and Canada; contributed also to leading British, S African and Canadian farming periodicals on bovine matters, particularly those appertaining to non-pulmonary tuberculosis among human beings. *Recreations:* literary. *Heir:* cousin, 2nd Baron Killearn. *Address:* 2 The Square, Burwash, Sussex. *T:* Burwash 574.
[*Died 28 Aug.* 1971.

LANCASTER, Col Claude Granville; Chairman, The Bestwood Co. Ltd; *b* 1899. *Educ:* Eton; RMC. Royal Horse Guards, 1918; served Sherwood Foresters, 1939-43 (despatches). Hon. Colonel, 112th Regt, RAC (Foresters). MP(C) Fylde, 1938-50, South Fylde, 1950-70. *Address:* 11 St Leonard's Terrace, SW3. *T:* 01-730 9272; Kelmarsh Hall, Northampton. *T:* Maidwell 276; Langford Grove, Maldon, Essex. *T:* Maldon 53567. *Club:* White's. [*Died 25 July* 1977.

LANCASTER, Brig. Edmund Henry, CB 1936; Indian Army, retired; *b* 1881; *s* of William Henry Lancaster, Epsom; *m* 1905, Alice (*d* 1966), *d* of Charles J. Grahame; one *s* one *d. Educ:* United Services Coll., Westward Ho! Queen's Royal West Surrey Regt, 1900; 25th Cavalry (FF) Indian Army, 1902-05; Indian Army Service Corps, 1905-30; Colonel DDS and T,

AHQ, India, 1930-32; Inspector RIASC Services, India, 1932-36; served NWFP, 1908 (despatches, medal with clasp); European War, 1914-18 (despatches, medals); Iraq, 1920 (medal with clasp). *Address:* c/o National and Grindlays Bank, 13 St James's Square, SW1. *[Died 6 April 1975.*

LANDAU, Muriel Elsie, (Mrs Samuel Sacks); Hon. Cons. Gynæcologist, Elizabeth Garrett Anderson Hospital, London Jewish Hospital and Marie Curie Hospital; *b* 21 Jan. 1895; *d* of Marcus and Caroline Landau; *m* 1922, Dr Samuel Sacks; four *s*. *Educ:* Dame Alice Owen's Sch., (Foundation Schol., Owen's Leaving Exhibn, Isabel Thorne Entrance Schol. to London Sch. of Medicine); London School of Medicine; Royal Free Hospital. During student career won prizes in Anatomy, Surgery (incl. Gant Medal for operative surgery), Gynæcology, Venereology and diseases of Ear, Nose and Throat; MRCS, LRCP 1918; Helen Prideaux Post Graduate Prize, 1918; MB, BS London 1918; FRCS, 1920; MD London 1921. Various resident hosp. appts, 1918-21; Royal Free Hospital; Tite Street Children's Hosp.; Hosp. for Women, Soho Sq.; Queen Charlotte's Hosp., RMO; Registrar, Hosp. for Women, 1921-22; Asst Surg. Eliz. Garrett Anderson Hosp., 1922, subseq. Sen. Surg.; Surg., Marie Curie Hosp., 1926; Sen. Gynæcologist, London Jewish Hosp., 1929. *Publications:* Women of Forty, 1956; contrib. Lancet. *Recreations:* cooking, gardening. *Address:* 37 Mapesbury Road, NW2. *T:* 01-452 6381. *[Died 13 Nov. 1972.*

LANDAU, Rom; Author, Sculptor; *b* 17 Oct. 1899. Professor of Islamic and North African Studies, University of the Pacific, 1952-67 (and American Academy of Asian Studies, San Francisco, 1952-58). Weekly lectures on Islam and Islamic Culture, Radio in English, Radiodiffusion Marocaine, Rabat, 1969-. Mem., Executive Cttee of World Congress of Faiths, London, 1936-44; RAF Liaison Officer, Air Gunner, 1939-41; Senior Specialist Middle East Div. of Ministry of Information, 1941; Mem. of Arab. Cttee, Political Intelligence Dept. of F.O. 1941-44; lectured Princeton, Yale, Columbia, Harvard, Stanford and other American Universities, 1952-55. A Rom Landau Collection (of his MSS) made at University of Syracuse (New York), 1964; a Rom Landau Moroccan Collection made at University of the Pacific (California) 1967. Dir, Peace Corps, Area Studies, Morocco Project 1, 1962-63. Hon. LHD University Pacific, 1967. Comdr of Ouissam Alaouite Order (Morocco), 1956. *Publications:* Minos the Incorruptible, 1925; Pilsudski, Hero of Poland, 1929; Paderewski, 1934; God is my Adventure, 1935 (revised and brought up to date, paperback, 1964); Seven, 1936; Thy Kingdom Come, 1937; Search for Tomorrow, 1938; Arm the Apostles, 1938; Love for a Country, 1939; Of No Importance, 1940; We Have Seen Evil, 1941; Hitler's Paradise, 1941; The Fool's Progress, 1942; Islam Today (co-edited with Prof. A. J. Arberry and contributed the chapter on Saudi Arabia), 1943; Letter to Andrew, 1943 (3rd edn); The Brother Vane, 1944; The Wing, 1945; Sex, Life and Faith, 1946; The Merry Oasis, 1947; Odysseus, 1948; Human Relations, 1949; Personalia, 1949; Invitation to Morocco, 1950; The Beauty of Morocco, 1951; The Sultan of Morocco, 1951; Moroccan Journal, 1952; The Moroccan Problem (in the Year Book of World Affairs), 1952; Morocco (survey written for and publ. by Carnegie Endowment for Internat. Peace, New York), 1952; Portrait of Tangier, 1952; Among the Americans, 1954; France and the Arabs (for Can. Inst. of Internat. Affairs), 1954; The Arabesque-The Abstract Art of Islam, 1955; Moroccan Drama 1900-1955, 1956; An Outline of Moroccan Culture, 1957; Mohammed V, King of Morocco, 1957; Arab Contribution to Civilization, 1958; Islam and the Arabs, 1958; The Philosophy of Ibn Arabi, 1959; Morocco-Independent, 1961; The Arab Heritage of Western Civilization, 1962; Hassan II, King of Morocco, 1962; The Moroccans-Yesterday and Today, 1963; History of Morocco in the Twentieth Century (in Arabic), 1963; Morocco: Marrakesh, Fez, and Rabat, 1967; The Kasbas of Southern Morocco, 1969; Al Hassan al Thani Malik al Maghrib (in Arabic), 1969; The Alaouites: the cultural contribution of King Hassan II, 1970. *Recreations:* the countryside, talking to dogs. *Address:* c/o Faber & Faber, 3 Queen Square, WC1; Marrakesh, Morocco. *[Died 2 March 1974.*

LANE, Ernest Olaf, CBE 1975; DFC 1943; AFC 1945; Solicitor to the Metropolitan Police 1965-76; *b* 26 April 1916; *s* of James and Margaret Beatrice Lane; *m* 1949, Nancy Eileen Fairbairn (*d* 1974); one *d*. *Educ:* University of Sydney, NSW (LLB). Private practice, 1938-39. Pilot, RAAF, 1940-45. Solicitor's Dept, New Scotland Yard, 1946-; apptd Head of Dept, 1965. *Recreation:* golf. *Address:* Grey Cottage, Whitmoor Vale, near Hindhead, Surrey. *T:* Hindhead 880. *Clubs:* MCC; Hindhead Golf. *[Died 29 Dec. 1976.*

LANE, H(enry) J(errold) Randall, CBE 1963; Legal Adviser to the British Council, 1940-64; retired; Honorary Member, British

Council, since 1964; *b* 29 April 1898; *e s* of Henry Lane, Polegate House, Cranleigh, Surrey; *m* 1926, Elizabeth Kathleen Coulborn; one *s* decd. *Educ:* privately; Manchester Univ. Served as cadet in Merchant Fleet Aux., 1916-17 and in Canadian Army Med. Corps, 1917-19. Lived in Canada and Italy, 1919-26. MA 1929, but remained at Manchester Univ. for a further year's research. Admitted a student of Inner Temple, 1936; called to Bar, 1944. Lectr in Eng. Lang. and Lit. Extra-Mural Dept, Leicester Univ. Coll., 1930-40; Dir, British Inst. of Milan (British Council), 1940; returned to England as Legal Officer (British Council); title of post changed to that of Legal Adviser, 1944. Legal Chairman, London Rent Assessment Cttees (Lord Chancellor's Panel), 1966-71; Chm., Brent and Harrow Rent Tribunal, 1970-71. Mem. Adv. Bd (Comparative Law), British Inst. of Internat. and Comparative Law, 1959-64. *Recreations:* tennis, walking, travel. *Address:* 4 King's Bench Walk, Temple, EC4. *T:* 01-353 1317. *Club:* Reform. *[Died 16 Aug. 1975.*

LANE, Jane, (Mrs Andrew Dakers); author; (Elaine) *y d* of late Mason Kidner; *m* 1937, Andrew Dakers; one *s*. Adopting pseudonym of Jane Lane (maiden name of maternal grandmother), wrote first novel at age of seventeen. *Publications:* Undaunted, 1934; Be Valiant Still, 1935; King's Critic, 1935; Prelude to Kingship, 1936; Come to the March, 1937; Sir Devil May Care, 1937; You Can't Run Away, 1940; England for Sale, 1943; He Stooped to Conquer, 1944; Gin and Bitters, 1945; His Fight is Ours, 1946; London Goes to Heaven, 1947; Parcel of Rogues, 1948; Fortress in the Forth, 1950; Dark Conspiracy, 1952; The Sealed Knot, 1952; The Lady of the House, 1953; Thunder on St Paul's Day, 1954; The Phœnix and the Laurel, 1954; Conies in the Hay, 1957; Command Performance, 1957; Queen of the Castle, 1958; Ember In the Ashes, 1960; Sow the Tempest, 1960; Farewell to the White Cockade, 1961; The Crown for a Lie, 1962; A State of Mind, 1964; The Wind through the Heather, 1965; From the Snare of the Hunters, 1968; The Young and Lonely King, 1969; The Questing Beast, 1970; A Call of Trumpets, 1971; The Severed Crown, 1972; Bridge of Sighs, 1973; Heirs of Squire Harry, 1974; A Summer Storm, 1976; A Secret Chronicle, 1977; in addition to these: *books for children:* The Escape of the King, 1950; The Escape of the Prince, 1951; Desperate Battle, 1953; The Escape of the Queen, 1957; The Escape of the Duke, 1960; The Escape of the Princess, 1962; The Trial of the King, 1963; The Return of the King, 1964; The March of the Prince, 1965; The Champion of the King, 1966; *biographies and history:* King James the Last, 1943; Titus Oates, 1949; Puritan, Rake and Squire, 1950; The Reign of King Covenant, 1957; Cat among the Pigeons, 1959. *Recreations:* riding and embroidery. *Address:* Kingsbury, 97 Sea Road, Angmering-on-Sea, Sussex. *[Died 6 Jan. 1978.*

LANE, Sir William Arbuthnot, 2nd Bt *cr* 1913; CBE 1954; *b* 7 July 1897; *o s* of Sir Arbuthnot Lane, 1st Bt; *S* father, 1943; *m* 1937, Fritzi, *yr d* of Capt. F. Számvald; one *d*. *Educ:* Winchester Coll. Served European War, 1914-18; French and British Red Cross Societies, France, 1915-16; joined RFC, 1917; RAF Airship Pilot, 1918; War of 1939-45, RAF, 1940; Staff Captain and DAPM to Provost Marshal of the UK, War Office, 1941-45. Metropolitan Special Constabulary, 1926, Commandant, D Div., 1939, Y Div., 1947, Comdt-in-C., 1950-58, retd. Man. Dir, Kaylene (Chemicals) Ltd., retd 1961; Dir, Lothbury Estates Ltd. Governor, Nat. Heart Hosp., 1948-67. OStJ. *Address:* 72 Drayton Gardens, SW10 9SB. *T:* 01-373 2497. *Club:* Royal Air Force. *[Died 26 Feb. 1972 (ext).*

LANE-POOLE, Vice-Admiral Sir Richard Hayden Owen, KBE, *cr* 1944 (OBE 1919); CB 1936; *b* 1 April 1883; *s* of Stanley Lane-Poole, Author and Oriental scholar, and Charlotte Wilson, Ballymoney, Co. Antrim; *m* Sigrid, *d* of Col E. H. Haig; one *d*. *Educ:* France; Bedford Sch. Commanded Cambrian, 1927-29; RN Coll., Greenwich, 1929-31; Commodore commanding S American division, 1932-33; Commodore, Devonport, 1934-35; commanded HM Australian Squadron, 1936-38; retired list, 1939; War of 1939-45, served as Commodore of Convoys and Dir of Demagnetisation. Hon. DLitt, University of New England, Australia, 1962. *Recreations:* fishing and shooting. *Address:* Spyway, Armidale, NSW, Australia. *Club:* United Service. *[Died 25 March 1971.*

LANG, Air Vice-Marshal Albert Frank, CB 1946; MBE 1919; AFC 1936; *b* 1895; *m* 1920, Martha Eiluned Roberts; one *d*. Joined RFC, 1912; Dir of Signals, Air Commission, Washington, 1941-45; Controller of Signals Equipment, British Air Commission, Washington, 1945; retired, 1946. US Legion of Merit, 1946. *Address:* 1223 Garden Street, Santa Barbara, Calif 93101, USA. *[Died 20 June 1977.*

LANG, Col Bertram John, CB 1919; CMG 1918; DSO 1916; late Argyll and Sutherland Highlanders; President, South African

War Veterans Association, 1967 until its closure, after 70 years, in 1971, when the few remaining veterans were handed over to the care of the Army Benevolent Fund; *b* London, 14 Jan. 1878; 2nd *s* of late Basil Lang, Advocate-Gen., Bombay, and late Mrs Basil Lang, *d* of Colonel Trenchard Haggard, RA; *m* 1st, 1904, Mrs Montgomery Bartlett (decd); 2nd, 1924, Mrs Ruby Julia Hunter (decd); (one *s* decd); 3rd, 1951, Catherine Macdonald (*d* 1964), Hougharry, N Uist, Outer Hebrides. *Educ:* Harrow; Royal Military College, Sandhurst. Joined 1st Batt. Argyll and Sutherland Highlanders, 1898; served in South African War (Queen's medal with 5 clasps); Adjutant 3rd Vol. Batt. Argyll and Sutherland Highlanders and 4th (TF) Batt. Leicestershire Regiment, 1905-11; passed into Staff Coll., Camberley, 1913; went out to France with Expeditionary Force, 10 Aug. 1914, as Staff Capt., Boulogne Base; served on Staff of HQ L of C as DAQMG; at GHQ as DAQMG; with 8th Corps HQ as AQMG; and 7th Div. as AA and QMG; served in France, Aug. 1914-Nov. 1917, and in Italy, Nov. 1917 to end of war (despatches seven times, CB, CMG, DSO, Bt Lt-Col, 1914 Star, French Croix de Guerre with Palm, and Officier Mérite Agricole; Officer of the Order of the Crown of Italy, Italian Croce di Guerra); AQMG Army HQ, India, 1930-34; retired, 1934. *Clubs:* Army and Navy, Royal Automobile.
[Died 3 Nov. 1975.

LANG, Hon. John Thomas; Managing Editor, Century newspaper, since 1950; former Premier of New South Wales; *b* Sydney, 21 Dec. 1876; *m d* of late Mrs Bertha Macnamara, Sydney; five *c*. Mayor of Auburn two years; MLA Granville, 1913-20, Parramatta, 1920-27, and Auburn, 1927-46; Colonial Treasurer, 1920-22; Premier and Treasurer of New South Wales, 1925-27, and 1930-32; MHR for Reid, 1946-49. *Publication:* The Turbulent Years, 1970. *Address:* 95 Rawson Street, Auburn, NSW 2144, Australia. *[Died 27 Sept. 1975.*

LANG, Rt. Rev. Leslie Hamilton, MA, Hon. CF; *b* 27 May 1889; *s* of Alex. Lang, CMG, and Mary Susan Lang; *m* 1918, Janette Catharine Todd (*d* 1964); two *s*. *Educ:* Repton; Trinity Coll., Cambridge. Curate of Portsea, 1915-17; Chaplain to Forces, 1917-18; Domestic Chaplain to Archbishop of York, 1918; Chaplain to Returned Soldiers in Diocese of Edmonton, Canada, 1919-20; Vicar of All Saints, Swanscombe, 1920-22; Warden of Trinity Coll. Mission and Vicar of St George's Camberwell, 1922-27; Vicar of Kingston-upon-Thames, 1927-34; Rural Dean of Kingston, 1932-34; Canon Residentiary of Winchester and Diocesan Missioner, 1934; Bishop of Woolwich, 1936-47; Archdeacon of Lewisham, 1936-47; Canon Residentiary of Winchester Cathedral, Archdeacon of Winchester and Asst Bishop, 1947-62, retd. Select Preacher Cambridge Univ., 1937. *Recreations:* golf, fishing. *Address:* The Friary, 19 St Cross Road, Winchester, Hants. *[Died 12 March 1974.*

LANGDON, Air Commodore William Frederick, CBE 1950; RAF retired; Director of British Atlantic Committee, 1955-72; *b* 11 Feb. 1898; *s* of late William Frederick Langdon, Sunningdale, Berks; *m* 1925, Eneid Mary Eleanor, *d* of late Major E. J. W. Platt, Llanfairfechan, N Wales; no *c*. *Educ:* City of London Sch. Served European War, with Royal Naval Div., 1915-19 (wounded); served with Army, Iraq, 1919-23; trans. to RAF, 1923; 14 Sqdn, Palestine, 1925; attached RAuxAF, 1926-31; 30 Sqdn RAF Mosul, 1933-35; Air Min., 1936-39; served War of 1939-45, Wing Comdr 1940. Middle East, 1943; Group Capt. 1943; Asst Air Attaché, Ankara, 1943-45. Air Cdre 1952; SASO 41 Grp, 1952-55; retired, 1955. Freeman, City of London, 1919. *Recreations:* lawn tennis, travel, shooting. *Address:* 2 Grosvenor Court, 99 Sloane Street, SW1. *T:* 01-235 1609. *Clubs:* White's, RAF, Queen's. *[Died 22 July 1976.*

LANGDON-DAVIES, John, MBE; Author; *b* 1897; *s* of late Rev. Guy Langdon-Davies; *m* 1st, 1918, Constance, *d* of D. H. Scott, FRS; two *s*; 2nd, 1933, Elizabeth Barr; one *d*; 3rd, 1949, Patricia Kipping; three *s* one *d*. *Educ:* Tonbridge Sch. (New Judd Schol.); St John's Coll., Oxford (Smythe Exhibitioner, Kent County Senior Scholar and Sir Thomas White Scholar). Did not take a degree. Lectured throughout USA annually, 1924-36; War Corresp. in Spain, 1936-38; in Finnish War, 1940. Hon. Comdt of South-Eastern Army Fieldcraft Sch., 1941-44. Founder of Foster-Parents Scheme for European children; Inventor and Ed. Jackdaw collections of historical documents for Schs, 1963-. Science Correspondent of various daily newspapers, 1936-48. *Publications:* New Age of Faith, 1925; Short History of Women, 1928; Dancing Catalans, 1929; Man and His Universe, 1930; Science and Common Sense, 1931; Inside the Atom, 1934; How Wireless Came, 1935; Short History of the Future, 1936; Behind the Spanish Barricades, 1937; Air Raid, 1939; Finland, the First Total War, 1940; Nerves versus Nazis, 1940; Fifth Column, 1940; Home Guard Warfare, 1941; Home Guard Training Manual, 1941; Home Guard Fieldcraft Manual, 1942; American Close Up, 1943; Life-Blood, 1945; British Achievement in the Art of Healing, 1946; Conquer Fear, 1948; Russia Puts the Clock Back, 1949; NPL Jubilee Book of the National Physical Laboratory, 1951; Westminster Hospital, 1719-1948, 1952; Gatherings from Catalonia, 1958; Sex, Sin and Sanctity, 1954; Seeds of Life, 1955; (with E. J. Dingwall) The Unknown is It Nearer?, 1956; Man the Known and Unknown, 1961; Carlos the Bewitched (as John Nada), 1963; Cato Street Conspiracy (as John Stanhope), 1963. *Address:* Holly Place, Shoreham, near Sevenoaks, Kent. *T:* Otford 3874. *[Died 5 Dec. 1971.*

LANGFORD-SAINSBURY, Air Vice-Marshal Thomas Audley, CB 1945; OBE 1940; DFC; AFC and 2 bars; Royal Air Force, retired; *b* 23 Nov. 1897; *s* of Emma and Thomas Hugh Langford-Sainsbury, Bath; *m* 1918, Maude Hamilton Russell-Mortimer; one *d*; *m* 1948, Dorothy (Prescott) Goodwin; one *d*. *Educ:* Radley Coll., Berks. Joined Royal Flying Corps, 1916; Wing Comdr, Royal Air Force, 1939; Group Capt., 1941; Air Commodore, 1944; Temp. Air Vice-Marshal, 1944; retired, 1949. OStJ 1964. *Recreations:* cricket and shooting. *Address:* Oakley Hay, Vincent Road, Selsey, Sussex. *T:* Selsey 2481. *Club:* Royal Air Force. *[Died 21 June 1972.*

LANGHAM, Sir John (Charles Patrick), 14th Bt, *cr* 1660; *b* 30 June 1894; *s* of Sir (Herbert) Charles Arthur Langham, 13th Bt, and Ethel Sarah (*d* 1951), *e d* of Sir William Emerson Tennent, 2nd Bt (*ext*); *m* 1930, Rosamond Christabel, MBE 1969, *yr d* of Arthur Rashleigh, Holy Well House, Malvern Wells, Worcs; one *s*. *Educ:* Rugby Sch.; Royal Military College, Sandhurst. *Heir:* *s* James Michael Langham [*b* 24 May 1932; *m* 1959, Marion, *d* of O. Barratt, Tanzania; two *s* one *d*]. *Address:* Tempo Manor, Co. Fermanagh, Ireland. *[Died 6 July 1972.*

LANGLEY, Brig. George Furner, CBE 1958; DSO 1919; State Film Appeal Censor, Victoria, retired; *b* 1 May 1891; *s* of Jabez and Fanny Langley; *m* 1918, Edmée Mary, *d* of late P. Plunkett, Cairo; two *d*. *Educ:* Melbourne Univ., BA, Diploma of Educn; FACE. Enlisted, Dec. 1914; 2nd Lt 1915; served Gallipoli, Torpedoed SS Southland, Evacuation; Gallipoli; transferred Imperial Camel Corps Jan. 1916; appointed CO 1st Battalion ICC Sept. 1916, commanded 1st Bn ICC to 30 June 1918, then commanded 14th Australian Light Horse; T/Command 5th A. L. H. Brigade Jan. 1919-Sept. 1919 (DSO, Serbian Order of White Eagle, despatches four times); commanded 20th ALH Regt and 4th ALH Regt of CMF; comd an Inf. Bde in 2 AIF, War of 1939-45; OStJ; ED; Red Cross Com. for Australia at Australia House, 1944-46. Formerly Principal, Melbourne High Sch. *Address:* 21 Arnold Street, Killara, NSW 2071, Australia. *Club:* Legacy. *[Died 24 Aug. 1971.*

LANGLEY, Vice-Admiral Gerald Maxwell Bradshaw, CB 1948; OBE 1919; *b* 1895; *s* of Admiral Gerald Charles Langley. *Educ:* Wellington. Joined Royal Navy, 1914; served European War, 1914-19; in Fleet Air Arm, 1923-39; Capt., 1936; Dir of Gunnery, Naval Staff, 1941-43; Chief Naval Staff Officer, Supreme Allied Command, South-East Asia, 1943-44; Rear-Admiral, 1946; Ministry of Defence, 1946-49; Vice-Adm. (retd), 1949. *Address:* Agecroft Mill, Milland, Liphook, Hants.
[Died 17 April 1971.

LANGLEY, Noel A.; author-playwright; *b* Durban, SA, 25 Dec. 1911; *m* 1937, Naomi Mary Legate (marriage dissolved, 1954); three *s* two *d*; *m* 1959, Pamela Deeming. *Educ:* Durban High Sch.; University of Natal, SA. Plays produced in London: Queer Cargo; For Ever; Edward My Son (with Robert Morley); Little Lambs Eat Ivy; Cage Me a Peacock; The Burning Bush; The Land of Green Ginger, 1966; The Snow Queen. Plays produced in New York: Farm of Three Echoes, 1939; The Walrus and the Carpenter, 1941. Films: Maytime, 1936 (USA); The Wizard of Oz, 1938 (USA); They Made Me a Fugitive, 1946; Cardboard Cavalier, Adam and Evalyn, 1948; Trio, Tom Brown's School Days, 1950; Scrooge, 1951; Ivanhoe (USA), Pickwick Papers (adaptation and direction), 1952; Knights of the Round Table (USA), 1953; Our Girl Friday (Adventures of Sadie) (screenplay and direction); Trilby and Svengali (screenplay and direction); Vagabond King (USA), 1954; The Search for Bridey Murphy (screenplay and direction), 1957. *Publications:* Cage Me a Peacock, 1935; There's a Porpoise Close Behind Us, 1936; Hocus Pocus, 1941; Land of Green Ginger, 1937; The Music of the Heart, 1946; The Cabbage Patch, 1947; Nymph in Clover, 1948; The Inconstant Moon, 1949; Tales of Mystery and Revenge, 1950; The Rift in the Lute, 1952; Where Did Everybody Go?, 1960; An Elegance of Rebels, 1960; The Loner, 1967; My Beloved Teck, 1970; A Dream of Dragon Flies, 1972; (jointly) There's a Horse in My Tree, Somebody's Rocking My Dream Boat, Cuckoo in the Nest. *Address:* c/o Eric Glass Ltd, 28 Berkeley Square, W1X 6HD.
[Died 4 Nov. 1980.

LANGRISHE, Capt. Sir Terence Hume, 6th Bt, *cr* 1775; *b* 9 Dec. 1895; *s* of Sir Hercules Robert Langrishe, 5th Bt, and Helen, (*d* 1955), *d* of Rt Hon. Fitzwilliam Hume-Dick, Humewood, Co. Wicklow; *S* father, 1943; *m* 1926, Joan Stuart, *e d* of Major Ralph Grigg, late 18th Hussars; three *s*. *Educ:* Eton. Served European War as Lt Irish Guards, attached to RFC/RAF; War of 1939-45 as Capt. in the Intelligence Corps. *Heir: s* Hercules Ralph Hume Langrishe, 9th Lancers [*b* 17 May 1927; *m* 1955, Hon. Grania Wingfield, *o d* of 9th Viscount Powerscourt; one *s* three *d*]. *Address:* Knocktopher Abbey, Co. Kilkenny. *Clubs:* Royal Yacht Squadron (Cowes); Kildare Street (Dublin); Bembridge Sailing (Bembridge).   *[Died 31 Dec. 1973.*

LANGTON; see Temple-Gore-Langton.

LARKING, Lt-Col Sir (Charles) Gordon, Kt 1970; CBE 1951; Chartered Accountant; *b* 31 Aug. 1893; *s* of late Charles Larking, Norwich; *m* 1917, Kathleen Ethel Pank (*d* 1970), Norwich; two *s* one *d*. *Educ:* Norwich. Served European War, 1914-19, Royal Fusiliers, Royal Sussex, MGC (Egypt and France); War of 1939-45, commanded 8th Bn E. Surrey Regt, 1939-42; British Legion: National Chairman, 1947-50 (visited Malaya, Burma, Australia, New Zealand, Kenya, Uganda, Tanganyika, S Africa, Canada and US); National Treasurer, 1962-70. Member of Maidstone Borough Council, 1922-74; Mayor, 1931-32, 1944-45, 1950-51; Alderman, 1941-74; Hon. Freeman, 1948. *Recreations:* cricket and football. *Address:* Pear Patch, Loose, Maidstone.   *[Died 10 Jan. 1978.*

LARSEN, Roy Edward; Vice-Chairman of Board, Time Incorporated, 1969-79 (Director, 1933-79, President, 1939-60, Chairman, Executive Committee, 1960-69); *b* 20 April 1899; *s* of Robert Larsen and Stella Belyea; *m* 1927, Margaret Zerbe; three *s* one *d*. *Educ:* Boston Latin Sch.; Harvard Univ. Circulation Manager, Time, 1922; Vice-President, Time Inc., 1927-39; Publisher Life, 1936-46. Overseer Harvard Univ., 1940-46, 1953-59; Chairman National Citizens Commn for Public Schools, 1949-56; Chairman of the Board of the Fund for the Advancement of Education, 1955-67; Member President's Cttee on Education Beyond the High School; Trustee, Ford Foundation, 1957-69; Chm. of Bd, Nantucket Conservation Foundn; Mem. Bd of Governors, Nature Conservancy; Hon. Trustee, New York Public Library. Chevalier, French Legion of Honour, 1950. Hon. LLD: Marietta Coll., 1946; Bucknell Univ., 1950; New York Univ., 1952; Harvard, 1953; Dartmouth Coll., 1954; Boston Univ., 1956; Hon. LHD, Kalamazoo Coll., 1951; Hon. LittD, Oberlin Coll., 1958. Hon. Phi Beta Kappa, 1957. *Address:* 4900 Congress Street, Fairfield, Conn 06431, USA. *Clubs:* Harvard, Century, River, University, Links (New York); Lyford Cay (Bahamas).   *[Died 9 Sept. 1979.*

LARTIGUE, Alexander Raphael C.; see Cools-Lartigue.

LASBREY, Rt. Rev. Bertram, MA, DD. *Educ:* Bedford Sch.; St Catharine's Coll., Cambridge; Ridley Hall, Cambridge. Deacon, 1904; Priest, 1905; Curate of St Andrew, Auckland, 1904-07; Chaplain, Weymouth Coll., 1907-11; Curate of St John, Melcombe Regis, 1907-11; Vicar of St Gabriel, Bishop Wearmouth, 1911-22; Bishop on the Niger, 1922-45; Assistant Bishop of Worcester and Rector of St Andrew's and All Saints with St Helen's, St Albans and St Michael's, Worcester, 1946-Jan. 1953. Hon. Canon of Worcester Cathedral, 1946-53; Public Preacher in the Diocese of Southwell, 1953-62. *Address:* Homes of St Barnabas, Dormans, Lingfield, Surrey.
    [Died 6 April 1976.

LASCELLES, Sir Francis (William), KCB 1954 (CB 1937); MC; MA; Clerk of the Parliaments, 1953-58; *b* 23 March 1890; *s* of late Lieut-Colonel H. A. Lascelles, Woolbeding, Midhurst; *m* 1924, Esmée Marion, *d* of late C. A. Bury, Downings, Co. Kildare; two *s*. *Educ:* Winchester; Christ Church, Oxford. Served in European War, 1914-19 with Sussex Yeomanry (wounded, MC). *Address:* Field House, Orford, Suffolk. *T:* Orford 361.   *[Died 16 May 1979.*

LASKEY, Francis Seward, MC; *b* 1886; *m* 1915, Elaine Dorothie Nancie (*d* 1971), *d* of William Procter Dilworth; two *s* (and one *s* killed in action, 1943). *Educ:* Merchant Taylors' Sch.; Oriel Coll., Oxford. Called to Bar, 1913; Recorder: Poole, 1939-41; Salisbury, 1941-61; served European War, 1914-19 (MC). *Address:* Queen Elizabeth Building, Temple, EC4. *T:* 01-353 5432. *Clubs:* Athenæum, Junior Carlton, Leander.
    [Died 3 Dec. 1972.

LATEY, William, CBE 1965 (MBE 1918); QC 1950; Special Divorce Commissioner, 1952-64 (continuously); *b* 12 Feb. 1885; *y s* of late John Latey, Editor of the Penny Illustrated Paper, 1860-1900 and later of The Illustrated London News, also of

The Sketch, and of late Constance Latey; *m* 1912, Anne Emily, *d* of late Horace G. Brinsmead; two *s*. *Educ:* Mercers' Sch. Writer and journalist; FJI 1915. War correspondent, Daily Chronicle, 1914-15; on Secretariat, Ministry of Munitions, Gun and Tank Supply, 1916-18; called to the Bar, 1916 (Oxford Circuit); practising since 1919, mainly in Probate and Divorce. War of 1939-45, Temple ARP Control Cttee and City Warden. Member General Council of the Bar, 1935-52; Chairman, Legal Board of National Marriage Guidance Council, till 1966; Member Archbishops' Commission on Law of Nullity of Marriage, 1950-54; HM Commissioner of Assize on various occasions, 1952-60; President, Medico-Legal Society, 1956-57; Member Councils of Law-Reporting, 1947-67, International Law Association, British Institute of International Law. Bencher of the Middle Temple, 1947; Lenten Reader, 1961; Treasurer, 1966. Freeman of the City of London. *Publications:* Latey on Divorce, 11th edn 1931-15th edn 1973; Probate and Conflict on Laws (Husband and Wife) in Halsbury's Laws of England, 1932; Family Law in Jenks' Civil Law Digest, 1947; Centenary of the Law Reports, 1965; The Tide of Divorce, 1970; and numerous other legal publications. *Recreation:* chess. *Address:* New Court, Temple, EC4. *T:* 01-353 1487. *Clubs:* Athenæum, Savage.
    [Died 28 Feb. 1976.

LATHAM, E(dward) Bryan, CBE 1964; MM 1915; BA 1974; Director, since 1921, President, since 1972, James Latham Ltd, Timber Importers, London (Managing Director, 1939-51, Chairman, 1951-71); *b* 7 May 1895; *s* of late E. Locks Latham, The Towers, Theydon Bois, Essex, and late Emily Latham (*née* Chappell); *m* 1927, Anne Arnot Duncan, Newton of Lathrisk, Fife; two *s*. *Educ:* Felsted, Essex; Open Univ. (BA Hons 1976). Served European War, 1914-18 (MM): France, Indian Frontier, Palestine; Lieut, 17th London Regt, later Captain, 19th Punjabi Regt. Governor Metropolitan Hosp., London, 1930-40; Chm., Nat. Sawmilling Assoc., 1942-43; Pres. Timber Trade Fedn of UK, 1945-47; Governing Council, Commonwealth Forestry Association, 1945- (Chm., 1961; Vice-Pres., 1964-); Gen. Council, British Standards Inst., 1946-48; Mem. Education Cttee, FBI, 1956-66; Founder-Pres., Inst. of Wood Science, 1956-58, Mem. Council, 1959-; Mem. Forestry Commn, 1957-63. Mem. British Delegs to Commonwealth Forestry Confs: London, 1947; Ottawa, 1952; to 5th World Forestry Congress, Seattle, 1960; Hon. Pres. Univ. of Edinburgh Forestry Assoc., 1962-63; Pres. Timber Research and Development Assoc. (TRADA), 1973- (Vice-Pres., 1963-69; Chm., 1943-44; Mem. Council, 1943-70); Pres., Timber Trade Benevolent Soc.; Member: Business Archives Council, 1962-68; Furniture and Timber Industry Training Board, 1965-71; F.Inst. of Wood Science, London, 1957-72; F.Forest History Foundation, Yale Univ., 1959-70; FRSA 1961. Mem. Royal Horticultural Soc., Surrey; Pres. Launceston Agric. Soc., 1967. *Publications:* Victorian Staffordshire Portrait Figures, 1953; Timber: Its Development and Distribution, 1957; Wood from Forest to Man, 1964; History of the Timber Trade Federation of the UK, 1965; Territorial Soldiers War, 1967; Trebartha, the House by the Stream: a Cornish history, 1970. Contributor to: Encyclopædia Britannica, Empire Forestry Review, Wood, Timber Trades Journal, Unasylva (FAO), etc. *Recreations:* fishing, riding, natural history, gardening; collector of Victorian Staffordshire Portrait figures. *Address:* Trebartha House, near Launceston, Cornwall. *T:* Coad's Green 336. *Club:* Army and Navy.   *[Died 7 Feb. 1980.*

LATHAM, Gustavus Henry, LLD, JP; Chairman and Managing Director, Whitehead Iron and Steel Co. Ltd, 1938-64 and other Companies; Director, Richard Thomas & Baldwins Ltd, retired 1964 (Deputy Chairman, 1955-64); Past Chairman: British Iron & Steel Corporation Ltd; British Steel Corporation Ltd; President, University College of South Wales and Monmouthshire, 1955-60; Past President British Iron and Steel Federation; Founder President, Newport and District Metallurgical Society, 1934; Vice-President Iron and Steel Institute; late Member of the Iron and Steel Board; *b* 29 Dec. 1888; *s* of Henry Charles Latham, Stoke-on-Trent, and Emma Fairall, Buxton; *m* 1st, 1916, Gwladys Gwen, *d* of Engr Rear-Admiral J. A. Lemon; one *s*; 2nd, 1953, Norah Priddey; one *d*. *Educ:* Secondary, High School and Technical Coll., Longton, Staffs. With L. & N.W. Railway for special training in Transport, 1901-04; joined L. D. Whitehead, Tredegar, to study and develop Continuous Rolling Mills for steel trade, 1905; started up first Semi-Continuous Rolling Mill in England and Europe, 1907; General Manager and Deputy Chairman Whitehead Iron and Steel Co. Ltd, 1931; appointed by Control Cttee set up by Bank of England as Managing Director Richard Thomas & Co. Ltd, 1939-45; Technical Adviser for steel trade for Finance Corporation for Industry, 1944; and to late Governor of the Bank of England (Lord Norman); Past President British Iron and Steel Research Association. Member

Newport Harbour Commissioners, 1941-64; Governor, Newport and Monmouthshire College of Technology; Chairman, Newport Council, Order of St John, 1951-68. KStJ. *Recreation:* continuous hot and cold rolling of steel. *Address:* Fields House, Newport, Gwent. *T:* 65743; Orchard Close, Broadway, Worcs.
[Died 21 April 1975.

LATHBURY, General Sir Gerald (William), GCB 1962 (KCB 1956; CB 1950); DSO 1943; MBE 1940; DSC (USA) 1944; Governor of Gibraltar, 1964-69; *b* 14 July 1906; *m* 1942, Jean Thin; two *d*; *m* 1972, Mrs Mairi Gibbs, *widow* of Patrick Somerset Gibbs. *Educ:* Wellington Coll.; Royal Military Coll., Sandhurst, 1924-25; gazetted to Oxfordshire and Buckinghamshire Light Infantry, 1926; Gold Coast Regt, 1928-33; Staff Coll., 1937-38; served throughout War of 1939-45 in France and Belgium, North Africa, Sicily, Italy and North-West Europe; Palestine, 1945-46; Imperial Defence Coll., 1948; GOC 16 Airborne Division (TA), 1948-51; Commandant, Staff Coll., Camberley, 1951-53; Vice-Adjutant-General, War Office, 1954; Commander-in-Chief, East Africa, 1955-57; Director-General of Military Training, War Office, 1957-60; General Officer Commanding-in-Chief, Eastern Command, 1960-61; Quartermaster-General to the Forces, 1961-65; ADC General to the Queen, 1962-65. Colonel, West India Regt, 1959; Jamaica Regt, 1962-68; Colonel Comdt, 1st Green Jackets, 43rd and 52nd, 1961-65; Colonel Comdt, The Parachute Regt, 1961-65. *Address:* Casa San Pedro, Gata de Gorgos, Prov. Alicante, Spain. *Club:* Army and Navy.   *[Died 16 May 1978.*

LATTER, Maj.-Gen. John Cecil, CBE 1944; MC; DL; *b* 6 May 1896; *o s* of late Dr Cecil Latter, Folkestone, Kent, and of late Ruth Beechey; unmarried. *Educ:* Cheltenham Coll. (Scholar); Trinity Coll., Oxford (Scholar). Served European War, 1914-18, 2/5 Lancs Fusiliers and Staff (MC). Diplomatic Service, 1919-21; resigned to take up permanent commission in Regular Army; psc, 1933; AAG, GHQ, BEF, Nov. 1939-June 1940 (despatches); Deputy Military Secretary (B), War Office, Aug. 1940-Jan. 1943; Deputy Military Secretary, GHQ Middle East Forces, Jan.-Dec. 1943; DAG, GHQ, Middle East Forces, Dec. 1943-July 1944; DA and QMG, 5th AA Group, July 1944-March 1945; Deputy Director, TA and Army Cadet Force, 1945-47; Colonel, 1944; retired 1947 (hon. Maj.-General); Secretary, Leeds Univ. Appointments Board, 1948-52; Chairman Combined Cadet Force Association, 1952-55; Assistant Director-General, Leeds Centenary Musical Festival, 1958. DL West Riding, 1952. *Publications:* edited (and partly wrote) Cadet Training Manual, for British National Cadet Association, 1933; The History of the Lancashire Fusiliers, 1914-18, 1949. *Address:* Riverside Cottage, Naburn, York YO1 4RR. *Club:* Army and Navy.   *[Died 7 July 1972.*

LAUDENBACH, Pierre; *see* Fresnay, Pierre.

LAUGHTON-SCOTT, Edward Hey, QC 1971; **His Honour Judge Laughton-Scott;** a Circuit Judge, since 1976; *b* 18 March 1926; *s* of Dr F. G. Laughton-Scott and Mrs R. Laughton-Scott (*née* Inskip); *m* 1952, Elizabeth Cecilia Macneece Foster; two *s* one *d. Educ:* Sunningdale Sch.; Tonbridge Sch.; Merton Coll., Oxford (MA). Served Life Guards, 1944-47 (Captain); Inns of Court Regt (TA), 1950-58 (Major). Called to Bar, Inner Temple, 1951; Mem. Bar Council, 1959-63 and 1968-72, Treasurer 1971; Mem. Senate, 1969-72; Bencher, Inner Temple, 1966. Dep. Chm., Hants QS, 1967-71; a Recorder of the Crown Court, 1972-76. Mem., Bar Cttee for Royal Commn on Assizes and Quarter Sessions, 1968-69; Chm., Bar Cttee on Rights of Audience in Crown Courts, 1971; Chm., Sub-Cttee of Bar Council on VAT and Fee Collection, 1972-76. Appeal Steward, British Boxing Bd of Control, 1972-; Assessor, GMC and GDC, 1973-76. Renter Warden, Skinners Co., 1973. *Recreations:* golf, sailing, shooting, bridge. *Address:* 4 Hobury Street, Chelsea, SW10. *T:* 01-352 4610. *Clubs:* Garrick; Hampshire (Winchester); Royal London Yacht.   *[Died 17 May 1978.*

LAURIE, Prof. Malcolm Vyvyan, CBE 1969 (OBE 1946); MA; DipFor; Professor of Forestry, University of Oxford, 1959-68; Emeritus Fellow of St John's College, Oxford; *b* 30 Aug. 1901; *s* of late Malcolm Laurie, DSc, FRSE and late Helena Agnes Laurie (*née* Phillips); *m* 1956, Margery Catherine Jackson. *Educ:* Edinburgh Academy; Sedbergh Sch.; King's Coll., Cambridge. BA Hons 1923; DipFor 1925; MA 1930. Indian Forest Service, 1925; served in various posts in Madras Province, 1925-35; Central Silviculturist, Forest Research Institute, Dehra Dun, UP, 1935-40; Dep. Dir, Timber Supplies, Dept of Supply, New Delhi, 1940-43; Director, Timber Supplies, New Delhi, 1943-46; retired from Indian Forest Service, 1946; Chief Research Officer, Forestry Commission, 1946-59. Mem., Natural Environment Research Council, 1965-68. Fellow, Inst. of Foresters. *Recreation:* gardening. *Address:* 11 Chadlington

Road, Oxford. *T:* Oxford 58520. *Clubs:* Royal Over-Seas League, Royal Commonwealth Society; Surrey Gliding (Lasham, Hants); Oxford Gliding (Weston-on-the-Green).
[Died 30 Nov. 1973.

LAVER, James, CBE 1951; Hon. RE; FRSA, FRSL; retired as Keeper, Departments of Engraving, Illustration and Design, and of Paintings, Victoria and Albert Museum, London (1938-59); author; *b* Liverpool, 14 March 1899; *o s* of A. J. Laver, Liverpool; *m* 1928, Bridget Veronica (*d* 1971), *d* of Martin Turley, Bray, Ireland; one *s* one *d. Educ:* Liverpool Institute; New Coll., Oxford. 2nd Lt King's Own (Royal Lancaster) Regiment, 1918. *Publications:* Cervantes (Newdigate Prize Poem), 1921; His Last Sebastian, 1922; Portraits in Oil and Vinegar, 1925; The Young Man Dances, 1925; A Stitch in Time, 1927; Design in the Theatre (with George Sheringham), 1927; The Circle of Chalk (translation), 1928, (produced by Mr Basil Dean at the New Theatre, 1929); Memoirs of Harriet Wilson, 1929; History of British and American Etching, 1929; Love's Progress, 1929; Nineteenth Century Costume, 1929; Macrocosmos, 1929; Etchings of Arthur Briscoe, 1930; Whistler, 1930; Eighteenth Century Costume, 1931; Nymph Errant, 1932 (produced by C. B. Cochran as a musical comedy at the Adelphi Theatre, 1933); Wesley, 1932; Works of Charles Churchill, 1933; Ladies' Mistakes, 1933; Stage Designs by Oliver Messel, 1933; Background for Venus, 1934; Winter Wedding, 1934; Forty Drawings by Horace Brodzky, 1935; Laburnum Tree (short stories), 1935; Tommy Apple, 1935; Panic Among Puritans, 1936; Tommy Apple and Peggy Pear, 1936; Vulgar Society (James Tissot), 1936; The House that Went to Sea (children's play), at Liverpool Repertory Theatre, 1936; French Painting and the Nineteenth Century, 1937; Taste and Fashion, 1937; The Heart was not Burned (play), Gate Theatre Studio, 1938; Swiss Family Robinson (children's play with Sir Barry Jackson), Birmingham Repertory Theatre, 1938; Poems of Baudelaire, 1940; Adventures in Monochrome, 1941; Nostradamus, 1942; Ladies of Hampton Court, 1942; Fashions and Fashion-Plates, 1943; XIXth Century French Posters, 1944; Isabella's Pageant, 1947; British Military Uniforms, 1948; Homage to Venus, 1949; Style in Costume, 1949; The Changing Shape of Things: Dress, 1950; Titian, 1950; Children's Costume in the Nineteenth Century, 1951; Tudor Costume, 1951; The Fertile Image, 1951; Drama: Its Costume and Décor, 1951; The Pleasures of Life: Clothes, 1953; The First Decadent, 1954; Victorian Vista, 1954; London as it is, 1954-55; Fragonard, 1956; Costume (Junior Heritage), 1956; Edwardian Promenade, 1958; Between the Wars, 1961; Costume, 1963; Museum Piece, 1963; Costume in the Theatre, 1964; Women's Dress in the Age of Jazz, 1964; The Age of Optimism, 1966; Victoriana, 1966; The Dandies, 1968; Modesty in Dress, 1969; A Concise History of Costume, 1969; English Sporting Prints, 1970; English Popular Prints, 1972; The Age of Illusion, 1972. *Address:* 4/10 The Glebe, SE3. *Clubs:* Beefsteak, Chelsea Arts (Hon.).
[Died 3 June 1975.

LAVERS, Sydney Charles Robert; *b* 4 June 1898; *m* 1915; one *s* two *d. Educ:* Oxford Street Board Schs, Plymouth, Devon. Miner prior to European War; served 3+ years in HM Forces. Returned to mines; became miners' official. Mem. of Parish Council at Birtley, 1927; RDC at Chester-le-Street, 1927; Durham CC since 1934; MP (Lab) for Barnard Castle Div. of Durham, 1945-50. Chairman: Northern Clubs Federation Brewery Ltd; Nat. Assoc. of Clubs Breweries Ltd. *Address:* 10 Station Road, New Penshaw, Houghton-le-Spring, Co. Durham.
[Died 9 April 1972.

LAVINGTON EVANS, L. G., *see* Evans, L. G. L.

LAW, Anastasia, (Mrs Nigel Law), CBE 1918; *d* of late M. Mouravieff, Imperial Russian Ambassador in Rome; *m* 1st, 1907, Sir Milne Cheetham (who obtained a divorce, 1923); one *s*; 2nd, 1929, Nigel Walter Law. Dame of Grace of Order of St John of Jerusalem. *Address:* High Trees, Chalfont St Peter, Bucks.
[Died 4 April 1976.

LAW, Sir Charles Ewan, Kt 1937; *b* 16 Feb. 1884; *s* of Charles Woodin and Janet Eliza Law; *m* 1st, 1909, Madeleine (*d* 1967), *yr d* of Albert Lagier, Perroy, Vaud, Switzerland; two *s* two *d*; 2nd, 1974, Florence Gloria, *widow* of his cousin Wyndham Law. *Educ:* High Sch., Croydon; Pembroke Coll., Cambridge. Called to Bar, Middle Temple, 1905; Burma Bar, 1905; Crown Counsel, Kenya, 1922; Resident Magistrate, Jamaica, 1925; Judge Kingston Court, Jamaica, 1927; Puisne Judge, Uganda, 1930; Chief Justice, Zanzibar, 1934-39; Mem., Court of Appeal for Eastern Africa, 1930-39; Chief Justice, Northern Rhodesia, 1939; Mem., Rhodesian (conjoint) Court of Appeal, 1939 retired, 1945. Chm. Brighton and Area Rent Tribunal, 1946-49 Chm. Medical Appeal Tribunal, London Region (Industrial

Injuries), 1948-57. Special Divorce Commissioner (Matrimonial Causes), 1949-57. JP Sussex, 1947. Order of the Brilliant Star of Zanzibar (2nd class), 1939. *Address:* 84 Offington Lane, Worthing, West Sussex. *T:* Worthing 61756.
[Died 11 Dec. 1974.

LAW, Margaret Dorothy, OBE 1951; MA; Consultant Editor, Chambers's Encyclopædia; *d* of Thomas Robert Evans, Shrewsbury, and Dorothy, *d* of late David Davies; *m* 1925, George Edward (decd), *s* of late Rev. William Law, Vicar of Rotherham; two *s. Educ:* St Leonards Sch., St Andrews; Girton Coll., Cambridge. Dir of Encyclopædia Britannica, 1925-43; Managing Editor Chambers's Encyclopædia, 1943-63; Mem. Cambridge Univ. Women's Appts Board, 1959-66. Consultant, Common Cents Foundation Center, Montreal, 1976-77. *Publication:* (contrib.) Indexers On Indexing, 1978. *Recreation:* reading. *Address:* 4 York Mansions, SW5. *T:* 01-373 8368.
[Died 27 Jan. 1980.

LAWES, Sir John (Claud Bennet), 4th Bt, *cr* 1882; *b* 9 Sept. 1898; *er s* of Sir John Lawes-Wittewronge, 3rd Bt, and Helena Ramsey (*d* 1961), *d* of Henry Ramsey Cox of Folkestone; relinquished surname of Wittewronge by deed poll, 1951; *S* father, 1931; *m* 1st, 1928, Kathleen Marjorie Livingstone (*d* 1938), *er d* of Gerald Tylston Hodgson; one *s*; 2nd, 1938, Naomi Constance Helen, *y d* of Lancelot Wykeham Badnall; one *d. Educ:* Blundell's Sch., Tiverton. *Heir: s* John Michael Bennet Lawes, *b* 24 Oct. 1932. *Address:* Le Clos du Coudré, St Pierre du Bois, Guernsey, CI.
[Died 9 Dec. 1979.

LAWLER, Wallace Leslie; *b* 15 March 1912; *s* of Stephen Lawler and Elizabeth Lawler (*née* Taylor); *m* 1943, Catherine Leticia (*née* Durcan); two *s* two *d. Educ:* St Paul's, Worcester; privately at Malvern. Founded Public Opinion Action Assoc., 1943. Contested Parly seats: Dudley, 1955; Perry Barr, 1959; Handsworth, 1964; Ladywood, 1966; MP (L) Ladywood Div. of Birmingham, June 1969-1970. First Liberal Councillor for 28 years, Birmingham City Council, 1962; re-elected, 1965 and 1968 (Leader of Council's Liberal Gp, 1968-); Vice-Chm., 1967, Vice-Pres., 1968, of the Liberal Party. Chm., Homeless Bureau, 1956-. *Publications:* Pensions for All, 1958; The Truth About Cathy, 1968. *Recreations:* politics, reading, camping. *Address:* 39 Tenbury Road, Birmingham 14. *T:* 021-444 1636. *Club:* National Liberal.
[Died 28 Sept. 1972.

LAWLEY, Edgar Ernest, CBE 1961; Chairman: Adderley Trading Co. (Pty) Ltd of S Africa; Afstral Investment Co. (Pty) Ltd of S Africa; Denton Heath Trading Co. Ltd; Jacobs Production & Distributing Co. Ltd; Lawley Estates Ltd; Joint Founder and Chairman, Lawley Group Ltd (now Royal Doulton Ltd), resigned 1952; Underwriter of Lloyd's; Director: Sandown Estates (Pty) Ltd, S Africa; Charnwood Estates (Pty) Ltd, S Africa; Trustee, Wright-Fleming Institute; Vice-President St Mary's Medical School; Member, General Council, King Edward's Hospital Fund for London; Chairman: Regent Street Association, 1947-49; St Mary's Hospital Medical School Centenary Appeal, 1956-57; St Mary's Hospital, 1957-64 (Vice-Chairman, 1945-57); *b* 4 Sept. 1889; *s* of Ernest Henry Lawley and Anne Elizabeth Jones; *m* Violet Victoria (*d* 1970), *d* of Arthur and Mary Moore; one *d. Educ:* King Edward's High Sch., Birmingham; Jena, Germany. *Recreation:* walking. *Address:* 41 Green Street, Mayfair, W1Y 3FH. *T:* 01-629 7551.
[Died 3 Sept. 1977.

LAWLOR, John, CVO 1969; QPM 1969; a Deputy Assistant Commissioner, Metropolitan Police, New Scotland Yard, 1969-70; *b* 16 March 1906; *s* of William and Janet Lawlor, Liverpool; *m* 1934, Ethel Guimaraes-Hackett; one *s* one *d. Educ:* St Margaret's Sch., Anfield, Liverpool. Joined Metropolitan Police, 1929; served principally in West End; passed through the ranks; Comdr No 1 Dist, 1965-68; on re-organisation of the Force (in 1968), became responsible for Uniformed Police opns throughout Metropolitan Police Dist, with specific responsibilities for commanding Police action in connection with ceremonial events, demonstrations, and public order, as a Comdr "A" Operations Dept, 1968-70, retd. *Recreations:* sport generally, football and fishing in particular. *Address:* Falcons, Netherhampton, Salisbury, Wilts SP2 8PU. *T:* Wilton 3557.
[Died 17 June 1975.

LAWRENCE, Alfred Kingsley, RA 1938 (ARA 1930); RP 1947; Figure Painter; *b* Southover, Lewes, Sussex, 4 Oct. 1893. *Educ:* Armstrong Coll., Newcastle upon Tyne; Royal College of Art, South Kensington. ARCA Travelling Scholarship, 1922. 19th Batt. Northumberland Fusiliers, 1914-18 (despatches); Prix de Rome Scholar, 1923; works: (Mural) The Altruists, Wembley Basilica, 1924; Building Pons Ælii, Newcastle; Queen Elizabeth Commissions Sir Walter Raleigh to discover unknown lands AD

1584, St Stephen's Hall, Houses of Parliament; Committee of Treasury of Bank of England, 1928, and other mural paintings in new Bank of England; County Hall, Chelmsford; The Resurrection, Altarpiece, Church of St James, Beckenham, Kent, etc.; other works: Return of Persephone, Cornish Venus, Leda, etc. Portrait painter, portrait draughtsman. Mem. of Faculty of Painting, British Sch. at Rome, 1926-50; Founder Mem. Council Abbey Scholarships for Mural Painting, 1926-53; Mem. Jury of award, Internat. Exhibition: Ghent, 1929; Carnegie Inst., Pittsburgh, USA, 1936. *Recreation:* the theatre. *Address:* 30 Holland Park Road, Kensington, W14. *T:* 01-937 8879. *Clubs:* Arts, Garrick, Chelsea Arts. *[Died 5 April 1975.*

LAWRENCE, Marjorie Florence, CBE 1977; dramatic soprano; Professor of Voice and Director of Opera Workshop, Southern Illinois University, Carbondale, Illinois, 1960-73, retired; Professor Emeritus; Professor of Voice: University of Arkansas at Little Rock, since 1974; Newcomb College, Tulane University, New Orleans, Louisiana, 1956-60; *b* Dean's Marsh, Vic., Australia; *d* of William Lawrence and Elizabeth Smith; *m* 1941, Dr Thomas Michael King, New York. *Educ:* privately. Studied voice with Mme Cécile Gilly, Paris, Louis Bachner, New York. Début with Monte Carlo Opera Co., as Elizabeth in Tannhäuser, 1932; début with Paris Grand Opera Co., as Ortrud in Lohengrin, 1932; début with Metropolitan Opera Co., as Brüennhilde in Die Walküre, 1935. Has appeared with Chicago, St Louis, and San Francisco opera companies, and in the Teatro Colon of Buenos Aires and Palacio de Belles Artes, Mexico City; has sung with leading symphony orchestras of the world. Stricken with infantile paralysis in Mexico City, June 1941; although unable to walk, made "come-back" as Venus in Tannhäuser at Metropolitan Opera, 1942, and as Isolde in Tristan und Isolde at Metropolitan Opera, 1943: in 1944 made a 50,000-mile troop concert tour of Australia and the South West Pacific; 1945, made two troop concert tours of England, Belgium, Germany, and France, and sang at Buckingham Palace for the King and Queen; 1946, returned to the Paris Opera. Marjorie Lawrence Opera Theater, S Illinois Univ., Carbondale, Ill, dedicated 26 Feb. 1971. FRSA 1969. Hon. DHL Ohio, 1969; Hon. DMus, S Illinois, 1978. Légion d'Honneur (France), 1946. *Publication:* Interrupted Melody, The Story of My Life (New York, Australia and New Zealand, London), 1949 (made into film, 1955; repr. 1969). *Address:* Route 5, Box 152, Hot Springs, Arkansas 71901, USA.
[Died 12 Jan. 1979.

LAWRENCE, Peter Frederick; Editor, Woman Magazine, since 1974; *b* 7 Aug. 1937; *s* of Frederick William Lawrence and Helen Fryer; *m* 1972, Sue Marie Shiret; two *s. Educ:* Clark's Coll.; St Martin's. Layout Artist, Vogue Magazine, 1956-59; Woman's Own: Layout Artist, 1959-64; Asst Art Editor, 1964-66; Art Editor, 1966-70; Art Dir, 1973-74. *Recreations:* cooking, darts, squash, motor racing. *Address:* 62 Donaldson Road, Shooters Hill, SE18. *Club:* Ladbroke's.
[Died 8 June 1976.

LAWRENCE, Lt-Col Richard Travers, CIE 1934; MC; Indian Army, retired; late Secretary to Governor of Punjab; *b* 7 July 1890; *m* 1st, 1933, Elisabeth Margaret (*d* 1937), *d* of Maj.-Gen. G. H. Addison, CB, CMG, DSO; two *d*; 2nd, 1940, Beryl Mary Dru, *d* of Dr Drury Pennington. Commissioned, 1910; Indian Army, 1911; Capt., 1915; Major, 1927; Lt-Col, 1936; retired, 1939. *Address:* Westdown, The Ridgeway, Guildford. *T:* Guildford 4730. *Club:* United Service & Royal Aero.
[Died 17 Feb. 1973.

LAWRENCE, Sir Russell; *see* Lawrence, Sir W. R.

LAWRENCE, Samuel Chave; *b* 9 June 1894; *s* of late John Lawrence, DLit, Prof. of English, Tokyo Univ.; *m* 1st, 1917, Dorothy Austen Storey (*d* 1943); two *d*; 2nd, 1955, Lucia Rosa de Maria. *Educ:* Collège Classique Cantonal, Lausanne; Universities of Tokyo and Berlin. Enlisted Queen's Westminster Rifles, Aug. 1914; 2nd Lt Leicestershire Regt 1915; Lt 1917; Consular Service, 1919; Vice-Consul, Washington, 1920; Cologne, 1924; Acting Consul, Mainz, 1925; Vice-Consul, Naples, 1926; Chicago, 1929; Consul (local rank), Santos, 1931; Acting Consul-Gen., São Paulo, in 1931; Consul at Pará, 1934; Chargé d'Affaires, Tegucigalpa, 1938; Consul, Curacao, 1939; Consul-Gen. (local rank) Duala, 1943; Consul, Turin, 1946-48, retd. *Recreation:* photography. *Address:* 55 Summerland Avenue, Minehead, Som TA24 5BN.
[Died 30 Jan. 1980.

LAWRENCE, Sydney, CBE 1961 (OBE 1951; MBE 1941); QPM; an Inspector of Constabulary for England and Wales, 1962-70; seconded as Commandant, Police College, Oct. 1963-Oct. 1966; *b* 18 Jan. 1905; *s* of Herbert and Margaret Lawrence; *m* 1929, Gladys Gregory; one *s. Educ:* Eccles Gram. Sch., Lancs. Articled clerk to City Treasurer Salford Corporation, 1922-26; joined Salford City Police, 1926, and left when Dep. Chief

Constable, 1945; Chief Constable, Reading, 1945-48; Chief Constable, Kingston upon Hull, 1948-62. Pres. Assoc. of Chief Police Officers, 1960-61. Queen's Police Medal for Distinguished Service, 1955. *Address:* 13 Richmond Grove, Bexhill-on-Sea, E Sussex TN39 3EQ. *T:* Bexhill 210377.
[Died 17 Oct. 1976.

LAWRENCE, Vernon, CBE 1959 (OBE 1942); JP; DL; Clerk of the County Council and Clerk of the Peace for Monmouthshire, 1937-66; also Clerk of the Lieutenancy; Hon. Secretary, Welsh Counties' Committee, 1949-66; *b* 29 Sept. 1899; *s* of William John and Annie Maud Lawrence; *m* 1st, 1919, Gertrude Mary Thomas (*d* 1969), Maesteg, Glam; one *s* one *d*; 2nd, 1971, Mrs Rosilla Vaughan-Trevitt. *Educ:* privately and University of S Wales and Monmouthshire; Cardiff Law Sch. Private Sec., 1919-29; Solicitor's Articled Clerk and Principal Clerk, Glamorgan County Council, 1929-32; Asst County Solicitor and Asst County Prosecuting Solicitor, Glamorgan, 1933-34; County Solicitor and County Prosecuting Solicitor, 1934-37. County ARP Controller for Monmouthshire, 1939-45. Mem., Welsh Advisory Cttee for Civil Aviation; Pres., Rent Assessment Panel for Wales. Mem., Tribunal of Inquiry into Aberfan Disaster, 1966-67. Former Chm., Law Cttee, Soc. of Clerks of the Peace of Counties and Clerks of County Councils. DL, County of Monmouth, 1965. *Recreations:* golf, gardening, motoring. *Address:* Greenover, Castleton, near Cardiff. *Club:* United Service and Royal Aero.   *[Died 29 Nov. 1971.*

LAWRENCE, Sir (William) Russell, Kt 1975; MA, LLB; QC 1973; Barrister-at-Law; Senior Master of the Supreme Court, Queen's Bench Division, and Queen's Remembrancer, 1970-75; *b* 14 Feb. 1903; 3rd and sole surv. *s* of late George Lawrence, Barrister-at-Law, and late Maria Hannah Russell; *m* 1st, 1940, Gertrude Emily Helene (*d* 1948), *d* of Carl Sanders; one *d*; 2nd, 1951, Barbara Mary Constance, *o d* of William Heathcote Morphett; one *s* one *d*. *Educ:* The Abbey Sch., Tipperary; Christ's Coll., Cambridge. Called to Bar, Gray's Inn, Jan. 1927; joined North Eastern circuit, Nov. 1927; practised in London and on NE circuit; Asst Recorder of Newcastle upon Tyne, 1946-51; Recorder of Pontefract, 1950-51; Master of Supreme Court, Queen's Bench Div., 1951-1975. Mem. of the Hendon Borough Council, 1947-51. Served War of 1939-45, Territorial Army 99th HAA Regt RA; active service in ranks until commissioned, May 1940; active service in UK, Iraq, India, and with Middle East Forces as Dep. Judge Advocate (Major), Office of Judge Advocate General of the Forces. Member: Civil Judicial Statistics Cttee, 1966-68; Lord Chancellor's Cttee on European Judgments Conventions, 1973. Pres., Medico-Legal Soc., 1971-73. *Recreations:* lawn tennis, golf, gardening. *Address:* 10 Gray's Inn Square, Gray's Inn, Holborn, WC1. *T:* 01-242 2796. *Clubs:* Junior Carlton; All England Lawn Tennis and Croquet.   *[Died 30 May 1976.*

LAWRIE, James Haldane; Director-General, Air Transport Users Committee; General Administrator, D'Oyly Carte Opera Trust Ltd; *b* 28 March 1907; *e s* of late Allan James Lawrie, KC, and late Ethel Annette Lawrie, *d* of Judge Richard Adams, QC. *Educ:* Newlands, Seaford, Sussex; Fettes Coll., Edinburgh (Open Schol.); University Coll., Oxford (Open Schol.). Lloyds Bank Ltd, 1930-37; Secretary, 1937-45, London Manager, 1940-45, National Bank of New Zealand Ltd; Chm., British Overseas Banks Assoc., 1944-45; Vice-Pres. British Bankers' Assoc., 1944-45; Council London Chamber of Commerce, 1944-48; Gen. Man., 1945-48, Industrial and Commercial Finance Corp. Ltd; Chm. and Man. Dir, National Film Finance Co. Ltd, 1948-49, when it became National Film Finance Corp.; Man. Dir, National Film Finance Corp., 1949-53; film producer and theatrical manager, including 59 Theatre Company, 1953-65; Chm., Air Transport Licensing Bd, 1971-72 (Mem., 1965, Dep. Chm., 1968); full-time Bd Mem. CAA, 1972-76. Mem., BBC Gen. Advisory Council, 1952-59; Chairman: Nat. Sch. of Opera, 1948-63; English Opera Gp, 1950-60; British Film Academy, 1958-59; Phoenix Opera, 1964-75; Sec., Soc. of Film and Television Arts, 1959-61; Member: Plant Cttee on Distribution and Exhibition of Cinematograph Films, 1949; Hutton Cttee on Purchase Tax, 1952. *Address:* Flat 2, 24 Palace Court, W2. *T:* 01-727 8349. *Club:* Savile.   *[Died 10 Dec. 1979.*

LAWS, Group Captain Frederick Charles Victor, CB 1946; CBE 1944 (OBE 1919); President Fairey Air Surveys Ltd; *b* 29 Nov. 1887; *yr s* of late William Laws, Thetford; *m* Grace, *d* of late Samuel Withers; one *d*. Served Coldstream Guards, 1905-12, RFC and RAF, 1912-33, retired; returned active list, 1939-46; reverted to retired list, 1946. Served European War, 1914-18 (despatches); Air Component BEF, 1939-40 (despatches); Air Ministry Air Staff Officer for the development of Air Photography, 1940-46; Managing Director, Race Finish Recording Co., 1946-63. Master Worshipful Company Coach

and Coach Harness Makers, 1955; Upper Freeman, Guild of Air Pilots, 1956. FRPS, 1920; President Photogrametric Society, 1955-57 (Vice-President, 1952); President's Medal, 1958; Hon. Member, 1962. Chairman National Cttee for Photogrametry, 1955-63. Legion of Merit, Degree of Officer (USA), 1945; Legion of Honour; Croix de Guerre (1939-45), with Palm (France). *Address:* 22 Dukes Lodge, Holland Park, W11. *T:* 01-727 9761. *Club:* Royal Air Force.   *[Died 27 Oct. 1975.*

LAWSON, George McArthur; *b* Edinburgh, 11 July 1906; *s* of Alexander Lawson and Euphemia Gordon McPherson McArthur; *m* 1939, Margaret Robertson Munro; two *s* (and one *s* decd). *Educ:* St Bernard's; North Merchiston elementary schools. Staff tutor with National Council of Labour Colleges, 1937-40; West of Scotland Organiser with NCLC, 1940-50; Secretary, Edinburgh Trades Council, 1950-54. MP (Lab) Lanarkshire, Motherwell, April 1954-Feb. 1974, Motherwell and Wishaw, Feb.-Oct. 1974, retired; an An Opposition Whip, 1959-64; Government Whip, 1964; Dep. Chief Government Whip, 1966-67. Mem., Scottish Adv. Cttee, Nature Conservancy Council; Exec. Mem., Nat. Trust for Scotland. Campaign Dir, Scotland is British Campaign, 1976-. *Address:* Brooklyn, 37 Burnblea Street, Hamilton, Lanarkshire. *T:* Hamilton 21691.
[Died 3 July 1978.

LAWSON, Sir Henry (Brailsford), Kt 1963; MC 1917; retired as Chief Legal Adviser and a Deputy Chief General Manager, Lloyds Bank Ltd, 1963; *b* 19 Feb. 1898; *s* of H. P. Lawson; *m* 1930, Mona Lilian, *e d* of Dr B. Thorne Thorne; three *s* one *d*. *Educ:* Lancing Coll.; Trinity Coll., Cambridge (BA, LLB). Member Council, 1943, Vice-President, 1961-62, President, 1962-63, of Law Society. *Address:* Churchmead, Pirbright, Surrey. *T:* Brookwood 4133.   *[Died 10 Dec. 1978.*

LAWSON, John, CB 1955; *b* 10 Nov. 1893; *y s* of late Thomas Lawson, Clapham; *m* 1933, Millicent Mary, *y d* of late Samuel White, Taunton, and *widow* of Lieut-Colonel T. W. Bullock. *Educ:* Dulwich Coll.; Merton Coll., Oxford (Postmaster). Served European War, 1914-18, Sherwood Foresters. 1st Class Lit. Hum. Oxford, 1920; MA. Admiralty, 1921; Principal Assistant Secretary, 1945; Under Secretary, Admiralty, 1948-56. *Address:* 2 Sefton House, Terminus Road, Bexhill-on-Sea, E Sussex TN39 3LR. *T:* Bexhill 1997.   *[Died 1 Feb. 1977.*

LAWSON, Colonel Sir Peter Grant, 2nd Bt, *cr* 1905; *b* 28 July 1903; *s* of 1st Bt and Sylvia (*d* 1962), *y d* of Charles Hunter, Selaby Hall, nr Darlington; *S father*, 1919; *m* 1940, Virginia, *d* of Sidney B. Dean, St Paul, Minn, USA, and Mrs Northup Dean, Burghfield, Berks. 2nd Lieut RHG, 1925; Lieut, 1927; Captain, 1934; Major, 1942; Lieut-Colonel, 1948; Colonel, 1952; retired, 1954. Served War of 1939-45 (despatches). Heir: none. *Address:* Venards House, North Gorley, Fordingbridge, Hampshire. *T:* Fordingbridge 53104.   *[Died 21 March 1973 (ext.)*

LAWSON, Sir Ralph Henry, 4th Bt, *cr* 1841; *b* 27 Sept. 1905; *s* of Sir Henry Joseph Lawson, 3rd Bt, and Ursula Mary, *o c* of late Philip John Canning Howard, Corby Castle, Carlisle; *S father*, 1947; *m* 1st, 1935, Lilyan Mary (*d* 1968), *e d* of Sir Edmund Chaytor, 6th Bt, and Isobel, Lady Chaytor; two *d*; 2nd, 1970, Mrs Helen Beresford Petre. *Educ:* Ampleforth. *Recreations:* all field sports. Heir: *b* William Howard Lawson [*b* 15 July 1907; *m* 1933, Joan Eleanor, *d* of late Major Arthur Cowie Stamer, CBE; three *s* one *d*]. *Address:* Wood House, Catterick, Yorks.
[Died 13 Feb. 1975.

LAWSON, Sir William (Halford), Kt 1962; CBE 1948; FCA; formerly Senior Partner in Binder, Hamlyn & Company, Chartered Accountants; *b* 21 March 1899; *s* of late H. P. Lawson; *m* 1931, Susan Elisabeth Bray; three *s* three *d*. *Educ:* Lancing; Trinity Coll., Cambridge. Pres., Institute of Chartered Accountants, 1957-58. Delegate on Austrian Treaty Commission in Vienna, 1947. Member: Transport Arbitration Tribunal, 1948-57; Purchase Tax (Valuation) Cttee, 1952; Royal Commission on Local Government in Greater London, 1957-60; Cttee to enquire into Company Law, 1959-62; Board of Trade Companies Act Accountancy Advisory Cttee, 1955-68; Chairman: (part-time) Iron and Steel Holding and Realisation Agency, 1962-67; Taxation Cttee, CBI, 1965-69; Arbitral Bodies for remuneration of Teachers, 1965-69; Min. of Technology (formerly BoT) Adv. Cttee under Local Employment Acts, 1966-; Review Bd for Government Contracts, 1969-. *Address:* Sands Lodge, Leigh Lane, Farnham, Surrey. *Clubs:* City of London, United University.   *[Died 3 Feb. 1971.*

LAWTHER, Barry Charles Alfred, CIE 1931; *b* 25 Aug. 1888. Indian Police Service in Punjab and NWF Province; retired 1934; Ministry of Home Security, 1941-42. *Address:* c/o National & Grindlay's Bank Ltd, 13 St James's Square, SW1. *Club:* Royal Commonwealth Society.   *[Died 3 March 1974.*

LAWTHER, Sir William, Kt 1949; JP; Past President National Union of Mineworkers; Past President Trades Union Congress; Past Secretary Miners' International; *b* Northumberland, 1889; *m* 1915, Lottie Laws (*d* 1962). *Educ:* Colliery Sch.; Central Labour Coll., London. Contested S Shields, 1922-23-24; MP (Lab) Barnard Castle, 1929-31; Durham CC, 1925-29; Member National Labour Party Exec. Cttee, 1923-26. TUC General Council, 1935-54. Chevalier of the Legion of Honour. *Recreation:* enjoyment in watching others enjoy themselves. *Address:* 6 Grange Close, Marden, Cullercoats, North Shields, Tyne and Wear. *T:* North Shields 72589. *[Died 1 Feb. 1976.*

LAYBOURNE, Rear-Adm. Alan Watson, CB 1955; CBE 1944 (OBE 1942); DL; a Governor and Almoner of Christ's Hospital; *b* 29 Nov. 1898; *s* of late William Watson Laybourne, Liverpool; *m* 1926, Helen, *d* of late George Gorrie Burnett, Toronto; one *s* one *d. Educ:* Christ's Hospital. Joined RN (Supply and Secretariat Branch), Jan. 1916. Served European War, 1916-19: Grand Fleet (Jutland), Mesopotamia; North Atlantic Convoys; served War of 1939-45: Scapa; Eastern Fleet and in USA (OBE, CBE). Promoted Captain 1947; Rear-Adm. 1952; retired 1955. Clerk to the Dean and Chapter of Durham, 1955-69; Member: House of Laity, Church Assembly, 1960-66; Cathedrals Commn, 1963-68. DL, Durham, 1967. OStJ 1968. *Recreation:* idleness. *Address:* 2 Vicar's Close, Chichester, W Sussex. *T:* Chichester 89219. *Club:* Naval and Military.
[Died 6 Feb. 1977.

LEA-COX, Maj.-Gen. Maurice, CB 1952; CBE 1946 (OBE 1941); *b* 8 Feb. 1898; *s* of Charles and Lizzie Maria Lea-Cox; *m* 1st, 1923, Joyce (*née* Duchesne); one *s* one *d*; 2nd, 1949, Ivy May Ashley (*née* Biggs). *Educ:* Eastbourne Coll.; RMA, Woolwich. 2nd Lieut, RA, 1916; Lieut, 1917; Captain, 1929; Bt Major, 1937; Major, 1938; Acting Lieut-Colonel, 1940; Colonel, 1944; transf. RAOC, 1945; Brig., 1948; Maj.-Gen., 1951. Served European War, France, Belgium, 1916-18 (British War and Victory Medals); NW Frontier (Mohmand), 1933 (Medal and Clasp); despatches, 1934; NW Frontier (Mohmand), 1935 (Clasp), France, 1940, AQMG 1940; Dep. Director Warlike Stores, DOS (W) War Office, 1941; DDOS (W) War Office, 1946; Commandant, BAOR, 1947; DOS BAOR, 1948; Commander, Mechanical Transport Organisation, 1951-April 1954, retired. Legion of Merit, USA, 1945. *Recreation:* gardening. *Address:* Tythe Barn, Fremington, Devon. *T:* Fremington 418. *[Died 23 May 1974.*

LEACH, Arthur Gordon, CIE 1933; late Indian Civil Service; *b* 16 March 1885; *s* of A. F. Leach, Charity Commissioner; *m* 1914, Margaret Sydney Woods (*d* 1969); one *d* (one *s* decd). *Educ:* Bradfield Coll.; New Coll., Oxford. Entered Indian Civil Service 1909; served in Madras as Sub-Collector, Special Settlement Officer, Collector and Sec. to Government in the Public Works and Labour Dept; retd 1934; Mem. Legislative Assembly, Delhi, 1933; IARO attached 9th Gurkha Rifles, 1917-19. *Address:* Cuttmill Rise, Puttenham, Guildford. *T:* Elstead 3147.
[Died 21 April 1978.

LEACH, Bernard (Howell), CH 1973; CBE 1962; Founder and Director of The Leach Pottery, St Ives, Cornwall, since 1920; *b* 5 Jan. 1887; *o s* of Andrew John Leach, Puisne Judge, Straits Settlements; *m* 1st, 1909, Edith Muriel, *o d* of Dr William Evans Hoyle, Dir of the Nat. Museum of Wales, Cardiff; two *s* three *d*; 2nd, 1936, Laurie Cookes; one adopted *s*; 3rd, 1955, Janet Darnell, American potter. *Educ:* Beaumont Coll.; Slade Sch. of Art. Studied at Slade Sch. of Art, 1903. Practised etching; went to Japan, 1909, studied pottery under Kenzan VI; returned to England, started The Leach Pottery at St Ives, Cornwall; revisited Japan and Korea, 1934-35; exhibited widely in England and abroad, and taught many students; lectured across USA, sponsored by Inst. of Contemp. Art, 1950, 1953, 1960; revisited Japan as guest of Nat. Craft Soc. Exhibitions: with Shoji Hamada, at Gallerie de France, Paris, 1964; Caracas, 1966; Crane Kalman Gall., London, 1967; Tokyo, Osaka, Okinawa and London, 1969, 1971; London, Tokyo, Okayama, 1973. Visited Venezuela and Columbia on Lectures and Exhibns for Brit. Council, 1966. Retrospective Exhibns: Arts Council, London, 1961; Tokyo, 1961; V&A 1977. Amer. Ceramic Soc., Binns Medal for 1950; Japanese Foundn Award, 1974. Fellow, UCL, 1974. Hon. DLitt Exeter, 1961. Order of the Sacred Treasure (Japan), 2nd Class, 1966. Freedom of the Borough of St Ives, 1968. *Publications:* A Potter's Book, 1940; A Potter's Portfolio, 1951; Japan Diary (in Japanese), 1953-54; (Eng. trans A Potter in Japan, 1960); Kenzan and His Tradition, 1966; (with J. P. Hodin) Bernard Leach: a potter's work, 1967; Drawings, Verse & Belief, 1973; Shoji Hamada, Potter, 1976; Bernard Leach: the potter's challenge, 1976; Beyond East and West: memoirs, portraits and essays, 1978. *Recreations:* cricket, tennis. *Address:* The Leach Pottery, St Ives, Cornwall. *T:* St Ives 6398.
[Died 6 May 1979.

LEACH, Charles Harold, CBE 1963; MA, FCA; retired; *b* 2 May 1901; *s* of late John Herbert Charles Leach; *m* 1928, Nora Eunice Ashworth (*d* 1975); two *s*; *m* 1975, Buntie Frith, Aldeburgh. *Educ:* Manchester Grammar Sch.; Brasenose Coll., Oxford. Articled Clerk, W. Bolton and Co., Manchester, 1923-26; Asst Sec., Alliance and Dublin Consumers Gas Co., Dublin, 1927-39; Gen. Manager and Sec., Liverpool Gas Co., Liverpool, 1939-49; Gen. Manager, Liverpool Group, North Western Gas Board, 1949-55; Chm., Southern Gas Board, 1956-61; Chm., West Midlands Gas Board, 1961-66. OStJ 1961. *Recreation:* bridge, previously lacrosse (Half Blue OU). *Address:* 6 Western Avenue, Branksome Park, Poole, Dorset BH13 7AL.
[Died 7 Oct. 1975.

LEACH, Thomas Stephen, CMG 1959; MC 1916; Chief Inspector of Fisheries, Ministry of Agriculture, Fisheries and Food, 1948-61, retired; *b* 20 Sept. 1896; *s* of Henry Robert Leach, Rickmansworth, Herts; *m* 1921, Eileen Isabel (*d* 1972), *d* of Sir Rowland Whitehead, 3rd Bt, Wallingford, Berks; two *s* one *d. Educ:* Aldenham. Joined 18th Royal Fusiliers, 1914; commissioned, 1916, 14th Hampshire Regt (MC). Joined Min. of Agriculture and Fisheries, 1919. *Recreations:* fishing and gardening. *Address:* Stockbridge Cottage, Tilford, Surrey. *T:* Frensham 2348. *[Died 17 Feb. 1973.*

LEADBITTER, Sir Eric Cyril Egerton, KCVO 1951 (CVO 1937); Kt 1946; *b* 8 June 1891; *y s* of late T. F. Leadbitter of Warden, near Hexham, Northumberland; *m* W. Irene, *d* of late Frederick Lloyd. *Educ:* Shrewsbury. Entered Public Trustee Office, 1910; Royal Naval Reserve, 1917-19; Asst Principal, Treasury, 1919; Private Sec. to Controller of Establishments, 1919-21; Private Sec. to Permanent Sec., 1921-28; Senior Clerk, Privy Council Office, 1928-34; Dep. Clerk of the Council, 1934-42; Clerk, 1942-51. *Publications:* Rain before Seven, 1915; The Road to Nowhere, 1916; Perpetual Fires, 1918; Shepherd's Warning, 1920; Dead Reckoning, 1922; The Evil that Men Do, 1923. *Address:* Oak Lodge, Bayhall Road, Tunbridge Wells.
[Died 25 Feb. 1971.

LEAK, Hector, CBE 1942; *b* 23 July 1887; *s* of late Dr Hector Leak and Miriam A. Bagott, Winsford, Cheshire; *m* 1916, Kathleen (*d* 1948), *d* of Capt. W. H. Ridgway, Birkenhead; four *s. Educ:* Berkhamsted Sch.; Caius Coll., Cambridge (Major Scholar). 9th Wrangler, 1908; BA 1909; entered Board of Trade, 1911; served on secretariat of International Conference on Safety of Life at Sea, 1914, of Imperial Conference, 1930, and of UK Delegation to International Monetary and Economic Conference, 1933; Asst Sec., 1932; Dir of Statistics, 1946; Adviser on Statistics, Board of Trade, 1948-51; Guy Medal, Royal Statistical Soc., 1939; Mem. of Council Royal Statistical Soc., 1933-49; Pres., 1941; Mem. of Internat. Institute of Statistics, 1937. *Publications:* Papers read before Royal Statistical Society. *Recreation:* gardening. *Address:* Bracondale, 8 Brook Barn Way, Goring-by-Sea, Sussex. *T:* Worthing 41091.
[Died 5 April 1976.

LEAKE, Hugh Martin-, ScD (Cambridge); *b* 28 Oct. 1878; *s* of late William Martin Leake, Ceylon; *m* 1914, Lois Millicent Frieda Bloxam; one *s* (elder son killed in action). *Educ:* Dulwich; Christ's Coll., Cambridge. Biologist, Bihar Indigo Planters' Association, 1901-4; Economic Botanist to Govt United Provinces, India, 1904-19; Dir of Agriculture, United Provinces, 1919-23; services to Egyptian Government, 1919; Sudan Government, 1923-24; Principal, Imperial Coll. of Tropical Agriculture, Trinidad, 1924-27. Agric. Editor, Internat. Sugar Jl, 1932-63. *Publications:* The Foundations of Indian Agriculture; Land Tenure and Agricultural Production in the Tropics; Unity, National and Imperial; Recent Advances in Agricultural Plant Breeding (with Dr H. H. Hunter); Things not Generally Said; numerous papers in scientific journals. *Recreation:* rifle shooting. *Address:* Wardington House, Wardington, near Banbury, Oxon. *[Died 29 April 1977.*

LEAKE, Sidney Henry, OBE 1918; retired, 1958, as Chairman and Senior Managing Director of Lewis's Investment Trust, Ltd and its Associated Companies, including Selfridge's; Chairman, Entre Rios (Pvt) Ltd, Bromley, Rhodesia, since 1963; *b* 31 May 1892; *s* of Henry and Elizabeth Leake; *m* 1924, Gertrude Elizabeth, *d* of Albert Burnell; two *s* one *d. Educ:* Model Sch. and Teachers' Training Coll., York. Ministry of Munitions, 1915-19, including service with Mil. Mission in Russia, 1917; War Office, 1919; Colonial Office, 1920; Crosse & Blackwell, 1921-23; joined Lewis's, 1923: Gen. Manager; Director; Managing Director; Dep. Chm. *Recreations:* golf, gardening. *Address:* Entre Rios, Bromley, Rhodesia. *Club:* Salisbury (Rhodesia). *[Died 28 Jan. 1973.*

LEAKEY, Louis Seymour Bazett, MA, PhD; FBA 1958; Hon. Director of the National Centre of Pre-History and Palæontology, Nairobi (Hon. Keeper, 1961 and 1962), since 1962; *b* Kabete, 7 Aug. 1903; *er s* of late Canon H. Leakey, of CMS Kabete, Kenya; *m* 1st, 1928, H. Wilfrida, 3rd *d* of late Henry Avern, Reigate, Surrey; one *s* one *d* ; 2nd, Mary Douglas, *o d* of late Erskine E. Nicol; three *s. Educ:* Weymouth Coll.; St John's Coll., Cambridge (Fellow, 1929-34; Hon. Fellow, 1966); FGS; FRAI. Leverhulme Res. Fellow, 1933-35. Major Lectures and Lecture Series include: Jane Ellen Harrison Meml, 1934; Munroe, Edinburgh Univ., 1936; Herbert Spencer, Oxford Univ., 1960-61; Huxley Meml, Birmingham Univ., 1961; Siliman Meml, Yale, 1963-64; Regents' Prof., Univ. of California at Riverside, 1963; George R. Miller Prof., Urbana, Illinois, 1965; Andrew D. White Prof. at Large, Cornell Univ., 1966-72; Hon. Prof. of Anatomy, Nairobi Univ., 1969-; research into customs of Kikuyu tribe for Rhodes Trustees, 1937-39 (Mem. Govt Cttee to report on Kikuyu Land Tenure, 1929). Mem., British Museum E African Expdn to Tanganyika Territory, 1924; Leader, E African Archeological Res. Expdns, 1926-27, 1928-29, 1931-32, 1934-35. CID Nairobi: OC special branch 6, 1939-45; hand-writing expert, 1943-51. Curator, Coryndon Meml Museum, Nairobi, 1945-61 (Hon. Curator, 1941-45); Pan-African Congress on Pre-history: Gen. Sec., 1947-51; Pres., 1955-59. Distinguished Lecture, Amer. Assoc. Advancement of Science Meetings, Philadelphia, Dec. 1971. Trustee: Motor Mart Trust, 1957; Royal Kenya Nat. Parks, 1948-62; Kenya Wild Life Soc., 1957; East Africa Kennel Club: Vice-Pres. and Chm. of Cttee, 1957; Judge of Grand Challenge Class, 1958; Pres., 1959-60; Pres., S African Archaeological Soc., 1960-61; Corresp. Mem., Zool. Soc.; Hon. Life Member: NY Acad. of Sci., 1962; Explorers' Club, 1964; Archaeological Survey Assoc. of S Calif., 1971. Hon. DSc: Oxford, 1953; E Africa, 1965; Hon. LLD: California, 1963; Guelph, 1969. Andrée Medal, Swedish Geog. Soc., 1933; Cuthbert Peek prize, RGS, 1933; Rivers Meml Medal, Royal Anthrop. Inst., 1952; Henry Stopes Meml Medal, Geolog. Assoc., 1955; (jtly with Mrs Leakey) Hubbard Medal, Nat. Geog. Soc., 1962; Viking Medal, Venner-Gren Foundn, 1962; Swedish Vega Medal, 1963; Royal Medal, RGS, 1964; Richard Hopper Day Meml Medal, Acad. of Nat. Scis of Philadelphia, 1964; Welcome Medal, Royal African Soc., 1968; Science Medal, Acad. for Biol. Scis, Italy, 1968; (jtly) Haile Selassie Award, 1968; (jtly with Dr M. D. Leakey) Prestwich Medal, Geol. Soc., 1969. Commander, Nat. Order of Senegal, 1968. *Publications:* New Classification of Bow and Arrow in Africa in the JRAI, 1930; The Stone-age Cultures of Kenya, 1931; Adam's Ancestors, 1934 (rev. edn, 1953); The Stone-age Races of Kenya, 1935 (new edn 1971); Stone-age Africa, 1936; Kenya Contrasts and Problems, 1936 (new edn 1969); White African, 1937 (new edn 1969); (with W. E. Owen) A Contribution to the Study of the Tumbian Culture in Kenya, 1945; Tentative Study of the Pleistocene Sequence and Stone-age Cultures of NE Angola, 1949; Olduvai Gorge, 1952; Mau Mau and the Kikuyu, 1952; (with Ylla) Animals in Africa, 1953; Defeating Mau Mau, 1954; The Pleistocene Fossil Suidæ of East Africa, 1958; First Lesson in Kikuyu, 1959; Olduvai Gorge, 1951-61, vol. 1: (with V. Goodall) Unveiling Man's Origins, 1968; Animals of East Africa, 1969; Gen. Editor, Fossil Vertebrates in Africa, 1969-; articles in scientific journals; contributions to: Encyclopædia Britannica; Chambers's Encyclopædia; The World Encyclopædia. *Recreations:* reading; tropical fish aquaria. *Address:* PO Box 15028, Langata, Nairobi, Kenya.   *[Died 1 Oct. 1972.*

LEAN, (Edward) Tangye, CBE 1952; Director, External Broadcasting, BBC, 1964-67 (Assistant Director, 1952-64); *b* 23 Feb. 1911; 2nd *s* of Francis William le Blount Lean and Helena Anne Tangye; *m* Doreen Myra Sharp; two *s* one *d. Educ:* Leighton Park; University Coll., Oxford. Editor, The Isis, 1932-33. Junior Leader Writer, News Chronicle, 1934, Leader Page Editor, 1936; Govt work in England and Scandinavia, 1939-40. Talks Asst, BBC German Service, 1941; News Commentator, 1942; Editor, BBC French Service for Europe, 1943; West European Services Dir, 1945; Principal Asst to Controller European Services, 1946; Editor, European Services, 1947; Controller, European Services, 1949. *Publications:* Of Unsound Mind, 1931; Spirit of Death, 1932; Storm in Oxford, 1933; Voices in the Darkness, 1943; A Study of Toynbee, 1947; The Napoleonists, 1970. *Address:* 89 Albert Street, NW1.   *[Died 28 Oct. 1974.*

LEASK, Air Vice-Marshal Kenneth Malise St Clair Graeme, CB 1945; MC 1918; MIMechE; RAF (retired); *b* 30 Oct. 1896; *s* of late John Leask, MB, CM, Boardhouse, Birsay, Orkney; *m* 1923, Lydia Alexandrovna, *d* of Alexander N. Modestoff of Tver (Kalinin); one *d. Educ:* St Bees Sch.; Victoria Coll., Jersey. 2nd Lt Devon Regt 1914; seconded to Machine-Gun Corps 1915 and to RFC 1916, and trained as pilot: with BEF France in Nos 42,

41 and 84 Sqdns, 1916, Lt 1917, Capt. 1917, regular Army commission in Devonshire Regt (MC and Bar). Permanent Commission in RAF as Flight Lt, 1919; at HQ Southern Area and Inland Area, 1919-20; in No 208 Squadron, Egypt and Turkey as Flight Comdr, 1921-23; in Directorate of Intelligence, Air Ministry, 1923-26; Squadron Leader, 1925; Senior Officers' Course, Sheerness, 1926; Officers' Long Engineering Course, 1926-28; CTO No. 4 Apprentices Wing, Halton, 1928-29; CTO Aircraft Depot, Karachi, India, 1929-32; OC No 60 Squadron, Kohat, 1932-33; Wing Comdr 1933; Senior Engineer Staff Officer, HQ, RAF, India, 1933-34; Senior Engineer Staff Officer HQ ADGB and Bomber Command, 1935-40 (despatches); Group Capt., 1938; AOC No 43 Group as Acting Air Commodore, 1940, and as Acting Air Vice-Marshal, 1942; Air Commodore and Air Vice-Marshal, 1946; Air Officer Commanding No 24 Group, RAF, 1944-47. Dir-Gen. of Engineering, Air Ministry, 1947-49. *Recreation:* photography. *Address:* Per Ardua, Vache Lane, Chalfont St Giles, Bucks.   *[Died 24 April 1974.*

LEAVIS, Frank Raymond, CH 1978; PhD; Hon. Visiting Professor of English, University of York, 1965; Hon. Fellow of Downing College, Cambridge, 1962-64 (Fellow, 1936-62); University Reader in English, 1959-62; Editor of Scrutiny, a Quarterly Review, 1932-53; *b* 14 July 1895; *s* of Harry Leavis; *m* 1929, Queenie Dorothy Roth; two *s* one *d. Educ:* Perse Sch.; Emmanuel Coll., Cambridge (Scholar). Historical Tripos and English Tripos; research and university teaching; one of the founders of Scrutiny, 1932. Cheltenham Lectr, 1968; Vis. Prof., Univ. of Wales, 1969; Churchill Prof. Dept of English, Bristol Univ., 1970. Hon. Mem. Amer. Acad. of Arts and Sciences, 1963. Hon. LittD: Leeds, 1965; York, 1967; QUB, 1973; Delhi, 1973; Hon. LLD Aberdeen, 1970. *Publications:* Mass Civilization and Minority Culture, 1930; D. H. Lawrence, 1930; New Bearings in English Poetry, 1932; For Continuity, 1933; Culture and Environment (with Denys Thompson), 1933; Revaluation: Tradition and Development in English Poetry, 1936; Education and the University, 1943; The Great Tradition: George Eliot, James and Conrad, 1948; The Common Pursuit, 1952; D. H. Lawrence: Novelist, 1955; Two Cultures?: The Significance of C. P. Snow, 1962; Retrospect of Scrutiny, 1963; Anna Karenina and Other Essays, 1967; (comp.) A Selection from Scrutiny, 1968; (with Q. D. Leavis) Lectures in America, 1969; English Literature in Our Time and the University, 1969; (with Q. D. Leavis) Dickens the Novelist, 1970; Nor Shall My Sword, 1972; Letters in Criticism, 1974; The Living Principle: English as a Discipline of Thought, 1975; Thought, Words and Creativity, 1976. Editor, Towards Standards of Criticism, 1933; Determinations, 1934; Mill on Bentham and Coleridge, 1950. *Address:* 12 Bulstrode Gardens, Cambridge.   *[Died 14 April 1978.*

LECKIE, Air Marshal Robert, CB 1943; DSO 1917; DSC 1916; DFC 1918; retired; *b* 16 April 1890; *o s* of late Samuel Leckie, Glasgow; *m* Bernice, *y d* of Mrs Douglas O'Kane, La Plata, Maryland, USA. *Educ:* Glasgow. Joined RNAS 1915; served in North Sea, European War, 1914-18 (despatches, DSC, DFC, DSO); Lieut-Colonel 1st Central Ontario Regt; commanded No. 1 Canadian Wing, RCAF; Director of Flying Operations, Canadian Air Board, 1920; Member Canadian Air Board, 1921-22; Boys' Training Wing, Halton (RAF), 1922; RN Staff Coll., England, 1922-23; HQ Staff Coastal Comd, 1923-25; commanded: (RAF) HMS Hermes (Aircraft Carrier), 1925-27; (RAF) HMS Courageous (Aircraft Carrier), 1927-29; RAF Station, Bircham Newton, 1929-31; at RAF Marine Experimental Station, Felixstowe, England, 1931; commanded: 210 Flying Boat Squadron, 1931; RAF Station, Pembroke Dock, 1931-33; RAF Station, Hendon, 1933-35; Supt RAF Reserve, i/c Elem. Civil Flying Schools, 1933-35; ADC to the King, 1936; Director of Training, Air Ministry, 1935-38; commanded RAF Medit. (HQ Malta), 1938-39; to Canada as Director of Training, RCAF, 1940; Member Air Council for Training, RCAF, 1940; Acting Chief of Air Staff, RCAF, 1943; Chief of Air Staff, RCAF, 1944; retired, 1947. Order of Polonia Restituta, 1st Class (Poland); US Legion of Merit, Degree of Commander; Order of White Lion, Class II (Czechoslovakia); Commandeur de la Légion d'Honneur (France). *Publications:* various articles, magazines and service journals. *Recreations:* golf, hunting and fishing. *Address:* 303 Acacia Avenue, Rockcliffe Park, Ottawa, Ontario K1M 0M1, Canada. *Clubs:* Royal Air Force; Gatineau Fish and Game.   *[Died 1 April 1975.*

LEDGER, Claude Kirwood, CBE 1943; retired; *b* Hereford, 1 Jan. 1888; 3rd *s* of Rev. Charles George Ledger and Isabel Mary Kirwood; *m* 1919, Elsie (*née* Litton) (*d* 1972); two *s* two *d. Educ:* Christ's Hospital; Hereford Cathedral Sch.; Wadham Coll., Oxford (BA 1911); Hannover and Marburg; Paris; Gray's Inn. Modern Languages Master at Leighton Park Sch., Reading,

1911-12, and at Haberdashers' Aske's Boys' Sch., Cricklewood, 1912-13; Vice-Consul, Antwerp, 1914; New York, 1914-20; Chargé d'Affaires, Dominican Republic, 1920-22; Consul, Belgian and French Congo, 1922-24; Madeira and Azores, 1924-31; Acting Consul-General, Monrovia, 1926-27; Consul, Bordeaux, 1931-37; Havre, 1937-40; Consul-General, Strasbourg, 1940; Lourenço-Marques, 1940-44; Léopoldville, 1944-46; Strasbourg, 1946-48; Tetuan, Spanish Morocco; retired, 1948. Coronation Medal, 1937. *Recreation:* philately. *Address:* Pendene, 22 Cunningham Hill Road, St Albans, Herts AL1 5BY. *[Died 19 Aug. 1974.*

LEDINGHAM, Colonel George Alexander, DSO 1940; MC; *b* 8 March 1890; *e s* of late Alexander Ledingham, SSC, Advocate in Aberdeen; *m* 1918, Ethel Curtis Thomson (marr. diss. 1952); one *d.* Served European War (despatches, MC, wounded); commanded 98th (Surrey and Sussex Yeomanry QMR) Field Regt, RA, 1937-42 (despatches twice, DSO); Colonel, 1942; Commander Military Government, South Brabant, on liberation, 1944, and Province of Westphalia occupation, 1945; Secretary-General United Nations War Crimes Commission, 1945-48. *Recreations:* croquet, handicraft; played Rugby football for Scotland, 1913; captained United Services *v* South Africans, 1917. *Address:* 63 Ridgeway North, PO Box BW 326, Borrowdale, Rhodesia. *T:* 884148. *[Died 8 Nov. 1978.*

LEDUC, Paul, BA, LLD; Barrister; *b* 28 Jan. 1889; *s* of Napoléon Leduc and Joséphine Béliveau; *m* 1917, Gabrielle Belcourt; one *s* one *d. Educ:* Collège Ste Marie, Montreal; Seminary of Quebec; Laval Univ. Called Quebec Bar, 1911; Practised Quebec until 1915, then moved to Ottawa; called Ontario Bar, 1916; practised law Ottawa, 1916-34, when retired from practice upon joining cabinet; MLA for Province of Ontario for the Riding of Ottawa East, 1934-40; Minister of Mines for Ontario, 1934-40; Attorney-General for Ontario, April to October 1937; Registrar Supreme Court of Canada, 1940-58. QC (Quebec), 1927; (Ontario), 1934. *Recreation:* reading. *Address:* 200 Rideau Terrace, Ottawa, Canada. *[Died 17 Dec. 1971.*

LEE, Maj.-Gen. Alec Wilfred, CB 1946; MC 1915; retired; *b* 20 Aug. 1896; *s* of late Wilfred Lee, Heathfield, Nailsea, Somerset; *m* 1938, Mary Alison Horn (*d* 1939); *m* 1947, Pamela Blanche Hammick, MBE (*d* 1969), *yr d* of late Capt. S. F. Hammick; *m* 1970, Margaret Lyndsey Norman, Te Puke, New Zealand. *Educ:* Clifton Coll. Commissioned S Stafford Regt, 1914; served France and Italy, 1915-19 (despatches 6 times); Captain, 1923; Bt Major, 1932; psc; Directing Staff, Staff Coll., 1933-36; Bt Lt-Col, 1936; transferred Royal Irish Fusiliers, 1937; Col, 1939; Brig., 1940; served France, 1939-40 (despatches); Libya, 1942-43; D/Comdr British Army Staff, Washington, 1944-47; Temp. Maj.-Gen., 1944; ADC to King, 1946-47. Colonel: S Stafford Regt, 1954-59; The Staffordshire Regt (The Prince of Wales's), 1959-61; retired, 1947. Commander Legion of Merit (USA). *Publications:* articles for Encyclopædia Britannica. *Recreations:* sailing, fishing, polo, travel. *Address:* Red Poulden, Tisbury, Wilts. *T:* Tisbury 287. *Clubs:* Naval and Military; Royal Dart Yacht. *[Died 5 July 1973.*

LEE, Alfred Morgan; Member, Press Council, 1961-73; Chairman, Joseph Woodhead & Sons Ltd, Huddersfield, 1972-74 (Director, 1949-74); Editor, The Huddersfield Examiner, 1965-67, retd (Joint Editor, 1959-65); *b* 11 Nov. 1901; *s* of John William and Sally Lee; *m* 1924, Nellie Brierley; one *s* one *d. Educ:* Huddersfield Coll. (secondary sch.). Joined staff of Huddersfield Examiner, 1915: Sports Editor, 1930-42; War Correspondent, 1942-45; News Editor, 1945. FJI 1962. *Address:* 8 Lightridge Road, Fixby, Huddersfield, W Yorks. *T:* Huddersfield 20511. *[Died 11 Aug. 1975.*

LEE, Air Vice-Marshal Arthur Stanley Gould, MC 1917; retired; *b* 31 Aug. 1894; *s* of late Arthur Lee, Nottinghamshire; *m* 1st, 1916, Gwyneth (*d* 1951), *d* of late Robert Lewis, Cheshire; one *d*; 2nd, 1953, Fay, *widow* of Sqdn-Leader M. R. Atkinson (killed air operations, 1942). Served European War, 1914-18: Sherwood Foresters, RFC (46 Fighter Sqn), RAF; Gen. Headquarters, Iraq, 1925-27; psa 1928; No. 10 (B) Squadron, 1929-30; Air Ministry (Air Staff), 1931-34; idc 1935; commanded RAF Station, Hornchurch (54, 65 and 74 Fighter Sqns), 1935-37; Group Captain, 1938; Air Commodore, 1942; Air Vice-Marshal, 1945; Chief Instructor, Turkish Air Force Staff Coll., 1937-40; SAO, British Air Forces, Greece, 1941 (despatches, Order of King George I of Greece, with crossed swords); Deputy SASO, Middle East HQ, 1941-42; SASO, No 12 Group, Fighter Command, 1943-44 (despatches); Chief of Air Section, British Armistice Control Commn, Roumania, 1944; Chief of British Military-Air Mission to Marshal Tito, Yugoslavia, 1945; retired, 1946. Chm., Anglo-Turkish Soc., 1958-62, Vice-Pres., 1962-. Order of Partisan Star, Yugoslavia,

1970. *Publications:* Special Duties in the Balkans and the Near East, 1946; The Royal House of Greece, 1948; Crown against Sickle (story of King Michael of Roumania), 1950; The Empress Frederick Writes to Sophie, Crown Princess of Greece (edited), 1955; Helen, Queen Mother of Roumania, 1956; The Son of Leicester, 1964; The Flying Cathedral (S. F. Cody), 1965; No Parachute (RFC, 1917), 1968; Open Cockpit, 1969; Aigua Blava and Xiquet, 1973; Fly Past, 1974; and some fiction. *Address:* 52 Queen's Gate Terrace, SW7 5PJ. *T:* 01-584 0929. *Club:* Royal Air Force. *[Died 21 May 1975.*

LEE, Mrs Asher; *see* Lee, Mollie Carpenter.

LEE, Rt. Hon. Sir Frank (Godbould), PC 1962; GCMG 1959 (CMG 1946); KCB 1950; Master of Corpus Christi College, Cambridge, 1962-June 1971; Hon. Fellow, Downing College, Cambridge; Fellow, London Graduate School of Business Studies, since 1966; *b* 26 Aug. 1903; *o s* of Joseph G. and Florence Lee, Brentwood, Essex; *m* 1937, Kathleen Mary Harris; three *d. Educ:* Brentwood Sch.; Downing Coll., Cambridge. Entered CS, 1926; Colonial Office, 1926-40; served in Nyasaland, 1931-33; Imperial Defence Coll., 1938; transferred Treasury, 1940; Treasury Delegation, Washington, 1944-46; transferred Ministry of Supply, 1946, Dep. Secretary, 1947; Minister at Washington, 1948; Permanent Secretary: Board of Trade, 1951-59; Min. of Food, 1959-61; Treasury (Joint), 1960-62; retired, Oct. 1962. Mem. Council, Univ. of E Anglia; Governor, LSE; Chm. Governors, Leys Sch., Cambridge. Hon. LLD, London. *Recreation:* walking. *Address:* The Master's Lodge, Corpus Christi College, Cambridge. *T:* 55345; Newnham Path, Church Rate Walk, Cambridge. *Clubs:* MCC; Hawks (Cambridge). *[Died 28 April 1971.*

LEE, Manfred B.; co-author with Frederic Dannay, under pseudonym Ellery Queen. *Publications:* Roman Hat Mystery, 1929; French Powder Mystery, 1930; Dutch Shoe Mystery, 1931; Greek Coffin Mystery, Tragedy of X, Egyptian Cross Mystery, Tragedy of Y, 1932; American Gun Mystery, Tragedy of Z, Siamese Twin Mystery, Drury Lane's Last Case, 1933; The Chinese Orange Mystery, Adventures of Ellery Queen, 1934; Spanish Cape Mystery, 1935; Halfway House, 1936; Door Between, 1937; Devil to Pay, Challenge to the Reader, Four of Hearts, 1938; Dragon's Teeth, 1939; New Adventures of Ellery Queen, 1940; 101 Years' Entertainment, 1941; Calamity Town, The Detective Short Story (a Bibliography), Sporting Blood, 1942; There was an Old Woman, Female of the Species, 1943; Misadventures of Sherlock Holmes, 1944; The Murderer is a Fox, Case Book of Ellery Queen, Rogues' Gallery, 1945; To the Queen's Taste, The Queen's Awards, 1946, 1946; The Queen's Awards, 1947, 1947; Murder by Experts, 1947; 20th Century Detective Stories, Ten Days' Wonder, The Queen's Awards, 1948, 1948; The Queen's Awards, 1949. Cat of Many Tails, 1949; Double, Double, The Queen's Awards 5th Series, The Literature of Crime, 1950; Queen's Quorum, 1951; The Origin of Evil, 1951; The Queen's Awards, 6th Series, 1951; Calendar of Crime, The King is Dead, The Queen's Awards, 7th Series, 1952; The Scarlet Letters, The Queen's Awards, 8th Series, 1953; The Glass Village, Ellery Queen's Awards, 9th Series, 1954; Queen's Bureau of Investigation, Ellery Queen's Awards, 10th Series, 1955; Inspector Queen's Own Case, Ellery Queen's Awards, 11th Series, 1956; In The Queen's Parlor, Ellery Queen's Awards, 12th Series, 1957; The Finishing Stroke, Ellery Queen's 13th Annual, 1958; Ellery Queen's 14th Annual, Ellery Queen's 1960 Anthology, 1959; Ellery Queen's 1961 Anthology, Ellery Queen's 15th Mystery Annual, 1960; Ellery Queen's 16th Mystery Annual, 1962; The Quintessence of Queen, 1962; To Be Read Before Midnight, 1963; The Player on the Other Side, 1963; Ellery Queen's Mystery Mix No 18, 1963; And on the Eighth Day, 1964; Ellery Queen's Double Dozen, No 19, 1964; Queens Full, 1965; Ellery Queen's 20th Anniversary Annual, 1965; The Fourth Side of the Triangle, 1965; Ellery Queen's Crime Carousel, 1966; Face to Face, 1967; Ellery Queen's All-Star Line-up, 1967; Poetic Justice, 1967; Ellery Queen's Mystery Parade, 1968; QED: Queen's Experiments in Detection, 1968; The House of Brass, 1968; Cop Out, 1969; Elllery Queen's Murder Menu, 24th Mystery Annual, 1969; Ellery Queen's Minimysteries, 1969; The Last Woman in His Life, 1970; Ellery Queen's Grand Slam, 1971. (Joint) Ellery Queen, Junior juvenile mysteries. Joint author of Radio and Television Programs: The Adventures of Ellery Queen; Joint editor of Ellery Queen's Mystery Magazine. *Address:* Roxbury, Connecticut, USA. *[Died 3 April 1971.*

LEE, May B.; *see* Stott, May, Lady.

LEE, Mollie Carpenter, (Mrs Asher Lee); Editor, Woman's Hour, BBC, 1967-71, retired; *b* 17 July 1911; *d* of Louis Hales and Florence (*née* Carpenter); *m* 1934, Asher Lee, OBE; one *d.*

Educ: Sittingbourne Co. Sch.; King's Coll., London Univ.; School of Slavonic Studies. BBC News Dept, External Services, 1943; BBC Woman's Hour, 1959. *Publications:* The Cat and The Medal, 1936; A Debt, 1949; Home for the Night, 1951; So Many Zeros, 1961; (ed) Woman's Hour: a Selection, 1967, 1969, 1971; Dying for Fun, 1971. *Recreations:* writing, cooking, theatre-going, travelling in France, making historical and literary pilgrimages. *Address:* 12 Malcolm Road, Wimbledon, SW19. *T:* 01-946 6391. *[Died 30 June 1973.*

LEE, Roger Malcolm; *b* 18 March 1902; *s* of late Lennox B. Lee; *m* 1935, Cecily Grace (*d* 1956), *d* of late Major Guy Mellor and of Mrs Mellor; two *s* one *d. Educ:* Eton; Pembroke Coll., Cambridge. In commerce in Argentine, 1927-29, and in India, 1930. Director of industrial companies in England and overseas, since 1933; Chairman, The Calico Printers' Association Ltd, 1947-64; Chairman, Lancashire Cotton Corporation, 1955-64. *Address:* How Caple Court, Hereford. *T:* How Caple 632. *Club:* Canning. *[Died 25 Sept. 1972.*

LEE, William Alexander, CBE 1920; Chevalier of Legion of Honour; Knight Officer of Order of the Crown of Italy; Director then Chairman, Mining Association of Great Britain, until 1954; *b* 1886; *s* of William Allan Lee, Grantham; *m* 1914, Edith Lydia, *d* of William Henry Grimwood, Willesden; two *s* two *d. Educ:* Royal Grammar Sch., Newcastle upon Tyne; London Univ. BA, BSc. Barrister, Inner Temple; entered Board of Trade, 1907; Secretary of Coal Mines Dept, 1918-19. *Publications:* Thirty Years in Coal, 1954; contributions to Historical Review of Coal Mining, 1925; etc. *Address:* White Croft, Littleworth Road, Esher, Surrey. *Club:* Junior Carlton. *[Died 13 July 1971.*

LEE, Rev. W(illiam) Walker; Chairman of the Bolton and Rochdale District of the Methodist Church, 1957-66; President, Conference of the Methodist Church, 1965; Chairman, Leeds District of Methodist Church 1966-78; *b* 1909; *s* of Matthew and Florence Lee; *m* 1935, Laura Annie Linsley; one *d* ; *m* 1975, Kathleen Burgess. *Educ:* King James I Grammar Sch., Bishop Auckland; Hartley Victoria Theological Coll., Manchester. Minister: Redditch Methodist Circuit, 1931-35; Birmingham Mission, 1935-40; Leeds Mission, 1940-44; Superintendent: Wednesbury Mission, 1944-49; Bolton Mission, 1949-57. Member of Methodist Delegation in Conversations between Church of England and Methodist Church, 1955-63. Hon. MA (Manchester). *Recreation:* gardening. *Address:* 574 Chorley Old Road, Bolton, Lancs BL1 6AA. *T:* Bolton 43609. *[Died 10 May 1979.*

LEE HOWARD, Leon Alexander, DFC 1944; writer and journalist; *b* 18 June 1914; *m* 1951, Sheila Psyche Black (marr. diss. 1973); *m* 1973, Madelon Dimont. *Educ:* privately. Served War of 1939-45: RAF Coastal Command, 1940-43; RAF Operational Film Production Unit, 1943-45. Editor: Woman's Sunday Mirror, 1955-59; Sunday Pictorial, 1959-61; Daily Mirror, 1961-71; Sub-editor, Rome Daily American, 1972-73. Hon. Knight of Mark Twain, 1977. *Publications: fiction: as Leigh Howard:* Crispin's Day, 1952; Johnny's Sister, 1954; Blind Date, 1955; *as Alexander Krislov:* No Man Sings, 1956. *Recreations:* writing, journalism. *Address:* 9 Hopefield Avenue, NW6. *[Died 4 Nov. 1978.*

LEECH, Clifford; Professor of English in University of Toronto, 1963-74; *b* 16 Jan. 1909; *s* of Edmund John Leech and Laura Mary Cumming; *m* 1942, Margaret Aldyth Clegg; *m* 1961, Gabriele Anspach. *Educ:* Clapham Coll.; Queen Mary Coll. (Univ. of London). Assistant Lecturer in English: University College of Swansea, 1933-36; Univ. of Durham, 1936-50; seconded to British Council in Turkey and Middle East, 1941-45; Principal of St Cuthbert's Society, Durham, 1946-52; Senior Lecturer in English, Univ. of Durham, 1950-54; Prof. of English Language and Literature, Univ. of Durham (Durham Division) 1954-63. Foyle Res. Fellow, The Shakespeare Institute, 1952; Vis. Univ. Prof., Connecticut Univ., 1974-75; Visiting Lectr, Free Univ. of Berlin, 1953; Research Fellow, Folger Shakespeare Lib., 1958; Commonwealth Prestige Fellow to Univs of NZ, 1967. Fellow, Royal Soc. of Canada, 1969. Dr (*hc*), Univ. of Clermont-Ferrand, 1962; Hon. DLitt Acadia Univ., NS, 1969. *Publications:* Mildmay Fane's Raguaillo d'Oceano and Candy Restored (ed), 1938; Shakespeare's Tragedies and Other Studies in Seventeenth Century Drama, 1950; John Webster: a Critical Study, 1951; A School of Criticism (inaugural lecture), 1955; John Ford and the Drama of his Time, 1957; The John Fletcher Plays, 1962; Shakespeare: The Chronicles, 1962; O'Neill, 1963; Webster: The Duchess of Malfi, 1963; John Ford, 1964; Twelfth Night and Shakespearian Comedy, 1965; Comedy in the Grand Style (W. D. Thomas Memorial Lecture), 1966; Tragedy (The Critical Idiom), 1969; The Dramatist's Experience with Other Essays in Literary Theory, 1970; Shakespeare's Tragic Fiction

(British Acad. Lecture, 1973); ed Marlowe (Twentieth Century Views), 1964; Shakespeare: The Tragedies, 1965; The Two Noble Kinsmen, 1966; The Two Gentlemen of Verona, 1969; (ed with J. M. R. Margeson) Shakespeare 1971, 1972; (ed with T. W. Craik) The Revels History of Drama in English, vols III and VI, 1975. General Editor, The Revels Plays, 1958-70. Contributions to Festschriften in honour of T. W. Baldwin, Baldwin Maxwell, Hardin Craig, Allardyce Nicoll, John Butt, G. Wilson Knight, Arthur Colby Sprague, Madeleine Doran, Mark Eccles. *Recreation:* getting angry. *Address:* 83 Elm Avenue, Apartment 107, Toronto M4W 1P1, Canada. *[Died 26 July 1977.*

LEECH-PORTER, Maj.-Gen. John Edmund, CB 1950; CBE 1945 (OBE 1944); OStJ; *b* 1896; *s* of Henry Leech-Porter, Winchester. *Educ:* Imperial Service Coll., Windsor. 2nd Lt RMA, 1914; served European War, 1914-19. Major, 1934; Lt-Col, 1941; Actg Brig., 1942-45; served in Sicily, 1943, and NW Europe, 1944-45; comdg Portsmouth Gp, 1949, Plymouth Gp, 1950-51, Royal Marines; retired list, 1951. Comdr Order of Leopold II with Palm; Croix de Guerre with Palm. *Recreations:* fishing, shooting, golf. *Address:* Broad Reach, Milford-on-Sea, Hants. *[Died 5 March 1979.*

LEEK, James, CBE 1941; lately Director BSA Co. Ltd, BSA Guns Ltd, BSA Motor Cycles Ltd; Ariel Motors Ltd, Birmingham; Monochrome Ltd; Triumph Engineering Co. Ltd, Coventry; President Birmingham Chamber of Commerce, 1949; *b* 12 Sept. 1892; *s* of Richard Harley and Annie Leek; *m* 1917, Kathleen Louise, *d* of J. E. Riley, Manufacturer, Bradford; one *s. Educ:* Newport Grammar School, Newport. *Address:* Sandown, 19 Banbury Road, Stratford-on-Avon, Warwicks. *T:* Stratford-on-Avon 3590. *[Died 23 Dec. 1978.*

LEES, Air Marshal Sir Alan, KCB, *cr* 1946 (CB 1943); CBE 1942; DSO 1937; AFC; *b* 23 May 1895; *e s* of late Maurice Lees, Park Bridge, Ashton-under-Lyne; *m* 1930, Norah Elizabeth, *y d* of late John Thomson, West Hartlepool; two *s* one *d. Educ:* Wellington Coll., Berks; RMC, Sandhurst. Served European War, 1914-18, with RFC; Iraq, 1923-26; NWFP, 1933-37; Air Officer Commanding-in-Chief, Reserve Command, 1946-49; retired list, 1949. *Address:* Home Close, Highclere, Newbury, Berks. *Clubs:* Royal Air Force, Queen's. *[Died 14 Aug. 1973.*

LEES, Rear-Adm. Dennis Marescaux, CB 1951; DSO 1940; *b* 28 Jan. 1900; *s* of Captain J. Lees, Royal W Kent Regt, and Gemma Lees (*née* Marescaux); *m* 1934, Daphne May Burnett; three *s. Educ:* Ludgrove Preparatory Sch.; RN Colls Osborne and Dartmouth. Fleet Gunnery Officer, Med. Fleet, 1934-36; in command HMS Calcutta, 1940-41, HMS Black Prince, 1943-45; Chief of Staff, Home Fleet, 1945-46; Dir of Naval Ordnance, 1946-49; Chief of Staff, Portsmouth, 1949-51; Dep. Chief of Naval Personnel (personal services), 1951-53; retired list, 1953. Greek War Cross, 1941; American Legion of Merit, 1945; French Croix de Guerre, 1948; French Legion of Honour, 1948. *Recreations:* cricket, golf, shooting. *Address:* 21 Selsey Avenue, Southsea, Hants. *T:* Portsmouth 33283. *Club:* United Service & Royal Aero. *[Died 4 Aug. 1973.*

LEES, Sir Hereward; *see* Lees, Sir W. H. C.

LEES, Lt-Col Lawrence Werner Wyld; *b* 11 Sept. 1887; *s* of late Rev. George Wyld Lees, Clifford, York, and Anna Werner, Dublin; *m* 1915, Gwendolen (*d* 1976), *d* of late R. T. Daniell, Colchester; one *s* one *d. Educ:* privately. Commissioned in Militia, Special Reserve, RA and RAF, 1906-21; served in France and East Africa, 1915-17; Dep. Asst Dir, War Office, 1917, and at Air Ministry, 1918; mem. of London and Liverpool Corn Trade Associations, 1924; of British Exec. Cttee Internat. Chamber of Commerce and British spokesman at Copenhagen Conference, 1939. High Sheriff of Shropshire, 1944-45. *Address:* Tunstall Hall Nursing Home, Market Drayton, Salop. *T:* Market Drayton 3768. *[Died 26 Aug. 1976.*

LEES, Stanley Lawrence, MVO 1952; Under-Secretary, Ministry of Transport, 1967-70, retired; *b* 1911; *yr s* of Dr Charlie Lees and Eveleen Lees, Tunbridge Wells; *m* 1938, Audrey, *d* of A. E. Lynam, Oxford; two *s* two *d. Educ:* Rugby Sch.; New Coll., Oxford. Solicitor, 1936; Solicitor's Office, Inland Revenue, 1936; Secretaries' Office, Inland Revenue, 1943; Royal Navy, 1944; HM Treasury, 1946; Under-Sec., 1958; Dir of Organisation and Methods, 1959-66. *Address:* 3 Malbrook Road, Putney, SW15. *T:* 01-788 6732. *[Died 1 June 1980.*

LEES, Walter Kinnear P.; *see* Pyke-Lees.

LEES, Sir (William) Hereward (Clare), 2nd Bt, *cr* 1937; retired as Director, Bleachers' Association Ltd; Director, Manchester District Board of Martin's Bank; *b* 6 March 1904; *o s* of Sir

William Clare Lees, 1st Bt, OBE, LLD, and Kathleen (*d* 1967), *d* of John Nickson, Liverpool; *S* father, 1951; *m* 1930, Dorothy Gertrude, *d* of Francis Alexander and Gertrude Florence Lauder; one *s* one *d*. *Educ:* Leys Sch., Cambridge. *Heir: s* William Antony Clare Lees, *b* 14 June 1935. *Address:* Ardeevin, Chapel-en-le-Frith, Stockport, Cheshire. *[Died 20 April 1976.*

LEESE, Sir Alexander (William), 4th Bt *cr* 1908; *b* 27 Sept. 1909; 3rd *s* of Sir William Hargreaves Leese, 2nd Bt and Violet Mary (*d* 1947), *d* of late Albert G. Sandeman; *S* brother, 1978. *Educ:* Eton. Formerly Captain, Supplementary Reserve, Coldstream Guards. *Heir: cousin* John Henry Vernon Leese, *b* 7 Aug. 1901. *Address:* 88 Cranmer Court, Sloane Avenue, SW3.
[Died 30 July 1979.

LEESE, Lt-Gen. Sir Oliver William Hargreaves, 3rd Bt, *cr* 1908; KCB 1943 (CB 1942); CBE 1940; DSO 1916; *b* 27 Oct. 1894; *e s* of 2nd Bt and Violet Mary (*d* 1947), 4th *d* of late Albert G. Sandeman; *S* father, 1937; *m* 1933, Margaret Alice (*d* 1964), *o d* of late Cuthbert Leicester-Warren. *Educ:* Ludgrove; Eton. Served European War, 1914-18 (wounded three times, DSO, despatches twice); Adj. 3rd Bn Coldstream Guards, 1920-22; Adj. OTC Eton, 1922-25; Staff Coll., Camberley, 1927-28; Bde Major, 1st Guards Brigade, 1929-32; DAA and QMG London District, 1932-33; Gen. Staff Officer, 2nd Grade, The War Office, 1935-36; commanded 1st Bn Coldstream Guards, 1936-38; Gen. Staff Officer, 1st Grade, Staff Coll., Quetta, 1938-40; Brigadier, 20th Guards Brigade, 1940; Dep. Chief of the Gen. Staff BEF, 1940; Brigadier, 29th Independent Brigade Group, 1940; Comdr West Sussex Div., 1941; Comdr, 15th (Scottish) Div., Comdr Guards Armoured Div., 1941; Commanding 30th Corps, 1942; Comdr, 8th Army, 1944; C-in-C Allied Land Forces South-East Asia, 1944-45; GOC-in-C Eastern Command, 1945-46; retired, 1946. Dep. Lt County of Salop, 1947. Hon. Col Shropshire Yeo., 1947-62; JP 1949-63; High Sheriff of Salop, 1958. Pres. Combined Cadet Force Assoc., 1950-71. Lieut, Tower of London, 1954. Pres. Warwickshire County Cricket Club, 1959-75; Nat. Pres., British Legion, 1962-70; Pres. Shropshire County Cricket Club, 1962-73; Chm., Old Etonian Assoc., 1964-73 (Pres., 1946); Pres. MCC, 1965-66; Pres. Cricket Soc., 1969-73. *Heir: b* Alexander William Leese, *b* 27 Sept. 1909. *Address:* Dolwen, Cefn Coch, Llanrhaeadr, Oswestry, Salop. *T:* Llanrhaeadr 411. *[Died 22 Jan. 1978.*

LEETE, Leslie William Thomas, CBE 1965 (MBE 1952); Chief Officer of the London Fire Brigade, 1962-70; *b* 18 Dec. 1909; *o s* of William Leete and Maud Evelyn Leete (*née* Cain), Luton, Beds; *m* 1941, Isabel, *yr d* of William Peover, Batchacre Hall, Adbaston, Salop; one *d*. *Educ:* Bedford Sch. Hat manufacturer, 1928-39. London Fire Brigade, 1939-: Senior Staff Officer: London Region, National Fire Service, 1944-48; London Fire Brigade, 1948-52; Dep. Chief Officer, London Fire Brigade, 1952-62. Fellow, Instn of Fire Engineers. *Recreations:* cabinet-making, gardening. *Address:* 3 Lansdowne Road, Luton, Beds. *Club:* Royal Automobile. *[Died 31 Aug. 1976.*

le FLEMING, Sir Frank Thomas, 10th Bt, *cr* 1705; *b* 27 Dec. 1887; *s* of Sir William Hudleston le Fleming, 9th Bt, and Martha, *d* of John Kelland, Crwys Morchard, Devon; *S* father 1945; *m* 1921, Isabel Annie Fraser, *d* of late James Craig, Manaia, NZ; three *s*. *Educ:* Napier Boys' High Sch., NZ. Served European War, 1914-18, in Engineer Corps. Landowner. *Heir: s* William Kelland le Fleming [*b* 27 April 1922; *m* 1948, Noveen Avis, *d* of C. C. Sharpe, Rukuhia, Hamilton, NZ; three *s* three *d*]. *Address:* Rydal Lovat, Auroa Road, RD Manaia, Taranaki, NZ. *T:* 41 Manaia. *[Died 5 July 1971.*

LEFSCHETZ, Prof. Solomon, PhD; ME; HB Fine Research Professor Emeritus, Princeton University; Professor, National University of Mexico, since 1944; *b* Moscow, 3 Sept. 1884; *m* 1913, Alice Berg Hayes. *Educ:* Ecole Centrale, Paris; Clark Univ., Worcester, Mass. With Westinghouse Electric & Manufacturing Co., Pittsburgh, 1907-10; Instructor of Maths, Nebraska Univ., 1911-13; University of Kansas: Instructor of Maths, 1913-16; Asst Prof., 1916-19; Assoc. Prof., 1919-23; Prof., 1923-25; Princeton University: Assoc. Prof., 1925-28; Prof., 1928-32; HB Fine Research Prof., 1933-53; Chm. Dept of Mathematics, 1945-53; Exchange Prof., Mexico City, 1945-46, 1947. Member: Nat. Acad. of Sciences; Amer. Math. Soc., (Pres. 1935-36); Math. Assoc. of Amer.; Amer. Philos. Soc.; Royal Society (For. Mem.); Acad. des Sciences de Paris (Associate Mem.), etc. Holds several hon. degrees. Decoration Aztec Eagle, 1964. Bordin Prize, French Academy, 1919; Bôcher Prize, Amer. Math. Soc., 1924; Feltrinelli Prize, Accad. dei Lincei, 1956. *Publications:* L'Analyse Situs et la géométrie algébrique, 1924; Surfaces et variétés algébriques, 1927; Topology, 1930; Algebraic Topology, 1942; Introduction to Topology, 1949; Algebraic Geometry, 1952; Differential Equations: geometric theory, 1958; editor, Annals of Mathematics. *Address:* 11 Lake Lane, Princeton, NJ 08540, USA. *[Died 5 Oct. 1972.*

LEGENTILHOMME, Général Paul Louis, Hon. KCB 1946; *b* at Valognes, Department of Manche (Normandy), 26 March 1884; *m* 1947, Marjorie M., *widow* of Comdr C. J. Smith, RN, and *o d* of late Alderman Sir Charles McRea. *Educ:* College of Le Havre. Military Sch. of St Cyr, 1905-7; Sub-Lt in the Colonial Infantry, 1907; Lt, 1909; Capt., 1915; Major, 1925; Lt-Col, 1928; Col, 1934; Général de brigade, 1938; Général de division, 1941; Général de Corps d'Armée, 1943; Général d'Armée, 1947; has served in Syria, in Indo-China, in Madagascar, and passed French, Staff Coll. and Centre des Hautes Etudes Militaires before the war; C-in-C in French Somaliland, 1938; C-in-C allied forces in French and British Somaliland, 1940; on 16 June, 1940 informed Foreign Office of his decision to carry on fight with Great Britain till victory, but was obliged to give in at Jibuti and escaped by night, 1 Aug. 1940, to join General de Gaulle; GOC Free French Forces in Sudan for operations against Erythrea, 1941; in command of allied forces operating in Syria and took Damascus, 1941; Haut Commissaire de France pour les possessions de l'Océan Indien et Gouvernement Général de Madagascar, 1942-43; Commissioner for National Defence, French Cttee of National Liberation, 1943; Commandant la 3ème Région Militaire, Rouen, 1944-45; Military Governor of Paris, 1945-47; retired 1947; Member, Assembly of French Union, 1952. Decorations: French: Médaille Militaire, Grande Croix de la Légion d'Honneur, Croix de la Libération, Croix de Guerre 1914-18 and 1939-45, etc. American: Commander of Legion of Merit. Belgian: Grand Officier de l'Ordre de la Couronne and Croix de Guerre. Czechoslovakian: Grand Officier du Lion Blanc. Brazilian: Grand Officier de l'Ordre de la Croix du Sud. Polish: Virtutis Militaris, 3rd Class. *Address:* Logis de la Plage, 06 Villefranche sur Mer, France.
[Died 23 May 1975.

LEGER, Alexis; *see* Leger, M.-R. A. St-L.

LEGER, Rt. Hon. Jules, CC (Canada) 1974; CMM; CD; PC 1979; Governor-General and Commander-in-Chief of Canada, 1974-79; Chancellor and Principal Companion, Order of Canada; Chancellor and Commander, Order of Military Merit; *b* 4 April 1913; *s* of Ernest Léger and Alda Beauvais; *m* 1938, Gabrielle Carmel; one *d*. *Educ:* Coll. of Valleyfield, PQ; Univ. of Montreal; Univ. of Paris (DLitt 1938). Associate Editor, Le Droit, 1938-39; Prof. of Diplomatic History and Current Affairs, Univ. of Ottawa, 1939-42; Dept of External Affairs, Canada: Third Sec., 1940; Santiago, 1943; Second Sec., 1944; First Sec., 1946; London, 1947-48; UN Gen. Assembly, Paris, 1948-49; seconded to Prime Minister's Office, 1949-50; Asst Under-Sec. of State, 1951-53; Ambassador to Mexico, 1953-54; Under-Sec. of State, 1954-58; Perm. Rep. to NATO Council, 1958-62; Ambassador to: Italy, 1962-64; France, 1964-68; Under-Sec. of State, 1968-73; Ambassador to Belgium and Luxembourg, 1973. KStJ 1974. *Address:* (home) 20 Driveway, Apt 1101, Ottawa, Canada; (office) 3-B-132 Pearson Building, Sussex Drive, Ottawa, Canada. *[Died 22 Nov. 1980.*

LEGER, (Marie-René) Alexis Saint-Leger (*pseudonym* St-John Perse); Grand Officier de la Légion d'Honneur; Commandeur des Arts et des Lettres; poet; *b* Guadeloupe, 31 May 1887; *s* of Amédée Leger, lawyer; *m* 1958, Dorothy Milburn Russell, USA. *Educ:* Universities of Bordeaux and Paris. Joined French Foreign Service, 1914; Sec., French Embassy, Peking, 1916-21; Chef de Cabinet, Ministry of Foreign Affairs, 1925-32; Counsellor, 1925; Minister, 1927; Ambassadeur de France and Sec.-Gen., Min. of Foreign Affairs, 1933-40. Left France for America, 1940. Consultant on French Literature, Library of Congress, 1941-45. Member: Amer. Acad. of Arts and Letters; Bayerischen Akademie Der Schönen Künste. Doctor (*hc*), Yale University. Hon. Mem., Modern Language Assoc. Grand Prix National des Lettres, Paris, 1959. Nobel Prize for Literature, 1960. Hon. Mem. American Academy of Arts and Sciences, 1963. KCVO (Hon.), 1927; GBE (Hon.), 1938; KCB (Hon.), 1940. *Publications:* Anabase, 1924 (Eng. trans., 1930, rev. edn, 1938, 1949); Eloges, 1911 (Eng. trans., 1944, rev. edn, 1956); La Gloire des Rois, 1925; Exil, 1944 (Eng. Trans., 1949); Vents, 1946 (Eng. trans., Winds, 1953); Amers, 1957 (Eng. trans., Seamarks, 1958); Chronique, 1960 (Eng. trans., 1961); Oiseaux, 1962 (Eng. trans., 1963); Pour Dante, 1965; Collected Poems, 1971; Œuvres Complètes, 1972; *posthumous publication:* Chant pour un équinox, 1976. *Address:* 1621, 34th Street NW, Washington, DC 20007, USA; Les Vigneaux, 83 Giens, France.
[Died 20 Sept. 1975.

LEGGATT, Maj.-Gen. Charles St Quentin Outen Fullbrook-, CBE 1945; DSO 1914; MC; *b* 16 Aug. 1889; *m* 1917, Mary Katharine, *d* of late Col G. H. Bittleston, RA, of Ashleigh,

Whitchurch, Devon; two *d. Educ:* Bath Coll.; RMC, Sandhurst. Entered Army, 1909; Capt., 1915; Bt Maj., 1918; Major, 1924; Lt-Col, 1932; Col, 1936; served European War, 1914-18 (wounded twice, despatches four times, DSO, Military Cross, Bt Maj.); commanded 2nd Bn Royal Berks Regt, 1932-36; Instructor Senior Officers' Sch., Sheerness, 1936-39; Comdr Inf. Brigade, TA, 1939-41; Div., 1941-42; Tunisia, 1943-44; 61 Area, Ancona, N Italy, 1944-46; retired pay, 1946. Officier Légion d'Honneur, 1947. *Address:* c/o Barclays Bank Ltd, Tucker Street, Cromer, Norfolk.   *[Died 29 May 1972.*

LEGGE, Maj.-Gen. Stanley Ferguson, CBE 1952; Master General of the Ordnance, Australia, 1954-57; *b* 24 April 1900; *s* of late Lt-Gen. J. G. Legge, CB, CMG; *m* 1929, Joyce Y. Walker, Melbourne, Aust.; one *s* one *d* (and one *d* decd). *Educ:* Melbourne Gram. Sch.; St Paul's, London. Lt, Aust. Staff Corps, 1920; various postings; DAQMG, 7 Aust. Div., AIF, 1940; held various positions in Middle East, Australia, New Guinea, Solomon Islands, until 1946; retired. QMG 1953. *Address:* Russets, Ivy Avenue, Kallista, Vic 3791, Australia.
                                                          [Died 25 July 1977.

LEGGE-BOURKE, Major Sir (Edward Alexander) Henry, (Sir Harry), KBE 1960; DL; MP (C) Isle of Ely, since 1945; *b* 16 May 1914; *o s* of late N. W. H. Legge-Bourke, Coldstream Guards, and Lady Victoria Forester; *m* 1938, Catherine Jean, 3rd *d* of Col Sir Arthur Grant, DSO, 10th Bt of Monymusk; two *s* one *d. Educ:* Eton; RMC, Sandhurst. 2nd Lt RHG 1934; served War of 1939-45 (wounded). Chairman: 1922 Cttee, 1970-72; Parly and Scientific Cttee, 1971-. Chm. Grant Production Co. Ltd. DL Cambridgeshire, 1955. Hon. Freeman, Borough of Wisbech, 1971. *Publications:* Defence of the Realm, 1949; Master of the Offices, 1950; The King's Guards, Horse and Foot, 1951; The Queen's Guards, 1965. *Address:* 9 Wilbraham Place, SW1. *Club:* Carlton.   *[Died 21 May 1973.*

LEHMANN, Beatrix; Actress; *b* 1 July 1903; 3rd *d* of late Rudolph Chambers Lehmann. *Educ:* home; Paris. Trained for stage at Royal Academy of Dramatic Art. First professional engagement, Sidney in The Bill of Divorcement on a tour of South Coast Village Halls. First London appearance, Lyric Theatre, Hammersmith, 1924, as Peggy in The Way of the World; subsequently played numerous West End parts. Appearances include: Lavinia in Mourning Becomes Electra; Abbie in Desire Under the Elms; Mrs Alving in Ghosts; Family Reunion; No Sign of the Dove; Blood Wedding; Waltz of the Toreadors; Garden District; Lady Macbeth in Macbeth, Old Vic; Miss Bordereau in The Aspern Papers; A Cuckoo in the Nest; Marfa Kabanova in The Storm, Old Vic; Hecuba, Mermaid; The Night I Chased the Women with an Eel; Peer Gynt, Chichester, 1970; Reunion in Vienna, Chichester, 1971; Mother Adam, Arts, 1971; Romeo and Juliet, Stratford-on-Avon, 1973. Entered films, 1935, The Cat and the Canary, 1977. TV appearances include series Love for Lydia, 1977; Crime and Punishment, 1979. Radio Actress of the Year award, 1976. *Publications:* two novels; a number of short stories. *Recreations:* swimming and history. *Address:* c/o International Creative Management, 22 Grafton Street, W1.   *[Died 31 July 1979.*

LEHMANN, Lotte; Opera, Concert and Radio Singer (Soprano), retired; *b* Perleberg, Germany, 27 Feb. 1888; *d* of Carl Lehmann and Marie Schuster; *m* Otto Krause (*d* 1939). *Educ:* Royal Academy of Music, Berlin. Has sung in opera and concert in the principal cities of Europe, USA, South America, Australia, New Zealand. Hon. Pres., Music Acad. of West, Santa Barbara, Calif.; Hon. mem. Vienna State Opera; Hon. mem. Music Academy, Vienna. Medals: Legion of Honour, France; Golden Palm, France; Golden Medal, Sweden; Golden Medal, Austria; Golden Medal, Germany; Rings of Honour: Viennese Philharmonic Orchestra; Soloists of Vienna Opera House; Ring of City of Vienna. Holds four doctorates in music and humane letters. *Publications:* Eternal Flight (novel); Midway in my Song (biography); More than Singing (song interpretation); My Many Lives (book on opera); Five Operas and Richard Strauss, 1964 (Eng. edn as: Singing with Richard Strauss); Eighteen Song Cycles, 1971. *Address:* 4565 Via Huerto, Hope Ranch, Santa Barbara, Calif 93105, USA. *T:* Santa Barbara 93105.
                                                          [Died 26 Aug. 1976.

LEI WANG-KEE, Most Rev. Peter; Bishop (RC) of Hong Kong, since 1973; *b* 29 March 1922. Ordained priest 1952; consecrated Bishop, 1971. *Address:* Bishop's House, 16 Caine Road, Hong Kong. *T:* 5-232487/221009/241633.   *[Died July 1974.*

LEICESTER, 5th Earl of, *cr* 1837; **Thomas William Edward Coke,** MVO 1937; Viscount Coke, 1837; an Hereditary Sub-Postmaster, 1733; Major Scots Guards (retired); Extra Equerry to the Queen since 1952 (to King George VI, 1937-52); DL

Norfolk; *b* 16 May 1908 (King Edward VII was sponsor); *o* surv. *s* of 4th Earl and Marion Gertrude (*d* 1955), *d* of late Colonel Hon. W. R. Trefusis; *S* father 1949; *m* 1931, Lady Elizabeth Yorke, DCVO 1973 (CVO 1965), Lady of the Bedchamber to the Queen, 1953-73, *o d* of 8th Earl of Hardwicke; three *d. Educ:* Eton; RMC Sandhurst. Joined Scots Guards in 1928; Captain, 1938; Major, 1945; served War of 1939-45; ADC to Field Marshal Earl Wavell, 1941. Equerry to the Duke of York (later King George VI), 1934-37. Lieut-Colonel Home Guard, 1952-56; Hon. Colonel, 1st Cadet Battalion, Royal Norfolk Regt. Local Director, Royal Insurance Co. Member Board of Governors, Gresham's School, Holt. President: Royal Norfolk Agricultural Assoc., 1958; CLA, Norfolk Branch, 1958-61. Royal Order of George I, Greece, 1963. *Heir: cousin* Anthony Louis Lovel Coke, RAF [*b* 11 Sept. 1909; *m* 1st, 1934, Moyra Crossley (marr. diss., 1947); two *s* one *d* ; 2nd, 1947, Vera Haigh, Salisbury, Rhodesia]. *Address:* Holkham Hall, Norfolk. *Clubs:* Turf, MCC.   *[Died 3 Sept. 1976.*

LEICESTER, James, MSc, MScTech, PhD, FRIC; Deputy Director, Polytechnic of North London, since 1971; *b* 23 Dec. 1915; *o s* of late James Leicester, Lancs; *m* 1943, Doris Waugh; two *s. Educ:* Cowley Sch., St Helens; Sheffield Univ. BSc (Hons. Chemistry) Sheffield, 1936; MSc Sheffield, 1937; MScTech, Manchester, 1939; PhD London, 1952. Demonstrator, Manchester Univ., 1937-40; Chemical Inspectorate, Ministry of Supply, 1940-45; Lecturer, Medway College of Technology, 1946-47; Lecturer and Senior Lecturer, Woolwich Polytechnic, 1948-56; Head of Dept of Chemistry, Northampton College of Advanced Technology, London, 1956-61; Principal, Northern Polytechnic, 1961-71. Member Court, City Univ. *Recreation:* map collecting. *Address:* 28 Broomfield Road, Bexleyheath, Kent. *T:* Crayford 521758.   *[Died 11 Nov. 1976.*

LEICESTER-WARREN, Lt-Col John Leighton Byrne, TD 1945; Land Owner; Vice-Lieutenant of Cheshire, 1968-74; *b* 25 Sept. 1907; *s* of Cuthbert and Hilda Leicester-Warren; *heir-pres.* to *cousin* Sir M. J. B. Leighton, 11th Bt; unmarried. *Educ:* Eton; Magdalen Coll., Oxford. BA 1928, MA 1933. Barrister-at-law, Inner Temple, 1933; N Wales and Chester Circuit, 1935-39. Served War of 1939-45, Cheshire Yeomanry and Staff 6 Cavalry Bde, GSO 3 Athens Area, 1940; captured 1941, POW; ADJAG (War Crimes) BAOR, 1946; Lieut-Colonel Comdg Cheshire Yeomanry, 1949-52. JP 1948, DL 1955, Cheshire; High Sheriff of Cheshire, 1965. *Address:* Tabley House, Knutsford, Cheshire. *T:* Knutsford 3021. *Club:* Pratt's.   *[Died 10 Aug. 1975.*

LEIGH, 4th Baron *cr* 1839; **Rupert William Dudley Leigh;** TD; DL; *b* 14 March 1908; *o s* of late Major Hon. Rupert Leigh; *S* uncle, 1938; *m* 1931, Anne (*d* 1977), *d* of Ellis Hicks Beach, Witcombe Park, Glos; four *s. Educ:* Eton; RMC, Sandhurst. 11th Hussars, 1928-36, Royal Gloucestershire Hussars, 1937-44 (Lieut-Colonel, 1st RGH, 1943). Served with Notts (Sherwood Rangers) Yeomanry in NW Europe, 1944-45. CStJ 1969. *Heir: s* Hon. John Piers Leigh [*b* 11 Sept. 1935; *m* 1st, 1957, Cecilia Poppy (marr. diss. 1974), *y d* of late Robert Cecil Jackson, Redlynch, Wilts; one *s* one *d* ; 2nd, Susan, *d* of John Cleave, Whitenash, Leamington Spa; one *s*]. *Address:* Stoneleigh Abbey, Kenilworth, Warwickshire. *T:* Kenilworth 53981; Adlestrop House, Moreton-in-Marsh, Glos. *T:* Kingham 364. *Club:* Cavalry and Guards.   *[Died 24 June 1979.*

LEIGH, His Honour Christopher Thomas Bowes, OBE 1944; TD 1943; Hon. Lt-Col RA; County Court Judge 1962-70; *b* 3 Jan. 1905; 2nd *s* of His Honour Thomas Bowes Leigh, KC, formerly County Court Judge of Manchester, and Marta Leigh, Wilmslow; *m* 1936, Vida Mary, *d* of H. R. and Mary Brunt, Staffordshire; no *c. Educ:* Cheltenham Coll. (Scholar); Queen's Coll., Oxford (Scholar). Hons in Classics and Law. Called to Bar, Gray's Inn, 1928; practised on Northern Circuit. Commissioned 7th Bn Lancashire Fusiliers (TA), 1926; Major, 1935. Served War of 1939-45: at first with 39th (LF) SL Regt; transferred to RA, 1942; served N Africa and Italy, commanding 105 and 12th LAA Regts, RA. Chairman, Agricultural Land Tribunal for Yorkshire and Lancashire, 1947-62. *Recreations:* racquets, tennis, golf. *Address:* 60 King Street, Manchester. *T:* 061-834 6876. *Clubs:* Vincent's (Oxford); Manchester Tennis and Racquet.   *[Died 21 May 1971.*

LEIGH, Laurence Brian; Managing Director, Tesco Stores (Holdings) Ltd; *b* 26 May 1935; *s* of Leslie and Reita Leigh; *m* 1959, Letitia Lewis; one *s* two *d. Educ:* Highgate Public School. MBIM. Served RAOC, 1953-54, E. Africa (Lieut). Marks & Spencer Ltd, 1952-56; Allied Stores USA, 1956-57; Marks & Spencer Ltd, 1957-60; Tesco Stores (Holdings) Ltd, 1960-. *Recreations:* yachting, swimming, squash. *Address:* Tesco Stores (Holdings) Ltd, Tesco House, Delamare Road, Cheshunt, Herts.   *[Died 22 Aug. 1974.*

LEIGHTON, Margaret, CBE 1974; actress; *b* 26 Feb. 1922; *d* of George Leighton and Doris Evans; *m* 1947, Max Reinhardt (marr. diss.); *m* 1957, Laurence Harvey (marr. diss. 1961; he *d* 1973); *m* 1964, Michael Wilding. *Educ:* C of E Coll., Birmingham. Joined Birmingham Repertory Company, 1938, and remained for season; with Travelling Repertory Company and touring for CEMA and ENSA, 1940; re-joined Birmingham Rep. Co., 1941. Old Vic Theatre Co., 1944; season 1944-45: Arms and the Man; Peer Gynt; Richard III; Uncle Vanya; with Old Vic Co. on European Tour, season 1945-46: Henry IV parts 1 and 2; Arms and the Man; six weeks season in New York; season 1946-47: Cyrano de Bergerac; An Inspector Calls; King Lear; The Alchemist; Richard II; played in Old Vic production of King Lear in Paris. Played in A Sleeping Clergyman, Criterion, 1947; Philadelphia Story, Duchess, 1949; The Cocktail Party, New, 1950; Three Sisters, Aldwych, 1951; Memorial Theatre, Stratford-upon-Avon, 1952; The Apple Cart, Haymarket, 1953; The Confidential Clerk, Edinburgh Festival and Lyric, 1953; Separate Tables, St James's, 1954-56 and in New York from 1956; Variation on a Theme, Globe, 1958; Much Ado about Nothing, New York, 1959; The Wrong Side of the Park, Cambridge Theatre, 1960; The Lady from the Sea, Queen's, 1961; The Night of the Iguana, 1961, Tchin Tchin, 1962, The Chinese Prime Minister, 1964, New York; Cactus Flower, Lyric, 1967; Little Foxes, New York, 1968; Antony and Cleopatra, Chichester Festival, 1969; Girlfriend, Apollo, 1970; The Rivals, Reunion in Vienna, Chichester Festival, 1971, Piccadilly, 1972; A Family and a Fortune, Apollo, 1975. *Films include:* Bonnie Prince Charlie; The Winslow Boy; Under Capricorn; The Elusive Pimpernel; The Astonished Heart; Calling Bulldog Drummond; Home at Seven; The Holly and the Ivy; The Good Die Young; The Constant Husband; The Teckman Mystery; Carrington, VC; A Novel Affair; The Passionate Stranger; The Sound and the Fury; The Waltz of the Toreadors; The Loved One, 1965; Seven Women, 1966; The Mad Woman of Chaillot, 1968; The Go-Between, 1971 (Best Supporting Actress award, 1972, Soc. of Film and TV Arts); Zee and Co., 1972; Lady Caroline Lamb, 1972; Bequest to the Nation, 1973; From Beyond the Grave, 1974. TV series, The Upper Crusts, 1973. *Address:* London Management, 235 Regent Street, W1.   *[Died 14 Jan. 1976.*

LEINSTER, 7th Duke of, *cr* 1766; **Edward FitzGerald;** Baron of Offaly, 1205; Earl of Kildare, 1316; Viscount Leinster (Great Britain), 1747; Marquess of Kildare, 1761; Earl of Offaly, 1761; Baron Kildare, 1870; Premier Duke, Marquess, and Earl, of Ireland; Captain, late Argyll and Sutherland Highlanders; late 2nd Lieut Irish Guards and Lieut 8th Battalion West Riding Regt; *b* 6 May 1892; *s* of Gerald, 5th Duke, and Hermione, *d* of 1st Earl of Feversham; *S* brother, 1922; *m* 1st, 1913, May (from whom he obtained a decree of divorce, 1930; she *d* 1935), *d* of late Jesse Etheridge; one *s*; 2nd, 1932, Mrs Clare van Neck (Rafaelle Kennedy, who obtained a divorce, 1946), *d* of Mrs J. H. Patterson, New York; 3rd, 1946, Mrs Theodore Wessel (*d* 1960); 4th, 1965, Mrs Vivien Conner; one step *s.* Served European War, 1914-17 (wounded). *Heir: s* Marquess of Kildare. *Address:* Ford Manor, Dormansland, Lingfield, Surrey RH7 6NZ. *T:* Lingfield 832201.   *[Died 8 March 1976.*

LEIR, Rear-Admiral Ernest W., DSO 1916; Legion of Honour, 1917; Royal Navy, retired; *b* 1883; *s* of Rev. C. E. Leir of Ditcheat, Somerset; *m* 1st, 1905, Muriel Amyatt (*d* 1937), *o d* of Rev. E. Amyatt-Burney, and *g d* of Rev. Edward Burney of the Royal Academy, Gosport; two *s* one *d*; 2nd, 1938, Gwendolen Iliffe, *o d* of late Brig.-General J. A. Gibbon, CMG. *Educ:* King's Sch., Bruton. Entered navy, 1898; served as midshipman on China Station, 1899-1902; took part in the relief of the Legations in Pekin, 1900; Lieut, 1903; attached to the Submarine Service; specially promoted to Commander, for services in the Bight of Heligoland action, Aug. 1914 (DSO for services rendered in overseas submarine work, despatches); Captain of the Dockyard, Dep.-Superintendent and King's Harbour-master at Chatham, 1923-24; Senior Naval Officer in the Persian Gulf, 1924-26; Captain, Reserve Flotilla, Portsmouth, 1926-27; Captain-in-Charge and King's Harbour-master, Portland, 1929-31; Naval ADC to the King, 1931; retired list, 1931. Commodore of Convoys during War of 1939-45 (despatches). *Address:* South Hill House, Ditcheat, Shepton Mallet, Somerset.   *[Died 2 Aug. 1971.*

LEITH, Sir (Robert) Ian (Algernon) F.; *see* Forbes-Leith.

LEITH-BUCHANAN, Sir George Hector Macdonald, 6th Bt, *cr* 1775; JP; *b* 30 Jan. 1889; *s* of 5th Bt and Maude Mary (*d* 1956), *d* of late Alexander Grant; *S* father, 1925; *m* 1933, Barbara Leshure. *Heir: cousin,* Charles Alexander James Leith-Buchanan, *b* 1 Sept. 1939. *Address:* Drummakill, Alexandria, Dunbartonshire.   *[Died 1 Aug. 1973.*

LEJEUNE, Caroline Alice, (Mrs E. Roffe Thompson); Film Critic to the Observer, 1928-60; Broadcaster and Television script writer; *b* Manchester, 1897; *m* 1925, Ernest Roffe Thompson; one *s. Educ:* Manchester Univ. Hon. DLitt, Durham Univ., 1961. *Publications:* Cinema; Chestnuts in Her Lap; Thank You for Having Me; *television adaptations:* Sherlock Holmes Series; The Three Hostages; Clementina; *original television play:* (with son, Anthony Lejeune) Vicky's First Ball; completed Angela Thirkell's posthumous novel Three Score and Ten. *Address:* Lane End, Pinner Hill, Middlesex.
[Died 1 April 1973.

LEMASS, Seán Francis; *b* Dublin, 15 July, 1899; *m* 1924, Kathleen Hughes; one *s* three *d. Educ:* Christian Brothers' Schools. Participated in Easter Week Rising, 1916, and taken prisoner at GPO; served again with IRA on renewal of hostilities; taken prisoner and interned until the Truce of 1921; remained with IRA after the Anglo-Irish Treaty; taken prisoner on capture of Four Courts garrison during first week of Civil War, July 1922, but escaped; appointed to IRA Headquarters staff; again taken prisoner, Dec. 1922, and interned. Managing Director, The Irish Press, Ltd, 1948-51. Minister for Industry and Commerce, Ireland, 1932-39, 1941-48, 1951-54 and 1957-59; Minister for Supplies, 1939-45; Tánaiste (Deputy Prime Minister), 1945-48, 1951-54 and 1957-59; Taoiseach (Prime Minister), 1959-67. TD, Dublin South, 1924-48, Dublin South (Central), 1948-69. Chairman: United Breweries of Ireland; Ronald Lyon Estates (Ireland), 1966-; Irish Security Services, 1968-; MacDonagh and Boland, 1966-; Unidare Ltd; Director: Electrical Industries of Ireland Ltd; Ryans Tourist Holdings Ltd; Waterford Glass Ltd. Hon. degrees: LLD: New Rochelle (New York), 1953; Villanova (Philadelphia), 1963; University of Dublin, 1965; DEconSc, National Univ. of Ireland, 1954. Grand Cross of Order of Gregory the Great, 1948; Grand Cross of Order of Merit of Federal Republic of Germany, 1962. *Address:* Hillside Drive, Rathfarnham, Dublin.   *[Died 11 May 1971.*

le MAY, Reginald Stuart, PhD (Cantab); Hon. Member, Siam Society; retired; *b* 6 January 1885; *s* of Herbert le May and Harriet Jane Newman; *m* 1916, Dorothy Madeline Castle; one *d. Educ:* Framlingham Coll. Confidential Clerk to Consul-General, Zürich, 1903-04; Asst Master, Framlingham Coll., 1907; Consular Service, Siam, 1907; Vice-Consul, Chiengmai, 1915, Bangkok, 1917; Acting Consul-General, Saigon, 1920, resigned, 1922; Economic Adviser to Siamese Government, 1922-23; Editor of Official Journal, The Record; responsible for spread of Rural Credit Societies throughout Siam; Pembroke Coll., Cambridge, 1934-37 (PhD 1937). President, Society of Old Framlinghamians, 1947. Has lectured to learned societies for 40 years to interpret East to West; his collection of Buddhist Art from Siam exhibited at Cambridge, Oxford and London (India House); part is now in the British Museum. Silver Medallist, RSA. *Publications:* The Stamps of Siam, 1920; An Asian Arcady-Northern Siam, 1926; Siamese Tales, Old and New, 1930, 3rd edn, 1971; The Coinage of Siam, 1932 (re-published 1961); The Economic Conditions of North-Eastern Siam, 1932; The Ceramic Wares of North-Central Siam, 1933; Buddhist Art in Siam, 1938, 3rd edn, 1971; The Culture of South-East Asia, 1954 (2nd edn 1956, 3rd edn 1964; special Indian edn 1962, with foreword by late Pandit Nehru; German edn 1968); Response to Beauty, 1954; Records of the le May Family in England (1630-1950), 1958; contributions on SE Asia to Burlington Magazine, Indian Art and Letters, Asian Review, Oriental Art, Chambers's New Encyclopædia. *Recreations:* football (Capt. of School); cricket (Kent 2nd XI); golf (Bangkok championship); bridge (Kent County champion with late Lieut-Colonel Stopford, 1947 and 1950); ballet and art exhibitions. *Address:* Southview Guest House, 21 Rusthall Road, Tunbridge Wells, Kent. *Club:* West Kent (Tunbridge Wells).   *[Died 22 Jan. 1972.*

LE MAY, Group Captain William Kent, CBE 1943 (OBE 1942); RAF; *b* 29 June 1911; *s* of Percy Kent and Kate Le May (decd); *m* 1938, Greta Lettice Violet Blatchley; two *s* two *d. Educ:* Tonbridge Sch.; Agricultural Coll., Wye. Aux. Air Force, 1931-40, No. 500 County of Kent Squadron; permanent commission, 1946; retired, 1961. *Club:* Royal Air Force.
[Died 18 Sept. 1978.

LEMBERG, (Max) Rudolf, FRS 1952; FAA 1954 (Vice-President, 1957); PhD (Breslau); Professor Emeritus, Heidelberg University, since 1956; *b* 19 Oct. 1896; *s* of Justizrat Dr Arthur Lemberg and Margarethe (*née* Wendriner); *m* 1924, Hanna (Adelheid) Claussen. *Educ:* Johannes Gymnasium, Breslau, Silesia; Universities of Breslau, Munich, Heidelberg. PhD (Dr phil.) Breslau, 1921; habilitation as Lecturer (Privatdozent), Heidelberg Univ., 1930; Rockefeller Foundation Fellow, Sir William Dunn Institute of Biochemistry, Cambridge, 1930-31; Privatdozent, Heidelberg Univ. and Asst at Chemical

Inst., 1931-33; Academic Assistance Council (now Society for Protection of Science and Learning) Fellow, Sir William Dunn Institute of Biochemistry, Cambridge, 1933-35; Dir, Biochemical Labs and Asst Dir, Inst. of Med. Res., Royal North Shore Hosp., Sydney, NSW, 1935-72. Member, Advisory Research Cttee of Australian National Health and Med. Research Council, 1948-59. Visiting Professor, University of Pennsylvania, Philadelphia, 1966. Foreign Member, Heidelberg Acad. Science, 1956; Hon. Member: Accad. Anatomico-Chirurgica Perusina, 1959, and of several scientific societies in Australia and the United States. Hon DSc Sydney Univ., 1970. H. G. Smith Medal, Royal Australian Chem. Inst., 1948; James Cook Medal, 1965, Walter Burfitt Prize and Medal, 1971, Royal Soc. of NSW; Britannica Australia Award, 1966. *Publications:* The Disintegration of Haemoglobin in the Animal Body, in Perspectives in Biochemistry, 1937; Hematin Compounds and Bile Pigments (with J. W. Legge) (New York and London), 1949; Haematin Enzymes, Papers and Discussions of IUB Symposium, Canberra, 1959 (ed with J. E. Falk amd R. K. Morton), (London) 1961; The Cytochromes (with J. Barrett) (New York and London), 1973; numerous publications in Biochemical Journal, Proc. of Royal Society, Annual Review of Biochemistry (prefatory chap., 1965), Biochimica et Biophysica Acta, Australian Journal of Experimental Biology and Medical Science, etc. *Recreations:* bushwalking, motoring; relations of religion and science; work for international peace. *Address:* 57 Boundary Road, Wahroonga, NSW 2076, Australia. *T:* 48-3714.
[Died 10 April 1975.

LE MESURIER, Captain Edward Kirby, CBE 1961; MVO 1935; RN; gardener's mate (unskilled); *b* 11 Dec. 1903; *s* of Captain Charles Edward Le Mesurier, CB, RN, and Florence Kirby; *m* 1930, Eleanor, *d* of Lt-Col Norton Churchill; one *s* two *d. Educ:* RN Colleges. Served RN, 1917-53; War of 1939-45 (despatches). Sec., Nat. Rifle Assoc., 1953-68. *Address:* Glentworth, Wotton-under-Edge, Glos. *T:* 3227.
[Died 13 Feb. 1980.

LENANTON, Lady; *see* Oman, C. M. A.

LE NEVE FOSTER, F.; *see* Foster, Fermian Le N.

LENNARD, Sir Richard Barrett-; *see* Lennard, Sir T. R. F. B.

LENNARD, Lt-Col Sir Stephen Arthur Hallam Farnaby, 3rd Bt, *cr* 1880; late Scots Guards; formerly President, S. H. Lennard and Co. Ltd, Investment Dealers, Vancouver, BC (retired); *b* 31 July 1899; *o s* of Lt-Col Sir Henry Arthur Hallam Farnaby Lennard, 2nd Bt, and Beatrice (*d* 1948), *d* of Albemarle Cator, Woodbastwick Hall, Norfolk; *S* father, 1928; *m* 1st, 1928, Mary Isabel (*d* 1970), *er d* of Lawrence Bruce Latimer, Vancouver, BC; 2nd, 1970, Margaret Jean, *widow* of Group Captain William Neville Cumming, OBE, DFC, RAF, and *o d* of Daniel Hockin, Vancouver, BC. *Educ:* Winchester; RMC, Sandhurst. Lt Scots Guards, 1918-25; residing in Vancouver since 1925. Served War of 1939-45, with BEF, France, 1940; MEF and 8th Army, 1941-42; Persia and Iraq, 1943, and India, 1943-45; latterly on the Staff, retiring with rank of Lt-Col, 1945. 1939-45 Star and N African Star with 8th Army Clasp. *Recreations:* shooting and fishing. *Heir:* none. *Address:* Glenhead, Whonnock, BC. *T:* 462-7277. *Club:* Vancouver (Vancouver).
[Died 20 April 1980 (ext).

LENNARD, Sir (Thomas) Richard (Fiennes) Barrett-, 5th Bt, *cr* 1801; OBE 1970; *b* 12 Dec. 1898; *s* of 4th Bt and Lepel Julia (*d* 1959), *d* of late Rev. Henry Thornton Pearse; *S* father, 1934; *m* 1922, Kathleen Finora, *d* of late Hon. John Donohoe FitzGerald; one *d. Educ:* Brighton Coll.; Clare Coll., Cambridge. Norwich Union Insurance Gp: Dir, 1941; Vice-Pres., 1960; Senior Vice-Pres. and Vice-Chm., 1963; retired 1973; East Anglia Trustee Savings Bank: Manager, 1938; Trustee, 1943; Vice-Chm., 1946; Chm., 1957; Vice-Chm., 1971; retired 1974. KStJ. *Heir:* cousin Rev. Hugh Dacre Barrett-Lennard [*b* 27 June 1917. *Educ:* Radley. Served War of 1939-45 (despatches), Capt. Essex Regt. Is a Priest of London Oratory]. *Address:* 31 Swallowfield Park, Reading, Berks. *Clubs:* Royal Automobile; Leander.
[Died 28 Dec. 1977.

LENSKI, Lois; *b* Springfield, Ohio, 14 Oct. 1893; *d* of Richard C. H. Lenski and Marietta Young; *m* 1921, Arthur S. Covey; one *s. Educ:* Ohio State Univ., Columbus; Art Students' League, NY; Westminster School of Art, London. Artist, painter; writer and illustrator of children's books. Hon. Doctor of Humane Letters, Women's Coll., University of North Carolina, USA 1962; Hon. LittD: Wartburg Coll., Iowa, 1959; Capital Univ., Ohio 1966; Southwestern Coll., Winfield, Kan, 1968. Regina Medal, Catholic Library Assoc., 1969; Special Children's Collection Silver Medallion, Univ. of Southern Mississippi, 1969. *Publications:* Skipping Village; A Little Girl of 1900; Jack

Horner's Pie; Alphabet People; Two Brothers and their Animal Friends; Two Brothers and their Baby Sister; Spinach Boy; The Wonder City; Washington Picture Book; Benny and his Penny; Grandmother Tippytoe; Arabella and her Aunts; The Little Family; Johnny Goes to the Fair; The Little Auto; Surprise for Mother; Gooseberry Garden; Sugar Plum House; Little Baby Ann; The Easter Rabbit's Parade; The Little Sail Boat; Phebe Fairchild Her Book; A-Going to the Westward; The Little Airplane; Bound Girl of Cobble Hill; Susie Mariar (repr. 1968); Ocean-Born Mary; The Little Train; Blueberry Corners; Indian Captive: The Story of Mary Jemison; Animals for Me; The Little Farm; Bayou Suzette; Davy's Day; Puritan Adventure; Let's Play House; Spring is Here; Strawberry Girl (awarded Newbery Medal, 1946); The Little Fire Engine; Blue Ridge Billy; Surprise for Davy; Judy's Journey (awarded Child Study Assoc. Award for 1947); Mr and Mrs Noah; Now It's Fall; Boom Town Boy, 1948; Cowboy Small; Cotton in My Sack, 1949; Texas Tomboy, 1950; I Like Winter, 1950; Prairie School, 1951; Papa Small, 1951; We Live in the South; Peanuts for Billy Ben; We are Thy Children; Hymn Book for Boys and Girls, 1952; On a Summer Day; Mama Hattie's Girl, 1953; Project Boy; We Live in the City; Songs of Mr Small; Corn-Farm Boy, 1954; San Francisco Boy; A Dog Came to School, 1955; We Live by the River; Berries in the Scoop; Songs of the City; Big Little Davy; Flood Friday, 1956; Houseboat Girl; Davy and His Dog, 1957; Little Sioux Girl, 1958; I went for a Walk, 1958; At our House, 1959; Coal Camp Girl, 1959; When I Grow Up, 1960; We Live in the Country, 1960; Davy Goes Places, 1961; Policeman Small, 1962; We Live in the Southwest, 1962; Shoo-Fly Girl, 1963; The Life I Live: Collected Poems, 1965; We Live in the North, 1965; High-Rise Secret, 1966; To Be a Logger, 1967; Debbie and her Grandma, 1967; Lois Lenski's Christmas Stories, 1968; Adventures in Understanding, 1968; Deer Valley Girl, 1968; Debbie Herself, 1969; Debbie and her Family, 1969; Debbie and her Dolls, 1970; Debbie Goes to Nursery School, 1970; City Poems, 1971; Florida, My Florida (poems), 1971; Journey into Childhood: autobiography, 1972. *Address:* Lutean Shores, Tarpon Springs, Florida 33589, USA. *[Died 11 Sept. 1974.*

LEON, His Honour Henry Cecil, MC 1942; County Court Judge, 1949-67; Chairman, British Copyright Council, since 1973; *b* 19 Sept. 1902; *y s* of late J. A. Leon and late Mrs Leon, of 4 Cleveland Gardens, Bayswater, W2; *m* 1st, 1935, Lettice Mabel (*d* 1950), *o d* of late H. D. Apperly and of Mrs Apperly, late of Chalfont St Peter, Bucks; no *c* ; 2nd, 1954, Barbara Jeanne Ovenden (*née* Blackmore); one step *s. Educ:* St Paul's Sch.; King's Coll., Cambridge. Called to the Bar, 1923. Served War 1939-45, 1/5 Queen's Regt. *Publications,* under pseudonym Henry Cecil: *fiction:* Full Circle, 1948; The Painswick Line, 1951; No Bail for the Judge, 1952; Ways and Means, 1952; Natural Causes, 1953; According to the Evidence, 1954; Brothers in Law, 1955 (filmed 1957); Friends at Court, 1956; Much in Evidence, 1957; Sober as a Judge, 1958; Settled out of Court, 1959; Alibi for a Judge, 1960; Daughters in Law, 1961; Unlawful Occasions, 1962; Independent Witness, 1963; Portrait of a Judge and Other Stories, 1964; Fathers in Law, 1965; The Asking Price, 1966; A Woman Named Anne, 1967; No Fear or Favour, 1968; Tell You What I'll Do, 1969; The Buttercup Spell, 1971; The Wanted Man, 1972; Truth with her Boots On, 1974; Cross Purposes, 1976; *non-fiction:* Brief to Counsel, 1958; Not Such an Ass, 1961; Tipping the Scales, 1964; Know About English Law, 1965; A Matter of Speculation, 1965; The English Judge (Hamlyn Lectures), 1970; *autobiography:* Just Within the Law, 1975; a number of short stories and articles; under pseudonym Clifford Maxwell: I Married the Girl, 1960. *Plays:* Brothers in Law (with Ted Willis), 1959; Settled Out of Court (with William Saroyan), Strand, 1960; Alibi for a Judge (with Felicity Douglas and Basil Dawson), Savoy, 1965; According to the Evidence (with Felicity Douglas and Basil Dawson), Savoy, 1967; No Fear or Favour, 1967; Hugo (with C. E. Webber), 1969; A Woman Named Anne, Duke of York's, 1970; The Tilted Scales, 1970; *TV Series:* with Frank Muir and Denis Norden: Brothers in Law, Mr Justice Duncannon; numerous radio plays. *Address:* 6 Gray's Inn Square, Gray's Inn, WC1. *T:* 01-242 7595. *Clubs:* Garrick, MCC. *[Died 21 May 1976.*

LEON, Prof. Philip, MA Oxon; Professor of Classics, University of Leicester, 1954-60, retired; Professor Emeritus, 1966; *b* 10 April 1895; *s* of Meyer and Taube Leon; *m* 1st, 1927, Mariette Eileen Soman (*d* 1941); two *d*; 2nd, 1948, Elizabeth Palmer Elliott; one *s. Educ:* Manchester Grammar Sch.; New Coll., Oxford. Asst Lecturer at University Coll., London, Dept of Latin, 1921-23; Lecturer in charge of Dept of Classics, University Coll., Leicester, 1923-54. Visiting Prof., University Coll. of Rhodesia and Nyasaland, Salisbury, 1961-63. *Publications:* The Ethics of Power, 1935; The Philosophy of Courage, 1939; Plato, 1939; Body, Mind and Spirit, 1948; The Professors, 1955; (trans.) Gandhi to Vinoba, 1957; Beyond Belief

and Unbelief, 1965; The Gospel according to Judas, 1968. Contrib. to Mind, Philosophy, The Hibbert Jl, Classical Quarterly, The Listener, Time and Tide, etc. *Recreations:* tennis, walking, climbing, swimming, chess, mathematics. *Address:* 12 Sackville Gardens, Leicester LE2 3TH. *T:* Leicester 704355.
[Died 15 Dec. 1974.

LEON TROUT, Sir H.; *see* Trout, Sir H. L.

LE PATOUREL, Brig. Herbert Wallace, VC 1943; DL; Director, Harveys of Bristol, since 1969; *b* 20 June 1916; *yr s* of late Herbert Augustus Le Patourel (Attorney-General for Guernsey) and Mary Elizabeth Daw; *m* 1949, Babette Theresa Beattie; two *d. Educ:* Elizabeth Coll., Guernsey. Bank Clerk, 1934-37; 2nd Lt Royal Guernsey Militia, 1936; transferred to The Hampshire Regt, 1937; served War of 1939-45 (despatches, VC); Instructor at Staff Coll., Quetta, 1945-47; Instructor, School of Infantry, Warminster, 1948-50; Parachute Regt, 1950-53; CO, 14th Para Bn and 5th Bn The Royal Hampshire Regt TA, 1954-57; GSO1, British Joint Services Mission, Washington, DC, 1958-60; Dep. Comdr, Ghana Army, 1960-61; Dep. Comdr, 43 Div./District, 1961-62; retired 1962. Executive Asst to the Directors of Showerings Vine Products and Whiteways Ltd, 1965-69. DL Avon, 1974. *Recreations:* sailing, small holding. *Address:* Ford Farm, Chewton Mendip, Bath. *T:* Chewton Mendip 576. *Clubs:* Army and Navy; Royal Channel Islands Yacht.
[Died 4 Sept. 1979.

LE ROUGETEL, Sir John Helier, KCMG, *cr* 1946 (CMG 1943); MC, 1917 and bar 1918; *b* 19 June 1894; *s* of Daniel Le Rougetel; *m* 1925, Mary Penrose-Thackwell; one *s* one *d. Educ:* Rossall; Magdalene Coll., Cambridge (Hon. Fellow 1952). Army, 1914-19. Entered Diplomatic Service, 1920; served at Vienna, Budapest, Ottawa, Tokyo, Peking, The Hague, Bucharest, Moscow, Shanghai, and at Foreign Office; Ambassador to Persia, 1946-50; Ambassador to Belgium, 1950-51; High Commissioner for the UK in South Africa, 1951-55; retired from Foreign Service, 1955. *Recreations:* fishing, golf. *Address:* Borovere Cottage, Alton, Hants.
[Died 3 Jan. 1975.

LESLIE, Sir Francis (Galloway), KCVO 1965 (CVO 1956); Physician in Ordinary HRH the late Princess Royal, 1951-65; *b* 10 April 1902; *e s* of late Lewis Francis Leslie, OBE, Haslemere; *m* 1929, Enid Mary, *o d* of Arthur Powell Simon, London; one *s* one *d. Educ:* Shrewsbury Sch.; Trinity Coll., Cambridge; The London Hospital. BA Cantab 1923; MRCS, LRCP, 1927; DCH Eng. 1943; MA Cantab 1959. Gen. Practitioner: Chichester, Sussex, 1928-36; London, 1937-39; Eton, Windsor (Mem. Eton Coll., Medical Board), 1941-44; Gen. Physician, London, 1944-. War of 1939-45, Lt, RAMC (Dep. Med. Specialist i/c Female Personnel), Aldershot Comd, 1939-40. Past Pres. Hunterian Soc., 1958-59. *Recreations:* various. *Address:* 24 Napier Avenue, Hurlingham, SW6. *T:* 01-736 4105.
[Died 2 Jan. 1971.

LESLIE, James Campbell, OBE 1943; MA, BSc(Agr); Livestock Consultant; *m* 1926; one *d. Educ:* Stonehaven Mackie Acad.; Aberdeen Univ.; North of Scotland Coll. of Agriculture, Teacher of Science, Mathematics and Agriculture, Annan Acad., Dumfriesshire; Lectr in Agriculture, Leeds Univ.; Organiser of Agricultural Educn to the Lindsey (Lincs) CC; Organiser of Agricultural Education to the Cambridgeshire County Council; Principal, Essex Institute of Agriculture, Chelmsford; Executive Officer, Essex War Agricultural Cttee; Dep. Gen. Sec., National Farmers' Union; Agricultural Adviser, Edmundsons Electricity Corporation, Ltd; Agricultural Adviser British Oil and Cake Mills Ltd, retired. *Publications:* contributed to various Agricultural Journals and Weekly Papers and the Scientific Cyclopædia of Agriculture. *Address:* Lightoaks, Fryerning, Ingatestone, Essex. *Club:* Chelmsford.
[Died 25 July 1974.

LESLIE, Sir (John Randolph) Shane, 3rd Bt, *cr* 1876; LLD (Notre Dame University, USA); Member Irish Academy; Author and Professor; *b* 1885; *er s* of Sir John Leslie, 2nd Bt, CBE, and Léonie Blanche (*d* 1943), *d* of Leonard Jerome of New York; *S* father, 1944; *m* 1912, Marjorie (*d* 1951), *y d* of Henry C. Ide, of Vermont, USA, late Gov.-Gen. of the Philippines and US Ambassador to Spain; two *s* one *d*; *m* 1958, Iris, *y d* of C. M. Laing, barrister, Bury Knowle, Headington, Oxford. *Educ:* Eton; King's Coll., Cambride (MA). Knight Comdr of St Gregory. *Publications:* Songs of Oriel; The Isle of Columcille; The End of a Chapter, 1916; Verses in Peace and War; The Oppidan, 1922; Life of Cardinal Manning; The Skull of Swift, 1928; The Greek Anthology, 1929; The Anglo-Catholic, 1929; A Ghost in the Isle of Wight, 1929; Memoir of J. E. C. Bodley,

1930; The Epic of Jutland, 1930; Sublime Failures, 1932; The Oxford Movement, 1933; Poems and Ballads, 1933; The Passing Chapter, 1934; The Script of Jonathan Swift and other Essays, 1935; American Wonderland, 1936; Men were Different: Studies in Late Victorian Biography, 1937; Sir Evelyn Ruggles-Brise, 1938; The Film of Memory, 1938; The Life of Mrs Fitzherbert, 1939; Letters of Mrs Fitzherbert, 1940; From Cabin Boy to Archbishop, 1942; Letters of Cardinal Vaughan to Lady Herbert of Lea, 1943; The Irish Tangle for English Readers, 1946; Salutation to Five, 1951; Memoir of Cardinal Gasquet, 1954; Shane Leslie's Ghost Book, 1955; Long Shadows, 1966. *Recreations:* Irish archæology and forestry. *Heir: s* John Norman Ide Leslie, *b* 6 Dec. 1916. *Address:* 16b Palmeira Court, Hove, Sussex.
[Died 13 Aug. 1971.

LESLIE, Samuel Clement, CBE 1946; Consultant on information policy to industrial and official bodies, since retirement as Head of the Information Division of the Treasury, 1959; Member, Northern Ireland Development Council, 1955-65; *b* Perth, Western Australia, 15 July 1898; *m* 1924, Doris Frances Falk; one *s* two *d. Educ:* Melbourne C of E Gram. Sch.; Melbourne Univ. (MA); Balliol Coll., Oxford (Rhodes Scholar, DPhil). Post-graduate work in philosophy; Lecturer in Philosophy, University Coll. of North Wales, 1922-23; Senior Lecturer in Philosophy, Melbourne Univ., 1924-25; accompanied Mr S. M. Bruce (Australian Prime Minister) to Imperial Conference of 1926; remained in Britain and entered business; Publicity Manager to Gas Light & Coke Co., 1936-40; Director of Public Relations, Ministry of Supply, 1940, Home Office and Ministry of Home Security, 1940-43; Principal Asst Sec., Home Office, etc., 1943-45; Dir, Council of Industrial Design, 1945-47. *Publications:* Front Line 1940-41, 1942 (official publication, anon.); The Rift in Israel, 1971. *Address:* 9 Southwood Heights, Southwood Lawn Road, N6. *Club:* Reform. [Died 7 Jan. 1980.

LESLIE, Sir Shane; *see* Leslie, Sir John R. S.

LETCHWORTH, Thomas Edwin, CMG 1959; Colonial Administrative Service, retired; *b* 1 April 1906; *m* 1936, Marjorie Danvers Bayliffe, *d* of late Col A. D. Bayliffe, CMG. *Educ:* Downside; Christ's Coll., Cambridge. Winning Cambridge crews, 1927, 1928 (stroke). Administrative Service, Nigeria, 1928; seconded Gambia, 1943-45; Resident, Bornu Province, 1955-58; retired, 1959. Mem., New Forest RDC, 1969-. *Address:* Quarr Coach House, Sway, near Lymington, Hants SO4 0EB. *T:* Sway 2593. *Clubs:* Royal Commonwealth Society; Leander, Royal Lymington Yacht. [Died 3 Feb. 1973.

LETHAM, James; Treasurer and General Manager, Bank of Scotland, 1966-70, Director, 1967-71; *b* 6 Aug. 1907; *s* of Robert Letham, Ironfounder, Airdrie, and Bethia McHutchison; *m* 1935, Williamina Margaret Robb (*d* 1969); one *s. Educ:* Airdrie and Glasgow High Schs. Entered service of Bank of Scotland, 1923; Asst Treasurer, 1955; Dep. Treasurer, 1965. Pres., Inst. of Bankers in Scotland; Chm., Cttee of Scottish Bank General Managers, 1968-70. Mem. of Court, Heriot-Watt Univ., 1966-; Vice-Pres. and Dir, Edinburgh Chamber of Commerce and Manufactures; Member: British Computer Soc. (papers on Computer Accountancy to professional and commercial bodies); Organising Cttee for British Commonwealth Games, 1970; Exec. Cttee, Scottish Council (Develt and Industry), 1967-69; Board, Forth Ports Authority; Scottish Regional Council, CBI; Scottish Hosp. Trust, 1971-. Hon. DLitt, Heriot-Watt, 1970. *Recreations:* golf, curling and gardening. *Address:* The Dykes, 89 Ravelston Dykes, Edinburgh 12. *T:* 031-337 7749. *Clubs:* Caledonian; Caledonian (Edinburgh). [Died 16 Jan. 1972.

LETHBRIDGE, Captain Sir Hector (Wroth), 6th Bt, *cr* 1804; *b* 26 Aug. 1898; *s* of Sir Wroth Periam Christopher Lethbridge, 5th Bart, and Alianore (*y d* of late Edward Chandos Pole, Radbourne Hall, Derby, and Lady Anne Chandos Pole, *d* of 5th Earl of Harrington); *S* father, 1950; *m* 1946, Diana, widow of Major John Vivian Bailey, The Royal Scots Fusiliers, and *er d* of Lt-Col Frank Noel, Hopton Hall, Great Yarmouth; one *s* one *d. Educ:* Radley. Served European War, 1914-18: Officers Cadet Bn, 1916; commissioned, The Rifle Brigade, 1917; France, 1917-18 (POW); India, 1919-20; RARO, 1920; recalled, 1939; served War of 1939-45, in Gold Coast, 1941; invalided home, 1941; demobilized, 1945. *Recreations:* tennis, shooting, golf. *Heir: s* Thomas Periam Hector Noel Lethbridge [*b* 17 July 1950; *m* 1976, Susan Elizabeth Rocke; one *s*]. *Address:* Long Sutton House, Langport, Somerset. *T:* Long Sutton 284. *Clubs:* Carlton; Somerset County (Taunton). [Died 29 June 1978.

LETHBRIDGE, Thomas Charles, MA, FSA; *b* 23 March 1901; *s* of Ambrose Y. Lethbridge and Violet Murdoch; *m* 1st, 1923, Sylvia Frances Robertson (marriage dissolved, 1944); one *s* one *d* (and one *s* decd); 2nd, 1944, Mina Elizabeth Leadbitter. *Educ:*

Wellington Coll.; Trinity Coll., Cambridge. Cambridge Expedition to Jan Mayen, 1921, to East Greenland, 1923; Excavator for Cambridge Antiquarian Soc., 1925-56; Hon. Keeper, Anglo-Saxon Collections, University Museum of Archæology and Ethnology, Cambridge; Cambridge Expedition to Baffin Bay etc, 1937. Hon. Mem., Cambridge Antiquarian Soc., 1957. Served War of 1939-45, RNVSR, NID, Major HG. *Publications:* Merlin's Island, 1945; Herdsmen and Hermits, 1950; Boats and Boatmen, 1952; Coastwise Craft, 1952; The Painted Men, 1954; Gogmagog, 1957; Ghost and Ghoul, 1962; Witches, 1962; Ghost and Divining-rod, 1963; ESP, 1965; A Step in the Dark, 1967; The Monkey's Tail, 1969; The Legend of the Sons of God (posthumous, 1972;) numerous papers and monographs on Anglo-Saxon, Scottish and Eskimo archæology. *Recreations:* boats, natural history, water-colour painting, curiosity. *Address:* Hole House, Branscombe, Seaton, Devon. *T:* Branscombe 229.   *[Died 30 Sept. 1971.*

LETTS, Winifred M.; *b* Feb. 1882; *y d* of late Rev. E. F. Letts, MA; *m* 1926, W. H. F. Verschoyle. *Educ:* St Anne's, Abbots Bromley; Alexandra Coll., Dublin. Contributions in prose and verse to the Spectator, Cornhill, Punch, Yale Review, etc; two plays, Eyes of the Blind, and The Challenge, performed at Abbey Theatre, Dublin; 3 act play, Hamilton & Jones, Gate Theatre, Dublin, 1941. *Publications:* Songs from Leinster (new edn illus., 1944); Hallowe'en and Poems of the War; More Songs from Leinster; Diana Dethroned; The Rough Way; Christina's Son; Naughty Sophia; other books for children; Corporals' Corner; Saint Patrick, the Travelling Man, 1932; Knockmaroon, 1933; Pomona & Co., 1934; Pomona's Island; The Gentle Mountain, 1938. *Recreations:* hunting wild flowers, gardening. *Address:* Beech Cottage, Killiney, Co. Dublin.   *[Died June 1972.*

LEVEEN, Jacob; Senior Member, Wolfson College (formerly University College), Cambridge; Keeper of Department of Oriental Printed Books and Manuscripts, British Museum, 1953-56; retired; *b* 24 Dec. 1891; *o* surv. *c* of late David and Rose Leveen; *m* 1928, Violet Egerton (marr. diss. 1963), *yr d* of late Capt. George Egerton Pearch; one *s* decd. *Educ:* Jews' Coll.; University Coll., London (Prizeman in Greek, and Hollier Scholar in Hebrew); School of Oriental and African Studies (BA with First Class Honours in Arabic; Ouseley Scholar in Arabic). Entered British Museum, 1914; Deputy Keeper, Dept of Oriental Printed Books and Manuscripts, 1944. War Service, 1916-20. *Publications:* Part IV of Catalogue of Hebrew and Samaritan Manuscripts in British Museum, 1935; The Hebrew Bible in Art (Schweich Lectures in Biblical Archæology, British Academy), 1944; (ed) A Digest of Commentaries on the Babylonian Talmud, British Museum, 1961; studies in the text of the Psalms (in Journal of Theological Studies and *Vetus Testamentum*); occasional articles and reviews in learned, art and popular journals. *Recreations:* talking, music, art and literature. *Address:* 5 Brookside, Cambridge. *T:* 50619. *Club:* Athenæum.   *[Died 1 Aug. 1980.*

LEVER, Baron *cr* 1975 (Life Peer), of Ardwick in the City of Manchester; **Leslie Maurice Lever,** Kt 1970; JP; Solicitor since 1927; *b* 29 April 1905; *e s* of late Bernard Lever and Mrs Bertha Lever; *m* 1939, Ray Rosalia, JP, Lancs, *o c* of late Dr Leonard Levene, formerly RAMC, Leicester; one *s* one *d*. *Educ:* Elementary Sch.; Manchester Grammar Sch.; University of Leeds. LLB (Hons) 1925; Solicitor (Hons) 1927; senior partner in firm of solicitors, Leslie M. Lever & Co.; Commissioner for Oaths, 1933. CC Manchester, 1932-; Alderman, 1949-74, Hon. Alderman, 1974; Lord Mayor of Manchester, 1957-58; JP 1957 (Chairman Manchester Magistrates). MP (Lab) Ardwick Div. of Manchester, 1950-70. Governor, Manchester Univ.; President: Manchester and Salford (East) Corps, St John Ambulance Bde; N Western Counties Horticultural Soc.; N Western Brass Bands Federation; Assoc. of Lancastrians in London, 1968-69; Patron Manchester and Salford Savings Bank; Member Council, Lancashire and Cheshire Industrial Development Assoc.; Hon. Life Member Dunkirk Veterans' Assoc.; Life Vice-President, Navy League, 1960-; President, India League; President, Manchester and District Liaison Cttee of all Ex-Servicemen's Assocs, Army, Navy and Air Force, in the area; Hon. President, Manchester Branch Brit. Limbless Ex-Servicemen's Assoc. (BLESMA) and Hon. Secretary All Party Parliamentary Cttee. Past Chairman, Manchester Univ. Settlement. Hon. Solicitor to various organisations. Holds or has held office as President or Vice-President in various local organisations to do with welfare, sports, etc. Mem., Nat. Council, Royal Institute for the Deaf, 1961. A representative of British Parliament at World Interparliamentary Convention, Brussels, 1961. Vice-President: Disabled Drivers' Assoc.; British Assoc. at Manchester, 1962. Patron, National Assoc. of Education Welfare Officers. FRSA 1935 (former President, NW Centre). Coronation Medal, 1953. Knight Grand Cross, Order of St Gregory the Great, 1968 (Kt

Comdr, 1960). Associate Serving Brother, O St John, 1967. Hon. LLD (Leeds), 1963. *Recreations:* reading and social work. *Address:* 16 John Dalton Street, Manchester M2 6HK. *T:* 061-832 5841-4. *Club:* Manchester Press (Hon. Life Member).
                                            [Died 26 July 1977.

LEVER, Sir Tresham (Joseph Philip), 2nd Bt, *cr* 1911; MA Oxon; FRSL; President, since 1974, Council Member, 1963-74, Brontë Society; *b* 3 Sept. 1900; *o c* of 1st Bt and Beatrice Hilda (*d* 1917), 3rd *d* of late Philip Falk, Kensington Palace Gardens; *S* father, 1924; *m* 1st, 1930, Frances Yowart (*d* 1959), *yr d* of late Lindsay Hamilton Goodwin and *widow* of Cecil Parker, Walton Hall, Lancs; one *s*; 2nd, 1962, Pamela, Lady Malcolm Douglas-Hamilton, *o d* of late Lieut-Colonel the Hon. Malcolm Bowes Lyon. *Educ:* Harrow; University College, Oxford. Called to Bar, 1925. Contested (C) S Hackney, 1929. High Sheriff of Leics, 1962-63. Equipped and furnished Brontë Memorial Chapel, St Michael and All Angels, Haworth, 1964. *Publications:* Profit and Loss, 1933; The Life and Times of Sir Robert Peel, 1942; The House of Pitt: a Family Chronicle, 1947; Godolphin, his Life and Times, 1952; The Letters of Lady Palmerston (ed), 1957; The Herberts of Wilton, 1967; Lessudden House, Sir Walter Scott and the Scotts of Raeburn, 1971; Clayton of Toc H, 1972; articles in Times Literary Supp., History To-day, etc. *Recreations:* shooting, fishing. *Heir: s* Tresham Christopher Arthur Lindsay Lever [*b* 9 Jan. 1932. *Educ:* Eton; Trinity Coll., Cambridge]. *Address:* Lessudden, St Boswells, Roxburghshire. *T:* St Boswells 2746.*Clubs:* St James', Beefsteak; New (Edinburgh).   *[Died 30 April 1975.*

LEVY, Aaron Harold, BA, MD, CM, FRCS; Consulting Surgeon, Moorfields Eye Hospital; Consulting Ophthalmic Surgeon, British Home and Hospital for Incurables and St Monica's Hospital, etc; Consulting Ophthalmic Surgeon, Willesden General Hospital, London Jewish Hospital, and Putney Hospital; *b* Montreal; *m* 1908, Lena (*d* 1965), *d* of I. Samuel, JP, Cardiff; one *s* one *d*. *Educ:* McGill Univ., Montreal; St Bartholomew's Hospital. Late Ophthalmic Surgeon, Tooting Military Hospital, Mitcham Military Hospital; Captain, RAMC; Fellow of the Royal Society of Medicine; Member of the Royal Institution; Fellow of the Royal Geographical Society. *Publications:* various articles on Ophthalmic Medicine and Surgery. *Address:* 19 Campden Hill Court, Campden Hill Road, W8. *T:* 01-937 9946. *Club:* Roehampton.
                                            [Died 31 March 1977.

LEVY, Benn Wolfe, MBE; farmer and dramatist; *b* March 1900; *o s* of late Octave G. Levy and Nannie Levy, *gs* of late Hon. L. W. Levy, Sydney, NSW, Australia; *m* 1933, Constance Cummings; one *s* one *d*. *Educ:* Repton; University College, Oxford. Royal Air Force, 1918. Publisher, 1923; Royal Navy, War of 1939-45. MP (Lab) Eton and Slough Division of Bucks, 1945-50. Arts Council Executive, 1953-61. *Publications:* This Woman Business; A Man with Red Hair (from the novel by Hugh Walpole); Mud and Treacle; Mrs Moonlight; Art and Mrs Bottle; The Devil; Topaze (from the French of Marcel Pagnol); Evergreen; Hollywood Holiday (with John van Druten); Springtime for Henry; Madame Bovary (from the French dramatization); The Poet's Heart; Young Madame Conti (adapted, from German of Bruno Frank, with Hubert Griffith); The Jealous God; Clutterbuck; Return to Tyassi; Cupid and Psyche; The Rape of the Belt; The Tumbler; Public and Confidential; The Marriage. *Address:* Cote House, Aston, Oxon. *T:* Bampton Castle 249.   *[Died 7 Dec. 1973.*

LEVY, Hyman, MA, DSc, FRSE; Professor of Mathematics, Imperial College of Science and Technology, SW, 1923-54; Emeritus Professor, 1954; Head of Department of Mathematics and Mechanics, 1946; Dean of Royal College of Science, 1946-52; Fellow, Imperial College, 1955; *b* Edinburgh, 7 March 1889; *m* 1918, M. A. Fraser, MA; two *s* one *d*. *Educ:* George Heriot's Sch., Edinburgh; Universities of Edinburgh, Oxford, and Göttingen. Graduated at Edinburgh, First Class Hons, Mathematics and Physics, 1911; awarded Ferguson Scholarship, 1851 Exhibition, Carnegie Research Fellowship; Member of Aerodynamics Research Staff of the National Physical Laboratory, 1916-20; Assistant Professor of Mathematics at Royal College of Science, 1920-23; Member of Council of London Mathematical Society, 1929-33; Vice-President, 1931-32; Chairman Science Advisory Cttee of Labour Party, 1924-30. Hon. ARCS. *Publications:* Aeronautics in Theory and Experiment; Science in Perspective; Science in the Changing World; The Universe of Science, 1932; Science in Edwardian England; Makers of the Modern Spirit, Newton, 1933; Science in an Irrational Society; The Web of Thought and Action; Numerical Studies in Differential Equations, 1934; Thinking, 1935; Elements of the Theory of Probability, 1936; A Modern Philosophy, 1937; Modern Science, 1939; Science, Curse or

Blessing? 1940; Social Thinking, 1945; Literature in an Age of Science, 1953; Jews and the National Question, 1957; Finite Difference Equations, 1958; Journeys in Belief, 1968; several mathematical text-books and a number of original memoirs on mathematical and aeronautical subjects; numerous articles on science and scientific philosophy in weekly and monthly periodicals. *Recreations:* scientific and political journalism, chess. *Address:* 25 Home Park Road, SW19. *T:* 01-946 7379.
[*Died* 27 *Feb.* 1975.

LEWEY, Hon. Sir Arthur Werner, Kt 1954; QC (Jamaica), 1939; MA (Cantab); *b* 2 Sept. 1894; *s* of late Arthur Lewey and Frances Helena Moorcroft Williams; *m* 1928, Kitty, *y d* of late Trevelyan Arnold Pope; one *s. Educ:* St Pauls; Trinity Hall, Cambridge. Gazetted Middlesex Regt, 1914, and served in Egypt, Flanders, Gallipoli, and Palestine (wounded twice); served with Territorial Army (8th Bn, Middlesex Regt), 1920-29; Called to Bar, Inner Temple, 1920, and joined South-Eastern Circuit; entered Colonial Service, 1929; Police Magistrate, Gambia, 1930; Crown Counsel, Kenya, 1932; Solicitor-General, Uganda, 1936; Attorney-General, Jamaica, 1939; Attorney-General, Gold Coast, 1943-48; Legal Adviser to the Resident Minister, West Africa (Viscount Swinton), 1944, and to West African Council, 1946; a Justice of Appeal, West African Court of Appeal, 1948-51 and Rhodesia and Nyasaland Court of Appeal, 1952; Chief Justice, N Rhodesia, 1952-55; Member, Judicial Commission on Central African Federation, 1952; A Federal Justice of the Supreme Court of the Federation of Rhodesia and Nyasaland, 1955-58, retired; acted as Chief Justice of the Federation for various periods. *Address:* Little Stodham House, Liss, Hampshire. *Clubs:* United Service & Royal Aero, MCC.
[*Died* 26 *Oct.* 1973.

LEWIN, Walpole Sinclair, CBE 1978; Consultant Neurological Surgeon to Addenbrooke's Hospital, Cambridge, since 1955; Associate Lecturer in Medicine, University of Cambridge, since 1976; *b* 20 Aug. 1915; *s* of Eric Sinclair Lewin, London; *m* 1947, Marion Cumming (*d* 1979); one *s* one *d. Educ:* University College, and University College Hospital, London. MRCS, LRCP 1939; MB, BS 1939; MS (London) 1942; FRCS 1940; MA (Cantab) 1970. University College First Entrance Exhibn, 1934; Magrath Clin. Schol., and Atkinson Morley Surgical Schol., 1939; Leverhulme Research Grant, RCS, 1947. Sometime House Physician, House Surgeon, Cas., Surgical Officer, Harker Smith Surgical Registrar, UCH; First Asst, Nuffield Dept of Surgery, Oxford; Clinical Lectr in Neurosurgery, Univ. of Oxford; Asst Neurological Surgeon, Radcliffe Infirmary, Oxford, 1949-61; Consultant Neurological Surgeon to Army. Hunterian Professor, RCS, 1948; Erasmus Wilson Demonstrator, RCS, 1965; Mem. Council, RCS, 1970-(Vice Pres., 1976-77, 1978-79). Mem. Scientific Adv. Council, Huntingdon Res. Centre, 1974-. Examnr in Surgery, Univ. of Cambridge, 1979-. Ruscoe Clarke Lectr, Birmingham, 1967; Victor Horsley Meml Lectr, 1975. Fellow: Assoc. of Surgeons; Royal Soc. Med.; Soc. of British Neurological Surgeons; Cambridge Phil. Soc.; Member: BMA; Internat. Soc. of Surgeons. Chm., Central Cttee, Hosp. Med. Services, 1968-71; Vice-Chm., Jt Consultants Cttee, 1967-71; Member: Central Health Services Council, 1966-76; General Med. Council, 1971-; Council, BMA, 1968- (Chm., 1971-76; Vice-Pres., 1979-; Gold Medallist, 1979); deleg., Gen. Assembly World Med. Assoc., 1971-, Council Mem., 1974- (Chm., 1977-); Council, World Fedn of Medical Educn; Delegate, Standing Cttee Doctors of EEC, 1971- (Pres., 1974-77); Vice President: Commonwealth Med. Assoc., 1972-; Internat. Soc. Psychiatric Surgery; Corres. Member: Amer. Assoc. of Neurological Surgeons; Amer. Acad. of Neurological Surgery; Deutsche Gesellschaft für Neurochirurgie; Hon. Mem., Brazil Med. Assoc. Served Army, 1942-47; Lieut-Colonel, RAMC; OC Surgical Div., MEF. Fellow: University Coll. London; Darwin Coll., Cambridge. Hon. DSc Hull, 1974. *Publications:* The Management of Head Injuries, 1966; Section, British Surgical Progress, 1958; papers to Medical Journals on Neurosurgical subjects. *Recreations:* tennis, gardening. *Address:* Martins Lodge, 4 Babraham Road, Cambridge. *T:* Cambridge 48843; (Addenbrooke's Hospital), Cambridge 45151. *Club:* Athenæum. [*Died* 23 *Jan.* 1980.

LEWIS, A(lfred) Neville; *see* Lewis, Neville.

LEWIS, Sir Aubrey Julian, Kt 1959; MD, FRCP; Professor of Psychiatry, University of London, 1946-66; *b* Adelaide, South Australia, 8 Nov. 1900; *s* of George Lewis, Adelaide; *m* 1934, Hilda Stoessiger, MD, FRCP (*d* 1966); two *s* two *d. Educ:* Christian Brothers' Coll., Adelaide; University of Adelaide. Medical Registrar, Adelaide Hospital, 1924-26; Rockefeller Medical Fellow, 1926-28; Clinical Director, Maudsley Hospital, 1936-48; President Section of Psychiatry, RSM, 1946; Consultant in Psychological Medicine British Post-Graduate

Medical Sch., 1932-45; Civilian Consultant in Psychiatry, RAF, 1945-67. Manson Lecturer, British Institute Philosophy, 1949; Maudsley Lecturer, RMPA, 1951; Bradshaw Lecturer, RCP, 1957; Galton Lecturer, Eugenics Society, 1958; Hobhouse Lecturer, University College, London, 1960; Bertram Roberts Lecturer, Yale, 1960; Maurice Bloch Lecturer, 1962; Harveian Orator, RCP, 1963; Linacre Lectr, Cambridge, 1967; Mapother Lectr, Inst. of Psychiatry, 1969. Member American Philosophical Society, 1961. Hon. FRCPsych, 1972. Hon. DSc Belfast, 1966; Hon. LLD Toronto, 1966. Ambuj Nath Bose Prize, RCP, 1968. *Publications:* Inquiries in Psychiatry, 1967; The State of Psychiatry, 1967; articles on medical topics. *Address:* Caversham Lodge, Barnes, SW13. *Club:* Athenæum.
[*Died* 21 *Jan.* 1975.

LEWIS, Cecil D.; *see* Day-Lewis.

LEWIS, Brig. Sir Clinton (Gresham), Kt 1941; OBE 1928; *b* 25 Nov. 1885; *s* of J. Hardwicke Lewis, late of Veytaux, Switzerland; *m* 1916, Lilian Eyre (*d* 1962), *d* of late Rev. Walter Wace; one *s* one *d* (and one *s* decd). *Educ:* privately, Montreux, Switzerland. Royal Military Acad., Woolwich, 1903-04 (Sword of Honour); Commission RE 1904; joined Survey of India, 1907; in charge Miri Mission Survey, NE Frontier, 1911-12; served European War, 1914-18 (despatches, Bt Major); Afghan War, 1919; Indo-Afghan Boundary Commission, 1919; with Turco-Iraq frontier delimitation commission, 1927; Surveyor-Gen. of India, 1937-41; employed with Ord. Survey, 1942-45. Hon. Sec. RGS, 1944-46, Vice-Pres. 1946-50. Founders' Gold Medal RGS 1937. *Publication:* (co-editor) first edition The Oxford Atlas, 1951. *Address:* 10 Gainsborough Gardens, Hampstead, NW3. *T:* 01-435 4478.
[*Died* 16 *June* 1978.

LEWIS, Mrs Dorothy; *see* Lewis, Mrs M. D.

LEWIS, E(dward) Daly; His Honour Judge Daly Lewis; a Circuit Judge (formerly Judge of County Courts), since 1960; *b* 14 Nov. 1908; *s* of Ernest Edward Lewis, MD, Weymouth Street, W1; *m* 1941, Nancy Ruth, *d* of Harold Margetson, Wingham, near Canterbury; two *d. Educ:* Harrow; Magdalen Coll., Oxford (MA). Called to Bar, Middle Temple, 1932; Midland Circuit. Joined RE (TA), 1938. Served War of 1939-45: Major, 1942; GSO2 Southern Command, DAAG War Office, 1943; Allied Force HQ in N Africa and Italy, 1944-45. Chm. Agricultural Land Tribunal for Yorks, 1954-60. Chm. Quarter Sessions for Parts of Holland, 1961; Dep. Chm., Quarter Sessions for Parts of Kesteven, 1962. *Recreations:* walking, golf. *Address:* Kettlethorpe Hall, near Lincoln. *T:* Torksey 279.
[*Died* 3 *April* 1977.

LEWIS, Sir Edward (Roberts), Kt 1961; Member of London Stock Exchange since 1925; Chairman: Decca Ltd; The Decca Record Co. Ltd; The Decca Navigator Co. Ltd; Decca Radar Ltd; Decca Survey Ltd; *b* 19 April 1900; *s* of late Sir Alfred Lewis, KBE; *m* 1st, 1923, Mary Margaret Hutton (*d* 1968), *d* of late Rev. George Dickson Hutton; one *s* (and one *s* decd); 2nd, 1973, Jeanie Margaret Smith. *Educ:* Rugby Sch.; Trinity Coll., Cambridge. Gold Albert Medal (RSA) 1967. *Address:* 69A Cadogan Place, SW1; Bridge House Farm, Felsted, Essex. *Club:* United Oxford & Cambridge University. [*Died* 29 *Jan.* 1980.

LEWIS, Eiluned; Writer; 2nd *d* of late Hugh Lewis, MA Cantab, JP, and Eveline Lewis, MA, JP, Glan Hafren, Newtown, Montgomeryshire; *m* 1937, Graeme Hendrey (*d* 1972), MIEE; one *d. Educ:* Levana, Wimbledon; Westfield Coll., University of London. Editorial Staff, News-Chronicle; Editor's Asst, Sunday Times, 1931-36. *Publications:* Dew on the Grass (Book Guild gold medal), 1934; (with Peter Lewis) The Land of Wales, 1937; The Captain's Wife, 1943; In Country Places, 1951; The Leaves of the Tree, 1953; Honey Pots and Brandy Bottles, 1954; Selected Letters of Charles Morgan, with Memoir, 1967; and two books of verse; regular contributor to Country Life. *Address:* Rabbits Heath Cottage, Bletchingley, Surrey.
[*Died* 15 *April* 1979.

LEWIS, Captain Henry Edward, CBE 1942; RN (retired); *b* 24 Sept. 1889; *s* of W. C. Lewis, Plymouth, Devon; *m* 1911, E. E. Rice, Plympton, Devon; one *d. Educ:* Plymouth. *Recreations:* tennis, etc. *Address:* Forestside Residential Home, Forestside, Rowlands Castle, Hants. [*Died* 16 *July* 1979.

LEWIS, Ivor Evan Gerwyn; former Puisne Judge, High Court of Uganda; *b* 1904; *er s* of late Dr Lionel H. Lewis, Porth, Glamorgan; *m* 1940, Winifred M. Hill; one *s. Educ:* Malvern Coll. Solicitor of the Supreme Court of Judicature, 1929; practised in UK and Straits Settlements. Called to the Bar, Gray's Inn, 1945 (Hons). Magistrate, Singapore, 1937; Registrar, High Court, Zanzibar, 1937; Resident Magistrate,

1938-46; Crown Counsel, 1947-48; Uganda, 1948. *Recreations:* cricket, golf. *Address:* Carvai, West Drive, Porthcawl, Mid Glam. *Club:* East India, Sports and Public Schools.
[*Died 25 April* 1977.

LEWIS, J(ack) Haydon, CMG 1958; OBE 1955; Commissioner of Prisons, Kenya, 1951-59, retired; *b* 18 Oct. 1904; British; *m* 1935, Doris Gwendoline; one step-*s*. *Educ:* Plumtree Sch., S Rhodesia; Rhodes Univ., S Rhodesia; Cambridge Univ. Cadet, Kenya, 1931; District Officer, 1934; District Commissioner, 1949; Senior District Commissioner, 1950. *Recreations:* cricket, golf. *Address:* Hill Rise, The Lane, West Mersea, Essex. *Club:* West Mersea Yacht (Hon. Sec.).   [*Died 14 Sept.* 1971.

LEWIS, Sir John Duncan; *see* Orr-Lewis.

LEWIS, Sir John (Todd), Kt 1970; OBE 1946; Chairman: Davenports CB & Brewery (Holdings) Ltd, 1952-74; HP Sauce Ltd, 1954-69; Lea & Perrins Ltd, 1954-69; Director: Express & Star (Wolverhampton) Ltd, since 1964; Grindlays Bank (Jersey) Ltd, since 1971; and other Companies; *b* 25 July 1901; *s* of George Lewis; *m* 1st, 1926, Lydia Mary Hall Beebee (*d* 1961); no *c*; 2nd, 1965, Marjorie Jean Hardy. *Educ:* Wolverhampton Gram. Sch. Qual. as Chartered Accountant, 1924. Partner in Agar, Bates, Neal & Co., 1925-62. Chm., Midland Caledonian Investment Trust Ltd, 1951-73. Life Governor, Birmingham Univ., 1956-; Chm. Birmingham Regional Hospital Bd, 1963-70. JP, Wolverhampton, 1950-70. Hon. LLD Birmingham, 1971. *Recreation:* golf. *Address:* Clos des Pins, Gorey, Jersey. *T:* Jersey Central 52207.   [*Died 10 Aug.* 1977.

LEWIS, Mrs (Mary) Dorothy, CBE 1961 (MBE 1953, OBE 1957); JP; Lord Mayor of Cardiff, 1960-61; *b* 5 Jan. 1894; *d* of George and Helena Lovell; *m* 1917, David Aubrey Lewis (*d* 1946); one *s. Educ:* Severn Road Sch.; Canton High Sch., Cardiff. Foundation Mem., first Branch of Conservative Women, Cardiff (formed after women granted parliamentary vote), Sept. 1919; Hon. Officer of Cardiff Conservative and Unionist Assoc. 1924-, and Life Vice-Pres. of Cardiff West Assoc.; Mem., Cardiff City Council, May 1944-; CC, 1944-55; Alderman, 1955-74. Holder of Souvenir Cert. for vol. work for St Dunstans; Souvenir Brochure for vol. services, Glamorgan Welfare for Troops Cttee, 1946. Vice-Pres. Weights and Measures Admin. for GB, subseq. Inst. of Trading Standards Admin, 1960. JP 1946. OStJ 1962. *Recreations:* reading, charitable social work. *Address:* 6 High Street, Llandaff, Cardiff. *T:* Cardiff 562731.   [*Died 29 Dec.* 1975.

LEWIS, Prof. Morris Michael; Professor Emeritus, University of Nottingham, since 1963; Director, Institute of Education, 1947-63, and Professor of Education, 1956-63; *b* 27 June 1898; *m* 1921, Hilda Winifred Maizels (Hilda Lewis, novelist); one *s. Educ:* University Coll., London. University Scholarship in English; Morley Medallist in Eng. Lit.; BA 1st Cl. Hons English; MA Educ, with Distinction; PhD. Senior English Master, Newport Gram. Sch., 1918-19, William Ellis Sch., 1919-24; Lecturer, University Coll., Nottingham, 1924-29, Sen. Lecturer, 1929-40; Vice-Principal, Goldsmiths' Coll., London, 1940-47. Chairman: Soc. of Teachers of Speech and Drama, 1942-57; Dept of Educn and Science Cttee on Educn of Deaf Children. Fellow British Psychological Soc. *Publications:* Infant Speech (Internat. Library of Psych.) 1936, 2nd edn 1951; Language in School, 1942; Language in Society, 1948; The Importance of Illiteracy, 1953; How Children Learn to Speak, 1957; Language, Thought and Personality, 1963; Language and Personality in Deaf Children, 1968; Language and the Child, 1969; papers on education and psychology in various journals. *Address:* 38 Wollaton Hall Drive, Nottingham. *T:* Nottingham 76417.
[*Died 23 Sept.* 1971.

LEWIS, Neville, RP; Artist; Member New English Art Club; *b* Cape Town, 8 Oct. 1895; *s* of Rev. A. J. S. Lewis, Cape Town; *m* 1st, 1916, T. M. C. Townshend; two *s* one *d*; 2nd, 1932, Vera Player; one *s* one *d*; 3rd, 1955, Countess Rosa Cécile, *d* of late Prince zu Solms-Baruth and of H. H. Princess zu Solms-Baruth, Mariental, SW Africa; one *s* one *d. Educ:* South African Coll. Sch., Cape Town; Slade Sch. of Fine Arts, University of London. Served European War, France, Belgium, Italy; worked some years in South Africa, painting native life; painted portraits in Spain, USA and England; offical War Artist SA Forces, 1940-43. Pictures have been acquired by National Gallery of British Art (Tate Gallery), Galleria Nacional del Arte Moderno (Madrid), Imperial War Museum, Corporation Galleries: Oldham, Manchester, Liverpool, Sheffield, Belfast, Leeds, Bradford, Birmingham etc.; SA National Gallery, Cape Town, Johannesburg, Durban. Has painted portraits of the following: Sir Winston Churchill, Air-Marshal Tedder, Solly Joel, HM King of Spain (late Alfonso XIII), HM King of Greece (late

George II), The Earl of Athlone, Princess Alice, and Field-Marshals Smuts, Montgomery and Alexander, Sobhuza II, King of the Swazis, State President of SA Republic, etc. *Publication:* Studio Encounters, 1963. *Address:* 42 Rowan Street, Stellenbosch, South Africa. *Clubs:* Chelsea Arts; Stellenbosch (S Africa).   [*Died 26 June* 1972.

LEWIS, Peter Edwin; His Honour Judge Peter Lewis; Circuit Judge on South Eastern Circuit since 1972; *b* 8 Dec. 1912; *s* of Frederick Herbert Lewis; *m* 1948, Mary Ruth Massey; three *s* one *d. Educ:* Malvern Coll.; University Coll., Oxford (BA, BCL). Called to Bar, Inner Temple, 1937; subseq. practised at Bar. Served RAF, 1940-47. *Recreation:* golf. *Address:* Saxon Lodge, Seaford, East Sussex BN25 1QL. *T:* Seaford 892785. *Club:* Union (Seaford).   [*Died 7 Jan.* 1976.

LEWIS, Wilmarth Sheldon, FSA, FRSA, FRSL; Hon. MA (Yale 1937); Hon. LittD (Brown, 1945, Rochester, 1946, Delaware, 1961, Cambridge 1962); Hon. LHD (Trin. Coll., Hartford, 1950, Bucknell 1958, Melbourne, 1972); Hon. DLitt (NUI, 1957); Hon. LLD (Yale 1965, Hartford 1972); Yale Medal, 1965; Founder and Editor Yale Edn of Horace Walpole's Correspondence since 1933; *b* 14 Nov. 1895; *s* of Azro N. and Miranda Sheldon Lewis; *m* 1928, Annie Burr Auchincloss (*d* 1959). *Educ:* Thacher Sch.; Yale Univ. (BA 1918). Served European War as 2nd Lt 144 Field Artillery, 1917-19; War of 1939-45 as Chief, Central Information Div., Office of Strategic Services, 1941-43; Research Assoc., Yale Univ., 1933-38; Fellow of Yale Univ., 1938-64; Fellow Amer. Acad. of Arts and Sciences; Mem., Amer. Philosoph. Soc. Chairman: Yale Library Assoc., 1933-45; Librarian's Council, Library of Congress, 1941-47; John Carter Brown Library Assoc., 1943-46; Hon. Fellow, Pierpont Morgan Library, 1970. Trustee: Institute for Advanced Study, Princeton, 1945-; Thacher Sch., 1940-46, 1954-74; Brooks Sch., 1946-49; Miss Porter's Sch., 1941-65; Watkinson Library, 1941-; Redwood Library, 1946-74; Henry Francis duPont (Winterthur) Museum, Delaware, 1954-76; John Carter Brown Library, 1955-75; Heritage Foundn, 1962-76; John F. Kennedy Library, 1964-; Mem. Commission: on National Portrait Gallery (Washington), 1964-76; National Coll. of Fine Arts, 1958-73. FSA 1967. Donald F. Hyde Award (Princeton), 1968; Benjamin Franklin Medal, RSA, 1975. *Publications:* Tutor's Lane, 1922; Three Tours Through London, 1748, 1776, 1797 (Colver Lectures, Brown Univ.), 1941; The Yale Collections, 1946: Collector's Progress, 1951; Horace Walpole's Library (Sandars Lectures), 1957; Horace Walpole (A. W. Mellon Lectures), 1960; One Man's Education, 1967; See for Yourself, 1971; Read As You Please, 1977; Rescuing Horace Walpole, 1978. Editor: A Selection of Letters of Horace Walpole, 1926, 1951, 1973; Horace Walpole's Fugitive Verses, 1931; (with Ralph M. Williams) Private Charity in England, 1747-57, 1938; Yale Edition of Horace Walpole's Correspondence, 39 vols, 1937-74, with completion (50 vols) about 1980. *Address:* Farmington, Conn 06032, USA. *Clubs:* Athenæum (London); Century, Grolier, Yale (New York); Tavern (Boston); Metropolitan (Washington); Pacific Union (San Francisco); Rowfant (Cleveland).   [*Died 7 Oct.* 1979.

LEWTHWAITE, Raymond, CMG 1955; OBE 1945; Medical Research Adviser, Ministry of Overseas Development, 1964-68; retired; *b* 18 Nov. 1894; *s* of late Charles A. Lewthwaite, Kendal; *m* 1926, Gladys (*d* 1964), *d* of Harry Johnson, Kendal; one *s* one *d. Educ:* Kendal Sch.; Magdalen Coll., Oxford; Middlesex Hosp. (Leopold Hudson prizeman). Served European War, 1916-19, Lt Border Regt; Capt. 1919-23. BA 1922; MA 1930; BM, BCh, 1925; DM 1930; North Persian Forces Memorial Medal for Medical Research, 1936; MRCP 1939; FRCP 1948. Institute for Medical Research, Malaya: Research Student, 1926, Senior Pathologist, 1931; Dir 1945. Field Dir, Med. Res. Council's Scrub-typhus Commission, South-East Asia Command, 1944-45. Dir of Colonial Medical Research, Colonial Office, 1949-61; Medical Research Adviser, Dept of Technical Co-operation, 1961-64. Assessor, Tropical Medicine Research Bd. *Publications:* sundry articles on tropical diseases, especially typhus group of fevers, in medical literature. Contributor to Modern Practice in Infectious Fevers. *Recreations:* reading and music. *Address:* 121 Erskine Hill, NW11. *T:* 01-458 3713.
[*Died 20 March* 1972.

LEY, Sir Gerald Gordon, 3rd Bt, *cr* 1905; TD; Captain, 1st Derbyshire Yeomanry; *b* 5 Nov. 1902; *e s* of Major Sir Henry Gordon Ley, 2nd Bt, and late Rhoda Lady Ley, *d* of Herbert Prodgers, Kington St Michael, Chippenham, Wilts; *S* father 1944; *m* 1st, 1936, Rosemary Catherine Cotter (marr. diss. 1956), *d* of late Captain Duncan Macpherson, Royal Navy; three *d*; 2nd, 1958, Grace Foster (marr. diss. 1968). *Educ:* Eton; Oxford Univ., BA Agriculture. Manages estates in Cumberland; High Sheriff of Cumberland, 1937. Lord of the Manors of

Lazonby, Kirkoswald, Staffield and Glassonby. Served Duke of Lancaster's Own Yeomanry, 1927-39; War Service, 1939-40; 1st Derbyshire Yeomanry, 1940-45. *Heir:* b Francis Douglas Ley. *Recreations:* fishing, salmon in particular; shooting. *Address:* Lazonby Hall, near Penrith, Cumbria CA10 1AZ. *TA:* Lazonby, Cumbria. *T:* Lazonby 218.   [*Died* 24 *March* 1980.

LEYLAND, Peter; *see* Pyke-Lees, Walter K.

LIBBY, Dr Willard Frank; Professor of Chemistry, University of California, since 1959; Director, Institute of Geophysics, since 1962; b Grand Valley, Colorado, 17 Dec. 1908; s of Ora Edward Libby and Eva May (*née* Rivers); m 1940, Leonor Hickey (marr. diss. 1966); twin d; m 1966, Dr Leona Marshall. *Educ:* Grammar and High Sch., near Sebastopol, California; Univ. of California, Berkeley. BS, 1931; PhD, 1933. Instr of Chemistry, Univ. of California, 1933-38; Asst Prof., 1938-45; Associate Prof., 1945; Guggenheim Meml Foundn Fellowship, Princeton Univ., 1941; War work in Manhatten District Project Columbia Univ., (on leave from Univ. of Calif), 1941-45; Prof. of Chemistry, Dept of Chemistry, and Inst. for Nuclear Studies, now Enrico Fermi Inst. for Nuclear Studies, Univ. of Chicago, 1945-59; Research Associate, Washington Geophysical Lab., Carnegie Instn, 1954-59; Vis. Professor: Univ. of Colorado, Boulder, 1967-70; Univ. of S. Florida, Tampa, 1972-; Atomic Energy Commission: Mem., 1954-59; Cttee of Sen. Reviewers, 1945-52; Gen. Advisory Cttee, 1950-54, 1960-62; Member: AEC's Plowshare Advisory Cttee, 1959-72; Cttee of Selection, Guggenheim Memorial Foundn, 1959-; Edit. Board, Science, 1962-70. Consultant, Douglas Aircraft Co., 1962-69. Member: Air Resources Bd, Calif, 1967-72; Earthquake Council, Calif, 1972-; President's Task Force on Air Pollution, 1969-70; US-Japan Cttee on Scientific Co-operation, 1970-73; Advisor and Consultant to various cos, commns and univs. Mem., Editorial Bd, Space Life Science, 1970-. Pres. and Dir, Isotope Foundn. Holds hon. doctorates in Science. Nobel Prize for Chemistry, 1960. Has received numerous awards from universities and scientific institutions. Member: National Academy of Science; Royal Swedish Academy of Science, American Phil. Society; American Academy of Arts and Sciences; Heidelberg Academy Science; Amer. Nuclear Soc.; Corres. Fellow, British Acad.; Mem. several professional societies and fraternities. *Publications:* Radiocarbon Dating, 1952 (2nd edn, 1955); author of numerous articles appearing principally in scientific journals (Journal American Chemistry Society, Phys. Review, Proc. National Academy Science, Journal Geophys. Research, Science, etc.). *Recreations:* swimming, golf. *Address:* (office) Department of Chemistry, University of California, 405 Hilgard Avenue, Los Angeles, California 90024, USA. *T:* 825-1968. *Clubs:* Metropolitan, Century Association (New York); Cosmos (Washington, DC); Explorer's (Los Angeles).
                                              [*Died* 8 *Sept.* 1980.

LICHINE, David; Choreographer; b 25 Dec. 1910; m 1942, Tatiana Riabouchinska; one d. *Educ:* in France. De Basil Champs-Elysées Ballet and then Marquis de Cuevas Ballet, 1932-49. Choreography: over 25 ballets. Last Ballets seen in London: La Création, La Rencontre (Ballets des Champs-Elysées); Infanta, Enchanted Mill (de Cuevas); Symphonic Impressions, Concerto Grosso, Graduation Ball, Nutcracker (London Festival Ballet). *Address:* 965 Oakhurst Drive, Los Angeles 49, California, USA.   [*Died* 26 *June* 1972.

LIDBURY, Sir Charles, Kt, cr 1941; Director of Westminster Bank Ltd, and of Westminster Foreign Bank Ltd, 1935-62; b 30 June 1880; s of Frank Albert Lidbury; m 1909, Mary (d 1939), d of George Moreton, Kinderton Hall, Middlewich, Cheshire; two d. General Manager Westminster Foreign Bank Ltd, 1928-47; General Manager, Westminster Bank Ltd, 1927-30; Chief General Manager Westminster Bank Ltd, 1930-47; President of Institute of Bankers, 1939-46. *Address:* Winter Field, Melbury Abbas, Shaftesbury, Dorset. *T:* Shaftesbury 2274.
                                              [*Died* 25 *July* 1978.

LIDBURY, Sir David John, KCMG 1948 (CMG 1941); CB 1943; DSO 1916; b 3 Oct. 1884; e s of late E. A. Lidbury, CBE; m 1923, Ethel (d 1942), d of late Charles Norbury; one d; m 1944, Alice (d 1952), d of late Matthew S. Morrison. *Educ:* Llandovery Sch.; Hertford Coll., Oxford. Assistant Surveyor, General Post Office, 1908. Served European War, 1914-18 (despatches, DSO); Controller, Money Order Department, 1929-34; Controller Post Office Savings Bank, 1934-35; Director of Army Postal Services to 1935; Assistant Secretary, Headquarters, GPO, 1935-38; Director, London Postal Region GPO, 1938; Principal Assistant Secretary, Ministry of Home Security, 1939-40; Assistant Director-General, GPO, 1941-47. President, 1st Commn at Postal Union Congresses at Buenos Aires (1939) and Paris (1947). Vice-President Exec. Commn of

Universal Postal Union, 1947-52. Chairman, Commn on Gold Coast Civil Service, 1950. Chairman East African Salaries Commission, 1953-54; Commissioner, Staff Revision Posts and Telegraphs Dept, Nigeria, 1955-56. Commander Order of Aviz (Portugal), 1917. *Address:* Flat 7, 37 Adelaide Crescent, Hove, Sussex. *T:* Brighton 731369.   [*Died* 21 *June* 1973.

LIDDELL, Peter John, DSC 1944; MA; Chairman, North West Water Authority, 1973-78; Member, National Water Council, since 1973; b 2 June 1921; s of Comdr Lancelot Charles Liddell, OBE, RN, and Rosalie Liddell (*née* Ballantyne); m 1st, 1948, Dorothy Priscilla Downes; two s one d; 2nd, 1960, Helen Ann, d of Rear-Adm. A. W. Laybourne, CB, CBE, and of Helen (*née* Burnett). *Educ:* Ampleforth; Wadham Coll., Oxford (MA). Served RNVR, 1940-46 (DSC). Farmed in Cumberland, 1959-76. Member: Cumberland River Board, 1954-65; Cumberland River Authority, 1964-74 (Vice-Chm., 1967-70, Chm., 1970-73); Chm., Assoc. of River Authorities, 1971-74 (Vice-Chm., 1969-71; Chm. Fisheries Cttee, 1966-71); Mem. Internat. Adv. Gp, Internat. Salmon Foundn, NYC, 1970- (Chm., 1970-72); President: Inst. of Fisheries Management, 1972- Vice-Pres. 1969-72); River Eden and District Fisheries Assoc., 1970- (Chm. 1956-70). Mem. Exec. Cttee: Central Council of Physical Recreation, 1968-73; Salmon and Trout Assoc.; Atlantic Salmon Res. Trust Ltd; Scottish Salmon Angling Fedn. Mem., The Sports Council, 1969-71; Chm., Northern Sports Council, 1971-74 (Dep. Chm., 1967-71); Vice-Chm., Standing Conf. of Northern Sport and Recreation, 1967-71; Member: Fisheries Adv. Cttee, Water Resources Bd, 1967-71; Inland Waterways Amenity Adv. Council, 1971-74; Water Cttee, Country Landowners Assoc., 1971-75, and 1977-; British Cttee, Internat. Water Supply Assoc., 1971- (Chm., 1974-); Water Space Amenity Commn; Council, Freshwater Biological Assoc. (Hon. Treas., 1975-); Council, Estuarine and Brackish Water Sciences Assoc. Membre d'Honneur, Assoc. Nat. de Défense des Rivières à Saumons, Paris. Winston Churchill Travelling Fellowship, 1968. Mem. RIPA, MBIM, FZS, FIFM, FRSA. Vis. Fellow, Univ. of Salford. Freeman: City of Newcastle upon Tyne, 1953; City of London, 1969. *Publications:* The Salmon Rivers of Eire: a report, 1971; articles in various jls, yearbooks, etc. *Recreations:* fishing, shooting, following all forms of sport and recreation. *Address:* Moorhouse Hall, Warwick-on-Eden, Carlisle CA4 8PA. *T:* Wetheral 60356; 30d Cadogan Square, SW1. *T:* 01-584 4660. *Clubs:* White's, Beefsteak, Flyfishers', MCC; The Brook (NY); County and Border (Carlisle).   [*Died* 11 *May* 1979.

LIESCHING, Sir Percivale, GCMG 1951 (KCMG 1944; CMG 1932), KCB 1947; KCVO 1953; b 1895; m 1924, Georgina, d of late James Williamson, Tunbridge Wells; three d. *Educ:* Bedford Sch.; Brasenose Coll., Oxford, MA. Served European War, 1914 and 1917-18 (despatches); East African Expeditionary Force, 1916; appointed to the Colonial Office, 1920; transferred to the Dominions Office, 1925; seconded to staff of High Commissioner for the United Kingdom in Canada, 1928-32; Political Secretary, Office of the High Commissioner for the United Kingdom in S Africa, 1933-35; Official Secretary, Office of the High Commissioner for the United Kingdom in Australia, 1936-38; Assistant Under-Secretary of State, Dominions Office, 1939-42; Second Secretary, Board of Trade, 1942-46; Permanent Secretary, Ministry of Food, 1946-48; Permanent Under-Secretary of State, Commonwealth Relations Office, 1949-55; High Commissioner for the UK in South Africa, and High Commissioner for Basutoland, Bechuanaland Protectorate, and Swaziland, 1955-58. *Address:* c/o Lloyds Bank Ltd, 6 Pall Mall, SW1. *Club:* Travellers'.   [*Died* 4 *Nov.* 1973.

LIGHTBOUND, Rt. Rev. Aloysius Anselm; Member Order of St Benedict; Titular Abbot of St Augustine's, Canterbury; Abbot of Belmont, 1948-53, resigned. *Address:* St Mary's Priory, 22 Church Road, Harrington, Cumberland. [*Died* 31 *May* 1973.

LILLEY, Francis James Patrick; b 24 July 1907; s of Francis John Charles Lilley; m 1937, Agnes Crossley Mackay, Glasgow; two s. *Educ:* Bellahouston Academy. Served with Argyll and Sutherland Highlanders, 1934-40; with 12th Battalion City of Glasgow Home Guard, 1941-45; Lieut-Colonel, 1942. Elected to Glasgow Corporation, 1957; has served on education and municipal transport cttees. Chairman, F. J. C. Lilley Ltd group of cos, civil engineering and public works contractors, etc. MP (C) Kelvingrove Division of Glasgow, 1959-64; PPS to Minister of Power, 1960-64, to Minister of Pensions, 1964. *Recreations:* golf and yachting. *Address:* 5 Le Boulevard, La Rocque, Jersey, CI. *T:* Jersey East 715. *Clubs:* Constitutional; Conservative (Glasgow); Royal Scottish Motor Yacht. [*Died* 21 *Aug.* 1971.

LIN YUTANG, MA (Harvard), PhD (Leipzig), LittD (Elmira and Rutgers, USA); Author; b 10 Oct. 1895; s of Lin Chiseng and Yang Sunming; m 1919, Lian Tsulfeng; three d. *Educ:* St

John's Univ., Shanghai; Harvard Univ. Prof. of English at Peking Univ., 1923-26; Sec. of Min. of Foreign Affairs, 1927; Chancellor, Nanyang Univ., Singapore, 1954-55. *Publications:* My Country and My People, 1935; History of the Press and Public Opinion, 1936; Importance of Living, 1937; Wisdom of Confucius (Modern Library), 1938; Moment in Peking, 1939; With Love and Irony, 1940; A Leaf in the Storm, 1941; Wisdom of China and India, 1942; Between Tears and Laughter, 1943; The Vigil of a Nation, 1945; The Gay Genius, 1947; Chinatown Family, 1948; (compiled and edited) The Wisdom of China, 1949; Peace is in the Heart, 1950; On the Wisdom of America, 1950; Widow, Nun and Courtesan, 1951; Famous Chinese Short Stories, 1952; The Vermillion Gate, 1953; The Unexpected Island, 1955; Lady Wu, 1956; The Secret Name, 1959; From Pagan to Christian, 1960; Importance of Understanding, 1961; Imperial Peking: Seven Centuries of China, 1961; The Red Peony, 1961; The Pleasures of a Nonconformist, 1962; Juniper Loa, 1963; The Flight of the Innocents, 1964; The Chinese Theory of Art, 1967. Edited: The Wisdom of Laotse, 1948; The Wisdom of Confucius, 1959; Lin Yutang's Chinese-English Dictionary of Current Usage (Hong Kong), 1972. *Recreation:* fishing. *Address:* William Heinemann Ltd, 15-16 Queen Street, Mayfair, W1.   *[Died 26 March 1976.*

LINDBERGH, Col Charles Augustus, AFC, DSC; Special Adviser on technical matters to Chief of Staff, US Air Force; nominated Brigadier-General by Mr Eisenhower; *b* Detroit, 4 Feb. 1902; *s* of late Charles Augustus Lindbergh and Evangeline Lodge Land; *m* 1929, Anne Spencer Morrow, *d* of late Dwight W. Morrow; three *s* two *d* (and one *s* decd). *Educ:* University of Wisconsin. Enrolled in Flying Sch., Lincoln, Nebraska, 1922; flew alone from New York to Paris, 1927; flew from America to Copenhagen via Greenland, Iceland and the Shetland Isles, 1933, with a view to establishing a Transatlantic air route. *Publications:* Flight and Life, 1948; The Spirit of Saint Louis, 1953 (Pulitzer Prize, 1954); *relevant publication:* The Hero, Charles A. Lindbergh: The Man and the Legend, by Kenneth S. Davis, 1960. *Address:* Scott's Cove, Darien, Conn 06820, USA.
                                                                [Died 26 Aug. 1974.

LINDELL, John Henry Stockton, CMG 1973; ED (CMF) 1971; MD, MS; retired as Chairman of Victorian Hospitals and Charities Commission, Australia, 1972; *b* 17 March 1908; *s* of John Lindell and Georgina Stockton; *m* 1941, Margaret Annie Rolland; two *s* two *d*. *Educ:* Melbourne High Sch.; Melbourne Univ. MB, BS 1940; MS 1946, MD 1948. Medical Supt, Royal Melbourne Hosp., 1943-53; Chm., Victorian Hospitals and Charities Commn, 1953-72. FPS 1948; FHA 1954. *Publication:* A Regional Plan for Hospitals, 1953. *Recreations:* reading, woodworking. *Address:* 13 Eaglemont Crescent, Eaglemont, Victoria 3084, Australia. *T:* 45 2039. *Clubs:* Beefsteak (Melbourne); Royal Automobile Club of Victoria.
                                                                [Died 24 Aug. 1973.

LINDGREN, Baron, *cr* 1961, of Welwyn Garden City (Life Peer); **George Samuel Lindgren,** DL; *b* 11 Nov. 1900; *s* of George William Lindgren, Islington, London; *m* 1926, Elsie Olive, *d* of Frank Reed, Chishill, Herts; one *s*. *Educ:* Hungerford Road LCC Elementary Sch. LNER Railway clerk. Mem. National Executive Cttee of Railway Clerks' Association, 1933-46; Chm. London Trades Council 1938-42. Mem. of Welwyn Garden City UDC, 1927-45; of Herts County Council, 1931-49; re-elected, 1952. Dep. Regional Commissioner, Midland Region, 1942-45. MP (Lab) Wellingborough Div. of Northamptonshire, 1945-Sept. 1959; Parly Sec. to: Ministry of: National Insurance, 1945-46; Civil Aviation, 1946-50; Town and Country Planning, 1950-51; Housing and Local Govt, Jan.-Oct. 1951; Joint Parly Sec., Min. of Transport, 1964-66; Parly Sec., Min. of Power, 1966-70. Treasurer, Transport Salaried Staffs Assoc., 1956-61. DL Herts, 1966. *Recreation:* swimming. *Address:* 4 Attimore Close, Welwyn Garden City. *T:* Welwyn Garden 22669.
                                                                [Died 8 Sept. 1971.

LINDNER, Doris Lexey Margaret; sculptress; *b* 8 July 1896. *Educ:* Norland Place, London; St Martin's Art School; Frank Calendron Animal Sch.; British Academy, Rome. Modelled animals for Royal Worcester Porcelain Co. for over 40 years. Has made bronzes of horses; also carved in stone, wood, concrete etc. *Recreation:* bridge. *Address:* Studio Cottage, Broad Campden, Glos. *T:* Evesham 840608.
                                                                [Died 20 April 1979.

LINDO, Sir (Henry) Laurence, OJ 1973; GCVO 1973; Kt 1967; CMG 1957; High Commissioner for Jamaica in London, 1962-73; *b* 13 Aug. 1911; *e s* of Henry Alexander and Ethel Mary Lindo (*née* Gibson); *m* 1943, Holly Robertson Clacken; two *d*. *Educ:* Jamaica Coll., Jamaica; Keble Coll., Oxford. Rhodes Scholar, 1931; OUAC 1934. Inspector of Schools, Jamaica,

1935; Asst Information Officer, 1939-43; Asst Sec., Colonial Secretariat, 1945; Principal Asst Sec., 1950. Administrator, Dominica, Windward Islands, 1952-59; Actg Governor, Windward Islands, 1957 and 1959; Governor's Sec., Jamaica, 1960-62; Ambassador to: France, 1966-72; Federal Republic of Germany, 1967-70. *Address:* c/o Royal Bank of Canada, Cockspur Street, SW1. *Clubs:* Travellers', Royal Commonwealth Society (West Indian), MCC, Royal Over-Seas League.   *[Died 8 May 1980.*

LINDON, Sir Leonard (Charles Edward), Kt 1964; MS, FRCS, FRCSE, FRACS; Hon. Surgeon and Neuro-Surgeon, Royal Adelaide Hospital; Associate Lecturer in Surgery, University of Adelaide; *b* Adelaide, 8 Feb. 1896; *s* of late J. H. Lindon, Adelaide; *m* 1921, Jean, *d* of late Dr H. Marten; two *s* one *d*. *Educ:* Geelong Gram. Sch.; St Peter's Coll., Adelaide; Universities of Adelaide and Oxford; London and Guy's Hospitals. Rhodes Scholar 1918. MB, BS 1919; MRCS LRCP 1920; FRCSEd 1922; FRCS 1922; MS Adelaide 1923; FRACS 1929. Served European War, 1914-18: Private, AIF, 1914-16; served War of 1939-45; Lt-Col, Australian Army Medical Corps, AIF, 1939-41 (despatches). Pres., Royal Australasian Coll. of Surgeons, 1959-61 (Vice-Pres., 1957-59); Mem., BMA (Pres. South Australian Branch, 1934-35). *Address:* 222 Brougham Place, North Adelaide, SA 5006, Australia. *Club:* Adelaide (Adelaide, SA).   *[Died 28 Aug. 1978.*

LINDSAY, Sir Daryl; see Lindsay, Sir E. D.

LINDSAY, Sir (Ernest) Daryl, Kt 1956; LLD; Director, National Gallery of Victoria, Australia, 1941-56, retired; Member, National Capital Planning Commission, Canberra; *b* 31 Dec. 1889; *s* of Robert Charles Lindsay, MD, and Jane Elizabeth Lindsay; *m* 1922, Joan A'Beckett, *d* of Mr Justice Weigall, Supreme Court of Victoria; no *c*. *Educ:* Creswick State Sch.; Creswick Gram. Sch. Bank clerk from 1907; pastoral pursuits, NSW, Queensland and Vic., 1908-14. Served European War, 1915-18 (war service medals); official War Artist, Med. Section, Queens Hosp., Sidcup, Kent (for Facial Restoration), 1918-19. Studied at Slade Sch. of Art, University of London, 1919; followed profession of painting. Australia, 1919-39; Keeper of the Prints, Nat. Gallery of Vic., 1939; appointed Dir of Gallery, 1941. Overseas Vice-Pres., National Trust for Scotland. ARWS 1937; medals for services to Art, 1952, 1956; Queen's Medal, 1955. Rep. by oil paintings and water colours, drawings, etc. in all Australian Nat. Galleries and at Victoria and Albert Museum, London. Hon. LLD Australian National Univ., Canberra. *Publications:* (with Lady Lindsay) The Story of the Red Cross, 1940; Historical Record of the Felton Bequests; The Leafy Tree, My Family, 1965. *Recreation:* farming. *Address:* Mulberry Hill, Baxter, Vic 3911, Australia. *T:* 777-735. *Clubs:* Melbourne, Victoria Racing (Melbourne). *[Died 25 Dec. 1976.*

LINDSAY, Sir William O'Brien, KBE 1955; Partner in Messrs Hamilton, Harrison and Mathews, Advocates, Nairobi; *b* Kent, 8 Oct. 1909; *s* of Col M. E. Lindsay, DSO, Craigfoodie House, Dairsie; *m* 1st, 1937, Janey Sevilla Glass Hooper (marr. diss., 1962); one *s* two *d*; 2nd, 1962, Elizabeth Sturman (marr. diss. 1975); one *d*; 3rd, 1975, Michaela, widow of Armand Denis. *Educ:* Harrow; Balliol Coll., Oxford (BA). Barrister, Gray's Inn. Sudan Political Service: Asst Dist Comr, 1932; Comdt, Administrators and Police Sch., 1936; Legal Dept, Dep. Asst Legal Sec., 1938; Police Magistrate, Khartoum, 1939-41; Chief Censor, Port Sudan, 1940; Bimbashi, Sudan Defence Force, 1942. Cyrenaica: Pres. of Courts, 1943. Judge of the High Court, Sudan, 1944; Dep. Legal Sec., 1948; Chief Justice, 1950; Acting Legal Sec., 1953-54; Mem. Executive Council, Chief Justice (Independent Judiciary), 1954-55. Retired as Chief Justice of the Sudan, Sept. 1955. Chief Representative, Petroleum Development (Oman) Ltd in Muscat and Oman, 1955-58. *Address:* PO Box 30333, Nairobi, Kenya. *[Died 20 Oct. 1975.*

LINDSAY-REA, R.; see Rea.

LINDSELL, Herbert George, CB 1952; retired public official; *b* 17 May 1903; *er s* of Henry George and Elizabeth Lindsell; *m* 1924, Dorothy, *d* of John and Mildred Watts; one *s*. *Educ:* elementary and secondary schs. Board of Trade, 1918-32; Import Duties Advisory Cttee, 1932-39; Principal, 1939; Ministry of Supply, 1939-; Asst Sec., 1941; Under-Sec., 1950-59; Principal Officer (Establishments), UKAEA, 1959-63, retd; Consultant to UKAEA, 1963-. *Address:* 105 Holland Road, Hove 2, Sussex. *T:* Brighton 734893; Wheelers Bank, Blackboys, Sussex. *T:* Framfield 279.   *[Died 13 May 1973.*

LINDSELL, Lt-Gen. Sir Wilfrid Gordon, GBE 1946 (KBE 1940; OBE 1919), KCB 1943 (CB 1942); DSO 1918; MC; retd pay, 1945; *b* 29 Sept. 1884; *s* of Col Robert F. Lindsell, CB, and

Kathleen, d of Richard Eaton of Mitchelstown, Ireland; m 1st, 1916, Marjorie (d 1957), OBE 1946; d of Adm. Swinton C. Holland, of Langley House, Chichester; two d; 2nd, 1958, Evelyn Nairn Butler, Hobart, Tasmania. *Educ:* Birkenhead Sch.; Victoria Coll., Jersey; Royal Military Academy, Woolwich. 2nd Lt Royal Artillery, 1903; Lt 1906; Capt. 1914; Major, 1918; Bt Lt-Col 1927; Bt Col and Col, 1931; served European War, 1914-18, as ADC to CRA 7th Div.; Staff-Capt. RA 7th Div.; Bde Major RA 62nd Div.; GSO, RA, 8 Corps (despatches four times, DSO, OBE, MC, Croix de Guerre Française); DAAG War Office, 1920; Instructor DAA and QMG. School of Military Administration, 1921-23; Instructor DAQMG Staff Coll., Camberley, 1925-28; GSO1 War Office, 1930-33; Commandant Senior Officers' Sch., Sheerness, 1934-35; Dep. Military Sec., War Office, 1935-36; Comdr, Royal Artillery, 4th Div., 1937-38; Maj.-Gen. in charge of Administration, Southern Command, 1938-39; Quartermaster-Gen. of BEF; Temp. Lt-Gen., 1940; Lt-Gen. 1941; Lt-Gen. in charge of Administration in the Middle East, 1942-43; Principal Administrative Officer to the Indian Command, 1943-45 (despatches thrice, KBE, KCB, GBE, American Order of Merit, degree of Commander). LLD (Hon.) Aberdeen Univ. *Publications:* Military Organisation and Administration, 29th edition; A and Q or Military Administration in War, 3rd edition. *Address:* Flat 6, 169 Queen's Gate, SW7. *Club:* Army and Navy.
[Died 2 May 1973.

LINEHAN, Prof. Patrick Aloysius, OBE 1969; DSc, MAgr, ARCScI; Senior Principal Scientific Officer, Field Botany Division, Ministry of Agriculture, Northern Ireland, 1948-69; Professor of Agricultural Botany, The Queen's University of Belfast, 1951-69; b 7 March 1904; s of late Senator Thomas Linehan, Ballinvarrig, Whitechurch, Co. Cork; m 1933, Teresa Josephine Gilmore (d 1966); two s (one d decd). *Educ:* Christian Brothers' Coll., Cork; Royal College of Science for Ireland; National University of Ireland; University of Cambridge. Research Demonstrator, Plant Breeding, University College, Dublin, 1927. Queen's Univ., Belfast: Asst, Dept of Agricultural Botany, 1930; Lecturer, 1944; Reader, 1950; Dean of Faculty of Agriculture, 1965-68. Min. of Agriculture for N Ireland: Research Asst, Seed Testing and Plant Disease Div., 1930; Dep. Head, Field Botany Div., 1938; Dep. Principal Officer (wartime), 1943; Principal Scientific Officer, Field Botany Div., 1946. President: Internat. Seed Testing Assoc., 1960-62; British Grassland Soc., 1954. *Publications:* scientific papers on grassland research, mainly in Journal of British Grassland Society; papers on seed research in Proc. International Seed Testing Assoc. *Recreation:* fishing. *Address:* 46 Ailesbury Road, Belfast BT7 3FH. *T:* Belfast 648013.   [Died 6 March 1973.

LINES, Dr Albert Walter, CBE 1974; Director, Engineering and Nuclear Physics, Science Research Council, 1972-74; b 14 Oct. 1914; s of Frederick Henry Lines and Amelia Lines (née Cleeton). *Educ:* King Edward VI Grammar Sch., Stratford upon Avon; Birmingham Univ. (BSc, PhD); Heslop Meml Medal 1936. Lectr, Northampton Polytechnic, 1939-40; Lectr, Anti-Aircraft Radio Sch., 1940-42; Telecommunications Res. Estabt, 1942-55; Guided Weapons Dept, RAE, 1955-61; Head of Space Dept, RAE, 1960-61; Dir, European Space Technology Centre, Techn. Dir, European Space Res. Organization, 1961-68; Dir, Eng. Div., SRC, 1969-72. Medal of Freedom with Bronze Palm, US, 1945. *Address:* 19 Ennismore Gardens, SW7. *T:* 01-584 7981.   [Died 1 Jan. 1976.

LINES, Walter; President, Lines Brothers Ltd (Chairman 1920-62); b 10 March 1882; s of Joseph Lines and Jane Lines (née Fitzhenry); m 1922, Henrietta Katherine Hendrey (d 1970); two s two d. *Educ:* Owen's Sch., EC1; Camden School of Art. Joined G. & J. Lines Ltd, 1896, Managing Director, 1908. Served European War, 1914-18: Honourable Artillery Company and RFA (Captain), France and Italy. Founded Lines Bros Ltd, with brothers W. J. and A. E. Lines, 1919. Was formerly Chairman and Managing Director, Lines Bros Ltd, and subsidiary Companies, Great Britain, Canada, Australia, New Zealand, S Africa, France, West Germany; Chairman Hamley Bros Ltd, Regent Street. Hon. Life President, Regent Street Assoc.; FRSA; FRGS. *Address:* Leigh Place, Godstone, Surrey.
[Died 23 Nov. 1972.

LINGHAM, Brig. John, CB 1948; DSO 1944; MC 1916; b 27 June 1897; s of Windeyer George Lingham; m 1924, Juliet Judd (d 1943); two d; m 1945, Jean Chisholm. *Educ:* City of London Sch.; Royal Military Coll., Sandhurst; Staff Coll., Camberley. Joined the Northamptonshire Regt, 1915; served European War, 1914-18, France, Mesopotamia, Egypt, Palestine, 1916-18; Pilot attached RAF, 1919. Served War of 1939-45, commanding 4th Bn Northamptonshire Regt, 1940-42; commanding 197 Infantry Bde, 1942-44; France, Belgium, Germany, 1944-45; retired from

Army, 1949; Control Commission, Germany, 1945; Land Commissioner, Lower Saxony, 1948, North Rhine-Westphalia, 1951; Consul-General, 1952; retired 1954. Colonel, The Northamptonshire Regt, 1956-60. *Recreation:* fishing. *Address:* 39 Gunters Mead, Queens Drive, Oxshott, Surrey.
[Died 23 March 1976.

LINKLATER, Eric, CBE 1954; TD; LLD (Aberdeen), 1946; b 1899; o s of late Robert Linklater, of Dounby, Orkney; m 1933, Marjorie, y d of late Ian MacIntyre; two s two d. *Educ:* Aberdeen Grammar Sch.; Aberdeen Univ. Sometime private in The Black Watch; studied medicine; MA, 1925; assistant editor, The Times of India, Bombay, 1925-27; assistant to Professor of English Literature, Aberdeen, 1927-28; Commonwealth Fellow in United States of America, 1928-30; Major, RE, commanding Orkney Fortress RE, 1939-41; in Directorate of Public Relations, War Office, 1941-45; Rector of Aberdeen Univ., 1945-48; Temp. Lieut-Colonel, Korea, 1951. DL Ross and Cromarty, 1968-73. FRSE 1971. *Publications:* White Maa's Saga, 1929; Poet's Pub, 1929 (filmed, 1949); A Dragon Laughed, 1930; Juan in America, 1931; Ben Jonson and King James, 1931; The Men of Ness, 1932; Mary Queen of Scots, 1933; The Crusader's Key, 1933; Magnus Merriman, 1934; The Revolution, 1934; Robert the Bruce, 1934; The Devil's in the News, 1934; Ripeness is All, 1935; The Lion and the Unicorn, 1935; God Likes Them Plain, 1935; Juan in China, 1937; The Sailor's Holiday, 1937; The Impregnable Women, 1938; Judas, 1939; The Man on My Back, 1941; The Cornerstones, 1941; The Raft and Socrates Asks Why, 1942; The Great Ship and Rabelais Replies, 1944; Crisis in Heaven (play), 1944; The Wind on the Moon (awarded Carnegie Medal), 1944; Private Angelo, 1946 (filmed 1949); The Art of Adventure, 1947; Sealskin Trousers, 1947; The Pirates in the Deep Green Sea, 1949; Love in Albania (play), 1949; A Spell for Old Bones, 1949; Mr Byculla, 1950; The Campaign in Italy, 1951; Laxdale Hall, 1951 (filmed, 1953); The Mortimer Touch (play), 1952; A Year of Space, 1953; The House of Gair, 1953; The Faithful Ally, 1954; The Ultimate Viking, 1955; The Dark of Summer, 1956; A Sociable Plover, 1957; Karina with Love, 1958; Position at Noon, 1958; Breakspear in Gascony (play), 1958; The Merry Muse, 1959; Edinburgh, 1960; Roll of Honour, 1961; Husband of Delilah, 1962; A Man Over Forty, 1963; The Prince in the Heather, 1965; Orkney and Shetland, 1965; The Conquest of England, 1966; A Terrible Freedom, 1966; The Survival of Scotland, 1968; The Stories of Eric Linklater, 1968; (with Edwin Smith) Scotland, 1968; The Royal House of Scotland, 1970; John Moore's England, 1970; Fanfare for a Tin Hat, 1970; The Corpse on Clapham Common, 1971; The Voyage of the Challenger, 1972. *Address:* The Mains of Haddo, Tarves, Aberdeenshire. *Clubs:* Savile; New (Edinburgh).   [Died 7 Nov. 1974.

LINNETT, John Wilfrid, FRS 1955; MA, DPhil (Oxon); Professor of Physical Chemistry, since 1965, Master of Sidney Sussex College, since 1970, Vice-Chancellor, 1973-75, University of Cambridge; b 3 Aug. 1913; s of late Alfred Thirlby Linnett and Ethel Mary Linnett (née Ward); m 1947, Rae Ellen Libgott; one s one d. *Educ:* King Henry VIII Sch., Coventry; St John's Coll., Oxford (Hon. Fellow, 1968). Henry Fellow, Harvard Univ., 1937-38; Junior Research Fellow, Balliol Coll., Oxford, 1939-45; Lectr, Brasenose Coll., Oxford, 1944-46; Fellow of Queen's Coll., Oxford, 1945-65, Hon. Fellow, 1971; University Demonstrator in Chemistry, Oxford, 1944-62; Reader in Inorganic Chemistry, Oxford, 1962-65; Fellow, Emmanuel Coll., Cambridge, 1965-70; Dep. Vice-Chancellor, Cambridge Univ., 1971-73. Council, Faraday Society, 1956-58, Vice-Pres., 1959-61, 1965-67, 1969-71, Pres., 1971-73; Council, Chemical Society, 1960-62, Hon. Sec., 1962, Vice-Pres., 1971-75, Pres.-elect, 1975-76, Pres., 1976-77; Council, RIC, 1970-73. Visiting Professor: Univ. of Wisconsin, 1950; Univ. of California, 1964, 1970; Victor Emmanuel, Cornell Univ., 1966; Technion Univ., Haifa, 1972; Vis. Lectr, Univ. of Minnesota, 1967. Hon. DSc Warwick, 1973. JP City of Oxford, 1964-65. Coventry Award of Merit, 1966. *Publications:* Wave Mechanics and Valency, 1960; The Electronic Structure of Molecules, a New Approach, 1964; scientific papers in Proc. Royal Society, Trans. Faraday Society, Journal Chemical Society, and other scientific journals. *Recreation:* cricket. *Address:* The Master's Lodge, Sidney Sussex College, Cambridge. *T:* Cambridge 61501. *Club:* Athenæum.   [Died 7 Nov. 1975.

LINSLEY, Ven. Stanley Frederick; Archdeacon of Cleveland and Canon of Bilton, 1965-74; Archdeacon Emeritus, since 1974; Chaplain to the Queen, 1964-73; b 19 Oct. 1903; o s of Frederick Linsley, Driffield, Yorks; m 1950, Joan, d of Horace Mulliner, Ellerdine, Shropshire; one s one d. *Educ:* Bridlington Sch.; Lichfield Theological Coll. Vicar of N Ormesby, Middlesbrough, 1932; Vicar of Tunstall, Stoke on Trent, 1937; Vicar of Cannock, Lichfield, 1943; Prebendary of Lichfield

Cathedral, 1945; Canon Missioner and Warden of Retreat House, Shallowford, Diocese of Lichfield, 1946; Vicar of Sambrook, Salop, 1951. General Director of Industrial Christian Fellowship and Vicar of Guild Church of St Katherine Cree, London, 1954; Vicar of Guild Church of St Botolph, Aldersgate, 1956; Vicar of Kidderminster, 1958; Rural Dean of Kidderminster, 1959; Rector of Thwing and Wold Newton, 1963-65; Rector of North and South Otterington, 1965-67; Vicar of Harome, 1967-71. Proctor in Convocation, Lichfield, 1946-51. *Publications:* contributions to theological journals. *Recreation:* agriculture. *Address:* Marton, Sinnington, York YO6 6RD.   [*Died* 14 *Dec.* 1974.

LINTERN, Bernard Francis; journalist; *b* 26 Nov. 1908; *e s* of late Rev. F. G. Lintern and Beatrice Golding; *m* 1931, Mary, *e d* of late Arthur Watts. *Educ:* Chigwell; University of London. Editor of Discovery, and Associate-editor of Television, 1932-34; Associate-editor of Industria Britanica, 1934; Editorial Director, Lawrence H. Tearle Publications, Cape Town and Johannesburg, 1950-60; Editor of The Stethoscope and Pharmacy News, Director, Marketing Publications Ltd, 1961-63. Seaman, RN, 1940; Lieut, RNVR, 1942; Combined Operations, 1941; attached, Fleet Air Arm, 1942-46. *Address:* 194 Russell Court, Woburn Place, WC1H 0LR. *Clubs:* Naval, Wig and Pen; Southern African Naval Officers' (Johannesburg).
                          [*Died* 1 *April* 1979.

LINTON, Sir Andrew, KBE 1964 (CBE 1953); Chairman, New Zealand Dairy Board, 1956-68 (formerly Deputy Chairman); *b* 1893; Scottish; *m* 1922, Catherine Shaw; one *s* two *d. Educ:* Otago and Southland. Elected NZ Dairy Board, 1935. Chairman: Dairy Research Institute (18 years); NZ Veterinary Council, 1947-57; NZ Superannuation Board (Dairy), 1952; formerly Member: NZ Meat Producers' Board, 1958-69; NZ Agricultural Council; NZ Trade Promotion Council; NZ Export Shipping Council; Director: Freezing Co., 1941-69; Trustee Co., 1958-69; member of many local bodies; Chairman of Dairy Companies, etc. *Address:* Glenavon, Greytown, Wairarapa, New Zealand. *Club:* Wellesley (Wellington, NZ).
                          [*Died* 9 *Jan.* 1971.

LINTON, Prof. David Leslie; Professor of Geography, University of Birmingham, since Oct. 1958; *b* 12 July 1906; *m* 1929, Vera Cicely Tebbs; three *s* one *d. Educ:* Haberdashers' Aske's Sch.; University of London, King's Coll. Demonstrator in Geography and Geology, University of London, 1927-29; Lecturer in Geography, University of Edinburgh, 1929-45; Professor of Geography, University of Sheffield, 1945-58; William Evans Visiting Professor, University of Otago, 1959. Served War with RAF (Photographic Intelligence), as Sqdn Leader, 1940-45. Hon. Editor of Geography, the Quarterly Journal of the Geographical Association, 1945-65 and Pres., 1964; Mem. Deutsche Akademie Leopoldina, 1961; Pres., Inst. of British Geographers, 1962, Geographical Assoc., 1964. FKC 1971. Murchison Award, Royal Geographical Soc., 1943. *Publications:* Structure, Surface and Drainage in South-East England (with S. W. Wooldridge), 1955; Sheffield and its Region (Ed.), 1956; papers in geographical journals. *Address:* 75 Wellington Road, Edgbaston, Birmingham 15. *T:* 021-440 2476.
                          [*Died* 11 *April* 1971.

LINZEE, Captain Robert Gordon Hood, CB 1944; CBE 1944 (OBE 1940); Royal Navy, retired; *b* Jan 1900; *o s* of Alexander Grosvenor Linzee; *m* 1929, Hon. Ellinor Aileen Cecil Craig, *d* of 1st Viscount Craigavon; one *s*; *m* 1946, Elizabeth, *d* of Percy Dawson, Shanghai, and *widow* of Rear-Admiral Philip Mack, DSO. *Educ:* West Downs, Winchester; Royal Naval Colls, Osborne and Dartmouth. Entered RN 1912; Comdr 1933; retd 1936; re-called 1939. *Clubs:* United Service & Royal Aero, MCC.   [*Died* 3 *Nov.* 1973.

LIPPMANN, Walter; writer; *b* 23 Sept. 1889; *s* of Jacob Lippmann and Daisy Baum; *m* 1st, 1917, Faye Albertson; no *c*; 2nd, 1938, Helen Byrne Armstrong. *Educ:* Harvard (AB). Associate Editor, New Republic, 1914-17; Assistant to Secretary of War, June-Oct., 1917; Captain, Military Intelligence, USA, 1918; Secretary of organisation directed by Colonel E. M. House to prepare data for Peace Conference; Editor, New York World, till 1931; special writer New York Herald Tribune Syndicate, 1931-62; syndicated by Washington Post and Los Angeles Times Syndicate, 1963; former Member Board of Overseers of Harvard Univ. Holds numerous Hon. Degrees. Overseas Press Club of America "Best Press Interpretation of Foreign News", 1953, 1955, 1960; Pulitzer Prize International Reporting, 1962; George Foster Peabody Television Award for Outstanding Contrib. to International Understanding, 1962; Medal of Freedom (US), 1964; Gold Medal for Essays and Criticism, American Inst. of Arts and Letters, 1965. Member of Institute of

Arts and Letters; American Academy of Arts and Letters; Senator, Phi Beta Kappa; Comdr, Legion of Honor; Officer Order of Crown of Leopold; Commander, Order of Orange-Nassau (Netherlands); Knight Cross First Class, Order of St Olav (Norway). *Publications:* A Preface to Politics; Drift and Mastery; Stakes of Diplomacy; The Political Scene; Liberty and the News; Public Opinion; The Phantom Public; American Inquisitors; Men of Destiny; A Preface to Morals; The US in World Affairs, Vol. I, 1932; Interpretations; The US in World Affairs, Vol. II, 1933; The Method of Freedom, 1934; The New Imperative, 1935; The Good Society, 1937; US Foreign Policy; Shield of the Republic, 1943; US War Aims, 1944; The Cold War, 1947; The Public Philosophy, 1955; The Communist World and Ours, 1959; The Coming Tests With Russia, 1961; Western Unity and the Common Market, 1962. *Recreations:* golf, tennis. *Address:* 28 East 63rd Street, New York, NY 10021, USA. *Clubs:* Harvard, Century, River (New York); Cosmos, Metropolitan, Tavern (Boston); National Press (Washington, DC).   [*Died* 14 *Dec.* 1974.

LIPTON, Marcus, CBE 1965 (OBE 1949); JP; MP (Lab) Lambeth Central, since 1974 (Lambeth, Brixton, 1945-74); *b* 29 Oct. 1900; *s* of late Benjamin Lipton and of Mary Lipton, Sunderland. *Educ:* Hudson Road Council Sch.; Bede Grammar Sch., Sunderland; Merton Coll., Oxford (Goldsmiths' Company Exhibitioner) MA. Barrister-at-law, Gray's Inn, 1926. Councillor, Stepney Borough Council, 1934-37. Contested (Lab) Brixton, 1935. Alderman, Lambeth Borough Council, 1937-56; Hon. Freeman, London Borough of Lambeth, 1974. JP County of London, 1939. Private, TA, 1939; Lieut-Colonel, 1944. Councillor, Binfield Parish Council, 1955-59. President: Lambeth Central Labour Party; Brixton Branch, British Legion; Southern Sunday Football League; Chairman, Anglo-Nepalese, Anglo-Bulgarian and Anglo-Haitian Parliamentary Groups. *Recreation:* giving advice. *Address:* 3 Wellington Court, Shelton Street, WC2. *T:* 01-836 7885.   [*Died* 22 *Feb.* 1978.

LISTER, Arthur, FRCS; Senior Ophthalmic Surgeon, London Hospital, 1948-70; Opthalmic Surgeon, Moorfields Eye Hospital, 1946-70; retired; *b* 12 Feb. 1905; *s* of Arthur Hugh Lister, Physician, and Sybil (*née* Palgrave); *m* 1937, Margaret Emily Pryor; three *s* two *d. Educ:* Lancing Coll.; Trinity Coll., Cambridge; London Hospital. BA Cambridge, 1927; MRCS, LRCP 1930; FRCS 1933; MB, BCh, Cambridge, 1934. House Surgeon and Senior Resident Officer, Moorfields Hospital, 1934-36; Asst Surgeon, Moorfields Hospital, 1939; Asst Ophth. Surgeon, London Hospital, 1939. Served War of 1939-45: Temp. Major (Ophthalmic Specialist), 1940; Temp. Lieut-Colonel, 1944; Adviser in Ophthalmology, 21 Army Group, NW Europe, 1944-45; Adviser in Ophthalmology, ALFSEA, 1945-46; demobilised, 1946. *Publications:* contributions to British Journal of Ophthalmology, Ophthalmic Literature, Trans. Ophthalmic Society UK, and Proc. Royal Society of Med. *Recreations:* fishing, gardening, model railway. *Address:* 89 Hamilton Terrace, NW8. *T:* 01-286 5732.   [*Died* 21 *March* 1975.

LISTER, Lt-Col Frederick Hamilton, DSO 1916; late of HM's Body Guard of the Honourable Corps of Gentlemen-at-Arms; late Royal Artillery; *b* 5 Dec. 1880; *yr s* of late Sir T. Villiers Lister, KCMG, and Lady Lister (sister of 10th Lord Belhaven and Stenton); *m* 1921, Mildred (*d* 1952), *yr d* of late Duncan Cameron, Springfield, Canterbury, NZ. *Educ:* Radley Coll.; RMA, Woolwich. Joined Royal Artillery, 1900; Captain, 1911; Major, 1915; Bt Lieut-Colonel, 1918; Lieut-Colonel, 1927; seconded for service in the Punjab Frontier Force, 1902-11; graduated at the Staff Coll., 1914; posted to General Staff, Aug. 1914; served European War and in South Russia, 1914-20 (despatches, DSO, Croix de Guerre, Bt Lieut-Colonel, Officer of Order of Leopold of Belgium, Order of St Vladimir of Russia); GSO 1 British Mission, Belgian GHQ, 1917; GSO 1 GHQ, British Forces, France, 1917-18; GSO i/c British Mission, 1st French Army, 1918; GSO 1 Supreme War Council, Versailles, 1918-19; GSO 1 Paris Peace Conference, 1919; GSO 1 British Mission to General Denikin in South Russia, 1919-20; Accompanied French operations in Rif Mountains in Morocco, 1926; retired pay, 1931. FRGS, FRHS. *Address:* Norman's Wood, Charles Hill, Tilford, Farnham, Surrey. *Clubs:* Geographical, Shikar.   [*Died* 9 *Nov.* 1971.

LISTON, Most Rev. James Michael, CMG 1968; Titular Archbishop of St Secundinus; *b* New Zealand, 1881. *Educ:* Holy Cross Coll., Dublin; Irish Coll., Rome. Priest 1904; Rector of Holy Cross Coll., Mosgiel, NZ, 1910-20; Co-adjutor to Bishop Cleary of Auckland, 1920-29; Bishop of Auckland, 1929-70. Asst at the Papal Throne, 1950; appointed to personal title of Archbishop, 1953. Chevalier Legion of Honour, 1939. *Address:* The Chaplaincy, Mater Misericordiae Hospital, Mountain Road, Auckland 3, NZ.   [*Died* 8 *July* 1976.

LITTEN, Maurice Sidney, RP 1968; portrait painter; *b* 3 May 1919; *s* of Sidney Mackenzie Litten and Margaret Lawson; *m* 1958, Alma Jean Thomson; one *s. Educ:* Skinners' Company's Sch.; St Martin's Sch. of Art; Goldsmiths' Sch. of Art. Served RAMC, 1939-46; 1st prize All India Services Art Exhbn, 1942. Exhibits at Royal Academy, Royal Soc. of Portrait Painters, Royal Soc. of British Artists. Principal commissions include: HM the Queen and HRH the Duke of Edinburgh for RMCS, 1954; Countess Bathurst; Maharanee of Cooch Behar; Sir Anthony Elkins; Arthur Wontner; Marchioness of Donegal; Lord Shawcross, 1970. *Recreations:* music, theatre, swimming, sailing. *Address:* Studio 6, 49 Roland Gardens, SW7. *T:* 01-373 0653. *Clubs:* Chelsea Arts, Hurlingham. *[Died 27 Dec. 1979.*

LITTLE, Sir Alexander; *see* Little, Sir R. A.

LITTLE, Admiral Sir Charles James Colebrooke, GCB 1945 (KCB 1935; CB 1919); GBE 1942; *b* Shanghai, 14 June 1882; *s* of Louis Stromeyer Little, FRCS, BA, FRAS; *m* 1st, 1908, Rothes Beatrix (*d* 1939), *d* of Colonel Sir Charles Leslie, 7th Bt; one *d*; 2nd, 1940, *cousin* Mary Elizabeth (Bessy), JP Sussex, *d* of late Ernest Muirhead Little, FRCS. *Educ:* Britannia, Dartmouth (1897). Specialised in Submarine Branch, 1903; commanded: H4, A7, B7, C5, C10, D1; Hibernia, 1907; St Vincent, 1910; HMS Fearless and Grand Fleet Submarine Flotilla, 1916-18 (CB civil); in command of HMS Cleopatra in the Baltic, 1919 (CB military); Director of Trade Div. Naval Staff, 1920-22; Member of British Delegation to the Washington Naval Conference, 1921; Captain of the Fleet, Mediterranean Station, 1922-24; SSO, RN War Coll., 1924-26; in command of HMS Iron Duke, 1926-27; Director Royal Naval Staff Coll., 1927-30; Rear-Admiral Second Battle Squadron, 1930-31; Rear-Admiral Submarines, 1931-32; Lord Commissioner of Admiralty and Deputy Chief of Naval Staff, 1932-35; Vice-Admiral, 1933; Commander-in-Chief, China Station, 1936-38; Admiral, 1937; a Lord Commissioner of the Admiralty and Chief of Naval Personnel, 1938-41; Head of British Joint Staff Mission in Washington, 1941-42; Commander-in-Chief, Portsmouth, 1942-45. Ex-Trustee of the National Maritime Museum; Ex-President, British Legion S. Area; Vice-President, Royal United Service Institution; Vice-President, Navy Records Society. Grand Officer Legion of Honour, Bronze medal, Royal Humane Society, Grand Cross Orange Nassau, Legion of Merit (Comdr), Grand Cross of St Olav. *Address:* The Old Mill, Ashurst, near Steyning, Sussex. *T:* Partridge Green 0461. *Clubs:* Army and Navy, Pilgrims. *[Died 20 June* 1973.

LITTLE, Sir (Rudolf) Alexander, KCB 1950 (CB 1946); *b* 23 May 1895; *s* of Charles Little; *m* 1925, Margaret Macnaughton; three *d. Educ:* Oundle; Caius Coll., Cambridge. Served European War, 1915-18; entered General Post Office, 1920; Director GPO, Scotland, 1942-44; Director of Postal Services, GPO, 1944-47, Dep. Director-General, 1947-49; Director-General, GPO, 1949-55, retired. *Recreation:* gardening. *[Died 27 Feb. 1977.*

LITTLER, Prince, CBE 1957; Chairman and Managing Director: Stoll Theatres Corporation Ltd; Associated Theatre Properties (London) Ltd; Theatre Royal, Drury Lane, Ltd; Chairman: Moss Empire Ltd; London Pavilion Ltd; Director: Ambassadors Theatre Ltd; Associated Television Ltd; Independent Television Corporation; *b* Ramsgate, Kent, 25 July 1901; *s* of F. R. and Agnes Littler; *m* 1932, Nora Delany. *Educ:* Stratford-on-Avon. For many years has presented Musical Comedies and Pantomimes in London, including Jack and the Beanstalk, Drury Lane, 1936; Cinderella, Coliseum, 1937; Brigadoon, Her Majesty's, 1950; Carousel, Drury Lane, 1951; Tea House of the August Moon, Her Majesty's, 1955; No Time for Sergeants, Her Majesty's, 1956; and over 200 Pantomimes in the Provinces. Member Council Theatrical Managers' Assoc.; Vice-President: Society of West End Theatre Managers; Denville Home for Aged Actors and Actresses; Variety Artistes Benevolent Fund. *Address:* Cranbourn Mansions, Cranbourn Street, WC2. *[Died 13 Sept. 1973.*

LITTLEWOOD, John Edensor, MA Cambridge; Hon. DSc, Liverpool; Hon. LLD, St Andrews; Hon. ScD Cambridge; FRS, FRAS; Hon. FIMA; Fellow of Trinity College, Cambridge, since 1908; Rouse Ball Professor of Mathematics in University of Cambridge, 1928-50; Fellow of the Cambridge Philosophical Society; Royal Medallist of the Royal Society, 1929, Sylvester Medallist, 1944; Copley Medallist, 1958; De Morgan Medallist, London Mathematical Society, 1939, Senior Berwick Prize, 1960; Corr. Member, French and Göttingen Academies; Former Member Royal Dutch, Royal Danish and Royal Swedish Academies; *b* Rochester, 9 June 1885. *Educ:* St Paul's Sch.; Trinity Coll., Cambridge (Scholar); Bracketed Senior Wrangler, 1905; Richardson Lecturer in Victoria Univ. of Manchester,

1907-10; Lecturer of Trinity Coll., 1910-28; Cayley Lecturer in the University of Cambridge, 1920-28. *Publications:* papers in various scientific journals. *Address:* Trinity College, Cambridge CB2 1TO. *TA:* Cambridge 58201. *[Died 6 Sept. 1977.*

LIVESEY, Roger; Actor; *b* 25 June 1906; *s* of Samuel Livesey and Mary Catherine Livesey (*née* Edwards); *m* 1936, Ursula Jeans (*d* 1973). *Educ:* Westminster City Sch. First stage appearance, St James's, 1917; West End parts, 1920-26; subsequently toured in W Indies and two seasons in S Africa, then continued London appearances; joined Old Vic-Sadler's Wells Company Sept. 1932, remaining there until May 1934; Alfred in Martine and Fontaney in The Poet's Secret, Ambassadors, 1933; Harold Parker in Meeting at Night, Globe, 1934; Jim Milburn in Sour Grapes, Apollo, 1934; Hsieh-Ping-Kuei in Lady Precious Stream, Little, 1934; Frank Burdon in Storm in a Teacup, Royalty, 1936; first stage appearance in New York as Mr Horner in The Country Wife, Henry Miller Theatre, 1936; Frank Burdon in Storm Over Patsy, Storm in a Teacup, Guild, 1937; Sir Richard Furze in Spring Meeting, Ambassadors, London, 1938; Dr Stockman in An Enemy of the People and Petruchio in The Taming of the Shrew, Old Vic, 1939; Anthony Anderson in The Devil's Disciple, Piccadilly, 1940; Matey in Dear Brutus, Globe, 1941; toured as Kurt Müller in Watch on the Rhine, and appeared in the same part at the Aldwych, 1943; Philip in The Fifth Column, Theatre Royal, Glasgow, 1944; Lt-Gen. Hume Banbury in The Banbury Nose, Wyndhams, 1944; toured Middle and Far East for ENSA in Dear Brutus, Watch on the Rhine, and Springtime for Henry; William in Ever Since Paradise, New, 1947; Hoerderer in Crime Passionel, Lyric, Hammersmith, 1948; George Bernard in Man of the World, Lyric, Hammersmith, 1950; toured Italy as Sir Toby Belch in Old Vic production of Twelfth Night, June 1950; Justice Overdo in Ben Jonson's Bartholomew Fair, Edinburgh Festival, 1950; 1950-51 Festival Season at reopened Old Vic: Sir Toby Belch in Twelfth Night, Justice Overdo in Bartholomew Fair, Chorus in Henry V, Captain Brassbound in Captain Brassbound's Conversion, Sir John Falstaff in The Merry Wives of Windsor; Hank Moreland in Third Person, Arts, 1951, and Criterion, 1952; Professor Mortimer in The Mortimer Touch, Duke of York's, 1952; Charley Delaney in The Teddy Bear, St Martin's, 1953; Marcus McLeod in Keep in a Cool Place, Saville, 1954; Stephen Leigh in Uncertain Joy, Royal Court, 1955; John Tarleton in Misalliance, Lyric, Hammersmith, 1956; Marcus Heatherington in A Lodging for a Bride, Westminster, 1960; Captain Shotover in Heartbreak House, Wyndhams, 1961; Inspector Gates in Kill Two Birds, St Martin's, 1962; Earl of Caversham in An Ideal Husband, Strand, 1965; First Player and Gravedigger in Hamlet, Round House, and New York, 1969; toured South Africa in Oh, Clarence!, 1970. Has played in numerous films including The Life and Death of Colonel Blimp, I Know Where I'm Going, A Matter of Life and Death, Vice Versa, That Dangerous Age, Green Grow the Rushes, The Master of Ballantrae, League of Gentlemen, No My Darling Daughter, Of Human Bondage. TV appearances include: The Winslow Boy, Amphitryon 38, The Canvas Rainbow, Adam's Apple, All Our Yesterdays, The Master Builder, The Entertainer, The Physicists. *Recreations:* golf, swimming, cricket, tinkering. *Address:* c/o London Management, 235 Regent Street, W1R 7AG. *Clubs:* Royal Automobile, Stage Golfing Society. *[Died 4 Feb. 1976.*

LIVINGSTON-HERBAGE, Julian; *see* Herbage.

LIVINGSTONE, Archibald Macdonald, CIE 1941; MC; MA, BSc (Agric.) Edinburgh; FRSA; *b* 1890; *s* of Archibald Livingstone, Civil and Mining Engineer, and Ann Watt Macdonald; *m* 1918, Gladys Mary, *d* of Harry Best, Customs and Excise; four *s* one *d.* Served European War, 1914-18; Major RFA (MC). Agricultural Marketing Adviser India and Burma (CIE) 1934-41. Lately Senior Marketing Officer, Ministry of Agriculture and Fisheries; retired, 1955. *Address:* 92 Marine Parade, Napier, New Zealand. *[Died 1 March 1972.*

LLEWELLYN, Lt-Col Sir Rhys, 2nd Bt, *cr* 1922; late Welsh Guards; *b* 9 March 1910; *e s* of Sir David Llewellyn, 1st Bt, LLD, and Magdalene (*d* 1966), *d* of Rev. H. Harries, DD, Porthcawl; *S* father, 1940; unmarried. *Educ:* Oundle; Trinity Coll., Cambridge, MA. Man. Dir, Graigola Merthyr Co. Ltd, Swansea, 1934-47. Master of Talybont Foxhounds, 1936-40; Supplementary Reserve of Officers, Welsh Guards, June 1939; War of 1939-45 (France and Germany, despatches); Regular Army Reserve of Officers, 1945-61. High Sheriff of Glamorgan, 1950-51. Comdr, Order of St John of Jerusalem. *Publication:* Breeding to Race, 1965. *Heir: b* Sir Henry Morton Llewellyn, CBE. *Address:* 80 Bedford Towers, Brighton BN1 2JG. *[Died 25 April 1978.*

LLEWELYN, Brig. Sir (Charles) Michael Dillwyn-V.; see Venables-Llewelyn.

LLOYD, see Selwyn-Lloyd.

LLOYD, Francis Nelson, CBE 1970; Managing Director, 1941-70, Chairman, 1949-71, F. H. Lloyd Holdings Ltd; Director Lloyds Bank, 1956-74; b 13 Aug. 1907; s of Daniel Charles Lloyd and Alice Hilda Lloyd, Bolton; m 1937, Pamela Mary Langley; two s two d. Educ: Charterhouse; Trinity Coll., Oxford. Graduated in Natural Science, 1928. With F. H. Lloyd & Co., Steel Founders, 1928-39; served in TA, RAOC, 1939-40; Man. Dir F. H. Lloyd & Co., 1941-69. Chm., Steel Castings Res. and Trade Assoc. Mem., Iron and Steel Adv. Cttee, 1967-. Recreations: golf and tennis. Address: 5 Eynsham Court, Tettenhall, Wolverhampton. [Died 27 June 1974.

LLOYD, Guy Vaughan, JP; Vice-Lieutenant of Dyfed (formerly of Carmarthenshire), 1968-73; b 12 Aug. 1901; y and o surv. s of late H. Meuric Lloyd, JP, and late Mrs Lloyd, Cynghordy, Llandovery; m 1948, Katherine, d of late A. Kenney Tyrer, Lower Carden Hall, Cheshire; one s. Educ: Malvern Coll.; New Coll., Oxford. JP 1950, DL 1965, Carmarthenshire. Recreations: farming, fishing. Address: Cynghordy, Llandovery, Dyfed. T: Cynghordy 202. [Died 12 Aug. 1975.

LLOYD, Huw Ifor, OBE 1921; MC 1916; MA; b 21 Nov. 1893; s of late I. T. Lloyd, Chelsea, and Aberdovey, Merionethshire; m 1919, Jessie, d of late T. C. Watson, DL, JP, Milton House, Morley, Yorks; one d. Educ: City of London Sch.; Emmanuel Coll., Cambridge (Exhibitioner), President Cambridge Union Society; History Tripos. Served European War, 1914-18, with 2nd Northamptonshire Regt in France and with 6th King's Own Royal Lancaster Regt in Mesopotamia; Military Governor and Political Officer, Baqubah, 1919-20; prisoner in Arab hands, Aug.-Sept. 1920; Assistant Adviser Ministry of Interior, 1921-23; Administrative Inspector, Iraq, 1923-30; attached as local expert to the British Delegation to the League of Nations, Geneva, respecting the Turko-Iraq Boundary, 1925-26; Called to the Bar, Gray's Inn, 1928; Judge of Civil Courts, Iraq, and Additional Member, Court of Cassation, 1930; President Civil and Criminal Courts, S. Iraq, 1931-38; Iraq Government Delegate to Round Table Conference on Palestine, London, 1939; served on Staff of General Wavell in Middle East, 1939-41; Director-General of Date Assoc., Iraq, 1939-46; Controller of Foreign Property, Iraq, 1939-41; Economic Adviser, Iraq Government, 1941-46; Trade Commr, Iraq Government in India, 1942; Controller of Cereals in Iraq, 1942; Iraq Government Delegate to UN Food and Agricultural Conf., Hot Springs, 1943; Asst Delegate Iraq Government to UN Conf., San Francisco, 1945; Legal Adviser: Iraq Government Deleg. to UN Conf., Lake Success, 1947; Iraq Embassy in London, 1947-58. Publications: The Geography of the Mosul Boundary in RGS Journal, 1926; reviews, and articles in journals and newspapers. Address: 50 Wood Vale, SE23.
[Died 10 June 1977.

LLOYD, John Davies Knatchbull, OBE 1957; MA; FSA; DL; JP; b 28 April 1900; e s of late John Maurice Edward Lloyd, Plas Trefaldwyn, Montgomery, Barrister-at-law, and Alice Norton, yr d of late Maj.-Gen. Charles Stirling Dundas (of Dundas), Bengal Artillery; unmarried. Educ: Winchester; Trinity Coll., Oxford. Secretary to the Council for the Preservation of Rural Wales, 1929-46; Secretary to Powysland Club, 1937-67; Mayor of Montgomery, 9 years, 1932-38, 1961, 1962; Commission in RAFVR, 1940; High Sheriff, Montgomeryshire, 1940; Chairman: Montgomeryshire Health Executive Council, 1948-51; Montgomeryshire Joint Planning Cttee, 1953-55; County Library Cttee, 1957-74; Member: Historic Buildings Council for Wales, 1953-75; Ancient Monuments Board for Wales, 1954 (Chairman, 1959-); Royal Commn on Ancient Monuments (Wales), 1967-74; Chairman, St Asaph Diocesan Faculty Advisory Cttee, 1961. JP 1934, DL 1960, Powys (formerly Montgomery). Hon. LLD Wales, 1969. Editor, Archæologia Cambrensis, 1956-69. Publications: various articles in Archæologia Cambrensis and in Montgomeryshire Collections (publication of Powysland Club); A Guide to Montgomery (published by the Corporation, 1936, 1948 and 1961); (Editor) Montgomeryshire Handbook (published by C. Council, 1949, 1958 and 1963); A Montgomery Notebook (privately printed), 1971; DoE Guide to Montgomery Castle, 1973. Recreations: music, archæology. Address: Bron Hafren, Garthmyl, Montgomery, Powys. T: Berriew 261. Club: Brooks's.
[Died 13 Dec. 1978.

LLOYD, (John) Selwyn (Brooke); see Selwyn-Lloyd, Baron.

LLOYD, Air Vice-Marshal Kenneth Buchanan, CB 1949; CBE 1943; AFC 1918; RAF (retired); b 8 Nov. 1897; s of late Major T. W. Lloyd; m 1924, Nellie Sanforth, d of late C. J. H. Jefferies; one s. Educ: St Bees; Royal Military Coll., Sandhurst; Royal Welsh Fusiliers; seconded RFC, 1914-18; RAF, 1918-49. Served War of 1939-45 (despatches); AOC, Iceland, 1942-43; AOC, Malta, 1944-47; SASO, HQ, Coastal Command, 1947-49; retired, 1949. Address: Sunnyside, Upper Swainswick, near Bath, Som. T: Bath 88332. [Died 8 Aug. 1973.

LLOYD, Colonel Pen; see Lloyd, Colonel Philip H.

LLOYD, Colonel Philip Henry, (Pen), CBE 1968; TD; DL; JP; Farmer, Landowner and Company Director; b 7 April 1905; s of late Samuel Janson Lloyd, JP; m 1943, Monica, d of W. C. Beasley-Robinson, and widow of H. R. Murray-Philipson, MP; no c. Educ: Oundle. Chairman: Breedon and Cloud Hill Lime Works Ltd; Breedon General Services Ltd; British Tar Products Ltd; Ironstone Royalty Owners Assoc., 1970-; Director: Cavendish Syndicate; Cocker Chemical Co.; Adv. Dir, Nottingham Local District, Barclays Bank, 1969-78; Hon. Mem., Trustee Savings Bank of Leicester and Notts, 1975. Member: County Councils Assoc.; Council for Small Industries in Rural Areas (Chm. for Leics); Local Authorities Mutual Investment Trust (Chm., 1974); Local Authorities Management Services and Computer Cttee (Vice-Chm., 1973-74); Governor: Brooksby Agricultural Coll.; Wyggeston Hospital; Member: East Midlands Economic Planning Council, 1965-72; Inter-Departmental Cttee on Coroners and Death Certification, 1965-71; Library Advisory Council (England), 1965-71; Board of Visitors, Gartree Prison (Chairman), 1966-75; Leicestershire Agricultural Exec. Cttee, 1960-71; Landowners' Standing Conference, Ironstone; Liveryman, Worshipful Company of Farmers. Military Mem., T&AFA, 1950-70. Chm., Leics Police Authority, 1974-; Mem., ACC Police Cttee, 1974-; Chm., No 4 Police Region, 1977; Vice-Chairman, Leicester and County Mission for the Deaf, 1961-75. DL Leicestershire, 1950; High Sheriff of Leicestershire, 1957; CA, 1960; Vice-Chm. Leicestershire CC, 1960-61, Chm., 1961-74. Farming approximately 1000 acres. FIMinE 1937. FRSA 1970. Hon. MA, Loughborough Univ. of Technology, 1969. Recreations: hunting (Joint Master Fernie Fox Hounds, 1946-62), shooting, breeding Springer spaniels, golf, tennis. Address: Stone House, Blaston, Market Harborough, Leics. T: Hallaton 234. Club: Boodle's. [Died 14 Sept. 1979.

LLOYD, Lt-Col Reginald Broughton, IMS retired; late Imperial Serologist and Chemical Examiner to Government of India, and Professor of Serology and Immunology, School of Tropical Medicine and Hygiene, Calcutta; b 31 Aug. 1881; e s of late Rev. L. W. Lloyd, MA; m 1912, Elizabeth (d 1961), e d of late Rev. J. W. Pratt, MA. Educ: Emmanuel Coll., Cambridge (Scholar); The London Hospital; MA Cambridge (1st Cl. Nat. Science Trip. Parts I and II), MB, BChir, 1907; Price Entrance Scholar, Anat. and Phys. Schol., Med. Schol.; Duckworth Nelson Prize for Med. and Surg., Wynne Baxter Prize for Medical Jurisprudence. Publications: Scientific papers on blood transfusion, medico-legal analysis of bloodstains and on the serology of tropical diseases. Recreations: fishing and gardening. Address: 91 Cooden Drive, Bexhill-on-Sea, East Sussex.
[Died 24 Sept. 1975.

LLOYD, Selwyn; see Selwyn-Lloyd, Baron.

LLOYD, William Ernest, MD, FRCP; Consulting Physician, Westminster Hospital, Brompton Hospital for Diseases of the Chest, and Bolingbroke Hospital. Educ: St Bartholomew's Hospital. Senior Scholar in Anatomy, Physiology and Chemistry; MB, BS (London), 1923; MD (London) 1925 (Univ. Gold Medal); MRCS 1921; FRCP 1934. Examiner in Medicine, Conjoint Board; Fellow Med. Soc. London; Mem., Assoc. of Physicians. Publications: contrib. to Medical journals. Address: Innisfree, Coppice Drive, Roehampton, SW15.
[Died 26 May 1975.

LLOYD, Wynne Llewelyn, CB 1962; MA (Cantab); Educational Consultant, since Oct. 1972; b 25 Jan. 1910; s of late Captain D. Ll. Lloyd, OBE, and E. A. Lloyd, Birchgrove, Pontardulais; m 1934, Kathleen Isobel Ormrod, Manchester; one d. Educ: Gowerton; Trinity Hall, Cambridge. Geographical Tripos, Parts I and II, Economics Tripos, Part II; Prizeman and Exhibitioner of Trinity Hall, 1930. Assistant Master, William Hulme's Grammar Sch., Manchester; Extra-mural Tutor, University College, Swansea; successively Asst Inspector, 1940, HM Inspector, Staff Inspector, 1950, and Chief Inspector (Wales), 1952-72, Min. of Education, DES, and Welsh Office. Member: Lockwood Cttee, 1964; Council, University Coll., Cardiff, 1970. Hon. Member, Royal Cambrian Acad., 1955; Hon. Fellow, Dept

of Educn, University Coll., Cardiff, 1971. *Publications:* Vol. VI of Social and Economic Survey of Swansea and District, 1940; contrib. to Pioneers of Welsh Education, 1964, and to various journals. *Recreation:* gardening. *Address:* Llain, Dimlands, Llantwit Major, Glam. *T:* Llantwit Major 2361. *Clubs:* United Oxford & Cambridge University, Cardiff and County.
[Died 20 April 1973.

LLOYD-BAKER, Olive Katherine Lloyd, CBE 1958; JP; *b* 1902; *d* of Capt. Michael G. Lloyd-Baker (killed in action, 1916) and late Blanche Verney, *d* of 18th Baron Willoughby de Broke, Compton Verney, Warwickshire. *Educ:* St James's, West Malvern. Member RDC, 1930-64; CC, 1943-51. County Chairman, NFU, 1942-43; County Chairman, CLA, 1953-56. Chairman Stroud Conservative Assoc., 1956-58, President, 1958-61. Prospective Conservative Candidate, West Glos, 1957-59. Landowner. JP Glos 1943; High Sheriff, Glos, 1970-71. *Recreations:* walking, collecting. *Address:* Hardwicke Court, Gloucester. *T:* Hardwicke 212. *Club:* Farmers'.
[Died 31 May 1975.

LLOYD GEORGE OF DWYFOR, Frances, Countess; (Frances Louise), CBE 1918; BA (London Classics Hons); Private Secretary to Rt Hon. D. Lloyd George, 1913-43; *d* of John and Louise Stevenson, Worthing; *m* 1943, 1st Earl Lloyd George of Dwyfor, PC, OM. *Educ:* Clapham High Sch.; Royal Holloway Coll. *Publications:* Makers of the New World, 1922; The Years that are Past, 1967; Lloyd George, a Diary, by Frances Stevenson (ed by A. J. P. Taylor), 1971. *Address:* Farm Cottage, Churt, Surrey.
[Died 5 Dec. 1972.

LLOYD JONES, Richard Francis, MA (Cantab), FICE, AFRAeS; Consulting Engineer and Consultant to Rendel and Dawbarn, Architects and Consulting Engineers; *b* 18 April 1908; *e s* of Cyril Walter Lloyd Jones; *m* 1938, Hester, *d* of late Henry Alan Ritchie; one *s* two *d*. *Educ:* Oundle; Trinity Coll., Cambridge. Assistant Engineer with Rendel, Palmer and Tritton, Consulting Engineers, 1929; Assistant to Resident Engineer, Royal Dock Approaches, Approaches Improvement Scheme, 1932; Assistant Engineer, 1934, Partner 1938-73, Norman & Dawbarn. Served in Royal Navy, 1942-45. Served on London Airport Advisory Panel, 1946. MConsE. *Address:* Shepherds' Close, Munstead, Godalming, Surrey GU8 4AR. *T:* Godalming 21561. *Club:* United Oxford & Cambridge University.
[Died 2 March 1975.

LLOYD-WILLIAMS, Dorothy Sylvia, MA (Cantab); Headmistress King Edward VI High School for Girls, Birmingham, 1953-64; *b* 2 Aug. 1901; *d* of late J. J. Lloyd-Williams, MA Oxon, and Ellen Augusta Crawley Vincent. *Educ:* Moreton Hall Sch., Shropshire; Girton Coll., Cambridge. Assistant mistress, Queen Mary's High Sch. for Girls, Walsall, 1924-26; Assistant mistress, Belvedere Sch., GPDST, Liverpool, 1926-29; Head of Science Dept, Roedean Sch., Brighton, 1929-40; Senior house mistress, Roedean Sch., Brighton, 1935-53. Member of Council, University of Birmingham. *Recreations:* reading, foreign travel, walking. *Address:* Brynele, Bwlchllan, Lampeter, Dyfed. *Club:* University Women's.
[Died 13 April 1977.

LLOYD-WILLIAMS, Commander Hugh, DSO 1941; VRD; CEng; MInstCE; FIEE; RNVR (retired); *b* 29 Aug. 1900; *s* of late Dr H. Lloyd-Williams, JP, Waenfawr, Caernarvonshire; *m* 1st, 1927, Emmy Lund (*d* 1933); two *s*; 2nd, 1935, Anne Marie Lomsdalen; one *d*. *Educ:* Mill Hill Sch.; Glasgow Univ., BSc (Eng). Served student apprenticeship with British Thomson Houston Co., Rugby; joined Metropolitan Electric Supply Co. Ltd, 1925; Sub-Area Engineer, 1948-57; District Manager, London Electricity Board, 1958-65. Joined London Division, RNVR in 1924; DSO for successful action against enemy submarine whilst in command of HMS Arbutus, 1941. *Address:* Brynmeredydd, Waenfawr, Caernarvon, Gwynedd LL55 4YY. *T:* Waenfawr 265. *Club:* Royal Welsh Yacht (Caernarvon).
[Died 22 Feb. 1977.

LLOYD-WILLIAMS, Katharine Georgina, CBE 1956; MD London; FFARCS; Consultant Anæsthetist to Royal Free Hospital Group, retired 1962; *b* 14 Feb. 1896; *d* of John Jordan Lloyd-Williams, MA Oxon, and Ellen Augusta Crawley Vincent. *Educ:* Queen Anne's Sch., Caversham; Bedford Physical Training Coll.; London (Royal Free Hospital) School of Medicine for Women. President, University of London Athletic Union (Women), 1922-23; Fellow, 1st Board of Faculty of Anæsthetists, RCS, 1948-53; President, Med. Women's Federation, 1958-59; Dean of Faculty of Med., University of London, 1956-60; Dean of Royal Free Hospital School of Medicine, 1945-62. Past President (now Hon. Fellow), Anæsth. Section of Royal Society of Med., 1956; Past President, Anæsth.

Section, BMA Annual Meeting, 1946; Member GMC, 1961-; Member NW Metropolitan Reg. Hospital Board, 1948-63; Visitor for King Edward VII Hospital Fund and Member King's Fund Aux. Cttee; Member Board of Management, Royal Med. Benevolent Fund and its Case Cttee, 1962-69. *Publications:* Anæsthesia and Analgesia in Labour, 1934; contrib. medical and dental journals. *Recreations:* travel, walking, gardening. *Address:* 8 Rosslyn Mansions, Goldhurst Terrace, NW6. *T:* 01-624 6486; Brynele, Bwlchllan, Lampeter, Cardiganshire. *T:* Aeron 466. *Club:* University Women's.
[Died 10 Jan. 1973.

LOCH, Colonel John Carysfort, CBE 1929; Member of the Royal Company of Archers, the Queen's Body Guard for Scotland; *b* Jamon Damoh District, CP, India, 25 Dec. 1877; *s* of Lieut-Colonel John Lowis Loch and Lucy Proby; *m* 1st, 1901, Violet Francis, *d* of Lieut-General Jenkin Jones; two *s* one *d* (and one *d* decd); 2nd, 1933, Helen Gladys Montgomery, *widow* of Spencer C. Thomson. *Educ:* Wellington Coll.; Sandhurst. Commissioned Unattached List for Indian Army, 1897; Attached 1st Bn Norfolk Regt 7th DCO Rajputs, 1898-1901; 1/3 QAO Gurkha Rifles, 1901-20; raised and commanded 1st Bn Nayar Bde, 1903-07; Commandant (Officiating) Nayar Brigade, 1907; raised and commanded 2/130 Baluchis, 1918-20; commanded 4/39 Garhwal Rifles, 1920; 3/152 Punjaubis, 1920-21; Kumaon Rifles, 1921-25; Officiating AAG Army HQ India, 1924-25; Director Military Prisons in India, 1925-29; retired, 1929; Chief Commandant, Mysore State Forces, 1929-35. Life Member, British Legion, Scotland, 1971. Served China, 1900-01 (medal and 2 clasps); European War, 1914-18, Mesopotamia (Staff) (despatches, brevet of Lieut-Colonel); Waziristan, 1920-21; Mahsud, 1920; Member, American Military Order of the Dragon (1901). *Recreation:* reading. *Address:* Pilgrims Progress, St Boswells, Roxburghshire. *T:* St Boswells 2262. *Clubs:* Army and Navy, Victory Ex-Service; Royal Bombay Yacht (Bombay).
[Died 26 May 1974.

LOCKETT, Richard Jeffery, CBE 1949; *b* 16 Sept. 1907; *s* of Richard Cyril Lockett and Beatrice (*née* Bell); *m* 1939, Mary Edna Crist, Oakland, California; one *s* one *d*. *Educ:* Winchester Coll.; Christ Church, Oxford. Sugar Planter and Cotton Merchant, Peru, 1928-50; responsible for procurement Peruvian Cotton for Ministry of Supply, 1941-45; Chairman, British Chamber of Commerce, Peru, 1943-44. Director: Cunard Steam Ship Co. Ltd, 1952-68; Royal Insurance Co. Ltd, 1954-74; Combined English Mills (Spinners) Ltd, 1961-64; Matthew Clark & Sons (Holdings) Ltd, 1962-72. Permanent Delegate of Peru to International Sugar Council, 1960-70. High Sheriff of Cheshire, 1967-68. *Recreations:* shooting, fishing, gardening. *Address:* Glassburn, by Beauly, Inverness-shire. *T:* Cannich 203.
[Died 25 Feb. 1980.

LOCKHART, Sir Allan R. E.; *see* Eliott Lockhart.

LOCKWOOD, James Horace; retired; *b* 25 May 1888; *s* of George Henry Lockwood, Woollen and Worsted Cloth Manufacturer, of Huddersfield. admitted a Solicitor, 1912; Captain RFA (T) European War; Pres., Bradford Law Soc., 1929; MP (C) Shipley Div. of Yorks, 1930-35; has taken a great interest in Bankruptcy Law Reform. *Recreations:* shooting and sailing. *Address:* 5 and 6 Stuart Court, Prince of Wales Mansions, Harrogate, Yorks. *T:* Harrogate 3780; Scutcheon House, Far Sawrey, Ambleside. *Clubs:* Union (Bradford); The Club (Harrogate).
[Died 29 Nov. 1972.

LOCMARIA, Marquis du P.; *see* Parc-Locmaria.

LODER, Sir Louis (Francis), Kt 1962; CBE 1953; retired; *b* 30 Dec. 1896; *s* of James Edward Loder and Marie Dorthea Loder (*née* Jensen); *m* 1924, Jean Arnot Maxwell; three *s*. *Educ:* Wesley Coll., Melbourne; Queen's Coll., University of Melbourne. Chief Engineer, Country Roads Board, Vic., 1928-40; Chm., 1940-44; Dir-Gen., Commonwealth Dept of Works, 1944-61. DEng, Perth, 1948. *Publications:* Papers in Proceedings of Institution of Engineers, Australia. *Recreation:* tennis. *Address:* PO Box 214, Healesville, Victoria 3777, Australia. *T:* Healesville 786. *Club:* Royal Automobile (Victoria).
[Died 11 Feb. 1972.

LOEWENTHAL, Sir John, Kt 1978; CMG 1975; ED 1965; FRCS, FRACS, FACS; Professor and Chairman, Department of Surgery, University of Sydney, 1956-79, now Emeritus; Consulting Surgeon: Royal Prince Alfred Hospital; Sydney Hospital; Royal North Shore Hospital; The Rachel Forster Hospital; Repatriation General Hospital, Concord; Westmead Hospital; Bowral and District Hospital; *b* 22 Dec. 1914; *s* of A. M. Loewenthal; *m* 1944, Anne June, *d* of Dr James Stewart; two *s* two *d*. *Educ:* Sydney Grammar School; Univ. of Sydney. MB, BS 1938; MS (Melbourne) 1946; FRCS 1946, FRACS 1956,

FACS 1965. Served War, 1939-46, AIF, Middle East and SW Pacific, Major AAMC. Nuffield Dominions Travelling Fellow, 1946-47; Chief Asst, St Bartholomew's Hosp., London, 1946-47; Sen. Lectr in Surgery, Manchester Univ., 1947-48; Hunterian Prof., RCS of Eng., 1948; Perpetual Student, Med. Coll. of St Bartholomew's, 1960; Col Cons. Surgeon, AAMC, 1963-73; Dean, Faculty of Med., Univ. of Sydney, 1966-71; Pres., Royal Australasian Coll. of Surgeons, 1971-74; Sims Commonwealth Travelling Prof., 1971; Nat. Pres., Nat. Heart Foundn of Aust., 1974-. Hon. Fellow: RCS of Edin., 1971; Coll. of Med. of S Africa, 1972; Amer. Coll. of Surgeons, 1969; Amer. Surgical Assoc., 1970; Assoc. of Surgeons of GB and Ire., 1971. *Publications:* in learned jls, on vascular, cancer and transplantation surgery, design of hospitals, control of surgical infection and medical education. *Recreation:* gardening. *Address:* Roberton Park, Glenquarry, via Bowral, NSW 2576, Australia. *T:* (048) 871 207; 8/45 Wharf Road, Birchgrove, NSW 2041. *T:* (02) 821277. *Clubs:* Australian, Legacy, Royal Commonwealth (Sydney); Bowral Golf. *[Died 25 Aug. 1979.*

LOGAN, Lt-Col Harry Tremaine; MC; MA; Professor Emeritus of Classics, University of British Columbia, retired; *b* Londonderry, Nova Scotia, 24 March 1887; *yr s* of Rev. John A. Logan, DD; *m* 1916, Gwyneth, *v d* of Sir James A. H. Murray, Editor, Oxford English Dictionary; one *s* one *d* (*er s* died of wounds, Normandy, 1944). *Educ:* BC Elementary Schs; Vancouver High Sch.; McGill; (Rhodes Scholar) St John's Coll., Oxford. Instructor in Classics, McGill Coll. of BC, 1913-15; Lt 72nd Seaforth Highlanders of Canada, 1915; served in Belgium and France in Canadian Machine Gun Corps, 1916-18 (despatches, MC); prepared Official History Canadian Machine Gun Corps, 1919; Mem. Classics Dept, University of British Columbia, 1915-36; Head, 1949-54; Special Lectr in Classics, 1954-67. Principal, Prince of Wales Fairbridge Farm Sch., 1936-45; Sec., The Fairbridge Soc., London, 1946-49. Mem., University of British Columbia Senate, 1930-48 and 1954-60; Board of Governors, 1941-45. Hon. LLD, University of British Columbia, 1965. *Publication:* Tuum Est, A History of the University of British Columbia, 1958. *Recreation:* gardening. *Address:* The University of British Columbia, Vancouver, BC, Canada. *[Died 25 Feb. 1971.*

LÖHR, Marie Kaye Wouldes; *b* Sydney, NSW, 28 July 1890; *d* of late Kate Bishop and Lewis J. Löhr; *m* Anthony Leyland Val Prinsep (whom she divorced, 1928; he died 1942); one *d*. *Educ:* Greycoat Sch. Made her first appearance on the stage at Sydney in The World Against Her, 1894; first appearance on the London stage at the Garrick, in Shockheaded Peter, and The Man who Stole the Castle, 1901; played with the Kendals, Sir Beerbohm Tree, and Sir John Hare; Manageress of the Globe Theatre, 1918-25, when she produced amongst other plays, Nurse Benson, A Voice from the Minaret, L'Aiglon, A Marriage of Convenience, etc. Has played many stage parts in the West End since then. Successes include: (Noël Coward's) Waiting in the Wings; The Silver Wedding; Ring Round the Moon; Treasure Hunt. Has also appeared on Television. Entered films in Aren't We All, 1932, and has appeared frequently. *Recreations:* golf, dancing, reading, music. *Address:* Flat 8, 199 Sussex Gardens, W2. *[Died 21 Jan. 1975.*

LOMAS, Harry, CBE 1972; QFSM 1970; Deputy County Director, St John Ambulance, Dorset, since 1979; *b* 9 June 1916; *s* of Harry Lomas, market gardener, Ashton-under-Lyne; *m* 1940, Ivy Mona Snelgrove; one *s* two *d*. *Educ:* Heginbotham Sch., Ashton-under-Lyne. Mem. Instn Fire Engrs. Manchester City Police Fire Bde, 1939; HM Royal Marines, 1942-46; Nat. Fire Service, 1946-48; Manchester City Fire Bde, 1948: Stn Officer, 1950; Asst Divisional Officer, 1955; Divisional Officer, 1957; Dep. Chief Officer, 1966; Chief Fire Officer, 1968-74. FIFE 1974. CStJ 1979 (OStJ 1970). *Recreations:* cine photography, gardening. *Address:* 5 Balfour Close, Highcliffe, Christchurch, Dorset BH23 4PN. *[Died 27 May 1980.*

LOMAX, Maj.-Gen. Cyril Ernest Napier, CB 1944; CBE 1941; DSO 1918; MC; *b* 28 June 1893; *s* of late Capt. and Adjutant D. A. N. Lomax, 41st (The Welch) Regt; *m* 1927, Constance Turberville Williams (*d* 1967); one *d*; *m* 1968, Mrs Edith May Mulcahy. *Educ:* Marlborough; RMC, Sandhurst. Served European War, 1914-19 (despatches five times, DSO and bar, MC, Italian War Cross); commanded 2nd Bn The Welch Regt, 1936-39; served Middle East, 1941 (second bar to DSO, CBE), in command 16th Inf. Brigade; Burma and on E Frontier, India (CB), in command 26th Indian Div.; GOC East Anglian District, 1946-48; Pres. No 1 Regular Commns Bd, 1948-49. Col The Welch Regt, 1949-58. *Address:* White Gates, Sea Lane, Ferring, Sussex. *T:* Worthing 43858. *[Died 30 Aug. 1973.*

LOMAX, Michael Roger T.; *see* Trappes-Lomax.

LOMBE, Vice-Adm. Sir Edward Malcolm E.; *see* Evans Lombe.

LONG, Sir Bertram, Kt 1957; MC; TD; Senior Registrar Principal Probate Registry, 1953-64 (Registrar, 1935-53); *b* 12 Sept. 1889; *s* of William Long, Horley, Surrey; *m* 1st, 1919, Beatrix Frederica Frances Mackay (who obtained a divorce, 1933; *d* 1958), *yr d* of late Sir Walter Grindlay Simpson, 2nd Bt of Strathavon and Balabraes, Ayton, NB (one *s* killed in action 1945); 2nd, 1940, Eleanora Carroll (*d* 1946), *o d* of late Dr and Mrs Dudley Morgan, Washington, DC; 3rd, 1947, Joan, *er d* of Walter Littleton. *Educ:* Dulwich Coll.; Worcester Coll., Oxford (MA). Called to Bar, Inner Temple, 1912; served with Oxfordshire and Buckinghamshire Light Infantry (TA), 1910-21, and 1924-31; mobilised, 1914-19, served France, Belgium, Italy (MC and Bar, 1914-15 Star, despatches thrice), TD 1928, served again with Oxfordshire and Buckinghamshire LI (TA), 1939-44; attached RAF, 1940-44; served England, France, Ireland; Lieut-Colonel; TED 1951. *Recreations:* walking, golf. *Address:* 23 Beechwood Crescent, Eastbourne, East Sussex. *T:* Eastbourne 26501. *Club:* Athenæum. *[Died 6 May 1975.*

LONGHURST, Henry Carpenter, CBE 1972; journalist, author, broadcaster, etc; *b* 18 March 1909; *s* of Henry William Longhurst, JP, and Mrs Constance Longhurst, Bedford; *m* 1938, Claudine Marie Sier; one *s* one *d*. *Educ:* Charterhouse (scholar); Clare Coll., Cambridge (BA Econ). Captain Cambridge Univ. Golf team, 1930 (and in USA 1931). Journalist: Sunday Times, etc since 1932. MP (Nat. C) Acton Division of Middlesex, 1943-45. Journalist of the Year Special Award, 1969; Walter Hagen Award for contrib. to Anglo-American golf relations, 1973. *Publications:* Candid Caddies, 1936; Golf, 1937; It Was Good While it Lasted, 1941; I Wouldn't Have Missed It, 1946; You Never Know Till You Get There, 1950; Golf Mixture, 1952; Round in Sixty-Eight, 1953; The Borneo Story, 1957; Adventure in Oil, 1959; Spice of Life, 1963; Only on Sundays, 1964; Never on Weekdays, 1968; My Life and Soft Times (autobiog.), 1971. *Recreations:* fishing, travel. *Address:* Clayton Windmills, Hassocks, Sussex. *Clubs:* Bath, Garrick; (Hon. Life Mem.) Royal and Ancient (St Andrews). *[Died 21 July 1978.*

LONGLAND, Austin Charles, CBE 1959; QC 1946; *b* 1888; *o s* of Rev. Charles Boxall Longland, MA; *m* 1915, Sybil, 3rd *d* of Rev. John Coker Egerton, MA; no *c*. *Educ:* Radley Coll.; Merton Coll., Oxford (Postmaster, MA). Barrister, Inner Temple, 1914; Bencher, 1955; Oxford Circuit. Served France and Macedonia, 1914-19, Wiltshire Regt (despatches). Referee Contributory Pensions Acts, 1927, Family Allowances Act, 1947; Vice-Chairman, Oxfordshire Quarter Sessions, 1947-54; Comr Agricultural Marketing Acts Inquiries 1948, 1950, 1951; Council Radley Coll., 1934-65 (Vice-Chairman 1949-59); Chairman House Cttee, Maida Vale Hospital, 1949-54. *Address:* Clanfield House, 16 Park Crescent, Abingdon, Berks. *T:* Abingdon 278; 4 Paper Buildings, Temple, EC4. *T:* 01-353 9568. *Club:* Athenæum. *[Died 2 July 1972.*

LONGMAN, Mark Frederic Kerr; President, Longman Group Ltd; Chairman, The Fine Art Society Ltd; Director, Longman Penguin Ltd; Vice-President of the Publishers Association, since 1971; *b* 12 Nov. 1916; *s* of Henry Kerr Longman and Margot Amy Cecil Russell; *m* 1949, Lady Elizabeth Mary Lambart, *d* of 10th Earl of Cavan; three *d*. *Educ:* Eton; Trinity Coll., Cambridge (BA). Joined staff of Longmans Green & Co. Ltd, 1938. Served in Army, in Africa and Europe, 1939-46; Captain, City of London Yeomanry. Rejoined Longmans Green & Co. Ltd, 1946; Dir, 1947. Mem. Council, Publishers' Assoc., 1963, Treas., 1967, Pres., 1969-71; Jt Hon. Treas., English-Speaking Union, 1964-70; Dep. Chairman, Nat. Book League, 1964-66, Chm., 1966-71. *Address:* Flat 8, 64 Rutland Gate, SW7. *T:* 01-589 6731; Bishopstone House, Salisbury, Wiltshire. *T:* Coombe Bissett 392. *Clubs:* Beefsteak, Buck's, Pratt's, Travellers', White's. *[Died 6 Sept. 1972.*

LONGMORE, Brigadier John Alexander, CB 1957; CBE (mil) 1946 (MBE (mil) 1927); TD; DL; Solicitor; *b* 7 May 1899; *s* of late Colonel Sir Charles Elton Longmore, KCB, VD, TD, DL, Porthill House, Hertford; *m* 1925, Marguerite Madeleine, *d* of late Major John Edward Chapman Mathews, and *g d* of Sir Richard Quain, Bt; one *s* two *d*. *Educ:* Harrow. Served European War with Coldstream Guards, 1917-19. 1st Bn Herts Regt, 1919-42 (Comdr, 1939-42, Hon. Col, 1952-61). Brigadier, and Dep. Director Home Guard and Territorial Army, War Office, 1942-46. Admitted Solicitor, 1922. Successively Vice-Chairman and Hon. Treasurer, now Vice-President, Army Cadet Force Assoc.; Chairman T&AFA for Co. of Hertford, 1953-64; Life Governor of Haileybury and Imperial Service Coll. DL Herts 1942. *Recreation:* gardening. *Address:* Great Amwell

House, Ware, Herts. *T:* Ware 870415; Point Head, Chapel Point, Mevagissey, Cornwall. *T:* Mevagissey 2217. *Clubs:* Guards; Royal Cornwall Yacht. [*Died 16 Aug. 1973.*

LONGMUIR, Very Rev. James Boyd, CBE 1973; TD 1950; Hon. DD; Moderator of the General Assembly of the Church of Scotland, May 1968-May 1969; Chaplain to the Queen since 1957; Dean of the Chapel Royal, since 1969; Chaplain to HM Bodyguard for Scotland (Royal Company of Archers), since 1969; *b* 26 April 1907; *s* of William Longmuir and Margaret Lohoar Boyd; *m* 1934, Bethia Liddell, *d* of Rev. Thomas MacGregor; one *s* one *d*. *Educ:* Dalziel High Sch.; Glasgow Univ. (MA and BL). Ordained to Swinton Parish, 1934. Scoutmaster 9th Berwickshire, and District Commissioner of Scouts, 1951. Commissioned Royal Army Chaplains Dept (TA), 1938; mobilised 1939; served in France, attached 4th Gordons, 1940; Italy, 5 Corps Troops, RE, 1944; SCF 5 Corps Troops; Staff Chaplain, HQ British Troops, Austria, 1945 (despatches). Clerk to Presbytery of Duns, 1949-53; Minister at Chirnside, 1952-61; Dep. Clerk, 1953, Principal Clerk, 1955-72, Sec. to Gen. Admin Cttee and Sec. to Moderator, Gen. Assembly of Church of Scotland. Governor of Esdaile; Trustee of Iona Cathedral; Chairman, Chalmers Lectureship Trust; General Trustee, Church of Scotland. Member: Broadcasting Council for Scotland, 1967-72; Commn on the Constitution, 1969. Hon. DD, Edinburgh, 1967. *Publications:* Simprim Church and Parish, 1947; Editor, Cox's Practice and Procedure in the Church of Scotland (5th edn), 1964. *Recreations:* history and gardening. *Address:* Viewfield, Gavinton, Berwickshire. *T:* Duns 2728. *Club:* Caledonian (Edinburgh). [*Died 22 Oct. 1973.*

LONGRIGG, Brigadier Stephen Hemsley, OBE 1927; DLitt (Oxon); *b* 7 Aug. 1893; *s* of W. G. Hemsley Longrigg; *m* 1922, Florence (*d* 1976), *d* of Henry Aitken Anderson, CSI, CIE; two *s* one *d*. *Educ:* Highgate Sch.; Oriel Coll., Oxford. Served Royal Warwickshire Regt, European War and after, 1914-21; Major 1918 (despatches twice). Govt of Iraq, 1918-31; Inspector-Gen. of Revenue, 1927-31; Iraq Petroleum Co., 1931-51; War of 1939-45: Gen. Staff, GHQ, Cairo, 1940-41; Chief Administrator of Eritrea, 1942-44, Brigadier, 1940-45 (despatches). Governor of Highgate Sch., 1946, Chairman of Governors, 1954-65. Chairman, British Petroleum Employers' Cttee for International Labour Affairs, 1946-51. Vice-President, Royal Central Asian Society; Member Council, Royal Institute of International Affairs, 1956-64; Lecture tours: Scandinavia, 1952; Germany, 1954; US and Canada, 1956 and annually, 1959-66. Visiting Professor: Columbia Univ., Summer, 1966; University of Colorado, 1967. Order of the Rafidain (Iraq), 1931; Lawrence of Arabia Medallist, 1962; Sir Richard Burton Memorial Medallist, 1969. *Publications:* Four Centuries of Modern Iraq, 1925; Short History of Eritrea, 1945 (repr. USA, 1975); Iraq, 1900 to 1950, 1953; Oil in the Middle East, 1954 (3rd edn 1968); Syria and Lebanon under French Mandate, 1958; (in collaboration) Iraq, 1958; The Middle East, a Social Geography, 1963 (2nd edn 1970). *Address:* Otara, Kingsley Green, East Sussex. *Clubs:* Athenæum, East India, Sports and Public Schools. [*Died 11 Sept. 1979.*

LONGSTRETH-THOMPSON, Francis, OBE 1948; BScEng London, FRICS, MICE; Past President and Member Council of Town Planning Institute, 1924-57; Planning Consultant in private practice, 1914-44; County Planning Adviser for Essex, 1944-55; Member Executive Committee, Council for the Preservation of Rural England; *b* 3 May 1890; *s* of Francis Thompson and Emma Florence Pepler (*née* Mills); changed his surname by deed poll, from Thompson to Longstreth-Thompson in 1964; *m* 1st, 1913, Mildred Grace Corder (*d* 1963); one *s* three *d*; 2nd, 1964, Olga Mary Radcliff. *Educ:* Bootham Sch., York; University College, University of London. Chadwick Gold Medallist in Municipal Engineering (University College, London); articled to Messrs Stothert and Pitt of Bath and W. T. Douglass, MInstCE, of Westminster; Asst Engineer Port of London Authority, 1912-13; Resident Engineer on Ridham Dock for Rendel, Palmer and Tritton, 1913-14; work in France for Friends War Victims Relief Cttee, 1917-18; Asst Architect Housing, Ministry of Health, 1919-21; in private practice as Town Planning Consultant in Westminster, 1922-44; Adviser to Witwatersrand and Pretoria Jt Town Planning Cttee (S Africa), 1934-39; and (with Prof. Thornton White) to Govt of Union of South Africa, in connection with Foreshore Reclamation Scheme at Cape Town, 1940; Member Advisory Cttee, appointed by LCC in 1930 in connection with proposed Charing Cross Bridge; Consultant for numerous Regional and Town Planning Schemes in England, Newfoundland, South Africa and Southern Rhodesia, 1923-40; appointed in 1943 by Minister of Town and Country Planning to prepare a planning scheme for Merseyside; Chairman Technical Cttee of Advisory Cttee for London Regional Planning; Member Terminal Railway Station Commission, Durban, 1948; Chairman County Planning Officers Society, 1947-54; Member Planning Cttee, County Councils Assoc., 1946-55. Coronation Medal, 1953. *Publications:* Site Planning in Practice, 1923; Cape Town Foreshore Scheme, 1940; Merseyside Plan, 1944; numerous Regional Planning Reports; articles on Town Planning, Encyclopædia of Local Government Law, 1940, and elsewhere. *Recreations:* books, sketching, The Times Crossword. *Address:* Bobbins, Hawksdown, Walmer, Kent. *T:* Deal 2904. *Club:* Athenæum. [*Died 19 March 1973.*

LONGWORTH, Sir Fred, Kt 1966; DL; retired Trade Union Secretary; Vice-Chairman, Lancashire County Council, 1967-73 (Chairman, 1964-67); *b* 15 Feb. 1890; *s* of James and Cresina Longworth; *m* 1916, Mary Smith. *Educ:* Tyldesley Upper George Street County Sch. Mem., Tyldesley UDC, 1940-70 (Chm., 1948-49, 1961-62); Mem., Lancs CC, 1946-73; CA, 1952; Mem., Educn Cttee, County Councils Assoc.; Mem., Council and Court, Lancaster Univ. DL Lancs 1968. *Recreations:* reading, music, politics, education. *Address:* 30 Crawford Avenue, Tyldesley, near Manchester. *T:* Atherton 2906. [*Died 29 Aug. 1973.*

LONGWORTH, Rt. Rev. Tom, DD; *b* Jan. 1891; *s* of late Thomas Longworth, JP, Oak Hill, Whalley, Lancs; *m* 1926, Dorothy, *er d* of Rev. Frank Conyers Hardy, Vicar of Edensor, Derbyshire; one *d*. *Educ:* Shrewsbury Sch.; University Coll., Oxford; Cuddesdon Coll. BA 1914; MA 1927; DD (Lambeth), 1949. Deacon, 1915; priest, 1916; Rector of Guisborough, 1927-35; Vicar of Benwell, 1935-39; Bishop Suffragan and Archdeacon of Pontefract and Canon of Wakefield, 1939-49; Bishop of Hereford, 1949-61. Mem. House of Lords, 1956-61. *Address:* Lichfields, Cripstead Lane, St Cross, Winchester, Hants SO23 9SF. [*Died 15 Oct. 1977.*

LONSDALE, Allister; His Honour Judge Lonsdale; a Circuit Judge, since 1972; *b* 4 Aug. 1926; 2nd *s* of late James Herbert Lonsdale, and Juanita Lonsdale; *m* 1955, Elizabeth Mary Alexandra (*née* Anning); one *s* three *d*. *Educ:* Watford Grammar Sch.; Wadham Coll., Oxford (MA). RAF, 1944-48; RAFVR, 1949-59 (Hon. Flt Lieut). Called to Bar, Inner Temple, 1952 (Yarborough-Anderson Scholar); NE Circuit. A Recorder, 1972. *Publications:* papers in Yorks Numismatic Soc. Trans, Thoresby Soc. Trans. *Recreations:* Numismatics (Pres. Yorks Numismatic Soc., 1971), recusant history. *Address:* c/o Lloyds Bank Ltd, East Parade, Leeds LS1 1RJ. *Club:* RAF Reserves. [*Died 29 July 1977.*

LONSDALE, Lt-Col Arthur H.; *see* Heywood-Lonsdale.

LONSDALE, Dame Kathleen, DBE 1956; FRS 1945; DSc; formerly Professor of Chemistry and Head of Department of Crystallography, University College, London, now Emeritus; *b* 28 Jan. 1903; 10th and *y c* of late Harry Frederick Yardley and late Jessie Cameron; *m* 1927, Thomas J. Lonsdale, MSc, PhD, FInstP; one *s* two *d*. *Educ:* Bedford Coll., London Univ. Research Asst to late Sir Wm Bragg, OM, 1922-27 and 1937-42; Amy Lady Tate Scholar, 1927-29 (at Leeds Univ.); Leverhulme Research Fellow, 1935-37; Dewar Fellow, Royal Institution, 1944-46; Special Research Fellow, US Federal Health Service, 1947; Fellow of University Coll. Vis. Prof., Michigan State Univ., 1958; Distinguished Vis. Prof.: Ohio State Univ., 1969; Harvard Univ., 1970. Vice-Pres., Royal Society, 1960-61; Pres., British Association, 1967-68, Hon. Sec., 1960-64, Pres., Section A, 1966-67. Pres., Internat. Union of Crystallography, 1966. Mem. Court, Univ. of Essex; Governor and Fellow, Bedford Coll., London Univ. Hon. DSc: Wales, 1960; Leicester, Manchester, 1962; Lancaster, 1967; Kent, 1968; Oxford, 1969; Bath, 1969; Hon. LLD: Leeds, 1967; Dundee, 1968. Hon. Fellow: Lucy Cavendish Coll., Cambridge; Somerville Coll., Oxford, 1969. Davy Medal, Royal Society, 1957. *Publications:* Structure factor tables, 1936; Crystals and X-rays, 1949; International Tables for X-ray Crystallography, Vol. I, 1952; Vol. II, 1959; Vol. III, 1962; Quakers Visit Russia, 1952; Removing the Causes of War (Swarthmore Lecture), 1953; Is Peace Possible? (Penguin Special), 1957; I believe... (Eddington Lecture), 1964; many papers in scientific periodicals, from 1925 onwards. *Address:* 125a Dorset Road, Bexhill-on-Sea, Sussex. *T:* Bexhill 3405. [*Died 1 April 1971.*

LOOMBE, Claude Evan, CMG 1961; *b* 9 Aug. 1905; *yr s* of late Arthur Thomas Loombe and Catherine Jane Jermy; *m* 1936, Zoë Isabella, *o d* of late R. D. Hotchkis, MD, and Penelope, *d* of late Alexander Ionides; three *d*. Entered Chartered Bank, 1925; service in Ceylon, China and India; seconded to Min. of Finance, Iraq Govt, 1941-45. Entered service of Bank of England as an Adviser, 1945; Adviser to the Governors, 1964-65; retired 1965; Dir, British Bank of the Middle East, 1965-77 (Chm., 1967-74);

Member: Kuwait Currency Bd, 1960-69; Jordan Currency Bd, 1948-65; Sudan Currency Bd, 1956-60; Libyan Currency Commn, 1952-56. Vice-Pres., Middle East Assoc. Iraqi Order of Al-Rafidain, 4th Class, 1946; Jordan Independence Order, 2nd Class, 1961; Order of Jordanian Star (1st Class), 1965. *Address:* 64 Shepherd's Way, Liphook, Hants. *T:* Liphook 722060. *Club:* Oriental.   *[Died 12 Feb. 1978.*

LORD, Sir Frank, KBE 1962 (OBE 1945); Kt 1954; MA; JP; DL; Mayor of Oldham, 1951-52; Master, Farriers' Company, 1962-63; Master, Paviors' Company 1971-72; JP 1940, High Sheriff, 1963, DL, 1968, County Palatine of Lancaster; JP County Borough of Oldham, 1935; Freeman, Co. Borough of Oldham, 1971; President, Oldham Conservative Association; Past Chairman, Oldham and District Hospital Management Committee; *b* 3 May 1894; *s* of Joseph Lord, Oldham; *m* 1923, Rosalie Jeannette, *d* of Clement Joseph Herent, Bruxelles; two *s*. *Address:* Parkfield, Werneth Hall Road, Oldham, Lancs OL8 1QZ; 3 Lord Court, Clayhall, Ilford, Essex. *Clubs:* City Livery, Carlton.   *[Died 9 April 1974.*

LORING, Sir (John) Nigel, KCVO 1964 (CVO 1953); MRCS, LRCP; Apothecary to the Household of Queen Elizabeth the Queen Mother, 1953, and to the Household of the Duke of Gloucester, 1959-66 (to the Household of King George VI and to that of The Princess Elizabeth and The Duke of Edinburgh, 1949-52; to that of Queen Mary, 1949-53; to HM Household, 1952-64); *b* 31 Aug. 1896; *s* of late Nele Loring, Market Drayton, Salop; *m* 1932, Sylvia (*d* 1978), 2nd *d* of late Col Blakeney-Booth, Billingham Manor, IoW; one *d* (and one *d* decd). *Educ:* RNC Osborne; Tonbridge Sch.; St Thomas's Hospital. Served European War 1914-19, RNR (Dover Patrol); War of 1939-45, Flight Lt 1941, Sqdn Ldr 1942 (despatches). Past Pres. of the Chelsea Clinical Soc.; Freeman, Worshipful Society of Apothecaries, London. *Recreations:* eighteenth century furniture, music. *Address:* The Grange, Goring-on-Thames, Oxon. *T:* Goring-on-Thames 2922.
[Died 22 July 1979.

LOTEN, Harold Ivens, MBE 1950; JP; Member of Council, 1945-76, Chairman of Council and Pro-Chancellor, 1950-71, University of Hull; *b* 28 June 1887; *s* of Arthur Richard and Caroline Loten; *m* 1914, Hilda Mary, *d* of John S. Kemp; two *d* (one *s* killed on active service, RNVR). *Educ:* St Bede's Sch., Hornsea. Served 1st Bn HAC Infantry, 1917-18. Sheriff of City and County of Kingston upon Hull, 1943-44, JP East Riding of Yorks, 1945; Pres. Hull Incorp. Chamber of Commerce and Shipping, 1946 and 1947. Manager, Midland Bank Ltd, Silver Street, Hull, 1937-49. Life Mem. Ct, Univ. of Hull. Fellow, Institute of Bankers; Pres., Rotary Club of Hull, 1943-44. Lay Preacher, 1905-76. Hon. LLD Hull, 1956. *Recreations:* gardening and reading. *Address:* Briar Garth, Atwick Road, Hornsea, North Humberside. *T:* Hornsea 3138.
[Died 17 March 1980.

LOTON, Sir Ernest Thorley, Kt 1965; JP (WA); *b* Perth, Western Australia, 26 Dec. 1895; *s* of E. W. Loton, Perth; *m* 1927, Grace M., *d* of H. Smith; two *s*. *Educ:* Hale Sch., Perth, WA. Mem. Council, Royal Agric. Soc. of W Australia since 1923 (Pres. 1932-33 and 1941-46); Hon. Org. Sec., Aust. Soc. Breeders of British Sheep, 1925-26 (Vice-Chm., 1926-53; Chm., 1953-55; Fed. Pres., 1949-50); Mem. Bd of Govs, Hale Sch., Perth, 1934-57 (Chm., 1947-57); Foundation Mem., Faculty of Agriculture, University of Western Australia, 1936-54; Mem., Commonwealth Banking Corporation, 1960-63. Director: Westralian Farmers Co-operative Ltd, 1936-65 (Chm., 1953-65); CSBP & Farmers Ltd, 1959-65; Australian Mutual Provident Soc., 1942-68; Cuming Smith and Mt Lyell Farmers' Fertilizers Ltd; WA Trustee & Exec. Company, 1952 (Chm. 1960-69); Chairman: Westralian Superphosphate Ltd, 1953-59; Kleenheat Gas Pty Ltd, 1960-65; Mem., Swan Road Board, 1929-61 (Chm., 1931-61); Pres. Swan-Guildford Shire, 1961-62. Pres., Co-op. Fedn of Aust., and Austn Rep. to SE Asia. Hon. Life Member: British Breeds Soc. of Aust., 1961; Austn Corriedale Assoc., 1961; Royal Agric. Soc. of WA, 1970. *Address:* 7 Jutland Parade, Dalkeith, WA 6009, Australia. *Club:* Weld (Perth, Western Australia).   *[Died 30 May 1973.*

LOUDOUN, Donaldson; Metropolitan Magistrate, 1961-76; Barrister-at-law; *b* 30 Jan. 1909; *m* 1st, 1933, Irene Charpentier; one *s* two *d*; 2nd, 1949, Clare Dorothy Bicgie (*d* 1980). Called to the Bar, Gray's Inn, 1934. Served War of 1939-45: BEF, 1939-40; Captain, Intelligence Corps (Parachute Section), 1944; Major, 1945; served in France, 1944; Belgium, 1945. *Recreation:* golf. *Address:* Broomhill, Dorking Road, Great Bookham, Surrey. *T:* Bookham 57469.   *[Died 12 June 1980.*

LOUGHLIN, Dame Anne, DBE 1943 (OBE 1935); General Secretary, Tailors and Garment Workers Trade Union, 1948-53; *b* 28 June 1894; *d* of Thomas Loughlin, Leeds. *Educ:* Leeds. General organiser, 1916-48; General Council, Trades Union Congress, 1929 (Pres. 1943). Retired.   *[Died 15 July 1979.*

LOVE, Enid Rosamond, (Mrs G. C. F. Whitaker), OBE 1973; Educational Consultant to Yorkshire Television Ltd, 1973-74 (Head of Educational Programmes, 1968-73); *b* 15 May 1911; *d* of late Cyril Maurice Love and late Louise Gaston (*née* Harrison), Reading, Berks; *m* 1965, Geoffrey Charles Francis Whitaker. *Educ:* Royal Masonic Sch. for Girls; University of London (Bedford Coll. and Institute of Historical Research). Teaching in various public and grammar schs, 1934-44; Head Mistress, County Grammar Sch. for Girls, Wokingham, Berks, 1944-49. Joined BBC, 1949, as Regional Education Officer for School Broadcasting Council; Asst Head of Sch. Broadcasting (Sound), 1951-56. Asst Head of School Broadcasting (Television), BBC, 1956-59; Head of School Broadcasting, Associated-Rediffusion Ltd, 1959-63; Head Mistress, Sydenham Sch., 1963-68. *Address:* The Corner House, 2 Hawkesdene, Shaftesbury, Dorset SP7 8NT.   *[Died 6 Nov. 1979.*

LOVE, Robert John McNeill, MS, London; FRCS; FACS; FICS; late Demonstrator of Anatomy and Physiology, late Surgical Assistant, London Hospital; Consulting Surgeon: Royal Northern Hospital; Metropolitan Hospital; Mildmay Mission Hospital; West End Hospital for Nervous Diseases; City of London Maternity Hospital; late Chairman, Court of Examiners, Erasmus Wilson Demonstrator, and Hunterian Professor, late member of Council, Royal College of Surgeons; Fellow, Royal Society of Medicine; Fellow, Association of British Surgeons; Member, Barbers' Company; *b* Plymouth, Devon, 2 May 1891; *s* of Alderman Joseph Boyd Love, JP, and Elizabeth Caroline Coleman; *m* 1930, Dorothy Borland (*d* 1961), Plymouth; one *d* (one *s* decd); *m* 1963, Rhoda Evelyn MacKie. *Educ:* Taunton Sch.; London Hospital. Qualified as doctor, 1914; commission in Royal Army Medical Corps, 1915; served at Gallipoli, in India, and Mesopotamia; returned to London Hospital and held resident appointments. *Publications:* Minor Surgery, 3rd edn, 1947; A Short Practice of Surgery (jointly), 16th edn, 1974; Surgery for Nurses (jointly), ninth edition, 1965; The Appendix, 1947; many articles in Medical Press. *Recreations:* phillumery, shooting; Hon. Commissioner Boy Scouts. *Address:* Sewards House, Brickendon, Hertford. *T:* Bayford 271. *Clubs:* East India, Sports and Public Schools; Hertford Constitutional.   *[Died 1 Oct. 1974.*

LOVELL, Reginald, DSc (Manchester); PhD (London); MRCVS; DVSM; Professor of Veterinary Bacteriology, University of London, at Royal Veterinary College, London, NW1, 1953-64; Professor Emeritus, since 1964; *b* 2 Jan. 1897; *s* of late Sidney and Mary Lovell, Wyke Regis; *m* Alice M. Orrell, MB, ChB (*d* 1969), *d* of late W. W. Orrell, OBE, Rochdale; one *s*. *Educ:* Hardye's Sch., Dorchester; Royal Veterinary Coll., Manchester Univ. QO, Dorset Yeomanry, 1914-19; Demonstrator in Bacteriology, University of Manchester, 1925-27; Research Asst and Lecturer in London Sch. of Hygiene and Tropical Medicine, 1927-33. Reader in Bacteriology, 1933, then Deputy Director of the Research Institute in Animal Pathology. President, Comparative Medicine Sect., Royal Society Med., 1949-50; Almroth-Wright Lecturer, 1951; Dalrymple-Champneys Cup and Medal, 1951; Hon. Treasurer Society Gen. Microbiology, 1951-61, President, 1961-63; Distinguished visiting lecturer, Michigan State Univ., USA, 1955; Benjamin Ward Richardson Lecturer, 1956. Ford Foundation Visiting Professor, University of Ibadan, 1964. Member of Council, RCVS, 1953-65. John Henry Steel Mem. Medal, 1965. *Publications:* The Aetiology of Infective Diseases, 1959; lectures, addresses, papers, etc, on Bacteriology, animal and human diseases in J. Path. Bact., J. comp. Path., Lancet and other learned journals. *Recreation:* books. *Address:* 4 Brookside Close, Kilmington, Axminster, Devon. *T:* Axminster 2765.
[Died 10 March 1972.

LOVELY, Percy Thomas; Member of Court of Common Council; Deputy of Tower Ward; Sheriff of the City of London, 1950; *b* 12 Dec. 1894; *s* of late Thomas Lovely; *m* 1919, Ethel Ada Rust (*d* 1970); five *d*. *Educ:* King's Coll., London. Volunteered for RNVR, 1914 (Prisoner of War, 1914-18). Underwriting Member of Lloyd's, 1948-; Director of Messrs. Ellis & Co., 1949-. Vice-Chm., Court of Arbitration, London. Member of the Worshipful Companies of: Bakers (Jun. Warden), Glaziers (Master, 1963), Horners (Master, 1973), Innholders, Painter Stainers and Basketmakers (1925-, Prime Warden, 1950); Past Master, Parish Clerks' Company; Past Master, Guild of the Freemen of the City of London (Master, 1958-). Churchwarden of St Margaret Pattens, London; Life Governor: St Bartholomew's Hospital,

Bridewell Royal Hospital, Queen Elizabeth Training College for the disabled; Hon. Treasurer, British Section: Council of European Municipalities; Council of Commonwealth Municipalities. FRSA. *Recreations:* travel, golf, chess. *Address:* Kings-Leigh, Westmoreland Road, Bromley, Kent. *T:* 01-460 4898. *Clubs:* City Livery (President, 1949-50), United Wards, Guild of Freemen, Entre Nous (Past President).

[Died 22 Jan. 1975.

LOVEMORE, Wing Comdr Robert Baillie, DSO 1919; RAFVR; late 3rd Battalion London Regiment (Royal Fusiliers), RFC and RAF; *e s* of late W. B. Lovemore, JP, of Swaziland; *m* Gwendolen Amy, *o d* of late H. C. Edwards, England; one *s. Educ:* Michaelhouse, Natal. Served European War, 1914-18 (despatches twice, DSO). Served as pilot Air Mail Lines, Union Airways, South African Airways and Wilson Airways (Kenya). Established and commanded E. African flying training scheme, 1939-40; 117 Squadron, Middle East Command, 1940-41; No 7, and subs. No 6, Air Schools in Training Command, Union of South Africa, 1942-46. *Address:* Blythe Glade, PO Emerald Hill, Port Elizabeth, South Africa. *[Died 27 July 1978.*

LOVERIDGE, Arthur John, CMG 1954; OBE 1947; Lecturer on Education in Tropical Areas, London University Institute of Education, 1959-72; *b* 1904; *e s* of late C. W. Loveridge, CB; *m* 1932, Marjorie Gertrude Coleman, Shepperton; one *d. Educ:* Emanuel Sch.; St John's Coll., Cambridge; Middle Temple. In Business, 1926-29; appointed Colonial Administrative Service, 1929. Chief Comr Gold Coast Colony, 1950, Northern Territories, 1953, Ashanti, 1954; retired 1956. Member of Commission of Enquiry into Disturbances in Sierra Leone, 1956, Uganda, 1960. *Publication:* (with L. J. Lewis), The Management of Education, 1965. *Recreations:* golf and dialectics. *Address:* Bird's Elm, Lower Road, Bookham, Surrey. *T:* Bookham 2369. *Club:* Travellers'. *[Died 11 Aug. 1975.*

LOW, David Morrice, FRSL; Writer; *b* 14 Sept. 1890; *o c* of late D. M. Low; *m* 1st, 1915, Heather Belle (*d* 1953), *d* of late Major A. T. Hancocks, DL, JP, Wolverley Court, Worcestershire; 2nd, 1956, Dorothy Margaret, *d* of R. W. Butters, Bury St Edmund's. *Educ:* Westminster Sch. (scholar); Oriel Coll., Oxford (scholar); 1st Class Mods, 1911; 2nd Class Lit. Hum., 1914; BA 1914; MA 1915; Assistant Master, Marlborough Coll., 1914-18; Westminster Sch., 1919-21; Rector of Kelvinside Academy, Glasgow, 1921-29; temp. Junior Asst Air Ministry, 1941-43; temp. Senior Assistant Foreign Office, 1943-45. Classical Lecturer and Sub-Dean Arts Faculty, King's Coll., London, 1945-57. Chairman, English Association, 1959-64. *Publications:* Kelvinside Academy, 1878-1928; Gibbon's Journal, 1929; Edward Gibbon, 1937; London is London, 1949; Norman Douglas, A Selection, 1955; A Century of Writers, 1855-1955, 1955; Essays and Studies Collected for the English Association, 1955; Gibbon's The Decline and Fall, abridged, 1960; Trends in English Pronunciation, 1960; contributor to: Cambridge Biblio. of English Literature; Encyclopædia Britannica; Encyclopædia Amer.; *trans:* N. Ginzburg, Voices in the Evening, 1963; Family Sayings, 1967; E. Patti, Roman Chronicle, 1965; *novels:* Twice Shy, 1933; This Sweet Work, 1935. *Address:* c/o Lloyds Bank Ltd, 15 Cheapside, EC2. *Club:* Garrick. *[Died 24 June 1972.*

LOW, Sir Francis, Kt 1943; *b* 19 Nov. 1893; *s* of late Francis Low, Finzean, Aberdeenshire, and Janet Harper; *m* 1926, Margaret H. Adams; two *s* one *d. Educ:* Robert Gordon's Coll., Aberdeen. Joined Aberdeen Free Press, 1910; commissioned 4th Bn Gordon Highlanders, 1916; served in Mesopotamia with 6th Bn Hampshire Regt, 1917-19; Intelligence Staff I Corps, 1918; Special Service Officer, GHQ Mesopotamian Expeditionary Force, 1919; Chief Reporter, Aberdeen Free Press, 1920; Sub-Editor, Times of India, 1922; Editor, Evening News of India, 1923; News Editor, Times of India, 1925; Assistant Editor, 1926; Editor, 1932-48; London Editorial Representative, 1948-53; Chairman, St Dunstan's War Appeal Cttee, Bombay, 1940-46; President, Bombay YMCA, 1943-48; Vice-President, Bombay Branch Royal Asiatic Society, 1944-48; Chairman, India Section, Empire Press Union, 1946-48; Leader, Indian delegation, Sixth Imperial Press Conference, London, 1946; FJI; President: Commonwealth Correspondents' Assoc., 1951; London Association of British Empire Newspapers Overseas, 1952-53; Hon. Secretary, East India Assoc., 1954-66; Vice-President, Royal Society for India, Pakistan and Ceylon; Chairman Cttee of Management, YMCA Indian Student Hostel, London; Patron, Woking Div. Cons. Assoc., Chm., 1957-60, Pres., 1962-71; Pres., London District, The Boys' Brigade, 1954-67. *Publications:* Struggle for Asia, 1955; articles on visits to the N. Africa, Malaya, and Burma war theatres, 1940-44. *Recreations:* golf and hill climbing. *Address:* High Gardens, 20 Tekels Avenue, Camberley, Surrey. *T:* Camberley 23192. *Clubs:* Athenæum; Royal Bombay Yacht, Willingdon Sports (Bombay). *[Died 18 Sept. 1972.*

LOW, Mabel Bruce, RBA 1919; artist; *d* of late Dr Robert Bruce Low, CB, MD; *m* 1933, Alexander Chisholm. *Educ:* Westminster School of Art; Edinburgh School of Art; Dresden. Colour print purchased by Contemporary Art Society for British Museum, 1939, and by Sunderland Corporation, 1940; Water Colours purchased by Bournemouth Corporation, 1940, 1953, 1961 and 1966. Past President, Southbourne Art Society. Vice-President, Society of Women Artists. *Address:* 14 Burford Court, Manor Road, Bournemouth, Dorset. *T:* Bournemouth 23815. *[Died 3 June 1972.*

LOWE, Sir David, Kt 1962; CBE 1950; DL; Chairman: Elvingston Estates Ltd, since 1962; British Society for the Promotion of Vegetable Research; *b* 12 May 1899; *s* of late Provost David Lowe, Musselburgh; *m* 1932, Katherine Cecile Jane, *d* of late Roderick Ross, CVO, CBE, Edinburgh; three *d. Educ:* Musselburgh Grammar Sch. President, National Farmers' Union of Scotland, 1948-49; President, Edinburgh Chamber of Commerce and Manufactures, 1958-60 and 1962-63; Governor, Edinburgh and East of Scotland College of Agriculture. Chairman: David Lowe & Sons Ltd, 1943-63; Thomson & Mathieson Ltd, 1959-65; Livingston Development Corporation (New Town), 1962-65; Scottish Horticultural Advisory Cttee, 1961-69. Director, National Seed Development Organisation Ltd. Member: Agricultural Research Council, 1954-64 (Dep. Chairman, 1958-64); Agricultural Marketing Development Exec. Cttee, 1962-68; Cinematograph Films Council, 1958-63. Chairman, Scottish Agric. & Horti. Apprenticeship Scheme, 1949-74. Vice-President, Scottish Council Development & Industry, 1963-68. Trustee, Scottish Country Industries Development Trust, 1960-66. VMH 1972. DL East Lothian, 1975. Hon. DSc Edinburgh, 1966. FRSE 1961; FRAgSs, 1970. *Recreation:* plant breeding. *Address:* Elvingston, Gladsmuir, East Lothian. *T:* Longniddry 52128. *Club:* Naval and Military. *[Died 2 Nov. 1980.*

LOWE, Sir (Francis) Gordon, 2nd Bt, *cr* 1918; Director Gordon Lowes Ltd; Lawn Tennis Journalist; *b* Edgbaston, 21 June 1884; *e s* of Rt Hon. Sir Francis William Lowe, 1st Bt, PC, MP; *S* father, 1929; *m* 1926, Honor Dorothy, *d* of late Lieut-Colonel H. S. Woolrych; one *s. Educ:* Charterhouse; Clare Coll., Cambridge. Gained International distinction at Lawn Tennis over a period of 25 years; has won innumerable championships, at home and abroad; was a member of the British team which brought the Davis Cup back from Australia in 1912; represented England against Spain in 1921, against Italy in 1922 and against Poland in 1925; reached semi-final of singles at Wimbledon 1911 and 1923; was in the final of the doubles with the late A. H. Lowe in 1914 and 1921; won covered Court Championship of the World, 1920; joined Indian Army Reserve of Officers in 1916, and went to Mesopotamia, 1917-19 (despatches). *Heir: s* Francis Reginald Gordon Lowe [*b* 8 Feb. 1931; *m* 1st, 1961, Francesca Cornelia Steinkopf (marr. diss., 1970); two *s*; 2nd, 1971, Helen Macaskie, *y d* of late Sandys Macaskie and Mrs R. Beresford-Peirse. *Educ:* Stowe; Clare Coll., Cambridge]. *Address:* 8 Seymour Walk, SW10. *T:* 01-352 6925; (business) Gordon Lowes Ltd, 173-174 Sloane Street, SW1. *T:* 01-235 8484/5/6. *Clubs:* Queen's, All England Lawn Tennis. *[Died 17 May 1972.*

LOWELL, Robert (Traill Spence), Jr, AB; poet and playwright; Professor of Literature, Essex University, 1970-72; *b* Boston, Mass, USA, 1 March 1917; *s* of Robert Traill Spence Lowell and Charlotte (*née* Winslow); *m* 1st, 1940, Jean Stafford (marr. diss. 1948); 2nd, 1949, Elizabeth Hardwick (marr. diss. 1972); one *d*; 3rd, 1972, Lady Caroline Blackwood; one *s. Educ:* Kenyon Coll., Ohio; Harvard Univ. Awarded the American Academy of Arts and Letters Prize and Pulitzer Prize, 1947; Guggenheim Fellowship and Consultant in poetry, Library of Congress, 1947-48; Vis. Fellow, All Souls Coll., Oxford, 1970. Guinness Poetry Award, National Book Award, 1959. Member of American Academy of Arts and Letters. *Publications:* Land of Unlikeness, 1944; Lord Weary's Castle, 1946; The Mills of the Kavanaughs, 1951; Life Studies: New Poems and an Autobiographical Fragment, 1959; Imitations, 1961; For the Union Dead, 1964; Old Glory (play), 1966 (US 1965); Benito Cereno (London 1967); Near the Ocean (poems), 1967; The Voyage (poems), 1968; Prometheus Bound (trans.), 1970; Notebook (poems), 1970; History, 1973; For Lizzie and Harriet, 1973; The Dolphin, 1973; *posthumous publications:* Day by Day (poems), 1978; The Oresteia of Aeschylus (trans.), 1979. *Address:* Castletown House, Celbridge, Co. Kildare. *[Died 12 Sept. 1977.*

LOWENFELD, Margaret Frances Jane, FRCPsych; Consultant Psychiatrist; Director of Training, The Institute of Child Psychology; *b* London, 4 Feb. 1890; *d* of Henry Lowenfeld and Alice E. Evens. *Educ:* Cheltenham Ladies' Coll. Entered London School (Royal Free Hospital) of Medicine for Women,

1912; Intermediate MB, BS, 1914; MRCS, LRCP, 1918; House
Surgeon, South London Women's Hospital, 1918; MO, British
Typhus Unit, Poland, MO to American YMCA working with
Polish Army and POW Dept, and Secretary, European Student
Relief, Warsaw, for students at work in reestablishment of
Universities, 1919-23; Medical Research Scholarship and
Muirhead Scholarship, held 1923-24 at Royal Hospital for Sick
Children, Glasgow, for work on Acute Rheumatism and Social
Conditions; Alfred Langton Research Scholarship; Obstetric
Dept, Royal Free Hospital, 1924-25. Founded Institute of Child
Psychology, 1928, Physician-in-charge, 1937; Consultant
Columbia University. Research in Contemporary Cultures, New
York, 1950. FBPsS; Foundation FRCPsych; FRSM; Member,
International Council of Psychologists. *Publications:* Play in
Childhood, 1935, repr. 1969; The Lowenfeld Mosaic Test, 1954.
Contributions, since 1939, to Journal of Mental Science,
American Journal of Orthopsych., American Journal
Psychotherapy, Proc. RSM, Lancet, etc. *Address:* 92 Harley
Street, W1. *T:* 01-935 3469; Eastwing, Cholesbury, Tring, Herts.
[Died 2 Feb. 1973.

LOWETH, Sidney Harold; retired architect; County Architect
for Kent, 1930-54 (formerly Deputy); *b* London, 10 Oct. 1893; *y*
s of William George Loweth and Helen Page; *m* 1920, Olive
Henrietta Gullett; no *c. Educ:* Parmiter's Foundn Sch.; privately
in London. FRIBA (ARIBA 1914); MIStrE 1920; FRSH 1920;
FRSA 1936 (Council, 1962); FSA 1942; MIRA 1962.
Responsible for design and erection of many County buildings;
also, in private practice, buildings in UK and Africa, banks,
churches, flats, commercial buildings for French and Greek
govts; Memorial to Pioneer Airmen of Gt Britain, Sheppy and
Invicta Memorial, Swanley. Hon. Consultant, MPBW. Mem.,
Franco-British Union of Architects, 1950 (Pres., 1962; Mem. Bd
of Examrs); Hon. Corr. Mem., Inst. des Architectos do Brazil,
1940; Vice-Pres., SE Soc. of Architects, 1946 (Chm. Educn
Cttee, Chm. Tunbridge Wells Chapter); Founder: Maidstone
Arts and Crafts Soc.; Civic Soc.; Bearsted and District Local
History Groups; Founder Mem., County Architects Soc., 1940;
Mem., many cttees of RIBA, SESA, Min. of Works, BSI, City
and Guilds of London. Worshipful Co. of Masons: Mem. Ct of
Assistants, 1946; Renter Warden, 1963; Upper Warden, 1964;
Master, 1965. 5 years on Bearsted Parish Council; 5 years on
Hythe Borough Council. Founder of St Paul's Watch.
Freemason (Provincial Grand Rank), Lodges in Colchester and
Maidstone. OStJ 1964. *Publications:* numerous articles.
Recreation: travelling abroad studying architecture. *Address:* 8
Southdown House, Silverdale Road, Eastbourne, East Sussex. *T:*
Eastbourne 31056. *Clubs:* Reynolds, St John's House; Cinque
Ports (Hythe); Devonshire (Eastbourne). *[Died 1 May 1977.*

LOWMAN, Rev. Canon Edward (Sydney Charles); Canon
Residentiary of Portsmouth Cathedral 1962-69, 1971-74, Hon.
Canon, 1969-71, Canon Emeritus 1974; *b* 20 Feb. 1908; *s* of
William Sydney George Lowman and Margaret Ellen Lowman
(née Ford); *m* 1947, Betty Margaret (née Jolly); one *d. Educ:*
Ashford Grammar Sch., Kent; King's Coll., London; Bishops'
Coll., Cheshunt. Royal Air Force, 1924-28. Deacon, 1938;
Priest, 1939; Curate of Heckmondwike, Yorks, 1938-41; Curate
of Bray, Berks, 1941-45; Vicar of Bray, Berks, 1945-57;
Cathedral Chaplain, Portsmouth, 1958-62. FRSA 1972.
Address: Semaphore House, Battery Row, Portsmouth. *T:*
Portsmouth 20470. *Club:* Royal Naval and Royal Albert Yacht
(Portsmouth). *[Died 4 Nov. 1974.*

LOWNDES, Alan; artist (painter); *b* 23 Feb. 1921; *s* of Samuel
and Jenny Lowndes; *m* 1959, Valerie (née Holmes); one *s* two *d.
Educ:* Christ Church C of E Sch., Stockport. Left school at 14;
apprenticed to a house decorator. Served War of 1939-45: joined
Cheshire Regt TA as Private, 1st Sept. 1939 (Africa Star, 8th
Army Clasp, etc); demobilised (still a Private) at end of War
after serving in the Desert and Italy. Attended life drawing and
painting evening classes at Stockport Coll.; worked as a textile
designer; painted in spare time; finally gave up job to paint full
time, 1949; lived in Cornwall up to 1970. First exhibited at
Crane Kalman Gallery, Manchester, 1950. *Exhibitions:*
England, America, Germany, Belgium, Italy; regular exhibitions
at Crane Kalman Gall., London. Paintings in the following
collections (amongst others): Arts Council; Nuffield
Foundation; Walker Art Gall., Liverpool; City Art Gall.,
Manchester; Coventry Art Gall.; Plymouth Art Gall.; Balliol
Coll. *Recreations:* observing the public in public places and
public houses. *Address:* 13 St George's Close, Upper Cam,
Dursley, Glos. *T:* Dursley 2014. *Club:* Chelsea Arts.
[Died 22 Sept. 1978.

LOWNDES, Brigadier Montacute W. W. S.; *see* Selby-Lowndes.

LOWRY, Laurence Stephen, RA 1962 (ARA 1955); RBA 1934;
Hon. MA (Manchester); Hon. LLD (Manchester) 1961;
Member National Society; Member London Group; *b*
Manchester, 1 Nov. 1887; *o s* of late R. S. M. Lowry and
Elizabeth Hobson, Manchester. Exhibited, Paris Salon
d'Automme and many places abroad; One Man Shows: Lefevre
Gallery, 1939, 1943, 1945, 1948, 1951, 1953, 1956, 1958, 1963,
1964, 1971; Sheffield Art Gallery, 1962; Retrospective
Exhibition, Tate Gallery, 1966; Stone Gallery, Newcastle, 1967;
Official purchases: Tate Gallery; Royal Scottish Academy;
Contemporary Art Society; Glasgow, Liverpool, Birmingham,
Manchester, Stoke, Aberdeen, Salford, Leeds, Leicester,
Nottingham, Southampton; Ministry of Information; Ministry
of Works; British Council; Arts Council; Royal Academy
(Chantrey Bequest). BBC Television Film, 1957. *Address:* The
Elms, Stalybridge Road, Mottram in Longdendale, Cheshire.
[Died 23 Feb. 1976.

LOWRY-CORRY, Lt-Col Sir Henry (Charles), Kt 1954; MC
1916; DL 1946; Vice Lieutenant in the County of Suffolk, 1957-
64; Chairman West Suffolk County Council, 1950-57; *b* 20 Feb.
1887; *er s* of Colonel the Hon. H. W. Lowry-Corry,
Edwardstone, Suffolk; *heir pres.* to 8th Earl of Belmore; *m* 1920,
Betty, *d* of Colonel D. J. Proby, Elton Hall, Peterborough; two *s*
two *d. Educ:* Eton; RMA, Woolwich. Served in RHA and RFA,
1906-35; served European War, 1914-18; retired as Major;
served War of 1939-45, in TA, as Lieut-Colonel, Middle East.
Chairman: Suffolk T & AFA, 1947-53; West Suffolk CC, 1950-
57. *Address:* Edwardstone Hall, Boxford, Suffolk. *T:* Boxford
233. *[Died 23 Dec. 1973.*

LOWSON, Sir Denys (Colquhoun Flowerdew), 1st Bt, *cr* 1951;
MA (Oxon); FCIS; *b* 22 Jan. 1906; *o s* of late J. G. Flowerdew
Lowson, JP, PhD, Balthayock, Perthshire, and Adelaide, *d* of
Col Courtenay Scott; *m* 1936, Patricia, OStJ, *yr d* of 1st Baron
Strathcarron, PC, KC, LLD; one *s* two *d. Educ:* Winchester;
Christ Church, Oxford (Hons in History and Law). Called to
Bar, Inner Temple, 1930; Member Royal Company of Archers
(Queen's Body Guard for Scotland), 1948; Sheriff of City of
London, 1939; Member for Coleman Street, Court of Common
Council, 1940; Alderman City of London, Vintry Ward, 1942-
68; transferred to the Ward of Bridge Without on becoming
Senior Alderman of the City of London (1968-73); one of HM
Lieutenants for City of London, 1942; Lord Mayor of London,
1950-51 (Festival of Britain year). A Church Commissioner for
England, 1948-62; Life Governor and Almoner of St
Bartholomew's Hospital and Chairman, Finance Cttee,
Governor of Bridewell and Bethlem Hospitals, and of the Royal
Hospitals, Vice-President, St Mary's Hospital, Paddington to
1948 and reappointed to Board of St Bartholomew's Hospital
under National Health Act, 1948-67; Hon. Treasurer, Princess
Louise Kensington Hospital for Children, 1938-48, and Vice-
President, League of Mercy to 1948; Master of Worshipful
Company of Glaziers, 1947-48, of Worshipful Company of
Loriners, 1950, of Gold and Silver Wyre Drawers, 1951; Hon.
Member Court of Assistants, Haberdashers Company, 1951;
Prime Warden, Shipwrights Company, 1955-56; Past Grand
Warden, United Grand Lodge of England; Vice-President St
John Ambulance Bde (Prince of Wales No 1 District), and Dep.
Commissioner, No 1 District, 1944-66; Member Exec. Council,
Lord Mayor's National Flood and Tempest Distress Fund, 1953;
Original Member, Victoria (Australia) Promotion Cttee, 1956;
Chairman: Commonwealth Producers' Organisation, 1957;
British section, Council of European Municipalities, 1965, Jt
Pres., 1971; Governor, The Honourable The Irish Society, 1958-
61; President, British Philatelic Assoc., Ltd, 1958-61; Life
Fellow, Royal Philatelic Soc., 1943-; Vice-President, Royal
Over-Seas League, 1959; President, Chartered Institute of
Secretaries, 1962-63. Hon. Colonel 290 Regt, City of London
RA, 1950; a member of London County Council for cities of
London and Westminster, 1949-52; a life Governor of University
College, Dundee, and of Royal Shakespeare Theatre; High
Steward of Stratford-upon-Avon, 1952; Hon. Freeman, Cities of
London (Ontario), Nanaimo (Vancouver Is.), Granby (Quebec),
Halifax (Nova Scotia), and Lewes (Sussex). Gold Medal, Order
of the Dogwood, BC, 1971. KJStJ; Order of Mercy; Grand
Officer Order of Orange Nassau (Netherlands); Kt Commander
Royal Order of the Dannebrog (Denmark); Kt Commander,
with Star, Royal Order of St Olaf (Norway); Kt Commander of
the Lion of Finland. *Recreations:* shooting, shot for Oxford
against Cambridge (Chancellor's Plate), Harvard and Yale;
travelling and philately. *Heir:* *s* Ian Patrick Lowson, OStJ, *b* 4
Sept. 1944. *Address:* 56 Gresham Street, EC2. *T:* 01-606 7131.
Clubs: Bath, Bucks, Caledonian, MCC; St James's (Montreal).
[Died 10 Sept. 1975.

LOWTHER, Col John George, CBE 1953; DSO 1919; MC; TD;
DL; JP Northants; *b* 1885; 2nd *s* of late G. W. Lowther of

Swillington House, Leeds, and *b* of late Lieut-Colonel Sir C. B. Lowther, 4th Bt, CB, DSO; *m* 1911, Hon. Lilah White (*d* 1976), *er d* of 3rd Baron Annaly; one *s* one *d* (and one *s* decd). *Educ:* Winchester. 2nd Lieut, Yorkshire Hussars, 1904; joined 11th Hussars, 1905; retired as Captain, 1919; served with Northamptonshire Yeomanry in European War (DSO, MC, despatches twice); Major in Northamptonshire Yeomanry, 1919; Major Commanding NY Armoured Car Coy, 1921; Col, 1928; Commanded 4th Bn Northamptonshire Regt, 1924-28, 1939-40; Infantry D. and M. School, 1940-41; Hon. Colonel 1st Northants Yeomanry, 1931-50; Sector Comdr, Home Guard, 1942-50; Joint Master of Pytchley Hounds, 1923-40 and 1949-60; County Councillor (Northants), 1939-49; County Alderman, 1949-70. Chairman, Little Bowden Justices (Petty Sessional Court), 1942-59. *Recreation:* hunting. *Address:* 2 Wesley Street, W1. *T:* 01-935 0741; Guilsborough Court, Northampton. *T:* Guilsborough 208. *Club:* Buck's.   *[Died 19 March 1977.*

LOYD, Gen. Sir (Henry) Charles, GCVO 1965 (KCVO 1947); KCB 1943 (CB 1941); DSO 1918; MC; DL; Colonel of Coldstream Guards, 1945-66; *b* 1891; *s* of late Edward Henry Loyd; *m* 1922, Lady Moyra Brodrick, *y d* of 1st Earl of Midleton, KP, PC; one *s* one *d*. Served European War, 1914-18 (despatches, MC, DSO); commanded 3rd Batt. Coldstream Guards, 1929-32; Officer Commanding Coldstream Guards Regt and Regimental District, 1932-34; General Staff Officer, 1st Grade, War Office, 1934-36; Brigadier, General Staff, British Troops in Egypt, 1936-38; Commander 1st Infantry Brigade (Guards), 1938-39; Commander 2nd Division, 1939-40; Chief of General Staff, Home Forces, 1941-42; GOC-in-C Southern Command, 1942-43; General 1946; GOC London District, 1944-47; retired pay, 1947. DL 1954, JP 1950, Norfolk. *Address:* Mettingham Pines, Bungay, Suffolk. *T:* Bungay 2516. *Club:* Guards.   *[Died 11 Nov. 1973.*

LUARD, Commander William Blaine, OBE 1945; FRIN; RN (retired); Naval Officer, Author and Inventor; *b* 2 Jan. 1897; *e s* of late Major William Du Cane Luard, RE, and late Maud, *d* of Sir Robert Blaine; *m* 1929, May Gladys Hayes. *Educ:* Mowden Sch., Brighton; RN Colleges, Osborne and Dartmouth. Invalided, 1917, as a Sub-Lieut. Contributor to numerous publications. Co-inventor, Addison-Luard Course and Distance Calculator; Sestral-Luard Navigator, and other navigational devices. Rejoined 1940; special duties (OBE, Croix de Guerre and palm). Co-inventor four devices in production during war. President Little Ship Club, 1944-54; Chairman, Cornwall Sea Fisheries Cttee, 1947-67. Special Study of French and English Fisheries. *Publications:* A Celtic Hurly-Burly, 1931; All Hands, 1933; Yachtsman's Modern Navigation and Practical Pilotage, 1933; Conquering Seas, 1935; Wild Goose Chase, 1936; ABC of Blue Water Navigation, 1936; Northern Deeps, 1937; Changing Horizons, 1946; Where the Tides Meet, 1948; The Little Ship Navigator, 1950; contrib. to numerous anthologies on the sea, inc. Secret Navies, 1978. *Recreations:* yachting, cruising. *Address:* Trelour, Mawnan Smith, near Falmouth, Cornwall TR11 5LE. *T:* Mawnan Smith 250328. *Clubs:* Little Ship (Hon. Life Mem.); Ocean Cruising (Hon. Mem.).
            [Died 29 June 1979.

LUCAS, Claude Arthur, TD 1950; Chairman Board of Governors, Hospital for Sick Children, Great Ormond Street, WC, 1953-67; *b* 5 Feb. 1894; *s* of late Sir Arthur Lucas; *m* 1928, Dorothy Hope, OBE 1950, *y d* of late Maj.-Gen. Sir John Hanbury-Williams, GCVO, KCB, CMG; no *c*. *Educ:* Wellington Coll.; University Coll., Oxford (MA). Served European War, 1914-18, 1/5 Hampshire Regt, NW Frontier, India, 1919; War of 1939-45, Middlesex Regt, Capt., seconded to Provost. Chartered Accountant; ACA 1925, FCA 1959; Mem. of Board, Hospital for Sick Children, 1921 (Vice-Chm., 1948); Member: House Cttee, Westminster Hosp. (Parkwood), Auxiliary Hosp. and Convalescent Home, 1921-63; Asthma Research Council, 1950- (Hon. Treas., 1950-60); Teaching Hosps Assoc., 1953-57 (a Dep. Chm.); Inst. of Child Health, 1955-67; Chm., London Postgraduate Hospitals Cttee, 1960-61 (Dep.-Chm., 1959-60). *Address:* 67 Melton Court, SW7. *T:* 01-589 8683. *Club:* United Oxford & Cambridge University.
            [Died 3 June 1974.

LUCAS, Major Sir Jocelyn (Morton), 4th Bt *cr* 1887; KBE 1959; MC; late 4th Battalion Royal Warwickshire Regt; *b* 27 Aug. 1889; 2nd *s* of Sir Edward Lingard Lucas, 3rd Bt and Mary Helen (*d* 1915), *d* of Henry Chance, Sherborne, Warwick; *S* father, 1936; *m* 1st, 1933, Edith (*d* 1956), *d* of late Very Rev. David Barry Cameron, DD, JP, Dundee, and *widow* of Sir Trehawke Herbert Kekewich, Bt, Peamore, Devon; 2nd, 1960, Mrs Thelma Grace de Chair (*d* 1974), *d* of Harold Dennison Arbuthnot, Field Place, Compton, Surrey. *Educ:* Eton; Royal Military Coll., Sandhurst. Joined 4th (Special Reserve Bn)

Royal Warwicks Regt, 1909; served European War, 1914-19 (wounded, prisoner, MC) Oct. 1914, subseq. ADC to Gen. Sir Sydney Lawford, Army of Occupation, Cologne; Vice-Pres., Royal Over-Seas League and Chm. of the Hospitality Cttee, 1938-; welfare liaison officer for Dominion troops, London District, 1940-48; founder and Chm. Allies Welcome Cttee, 1940-50; also of Returned Prisoners of War Advice Cttee, 1944-48. MP (C) Portsmouth, South, 1939-66; Member: Parly delegn to France, 1946 and 1957; Commonwealth Conf., Ottawa, 1952; led delegn to Denmark, 1955, to Sweden, 1962, and to France for 50th Anniversary of Anglo-French Condominion of the New Hebrides. Has hunted several packs of hounds; served as part-time auxiliary fireman, 1938-42 (Section Leader); broken back and other injuries while fire fighting; Chm. Empire War Memorial Fund (St Paul's); a Governor and Mem. Council of Royal Veterinary Coll.; a Vice-Pres., Kennel Club; Pres. Pitt Street Settlement; Chm. British Sportsman's Club, 1957-68; was responsible for legalisation of fishing on Serpentine, 1942 and holds Fishing Licence No. 1 for the Royal Parks; holds RAC Pilot's Certificate 893. Comdr, Order of Orange-Nassau. Czechoslovak Military Medal of Merit, 1st Class. *Publications:* Hunt and Working Terriers; Pedigree Dog Breeding; The Sealyham Terrier; the New Book of the Sealyham; Simple Doggie Remedies, etc. *Recreations:* travel, all equestrian and field sports, breeding pedigree dogs. *Heir:* cousin Thomas Edward Lucas [*b* 16 Sept. 1930; *m* 1958, Charmian (*d* 1970), *d* of Col J. S. Powell; one *s*]. *Address:* Michelmersh Court, Romsey, Hants SO5 0NS. *T:* Braishfield 68270. *Clubs:* Carlton, Kennel.
            [Died 2 May 1980.

LUCAS, Prof. Wilfrid Irvine, MA (Bristol), Drphil (Heidelberg); Professor of German, University of Southampton, 1954-71, now Emeritus; *b* 12 Dec. 1905; *m* 1930, Emmeli, *d* of Prof. Ludolph Brauer, Univ. of Hamburg; two *s* two *d*. *Educ:* Bristol Gram. Sch.; University of Bristol. Lecturer in English, University of Heidelberg, 1927-31; Lecturer in German, University of Southampton, 1931; Dean, Faculty of Arts, 1952-56; Public Orator, 1953, 1955; Dep. Vice-Chancellor, 1957-59. Mem., University Grants Cttee, 1964-69. *Publications:* (ed) Bergengruen's Das Hornunger Heimweh and other stories, 1957; revised and enlarged Twentieth Century of Robertson's History of German Literature, 1959; various articles and reviews. *Recreation:* photography. *Address:* 6 Highfield Close, Southampton SO2 1QZ. *T:* Southampton 54204. *Club:* Royal Commonwealth Society.   *[Died 7 May 1973.*

LUCE, Rev. Arthur Aston, MC; DD; LittD; Chancellor, St Patrick's Cathedral, Dublin, since 1936; Precentor, 1952-73; Captain late 12th Royal Irish Rifles; Senior Fellow, Trinity College Dublin; Professor of Moral Philosophy, 1934-49; retired 1949; Berkeley Professor of Metaphysics, 1953; Member, Royal Irish Academy; *b* 21 Aug. 1882; *s* of Rev. J. J. Luce, Vicar, St Nicholas, Gloucester; *m* 1918, Lilian Mary Thompson (*d* 1940); two *s*. *Educ:* Eastbourne Coll.; Trinity Coll., Dublin. Fellow, Trinity Coll., Dublin, 1912; served with 12th Royal Irish Rifles, 1915-18 (MC 1917). LittD (*hc*) Queen's Univ., Belfast, 1953. *Publications:* Monophysitism Past and Present, 1920; Bergson's Doctrine of Intuition, 1922; Berkeley and Malebranche, 1934; Berkeley's Philosophical Commentaries (Commonplace Book), 1944; Berkeley's Immaterialism, 1945; The Works of George Berkeley, Vol. I, 1948, Vol. IV, 1950, Vol. VII, 1955, Vol. VIII, 1956, Vol. IX, 1957; The Life of George Berkeley, 1948; Sense without Matter, 1954; Teach yourself Logic, 1958; Fishing and Thinking, 1959; (ed) The Book of Durrow, 1961; The Dialectic of Immaterialism, 1963; several articles on Berkeley. *Recreations:* salmon and trout angling. *Address:* Ryslaw, Bushy Park Road, Dublin. *T:* 970373. *Club:* Kildare Street and University (Dublin).   *[Died 27 June 1977.*

LUCE, Adm. Sir David; see Luce, Adm. Sir J. D.

LUCE, Rev. Canon Harry Kenneth; Headmaster, Durham School, 1932-58, retired; Examining Chaplain to Bishop of Birmingham since 1924; Hon. Canon of Durham since 1942; Canon Emeritus, since 1965; *b* 20 July 1897; *s* of Edmund and Margaret Eleanor Luce, Brighton; *m* 1925, Norah, *o d* of late Sir Sydney Chapman, KCB, CBE; three *d*. *Educ:* Eton (Scholar); King's Coll., Cambridge (Scholar); Westcott House, Cambridge. Bell Univ. Scholar, 1st class Classical Tripos Pt I, 1920; 2nd class Theological Tripos Pt II, 1921; BD Cambridge, 1933. Deacon, 1921; Priest, 1922; Curate of Holy Trinity, Cambridge, 1921; Master of King's Scholars in Westminster Sch., 1922-29; Headmaster, King Edward VI Sch., Southampton, 1929-32. *Publications:* S Matthew's Gospel in English for Schools; S Mark's Gospel in English for Schools; A Modern Confirmation Manual; The Creed of a Schoolboy; St Luke's Gospel, in Cambridge Greek Testament; Lift up your Hearts; St Luke's Gospel in English for Schools; St Luke's Gospel, in Cambridge

Bible; The Courage of God; The Acts of the Apostles, in English for Schools; To the School at War, 1944; The Life of Christ in the Four Gospels, 1953; St Paul, 1957; To Believe and to Do, 1959; Jesus of Nazareth, 1961; The Religions of Mankind, 1961. *Recreations:* gardening, music. *Address:* 44 Willow Road, Charlton Kings, Cheltenham, Glos. *T:* Cheltenham 21048.
[*Died 26 Nov.* 1972.

LUCE, Admiral Sir (John) David, GCB 1963 (KCB 1960; CB 1957); DSO 1940, and Bar, 1944; OBE 1942; Chief of Naval Staff and First Sea Lord, 1963-66; *b* 23 Jan. 1906; *s* of late Adm. John Luce, CB; *m* 1935, Mary Adelaide Norah Whitham; two *s.* *Educ:* RNC Dartmouth. Joined Submarines, 1927; Commanded HM Submarine H 44, 1936; Rainbow, 1939-40; Cachalot, 1940-41; Capt., 1945; RN Air Station, Ford, 1946-48; Dep. Dir, Plans Div., Admiralty, 1948-51; in comd of HMS Liverpool, 1951-52; HMS Birmingham, 1952-53; Dir of Royal Naval Staff Coll., 1953-54; Rear-Adm., 1955; Naval Sec. to the First Lord of the Admiralty, 1954-56; Flag Officer (Flotillas), Home Fleet, 1956-58; Vice-Adm. 1958; Flag Officer, Scotland, 1958-59; Adm., 1960; C-in-C, Far East Station, 1960-62; First C-in-C of British Forces in the Far East, 1962-63, and UK Military Adviser to SEATO. Pres. Royal Naval Assoc. *Recreations:* tennis, golf. *Address:* c/o Lloyds Bank Ltd, Devizes, Wilts; Monastery Garden, Edington, Westbury, Wilts. *Clubs:* Army and Navy, Royal Over-Seas League (Chm. Central Council).
[*Died 6 Jan.* 1971.

LUCE, Reginald William, CB 1947; MBE 1937; MSM; *b* 1893; *s* of P. J. Luce, Jersey, CI. *Educ:* Modern Sch., Jersey; Paris; King's Coll., London. Entered Civil Service by open competition, 1912, and appointed to Board of Trade. Served throughout European War, 1914-18, in Middx Yeomanry and RHA (MSM 1916). Sec. to BoT Cttee on Patent Law, 1929-31; to Bot Cttee on Trade Mark Law, 1932-33; Sec. to London Conf. of Industrial Property Union, 1934; to BoT Cttee on International Copyright, 1936; transferred to Min. of Labour and National Service, 1939; Asst Sec., Min. of Labour and National Service, 1942-45; seconded to Foreign Office as Chief, Manpower Div. Control Commn for Germany, 1945-48; Manpower Adviser to UK High Comr for Germany, 1949; Comr for Schleswig-Holstein, 1950-52; Counsellor (Labour), British Embassy, Paris, 1953-56; Adviser to Govt of Mauritius on Employment situation and wages of sugar plantation workers, 1957-58; to Govts of Windward Islands, on establishment of Employment Services, 1963 and 1965. *Address:* 266 Cooden Drive, Bexhill-on-Sea, Sussex. *T:* Cooden 3391.
[*Died 4 July* 1971.

LUCE, Sir William (Henry Tucker), GBE 1961 (KBE 1956; OBE 1947); KCMG 1957 (CMG 1954); DL; Personal Representative of the Foreign and Commonwealth Secretary for Persian Gulf Affairs, 1970-72; Political Resident in the Persian Gulf, 1961-66; *b* 25 Aug. 1907; *s* of late Adm. John Luce, CB; *m* 1934, Margaret, *d* of late Adm. Sir Trevylyan Napier, KCB; one *s* one *d. Educ:* Clifton Coll.; Christ's Coll., Cambridge. Sudan Political Service, 1930; Private Sec. to Governor-Gen., 1941-47; Dep. Governor, Equatoria Province, 1950; Governor, Blue Nile Province, and Dir of Sudan Gezira Board, 1951; Adviser to the Gov.-Gen. of the Sudan on Constitutional and External Affairs, 1953-56; Governor and C-in-C, Aden, 1956-60. Chm., Oryx Investments, 1974-77; Director: Eastern Bank, 1966-70, 1972-; Tilbury Overseas Contractors, 1967-70; Gray Mackenzie, 1967-70, 1972-; Chartered Bank, 1972-; Inchcape, 1973-77; Standard Chartered Bank, 1973-. Chm., Anglo-Arab Assoc., 1968-70. DL Wilts, 1972. *Address:* Brook House, Fovant, near Salisbury, Wilts. *T:* Fovant 254. *Club:* Bath.   [*Died 7 July* 1977.

LUCKER, Sydney Charles; *b* 5 Jan. 1897; *m* 1920, Florence Hardy (*d* 1966); one *d.* Editorial Advisor, National Sunday School Union's Business Dept, 1959-61 (Gen. Manager and Editor, 1939-59); Editor, Sunday School Chronicle, 1930-59; Editor, Graded Teacher Series of Lesson Helps (Quarterlies and Annuals), 1940-59; Chief London Correspondent, Religious News Service (USA), 1938-65; Chm., Religious Weekly Press Group, 1953-54; previous journalistic appointments at Bournemouth, Torquay and London. *Publication:* Answers to Life's Questions, 1939. *Recreation:* photography. *Address:* 55 Aynhoe Road, W14. *T:* 01-602 0971.   [*Died 27 Aug.* 1977.

LUCY, Major Sir Brian Fulke Cameron-Ramsay-F.; *see* Fairfax-Lucy.

LUDBROOK, Dr Samuel Lawrence, CMG 1970; FRCP; FRACP; retired; Medical Adviser to Auckland Branch of the New Zealand Crippled Children Society, 1952-70; *b* 20 Aug. 1895; *e s* of H. S. Ludbrook, Ohaewai, Bay of Islands, NZ; *m* 1927, Ailsa Hannah Burns; three *s. Educ:* Wanganui Collegiate

Sch.; Otago Univ. Medical Sch. MB, ChB, 1919; MRCP 1924. Major, NZ Medical Corps, 1945. Auckland Hosp., 1920; Royal Northern Hosp., London, 1922; St George's Hosp., London, 1923; SMO, Shadwell Children's Hosp., 1924-25; Hon. Physician, Auckland Hosp., NZ, 1926, Senior Paediatrician, 1930, Hon. Cons. Paediatrician, 1952. Foundation Fellow, Royal Australasian Coll. of Physicians, 1939; FRCP 1950. *Publications:* sundry articles in medical jls. *Recreation:* horticulture. *Address:* 165 Mellons Bay Road, Howick, New Zealand. *Clubs:* Northern, Auckland University (Auckland).
[*Died Aug.* 1976.

LUDLOW-HEWITT, Air Chief Marshal Sir Edgar Rainey, GCB 1946 (KCB 1933; CB 1928); GBE 1943; CMG 1919; DSO 1918; MC; DL; *b* 1886; *s* of Rev. Thomas Arthur Ludlow-Hewitt of Clancoole, Bandon, Co. Cork, and Minety, Wilts; *m* 1923, Albinia Mary (*d* 1972), *d* of Major Edward Henry Evans-Lombe of Marlingford Hall, Norwich, and *widow* of Capt. Francis Clerke, Coldstream Guards. *Educ:* Radley; Sandhurst. 1st Bn Royal Irish Rifles, 1905-14; Royal Flying Corps, 1914; served European War, 1914-19 (CMG, DSO, MC, despatches six times, Legion of Honour), Bt Major, Royal Irish Rifles, 1915; Comd 10th Bde RAF, 1918; Chief Staff Officer, Headquarters RAF in France, 1918-19; Commandant Royal Air Force Staff Coll., 1926-30; Air Officer Commanding Iraq Command, 1930-32; Dir of Operations and Intelligence, Air Ministry, 1933-35; Air Officer Commanding RAF, India, 1935-37; AOC-in-C, Bomber Comd, 1937-40; Inspector-Gen. of the RAF, 1940-45; retd 1945. Air ADC to the King, 1921-23; Principal Air ADC to the King, 1943-45. Chm. Board of Governors, College of Aeronautics, 1945-53; Pres., Southern Area British Legion, 1946-51. DL Wilts 1953. *Address:* Westbrook House, Bromham, Chippenham, Wilts. *T:* Bromham 345.
[*Died 15 Aug.* 1973.

LUDOVICI, Capt. Anthony M., late RFA; author; *b* 1882; *s* of late Albert and Marie Ludovici, London; *m* 1920, Elsie F. Buckley (*d* 1959). *Educ:* privately and abroad, but chiefly by his mother. Started life as an artist; illustrated various books; was for some time private sec. to late Auguste Rodin; ultimately left art for literature; lectured in London and elsewhere on Friedrich Nietzsche's philosophy, art, politics, etc; translated various foreign works, including six vols of Nietzsche's philosophy; served European War, 1914-19; fought at Armentières and the Somme; attached Intelligence Staff, War Office, April 1917; GSO3, March 1919; demobilised, Oct. 1919. Mem., Soc. of Authors. *Publications:* Who is to be Master of the World?, 1909; Nietzsche: His Life and Works, 1910; Nietzsche and Art, 1911; A Defence of Aristocracy, 1915; Man's Descent from the Gods, 1921; The False Assumption of Democracy, 1921; Woman: a Vindication, 1923; Lysistrata, 1924; Reminiscences of Rodin, 1926; Man, an Indictment, 1927; A Defence of Conservatism, 1927; The Night-Hoers, 1928; The Sanctity of Private Property, 1932; The Secret of Laughter, 1932; Health and Education through Self-Mastery, 1933; Violence, Sacrifice and War, 1933; Creation or Recreation, 1934; The Choice of a Mate, 1935; The Future of Woman, 1936; The Truth about Childbirth, 1937; English Liberalism, 1939; The Four Pillars of Health, 1945; Enemies of Women, 1947; The Child: An Adult's Problem, 1948; The Quest of Human Quality, 1952; Religion for Infidels, 1960; The Specious Origins of Liberalism, 1967; *novels:* Mansel Fellowes, 1918; Catherine Doyle, 1919; Too Old for Dolls, 1920; What Woman Wishes, 1921; The Goddess that Grew Up, 1922; French Beans, 1923; The Taming of Don Juan, 1924. *Recreations:* painting, conversation. *Address:* 197 Henley Road, Ipswich, Suffolk. *Club:* Naval and Military.
[*Died 3 April* 1971.

LUGG, Group Captain Sidney, CBE 1944; CEng; FIEE, FInstD, FIERE; Director of Vacuum Reflex Ltd, since 1956; RAF 1922-52, retired; *b* 20 May 1906. *Educ:* Bournemouth Secondary Sch. Officer, Legion of Merit (US), 1944. *Recreation:* cricket. *Address:* 36 Lenham Avenue, Rottingdean, near Brighton, Sussex.   [*Died 5 Oct.* 1972.

LUKE, Sir Kenneth George, Kt 1962; CMG 1954; JP 1945; Chairman and Managing Director: K. G. Luke Group Industries Ltd; Concentric Engineering Pty Ltd; Luke and Singer Pty Ltd; Chairman: F. L. Hudson & Co.; Terry Engineering; Director, Mercantile Mutual Insurance Co. Ltd; *b* 11 Nov. 1898; *s* of George Edwin Luke, Somerset, England; *m* 1939, Valda Letitia, *d* of Louis John A. Richardson, Melbourne, Vic.; one *d. Educ:* Melbourne and Ballarat, Vic. Hon. Consultant Dept of Supply, Australia. Public service includes holding of various offices in naval and civil clubs and assocs; Life Governor many hosps of all denominations; holds several records and championships in breeding Poll Hereford cattle and Dorset Horn sheep; Life Member, Councillor and Mem. Cttees,

Royal Agricultural Society. *Recreations:* interested in football, cricket, motor cycling, yachting, lawn tennis, golf, bowls, racing (breeder of bloodstock). *Address:* K. G. Luke Group Industries Ltd, 505 St Kilda Road, Melbourne, Victoria 3004, Australia. *T:* (business) 26.3654; (private) 81.3662. *Clubs:* Savage, Green Room (Melbourne). *[Died 13 June 1971.*

LUMLEY, Air Cdre Eric Alfred, CBE 1948; MC 1918; MD, BCh, DPH, DTM&H; RAF retired; lately Medical Officer to RAF Recruiting Centre, Birmingham; *b* 7 Dec. 1891; *s* of Joseph Alfred Lumley and Henrietta Lumley (*née* Barnes), Tullamore, King's County, Ireland; *m* 1920, Elsie Clift (*d* 1969), Redcar, Yorks; one *s* two *d. Educ:* Wesley Coll., Dublin; Dublin Univ. MB, BCh, BAO (Univ. of Dublin), 1914; LM Rotunda, 1914; DPH (London), 1930; DTM&H (London), 1946; MD (Dublin), 1948; Capt. RAMC, 1914-18 (MC); service with 8/10 Gordon Highlanders, No 138 Field Amb., 36th (Ulster) Divisonal Artillery, etc. Joined RAF, 1919; Group Capt. 1928; Air Cdre 1946; served in Egypt, Iraq (2 tours), Aden (2 tours), as well as home appts, 1919-38; War of 1939-45; PMO British Forces in Aden, 1938-40; OC, RAF Hosp., Ely, 1940-42; SMO Nos 27 & 28 Groups RAF, 1942-44; PMO Fighter Comd, 1944-46; PMO, RAF in India and Royal Indian Air Force, 1946-47; RAF Rep. on Govt of India Cttee (Roy. Cttee) on Integration of Medical Services of Indian Armed Forces, 1947; retd from RAF, 1950. Public Health Service MO, 1950-52; Civilian MO employed by Air Ministry, 1952-65. *Publications:* Army and Air Force Doctor, 1971; various, in BMJ, Jl Indian Med. Assoc. and Sports India. *Recreations:* cricket, golf, billiards, trout and salmon fishing. *Address:* Gindle's Cottage, Walmersley, Bury, Lancs. *T:* 061-764 2529. *[Died 6 Aug. 1979.*

LUNN, Sir Arnold, Kt 1952; Hon. DPhil (Zürich), 1954; Citoyen d'honneur of Chamonix, France, 1952; Grand Cross of Isabel la Catolica, Spain, 1959; *b* Madras, 18 April 1888; *e s* of late Sir Henry Lunn; *m* Lady Mabel (*d* 1959), *d* of late Rev. Hon. John Stafford Northcote, Chaplain to HM, and *sister* of 3rd Earl of Iddesleigh; two *s* one *d*; *m* 1961, Phyllis, *d* of late O. N. Holt-Needham. *Educ:* Harrow; Balliol Coll., Oxford. Sec., Oxford Union Soc.; Edited the Isis. Ex-President Ski Club of Great Britain, Founder and Ex-President of Alpine Ski, Kandahar Ski and Oxford Univ. Mountaineering Clubs; Mem. Cttee, Internat. Ski Federation, 1943-49; Chm., International Downhill Ski-racing Cttee, 1946-49; invented and obtained Olympic recognition for the modern Slalom race. During war of 1939-45, Press Correspondent Balkans, Chile, Peru. Lectured: in USA; for British Council, Spain, Rome, Malta; Lowell Lectr, Harvard Univ., 1960. Attached to Ministry of Information (SP), War Office, June 1941; to Amer. High Comr in Germany, April-July 1953. *Publications:* Guide to Montana, 1907; Oxford Mountaineering Essays (ed), 1912; The Englishman in the Alps, 1912; The Harrovians, 1913; Ski-ing, 1913; The Alps (Home Univ. Library), 1914; Loose Ends, 1919; Was Switzerland Pro-German? (*nom de plume* Sutton Croft), 1920; Auction Piquet (*nom de plume* Rubicon), 1920; Cross Country Ski-ing, 1920; The Alpine Ski Guides (Bernese Oberland), 1920; Alpine Ski-ing, 1921; Roman Converts, 1924; Ski-ing for Beginners, 1924; The Mountains of Youth, 1925; A History of Ski-ing, 1927; Things that have Puzzled Me, 1927; Switzerland (Kit-bag Travel Books), 1928; John Wesley, 1929; The Flight from Reason, 1930; The Complete Ski-runner, 1930; Family Name, 1931; Venice (Kitbag Travel Books), 1932; (with Rev. R. A. Knox) Difficulties, 1932; The Italian Lakes and Lakeland Cities, 1932; Within the Precincts of the Prison, 1932; (with C. E. M. Joad) Is Christianity True?, 1933; Public School Religion, 1933; Now I See, 1933; A Saint in The Slave Trade, 1934; (with Prof. J. B. S. Haldane, FRS) Science and the Supernatural, 1935; Within that City, 1936; Spanish Rehearsal, 1937; Communism and Socialism, 1938; Whither Europe?, 1940; Come What May: An Autobiography, 1941; And the Floods Came, 1942; Mountain Jubilee, 1943; The Good Gorilla, 1943; Switzerland and the English, 1944; The Third Day, 1945; Is the Catholic Church Anti-Social? (with G. G. Coulton), 1946; Switzerland in English Prose and Poetry, 1947; Mountains of Memory, 1948; The Revolt against Reason, 1950; The Cradle of Switzerland, 1952; The Story of Ski-ing, 1952; Zermatt and the Valais, 1955; Memory to Memory, 1956; Enigma, 1957; A Century of Mountaineering, 1957; The Bernese Oberland, 1958; And Yet So New, 1958; The Swiss and their Mountains, 1963; The Englishman on Ski, 1963; The New Morality (with Garth Lean), 1964; The Cult of Softness (with Garth Lean), 1965; Matterhorn Centenary, 1965; Unkilled for So Long (memoirs), 1968; (with Garth Lean) Christian Counter-attack, 1969; The Kandahar Story, 1969; contributed to Encyclopædia Britannica; Editor Georgian Stories, 1922, 1924, 1925; Co-Editor, Ski Survey, 1971- (Editor British Ski Year Book 1919-71). *Address:* c/o Ski Club of Great Britain, 118 Eaton Square, SW1. *Clubs:* Athenæum, Alpine (Hon. Mem.). *[Died 2 June 1974.*

LUNT, Alfred; actor; *b* Milwaukee, 1892; *m* Lynn Fontanne, actress. *Educ:* Carroll Coll., Waukesha. First appearance, Castle Square Theatre, Boston, 1913; toured with Margaret Anglin, 1914; with Mrs Langtry in vaudeville; Claude Estabrook in Romance and Arabella, New York, 1917; Clarence in Clarence, 1919-21; Charles II in Sweet Nell of Old Drury, 1923; The Guild Theatre, 1925-29; first appearance in London as von Echardt in Caprice at St James's Theatre; leading parts in: Reunion in Vienna, New York, 1931, London, 1934; Design for Living; Point Valaine; The Taming of the Shrew; Idiots' Delight; Amphitryon 38, New York and London, 1938; The Pirate, New York, 1943; There Shall Be No Night, New York and London, 1943; Quadrille, London, 1952; The Great Sebastians, New York, 1956; The Visit, London, 1960, etc; Dir Theatre Guild, 1935-. Presidential Medal of Freedom, 1964; Kt White Rose, Finland. Holds hon. degrees, incl. Hon. DLitt, Milwaukee, 1930. Emmy Award. *Club:* Players' (New York). *[Died 3 Aug. 1977.*

LUSCOMBE, Norman Percival, CB 1962; Director of Armament Supply, Ministry of Defence (Navy), 1964-66 (Admiralty, 1959-64); *b* 11 Oct. 1902; *s* of late Percival Wicks Luscombe and of Mary Elizabeth (*née* Knight); *m*; one *s* one *d. Educ:* Hereford High Sch. Joined Admiralty, 1923; Captain RNVR, 1944-48. *Recreation:* golf. *Address:* St Mellons, Court Park, Thurlestone, Devon. *[Died 4 Feb. 1976.*

LUSH, Sir Archibald (James), Kt 1969; Chief Inspector of Schools, Monmouthshire, 1944-64, retired; *b* 15 Sept. 1900; *s* of late James Lush, Tredegar, Mon; *m* 1st Ada (decd) *d* of Seth Williams; 2nd, Eusebia May Yendoll. *Educ:* Tredegar Grammar Sch.; Jesus Coll., Oxford. County youth organiser, Mon, 1940. Formerly Chm., Welsh Hosp. Bd. *Publication:* The Young Adult in South Wales, 1939. *Address:* Tremon, The Close, Gilwern, Abergavenny, Gwent. *T:* Gilwern 830671.
[Died 14 April 1976.

LUSTGARTEN, Edgar; author, journalist, broadcaster; *b* 3 May 1907; *s* of Joseph and Sara Lustgarten; *m* 1932, Joyce (*née* Goldstone) (*d* 1972); no *c. Educ:* Manchester Grammar Sch.; St John's Coll., Oxford. Pres., Oxford Union, 1930. Practising Barrister, 1930-40; Radio Counter-Propaganda, 1940-45; BBC Staff Producer, 1945-48; Organiser: BBC Television Programme, In The News, 1950-54; ATV Television Prog., Free Speech, 1955-61; Chm., ATV Television Prog., Fair Play, 1962-65; Narrator, BBC Focus Prog., 1965-68. Solo Broadcaster in many BBC series of Famous Trials, 1952-. *Publications: novels:* A Case to Answer, 1947; Blondie Iscariot, 1948; Game for Three Losers, 1952; I'll never leave you, 1971; Turn the Light Out as You Go, 1978; *studies in true crime:* Verdict in Dispute, 1949; Defender's Triumph, 1951; The Woman in the Case, 1955; The Business of Murder, 1968; The Chalk Pit Murder, 1975; A Century of Murderers, 1975; The Illustrated Story of Crime, 1976. *Address:* c/o Curtis Brown Ltd, 1 Craven Hill, W2.
[Died 15 Dec. 1978.

LUTTIG, Dr Hendrik Gerhardus; Ambassador of Republic of South Africa to the Court of St James's, 1967-72; *b* 26 Oct. 1907; *s* of David and Susanna Luttig; *m* 1939, Dr Marie van Castricum; one *s* one *d. Educ:* Wepener High Sch., SA; Grey University College, SA (MA); Leiden Univ., Holland (DLitt et Phil). MP for Mayfair, Johannesburg, 1949; served on Public Accounts Cttee and various other select cttees; Ambassador to Vienna, 1965-67. Director: Plessey South Africa, 1972-; Cadbury Schweppes (SA) Ltd; Mitchell Cotts Ltd; Rank Xerox (Pty) Ltd; Standard General Insurance Co.; Oerlikon Electrodes SA (Pty) Ltd. Past Pres. and Council Mem., SA British Trade Assoc. *Recreation:* golf. *Address:* 46 Valley Road, Westcliff, Johannesburg. *Clubs:* HERE XVII (Cape Town); Windsor Park Golf, Country (Johannesburg). *[Died 12 July 1975.*

LUWUM, Most Rev. Janani; Archbishop of Uganda, Rwanda, Burundi and Boga Zaire, and Bishop of Kampala, since 1974; *b* 1924; *m* 1947, Mary Lawil; four *s* four *d. Educ:* Gulu High Sch.; Boroboro Teacher Training Coll. Teaching, 1943-49; training for Ministry, 1950-55; ordained, 1956; London Coll. of Divinity, 1963-65 (ALCD). Principal, Buwalasi Coll., 1965-66; Provincial Secretary, 1966-68; Bishop, Northern Uganda, 1969-74. *Address:* PO Box 14123, Kampala, Uganda. *T:* (office) Kampala 46218; (home) 46177. *[Died 17 Feb. 1977.*

LUXFORD, John Hector, CMG 1953; Chairman War Pensions Appeal Board for New Zealand, 1951-65; *b* Palmerston North, New Zealand, 28 May 1890; *y s* of W. L. Luxford, JP; *m* Laura Dagmar, *y d* of John Otton, Numerella, Bega, New South Wales; two *s. Educ:* Wanganui Collegiate Sch., NZ. Admitted Solicitor of the Supreme Court of NZ, 1913; admitted Barrister of the Supreme Court of NZ, 1919; served in NZ Expeditionary Forces, attaining rank of Major (despatches); subsequently posted to Reserve of Officers, NZ Military Forces, with rank of Major; Stipendiary Magistrate, 1928; Chief Judge of Western Samoa, 1929-35; Stipendiary Magistrate, Wellington, 1935-41; Principal Stipendiary Magistrate, Auckland, NZ, 1941-51. Mayor of Auckland, NZ, 1953-56. Chairman, Transport Licensing Appeal Authority, Air Services Licensing Appeal Authority, 1966-68; Chm., No 2 town and Country Planning Appeal Board, 1968-. *Publications:* With the Machine Gunners in France and Palestine, 1922 (an official history of the NZ Machine Gun Corps); Liquor Laws of New Zealand, 3rd edn 1964; Police Law in New Zealand, 3rd edn 1966; Real Estate Agency in New Zealand, 4th edn 1964; Commercial Law in New Zealand, 2nd edn 1961; Domestic Proceedings, 1956, 2nd edn 1970. *Address:* Bega, 35 Orakei Road, Remuera, Auckland 5, NZ. *Club:* Northern (Auckland).   *[Died 8 April 1971.*

LYCETT, Brigadier Cyril Vernon Lechmere, OBE 1921; BA; *b* 14 May 1894; *s* of A. E. Lechmere and J. M. Lycett; *m* 1921, Alexandra Sandika Camarioto (*d* 1970); two *d. Educ:* King Edward VI Sch., Birmingham; Trinity Coll., Cambridge (Scholar). Entered army, Royal Engineers (SR) 1914; served European War, 1914-18 (despatches twice, OBE). Transferred Royal Corps of Signals, 1922; Chairman Wireless Telegraphy Board, 1938-42; served War of 1939-45; DD 'Y' War Office, 1943-44; Director of Signal Intelligence, India and SEAC, 1945-46, retired 1946. Sec. Royal Horticultural Soc., 1946-56. *Address:* 504 Plantation Place, Anaheim, Calif 92806, USA.
[Died 8 June 1978.

LYDFORD, Air Marshal Sir Harold Thomas, KBE 1954 (CBE 1945); CB 1948; AFC; Commander of Legion of Merit, USA; *b* 1898; *m* Isabel Broughton Smart. *Educ:* privately. Wing Comdr 1937; Group Capt. 1942; Air Cdre 1946; Air Vice-Marshal 1947; Air Marshal 1953; Dir of Organisation, Air Min., 1941; Mem. RAF delegn, Washington, DC, 1942-44; AOC No 28 Group, 1944; AOC British Forces, Aden, 1945-48; Comdt-General RAF Regiment, 1948-50; AOC No 18 Group, Coastal Command, and Senior Air Force Officer in Scotland, 1950-52; AOC-in-C Home Comd, 1952-March 1956, retd. *Address:* Merchiston, Hare Hatch, Twyford, Berks. *Clubs:* Naval and Military, Royal Air Force.   *[Died 20 Sept. 1979.*

LYELL, Sir Maurice (Legat), Kt 1962; Judge of the Queen's Bench Division, High Court of Justice, 1962-71; *b* 28 July 1901; 7th *s* of Alexander Lyell, Gardyne Castle, Angus; *m* 1937, Veronica Mary Luard (*d* 1950); one *s* one *d* (and one *d* decd); *m* 1955, Hon. Katharine, *y d* of 1st Viscount Runciman of Doxford, and *widow* of 4th Baron Farrer. *Educ:* Trinity Coll., Glenalmond; Keble Coll., Oxford (MA). Called to Bar, Inner Temple, 1926; Bencher, 1960; QC 1954. Dir of Press Censorship, Min. of Information, 1940-45. Gen. Council of Bar, 1953-57, 1958-62. Joint Master, with wife, of Aldenham Harriers. *Publication:* Law of Income Tax relating to Non-residents and Foreign Income, 1930. *Recreation:* idling. *Address:* Puddephats, Markyate, Herts. *T:* Markyate 317.   *[Died 27 May 1975.*

LYLE OF WESTBOURNE, 2nd Baron *cr* 1945, of Canford Cliffs; **Charles John Leonard Lyle;** Bt, 1932; JP; Director, Messrs Tate & Lyle Ltd, 1954-74; Managing Director, 1929-54, retired 1974; *b* 8 March 1905; *S* father, 1954; *m* 1927, Joyce Jeanne, *er d* of Sir (Joseph) John Jarvis, 1st Bt; no *c. Educ:* Harrow Sch.; Pembroke Coll., Cambridge (BA). Dep. Dir, Sugar Div., Min. of Food, 1939-50. JP Surrey, 1951-. *Recreations:* travel, lawn tennis. *Heir:* none. *Address:* Bakersgate, Pirbright, Woking, Surrey. *T:* Worplesdon 2120.
[Died 1 Aug. 1976 (ext).

LYLE, Sir Ian Duff, Kt 1959; DSC; President of Tate & Lyle Ltd, 1964-78 (Chairman 1954-64); *b* 1907; *s* of late Colonel Abram Lyle, OBE, TD, Barrington Court, Ilminster, Somerset; *m* 1935, Julia Margaret (*d* 1962), *d* of David McWhirter McKechnie, South Africa; one *s* two *d. Educ:* Shrewsbury Sch.; St John's Coll., Oxford. *Address:* Barrington Court, Ilminster, Somerset. *T:* South Petherton 243. *Clubs:* White's; Royal Thames Yacht.
[Died 3 June 1978.

LYLE, James Duncan, MB, BS, MRCS, LRCP; retired; *b* 1887; *o s* of late James Lyle, Hunter's Quay, Argyllshire; *m* 1918, Irene Violet, *o d* of late Henry Alabaster, Eastbourne; one *d.* James Anderson Prize in Clinical Medicine; late Emergency Officer, late assistant anæsthetist, London Hospital. *Address:* c/o Mrs G. T. Hesketh, Rose Island, Heyford Hill Lane, Littlemore, Oxford OX4 4YH. *T:* Oxford 79241.   *[Died 4 July 1972.*

LYMER, Brigadier Rymel Watts, CBE 1945 (MBE 1943); DSO 1943; TD 1951; DL; *b* 1909; *s* of late Charles Richard Lymer, Chorley, Lancs; *m* 1st, Shelagh Dorham (*d* 1954), *d* of late Frederick Dearden, Upton, Cheshire; two *s* one *d*; 2nd, 1957,

Edna, *d* of late Evan Dixon Robinson, Chorley, Lancs, an *widow* of George William Harper. *Educ:* William Hulme's Sch Served War of 1939-45: France, Middle East, Sicily, Italy an NW Europe (despatches thrice, MBE, DSO, CBE). ADS & T 1942, AQMG, 1943, Eighth Army; Brig. 'Q', 21st Army Group 1944. Hon. Col 42 Lancs Div. RASC, 1949-54; Vice-Chm. Lancs T & AFA, 1959-68; Mem., Lancs and Cheshir TA&VRA, 1968-. A Governor of Lyme Green Settlement fo Paraplegics, Macclesfield. Managing Director, North Britis Chemical Co. Ltd, 1946-58. Retired from Manchester Stoc Exchange, Sept. 1965. DL Lancs, 1961. *Recreations:* Territoria Army and travel. *Address:* Chynalls, Mobberley, Cheshire. *T* Mobberley 2100. *Club:* St James's (Manchester).
[Died 8 Oct. 1972

LYNAM, Jocelyn Humphrey Rickman, MA (Oxon); Headmaste Dragon School, Oxford, 1933-65; *b* 27 June 1902; *s* of Alfre Edmund and Mabel Agnes Lynam; *m* 1965, Barbara Frearson *Educ:* The Dragon School, Oxford; Rugby (Scholar); Hertfor Coll. (Exhibitioner), Oxford. Asst master at The Dragon Schoo 1925; Joint Headmaster, 1933. Served on Council o Incorporated Association of Preparatory Schools, 1936-38 1940-42, 1944-46, 1949-51, 1953-55, 1958-. Chairman o Council of IAPS, 1941 and 1942. *Recreations:* gardening formerly cricket (Rugby School XI) and hockey (Oxford Univ 1925). *Address:* 6 Chadlington Road, Oxford. *Club:* Vincent' (Oxford).   *[Died 20 Jan. 1978*

LYNCH, Francis Joseph, JP; Member, Industrial Tribunal, sinc 1975; *b* 15 March 1909; *s* of William Patrick and Agnes Mar Lynch; *m* 1952, Florence Petrie; one *s* one *d. Educ:* St John' Cathedral Sch., Salford, Lancs. Political Agent, Labour Party 1933-55; Salford City Council, 1935-49; JP, Salford, 1949-6 Surrey (now SW London), 1961-74, Derbyshire, 1974-. Serve War, RA, (Sgt), Italy, 1940-45. Confederation of Health Servic Employees: Organiser, 1945; Regional Sec., 1948; Nat. Office 1954; Asst Gen. Sec., 1967; Gen. Sec., 1969-74. *Recreation* walking. *Address:* 1 Low Meadow, Whaley Bridge, Stockpor Cheshire SK12 7AY. *T:* Whaley Bridge 2708.
[Died 10 May 198

LYNCH-BLOSSE, Sir David Edward, 16th Bt *cr* 1622; wit George Allen & Unwin Ltd, since 1960; *b* 24 Nov. 1925; *s* o Hely Richard Lynch-Blosse (*d* 1928), and Evangeline Margare Victoria, *d* of late Charles William Maitland Hudson; *S* uncl 1969; *m* 1950, Elizabeth, *er d* of Thomas Harold Payne, Welwy Garden City; one *s* two *d. Educ:* Marlborough; Jesus College Oxford. Administrative Officer, Northern Nigeria, 1950-5 *Heir: s* Richard Hely Lynch-Blosse, *b* 26 Aug. 1953. *Address:* 3 Elmwood, Welwyn Garden City, Herts. *[Died 15 Oct. 1971*

LYNDE, Professor Carleton J., BA, PhD; Professor of Physics Teachers' College, Columbia University, 1924-39; Professo Emeritus, since 1939; *b* Mitchell, Ontario, 1 Sept. 1872; *m* ; on *s. Educ:* University of Toronto, AB; University of Chichag PhD. Science Master, Auburn, NY, High Sch., 1896-9 Instructor in Physics, University High Sch., Chicago, 189 1906; Professor of Physics, Washington and Jefferson Coll Washington, Pa, 1906-07; Prof. of Physics, Macdonald Coll PQ, Canada, 1907-24. *Publications:* Effect of Pressure o Surface Tension; Home Waterworks; Osmosis in Soils: the soi acts as a Semipermeable Membrane; On Osmosis in Soils: th Efficiency of the Soil Constituents as Semipermeabl Membranes; On a New Method of Measuring the Capillary Li of Soils; Physics of the Household: an elementary text-book fo students of household science; Laboratory Manual on Physics o the Household; Hydraulic and Pneumatic Engineering for Boy Light Experiments for Boys; Experimental Glass-Blowing fo Boys; Everyday Physics; A Laboratory Course in Everyda Physics; Science Experiences with Home Equipment; Scienc Experiences with Inexpensive Equipment; Science Experience with Ten-Cent Store Equipment. *Recreations:* formerly tenni golf, fishing. *Address:* 809 Carlton Towers, 470 Third Street S St Petersburg, Florida 33701, USA. *[Died 31 Aug. 197*

LYNE, Arthur William, OBE 1939; *b* 21 July 1884; one *d. Educ* Kettering Road Elementary Sch., Northampton. Boot and Sho Operative until 1914. Served War of 1914-18 with Northam Regt as Sergeant. Officer National Union Boot and Sho Operative, 1919. A Chairman, Northampton Borough Counci 1920-64; Mayor of Borough, 1938 and 1939; Hon. Freeman o Borough, 1958. JP Northampton Borough, 1923-64. MP (Lab for Burton-on-Trent, 1945-50. *Address:* 52 Greenfield Roac Northampton. *T:* Northampton 42079. *[Died 30 Dec. 197*

LYNEN, Prof. Feodor, Dr phil; Pour le mérite, 1971; Directo Max-Planck-Institut für Biochemie, 1972-79; Professor o Biochemistry, University of Munich, since 1953; *b* 6 April 191

s of Wilhelm and Frieda Lynen; *m* 1937, Eva (*née* Wieland); two *s* three *d*. *Educ:* Univ. of Munich (Dr phil). Extraordinary Prof., Univ. of Munich, 1947-53; Dir, Max-Planck-Institut für Zellchemie, 1954-72. Foreign Member, Royal Society, 1975. Dr med *hc* Freiburg, 1960; Dr rer nat *hc* Seoul, 1968; DSc *hc* Miami, 1968; D*hc* Univ. René Descartes, Paris, 1976; Dr *hc* Univ. Regensburg, 1978; D*hc* Univ. of Pécs, 1979. Nobel Prize for Medicine, 1964. *Publications:* articles in Biochim. Biophys. Acta, Eur. J. Biochem., Hoppe-Seyler's Z. Physiologie. *Recreations:* skilaufen, wandern, schwimmen, radfahren. *Address:* Max-Planck-Institut für Biochemie, D-8033 Martinsried, Bundesrepublik Deutschland. *T:* 85 85 323.

             [Died 6 Aug. 1979.

LYNES, Rear-Adm. Charles Edward, CMG 1919; *b* 1875; *s* of late Edward Lynes, MD, JP, Coventry; *m* 1954, Muriel Vaughan. Entered Royal Navy, 1893; retired list, 1930. *Address:* 47 Southdown Road, Seaford, E Sussex. *Club:* Naval and Military.

             [Died 30 Jan. 1977.

LYON, Maj.-Gen. Sir Francis James Cecil B.; *see* Bowes-Lyon.

LYON, Robert, MA (Dunelm); RBA; RP; retired as Principal, Edinburgh College of Art (1942-60); *b* 18 Aug. 1894; 3rd *s* of Charles Lyon, Elgin, and Grace Mortimer Wood, Yorkshire; *m* 1924, Mabel Sansome Morrison, Blundellsands; one *s*. *Educ:* Royal College of Art, London; British School at Rome. Served with King's Liverpool Regt, 1914-19; Lecturer in Fine Art and Master of Painting, King's Coll., Newcastle upon Tyne (Univ. of Durham), 1932; Mem. Soc. Mural Painters; professional practice includes Mural Painting. Exhibitor: Royal Society of Portrait Painters; Royal Academy and New English Art Club. *Recent work includes:* murals for Western General Hosp., Edinburgh, and King's College Hosp. Dental Dept. *Recreation:* fishing. *Address:* Little Alliss, Rushlake Green, East Sussex. *T:* Rushlake Green 323.

             [Died 7 June 1978.

LYONS OF BRIGHTON, Baron *cr* 1974 (Life Peer), of Brighton, E Sussex; **Braham Jack Dennis Lyons;** Independent Public Relations Consultant, since 1976; *b* 11 Sept. 1918; *s* of late Ralph and Dena Lyons; *m* 1st, 1940, Laurie Adele Lion (marr. diss. 1957); two *s*; 2nd, 1961, Mary Priscilla Woolley (decd); one *d*. *Educ:* St Paul's School. Features Editor, Everybody's Weekly, 1946; Man. Director, Modern Features Ltd, 1951; Gen. Manager of Public Relations Div., Pritchard Wood & Partners (now part of Wasey Quadrant), 1952-63; Man. Director of Infoplan Ltd, 1963-68; Partner, Traverse-Healy Lyons & Partners, 1968-75; Dir, London Communications Consortium, 1976-. *Address:* 2 Clifton Terrace, Brighton BN1 3HA. *T:* Brighton 202346. *Club:* Reform. *[Died 18 Jan. 1978.*

LYONS, Eric (Alfred), CBE 1979 (OBE 1959); FRIBA; DistTP; FSIAD; architect in private practice since 1945; *b* 2 Oct. 1912; *s* of Benjamin and Caroline Lyons; *m* 1944, Catherine Joyce Townsend; two *s*. *Educ:* The Polytechnic Sch. of Architecture. DistTP, RIBA, 1961; Architecture Award, RIBA, 1966; Mem. RIBA Coun., 1960-63, 1964-; Vice-Pres., RIBA, 1967, 1968, Senior Vice-Pres. 1974, Pres., 1975-77. Eleven awards for Good Design in Housing by Min. of Housing and Local Govt; six awards by Civic Trust. In partnership with G. Paulson Townsend, 1945-50; Partner, Eric Lyons Cunningham Partnership, 1963-. Hon. Fellow, Amer. Inst. of Architects. Mem., Académie d'Architecture, France. *Principal works:* housing at Blackheath, Ham, Cambridge, Weybridge, new town of Vilamoura, Portugal, etc; Architect to the Worlds End Chelsea neighbourhood; other work includes housing and schools for various local authorities. *Recreations:* music, drama. *Address:* Mill House, Bridge Road, Hampton Court, Surrey. *T:* 01-979 6656.

             [Died 22 Feb. 1980.

LYSTER, Anthony St George, CSI 1943; Indian Service of Engineers, retired; *b* 13 March 1888; *e s* of Major Charles Bybie Lyster, Newsholme, West Malvern, Worcs; *m* 1921, Dorothy Prideaux, 2nd *d* of Dr John Delpratt Harris, 45 Southernhay, Exeter; two *s*. *Educ:* Harrow Sch.; Pembroke Coll., Cambridge. Asst Engineer Public Works Dept Punjab, India, 1911. Served in Mesopotamia and Persia, 1915-19 (two medals, despatches). Chief Engineer and Sec. for Irrigation to Punjab Govt, 1940-43; Pres. Punjab Engineering Congress, 1942; retired, 1943. Jubilee Medal, 1935; Coronation Medal, 1937; Civil Defence Long Service Medal. *Recreations:* attendance at rowing regattas and travel. *Address:* Southernhay, Cliff Road, Sidmouth, Devon. *T:* Sidmouth 2852. *Club:* Royal Over-Seas League.

             [Died 7 Jan. 1971.

LYTHGOE, Sir James, Kt 1951; CBE 1945; Hon. MA Manchester, 1948, Hon. LLD Manchester, 1970; *b* 21 Oct. 1891; *s* of James Clare Lythgoe; *m* 1918, Dorothy May Ashworth; one

s one *d*. *Educ:* Cheadle Hulme Schs; Stand Grammar Sch. Ex-Treasurer of the City, Manchester. Mem. Council, Inst. of Municipal Treasurers and Accountants, 1942-51 (Pres., 1947-48); Member: Rushcliffe Cttees (Nurses and Midwives Salaries), 1941-47; National Savings, 1941-43; Central Health Service Whitley Council, 1949-51; Home Office Cttees on Police Extraneous Duties, 1950, and Police Pensions, 1951; Colonial Office Advisory Panel on Local Govt, 1951-70; Hon. Treas., Hallé Concerts Soc., 1952-60; Interdepartmental Cttee on Concentration of Slaughter Houses, 1953; Departmental Cttee to review Salmon and Freshwater Fisheries Act, 1957; Public Works Loans Bd, 1956-68; Manchester Regional Hosps Bd, 1951-66 (Chm., 1962-66); Council, Manchester Univ. Ct, 1951-72; Feoffee Chetham's Hosp. Sch. and Library; Trustee, Municipal Mutual Insurance Ltd. *Publications:* various, on local government, public administration and finance. *Recreations:* golf, photography. *Address:* 34 Carrwood Road, Wilmslow, near Manchester. *T:* Wilmslow 3234. *Club:* National Liberal.

             [Died 17 Dec. 1972.

LYTTON SELLS, Arthur Lytton, MA (Cambridge), Docteur de l'Université de Paris, Lauréat de l'Académie française; Officier d'Académie; *b* Edgbaston, Birmingham, England, 28 May 1895; *s* of Arthur Sells and Elizabeth Whittaker; *m* 1929, Iris Esther, MA, *d* of F. T. Robertson, JP, formerly editor of Adelaide Advertiser, Adelaide, South Australia; one *s*. *Educ:* King Edward VII School; Univs of Cambridge and Paris. Scholar of Sidney Sussex Coll., Cambridge, 1914-15, 1919-21; served HAC, 1918-19; Lectr, Cambridge, 1923-29; Univ. Lectr in French, 1929; Prof. of French, Durham Univ., 1930-51; Prof. of English Literature, Padua Univ., 1946; Prof. of French and Italian at Indiana Univ., 1951; Research Prof. Emer., 1965. Visiting Professor: Harvard, 1953, New York Univ., 1954, Assumption Coll., Worcester, Mass, 1967, Wake Forest Univ., N Carolina, 1970-. *Publications:* Les Sources françaises de Goldsmith, 1924, awarded Prix Bordin of the French Academy; The Early Life of J. J. Rousseau, 1929; Molière and La Mothe le Vayer, 1933; The History of Francis Wills, 1935; (with I. Lytton Sells) Key to Manual of French Translation and Composition, 1937; contrib. France, ed by R. L. G. Ritchie, 1937; Earth of the Tarentines, 1940; Heredia's Hellenism, 1942; The Italian Influence in English Poetry, 1954; Animal Poetry in French and English Literature, 1955; (ed) The Military Memoirs of James II, 1962; The Paradise of Travellers, 1964; (trans.) Mollat and Wolff: The Popular Revolutions of the Late Middle Ages, 1974; Oliver Goldsmith: his life and works, 1975; (with I. Lytton Sells) Thomas Gray: his life and works, 1977. *Recreations:* reading, photography. *Address:* Dunster House, The Avenue, Durham. *T:* 2525. *Club:* Athenæum. *[Died 22 Dec. 1978.*

LYVEDEN, 5th Baron *cr* 1859; **Sydney Munro Vernon;** retired; *b* 21 Nov. 1888; *s* of Cecil Sydney Archibald Vernon (*g s* of 1st Baron) (*d* 1944) and Jessie Jane (*d* 1942), *d* of John Munro; *S* kinsman, 1969; *m* 1st, 1912, Ruby Shandley (*d* 1932); one *s* three *d* (and one *d* decd); 2nd, 1959, Gladys, *widow* of John Cassidy. *Educ:* Northland Private Boarding School. *Recreations:* bowling and motoring. *Heir:* *s* Hon. Ronald Cecil Vernon [*b* 10 April 1915; *m* 1938, Queenie Constance, *d* of Howard Ardern; three *s*]. *Address:* 2a Main Road, Day's Bay, Wellington, New Zealand. *T:* 86-86. *Clubs:* Petone Working Men's and Literary Institute; Central Bowling; Royal Automobile and AA Motor.

             [Died 19 Sept. 1973.

M

MACADAM, Sir Ivison (Stevenson), KCVO 1974 (CVO 1953; MVO 1937); Kt 1955; CBE 1935 (OBE 1919); FRSE; MIMechE; Editor, The Annual Register of World Events, 1947-73; *b* 18 July 1894; 2nd *s* of late Col W. Ivison Macadam, FRSE, Professor of Chemistry, Edinburgh; *m* 1934, Caroline Ladd, *e d* of late Elliott Corbett, Portland, Oregon, USA; two *s* two *d*. *Educ:* Melville Coll., Edinburgh; King's Coll., London; Christ's Coll., Cambridge. Mem., Council, 1957-74, Delegacy, 1960-74, Vice-Chm., 1971-74 and Fellow, King's Coll., London. Served European War, 1914-19, City of Edinburgh (Fortress) Royal Engineers; Officer commanding Royal Engineers, Archangel, North Russian Expeditionary Force (despatches thrice). Asst Dir-Gen. and Principal Asst Sec., Min. of Information, 1939-41; Sec. and Dir-Gen., Royal Inst. of Internat. Affairs, 1929-55. Founder Pres. and Trustee of the National Union of Students; Mem. Council, King George's Jubilee Trust, 1935-74 (Vice-Chm., 1972-74); Pres., Co. of Norfolk St John Ambulance Bde,

1972-74; a Dep. Pres., Victoria League. CStJ. *Address:* 16 Upper Belgrave Street, SW1X 8BL. *T:* 01-235 4417; Runton Old Hall, East Runton, Cromer, Norfolk. *T:* Cromer 2425. *Clubs:* Athenæum; Norfolk (Norwich). *[Died 22 Dec. 1974.*

McADAM, Prof. Robert, BSc, PhD, CEng, FIMinE, FRSE; Hood Professor of Mining Engineering, Heriot-Watt University, Edinburgh, 1967-75, now Emeritus; *b* 15 March 1906; *y s* of William McAdam, Broomieknowe, Midlothian; *m* 1933, Winifred Julia, *o d* of T. W. Dixon, Edinburgh; one *s. Educ:* Lasswade Secondary Sch.; Univ. of Edinburgh. Practical experience in coal mines in Scotland and gold mines in India; Tait research worker on Mine Ventilation, 1930. Sen. Lectr in Mining, Heriot-Watt Coll., Edinburgh, 1931-48; Hood Prof. of Mining, Univ. of Edinburgh and Heriot-Watt Coll., Edinburgh, 1948-67. Heriot-Watt Univ., Edinburgh: Dean of Faculty of Engineering, 1967-69; Vice-Principal, 1970-74. Carried out research work on errors affecting mine surveying operations, production of oil from coal, geophysical prospecting, and mine rescue work. *Publications:* Colliery Surveying, 1953, 1963; Mine Rescue Work, 1955; Mining Explosives, 1958; numerous papers on mining and scientific subjects in Trans of IMinE, Inst. Mining Surveyors, and in technical press. *Address:* Allermuir, Captains Road, Edinburgh EH17 8DT. *T:* 031-664 2770.
[Died 5 Nov. 1978.

MacADAM, William, MA, BSc, MD, FRCP; Professor of Medicine and Clinical Medicine, University of Leeds, 1932-46, Emeritus Professor since 1946; Hon. Consultant Physician, General Infirmary, Leeds; *b* 10 Dec. 1885; *s* of Archibald MacAdam, Corstorphine; *m* Irene M. H. Tincker, MB, ChB; two *s* one *d. Educ:* Glasgow Univ. MB, ChB Hons, with Brunton Memorial Prize, 1909. Formerly: Consulting Physician: United Leeds Hosp. Board; Leeds Regional Hosp. Board; Hon. Physician: General Hosp., Halifax; Clayton Hosp., Wakefield; General Hosp., Skipton; Lectr in Pathology and in Metabolic Medicine, Univ. of Leeds; McCunn and Carnegie Research Scholar, Univ. of Glasgow; Pres., British Gastro-Enterological Soc., FRCP, 1932; Fellow, BMA, 1959. *Publications:* numerous contribs and papers in various scientific and medical jls. *Address:* Lindores, 2 Foxhill Avenue, Leeds LS16 5PB. *Club:* Leeds (Leeds). *[Died 19 May 1976.*

McADDEN, Sir Stephen (James), Kt 1962; CBE 1959; MP (C) Southend East since 1950; Director, Butlins Construction Co. Ltd; *b* 3 Nov. 1907; *s* of William John McAdden and Elizabeth (*née* Mulhern); *m* 1951, Doris Hearle, *d* of Walter and Ethel Gillies, Leytonstone, and *widow* of Captain William Hearle, RAC. *Educ:* Salesian Sch., Battersea. Comd Hackney Bn, Home Guard, Lt-Col. Councillor: Hackney Borough Council, 1937-45; Woodford Borough Council, 1945-48; Essex County Council, 1947-48. Chairman: West Toxteth (Liverpool) Junior Imperial League, 1929-31, Hackney Branch, 1932-35; Grand Prior, Primrose League, 1955-58. Trustee Liverpool Victoria Friendly Society; National Pres. and Chm., Music Users Assoc.; Vice-Pres., National Chamber of Trade. Mem., Speaker's Panel of Chairman of Cttees, 1966-. Freeman of City of London, 1974. *Recreations:* tennis, cricket, debating. *Address:* 552 Woodgrange Drive, Thorpe Bay, Essex. *T:* Southend-on-Sea 588421; House of Commons, SW1. *Clubs:* St Stephen's; Alexandra Yacht (Southend), Thorpe Bay Yacht.
[Died 26 Dec. 1979.

MACAFEE, Prof. Charles Horner Greer, CBE 1961; DL; Emeritus Professor of Midwifery and Gynæcology, The Queen's University, Belfast, since 1963 (Professor, Oct. 1945-Oct. 1963, retired); Member of Senate; *b* 23 July 1898; *s* of Rev. Andrew Macafee, BA, and A. H. Macafee, MBE, JP; *m* 1930, Margaret Crymble (*d* 1968), *d* of Prof. C. G. Lowry; two *s* one *d. Educ:* Omagh Academy; Foyle Coll., Londonderry. MB, BCh, BAO, First Class Hons, 1921; FRCS 1927; FRCSI 1927; Foundation Fellow, 1929, and Mem. Council, RCOG; Past Pres., Ulster Obstetrical and Gynæcological Soc.; Chm. Adv. Cttee on the Maternity Services in Northern Ireland; Past Pres., Ulster Medical Soc.; Vice-Pres., RCOG, 1961-64; formerly Mem. Northern Ireland Hospitals Authority; formerly External Examiner: Oxford, Dublin, Glasgow and Leeds; Lichfield Lectr, Oxford, 1955; Sims-Black Travelling Prof. to Rhodesia and S Africa, RCOG, 1956; William Meredith Fletcher Shaw Memorial Lectr, London, 1961. DL, County Down, 1969. Hon. Fellow: Edinburgh Obstetrical Soc., 1972; Ulster Medical Soc., 1977; Hon. FRCPI, 1977. Hon. DSc Leeds, 1961; Hon. LLD Belfast, 1974. Blair Bell Memorial Medal, RSM, 1965; Eardley Holland Medal, RCOG, 1965. *Publications:* contributed to: Modern Trends in Obstetrics and Gynæcology; Modern Trends in British Surgery; many contribs to Jl of Obstetrics and Gynæcology, British Empire; Proc. RSocMed; Ulster Medical Jl. *Recreations:* reading, writing, gardening. *Address:* The

Cottage Stramore Lodge, 142 Warren Road, Ballywilliam, Donaghadee, Co. Down, Northern Ireland.
[Died 16 Aug. 1978.

MACAFEE, Colonel John Leeper Anketell, CBE 1964; RM; Director of Naval Security since 1961; *b* 24 July 1915; *s* of late Thomas Boyd Macafee, BA, Clonallen, Armagh, Northern Ireland, and late Muriel Kathleen Macafee; *m* 1939, Mary Ruth Noel Lewis, *d* of late Comdr G. J. W. Lewis, Green Court, Bredhurst, Kent; two *d. Educ:* Campbell Coll., Belfast. Entered RM (2nd Lieut), 1934; HMS Hood, 1937; PT Course, 1938; HMS Royal Sovereign, 1938-40; Naval Provost Marshal, Mediterranean Fleet, 1940-42; 3rd Bn RM, 1942-43; 44 Commando, RM, 1943-44; Holding Commando (overseas) (CO), 1944-45; HQ RM (Devon), 1945-46; Staff Coll., Camberley, 1947; Staff of Comdt General, RM, Admiralty, 1948-49; Instructor, Staff Coll., Camberley, 1950-52; Staff Officer (Intelligence) S Atlantic, 1953-55; Joint Services Amphibious Warfare Centre, 1955-57; 42 Commando RM (CO), 1957-59; HQ, RM, Plymouth, 1959; Fleet RM Officer, Mediterranean Fleet, 1960; Deputy Director, Naval Intelligence, 1961. ADC to the Queen, 1963-64. *Recreations:* tennis, gardening, carpentry. *Address:* Grove House, Bredhurst, Gillingham, Kent. *T:* Medway 32316. *[Died 20 Feb. 1974.*

McALISTER, Mary A., (Mrs J. Alexander McAlister), CBE 1968; *d* of late Charles McMackin and Winifred (*née* Deeney); *m* 1927, J. Alexander McAlister; four *d. Educ:* Franciscan Convent, Glasgow. Nurse by profession (fevers); trained Knightswood Hospital, Glasgow, 1923-26. Served during War of 1939-45, Civil Nursing Reserve and ultimately Postal Censorship. Member Glasgow Corporation (Labour), 1945-48; Convener, Health and Welfare Cttee, 1952-55. Formerly Member: Standing Advisory Cttee on Local Authority Services; Western Region Hospitals Board; General Nursing Council for Scotland; Central Midwives Board. JP Glasgow, 1947-51. MP (Lab) Kelvingrove Div. of Glasgow, March 1958-Sept. 1959. Hon. Pres., Royal College of Nursing (Glasgow Branch), 1956-58. Member: National Assistance Board, 1961-66; Supplementary Benefits Commn, 1966-67 (Dep. Chm., 1967). *Address:* 22 North Gardner Street, Glasgow G11 5BT. *T:* 041-339 1606. *[Died 26 Feb. 1976.*

McALISTER, Samuel, CBE 1944; retired banker; *b* 10 May 1896; *s* of late Francis McAlister, Dunlaoghaire, Co. Dublin, Ireland; *m* 1927, Jessie A., *er d* of late Fred Smith, CBE, JP, Pollard Hall, Gomersal, Yorks; two *s* one *d. Educ:* Wesley Coll., Dublin. Served European War, 1914-19, RN. Chm., British Chamber of Commerce in Brazil, 1941-44; Vice-Pres., Brazilian Bankers' Assoc., Rio de Janeiro, 1950-54. *Address:* Ashcroft, 114 Ashley Road, Walton-on-Thames, Surrey. *[Died 12 April 1971.*

MacANDREW, 1st Baron *cr* 1959; **Charles Glen MacAndrew;** PC 1952; Kt 1935; TD; DL; JP; Hon. LLD (St Andrews); *b* 13 Jan. 1888; *s* of F. G. MacAndrew; *m* 1918, Lilian Cathleen Curran (from whom he obtained a divorce 1938); one *s* one *d* ; *m* 1941, Mona, *d* of J. A. Ralston Mitchell, Perceton House, by Irvine; one *d. Educ:* Uppingham; Trinity Coll., Cambridge. MP (U) Ayr and Bute, Kilmarnock Div., 1924-29; MP (U) Partick Div., Glasgow, 1931-35; Dep. Chm. of Ways and Means, House of Commons, May-July 1945 and March 1950-Oct. 1951; MP (U) Bute and Northern div. of Ayr and Bute, 1935-59; Dep. Speaker of the House of Commons, 1951-59; Chm. of Ways and Means, 1951-59. Commanded Ayrshire Yeomanry, 1932-36; Hon. Col, 1951-55; DL, JP, Ayrshire. OStJ. *Heir: s* Hon. Colin Nevil Glen MacAndrew [*b* 1 Aug. 1919; *m* 1943, Ursula, *yr d* of Capt. Joseph Steel, Lockerbie, Dumfriesshire; two *s* one *d. Educ:* Eton; Trinity Coll., Cambridge]. *Address:* The White House, Monkton, Ayrshire. *T:* Prestwick 77872. *Clubs:* Carlton; Royal and Ancient Golf (St Andrews). *[Died 11 Jan. 1979.*

MacANDREW, Lt-Col James Orr, TD; DL; Ayrshire Yeomanry; *b* 22 June 1899; *s* of F. G. MacAndrew, Knock Castle, Largs; *m* 1944, Eileen, *o d* of Robin Butterfield; one *d. Educ:* Trinity Coll., Glenalmond; Trinity Hall, Cambridge. Served European War, 1914-18, joined RFC 1917; War of 1939-45. Hon. Col Ayrshire Yeomanry, 1955-60. MP (U) Ayr and Bute South Ayrshire Div., 1931-35. Jt Master, Eglinton foxhounds, 1939-40. DL Ayrshire, 1966. *Address:* South Park, Ayr. *T:* Ayr 64783. *Club:* Cavalry and Guards.
[Died 11 July 1979

MACARTHUR, Hon. Sir Ian (Hannay), Kt 1974; Judge of Supreme Court of New Zealand, since 1959; *b* 9 July 1906; *s* of James Smith Macarthur and Mary Margaret Corrie Hannay; *m* 1937, Enid de Castro Twigg, *d* of Samuel Twigg; three *d. Educ:* Scots Coll.; Victoria Univ. of Wellington (LLM). Served with 2 NZ Div., 1941-44. Practised as Barrister and Solicitor at

Wellington, NZ, 1935-40 and 1945-59; Pres., Wellington District Law Soc., 1956. *Recreation:* gardening. *Address:* 35 Macmillan Avenue, Cashmere, Christchurch 2, New Zealand. *T:* 327-115. *Club:* Christchurch (Christchurch, NZ).
[Died 19 Sept. 1975.

MacARTHUR, Neil, DL; *b* 20 March 1886; *s* of John MacArthur, Castleton, Glassary, Argyll; *m* 1916, Mary MacArthur, *d* of Capt. Malcolm Campbell, Ibrox, Glasgow; one *s* one *d.* *Educ:* Lochgilphead Sch.; Glasgow Univ. Qualified as Solicitor, 1911. Served European War, 1914-18, with 4th Bn QO Cameron Highlanders, and RAF (despatches). Lt-Col 1927; Bt Col 1931. DL Inverness-shire, 1954. Hon. Sheriff Substitute of Inverness, Moray, Nairn, and Ross and Cromarty. Formerly Director: Deltenne (Ceylon) Tea Estates Ltd, Highland Haulage Ltd. *Recreations:* shooting, fishing, golf. *Address:* Milnfield, Inverness. *T:* Inverness 33439. *Clubs:* Caledonian (Edinburgh); Highland (Inverness).   *[Died 17 Nov. 1973.*

MACARTNEY, Carlile Aylmer; FBA 1965; MA, DLitt, Oxon; *b* 1895; *s* of late Carlile Henry Hayes Macartney; *m* Nedella, *d* of late Col Dimitri Mamarchev, Bulgarian Army; no *c.* *Educ:* Winchester (scholar, Pitt Exhibitioner); Trinity Coll., Cambridge (scholar). Served European War, 1914-18; HBM Vice-Consul (acting), Vienna, 1921-25; with Encyclopædia Britannica, 1926-28; Intelligence Dept, League of Nations Union, 1928-36; Research Dept, Foreign Office, 1939-46; Montagu Burton Prof. of International Relations, Edinburgh Univ., 1951-57; Research Fellow, All Souls Coll., Oxford, 1936-65, Fellow Emeritus, 1976. Mem., Sch. of Slavonic Studies; Foreign Mem., Hungarian Acad., 1947-49; Corresp. Mem., Austrian Acad. of Sciences, 1974. Hon. DLitt Lancaster, 1977. Freeman, City of Cleveland, USA. Grand Decoration of Honour in Gold (Austria), 1974. *Publications:* The Social Revolution in Austria, 1926; Survey of International Affairs for 1925, Part II (with other authors) 1927; The Magyars in the Ninth Century, 1930 (2nd edn 1968); National States and National Minorities, 1934 (2nd edn 1968); Hungary (Modern World Series), 1934 (Hungarian edn, revised, 1936); Hungary and her Successors, 1937 (2nd edn 1965); Studies in the Earliest Hungarian Historical Sources, I-VIII, 1938-52; Problems of the Danube Basin, 1942 (Hungarian translation, 1943); The Mediæval Hungarian Historians, 1953; Oct. 15th, 1957 (2nd edn rev. 1961); (with A. W. Palmer) Independent Eastern Europe, 1961; Hungary: A Short History, 1962; The Habsburg Empire 1790-1918, 1969, 2nd edn 1971; Maria Theresa and the House of Austria, 1969; The Habsburg and Hohenzollern Dynasties in the Seventeenth and Eighteenth Centuries, 1970; contribs to Encyclopædia Britannica, 13th and 14th edns, Chambers's Encyclopædia, and to British and Central European Reviews; translations. *Recreation:* travel. *Address:* Hornbeams, Boars Hill, near Oxford. *T:* Oxford 735224.   *[Died 18 June 1978.*

MACAULAY, Hon. Leopold, QC (Canada); BA, LLB, DLS; Barrister, retired; Vice-President, Canadian Red Cross Society; *b* Peterboro, Ont., 25 Nov. 1887; *s* of Robert Macaulay and Agnes Giroux, Canadians; *m* ; two *s* one *d* ; *m* 1963, Kathleen H. Sherk, Midland, Mich., USA. *Educ:* Lindsay Public Sch.; Harbord Collegiate, Toronto; Univ. of Toronto; Osgoode Hall, Toronto. Provincial Sec. and Registrar of the Province of Ontario, Canada, 1930-31; Minister of Highways, Ontario, 1931-34, and Minister of Public Works, 1934; Pres. Univ. of Toronto Alumni Fedn, 1937-38; Conservative Mem. for South York Riding, Ont., 1926-43; retired 1943; Chm., National Council, Red Cross, Canada, 1951-52; Chm. Board of Regents, Victoria Univ., Toronto, 1951-58. *Recreation:* golf. *Address:* 95 River View Drive, Toronto, Ontario, Canada M4N 3C6. *Club:* Rosedale Golf.   *[Died 24 Dec. 1979.*

McAULIFFE, Gen. Anthony Clement, DSC (US); DSM (US) (with Oak Leaf Cluster); Silver Star; Legion of Merit and Bronze Star Medal; US Army retired; Vice-President, American Cyanamid Company, 1956-64, retired; *b* 2 July 1898; *s* of John J. and Alice K. McAuliffe; *m* 1920, Helen Willet Whitman; one *s* one *d.* *Educ:* US Military Academy, West Point, NY. Passed through grades 2nd Lt to Gen. in US Army, 1918-56. Combat operations, War of 1939-45, European Theatre as Dep. Div. Comdr and Acting Div. Comdr of 101st Airborne Div. and as Div. Comdr of 103rd Infantry Div.; retired, 1956. DSO and Bar (British), 1945 also decorations from governments of France, Belgium, Holland and Luxembourg. *Recreations:* golf, poker and bridge. *Address:* 4515 Willard Avenue, Chevy Chase, Md 20015, USA.   *[Died 11 Aug. 1975.*

McBAIN, Alexander Richardson, CB 1946; OBE 1968; Under-Secretary, Ministry of Supply, Jan. 1946-Dec. 1948, re-employed Oct. 1949; late Chairman, Southern Gas Board, 1952-55; *b* 1887; *s* of Alexander McBain, Glasgow; *m* 1925, Winifred Alice, *d* of

William Winton Davies. *Educ:* Glasgow High Sch. and Technical Coll. *Address:* Cherrygarth, Hillfield Square, Chalfont St Peter, Bucks. *T:* Gerrards Cross 84209.
[Died 15 Sept. 1971.

MacBRIDE, Geoffrey Ernest Derek, CMG 1971; MBE 1950; Counsellor, HM Diplomatic Service; retired 1975; *b* 16 April 1917; *s* of late Prof. E. W. MacBride, FRS, and late Constance Harvey (*née* Chrysler); *m* 1st, 1940, Shirley Margaret (*née* Evans) (marr. diss. 1959); one *s* ; 2nd, 1972, June Parker (*née* Moore). *Educ:* Westminster Sch.; Christ Church, Oxford. BA (MA) Mod. Hist. HM Forces, 1939-46; Control Commission for Germany, 1947-52; Foreign Office, 1952-54; HM Embassy, Vienna, 1954-57; FO, 1957-61; HM Consulate-General, Duesseldorf, 1961-66; FCO, 1966-75. *Recreations:* keyboard instruments (esp. harpsichord), sailing. *Address:* North Rampart, The Drive, Chichester, West Sussex. *T:* Chichester 527201.   *[Died 24 Dec. 1975.*

McBRIDE, Neil; MP (Lab) Swansea East since 1963; *b* Neilston, Renfrewshire, Scotland, 13 April 1910; *e s* of late Neil McBride, Senior, of Neilston; *m* 1937, Delia, 3rd *d* of late James Maloney, Paisley; no *c.* *Educ:* St Thomas' Sch., Neilston; continuation classes; National Council of Labour Colleges. Brass finisher; last employers, John Brown & Co. (Clydebank) Ltd. Formerly Member Paisley Corporation. Contested (Lab): Perth and Perth East, 1951, High Peak, Derbyshire, 1955. Asst Govt Whip, 1966-69; a Lord Comr, HM Treasury, Oct. 1969-1970; Opposition Whip, 1970-74; Chm., Welsh Lab. Parly Gp, 1972-73. *Recreations:* travel, reading, spread of Socialism. *Address:* 116 Eaton Road, Brynhyfryd, Swansea, Glam.
[Died 9 Sept. 1974.

McBURNEY, Prof. Charles Brian Montagu, FBA 1966; FSA, MA, PhD, ScD; Professor of Quaternary Prehistory, University of Cambridge, since 1977; Fellow, Corpus Christi College, Cambridge, since 1962; *b* 18 June 1914; *s* of Henry McBurney and Dorothy Lilian (*née* Rundall); *m* 1953, Anne Frances Edmonstone Charles; two *s* one *d.* *Educ:* privately; King's Coll., Cambridge (BA 1937). Research Fellow, King's Coll., Cambridge, 1940-53; Univ. Lectr in Archæology, 1953-67, Reader 1967-77, Prof. (personal chair), 1977-. Membre d'honneur, Soc. Jersiaise. Hon. Corresp. Mem. Istituto Italiano di Paleontologia Umana, Rome. Knight of Order of the Dannebrog (First Class), 1961. *Publications:* (with R. W. Hey) Prehistory and Pleistocene Geology of Cyrenaican Libya, 1955; The Stone Age of Northern Africa, 1960; The Haua Fteah (Cyrenaica) and the Stone Age of the SE Mediterranean, 1967; (ed jtly) France before the Romans, 1974; articles on early prehistory of Iran, Libya, Central and SW Europe, and Britain in Proc. Brit. Acad., Proc. Prehistoric Soc., Jl of Royal Anthropological Inst., L'Anthropologie, Encyclopædia Britannica, etc. *Recreations:* trout fishing, walking, travelling. *Address:* 5 Grange Road, Cambridge. *T:* Cambridge 51385. *Club:* United Oxford & Cambridge University.
[Died 14 Dec. 1979.

McCABE, Alasdair; Managing Director, Educational Building Society; Editor, Irish Year Book. MP (SF) South Sligo, 1918-22; Member Dail Eireann for Mayo East and Sligo County, 1921-23; Leitrim and Sligo, 1923-24. Commandant Army, 1921-23. *Recreation:* golf. *Address:* 33 Oakley Road, Ranelagh, Dublin. *T:* 974335.   *[Died 31 May 1972.*

McCALL, Sir Alexander, Kt 1947; MD, ChB; Fellow London Medical Society and Hunterian Society. MB, ChB, 1906; MD Glasgow (high commend.), 1909; late Asst Pathologist, London Homoeopathic Hosp.; Clinical Asst, West End Hosp. for Diseases of the Nervous System; Asst Physician, City of Glasgow Fever and Smallpox Hospitals. *Publications:* Diazo-Reaction and Bacilluria in Enteric Fever. *Address:* 30a Wimpole Street, W1. *T:* 01-935 7311.   *[Died 19 Dec. 1973.*

McCALL, Adm. Sir Henry (William Urquhart), KCVO 1953; KBE 1951; CB 1949; DSO 1942; retired; *b* 11 June 1895; *s* of Henry John McCall, Largs, Ayrshire, and Isobel Alston McCall (*née* Dykes); *m* 1926, Helen Mary Leycester; two *d.* *Educ:* RN Colleges, Osborne and Dartmouth. Entered RNC Osborne, 1908; Lieut 1917; Comdr 1931; Capt. 1937; Naval Attaché, Buenos Aires, 1938-40; comd HMS Dido, 1940-42; Chief of Staff to Head of British Admiralty Delegn, Washington, 1943; comd HMS Howe, 1944-46; Rear-Adm. 1946; Senior British Naval Officer, Middle East, 1946-48; Flag Officer Destroyers, Mediterranean Fleet, 1949-50; Vice-Adm. 1950; Vice-Adm. Commanding Reserve Fleet, 1950-53; adm. 1953; Retd Sept. 1953. *Address:* Wonston Lee, Wonston, near Winchester, Hants. *T:* Sutton Scotney 344. *Club:* Naval and Military.
[Died 23 March 1980.

MacCALLUM, Sir Peter, Kt 1953; MC; MSc (NZ and Melbourne), MA, MB, ChB(Ed), MD (hc Melbourne), DPH, FRCP(Ed), FRS(Ed), FRACP; MCPA; Professor Emeritus, University of Melbourne, 1951; *b* 1885; *s* of Peter MacCallum, Christchurch, NZ; *m* 1st, 1919, Bella Dytes McIntosh (*d* 1927), DSc, MA, *d* of late George Cross, Timaru, NZ; three *d*; 2nd, 1928, Ursula Lillie (*d* 1941), *d* of late Archdeacon T. Grace, of Blenheim, NZ; one *s*; 3rd, Frieda Maud (*d* 1953), *d* of late Rev. A. D. Davies, Camperdown, Victoria. *Educ:* Christ's Coll. and Canterbury Univ. Coll., Christchurch, NZ; University of Edinburgh. Lecturer in Pathology Univ. and Royal Colls, Edinburgh; Prof. of Pathology, University of Melbourne, 1925-50; Hon. Dir Clinical Studies, 1948-52; Chm.: Australian Red Cross, 1951-58; Australian National Research Council, 1948-51; Australian Coll. of Dentistry, Melbourne, 1941-63; Executive Anti-Cancer Council of Victoria, 1945-63; Pres. BMA (Vic. Branch), 1946; Pres. Victorian Cancer Congress, 1960; Chm. Consultative Council on Tuberculosis, 1945-48; Member: Dental Bd of Vic., 1928-33; University Council, 1931-50 and 1953-61; Med. Bd of Vic., 1945-63. Royal Commn on Bundaberg Fatalities, 1928. Served European War, 1914-18, Capt. RAMC(SR) 1915-19, France and Belgium (MC); War of 1939-45, Lt-Col AAMC, Dir of Pathology. *Publications:* articles on Pathology and Medical Education; Advisory Report to Govt of Western Australia on Medical School establishment. *Recreation:* fishing. *Address:* 91 Princess Street, Kew, Victoria 3101, Australia. *[Died 4 March 1975.*

McCALLUM, Ronald Buchanan; Master, Pembroke College, Oxford, 1955-67; Principal of St Catharine's, Cumberland Lodge, Windsor Great Park, 1967-71; *b* 28 Aug. 1898; 4th *s* of late Andrew Fisher McCallum and of Catherine Buchanan Gibson, Paisley; *m* 1st, 1932, Ischar Gertrude Bradley (*d* 1944), Wallasey, Ches; two *d*; 2nd, 1950, Evelyn Margaret, *er d* of Sir Douglas Veale, *qv*; two *s* one *d. Educ:* Paisley Grammar Sch.; Trinity Coll., Glenalmond; Worcester Coll., Oxford. Lt Labour Corps, BEF, France, 1917-19. 1st Cl. Hons School of Modern History, Oxford, 1922. Procter Visiting Fellow to Princeton Univ., 1923. Lectr in History, Glasgow Univ., 1924; Fellow of Pembroke Coll., Oxford, 1925; Statutory Comr for Univ. of St Andrews, 1953-58. Member: Oxford City Council, 1958-67; Council of Reading Univ., 1957-67; Chm. Adv. Cttee for Univ. of Dundee, 1964-66. Hon. Fellow: Worcester Coll., Oxford, 1961; Pembroke Coll., Oxford, 1968. Hon. LLD, Dundee, 1967. *Publications:* Life of Asquith, 1936; Public Opinion and the Last Peace, 1944; Britain and France, 1944; (with Alison Readman) The General Election of 1945, 1947; Supplementary Chapter to Halévy, History of the English People, Vol. IV; The Liberal Party from Earl Grey to Asquith, 1963. *Address:* The Old Vicarage, Letcombe Regis, Wantage, Berks. *Club:* National Liberal. *[Died 18 May 1973.*

McCANDLISH, Maj.-Gen. John Edward Chalmers, CB 1946; CBE 1942 (OBE 1941); CEng; MIEE 1961; psc; *b* 11 Oct. 1901; *s* of late E. J. McCandlish, WS; *m* 1st, 1924, Margaret Storey, JP (marr. diss.), *d* of late Rev. C. E. Julian; one *s*; 2nd, 1950, Pauline, *d* of late P. L. Squirrell, MC; one *d. Educ:* Wellington Coll.; RMA, Woolwich; Staff Coll., Camberley. 2nd Lt Royal Engineers, 1921; Major 1938; Col 1944; served War of 1939-45 (despatches five times), OBE, CBE, CB; Order of the House of Orange, 2nd class); Maj.-Gen. 1947; Dir of Personnel Administration, War Office, 1946-49; retired, 1949. Colonial Development Corp., 1949-56; Chief Executive, Scottish Electrical Training Scheme, 1957-68. Hon. Col, 80 (S) Port Regt RCT (TA), 1962-67. Master, RE Draghounds, 1930-32. *Address:* The White House, Buckland, Faringdon, Oxfordshire SN7 8RB. *T:* Buckland 268. *Club:* Army and Navy. *[Died 26 Aug. 1974.*

McCANN, John, CBE 1966; MP (Lab) Rochdale, since Feb. 1958; *b* 4 Dec. 1910; *s* of John and Margaret McCann; *m* 1939, Alice Nolan; one *s* one *d. Educ:* Beech Street Elementary Sch. Diesel engineer. Councillor, Eccles, 1945; Alderman, 1952; Mayor of Eccles, 1955-56. Contested (Lab) Rochdale, 1955; an Opposition Whip, 1961-64; Vice-Chamberlain of the Household, 1966-67; a Lord Commissioner of the Treasury, 1964-66 and 1967-69. *Recreations:* public works; watching Rugby; archery. *Address:* 7 School Road, Barton, Eccles, Lancs. *T:* 061-789 4024. *[Died 16 July 1972.*

McCARTHY, Sir Edwin, Kt 1955; CBE 1952; Chairman, Commonwealth Economic Committee, 1964-67; *b* 30 March 1896; *s* of late Daniel and Catherine McCarthy, Melbourne, Australia; *m* 1938, Marjorie Mary, *d* of George and Alice Graham, Sydney; one *s* one *d. Educ:* Christian Brothers' Coll., Melbourne; Melbourne Univ. Joined Australian Commonwealth Govt Service; Sec., Dept of Commerce, 1945-50. Austr. Shipping representative in USA, 1941-44; also during this period engaged

in other work associated with war activities in USA and UK; Australian Comptroller-Gen. of Food, 1945-46. Dep. High Comr for Australia in the United Kingdom, 1950-58; Australian Ambassador to the Netherlands, 1958-62 and to Belgium, 1959-62; Australian Ambassador to the European Economic Community, 1960-64. *Recreation:* golf. *Address:* 2 Gladswood Gardens, Double Bay, NSW 2028, Australia. *Club:* University (Sydney). *[Died 4 Sept. 1980.*

McCARTHY, Ralph; Deputy Chairman, Neilson McCarthy; last Editor of The Star, London, until its demise, Oct. 1960; *b* 30 Nov. 1906; 3rd *s* of late James McCarthy and Margaret McCarthy, Gourock; *m* 1933, Nan Graham, MA (*d* 1966); two *s* one *d. Educ:* Gourock; Greenock High Sch. Reporter, Glasgow Evening Times, 1926; Sub-editor, Daily Express, 1929; Asst Editor, Sunday Express, 1933; News Chronicle: Features Editor, 1936; Asst Editor, 1938; Northern Editor, 1949; Dir, 1955; Editor and Dir, The Star, March 1957. *Address:* 24 Bruton Place, W1X 7AB. *Club:* Caledonian. *[Died 12 Oct. 1976.*

McCAUGHEY, Sir (David) Roy, Kt 1963; CMG 1956; grazier; former Chairman New South Wales Board of Elder, Smith, Goldsbrough Mort Ltd (1963-69), with which is amalgamated The Commonwealth Wool & Produce Co. Ltd (Chairman, 1950; Chairman, Elder Smith & Co., 1958); *b* Jerilderie, NSW, 2 Oct. 1898; *s* of David and Lucilla McCaughey, Coree, Jerilderie; *m* 1944, Gwendoline Patricia Camille, *d* of Walter Thomas Phelan, Ireland; no *c. Educ:* Geelong Grammar Sch., Vic., Australia. Served War 1914-18, in AIF and BEF; 2nd Lt RFA, 1918. *Address:* Box 131, GPO Sydney, NSW 2001, Australia; The Astor Flats, Macquarie Street, Sydney, NSW 2000, Australia. *T:* 27-2143 and 28-6412; Coonong, Urana, NSW 2645. *Clubs:* Australian, Union (Sydney); (Life Mem.) Australian (Melbourne). *[Died 13 Sept. 1971.*

McCLEAN, Rt. Rev. (John) Gerard; Bishop of Middlesbrough, since 1967; *b* Redcar, Yorks, 24 Sept. 1914; *s* of Robert and Elizabeth McClean. *Educ:* Marist Coll., Middlesbrough; Ushaw Coll., Durham. Ordained, 1942. Titular Bishop of Maxita and Coadjutor of Middlesbrough, Feb. 1967; Bishop of Middlesbrough, June 1967. *Recreation:* golf. *Address:* Bishop's House, 16 Cambridge Road, Middlesbrough, Cleveland. *T:* Middlesbrough 88253. *[Died 27 Aug. 1978.*

McCLELLAND, William, CB 1923; OBE; MIEE; retired; *b* 1873; *m* 1898, Isabella Shepherd (*d* 1933), Manchester; two *s* one *d. Educ:* Manchester. Asst to C. H. Wordingham, MICE, Consulting Engineer, 1901-03; Electrical Engineer, Admiralty, on design and inspection of Warship Construction, 1903-06; Electrical Engineering Asst to Dir of Dockyards, Admiralty, 1906-18; Dir of Electrical Engineering, Admiralty, SW1; Principal Electrical Adviser to Board of Admiralty, 1919-34; responsible for designs and equipment of electrical installations in all HM ships; served on Defence Cttees; Ex-Hon. Treas. and Mem. Council of Instn of Electrical Engineers; Gen. Board of National Physical Laboratory, 1930-36; responsible for repair of electrical installations in all HM ships during the war in 1914-18; also for electrical equipment for many naval bases and emergency dockyards. *Publication:* The Applications of Electricity in Warships. *Address:* 76 Marine Court, St Leonards-on-Sea, Sussex. *T:* Hastings 639. *[Died 24 Jan. 1971.*

McCLEMENS, John Henry; formerly Chief Judge at Common Law, an additional Judge of Appeal, Supreme Court of New South Wales; *b* 7 March 1905; *m* Joan Raymunde Delaney (Principal, Petersham Girls' High Sch.), *d* of J. A. Delaney. *Educ:* N Sydney Boys' High Sch.; Sydney Univ. (BA, LLB). Admitted Solicitor, Supreme Court of NSW, 1929; Barrister, 1930; KC 1945; practised largely in Common Law and Appeal work until appt to Bench; Justice of Supreme Ct of NSW, 1951. Chm. Bd of Management, Mater Misericordiæ Gen. Hosp., N Sydney; Former Pres. Prisoners Aid Assoc. (NSW); Dep. Chm. Adv. Cttee, Dept of Criminology, Sydney Univ.; rep. Australia at UN Conventions on Crime and Treatment of Offenders; led delegn to Stockholm Convention, 1965; former Pres., Australian Prison After-Care Council; former Pres., Australian Council of National Trusts and Nat. Trust of Aust. (NSW); former Pres., Australian Crime Prevention Council. Australian Governmental participant, United Nations Seminar on the Role of the Police in the Protection of Human Rights, Canberra, 1963; Mem., Ministerial Working Party to review Penal Legislation; Chm., Papal Welcome Cttee, 1970. KCSG 1960. *Publications:* Report of Royal Commission on Callan Park Mental Hospital, 1961; contribs to Australian Law Jl, Sydney Law Review, Australian Jl of Criminology, Social Service (Review). *Recreation:* gardening. *Address:* 7 Sugarloaf Crescent, Castlecrag, NSW 2068, Australia. *Club:* University (Sydney). *[Died 3 Nov. 1975.*

MACCLESFIELD, 7th Earl of *cr* 1721; **George Loveden William Henry Parker;** Baron Parker, 1716; Viscount Parker, 1721; Lord Lieutenant of County of Oxford, 1954-63; *b* 24 May 1888; *g s* of 6th Earl, and *o c* of Viscount Parker (*d* 1895) and Carine Agnes (*d* 1919), *d* of late Pryse Loveden, Gogerddan, Cardigan (she *m* 2nd, 1897, Capt. L. W. Matthews, 5th Dragoon Guards); *S* grandfather, 1896; *m* 1909, Lilian Joanna Vere (*d* 1974), *d* of Major Charles Boyle, The Priory, Great Milton, Oxon; two *s.* Chm., Oxfordshire CC, 1937-70. DL 1935, JP 1911, Oxon. *Heir: s* Viscount Parker. *Address:* Shirburn Castle, Watlington, Oxon. *Club:* Royal Yacht Squadron (Cowes).   [*Died* 20 *Sept.* 1975.

McCLINTIC, Mrs Guthrie; *see* Cornell, Katharine.

McCLOUGHRY, Air Vice-Marshal Edgar J. K.; *see* Kingston-McCloughry.

MacCOLL, James Eugene, JP; MP (Lab) Widnes Division of Lancashire since 1950; *b* 27 June 1908; *y s* of late Hugo MacColl and Maude Macarthy, Sunderland. *Educ:* Sedbergh Sch.; Balliol Coll., Oxford (Exhibitioner); Univ. of Chicago. Librarian, Oxford Union, 1930; Commonwealth Fund Fellow, 1930-32; Barrister, Inner Temple, 1933; Co-opted Mem., LCC Education Cttee, 1936-46; Paddington Metropolitan Borough Council, 1934 (Mayor of Paddington, 1947-49); JP County of London, 1938. Jt Parly Sec., Min. of Housing and Local Govt, 1964-69. Research Asst, Polit. and Economic Planning Trust, 1945-50; Chm.'s Panel, London Juvenile Courts, 1946-64; Hemel Hempstead New Towns Corporation, 1946-50; Domestic Coal Consumers Council, 1947-50. *Publications:* (with E. C. R. Hadfield) Pilot Guide to Political London, 1945; British Local Government, 1948; articles in Political Quarterly, Fortnightly, Public Administration. *Address:* 21 Randolph Road, W9. *T:* 01-286 4347.   [*Died* 16 *June* 1971.

MacCOLL, René; author; Chief Foreign Correspondent, The Daily Express, 1959-69; *b* 12 Jan. 1905; *yr s* of Dugald Sutherland MacColl and Andrée Zabé; *m* 1st, 1928, Helen (*d* 1945), *o d* of Walter Edwards, Boyertown, Pa, USA; one *s* one *d*; 2nd, 1946, Margaret Hermione, *e d* of Lt-Col Kenneth H. Bruce, DSO, and Lorna Burn-Murdoch. *Educ:* University College Sch., London; Lincoln Coll., Oxford. Sec. to late Van-Lear Black, Baltimore, Md, 1926-29 (with whom flew on his pioneering flights, incl. London-Capetown-London, Jan.-Apr. 1929). Reporter on Baltimore Sun, 1927-28; joined Daily Telegraph, 1929 (Correspondent in Spanish Civil War, Franco side, 1939). Press Liaison, RAFVR (Sqdn Ldr) in France, 1939-40: Dir, Press and Radio Div., British Information Services, New York, 1941-45. Washington Correspondent, Daily Express, 1946-48; Paris Correspondent, 1949-50; Chief American Correspondent, 1951-52; Roving Reporter, 1953-58. *Publications:* A Flying Start, 1939; Assignment Stuffed Shirt, 1952; Just Back from Russia, 1955; Roger Casement: A New Judgement, 1956; Deadline and Dateline, 1956; Land of Ghengis Khan, 1963. *Recreation:* numismatics. *Address:* Clock Lodge, Crowborough, Sussex. *T:* Crowborough 61364. *Clubs:* Garrick; National Press (Washington, DC).   [*Died* 20 *May* 1971.

McCOLVIN, Lionel Roy, CBE 1951; FLA; Librarian, City of Westminster Public Libraries, 1938-61; *b* Newcastle upon Tyne, 30 Nov. 1896; 2nd *s* of late John Andrew McColvin, artist; *m* 1922, Mary Carter; two *s* two *d. Educ:* Croydon. Reference Librarian, Croydon Public Libraries, to 1921; Dep. Librarian, Wigan Public Libraries, 1921-24; Chief Librarian, Ipswich Public Libraries, 1924-31; Chief Librarian, Hampstead Public Libraries and Curator of the Keats House and Museum, Hampstead, 1931-38; Fellow and Hons Diplomate of Library Assoc.; Councillor, 1925-, Pres., 1952 (Hon. Sec., 1934-51), Library Assoc.; visited USA to study library administration on behalf of the Library Assoc., 1936, Middle East, Australia, NZ and USA, 1946-47, Germany, 1950 and 1956, Sweden, Norway, etc; Pres., Soc. of Municipal and County Chief Librarians, 1953-; Pres., Internat. Fedn of Library Assocs, 1953-; Mem. Exec. Cttee of Nat. Central Library, UNESCO; Nat. Cooperating Body for Libraries, Cen. Music Library, Brit. Council Advisory Panel on Books and Libraries, etc. *Publications:* Music in Public Libraries, 1924; The Theory of Book Selection, 1925; Euterpe or the future of art, 1926; Library Extension Work and Publicity, 1927; How to Find Out, 1933, new edn 1947; How to Use Books, 1933, new edn 1947; How to Enjoy Music, 1934; How to Enjoy Plays, 1934; Library Stock and Assistance to Readers, 1936; Libraries and the Public, 1937; Music Libraries (with Harold Reeves), 1937-38; Library Staffs, 1939; The Public Library System of Great Britain, 1942; British Libraries (with J. Revie), 1946; Public Libraries in Australia, 1947; Library Extension (for UNESCO), 1950; The Personal Library, 1953; Reference Library Stock, 1952; The Chance to Read, 1956; Library Service for Children (for UNESCO), 1957;

Ed. 'Librarian' Subject Guide to Books, 1958. *Recreations:* music, painting, letter-writing, talking. *Address:* 17 Seymour Court, Eversley Park Road, N21.   [*Died* 16 *Jan.* 1976.

McCONNELL, Adams Andrew, MA, MCh (Hon.) Dublin; FRCSI; Hon. FRCS; Regius Professor of Surgery, Dublin University, 1946-61; Surgeon Richmond Hospital, Dublin; Consulting Surgeon to Dr Steeven's Hospital, Dublin, National Children's Hospital, Dublin, Stewart Institution, Palmerstown, Co. Dublin; Consulting Neurological Surgeon to the Royal Victoria Eye and Ear Hospital, Dublin; FRSM; Hon. Fellow Trinity College, Dublin; Ex-President and Emeritus Member, Society of British Neurological Surgeons; late Professor of Surgery and Ex-President RCS in Ireland; *b* 1884; *s* of Dr Andrew McConnell, Belfast; *m* 1st, 1914, Nora (*d* 1968), *d* of S. P. Boyd, DL, Dublin; 2nd, 1969, Gladys Danefield, *d* of David Hopkins, Dublin. *Educ:* Royal Academical Institution, Belfast; Trinity Coll., Dublin. First Prizeman in Anatomy and Physiology, Trinity Coll.; Medical Scholar in Anatomy and Institutes of Medicine. First Senior Moderator (large Gold Medal) in Natural Science; Demonstrator in Zoology and Physiology; Asst to Prof. of Anatomy, Trinity Coll., 1910-12; Anæsthetist and Lectr on Anæsthetics, Sir Patrick Dun's Hosp., Dublin, 1909-10; Anæsthetist Incorporated Dental Hosp., 1910-12; Fellow (Pres. 1946, 1947) Royal Academy of Medicine in Ireland; Ex-Pres. Dublin Univ. Biological Assoc.; Hon. member: Société de Neuro-Chirurgie de Langue Française; Nordisk Neurokirurisk Förening; La Real Academia Nacional de Medicina; Asociación Española de Neuropsiquiatria; late Lectr on Applied Anatomy Trinity Coll., Dublin. *Publications:* many papers on neurosurgery to medical journals. *Address:* Conna, Shankill, Co. Dublin. *T:* Dublin 851607. *Clubs:* University, Friendly Brothers (Dublin).   [*Died* 5 *April* 1973.

McCORMACK, John William; Member US House of Representatives 1927-70; House Majority Leader (Democrat) 1955-70 (with exception 4 years Democrat Whip); Speaker, 1962-70; lawyer; *b* Boston, Mass., 21 Dec. 1891; *s* of Joseph H. McCormack and Mary E. O'Brien; *m* 1920, M. Harriet Joyce (*d* 1971). *Educ:* public schools. Admitted Massachusetts Bar, 1913, practised law, Boston, firm of McCormack & Hardy; Mem. Mass Const. Conv., 1917-18, House of Representatives, 1920-22, State Senate, 1923-26. Holds hon. degrees. Kt of Malta, 1st class; Kt Comdr, with star, St Gregory the Great. *Address:* 111 Perkins Street, Jamaica Plain, Mass 02130, USA.
          [*Died* 22 *Nov.* 1980.

McCORMACK, Percy Hicks, FIA; General Manager and Actuary, Provident Mutual Life Assurance Association, 1938-51, Director, 1951-66; *b* 23 Aug. 1890; *s* of late Martin McCormack, formerly of Knutsford, Cheshire, and Elizabeth Ann, *d* of Edmund Hicks; *m* 1926, Marjorie Vera Stewart, *d* of Charles A. Norris, Frittenden; two *s. Educ:* Bickerton, Birkdale; Liverpool Univ. Joint Asst Actuary, Provident Mutual Life Assurance Assoc., 1920; Joint Actuary, 1928; Consulting Actuary, London, Midland & Scottish Railway Co. and British Railways (Midland Region), 1938-55; Dir, London & Lomond Investment Trust Ltd, 1938-68. *Publications:* contribs to jls on actuarial and other subjects. *Address:* 12B Bedford Towers, Brighton, East Sussex. *Club:* Athenæum. [*Died* 12 *Feb.* 1980.

McCORQUODALE OF NEWTON, 1st Baron *cr* 1955, of Newton-le-Willows; **Malcolm Stewart McCorquodale,** PC 1945; KCVO 1965; *b* 29 March 1901; 2nd *s* of late Norman McCorquodale, Winslow Hall, Bucks; *m* 1st, 1931, Winifred (*d* 1960), *d* of late J. O. M. Clark; two *d*; 2nd, 1962, Hon. Mrs Gibb. *Educ:* Harrow; Christ Church, Oxford (scholar, MA). MP (Nat C) Sowerby Div. of Yorks, 1931-45; Parly Sec., Min. of Labour and National Service, 1942-45; MP (C) Epsom Div. of Surrey, Nov. 1947-55. Served War of 1939-45, RAFVR. Chm., McCorquodale & Co. Ltd, and other printing companies till 1942, and again 1945-67, Pres., 1968-; Director: United Kingdom Provident Institution; Bank of Scotland Ltd, 1960-71; Pres., British Employers' Confederation, 1960 (Vice-Pres. 1955). Governor of Harrow School, 1962-71, Chm., 1964-71. *Heir:* none. *Address:* 30 Jay Mews, SW7; Cotswold Park, Cirencester, Glos. *Clubs:* Carlton, Royal Automobile.
          [*Died* 25 *Sept.* 1971 (*ext*).

McCOY, William Frederick, QC; Senior Crown Prosecutor for the City of Belfast, 1949-67; retired; *s* of late William and C. L. McCoy, Fivemiletown, Co. Tyrone; *m* 1940, Margaret Edna Earls; two *s. Educ:* Clones High Sch. Admitted Solicitor of Supreme Court of Judicature, Ireland, 1907; called to Irish Bar, 1920; joined NW Circuit and, on establishment of Northern Ireland, became member of Circuit of N Ireland; Resident Magistrate, City of Belfast, 1937-43; called to Inner Bar, 1939, Bencher, 1942. MP (U) South Tyrone, Northern Ireland House of Commons, 1945-65. Elected Speaker Northern Ireland House of Commons, Jan. 1956; resigned April 1956. *Recreations:* hunting and shooting. *Address:* Knockballymore, Magheraveely, Co. Fermanagh. *T:* Newtownbutler 211. *Club:* Tyrone County (Omagh). [*Died 4 Dec.* 1976.

McCRACKEN, Esther Helen; wrote for stage and screen; Member of Court, Newcastle University; Member, Alnwick and Rothbury Hospital Management Committee; *b* 25 June 1902; *d* of Henry Armstrong and Maud Clapham; *m* 1st, 1926, Lt-Col Angus Murray McCracken, DSO, MC, RA (died of wounds in Italy, 1943); two *d*; 2nd, 1944, Mungo Campbell; (one *d* decd). *Educ:* Central Newcastle High Sch. War of 1939-45, discharged from WRNS, 1942, on compassionate grounds. Eight years with Newcastle Repertory Theatre Company; Playhouse, Newcastle, 1929-; fairly regular broadcasting of own songs, sketches, etc (and other people's), 1935-; first attempt at writing short story, The Willing Spirit, published by Daily Herald, 1936, quickly followed by broadcast version and then by stage version produced by herself, acted by YWCA team and winning Drama Festival at Old Vic; first 3-act play, Quiet Wedding, Richmond Theatre, spring 1938, Wyndham's, Oct. 1938; Counter Attraction, Richmond, 1938; White Elephants, Richmond, 1940; Quiet Weekend, Wyndham's, 1941; Living Room, Garrick Theatre, 1943; No Medals, Vaudeville, 1944; Cry Liberty, Vaudeville, 1950. *Publications:* The Willing Spirit (1-Act Play), 1937; Behind the Lace Curtains (1-Act Play), 1937; North Country Lullaby (Song), 1937; Quiet Wedding (3-Act Play), 1938; Living Room; Quiet Weekend. *Recreations:* reading, writing, sailing. *Address:* Rothley Lake, Hartburn, Morpeth, Northumberland. *T:* Scots Gap 255. *Club:* English-Speaking Union. [*Died 9 Aug.* 1971.

McCRIE, John Gibb, OBE 1945; TD 1947; (part-time) Associate Dean of Faculty of Medicine, University of Nottingham, since 1969; *b* 24 Nov. 1902; *o c* of C. G. McCrie and J. W. Gibb, Edinburgh; *m* 1947, Margaret Isabella, *d* of Walter Forrest and Margaret Logan. *Educ:* George Watson's Coll., Edinburgh; Univ. of Edinburgh. MB, ChB (1st Class Hons), Edinburgh, 1925; MRCPE 1928; FRCPE 1931; Lectr in Medicine, Univ. of Edinburgh, 1931-46; Asst Physician, Royal Infirmary, Edinburgh, 1936-38; Physician, and Dep.-Director of the Medical Unit, Edinburgh Municipal Hospitals, 1938-46; Senior Administrative Officer, School of Medicine, University of Leeds, 1946-47; Dean of the Faculty of Medicine, 1947-68, Hon. Lectr in History of Medicine, 1962-72, Univ. of Sheffield; (part-time) Associate Dean of Faculty of Medicine, Univ. of Nottingham, 1969-76. Former Member, Sheffield Regional Hospital Board and Board of Governors, United Sheffield Hospitals; former Hon. Consultant (Adviser in Medical Teaching), United Sheffield Hospitals; former (Co-opted) Mem., N Midlands (Sheffield) Faculty, Royal Coll. of General Practitioners. Representative of Univ. of Sheffield on GMC, 1947-72; Vice-Pres., Assoc. for Study of Medical Education; Hon. Vice-Pres., S Yorks Branch, British Red Cross Society. Hon. Lt-Col, RAMC (TA). Served War of 1939-45 with BEF, 1940, and BNAF and CMF, 1942-45 (Lieut-Colonel, Acting Colonel). Hon. MD Sheffield, 1974. *Publications:* various papers on clinical subjects in medical jls. *Address:* 14 Ireton Grove, Attenborough, Nottingham NG9 6BJ. *T:* Nottingham 255132.
[*Died 24 Jan.* 1977.

McCRINDLE, Major John Ronald, CMG 1950; OBE 1919; MC; Chairman Breaches Commission International Air Transport Association, 1959-68; *b* 29 Nov. 1894; *s* of J. R. Ronald McCrindle, MB, CM, Kingston, Jamaica; *m* 1st, 1921, Odette, *d* of J. F. Feder, New York; one *s*; 2nd, 1932, Susan Ertz, FRSL, *d* of Charles Edward and Mary Gertrude Ertz. *Educ:* Jamaica Coll.; Glasgow Univ.; Harvard Univ. 2nd Lieut, Gordon Highlanders TF, Aug. 1914; seconded Royal Flying Corps, Nov. 1914; served France, Mesopotamia, Egypt, Palestine (OBE, MC, despatches thrice); Permanent Commission, Royal Air Force, 1919; Commanded London-Paris Communication Squadron during Peace Conference, 1919; Asst to British Air Representative in Paris on Council of Ambassadors, Marshal Foch's Cttee and Aeronautical Adv. Cttee, 1919-22; Mission of Supreme Council of Peace Conference to Bucharest and Budapest, 1919; retired, 1922. Called to Bar, Lincoln's Inn, 1927; practised Chancery Bar, 1927-35; Managing Director, British Airways Ltd, 1935-40; Dep. Director-General, BOAC, 1940-47; Adviser on international affairs to BOAC, 1948-58; Managing Director (External Affairs) BOAC, 1947-49; Member of the Board, 1946-58. Mem. Exec. Cttee International Air Transport Assoc., 1945-58; Adviser: UK Delegn, Chicago Civil Aviation Conference, 1944; Civil Aviation Conference, Bermuda, 1946; other internat. aviation confs, 1944-58. Officer of the Crown (Belgium); Commander of Order of Orange Nassau; Officer of Legion of Honour; Commander, 2nd Class of

Order of Vasa (Sweden). *Address:* 17 Sloane Court West, SW3. *T:* 01-730 6361; Lossenham Manor, Newenden, Hawkhurst, Kent. *T:* Northiam 2196. *Clubs:* Athenæum, Naval and Military. [*Died 12 March* 1977.

McCULLAGH, Sir (Joseph) Crawford, 2nd Bt *cr* 1935; *b* 25 Sept. 1907; *s* of Sir Crawford McCullagh, 1st Bt, PC (N Ireland), DL, and Margaret Craig, CBE (*d* 1944), *d* of William Brodie, Bolton-le-Moors; *S* father, 1948; *m* 1937, Elizabeth Green. *Educ:* Campbell Coll., Belfast. Ex-Councillor Belfast Corporation, Clifton Ward. *Recreation:* aviculture. *Heir:* none. *Address:* Lismara, Whiteabbey, Co. Antrim. *T:* Whiteabbey 2220. *Clubs:* Royal Ulster Yacht (Bangor, Co. Down); North of Ireland Cricket and Football (Belfast). [*Died 16 Jan.* 1974 (*ext*).

McCULLOUGH, Donald; see McCullough, W. D. H.

McCULLOUGH, (William) Donald (Hamilton), MA; advertising and public relations consultant, writer and broadcaster; *b* 15 Aug. 1901; *s* of late Rev. W. C. McCullough, BA, LLB, St Margaret's Manse, Hawick; *m* Nan, *yr d* of late Captain H. L. Watts-Jones, RN; three *s* two *d*. *Educ:* Watson's Coll.; Edinburgh Univ. RAFVR, 1939-40. National Trust: Mem., Exec. and Neptune Cttees, 1950-69; Chm., Publicity Cttee; Mem., CPRE; Mem., Cttee, Norfolk Soc. *Publications:* How to Run a Brains Trust, 1947; with Fougasse: Aces Made Easy, 1934; You Have Been Warned, 1935; Many Happy Returns, 1936; Fancy Meeting You, 1947; Question Mark, 1949; with Ernest Clegg: Countryman County Maps, 1946. *Recreations:* golf, sailing. *Address:* Flagstaff House, Burnham Overy Staithe, Norfolk. *TA* and *T:* Burnham Market 248. *Clubs:* Bath; Brancaster; Pilgrims. [*Died 19 Jan.* 1978.

McDAVID, Sir Edwin Frank, Kt 1953; CMG 1948; CBE 1942 (MBE 1933); retired; *b* 26 Oct. 1895; *s* of late E. N. McDavid, Company Secretary, and Elizabeth McDavid; *m* 1920, Elma Hildred Delph; no *c*. *Educ:* Queen's Coll., British Guiana. Served with Fitzpatrick, Graham and Co., Chartered Accountants, 1914-20; Secretary, Excess Profits Tax Board of Assessment, British Guiana, 1920; Chief Accountant, British Guiana Govt Railway and Steamer Services, 1923; acted as Man. Dir of above Services, 1928; Deputy Colonial Treas., British Guiana, 1929; Commissioner of Income Tax, 1929-53; Financial Secretary (formerly Colonial Treasurer) and Member of Executive and Legislative Councils, 1935-53; Chairman: British Guiana Rice Marketing Board, 1939-46; British Guiana Rice Development Co., 1952-60; President, State Council, 1953; MEC, MLC, Minister of Lands and Agriculture, 1954-57. Managing Director, Demerara Mutual Life Assurance Society Ltd, 1960-62 (Chairman, 1957-59). Chairman, British Guiana Public Library, 1941-61; Hon. Colonel British Guiana Volunteer Force, 1954-62. *Address:* c/o Barclays Bank Ltd, 21 High Street, Winchester, Hants. [*Died 1 Aug.* 1980.

MacDERMOT, The, (Charles John), styled Prince of Coolavin; *b* 20 Feb. 1899; 2nd and *e* surv. *s* of late Charles E., The MacDermot, and Caroline MacDermot; *m* 1954, Felicity, *d* of Edward T. MacDermot, MA, JP, Lillycombe, Porlock, Somerset. *Educ:* Stonyhurst Coll.; Trinity Coll., Dublin. *Heir: b* Sir Dermot F. MacDermot, KCMG, CBE. *Address:* Coolavin, Ballaghaderreen, Co. Roscommon. [*Died 7 May* 1979.

MacDERMOTT, Baron (Life Peer), *cr* 1947, of Belmont; **John Clarke MacDermott,** PC 1947, PC (Northern Ireland), 1940; MC; LLD; Lord Chief Justice of Northern Ireland, 1951-71; *b* 12 April 1896; *s* of late Rev. John and Lydia Allen MacDermott, Belmont, Belfast; *m* 1926, Louise Palmer, *o d* of Rev. J. C. Johnston, MA, DD; two *s* two *d*. *Educ:* Campbell Coll., Belfast; Queen's Univ. of Belfast. Foundation Scholar, 1914. Served in European War in France: Lieut, 51st Bn MGC (MC). LLB First Class Honours, 1921; Victoria Prizeman and Exhibitioner, King's Inns, Dublin; called to Irish Bar, 1921; Lecturer in Jurisprudence, Queen's Univ. of Belfast, 1931-35; appointed to determine Industrial Assurance Disputes in Northern Ireland, 1929-38; KC (Northern Ireland), 1936; MP (U) Queen's University of Belfast, Parliament of Northern Ireland, 1938-44; Governor, Campbell Coll., 1934-59; Chairman Joint Select Cttee on Road and Rail Transport in Northern Ireland, 1939; Sept. 1939, Major RA; Minister of Public Security for Northern Ireland, June 1940-Nov. 1941; Attorney-General, 1941-44; Judge, High Court of Justice, Northern Ireland, 1944-47; a Lord of Appeal in Ordinary, 1947-51; Chairman, National Arbitration Tribunal, Northern Ireland, 1944-46; Bencher Inn of Court of Northern Ireland; Hon. Bencher Gray's Inn, 1947 Hamlyn Lectures on Protection from Power, 1957; Chairman Commission on Isle of Man Constitution, 1958. Pro-Chancellor Queen's Univ. of Belfast, 1951-69. Hon. LLD: QUB, 1951 Edinburgh, 1958; Cambridge, 1968. *Address:* Glenburn, 8

Cairnburn Road, Belfast 4. *T:* Belfast 63361. *Clubs:* Athenæum; Ulster (Belfast).   [*Died* 13 *July* 1979.

McDERMOTT, Geoffrey Lyster, CMG 1957; diplomat, author and journalist; retired from Foreign Service, 1962; *b* 7 Oct. 1912; *o s* of late Captain J. W. McDermott, CIE, and Mrs G. E. McDermott; *m* 1st, 1937, Ruth Mary, *d* of late Sir Arthur Fleming, CBE; one *s* one *d*; 2nd, 1947, Elizabeth Marion Robertson; two *s* (and one step *s*). *Educ:* Marlborough Coll. (scholar); King's Coll., Cambridge. Scholar in Mod. Langs at King's, 1930; 1st class hons both parts of Mod. Langs tripos, 1931 and 1933. Entered Diplomatic Service, 1935; 3rd Sec., FO, 1935; Sofia, 1938; 2nd Sec., Ankara, 1941; FO, 1943; 1st Sec., FO, 1944; Cairo, 1946; Santiago, 1948; Chargé d'Affaires there, 1949, 1950, 1951; Counsellor and Head of Permanent Under-Secretary's Dept in the Foreign Office, 1953-56; Minister HM Foreign Service, employed in Foreign Office, 1956-58; ambassadorial rank as Political Representative with Middle East Forces, Cyprus, 1958-61, and as HM Minister in Berlin, 1961-62. Chm., Cttee for the Recognition of German Democratic Republic, 1971-73. FRSA 1958. *Publications:* Berlin: Success of a Mission?, 1963; The Eden Legacy and the Decline of British Diplomacy, 1969; Leader Lost: a biography of Hugh Gaitskell, 1972; The New Diplomacy, 1973; numerous articles. *Recreations:* walking, motoring, and the arts. *Address:* 22 Queen Street, W1X 7PJ. *T:* 01-499 1466; The Old Rectory, Ripple, near Tewkesbury, Glos. *T:* Upton-upon-Severn 2444. *Clubs:* Boodle's, Garrick.   [*Died* 29 *Nov.* 1978.

McDIARMID, Hugh; *see* Grieve, C. M.

MACDIARMID, Niall Campbell; Chairman: Sanderson Kayser Ltd, since 1974; CompAir Ltd, since 1974; Director: Sketchley Ltd (Chairman, 1975-77); Provincial Insurance Co. Ltd; Baker Perkins Holdings Ltd; Unicorn Industries Ltd; *b* 7 June 1919; *y s* of Sir Allan Campbell Macdiarmid, and Grace Buchanan (*née* McClure); *m* 1946, Patricia Isobel Mackie-Campbell, *yr d* of Geordie Osmonde Lorne Campbell and Jessie Isobel (*née* Mackie); two *d* (and one *d* decd). *Educ:* Uppingham Sch.; Magdalen Coll., Oxford. Served War of 1939-45 with The Argyll and Sutherland Highlanders (despatches three times). Man. Dir, The Stanton Ironworks Co. Ltd (later Stanton and Staveley Ltd), 1957-62, Chm., 1962-64; Chm., Stewarts and Lloyds Ltd, 1964-69; Dir, The United Steel Companies Ltd, 1964-67; Man. Dir, Northern and Tubes Group, BSC, 1967-69; Dep. Chm., Vickers Ltd, 1970-71. Member: Iron and Steel Board, 1961-67; BSC, 1967-69; E Midlands Gas Board, 1962-67; Pres., Iron and Steel Inst., 1969-70. Trustee of Uppingham School (Chairman, 1967-77); Trustee, Duke of Edinburgh's Award, 1963-71. *Address:* Hillside House, Tinwell Road, Stamford, Lincs. *T:* Stamford 3075. *Club:* Lansdowne.   [*Died* 12 *May* 1978.

MACDONA, Brian Fraser, CBE 1967; Director, Barclays Bank DCO and Barclays Export Finance Co. Ltd, since 1964; *b* 26 Jan. 1901; *o s* of late G. Bagot Macdona, Streatham, and Hannah Mary (*née* Gomersall); *m* 1923, Elsie May, *d* of late E. W. Fellgate, Ealing; no *c*. *Educ:* Modern Sch., Streatham. FIB 1951. Jun. Clerk, Van den Berghs Ltd, 1915-17; joined Barclays Bank Ltd, Head Office, 1917; served in Suffolk, 1920-22; attached Barclays Bank (Dominion, Colonial and Overseas), London, Sudan, S Africa, Rhodesia, E Africa, 1927-29; transf. in 1929 to that bank and appointed Bank Manager at Nairobi, Mombasa, Eldoret and Kampala, 1929-37; Supt, E African Brs and Local Dir's Asst, Nairobi, 1937; Local Dir, E Africa, 1942-45, Egypt, Sudan and Libya, 1945-48; Asst Gen. Man., Head Office, London, 1948; Gen. Man. 1951; Sen. Gen. Man. 1959-64. Dir, Bank of London & Montreal Ltd, 1964-70. Served as govt nominee, various projects, and as office-bearer, numerous assocs, cttees, bds, etc in E Africa and Egypt. Hon. Treasurer: 20th Congress, IGU, 1964; Brit. Inst. History and Archaeology in E Africa, 1965-; Royal African Soc., 1951-53 (Vice-Chm. of Council, 1953-65, Chm. 1965-); Mem. Council: Mount Everest Foundn, 1964-69; RSA, 1965 (Jt Treas. 1968-); Hakluyt Soc., 1967-; RGS, 1960-70 (Hon. Treas. 1970-); Internat. Students Trust, 1961 (Dep. Chm. of Govs, 1964-); Royal Commonwealth Soc., 1960-69 (Chm., 1969-). Gov., Victoria Coll., Alexandria, 1945-. Mem. Adv. Commn: of FBI, on possibilities of Nigerian Industrialisation, 1961; of Western Hemisphere Export Council, on British Exports and W Indies Industrialisation, 1962. Has lectured on African affairs in N America and UK. Visited Africa and the Caribbean frequently from 1950, also Moscow, Australasia and the Americas. Liveryman, Scriveners' Co., 1955-; Freeman, City of London, 1955. Lord Mayor's medal for services to export, 1964. Hon. FRGS 1967. *Recreations:* motoring, watching cricket, admiring other people gardening, writing and talking about Africa and Commonwealth problems. *Address:* Square Cottage, East Road, St George's Hill,

Weybridge, Surrey. *T:* Weybridge 42115. *Clubs:* Overseas Bankers, City Livery, MCC, Royal Commonwealth Society; Nairobi, Kenya Kongonis (Kenya); Kampala (Uganda).
[*Died* 22 *May* 1971.

MACDONALD, Adam Davidson, MA, MSc, MD; retired as Leech Professor of Pharmacology in the University of Manchester, Sept. 1964; *b* Perth, Scotland, 17 Oct. 1895; *s* of Robert Macdonald, schoolmaster; *m* 1927, Helen Muriel Anderson, Edinburgh; one *s* two *d*. *Educ:* High School of Dundee; Univ. of Edinburgh (Neill Arnott Scholar and Goodsir Fellow). Demonstrator in Physiology, Univ. of Edinburgh; Lectr in Experimental Physiology and Reader in Pharmacology, Univ. of Manchester. *Publications:* various papers in physiological and pharmacological journals. *Recreations:* golf, gardening. *Address:* 2 Broadway Avenue, Cheadle, Cheshire. *T:* 061-428 2435.   [*Died* 21 *May* 1978.

McDONALD, Alexander Hugh, FBA 1967; MA, PhD; LittD; Life Fellow of Clare College, Cambridge, 1973; Honorary Research Fellow, University of Western Australia, since 1975; *b* 19 May 1908; *s* of Rev. William and Mary McDonald; *m* 1941, Joan Urey, *d* of Sir Martin and Ada McIlrath. *Educ:* Auckland Grammar Sch.; Auckland Univ. Coll., NZ; Clare Coll., Cambridge. Univ. of NZ: BA, Sen. Schol. in Greek, 1928; MA, Double First in Latin and Greek, Travelling Scholarship in Arts, 1929; Clare Coll., Cambridge: Exhibitioner, First in Classical Tripos, Part II, 1932; Research at Göttingen Univ., 1933; Senior Research Student, Clare Coll., 1934; PhD (Cambridge) 1936. Lecturer in Ancient History, Nottingham University Coll., 1934-38; Sydney Univ., Australia: Reader in Ancient History, 1939-44; Acting Prof. of Latin, 1945, Prof. of Ancient World History, 1945-51; Lectr in Ancient Hist., Univ. of Cambridge, 1952-73; Fellow, 1952-73, Sen. Tutor, 1954-57, and Steward, 1963-65, Clare Coll., Cambridge. Editor, Current Affairs Bulletin, Australian Army, 1943-46; News Commentator, ABC, 1943-51; Liaison Officer (NSW) for Colonial Service appointments, 1946-51. Acting Prof. of Ancient History, Chicago Univ., 1954. Mem. Inst. Advanced Study, Princeton, NJ, 1966; Chairman Archæol. Faculty, British School at Rome, 1967-70; President: Cambridge Philological Soc., 1968-70; Roman Soc., 1971-74. Hon. LLD Glasgow, 1948; Hon. LittD Auckland, 1967. Hon. FAHA 1975. *Publications:* Japanese Imperialism, 1944; (ed) Trusteeship in the Pacific, 1948; (ed) Oxford Text of Livy, 1937, Vol. V, 1965; Republican Rome, 1966; papers and reviews in Jl of Roman Studies; reviews in Classical Review. *Recreations:* golf, theatre. *Address:* 13A Strathearn, 16 Kings Park Avenue, Crawley, WA 6009, Australia. *T:* Perth (WA) 386.3391. *Club:* University (Sydney).
[*Died* 9 *July* 1979.

McDONALD, Air Comdt Ann Smith, CB 1972; RRC 1972 (ARRC 1958); QHNS 1970; Matron-in-Chief Princess Mary's Royal Air Force Nursing Service, since Sept. 1970; *b* 21 Oct. 1914; *d* of late Archibald McDonald. *Educ:* Queen's Park Sch., Glasgow. SRFN, Belvidere Hosp. Glasgow, 1935; SRN, Victoria Infirmary, Glasgow, 1939. Joined PMRAFNS, 1941; Matron, 1959; Senior Matron, 1966; Principal Matron, 1968 (having served in Hospitals and Med. Centres in UK, West Africa, India, Aden, Germany). OStJ 1960. *Address:* Ministry of Defence NSB(RAF), 1-6 Tavistock Square, WC1. *T:* 01-387 5040 (Ext. 203). *Club:* Royal Air Force. [*Died* 30 *May* 1972.

MACDONALD of Sleat, Miss Celia Violet Bosville, CBE 1937 (OBE 1919); *b* Thorpe Hall, Bridlington, 28 Jan. 1889; *d* of Sir Alexander Wentworth Macdonald Bosville Macdonald of the Isles, 14th Bt, and 21st Chief of Sleat. *Educ:* home. At one time Scoutmaster and Commissioner for Girl Guides in E Riding, Yorks; OBE in 1919 for War Work; in 1921 joined Lady Frances Ryder in her private scheme for hospitality for Dominion Students, and became Chairman of The Dominions Fellowship Trust formed out of that work in 1948. Retired 1961. Coronation Medal, 1953. Hon. MA Oxford, 1959. *Recreations:* music, travelling. *Address:* 90 Whitelands House, Cheltenham Terrace, SW3.   [*Died* 4 *Jan.* 1976.

MACDONALD, Maj.-Gen. Harry, CB 1940; CIE 1946; DSO 1918; DL Inverness-shire, 1948; *b* 3 May 1886; *s* of late John Macdonald, Redcliff, Portree, Isle of Skye, and late Anne Marjory Walker; *m* 1934, Sheila Mairi Adelaide, *d* of late Brig.-Gen. Sir Walter C. Ross, KBE, Cromarty; three *d*. *Educ:* Fettes Coll., Edinburgh; RMC Sandhurst. Joined Indian Army, 1906; served European War, 1914-19 (despatches five times, Bt Major, DSO, Croix de Guerre avec palmes); graduated at Staff Coll., Camberley, 1919; Gen. Staff, War Office, 1920-24; Major, 1921; Bt Lt-Col, 1929; Lt-Col, 1932; Col 1935; Maj.-Gen., 1940; Gen. Staff Officer, Western Command, India, 1928-31; Commandant, Probyn's Horse (5th KEO Lancers) Indian Army, 1933-35; Gen.

Staff Officer, 1st Grade, Lahore District, 1935-36; commanded 1st (Risalpur) Cavalry Bde, India, 1936-39; Maj.-Gen. Cavalry, India, 1939-40; Comd, Meerut District, India, 1940-43; retd, 1943; re-employed as Chief Civil Liaison Officer and Dep. Dir of Recruiting, N Area, India, 1943-46; retired, 1946. Hon. Sheriff Substitute, Inverness, Moray, Nairn and Ross and Cromarty, 1949-71. *Recreations:* shooting, fishing, polo. *Address:* Redcliff, Portree, Isle of Skye. *T:* Portree 14. *Club:* Cavalry and Guards.
[Died 15 Oct. 1976.

MACDONALD, Maj.-Gen. John Frederick Matheson, CB 1959; DSO 1951; OBE 1945; *b* 7 Nov. 1907; *e s* of late Major Eric William Macdonald, Ringmer, Sussex; *m* 1st, 1933, Joan Drayson (*d* 1961), *d* of late Norval H. Prentis, East Bergholt, Suffolk; one *s*; 2nd, 1964, Kathleen Flora, *widow* of Lieut-Col D. W. Mac L. Prinsep, Skinner's Horse. *Educ:* Marlborough Coll.; Royal Military Coll., Sandhurst. 2nd Lt KOSB 1927; Lt (Adjt) 1 KOSB 1935-37; Lt-Col 1 KOSB, 1944; Lt-Col (GSO1) HQ 3 Brit. Inf. Div., 1944-45, France, Belgium, Germany. Lt-Col (AQMG) West Africa Comd, 1948-49; Lt-Col 1 KOSB, Hong Kong and Korea, 1949-51; Lt-Col 1949; Brig. 28 British Commonwealth Brigade, Korea, 1951-52; Brig. 31 Lorried Inf. Brigade, Germany, 1952-54; Imperial Defence Coll., 1955; Brig. 1956; Maj.-Gen., Chief of Staff Scottish Command, 1957-1958; Maj.-Gen. 1957; GOC 52 (Lowland) Division/District, 1958-61; retired, 1961. Hon. Col 4/5 Bn KOSB, TA, 1962-67. County Comr, Boy Scouts, Suffolk, 1962-67. Chevalier, Order of Leopold, with Palm, and Croix de Guerre, 1940, with Palm, Belgium, 1947; Officer, Legion of Merit, USA, 1953. *Address:* The Grange, Elmswell, Bury St Edmunds, Suffolk. *T:* Elmswell 40270.
[Died 29 May 1979.

McDONALD, Hon. Sir John (Gladstone Black), Kt 1957; retired from Parliament of Victoria, Australia; *b* 6 Dec. 1898; *s* of Donald McDonald, Falkirk, Scotland; *m* 1932, Mary Cosser Trotter; one *s* two *d*. *Educ:* Camelon, Scotland. MLA for Shepparton, Victoria, 1936-55. Minister for Water Supply and Minister for Electricity, 1943-45; Minister for Lands etc., 1947-48; Leader of the Opposition, 1945-47; Premier and Treasurer, 1950-52. Served in 37th Bn AIF, in France, 1916-18. Director: Goulburn and Murray Television Co.; Farmers Co-operative Fertilisers Euroa Ltd. *Address:* PO Box 101, Shepparton, Vic 3630, Australia. *T:* 219004.
[Died 23 April 1977.

MacDONALD, Robert, CBE 1965; Sheriff-Substitute of Dumfries and Galloway at Dumfries, 1965-70; *s* of John Robert MacDonald and Isabella Sinclair; *m* 1948, Elizabeth Grant, JP. *Educ:* Wick High Sch.; Edinburgh Univ. Grad. Law with dist., Edinburgh 1930. Procurator-Fiscal, Glasgow, 1951-65; Lectr in Law, Glasgow Univ., 1946-52; Examiner in Law to Law Soc. of Scotland, 1960-65; Examiner in Medical Jurisprudence, Law Faculty, Glasgow Univ. *Address:* Maryfield, Auldgirth, Dumfries. *T:* Auldgirth 225. *Clubs:* Royal Over-Seas League; Royal Scottish Automobile, Glasgow University College (Glasgow).
[Died 30 May 1971.

MACDONALD, Air Vice-Marshal Somerled Douglas, CB 1951; CBE 1945; DFC 1920; retired; *b* 1899; *s* of late Dr D. Macdonald, of Glen Urquhart, Inverness-shire; *m* 1931, Mary Laura, *d* of Sir Osborn George Holmden, KBE; *m* 1949, Hon. Margaret Anne, *d* of 2nd Baron Trent, KBE. *Educ:* George Watson's Coll., Edinburgh. Served European War, 1914-19: joined RFC, 1917, transferred to RAF, 1918; served in Mesopotamia and Persia; served in Iraq and ME (Egypt), 1924-27, and 1936-37; attached HQ Sudan Defence Force, 1937-39; served War of 1939-45: commanded 3 Wing (Sudan), 263 Wing (Palestine), 213 Wing (Lebanon), 217 Wing (Persia), and Bomber detachment in Iraq during rebellion, 1941; SASO No 9 (Fighter) Group, Fighter Comd, 1944; SASO No 12 (Fighter) Group, 1945; AOC No 11 (Fighter) Group, 1946-48; Assistant Chief of Air Staff (Training), 1948; Inspector-Gen. of Air Training, Western Union, 1950. Head of Air Training Advisory Group, NATO, 1952-54, retired. *Address:* Inglewood Lodge, Kintbury, Berks. *T:* Kintbury 446. *Club:* Royal Air Force.
[Died 23 Nov. 1979.

MACDONALD, Hon. Sir Thomas (Lachlan), KCMG 1963; High Commissioner for New Zealand in London, 1961-68; New Zealand Ambassador to the European Economic Community, 1961-67; New Zealand Ambassador to Ireland, 1966-68; *b* 14 Dec. 1898; *s* of Thomas Forsaith and Margaret Ann Macdonald; *m* 1925, Elsie Ann Stuart; one *d*. *Educ:* South Sch. and Southland Boys' High Sch., Invercargill, NZ. Union Steamship Co. of New Zealand Ltd, 1915-18. Served NZ Mounted Rifles, Egypt and Palestine, 1918-19. Farming in New Zealand, 1919-37 and 1945-55. MP for Mataura, NZ, 1938-46; MP for Wallace, NZ, 1946-57. Min. of Defence, 1949-57, and of External Affairs, 1954-57. Served overseas, North Africa, 2nd NZEF, 1940-43.

Recreations: tramping, photography, swimming, gardening. *Address:* 1 Camellia Grove, Parklands, Waikanae, New Zealand.
[Died 11 April 1980.

McDOUALL, John Crichton, CMG 1966; HM Overseas Civil Service, retired; *b* 26 April 1912; *s* of late Rev. Crichton Willoughby McDouall; *m* 1946, Kathleen Glover Moir, *d* of late A. B. Moir, Taikoo, Hong Kong; one *s* two *d*. *Educ:* Monkton Combe Sch.; Jesus Coll., Cambridge; Birmingham Univ. Colonial Administrative Service, Hong Kong, 1934-39; served War of 1939-45, Hong Kong RNVR and POW; Brit. Mil. Administration, Hong Kong, 1945-46; Administrative Service, Hong Kong, 1946-52; Chief Social Welfare Officer, Fedn of Malaya, 1952-57; Sec. for Chinese Affairs, Hong Kong, 1957-67; retired, 1967. Coronation Medal, 1953. *Address:* The Old School, Souldern, Bicester, Oxfordshire. *T:* Fritwell 217.
[Died 13 Dec. 1979.

MACDOUGALL, Maj.-Gen. Alastair Ian, CBE 1943; DSO 1919; MC; *s* of late Col James William Macdougall, Edinburgh; *b* 1888; *m* 1922, Constance, *d* of late S. St Barb Emmott, Havant, Hants; (one *s* died of wounds, 1945) one *d*. *Educ:* Wellington Coll.; RMC, Sandhurst. Served European War, 1914-19 (despatches, MC, DSO, Brevet Major, Brevet Lt-Col); commanded Royal Scots Greys, 1928-32; Comdr 6th (Midland) Cavalry Brigade TA 1932-34; Instructor (Class Y) Senior Officers' Sch., Sheerness, 1934; Gen. Staff, War Office, 1936-39; Area Comdr 1939; Maj.-Gen., Gen. Staff, 1940; DCGS 1940; District Comdr, 1940-44; ADC to the King, 1939-44; retired, 1944. Chm., Argyll TA Assoc., 1946-55. *Address:* Home Close, Beaulieu, Hants. *T:* 284. *Club:* Army and Navy.
[Died 13 March 1972.

MacDOUGALL, Leslie Grahame, RSA 1946 (ARSA 1937); FRIBA 1937 (ARIBA 1926); PPRIAS; FSA (Scotland); Architect; *b* Edinburgh, 14 Aug. 1896; *s* of late Patrick William Thomson, Edinburgh; *m* 1st, 1933, Barbara Mary Henderson (against whom he obtained decree of divorce (undefended) 1943); 2nd, 1949, Coline Helen Elizabeth, Madam MacDougall of MacDougall, *e d* of late Col A. J. MacDougall of MacDougall, CMG. Assumed the surname of MacDougall in lieu of Grahame-Thomson on accession of his wife to Chiefship of Clan MacDougall, 1953. *Educ:* Merchiston Castle Sch.; Edinburgh Univ. and School of Architecture, Edinburgh Coll. of Art. Served Great War, 1914-18, HLI and Army Pay Dept, Overseas with Egyptian Expeditionary Force, 1917-19; Edinburgh Coll. of Art, 1920-26; entered office of late Sir Robert Lorimer, KBE, ARA, RSA, as pupil, 1921; commenced private practice, 1926; works: National Bank of Scotland new head office, Caledonian Insurance Company's new head office, Reid Memorial Church, Edinburgh, Fairmilehead Parish Church, Moncur Memorial Church, Isle of Stronsay, Orkney, Christ's Church, Oban, other Banks and Churches, Domestic and Hotel work. *Recreations:* foreign travel, hill-climbing, gardening. *Address:* Dunollie Castle, Oban, Argyll. *T:* Oban 2012; 6 Ainslie Place, Edinburgh, 3. *T:* 031-225 8129. *Clubs:* Savage, Caledonian, New (Edinburgh), Scottish Arts; Royal Highland Yacht.
[Died 3 June 1974.

McDOWALL, Roger Gordon, CIE 1935; *b* 9 Nov. 1886; *s* of Rev. William McDowall, MA, and Jessie Crocket; *m* 1913, Martha Law Howie; one *s*. *Educ:* Duncow; Dumfries Academy; Glasgow Univ.; Christ Church, Oxford. Entered Indian Civil Service, 1911; Assistant Commissioner in Burma, 1911-16; Assistant Secretary to Government of Burma, 1916-19; Registrar of Chief Court (and later of High Court), Rangoon, 1920-23; Deputy Commissioner, Bassein, 1923-27; Tharrawaddy, 1927-28; Finance Secretary to Government of Burma, 1929-32; Reforms Secretary to Government of Burma, 1932-37; Secretary to the Governor of Burma, 1937-39; retired, 1941. *Recreation:* gardening. *Address:* Old Mill, Dunlop, Ayrshire. *T:* Dunlop 277.
[Died 18 March 1972.

MACE, Cecil Alec, MA Cantab, DLit London; Emeritus Professor of Psychology, University of London, since 1961; Hon. Fellow, Birkbeck Coll.; Hon. Fellow, British Psychological Society; *b* 22 July 1894; *s* of Walter and Mary Mace, Norwich; *m* 1922, Marjorie, *d* of Harris Lebus; two *s*. *Educ:* King Edward VI Middle Sch.; City of Norwich Sch.; Queens' Coll., Cambridge. Lectr, University Coll., Nottingham, 1922-25; Lectr, Univ. of St Andrews, 1925-32; Reader, Bedford Coll., Univ. of London, 1932-44; Prof. of Psychology, Birkbeck Coll., Univ. of London, 1944-61. Tarner Lectr, Trinity Coll., Cambridge, 1940-41; Manson Lectr, Royal Inst. of Philosophy, 1965. Hon. Mem. Aristotelian Soc. (Pres., 1948-49); Pres. Psychological Section, British Assoc. 1951; Pres., British Psychological Soc., 1952-53. *Publications:* The Psychology of Study, 1932 (Rev. paperback edns 1968, 1970); The Principles of Logic, 1933; Incentives:

Some Experimental Studies, 1935; Articles in Times Lit. Supp., Encyclopædia Britannica, Chambers's Encyclopædia and Encyclopedia of Philosophy; Ed. and Contrib., British Philosophy in the Mid Century, 1957 (rev. edn, 1966); various articles and papers in Proc. Aristotelian Society, British Journal of Psychology, and other journals of Philosophy and Psychology. For some years Editor of Methuens Manuals of Psychology and of the Pelican Psychology Series. *Address:* 105 Roebuck House, Palace Street, SW1. *T:* 01-828 2764; Vale Farm, Hollesley, Woodbridge, Suffolk. *T:* Shottisham 258.
[Died 7 June 1971.

McELLIGOTT, James, MA, LLD; Secretary, Department of Finance, 1927-53; Governor, Central Bank of Ireland, 1954-60; President of Economic and Social Research Institute; *b* Tralee, Co. Kerry, 1893; *m* 1927, Annie Gertrude, *d* of James Fay, of Edenderry, Offaly. *Educ:* University College, Dublin, National University of Ireland; BA (hons) Classics, 1913; MA Economics, 1917. Passed for Indian Civil Service; left Service for financial journalism; Managing Editor, The Statist, London, 1921; returned to Ireland as Financial Adviser to Irish Government, 1923, and acted on many important Commissions and Cttees. *Publications:* papers, economic and financial subjects. *Recreation:* travelling. *Address:* Central Bank of Ireland, Dublin.   [Died 23 Jan. 1974.

McELROY, Neil H.; Chairman, The Procter & Gamble Co., since 1959 (Chairman, Executive Committee, since 1971); *b* 30 Oct. 1904; *s* of Malcolm Ross McElroy and Susan Hosler McElroy; *m* 1929, Mary Camilla Fry; one *s* two *d*. *Educ:* Harvard Coll. Joined The Procter & Gamble Co., Cincinnati, Ohio, 1925; Advertising Dept, 1925; Manager, Promotion Dept, 1929-40; Manager, Advertising and Promotion, 1940-43; Dir, and Vice-Pres. in charge Advertising, 1943-46; Vice-Pres., Gen. Man., 1946-48; Pres., 1948-57. Secretary of Defense, USA, 1957-59. Dir, Gen. Electric Co., Chrysler Corp.; Dir, Equitable Life Assurance Soc. of the United States. Dir, Atlantic Council of US; Mem., Exec. Cttee, The Business Council; Chm., Cttee on Univ. Resources, Harvard Univ.; Mem. of 2 Harvard visiting cttees; Member: United Negro Coll. Fund Council; Cttee for Corporate Support of American Univs; Nat. Adv. Council, Girl Scouts of America; Exec. Cttee, Cincinnati Inst. of Fine Arts. Trustee, National Safety Council; Founding Mem., Business Cttee for the Arts, Inc.; Pres., Board of Overseers, Harvard Univ., 1963-66; Chairman: Council for Financial Aid to Education, 1963-66; White House Conference on Education, 1954-55; President's Commn on School Finance, 1970-72; Pres., Soap and Detergent Assoc., 1950; various positions, Nat. Industrial Conf. Bd, 1953-64. Holds several Hon. degrees. Medal of Freedom (USA), 1959. *Address:* PO Box 599, Cincinnati, Ohio 45201, USA. *Clubs:* Cincinnati Country, Commonwealth, Commercial (Pres., 1960-61), Camargo, Queen City (Cincinnati); Links, 29 (New York); Chevy Chase, 1925 F Street (Washington, DC); Bohemian (San Francisco); Harvard (Boston and New York).   [Died 30 Nov. 1972.

MacEOIN, Lt-Gen. Seán; *b* County Longford, 30 Sept. 1893; *e s* of Andrew MacEoin and Catherine Treacy, Kilshruley, Ballinalee, Co. Longford; *m* 1922, Alice Christina, *e d* of Mr Cooney, Gurteen House, Killashee, Co. Longford. *Educ:* Ballinalee National School; correspondence course. Co. Captain Irish Volunteers at 21 years of age, 1914-17; Batt. Commander 1st Batt. Longford Brigade Irish Volunteers, 1917-20; Vice-Brigadier Longford Brigade, 1920-21; OC 1st Midland Divison rank Comdt General, 1921-22; GOC Western Command rank Maj.-Gen., 1922-23; GOC Athlone Command, 1923-24; GOC Reformed Western Command, 1924-25; GOC Curragh Training Camp, 1925-27; Quartermaster-General, 1927-29; Chief of Staff, 1928-29; resigned June 1929; Lt-Gen. 1929 (R of O); Dáil Deputy, 1921-23; seconded motion for Ratification Treaty between Great Britain and Ireland, 1921; Member of the Dáil for Athlone-Longford, 1929-65; Minister for Justice, 1948-51; Minister for Defence, March-June 1951, and 1954-57. Candidate Presidential Elections, 1945-59. Retired active politics, 1965. Grand Cross and Commander Merit, Argentine, 1957; Silver Sword of Light, Ireland, 1965. *Recreations:* hunting, golf. *Address:* Cloncoosc, Stillorgan Road, Donnybrook, Dublin.
[Died 7 July 1973.

McEWEN, Sir James Napier Finnie, 2nd Bt, *cr* 1953; *b* 14 Dec. 1924; *s* of Sir John Helias Finnie McEwen, 1st Bt; *S* father, 1962; *m* 1958, Clare, *d* of J. E. W. G. Sandar; three *d*. *Educ:* Eton. Served War of 1939-45 with Grenadier Guards in France. *Heir:* *b* Robert Lindley McEwen [*b* 23 June 1926; *m* 1954, Brigid Cecilia Laver; two *s* four *d*]. *Address:* Bardrochat, Colmonell, Ayrshire. *Club:* New (Edinburgh).   [Died 2 July 1971.

McEWEN, Rt. Hon. Sir John, PC 1953; GCMG 1971; CH 1969; Australian former politician and farmer; *b* Chiltern, Victoria, 29 March 1900; *s* of David James McEwen and Amy Ellen (Porter) McEwen; *m* 1st, 1921, Annie McLeod, DBE 1966 (*d* 1967), *d* of John McLeod, Tongala, Victoria; 2nd, 1968, Mary Eileen, *d* of Patrick Aloysius Byrne, Adelaide. Enlisted Australian Imperial Forces, 1918; farmer at Stanhope, Victoria, 1919-76; MHR Echuca, 1934-37, Indi, 1937-49, Murray, 1949-71 (retd); Minister for: the Interior, Australia, 1937-39; External Affairs, 1940; Air and Civil Aviation, 1940-41; Member: War Cabinet, 1940-41; Advisory War Council, Australia, 1941-45; Australian Delegation, UNCIO, San Francisco, 1945; Minister for: Commerce and Agriculture, Australia, 1949-56; Trade, 1956-63; Trade and Industry, 1963-71; led numerous delegns to GATT talks, Geneva; Dep. Leader, Australian Parly Country Party, 1943-58, Leader, 1958-71; Deputy Prime Minister, 1958-71; Prime Minister, Dec. 1967-Jan. 1968. Order of the Rising Sun, 1st Class (Japan), 1973. *Recreation:* reading. *Address:* (office) 367 Collins Street, Melbourne, Vic. 3000, Australia. *T:* Melbourne 62-1734. *Club:* Melbourne (Melbourne).
[Died 21 Nov. 1980.

McEWEN, Sir Robert (Lindley), 3rd Bt *cr* 1953; *b* 23 June 1926; 2nd *s* of Sir John McEwen, 1st Bt, of Marchmont and Bardrochat, and of Bridget Mary, *e d* of late Rt Hon. Sir Francis Lindley, GCMG, CB, CBE; *S* brother, 1971; *m* 1954, Brigid Cecilia, *o d* of late James Laver, CBE; two *s* four *d*. *Educ:* Eton (scholar); Trinity College, Cambridge (scholar). Starred 1st Cl. Law Trip. Part II, 1950 (Senior Scholar). Served Grenadier Guards, 1944-47 (Lieut). Barrister, Inner Temple, 1951. Sublector, Trinity College, Cambridge, 1953-55. Contested (C): East Edinburgh, 1964; Roxburgh, Selkirk and Peebles, 1965. Hon. Sheriff, Roxburgh, Berwick and Selkirk, 1971-. Chm., Berwickshire Civic Soc., 1973-75. *Publications:* The Law of Monopolies, Restrictive Practices, and Resale Price Maintenance (with Lord Hailsham), 1956; Gatley on Libel and Slander, 7th edn 1973; contrib. to Halsbury's Laws of England; Listener, Spectator, etc.; illustrations in: Iris Origo, Giovanna and Jane; Gavin Maxwell, Ring of Bright Water, and Raven Seek Thy Brother. *Heir:* *s* James Francis Lindley McEwen, *b* 24 Aug. 1960. *Address:* Marchmont, Berwickshire. *T:* Duns 2321. *Clubs:* Brooks's, Beefsteak; Puffins (Edinburgh).
[Died 18 May 1980.

McFADYEAN, Sir Andrew, Kt 1925; *b* 23 April 1887; *e s* of late Sir John McFadyean; *m* 1913, Dorothea Emily, *y d* of late Charles Kean Chute; one *s* three *d*. *Educ:* University College School., London; University College, Oxford (Scholar); First Class Final Honour School, Lit. Hum., 1909. Entered Treasury, 1910, by open competition; Private Secretary, 1913, to Mr Masterman and successively to Mr Montagu, Mr Acland, Sir John Bradbury, Mr McKinnon Wood, Sir Hardman Lever and Mr Stanley Baldwin; accompanied Sir H. Lever to USA on special financial mission, 1917; Treasury representative, Paris, Sept. 1919-Jan. 1920; Sec. to British Delegn Reparation Commn, 1920-22; Gen. Sec. to Reparation Commn, 1922-24, and Sec. to Dawes Cttee, 1924; Comr of Controlled Revenues, Berlin, 1924-30; Member, Executive National Liberal Federation, 1933-36; Joint Treasurer, Liberal Party Organisation, 1936-48, Pres., 1949-50; Vice-Pres., 1950-60; Pres., Free Trade Union, 1948-59; Vice-Pres., Liberal Internat., 1954-67; Vice-Pres., Anglo-Israel Assoc. (Chm. Council, 1950-60). Mem. Council, Royal Inst. of Internat. Affairs, 1933-67, President, 1970. Contested (L) City of London, 1945; Finchley, 1950. *Publications:* Reparation Reviewed, 1930; The Liberal Case, 1950; Recollected in Tranquility, 1964; trans. Count Coudenhove-Kalergi's The Totalitarian State Against Man, 1938, Europe Must Unite, 1939. *Address:* 28 St Stephens Close, Avenue Road, NW8 6DB. *T:* 01-722 6065. *Club:* Travellers'.
[Died 2 Oct. 1974.

MACFARLANE, Janet Alston, MA, LLD (St Andrews); Headmistress of St Leonards and St Katharines Schools, St Andrews, Fife, 1938-55; *e d* of late Charles Macfarlane, JP, Hutton Avenue, West Hartlepool, Co. Durham. *Educ:* Dundee High Sch.; St Andrews Univ. Senior French Mistress, Cheltenham Ladies' Coll., 1927; Vice-Principal, 1931-38; Acting Principal, May-Dec. 1936. *Address:* 33 Town Wall, Hartlepool, Cleveland. *T:* Hartlepool 74304.   [Died 9 Feb. 1980.

MACFIE, Prof. Alec Lawrence, MA, LLB, DLitt (Glasgow); Hon. LLD (Glasgow); Professor of Political Economy, University of Glasgow, 1946-58, now Emeritus; *b* 29 May 1898; *s* of Rev. W. G. Macfie, Mowbray, Cape Town; unmarried. *Educ:* High School of Glasgow; University of Glasgow. Served European War, 1917-18, The 2nd Bn The Gordon Highlanders. Lecturer in Political Economy, Glasgow Univ., 1930-45. *Publications:* Theories of the Trade Cycle, 1934; An Essay on

Economy and Value, 1936; Economic Efficiency and Social Welfare, 1943; The Individual in Society: Papers on Adam Smith, 1967. *Address:* 21 Tannoch Drive, Milngavie, Glasgow.
[Died 10 *April* 1980.

McGARVEY, Sir Daniel, Kt 1977; CBE 1970; President, Amalgamated Society of Boilermakers, Shipwrights, Blacksmiths and Structural Workers, since 1965; *b* 16 Sept. 1919; British parentage; *m* 1942, Jean Scullion; two *d. Educ:* Our Holy Redeemer's RC Sch., Clydebank; St Patrick's High Sch., Dumbarton. Elected Mem., Exec. Council, Amalgamated Soc. Boilermakers etc., 1951; Exec. Council of Confederation of Shipbuilding and Engineering Unions, 1954; Chm. Boilermakers' Executive Council, 1954; National Executive of the Labour Party, 1958-65; Gen. Sec. Soc. Boilermakers Section of Amalgamated Soc., 1964. Mem., Gen. Council, TUC, 1965-, Chm., 1976. Member: Manpower Services Commn, 1974-; North East Post Office Exec. Bd, 1974-; NEDC, 1975-. *Recreations:* gardening, football, reading. *Address:* (home) 5 Coldstream Road, Newcastle upon Tyne NE15 7DN. *T:* Newcastle upon Tyne 741564; (office) Lifton House, Eslington Road, Newcastle upon Tyne NE2 4SB. *T:* Newcastle upon Tyne 813205. *[Died* 26 *April* 1977.

McGAW, William Rankin, CB 1955; *b* 17 Jan. 1900; *er s* of late William McGaw; *m* 1928, Agnes Hannah Scott; no *c. Educ:* Allen Glen's Sch., Glasgow; Glasgow Univ. (BSc). Entered Civil Service, Air Ministry Development staff, 1924. Served Royal Aircraft Establishment, Farnborough, 1924-39. Appointed Dir of Aircraft Equipment Production, 1941, Ministry of Aircraft Production and later Ministry of Supply. Director: of Aircraft Supplies (General), 1946-48; of Production, 1948-52; Dir-Gen. of Aircraft Production, Ministry of Supply, 1952-61. *Recreations:* fly-fishing, gardening. *Address:* Orchard Lodge, Sycamore Road, Farnborough, Hants. *T:* Farnborough, Hants 41013. *[Died* 15 *March* 1974.

McGINNETY, Frank Edward, CBE 1961; *b* 29 March 1907; *s* of William Henry and Margaret McGinnety; *m* 1949, Doris Marie Grigson. *Educ:* Rutherford Coll., Newcastle upon Tyne; Armstrong Coll., University of Durham (MSc). Min. of Supply: Signals Research and Development Establishment, 1929-54; asst Dir, Electronics Research and Development, 1954-55; Dir of Inspectorate of Electrical and Mechanical Equipment, 1955-57; Dep. Dir-Gen. of Inspection, Min. of Supply, 1957-59, Min. of Aviation, 1959-60; Dir-Gen. of Inspection, Min. of Aviation, 1960-66. CEng, FIEE; Fellow and Past Pres., Instn of Engineering Inspection. *Recreations:* sailing, horticulture, painting, photography. *Address:* Broadlands, Malmains Way, Beckenham, Kent BR3 2SB. *T:* 01-650 7503.
[Died 12 *Aug.* 1973.

McGLASHAN, Rear-Adm. (retd) Sir Alexander Davidson, KBE 1954; CB 1953; DSO 1946; FIMechE; *b* 8 Oct. 1901; *s* of Dugald and Margaret Neilson McGlashan (*née* Davidson); *m* 1926, Irene Margaret Cooke; two *s* one *d. Educ:* Perth Acad. Cadet, RN, 1919; Midshipman, 1921; Sub-Lt, 1922; Lt (E) 1923; Lt-Comdr (E), 1931; Comdr (E), 1935; Capt (E), 1944; Rear-Adm. (E), 1951. Retired, 1955. *Recreations:* gardening, carpentry. *Address:* Rotherway, Potterne Wick, Devizes, Wilts. *T:* Devizes 2950. *Club:* Royal Automobile. *[Died* 4 *March* 1976.

McGLASHAN, Archibald A., RSA 1939 (ARSA 1935); RGI 1977; Artist Painter; *b* 16 March 1888; *s* of John Crooks McGlashan and Agnes Thomson; *m* 1922, Teresa Giuliani (*d* 1971); one *s* two *d. Educ:* Paisley; Glasgow. Trained at Glasgow Sch. of Art; travelled extensively on the Continent, visiting chief Art centres. Pictures purchased by:-Scottish Modern Art Assoc.; Glasgow, Belfast, Newcastle, Aberdeen, Paisley, Perth, Dundee, and Edinburgh Corporations; Glasgow Univ., Arts Council of Great Britain. Has exhibited pictures at Royal Scottish Acad., Royal Acad., The Royal Glasgow Institute of the Fine Arts, The Paisley Art Institute, Walker Art Gallery, Liverpool and in America and Canada. *Address:* 35 Roddinghead Road, Whitecraigs, Glasgow G46 6TN. *T:* 041-639 4684. *Club:* Art (Glasgow). *[Died* 3 *Jan.* 1980.

McGONIGAL, Rt. Hon. Sir Ambrose Joseph, PC 1975; Kt 1975; MC 1943 and bar 1944; **Rt. Hon. Lord Justice McGonigal;** Lord Justice of Appeal, Supreme Court of Judicature, Northern Ireland, since 1975 (Judge of High Court of Justice, N Ireland, 1968-75); *b* 22 Nov. 1917; 2nd *s* of Judge John McGonigal, KC and Margaret McGonigal; *m* 1941, Patricia, *o d* of Robert Taylor; two *s* two *d. Educ:* Clongowes Wood Coll.; Queen's Univ., Belfast. Served HM Forces, 1939-46; commnd RUR, 1940; 12th Commando, 1943-44 (wounded); Special Boat Service, 1944-45 (despatches). Called to Bar, N Ireland, 1948; to Inner Bar of N Ireland, 1956; Bencher, The Inn of Court of N

Ireland, 1964. Member: Cttee on Public Library Service in N Ire.; Cttee on Adult Education in N Ire.; N Ire. Charities Central Investment Fund Advisory Cttee, 1966-74; Senate, QUB, 1969-74. Governor: Armagh Observatory, 1968-; St Joseph's Coll. of Education, 1969-74. *Recreations:* various. *Address:* Bishops Court House, Bishops Court, Co. Down BT30 7EY. *Club:* Special Forces. *[Died* 22 *Sept.* 1979.

MacGONIGAL, Maurice, PPRHA; Hon. RA; Hon. RSA; Professor of Painting, Royal Hibernian Academy; Member of Board of Governors, National Gallery of Ireland; Member of Advisory Committees: of Municipal Gallery of Modern Art; for Wolfe Tone Memorial; Coun. of Industrial Design, Ireland; Currency Design Council; *b* Dublin, Jan. 1900; *s* of Frank MacGonigal and Caroline Lane; *m*; two *s*. Studied at Dublin Metropolitan Sch. of Art; Taylor Scholarship in Painting, 1924; interested in Irish Landscape and Genre Painting; exhibited London, America, etc.; is represented by pictures: Municipal Gallery of Modern Art, Dublin, Cork, Belfast and Limerick Galleries; Senate Chambers, Leinster House, Dublin RCP, Nat. Mus. of Ireland. LLD *hc* NUI, 1970. *Address:* 2 Templemore Avenue, Rathgar, Dublin 6, Ireland. *T:* 01-973504.
[Died 31 *Jan.* 1979.

McGOUGAN, Malcolm; Barrister-at-law; Recorder of Poole, 1954-71; *b* 19 Aug. 1905; *s* of late Angus McGougan, Nottingham; *m* 1929, Enid Monica, *y d* of late Albert Hopkinson, Cambridge; two *s. Educ:* Nottingham High Sch.; Pembroke Coll., Cambridge (MA). Called to the Bar, 1929. Western Circuit and Wilts Sessions. Served RAFVR, Middle East, North Africa and UK, 1940-45 (despatches four times); Wing Comdr. Recorder of Andover, 1948-54; Dep. Chm., Surrey QS, 1956-71. *Recreation:* fishing. *Address:* 1 Paper Buildings, Temple, EC4; Stubbetts, Forest Green, near Dorking, Surrey. *Club:* United Oxford & Cambridge University.
[Died 12 *Feb.* 1976.

McGOVERN, Sir Patrick (Silvesta), Kt 1959; CBE 1954; company director; *b* 4 April 1895; *s* of late John and Elizabeth McGovern; *m* 1922, Henrietta Rose, *d* of late John Laurissen and of Matilda Laurissen; two *d. Educ:* State Schs, Vic.; Beechworth Coll. Entered Commonwealth Public Service, 1911; Income Tax Assessor, 1925-30; Chief Investigation Officer, Sales Tax, 1930-39; Dep. Comr of Taxation, Canberra, 1939-42; Second Comr of Taxation, 1942-46; Commissioner of Taxation, Commonwealth of Australia, 1946-61. *Recreation:* golf. *Address:* 4 Barkly Crescent, Forrest, Canberra, ACT 2603. *T:* 73-1850. *Clubs:* Commonwealth (Canberra); Melbourne (Melbourne); Union (Sydney). *[Died* 18 *March* 1975.

McGRATH, Raymond, BArch (Sydney); FRIBA; FRIAI; RHA; FSIA; architect; Professor of Architecture, Royal Hibernian Academy, 1968; *b* Sydney, NSW, 7 March 1903; *s* of Herbert Edgar McGrath, NZ, and Edith Sorrell, NSW; *m* 1930, Mary Catherine Crozier, Dallas, Texas; one *s* one *d. Educ:* Fort Street Boys Schs; Univ. Sydney (University Medal for English Verse. BArch with first class hons and University Medal, 1926, Wentworth Travelling Fellowship, 1926); Clare Coll., Cambridge (Research Student of Architecture, 1927-29). Australian Medallion of Board of Architects of NSW, 1928; Consultant to the British Broadcasting Corporation, 1930-35; in private practice in London, 1930-39; Principal Architect, Office of Public Works, Dublin, 1948-68; in private practice in Dublin, 1968-. Pres., Soc. of Designers in Ireland, 1972. *Architectural works:* Finella, Cambridge, 1928; studios, furniture and equipment for BBC, 1930-34; interiors of Aircraft for Imperial Airways, 1932; various restaurants, showrooms and exhibitions; The Cenotaph, Leinster Lawn, Dublin, 1950. Appointed architect for The Kennedy Memorial Concert Hall, Dublin, 1964, and Royal Hibernian Acad. of Arts new galleries, Dublin, 1970. Domestic work: Frognal House, Hampstead, St Ann's Hill, Chertsey; various commercial buildings; official works: remodelling of President's House, Dublin; adaptation of Irish Embassies in London and Paris, etc. *Drawings and paintings:* Wood engravings for illustrations; various topographical drawings; paintings in water-colour, gouache and oil. Commissioned as official War Artist, Feb. 1940, to make drawings of Aircraft Production. *Industrial Design:* Furniture, glassware, carpets. *Publications:* Twentieth Century Houses (in Basic English), 1934; Glass in Architecture and Decoration (with A. C. Frost), 1937 (new edn 1961). *Address:* Somerton Lodge, Rochestown Avenue, Co. Dublin. *T:* 854032.
[Died 2 *Dec.* 1977.

MACGREGOR, Prof. Alastair Goold, MD, BSc, FRCP, FRCPE, FRCPGlas; Regius Professor of Materia Medica, Department of Therapeutics and Pharmacology, University of Aberdeen, since 1959; Hon. Physician, Royal Infirmary,

Aberdeen; *b* 23 Dec. 1919; *er s* of late Prof. George H. C. Macgregor, DD; *m* 1944, Janet Elizabeth, *e d* of late Andrew McPherson, Sec., Boys' Brigade, Scotland; three *s* one *d. Educ:* Fettes Coll., Edinburgh; University of Glasgow. BSc 1941; MB, ChB 1943; MD (High Commendation) 1951; FRCPGlas 1947; FRCPE 1957; FRCP 1963. Surgeon Lt RNVR, 1944-46. Clinical Asst, Western Infirmary, Glasgow, 1946-48; Lecturer in Therapeutics, University of Sheffield, 1948-52; Senior Lecturer in Therapeutics, University of Edinburgh, 1952-59. Member: Assoc. of Physicians of Great Britain; Med. Research Soc.; British Pharmacological Soc. *Publications:* Practical Prescribing, 1953; chapters in books on therapeutics, genetics and endocrine disorders; various contributions to medical and pharmacological literature, chiefly on thyroid function and metabolic disease. *Recreations:* gardening, golf, travel and photography. *Address:* Ardruighe, Milltimber, Aberdeenshire. *T:* Aberdeen 47480; Department of Therapeutics and Pharmacology, Foresterhill, Aberdeen. *T:* Aberdeen 23423.
[Died 31 May 1972.

McGREGOR, Hon. Sir George Innes, Kt 1967; Judge of the Supreme Court of New Zealand, 1953-69; *b* 14 May 1899; *s* of Arthur Eldred McGregor, Akaroa, NZ; *m* 1930, Elizabeth Isabella Muriel Young; two *d. Educ:* Waitaki Boys' High Sch.; University of Otago. BA, LLB, 1920; LLM hons (NZ), 1922. Barrister and Solicitor, Palmerston North, NZ, 1922-53; Crown Solicitor, Palmerston North, 1946-53. *Publications:* contribs to New Zealand Law Jl. *Recreation:* golf. *Address:* 3 Gladstone Terrace, Kelburn, Wellington W1, NZ. *Clubs:* Wellington, Hawke's Bay, Manawatu (New Zealand). *[Died 7 April 1976.*

MacGREGOR of MacGREGOR, Hon. Lady; (Gylla Constance Susan), OBE 1948; *y d* of late Hon. Eric Norman Rollo; *m* 1925, Capt. Sir Malcolm MacGregor of MacGregor, 5th Bt, CB, CMG (*d* 1958); one *s* one *d. Educ:* privately. Three months' training in theatres at Guy's Hospital; in charge of Plaster Dept, Edmonton Special Military Hospital, 1917-19; private sec. to late Ian Colvin, Morning Post, 1921-24; Chm. National Exhibition of Needlework, Edinburgh, 1934; Mem. of Council of Management Empire Exhibition, Glasgow, 1938; Mem. Executive of Scottish Development Council, 1934-46; Vice-Chm. Scottish Cttee of Council for Art and Industry, 1934; Mem. Scottish Housing Advisory Cttee, 1939-42; Mem. of Council of National Trust for Scotland, 1937-46; Chairman of Women's Land Army Cttee Perth West; Mem. of Scottish Tourist Cttee; Mem. of Executive Cttee of Enterprise Scotland, 1947; Chairman Amenity Cttees: North of Scotland Hydro-Electric Board and S of Scotland Electricity Bd, 1964-71; Member: Scottish Cttee of Council of Industrial Design, 1941-49; Royal Fine Art Commission for Scotland, 1943-63. Order of the Vasa, 1st Cl., 1954. *Address:* Craggan House, Lochearnhead, Perthshire. *T:* Lochearnhead 250. *[Died 1 Feb. 1980.*

McGREGOR, Air Marshal Sir Hector (Douglas), KCB 1960 (CB 1953); CBE 1945; DSO 1940; *b* 15 Feb. 1910; *m* 1931, Jean Martin; one *s* three *d. Educ:* Napier, New Zealand. Joined RAF, 1928; OC 33 (F) Squadron, 1938-39; OC 213 (F) Squadron, 1940; Special Planning Staff, 1941; OC Tangmere Sector, 1942-43; Dep. Dir Operations, Intelligence and Plans, Mediterranean Allied Air Forces, 1943-44; AOC Levant, 1945-46; idc 1947; Air Ministry, 1948-49; NATO Standing Group Staff, Washington, 1950-51; AOC 2 Group, Germany, 1951-53; Director of Guided Missile Development, at Ministry of Supply, 1953-55; Assistant Controller Aircraft, Ministry of Supply, 1956; Chief of Staff (Air Defence) SHAPE, Paris, 1957-59; Air Officer Commanding-in-Chief: Fighter Command, RAF, 1959-62; Far East Air Force, 1962-64. Retired from RAF, 1964. Chm., New Zealand News Consultative Board, 1968-. US Legion of Merit, 1945. *Recreations:* sailing, fly-fishing. *Address:* Bull's Cottage, Old Bosham, West Sussex. *Club:* Royal Air Force.
[Died 11 April 1973.

McGREGOR, Sir James Robert, KBE 1956; Proprietor J. W. McGregor and Co., and of J. R. McGregor Pty Ltd, wool exporters, Australia, since 1908; *b* 1889; *s* of James Wigham McGregor; *m* 1921, Freda Bruce Taylor (*d* 1941), Queensland. Formerly Chairman Australian Council of Wool Buyers; Technical Member of Central Wool Cttee during War of 1939-45. *Address:* Neidpath, 2 Carthona Avenue, Darling Point, Sydney, NSW 2706, Australia. *[Died 3 Aug. 1973.*

MACGREGOR, Lewis Richard, CBE 1938; LLB (Glasgow); Certified Public Accountant (Australia); Australian Foreign Service Official; Company Director; *b* 1886; *s* of late Thomas Macgregor, HM Royal Marines, Aberfeldy, Scotland and Portsmouth, England; *m* Mary Hannah, *d* of late Joseph White, Bournemouth, and niece of late H. Brashaw, JP, Mayor of Bunbury, Western Australia; one *s* one *d. Educ:* Allan Glens

School; Glasgow and West Scotland Technical Coll.; Chicago Sch. of Law (LLB). Wheat Export Control for Western Australian Government during European War, 1914-18; special mission to United Kingdom on behalf of Western Australia, 1919; Director of Agricultural Organization, Queensland Govt, 1922; Director of Marketing, Queensland Government, 1926; Queensland Government Representative on various Boards and Commissions, 1922-30; Australian Government Commissioner in Canada, 1930-38; negotiated first commercial agreement between Canada and Australia (still in force); Australian Delegation to Imperial Conference, London, 1930, and Ottawa, 1932; Special Trade Missions on behalf of Australia to Newfoundland, 1932, British West Indies, 1933, Far East, 1934, Union of South Africa and Rhodesia, 1937; Australian Government Trade Commissioner in USA, 1938-41; Commissioner General for Australian Government to New York World's Fair, 1939; Director-General, Commonwealth of Australia War Supplies Mission, Washington and Ottawa, 1941-45; HM Australian Minister to Brazil, 1945-49; Member: USAF Contract Review Board, Korean War, 1950-54. JP 1928-30. *Address:* Casuarina, Sandy Lane, St James, Barbados, West Indies; PO Box 371, Millbrook, New York 12545, USA. *Clubs:* Canadian (NY); Bridgetown (Barbados). *[Died 28 Feb. 1973.*

MacGREGOR, Robert Barr, CMG 1946; MB, ChB, FRCPEd; *b* 14 July 1896; *s* of Patrick MacGregor; *m* 1st, 1921, Helen May Harper (*d* 1964); one *s*; 2nd, 1970, Edith Rushbrooke, *e d* of Thomas Crook, OBE. *Educ:* Dunbar Sch.; Edinburgh University. Served in RAMC, 1918-20; joined Straits Settlements Medical Service, 1920; Director, Medical Services, Straits Settlements and Adviser, Medical Services, Malay Straits, 1940; Director, Medical Services, Federation of Malaya, retired 1951; SMO, Malacca Agricultural Medical Board, 1951-58; RMO, Wooley Hosp., 1965-67; Ship's Surgeon, Royal Fleet Auxiliary, 1967-75. CStJ. *Address:* 9 Camden Hurst, Milford-on-Sea, Hants. *[Died 9 Nov. 1979.*

MacGREGOR, William Duncan, CIE 1933; FIEE; *b* 20 Oct. 1878; *s* of Alexander Downie MacGregor and Jessie Steel Proudfoot; *m* 1906, Marie Adelaide Achard (*d* 1942); (*s* killed in action in New Guinea, 1943; *d* decd 1946); *m* 1948, Christine Johanne Aschehoug (*d* 1963), Oslo, Norway. *Educ:* George Heriot's School and Heriot-Watt Coll., Edinburgh; appointed to Indian Posts and Telegraphs Department, 1900; Divisional Engineer, 1910; Deputy Chief Engineer, 1921; Officiating Postmaster-General, Central Provinces, 1922; PMG Burma, 1925; Officiating Chief Engineer Posts and Telegraphs, 1931; PMG Bengal and Assam, 1932; retired, 1933. *Address:* The Grange, Yockleton, near Shrewsbury, Salop.
[Died 4 Jan. 1974.

McGUFFIE, Kenneth Cunningham; Admiralty Registrar, Royal Courts of Justice, London, since 1957; Registrar of the Shipping Claims Tribunal, since 1958; *b* 30 June 1913; *y s* of late Thomas Chalmers McGuffie and Jenny (*née* Dunlop). *Educ:* Windlesham House Sch.; Harrow; Christ Church, Oxford; Geneva Univ.; Glasgow Univ (BL). Called to Bar, Gray's Inn, 1946; admitted Advocate, Scots Bar, 1946; Councillor (Co.) Walton and Weybridge UDC (St George's Hill Ward), 1947 until resigned, 1948; practised in London, Admiralty and Scots Law, 1946-57; Dep. Admiralty Registrar (during Registrar's illness), 1956. *Publications:* ed 10th edn, Marsden's Law of Collisions at Sea, 1953, 11th edn, 1961 (Vol. 4 of British Shipping Laws), and First Cumulative Supplement, 1965, and Jt Editor, Second Cumulative Supplement, 1970; ed 4th edn, Kennedy's Law of Civil Salvage, 1958; contributor to Encyclopædia Britannica and Halsbury's Laws of England, 3rd edn, shipping law; Joint Editor, British Shipping Laws, 1961- (new encyclopædic work, to be in 14 vols); author, Notes on Four Admiralty Registry Letter Books, 1795-1810, 1853-54, 1854-55, 1855-56, 1st edn, 1964; joint author, McGuffie, Fugeman and Gray's Admiralty Practice, 1st edn, 1964 (vol. 1 of British Shipping Laws) and Supplements, 1965, 1970; joint Editor (Admiralty practice) The Annual Practice, 1964, 1965, and 1966 and Supplements; The Supreme Court Practice, 1967, 1970 and Supplements. *Address:* 202 Cranmer Court, SW3 3HG. *T:* 01-584 7177. *[Died 29 Nov. 1972.*

McGUIGAN, His Eminence Cardinal James Charles, DD; *b* Hunter River, PEI, 1894. *Educ:* Prince of Wales College and St Dunstan's Coll., Charlottetown, PEI; Grand Seminary and Laval Univ., Quebec; DD, PhD, JCD, LLD; course at Catholic Univ. of America, Washington, 1927. Priest, 1918; Prof. at St Dunstan's Coll., 1918-19; Sec. and Chancellor of Charlottetown, 1919-20; and of Edmonton, 1920-25; Vicar-Gen. of Edmonton, 1923-30; Rector of St Joseph's Cathedral, Edmonton 1925-27; Rector St Joseph's Seminary, Edmonton, 1927-30; RC Archbishop of Regina, 1930-34; Archibishop of Toronto, 1934-

71; Cardinal, 1946. *Address:* c/o Archbishop's House, Old Yonge Street, Willowdale, Ont, Canada. *[Died 8 April 1974.*

McHARDY, Rev. Archibald, CB 1950; CBE 1945; MC 1919; DL; *b* 6 April 1890; *y s* of late Archibald McHardy, Edinburgh; unmarried. *Educ:* George Heriot's Sch., Edinburgh; Edinburgh Univ. MA Edinburgh, 1911; DD Edinburgh, 1944. Served European War, RAMC Field Ambulance. Sergeant RAMC, 1914-17; France, 1915-17 (wounded, Ypres, 1917); Army Chaplain, France and Germany, 1917-19; RAF Chaplain, 1919-50; Principal Chaplain (Church of Scotland) RAF, 1928-50; retired, 1950. Served at home, also tours of duty in Egypt, Palestine, Iraq, Far East, etc. Hon. Chaplain to the King, 1942-50. Vice-President of National Council of the YMCA. DL County of City of Edinburgh, 1960. *Recreation:* golf. *Address:* 51 Lauderdale Street, Edinburgh 9. *Clubs:* Royal Air Force, Royal Commonwealth Society.   *[Died 7 April 1973.*

MACHTIG, Sir Eric Gustav, GCMG, *cr* 1948 (KCMG, *cr* 1939; CMG 1935); KCB, *cr* 1943; OBE 1926 (MBE 1918); *b* 1889; *s* of late F. G. Machtig, Wimbledon; *m* 1941, Norah Marguerite Friend (*d* 1943). *Educ:* St Paul's Sch. (Scholar); Trinity Coll., Cambridge (Scholar). 1st Class 2nd Division Classical Tripos, 1911; entered Colonial Office 1912; transferred to Dominions Office (later Commonwealth Relations Office) as Assistant Secretary, 1930; Assistant Under-Secretary of State, 1936; Dep. Under-Secretary of State, 1939; Permanent Under-Secretary of State for Commonwealth Relations, 1940; seconded for special duties, Dec. 1948; retired from Service, 1949. A Dir, Barclay's Bank (DCO), 1949-69. Chm. Working Cttee, Lord Mayor's Nat. Thanksgiving Fund, 1950; Chm., Sister Trust, 1950-65; a Vice-Chm. Victoria League, 1950-62. *Recreations:* music, travelling. *Address:* 11 Belvedere Drive, SW19. *T:* 01-946 3241.
                                               [Died 24 July 1973.

MacINNES, Rt. Rev. Angus Campbell, CMG 1961; Master of St Nicholas Hospital, Salisbury, since 1968; *b* 18 April 1901; *s* of late Rennie MacInnes, DD, Bishop in Jerusalem, 1914-31, and late Janet Waldegrave Carr, MRCS, LRCP; *m* 1928, Florence Isabella Joy Masterman, MB, BS, *d* of E. W. G. Masterman, MD, FRCS, FRGS; two *s* two *d. Educ:* Harrow; Trinity Coll., Cambridge. BA 1923; MA 1927. Teacher Jerusalem Men's Coll., 1923-25; Westcott House, Cambridge, 1925-26; Deacon, 1926; Curate, St Mary Magdalene, Peckham; Priest, 1927; CMS Missionary, Palestine, 1928; Principal, Bishop Gobat Sch., Jerusalem, 1930-44; Secretary of CMS Palestine Mission, 1940-50; Archdeacon in Palestine and Transjordan and Exam. Chaplain to Bishop in Jerusalem, 1943-51; Vicar of St Michael's, St Alban's, 1951-54; Rural Dean of St Albans, 1953-57; Residentiary Canon, St Alban's Abbey, 1953-57; Bishop Suffragan of Bedford, 1953-57; Archbishop in Jerusalem and Metropolitan, 1957-68; Asst Bishop of Salisbury, 1968-73. Sub-Prelate and Chaplain, Order of St John of Jerusalem, 1957. Coronation Medal, 1937. DD (Lambeth) 1957. *Address:* St Nicholas Hospital, Salisbury, Wilts SP1 2SN. *T:* Salisbury 6874.
                                               [Died 29 April 1977.

MacINNES, Charles Malcolm, CBE 1959; Hon. LLD Dalhousie, 1952; Hon. LLD Alta, 1958; Emeritus Professor of Imperial History, University of Bristol; *b* Calgary, Alberta, 21 Dec. 1891; *s* of Malcolm MacInnes, Calgary, and Catherine MacArthur; *m* 1926, Violet Ethel (*d* 1969), *d* of Dr A. W. Peake, South Lodge, Druid Stoke, Bristol; one *s. Educ:* Dalhousie Univ., Halifax, Nova Scotia; Balliol Coll., Oxford. Assistant Lecturer in History, University of Bristol, 1919, Lecturer, 1922, Reader in Imperial History, 1930; Professor of Imperial History, University of Bristol, 1943-57; Dean of Faculty of Arts, 1952-55; Editor of Universities Review, 1924-62; President, Assoc. of University Teachers of UK, 1950-51; Vice-Pres., Historical Assoc.; Vice-Chairman Royal Empire (later Commonwealth) Society, Bristol Branch, 1934-52, Chairman, 1952-; Vice-Pres., Royal Commonwealth Soc., 1969-. Emergency Information Officer for the City of Bristol, 1941-45. Commander of Order of Orange Nassau, 1952; Commandeur de l'Ordre de l'Etoile Noire, 1956. *Publications:* The British Commonwealth and its Unsolved Problems, 1925; The Early English Tobacco Trade, 1926; In the Shadow of the Rockies, 1930; England and Slavery, 1934; An Introduction to the Economic History of the British Empire, 1935; A Gateway of Empire 1939 (2nd edn, 1968); The British Empire and Commonwealth, 1815-1949, 1951; The British Empire and the War, 1941; (Jt Editor) Bristol and its Adjoining Counties (for British Assoc.), 1955; (ed) Principles and Methods of Colonial Administration, 1950; Bristol at War, 1962; contrib. to other books, pamphlets and articles. *Recreations:* riding, rowing. *Address:* 5 Queen's Court, Clifton, Bristol, 8. *Clubs:* Savile, Royal Commonwealth Society; Savages (Bristol).   *[Died 5 March 1971.*

MacINNES, Colin; Author; *b* 1914; *s* of J. Campbell MacInnes and Angela (novelist, as Angela Thirkell, who *m* 2nd, G. L. Thirkell), *d* of J. W. Mackail, OM. *Educ:* in Australia. Served War of 1939-45: Sergeant, Intelligence Corps. *Publications:* To the Victors the Spoils, 1950; June in Her Spring, 1952; City of Spades, 1957; Absolute Beginners, 1959; Mr Love and Justice, 1960; England, Half English, 1961; All Day Saturday, 1966; Sweet Saturday Night, 1967; Westward to Laughter, 1969; Three Years To Play, 1970; Out of the Garden, 1974; No Novel Reader, 1975; Out of the Way: later essays, 1980 (published posthumously). *Address:* c/o MacGibbon & Kee Ltd, 3 Upper James Street, Golden Square, W1R 4BP. *[Died 22 April 1976.*

McINNES, James, MBE 1941; JP; *b* 19 May 1901; *s* of James William McInnes, Engineer, and Jean McKirdy, Restaurateur; *m* 1925, Elizabeth Hislop Cowie (*d* 1963); one *s. Educ:* Glasgow (Lambhill Street Secondary Sch.). Member Glasgow Town Council, 1933-50, Leader Labour Group, 1949; Magistrate, City of Glasgow, 1937; Principal Administrative Officer, Western Region, NFS, 1941; Member of Fire Service Commission, 1941; Member of Scottish Building Costs Commission, 1947; Chairman Scottish Housing and Town Planning Council, 1948. MP (Lab) Glasgow Central, 1950-66, retired. JP Glasgow 1941. *Recreations:* golf, bowling. *Address:* 94 Bellahouston Drive, Glasgow SW2. *T:* 041-882 2576.   *[Died 14 April 1974.*

MacINNES, Robert Ian Aonas, QC (Scotland), 1946; Sheriff Substitute of Lanarkshire at Hamilton, 1953-55; *b* 23 July 1902; *yr s* of late Rev. Dr Alexander MacInnes, Kirkliston, Edinburgh; *m* 1937, Mary Galloway, *d* of Rev. T. Angus Morrison; one *d. Educ:* privately; Edinburgh Univ. Contested (L) W Stirlingshire, 1923; called to Scottish Bar, 1924; Sheriff Substitute of Ross and Cromarty and Sutherland at Stornoway, 1934-40; of Argyll at Dunoon, 1940-41; of Bute at Rothesay, 1940-41; of Lanarkshire at Glasgow, 1948-53. Contested (Lab) Caithness and Sutherland, 1945. *Recreation:* fishing. *Address:* c/o The National Westminster Bank Ltd, 6 Cambridge Crescent, Harrogate, Yorkshire.   *[Died 14 Jan. 1972.*

MacINNES, William Alexander, MC, MA (Glasgow), DèsL (Paris); Officier d'Académie; Professor of French, Hull University, 1932-57; retired; Emeritus Professor since 1958; *b* 11 April 1892; *s* of William and Jemima MacInnes; *m* 1918, Madeleine Elizabeth Bauer; one *d. Educ:* Glasgow High Sch., Univs of Glasgow, Paris, Grenoble, Florence. Private in Artists' Rifles; 2nd Lieut, 4th Bn Highland Light Infantry; Lieut and Captain, 11th Border Regt (MC and Bar, wounded); Head of Modern Language Dept, Senior War Office School of Education, Cambridge and Newmarket, 1919; studied in Paris and Grenoble, 1920-24; Assistant Lecturer in French, The Victoria Univ., Manchester, 1924-29; Assistant Lecturer in French, The University, Glasgow, 1930-32. *Publications:* edited Swinburne's Ballads of the English Border, 1925; L'Œuvre française de Swinburne, 1933; Thomas Gray en France, 1933; contributor to various French literary reviews and periodicals. *Recreation:* writing. *Address:* 201 Victoria Avenue, Hull, North Humberside. *T:* Hull Central 443949.   *[Died 21 Oct. 1977.*

McINTOSH, Alastair (James), CMG 1960; OBE 1953; retired as Principal Adviser to the High Commissioner, Aden (1963-July 1964); *b* 5 Aug. 1913; *s* of Alexander McIntosh, Dundee. *Educ:* Merchant Taylors' Sch.; St John's Coll., Oxford; Bonn Univ.; American Univ., Beirut. Asst Lectr, Manchester Univ., 1939-40. Served War of 1939-45, 1940-47. Political Officer, Aden Protectorate, 1947; Dep. British Agent, Eastern Aden Protectorate, 1954; Asst Chief Sec., Aden, 1955; Res. Adviser and British Agent, Eastern Aden Protectorate, 1958; Protectorate Sec., Aden, 1960. Merchant Taylor and Citizen of London. *Recreation:* music. *Address:* Latchets, Barford St Martin, Wilts. *T:* Wilton 2159.   *[Died 1 July 1973.*

McINTOSH, Sir Alister (Donald), KCMG 1973 (CMG 1957); Chairman of Trustees, National Library of New Zealand, since 1970; *b* Picton, NZ, 29 Nov. 1906; *e s* of Harry Hobson and Caroline McIntosh; *m* 1934, Doris Hutchinson Pow; one *s. Educ:* Marlborough Coll., Blenheim; Victoria University, Wellington, NZ (MA); University of Michigan, Ann Arbor, USA. Labour Dept, 1925; Parliamentary Library, 1926-34; Carnegie Travelling Fellowship, 1932-33; Prime Minister's Dept, New Zealand, 1935-66; Secretary of War Cabinet, 1943-45; Sec. of External Affairs, NZ, 1943-66; Permanent Head, Prime Minister's Dept, 1945-66; New Zealand Ambassador to Italy, 1966-70; Chm., Broadcasting Council of NZ, 1973-76. Attended many Commonwealth Prime Ministers' conferences and United Nations Assemblies as adviser or delegate, 1944-66. Chm., NZ Historic Places Trust, 1973-78. Hon. LLD, Univ. of Canterbury, NZ, 1965. *Publication:* Marlborough Provincial History, 1939. *Address:* 11 Wesley Road, Wellington, New Zealand. *Club:* Wellington.   *[Died 30 Nov. 1978.*

McINTOSH, Ian Donald, MA; Headmaster of Fettes College, Edinburgh, 1958-July 1971; *b* 4 July 1908; *o s* of late Donald McIntosh, Inverness, and of Lilian Barritt; *m* 1942, Florence Anne, *d* of late Lockhart Boyne, Inverness; one *s* two *d. Educ:* Inverness Academy; Aberdeen Univ. 1st Class Mod. Lang., 1930; Open Schol., Trinity Coll., Cambridge, 1932, 1st Class Mod. Lang. Trip. Part 2, 1934. Assistant Master, Bradfield Coll., 1934-37; Assistant Master, Winchester Coll., 1937-53 (Senior Mod. Lang. Master from 1945). Head Master, George Watson's Coll., Edinburgh, 1953-58. Hon. LLD Aberdeen 1962. *Recreations:* cricket, football, golf, light verse, motoring. *Address:* 22 Comely Bank, Edinburgh. [Died 18 Jan. 1975.

McINTOSH, Robert, CSI 1947; MBE 1937; BSc, MIE(Ind); *b* 1894; *s* of D. H. McIntosh; *m* 1925, Isabella Davidson, *d* of A. Butchart; one *d. Educ:* Edinburgh and St Andrews Universities. Joined Indian Service of Engineers, 1920; Chief Engineer, Public Works Dept (General and Defence), Madras, 1945; retired. *Address:* 2 Bingham Terrace, Dundee. *T:* Dundee 44555. *Club:* Madras (Madras). [Died 15 Aug. 1972.

MACINTYRE, Hon. Sir Donald, Kt 1961; CBE 1947; MP Bulawayo, Federation of Rhodesia and Nyasaland, 1954-63 (MP Bulawayo Central, Southern Rhodesia, 1934-53); *b* Glasgow, 9 Sept. 1891; *s* of Peter Macintyre; *m* 1st, 1912, Gertrude Gill (*d* 1976), Redruth, Cornwall, England; 2nd, 1976, Blanche Gwendoline Fikuart (*née* Horn). *Educ:* Downahill Sch., Glasgow. Councillor of Bulawayo (Mayor, various periods). Chairman: Osborn's Bakeries Ltd (also Managing Director); Rhodesian Investment Trust Co. Ltd; Founder and Director McIntyre & Son; Director: Rhobank; Phillips (Rhodesia). Minister of Finance, Federation of Rhodesia and Nyasaland, 1953-62. JP Southern Rhodesia, 1935; 1st Alderman, City of Bulawayo, 1950; Freedom of City of Bulawayo, 1955. *Address:* 12 Hall Road, Kumalo, Bulawayo, Rhodesia. [Died 24 Aug. 1978.

McINTYRE, Rev. Canon James; Canon Emeritus of Gloucester Cathedral, since 1968; Fellow, University College, Durham, since 1950; working in Trinity College, Toronto, since 1968; *b* 26 Oct. 1888; *e s* of late Robert and Matilda Anne McIntyre, Auchterarder, Scotland; *m* 1st, 1915, Sybil Mary (*d* 1960), *d* of late Sir H. F. Norbury, KCB, KHS, RN; one *d*; 2nd, 1961, Isolde Meinhardt, *d* of late Gustav Adolf Meinhardt and Marie Dorothea Meinhardt. *Educ:* Merchant Taylors' Sch.; University College, Durham (BA, MLitt); Ely Theological Coll.; S John's Coll., University of Manitoba (BD 1st class); Trinity Coll., University of Toronto (DD). Deacon, 1913; Priest, 1914; Curate of Holy Trinity, Eltham, 1913-15; Incumbent of S Mary, Edmonton, Canada, 1915-16; Minister of S Barnabas, Epsom, 1916-18; Rector of Washford Pyne, 1918-21; Curate in charge of S Paul's, Newton Abbot, 1922-25; Vicar of Bishop's Teignton, 1925-30; Rector of Holy Trinity, Bath, 1930-32; of Lympstone, 1932-46. Chapter Librarian, Gloucester Cathedral, 1946-52; Receiver, 1955-68. Proctor in Convocation (Diocese of Exeter), 1929-31 and 1936-45. Canon Residentiary of Gloucester Cathedral, 1946-68, Canon Emeritus, 1968-. JP for City of Gloucester, 1950-68. Examining Chaplain to Bishop of Worcester, 1953-68; Chaplain to City High Sheriff, Gloucester, 1953. *Recreations:* sea lore and life. [Died 24 July 1978.

McINTYRE, Cardinal, His Eminence James Francis Aloysius; Archbishop of Los Angeles, California, 1948-70; *b* New York, 25 June 1886; *s* of late James F. McIntyre and Mary (*née* Pelley). *Educ:* Public Sch. 70; Cathedral Coll. and St Joseph's Seminary, New York. Began work as runner at New York Curb Exchange, 1899; with H. L. Horton Co., Wall Street, 1902-15, rising to Office Manager; studied at evening schs and left business world, 1915. Graduated from Cathedral Coll., 1916; Priest, 1921; Curate of St Gabriel's Church, 1921-23; Asst Chancellor and Asst Diocesan Sec., New York, 1923; Chancellor, 1934; Papal Chamberlain, 1934; Domestic Prelate, 1936; Mem. Diocesan Board of Consultors, 1939; Titular Bishop of Cyrene and Auxiliary Bishop of New York, 1941; a Vicar-Gen., Diocese of New York, 1945; Coadjutor Archbishop and Titular Archbishop of Paltus, 1946; Cardinal, 1953. Knight Grand Cross of the Holy Sepulchre, 1946. *Address:* 637 South Kingsley Drive, Los Angeles, Calif 90005, USA. [Died 16 July 1979.

MacIVER, Alan Squarey, CBE 1960; MC 1918; *b* 2 Aug. 1894; *y s* of late David MacIver, MP; *m* 1922, Lois Katharine Scott-Moncrieff (*d* 1975); two *s* two *d. Educ:* Shrewsbury Sch.; Christ Church, Oxford (MA). Served European War, 1914-18; commd Lancashire Fusiliers (wounded). Called to Bar (Inner Temple), 1922. Managing Dir, David MacIver & Co., Ltd, Steamship Owners, 1925-32. Institute of Chartered Accountants in England and Wales: Asst Sec., 1935, Dep. Sec., 1945, Sec., 1950-62. War of 1939-45, Gen. Staff, War Office, 1940-45. Sec. Sixth

International Congress on Accounting, London, 1952. *Address:* 3 Ravenscroft Road, Henley-on-Thames, Oxon. *Club:* Leander. [Died 5 May 1975.

MacIVER, Prof. Arthur Milne; Professor of Philosophy, University of Southampton, 1960-70; *b* Liverpool, 24 March 1905; *s* of Andrew T. S. MacIver, shipowner, Birkenhead; *m* 1st, 1932, Margaret Willoughby Moon (*d* 1937); one *d*; 2nd, 1944, Miriam Frances Round; one *s* one *d* (and one *s* decd). *Educ:* Winchester Coll.; New Coll., Oxford. BA 1928, MA 1931. Asst in Philosophy, University of Edinburgh, 1931-32; Temp. Lecturer, University of Leeds, Nov.-April 1932-33; Asst Lecturer, University of Birmingham, 1933-34; Lecturer, University of Leeds, 1934-38. Served War of 1939-45, with Political Warfare Exec., 1942-45. Sen. Lecturer, University Coll. (now University of Southampton), Southampton, 1949-60. Pres. Mind Association, 1958; Pres. Aristotelian Soc., 1961-62. *Publications:* articles and reviews in Proc. Aristotelian Soc., Analysis, Philosophy, Mind, etc. *Address:* Oakhill, 126 Highfield Lane, Southampton. *T:* Southampton 54669. [Died 15 June 1972.

MACK, Sir Henry; see Mack, Sir W. H. B.

MACK, Hon. Sir William (George), KBE 1967; Chief Justice of the Supreme Court of Queensland, Australia, 1966-71, retired (Acting Chief Justice, 1965); Chairman, Central Sugar Cane Prices Board, 1957; *b* 2 Nov. 1904; *s* of late A. G. Mack; *m* 1937, Ida, *d* of H. W. Mocatta; one *s* one *d. Educ:* Maryborough Grammar Sch., Australia. Called to the Bar, Queensland, 1930; associate to Mr Justice Henchman; served War of 1939-45 (Major), New Guinea and Pacific Islands: Lecturer in Probate, Divorce and Admiralty Law, University of Queensland; Judge of the Supreme Court of Queensland, 1950-66. President: Land Appeal Court, 1963-71; Med. Assessment Tribunal, 1964-71. *Address:* 60 Alexandra Road, Ascot, Qld 4007, Australia. *Club:* Queensland, Queensland Turf (Life member) (Brisbane). [Died 26 July 1979.

MACK, Sir (William) Henry (Bradshaw), GBE 1952; KCMG 1947 (CMG 1942); LLD (Dublin) 1948; HM Diplomatic Service, retired; *b* 21 Aug. 1894; 2nd *s* of late Rev. A. W. Bradshaw Mack, Dalkey, Co. Dublin; *m* 1921, Lilian May (*d* 1971), *o d* of late F. Lonsdale North, JP, Dublin; one *s. Educ:* The High Sch., Dublin; Trinity Coll., Dublin (Scholar, double Sen. Mod. BA). Served European War (RA) in France and Flanders, 1916-19; temporarily employed Treasury, 1920; entered Foreign Office and Diplomatic Service, 1921. Served at Istanbul, Berlin, Foreign Office, Cairo, Prague, Vienna, Rome, and Paris to 1940. Head of French Dept, Foreign Office, 1940. British Civil Liaison Officer to Allied Comdr-in-Chief in North Africa in 1942 and accompanied Gen. Dwight D. Eisenhower to North Africa, Nov. 1942 (Asst Under-Sec. of State in Foreign Office while so employed); returned to Foreign Office, 1943; Dep. Commissioner (Civil) Allied Commission for Austria, 1944; UK Political Representative in Austria and Political Adviser to British High Commissioner and GOC-in-C British Troops in Austria, 1945; HM Minister to Austria, 1947-48; Ambassador to Iraq, 1948-51; Ambassador to the Argentine Republic, 1951-54 retired, 1955. *Address:* Rose Lawn, Ballybrack, County Dublin, Ireland. *Club:* Royal Irish Automobile (Dublin). [Died 9 March 1974.

MACKAIL, Denis George, FRSL; *b* 3 June 1892; *o s* of late J. W. Mackail, OM; *m* 1917, Diana (*d* 1949), *o c* of Sir Guy Granet, GBE; two *d. Educ:* St Paul's Sch.; Balliol Coll., Oxford. *Publications:* What Next?, 1920; Romance to the Rescue, 1921; Bill the Bachelor, 1922; According to Gibson; Summertime, 1923; The *Majestic* Mystery, 1924; Greenery Street, 1925; The Fortunes of Hugo, 1926; The Flower Show, 1927; Tales from Greenery Street, 1928; Another Part of the Wood; How Amusing!, 1929; The Young Livingstones; The Square Circle, 1930; David's Day; Ian and Felicity, 1932; Having Fun, 1933; Chelbury Abbey; Summer Leaves, 1934; The Wedding, 1935; Back Again, 1936; Jacinth, 1937; London Lovers; Morning, Noon and Night, 1938; The Story of J.M.B.: A Biography, 1941; Life with Topsy, 1942; Upside-Down, 1943; Ho!; Tales for a Godchild, 1944; Huddleston House, 1945; Our Hero; We're Here!, 1947; Where Am I?, 1948; By Auction; Her Ladyship, 1949; It Makes the World Go Round, 1950; numerous short stories in various periodicals. *Address:* 10/74 Elm Park Gardens, SW10. *Club:* Athenæum. [Died 4 Aug. 1971.

McKAY, Andrew Foggo; Director-General, Greater Glasgow Passenger Transport Executive, since 1976; *b* 13 March 1923; *s* of William McKay and Janet Foggo McKay; *m* 1945, Elise Katherine Love; one *s* one *d. Educ:* Kirkcaldy High Sch. Joined salaried staff, LNER, 1939. Served war in Royal Navy, 1942-46.

Returned to salaried staff, LNER, 1946. British Rail: Traffic Apprentice, 1952; Asst to Traffic Manager, 1956; Asst Dist Passenger Manager, 1960; Asst Dist Goods Manager, 1962; Divl Officer (Finance), 1964; Divl Manager, Glasgow, 1966; Passenger Manager, 1968, Asst to Gen. Manager, 1970, and Passenger Manager, 1972, Scottish Region. Director of Planning, GGPTE, 1973. *Recreations:* golf, walking, gardening. *Address:* 9 Brandon Drive, Bearsden, Glasgow G61 3LN. *T:* (home) 041-942 7310; (office) 041-248 5971.

[Died 11 May 1979.

McKAY, Sir Charles Holly, Kt 1963; CBE 1956; formerly: State President, Returned Sailors', Soldiers' and Airmen's League of Australia, Victoria; Commissioner, Melbourne Harbour Trust; *b* Great Western, Victoria, 19 Aug. 1896; *m* 1934, Frances E., *d* of W. Deans. *Educ:* Church of England Grammar Sch., Ararat, Victoria. Served 12th Infantry Bn. *Address:* 2 Banfield Street, Ararat, Victoria 3377, Australia. *Club:* Naval and Military (Melbourne). *[Died 8 Nov. 1972.*

MACKAY, Brigadier Kenneth, CBE 1955 (OBE 1941); DSO 1942; *b* 26 June 1901; *s* of William Mackay, Herne Bay, Kent; *m* 1923, Eve, *d* of E. Ll. Ingram, Parkstone, Dorset; three *s. Educ:* Imperial Service Coll.; Royal Military Academy. Commissioned, Royal Engineers, 1921; Captain, 1932; Major, 1938. Served War of 1939-45 (despatches twice): Greece, Crete, Western Desert, N Africa, NW Europe; CRE 1st Armoured Div. and Chief Engineer, Airborne Corps. Colonel, 1948; Brigadier, 1952; retired, 1954. Chief Administrative Engineer, Eastwoods' Group, 1958-63. Bronze Star Medal (USA), 1944. *Recreations:* painting and gardening. *Address:* 3 Fairfield Close, Lymington, Hants SO4 9NP. *T:* Lymington 77363.

[Died 7 Nov. 1974.

McKEAG, Major William; *b* 1897; *s* of William McKeag, Belmont, Durham; *m* 1922, Marie Elizabeth, *d* of William Corn Crowe, Newcastle upon Tyne; two *s* one *d. Educ:* Belmont School and Johnston's School, Durham; privately. Solicitor; Partner in firm of Molineux McKeag and Cooper, Newcastle upon Tyne and Durham; Director of various companies; served European War, 1914-18, various theatres, and in Russia with Denikin and Wrangel (MSM, Russian Orders of St Stanislaus and St Anne). Served War of 1939-45, Deputy Assistant Adjutant General. Contested Durham at General Elections, 1924 and 1929; MP (L) Durham Division, 1931-35; contested Newcastle North, Gen. Election, 1945; Newcastle East, Gen. Election, 1950; Alderman of City of Newcastle upon Tyne; Deputy Lord Mayor of City of Newcastle upon Tyne, Lord Mayor, 1951-52 and 1953-54; President Newcastle upon Tyne Law Students Assoc.; Member of Newcastle upon Tyne Law Society Council; Under Sheriff, Newcastle upon Tyne; Governor of Royal Victoria Infirmary, Newcastle upon Tyne; Governor Newcastle Royal Grammar Sch.; Chairman, Parliamentary Cttee, Newcastle Corporation; Chairman, Progressive Party, Newcastle upon Tyne; Member: Tyneside Industrial Development Board; Cttee, Inst. of Directors, Newcastle upon Tyne; Tyne Improvement Commissioner; President: Tynemouth Liberal Assoc.; Elswick British Legion; Skal Club of NE England; Newcastle Br. United Commercial Travellers' Assoc.; NE Sporting Club; Boys Club and Kindred Assoc.; Member, Management Cttee, Matfen Hall, Northumberland Cheshire Home; Chairman, Newcastle United FC. Consul for Iceland; President, Consular Corps of Newcastle; Hon. Freedom, City of Newcastle upon Tyne, 1966; Member Society of Antiquaries. Médaille d'Argent de la Ville de Paris; Commander, Order of the Falcon, Iceland. *Publications:* The Evils of Legislation by Regulation; various articles, Sociology, Foreign Affairs, European Problems, etc. *Recreations:* world travel, golf, riding. *Address:* 30 Jesmond Road, Newcastle upon Tyne. *T:* Newcastle 81-1212; 60 Sadler Street, Durham City. *T:* Durham 4011; 19 Windsor Terrace, Newcastle upon Tyne. *T:* 811948. *Clubs:* Pilgrims, Pen and Palette (Newcastle). *[Died 4 Oct. 1972.*

McKEE, His Honour Sir Dermot St Oswald, Kt 1974; a Circuit Judge (formerly Judge of County Courts), 1952-74; *b* 22 Sept. 1904; *o s* of Rev. W. S. McKee, Bradford; *m* 1st, 1928, Violet, *d* of late Eli Dalton, Leeds; no *c* ; 2nd, 1970, Mary K. Wallace, *d* of late Eli Dalton. *Educ:* privately; Leeds Univ. (LLB). Called to Bar, Gray's Inn, 1926. Practice, NE Circuit. Served War of 1939-45; Sqdn Leader, RAF, 1940-45. West Riding Quarter Sessions: Deputy Chairman, 1952; Chairman, 1957; Chairman: Cttee Reorganisation of Parishes Measure for Northern Province, 1957; Conscientious Objectors Tribunal, NE Area, 1958; County Court Rules Cttee, 1969-74 (Mem. 1956-). *Recreation:* fly-fishing. *Address:* Thatched Cottage, Tockwith, York. *T:* Tockwith 281. *[Died 3 April 1980.*

McKEEFRY, His Eminence Cardinal Peter Thomas Bertram; Archbishop of Wellington (NZ), since 1954; *b* 3 July 1899; 5th *s* of late Michael and Mary McKeefry. *Educ:* Christian Brothers, Dunedin; Holy Cross College, Mosgiel; Propaganda Fide, Rome. Ordained, Rome, 1926. Curate, St Patrick's Cathedral, Auckland, 1926; Secretary to late Bishop Cleary, 1926; Assistant Editor, The Month (NZ), 1926; Editor, 1930; Editor and Manager, Zealandia, 1936; Secretary to Archbishop Liston, 1930; Diocesan Secretary, Auckland, 1935; Titular Archbishop of Dercos and Coadjutor-Archbishop to Wellington, with right of succession, 1947. Cardinal, 1969. *Publications:* miscellaneous historical articles; edited pioneer NZ records. *Address:* 10 Guilford Terrace, Wellington 1, NZ. *T:* 42-166.

[Died 18 Nov. 1973.

Mac KEITH, Ronald Charles, MA, DM, FRCP; Editor, Developmental Medicine and Child Neurology, since 1959, and Director, Medical Education and Information Unit, Spastics Society, since 1958; formerly Paediatrician, from 1948, and Director Newcomen Clinic, from 1964, Guy's Hospital; Hon. Pædiatrician: Tavistock Clinic, since 1948; Cassel Hospital, since 1960; *b* 22 Feb. 1908; 6th *s* of Alexander Arthur Mac Keith, MB, ChM, and of Alice, *d* of H. Gadd; *m* 1943, Elizabeth Mary, *er d* of Clement Osborn Bartrum, BSc, FRAS, and of Kate, *d* of F. F. Shattock; two *s* two *d. Educ:* King Edward VI Sch., Southampton; Queen's Coll., Oxford; St Mary's Hospital; Bellevue Hospital, New York. Radcliffe Travelling Fellow, University of Oxford, 1935-36. Temp. acting Surgeon Lieut-Commander, RNVR, 1940-45. Lecturer, WHO Seminar, Sydney, 1953; WHO Study Group, Stockholm, 1954; Secretary, Child Health Sect., BMA, 1956; organised Internat. Study Groups on Child Neurology, Oxford, 1958-76; Member: British Pædiatric Assoc. (James Spence Medal 1972); Soc. for Psychosomatic Research. Joint Sec., Little Club; FRSocMed (Sec., Section of Pædiatrics 1954; Pres. 1970); Chm. Assoc. Child Psychology and Psychiatry, 1961-63; Jt Sec., European Study Gp, Child Neurology. Corresp. Mem., Soc. française de Pédiatrie; Pædiatric Soc., Catalonia; world commn on Cerebral Palsy; Mem. Comité de patronage, Revue de Médicine psychosomatique. Hon. Mem., Amer. Acad. Pædiatrics; Hon. Mem., Amer. Acad. Cerebral Palsy; Rosén von Rosenstein medallist, Swedish Pædiatric Soc., 1974. *Publications:* Infant Feeding and Feeding Difficulties, 3rd edn (with P. R. Evans), 1958, 5th edn (with C. B. S. Wood), 1976; (with J. Sandler) Psychosomatic Aspects of Pædiatrics, 1961; (with J. Apley) The Child and his Symptoms, 1962, 2nd edn 1969; (with M. C. O. Bax) Minimal Cerebral Dysfunction, 1963; (with M. C. Joseph) New Look at Child Health, 1966; (with Peter Gardiner and Vernon Smith) Aspects of Paediatric Ophthalmology, 1969; (with Dorothy Egan and Ronald Illingworth) Developmental Screening 0 to 5 years, 1969; (with I. Kolvin and R. Meadow) Bladder Control and Enuresis, 1973; papers, chapters, articles, films and broadcasts on medical and other subjects. *Recreations:* reading, cooking. *Address:* 35 Bloomfield Terrace, SW1W 8PQ. *T:* 01-730 8164. *Club:* Athenæum. *[Died 30 Oct. 1977.*

MacKENZIE, Alasdair Francis, CMG 1961; *b* 11 April 1910; *e s* of Alexander MacKenzie; *m* 1937, Elizabeth Medea Haynes; one *s* one *d. Educ:* Archbishop Tenison's Sch.; Royal College of Science; Downing Coll., Cambridge; Imperial College of Tropical Agriculture. Agricultural Officer, Sierra Leone, 1935; Senior, 1946; Deputy Director, 1951; Director of Agriculture, British Guiana, 1954; Agricultural Adviser, West Indies, 1958; General Adviser on Tropical Agriculture to Govt of Bolivia, 1962-65. *Publications:* various reports on Commissions of Inquiry on Sugar Industry in West Indies. *Recreations:* fishing, shooting, golf. *Address:* The Knoll, London Road, Liphook, Hants. *Clubs:* West Indian, Flyfishers'. *[Died 17 May 1971.*

MACKENZIE, Sir Compton, Kt 1952; OBE 1919; FRSL; CLit, 1968; Hon. LLD (Glasgow, St Francis Xavier University, Antigonish, NS); Hon. RSA; author; *b* West Hartlepool, 17 Jan. 1883; *e s* of Edward Compton (Mackenzie) and Virginia Bateman; *m* 1st, 1905, Faith (*d* 1960), *y d* of late Rev. E. D. Stone, sometime Master of Eton Coll.; 2nd, 1962, Christina MacSween (*d* 1963), *e d* of late Malcolm MacSween, Tarbert, Harris; 3rd, 1965, Lilian MacSween, *y d* of late Malcolm MacSween, Tarbert, Harris. *Educ:* St Paul's Sch.; Magdalen Coll., Oxford, BA; 2nd Class Modern History, 1904. 2nd Lieut, 1st Herts Regt, 1900-01; Lieut, Royal Marines, 1915; Captain, 1916; served with RND in Dardanelles Expedition, 1915; invalided Sept. 1915; Military Control Officer, Athens, 1916; Director Ægean Intelligence Service, Syra, 1917 (OBE, 1915 Star, Chevalier of the Legion of Honour and of the Redeemer, 4th class of the White Eagle with swords); Captain, Home Guard, 1940-44; President: Wexford Festival, 1951-; Croquet Association, 1954-66; Songwriters' Guild, 1956-; Patron, Poetry Society, 1964- (Pres., 1961-64); Governor-General of the Royal

Stuart Society, 1961-; Rector of Glasgow University, 1931-34; Literary critic of the Daily Mail, 1931-35; President: Dickens Fellowship, 1939-46; Guild of Independent Publishers, 1969. Invited by the Indian Government to visit all the battlefields of the Indian Army during War of 1939-45, 1946-47. Kt Comdr, Royal Order of the Phoenix (Greece), 1966. *Publications:* Poems, 1907; The Passionate Elopement, 1911; Carnival, 1912; Kensington Rhymes, 1912; Sinister Street, vol. i, 1913; Sinister Street, vol. ii, 1914; Guy and Pauline, 1915; Sylvia Scarlett, 1918; Sylvia and Michael, 1919; Poor Relations, 1919; The Vanity Girl, 1920; Rich Relatives, 1921; The Altar Steps, 1922; The Seven Ages of Woman, 1922; The Parson's Progress, 1923; Gramophone Nights (with Archibald Marshall), 1923; The Heavenly Ladder, 1924; Santa Claus in Summer, 1924; The Old Men of the Sea (Paradise for Sale, 1963), 1924; Coral, 1925; Fairy Gold, 1926; Rogues and Vagabonds, 1927; Vestal Fire, 1927; Extremes Meet, 1928; Extraordinary Women, 1928; The Three Couriers, 1929; Gallipoli Memories, 1929; April Fools, 1930; Told, 1930; Athenian Memories, 1931; Buttercups and Daisies, 1931; Our Street, 1931; Unconsidered Trifles, 1932; Greek Memories, 1932 (withdrawn, reissued, 1940); Prince Charlie, 1932; Water on the Brain, 1933; Literature in my Time, 1933; Reaped and Bound, 1933; The Darkening Green, 1934; Marathon and Salamis, 1934; Prince Charlie and his Ladies, 1934; Catholicism and Scotland, 1936; The Book of Barra (with J. L. Campbell), 1936; Figure of Eight, 1936; Pericles, 1937; The Four Winds of Love; The East Wind, 1937; The South Wind, 1937; The West Wind, 1940; West to North, 1940; The North Wind, Vol. I, 1944; The North Wind, Vol. II, 1945; The Windsor Tapestry, 1938; A Musical Chair, 1939; Aegean Memories, 1940; The Red Tapeworm, 1941; The Monarch of the Glen, 1941; Calvary, 1942; Wind of Freedom, 1943; Keep the Home Guard Turning, 1943; Mr Roosevelt, 1943; Brockhouse, 1944; Dr Benes, 1946; The Vital Flame, 1946; Whisky Galore, 1947; All Over the Place, 1949; Hunting the Fairies, 1949; Coalport, 1951; Eastern Epic, Vol. I, 1951; I Took a Journey, 1951; The Rival Monster, 1952; The Queen's House, 1953; Echoes, 1953; Realms of Silver, 1953; The Savoy of London, 1953; Ben Nevis Goes East, 1954; My Record of Music, 1955; Thin Ice, 1956; Sublime Tobacco, 1957; Rockets Galore, 1957; The Lunatic Republic, 1959; Cats' Company, 1960; Greece in My Life, 1960; Mezzotint, 1961; Catmint, 1961; On Moral Courage, 1962; Look at Cats, 1964; Little Cat Lost, 1965; The Stolen Soprano, 1965; Paper Lives, 1966; Robert Louis Stevenson, 1968; The Strongest Man on Earth, 1968; The Steps that Kept Going Down, 1968; The Secret Island, 1969; Butterfly Hill, 1970; My Life and Times: Octave One 1883-91, 1963; Octave Two 1891-1900, 1963; Octave Three 1900-07, 1964; Octave Four 1907-14, 1965; Octave Five 1915-23, 1966; Octave Six 1923-30, 1967; Octave Seven 1930-38, 1968; Octave Eight 1939-46, 1969; Octave Nine 1946-52, 1970; Octave Ten 1953-63, 1971. *Plays:* The Gentleman in Grey, 1906; Carnival, 1912; Columbine, 1920; The Lost Cause, 1931. *Recreations:* gramophone: Editor of The Gramophone, 1923-61; cats: President of the Siamese Cat Club, 1928-. *Address:* 31 Drummond Place, Edinburgh 3. *Clubs:* Savile, Pratt's, Authors' (President); Scottish Arts (Edinburgh). *[Died 30 Nov. 1972.*

MACKENZIE, Brig. David Alexander Laurance, CBE 1944; DSO 1937 (bar 1945); Brigadier, retired, Indian Army; *b* 2 May 1897; *s* of late David Mackenzie, Killen, Fortrose, Ross-shire; *m* 1st, 1927, Muriel Edith Gertrude McIntyre (*d* 1947); three *s*; 2nd, 1950, Francesca Cristine Boileau-Lessy; two *d* (one *s* decd). *Educ:* Dunblane, Perthshire; RMC, Sandhurst. Served European War in 1st Bn Grenadier Guards, BEF France, 1916-17 (two medals). Commissioned into 12 Frontier Force Regt, IA, 1918; EEF, Palestine, 1919-20. NWF Campaign, Waziristan, 1923-24 (Medal and clasp); psc 1932. Staff (Captain) Quetta Bde, 1935-36; Bde Major, Rawalpindi Bde, 1936-39; NWF Campaigns: 1936-37, 1937-38 (Medal and clasp, DSO). War of 1939-45: GSO1, War Office, 1939-42; Comd 9/12 FF Regt, 1943; Burma Campaign: Bde Comdr, 32 Ind. Infantry Bde, 1943-45 (CBE, Bar to DSO, 5 medals). Brigadier Infantry and Dep. Director Military Training at GHQ, India, 1945 (May)-1946; Comdt Tactical and Admin. School, India, 1947; Director, Military Training, AHQ, India, 1948; Military Adviser to High Commissioner for India in London, 1948-50. Commandant, Surrey Army Cadet Force, 1949-52. Commandant, Home Office Civil Defence Experimental Mobile Column, 1951-54; Commandant, Home Office Civil Defence School, Falfield, Glos, 1955-62. Adviser in Civil Defence to Cento, 1962-66. *Recreations:* motoring, gardening and cricket. *Address:* The White House, Spetisbury, Blandford, Dorset. *T:* Sturminster Marshall 366. *[Died 6 Jan. 1976.*

MACKENZIE, Col Eric Dighton, CMG 1935, CVO 1939; DSO 1917; *b* 22 Aug. 1891; *s* of Sir Allan Mackenzie, 2nd Bt of Glenmuick, Aberdeenshire; *m* 1948, Elizabeth, *d* of late Capt. J.

W. G. Innes, CB, RN, and late Marchioness of Aberdeen; two *s* one *d*. *Educ:* Eton Coll. Joined Scots Guards, 1911; served European War (wounded thrice, DSO, despatches twice); retired, 1926; re-employed, 1939-44; Comptroller of the Household to Gov.-Gen. of Canada, 1931-39; JP (Argyll); OStJ. *Address:* Calgary House, Tobermory, Isle of Mull. *Club:* St James'. *[Died 8 Aug. 1972.*

MacKENZIE, Prof. Fraser; Professor of French Language and Literature, University of Birmingham, 1946-73; *b* Wellington, NZ, 3 Nov. 1905; *s* of late Hugh MacKenzie, CMG, Prof. of English Language and Literature, Victoria UC, Wellington, NZ, and late Annie Catherine Watson Stewart. *Educ:* Wellington Coll., NZ (Bristol Pianoforte Scholarship, 1923); Victoria University Coll., NZ; Sorbonne, Paris. Asst Lecturer in French, Univ. of St Andrews, 1934-39; Sen. Lecturer in French, Univ. of Aberdeen, 1939-46. Exchange Prof. of French, Univ. of Montpellier, France, March 1948, 1950, 1952, 1954; Guest Prof. of English, Univ. of Toulouse, 1954; Guest Prof. of Mod. Langs, Victoria University Coll., Wellington, NZ, 1955. Hon. Life Mem., Académie des Jeux Floraux, Toulouse, 1954. Hon. President: Birmingham Univ. Mathematical Soc., 1961-62; Birmingham Univ. Electrical Engineers Soc., 1962-63; Hon. Vice-Pres., Salford Univ. Chem. Soc., 1972-73. DèsL (Paris), 1946; Doctorate (*hc*): Univ. of Montpellier, 1952; Univ. Laval, Quebec, 1967. Chevalier de la Légion d'honneur, 1954. *Publications:* Les Emprunts réciproques de l'anglais et du français, 2 vols (Paris), 1946; (ed) Studies in French Language, Literature and History offered to Prof. R. L. Graeme Ritchie, 1950. *Recreations:* swimming, travel. *Address:* 3 Braithwaite Street, Karori, Wellington 5, New Zealand.

[Died 21 Dec. 1978.

MACKENZIE, James Young; HM Diplomatic Service, retired; *b* 13 Jan. 1914; *s* of late J. A. Mackenzie; *m* 1953, Edith, *d* of late Air Commodore F. Beaumont, CB; two *s*. *Educ:* Kelvinside; Christ Church, Oxford. Entered Diplomatic Service, 1938; Montevideo, 1941; Beirut and Damascus, 1942; Chungking, 1945; Nanking, 1946; Foreign Office, 1948; Baghdad, 1953; Athens, 1954; Vienna, 1959; Seville, 1963-67. *Address:* 51 Pienzenauerstrasse, Munich 81, Germany. *Club:* St James'.

[Died 16 Sept. 1971.

MACKENZIE, John Gurney, CMG 1955; Colonial Administrative Service, retired; *b* 6 Oct. 1907; *s* of William Cossar Mackenzie DSc, and Mary Ann Mackenzie (*née* Sheppard); *m* 1939, Kathleen Hope Harris; one *s* one *d*. *Educ:* Fettes Coll. Edinburgh; Magdalene Coll., Cambridge (BA Hons). Colonial Administrative Service, Nigeria, 1929-56. Financial Sec., Eastern Region, 1951; Civil Sec., 1952. Chm. Public Service Commission, Eastern Region, Nigeria, 1954-Dec. 1956. Retired, 1956. Chm., Civil Service Commission, Bahamas, 1961-64. *Address:* Ardloch, Lochearnhead, Perthshire.

[Died 12 Sept. 1975.

MACKENZIE, Sir (Lewis) Roderick Kenneth, 9th Bt of Scatwell, *cr* 1703 (Nova Scotia); and presumably 11th Bt of Tarbat, *cr* 1602 (Scotland); *b* 8 Aug. 1902; *o s* of Sir Kenneth D. Mackenzie, 8th Bt, and Stephanie Corinne (*d* 1921), *y d* of Dr J. Espinet, MD, Trinidad; *S* father, 1930. *Educ:* The School House, Oakham. Formerly with Empire Cotton Growing Corporation, Southern Rhodesia. *Heir:* kinsman, Roderick Campbell Mackenzie, *b* 15 Nov. 1954. *[Died 10 Dec. 1972.*

McKENZIE, Malcolm George, MBE (mil.) 1944; solicitor; Secretary, Commission for the New Towns, 1974-78; *b* 11 July 1917; *s* of Captain Simon McKenzie and Hilda Warner; *m* 1945, Flora, *d* of T. Harris, S Shields; one *s* two *d*. *Educ:* Ealing Grammar Sch.; Coll. of Law. 26th (LEE) RE, TA, 1938; served War, incl. Europe, 1939-46 (MBE); 124th LAA Regt, RA (Major). Administrator, Mddx CC, 1935-59; Under-Sec., County Councils Assoc., 1959-62; Chief Admin. Officer, Commn for the New Towns, 1962-73 (Advisory Tour, Venezuela, 1969). *Recreations:* Welcare (Christian Housing Assoc.), travel. *Address:* 16 Heronsforde, Ealing W13 8JE. *T:* 01-997 6957. *[Died 22 Aug. 1979.*

MACKENZIE, Melville Douglas, CMG 1947; MD (London), DTM, DTH (Cambridge), DPH; retired as Principal Medical Officer, Ministry of Health; Chief UK Delegate to first, second, third, fourth, fifth and sixth World Health Assemblies; Chairman of Executive Board, 1953-54; *b* 29 June 1889; *s* of Frederick Lumsden Mackenzie, MD, North House, Lockwood, Huddersfield; *m* 1934, Caroline Faith, *d* of Capt. R. H. R. Mackay, OBE, JP, RN, Petham, Kent; two *s* one *d*. *Educ:* Epsom Coll.; St Bartholomew's Hosp., London. MB, BS (London), 1911; MD (London) 1920; DTM, DTH (Cambridge) 1920; DPH 1921; served European War 1914-18, Capt. RAMC

1917-19 (despatches); Sen. MO to Russian Famine Relief Administration, 1921-23; sometime Special Comr of Council of League of Nations to Governments of Liberia and China, Acting-Dir of League of Nations Epidemiological Bureau, Singapore, and Chm. of European Health Cttee of UNRRA; British Delegate with Plenipotentiary powers to World Health Conference, NY, 1946. *Publications:* various articles in medical journals. *Address:* Petham Lodge, near Canterbury, Kent. *T:* Petham 214. *[Died 1 Dec. 1972.*

MACKENZIE, Sir Roderick; *see* Mackenzie, Sir L. R. K.

MacKENZIE, William Forbes, CMG 1955; CBE 1951 (OBE 1946); *b* 5 June 1907; *e s* of late Dr A. J. MacKenzie, Salisbury, S Rhodesia; *m* 1934, Marion Elizabeth, *d* of late F. H. Glenton, Johannesburg, S Africa; no *c. Educ:* Merchiston Castle Sch.; Caius Coll., Cambridge. Native Affairs Dept, S Rhodesia, 1927-36; District Officer, Bechuanaland Protectorate, 1937-48; Asst Administrative Sec. to High Comr for Basutoland, Bechuanaland Protectorate and Swaziland, 1948-49; Dep. Resident Comr and Govt Sec., Swaziland, 1949-51; Dep. Res. Comr and Govt Sec., Bechuanaland Protectorate, 1951-53. Res. Comr, Bechuanaland Protectorate 1953-56, retired. *Recreations:* fishing, shooting and golf. *Address:* 9 Kevin Avenue, Chisipite, Salisbury, Zimbabwe. *Clubs:* Country (Johannesburg); Bulawayo, Salisbury (Zimbabwe). *[Died 1 Aug. 1980.*

McKERRON, Robert Gordon; Emeritus Professor of Law, Rhodes University, South Africa; *b* 20 March 1900; *yr s* of late Prof. R. G. McKerron; *m* 1st, 1928, Nancy (*d* 1937), *o d* of H. A. Green, Johannesburg; one *s*; 2nd, 1939, Elsie, *d* of late J. E. Healey; one *d* (and one *s* decd). *Educ:* Aberdeen Grammar Sch.; Fettes Coll., Edinburgh; Aberdeen Univ. (1st cl. Hons Classics); Oriel Coll., Oxford (1st cl. Hons BA, Hons Sch. of Jurisprudence, 1924; 1st cl. BCL, 1925) (Hon. Fellow 1971); Vinerian Law Schol., 1926; Bacon Scholarship, Gray's Inn, 1926; DCL Oxon, 1947. QC (SA), 1955; Advocate, Supreme Ct of SA; Barrister-at-law, Gray's Inn. Prof. of Law and Dean of the Faculty in University of the Witwatersrand, 1926-46; practised Johannesburg Bar, 1947-54; Prof. and Dean of Faculty of Law, Rhodes Univ., 1955-68. For duration of War, Major SA Defence Force (despatches, POW, Italy). *Publication:* Law of Delict, 7th edn, 1971. *Recreations:* formerly playing, now watching, cricket, golf and tennis. *Address:* 401 Ashbourne, Main Road, Kenilworth, Cape Province, S Africa. *Clubs:* Rand (Johannesburg); Kelvin Grove (Cape Town).
[Died 14 April 1973.

MACKIE, Edwin Gordon; Hon. Ophthalmic Surgeon, United Sheffield Hospitals; Ophthalmic Medical Referee to County Courts; *b* 1896; *e s* of late David Cable Mackie, FSA (Scotland), and Charlotte Fyffe McDonald; *m* 1st, 1931, Mary Owen (*d* 1968), *y d* of F. P. Stokes, Melbourne, Australia; one *s* two *d*; 2nd, 1970, Peggy Lever Brundell Bovill, *o d* of Basil Pickering, MC, JP, East Markham. *Educ:* Madras Coll.; St Andrews Univ.; Birmingham. Served European War: MEF, BEF, Lt The Royal Scots. MA 1919; MB, ChB, 1924 (Medal Ophthalmology). Resident Posts: Dundee Royal Infirm.; Birmingham and Midland Eye Hospital; DOMS (England), FRCSGlas. Temp. Tutor, Edinburgh, 1927; Asst Surgeon, Royal Hosp., Sheffield, 1927, Surg. 1935. Formerly: Surg., Beckett Hosp., Barnsley; visiting oculist, State Instn, Rampton, etc; Clin. Lectr in Ophthalmology; Lectr in Applied Anat., University of Sheffield; Ext. Examr Queen's Univ., Belfast, and Examr for Dipl. in Ophthalmology, Examining Bd in England; Mem. Council, Sheffield Univ., 1949-51; Mem. Bd of Govs, United Sheffield Hosps, 1954-57. Served War of 1939-45: RAMC; France, Comd Ophthalmologist UK, Lt-Col OC Hosp. MEF. President: N of England Ophthalmological Soc., 1947; Sheffield Medico Chirurgical Soc., 1957. Member: Oxford Ophthalmological Congress; Ophthal. Soc. of UK (Vice-Pres., 1962-65; Life Mem. 1973); Ophthal. Gp Cttee, BMA, 1945-65; Council, Faculty of Ophthalmologists, 1946-66 (Pres., 1959-61, Hon. Mem., 1971); Court, University of Sheffield, 1963-75. Life Trustee, Zachary Merton Charity for Convalescents (Chm., 1966-76). Ophthalmic Lecture Tour, Australia and India, 1955. Middlemore Memorial Lectr, 1955. Convenor, Ophth. Adv. Cttee, Sheffield Region, 1948-63; Visitor, Educational Establishments and Examinations, General Optical Council, UK. *Publications:* articles and papers to: Brit. Jl of Ophthalmology; Trans. Ophthalmolog. Soc. of UK, etc. *Recreations:* heraldry, fishing. *Address:* 357 Fulwood Road, Sheffield S10 3BQ. *T:* Sheffield 662206. *Club:* Sheffield (Sheffield). *[Died 30 Aug. 1980.*

MACKIE, John Duncan, CBE 1944; MC, MA, Hon. LLD St Andrews and Glasgow; HM Historiographer in Scotland since 1958; Professor of Scottish History and Literature in the University of Glasgow, 1930-57, retired; Dean of Faculties

(Deputy-Principal), 1940-45; visiting Canadian and S African Universities on British Council travel grants; Member Scottish Records Advisory Council and Chairman, Scottish National Register of Archives; a Vice-President, of Society of Antiquaries of Scotland, 1949-53; President of Scottish History Society; President of Historical Association of Scotland, 1949-53; Member, Scottish National Portrait Gallery Advisory Committee; President of Glasgow Archæological Society, 1936-39; *b* 1887; *e s* of late John Beveridge Mackie of the Dunfermline Journal and Lilias Agnes, *d* of James Robb; *m* 1917, Cicely Jean (*d* 1976), *e d* of Alexander Stephen Paterson, Advocate, Edinburgh; two *s* one *d. Educ:* Middlesbrough High Sch.; Jesus Coll., Oxford. 2nd Cl. Classical Mods; 1st Cl. History Finals; Lothian Essay Prize; Hon. LLD (St Andrews), 1950; Hon. LLD (Glasgow), 1959. Lecturer in Modern History, and head of the Dept of Modern History in the University of St Andrews, 1908-26; Prof. of Modern History in the University of London (Bedford Coll.), 1926-30. Served European War, 1914-19, with 14th Battalion Argyll and Sutherland Highlanders, Capt. (Acting Major, twice wounded); Chm. of Glasgow Joint Recruiting Board, 1939-46. Chevalier de la Légion d'Honneur, 1946; KStJ 1955 (CStJ 1948). *Publications:* essays and reviews in the Scottish Historical Review, English Historical Review, History, Encyclopædia Britannica, etc; The Sixteenth Century, in Cassell's History of the British People (1925); Negotiations between James VI and I and Ferdinand I of Tuscany (1927); The Estate of the Burgesses in the Scots Parliament (1923) (with Dr G. S. Pryde); Cavalier and Puritan, 1930; Andrew Lang and House of Stuart, 1935; Thomas Thomson's Memorial on Old Extent (Stair Soc.), 1946; The Earlier Tudors, 1485-1558, 1952; The University of Glasgow, 1451-1951: A Short History, 1954; Scottish History (Readers' Guide), 1956; A History of the Scottish Reformation, 1960; Introd. to Polwarth Papers, V, 1962; A History of Scotland (Pelican), 1964; (ed) Calendar of State Papers relating to Scotland and Mary Queen of Scots, Vol. XIII, 1597-1603, 1969. *Address:* Marley Manor Nursing Home, near Haslemere, Surrey. *[Died 22 Sept. 1978.*

McKIE REID, Col Andrew; *see* Reid.

MACKILLIGIN, Robert Springett, CMG 1944; OBE 1919; MC 1916; MIMM; *b* 23 March 1890; *s* of Robert Marquis Mackilligin; *m* 1938, Patricia Margaret Elizabeth, *d* of late Lt-Col F. S. Waldegrave, OBE, MC, QO Cameron Highlanders; one *s* one *d. Educ:* Cranbrook Sch., Kent; Camborne Sch. of Mines, Cornwall. Mining Engineering in Burma and West Africa, 1910-15; served in France, Capt. RE, 1915-17; N Russia, RE, 1917-19 (despatches twice, MC and bar, OBE); with Anglo-Iranian Oil Co. in Persia and Patagonia, 1920-36; Inspector of Mines and Petroleum Technologist, Trinidad, 1936-46. *Address:* c/o Lloyds Bank Ltd, 6 Pall Mall, SW1. *[Died 31 Dec. 1972.*

MACKINLAY, Sir George Mason, Kt 1955; Director, McLeod Russel and Co. Ltd, since 1957, etc.; *b* 18 Oct. 1906; *s* of late Charles Alexander Mackinlay; *m* 1936, Ellen Margaret Greaves; one *s. Educ:* Loretto. Pres. of the Associated Chambers of Commerce and of the Bengal Chamber of Commerce, 1954-55. Lately Chm. and Man. Dir Jardine Henderson Ltd, Calcutta, and Dir of State Bank of India. *Address:* Cross Keys, East Meon, near Petersfield, Hants. *Club:* Oriental.
[Died 12 June 1973.

McKINNEY, Sir William, Kt 1964; CBE 1956; *b* 14 Nov. 1897; *s* of James and Edith McKinney; *m* 1st, 1925, Lisla Chesney, *d* of Robert Clyde; one *s*; 2nd 1936, Mary E., *d* of William T. Unsworth. *Educ:* Belfast Royal Academy. Joined Board of Management of Royal Victoria Hospital, Belfast, 1931; subsequently Hon. Sec. First Vice-Chm., Northern Ireland Hospitals Authority, 1948-50 and 1953-55. Custodian Trustee, Belfast Savings Bank (Chm., 1946 and 1967). Chm., Northern Ireland Hospitals Authority, 1956-65. Hon. Treasurer, Queen's Univ., 1966. Hon. LLD Queen's Univ., 1966. *Address:* 5 Deramore Park South, Belfast BT9 5JY. *T:* Belfast 666396.
[Died 20 Nov. 1979.

MacKINNON, Georgina Russell Davidson, (Gena MacKinnon), OBE 1964; Chairman of Drambuie Liqueur Co.; *b* 1885; *d* of John and Margaret Davidson; *m* 1914, Malcolm MacKinnon; one *s* one *d. Educ:* James Allen's Girls' Sch., London; Wick Acad., Caithness. Company Chm. and Farmer of pedigree Jersey cattle. *Address:* Williamcraigs, Linlithgow, West Lothian, Scotland. *T:* Linlithgow 2072. *Clubs:* White Elephant, Siegis, 21. *[Died 11 April 1973.*

McKINNON, Sir James, Kt 1956; Chief Inspector, Board of Customs and Excise, 1954-59; retired Dec. 1959; *b* 24 Sept. 1894; *m* 1919, Margaret Simpson; two *s* one *d. Educ:* Rothesay Academy. Entered Bd of Customs and Excise, 1914; Collector,

Customs and Excise, Belfast, 1950-52; Dep. Chief Inspector, Bd of Customs and Excise, 1952-54. *Address:* 3 Gainsborough Terrace, Manor Road, Cheam, Surrey. *T:* 01-642 1659.
[Died 8 Dec. 1971.

MACKINNON, Col Lachlan, CBE 1956; DSO 1919; TD; DL; MA, LLB; Advocate in Aberdeen; *b* 9 Sept. 1886; *s* of Lachlan Mackinnon and Theodora Thompson; *m* 1st, 1914, Marjory Gordon (*d* 1940); two *s* one *d*; 2nd, 1950, Ann Paul Scott. *Educ:* Robert Gordon's Coll. and University, Aberdeen; partner, 1909-66, in firm of L. Mackinnon and Son; Hon. Sheriff-Substitute for Aberdeenshire; Lecturer in International Law, University of Aberdeen, 1936-51. Commissioned to 4th Batt. Gordon Highlanders TA. 1905; Lt, 1906; Capt., 1910; served European war in France and Flanders for 35 months, Temp. Lt-Col comdg 14th (S) Batt. Argyll and Sutherland Highrs, 1918 (despatches twice, DSO, TD, Croix de Guerre, 1914-15 star); commanded 4th Gordon Highrs, 1920-23; Brevet Col; Chm. City of Aberdeen TA Assoc., 1934-37; Palmes d'Officer d'Académie, 1939; Médaille d'honneur, 1950; Médaille Civique, 1st class (Belgian), 1954. Chevalier de l'ordre de Léopold, 1956; Chevalier de la Légion d'Honneur, 1956. DL County of the City of Aberdeen, 1959. *Publications:* Leading Cases in the International Private Law of Scotland, 1934; Manual of Company Law and Conveyancing (Joint), 1939. *Recreations:* golf and fishing. *Address:* Woodcote, Torphins, Aberdeenshire. *T:* Torphins 292. *Club:* Royal Northern (Aberdeen).
[Died 10 Aug. 1973.

MACKINTOSH OF HALIFAX, 2nd Viscount, *cr* 1957; Baron, *cr* 1948; Bt, *cr* 1935; **John Mackintosh,** OBE 1976; BEM 1946; FInstM 1968; Director, John Mackintosh & Sons Ltd, 1950-76; *b* 7 Oct. 1921; *s* of Harold Vincent Mackintosh (1st Viscount, Baron and Bt) and Constance (*née* Stoneham) (*d* 1975); *S* father, 1964; *m* 1st, 1946 (marr. diss., 1956); two *d*; 2nd, 1956, Gwynneth, *yr d* of Charles H. Gledhill, Halifax, Yorkshire; two *s. Educ:* Bedales Sch.; Trinity Coll., USA. RAOC, 1942-47. Director: Tom Smith & Co. Ltd, 1956-76; Tudor Auto Services, 1961-72; Thickthorn Farm Ltd, 1955- (Chm., 1965-). President: Confectioners' Benevolent Fund, 1959-60 (Vice-Chm., 1964-67, Chm., 1967-76); Leeds Inst. of Marketing, 1966-68; Chairman: Norfolk Savings Cttee, 1975-78; Norwich Savings Cttee, 1965-75; Inst. of Directors (Norfolk and Suffolk Branch), 1968-78 (Pres., 1978-); Governor, Town Close Preparatory Sch., Norwich; Vice-Chairman: Eastern Region Nat. Savings Cttee; Industrial Savings Cttee, Eastern Region. Hon. Treasurer: London Cttee, World Council Christian Education, 1965-72; Nat. Christian Educn Council, 1972-. *Recreations:* cricket, football. *Heir: s* Hon. (John) Clive Mackintosh, *b* 9 Sept. 1958. *Address:* The Old Hall, Barford, Norwich, Norfolk NR9 4AY. *T:* Barnham Broom 271. *Clubs:* Royal Automobile, MCC.
[Died 2 Nov. 1980.

MACKINTOSH, Hon. Lord; Charles Mackintosh, MC; Hon. LLD (Edinburgh); Hon. Fellow, Wadham College, Oxford; one of the Senators of the College of Justice in Scotland, 1944-64; *b* 28 May 1888; *s* of Hugh and Henrietta I. Mackintosh; *m* 1921, Mary Lawrie Prosser; four *d. Educ:* Edinburgh Academy; Wadham Coll., Oxford; Edinburgh Univ. Called to Scots Bar, 1914; served European War, Gallipoli, Palestine, France, 1914-19; KC 1935; Sheriff of Argyll, 1937-42; Sheriff of Inverness, Elgin and Nairn, 1942-44. *Recreation:* golf. *Address:* 55 Northumberland Street, Edinburgh. *T:* 031-556 3681. *Club:* New (Edinburgh).
[Died 2 Aug. 1978.

MACKINTOSH, Charles; *see* Mackintosh, Hon. Lord.

MACKINTOSH, (Charles Ernest Whistler) Christopher, BA; Director: International Publicity and Advertising Ltd; Gillon & Co. Ltd; Five Ocean Film Co. Ltd; *b* 31 Oct. 1903; *e s* of late Charles E. Mackintosh, Chaville, France; *m* 1st, 1927, Lady Jean Douglas-Hamilton (divorced 1946), *e d* of 13th Duke of Hamilton; two *s* two *d*; 2nd, 1946, Irene, *d* of Colonel Mann Thomson, Melton Mowbray; one *s* one *d. Educ:* Eastbourne Coll.; University College, Oxford. Honours School of Mod. Hist.; Public Schools Doubles Tennis Champion, 1921; Oxford Rugby Blue and Athletic Blue; Scottish International Rugby; Olympic Games, 1924; Member of British Bobsleigh Team winning World Championships, 1937; Oxford University Ski Team; British Ski Team. Chairman and Managing Director of Sir Henry Lunn Ltd, and Alpine Sports Ltd, 1931-44. *Recreations:* Rugby football, cricket, athletics, golf, ski-ing, tennis, shooting, fishing. *Address:* The Lodge, Linplum, Haddington, East Lothian. *Clubs:* Queen's, Royal Automobile.
[Died 12 Jan. 1974.

MACKINTOSH, Christopher; *see* Mackintosh, C. E. W. C.

MACKINTOSH, Eric Donald, CBE 1949; JP; DL; Trustee: East Anglian Trustee Savings Bank, since 1942; Trustee Savings Bank of Eastern England, since 1976 (Chairman, 1976-77); *b* 1906; *s* of late John Mackintosh, JP, Halifax; *m* 1928, Gwendolyn, *d* of H. L. France, Halifax; two *s* one *d. Educ:* Halifax New Sch.; Manchester Univ. Director, Cocoa Chocolate and Confectionery Division, Ministry of Food, 1942-45; President, Cocoa, Chocolate and Confectionery Alliance Ltd, 1946-48 (Vice-Pres., 1949-51; Treas., 1957-72). Formerly Director: Norwich Union Fire Insurance Soc.; Norwich Union Life Insurance Soc.; Scottish Union & National Insurance Co. Ltd; Maritime Insurance Co. Ltd; Tom Smith & Co. Ltd (Chm., 1951-71). JP, 1949, DL 1974, High Sheriff, Norfolk, 1971-72. *Recreations:* music, fishing. *Address:* Brooke House, Brooke, Norwich NR15 1JN. *Clubs:* Royal Automobile; Norfolk (Norwich).
[Died 25 April 1978.

MACKINTOSH, John Pitcairn; MP (Lab) Berwick and East Lothian, 1966-Feb. 1974 and since Oct. 1974; part-time Professor and Head of Department of Politics, Edinburgh University, since 1977; freelance writer; television commentator; *b* 24 Aug. 1929; *s* of Colin M. Mackintosh and Mary Victoria (*née* Pitcairn); *m* 1957, Janette M. Robertson (marr. diss. 1963); one *s* one *d*; *m* 1963, Catherine Margaret Una Maclean; one *s* one *d. Educ:* Melville Coll., Edinburgh; Edinburgh, Oxford and Princeton Univs. DLitt Edinburgh, 1967. Asst Lectr, Glasgow Univ., 1953-54; Lectr in History, Edinburgh Univ., 1954-61; Sen. Lectr in Government, University of Ibadan, Nigeria, 1961-63; Senior Lecturer in Politics, Glasgow Univ., 1963-65; Professor of Politics, Univ. of Strathclyde, 1965-66. Vis. Prof., Birkbeck Coll., London, 1972-. Member, Select Cttees on Agriculture, 1967-69; Scottish Affairs, 1968-70, Procedure, 1966-72, Scrutiny of European Secondary Legislation, 1974-; Vice-Chm., GB/East Europe Centre; Mem., Exec. Cttee, British Council, 1968-73. Chm., Hansard Soc., 1974-78. Joint Editor, The Political Quarterly, 1975-. *Publications:* The British Cabinet, 1962; Nigerian Politics and Government, 1966; The Devolution of Power, 1968; British Government and Politics, 1970; (ed) British Prime Ministers in the Twentieth Century, vol. I: Balfour to Chamberlain, 1977, vol. II: Churchill to Callaghan, 1978. *Recreation:* gardening. *Address:* Nether Liberton House, Gilmerton Road, Edinburgh. *T:* 031-664 3911. *Clubs:* Reform; Edinburgh University.
[Died 30 July 1978.

MACKINTOSH, Captain Sir Kenneth Lachlan, KCVO 1966; Royal Navy (retired); Serjeant at Arms, House of Lords, 1962-71; Yeoman Usher of the Black Rod, 1953-71; Secretary to the Lord Great Chamberlain, 1953-71; *b* 6 July 1902; *s* of Stewart Mackintosh and Alice Ballard; *m* 1st, 1929, Elizabeth (*d* 1960), *d* of Captain Bertram Fawcett; one *s* one *d* (and two *s* decd); 2nd, 1962, Yolande, *d* of Leonard Bickford-Smith. *Educ:* RN Colleges, Osborne and Dartmouth. Directing Staff of RN Staff Coll., 1938; served in: French Fleet, 1939; HMS Duke of York, 1940; HMS Fencer (comd), 1945; HMS Liverpool (comd), and as Chief of Staff to Earl Mountbatten, 1948; Naval Attaché, Paris, 1950; retired, 1953. *Address:* Windalls, Slinfold, Sussex. *T:* Slinfold 242.
[Died 12 Jan. 1979.

MACKLIN, Sir (Albert) Sortain (Romer), Kt 1946; Indian Civil Service (retired); *b* 4 March 1890; *s* of late Albert Romer Macklin, County Court Judge, and Kate, *d* of Benjamin Warren, of Deal; *m* 1st, 1920, Marjorie Vivian (*d* 1971), MBE 1943, *d* of late G. H. Kent; one *d*; 2nd, 1972, Lilian Margaret, *widow* of Rev. R. C. Herring. *Educ:* Westminster; Christ Church, Oxford. Entered ICS, 1913; posted to Bombay Presidency; Puisne Judge, High Court, Bombay, 1935-47. Chairman Medical Appeal Tribunal, Liverpool, 1952-62. *Recreations:* fishing, sailing. *Address:* 32b St John's Road, Eastbourne, East Sussex. *Club:* Flyfishers'.
[Died 28 Dec. 1976.

McLACHLAN, Donald Harvey, OBE 1945; author and journalist; *b* 25 Sept. 1908; *s* of David James McLachlan, London; *m* 1934, Katherine, *d* of late N. Bishop Harman, FRCS; three *s* one *d. Educ:* City of London School; Magdalen Coll., Oxford. 1st class PPE, 1930; Laming Fellow, Queen's Coll., Oxford, 1932-33; Editorial staff of The Times, 1933-36; Assistant Master, Winchester Coll., 1936-38; Editor, The Times Educational Supplement, 1938-40. Naval Intelligence, 1940-45; Assistant Editor (Foreign), The Economist, 1947-54; Deputy Editor of the Daily Telegraph, 1954-60; Editor, Sunday Telegraph, 1961-66. Visiting Fellow of Nuffield Coll., Oxford, 1960-68. Member, General Advisory Council, BBC, 1961-65. *Publications:* Room 39: A Study in Naval Intelligence, 1968; In the Chair: Barrington-Ward of The Times, 1970. *Recreations:* music, walking. *Address:* Coneycroft, Selborne, Hants. *T:* Selborne 224, (in London) 01-834 2012. *Club:* Brooks's.
[Died 10 Jan. 1971.

MacLACHLAN, Robert Boyd, CIE 1935; MInstCE; Superintending Engineer, Indian Service of Engineers (retired); *b* 5 Sept. 1880; *s* of James Boyd and Mary Sinclair MacLachlan; unmarried. *Educ:* Rutland Coll., Dublin; Queen's Coll., Galway. Graduated from the Royal University of Ireland in Degrees of Arts and Engineering in 1902, and 1903; Assistant Engineer in the Indian Public Works Department, 1905; served in the Irrigation Department in the Bombay Presidency and in Sind, 1905-22; Under Secretary to Government in the Public Works Department, 1923; Superintending Engineer in charge of the Western Circle of the Lloyd Barrage and Canal Construction Project, 1923-33; a Member of the Sind Administrative Cttee, 1934. *Recreations:* shooting, fishing, riding. *Address:* c/o Bank of Ireland, Main Street, Wicklow, Ireland. *Clubs:* East India, Sports and Public Schools; Sind (Karachi). *[Died* 4 Feb. 1975.

MACLACHLAN, Thomas Kay, MA, MB, BCh (Cambridge), FRCPE, FRFP&S; late Area Consultant Physician, Counties of Stirling, Clackmannan and West Perth; Member Associations of: Physicians of Great Britain; British Neurologists; International Society of Internal Medicine; Physician for Diseases of the Nervous System, Victoria Infirmary, Glasgow; Senior Assistant Physician, Glasgow Royal Infirmary; Consulting Neurologist, Glasgow Eye Infirmary; Physician, Glasgow Royal Cancer Hospital; Medical Specialist to Ministry of Pensions; Examiner in Neurology and Psychiatry for Fellowship of Royal Faculty of Physicians and Surgeons; *b* 17 Feb. 1895; *s* of Lachlan Maclachlan, Dalnabruaich, Helensburgh; *m* Sarah, *yr d* of John Nelson, Eaglesfield, Dumfriesshire; one *s* one *d*. *Educ:* Merchiston Castle Sch.; Pembroke Coll., Cambridge; London, Strassburg, Paris. Fearnsides Research Scholar in Nervous Diseases, Cambridge Univ.; Foulis Memorial Scholar, Glasgow Univ. Served European War, 1914-17, Argyll and Sutherland Highlanders (wounded). *Publications:* Familial Periodic Paralysis; Disseminated Encephalomyelitis after Spinal Anæsthesia; Narcolepsy; The Liver Treatment of Pernicious Anæmia; Diabetes and its Complications since the Institution of Insulin Therapy. *Recreations:* golf and gardening. *Address:* Leewood House, Dunblane, Perthshire. *T:* Dunblane 2161.
[Died 6 Sept. 1972.

MACLAGAN, William Gauld, MA (Oxford), PhD (Edinburgh); Professor of Moral Philosophy, University of Glasgow, 1946-69; *b* 22 April 1903; 2nd *s* of Rev. P. J. Maclagan, DD, and of Emily Elizabeth Gauld; *m* 1943, Catharine Hannah Mair; one *s* one *d*. *Educ:* City of London Sch.; Exeter Coll., Oxford; Edinburgh Univ. Assistant, Department of Logic and Metaphysics, Edinburgh Univ., 1928-29; Lecturer in Philosophy, Oriel Coll., Oxford, 1930-46; Fellow, 1931-46. Temporary Civil Servant, HM Treasury, 1940-46. Edward Cadbury Lecturer, Birmingham Univ., 1955-56. *Publications:* The Theological Frontier of Ethics, 1961; papers in various philosophical journals. *Address:* Dunrivach, Aberfoyle, Stirling. *T:* Aberfoyle 332. *[Died* 14 Dec. 1972.

MacLAREN, Andrew; *b* 1883; *s* of John MacLaren of Glasgow; two *s*. *Educ:* Technical Coll. and School of Art, Glasgow. MP (Lab) Burslem Div. of Stoke-on-Trent, 1922-23, 1924-31 and 1935-45. *Address:* 14 Harbledown Road, SW6. *T:* 01-736 0649. *Clubs:* Beefsteak, Garrick. *[Died* 11 April 1975.

McLAREN, Martin; Director: English China Clays Ltd, since 1973; Archway Unit Trust Managers Ltd, since 1973; *b* 11 Jan. 1914; *s* of late Hon. Francis McLaren; *m* 1943, Nancy Ralston, *d* of late Rt Hon Philip Cator; two *s* (and one *s* decd). *Educ:* Eton Coll. (Scholar); New Coll., Oxford; Harvard Univ. (Henry Fellow). Asst Principal, Home Office, 1938. Served War of 1939-45, Grenadier Guards, Major. Principal, Home Office, 1946-47. Barrister, Middle Temple, 1948. MP (C) Bristol North-West, 1959-66, 1970-Sept. 1974; an Asst Govt Whip, 1961-63; a Lord Comr of the Treasury, 1963-64; an Opposition Whip, 1964-66; PPS to Sec. of State for Foreign and Commonwealth Affairs, 1970-74. *Recreations:* squash rackets (half-blue), looking at pictures and buildings. *Address:* 30 Smith Square, SW1. *T:* 01-222 6626; Old Rectory, Inkpen, Newbury, Berks. *Clubs:* Brooks's, Buck's. *[Died* 27 July 1979.

McLAREN, Moray David Shaw; Author; *b* 24 March 1901; *s* of John Shaw McLaren, MD, FRCS, and Eva Helen Inglis; *m* 1946, Lennox Milne (OBE 1956). *Educ:* Merchiston Castle; Corpus Christi Coll., Cambridge. Studied in Paris, 1924-25. Asst editor, The London Mercury, under Sir John Squire; joined BBC staff, 1928; first asst editor upon foundation of The Listener, 1929; first Programme Director for Scotland, 1933; Asst Dir talks, then Features and Drama, 1935-40; attached to Foreign Office as Head of Polish Region Political Intelligence Dept, 1940-45; then returned to live in Edinburgh and write.

Publications: Return to Scotland; A Wayfarer in Poland; The Noblest Prospect (novel); Poland's Progress; Escape and Return (novel); A Dinner with the Dead (Short Stories); Stern and Wild; By Me... (A Shakespearean Study); The Unpossesed (novel); The Capital of Scotland; Stevenson and Edinburgh; A Small Stir-Letters on the English (with James Bridie); The Scots (Pelican); A Singing Reel; Scotland in Colour; The Highland Jaunt; Lord Lovat of The '45; Understanding the Scots; The Pursuit (novel); Fishing As We Find It (with Gen. R. N. Stewart); The Wisdom of the Scots; Union Compleat (satire); If Freedom Fail; The Shell Guide to Scotland; Corsica Boswell; Rivers and Lochs of Scotland (with W. B. Currie); Walter Scott, Man and Patriot: A Biographical Study; The Intuitive Prince (biography); plays: One Traveller Returns; Heather on Fire (award Foyle Trust); The Non-Resident; Muckle Ado. Author of many radio plays and feature programmes. Regular literary reviewer, The Glasgow Herald, The Scotsman, and other jls. *Recreations:* trout-fishing, travel and croquet (Founder and first Pres. of Edinburgh Croquet Club). *Address:* Peg de Lone, Station Avenue, Haddington, East Lothian. *Clubs:* Savile; Scottish Arts, Edinburgh Croquet (Edinburgh). *[Died* 11 July 1971.

McLAREN, Ross Scott, DSO 1940; OBE 1964 (MBE 1945); TD 1944; DL; JP; BSc; retired as Production Director, Northumberland and Durham Division, National Coal Board, 1966; *b* 3 March 1906; *s* of late H. B. McLaren, Lumley Grange, Fence Houses, Co. Durham; *m* 1935, Marjorie Stratton; two *d*. *Educ:* Rossall Sch.; King's Coll., Durham Univ. Mining Engineer (MIME). DL 1948, JP 1950, Co. Durham. *Address:* The Dene, Riding Mill, Northumberland. *[Died* 6 June 1975.

McLAUGHLIN, Charles Redmond, MA, MB, ChB, BChir, FRCSE; Consultant Plastic Surgeon: Queen Victoria Hospital, East Grinstead, 1948-69; Kent and Canterbury Hospital, Canterbury, 1953-69; St Bartholomew's Hospital, Rochester, 1962-69; *b* 1 Oct. 1909; *s* of late W. H. McLaughlin, JP, DL and Emma Margaret Brough (née Warren); *m* 1936, Rosemary Macdonald; one *s* one *d* (and one *s* decd). *Educ:* Rugby Sch.; Emmanuel Coll., Cambridge; University of Edinburgh. House Phys, Royal Infirmary, Edinburgh; House Surg., Royal Hants County Hosp., Winchester, 1935; Hon. Surg. to Out-patients, Royal Surrey County Hosp., Guildford, 1937-38. Served with RAFVR, Medical Br., 1940-45; Wing Comdr i/c surgical div., 1945. EMS Surg., Queen Victoria Hosp., E Grinstead, 1946-48; Cons. Surg. to SE Metrop. Regional Hosp. Bd, 1948-69. Founder Mem. Brit. Assoc. of Plastic Surgeons, 1948 (Hon. Sec., 1957-59; Mem. Coun., 1960-62); Mem. Ed. Bd, Brit. Jl of Plastic Surgery, 1950-69; Chm. of Adv. Cttee on Plastic Surgery to Regional Bd, 1964-69. *Publications:* Plastic Surgery, 1951; The Royal Army Medical Corps, 1971; The Escape of the Goeben, 1974; chapters in several surgical textbooks; articles in British, American and French jls; editorials in Lancet. *Recreations:* music; writing and reading naval and military history. *Address:* The Oast, Mayfield, East Sussex. *T:* Mayfield 3064.
[Died 29 June 1979.

MacLEAN, Col Charles Allan, CBE 1941 (MBE 1918); MC; *b* 22 May 1892; *s* of John MacLean, Tobermory, Isle of Mull, Scotland; *m* 1920, Mabel Elsie (*d* 1976), *y d* of Alfred Matthews, Sherborne St John, Hants; three *s* one *d*. *Educ:* Tobermory and Kingussie Sch.; Edinburgh Univ. MA 1914; BSc (Agric) 1920; in France with 11th Argyll and Sutherland Highlanders, 1915-19 (MBE, MC, Croix de Guerre, despatches). Joined Indian Agricultural Service, 1920; Cane Commissioner, Bihar, 1939-43; Dir of Agriculture, 1943-46; Commissioner of Agriculture, Baroda, 1946-49; Field Agricultural Officer, Jordan, with UN Relief and Work Agency, 1951-55. Commanded Chota Nagpur Regt AF(I), 1934-38, and Bihar Light Horse AF(I), 1939-41. Mem., Tobermory Town Council, 1958-62; Provost of Tobermory, 1959-62. Pres. Mull and Iona Council of Social Service, 1959-66. Freeman, Burgh of Tobermory, 1975. *Address:* Ulva Cottage, Tobermory, Scotland. *T:* Tobermory 2044.
[Died 30 March 1978.

McLEAN, John, CBE 1947; Member, Council of Foreign Bondholders, 1948-74; a UK Representative on Commonwealth Economic Committee, 1950-62; a General Commissioner of Income Tax for City of London, 1956-68; *b* 19 April 1893; *s* of late Thomas Crawford McLean; *m* 1915, Catherine Kydd Strachan; one *s* two *d*. *Educ:* Hyndland Sch., Glasgow. Company Director; Chm., George Wills & Sons Ltd, Exporters and Importers, 1949-59, retired. Vice-Pres., London Chamber of Commerce, 1946 (Chm. 1944-46); Vice-Pres., Fedn of Commonwealth Chambers of Commerce, 1951 (Chm. 1948-51); Pres. Assoc. of British Chambers of Commerce, 1948-50; Member: Export Credits Guarantee Advisory Council, 1952-63; Port of London Authority, 1955-64. *Recreation:* golf. *Address:* Glenesk, 57 Brookmans Avenue, Brookmans Park, Hatfield,

Herts. *T:* Potters Bar 53336. *Club:* East India, Devonshire, Sports and Public Schools. *[Died* 30 *April* 1978.

McLEAVY, Baron (Life Peer), *cr* 1967, of City of Bradford; **Frank McLeavy;** *b* 1 Jan. 1899; *y s* of late John McLeavy, Congleton, Cheshire; *m* 1924; one *s* one *d* (and one *s* decd). *Educ:* Elementary Sch. and Evening Institutes. Road Passenger Transport Officer; Mayor of Bebington, 1939-41; formerly: JP Co. of Chester; Alderman Cheshire County Council; Chairman, Bebington ATC Cttee; MP (Lab) Bradford East Div., 1945-66, retired. Mem. of Cheshire Standing Joint Cttee; Chm. of all-party Cttee which organised Parliamentary Presentation to Sir Winston Churchill on his eightieth birthday. Mem. of Cheshire Police Authority. JP Co. Middlesex, 1951-. *Address:* 9 Sheridan Terrace, Whitton Avenue, Northolt, Mddx. *[Died* 1 *Oct.* 1976.

MacLENNAN, Sir Hector, Kt 1965; MD, FRCP, FRCPGlas, FRCOG; Chairman, Advisory Committee on Distinction Awards, since 1971; Director, Inveresk Research International; *b* 1 Nov. 1905; *s* of Robert Jackson MacLennan and Amy Florence Ross; *m* 1st, 1933, Isabel Margaret Adam (*d* 1973); three *s* one *d*; 2nd, 1976, Jean Elspeth Duncan Lackie. *Educ:* Glasgow High Sch.; University of Glasgow. President Glasgow Univ. Union, 1927. Cons. Surgeon, Glasgow Royal Maternity and Women's Hospital, 1934-71; Senior Cons. Gynæcologist, Victoria Infirmary, Glasgow, 1948; Mem. W Regional Hosp. Bd, 1950-56. Mem. GMC, 1965-69. Lately External Examr in Obst. and Gynæc., Univs of Birmingham, Newcastle, Aberdeen, Edinburgh, Oxford, Dundee and Cambridge, and, at present, Dublin. Blair-Bell Lectr, 1944; Lloyd-Roberts Lectr, 1964; Osler Lectr, 1966; Arthur Wilson Oration, 1966; Joseph Price Oration, 1966; Harveian Oration, Edinburgh, 1970. President: RCOG, 1963-66; RSM, 1967-69; Chairman: Medico-Pharmaceutical Forum, 1968-70; Scottish Tourist Bd, 1969-74. Lord High Comr to General Assembly of Church of Scotland, 1975 and 1976. Hon. FACOG, 1964; Hon. FCSOG 1965; Hon. FRCSE, 1967; Hon. Fellow, American Assoc. of Obsts and Gynæcs, 1967. Hon. Alumnus: Sloane Hosp. for Women, NY; Nat. Maternity Hosp., Dublin; Master of Midwifery, Royal Society of Apothecaries, 1968. Hon. FRCPGlas 1971; FRCP 1973; Hon. Member: Royal Medico-Chirurgical Soc., Glasgow, 1971; Section of Medical Educn, RSM, 1971. Hon. LLD Glasgow, 1974. *Publications:* contribs to Combined Textbook of Obstetrics and Gynæcology and British Practice of Obstetrics and Gynæcology (1st edn), and sundry others. *Recreations:* fishing, shooting. *Address:* Invercorry, Rogart, Sutherland. *T:* Rogart 344. *[Died* 6 *Jan.* 1978.

MacLENNAN, Sir Robert Laing, Kt 1947; CIE 1943; Chairman of Assam Valley Branch, Indian Tea Association, Assam, 1937-47, retired 1949; *b* 1888; *s* of Donald McLennan, Inverness-shire and Aberdeen; *m* 1st, 1924, Anne Williamson (*d* 1929); 2nd, 1932, Christina Comniti (*d* 1977), *d* of Walter Taylor, Aberdeen. Hon. Pres. Clan MacLennan Assoc. *Address:* Bridgebank, Milltimber, Aberdeenshire, Scotland. *[Died* 30 *June* 1977.

MacLEOD, (Alexander) Cameron, FRCS; Hon. Consulting Surgeon: Charing Cross Hospital; Hampstead General Hospital; Connaught Hospital, Walthamstow; formerly: Consultant Surgeon, Wanstead Hospital; Surgical Registrar and Assistant, Bland-Sutton Institute of Pathology, Middlesex Hospital; *b* London, 7 Dec. 1899; *e s* of late C. E. Alexander MacLeod, FRCS; *m* 1934, Jean Marjorie, *o d* of late Col Arthur Charles Fergusson, CMG, DSO, RA; one *s* two *d*. *Educ:* Haileybury Coll.; Middlesex Hosp. MB, BS (London). Served with HM Land Forces, 1918-19, temporary 2nd Lieut RH and RFA. Senior Fellow Assoc. of Surgeons of Great Britain and Ireland; Late Mem. Bd of Examiners in Dental Surgery (Surgical Sect.), RCS. Served RAMC, 1940-45, temp. Lt-Col officer i/c Surgical Div., Cambridge Hosp., Aldershot, 1940-42; MEF, 1942-45. *Publications:* The MacLeods of St Kilda (Clann Alasdair Ruaidh), 1968; papers on surgical subjects in medical journals. *Recreations:* genealogy, fly-fishing, music, gardening, walking. *Address:* 41 Downshire Hill, NW3. *T:* 01-435 1625. *[Died* 9 *Nov.* 1971.

MacLEOD, Cameron; see MacLeod, A. C.

MacLEOD of MacLeod, Dame Flora, DBE 1953; JP; 28th Chief of MacLeod; *b* 3 Feb. 1878; *d* of Sir Reginald MacLeod of MacLeod, KCB, 27th Chief, and Lady Agnes Northcote; *m* 1901, Hubert Walter (*d* 1933); two *d. Heir: g s* John MacLeod yr of MacLeod, 2nd *s* of late Captain Robert Wolrige Gordon, MC, and Joan Walter. *Address:* Dunvegan Castle, Isle of Skye. *T:* Dunvegan 206. *[Died* 4 *Nov.* 1976.

McLEOD, (James) Walter, OBE; FRS 1933; FRSE 1957; Hon. ScD (Dublin), 1946; Hon. LLD (Glasgow), 1961; Emeritus Professor, University of Leeds, since 1952; *b* 2 Jan. 1887; *s* of John McLeod and Lilias Symington McClymont; *m* 1st, 1914, Jane Christina Garvie, MA (Glasgow) (*d* 1953); one *s* five *d*; 2nd, 1956, Joyce Anita Shannon, MB ChB (St Andrews). *Educ:* George Watson's Coll., Edinburgh; Collège Cantonal, Lausanne; Mill Hill Sch.; Glasgow Univ., Coates Scholar, 1909-10, Carnegie Scholar, 1910-11. Research work in Bacteriology, Glasgow Univ. Assistant Lecturer in Pathology, Charing Cross Hospital, London, 1912-14; Temp. Lieut and Captain, RAMC, 1914-19 (despatches four times, OBE); Leeds University: Lecturer in Bacteriology, 1919, Dean of Medical Faculty, 1948-52, Brotherton Prof. of Bacteriology, 1922-52; research work under Scottish Hospital Endowments Research Trust, in the Dept of Surgery, Edinburgh Univ., 1954-63; research work, Central Microbiological Laboratories, Western General Hospital, Edinburgh, 1963-73; President of the Society for General Microbiology, 1949-52. Hon. FRCPath, 1970. Corresponding member of the Société de Biologie, Paris, 1928; Hon. Mem. Scottish Soc. for Experimental Medicine, 1957; Hon. Mem., Pathological Soc. of Great Britain and Ireland, 1961. Worked with Boys Brigade in Leeds, 1919-52, and later in Edinburgh. *Publications:* papers on Bacteriology, etc, in Journal of Pathology, Biochemical Journal, Journal of Hygiene, and Lancet; chapter on bacterial oxidations and reductions in Newer Knowledge of Bacteriology, 1928; chapters on bacterial oxidations, etc, System of Bacteriology, MRC, 1931; Section on Diphtheria, Encyclopædia Britannica, 1961. *Recreations:* golf, fishing. *Address:* 30 Ravelston Gardens, Edinburgh EH4 3LE. *T:* 031-337 1524. *[Died* 11 *March* 1978.

MACLEOD, Robert Duncan; Founder and Past Editor of the Library Review; *b* Greenock, Renfrewshire; unmarried. Served in public libraries at Greenock and Glasgow; first librarian to Carnegie United Kingdom Trustees; Fellow of the Library Association, with honours in classification and cataloguing; helped to start official library training classes in Glasgow, and promoted other library activities; founder of County Library Circle, and of Strathclyde Librarians' Club; declined Presidency of the Scottish Library Association; past Hon. Secretary, Scottish PEN. *Publications:* Rural Libraries and Rural Education, 1922; County Rural Libraries: Their Policy and Organisation, 1923; The Scottish Publishing Houses, 1953; Morris without Mackail, 1954, new edn, 1957; John Davidson, 1956; Poems and Ballads by John Davidson, 1958; The Anglo-American Library Associations, 1958; editor of various catalogues, including Modern Scottish Literature: a Guide Book, 1933; contributor to British, American, and Indian periodicals. *Clubs:* Savage, Press; Western, Art (Glasgow). *[Died* 4 *Aug.* 1973.

McLEOD, Gen. Sir Roderick (William), GBE 1964 (CBE 1945); KCB 1958 (CB 1952); DL; *b* 15 Jan. 1905; *s* of Col Reginald George McQueen McLeod, DSO, late RA, and Cicely Knightley (*née* Boyd); *m* 1st, 1933, Camilla Rachel Hunter (*d* 1942), *d* of late Sir Godfrey Fell, KCIE, CSI, OBE; one *d*; 2nd, 1946 Mary Vavasour Lloyd Thomas, MBE (*née* Driver), *widow* of Major R. J. H. Thomas, MVO, RHA. *Educ:* Wellington Coll., Berks; RMA, Woolwich. Commissioned 1925, operations, NW Frontier, India, 1931-32; Staff Coll., 1938. Comdr SAS Troops, 1944-45; Dir Military Operations, India, 1945-46; idc 1947; Asst Comdt, Staff Coll., 1948-49; CRA 7th Armoured Div., 1950; Dir of Military Operations, War Office, 1951-54; GOC 6th Armoured Div., 1955-56; Chief Army Instructor, Imperial Defence Coll., Jan.-Dec. 1957; Dep. Chief of Defence Staff, 1957-60; Comdr British Forces, Hong Kong, 1960-61; Gen. 1961; GOC-in-C, Eastern Comd, 1962-65; ADC (Gen.) to the Queen, 1963-65. DL Surrey, 1967. Comdr Order of Leopold II, 1946; Chevalier Legion of Honour, 1945; Croix de Guerre avec Palme, 1945. *Recreations:* ski-ing, sailing. *Address:* Fairhill, The Hockering, Woking, Surrey. *T:* Woking 61477. *Clubs:* Army and Navy, Ski Club of Great Britain, Eagle Ski Club.
[Died 6 *Dec.* 1980.

MacLEOD, Walter; see MacLeod, J. W.

Mac LIAMMÓIR, Micheál; actor, designer, playwright; Director of Dublin Gate Theatre Productions since 1928; *b* Cork, Ireland, 25 Oct. 1899; *s* of Alfred Antony Mac Liammóir and Mary Elizabeth (*née* Lawler Lee). *Educ:* privately. First appearance on stage (as child) at Little Theatre, London, in The Goldfish, 1911; West End parts, 1911-15; studied painting at Slade Sch., 1915-16. Painted and designed for Irish Theatre and Dublin Drama League; lived abroad studying painting till 1927; returned to Ireland and joined Anew McMaster's Shakespearean Co. With Hilton Edwards: opened Galway Gaelic Theatre; they also estab. Dublin Gate Theatre, 1928; has since acted in, and designed for, over 300 prodns there; apptd Dir of Govt subsidized Dublin Gaelic Theatre, 1928; with Dublin Gate

Theatre Co., London, 1934; toured in Egypt, 1936-38, Balkan States, 1939. With Hilton Edwards and Gate Co. he played in (his own) Ill Met by Moonlight, Vaudeville, London, 1947; season, Embassy, 1947. First appearance on New York Stage as Larry Doyle in John Bull's Other Island, Mansfield, 1948. Iago in film Othello, 1949; in (his own) Home for Christmas, Gate, 1950; Hedda Gabler, Lyric, Hammersmith, 1954; in revue Gateway to Gaiety (setting, costumes, and contrib. material), Gaiety, Dublin, 1956; The Hidden King, Edinburgh Fest., 1957. The Key of the Door, The Heart's a Wonder (setting and costumes), Lyric, Hammersmith, 1958; appeared in The Informer (adaptation and décor), Dublin, 1958; Much Ado About Nothing, NY, 1959. One-man entertainment, The Importance of Being Oscar, Dublin, 1960, London, 1960 (1966), since 1960 in this programme in Europe, USA, S America, Australia, New Zealand, etc.; One-Man programmes: I Must be Talking to my Friends and Talking about Yeats, in Dublin, subseq. London; film: What's the Matter with Helen, 1971. Various Irish awards for plays, etc. Kronborg Gold Medal, Elsinore, 1952. Hon. LLD, TCD, 1962. Freeman, City of Dublin, 1973. Publications: in Irish: Oíicheanna Sidhe (faery tales), 1922; OícheBhealtaine (play), 1933; Lá agus Oíche (short stories), 1934; Diarmuid agus Gráinne (play), 1935; Ceo Meala Lá Seaca (essays), 1952; Áisteoirí faoi dhá Sholas (memoirs), 1956; Bláth agus Taibhse (poems), 1964; in English: All for Hecuba (autobiography), 1946; Put Money in thy Purse (diary), 1954; Ill Met by Moonlight (play), 1957; Each Actor on his Ass (memoirs), 1960; Where Stars Walk (play), 1961; The Importance of Being Oscar, 1963; Ireland (a study of the country and its people), 1966; An Oscar of No Importance (autobiography and study of Wilde), 1968; (with Eavan Boland) W. B. Yeats and His World, 1971; Prelude in Kazbek Street (play), 1973; Enter, a Goldfish: memoirs of an Irish actor, young and old, 1977. Recreations: travel, balletomania. Address: 4 Harcourt Terrace, Dublin, Ireland. T: Dublin 6.7609. Club: Arts (Dublin).											[Died 6 March 1978.

McLUHAN, Prof. (Herbert) Marshall, CC (Canada) 1970; PhD, LLD; FRSC 1964; Professor of English, St Michael's College, University of Toronto, since 1952, Director, Centre for Culture and Technology, since 1963; b Edmonton, Alberta, 21 July 1911; s of Herbert Ernest and Elsie Naomi McLuhan; m 1939, Corinne Keller Lewis, Fort Worth, Texas; two s four d. Educ: Univ. of Manitoba (BA 1932, MA 1934); Trinity Hall, Cambridge (BA 1936, MA 1939, PhD 1942). Teacher: Univ. of Wisconsin, 1936-37; Univ. of St Louis, 1937-44; Assumption Univ., Ontario, 1944-46; St Michael's Coll., Toronto, 1946-. Albert Schweitzer Prof. in Humanities, Fordham Univ., New York, 1967-68. Jt Editor, Explorations Magazine, 1954-59. Dir, media project for US Office of Educn and Nat. Assoc. of Educnl Broadcasters, 1959-60; Consultor to the Vatican Pontifical Commn for Social Communications, 1973. Many hon. degrees and awards from univs and colleges. Carl Einstein Prize, Young German Art Critics of W Germany, 1967; Molson Award, Canada Council, 1967; IPR President's Award (GB), 1970; Christian Culture Award, Assumption Univ., 1971. Gold Medal of Italian Republic, 1971. Publications: The Mechanical Bride: folklore of industrial man, 1951; (ed with E. S. Carpenter) Explorations in Communications, 1960; The Gutenberg Galaxy: the making of typographic man, 1962 (Governor-Gen.'s Award for critical prose, 1963); Understanding Media: the extensions of man, 1964; (with R. J. Schoeck) Voices of Literature, vols I-III, 1964, 1965, 1970; The Medium is the Massage: an inventory of effects, 1967; War and Peace in the Global Village, 1968; (with H. Parker) Through the Vanishing Point: space in poetry and painting, 1968; Counterblast, 1969; The Interior Landscape: selected literary criticism (ed E. McNamara), 1969; Culture is our Business, 1970; From Cliché to Archetype, 1970; Take Today: the executive as drop-out, 1972; (jtly) The City as Classroom, 1977; D'œil à oreille, 1977; (with P. Babin) Autre homme, autre chrétien à l'âge électronique, 1977. Recreation: media study. Address: Centre for Culture and Technology, University of Toronto, Toronto, Ontario M5S 1A1, Canada. T: 416-978-3328; 3 Wychwood Park, Toronto, Ontario M6G 2V5, Canada.											[Died 31 Dec. 1980.

MACLURE, Lt-Col Sir John William Spencer, 3rd Bt, cr 1898; OBE 1945; b 4 Feb. 1899; er s of Col Sir John Maclure, 2nd Bt, and Ruth Ina Muriel (d 1951), e d of late W. B. McHardy, Comdr, RN, and Chief Constable of Lanarkshire; S father, 1938; m 1929, Elspeth King, er d of late Alexander King Clark, Wykeham Hatch, West Byfleet; two s one d. Educ: Wellington Coll.; Royal Military College, Sandhurst. Joined KRRC 1917; Lt-Col 1939; served in France and Flanders, 1918; North Russia, 1919; India, 1920-22 and 1925-28; Burma, 1936-38; commanded Rifle Depôt, 1939-40 and 1941-44; commanded 37 Reinforcement Holding Unit, BWEF, 1944 (OBE); commanded 113 Transit Camp, BLA; at Osnabruck; Comdr British Troops

Holland, and 41 (Hook) Garrison, Holland, 1946; RARO 1949-54. Heir: s John Robert Spencer Maclure [b 25 March 1934; m 1964, Jane Monica, d of Rt Rev. T. J. Savage, MA; four s]. Address: Flat 2, 25 Christchurch Road, Winchester, Hants SO23 9SU. T: Winchester 4147.							[Died 1 March 1980.

McMAHON, Sir Patrick; see McMahon, Sir W. P.

MACMAHON, Lt-Gen. Peadar; retired as Secretary, Department of Defence, Ireland, 1958; b 10 Jan. 1893; m 1924, Anne Parkinson; three s one d. Gen. Officer Commanding Curragh Training Camp, 1922-24; Chief of Staff, 1924-27. Address: Gracemount, Howth, Co. Dublin. T: 322832.							[Died 27 Feb. 1975.

McMAHON, Sir (William) Patrick, 7th Bt, cr 1817; in private practice as Land Agent; b 24 April 1900; s of Lt-Col Sir Eyre McMahon, 6th Bt, and Lydia Mary (d 1933), widow of Slingsby Cradock and d of Major W. P. Hoey, Co. Wicklow; S father 1935; m 1939, Ruth Stella Hahlo (marr. diss. 1960), yr d of late P. R. and late Mrs Kenyon Slaney; two s. Educ: Wellington Coll. Fellow of the Land Agents Soc.; Professional Associate of Surveyors Institution. Heir: s Brian Patrick McMahon, b 9 June 1942. Address: Les Buttes, St Martin, Jersey, CI. T: Central 53367. Club: Victoria (Jersey).							[Died 5 Jan. 1977.

MacMANUS, Emily Elvira Primrose, CBE 1947 (OBE 1930); SRN, SCM, retired; b 18 April 1886; d of Leonard Strong McManus, MD, of Battersea, London, and Killeaden House, Kiltimagh, Co. Mayo, Eire, and Julia Emily Boyd, Howth, Co. Dublin. Educ: Governess and private schs. Gen. Nursing Training, Guy's Hosp., 1908; Midwifery Training, East End Mothers' Home, 1912; Sister, Kasr en Aini Hospital, Cairo, and Private Nursing, Egypt; Sister, King's Lynn; Sister, Guy's Hospital; Sister, QAIMNSR, France, 1915-18 (despatches twice); Asst Matron, Guy's Hosp., 1919; Asst Medical Research Council, Food Experiment, Dr Barnardo's Boys' Garden City, 1922; Matron, Bristol Royal Infirmary, 1923; Matron, Guy's Hosp., 1927-46; Sector Matron, Sector 10, EMS, 1939-46; Principal Matron, TANS, 1923-46; late Mem. Gen. Nursing Council; Chm., Voluntary Advisory Nursing Board for HM Prisons, 1936-46; Mem. Council Queen's Dist Nursing Assoc., Eire; late Mem. Council Queen's Dist Nursing Assoc., and Overseas Nursing Assoc.; Pres. Royal College of Nursing, 1942-44; Nursing Missions: British West Indies, 1946-47; Persia 1948, Turkey, 1949, Holland 1952. Broadcast series, BBC, Mary and her Furry Friends, 1964; Broadcasts, BBC: Silver Lining in series Home this afternoon, 1965; Desert Island Discs, 1966. Publications: Hospital Administration for Women, 1934; Nursing in Time of War (Jt), 1939; Matron of Guy's 1956. Recreations: fishing, gardening, literature. Address: Terry Lodge, Terrybawn, Bofeenaun, Ballina, Co. Mayo, Eire. T: Foxford 104. Club: Royal Irish Automobile (Dublin).							[Died 22 Feb. 1978.

McMASTER, Ian, OBE 1960; b 28 Jan. 1898; s of Rev. Kenneth McMaster and Gertrude Lucy Strachan; m 1924, Jane Harvey, MA, FRHistS (d 1958); one d; m 1963, Mary Isabella Blewitt Neville, Warden, St Luke's Home, Oxford. Educ: King's Sch., Canterbury; University Coll. Sch., London; Queen's Coll., Oxford (Scholar); Grenoble Univ. Chief History Master, King Edward VI Sch., Birmingham, 1922-35; History Master, Eton Coll., 1935-40; Consul in Florence and Consul-Gen. to Republic of San Marino, 1952-60; HM Foreign Service, retd 1960. Warden, Sheffield Diocesan Conference House, 1960-64. Formerly Mem. Archbishop's Council for Inter-Church Relations; Diocesan Lay Reader. Recreation: human problems. Address: 3 Garford Road, Oxford. T: Oxford 58017.							[Died 2 Feb. 1978.

McMENEMEY, William Henry, MA, DM, FRCP, FRCPath, FRCPsych; Emeritus Professor of Pathology, Institute of Neurology, University of London, and Hon. Consulting Pathologist, National Hospitals for Nervous Diseases; b 16 May 1905; s of William Henry McMenemey and Frances Annie (née Rankin), MD (Aberdeen); one s one d. Educ: Birkenhead Sch.; Merton Coll., Oxford; St Bartholomew's Hospital. Formerly: House Physician and Junior Demonstrator in Pathology, St Bart's Hosp.; Registrar in Neurology, Maida Vale Hosp.; Pathologist, Napsbury and Shenley Hosps and Asst Pathologist, West End Hosp. for Nervous Diseases, 1934-37; Asst Pathologist, Radcliffe Infirmary, Oxford, 1937-40; Pathologist, Royal Infirmary, Worcester, 1940-49; Pathologist, Maida Vale Hosp., 1949-70; Prof. of Pathology, Inst of Neurology, 1965-70. Savill Prize, 1932; Charles Hastings Memorial Lectr, 1951; Pres., International Soc. of Clinical Pathology, 1966-69; Sec., Internat. Soc. of Neuropathology, 1967-70; President: Assoc. of Clinical Pathologists, 1958 (Sec.

1943-57); Brit. Neuropathological Soc., 1957-60; Sect. of Neurology, 1960-61 and Sect. of History of Medicine, 1962-64, Royal Soc. Med.; Hon. FRCPath (Australia); Hon. Member: Amer. Soc. of Clinical Pathology; Amer. Assoc. of Neuropathologists; Soc. Française de Biologie Medicale; Romanian Soc. of Medical Sciences; Assoc. Español. Biopatolog. Clin.; John Shaw Billings Hist. of Medicine Soc.; Corresp. Member: Vereinigung Deutsch. Neuropathologen u. Neuroanat.; Soc. Française de Neurologie. *Publications:* History of Worcester Royal Infirmary, 1947; James Parkinson, 1955; The Life and Times of Sir Charles Hastings, 1959; various writings on neuropathology, clinical pathology and medical history. *Recreations:* music, gardening. *Address:* Manor House, London Road, Morden, Surrey. *Club:* Athenæum.
[*Died* 24 *Nov.* 1977.

MacMILLAN, Sir Ernest Campbell, CC 1969; Kt 1935; MusD, LLD, LittD, Hon. RAM, FRCM, FRCO; Dean Faculty of Music, University of Toronto, 1927-52; Principal, Toronto Conservatory of Music, 1926-42; Conductor: Toronto Symphony Orchestra, 1931-56; Toronto Mendelssohn Choir, 1942-57; President: Composers, Authors and Publishers Association of Canada, 1947-69; Canadian Music Centre, 1959-70; Canadian Music Council, 1949-66; Member Canada Council, 1957-63; *b* near Toronto, 18 Aug. 1893; *s* of Rev. Alexander MacMillan, DD, and Winifred Ross; *m* 1919, Laura Elsie Keith; two *s*. *Educ:* Toronto; Edinburgh. At an early age took an interest in music, especially the organ, making many public appearances from the age of nine onwards, passed Associateship Royal College of Organists at age of 13, Fellowship at age of 17 (winning Lafontaine Prize) and graduated as MusB at Oxford the same year; Arts course (Hons in Mod. History) Univ. of Toronto; was in Germany in summer of 1914 and after outbreak of war interned in Ruhleben Camp; while there, wrote a setting (chorus and orchestra) of Swinburne's England, which was accepted for the degree of MusD, Oxford, 1918; after release returned to Canada. Richard Strauss Medal, 1957; Canada Council Medal, 1964. *Publications:* England, an Ode for Chorus and Orchestra; String Quartet in C Minor; two Sketches for String Quartet; Songs; Choral Compositions; Canadian Song Book; various arrangements of French Canadian Songs for Voice and Piano, male voice choir, etc.; Six Bergerettes du Bas Canada (Voices with Oboe, Violin, Cello and Harp). Various educational publications. Ed, Music in Canada, 1955. *Address:* 115 Park Road, Toronto 289, Canada. *T:* 921-9787. *Clubs:* Arts and Letters (Past Pres.), (Toronto), Faculty (Univ. of Toronto).
[*Died* 6 *May* 1973.

MacMILLAN, Harvey Reginald, CC (Canada) 1970; CBE 1943; company director; *b* 9 Sept. 1885; *s* of John Alfred MacMillan and Joanna Willson; *m* 1911, Edna, *d* of C. Mulloy; two *d*. *Educ:* Toronto Univ. (BScA); Yale Univ. (MScF). Chief Forester of British Columbia, 1912; Founder and Pres., H. R. MacMillan Export Co. Ltd, 1919; Timber Controller for Canada, 1940; Pres., Wartime Merchant Shipbuilding Ltd for Canada, 1941. Hon. Dir, MacMillan, Bloedel Ltd; Mem., International Chamber of Commerce; Hon. DSc, Univ. of British Columbia, 1950; Hon. LLD: Univ. of Toronto, 1957; Univ. of Guelph, 1966. Hon. Patron of the Vancouver Public Aquarium. *Recreations:* shooting and fishing. *Address:* (office) 1075 West Georgia Street, Vancouver V6E 3R9, BC, Canada; (home) 3741 Hudson Street, Vancouver V6H 3A6, BC, Canada. *Clubs:* University, Terminal City, Vancouver, Faculty (Vancouver, BC); Union (Victoria, BC). [*Died* 9 *Feb.* 1976.

McMILLAN, James Athole, CBE 1957 (OBE 1945); BSc (Agric.); Director, National Agricultural Advisory Service, Ministry of Agriculture, Fisheries and Food, 1959-Feb. 1961, retired; *b* 25 Feb. 1896; *m* 1949, Marian R. Watson; three *s* one *d*. *Educ:* George Watson's Coll., Edinburgh; Edinburgh Univ. BEF France, 1916-18. Asst Agricultural Organiser, Derbys CC, 1919-20; Lecturer in Agriculture, Leeds Univ., 1921-27; Agricultural Organiser, Lindsey CC, 1927-30; Agricultural Organiser, Cambs CC, 1930-39; Executive Officer, Cambs War Agricultural Executive Cttee, 1939-46; Provincial Dir, National Agricultural Advisory Service, 1946-48; Senior Education and Advisory Officer, Nat. Agric. Adv. Service, Min. of Agric., Fisheries and Food, 1948-59. *Recreations:* Rugby and cricket interests. *Address:* 7 Bonaly Drive, Edinburgh EH13 0EJ. *T:* 031-441 3869. [*Died* 9 *Sept.* 1977.

MACMILLAN, Malcolm Kenneth; journalist; *b* 21 Aug. 1913; *s* of Kenneth Macmillan and Mary Macaulay; married. *Educ:* Edinburgh Univ. Served as Private, Infantry, 1939-40. MP (Lab) Western Isles, 1935-70; Chm., Scottish Parliamentary Labour Party, 1945-51; Chm., Govt Advisory Panel on Highlands and Islands, 1947-54; Mem. Post Office Advisory Council, 1946-51;

Mem. Scottish Advisory Council on Civil Aviation, 1947-53; Mem. Scottish Economic Conf., 1949-. Chm., Parly Cttee for East West Trade, 1965-70. Contested (United Lab Party) Western Isles, 1974. *Address:* 11 Cross Street, Coulregrein, Stornoway, Isle of Lewis; 69 St Vincent Crescent, Glasgow G3 8NQ. [*Died* 17 *Nov.* 1978.

MACMILLAN, Norman, OBE 1956; DL; author; Wing Comdr RAFVR (T), retired 1958; first Air Force Member, Cornwall TAAFA, 1947-61, Vice-Chairman (Air), 1953-54 and 1956-57, Chairman for Buildings and Ranges, 1957-61; *b* Glasgow, 9 Aug. 1892; 2nd *s* of John Campbell Macmillan, Carsphairn, Kirkcudbrightshire, and Jeanie Hamilton, Hamilton, Lanarkshire; *m* Gladys Mary Peterkin, *d* of James Alfred Peterkin Mitchell, Dundee. *Educ:* Allan Glen's Sch.; Royal Technical Coll.; RAF Officers' Engrg Course. Served European War, HLI, Belgium and France, 1914-16; RFC and RAF, France and Italy, 1916-19 (MC, AFC, 1914 Star; retains rank of Captain); commanded Special Mobile Flight, RAF, 1921 (Retains rank of Flt Lieut RAF); Royal Aero Club Aviator's Certificate, 1917; Pilot's B Licence, 1919; Air Ministry approved test pilot; Founder Assoc. MIAeE, 1919; consultant test pilot, 1919-23, to various companies; Instructor Spanish naval and military aviation schs, 1922; pilot of first attempt to fly round world, 1922; first flight London-Sweden in one day, 1923; winner speed prize first international light aeroplane competition, 1923; chief test pilot, Fairey Aviation Co., 1924-30; AFRAeS, 1928; MRAeS, 1973; Founder Mem. and Warden Guild of Air Pilots, 1929-34, Dep. Master, 1934-35, Upper Freeman, 1956, Liveryman, 1958; Air Navigator's Licence, 1929; Chief Consultant Test Pilot and a principal foreign representative Armstrong Siddeley Development Co., 1931-33; first British pilot to fly over Andes Mountains, 1931, and first pilot to fly route Bahia Blanca to Neuquen-Chillan; publicly advocated powerful British air rearmament from 1934 onwards, on platform and in Press; Pres. Nat. League of Airmen, 1935-38; FRSA 1936-57; Special Aviation and Air Corres. Daily Mail, 1936-39; served War of 1939-45 with RAFVR(T), (Sqdn Ldr), and as War Correspondent; Founder Mem. Circle of Aviation Writers, 1941; Dist Inspecting Officer, ATC Cornwall, 1945-47 and OC Cornwall Wing, ATC, 1947-58. Flew on operational flights during Malayan emergency, 1958. Pres., No 45 Sqdn RFC/RAF Assoc., 1961-73. DL Cornwall, 1951. Hon. Mem., Mark Twain Soc., 1975. Special contributor to Aeronautics from its inception in 1939. UK Special Correspondent, Aircraft, Melbourne, Aust.; Contribs to: numerous magazines and aerospace jls; Grolier Encyclopedia, New York; Shell Aviation News. *Publications:* The Art of Flying, 1928; Into the Blue, 1929, rev. augmented edn with new illustrations, 1969; The Air Tourist's Guide to Europe, 1930; An Hour of Aviation, 1931; The Romance of Flight, 1934; Sefton Brancker, 1935 (proceeds founded Guild of Air Pilots and Navigators Benevolent Fund); The Romance of Modern Exploration and Discovery, 1936; Freelance Pilot, 1937; The Chosen Instrument, 1938; (ed) How We Fly, 1939; (ed) Best Flying Stories, Air Strategy, 1941; How to Pilot An Aeroplane, 1942; The Pilot's Book on Advanced Flying, 1943; Aeroplanes section of Railways, Ships and Aeroplanes, 1944; The Royal Air Force in the World War, Vol. 1, 1942; Vol. 2, 1944; Vol. 3, 1949; Vol. 4, 1950; Great Airmen, 1955; Great Aircraft, 1960; Tales of Two Air Wars, 1963; Great Flights and Air Adventures, 1964 (also as Talking Book for the Blind); Wings of Fate, Strange True Tales of the Vintage Flying Days, 1967; Offensive Patrol: the first full-length account of the RFC/RAF in Italy 1917-18, 1973. *Address:* Trecara Lodge, 2 Edward Street, Truro, Cornwall TR1 3AJ. *T:* Truro 3602. *Club:* Royal Air Force. [*Died* 5 *Aug.* 1976.

McMILLAN, Thomas McLellan; MP (Lab) Glasgow Central since 1966; *b* 12 Feb. 1919; *s* of James and Isabella McMillan; *m* 1946, Mary Elizabeth Conway; one *s* one *d*. *Educ:* secondary sch. Glasgow City Councillor, 1962; Magistrate and Bailie of Burgh, 1964. *Address:* House of Commons, SW1. *T:* 01-219 3000. [*Died* 30 *April* 1980.

McMILLAN, William, CVO 1956; RA 1933 (ARA 1925); RBS 1932 (ARBS 1928); sculptor; *b* Aberdeen, 31 Aug. 1887; *m* 1916, Dorothy Williams (*d* 1964), Carlisle. *Educ:* Gray's School of Art, Aberdeen; Royal College of Art. *Works:* George V Statue, Calcutta; Earl Haig at Clifton Coll., Bristol; Hugh Oldham, Bishop of Exeter, founder of Manchester Grammar Sch.; Beatty Memorial Fountain, Trafalgar Square; Statue of King George VI, Carlton Gardens, London; Statue of Sir Walter Raleigh, Whitehall, SW1; Statue of Lord Trenchard, Victoria Embankment; Alcock and Brown group, London Airport. Great War Medal, Victory Medal, and various other medals, busts, etc. Works in Tate Gallery, etc. *Address:* 3 Cholmondeley Walk, Richmond, Surrey. *Club:* Chelsea Arts. [*Died* 25 *Sept.* 1977.

MACMILLAN, Prof. William Miller, MA; Hon. DLitt, Oxford, 1957, Natal, 1962, Edinburgh, 1974; *b* Aberdeen, 1885; *s* of late Rev. John Macmillan, MA, formerly of Madras; *m* 1st, Jean, *d* of late John Sutherland, MA; 2nd, Mona, *e d* of late Admiral Sir Hugh J. Tweedie, KCB; two *s* two *d*. *Educ:* Stellenbosch, SA; Merton Coll., Oxford. Rhodes Scholar, 1903-06; studied in Aberdeen, Glasgow, and Berlin, 1906-10; Lecturer in History and Economics, Rhodes Univ. Coll., Grahamstown, SA, 1911; Prof. of History, University of the Witwatersrand, Johannesburg, SA, 1917-34; Assoc. Member of All Souls Coll., Oxford, 1926-27 and 1933; Membre de l'Institut Colonial Internat., 1931; African Travel, 1930-33, 1938, 1958-59, 1962, 1964; USA and W Indies, 1934-35; Hon. Life Member Royal African Society, 1935; African Studies Assoc. of UK, 1966; Hon. Vice-President, Anti-Slavery and Aborigines Protection Society, 1965. Heath Clark Lecturer (joint), University of London, 1938-39; Member of Advisory Cttee on Education in the Colonies, 1938-41; Empire Intelligence Section, BBC, 1941-43; Senior Representative of the British Council in West Africa, 1943-46; Colonial Labour Advisory Cttee, 1946-52; Director of Colonial Studies, Univ. of St Andrews, 1947-54. Hoernlé Memorial lecturer, SA, 1949; Mission to Tanganyika for Tanganyika Government, 1950; Observer Mission to Bechuanaland Protectorate, 1951; Central Africa, 1952; acting Prof. of History, Univ. Coll. of the West Indies, Jamaica, 1955. Coronation Medal, 1953; Chevalier, Royal Belgian Order of the Lion, 1953. *Publications:* The South African Agrarian Problem, 1919; The Cape Colour Question: a Historical Survey, 1927, 1969; Bantu, Boer, and Briton: the Making of the SA Native Problem, 1929 (new edn, 1963); Complex South Africa, 1930; Warning from the W Indies, 1936, reissued in Penguin Series, 1938; Africa Emergent, 1938 (Pelican 2nd edn 1948); Europe and West Africa, 1940; Democratize the Empire, 1941; The Road to Self-Rule, A Study in Colonial Evolution, 1959 (Italian edn 1963, Amer. edn 1971); My South African Years, 1974. *Recreation:* walking. *Address:* Yew Tree Cottage, Long Wittenham, Abingdon, Berks. *T:* Clifton Hampden 358. *Club:* Royal Commonwealth Society. *[Died 23 Oct. 1974.*

MACMORRAN, Kenneth Mead, QC 1932; *b* 1883; *o s* of late Alexander Macmorran, KC; *m* 1920, Freda Mary, *y d* of late W. F. Knight, of The Mount, Duppas Hill, Croydon; no *c*. *Educ:* Westminster; King's Coll., Cambridge (MA, LLB). Barrister (Middle Temple), 1907; served European War, 1915-20; Staff Captain to Judge Advocate-General, 1919; mentioned, Secretary of State's list for War Services, 1919; Chancellor: Dioceses of Chichester, 1922-64, St Albans, 1922-62, Ely, 1924-65, Guildford, 1927-68, Lincoln, 1937-69, and Newcastle, 1942-69; JP (Surrey) 1933; Dep. Chairman, Surrey Quarter Sessions, 1941-44, Assistant Chairman, 1944-48; Member of Church Assembly, 1930-37; Bencher, Middle Temple, 1937; Member, Enemy Aliens Tribunal (Germans and Austrians), 1940; Probation Advisory Cttee (Home Office), 1946; a Referee under National Health Insurance, Widows and Orphans (etc.) Pensions and Family Allowances Acts, 1926-50; Master Treasurer of the Middle Temple, 1956. *Publications:* A Handbook for Churchwardens and Parochial Church Councillors; Cripps on Church and Clergy, 8th edn. *Address:* c/o Lloyds Bank, Chichester, Sussex. *[Died 9 Jan. 1973.*

MacMULLAN, Charles W. Kirkpatrick, CBE 1947; (Writer under the name of C. K. Munro); *b* 17 Feb. 1889; *o s* of Professor S. J. MacMullan, Queen's Coll., Belfast, and Anne Marshall Weir, Cookstown, Co. Tyrone; *m* Mary Sumner (*d* 1956), *d* of H. A. Sumner, Birmingham; one *s*. *Educ:* Harrow; Pembroke Coll., Cambridge. Under Secretary, Ministry of Labour (retired). *Plays:* Wanderers, 1915; At Mrs Beam's, 1922; The Rumour, 1923; Storm, 1924; The Mountain, 1926; Cocks and Hens, 1927; Mr Eno, 1928; Veronica, 1930; Bluestone Quarry, 1931; Ding & Co., 1934. *Broadcast Plays:* The New Vicar, 1963; Jonsen, 1964. *Publications: essays:* The True Woman, 1931; Watching a Play (Shute Lectures), 1933; The Fountains in Trafalgar Square, 1952. *Address:* 2 The Rosery, South Heath, Great Missenden, Bucks. *[Died 18 July 1973.*

McMULLEN, Col Denis, CBE 1966; consultant; Chief Inspecting Officer of Railways, Ministry of Transport, 1963-68 (Inspecting Officer, 1948); retired; *b* 21 April 1902; *e s* of Norman McMullen and Helen Mary McMullen (*née* Macpherson); *m* 1928, Ida Wilhelmina Taylor; two *s* one *d* (and one *s* decd). *Educ:* Cheltenham Coll.; Royal Military Academy (Woolwich). Commissioned in Royal Engineers, 1921; posted India, 1924; seconded Indian State Railways (NW Railway), 1925-39. Served in France, Iraq and India (despatches), 1940-45. Controller of Railways, Allied Commn, Austria, 1945-46; seconded to Indian State Railways (NW Railway), 1946-47; seconded to Pakistan State Railways (NW Railway) (Chief Operating Superintendent), 1947-48. CEng, FICE; FCIT;

Fellow, Instn Railway Signal Engineers, 1949. *Recreations:* fishing, gardening. *Address:* Merlewood, Woodham Road, Woking, Surrey. *T:* Woking 65955. *Club:* United Service and Royal Aero. *[Died 3 June 1973.*

MACMURRAY, John, MC; MA (Glasgow and Oxon); LLD (Glasgow); retired as Professor of Moral Philosophy, University of Edinburgh (1944-58); *b* Maxwellton, Kirkcudbrightshire, 16 Feb. 1891; *s* of James Macmurray, Civil Servant; *m* 1916, Elizabeth Hyde, *d* of George Campbell of Umsinga, Natal, and Banchory, Kincardineshire; no *c*. *Educ:* Grammar Sch. and Robert Gordon's Coll., Aberdeen; Glasgow Univ.; Balliol Coll., Oxford. Graduate of Glasgow Univ., 1913; Snell Exhibitioner and Newlands Scholar of Balliol Coll., 1913; War Service, 1914-19: as private, RAMC 1914; Lieut, QO Cameron Highlanders, 1916 (MC); John Locke Scholar in Mental Philosophy of the University of Oxford, 1919; Lecturer in Philosophy, University of Manchester, 1919; Professor of Philosophy in the University of the Witwatersrand, Johannesburg, S. Africa, 1921; Fellow and Classical Tutor and Jowett Lecturer in Philosophy, Balliol Coll., Oxford, 1922-28; Grote Professor of the Philosophy of Mind and Logic, University of London, 1928-44. Gifford Lectr, Glasgow Univ., 1953-54. *Publications:* Freedom in the Modern World, 1932; Interpreting the Universe, 1933; Philosophy of Communism, 1933; Creative Society, 1935; Reason and Emotion, 1935; Structure of Religious Experience, 1936; The Clue to History, 1938; The Boundaries of Science, 1939; Challenge to the Churches, 1941; Constructive Democracy, 1943; Conditions of Freedom, 1949; The Self as Agent, 1957 (Gifford Lect. 1953); Persons in Relation, 1961 (Gifford Lect. 1954); Science, Art and Religion, 1961; Search for Reality in Religion, 1965; (with other contributors) Adventure, 1927; Some Makers of the Modern Spirit, 1933; Marxism, 1934; Aspects of Dialectical Materialism, 1934. *Recreation:* gardening. *Address:* 8 Mansionhouse Road, Edinburgh EH9 1TZ. *T:* 031-667 5784. *[Died 21 June 1976.*

MACNAB, Brigadier John Francis, CBE 1957 (OBE 1943); DSO 1945; *b* 15 Sept. 1906; *o* surv. *s* of late Colonel Allan James Macnab, CB, CMG, FRCS, IMS, and Nora, *d* of Lieut-General Sir Lewis Dening, KCB, DSO; *m* 1938, Margaret, *d* of C. M. Treadwell; one *s* one *d*. *Educ:* Wellington Coll., Berks; RMC Sandhurst. Joined Queen's Own Cameron Highlanders, 1926; Lieut, 1929; seconded for service with KAR, 1929-35 and 1937; served with Cameron Highlanders, Catterick, and Regimental Depôt, Inverness, 1935-37; served War of 1939-45, Italian Somaliland, Abyssinia, Madagascar, Burma (despatches twice); Comd 1st Nyasaland Bn, KAR, 1941-43; Commander: 30th E African Inf. Bde, 1943; 21 (E African) Inf. Bde. Monsoon Campaign, Burma, 1944. Dep. President Regular Commissions Board, 1946; Comd 2nd Bn The Seaforth Highlanders, 1947; Colonel, Vice-President Sandhurst Selection Board, 1948; Comd: 6th Highland Bde, 2nd Div. BAOR, 1949-51; 153 Highland Bde, Highland Div., 1951-54; GHQ Troops, E Africa, 1954-57; Dep. Commander East Anglian District, Nov. 1957-Dec. 1959, retired. Late Hon. Colonel, Tanganyika Rifles and late Hon. Colonel, 6th and 2/6th Bn, KAR. Representer of House of Barravorich in Clan Macnab. *Recreations:* fishing and piping. *Address:* c/o Williams & Glyn's Bank Ltd, (Holt's Branch), Kirkland House, Whitehall, SW1; 45/4 Marina Street, Pieta, Malta, GC. *Club:* Army and Navy. *[Died 13 Nov. 1980.*

MACNAGHTEN, Sir Antony, 10th Bt, *cr* 1836; Chairman, London Discount Market Association, 1957-59; Manager, Alexanders Discount Co. Ltd, 1946-60; *b* 15 Nov. 1899; *s* of Rt Hon. Sir Malcolm Martin Macnaghten, KBE (*d* 1955) and Antonia Mary (*d* 1952), *e d* of Rt Hon. Charles Booth, FRS; *s* uncle, Hon. Sir Frederic Fergus Macnaghten, 9th Bt, 1955; *m* 1926, Magdalene, *e d* of late Edmund Fisher; three *s* one *d*. *Educ:* Eton Coll.; Trinity Coll., Cambridge. *Heir: s* Patrick Alexander Macnaghten [*b* 24 Jan. 1927; *m* 1955, Marianne, *d* of Dr Erich Schaefer, Cambridge; three *s*]. *Address:* Dundarave, Bushmills, Co. Antrim, N Ireland. *T:* 215. *Club:* United Oxford & Cambridge University. *[Died 12 Dec. 1972.*

McNAIR, 1st Baron, *cr* 1955, of Gleniffer; **Arnold Duncan McNair,** Kt 1943; CBE 1918; FBA 1939; LLD, Cambridge; Hon. LLD, Glasgow, Liverpool, Birmingham, Salonika, Brussels; Hon. DCL, Oxford; Hon. DLitt, Reading; QC; Fellow of Gonville and Caius College, Cambridge, since 1912; Bencher of Gray's Inn, Treasurer, 1947; *b* 4 March 1885; *e s* of late John McNair, of Lloyds, and Jeannie Ballantyne, both of Paisley; *m* 1912, Marjorie (*d* 1971), *yr d* of late Sir Clement M. Bailhache; one *s* three *d*. *Educ:* Aldenham; Gonville and Caius Coll., Cambridge. Admitted solicitor, 1906; Law Tripos, 1908, 1909; President of Cambridge Union, 1909; Secretary of Advisory Board of Coal Controller, 1917-19; Secretary of Coal Industry (Sankey) Commission, 1919; Chairman: Cttee on Supply and

Training of Teachers, 1942-44; Palestine Jewish Education Commn, 1945; Cttee on Recruitment to the Dental Profession, 1955-56; Burnham Cttee, 1956-58. Reader in International Law in the University of London, 1926-27; Tagore Professor in the University of Calcutta, 1931; Whewell Professor of International Law, University of Cambridge, 1935-37; Vice-Chancellor, Liverpool University, 1937-45; KC 1945. British Member, Permanent Court of Arbitration at The Hague, 1945-65; President of the International Court of Justice, 1952-55 and Judge, 1946-55; President of the European Court of Human Rights, 1959-65. Manley Hudson Gold Medal, American Society of International Law, 1959. *Publications:* Legal Effects of War, 1920, 4th edn (with A. D. Watts), 1966; Law of the Air, 1932, 3rd edn (by M. R. E. Kerr and A. H. M. Evans), 1964; (with W. W. Buckland) Roman Law and Common Law, 1936, 2nd edn 1952; Law of Treaties, 1938 and 1961; Dr Johnson and the Law, 1949; International Law Opinions, 1956; Expansion of International Law, 1962. *Heir:* s Hon. Clement John McNair [b 11 Jan. 1915; m 1941, Vera, d of Theodore James Faithfull; two s one d]. *Address:* 25 Storey's Way, Cambridge. *T:* Cambridge 53595.   [Died 22 May 1975.

McNAIR, Brigadier John Kirkland, CBE 1942; b 21 Oct. 1893; s of late Rev. H. B. McNair, Vicar of Aylesbury, Bucks; m 1st, 1915, Evelyn Dorothy Rastricke, er d of late E. R. Hanson, Chulmleigh, N. Devon; one d; 2nd, 1944, Nancy Adeleiza, er d of late W. A. Della Gana, Little Sunte, Lindfield; one s one d. *Educ:* Rugby; RMA, Woolwich. First Commission, Royal Regt of Artillery, 1913; Captain, 1917; Bt-Major, 1930; Major, 1931; Bt Lieut-Colonel, 1935; Lieut-Colonel, 1938; Colonel, 1938; Temp. Brigadier, 1940; served European War, 1914-18, in France in RFA (wounded twice); Staff Coll., Quetta, 1923-24; GSO 2 India, 1925-27; DAQMG India, 1927-29; RAF Staff Coll., Andover, 1931; GSO 2 Air Co-operation, 1932-34; GSO 2 War Office, 1934-36; idc, 1938; GSO 1 War Office, 1939-40; Dep. Director Military Operations War Office, 1940-41; Brig., RA Southern Command, 1941-42; Brigadier General Staff (Operations and Plans), Joint Staff Mission, Washington, 1942-44; retired, 1946; late Senior Administrative Officer, Imperial War Graves Commission; Officer Legion of Merit. *Address:* Little Putlands, Fairwarp, Uckfield, Sussex. *T:* Nutley 2676. *Club:* Naval and Military.   [Died 8 Aug. 1973.

McNAIR, Sir William Lennox, Kt 1946; Judge of the Queen's Bench Division, High Court of Justice, 1950-66; b 18 March 1892; s of late John McNair of Lloyds; unmarried. *Educ:* Aldenham (Schol.); Gonville and Caius Coll., Cambridge (Classical Schol.). First Class Law Tripos, Part I, 1913; Part II, 1914; LLM, 1919; Whewell Exhibitioner in International Law, 1919. Called to Bar, Gray's Inn, 1917; Bencher, 1938; KC 1944; Treasurer, 1951; Vice-Treasurer, 1952. Served with Royal Warwicks. Regt, 1914-18, Captain (despatches). Legal Adviser, Ministry of War Transport, 1941-45. Hon. Fellow Gonville and Caius College, Cambridge, 1951. *Publications:* Joint Editor of Temperley's Merchant Shipping Acts, 1925-72; Joint Editor of Scrutton on Charterparties and Bills of Lading. *Address:* 130 Court Lane, Dulwich, SE21.   [Died 19 Feb. 1979.

McNAIRN, Edward Somerville, CB 1962; Member, London Rent Assessment Panel, since 1974; b 5 Sept. 1907; er s of Edward B. McNairn and Mary Craig Sharp; m 1934, Nancy Stevenson; three d. *Educ:* Hutchesons' Grammar Sch., Glasgow; Glasgow Univ. Inland Revenue, 1929-69 (a Commissioner, 1958-69). Chm., Cttee on Rating of Plant and Machinery, 1971-72; Sec., PO Users' Nat. Council, 1971-72; Sec., Company Affairs Cttee, CBI, 1972-73. *Recreations:* gardening; theatre; anything to do with railways. *Address:* 31 Woodcote Avenue, Wallington, Surrey. *T:* 01-647 6229.   [Died 24 July 1975.

McNAMARA RYAN, Patrick John; see Ryan.

McNARNEY, Gen. Joseph T., Hon. KCB 1946; Director, General Dynamics Corporation; b Emporium, Pa, 28 Aug. 1893; s of James Pollard McNarney and Helen Taggart; m 1917, Helen Wahrenberger; one d. *Educ:* US Military Academy (BS 1915). Graduate Air Corps Tactical Sch., 1921, Command and General Staff Sch., 1926, Army War Coll., 1930. Comd 2nd Lieut, US Army, 1915, through grades to General, 1945; with Aviation Section, Army Signal Corps, 1916; comdg corps observation groups, overseas, 1917-19; Instructor Air Corps Tactical Sch., 1920-25; General Staff, War Dept, 1926-29; comdg March Field, California, 1930-31, 7th Bombardment Group, 1932-33; Instructor Army War Coll., 1933-35; Asst Chief of Staff, GHQ Air Force, 1935-38; comdg 7th Bomber Group, 1939; General Staff, War Dept, 1939-41; Chairman War Dept Reorganization Cttee, Jan. 1942; Dep. Chief of Staff, US Army, March 1942; Dep. Supreme Allied Commander, Mediterranean Theatre of Operations, 1944; Military Governor of Germany and

Commanding General, US Forces in Europe, 1945-47; commanding General, US Air Force Materiel command, 1947; Senior US Army Representative on Military Staff Cttee of United Nations, 1947; Chairman Dept of Defense Management Cttee, 1949-52; retired, 1952. President Convair, a Division of General Dynamics Corporation, 1952-58. *Address:* 1225 North Granada Avenue, Apt 12, Alhambra, Calif 91801, USA.   [Died 1 Feb. 1972.

MacNEECE, William Foster; *see* Foster, Air Vice-Marshal W. F. MacN.

McNEIL, Sir Hector, Kt 1969; CBE 1966; President, Babcock & Wilcox Ltd, 1972-73 (Chairman, 1968-71, Managing Director, 1958-68); b 20 July 1904; s of late Angus McNeil, New Zealand, and late Mary McNeil; m 1939, Barbara J. Turner, d of late P. S. Turner; one s one d. *Educ:* Christchurch, NZ. University of New Zealand (BE). Public Works Dept, New Zealand, 1927-29; State Electricity Commission of Victoria, Australia, 1929-31; joined Babcock & Wilcox Ltd, 1931; General Manager, 1947; Director, 1950; Dep. Managing Director, 1953; Director, National Bank of New Zealand, 1959-77. Chm., Export Council for Europe, 1966-69; Member: Export Guarantees Advisory Council, 1968-73; Council BIM, 1971-. President of Inst. of Fuel, 1957-58; FIEE; FIMechE; CIMarE. *Recreations:* shooting, golf. *Address:* Bramber, St George's Hill, Weybridge, Surrey. *T:* Weybridge 48484.   [Died 30 Dec. 1978.

McNEILL, Maj.-General Alister Argyll Campbell, CB 1943; MB, ChB; IMS retired; b 21 Nov. 1884; s of late Alexander McNeill, JP. *Educ:* High Sch., Glasgow; Glasgow Univ. (MB, ChB, 1906); Lieut, IMS, 1908; Captain, 1911; Major, 1920; Lieut-Colonel, 1928; Bt Colonel, 1935; Colonel, 1937; Maj.-General, 1941. Served European War, 1914-19 (despatches twice); KHS 1935-43. *Address:* c/o National and Grindlay's Bank Ltd, 13 St James's Square, SW1. *Club:* Royal and Ancient (St Andrews).   [Died 19 Jan. 1971.

McNEILL, Florence Marian, MBE 1962; Author, Journalist, Lecturer and Broadcaster; b Orkney, 26 March 1885; d of Rev. Daniel McNeill, MD, and Janet McNeill (née Dewar). *Educ:* Orkney; Glasgow (MA); Paris; Rhineland. Spent a period as art student. Social work, London, 1913-17. Founded Clan MacNeil Assoc. of Scotland, 1932. Scottish Secretary of State's Advisory Cttee on Rural Housing, 1944-45. *Publications:* Iona: a History of the Island, 1920; The Scots Kitchen: its Traditions and Lore, with Old-Time Recipes, 1929; The Road Home (novel), 1932; Recipes from Scotland, 1946; An Iona Anthology, 1947; The Scots Cellar, 1956; The Silver Bough: a Four-volume Study of the National and Local Festivals of Scotland, 1956-61, 1970; Hallowe'en, 1970; (In collaboration with F. J. Wakefield) An Inquiry in Ten Towns in England and Wales into the Protection of Minor Girls, 1916. *Recreations:* clarsach (Celtic harp), ceilidh (Highland social gathering), kitchen. *Address:* 31 St Alban's Road, Edinburgh 9. *T:* 031-667 4160. *Club:* Scottish PEN.   [Died 22 Feb. 1973.

McOWAN, George, MA, BSc, PhD; retired; b Alva, 1894; m 1928, Jan D. M., MA, yr d of A. Gibson, MB, ChB, FRCSE, FSA (Scotland), JP, Baillieston, Scotland; three d; m 1958, Graeme Lambert, yr d of late A. T. Wilson, Rangoon. *Educ:* St Andrews Univ. Lt 8th Royal Scots Fusiliers, 1914-18; Captain and Officer-Commanding St Andrews Univ. OTC, 1921-27; Lecturer in Chemistry, Univ. of St Andrews, 1923-27; Prof. of Chemistry, Raffles Coll., Singapore, 1927; Principal, Raffles Coll., 1938. *Publications:* contributions to Journal of Chemical Society. *Recreations:* golf, tennis. *Address:* 11 Marchhall Crescent, Edinburgh.   [Died 25 Jan. 1972.

MacOWAN, Michael Charles Henry, CBE 1976; Artistic Director, London Academy of Music and Dramatic Art, 1972-73 (Principal, 1954-66); b 18 April 1906; s of Norman MacOwan and Violet (née Stephenson); m 1932, Alexis McFarlane (Alexis France); one d. *Educ:* Haileybury Coll. Started as an actor, in 1925; abandoned acting for production; apptd producer Hull Repertory, 1931; Asst Producer and Master of Students, Old Vic, 1933-35; Producer, Westminster Theatre, 1936-39; A Month in the Country, Mourning Becomes Electra, Troilus and Cressida (in modern dress), etc. War service, 1939-45. Apptd Drama Dir Arts Council of Great Britain, 1945; produced Macbeth, Stratford-on-Avon, 1946. London productions include: The Linden Tree, 1947; Cockpit, 1948; A Sleep of Prisoners, 1951; The River Line, 1952; The Applecart, 1953; The Burning Glass, 1954; The Seagull, 1956; The Potting Shed, 1958. Has also undertaken radio and television productions and extensive lecturing and teaching, at home and abroad. *Recreations:* gardening, photography and country pursuits. *Address:* 3 Blake Gardens, SW6 4QA. *T:* 01-736 3520.   [Died 21 Aug. 1980.

McPHERSON, Brig. Alan Bruce, CBE 1944; MVO 1933; MC 1915; Indian Army, retired; *b* 6 Jan. 1887; *s* of late Donald William McPherson, Dunvegan, Isle of Skye; *m* 1915, Gladys Lawrie (*decd* 1972), *d* of late Col W. H. Riddell, Bedfordshire Regt; one *d. Educ:* Bedford Sch.; RMC Sandhurst. 2nd Lt IA 1906; Lt, 1909; Captain 1915; Major, 1921; Brevet Lt-Col, 1930; Substantive Lt-Col, 1931; Col, 1933; Served European war in France, 1914-15; Egypt, 1915; Mesopotamia, 1915-16 (wounded, despatches twice, MC); DAAG (Demobilization) Bombay 1918-19; Staff Coll. 1920-21; GSOII (Intelligence) 1922; DAAG 1922-26 and 1928-30; Officer in Command Indian War Memorial contingent, Neuve Chapelle, France, 1927; Commandant, 2/9th Jat Regt, 1931-34; Officer in charge the King's Indian Orderly Officers, 1933; AAG Northern Command, India, 1935-37; Operations NWF India, 1936-37; Comdr 11th (Ahmednagar) Infantry Brigade, India and Egypt, 1937-40; Dep. Dir of Mobilization, War Office, 1940-46; retired 1947; re-employed War Office 1947-49, 1950-57. *Publications:* Official Historical Monographs (2nd World War), on Mobilization and Discipline. *Address:* c/o Lt-Col D. J. Cable, OBE, MC, 6 Lammas Park Road, Ealing, W5. *Club:* Naval and Military. *[Died 14 Dec. 1978.*

MACPHERSON of Pitmain, Lt-Col Alexander Kilgour, MVO 1928; Senior Chieftain of the Clan Macpherson; *b* 6 March 1888; *er s* of late Dr F. A. Macpherson and Florence, *d* of late Archdeacon W. F. Taylor, DD, Liverpool, and Abergele; *m* 1st, Margaret G. Moore (*d* 1920); 2nd, 1924, Margaret M. Ramsay Crowley (*d* 1965); two *d. Educ:* Liverpool; Royal Military Coll., Sandhurst. Commissioned, 1908; attached 2nd Royal Berks Regt; posted 12th Pioneers, Indian Army, 1909; served France, 1914 (wounded), Waziristan, 1917, and with Marri Field Force, 1918; Captain 1915; Major, 1924; Lt-Col, 1932; commanded 1st Bn Corps of Bombay Pioneers, Indian Army, 1932-34; retired, 1934; called up active service Sept. 1939; commanded Nabha Akal Infantry, Eritrea and Cyprus, Middle East Force; Col (AQMG), GHQ, India; returned to pension establishment, Dec. 1943. DL, Inverness-shire, 1950-53. *Publication:* The Darkening Scene, 1967 (2nd edn 1968). *Recreations:* big-game shooting, riding, mountaineering. *Address:* Mains Hotel, Newtonmore, Inverness-shire. *Club:* United Service & Royal Aero. *[Died 12 Aug. 1974.*

MACPHERSON, Hon. Campbell Leonard, OBE 1949; Lieutenant-Governor of Newfoundland, 1957-63; *b* 4 July 1907; *s* of late Cluny Macpherson, CMG; *m* 1932, Faith Vilas; two *s* one *d. Educ:* Westminster Sch., London, England. Chairman, The Royal Stores Ltd, and associated companies, 1963. Mem. Bd of Regents: Memorial Univ. of Newfoundland, 1949-57; Mount Allison Univ.; Chm., Children's Hosp. Corp. Pres., Newfoundland Grenfell Assoc.; Dir, Internat. Grenfell Assoc. KJStJ, 1958. Hon. LLD: Mount Allison Univ., 1962; Memorial Univ. of Newfoundland, 1963. *Recreations:* motoring, golf. *Address:* Westerland, St John's, Newfoundland (PO Box 5847). *Clubs:* Naval and Military; Canadian (New York); Bally Haly Golf (St John's); Mount Royal (Montreal).
[Died 28 June 1973.

McPHERSON, Donald George; Assistant Under-Secretary of State, responsible for Health, Welsh Office, since 1969; *b* 5 Jan. 1914; *s* of George and Catherine McPherson; *m* 1943, Sybil Jean Blackley; two *s. Educ:* Newport (Mon) High Sch. Entered Estate Duty Office, 1932; called to Bar, Gray's Inn, 1937. Asst Sec., Board of Inland Revenue, 1950; Mem., Ceylon Taxation Commn, 1954-55; Establishment Officer, UKAEA, 1959-61; Sec., War Damage Commn, 1961-65; UN Adviser on Taxation, Cyprus, 1963; Sec., Royal Mint, 1966-67; Asst Sec., Min. of Health, 1967-69; Chm., Welsh Board of Health, 1969 (until Welsh Office take-over). OStJ 1972. *Recreation:* sport (particularly sailing and tennis) (Life Mem., CS Sports Council, Vice-Pres., CS LTA, Chm. Cardiff Area, CS Sports Council). *Address:* Robin Hill, Twyncyn, Dinas Powis, Glam. *T:* Dinas Powis 2339. *Clubs:* Royal Commonwealth Society, Wig and Pen. *[Died 25 Sept. 1973.*

MACPHERSON, Sir John (Stuart), GCMG 1951 (KCMG 1945; CMG 1941); Vice-Chairman, Advisory Committee on Distinction Awards for Consultants, since 1962; *b* 25 Aug. 1898; *er s* of late James P. Macpherson, JP; *m* 1928, Joan, *er d* of late Dr W. E. Fry, CStJ; one *s. Educ:* Watson's Coll., Edinburgh; Edinburgh Univ. (MA 1921). Served European War, 1917-19, France, Commissioned in Argyll and Sutherland Highlanders; Malayan Civil Service, 1921-37 (Seconded Colonial Office, 1933-35); Principal Asst Sec., Nigeria, 1937-39; Chief Sec., Palestine, 1939-43; Head of British Colonies Supply Mission in Washington, and Member of Anglo-American Caribbean Commission, 1943-45; Comptroller for Development and Welfare in the West Indies and British co-Chairman Caribbean

Commission, 1945-48; Governor of Nigeria, 1948-54; Gov.-Gen., Federation of Nigeria, 1954-55. Chm., UN Visiting Mission to Trust Territories of the Pacific, 1956; Permanent Under-Sec. of State for the Colonies, 1956-59; Chairman: Cable & Wireless Ltd, 1962-67; Basildon Develt Corp., 1964-67 (Dep. Chm., 1960-64). A Vice-President: Royal Commonwealth Soc.; Royal African Soc.; Mem. Council, Voluntary Service Overseas. Hon. Associate, Univ. Coll., Ibadan, 1950. Hon. LLD Edinburgh, 1957. KStJ 1952. *Address:* 141 Marsham Court, Westminster, SW1. *T:* 01-834 8807. *Club:* Athenæum.
[Died 5 Nov. 1971.

MacPHERSON, Malcolm, MBE 1945; MP (Lab), Stirling and Falkirk Burghs, since 1948; Vice-Chairman, Parliamentary Labour Party, 1964-67; *b* 1904; *s* of late John MacPherson and late Mary MacKay; *m* 1929, Janet Elder (*d* 1961), *d* of late William McKay; two *s* two *d. Educ:* Trinity Acad., Edinburgh; Univ. of Edinburgh. Taught in George Heriot's Sch., Edinburgh, 1926-28; Univ. of New Brunswick, Canada, 1928-38; University Coll., Exeter, 1938-40; Canadian Army, 1940-45; Labour Candidate, Yeovil Div., Gen. Election, 1945. *Address:* Airlie Mount, Alyth, Perthshire. *T:* Alyth 515. *[Died 24 May 1971.*

MACPHERSON, Very Rev. William Stuart, MA Cantab; Dean of Lichfield, 1954-69, Dean Emeritus, 1969; Hon. Canon, Ripon Cathedral, 1953-54; *b* 30 Sept. 1901; *s* of late Henry Macpherson, Headingley Hall, Leeds; *m* 1937, Peggy Josephine Wilton; two *s* one *d. Educ:* Sedbergh Sch.; Pembroke Coll., Cambridge. BA Cambridge, 1923. Priest, 1932; Curate of Richmond, Yorks, 1932-37; Minor Canon, Ripon Cathedral, 1937-39; Chaplain RNVR, 1939-45; Archdeacon of Richmond, 1951-54, Rector of Richmond, 1945-54. Proctor in Convocation, 1949. *Address:* Yew Tree Cottage, Hawkchurch, Axminster, Devon. *T:* Hawkchurch 485. *[Died 7 July 1978.*

McQUAID, Most Rev. John Charles, DD, MA, DLitt, MRIA; FRSAI; *b* Cootehill, Co. Cavan, 28 July 1895; *e s* of late Dr Eugene Ward McQuaid. *Educ:* St Patrick's Diocesan Coll., Cavan; Blackrock Coll.; Clongowes Wood Coll.; National Univ. of Ireland; Rome. Entered Novitiate of Holy Ghost Fathers at Kimmage Manor, 1913; professed, 1914; ordained priest, 1924. Pres., Blackrock Coll., 1931-39. Archbishop of Dublin and Primate of Ireland, 1940-72; retired. Chm. Catholic Headmasters' Assoc. for many years; represented Ireland at International Education Congresses in Brussels, The Hague, Luxembourg, and Fribourg; Rector of Catholic Univ., Ireland. *Address:* Notre Dame des Bois, Ballybrack, Co. Dublin.
[Died 7 April 1973.

MacQUARRIE, Hon. Josiah H., Justice of the Supreme Court of Nova Scotia, Canada, 1947-66; *b* 12 Nov. 1897; *s* of James T. and Agnes MacWhinnie MacQuarrie; *m* 1921, Mattie, *d* of Ethelbert and Annie Atkinson; one *s* two *d. Educ:* Pictou Academy; Acadia Univ.; Dalhousie Univ. Practised law at Pictou, Nova Scotia, with firm of Macdonald and MacQuarrie, 1921-32; Head of Legal firm New Glasgow, Nova Scotia, of MacQuarrie and MacQuarrie, 1932-40; Mem. Parliament of Nova Scotia, Attorney Gen. and Min. of Lands and Forests of Nova Scotia, 1933-47; Min. of Municipal Affairs, Prov. of Nova Scotia (from beginning of Dept), 1937-47. *Recreations:* golf, swimming. *Address:* Halifax, Nova Scotia. *TA:* Halifax Nova Scotia. *T:* Halifax 2-2087. *Clubs:* Scotia, (New Glasgow); Halifax (Halifax). *[Died 7 April 1971.*

MacQUEEN, Maj.-Gen. John Henry, CBE 1943; CD; retired; *b* Canada, 19 Sept. 1893; *s* of John T. and Emma Olding MacQueen; *m* 1917, Aimee Olive Miller Roy; no *c. Educ:* New Glasgow High Sch.; Royal Military College of Canada; Military Coll. of Science, England. Commissioned RCOC 1914; European War, 1914-19, Canada and England; District Ordnance Officer, Military District No. 10, Winnipeg, Manitoba, 1929-38; Dir of Ordnance Services, Canada, 1938-39; Senior Ordnance Officer, 1939, and Asst Quartermaster-Gen. (Ordnance Services), 1940, Dep. Quartermaster Gen., Canadian Military Headquarters, London, England, 1941-45; Master Gen. of the Ordnance, 1945. Pres. Canadian Arsenals Ltd, 1947-61. Served War of 1939-45, Canada, England, France, Italy. Legion of Merit, USA, 1948. Coronation Medal, 1937. *Recreations:* shooting, fishing, golf, bridge. *Address:* 33 Loch Isle Road, Ottawa, Ont K2H 8G5, Canada. *Clubs:* Rideau (Ottawa); Royal Ottawa Golf (Hull, PQ). *[Died 1 March 1980.*

MACRAE, Angus; Vice-President, British Medical Association, since 1960; *b* 1893; *s* of late Rev. Duncan Mackenzie Macrae, Minister at Helmsdale and at Lochearnhead; *m* 1926, Marjorie Isobel, *d* of late G. M. Brotherston; one *s* (and one *s* decd). *Educ:* George Watson's Coll. and Univ. of Edinburgh (MA 1919; MB, ChB, 1924). Served European War, 4th Seaforth Highlanders,

1915-19. Investigator, Nat. Institute of Industrial Psychology, 1925. Asst Sec., 1935, Dep. Sec., 1948, BMA; Sec., Central Medical Recruitment Cttee, 1950-58; Hon. Sec., British Commonwealth Medical Conference, 1950-58; Sec., BMA, 1950-58; retd; Information Officer, Nat. Inst. of Indust. Psychol., 1958-63. Hon. MD (NUI), 1952; Hon. LLD, Edinburgh, 1959. *Publications:* Talents and Temperaments, 1932; various articles on psychological subjects. *Address:* The Long Yard, Wickham St Paul, Halstead, Essex C09 2PT. *T:* Twinstead 365. *[Died 21 Feb. 1975.*

McROBERT, Sir George Reid, Kt 1947; CIE 1942; Col IMS (retired); Consulting Physician, Hospital for Tropical Diseases, University College Hospital, London; *b* 21 Jan. 1895; *s* of late A. T. McRobert, Aberdeen; *m* 1919, Catherine Ellen (*d* 1969), *d* of late G. T. C. Gregory, New Malden, Surrey; two *d. Educ:* Gordon's Coll., Aberdeen; Aberdeen Univ. MB 1917; MD 1923; MRCP 1923; FRCP 1935; DTM&H Eng 1924; Hon. FRCPEd 1970. RAMC (SR) 1917-20. France and Mesopotamia; IMS 1920; Waziristan Campaign; entered Civil side of IMS 1925; Prof. of Physiology, Rangoon Univ., 1925-30; Prof. of Medicine and Senior Physician, Madras, 1934-45; Inspector-Gen. of Hospitals, Bihar, 1945-47; Mem. Medical Bd, India Office and Commonwealth Relations Office, 1947-58; Medical Adviser to Sec. of State for Commonwealth Relations, 1958-62; Consulting Physician to Colonial Office and to Officers Convalescent Home, Osborne, 1951-60; Mem. Bd of Governors, University Coll. Hosp., 1955-63; Mem. of Governing Council, Epsom Coll., 1955-67; Physician, Tropical Diseases Hosp., London, 1951-60; Adviser for Colombo Plan Affairs, Dept of Technical Co-operation, 1961-62; Pres., Royal Society of Tropical Medicine and Hygiene, 1961-63. Jubilee and Coronation Medals. *Publications:* numerous in Professional Journals; part author Rogers and Megaw's Tropical Medicine. *Recreation:* writing. *Address:* 3 Stoke Road, Nayland, by Colchester, Essex. *T:* Nayland 262832. *Club:* Athenæum. *[Died 6 June 1976.*

MacROBERT, Norman Murie, CMG 1952; retired; *b* 30 May 1899; 3rd *s* of George Findlay MacRobert and Mabel Louisa, *d* of late Gen. Nugent; unmarried. *Educ:* Shrewsbury Sch. Lt Rifle Brigade, 1918-20. Colonial Administrative Service, 1927. Served in Royal West African Frontier Force, Sierra Leone, 1940; Major, 1941-42. Provincial Commissioner, 1946; Acting Chief Comr, 1952 and 1953; retired 1954. *Recreations:* gardening, photography. *Address:* 8 Rowans Court, Prince Edwards Road, Lewes, Sussex. *[Died 16 Nov. 1972.*

McSHANE, John J., JP; Retired Secondary School Headmaster, Walsall; *b* Wishaw, Lanarkshire, 1 Oct. 1882; *s* of Philip McShane, miner; *m* Annie, *d* of Fred W. Bromwich, Walsall; one *s* two *d. Educ:* St Ignatius RC Sch., Wishaw; Glasgow Univ. Training Coll. Left Elementary Sch. at 14 years; went to work at railway wagon works; studied at night sch. and worked during day; ultimately passed to coll.; Headmaster, Armadale RC Sch. (West Lothian), 1909; after six years, went to Walsall; Headmaster, St Mary's RC Sch., Walsall, 1922-29; MP (Lab) Walsall Borough, 1929-31; mem. of NUT; Pres., South Midland Federation Class Teachers, 1920; Pres., Walsall Debating Soc., 1924; Pres., Walsall Labour Party, 1921-22; Chm., Walsall Board of Guardians, 1929. Dir Walsall Co-op Soc. 1933-55; Chm. Midland Section, CWS Representation Cttee, 1944-55. *Recreations:* tennis, golf, reading, and politics. *Address:* 3 Glenelg Mews, Beacon Road, Walsall, West Midlands. *T:* 021-360 4445. *[Died 26 May 1972.*

McSHEEHY, Maj.-Gen. Oswald William, CB 1943; DSO 1915; OBE 1919; MB, BS, London; RAMC, retired; *b* 27 Nov. 1884; *y s* of late Surgeon-Major E. L. McSheehy, MD, FRCSI, JP, Limerick, and Teresa, *d* of Joseph Hirst, JP, Huddersfield; *m* 1911, Caroline, (*d* 1950), *e d* of late Col H. Paterson, Indian Army; two *s* three *d*; *m* 1954, Teresa Delaine. *Educ:* St Edmund's Coll., Ware; St Thomas's Hospital. Entered army, 1909; Capt.; Major, 1921; Bt Lt-Col 1926; Lt-Col 1934; Col 1937; Brig. 1940; Maj.-Gen. 1941; served European War, 1914-18 (despatches twice, DSO, OBE); Dep. Asst Dir-Gen., War Office, 1922-26; Dep Dir-Gen. Army Medical Services, War Office, 1938-41; served S Africa, India and Malaya; Dep. Dir of Medical Services, SE and E Cd at home, 1941-45; Hon. Surgeon to the King, 1941-44; retired pay, 1945; Dep Dir of Health, UNRRA, London, 1945-46; Col Comdt, RAMC, 1946-50, Rep. Comdt, 1948. *Address:* Creagh, 26 Waverley Lane, Farnham, Surrey. *[Died 21 July 1975.*

MacTAGGART, Sir Andrew (McCormick), Kt 1951; Civil Engineer; Company Director, 1928-66; *b* 13 July 1888; *s* of Matthew MacTaggart, Waterside House, Fenwick, Ayrshire; *m* 1st, 1919, Marie Louise (marr. diss. 1961), *d* of Gaston Petit, France; 2nd, 1961, Irene Countess of Craven. *Educ:*

Kilmarnock; Glasgow. Completed a 4-year pupilage with Warren & Stewart, Glasgow, 1904-8; Asst Engineer on Nigerian Railways, 1912-16, promoted to permanent staff, resigned, 1916. Served European War, 1914-18, joined Royal Engineers with commission in France, 1917. Rejoined Balfour, Beatty & Co. Ltd in 1919. Responsible for the design and construction of Grampian Company's hydro-electric development in Scotland; in charge of construction of Lochaber Hydro-Electric Scheme in Scotland; responsible for construction of hydro-electric developments in Italy, India, and E Africa, and construction of large irrigation and railway works in Iraq. Pres., Power Securities Corp.; Pres. Fedn of Civil Engineering Contractors, 1948-49, 1949-50, 1950-51; Mem. of Council, British Employers' Confederation, 1940-62. *Recreations:* shooting and fishing. *Address:* Clatfields, Marsh Green, Edenbridge, Kent. *T:* Edenbridge 862819. *Club:* Caledonian. *[Died 20 June 1978.*

McVEIGH, Rt. Hon. Sir Herbert Andrew, PC (N Ireland) 1965; Kt 1964; Lord Justice of Appeal, Supreme Court of Judicature, N Ireland, 1964-73 (Judge of High Court of Justice, N Ireland, 1956-64, also Judge of the Restrictive Practices Court, 1957-73, and Deputy-Chairman Boundaries Commission, N Ireland, 1957-64); *b* 8 Dec. 1908; *s* of late John McVeigh, JP, Londonderry; *m* 1940, Mary Elizabeth Mabel, *e d* of late Adam Reade, Portstewart, Co. Londonderry; two *d. Educ:* Foyle Coll., Londonderry; Queen's Univ., Belfast (BA). Pres. Students' Representative Council, 1929-30. Junior Crown Counsel, Co. Antrim; Senior Crown Counsel: Co. Fermanagh; Co. Tyrone; Co. Antrim; Member: Bar Council, 1938-56; Nat. Arbitration Tribunal; Distinction Awards Cttee (NI) relating to Hosp. Authority Consultants; several official cttees on legal questions. Dep. Umpire under Insurance and Employment Acts. Barrister, Inn of Court, NI, 1931, KC (NI) 1948, Bencher, 1954; mem. of Gray's Inn; Chairman: Education Cttee of Benchers; Finance and Libraries Cttee of Benchers; N Ireland Assoc. for Mental Health. President: Queen's Univ. Assoc.; Foyle Coll. Old Boys Assoc.; Belvoir Park Golf Club; Gov., Victoria Coll., Belfast. *Publication:* Law of Valuation, 1935. *Recreations:* swimming, golf. *Address:* 25 Cambourne Park, Belfast BT9 6RL. *T:* 660927. *Club:* Northern Counties (Londonderry). *[Died 3 Oct. 1977.*

McVEY, Sir Daniel, Kt 1954; CMG 1950; MIE (Australia); President, Dunlop Australia Ltd; also Director several other cos; *b* 1892; *s* of Daniel McVey, Falkirk, Stirlingshire, and Jeanie, *d* of Robert Cunningham Kay; *m* 1919, Margaret Gardiner, *d* of Thomas Packman, Brisbane; two *s* one *d. Educ:* Falkirk High Sch., Scotland. Joined Commonwealth Public Service, 1914; served with AIF, 1915-19; Lt, 45th Battery, AFA; Communications Engineer, 1914-30; Asst Supt of Mails, NSW, 1930-33; Supt of Mails, NSW, 1933-37; Asst Commissioner, Commonwealth Public Service Board, 1937-38; Commissioner, National Insurance Commission, 1938-39; Sec., Dept of Supply and Development, May-Dec. 1939; Dir-Gen. of Posts and Telegraphs, 1939-46; Dir of War Organisation of Industry, 1941-42; Sec. Dept of Aircraft Production, Dep. Chm., Aircraft Advisory Cttee, 1942-45; Dir-Gen. of Civil Aviation, Australia, 1943-46; Dir-Gen. of Aircraft Production, 1945-46; Chm. Radiophysics Advisory Board and Mem. Radio Research Board until June 1946. Commissioner, Australian National Airlines Commission, Feb.-June 1946. Leader of Australian Air Mission to the USA, Canada, and the UK, Jan.-May 1942; Leader of delegation to British Commonwealth Communications Council, London, April-July 1944; Adviser to Australian Prime Minister on Civil Aviation and Telecommunications at Prime Ministers' Conference, London, May 1944; Delegate to Civil Aviation Conference, Wellington, NZ, Oct. 1944; Delegate to International Civil Aviation Conference, Chicago, USA, Nov.-Dec. 1944; Delegate to British Commonwealth Civil Aviation Conference, Montreal, Dec. 1944; Leader of Australian Delegation at British Commonwealth Air Transport Conference, London, July 1945; Leader of Australian Delegation at British Commonwealth Telecommunications Conference, London, July-Aug. 1945; Delegate to British Commonwealth Civil Aviation Conference, Wellington, NZ, March 1946. Mem. Bd of Trustees, Nat. Museums of Victoria, 1945-46; Chm. and Man. Dir, STC Pty Ltd, 1946-49; Man. Dir Metal Manufactures, Ltd and Austral Bronze Co. Pty Ltd, 1949-62; Chm. Commonwealth-State Consultative Cttee on Electric Power, 1951-52; Chm. Materials Industry Advisory Cttee to Minister of Defence Production, 1953-66; Mem. Australian Atomic Energy Commission Business Advisory Group, 1954-64. Kernot Memorial Medal, Univ. of Melbourne, 1945. Hon. Life Gov., Alfred Hospital, Melbourne. *Recreation:* golf. *Address:* 12 Cleeve Court, Toorak, Victoria 3142, Australia. *Clubs:* Melbourne, Savage (Melbourne); Australian (Sydney). *[Died 24 Dec. 1972.*

McVITTIE, Wilfrid Wolters, CMG 1958; *b* 24 May 1906; *s* of Francis McVittie and Emily McVittie (*née* Weber); *m* 1938, Harriett Morna Wilson, *d* of Dr G. Wilson, Toronto; one *s* two *d. Educ:* abroad; King's Coll., Univ. of London. Entered Japan Consular Service, 1930; Consul at Yokohama, 1938; 1st Sec. (Commercial), Buenos Aires, 1946; Counsellor (Commercial), British Embassy, Mexico City, 1948; Counsellor (Commercial) and Consul-Gen., British Embassy, Lisbon, 1952; HM Ambassador to the Dominican Republic, 1958-62. Comendador, Military Order of Christ (Portugal), 1957. *Recreation:* ornithology. *Address:* White House, Itchenor, Sussex.
[*Died* 17 *Sept.* 1980.

McWHIRTER, (Alan) Ross; author, compiler, publisher; *b* 12 Aug. 1925; *yr (twin) s* of William Alan McWhirter, Managing Director of Associated Newspapers and Northcliffe Newspapers Group, and Margaret Williamson; 1957, Rosemary Joy Hamilton, *d* of Leslie C. H. Grice; two *s. Educ:* Marlborough; Trinity Coll., Oxford. MA (Jurisprudence). Served RN, 1943-46: Sub-Lieut RNVR, HM Minesweepers, North Sea and Mediterranean (medal with clasp). Dir, McWhirter Twins Ltd, 1950; co-founder, Redwood Press, 1966. Editor and compiler, Guiness Book of Records, 1955-, 81 edns in 15 languages, with global sales of 23.9 million copies. Sports Correspondent: Star, 1951-60; Evening News, 1960-62; Chm., Sports Writers' Assoc., 1959; Campaign Dir, Current Affairs Press, 1975. Contested (C) Edmonton, 1964. *Publications:* Get To Your Marks, 1951; (ed 1952-56) Athletics World; Dunlop Book of Facts, 1964, 1966; (with Sir Andrew Noble, Bt) Centenary History of OURFC, 1969; (with U. A. Titley) Illustrated Centenary History of the RFU, 1972; (ed) 'Gainst All Disaster, 1975. *Recreations:* ski-ing; formerly athletics (Oxford v Cambridge relays, 1946; AAA 4×110 yds championship, 1948). *Address:* c/o 2 Cecil Court, London Road, Enfield, Mddx EN2 6DJ. *T:* 01-366 4551. *Clubs:* Vincent's (Oxford); Achilles.   [*Died* 27 *Nov.* 1975.

MACWHIRTER, Clara Elizabeth Littlewort, OBE 1957; Headmistress, Central High School for Girls, Manchester, 1931-59; *d* of Francis Littlewort Macwhirter and Isobel Macwhirter (*née* Stewart). *Educ:* University of Edinburgh; University of Rennes, France. Teacher of French: at Leith Academy, 1919-22; at Holly Lodge High Sch., Liverpool, 1922-31. *Recreations:* languages, travel. *Address:* 150a Barlow Moor Road, West Didsbury, Manchester 20.   [*Died* 30 *Nov.* 1971.

McWHIRTER, Ross; *see* McWhirter, A. R.

McWILLIAM, Sir John, Kt 1970; HM Lieutenant, County of Fife, since 1965; *b* 3 April 1910; *s* of James McWilliam and Flora Campbell Elgin; *m* 1935, Ann Tyson McPherson; one *s* two *d. Educ:* Radnor Park and Clydebank High Schs. Convener, County Council of Fife, 1961-70; Vice-Chairman, Forth Road Bridge Board, 1961-70; Vice-Chairman, Tay Road Bridge Board, 1961-70; Member, Glenrothes Development Corp., 1962-70 (Dep. Chairman, 1964-70); Chairman: Countryside Commn for Scotland, 1968-72; Forth Ports Authority, 1969-73. Member, Police Council of Great Britain, 1960-70; Vice-Chairman, Assoc. of County Councils in Scotland, 1962-70; Member, several Government Cttees of Inquiry relative to Local Government. *Recreations:* reading, public service. *Address:* Kilbowie, Kinghorn, Fife. *T:* Kinghorn 555. *Clubs:* Royal Automobile, Royal Scottish Automobile (Glasgow).
[*Died* 7 *Aug.* 1974.

MADARIAGA, Don Salvador de, MA; Honorary President, International Liberal Union and Congress for Freedom of Culture; Founder President, College of Europe (Bruges); Hon. Fellow of Exeter College, Oxford; Member: Spanish Academy of Letters and of Moral and Political Sciences; French Academy of Moral and Political Sciences; Academy of History of Caracas and many other Spanish-American Institutions of Learning; *b* Corunna, Spain, 23 July 1886; *s* of Don Jose de Madariaga, Colonel, Spanish Army, and Dona Ascension Rojo de Madariaga; *m* Constance Archibald, MA Hons (Glasgow) (*d* 1970); two *d*; *m* 1970, Emilia Szekely-Rauman (*b* Budapest). *Educ:* Institute del Cardenal Cisneros, Madrid; Collège Chaptal, Paris; Ecole Polytechnique, Paris; Ecole Nationale Supérieure des Mines, Paris. Technical Adviser to Superintendent of Line, Spanish Northern Railway, 1911-16; Journalist, Publicist and Literary Critic, London, 1916-21; Member of Press Section League of Nations Secretariat, Geneva, 1921-22; Director of Disarmament Section of League of Nations Secretariat, 1922-27; King Alphonso XIII Prof. of Spanish Studies, Oxford, 1928-31; Secretary of the Temporary Mixed Commission for Disarmament, then of the Preparatory Commission for a Disarmament Conference; Secretary of the Third (Disarmament) Commission of the Assembly of the League of Nations, 1922-27; Secretary General of the International

Conference for the Supervision of the Trade in Arms, Geneva, April-May 1925; Spanish Ambassador to USA, 1931, to France, 1932-34; Spanish Permanent Delegate to the League of Nations, 1931-36; Visiting Prof. of Spanish, Princeton Univ., 1954. Hans Deutsch European Prize, 1963; Hanseatic Goethe Prize, 1967. MA by Decree of University of Oxford, 1928; Hon. Doctor Universities of Arequipa, Lima, Oxford, Poitiers, Princeton, Liége, Lille; Matricula d'Onore, University of Pavia, 1966. Charlemagne Prize, 1973. Knight Grand Cross of Orders of the Spanish Republic, Légion d'Honneur (France), Jade-in-Gold of China, White Lion of Tchecoslovakia, Aztec Eagle of Mexico, Boyacá of Colombia, Merit of Chile, Sun of Peru, Grand Cross of Order of Merit of Federal Republic of Germany, etc. *Publications:* apart from several publications in Spanish and French, has published: Shelley and Calderon and other Essays on Spanish and English Poetry, 1920; Spanish Folksongs, 1922; The Genius of Spain, 1923; The Sacred Giraffe, 1926; Englishmen, Frenchmen, Spaniards, 1928, 2nd edn 1970; Disarmament, 1929; Sir Bob, 1930; I, Americans, 1930; Don Quixote, 1934; Anarchy or Hierarchy, 1937; Theory and Practice in International Relations, 1938; The World's Design, 1938; Christopher Columbus, 1939; Hernán Cortés, 1941; Spain, 1942; The Heart of Jade, 1944, new edn 1956; Victors, Beware, 1946; The Rise of the Spanish American Empire, 1947; The Fall of the Spanish American Empire, 1947; On Hamlet, 1948; Bolivar, 1952; Portrait of Europe, 1952; Essays with a Purpose, 1953; A Bunch of Errors, 1953; War in the Blood, 1957; Democracy versus Liberty?, 1958; Latin-America between the Eagle and the Bear, 1962; Portrait of a Man Standing, 1967; Morning Without Noon (autobiog.), 1973; frequent contributions to the English, American, Spanish, and Spanish-American press. *Recreation:* a change of work. *Address:* La Palma, CH 6000, Locarno, Switzerland. *Clubs:* Reform (London); Ateneo (Madrid).   [*Died* 14 *Dec.* 1978.

MADDAN, Martin; MP (C) Hove, since 1965; Chairman, AGB Research Ltd, since 1962; *b* 1920; *s* of late James Gracie Maddan, CBE; *m* 1958, Susanne, *d* of late R. C. Huband, JP; two *s* two *d. Educ:* Fettes Coll., Edinburgh; Brasenose Coll., Oxford. Served Royal Marines, 1939-46; Major, 1944. Contested (C) North Battersea, 1950. MP (C) Hitchin Division of Herts, 1955-64; PPS to Minister of Health, 1961-63. Joint Hon. Treasurer, European Movement (earlier Britain in Europe group), 1956-; UK Sponsor, Declaration of Atlantic Unity, 1958-; Council Oxford and Bermondsey Club, 1952-; Fellow, St Michael's Coll., Tenbury, 1964-; Mem., Market Research Society, 1953-. *Publications:* Profitable Export Marketing, 1955. *Address:* House of Commons, SW1.   [*Died* 22 *Aug.* 1973.

MADDOCKS, His Honour George; County Court Judge, retired; *b* 5 April 1896; *s* of William and Sarah Alice Maddocks, Southport; *m* 1928, Harriet Mary Louisa Day; two *s* one *d. Educ:* Christ Church Hall, Southport; Manchester Univ. Called to Bar, Middle Temple, 1923. *Address:* 104 Roe Lane, Southport, Lancs.   [*Died* 3 *April* 1980.

MADDOX, Samuel; General Secretary, Bakers, Food and Allied Workers' Union, since 1975; *b* 16 June 1930; *s* of Samuel and Jane Maddox; *m* 1952, Doreen Greenham; two *s* one *d. Educ:* Broad Meadow Sec. Sch., Chesterton, Staffs. Served Army, Queen's Horse Guards, 1947-49. Mem. Exec. Council, Bakers' Union, 1967-68; Dist Sec., 1968-75. *Publication:* Our History: a complete history of the Bakers' Union from 1849 to 1975, 1975. *Recreation:* coarse, salmon and trout fishing. *Address:* Stanborough House, Stanborough, Welwyn Garden City, Herts. *T:* Hatfield 60150.   [*Died* 29 *April* 1979.

MAGNANI, Anna; Italian stage and film actress; *b* Rome, Italy, 7 March 1908; *m* Goffredo Alessandrini; one *s. Educ:* Academy of Dramatic Art, Rome. First appeared on legitimate stage and worked in repertory companies. First film appearance in Blind Woman of Sorrento, 1934. Films include: Open City, 1946; Before Him All Rome Trembled, 1947; Angelini, 1947; Love, 1947; Volcano, 1953; Bellissima, 1953; The Gold Coach, 1954; The Rose Tattoo, 1955; Suor Letizia, 1958; Awakening, 1958; Nella Città l'Inferno, 1959; The Fugitive Kind, 1960; And the Wild, Wild Women, 1961; Mamma Roma, 1963; The Secret of Santa Vittoria, 1968. Returned to the stage in La Lupa, Florence, 1965, London, 1969. Many awards, including Venice Film Festival Award, Italian Ribbon of Silver and Oscar (USA). *Address:* c/o Ercole Graziadei, Via Veneto 96, Rome, Italy.
[*Died* 26 *Sept.* 1973.

MAGNAY, Harold Swindale; Consultant, OECD, Paris, since 1964; *b* 24 Jan. 1904; *e s* of late Andrew Magnay and late Phœbe Elizabeth Swindale, Newcastle upon Tyne; *m* 1931, Meg, *e d* of late Thomas Wood and Meggie Huntley, Felling-on-Tyne; one *s. Educ:* Elswick Road Council Sch. and Royal Grammar Sch.,

Newcastle upon Tyne; St John's Coll., Cambridge (Exhibitioner in History, Law Schol.). Game Ranger and District Reclamation Officer, Tanganyika, 1925-27; Asst Master, RGS, 1927-30; Asst Director of Education, Newcastle upon Tyne, 1930-34; Director of Education: Barnsley, 1934-40; Leicester, 1940-46; Liverpool, 1946-64. Past President Assoc. of Education Officers; Past Chairman, Assoc. of Art Institutions. Hon. Secretary various educational cttees, etc; National Council Boy Scouts' Assoc.; Past Chairman, BBC Northern Advisory Council; formerly President, Liverpool Sunday School Union; Member: Percy Cttee on Higher Technological Education; Reynolds Cttee on Remand Homes and Approved Schools; Fulton Commn on Education in Sierra Leone. Member: University Grants Cttee, 1946-53; Advisory Cttee on Education in the Colonies, 1955-58; Hospital Radio (Pres.); Christian Aid, Bishop's Stortford (Chm.). Hon. FRIBA. Hon. MA Liverpool, 1959. Silver Medal of Honour, City of Amsterdam, 1964. *Recreations:* walking and talking. *Address:* 25 Grange Park, Bishop's Stortford, Herts. *T:* Bishop's Stortford 2588. *Clubs:* United University; University (Liverpool). *[Died 24 Oct. 1971.*

MAGNER, Jeremiah John, CB 1948; MC 1918; Major-General (late RAMC), retired; Medical Director, National Mass Radiography Association, since 1951; *b* 26 June 1891; 2nd *s* of late David Magner, Carrigville, Cork; *m* 1927, Sarah Gabriel, *d* of John Magner, Clonmel; no *c. Educ:* National University of Ireland; London Univ. MB, BCh, BAO (NUI) 1914; DMR (London) 1935. FFR, RCS(I), Founder Fellow. Served European War, 1914-19, France, Belgium, Balkans, Russia (despatches, MC, 1914 Star and two medals); War of 1939-45, 8th Army, Desert Campaign, Italy (despatches twice, CB). KHP 1948-51; DDMS, HQ Northern Command, York, 1948-51; retired pay, 1951. *Recreations:* hunting, golf, fishing. *Address:* 6 Herbert Park, Ballsbridge, Dublin. *T:* 684740.
[Died 23 July 1973.

MAGOWAN, Joseph Irvine, CB 1956; DL; Permanent Secretary, Ministry of Agriculture, Northern Ireland, 1953-56, retired; President, Alliance Party of Northern Ireland, since 1971; *b* 16 Jan. 1901; *s* of Wm H. Magowan, Mountnorris, and S. A. Magowan; *m* 1933, Mima Hazlett Kennedy; one *s* three *d. Educ:* Mountnorris; privately; Dublin; Edinburgh. Member RCVS, 1924; private practice, 1924-27; Diploma of Veterinary State Medicine, 1928; Min. of Agriculture, NI, 1929, Dep. Chief Veterinary Officer, 1940-47; Asst Secretary, Ministry of Agriculture, Northern Ireland, 1947-53. DL Co. of Armagh. *Recreations:* field sports, pigeon racing, gardening. *Address:* Mountnorris, Armagh, N Ireland. *T:* Glenanne 209. *Club:* City (Armagh). *[Died 31 May 1977.*

MAGUIRE, Conor Alexander; Member, European Court of Human Rights, 1965-71; Chief Justice of Eire, 1946-61; *b* 16 Dec. 1889; *s* of C. J. O'L. Maguire, MD, and Florence O'Neill; *m* 1921, Nora Whelan; three *s. Educ:* Clongowes Wood Coll.; Univ. Coll., Dublin. MA, LLB National University of Ireland; Solicitor, 1914; Judge and Land Settlement Commissioner Dail, 1920-22; Called to Bar of Ireland, 1922; Inner Bar, 1932; prominent in the Sinn Fein movement; Member of Dail Eireann for National University of Ireland; Attorney-General, Irish Free State, 1932-36; Judge of the High Court and Judicial Commissioner, 1936; President of the High Court, 1937-46; Chairman Central Council, Irish Red Cross Society, 1940-46; President International Celtic Congress, 1957-61; Irish Representative European Commission of Human Rights, Strasbourg, 1963-65. Commandeur Légion d'Honneur; Order of St Raimon de Penafort (Spain); Grosse Verdienstkreuz (Federal Republic of Germany). LLD (*hc*): NUI; Dublin University. *Recreations:* fishing and shooting. *Address:* St Alban's, Albany Avenue, Monkstown, Co. Dublin. *[Died 26 Sept. 1971.*

MAHALANOBIS, Prasanta Chandra, FRS 1945; Hon. FSS 1954; FNA; BSc Calcutta, MA Cantab; Statistical Adviser to Cabinet, Government of India, since 1949; Member, Planning Commission, Government of India, 1955-67; Hon. President Internat. Statistical Institute, 1957 (Member 1937, Hon. Member 1952); Secretary and Director, Indian Statistical Institute, Calcutta, since 1931; Founder Editor, Sankhyā: the Indian Journal of Statistics, since 1933; *b* 29 June 1893; *s* of late Probodh Chandra Mahalanobis and late Nirodbasini Mahalanobis; *m* 1923, Nirmal Kumari Maitra; no *c. Educ:* Brahmo Boys' Sch. and Presidency Coll., Calcutta; King's Coll., Cambridge (Senior Scholar, 1915). BSc (Hons Physics) Calcutta Univ. 1912; Cambridge Mathematical Tripos, Part I, 1914; Nat. Sci. Tripos, Part II (Physics), 1915. Indian Educational Service, 1915-48; Head of Dept of Physics, Presidency Coll., 1922-45; Principal, 1945-48, Prof. Emeritus, 1948-; Lecturer, Calcutta Univ. Postgraduate Dept, 1917-40, Hon. Head of its Postgraduate Dept of Statistics, 1941-45; Meteorologist,

Calcutta, in charge of Alipore Observatory (in addition to duties in Presidency Coll.), 1922-26; Lectures and Scientific tours in many countries; also delegate to internat. conferences and representative at meetings and on commns, from 1946. Chm. UN Sub Commns on Statistical Sampling, 1947-51. Foundation Fellow, Indian Nat. Science Acad., formerly Nat. Inst. of Sciences of India (Pres. 1957-58); Fellow, Indian Acad. of Sciences, Nat. Acad. of Sciences, India, Royal Statistical Soc., London; Foundation Vice-Pres., International Biometric Soc., 1947; Mem., Int. Population Union. Presided over Anthropology Section, 1925, and Mathematics and Statistics Section, 1942, of Indian Science Congress; Gen. Sec., Indian Science Congress, 1945-48; Treas., 1952-55; Pres. 1950; Mem. UN Statistical Commn, 1946- (Chm. 1954-58); Hon. Gen. Sec., Rabindranath Tagore's Visvabharati from its inception, 1921 to 1931; Past Ed., Visvabharati Quarterly. Awarded Weldon Medal and Prize by Univ. of Oxford, 1944. Deva Prasad Sarbadhikari Gold Medal and Hon. DSc, Calcutta Univ., 1957; Gold Medal, Czechoslovak Acad. of Sciences, 1964; Durga Prasad Khaitan Meml Gold Medal, Asiatic Soc., 1968; For. Mem., USSR Acad. of Sciences, 1958. Hon. Fellow, King's Coll., Cambridge, 1958; Hon. Desikottama, Visvabharati, 1961; Hon. DSc: Sofia State Univ., 1961; Delhi Univ., 1964; Stockholm Univ., 1965. Padma Vibhushan, 1968. *Publications:* Experiments in Statistical Sampling in the Indian Statistical Institute, 1961; Talks on Planning, 1961; An Approach of Operational Research to Planning in India, 1963; Sample Census of Area under Jute in Bengal (1940), 1968; about 200 research papers and publications on statistical subjects; literary and philosophical essays and articles in English and Bengali. *Address:* 204 Barrackpore Trunk Road, Calcutta 35. *T:* 56-3223; The Cabinet Secretariat, Government of India, 8 King George Avenue, New Delhi. *[Died 28 June 1972.*

MAHEU, René G.; Director-General, United Nations Educational Scientific and Cultural Organization (Unesco), 1962-74; *b* Saint-Gaudens, France, 28 March 1905; *s* of Joseph Maheu and Madeleine Roucoule; *m* 1928, Inès Allafort du Verger; one *s. Educ:* Lycée de Toulouse, Lycée Louis-le-Grand, Paris; Ecole Normale Supérieure; Sorbonne, Paris. Prof. of philosophy: Lycée de Coutances, France, 1930; Univ. of Cologne (Romanisches Seminar), Germany, 1931-33; Institut Français du Royaume Uni, London, 1933-39; Collège Franco-Musulman Moulay-Idriss, Fès, Morocco, 1940-42; attached to Cabinet Civil of French Resident-Gen., Rabat, Morocco, 1944-46; joined Secretariat of Unesco, Sept. 1946; Head, Div. of Free Flow of Information, 1946-48; Dir, Cabinet of Dir-Gen., 1949-53; Asst Dir-Gen., 1954-59 (Rep. to UN, 1955-58); Dep. Dir-Gen., 1960-61; Acting Dir-Gen., 1961-62. *Publication:* La civilisation de l'universel, 1966. *Address:* 14 rue Wilhelm, Paris 16e, France. *Club:* Union Interaliée (Paris). *[Died 19 Dec. 1975.*

MAIN, Brig. John Walter, CBE 1943; ED 1944; *b* 30 May 1900; *s* of late Chas F. and Hilda S. Main, Glenelg, Woodville, S Australia; *m* 1st, 1923, Violet Plunket (*d* 1937), Adelaide, S Australia; one *s* (and one *s* decd); 2nd, 1940, Hilda R. Pender, Maitland, New South Wales. *Educ:* High Sch. and Univ., Adelaide. Draughtsman, J. S. Bagshaw & Sons, Engineers, Adelaide, Munitions Supply Board, Melbourne, 1924-25; Chief Draughtsman, Melbourne Tramway Board, Rolling Stock and Wksp Branch, 1925-36; Design Engineer, Broken Hill Pty Steelworks, Newcastle, NSW, 1936-39. Citizen Military Forces, 1921-40; AIF 1940; Middle East: Major and Fd Coy Comd, 1940-41; Lt-Col and CRE Corps, 1941-42; New Guinea, Brig. and Chief Engr, Corps, and Army, 1942-44; R of O, 1945-49; Citizen Military Forces, 1950-55, as Brigade Comdr; R of O 1955; Retired List, 1956. Engineer and Supt, Newcastle Steelworks, from 1945 and Gen. Supt of Transportation from 1953, retd 1965. FCIT; FAIM. *Recreations:* motoring, caravan, bowls. *Address:* 3 Hillcrest Road, Merewether, NSW 2291, Australia. *Clubs:* Imperial Service (Sydney); Newcastle; United Service; Newcastle Masonic; Legacy (Past Pres.) (Newcastle, NSW). *[Died 26 Sept. 1971.*

MAINE, Rev. Basil Stephen, MA; Hon. Member, Royal Society of Musicians of GB; Life Member, Royal College of Organists; Hon. Member, Incorporated Society of Musicians; *b* Norwich, 4 March 1894; *e s* of Stephen Frederick Maine and Kate Elizabeth Maine. *Educ:* City of Norwich Sch.; Queens' Coll., Cambridge (Organ Scholar); Winchester Reading Prize, Ryle Reading Prize, and Hughes Essay Prize, History Tripos; studied music under Dr Charles Wood and Sir Charles Stanford; Music and Mathematics Master at Durnford Sch., Langton Matravers; later Asst Organist Durham Cathedral; one of the Music Critics of the Daily Telegraph, 1921-26; later joined the Morning Post Staff; gave Weekly Talks on Music for BBC, 1927-28; Editor of the Music Bulletin, 1925-29; created the rôles of the Young King in Laurence Binyon's The Young King, of Jesus in John

Masefield's The Trial of Jesus, and of the Prophet in Masefield's A King's Daughter; performed the rôle of the Soldier in first broadcast performance (here) of Stravinsky's Soldier's Tale (Glasgow, 1927); performed the rôle of the Narrator in Honegger's King David, given at Three Choirs' Festival, Gloucester, 1928; has lectured on British Music throughout this country, in USA, Canada, and at the Conservatoire of Music, Prague; was the Orator in first performance of Arthur Bliss' Morning Heroes, Norwich Fest., 1930; also 1961; also in first London performance of the same work, Queen's Hall, 1931; and first performance in America, 1931; one of English reps at First International Congress of Music at Florence, 1933. Ordained 1939. Gave Bach Commemoration Lecture, Norwich Cathedral, 1950. Publications: Receive It So (Essays); Reflected Music (Essays); Rondo (novel), 1930; Plummers Cut (novel), 1932; Life and Works of Elgar, 1933; Life of Chopin, 1933; Study of Paderewski, 1934; Edward VIII, Duke of Windsor, 1937; The Best of Me (Autobiography), 1937; People are Much Alike, 1938; Franklin Roosevelt, 1938; The BBC and its Audience, 1939; New Paths in Music, 1940; Maine on Music, 1946; Music and the BBC, 1948; Twang with our Music, 1957. Songs, Orchestral, Organ and Choral Music and Works for Violoncello; Te Deum (first performed at Colchester Festival of Britain, 1951); Shakespearean Speeches recorded for HMV and Decca. Address: Beacon Lodge, Overstrand Road, Cromer, Norfolk.
[Died 13 Oct. 1972.

MAINSTONE, Mrs Madeleine Françoise; Keeper, Department of Education, Victoria and Albert Museum, since 1965; b 19 Sept. 1925; d of Johan Th. L. Rozendaal and Elizabeth M. Rozendaal (née Bol); m 1954, Rowland J. Mainstone; one s two d. Educ: Leiden Univ. (LittDra 1953); Harvard Univ. (MA 1949). Assistant at Leiden Univ. Printroom, 1945-47; WEA and Univ. Extra Mural Lectr, 1961-65; has represented V&A Museum at Internat. Museum Meetings in France, Denmark, Sweden and Russia; lectures on Dutch painting, Italian Renaissance and German 16th century art. Recreations: dressing up and taking it easy. Address: 20 Fishpool Street, St Albans, Herts AL3 4RT. T: St Albans 57485.
[Died 30 Oct. 1979.

MAINWARING, Brig. Hugh Salusbury Kynaston, CB 1945; CBE 1944; DSO 1942; TD; Lord-Lieutenant of Clwyd, since 1974 (Lord Lieutenant of Flintshire, 1951-74); b 22 Jan. 1906; s of late Col Sir W. R. K. Mainwaring, CB, CBE, Hafod-y-Coed, St Asaph; m 1935, Diana (d 1967), d of late Major W. M. Dugdale, CB, DSO; three s one d. Educ: Eton; Christ Church, Oxford. Served 10th Royal Hussars, 1928-35; 5th Bn RWF (TA), 1936 onwards (converted to RA 1939); War of 1939-45, Middle East, Italy, Greece, 1940-45; GSO1 Eighth Army; BGS Allied Armies in Italy; BGS Land Forces, Greece; BGS Southern Command. DL 1945; JP 1945. KStJ 1970. Address: Hafod-y-Coed, St Asaph, Clwyd. T: Trefnant 655. Club: Cavalry and Guards.
[Died 6 July 1976.

MAINWARING, William Henry; b 1884; s of William Mainwaring, Swansea. Educ: Central Labour Coll., London. Lecturer in Economics and Vice-Principal, Central Labour Coll., 1919; miners' agent for the Rhondda district, 1924. MP (Lab) East Rhondda, 1933-Sept. 1959. Address: 38 Harbord Road, Oxford. T: 57042.
[Died 18 May 1971.

MAINWARING-BOWEN, Arthur Charles; practising solicitor; Legal Adviser to British Rheumatism & Arthritis Association Charity Group, since 1976, Life Vice-President 1949; b Pentrebach, Carmarthen, 24 March 1922; o s of Major Arthur Pendragon (Mainwaring) Bowen, RE, mil. architect, SDF (died on active service 1942), and Edith Helena, d of Alderman Charles Stephenson, Newark; m 1953, Helen Patricia Cope, MBAOT, Monken Hadley; one s one d. Educ: Ysgol Ramâdeg Gwendraeth; University Coll., Aberystwyth (Welsh Church Scholar in History, 1941, for Oxford; BA, LLB London); Architectural Assoc. Sch.; Coll. of Law, Law Soc. Solicitor 1950. Univ. OTC; Home Guard (disabled, 1942); campaigned for further educn for disabled ex-servicemen, 1943-45. Founded British Rheumatism & Arthritis Assoc., 1946-47, Hon. Sec., 1947-49; initiated: BRA holiday hotel scheme, 1956; Rehabilitation and BRA Welfare Funds, 1965; BRA Home (SW), 1973; National Disabled Youth Centre Trust, 1975. Chairman: Torbay and Dist Disablement Adv. Cttee, Dept of Employment, 1969-75 (initiated Torbay Arthritis Clinic, 1970; established Torbay Sheltered Workshop, 1972); Legal Gp Practice Study Cttee, 1972-. Mem., Council for Care of Disabled (now Royal Assoc. for Disability and Rehabilitation), 1949-; Hon. Mem., British Legion, 1970. Trustee: Pinder Children's Centre; Open Univ. Med. Soc.; trusts for rehab. of handicapped, and for convalescent homes. Publications: articles on problems of disability, charitable work, the laity in pastoral care, local history and geography, group practice and managerial problems.

Recreations: gardening, sketching, genealogy, country pursuits. Address: 2 St George's Crescent, Torquay, Devon. T: Torquay 37767; Pentrebach, Carmarthen, Dyfed; c/o British Rheumatism & Arthritis Association, 6 Grosvenor Crescent, SW1X 7ER. T: 01-235 0902. Clubs: Law Society's Hall, English-Speaking Union, Royal Societies; Royal Torbay Yacht, Museum Society (Torquay).
[Died 31 Jan. 1980.

MAIS, Stuart Petre Brodie, MA; FRSA, broadcaster; televiser; novelist; lecturer on books, travel and the countryside; free-lance journalist; late Professor of English at RAF Cadet College; Examiner and Lecturer to University of London; b 4 July 1885; o c of late Rev. Brodie Mais, Tansley Rectory, Matlock; m; four d. Educ: Denstone; Christ Church, Oxford. Blue for three-mile race, 1907, 1909; blue for cross-country running, 1906, 1908; hons in Math. Mods, 1907, and in English Literature Finals, 1909; BA 1909; MA 1913; Schoolmaster: Rossall, 1909-13; Sherborne, 1913-17; Tonbridge, 1917-20; Radley, 1941-45; Literary Critic to the Evening News, 1918; Literary Critic to Daily Express, 1921-23; Literary Editor of Daily Graphic, 1923-26; leader-writer and book-reviewer to Daily Telegraph, 1926-31. Publications: several school text-books; April's Lonely Soldier, 1916; Interlude, 1917; Rebellion, 1917; From Shakespeare to O. Henry, 1917; A Schoolmaster's Diary, 1918; Lovers of Silver, 1918; The Education of a Philanderer, 1919; Books and their Writers, 1919; Uncle Lionel, 1920; Colour Blind, 1920; Why we should Read, 1920; Breaking Covert, 1921; Caged Birds, 1922; Quest Sinister, 1922; Oh! To Be in England, 1922; Prunello, 1923; Some Modern Authors, 1923; Perissa, 1924; Eclipse, 1925; Orange Street, 1926; See England First, 1927; Do You Know? 1927; Glorious Devon, 1928; The Cornish Riviera, 1928; First Quarter, 1929; Sussex, 1929; Frolic Lady, 1930; It Isn't Far from London, 1930; England of the Windmills, 1931; Delight in Books (BBC talks), 1931; Southern Rambles, 1931; This Unknown Island (BBC talks), 1932; The Highlands of Britain, 1932; Some Books I Like (BBC talks), 1932; These I have Loved, 1933; SOS Talks on Unemployment (BBC talks), 1933; Week-Ends in England, 1933; A Modern Columbus (BBC talks), 1934; Isles of the Island (BBC talks), 1934; More Books I Like (BBC talks), 1934; Round About England, 1935; England's Pleasance, 1935; The Writing of English (BBC talks, 1935); Walking at Week-Ends, 1935; A Chronicle of English Literature, 1936; England's Character, 1936; All the Days of My Life, 1937; The Three-Coloured Pencil, 1937; Let's Get Out Here, 1937; Light over Lundy, 1938; Old King Coal, 1938; Walking in Somerset, 1938; Britain Calling, 1938; Highways and Byways in the Welsh Marches, 1939; Listen to the Country, 1939; Hills of the South, 1939; Fifty years of the LCC, 1939; Raven among the Rooks, 1939; Men in Blue Glasses, 1940; There'll Always be an England, 1940; A Cluster of Grapes, 1941; Diary of a Citizen in War-Time, 1941; Black Spider, 1941; Youth after the War, 1943; Caper Sauce, 1947; I Return to Scotland, 1947; I Return to Switzerland, 1948; I Return to Ireland, 1948; Who Dies?, 1948; The Story of Oxford, 1949; I Return to Wales, 1949; What to see in Britain, 1949; The English Scene Today, 1949; We Wander through the West, 1949; The Land of the Cinque Ports, 1949; Little England Beyond Wales, 1949; I Loved You Once, 1949; The Best in their Kind, 1949; The Riviera, New Look and Old, 1950; Arden and Avon, 1950; Madeira Holiday, 1951; Britannia 1651-1951, 1951; Norwegian Odyssey, 1951; Come Love, Come Death, 1951; Winter Sports Holiday, 1951; Austrian Holiday, 1952; Buffets and Rewards, 1952; The Channel Islands, 1953; The Happiest Days of My Life, 1953; Italian Holiday, 1954; The Isle of Man, 1954; Spanish Holiday, 1955; Majorcan Holiday, 1956; Our Village Today, 1956; Roman Holiday, 1957; Mediterranean Cruise Holiday, 1958; South American Holiday, 1959; Continental Coach Holiday, 1960; Dutch Holiday, 1960; Round Africa Holiday, 1961; Greek Holiday, 1962; Caribbean Cruise Holiday, 1963; Round Britain Coach Holiday, 1963; Round the World Cruise Holiday, 1965; An English Course for Everybody, 1968; This Delicious Madness, 1968. Recreation: travel of any sort anywhere. Address: Flat 20, Bliss House, Finches Gardens, Lindfield, Haywards Heath, West Sussex. T: Lindfield 3529. Clubs: Achilles, Sette of Old Volumes; Vincent's.
[Died 21 April 1975.

MAISKY, Ivan Mikhailovich; Member of Academy of Sciences of USSR, 1946; b Kiriloff, Novgorod Province, 19 Jan. 1884; m 1922, Agnes Alexandrovna Skippin; no c. Educ: Secondary Sch., Omsk, Siberia; St Petersburg and Munich Univs. Journalist; entered Soviet Diplomatic Service; Chief of Press Dept, Moscow Foreign Office, 1922; Counsellor at Soviet Embassy in London, 1925-27; Counsellor at Soviet Embassy in Tokio, 1927-29; Minister to Finland, 1929-32; Ambassador of USSR in Great Britain, 1932-43; Asst People's Commissar for Foreign Affairs, USSR, 1943-46; negotiated and signed Non-Aggression Treaty with Finland, 1932; Temporary Trade Agreement with Great

Britain, 1934; Anglo-Soviet Naval Treaty, 1937; Soviet-Polish Pact of Mutual Assistance, 1941, Soviet-Czechoslovak Pact of Mutual Assistance, 1941, Soviet-Canadian Agreements on the establishment of Diplomatic and Consular Relations, 1942; The Agreement on the establishment of Consular Relations between the USSR and South Africa, 1942; The Canadian-Soviet Credit Agreement, 1942; The Agreements on the establishment of Diplomatic Relations with (a) Holland, (b) Ethiopia, (c), Egypt, 1943. Order of Lenin, 1942; Order of Labour Red Banner, 1944; Order of Labour Red Banner, 1945; Order of Labour Red Banner, 1964. *Publications:* Germany and the War, 1916; Political Germany, 1917; Modern Mongolia, 1921; Foreign Policy of RSFSR, 1922; Before the Storm, 1944; Spain (1808-1917), 1957; So Near and Yet So Far (novel), 1958; Mongolia on the Eve of Revolution, 1959; Reminiscences of Soviet Ambassador in Britain, 1960; Journey into the Past, Reminiscences, 1960; Spanish Notebooks, Reminiscences, 1962; Who helped Hitler, Reminiscences, 1962; Memoirs of a Soviet Ambassador (3 vols), 1964-65, new edn in one vol. 1971; Bernard Shaw and the Others, Reminiscences, 1967. *Address:* Academy of Sciences, Moscow, USSR.   *[Died 4 Sept. 1975.*

MAITLAND, Hugh Bethune, MD (Toronto); MSc (Manchester); MRCS; LRCP; Professor Emeritus of Bacteriology, University of Manchester; *b* Port Perry, Ont., Canada, 1895; *m* 1926, Mary Logan Cowan, BA, MB (Toronto); one *s* one *d. Educ:* Univ. of Toronto. Temporary Surgeon-Lt RN, 1917-19; Lecturer and Asst Prof. in Bacteriology, Univ. of Toronto, 1919-24; Research work in Germany, 1924-25; Bacteriologist to the Scientific Advisory Cttee on Foot-and-Mouth Disease of the Ministry of Agriculture and Fisheries, working at the Lister Institute of Preventive Medicine, 1925-27; Mem. of the Bacteriological Staff of the Lister Institute, 1927; Prof. of Bacteriology, Univ. of Manchester, 1927-62; Colombo Plan Bacteriologist, Inst. for Med. Res., and Med. Faculty, Univ. of Malaya, Kuala Lumpur, 1962-66. *Address:* 9 Rowbury Drive, Ashby Road, Burton-upon-Trent, Staffs.   *[Died 13 Jan. 1972.*

MAITLAND, Comdr Sir John (Francis Whitaker), Kt 1960; *b* 1903; *o s* of late William Whitaker Maitland, CVO, OBE, Loughton Hall, Essex; *m* 1930, Bridget, *er d* of E. H. M. Denny, Staplefield Place, Sussex; four *s* one *d. Educ:* Osborne, Dartmouth. Royal Navy: retired 1934, rejoined 1939-45; Comdr, 1943. MP (C) Horncastle Div. of Lincolnshire, 1945-66. Pres. Institute of Patentees and Inventors, 1966-75. DL Essex, 1934; JP Essex, 1935; DL Lincolnshire, 1957. Mem. Lindsey CC, 1967. Chm. Council of St John for Lincolnshire, 1966-71; OStJ. FRSA. *Address:* Harrington Hall, near Spilsby, Lincs. *T:* Spilsby 2281.   *[Died 17 Nov. 1977.*

MAITLAND, Col Mark Edward Makgill Crichton, CVO 1952; DSO 1917; 3rd *s* of late Maj.-Gen. D. M. and Lady Margaret Crichton Maitland; *b* 1882; *m* 1924, Patience Irene Fleetwood, 2nd *d* of late Sir John Fuller and late Mrs H. Forestier-Walker, of Cottles, Melksham, Wilts; two *s* one *d. Educ:* Eton; RMC, Sandhurst. 2nd Lieut, Grenadier Guards, 1901; Lieut, 1904; Captain, 1910; Major, 1915; (Temp.) Lieut-Colonel in command 1st Batt. 1916; 2nd Batt. 1919; 3rd Batt. 1923-27; Colonel commanding The Regt, 1939; ADC Governor, New Zealand, 1910 and 1911; served S African War, 1902 (medal and clasp); European War, 1914-18 (wounded, DSO, Croix de Guerre); retired pay, 1928; HM Bodyguard, Hon. Corps of Gentlemen-at-Arms, 1928-52; HM Body Guard for Scotland, Royal Company of Archers, retired Dec. 1960. JP, DL Wiltshire. *Address:* The Island House, Wilton, Salisbury, Wilts. *T:* Wilton 3241. *Club:* MCC.   *[Died 30 Jan. 1972.*

MAIZELS, Prof. Montague, FRS 1961; MD, FRCP; Professor in Clinical Pathology, University of London, 1951-64, now Emeritus; *b* 30 Sept. 1899; *s* of Joseph and Deborah Maizels; *m* 1938, Dulcie Speight; one *d. Educ:* Guy's Hospital. Clinical Pathologist, University College Hospital, 1931. *Publications:* in Journal of Physiology, Lancet, etc. *Recreation:* photography. *Address:* 15 Southwood Heights, 29 Southwood Lawn Road, Highgate, N6 5SD. *T:* 01-340 9477.   *[Died 10 Feb. 1976.*

MAKARIOS III, Archbishop; Archbishop and Ethnarch in Cyprus, Oct. 1950; elected President of Cyprus in 1959 and took up official duties when Cyprus became a Republic in 1960; re-elected, 1968, 1973; *b* Panayia, Paphos, Cyprus, 13 Aug. 1913; *s* of a farmer. *Educ:* Kykko Monastery; secondary sch., Nicosia; Schools of Theology and Law, Athens Univ.; School of Theology, Boston Univ., USA (awarded schol. by World Council of Churches). Deacon, 1938; Grad. Theology, 1942; Priest, 1946. Bishop of Kitium, 1948 (elected while still student at Boston). Suggested Pancyprian plebiscite in which Greek Cypriot population voted 97 per cent in favour of union with Greece (Enosis), 1950; attended General Assembly of UNO, New York, 1952; press conferences in USA, London and

Athens; visited Athens, and persuaded Greek Government to place Cyprus question before UN, 1954; attended 9th Session General Assembly, New York, when Cyprus was discussed, 1954; supported revolutionary armed struggle led by Nat. Organisation of Cypriot Fighters (EOKA), lasting 1955-59. He attended 1st Afro-Asian Conference, Indonesia, 1955; had meetings with the Secretary of State for the Colonies, Mr Lennox-Boyd (now Lord Boyd of Merton), in Cyprus, and with the Governor of Cyprus, Field-Marshal Sir John Harding (now Lord Harding of Petherton), in which they discussed the future of the Island, without agreement, and as a consequence the Archbishop was exiled to the Seychelles Islands, 1956; visited there by delegates of the British Government, who asked him to accept the proposed Radcliffe Constitution, he rejected it; released, on condition that he should not return to Cyprus, he then went to Athens, 1957; continued to attend General Assemblies, UN, where the Cyprus question was discussed; invited to London for talks, 1959; these resulted in signing of London Agreement (continuation of Zürich Agreement) by Great Britain, Greece and Turkey, under which Cyprus would be declared an Independent Republic (Sir Hugh Foot being the last Governor); returned to Cyprus, March 1959; talks on implementation of the agreements followed, at a five-partite conference, on ceding of bases, etc., in London and in Cyprus, 1960; Cyprus was admitted a member of the Commonwealth, and the Archbishop represented the Island at the Commonwealth Prime Ministers' Conference, March 1961, and subsequently. Represented Cyprus, Conferences Non-Aligned Countries, Belgrade, 1961, Cairo, 1964, Lusaka, 1970. Has made official visits abroad and was awarded several hon. doctorates by universities. Holds foreign decorations and has been awarded gold medals of cities. *Address:* Presidential Palace, Nicosia, Cyprus.   *[Died 3 Aug. 1977.*

MAKINS, Sir (Alfred) John (Ware), Kt 1950; General Manager Commercial Union Assurance Co. Ltd, 1938-58, retired; Director, 1958-65; *b* 31 Aug. 1894; *e s* of late Alfred William Bayley Makins, and of Lucy Jane (*née* Arnold); *m* 1927, Barbara Lilla, *surv d* of late Charles and Lilla Copland; one *s* one *d. Educ:* St Paul's Sch., West Kensington; abroad. Entire career with Commercial Union Group; Germany and France, 1910-13; Foreign Fire Dept at Head Office, 1919-24; Manager in Japan, 1925; Asst Manager in China, 1926; Asst US Manager at New York, 1927-31; Fire Manager at Head Office, 1931-35; Manager, 1935-38. President, Insurance Institute of London, 1944-45; President, Insurance Orphans' Fund, 1951-52; Chairman: British Insurance Assoc., 1947-48, 1948-49; British Aviation Insurance Co. Ltd, 1949-58; Trade Indemnity Co. Ltd, 1951-58; formerly Member, Cttee of Management, Institute of Cardiology, retd 1969. Served European War, 1914-18. RFA (TF), Captain. *Address:* 9 Hampstead Way, NW11. *T:* 01-455 4710. *Clubs:* Oriental, The Pilgrims, Ends of the Earth.   *[Died 17 Nov. 1972.*

MAKINS, Sir John; *see* Makins, Sir (Alfred) J. (W.).

MALALASEKERA, Gunapala Piyasena, OBE 1949; DLitt (London); Chairman, Sri Lanka National Council for Higher Education, since 1967; *b* 1899; *m* 1933, Lyle Wijewardene; three *s* three *d. Educ:* St John's Coll., Ceylon; University of London. Head of Department of Oriental Languages, University Coll., Colombo, 1927-42; Prof. and Head of Dept of Pali and Buddhist Civilisation, Univ. of Ceylon, 1942-57; Ambassador for Ceylon to USSR, 1957-61; High Commissioner to Canada, 1961-63; Permanent Rep. of Ceylon to UN, 1961-63; High Commissioner to Great Britain, 1963-66. President, World Fellowship of Buddhists, 1950-58. General President Indian Philosophical Congress, 1957. Chief Editor, Encyclopædia of Buddhism, 1956-. Hon. DPhil (Moscow). *Publications:* Dictionary of Pali Proper Names (2 vols), 1938; The Pali Literature of Ceylon; The Buddha and his Teaching, 1957, etc. *Recreations:* reading, meeting people of all types. *Address:* 12 Longden Terrace, Colombo 7, Sri Lanka. *T:* 85808, 86123. *[Died 23 April 1973.*

MALCOLM, Angus (Christian Edward), CMG 1952; Director, Bath Preservation Trust, since 1971; *b* 6 Oct. 1908; 3rd *s* of late Sir Ian Malcolm, KCMG, of Poltalloch; *m* 1947, Jacqueline Marie (marr. diss. 1967), *o d* of late Maj.-Gen. F. H. Theron, CB, CBE; four *d. Educ:* Eton; New Coll., Oxford. Entered Foreign Office, 1933; Madrid, 1936; Washington, 1938; Foreign Office, 1942; Rome, 1944; Mexico City, 1947; Prague, 1949; Foreign Office, 1950; Minister, Vienna, 1953; HM Ambassador and Consul-General, Tunis, 1956-60. Retired, 1961. Rootes Ltd, 1961-67; Bursar, The American Museum in Britain, 1968-71. *Recreation:* sightseeing. *Address:* 14 Royal Crescent, Bath, Somerset. *T:* Bath 26493.   *[Died 19 Oct. 1971.*

MALCOLM of Poltalloch, Lieut-Colonel George Ian, DL, JP; 18th Laird and Hereditary Chief of the Clan; farmer; Breeder of PB Arabs; *b* 26 April 1903; *e s* of Sir Ian Malcolm, KCMG (*d* 1944) and Jeanne Marie (decd), *o c* of Edward Langtry, Jersey, and Emily le Breton, afterwards Lady de Bathe; *m* 1st, 1929, Enid Sybil, *d* of Maj.-Gen. H. S. Gaskell, CB, DSO (marr. diss. 1944); one *s* one *d*; 2nd, 1946, Muriel Hobhouse, BEM, *d* of Ernest Presgrave Hebblethwaite. *Educ:* Eton; RMC Sandhurst. Joined Argyll and Sutherland Highlanders, 1923; ADC (India), 1927-28; Adjutant 8th (Argyllshire) Bn, 1933-37; Lieut-Col, 1943; Comd 8th Bn in Austria, 1945-46 (Bn disbanded); retired, 1947. Service in India, Egypt, Sudan, Palestine (despatches). War of 1939-45: with 1st Bn A and SH, on Staff, and in Combined Operations in Middle East and Central Pacific; Staff Coll., Haifa, 1940. Member Royal Company of Archers (Queen's Body Guard for Scotland), 1935. Producer: Vienna Tattoo, 1946; Revue Order, Glasgow, 1948; Edinburgh Tattoo, 1949-50-51; London District Tattoo, 1950-51; Organizer of Clan Gathering at Festival of Britain, 1951; Producer, Royal Tournament, 1953, Stirling Castle Tattoo, 1953; The Queen's Volunteers, Kelvin Hall, 1958; Cowal Military Display, 1959-61. Chm. Argyll T&AFA, 1957-67; Rep. Chm. Scotland Council of T&AFA, 1961-66; Hon. Colonel Glasgow Univ. OTC, 1962-67. Dir. Royal Highland Agricultural Soc., 1955-66 (Hon. Vice-Pres., 1974); Mem. Scot. US Museum Adv. Cttee, 1955; Gen. Commr Income Tax, Mid-Argyll Division, 1960; Mem., Exec. Cttee, Nat. Army Museum, 1966; Chm., Mid Argyll Savings Gp. 1967. Lay Reader, Diocese of Argyll; Patron of living of Holy Trinity, Lamorbey. Chm. N Argyll Scout Cttee, 1963-71. FSA Scotland 1942. DL 1948, JP 1949, Vice-Lieutenant 1958, Argyll. *Publications:* History of the Argyll and Sutherland Highlanders, 1794-1972; Argylls in Korea, 1952; Historical Record of the British Legion, Scotland, 1959; Argyllshire Highlanders, 1860-1960, 1960; Argyllshire Gathering 1871-1971, 1971; articles and verse in Punch, The Field, Blackwood's Magazine, and other periodicals; songs. *Recreations:* shooting, military history. *Heir: s* Robin Neill Lochnell Malcolm, *b* 1934. *Address:* Duntrune Castle, Lochgilphead, Argyll. *T:* Kilmartin 276 and 283; 6 Malta Terrace, Edinburgh EH4 1HR. *T:* 031-332 3499. *Clubs:* Naval and Military; New (Edinburgh); Royal Scottish Automobile (Glasgow); Royal Highland Yacht (Oban) (Commodore 1968-70); Western Meeting (Ayr).
[Died 20 March 1976.

MALCOLM, Sir Michael Albert James, of Balbedie, Innertiel and Lochore, 10th Bt, *cr* 1665; Director of the Lothian Coal Co. Ltd, until Nationalisation; *b* 9 May 1899; *s* of 9th Bt and Evelyn Alberta (*d* 1947), 3rd *d* of Albert George Sandeman, and *g d* of Viscount de Moncorvo; *S* father, 1927; *m* 1st, 1918, Hon. Geraldine M. Digby (marr. diss. 1946; she *d* 1965), *d* of 10th Baron Digby; one *s* two *d*; 2nd, 1947, Kathleen Melvin, *d* of late G. J. Gawthorne, Commander, RN. *Educ:* Eton. Major, Scots Guards; served European War, 1914-18 (severely wounded); ADC to GOC in C, Scottish Command, 1919-23; ADC to Lord High Commissioner, General Assembly of Church of Scotland, 1924-25; employed War Office in AG Dept, 1940-41; MS Branch, 1941-42 and 1945; PID Foreign Office, 1944. Member of Royal Company of Archers (HM Body Guard for Scotland). Member: Cttees Earl Haig Fund (Scottish Branch); The Economic League, Central Council; Chairman East of Scotland Sub-Area; Standing Council of Baronetage. *Heir: s* David Peter Michael Malcolm, CA, Major, Scots Guards [*b* 7 July 1919; *m* 1959, Hermione, *d* of Sir David Home, 13th Bt; one *d*]. *Address:* Milton Lodge, North Berwick, East Lothian. *Clubs:* Guards; New (Edinburgh).
[Died 10 Jan. 1976.

MALIK, Yakov Alexandrovich; Order of Lenin, 1944 and 1945; Deputy Foreign Minister of the USSR, since 1960; Permanent Representative of the USSR at the United Nations, 1968-76; *b* 11 Ukraine, 6 Dec. 1906; *m*; one *s* one *d* (and one *s* decd). *Educ:* Kharkov Inst. of Economics; Inst. for Diplomatic and Consular Staffs, Moscow. Dep. Chief, Press Dept, Ministry of Foreign Affairs, 1937; Counsellor, 1939, Ambassador, 1942-45, at Tokyo; Political Adviser, Allied Council for Japan, 1946; Deputy Foreign Minister, 1946-53, and Permanent Representative of USSR to United Nations, 1948-52; Soviet Ambassador to the Court of St James's, 1953-60. *Address:* Ministry of Foreign Affairs, Smolenskaya Ploshchad, Moscow, USSR.
[Died 12 Feb. 1980.

MALIPIERO, G. Francesco; composer; Professor of History of Music at University of Padua; *b* Venice, 18 March 1882. *Educ:* under Stefan Stocker, Vienna, and Enrico Bossi, Venice. Formerly Director of the Conservatorio Musicale, Venice. Member American Academy Arts and Letters, New York. Member Royal Flemish Academy of Belgium, Brussels. Works for theatre: L'Orfeide, Tre Commedie Goldoniane, Filomelae l'Infatuato, Torneo Notturno, Pirandello's Favola del Figlio

Cambiato, Shakespeare's Julius Cæsar and Antony and Cleopatra, Ecuba, La Vita è Sogno, I Capricci di Callot, Allegra Brigata, Mondi celesti e infernali, Vergilii Aeneis, Don Giovanni, as operas, etc. Symphonic works: 3 series of Impressioni dal Vero, Pause del Silenzio, Concerti, 11 Symphonies, Fantasie Concertanti, Dialoghi; 6 piano concertos; 2 violin concertos; Eight Quartets (first one winner of Coolidge Prize, 1920) Sonate a tre, a quattro, a cinque; great deal of piano music and songs; edited and published himself complete works of Claudio Monteverdi and Antonio Vivaldi. Written several books on musical subjects. *Relevant publication:* L'Opera di Gian Francesco Malipiero. *Address:* 9 Forestovecchio, Asolo 31011, Treviso, Italy.
[Died 1 Aug. 1973.

MALKIN, H(arold) Jordan, CBE 1964; Director of Postgraduate Studies, Royal College of Obstetricians and Gynæcologists, 1967-75, retired; *b* 27 April 1898; *s* of late Sydney and Edith Jordan Malkin (*née* Stormer); *m* 1932, Theresa Joyce Ferris Bearder, *d* of late Cyril Horner Bearder and Mrs Dora Christiana Bearder, Abingdon, Berks; two *d*. *Educ:* Epworth Coll.; University Coll. and Hospital, London. Royal Field Artillery, 1916-19. University Coll., University Coll. Hospital, 1916 and 1919-24. Consultant Obstetrician and Gynæcologist, Nottingham, 1928-67. Rockefeller Travelling Fellowship, 1926. MD London, 1926; FRCSEd 1925; FRCOG 1938; Hon. LLD Nottingham, 1970. *Address:* 19 Cavendish Crescent South, The Park, Nottingham. *T:* Nottingham 47015; Ivy Cottage, Wargrave Road, Henley-on-Thames, Oxon. *T:* Wargrave 2453. *Club:* Oriental.
[Died 13 Dec. 1978.

MALLABY, Sir (Howard) George (Charles), KCMG 1958 (CMG 1953); OBE 1945; *b* 17 Feb. 1902; *s* of William Calthorpe Mallaby and Katharine Mary Frances Miller; *m* 1955, Elizabeth Greenwood Locker (*née* Brooke), one *step s* two *step d*. *Educ:* Radley Coll.; Merton Coll., Oxford. BA 1923; MA 1935; MA (Cantab) 1965; Asst Master Clifton Coll., 1923-24; Diocesan Coll., Rondebosch, S Africa, 1926; Assistant Master and House Master, S Edward's Sch., Oxford, 1924-26 and 1927-35; Headmaster, St Bees Sch., Cumberland, 1935-38; District Commissioner for the Special Area of West Cumberland, 1938-39; Dep. Regional Transport Commissioner for North Western Region, 1939-40; Captain, Gen. List, 1940; Major, 1941; Lieut-Col, 1943; Colonel, 1945; served in Military Secretariat of War Cabinet, 1942-45; US Legion of Merit (Degree of Officer), 1946. Secretary, National Trust, 1945-46; Asst Secretary, Ministry of Defence, 1946-48; Secretary-General Brussels Treaty Defence Organisation, 1948-50; Under Secretary, Cabinet Office, 1950-54; Secretary, War Council and Council of Ministers, Kenya, 1954; Dep. Secretary, University Grants Cttee, 1955-57; High Commissioner for the United Kingdom in New Zealand, 1957-59; First Civil Service Commissioner, 1959-64, retired. Chairman of Council of Radley Coll., 1952-57. Governor: St Edward's Sch.; Bedford Coll., London Univ.; Chairman: Cttee on the Staffing of Local Government, 1967; Hong Kong Govt Salaries Commn, 1971; Special Cttee on Structure of Rugby Football Union, 1972-73. Extraordinary Fellow, Churchill Coll., Cambridge, 1964-69. *Publications:* Wordsworth (Extracts from the Prelude with other Poems), 1932; Wordsworth: A Tribute, 1950; From My Level, 1965; Each in his Office, 1972; (ed) Poems by William Wordsworth, 1970. *Address:* Down The Lane, Chevington, W Suffolk. *T:* Chevington 308.
[Died 18 Dec. 1978.

MALLALIEU, Sir Edward Lancelot, (Sir Lance), Kt 1974; QC 1951; Barrister-at-law; Governor Royal Agricultural Society of England; *b* 14 March 1905; *s* of County Alderman F. W. Mallalieu, MP, JP; *m* 1934, Betty Margaret Oxley, *d* of Dr Pride, late of Bridlington, *g d* of late J. W. Oxley of Leeds; one *s* two *d*. *Educ:* Dragon Sch., Oxford; Cheltenham Coll.; Trinity Coll., Oxford. MA 1930. Called Bar, Inner Temple, 1928; NE Circuit. Sometime farmer in Co. Wicklow, and Dir of Farming Coll. of St Columba. MP (L) Colne Valley, Yorks, 1931-35; PPS to Rt Hon. Sir Donald Maclean, President Board of Education, 1931-32; MP (Lab) Brigg, Lincs, 1948-Feb. 1974; Senior Member, Speaker's Panel of Chairmen, 1964-71; Second Dep. Chm., 1971-73, First Dep. Chm., 1973-74, of Ways and Means. Member Exec., Inter-Parliamentary Union (Geneva), Chairman British Group; Secretary-General, World Assoc. of World Federalists, The Hague (Parliamentary Adviser, 1966); Hon. Vice-Pres., Franco-British Parly Relations Cttee. Hon. Vice-President, Parly Group for World Government. A Director of the French Hospital, Rochester. Second Church Estates Comr, 1965-70. Chevalier, Legion of Honour, 1957. *Address:* 5 Woodstock Close, Oxford OX2 8DB. *Club:* Royal Cruising.
[Died 11 Nov. 1979.

MALLALIEU, Sir (Joseph Percival) William, Kt 1979; *b* 18 June 1908; 3rd *s* of late County Alderman F. W. Mallalieu, MP; *m*

1945, Harriet Rita Riddle Tinn; one *s* one *d. Educ:* Dragon Sch., Oxford; Cheltenham; Trinity Coll., Oxford; University of Chicago. Oxford Rugger Blue, 1927; President Oxford Union, 1930; Commonwealth Fellow, University of Chicago, 1930-32; Col, Governor of Kentucky's Bodyguard, 1933; worked on London newspapers, 1933-41; served in Royal Navy, 1942-45. MP (Lab) Huddersfield, 1945-50, Huddersfield E, 1950-79; PPS to Under-Sec. of State for Air, 1945-46, to Minister of Food, 1946-49; Under-Secretary of State for Defence (Royal Navy), 1964-66; Minister: of Defence (Royal Navy), 1966-67; of State, Board of Trade, 1967-68, Min. of Technology, 1968-69. Member, Management Committee: RNLI, 1959-63; Royal Hosp. Sch., Holbrook, 1947-66. Life Mem., NUJ, 1973. *Publications:* Rats, 1941; Passed to You, Please!, 1942; Very Ordinary Seaman, 1944; Sporting Days, 1955; Extraordinary Seaman, 1957; Very Ordinary Sportsman, 1957. *Recreations:* walking, gardening; watching Huddersfield Town. *Address:* Village Farm, Boarstall, Aylesbury, Bucks. *T:* Brill 454. *Club:* Press.   *[Died 13 March 1980.*

MALLALIEU, Sir Lance; *see* Mallalieu, Sir E. L.

MALLALIEU, Sir William; *see* Mallalieu, Sir J. P. W.

MALLAM, Lieut-Colonel Rev. George Leslie, CSI 1947; CIE 1943; *b* 13 Dec. 1895; *o s* of late George Mallam, Parkstone, Dorset; *m* 1st, 1934, Constance Marie (KIH, silver) (*d* 1944), *d* of late Dr E. J. W. Carruthers; two *s* ; 2nd, 1950, Mary Sophronia, *o d* of Canon Cory, St Audrey's, Wilden; one *d. Educ:* Malvern. Commissioned IA, 1916; joined Political Dept, 1921; Counsellor British Legation, Kabul, Afghanistan, 1932. Financial Secretary to Government North-West Frontier Province, 1939; then Chief Secretary, Planning and Development Comr and Revenue and Divisional Comr. Called to Bar, Gray's Inn, 1926. Deacon, 1949; Priest, 1950; Vicar of Eckington, near Pershore, Worcs, 1952-65, retired 1965. *Address:* Abbey Place, Defford Road, Pershore, Worcs. *T:* Pershore 2223.   *[Died 17 Oct. 1978.*

MALLESON, Lady Constance; (Colette O'Niel); *b* Castlewellan, County Down, 1895; *y d* of 5th Earl Annesley and his cousin, Priscilla Cecilia Armytage Moore, Anmore, Co. Cavan; *m* 1915, W. Miles Malleson, (from whom she obtained a divorce, 1923; he *d* 1969). *Educ:* Dresden; Paris; RADA, London. Professional appearances: lead in Le monde ou l'on s'ennui, Queen's; lead in L'Enfant Prodigue, Kingsway; The Quaker Widow in Abraham Lincoln, Lyceum; lead in Orphans of the Storm, Lyceum; Helen, in Euripides' The Trojan Women; lead in Masefield's The Faithful (Stage Society); leading lady at various Repertory theatres and at Scala; lead in Miles Malleson's Young Heaven, Hull and London, 1925; toured S Africa, the Rhodesias, Egypt, Palestine, with Dame Sybil Thorndike and Sir Lewis Casson; leading lady on Sir Frank Benson's Farewell Tour, playing Portia, Olivia, Kate Hardcastle, Lady Teazle, Lydia Languish. Member: Howard League for Penal Reform; Summerhill Society; Private Libraries Assoc.; Anti-Slavery Society; Society for the Preservation of Ancient Buildings; Suffolk Preservation Society; National Trust; Conservation Soc.; Nat. Council for Civil Liberties. Worked for English Mental Hospital Reform, and for British Army Blood Supply Depot (1939); lectured in Sweden, 1936-37, and in Finland, 1941 and 1946; volunteered for service in Finland during Russian Invasion, 1939-40. *Publications:* After Ten Years, 1931; Fear in the Heart, 1936; In the North: Autobiographical Fragments, in Norway, Sweden and Finland, 1936-46, 1947; Queen Margaret of Norway (trans. from Norwegian of Trygve Kielland's Historical play), 1954; (ed) As the Sight is Bent: the Unfinished Autobiography of Mabel M. Annesley, 1964; Contrib. to Bertrand Russell: Philosopher of the Century, 1967. Contrib. to Guardian, The Countryman, Helsingin Sanomat. *Address:* Lavenham, Suffolk.   *[Died 5 Oct. 1975.*

MALLESON, Comdr Wilfrid St Aubyn, VC 1915; RN, retired; *m* 1927, Cecil Mary Collinson. Served Dardanelles, 1914-15 (VC), during landing of Expeditionary Force swam with line from lighter to lighter; retired list, 1941.   *[Died 21 July 1975.*

MALLETT, Richard; Film Critic for Punch, since 1938; *b* 3 April 1910; *s* of Alfred Edward Mallett and Bertha Ann Richards. *Educ:* Lowestoft Secondary Sch. Contributor to Punch since 1928; Evening News editorial staff, July 1931-Aug. 1934; Punch editorial staff, 1937-; Acting Assistant Editor during much of War of 1939-45; member of Punch Table, 1945-. *Publications:* Doggerel's Dictionary, 1946; Amos Intolerable, 1948; Literary Upshots, 1951. *Recreation:* sketching. *Address:* 103 Cliffords Inn, EC4A 1BX. *T:* 01-405 3641. *Club:* Savage.   *[Died 29 Nov. 1972.*

MALLOCK, Brig. Arthur Richard Ogilvie, CIE 1939; Indian Army, retired; *b* 21 Oct. 1885; *m* 1910, Dulce, *y d* of J. T. R. de Havilland. Entered Indian Army, 1905; DAAG India, 1924-28; GSO 1st Grade, India, 1932-36; Brigade Commander 12th (Secunderabad) Inf. Brigade, 1936; retired, 1939. *Address:* 56 Queen's Park, West Drive, Bournemouth, Hants.
                                    [Died 31 May 1972.

MALLOWAN, Dame Agatha; *see* Christie, Dame Agatha.

MALLOWAN, Sir Max (Edgar Lucien), Kt 1968; CBE 1960; MA, DLit; FBA 1954; FSA; Fellow of All Souls College, Oxford, 1962-71, Emeritus Fellow, 1976; Professor of Western Asiatic Archæology, University of London, 1947-62, now Emeritus Professor; *b* London, 6 May, 1904; *s* of Frederick Mallowan, London; *m* 1st, 1930, Agatha Mary Clarissa Miller (Dame Agatha Christie, DBE (*d* 1976); 2nd, 1977, Barbara Parker. *Educ:* Lancing; New Coll., Oxford (Hon. Fellow, 1973). Archæologist. Assistant on staff of British Museum and of Museum of University of Pennsylvania Expedition to Ur of the Chaldees, 1925-30 and on staff of British Museum Expedition to Nineveh, 1931-32. Subsequently directed excavations on behalf of British Museum and British School of Archæology in Iraq, at Arpachiyah, 1933; in Syria, at Chagar Bazar, 1934-36, at Brak and at various sites in the Balikh valley, 1937-38. During War of 1939-45 served in RAFVR with rank of Wing Commander; posted for duty with British Military Administration in Tripolitania 1943-44 and served as Adviser on Arab Affairs and subsequently as GSO 1, Deputy Chief Secretary. Director, British School of Archæology in Iraq, 1947-61 (Chairman, 1966-70, Pres., 1970-); President British Institute of Persian Studies, 1961-; Vice-President: British Academy, 1961-62; Egypt Exploration Soc., 1968-. Excavated in Zab valley, 1948, 1955, at Nimrud, 1949-58. Mem. Governing Body, SOAS, 1967-75; a Trustee, British Museum, 1973-78. Schweich Lectr, 1955, Albert Reckitt Archaeological Lectr, 1969, British Academy. FBA, and corresp. Member: Arab Acad., Baghdad, 1954; German Archæological Inst., 1962; Foreign Member: Académie des Inscriptions et Belles-Lettres, Paris, 1964; Royal Danish Acad. of Letters and Scis, 1974. Museum of Univ. of Pennsylvania, Lucy Wharton Drexel Gold Medal, 1957; Hon. Fellow Metropolitan Museum of Art, New York, 1958. Lawrence of Arabia Meml Medal, RCAS, 1969; Order of Homayoon Class 2, 1977. Editor: Near Eastern and Western Asiatic series of Penguin books, 1948-65; Iraq, 1948-71. *Publications:* Prehistoric Assyria; Excavations at Chagar Bazar; Excavations in the Balikh Valley; Excavations at Brak: archæological articles in Iraq, Antiquity, The Times, Illustrated London News, etc; Twenty-five Years of Mesopotamian Discovery, 1932-56; (with Sir Leonard Woolley) Ur Excavations, The Neo-Babylonian and Persian Periods, 1962; Early Mesopotamia and Iran, 1965; Nimrud and its Remains, 2 Vols, 1966; contrib. chapters to Cambridge Ancient History, 1967; Elamite Problems, 1969; (with L. G. Davies) Ivories in Assyrian Style, 1970; (with G. Herrmann) Ivories from Nimrud Fascicule III Furniture from SW7 Fort Shalmaneser, 1974; Mallowan's Memoirs, 1977; The Nimrud Ivories, 1978. *Recreations:* trees, travel. *Address:* Winterbrook House, Wallingford, Oxon OX10 9DX. *Clubs:* Athenæum, Boodle's.   *[Died 19 Aug. 1978.*

MALRAUX, André; Compagnon de la Libération; Officier de la Légion d'Honneur; Author; Minister of State for Cultural Affairs, Fifth Republic of France, 1960-69; *b* 3 Nov. 1901; *s* of Fernand Malraux and Mme (*née* Lamy); *m* 1st; one *d* (two *s* decd); *m* 2nd, 1948, Madeleine Lioux. *Educ:* Paris. Studied archæology and orientalism; first Asian visit, China and Indo-China, 1923-25. Pres. World Cttee for liberation of Dimitroff; responsible for taking protests to Hitler against trial of Reichstag offenders; served with Spanish Republican Government as organiser and head of foreign aviation, 1936. Served War of 1939-45 (wounded, taken prisoner, escaped 1940); Chef des services de dynamitage in the Corrèze-Dordogne-Lot inter-regional centre; comdr, attack against German div. Das Reich; Col Comdt, Alsace-Lorraine Bde; Minister of Information, 1945-46; Mem., Council of Musées de France: Ministre délégué à la Présidence du Conseil, France, June 1958-Jan. 1959 (was also in charge of Information from 1 June to 7 July). Minister of State, Fifth Republic, 1959-60. Mem., Amer. Acad. of Arts and Sciences; Hon. DCL Oxon, 1967. DSO; Commandeur de la République Espagnole. *Publications:* La Tentation de l'Occident; La Voie Royale; Les Conquérants, 1926-30; La Condition Humaine, 1933 (trans. in 18 languages); Le Temps du Mépris, 1935; L'Espoir (novel and film), 1938; Les Noyers de l'Altenburg, 1941 (Eng. trans.: The Walnut Trees of Altenburg, 1952); Saturne, Essai sur Goya, 1949; Psychologie de l'Art, 1950 (Eng. trans.: Psychology of Art, 1949-51); Les Voix du Silence, 1951 (Eng. trans.: The Voices of Silence, 1954); La Métamorphose des Dieux: vol. I, Le Surnaturel, 1957 (Eng.

trans., The Metamorphosis of the Gods, 1960), vol. II, L'Irreél, 1974, vol. III, L'Intemporel, 1976; Le Miroir des Limbes: vol. I, Antimémoires, 1967 (Eng. trans., Antimemoirs, 1968), vol II, La Corde et les Souris, 1975, composed of (i) Les Chênes qu'on abat, 1971 (Eng. trans., Fallen Oaks, 1972), (ii) La Tête d'Obsidienne, 1974, (iii) Lazare, 1974 (Eng. trans., Lazarus, 1977); Oraisons funèbres, 1971; *posthumous publication:* L'homme précaire et la littérature, 1977. *Relevant Publication:* Malraux: life and work, by Martine Courcel, 1976. *Address:* 2 rue d'Estienne d'Orves, 91370 Verrières-le-Buisson, France.
[*Died 23 Nov. 1976.*]

MALTBY, Maj.-Gen. (Christopher) Michael, CB 1946; MC; DL; retired pay; *b* 13 Jan. 1891; *er s* of late Christopher James Maltby, Felmersham, Beds; *m* 1927, Hélène Margaret Napier-Clavering (*d* 1974); two *d. Educ:* King's Sch., Canterbury; Bedford Sch.; RMA, Woolwich. Commissioned 1910; joined Indian Army, 1911; Capt., 1915; Bt Major, 1919; Major, 1927; Bt Lt-Col 1933; Lt-Col 1935; Col 1938; Brig. 1939; Maj.-Gen. 1941. Passed Staff Coll., Quetta, 1923-24; passed RAF Staff Coll., Andover, 1927-28; GSO2 and DAAG AHQ India; GSO1, Quetta Staff Coll. and Baluchistan Dist; Comdr 3rd Jhelum Bde, Calcutta Bde, 19th Indian Inf. Bde, Deccan Dist and British Troops in China. Served Persian Gulf, 1913-14. European War, 1914-18 (wounded, despatches thrice, MC, Bt Maj.); NWF India, 1923-24, 1937 (despatches); commanded in Hong Kong, 1941. DL Somerset, 1953. *Recreation:* shooting. *Address:* c/o Southfield, Millcross, Kingston-St-Mary, Taunton, Somerset. *Club:* Naval and Military. [*Died 6 Sept. 1980.*]

MALTBY, Air Vice-Marshal Sir Paul (Copeland), KCVO 1962; KBE 1946; CB 1941; DSO 1917; AFC; RAF retired; DL; *b* 5 Aug. 1892; 2nd *s* of C. J. Maltby, Felmersham, Beds; *m* 1921, Winifred Russell, *d* of late J. H. Paterson, 6 Moray Place, Edinburgh; one *s* (and *e s* killed in action 1945) one *d. Educ:* Bedford Sch. Royal Military College, Sandhurst. Gazetted to Royal Welch Fusiliers, serving in India, 1911-14; France, 1914-15; transferred to RFC, 1915, serving in France and England to end of the European War; with RAF in India, 1919-24; RAF Staff Coll., 1926; Imperial Defence Coll., 1931; Commandant of the Central Flying Sch., 1932-34; AOC RAF in Mediterranean, 1935-38; AOC 24 (Training) Group, 1938-40; 71 (AC) Group, 1940-41; AOC RAF in Java, 1942; retired, 1946; Serjeant-at-Arms, House of Lords, 1946-62. DL Southampton, 1956-. Grand Officer of Order of Orange Nassau (Netherlands). *Address:* Froglanes, Rotherwick, Basingstoke, Hants.
[*Died 2 July 1971.*]

MALTBY, Sir Thomas Karran, Kt 1949; Commissioner of Public Works, Victoria, Australia, 1955-61; *b* Oct. 1891; *s* of Thomas Karran and Ada Agnes Maltby; *m* 1913, Margaret McDonald; one *s* two *d. Educ:* School of Mines, Bendigo, Victoria, Australia. Served European War, 1914-18 (despatches); commissioned Australian Imperial Forces, 1914; Gen. Staff, 1918. Legislative Assembly, 1929-. Opposition Whip, 1929; Government Whip, 1930; Sec. to Cabinet, 1933-34; Hon. Minister, 1934; Minister for Lands and Forests, 1935; AA & QMG, 1942; Dep. Premier, Chief Sec., Minister in Charge Elec. Undertakings, 1945; Speaker, Legislative Assembly, Victoria, 1947-49. *Address:* 10 Culbin Avenue, Belmont, Geelong, Victoria 3216, Australia. *T:* 433931. [*Died 2 June 1976.*]

MALVERN, 1st Viscount *cr* 1955, of Rhodesia and of Bexley; **Godfrey (Martin) Huggins,** PC 1947; CH 1944; KCMG 1941; DCL (Oxon) 1951; (Rhodes) 1957; LLD (Witwatersrand) 1953, (London) 1955; Prime Minister, Federation of Rhodesia and Nyasaland, 1953-56 (of Southern Rhodesia, 1933-53); Director of: Merchant Bank of Central Africa; Rothman's (of Pall Mall) Rhodesia Ltd; *b* 6 July 1883; *e s* of late Godfrey Huggins and late Emily Blest; *m* 1921, Blanche Elizabeth, *d* of late James Slatter, Pietermaritzburg, South Africa; two *s. Educ:* Malvern Coll.; St Thomas's Hosp., MRCS, LRCP, 1906; FRCS 1908. Hon. FRCPE 1959. After 2+ years holding post-grad. appts at St Thomas's Hosp. became House Physician and subsequently Medical Superintendent at the Hospital for Sick Children, Great Ormond Street, London; came to Southern Rhodesia, 1911; general practitioner and surgeon, S Rhodesia, until 1921; since that date only as consultant surgeon; served with RAMC, England, Malta, France, European War, 1914-17; MLA, Southern Rhodesia, representing Salisbury North, 1923-33; Salisbury District, 1934-39, Salisbury North, 1939-53; Salisbury Suburbs (Federal), 1953-58. Minister of Native Affairs, 1933-49; Minister of Defence, 1948-56. KGStJ. *Publications:* Amputation Stumps: Their Care and After-Treatment; technical and other articles in various publications. *Recreation:* horticulture. *Heir: er s* Hon. John Godfrey Huggins [*b* 26 Oct. 1922; *m* 1946, Patricia Marjorie, *d* of Frank Renwick-Bower, Durban, S Africa; two *s* one *d. Educ:* Winchester. Joined RAF 1940; Flight

Lt 1944; retd 1945; re-joined RAF, 1952]. *Address:* Craig Farm, PO Highlands, Salisbury, Rhodesia. *Clubs:* Athenæum, No 10; Salisbury, New (Salisbury); Mashonaland Turf; numerous Country (Rhodesia). [*Died 8 May 1971.*]

MALVERN, 2nd Viscount *cr* 1955, of Rhodesia and of Bexley; **John Godfrey Huggins;** *b* 26 Oct. 1922; *er s* of 1st Viscount Malvern, PC, CH, KCMG and Blanche Elizabeth (*d* 1976), *d* of late James Slatter, Pietermaritzburg, S Africa; *S* father, 1971; *m* 1949, Patricia Marjorie, *d* of Frank Renwick-Bower, Durban, S Africa; two *s* one *d. Educ:* Winchester. Joined RAF 1940; Flight Lt 1944; retd 1945; re-joined RAF, 1952. *Heir:* son. *Address:* PO Box AP50, Salisbury Airport, Rhodesia. [*Died 28 Aug. 1978.*]

MAN, Maj.-Gen. Patrick Holberton, CB 1966; CBE 1962 (OBE 1946); DSO 1956; MC 1940; *b* 17 March 1913; *s* of Colonel Hubert William Man, CBE, DSO, and Mrs Beryl Man (*née* Holberton); *m* 1938, Barbara Joan Marion Marsh; two *d. Educ:* Rugby Sch.; RMC, Sandhurst. Commissioned into The Hampshire Regt, 1933. Served France and Belgium, 1939-40; Staff Coll., Camberley, 1941; served South-East Asia, 1943-45. RAF Staff Coll., 1946-47; served Middle East, 1950-52; Imperial Defence Coll., 1953; served Malaya, 1954-56, and BAOR, 1959-63; GOC Aldershot District, 1963-66; Dir of Personal Services (Army), 1966-68, retd. Colonel Comdt, Military Provost Staff Corps, 1967-72. MBIM. Bronze Star, 1945; Selangor Meritorious Service, 1956. *Recreation:* ski-ing. *Address:* Quill Farm, Campsea Ashe, near Woodbridge, Suffolk.
[*Died 10 Oct. 1979.*]

MANCHESTER, 10th Duke of, *cr* 1719; **Alexander George Francis Drogo Montagu,** OBE 1940; Earl of Manchester, 1626; Viscount Mandeville, Baron Montagu of Kimbolton, 1620; Commander, Royal Navy, retired; *b* 2 Oct. 1902; *er s* of 9th Duke of Manchester and late Helena (who obtained a divorce, 1931 and *m* 1937, 11th Earl of Kintore), *d* of late Eugene Zimmerman, USA; *S* father, 1947; *m* 1st, 1927, Nell Vere Stead (*d* 1966), Melbourne; two *s*; 2nd, 1969, Mrs Elizabeth Crocker, Pebble Beach, Calif. *Educ:* Osborne; Dartmouth. Retired from Royal Navy, 1930. *Recreations:* shooting, etc. *Heir: s* Viscount Mandeville. *Address:* Kapsirowa, Hoey's Bridge PO, Kenya. *Club:* Junior Naval and Military. [*Died 23 Nov. 1977.*]

MANDLEBERG, J. Harold; *b* 2 Sept. 1885; *e s* of late Sir G. Charles Mandleberg; *m* 1921, Jessie, *d* of late Arthur Entwisle, Bolton; one *d. Educ:* Harrow; Trinity Coll., Cambridge. Hons in Natural Science, MA 1910; FRIC; FIRI; FCS. European War, 1914-18, and War of 1939-45, in Army. Chairman, NW Regional Board for Industry, Dec. 1947-April 1949 (apptd by Chancellor of Exchequer); Director: North-Western Industrial Estates Ltd (appointment by President of Board of Trade), 1946-54. Ex-Chairman, NW Regional Council FBI. *Publication:* Physical Chemistry made Plain, 3rd edn, 1966. *Address:* Flat 4A, Harcourt House, 19A Cavendish Square, W1. *Clubs:* White's; Leander (Henley-on-Thames). [*Died 12 March 1973.*]

MANDLEBERG, Brig. Lennard Charles, CBE 1938; DSO 1919; MC and bar; late 8th Battalion Lancashire Fusiliers; *b* 1893; *y s* of late Sir G. Charles Mandleberg; *m* 1919, Marjorie Helen, *y d* of late John Craig; one *s. Educ:* Harrow; Trinity Coll., Cambridge. Served European War, 1914-19 (despatches, DSO, MC and bar); Commander 164th (North Lancashire) Infantry Brigade, TA, 1936-39; Commander Infantry Brigade, 1939. *Address:* Oldany Lodge, nr Lochinver, By Lairg, Sutherland. *Club:* White's. [*Died 13 Jan. 1975.*]

MANIFOLD, Hon. Sir (Thomas) Chester, KBE 1965; Kt 1953; Grazier, Australia; *b* 1897; *s* of Hon. J. Chester and Lilian E. Manifold; *m* 1923, Gwenda, *d* of Maj.-Gen. H. W. and Winifred Grimwade; three *d. Educ:* Geelong Grammar Sch., Victoria; Jesus Coll., Cambridge. Served European War, RFA, 1916-19; War of 1939-45: 2nd AIF, 1940-43 (despatches), VDC, 1943-45. Councillor, Shire of Hampden, 1926-41; Member for Hampden, State Parliament, 1929-35; Hon. Minister, Argyle Government, 1932-33. Chairman, Totalizator Agency Bd of Victoria, 1960-68. Chairman, Victoria Racing Club, 1952-62, Vice-Chairman, 1943-52 and 1962. *Recreations:* racing, golf, tennis. *Address:* Talindert, Camperdown, Victoria 3260, Australia. *T:* Camperdown 31004. *Clubs:* Melbourne, Naval and Military (Melbourne, Victoria). [*Died 6 Jan 1979.*]

MANKTELOW, Sir (Arthur) Richard, KBE 1957; CB 1948; retired as Deputy Secretary, Ministry of Agriculture, Fisheries and Food (1954-60); *b* 8 April 1899; *s* of late Richard Manktelow, Worthing; *m* 1st, 1926, Edith Helen (*d* 1965), *d* of late Harry Saxby, Grove Park; three *s* one *d*; 2nd, 1967, (Mrs Dorothea Taylour. *Educ:* King Charles the Martyr Sch., Tunbridge Wells; London School of Economics. Entered Civil

Service as boy clerk, 1914. Served European War, 1917-19, London Irish Rifles and Machine Gun Corps. Asst Secretary, 1937; Principal Asst Secretary, 1945; Under-Secretary, 1946; Principal Finance Officer, 1951-54. Chm., Alexander Duckham & Co., 1969-71. Trustee of National Society for Cancer Relief, 1959-; Sponsor, Colostomy Welfare Gp. Director, Agricultural Mortgage Corporation, 1961-73; Member, Council, Royal Veterinary College, 1960-71. Chairman: Regional Public Services Survey Commission for West Indies, 1961-62; East Caribbean Civil Service Commission, 1962-63. Knight Order of St Olav of Norway, 1947. *Address:* Careys, Abinger Common, Dorking, Surrey. *T:* Dorking 730754. *Club:* Royal Commonwealth Society. [*Died 14 Jan. 1977.*

MANLEY, Prof. Gordon; Emeritus Professor and Research Associate since 1968, University of Lancaster, (Professor of Environmental Sciences, 1964-68); *b* 3 Jan. 1902; *s* of Valentine Manley, Chartered Accountant; *m* 1930, Audrey Fairfax, *d* of late Professor Arthur Robinson, MA, DCL, Master of Hatfield Coll., Durham; no *c*. *Educ:* Queen Elizabeth's, Blackburn; Manchester Univ.; Caius Coll., Cambridge; MA (Cantab), DSc (Manchester). Meteorological Office, 1925; Greenland Expedition, 1926; Asst Lectr, Birmingham, 1926; Lectr and Head of Dept, Durham, 1928; Univ. Demonstrator and Lectr, Cambridge, 1939-48; Prof. of Geography, Univ. of London (Bedford Coll.), 1948-64. President, Royal Meteorological Society, 1945-46 (Hon. FRMetS, 1976). Leverhulme Award for work on Pennines, 1937; Buchan Prize (Royal Met. Society), 1943; Symons Lecturer, 1944; Murchison Grant (RGS), 1947; Vis. Lectr, Univ. of Oslo, 1957; Vis. Prof., Texas A&M Univ., 1969. Flt-Lieut, Cambridge University Air Squadron, 1942-45. Correspondent for glaciology, British National Ctte for the International Geophysical Year, 1955-61. Air Ministry, Sub-Cttee for Meteorological Research, 1958-62. Ministry of Technology Visitor, 1964-69. External Examiner, Universities of Bristol, St Andrews, and others. Hon. DSc Dunelm, 1979. *Publications:* Climate and the British Scene, (5th imp. 1972); papers, chiefly on British and Polar climatology, also on history of cartography, etc, in scientific journals. *Recreation:* travel among mountains. *Address:* 3 Whitwell Way, Coton, Cambridge. [*Died 29 Jan. 1980.*

MANN, Arthur Henry, CH 1941; Honorary LLD Leeds; *b* Warwick, 1876. Editor of Yorkshire Post, 1919-39; formerly Editor of the Evening Standard; Member of Board of Governors of BBC, 1941-46. *Address:* 180 Sandgate Road, Folkestone, Kent. *Club:* Devonshire. [*Died 23 July 1972.*

MANN, Sir (Edward) John, 2nd Bt, *cr* 1905; *b* 26 Jan. 1883; *e s* of Sir Edward Mann, 1st Bt, and Anna Jane (*d* 1928), *d* of Paul Bell, Stiffkey, Norfolk; *S* father 1943; *m* 1951, Clare Helen, *d* of Robert Graham Dryden Alexander, Brentwood, Essex. *Educ:* Marlborough Coll.; Pembroke Coll., Cambridge, BA; High Sheriff of Norfolk, 1939-40. *Heir: g n* Rupert Edward Mann, *b* 11 Nov. 1946. *Address:* Thelveton Hall, Diss, Norfolk. *T:* Dickleburgh 213. *Club:* Norfolk (Norwich). [*Died 17 Sept. 1971.*

MANN, Sir John; see Mann, Sir E. J.

MANN, Keith Cranston, CBE 1953; *b* 23 Sept. 1903; *s* of Frederick Thomas Mann, Dublin; *m* 1930, Millicent Grace, *d* of late G. Philip Girling, Portadown, Co. Armagh, N Ireland; three *d*. *Educ:* St Stephen's Green Sch., Dublin; Trinity Coll., Dublin Univ. Asst Civil Engineer, Public Works Office, Ireland, 1926-29; entered Air Min. as Asst Civil Engr, Directorate Gen. of Works, 1929; Superintending Engr, 1939-42; Chief Engr, RAF Maintenance Command, 1942-46; Chief Engr, Middle East Air Force, 1946-48; Dep. Dir of Works, Air Min., 1948-50; Dir of Works, Overseas Dept, 1950-58; Dep. Dir Gen. of Works, Air Min., 1958-63; Chief Civil Engr, Min. of Public Building and Works, 1963-64. *Publications:* contributor to Proc. Instn of Civil Engrs on Airfields. *Recreations:* country pursuits and music. *Address:* Field Cottage, Chedworth, Cheltenham, Glos. *T:* Fossebridge 279. [*Died 7 Feb. 1972.*

MANNERING, Rev. Ernest; *b* 28 Sept. 1882; 2nd *s* of George Willshar and Annie Southey Mannering, of Beckenham, Kent; *m* 1921, Irene, *y d* of late Rt Rev. J. Denton Thompson, Bishop of Sodor and Man. *Educ:* Dulwich Coll.; BNC, Oxford (Scholar); 2nd class Classical Moderations, 3rd class Lit. Hum.; BA 1905, MA 1908; Wycliffe Hall, Oxford, 1906. Deacon, 1906; Priest, 1907; Curate of Holy Trinity, S Marylebone, 1906-11; Christ Church, Woking, 1911-13; Temporary Chaplain to the Forces, 1915-19; Principal of Bishop Wilson Theological Coll., Isle of Man, and Domestic Chaplain to the Bishop of Sodor and Man, 1913-15 and 1919-20; Vice-Principal of St Aidan's Coll., Birkenhead, 1920-21; Vicar of St Mark's, Sheffield, 1921-30;

Vicar of St Peter's, Brockley, 1931-35; Vicar of Wadhurst, 1935-46; Rural Dean of Etchingham, 1935-46; Rector of Westonbirt with Lasborough and Chaplain to Westonbirt Sch., 1946-50; Vicar of Hanmer Springs, New Zealand, 1950-52. *Address:* The Firs, 243 West Malvern Road, Malvern, Worcs WR14 4BE. [*Died 24 Oct. 1977.*

MANNERING, Rev. Canon Leslie George, MC; MA; Canon Residentiary, Bristol Cathedral, 1932-53, now Canon Emeritus, 1953; Chaplain to the Queen, 1952-69 (to King George VI, 1951-52); *b* 27 Oct. 1883; *s* of George Willsher Mannering and Annie Southey Mannering; *m* 1919, Constance Marguerite Douthwaite; no *c*. *Educ:* Dulwich Coll.; Sidney Sussex Coll., Cambridge (Scholar). 2nd Class Classical Tripos, BA; Ridley Hall, Cambridge; 3rd Class Theological Tripos; MA; Deacon, 1907; Priest, 1908; Curate, Emmanuel, West End, Hampstead, 1907-10; Curate, Holy Trinity, Cambridge, 1910-14; Chaplain, Pembroke Coll., Cambridge, 1912-14; Chaplain to the Forces, 1914-19; Senior Chaplain 17th Div. BEF, 1916-17 (MC); Vicar, St Matthew's, Brixton, SW2, 1920-26; St John the Evangelist, Redhill, Surrey, 1926-32; Rural Dean, Reigate, 1929-32; Commissary to Bishop of Victoria, Hong Kong, 1924-32; Founder of the Bible Reading Fellowship; Select Preacher, Cambridge Univ., 1937; Lecturer in Pastoral Theology, Cambridge Univ., 1939. *Address:* 3 Court Road, Malvern, Worcs WR14 3BU. *T:* Malvern 2271. [*Died 25 July 1974.*

MANNERS, 4th Baron, *cr* 1807; **Francis Henry Manners,** MC; DL; JP; Hants CC; late Captain Grenadier Guards; Brevet Colonel late 5/7 Battalion Hampshire Regiment, TF; *b* 21 July 1897; *s* of 3rd Baron and Constance (*d* 1920), *d* of Col Henry E. H. Fane, MP, of Clovelly Court, Devon; *S* father, 1927; *m* 1921, Mary Edith, *d* of late Rt Rev. Lord William Cecil, Bishop of Exeter; three *s* one *d*. *Educ:* Eton. Served European War, 1914-19 (wounded MC). *Heir: s* Flight Lt Hon. John Robert Cecil Manners, RAFVR [*b* 13 Feb. 1923; *m* 1949, Jennifer Selena, *d* of Ian Fairbairn, 4 More's Garden, Chelsea, and of Mrs C. Fairbairn; one *s* two *d*]. *Address:* North End House, Avon, Christchurch, Hants. *T:* Bransgore 317. [*Died 25 Nov. 1972.*

MANNHEIM, Hermann, OBE 1959; Dr juris; Reader in Criminology, University of London, 1946-55, retired; Hon. Director, Criminological Research Unit, London School of Economics, 1956-61; naturalised British subject, 1940; *b* 26 Oct. 1889; *s* of Wilhelm Mannheim and Clara Marcuse; *m* 1919, Mona Mark. *Educ:* Munich, Freiburg, Strasbourg, Koenigsberg Univs. Judge in Criminal Courts and Court of Appeal (Kammergericht), Berlin, 1923-33 (Promoted by West German Govt to rank of retd Pres. of Div. of Court of Appeal, 1952); Lectr and Prof. in Faculty of Law, Berlin Univ., 1923-33; Lecturer in Criminology, London Sch. of Economics, 1935-46; Visiting Prof., Univs of Oregon and Pennsylvania, 1953. Leon Fellow Univ. of London, 1936-37; Pres. Scientific Cttee, Internat. Soc. of Criminology until 1962; Vice-President: Inst. for Study and Treatment of Delinquency; British Soc. of Criminology; Mem. Joint Cttee on Psychiatry and the Law of BMA and Magistrates' Assoc., resigned 1956; Mem., Colonial Office Advisory Cttee on Treatment of Offenders, until 1961; Chm. Programme Cttee, Third Internat. Congress on Criminology, London, 1955; Jt Dir Fourth Internat. Course in Criminology, London, 1954. Chm. Scientific Group for the Discussion of Delinquency Problems, 1956-58; Lecture tours, Holland, 1949, Norway and USA, 1953, Western Germany, 1956, USA and Canada, 1957. Hon. Dr of Law, Utrecht, 1957; Hon. DSc Econ Wales, 1970. Hon. Fellow, London Sch. of Economics, 1965. Coronation Medal, 1953; Grosses Verdienstkreuz der Bundesrepublik Deutschland, 1965; Golden Beccaria Medal of German Society of Criminology, 1965. *Publications:* Der Masstab der Fahrlässigkeit im Strafrecht, 1912; Die Revision im Strafverfahren, 1925; Pressrecht, 1927; The Dilemma of Penal Reform, 1939; Social Aspects of Crime in England between the Wars, 1940; War and Crime, 1941; Criminal Justice and Social Reconstruction, 1946; Juvenile Delinquency in an English Middletown, 1948; (with A. M. Carr-Saunders and E. C. Rhodes) Young Offenders, 1942; (with L. T. Wilkins) Prediction Methods in relation to Borstal Training, 1955; Group Problems in Crime and Punishment, 1955, enl. edn 1972; (Co-author) The Teaching of Criminology (UNESCO), 1957; Courts for Adolescents, 1959; (Co-author) Law and Opinion in England in the Twentieth Century, 1959; Deutsche Strafrechtsreform in englischer Sicht, 1960. Editor Pioneers in Criminology, 1960, enl. edn 1972; Comparative Criminology (2 vols), 1965 (German and Italian edns, 1974). Joint Editor British Journal of Criminology (resigned 1966); Joint Editor Library of Criminology, 1960-66. *Recreations:* music and travelling. *Address:* 16 Heathfielde, Lyttelton Road, N2. [*Died 20 Jan. 1974.*

MANNHEIM, Lucie; actress; *b* Berlin, 30 April 1905; *d* of late Louis Mannheim and Gertrud Mannheim (*née* Zander); *m* 1941, Marius Goring. *Educ:* Dorothean Schule and Eupel Schule, Berlin. Made first appearance at age of twelve, 1917, as Kaethie in Alt Heidelberg; joined Berlin Volksbuehne, 1919, playing among other parts Cordelia in King Lear, Aman in Tagore's Post Office, Agafia in Gogol's Marriage. Became leading actress at Berlin State Theatre, playing among other parts, 1924-33: Nora in Ibsen's Doll's House, Juliet in Romeo and Juliet, Irina in Chekov's Three Sisters, Kaetchen in Kleist's Kaetchen von Heilbronn. Played concurrently, in many other theatres, musical plays, comedies, farces in Berlin dialect and straight plays such as Verneuil's Monsieur Lamberthier, The Trial of Mary Dugan. Left Germany, 1933. First appearance in London in Nina, Criterion, 1935; Girl Unknown, New, 1936; The Last Straw, Comedy, 1937; in management at Duke of York's Theatre with Marius Goring producing Doll's House, revival of Nina, 1938-39. Worked for BBC German Service, 1940-46. Toured Germany with Monsieur Lamberthier, playing in English and German, 1947. Arts Theatre Festival 1948: playing Rebecca West in Ibsen's Rosmersholm, Sweetie in Shaw's Too True to be Good, Madame Popof in Chekov's Bear, Fyokla in Gogol's Marriage, Germaine in Monsieur Lamberthier (also produced last 3 plays). Daphne Laureola and The Corn is Green, in Berlin, 1949-50; Rose Tattoo, Berlin, 1952; Relative Values, Berlin, 1953; Hauptmann's Ratten, 1954; Tolstoy's Light Shines in Darkness, 1956; Look Homeward Angel, 1958; Biberpelz, 1959; Tonight at 8.30, 1960; La Voix Humaine, 1960; Anouilh's The Grotto, 1962; Ratten, Hamburg, 1965; The Skin of our Teeth, Hamburg, 1966; two Berlin musicals (also prod Hamburg), 1967; Anouilh's Pauvre Antoine, Berlin, 1967. Has done many broadcasts for BBC and made several films in Berlin, Paris and London; has appeared on TV in England and Germany. Awarded Verdienst Kreuz, 1953 and Grand Cross of Merit, 1959, by President of German Federal Republic for services to the theatre. Made Berlin State Actress by Berlin Senate, 1963. *Recreations:* skating, sun-bathing. *Address:* Middle Court, The Green, Hampton Court, Surrey. *T:* 01-977 4030.
[Died 17 July 1976.

MANNING, Prof. Charles Anthony Woodward; Montague Burton (formerly Cassel) Professor of International Relations, London School of Economics, University of London, 1930-62, now emeritus; *b* 18 Nov. 1894; *s* of Dumaresq Williamson Manning and Helena Isabella Bell; *m* 1939, Marion Somerville (Maisie) Johnston (*d* 1977). *Educ:* Diocesan Coll (Bishops), Rondebosch; South African Coll., Cape Town; Brasenose Coll., Oxford. Bishops Rhodes Schol., 1914. Enlisted 18th Royal Fusiliers, 1914; commissioned 7th Oxford and Bucks Lt Inf., 1915; active service France and Salonika, 1915-17 (wounded, despatches twice); Instr 11th Officer Cadet Bn (Actg Capt.), 1917-18; BA Oxon Greats (distinction), 1920; BA Oxon Jurisprudence (1st Cl.), 1921; BCL (1st Cl.), 1922; Sen. Hulme Schol., 1921; Barr., Middle Temple, 1922; ILO (Diplomatic Div.), 1922; League of Nations (Personal Asst to Sec.-Gen.), 1922; Fellow, New Coll., and Law Lecturer, New and Pembroke Colls, Oxford, 1923; Laura Spellman Rockefeller Fellow (Harvard), 1925-26; Dep. Prof. of Internat. Law and Diplomacy, Oxford, 1927; Examiner in Roman Law to Council of Legal Education, 1927-32. Tutor, Zimmern Sch. of International Studies, Geneva, 1925 and subs. summers. Sen. Specialist, Wartime Chatham House, 1939-43. Chm., South Africa Soc., 1964-. Hon. DPhil Pretoria, 1971. *Publications:* The Policies of the British Dominions in the League of Nations, 1932; (trans.) Völkerrecht im Grundriss by Hatschek, 1930; (editor) Salmond's Jurisprudence, 8th edn, 1930; (edited and contrib. to) Peaceful Change, 1937; University Teaching of Social Sciences, International Relations (Unesco), 1952; The Nature of International Society, 1962; Empire into Commonwealth (in Promise of Greatness), 1968; Austin To-day (in Modern Theories of Law), 1933, and other articles. *Recreations:* watercolour, gardening, music. *Address:* Westcliff, Spaanschemat River Road, Constantia, Cape, 7800, South Africa. *[Died 10 March 1978.*

MANNING, Dame (Elizabeth) Leah, DBE 1966; *d* of Charles and Margaret Perrett, Rockford, Ill; *m* 1914, William Henry Manning (decd), The Observatory, Cambridge. *Educ:* St John's Sch., Bridgwater; Homerton Coll., Cambridge. Past Organising Sec. of Nat. Union of Teachers; Past Headmistress of Open Air Sch., Cambridge; Past Pres. of National Union of Teachers; MP (Lab.) East Islington, Feb.-Oct. 1931; Epping Div. of Essex, 1945-50. Company Dir from 1955, now retired. *Publications:* What I Saw in Spain, 1933; A Life for Education (autobiography), 1970. *Recreations:* travelling, swimming, motoring. *Address:* Willow Cottage, Hatfield Broad Oak, Essex. *T:* Hatfield Broad Oak 247. *[Died 15 Sept. 1977.*

MANNING, Sir George, Kt 1967; CMG 1960; MA; DipSocSci; Mayor of Christchurch, NZ, 1958-68; *b* 11 Feb. 1887; *s* of Richard Manning; *m* 1923, S. E. Willmore; one *s*. *Educ:* Gowerton Gram. Sch., Wales; Canterbury Univ., NZ. Steelworker, 1906-10; emigrated to NZ, 1910; Secretary: Canterbury WEA, 1921-48; New Zealand WEA, 1923; Dominion Pres., WEA, 1946-49; Adult Education and WEA Lecturer, 1948-58. Councillor, Christchurch City Council, 1927-29 and 1936-58. Member: Christchurch Tramway Board, 1933-50; Lyttelton Harbour Bd, 1939-40, 1946-71; Council, Univ. of Canterbury, 1958-68. Hon. DCL Canterbury, 1972. *Recreations:* bowls, gardening. *Address:* 7 Bletsoe Avenue, Christchurch 2, New Zealand. *[Died 29 Dec. 1976.*

MANNING, Hon. Sir (James) Kenneth, Kt 1972; Judge of the Supreme Court, New South Wales, 1955-73; Member, Court of Appeal, 1969-73; *b* Sydney, 26 May 1907; *s* of late H. W. Manning, Sydney; *m* 1967, Sheila, *d* of late R. F. Barker. *Educ:* Sydney Grammar Sch. Served War of 1939-45 (despatches): RAAF, 1941-46; New Guinea, 1942; subseq. Dep. Dir of Personal Services (Wing Comdr). Solicitor, NSW, 1930; Barrister, 1940; QC 1953. Chm., Law Reform Commn of NSW, 1966-69. Hon. Treas., Bar Assoc. of NSW, 1950-53; Challis Lectr, Sydney Univ., 1950-55. *Publications:* co-author: The Law of Banker and Customer in Australia, 1947; Australian Bankruptcy Law and Practice, 3rd edn, 1953. *Address:* 71 The Esplanade, Balmoral Beach, NSW 2088, Australia.
[Died 11 Aug. 1976.

MANNING, Dame Leah; *see* Manning, Dame E. L.

MANNING, Olivia (Mary), (Mrs R. D. Smith), CBE 1976; author; *b* 1915; *o d* of late Oliver Manning, Commander, RN, and Olivia, *e d* of late David Morrow, Down, Ireland; *m* 1939, Emeritus Prof. Reginald Donald Smith, New Univ. of Ulster (Vis. Prof., Univ. of Surrey). *Publications:* novels: The Wind Changes, 1938; Artist Among the Missing, 1949; School for Love, 1951; A Different Face, 1953; The Doves of Venus, 1955; The Balkan Trilogy (The Great Fortune, 1960; The Spoilt City, 1962; Friends and Heroes, 1965); The Play Room, 1969; The Rain Forest, 1974; The Danger Tree, 1977; The Battle Lost and Won, 1978; The Sum of Things, 1980; *short stories:* Growing Up, 1948; A Romantic Hero, 1966; *history:* The Remarkable Expedition, 1947; *travel:* The Dreaming Shore, 1950; *humour:* My Husband Cartwright, 1956; *general:* Extraordinary Cats, 1967. Contributed to Horizon, Windmill, Spectator, New Statesman, Punch, The Observer, Sunday Times, Sunday Telegraph, The Times, Times Literary Supplement, Vogue, Harper's, The Queen, Saturday Book, Best Short Stories, Winter's Tales, Transatlantic Review, Encounter, Adam, Books and Bookmen. *Recreation:* cats. *Address:* 3/71 Marlborough Place, NW8. *T:* 01-624 1025. *[Died 23 July 1980.*

MANNING, Richard Joseph; *b* 28 March 1883; *s* of Richard Manning; *m* 1912, Ada Agnes Baird, 2nd *d* of Capt. James Brown; two *s* (and one *s* lost in the War of 1939-45) three *d*; *m* 1939, Margaret Asher, *o d* of John Wilson, Blundellsands. *Educ:* Clongowes Wood Coll.; University Coll., Blackrock. Inspector of Police, British Guiana, 1909-20; Resident Magistrate, Tanganyika, 1920-25; Resident Magistrate, Jamaica, 1925-27; Police Magistrate, Gold Coast, 1927-32; Puisne Judge, Trinidad and Tobago, 1932-36; Senior Puisne Judge, Palestine, 1936-39; Puisne Judge, SS, 1939; seconded as Puisne Judge, Uganda, 1942-46; retired, 1946. Chm. Advisory Cttee on Detainees, Palestine, 1947 and 1948; Additional Judge, British Guiana, 1948-50. Commissioner, Caura Inquiry, Trinidad, 1950. Acting Judge, Windward and Leeward Islands, 1950-54, 1959, 1960; Chm. Public Utilities Bd, Barbados, 1955-58. Jubilee Medal, 1935; Coronation Medals, 1937 and 1953; Palestine Gen. Service Medal, 1939. *Publication:* British Guiana Police Manual. *Address:* Red Rocks Private Home, Hoylake, Cheshire.
[Died 2 April 1979.

MANSBRIDGE, Very Rev. Harold Chad; Provost of St Mary's Cathedral, Glasgow, since 1970; Priest-in-charge, St George's, Maryhill, Glasgow, since 1976; *b* 4 March 1917; *s* of Tom Standish and Lotty Mansbridge; *m* 1945, Margaret Edythe Clark; one *s* one *d*. *Educ:* Price's School, Fareham, Hants; Kelham Theological College. Deacon 1941, priest 1942, Southwell; Curate of St George, Nottingham, 1941-44; Cullercoats, 1944-45; Stratfield Mortimer, 1945-48; Rector of Shellingford, 1948-60; Priest-in-charge, Fernham 1948-58, and of Longcot with Fernham, 1958-60; Rector of St Devenick's, Bieldside, Aberdeen, 1960-70; Canon, St Andrew's Cathedral, Aberdeen, 1970. *Recreation:* cooking, and in particular cake making. *Address:* Cathedral House, 39 Kirklee Road, Glasgow G12 0SP. *[Died 15 July 1980.*

MANSFIELD AND MANSFIELD, 7th Earl of, *cr* 1776 and 1792, Gt Britain; **Mungo David Malcolm Murray,** MA Oxon; FLS, FZS, FZS (Scotland), FRHS, MBOU; Lord Lieutenant of Perthshire since 1960; JP Perthshire and Dumfriesshire; Baron Scone, 1605; Viscount Stormont, 1621; Baron Balvaird, 1641; (Earl of Dunbar, Viscount Drumcairn, and Baron Halldykes in the Jacobite Peerage); Hereditary Keeper of Bruce's Castle of Lochmaben; Chairman, Edinburgh Board of Royal Insurance Company; President: Perthshire Agricultural Society; Wildfowlers Association of Great Britain and Ireland; Perth Division Conservative and Unionist Association, 1935; Past President, British Empire Union; Chairman, Perth Division Unionist Association, 1945-60; Mem. of Perth County Council since 1935; Mem. of Executive of West India Committee; DL Perthshire, 1947; Brig. Royal Company of Archers (Queen's Body Guard for Scotland); late Lt 6/7th Black Watch; TA; Major in Home Guard, 1940-43; *b* 9 Aug. 1900; *o s* of 6th Earl and Margaret Helen Mary (*d* 1933), *d* of late Rear-Adm. Sir Malcolm MacGregor of MacGregor, 4th Bt; *S* father, 1935; *m* 1928, Dorothea Helena, *y d* of late Rt Hon. Sir Lancelot Carnegie, GCVO, KCMG; one *s* two *d. Educ:* privately; Christ Church, Oxford (BA (Hons) 1922, MA). Mem. of Perthshire Education Authority, 1925-30; MP (U) Perth, 1931-35; contested (U) N Lanark March (bye-election) and again May 1929; Gov. of Edinburgh and East of Scotland Coll. of Agriculture, 1925-30; Founder of Imperial Policy Group, 1934; Chm. of Directors of James Murray's Royal Asylum, Perth, 1935-48; Chm., Perthshire Mental Hosp. Bd, 1948-51; ex-Chm. Royal Scottish Society for Prevention of Cruelty to Children; Hon. Sec., British Group, Interparliamentary Union, 1932-35; First Chm. of British Trust for Ornithology, 1933-39; Hon. Pres., Scottish Chamber of Agriculture, 1936-38; Mem. Perthshire Agricultural Exec. Cttee, 1940-47; Vice-Preses, the Perth Hunt, Preses, 1929 and 1953; Member: Departmental Cttee on Scottish Farm Buildings, 1943-45; Advisory Cttee on Conservation of the Water Supplies of Scotland; has sat on many Scottish Provisional Order Commissions; Mem. Tay Salmon Fisheries Board and Tay Pollution Prevention Board; President: Scottish Association of Salmon Fishing Boards; Scottish Section, Franco-Scottish Soc. Mem. Council, Zoological Soc. of London (Vice-Pres., 1960-1963). Vice-Lieutenant of Perthshire, 1959-60. An Elder of the Church of Scotland; Lord High Commissioner to the Gen. Assembly of Church of Scotland, 1961 and 1962. Ex-Pres. The Cactus Soc. of Great Britain; Vice-Pres. Scottish League for European Freedom; Past Pres., Soc. for Individual Freedom; Member: Coun. of Royal Highland and Agric. Soc. of Scotland (Vice-Pres., 1948-49, 1964-65); Sec. of State for Scotland's Adv. Cttee on Protection of Birds; Adv. Cttee on JPs for Scotland. Chevalier, Legion of Honour; Medal of City of Paris. *Publications:* Articles on Ornithology, Shooting, Wildfowling, Agriculture, Forestry, Politics, and the West Indies, especially Jamaica. *Heir: s* Viscount Stormont. *Address:* Scone Palace, Perthshire. *Clubs:* Pratt's, Carlton, Lansdowne, MCC; New (Edinburgh); Jamaica (Kingston).
[Died 2 Sept. 1971.

MANSFIELD, Henry, OBE 1976; IPFA, FBCS, DPA; Chief Executive, Cardiff City Council, since 1974; *m* 1944, Laura Evelynne (*née* Dykes); three *s* two *d. Educ:* Canton High Sch., Cardiff. Served Cardiff CC, 1930-; City Treasurer and Controller, 1966-74. Pioneered develt of computers in Welsh local govt; Chm., Welsh Local Govt Computer Steering Cttee; represents Assoc. of Dist Councils on LAMSAC (Mem., LAMSAC Computer Adv. Panel), Local Govt Operational Research Cttee, Royal Inst. of Public Admin and Jt Cttee on Use of Computers in Bldg Industry. Mem. (of former) IMTA, 1938 (past Chm., Associates Section and Students' Soc.); Course Pres. for some years at IMTA/IPFA Nat. Residential Courses, Cardiff. Many lectures to student socs and professional bodies, etc. Chm., Wales Local and Public Authorities Savings Cttee; Member: Nat. Local and Public Authorities Savings Cttee; Wales Savings Cttee; Cardiff Savings Cttee. Hon. FBCS, 1975. *Publications:* articles in local govt press. *Recreation:* church work. *Address:* Briarwood, Pwllmelin Lane, Llandaff, Cardiff CF5 2NQ. *T:* Cardiff 562521.   *[Died 8 March 1979.*

MANSFIELD, Philip Theodore, CSI 1941; CIE 1936; late ICS; *b* 1 Feb. 1892; 2nd *s* of G. J. Mansfield, Blackheath, SE, formerly of Singapore; *m* 1922, Helen Rosamund, *d* of H. E. Aked, Harrogate; three *s* one *d. Educ:* Charterhouse; Pembroke Coll., Cambridge (MA). ICS, 1915; 2nd Lt IARO, 1918; Chief Sec. Orissa Govt, 1936, Bihar Govt, 1944; Retired, 1946. Asst Sec. Ministry of Town and Country Planning, 1946-47. *Address:* Knockronan, Church Road, Wickham Bishops, Witham, Essex. *T:* Wickham Bishops 178. *Clubs:* Royal Over-Seas League, English-Speaking Union.   *[Died 17 May 1975.*

MANTON, Sidnie Milana, FRS 1948; MA, PhD, ScD (Cantab) **(Mrs J. P. Harding);** retired as Research Fellow, Queen Mary College, London, 1967; Hon. Research Associate, British Museum (Natural History), since 1948; *b* 4 May 1902; *d* of George S. F. Manton, LDS, RCS, and Milana Manton, London; *m* 1937, J. P. Harding, PhD; one *s* one *d. Educ:* St Paul's Girls' Sch., Hammersmith; Girton Coll., Cambridge. Scholar, 1921-25; Research Student, 1925-28; Fellow, 1928-48; Director of Studies in Natural Sciences, Girton Coll., 1935-42; Demonstrator in Comparative Anatomy, University of Cambridge, 1927-35; Visiting Lecturer, King's Coll., London, 1943-46, Asst Lecturer, 1946-49; Reader in Zoology, University of London, 1949-60. Hon. Dr, Lund, Sweden, 1968. Linnean Gold Medal, 1963; Frink Medal, Zoological Soc., 1977. *Publications:* Colourpoint, Longhair and Himalayan Cats, 1971; The Arthropoda: habits, functional morphology and evolution, 1977; papers in scientific journals on zoological subjects. *Recreation:* cat breeding (new varieties). *Address:* 88 Ennerdale Road, Richmond, Surrey. *T:* 2908.   *[Died 2 Jan. 1979.*

MANUEL, Archibald Clark, JP; *b* 1 March 1901. Joined Labour Party, 1927. Engine driver; member Associated Society of Locomotive Engineers and Firemen. MP (Lab) Central Ayrshire Div. of Ayrshire and Bute, 1950-55, 1959-70. Formerly executive member Scottish Housing and Town Planning Council. Member: Ayr County Council; Ardrossan Town Council; Western Regional Hospital Board; Ayrshire Exec. Council (Health Service). JP 1938. *Address:* Eorna Cottage, Salen, Acharacle, Argyll.   *[Died 10 Oct. 1976.*

MANUWA, Chief the Honourable Sir Samuel (Layinka Ayodeji), Kt 1956; CMG 1953; OBE 1948; MD, ChB; LLD; DSc; DLitt; FRCS; FRCP; FRSE; FACS; FACP; FICS; The Oloye (Chief) Iyasere of Itebu-Manuwa, The Obadugba of Ondo, and The Olowa Luwagboye of Ijebu Ode; Chief Medical Adviser to the Federal Government of Nigeria (Colonial Medical Service), 1954-59, retired; Pro-Chancellor and Chairman of Council, University of Ibadan; *b* 4 March 1903; *e s* of Rev. Benjamin Ilowo Manuwa (Church Missionary Society), *s* of late Alaiyeluwa Oba Kuehin, Elero (Head Chief) of Itebu-Manuwa, and Matilda Omolara Thomas, Ondo; *m* 1st, Theodora Obafunmilayo (marr. diss.), *y d* of late Rt Rev. Bishop Oluwole, MA, DD; one *d*; 2nd, Isabella Inyang, *y d* of Prince Ibok Eyo Ita, *s* of late Eyo Honesty III, Obong (Head Chief) of Creek Town, Calabar; two *s* one *d. Educ:* CMS Grammar Sch. and King's Coll., Lagos; Universities of Edinburgh and Liverpool. MB, ChB (Edinburgh) 1926; LM (Dublin) 1926; DTM (Liverpool) 1926; MD (Edinburgh) 1934; DTH (Liverpool) 1934; FRCSE 1938; FRCPE 1960 (MRCPE 1957); FACP 1963; FRSE 1967; FACS 1971; FICP 1974. Edinburgh University: Robert Wilson Memorial Prize and Medal (Chemistry), Wellcome Prize and Medal (Medicine); Demonstrator in Human Anatomy, 1925-26. MO, subs. Surgical Specialist and Senior Specialist in Colonial Medical Service, Nigeria, 1927-48; DDMS, 1948-51; DMS, 1951; Inspector-General of Medical Services, 1951-54. Member, W Nigeria House of Assembly, 1948-51; MLC and MEC 1951-52; Member, Governor's Privy Council, 1952-54; PC Federation of Nigeria, 1954-60; Member Federal Advisory Council on the Prerogative of Mercy, 1960-66; President, Assoc. of Surgeons of West Africa, 1960-62; Pres., Assoc. of Physicians of W Africa, 1962-68; Representative of grouped African, Mediterranean and Middle East Branches on Central Council of BMA, 1961-64; First Comr, Federal Public Service Commn. Formerly Examiner in Anat. and Surgery, Yaba Medical School; Hon. Assoc. University Coll. of Ibadan, Nigeria; Member Council, Univ. of Ife, Western Nigeria, 1961-66; Council, Imperial Society of Knights Bachelor, 1957-. FRSA London; Member New York Acad. Sciences; Fellow: American Public Health Assoc.; Internat. Coll. of Surgeons. Vice-President at 6th International Congress on Tropical Medicine and Malaria, Lisbon, 1958, Hon. Pres., Athens, 1973; Vice-President, 1964-65, President, 1965-66, World Federation for Mental Health. Hon. FRSTMH, 1974. CStJ. Hon. LLD Edinburgh 1953; Hon. DSc: University of Nigeria, 1963; Ibadan, 1965. Hon. DLitt, University of Ife, 1967. John Holt Medal, University of Liverpool, 1959, for services to Tropical Medicine. Director: May and Baker (West Africa) Ltd; Law Union and Rock Insurance Co. of Nigeria Ltd. *Publications:* various papers in scientific journals dealing with tropical medicine, surgery and mental health. *Recreations:* walking, gardening. *Address:* Federal Public Service Commission, Lagos, Nigeria, (*T:* 27096); 2 Alexander Avenue, Ikoyi (*T:* 53588), Lagos, Nigeria; Pro-Chancellor's Lodge, University of Ibadan, Nigeria (*T:* Ibadan 62550). *Clubs:* Royal Commonwealth Society; Island, Metropolitan (Lagos); University Union (Edinburgh).
[Died 16 Sept. 1975.

MANZONI, Sir Herbert (John Baptista), Kt 1954; CBE 1941; City Engineer and Surveyor, Birmingham, 1935-63; Consultant W. V. Zinn and Associates, Consulting Engineers; *b* 21 March 1899; *s* of Giovanni Carlo Manzoni, Milan and Birkenhead; *m* 1923, Lilian May, *d* of A. N. Davies of Birkenhead; two *s* (and one *s* decd). *Educ:* Birkenhead; Liverpool Univ. Served European War, 1914-18, 12th Lancer Regt and 7th Middlesex Regt; Chief Engineer, Sewers and Rivers, Public Works Dept, Birmingham, 1927-29; Dep. City Surveyor, Birmingham, 1929-35. President, Institute Civil Engineers, 1960-61; Past President, Institute Municipal Engineers; Member, Town Planning Institute; FRSH; Registered Architect. Chairman: Building Research Board, DSIR 1954-60; Elford Internal Drainage Board, 1944-; President British Standards Institution, 1956-58; Member: West Midland Group on Post-War Reconstruction and Planning; Member of Court, Loughborough Univ. of Technology; Life Governor, Birmingham Univ.; Nat. President, Federation of Master Builders, 1964-70; Chairman: Civil Engineering Research Assoc., 1964-67; Construction Industry Research and Information Assoc., 1967-70. Hon. Assoc. University of Aston. Hon. Member Institution of Royal Engineers. Hon. DSc (Birmingham), 1961; Hon. DTech (Loughborough), 1967. *Publications:* papers and communications to professional bodies. *Recreation:* fishing. *Address:* 20 Viceroy Close, Bristol Road, Birmingham 5. *T:* 021-440 2371.
[Died 18 Nov. 1972.

MAPP, Charles; JP; *b* 1903. *Educ:* elementary and grammar schools. Railway goods agent (retired). Member, Sale Borough Council, 1932-35, 1945-46. Contested: Northwich, 1950; Stretford, 1951; Oldham East, 1955; MP (Lab) Oldham East, Oct. 1959-70, retired. JP 1949-. *Address:* 21 Fairhaven Road, Southport, Merseyside.
[Died 3 May 1978.

MAPPIN, Sir Frank Crossley, 6th Bt, *cr* 1886; *b* 15 Aug. 1884; *s* of Sir Samuel Wilson Mappin, 5th Bt, and Laura (*d* 1937), *d* of William Morton; *S* father 1942; *m* 1909, Ruby, *d* of George Lamberton Thomson, Auckland, NZ; three *d*. *Educ:* Felsted; Gonville and Caius Coll., Cambridge. KStJ 1952. *Heir:* none. *Address:* 450 Remuera Road, Auckland 5, New Zealand.
[Died 25 Jan. 1975 (ext).

MAR, 30th Earl of (ante 1404); **James (Clifton) of Mar;** Premier Earl of Scotland; Baron Garioch, 1336; (recognised in the surname "of Mar" by warrant of Court of Lord Lyon, 1959, in lieu of that of Lane); *b* 22 Nov. 1914; *o* surv. *s* of Charles Macdonald Lane, CSI (*d* 1956); *S* kinsman (Lionel Walter Young Erskine, 29th Earl) 1965; *m* 1st, 1939, Millicent Mary Salton (marr. diss., 1958); two *d* (one *s* decd); 2nd, 1960, Marjorie Aileen Grice, *d* of late J. R. Miller, and *widow* of Major C. W. S. Grice, Central India Horse. *Educ:* Marlborough. *Recreations:* gardening, fishing, kicking pigeons. *Heir:* er *d* Mistress of Mar. *Address:* Princes Court, Brompton Road, SW3.
[Died 21 April 1975.

MARCEL, Gabriel; French philosopher and author; Membre de l'Institut; *b* Paris, 7 Dec. 1889; *s* of Henry Marcel and Laure Meyer; *m* 1919, Jacqueline Boegner; one *s*. *Educ:* Lycée Carnot, Sorbonne, Paris (agrégé de philosophie). Several years of teaching; later worked in collaboration with publishers Plon and Grasset; contributed dramatic and literary criticism to numerous periodicals, including Nouvelle Revue Française, Europe Nouvelle, Nouvelles Littéraires, etc. Gifford Lecturer, Aberdeen, 1949-50. Grand Prix de Littérature de L'Académie Française, 1948; Peace Prize, Frankfurt, 1964; Erasmus Prize, 1969. Officer, Legion of Honour. *Publications:* Journal métaphysique, 1927; Etre et avoir, 1934; Du refus à l'invocation, 1940; Homo Viator, 1945; La Métaphysique de Royce, 1945; Le Mystère de l'être (Gifford Lectures), 1951; Les Hommes contre l'humain; La Dignité Humaine, 1964; Pour Sagesse Tragique, 1968; En Chemin vers quel Eveil, 1971, etc; *plays:* Un Homme de Dieu, 1929; Le Chemin de Crête, 1936; Le Fanal, 1936; Le Dard, 1937; La Soif, 1938; L'Horizon, 1945; L'Emissaire-Le Signe de la croix, 1949; Rome n'est plus dans Rome, 1951; Mon Temps n'est pas le vôtre, 1955; Croissez et multipliez, 1955; Fragments philosophiques, 1909-1914, 1963. *Relevant publication:* Gabriel Marcel, by Seymour Cain, 1963. *Address:* 21 rue de Tournon, Paris 6e, France. *T:* Danton 29.28.
[Died 8 Oct. 1973.

MARCHANT, Ernest Cecil, CIE 1946; *b* 27 Sept. 1902; *s* of E. J. Marchant, Cambridge; *m* 1933, Margaret Glen, *d* of Major George Lamb, IMS; two *d*. *Educ:* Perse Sch.; St John's Coll., Cambridge (Scholar). Asst Master, Oakham Sch., 1925-28; Mem., Royal Soc. Expedn to Great Barrier Reef, 1928-29; Asst Master, Geelong Sch., Australia, 1929-30; Asst Master, Marlborough Coll., 1931-38; Principal, The Daly Coll., India, 1939-46; HM Inspector of Schools, 1947-66, Staff Inspector,

1952-66. *Address:* Burford House, The Common, Chipperfield, Herts WD4 9BY. *T:* Kings Langley 62549.
[Died 13 Sept. 1979.

MARCHWOOD, 2nd Viscount, *cr* 1945, of Penang and of Marchwood, Southampton; **Peter George Penny,** Baron *cr* 1937, Bt, *cr* 1933; MBE (mil.) 1944; *b* 7 Nov. 1912; *s* of 1st Viscount Marchwood, KCVO; *S* father, 1955; *m* 1935, Pamela, *o d* of John Staveley Colton-Fox, JP, Todwick Grange, nr Sheffield; two *s* one *d*. *Educ:* Winchester. Editorial Staff, Sheffield Daily Telegraph and Daily Telegraph and Morning Post, 1929-35; Financial Advertising Staff, Daily Telegraph and Morning Post, 1935-47. Served War of 1939-45, Major, RA. Joined Vine Products Ltd, as General Manager, 1947; Dep. Managing Director, 1951; Chairman and Managing Director, 1955-59; Exec. Dir, Geo. Wimpey & Co (Contractors), 1960-71. *Recreations:* racing, shooting. *Heir: s* Hon. David George Staveley Penny [*b* 22 May 1936; *m* 1964, Tessa Jane, *d* of W. F. Norris; three *s*]. *Address:* Manor House, Cholderton, near Salisbury, Wilts. *T:* Cholderton 200. *Club:* White's.
[Died 6 April 1979

MARCUSE, Herbert, PhD; Professor of Philosophy, University of California at San Diego, since 1965; *b* Berlin, 19 July 1898; *m* Sophie (*d* 1951); one *s*; *m* 1955, Inge Werner (*d* 1973); two step-*s*; *m* 1977, Erica Sherova; American nationality, 1940. *Educ:* Univs of Berlin and Freiberg. Went to USA, 1934; Inst. of Social Research, Columbia Univ., 1934-40; served with Office of Strategic Services and State Dept, 1941-50; Russian Inst., Columbia and Harvard Univs, 1951-53; Prof. of Politics and Philosophy, Brandeis Univ., 1954-65. *Publications:* Reason and Revolution, 1941; Eros and Civilization, 1954; Soviet Marxism, 1958; One-Dimensional Man, 1965; The Ethics of Revolution 1966; Negations, 1968; An Essay on Liberation, 1969; Counterrevolution and Revolt, 1972; Studies in Critical Philosophy, 1972; The Aesthetic Dimension, 1978. *Address* University of California, San Diego, Calif 92038, USA.
[Died 29 July 1979

MARDER, Prof. Arthur (Jacob), CBE (Hon.) 1971; Professor of History, University of California at Irvine, 1964-77, now Emeritus Professor; *b* 8 March 1910; *s* of Maxwell J. Marder and Ida (*née* Greenstein); *m* 1955, Jan North; two *s* one *d*. *Educ:* Harvard Univ. BA 1931; MA 1934; PhD 1936. MA Oxon, 1969; Hon. DLitt Oxon, 1971. Asst Professor of History, University of Oregon, 1936-38; Research Assoc., Bureau of International Research, Harvard Univ., 1939-41; Research Analyst, Office of Strategic Services, 1941-42; Assoc. Professor, Hamilton Coll. 1943-44; Assoc. Professor, University of Hawaii, 1944-51 Professor, 1951-58; Sen. Professor, 1958-64. Visiting Prof. Harvard Univ., 1949-50; Eastman Prof., Oxford, and Fellow of Balliol Coll., 1969-70; Australian-American Educnl Foundn Dist. Visitor, 1979. FRHistS 1966; Fellow, J. S. Guggenheim Foundation, 1939, 1945-46, 1958; grantee, American Philosophical Society, 1956, 1958, 1963, 1966, Rockefeller Foundation, 1943; UK Fulbright Fellow Alt., 1954. Corresp FBA, 1970. Member: American Philosophical Soc., 1972 Council, Amer. Hist. Assoc., 1972-75 (Pres., Pacific Coast Br. 1971-72); Phi Beta Kappa (Foundn Mem., Univ. of Calif Irvine), 1974. Fellow: American Acad. of Arts and Sciences 1972; Japan Foundn, 1976; RUSI, 1977; Nat. Endowment for Humanities, 1978-79. Chesney Memorial Gold Medal of RUSI 1968; Admiralty Board citation, 1970; Dist. Faculty Lectureship Award, Univ. of California, Irvine, 1977. *Publications:* The Anatomy of British Sea Power, 1940 (G. L. Beer Prize, Amer Hist. Assoc., 1941); Portrait of an Admiral, 1952; Fear God and Dread Nought, 3 vols, 1952, 1956, 1959; From the Dreadnought to Scapa Flow, vol 1, 1961, vol 2, 1965, vol 3, 1966 (2nd edn 1978), vol 4, 1969, vol 5, 1970; From the Dardanelles to Oran 1974; Operation Menace, 1976; Old Friends, New Enemies 1981; contributions to American Hist. Review, Journal o Modern History, English Hist. Review, etc. *Recreations:* golf hiking, Chinese cooking. *Address:* 730 Woodland Drive, Santa Barbara, Calif 93108, USA. *T:* (805) 969-4491.
[Died 25 Dec. 1980

MAREK, Kurt W. (pseudonym **C. W. Ceram**); Writer (free-lance 1934-45, and since 1952); *b* Berlin, 20 Jan. 1915; *s* of Max Marek and Anna Marek (*née* Mistol); *m* 1952, Hannelore Schipmann one *s*. *Educ:* Hohenzollern Upper Secondary Sch.; Lessing High Sch.; Berlin Univ. Began journalistic career, 1932; lit. theatre critic, Berlin Newspapers, 1935; staff Die Welt, 1946-50; editor in-chief Rowohlt publ. Hamburg, 1946-52; co-owner and co publ. of Benjamin (weekly for young people), Hamburg, 1946 49. Served from Private to 1st Lieut, Anti-Aircraft Unit German Army, 1938-45. Wrote and directed 6 documentaries about archæology for international television (German production) 1961-62. Member: Archaeological Inst. of America

Amer. Anthropological Assoc. (With Ernest Hemingway) Roman Bancarella Book Award, 1953. *Publications:* (his books have been translated into 26 languages): Gods, Graves and Scholars, 1951; Narrow Pass, Black Mountain, 1955; (ed and Introd.) Diary of an Anonymous Woman: A Woman in Berlin, 1955; Archæology of the Cinema, 1955; A Picture History of Archæology, 1957; Yestermorrow, Notes on Man's Progress, 1965; The World of Archæology, ed. and introd. C. W. Ceram, 1966; The First American, 1971; contribs to professional publications. *Recreation:* travelling. *Address:* (home) Reinbek bei Hamburg, Germany. *T:* 722 2360. *Club:* PEN (Member in Germany and USA). *[Died 12 April 1972.*

MARGAI, Sir Albert (Michael), Kt 1965; Lawyer and Politician, Sierra Leone; *b* 10 Oct. 1910; 6th *s* of late M. E. S. Margai and Ndaneh Margai, Gbangbatoke and Bonthe; *m* 1949, Esther; ten *c. Educ:* St Patrick's Roman Catholic Sch., Bonthe; St Edward's Secondary Sch., Freetown; Middle Temple, London. Male Nurse and Dispenser, 1932-44. Practising Barrister, 1948; Sierra Leone Government: MLC and Minister of Education and Local Government and Welfare, 1950-57; MP 1957; Min. of Natural Resources, 1960; Minister of Finance, 1962; Prime Minister of Sierra Leone and Minister of Defence, 1964-67. Founder Member, People's National Party, 1958-67. Knight Grand Cross of St Gregory (Vatican), 1962. *Recreation:* tennis.
[Died 18 Dec. 1980.

MARION, Dr Léo Edmond, CC (Canada) 1967; MBE 1946; FRSC 1942; FRS (London), 1961; Hon. Professor of Biochemistry; Dean, Faculty of Pure and Applied Science, University of Ottawa, 1965-69, retired; *b* 22 March 1899; *s* of Joseph Marion and Emma Vezina; *m* 1933, Paule Lefort; no *c. Educ:* Queen's (BSc 1926, MSc 1927); McGill (PhD 1929); University of Vienna. Research chemist, National Research Council, 1929-42; Head, Organic Chemistry Section, 1943; Editor in Chief of all Canadian Journals of Research, 1947-65; Vice-President (scientific), National Research Council, Ottawa, 1960-65, Dir, Div. of Chemistry, 1952-63. Hon. Member: Société Chimique de France, 1957; Royal Canadian Inst., Toronto, 1971; President, Chemical Institute of Canada, 1961. President Royal Society of Canada, 1964. Hon. degrees: DSc: Laval, 1954; Ottawa, 1958; Queen's, 1961; British Columbia, 1963; Royal Military Coll., 1965; Carleton, 1965; McGill, 1966; Poznan, 1967; D. de l'U: Montreal, 1961; Paris, 1962; LLD: Toronto, 1962; Saskatchewan, 1968; DCL, Bishop's, 1966. Member American Chemical Society; Association Canadienne-Française pour l'Avancement des Sciences Medal, 1948; Chem. Inst. of Canada Medal, 1956; City of Paris Medal, 1957; Professional Institute of Canada Medal, 1959; Chem. Inst. of Canada Montreal Medal, 1969. *Publications:* chapters in: The Alkaloids; 195 papers on chemistry of alkaloids. *Address:* 211 Wurtemburg Street, Apartment 1413, Ottawa K1N 8R4, Canada. *[Died 16 July 1979.*

MARITAIN, Jacques; Professor Emeritus of Philosophy, Princeton University; Professor of Philosophy, Princeton University, 1948-52; Docteur en Philosophie; Agrégé de l'Université; *b* 18 Nov. 1882; *s* of Paul and Geneviève Maritain; *m* Raissa Oumançoff (decd). *Educ:* Université de Paris. Late Professeur de philosophie à l'Institut Catholique de Paris et à l'Institut d'études médiévales de Toronto. Visiting Prof. at Columbia Univ. and at Princeton Univ., 1940-44; French Ambassador to the Holy See, 1945-48. Grand Prix de Littérature, Académie Française, 1961; Grand Prix National des Lettres, 1963. *Publications:* Art et Scolastique, 1920, 3e édn, 1935, trad., en anglais, 1927; Frontières de la Poésie, 1935; La Philosophie bergsonienne, 1914, 1930; Introduction à la philosophie, 1920, trad. anglaise, 1930; Théonas, 1921, trad. anglaise, 1933; Réflexions sur l'Intelligence, 1923, 1930; Trois Réformateurs, 1925, 1931, trad. anglaise, 1928; Réponse à Jean Cocteau, 1926; Quelques pages sur Léon Bley, 1927; Primauté du Spirituel, 1927, trad. anglaise, 1930; Le Docteur Angélique, 1930, trad. anglaise, 1931; Religion et Culture, 1931, trad. anglaise, 1931; Le Songe de Descartes, 1932; Distinguer pour unir ou Les Degrés du Savoir, 1932; Du Régime temporel et de la Liberté, 1933, trad. anglaise, 1935; Sept Leçons sur l'être, 1934 (trad. anglaise: A Preface to Metaphysics, 1940); La Philosophie de la Nature, 1935; Questions de Conscience, 1938; Humanisme Intégral, 1936 (trad. anglaise: True Humanism, 1939); Anti-semitism; The Living Thoughts of St Paul; A travers le Désastre; Redeeming the Time; The Rights of Man and Natural Law; Christianity and Democracy; De Bergson à Thomas d'Aquin; Principes d'une Politique humaniste; Messages; Pour la Justice; Education at the Crossroads, 1939-45; La Personne et le Bien commun; Court Traité de l'Existence et de l'Existant, 1947; Man and the State, 1951; The Range of Reason, 1952; Creative Intuition in Art and Poetry, 1953; On the Philosophy of History, 1957; Reflections on America, 1958;

The Responsibility of the Artist, 1960; La Philosophie Morale, 1960; Eng. trans. (Moral Philosophy), 1964; On the Use of Philosophy, 1961; Dieu et la permission du mal, 1963, Eng. trans. 1966; Carnet de Notes, 1965; Le Paysan de la Garonne, 1966, Eng. trans. 1968; De la grâce et de l'humanité de Jésus, 1967; De l'Eglise du Christ, 1971. With Madame Raïssa Maritain: De la vie d'Oraison, 1925, 1933, Eng. trans., 1928; Situation de la poésie, 1938. *[Died 28 April 1973.*

MARK-WARDLAW, Rear-Adm. (retired) Alexander Livingston Penrose; Governing Director, Loseberry Enterprises; UK Representative, 1st Genoa International Nautical and Telecommunications Exhibition, 1963; President of Honour, International Cargo Handling Co-ordination Association (ICHCA), since Sept. 1959 (Co-Founder and President Executive, 1951-59); UK Representative: CRM Milan; Autronica Norway; Werkspoor NV; Vredestein-International of The Hague; Rudolf Bauer, Austria; *b* 9 March 1891; *s* of late Colonel W. L. P. Mark-Wardlaw, North Staffordshire Regt, and late Mrs Florence Emily Mark-Wardlaw; *m* 1916, Irene Marjorie Cochran Carr (*d* 1961); one *s* one *d. Educ:* Fosters, Stubbington; RN Colleges, Osborne and Dartmouth. Comd submarines during European War, 1914-18; selected as 1st specialist (E,) from Exec. Branch under Selborne Fisher Scheme, 1918, with permanent retention of Military Command status. Asst Naval Attaché, Washington, 1934-37; served War of 1939-45, with Home Fleet; Combined Operations HQ, as acting Rear-Admiral, 1942-44; ADC to the King, 1943; served on staff of Allied Naval C-in-C X Force and subs. Allied Naval C-in-C Germany, 1944-46; promoted for war services of particular merit to rank of Rear-Admiral, 1946; Control Office for Germany and Austria, 1946; Shipping Adviser Foreign Office, 1949, Military Security Board, Germany, 1950. MRINA, 1937. MIMechE 1948. MIMarE 1951; Assoc. Institute of Transport. Member: Fertilizer Society; Inst. of Navigation; Inst. of Directors. Military Medal for Greece, Order of the Redeemer, Greece, 1931. *Recreation:* gardening. *Address:* Loseberry, Claygate, Surrey. *T:* Esher 62882. *Club:* Naval and Military.
[Died 9 Dec. 1975.

MARKELIUS, Sven Gottfrid; Architect; Professor *hc* ; *b* Stockholm 25 Oct. 1889; *m* 1938, Ka (*née* Simon); three *s* two *d. Educ:* Stockholm Institute of Technology; Dept of Architecture, Royal Academy of Fine Arts. Chief of Planning Section, Royal Board of Building, Stockholm, 1938-44; City Planning Director, Stockholm, 1944-54. Visiting Professor: Yale, 1949; MIT 1962; University of California, Berkeley, 1962. Member, Swedish Royal Academy of Fine Arts, 1942; President Federation of Swedish Architects Societies, 1953-56; Member World Academy of Art and Science; Member Group of Consultants of UN Headquarters in New York, 1947; Member Advisory Cttee of UNESCO Headquarters in Paris, 1952- (Member Art Cttee, 1954-56). Works include: Student's Clubhouse, Stockholm Inst. of Technology, 1929; Hälsingborg Concert Hall, 1932; Cooperative Apartment Hotel, Stockholm, 1935; Office Bldg for Stockholm Builders' Assoc., 1937; Swedish Pavilion, New York World Fair, 1939; Trade Union Centre, Linköping, 1953; Trade Union Centre, Stockholm, 1960; Forest Industries Centre, Stockholm, 1961; Bürgerhaus, Giessen, W Germany, 1965; Park Hotel, Stockholm, 1967; Sweden House, Stockholm, 1968; private and apartment houses. Howland Memorial Prize, Yale Univ., 1949; Medal of St Erik, 1959; Medal of Prince Eugen, 1961; Royal Gold Medal, RIBA, 1962. Dr ing *hc* Techn. Hochschule Aachen, 1966. *Publications:* Acceptera (in collaboration), 1930. Articles in professional journals. *Address:* Kevingestrand 5, Danderyd, Sweden. *T:* 755 4466.
[Died 27 Feb. 1972.

MARKER, Edwin Henry Simon, CB 1946; Under-Secretary, Board of Trade, 1946-52; retired from Civil Service, 1952; *b* 22 Jan. 1888; *s* of late Alfred H. Marker, Parkwood, Sevenoaks, Kent; *m* 1931, Christina, *er d* of late G. J. Francis; two *s* two *d. Educ:* St Paul's Sch.; Wadham Coll., Oxford. First Class Classical Mods., 1909; First Class Lit. Hum., 1911; entered Board of Trade, 1912; Secretary to Cttee on Shipping and Shipbuilding, 1916; Comptroller, Companies Dept; 1934; Member of Cttee on Compulsory Insurance, 1936; Principal Assistant Secretary, Insurance and Companies Dept, 1941; Member of Cttee on Shares of No Par Value, 1952-53. Visited India as Adviser to Government of India in connection with Indian Company Law amendment, 1953, 1955-56. Elected Hon. Member, Inst. of Directors, 1960. *Address:* 35 Hazlewell Road, Putney, SW15. *T:* 01-788 6728. *Club:* United University.
[Died 13 Feb. 1973.

MARKHAM, Sir F.; see Markham, Sir S. F.

MARKHAM, Roy, FRS 1956; MA, PhD; John Innes Professor of Cell Biology and Director, John Innes Institute, University of East Anglia, Norwich, since 1967; Director, Agricultural Research Council Virus Research Unit, 1960-67 (Hon. Director, 1967-68); *b* 29 Jan. 1916; *m* 1940, Margaret Mullen. *Educ:* St Paul's; Christ's Coll., Cambridge. Fellow of Christ's Coll., Cambridge, 1965-67. Mem. of Council, John Innes Inst., 1964-67. Hon. Mem., Amer. Soc. of Biological Chemists. *Publications:* various. *Address:* John Innes Institute, Colney Lane, Norwich NR4 7UH. *T:* Norwich 52571; 10 Daniels Road, Norwich NR4 6Q2. *T:* Norwich 53429.   *[Died 16 Nov. 1979.*

MARKHAM, Sir (Sydney) Frank, Kt 1953; DL; Company Director; Major psc on General List (served with 3rd Army Corps in France and with 1st Army in N Africa, 2nd Army in Germany); *b* 19 Oct. 1897; *m* 1928, Frances, *d* of S. F. Lowman; three *s* two *d. Educ:* Wadham Coll., Oxford. MA, BLitt, Dip. Econ. MP (Lab) Rochester (Chatham Div.), 1929-31; MP (Nat) S Nottingham, 1935-45; MP (C) Buckingham Div. of Bucks, 1951-64. Parliamentary Private Sec. to Prime Minister, 1931-32, to the Lord Pres. of the Council, 1936-37; Pres. Museums Association, 1939-42; Chm. Parliamentary Science Cttee, 1938-41; Mem. Select Cttee on Estimates, 1953-62, Chm., 1962-64; Chm. Parliamentary Delegation to Kenya, 1961, to Malta, 1963 and to Far East, 1964. DL Beds, 1966. *Publications:* Climate and the Energy of Nations, 1942 (American edn, 1944); A History of Stony Stratford, 1951; A History of Milton Keynes and District, 1973. *Address:* Heath Park Road, Leighton Buzzard, Beds. *T:* Leighton Buzzard 67103.   *[Died 13 Oct. 1975.*

MARKS, Derek John; Director, since 1965, and Special Adviser to the Chairman, since 1971, Beaverbrook Newspapers; *b* 15 Jan. 1921; *e s* of late Mr and Mrs H. J. Marks; *m* 1942, Jean, *d* of Edward Greenhalgh and late Mrs Emily Greenhalgh, Edgerton, Huddersfield; one *s* two *d. Educ:* Seaford Coll. RAF, 1940-46. Huddersfield Examiner, 1946-48; East African Standard (Nairobi), 1948-49; Yorkshire Post (London), 1950-52; Daily Express, 1952. Various appts within Beaverbrook Newspapers; finally Dep. Editor, Evening Standard until 1965; Editor of Daily Express, 1965-71. Hon LLD New Brunswick, 1971. *Address:* 121-128 Fleet Street, EC4. *T:* 01-353 8000. *Club:* Press.   *[Died 8 Feb. 1975.*

MARLAR, Edward Alfred Geoffrey, MBE 1944; MA, LLB Cantab; retired as Headmaster of Whitgift School, Croydon (1946-July 1961); *b* 2 Jan. 1901; *s* of J. F. Marlar; *m* 1924, Winifred Stevens; one *s* one *d. Educ:* Brighton Coll.; Selwyn Coll., Cambridge (Hons History and Law). Senior History Master, Dunstable Gram. Sch., 1922-27; Senior History and VIth Form Master, Worksop Coll., 1927-34; Headmaster, Moulton Gram. Sch., 1934-37; Headmaster, King Edward VI Sch., Lichfield, 1937-46. *Address:* Warren Edge, Salisbury Road, Eastbourne, E Sussex.   *[Died 24 April 1978.*

MARLBOROUGH, 10th Duke of, *cr* 1702; **John Albert Edward William Spencer-Churchill;** Baron Spencer, 1603; Earl of Sunderland, 1643; Baron Churchill, 1685; Earl of Marlborough, 1689; Marquis of Blandford, 1702; Prince of the Holy Roman Empire; Prince of Mindelheim in Suabia; Captain, 1st Life Guards, 1916; retired, 1927; Military liaison officer to Regional Commander, Southern Region, 1942; Lt-Col liaison officer, US Forces, 1942-45; *b* 18 Sept. 1897; *e s* of 9th Duke and Consuelo (*d* 1964), *d* of late W. K. Vanderbilt, New York; *S* father, 1934; *m* 1st, 1920, Hon. Mary Cadogan, CBE 1953 (*d* 1961), *d* of late Viscount Chelsea, and late Lady Charles Montagu; two *s* three *d*; 2nd, 1972, Mrs F. Laura Canfield. *Educ:* Eton. Mayor of Woodstock, 1937-38, 1938-39. *Heir: s* Marquess of Blandford. *Address:* Blenheim Palace, Woodstock, Oxon.
   [Died 11 March 1972.

MARLING, Lt-Col Sir John Stanley Vincent, 4th Bt, *cr* 1882; OBE 1945; *b* 26 July 1910; *s* of Sir Charles Murray Marling, GCMG, CB, and Lucia, CBE (*d* 1927), *o c* of late Maj.-Gen. Sir John Ramsay Slade, KCB; *S* uncle, 1936; *m* 1st, 1939, Georgina Brenda (Betty) (marr. diss., 1957, she *d* 1961), *o c* of late Henry Edward Fitzroy-Somerset; one *s* three *d*; 2nd, 1957, Marjorie Frances Esclairmonde, *widow* of Major Gustavus March-Phillipps, and 3rd *d* of late Sir Francis Hugh Stewart, CIE. *Educ:* Winchester Coll.; RMC, Sandhurst. Joined 17th/21st Lancers, 1930; retired 1947. *Heir: s* Charles William Somerset Marling, *b* 2 June 1951. *Address:* Woodcray Manor Farm, Wokingham, Berks.   *[Died 20 Sept. 1977.*

MARPLES, Baron *cr* 1974 (Life Peer), of Wallasey; **Alfred Ernest Marples,** PC 1957; FCA; *b* 9 Dec. 1907; *s* of late Alfred Ernest Marples and late Mary Marples; *m* 1956, Mrs Ruth Dobson. *Educ:* Stretford Gram. Sch. Chartered Accountant, 1928; joined London Scottish, July 1939; 2nd Lt Royal Artillery,

Jan. 1941; Captain, 1941. MP (C) Wallasey, 1945-Feb. 1974; Parly Sec., Ministry of Housing and Local Government, 1951-54; Joint Parliamentary Sec., Ministry of Pensions and National Insurance, Oct. 1954-Dec. 1955; Postmaster-Gen., 1957-59; Minister of Transport, Oct 1959-64, and Chm., Nationalized Transport Advisory Council, 1963-64; Shadow Minister of Technology, 1964-66; Sponsor, Conservative Party Public Sector Research Unit, 1967-70. Internat. Dir, Purolator Services Inc. (USA), 1970-76; Dir, Purolator Services Ltd (UK), 1970-76. Hon. Freeman, Borough of Wallasey, 1970. *Publication:* The Road to Prosperity, 1947. *Recreations:* tennis, mountaineering. *Address:* Les Laverts, Fleurie 69820, France.
   [Died 6 July 1978.

MARQUAND, Rt. Hon. Hilary Adair, PC 1949; MA, DSc; Deputy Chairman, National Board for Prices and Incomes, 1965-68; *b* 24 Dec. 1901; *s* of Alfred Marquand and Mary Adair; *m* 1929, Rachel Eluned, BA, *d* of D. J. Rees, Glanyronen, Ystalyfera; two *s* one *d. Educ:* Cardiff High Sch.; University Coll., Cardiff (State Scholar). BA Wales (1st Cl. Hons History, 1923; 1st Cl. Hons Economics, 1924); Gladstone and Cobden prizeman; MA (with Distinction), 1928; DSc 1938; Laura Spelman Rockefeller Fellow in Social Sciences in the USA, 1925-26; Lecturer in Economics, Univ. of Birmingham, 1926-30; Prof. of Industrial Relations, University Coll., Cardiff, 1930-45, Mem. Council, 1967-; Dir of Industrial Surveys of South Wales, 1931 and 1936; Mem. Cardiff Advisory Cttee UAB; spent a year in the USA in the study of Industrial Relations, 1932-33; Visiting Prof. of Economics, Wisconsin Univ., 1938-39; Acting Principal, Board of Trade, 1940-41, and Dep. Controller, Wales Div., Ministry of Labour, 1941-42; Labour Adviser Ministry of Production, 1943-44; MP (Lab) East Cardiff, 1945-50, East Div. of Middlesbrough, 1950-61; Sec. for Overseas Trade, 1945-57; Paymaster-Gen., 1947-48; Min. of Pensions, 1948-51; Min. of Health, Jan.-Oct. 1951. Hon. Mem. Phi Beta Kappa; Mem. Labour Party since 1920; Lecture Tours for Brit. Council in India, Pakistan and Ceylon, 1952-53, in WI, 1954 and 1959 and in Finland, 1957. Chm. Information Cttee Inter-Parl. Union, London Conf., 1957 and Mem. delegns to Turkey, 1953 and Finland, 1955; Representative at Assemblies of Council of Europe and W European Union, 1957-59. Mem. Commonwealth Parl. Assoc. Conf., 1961; Leader delegn to Gambia and Sierra Leone. Sidney Hillman Lecturer, Univ. of Wisconsin, 1956. Dir, Internat. Inst. for Labour Studies (Geneva), Dec. 1961-April 1965. *Publications:* Dynamics of Industrial Combination, 1931; Industrial Survey of South Wales (part author), 1932; Industrial Relations in the USA 1934; South Wales Needs a Plan, 1936; Second Industrial Survey of South Wales (joint), 1937; Organized Labour in Four Continents (joint), 1939; Articles and Reviews in Political Quarterly, The Times, Manchester Guardian, Economic Journal, Observer, etc. *Recreations:* travel, gardening.   *[Died 6 Nov. 1972.*

MARRACK, Rear-Adm. Hugh Richard, CBE 1943; DSC 1918; Rear-Admiral, retired; *b* 5 July 1888; *s* of late John Reed Marrack, Tiverton, N Devon; *m* 1917, Christine (*d* 1969), *widow* of Lt George Pilkington, RN, and *d* of late A. M. Hallett; no *c. Educ:* Blundell's Sch., Tiverton; HMS Britannia. Joined HMS Britannia, 1902; Sub-Lt, Submarine Branch of Navy, 1908; Commanded HM Submarine A10, 1911-12; European War, 1914-18, Commanded HM Submarines C19 and E51 (minelayer), 1912-19; Commanded HM Submarines L71, K8, M3 and HM Australian Submarine Oxley, 1918-28; Commanded Portland Submarine Flotilla, 1929-31; Commanded China Submarine Flotilla, 1931-33; Commanded HMS Carlisle, 1934-37; Commodore i/c and Supt Sheerness, 1939-43; Commodore Supt Gibraltar, 1943-45; Comdr, 1923; Captain, 1931; ADC to the King, 1940; Rear-Adm., 1941; retired, 1941. *Address:* Flat 2, Chessington, Craneswater Park, Southsea, Hants.   *[Died 12 Feb. 1972.*

MARRACK, Prof. Emeritus John Richardson, DSO 1917; MC; Emeritus Professor of Chemical Pathology, London University; *b* 26 Nov. 1886; *s* of late John Reed Marrack; *m* 1st, 1913, Bertha Ada Fitzgerald Whiddington; one *s*; 2nd, 1922, Alice May Swaffield Milward; three *s. Educ:* Blundell's Sch., Tiverton; Cambridge Univ. (MA, MD); London Hosp. Late Prof. of Chemical Pathology at London Hosp. Medical Coll. and Univ. Lecturer Chemical Pathology, Cambridge Univ.; late Visiting Prof., University of Texas; John Lucas Walker Student, Cambridge Univ., Beit Memorial Fellow, Fellow St John's Coll., Cambridge. Served European War, 1914-19 (despatches, DSO, MC). *Publications:* The Chemistry of Antigens and Antibodies, MRC Report; (with Dr Panton) Clinical Pathology; Food and Planning, 1942. *Recreation:* walking. *Address:* 420 Mulberry Lane, Bellaire, Texas 77401, USA.   *[Died 13 June 1976.*

MARRIC, J. J.; *see under* Creasey, John.

MARRIOTT, Cyril Herbert Alfred, CBE 1949; *b* Chambly, Quebec, 28 Sept. 1897; *s* of Basil Sterling Talbot Marriott and Daisy Cecilia Bareham; *m* 1919, Helen Milne (*d* 1964); one *s* two *d*. *Educ:* Trent Coll. Entered Royal Navy as Asst Clerk, 1915; served in HMS Africa and as Secretary's Clerk to Admiral Sir John R. Jellicoe in HMS Iron Duke and to Admiral Sir David Beatty in HMS Iron Duke and Queen Elizabeth, and to Rear-Admiral Sir Wm E. Goodenough in HMS Orion, and to Rear-Admiral Maurice Woollcombe in HMS Colossus, and as Sec. to Flag Captain Arthur J. Davies in HMS King George V; left Navy 1919, as Acting Paymaster Sub-Lt to enter Consular Service; Vice-Consul Copenhagen, 1919; Braila, 1921; Acting Consul, Stockholm, 1924; Vice-Consul, New York, 1924; Antwerp, 1927; Panama (Chargé d'Affaires in 1933), 1931; Consul-General, Galatz, and Deputy British Commissioner on European Commission of the Danube, 1934; Consul, Bahia, 1937-41; Consul, Porto Alegre, 1941-44; Consul-General, Counsellor, and Counsellor (Commercial), Copenhagen, 1945-48; Political Adviser to GOC British Forces in Palestine, April-June 1948; Consul-General Haifa, 1948-49. Consul-General, Zürich, 1949-57. Appeals Sec., Crusade of Rescue, 1957-66. *Address:* Rivermead, The Street, Castle Eaton, Wilts SN6 6JZ. *T:* Kempsford 298.   [*Died* 8 *Sept.* 1977.

MARRIOTT, Maj.-Gen. Sir John (Charles Oakes), KCVO 1950 (CVO 1937; MVO 1935); CB 1947; DSO 1917; MC; *b* 1895; *s* of late Charles Marriott of Stowmarket, Suffolk; *m* 1920, Maud (*d* 1960), *d* of Otto Kahn, New York; one *s*. *Educ:* Repton. Entered Northants Regt, 1914; served European War, 1915-18 (wounded, despatches, MC, DSO, Croix de Guerre); Military Attaché's Staff, Washington, 1919-20; transferred to Scots Guards, 1920; DAA & QMG London District, 1933-37; commanded 2nd Bn Scots Guards, 1938; served Middle East, 1940-42 (Bar to DSO); commanded 29 Indian Inf. Bde and 201 Guards Bde. Commander Guards Div. 1945-47; GOC London District, 1947-50; retd pay, 1950. *Address:* 7 Pelham Crescent, SW7. *Clubs:* Cavalry and Guards, Turf. [*Died* 11 *Sept.* 1978.

MARRIOTT, Patrick Arthur; retired as Governor, HM Prison, Parkhurst, Isle of Wight (1951-59); *b* 20 July 1899; *s* of late Canon P. A. R. Marriott, St George's Coll., Jerusalem, and late Gertrude E. Marriott; *m* 1929, Honor Chalfont, *d* of late Major W. W. Blackden, Royal Munster Fusiliers, and Mrs Blackden, Byways, Yateley, Hants; two *s*. *Educ:* Christ's Hospital. Sub. Lieut RNAS and Lieut RAF, 1917-21; Lieut British North Borneo Armed Constabulary, 1924-29; joined HM Prison Service as Governor, Class IV, 1929, and has been Governor of Nottingham, Lincoln, Brixton, Pentonville and Parkhurst Prisons. Captain, Hampshire Yeomanry, 1929-35; Major, Royal Artillery, 1939-45. *Address:* Hunters Lodge, Virginstowe, Beaworthy, Devon.   [*Died* 3 *June* 1980.

MARRIOTT, Richard Michael Harris; Director, Williams de Broe Hill Chaplin & Co., since 1967; *b* 24 Nov. 1926; *s* of Reginald Harris Marriott and Olive Barbara Marriott (*née* Mason); *m* 1951, Anne Unity Alice Brine; three *s*. *Educ:* Tonbridge School. Commnd KRRC, served 1945-47; re-called to Army for Korean Emergency, 1950-51. Member of Stock Exchange, 1949; Mem. Stock Exchange Council, 1971; Chairman of Stock Exchange, 1975. *Recreations:* cricket, vintage cars. *Address:* Barrwood, Shipbourne, Kent. *Clubs:* Bath, City of London.   [*Died* 11 *Dec.* 1975.

MARRIS, Eric Denyer, CB 1950; *b* 27 July 1891; 2nd *s* of late George Suffield Marris, Birmingham, and late Mary Twining, *d* of William Denyer George; *m* 1921, Phyllis (*d* 1970), *d* of late T. H. F. Lapthorn, JP, Portsmouth; two *s* one *d*. *Educ:* Bromsgrove Sch., Worcs; Emmanuel Coll., Cambridge. Mathematical Tripos, 1913. Lieut, Warwicks Regt, 1915-19. Board of Education and Ministry of Education, 1919; Under-Sec., Ministry of Education, 1947-51; seconded to Ministry of Food, 1939-40; retired, 1951. *Address:* 78 Heath Road, Petersfield, Hants.   [*Died* 16 *April* 1976.

MARSH, Rt. Rev. Donald Ben, DD; Bishop of the Arctic, since 1950; *b* 24 Nov. 1903; *s* of William John Marsh and Kathleen Daisy (*née* Peters); *m* 1933, Winifred Florence (*née* Petchey); one *s* two *d*. *Educ:* Emmanuel Coll., Saskatchewan; Hon. DD 1950. Deacon, 1926; priest, 1929, Keewatin. Missionary at Eskimo Point, 1926-44; Incumbent of All Saints Cathedral, Aklavik, Diocese of the Arctic, 1944-47; Archdeacon of Baffin Land, 1939-44; Archdeacon of Aklavik, 1944-50; Administrator of Diocese of the Arctic, 1949-50. *Recreation:* photography. *Address:* 30 Westwood Lane, Thornhill, Ont., Canada; 1055 Avenue Road, Toronto, Ont., Canada. *T:* 481.2263.
                                          [*Died* 5 *Feb.* 1973.

MARSH, Maj.-Gen. Edward Bertram, MC 1918; Retired Army Officer; Chairman, RAMC Charities General Fund, 1958-71; *b* 3 March 1890; *s* of late Dr N. Percy Marsh, Liverpool; *m* 1920, Stephanie Maud, *o c* of late Sir Edward A. Gait, KCSI, CIE; one *s* (and one *s* decd). *Educ:* Liverpool Coll.; Liverpool Univ.; Guy's Hospital. MB, ChB (Hons) Liverpool, 1913; MRCP 1925. Served in 1st W Lancs Field Amb. (TA) as Driver, 1908-12; Lieut RAMC (SR) Sept. 3, 1914; Reg. Commn, 1918. Served European War, 1914-18, BEF (despatches twice). Served Waziristan Field Force, 1919-20 (Medal and two clasps); Lieut-Col 1937; Cons. Phys. Middle East, 1938-39. Served War of 1939-45; Middle East, UK, and as DDMS Gibraltar, 1942-44; Col 1943, Temp. Maj.-Gen. 1946. Comdt, Royal Army Med. Coll., 1946-48; retired 1949 with hon. rank Maj.-Gen. *Recreations:* golf, gardening. *Address:* 14 Orchard Rise, Kingston Hill, Surrey. *T:* 01-942 8688.   [*Died* 7 *April* 1976.

MARSH SMITH, Reginald Norman, CSI 1946; CIE 1942; KPM; *b* 1891; *s* of Capt. S. Marsh Smith, RAVC; *m* 1919; one *s*. *Educ:* Bromsgrove Sch. Indian Police, 1911; Inspector-General Police, Gwalior State, 1936 and 1946; Deputy Inspector-General Police, UP, 1939; Sec. to Govt United Provinces Rationing Dept; Inspector-General Police; Madhya Bharat, India, 1948; retired, 1949. KPM 1925; Indian Police Medal, 1932; Bar to King's Police Medal, 1934. *Address:* The Croft, Nunthorpe, Teesside, Yorks.   [*Died* 18 *May* 1975.

MARSHALL, Comdr Sir Douglas, Kt 1963; RNVR; *b* 2 Oct. 1906; *s* of Captain William Worth Marshall, 63rd Punjab LI; *m* 1st, 1929, Joan Annette Sherry (*d* 1952); one *d*; 2nd, 1953, Mrs Peter Symons; one *d*. *Educ:* Plymouth Coll. Director: Alfred Booth & Co. Ltd; Friends Provident Ltd. Joined Trade Division, Admiralty, Sept. 1939; Lieut RNVR 1939; Commander, 1944; on Staff of Allied Naval Commander Expeditionary Force, 1944-45; Post-Hostilities Plans War Cabinet Sub-Cttee, 1943. MP (C) Bodmin Div. of Cornwall, 1945-64. Mem. Public Accounts Cttee, 1951-53; Mem. Inter-Parliamentary Delegn to Yugoslavia, 1950, to Turkey, 1959; Hon. Mem., Commonwealth Parly. Assoc. (Leader, Delegns to WI 1953 and 1963; also Leader Delegn to Basutoland, Bechuanaland and Swaziland, 1964). Member: FZS; RHS; Council of Salmon and Trout Assoc.; Marine Biological Assoc. of UK; Vice-Pres., The Men of the Trees. Licensed Reader of Diocese of Cornwall. Hon. Freeman, Borough of Bodmin, 1965. Coronation Medal, 1953. *Recreations:* fishing, shooting and travel. *Address:* Hatt House, near Saltash, Cornwall. *T:* Saltash 2669; Pembroke Cottage, Fowey, Cornwall. *Clubs:* Carlton, Beefsteak, MCC, Naval; (Hon. Mem.) House of Commons Yacht; Royal Fowey Yacht (Fowey).   [*Died* 24 *Aug.* 1976.

MARSHALL, Rt. Rev. Guy, MBE 1943; Vicar of Blakesley with Adstone and Hon. Assistant Bishop, Diocese of Peterborough, since 1974; *b* 5 Nov. 1909; *s* of Edgar Breedon Marshall and Marion (*née* Worsley); *m* 1st, 1936, Dorothy Gladys Whiting (*d* 1975); three *s* one *d*; 2nd, 1977, Harriet Ethel, *d* of Rev. J. J. Moore. *Educ:* Prince Henry's Grammar Sch., Otley; University Coll., Durham; King's Coll., London. AKC 1936. Deacon 1936, Priest 1937. Curate, St Andrew's, Stoke Newington, 1936-38; Chaplain, Missions to Seamen in Southampton, Buenos Aires and Rosario, 1938-42; Chaplain, St Andrew's Seafarers' Chapel, Rosario, 1942-44; Rector, Canon and Sub-Dean, St John's Cath., Buenos Aires, 1944-52; Rector, Stoke Bruerne with Grafton Regis and Alderton, 1953-56; Chaplain, Missions to Seamen, Toronto, 1956-67 and Rector, St Stephen's, Toronto, 1958-67; Bishop Suffragan of Trinidad and Tobago for work in Venezuela, 1967; Bishop in Venezuela, 1972, resigned 1974. *Recreations:* reading, bridge, Rugby Union football, cricket. *Address:* The Vicarage, Blakesley, Towcester, Northants. *T:* Blakesley 507. *Club:* Royal Commonwealth Society.
                                          [*Died* 3 *Aug.* 1978.

MARSHALL, Howard Percival; *b* 22 Aug. 1900; *o s* of Percival Marshall; *m* 1st, 1925, Ruth ffolliott Shackle; two *s*; 2nd, 1944, Nerina Wentworth Day, *d* of late Major Cameron Shute. *Educ:* Haileybury Coll.; Oriel Coll., Oxford. Special correspondent Westminster Gazette, Daily Telegraph, Daily Mail, etc; Asst News Editor BBC, 1928; BBC Sports and Special Events Commentator, 1930-; Director of Public Relations, Ministry of Food, 1940-43; Dir of War Reporting and War Correspondent, BBC, 1943-45 (N Africa and Invasion of Europe); Dir, Personnel and Public Relations, Richard Thomas and Baldwins Ltd, 1945-64. *Publications:* Slum (book on housing); With Scott to the Pole; (with W. W. Wakefield) Rugger; (with H. R. L. Sheppard) Fiery Grains; Under Big Ben; Over to Tunis; Oxford v. Cambridge: the Story of the University Rugby Match; Coronation Day; Men Against Everest; Anthologies of Boxing, Cricket, Rugger; Reflection on a River; ed, Dent's Modern Sports Series; Co-Founder, The Angling Times and Trout and

Salmon. *Recreation:* fishing. *Address:* Easton Lodge, Easton, near Newbury, Berks. *T:* Boxford 229. *Club:* Savile.
[*Died* 27 *Oct.* 1973.

MARSHALL, Sir James, Kt 1953; DL; JP; *b* 23 Oct. 1894; *s* of James and Julia Harriet Marshall, Hounslow, Middlesex; *m* 1939, May Florence Kent (*d* 1972); two *s* two *d. Educ:* Whitgift, Croydon. Croydon Borough: Councillor, 1928; Alderman, 1936-68; Mayor, 1945-46. Chm., Croydon Food Control Cttee, 1939-53; Mem. Crawley Development Corporation, 1945-61; Chm. Whitgift Governors, 1944-69. JP 1937; DL Surrey, 1952; DL Greater London, 1966. FRPSL. *Recreations:* lawn tennis, horticulture, philately. *Address:* 66 Croham Road, South Croydon, Surrey. *T:* 01-680 8964. *Club:* Royal Automobile.
[*Died* 20 *Feb.* 1979.

MARSHALL, Norman, CBE 1975; play producer; *b* 16 Nov. 1901; *s* of Lt-Col D. G. Marshall, IMS, and Elizabeth Mackie. *Educ:* Edinburgh Academy; Worcester Coll., Oxford. Producer, Cambridge Festival Theatre, 1926-33; directed Gate Theatre, 1934-40. Produced many plays in West End, including Parnell, 1936, Victoria Regina, 1937, Of Mice and Men, 1939, The Petrified Forest, 1942, Uncle Vanya, 1943, The First Gentleman, 1946, The Indifferent Shepherd, 1948. Later did a series of productions in countries abroad, including France, Germany, Italy, Israel, India and Pakistan. Shute Lecturer on the Art of the Theatre, Liverpool Univ., 1951. Head of Drama for Associated-Rediffusion Television, 1955-59. Chairman: British Council's Adv. Cttee on Drama, 1961-68; British Theatre Assoc., 1965-76; Joint Chm., National Theatre Building Cttee; Vice-Chm., Theatre's Advisory Council, 1963-74; Pres., Assoc. of British Theatre Technicians (Chm., 1961-73). Governor, Old Vic. Lectures: tours of Canada and Australia, 1961 and 1962; Univs of Cape Town and Natal, 1964; tour of Norway, Sweden, Denmark and Finland, 1973. Directed Romeo and Juliet, and Hamlet, South Africa; Directed: at Chichester Theatre Festival, 1966; at Canterbury Festival, 1970. Midsummer Prize, Corp. of London, 1971. *Publications:* The Other Theatre, 1948; The Producer and the Play, 1957, 3rd edn 1975. *Address:* 9 Arundel Court, Jubilee Place, SW3. *T:* 01-352 0456. *Club:* Garrick.
[*Died* 7 *Nov.* 1980.

MARSHALL, Robert, MD (with distinction), DPH Queen's University, Belfast; FRCP; FRCPI; FRCPS (Hon.); retired; Hon. Governor and Consulting Physician at the Royal Victoria Hospital and Ulster Hospital, Belfast; *b* 9 Sept. 1889; *s* of late W. J. Marshall, JP, Belfast, and Bertha Shaw; *m* 1916, Evelyn Mary, *d* of William Marshall, Bangor, Co. Down; (one *s* killed on active service, 1945) one *d. Educ:* Methodist Coll. and Queen's Univ., Belfast. MB with Hons and 1st place in medicine, 1912; Resident Medical Officer, National Hosp. for Diseases of Heart, London, 1914; joined RAMC Aug. 1914; served in France with 1st and 3rd Cavalry Divisions; Mem., Royal College of Physicians of Ireland, 1920, Fellow, 1921 and Censor to the Coll., 1930-33; FRCP; formerly: Mem. of Senate and Clinical Lectr in Medicine Queen's Univ. of Belfast; External Examiner in Medicine of University of Glasgow and Trinity Coll., Dublin. Hon. Mem. of the Post-Graduate Medical Assoc. of America; Hon. Fellow of the Royal College of Physicians and Surgeons of Glasgow; Senior Mem., Assoc. of Physicians of Great Britain and Ireland, British Cardiac Soc., and British Paediatric Assoc.; Hon. Fellow, Ulster Medical Soc. (Pres., 1942-43); Fellow, British Medical Assoc. OStJ. Hon. LLD Queen's University, Belfast, 1970. *Publications:* The Book of Belfast, British Medical Association, 1937; The Royal Victoria Hospital, Belfast, 1903-53; and various papers on medical and cardiological subjects. *Recreations:* reading, photography. *Address:* 3 Harberton Avenue, Belfast BT9 6PH. *T:* Belfast 665853.
[*Died* 24 *March* 1975.

MARSHALL, Robert Smith, CBE 1954; Animal Health Adviser, Department of Technical Co-operation, 1961-63 (to the Secretary of State for the Colonies, 1955-61), retired; *b* 5 April 1902; *s* of late Rev. Thomas Marshall, Dalziel North Manse, Motherwell; *m* 1937, Agnes Inglis Melville; one *d. Educ:* Hamilton Academy; West of Scotland Agricultural Coll.; Glasgow Veterinary Coll. NDA, NDD, 1923; MRCVS 1926; DVSM (Edinburgh) 1927; Academic Diploma of Bacteriology (London) 1929. Asst Veterinary Pathologist, Nigeria, 1929-38; Sen. Veterinary Research Officer, Nigeria, 1938-44; Principal, Veterinary Sch., Nigeria, 1944-48; Dep. Dir Veterinary Services, Nigeria, 1948-51; Inspector-Gen., Animal Health Services, Nigeria, 1951-55. *Publications:* scientific papers in Jl of Bacteriology and Jl of Comparative Pathology. *Recreations:* golf, fishing. *Address:* Hazelrig, Victoria Road, Lundin Links, Fife. *T:* Lundin Links 297.
[*Died* 27 *Sept.* 1976.

MARSHALL, Sheina Macalister, OBE 1966; FRS 1963; FRSE; DSc (Glasgow); Zoologist at the Marine Station, Millport, 1922-64; *b* 20 April 1896; *d* of John Nairn Marshall, MD, and Jean Colville Binnie. *Educ:* home; Rothesay Academy; St Margaret's Sch., Polmont; Glasgow Univ. Carnegie Fellowship, 1920-22; Zoologist, Millport, 1922. Mem., Great Barrier Reef Expedition, 1928-29. *Publications:* (with Dr A. P. Orr): The Biology of a Marine Copepod, *Calanus finmarchicus,* 1955; Seashores, 1965; The Fertile Sea, 1969; papers in Jl Marine Biological Assoc. of the UK and elsewhere. *Recreations:* walking, embroidery. *Address:* Bellevue, Millport, Isle of Cumbrae. *T:* Millport 406.
[*Died* 7 *April* 1977.

MARSHALL, Sir Sidney Horatio, Kt 1952; JP; DL; Alderman Surrey County Council, since 1941 (Chairman, 1947-50; Chairman Education Committee since 1942); Alderman Sutton and Cheam Boro' Council; Hon. Freeman of Sutton and Cheam, 1948; *b* 17 July 1882; *s* of William Robert Marshall, Mitcham; unmarried. *Educ:* Elementary and Private Schs. In industry in Food, Chemical and Dye Industry. Chm. several companies. JP 1937; Surrey County Councillor, 1931; Chm. Sutton and Cheam UDC, 1932-34; Charter Mayor, 1934; Mayor, 1936-37, Dep. Mayor, 1935 and 1937-38; Chm. Surrey assistance board advisory cttee; Sutton and District juvenile advisory cttee; Member: Surrey agricultural wages cttee; London tribunal for hearing conscientious objectors; Educational Trust for Visual Aids. DL Surrey, 1950. MP (C) for Sutton and Cheam, 1945-54. *Recreations:* mainly own work, plus listening to good music and reading. *Address:* 66 The Crescent, Belmont, Surrey. *T:* 01-642 1417; Headley Grove Farm, Epsom. *T:* Headley 95. *Club:* Constitutional.
[*Died* 28 *March* 1973.

MARSHALL, Prof. William Thomas; Regius Professor of Civil Engineering, University of Glasgow, since 1952; *b* 14 Oct. 1907; *s* of Thomas and Edith Marshall; *m* 1939, Margaret Ewing Adam; one *s* one *d. Educ:* Westminster City Sch.; Imperial Coll. of Science. Reinforced Concrete Designer with British Reinforced Concrete Eng. Co. Ltd, Stafford, 1929-34; Engineering Asst with F. A. Macdonald & Partners (Glasgow) Ltd, 1934-36; Lecturer in Civil Engineering, Imperial Coll. of Science, 1936-45; Technical Officer, Instn Struct. Engrs, 1945-46; Prof. of Engineering, St Andrews Univ., 1946-52. Visiting Professor: Northwestern Univ., Ill., 1960; University of Western Australia, 1967. *Publications:* Fundamental Principles of Reinforced Concrete Design, 1951; Solutions to Problems in Structures, 1958; (with H. M. Nelson) Structures, 1969; a number of papers on structural engineering. *Recreations:* cricket, youth organisations. *Address:* James Watt Engineering Laboratories, The University, Glasgow. [*Died* 31 *Dec.* 1975.

MARSHALL-REYNOLDS, Clyde Albert, QC 1962; retired; *b* 11 March 1898; *o c* of late Leslie Clyde Reynolds and Amy Maud Marshall-Reynolds (*née* Marshall); unmarried. *Educ:* Sydney Grammar Sch., Australia; private tutor in England; Wadham Coll., Oxford. Called to Bar, Middle Temple, 1926; Mem. Middle Temple and Inner Temple. Bencher, Middle Temple, 1958. Special Commissioner in Divorce, 1965, 1966, 1967 and 1968. Parish Clerk, St Leonards, Eastcheap; Church Warden, St Botolph, Billingsgate. Freeman, City of London, 1954. *Recreations:* motoring, gardening. *Address:* 16 Gledhow Gardens, SW5. *T:* 01-373 6935; Yews Farm, Blackboys, East Sussex.
[*Died* 15 *Aug.* 1977.

MARSHAM, Brig. Francis William Bullock-, DSO 1918; MC; late 19th Royal Hussars; *b* 1883; *m* 1922, Mrs Cordy-Simpson, widow, Hope Court, Crowborough, *o d* of Sir Fitzroy Maclean, 10th Bt. *Educ:* Eton. Served European War, 1914-19 (despatches, DSO, MC); Lt-Col 1927; Bt-Col 1931; Col 1931; commanded 3rd Carabiniers, 1927-31; 5th Cavalry Brigade, 1931-32; Comdr 1st Cavalry Brigade, 1932-36; Aide-de-camp to the King, 1935-38; retired with rank of Brig., 1938. Chief Umpire 1st Armd Div., 1939-40; GSO1 Home Guard, 1940-42; County Cadet Comdt, Berks Cadets, 1942-46. *Address:* Overblow, Shorne, Kent. *T:* Shorne 2254. *Clubs:* Cavalry, Royal Automobile.
[*Died* 22 *Dec.* 1971.

MARSHAM, Dame Joan, (Hon. Mrs Sydney Marsham), DBE 1945 (CBE 1937; OBE 1918); Chairman: The Personal Service League; National Women's Auxiliary, YMCA; *b* 4 Jan. 1888; *d* of William Warry, ISO, Shapwick, Somerset; *m* 1911, Hon. Sydney Marsham (*d* 1952), *y s* of 4th Earl of Romney; one *s. Address:* c/o Coutts & Co., 440 Strand, WC2.
[*Died* 13 *March* 1972.

MARTIN, Sir Alec, KBE 1959; Kt 1934; LLD 1960; *b* London, 25 Nov. 1884; *s* of Samuel and Rosina Martin; *m* 1909, Ada Mary Fell; three *s* two *d. Educ:* All Saints Church Sch., Knightsbridge. Started at Christies at the age of twelve, and was

Managing Dir of the firm, 1940-58; Governor and Guardian of the Nat. Gallery of Ireland, Dublin; Chm. of Trustees of the Wallace Collection; Hon. Sec. Nat. Art-Collections Fund; a Governor of the Foundling Hosp. KStJ 1958. *Recreations:* lots. *Address:* 16 Dover Park Drive, Roehampton, SW15. *T:* 01-788 0376.   [*Died* 15 *April* 1971.

MARTIN, Charles Emanuel; Professor of International Law and Political Science, University of Washington, Seattle, Washington, 1925-62; Director University of Washington Institute International Affairs, 1935-62; Emeritus Professor of International Law and Political Science since 1962; *b* Corsicana, Texas, 11 Sept. 1891; *s* of Emanuel Cobb Martin and Roxie Annie Moon; *m* 1921, Jewell Boone; no *c. Educ:* University of California, Berkeley (BA 1914, MA 1915); Columbia Univ. (PhD 1918); Hon. LLD University S Cal. 1942; Columbia Univ, Fellow Int. Law, 1916-17; War Trade Bd and Food Adm. US Govt 1917-18; Coast Artillery Corps, US Army, 1918; Carnegie Endowment Fellow Int. Law, 1918-19; Lecturer on Int. Law and Politics and Sec. Bureau Int. Relations, University Calif., Berkeley, 1919-20; Head Dept Pol Science, University Cal. at Los Angeles, 1920-25; Dean Faculty Social Science, University of Washington, 1926-29 and Head Political Science Dept, 1925-52; mem. Carnegie Endowment European Int. Law Conference, 1926; visiting Prof. Int. Relations, University of Hawaii, 1929; Carnegie Endowment Prof. Int. Relations accredited to universities in Orient and Antipodes, 1929-30; Dir Sch. Pacific and Oriental Affairs, University of Hawaii, 1932; Mem. Govt Bd on Immigration and Naturalization Service, US Dept Labor, 1933; Exchange Prof. Int. Law and Adm., American Univ., Washington, DC, 1942-43; Ednl consultant, Nat. Inst. Public Affairs, Washington, DC, 1942-43; Special Expert to Sec. of US Army and Chm. Bd of Consultants of US Cultural and Social Science Mission to Japan, Sept. 1948-Jan. 1949. Deleg. Inst. Pacific Relations Confs, 1929, 1936, 1950, 1954; in Japan, US, and India. University of Washington and Rockefeller Foundation Research professorship, East and SE Asia, 1954-55; Lectr, Inter-Amer. Acad. of Comparative and Internat. Law, Havana, Cuba, Feb. 1957; Prof. of Amer. Studies, University Philippines, 1962-63; Haynes Prof. Internat. Law, Whittier Coll., Calif., 1964. United States-Mexican pre-recognition Conference, Mexico City, 1923; Summer Sessions at California, Harvard, Texas, Michigan, George Washington, Stanford, Southern California, Hawaii Univs; Special Lecturer at Miss., Emory, La, and NC Univs; Lecturer Canadian Inst. Int. Affairs, 1933, 1943, 1951, 1953; Trustee Am. Inst. Pacific Relations; Dir and Ex Comm., Inst. World Affairs; Ex Comm., Council For. Relations (Seattle Comm.); Am. Commission on Org. of Peace; Pres. World Affairs Symposium (Seattle). Late Pres. and Chm. Board Trustees Seattle World Affairs Council; Trustee Seattle Art Museum, 1940-52. Pres., American Soc. of International Law, 1960-61; Member: Amer., Western, and Pacific NW Political Science Assocs; American Section, Internat. Law Assoc.; Asiatic Soc. of Japan. *Publications:* Policy of the US as Regards Intervention, 1921; An Introduction to the Study of American Constitution, 1926; American Government and Citizenship (with W. H. George), 1927; Politics of Peace, 1929; Permanent Court of International Justice and Question of American Adherence, 1932; various articles on civic, political, public and international affairs; Report of US Cultural and Social Science Mission to Japan (in collaboration), 1949; South and South-east Asia, 1951; Rebirth of a Nation (Japan), 1953; Universalism and Regionalism in International Law and Organization, 1959. Edited: The Pacific Area, 1929; Pacific Problems, 1932; War and Society, 1941; Problems of the Peace, 1945; San Francisco Conference and the UN Organization, 1946; The World in Crisis, 1948; Prospects for World Stability, 1950; New Weapons for the New Diplomacy, 1953. *Recreations:* foreign travel, teaching assignments abroad; organizing internat. relations institutes as an avocation. *Address:* 3828 48th Avenue NE, Seattle, Washington 98105, USA; Dept Political Science, University of Washington, Seattle, Washington 98105. *T:* Lakeview 4-1117, (office) 543-2780. *Clubs:* Rainier, Monday, Faculty, China (Seattle); Cosmos (Washington, DC); Army and Navy (Manila, RP).   [*Died* 12 *Jan.* 1977.

MARTIN, Rt. Rev. Clifford Arthur, MA Cantab; DD Lambeth; LLD Liverpool; *b* 11 Nov. 1895; *s* of Arthur Henry Martin; *m* 1926, Margaret La Trobe (*d* 1972), *d* of late Rev. Frederick La Trobe Foster; one *s* three *d. Educ:* Fitzwilliam Coll., Cambridge; Ridley Hall, Cambridge. Served as an officer in Royal Sussex Regt 1915-19; ordained 1920, to Christ Church, Croydon; Sec. Young People's Dept, Church Missionary Soc., 1924-27; Vicar Christ Church, Croydon, 1927-33; Vicar Christ Church, Folkestone, 1933-39; Vicar St Andrew, Plymouth, 1939-44; Chaplain to the King, 1941-44; Bishop of Liverpool, 1944-65. Select Preacher Cambridge Univ., 1945. Hon. Fellow, St Peter's Coll., Oxford, 1965. *Address:* School Lane, Middle Littleton,

near Evesham, Hereford and Worcester. *T:* Evesham 830698. *Club:* Royal Commonwealth Society.   [*Died* 11 *Aug.* 1977.

MARTIN, Brig. Cyril Gordon, VC 1915; CBE 1938; DSO 1914; *b* 19 Dec. 1891; *s* of late Rev. John Martin, Foochow, China; *m* 1917, Mab (*d* 1973), *o d* of late Major E. Hingston, RE; one *s* (and one killed in action 1944) one *d. Educ:* Bath Coll.; Clifton Coll. Entered army, 1911; Major, 1928; Lt-Col, 1936; Col, 1939; served European War, 1914-15 (despatches, VC, DSO); EEF Palestine, 1918; NW Frontier of India, 1930-31 (despatches, Bt Lt-Col); Waziristan, 1937 (CBE); Dep. Chief Engineer, Northern Command, India, 1939; Chief Engineer British Troops in Iraq, 1941 (despatches); Chief Engineer NW Army, India; ADC to the King, 1945-47; retired pay, 1947. *Address:* 3 Pinelands Close, St John's Park, Blackheath, SE3 7TF. *T:* 01-858 6620.   [*Died* 14 *Aug.* 1980.

MARTIN, Sir David (Christie), Kt 1970; CBE 1960; FRSE, FRIC; Executive Secretary, The Royal Society, since 1947; *b* 7 Oct. 1914; 3rd *s* of late David Christie Martin and Helen Linton; *m* 1943, Jean MacGaradh Wilson, *d* of late Thomas Hay Wilson, Edinburgh. *Educ:* Kirkcaldy High Sch.; Edinburgh Univ. BSc (Chemistry) 1937, PhD 1939, Edinburgh. Asst Sec., Royal Society of Arts, 1939-45; seconded to Dept of Research and Develt, Min. of Supply, 1939-45; Gen. Sec., Chemical Soc., 1945-47; Comr for Gen. Purposes of Income Tax, 1950-; Sec., 1950-54 and Recorder, 1955-58 of Chemistry Sect. of Brit. Assoc. for Advancement of Science, and Mem. Coun., 1959-69, 1970-; Manager, Royal Instn, 1951-52; Mem. Exec. Coun., Ciba Foundn, 1967-; Member: Special Cttee on Solar-Terrestrial Relationships of Internat. Council of Scientific Unions, 1967-; Council of Management, Soc. for Protection of Science and Learning, 1967-; Chm., BBC Science Consultative Gp, 1968-; Mem., BBC Gen. Adv. Council, 1968-; Chm., Standing Cttee on Statutes, Internat. Union of Pure and Applied Chem., 1971-75, Mem., GB/China Cttee, 1973-; Member: Soc. of Chem. Industry; Council, RSA, 1972-; Adv. Council, Charities Aid Foundn, 1975-. Hon. FCS. Hon. DSc Edinburgh, 1968; Hon. DCL Newcastle upon Tyne, 1973. *Publications:* contrib. to The Royal Society: Its Origins and Founders; papers and articles in scientific jls. *Recreation:* fishing. *Address:* Flat 1, 6 Carlton House Terrace, SW1. *T:* 01-839 5260. *Club:* Athenæum.
                                                              [*Died* 16 *Dec.* 1976.

MARTIN, Adm. Sir Deric Douglas Eric H.; *see* Holland-Martin.

MARTIN, Lt-Col Edward C. de R.; *see* De Renzy-Martin.

MARTIN, Edward Kenneth; Consulting Surgeon, University College Hospital; Fellow of University College, London; *b* 21 Sept. 1883; *s* of Dr Edward Fuller Martin, Weston-super-Mare; *m* 1923, Philippa Parry Pughe, FRCS; three *d. Educ:* Charterhouse; University Coll., London. MS, FRCS (Mem. of Court of Examiners); BEF, 1914-18; Temp. Major RAMC. *Publications:* various contributions to medical journals. *Recreation:* travelling. *Address:* 97 Dorset House, Gloucester Place, NW1 5AF. *T:* 01-935 6322.   [*Died* 19 *Jan.* 1980.

MARTIN, Frank, Dr *hc* ; Composer; *b* Geneva, 1890; *s* of Charles Martin and Pauline Duval; *m* 1940, Maria Boeke; two *s* four *d. Educ:* Gymnasium, Geneva. Studied under M. Joseph Lauber. Compositions include: Le Vin herbé; In Terra Pax (oratorio breve); Golgotha (oratorio); Der Cornet (mezzo-soprano and small orch.); 6 Monologues from Hofmannsthal's Jedermann (baryton and piano or orch.); Petite symphonie concertante (harp, harpsichord, piano and double string orch.); 8 Preludes (piano); Concerto (7 wind instrs); Ballades for: 'cello and piano or orch.; flute and piano or orch.; saxophone and orch.; trombone and piano or orch.; piano and orch.; viola and orch.; Der Sturm (opera, The Tempest); 4 Etudes (string orch.); Concerto (violin and full orch.); Ouverture en Rondeau (full orch.); Pseaumes (mixed choir and orch.); Concerto (harpsichord and small orch.); Mystère de la Nativité (9 soloists, 2 mixed choirs, orch.; mediaeval text); Monsieur de Pourceaugnac (opera; Molière); Les 4 Eléments, études symphoniques (full orch.); Pilate (oratorio breve, 4 soloists, choirs, orch.); Concerto (cello and small orch.); String Quartet; String Trio; Maria-Triptychon (soprano, violin and orch.); Erasmi Monumentum (full orch. and organ); Concerto (piano and orchestra), 1970; Trois Danses (oboe, harp, string orchestra), 1970; Poèmes de la Mort (3 male voices and 3 electric guitars; Villon), 1971; Requiem (4 soloists, mixed choir, orch. and organ), 1972; Polyptyque (violin, string orch.), 1973; Fantaisie sur des rythmes Flamenco (piano), 1973. His music is frequently performed in England. Many years resident in Holland. *Address:* Bollelaan 11, Naarden (NH), Netherlands. *T:* Bussum 42781.   [*Died* 21 *Nov.* 1974.

MARTIN, Sir George William, KBE 1935; JP; LLD (Leeds), 1951; Chairman of Directors, Wilkinson and Warburton Ltd; Underwriting Member of Lloyd's; Chairman Leeds Musical Festival, 1942-54; Member National Assistance Board, 1948-56; *b* 24 June 1884; *s* of Edward and Ester Margret Martin; *m* 1913, Doris Dixon Marshall (*d* 1966); no *c*. Chairman of the PAC Cttee of Assoc. of Municipal Corporations, 1931-33 and 1935-44, and of its Health Cttee, 1942-45; Vice-Chm Finance Cttee, City of Leeds, 1929-30; Mem. of National Radium Commission, and Central Cttee for Refugees; Mem. and Chm. of Employers Panel Rushcliffe Cttee on Nurses Salaries, 1941-47; Chm. Nuffield Provincial Hospital Trust Regionalization Cttee, Chm. Yorks Regionalization Cttee; Chm. of Leeds Public Dispensary and Hosp. and Mem. of the Board of the General Infirmary at Leeds, 1929-48, and Leeds Tradesmen's Benevolent Institution; Chm. City of Leeds Health Cttee, 1935-45, 1951-52; Lord Mayor City of Leeds, 1946-47; Chm. United Leeds Hospital Board, 1948-61; Mem. Advisory Cttee of National Fitness Council; Mem. of the Court and Council, Leeds Univ., 1948-58. Pres. Leeds Chamber of Commerce, 1948-52; Vice-Chm., Teaching Hosp. Association; Chm. Wartime Trading Cttee of Chamber of Commerce; Chm. of the Leeds Convalescent Soc.; Founder Mem., 1945, and former Chm., Methodist Homes for the Aged; Master of Court Company of Feltmakers, 1951-52; Trustee of Thomas Wade; Chairman of Governors: East Moor Sch.; Woodhouse Grove Sch.; Mem. of the Council of the Wholesale Textile Assoc., London, 1938-60; Mem. of Departmental Cttee to consider Laws relating to Rag Flock, 1938-39; Treasurer and Chm. Yorks Council British Empire Cancer Campaign. JP Leeds 1932; High Sheriff of Yorks, 1954. Pres. Leeds YMCA. Contested (C) West Leeds, 1929. Hon. Freeman, City of Leeds, 1966. *Recreation:* shooting. *Address:* Adel Lodge, Adel, Leeds. *T:* 673216. *Clubs:* Carlton; Leeds, Leeds County Conservative (Leeds); Alwoodley Golf.
[Died 13 Oct. 1976.

MARTIN, Rt. Rev. Henry David, DD; Hon. Assistant Bishop, Diocese of British Columbia; *b* London, England, 30 June 1889; *s* of H. W. and M. E. Martin; *m* 1919, Margaret Kathleen Wilson; two *d. Educ:* St Paul's Sch., London; University of Toronto; Wycliffe Coll., Toronto. Deacon 1915, Curate, St Luke's Church, Saint John, NB; Priest 1916, Curate, St James' Cathedral, Toronto; Priest-in-Charge, Holy Trinity Church, Winnipeg, 1917-18; Rector, St George's Church, Winnipeg, 1918-39; Canon of St John's Cathedral, Winnipeg, 1932; Bishop of Saskatchewan, 1939-59. *Recreations:* swimming, golf, walking. *Address:* 2715 Beach Drive, Victoria, BC, Canada.
[Died 27 March 1971.

MARTIN, Maj.-Gen. John Simson Stuart, CSI 1945; MB, MRCP (Edinburgh); VHS 1939; KHS 1942; IMS, retired; *b* 18 June 1888; *s* of Rev. D. J. Martin and Letitia Tennant Stuart; *m* 1924, Caroline Lorna Halkett; two *s* two *d. Educ:* Oban High Sch.; Rockhampton Grammar Sch. (Queensland); Edinburgh Univ. MB, ChB 1911; MRCP (Edinburgh) 1928; Lt IMS 1912; Capt. 1915; Major, 1923; Lt-Col 1931; Col 1938; Acting Brig., later Acting Maj.-Gen. 1942; Subst. Maj.-Gen. 1943; retired, 1945. Served European War, 1914-18 (despatches). Owns about 5000 acres. *Address:* Glendale, Isle of Skye. *T:* Glendale 206.
[Died 24 Dec. 1973.

MARTIN, Leonard Cyril, MA; BLitt; King Alfred Professor of English Literature, University of Liverpool, until Oct. 1951; *b* Leyton, Essex, 21 March 1886; 2nd *s* of Edward John Martin and Ellen Heavens; *m* 1920, Dorothy Mary, *y d* of late John and Martha Green, Peebles. *Educ:* Chigwell Sch., Essex; Keble Coll., Oxford. Lecturer in English, Trinity Coll., University of Toronto, 1909-13; University of Lund, 1913-15; Asst Commercial Attaché, British Legation, Copenhagen, 1915-18; Representative in Denmark of Ministry of Information, 1918-19; Lecturer in English, University Coll., Reading, 1919; Maître de Conférences, Sorbonne, 1920-22; Senior Lecturer in English Literature, University of Liverpool, 1923-29 (in charge of Dept, 1926-29); Foyle Research Fell. Shakespeare Inst., Stratford-on-Avon, 1953-55; Hon. Mem. Modern Language Assoc. of America, 1965. *Publications:* Editor: The Works of Henry Vaughan; The Poems of Richard Crashaw; Milton's Paradise Regained; The Poems of Nathaniel Wanley; The Poems of Marlowe; Cowley, Poetry and Prose; The Poems of Herrick; Religio Medici and other works of Sir Thomas Browne. Contributions to Modern Language Review, etc. *Address:* Glencairn, Peebles EH45 9DL. *T:* Peebles 20393.
[Died 27 Jan. 1976.

MARTIN, Hon. Sir Norman (Angus), Kt 1949; Resident Director in Australasia for Thomas Cook and Son, since 1950; Director several cos; Chairman: Victorian Inland Meat Authority, 1958-73; Australia Day Council; *b* 24 April 1893; *s* of Angus Martin,

Portland, Vic; *m* 1919, Gladys, *d* of Captain Barrett, MC; one *s* one *d. Educ:* Werribee. Minister of Agriculture, Victoria. A Vice-Pres. of Land and Works, 1943-; MLA for Gunbower, 1934-. Served European War, AIF, 1914-18. Councillor of Cohuna Shire since inauguration of Shire, Pres. 1930-31 and 1939-40; Agent-General for Victoria in the UK, 1945-50. Pres. Leitchville Branch United Country Party, Vic, for fifteen years. *Recreations:* golf, tennis, shooting. *Address:* Longleat, 133 Alexandra Avenue, South Yarra, Victoria 3141, Australia; c/o Thomas Cook and Son, 267 Collins Street, Melbourne, Victoria 3000, Australia. *Clubs:* Royal Automobile; Australian, Savage, VRC (Melbourne).
[Died 1978.

MARTIN, Col Reginald Victor, CIE 1938; IMS, retired; MRCS, LRCP, DOMS; *b* 20 March 1889; *s* of B. R. Martin, MB, Killeshandra, Cavan, Ireland; *m* 1913, Katherine (*d* 1968), *d* of Maj.-Gen. R. M. Clifford; two *s* two *d. Educ:* St Paul's Sch., Kensington; St Mary's Hospital, Paddington. Entered Indian Medical Service, 1913; war service 1914-18 (despatches). Waziristan, 1923; Inspector-General of Prisons, Province of Bombay, 1936-38; Waziristan, 1940-41; VHS, 1942-43; ADMS, 1941-44 (Brigadier 1942-43); KHP, 1943-44; retired 1944; re-employed, 1944-46. *Recreations:* golf, tennis. *Address:* 35 Manor Orchard, Taunton, Somerset.
[Died 26 Feb. 1973.

MARTIN, Thomas, MSc; DIC; FInstP; *b* Norwood, 26 July 1893; *er s* of late Thomas Martin; *m* 1918, Dorothy Sylvia, *yr d* of late Frederick Vernon, Dulwich; two *s. Educ:* Alleyns Sch.; University Coll., London. Served in Royal Artillery, 1914-19 and 1939, Captain RA. Metallurgical research, Royal School of Mines, 1919-23; Sec., Brit. Empire Exhibition Cttee of Royal Society, 1923-25; Sec., Optical Convention, 1926; Sec., Institute of Physics, 1926-29, and Editor, Journal of Scientific Instruments, 1928-29; General Sec., Royal Institution of Great Britain, 1929-50; Sec., Royal Institution Cttee, Faraday Celebrations, 1931; Asst and later Deputy Dir of Instrument Production, Ministry of Supply, 1939-46; Principal Scientific Officer, Home Office, 1951-64; Consultant, Ministry of Defence, Navy Dept, 1964-65. Chm. Cinematograph Equipment Allocation Cttee, 1941-46; Mem. Anglo-American Mission to European Countries on Instrument Requirements, 1946; Chm. Film Sub-Commn, UNESCO Commn on Technical Needs, Paris, 1947; Pres. British Soc. for the History of Science, 1962-64. *Publications:* Faraday, 1934; ed. Faraday's Diary, 1932-36; The Royal Institution (for British Council), 1942; Faraday's Discovery of Electro-Magnetic Induction, 1949; articles in scientific journals. *Address:* 8 Bramerton Street, Chelsea, SW3. *T:* 01-352 1116. *Clubs:* Athenæum, Savile.
[Died 11 Sept. 1971.

MARTIN-LEAKE, Hugh; *see* Leake.

MARTINSON, Harry E.; Swedish author and poet; *b* Jämshog, Sweden, 6 May 1904; *s* of Sea Captain Martin Olofsson and Betty Olofsson; *m* 1st, 1929, Moa Martinson (*née* Swartz); 2nd, 1942, Ingrid Lindcrantz. Member, Swedish Academy. Spent early life at sea; many of his subsequent prose and verse compositions deal with nomadic existence. Nobel Prize for Literature (jtly), 1974. Autobiographical work: Flowering Nettles; Cape Farewell; The Road; Aniara (later set to music as opera by Karl-Birger Blondahl). *Publications:* Spökskepp, 1929; Nomad, 1931; Resor utan mäl, 1932; Kap Farväl, 1933; Nässlorna blomma, 1935; Vägen ut, 1936; Svärmare o harkrank, 1937; Midsommeardalen, 1938; Det enkla o det svära, 1939; Verklighet till döds, 1940; Den förlorade jaguaren, 1941; Passad, 1945; Vägen till Klockrike, 1948; Cikada, 1953; Aniara, 1956; Gräsen i Thule, 1958; Vagnen, 1960; Utsikt från en grästuva, 1963; Tre Knivar från Wei, 1964; Dikter om ljus o mörker, 1971; Tuvor, 1973.
[Died 11 Feb. 1978.

MARYON-WILSON, Sir Hubert (Guy Maryon), 13th Bt *cr* 1661; *b* 27 July 1888; *s* of Rev. George Maryon Wilson (*d* 1906), 5th *s* of 9th Bt, and Albinia Frances Short (*d* 1920); assumed surname of Maryon by deed poll; *S* kinsman 1965; *m* 1923, Janet Mary, *d* of late Rev. Ernest Arthur Moxon, Lincs. *Educ:* Radley. *Heir:* none. *Address:* The Grange, Great Canfield, Dunmow, Essex.
[Died 13 Sept. 1978 (ext).

MASIH, Rt. Rev. Inayat; Bishop of Lahore, since 1968; *b* 14 Sept. 1918; *m* 1952, Farkhanda; one *d. Educ:* Punjab Univ., Lahore; Bishop's Coll., Calcutta; Serampore Univ. Curate, Holy Trinity cum Lahore Cathedral Parish, 1947-50; Vice-Princ., St John's Divinity Sch., Narowal, Dio. of Lahore, 1950-52; Priest i/c Pattoki District, 1952-53; higher studies in USA, 1953-55; Priest i/c Gojra District, Lahore Dio., 1955-59; Exec. Sec., West Pakistan Christian Coun., 1959-65; Archdeacon of Lahore, 1965-68. Moderator, Church of Pakistan, 1971-74. *Recreations:* reading, badminton. *Address:* Bishopsbourne, Cathedral Close,

The Mall, Lahore, Pakistan. *T:* Lahore 53790.
[Died 7 June 1980.

MASON, Hon. Henry Greathead Rex, CMG 1967; QC (NZ) 1946; *b* 3 June 1885; *s* of Harry Brooks and Henrietta Emma Mason; *m* 1912, Dulcia Martina Rockell (*d* 1971); one *s* two *d* (and one *s* decd). *Educ:* Wellington Coll., New Zealand (Scholar); Victoria University Coll., Wellington (Scholar). BA (NZ) 1906; MA (Hon. Maths and Math. Physics), 1907; LLB 1910; admitted Solicitor, 1909; Barrister, 1923; Practised as Solicitor, Pukekohe, 1911, Auckland, 1923, 1924-42 in partnership with brother, Spencer R. Mason; MP New Zealand, 1926-66 (Eden, 1926-28; Auckland Subs., 1928-46; Waitakere, 1946-63, New Lynn, 1963-66). National President New Zealand Labour Party, 1931; Attorney-General and Minister of Justice, New Zealand, 1935-49; Minister of Education, 1940-47; Native Minister, 1943-46; Attorney-General, Minister of Justice and Minister of Health, 1957-60. Mayor of Pukekohe, 1915-19; Mem. Auckland Transport Board, 1930; Chm., 1935-39. Head of New Zealand Delegation to Paris Peace Conference, 1946. Fellow, Royal Numismatical Soc. of NZ (Inc.). Hon. LLD Victoria Univ., Wellington, NZ. *Address:* Flat 12, Newman Court, 16/20 Tinakori Road, Wellington 1, NZ. *T:* 42538.
[Died 2 April 1975.

MASON, Lt-Col Kenneth, MC; late RE; MA; Professor of Geography, Oxford University, 1932-53; Hon. Fellow of Hertford College, Oxford, 1953; late Superintendent, Survey of India; *b* 10 Sept. 1887; *s* of late Stanley Engledue Mason of Oakhurst, Crofton, Orpington; *m* 1917, Dorothy Helen Robinson (*d* 1974), *d* of late Captain Arthur Robinson, Knowsley Park, Lancs; two *s* one *d. Educ:* Homefield, Sutton; Cheltenham Coll.; Royal Military Academy, Woolwich. 2nd Lieut Royal Engineers, 1906; Lieut., 1907; Capt., 1914; Brev.-Maj., 1918; Subs.-Maj., 1925; Lieut-Col, 1933; joined Survey of India, 1909; in charge of expedition connecting Indo-Russian Surveys on Pamirs, 1913; in charge Shaksgam Exploration, 1926; awarded Cuthbert Peek Grant by Royal Geographical Society, 1926, and Royal Founders Gold Medal, 1927; Hon. Mem. French Alpine Club, 1930; Councillor Royal Geographical Soc., 1932-45, 1952-54; Vice-Pres., 1937-42; Hon. Fellow, 1965; Mem., Mount Everest Cttee, 1933-40. Served European War Western Front, 1914-15 (wounded); Mesopotamia, Persia, etc., 1916-19 (MC, Brevet-Majority, despatches thrice); Attached NID Admlty, 1940-46. Founder and Hon. Editor: The Himalayan Journal, 1928-45. Freeman and Mem. of Court of Drapers' Company, City of London, Master, 1949. Life Mem. of Council, Cheltenham Coll.; Pres., Cheltonian Soc., 1958. Governor: Howells' Sch., Denbigh; Bancroft's Sch. *Publication:* Abode of Snow, 1955. *Recreations:* mountaineering, travel. *Address:* Sylvanway, West End Road, Mortimer, near Reading, Berks. *T:* Mortimer 332, 753. *Clubs:* Alpine (elected 1914, Hon. Mem. 1973); Himalayan (Calcutta) (founder, 1928).
[Died 2 June 1976.

MASON, Leonard Ralph; Special Assistant to the General Manager, General Motors Overseas Operations Division, since 1974; *b* 31 Oct. 1910; *s* of late Leonard Tyree Mason and late Beulah Mason; *m* 1st, 1939, Cleo Elizabeth Manzer (decd); one *s* two *d*; 2nd, 1966, Rena Lehr Gordon, *widow*; one step *s* one step *d. Educ:* Virginia Polytechnic Inst., Blacksburg. Chevrolet Motor Co.: Prodn Foreman, Baltimore, 1935; Shift Supt, Mil. Prodn, Baltimore, 1943; Divi Supt, Prodn, Baltimore, 1945; Gen. Supt, Kansas City, 1949; Plant Man., Atlanta, 1954; Plant Man., St Louis, 1956; Regional Man., Chevrolet Manufrg, Detroit, 1957; Gen. Manufrg Man. for all Chevrolet Plants, 1964; Man. Dir, Adam Opel, 1966; Gen. Dir, European Operations, Gen. Motors Overseas Corp., 1970-74. Grand Cross, Legion of Merit, Germany, 1971. *Recreations:* golf, reading, walking, hunting and trap shooting. *Address:* 72 Chester Square, SW1W 9DU. *T:* 01-730 5935. *Clubs:* Les Ambassadeurs; Bloomfield Hills Country (Michigan).
[Died 12 May 1974.

MASON, Michael; *see* Mason, R. M.

MASON, Sir Paul, KCMG 1954 (CMG 1947); KCVO 1958; HM Diplomatic Service, retired; *b* 11 June 1904; *m* 1938, Roberta, *d* of late J. Lorn McDougall, KC, Ottawa; one *s* one *d. Educ:* Eton; King's Coll., Cambridge. 1st Cl. Hons Modern History, 1926. Entered Foreign Service, 1928; has served at Brussels, Prague, Ottawa, Lisbon and in Foreign Office; Asst Private Sec. to Sec. of State, 1934-36; Private Sec. to Parliamentary Under Sec. of State, 1936-37; Acting Counsellor, 1945; Minister at Sofia, 1949-51; Asst Under Sec. of State, Foreign Office, 1951-54; Ambassador to The Netherlands, 1954-60; UK Permanent Rep. on N Atlantic Council, 1960-62; Alternate Delegate to Minister of State in Geneva Delegation on Disarmament and

Nuclear Tests, 1962-64. Treas., Univ. of Nottingham, 1972-. High Sheriff of Notts, 1970. Chev. Order of Leopold; Gd Cr., Order of House of Orange, 1958. *Recreations:* various. *Address:* Morton Hall, Retford, Notts. *Club:* Lansdowne.
[Died 14 May 1978.

MASON, Dr (Richard) Michael; MA, DM; FRCP; Senior Physician, Department of Rheumatology, The London Hospital; Physician in Rheumatic Diseases, King Edward VII Hospital for Officers, since 1960; Civil Consultant in Rheumatology, RAF, since 1970; *b* 27 Sept. 1917; *o s* of Sir Laurence Mason, CIE, OBE, MC; *m* 1943, Heather, *d* of Lt-Col R. H. Johnston, OBE; one *s* one *d* (and one *d* decd). *Educ:* Marlborough; Christ Church, Oxford; St Bartholomew's Hosp., London. BM, BCh 1942; MA 1943; DM 1953; FRCP 1962. Med. Officer (Flt-Lt), RAFVR, 1943-46 in UK and W Europe; later Sqdn MO 604 Sqdn RAuxAF. Apptd London Hospital, 1957. Hon. Consultant, Osborne House, IOW, 1963-68; Vis. Prof., Sydney Univ., 1967; Hon. Med. Sec. 1955-71, Chm. Exec. Cttee 1971-, Arthritis and Rheumatism Council; Mem., Armed Forces Med. Adv. Bd, 1975-; Examr in Medicine, RCP, 1972-75; President: Heberden Soc., 1974; British League against Rheumatism, 1974-77. *Publications:* (ed jtly) An Introduction to Clinical Rheumatology, 1971, 2nd edn, 1975; many papers in scientific jls. *Recreations:* ski-ing, yachting. *Address:* 44 Harley House, NW1 5HH. *T:* 01-935 5639. *Clubs:* Athenæum; Royal Harwich Yacht; Kandahar Ski.
[Died 30 June 1977.

MASSEY, Sir Arthur, Kt 1956; CBE 1941; Chief Medical Officer, Ministry of Pensions and National Insurance, 1947-59, retired; *b* 1894; *s* of late Albert Massey, Keighley, Yorks; *m* 1924, Dorothy Blanche Ince, *d* of late Rev. H. H. T. Cleife, MA Cantab; one *d. Educ:* University of Leeds, MD, etc; Hon. Fellow, American Public Health Assoc.; Vice-President: Royal Society Health; Vocational Guidance Assoc.; KHP, 1950-52; QHP, 1952-53; Examiner in Public Health, Universities of London and Bristol, 1947-50, and Birmingham, 1952-55; MOH, City of Coventry, 1930-47. Chairman: Chadwick Trust, 1969-79 (Trustee, 1961-); Central Council for Health Educn, 1944-46. Lecturer in USA 1944, Yale Univ. 1954. Served 1915-18 in RFA (Lt), and 1943-45 in HG (Lt-Col, Zone Medical Adviser). *Publications:* Epidemiology and Air Travel, 1933; (ed) Modern Trends in Public Health, 1949; various contributions to the medical literature on hospital policy, public health and social insurance. *Recreations:* bridge, gardening, watching cricket. *Address:* 93 Bedford Gardens, W8 7EQ. *T:* 01-727 6951. *Club:* Athenæum.
[Died 13 April 1980.

MASSIAH, Sir (Hallam) Grey, KBE 1966 (CBE 1956); Kt 1960; President of Legislative Council, Barbados, 1958-66; MLC Barbados, 1943-66; *b* 18 July 1888; *s* of Hon. Hallam Massiah, MD, Barbados, and Florette Massiah; *m* 1915, Enid Leger (decd), Montreal; one *s* one *d. Educ:* Lodge Sch., Barbados; Durham Univ.; McGill Univ., Montreal. BA 1910, MA 1932, Durham; MD, CM 1915, McGill. Police Surg., Barbados, 1918-48; Visiting Surg., Gen. Hosp., Barbados, 1919-48. *Recreations:* book collecting, shooting. *Address:* Merton Lodge, Highgate Gardens, Barbados, West Indies. *T:* Barbados 7644. *Clubs:* Royal Commonwealth Society; Savannah, Bridgetown, Royal Barbados Yacht (Barbados).
[Died 20 April 1972.

MASSINE, Léonide; Choreographer; *b* Moscow, 27 July 1896; *s* of Teodor Affanasievitch and Eugenia Nikolaevna Gladkova; *m* 1939, Tatiana Vladimirovna Milisnikova; one *s* one *d. Educ:* Imperial Ballet Sch., and Maly Theatre, Moscow; pupil of Domashoff, Enrico Cecchetti and Nicolas Legat. Choreographer and principal dancer, Diaghilev Ballet Russe, 1914-20; choreographer, dancer, and artistic dir, Ballet de Monte Carlo, 1932-41; National Ballet Theatre, NY, 1941-44; organized Ballet Russe Highlights, 1945-46; guest artiste and choreographer: Sadler's Wells Ballet, Covent Garden, Royal Opera House, Copenhagen, Teatro Alla Scala, Milan, Opéra-Comique, Paris, 1947-51. Edinburgh Festival 1960; Ballets Européens de Nervi, 1960. *Ballets:* Soleil de Nuit, 1915; Las Meninas, 1916; Good Humoured Ladies, Contes Russes, Parade, 1917; La Boutique Fantasque, Le Tricorne, 1919; Le Sacre du Printemps, Les Astuzie Feminili, Pulcinella, Le Rossignol, 1920; Salade, Gigue, Le Beau Danube, 1924; Les Facheux, Les Matelots, Zephire et Flore, 1925; Cimarosiana, 1926; Le Pas d'Acier, Ode, Mercure, 1927; Les Enchantements d'Alcine, Le Roi David, Amphion, 1929-30; Le Beau Danube (2nd version), Belkis, Vecchia Milano, La Belle Hélène, 1932; Les Présages, Les Jeux d'Enfants, The Miracle, 1933; Choreartium, Scuola di Ballo, 1933-34; Le Bal, Union Pacific, Jardin Public, 1935; Symphonie Fantastique, 1936; Gaité Parisienne, Seventh Symphony, St Francis (Nobilissima Visione), 1938; Capriccio Espagnol, Rouge et Noir, Bogatyri, Bacchanal, 1939; Wien 1814, The New Yorker, 1940; Labyrinth, Saratoga, 1941; Aleko, Don Domingo,

1942; Mlle Angot, 1943; Antar, Daphnis et Chloe, Unfortunate Painter, Rêverie Classique, Moonlight Sonata, Mad Tristan, 1944; Bullet in the Ballet, Les Arabesques (revived), Les Matelots (rev.), 1945-46; Boutique Fantasque, Tricorne (rev.), 1946; Mam'selle Angot (2nd version), 1947; Capriccio (de Stravinsky), Episode de la Vie d'un Artiste, Clock Symphony, Sacre du Printemps (rev.), 1948; Quattro Stagioni, Mad Tristan (rev.), Good Humoured Ladies (rev.), Suite Bergamasque, Le Peintre et son Modèle, 1949; La Valse (de Ravel), 1950; Le Bal du Pont du Nord, Symphonie Allégorique (Les Saisons), Donald of the Burthens, Capriccio Espagnol (rev.), 1951; (created) Laudes Evangelli, M'selle Angot (rev.), dances for: Wilhelm Tell, Armida, Didone, Gioconda, 1952; Rezurrezione e Vita, 1954, Arianna, 1954; Commedia Umana, 1960; Le Bal des Voleurs, 1960; The Three Cornered Hat (rev.), 1973; *Staged:* for Royal Ballet, 1968: Boutique Fantasque; Mam'selle Angot. *Films:* (prod. dances and appeared) Carnival in Costa Rica, 1945; (comp. and danced his part): Red Shoes, 1948; Tales of Hoffmann, 1951; Carosello Napoletano, 1953. *Publications:* My Life in Ballet, 1968; Massine on Choreography, 1976.
[Died 17 March 1979.

MASSY, Brig. Charles Walter, CBE 1940; DSO 1918; MC; *b* 2 May 1887; *s* of late Arthur W. Massy, Cuffern, Roch, Pembrokeshire, and Cottesmore, Haverfordwest; *m* 1st, 1920, Muriel Lorna, *d* of J. A. Hallinan, Glandalane, Fermoy; two *s*; 2nd, 1958, Irene Gillbee, *d* of late Richard Gillbee Thorold, and widow of Clifford Hackney, MRCS. *Educ:* Cheltenham Coll.; RMA Woolwich. 2nd Lt RFA, 1907; Lt 1910; Captain 1914; Major, 1917; Lt-Col 1935; Col 1938; retired pay, 1942; served in France in RHA and RFA, 1914-18 (DSO, MC, despatches twice). Served in France, 1940. DL Monmouthshire, 1948-55. *Recreation:* fishing. *Address:* Tiddler's Well, Dalditch Lane, Budleigh Salterton, Devon. *Club:* Pembrokeshire County (Haverfordwest).
[Died 1 June 1973.

MASTER, Alfred, CIE 1931; DPhil; ICS (retired); Assistant Keeper, India Office Library, 1951-57; *b* 12 Feb. 1883; *s* of George Reginald Master, MRCS, late of Sheringham; *m* 1909, Dorothy Amy (*d* 1952), *d* of Rev. H. A. Thorne; three *d*. *Educ:* King Edward VI Sch., Norwich; Epsom Coll.; BNC, Oxford (MA; DPhil 1962). Entered ICS, 1906; Municipal Commissioner, Ahmadabad, 1917; Temp. Major, GSO2; Military Mission to Turkestan, Persia, 1918; officiating Sec. to Government of Bombay, General Dept, 1925; Collector of Bombay City and Suburbs, 1932-34; Lecturer: in Marathi, 1937-38; in Gujarati, 1938-39, in Indian Philology, 1944-50, at the School of Oriental and African Studies, London Univ.; Asst Keeper, India Office Lib., 1951-57; Member Governing Body, School of Oriental and African Studies, 1952-60. *Publications:* Introduction to Telugu Grammar, 1947; Catalogue of the Gujarati & Rajasthani Manuscripts in the India Office Library by J. F. Blumhardt, revised and enlarged, 1954; A Grammar of Old Marathi, 1964; English edn of L'Indo-Aryen, by Jules Bloch, 1965; articles in journals on Local Government, Linguistics, and Numismatics. *Address:* Woodchurch, Burleigh Road, Ascot, Berks. *T:* 22897.
[Died 16 June 1978.

MASTERMAN, Sir John (Cecil), Kt 1959; OBE 1944; Royal Order of Crown of Yugoslavia (3rd cl.), 1945; Provost of Worcester College, Oxford, 1946-61; MA; Hon. LLD Toronto; Hon. DCL University of King's College, Halifax, NS; Hon. DLitt Heriot-Watt University; Hon. Fellow Worcester College, Oxford; Hon. Student of Christ Church, Oxford; Hon. Fellow St Catharine's College, Cambridge; *b* 12 Jan. 1891; *s* of late Captain J. Masterman, Royal Navy, JP. *Educ:* Royal Naval Colleges, Osborne and Dartmouth (Midshipman, 1908); Worcester Coll., Oxford (Sch.); Freiburg Univ. First Class Mod. Hist. Sch., Oxford, 1913; Lecturer, Christ Church, 1913; Student of Christ Church, 1919-46; Censor of Christ Church, 1920-26; Interned in Germany, 1914-18. Lieut Intelligence Corps, 1940; Major (Local) and specially employed, 1941-45. Represented OUAC v. Cambridge, 1912-13; represented England at lawn tennis v. Ireland and Scotland, 1920; represented England at hockey v. Scotland, Ireland, and France, 1925, and v. Scotland, 1927; MCC Canadian Tour, 1937. Governor, Wellington Coll., 1944-65; Fellow of Eton, 1942-64. Mem. Governing Body: Cranleigh Sch., 1935-47; Eastbourne Coll., 1926-57; Atlantic Coll., 1962-68; Governor, St Edward's Sch., 1944-58. Chm. of Cttee on the Political Activities of Civil Servants, 1948; Chm. Army Education Advisory Board, 1952-56; Mem. BBC Gen. Advisory Council, 1952-59; Chm., ATV Educnl Adv. Cttee, 1961-67. Adviser on personnel matters to Birfield Ltd, 1961-68. Vice-Chancellor, Oxford Univ., 1957-58. Pres. Oxfordshire County Cricket Club, 1956-65. *Publications:* An Oxford Tragedy, 1933; Fate Cannot Harm Me, 1935; Marshal Ney, 1937; To Teach the Senators Wisdom or An Oxford Guide Book, 1952; The Case of the Four Friends, 1957; Bits and Pieces, 1961; The XX System

in the War of 1939 to 1945, 1972; On the Chariot Wheel (autobiog.), 1975. *Recreations:* cricket and other games. *Address:* 6 Beaumont Street, Oxford OX1 2LR. *Clubs:* United Oxford & Cambridge University, MCC; Vincent's (Oxford).
[Died 6 June 1977.

MASTERTON, William, CA; Finance Director, British Aircraft Corporation (Holdings), since 1960; *b* 20 April 1913; *s* of John Crichton Masterton, Solicitor, and Margaret Bower Masterton (*née* Hunter); *m* 1955, Kathlyn Aimee Milligan. *Educ:* Waid Academy; Edinburgh University. Qualified CA, Edinburgh, 1935; Thomson McLintoch & Co., London, 1935-39; joined Bristol Aeroplane Co., 1939; Sec., 1946; Finance Dir, 1952; Dep. Chm., 1964; Chairman: Bristol Aeroplane Co., 1968-69; Bristol Aerojet, 1967-69; Dep. Chm., British Aircraft Corp., 1965-; Director: Bristol Siddeley Engines, 1959-67; Short Bros & Harland, 1964-69; Rolls Royce Ltd, 1966-69; Rolls Royce Holdings, Canada, 1968-69; Lloyds Bank, Regional Board, 1967-. *Recreations:* golf, gardening. *Address:* Mount Elton, Clevedon, Som. *T:* Clevedon 3238.
[Died 22 Dec. 1971.

MATHER, Loris Emerson, CBE 1945; FIMechE; retired as Chairman Mather & Platt, Ltd, 1960; *b* Manchester 1886; *s* of late Rt Hon. Sir William Mather, LLD, MICE; *m* 1912, Leila (*d* 1976), *d* of late John S. Morley; two *s* one *d*. *Educ:* Harrow; Trinity Coll., Cambridge; Germany. Commission in RE (TA), 1909-19 (Captain); Member, Royal Commission of Awards to Inventors, 1953-55. *Address:* Meadow Croft, Parkside, SW19. *T:* 01-946 4672.
[Died 16 April 1976.

MATHER-JACKSON, Sir (George) Christopher (Mather), 5th Bt, *cr* 1869; *b* 12 March 1896; *s* of William Birkenhead Mather Jackson (*d* 1934) (2nd *s* of 2nd Bt) and Georgiana Catherine (*d* 1932), *d* of Rev. Brabazon Hallowes. *S* cousin, Sir Edward Arthur Mather-Jackson, 4th Bt, 1956; assumed additional surname of Mather-, 1957; *m* 1941, Victoria Emily Ford, *d* of Indrick Freyberg, Mitau, Latvia. *Educ:* Wellington Coll. Formerly Managing Dir of coal, iron and engineering companies and Dir of other companies; now retired. Served European War, 1914-18 (despatches). *Recreations:* golf, shooting, motoring. *Heir: b* Anthony Henry Mather Jackson [*b* 9 Nov. 1899; *m* 1923, Evelyn Mary, *d* of Lieut-Col Sir Henry Kenyon Stephenson, 1st Bt, DSO; three *d*]. *Address:* West Court, Crondall, near Farnham, Surrey. *T:* Aldershot 850448. *[Died 19 Nov. 1976.*

MATHESON, Captain Alexander Francis, RN (retired); Lord-Lieutenant of Ross and Cromarty, since 1968; *b* 6 Feb. 1905; *e s* of late Hugh Mackay Matheson; *m* 1937, Frances Mary, *d* of late Col J. P. Heywood Lonsdale, DSO, OBE and Hon. Mrs Heywood Lonsdale; one *s* two *d*. *Educ:* RN Colleges, Osborne and Dartmouth. Entered RN, 1918; served War of 1939-45; Captain, 1946; retired, 1949. Mem., Queen's Body Guard for Scotland (Royal Company of Archers). DL 1956. Convener, 1961-66, Vice-Lieutenant, 1957-68, Ross and Cromarty. *Address:* Brahan, Conon Bridge, Ross-shire. *T:* Conon Bridge 284. *Club:* New (Edinburgh).
[Died 20 Aug. 1976.

MATHESON, Donald Macleod, CBE 1945; Director, John Smedley Ltd, retired, 1967; *b* 20 June 1896; *o s* of Rev. Donald Matheson; *m* 1931, Enid Futvoye, *e d* of John Marsden-Smedley, Lea Green, near Matlock; no *c*. *Educ:* St George's, Harpenden; Balliol Coll., Oxford. RGA, 1915-18; BEF France, Captain (Acting) Major. Trustee Ernest Cook Trust, 1952-65. Treasurer, Peabody Fund, 1952-62. USA 1919-20; Gas Light & Coke Co., 1921-34, Asst Sec., etc. Sec. National Trust, 1934-45, mem. Cttees, 1945-52. Mem., War Works Commn, 1945-64. *Publications:* translations from French published in UK, India, and Pakistan, 1959-69. *Address:* Grimsbury Bank, Hermitage, Berks.
[Died 14 Jan. 1979.

MATHEW, Rev. Anthony Gervase, MA; STL; FSA; *b* 14 March 1905; 2nd *s* of Francis Mathew and Agnes, *d* of James Tisdall Woodroffe. *Educ:* privately; Balliol Coll., Oxford. Joined the Dominican Order, 1928; ordained, 1934; degree of Lector in Theology, 1936; Lecturer in Greek Patristics and on Byzantine art and archaeology, University of Oxford, 1937; Mem. of History Faculty at Oxford, and Lecturer on Medieval Social Theory, 1938; Mem. of the English Faculty and Lecturer on 14th century English literature, 1945; University Lecturer in Byzantine Studies, Oxford, 1947-71. Archæological survey for Government of Tanganyika, 1950, for the Government of British Somaliland Protectorate, 1951, for the Govt of Uganda, 1953, in South Arabia, 1962. Mem. of Sub-Faculty of Anthropology, Oxford, 1956-; Visiting Prof. of History, University of California, 1965. *Publications include:* The Reformation and the Contemplative Life (with David Mathew), 1934; Byzantine Painting, 1950; Byzantine Aesthetics, 1963; The Court of Richard II, 1967; contrib. to Cambridge Mediaeval

History, Journal of Roman Studies, Journal of Hellenic Studies, Antiquity, Oriental Art. *Address:* Blackfriars, St Giles, Oxford OX1 3LY.   *[Died 4 April 1976.*

MATHEW, Most Rev. David, MA, LittD, FSA; FRSL; Archbishop of Apamea; Assistant at the Pontifical Throne; *b* 15 Jan. 1902; *e s* of late Francis Mathew and Agnes, *d* of James Tisdall Woodroffe, Advocate-General of Bengal. *Educ:* Osborne and Dartmouth (Midshipman RN 1918-19); Balliol Coll., Oxford. Research Student at Balliol, 1923-24; Preston Read Scholar, 1924-25; ordained priest, 1929; assistant priest at St David's Cathedral, Cardiff, 1930-34; Chaplain to the Catholics in University of London, 1934-44; Conventual Chaplain of the Knights of Malta since 1936; mem. of Catholic Education Council; titular Bishop of Aelia and Bishop Auxiliary of Westminster, 1938-46; Apostolic Visitor to Ethiopia, 1945; Apostolic Delegate in Africa, 1946-53; Bishop-in-Ordinary (RC) to HM Forces, 1954-63; Sec., Pontifical Commn on the Missions, 1960; Consultor of the SC de Propaganda Fide; LittD, Trinity Coll., Dublin, 1933; Ford's Lectr in English History, Oxford, 1954; James Mathews Lectr in University of Wales, 1952. Hon. LLD Glasgow, 1958. Grand Officer of Order of Polonia Restituta. *Publications:* The Celtic Peoples and Renaissance Europe, 1933; The Reformation and the Contemplative Life, 1934 (with Gervase Mathew); Catholicism in England, 1936; The Jacobean Age, 1938; British Seamen, 1943; The Naval Heritage, 1944; Acton, 1945; Ethiopia, 1946; The Social Structure in Caroline England (Ford Lectures), 1947; Sir Tobie Mathew, 1950; The Age of Charles I, 1951; Scotland Under Charles I, 1955; James I, 1967; Lord Acton and His Times, 1968; The Courtiers of Henry VIII, 1970; Lady Jane Grey, 1972; *novels:* Steam Packet, 1936; In Vallombrosa, trilogy, 1950-53. *Club:* Athenæum.   *[Died 12 Dec. 1975.*

MATHIAS, Brig. Leonard William Henry, DSO 1918; late IA; *b* 31 Oct. 1890; *s* of late Col Leonard John Mathias, IA, and *g s* of late Maj.-Gen. Henry Vincent Mathias, B Staff Corps; *m* 1920, Winifrede Violet, *d* of late David Landale Johnston, Esq., ICS, Norfolk, and *g d* of late Rev. Maurice Howard Marsden of Moreton Rectory, Dorset; one *s* one *d. Educ:* private sch.; RMC Sandhurst. Received 1st Commission, 1910; attached Royal Warwickshire Regt, Bombay; appointed 128th Pioneers, 1911; proceeded Mesopotamia, 1915; besieged Kut-el-Amara, 1915-16, attached 22nd Coy. 3rd Sappers and Miners (despatches, DSO); taken prisoner by Turks, 1916, and interned at Yozgad, Asia Minor; released from captivity, Dec. 1918; Deputy Dir of Transport, QMG's Branch, India, 1939; Brig., 1940-43; ADC to the King, 1941-43; Area Comdr, 1943-45; Control Commission for Germany (BE), 1945-49; Comdt 5th C/Bn The Gloucestershire Regt, 1949-59. *Recreations:* shooting, sailing. *Address:* Falkland House, Painswick, Glos. *T:* Painswick 3466. *Club:* United Service & Royal Aero.   *[Died 22 Dec. 1972.*

MATHYS, Sir (Herbert) Reginald, Kt 1974; TD; Deputy Chairman, Courtaulds Ltd, 1961-73 (Director, 1954-73); *b* 28 March 1908; *s* of Albert William Mathys and Minnie (*née* Bullen); *m* 1939, Marjorie Kay; one *s* one *d. Educ:* Cranleigh Sch.; Birkbeck Coll., London Univ. Chartered Patent Agent in gen. practice, 1926-39. Served War of 1939-45, RE, England (Anti-Aircraft) and India. Joined Courtaulds Ltd as Head of Patent Dept, 1946; Chm., British Cellophane Ltd (part-owned subsid.), 1956-65; Dir, British Nylon Spinners Ltd, 1961-64, Chm. 1964. Vice-Pres., Trade Marks, Patents and Designs Fedn, 1954-75; Chairman: Standing Adv. Cttee on Patents, 1967-72; EDC for Newspaper, Printing and Publishing Industry, 1966-67; Industrial Property Commn, ICC, Paris, 1969-73; Deptl Cttee on British Trade Mark Law and Practice, 1972-73; Member: Deptl Cttee on Patent Law, 1967-70; Council, FBI, 1959-65; Council, CBI, 1965-73; BNEC, 1964-71; British Library Organizing Cttee, 1971-73; Nat. Savings Cttee, 1966-70; Vice-Pres., ASLIB, 1971-74; a Governor: Birkbeck Coll., 1967-74 (Hon. Fellow, 1974); Cranleigh Sch., 1968-77. Mem. Livery Founders' Company. *Publications:* articles in journals, primarily on matters relating to Letters Patent for Invention. *Recreation:* sailing small boats. *Address:* Catherine's Cottage, Lymore Valley, Milford-on-Sea, Lymington, Hants. *T:* Milford-on-Sea 2634. *Clubs:* Royal Thames Yacht, Keyhaven Yacht.
                                                    [Died 11 June 1977.

MATTERS, Sir (Reginald) Francis, Kt 1961; VRD; MS, MD (Adelaide); FRCS (Edinburgh), FRACS, FRCOG; Hon. Cons. Gynaecologist, Royal Adelaide Hospital; Hon. Cons. Obstetrician, Queen Elizabeth Hospital; Hon. Cons. Obstetrician, Queen Victoria Hospital; *b* 23 July 1895; *s* of late Thomas James Matters, Adelaide; *m* Elbe Cornwall, *d* of late John Mitchell, Sydney; one *s* one *d. Educ:* Prince Alfred Coll., Adelaide; Universities of Sydney and Adelaide. Served European War, AAMC France and Belgium (Captain, wounded

twice); War of 1939-45, Surg. Comdr RAN, SW Pacific, wounded in action. Studied in London, Edinburgh and Vienna. Aust. representative: Internat. Gynaecological Congress, London, 1949; Internat. Hosp. Fedn, Edinburgh, 1959; on Govt Commn to enquire into diagnosis and treatment of cancer, 1935; studies of same in UK, USA, Canada and Europe, 1949, 1951 and 1959. Was Mem. two Anthropological expedns to study Australian Aborigines in N Australia. SA Past Fellows rep., Aust. Regional Council of RCOG (Co-opted Councillor, RCOG, London, 1951 and 1959). Past President: Navy League of SA Div.; Royal Society of St George (SA); Camellia Res. Soc. of SA; Past Chm. SA Council of Fairbridge Soc. of London; Past Chm., Royal College of Obstetricians and Gynaecologists SA State Cttee. Pres. Debating Club. Vice-Pres. Council of St John; OStJ. *Publications:* The Cervix Uteri; many papers in Med. and Sci. jls; several papers of original research especially referring to cancer investigation; papers on surgical operative procedure. *Recreations:* walking, golf, bowls, shooting until recently, yachting. *Address:* 8 Carter Street, Thorngate, SA 5082, Australia. *T:* 441859. *Clubs:* Naval, Military and Air Force, Legacy (Past Pres.) (Adelaide); Royal Adelaide Golf; Senior Golfers' Society.   *[Died 14 Oct. 1975.*

MATTHEW, Sir Robert (Hogg), Kt 1962; CBE 1952; PPRIBA; FRTPI; FRIAS; FRSE; ARSA; MA; Chairman, School of the Built Environment, University of Edinburgh, since 1968; Consultant adviser on building conservation policy to Secretary of State for Scotland, since 1970; *b* 12 Dec. 1906; *s* of late John F. Matthew and Annie B. Matthew (*née* Hogg); *m* 1931, Lorna Louise Pilcher; one *s* two *d. Educ:* Melville Coll., Edinburgh. Chief Architect and Planning Officer, Dept of Health for Scotland, 1945; Architect to the London County Council, 1946-53; Forbes Prof. of Architecture, Univ. of Edinburgh, 1953-68. Member: Royal Fine Art Commission for Scotland; Historic Buildings Council, Scotland; Inquiry Team to advise on standards of design in Govt buildings, DoE, 1972-. President: International Union of Architects, 1961-65; Commonwealth Assoc. of Architects, 1965-68; RIBA; Pres., RIBA, 1962-64; Mem., BBC Gen. Adv. Council, 1963-67. Hon. Fellow: Amer. Inst. of Architects, 1951; NZ Inst. of Architects, 1959; Royal Architectural Inst. of Canada, 1964. Hon. LLD Sheffield, 1963; Hon. Dr Ion Mincu Inst. of Architecture, Bucharest, 1971. Soane Medal, 1932; Bossom Gold Medal, 1936; Distinction in Town Planning, 1949, Royal Gold Medal for Architecture, 1970; Gold Medal, Danish Architectural Assoc., 1965. *Address:* Keith Marischal, Humbie, East Lothian; 24 Park Square East, NW1; 31 Regent Terrace, Edinburgh 7. *T:* 031-556 5621. *Club:* Reform.   *[Died 21 June 1975.*

MATTHEWS, Sir Arthur, Kt 1941; OBE; Retired; *b* 15 June 1886; *s* of late Robert Matthews, Heaton Mersey, near Manchester; *m* 1914, Josephine Mason Hutchinson (*decd*); one *s* one *d*; *m* 1933, Constance Dorothy Morris. *Educ:* The Leys Sch., Cambridge; Jesus Coll., Cambridge. Apprentice rising to Works Manager of Armstrong Whitworth and Co., Ltd, Openshaw, Manchester, 1908-22; Works Manager and Local Dir Thos. Firth and Sons, Sheffield, 1922; General Works Manager and Dir Thos Firth and John Brown, Ltd, Sheffield, 1930, Managing Dir, 1944-51. Past Dir of other companies. *Address:* Spring Bank, 60 Stumperlowe Crescent Road, Sheffield 10. *T:* Sheffield 31058.   *[Died 27 April 1971.*

MATTHEWS, Maj.-Gen. Francis Raymond Gage, CB 1949; DSO 1945; *b* 26 Jan. 1903; *s* of late H. F. Matthews, MA, ICS, Nicholas Nymet, North Tawton, Devon, and of late Mrs H. B. Jones (she *m* 2nd, 1914, Col H. B. Jones, CB; he died 1952); *m* 1st, 1936, Jean Frances Graham (*d* 1961), *d* of Gen. Sir David Campbell, GCB; one *s* ; 2nd, 1970, Heather Rosalie Shackleton, Dublin; one *s. Educ:* Cheltenham Coll.; RMC, Sandhurst. Commissioned 1923 into York and Lancaster Regt; promoted into The South Wales Borderers, 1935; Staff Coll., 1937-38; GSO2, 1939-40; GSO1 Div., 1940-41; Bn Comd, MEF, 1941; DMT, Middle East, 1943; Bde Comd, Italy and NW Europe, 1943-44; Div. Comd, BAOR, 1945; First Comdt, RMA, Sandhurst, 1946-48; GOC Land Forces, Hong-Kong, 1948-49. Pres., No 1 Regular Commissions Board, War Office, 1949-50; Commander, 1st Infantry Division, 1950-52; Dir of Infantry, War Office, 1952-55; Comdt, Civil Service Defence Coll., 1956; Dir, Civil Defence, SW Region, 1960-66. Col The South Wales Borderers, 1954-61. Joint Master, South and West Wilts Foxhounds, 1966-71. *Recreation:* riding. *Address:* Horseshoe Cottage, Crockerton, Warminster, Wilts. *Club:* Naval and Military.   *[Died 26 May 1976.*

MATTHEWS, Ven. Hubert John, MA; Archdeacon Emeritus of Hampstead, since 1962, Archdeacon, 1950-62; Rector of St Andrew Undershaft, 1954-62; Chaplain of the Order of St John of Jerusalem, 1946; Examining Chaplain to the Bishop of

London, 1950-62; *b* 18 June 1889; *s* of Henry Arthur and Edith Kate Matthews; *m* 1920, Kathleen Frances, *d* of A. M. Cawthorne; one *s* two *d. Educ:* Winchester; St John's Coll., Oxford. Originally intended for legal career; articled to Ellis Peirs & Co., solicitors, 1911; Cuddesdon Theol Coll., 1913; Curate of St Martin-in-the-Fields, 1914-21; Temp. Chaplain RN (HMS Malaya), 1917-19; Vicar of All Hallows, East India Docks, 1921-25; Curate-in-Charge, Christ Church, Kensington, 1925-30; Vicar of St Jude's, South Kensington, 1930-42; Rector of St Marylebone, 1942-54; Chaplain to Grocers' Company, 1944; Rural Dean of St Marylebone, 1946-50; Prebendary of St Paul's Cathedral, 1948-50; clerical sec. of London Diocesan Conf., 1948-50; on HQ Cttee of Emergency Help Scheme of British Red Cross and Order of St John, 1926-62 (vice-chm. 1944-62). *Recreations:* reading, travel. *Address:* Martyn House, Baldric Road, Folkestone, Kent. *Club:* Radnor (Folkestone).
[*Died* 28 *April* 1971.

MATTHEWS, Prof. James Robert, CBE 1956; LLD; MA, FRSE, FLS; Regius Professor of Botany, University of Aberdeen, and Keeper of Cruickshank Botanic Garden, 1934-59; Chm. Macaulay Institute for Soil Research, 1947-59; Chm. Scottish Horticultural Research Inst., 1952-59; Member, Nature Conservancy (Scottish Cttee) (ex-Chm.), 1949-61; Gov., North of Scotland Coll. of Agriculture, 1937-59; Member: Aberdeen Coll. of Education Cttee, 1945-55; Cttee for Brown Trout Research, 1948-59; Governing Body, Rowett Research Institute, 1955-59; Vice-Pres. Royal Society of Edinburgh, 1958-61; *b* 8 March 1889; *yr s* of Robert Matthews, Dunning, Perthshire, and Janet McLean; *m* 1st, 1916, Helen Donaldson, Milnathort (*d* 1926); 2nd, 1928, Christine Young Blackhall, Edinburgh; two *s. Educ:* Perth Acad.; Edinburgh Univ. Lecturer in Botany, Birkbeck Coll., London, 1913-16; Temp. Protozoologist at Liverpool Sch. of Tropical Medicine (Western Command), 1916-19; Lecturer in Botany, University of Edinburgh, 1920-29; Prof. of Botany, University of Reading, 1929-34. Veitch Memorial Medal in Horticulture, 1958; Neill Prize and Medal for Natural History, Royal Society Edinburgh, 1964. *Publications:* Origin and Distribution of the British Flora, 1955; various papers on the Taxonomy of British Plants (especially Rosa), on Plant Distribution, and on Plant Morphology; also numerous papers on the Protozoology of Dysentery. *Recreations:* gardening, music. *Address:* Duncrib, Banchory, Kincardineshire AB3 3SQ.
[*Died* 12 *April* 1978.

MATTHEWS, Norman Derek, OBE 1963; Governor of Montserrat, since 1974; *b* 19 March 1922; *s* of late Dr Horatio Matthews, ophthalmic surgeon, and of Mrs Ruth Fryer Matthews; *m* 1st, 1944, Pamela Elaine (*née* Matchett) (marr. diss.); one *s* one *d*; 2nd, 1951, Muriel Elisabeth (*nee* Knott); one *s* one *d. Educ:* Epsom Coll.; London Univ. RN, 1940-46. Colonial Administration, Nyasaland, 1946-64; Permanent Secretary, Malawi Govt, 1964-67; joined FCO, 1967. *Recreations:* fishing, sailing. *Address:* Government House, Montserrat, West Indies. *Clubs:* Army and Navy; Montserrat Yacht (Montserrat).
[*Died* 21 *July* 1976.

MATTHEWS, Rt. Rev. Seering John, OBE 1967; *b* 26 March 1900; *s* of Seering Frederick and Sarah Jane Matthews; *m* 1944, Barbara, *d* of Rev. H. G. Browning, Althorne, Essex; two *s* two *d. Educ:* St John's Coll., Auckland; Fort Street High Sch., Sydney; Moore Theol Coll., Sydney. ThL 1925. Deacon, 1925; Priest, 1926. Curate, Christ Church, Sydney, 1925-29; permission to officiate Dio. Canterbury, 1930; Priest-in-Charge, St Mary's Fitzroy, Melbourne, 1931-32; Vicar, St James', Calcutta, 1933-38; Principal, Bp Westcott Sch., Namkum, 1938-42; Chap. RAF (India), 1942-46; Vicar, St Bartholomew's, Ipswich, Suffolk, 1946-51; Chap. Southport Sch., Brisbane, 1951-54; Rector, St Paul's Cathedral, Rockhampton, 1954-60; Archdeacon of Rockhampton, 1954-60; Bishop of Carpentaria, 1960-68. *Recreation:* fishing. *Address:* 71 Kalimna Drive, Moana Park, Qld 4217, Australia. *Club:* United Service (Brisbane).
[*Died July* 1978.

MATTHEWS, Very Rev. Walter Robert, KCVO 1935; CH 1962; DD, DLit (London), Hon. DD (Cambridge, St Andrews, Glasgow, Trinity College, Dublin, Trinity College, Toronto), Hon. STD (Columbia University, USA); Hon. STP (St John's College, Winnipeg); Hon. LLD (London), 1969; FRSL 1948; Dean of St Paul's, 1934-67; Dean Emeritus since 1967; Dean of Order of the British Empire, 1957-67; Hon. Bencher, Gray's Inn; *b* 1881; *s* of P. W. Matthews, Chief Inspector, Bankers' Clearing House; *m* 1912, Margaret Bryan, BSc (*d* 1963); one *s* one *d* (and one *s* killed in action, 1940). *Educ:* Wilson's Grammar Sch., Camberwell; King's Coll., London. Curacies St Mary Abbots, Kensington, and St Peter, Regent Square; Asst Chaplain Magdalen Hosp.; Lecturer in Philosophy at King's Coll., 1908-18, also in Dogmatic Theology, 1909-18; Vicar of

Christ Church, Crouch End, 1916-18; Dean of King's Coll., London, 1918-32 (now Fellow); Prof. of the Philosophy of Religion, King's Coll., 1918-32; Dean of Exeter, 1931-34; Canon Theologian of Liverpool Cathedral, 1930; Chaplain to Gray's Inn, 1920; Preacher to Gray's Inn, 1929; examining Chaplain to the Bishop of Oxford; Boyle Lecturer, 1920-22; Chaplain to the King, 1923-31; White Lecturer, 1927; Noble Lecturer, 1928; Wilde Lecturer, 1929; Warburton Lecturer, 1938. FRSL 1948; Fellow Westfield Coll., University of London, 1948. Freedom Cross of King Haakon VII (Norway), 1947; Order of White Lion (3rd class) Czechoslovakia, 1947. *Publications:* Studies in Christian Philosophy, 1921; 2nd edition, 1928; an edition of Butler's Ethical Writings in Bohn Library; The Idea of Revelation, 1924; The Psychological Approach to Religion, The Gospel and the Modern Mind, 1925; God and Evolution, 1926; joint editor, Library of Constructive Theology; Editor, Dogma in History and Thought, 1929; God in Christian Thought and Experience, 1930; 7th edn 1942; Seven Words, 1933; The Adventures of Gabriel in his Search for Mr Shaw, 1933; Essays in Construction, 1934; Hope of Immortality; The Purpose of God, 1935; Our Faith in God, 1936; The Christian Faith, 1936; Signposts to God, 1938; Teaching of Christ, 1939; Following Christ; Moral Issues of the War, 1940; The Foundations of Peace, 1942; Strangers and Pilgrims, 1945; St Paul's in Wartime, 1946; The Problem of Christ in the 20th Century, 1951; Some Christian Words, 1956; joint editor, A History of St Paul's Cathedral and the Men Associated with it, 1957; The Search for Perfection, 1957; The Lord's Prayer, 1958; The Thirty-Nine Articles, 1961; Memories and Meanings, 1969; The Year Through Christian Eyes, 1970. *Address:* 6 Vincent Square, SW1. *Club:* Athenæum.
[*Died* 5 *Dec.* 1973.

MATTHEWS, Prof. William; Visiting Distinguished Professor, English Department, University of Pittsburgh, since 1972; *b* London, 25 June 1905; *s* of William Eldridge Matthews and Annie Louise (*née* Rodwell); *m* 1948, Lois Nicholson Emery; no *c. Educ:* Birkbeck Coll., Univ. of London. BA 1929, MA 1931, PhD 1934. Clerk in Parliamentary Solicitors' Office, 1919-29; Lectr, Westfield Coll., 1936; Instructor, Univ. of Wisconsin, 1938-39; Prof. of English, Univ. of California at Los Angeles, 1939-72, retd; Dir, Center for Medieval and Renaissance Studies, UCLA, 1970-72. Pres., Philological Assoc. of Pacific Coast, 1964-65; Pres., Internat. Assoc. of Univ. Profs of English, 1971-74. Hon. DLett Claremont Graduate Sch., 1967. Prize for Distinguished Graduate Teaching; Faculty Research Lectureship, UCLA, 1968; twice Guggenheim Fellow. *Publications:* Cockney Past and Present, 1938; Diary of Dudley Ryder, 1939; Our Soldiers Speak, 1943; American Diaries, 1945; British Diaries, 1950; British Autobiographies, 1955; The Tragedy of Arthur, 1960; Later Medieval English Prose, 1963; The Ill-Framed Knight, 1966; Charles II's Escape from Worcester, 1966; Medieval Secular Literature, 1966; Old and Middle English Literature, 1968; Autobiography, Biography and the Novel, 1973; American Diaries in Manuscript, 1974; (with Robert Latham) The Diary of Samuel Pepys, Vols I-VIII, 1970-74 (in continuation), etc; numerous articles in scholarly jls. *Recreations:* gardening, book-collecting, swimming. *Address:* 189 Greenfield Avenue, Los Angeles, California 90049, USA. *T:* Los Angeles 476-2715.
[*Died* 11 *June* 1975.

MAUDE, Col Alan Hamer, CMG 1919; DSO 1917; TD; *b* Highgate, 18 Aug. 1885; *e s* of Edmund Maude and Claudine Ina, *d* of G. A. Pridmore, JP, Coventry; *m* 1910, Dorothy Maude (*d* 1960), *o d* of Frederic Upton; one *s. Educ:* Rugby (scholar); Oriel Coll., Oxford (exhibitioner, MA). Sub-Editor Daily Chronicle, 1912-14; on Editorial Staff of The Times, 1920-50. Joined Army Service Corps (TF), 1909; served in France and Belgium, 1915-19 (despatches twice, CMG, DSO); Commanded 47th (London) Divl Train, 1918-19 and 1924-29, and 59th Divl Train, 1919; Bt-Col 1928; Col (TA), 1929; ADS&T, GHQ, BEF, 1939; AQMG and Controller, Central Purchase Bd, BEF, 1940; CRASC, Bordon District, 1940-43, and Kent District, 1943-45; Hon. Col 56th (London) Armoured Divl Column, RASC, TA, 1947-53. Pres. Old Rugbeian Soc., 1952-53. DL London, 1937-76. *Publications:* Edited War History of the 47th Division, 1914-19; Rugby School Register, 1911-46; and many special numbers of The Times. *Recreations:* formerly rifle-shooting (Captain, Rugby and Oxford teams); gardening, photography, genealogy. *Address:* Stone House, Petworth, West Sussex. *T:* Petworth 42314.
[*Died* 6 *June* 1979.

MAUDE, Brig. Christian George, DSO 1918; OBE 1919; MC; *b* 4 Sept. 1884; *s* of late Lt-Col A. Maude, 8 Pelham Street, SW7; *m* 1st, 1920, Patience (from whom he obtained a divorce, 1930; she *d* 1935), *e d* of 1st Baron Rochdale, CB; one *d* (and one *s* decd); 2nd, 1931, Hester Joan, *y d* of late Charles and Lady Mabelle Egerton; three *d. Educ:* Rugby; RMC Sandhurst. Joined 5th Fusiliers, 1904; transferred to Royal Fusiliers, 1908; to Army

Educational Corps, 1920; served Mohmand Expedition, NW Frontier, India, 1908; European War, France and Palestine, 1915-19 (despatches, DSO, OBE, MC); Inspector, Army Educational Corps, War Office, 1937, and Controller AEC, 1943-44; retired pay, 1945; employed with CCG, 1946-54. *Recreation:* fishing. *Address:* The Downs, Broad Oak, Heathfield, Sussex. *T:* Heathfield 3681. *Club:* Boodle's.
                                                    [*Died* 13 *Dec.* 1971.

MAUDE, Evan Walter, CB 1968; a Deputy Secretary, Ministry of Agriculture, Fisheries and Food, 1970-79; *b* 11 Feb. 1919; *s* of late Sir E. John Maude, KCB, KBE; *m* 1949, Jennifer, *d* of Sir Edward Stanley Gotch Robinson, CBE, FSA, FBA, and of Pamela, *o d* of Sir Victor Horsley, CB, FRS, and *widow* of Capt. O. T. Bulmer; three *d*. *Educ:* Rugby; New Coll., Oxford. Served in RNVR (Fleet Air Arm), 1940-45 (despatches). Entered HM Treasury, 1946; Asst Private Sec. to Chancellor of the Exchequer and Economic Sec., 1947-48; Private Sec. to Sec. of State for Co-ordination of Transport, Fuel and Power, 1951-53; Principal Private Sec. to Chancellor of Exchequer, 1956-58; Asst Under-Sec. of State, Dept of Economic Affairs, 1964-66; Dep. Under-Sec. of State, 1966-67; Economic Minister in British Embassy, Washington, 1967-69; Third Sec., Treasury, 1969-70. Mem. ARC, 1974-79. *Recreations:* sailing, ski-ing, music. *Address:* 5 Downshire Hill, NW3.   [*Died* 11 *Feb.* 1980.

MAUDLING, Rt. Hon. Reginald, PC 1955; MP (C) Barnet, Chipping Barnet, since 1974 (Herts, Barnet, 1950-74); Hon. Fellow Merton College, Oxford, 1958; *b* 7 March 1917; *m* 1939, Beryl Laverick; three *s* one *d*. *Educ:* Merchant Taylors'; Merton Coll., Oxford. 1st Class in Greats. Called to the Bar, Middle Temple, 1940. Contested Borough of Heston and Isleworth, 1945. Parly Sec. to Minister of Civil Aviation, 1952; Economic Sec. to the Treasury, Nov. 1952-April 1955; Minister of Supply, April 1955-Jan. 1957; Paymaster-Gen., 1957-59; Pres. of the Board of Trade, 1959-61; Sec. of State for the Colonies, Oct. 1961-July 1962; Chancellor of the Exchequer, July 1962-Oct. 1964; Home Secretary, 1970-72. Pres., Nat. Union of Cons. and Unionist Assocs., 1967. *Publication:* Memoirs, 1978. *Address:* Bedwell Lodge, Essendon, Herts.   [*Died* 14 *Feb.* 1979.

MAUFE, Sir Edward, Kt 1954; RA 1947 (ARA 1938); MA Oxon, FRIBA; architect; Hon. Fellow of St John's College, Oxford; Hon. LLD The Queen's University, Northern Ireland; Hon. Master of the Bench, Gray's Inn; *b* 1883; *s* of Henry Maufe, Red House, Bexley Heath, Kent; *m* Gladys Prudence, *d* of Edward Stutchbury, Geological Survey of India; (one *s* decd). Educ: St John's Coll., Oxford; articled to W. A. Pite, FRIBA. Served Salonica Forces, Capt. RA, ADC to GOC, RA XIIth Corps. Vice-Pres., RIBA, 1939-43. Chief Architect and Artistic Adviser to Commonwealth War Graves Commission, 1943-69; Royal Fine Art Commission, 1946-53; Treasurer of the Royal Academy, 1954-59; Mem. of Lloyd's; Medallist, Paris Exhibition, 1925; Royal Gold Medal for Architecture, 1944. *Works include:* Guildford Cathedral; The Runnymede Memorial; buildings for Trinity and St John's Colls, Cambridge, and St John's and Balliol, Oxford; Morley Coll., London Hosp. Students' Hostel; Kelling Hall, Norfolk; Yaffle Hill, Dorset; BBC Chapel; St Saviour's, Acton; St Thomas's, Hanwell; Festival Theatre, Cambridge; Playhouse, Oxford; The Magna Carta Memorial. Architect for Reconstruction of: Gray's Inn; Middle Temple; St Columba, Pont St. *Address:* Shepherd's Hill, Buxted, Sussex. *Clubs:* Arts, Chelsea Arts.
                                                    [*Died* 12 *Dec.* 1974.

MAUNDRELL, Captain Arthur Goodall, CB 1937; CIE 1935; Royal Indian Navy, retired; *b* 1884; *y s* of late Ven. Archdeacon H. Maundrell, Japan and Winchester; *m* 1916, Amy Florence Mary, *o d* of late Capt. George B. Graham, Duke of Wellington's Regt. Joined RIN, 1906; served European War, 1914-19; Port Officer, Akyab, Burma, 1923-26; Chief of Staff, Navy Office, and Capt. Superintendent Dockyard, Bombay, Hon. ADC to Viceroy of India, 1934-38; retired, 1938; recalled to service Sept. 1939 to Sept. 1945 as Commodore of Convoys and RINLO Admiralty for 2+ and 3+ years respectively. *Address:* St Elmo, Grouville, Jersey, CI. *Club:* United Service & Royal Aero.   [*Died* 9 *Nov.* 1972.

MAUNSELL, Mark Stuart Ker, CBE 1952 (OBE 1944); DSO 1943; Vice-Chairman, Brooke-Bond Liebig Ltd, 1976-79 (Director, 1973-80); Director: Liebig Meat Co., 1974-78; Baxters (The Butchers) Ltd, 1975-79; *b* 24 July 1910; *s* of Ernest Oliver Henry Maunsell, Flamsteadbury, Redbourn; *m* 1939, Ruth Hunter Mason, *d* of T. A. C. Mason, Headley, Surrey; one *s* one *d*. *Educ:* Cheltenham; RMA, Woolwich. Commissioned, RA, 1930; RHA Palestine (Clasp, 1934-35). Served War of 1939-45, 2nd Div., Burma; Chief of Staff, Control Commn, Saigon, FIC, 1945; Asst Comdt, RMA, Sandhurst, 1946; Chief

of Staff, Allied Forces Hong Kong, 1949; Chief of Staff, 1 (Br) Corps, 1954. Dir of Trading, John Lewis Partnership, 1957-63; Dir, Gallaher Ltd, 1963-76. Inspector-General of Prisons, 1967-70. Chm., Nat. Trust Trading, 1978-. Croix de Guerre (France); Commandeur, Légion d'Honneur, 1947. *Address:* Hurst Lodge, Hurstbourne Tarrant, near Andover, Hants SP11 0AH. *T:* Hurstbourne Tarrant 304. *Clubs:* Jockey, Cavalry and Guards.
                                                    [*Died* 30 *July* 1980.

MAUNSELL, Brig. Raymund John, CBE 1944 (OBE 1941); late Brigadier General Staff, SHAEF; *b* 25 Nov. 1903; *y s* of Major M. C. Maunsell; *g s* of Gen. Sir Frederick Maunsell, KCB, RE; *m* 1st, 1931, Nora Constance Richmond (*d* 1956); one *s* one *d*; 2nd, 1960, Mrs Beryl Preston. *Educ:* Beaumont Coll.; RMC, Sandhurst. Commissioned into Royal Tank Corps, 1923; served with Trans-jordan Frontier Force, 1930-31; Gen. Staff, HQ British Troops in Egypt, 1932-37; Major special appointment, 1937-39; at GHQ Middle East and SHAEF: Lt-Col GS 1939-42; Col GS 1942-43, Brig. GS, 1943-46, retd 1946. Company Official, 1948-63. US Legion of Merit, 1946. *Address:* La Maison Haute, Mont de la Rocque, St Aubin, Jersey, Channel Islands. *T:* Central 41802. *Clubs:* Army and Navy; Victoria (Jersey); Royal Channel Islands Yacht.   [*Died* 14 *Oct.* 1976.

MAWBY, Sir Maurice (Alan Edgar), Kt 1963; CBE 1959; Chairman, Queensland Alumina Ltd; Director, Guardian Royal Exchange Assurance Co.; *b* 31 Aug. 1904; *s* of Charles Curtis and Alice Maud Mawby (*née* Smith); *m* 1929, Lena White; one *s*. *Educ:* Broken Hill High Sch. and Broken Hill Technical Coll., NSW, Australia. Chairman: Conzinc Riotinto of Australia Ltd, 1962-74 (Dir, 1974-77); Hamersley Holdings, 1965-71; Bougainville Mining, 1967-71. FAA 1969; Fellow, Aust. Acad. of Technology and Science, 1975. Hon. DSc, NSW University of Technology, Sydney, 1955; Hon. DASc, Victoria Inst. of Colleges, 1975. *Publications:* technical papers. *Address:* 102 Mont Albert Road, Canterbury, Victoria 3126, Australia. *T:* 836 8888. *Clubs:* Melbourne, Athenæum (Melbourne); Broken Hill (Broken Hill, NSW).   [*Died* 4 *Aug.* 1977.

MAXSE, Dame Marjorie, DBE 1952 (CBE 1941; MBE 1918); *b* 1891; *d* of late E. G. B. Maxse, CMG, and Alice, *o d* of T. N. Miller. Administrator, subsequently Chief Organisation Officer, Conservative Central Office, 1921-39; Dir Children's Overseas Reception Board, Vice-Chm. WVS, 1940-44; Vice-Chm. Conservative Party Organisation, 1944-51. *Address:* Court House, Barcombe, Lewes, Sussex. *Club:* University Women's.
                                                    [*Died* 3 *May* 1975.

MAXWELL, Sir Alexander Hyslop, KCMG 1951; Kt 1943; *b* 21 April 1896; *s* of late Judge A. Hyslop Maxwell; *m* 1st, 1924, Doris Galbraith (marriage dissolved 1957), *d* of late Henry Pattinson, Liverpool; one *s* one *d*; 2nd, 1958, Phyllis Hargreaves (*d* 1971), New Zealand. *Educ:* Moorland House, Heswall; Trinity Coll., Glenalmond; Switzerland. Served European War of 1914-18; in Royal Naval Div.; interned in Holland after fall of Antwerp, Oct. 1914. Joined family business of W. A. & G. Maxwell & Co. Ltd, Tobacco Importers, of Liverpool, 1919; Dir, 1924; Man. Dir Macmillan Maxwell & Co. Ltd, 1931, Chm., 1946-; Chm. British India Tobacco Corporation. Director: Ronson Products, Ltd; Knott Hotels (London) Ltd. Govt Delegate to Greece and Turkey, 1940 and 1946; Tobacco Adviser Board of Trade, 1940; Tobacco Controller, Board of Trade, 1940-45, remaining at Board of Trade as Adviser to Govt and Chm. of Tobacco Advisory Cttees. Chm. British Travel and Holidays Assoc., 1950-54 (British Tourist and Holidays Bd, 1947-50). Pres. Inst. of Travel Managers, 1959-66; Pres. Hosp. Caterers' Assoc., 1951-66; Mem. Bd of Govs, University Coll. Hosp., 1945 (Vice-Chm., 1948-51, Chm. 1951-63). Officer Legion of Honour; Comdr Order of Orange Nassau; Comdr Order Ouissam Alaouite (Morocco). *Address:* 61 Cadogan Square, SW1. *T:* 01-235 8422. *Clubs:* American, Pilgrims; Salisbury (Rhodesia).   [*Died* 15 *Oct.* 1971.

MAXWELL, Hon. Allan Victor, CMG 1967; retired Australian Judge; *b* 12 May 1887; *s* of late Francis Augustus Maxwell; *m* 1919, Margaret Lawless; one *s* three *d*. *Educ:* Birchgrove; Fort Street; University of Sydney (BA, LLB). Called to Bar, 1913; KC 1929. Justice, Supreme Court, NSW, 1934-55; Senior Puisne Judge, 1950. Royal Commissioner (Federal and State). NSW delegate to First Australian Law Convention, 1933. President: Royal Blind Soc. of NSW, 1945-61; Aust. Nat. Council for the Blind, 1959-; NSW Rowing Assoc., 1943-. *Recreation:* golf. *Address:* 452 Edgecliff Square, Edgecliff, Sydney, NSW 2027, Australia. *T:* 32.2724. *Clubs:* Australian (Sydney); Royal Sydney Golf (Rose Bay).   [*Died* 5 *Oct.* 1975.

MAXWELL, Maj.-Gen. Sir Aymer, Kt 1957; CBE 1941; MC; JP; Vice-Lieutenant of Stewartry of Kirkcudbright since 1956; *b* 27

Dec. 1891; *s* of Wellwood Maxwell of Kirkennan; *m* 1915, Isobel Frances Hawthorn, *d* of Maj.-Gen. D. G. L. Shaw. *Educ:* Cheltenham; RMA, Woolwich. Commissioned in Royal Artillery, 1911; served European War, France, 1914-18; War of 1939-45, Middle East; retd pay, 1944. Chm. British Legion, Scotland, 1954-58. Mem. of the Queen's Body Guard for Scotland (The Royal Company of Archers); Convener, County Council of Stewartry of Kirkcudbright, 1959-64 (Vice Convener, 1956-59). *Address:* Kirkennan, Dalbeattie, Kircudbrightshire. *T:* Palnackie 211. [*Died* 16 *Oct.* 1971.

MAXWELL, **Bertram Wayburn**, BA, MA, PhD; Adjunct Professor of History and Political Science, Wagner College, Staten Island, New York, and Literary Adviser to Macmillan Publishing Co., New York, USA; *b* 14 Jan. 1891; *s* of Mark Maxwell and Sarah Martha Bender; *m* 1936, Margaret Evelyn Wright. *Educ:* Privately; Hamline Univ.; State Univ. of Iowa. Served in US Army, 1918-19; Mem. of American Political Science Association. *Publications:* Contemporary Municipal Government of Germany, 1928; The Soviet State, 1935; Co-Author of Propaganda and Dictatorship, 1936; Comparative Local Government (joint), 1938; International Relations, 1938; trans. (with Margaret Maxwell) Hombu, Indian Life in the Brazilian Jungle, 1963, etc; contributes to various academic journals. *Address:* 81 Charles Street, New York, NY 10014, USA. [*Died* 16 *Jan.* 1972.

MAXWELL, **Denis Oliver**; Director: Barclays Bank Trust Co. Ltd, since 1971; Barclays Bank DCO, since 1968; *b* 27 Feb. 1906; 2nd *s* of William and Sarah Maxwell; *m* 1932, Lilian Hannah Sheppard; two *s*. *Educ:* St Ignatius Coll., London. Entered Martins Bank Ltd, London, 1924; Jt Gen. Manager, 1954; Dep. Chief Gen. Manager, 1961; Director, 1965; Chief Gen. Manager, 1966. *Recreation:* golf. *Address:* Windle Wood, Vyner Road North, Bidston, Birkenhead, Cheshire, L43 7PY. *T:* 051-652 4411. *Club:* Royal Liverpool Golf.
[*Died* 22 *Dec.* 1971.

MAXWELL, **Rt. Rev. Harold Alexander**; *b* 17 Dec. 1897; *s* of J. Maxwell; *m* 1929, Grace, *d* of Bishop W. W. Cassels, W China; one *s* one *d*. *Educ:* Liverpool Coll.; Liverpool Collegiate Sch.; Liverpool Univ. (BA in Philosophy, Hon. MA 1946); Ridley Hall, Cambridge (Theology). Deacon, 1924; Priest, 1925; joined CMS and sailed for China, 1926; engaged in educational and pastoral work for eleven years; Lecturer at Union Theological Coll., Chengtu, 1940-43; Sec. of Church Missionary Soc., W China, 1940-50; Elected to Exec. Cttee National Christian Council, China, 1942; Vice-Chm. Board of Managers W China Univ., 1949; Asst Bishop of West Szechwan Diocese, China, 1943-50; Vicar of Copt Oak, Leicester, 1950-52; Ab-Kettleby with Wartnaby and Holwell, 1952-59; Rector of Swithland, 1959-65; an Asst Bishop of Leicester, 1950-65; retired 1965. *Publications:* Vital Truths (in Chinese), 1939; Confronted with Christ (Chinese and English), 1944. *Address:* 4 Wessex Avenue, New Milton, Hants. [*Died* 30 *Dec.* 1975.

MAXWELL, **Herbert William**; *b* 24 March 1888; *s* of James Ward Maxwell and Charlotte Eleanor Morris; *m* 1915, Winifred J. Coysh (*d* 1961); one *s* one *d*. *Educ:* Kent Coll., Canterbury. Surveyor and Land Agent, 1906-14; Sergeant 1/25th London Cyclist Battalion, 1908-16; Lieut Royal Engineers, 1916-19; Secretary: British Institute of Industrial Art; Palace of Arts, BEE Wembley; Exhibition of Flemish and Belgian Art; Advisory Cttee, Royal Mint, 1920-27; Curator, Stoke-on-Trent Museums, 1927-30; Dir Bristol Museum and Art Gallery, 1930-45; Fellow, Royal Society of Arts; Mem. of Council, Museum Association, 1930-32; Pres., South-western group of Museums and Art Galleries 1931-32; Hon. Sec., Council for the Preservation of Ancient Bristol; Hon. Gen. Sec. Theatre Royal, Bristol, Preservation Fund, 1938-48. In South America with exhibition of British Contemporary Art for British Council, 1943-44; Mem. Advisory Council, Victoria and Albert Museum, 1945-50, Acting Hon. Sec. Royal West of England Academy, 1946-51; Dir, City Art Gallery, Bristol, 1945-52; Curator, Snowshill Manor, Glos (The National Trust), 1952-62. Elected to Morden Coll., 1967. *Publications:* Exhibition Catalogues, Magazine articles, etc. *Address:* Morden College, Blackheath, SE3 0PW. [*Died* 20 *Feb.* 1979.

MAXWELL, **Surgeon Rear-Adm. Joseph Archibald**, CB 1950; CVO 1939; CBE 1944 (OBE 1938); *b* 1890; *s* of Thomas Henry Maxwell, KC, LLD; *m* 1919, Dorothy Anna, ARRC (*d* 1979), *d* of John Arthur Perkin, The Grange, Matfield, Kent; two *s* two *d*. *Educ:* Trinity Coll., Dublin (MB, BCh 1912); FRCS Edinburgh 1926. Surgeon Rear-Adm. 1946; in charge: Hospital Ship Oxfordshire, 1943-44; RN Aux. Hosp. Sydney, 1944-46; RN Aux. Hosp. Sherborne, 1946-48; RN Hosp. Haslar, 1948-49; formerly Surgical Specialist, RN Hosps, Haslar, Malta,

Chatham, and Plymouth; retired, 1949; CStJ 1949, KHS 1946-49. Medical Superintendent, St Mary's Hospital, Portsmouth, retired 1955. *Address:* The Old Vicarage, Compton Chamberlayne, Salisbury, Wilts. [*Died* 12 *July* 1980.

MAXWELL, **Mrs Patrick Perceval-**; *see* King-Hall, Magdalen.

MAY, **Surgeon Vice-Adm. Sir Cyril**; *see* May, Surgeon Vice-Adm. Sir R. C.

MAY, **Major Frederick, (Fred May)**, MBE 1939; TD; CStJ; Artist and Caricaturist; Chevalier Légion d'Honneur; Officier Palmes d'Académie; Médaille au Mérite (Française); *b* 25 Jan. 1891; *s* of late John Morritt May and Annie (*née* Gittins); *m* 1916, Amy Kidger (*d* 1973); one *s* one *d*. *Educ:* Wallasey Coll. of Art; Reading Univ. Major, late The Green Howards; served: European War, 7 Bn France, 1916-17 (wounded); War of 1939-45, The 4th Bn Green Howards, GSO, GHQ 21 Army Gp (MI), HQ Fighter Command and SHAEF G3 Div., France and Germany, 1944-46. Formerly artist on North Eastern Daily Gazette, Middlesbrough, Liverpool Daily Post and Echo, and later The Tatler, Graphic, and Weekly Sketch for 60 years. Rejoined new edn of The Tatler, 1968. Contrib. to several jls, from New Zealand to Vancouver; successful Loan Exhibn of own paintings and sketches, Municipal Libraries, Middlesbrough, Nov. 1930; permanent collections in Sir John Hunt Art Section, City Library, York, Artists' Club, Liverpool, Bentley Priory, Stanmore, Mddx, Polo Museum, Midhurst, RAF Museum, Hendon, and several City Art Galls, Libraries and Museums; work chosen by Japanese Govt, as being correct representative of British Caricature and to contribute to permanent Art Collection at Tokyo, 1921; King George VI Coronation Medal; Staff Officer to Gen. Sir Eric S. Girdwood, Chief Gold Stick Officer, Westminster Abbey, 12 May 1937. *Publications:* The 4th Battalion, Green Howards; The York and Lancaster Regiment; City Lights. *Recreations:* walking, swimming. *Address:* Old Green Cottage, Hillside, Odiham, Hants. *T:* Odiham 2239. *Club:* Artists (Liverpool).
[*Died* 31 *Oct.* 1976.

MAY, **Percy**; DSc (London), FRIC; Consulting Chemist; *b* London, 1886; 4th *s* of late William and Emma May; *m* 1942, Marjorie Stone, *o d* of late T. R. Maynard; one *s* one *d*. *Educ:* Tollington Park Coll.; University Coll., London; Tuffnell Scholarship, 1908; BSc, 1908 (first-class hons), DSc, 1916; Research Work, 1908; Lecturer and Demonstrator in Chemistry, University of Birmingham, 1911-12; Chemical Research Work in London, 1912-16; at Oxford 1916-21. *Publications:* various papers in Journal of Chemical Society and other scientific journals; Chemistry of Synthetic Drugs, 1st edn 1911, 4th edn 1939, 5th edn 1959. *Recreations:* reading, music, photography. *Address:* 36 Woodstock Road North, St Albans, Herts. *T:* St Albans 51619. [*Died* 1 *Nov.* 1974.

MAY, **Surgeon Vice-Adm. Sir (Robert) Cyril**, KBE 1958 (OBE 1942); CB 1956; MC 1918; FRCS 1957; Medical Director-General of the Navy, 1956-60; *b* 12 June 1897; *yr s* of Robert May, Belgrave Road, London; *m* 1925, Mary (*d* 1977), *d* of Patrick James Robertson, Cupar, Fife; one *s*. *Educ:* Westminster Sch.; Guy's Hospital. Served European War, 1916-18; 2nd Lieut RGA 1915; Actg Major 1917; comd 139 Siege Battery. MRCS, LRCP 1925. Surgeon Lieut RN, 1925; Surgeon Comdr, 1937; Asst to Med. Dir.-Gen., 1938-46; Surgeon Capt., 1946; Senior Medical Officer (Surgical Sect) RN Hosp., Chatham, 1946-49 and 1951-53; Fleet Medical Officer, Home Fleet, 1949-50; Surgeon Rear-Adm., 1953; Medical Officer-in-Charge, RN Hosp., Malta, and Medical Adviser to C-in-C, AFMed., 1953-56; QHS, 1953-60; Surg. Vice-Adm., 1956. KStJ 1959. *Recreations:* cricket, lawn tennis, golf. *Address:* 45 Belsize Court, Lyndhurst Gardens, NW3. *T:* 01-435 5233.
[*Died* 17 *Sept.* 1979.

MAYCOCK, **Rev. Francis Hugh**; Principal of Pusey House, Oxford, 1952-70; Tutor, St Augustine's College, Canterbury, 1970-74; *b* 4 Oct. 1903; *s* of Canon H. W. Maycock and Mrs M. M. Maycock; unmarried. *Educ:* Tonbridge Sch.; Christ Church, Oxford; Cuddesdon Theological Coll. Christ Church, Forest Hill, SE 23, 1927-29; Corpus Christi Mission, Camberwell, 1929-31; Chaplain, Sidney Sussex Coll., Cambridge, 1931-36; Diocese of Borneo, 1936-40; Chaplain of Westcott House, Cambridge, 1940-44; Vicar of St Mary's the less, Cambridge, 1944-52. Examining Chaplain to the Bishop of Ripon, 1959-70. *Publication:* Original Sin (Mirfield Series), 1948. *Address:* 5 Bernard, Burwash, East Sussex. [*Died* 25 *May* 1980.

MAYDON, **Lt-Comdr Stephen Lynch Conway**, RN retired, DSO 1942 (and Bar 1943); DSC 1945; *b* 15 Dec. 1913; *y s* of J. G. Maydon, one time MLA, and Min. of Railways and Harbours,

Natal, S Africa, and Dorothy Isabel Cope; *m* 1938, Joan Mary Doligny Baker, *d* of C. V. Baker, Betchworth, Surrey; three *s*. *Educ:* Twyford Sch., near Winchester; Royal Naval College, Dartmouth. Served in submarines throughout 1939-45 War. Retired from Royal Navy, 1949. Contested (C) Bristol South, 1950; MP (C) Wells Division of Somerset, 1951-70; Jt Parly Sec., Min. of Pensions and Nat. Insce, 1962-64. *Address:* Bruin Wood, Wraxall, near Bristol BS19 1PN. *Club:* Army and Navy.
[*Died 2 March* 1971.

MAYER, Col Edward Rudolph, TD; DL; Member, Thames Conservancy, since 1970; *b* 9 Aug. 1902; *s* of Max Mayer; *m* 1936, Rosemary, *d* of Thomas Craven. *Educ:* Harrow; Trinity Coll., Cambridge (MA, LLB). TA Commission, 1924, Brevet Col, 1950. Served War of 1939-45, E Africa, India and Burma (despatches); Commanded: 304 LAA/A Tank Regt East African Artillery, 1943; 264 (7th London) Field Regt RA (TA), 1947-50; Hon. Col 1953-61; Hon. Col 254 (City of London) Regt RA (TA), 1961-63; Mem. County of London T&AFA, 1947-58. Mem. Board of Trade Advisory Cttees: Revolving Fund for Industry, 1953-58 (Chm. 1958) and Census of Production, 1955-65; Member: Consultative Council for Industry, 1961-67; Export Council for Europe, 1963-66. Pres., National Association of British Manufacturers, 1960-63; Mem. Council CBI, 1965-72. DL County of London, 1954; Hants CC, 1970-. *Recreation:* shooting. *Address:* The Old House, Rotherwick, near Basingstoke, Hants. *T:* Hook 2167. *Clubs:* St James'; Hampshire (Winchester).
[*Died 5 June* 1973.

MAYER, Prof. Maria Goeppert; Professor of Physics, University of California at San Diego, since 1960; *b* Kattowitz, Upper Silesia, 28 June 1906; *o c* of Friedrich Goeppert and Maria (*née* Wolff); became US citizen, 1933; *m* 1930, Joseph Edward Mayer; one *s* one *d*. *Educ:* public and private schs, Göttingen; University of Göttingen (PhD). Volunteer Associate, Johns Hopkins Univ., 1931-39; Lecturer in Chemistry: Columbia Univ., 1939-46; Sarah Lawrence Coll., 1942-45; Physicist, SAM Laboratories, Columbia Univ., 1942-45; Senior Physicist, Argonne National Laboratory, 1946-60; Professor of Physics, University of Chicago, and Enrico Fermi Institute for Nuclear Studies, 1946-60. Member: Nat. Acad. of Sciences; Amer. Physical Soc.; Amer. Philosophical Soc.; Amer. Acad. of Arts and Sciences; Sigma Xi; Corresp. Mem., Akademie der Wissenschaften, Heidelberg. Hon. DSc: Russell Sage Coll., 1960; Mount Holyoke Coll., 1961; Smith Coll., 1961; University of Portland, 1968; Ripon Coll., 1970. Nobel Prize for Physics (jointly), 1963. *Publications:* (with J. E. Mayer) Statistical Mechanics, 1940; (with J. D. Jensen) Elementary Theory of Nuclear Shell Structure, 1955. *Address:* Department of Physics, University of California, San Diego, Calif 92037, USA; 2345 Via Siena, La Jolla, Calif 92037.
[*Died 20 Feb.* 1972.

MAYER, René; Grand Officier de la Légion d'Honneur; Croix de Guerre, 1914-18; Médaille des Evadés; Commandeur du Mérite Maritime; President of the High Authority of European Coal and Steel Community, 1955-57, resigned; *b* Paris, 4 May 1895; *m* 1921 Denise Bloch; one *d* (one *s* killed in War of 1939-45). *Educ:* University of Paris (Licencié en lettres et en droit). Maitre des Requétes, Conseil d'Etat; Vice-Prés., Chemins de Fer du Nord, 1930; Administrateur and Membre du Comité de Direction, SNCF, 1938; Deputy for Constantine, French National Assembly, 1946-56; Commr for Communications, French Cttee for National Liberation, Algiers, 1943; Minister of Public Works and Transport, 1944; Minister of Finance and Economic Affairs, 1947, 1951; Minister of National Defence, 1948; Keeper of the Seals, Ministry of Justice, 1950; Premier, Jan. 1953. Medal of Freedom with silver palm (USA); Grand Cross: of Orange Nassau (Netherlands); of Order of Pahlevi (Iran); of Order of George I (Greece); of Merit of the Republic of Italy; of Order of Crown of Oak (Luxembourg); of Order of Crown (Belgium). *Publication:* Le Pacte Atlantique, (Paris) 1950. *Address:* 9 Rue Vaneau, Paris 7e, France.
[*Died 13 Dec.* 1972.

MAYFIELD, Rev. Canon Guy; Hon. Canon of Chichester; Archdeacon of Hastings, 1956-75; *b* 23 June 1905; *yr s* of late Alfred and Beatrice Mayfield, Hull; *m* 1932, Thelma R., *e d* of late Engineer-Captain M. Johnson; three *s*. *Educ:* Lancing Coll.; Magdalene Coll., Cambridge (MA). 2nd Class Hons Law Tripos; ordained, 1930; Curate: St John's, Fitzroy Square; St Saviour's, Walton Street, SW; Hurstpierpoint. Asst Editor, The Guardian, 1936-39; Chaplain, RAFVR, 1939, Duxford, Gibraltar; Sen. Chaplain, Egypt and The Sudan, 1943. Rector: St Paul's, St Leonards-on-Sea, 1946; Little Horsted, 1948; Dir of Religious Education, Chichester Diocese, 1948; Dep. Diocesan Sec., Press Sec., 1950; Prebendary in Chichester Cathedral, 1956. Select Preacher, Cambridge Univ., 1964. *Publications:* The Church of England: its members and its business, 1957; Towards Simplicity in Prayer, 1964; Like Nothing on Earth,

1965. *Recreation:* painting. *Address:* Curls Cottage, Ripe, Lewes, East Sussex. *Club:* Royal Commonwealth Society.
[*Died 19 July* 1976.

MAYHEW, Capt. George Henry, CBE 1959; Group Marine Superintendent, British and Commonwealth Shipping Group, 1961-64, retired; Director, Union-Castle Line, 1961-64, retired; Commodore, Union-Castle Line, 1953-60; Commodore Master, RMS Windsor Castle (including maiden voyage) during 1960, retired from Sea Service, 1960; *b* 16 Jan. 1901; *s* of George H. and Winifred Mayhew; *m* 1934, Betty, *er d* of Major H. Cardwell, Bowden, Cheshire; one *s*. *Educ:* Blyth Grammar Sch. Joined Union Castle Line as cadet, 1917. War service, 1917-18 and 1939-45. Commanded: Pretoria Castle, Coronation Spithead Review; Pendennis Castle, maiden voyage, 1959. *Address:* A431 St Martini Gardens, Cape Town, S Africa. *Club:* South African Master Mariners (Capetown).
[*Died 8 Oct.* 1973.

MAYLE, Norman Leslie, CMG 1951; Assistant Secretary, Colonial Office, 1944-59; *b* 1899; *m* 1934, Dorothy, *d* of William Whalley; one *s*. Served European War, 1917-19 (Lieut, RFC and RAF). Appointed Colonial Office, 1917; asst principal, 1928; Private Sec. to Under-Sec. of State for the Colonies, 1932; principal, 1936; Mem. British delegation to United States bases Conference, 1941. Federal Service Comr, Aden, 1959-60; Salaries Comr, Fiji and W Pacific, 1961. *Address:* 310 Hood House, Dolphin Square, SW1V 3LX. *T:* 01-834 3800.
[*Died 7 March* 1980.

MAYNARD, Air Vice-Marshal Forster Herbert Martin, CB 1941; AFC 1919; Commander Legion of Merit, USA, 1945; Manager to the Conservative Central Board of Finance, 1946-51; *b* 1 May 1893; *s* of late Rev. H. M. Maynard; *m* 1920, Irene, *d* of late Dr J. H. Pim; one *s* (one *s* decd). *Educ:* St John's Sch., Leatherhead; University Coll., London. Sapper and Corporal Royal Naval Division, Aug. 1914-April 1915; Flight Sub-Lieut RNAS, May 1915; served France, and UK during European War, with RNAS and RAF; permanent commission, Flight-Lieut, 1919; Air Commodore, 1940; Air Vice-Marshal, 1941; RAF Staff Coll., 1924-25; Imperial Defence Coll., 1931; commanded 12 (Bomber) Squadron, 1929-30, and University of London Air Squadron, 1935-36; Air Officer Commanding RAF, Malta, 1940-41; Air Officer in charge of Administration, Coastal Command, 1941-44; Air Officer Commanding 19 Group, 1944-45; retired Nov. 1945. *Recreations:* market gardening, croquet, golf. *Address:* Overdale, West View, Colyford, E Devon. *T:* Colyton 487.
[*Died 26 Jan.* 1976.

MAYNARD, Brig.-Gen. Francis Herbert, CB 1937; DSO 1937; MC 1916; Squadron Leader RAFVR; *b* Ottawa, Canada, 21 Dec. 1881; *s* of M. W. Maynard, Canadian Civil Service, and Ellen, *d* of Senator Hon. R. B. Dickey, Father of Confederation; *m* 1914, Ethel Bates; three *d*. *Educ:* RMC Kingston, Canada (Hon. DScMil 1976; in his capacity as oldest surviving graduate attended centenary celebrations of RMC Canada, Oct. 1976, took salute at paarade of about 1000 serving and ex-cadets, unveiled commemorative statue and received hon. degree). Commissioned to Indian Staff Corps; joined 2nd Battalion Oxf. and Bucks in Bombay, 1902, 25th Bombay Rifles, 1903; served in European War with 5/6 Rajputana Rifles, 57th Wildes Rifles, 4th Suffolks, 4th Black Watch, 2/30th Punjabis (despatches twice, MC); 3rd Afghan War; with Wana Column, operations in Waziristan, 1936-37 (CB); Waziristan 1937 (despatches twice, DSO); operations Waziristan, 1938 (despatches); Commanded 5/6 Rajputana Rifles; held appointment Inspector of PT India; Commander Bannu Brigade, Bannu, NWFP, India, 1934-38; ADC to HM George VI, 1937-38; retired, 1938, awarded good service pension; Hon. Col 5/6 Rajputana Rifles, 1939; Jubilee medal; Coronation medal; served as Flt-Lieut, RAFVR, 1939-40; successively PO, Sqn Ldr and Wing Comdr, RAF, 1940-45. *Recreations:* riding, shooting, and golf. *Address:* 6 York Place Mansions, 117 Baker Street, W1.
[*Died 30 March* 1979.

MAYNE, Cuthbert Joseph, CMG 1954; *b* 3 July 1902; *s* of late Captain Jasper Graham Mayne, CBE, late Inniskillen Fusiliers, Sec. Army Rifle Association, and Chief Constable, E Suffolk, and Cecily Weld; *m* 1948, Joanna, *d* of F. Walsh. *Educ:* Ampleforth Coll., Yorks. Joined Nigerian Administrative Service as Cadet, 1926, District Officer, 1936; Senior District Officer, 1945; Resident, 1946; Senior Resident, 1950. Acted Chief Commissioner once, acted Lieut-Gov. twice and acted Gov. twice, Eastern Region, 1950-56; Deputy Governor, Eastern Nigeria Administrative Service, 1954-56, retired. *Recreations:* trout fishing, shooting. *Address:* Penrhiw Cerrig, Crickadarn, Builth Wells, Breconshire.
[*Died 7 March* 1972.

MAYNE, Dr Gerald Outram; Chief Medical Adviser, Department of Health and Social Security, since 1978; *b* 29 May 1919; *s* of W. J. F. Mayne, MD and Cora Mayne, ARRC; *m* 1943, Hon. Helena Stewart Keith, *d* of late Baron Keith of Avonholm, PC (Life Peer); two *s*. *Educ:* Leeds Grammar Sch.; Univ. of Edinburgh. MB, ChB 1942, DPH 1948, MFCM 1972. House Phys., Edinburgh Royal Infirmary, 1942-43; commnd in RAMC, 1943-47; Asst Med. Officer of Health, County of Roxburgh, 1949-50; Asst Physician, Edinburgh Royal Infirmary, 1950-58; Med. Officer and Sen. Med. Officer, DHSS, 1958-73; Dep. Chief Med. Advr, 1973-78. QHP, 1977-. *Publications:* papers in BMJ, Brit. Jl Venereal Diseases, etc. *Recreations:* hill walking, gardening. *Address:* 47B Fairdene Road, Coulsdon, Surrey CR3 1RG. *T:* Downland 56944. *Clubs:* Civil Service; University Union (Edinburgh).
[Died 13 April 1980.

MAYO, Hon. Sir Herbert, Kt 1948; Senior Puisne Justice of Supreme Court of SA, 1942-66; *b* Adelaide, S Australia, 3 June 1885; *s* of George Gibbes Mayo, Adelaide, Civil Engineer; *m* 1st, 1911, Clarice Gwendoline Thomson Melrose (*d* 1957), Aldgate, SA; one *s* (and one lost at sea, HMAS Sydney, 1941) three *d*; 2nd, 1958, Gwen Alister Brookes, *d* of John MacInnes, Naracoorte, SA. *Educ:* St Peter's Coll., Adelaide; Trinity Coll., Melbourne Univ.; Adelaide Univ. LLB 1909; admitted to SA bar, 1909; KC 1930; Justice Supreme Court, 1942. Actg Chief Justice, May-Dec. 1957. Pres., Phœnix Soc. of S Australia; Pres. British and Foreign Bible Society (SA Auxiliary); Deleg. to London Conf., E-SU, 1951. Formerly: Chancellor of Dioceses of Adelaide and of Willochra (Anglican); Pres. Law Council of Australia, 1933-34, Vice-Pres. 1940-42; Pres. Law Soc. of SA Inc., 1932-33, 1934-35, 1939-40, and 1940-41. Pres. (SA br.), Fellow (Qld br.), Royal Geographical Society of Australasia; Pres. (SA br.), English-Speaking Union; Lectr in Jurisprudence, and in Commercial Law II, University Adelaide; Bd of Govs St Peter's Coll., Adelaide; Jt Ed for SA of Australian Law Jl. *Address:* 90 Northgate Street, Unley Park, Adelaide, SA 5061, Australia. *Clubs:* Adelaide (Adelaide); Australasian Pioneers (Sydney); Royal SA Yacht Squadron.
[Died 1 Oct. 1972.

MAZE, Paul Lucien, DCM 1919, MM 1916 and Bar 1917; Légion d'Honneur, Croix de Guerre; Painter; *b* Havre, 21 May 1887; *s* of Georges Henry Maze and Catherine Branchard; *m* 1st, 1921, Mrs T. A. Nelson (Margaret Balfour) (marr. diss., 1949; she *d* 1967); one *s* (one *d* decd); 2nd, 1950, Jessie Lawrie. *Educ:* Havre and England. Served War of 1914-18, unofficially with Royal Scots Greys, later with French Army on reconnaissance work (despatches thrice); served War of 1939-45 in Home Guard and as personal Staff Officer to Air Marshal Sir Arthur Harris. Rounded Cape Horn in square rigged ship; since when he has established international reputation as painter; Jubilee exhbn of over 100 paintings, Wildenstein Gallery, 1977. *Publication:* A Frenchman in Khaki, 1934. *Address:* Mill Cottage, Treyford, Midhurst, W Sussex. *T:* Harting 464. *[Died 17 Sept. 1979.*

MBANEFO, Sir Louis (Nwachukwu), Kt 1961; Chief Justice of Eastern Region of Nigeria, 1959-67; *b* 13 May 1911; *s* of Chief Mbanefo, the Odu of Onitsha; *m* 1943, Elizabeth Bona Coker; three *s*. *Educ:* King's Coll., Lagos; University Coll., London (LLB 1935; Fellow, 1972); King's Coll., Cambridge (BA (Hist. Tripos) 1937). Set up in Legal Practice, Nigeria, 1937; Mem. of Eastern Nigeria House of Assembly, 1950-52; Mem. of Nigerian Legislative Council, 1950-51; Judge of Supreme Court of Nigeria, 1952, of E Region, 1956; Judge of Federal Supreme Court of Nigeria, 1958-59. Pro-Chancellor, University of Ibadan, Nigeria, 1965-67. Hon. LLD University of Nigeria, 1963. *Recreations:* tennis and golf. *Address:* PMB 1773, Onitsha, Nigeria. *Clubs:* Athenæum; Metropolitan (Lagos).
[Died 28 March 1977.

MEAD, Sir Cecil, Kt 1967; Director, Software Sciences International Ltd, since 1970 (Chairman, 1970-76); *b* 24 Dec. 1900; *s* of James Frederick Mead; *m* 1929, Anne Muriel (*d* 1977), *d* of William Tysoe Boyce; three *d*. Joined Guest, Keen & Nettlefolds Ltd, 1916. Served War of 1914-18, RNVR. The British Tabulating Machine Co. Ltd: joined Tech. Service org., 1924; Sales Man., 1939; Dep. Man. Dir, 1949-55; Man. Dir, 1955-59; ICT (formed by merger of Br. Tabulating Machine Co. Ltd and Powers-Samas Accounting Machines Ltd): Man. Dir, 1959-60, 1964; Dep. Chm., 1960-65; Chm. and Chief Exec., 1965-67. Dir, Internat. Tutor Machines, 1962. Chm., BIM, 1963-64. *Address:* 20 Wolsey Road, East Molesey, Surrey.
[Died 9 Dec. 1979.

MEAD, Dr Margaret; American Anthropologist; Adjunct Professor of Anthropology, Columbia University; Curator Emeritus of Ethnology, American Museum of Natural History, New York (Curator, 1964-69); *b* Philadelphia, 16 Dec. 1901; *d* of Edward Sherwood Mead and Emily (*née* Fogg); *m* 1923, Luther Cressman; *m* 1928, Reo Franklin Fortune; *m* 1936, Gregory Bateson; one *d*. *Educ:* Doylestown High Sch. and New Hope Sch. for Girls, Pennsylvania; De Pauw Univ., Greencastle Indiana; Barnard Coll. (BA); Columbia Univ. (MA; PhD 1929). Nat. Research Council Fellow for Study of Adolescent Girls in Samoa, Associate at Bishop Museum, Honolulu, 1925; Asst Curator of Ethnology, Amer. Museum of Nat. History, 1926-42; Social Science Research Council Fellow for Study of Young Children, Admiralty Is., 1928-29, and extensive field work in New Guinea, etc., during subsequent years; Visiting Lectr in Child Study, Vassar Coll., 1939-41; Exec. Sec., Cttee on Food Habits, Nat. Research Council, 1942-45; Associate Curator of Ethnology, American Museum of Natural History, New York, 1942-64. Lectr, Teachers Coll., 1947-51; Dir Columbia Univ. Research in Contemporary Cultures, 1948-50; Adjunct Prof. of Anthropology, Columbia Univ., 1954-; Consultant, 1968, Chm. (and Prof. of Anthropology), 1969-71, Social Sciences Div., Fordham Univ. Liberal Arts Coll., Lincoln Center, NY; Pres. World Federation for Mental Health, 1956-57; Visiting Prof., Dept of Psychiatry, University of Cincinnati, 1957-; Sloan Prof., Menninger Foundation, 1959-63; Pres., Amer. Anthropological Assoc., 1960; Chairman of Board, Amer. Assoc. for Advancement of Sci., 1976; Mem., Nat. Acad. of Scis, 1975. TV film, Margaret Mead's New Guinea Journal 1928-68, 1968. Arches of Science Award, 1971; Kalinga Prize, 1971; Wilder Penfield Award, 1972. Hon. DSc of several univs. *Publications:* An Inquiry into the Question of Cultural Stability in Polynesia, 1928; Coming of Age in Samoa, 1928; Growing Up in New Guinea, 1930; The Changing Culture of an Indian Tribe, 1932; Sex and Temperament in Three Primitive Societies, 1935; Ed. Cooperation and Competition among Primitive Peoples, 1937; (with Gregory Bateson) Balinese Character: A Photographic Analysis, 1942; And Keep Your Powder Dry, 1942; Male and Female: A Study of the Sexes in a Changing World, 1949; Soviet Attitudes Toward Authority, 1951; (with Frances Macgregor) Growth and Culture: a Photographic Study of Balinese Childhood, 1951; ed, (with Rhoda Metraux): Study of Culture at a Distance, 1953, also Themes in French Culture, 1954; (with Nicolas Calas) Primitive Heritage, 1953: ed Cultural Patterns and Technical Change, 1953; (with Martha Wolfenstein) Childhood in Contemporary Cultures, 1955; New Lives for Old: Cultural Transformation, Manus, 1928-1953, 1956; An Anthropologist at Work: Writings of Ruth Benedict, 1959; People and Places, 1959; Continuities in Cultural Evolution, 1964; Anthropologists and What They Do, 1965; (With Ken Heyman) Family, 1965; (ed, with Th. Dobzhansky and E. Tobach) Science and the Concept of Race, 1968; (with Paul Byers) The Small Conference: an innovation in communication, 1968; Culture and Commitment, 1969; (with Rhoda Metraux) A Way of Seeing, 1970; (with James Baldwin) A Rap on Race, 1971; Blackberry Winter: my earlier years (memoirs), 1972; Twentieth Century Faith, 1972; Ruth Benedict: an autobiography, 1974; (with Ken Heyman) World Enough: rethinking the future, 1975. *Address:* American Museum of Natural History, Central Park West at 79th Street, New York, NY 10024, USA.
[Died 15 Nov. 1978.

MEAD, Brig. Stephen, DSO 1918; *s* of F. Mead, Metropolitan Magistrate; *b* 1882; *m* 1910, Beatrice Eleanor (*d* 1953), *d* of Commander L. P. Willan, RN; one *s* (and one killed in action). *Educ:* Tonbridge School; RMA Woolwich. Commission, RA 1901; Adjutant of Territorials; Instructor in Gunnery; Adjutant (regular) twice; Served European War, France and Flanders, 1916-19; Brigade Major 22nd Corps Heavy Art. 1917-19 (despatches twice, DSO); Comdr, Royal Artillery, 54th (East Anglian) Div., TA, 1935-39; retired pay, 1939. *Address:* c/o Lloyds Bank Ltd, Cox's and King's Branch, 6 Pall Mall, SW1.
[Died 10 May 1972.

MEAGHER, Sir Thomas, Kt 1947; MB, BS; JP; medical practitioner, Victoria Park, since 1927; *b* Menzies, W Australia, 26 March 1902; *s* of Philip Francis and Ann Agnes Meagher, Bendigo, Victoria, Australia; *m* 1927, Marguerite Winifred Hough (*d* 1952); four *s* two *d*; *m* 1953, Doris Ita Walsh. *Educ:* Christian Brothers Coll., Perth; University of Western Australia; Newman Coll.; Melbourne Univ. Graduated 1925; House Surg., Royal Perth Hospital and Children's Hosp., 1925-26; in practice Victoria Park since 1927; Councillor, City of Perth, 1937-38; Lord Mayor, City of Perth, 1939-45; Past-Pres. RAC, W Australia; Past-Pres. Australian Automobile Assoc.; Pres. and Life Mem., Amateur Athletic Assoc., WA; Olympic Fed. Brit. Empire and Commonwealth Games Assoc., Pentathlon Assoc.; Pres. Industrial Fund for Advancement of Science Education in Schools; Pres. King's Park Board; KStJ. Mem. of Chapter, Commandery of St John of Jerusalem and Ambulance Assoc. of WA; Past Pres. Royal Commonwealth Society; Chm. Museum Bd of WA; Trustee and Past Pres.

Coun., Justices' Assoc. of WA; Pres. Nat. Safety Council; Vice-Patron Nat. Rose Soc.; Trustee Police Boys' Clubs; Life Member, Old Aquinians, Ex-Naval-Men's Assoc., Greek Ex-Service Men's Assoc.; Hon. Mem. Rotary Club, Perth. *Recreations:* fishing, gardening, sport. *Address:* Boolah Mia, 787 Albany Highway, East Victoria Park, WA 6101, Australia; Saranna, The Esplanade, Rockingham, Qld.
[Died 27 June 1979.

MEANY, George; President, American Federation of Labor and Congress of Industrial Organizations, 1955-79; *b* 16 Aug. 1894; *s* of Michael Meany and Anne Cullen; *m* 1919, Eugenie A. McMahon (*d* 1979); three *d. Educ:* American public schs. Mem., Journeymen Plumbers Union, 1915; Business Agent, Local 463 of Plumbers Union, 1922; Pres. NY State Federation of Labor, 1934-39; Sec.-Treasurer, American Federation of Labor, 1940-52, Pres., 1952-55. Chm. Mem., or Adviser numerous bds and cttees. Laetare Medallist, University of Notre Dame, Ind., 1955; Hon. Dr of Laws of several American Univs; Rerum Novarum Award, St Peter's Coll., Jersey City, NJ, 1956; Presidential Medal of Freedom, US, 1963. Holds, also, foreign decorations. *Recreations:* golf, painting. *Address:* 4201 Cathedral Avenue NW, Washington, DC 20016, USA. *Clubs:* Columbia Country, University, International, National Press (Washington, DC).
[Died 10 Jan. 1980.

MEARS, Brig. Gerald Grimwood, CBE 1945; DSO 1944; MC 1918; *b* 15 Oct. 1896; *o s* of late Sir Grimwood Mears, KCIE; *m* 1925, Margaret (MBE 1946), *y d* of late Maj.-Gen. Sir Gerald Giffard; two *d. Educ:* St Paul's Sch. RA temp. commission Sept. 1914, regular Oct. 1915; BEF France, 1915-19 (1914-15 Star, Gen. Service and Victory medals, MC and Bar); India Frontier, 1919; ADC to Viceroy, 1921-22; Razmak Field Force, 1923; Staff Coll., Quetta, 1928-29; GSO 3 Sch. of Army Co-operation, Old Sarum, 1931-33; Staff Officer RA Southern Command, 1933-35; GSO 2 War Office, 1936-39; GSO 2 Allied Military Cttee, 1939-40; GSO 1 War Office and Home Forces, 1940-41; BGS Northern Command, 1942-43; CRA 3rd British Infantry Div., 1943-45 (DSO, CBE); CCRA and Chief of Staff, 1st British Corps, BRA, ALFSEA, 1946; BRA Southern Command, 1947; Commandant, Sch. of Artillery, 1947-49; ADC to the King, 1947-49; retd 1949. *Recreations:* yachting, fly-fishing, shooting. *Address:* Driftway, Steeple Langford, Salisbury, Wilts. *T:* Stapleford 461.
[Died 19 Nov. 1979.

MEASHAM, Richard John Rupert, CMG 1944; OBE 1919; *b* 2 June 1885; *s* of Rev. Richard Measham, MA, RN, and Frances Sarah, *d* of Capt. J. Woon, RMLI; *m* 1914, Beatrice Louisa Baynham (*d* 1972); one *d* (and one *d* decd). *Educ:* RN Sch., Eltham; Wadham Coll., Oxford (scholar). 1st Class Classical Mods; 2nd class Lit Hum; Asst Surveyor, Class II, GPO, 1907; Class I, 1919; Surveyor, Eastern Scotland, 1930; Postal Controller Scottish Region, 1935; Regional Dir, Scottish Region, 1939; Dir of Postal Services, 1942-44; Regional Dir, Scottish Region, GPO, 1944-45; served European War with Royal Engineers (Postal Section), 1914-19 (despatches twice, OBE). *Address:* c/o Lloyds Bank, The Strand, Exmouth; 1 Clwyn Road, The Strand, Exmouth. *[Died 17 April 1976.*

MEDLEY, Brig. Edgar Julius, DSO 1940; OBE 1938; MC 1916; *b* 16 Dec. 1893; 2nd *s* of late Prof. D. J. Medley; *m* 1929, Norah Templer; one *s. Educ:* Sedbergh; RMA, Woolwich. Commissioned Royal Artillery, 1914; served European War, 1914-18, with 6th and 29th Divs; in India, 1919-27, with 37th Field Battery RA; Staff Coll., Camberley, 1927-28; Staff Officer RA Aldershot, 1929-32; Gen. Staff (GSO 3) War Office, 1932-33; RAF Staff Coll., Andover, 1934; Gen. Staff, Malaya, 1936-38; Comdr 19th SL Militia Depot, June-Oct. 1939; Comdr 53 A/Tk Regt RA (Worcs Yeomanry), Nov. 1939; served in France, Jan.-June 1940; Brig. and Comdr Corps Medium Artillery, July 1940; Comdr Corps RA, Feb. 1941; went to MEF, June 1941; Brig. RA, Sept. 1941; GSO 1 Senior Officers Sch., 1942; Asst Commandant Staff Coll., 1943-44; Dep. Military Sec., War Office, Nov. 1944-46; retired Dec. 1946. *Address:* 1 Thanes House, Shaftesbury, Dorset.
[Died 21 June 1972.

MEDLICOTT, Sir Frank, Kt 1955; CBE 1945; Treasurer of the Liberal Party, 1969-71; Director: Wembley Stadium Ltd; Temperance Permanent Building Society; Solicitor; *b* 10 Nov. 1903; *s* of John James and Ethel Laura Medlicott; *m* 1931, Helen Elizabeth, *d* of Rev. Walter T. Penny; two *s. Educ:* North Town Elementary Sch., and Huish's Grammar Sch., Taunton. Contested (L) Acton, 1929; MP (LNat) E Norfolk, 1939-50, (Nat L and C) Central Div. of Norfolk, 1950-59. Parly Private Sec., Min. of Health, 1943. Mem. Norfolk CC, 1942-46, 1950-58. Gunner, RA, Sept. 1939; Captain, Aldershot Command HQ, 1940; Col South-Eastern Command Staff, 1941; Brig., 21st

Army Gp, 1944-45 (CBE, despatches); Bronze Star Medal (USA). Pres., London Embankment Mission; Treasurer, UK Band of Hope Union. *Recreations:* Rugby football (Somerset and Harlequins), music. *Address:* Carlton House, Lower Regent Street, SW1. *Clubs:* Royal Commonwealth Society, New Arts.
[Died 9 Jan. 1972.

MEECH, Sir John Valentine, KCVO 1967 (CVO 1963); JP (NZ); retired Civil Servant, New Zealand Government; *b* 25 Jan. 1907; *s* of Edwin Arthur Wilton Meech and Jane Meech; *m* 1938, Rachel Crease Anderson; no *c. Educ:* Island Bay and Eastern Hutt Schs; Hutt Valley High Sch.; Public Service Coll. Sec. for Internal Affairs, Sec. of Civil Defence and Clerk of the Writs, NZ Govt, 1959-67; Mem. various Bds and Cttees, 1959-67; New Zealand Sec. to the Queen, 1962-63; Dir of Royal Visits, Heads of State etc., 1959-67. JP 1949-; Mem. Council of Duke of Edinburgh's Award in New Zealand, 1963-69. Chm. of Bd of Trustees, Nat. Sch. of Ballet, 1969-; Member: Music Advisory Cttee, Queen Elizabeth II Arts Council, 1969-; Electricity Distribution Commn, 1968- (Dep. Chm); Life Mem., NZ Inst. of Town Clerks and Municipal Treasurers. *Recreations:* golf, racing, gardening, reading, arts. *Address:* 205 Barnard Street, Highland Park, Wellington 1, New Zealand. *T:* 47-280. *Clubs:* Civil Service, Miramar Golf (Wellington). *[Died 11 Oct. 1971.*

MEHTA, Dr Jivraj Narayan, MD (London), MRCP; Member for Amreli, in Lok Sabha, since March 1971; *b* 29 Aug. 1887; *m* 1924, Hansa Manubhai Mehta; one *s* one *d. Educ:* Amreli High Sch., Gujarat State; Grant Med. Coll., Bombay; London Hosp. Med. Coll., London. Actg Asst Dir, Hale Clinical Lab., London Hosp., 1914-15; Chief MO, Baroda State, 1923-25; Dean, Seth GS Med. Coll. and KEM Hosp., Bombay, 1925-42; Dir-Gen. of Health Services, and Sec. to Govt of India in Min. of Health, 1947-48; Dewan, Baroda State, 1948-49; Elected Pres., Indian Med. Assoc., 1930, 1943, 1945; Mem. Syndicate, University of Bombay, 1928-29; Mem. Academic Coun., University of Bombay, 1934-43; Mem. Syndicate, University of Baroda, 1949-60; Fellow, Shrimati Nathibhai Thackersey Univ. for Women, 1916-60; Pres., Indian Conf. on Social Work, 1950, 1952-54; Mem. Governing Body, Indian Research Fund Assoc., 1931-32, 1937-39, 1946-51; Mem. Scientific Adv. Bd, Indian Coun. of Med. Research, 1946-51, 1953-56; Mem. Bd of Trustees, Kamala Nehru Memorial Hosp., Allahabad, 1940-; Vice-Pres., Bombay Nurses, Midwives and Health Visitors Coun., 1942; Mem. Bd of Scientific and Industrial Research, India, 1944-63; Chm., Pharmaceutical and Drugs Cttee, Coun. of Scientific and Industrial Research, 1954-60; Mem. Atomic Research Cttee, Coun. of Scientific and Industrial Research, 1951-60; Mem. Adv. Cttee, All India Med. Inst., New Delhi, 1955-57; Mem. Governing Body, All India Inst. of Med. Sci., 1957-63, 1971-; Chm., Children's Aid Soc., Bombay, 1949; Vice-Chm., Gandhi Memorial Leprosy Foundn, 1952-; Chm. Executive Council: Central Drug Research Institute, Lucknow, 1958-63; Central Salt and Marine Chemicals Research Institute at Bhavnagar, 1961-63, 1967-. Vice-Pres., All India Prohibition Council, 1968-. Mem. Medical Council of India, 1938-43, 1947-64 (Chm. Post-Grad. Cttee, 1962-64); Mem. Constituent Assembly, New Delhi, 1948-49; MLA Bombay, 1946-47 and 1949-60; Minister for Public Works, Bombay Govt, 1949-51; Finance Minister, Bombay Govt, 1952-60; Chief Minister, Gujarat State, 1960-63; High Comr for India in UK, 1963-66. Mem. Nat. Cttee Mahatma Gandhi Centenary Celebrations, 1966-70. Imprisoned for participation in Nat. Independence movt, 1932 (for 2 years) and 1942 (for 2 years). Awarded Padma Vibhushan, India, 1972. *Publications:* articles in Lancet and Jl of Indian Med. Assoc. *Address:* Everest House, 14 Carmichael Road, Bombay 26, India. *T:* 364159. *Clubs:* National Sports; Willingdon Sports (Bombay). *[Died 7 Nov. 1978.*

MEIKLE, Alexander, CBE 1964; CA; Chairman, 1969-76 (General Manager 1943-66, Director 1958), Woolwich Equitable Building Society; *b* 22 Oct. 1905; *s* of David and Marion Meikle; *m* 1935, Margaret Alice, *d* of Wilfred G. Wallis; three *s. Educ:* Shawlands Academy; Glasgow Univ. CA 1928. Asst Sec., Woolwich Equitable Building Soc., 1929. Vice-Pres. 1970 (Mem. Council, 1947-70, Chm., 1958-60), Building Societies Assoc.; Vice-President: Metropolitan Assoc. of Building Socs; Building Socs Inst.; Vice-Pres. and Mem. Council, Internat. Union of Building Socs; Vice-Pres., Nat. House Building Council. *Address:* Pilgrims, Church Road, Sundridge, near Sevenoaks, Kent. *T:* Westerham 62558. *Club:* Caledonian. *[Died 14 July 1980.*

MEIKLEJOHN, Ven. Robert; Archdeacon Emeritus; *b* 20 Dec. 1889; *s* of John Robert Meiklejohn and Emma Madeleine Wharton; *m* 1915, Lisa Lockyer (*d* 1953); no *c. Educ:* Haberdashers' Aske's Hampstead Sch.; King's Coll., London (LLB, BD, AKC). Ordained, 1914; temp. Chaplain, RN, 1915-

19; Vicar of Dorrington, Salop, 1920-25; Chaplain Missions to Seamen, 1926-29; Rector, Felbrigg with Metton, 1930 (and Sustead, 1947) until 1961, Rural Dean of Repps, dio. of Norwich, 1945-54; Hon. Canon of Norwich Cathedral, 1948-54; Archdeacon of Norwich, 1954-61, emeritus, Oct. 1961. *Address:* 3 Metton Hall, Roughton, Norwich. *T:* Hanworth 292.
[Died 7 July 1974.

MEIR, Mrs Golda; Member of Mapai (Israel Labour Party) since 1939, and member of its Leadership Forum and Party Executive, since 1976; Prime Minister of Israel, 1969-74; Member of Parliament, 1948-74; *b* Kiev, SW Russia, 3 May 1898; *d* of Moshe and Bluma Mabovitz; *m* 1917, Morris Myerson (*d* 1951); one *s* one *d*. *Educ:* Teachers' Seminary, Milwaukee, Wis. Teacher, and leading mem. Poalei Zion (Zionist Labour Party), Milwaukee. Delegate US section World Jewish Congress until 1921 when immigrated Palestine, joined Merhavia collective farm village; with Solel Boneh, Labour Federation (Histadruth) Contracting and Public Works Enterprise, 1924-26. Apptd Sec. Women's Labour Council of Histadruth, 1928; Mem. Exec. and Secretariat Fedn of Labour, 1929-34; Chm. Board of Directors Workers Sick Fund, also Head Political Department Fedn of Labour. Mapai (Labour Party) delegate Actions Cttee, World Zionist Organization, 1936; Mem. War Economic Advisory Council of Palestine Govt. Leading Mem. Hagana struggle. Head Political Dept Jewish Agency for Palestine, Jerusalem, 1946-48; Israel Minister to Moscow, Aug. 1948-April 1949; Minister of Labour and Social Insurance in Israeli cabinet, 1949-56; Minister for Foreign Affairs, 1956-66; Gen. Sec. of Mapai (Israel Labour Party), 1966-68. Leading figure at numerous Zionist, Internat. Labour and Socialist congresses. *Publications:* This is Our Strength (selected papers), 1962; My Life, 1975. *Address:* Tel-Aviv, Israel. *[Died 8 Dec. 1978.*

MEISS, Prof. Millard; Professor of the History of Art, Institute for Advanced Study, Princeton, NJ, since 1958; *b* 25 March 1904; *s* of Leon Meiss and Clara (*née* Loewenstein); *m* 1928, Margaret Louchheim; one *d* (one *s* decd). *Educ:* Princeton Univ. (BA); New York Univ. (MA, PhD). Lectr, History of Art, New York Univ., 1931-33; Lectr, Asst Prof., Associate Prof., Prof., Fine Arts and Archæol., Columbia Univ., 1934-53; Prof. of Fine Arts, Curator of Paintings, Fogg Museum, Harvard Univ., 1954-58. Hon. Trustee, Met. Museum of Art; Member: Amer. Acad. of Arts and Sciences; Amer. Philosophical Soc.; Medieval Acad. of America, Fellow and Haskins Medal, 1953; Corresp. Member: Accademia Senese degli Intronati; British Acad.; Soc. des Antiquaires de France; Accademia delle Arti del Disegno, Florence; Accademia Clementina, Bologna. Morey Award, College Art Assoc., 1969. Stella della Solidarietà (Italy), 1949. Hon. DLitt: Florence, 1968; Princeton, 1973. *Publications:* Painting in Florence and Siena after the Black Death, 1951; Andrea Mantegna as Illuminator, 1957; Giotto and Assisi, 1960; The Painting of the Life of St Francis in Assisi (with Leonetto Tintori), 1962; Giovanni Bellini's St Francis, in the Frick Collection, 1964; French Painting in the Time of Jean de Berry: The Late XIV Century and the Patronage of the Duke, 1967; The Boucicaut Master, 1968; Illuminated Manuscripts of the Divine Comedy (with P. Brieger and C. Singleton), 1969; (with J. Longnon and R. Cazelles) The Très Riches Heures of Jean, Duke of Berry, 1969; The Great Age of Fresco, 1970; La Sacra Conversazione di Piero della Francesca, 1971; French Painting in the Time of Jean de Berry: the Limbourgs and their contemporaries, 1974; (with M. Thomas) The Rohan Book of Hours, 1974. *Address:* Institute for Advanced Study, Princeton, NJ 08540, USA. *[Died 12 June 1975.*

MEKIE, Eoin Cameron, CBE 1955; BL, CompIEE, FCIT; *b* 3 Nov. 1906; *s* of Dr D. C. T. Mekie and Mary Cameron; *m* 1932, Margaret Blench; two *s* two *d*. *Educ:* George Watson's College, Edinburgh; Edinburgh Univ.; Lincoln's Inn, London. Scottish Solicitor, 1929; Balfour Beatty & Co. (London and Edinburgh), 1930-35; Legal Adviser, Edmundsons Electricity Corp., 1935-39. Served 3rd Bn London Scottish, 1939-41. Sec., Legal Adviser and Joint General Manager to the Edmundsons Electricity Supply Group of Companies, 1941 until Nationalisation in 1948; Chm., Silver City Airways, 1950-62; Dir of increasing number of Cos., 1948; Chairman: Mekie and Co. Ltd; J. B. Holdings Ltd; Mekie Howard & Co. Ltd; Grampian Chemicals Ltd. Contested (U and Nat. L) Leith Div. of Edinburgh, 1950, 1951. Underwriter of Lloyd's; Liveryman of Worshipful Guild of Air Pilots and Navigators of the British Empire. *Publications:* Electricity (Supply) Acts 1882-1935 (with D. H. James), 1935; Town and Country Planning Law (with Harold B. Williams), 1948. Miscellaneous political articles and pamphlets. *Recreations:* fishing and golf. *Address:* 126 Sandy Lane, Cheam, Surrey. *T:* 01-642 7759. *Club:* Caledonian. *[Died 4 Aug. 1977.*

MELCHETT, 3rd Baron, *cr* 1928, of Landford; **Julian Edward Alfred Mond;** Bt, *cr* 1919; Chairman: British Steel Corporation, since 1967; British Field Products Ltd; *b* 9 Jan. 1925; 2nd *s* of 2nd Baron and Amy Gwen Wilson, Klerksdorp, Transvaal; *S* father, 1949; *m* 1947, Sonia Elizabeth, *er d* of Lieut-Col R. H. Graham; one *s* two *d*. *Educ:* Eton Coll. Served War of 1939-45: Air Br., RNVR. Dir, Orion Bank Ltd, 1972-. Member: NEDC, 1969-; Council, CBI, 1969-. Governor, London Business Sch., 1973-. *Heir: s* Hon. Peter Robert Henry Mond, *b* 24 Feb. 1948. *Address:* 16 Tite Street, Chelsea, SW3. *T:* 01-352 7645. *Club:* Brooks's. *[Died 15 June 1973.*

MELCHIOR, Lauritz L. H.; Singer to the Royal Court of Denmark (Kgl. Kammersanger); Leading Dramatic Tenor, Metropolitan Opera, New York, Covent Garden Opera, London, Grand Opera, Paris, San Francisco, Chicago, Royal Opera, Copenhagen, Metro-Goldwyn-Mayer Pictures, Paramount Pictures; *b* Copenhagen, Denmark, 20 March 1890; *s* of Rector (Skolebestyrer) Jörgen Melchior and Julie Möller; *m* 1925, Maria Hacker (*d* 1963); one *s* one *d*; *m* 1964, Mary Markham (marriage dissolved). *Educ:* Melchoir Sch., Copenhagen; Royal Opera Sch., Copenhagen. Debut as Silvio in Pagliacci at the Royal Opera, Copenhagen, 1913; later Tenor, sang 8 years in the Wagner Festivals in Bayreuth (Sigmund, Siegfried, Parsifal, Tannhauser, Lohengrin, Tristan); since 1924, Covent Garden Opera, London, 1926, Metropolitan Opera, New York, 1930, Grand Opera Paris; Guest Performances at Buenos Aires, San Francisco, Berlin, Hamburg, Vienna, Copenhagen, Chicago, Barcelona, Bruxelles, etc. Holds several hon. degrees. Pres. Royal Danish Guards, Societies (abroad). Vassar College gold medal for outstanding service to music in America; Outstanding Achievement Grand Lodge Medal, 1944. Commander: Dannebrog (Denmark); White Rose of Finland; El Merito of Chili; Grand Cross, Order of St Brigitte (Catholic); Legion of Honour, France; Grand Cross of Merit of Federal Republic of Germany, etc; Knight of Malta; Knight of St Hubert. *Recreations:* hunting and others. *Address:* The Viking, 13671 Mulholland Drive, Beverly Hills, California 90210, USA. *Clubs:* Danish; Bohemian (San Francisco); Liederkranz (New York). *[Died 18 March 1973.*

MELLANBY, Lady; May; MA, ScD Cantab; Hon. DSc Sheffield, 1933; Hon. DSc Liverpool, 1934; Charles Mickle Fellow, Toronto University, 1935-36; Member of the Empire Marketing Board Research Grants Committee until disbanded; formerly Investigator for Medical Research Council; *b* London, 1882; *e d* of late Rosa and George Tweedy, London; *m* 1914, Sir Edward Mellanby, GBE, KCB, FRS, FRCP (*d* 1955). *Educ:* Hampstead and Bromley High Schs; Girton Coll., Cambridge. Natural Science Tripos Parts I and II; Research Scholar and Lecturer, London Univ. (Bedford Coll.), 1906-14; Hon. Fellow, Girton Coll., 1958; Hon. Member: Internat. Assoc. for Dental Research (Science Award of Assoc., 1975, in recognition of outstanding basic research in biological mineralization); British Dental Assoc.; Stomatological Soc. of Greece. *Publications:* many publications of a scientific nature principally dealing with conditions affecting the structure of the teeth and related tissues and their resistance to disease including MRC Special Report Series 140, 153 and 191. *Address:* 5 East Heath Road, Hampstead, NW3. *T:* 01-435 2874. *Club:* English-Speaking Union. *[Died 5 March 1978.*

MELVILLE, 8th Viscount *cr* 1802; **Henry Charles Patric Brouncker Dundas;** Baron Dunira, 1802; *b* 5 March 1909; *er s* of 7th Viscount and Agnes Mary Florence (*d* 1954), *e d* of Henry Brouncker, Boveridge Park, Cranbourne; *S* father, 1935. *Educ:* King's Sch., Canterbury. *Heir: n* Robert David Ross Dundas, *b* 28 May 1937. *Address:* Melville Castle, Lasswade, Midlothian. *[Died 26 March 1971.*

MELVILLE, Henry Edward; Director of National Provident Institution for Mutual Life Assurance, 1941-63 (its Manager and Actuary until end of 1945); *b* 6 Dec. 1883; *e s* of Thomas and Mary E. Melville; *m* 1911, Edith Ann (*d* 1973), *d* of late Thomas Bagnall Read; three *s*. *Educ:* City of London Sch. FIA 1908; Assistant Actuary, Star Assurance Society, 1913; Life Manager, Eagle Star and British Dominions Insurance Co., Ltd, 1921; Actuary and Secretary, National Provident Institution, 1931; Chairman, Life Offices' Association, 1935-37; Chairman, Investment Protection Committee, of British Insurance Association, 1940-42; President, Institute of Actuaries, 1942-44. *Address:* The Spa Hotel, Tunbridge Wells, Kent.
[Died 9 Feb. 1976.

MENDELSON, John Jakob; MP (Lab) for Penistone Division of West Riding of Yorkshire since June 1959; *b* 1917; *s* of late J. C. Mendelson. *Educ:* in London and abroad; University of London (BSc Econ). Lecturer in Economics and Public Administration,

Extra Mural Studies, University of Sheffield, 1949-59; formerly, Vice-Pres., Sheffield Trades and Labour Council; Member: Public Accounts Cttee, 1964-66; Mr Speaker's Conf., 1973-. Mem. Consultative Assembly, Council of Europe, 1973-. *Publications:* (jointly) The History of the Sheffield Trades and Labour Council; (jt) The Growth of Parliamentary Scrutiny, 1970; articles in various national weekly papers. *Recreations:* book-collecting, music, Association football, chess. *Address:* House of Commons, SW1; 114 Riverdale Road, Ranmoor, Sheffield, S10 3FD; Flat 15a, Dunrobin Court, 391 Finchley Road, NW3. *T:* 01-794 5472.   *[Died 20 May 1978.*

MENDELSSOHN, Kurt Alfred Georg, FRS 1951; MA Oxon; MA, DPhil Berlin; Reader in Physics, Oxford University, 1955-73, Emeritus Reader, 1973; Emeritus Professorial Fellow of Wolfson College, 1973 (Professorial Fellow, 1971-73); *b* 7 Jan. 1906; *s* of Ernst Mendelssohn and Eliza Ruprecht, Berlin; *m* 1932, Jutta Lina Charlotte Zarniko, Heiligenbeil; one *s* four *d*. *Educ:* Goethe-Sch., Berlin; Berlin Univ. Research and teaching appointments: Berlin Univ., 1930; Breslau Univ., 1932; Oxford Univ., 1933; Fellow, Wolfson Coll., 1966. Visiting Professor: Rice Institute, Texas, 1952; Purdue Univ., 1956; Tokyo Univ., 1960; Kumasi, Ghana, 1964; Tata Inst., Bombay, 1969; Acad. Sinica, Peking, 1971; Penang Univ., 1972; Coimbra Univ., 1973; Cairo Univ., 1975. Pres., A2 Commn, Internat. Inst. of Refrigeration, 1972-76. Consultant, UKAEA, 1973-. Vice-Pres. Physical Soc., 1957-60; Chm., Internat. Cryogenic Engineering Cttee, 1969-. Editor, Cryogenics, 1960-. Hughes Medal, Royal Society, 1967; Simon Memorial Prize, 1968. *Publications:* What is Atomic Energy?, 1946; Cryophysics, 1960; The Quest for Absolute Zero, 1966, 2nd edn 1977; In China Now, 1969; The World of Walther Nernst, 1973; The Riddle of the Pyramids, 1974; Science and Western Domination, 1976; in Proc. Royal Society and other scientific and med. jls, mainly on low temperature research, medical physics and Egyptology. *Recreations:* Egyptology, oriental art. *Address:* Wolfson College, Oxford; 235 Iffley Road, Oxford. *T:* 43747. *Club:* Athenæum.   *[Died 18 Sept. 1980.*

MENECES, Maj.-Gen. Ambrose Neponucene Trelawny, CB 1963; CBE 1944; DSO 1945; MD; *b* London, 19 March 1904; *s* of Joseph and Amy Meneces, London; *m* 1st, 1934, Elsie Gertrude Hunt (*d* 1976); 2nd, 1977, Cecilia Ethel Parker. *Educ:* St Benedict's; Westminster Cathedral Sch.; Univ. Coll. Hosp. MB, BS London 1928; MD London 1946; FRCP 1960; DTM&H London 1948. Commissioned into RAMC 1928; served on North-West Frontier, 1935-36; Burma, 1942-45 (despatches three times); Korea, 1952-54. Prof. of Tropical Medicine, Royal Army Medical College, 1949-52; Chief of Medical Divs, SHAPE, 1956; Dir of Medical Services, Western Command, 1958-61, BAOR, 1961-62; Commandant and Dir of Studies, Royal Army Medical College, 1963-66; MO, DHSS, 1966-71. Fellow of University Coll., London, 1964-. Fitzpatrick Lectr, RCP, 1969-70. Chadwick Medal, 1964. OStJ 1954; QHP, 1960-66. *Publications:* Transport of Casualties by Air, 1949; Heat Stroke and Heat Exhaustion, 1950; First Aid for Nuclear Casualties, 1956; Life of Sir Edwin Chadwick, 1972; contribs to British Encyclopædia of Medicine, etc. *Recreation:* fishing. *Address:* 2 Bracken Road, Seaford, E Sussex BN25 4HR. *Club:* Athenæum.   *[Died 28 May 1979.*

MENGES, Herbert, OBE 1963; Conductor and Composer; *b* 27 Aug. 1902; *s* of John George Menges and Katherine Whitcher, both musicians; *m* Evelyn Stiebel (marr. diss.); two *s* one *d*. First public appearance, aged 4, at Hove, as violinist; afterwards studied piano with Mathilde Verne and Arthur de Greef and later composition at the Royal College of Music under Gustav Holst and Vaughan Williams. Appointed Musical Director and Conductor in Chief to the Brighton Philharmonic Society in 1925, and has now completed 45 years in the position. Dir of Music to the Old Vic and to the Old Vic Theatre Company, 1931-50, for which he wrote or arranged music for many plays, notably for the Shakespeare productions. Associate Conductor, Sadler's Wells Opera Co., 1940-44; appointed Dir of Music to Laurence Olivier Productions Ltd, 1950, and to Chichester Festival Theatre, 1962. In the symphonic field he appears as guest conductor with all of the leading British Orchestras and Societies, including the Royal Philharmonic Society, London Philharmonic Orchestra, BBC Symphony Orchestra, New Philharmonia Orchestra, London Symphony Orchestra, Royal Liverpool Philharmonic Society, Hallé Society, etc.; and in America with Columbia Broadcasting System Orchestra. Records for HMV and Mercury Records (USA), etc. *Recreations:* books, gardening. *Address:* 64 Belsize Park Gardens, NW3. *T:* 01-722 1953.   *[Died 20 Feb. 1972.*

MENGES, Isolde; Hon. FRCM; violinist; Professor of Violin, Royal College of Music, from 1931, retired; *b* 1893; *m* 1920, Tod Boyd; one *s. Educ:* under Prof. Leopold Auer. First Orchestral Concert in London, 1913; founded Menges String Quartet, 1931. *Address:* 69 Castelnau, SW13. *T:* 01-748 3787.   *[Died 13 Jan. 1976.*

MENON, Vengalil Krishnan K.; *see* Krishna Menon.

MENZIES, Rt. Hon. Sir Douglas (Ian), PC 1963; KBE 1958; Justice of the High Court of Australia since 1958; *b* 7 Sept. 1907; *s* of Rev. Frank Menzies; *m* 1936, Helen Jean, *d* of late Rev. Dr William Borland; one *s* three *d. Educ:* University of Melbourne (Jessie Leggatt Schol., J. B. Nunn Prize, Supreme Court Prize); Fellow of Queen's Coll., Melbourne. Sec., Australian Defence Cttee and Chiefs of Staff Cttee, 1941-45; QC (Australia) 1949; Pres. Medico-Legal Soc., Victoria, 1956; Pres. Law Council of Australia, 1957-58; Chm. Victorian Bar Council, 1958; Vice-Pres. Internat. Bar Assoc., 1958; Pres. National Heart Foundation of Australia, 1964; Chancellor, Monash Univ., 1968. Hon. Bencher, Inner Temple, 1971. *Publication:* (jointly) Victorian Company Law, 1940. *Recreation:* farming. *Address:* Cambridge, 165 Hotham Street, East Melbourne, Victoria 3002, Australia. *Clubs:* Union (Sydney); Melbourne, Savage (Melbourne).   *[Died 29 Nov. 1974.*

MENZIES, Rt. Hon. Sir Robert (Gordon), KT 1963; AK 1976; PC 1937; CH 1951; QC 1929; FRS 1965; LLM; MHR for Kooyong, 1934-66; Prime Minister, Australia, 1939-41 and 1949-66 (also Minister for External Affairs, 1960-61; led Mission to Pres. Nasser on Suez Canal, 1956); *b* Jeparit, 20 Dec. 1894; *s* of late James Menzies; *m* 1920, Pattie Maie (Dame Pattie Menzies, GBE), *d* of late Senator J. W. Leckie; one *s* one *d* (and one *s* decd). *Educ:* State Schs; Grenville Coll., Ballarat; Wesley Coll., Melbourne; Melbourne Univ. (first class Final Hons). First Australian Hon. LLD Melbourne Univ., also Hon. LLD: QUB, Bristol Univ., Universities of BC Sydney, McGill, Laval, Montreal, Harvard, Royal University of Malta, Tasmania, Cambridge, Leeds, Adelaide, Edinburgh, Birmingham, Aust. Nat. Univ. Canberra, Sussex; Hon. DCL, Oxford and Univ. of Kent at Canterbury; Hon. DSc, University of NSW. Hon. Fellow, Worcester Coll., Oxford, 1968. Practised as a Barrister at the Victorian Bar; entered Victorian Parliament, 1928; MLC East Yarra, 1928-29; MLA Nunawading, 1929-34; Hon. Minister, McPherson Government, 1928-29; Attorney-Gen., Minister for Railways and Dep. Premier of Victoria, 1932-34; Attorney-Gen., Commonwealth of Australia, 1934-39; Treasurer, 1939-40; Minister: for Trade and Customs, Feb.-March 1940; for Co-ordination of Defence, 1939-42; for Information and for Munitions, 1940; Prime Minister, 1939-41; Leader of Opposition, 1943-49. Chancellor, Melbourne Univ., 1967-72. Freeman of Cities of Swansea, 1941; Edinburgh, 1948; London, 1952; Oxford, 1953; Athens, 1955; Melbourne, 1966; Hastings, 1966; Sandwich, 1967; Deal, 1969; Hon. Master of Bench, Gray's Inn, 1935; FRSA; Hon. FRACP, 1955; Hon. FRAIA, 1956; Hon. FInstM, 1957; Hon. FAA, 1958; Hon. FRCPEd 1960; Hon. FRCOG 1961; Hon. FRCS 1965; Hon. Freeman: Clothworkers' Co.; Goldsmiths' Co.; Trustee, Melbourne Cricket Ground. Constable of Dover Castle, Lord Warden of the Cinque Ports, 1965-; Pres., Dover Coll., 1966-; Pres., Kent County Cricket Club, 1969. Chief Commander, Legion of Merit (US), 1950; Order of Rising Sun, First Class (Japan), 1973. *Publications:* The Rule of Law during War, 1917; To The People of Britain at War from the Prime Minister of Australia, 1941; The Forgotten People, 1943; Speech is of Time, 1958; Afternoon Light (Memoirs), 1967; Central Power in the Australian Commonwealth, 1967; The Measure of the Years, 1970; (jt) Studies in Australian Constitution; contribs to contemporary art and legal jls. *Recreations:* walking and watching first-class cricket. *Address:* 2 Haverbrack Avenue, Malvern, Melbourne, Vic 3144, Australia; (Business) 95 Collins Street, Melbourne, Vic. 3000. *Clubs:* Athenæum, Savage, Pratt's, MCC, (Pres. 1962) Lord's Taverners'; Athenæum, Australian, Savage, (Pres.) Melbourne Scots, West Brighton (all Melbourne).   *[Died 15 May 1978.*

MENZIES ANDERSON, Sir Gilmour, Kt 1962; CBE 1956 (MBE 1943); solicitor; *b* 29 April 1914; *s* of William Menzies Anderson, DSO, MC, and Jessie Jack Gilmour; *m* 1943, Ivy Beryl Shairp (*née* Chadwick); one *d. Educ:* Glasgow High Sch.; Glasgow Univ. (LLB). Solicitor, 1939. Mem. Glasgow Corporation, 1938-39 and again, 1945-47. Commissioned 6th HLI (TA), 1939; served with "Chindits", India and Burma, 1942-45; in comd 16th Inf. Bde, 1945; demob., 1945, with rank Hon. Brig. Chm., Glasgow Unionist Assoc., 1954-57; Pres., Scottish Unionist Assoc., 1960-61; Chm. Conservative Party in Scotland, 1967-71 (Dep. Chm. 1965-67). *Recreations:* fishing and shooting. *Address:* Craigievern Cottage, Balfron Station, Glasgow G63 0NQ. *T:* Drymen 320. *Club:* Western (Glasgow).   *[Died 12 Dec. 1977.*

MERCER, David; Playwright since 1961; *b* 27 June 1928; has one *d. Educ:* King's Coll., Newcastle upon Tyne. Writers' Guild Award (Best Teleplay): A Suitable Case for Treatment, 1962; In Two Minds, 1967; Let's Murder Vivaldi, 1968; Evening Standard Drama Award (Most Promising Dramatist): Ride a Cock Horse, 1965; British Film Academy Award (Best Screen Play): Morgan, 1965. *Screenplays:* Family Life, 1970; Providence, 1977 (French Film Academy Award). *Publications:* The Generations, 1964; Three TV Comedies, 1966; Ride a Cock Horse, 1966; The Parachute and Other Plays, 1967; Belcher's Luck, 1967; The Governor's Lady, 1968; On the Eve of Publication and Other Plays, 1970; After Haggerty, 1970; Flint, 1970; Duck Song, 1974; The Bankrupt and other plays, 1974; Huggy Bear and other plays, 1977; Shooting the Chandelier, 1978; Cousin Vladimir, 1978; Then and Now, 1979; Collected TV Plays, 1980. *Recreation:* travel. *Address:* c/o Margaret Ramsay Ltd, 14a Goodwin's Court, WC2. *[Died 8 Aug. 1980.*

MERCER, Howard, CBE 1951; MC 1917; DFC 1919; *b* 14 May 1896; 2nd *s* of E. J. Mercer; *m* 1940, Mary Noble; two *s. Educ:* Elstow Sch., Bedford. Served European War, 1914-18, France and Salonika: commissioned to Devonshire Regt, 1916 (despatches); seconded to Royal Air Force, 1918; with RAF in S Russia, 1919; appointed to Administrative Service, Nigeria, 1921; seconded to British Military Administration, Tripolitania, 1942; Chief Sec., 1945-51, with Rank of Col. Dir of Establishments to Government of Tripolitania; retired from Colonial Service, 1951, and from Tripolitania, 1952. Order of St Stanislaus (Russia), 1919; Cross of St George (Russia), 1919. *Recreation:* golf. *Address:* 3a Parkside Road, Parkstone, Dorset. *[Died 21 Dec. 1973.*

MERCER, Sir Walter, Kt 1956, FRCS, FRS (Edinburgh), FACS (Hon.); FRCS (Hon.); FCSSoAf (Hon.); FRoyMedSoc, Edinburgh (Hon.); MChOrth (Liverpool) (Hon.); FRCSI (Hon.); FRCS (Can.) (Hon.); DL; Emeritus Professor of Orthopædic Surgery, University of Edinburgh; late Director of Orthopædic Services, South-East region of Scotland; Past President, Royal College of Surgeons of Edinburgh; Past Chairman Standing Advisory Committee on Artificial Limbs, Ministry of Health; Chairman, Editorial Board, Journal of Royal College of Surgeons of Edinburgh; *b* 19 March 1890; 2nd *s* of E. B. Mercer, Stow, Midlothian; *m* 1923, Helen Maisie Lunan; one *s. Educ:* George Watson's Coll., Edinburgh; University of Edinburgh, MB, ChB (Edinburgh), 1912; FRCS (Edinburgh), 1921; FRS Edinburgh, 1935; FACS, 1954; Asst Surgeon, Royal Infirmary, Edinburgh, 1925; Surgeon, Chalmers Hosp., Edinburgh, 1931; Consultant Surgeon, Ministry of Pensions, Edinburgh, 1924; Surgeon, South-Eastern Counties of Scotland Sanatorium, 1926; Surgeon, Royal Infirmary, Edinburgh, 1943; Prof. of Orthopædic Surgery, University of Edinburgh, 1948; Fellow Royal Society of Medicine; Fellow Assoc. of Surgeons of Great Britain and Ireland, 1930; Fellow British Orthopædic Assoc., 1925; Mem. International Soc. of Surgery, 1948; Hon. Mem., Société Internationale de Chirurgie Orthopédique et de Traumatologie, 1950; Corres. Mem. American Orthopædic Assoc., 1954; Hon. Fellow: Royal College of Surgeons of England, 1956; Alberta Orthopædic Soc.; Hon. Member: Canadian Orthopædic Assoc., 1959; Société Française d'Orthopédie et de Traumatologie, 1960. Served European War, 1915-20, as Capt. RAMC, in France, Italy and the Mediterranean. DL County of City of Edinburgh, 1960. *Publications:* Textbook, Orthopædic Surgery (6th edn), 1963; contrib. to jls, including: Lancet, BMJ, Br. Jl of Surgery, Edinburgh Medical Jl, The Practitioner, The Prescriber, Journal of Chartered Society of Massage, Journal of Bone and Joint Surgery; contrib. to Maingot's Techniques of British Surgery, Illingworth's Surgical Treatment, Thomson & Miles' Manual of Surgery, McIntosh's War and the Doctor, Handfield-Jones and Porritt's Essentials of Modern Surgery. *Recreations:* golf, curling, shooting, postal history, photography, reading. *Address:* Bidston, 7 Easter Belmont Road, Edinburgh. *T:* 031-337 4923. *Clubs:* Golfers'; New (Edinburgh).
[Died 23 Feb. 1971.

MERCHANT, Livingston Tallmadge; *b* New York City, 23 Nov. 1903; *s* of Huntington Wolcott Merchant and Mary Floyd Tallmadge; *m* 1927, Elizabeth Stiles; one *s* one *d. Educ:* Hotchkiss Sch.; Princeton Univ. AB cum laude, 1926; Hon. LLD 1960; Hon. LLD: Hofstra Univ., 1959; Queen's Univ., Canada, 1961; Harvard, 1968; Hon. DCL, Bishop's Univ., Quebec, 1962; Associate in firm of Scudder, Stevens and Clark (Boston), 1926-30; General partner Scudder, Stevens and Clark (New York), 1930-42. Dir of several insurance companies, investment trusts, and a national bank. Joined Dept of State, 1942; Asst Chief, Div. of Defense Materials, 1942-43; Chief, War Areas Economic Div., 1944-45; Economic Counselor with personal rank of Minister, Paris, 1945; Chief Aviation Div.,

Dept of State, 1946; Foreign Service Officer, Cl. 2, 1947; Class 1, 1950; Career Minister, 1954; Career Ambassador, 1960. Counselor of Embassy, Nanking, 1948-49; Dep. Asst Sec. of State for Far Eastern Affairs, 1949-51; Dep. to US Special Rep. in Europe with Personal Rank of Ambassador, and US Alternate Perm. Rep. on NATO, 1952-53; Asst Sec. of State for European Affairs, 1953-56, 1958-59, United States Ambassador to Canada, 1956-58, 1961-62; Under Sec. of State for Political Affairs, State Dept, Washington, 1959-61. Delegate, or Senior Adviser, Bermuda, Berlin, Geneva, London, Paris and NATO Confs, 1953-60. Former Director: Glens Falls Insce Co.; Research Analysis Corp.; Nat. Life Assce Co. of Canada. US Director of The World Bank, 1965-68. *Address:* 4101 Cathedral Avenue, NW, Washington, DC 20016, USA. *Clubs:* Princeton, Metropolitan, Alfalfa, The Alibi (Washington); Princeton (New York); Chevy Chase (Chevy Chase, Md); University Cottage (Princeton, NJ).   *[Died 15 May 1976.*

MEREDITH, Air Vice-Marshal Sir Charles Warburton, KBE 1947 (CBE 1941); CB 1943; AFC 1918; RAFVR retd; *b* 1896; *s* of late C. J. Meredith; *m* 1926, Honoria Druce, *d* of J. T. Davidson; one *s* one *d. Educ:* Wynberg High Sch. Grad. RAF Staff Coll., Andover, England. Formerly Comdt-Gen. SR Forces. *Club:* Salisbury (Rhodesia).   *[Died 19 April 1977.*

MEREDITH, George Patrick, MSc, MEd (Leeds); PhD (London); FBPsS; Professor of Psychophysics, University of Leeds, 1967-69; retired 1969; now Professor Emeritus; Director of Epistemic Communication Research Unit, retired 1969; *b* 10 May 1904; *s* of Edgar and Helen Meredith; *m* 1942, Gillian Tremaine; one *s. Educ:* Wolverley Sch.; University of Leeds; University Coll. and Institute of Education, University of London. Taught science in Switzerland, London and Gloucestershire, 1926-38; Lecturer in Educational Psychology and Visual Education, UC, Exeter, 1938-47; established and directed Visual Education Centre, Exeter; Research Grants: Leon Trust, 1945; DSIR, 1954; Dept of Educ. and Science, 1965; Dept of Environment, 1970. Lecturer in Educational Psychology, University of Leeds, 1947-49; Professor of Psychology, 1949-67. Editor-in-Chief, International Jl of the Educational Sciences, 1967-70. *Publications:* Visual Education and the New Teacher, 1946; Materials for Visual Aids, 1947; The Method of Topic Analysis, 1948; Algebra by Visual Aids (4 vols), 1948; The Modular Calculus, 1958; Semantic Matrices, 1959; Learning, Remembering and Knowing, 1961; Instruments of Communication, 1966; Dyslexia and the Individual, 1972; articles in Forum of Education, Occupational Psychology, New Era, Nature, Times Ed. Supp., Jl of Ed., Brit. Jl of Psychology, 20th Century, Proc. of Aristotelian Soc., BMJ, etc. *Recreations:* astronomy, walking, climbing, dramatics. *Address:* 7 Grosvenor Mount, Leeds LS6 2DX. *T:* Leeds 755997. *Club:* Athenæum.
[Died 2 April 1978.

MEREDITH, Leonard Arthur De Lacy, CMG 1933; OBE 1923; BA; *b* 1888; *s* of late Arthur Meredith, CSI, ICS. *Educ:* Eton; Balliol Coll., Oxford. Solicitor, 1914; Lieut 3rd Glos Regt, 1914; invalided, 1915; entered Department of Overseas Trade, 1918; General Manager, Travel Association of Great Britain and Ireland, 1930-39; Ministry of Supply, 1939; Board of Trade, 1946-52. *Clubs:* Boodle's, MCC.   *[Died 23 May 1971.*

MERIVALE, Dame Gladys; *see* Cooper, Dame Gladys.

MERRIMAN, Sir Walter Thomas, Kt 1954; Managing Director, Merryville Pty Ltd, Stud Merino Sheep and Beef Cattle Breeders, Yass, New South Wales, Australia; *b* Ravensworth, 18 May 1882; *s* of late George Merriman, Ravenswoth, Yass; *m* 1908, Kate, *d* of Samuel Sleeman; two *s* four *d. Educ:* Murrumbateman State Sch., New South Wales. Life Mem. Royal Agric. Society of NSW and of Pastoral and Agric. Socs of Yass, Cootamundra and Boorowa; formerly: Councillor Goodradigbee Shire; Pres. Yass and Dist Soldiers' Memorial and Literary Inst.; Chm., Yass Pastures Protection Bd; Pres. Yass Pastoral and Agric. Assoc.; Dir, Yass Dist Hosp.; Master Yass Masonic Lodge of Concord; Dist Grand Inspector. *Address:* Merryville, Yass, NSW 2582, Australia.   *[Died 25 Jan. 1972.*

MERSEY, 3rd Viscount, *cr* 1916, of Toxteth; **Edward Clive Bigham;** DL; Baron, *cr* 1910; *b* 5 June 1906; *e s* of 2nd Viscount Mersey, PC, CMG, CBE, and Mary (*d* 1973), *d* of late Horace Seymour, CB (nominated, but not invested as KCB); *S* father 1956; *m* 1933, Lady Katherine Fitzmaurice (Lady Nairne), *er d* of 6th Marquess of Lansdowne (she succeeded Aug. 1944, on the death of her brother, 7th Marquess, to the Lordship of Nairne); three *s. Educ:* Eton Coll.; Balliol Coll., Oxford (BA). Served Irish Guards, 1940-45. Mem. LCC, 1955-65. DL West Sussex, 1977. *Heir: s* Master of Nairne. *Address:* Bignor Park, Pulborough, W Sussex; Derreen, Lauragh, Killarney, Ireland.

Clubs: Brooks's, Pratt's, MCC, White's, Beefsteak.
[Died 2 *Aug.* 1979.

MERTHYR, 3rd Baron, of Senghenydd, Co. Glamorgan, *cr* 1911; **William Brereton Couchman Lewis,** PC 1964; KBE 1969; TD; Bt *cr* 1896; Barrister-at-Law, Inner Temple, 1927; *b* Saundersfoot, 7 Jan. 1901; *o s* of 2nd Baron and Elizabeth Anna (*d* 1925), *d* of late Maj.-Gen. R. S. Couchman; *S* father, 1932; *m* 1932, Violet, *y d* of late Brig.-Gen. Sir Frederick Charlton Meyrick, 2nd Bt, and Mary, Lady Meyrick, of Bush, Pembroke; five *s. Educ:* Sunningdale Sch.; Eton Coll.; Magdalen Coll., Oxford (MA). JP, Co. Pembroke, 1925; DL 1932; Vice-Lieutenant, 1959-74; Pres. National Association of Local Councils, 1965-74; Vice-President: National Marriage Guidance Council; Family Planning Assoc.; Mem. Pembrokeshire CC, 1928-39; OC 185th Heavy Battery, RA (TA) 1930-40; Mem. Royal Commission on Local Govt on Tyneside, 1936; Mem. Deptl Cttee on Justices' Clerks, 1938; Chm. Deptl Cttee on Rag Flock Acts, 1938; Chm. Narberth RDC, 1939; Mem. Royal Commission on Justices of the Peace, 1948; Pres., Royal Forestry Soc. of England and Wales, 1948-50; a Nat. Parks Comr, 1950-53. Dep.-Chm. Haverfordwest QS, 1948-51; Chairman: Pembrokeshire QS, 1950-71; Nat. Marriage Guidance Council, 1951-57; Magistrates' Assoc., 1952-70; RSPCA, 1953-57; Hon. Treas. NSPCC, 1952-57; Chm. Deptl Cttee on Hedgerow and Farm Timber, 1953; Chm. Constituency Delineation Commission: Malaya, 1954; Nigeria, 1957-58; Lord Chm. of Cttees and Deputy Speaker, House of Lords, 1957-74. Chm., Dyfed-Powys Police Authority, 1968-72. Hon. Mem., Justices' Clerks' Soc., 1971. Served War of 1939-45 (PoW Hong Kong, 1941-45). CStJ. *Heir: s* Hon. Trevor Oswin Lewis. *Address:* Churchton, Saundersfoot, Dyfed SA69 9BB. *Clubs:* Royal Cruising; Leander.   *[Died* 5 *April* 1977.

MERZ, Charles; Editor, The New York Times, 1938-61, Editor Emeritus since 1961; *b* 23 Feb. 1893; *m* 1924, Evelyn Scott. *Educ:* Yale Univ. Associate Editor, New York World, 1924-31; Mem. of the Editorial Staff of the New York Times, 1931-38. LittD: Colgate Univ., 1939; Wooster Coll., 1939; Yale Univ., 1942; Columbia Univ., 1945. *Publications:* The Great American Bandwagon, 1928; The Dry Decade, 1931. *Address:* 10 Gracie Square, New York, NY 10028, USA. *T:* RE 7-4118. *Clubs:* Century, Yale (New York); Elizabethan (New Haven).
[Died 31 *Aug.* 1977.

MESSEL, Oliver Hilary Sambourne, CBE 1958; *b* 13 Jan. 1904; 2nd *s* of Lieut-Col Leonard Messel, OBE, TD, Homestead, Cuckfield, Sussex, and Maud Frances, *o d* of Edward Linley Sambourne. *Educ:* Eton; Slade School of Art. *Theatrical Productions:* plays: Cochran Revue, 1926, This Year of Grace, 1928, Wake Up and Dream, 1929, Cochran Revues, 1930-31, all at London Pavilion; Helen, Adelphi; The Miracle, Lyceum, 1932; Glamorous Night, Drury Lane, 1935; The Country Wife, Old Vic and New York, 1936; A Midsummer Night's Dream, Old Vic, 1937; The Tempest, Old Vic; The Infernal Machine, Arts, 1940; Big Top, His Majesty's, 1942; The Rivals, Criterion, 1945; Tough at the Top, Adelphi, The Lady's Not for Burning, Globe and New York, 1949; Ring Round the Moon, Globe and Copenhagen, The Little Hut, Lyric and New York, 1950; Romeo and Juliet, New York, 1951; Under the Sycamore Tree, Aldwych, Letter from Paris, Aldwych, 1952; The Dark is Light Enough, Aldwych and New York, The House of Flowers, New York, 1954; The School for Scandal, Copenhagen, 1958; Rashomon, New York, 1958; costume designs for Gigi, 1973; *operas:* The Magic Flute, Covent Garden, 1947; Ariadne auf Naxos, Glyndebourne; Queen of Spades, Covent Garden, 1950; Idomeneo, Glyndebourne, 1951; La Cenerentola, Glyndebourne, 1952; Il Barbiere di Siviglia, Le Comte Ory, Glyndebourne, La Cenerentola, Glyndebourne, Berlin, 1954; Zemire et Azore, Bath Festival, Le Nozze di Figaro, 1955; Die Entführung aus dem Serail, Die Zauberflöte, Glyndebourne, 1956; Samson, Covent Garden, 1958; Der Rosenkavalier, Glyndebourne, 1959; Le Nozze di Figaro, Metropolitan, New York, 1959; Ariadne, Metropolitan, New York, 1962; *ballets:* Francesca da Rimini, Covent Garden and New York, 1937; Comus, New Theatre, 1942; Sleeping Beauty, Covent Garden and New York, 1946; Homage to the Queen, Covent Garden and New York, 1953. *Films:* Private Life of Don Juan, 1934; Romeo and Juliet, 1936; Caesar and Cleopatra, 1945; The Queen of Spades, 1949; Suddenly Last Summer, 1959. *Exhibitions:* Masks, Claridge Galls, 1925; Designs and Maquettes, Lefevre Galls, 1933; Leicester Galls, 1936; Portrait Paintings, Leicester Galls, 1938; Paintings and Designs, Carol Carstairs Galls, New York, 1938; Designs for film Queen of Spades, Leicester Galleries, 1949; Paintings and Designs, Redfern Galleries, 1951; Sagittarius Gallery, New York, 1959; O'Hana Gallery, 1962. *Decorations:* for Royal Command Performance, Covent Garden, for Reprodent of France, 1950, and Gala Performance

for King of Sweden, 1954. *Architectural design:* reconstruction of Flaxley Abbey, Glos, 1958-65; Queen's Park Theatre, houses, and garden, Bridgetown, Barbados, 1967-75; designed all initial buildings for develt of island of Mustique; also about 15 houses, 1968-75. Served in HM Forces, Captain, 1940-44. Fellow of University Coll. London, 1956. Hon. Associate, Regional Coll. of Art, Manchester, 1960. *Publications:* Stage Designs and Costumes, 1933; Designs for (Batsford) Romeo and Juliet, 1936; Designs for (Folio Society) A Midsummer Night's Dream, 1957; Designs for (Adrianne Allen and Marjorie Salter) Delightful Food, 1958. *Recreation:* gardening. *Address:* Maddox, St James', Barbados, West Indies.   *[Died* 13 *July* 1978.

MESSENT, Sir Philip (Santo), Kt 1951; Hon. Consulting Surgeon, Royal Adelaide Hospital, since Nov. 1953; President, World Convention, Churches of Christ, Adelaide, 1970; Chairman, Churches of Christ Federal Overseas Mission Board of Australia, since 1942; *b* 22 Feb. 1895; *s* of late P. S. Messent, ISO, and late A. E. Messent; *m* 1920, Agnes May Rich; one *s* three *d. Educ:* Kyre Coll., Unley Park; University of Adelaide. MB, BS 1918, MS 1923, University of Adelaide; FRACS 1927. Hon. Asst Surgeon, 1928, Hon. Surgeon, 1933, Royal Adelaide Hospital; retd 1953, Hon. Consulting Surgeon, 1953. Associate Lecturer in Surgery, Univ. of Adelaide; Dir of Surgical Studies, 1950-53, retired. Pres. Med. Bd of SA, 1953-70; Governor, Scotch Coll., Adelaide. *Recreations:* tennis, gardening. *Address:* 26 Westall Street, Hyde Park, SA 5061, Australia.
[Died 5 *Feb.* 1976.

MESSER, Sir Frederick, Kt 1953; CBE 1949; JP; Middlesex County Alderman, 1938-52, retired; Vice-President Medical Superintendents' Society; *b* 12 May 1886; father, Poor Law Officer; *m* 1908, Edith B. Chapman; one *s* (and one *d* decd). Mem. of French Polishers Union, 1909-; Mem. of EC of Union, 1915-21; Gen. Treas. of Union, 1917-21; Chm., S Tottenham Labour Party, 1920-29; Middx County Council for Town Hall Ward, 1925; JP 1928; Chm. County Labour Group, 1925-40. MP (Lab.) South Tottenham, 1929-31, and 1935-50, MP (Lab.-Co-op.) Tottenham, 1950-Sept. 1959. Chm. Industrial Orthopædic Soc. Southern Area (Council, 1919-22, Acting General Sec., 1922-24); formerly Chm. North-West Metropolitan Regional Hospital Board; Chm. Central Health Services Council, 1948-57; Chm. Ministry of Education Advisory Cttee on Handicapped Children, 1944-56; Chm. Croydon Hosp. Management Cttee, 1961-64. Freeman of Borough of Tottenham, 1955. *Address:* 189 Kingsdown Avenue, Croydon, Surrey. *T:* 01-660 4712.   *[Died* 8 *May* 1971.

MESSERVY, Gen. Sir Frank Walter, KCSI 1947; KBE 1945; CB 1942; DSO 1941 (and Bar, 1944); late IAS; *b* 9 Dec. 1893; *s* of W. J. Messervy and Myra Naida de Boissiere; *m* 1927, Patricia, *d* of Col E. Waldegrave Courtney, Silksworth, Camberley; one *s* one *d* (and one *s* decd). *Educ:* Eton; Royal Military College, Sandhurst. 2nd Lieut IA 1913; 9th Hodson's Horse, 1914; served European War, France, Palestine, and Syria; Kurdistan, 1919; Staff Coll., Camberley, 1925-26, psc; Bt Major, 1929; Bt Lt-Col 1933; commanded 13th DCO Lancers, 1938-39; GSO1, 5th Indian Division, 1939-40; Col 1939; comd Gazelle Force, Sudan and Eritrea, 1940-41; comd 9 Ind. Inf. Bde at Keren, 1941; comd 4 Ind. Div. Western Desert and Cyrenaica, 1941-42; comd 1 Armd Div. Cyrenaica, 1942; comd 7 Armd Div. Western Desert, 1942; DCGS, GHQ, MEF 1942; comd 43 Ind. Armd Div. 1942-43; DAFV, GHQ India Command, 1943; Maj.-Gen. 1943; commanded 7th Indian Division in Arakan and at Kohima, 1944; commanded 4th Corps, Burma, Tamu to Rangoon, 1944-45; Lieut-Gen. 1945; GOC-in-C Malaya Command; GOC-in-C Northern Command, India, 1946-47; Commander-in-Chief Pakistan Army, 1947; retired, 1948; despatches 4 times. Col 16th Lt Cav., 1946-49; Col The Jat Regt, 1947-55; Deputy Chief Scout, April 1949-50. Berks County Councillor, 1953-56. Legion of Merit, USA, Commander; Order of the Nile 4th Class. *Recreations:* shooting, gardening. *Address:* North End House, Heyshott, Midhurst, Sussex. *T:* Midhurst 2069.   *[Died* 2 *Feb.* 1974.

METCALF, Maurice Rupert, CMG 1954; OBE 1945; seconded to Central African Office, 1962 (from CRO), retired, 1964; *b* 5 May 1905; *s* of late Henry E. Metcalf; *m* 1928, Dorothy Stuart (*d* 1963), *d* of George S. Ring, New York, USA; two *s*; *m* 1964, Joan Mary Reed. *Educ:* Oundle Sch.; Sidney Sussex Coll., Cambridge. Horace Plunkett Foundation, 1927-32; National Farmers' Union, 1932-41; Ministry of Food, 1941; Prin. Private Sec. to Minister, 1943; Prin. Private Sec. to Minister of Reconstruction, 1943; Personal Asst to Lord President of the Council, 1945; Ministry of Food, 1945; transf. to Commonwealth Relations Office, 1949; Dep. UK High Commissioner in Ceylon, 1950-53; Establishment Officer, 1954; UK High Commissioner for Federation of Rhodesia and

Nyasaland, 1955-61; Asst Under-Sec. of State, CRO, 1961. *Address:* Flat 1, 4 Milnthorpe Road, Eastbourne, Sussex.
							[Died 6 Jan. 1972.

METCALFE, Maj.-Gen. John Francis, CB 1960; CBE 1954; *b* 30 June 1908; *s* of late Brigadier-General F. H. Metcalfe, DSO; *m* 1938, Natalia Eleanor, *d* of late Col N. E. Margetts, US Army; one *d*. *Educ:* Radley Coll.; Royal Military Coll., Sandhurst. Commissioned, Queen's Royal Regt, 1928; served in India and Burma, 1939-45; Instructor, Staff Coll., Quetta, 1942-43; OC 2nd Bn Queen's Royal Regt, 1944; Brigadier, Q, HQ ALFSEA, 1945; Col i/c Administration, South Wales District 1946; Instructor, Joint Services Staff Coll., 1947-49; OC 1st Bn East Surrey Regt, 1949-51; Brigadier General Staff, HQ Western Command, 1952-53; Imperial Defence Coll., 1954; Commander 2nd Federation Infantry Brigade, Malaya, 1955-57; Dir of Personnel Administration, War Office, 1958-61; GOC Aldershot District, 1961-63, retd. Col, The Queen's Royal Surrey Regiment, 1959-64. *Recreation:* golf. *Address:* Windlesham, Littlestone, New Romney, Kent. *Club:* Army and Navy.							*[Died 11 June 1975.*

METCALFE, Sir Ralph Ismay, Kt 1943; Director of Wm Cory & Son Ltd, and Associated Companies until 1961; Director, Petrofina (Great Britain) Ltd, until 1968; *b* 20 May 1896; *s* of George Metcalfe, Maryport, Cumberland, and Southampton; *m* 1st, 1920, Betty, *d* of E. H. Pelling; 2nd, 1947, Dorothea, *d* of C. E. Gibbs. *Educ:* King Edward VI Sch., Southampton. Entered Civil Service (Admty), 1915; resigned, 1920, on joining Wm Cory & Son Ltd; Dir of Tanker Division, Ministry of War Transport, 1939-42, and Dir of Sea Transport, 1942-45; Mem., Port of London Authority, 1949-67. Master, Company of Watermen and Lightermen of the River Thames, 1959-60; Prime Warden, Worshipful Co. of Shipwrights, 1963-64. Served European War, 1914-18, in RFC and RAF. Chevalier Légion d'Honneur (France); US Medal of Freedom with Gold Palm; Commander: Order of Orange-Nassau; Order of St Olav; Ordre de la Couronne, Belgium. *Address:* Elmtree House, Coast Road, West Mersea, Essex. *T:* West Mersea 2934. *Clubs:* Athenæum, Alpine, Travellers'.					*[Died 2 Nov. 1977.*

METCALFE, Sir Theophilus (John), 8th Bt, *cr* 1802; *b* 14 Oct. 1916; *s* of late Lieut-Col Eric Debonnaire Theophilus Metcalfe, OBE, MC, Indian Army, half-brother of 7th Bt, and Winifred Crampton, *d* of E. Neild Shackle, Hayes, Middx; *S* uncle, 1950. *Educ:* Haileybury. *Heir:* none. *Address:* 3 Kensington House, 35 Kensington Court, W8.				*[Died 11 Feb. 1979 (ext).*

METHUEN, 4th Baron *cr* 1838; Paul Ayshford Methuen, MA Oxon; DipAg; RA 1959 (ARA 1951); RWS; FSA; Hon. FRIBA; painter and zoologist; Member Royal Fine Art Commission, 1952-59; Trustee of National Gallery, and of Tate Gallery, 1938-45; Trustee Imperial War Museum, 1950-52; *b* 29 Sept. 1886; *e s* of 3rd Baron and Mary Ethel, CBE (*d* 1941), *d* of late William Ayshford Sanford, Nynehead Court; *S* father, 1932; *m* 1915, Eleanor (Norah) (*d* 1958), *d* of late W. J. Hennessy of Rudgwick, Sussex. *Educ:* Eton; New Coll., Oxford. 2nd Class Hons Nat Sc. 1910; MA 1914; DipAg 1920. Asst Transvaal Museum, Pretoria, 1910-14; Lieut Scots Guards (SR), 1914-19 (seeing active service in France); Ministry of Agriculture as Live Stock, and later as Marketing, Officer, 1925-32. Has held eleven one-man Exhibitions at the Leicester Galleries, etc.; retrospective exhibn, Fieldborne Galls, 1973; has had works acquired by BM, Tate Gallery, Victoria and Albert Museum, Cont. Art Soc., Imp. War Museum, Musée Nat. d'Art Moderne, Paris. Staff Capt. HQ London District, 1940-44 and Major as Monuments and Fine Arts Officer, CA 21 Army Group, AEF, 1944-45. Hon. LLD: Bristol, 1963; Bath, 1970. Chevalier, Legion of Honour, France. *Publications:* Normandy Diary, 1952; A Catalogue of the Methuen Miniatures, 1970; several scientific articles. *Heir:* *b* Captain Hon. Anthony Paul Methuen. *Address:* Corsham Court, Wilts. *T:* Corsham 712214; 6 Primrose Hill Studios, NW1.				*[Died 7 Jan. 1974.*

METHUEN, 5th Baron *cr* 1838; Anthony Paul Methuen; Captain; *b* 26 June 1891; 2nd *s* of Field-Marshal Lord Methuen, GCB, GCMG, GCVO (*d* 1932), and Mary Ethel, CBE (*d* 1941), *d* of late William Ayshford Sanford; *S* brother, 4th Baron Methuen, 1974; *m* 1920, Grace (*d* 1972), *d* of Sir Richard Holt, 1st Bt; two *s* one *d*. *Educ:* Wellington; New Coll., Oxford. SR Scots Guards, 1914-18; Chartered Architect. *Heir:* *s* Hon. Anthony John Methuen, *b* 26 Oct. 1925. *Address:* Ivy House, Corsham, Chippenham, Wilts. *T:* Corsham 712263.
							[Died 21 June 1975.

METHVEN, Sir (Malcolm) John, Kt 1978; Director General, Confederation of British Industry, since 1976; *b* 14 Feb. 1926; *s* of late Lt-Col M. D. Methven, OBE and late Mrs H. M.

Methven; *m* 1st, 1952, Margaret Field Nicholas; three *d*; 2nd, 1977, Karen Jane Caldwell. *Educ:* Mill Hill Sch.; Gonville and Caius Coll., Cambridge (Tapp Exhibn in Law; Tapp Post-Grad. Schol. in Law; MA, LLB). Admitted Solicitor, 1952; Solicitor, Birmingham Corp., 1952-57; ICI (Metals Div.), 1957; ICI (Legal Dept), 1957-68; Head of Central Purchasing Dept, ICI, 1968-70; Dep. Chm., ICI Ltd, Mond Div., 1970-73; Dir-Gen. of Fair Trading, 1973-76. Member: Monopolies Commn, 1972; NEDC, 1976-. Custodian Trustee, Nat. Assoc. of Citizens' Advice Bureaux. Vice Pres., Inst. of Trading Standards Admin. *Recreations:* music, sailing, gardening. *Address:* 20 Bushwood Road, Richmond, Surrey.				*[Died 23 April 1980.*

MEXBOROUGH, 7th Earl of, *cr* 1766; John Raphael Wentworth Savile, DL; Baron Pollington, 1753; Viscount Pollington, 1766; *b* 11 Oct. 1906; *o s* of 6th Earl and Hon. Marjorie Knatchbull-Hugessen, *d* of 2nd Baron Brabourne; *S* father 1945; *m* 1930, Josephine, *d* of Capt. Fletcher of Saltoun; two *s* one *d*. *Educ:* Downside Sch.; Pembroke Coll., Cambridge (MA). JP North Riding of Yorks; DL, North Riding of Yorks, 1967. Capt., Intelligence Corps, 1942; in India, May 1941-Jan. 1945; ADC to Governor of Bihar, 1944-45. *Heir:* *s* Viscount Pollington. *Address:* Arden Hall, Hawnby, York. *T:* Bilsdale 213. *Clubs:* Brooks's, All England Lawn Tennis.			*[Died 15 May 1980.*

MEYER, Heinerich Carl, CMG 1956; ISO 1950; MM 1917; BSc; retired as Commissioner, The South Australian Harbors Board (1950-65); *b* 3 March 1896; *s* of late Henry and Lavinia Meyer, Adelaide, South Australia; *m* 1st, 1924, Jessica Chilman (*d* 1936); two *d*; 2nd, 1940, Monica, *d* of late Jas. B. Thompson; one *s*. *Educ:* University of Adelaide. Apptd to staff of S Australian Harbors Bd when just constituted, 1914; Chief Engineer, 1935-50; General Manager, 1942-61. Served European War, 1914-18, AIF in Egypt, Gallipoli (took part in landing, April 1915), and France (wounded); Australian Naval and Mil. Expeditionary Force and Admin. of Mandated Territory of New Guinea, 1920-22. Sent abroad by S Australian Govt to investigate port ops equipment and develt in world ports, 1946-47 and 1959. *Address:* 15 Myrtle Avenue, Myrtle Bank, S Australia 5064. *T:* 79.4753. *Club:* Naval, Military and Air Force of South Australia.					*[Died 6 Aug. 1972.*

MEYER, John Mount Montague, CBE 1967; Chairman and Managing Director, Montague L. Meyer Ltd; *b* 6 July 1915; *s* of late Montague L. Meyer and Muriel G. Meyer; *m* 1942, Denise Georgina Saunders; two *s*. *Educ:* Sherborne School. Joined Montague L. Meyer Ltd, 1933: Dir 1938; Asst Man. Dir and Gen. Man. 1939; Vice-Chm. 1951; Chm. and Man. Dir 1961. Man. Dir, MacMillan Bloedel Meyer Ltd, 1966-; Director: MacMillan Bloedel Ltd, Vancouver, 1972-; Hallam Group of Nottingham Ltd, 1973-. Vice-Chm., Bd of Port of London Authority, 1976- (Mem., 1961-). *Recreations:* golf, fishing. *Address:* 52 Northgate, Regent's Park, NW8 7EH. *T:* 01-722 5678. *Club:* MCC.				*[Died 26 Sept. 1979.*

MEYNELL, Sir Francis (Meredith Wilfrid), Kt 1946; RDI; book designer, publisher and poet; Director, Nonesuch Press Ltd; typographic adviser (unpaid) to HM Stationery Office, 1945-66; Hon. Member Art Workers Guild; Society of Typographic Designers (President, 1958-62); Member Council, Royal College of Art, 1959-61; *b* 12 May 1891; *y s* of late Wilfrid Meynell, CBE and late Alice Meynell; *m* 1st, 1914, Hilda Saxe; one *d*; 2nd, 1925, Vera Mendel; one *s*; 3rd, 1946, Alix Hester Marie Kilroy (Dame Alix Meynell, DBE). *Educ:* Downside; Trinity Coll., Dublin. Dir, Daily Herald, 1918-20; Founder, and designer for Nonesuch Press, 1923-; regular contributor to News-Chronicle, 1934; on loan from Mather and Crowther Ltd, of which he was a Dir, to Bd of Trade for wartime duties as Adviser on Consumer Needs, 1940; Royal Designer for Industry, 1945; one-time Member, Coun. of Industrial Design, and of Advisory Council Victoria & Albert Museum; Mem. Royal Mint Adv. Cttee, 1967-70. Dir-Gen. Cement and Concrete Assoc., 1946-58. Vice-Pres., Poetry Soc., 1960-65. Hon. DLitt Reading, 1964. *Publications:* The Typography of Newspaper Advertisements, 1929; The Week-End Book, 1923; The Nonesuch Century, 1936; Seventeen Poems, 1945; English Printed Books, 1946; Poems and Pieces, 1961; By Heart, 1965; My Lives, 1971; (with H. Simon) Fleuron Anthology, 1973. *Recreation:* family bridge. *Address:* The Grey House, Lavenham, Suffolk. *Clubs:* Double Crown, Saintsbury, Savile.					*[Died 9 July 1975.*

MEYNINK, John Fitzsimmons, CMG 1958; *b* 4 June 1887; Australian; *s* of late J. E. Meynink, Sydney and Moree, NSW; *m* 1919, Jane Ellen Crothers; two *s*. *Educ:* Maitland High Sch., NSW. Began career as Grazier (Qld). Served 3 years in Field Artillery, 1st Div. AIF, France, 1916-18. Pres. United Graziers Assoc. of Qld, Aust., 1939-41 (now Trustee); Mem. for 10 years of Graziers Federal Council of Aust., and Aust. Wool Council;

Mem. for 5 years of State Cttee of Aust. Central Wool Cttee, handling Australia's complete wool clip throughout War of 1939-45; Dir of Qld Trustees, 1938, Dep. Chm., 1953, Chm., 1960 (retired from Board, 1962). Mem. Cttee Qld Turf Club, 1938-. Chm. Licensing Cttee and Trustee, Vice-Chm., 1966-; Mem. Adv. Bd of Aust. Comforts Fund, Qld Div., throughout War of 1939-45; Councillor, 1945-, Trustee and Treasurer, Patriotic Fund of Qld. *Recreation:* racing. *Address:* Unit 1A, Camden, Toorak Road, Hamilton, Qld 4007, Australia. *Clubs:* Queensland, Tattersalls (Brisbane).   *[Died 13 April 1972.*

MEYRICK, Adm. Sir Sidney Julius, KCB 1938 (CB 1934); *b* 28 March 1879; *e s* of late Julius Meyrick; *m* 1901, Judith (*d* 1963), *e d* of late Admiral Sir John R. T. Fullerton; two *s* (and one killed in action, 1942). *Educ:* HMS Britannia. Entered Navy, 1893; Lieut, 1899; Commander, 1915; Commander, HMS Resolution, Grand Fleet, 1916-18; Captain, 1919; Flag-Captain and Chief Staff Officer, HMS Courageous, Reserve Fleet, 1920-21; Captain (D), Sixth Destroyer Flotilla, 1921-22; Flag-Captain and Chief Staff Officer, HMS Revenge, Atlantic Fleet, 1922-23; Staff of War Coll., Greenwich, 1923-26; Dir of Training and Staff Duties, Admiralty, 1926-27; Flag-Captain and Captain of the Fleet, HMS Nelson, Atlantic Fleet, 1927-29; Captain Royal Naval College, Dartmouth, 1929-32; Naval ADC to the King, 1931-32; Rear-Adm., 1932, Naval Sec. to the First Lord of the Admiralty, 1932-34; Commanding Second Cruiser Squadron, 1934-36; Vice-Adm., 1936; Admiral, 1940; Commander-in-Chief America and West Indies Station, 1937-40; retired list, 1941. *Address:* Norton House, near Chichester, Sussex. *T:* Eastergate 2198.   *[Died 18 Dec. 1973.*

MICHAELIS, Sir Archie, Kt 1952; *b* 19 Dec. 1889; *s* of Frederick David and Esther Zillah Michaelis, St Kilda, Australia; *m* 1920, Claire Esther Hart; three *d. Educ:* Wesley Coll., Melbourne; Harrow Sch., England. Served European War, 1914-18, with HAC in Egypt and Aden, and afterwards in Salonika with RA (SR). Mem. State Parliament of Vic., Legislative Assembly, 1932-52, as Mem. for St Kilda; Hon. Minister Macfarlan Administration, 1945, Speaker, 1950-52. Connected with various Jewish and charitable activities; former Chm., Michaelis, Hallenstein & Co. Pty Ltd, and Associated Leathers Ltd, Melbourne. Vice-Pres., Kipling Society, London. *Recreation:* reading. *Address:* 281 Williams Road, South Yarra, Victoria 3141, Australia. *T:* 24.3866. *Clubs:* Royal Automobile (Victoria); Naval and Military (Melbourne).
                                    [Died 27 April 1975.

MICHELL, Harry Denis, DFC 1945; Senior Directing Staff (Civil), Joint Services Staff College, Latimer, since 1969; *b* 29 Oct. 1923; *s* of late Henry Michell and Belle Emslie Ledingham; *m* 1951, Jillian, *d* of A. S. Green; one *s* one *d* (and one *s* decd). *Educ:* Royal Grammar Sch., Colchester; St Edmund Hall, Oxford. RAFVR, 1942-46. Joined Foreign Service (now Diplomatic Service), 1949; Vice-Consul, Alexandria, 1949-50; Asst Political Agent, Kuwait, 1950; Political Officer, Trucial Coast, 1950-51; Asst Political Agent, Kuwait, 1951-52; FO, 1952-53; 2nd, later 1st Sec., Cape Town/Pretoria, 1953-57; Middle East Centre for Arab Studies, Lebanon, 1957-58; Private Sec. to Minister of State, FO, 1959-62; Head of Chancery, Damascus, 1962-63; FO, later DSAO, 1963-65; Counsellor, Prague, 1965-69; Civil Service Fellow Commoner, Downing Coll., Cambrdige, 1969. *Recreations:* music, cookery. *Address:* Bosky Dean, Jordans, Bucks. *T:* Chalfont St Giles 4152. *Clubs:* Pathfinder, Royal Air Force.   *[Died 1 Jan. 1971.*

MICKLEM, Rev. Nathaniel, CH 1974; MA Oxon; Principal and Professor of Dogmatic Theology, Mansfield College, Oxford, 1932-53, Hon. Fellow, 1972; *b* 10 April 1888; *s* of late Nathaniel Micklem, QC, and Ellen Ruth Curwen; *m* 1916, Agatha Frances (*d* 1961), *d* of Thomas Ball Silcock, JP, Bath; three *s. Educ:* Rugby; New Coll., Oxford. Professor of Old Testament Literature and Theology at the Selly Oak Colleges, Birmingham, 1921-27; Professor of New Testament Literature and Criticism, Queen's Theological Coll., Kingston, Ont., 1927-31; Wilde Lectr in Natural and Comp. Religion, Oxford, 1948-51. Select Preacher, Oxford Univ., 1960. President: Liberal Party, 1957-58; Liberal Internat. (British Gp), 1959-71; Patron, World Liberal Union, 1973. Hon. LLD Queen's Univ.; Hon. DD: Queen's, Ont.; Glasgow. *Publications:* The Theology of Politics, 1941; Law and the Laws, 1952; The Box and the Puppets 1888-1953, 1957; Behold the Man, 1969. *Address:* Sheepstead House, Abingdon, Oxon. *T:* Frilford Heath 390752. *Club:* Authors'.
                                    [Died 26 Dec. 1976.

MICKLEM, Brig. Ralph, CMG 1918; CBE 1945; late RE; *b* 30 Jan. 1884; *s* of late Leonard Micklem; *m* Eva May, *y d* of late Commander Sir Trevor Dawson, 1st Bt, RN; one *s* (and one *s* killed on active service, 1944). *Educ:* Eton (scholar); RMA,

Woolwich. Entered RE, 1902; Captain 1913; Major, 1917; served Egyptian Army, 1907-15; 4th Medjidieh, 1912; 4th Nile, 1917; European War, 1914-18 (wounded, despatches, CMG); retired, 1919; Lieut-Col R of O, 1927; re-employed, 1939-45, War Office; Brig. 1941. *Address:* Heriots, Stanmore, Mddx.
                                    [Died 21 March 1977.

MICKLETHWAIT, Rear-Adm. St John Aldrich, CB 1952; DSO 1939, and Bars 1940 and 1942; DL; Royal Navy Retired; *b* 4 March 1901; *e s* of late St J. G. Micklethwait, KC; *m* 1929, Clemence Penelope Olga Welby-Everard; two *s* one *d. Educ:* Osborne; Dartmouth. Midshipman, 1917; Comdr, 1935; Capt., 1940; Rear-Adm., 1950. Served War of 1939-45 (DSO and two Bars, prisoner). Flag Officer, Training Squadron, 1950-51; Flag Officer, Gibraltar, 1952-53; retired Dec. 1953. High Sheriff of Monmouthshire, 1959; DL, 1960. *Address:* Penhein, near Chepstow, Gwent. *T:* Penhow 210.   *[Died 31 July 1977.*

MIDDLEBROOK, Sir Harold, 2nd Bt, *cr* 1930; *b* 5th Oct. 1887; *s* of Sir William Middlebrook, 1st Bt, and Alma Jackson; *S* father 1936; *m* 1914, Mabel Vasey. Solicitor, 1911. *Heir:* none. *Address:* 8 Park Road, Harrogate, Yorks.
                                    [Died 27 Feb. 1971 (ext).

MIDDLETON, George Walker, CBE 1952; retired as General Secretary of the Scottish Trades Union Congress (1949-63); Chairman, Herring Industry Board; Vice-Chairman, Economic Planning Council for Scotland; *b* 4 April 1898; *s* of William and Margaret Middleton; *m* 1935, Marjorie Murray. *Educ:* Rockvilla Elementary and Keppochhill Schs. Mem. of National Union of Shop, Distributive and Allied Workers. *Address:* 58 Castlebay Street, Glasgow, N2.   *[Died 8 Aug. 1971.*

MIDDLETON, Mrs Peggy Arline; Chairman, Finance Board, Greater London Council, since 1973; *b* 3 Jan. 1916; *d* of William and Nellie Loughman; *m* 1st, 1932, Edward Richardson Brown; 2nd, 1941, Alexander Robert Middleton; three *s* one *d. Educ:* privately; Kingswood Grammar Sch., Bristol. Teaching Diploma, Borthwick Coll. (post-war). BBC Features until 1940; Preston Record Office, 1941-42; babies, 1943-48; Organiser, Family Planning, 1948-50; teaching and free-lance writing, US National Guardian, 1950-55; local govt from 1952. *Recreations:* entertaining, theatre, travelling, gardening, writing, dogs (wolfhound). *Address:* 19 Kidbrooke Park Road, SE3. *T:* 01-856 0418.   *[Died 26 Aug. 1974.*

MIDLETON, 2nd Earl of, *cr* 1920; **George St John Brodrick**, MC; Viscount Midleton, *cr* 1717, of Midleton, Ireland; Viscount Dunsford of Dunsford, Surrey, 1920; Baron Brodrick, Midleton, Ireland, 1715; Baron Brodrick, Peper Harow, 1796; late Capt., Surrey Yeomanry; *b* 21 Feb. 1888; *e s* of 1st Earl of Midleton and Lady Hilda Charteris (*d* 1901), *d* of 9th Earl of Wemyss; *S* father, 1942; *m* 1st, 1917, Margaret (marr. diss. 1925), *d* of J. Rush, Cromer, Norfolk; 2nd, 1925, Guinevere (marr. diss. 1975, she *d* 1978), *widow* of George J. Gould and *d* of Alexander Sinclair, Dublin; 3rd, 1975, Irene Creese, (Rene Ray). *Educ:* Eton; Balliol Coll., Oxford. Served World War I, 1914-17 (despatches, Legion of Honour, Military Cross). Served World War II, 1939-45 (ADC to C-in-C Home Forces). *Heir:* (to Viscountcy of Midleton and Barony of Brodrick only) *cousin*, Trevor Lowther Brodrick [*b* 7 March 1903; *m* 1940, Sheila Campbell, *d* of Charles Campbell Macleod]. *Address:* Martello Lodge, St Brelade's Bay, Jersey, Channel Islands. *T:* Central 41171.   *[Died 2 Nov. 1979 (Earldom ext).*

MIEVILLE, Arthur Leonard, DSO 1919; MC; freelance research for a company in Britain, and foreign patents, since 1971; *b* 31 Oct. 1879; *s* of Frederick Louis Mieville and Fanny Stokes Richardson; *m* 1915, Emma Plimsoll Vaux, SStJ; one *s* one *d. Educ:* Horton; Bedford County Sch., Elstow; London University. Life Mem. Civil Engineering Inst. of Canada; FIMechE. Formerly: Development Engineer, The Cementation Co. Ltd (1954-71); Man. Dir, Associated Cos throughout Asia of John Blackwood Hodge Ltd; Managing Dir Bailimo Ltd; Vice-Pres. British American Industries Ltd, New York; Dep. Dir opencast coal production, Ministry of Fuel, and representative of the Ministry at Washington; Gen. Man. of General Aircraft Ltd; Adviser to Ministry of Aircraft Production; Senior Technical Officer, Ministry of Labour HQ; Consulting Engineer in Canada; War Service with Canadian Engineers; Gen. Manager Montevideo Tramways; served European War, 1914-19 (DSO, MC, despatches). Inventions: Roller Bearings, Wind Tunnel. *Publication:* Astronomical Navigation without Mathematics, 1945 (New York). *Address:* 17 Allington Court, Allington Street, SW1. *T:* 01-834 2064. *Clubs:* Bengal, Royal Calcutta Golf (Calcutta).
                                    [[Died 12 Nov. 1976.

MIEVILLE, Sir Eric Charles, GCIE 1947 (KCIE 1936); KCVO 1943; CSI 1933; CMG 1930; *b* 31 Jan. 1896; *s* of Charles Ernest Miéville; *m* 1922, Dorothy (*d* 1962), *d* of G. C. A. Hasloch. *Educ:* St Paul's Sch. Student Interpreter in the Far Eastern Consular Service, 1919; Local Vice-Consul, 1921; Private Sec. to successive British Ministers in Peking, 1920-27; Sec. to the Governor-Gen. of Dominion of Canada, 1927-31; Priv. Sec. to the Viceroy of India, 1931-36; Sec. to Executive Council of Governor-Gen. of India, 1935-36; Private Sec. to the Duke of York, 1936; Asst Private Sec. to the King, 1937-45; a senior mem. of staff of Viceroy of India, 1947. *Recreations:* golf, tennis, etc. *Clubs:* White's, Buck's.   *[Died 16 Sept. 1971.*

MIKKELSEN, Captain Ejnar; Knight of Dannebroge; Hon. PhD Copenhagen, 1956; *b* 23 Dec. 1880; *s* of Aksel Mikkelsen, Government Inspector of Danish Slöjd; *m* 1st, 1913, Naja (*d* 1918), *d* of Captain Gustav Holm, RN; 2nd, Ella, *d* of Barrister Holm-Jensen; two *s. Educ:* Copenhagen. Went to Sea, 1894; travelled all about the world; Mem. of the Amdrups Expedition to East Coast of Greenland, surveying from Scoresby Sound to Angmasalik, 1900; Mem. of the Baldwin-Ziegler Polar Expedition to Franz Joseph's Land, 1901-02; Chief Officer on the International Hydrographic Expedition to Northern Atlantic, 1903-04; Jt Comdr with Mr Ernest de K. Leffingwell of Expedition to the North of Alaska, 1906-08; Commander of Expedition to North-Eastern Greenland, 1909-12; Commander, Colonizing Expedition to Scoresby Sound, 1924; Commander of experimental fishing cruise to West Greenland, 1925; Commander of Expedition to SE Greenland, 1932; Manager of the Faroe Whaling Co. Ltd; Pres. of the Scoresby Sound Cttee; Expert-Mem. of Government Delegation about Danish sovereignty, East Greenland before Internat. Court in The Hague, 1932; Inspector-Gen. of E Greenland, 1933, retd 1951. Pres. Greenland Soc., 1934-56; attached Danish Legation in Washington as Adviser in Greenland Matters, 1944; Governor of Arctic Inst. of North America, 1948 (hon. mem. 1956); Chm. Danish Arctic Institute, 1954. Awarded medals from Belgian, Scottish, Danish, and French Geog. Socs; Medal of Merit in silver and gold; Patron's Gold Medal, RGS, 1934; Livingstone Gold Medal, RSGS, 1948. Officer of French Legion of Honour. *Publications:* Conquering the Arctic Ice; Lost in the Arctic; Report on the Alabama Expedition; Frozen Justice; John Dale; Danes in Argentine; Med Grónland til Scoresby Sound; Nachbarn des Nordpols, De ostgrónd landske Eskimoirs Historie; The East Greenlanders-Possibilities of Existence, their Production and Consumption, and different papers to Meddelelser om Gronland. Fra Hündevagt til Hündeslade, 1953; Mirage in the Arctic, 1955; Farlig Tomandsfárd, 1956; Two Against the Ice, 1957; Fra Fribytter til Embedsmand, 1957; Svündne Tider Tider i Ost-Grónland, 1960. *Address:* Vilhelmshaabsvej, Charlottenlund, Denmark. T: Ordrup 1414; (summer) Gudhjem, Bornholm.   *[Died 4 May 1971.*

MIKOYAN, Anastas Ivanovich; five Orders of Lenin; Order of the October Revolution, 1970; Order of the Red Banner; Hero of Socialist Labour; Hammer and Sickle Gold Medal, etc; Member of the Presidium of the Supreme Soviet, USSR, since 1965; Member of the Presidium of the Central Committee of the Communist Party of Soviet Union, 1952-66; Member Supreme Soviet since 1937; *b* Sanain, Armenia, 25 Nov. 1895; *m* ; one *s. Educ:* Armenian Ecclesiastical Seminary, Tiflis. Joined Communist Party, 1915; fought in Revolution, Baku (imprisoned and escaped thrice), 1917-19; Mem. All-Russian Central Exec. Cttee, 1919-23; Mem. All-Union Central Exec. Cttee, 1923-27; Mem. Central Cttee, Communist Party, 1923-; Peoples' Commissar of Trade, 1926; Mem. Council of Labour and Defence, 1926; Peoples' Commissar of Supply, 1930-34, of the Food Supply Industry, 1934-38; Mem. Political Bureau of the Central Cttee, 1935- (Candidate, 1926-35); Dep. Chm., Council of People's Commissars, 1937-46; People's Commissar of Foreign Trade, 1938-46; Mem. State Defence Cttee, 1942-45; Vice-Chm., Council of Ministers of USSR, 1946 and simultaneously Minister of Foreign Trade, 1946-49; Minister of Trade, 1953; First Vice-Chm., Council of Ministers of the USSR, 1955-64; Chm., Presidium of the USSR Supreme Soviet, 1964-65. *Address:* Presidium of the Supreme Soviet of the USSR, Kremlin, Moscow, USSR.   *[Died 21 Oct. 1978.*

MILES, Maj.-Gen. Eric Grant, CB 1943; DSO 1917; MC 1915; *b* 1891; 2nd *s* of late George H. Miles, Homestall, Welwyn, Herts; *m* 1924, Lady Marcia Valda, (*d* 1972), *y d* of 7th Earl of Roden; one *d. Educ:* Harrow; RMC. Joined King's Own Scottish Borderers, 1911; served European War, 1914-19 (wounded, despatches 5 times, DSO, MC); Capt. KOSB, 1916; Brevet Major, 1919; psc 1922; GSO 3 War Office, 1923; Brigade Major Shanghai Defence Force, 1927-28; Major, 1927; General Staff Officer, 2; War Office, 1930-33; Bt Lt-Col 1931; Imperial Defence Coll., 1934; Lt-Col 1936; commanded 1st Bn Royal

Berks Regt, 1936-38; Col 1934; Gen. Staff Officer, 1st Grade, Malaya, 1938-39; Brig., 1940; Maj.-Gen., 1940; served in Flanders, 1940 (despatches); North Africa, 1943 (wounded); commanded 126th Inf. Bde 1940, 42nd (East Lancs) Div. 1941, 56th (London) Div. 1941-43; GOC Kent and South-Eastern Districts, 1943-46; Actg Lt-Gen., Sept.-Nov. 1944, as GOC-in-C South-Eastern Command; retired pay, 1946; Col KOSB, 1944-54. A Mem. of the House of Laity, Church Assembly, 1955-60; Dep. Chm. Lichfield Diocesan Board of Finance, 1954-60, Chm., 1960-71. *Address:* The Rope Walk, Lyth Hill, Shrewsbury. *T:* Bayston Hill 2053.   *[Died 3 Nov. 1977.*

MILES, Frederick George, FRAeS; MSAE; Chairman and Managing Director: F. G. Miles Engineering Ltd; Miles-Hivolt Ltd; Chairman: Miles Nautical Instruments Ltd; Hivolt Ltd; Freeman of the Guild of Air Pilots and Air Navigators; *b* 22 March 1903; *m* 1932, Maxine, *d* of Sir Johnston Forbes-Robertson; one *s* (and one *d* decd). *Educ:* Brighton. Career: mostly flying. *Address:* Batts, Ashurst, Steyning, W Sussex.
                                                    [Died 15 Aug. 1976.

MILES, Richard; President, F.C. Construction (Holdings) Co.; former Director of a number of companies (chiefly engineering) in UK and abroad and Chairman, Head Wrightson & Co. Ltd, retired 1959; *b* 3 Feb. 1893; *s* of Thomas Vivian and Elizabeth Miles; *m* 1917, Alice Miller; one *s* one *d. Educ:* Nottingham High Sch.; Sheffield Univ. (MechEng). Major KOYLI and Machine Gun Corps, 1914-18. Major, Home Guard, 1939-44. Asst Gen. Manager, 1919-28, and Gen. Manager, 1928-32, Newton Chambers & Co. Ltd, Thorncliffe Ironworks, near Sheffield. Past-Pres., Institute of British Foundrymen, 1941-42. MIMechE. Former Dir, North Eastern Trading Estates Ltd; Former Mem. of Council, University of Newcastle upon Tyne, and Mem., National Research Development Corp.; Past Pres. Brit. Cast Iron Research Assoc. *Publications:* contrib. to financial, technical, and similar periodicals. *Recreations:* gardening, music. *Address:* Borth Wen Farm, Llandegfan, Menai Bridge, Gwynedd. *T:* Menai Bridge 713381.
                                                    [Died 26 May 1976.

MILFORD, Maj.-Gen. Edward James, CB 1947; CBE 1945; DSO 1919; psc; Australian Military Forces: Dir of Artillery, 1938-39; CRA Australian Division AIF, 1940; Master-General of the Ordnance, 1941; Divisional Commander, 1942; Adjutant-General, 1946; retired from Australian Military Forces, 1948. *Address:* Mornington, Vic 3931, Australia. *Club:* Naval and Military (Melbourne).   *[Died 10 June 1972.*

MILHAUD, Darius; Grand Officier, Légion d'Honneur, 1965; composer; Hon. Professor of Composition, Conservatoire de Musique, Paris, 1947; *b* Aix-en-Provence, 4 Sept. 1892; *m* 1925, Madeleine Milhaud; one *s. Educ:* Paris Conservatory. Attached to French Legation, Brazil, 1917-18. Prof. of Music, Mills Coll., California, 1940-. Mem., Acad. des Beaux Arts, 1972. *Works:* La Brébis Egarée, L'Homme et son Désir; La Création du monde; Le Retour de l'enfant prodigue; Protée; L'Orestie d'Eschyle; Le Bœuf sur le toit; Le Train Bleu; Salade; Les Malheurs d'Orphée; Esther de Carpentras; Le pauvre Matelot; Christophe Colomb; Maximilien; Les Songes, La Sagesse, Bolivar, David, La Mère Coupable, etc. *Publications: autobiography:* Notes sans musique, 1949, enl. 2nd edn 1962; Ma vie heureuse, 1974. *Address:* 10 Boulevard de Clichy, Paris. *T:* Montmartre 67-66.   *[Died 22 June 1974.*

MILL IRVING, David Jarvis, CBE 1955; Founder Member, and Hon. President, 1966, Scottish National Party in East Lothian; Ambassador to Costa Rica, 1956-61, retired; *b* 11 April 1904; 2nd *s* of late W. Mill Irving, LDS, RCSE, Langholm and Edinburgh, and Mary Low Jarvis; *m* 1934, Margaret Estella Orchardson, *d* of late W. Moxon, Edinburgh and Tangier; one *s. Educ:* Daniel Stewart's Coll., Edinburgh; Edinburgh Univ.; Pembroke Coll., Cambridge. MA (Hons) Edinburgh, 1929. Entered HM Diplomatic Service as Probationer Vice-Consul in former Levant Consular Service, 1927; served in Egypt, 1929-32, and in Morocco, 1932-34; Vice-Consul at Suez, 1934; a Judge of HBM Consular Court for Egypt, 1934-37; Vice-Consul at Rabat, 1940; Asst Oriental Sec. at Cairo with rank of 1st Sec., 1941; Consul at Fez, 1945; served as 1st Sec. in Foreign Office, 1945-49. Mem. UK Deleg. to Internat. Conf. for revision of Conventions relating to War Victims, 1949; Special Ambassador for Inauguration of President of Hayti, 1950; Minister to Hayti, 1950-53; Ambassador, 1953-55; Consul-Gen. for Algeria, 1955. Special Ambassador for the Inauguration: of the President of Honduras, 1957; of the President of Costa Rica, 1958. Member: Saltire Soc.; Scottish Genealogy Soc.; Andrew Fletcher Soc.; Sir Walter Scott Club. FSAScot; FAMS. Coronation Medal, 1953. *Recreation:* Scottish historical research. *Address:* Langlaw, East Saltoun, Pencaitland, East Lothian EH34 5EB. *T:* Pencaitland

340266. *Club:* Scottish National (Edinburgh).
[*Died* 16 *Aug.* 1978.

MILLAR, John, CBE 1977; FIOB; DL; Lord Provost and Lord Lieutenant of the City of Edinburgh, 1975-77; Member: Falkirk Town Council, 1938-44; Edinburgh Town Council, 1961-75; *b* 18 June 1905; *m* 1932, Janet Calder Williamson; three *s* one *d*. *Educ:* Falkirk High Sch. Retired. Dir, Border Concrete Products Ltd. Chm., Edinburgh Festival Guild. DL Edinburgh, 1977. Royal Order de l'Étoile Polaire (Sweden), 1975; Commandeur de l'Ordre National du Mérite (France), 1976. *Recreations:* golf, walking. *Address:* 8 Northlawn Court, Easter Park Drive, Edinburgh EH4 6JR. [*Died* 15 *Oct.* 1978.

MILLBOURN, Rev. Arthur Russell; Canon Emeritus; *b* 10 May 1892; 2nd *s* of Arthur and Harriet Lucie Millbourn, London; *m* 1st, 1920, Ethel Mary (*d* 1960), *d* of John and Mary Congreve, Cambridge; 2nd, 1962, Eleanor Mary, widow of T. D. Fairgrieve and *d* of late P. B. Halcombe, Bournemouth. *Educ:* Christ's Hospital; Pembroke Coll., Oxford (Classical Scholar). Class. Hon. Mods II, 1913; Lit. Hum. II, 1915; Asst Master, S. John's Sch., Leatherhead, and House Tutor, 1915-22; Headmaster, Colston's Sch., Stapleton, Bristol, 1923-39; Deacon 1928; Priest 1929; Canon Residentiary of Bristol Cathedral, 1939-61. *Recreations:* music, foreign travel, railway engineering. *Address:* Feock, Truro, Cornwall. *T:* Devoran 862498.
[*Died* 8 *April* 1973.

MILLER, Alexander James Nicol, CB 1959; Commissioner of Inland Revenue, 1957-71; *b* 24 April 1911; *s* of late James John Miller; *m* 1940, Doris Martha Hankins; no *c*. *Educ:* Queen Mary's Grammar Sch., Walsall; Jesus Coll., Oxford. Entered Inland Revenue Dept, 1934. *Address:* 22 Waverley Lane, Farnham, Surrey. [*Died* 18 *May* 1974.

MILLER, Archibald Elliot Haswell, MC; Hon. MA Edinburgh 1951; RSW; Keeper and Deputy Director, National Galleries of Scotland, 1930-52 (retired); Secretary, Royal Fine Art Commission for Scotland, 1930-52 (retired); Secretary (later Director) National Buildings Record, Scottish Council, 1945-53 (retired); *b* Glasgow, 10 June 1887; *s* of William Miller and Elizabeth Haswell; *m* 1916, E. Josephine Cameron (Josephine Haswell Miller, ARSA); one *d*. *Educ:* Glasgow Academy. Studied Munich, Berlin, Vienna and Paris; Asst Professor in Glasgow Sch. of Art, 1910-14 and 1919-30; war services 1914-19 with 7th Bn Highland Light Infantry (MC), and 1939-45 with Intelligence Corps. Represented by works in Glasgow Art Gallery, National Gallery of New South Wales, and Imperial War Museum (Series of drawings representing all types of dress and equipment of the 1914-18 war period); has made a special study of military uniforms and Highland dress. Retrospective Exhibn 1908-71, Imperial War Museum, 1971. Consultant Art Historian, Army Museums Ogilby Trust. Mem. of Soc. of Mural Decorators and Painters in Tempera; has carried out mural paintings in Livingstone Memorial Museum, Blantyre. *Publication:* Military Drawings and Paintings in the Royal Collection, vol i, 1966, vol ii, 1970. *Address:* Yew Tree Cottage, Kington Magna, Gillingham, Dorset. *T:* East Stour 326.
[*Died* 25 *March* 1979.

MILLER, Maj.-Gen. Charles Harvey, CB 1942; CBE 1941; DSO 1943; Legion of Honour, 1943; Croix de Guerre avec Palmes; Legion of Merit, Degree of Commander, 1945; *b* 11 Sept. 1894; *s* of late Robert Miller, Dummer Grange, Basingstoke; *m* 1923, Hon. Bridget Violet Douglas-Pennant, *d* of 5th Baron Penrhyn; one *d*. *Educ:* Winchester; RMA, Woolwich. Joined 18th Hussars, 1914; served European War, 1914-19 (wounded twice). Staff Coll., Camberley, 1927-29; Comd Transjordan Frontier Force, 1932-36; Brevet Col, 1936; commanded 13/18 Hussars, 1937-38; commanded 5 Cavalry Brigade, 1940; on the staff HQ BTE (despatches) 8th Army, 1941-42; MGA 18 Army Group and 15 Army Group, 1943, served in Western Desert, Tunis, Sicily, and Italy; MGA Southern Command, 1943-45; Temp. Maj.-Gen. 1943; Maj.-Gen. 1944; retired pay, 1946; Chief of Staff to the Duke of Gloucester, in Australia, 1946-47; Fellow of Royal Commonwealth Society and Royal Geographical Society. DL Suffolk, 1953. *Address:* Old Rectory, Badingham, Suffolk. *T:* Badingham 222. *Club:* Cavalry. [*Died* 23 *Dec.* 1974.

MILLER, Henry George, MD,, FRCP; Vice-Chancellor of University of Newcastle upon Tyne, since 1968 (Dean of Medicine, 1966-68, and Professor of Neurology, 1964-68); *b* 13 Dec. 1913; *s* of John Miller, Stockton-on-Tees, Co. Durham; *m* 1942, Eileen Cathcart Baird, MRCOG; two *s* two *d*. *Educ:* University of Durham. MB 1937, MD 1940, MRCP 1940, DPM 1943, FRCP 1953. Asst Resident Pathologist, Johns Hopkins Hospital, Baltimore, 1938; clinical appts at Hospital for Sick Children, Gt Ormond Street, 1939; Neuropsychiatric Specialist,

RAF Med. Service, 1942-46; Hammersmith Hosp. and Nat. Hosp. Queen Square, 1946-47; Asst Physician, Royal Victoria Infirmary, Newcastle upon Tyne, 1947-64. Examiner in Medicine, University of Liverpool; Vis. Prof. of Medicine, University of Queensland, 1963. Mem., Assoc. of Physicians of GB and Ireland (Pres., 1974-75); Hon. For. Mem., Soc. Française de Neurologie; American Neurological Assoc. *Publications:* Early Diagnosis, 1960; Modern Medical Treatment, 1962, new edn with R. Hall, 1975; (ed with R. Daley) Progress in Clinical Medicine, 1948, 6th edn 1971; (with W. B. Matthews) Diseases of the Nervous System, 1972, new edn 1975; Medicine and Society, 1973; many papers on medical and neurological subjects. *Address:* Vice-Chancellor's Lodge, Adderstone Crescent, Newcastle upon Tyne NE2 2HH. *T:* Newcastle 813021. *Clubs:* Athenæum, Garrick.
[*Died* 25 *Aug.* 1976.

MILLER, Henry (Valentine); author and painter; *b* New York City, 26 Dec. 1891; *m*; one *s* two *d* by former *ms. Educ:* City Coll., NY; Cornell Univ. Worked in US until 1930; lived in Paris and was employed on editorial work on Phoenix, Booster and Volontés, 1930-38; visited Greece, 1939; returned to US, 1940. Mem., Amer. Inst. of Arts and Letters, 1958. *Publications:* Tropic of Cancer, 1931 (US 1961, UK 1964); Aller Retour New York, 1935; Tropic of Capricorn, 1935 (US 1962, UK 1964); Black Spring, 1936 (UK 1965); Max and the White Phagocytes, 1938 (UK 1970); The Cosmological Eye, 1939 (UK 1946); The World of Sex, 1940 (US 1957, UK 1970); The Colossus of Maroussi, 1941; The Wisdom of the Heart, 1941 (UK 1947); Sunday After the War, 1944 (UK 1946); The Air-Conditioned Nightmare, 1945 (UK 1947); Murder the Murderer, 1946; Maurizius Forever, 1946; Remember to Remember, 1947 (UK 1952); The Smile at the Foot of the Ladder, 1948 (UK 1966); Rosy Crucifixion, 1965: Sexus, 1949; Plexus, 1953; Nexus, 1959; The Books in My Life, 1952; Quiet Days in Clichy, 1956 (UK 1966); The Time of the Assasins, 1956 (UK 1959); Big Sur and the Oranges of Hieronymous Bosch, 1956 (UK 1958); The Red Notebook, 1958; Reunion in Barcelona, 1959; Stand still like the Mockingbird, 1962; A Letter, 1962; Watercolours, 1962; Just Wild About Harry, 1963 (UK 1964); (with Lawrence Durrell) A Private Correspondence, 1963; (with M. Fraenkel) Hamlet: correspondence, 1963; Greece, 1964; Letters to Anais Nin, 1965; What are you going to do about Alf?, 1971; My Life and Times, 1972; The Immortal Bard, 1973; On Turning Eighty, 1973; First Impressions of Greece, 1974; Journey to an Antique Land, 1974; The Waters Reglitterized, 1974; Henry Miller's Book of Friends, 1978. Exhibition of paintings, Los Angeles, 1966. *Address:* c/o Grove Press, 80 University Place, New York, NY 10013, USA; c/o Edward P. Schwartz, Henry Miller Literary Society, 121 N 7th Street, Minneapolis, Minn 55403, USA. [*Died* 7 *June* 1980.

MILLER, Rear-Adm. (retd) Hugh, CB 1935; DSO 1918; *b* 1880; *s* of late Joseph Charles Miller, Beckenham, Kent; *m* 1919, Muriel, *d* of late Dr Edward Baines Holwell, Leeds. *Educ:* Whitgift Sch. Legion of Honour and Orders of Sacred Treasure of Japan, Nile of Egypt, and Striped Tiger of China; retired list, 1935. *Address:* Highbury, Tilmore, Petersfield, Hants. *T:* Petersfield 3473. *Club:* Army and Navy. [*Died* 21 *Aug.* 1972.

MILLER, Sir James, GBE 1965; Kt 1953; DL, JP; *b* 16 March 1905; *s* of James Miller, Architect, Edinburgh; *m* 1933, Ella Jane Stewart; two *s* one *d* (and one *s* decd). *Educ:* George Heriot's Sch., Edinburgh. Trained as Architect, thereafter Man. Dir James Miller & Partners Ltd, Building & Civil Engineering Contractors, Edinburgh, London and Wakefield, until 1973. Edinburgh Town Council, Nov. 1936-54; Lord Provost of the City of Edinburgh, May 1951-54; Sheriff, City of London, 1956; Alderman of Bishopsgate, 1957-72; Lord Mayor of London, 1964-65. DL Edinburgh, 1955. Master of the Worshipful Company of Coachmakers and Coach Harness Makers, 1964. Hon. LLD Edinburgh, 1953; Hon. DSc City Univ., 1966. KStJ. *Recreations:* yachting, golf, etc. *Address:* Belmont, Ellersly Road, Edinburgh. *T:* 031-337 1822. *Clubs:* Royal Automobile, City Livery; Caledonian, Royal Forth Yacht (Edinburgh).
[*Died* 20 *March* 1977.

MILLER, Bt Col Sir James (MacBride), Kt 1958; MC; TD; DL; *b* 18 June 1896; *s* of Rev. John Miller, Eyemouth, Berwickshire; *m* 1925, Jane Elizabeth Simson Elliot, *d* of Francis Elliot, Middlestots, Duns, Berwickshire. *Educ:* Berwickshire; George Watson's Coll., Edinburgh. Royal Artillery, TA, 1915-36. Convener, Berwickshire County Council, 1949-61; President of the Association of County Councils of Scotland, 1956-58. DL Berwickshire, 1948. Hon. Sheriff Substitute, Duns. *Address:* Duneaton, West Bay Road, North Berwick.
[*Died* 9 *Nov.* 1977.

MILLER, John, RSA 1966 (ARSA 1958); PRSW 1970-74 (RSW 1952); Senior Lecturer (Drawing and Painting), Glasgow School of Art, since 1972 (Lecturer, 1944-72); *b* 21 March 1911; *s* of John Miller; *m* 1954, Barbara Neilson Brodie, BArch (Strathclyde); two *s* one *d. Educ:* Glasgow Sch. of Art (Dipl. and Post-Dipl.); Hospitalfield Art Coll., Arbroath. Exhibited at: Royal Acad.; Royal Scottish Acad.; Soc. of Scottish Artists; Royal Glasgow Inst.; Royal Scottish Society of Painters in Water Colours. Work in Permanent Collections: Glasgow Art Galls; Dundee Art Gall.; Paisley Art Gall.; Newport Art Gall.; Arts Coun.; Corp. of Edinburgh (Watson Bequest). *Recreation:* walking. *Address:* 15 Ardenconnel Way, Rhu, Dunbartonshire. *T:* Rhu 326. *Club:* Art (Glasgow). 			*[Died 18 Jan. 1975.*

MILLER, John Duncan, CMG 1968; *b* 6 April 1902; *e s* of late Hubert James Miller and Elsa Mary (*née* Collmann), Old Court House, Knutsford; *m* 1926, Leila Madeline (*d* 1973), *o d* of late Gen. Sir John Asser, KCB, KCMG, KCVO; one *s. Educ:* Wellington Coll.; Trinity Hall, Cambridge. Served War of 1939-45: War Office, 1940-41; British Army Staff, Washington, 1941-43; HQ 11th Army Gp and Allied Land Forces, SE Asia, 1943-45. Dir, British Information Services, Middle West of USA, 1945-47; Washington Corresp. of The Times and The Economist, 1947-54; Special Representative in Europe of Internat. Bank for Reconstruction and Develt, 1955-68; Rep. in Continental Europe for Baring Brothers & Co. Ltd, 1968-71. Order of Legion of Merit (US), 1946. *Publication:* Who's Who in the Wars, 1940. *Recreations:* music and water. *Address:* Le Petit Large, Saumane, 84800 L'Isle-sur-Sorgue, France.
			[Died 20 May 1977.

MILLER, Dame Mabel (Flora), DBE 1967; LLB; JP; Barrister: Australian Representative to Status of Women Commission, United Nations, since 1967; Member, Metric Conversion Board, since 1970; *b* Broken Hill, NSW; *d* of J. C. Goodhart, Victor Harbour, S Australia; *m* 1930, Alan Miller; one *d. Educ:* Girton House, Adelaide; University of Adelaide. Joined WAAAF, 1941; Dep. Dir, WAAAF, 1942-43 (Sqdn Officer); Staff Officer, WAAAF, North Eastern Area, 1944. Alderman, Hobart, 1952- (Dep. Lord Mayor, 1954-56, 1964-66, 1966-68); MHA for Franklin, Tasmania, 1955-64. Pres., Right to Life Assoc., Tasmania; Foundn Mem., Tasmanian Women's Air Trng Corps (Women's Vol. Auxiliary); Member: Interim Cttee, Austr. Nat. Gall. in Canberra; Aust.-Amer. Assoc.; Member Committee: Aust.-British Assoc.; Queen Alexandra Hospital Country Women's Assoc.; Red Cross; Girl Guides Assoc. (Exec. Mem.); Past Pres., Nat. Coun. of Women. *Recreations:* golf, reading. *Address:* 403 Sandy Bay Road, Hobart, Tasmania. *T:* 252084. *Clubs:* University Women's; Queen Mary, Air Force, Royal Automobile, Business and Professional Women's, (Assoc. Mem.) Naval, Military and Air Force (Hobart); Lyceum (Melbourne); Royal Over-Seas League, Tasmanian Assoc. of University Women Graduates (Tasmania). *[Died 29 Dec. 1978.*

MILLER, Mrs Millie; MP (Lab) Redbridge, Ilford North, since Oct. 1974; social worker; *b* April 1923. *Educ:* Dame Alice Owen's Girls' School. Mayor of Stoke Newington, 1957-58, Camden, 1967-68; Leader, Camden Council, 1971-73. Contested (Lab) Ilford, North, Feb. 1974. Mem., G&MWU. *Address:* House of Commons, SW1A 0AA; 105 Highgate West Hill, N6 6AP. 			*[Died 29 Oct. 1977.*

MILLER, Rev. Norman, MA; *s* of late E. Banbury Miller, Bristol; *m* 1942, Annette Daukes, *e d* of late Rt Rev. F. W. Daukes, sometime Bishop of Plymouth; two *s. Educ:* Clifton Coll.; Queen's Coll., Cambridge (Schol.); University Stewart of Rannoch Schol. for Classics. Sixth Form Master, Berkhamsted Sch.; ordained, 1914; Asst Master in Haileybury Coll.; House-Master, 1919-26; Headmaster of Kelly Coll., Tavistock, 1926-38; Vicar of St Albans, Bristol, 1939-51; Rector of Swanage, Dorset, 1951-61. *Address:* Barn Cottage, Quenington, Glos.
			[Died 28 March 1980.

MILLER, Rev. Peter Watters, MA, BD, DD (Edinburgh); Professor of Old Testament Language and Literature, Free Church College, Edinburgh, 1936-66, Principal, 1945-66, Principal Emeritus since 1966; *b* 10 May 1890; *s* of Donald Miller and Christina Watters; *m* 1918, Annie Smith (*d* 1961). *Educ:* Castletown Sch., Caithness; Edinburgh Univ.; Free Church Coll., Edinburgh. Ordained in 1915 and settled as Minister of Free Church in Campbeltown, Argyllshire; served abroad during European War for two years as a Chaplain to the Forces in France and Germany; Minister of Partick Congregation of Free Church of Scotland, 1923-36; Lecturer in Religious Instruction in the Teachers' Training Centre (later Coll. of Educn) at Jordanhill, Glasgow, 1931-36; Moderator of General Assembly of Free Church, 1936. *Address:* 69 Arden Street, Edinburgh EH9 1BT. 			*[Died 11 May 1976.*

MILLER, Sir Roderick (William), Kt 1970; CBE 1962; Chairman and Managing Director, R. W. Miller (Holdings) Ltd and associated companies since 1958; *b* 12 Nov. 1911; *s* of R. W. Miller, Queensferry, Scotland; *m* 1957, Elizabeth, *d* of C. E. Barberie; two *s* two *d. Educ:* Scots Coll., Sydney. Sales Manager, R. W. Miller & Co., 1931, Director from 1931. Served 1940-45, Gunner 2/1st Aust. AA Regt; Lieut 1942; Captain 1945. *Recreations:* golf, boating, fishing, swimming; formerly prominent in GPS football, rowing, athletics, rep. NSW in Rugby Union. *Address:* 9 Hillside Avenue, Vaucluse, NSW 2030, Australia. *T:* (office) 27-4361. *Clubs:* Royal Automobile of Australia, Tattersalls, Victoria (Melbourne); Royal Motor Yacht; Manly Golf; Sydney Turf; Australian Jockey.
			[Died 26 April 1971.

MILLER, Sir Stanley N.; *see* Norie-Miller.

MILLER, William Christopher; retired as Director of Equine Research Station of the Animal Health Trust, Newmarket (1946-66); Courtauld Professor of Animal Husbandry, Royal Veterinary College, 1935-46; *b* 19 May 1898; *s* of late William Warden Miller and Annie Riddle Bell; *m* 1926, Margaret Alice Munro; two *s. Educ:* Colchester Royal Grammar School; Royal (Dick) Veterinary College, Edinburgh. Mem., Royal College of Veterinary Surgeons, 1919; Lecturer, Zootechny and Animal Management, Royal (Dick) Veterinary College, 1919; Lecturer, Veterinary Hygiene, Edinburgh and East of Scotland Coll. of Agriculture, 1920; University Lecturer and Research Asst, Institute of Animal Genetics, University of Edinburgh, 1928; Fellow Royal Society of Edinburgh, 1929; Pres. Nat. Vet. Med. Assoc., 1944-45; Steele Memorial Gold Medal, 1956; Victory Gold Medal, Central Vet. Soc., 1958; awarded Fellowship of RCVS, by election, 1964. Hon. Mem. RSM, 1967. *Publications:* Parasites of British Sheep; Editor, Black's Veterinary Dictionary (with West); Practical Animal Husbandry (with Robertson); Care and Management of Horses on Thoroughbred Studs, 1964; Feeding of Ponies, 1966. Articles and papers in Veterinary Record; Veterinary Jl, Jl of Agricultural Science; The British Racehorse; Empire Jl of Experimental Agriculture; Jl of Textile Institute; Proceedings of Royal Society; Proceedings of Royal Society Medicine; Animal Health; Handbuch der Tierzüchtung, etc. *Address:* 32 Crofton Avenue, Walton-on-Thames, Surrey.
			[Died 17 Dec. 1976.

MILLER JONES, Keith; Chairman, Board of Governors of the National Hospitals for Nervous Diseases, 1963-74; Solicitor; *b* 7 April 1899; *o s* of late Frank W. Jones, Headingley, Leeds; *m* 1950, Hon. Betty Ellen Askwith, *o d* of late Baron Askwith, KCB, KC, LLD. *Educ:* privately; New Coll., Oxford (Hon. Exhibr); Leeds Univ. Admitted Solicitor, 1925; Mem., firm of Braby & Waller, 1925-62. Mem., Paddington Group HMC, 1948-60; Dep. Chm., Georgian Group, 1955-71 (Mem. Council); Founder Mem., Hansard Soc. for Parly Govt, 1944 (Mem. Council, 1944-75); Founder Mem., Wildfowl Trust, 1946 (Mem. Coun., 1946-67). *Recreations:* music, golf. *Address:* Flat 9, 105 Onslow Square, SW7. *T:* 01-589 7126. *Clubs:* Brooks's; Richmond Golf. 			*[Died 11 July 1978.*

MILLIGAN, Rt. Hon. Lord; Rt. Hon. William Rankine Milligan, PC 1955; Senator of College of Justice in Scotland, 1960-73; *b* 12 Dec. 1898; *er s* of late Very Rev. George Milligan, DD, Glasgow; *m* 1925, Muriel Jean, *er d* of late James MacLehose, LLD; one *s* three *d. Educ:* Sherborne; University Coll., Oxford; University of Glasgow. Served HLI 1917-19; represented Oxford in the Inter-University sports, 1920-23; Pres. OUAC 1923; represented Scotland against England and Ireland 1920; admitted to Faculty of Advocates, 1925; QC Scot. 1945; Solicitor-Gen. for Scotland, 1951-54; Lord Advocate, Dec. 1954-March 1960; MP (C) Edinburgh North, 1955-60. Pres., Scottish Amateur Athletic Assoc., 1936; Mem. Queen's Body Guard for Scotland (Royal Company of Archers); Chm. of Cttee Edinburgh and East of Scotland Branch of Overseas League, 1938-46; Hon. President: Scottish Amateur Athletic Assoc., 1959-71; Scottish Basketball Assoc., 1973-; Atalanta Club. *Recreations:* gardening, golf, fishing. *Address:* 38 India Street, Edinburgh. *T:* 031-225 4937. *Clubs:* New (Edinburgh); Western (Glasgow). 			*[Died 28 July 1975.*

MILLIGAN, Patrick Ward, DL; Chairman: Sedgwick Collins & Co., 1967-72; Sedgwick Forbes (Holdings) Ltd, 1972-74; a General Commissioner for Income Tax, since 1975; *b* 27 May 1910; 2nd *s* of James Knowles Milligan, MRCS, LRCP and Arabella Milligan; *m* 1934, Betty Mavis, *yr d* of Frank Rogerson; one *s* one *d. Educ:* Winchester Coll. Joined Lloyd's, 1928; underwriting mem., 1932. Served War of 1939-45, Queen's Royal Regiment; AQMG, BTE, 1945, Lt-Col. Member: Cttee Non Marine Assoc., Lloyd's, 1949-62 (Chm., 1958); Cttee of Lloyd's, 1954-57 and 1959-62; Dep. Chm. of Lloyd's, 1957,

1960, Chm., 1962; Chm., Lloyd's Brokers' Assoc., 1967. Chm. Transport Users Consultative Cttee (SE Area), 1966-76. DL Surrey 1976. *Recreations:* golf, cricket. *Address:* The Coach House, Eashing, Surrey. *T:* Godalming 5459. *Club:* Gresham.
[Died 17 Dec. 1978.

MILLIGAN, Rt. Hon. William Rankine; *see* Milligan, Rt. Hon. Lord.

MILLINGTON-DRAKE,   Sir   Eugen   (John   Henry Vanderstegen), KCMG 1942 (CMG 1938); Vice-President: Hispanic Council, since 1948; Anglo-Spanish Society, since 1953; Poetry Society, since 1942; Member, Comité d'Honneur, since 1955, and Council, since 1950, Fédération Britannique de l'Alliance Française; *b* 26 Feb. 1889; *o s* of late Henry Millington-Drake; *m* 1920, Lady Effie Mackay, 4th *d* of 1st Earl of Inchcape; two *s* one *d* (and one *d* decd). *Educ:* Eton; Magdalen Coll., Oxford (MA, Hons in Hist.); Berlin Univ. HM Diplomatic Service, 1912; St Petersburg, 1913; Buenos Aires, 1915; Paris (Peace Delegation, 1919, and Embassy, 1920); First Sec. and at times Chargé d'Affaires at Bucharest, 1921-24; at Brussels, 1924-27; at Copenhagen, 1927-28; Counsellor of Embassy, Buenos Aires, 1929-33; Minister to Uruguay, 1934-41. Hon. Pres. Uruguayan Delegation to Olympic Games, 1936; Special Ambassador for inauguration of new President of Uruguayan Republic, 1938; Founding Pres. Friends of Uruguay Soc., 1940; seconded from FO as Chief Representative of British Council in Spanish America, 1942-46. Rep. Oxford, Cambridge and London Univs, at Centenary of Univ. of Santiago de Chile, 1942. Hon. Dr Catholic Univ. of Chile, 1943; Hon. Dr Univ. of Buenos Aires and Hon. Prof. Univ. of Montevideo, 1946. Hon. Citizen of Montevideo. Founder, Hudson Institute, 1947; Chm. Reception Cttee of XIV Olympiad, London, 1948; represented Hispanic Council at San Martin Centenary, Boulogne, 1950; Vice-Pres. Council, Royal India, Pakistan and Ceylon Society for which visited the East on Cultural Missions, 1949-50 and 1960; Lecture tours of Africa, Madagascar, Mauritus and Reunion, representing various cultural and sports institutions, 1952 and 1953; lectured on Graf Spee: at Naval Acad., Annapolis; at Naval War Sch., Newport, RI, 1968; in Spanish, in Venezuela, Colombia, Peru, Chile, Argentina, 1969. Medal of Société des Poètes Français for services to French culture overseas, 1953. FRSA 1960. Liveryman of Grocers' Company. Donated Macnaghten War Memorial Library to Eton Coll., and instituted French Declamation Prize, 1938; also Latin-American Prizes at Eton and Harrow, 1947; founded Sir John O'Conor Memorial Scholarship for doctors of British Hospital, Buenos Aires, to study in Britain, 1946; Donor with Lady Effie of site of Royal Air Force Memorial on Coopers Hill by Runnymede. Presented: Leclerc Prize for Shooting for NATO Armies, 1950; Canning Prize for general knowledge of Latin America, open to teams of three from all Secondary Schs in the UK; Harwood Prize for Spanish at Dartmouth; Bourne Cup for public schs at Reading Head of River Regatta. *Publications:* Hugh Macnaghten's House Record, 1899-1920, 1932; Joyas de la Poesia Inglesa (Anthology of Spanish-American translations of English Poetry), 1941; Poesias de las Provincias que he conocido (Anthology of Poetry of Argentine Provinces), 1949; Walter Owen: Interpreter of Hispanic Epic Poetry to the English-Speaking World, 1954; A Round the World Goodwill Lecture Tour, 1961-62; The Drama of Graf Spee and the Battle of the Plate, 1964; Entente Cordiale (trans.), 1971. *Recreations:* rowing, Eton VIII, 1905-08 (winners of Ladies Plate 1905); rowed in Magdalen Coll. crews head of river and winners of the Grand at Henley 1910, winners Oxford University Boat Club Fours, 1909-10, Oxford VIII 1911 (winners in then record time). Vice-Pres. National Amateur Rowing Assoc., 1950-55; Mem. Exec. Cttee Assoc. Internat. de Boxe Amateur, 1946-54; Rep. Uruguay on Fedn Internat. Socs d'Aviron and Internat. Lawn Tennis Assoc. *Address:* Palazzo Taverna, Via di Monte Giordano 36, Rome. *Clubs:* Garrick, Leander, All England Lawn Tennis, Internat. Lawn Tennis, Vincent's (Oxford).
[Died 12 Dec. 1972.

MILLN, Rear-Adm. William Bryan Scott, CB 1969; *b* 15 March 1915; *e s* of late Surg.-Captain James Duff Scott Milln; *m* 1944, Maureen Alice Gardner; four *d. Educ:* Mount House, Plymouth; RNC Dartmouth. RNEC, 1933-36 and 1942-44; RNC Greenwich, 1937-39; served in HMS: Royal Oak, 1932-33; Apollo, 1936-37; Birmingham, 1939-42; Tumult, 1944-46; Glory, 1952-54; Thunderer, 1954-57; Victorious, 1957-59; Engr-in-Chief's Dept, Admty, 1946-52; Staff of C-in-C Far East, 1959-61; Dep. Dir of Marine Engrg, 1961-64; Captain, HMS Thunderer, 1964-67; Asst Chief of Staff (Logistics), SHAPE, 1967-69, retired. Lt 1937; Lt-Comdr 1944; Comdr 1948; Captain 1959; Rear-Adm. 1967. *Recreations:* practically everything, now reduced to golf. *Address:* Burhill Golf Club, Walton-on-Thames, Surrey.
[Died 11 Jan. 1979.

MILLS, Air Chief Marshal Sir George (Holroyd), GCB 1959 (KCB 1954; CB 1945) DFC 1940; Gentleman Usher of the Black Rod, House of Lords, 1963-70; *b* 26 March 1902; *s* of late W. B. S. Mills, The Priory, Swanley, Kent; *m* 1926, Mary, *d* of late S. Austen Smith, The Old Place, Swanley, Kent; two *s* one *d. Educ:* Berkhamsted; Royal Air Force Coll., Cranwell. Commissioned, 1921; Iraq, 1922-24; India, 1930-34; RAF Staff Coll., 1935-39; Air Ministry, 1935-39; Served War of 1939-45 in Bomber Command, Staff Coll., Air Ministry, and as AOC Balkan Air Force, 1945; Egypt, 1945-46; Dir of Plans, Air Ministry, 1946-48; Air Officer Commanding No. 1 Group, 1949-50; Head of United Kingdom Military Delegation to Western Union Military Staff Cttee, 1950-51; AOC, Malaya, 1952; AOC-in-C, Bomber Comd, 1953-55; Comdr, Allied Air Forces, Central Europe, 1956-69; Chm., British Defence Staffs, Washington, DC, and UK Representative on Standing Group of NATO Military Cttee, 1959-62; Air ADC to the Queen, 1956-62; retired, 1962. Trustee, Imperial War Museum, 1963-70. *Address:* c/o Lloyds Bank Ltd, 6 Pall Mall, SW1.
[Died 14 April 1971.

MILLS, Col Sir John (Digby), Kt 1958; TD, DL, JP; Member of House of Laity, 1944-60; Church Commissioner, 1948-58; 2nd and *o surv s* of late Rev. Cecil Mills, Bisterne, Ringwood, Hants, and Taverham Hall, Norfolk, and Anne H. F., *e d* of late Capt. F. H. G. Nicolls, 4th Dragoon Guards; *b* 1879; *m* 1918, Carola (JP (Hants), 1937); *o d* of late Judge S. P. Tuck, International Court of Appeals, Alexandria, Egypt, and of Maryland, USA; three *s. Educ:* Charterhouse; Oriel Coll., Oxford, BA. Joined Warwicks Yeomanry as 2nd Lieut, 1901; Major, 1911-20; served with WY in Egypt, Gallipoli, and France (despatches 3 times); MP (C) New Forest and Christchurch Division (Hants), Feb. 1932-July 1945; Second Church Estates Commissioner, 1943-45; Mem. of Hants County Council, 1907-64; County Alderman, 1925-64; a Verderer of the New Forest, 1922-38 and 1945-55; Chm., New Forest and Christchurch Div. Conservative Assoc., 1925-32; Chm., Winchester Diocesan Bd of Finance, 1948-54. Lt 8th (HD) Bn, Hants Regt, Sept. 1939-May 1940; Group Organiser LDV, 1940; Col and Comdr, New Forest Group, Home Guard, 1941-43, 2 i/c Hants Zone, 1943-45. Hon. Col Home Guard. *Recreations:* formerly shooting and fishing. *Address:* White House, Hangersley, Ringwood, Hants. *T:* Ringwood 3653. *Club:* Cavalry.
[Died 2 July 1972.

MILLS, Prof. John Norton, MA, DM Oxon, MD Cantab; Brackenbury Professor of Physiology, University of Manchester since October 1965; *b* 28 June 1914; *s* of George Percival Mills, Consultant Surgeon, and T. M. Cristabel (*née* Humphreys); *m* 1942, June Rosemary Jill Brenan; one *s* two *d. Educ:* Winchester; New Coll., Oxford; Christ Church, Oxford. Lecturer, New Coll., Oxford, 1941-46; Fellow and Lecturer, Jesus Coll., Cambridge, 1946-50; University of Manchester: Lecturer in Human Physiology, 1950; Sen. Lecturer, 1955; Reader in Physiology, 1959. *Publications:* (with R. T. W. L. Conroy) Human Circadian Rhythms, 1969; Chapters in: Recent Advances in Physiology (ed R. Creese), 1962; A Companion to Medical Studies (ed Passmore and Robson), 1968; Modern Trends in Physiology (ed C. B. B. Downman), 1972; Scientific Foundations of Paediatrics (ed Davis and Dobbing), 1974; ed and contrib. Biological Aspects of Circadian Rhythms, 1973; papers in Jl Physiol., Clin. Sci., Jl Endocrin., Brit. Med. Bulletin, Chronobiologia, Internat. Jl Chronobiol., etc. *Recreations:* rock climbing, walking, field botany. *Address:* 4 Lancaster Road, Didsbury, Manchester M20 8TY. *T:* 061-445 2949.
[Died 3 Dec. 1977.

MILLS, John Spencer, CBE 1976; MC 1944; Chief Executive and Clerk, Essex County Council, since 1971; *b* 12 May 1917; *s* of Samuel and Edith Mary Spencer Mills; *m* 1951, Olga Esme Smith; two *d. Educ:* Rossall Sch.; Manchester Univ. (LLB). Solicitor. Asst Solicitor, NR CC, 1946-51; Chief Asst Solicitor, Lancs CC, 1951-54; 2nd Dep. Clerk, Essex CC, 1954-67, Dep. Clerk 1967-70. *Recreations:* gardening, travel. *Address:* Nutters, Hopping Jack's Lane, Danbury, Chelmsford, Essex. *T:* Danbury 2381.
[Died 24 Sept. 1976.

MILLS, Maj.-Gen. Percy Strickland, CIE 1938; IMS, retired; *s* of William James Mills, London, and Helen Anne Mills; *m* 1920, Norah Catharine Lake; one *s* one *d. Educ:* Dulwich Coll.; Guy's Hosp. Entered Indian Medical Service, 1906; served Mohmand Campaign, 1908, and European War, 1914-20 (despatches twice); Lt-Col, 1925; Col., 1935; Maj.-Gen., 1937; Hon. Physician to the King, 1938-41. Served in India in War of 1939-45; retired, 1941. *Recreations:* golf, bridge. *Address:* c/o Standard Bank of South Africa, George, South Africa.
[Died 2 Aug. 1973.

MILLS BALDWIN, Nelson; see Baldwin, N. M.

MILMAN, Lt-Col Octavius Rodney Everard, DSO 1917, Hon. MA Oxford, 1930; late Royal Artillery; sometime Fellow and Bursar of Keble College, Oxford; *b* 23 April 1882; *y s* of late Lt-Col Everard Stepney Milman, Royal Artillery; *m* 1911, Mary Freya, *d* of late Rev. Canon W. E. Haigh; two *d*. *Educ:* Uppingham; Merchant Taylors'; RMA, Woolwich. Commissioned Royal Artillery, 1900; retired, 1921; served European War, 1914-18, Egypt, Gallipoli, and France; Administrative Staff Army and General Headquarters (despatches, Brevet majority, DSO). *Address:* 84 Greenhill, Prince Arthur Road, NW3.   [*Died* 19 *June* 1971.

MILNE, Archibald George, CBE 1975; CEng, FIMechE, FIEE; Chairman: British Approvals Service for Electric Cables, since 1974; British National Committee, International Conference on Electricity Distribution, since 1975; *b* 19 Feb. 1910; British; *m* 1937, Margaret Delia Salmon; two *s*. *Educ:* Faraday House Electrical Engrg Coll., London (Hons Dipl.). Asst Works Man., Thomas Firth & John Brown Ltd, Sheffield, 1934-36; various engrg posts, Yorks Electric Power Co., 1936-45; Techn. Supt, Blackburn Corp., 1945-46; Dep. City Electrical Engr, Bath, 1946-48; South Western Electricity Board: Man., Bath District, 1948-51; Dep. Chief Engr, 1951-58; Man., Bristol District, 1958-60; Chief Engr, London Electricity Bd, 1960-65; Dep. Chm., 1966-74, Chm., 1974-76, South Eastern Electricity Bd. Pres., IEE, 1973-74. *Publications:* numerous papers and lectures. *Recreations:* golf, sculpture, painting. *Address:* 2a Shirley Drive, Hove, E Sussex BN3 6UA. *T:* Brighton 504947. *Club:* Dyke Golf.   [*Died* 16 *Dec.* 1980.

MILNE, Sir David, GCB 1958 (KCB 1947; CB 1942); retired as Permanent Under-Secretary of State for Scotland (1946-59); *b* Edinburgh, 11 March 1896; *s* of late Rev. David Munro Milne, BD; *m* 1928, Winifrede (*d* 1970), *e d* of late Surgeon-Capt. L. Kilroy, RN; one *s* one *d*. *Educ:* Daniel Stewart's Coll.; Edinburgh Univ. Military Service, 9th Royal Scots, 1915-19. Entered Scottish Office, 1921; Private Sec. to successive Secs of State for Scotland, 1930-35; Asst Sec., 1935; Deputy-Sec., Scottish Home Dept, 1939; Sec., 1942-46. National Governor for Scotland, BBC, 1960-65; Mem. Cttee Inquiry into Security Procedures and Practices, 1961. *Publication:* The Scottish Office, 1958. *Address:* 36 Greenhill Gardens, Edinburgh. *T:* 031-447 3574. *Clubs:* Athenæum, Savile; New (Edinburgh).
                    [*Died* 4 *Feb.* 1972.

MILNE-THOMSON, Louis Melville, CBE 1952; MA, DSc; FRSE; Professor of Applied Mathematics, University of Arizona, 1961-70, now Emeritus; *b* 1891; *e s* of Col A. Milne-Thomson, CMG; *m* Gertrude, *e d* of Dr Karl Frommknecht; three *d*. *Educ:* Clifton Coll. (Classical Scholar); Corpus Christi Coll., Cambridge (Mathematical Scholar). First Class, Mathematical Tripos Pt I; Wrangler with distinction Mathematical Tripos Pt II; Asst Master, Winchester Coll., 1914-21; Professor of Mathematics, RN Coll., Greenwich, 1921-56; Gresham Professor of Geometry; Visiting Professor of Applied Mathematics, Brown Univ., Rhode Island; Mathematics Research Center, Univ. of Wisconsin; Visiting Professor: Univ. of Rome, 1968; Univ. of Queensland, 1969; Univ. of Calgary, 1970; Otago, 1971. Mem. of British Assoc. Mathematical Tables Cttee; External Examiner in the University of London; Examiner for the Universities of Bristol and Nottingham, Oxford and Cambridge Joint Board, Civil Service Commission, etc; Fellow of: the Royal Astronomical Soc.; the Cambridge Philosophical Soc.; Inst. of the Aerospace Sciences; Mem. of the London Mathematical Soc., the American Mathematical Soc., and of the Circolo Matematico di Palermo. MAIAA. Hon. ScD, Bucharest, 1968. *Publications:* Standard Table of Square Roots; Standard Four Figure Mathematical Tables; Elliptische Funktionen, 1931; The Calculus of Finite Differences, 1933; Theoretical Hydrodynamics, 1938 (5th edn, 1968); Theoretical Aerodynamics, 1948 (4th edn, 1968); Jacobian Elliptic Function Tables, 1950; Hidrodinámica Teórica, 1951; Plane Elastic Systems, 1960 (2nd edn 1968); Antiplane Elastic Systems, 1962; Russian-English Mathematical Dictionary, 1962; Systèmes élastiques plans, 1968; Elliptic Functions, 1971. Papers on Mathematics, in scientific periodicals. *Recreations:* sailing, foreign travel. *Address:* Mathematics Department, University of Arizona, Tucson, Arizona 85721, USA; 2 Bullfinch Lane, Riverhead, Sevenoaks, Kent. *T:* Sevenoaks 53366. *Clubs:* Athenæum, Carlton; Hope (Providence, RI).   [*Died* 21 *Aug.* 1974.

MILNES, G. Turquet; see Turquet, Gladys.

MILNES, Nora, LLD (Hon.); BSc (London); Reader Emeritus in Social Study, University of Edinburgh (Director, Edinburgh School of Social Study, 1918-28, Department of Social Study, 1928-51); Reader in Social Study, 1946; *b* 1882; 3rd *d* of Alfred Milnes, DLit. *Educ:* North London Collegiate Sch. for Girls; and privately. Worked for London COS, 1911-13. Tutor and Lecturer, Social Science Dept, London Sch. of Economics, 1913-18; Lecturer in Economics, King's Coll. for Women, Household and Social Science Dept, 1915-18; awarded Commonwealth Grant to study Child Guidance in USA, 1929; Visiting Lecturer, Dept of Social Science and Administration, University of Chicago, 1929. Mem. apptd. by Scottish Educ. Dept, to Gen. Nursing Council for Scotland, 1920-23; re-appointed until resigned, 1942; organized for Ministry of Labour, short courses of training to qualify Personnel Managers for wartime industries ("Bevin Babies"), 1940-44; Mem. Selection Cttee for Supplementary Register, Min. of Labour; Mem. Appeals Tribunal for Scotland under Further Education and Training Scheme, Min. of Labour, 1946-52. Hon. LLD Edinburgh 1958. *Publications:* Child Welfare, from the Social Point of View, 1920; Economics of Wages and Labour, 1926; A Study of Industrial Edinburgh, 1923-34, Vol. I, 1936; contributions to various journals. *Recreation:* listening to music. *Address:* 9 Vale Court, Mallord Street, Chelsea, SW3. *T:* 01-352 5664.
                    [*Died* 13 *Nov.* 1972.

MILNES-COATES, Sir Clive; see Coates.

MILSOM, Hilda Maud, CVO 1946; CBE 1935 (OBE 1927); *d* of William Griffith Milsom, Reading. *Educ:* Polam Hall, Darlington. Clerk in His Majesty's Private Secretary's Office, 1915-45; Chief Clerk 1919-45. *Address:* Southcot, Lester Point, Combe Martin, Ilfracombe, N Devon. *T:* Combe Martin 2234.
                    [*Died* 20 *April* 1972

MILTON, Ernest; Actor; *b* 10 Jan. 1890; *m* 1926, Naomi Royde Smith (*d* 1964). His parts have included Rupert Cadell in Rope, Ferdinand De Levis in Loyalties, Dr Oetternschlag in Grand Hotel, Lord Beaconsfield in Victoria Regina, the name part in Pirandello's Henry IV (The Mock Emperor); the title part in Francis Thompson; the leading character in Night's Candles, an English version of De Musset's Lorenzaccio; Hamlet in entire version, 23 April 1934, at Sadlers Wells; Evan in wife's play, A Balcony; among his Shakespearean parts at the Old Vic have been Hamlet, Shylock, King Lear, Macbeth, Romeo, Orsino, Richard II, Oberon, and Armado; Old Vic Company, playing Sir Andrew Aguecheek and Svengali, and visiting the mining villages of County Durham as Shylock in the Merchant of Venice. Later parts have been King John, Sir Giles Overreach, Macbeth, Father Zossima in The Brothers Karamazov, Count Mancini in He Who Gets Slapped, Hugo von Gerhardt in The Compelled People, and Malvolio in the Old Vic's Italian tour of Twelfth Night, 1950; Lodovico in Othello, Old Vic, 1951; The Duke in The Comedy of Errors, Royal Court Theatre, 1952; Lorenzo Querini in The Strong are Lonely, Piccadilly Theatre 1955, also at Haymarket Theatre, 1956; Pope Paul in Malatesta Lyric, Hammersmith, 1957; The Narrator in the Finsbury Story, Sadler's Wells Theatre, 1960; King Philip II of Spain in Teresa of Avila, Dublin Festival and Vaudeville, 1961; The Lord Cardinal in Women Beware Women, Arts, 1962; Bishop Tihon in The Possessed, Mermaid, 1963; Nicodemus in This is For Now, Westminster Cathedral, 1966; Joseph Piller in The Deadly Game, Savoy, 1967. *Publications:* Christopher Marlowe, a play To Kiss the Crocodile, a novel; has written and produced his own play, Paganini, and his play Mary of Magdala, in which he played the rôle of Quintus; Two Novelettes by Quite a Gentleman. *Address:* Barclays Bank Ltd, 52 Regent Street, W1
                    [*Died* 24 *July* 1974

MILTON, Sir Frank, Kt 1970; MA; Chief Metropolitan Magistrate, 1967-75; *b* 6 Jan. 1906; *s* of late G. Lowenstein. Director of S. Japhet & Co. Ltd of London; *m* 1st, 1940, Barbara McFadyean (marr. diss. 1945); 2nd, 1954, Iris Averil, *e d* of late Sheffield Airey Neave, CMG, OBE; two *s* (adopted). *Educ:* Bembridge Sch.; St John's Coll., Oxford. Called to Bar Lincoln's Inn, 1930 (Bencher, 1967); on the south-eastern circuit; contested (L) South Islington, 1929. Served War of 1939-45, Royal Artillery, Major. Metropolitan Magistrate, 1952-67 Chm. Epping Group Hosp. Management Cttee, 1958-63 Member: Standing Cttee on Criminal Law Revision, 1959-Cttee on Immigration Appeals, 1966-67; Cttee on Distribution of Criminal Business, 1974-. Dep. Chm., Herts QS, 1965-71 *Publications:* In Some Authority, 1959; More Than a Crime 1962; The English Magistracy, 1967. *Recreations:* watching village cricket, chess. *Address:* 7 Stone Buildings, Lincoln's Inn WC2. *T:* 01-405 0304; Riverside, Hewish, Crewkerne, Som. *T* Crewkerne 3465. *Club:* Garrick.   [*Died* 8 *Jan.* 1976

MILVERTON, 1st Baron, *cr* 1947, of Lagos and of Clifton Arthur Frederick Richards, GCMG 1942 (KCMG 1935; CMG

1933); KStJ 1945; Freedom Medal (USA), with silver palm, 1946; retired 1975; *b* 21 Feb. 1885; 2nd *s* of late W. Richards; *m* 1927, Noelle Benda Whitehead; two *s* one *d*. *Educ:* Clifton Coll.; Christ Church, Oxford. Cadet, Malayan Civil Service, 1908; in various district posts in the Federated Malay States, Kelantan and Kedah, 1910-20: 2nd Asst Colonial Sec., Straits Settlements, 1920; Sec. to Select Cttee on Constitution of Legislative Council, 1921; 1st Asst Colonial Sec. SS; and Clerk of Councils, Sec. to Trade Commissions, Straits Settlements and Federated Malay States; General Sec., Straits Settlements Retrenchment Cttee, 1922; Sec. to High Commissioner for Malay States, 1923; Chm., Executive Cttee, British Malaya, British Empire Exhibition, 1924; Sec., Opium Cttee, British Malaya; Sec. Cttee to enquire into organisation of Postal Services, Straits Settlements, Federated Malay States and Unfederated Malay States, 1924; Under-Sec. to Government FMS, 1926; Acting General Adviser to Government of Johore, 1929; Governor of North Borneo, 1930-33; Governor and Commander-in-Chief, Gambia Colony, 1933-36; Governor and Commander-in-Chief of Fiji and High Commissioner for Western Pacific, 1936-38; Capt.-Gen. and Governor-in-Chief of Jamaica, 1938-43; Governor and C-in-C, Nigeria, 1943-47. A part-time Dir, Colonial Development Corp., 1948-51; Chm. of Council, London Sch. of Hygiene and Tropical Medicine, 1948-51; a Vice-Pres. of Royal Empire Society; Mem. of Board of Governors of Clifton Coll. Pres. Assoc. of British Malaya, 1948-50. Chairman: Empire Day Movement, 1948-50; British Empire Leprosy Relief Assoc., 1948-50; Royal African Soc., 1963-65; Director: West Indies Sugar Co. Ltd; Bank of West Africa, 1950-65; Kamuning (Perak) Rubber & Tin Co. Ltd, 1956-65. *Recreations:* golf, sailing. *Heir: s* Rev. Hon. Fraser Arthur Richard Richards [*b* 21 July 1930; *m* 1957, Mary Dorothy, *d* of Leslie Fly, Bickley, Kent; two *d*]. *Address:* The Lodge, Cox Green, Maidenhead, Berks. *T:* Maidenhead 20040. *Clubs:* Athenæum, United Oxford & Cambridge University, Royal Commonwealth Society (West Indian), Number 10.
[Died 27 Oct. 1978.

MINFORD, Rt. Hon. Nathaniel Owens, PC (N Ireland) 1969; Member for South Antrim, and Speaker, Northern Ireland Assembly, 1973-75; *b* 2 Dec. 1912; *s* of Hugh Minford, Templepatrick, Co. Antrim; *m* 1951, Maureen Helena, *d* of Dr T. F. Minford, Randalstown; two *s*. *Educ:* Belfast Royal Academy. MP (U) Antrim, NI Parlt, 1951-72; Minister of State, Min. of Devell, 1969-72; Leader, House of Commons, 1971-72; elected (U) to NI Assembly, 1973. *Address:* 2 Birch Hill Avenue, Antrim, Co. Antrim, N Ireland. *[Died 5 Sept. 1975.*

MINNEY, Rubeigh James; Novelist, Biographer, Playwright, Film Producer; *b* 29 Aug. 1895; *s* of late J. R. Minney; *m* 1st, Edith Fox (marr. diss.); one *s* one *d* ; 2nd, Hetty (*née* Bolsom). *Educ:* King's Coll., London. Editorial Staff, Pioneer, Allahabad; Englishman, Calcutta; represented The Times in Calcutta; special representative with Duke of Connaught to India, 1920; Daily Express, London; Asst Editor, Sunday News, London; Editor, Everybody's Weekly, 1925-35; Dir Everybody's Publications, Ltd, until 1935; Dir Chapman and Hall, Ltd, 1934-36; Editor, Sunday Referee, 1935-39; Editor, The Era; Editor The War Weekly, 1939-41; Editor The Strand Magazine, 1941-42. In films since 1942. Hon. Pres. London Sch. of Economics Film Soc., 1948-49; Mem. of Executive and General Council, Association of Cine-Technicians, 1953-56; Vice-Chm. ACT Films Ltd, 1951-68, Chm. 1968-. Parly Candidate (Lab) for Southend East, 1950, for Bexley, 1955. Went to Peking to speak at George Bernard Shaw Centenary celebration, July 1956. *Publications:* novels: Maki, 1921; The Road to Delhi, 1923; Distant Drums, 1935; Governor General, 1935; How Vainly Men..., 1940; A Woman of France, 1945; Nothing to Lose, 1946 (filmed as Time Gentlemen Please, 1952); Bring out the Drum, 1950; The Governor's Lady, 1951; (with Margot Duke) Anne of the Sealed Knot, 1972; *biographies, etc:* Clive of India, 1931; Shiva, or The Future of India; Midst Himalayan Mists; Excursions in Ink; Across India by Air; The Journalist; Night Life of Calcutta; India Marches Past, 1933; Hollywood by Starlight, 1935; Talking of Films, 1947; Chaplin, The Immortal Tramp, 1954; Viscount Southwood, 1954; Carve Her Name with Pride, 1956 (filmed 1957); Next Stop Peking, 1957; Viscount Addison, Leader of the Lords, 1958; The Private Papers of Hore-Belisha, 1960; Fanny and the Regent of Siam, 1962; No 10 Downing Street: A House in History, 1963; The Film Maker and his World, 1964; The Edwardian Age, 1964; I Shall Fear No Evil: the story of Dr Alina Brewda, 1966; The Two Pillars of Charing Cross, 1967; The Bogus Image of Bernard Shaw, 1969 (US, Recollections of George Bernard Shaw); The Tower of London, 1970; Hampton Court, 1972; Rasputin, 1972; Puffin Asquith, 1973; Lola Montez, 1976; *plays:* Clive of India (with W. P. Lipscomb), first prod. by village players of Great Hucklow in Derbyshire, 1933; filmed by Twentieth Century, Hollywood, 1934; They Had His Number (with Lady Rhys-Williams), first

produced at Hippodrome, Bolton, 1942; Gentle Caesar (with Sir Osbert Sitwell), first produced Alexandra Theatre, Birmingham, 1943; The Voice of the People, first produced Southend, 1950. *Films:* (as producer): Madonna of the Seven Moons; Osbert Sitwell's A Place of One's Own; The Wicked Lady; The Magic Bow; The Idol of Paris; Terence Rattigan's The Final Test, etc. *Address:* Hook House, Cousley Wood, Wadhurst, Sussex. *Club:* Savage. *[Died 5 Jan. 1979.*

MINNIS, Samuel Ellison, CBE 1941; *b* March 1882; *s* of late Rev. Alexander Minnis, Saltersland, Co. Londonderry; *m* 1906, Mary Rose Davidson, *d* of late James Eakin; three *d*. *Educ:* Rainey Sch., Magherafelt; Queen's Coll., Galway; Royal University of Ireland (Scholar Mod. Lang.). Entered Civil Service, Inland Revenue Dept, 1904; Comptroller of Stamps and Income Tax and Asst Registrar of Joint Stock Companies for Ireland, 1919; Asst Sec., Board of Inland Revenue, 1922. *Address:* 16 Deansway, East Finchley, N2. *T:* 01-883 8166. *[Died 2 April 1971.*

MINTER, Sir Frederick (Albert), GCVO 1959 (KCVO 1935; CVO 1931); JP; President F. G. Minter, Ltd, Berkeley Electrical Engineering Co. Ltd, *b* 11 July 1887; *s* of late F. G. Minter; *m* 1912, Greeta Constance West (*d* 1973); three *s*. *Educ:* Framlingham Coll. Capt. Royal Marines, 1916-19; Engineer, Otira Gorge Tunnel, New Zealand, 1908; restored The King's Beasts, St George's Chapel, Windsor Castle; Dir Ancient Buildings Trust, Ltd; Fellow of Institute of Builders; FIStructE. Chm. the Royal Alexandra and Albert Sch., 1952-63; Mem. of Governing Body, Framlingham Coll.; Vice-Pres. London Police Court Mission; Mem. of British Commonwealth Relations Conference in Sydney, 1938; Chm. Board of Governors, Queen Charlotte's and Chelsea Hosp. for Women, 1948-54; Mem. Gen. Council, King Edward's Hosp. Fund for London. JP Surrey, 1935. *Recreation:* fishing. *Address:* Old Ford Cottage, Warnford, Southampton. *Clubs:* Carlton, Flyfishers', Royal Automobile. *[Died 12 July 1976.*

MINTO, 5th Earl of, *cr* 1813; **Victor Gilbert Lariston Garnet Elliot (-Murray-Kynynmound);** Baron of Nova Scotia; Bt 1700; Baron of Minto, 1797; Viscount Melgund, 1813; *b* 12 Feb. 1891; *s* of 4th Earl and Mary (author of India: Minto and Morley, 1905-10, 1934; she *d* 1940), *d* of Gen. Hon. Charles Grey; *S* father, 1914; *m* 1921, Marion, OBE 1956 (*d* 1974), *d* of G. W. Cook, Montreal; two *s* two *d*. Late Lieut Lothians and Border Horse Yeomanry; Capt. Scots Guards. *Heir: s* Viscount Melgund, MBE. *Address:* Minto, Hawick, Scotland. *T:* Denholm 321. *[Died 11 Jan. 1975.*

MISSENDEN, Sir Eustace James, Kt 1944; OBE 1937; Chairman, Railway Executive, 1947-51; *b* 3 March 1886; *s* of late James Missenden; *m* 1912, Lilian Adeline Gent (*d* 1959); no *c*. *Educ:* Folkestone, Kent. Entered Service SE and C Rly, 1899; SR Docks and Marine Manager, 1933; Traffic Manager, 1936; Gen. Manager, 1939; Col-Comdt, Engineer and Railway Staff Corps, RE (TA), 1949-51. KStJ; Officer of Legion of Honour (France); Chevalier, Order of Leopold (Belgium); American Medal of Freedom with Gold Palm. *Recreations:* golf, gardening. *[Died 30 Jan. 1973.*

MITCHELL, Andrew Park, CMG 1948; *b* 23 Aug. 1894; *s* of Andrew John Mitchell, Kew, Surrey; *m* 1922, Evangeline (*d* 1957), *d* of William Morris, Edinburgh; (one *s* killed in action, 1944), one *d*. *Educ:* St Paul's Sch.; London Univ. Survey of Egypt, 1919-27; Dir of Lands and Surveys, Transjordan, 1927-40; Dir of Surveys, Palestine, 1940-48; Dir of Surveys, Nigeria, 1948-51, Inspector-Gen., 1951-53. Served European War, 1914-19, in India, Egypt and France: Pilot RFC. Mem. of Cttee of enquiry into application of Land Transfer Regulations, 1945; Dir of Surveys, Land Officer and Comr of Mines, Uganda, 1954-57; Mem. Land Admin. Commn, Malaya, 1957; Survey Enquiry, Cyprus, 1958; Land Registration and Survey Enquiry, Seychelles, 1959. 2nd Class Order of Istiqlal, Transjordan. Represented England in athletics, 1914. *Recreations:* golf, bridge. *Address:* 36 Pensford Avenue, Kew Gardens, Richmond, Surrey. *[Died 6 June 1975.*

MITCHELL, Bertram, CB 1963; retired as Chief Inspector, Board of Customs and Excise (1960-63); *b* 19 Sept. 1898; *s* of James and Mary A. Mitchell; *m* 1931, Dora M. Alway. *Educ:* Newton Abbot Grammar Sch. Collector, Customs and Excise, Manchester, 1956-58; Dep. Chief Inspector, Board of Customs and Excise, 1958-59. *Address:* 14 Mildenhall, West Cliff Road, Bournemouth, Dorset. *T:* Bournemouth 760400. *[Died 28 June 1978.*

MITCHELL, Craig, CB 1949; *b* Loanhead, Midlothian, 5 Oct. 1896; *m* 1921, Jean Manson McDonald; one *s* one *d* (and one *s*

decd). *Educ:* George Heriot's Sch.; University of Edinburgh. Served European War, Argyll and Sutherland Highlanders, 1915-19. Entered Civil Service, 1912; Private Sec. to Parly Under-Sec. of State for Scotland, 1934; Asst Sec., Dept of Health for Scotland, 1939; Principal Officer, Scotland Civil Defence Region, 1941-43; Principal Asst Sec., Dept of Health for Scotland, 1943-44; Dep. Sec. Dept of Health for Scotland, 1944-59; Member: Gen. Dental Council, 1959-69; Bd of Management, Royal Edinburgh Hosp., 1962-66; Chairman: Scottish Water Adv. Cttee, 1962-69; Building Standards Adv. Cttee, 1959-70. *Address:* 11 Pentland Avenue, Colinton, Edinburgh 13. *T:* 031-441 2630. *Club:* Royal Commonwealth Society.
[Died 8 Dec. 1975.

MITCHELL, Air Vice-Marshal Frederick George Stewart, CB 1956; CBE 1953 (OBE 1942); *b* Simonstown, S Africa, 14 Dec. 1901; *s* of Capt. F. Mitchell; *m* 1932, Beryl Barley; one *s* one *d*. *Educ:* Brighton Technical Coll.; RAF Coll., Cranwell. Pilot Officer, 1921; squadron duties at home and India, 1922-25; Armament and Gunnery Sch., Eastchurch, 1926-29; Armament officer duties at home and in Egypt, 1929-31 and 1935-39; Directorate of Trng, Air Min., 1931-33; No 4 (AC) Squadron, Farnborough, 1933-35; Air Force Experimental Officer, Chem. Defence Experimental Station, Porton, 1939-42; Directorate of Armament Research and Develt, Min. of Supply, 1942-46; Br. Jt Services Mission (Tech. Services), Washington, 1946-48; Vice-Pres. (Air) Ordnance Bd, 1948-50; Air Cdre, 1949; Director of: Armament, 1950, Tech. Requirements, 1951, Armament Engineering, 1952, all at Air Min.; AOC No 43 Group, 1952-55; Air Officer i/c Administration, Maintenance Command, 1955-58. Air Vice-Marshal, 1956; retired 1958. Officer, Legion of Merit (US), 1947. *Address:* 10 Amberley Close, Highcliffe, Christchurch, Hants BH23 5AR. *[Died 13 Feb. 1974.*

MITCHELL, Rt. Rev. Frederick Julian, DD; *b* 30 July 1901; *s* of late Rev. R. J. Mitchell, MA, The Rectory, Trillick, Co. Tyrone; *m* Kathleen Louise, *d* of Rev. R. Watson, BD, Castle Archdale, Co. Fermanagh. *Educ:* Campbell Coll.; Trinity Coll., Dublin. Deacon, 1924, St Mary's, Belfast; Priest, 1925; Incumbent of S Polycarp, Finaghy, Belfast, 1928; Dean of Residences, QUB, 1934; Incumbent of Kilconriola and Ballyclug, 1936; Rural Dean of Ballymena, 1945; Canon and Prebendary of Kilroot in Chapter of S Saviour of Connor, and Bishop of Kilmore, Elphin and Ardagh, 1950-55; Bishop of Down and Dromore, 1955-69. *Publications:* A Pageant of the Book of Common Prayer (for Quater Centenary of 1549 Prayer Book); Pageant of the Holy Bible (in connection with Festival of Britain); Hail Caesar!; It Happened in Nazareth. *Address:* Glen Lodge, Belmont Road, Belfast 4, Northern Ireland. *[Died 3 June 1979.*

MITCHELL, George Hoole, CBE 1967; FRS 1953; FRSE 1955; formerly Assistant Director (Scotland), Geological Survey of Great Britain; *b* 31 Dec. 1902; *s* of George Richard and Emma Mitchell; *m* 1930, Vera Margaret Richardson; two *s*. *Educ:* Liverpool Coll.; Liverpool Univ. (DSc); Imperial Coll. of Science and Technology. Beit Scientific Research Fellow, 1926. Wollaston Fund, 1936, Bigsby Medal, 1947, Murchison Medal, 1964, Geological Soc. of London; Liverpool Geological Soc. Medal, 1951; Pres., Yorks Geological Soc., 1955-56, Sorby Medal; Pres., Section C, British Assoc., 1957; Pres., Edinburgh Geological Soc., 1961-63 (Clough Medal, 1969-70). Geological Survey of Great Britain, 1929-67. Fellow, Imperial Coll., 1967. *Address:* 115 Octavia Terrace, Greenock, Renfrewshire PA16 7PZ. *T:* Greenock 31278. *[Died 11 March 1976.*

MITCHELL, Sir George (Irvine), Kt 1976; CB 1970; QC (Scot.) 1972; Legal Secretary to Lord Advocate and First Parliamentary Draftsman for Scotland, 1969-76; an Assistant Legal Secretary and Parliamentary Draftsman, Lord Advocate's Department, since 1976; *b* 18 Feb. 1911; *e s* of late John Irvine Mitchell and Mrs L. J. Mitchell; *m* 1945, Elizabeth, *d* of late Charles and Anna Norman Leigh Pemberton; one *s* one *d*. *Educ:* George Watson's Coll.; Edinburgh Univ. MA 1932; LLB 1935; Vans Dunlop Scholarship in Law, 1937. Admitted to Faculty of Advocates, 1937; called to English Bar, Inner Temple, 1945. Served War of 1939-45, Border Regt, War Office. Draftsman in Lord Advocate's Dept, 1946. *Address:* 14 Rodway Road, Roehampton, SW15. *T:* 01-788 6649. *[Died 10 July 1978.*

MITCHELL, Prof. John David Bawden, CBE 1972; PhD; LLB (London); LLD (Edinburgh); Solicitor; Salvesen Professor of European Institutions, University of Edinburgh, since 1968; *b* 28 May 1917; *s* of A. Mitchell, OBE; *m* 1945, Jeanne Rosamund, *d* of late Maj-Gen. W. H. S. Nickerson, VC, CB, CMG; two *d*. *Educ:* Colfe's Grammar Sch.; London Sch. of Economics and Political Science, Univ. of London (Whittuck Schol.). Served War of 1939-45: commissioned North Staffs Regt, 1939; BEF 1940 (despatches); Staff Officer, 1943; released 1946. Admitted

Solicitor, 1947; Lectr in Law, University Coll. of Wales, 1947-48; Lectr, Law Soc.'s Sch., 1948-49; Lectr 1949, Reader in English Law in the Univ. of London, 1952, at LSE; Prof. of Constitutional Law, Univ. of Edinburgh, 1954-68. Member: Vedel Cttee (EEC), 1971-72; Hansard Soc. Commn on Electoral Reform, 1975-76; Political Scis and Internat. Relns Cttee, SSRC, 1975-79. Hon. Pres., Univs Assoc. for Contemp. European Studies. Docteur de l'Université (*hc*), Lille, 1965; Hon. LLD Amsterdam, 1975. *Publications:* Contracts of Public Authorities, 1954; Constitutional Law, 1964 (2nd edn 1968). Articles in various legal periodicals. *Recreations:* talking and walking. *Address:* 28 Murrayfield Avenue, Edinburgh EH12 6AX. *T:* 031-337 6189. *Club:* Edinburgh University Staff (Edinburgh). *[Died 19 Dec. 1980.*

MITCHELL, Sir Mark (Ledingham), Kt 1957; BSc (Hons, Adelaide), MSc Cantab; FRACI; FACE; First Chancellor, Flinders University of South Australia, 1966-71; *b* Adelaide, South Australia, 13 June 1902; *s* of late Sir William Mitchell, KCMG. *Educ:* Queen's Sch., Adelaide, SA; University of Adelaide; Cambridge Univ. Lecturer in Biochemistry, University of Adelaide, 1927-38; Prof., 1938-63; Dep. Vice-Chancellor 1950-65. Editor-in-Chief, Australian Journal of Experimental Biology, 1935-63. Hon. DSc Flinders. *Address:* 11 Fitzroy Terrace, Fitzroy, SA 5082, Australia. *Clubs:* Adelaide (Adelaide); Royal South Australian Yacht Squadron.
[Died 8 July 1977.

MITCHELL, His Honour Norman Frederick, CMG 1960; Judge of County Courts (Civil and Criminal), State of Victoria, Australia, 1946-70; Chairman, County Court Judges, State of Victoria, 1965-70; *b* 19 Feb. 1900; *s* of Frederick John and Catherine Mabel Mitchell; *m* 1927, Jennie Moffitt Graham; one *d* (one *s* decd). *Educ:* University High Sch.; Melbourne Univ. On Staff of Melbourne C of E Grammar Sch., 1918-25; BA 1921; Diploma of Education, 1922; LLB, 1925; admitted to Victorian Bar, 1926. Served War of 1939-45, Area and Group Law Officer, RAAF, 1941-45. Dep. Chm., Workers Compensation Board, 1946; Mem. of Trotting Control Board, 1946-56, Chm., 1953-56; Dep. Pres., Court of Industrial Appeal, 1963-70. Trustee, 1949-, Vice-Pres., 1953-55, Pres., 1956-64, Royal Agricultural Society of Victoria. *Recreations:* cricket, football. *Address:* 183 Kooyong Road, Toorak, Vic. 3142, Australia. *T:* 20 8012.
[Died March 1972.

MITCHELL, Yvonne; actress and novelist; Member, National Theatre Board, since 1976; *d* of Bertie Joseph and Madge Mitchell; *m* 1952, Derek Monsey (*d* 1979); one *d*. *Educ:* St Paul's. First stage appearance as the child Estella in Great Expectations, 1940; plays include: Ophelia in Hamlet, Old Vic and Elsinore, 1950; Katherine in the Taming of the Shrew and Cordelia in King Lear, Stratford upon Avon, 1952; The Wall, Billy Rose Theatre, New York, 1960; Anna Petrovna in Ivanov, Phœnix, 1965; Children of the Wolf, Apollo, 1971; Pirandello's Henry IV, Her Majesty's, 1974; Bloomsbury, Phœnix, 1974; films include: Queen of Spades, 1949; The Divided Heart (Brit. Film Acad. Award), 1954; Woman in a Dressing-Gown (Berlin Fest. Award and Variety Club of Gt Britain Award), 1957; Sapphire, 1958; Trials of Oscar Wilde, 1959; Genghis Khan, 1965; Velvet House, 1968; many appearances on TV, incl. Chéri (BBC TV series), 1973. *Publications:* plays: The Same Sky (Produced Duke of York's Theatre, 1951) (Arts Council Award); Actress, 1957; (trans. from the French) Measure of Cruelty, 1964; *novels:* The Bedsitter, 1959; Frame for Julian, 1960; A Year in Time, 1964; The Family, 1967; Martha on Sunday, 1970; God is Inexperienced, 1974; But Answer Came There None, 1977; *for children:* Cathy Away, 1964; Cathy at Home, 1965; But Wednesday Cried, 1974; *biography:* Colette: a Taste for Life, 1975. *Address:* c/o Adza Vincent, 11a Ivor Place, NW1. *[Died 24 March 1979*

MITCHELL-HEGGS, Gordon Barrett, OBE 1944; ERD 1972 TD; MD, BS, FRCP, MRCS; Consultant Physician (Physician-in-Charge Skin Department, and Dean of the Medical School 1960-67), St Mary's Hospital, W2; Hon. Physician to St John's Skin Hospital and to St Mary's Hospital Medical School; formerly Hon. Dermatologist to the Royal Masonic Hospital, St Luke's Hostel for Clergy, Hospital of St John and St Elizabeth etc.; formerly Hon. Consultant in Dermatology to the Army; *b* 10 June 1904; *e s* of late Francis Raymond Mitchell Heggs MRCS, LSA; took name of Mitchell-Heggs by deed poll, 1939 *m* 1937, Nora, *d* of late Rev. H. C. Finch, Abbotts Langley Herts; one *s*. *Educ:* Nottingham High Sch.; St Mary's Hosp Medical Sch. (Public Schs and Lord Kitchener Memoria Scholar); Strasbourg, Vienna, Budapest. Hon. Medallist o University of Louvain. Formerly CO, and subsequently Hon Col, 17th (London) Gen. Hosp., RAMC, TA, until 1960. Serve War of 1939-45, BEF France, Madagascar, Middle East Forces

Sicily, Normandy and Belgium campaigns (despatches); Officer i/c Med. Div., Gen. Hosp. Past-President: Hunterian Soc. of London; St John's Hosp. Dermatological Soc.; Section of Dermatology, Royal Society of Medicine; Council Mem., Royal College of Physicians; Mem., and Past Pres., British Assoc. of Dermatology; Hon. Mem. Dermatological Socs of Austria, Iran, Venezuela and Yugoslavia; Corresp. Mem. Dermatological Socs of Belgium, Denmark, France, Holland, Sweden and USA. Hon. Mem. (Rep. for GB, 1952-72), Internat. Cttee of Dermatology. Master, Apothecaries' Soc., 1974. Hon. FRIPHH. *Publications:* Modern Practice in Dermatology, 1950. Chapters in: Penicillin (Fleming, 1946 and 1950), and ACTH and Cortisone (Copeman, 1953). Medical papers and articles on Diseases of the Skin. *Recreations:* gardening, fishing. *Address:* 31 Weymouth Street, W1. *Clubs:* Athenæum, Garrick. [*Died 15 Dec. 1975.*

MITCHESON, Prof. J(ames) Cecil, CBE 1961; BSc; Hon. ARSM; Fellow, Imperial College of Science and Technology; Professor Emeritus of Mining, London University, since 1963; *b* 18 May 1898; *s* of late G. A. Mitcheson; *m* 1928, Jean Hyndman, *d* of late D. S. Macpherson; one *s* one *d*. *Educ:* Bootham Sch.; RMA Woolwich; University of Birmingham. Lecturer in Coal Mining, Birmingham Univ., 1923-24; Agent and later Man. Dir, Morris & Shaw, Ltd, 1934-46; Dir of Production for Min. of Fuel and Power, for Warwicks Coalfield, 1944-45; Divl Mining Development Engineer, W Midlands Div., NCB, 1947; Cons. Mining Engineer, 1947-52; Prof. of Mining, Imperial Coll., Royal School of Mines, London Univ., 1953-63. Mem., Mining Qualifications Board, 1950-69; Chm., Safety in Mines Research (Advisory) Bd, 1960-69. Hon. FInstME (Pres. 1953-54); FIMM. Chm., Geological Survey Board, 1961-65 (Mem. 1959-); Mem., Natural Environment Research Council, 1965-69. Lt RFA, with 33rd Div., France and Flanders, 1918. *Publications:* papers in Proceedings Instn of Mining Engineers and other technical jls. *Address:* The Croft, Knotty Green, Beaconsfield, Bucks. [*Died 22 Sept. 1979.*

MITFORD, Nancy, (Hon. Mrs Peter Rodd), CBE 1972; *b* 1904; *d* of 2nd Baron Redesdale; *m* 1933, Hon. Peter Rodd (marr. diss. 1958; he *d* 1968). *Educ:* home. Légion d'Honneur, 1972. *Publications:* Pursuit of Love, 1945; Love in a Cold Climate, 1949; The Blessing, 1951; Madame de Pompadour, 1953, new edn 1968; Voltaire in Love, 1957; Don't Tell Alfred, 1960; The Water Beetle, 1962; The Sun King, 1966; Frederick the Great, 1970; edited: The Ladies of Alderley, 1967; The Stanleys of Alderley, 1968; (ed) Noblesse Oblige, 1973. *Address:* 4 rue d'Artois, 78000 Versailles, France. [*Died 30 June 1973.*

MITFORD, Prof. Terence Bruce, DLitt; FBA 1974; FSA; Professor and Research Fellow, University of St Andrews, 1974-77 (Reader in Humanity and Classical Archaeology, 1959-74); *b* Yokohama, Japan, 11 May 1905; *e s* of late C. E. Bruce Mitford, writer, Madras, and late Beatrice (née Allison), Princeton, BC; *m* 1936, Margaret, *d* of late Prof. P. T. Herring; four *s* one *d*. *Educ:* Dulwich Coll.; Jesus Coll., Oxford (Sen. Classical Scholar). DLitt Oxon, 1973. FSA 1940. Served War: Officers Emergency Reserve, 1938; commnd Dorset Regt, 1939; seconded to SOE and SAS, ME; Crete, 1940-41 and 1944-45; Syria, SE Persia, Sicily and Aegean, 1943. Univ. of St Andrews: Asst in Humanity, 1928; Warden of St Salvator's Coll., 1932-36; Lectr in Humanity and Class. Archaeol., 1936-59. Leverhulme Vis. Prof., Vienna, 1976. Corres. Fellow, Austrian Acad. Corres. Member: German Archaeol. Inst.; Austrian Archaeol Inst. Member: Inst. of Advanced Study, Princeton, NJ, 1961 and 1967; British Ornithol. Union. *Publications:* Studies in the Signaries of SW Cyprus, 1961; (with G. E. Bean) Journeys in Rough Cilicia, 1970; The Inscriptions of Kourion, 1971; (with I. Nicolaou) The Inscriptions of (the Cypriot) Salamis, 1974; The Nymphaeum of Kafizin, 1979; some sixty papers in learned periodicals. *Recreations:* travel at grass-root level in SE Europe, Turkey, Cyprus; ornithology. *Address:* Ardlogie, by Cupar, Fife. *T:* Balmullo 262. *Club:* Athenæum. [*Died 8 Nov. 1978.*

MITFORD-BARBERTON, I. G.; see Barberton.

MITHA, Hon. Sardar Sir Suleman Cassum, Kt 1933; CIE 1915; MCS; JP; banker and general merchant; five *s* three *d*. *Address:* Lands End Road, Malabar Hill, Bombay, 6. *TA:* Minerva. *T:* 25904 and 40756. *Club:* Orient (Bombay).

MITRANY, David, PhD, DSc (London); Professor in School of Economics and Politics, Institute for Advanced Study, Princeton, New Jersey, since 1933; also Adviser on International Affairs to Board of Unilever & Lever Bros Ltd, since 1943; *b* Bucharest, Rumania, 1 Jan. 1888; *s* of Moscu and Jeannette Mitrany, Bucharest; *m* 1923, Ena Victoria, *d* of Alfred J. Limebeer, London; no *c*. *Educ:* London Sch. of Economics and Political Science. Editorial Staff of Manchester Guardian, 1919-

22; Asst European Editor of Economic and Social History of the World War (Carnegie Endowment for International Peace), 1922-29; Visiting Professor at Harvard Univ. 1931-33; Dodge Lecturer Yale Univ. 1932; Nielsen Research Professor, Smith Coll., 1951; Mem. British Co-ordinating Cttee for Internat. Studies, 1927-30. *Publications:* The Problem of International Sanctions, 1925; Marx v the Peasant, 1927; The Land and the Peasant in Rumania, 1928; The Progress of International Government (Dodge Lectures), 1934; The Effect of the War in South-Eastern Europe, 1937; American Policy and Opinion (Survey of International Affairs), 1940; A Working Peace System, 1943; American Interpretations, 1946; Marx against the Peasant, 1951 (six foreign edns); A Working Peace System (Essays), 1966. Articles in Encyclopædia Britannica, Encyclopædia of the Social Sciences (USA), The Sociological Review, Political Quarterly, Round Table, International Affairs, Agenda, etc. *Recreations:* walking, gardening. *Address:* Lower Farm, Kingston Blount, Oxford. *T:* 236. [*Died 25 July 1975.*

MOBERLY, Rt. Rev. Robert Hamilton; *b* 1884; *s* of Canon R. C. Moberly, DD, and Alice Sidney Moberly; *m* 1917, Rosamund Vere, *d* of late Rev. B. B. Smyth and late Grace Elizabeth Augusta Massy Smyth; one *s* (and one *s* killed in War, 1942). *Educ:* Winchester; Oxford, 1st class in Mods, Greats and Theology; Cuddesdon. Asst curate, St Margaret's-at-Cliffe, near Dover, 1909-14; Benoni, Transvaal, 1914-25; CF 1917-19; Principal, Bishops' Coll., Cheshunt, 1925-36; Bishop Suffragan of Stepney and Rector of St Margarets, Lothbury, 1936-52; Dean of Salisbury, 1952-60. White Lecturer, 1930. *Publication:* The Great Friendship, 1934. *Address:* Wadhurst, Pound Road, West Wittering, Sussex. [*Died 16 Sept. 1978.*

MOBERLY, Sir Walter (Hamilton), GBE 1949; KCB 1944; Kt 1934; DSO 1917; MA; Hon. LLD (Belfast); Hon. DLitt (Manchester, Nottingham and Keele); Hon. Fellow of Lincoln College, Oxford, 1930; Hon. Fellow of Merton College, 1937; Hon. Fellow of New College, 1942; Fellow of Winchester College, 1942-66; *b* 20 Oct. 1881; *s* of late R. C. Moberly, DD, Canon of Christ Church, Oxford, and Alice Sidney, *d* of Walter Kerr Hamilton, Bishop of Salisbury; *m* 1921, Gwendolen, *d* of late W. M. Gardner; four *s*. *Educ:* Winchester; New Coll., Oxford (Scholar). First Class Lit. Hum., 1903; Fellow of Merton Coll., 1904-7; Lecturer in Political Science, Aberdeen, 1905-6; Fellow of Lincoln Coll., 1906-21; Prof. of Philosophy, Birmingham Univ., 1921-24; Principal of University Coll. of the South-West of England, Exeter, 1925-26; Vice-Chancellor of University of Manchester, 1926-34; Chm. of University Grants Cttee, 1935-49; Principal of St Catherine's, Cumberland Lodge, Windsor, 1949-55. Served European War, Oxford and Bucks Light Infantry, France and Belgium (DSO, despatches, twice). *Publications:* The Crisis in the University, 1949; two essays in Foundations, 1912; Responsibility (Riddell Lecture), 1956; The Ethics of Punishment, 1968. *Address:* 7 Fyfield Road, Oxford. [*Died 31 Jan. 1974.*

MOCKETT, Sir Vere, Kt 1943; MBE 1918; *b* 25 July 1885; *y s* of Brooke Mockett and Blanche Marion Walker; *m* 1918, Ethel Nora Gaddum Tomkinson (*d* 1969); one *s* two *d*. *Educ:* Marlborough; Worcester Coll., Oxford. BA 1907; MA 1910; called to Bar, Inner Temple, 1908; North Eastern Circuit, 1908-14; practised at Madras Bar, 1921-32; officiated as Judge, High Court, Madras, 1932; Lecturer at Kings Coll., London, Faculty of Law, 1933-34; Judge, High Court of Judicature at Madras, 1934-45; officiated twice as Chief Justice; served European War, 1914-19, 4th and 5th Buffs; Aden Field Force and Mesopotamia, 1915-19; Staff Capt., 1917-19 (MBE, despatches). *Recreations:* shooting, fishing, reading. *Address:* c/o Lloyds Bank Ltd, 222 Strand, WC2. *Club:* United Oxford & Cambridge University. [*Died 13 Jan. 1977.*

MOCKLER-FERRYMAN, Col (Hon. Brig.) Eric Edward, CB 1945; CBE 1941; MC; FZS; Hon. MA London; *b* 27 June 1896; *s* of late Col A. F. Mockler-Ferryman, 43rd LI; unmarried. *Educ:* Wellington; RMA, Woolwich. Commissioned RA, 1915; France and Flanders, 1915-19 (MC); seconded to AMF, 1937-39; served, 1939-45; Brig., 1940; Control Commission, Hungary, 1945-46; retired pay, 1947; Comdr Legion of Merit (US), Chevalier, Légion d'honneur and Fr. Croix de Guerre; Comdr Order of Leopold II and Belgian Croix de Guerre; Comdr Order of Orange Nassau. *Address:* c/o Lloyds Bank, 6 Pall Mall, SW1. *Club:* Army and Navy. [*Died 19 Nov. 1978.*

MOE, Henry Allen; Foundation Officer; First Chairman of National Endowment for the Humanities, 1965-66; *b* Minnesota, 2 July 1894; *s* of Christian and Sophia Martha Moe; *m* 1925, Edith Louise (née Monroe, BA); one *s*. *Educ:* Hamline Univ., Minnesota (BS); Brasenose Coll., Oxford (BA jurisprudence, 1st cl. Hons, BCL). Called to Bar, Inner Temple, London, 1924.

Hulme Lectr in Law for Brasenose and Oriel Colls, Univ. of Oxford, 1923-24; Lectr in Law, Columbia Univ. (NYC), Sch. of Law, 1927-29; John Simon Guggenheim Memorial Foundation: Sec., 1925-60; Sec. Gen., 1937-61; Pres. 1961-63; Pres. Emeritus, 1970; Pres. Harry Frank Guggenheim Foundation, 1970; retired as Pres. Amer. Phil. Soc., 1970; Vice-Chm., Museum of Modern Art (NYC); also is a Trustee of several US instns; was Trustee of Rockefeller Foundn, 1945-60. Hon. Fellow, Brasenose Coll., Oxford, 1955-. Holds numerous hon. degrees, both in USA and abroad, including DCL, Oxford, 1960. Award of Nat. Inst. of Arts and Letters (NYC), 1955; Public Service Medal, Nat. Academy of Sciences (Washington, DC), 1958; Special Citation, NY State Council on the Arts, 1971. *Publications:* articles in Proc. Amer. Phil. Soc., Science, New York History, Physics Today. *Recreations:* gardening, carpentry, stone masonry. *Address:* (office) 30 Wall Street, New York, NY 10005, USA. *T:* 269-1833; (homes) Sherman, Conn 06784; Riverdale-on-Hudson, New York, NY 10471. *Club:* Century (Hon. Mem.) (New York).   *[Died 2 Oct. 1975.*

MOFFAT, John; *b* Jarrow-on-Tyne, 19 Nov. 1891; *o s* of late James Moffat, Morpeth and Jarrow, and late Frances Richley Moffat, Peebles; *m* 1927, Jean Wilson, *e d* of late Charlotte and late John Main, Edinburgh. Served European War, 1914-18 and War of 1939-45; retd, 1947, with rank of Major; served on editorial staffs of Scotsman, Glasgow Herald, Daily Express, Manchester Guardian and Manchester Evening News, Yorkshire Post, Manchester Evening Chronicle. Editor-in-Chief, Yorkshire Herald Newspaper Co., 1930-36; GS Publications Officer, Northern Command, 1940-45. Press Chief, British Sector, Berlin, July 1945-April 1946; started Der Berliner, first British newspaper in Berlin in July 1945 and edited it till its cessation in April 1946; Editor, British Zone Review, May 1946-June 1949. Press Officer, War Office, Aug. 1951-Nov. 1958, retired. *Address:* The Old Vicarage, Keyingham, East Yorkshire. *T:* Keyingham 2343.
                                                  [Died 30 Sept. 1973.

MOFFAT, Rennie John, CBE 1956 (MBE 1918); Consultant on development plans, Cawood, Wharton and Co., 1958-70, retired; *b* 23 May 1891; *o s* of late John and Susan Moffat; *m* 1918, Lottie May (*d* 1974), 4th *d* of late Robert and Edith Mizen; one *s*. *Educ:* Central Foundation Sch., London; King's Coll., London. Entered Civil Service, (Patent Office), 1906; Ministry of Munitions, 1915-16; served European War, Inns of Court OTC, 1916-18. Sec., Road Transport Board, 1918; Coal Mines Dept (later Mines Dept), Bd of Trade, 1919-39 (latterly head of Inland Trade Branch); resigned from Civil Service, 1939. General Manager, Midland Coal Mines Schemes, 1939-46; Dep. Dir-Gen. of Marketing, NCB, 1946-55; Dir-Gen. of Marketing, 1955-58. *Address:* 6 Henley Court, Chase Side, Southgate, N14. *T:* 01-882 1233.   *[Died 23 Feb. 1978.*

MOFFETT, John Perry, CMG 1959; *b* 8 March 1909; *s* of John Moffett and Beatrix Heron; *m* 1933, Phyllis M. Brittain, *d* of John Wesley Brittain; one *s* two *d*. *Educ:* Cork Gram. Sch.; Trinity Coll., Dublin (BA, LLB). Provincial Administration, Colonial Service, Tanganyika, 1932-48; Local Courts Adviser, 1948; Commissioner for Social Development, 1953-58. *Publications:* (ed): Tanganyika: A Review of its Resources and their Development, 1956; Handbook of Tanganyika, 1958; Tanganyika Notes and Records, 1950-56. *Recreations:* golf, bird-watching. *Address:* Hill House, Roundhill Drive, Old Woking Road, Woking, Surrey. *T:* Woking 62812. *Club:* Worplesdon Golf.   *[Died 8 July 1972.*

MOHAMED, Hon. Sir Abdool Razack, Kt 1970; Member, Legislative Council, Mauritius, since 1953; Minister of Housing, Lands and Town and Country Planning, since 1959; *b* Calcutta, India, 1906; *m* ; nine *c*. *Educ:* India. Arrived in Mauritius, 1925; Municipal Councillor, 1943-56; Mayor of Port Louis, 1949, 1953 and 1956; Deleg. to London Constitutional Talks, 1955, 1957, 1961 and 1965. *Address:* Avenue Belle Rose, Quatre Bornes, Mauritius.   *[Died 8 May 1978.*

MOIR, Rt. Rev. Francis Oag H.; *see* Hulme-Moir.

MOIR, John Chassar, CBE 1961; MA, DM, FRCSE, FRCOG; Visiting Professor, Royal Postgraduate Medical School; Nuffield Professor of Obstetrics and Gynæcology, University of Oxford, 1937-67, now Emeritus; Fellow, Oriel College, 1937-67, Hon. Fellow, 1974; *b* 1900; *s* of late John and I. Moir (née Pirie), Montrose; *m* 1933, Grace Hilda Bailey; two *s* two *d*. *Educ:* Montrose Academy; Edinburgh University. MB, ChB (Edinburgh), 1922; MD, Gold Medal (Edinburgh), 1930; Asst Surgeon, East Surrey Hospital; 1st Asst Obstetric Unit, University Coll. Hospital, London; Reader in Obstetrics and Gynæcology, University of London (British Postgraduate

Medical Sch.); Rockefeller Travelling Fellowship, 1932; Visiting Professor, Queen's Univ., Ontario, 1950; Examiner in Obstetric and Gynæcology, University of Oxford, etc; late Pres., section Obstetrics and Gynæcology, Royal Society Medicine; Hon. Fellow, 1974; Hon. Fellow, American Association of Obstetricians and Gynecologists; Hon. Fellow, Amer Gynecological Soc.; Corresponding Fellow, New York Acad. of Medicine; Hon. LLD Queen's Univ., Ont; Hon. DSc Edinburgh, 1970; Manchester, 1972; Master of Midwifery, hc Soc. Apothecaries, London. *Publications:* 5th edn, Munro Kerr's Operative Obstetrics, 1949, 8th edn, 1967; The Vesicovaginal Fistula, 1961, 2nd edn, 1967; contributions to scientific journals, and to textbooks on obstetrics and gynæcology. *Address:* Farnmore, Woodstock Road, Charlbury, Oxford.   *[Died 24 Nov. 1977*

MOIR, Percival John; retired as Professor of Surgery and Dean of the Faculty of Medicine, University of Leeds, 1952-60 Emeritus Professor since 1960; *b* July 1893; 2nd *s* of late Frederick R. Moir; *m* 1926, Joan Evelyn Lander Whitehead; on *s*. *Educ:* Kelvinside, Glasgow; Univ. Glasgow; London Hospital MB, ChB Glasgow Univ., 1914; FRCS, 1923; Capt. RAMC 1914-18, served in Gallipoli, Egypt, Palestine, and France (despatches, MC). Formerly: Senior Hon. Surgeon, General Infirmary at Leeds; Surgeon Leeds Regional Hospital Board and United Leeds Hospitals Board; Mem. Board of Governors Leeds United Hospitals; Mem., Leeds Regional Hospital Board Mem., General Medical Council. Hon. Consulting Surgeon Dewsbury, Pontefract, Mirfield, and Ilkley Hospitals; Cons Surg. WRCC; Prof. of Surgery, University of Leeds, 1940-46 Mem. Court of Examiners, Royal College of Surgeons of England, 1941-47. Fellow, Association of Surgeons of Great Britain and Ireland. *Publications:* contributed articles to Medical Journals. *Address:* 10 Windermere Avenue, SW19. *T* 01-540 5505.   *[Died 8 Dec. 1980*

MOLESWORTH, Hender Delves; *b* Raptsgate Park Cirencester, 10 Feb. 1907; *s* of late Lionel Charles Molesworth and Saba Maud, *d* of Sir Henry Delves Broughton, 9th Bt; *m* 1934, Evelyn Carnegy, *d* of late M. W. and Edith Galloway Shelley Hall, Ongar. *Educ:* Stubbington; Oundle; Universit Coll., Oxford. Joined staff of Victoria and Albert Museum, 1931 Curator of Institute of Jamaica, 1936-38; Ministry of Information, 1940; Press Attaché British Legation, Addis Ababa, 1942-45. Victoria and Albert Museum: Keeper of Sculpture, 1946; Keeper of Woodwork, 1954; retd 1966 *Publications:* European Sculpture, 1965; The Princes, 1969 (with J. Kenworthy-Browne) Three Centuries of Furniture Design, 1972; articles on art, etc. *Recreations:* travel, painting *Address:* The Orangery, Langley Park, Wexham, Bucks. *T* Slough 28815.   *[Died 20 April 1978*

MOLINE, Most Rev. Robert William Haines, MC; MA; DD (Lambeth), 1948; *b* Sudbury, Suffolk, 20 Oct. 1889; *s* of late Canon R. P. Moline and Alice Price; *m* 1929, Mirabel Mathilde (*d* 1978), *d* of Thomas Rookley Parker, Townsville. *Educ:* King's Sch., Canterbury; Emmanuel Coll., Cambridge (Scholar). BA 1912, MA 1919. Asst Master, Cranleigh Sch Surrey, 1912-14; served in Rifle Brigade and Machine Gun Corps, 1914-19; granted rank of Major on demobilisation, 1919 Bishop's Coll., Cheshunt, 1919. Deacon, 1920; Priest, 1921; Asst Curate, St Matthew's, Bethnal Green, 1920-22; joined Brotherhood of St Barnabas, North Qld, 1922; Warden of Brotherhood, 1925-27; Archdeacon of North Qld, 1926-29 Rector of North Cadbury, Som, 1929-34; Rector of Popla 1934-40; Vicar of St Paul's, Knightsbridge, 1940-47; Archbishop of Perth (Australia), 1947-62, resigned. *Address:* 70 Hipwood Road, Hamilton, Brisbane, Qld 4007, Australia.
                                                  [Died 8 Aug. 1979

MOLOHAN, Michael John Brew, CMG 1957; MBE 1936 formerly Member of HM Overseas Civil Service; *b* 30 May 1906 *s* of late George Brew Molohan, New Milton, Hants; *m* 1951 Alice Kathleen Branson Wilkinson; no *c*. *Educ:* Cheltenham Coll.; Trinity Coll., Oxford (BA). Entered Colonial Servic (Tanganyika) as Administrative Officer, 1929; Labour Com Tanganyika, 1948-53; Senior Prov. Comr, 1953-61. *Recreations* Rugby football, cricket, golf. *Address:* 4 Eversleigh Buckingham Close, London Road, Guildford, Surrey. *Club* Royal Commonwealth Society.   *[Died 25 Jan. 1980*

MOLONY, Sir Hugh (Francis), 2nd Bt, *cr* 1925; MA, MA FICE, FIEI; MConsEI; Chartered Engineer, also a Consulting Engineer; Director of companies; *b* 2 Sept. 1900; *e s* of Rt Hon Sir Thomas Francis Molony, 1st Bt, PC (Ireland), KC, and Pauline Mary (*d* 1951), *o d* of Bernard Rispin, Eccles Street Dublin; *S* father 1949; *m* 1936, Alexandra Campbell Cooper, *d* of late John Alexander Todd, Glasgow, and *widow* of M.

Cooper; one s. *Educ:* St Benedict's Sch., Ireland; Trinity Coll., Dublin. University of Dublin; BA 1921; MA 1930; Bachelor of Engineering, 1922, Master, 1945. Associate Mem. of Institution of Civil Engineers, 1926, Mem. 1938, Fellow 1968. Pupil in Civil Engineering of late Sir Basil Mott, Bt. Asst and Resident Engineer for Messrs Mott, Hay & Anderson, MMICE, on bridges and tunnel works in England, 1922-27; Bridge Engineer to the Entre Rios & Argentine NE Railways, 1927-38; Engineer on tunnel construction in London, 1938; Engineering Inspector, Ministry of Health and, subsequently, Ministry of Housing and Local Government for Public Health and Civil Engineering Works, 1938-55, including wartime service as Regional Engineer, Min. of Health, Northwestern Region, 1940-46. *Publications:* professional papers for the Institution of Civil Engineers and articles in technical jls. *Heir: s* Thomas Desmond Molony [*b* 13 March 1937; *m* 1962, Doris, *d* of late G. E. Foley, Cork; four *d*]. *Address:* Hobjohn's Croft, Heathfield Copse, West Chiltington, Pulborough, West Sussex. *Club:* Kildare Street and University (Dublin). *[Died 31 March 1976.*

MOLONY, Sir Joseph (Thomas), KCVO 1970; Kt 1967; QC 1955; a Recorder, since 1972 (Recorder of Bristol, 1964-71); Judge of the Courts of Appeal, Jersey and Guernsey, 1972-75; *b* 8 Dec. 1907; 2nd *s* of Rt Hon. Sir T. F. Molony, 1st Bt, PC, Lord Chief Justice of Ireland; *m* 1936, Carmen Mary, *o d* of late Frankland Dent, PhD, MSc, FIC (Colonial Civil Service Singapore); two *s* two *d*. *Educ:* Downside; Trinity Coll., Cambridge (Senior Scholar). MA, LLM 1933; Barrister, Inner Temple, 1930 (Cert. of Honour, Barstow Scholar, Yarborough-Anderson Scholar); Master of the Bench, 1961. Leader of the Western Circuit, 1964-75; Mem. Bar Council, 1954-58, 1962; Commissioner of Assize: Midland and South-Eastern Circuits, 1958; North-Eastern Circuit, 1960; Western Circuit, 1968; Recorder: Devizes, 1951-54; Exeter, 1954-60; Southampton, 1960-64. Attorney General to the Duchy of Cornwall, 1960-69. Chairman: General Council of the Bar, 1963-64, 1964-65, 1965-66; Board of Trade Departmental Cttee on Consumer Protection, 1959; Code of Practice Cttee, Pharmaceutical Industry, 1967. Served War of 1939-45, Sqdn Leader, RAF, 1940-45. *Address:* 4 Parkside Gardens, Wimbledon Common, SW19. *T:* 01-946 3440. *[Died 28 May 1978.*

MONAHAN, Hon. Sir Robert (Vincent), Kt 1967; Supreme Court Judge, State of Victoria, Australia, 1955-70; *b* 11 April 1898; *s* of Patrick Martin Monahan, Victoria, and Mary Frances Monahan (*née* Nolan); *m* 1929, Lillie Elevia, *d* of Peter Donald Bowman, Adelaide; three *s* one *d*. *Educ:* St Patrick's Coll., Ballarat; Newman Coll., Univ. of Melbourne. Admitted to: Victorian Bar, 1922; New South Wales Bar, 1942; Tasmanian Bar, 1948; KC 1947; practised at Common Law and Criminal Law Bar throughout professional career. *Recreations:* golf, racing, fishing. *Address:* 99 Spring Street, Melbourne, Vic 3000, Australia. *T:* 26-2016. *Clubs:* Australian; Athenæum, Melbourne (Melbourne); Melbourne Cricket; Lawn Tennis Association of Victoria; all Melbourne racing; Victoria Golf. *[Died 10 May 1975.*

MONCKTON, Reginald Francis Percy, TD; DL; *b* 3 June 1896; *y* and *o* surv. *s* of late Francis Monckton of Stretton Hall and Somerford Hall, Staffs; *m* 1931, Sheila, *y d* of H. G. Stobart of Thornton Hall, Yorks; one *s* one *d* (and one *s* one *d* decd). *Educ:* Eton. Joined Montgomeryshire Yeomanry, 1914; saw service in Palestine; survived the sinking of HMS Aragon off Alexandria, 1918; Dep. Military Governor of Jericho, 1918-20; ADC and Private Sec. to 1st High Comr for Palestine, 1920-25; transferred to Staffs Yeomanry, 1925; saw service in Middle East, 1940-41, with Public Relations Unit. DL Staffs; High Sheriff of Staffs, 1937; Vice-Lieutenant, Co. of Staffs, 1962-67; MFH Albrighton, 1929-35, Goathland, 1936-38; Mem. Church Assembly (House of Laity), 1950-71; Church Commissioner, 1958-68. *Publications:* Hunting Reflections, 1936; The Key of Gold, 4th edn, 1965. *Recreations:* hunting, fishing, shooting. *Address:* Stretton Hall, Stafford. *[Died 30 Dec. 1975.*

MONCRIEFF; *see* Scott-Moncrieff.

MONCRIEFF, Sir Alan (Aird), Kt 1964; CBE 1952; MD; FRCP; FRCOG; Emeritus Professor of Child Health, University of London; late Physician, Hospital for Sick Children, Great Ormond Street, 1934-64; Consulting Physician, Children's Department, Middlesex Hospital, London; *b* Bournemouth, 9 Oct. 1901; *e surv. s* of Rev. William Moncrieff; *m* 1928, Honor (*d* 1954), *o d* of Cecil Wedmore, Clevedon, Som.; two *s* one *d*; *m* 1955, Mary Katherine, *er d* of Ralph Wedmore. *Educ:* Caterham Sch.; Univ. of London, Middlesex Hosp. Medical Sch. Qualified as a medical practitioner, 1922; Post-Graduate experience in various resident appointments at this Hosp. and at the Hosp. for Sick Children, Great Ormond Street; studied in

Paris while working in the Health Div. of the League of Red Cross Socs, 1923-24; studied in Hamburg and other parts of Germany in 1930-31 while holding a Rockefeller Travelling Medical Fellowship; Goulstonian Lectr, RCP, 1935; Charles West Lectr, RCP, 1952; Newsholme Lecturer, London Sch. of Hygiene, 1953; Harben Lecturer, 1962. James Spence Gold Medallist, 1961. Hon. Fellow, American Academy of Pediatrics; Corr. étrang. Académie Nat. de Médecine, France; Mem. Corr. Soc. de Pédiatrie de Paris and Sociedade Portuguesa de Pediatria; Hon. Mem. American and Canadian Pediatric Socs. Chevalier de la Légion d'Honneur, 1968. *Publications:* contribs to scientific and medical journals on matters relating to diseases of children and respiration. *Recreations:* music, reading, and writing. *Address:* Waterford Lodge, Waterford, Hertford. *T:* Hertford 4391. *[Died 24 July 1971.*

MONIER-WILLIAMS, Clarence Faithfull, CB 1952; MBE 1934; *b* 5 May 1893; 2nd *s* of late Dr M. S. Monier-Williams; *m* 1944, Muriel Leonie, *o d* of late J. A. Edwards; no *c*. *Educ:* Westminster Sch.; Lincoln Coll., Oxford (BA). Entered Army, 1914; seconded from Army for service in the Foreign Office, 1917; transferred to Dept of Overseas Trade, 1919, Board of Trade, 1939; Under-Sec., Board of Trade, 1948-54, retired 1954. *Recreations:* travelling, gardening. *Address:* Broad View, Wonham Way, Gomshall, Surrey. *T:* Shere 2286. *[Died 15 Sept. 1974.*

MONK, Albert Ernest, CMG 1966; Permanent President, Australian Council of Trade Unions, 1949-69 (Secretary, 1945-49; President, 1934-43); *b* 1900. Clerk, Transport Workers' Union, 1919; Clerk, Asst Sec. and Sec., Trades Hall Council, Melbourne, 1924-39. Chm., Victoria State Relief Cttee, 1934-44, 1954-. Member: Governing Body, ILO; Exec. Council, WFTU, 1945-49; Mem. Exec. Bd, Internat. Confederation, Free Trade Unions, 1949-. *Address:* 17-25 Lygon Street, Carlton, Vic 3053, Australia. *[Died 11 Feb. 1975.*

MONKHOUSE, Prof. Francis John; Professor of Geography, University of Southampton, 1954-66; *b* 15 May 1914; *s* of late Alderman Joseph Monkhouse and Mrs E. L. Monkhouse, Workington; *m* 1938, Bertha Greensmith; one *s* one *d*. *Educ:* Workington Grammar Sch.; Emmanuel Coll., Cambridge (MA). Teaching, 1936-40. Intelligence Div., Naval Staff, 1941-44; Inter-Services Topographical Div., South-East Asia, 1944-45. Univ. of Liverpool, Depts of Geography and Education, 1946-54. Visiting Professor: Miami Univ., Ohio, 1960-61; Univ. of Southern Illinois, 1965-66; Univ. of Maryland, USA, 1968. Hon. DSc Miami Univ., Oxford, Ohio. *Publications:* The Belgian Kempenland, 1949; (with H. R. Wilkinson) Maps and Diagrams, 1952; Principles of Physical Geography, 1954; A Study Guide in Physical Geography, 1956; Landscape from the Air, 1958; A Regional Geography of Western Europe, 1959; The English Lake District, 1960; Europe, 1961; A Dictionary of Geography, 1965; The Countries of North-Western Europe, 1965; (with A. V. Hardy) The American Landscape, 1965; (with H. R. Cain) North America, 1970; The Material Resources of Britain, 1971; (with J. S. Williams) Climber and Fellwalker in Lakeland, 1972; (with A. V. Hardy) The Man-made Landscape, 1974. *Recreation:* mountaineering. *Address:* Crag Farm House, Ennerdale, Cleator, Cumbria. *T:* Lamplugh 214.
[Died 1 March 1975.

MONKS, Air Vice-Marshal Alfred Thomas, CB 1957; *b* 15 March 1908; *s* of late William Patrick Monks; *m* 1937, Emily Irene, 2nd *d* of late George S. Overton, Navenby, Lincs; no *c*. *Educ:* Sir Joseph Williamson's Mathematical Sch., Rochester, Kent. Aircraft Apprentice, RAF, 1924-26; flying course, 1931; commissioned, 1932; specialised in signals, 1934-35; Chief Signals Officer: AHQ, E Africa, 1943; AHQ, Eastern Mediterranean, 1943-44 (despatches 1944); Dep. Dir of Telecommunications, Air Ministry, 1944-46; commanded: No 4 Radio Sch., 1946; No 1 Radio Sch., 1946-48, and 1952-53; Dep. Dir of Signals, Air Ministry, 1949-51; Chief Signals Officer, Allied Air Forces (NATO), Northern Europe, 1953-55; Controller, RAF Telecommunications, 1955-60; SASO Technical Training Command, 1960-63, retired 1963. CEng, FIEE. *Address:* The Grange, Navenby, Lincoln. *Club:* Royal Air Force. *[Died 30 Jan. 1972.*

MONNET, Jean; European political figure; *b* Cognac, Charente, 9 Nov. 1888; *s* of J. G. Monnet. *Educ:* Cognac Coll. French representative, Allied Exec. Cttees for re-allocation of common resources, European War; Dep. Sec.-Gen., League of Nations, 1918; returned to family business; took part in re-organisation of Chinese Railways, 1932; Chm., Franco-British Economic Co-ordination Cttee, 1939; took part in organisation of common defence programme, 1940; Mem. British Supply Council, Washington, 1940-43; Comr for Armament, Supplies and

Reconstruction, French National Liberation Cttee, Algiers, 1943-44; created Plan Monnet, 1946; Gen. Comr, Plan for Modernisation and Equipment of France, 1946; Pres. Preparatory Conf. of Schuman Plan, 1950; Pres. European Coal and Steel Community, 1952-55; Chm., Action Cttee for the United States of Europe, 1956-75. Hon. Mem., RGS, 1972. Holds hon. doctorates of following universities: Columbia, 1953; Glasgow, 1956; Princeton, 1959; Yale, 1961; Cambridge, 1961; Oxford, 1963. Wateler Peace Prize, 1951; Charlemagne Prize, 1953; Grand Cross of Merit of German Federal Republic, 1958; Freedom Award, 1963; Prize of Foundation Gouverneur Emile Cornez, 1963; US Presidential Medal of Freedom, 1963. Hon. GBE 1947; Hon. CH 1972. *Publications:* Les Etats Unis d'Europe ont commencé (collection of extracts from speeches); Memoirs, 1976. *Address:* Houjarray, par Montfort l'Amaury (Seine-et-Oise), France. *[Died 16 March 1979.*

MÖNNIG, Hermann Otto, BA, DrPhil, BVSc, DSc (*hc*); Chairman, Agricura Laboratoria Ltd, 1945-70, now Adviser; formerly Chairman, Science Advisory Council; Scientific Adviser to Prime Minister, 1962; National Parks Board, 1952; *b* Cape Town, 27 Jan. 1897; *s* of C. J. O. Mönnig and A. H. Schmidt; *m* 1923, Everdina Maria Koning; two *s. Educ:* Gymnasium, Paarl; Univs of Stellenbosch, Amsterdam, Zürich, Neuchâtel, SA. Research Officer at Onderstepoort, S Africa, 1922; Graduated in Veterinary Science, Univ. of South Africa, 1926; Pretoria Univ.: Lectr in Helminthology, 1928; Prof. of Parasitology, 1930; Mem. of Council, 1949-70. *Publications:* Veterinary Helminthology and Entomology, 1934; various scientific articles on parasitology. *Recreation:* wood-carving. *Address:* 246 Hay Street, Pretoria, Transvaal, South Africa. *TA:* Agrilab, Silverton. *T:* Pretoria 74-2674. *[Died 27 Nov. 1978.*

MONNINGTON, Sir (Walter) Thomas, Kt 1967; PRA (RA 1938; ARA 1931); painter; President of the Royal Academy since 1966; Fellow of University College, London; *b* 1902; *s* of Walter Monnington, Barrister; *m* 1924, Winifred (*d* 1947), *d* of W. H. Knights; one *s*; *m* 1947, Evelyn Janet, 3rd *d* of Bernard Hunt; one *s. Educ:* University Coll., London; Slade Sch. (scholar). Trustee, British Museum, 1963-69. Mem. Exec. Cttee National Art Collections Fund. Commander, Order of Polonia Restituta, 1971; Commander, Order of the Crown, Belgium, 1972; Grand Decoration of Honour in Gold, Austria, 1972. *Address:* Leyswood, Groombridge, Tunbridge Wells, Kent. *T:* Groombridge 205; Royal Academy of Arts, Burlington House, Piccadilly, W1V 0DZ. *T:* 01-734 9052. *Clubs:* Athenæum, Arts. *[Died 7 Jan. 1976.*

MONOD, Jacques Lucien, Officier de la Légion d'Honneur; Commandeur de l'Ordre National du Mérite; French molecular biologist; Director, Pasteur Institute, Paris, since 1971; Honorary Professor of Molecular Biology at the Collège de France, since 1973; *b* 9 Feb. 1910; *s* of Lucien Monod, painter and Charlotte Todd MacGregor; *m* 1938, Odette Bruhl; two *s. Educ:* Cannes Lycée; Univ. of Paris. War service, 1939-45; Croix de Guerre, Chevalier de la Légion d'Honneur, Bronze Star Medal. Zoology Asst, 1931, Head of Laboratory, 1945, Head of Dept of Cellular Biochemistry, 1954, Institut Pasteur; Prof., Faculty of Sciences, Univ. of Paris, 1959-67; Prof. of Molecular Biology, Collège de France, 1967-72. Rockefeller Foundation Fellow, 1936; non-resident Fellow, Salk Inst. Member: American Academy of Arts and Sciences; Deutsche Akademie der Naturforscher Leopoldina. For. Member: Royal Society, 1968; Nat. Acad. of Sciences of Washington, 1968; Royal Swedish Acad. of Sciences, 1973; Accademia Nazionale dei XL, 1975; Royal Netherlands Acad. of Arts and Sciences, 1975. Hon. DSc: Univ. of Chicago, 1965; Rockefeller Univ., 1970; Oxford Univ., 1973; Univ. Libre, Bruxelles, 1975. Charles-Leopold Mayer Prize, 1964; Nobel Prize for Medicine and Physiology (jointly), 1965. *Publications:* Chance and Necessity, 1972; papers on molecular biology. *Recreations:* music (cello), sailing. *Address:* Institut Pasteur, 28 rue du Dr Roux, Paris 15, France. *[Died 31 May 1976.*

MONRO, Hon. Lady, DBE 1919; **Mary Caroline;** *y d* of 1st Baron O'Hagan; *m* 1912, General Sir Charles Carmichael Monro, 1st Bt, GCB, GCSI, GCMG (*d* 1929); no *c. Address:* Flat 7, Belgravia House, 2 & 5 Halkin Place, SW1X 5TF. *T:* 01-245 9474. *Clubs:* Sesame Pioneer and Lyceum, Anglo-Belgian. *[Died 28 Aug. 1972.*

MONSARRAT, Nicholas John Turney, FRSL; author; *b* Liverpool, 22 March 1910; *s* of late K. W. Monsarrat; *m* 1st, 1939, Eileen Rowland (marr. diss. 1952); one *s*; 2nd 1952, Philippa Crosby (marr. diss. 1961; she *d* 1979); two *s*; 3rd, 1961, Ann Griffiths. *Educ:* Winchester Coll.; Trinity Coll., Cambridge (BA 1931). Heinemann Foundation Prize for Literature, 1951. Coronation Medal, 1953. War of 1939-45; in RN 1940-46; Lt-

Comdr RNVR (despatches). Councillor, Kensington Borough Council, 1946. Dir, UK Information Office, Johannesburg 1946-53; Ottawa, 1953-56. Chm. Nat. War Memorial Health Foundation (South Africa), 1951-53. Board of Governors Stratford Shakespeare Fest. of Canada, 1956; Bd of Dirs, Ottawa Philharmonic Orchestra, 1956. Chevalier, Sovereign Order of St John of Jerusalem, 1973. *Publications:* Think of Tomorrow 1934; At First Sight, 1935; The Whipping Boy, 1936; This is the Schoolroom, 1939; Three Corvettes, 1945; Depends What You Mean by Love, 1947; My Brother Denys, 1948; The Cruel Sea 1951; HMS Marlborough Will Enter Harbour, 1952; The Story of Esther Costello, 1953; Boys' Book of the Sea, 1954; Canada Coast-to-Coast, Castle Garac, 1955; The Tribe that Lost its Head, 1956; Boys' Book of the Commonwealth, 1957; The Ship that Died of Shame, 1959; The Nylon Pirates, 1960; The White Rajah, 1961; The Time Before This, 1962; Smith and Jones 1963; To Stratford with Love, 1963; A Fair Day's Work, 1964 The Pillow Fight, 1965; Something to Hide, 1965; Richer Than all His Tribe, 1968; The Kappillan of Malta, 1973; Monsarrat at Sea, 1975; The Master Mariner: vol. I, Running Proud, 1978; vol II, Darken Ship, 1980 (published posthumously) *autobiography:* Life is a Four-Letter Word, Vol. I, 1966, Vol. II 1970; *play:* The Visitor (Daly's Theatre, 1936); *films:* The Cruel Sea, 1953; The Ship That Died of Shame, 1955; The Story of Esther Costello, 1957; The Way of a Ship (Narration), 1965 Something to Hide, 1972. *Recreations:* sailing, music. *Address:* c/o Campbell Thomson & McLaughlin Ltd, 31 Newington Green, N16 9PU. *T:* 01-249 2971; San Lawrenz, Gozo, Malta. *T:* 556977. *Clubs:* Naval, Lansdowne; Rideau (Ottawa). *[Died 8 Aug. 1979.*

MONSEY, Yvonne, (Mrs Derek Monsey); *see* Mitchell, Yvonne.

MONTAGU, Ainsley Marshall Rendall, CIE 1945; FCGI; FICE MIWE; *b* 6 Nov. 1891; *s* of Alfred John Montagu and Hester Vaudrey (*née* Holland); *m* 1st, 1918, Margaret Violet Rumsby two *s*; 2nd, 1940, Phyllis Henley Marion Moreton; one *d. Educ* St Paul's Sch.; City and Guilds Engineering Coll., London Joined PWD India, 1914; served European War, 1914-18, with KGO Bengal Sappers and Miners and RFC (despatches Returned to PWD, 1920; Chief Engr and Sec. to Govt, Punjab PWD (Irrigation Br.), 1943; retd, 1947. Engineering Adviser to UNRWA for Palestine Refugees, 1950-52; Dep. Dir, Public Works Dept, Sudan Government, Khartoum, 1952-54 Consultant, Sir Murdoch MacDonald & Partners, 1954-68 retired. Fellow of City and Guilds of London Institute (FCGI) 1957. *Publications:* papers on hydraulics and hydraulic engineering for learned societies and journals. *Address:* c/o Lloyds Bank Ltd, 6 Pall Mall, SW1. *[Died 26 Dec. 1977.*

MONTANARO, Brig. Gerald Charles Stokes, DSO; MA, CEng FICE, FIMechE, FIEE, MRAeS, MBIM, FCIS, MNSE company director; *b* 16 Sept. 1916; *s* of late Col C. A. H. Montanaro, OBE; *m* 1946, Valerie Frances (*née* Bensted); two four *d* (and one *s* one *d* decd); *m* 1965, Judith Mary (*née* Newington). *Educ:* Bedford Sch.; RMA and Cambridge Univ. Commissioned, RE, 1936; BEF, France, 1939-40; Commandos Special Canoe Troop, 1940-42 (DSO); commissioned Lieut-Comdr, RN, 1942-45, in comd flotilla of submersible craft; Staff Coll., 1947; GSO2 and GSO1 (ops) GHQ, MELF, 1947-48 Tech. Staff Course, 1948-49; Mil. Comdg Officer RAE, 1949-52 OC Sqdn and Regt, Hong Kong and Korea, 1952-54; GSO1 War Office, 1954-57; Comd of Regt and CRE, BAOR, 1957-60; Ass Dir Devel., WO, 1960-61; Brig., Gen. Staff, WO, 1962-63; Brig IDC, 1963-64; Brigadier A/Q HQ ME, Aden, 1964-65. Man Dir Reed Develt Services Ltd, and Dep. Chm. Reed Transport Ltd, Reed Paper Gp, 1965-66; Dep. Man. Dir, Norton Villiers Ltd, 1967-68; Dir, Fairline Engineering Ltd, 1968-70; Man. Dir Alistair McCowan & Associates, Nigeria, retired. *Recreations* deer stalking, shooting, sailing. *Address:* Ferh, Transfiguration Square, Lija, Malta. *T:* Malta 41896. *Clubs:* Naval and Military Malta Union, St Hubert. *[Died 24 April 1979.*

MONTGOMERY OF ALAMEIN, 1st Viscount *cr* 1946, of Hindhead; **Field-Marshal Bernard Law Montgomery,** KG 1946 GCB 1945 (KCB 1942; CB 1940); DSO 1914; DL; Colonel Commandant: The Parachute Regiment, 1945-55; Royal Tank Regt, 1946-56; Army Physical Training Corps, 1946-61 Colonel, Royal Warwickshire Regiment, 1946-63; *b* 17 Nov. 1887; *s* of late Rt Rev. H. H. Montgomery, KCMG; *m* 1927 Elizabeth (*d* 1937), *widow* of Capt. O. A. Carver, RE; one *s Educ:* St Paul's. Entered Army, 1908; Lieut-Col 1931; Col 1934 Maj.-Gen. 1938; Lt-Gen. 1942; Gen. 1942; Field-Marshal 1944 served European War, 1914-18 (despatches, DSO, Bt Major War Medals); comd 1st Bn Royal Warwickshire Regt, 1931-34 GSO1, Staff Coll., Quetta, 1934-37; Comdr, 9th Infantry Bde Portsmouth, 1937-38; comd 8th Div., 1938-39; War of 1939-44 (War Medals); 3rd Div., 1939-40; 5th Corps, 1940; 12th Corps

1941; SE Comd, 1942; Comdr Eighth Army from July 1942 during campaigns in N Africa, Sicily and Italy; C-in-C Br. Group of Armies and Allied Armies, N France, 1944; comd 21st Army Group, 1944-45; comd BAOR, 1945-46; CIGS, 1946-48; Chm. of Western Europe Commanders' in Chief Cttee, 1948-51; Deputy-Supreme Allied Comdr, Europe, 1951-58; DL Southampton, 1959. Hon. Freeman City of London and many other cities and towns at home and abroad; Freeman of: Mercers' Co., Co. of Fletchers, and Carpenters' Co., London; Bonnetmakers and Dyers, Glasgow; former Governor of St Paul's Sch., London. Pres. and Vice-Pres., Patron, Vice-Patron and Hon. Patron, and Hon. Mem. of numerous socs. Hon. DCL: Oxford; Edinburgh; Dalhousie, Halifax; Newfoundland; Hon. LLD: Cambridge; Queen's, Belfast; Glasgow; St Andrews; Toronto; McGill; British Columbia; Hon. Dr of Science: Louvain; Liège. Has many foreign orders and decorations. *Publications:* Ten Chapters, 1946; Forward to Victory, 1946; Normandy to the Baltic, 1947; Forward from Victory, 1948; El Alamein to the River Sangro, 1948; Memoirs, 1958; An Approach to Sanity: a Study of East-West Relations, 1959; The Path to Leadership, 1961; Three Continents, 1962; History of Warfare, 1968. *Relevant publication:* A Field-Marshal in the Family, by Brian Montgomery, 1973. *Heir: s* Hon. David Montgomery, CBE. *Address:* Islington Mill, Alton, Hants. *Clubs:* Athenæum, Savage, Cavalry, Bath.
[*Died* 24 *March* 1976.

MONTGOMERY, Brig. Ernest John, CB 1953; CBE 1950 (OBE 1944; MBE 1940); JP; retired; *b* 24 March 1901; *s* of late Herbert Elphinstone Montgomery, AMICE; *m* 1931, Rosemary Elizabeth, *d* of Sir John Noble, 1st Bt, of Ardkinglas; one adopted *d. Educ:* Rugby Sch.; RMC, Sandhurst. Commnd HLI, 1920; served in Egypt, Palestine, Turkey and India, 1920-34. Personal Asst to Resident, Mysore, 1927; Private Sec. to Governor of Bihar and Orissa, 1928-31, Adjt 2nd Bn, HLI, 1931-34; DAAG, HQ, Scottish Command, 1937-40 (MBE); Staff Coll., 1940; DAAG 52nd Lowland Div., 1940; Comd 1st Bn HLI, 1940-42; AA&QMG, 45th West Country Div., 1942; AQMG 1st Corps, 1942-43; AA&QMG 3rd Div., 1943; Comdr 101 Beach Sub Area, 1943; served in France and Holland, 1944-46 (despatches, OBE); Dep. Asst Chief-of-Staff Organization, CCG, Berlin, 1946-47; Comdr Scottish Beach Bde (TA), 1947-50 (CBE); Brigadier in Charge of Administration, Singapore Base District, 1951-54 (CB), retired. Mem. Royal Company of Archers (Queen's Body Guard for Scotland). JP Argyll. Hon. Sheriff Substitute, 1960. *Recreations:* gardening, shooting, sailing. *Address:* Kinlochruel, Colintraive, Argyll. *Clubs:* Army and Navy; New (Edinburgh). [*Died* 10 *Oct.* 1972.

MONTGOMERY, Sir Frank (Percival), Kt 1953; MC 1916; retired; Hon. Consulting Radiologist: Royal Victoria Hospital; Belfast City Hospital; Ulster Hospital for Children; Pro-Chancellor, Queen's University, Belfast, 1956-67, and Member of Senate, 1942-67; *b* 10 June 1892; *y s* of late Very Rev. Henry Montgomery, MA, DD, Belfast; *m* 1925, Joan, *er d* of late W. Christopherson, Ipswich, Suffolk; two *s* two *d. Educ:* Campbell Coll., Belfast; Queen's Univ., Belfast (MB, ChB). Served European War, 1914, RAMC, 1915-19, French Croix de Guerre, 1917. Divisional Inspector, Dept Public Health Egyptian Govt, Cairo, 1919-23; DMRE Cantab, 1924. Consulting Radiologist, Belfast, 1925-68. Mem. Health Advisory Council, N Ireland, 1944-47; Chm. Northern Ireland Hospitals Authority, 1948-56; Hon. Governor, Ulster Hospital, Dundonald, 1956. FFR (London), 1938; Hon. FFR, RCS(I), 1962. Hon. LLD Queen's Univ., Belfast, 1968. *Recreation:* golf. *Address:* 19 Broomhill Park, Belfast. *T:* Belfast 666984. *Club:* Royal County Down Golf (Captain, 1957).
[*Died* 11 *Aug.* 1972.

MONTGOMERY, Ian, CB 1963; Deputy Under-Secretary of State (Army), Ministry of Defence, since 1964 (War Office, 1963-64); *b* 25 March 1913; *o s* of John and Mary Montgomery; *m* 1945, Marguerite Dorothy Bryan; one *d. Educ:* Newcastle-under-Lyme High Sch.; Magdalen Coll., Oxford. Entered Administrative Class of Home Civil Service, 1936, assigned to Ministry of Labour; HM Treasury, 1938; Private Secretary: to Second Sec., 1940-41, to Financial Sec., 1941-42; Principal, 1942; Grenadier Guards, 1942-44; Offices of the War Cabinet, 1944-45; Private Sec. to Sec. to the Treasury, 1945-46; MoD, as Asst Sec., 1947; Principal Private Sec. to Minister of Defence, 1950-51; Imperial Defence Coll., 1952; Under-Sec., MoD, 1957-63. *Address:* Burcot, Icklingham Road, Cobham, Surrey. *Club:* Athenæum. [*Died* 4 *Nov.* 1971.

MONTGORGE, Alexis Jean; *see* Gabin, Jean.

MONTHERLANT, Henry de; writer; Member of the French Academy since 1960; *b* Paris, 21 April 1896; *s* of Joseph Millon

de Montherlant and Marguerite (*née* Camusat de Riancey). *Educ:* Lycée Janson-de-Sailly; Ecole Ste-Croix de Neuilly. Served European War, 1914-18 (Croix de Guerre, Médaille des Combattants Volontaires). Served War of 1939-45, as War Correspondent. Grand Prix de Littérature of French Academy, 1934. Several plays prod. Comédie Française. *Publications:* La Relève du Matin, 1920; Le Songe, 1922; Les Olympiques, 1924; Les Bestiaires, 1926; Aux Fontaines du Désir, 1927; La Petite Infante de Castille, 1929; Mors et Vita, 1932; Encore un Instant de Bonheur, 1934; Les Célibataires, 1934; Service Inutile, 1935; Les Jeunes Filles (4 vols): Les Jeunes Filles, 1936, Pitié pour les Femmes, 1936, Le Démon du bien, 1937, Les Lépreuses, 1939; l'Equinoxe de Septembre, 1938; La Solstice de Juin, 1941; La Reine Morte, 1942; Fils de Personne, 1944; Malatesta, 1946; Le Maître de Santiago, 1947; Demain il fera Jour, 1949; Celles qu'on prend dans ses bras, 1950; La Ville dont le Prince est un Enfant, 1951; Port-Royal, 1954; Carnets, 1958; Don Juan, 1958; Le Cardinal d'Espagne, 1960; La Guerre Civile, 1965; La Rose de Sable, 1968; Les Garçons, 1969. *Address:* Société des Gens de Lettres, Hôtel Massa, 38 rue du Faubourg-Saint-Jacques, Paris 14e, France. [*Died* 21 *Sept.* 1972.

MOODY, Arthur Seymour; Member Amalgamated Society of Woodworkers since 1912; *b* 6 June 1891; *s* of William Henry and Elsey Elizabeth Moody; *m* 1937, Edith Mary Coney; one *s* one *d. Educ:* Hull Council Schs; Hull Technical Coll. Mem. of Court of Referees, ten years; on Hull City Council, 1934-37. Mem. National Executive of Labour Party, 1942-46. MP (Lab) for Fairfield Div. of Liverpool, 1945-50, Gateshead East, 1950-64. *Recreations:* Rugby football, swimming. [*Died* 12 *Dec.* 1976.

MOODY, Sydney, CMG 1942; OBE 1932; Colonial Secretary, Mauritius, 1939-48; *b* 1889; *s* of Jonathan Moody; *m* 1921, Flora Marion, *e d* of late Rev. William Ewing, MC, DD, Edinburgh; two *d. Educ:* Oxford (BA). Served European War, 1914-20. *Address:* The Brae, Alyth, Perthshire. [*Died* 5 *June* 1979.

MOODY-STUART, Sir Alexander, Kt 1960; OBE 1945; MC 1918; *b* 28 Jan. 1899; *yr s* of late George Moody-Stuart, CBE; *m* 1925, Judith, *d* of late L. I. Henzell, OBE, Antigua; three *s* three *d. Educ:* Winchester; Christ's Coll., Cambridge (BA); Imperial Coll. of Tropical Agriculture, Trinidad. RFA 1917. Became resident of Antigua, 1924; Mem. of Executive and Legislative Councils of Antigua and Leeward Islands for many years. *Address:* Grey House Cottage, Albrighton, near Wolverhampton. [*Died* 12 *Dec.* 1971.

MOON, Sir John (Arthur), 4th Bt, *cr* 1887; Master (retired) Merchant Navy; *b* 27 Oct. 1905; 3rd *s* of Reginald Blakeney Moon (*d* 1927; *g s* of 1st Bt) and Lucy Annie (*d* 1935), *d* of J. Crowther; *S* brother, Sir Richard Moon, 3rd Bt, 1961; *m* 1939, René Henriette Maria Dolores (*d* 1949), *o d* of late Joseph Amédée Amedet, Le Mans, France; no *c. Heir: cousin* Edward Moon, MC [*b* 23 Feb. 1911; *m* 1947, Mary, *o c* of late Captain B. D. Conolly]. *Address:* BP 2710, Papeete, Tahiti, French Polynesia. [*Died* 22 *Feb.* 1979.

MOORE, Archie Murrell Acheson, FRCS; Hon. FICS, 1962; FRSH; formerly Senior Surgeon and Associate Director, Surgical Unit, London Hospital, Hon. Consultant Surgeon, since 1968; Hon. Consultant Surgeon: Poplar Hospital; King George Hospital, Ilford; Dr Barnardo's Homes; St Luke's Nursing Home for the Clergy; Arthur Stanley Institute for Rheumatism; *b* 14 Aug. 1904; *s* of Archie Moore, Aughnacloy, NI; *m* Marjorie Aitken (*d* 1977); one *s* two *d. Educ:* Boys' High Sch., Pretoria, SA; London Hosp. (Surgical Scholar; Buxton, Lethby and minor surgical prize); King's Coll. FRCS 1930; MRCS, LRCP 1927; FDSRCS 1973. Formerly: Surgeon Southend Gen. Hosp. and Essex CC. Examiner in Surgery: Univs of London and Durham; RCS; GDC. Past Mem. Bd of Examiners for primary FRCS; Vice-Pres. and Fellow and Past Treas., BMA; Past Pres. Metropolitan Counties Br. and Chm. Marylebone Div. BMA; Past Chm. Conf. of Consultants and Specialists, and Chm. Adv. Cttee, Commonwealth Medical Adv. Bureau; Chm. Library sub-Cttee BMA; Chm. Cttee on Accidents in Home. Pres. Bd of Registration of Medical Auxiliaries; Mem. Statutory Chiropodists' Bd; Mem. Governing Body British Post Graduate Medical Fedn; Mem. Bd of Governors, London Hosp.; Past Pres., British Supporting Gp, World Medical Assoc.; Past Hon. Pres. British Medical Students Assoc. Chairman: Academic Bd, London Hosp. Medical Coll.; Cttee of Management Medical Insurance Agency; British Medical Students Trust. Mem., Academy of Forensic Sciences; Visitor for GDC. James Sherren Centenary Meml Lectr, 1972. Gen. Comr of Income Tax. Past Master, Worshipful Soc. of Apothecaries, 1961-62, and Hon. Treas.; Liveryman Worshipful Co. of Barbers; Freeman City of London. Hon. Mem. Assoc. of Police Surgeons; FRSM; Fellow: Assoc. of Surgeons; Medical

Soc. London. FZS. CStJ 1968. *Publications:* contribs to medical jls. *Recreation:* fencing. *Address:* 18 Millers Close, Cleeve Road, Goring-on-Thames, near Reading, Berks RG8 9BS. *T:* Goring-on-Thames 3932. *Club:* Athenæum. *[Died* 16 *April* 1979.

MOORE, Maj.-Gen. Francis Malcolm, CSI 1947; CIE 1946; IA (retired); *b* 2 Feb. 1897; *s* of late D. F. Moore, LLD, and M. O. Moore; *m* 1927, Helen Marian Dunn; no *c. Educ:* St Columba's Coll.; Trinity Coll., Dublin. Commissioned 1915, Royal Irish Rifles (wounded in France); transferred to Indian Army, 1917; served with 52nd Sikhs (Frontier Force) in Mesopotamia for 3 years (despatches); after 23 years' service with 2/12th Frontier Force Regt commanded 2/16th Punjab Regt in Malaya, 1940; raised and commanded 100th Indian Infantry Brigade, 1941; commanded 34th Indian Div. 1942 until April 1943, when transferred to command 14th Indian Div. (4 weeks only) and then to command 39th Indian Div. until March 1945; Dir of Selection of Personnel, 1945-46; Military Adviser-in-Chief Indian States Forces, 1946; retd, 1948. *Publications:* numerous articles on military subjects and short stories under nom-de-plume Fan Tan. *Recreations:* Rugby football; boxing (runner-up in Irish Command Heavyweights, 1915); rowing (open Sculls Champion, India, 1925); golf. *Address:* c/o Allied Irish Banks, Foster Place, Dublin; Corofin, Greystones, Co. Wicklow, Ireland. *[Died* 6 *Sept.* 1974.

MOORE, Rear-Adm. (retired) George Dunbar, CBE 1944; *b* 10 Oct. 1893; *s* of Dr John Irwin and Susan Moore; *m* 1923, Doretta Ziele Russell; one *d. Educ:* The Southport Sch., Queensland; Brisbane Grammar Sch.; HMS Conway. Sub-Lt RAN 1914; Lt 1916; Comdr 1928; Capt. 1935; Commodore, 1942; Acting Rear-Adm., 1944; commanded: HMS Dunoon, 1932-33; HMAS Penguin, 1934-35; HMAS Yarra, 1936-37; HMAS Stuart, 1937-38; HMS Curaçoa, 1939; HMS Dauntless, 1939-41; HMAS Australia, 1941; HMAS Canberra, 1942. 2nd Naval Mem., Australian Commonwealth Naval Board, 1942-44; Flag Officer-in-Charge, New South Wales, 1944-50; Minister for Australia in the Philippines, 1950-55, retired. *Address:* Bank of New South Wales, King Street and George Street, Sydney, NSW 2000, Australia. *Club:* Royal Sydney Golf (Sydney). *[Died* 27 *July* 1979.

MOORE, Harold, CBE 1932; DSc (London); PhD, FRIC, FInstP; *b* 5 Jan. 1878; *m* 1st, 1908, Grace Dora (*d* 1921), *d* of late R. J. Read, Norwich; two *d* (and one *d* decd); 2nd, 1922, Una Katharine, *d* of late A. W. Yeo; one *d* (and one *s* decd). Chemist to Islip Iron Co., Northants, 1899-1901; metallurgist to William Beardmore & Co., Parkhead Steel Works, 1901-04; joined Research Dept, Woolwich, as chief metallurgist, 1904; Dir of Metallurgical Research in that dept, 1919-32; Dir of British Non-Ferrous Metals Research Assoc., 1932-44; Editor, Transactions of the Society of Instrument Technology, 1949-56; Past Pres. Institute of Metals and of Institution of Metallurgists. *Publications:* papers on metallurgical and related subjects in journals of Institute of Metals, Iron and Steel Institute, Faraday Society, and other scientific institutions. *Recreation:* music. *Address:* Riverside House, Shoreham, Sevenoaks, Kent. *T:* Otford 3260. *Club:* Athenæum. *[Died* 29 *Aug.* 1972.

MOORE, Sir Harold (John de Courcy), Kt 1922; *s* of late Hobart Moore of Bengeo, Herts; *b* 8 June 1877; *m* 1st, 1906, Jeanne Germaine, *d* of late Eugene Gokel; two *s* one *d*; 2nd, 1924, Mary (*d* 1965), *d* of late J. C. Cuthbertson; 3rd, 1965, Winifred (*d* 1974), *d* of late Edwin Atkin. Alderman of the City of London (Walbrook Ward), 1921-29; Senior Sheriff of the City of London, 1921-22; Lieut of the City of London; Fellow, Inst. of Chartered Accountants; Fellow, Inst. of Arbitrators. Served European War with Royal Flying Corps and Royal Air Force (rank, Major); sometime a Mem. of Board of Financial Control, Air Ministry. Senior Grand Deacon of English Freemasons, 1927-28. *Address:* Hillcroft, Burley, Hants. *Club:* Bath (Johannesburg). *[Died* 6 *Dec.* 1976.

MOORE, Henry Ian, CBE 1964; MSc, PhD, NDA, Dipl. Agric. Cantab; FRAgSs; Principal of Seale-Hayne Agricultural College, Newton Abbot, Devon, 1948-71; *b* 6 Oct. 1905; *s* of William Henry and Annie Ellen Moore; *m* 1931, Gwendolen Robinson. *Educ:* University of Leeds; Univ. of Cambridge. Senior Lecturer in Agriculture and Hon. Reader in Crop Husbandry, Univ. of Leeds, 1930-48; Governor: Plant Breeding Inst., Cambridge, 1954-62; Grassland Research Inst., Hurley, 1960-70; Member: Grassland Utilisation Ctte, 1957-58; Adv. Ctte on Agricultural Education, 1964; President: Agricultural Education Assoc., 1963-64; British Grassland Soc., 1953-54. *Publications:* Silos and Silage, 1942; Crops and Cropping, 1943; Grassland Husbandry, 1943; Good Husbandry, 1946; Background to Farming, 1947; Root Crops, 1948; Science and Practice of Grassland Farming, 1949; Science and Practice in

Cropping for Meat and Milk Production, 1952; Silage and Haymaking, 1959; Winter Keep on the Farm, 1960; Grass and Grasslands, 1966; (ed) McConnell's Agricultural Notebook, 12th to 16th editions. *Recreations:* country pursuits, photography. *Address:* Chaceley, Church Road, Bishopsteignton, Devon. *T:* Teignmouth 5389.
[Died 24 *Sept.* 1976.

MOORE, Adm. Sir Henry Ruthven, GCB 1946 (KCB 1942; CB 1939); CVO 1937; DSO 1916; DL; *b* 29 Aug. 1886; *e s* of late Col Henry Moore, JP, late King's Own Royal Regiment; *m* 1908, Katherine Henley Joan (*d* 1945), *d* of late H. J. Gillespie, barrister-at-law, The Gables, Windsor; one *s* one *d*; *m* 1948, Catherine Harlow Wilkinson, *widow* of Vice-Adm. T. S. Wilkinson, USN, and *d* of late Richard Austin Harlow, Hockley, Arlington, Virginia. *Educ:* Sherborne. Entered HMS Britannia as Naval Cadet, 1902; Lt, 1908; Comdr, 1919; Capt., 1926; Rear-Adm., 1938; Vice-Adm., 1941; Adm., 1945; served on staff of Royal Naval Staff Coll., 1919-21; Naval Asst Sec. to the Cttee of Imperial Defence, 1921-24; Asst Sec. to British Delegation to Conference for Limitation of Armament, Washington, 1921-22, and at Geneva, 1927; attended Imperial Defence Coll., 1927; Dep. of Dir of Plans Div., Admiralty, 1930-32; Dir, 1932-33; HMS Neptune, 1933-35; Cdre 1st Class and Chief of Staff to C-in-C Home Fleet, 1936-38; ADC to the King, 1937-38; Chief of Staff to Comdr-in-Chief, Portsmouth, 1938-39; Rear-Adm. Commanding 3rd Cruiser Sqdn, 1939-40; Asst Chief of Naval Staff (Trade), 1940-41; Vice-Chief of Naval Staff, 1941-43; Second-in-Command Home Fleet, 1943-44; C-in-C Home Fleet, 1944-45; Head of British Naval Mission, Washington, DC, Dec. 1945-Sept. 1948; Naval Representative of British Chiefs of Staff on Military Staff Cttee of Security Council, UN, 1946-48; Comdr-in-Chief, The Nore, 1948-50; First and Principal Naval ADC to the King, 1948-51; retired list, 1951. Served in Grand Fleet in European War of 1914-18 (despatches, DSO); War of 1939-45 (despatches). DL Kent, 1957; High Sheriff of Kent, 1959-60. OStJ. Chief Comdr, Legion of Merit (USA). *Address:* The Beck, Wateringbury, Kent. *T:* Maidstone 812566. *[Died* 12 *March* 1978.

MOORE, Miss Jocelyn Adelaide Medway, (Mrs David Symon), FRCS; FRCOG; retired; Professor of Obstetrics and Gynæcology, Ahmadu Bello University Hospital, Zaria, Nigeria, 1969-73; Hon. Consultant Obstetrician and Gynæcologist, Royal Free Hospital; Emeritus Consultant, South London Hospital for Women; *b* 29 Aug. 1904; *e d* of Maj.-Gen. Sir John Moore, KCMG, CB, FRCVS; *m* 1941, David Symon (decd); no *c. Educ:* Wycombe Abbey Sch., Bucks; Royal Free Hospital School of Medicine. Served RAMC, 1941-45, as Specialist in Gynaecology, in the UK, Belgium and Germany. Mem. BMA; Mem. Medical Women's Fedn. *Address:* The Boot, 6 Upper Street, Quainton, Aylesbury, Bucks. *T:* Quainton 229. *[Died* 6 *Feb.* 1979.

MOORE, Kenneth Alfred Edgar, FCA; Director: National Mutual Life Assurance Society, 1935-70 (Chairman, 1941-69); St Austell Brewery Co. Ltd; Lymington Marina Ltd; *b* 30 Dec. 1894; *er s* of late Edgar Richardson Moore and Rose Salter, Barnet, Herts; *m* 1918, Doris (*d* 1966), *d* of late George Arthur Edell; one *s* three *d. Educ:* Highgate Sch. Served European War, HAC and Middlesex Regt. Partner in firm of Edward Moore & Sons, Chartered Accountants, 1921-36; Chm., Trinidad Petroleum Development Co. Ltd, 1937-54; Dep. Chm., Ranks, Hovis-McDougall, 1962-64 (Chm., 1935-57, McDougalls Trust Ltd, merged with Hovis Ltd, 1957; Chm., 1957-64, Hovis-McDougall Ltd). Mem. Council, Inst. of Chartered Accountants, 1951-56. Inventor, Sestrel-Moore Compass, and other navigational equipment. *Publication:* (with Michael Moore, FCA) Company Accounts and Balance Sheets, 1931. *Recreations:* fishing, sailing. *Address:* West Timber, Bucklers Hard, Beaulieu, Hants. *T:* Bucklers Hard 237. *Clubs:* Royal Yacht Squadron (Cowes); Royal Cruising; Royal Lymington Yacht. *[Died* 25 *July* 1976.

MOORE, Marianne Craig; *b* St Louis, Mo, 15 Nov. 1887; *d* of John Milton Moore and Mary (*née* Warner). *Educ:* Bryn Mawr Coll.; Carlisle Commercial Coll. (Pa). Teacher, Carlisle US Indian Sch., 1911-15; Asst, NY Public Libr., 1921-25; Actg Ed., The Dial, 1925-29. Guggenheim Memorial Foundn Fellowship, 1945; Bollingen Prize in Poetry, 1952; Pulitzer Prize in Verse, 1952; Nat. Medal for Literature, 1968, etc. Holds several hon. doctorates, incl. LittD: Washington Univ., St Louis, 1967; New York Univ., 1967; Harvard, 1969. *Publications:* Poems, 1921; Observations, 1924; Selected Poems, 1935; The Pangolin and Other Verse, 1936; What Are Years?, 1941; Nevertheless, 1944; Collected Poems, 1951; The Fables of La Fontaine (trans.), 1954; Predilections, 1955; Like a Bulwark, 1956; O to be a Dragon, 1959; A Marianne Reader, 1961; The Arctic Ox, 1965;

Tell me, Tell me, 1966; The Complete Poems of Marianne Moore, 1968; Selected Poems, 1969. *Address:* 7b 35 West 9th Street, New York City, NY 10011, USA. *[Died 5 Feb. 1972.*

MOORE, Lt-Col Sir Thomas (Cecil Russell), 1st Bt *cr* 1956; Kt 1937; CBE 1920 (OBE 1918); Chairman, Sarakan Products Ltd; *b* 16 Sept. 1886; *y s* of John Watt Moore, Fintona, Co. Tyrone, and Mary, *d* of late Alexander Kirkpatrick, Closeburn Castle, Dumfriesshire; *m* 1925, Jean (*d* 1945), *yr d* of late William Gemmill, Glasgow, and *widow* of John Hislop Pettigrew, Glasgow; *m* 1950, Penelope, *widow* of R. L. Angus, Ladykirk, Monkton, Ayrshire. *Educ:* Portora Royal Sch.; Trinity Coll., Dublin. Joined Regular Army, 1908; served in France, 1914; on General Headquarters Staff in Ireland, 1916-18; in Russia, 1918-20; in Ireland, 1920-23 (Brevet Major, OBE, Order of White Eagle of Serbia, 4th Class, St Anne of Russia, 2nd Class, St Vladimir of Russia, 4th Class, Hungarian Order of Merit, 2nd class, CBE, despatches twice); retired from Regular Army, 1925; contested (U) Coatbridge Div. of Lanarkshire, 1924; MP (U) Ayr Burgh, 1925-50, Ayr Div. of Ayrshire and Bute, 1950-64. Has sponsored nine Acts of Parliament, including Slaughter of Animals Act and Architects Registration Act. Chm. Home Guard Joint Parly Cttee for both Houses of Parliament during entire period that HG existed during War. Vice-Pres., RSPCA; Trustee, International League for the Protection of Horses; Chm. Anglo-Italian Soc. for the Protection of Animals; Chm. Anglo-Hungarian Fellowship; associated with all leading animal protection socs in this country. Formerly Chm., Eastwoods Ltd and subsids. FRGS; Freeman of City of London; Hon. ARIBA; Past Master Needlemakers' Company. *Recreations:* books, golf. *Address:* 87 Harley House, Regent's Park, NW1. *T:* 01-935 7317; Bogside House, Monkton, Ayrshire. *T:* Prestwick 7417. *Clubs:* St James', Carlton, Garrick; Conservative (Glasgow); County (Ayr).   *[Died 9 April 1971 (ext).*

MOORE, Sir William Samson, 2nd Bt, *cr* 1932; *b* 17 April 1891; *s* of Rt Hon. Sir William Moore, 1st Bt, PC, LLD, DL, JP; *S* father, 1944; *m* 1915, Ethel (Grig) (*d* 1973), *d* of W. L. Wheeler, Lennoxvale, Belfast; one *s* (one *d* decd). *Educ:* RNA, Gosport; Marlborough. Served European War, 1914-18. High Sheriff, Co. Antrim, 1944. DL, JP, Co. Antrim. *Heir: s* William Roger Clotworthy Moore, TD [*b* 17 May 1927; *m* 1954, Gillian, *d* of John Brown, Co. Antrim; one *s* one *d. Educ:* Marlborough. High Sheriff, Co. Antrim, 1964]. *Address:* Moore Lodge, Ballymoney, Northern Ireland. *T:* Kilrea 322.   *[Died 27 July 1978.*

MOOS, Sorab Nanabhoy, CIE 1943; MA Cantab; FRSA; IES (retired); *b* 25 Sept. 1890; *s* of Dr N. A. F. Moos, DSc (Edinburgh), FRSE; *m* 1916, Makee Petit; two *s* one *d. Educ:* Elphinstone Coll., Bombay; King's Coll., Cambridge. Professor Mathematics and Physics, Victoria Jubilee Technical Coll., 1915-18; Inspector of Schs, 1918-32; Dep. Dir Public Instruction, 1932-39; Dir, Public Instruction, Bombay Province, 1939-45; Mem. Public Service Commission, Bombay-Sind, 1946-47. *Publications:* various articles and reports on Education. *Recreations:* golf, tennis. *Address:* Emsworth, Pali Hill, Bandra, Bombay, India. *T:* Bombay 534003. *Clubs:* Poona, Turf Club of Western India (Poona); Ripon, Willingdon (Bombay).
                                        [Died 16 Dec. 1974.

MORAN, 1st Baron, *cr* 1943, of Manton; **Charles McMoran Wilson,** Kt 1938; MC; Consulting Physician, St Mary's Hospital; *b* Skipton-in-Gaven, Yorks, 10 Nov. 1882; *s* of John Forsythe Wilson, MD; *m* 1919, Dorothy, MBE, *d* of late Dr S. F. Dufton; two *s.* MD London (Gold Medal), 1913; Formerly: Mem. of Senate and Hon. Sec. Faculty of Medicine, Univ. of London; Examiner in Medicine, Univs of Cambridge and Birmingham; Consultant Adviser, Ministry of Health; Chm. Advisory Cttee on Distinction Awards for Consultants. Mem., Association of Physicians; Fellow of Royal Society of Medicine; Mem., Med. Soc. of London and of Harveian Soc.; Medical Officer attached 1st Batt. Royal Fusiliers, 1914-17; Medical Officer i/c medical side, 7th Stationary Hospital, Boulogne, 1917-18; Major RAMC (MC, Italian Silver Medal for Military Valour, despatches twice); Dean, St Mary's Hospital Medical Sch., 1920-45; Pres., Royal College of Physicians, 1941-50. Chm. Army Med. Advisory Bd. Hon. FRCPE; Hon. FFPSG; Hon. FACP; Hon. FRACP. *Publications:* The Anatomy of Courage, 1945; Winston Churchill, The Struggle for Survival, 1966; med. papers and articles on medical education. *Heir: s* Hon. (Richard) John (McMoran) Wilson, CMG. *Address:* Newton Valence Manor, near Alton, Hants. *T:* Tisted 336.
                                        [Died 12 April 1977.

MORAN, Prof. Frances Elizabeth; Regius Professor of Laws, Trinity College, Dublin, 1944-63, retired; Professor of Equity Pleading and Practice, King's Inns, Dublin, 1932-68, retired; Professorial Representative on Board of Trinity College, 1958-

62; Senior Counsel; Past President, International Federation of University Women; *b* Dublin, 6 Dec. 1893; 2nd *d* of late Senator James and late Elizabeth Moran, St James', Clontarf, Dublin; unmarried. *Educ:* Dominican Coll. and Trinity Coll., Dublin. Called to Bar, 1924; took silk, 1941; Reid Prof. in Law Sch., Trinity Coll., 1925-30; Lecturer in Law, 1930-34; Prof. of Laws, 1934-44; Hon. Fellow, 1968. Hon. Bencher, King's Inns, 1969. Hon. LLD, Queen's Univ., Belfast, 1957. *Recreations:* walking, reading, and foreign travel. *Address:* St James', Howth Road, Clontarf, Dublin 3. *T:* 339516.   *[Died 7 Oct. 1977.*

MORAN, Joseph Michael, CB 1978; QC (Scot.) 1976; Legal Secretary to the Lord Advocate and First Parliamentary Draftsman for Scotland since 1976; *b* 27 June 1925; *s* of late Michael Moran and Catherine Stevenson; *m* 1959, Margaret, *d* of late John Barry, Sugarstown House, Co. Kilkenny; one *s* two *d. Educ:* St Aloysius' Coll., Glasgow; Holy Cross Acad., Edinburgh; Univ. of Edinburgh (MA 1945, LLB (with distinction) 1947). Admitted to Faculty of Advocates and called to Scottish Bar, 1948; entered Lord Advocate's Dept, 1949. Dep. Legal Sec. to Lord Advocate, 1969-76. *Recreations:* reading, bridge, golf. *Address:* 1 Coombe Gardens, West Wimbledon, SW20 0QU. *T:* 01-946 7421.   *[Died 21 Oct. 1978.*

MORAND, Paul; *b* Paris, 1889; *m* Helen Chrissoveloni. *Educ:* in Paris; Oxford Univ. In Diplomacy, 1912-44 (France); Secretary of Embassy in London, 1913-16; Rome, 1917-18; Madrid, 1918-20; French Chargé d'Affaires in Bangkok, 1925; French Commissioner on the Danube, 1938; Head of French Mission in England of Economic Warfare, Sept. 1939; Minister Plenipotentiary in London, 1940; Minister at Bucarest, 1943; Ambassador at Berne, 1944; started a literary career in 1920. Mem., Académie Française, 1968. *Publications:* Poems (1919-21), repr. 1973; Green Shoots, 1922; Open all Night, 1923; Closed all Night, 1924; Europe at love, 1925; Lewis and Irene, 1926; A Frenchman's London, 1933; Bucarest, 1935; L'Homme pressé, 1941; Life of Maupassant, 1942; Montociel, 1945; Journal d'un attaché d'ambassade, 1948, repr. 1970; The Flagellant of Seville, 1951; Fouquet, 1961; The New London, 1962; The Habsburg, 1963; Tais-toi, 1965; Nouvelles des yeux, Nouvelles du cœur, 1965; Sophie de Celle, 1968; Venises, 1971; Les écarts amoureux, 1975. *Posthumous publication:* L'Allure de Chanel, 1976. *Relevant publication:* Morand, by M. Schneider, 1972. *Address:* Château de l'Aile, Vevey, Switzerland. *Club:* Automobile of France. *[Died 27 Feb. 1975.*

MORAY, 19th Earl of, *cr* 1561; **Archibald John Morton Stuart;** Lord Abernethy and Strathearn, 1562; Lord Doune, 1581; Baron of St Colme, 1611; Baron Stuart (G. Brit.), 1796; *b* 14 Nov. 1894; 2nd *s* of 17th Earl and Edith Douglas (*d* 1945), *d* of late Rear-Adm. George Palmer; *S* brother 1943; *m* 1922, Mabel Helen Maud Wilson (*d* 1968); three *s* (one *d* decd). *Educ:* RNC Osborne and Dartmouth. Entered RN 1907; Lieut-Comdr (retired) 1923. Lived and farmed in Bechuanaland Protectorate, 1923-43. *Heir: s* Lord Doune. *Address:* Darnaway Castle, Forres, Morayshire. *T:* Forres 2101. *Clubs:* White's, Naval and Military; New (Edinburgh); Rand (Johannesburg).
                                        [Died 27 March 1974.

MORAY WILLIAMS, Barbara, ARE, ARCA; **(Frú Barbara Arnason)**; Artist; *b* Petersfield, Hants, 19 April, 1911; *d* of A. Moray Williams, OBE, MA, and Mabel Lizzie Williams; *m* 1937, Magnús A. Arnason, artist; one *s. Educ:* Privately. *Address:* Kopavogi, Iceland. *T:* Reykjavik 40218.
                                        [Died 30 Dec. 1975.

MORDAUNT, Lt-Col Sir Nigel John, 13th Bt, *cr* 1611; MBE 1945; RA; Member of London Stock Exchange, since 1929; *b* 9 May 1907; *e s* of late E. C. Mordaunt and Cicely Marion, 2nd *d* of Henry Tubb; *S* uncle 1939; *m* 1938, Anne, *d* of late Arthur F. Tritton, Denford Mill, Hungerford, Berks; three *s* one *d. Educ:* Wellington Coll.; Christ Church, Oxford. Served War of 1939-45 (MBE). *Heir: s* Richard Nigel Charles Mordaunt [*b* 12 May 1940; *m* 1964, Myriam Atchia; one *s* one *d*]. *Address:* Elsenham Place, Bishops Stortford, Herts. *T:* Stansted 2344. *Clubs:* City of London, Buck's.   *[Died 4 Aug. 1979.*

MORDELL, Louis Joel, MA Cantab; MSc Manchester; FRS; Emeritus Professor of Pure Mathematics in the University of Cambridge (Sadleirian Professor of Pure Mathematics, 1945-53); Fellow of St John's College since 1945; *b* Philadelphia, Pa, USA, 28 Jan. 1888; *m* ; one *s* one *d. Educ:* Central High Sch., Philadelphia; St John's Coll., Cambridge. Formerly lecturer at Birkbeck Coll., London, and lecturer and reader in Mathematics at Manchester Univ.; Visiting Prof. at Chicago Univ., Summer Term, 1923, and at Univ. of Pennsylvania, Fall Term, 1950; Fielden Prof. of Pure Mathematics in the Univ. of Manchester, 1923-45; Lecturer at Summer Seminar of Canadian Math.

Congress, Toronto, 1947; Visiting Prof., Univ. of Toronto, 1953-55; Visiting Lecturer, Italian Internat. summer course, Varenna, Lake Como, 1955; Visiting Prof., Univ. Coll. of Ghana, 1957. Nuffield Visiting Professor: University Coll., Ibadan, 1957, Mount Allison Univ., NB, Canada, 1958-59; Visiting Professor: Colorado Univ., 1959-60; Notre Dame Univ., 1960-61; Univ. of Arizona, from 1961 to Spring Semester, 1964; Univ. of Illinois, 1964-65; Catholic Univ. of America, 2nd Semester, 1965-66; Waterloo Univ., Ontario (2nd Semester), 1966-67, 1969; Univ. of Toronto, 1st Semester, 1968-69; Calgary Univ., 1970-71. In recent years has lectured in maths at 190 Univs and Instns in Europe, India, E and W Africa, Canada and USA; De Morgan Medal, 1941, and Berwick Prize, 1946, London Mathematical Soc. Pres. London Mathematical Soc., 1943-45; Sylvester Medal of the Royal Soc., 1949. Foreign member: Norwegian Academy of Science at Oslo; Academy of Science at Bologna; Acad. of Science at Uppsala. Hon. LLD Glasgow, 1956; Hon. DSc Mount Allison Univ., 1959; Hon. DMath Waterloo Univ., 1970. *Publications:* Three Lectures on Fermat's Last Theorem, 1921; A Chapter on the Theory of Numbers, 1947; Reflections of a Mathematician, 1958; Diophantine Equations, 1969; numerous papers on the Theory of Numbers and allied subjects in many math. jls. *Recreations:* walking, swimming, and bridge. *Address:* St John's College, Cambridge; 1 Bulstrode Gardens, Madingley Road, Cambridge. *T:* Cambridge 54281. *Club:* Athenæum.
[Died 12 March 1972.

MOREING, Captain Algernon Henry; formerly partner in Bewick, Moreing & Co., mining engineers, London; *b* 30 Sept. 1889; *s* of late Charles Algernon Moreing and Helena Marian, *d* of Edward Harcourt Longden, HEICS; *m* 1925, Dorothy Maude, *er d* of late J. Holman, JP, of Roswarne, Camborne. *Educ:* Winchester; Trinity Coll., Cambridge, MA. Captain RA (TA); served in France, 1915-18 (despatches); MP (Coalition L) Buckrose Div. of Yorks, Dec. 1918-22; (NL) Camborne Div. of Cornwall, 1922-23; (Constitutional) Camborne, 1924-29; Parliamentary Private Sec. to Rt Hon. Sir Eric Geddes, Minister of Transport, 1920; recalled for military duty, 1940. Past-Master of the Merchant Taylors' Company. *Address:* Fysh House, Bures, Suffolk. *T:* Bures 324. *[Died 22 Oct. 1974.*

MORGAN, Arthur Eustace, MA; Hon. LLD; FRSC; Warden, Toynbee Hall, 1954-63; Chairman, Purimachos, Ltd, 1956-70; President, The National Boys' Club, 1963-65; *b* Bristol, 26 July 1886; 5th *s* of John Charles Morgan, of HBM Consular Service, and Elizabeth Reid Livingstone-Learmonth; *m* 1909, Mabel Eugénie, *d* of Thomas Walter Warren Melhuish; four *d*. *Educ:* University Coll., Bristol; Trinity Coll., Dublin. Asst Lectr, Univ. of Bristol, 1909-10; Lectr in English Language and Literature, University Coll., Exeter, 1910-19; Professor, 1919-24; Professor of English Language and Literature, Univ. of Sheffield, 1924-26; Principal of the University Coll., Hull, 1926-35; Principal and Vice-Chancellor of McGill Univ., Montreal, 1935-37; Chief Special Officer for National Service, Ministry of Labour, 1939; District Commissioner for the Special Areas (Durham and Tyneside) 1939; Regional Information Officer, Ministry of Information, Newcastle on Tyne, 1939-41; Asst Sec., Ministry of Labour and National Service, 1941-45; Educational Controller, British Council, 1945-50; RA, 1915-19; Captain, Gunnery Instructor No 2 RFA Cadet Sch. (despatches). Has lectured in many parts of the world. *Publications:* Scott and his Poetry; Tendencies of Modern English Drama; First Part of Henry IV, Arden Edition of Shakespeare (with R. P. Cowl); English Plays, 1660-1820; The Needs of Youth (Report to King George's Jubilee Trust), 1939; Young Citizen, 1943; sundry literary and educational pamphlets, papers and articles. *Recreations:* reading, playing with great-grandchildren. *Address:* 34 Downs Park West, Bristol 6. *T:* 626009. *[Died 3 Feb. 1972.*

MORGAN, David Loftus, CMG 1952; MBE 1943; *b* 21 Nov. 1904; *s* of late George Morgan, CIE; *m* 1929, Phyllis Douglas Russell; one *d*. *Educ:* Harrow; Trinity Coll., Cambridge. District Officer, Kenya, 1926: Dep. Provincial Commissioner, 1945; Provincial Commissioner, 1947-51; Resident Commissioner, Swaziland, 1951-56, retired. Member: Swaziland Railway Board, 1961-74; Swaziland Public Service Commission, 1963-69. Dir of cos. *Recreation:* golf. *Address:* PO Box 84, Mhlambanyati, Swaziland. *Clubs:* Caledonian; Nairobi (Kenya). *[Died 8 July 1976.*

MORGAN, Rt. Rev. Edmund Robert, DD; resigned as Bishop of Truro (1951-60. 1959); *b* London, 28 July 1888; *s* of Joseph John Morgan, solicitor, and Adelaide Holberton; *m* 1916, Isabel Charlotte (*d* 1964), *y d* of Joseph Jupp of Mowbray House, Malvern; one *s* (and two who died in the war). *Educ:* Winchester; New Coll., Oxford; Liverpool Univ. (Dip. in Educn). Curate, Farnham, 1913-15; Eastleigh, 1915-19; Domestic Chaplain to Bishop Talbot of Winchester, 1919-23;

Warden, Coll. of the Ascension, Selly Oak, Birmingham, 1923-36; Rector of Old Alresford, 1936-42; Archdeacon of Winchester, 1936-43; Suffragan Bishop of Southampton, 1943-51; Canon of Winchester Cathedral, 1942-51. DD (Lambeth) 1955. Editor, The East and West Review, 1935-46. *Publications:* (ed) Essays Catholic and Missionary, 1928; The Catholic Revival and Missions, 1933; The Mission of the Church, 1946; (ed) The Mission of the Anglican Communion, 1948; The Undiscovered Country, 1962; Reginald Somerset Ward: A Memoir, 1963; The Ordeal of Wonder, 1964. *Recreations:* music, gardening, carpentry. *Address:* Moor Farm, Whiteparish, Salisbury, Wilts. *[Died 21 Sept. 1979.*

MORGAN, Hon. Sir Edward James Ranembe, Kt 1952; *b* Warwick, Queensland, 25 March 1900; *s* of Edward Ranembe Morgan, Adelaide, and Jean McMillan, *d* of John Brown, Culver Lodge, Much Hadham, Herts; *m* 1924, Dorothy Millar, *o c* of James Waite, MBE; two *s* one *d*. *Educ:* St Peter's Coll., Adelaide; The University of Adelaide (LLB). Called to South Australian Bar, 1921; Stipendiary Magistrate, Adelaide Police Court, 1934-41; Pres. of Industrial Court (South Australia), 1941-52; Judge of Commonwealth Court of Conciliation and Arbitration, 1952-56; Judge, Commonwealth Industrial Court, 1956-60; Judge, Supreme Court of Australian Capital Territory, 1958-60. Mem., Board of Trustees, Art Gallery of S Australia, 1940-44, and 1961-63, Chm., 1944-55, and 1963-70; Pres. Nat. Trust of S Australia, 1960-62; *Publications:* The Adelaide Club, 1863-1963; (with S. H. Gilbert) Victorian Adelaide, 1968; (with S. H. Gilbert) Early Adelaide Architecture, 1969. *Address:* 155 Kermode Street, North Adelaide, SA 5006, Australia. *Clubs:* Adelaide (Adelaide), Melbourne (Melbourne).
[Died 11 Sept. 1977.

MORGAN, Col Farrar Robert Horton, DSO 1940; OBE 1946; late Border Regiment; *b* 12 Sept. 1893; *e s* of late Robert Upton Morgan, MBE; *m* 1st, 1915, Alice Winifred May (*d* 1955), *d* of late Thomas R. Cross; two *s* two *d*; 2nd, 1957, Frances Maud (*d* 1977), 4th *d* of late Harold and Ida Blackborow and *widow* of Sidney Turner. *Educ:* University Coll. Sch.; Sch. of Oriental Studies, London Univ. First commissioned, 1914, Border Regt; served in France, 1915-16 (despatches, 1915 Star, British War and Victory Medals); King's African Rifles, E Africa, 1917-24; Somaliland, 1920 (Medal and Clasp); Adjt Glasgow and Aberdeen Univs OTC, 1931-35; Lt-Col 1940; Col, 1941; served in China, 1927; Palestine, 1937-39 (Medal and Clasp); war of 1939-45, France, 1939-40 (despatches, DSO); Comd British Troops in Syria, 1944-46 (OBE); retired pay, 1946. Syrian Order of Merit (1st Class). Principal Control Officer, Germany, 1946-49. *Recreation:* painting. *Address:* Greystones, Bath Road, Bradford-on-Avon, Wilts. *T:* Bradford-on-Avon 3418.
[Died 31 May 1978.

MORGAN, Sir Frank William, Kt 1948; MC; President, Prudential Assurance Co. Ltd, 1965-70; *b* 23 June 1887; *o s* of Alfred and Mary Anne Morgan; *m* 1926, Beatrice Agnes (*d* 1973), *widow* of Frederick Christian Dietrichsen, Barrister; no *c*. *Educ:* Parmiter's Sch. Since 1903 with Prudential Assurance Co.; Manager for India, Burma and Ceylon, 1928-33; Man. for Near East, 1933-34; Gen. Man., Prudential Assurance Co. Ltd, 1941-50, Dir, 1950-53, Chm., 1953-65. Served European War, 1914-18 with Hon. Artillery Company (A Battery), and Royal Field Artillery-commanded 99th Battery RFA (MC). *Recreations:* gardening and fishing. *Address:* Hyde Heath Farm, near Amersham, Bucks. *T:* Chesham 3028. *Club:* Oriental.
[Died 21 April 1974.

MORGAN, His Honour H(opkin) Trevor; *see* Morgan, His Honour Trevor.

MORGAN, Capt. Horace Leslie, CMG 1931; DSO 1920; RN, retired; *b* 1888; *s* of Capt. H. H. Morgan, RMLI; *m* 1933, Kathleen Hilda, *o d* of late M. G. Bellhouse and of Mrs Hunter, wife of Lt-Col C. F. Hunter, DSO; three *s*. Served European War, 1914-19 (despatches, DSO); received thanks New Zealand Government for services during the earthquake at Napier (CMG); retired list, 1934. Served War of 1939-45 as a Sea Transport Officer. *Address:* Century Field, Bay View Road, Northam, N Devon. *[Died 30 July 1973.*

MORGAN, James Conwy, CMG 1966; HM Diplomatic Service, retired; *b* 16 April 1910; *e s* of late Dr Conwy Llewellyn Morgan, MD, and of Mary Morgan (*née* Cowtan); *m* 1933, Cicely Mary Norman Cobb; one *s* two *d*. *Educ:* Malvern Coll.; Brasenose Coll., Oxford. Cadet, Colonial Service, Tanganyika, 1934; Asst District Officer, 1936 (DO *in absentia*), 1946). Commissioned SR of O, The Royal Sussex Regiment, 1930; subseq. RARO and KAR, RO; called up Sept. 1939, 2/6 KAR (Tanganyika); subseq. Brit. Mil. Admin., Somalia, 1941; Major and GSO 2,

1942 (despatches); Lt-Col and Sen. Civil Affairs Officer, 1945; demob. 1947; cont. in RARO, Major, until retd as Lt-Col, 1958. Transf. from Colonial to Home CS, 1947. Colonial Office: Principal; Asst Sec., 1955; att. to Monckton Commn, 1960; transf. to CRO, 1962; Chief of Staff to Chm. of Dissolution Cttee A, in Salisbury, SR, 1963; Head of Medit. Dept, CRO, 1964; Asst Under-Sec. of State, 1965; British Dep. High Comr, Canberra, 1966-67; Asst Under-Sec. of State, Dependent Territories Div., CO, 1967-68, FCO, 1968-70, retired 1970. Conducted Review Body of Professional and Administrative Salary Scales, Hong Kong, 1970; Adviser to Hong Kong Salaries Comr, 1971; Tech. Assistance Advr, Biennial Pay Review, Gibraltar, 1972; Chm., Working Gp, Certificated Masters Pay Scale, Hong Kong, 1972; Foreign Secretary's Rep. on Hong Kong Govt London Selection Bd for Police Inspectors, 1974-; Independent Comr on Top Salaries, Gibraltar, Oct.-Dec. 1975. *Recreations:* walking, reading, golf. *Address:* Oak Bank, Ashurst, near Tunbridge Wells, Kent. *T:* Fordcombe 388.
[Died 24 June 1977.

MORGAN, Col Kevern Ivor, CBE 1955 (OBE 1934); Chartered Accountant since 1924; Director of Companies; *b* 22 Sept. 1894; *s* of William Morgan, Wolfs Castle, Pembs; *m* 1954, Claudia Jean, *er d* of late Capt. Charles Trueman, MN, Barry Island, Glamorgan; no *c*. *Educ:* Dynevor Gram. Sch.; Swansea Tech. Coll. Served with RAPC (UK), 1939-47. Hon. Col 108 (Welsh) Field Engineer Regt, 1955-59. Chairman: Whole Body of Swansea Justices; Swansea Licensing Magistrates; Swansea Licensing Planning Cttee; Swansea Coun., Order of St John; Minister's Appointee, Swansea Health Service Exec. Coun. (Chm. Med. Service Cttee and Dental Service Cttee); Mem. Management Cttee, Trustees of Swansea Savings Bank. High Sheriff of Breconshire, 1958; JP Swansea, 1939. CStJ. *Recreations:* fishing, shooting. *Address:* 15 Hawthorne Avenue, Uplands, Swansea. *T:* 56218. *Club:* Ffynone (Swansea).
[Died 14 July 1971.

MORGAN, Montagu Travers, CMG 1949; MC; MD; *b* 14 Nov. 1889; *s* of Llewellyn A. Morgan, MD, and Dorothy (*née* Hankin); *m* 1914, Maud Elizabeth Bateman (*d* 1949); two *s*; *m* 1949, Marguerite Juliette Félicie Jolly. *Educ:* Liverpool Coll. and Univ. Resident MO City Fever Hosp., Liverpool; Dep. County MOH and Tuberculosis Officer, Herefordshire; RAMC 1915-18 (despatches, MC); County MOH, Pembs; Medical Officer, Board of Education; Medical Officer, Ministry of Health; MOH, Port of London, 1938-54; formerly Pres., International Health Office, Paris; mem. expert Commissions on Mecca Pilgrimage and quarantine, World Health Organisation. Officer, Légion d'Honneur, 1948. Smith Award, 1949. *Publications:* Numerous contributions, reports, etc, to Government Depts; Ergot Poisoning in Rye Bread (Jl Hyg. 1929); (Jointly) Epidemic Jaundice, Min. of Health Medical Series, 1927. *Recreation:* fishing. *Address:* Brandy Mount House, Alresford, Hants. *T:* Alresford 2189.
[Died 17 June 1974.

MORGAN, Sir Morien Bedford, Kt 1969; CB 1958; MA; FRS 1972, CEng, Hon. FRAeS; Master, Downing College, Cambridge, since 1972; *b* 20 Dec. 1912; *s* of late John Bedford and Edith Mary Morgan, Bridgend, Glam; *m* 1941, Sylvia Axford; three *d*. *Educ:* Rutlish, Merton; St Catharine's Coll., Cambridge (Hon. Fellow, 1973). John Bernard Seely Prize in Aeronautics, 1934; apprenticed to Mather & Platt Ltd, 1934-35; joined Aerodynamics Dept, Royal Aircraft Establishment, 1935, and for some years was engaged on flight research and develt, specialising in problems of aircraft stability and control. Pilot's "A" licence, 1944. Head of Aero. Flight Section, RAE, 1946-48. Head of Guided Weapons Dept, RAE, 1948-53; Dep. Dir, RAE, 1954-59; Scientific Adviser, Air Ministry, 1959-60; Dep. Controller of Aircraft (R&D), Min. of Aviation, 1960-63; Controller of Aircraft, 1963-66; Controller of Guided Weapons and Electronics, Min. of Technology, 1966-69; Dir, RAE, 1969-72. Member: Airworthiness Requirements Bd, 1973-; Air Warfare Adv. Bd, 1974-; PO Bd (part time), 1975-77. Chm., Air Traffic Control Bd, 1975-; Pres., Royal Aeronautical Society, 1967-68, Hon. Fellow, 1976. Founder Fellow, Fellowship of Engineering, 1976. Hon. DSc: Cranfield, 1976; Southampton, 1976. Silver Medal of the Royal Aeronautical Society, 1957, Gold Medal 1971, Busk Prize 1972. *Publications:* Reports and Memoranda of Aeronautical Research Council. Lectures to Royal Aeronautical Society. *Recreation:* music. *Address:* The Master's Lodge, Downing College, Cambridge. *T:* Cambridge 56338. *Club:* Athenæum.
[Died 4 April 1978.

MORGAN, Paul Robert James, CIE 1947; retired; *b* 1 Feb. 1898; *s* of late W. A. Morgan of the Stock Exchange, and of late Mrs W. A. Morgan, Nice, France; *m* Beatrice Helen Carteret, *o d* of late Lt-Col Hugh Stewart, CIE, Indian Political Dept, and late

Mrs D. M. Stewart, Tunbridge Wells, Kent; two *d* (one *s* decd). *Educ:* Sherborne. Commissioned Sept. 1914 with RE (TF); served in Gallipoli, France and Belgium; transferred to 3/8 Gurkha Rifles, Indian Army, 1917 (Captain). Entered India Police, 1920, and attached to Punjab. Had various district appointments; posted to Provincial Additional Police, 1929-32 and 1939-47, as Commandant Provincial Additional Police, Punjab. Indian Police Medal, 1934. *Recreations:* shooting, tennis, golf. *Address:* Fairway, Headland Avenue, Seaford, Sussex. *T:* Seaford 893934.
[Died 19 June 1974.

MORGAN, His Honour Trevor, MC; QC 1936; DL; JP County of Glamorgan; MA, LLB; County Court Judge, Circuit No 31, 1948-64, retired; Chairman Carmarthenshire QS, 1951-66; retired; Deputy Chairman Glamorgan Quarter Sessions, 1948-59; *b* 19 June 1892; *s* of Hopkin Morgan, JP, and Sarah Morgan, Pontypridd; *m* 1932, Leslie, *d* of Col W. D. Phillips, TD, Llwydcoed, Aberdare; two *s*. *Educ:* Mill Hill Sch.; Gonville and Caius Coll., Cambridge. Served War, 1914-19, with 5 Bn The Welch Regt and 1 Bn The Wiltshire Regt (despatches). Called to Bar, Inner Temple, 1920. Chm. of Council, University Coll. of Swansea, 1966-70, Vice-Pres., 1969. Hon. LLD Univ. of Wales, 1975. DL Glamorgan, 1958. *Address:* Pilgrim Cottage, Brynfield Road, Langland, Swansea. *Club:* Glamorgan County (Cardiff).
[Died 25 Oct. 1976.

MORGAN, Gen. Sir William Duthie, GCB 1949 (KCB 1945; CB 1944); DSO 1919; MC; Hon. LLD (Edinburgh); *b* Dec. 1891; *s* of late Alexander Morgan, OBE, MA, LLD, DSc, Edinburgh; *m* 1921, Amy (*d* 1976), *d* of Cromwell Varley of the Manor House, Chislehurst; one *s* one *d*. Served European War, 1914-19 (despatches, MC, DSO, Belgian Croix de Guerre); Waziristan, 1922-23; Military Attaché, Budapest, 1929-31; Chief Instructor RM Academy, 1934-38; served in France, 1939-40, as Regimental Comdr and GSO 1 1st Div.; BGS 1st Corps, 1940; Comdr 55 Div. 1941; Chief of General Staff, Home Forces, 1942-43; GOC-in-C Southern Command, 1944; Chief of Staff to Supreme Allied Comdr, Mediterranean, 1945; Supreme Allied Comdr, Mediterranean Theatre, 1945-47; Comdr, British Army Staff, Washington, and Army Mem. of Joint Staff Mission, 1947-50; retired 1950. Col Comdt RA, 1947-56. Chairman: Siemens Brothers & Co. Ltd, London, 1953-57; Gloucester Railway Carriage & Wagon Co. Ltd, 1957-62. DL County of London, (later Greater London), 1958-76, Vice-Lieutenant, Co. London 1958, Greater London 1965-70. *Address:* c/o Lloyds Bank Ltd, Cox's and King's Branch, 6 Pall Mall, SW1. *Club:* Carlton.
[Died 13 May 1977.

MORGAN, William Matheson, CMG 1971; Managing Director of Western Mining Corporation Ltd, 1962-71; *b* 9 Nov. 1906; *s* of late Alexander M. Morgan and Myrtle E. Morgan (*née* Green); *m* 1935, Agnes M. Davis; two *s*. *Educ:* Geelong Grammar Sch., Victoria; Adelaide Univ. Bachelor of Engrg (Civil) 1930. RAAF, Airfield Construction Units, 1942-44 (Flt-Lt). State Electricity Commn of Victoria: Engr i/c Brown Coal Investigation, 1945-49; i/c Coal Production, 1949-56; Gen. Manager, Western Mining Corp., 1957-62. Director: Alcoa of Australia Ltd, 1962; Gold Mines of Kalgoorlie (Aust.) Ltd, 1956; Central Norseman Gold Corp. NL, 1965. Pres., Australian Mining Industry Council, 1970. *Recreations:* fishing, ski-ing, golf. *Address:* 6 Kenley Court, Toorak, Victoria 3142, Australia. *T:* 20-1501. *Clubs:* Melbourne, Australian, Royal Melbourne Golf (Melbourne); Weld (Perth); Adelaide (Adelaide); Commonwealth (Canberra).
[Died 2 Feb. 1972.

MORISON, Lt-Col John, CIE 1932; MB, ChB, DPH, FRS Edinburgh; IMS (retired); *b* 6 Nov. 1879; *s* of Donald Morison, MD, EP, Mission, Rajshahi, Bengal; *m* 1907, Annie Macdonald, *d* of late Hugh Maclean, Glasgow. *Educ:* High Sch., Glasgow; George Watson's Coll., Edinburgh; Glasgow Univ. House Surgeon, Western Infirmary, Glasgow; Asst Medical Officer, Lugar Iron Works; Asst Medical Officer, Asylums Board; entered Indian Medical Service, 1906; retired 1934; served European War (despatches); Research Dept of Government of India, 1912; Dir, King Edward VII Memorial Pasteur and Medical Research Institute, Shillong, Assam. *Publications:* papers on Enteric fever, Purification of Water Supplies, Bacteriophage in Cholera and Dysentery. *Recreation:* golf. *Address:* 13 Cluny Drive, Edinburgh, 10. *T:* 031-447 4676.
[Died 21 Feb. 1971.

MORISON, Sir Ronald (Peter), Kt 1960; QC (Scotland) 1936; MA; LLB; *b* 3 June 1900; *e s* of Rt Hon. Lord Morison, PC; *m* 1st, 1925, Frances Isabelle, *d* of Rt Hon. Lord Salvesen, PC; two *s* one *d*; 2nd, Johanna Maria Magdalena, *d* of late Peter Hoorweg, Capt. Netherlands Artillery. *Educ:* Winchester Coll.; Edinburgh Univ. (MA; LLB with distinction). Admitted to Scottish Bar, 1923; to English Bar, 1940; 2nd Lt Scots Guards,

Sept. 1940; Major, Deputy Judge Advocate, 1942; resumed civilian work in Aug. 1944; Sheriff of Inverness, Elgin and Nairn, 1944-45; Dean of the Faculty of Advocates, 1944-45. Mem. of Industrial Disputes Tribunal, 1944-54; Independent Chm., Executive Cttee of the British Iron and Steel Federation, 1955-62, Legal Consultant to Federation, 1962-67. Chairman: Departmental Cttee on the Probation Service, 1959-62; Commission of Inquiry into labour difficulties in the copper belt, N Rhodesia, 1962; Railway Staff National Tribunal, 1960; Police Arbitration Tribunal, 1956-73; Dep. Chm., Criminal Injuries Compensation Board, 1964. *Recreations:* fishing, golf. *Address:* Old Tudor, Iden, Rye, East Sussex. *T:* Iden 202. *Club:* White's. *[Died 11 Feb. 1976.*

MORISON, Samuel Eliot, FBA; Hon. LittD Oxford 1951; historian; Professor of History, Harvard University, 1925-55; served as Historian of Naval Operations with rank of Rear-Admiral in US Naval Reserve, 1942-51; *b* Boston, Mass, 9 July 1887; *s* of John H. Morison and Emily Eliot; *m* 1st, 1910, Elisabeth S. Greene (*d* 1945); three *d* (one *s* decd); 2nd, 1949, Priscilla Barton (*d* 1973). *Educ:* Harvard Univ. (AB 1908, PhD 1912, LittD); Ecole des Sciences Politiques, Paris, France. Harold Vyvyan Harmsworth Prof. of American History, Oxford Univ., 1922-25; Attaché, American Commission to Negotiate Peace, 1919; mem. Baltic Commission of Paris Conference, 1919; Jusserand Medal and Loubat Prize, 1938; Commodore of Harvard Columbus Expedition, 1939-40. Corresp. FBA, 1954. Fellow, Amer. Philos. Soc., FSA. Balzan Award, 1963; Presidential Medal of Freedom. *Publications:* Life and Letters of H. G. Otis, 1913; Maritime History of Massachusetts, 1921; Oxford History of the United States, 1927; Tercentennial History of Harvard University; (with H. S. Commager) Growth of the American Republic, 1950 (6th edn 1969); Admiral of the Ocean Sea: a Life of Christopher Columbus, 1942; Christopher Columbus, Mariner, 1955; History of US Naval Operations, World War II, 15 vols, 1947-62. American Contributions to Strategy of World War II, 1958; Paul Jones, a Sailor's Biography, 1960; One Boy's Boston, 1962; (with Mauricio Obregón) The Caribbean as Columbus Saw It, 1964; Vistas of History, 1964; Spring Tides, 1965; Oxford History of the American People, 1965; Old Bruin, the Life of Commodore M. C. Perry, 1967; H. G. Otis, Urbane Federalist, 1969; The European Discovery of America: the Northern Voyages, 1971; Samuel de Champlain, 1972; The European Discovery of America: the Southern Voyages, 1974. *Recreation:* sailing. *Address:* Good Hope, Northeast Harbor, Maine 04662, USA. *Club:* Athenæum. *[Died 15 May 1976.*

MORLAND, Sir Oscar Charles, GBE 1962; KCMG 1959 (CMG 1949); HM Ambassador to Japan, 1959-63, retired; *b* 23 March 1904; *s* of Harold John Morland, MA, FCA; *m* 1932, Alice, *d* of late Rt Hon. Sir F. O. Lindley, PC, GCMG; four *s. Educ:* Leighton Park Sch.; King's Coll., Cambridge. Joined HM Consular Service, 1927. Served in Japan, Manchuria, London. Under Sec., Cabinet Office, 1950-53; Ambassador to Indonesia, 1953-56; Asst Under-Sec., FO, 1956-59. Mem., Leeds Regional Hosp. Bd, 1965-74 (Chm. Mental Health and Geriatrics Cttee, 1972-74). *Address:* The High Hall, Thornton-le-Dale, Pickering, North Yorks. *T:* Thornton-le-dale 371. *Club:* Travellers'. *[Died 20 May 1980.*

MORLEY, Sir Alexander (Francis), KCMG 1959 (CMG 1955); CBE 1948; retired from HM Diplomatic Service; re-employed in Foreign and Commonwealth Office; *b* 6 Jan. 1908; *s* of late Arthur S. Morley, FRCS; *m* 1939, Hedy, *e d* of late Prof. Julius von Landesberger-Antburg, Vienna; one *d. Educ:* Rugby; Queen's Coll., Oxford. Appointed to India Office, 1930; Private Sec. to Parl. Under-Sec. of State, 1933-36; served in Burma Office, 1938-40 and again 1945-47; seconded to Min. of Aircraft Production, 1940-42; Economic Adviser to Lord Privy Seal, 1947-49; with Commonwealth Relations Office, 1949-65; Dep. High Comr for UK in New Zealand, 1950-52 (Actg High Comr March-Nov. 1951). Asst Under-Sec. of State, 1954; Dep. High Comr for UK, Calcutta, 1956-57; British High Commissioner in Ceylon, 1957-62; British High Commissioner in Jamaica, 1962-65; HM Ambassador to Hungary, 1965-67. *Publication:* The Harrap Opera Guide, 1970. *Address:* 47 Campden Hill Square, W8. *Club:* Travellers'. *[Died 19 Sept. 1971.*

MORLEY, Air Vice-Marshal George Henry, CB 1968; CBE 1961 (OBE 1944); Senior Consultant of the Royal Air Force, since 1966; RAF Senior Consultant in Plastic Surgery since 1950, in Surgery since 1966; *b* 22 Feb. 1907; *s* of late Dr G. F. Morley, Portsmouth, Hants; *m* 1944, Kathleen Joan Elizabeth, *d* of late Robin Green, Felmersham, Beds; one *s* one *d. Educ:* St Helen's Coll., Southsea; Middlesex Hosp., W1. MRCS, LRCP 1929; FRCS 1935. Hon. Surg. to the Queen, 1958. Pres., British Assoc. of Plastic Surgeons, 1961; Fellow, Assoc. of Surgeons of Gt

Britain and Ireland; Royal Society Medicine; Mem., British Club for Surgery of the Hand. First McIndoe Memorial Lecturer, Royal College of Surgeons of England, 1962; Ruscoe Clarke Memorial Lecturer, Birmingham, 1965. Hon. Member: Institute of Accident Surgery, Birmingham, 1965; Assoc. of Mil Surgeons, USA, 1949; Divisional Pres., Wendover Cadets Div., St John Ambulance Brigade, 1962. CStJ 1960. Lady Cade Medal, RCS, 1967. *Publications:* First Aid and Early Treatment of Burns in the Royal Air Force, 1957; several papers on plastic and general surgery, burns and hand injuries. *Address:* South Coombe, Wendover, Bucks. *T:* Wendover 3178. *Clubs:* Guinea Pig, Royal Air Force; Nuffield United Services Officers' (Portsmouth). *[Died 26 May 1971.*

MORLEY, John, ChM, FRCS; Captain RAMC (T); awarded Croix de Chevalier Legion of Honour for distinguished services in Gallipoli; Hon. Consulting Surgeon, Ancoats Hospital, Manchester, and Manchester Royal Infirmary; Consulting Surgeon for Children, St Mary's Hospital, Manchester; Professor of Surgery (Emeritus), Manchester University; Fellow, Association of Surgeons; Fellow (Hon. Member section of Surgery) Royal Society of Medicine. Ex-President, Manchester Medico-Legal Manchester Surgical, Manchester Medical and Manchester Pathological Societies; formerly External Expert Adviser in Surgery, London University; External Examiner in Surgery, Cambridge, Edinburgh, Birmingham and Durham Universities, etc; *s* of Rev. J. S. Morley, MA; *m* 1st, Mary O. Simon (decd), Stowmarket; two *s* one *d* (and one *s* decd); 2nd, Margaret Hyde Greg, Norcliffe Hall, Handforth. *Educ:* Bishop's Stortford Coll.; Manchester Univ. Formerly Hon. Surg., Ancoats Hosp. and Royal Manchester Children's Hospital; House Surg. and Surgical Registrar, Manchester Royal Infirmary, Demonstrator of Anatomy, and Lecturer in Clinical Anatomy, Manchester Univ.; Tom Jones Surgical Scholar; Ashby Memorial Scholar for Research in Diseases of Children; University Graduate Scholar; etc.; First Class Hons, Manchester Univ., MB, ChB Examination, 1908. *Publications:* Abdominal Pain, 1931; Abdominal Pain and Acute Abdominal Emergencies, Encyclopædia of Practical Medicine, 1936; Reviser, Surgical and Topographical Section, Morris's Anatomy; Jackson's Pericolic Membrane: Its Nature, Clinical Significance and Relation to Abnormal Mobility of the Proximal Colon, Lancet, 1913; Traumatic Intramuscular Ossification, British Medical Journal, 1913; (with N. Monk-Jones) Bishop's Stortford College, 1868-1968: a centenary chronicle, 1969; numerous other articles. *Recreations:* fishing and shooting. *Address:* Edenview, Langwathby, Penrith, Cumberland. *T:* Langwathby 210. *Club:* St James's (Manchester). *[Died 9 March 1974.*

MORO, Aldo; Prime Minister of Italy, 1963-68 and 1974-76; President, Christian Democrat Party, since 1976; *b* 23 Sept. 1916; *s* of Aida and Renato Moro. *Educ:* Bari University. Member: Italian Constituent Assembly, 1946; Co-ordination Cttee for drafting of new Constitution of Republic of Italy; elected to Chamber of Deputies, 1948, reelected 1953, 1958, 1963, 1968, 1976; Under-Sec. of State, Foreign Affairs, 1949; Pres., Christian Democrat Party Gp, Chamber of Deputies, 1953-55; Minister of Justice, 1955-57; Minister of Educn, 1957-59; Political Sec., Christian Democrat Party, 1959-63; Minister of Foreign Affairs, Italy: Dec. 1965-Feb. 1966; Aug. 1969-June 1972; July 1973-Oct. 1974; Chm., Council of Ministers of the Common Market, July-Dec. 1971; Pres., Foreign Affairs Commn, Chamber of Deputies, Italy, 1972-73. *Publications:* La capacità giuridica penale, 1939; Lo Stato, 1943; L'Antigiuridicità, 1947; Unita e pluralitá de reati, 1951. *Address:* Camera dei Deputati, Rome, Italy. *[Died 9 May 1978.*

MORRAH, Dermot Michael Macgregor, Arundel Herald Extraordinary, since 1953; *b* 26 April 1896; *er s* of late Herbert Arthur Morrah and late Alice Elise, *d* of Major C. A. Macgregor, RE; *m* 1923, Ruth, *er d* of late Willmott Houselander; two *d. Educ:* Winchester; New Coll., Oxford. Served European War in Royal Engineers, 1915-19. 1st class, Modern History, 1921; MA 1921; Fellow of All Souls Coll., 1921-28; FRHistS, 1922-57; Home Civil Service, 1922-28; Leader-writer, Daily Mail, 1928-31, The Times, 1932-61, The Round Table, 1942-44; The Daily Telegraph, 1961-67; Editor, The Round Table, 1944-65. Represented The Times at Coronation, 1937, 1953; royal tour of South Africa, 1947; Mem. Council Commonwealth Press Union, 1945-, and Chm., Press Freedom Cttee, 1956-71; Chm., IEC Wine Soc., 1959-63; Chm., Circle of Wine Writers, 1964-66, Vice-Pres., 1972; Hon. Life Mem., Brit. Red Cross Soc., 1945. Freeman of the City of London, 1960. *Publications:* If It Had Happened Yesterday, 1930; The Mummy Case, 1933; The British Red Cross, 1944; Most Excellent Majesty, 1953 (revised as Crown and People,

1959); History of Industrial Assurance, 1955; The Work of the Queen, 1958; To Be a King, 1968. For King George's Jubilee Trust: The Royal Family in Wartime, 1945; Princess Elizabeth, 1947; The Royal Family in Africa, 1947; The Royal Family, 1950; Princess Elizabeth, Duchess of Edinburgh, 1950. *Plays:* Caesar's Friend (with late Campbell Dixon), 1933; Chorus Angelorum, 1937. *Films:* Royal Heritage, 1953; The Coronation Ceremony, 1953. *Recreations:* chess (for Oxford against Cambridge, 1920), ombre, wine. *Address:* 3 Kennington Palace Court, Sancroft Street, SE11. *T:* 01-582 1894. *Club:* United Oxford & Cambridge University.   *[Died 30 Sept. 1974.*

MORRELL, A(rthur) Claude, CBE 1952; MC 1917; Chairman, John Morrell & Co. Ltd, 1929-69; *b* 3 April 1894; *s* of Alfred Morrell, CBE, Liverpool; *m* 1931, Laura May (*d* 1976), *d* of Andrew D. Mearns, Blundellsands, Lancs; no *c. Educ:* Malvern Coll. Served European War, 1914-19 (MC): with the King's (Liverpool) Regt and on General Staff, Fourth Army, Dir, Martins Bank, 1944-68. JP (Cheshire), 1945. *Recreations:* golf, music. *Address:* Cloverly Nursing Home, Brimstage Road, Bebington, Merseyside L63 6HF. *T:* 051-342 3816.
                                                          [Died 11 April 1978.

MORREN, Sir William Booth Rennie, Kt 1952; CBE 1943; MVO 1937; Chief Constable of the City of Edinburgh, 1935-55, retired: ARP Controller of City of Edinburgh, 1940-45; *b* Aberdeen, 3 July 1890; *s* of late John Morren, OBE, Rhynie, Aberdeenshire, Chief Constable of Counties of Roxburgh, Berwick, and Selkirk; *m* 1916, Grace Evelyn Thorburn, *o d* of John T. Falconer; two *s* one *d.* Served in European War with Royal Scots (Capt.). Pres. Chief Constables Assoc. of Scotland, 1947. Chm., British Police Athletic Assoc., 1950-54; 1st Pres., European Police Sports Union, 1950-56; Life Pres., 1956-. Joint Chm. St Andrews Ambulance Assoc. SE Scotland and Chm. Scottish Ambulance Cttee for Edinburgh, 1960-65. Appointed Dep. Lord High Constable of Scotland during Royal State Visit to Scotland, 1953. Fellow Ancient Monuments Soc., 1957. King Haakon VII Liberty Cross of Norway, 1947; Swedish Police Sports Assoc. Gold Medal of Hon., 1952; Norwegian Police Sports Assoc. Medal of Hon., 1956. Gold Medal of Hon., European Police Sports Union, 1964. *Address:* 9 Murrayfield Drive, Edinburgh.   *[Died 15 Dec. 1972.*

MORRIS, 2nd Baron, *cr* 1918; **Michael Morris,** MA Cantab; Squadron Leader, RAFVR (retired); Solicitor; Senior Partner in Blount Petre & Co.; Director, Bacal Construction Ltd; *b* 12 April 1903; *s* of 1st Baron and Isabel Langrishe (*d* 1934), *d* of Rev. William Legallais; *S* father 1935; *m* 1st, 1933; two *s* two *d*; 2nd, 1960, Mary, *yr d* of late Rev. A. R. Langhorne, and of Mrs Langhorne. *Educ:* Downside; Trinity Coll., Cambridge. Called to Bar, Inner Temple, 1925. Served RAFVR 1939-43; Legal Staff Officer to RAF, Middle East Command, and Military Prosecutor of Palestine, 1940-42. Dir and some time Chm. of Solicitors Benevolent Assoc.; Mem. of Conservative Sub-Cttee on Reforms in the Administration of Justice. Has taken part in the BBC Brains Trust. *Recreation:* racing. *Heir: s* Hon. Michael David Morris, *b* 9 Dec. 1937. *Address:* 8 Carlos Place, Grosvenor Square, W1. *T:* 01-499 2807; The Old Farmhouse, Lower Denford, Hungerford, Berks.   *[Died 11 March 1975.*

MORRIS OF BORTH-Y-GEST, Baron (Life Peer) *cr* 1960; **John William Morris,** PC 1951; CH 1975; Kt 1945; CBE 1945; MC; *b* 11 Sept. 1896; *s* of Daniel and Ellen Morris, Liverpool and Portmadoc. *Educ:* Liverpool Institute, Liverpool; Trinity Hall, Cambridge (MA, LLB, Hon. Fellow, 1951); Harvard Law Sch., Harvard Univ., USA. Served in Royal Welch Fusiliers, 1916-19; two years in France (Captain); Pres. Cambridge Union Soc., 1919; Joseph Hodges Choate Memorial Fellowship, Harvard Univ., USA, 1920-21; called to Bar, Inner Temple, 1921; Bencher, 1943; Reader, 1966; Treasurer, 1967; Northern Circuit; KC 1935; Judge of Appeal, IOM, 1938-45; a Judge of the High Court, King's Bench Division, 1945-51; a Lord Justice of Appeal, 1951-60; a Lord of Appeal in Ordinary, 1960-75. Contested Ilford Div. (L) in 1923, 1924; Hon. Standing Counsel to the Univ. of Wales, 1938-45; HM Commissioner of Assize, Northern Circuit, 1942, and at Birmingham, Dec. 1944; Dep. Chm., Home Office Adv. Cttee, under Defence Regns, 1940-45; prepared Report for Treasury on Requisitioning, 1941; Chm., Home Office Cttee on War Damaged Licensed Houses, 1942-43; Chm., Cttee on the Selling Price of Houses, 1945; Chm., Courts of Inquiry into Engineering and Shipbuilding Wages Disputes, 1954; acted as Referee to decide the wage questions upon Settlement of Railway Strike, 1955; Chm. of National Reference Tribunal under the Coal-Mining Industry Conciliation Scheme, 1955-65; Chm., Home Office Cttee on Jury Service, 1963-64. Pres., London Welsh Assoc., 1951-53; Hon. Mem., Canadian and American Bar Assocs; Member: Pilgrims Soc.; Univ. Grants Cttee, 1955-69; Charing Cross Hosp. Council of Management,

1941-48 and of Board of Governors of Group, 1948-68; Pro-Chancellor of Univ. of Wales, 1956-74; Mem., the Gorsedd. Commissary of the Univ. of Cambridge, 1968-. JP 1939, DL 1951, Caernarvonshire; Dep.-Chm., Caernarvonshire QS, 1939-43, and Chm., 1943-69. Hon. LLD: Wales, 1946; British Columbia, 1952; Liverpool, 1966; Cambridge, 1967. *Address:* House of Lords, SW1; Bryn Gauallt, Portmadoc, Gwynedd. *Clubs:* Athenæum, Reform, MCC.   *[Died 9 June 1979.*

MORRIS, Most Rev. (Alfred) Edwin, DD; retired as Archbishop of Wales (1957-67) and Bishop of Monmouth (1945-67); *b* 8 May 1894; *s* of Alfred Morris, 42 Stourbridge Road, Lye, Stourbridge; *m* 1925, E. L. Davis (*d* 1968); four *s* one *d. Educ:* St David's Coll., Lampeter (Senior Scholar); BA 1922 (1st Class Hons Theol); St John's Coll., Oxford (Exhibitioner); BD Lampeter, 1932; DD (Lambeth) 1950; Junior Septuagint Prize, Oxford, 1923; Junior Greek Testament Prize, Oxford, 1924; 1st Cl. Hons in Theology and BA Oxon, 1924; Prof. of Hebrew and Theology at St David's Coll., Lampeter, 1924-45; MA Oxon, 1928; served in France with RAMC (9th Div.), European War; Examining Chaplain to the Bishop of Bangor, 1925-28; Examining Chaplain to the Bishop of Llandaff, 1931-39; Lloyd Williams Fellow of St David's Coll., Lampeter, 1931-45; Hon. Fellow, St John's Coll., Oxford, 1958. Hon. Canon, St David's Cathedral, 1968. Sub-Prelate, OStJ, 1958. Hon. DD Wales, 1971. *Publications:* The Church in Wales and Nonconformity, 1949; The Problem of Life and Death, 1950; The Catholicity of the Book of Common Prayer, 1952; The Christian Use of Alcoholic Beverages, 1961. *Recreations:* gardening, oil painting. *Address:* Noyadd, Llanfair Clydogau, Lampeter, Cards. *T:* Llangybi 278; Llyndir, Porth Sele, St David's, Pembs.
                                                          [Died 19 Oct. 1971.

MORRIS, Brig. Arthur de Burgh, CBE 1949 (OBE 1948); DSO 1944; retired; *b* 11 Dec. 1902; *s* of late Lt-Col G. M. Morris, 8th Gurkha Rifles; *m* 1928, Doreen, *d* of late Sir Henry Miller, Londonderry; one *d. Educ:* Wellington Coll.; RMC, Sandhurst. Commissioned 2nd Lt, into 1st Sherwood Foresters, 1922; Adjt, 8th Sherwood Foresters, 1930-34; transferred to 8th Gurkha Rifles, 1936; Bde Major, Thal Bde NWFP, 1941-42; Temp. Lt-Col and Comd 1/8 Gurkha Rifles, 1943; served in Arakan and Burma, 1944 (DSO); Temp. Col and 2nd i/c 37 Inf. Bde (Gurkha), 1945; Temp. Brig. and Comd 49 Indian Inf. Bde, Nov. 1945; served in Java, 1946-47 (OBE); Comd North Malaya Sub. Dist, 1947-48 (CBE); Comdr Kowloon Inf. Bde, 1948; Brigade of Gurkhas, 1948; Comdr 48 Gurkha Inf., Bde, Malaya, 1950-53 (despatches); Perak Meritorious Service Medal (Malaya), 1953; retired, 1953. High Sheriff, City of Londonderry, 1964. *Recreations:* hunting and shooting. *Address:* Moyola Park, Castledawson, County Londonderry, Northern Ireland.   *[Died 14 Sept. 1978.*

MORRIS, Rt. Rev. Arthur Harold, DD (Lambeth), 1954; *b* 20 Feb. 1898; *s* of E. H. Morris, Ross-on-Wye, Herefordshire; *m* 1924, Evelyn Ethel Woods (*d* 1953); three *s. Educ:* Cambridge and County High Sch. for Boys; Fitzwilliam Hall, Cambridge; Ridley Hall, Cambridge. 2nd Lt, The King's (Liverpool Regt), 1917. Took degrees BA and LLB, Cambridge, 1920 (Law Tripos); MA 1924. Deacon, 1922, Priest, 1923. Vicar of Great Clacton with Little Holland, 1926; Metropolitan Sec., Church Pastoral-Aid Soc., 1930; Vicar of St Mark's, Hamilton Terrace, London, 1933; Rural Dean of St Marylebone, 1940; officiating chaplain RAF, 1940-45; Proctor in Convocation for Diocese of London, 1945; Archdeacon of Halifax and Canon of St Hilda in Wakefield Cathedral, 1946; Proctor in Convocation, Diocese of Wakefield, 1946; Bishop Suffragan and Archdeacon of Pontefract, and Canon of St Chad in Wakefield Cathedral, 1949-54; Bishop of St Edmundsbury and Ipswich, 1954-65. Mem. Leeds Regional Hosp. Bd, 1951; Church Commissioner, 1952; Mem. Bd of Governors, Church Comrs, 1954; Chm., Council for Women's Ministry in the Church (called Central Council for Women's Church Work until 1960), 1955-60: Mem. Admin. Cttee, Church Comrs, 1956-64; Vice-Chm. Pastoral Cttee, 1964-65; Mem. of the House of Lords, 1959-65; Chm., Board of Governors, Felixstowe Coll., 1960. *Recreation:* Rotary (President, St Marylebone Club), 1944). *Address:* Shepherds, The Heath, Holbrook, Ipswich, Suffolk IP9 2QB.
                                                          [Died 15 Oct. 1977.

MORRIS, Brig. Arthur Henry Musgrave, CBE 1957; DSO 1945; MC 1940; GM 1940; Royal Engineers, retired; Director-General, British Quarrying and Slag Federation; *b* 22 Oct. 1904; *s* of late Col A. E. Morris, Edenderry, Offaly, Ireland; *m* Marianne Müller, Karlsbad; two *d. Educ:* Cheltenham; RMA Woolwich. Commd RE (2nd Lt), 1924; service in: India, Burma, 1926-32; UK, 1932-39; France (BEF), 1940; USA (Joint Staff Mission), 1941; Italy, 1943-45 (despatches twice); Austria, 1945-46; Palestine, 1947; Germany, 1948-51; Korea, 1953-54. Col

1951; Brig. 1955; retd 1957. *Recreations:* painting, writing. *Address:* 15 Fort Road, Guildford, Surrey. *T:* 62998. *Club:* United Service & Royal Aero.   [*Died* 20 *Nov.* 1972.

MORRIS, Charles John; *see* Morris, J.

MORRIS, Most Rev. Edwin; *see* Morris, Most Rev. A. E.

MORRIS, Captain George Horace Guy, CBE 1960; retired; *b* 21 Feb. 1897; *o s* of late H. W. T. Morris of Litherland, County of Lancaster; *m* 1919, Nancy (*d* 1963), *o c* of late Josiah Meir, Tunstall, Staffs; one *s* one *d. Educ:* Liverpool. Went to sea as apprentice with W. Lowden & Co., Liverpool, 1912; served as Lt RNR, 1916-20; joined Cunard Line as Junior Officer, 1922; Captain, 1947. Commanded: SS Vasconia, SS Arabia, SS Assyria, RMS Parthia, RMS Media, RMS Scythia, RMS Georgic, RMS Britannic, RMS Caronia, RMS Mauretania. Appointed Relieving Captain Queen Liners, 1956; Captain RMS Queen Mary, 1957; Captain RMS Queen Elizabeth, 1958; Commodore Cunard Line, 1958; retired, 1960. *Recreation:* motoring. *Address:* 6 Archers Court, Arrowe Park, Birkenhead, Merseyside. *T:* 051-677 6723.   [*Died* 13 *June* 1979.

MORRIS, Sir George P.; *see* Morris, Sir Parker.

MORRIS, John, (C. J. Morris), CBE 1957; *b* 27 Aug. 1895; *e s* of late Frank Morris. *Educ:* King's Coll., Cambridge (MA, MSc, Diploma in Anthropology). Served with Leicestershire Regt and 3rd QAO Gurkha Rifles, 1915-34; served European War: France and Belgium, 1915-17 (wounded), Palestine, 1918; Afghanistan, 1919; Waziristan and NW Frontier of India, 1919-21 and 1921-24; travelled extensively in Central Asia, Tibet, Nepal, Bhutan, Africa, the Far East, etc; mem. of 1922 and 1936 Mount Everest Expeditions; Murchison Memorial of Royal Geographical Society, for explorations in Chinese Turkestan, 1929; William Wyse studentship in Social Anthropology, Univ. of Cambridge, 1934-37. Prof. of English Literature at Keio Univ., Tokyo, and Lecturer at Imperial and Bunrika Univs, Tokyo; concurrently adviser on English language to Japanese Dept of Foreign Affairs, 1938-42; BBC: Head of Far Eastern Service, 1943-52; Controller, Third Programme, 1952-58. *Publications:* The Gurkhas (with Major W. Brook Northey), 1928; Handbooks for the Indian Army: Gurkhas, 1935; Living with Lepchas, 1938; Traveller from Tokyo, 1943; The Phœnix Cup, 1947; From the Third Programme (Edited), 1956; Hired to Kill, 1960; A Winter in Nepal, 1963; Eating the Indian Air, 1968. *Recreations:* travel, reading, music. *Address:* 21 Friday Street, Henley-on-Thames, Oxon. *T:* Henley-on-Thames 4369. *Clubs:* Savile, Alpine; University Alpine (Cambridge); Japan Alpine (Tokyo); Himalayan (Calcutta).   [*Died* 13 *Dec.* 1980.

MORRIS, John David, CB 1947; OBE 1937; *b* 1895; *yr s* of late James Thomas Morris, Newport, Mon; *m* 1950, Marjorie, *o d* of Capt. S. V. Bowden, Kensington, W14. *Educ:* Newport High Sch. Joined Civil Service, 1913; Admiralty, 1914; commnd RM and served overseas, 1917-19; Mem. of British Delegn to Disarmament Conf., Geneva, 1932-34; Dir of Finance, Admty, 1944; Under-Sec., 1946-51; Prin. Under-Sec., 1951-56; Dep. Sec., Admty, 1956-58, retd. *Recreations:* tennis and walking. *Address:* 57 Holland Park, W11 3RS. *T:* 01-727 8132. *Club:* Royal Automobile.   [*Died* 31 *July* 1972.

MORRIS, Hon. Sir Kenneth (James), KBE 1968; CMG 1964; Senator, Australian National Parliament, 1963-68, retired; *b* 22 Oct. 1903; *s* of J. R. Morris; *m* 1931, Ettie L., *d* of W. H. Dunlop; three *s* one *d* (and one *s* decd). *Educ:* Brisbane Gram. Sch. Business Company Dir prior to 1939. Enlisted AIF, 1939; served in England with 6th Australian Division, then original mem. of 9th Australian Division; served Tobruk, Alamein, New Guinea; transferred to R of O, Major, 1944. Elected Qld Parliament, 1944, as MLA Enoggera (later Mt Coot-tha); served as Whip, 1944-49; Deputy Leader, 1949-53, Leader, 1953-62. Parliamentary Liberal Party; Deputy Premier, Minister of Labour and Industry, 1957-63. *Recreations:* bowls, fishing. *Address:* 20/45 Moray Street, New Farm, Brisbane, Qld 4005, Australia. *T:* 358 1289. *Clubs:* United Service, Masonic (Brisbane).   [*Died* 1 *June* 1978.

MORRIS, Air Marshal Sir Leslie D.; *see* Dalton-Morris.

MORRIS, Malcolm John, QC 1959; **His Honour Judge Malcolm Morris;** a Circuit Judge, since 1972; *b* 11 Sept. 1913; *s* of late Sir Harold Morris, MBE, QC; *m* 1949, Betty Rene, *d* of E. Russ; one *s* one *d. Educ:* Eton; Magdalen Coll., Oxford. Served with Royal Artillery, 1939-46; Hon. Lt-Col. Barrister, Inner Temple, 1937; Master of the Bench, Inner Temple, 1965; Treasurer of Senate, Four Inns of Court, 1970-. Recorder of Margate, 1952-62; Recorder of Croydon, 1962-65; Recorder of Southend, 1966-

71; Dep. Chm., Berks QS, 1966-71. Mem. of the Criminal Law Revision Cttee, 1965-. *Address:* 53 Drayton Gardens, SW10. *T:* 01-373 1335; Lower Dean, Watlington, Oxford OX9 5ET. *T:* Watlington 2758; Farrar's Building, Temple, EC4. *T:* 01-353 3598. *Clubs:* MCC; Leander.   [*Died* 15 *Oct.* 1972.

MORRIS, Sir Parker, Kt 1941; Town Clerk of Westminster, 1929-56, retired; *b* 15 Sept. 1891; *s* of David and Annie Kent Morris, Manchester; *m* 1918, Dorothy Aylmer Hale, Manchester; one *s* one *d. Educ:* Retford; Manchester Univ. LLB (London). Served in European War, 1914-19, in Manchester Regt and Machine Gun Corps. Admitted Solicitor of Supreme Court, Jan. 1919. Deputy Town Clerk of Salford, 1919-23; Town Clerk of Chesterfield, 1923-29; Hon. Clerk to Metropolitan Boroughs Standing Joint Cttee, 1929-56; Jt Sec. Departmental Cttee on London Cleansing, 1929; Mem. Central Valuation Cttee for England and Wales, 1937-49; Mem. Royal Commn on Location of Industry, 1937-39; Chairman: Nat. Fedn of Housing Socs, 1956-61; Cttee for Old People's Housing Socs, 1961-67; Archway Group Hosp. Management Cttee, 1956-63; Study Group on Building Contracts of Local Authorities, Royal Inst. of Public Administration; Mem. Housing Management Sub-Cttee, 1956-59; Chm. Greater London Citizens' Advice Bureaux Advisory Cttee, 1957-67; Mem. Central London Valuation Panel, 1957-58; Member: Central Housing Advisory Cttee, 1957-62; Chm., Housing Standards Sub-Cttee, 1959 (a Report, Homes for Today and Tomorrow, 1961); Mem. NW Metropolitan Regional Hosp. Bd and Chm. of Establishment Cttee, 1960-63. ARP Controller of Westminster, 1939-45. Hon FRIBA, 1970. Chevalier of: Legion of Honour, France, 1950; Order of Orange-Nassau, Netherlands, 1950; Order of the Dannebrog, Denmark, 1951; Order of the North Star, Sweden, 1954; Order of the Star of Ethiopia, 1954; Military Order of Christ, Portugal, 1955; Order of Al Rafidain, Iraq, 1956. *Recreation:* golf. *Address:* Berwyns, One Tree Hill, Guildford, Surrey. *T:* 3678.   [*Died* 22 *Jan.* 1972.

MORRIS, Sir Philip (Robert), KCMG 1960; Kt 1946; CBE 1941; MA Oxon; Hon. LLD: Rhodes, 1950; Bristol, 1951; McGill, 1955; Windsor, 1958; NUI, W Ontario, 1960; London, 1965; Bath, 1966; Hon. ARCVS 1958; FRSA 1961; Hon. FRCS 1966; Vice-Chancellor Bristol University, 1946-66; *b* 6 July 1901; 2nd *s* of late M. C. Morris, HM Inspector, and late J. Morris, Sutton Valence; *m* 1926, Florence Redvers Davis, 2nd *d* of Walford Davis Green, Barrister-at-law, and Annie L. Green; two *s* one *d* (and one *d* decd). *Educ:* Tonbridge Sch.; St Peter's, York; Trinity Coll., Oxford. Modern Greats, 1923; Teachers' Diploma, London Univ., 1924; Lectr in History and Classics, Westminster Trng Coll., 1923-25; Administrative Officer, Kent Education Cttee, Asst Dir, 1932; Dir, 1938-43; Dir-Gen. of Army Education, 1944-46; Educational Adviser, HM Prison, 1938-44; Mem. Board of Education Cttee on Training of Teachers and Youth Leaders, 1942-44. Life Trustee of Carnegie UK Trust; UK Deleg. First Conf. of UNESCO, 1946; Chm., Army Educ. Advisory Bd, 1946-48; Vice-Chm., British Council, 1946-59; Chm., Secondary Sch. Examinations Council, 1948-51 (Actg Chm. 1947-48); Chairman: Nat. Advisory Council on Training and Supply of Teachers, 1946-59; Cttee of Vice-Chancellors and Principals, 1955-58; Miners' Welfare Nat. Scholarship Scheme Selection Cttee, 1948-49; Anglo-Czechoslovak Cultural Commn, 1949; Chm. Conference on African Education, 1952; Theatre Royal, Bristol, Management Cttee, 1946-63; Chm. Commonwealth Education Conference, 1959; Chm. Commonwealth Education Liaison Cttee, 1959-62; Vice-Chm., United Bristol Hosps Bd of Govs, 1948-66; Member: BBC Gen. Adv. Council, 1947-52; Vice-Chm. of BBC, 1954-60 (a Governor, 1952-60); BBC West Reg. Adv. Council, 1961-68 (Chm. 1947-52); SW Regional Hosp. Bd, 1948-53; Central Adv. Council for Educn (England), 1944-48; Adv. Cttee for Educn in the Colonies, 1945-48 and 1949-52, 1953-56, 1959-62; General Nursing Council, 1954-55; Advisory Cttee on Recruiting, 1958; Cttee on Higher Education, 1961-64. Mem. Council, Boy Scouts' Assoc., 1946-59; Vice-Chm. Assoc. Univs of British Commonwealth, 1951-55; Pres., Library Association, 1955; Mem., Governing Bd of National Institute for Research in Nuclear Science, 1957-58; Hon. Mem., Bristol Medico-Chirurgical Soc., 1963-. Hon. Fellow, Bristol Univ., 1966. *Publications:* Christianity and the World of Today, 1961; articles, published addresses etc, on educational subjects. *Recreations:* music, golf. *Address:* Bryncoedifor Vicarage, Rhydymain, Dolgellau, Gwynedd LL40 2AN. *T:* Rhydymain 237. *Club:* Athenæum.   [*Died* 21 *Nov.* 1979.

MORRIS, Dr Richard Murchison, CMG 1958; OBE 1949; *b* 14 Sept. 1898; *s* of Richard Henry Morris, Capetown, S Africa; *m* 1928, Kathleen, *d* of Lt-Col C. H. Divine, DSO; one *d* (and one *s* decd). *Educ:* Diocesan Coll., Rondebosch, Cape; London

Hospital, Univ. of London. 2nd Lt (Pilot) RAF, 1918. MRCS, LRCP, 1923; House-Surgeon, Poplar Hosp.; MB, BS, 1924; House Physician, etc, London Hosp.; House Physician, Tropical Diseases Hosp.; MD (Gold Medal), 1926; DTM and H, 1926; S Rhodesian Medical Service, 1926; DPH (London, 1932); Sen. Govt MO, 1934; DMS, 1946; Sec. for Health, 1948; Sec. to Ministry of Health, Fedn of Rhodesia and Nyasaland, 1954-58, retired. Councillor, Salisbury City Council, 1961-75; Alderman, City of Salisbury, Rhodesia, 1971. Surg.-Col British S Africa Police, 1946; Col and ADMS Matabeleland, 1939-45; Consultant Physician, RAF Training Group, S Rhodesia, 1940-45. External Examiner in Medicine, Univ. of Capetown, 1950-51. Vice-Chm. Council, University of Rhodesia, 1968-. KStJ 1963. Hon. LLD, Univ. of Rhodesia, 1977. *Publications:* medical papers in Lancet and Central African Jl of Medicine. *Address:* 2 Denmark Avenue, PO Belvedere, Salisbury, Rhodesia. *T:* Salisbury 21351. *Clubs:* Bulawayo (Bulawayo); Salisbury (Salisbury). *[Died 19 March 1979.*

MORRIS, William Alexander, CMG 1956; *b* 15 June 1905; *e s* of late William G. Morris, Cheam, Surrey; *m* 1938, Cecilia Mary, *d* of late James M. Anderson, of Istamboul, and Oxted, Surrey; four *d. Educ:* St Paul's Sch.; Univ. of London. BSc (Econ.) Hons 1929. Economic Asst to High Comr for Australia, 1935-39; entered Bd of Trade, 1940; transferred to Colonial Office, 1942; seconded to Foreign Office, 1963; HM Consul-Gen., Rotterdam, 1963-65; Dept of Economic Affairs and Cabinet Office, 1966-70, retired 1970. *Address:* 30 Bridewell Street, Devizes, Wilts. *T:* Devizes 5249. *[Died 10 March 1979.*

MORRIS, William Alfred, MVO (4th Class) 1942; late 12th Royal Lancers; *b* 26 Nov. 1912; *s* of late Alfred William Johnson Morris and Adeline Gonthier; *m* 1st, 1939, Patricia Beryl Robertson; one *s* one *d*; 2nd, 1953, Lesley Dade Spurr. *Educ:* Eton. Served War of 1939-45 (Croix de Guerre 1943); retired, 1948. *Address:* The Manor House, Culworth, near Banbury, Oxon. *T:* Sulgrave 323; 21 Ennismore Mews, SW7. *T:* 01-589 1733. *Club:* Cavalry. *[Died 16 April 1973.*

MORRIS-JONES, Sir (John) Henry, Kt 1937; MC; LRCP and S (Edinburgh); DL Denbigh; JP; Hon. Captain, RAMC; *b* Waenfawr, Caernarvonshire, 2 Nov. 1884; *s* of Capt. Morris Jones and Ann Jones; *m* 1931, Leila Augusta Paget-Marsland, widow of J. Illidge Marsland. *Educ:* Menai Bridge Grammar Sch.; St Mungo's Coll., Glasgow. For twenty years practised as a general medical practitioner at Colwyn Bay, and took an active part in its public life and in that of the County of Denbigh; Mem. and ex-Chm., UDC, High Sheriff Designate of the County, 1929-30, and Mem. of County Council; MP (L) Denbigh Div., 1929-31, (L Nat), 1931-50; retd 1950; Chm. Exec. Nat. Lib. Party, 1953-54. Chm., Welsh Parliamentary Party, 1941-42; Asst Govt Whip, 1932-35; Lord Commissioner of the Treasury, 1935-37; served as Chm., Div. BMA and Colwyn Bay Medical Soc.; Hon. Treas. and Joint Hon. Sec. Reception Cttee Royal Visit to North Wales, 1937; Mem. of official Parly Delegn to Australia for Sesqui-centenary celebrations, 1938; Mem. of Parly Delegn to Buchenwald Concentration Camp, April 1945; Mem. of Gorsedd under Bardic title of Rhoslanydd; Mem. of Governing Body and Representative Body, Church in Wales, 1950-62. Served in France, with 2nd Bn Worcester Regt, 1914-18 (MC); travelled extensively. Hon. Freedom of Colwyn Bay, 1956. *Publications:* Surgical Experiences at Wimereux, France (with Hugh Lett); Doctor in the Whips' Room, 1955. *Recreation:* walking. *Address:* Bryndyfnog, Llanrhaldr, near Denbigh, North Wales. *T:* Llanynys 236. *Club:* Reform. *[Died 9 July 1972.*

MORROGH BERNARD, Rt. Rev. Mgr. Canon Eustace Anthony, LCL; Vicar-General, 1939-63, of Archdiocese of Westminster; *b* Killarney, 1893; *s* of Eustace Morrogh Bernard, Flesk House, Killarney, Co. Kerry, and Mary Anne, 5th *d* of Samuel Jas Brown, Loftus Hill, Yorks. *Educ:* Ampleforth; St Edmund's Ware; Angelico Univ., Rome (LCL). Ordained Catholic Priest, 1918; Asst Dioc. Chancellor of Westminster, 1919-37; Chancellor, 1937-44; Privy Chamberlain to the Pope, 1933; Domestic Prelate, 1938; Protonotary Apostolic *ad instar,* 1960; Canon of Metropolitan Cathedral of Westminster, 1941. *Address:* Nazareth House, Hammersmith Road, W6. *[Died 11 Jan. 1972.*

MORROW, Sir (Arthur) William, Kt 1959; DSO 1942; ED 1949; FRCP, FRACP; Hon. Consultant Physician, Royal Prince Alfred Hospital, Sydney, since 1963 (Hon. Physician, 1951-63); *b* 12 July 1903; *s* of Arthur John Morrow and Helonar (*née* Harkin); *m* 1st, 1937, Jean Buchanan Brown (*d* 1970); three *d*; 2nd, 1974, Margaret Mary, *d* of late Dr E. Wilfred Fairfax and Mary Fairfax (*née* Lamb). *Educ:* Newington Coll., Sydney; Sydney Univ. MB, BS Sydney 1927; FRCP 1949; FRACP 1938;

Hon. FACP 1968. First Cl. Hons in Medicine at graduation, 1927; RMO, Royal Prince Alfred Hospital, Sydney, 1927; Dep. Supt 1932; Hon. Asst Phys., 1934. Hon. Cons. Phys., Canterbury District Memorial Hosp., Sydney, 1938; Marrickville Dist Hosp., 1939; Western Suburb Hosp., 1937; Lectr in Therapeutics, Univ. of Sydney, 1938-63. Served in AIF, War of 1939-45 (finishing rank Col); final posting, Cons. Phys. Advanced HQ (despatches, DSO). Now RAAMC Reserve. Pres. NSW Branch, BMA, 1958-59. Council, RACP, 1957- (Censor, 1953-, Censor-in-Chief, 1962-66, Pres. 1966-68). *Publications:* numerous medical scientific articles, mainly applied to gastro-enterology. *Recreation:* golf. *Address:* 7 Rupertswood Avenue, Bellevue Hill, NSW 2023, Australia; (professional) 187 Macquarie Street, Sydney, NSW 2000. *T:* 221 1539. *Clubs:* Australian, Royal Sydney Golf (Sydney); Australian Jockey. *[Died 22 Aug. 1977.*

MORROW, Sir William; *see* Morrow, Sir A. W.

MORSE-BOYCOTT, Rev. Desmond; Co-founder with his wife, in 1932, and Hon. Principal and Director of the Music, of St Mary-of-the-Angels Song School, now Administrator of the Trust's Morse-Boycott Bursaries relative to Choir Schools; Assistant Curate of St Mary the Virgin, Somers Town, 1919-35; *b* 10 Dec. 1892; *y s* of late Frederic Augustus Morse-Boycott, Sennowe, Norfolk, and Octavia Mary, 5th *d* of Matthew John Anketell, Anketell Grove, JP and DL Co. Monaghan; *m* Marguerite Harriet Sandford (*d* 1959), Chailey, Sussex; one *d. Educ:* privately; Lichfield Theological Coll. At the age of 16 entered the service of the West Sussex County Education Cttee; during this period studied commercial subjects and became an expert shorthand teacher; became asst curate at Mayfield in Sussex; Bognor; then Somers Town; entered journalism, teaching himself the craft; became a contributor to all the leading newspapers; conducted a Test Centre for young aspirants to the ministry. Has supplied boys' choirs for various films as well as for Church and secular occasions of importance. LTh (Durham); FRSA. Hon. Fellow, Tonic Sol-Fa Coll. of Music, 1969. *Publications:* Alleluia; Three Holy Fruits; Seven Words of Love; Simplicitas and His Brethren, 1920; The Pilgrim's Way; Holy Communion; Ten Years in a London Slum, 1929; God and Everyman; Mystic Glow; Wayside Words; We do see Life; Saith the Preacher, 1931; Fields of Yesterday, 1932; Lead, Kindly Light; Credo, etc; The Secret Story of the Oxford Movement, 1933; Is it a Sin?, 1935; Great Crimes of the Bible, 1936; A Tramping Parson's Message, 1936; How can I be Happy?, 1937; Fear Not, 1939; They Shine Like Stars, 1948; A Golden Legend of the Slums, 1951; A Tapestry of Toil (autobiog.), 1970; A Pilgrimage of Song, 1972. Edits The Angel. *Recreations:* painting, music, philately. *Address:* Walnut Tree Cottage, 79 Ashacre Lane, Offington, Worthing, West Sussex. *T:* Worthing 60927. *[Died 9 Aug. 1979.*

MORSHEAD, Sir Owen (Frederick), GCVO 1958 (KCVO 1944; CVO 1937; MVO 1933); KCB 1953; DSO 1917; MC; Librarian, Windsor Castle, 1926-58, after which date appointed Emeritus Librarian; also formerly Assistant Keeper Royal Archives; Fellow Magdalene College, Cambridge, since 1920; Chairman Dorset Historic Churches Trust, 1959-73; *b* 1893; *y s* of late Reginald Morshead, Hurlditch Court, Tavistock, Devon; *m* 1926, Paquita, *d* of J. G. Hagemeyer, Florence, Italy; one *s* two *d. Educ:* Marlborough; RMA, Woolwich; Magdalene Coll., Cambridge. Served European War, 1914-19 (despatches five times, DSO, Bt Major, MC, Croce di Guerra); Legion of Honour (Officier). Comd 9th Berks Bn Home Guard, 1941-45. DL Berks, 1946-58. *Publications:* Everybody's Pepys, 1926; Windsor Castle, 1951; George IV and Royal Lodge, 1965. *Address:* Lindens, Sturminster Newton, Dorset. *T:* Sturminster Newton 209. *[Died 1 June 1977.*

MORSON, A(lbert) Clifford, OBE, FRCS; Consulting Urologist, St Peter's Hospital for Urinary Diseases, Hampstead General Hospital, Whipps Cross Hospital and NW Metropolitan Regional Hospital Board; *s* of Thomas Pierre and Florence Morson; *m* 1917, Adela Frances Maud, *o d* of late Lincoln Phené and Alice Phené; three *s. Educ:* Haileybury Coll. Qualified as a Medical Practitioner at the Middlesex Hosp., 1906; as a student obtained Lyall Gold Medal and Scholarship for practical surgery; Capt. Rugby Football Club; Original Mem., Royal Naval Volunteer Reserve (London Div.), 1903; Various resident Medical appointments, 1907-12; Middlesex Hosp. and St Peter's Hosp. for Urinary Diseases, Registrar and Research Scholar, Cancer Laboratories, Middlesex Hosp., 1912-14; received temporary commission as Surgeon in HM Navy, August 1914; served in HMS Zealandia, and HMS Centurion of Grand Fleet; Surgeon, Hospital Ships Somali and Karapara throughout Gallipoli campaign (OBE, 1914-15 star, general service and Victory medals); demobilised 1919. Pres., 1933-34,

Section of Urology, RSM; Hon. Pres. International Soc. of Urology; Past Pres. British Assoc. of Urological Surgeons; lately Mem. Regional Hosp. Bd NW Metropolitan Area. Hon. Member: Brit. Assoc. of Urological Surgeons, Canadian Urological Assoc., Finnish Urological Soc.; Mem. Cttee of Management, Inst. of Urology (London Univ.). Hon. Fellow RSM. *Publications:* A Guide to Urinary Diseases (with Adolphe Abrahams); Urinary Infections, Pocket Monograph series; numerous articles in medical and scientific journals. *Recreations:* all outdoor sports. *Address:* 66 Northway, NW11. *T:* 01-455 0264.   *[Died 5 Jan. 1975.*

MORSON, Clifford; *see* Morson, A. C.

MORTIMER, Sir Charles Edward, Kt 1950; CBE 1943; *b* 1 Jan. 1886; *s* of Joseph Mortimer; *m* 1920, Winifred Whitehouse (*d* 1973); two *s*. *Educ:* Hartley Coll., Manchester. Methodist Minister, 1910-16; entered Land Dept, Kenya, 1917, as Clerk; Land Asst, 1920-27; Lands Sec., 1928-38; Commissioner of Lands and Settlement, 1938-39; Commissioner for Local Govt, Lands and Settlement, 1939-46; Mem. for Health and Local Government, Kenya Colony, 1946-50, and 1952-54. KStJ 1965. *Address:* 20 Ludlow Street, Kenmore, Qld 4069, Australia.
                                    [Died 3 Sept. 1974.

MORTIMER, Charles Raymond Bell; *see* Mortimer, Raymond.

MORTIMER, Raymond, CBE 1955; Officier de la Légion d'Honneur; *b* 25 April 1895; *s* of Charles Edward Mortimer and Marion Josephine Cantrell. *Educ:* Malvern; Balliol Coll., Oxford. French Red Cross, 1915-18. Temp. Mem., FO, 1918-19. Reviewer for New Statesman, Nation (later Literary Editor), and The Sunday Times; contributor to The Times, TLS, and Horizon. Former Mem., Royal Fine Art Commn. *Publications include:* (with Hamish Miles) The Oxford Circus, 1922; The French Pictures: a letter to Harriet, 1932; Channel Packet, 1942; (compiled) Poems by Tennyson, 1958; Try Anything Once, 1976. *Recreations:* travel, bridge. *Address:* 5 Canonbury Place, N1. *T:* 01-226 3548; Long Crichel House, Wimborne, Dorset. *T:* Tarrant Hinton 250. *Club:* Travellers'.   *[Died 9 Jan. 1980.*

MORTIMER, Rt. Rev. Robert Cecil; *b* Bristol, 6 Dec. 1902; *y s* of Rev. E. Mortimer; *m* 1933, Mary Hope, *d* of J. R. Walker, Barrister-at-Law; two *s* two *d*. *Educ:* S Edward's Sch., Oxford; Keble Coll., Oxford; Wells Theological Coll. 1st Class Hon. Mods 1923; 1st Class Lit Hum 1925; BA 1925, MA 1929, BD 1939; DD 1947; Curate S Mary Redcliffe, Bristol, 1926-29; Deacon, 1926; Priest, 1927; Lecturer Christ Church, Oxford, 1929; Student and Tutor, 1930-44; University Lecturer in Early Canon Law, 1935-43; Junior Censor of Christ Church, 1940-44; Canon of Christ Church, Oxford, and Regius Prof. of Moral and Pastoral Theology, 1944-49; Bishop of Exeter, 1949-73. Examining Chaplain to the Bishop of Ripon, 1931-46, to Bishops of Salisbury and Bristol, 1946-49; Proctor of University of Oxford in the Convocation of Canterbury, 1943-49; Select Preacher to University of Oxford, 1939-41; Select Preacher to Cambridge University, 1947; Provost of Denstone, 1948; Chancellor of the Diocese of Blackburn, 1948. Hon. Fellow, Keble Coll., 1951; Hon. Student, Christ Church, Oxford, 1968. *Publications:* Gambling, 1933; Origins of Private Penance, 1939; The Elements of Moral Theology, 1947; Marriage in Church and State (Revised and Supplemented), 1947; Christian Ethics, 1950; The Duties of a Churchman, 1951; Western Canon Law, 1953. *Recreations:* hockey (played for West of England, 1927-29) and other games. *Address:* The Old Rectory, Newton Reigny, Penrith, Cumbria. *Club:* Athenæum.   *[Died 11 Sept. 1976.*

MORTON, 21st Earl of, *cr* 1458 (*de facto* 20th Earl, 21st but for the Attainder); **Sholto Charles John Hay Douglas;** Lord Dalkeith and Aberdour, 1458; Flight Lt, late RAFVR; *b* 12 April 1907; *s* of Lord Aberdour (*d* 1911; *e s* of 20th, *de facto* 19th, Earl of Morton) and Brenda (*d* 1954), *d* of Lord Ruthven, Fulmer Place, near Slough; *S* grandfather, 1935. *Educ:* Magdalen Coll., Oxford (MA). Fellow of the Linnæan Soc. VMH, RHS, 1967. *Heir: c* John Charles Sholto Douglas [*b* 19 March 1927; *m* 1949, Sheila Mary, *d* of late Rev. Canon John Stanley Gibbs, MC, Didmarton House, Badminton, Glos; two *s* one *d*]. *Address:* The Hatch, Churt, Surrey.
                                    [Died 13 Feb. 1976.

MORTON OF HENRYTON, Baron (Life Peer) *cr* 1947, of Henryton; **Fergus Dunlop Morton,** PC 1944; Kt 1938; *b* 17 Oct. 1887; *y s* of late George Morton of Lochgreen, Troon, Ayrshire; *m* Margaret Greenlees, *er d* of James Begg; one *d*. *Educ:* Kelvinside; St John's Coll., Cambridge. Hon. Foundation Scholar, classics; First Class Law Tripos; MA, LLB. Called to Bar, 1912; temp. commission as Lt Highland Light Infantry, Sept. 1914; Capt., 1915; active service, 1916-18 (MC); War

Office, 1918-19; returned to practice at the Bar, Sept. 1919; KC 1929; Judge of Chancery Div., High Court of Justice, 1938-44; a Lord Justice of Appeal, 1944-47; a Lord of Appeal in Ordinary, 1947-59. Bencher of Lincoln's Inn, 1932; Treas., 1953. Hon. Fellow of St John's Coll., Cambridge, 1940. Chairman: Black List Cttee, Min. of Economic Warfare, 1941-46; Council of Legal Educn, 1949-53; Cttee on the Law of Intestate Succession, 1950; Royal Commn on marriage and divorce, 1951. Dep. High Steward, Cambridge Univ. Hon. Mem., Faculty of Advocates; Hon. Mem. Cdn and Amer. Bar Assocs; Hon. LLD: Cambridge, 1951; Glasgow, 1951; St Andrews, 1956; Sydney, 1957. *Recreations:* playing golf and watching every kind of outdoor ball game. *Address:* 78 Melton Court, SW7. *T:* 01-589 8989; Grey Thatch, Winter Hill, Cookham, Berks. *T:* Bourne End 20 233. *Club:* Athenæum.   *[Died 18 July 1973.*

MORTON, Anthony; *see* Creasey, John.

MORTON, Major Sir Desmond John Falkiner, KCB, *cr* 1945 (CB 1941); CMG 1937; *b* 13 Nov. 1891; *o s* of late Col Charles F. Morton, Royal Dragoons, and Edith, *d* of John Tolerton Leather, of Middleton Hall, Northumberland; unmarried. *Educ:* Eton; Royal Military Academy, Woolwich. 2nd Lt RH and RFA, 1911; fought in European War with regiment and on the Staff; ADC to FM Earl Haig, 1917 (despatches, MC, French Croix de Guerre and Médaille d'honneur, Brevet of Major; seconded under Foreign Office, 1919; Dir of Industrial Intelligence Centre, 1930; Principal Asst Sec., Min. of Economic Warfare, 1939; Personal Asst to Prime Minister, 1940-46; UK delegate to Inter-Allied Reparation Agency; UK Comr for Restitution of Monetary Gold, 1946; Vice-Chm. of UN Economic Survey Mission for the Middle East, 1949; lent by Treasury to Ministry of Civil Aviation, 1950; retired 1953. Governor of St Luke's Hosp., Woodside, 1946-48, Middlesex Hosp., 1947-66; Chm. Hammersmith Post-Graduate Group, 1954-66; Chm. London Post-Graduate Cttee, 1964-66. Officier Légion d'Honneur, 1946; Grand Officer Order of Orange-Nassau, 1947. *Address:* 22 Kew Green, Richmond, Surrey. *T:* 01-940 4168. *Clubs:* United Service & Royal Aero, Challoner.
                                    [Died 31 July 1971.

MORTON, George F., MA, BSc, DésL; Retired Head Master, Leeds Modern School; *b* 31 Dec. 1882; *s* of J. B. Morton and S. E. Figgins; *m* 1915, J. C. B. Templeton, MA, BSc; two *s* one *d*. *Educ:* Macclesfield Grammar Sch.; Emmanuel Coll., Cambridge; Sch. of Economics, London; Faculté de Rennes. Head Master: Katharine Lady Berkeley's Grammar Sch., Wotton-under-Edge, Glos. *Publications:* Childhood's Fears; Hike and Trek; Hike and Hero; La Psychanalyse et l'Education Morale de l'Enfant; Madhouse for the Million, 1939; Highlands and Backwoods, 1958. *Recreations:* walking and camping. *Address:* Uplands, Shipham, near Winscombe, Somerset. *T:* Winscombe 3234.   *[Died 9 April 1975.*

MORTON, Major Harold Trestrail; Member, Agricultural Land Tribunal, 1948-65; *b* 8 Nov. 1894; *s* of late Thomas Morton, JP, Aston Dene, Stevenage, Herts; *m* 1916, Beatrice Nathalie, *d* of late Capt. James Edward Shaw and Adela C. A. Shaw, CBE, JP; one *s* two *d*. *Educ:* Bradfield Coll. Served European War, 1914-19, with East Riding Yeomanry, Capt. 1917, and Royal Horse Guards; Major, 1940, Home Guard. Master of Whaddon Chase Hounds, 1940-47; JP Bucks 1931; High Sheriff of Bucks, 1943. Chairman: Aylesbury Div. Conservative and Unionist Assoc., 1946-55; Bucks Branch of Country Landowners' Assoc., 1944-47 (Pres., 1947-50). Order of the White Lion, Czechoslovakia, 1946. *Recreations:* hunting, shooting, and fishing. *Address:* The Abbey, Aston Abbotts, Aylesbury, Bucks. *T:* Aston Abbotts 202; 97 Gresham Street, EC2. *T:* 01-638 9991; Glenfiddich Lodge, Dufftown, Banffshire. *T:* Dufftown 327. *Clubs:* Gresham, Kennel.   *[Died 31 May 1972.*

MORTON, Henry Vollam, FRSL; author and journalist. Entered journalism, Birmingham Gazette and Express, 1910; assistant editor, 1912; edited Empire Magazine, London, 1913; sub-editor, Daily Mail, 1913-14; served in Warwicks Yeomanry during War; joined editorial staff Evening Standard in 1919; Daily Express, 1921; special writer, Daily Herald, 1931-42. Comdr, Order of the Phœnix (Greece), 1937; Cavaliere, Order of Merit (Italy), 1965. *Publications:* The Heart of London, 1925; The London Year, 1926; London, 1926; The Spell of London, 1926; The Nights of London, 1926; In Search of England, 1927; The Call of England, 1928; In Search of Scotland, 1929; In Search of Ireland, 1930; In Search of Wales, 1932; Blue Days at Sea, 1932; In Scotland Again, 1933; In the Steps of The Master, 1934; Our Fellow Men, 1936; In the Steps of St Paul, 1936; Through Lands of the Bible, 1938; Ghosts of London, 1939; Women of the Bible, 1940; H. V. Morton's London, 1940; Middle East, 1941; I, James Blunt, 1942; I Saw Two Englands,

1942; Atlantic Meeting, 1943; In Search of South Africa, 1948; In Search of London, 1951; In the Steps of Jesus, 1953; A Stranger in Spain, 1954; A Traveller in Rome, 1957; This is Rome, 1960; This is the Holy Land, 1961; A Traveller in Italy, 1964; The Waters of Rome, 1966; A Traveller in Southern Italy, 1969; H. V. Morton's England, 1975; The Splendour of Scotland, 1976. *Address:* PO Box 67, Somerset West, Cape Province, South Africa. *[Died 18 June 1979.*

MORTON, John Cameron Andrieu Bingham Michael, (J. B. Morton), CBE 1952; Journalist; Beachcomber of the Daily Express, 1924-75; *b* 7 June 1893; *s* of Edward Morton, journalist and dramatist, and Rosamond, *d* of Capt. Devereux Bingham, Wartnaby Hall, Leics; *m* 1927, Dr Mary O'Leary (decd), Cappoquin, Co. Waterford. *Educ:* Park House, Southborough; Harrow; Worcester Coll., Oxford. Enlisted, 1914; fought in France; Commission, 1916; Intelligence, MI7b, 1917; received into Catholic Church, 1922. *Publications:* The Barber of Putney, 1919; Enchanter's Nightshade, 1920; Penny Royal, 1921; Tally-Ho!, 1922; Old Man's Beard, 1923; The Cow Jumped Over the Moon, 1924; Gorgeous Poetry, 1924; Mr Thake, 1929; Mr Thake Again, 1930; By the Way, 1931; Maladetta, 1932; Drink Up, Gentlemen, 1932; 1933 and Still Going Wrong; Sobieski, King of Poland, 1932; Hag's Harvest, 1933; Morton's Folly, 1933; Who's Who at the Zoo, 1933; The Adventures of Mr Thake, 1934; The Death of the Dragon, and other fairy tales, 1934; Skylighters, 1934; Vagabond, 1935; Stuff and Nonsense, 1935; Mr Thake and the Ladies, 1935; The Bastille Falls (Studies of the French Revolution), 1936; Gallimaufry, 1936; The Dauphin (Louis XVII), 1937; Sideways through Borneo (an Unconventional Journey), 1937; The New Ireland, 1938; A Diet of Thistles, 1938; The Dancing Cabman (Collected Verse), 1938; Pyrenean, 1938; Saint-Just, 1939; A Bonfire of Weeds, 1939; I Do Not Think So, 1940; Fool's Paradise, 1941; Captain Foulenough & Company, 1944; The Gascon, 1946; Brumaire; The Rise of Bonaparte, 1948; Here and Now, 1948; The Misadventures of Dr Strabismus, 1949; The Tibetan Venus, 1951; Camille Desmoulins: and Other Studies of the French Revolution, 1951; St Thérèse of Lisieux: The Making of a Saint, 1954; Hilaire Belloc: A Memoir, 1955; Springtime: Tales of the Cafe Rieu, 1956; Marshal Ney, 1958; Merry-go-Round, 1959; The Best of Beachcomber (selected by Michael Frayn), 1963. TV Series: The World of Beachcomber, BBC, 1969-70. *Address:* Melleray, Sea Lane, Ferring, West Sussex. *Club:* St Stephen's Green (Dublin). *[Died 10 May 1979.*

MORTON, Professor Richard Alan, FRS 1950; PhD, DSc, CChem, FRIC; Johnstone Professor of Biochemistry, University of Liverpool, 1944-66; Emeritus Professor since 1966; *b* 22 Sept. 1899; *m* 1926, Heulwen Roberts; one *d. Educ:* Oulton Sch.; Univ. of Liverpool. Lecturer in Chemistry, 1924; Special Lecturer in Spectroscopy, 1931; Visiting Professor, Ohio State Univ., 1930; Meldola Medallist, 1930. Mem. of Council, The Royal Society, 1959-61, 1970-72, Leverhulme Emeritus Fellow, 1970; Chm. Scientific Publications Board, 1961-62; Mem., Editorial Board: Biochem. Society for 7 years; Nutrition Soc., 1963-67; Chm. Cttee Biochem. Soc., 1959-61 (Hon. Mem., 1966); Mem. Scientific Advisory Cttee, British Egg Marketing Board, 1961-70; Mem. Research Grants (Biology Sub-Cttee), DSIR (SRC), 1962-68, subseq. Biology Cttee of Univ. Science and Techn. Bd. Chm., British Cttee for Chemical Education, 1962-65. Chm. Bd of Governors: Liverpool Institute High Sch. for Boys and Blackburne House High Sch. for Girls, 1960-67; Vice-Chm. Board of Governors, Liverpool Coll. of Technology, 1961-67; Mem. of Council, Royal Inst. of Chemistry, 1958-60, Vice-Pres. and Chm. Education Cttee, 1960-62. Mem. Cttees and Panels concerned with vitamins, bread, flour and nutrition generally; Chm., Cttee on Food Additives, 1963-68; Member: Oceanography and Fisheries Cttee, Natural Environment Research Council, 1965-69; Council, Marine Biological Assoc. of UK, 1967-70; Anglo-Portuguese Mixed Commn, 1967-, 1969; Hon. Mem., Amer. Inst. of Nutrition, 1969; Scientific Governor, Brit. Nutrition Foundn, 1967-. Babcock Lecturer, Univ. of Wisconsin, 1960; Hanau W. Loeb Lectr, St Louis Univ., 1960; Redfearn Lectr, Univ. of Leicester, 1971; Royal Society Leverhulme Vis. Prof., Royal Univ. of Malta, 1969. Hon. DSc: Coimbra, 1964; Wales, 1966; Hon. ScD TCD, 1967. *Publications:* Absorption Spectra of Vitamins and Hormones, 2nd edn, 1942; ed, Biochemistry of Quinones, 1965; ed, Protein Utilization by Poultry; ed, An International Encyclopædia of Food and Nutrition, Vol. 9, Fat-soluble Vitamins, 1969; History of the Biochemical Society, 1969; Biochemical Spectroscopy, 1975; contributions to chemical and biochemical jls. *Address:* 39 Greenhill Road, Liverpool L18 6JJ. *T:* 051-724 1331. *[Died 21 Jan. 1977.*

MORTON, Sir Stanley (William Gibson), Kt 1973; Chairman, since 1971, and Managing Director, since 1968, Abbey National

Building Society; *b* 1911. Joined National (later Abbey National) Building Soc., 1927: Estabt Officer, 1945; Jt Gen. Manager, 1958; Gen. Manager, 1962; Chief Gen. Manager, 1964; Dir, 1965; Dep. Chm., 1969. Chm., Nat. House Builders' Registration Council, 1970-73; Member: Milton Keynes Develt Corp.; Housing Corp., 1972-. Director: Metropolitan Bd, Legal & General Assce Soc. Ltd; London Brick Co. Ltd, 1972-. Chm., Building Socs Assoc., 1971-73; Member: Council, Internat. Union Building Socs and Savings Assocs (Chm., Develt Cttee); Council, Chartered Inst. of Secretaries (Hon. Treas.); Exec. Cttee, Metropolitan Assoc. Building Socs (Chm.); Inst. Arbitrators (Pres.); Building Socs Inst. (Pres.); Managing Cttee, London Housing Trust; Managing Cttee, White Ensign Assoc. *Address:* Abbey National Building Society, Abbey House, Baker Street, NW1; 105 Century Court, St John's Wood, NW8. *Clubs:* Caledonian, City Livery. *[Died 18 Dec. 1975.*

MORTON, William Cuthbert, CBE 1919; MD; late Captain RAMC; *b* 1875; *s* of Rev. John Morton, DD, missionary of Presbyterian Church in Canada, to East Indians in Trinidad, and Sarah Etter, *d* of William Silver, Halifax, NS. *Educ:* Queen's Royal College, Trinidad, WI; Edinburgh Univ. MA (Classical First) 1896, MD 1910; Univs of Berlin and Freiburg. Retired. *Publications:* Principles of Anatomy: The Abdomen Proper, 1911; The Language of Anatomy (ed Dr Robert Bridges), 1922; The Harmony of Verse, 1968. *Address:* 55 Thornton Hill, Exeter. *T:* Exeter 77720. *[Died 4 Feb. 1971.*

MOSLEY, Brig. Henry Samuel, DSO 1916; MRCVS; Colonel Commandant RAVC, 1943-48; *b* 3 Feb. 1879; *m* 1915, Marcia Constance Emmeline (*d* 1966), *d* of late Rev. Dixon Dixon-Brown, Unthank Hall, Northumberland. Entered Army Veterinary Dept, 1902; Col, 1929; served South African War, 1901-02 (Queen's medal with four clasps); European War, 1914-18 (despatches 4 times, DSO, Orders of St Maurice and St Lazarus of Italy and of Crown of Italy); NW Frontier, 1924; commandant of the Royal Army Veterinary Sch. and Sch. of Farriery at Aldershot, 1928-29; Dir of Veterinary Services, Army, Headquarters, India, 1932-36; retired pay, 1936. *Club:* Naval and Military. *[Died 10 April 1975.*

MOSLEY, Sir Oswald Ernald, 6th Bt, *cr* 1781; late 16th Lancers; *b* 16 Nov. 1896; *e s* of Sir Oswald Mosley, 5th Bt; *S* father, 1928; *m* 1st, 1920, Lady Cynthia Curzon (*d* 1933), 2nd *d* of 1st Marquess Curzon of Kedleston; two *s* one *d*; 2nd, 1936, Hon. Diana Mitford, 3rd *d* of 2nd Baron Redesdale; two *s*. *Educ:* Winchester; RMC, Sandhurst. Served in France during European War with his regt and also the RFC; MP (CU) Harrow Division of Middx, Dec. 1918-22; (Ind) 1922-24; (Lab) 1924; Smethwick 1926-31; Chancellor of Duchy of Lancaster, 1929-30. Founded British Union of Fascists 1932, imprisoned under Regulation 18B during Second World War. Appears on TV in Britain, Germany and America. *Publications:* The Greater Britain, 1932; My Answer, 1946; The Alternative, 1947; Europe: Faith and Plan, 1958; 300 Questions Answered, 1961; (autobiography) My Life, 1968; pamphlets, articles. *Heir:* s 3rd Baron Ravensdale. *Address:* 1 Rue des Lacs, 91400 Orsay, Essonne, France. *T:* (Paris) 0104211. *Club:* White's. *[Died 3 Dec. 1980.*

MOSS, Col Edward Lawton, CMG 1919; MC; FRCOG; FRSM; MRCS, LRCP; late RAMC; *b* Portsmouth, 1880; *s* of late E. L. Moss, RN, MD, FRCSI; *m* Eileen, *d* of late Col R. Parker, RE; two *s* one *d. Educ:* Dover Coll.; St Thomas's Hospital. Entered RAMC 1905; served European War, 1914-18; France, Salonika, and N Russia (despatches thrice, 2nd class Order of St Anne with Crossed Swords); ADMS N Russian Syren Force; late Officer in charge of Louise Margaret Hospital for Women, 1920-24; and Examiner to War Office in Obstetrics and Gynæcology; retired from Army, 1925. *Recreation:* fly-fishing. *Address:* Donaghmore, Co. Leix, Eire. *[Died 12 Feb. 1975.*

MOSS, John, CBE 1946; *b* 12 June 1890; *m* Grace Elizabeth Bullard; two *s. Educ:* Loughborough Grammar Sch. 4th Bn Buffs TA, 1919-31. Called to Bar, Gray's Inn, 1915. Mem. Govt Cttee on Care of Children, 1945-46; Public Assistance Officer for Kent, 1930-48; Chm. of the Nat. Old People's Welfare Council, 1951-67. Lectured in United States, Canada, Australia, New Zealand and South Africa on Brit. Social Services. *Publications:* editor and author of various works on local government law and practice; contributor to periodicals in Great Britain and overseas, Halsbury's Laws of England, Macmillan's Local Government Law and Administration, and Encyclopædia Britannica; Editor, Local Government Law and Legislation. *Address:* 2 Westlea Court, Dixwell Road, Folkestone, Kent. *T:* Folkestone 54965. *Club:* Reform. *[Died 15 Feb. 1976.*

MOSS, Hon. Alderman Robert; Manchester City Council, 1930-66; Lord Mayor of Manchester, 1949-50; late Deputy Mayor of Manchester; Chairman, 1947, and 1949-52, Manchester Corporation Transport Committee. Formerly Chairman: Wythenshawe Estate Committee; Young People's Committee; Town Hall Committee, Manchester Corporation; City of Manchester Development Committee. *Recreations:* outdoor sports. *Address:* 7 Alwen Drive, Rhos-on-Sea, Denbighshire.
[*Died* 21 *Feb.* 1973.

MOTTRAM, Ralph Hale, JP; FRSL; *b* Norwich, 30 Oct. 1883; *m*; two *s* one *d. Educ:* Norwich; Lausanne. HM Forces, 1914-19; Home Guard, 1940-44. Hon. Doctorate, East Anglia Univ., 1966. *Publications:* The Spanish Farm; Sixty-Four, Ninety-four; The Crime at Vanderlynden's; The Spanish Farm Trilogy; Our Mr Dormer; The English Miss; Ten Years Ago; The Boroughmonger; A History of Financial Speculation; Europa's Beast, 1930; Miniature Banking Histories; The New Providence, Poems Old and New, 1930; Castle Island, 1931; The Headless Hound, 1931; John Crome of Norwich, 1931; Home for the Holidays, 1932; Dazzle, 1932; Through the Menin Gate; The Lame Dog, 1933; East Anglia, 1933; Bumphrey's, 1934; Strawberry Time and the Banquet, 1934; Early Morning, 1935; Flower Pot End, 1935; Journey to the Western Front, 1936; Portrait of an Unknown Victorian, 1936; Time To Be Going, 1937; Success to the Mayor, 1937; Old England, 1937; Noah; There was a Jolly Miller, 1938; Autobiography with a Difference; You Can't have it Back, 1939; Traders' Dream, 1939; Miss Lavington, 1939; Bowler Hat, 1940; The Ghost and the Maiden, 1941; The World turns Slowly Round, 1942; The Corbells at War, 1943; Visit of the Princess, 1946; Buxton the Liberator, 1946; The Gentleman of Leisure, 1947; Come to the Bower, 1949; One Hundred and Twenty-Eight Witnesses, 1951; The Broads, 1952; The Part that is Missing, If Stones Could Speak, 1953; The Window Seat, 1954; Over the Wall, 1955; Scenes that are Brightest, 1956; For Some We Loved, 1956; Another Window Seat, 1957; No-one Will Ever Know, 1958; Vanities and Verities, 1958; Young Man's Fancies, 1959; Musetta, 1960; Time's Increase, 1961; To Hell, with Crabb Robinson, 1962; Happy Birds, 1963; Maggie Mackenzie, 1965; Speaking Likeness, 1967; Behind the Shutters, 1968; The Twentieth Century: a Personal Record, 1969. *Address:* 4a Queensway, King's Lynn, Norfolk.   [*Died* 16 *April* 1971.

MOTTRAM, Vernon Henry, MA; late Professor of Physiology in the University of London (Queen Elizabeth, formerly King's, College of Household and Social Science, Kensington, W8); *b* 14 March 1882; *s* of late Rev. Wm Mottram and Elizabeth Fruen; *m* 1921, Elsie Bulley (*d* 1970), *d* of late H. S. King, St Albans; three *s. Educ:* Caterham and St Olave's Schs; Trinity Coll., Cambridge (Sizar, Scholar, and Fellow). Research under Carl Voit in Munich; Senior Demonstrator and Lecturer in Chemical Physiology in the Univ. of Liverpool; Lecturer in Physiology in McGill Univ. and in the Univ. of Toronto. *Publications:* Manual of Histology, 1923; Food and the Family, 1925, 6th rev. edn 1938; Functions of the Body, 1926; (with J. Lindsay) Manual of Modern Cookery, 1927, 7th edn 1943; (with W. M. Clifford) Properties of Food, 1929; (with Mrs V. H. Mottram) Sound Catering for Hard Times, 1932; (with E. M. Radloff) Food Tables, 1937; Healthy Eating, 1940; The Physical Basis of Personality, 1944; Human Nutrition, 1948, new edn 1972; (with Sir R. Hutchison) Food and Principles of Dietetics, 1948, new edn 1956; (with N. Heaton) Cooking for the Sick and Convalescent, 1951; (with G. M. Chappell and others) Food Sense, 1953; various articles in journals of physiology on the metabolism of fat. *Recreation:* reading. *Address:* Waterhouse, Monkton Combe, near Bath, Avon. *Club:* Penn.
[*Died* 11 *March* 1976.

MOULD-GRAHAM, Colonel Robert, OBE 1944; MC 1918; TD 1930; DL; FCA; Consultant, Graham Proom & Smith, Chartered Accountants, Newcastle upon Tyne and Sunderland, 1966-76; Secretary, Royal British Legion Attendants Co. Ltd; Director: Cold Rolling Mills Ltd; A. M. Forster Ltd, 1951-76; Guardian Assurance Co. Ltd (Local Board), 1930-68; Northern Rock Building Society, 1939-71 (Chairman, 1954-67); W. E. Moffett and Co. Ltd, 1946-69 (Chairman); Part-time Member North Eastern Electricity Board, 1956-65; President Tyneside Chamber of Commerce, 1963-65; *b* 1895; *s* of late Joseph Graham, BSc, Corbridge, Northumberland; *m* 1st, 1922, Beatrice (*d* 1931), *d* of late H. S. Vincent; (one *d* decd); 2nd, 1937, Jocelyn Edith Katherine, MBE 1946, Col Comdt, Church Girls Brigade, 1967-, *d* of late Comdr F. P. Saunders, RN; one *s* one *d* (and one *d* decd). *Educ:* Rutherford Coll., Newcastle upon Tyne. Served European War, 1914-18, with 72 Field Regt, RA (France and Belgium); War of 1939-45 (despatches twice); with 272 Field Regt, RA (TA) and Staff, France, Belgium, N Africa and Italy. Hon. Col 272 Field Regt, 1949-65. A mem. of House

of Laity Church Assembly, 1952-60; Newcastle Diocesan Soc., and Diocesan Bd of Finance, 1948-66; Mem., Salisbury Diocesan Bd of Finance, 1967-73. Chm., Buckland Newton Br., Brit. Legion, 1966-; Mem., Dorset County Cttee, 1967-, Vice-Pres., 1974. Alderman of Newcastle upon Tyne, 1949-61; Pres. Newcastle Central Br., Royal Brit. Legion, 1948-65; Tyne Improvement Comr, 1947-58; Sheriff of Newcastle upon Tyne, 1951-52, Lord Mayor 1954-55. JP 1948; DL Northumberland, 1953, Tyne and Wear, 1974. *Address:* The Manor House, Alton Pancras, Dorchester, Dorset DT2 7RW. *T:* Piddletrenthide 354. *Clubs:* Army and Navy; Northern Counties (Newcastle).
[*Died* 28 *Jan.* 1979.

MOULT, Thomas; Poet, Critic, Editor, Novelist, Lecturer; President Poetry Society, 1952-61; *b* Mellor Hall, Derbyshire; *m* Bessie Boltanskye; one *d. Educ:* Marple; Manchester. Associated with late Charles E. B. Russell of Heyrod Street Lads' Club, Manchester, in Borstal and convict prison work; associated with Harold Wood of Manchester and C. E. Heald in boys' club work in Manchester and London; Music criticism with Manchester Guardian and Manchester City News; art and drama criticism with The Athenæum, The English Review, etc.; Literary Editor and Advisory Sports Editor, Sunday Referee; founded Voices (Magazine of the Arts), 1919; edited Modern Writers and Playwrights series of Critical Biographies, 1929; Chairman, Editorial Board, The Poetry Review, 1952-62. *Publications:* Snow over Elden (novel), 1920; Down Here the Hawthorn (poems), 1921; Brown Earth (choral poem), 1922 (Carnegie Prize-winner); The Best Poems of 1922 (Anthology), 1923; Forty Years in My Bookshop (edited), 1923; The Comely Lass (novel), 1923; Cenotaph (Anthology), 1923; The Best Poems of 1923 (Anthology), 1924; The Best Poems series continued yearly; The Man who was Born Again (translation with Prince Mirsky), 1926; Poems from Books (Anthology), 1927; Barrie (criticism), 1928; Derbyshire in Prose and Verse, 1929; Sally Go Round the Moon (children's novel), 1931; Saturday Night (novel), 1931; Playing for England, by Jack Hobbs (edited), 1931; Sport's Great Stories (anthology), 1931; Mary Webb, a biography and a criticism, 1932; W. H. Davies (criticism), 1934; Bat and Ball: a New Book of Cricket, 1935; Willow Pattern (cricket poems), 1936; Robin of Sherwood (radio musical play), 1937; Master Showman (autobiography of a Circus King, edited), 1937; Down North: by Tony Onraet, Canadian Trapper (edited), 1942; (editor) Cricket is my Life, by Len Hutton, 1949; All-Sports Special! (autobiographical fragment); Bat and Ball (new edn with Foreword by Lord Birkett); I Love England. *Recreations:* moorland walks, chess, cricket. *Address:* The Mill House, Finchingfield, Braintree, Essex. *T:* Gt Bardfield 357. *Clubs:* Savage, Paternosters, Cricket Society, Football Writers, PEN.   [*Died* 19 *Nov.* 1974.

MOUNTAIN, Lt-Col Sir Brian (Edward Stanley), 2nd Bt, *cr* 1922; President, Eagle Star Insurance Co. Ltd (Chairman, 1948-74); Chairman: Bernard Sunley Investment Trust Ltd; English Property Corporation Ltd; United Racecourses Ltd; Chairman or President of overseas companies; Director: Air Holdings Ltd; Airwork Services Ltd; British Air Transport (Holdings) Ltd; *b* 22 Aug. 1899; *o s* of Sir Edward Mortimer Mountain, 1st Bt, and Evelyn Ellen (*d* 1950), *d* of A. Siegle; *S* father 1948; *m* 1926, Doris Elsie, *e d* of E. C. E. Lamb, 2 Queen Street, Mayfair, W1; two *s* one *d. Educ:* Charterhouse; RMC Sandhurst. Served European War, 1914-19, as Lt 9th Lancers and later 96th Royal Devon Yeo. Field Bde; recalled War of 1939-45, served France. Late Gen. Man., Eagle Star Insce Co. Mem. Council, Racehorse Owners Assoc. Ltd. *Recreations:* fishing, shooting, racing. *Heir:* *s* Denis Mortimer Mountain. *Address:* Dunley Manor, Whitchurch, Hants. *T:* Whitchurch 2475; 75 Eaton Square, SW1. *T:* 01-235 5599. *TA:* Eaglestaco, London; *Telex:* 885867. *Clubs:* Carlton, Boodle's, Royal Automobile, Jockey.
[*Died* 17 *Feb.* 1977.

MOUNTAIN, Surgeon Rear-Adm. (D) William Leonard, CB 1966; OBE 1953; LDSRCS 1931; Director of Naval Dental Services, Ministry of Defence, 1964-68; *b* 29 Feb. 1908; *s* of William Mountain, LDS, Cowes, IoW; *m* 1946, Glenda Fleming, *d* of late Cyril Fleming, Groombridge, Sussex; one *d. Educ:* Sherborne Sch.; Guy's Hosp. Joined Royal Navy in rank of Surg.-Lt (D), 1933; Surg. Lt-Comdr (D) 1939. Served in HM Ships: Glasgow, Woolwich, Duke of York, Furious and Rodney, 1939-45; Fleet Dental Surg., Home Fleet, 1943-45; Surg. Comdr (D), 1948; Asst Dep. Dir-Gen. Dental Services, 1948-55; Surg. Captain (D), 1955; Command Dental Surg., The Nore, 1955-59; Fleet Dental Surg., Mediterranean, 1960; Command Dental Surg., Portsmouth, 1961-64; Surg. Rear-Adm. (D) 1964. QHDS, 1961-68. *Recreation:* golf. *Address:* 20 Yew Tree Road, Southborough, Tunbridge Wells, Kent. *T:* Tunbridge Wells 28378. *Club:* Royal Ashdown Forest.   [*Died* 19 *Feb.* 1980.

MOUNTBATTEN OF BURMA, 1st Earl, *cr* 1947; Baron Romsey, *cr* 1947; Viscount Mountbatten of Burma, *cr* 1946; **Admiral of the Fleet Louis (Francis Albert Victor Nicholas) Mountbatten,** KG 1946; PC 1947; GCB 1955 (KCB 1945; CB 1943); OM 1965; GCSI 1947; GCIE 1947; GCVO 1937 (KCVO 1922; MVO 1920); DSO 1941; FRS 1966; Hon. DCL (Oxford); Hon. LLD (Cambridge, Leeds, Edinburgh, Southampton, London, Sussex); Hon. DSc (Delhi and Patna); AMIEE 1927; AMRINA 1939; Governor of the Isle of Wight, 1965; Lord-Lieutenant of the Isle of Wight, since 1974; Personal ADC to the Queen since 1953 (Personal Naval ADC to King Edward VIII, 1936, and to King George VI, 1937-52); Col of the Life Guards, 1965; Col Commandant of the Royal Marines, 1965; Hon. Lt-Gen. and Air Marshal, 1942, and Hon. Colonel: Calcutta Light Horse, 1947; 292 Airborne Field Regt, 1947-55; 428th The Princess Beatrice IoW Rifles Heavy AA Regt, RA(TA), 1950-55; 289 Parachute Regt, RHA(TA), 1956; 4/5th Bn The Royal Hampshire Regiment (TA), 1964-71; an Elder Brother of Trinity House; Grand President: Brit. Commonwealth Ex-Services League, 1946-74; Royal Life Saving Society; Royal Over-Seas League; Pres. of Council of SSAFA; King George's Fund for Sailors; Royal Naval Film Corporation, Royal Naval Saddle Club, Sailors Home and Red Ensign Club, Gordon Smith Inst., Liverpool, Training Ship Mercury and Commando Benevolent Fund; Society of Genealogists; Britain-Burma Soc.; Past Pres., Soc. of Film and Television Arts; Mem. and Past Pres., Inst. of Electronic and Radio Engineers; Chm. and Founder, National Electronics Research Council; Commodore Sea Scouts; Hon. Mem. Honourable Company of Master Mariners; Mem. Mercers', Vintners' and Grocers' Companies; Royal Swedish Naval Soc.; Inner Magic Circle; Sword of Honour and Freedom of City of London, 1946; High Steward, 1940, and First Freeman, 1946, of Romsey; Freedom of City of Edinburgh, 1954; Freedom of Paimpol, 1961; *b* Frogmore House, Windsor, 25 June 1900; *yr s* of Adm. of the Fleet 1st Marquess of Milford Haven and Princess Victoria, *d* of Louis IV, Grand Duke of Hesse, KG, and of Princess Alice, Queen Victoria's Daughter; was known as Prince Louis Francis of Battenberg until, in 1917, his father relinquished title and assumed surname of Mountbatten; *m* 1922, Hon. Edwina Cynthia Annette Ashley (*d* 1960, in North Borneo, on tour as Superintendent-in-Chief, St John Ambulance Brigade), *d* of Lord Mount Temple, PC (Countess Mountbatten of Burma, CI, GBE, DCVO, LLD); two *d. Educ:* Locker's Park; Osborne and Dartmouth; Christ's Coll., Cambridge (Hon. Fellow, 1946). Naval Cadet, 1913; Midshipman, 1916; Sub-Lt, 1918; Lt, 1920; Lt-Comdr, 1928; Comdr, 1932; Capt., 1937; Cdre 1st Cl., 1941; Actg Vice-Adm., 1942; Actg Adm., 1943; Rear-Adm., 1946; Vice-Adm., 1949; Actg Adm., 1952; Adm. 1953; Adm. of the Fleet, 1956. Served in HMS Lion, 1916; HMS Queen Elizabeth, 1917; HM Sub. K6, 1918; HMS P31, 1918; HMS Renown, 1920 (Prince of Wales' Tour, Australia and New Zealand); HMS Repulse, 1921; HMS Renown, 1921 (Prince of Wales' Tour to India, Japan, and the Far East); HMS Revenge, 1923; Signal Sch., Portsmouth, 1924; RN Coll., Greenwich, 1925; Reserve Fleet Wireless and Signal Officer, 1926; Asst Fleet Wireless Officer, Mediterranean Fleet, 1927-28; 2nd Destroyer Flotilla Signal and Wireless Officer, 1928-29; Senior Wireless Instructor, Signal Sch., Portsmouth, 1929-31; Fleet Wireless Officer, Mediterranean Fleet, 1931-33; qualified as interpreter in French and German, 1933; in command of HMS Daring, 1934; and of HMS Wishart, 1935; Admiralty (Naval Air Div.), 1936; in command of HMS Kelly, and of the 5th Destroyer Flotilla, 1939 (despatches twice); in command of HMS Illustrious, 1941; Commodore Combined Ops, 1941-42; Chief of Combined Ops, 1942-43, and mem. of British Chiefs of Staff Cttee, 1942-43; Supreme Allied Comd, SE Asia, 1943-46; Viceroy of India, March-Aug. 1947; Governor-Gen. of India, Aug. 1947-June 1948; Flag Officer, Commanding 1st Cruiser Sqdn, Mediterranean Fleet, 1948-49; Fourth Sea Lord, 1950-52; Comdr-in-Chief, Mediterranean, 1952-54; concurrently C-in-C, Allied Forces, Mediterranean, 1953-54; First Sea Lord, 1955-59; Chief of UK Defence Staff and Chm. of Chiefs of Staff Cttee, 1959-65. Designated by the Home Sec. to examine into and report on prison security, Oct. 1966-. Chm., Council of Atlantic Colls, 1968-. For War Service: Legion of Merit, 1943, DSM, 1945 (US); Greek Mil. Cross (Crete), 1941; Grand Cross of Order of George I (Greece), 1946; Special Grand Cordon of the Cloud and Banner (China), 1945; Grand Cross of the Legion of Honour and Croix de Guerre (France), 1946; Grand Cross of: Star of Nepal, 1946; Order of White Elephant of Siam, 1946; Order of the Lion of the Netherlands, 1947. Not for War Service: KStJ 1943; Grand Cross of: Isabella Catolica (Spain), 1922; Crown of Rumania, 1924; Star of Rumania, 1937; Mil. Order of Avis (Portugal), 1951; The Seraphim (Sweden), 1952; Agga Maha Thiri Thudhamma (Burma), 1956; Grand Cross, Order of Dannebrog (Denmark), 1962; Grand Cross of the Order of the

Seal of Solomon of Ethiopia, 1965. *Publications:* Time only to Look Forward (Speeches), 1949; Report to the Combined Chiefs of Staff by the Supreme Allied Commander SE Asia (1947), 1950; Reflections on the Transfer of Power and Jawaharlal Nehru, 1968. *Recreations:* polo, shooting and underwater-fishing. *Heir:* (by special remainder to the Earldom) *d* Lady Patricia Mountbatten [*b* 14 Feb. 1924; *m* 1946, 7th Baron Brabourne; five *s* two *d*]. *Address:* 2 Kinnerton Street, SW1. *T:* 01-235 0081; Broadlands, Romsey, Hants. *T:* Romsey 3333; Classiebawn Castle, Cliffoney, County Sligo. *T:* Cliffoney 6. *Clubs:* Royal Automobile (Pres.), Royal Thames Yacht (Admiral of the Cumberland Fleet, Cdre, 1944-69), Royal Motor Yacht (Vice-Adm.), Naval and Military, Royal Air Force, East India, Devonshire, Sports and Public Schools, Savage, MCC, Buck's; Royal Yacht Squadron; Royal Southampton Yacht (Admiral); Royal and Ancient; Hampshire Aeroplane (Pres.); Hawks, Cambridge Union.
                                                        [Died 27 Aug. 1979.

MOUNTEVANS, 2nd Baron, *cr* 1945, of Chelsea; **Richard Andvord Evans;** formerly Director, International Federation of the Periodical Press; *b* 28 Aug. 1918; *er s* of 1st Baron Mountevans, KCB, DSO, LLD, and of his 2nd wife, Elsa, *d* of Richard Andvord, Oslo, Norway; *S* father 1957; *m* 1940, Deirdre Grace, *d* of John O'Connell, Buxton House, Buxton Hill, Cork, Ireland; two *s* one *d. Educ:* Cranbrook Sch.; Sydney; Stowe. Served War of 1939-45, Lt (S) RNVR; in Holland during German invasion, also in Bombay on the staff of the Senior RN Officer, 1942-45. Subsequently on staff of ICI Ltd, 1946-61. Chm. Anglo-Swedish Group and Vice-Chm., Anglo-Norwegian Group of IPU. Kt Comdr, Royal Order of Vasa of Sweden. *Recreations:* music, literature, travel. *Heir:* *s* Hon. Edward Patrick Broke Evans, *b* 1 Feb. 1943.   *[Died 12 Dec. 1974.*

MOUNTFORD, Sir James (Frederick), Kt 1953; MA Oxon, DLitt Birmingham, Hon. DCL Oxon; Vice-Chancellor, University of Liverpool, 1945-63, retired; *b* 15 Sept. 1897; *s* of Alfred Mountford, West Bromwich, Staffs; *m* 1922, Doris May, *e d* of Harry Edwards, Handsworth, Birmingham; three *d. Educ:* West Bromwich Grammar Sch.; Univ. of Birmingham and (as a research student) Oriel College, Oxford; Cromer Greek Prize (British Academy), 1919; Fereday Fellow, St John's Coll., Oxford, 1924-27; Lecturer in Classics, King's Coll., Newcastle, 1918; Lecturer in Latin, Edinburgh Univ., 1919-24; Schiff Lecturer, Cornell Univ., 1924; Prof. of the Classics, Cornell Univ., 1924-27; Prof. of Latin, University Coll. of Wales, Aberystwyth, 1928-32; Prof. of Latin, Univ. of Liverpool, 1932-45, and Dean of Faculty of Arts, 1941-45; sometime External Examiner to Univs of Durham, Leeds, Manchester, St Andrews, and Wales; Chm. Cttee Vice-Chancellors and Principals, 1948-49; Mem. Advisory Cttee, Leverhulme Research Awards, 1948-70 (Chm., 1958-70); Chm. of Governors, Birkenhead Sch., 1944-49; Chm. of Governors, Birkenhead High Sch. for Girls, 1953-60; Chm., Northern Univs. Jt Matric. Board, 1947-49; Vice-Chm. Liverpool Regional Hosp. Board, 1948-70; Chm. of Govs, Burton Manor Residential Coll., 1946-66; Chm. of Govs, Malayan Federation Teachers' Training Coll., Kirby, 1951-63; Gov., Shrewsbury Sch., 1951-62; Dir, Liverpool Playhouse, 1952-66; Mem., Governing Bd of National Institute for Research in Nuclear Science, 1957-61; Chm., Univ. Cttee, British Council, 1953-60. President: Classical Assoc., 1962-63; Virgil Soc., 1966-69. Hon. LittD, TCD; Hon. DLitt, Hull, Keele; Hon. LLD, Alberta, Birmingham, Liverpool, London, Manchester, Wales. *Publications:* Quotations from Classical Authors in Medieval Latin Glossaries, 1925; 'Abavus' Glossarium, 1926; Greek Music in Papyri and Inscriptions (in New Chaps in Greek Lit.), 1929; The Scholia Bembina to Terence, 1934 (repr. 1969); British Universities, 1966; Keele: an historical critique, 1972; edn of Kennedy's Revised Latin Primer, 1930; edn of Arnold's Latin Prose Composition (and Latin Versions), 1938-40; edn of Sidgwick's Greek Prose Composition, 1951; joint author of: Glossarium Ansileubi, 1926; Post-Classical Latin Unseens, 1928; Index to Scholia of Servius and Donatus, 1930 (German reprint, 1962); Outline of Latin Prose Composition, 1942; contributions to learned periodicals and articles on education. *Recreations:* music, the theatre, and photography. *Address:* 11 The Serpentine, Liverpool L19 9DT. *T:* 051-427 3199.   *[Died 18 June 1979.*

MOWRER, Edgar Ansel; Newspaper Columnist; *b* Bloomington, Illinois, USA, 8 March 1892; *s* of Rufus Mowrer and Nellie Scott; *m* 1916, Lilian Thomson, London, England; one *d. Educ:* Univ. of Chicago, Chicago, Ill.; Sorbonne, Paris; Univ. of Michigan (AB). Joined Chicago Daily News outbreak world war, serving French and Italian Fronts; later Rome correspondent, subsequently Berlin correspondent during 10 years; Paris correspondent until June 1940. Pulitzer Prize, 1932. Writer on foreign affairs from Washington, DC; Dep. Dir of the

Office of Facts and Figures (later called Office of War Information), 1942-43. Amer. Editor, Western World Magazine, 1957-60; *Publications:* Immortal Italy, 1923; This American World, 1928; The Future of Politics, 1930; Germany Puts the Clock Back, 1932; Mowrer in China, 1938; Global War, 1942; The Nightmare of American Foreign Policy, 1948; Challenge and Decision, 1950; A Good Time to be Alive, 1959; An End to Make-Believe, 1961; Triumph and Turmoil, A Personal History of Our Time, 1968; (with Lilian T. Mowrer) Umano and the Price of Lasting Peace, 1972. *Recreations:* walking, canoeing. *Address:* Wonalancet, New Hampshire 03897, USA. *Clubs:* Century (New York); Adventurers (Chicago). *[Died 2 March 1977.*

MOYES, Rt. Rev. John Stoward, CMG 1962; DD (Trinity College, Toronto); MA (Adelaide), ThD (Australian College of Theology); retired as Bishop of Armidale, (1929-64); Episcopal Canon of St George's Cathedral, Jerusalem, 1962-65; *b* Koolunga, S Australia, 25 July 1884; *s* of John Moyes and Ellen Jane Stoward; *m* 1909, Helen Margaret, *e d* of late Sir Richard Butler, Premier and Treasurer of SA; four *s* two *d. Educ:* St Peter's Coll., Adelaide (Dux); Univ. of Adelaide; St Barnabas Theological Coll., Adelaide; 1st Class Honours in ThL of Aust. Coll. of Theology; course in hons Maths, gaining BA, 1905; supplemented this with course in Classics, gaining MA degree, 1907. Asst Curate, Port Pirie, 1907-10; S Mary, Lewisham (Southwark), 1911-13; Rector of S Cuthbert's, Prospect, 1913-19; S Paul's, Port Pirie, 1919-21, S Bartholomew's, Norwood, 1921-29; Archdeacon of Adelaide, 1925-29; Examining Chaplain, Bishop of Adelaide, 1925-29; Chaplain Commonwealth Forces, 1918-20. Episcopal Canon, St George's, Jerusalem, 1961-65. 1st Freeman of: City of Armidale, 1954; City of Tamworth, 1964. Dep. Chancellor, Univ. of New England, 1960-67. DLitt (*hc*) Univ. of New England, 1961. *Publications:* Marriage and Sex; The Church and The Hour; Australia, the Church and the Future (Moorhouse Lectures), 1941; American Journey, 1944; In Journeyings Often (Oxford Univ. Press), 1949; The Communist Way of Life and The Christian's Answer, 1951; America Revisited, 1955; Third Time of Asking, 1959; Coventry Campaign, 1959. *Recreation:* music. *Address:* Warrina Village, Castle Hill, NSW 2154, Australia.
[Died 29 Jan. 1972.

MOYLE, Baron *cr* 1966 (Life Peer), of Llanidloes; **Arthur Moyle**, CBE 1951; JP; Governor, Birmingham University; *b* 25 Sept., 1894; *s* of David and Mary Moyle; *m* 1st, 1921, Elizabeth Evans (*d* 1949); one *s*; 2nd, 1951, Lena Bassett. *Educ:* Elem. Sch., Llanidloes; Fircroft Coll., Bournville. MP (Lab) Stourbridge Div. of Worcs, 1945-50; Oldbury and Halesowen, 1950-64; Parliamentary Private Sec. to Rt Hon. Clement Attlee, May 1946-Dec. 1955. Chm. of Nat. Joint Council for Local Authorities' Non-Trading Services (Manual Workers), 1936 and 1937; Mem. of Nat. Joint Council for Local Authorities' Administrative, Professional, Technical and Clerical; Mem. of Rushcliffe Cttee for Nurses' Salaries from its inception to 1946, and of the following bodies from their inception until 1945: TUC Local Govt Advisory Cttee; Nat. Joint Council for County Council Roadmen; Nat. Joint Council for Staffs of Hospitals and Allied Instns; Nat. Officer, Nat. Union of Public Employees. Former Pres. and Vice-Pres. Poultry Assoc. of Great Britain Ltd. *Address:* Hafod, The Bungalow, Grassy Lane, Sevenoaks, Kent. *[Died 23 Dec. 1974.*

MOYNIHAN, Most Rev. Denis, DD; Bishop of Kerry, 1953-69; *b* 16 June 1885. *Educ:* St Brendan's Seminary, Killarney; Irish College, Paris. Served in Archdiocese of Liverpool and in Diocese of Kerry. Was Administrator of the Cathedral, Killarney, for fourteen years before appointment to Diocese of Ross; Bp of Ross (RC) 1941-53. *Address:* Bon Secours Hospital, Tralee, Co. Kerry, Eire. *[Died 5 Dec. 1975.*

MUCKLOW, Prof. Graham Fernie, DSc, FIMechE; Professor of Mechanical Engineering, Birmingham University, 1940-59; *b* 2 Jan. 1894; 3rd *s* of Edward Mucklow, Bury, Lancs; *m* 1936. Antonia Mary (*d* 1962), *d* of Col G. A. Kay, Wall, Staffs; two *s. Educ:* Rugby Sch.; McGill Univ.; Manchester Univ. Served European War, Northumberland Fusiliers and Anti-Gas Service, 1915-19. Research Asst, Research Assoc. of British Motor and Allied Manufacturers (now Motor Industries Research Assoc.), 1921-22; Lecturer in Engineering, Manchester Univ., 1922. Chm., Midland Branch, Instn of Mech. Engineers, 1951-53. *Publications:* various papers on problems relating to the internal combustion engine, wave-action in gases, etc, ProcIMechE, etc. *Recreation:* sailing. *Address:* 6 Cherry Hill Avenue, Barnt Green, Worcs. *T:* 021-445 1364.
[Died 14 June 1973.

MUDALIAR, Diwan Bahadur Sir Arcot Lakshmanaswami, Kt 1945; BA; MD; LLD; DSc; DCL Oxon; FRCOG; FACS; Vice-Chancellor, University of Madras, 1942-69; *b* 14 Oct. 1887; *s* of A. Kuppuswami Mudaliar; *m* 1916, Ratha Bai, *d* of V. Damodara Mudaliar; three *s* one *d. Educ:* Madras Christian Coll., Madras; Medical Coll., Madras. Prof. of Obstetrics and Gynæcology, Madras Medical Coll., and Superintendent of Govt Hosp. for Women and Children, 1934-42; Principal, Medical Coll., Madras, 1939-42; Hon. Lt-Col, Madras Univ. OTC; Mem., Indian Medical Council, 1931-70; ex-Mem., Univ. Commission, 1948; Chm., Secondary Educ. Commission, 1952-53; Mem., Indian deleg., Unesco, 1951-56; Mem., Exec. Bd, Unesco, 1950- (Chm., 1954-56); Chairman: Standing Cttee, Inter-Univ. Bd, 1949; Exec. Assoc. of Commonwealth Univs, 1951-52 (Mem., 1948-58); Mem., Legislative Council, Madras, 1946-70. President: WHO, 1961-62; Third World Conf. on Med. Educn, New Delhi, 1966. Hon. Fellow, RCPEd, 1966. Centennial Award, Massachusetts Dept of Public Health, 1969; Leon Bernard Foundn Medal and Prize, WHO, 1971. Padma Vibushan, 1963. *Publications:* Ante-natal, Natal, and Neo-natal Mortality of Infants; Clinical Obstetrics; Midwifery Casebook for Midwives. *Address:* Kensington, Poonamallee High Road, Kilpauk, Madras, India. *T:* (Office) 3854, (residence) 3263. *Clubs:* Cosmopolitan (Madras); Kodaikanal Boat.
[Died 15 April 1974.

MUDALIAR, Diwan Bahadur Sir Arcot Ramaswami, KCSI 1942; Kt 1937; Hon. DCL: Oxon 1946; Durham, 1953; formerly Vice-Chancellor, University of Travancore; *b* 14 Oct. 1887; *s* of A. Kuppuswami Mudaliar; *m* 1910, Kamammal, *d* of V. Damodara Mudaliar; two *s* two *d. Educ:* Madras Christian Coll.; Law Coll., Madras. Advocate, Madras; Mem., Legislative Council, Madras, 1920-26; Parly Sec. to Minister Education, 1920-23; Pres. of Corporation of Madras, 1928-30; Mem., Council of State, 1930; Mem., Indian Legislative Assembly, 1931-34 (Dep. Leader of Opposition); Member: Age of Consent Cttee, 1929; Round Table Conference Federal Structure Cttee, Army Retrenchment Cttee (Chm.), Indian Franchise Cttee, NW Frontier Subject Cttee and Special Textile Tariff Board, 1933; Mem., India Council, 1936-37; Reserve Bank Cttee; Statutory Railway Cttee, 1936; a corresp. mem. of Economic Cttee of League of Nations and a Mem. of Imp. Economic Cttee, 1937; Adviser, Sec. of State for India, 1937-39; Commerce Mem. of Governor-General's Executive Council, 1939-42; a representative of India at War Cabinet and Pacific War Council in London, 1942-43; Mem. of Viceroy's Executive Council without portfolio, 1942-43; Dewan of Mysore, 1946-49; Leader Indian Delegation to British Commonwealth Relations Conference, Toronto, 1933; India Delegate, Nine Power Conference, Brussels, 1937; Leader Indian Deleg. UN Conf., San Francisco, 1945, and 1st Gen. Assembly, 1946; Leader, India Delegation IPR, Mont Tremblant, Dec. 1942; Hon. Editor, Justice, 1927-35; Mem. for Supply, 1943-46, for Planning and Development, 1946, Gov.-Gen's Exec. Council, India; Pres., Economic and Social Council, UN, 1946, re-elected 1947; Leader, Ind. Deleg., UN Maritime Conf., 1948, and Freedom of Information Conf., 1948; Mem., Internat. Civil Service Bd, 1949; Senior Vice-Pres. of the Economic and Social Council, United Nations, 1950, 1951. *Recreation:* golf. *Address:* Kensington, Kilpauk, Madras, S India. *Clubs:* National Liberal, Royal Over-Seas League; Cosmopolitan, Madras, Social (Madras). *['Died 17 July 1976.*

MUDIE, Sir (Robert) Francis, KCSI 1945 (CSI 1941); KCIE 1944 (CIE 1935); OBE 1919; *b* 24 Aug. 1890; *s* of Patrick Spence Mudie, Dundee, and Margaret Lind Heron; *m* 1st, 1919, Mary Spencer (*d* 1960); one *d*; 2nd, 1960, Mary Elizabeth Abercromby (Kaisar-I-Hind Silver Medal, OStJ, Ghazi-i-Azad Kashmir), *d* of late John Ellison Macqueen. *Educ:* Fettes Coll., Edinburgh; King's Coll., Cambridge. Wrangler, 1911; Asst Master, Clifton, 1911; Eton Coll., 1912-13; entered ICS in 1914 and appointed to Bengal; 2nd Lt 6th City of London Rifles, 1914; Indian Army Reserve of Officers, 1915; Asst Magistrate Jhansi, 1919; Joint Magistrate Benares, 1920; Magistrate and Collector, Agra, Sultanpur, Partabgarh, Fatehgarh, 1922-26; Settlement Officer Agra, 1926-29; Sec. Round Table Conference, 1930-31; Magistrate and Collector, Allahabad, Bulandshahr, Cawnpore, 1931-36; Government of India Secretariat, 1936 and 1937; Collector, Agra, 1937-38; Revenue Sec., UP Govt, 1938-39; Chief Sec. UP Govt, 1939-43; Acting Governor of Bihar, 1943-44; Home Mem., Viceroy's Executive Council, 1944-45; Governor of Sind, 1946-47; Governor of West Punjab, 1947-49; Head of British Economic Mission to Yugoslavia, 1951-54; Chm., Mission of Inquiry into Rubber Industry of Malaya, 1954, of the Commission on the Desert Locust Control Organisation, 1955, and of the British Caribbean Federal Capital Commission, 1956; Mem. of the Commission on the Constitution of the Isle of Man, 1958. *Publications:* Agricultural Debt in the Agra District;

(with Comdr I. M. N. Mudie, RN) The Mudies of Angus; (with D. M. Walker) Mains Castle and the Grahams of Fintry; (with D. M. Walker and others) Broughty Castle and the Defence of the Tay. *Recreations:* formerly riding, motoring, mathematics; now crosswords, patience, local history. *Address:* Easter Cott, Broughty Ferry, Angus. *Club:* Caledonian.
[Died 15 Sept. 1976.

MUIR, Sir Edward (Francis), KCB 1956 (CB 1950); FSA 1959; *b* 29 June 1905; *o s* of late W. E. Muir, JP; *m* 1928, Evelyn Mary Whitfield (*d* 1964); one *s* one *d. Educ:* Bradfield Coll.; Corpus Christi Coll., Oxford. BA, 1927, MA 1930; entered HM Office of Works, 1927; Under-Sec., 1946-51; Deputy Sec., Ministry of Materials, 1951-54; Ministry of Works, 1954-56; Permanent Secretary: Ministry of Works, 1956-62; Ministry of Public Building and Works, 1962-65. Chm., Assoc. of First Div. Civil Servants, 1948-49; Liveryman of the Worshipful Company of Fan Makers, 1936; Master, 1958. Governor, Central Foundation Schs of London, 1958-68. Pres., Haslemere Educational Museum, 1964; Mem. Standing Commission on Museums and Galleries, 1965-72; Chairman: Ancient Monuments Board for England, 1966-78; Conf. on Training Architects in Conservation, 1969; A Trustee, Oxford Historic Buildings Fund, 1967; Vice-Pres., Fedn of Sussex Amenity Socs, 1977- (Vice-Chm., 1968-77); Mem., Redundant Churches Fund, 1969-76. Hon. Fellow Corpus Christi Coll., Oxford, 1965-. *Address:* Muirfield, Haslemere, Surrey. *T:* Haslemere 2931. *Clubs:* Athenæum, United Oxford & Cambridge University.
[Died 26 Aug. 1979.

MUIR, Sir Edward (Grainger), Kt 1970; Sergeant Surgeon to The Queen, 1972-73 (formerly Surgeon to HM Household, and to the Queen, 1964-71); Consulting Surgeon: King's College Hospital; Queen Victoria Hospital, East Grinstead; King Edward VII Hospital for Officers; *b* 18 Feb. 1906; *s* of Dr D. D. Muir; *m* 1929, Estelle Russell; two *s. Educ:* Eltham Coll.; Middlesex Hospital. MRCS, LRCP, 1927; MBBS, 1928; FRCS, 1931; MS(London) Gold Medal, 1932; Hon. FRACS. Served in RAMC, 1940-45. Fellow and Hon. Treas. Royal Society of Medicine; Fellow and late Pres., Med. Soc. London. Mem. Court of Examiners and Mem. of Council, RCS (Vice-Pres., 1971, Pres., 1972); Examiner in Surgery to Univs of Oxford, Cambridge and London; Mem. Army Medical Advisory Board; Cons. Surgeon to the Army. *Publications:* Carcinoma of the Colon, 1961; articles in various medical journals and textbooks. *Address:* 149 Harley Street, W1. *T:* 01-935 4444. *Club:* Athenæum.
[Died 14 Oct. 1973.

MUIR, Ernest, CMG 1948; CIE 1937; MD, FRCSE; LLD (Hong Kong); retired; Hon. Medical Adviser British Leprosy Relief Association, 1947-65 (Medical Section, 1935-47); *b* 17 June 1880; *s* of Rev. G. S. Muir; *m* Sophie Vartan (*d* 1961); one *s* one *d. Educ:* George Watson's Coll. and University, Edinburgh. Medical Missionary of UFC Church in Kalna, Bengal, 1905-20; Research Worker in Leprosy, Sch. of Tropical Medicine, Calcutta, 1920-35; Medical Superintendent Leper Settlement, Chacachacare, 1940-45. Hon. Sec. Internat. Leprosy Assoc., 1935-54, 1956-58. Kaisar-i-Hind, 1st Class, 1921, and bar, 1932. *Publications:* Handbook of Kala Azar; Handbook of Leprosy; Kala Azar (with Dr Napier); Leprosy (with Sir L. Rogers) 3rd edn 1946; Manual of Leprosy, 1948. *Address:* 1 Ingram House, Whiteley Village, Walton-on-Thames, Surrey.
[Died 1 Nov. 1974.

MUIR, Percival Horace; Managing Director, Elkin Mathews Ltd, since 1939, Director since 1930; *b* 17 Dec. 1894; *s* of Charles Henry Muir and Annie Hancock; *m* 1935, Barbara Kenrick Gowing (pen-name Barbara Kaye); one *s* one *d. Educ:* LCC primary and secondary Schs. After varied career in business and as lecturer, journalist and actor, set up on own account as antiquarian bookseller, 1920; joined Dulau & Co. Ltd, as Dir, 1927; Elkin Mathews Ltd, 1930. Chm., Collector Ltd. President: Antiquarian Booksellers' Assoc., 1945-47 (Hon. Life Mem.); Internat. League of Antiquarian Booksellers, 1948-50, thereafter life Pres. of Honour; Hon. Life Member: Nat. Book League; Société de la Librairie Ancienne et Moderne. *Publications:* Points, being extracts from a bibliographer's scrapbook, 1931, 2nd series 1934; Book Collecting, Vol. I, 1944, Vol. II, 1949; English Children's Books, 1954 (new edn, 1979); Minding My Own Business, 1956; Printing and the Mind of Man, 1967; Victorian Illustrated Books, 1971; ed, and part-author, Talks on Book Collecting, 1952; (with J. H. Hall) Some Printers and Publishers of Conjuring Books and other ephemera 1800-1850, 1976. *Recreations:* bibliography, music, gardening. *Address:* Scriveners, Blakeney, Holt, Norfolk. *T:* Cley 974475.
[Died 24 Nov. 1979.

MUIR, Ronald John K.; *see* Kerr-Muir.

MUIRHEAD, Sir John (Spencer), Kt 1953; DSO 1918; MC; TD; Vice-Lieutenant of Stirlingshire, 1960-64; Brigadier (retired); solicitor; Hon. President George Outram and Co. Ltd (late Chairman); President, Law Society of Scotland, 1950; Dean Royal Faculty of Procurators in Glasgow, 1952; Member Royal Commission on University Education in Dundee, 1951; Member Royal Commission on Scottish Affairs, 1952; Chairman St Andrews University Statutory Commissioners, 1953; Member of the Queen's Body Guard for Scotland (The Royal Company of Archers); Chairman City of Glasgow T&AFA, 1950; Lecturer in Roman Law, Glasgow University, 1920-54; Secretary Glasgow University Court, 1937-45; *b* 19 April 1889; *s* of James Muirhead and Robina Spencer; *m* 1917, Geraldine, *d* of late Maxwell Hedderwick, Glasgow; two *s* one *d* (and one *s* decd). *Educ:* St Ninians, Moffat; Fettes Coll., Edinburgh; Oriel Coll., Oxford (Classical Scholar); Glasgow Univ. BA Oxon 1912 (1st Class Class. Mods; 1st Class Lit. Hum.), MA Oxon 1952, LLB Glasgow 1919, Hon. LLD: Edinburgh, 1951; St Andrews, 1968; Hon. Fellow, Oriel Coll., Oxford, 1962. 2nd Lt RE, TF, 1912; OC VI Corps Signals, 1915, 51st (Highland) Div. Signals, 1917; served with BEF, 1915-19 (despatches thrice); OC 52nd (Lowland) Division Signals, 1922-29, Dep. CSO, Scottish Comd, 1929-32; OC Glasgow Univ. OTC, 1931-33; OC 74th HAA Regt RA, 1938; Brig. Comdg 2nd, 4th and 1st AA Bdes, in MEF, 1940-42 (despatches twice); BAS, Washington, USA, 1942-44. DL Stirlingshire, 1936. *Address:* 10 Clarendon Place, Stirling. *T:* Stirling 343. *Clubs:* Western (Glasgow); New (Edinburgh).
[Died 17 Feb. 1972.

MUIRHEAD, (Litellus) Russell, MA; FSA; FSG; Consulting Editor of the Blue Guides, 1963-65 (Editor, 1930-63); Director Ernest Benn Ltd, 1951-63; *b* 1896; *s* of late Findlay Muirhead, Edinburgh and London, and Mary Clench, St Mary's, Ontario, Canada; *m* 1923, Benedetta, *o d* of Didier Lagneau, Paris; one *s. Educ:* University Coll. Sch.; Christ's Coll., Cambridge. Served in Gallipoli, Macedonia, Palestine, France (Royal Irish Fusiliers), 1915-19; Asst Editor of the Blue Guides, 1921; Editor of Discovery, 1934-38; Editor of The Chemical Age, 1939-46; Editor of the Penguin Guides, 1938-49; Broadcast series of talks and television programmes on exploring London, etc., 1938-39 and 1949. Served in London Home Guard, 1940-44; Member Council: British Archæological Assoc., 1950-60, 1962, 1972-74; Soc. of Genealogists, 1955-62, 1963-67; Brit. Record Soc., 1959; London Topographical Soc., 1969-75. *Publications:* Blue Guides to England, Scotland, Wales, Ireland, France, Italy, Spain, Holland, Switzerland, others of the series with late Findlay Muirhead; articles and book reviews in the Fortnightly, the Times, Sunday Times, etc. *Recreations:* archaeology, travel. *Address:* 87 Addison Road, W14 8ED. *T:* 01-603 8150.
[Died 6 Feb. 1976.

MULCAHY, General Richard; *b* Waterford, 10 May 1886; *m* 1919, Mary Josephine, *d* of John Ryan, Tomcoole, Wexford; three *s* three *d. Educ:* Irish Christian Brothers. Civil Service, 1903-16; took part in Irish Rising, 1916; Chief of Staff, Irish Volunteers, 1918-21; Minister for Defence, Ireland, 22 Jan.-2 April 1919; Asst Minister for Defence, 1919-21; Minister for Defence, 1922-24; Commander-in-Chief, National Forces, 1922-23; Minister for Local Government and Public Health, 1927-32; Pres. Fine Gael Party, 1944-60; Minister for Education, 1948-51; Minister for Education, 1954-57, and Minister for Gaeltacht, 1956-57. MP (SF) Clontarf Division of Dublin, 1918-22; Mem. of Dail, North City, Dublin, 1921-37, 1938-43, Co. Tipperary, 1944-61; Chm. of Commission of Enquiry into Irish Speaking Districts, 1925. *Address:* 1 Temple Villas, Palmerston Road, Dublin.
[Died 16 Dec. 1971.

MULHALL, John Archibald, CMG 1953; OBE 1947; retired; *b* 19 July 1899; *s* of late Robert Mulhall, Southampton; *m* 1936, Eleanor Beatrice Olive, *e d* of late Harry Arthur Webb; no *c. Educ:* University Coll., London (BSc). Served European War, 1916-18, 8th City of London Regt. Entered Ceylon Civil Service, 1921; Asst Colonial Sec., Ceylon, 1928; Asst Chief Sec., 1931; Actg Dep. Chief Sec., 1943; Sec. to C-in-C, Ceylon, 1943; Sec. to Governor, Ceylon, 1944; Sec. to Governor-General, Ceylon, 1948; Chm., Public Service Commission, Ghana, 1951; retired, 1957; reported on establishment of a Public Service Commission in Cyprus, March 1957. *Publication:* The Public Service Commission in Overseas Territories, 1962. *Recreations:* golf and ski-ing. *Address:* Banister's, Burley, Ringwood, Hants. *Clubs:* East India and Sports, Royal Commonwealth Society.
[Died 16 April 1971.

MULHOLLAND, Rt. Hon. Sir Henry George Hill, PC (NIre) 1930; 1st Bt, *cr* 1945; MP County Down, Northern Ireland, 1921-29, Ards since 1929; HM Lieutenant for Co. Londonderry,

1961-65; *b* 20 Dec. 1888; 2nd *surv. s* of 2nd Baron Dunleath and *heir-pres.* to 4th Baron Dunleath, TD; *m* 1914, Sheelah, *d* of Sir Douglas Brooke, 4th Bt of Colebrooke, Co. Fermanagh; one *s* one *d. Educ:* Eton; Trinity Coll., Cambridge, BA. Served European War, 1914-19; Lt RAF; Asst Parliamentary Sec. to Ministry of Finance, Northern Ireland, 1926-29; Speaker House of Commons of Northern Ireland, 1929-45; National Governor, BBC, for Northern Ireland, 1952-58, retired. *Recreations:* cricket, golf, shooting. *Heir: s* Major Michael Mulholland, Oxford and Bucks Light Infantry [*b* 15 Oct. 1915; *m* 1st, 1942, Rosemary Ker (marriage dissolved, 1948); 2nd, 1949, Elizabeth Hyde; one *s*]. *Address:* Ballyscullion Park, Bellaghy, Co. Derry. *T:* Bellaghy 235. *[Died* 5 *March* 1971.

MULHOLLAND, Sir (William) Walter, Kt 1956; OBE 1946; retired Sept. 1961; Member: New Zealand Meat Producers' Board, 1943-61; Wheat Committee, 1936-70; Director, Meat Export Development Co., 1960-61; *b* Darfield, 1887; *s* of D. Mulholland; *m* 1915, Daisy Eveline Campbell; two *s* one *d* (and one *s* one *d* decd). *Educ:* Darfield. Managed father's farm until 1913 when started farming own 506-acre farm at Darfield; bought land and built new homestead at Ladybank, Darfield, 1920. Branch Sec., Farmers' Union, 1904; served continuously in various offices in this, and its successor, Federated Farmers of NZ (Life Mem.). Formerly Dir NZ Wheatgrowers Co-operative Assoc. (Chm.); Dir, United Wheatgrowers (NZ) Ltd (past Chm.); Dominion President: NZ Farmers' Union (1936 until dissolution); NZ Federated Farmers (1946) and Mem. Dominion Council from its formation, 1944; Chm. Cttee of Meat Industry Research Inst. of NZ, 1955-62; Foundn Mem. Cttee of Wheat Research Inst. of NZ. *Publications:* articles, letters and reports on farm politics, economics and practice. *Recreations:* fishing, photography. *Address:* 6 Maxwell Street, Darfield, Canterbury, New Zealand. *T:* 272 Darfield.
[Died 9 *Nov.* 1971.

MULLENS, Sir Harold (Hill), Kt 1963; FIEE; FRSA; President, Reyrolle Parsons Ltd; Deputy Chairman, The Nuclear Power Plant Co. Ltd; *b* 19 Feb. 1900; *s* of Harry Joseph Mullens and Gertrude Charlotte (*née* Hill); *m* 1932, Winifred McConnell; one *s* one *d. Educ:* Merchant Taylors' Sch.; Durham Univ. (BSc). Joined North Eastern Electric Supply Co. Ltd, 1926 and held various appointments from asst engineer to deputy General Manager until nationalisation of electricity supply industry. Chm. of North Eastern Electricity Board, 1948-54, when resigned to become Managing Dir of A. Reyrolle & Co. Ltd; Chairman: A. Reyrolle & Co. Ltd, 1958-68; C. A. Parsons & Co. Ltd, 1960-68; Reyrolle Parsons Ltd, 1968; Anglo Great Lakes Corp. Ltd, 1959-68; Sir Howard Grubb Parsons & Co. Ltd, 1960-66; The Bushing Co. Ltd, 1958-70; Director: Parolle Electrical Plant Co. Ltd, 1959-68; Pyrotenax Ltd, 1959-67; Dorman Long & Co. Ltd, and subsids, 1955-67; Internat. Research & Develt Co., 1963-68; The Nuclear Power Group Ltd, 1965-68. Mem. of British Electricity Authority, 1952-53. Vice-Pres. of British Electrical Development Assoc., 1956-59. Pres., British Electrical and Allied Manufacturers' Association, 1962-63; Pres., British Electrical Power Convention, 1963-64. Chm. Governors, Rutherford Coll., 1959-61. Hon. Col 105 Corps Engineer Regt Royal Engineers (TA), 1955-57. *Publications:* technical papers. *Recreations:* gardening and golf. *Address:* 4 Westfield Grove, Gosforth, Newcastle upon Tyne. *T:* Gosforth 854297. *Club:* Northern Counties (Newcastle).
[Died 19 *Feb.* 1980.

MULLENS, Sir William (John Herbert de Wette), Kt 1963; DSO 1940 and Bar, 1945; TD 1944; DL; Senior Government Broker, 1950-62; Vice-Lieutenant of Surrey, since 1973; *b* 21 July 1909; *s* of late William Herbert Mullens, DL, JP; *m* 1948, Bridget, *d* of D. W. Berdoe-Wilkinson; one *s* one step *d. Educ:* Harrow. Served War of 1939-45 in Kent Yeomanry (despatches twice, DSO and Bar), commanded 1943-45, 1947-50. Treas., Univ. of Surrey, 1966-; Chm., Ecclesiastical Insurance Office Ltd, 1971-. Prime Warden, Goldsmiths' Company. High Sheriff of Surrey, 1964; DL 1966. Chm., SE TA&VRA; Hon. Col Kent and Co. of London Yeomanry Sqdn, Royal Yeomanry, 1970-74. *Recreations:* shooting, golf. *Address:* Lower Eashing Farmhouse, Eashing, near Godalming, Surrey GU7 2QF. *T:* Godalming 21436. *Clubs:* Carlton, Boodle's, Turf, Pratt's.
[Died 10 *Feb.* 1975.

MUNBY, Alan Noel Latimer, TD 1945; LittD 1962; Fellow of King's College, Cambridge since 1948; *b* 25 Dec. 1913; *s* of Alan Edward Munby and Ethel Annie (*née* Greenhill); *m* 1st, 1939, Joan Edelsten (*d* 1945); 2nd, 1945, Sheila Rachel Crowther-Smith; one *s. Educ:* Clifton Coll.; King's Coll., Cambridge. In antiquarian book-trade with Bernard Quaritch Ltd, 1935-37; Sotheby & Co., 1937-39, 1945-47. Queen Victoria's Rifles, KRRC, 1936-45 (Capt., despatches, POW). Librarian, King's

Coll. Cambridge, 1947-; J. P. R. Lyell Reader in Bibliography, Univ. of Oxford, 1962-63; Arundell Esdaile Lecturer, English and Library Associations, 1964; David Murray Lectr, Univ. of Glasgow, 1965; Visiting Fellow, All Souls Coll., Oxford, 1968; Sandars Reader in Bibliography, Univ. of Cambridge, 1969-70. Mem., British Library Bd, 1973-. Trustee, British Museum, 1969-. Pres., Bibliographical Soc., 1974. Hon. Fellow, Pierpont Morgan Library, New York. *Publications:* Letters to Leigh Hunt (edited), 1934; English Poetical Autographs (with Desmond Flower), 1938; The Alabaster Hand and other Ghost Stories, 1949; Phillipps Studies, 5 vols, 1951-60; Cambridge Coll. Libraries, 1959; The Cult of the Autograph Letter in England, 1962; The Libraries of English Men of Letters, 1964; Macaulay's Library, 1966; Sir Thomas Phillipps, Portrait of an Obsession (with N. Barker), 1967; Connoisseurs and Medieval Miniatures, 1972. Gen. Editor, Sale Catalogues of Libraries of Eminent Persons. *Recreations:* book collecting, shooting. *Address:* 24 Millington Road, Cambridge. *T:* 57632. *Clubs:* United Oxford & Cambridge University, Roxburghe. *[Died* 26 *Dec.* 1974.

MUNCASTER, Claude, Hon. RBA 1974; RWS 1936 (ARWS 1931); Hon. ROI 1974; Hon. PPRSMA 1974; landscape and marine painter; author, lecturer and broadcaster; *b* 4 July 1903; *s* of late Oliver Hall; adopted name of Claude Grahame Muncaster by deed poll, Nov. 1945; *m* 1933, Primrose Keighley, *y d* of 1st Baron Riverdale, GBE, LLD, JP; two *s. Educ:* Queen Elizabeth's Sch., Cranbrook. RBA, 1946-74; ROI, 1948-74; SMA 1939, PSMA 1958. First exhibited at RA, 1919; first one-man exhibition at Fine Arts Soc., Bond Street, 1926; subsequent one-man exhibitions most years in London, the Provinces and overseas; Public Purchases: Tate Gallery, Birmingham, Glasgow, Sheffield, Brighton, Worthing, Eastbourne, Plymouth, Hull, Newcastle, Bradford, Sunderland, Cape Town, New Zealand, Australia Art Galleries. Oil Painting, Shipyard at Palma in Majorca, purchased by Royal Academy under Edward Stott Fund, 1946; series of watercolours of Windsor, Sandringham and Balmoral commissioned by the Queen, 1946-47; One Man Exhibition; Association of Arts, Cape Town, 1948. Lt-Comdr RNVR 1940-44. Acted as adviser on camouflage of ships at sea to Division at Admiralty responsible for Naval Camouflage. Pres. RWS Art Club, 1951-60; Art Adviser to Worthing Corp., 1954-59; Pres. St Ives Soc. of Artists, 1955-63; Pres. Royal Soc. of Marine Artists, 1957. Awarded de Lazio Medal, 1957. *Publications:* Rolling Round the Horn, 1933; Students' Book of Watercolour Painting, 1938; Landscape and Marine Painting, 1958. *Address:* Whitelocks, Sutton, near Pulborough, Sussex. *T:* Sutton, Sussex 216. *Clubs:* Lansdowne; Conway, Naval (Hon. Member). *[Died* 30 *Nov.* 1974.

MUNDY, John Cloudesley, CMG 1947; Director: International Aeradio (East Africa) Ltd; Kenya Power Co. Ltd; (Past Chairman) East African Power and Lighting Co. Ltd; Local Chairman, South African Mutual Life Assurance Society, since 1957; *b* 9 Sept. 1900; *s* of late William Peckham and Amelia Beatrice Mundy, Brighton, Sussex; *m* Annie (decd), *o d* of late Arthur Holden, Skipton, Yorks, and Mary Holden; no *c. Educ:* Varndean, Brighton. Served European War, 1914-18, in RAF, 1918; joined Inland Revenue Dept in UK as Asst Inspector of Taxes; seconded to Kenya as Commissioner of Income Tax, 1937; Mem. for Finance, East Africa High Commission, 1948-57; Mem. of East Africa Central Legislative Assembly, 1948-57. *Recreation:* golf. *Address:* PO Box 763, Nairobi, Kenya. *T:* Nairobi 65360. *Clubs:* East India and Sports; Nairobi (Nairobi).
[Died 8 *Nov.* 1971.

MUNRO, Sir Arthur (Herman), 14th Bt, *cr* 1634; retired; *b* 10 Sept. 1893; *o s* of Sir Arthur Talbot Munro, 13th Bt, and Frances Emily Emmeline, *d* of William March; *S* father 1953; *m* 1919, Violet Beatrice, *d* of Henry Powles, Nunhead, SE15; two *d* (and one *s* Royal Navy, died on active service, 1945; one *d* decd). *Educ:* Wilson's Grammar Sch., Camberwell, SE. Served European War, 1914-18, with 47th Div. (France and Germany). *Recreation:* golf. *Heir: cousin* Ian Talbot Munro, *b* 28 Dec. 1929. *Address:* 276 Wokingham Road, Reading, Berks. *T:* Reading 61365. *[Died* 27 *March* 1972.

MUNRO, C(harles) K.; see MacMullan, C. W. K.

MUNRO, Lt-Col David Campbell Duncan, DSO 1918; MC; DCM; late Gordon Highlanders; *b* Cairnie, Aberdeenshire, 13 Dec. 1885; *m* 1917, Grace (*d* 1974), *e d* of C. T. Studd and *widow* of Martin J. Sutton, Wargrave Manor, Berks; one *s. Educ:* Ruthven Public Sch.; Edinburgh. Entered Army, 1903; served in the ranks, Gordon Highlanders; served in India, and commanded Hood Battalion and Liverpool Scottish; European War in France and Belgium (DSO, MC, DCM, medal of St George of Russia, 1st Class, 1914-15 Star, War and Victory medals, despatches twice); Adjutant, 1st Gordon Highlanders,

1916; retired rank, Lt-Col, 1920; Southern Rhodesia Defence Force, 1922-28; Mem. S Rhodesia Legislative Assembly, 1924-28. Served War of 1939-45 (Defence and War Medals). *Recreations:* golf, tennis. *Address:* Glenhaze, Tidworth Road, Porton, Salisbury, Wilts. *Clubs:* United Service & Royal Aero; Salisbury (Rhodesia). *[Died 24 March 1974.*

MUNRO, Sir Leslie (Knox), KCMG 1955; KCVO 1957; MP (National) for Hamilton West, New Zealand, 1969-72 (for Waipa, 1963-69); *b* 26 Feb. 1901; *s* of Colin Robert and Marie Caroline Munro; *m* 1st, 1927, Christine Mary Priestley (*d* 1929); one *d*; 2nd, 1931, Muriel Olga Sturt; one *d. Educ:* Auckland Grammar Sch.; Auckland Univ. Coll. (LLM 1923; Senior Schol.). Auckland Univ. College: Lecturer in Constitutional Law and Roman Law, 1925-38, Dean of Faculty of Law, 1938. Pres. Auckland District Law Soc., 1936-38; Mem. Council, NZ Law Soc., 1936-39; Associate Editor, New Zealand Herald, 1941, Editor, 1942-51; New Zealand Ambassador to the United States, 1952-58; New Zealand Permanent Representative to the United Nations, 1952-58. Pres., Trusteeship Council, 1953-54; NZ Delegate to Security Council, 1954-55; Chm., First Political Cttee, UN, 1957; Pres. of the United Nations, 1957-58; UN Rep. on Implementation of Hungarian Resolutions, 1958-62. Sec.-Gen., International Commission of Jurists, 1961-63. Hon. LLD: Harvard, Bradley, Colgate, Michigan, Brooklyn, Hobart, Syracuse, Fairleigh Dickinson, Far Eastern (Manila), Birmingham, England, and Auckland Univs. *Publications:* United Nations: Hope for a Divided World, 1960; articles in Foreign Affairs and in NZ Law Journal. *Eecreations:* golf, tennis, walking. *Address:* 24 Pollock Drive, Hamilton, New Zealand. *Clubs:* Northern (Auckland); Hamilton (Hamilton).
[Died 13 Feb. 1974.

MUNROW, David John; Founder and Director, Early Music Consort of London, since 1967; part-time Lecturer in History of Music, Leicester University, since 1967; *b* Birmingham, 12 Aug. 1942; *s* of Albert Davis Munrow and Hilda Ivy Munrow (*née* Norman); *m* 1966, Gillian Veronica Reid; no *c. Educ:* King Edward's Sch., Birmingham; Pembroke Coll., Cambridge (MA); Birmingham Univ. British Council Sch. Leavers teaching appt, Markham Coll., Lima, 1960-61; Cambridge, 1961-64; research, Birmingham, 1964-65; Mem. Royal Shakespeare Theatre Wind Band, 1966-68; Prof., Royal Academy of Music, 1969-73; London debut, Wigmore Hall, 1968; composed and arranged incidental music for: TV series Six Wives of Henry VIII, Elizabeth R, 1970-71; part of Ken Russell's The Devils, 1971; film Henry VIII and his Six Wives, 1972; John Boorman's Zardoz, 1974; La Course en Tête (film), 1974; musical adviser to Michel Legrand on The Three Musketeers (film), 1974; inaugurated BBC radio 3 series Pied Piper, introducing music for children, 1971. Has made numerous recordings. Hon. ARAM 1970. *Publication:* Instruments of the Middle Ages and Renaissance, 1976. *Recreations:* collecting musical instruments, sailing, travel, collecting antiques. *Address:* c/o Harrison/Parrott Ltd, 22 Hillgate Street, W8 7SR. *T:* 01-229 9166. *[Died 15 May 1976.*

MUNSTER, 5th Earl of, *cr* 1831; **Geoffrey William Richard Hugh FitzClarence,** PC 1954; KBE 1957; Viscount FitzClarence, Baron Tewkesbury, 1831; HM Lieutenant, Surrey, 1957-72; *b* 17 Feb. 1906; *o s* of late Major the Hon. Harold E. FitzClarence, 7th *s* of 2nd Earl; *S* uncle, 1928; *m* 1928, Hilary, *o d* of Kenneth Wilson of Cannizaro, Wimbledon. *Educ:* Charterhouse. A Lord-in-Waiting, 1932-38; Mem. LCC for North Paddington, 1931-37; Paymaster-Gen., 1938-39; Parliamentary Under-Sec. of State for War, Feb.-Sept. 1939; Parliamentary Under-Sec. of State for India and for Burma, 1943-44; Parliamentary Under-Sec. of State, Home Office, 1944-45; Parliamentary Under-Sec. of State, Colonial Office, 1951-54; Minister without Portfolio, 1954-57. Chairman, Uganda Relationships Commission, 1960-61. ADC and Military Asst to Gen. Viscount Gort, VC, 1939-41; GSO 2 Malta, 1942; Capt. Grenadier Guards. Chm. Assoc. of Conservative Clubs, 1949-61. Dep. Chm., UK Branch, Commonwealth Parliamentary Assoc., 1955-62. *Heir: cousin,* Edward Charles FitzClarence [late Irish Guards, *b* 3 Oct. 1899]. *Address:* Sandhills, Bletchingley, Surrey. *T:* Godstone 3204. *Club:* Turf.
[Died 27 Aug. 1975.

MURDOCH, Charles; Chief Executive, City of Glasgow District Council, since 1974; *b* 16 June 1925; *s* of Charles and Christina Murdoch; *m* 1950, Irene Moffat Shannon. *Educ:* Whitehill Sch.; Glasgow Univ. Served War: RNVR, 1943-47. Corporation of Glasgow, 1941-75 (Town Clerk Depute, 1965-75). *Recreations:* sailing, walking, reading. *Address:* 21 Merrylee Road, Glasgow G43 2SH. *T:* 041-637 2022. *Club:* RNVR (Scotland).
[Died 28 March 1979.

MURDOCK, Kenneth Ballard; Francis Lee Higginson Professor of English Literature, Emeritus, Harvard University, USA and Master Emeritus of Leverett House, since 1964; *b* 22 June 1895; *s* of Harold Murdock and Mary Lawson; *m* 1922, Laurette Eustis Potts; two *d*; *m* 1942, Eleanor Eckhart McLaughlin. *Educ:* Harvard Univ., AB, AM, PhD. Asst in English, Harvard, 1916-17, 1919-20; Asst Dean, Harvard, 1919-24; Instr. in English, Harvard, 1923-26; Asst Prof. English, 1926-30; Associate Prof., 1930-32; Prof., 1932-64; Master of Leverett House, 1931-41; Dean of Faculty of Arts and Sciences, 1931-36; Dir Harvard Centre for Renaissance Culture, 1961-64; Editor of New England Quarterly, 1928-38 and 1939-61, of American Literature, 1929-38 and 1939-49; Editor of Publications of Colonial Soc. of Massachusetts, 1925-30. A trustee of the American-Scandinavian Foundation, USA. Honorary degrees: LittD Middlebury Coll., 1930; LHD Trinity Coll., 1932; LLD Bucknell Univ., 1933; LHD Univ. of Vermont, 1938; FilD Univ. of Uppsala, Sweden, 1950; LittD, Harvard Univ., 1960. Knight of Order of the North Star (Sweden). *Publications:* Portraits of Increase Mather, 1924; Increase Mather, the Foremost American Puritan, 1925; Selections from Cotton Mather (ed), 1926; Handkerchiefs from Paul (ed), 1927; A Leaf of Grass from Shady Hill (ed), 1928; The Day of Doom (ed), 1929; C. Mather, Manuductio ad Ministerium (ed), 1938; The Sun at Noon, 1939; The Notebooks of Henry James (ed), with F. O. Matthiessen), 1947; Literature and Theology in Colonial New England, 1949; Pt I of The Literature of the American People (ed A. H. Quinn), 1951. *Address:* 301 Berkeley Street, Boston, Mass 02116, USA. *Clubs:* Harvard, Odd Volumes, Somerset, Tavern (Boston); Harvard, Century (NY). *[Died 15 Nov. 1975.*

MURE, Geoffrey Reginald Gilchrist, Hon. LLD (St Andrews); Warden of Merton College, Oxford, 1947-63; Hon. Fellow, Merton College, since 1963; Fellow of Wye College; *b* 8 April 1893; *s* of Reginald James Mure and Anna Charlotte Neave; *m* 1927, Kathleen Mary Seton (marr. diss. 1963), *d* of Seton de Winton; one *d* decd; *m* 1964, Mrs Josephine Browne (*d* 1974). *Educ:* Eton Coll.; Merton Coll., Oxford. 1st Cl. Hon. Mods, 1913; Warwicks RHA (T), 1914-19; served France and Belgium, 1915-18 (MC, despatches, Chevalier Ordre de la Couronne, Croix de Guerre); Fellow and Tutor of Merton Coll., 1922; University Lecturer in Philosophy, 1929-37. Served on Gen. Staff War Office, 21 Army Group, SHAEF in connexion with propaganda, 1939-45; Pro-Vice-Chancellor, Univ. of Oxford, 1957. *Publications:* Translation of Aristotle, Posterior Analytics, 1925; Aristotle, 1932; Josephine, a Fairy Thriller, 1937; The Boots and Josephine, 1939; Introduction to Hegel, 1940; A Study of Hegel's Logic, 1950; Retreat from Truth, 1958; The Philosophy of Hegel, 1965; Idealist Epilogue, 1978; articles. *Recreations:* formerly rowing, fox-hunting and miscellaneous ball games, now sketching. *Address:* 105 Bryanston Court, W1. *T:* 01-262 5724. *Clubs:* Savile, Leander. *[Died 24 May 1979.*

MURE, William, CBE 1945; *b* 9 Aug. 1898; *s* of Col William Mure, Caldwell, Ayrshire, and Georgina, *e d* of 15th Earl of Eglinton and Winton; *m* 1921, Nancy Margaret (*d* 1944), *d* of Col Garton Unwin; one *d* (one *s* decd); 2nd, 1946, Mrs Cecily Vian, (*née* Gordon Cumming) (*d* 1970). *Educ:* Wellington; RMA, Woolwich. Served European War, RFA and RHA. Joint Controller of Non-Ferrous Metals, 1940-45; British Metal Corp. Ltd, Managing Dir, 1963, Dep. Chm., 1964, retired 1972. *Recreation:* racing. *Address:* 16 Selwood Place, SW7 3QL. *T:* 01-370 1560. *[Died 26 April 1977.*

MURNAGHAN, Francis Dominic; Mathematical Consultant; *b* Omagh, Co. Tyrone, Ireland, 4 Aug. 1893; *s* of George Murnaghan and Angela Mooney; *m* 1919, Ada May Kimbell; one *s* one d. *Educ:* Christian Bros Sch., Omagh; Univ. Coll., Dublin. BA, MA, DSc (hon.) National Univ. of Ireland; Travelling Student in Mathematical Physics, 1914-16; PhD The Johns Hopkins Univ., Baltimore. Instructor in Mathematics, The Rice Institute, 1916-18; Associate The Johns Hopkins Univ., 1918-21; Associate Prof., 1921-28; Prof. 1928-48; Dir Mathematics Institute, Rutgers, 1926; Visiting Prof. Univ. of Chicago, 1928 and 1930; Prof., Centro Técnico de Aeronáutica, Brazil, 1948-60; MRIA; MNAS. *Publications:* Vector Analysis and the Theory of Relativity, 1922; Theoretical Mechanics (with J. S. Ames), 1929; Hydrodynamics (with H. L. Dryden and H. Bateman), 1932; Theory of Group Representations, 1938; Analytic Geometry, 1946; Differential and Integral Calculus, 1947; Applied Mathematics, 1948; Finite Deformation of an Elastic Solid, 1951; Algebra elementar e trigonometria, 1954; Cálculo avancado, 1954; Equações diferenciais, 1955; The orthogonal and symplectic groups, 1957; The Laplace Transformation, 1962; The calculus of variations, 1962; The unitary and rotation groups, 1962. *Address:* 6202 Sycamore Road, Baltimore, Md 21212, USA. *[Died 24 March 1976.*

MURNAGHAN, Hon. James Augustine, MA, LLD; retired, as Judge of Supreme Court (formerly Judge of High Court) Irish Free State; *b* 1881; 2nd *s* of late George Murnaghan, Lisanelly House, Omagh; *m* 1919, Alice, *d* of Thomas Davy, Beaumont, Terenure. Barrister-at-Law (Irish Bar), 1903; Northern and Midland Circuits; on Board of Governors, National Gallery of Ireland, 1925-; Chm., 1962; Prof. of Jurisprudence, Roman Law and International Law, National Univ. of Ireland, 1910-24. *Address:* 25 Upper Fitzwilliam Street, Dublin.
[*Died* 13 *Nov.* 1973.

MURPHY, Sir Alexander (Paterson), Kt 1954; MC 1918; Medical Consultant; *b* 25 Oct. 1892; *s* of George Sylvester Murphy and Jessie Watson Murphy; *m* 1921, Esme Park Hobson; three *d* (one *s* decd). *Educ:* Brisbane Grammar Sch.; St Andrew's Coll., Sydney Univ. MB, ChM 1916. MD 1947. FRCP, FRACP. Served War of 1917-19, France and Belgium, with AMC, AIF; practice, Brisbane, 1920; First Head, Dept of Medicine, and First Prof. of Medicine, University of Queensland, 1937-50. President: Queensland Branch of BMA, 1933; 7th Session, Australasian Medical Congress, 1950; Mem. Council and Board of Censors of RACP, 1939-52 (Pres.), 1952-54). Patron, Aust. Post-Grad. Fedn in Medicine. Bancroft Orator (Brisbane), 1954; Listerian Orator (Adelaide), 1955; Syme Orator, Sydney, 1959. Hon. DSc, Univ. of Tasmania, 1958; Hon. MD, Univ. of Queensland, 1967. *Publications:* contribs to med. jls. *Recreations:* golf, fishing. *Address:* Forres, Whyenbah Street, Hamilton, Brisbane, Qld 4007, Australia. *Clubs:* Queensland (Brisbane); Union (Sydney).
[*Died* 1 *Oct.* 1976.

MURPHY, Prof. Alfred John, CBE 1964; DSc; FIM, FRAeS; Vice-Chancellor, Cranfield Institute of Technology, 1969-70, retired; *b* 26 Feb. 1901; *s* of late William and Martha Murphy; *m* 1927, Helen Eulalie Blanche (*d* 1974), *d* of late Rev. Herbert Findlay Millar, Jamaica, British West Indies; two *s*. *Educ:* Altrincham High Sch.; Univ. of Manchester. 1st Cl. Hons Chemistry, Manchester, 1920. Metallurgical Research, Univ. Coll., Swansea, 1920-23 and National Physical Laboratory, 1923-31; Chief Metallurgist, J. Stone & Co. Ltd, London, 1931-49; Dir, J. Stone & Co. Ltd, Light-Metal Forgings Ltd, Chm. Stone-Fry Magnesium Ltd, 1946-49; Prof. of Industrial Metallurgy, Univ. of Birmingham, 1950-55, and Dir of the Depts of Metallurgy, 1953-55; Principal, Coll. of Aeronautics, Cranfield, Bedford, 1955-69. Past Pres. Instn of Metallurgists; Past Pres. Inst. of Metals (Platinum Medallist, 1971); Pres., Brit. Cast Iron Res. Assoc., 1968-70; Vice-Chm., British Non-Ferrous Metals Research Assoc.; Member Council: Inter-Service Metallurgical Research Council, 1949-55 (Chm.), 1962-65; Aeronautical Research Council, 1961-64 (Materials Sub-Cttee, 1968-71). *Publications:* Non-Ferrous Foundry Metallurgy, 1954; numerous papers on metallurgical subjects. *Recreation:* music. *Address:* 4 Riverside Towers, St Mary's Street, Bedford. *T:* Bedford 59938. *Club:* Savage.
[*Died* 25 *Sept.* 1980.

MURPHY, Sir Dermod (Art Pelly), Kt 1969; CMG 1960; OBE 1955; Governor and Commander-in-Chief, St Helena, 1968-71; *b* 10 Aug. 1914; *s* of John J. L. Murphy, Solicitor, Dublin, and Anne Murphy (*née* Pelly), Dublin. *Educ:* Trinity Coll., Dublin (LLB, MA); Oriel Coll., Oxford. Colonial Service, 1938; Western Nigeria: Resident (Provincial Comr), Ibadan Prov., 1954; Perm. Sec., Min. of Local Govt, 1957; Actg Dep. Gov., 1958-60; Actg Gov., 1960; Commissioner for Special Duties, Western Nigeria, 1958-60; Colonial Office, 1960-63. *Recreations:* music, travel, literature. *Address:* 7 Radnor Mews, W2. *Club:* East India, Sports and Public Schools.
[*Died* 21 *Oct.* 1975.

MURPHY, Lt-Col Gerald Patrick, CIE 1943; IA and Indian Political Service (retired); *b* 8 May 1888; *y s* of Lt-Col Patrick Murphy, IMS, and Helen, *d* of Surgeon James McCraith, FRCS, RN; *m* 1926, Charlotte, *d* of Charles Nelson, Gloucester, Mass, USA; one *s*. *Educ:* Brighton Coll.; RMC, Sandhurst. 2nd Lt IA 1908; Political Service, 1913; reverted to military employ for European War, 1914-19; served NW Frontier 1915 and in Mesopotamia, 1916-18; held various appointments as Asst Political Agent and Asst Resident till 1926; HBM Consul, Muscat, 1926-30; Political Agent, West India States and Orissa States, 1930-37; Resident: Kolhapur and the Deccan States, 1937-38; for the Madras States, 1939-43; retired. *Address:* 13 Millais Park, St Helier, Jersey, CI.
[*Died* 7 *Dec.* 1978.

MURPHY, Most Rev. Henry, DD; *b* 19 May 1912; *s* of Patrick Murphy and Mary Nash. *Educ:* St Patrick's Coll., Maynooth. BSc 1932; DD 1938 (Maynooth, postgraduate studies). Ordained Priest 1936. Prof., St Munchin's Coll., Limerick, 1938-58; Bishop of Limerick, 1958-. *Address:* Kilmoyle, North

Circular Road, Limerick, Ireland. *T:* Limerick 44974.
[*Died* 8 *Oct.* 1973.

MURPHY, (John) Pelly; Resident Judge of HM Court of The Sovereign Base Areas of Akrotiri and Dhekelia, Cyprus, 1969-72, retired 1972; *b* 19 March 1909; *s* of late J. J. L. and late Anne Murphy. *Educ:* Mount St Mary's Coll.; Trinity Coll., Dublin. Barrister-at-Law: King's Inns, Dublin; Inner Temple. Asst Crown Solicitor, Hong Kong, 1936; Attorney-General: Gambia, 1947; Zanzibar, 1950; Puisne Judge, Supreme Court, Kenya, 1956-64; Asst Legal Adviser, FO, 1966-69. *Recreation:* idling. *Address:* c/o Allied Irish Banks, 8 Throgmorton Avenue, EC2. *Clubs:* East India, Devonshire, Sports and Public Schools; Royal Irish Yacht (Dun Laognaire).
[*Died* 20 *July* 1979.

MURPHY, Neville Richard, MA; Principal, Hertford College, Oxford, 1939-59; *b* 3 March 1890. *Educ:* Christ's Hosp.; Brasenose Coll., Oxford. Capt. (SR) Royal Irish Fusiliers and Tank Corps, 1914-18; Fellow of Hertford Coll., Oxford, 1919, Hon. Fellow, 1959; Hon. Fellow of Brasenose Coll., Oxford, 1960. *Publications:* The Interpretation of Plato's Republic, 1951; articles on Plato in Classical Quarterly. *Address:* 22 Walden Way, Hornchurch, Essex.
[*Died* 15 *July* 1971.

MURPHY, Maj.-Gen. Richard, CB 1954; CBE 1950; MB, BCh; *b* 1896; *s* of late Richard Paul Murphy, Killarney, County Kerry; *m* 1938, Florence Helen, *d* of late Joseph Patrick Tyndall, Stillorgan, County Dublin; one *s*. *Educ:* Clongowes Wood Coll.; Trinity Coll., Dublin. Lt RAMC 1920; DADGAMS, War Office, 1937-40; served War of 1939-45 (despatches); DDMS, MELF, 1943-46; Comdt Depot, RAMC, 1948-51; DDMS, Scottish Command, 1952. Lt-Col 1944; Col 1948; Brig. 1952; Maj.-Gen. 1953; QHS 1953-56; Dep. Dir Medical Services, Southern Command, 1953-56, retired. CStJ. *Address:* 95 Shirley Drive, Hove, Sussex BN3 6UE.
[*Died* 1 *May* 1971.

MURPHY, Robert Daniel; Statesman; Chairman, Intelligence Oversight Board; Member, President's Foreign Intelligence Advisory Board; *b* Milwaukee, Wisconsin, 28 Oct. 1894; *s* of Francis Patrick Murphy and Catherine Louise Schmitz; *m* 1921, Mildred Claire Taylor; three *d*. *Educ:* Marquette Academy and Univ.; George Washington Univ., LLB 1920; LLM 1928; clerk Post Office Dept, 1916-17; clerk American Legation, Bern, 1917-19; Asst Chief Treas. Dept, 1919-20; vice-consul, Zürich, 1921; Munich, 1921-25; Consul, Seville, 1925; Dept of State, 1926-30; Consul, Paris, 1930-36; First Sec. Paris, 1936-39; Counsellor, Paris, 1940; Chargé d'Affaires, Vichy, July 1940; detailed Nov. 1940 by President Roosevelt to investigate conditions in French N Africa; concluded economic accord with General Maxime Weygand, Feb. 1941; effected preparations for Allied landings in N Africa, Nov. 1942; conducted negotiations for entry of French W Africa into war, Dec. 1942; appointed President's Personal Rep. with rank of Minister to French N Africa; chief civil affairs officer on staff of Supreme Commander Allied Forces HQ, 1942; DSM (American), 1942; participated in negotiations for Italian armistice, July-Aug. 1943; mem. Mediterranean Advisory Commission with rank of Ambassador, Sept. 1943; US Polit. Adviser with rank of Ambassador, Allied Forces HQ 1943; US Polit. Adviser for Germany with rank of Ambassador, SHAEF, 1944; Political Adviser to the Office of Military Government for Germany (US), 1945-49; Dir, Office of German and Austrian Affairs, US, 1949; US Ambassador in Brussels, 1949-52; US Ambassador in Tokyo, 1952-53; Asst Sec. of State for UN Affairs, 1953; Deputy Under Sec. of State, US, 1954-59; Under Sec. of State for Political Affairs, 1959. Hon. Chm., Corning Glass International, 1967. *Publication:* Diplomat among Warriors, 1964. *Recreations:* golf, etc. *Clubs:* Metropolitan (Washington); University, Links (New York); Chevy Chase (Maryland).
[*Died* 9 *Jan.* 1978.

MURRANT, Sir Ernest Henry, KCMG 1945; MBE; retired as Chairman of Furness Withy & Co. Ltd and other Cos; *b* 1889; *o s* of Henry John Murrant; *m* 1914, May (*d* 1973), *y d* of John Archer, Belfast; one *s*. Min. of War Transport Rep. in Middle East, 1941-44; Pres. (1947) Council of Chamber of Shipping; Chm. General Council of British Shipping, 1947-48. Retired as: Dir of Barclays Bank Ltd, 1960; Chm. Bd of Management, Seamen's Hosp., 1967; Hon. Treas. Royal Alfred Merchant Seamen's Soc., 1969; Prime Warden Shipwrights' Co., 1957; Hon. Member: Hon. Co. of Master Mariners; Assoc. of Old Worcesters. *Recreation:* golf. *Address:* Browning's Manor, Blackboys, Sussex. *T:* Framfield 207. *Club:* Royal Eastbourne (Eastbourne).
[*Died* 29 *March* 1974.

MURRAY OF GRAVESEND, Baron *cr* 1976 (Life Peer), of Gravesend; Albert James Murray; Member, European Parliament, Oct. 1976-Feb. 1978, and July 1978-1979 (Secretary, Labour Group, 1978-79); *b* 9 Jan. 1930; *s* of

Frederick Clifton Murray and Catherine Murray; *m* 1960, Margaret Anne (*née* Wakeford); one *s* one *d*. *Educ:* Elementary. LCC Southwark Borough Council, 1953-62; LCC 1958-65 (Chm., LCC Schs Planning Cttee, 1961-65). MP (Lab) Gravesend, 1964-70; Mem., Estimates Cttee, 1966-; PPS to: Minister of Defence (Navy), 1965-66; Minister of State, Board of Trade, 1966-68; Minister of State, Min. of Technology, 1968-69; Parly Sec., Min. of Transport, Oct. 1969-June 1970. Mem., Governing Council, Nat. Soc. of Operative Printers and Assistants, 1971-73. Private Sec. to the Prime Minister, 1974-76. *Recreations:* reading, fishing, watching Association football. *Address:* 13 Parrock Road, Gravesend, Kent. *T:* Gravesend 65958.   *[Died 10 Feb. 1980.*

MURRAY of Blackbarony, Sir Alan (John Digby), 14th Bt, *cr* 1628; Hereditary Secretary for Scotland; engaged in livestock-raising and agriculture in Argentina; *b* 22 June 1909; *s* of late Alan Digby Murray and late Eileen Muriel Shaw; *S* cousin, Sir Kenelm Bold Murray, 13th Bt, 1959; *m* 1943, Mabel Elisabeth, *d* of Arthur Bernard Schiele, Arias, Argentina; four *s*. *Educ:* Brighton Coll., Sussex. *Recreations:* golf, tennis, riding. *Heir: s* Nigel Andrew Digby Murray, *b* 15 Aug. 1944. *Address:* (Residences): Estancia La Linda Mora, Arias, Argentina; Four Winds, Los Cocos, Sierras de Cordoba, Argentina. *Clubs:* English, Tigre Boat, Dorado Fishing (Buenos Aires); Strangers' (Rosario).   *[Died 9 May 1978.*

MURRAY, Sir Alistair; *see* Murray, Sir Robert Alistair.

MURRAY, Sir Andrew (Hunter Arbuthnot), Kt 1949; OBE 1945; DL, JP; *b* Edinburgh, 19 Dec. 1903; *s* of late Alfred Alexander Arbuthnot Murray, MA, LLB, WS, JP, FRSE and Mary Moir; unmarried. *Educ:* Daniel Stewart's Coll.; George Heriot's Sch. Councillor of Edinburgh, 1929; (Hon.) City Treasurer, 1943-46; Lord Provost of Edinburgh, 1947-51. Hon. LLD (Edinburgh); DL County of City of Edinburgh. Outstanding interest is Social Services, mainly among Youth and Aged. Former President of Liberal Party Organisation, 1961-65. KStJ 1954, Chancellor of the Priory of Scotland and Preceptor of Torphichen. *Address:* 1 Randolph Place, Edinburgh EH3 7TQ. *T:* 031-225 5698.
[Died 21 March 1977.

MURRAY, Catherine Joan Suzette; *see* Gauvain, C. J. S.

MURRAY, Charles de Bois; formerly Sheriff in Renfrewshire and Berwickshire, retired 1963; *b* 1891, *e s* of late C. R. Murray, Merchant, Glasgow; *m* 1929, Hope (*d* 1963), 3rd *d* of late James Cruickshank Smith, CBE, LLD; one *d* (one *s* decd). *Educ:* Glasgow Acad.; Glasgow Univ. (MA with 1st class hons in classics, 1912; LLB 1919). During European War, 1914-18, served in France and Belgium with the infantry, and from 1916 with tank corps; demobilised, 1919. with rank of Capt.; called to Scottish Bar, 1919, and to English Bar (Inner Temple), 1922. Contested (L) Tradeston, Glasgow, 1922, and North Midlothian, 1923. *Publications:* Forbes of Culloden, 1936; How Scotland is Governed, 1938 (second ed. revised, 1947); Rebuilding Europe, 1944; The Law of Wills in Scotland, 1945; The Future of Scots Law, 1961; also many articles to legal and literary journals and reviews. *Address:* 92 Hamilton Place, Aberdeen. *T:* Aberdeen 51797.   *[Died 19 March 1974.*

MURRAY, Colin Robert Baillie, CIE 1946; *b* 1892; *s* of late A. A. Murray, Kilcoy, Black Isle, Ross-shire; *m* 1917, Margaret (*d* 1971), *d* of E. G. Drake-Brockman, ICS; one *s* one *d*. *Educ:* Cargilfield Sch., Edinburgh; Clifton. Entered Indian Police, 1911; served European War, 8th Cavalry, Indian Army, 1915-19. Deputy Dir of Intelligence, Govt of India, 1938; Inspector-General of Police, Orissa, India, 1944-46; retired, 1947. *Address:* 51 Seabrook Road, Hythe, Kent. *T:* 67008.
[Died 13 Dec. 1979.

MURRAY, Edward C.; *see* Croft-Murray.

MURRAY, Ian, MD, FRCPGlas, FRCPE; Consulting Physician, retired; late Visiting Physician and Physician in charge of Department for Metabolic Diseases, Victoria Infirmary, Glasgow; Hon. Lt-Col RAMC; Professor of Physiology, Anderson College, Glasgow; *b* 26 April 1899; *s* of late John and Elizabeth Murray; *m* 1924, Annabel M. T. Tully, MA, PhD; one *s* one *d*. *Educ:* Glasgow Academy; Glasgow Univ. (Carnegie Research Scholar in physiology). Retired from Victoria Infirmary, Glasgow, Oct. 1964. Vice-Pres., Brit. Diabetic Assoc.; Hon. Associate, Brit. Dietetic Assoc. *Publications:* Good Health with Diabetes, 4th edn 1963; The Victoria Infirmary of Glasgow, 1890-1948, 1967; papers in medical jls on nutritional and metabolic subjects and medical history. *Address:* Bluerisk, Strathblane, near Glasgow. *T:* Blanefield 70214. *Clubs:* Art, Royal Scottish Automobile (Glasgow).   *[Died 7 March 1974.*

MURRAY, Sir (Jack) Keith, KBE 1978 (OBE 1959); ED; BA, BScAgr, NDD, DipMilSc; retired as Administrator, Territory of Papua and New Guinea, (1949-52), and President Executive Council, also of Legislative Council of Papua and New Guinea; Hon. Life Member, RSSAILA; *b* Brighton, Vic., 8 Feb. 1889; *s* of late John Murray, Coburg, Melbourne; *m* 1924, Evelyn, BSc Agr., *d* of late Ernest Andrews. *Educ:* Univ. of Sydney; Dairy Sch. for Scotland. Formerly Lecturer in Bacteriology and Dairy Technology, Hawkesbury Agric. Coll., NSW; Principal Qld Agric. Coll., 1923-45; Prof. of Agric., Univ. of Queensland, 1927-45, Emeritus Prof., 1975; Mem. Federal Dairy Investigation Cttee, 1930; Fellow Aust. Nat. Research Council; Fellow, Aust. and NZ Assoc. for Advancement of Science (Pres. Section "K" Melbourne meeting, 1935); Pres. Royal Society of Queensland, 1936. Served with 1st and 2nd AIF; Lt-Col, CO 25th (Darling Downs) Bn, AMF, 1940; Lt-Col, GSO2 (Training) Northern Command, 1940; Col comdg AIF Training Depots, Northern Comd, 1941-42; Col Comdg 5th Aust. Training Bde, 1943; Research Officer, Directorate of Research, HQ, Allied Land Forces, 1944; Chief Instructor, Allied Land Forces Sch. of Civil Affairs, Duntroon, 1945. Hon. Col, retired list, 1951. Administrator, Provisional Administration of Papua-New Guinea, 1945-49. Macrossan Memorial Lecturer, Univ. of Queensland, 1946. Mem. Australian Delegation to South Seas Conference (South Pacific Commn), 1947. Adviser, under Colombo Plan, in Agricultural Education to Ceylon Dept of Agriculture, 1956-57; Actg Warden, Internat. House, Univ. of Melbourne, 1959; Mem. of Senate, Univ. of Queensland, 1953-68; Mem. Nat. Council, Australian Boy Scouts Assoc., 1959-70. Hon. Life Member: Royal Society Queensland; Queensland Univ. Union; FAIAS. Hon. DSc Queensland. *Recreation:* walking. *Address:* 49 Dell Road, St Lucia, Qld 4067, Australia. *Clubs:* United Services (Brisbane); Public Service, Konedobu (both at Port Moresby, Papua).   *[Died 10 Dec. 1979.*

MURRAY, Hon. Sir John Murray, Kt 1958; QC; *b* 9 March 1888; *s* of Charles Murray and Marian Dale; *m* 1916, Izobel Booysen; three *s* one *d*. *Educ:* Victoria Coll., Stellenbosch, S Africa; Worcester Coll., Oxford. Union of S Africa Civil Service, 1911; Advocate of Supreme Court, S Africa, 1914; Judge of Supreme Court of S Africa (Transvaal Provincial Division), 1937; Chief Justice, High Court of Southern Rhodesia, 1955-61. *Address:* PO Box 114, Plettenberg Bay, South Africa. *Clubs:* Pretoria (S Africa); Salisbury (Rhodesia). *[Died 11 May 1976.*

MURRAY, Sir (John) Stanley, Kt 1957; BA; Pastoralist; Past Chairman, The News Ltd, Adelaide; retired 1964; Chairman and Director of companies; *b* 27 March 1884; *s* of late John Murray, Wirrabara, SA; *m* 1910, Winifred Olive, *d* of late Dr A. E. Wigg; two *d*. *Educ:* Trinity Coll., Glenalmond; Collegiate Sch. of St Peter, Adelaide; Trinity Coll., Cambridge. Called to Bar, Inner Temple, 1909. Was Chm., Adelaide Electric Supply Co. Ltd, for ten years prior to its acquisition by the Electricity Trust of SA. *Recreations:* golf, racing. *Address:* Rosebank, Mt Pleasant, SA 5235, Australia. *T:* Mt Pleasant 2. *Clubs:* Adelaide (Adelaide); Australian (Melbourne).   *[Died 30 May 1971.*

MURRAY, Sir Keith; *see* Murray, Sir J. K.

MURRAY, Sir Kenneth, Kt 1958; JP, DL (Ross and Cromarty); *b* 23 Aug. 1891; *o s* of T. M. Murray, Geanies, Fearn, Ross-shire; *m* 1919, Edith Maud, *y d* of W. J. Tustin; one *s* three *d*. *Educ:* Winchester; New College, Oxford (BA). Served European War, 1914-18, with Lovat Scouts; discharged early 1918 with rank of Captain on account of ill-health caused by wounds. Mem. of HM's Body Guard for Scotland (Royal Company of Archers). Chm. of the Court, Royal Bank of Scotland, 1946-55 (Dir, 1935-57); Chm. and Dir of various other institutions and companies, 1930-67. Succeeded, in 1936, to the property of Geanies, Fearn, Ross-shire. *Recreation:* gardening. *Address:* Geanies, Fearn, Ross-shire. *T:* Portmahomack 247. *Club:* New (Edinburgh).
[Died 11 April 1979.

MURRAY, Rear-Adm. Leonard Warren, CB 1944; CBE 1943; RCN (retired); Barrister at Law, Middle Temple; *b* 22 June 1896; 2nd *s* of Simon Murray; *m* 1st, 1921, Jean Chaplin Scott (*d* 1962); two *s*; 2nd, 1963, Mrs Nina Sergeievna Shtetinin Seaford Warwick, Buxton. Entered RCN, 1911; Lt 1917; served European War, 1914-18, in Atlantic Convoys and Grand Fleet; Commander, 1929; Capt. 1938; Rear-Adm. 1941; commanded HMC Ships Naden, Saguenay, Stadacona and Assiniboine; Senior Naval Officer, Esquimalt, 1929-31; Dir Naval Ops (Can.), 1931-32; Senior Naval Officer Halifax, 1934-36; Deputy Chief of Naval Staff (Can.), 1939-40 and a founding mem. of Canada-US Permanent Joint Defence Board; Command of Canadian Naval Forces Overseas, 1941; Flag Officer, Newfoundland, 1941-42; Comdg Officer Atlantic Coast (Can.), 1942; C-in-C Canadian Northwest Atlantic, 1943-45; retired,

1946. Admitted Middle Temple, 1947; Pres., Inns of Court Students' Union, 1948-49. Called to the Bar, 1949. Commander Legion of Honour, and Croix de Guerre (with palms), 1946; Commander, Legion of Merit (USA), 1946; Cross of Liberation (Norway), 1948. *Recreations:* sailing, ski-ing. *Address:* 6 The Square, Buxton, Derbyshire. *Clubs:* United Service & Royal Aero; Bar Yacht.   [*Died 25 Nov. 1971.*

MURRAY, (Malcolm) Patrick, CB 1954; *b* 10 July 1905; *s* of late Sir Oswyn Murray, GCB, and Lady Mildred Octavia Murray; *m* 1st, 1934, Betty (*d* 1955), *er d* of A. M. Black, Richmond, Surrey; one *s* one *d* (and one *s* decd); 2nd, 1956, Richilda, *d* of Walter Hemingway, Wakefield, Yorks. *Educ:* Uppingham; Exeter Coll., Oxford (Open History Scholar). MA Honour Schools of Modern History and of Jurisprudence. Entered Home Civil Service as Asst Principal, Air Ministry, 1929; Private Sec. to Permanent Sec., 1931-37; graduated Imperial Defence Coll., 1938; Asst Sec., 1939; seconded for special duty, 1943; transferred to Ministry of Fuel and Power, 1946; Under-Sec., Electricity Division, Ministry of Fuel and Power, 1947-59; Dir of Establishments, Ministry of Power, 1959-61; a Deputy Sec., Ministry of Power, 1961-65, retd. *Address:* Gorley Green Cottage, South Gorley, Fordingbridge, Hants SP6 2PP. *Club:* Special Forces.   [*Died 21 July 1979.*

MURRAY, Margaret Mary Alberta, DSc (London); Professor Emeritus in the University of London since 1959; Professor of Physiology, Bedford College, University of London, 1947-59. *Address:* 42 Wilton Crescent, Wimbledon, SW19.
                          [*Died 6 March 1974.*

MURRAY, Patrick; *see* Murray, M. P.

MURRAY, Sir (Robert) Alistair, Kt 1961; OBE 1957; retired as Manager of three Investment Trust Companies; *b* 3 July 1896; *s* of late Robert Alexander Murray, CA, Pirniehall, Drymen Station, Stirlingshire; *m* 1924, Ottilie Grahame, *d* of late Tom Anderson, 4 Cleveden Cres., Glasgow, C2; one *s* two *d*. *Educ:* Cargilfield Sch. and Fettes Coll., Edinburgh. Served European War, 1914-18, 2nd Lt, 4th Bn Argyll and Sutherland Highldrs, 1915; Salonika, 1915; posted to 1st Bn Argyll and Sutherland Highldrs, 1916, Salonika and Constantinople; regular commission with effect from March 1915; returned to UK, 1919 (despatches); retired from Army, 1919; War of 1939-45, with two searchlight Regts one of which was converted to LAA, also with 11th Argyll and Sutherland Highlanders; demobilised, 1945 (Major). After training, became active in assisting to manage a group of Investment Trust Cos (Man. 1935-61); Dir, various other companies. *Recreations:* golf; race-horse owner. *Address:* 10 Beechwood Court, Bearsden, by Glasgow. *Clubs:* Caledonian; Western (Glasgow); Prestwick Golf (Ayrshire); Royal and Ancient (St Andrews); Hon. Company of Edinburgh Golfers, New (Edinburgh).   [*Died 10 Jan. 1973.*

MURRAY, Rear-Adm. Ronald Gordon, CB 1950; CBE 1946; Royal Navy (retired); *b* 24 March 1898; *s* of late Charles Murray, Consulting Engineer and Naval Architect; *m* 1926, Marjorie Coldicott; one *s*. *Educ:* Whitgift, Croydon; HMS Conway; RN Coll., Dartmouth; Emmanuel Coll., Cambridge. Went to sea, 1 Aug. 1914; commanded RN Lewis Gun Detachment, E Africa, 1916-17; Submarine Service for 8 years; Rear-Adm., 1947; Dir, Aircraft Maintenance and Repair, Admiralty, 1947-49; Manager, Engineering Dept, HM Dockyard, Chatham, Dec. 1949-51; retired 1951. *Address:* 11 School Lane, Emsworth, Hants.   [*Died 7 Sept. 1975.*

MURRAY, Sir Stanley; *see* Murray, Sir J. S.

MURRAY, Sir William (Patrick Keith), 11th Bt *cr* 1673; theatre designer, technician and impresario; *b* 7 Sept. 1939; *s* of Sir Patrick (Ian Keith) Murray, 10th Bt, and Liska, *d* of A. T. Creet, Ghusick, Kalipahari, India; *S* father, 1962; *m* 1st, 1963, Susan Elizabeth (marr. diss. 1973), *d* of Stacey Jones, Penyrwlodd, Hay-on-Wye, Herefordshire; one *s*; 2nd, 1975, Deidre Wood. Founder and Dir, Ochtertyre Theatre; Chm., Film Enterprises (Scotland) Ltd; Director: Scottish Ballet; Temdron Ltd; Monsoon Films Ltd; Rochester Films Ltd, etc. *Heir:* *s* Patrick Ian Keith Murray, *b* 22 March 1965. *Address:* Ochtertyre, Crieff, Perthshire (Seat).   [*Died 2 Nov. 1977.*

MURRELL, William Lee, CIE 1947; OBE 1941; BCE (Melb.); FICE; retired from Indian Service of Engineers; *b* 26 Feb. 1893; *s* of Charles Murrell and Mary Fowler; *m* 1919, Sibyl Hall; two *s*. *Educ:* Caulfield Grammar School, Melbourne; University of Melbourne. BCE 1915; served European War, 1914-18, with AIF 3 years; Lieut 2nd Aust. Pioneer Bn Indian Service of Engineers, 1919-48. On foreign service as State Engineer, Mayurbhanj State, 1923-26; service was with Govt of Bihar.

Superintending Engineer, 1935. Addtl Chief Engr, Mil. Works, and Dep. Sec. Bihar Govt, 1943-45; Chief Engr and Sec. to Govt of Bihar, 1947-48. Member: Nat. Trust of Aust. (Vict); Royal Victorian Historical Society. *Address:* 1 Dalgetty Road, Beaumaris, Victoria 3193, Australia. *T:* 99-2886. *Clubs:* Beaumaris Yacht, Beaumaris Bowling.   [*Died 2 Sept. 1971.*

MUSGRAVE, Noel Henry; Editor, Journal of the Royal Institute of British Architects, 1956-64, retired; *b* 15 Jan. 1903; *s* of Harry Musgrave and Mabel Flinn; *m* 1929, Jennie Elizabeth Sharp; no *c*. *Educ:* St Paul's Sch.; Architectural Association Sch. of Architecture. Editor of The Architect and Building News, 1946-56. *Recreations:* painting, sailing, bird watching. *Address:* The Black Cabin, South Wootton, King's Lynn, Norfolk.
                          [*Died 19 March 1971.*

MUSPRATT, Gen. Sir Sydney Frederick, KCB 1937 (CB 1930); CSI 1922; CIE 1921; DSO; Indian Army, retired; *b* 1878; *s* of late H. Muspratt, ICS; *m* 1925, Rosamonde, *y d* of late Sir Edward Barry, 2nd Bt; two *s*. *Educ:* US Coll.; Sandhurst. Served NW Frontier Expedition, 1908; European War in France, 1914-18 (DSO, Brevet Lt-Col, Legion of Honour); Commanded 4th Indian Infantry Brigade, Nowshera, 1925-27; Dir of Military Operations, AHQ, India, 1927-29; Maj.-Gen., 1929; Dep. Chief of the Gen. Staff, AHQ, India, 1929-31; Sec. Military Dept, India Office, 1931-33 and 1937-41; Comdr Peshawar District, 1933-36; Lt-Gen., 1936; Gen. 1938; ADC Gen. to the King, 1940-41; retired, 1941. *Address:* 22 East Street, Alresford, Hants. *Club:* United Service & Royal Aero.
                          [*Died 28 Nov. 1972.*

MUSTO, Sir Arnold (Albert), Kt 1932; CIE 1923; MInstCE; *b* 4 Oct. 1883; *s* of late J. J. Musto, Alderman of London; *m* 1922, Margaret (*d* 1965), 2nd *d* of W. J. McCausland of Magherafelt, Co. Derry, N Ireland; four *d* (one *s* decd). *Educ:* Birkbeck Coll., Univ. of London. Rotherhithe Tunnel Construction, 1905-06; Asst Engineer, Public Works Dept (Indian Service of Engineers), Government of Bombay, 1907; Indus River Commission, 1907-09; Mechanical and Agricultural Engineer to the Govt of Bombay, 1909-12; reverted to PWD and designed Lloyd Dam, Poona District; Fuleli Canal District, 1913-14; Executive Engineer, Nasrat Canals District, 1914-15; Indus River Commission, 1915-16; served European War, in Mesopotamia, IARO, 1916-18; Controller of Munitions, Karachi (declined remuneration), 1918; in addition was Executive Engineer, Sukkur Barrage Project District, 1918-20, when he designed and submitted the Complete Project for the Sukkur Barrage and its allied Canal Systems; deputation in England on Barrage Project, 1921; Executive Engineer, Sukkur Barrage Project Div., 1921-23; a Nominated Mem. of the Bombay Legislative Council, 1923; Superintending Engineer, Lloyd Barrage Circle, to construct the Barrage and the Headworks of the Seven Canal Systems, 1923-32; Chm., Planning and Housing Commission, Trinidad, 1939; Regional Transport Commissioner for Midland Region, 1940-46, for Western Area, 1946-53. *Publications:* The Future of Sind; The Sukkur Barrage and Sind Canals. *Address:* Danny, Hurstpierpoint, Hassocks, Sussex. *T:* Hurstpierpoint 2299. *Clubs:* Royal Commonwealth Society; Royal Bombay Yacht; Sind (Karachi).   [*Died 29 May 1977.*

MUSTOE, Nelson Edwin, QC 1952; *s* of Edwin and Edith Mustoe, Wynberg, Cape, SA; *m* 1st, 1929, Edith Lake Patra (*d* 1955), *d* of Carroll Ethelbert Hamby, Sherrill, Missouri, USA; three *s*; 2nd, 1960, Anne, *d* of H. W. Revill, Lenton, Nottingham. *Educ:* High Sch. Wynberg; Trinity Coll., Dublin (MA, LLB, University Prizeman in Economics). Served European War, 1915-18, in South African Field Artillery and RAF, in East Africa and Egypt; formerly on unattached list, TA. Entered Inland Revenue Solicitor's Dept, 1925, leaving in 1939 for private practice. Advocate, Supreme Court of South Africa, 1936. Chm. S Africa Settlement Assoc. (1820 Assoc.), 1954-65; Vice-Chm., Royal African Society, 1966-69; Member: Exec. Cttee, Anglo-Ethiopian Soc., 1956-70 (Chm., 1956-62); Chm., Britain and South Africa Forum, 1965-75; Master, Worshipful Co. of Glaziers, 1970-71. *Publications:* Income Tax on Landed Property; Close Companies; Agricultural Law and Tenant Right; Gen. Ed., Simon's Income Tax, 2nd and 3rd edns; Cons. Ed., British Tax Encyclopædia. *Recreations:* foreign travel, political science, family interests. *Address:* 5 Paper Buildings, Temple, EC4. *T:* 01-353 8494; 31 Circus Lodge, NW8. *T:* 01-286 5023. *Clubs:* Athenæum, City Livery.
                          [*Died 8 April 1976.*

MUTCH, Air Cdre James Richard, CB 1946; Dir of Technical Training at the Air Ministry, 1956-59, retired; *b* 21 July 1905; Scottish; *m* 1938, Beatrice Alexandra Caroline Rae-Smith (*d* 1956); one *s* one *d*. *m* 1960, Dorothy Mona Sadler (*widow*), *née*

Longbottom. *Educ:* Aboyne Sch., Aberdeenshire; Royal Air Force Apprentice Sch., Cranwell; Royal Air Force College, Cranwell. RAF apprentice training, 1921-24; RAF cadet training, 1925-26; Pilot Officer, 1926; Flying Officer, 1928; Flight Lt 1932; Sqdn Leader, 1937; Wing Comdr 1940; Group Capt. 1942; Air Commodore (Acting), 1944-46 and 1951-54; Air Cdre (Subs.), 1954; Senior Technical Staff Officer, Headquarters Flying Training Command, 1953-56. Qualified as Engineer Specialist Officer at RAF Sch. of Aeronautical Engineering, 1931-33; psa 1938. *Recreations:* gardening, shooting. *Address:* c/o Lloyds Bank, Cox & King's Branch, 6 Pall Mall, SW1.
[Died 12 Aug. 1973.

MYLES, Captain Edgar Kinghorn, VC 1916; DSO 1917; late The King's Regiment and Worcestershire Regiment; *b* 23 July 1894; married. Served European War, Egypt, Gallipoli 1915; Mesopotamia, 1916-18 (VC, DSO). *Address:* Huntly, Bishopsteignton, South Devon. *T:* Teignmouth 5201.
[Died 31 Jan. 1977.

MYSORE, HH the Maharaja Sri Jaya Chamarajendra Wadiyar Bahadur, GCB 1946; GCSI 1945; Hon. LLD Benares Hindu University, 1942; DLitt Annamalai University, 1955; Governor of Mysore; formerly Chancellor of Mysore University; Chancellor of Karnatak University; *b* 18 July 1919; *o s* of late Sri Kanteerava Narasimharaja Wadiyar, Yuvaraja of Mysore. *Educ:* privately; Univ. of Mysore; BA 1938. Hon. FTCL 1946. The area of the State is over 70,000 square miles and it has a population of over 19 millions. *Recreations:* music, riding, tennis, racquets, big game shooting, golf. *Address:* The Palace, Mysore.
[Died 23 Sept. 1974.

N

NABARRO, Sir Gerald (David Nunes), Kt 1963; MP (C) South Worcs, since 1966; director of companies; broadcaster, televiser, journalist, publisher and author; *b* 29 June 1913; *e* surv. *s* of S. N. Nabarro, London; *m* 1943, Joan Maud Violet im Thurn, *e d* of late Col B. B. von B. im Thurn, DSO, MC, Dawn House, Winchester, Hants; two *s* two *d*. *Educ:* LCC Sch. until age of 14. Regular Army, 1930-37; Territorial Army, 1937-43; TARO, 1943-63. Worked in all grades in industry, mostly engineering and sawmilling, from labourer to Managing Dir. Contested (C) West Bromwich Div. of Staffs, 1945; MP (C) Kidderminster Div. of Worcs, 1950-64. Chm. West Midlands Fedn (56 Constituencies) of Young Conservatives, 1946-48 (Pres., 1948-50); Author of Parliamentary legislation for: Clean Air, 1955; Coroners' Act, 1953; Thermal Insulation (Industrial Buildings) Act, 1957; Oil Burners (Standards) Act, 1960. Governor, Univ. of Birmingham; Mem., Convocation, Univ. of Aston. President: Road Passenger and Transport Assoc., 1951-55; Nat. Union of Manufacturers, Merseyside, 1956-62; Inst. of Marketing (London Branch) 1968-70; British Direct Mail Advertising Assoc., 1968-72; Chm., Council for Independent Education; MInstF; FRSA; Member: Soc. of Authors; Inst. of Dirs; Amer. Fedn of Television and Radio Artists (AFTRA). Trustee, Elgar Birthplace Trust. Pres., Internat. Coil Winding Assoc., and numerous sporting, cultural, and welfare organisations in Worcs. Motto, Audax et Fidelis. *Publications:* Portrait of a Politician, 1970; Severn Valley Steam, 1971; Steam Nostalgia, 1972; Learners at Large, 1973; Exploits of a Politician, 1973; numerous contributions on economics, finance, and industry. *Recreations:* travel, book collecting, railways, walking. *Address:* The Orchard House, Broadway, Worcs; House of Commons, SW1. *T:* 01-219 3000. *Clubs:* Carlton, Army and Navy.
[Died 18 Nov. 1973.

NABOKOV, Vladimir; American author and lepidopterist; *b* St Petersburg (now Leningrad), Russia, 23 April 1899; *s* of Vladimir Nabokov and Hélène Rukavishnikov; *m* 1925, Véra Slonim; one *s*. *Educ:* St Petersburg; Trinity Coll., Cambridge (BA). He then rejoined his family (in exile from Russia) in Berlin, 1922; there, he trans. some English literary works into Russian, including Alice in Wonderland (publ. 1923), and between 1923 and 1940 he wrote in Russian (in Berlin and Paris) novels, poetry, short stories and plays; much of this work has now been published in England and USA (trans. by him, mostly with his son, Dmitri, also with Michael Scammell and M. Glenny). In 1940 he settled in USA (becoming a US Citizen, 1945). Lecturer, Wellesley Coll., 1941-48; Research Fellow in Lepidoptera, Harvard Univ. Museum of Comparative Zoology, 1942-48; Prof. of Russian Literature, Cornell Univ., 1948-59.

Grant in Literature, Amer. Acad. Arts and Letters, 1951; Guggenheim Fellow, 1943 and 1953; Brandeis Univ. Medal, 1964; Award, Amer. Acad. of Arts, 1969; Nat. Medal for Literature, USA, 1973. *Publications: novels:* The Real Life of Sebastian Knight (USA, 1941, 1959; Eng., 1945, 1960); Bend Sinister (USA, 1947; Eng., 1960, 2nd edn 1972); Pnin (USA and Eng., 1957); Lolita (USA, 1958; Eng., 1959; filmed, 1962); Pale Fire (USA and Eng., 1962); Ada (USA and Eng., 1969); Transparent Things (USA 1972; Eng. 1973); Look at the Harlequins (USA, 1974; Eng. 1975); *novels trans. from his Russian:* Camera Obscura (Eng., 1936; USA, as Laughter in the Dark, 1938; Eng., thus, 1961; filmed 1969); Despair (Eng., 1937; USA, 1966); Invitation to a Beheading (USA and Eng., 1960); The Gift (USA and Eng., 1963); The Defense (USA, 1964; Eng., as The Defence, 1964); The Eye (USA, 1965; Eng., 1966); King, Queen, Knave (USA and Eng., 1968; filmed 1971); Mary (USA 1970, Eng. 1971); Glory (USA and Eng., 1971); *poetry:* Poems (USA, 1959; Eng., 1961); Poems and Problems (USA 1971; Eng. 1972); *biography:* Nikolai Gogol (USA, 1944; Eng., 1947, repr. 1973); *short stories:* Nine Stories (USA, 1947); Nabokov's Dozen (13 stories, some from his Russian or French, USA, 1958; Eng., 1959); Nabokov's Quartet (USA, 1966; Eng., 1967); A Russian Beauty and other stories (USA and Eng. 1973); Tyrants Destroyed and other stories, 1975; Details of a Sunset, 1976; *anthology:* Nabokov's Congeries (USA, 1968); *essays:* Strong Opinions, 1974; *plays:* several, written from 1923 to 1938, inc. The Waltz Invention (publ. USA, 1966, produced USA and Oxford); *screenplay:* Lolita (Eng. and USA, 1974); *memoirs:* Conclusive Evidence (USA and Eng., 1951; rev. edn, as Speak, Memory, USA and Eng., 1967); *translations from other writers include:* Three Russian Poets (USA, 1945; Eng., 1947); A Hero of Our Time (with D. Nabokov, by M. Lermontov) (USA, 1958); Song of Igor's Campaign (12th century epic) (USA and Eng., 1960); Eugene Onegin (by A. Pushkin) 4 vol. project, begun by him in 1949: vol. 1, introd. and text; vols 2-4, commentaries, appendix, index (USA, 1964; Eng., 1964); *lepidopterology:* The Nearctic Members of the Genus Lycaeides Hübner (Harvard, 1949) and others. *Recreation:* butterfly hunting. *Address:* c/o Weidenfeld & Nicolson, 11 St John's Hill, SW11 1XA.
[Died 2 July 1977.

NAIRN, Bryce James Miller, CBE 1960 (OBE 1944); Consul-General, Tangier, 1957-63, retired; *b* 9 July 1903; *s* of Cuthbert and Mary Nairn; *m* 1928, Margaret Mary, *d* of T. R. White, Orkney; one *d* (and one *d* decd). *Educ:* Pollokshields Academy, Glasgow. After taking MRCVS, farmed in French Morocco, 1926-32; joined Foreign Service, 1933; served Marrakesh and Tangier, 1933-40; Brazzaville, 1941-43; Marrakesh and Casablanca, 1943-44; Consul: Bordeaux, 1944-48, Madeira, 1948-50, St Paul-Minneapolis, 1950-53; Consul-General, Lourenço-Marques, 1953-57. *Recreations:* riding, shooting, fruit farming, golf. *Address:* 29 The Crescent, Nunthorpe, Middlesbrough, Cleveland TS7 0JW. *T:* Middlesbrough 316667.
[Died 15 Sept. 1978.

NAIRN, George Alexander Stokes, MBE 1918; FRSA 1950; *b* 27 Aug. 1889; *s* of George McKie Nairn; *m* 1925, Doreen Mann Watson; one *s* one *d*. *Educ:* Liverpool Coll. Commissioned (TA), 1913; served European War, 1914-18, 9th Battalion, The King's Liverpool Regt, rank of Major. Joined Lever Brothers, 1919; Dir, William Gossage & Sons, Widnes, 1919-32, Chm., 1932-34; Lever Brothers & Unilever Ltd. Continental Liaison Cttee, London and Rotterdam, 1934-40; Pres. Lever Brothers, Canada, 1940-44; Unilever UK Food Executive, 1945-46; Chm., Lever Brothers, Port Sunlight, Ltd, 1947-54; Dir, North-Western Industrial Estates Ltd, 1949-59. Mem. Mersey Docks and Harbour Board, 1949-55; Mem. Merseyside and North Wales Electricity Board, 1949-56. Chm. Liverpool Collegiate Sch. Bd of Governors; Governor, Liverpool Coll.; Council, Manchester Coll. of Sci. and Tech.; Member: Exec. and Finance Cttee, Liverpool Cathedral; Central Board of Finance, Church of England, 1955-65. Former Member: NW Regional Academic Bd for Advanced Technology, also NW Regional Advisory Coun. on Educ. for Industry and Commerce, 1948-57. Central Electricity Authority, 1956-57; Pt-time Mem. of the Central Electricity Generating Bd, 1957-60. *Recreations:* gardening and photography. *Address:* Highlawn, Mill Road, Bromborough, Cheshire. *T:* 051-334 2244.
[Died 13 July 1974.

NAISH, Lieut-Commander George Prideaux Brabant, VRD 1965; RNR; Keeper, National Maritime Museum, Greenwich, 1969-71, Historical Consultant to Director, since 1971; *b* 6 April 1909; *s* of Rev. Francis Clement Prideaux Naish and Irene Stainforth Brabant; *m* 1937, Elizabeth Joan, *o c* of Henry Mills Goldsmith; two *s*. *Educ:* St Edward's School, Oxford; University College, Southampton. Joined Staff of newly constituted National Maritime Museum, 1935. Served in RNVR during War of 1939-45; transferred to permanent RNVR and RNR shortly after demobilization. Pres., Council for Nautical Archæology; Hon. Sec., Soc. for Nautical Research; FSA. *Publications:* Nelson's Letters to his Wife (ed for Navy Records Soc.), 1958; Spanish Armada Documents (ed for Navy Records Soc.), 1952; Ships and Shipbuilding, chapters in A History of Technology, ed Singer, vol. 3, 1957 and vol. 4, 1958; (jtly) The Age of Sailing Ships, 1976, etc. *Recreation:* yacht cruising. *Address:* 5 Hardy Road, Blackheath, SE3. *T:* 01-858 1333. *Club:* Royal Cruising. *[Died 30 July 1977.*

NALDER, Major-General Reginald Francis Heaton, CB 1944; OBE 1941; BSc; retired; *b* 2 Feb. 1895; *s* of late Francis Henry Nalder; *m* 1916, Kathleen, *d* of late William Heaton Jacob; one *s* one *d. Educ:* Dulwich Coll.; London University. Commissioned Loyal North Lancashire Regt, 1914; E Surrey Regt, 1915; served European War, France, Belgium and Italy, 1916-18; transferred to Royal Signals, 1922; North-West Frontier of India, 1930-31; at War Office, 1935-39; served War of 1939-45: in France and Belgium, 1939-40; Chief Signal Officer, Allied Armies in Italy, 1943-45, and AFHQ, 1945 (despatches, OBE, CB, Commander Legion of Merit, Officer Legion of Honour, French Croix de Guerre). Signal Officer-in-Chief, India, 1946-47; retired, 1947; Colonel Commandant Royal Signals, 1955-60. Princess Mary Medal (Royal Signals Institution), 1966. *Publications:* British Army Signals in the Second World War, 1953; The Royal Corps of Signals, 1958. *Address:* 23 Alexandra Road, Epsom, Surrey KT17 4BP. *T:* Epsom 22041. *Clubs:* Naval and Military, Royal Automobile. *[Died 12 April 1978.*

NAN KIVELL, Sir Rex de Charambac, Kt 1976; CMG 1966; Director of the Redfern Gallery, London, since 1925; *b* 9 April 1899; *s* of George Henry and Mary Louise Nan Kivell. *Educ:* New Brighton School and Canterbury College, New Zealand; Royal College of Science, London. New Zealand Army, 1915-18. Judge's Marshal to the High Court Judges, London, 1920-35. Publisher, books and art publications. Archæologist, working chiefly on Romano-British sites in Wiltshire. Formed the extensive Australasian Collection of early manuscripts, books, paintings, drawings, prints, maps, log-books, etc, now housed in the National Library, Canberra, Australia. Order of Dannebrog, 1935. *Publications:* The La Tene occupation of Britain, 1935; Portraits of the Famous and Infamous, 1970; archæological researches; books on English artists; articles for Wiltshire archæological magazines. *Recreations:* studying architecture, gardening, collecting modern paintings. *Address:* 20 Cork Street, Burlington Gardens, W1. *T:* 01-734 1732.
[Died 7 June 1977.

NAPIER, Hon. Sir Albert (Edward Alexander), KCB 1945 (CB 1922); KCVO 1954; QC 1947; *b* 4 Sept. 1881; *y s* of F. M. 1st Lord Napier of Magdala and late Mary Cecilia, CI, *d* of Major-Gen. E. W. S. Scott; *m* 1917, Amy Gladys Stuart, *d* of late F. M. Sir George Stuart White; one *d* (*o s* killed on active service, 1942). *Educ:* Temple Grove; Eton (King's Scholar); New College, Oxford (Exhibitioner); 1st Class Lit. Hum. 1904. Eldon Law Scholar, 1906; called to the Bar, Inner Temple, 1909; Private Secretary to the Lord Chancellor, 1915-19; Deputy Serjeant-at-Arms in the House of Lords, 1916-19; Assistant Secretary in the Lord Chancellor's office and Deputy Clerk of the Crown, 1919-44; Clerk of the Crown in Chancery and Permanent Secretary to the Lord Chancellor, 1944-54. Bencher of the Inner Temple, 1949. *Address:* 12 Carlyle Mansions, Cheyne Walk, Chelsea, SW3. *T:* 01-352 8378. *Club:* Travellers'.
[Died 18 July 1973.

NAPIER, Charles (Goddard), RSW; artist; *b* 1 Aug. 1889; 2nd *s* of late Andrew Nelson Napier, herbalist, Edinburgh; *m* 1934, Hazel May Eadie (*d* 1960), *d* of late Arthur William Ballance, Herringswell. *Educ:* George Watson's Coll., Edinburgh. Studied Edinburgh College of Art; works mostly in water-colours; attracted by architectural subjects; did a series of black and white drawings of prominent Edinburgh buildings; painted in Holland, France and Italy; exhibited RSA, Glasgow Institute, USA, Canada, and New Zealand; first London exhibition of water-colours, Brook Street Art Gallery, Feb. 1934; exhibition of water colours, British Council, Oxford, 1949; second exhibition of water colours, Phantasy and Dream, British Council, 1952. Marlborough in Wiltshire purchased 1937, and In Wells Harbour, Norfolk, 1940, for Scottish Modern Arts, Edinburgh. *Address:* Nursing Home, 4 East Castle Road, Edinburgh EH10 5AR. *T:* 031-229 5281. *[Died 20 July 1978.*

NAPIER, Ian Patrick Robert, MC; *b* 24 July 1895; *yr s* of Henry Melvill Napier, JP, Milton House, Bowling, Dunbartonshire; *m* 1st, 1927, Frieda, *o d* of 1st Baron Essendon; two *s* ; 2nd, 1942, Nora, *d* of John R. Moore; one *s. Educ:* Eton College (rowed in Eton eight, 1912, 1913, 1914). Served European War, 1914-18: Argyll and Sutherland Highlanders, Capt. 1916; seconded to

RFC, 1916; attached Aviation French Army, June-Dec. 1917. Shipbuilding (in family firm) and Shipowning. Director: Napier & Miller Ltd, 1925-34; Hudson's Bay Co., 1934-68; Coast Lines Ltd, 1949-66; Chairman, David MacBrayne Ltd, 1953-66. Member Scottish Transport Council, 1951-63. A Governor, Cutty Sark Soc., 1954-75. Mem. Royal Company of Archers (HM Body Guard for Scotland). Mem., Inst. of Hammermen and a Freeman of City of Glasgow. OStJ. Legion of Honour; Croix de Guerre (France). *Recreations:* shooting, fishing. *Address:* 169 Queen's Gate, SW7 5HE. *T:* 01-589 3544.
[Died 9 May 1977.

NAPIER, Hon. Sir (John) Mellis, KCMG 1945; Kt 1943; KStJ; Chief Justice of South Australia, 1942-67; Lieutenant-Governor of South Australia, 1942-73; Chancellor of the University of Adelaide, 1948-61; *b* Dunbar, Scotland, 24 Oct. 1882; *s* of late Alexander Disney Leith Napier, MD, MRCP, FRSE; *m* 1908, Dorothy Bell (*d* 1959), *d* of Edward Kay, Adelaide; two *s* (and one missing, presumed died, on active service). *Educ:* City of London School; Adelaide University; LLB 1902; LLD (*hc*) Melbourne 1956; LLD (*aeg*) 1959. Called SA Bar, 1903; KC 1922; Puisne Judge of Supreme Court of S Australia, 1924-42; Chairman of Royal Commission on Monetary and Banking Systems of Australia, 1936-37. *Address:* 49 Kanmantoo Road, Aldgate, South Australia. *[Died 22 March 1976.*

NAPPER, Prof. Jack Hollingworth, CBE 1968; Professor of Architecture and Head of the School of Architecture in the University of Newcastle upon Tyne, 1963-70, now Emeritus; *b* 23 Dec. 1904; *s* of Frederick George Napper, Headmaster, and Edna Napper; *m* 1935, Mary Whitehead; two *s* one *d. Educ:* Oldham High Sch.; Univ. of Manchester. Clerk in cotton industry 1918-31; Architectural Assistant (Oldham, Bolton, London), 1935; Lecturer in Architecture, Hull, 1935-38; University of Durham, King's College, Newcastle upon Tyne: Lectr in Architecture, 1938-59; personal chair of Architecture, 1959-60; Head of School of Architecture, 1960-70. Private Practice, 1944-. President, Northern Architectural Association, 1958-59; Mem. Council, RIBA, 1958-63, 1963-69, and 1970-74, Vice-Pres., 1973-74. *Publications:* (with Prof. W. Fisher Cassie) Structure in Building, 1952; reviews in Jl of RIBA. *Address:* 15 Brandling Park, Newcastle upon Tyne NE2 4RR. *T:* Newcastle upon Tyne 810724. *[Died 12 June 1978.*

NASH, Gilbert John, CB 1951; Under-Secretary, Ministry of Labour, 1948-66; *b* 2 Dec. 1905; *s* of Ebenezer Thorp and Alice Nash; *m* 1940, Marguerite Lilian Braisher; one *d. Educ:* Royal Grammar Sch., Henley-on-Thames; St Catharine's College, Cambridge (Wrangler, 1927). Asst master, King's Sch., Peterborough, 1928. Entered Ministry of Labour as asst principal, 1928; Principal, 1934; Asst Sec. 1940; Under-Secretary, 1948-66. *Recreations:* pottery, painting in oils, writing verse. *Address:* 3 St Margaret's Close, Penn, High Wycombe, Bucks. *T:* Penn 2612. *[Died 18 Jan. 1974.*

NASH, John Northcote, CBE 1964; RA 1951 (ARA 1940); artist; *b* London, 11 April 1893; 2nd *s* of late W. H. Nash; *m* Dorothy Christine (*d* 1976), *o d* of Mr Kühlenthal, Gerrard's Cross, Bucks. *Educ:* Wellington College. Joined Artists' Rifles, September 1916; France, 1916-18, when he was commissioned to paint war pictures for the Imperial War Museum; was 2nd Lt in this connection; Hon. Commission in Royal Marines, 1940, as one of official War Artists to the Admiralty; Capt. RM 1941; Acting Temp. Major, 1943; reverted to rank of Temp. Capt. on discharge in Nov. 1944. Hon. Member of Society of Wood Engravers; Assistant Teacher of Design, Royal College of Art, 1934-57; Fellow RCA. Hon. DUniv, Essex, 1967. Paintings purchased for public galleries: The Tate Gallery, Manchester, Bath, Leeds, Dublin, Victoria and Albert Museum, South Kensington, Sheffield, also Walker Art Gallery, Liverpool and Bristol. Retrospective exhibn, Royal Academy, 1967. *Address:* Bottengoms Farm, Wormingford, near Colchester, Essex. *T:* Great Horkesley 308. *[Died 23 Sept. 1977.*

NASH, Ogden; author; *b* 19 Aug. 1902; *s* of Edmund Strudwick Nash and Mattie Chenault; *m* 1931, Frances Rider Leonard; two *c. Educ:* St George's School, Newport, RI; Harvard University. *Publications:* Hard Lines (poems), 1931; Free Wheeling, 1931; Happy Days, 1933; The Primrose Path (poems), 1935; The Bad Parents' Garden of Verse, 1936; I'm a Stranger Here Myself, 1938; The Face is Familiar, 1941; Good Intentions, 1942; Many Long Years Ago (poems), 1945; Versus, 1949; Family Reunion, 1951; The Private Dining Room, 1953; You Can't Get There From Here, 1957; The Christmas That Almost Wasn't, 1957; Collected Verses from 1929 on, 1961; Everyone But Thee and Me, 1963; The Untold Adventures of Santa Claus, 1965; An Ogden Nash Omnibook, 1967; Santa, Go Home, 1968. (Jt) One Touch of Venus (mus. comedy), 1943. Verses to magazines.

Address: c/o Curtis Brown Ltd, 60 East 56th Street, New York, NY 10022, USA.   *[Died* 19 *May* 1971.

NASON, Rev. (George) Stephen, MA; *b* 30 March 1901; *s* of Edward Noel Nason, MD, Nuneaton, Warwickshire; *m* 1930, Edna Hartley; one *d. Educ:* Shrewsbury; Pembroke Coll., Cambridge. Metropolitan Vickers, Manchester, 1922-25; Humphreys & Glasgow, London, 1925-26; Ely Theological College, 1926-27; St Luke's, Battersea (Curate), 1927-29; Richmond Parish Church (Curate), 1929-33; Rector of Bamford-in-the-Peak, 1933-45; Chaplain RNVR, 1939-45; Dean of Gibraltar, 1945-50; Vicar of St Alfege, Greenwich, 1950-58; Rural Dean of Greenwich and Deptford, 1954-58; Vicar of St Peter and St Paul, Hambledon, Hants, 1958-64; Curate of St John's Meads, Eastbourne, 1964-69. *Address:* 16 The Village, Meads, Eastbourne, Sussex. *Clubs:* Leander, Achilles.
                                      [Died 13 *March* 1975.

NATHAN, (Rt. Hon.) Eleanor Lady; Eleanor Joan Clara Nathan; *b* 28 Oct. 1892; *d* of late C. Stettauer, LCC; *m* 1919, Major H. L. Nathan (later 1st Baron Nathan, PC, TD, FBA, DL, JP; *d* 1963); one *s* (*see* 2nd Baron Nathan) one *d. Educ:* Queen's Coll., London; Girton Coll., Cambridge (MA Cantab). Chairman of Governors: Avery Hill Coll. of Education; Warnham Court Sch.; Coombe Hall Sch.; Governor: Bedford Coll.; JFS Sch.; King Edward's Sch., Witley. Vice-President Royal Geographical Society. JP County of London 1928 (Juvenile Court Panel, 1937-52); President: Women's Farm and Garden Assoc., 1950-70; E London Nursing Assoc.; Central Council for District Nursing in London, 1950-66. Mem. of LCC (NE Bethnal Green, 1928-34) (C Wandsworth, 1937-49); Chm. of LCC, 1947-48; Alderman of LCC, 1951-65; Mem., LCC and ILEA Educn Cttees, 1937-67. FRSA. Pres. Union of Jewish Women, 1945-55. First Chm. of Governors, Holland Park Sch., 1958-67; Former Governor: Girton Coll., Cambridge; Royal Holloway Coll., Univ. of London; former Member, Cambridge University Women's Appointments Board. First Woman Member of Metropolitan Water Board, 1937-46; Member of Home Office Committee of Enquiry into Closing Hours of Shops (Gowers Committee), 1946-49. *Address:* 80 Portman Towers, George Street, Montagu Square, W1. *T:* 01-935 7699.
                                      [Died 6 *June* 1972.

NATTA, Prof. Giulio; Director, Institute of Industrial Chemistry, Polytechnic of Milan, since 1938; *b* 26 Feb. 1903; *m* 1936, Rosita Beati; one *s* one *d. Educ:* Polytechnic Institute of Milan. Degree in Chemical Engineering, 1924; Professor in General Chemistry, 1927. Assistant Prof. in Analytical Chemistry, Polytechnic of Milan, 1925-32; Full Prof. and Director, Inst. of General Chemistry, Univ. of Pavia, 1933; Full Prof. of Physical Chemistry, Univ. of Rome, 1935-37; Full Prof. of Industrial Chemistry, Polytechnic of Turin, 1937-38. Doctor *hc* in Chemistry, Univ. of Turin, 1962; also holds honorary doctorates from foreign universities, etc; 16 gold medals from Italian and foreign Chemical Societies, among them Nobel Prize for Chemistry (jtly), 1963. *Publications:* about 450 articles mainly published in: Die Makromol. Chemie; Jl of Polymer Science; Chimica e Industria; Jl of Amer. Chem. Soc.; Tetrahedron; Rend. Accademia Nazionale Lincei. *Address:* Via S Sebastiano 11, 24100 Bergamo, Italy. *T:* 221100. *Club:* Rotary (Milan).
                                      [Died 2 *May* 1979.

NATTRASS, Frederick John, MD Durham, FRCP; Emeritus Professor of Medicine, Universities of Durham and Newcastle upon Tyne; Hon. Consulting Physician, Royal Victoria Infirmary, Newcastle upon Tyne; Hon. Life President, formerly Chairman, Muscular Dystrophy Group of Great Britain; *b* 6 August 1891; *s* of Rev. J. Conder Nattrass, BA, BD; *m* 1st, 1915, Gladys (*d* 1951), *d* of Benjamin Vickers, Lincoln; two *d* (one *s* decd); 2nd, 1963, Helen Byrne Bryce (*d* 1971), Burford, Oxford. *Educ:* King Edward's Sch., Birmingham; Univ. of Durham, MB, BS (1st Class Honours) Durham, 1914; MD (gold medal), 1920; Capt., RAMC, 1915-20 (BEF, France; POW). Physician, Royal Victoria Infirmary, Newcastle, 1921-56; Prof. of Medicine, Univ. of Durham, 1941-56; Prof. of Medicine, Univ. of Lagos, Nigeria, 1962-63. Sometime Examiner in Medicine, University of Bristol, Trinity College, Dublin, Univs. of Manchester, Queen's Belfast, St Andrews, Nat. Univ. of Ireland. Censor Royal College of Physicians, 1950-52; Senior Censor, 1955-56; Lumleian Lecturer, RCP, 1948; Pres., Newcastle and Northern Counties Med. Soc., 1948-49. President: Assoc. of Physicians of GB and Ireland, 1953-54; Assoc. of British Neurologists, 1957-59; Section of Neurology, Royal Society of Medicine, 1954-55. Pres., 3rd Internat. Congress on Muscle Diseases, 1974. Hon. DCL Newcastle, 1974. *Publications:* The Commoner Nervous Diseases, 1931; section on nervous diseases in Chamberlain's Textbook of Medicine, 1951; papers and addresses chiefly on disorders of the nervous and muscular systems. *Recreations:*

ornithology, music. *Address:* Little Cocklands, Burford, Oxford. *T:* Burford 2110.   *[Died* 19 *Jan.* 1979.

NAYLOR, Margot, (Margaret Ailsa); free-lance financial journalist; regular contributor to Daily Mail and The Director since 1967; *b* 28 Sept. 1907; *e d* of late Thomas Lodge, CB and Isobel (*née* Scott); *m* 1st, 1927, M. F. Wigham Richardson; 2nd, 1937, Guy Naylor; one *d. Educ:* Hornsey High Sch., London; Godolphin Sch., Salisbury; Lycée Molière, Paris; Ecole Vinet, Lausanne; Berlin Univ.; Girton Coll., Cambridge; London Sch. of Economics. Min. of Information, 1940-42; Cabinet Offices, 1942-45; Investors Chronicle, 1954-61; Investment Editor, The Statist, 1961-63; Financial Editor, The Observer, 1963-67. *Publications:* (with Ralph Harris and Arthur Seldon) Hire Purchase in a Free Society, 1958; Your Money, 1966; How to Reduce Your Tax Bill, 1968, 2nd edn, 1969; (ed) Financial Times Yearbook of Business Information, 1969; The Truth About Life Assurance, 1971; Margot Naylor's Guide to Money, Savings and Investment, 1972. *Recreations:* cooking, compound interest. *Address:* 107 New Kings Road, SW6. *T:* 01-736 4875. *Club:* Temple Bar.   *[Died* 22 *Sept.* 1972.

NAYLOR, Maj.-Gen. Robert Francis Brydges, CB 1942; CBE 1941; DSO 1919; psc 1922; *b* 6 Oct. 1889; 2nd *s* of C. T. Naylor, Barton End House, Nailsworth, Glos; *m* 1927, Lady Mary Byng, *yr d* of 6th Earl of Strafford; two *s* one *d. Educ:* Charterhouse; Sandhurst. Entered Army, 1909; joined 1st Battalion South Stafford Regiment, 1909; seconded to Royal Engineers (Signal Service), 1912; transferred Royal Signals, 1920; Brevet Major, 1918; Major, 1924; Lt-Col, 1931; Col, 1935; Temp. Maj.-Gen., 1940; Maj.-Gen., 1941; served European War, 1914-18, France and Flanders (despatches seven times, DSO, MC, Bt Major; Chevalier Légion d'Honneur); Brigade Major Signal Training Centre, 1923-25; General Staff Officer, Malta, 1925-27. Instructor, School of Signals, 1927-28; employed with Royal West African Frontier Force, 1928-31; commanded 3rd Divisional Signals, Bulford, 1931-35; GSO1 Scottish Command, 1935-38; Brigadier in charge of Administration, Western Command, 1938-39; Served War of 1939-45 (despatches, CB, CBE); Maj.-Gen. in charge of Administration, 1939-41; Deputy Quartermaster-General, 1941-43; Vice-Quartermaster-General, 1943; Commander L of C 21 Army Group, 1944; Commander Northumbrian District, 1945-46; retired pay, 1946. Col Comdt Royal Corps of Signals, 1944-53. Pres., Royal National Rose Society, 1963-64 and 1967-68. *Address:* Dancers Hill House, Barnet, Herts. *Club:* Army and Navy.   *[Died* 23 *Dec.* 1971.

NEAL, Harold; *b* 23 July 1897; two *s* one *d. Educ:* Church of England School, Langley Mill. Began work in a coal mine at age of 13. Studied mining at Nottingham University Coll.; Mem. of Heanor UDC, 1930-44, Chm., 1939-40; MP (Lab) for Clay Cross, 1944-50, for Bolsover, 1950-70; travelled extensively in Europe and the Middle East; Mem. Imperial War Graves Commn, 1947-51; Parly Sec., Min. of Fuel and Power, 1951. Active in Co-operative Movement for many years; Dir of Langley Mill Co-op. Soc. First miner MP to represent Clay Cross; formerly Vice-Pres. Derbyshire Miners Association; Chairman: East Midland Group of Labour MPs; Steel and Power Cttee, Parly Labour Party. *Recreations:* gardening and reading. *Address:* Riseholme, Aldreds Lane, Langley, Heanor, Derbyshire. *T:* Langley Mill 3366.   *[Died* 25 *Aug.* 1972.

NEALE, Folliott Sandford; *b* 11 Nov. 1901; *y s* of Rev. John Neale, Hardingstone Grange, Northants, and of Ada Rossall, *d* of late Humphrey Sandford, Isle of Rossall, Salop; *m* 1929, Gwendolyn (*d* 1970), *o surv. c* of W. W. G. Phillipps, Berwick House, Salop; one *d* (and one *s* decd). *Educ:* Marlborough; Loughborough Engineering Coll. Member: Co. Probation Cttee, 1939-71; Magistrates Courts Cttee, 1956-; Visiting Cttee, HM Prison, Shrewsbury, 1949-72; Hospital Boards, 1937-; Diocesan Assessor, Lichfield Diocese, 1958-; Chm., County Licensing and Compensation Cttee. Chm. Welsh and Shropshire Jersey Breeders Assoc., 1956-; Pres. Shropshire and West Midland Agricultural Soc., 1961. Chm., Shropshire Antiques Soc., 1968-; JP Salop, 1937 (Chm., Mid-Shropshire Bench, 1956-); High Sheriff of Shropshire, 1948-49. *Recreations:* breeder of pedigree Jersey cattle (Berwick Herd); gardening; forestry. *Address:* Berwick House, near Shrewsbury. *T:* Shrewsbury 2941. *Club:* Shropshire (Shrewsbury).   *[Died* 24 *Aug.* 1972.

NEALE, Sir John (Ernest), Kt 1955; MA; Hon. DLitt (Wales), 1948, Birmingham 1954, Leeds 1960, Cambridge 1960); Hon. LittD (Liverpool 1956); Hon. DLit (London 1960); Hon. LHD (Amherst 1958); FBA; Astor Professor of English History, University of London, 1927-56; retired; Professor Emeritus, 1956; Fellow of University College, London; *b* Liverpool, 7 Dec. 1890; *m* 1932, Elfreda, *d* of William Skelton, Harrogate; one *d. Educ:* Liverpool University; University College, London. Asst in

the Department of History, University College, London, 1919-25; Prof. of Modern History, Univ. of Manchester, 1925-27; Member Treasury Cttee on House of Commons Records, 1929; Lectures: Lady Ardilaun, Alexandra College, Dublin, 1938; Ford's, in English History, Oxford Univ., 1941-42; Ballard Mathews, University Coll. of N Wales, 1942; Raleigh, British Academy, 1948; Creighton, Univ. of London, 1950; annual Neale public lecture in English History instituted at University Coll., London, 1970, on 80th birthday. Trustee, London Museum, 1945-70. Foreign Hon. Member: American Acad. of Arts and Sciences, 1950; American Historical Assoc., 1968; former Mem., Editorial Bd of History of Parliament. *Publications:* various papers on Tudor History in the English Historical Review, History, Transactions of the Royal Historical Society, and Tudor Studies (ed. R. W. Seton-Watson, 1924); Queen Elizabeth, 1934 (awarded James Tait Black Memorial Prize); The Age of Catherine de Medici, 1943; The Elizabethan House of Commons, 1949; Elizabeth I and Her Parliaments, 1559-1581, 1953; Elizabeth I and Her Parliaments, 1584-1601, 1957; Essays in Elizabethan History, 1958. *Address:* Adare, 57 Penn Road, Beaconsfield, Bucks. *T:* Beaconsfield 4466.
[Died 2 Sept. 1975.

NEAME, Lt-Gen. Sir Philip, VC 1914; KBE 1946; CB 1939; DSO 1916; psc; idc; DL; Colonel Commandant, RE, 1945-55; Hon. Colonel 131 Airborne Regiment RE (T), 1948-58; Hon. Colonel Kent ACF Regiment RE, 1952-58; President of the Institution of Royal Engineers, 1954-57; *b* 12 December 1888; *y s* of late F. Neame, JP, of Luton, Selling, Faversham; *m* 1934, H. Alberta Drew; three *s* one *d*. *Educ:* Cheltenham Coll.; RMA Woolwich. Entered Army, 1908; Capt. 1914; Bt Major 1917; Bt Lt-Col 1922; Major, 1925; Col 1926; Maj.-Gen. 1937; Temp. Lt-Gen., 1940; Lt-Gen., 1947; served European War, 1914-18, 15th Field Coy, RE, Adjt Divl Engineers; Brig.-Maj. Inf. Bde, Gen. Staff of Division, Corps and Army (despatches five times, VC, DSO, Chevalier of the Legion of Honour, French Croix de Guerre, Belgian Croix de Guerre); on the Directing Staff, Staff College, Camberley, 1919-23; served in India with KGO Bengal Sappers and Miners, 1925-29; Imperial Defence College, 1930; General Staff Officer, 1st Grade, Waziristan District, India, 1932-33; Brigadier, General Staff, Eastern Command, India, 1934-38; went to Lhasa, Tibet, with political-military mission, 1936; Commandant Royal Military Academy, Woolwich, 1938-39; Deputy Chief of the General Staff, BEF France, 1939-40; Commander 4th Indian Division, Western Desert, 1940; GOC (Lt-Gen.) Palestine, Transjordan, Cyprus, 1940; GOC-in-C and Military Governor, Cyrenaica, 1941 (despatches twice); Commanded British, Australian, and Indian Forces against Rommel's first attack in Cyrenaica, Mar.-Apr. 1941; prisoner of war, 1941, escaped from Italy 1943; retired pay, 1947. Lieutenant-Governor and Commander-in-Chief of Guernsey and its dependencies, Channel Islands, 1945-53. Mem., Governing Body of Gordon Boys School; Vice-Pres., Nat. Rifle Assoc.; Pres. North London Rifle Club. DL Kent, 1955. FRGS. KStJ; Knight of Order of White Lion, Czechoslovakia. *Publications:* German Strategy in the Great War, 1923; Autobiography, Playing with Strife, 1946; also various articles on big-game shooting, Tibet, North West Frontier, etc. *Recreations:* gardening and fruit growing, polo, hunting, point to point racing, big and small game shooting, rifle and revolver shooting (in British Olympic Sporting Rifle Team, Gold and Bronze Medals, France, 1924; in Army Revolver VIII and Army Rifle Twenty). *Address:* The Kintle, Selling Court, Faversham, Kent.
[Died 28 April 1978.

NEAME, Sir Thomas, Kt 1960; MBE 1918; FSA; VMH; Farmer and Fruit-grower; *b* 23 Dec. 1885; *s* of late Frederick Neame, Luton, Selling, Faversham; *m* 1920, Gwendolyn Mary, *d* of George Thomson, Torquay (*see* Astra Desmond); two *s* (and one *s* decd). *Educ:* Cheltenham Coll.; Gonville and Caius Coll., Camb. Studied in Germany; at Stewarts & Lloyds Tube Works till 1914. Served European War, 9th Bn Worcestershire Regt, Gallipoli. Joined family farming business, 1919, growing hops and fruit on a large scale; won many prizes at Imperial Fruit Show and in Dairy Herd competitions. Chm., East Malling Research Station, 1945-60. A Trustee Royal Agricultural Soc. of England; Master of the Farmers' Co., 1958-59; Pres., Kent Archaeological Soc., 1959-66; Vice-Pres., RHS. High Sheriff of Kent, 1948-49. *Recreation:* horticulture. *Address:* Preston Lea, Faversham, Kent. *T:* Faversham 2012. *Club:* Athenæum.
[Died 28 Aug. 1973.

NEAME, Lady (Thomas); *see* Desmond, Astra.

NEAVE, Airey Middleton Sheffield, DSO 1945; OBE 1947; MC 1942; TD (with 1st clasp) 1945; MP (C) Abingdon Division of Berkshire since July 1953; Director, Clarke Chapman Services Limited, since 1971; Barrister-at-Law; *b* 23 January 1916; *e s* of

late Dr Sheffield Neave, CMG, OBE; *m* 1942, Diana Josceline Barbara, *d* of Thomas A. W. Giffard, MBE, JP, of Chillington Hall, Wolverhampton; two *s* one *d*. *Educ:* Eton; Merton Coll., Oxford. BA (Hons) Jurisprudence, 1938, MA 1955. Called to the Bar, Middle Temple, 1943. Served War of 1939-45 (despatches, MC, DSO); with RA (TA) in France, 1940; wounded and prisoner, 1940; escaped, 1942; MI9, 1942-44; GSO(2) (I), 21 Army Group, 1944-45. Lieut-Col AAG, British War Crimes Executive, 1945-46; served indictments on Goering and major Nazi War Criminals, 1945; Comr for Criminal Organizations. Internat. Mil. Tribunal, Nuremburg, 1946; OC Intell. Sch. no 9 (TA), 1949-51. Contested Thurrock (C), 1950, Ealing North (C) 1951; PPS to Minister of Transport and Civil Aviation, 1954; PPS to Secretary of State for Colonies, 1954-56; Joint Parly Sec., Min. of Transport and Civil Aviation, 1957-59; Parly Under-Sec. of State for Air, 1959. Dep. Chm., Parly and Scientific Cttee, 1971-74; Mem., Select Cttee of House of Commons on Science and Technology, 1965-75 (Chm., 1970-74); Head of Leader of Opposition's private office, 1975-; opposition spokesman on N Ireland, 1975-. Hon. Sec., Assoc. of British Chambers of Commerce, 1960-62; a Governor, Imperial College of Science and Technology, 1963-71. UK delegate to UN High Comr for Refugees, 1970-75; Chm., Standing Conf. of British orgns for aid to refugees, 1972-74. French Croix de Guerre, American Bronze Star and Officer Order Orange Nassau, Holland, 1945; Knight, Order Polonia Restituta (Poland), 1977 (Comdr, 1971). *Publications:* They Have Their Exits, 1953; Little Cyclone, 1954; Saturday at MI9, 1969; The Flames of Calais, 1972; Nuremberg, 1978. *Address:* c/o Northern Engineering Ltd, Tavistock House East, Woburn Walk, Tavistock Square, WC1. *T:* 01-387 9393. *Club:* Carlton.
[Died 30 March 1979.

NEDEN, Sir Wilfred (John), Kt 1955; CB 1949; CBE 1946; retired as Chief Industrial Commissioner, Ministry of Labour and National Service, (1954-58); Deputy Chairman, BOAC, 1960-63; *b* 24 August 1893; *s* of John Thomas and Margaret Neden; *m* 1st, 1925, Jean Lundie (*d* 1965); one *s* one *d*; 2nd, 1967, Mrs L. Violet Ryan, Hove, Sussex. *Educ:* St Olave's Gram. Sch. Army, 1914-22, Lieut RFA (Regular Commission); served European War, 1914-18, severely wounded, 1918 (despatches). Entered Ministry of Labour, 1922; Under Secretary, 1946; Director of Organisation and Establishments, 1948-54. *Address:* Courtneys, 36 Forest Drive, Keston Park, Keston, Kent BR2 6EF. *T:* Farnborough 51936.
[Died 11 April 1978.

NEELANDS, Abram Rupert, MC, BA, ME, DLS, CEng, MIMM, MIME, MIStructE, FRSA; President, The Cementation Co. Ltd; *b* Winnipeg, Canada; *s* of James Adam Neelands and Jane Oliphant Butchart; *m* Kathleen Agnew (*d* 1941); one *s* two *d*. *Educ:* Wheatland Public School; Brandon Collegiate; Manitoba Univ. (BA); Toronto Univ. (Mining Engineer). Engrg work with Canadian Pacific Rly, British Columbia Copper Company; Private Practice in Engineering and Contracting; Topographical Surveys Dominion Government, Mexican Corporation, Persian Mining Syndicate; served European War with 1st Field Company Canadian Engineers (MC, despatches); rank of Major. *Address:* 66 Chelsea Square, SW3. *T:* 01-352 0602. *Clubs:* Carlton, Constitutional, Mining and Metallurgical, Royal Over-Seas League, Anglo-Spanish.
[Died 19 Oct. 1971.

NEEP, Edward John Cecil, QC; *b* 13 Oct. 1900; *e s* of late Rev. Edward Neep, Rector of St George's, Southwark, and Florence Emma Neep; *m* 1926, Evelyn, *e d* of late Sir Harry Pritchard. *Educ:* Westminster School (King's Scholar). Works chemist, 1917-20; tutor and journalist, 1920-23; called to Bar, Middle Temple, 1923; practised for twenty-nine years at the Bar and at the Patent and Parliamentary Bars for twenty years. Contested (Lab) Woodbridge 1922 and 1923, Central Leeds 1924, Lowestoft 1931; KC 1946; QC 1952. Deputy Speaker and Chairman of Committees, Kenya Legislative Council, 1952. *Publications:* Seditious Offences; (part author of): A Handbook of Church Law; Pons Asinorum, or the Future of Nonsense; Horatio Nelson; Gladstone: a spectrum. *Address:* 31 Rua de Santo Antonio à Estrela, Lisbon, Portugal. *[Died 3 Oct. 1980.*

NEGUS, Sir Victor (Ewings), Kt 1956; Hon. DSc Manchester; MS (University Medal), FRCS, Hon. FRCS, Edinburgh and Ireland; Consulting Surgeon to Ear, Nose, and Throat Department, King's College Hospital, London; *b* London, 1887; *s* of William Negus, DL, JP; *m* 1929, Gladys Rennie; two *s*. *Educ:* King's Coll. School; King's Coll., London; King's Coll. Hospital. House Surgeon and House Physician, King's College Hospital; Fellow of King's College, London; Arris and Gale Lectr, Hunterian Professor, Hunterian Prizeman and Medallist and Lister Medallist, Royal Coll. of Surgeons of England; Semon Lecturer; Trustee of the Hunterian Collection; Hon. Gold

Medal, RCS, 1969. Served European War, RAMC, 1914-19 (Mons Star, despatches); EMS, 1939-46. Late Co-opted Member Council and Member Court of Examiners, RCS; Hon. Fellow American Laryngological, Rhinological and Otological Soc. and Swedish Med. Soc.; Hon. Fellow, Amer. Laryngological Assoc.; Hon. Mem. Amer. Broncho-Esophagological Assoc. and Canadian Otolaryngological Soc. Corresp. Mem. Danish Society of Oto-Laryngology; Hon. Mem. Italian Society of Laryngology, Otology and Rhinology; scientific section of Hungarian Oto-rhino-laryngologists; Austrian Oto-laryngological Society; Turkish Oto-rhino-laryngological Society; and of Laryng. Soc. of New York; Corresp. Mem. Laryngo-Rhinological Soc. of Vienna and of Soc. of Laryngology of the Hosps of Paris; Hon. Mem.: Scottish Otol. Soc., Manchester Med. Soc. and Harveian Soc.; Life Member Anat. Soc.; President International Congress Otolaryngology, London, 1949; Pres. Thoracic Soc., 1949-50; Past Pres. Sect. of Laryngol., RSM; Hon. DSc Manchester; Hon. Fellow, RSM; lately Hon. Treas. Collegium Oto-rhino-larygologicum (Pres., 1954); Past Pres. British Assoc. of Otolaryngologists and Asst-Sec. of Aux. RAMC Funds. *Publications:* The Mechanism of the Larynx, 1929; Diseases of the Nose and Throat (with Sir St Clair Thomson), 1937, 6th Edn 1955; Comparative Anatomy and Physiology of the Larynx, 1949; A Hitherto Undescribed Function of the Vocal Cords, Journal of Laryngology and Otology, 1924; Observations on the Evolution of Man from the Evidence of the Larynx, Acta Oto-laryngologica, 1928; Comparative Anatomy and Physiology of the Nose, 1958; The Biology of Respiration, 1965; The History of the Trustees of the Hunterian Collection, 1965; Artistic Possessions at the Royal College of Surgeons of England, 1967. *Address:* 4 Nutcombe Height, Hindhead, Surrey.
[Died 15 July 1974.

NEIL, Rev. William, MA, BD, PhD, DD; Warden of Hugh Stewart Hall, 1953-75, Reader in Biblical Studies 1965-75, in the University of Nottingham; *b* 13 June 1909; *s* of William Maclaren Neil and Jean Chalmers Hutchison; *m* 1936, Effie Lindsay Park, *d* of late Rev. Graham Park, MA, and Euphemia Lindsay, MA; two *s. Educ:* Glasgow Acad.; Univs of Glasgow and Heidelberg. Black Fellow, 1932-33, Faulds Fellow, 1934-37, Univ. of Glasgow. Minister at Bridge of Allan, 1937-46. Chaplain to 4/5 Royal Scots, 1940-43, and 5 Survey Regt RA, CMF 1943-45 (despatches, Italy). Head of Dept of Biblical Study, Univ. of Aberdeen, 1946-53. Croall Lecturer, Univ. of Edinburgh, 1967. Vis. Prof. of Theology, Univ. of Rhodesia, 1978-79. Hon. DD Glasgow, 1961. *Publications:* St Paul's Epistles to the Thessalonians (Moffatt Commentaries), 1950; The Rediscovery of the Bible, 1954; The Epistle to the Hebrews, 1955; The Plain Man Looks at the Bible, 1956; I and II Thessalonians (Torch Commentaries), 1957; One Volume Bible Commentary, 1962; Jeremiah and Ezekiel (Bible Guides), 1964; The Life and Teaching of Jesus, 1965; Apostle Extraordinary: The Life and Letters of St Paul, 1966; The Christian Faith in Art (with Eric Newton), 1966; Galatians (Cambridge Bible Commentaries), 1967; The Truth About Jesus, 1968; The Truth about the Early Church, 1970; The Bible Story, 1971; The Truth about the Bible, 1972; The Acts of the Apostles (New Century Bible), 1973; Concise Dictionary of Religious Quotations, 1974; The Difficult Sayings of Jesus, 1975; Good News in Corinthians, 1977; translations: The Bible as History, 1956; Jesus Lived Here, 1958; Editor, The Bible Companion, 1959; General Editor, Knowing Christianity, 1964-; contributor to: Interpreter's Dictionary of the Bible, Peake's Commentary on the Bible, Cambridge History of the Bible, etc. *Address:* 590 Derby Road, Adams Hill, Nottingham NG4 2GZ. *T:* Nottingham 781818.
[Died 10 Nov. 1979.

NEILL, Alexander Sutherland, MA; MEd (Newcastle) 1967; author and child psychologist; *b* 17 Oct. 1883; *s* of late George Neill and Mary Sinclair Sutherland Neill, Forfar; *m* 1st, Ada Lilian Lindesay-Neustatter (*d* 1944); 2nd, 1945, Ena May Wood; one *d. Educ:* father's village school (Kingsmuir); Edinburgh University. Office boy, then draper, teacher, journalist, educator; joint-founder of International School, Hellerau, Dresden, 1921. Founder, Summerhill School, 1924. Hon. LLD Exeter, 1968; Hon. DUniv, Essex, 1971. *Publications:* A Dominie's Log, 1915; A Dominie Dismissed, 1916; The Booming of Bunkie, 1919; A Dominie in Doubt, 1920; Carroty Broon, 1921; A Dominie Abroad, 1922; A Dominie's Five, or Free School, 1924; The Problem Child, 1926; The Problem Parent, 1932; Is Scotland Educated, 1936; That Dreadful School, 1937; The Last Man Alive, 1938, repr. 1971; The Problem Teacher, 1939; Hearts, not Heads, 1945; The Problem Family, 1948; The Free Child, 1953; Summerhill (a compilation), 1962; Talking of Summerhill (in USA, Freedom, not Licence), 1967; Neill! Neill! Orange Peel! (autobiog.), 1973. *Address:* Summerhill School, Leiston, Suffolk. *T:* Leiston 830540.
[Died 23 Sept. 1973.

NEILSON JONES, W.; see Jones.

NEILSON-TERRY, Phyllis, FRAM; Actress; *b* 15 Oct. 1892; *d* of late Fred Terry and late Julia Neilson; *m* 1958, Heron Carvic. *Educ:* Waterside, Westgate-on-Sea; Paris; Royal Academy of Music. Played with her father and mother in 1909; Viola in Twelfth Night with Sir Herbert Tree, 1910; Rosalind and Juliet in her father's productions at the New Theatre; Trilby, Portia, Desdemona with Sir Herbert; later was with Charles Frohman, and Sir George Alexander; toured America, 1914-19; went into management on return to England, produced J. B. Fagan's The Wheel, and Temple Thurston's A Roof and Four Walls, at the Apollo, London; toured S Africa, 1927; Candida with Sir Barry Jackson, Malvern Festival; has played at the Open Air Theatre, The Memorial Theatre, Stratford, Queen Katherine and Lady Macbeth. Has broadcast Macbeth, Trilby, Candida, The Scarlet Pimpernel and many other plays. In management with Heron Carvic in his plays The Widow of 40 and The Beggars' Union. Played Mrs Railton-Bell in Separate Tables, St James's, and Music Box Theatre, New York. *Recreation:* reading. *Address:* Upton, Appledore, Kent. *T:* Appledore 355.
[Died 25 Sept. 1977.

NEISH, Arthur Charles, OC 1972; MSc, PhD; FRS 1971; Distinguished Research Scientist, National Research Council, Canada, since 1972; *b* 4 July 1916; *s* of Rev. C. W. Neish, Nova Scotia; *m* 1944, Dorothy Ann Ray; three *s* one *d. Educ:* McGill University, Montreal. BSc(Agr) 1938, MSc 1939, PhD 1942. Sessional Lectr, McGill Univ., 1942-43; National Research Council Laboratories, Canada: Research Officer (bacterial fermentations), Ottawa, 1943-48; Prairie Regional Laboratory, Saskatoon (biochemistry of plants and microorganisms), 1948-61; apptd to Atlantic Regional Laboratory, Halifax, NS, 1961 (plant biochemistry and cultivation of marine plants), Dir, 1962-72. Hon. DSc: Mount Allison, 1967; McGill, 1972. *Publications:* Constitution and Biosynthesis of Lignin (with K. Freudenberg), 1968 (Germany); over 100 original contribs in various scientific jls. *Recreations:* golf, curling, gardening. *Address:* Rural Route No 2, Granville Ferry, Anna. Co., Nova Scotia, Canada. *T:* 902-532-2882.
[Died 7 Sept. 1973.

NELSON, 7th Earl, *cr* 1805, of Trafalgar and of Merton; **Henry Edward Joseph Horatio Nelson;** Baron Nelson of the Nile and of Hilborough, Norfolk, 1801; Viscount Merton of Trafalgar and of Merton, 1805; formerly tea planter, Ceylon and India; *b* 22 April 1894; second *s* of 5th Earl Nelson and Geraldine (*d* 1936), *d* of late Henry H. Cave, Northampton; *S* brother 1957; unmarried. *Educ:* Maredsous, Belgium; HMS Conway. Served European War, 1914-18, with Australian Imperial Force; War of 1939-45 with Merchant Navy and as Major, Indian Army. *Recreations:* formerly yachting and boxing. *Heir: b* Hon. George Joseph Horatio Nelson [*b* 20 April 1905; *m* 1945, Mary Winifred, *d* of G. Bevan, Swansea; one *d*]. *Address:* Richmond House, 27 Rabling Road, Swanage, Dorset BH19 1ED. *T:* 2832.
[Died 8 Aug. 1972.

NELSON, John Howard, CB 1979; Deputy Under-Secretary of State (Air), Ministry of Defence, since 1976; *b* 23 May 1925; *s* of late Rev. S. T. Nelson and of Mrs Nelson; *m* 1949, Hazel Dent; one *s* one *d. Educ:* Methodist Coll., Belfast; Pembroke Coll., Cambridge (Scholar). BA 1948. War Service 1943-46, Sub-Lt RNVR. Asst Principal, Air Ministry, 1949; Principal, 1954; Asst Sec., 1962; attended Imperial Defence Coll. course, 1968; Asst Under-Sec. of State, 1972. *Recreations:* unremarkable. *Address:* 2 Ingleside Grove, Blackheath, SE3. *T:* 01-858 2716.
[Died 22 Feb. 1979.

NERUDA, Pablo; poet; Chilean Ambassador to France, since 1970; *b* Chile, 12 July 1904; *s* of late José del Carmen Reyes and Rosa de Basoalto; *m* 1st, Maruca Hagenaar Vogelzang; 2nd, 1951, Matilde Urrutia. *Educ:* Instituto Pedagógico; Univ. of Chile. Joined Chilean consular service, 1927; Consul: Burma, Ceylon, Dutch EI, 1927-32; Buenos Aires, 1933-37; Mexico City, 1941-44; Mem., Chilean Senate, 1945-47; exiled in Mexico, 1947-53. Editor, El Caballo verde para la Poesia, 1935. Mem., World Peace Council, 1950-; Pres., Unión de Escritores de Chile, 1959-. Hon. Mem., Amer. Acad. of Arts and Scis. Hon. DLitt Oxon, 1965. Premio Municipal de Literatura, Chile, 1944; Premio Nacional de Literatura, Chile, 1945; International Peace Prize, 1950; Lenin and Stalin, Peace Prizes, 1953; Order of Merit, Czechoslovakia, 1966; Nobel Prize for Poetry, 1971. *Publications:* Crepusculario, 1923; Veinte poemas de amor y una canción desesperada, 1924; Tentative de un hombre infinito, 1925; Prosas de Pablo Neruda, El habitante y su esperanza (stories), Anillos, 1926; El hondero entusiasta, 1933; Residencia en la tierra (2 vols), 1933-35; Cantos materiales, 1935; España en el corazón, 1937; Las furias y las penas, 1939; Un canto para Bolivar, 1941; Nuevo canto de amor a Stalingrado, 1943; Viajes,

1947; González Videla: el laval de la America Latina, 1949; Canto general, 1950; Los versos del capitán, 1952; Odas elementales, 1955; Obras completas, 1957, 3rd edn 1961; Tercer libro de las odas, 1957; Estravagario, 1958; Cien sonetos de amor, Navigaciónes y regresos, 1959; Canción de gesta, 1960; Las piedras de Chile, Cantos ceremoniales, 1961; Plenos poderes, 1962; Memorial de Isla Negra (autobiog.), 1964; Arte de pájaros, Una casa en la arena, 1966; La barcarola, Fulgor y muerte de Joaquin Murieta (play), 1967; Las manos del dia, 1968; Aún, 1970; Antología esencial, 1973; Geografia infructuosa, 1973; Incitación al Nixonicidio y alabanza de la revolución Chilena, 1973. *Address:* Chilean Embassy, Rue de la Motte-Picquet, Paris 7e, France; Correo de Isla Negra, Chile; Marquez de la Plata 0192, Santiago, Chile.
[Died 23 *Sept.* 1973.

NERVI, Pier Luigi; Structural engineer, Italy; Partner of and consultant adviser to Nervi & Bartoli, Engineers, since 1932; *b* 21 June 1891; *s* of late Antonio and Luisa Bartoli; *m* 1924, Irene Calosi; four *s. Educ:* Univ. of Bologna (Degree in Civil Engineering). Engineer, Società per Costruzione Cementizie, Bologna, 1913-15, and 1918-23; Officer, Engineering Corps, 1915-18; Partner, Nervi & Nebbiosi, Engineers, 1923-32. Prof. of Technology and Technique of Construction, Faculty of Architecture, Rome, 1947-61; Charles E. Norton Prof., Harvard, 1961-62. Life Mem., Internat. Inst. Arts and Letters, Zürich, 1961; Hon. Member: Amer. Acad.-Inst. of Arts and Letters, 1957; Amer. Acad. Arts and Sciences, 1960; Foreign Mem., Royal Acad. of Fine Arts, Stockholm, 1957; Corresponding Member: Academia Nacionale de Ciencias Exactas Fisicas y Naturales, Buenos Aires, 1959; Bayrische Akademie der Schönen Künste, 1960; Accademico Nazionale, and Accad. di San Luca, Roma, 1960; Special Mem., Architectural Section, Academy of Arts of Berlin, 1964. Holds Hon. Degrees at Universities of Buenos Aires, 1950, Edinburgh, 1960, Warsaw, 1961, Harvard, 1962, at Technische Hochschule, München, 1960, and at Dartmouth Coll., 1962, Univ. of London, 1969. Hon. FAIA 1956; Hon. RA (London), 1967. Alfred Lindau Award, Amer. Concrete Inst., 1963; E. Mörsch Award, Deutsche Beton Verein, 1963; Feltrinelli Award, Rome, 1968. Frank P. Brown Medal, 1957; Royal Gold Medal for Architecture, 1960; Gold Medal: AIA, 1964; IStructE, 1968. Cavaliere di Gran Croce al Merito della Repubblica Italiana; Cavaliere al Merito del Lavoro, Rome, 1962. *Publications:* Arte o scienza del costruire, 1945; El linguaje arquitectonico (Buenos Aires), 1952; Costruire correttamente, 1954; New Structures, 1963; Aesthetics and Technology in Building, 1965; various articles on architecture in Italian, French, English and American technical journals. *Recreation:* sailing. *Address:* Lungo Tevere Arnaldo da Brescia 9, Rome, Italy. *T:* 350292. *Club:* Rotary (Rome). *[Died* 9 *Jan.* 1979.

NESBITT, Maj.-Gen. Frederick G. B.; *see* Beaumont-Nesbitt.

NETHERTHORPE, 1st Baron, *cr* 1959; **James Turner;** Kt 1949; Director: Fisons Ltd, 1960-78 (Chairman 1962-73); Lloyds Bank Ltd, 1957-78; Abbey National Building Society; Steetley Co. Ltd, 1965-78; Film Development and Research Ltd; Unigate (Vice-Chairman, since 1976); J. H. Fenner & Co. (Holdings) Ltd; The National Bank of New Zealand Ltd, 1976-79; *b* 6 Jan. 1908; *s* of late Albert Edward Mann Turner, Anston, Sheffield, and Lucy, *d* of Henry Helliwell; *m* 1935, Margaret Lucy, *d* of James Arthur Mattock; three *s* (and one *s* decd). *Educ:* Knaresborough; Leeds University. BSc Leeds, 1928. Chairman of Notts County Branch, NFU, 1937; Notts Council Deleg., NFU, 1943; Vice-Pres., NFU, 1944; Pres., NFU, 1945-60. Pres. Internat. Fedn of Agricultural Producers, 1946-48; Member: Brit. Productivity Council (Chm., 1963); Commn of Inquiry into Industrial Representation, 1971-72; NEDC, 1971-75; Pay Bd, 1974; Animal Health Trust; Council, Royal Assoc. of British Dairy Farmers (Pres. 1964); Council Royal Agricultural Society of England (Pres. 1965); Liveryman of Painter-Stainers Co. and of Farmers Co. LLD (Hon.), Leeds, 1952; LLD (Hon.) Birmingham, 1959. *Recreations:* shooting and golf. *Heir:* s Hon. James Andrew Turner. *Address:* The Garden House, Hadley Hurst Cottages, Hadley Common, Barnet, Herts EN5 5QF. *T:* 01-449 9017. *Club:* Farmers'. *[Died* 8 *Nov.* 1980.

NEVADA, Mignon; British soprano; teacher of singing and operatic technique; *b* Paris, 1888; *d* of late Emma Nevada and late Dr R. S. Palmer; made professional *début* at the Costanzi Theatre, Rome, as Rosina in Il Barbiere di Siviglia; appeared in Covent Garden, 1910; since then has appeared in nearly all the leading Opera houses of Europe, many times at Covent Garden; and at the Paris Grand Opera. Was in Government Service through whole of War of 1939-45. *Address:* Montgomery House, Long Melford, Sudbury, Suffolk. *T:* Long Melford 380.
[Died 25 *June* 1971.

NEVEN-SPENCE, Col Sir Basil Hamilton Hebden, Kt 1945; Landowner (Udaller); FRGS; *b* 12 June 1888; *e s* of late T. W. L. Spence, CB, JP, Uyea, Shetland, and Henrietta Fanny, *d* of R. J. Hebden, DL, JP, Eday, Orkney; *m* 1st, 1917, Margaret Alice (*d* 1961), *d* of G. H. Mackenzie, MD, Edinburgh; one *d* (and one *s* one *d* decd); 2nd, 1963, Constance Eila, *widow* of Maj.-Gen. Sir Hubert Jervoise Huddleston, GCMG, GBE, CB, DSO, MC (she *d* 1967), *d* of late F. H. M. Corbet. *Educ:* Edinburgh Acad.; Univ. of Edinburgh. MB, ChB, 1911; MD, 1924; MRCPEd, 1924; FRCPEd, 1927; Lieutenant RAMC, 1911; seconded to Egyptian Army and Sudan Government, 1914; served Darfur and Palestine (despatches twice, British and Sudan General Service Medals, Victory Medal, Order of the Nile, Fourth Class); Magistrate; Organiser of sleeping sickness campaign, Bahr El Ghazal; Govt Bacteriologist; Reverted to British Army, 1924; Specialist Physician, Aldershot Command; retired 1927. Vice-Convener of Shetland, 1934-35. MP (U) Orkney and Shetland, 1935-50. Hon. Col 430 Coast Regt RA (Orkney and Shetland) TA, 1950-56. Granted Hon. rank of Colonel 1956. Col comdg A1 Sector Home Guard, 1952-56. Hon. Col 861 (Indep.) LAA Battery, RA (Orkney and Zetland) TA 1957-58. Mem. Scottish Cttee The Nature Conservancy 1948-62 and of The Nature Conservancy, 1955-62, Chairman of the Scottish Cttee, 1955-62. Lord Lieutenant for the County of Zetland, 1952-63. *Address:* Busta House, Brae, Shetland. *T:* Brae 209. *Club:* Caledonian. *[Died* 13 *Sept.* 1974.

NEVILL, Col Charles William, OBE 1943; TD and Clasps, 1943; JP; Lord Lieutenant for Carmarthenshire, since 1967; *b* 16 Aug. 1907; *o s* of late Col R. A. Nevill, DSO, TD, JP, DL; *m* 1947, Philippa (JP 1968), *o d* of late Capt. H. P. Farrel, sometime Principal of Sinde Univ. Karachi; two *s. Educ:* Clifton College. Man. Dir, Nevill's Dock & Railway Co. Ltd; Gen. Comr of Income Tax for Kidwelly Div., 1961; Mem., T&AFA (Carms), 1945 (Chm., 1960-66); Trustee, SW Wales Savings Bank; Patron: Carms Co. Br., British Legion; Carms Red Cross Soc.; Carms Young Farmers Club. President: Carms County Scout Council; Forces Help Soc. and Lord Roberts Workshops for Carms; Sailors', Soldiers' and Airmen's Society for Carms; NSPCC for Carms; St John Council for Carms; Carms Community Council. Sec. and Treasurer, Ferryside Lifeboat Stn RNLI, 1949-60 (when closed). JP 1950, DL 1956, Vice-Lieut 1967, Carmarthenshire. 2nd Lt 4th (Carms) Bn The Welch Regt TA, 1926; Capt. 1931; psc Camberley, 1939; Maj. 1940; Lt-Col 1942. Served War of 1939-45: Norway, 1940; Middle East, Persia and Iraq, N Africa, Corsica, Italy, 1940-45; AQMG British Troops in Egypt, 1942, AFHQ 1943. Hon. Col, 4th (Carms) Welch Cadet Force, 1963-69; Hon. Col, 4th (V) Bn, Royal Regt of Wales, 1972. KStJ 1973. *Address:* Brondeg, Ferryside, Carmarthenshire. *T:* Ferryside 238.
[Died 2 *Jan.* 1973.

NEVILL, Rev. Thomas Seymour, FRSA; *b* 30 Oct. 1901; *s* of late T. G. Nevill, FSA and late Mrs Nevill; *m* 1966, Muriel Pite (*née* Tasker), *widow* of A. G. Pite. *Educ:* Dover Coll.; Jesus Coll., Cambridge. Westcott House, Cambridge, 1956. BA, 1923; MA, 1926; 2nd Class Honours Mod. and Med. Languages Tripos and Historical Tripos; Asst Masterships at Llandovery Coll., Dover Coll. and Weymouth Coll.; Assoc. Member of Headmasters' Conference; Welsh Hockey XI, 1927, 1929 and 1930; Schools' Secretary of Student Christian Movement, 1934-37; Headmaster of Wellingborough School, 1940-56. Ordained Deacon, 1956; Priest, 1957. Curate at Fareham Parish Church, 1956-58; Charterhouse Missioner in Southwark, 1958-62; Master of Charterhouse, 1962-73; Speaker's Chaplain, 1969-72. Pres., Sion College, 1967-68. Chaplain, Royal Masonic Hosp., 1973-78. *Recreations:* rock-climbing and photography. *Address:* Davenham, Graham Road, Malvern, Worcs WR14 2HY. *T:* Malvern 5174. *Club:* Hawks (Cambridge). *[Died* 17 *Aug.* 1980.

NEVILLE, Bertie Aylmer Crampton, CIE 1941; *b* 7 Oct. 1882; *s* of Col W. B. Neville, Inniskilling Fus., Moyfin, Co. West Meath; *m* 1911, Mabel Jess (*d* 1957), *d* of J. O'B. Sceales, Bankura, Bengal; two *s. Educ:* Corrig School, Kingstown; Royal College of Surgeons, Ireland. Five years with Bank of Ireland; joined Bank of Bengal, 1906; and Imperial Bank of India, 1921, on amalgamation of Presidency Banks; Sec. and Treas., Calcutta, and a Director of the Bank, 1933-41. *Recreations:* golf, photography, fishing. *Address:* C'an Neville, Atalaya Estate, Paguera, Majorca. *Clubs:* East India, Sports and Public Schools; Bengal (Calcutta). *[Died* 1973.

NEVILLE, Captain Philip Lloyd, CVO 1954; *b* 7 Oct. 1888; 2nd *s* of late Admiral Sir George Neville, KCB, CVO; *m* 1942, Eleanor Fellowes (*d* 1972), Toronto, Canada; two *s. Educ:* HMS Britannia. Served European War, 1914-18, and War of 1939-45. Gentleman Usher to King George VI, 1937, to The Queen, 1953-66; Extra Gentleman Usher, 1967-. Order of the Nile,

Egypt, 4th Class. *Recreations:* shooting, country life. *Address:* Henstridge, Templecombe, Somerset. *T:* Stalbridge 62253.
[Died 23 Aug. 1976.

NEVIN, Robert Wallace, TD 1948; FRCS; Consulting Surgeon: St Thomas' Hospital; Treloar's Hospital, Alton, Hants; *b* Burton-on-Trent, Nov. 1907; *s* of Robert Nevin, medical practitioner, and Florence, *d* of Joseph Chamberlain, Burton-on-Trent; *m* 1947, Rosalind Audrey Leeson, *d* of late Rt Rev. Spencer Leeson, DD, Bishop of Peterborough, 1949-56; one *s* two *d. Educ:* Clifton; Emmanuel College, Cambridge. BA (Nat. Scis tripos) Cantab, 1929; MB, BChir Cantab, 1932; MRCS, LRCP 1932; FRCS 1933; MA Cantab 1933. Teacher of Surgery in Univ. of London, 1949; Dean, St Thomas's Hosp. Med. Sch., 1957-68; Chief Surgeon to Metropolitan Police, 1957-77; Member: Bd of Governors, St Thomas' Hosp., 1955-70; Senate, Univ. of London, 1966-69. Examiner in Surgery, Universities of Cambridge, London, Glasgow, Oxford; Mem. Ct of Examrs, RCS; Hunterian Professor Royal College of Surgeons, 1947; Col RAMC (TA), 1947. *Publications:* numerous papers in medical and surgical jls. *Recreations:* gardening, fishing. *Address:* The Old Forge, Greywell, Basingstoke, Hants. *T:* Odiham 2217. *Club:* Athenæum.
[Died 20 Dec. 1980.

NEVIN, Samuel, FRCP; retired as Physician, Maida Vale Hospital, and Neurologist, King's College Hospital; *s* of Samuel Nevin, District Inspector, Royal Ulster Constabulary; *m* 1950, Margaret Esch; one *s* one *d. Educ:* Methodist College, Belfast, Queen's Univ., Belfast. BSc (1st Cl. Hons) 1929; MB, BCh, BAO (1st Cl. Hons) Belfast 1927; MD (Gold Medal) 1930; MRCP 1934; FRCP 1941. Formerly: House Physician, National Hospital, Queen Square; Director Research Laboratory, Inst. Psych., Maudsley Hosp.; Prof. Mental Pathology, Univ. of London. Hon. Lt-Col RAMC. *Publications:* contributions to medical journals. *Address:* 4 Parkside, 14 Court Downs Road, Beckenham, Kent BR3 2TN. *T:* 01-650 1530.
[Died 13 Sept. 1979.

NEVINS, Prof. Allan; author and teacher, USA; formerly Distinguished Senior Research Associate, Huntington Library, San Marino, California; *b* 20 May 1890; *s* of Joseph A. Nevins and Emma Stahl; *m* 1916, Mary Fleming Richardson; two *d. Educ:* University of Illinois; Columbia University. Instructor in English Literature, Univ. of Illinois, 1912-13; editorial staff NY Nation, 1913-18; editorial staff, NY Evening Post, 1913-23; Literary Editor NY Sun, 1923-25; editorial staff NY World, 1925-27; professor of history, Cornell Univ., 1927-28; associate in history at Columbia Univ. and asst editor NY World, 1928-31; holder of Sir George Watson Chair in British universities, 1934-35; visiting professor California Institute of Technology, 1937; Harmsworth professor of American history at Oxford, 1940-41, 1964-65; De Witt Clinton Professor of American History, Columbia University, 1931-58; staff Huntington Library, 1958-69; Pres. Amer. Acad. of Arts and Letters, 1965-68; special representative Office of War Information in Australia and NZ, 1943-44; Chief Public Affairs Officer Amer. Embassy, London (summers), 1946-47; visiting prof., Univ. of Jerusalem, 1951-52; Prof., Claremont Colls, 1968-69. Founder: Oral Hist. Research Office, Columbia Univ., 1948; Nevins Chair in Economic History, Columbia Univ., 1965. Chm., US Civil War Centennial Commn, 1961-66; Editor-in-Chief, 15 vol Impact Series for Civil War Centennial Commn; Life Mem., Bd of Dirs of Woodrow Wilson Internat. Center for Scholars, 1969. Hon. DLitt Oxford, 1965. Alexander Hamilton Award, Columbia Univ., 1968. *Publications:* Life of Robert Rogers, 1914; History of the University of Illinois, 1918; American Social History Recorded by British Travellers, 1923; The American States During and After the Revolution, 1925; The Evening Post: A Century of Journalism, 1925; The Emergence of Modern America, 1927; Henry S. White: Thirty Years of American Diplomacy, 1930; Grover Cleveland: A Study in Courage, 1932 (Pulitzer Prize for best biography of the year); Abram S. Hewitt, With Some Account of Peter Cooper, 1935; Life of Hamilton Fish, 1936 (Pulitzer prize for best biography of year); The Gateway to History, 1938; Frémont, Pathmaker of the West, 1939; John D. Rockefeller, The Heroic Age of American Business, 1940; American Foreign Policy in the Light of its Recent History, 1941; A Brief History of the United States, 1941; This is England To-Day, 1941; (with J. B. Brebner) The Making of Modern Britain, 1943; (with H. S. Commager) America, The Story of a Free People, 1944; The Ordeal of the Union (awarded Scribner Centenary Prize and Bancroft Prize, 1947); America Through British Eyes, 1948; The Emergence of Lincoln, 1950; (with Frank E. Hill) Ford: the Times, the Man, the Company, 1953; Study in Power: John D. Rockefeller, Industrialist and Philanthropist, 1953; Ford: Expansion and Challenge, 1957; The War for the Union: The Improvised War, 1861-1862, 1959; The War for the Union: War Becomes Revolution, 1862-1863, 1960; The State Universities and Democracy, 1962; Ford: Decline and Rebirth, 1962; Herbert H. Lehman and His Era, 1962; (with Ralph Hidy and Frank E. Hill) Timber and Men-The Weyerhaeuser Story, 1963; James Truslow Adams: Historian of the American Dream, 1968; also Editor: Polk, The Diary of a President, 1845-1849, 1929; The Diaries of Philip Hone, 1936; Letters and Journal of Brand Whitlock, 1936; (with J. Mirsky) The World of Eli Whitney, 1952; Diary of the Civil War, 1860-1865: George Templeton Strong, 1952; Statesmanship of the Civil War, 1953; John C. Frémont, Narratives of Exploration and Adventure, 1956; A Portion of that Field: The Centennial of the Burial of Lincoln, Commemorative Papers by Various Authors, 1957; A Diary of Battle: The Personal Journals of Col Charles S. Wainwright, 1861-1865, 1966; Leatherstocking Saga: James Fenimore Cooper, 1966; The Burden and the Glory: Speeches of John F. Kennedy, 1964; Frémont's Geographical Memoir, 1964. *Recreations:* golf, fishing. *Address:* 1820 White Oak Drive, Menlo Park, California, USA. *Clubs:* Athenæum; Century, Lotos, Columbia Faculty (New York); National Press (Washington).
[Died 5 March 1971.

NEWARK, Prof. Francis Headon, CBE 1960; QC (NI) 1972; BCL, MA (Oxon); *b* 25 Sept. 1907; *yr s* of late Herbert Hardwick Newark, Leamington Spa; *m* 1934, Kathleen Mary Bainbridge; two *s* one *d. Educ:* Warwick School; Exeter College, Oxford. Barrister-at-Law, Lincoln's Inn; Lecturer in Law, Queen's University, Belfast, 1937, Prof. of Jurisprudence, 1946, Prof. of Civil Law, 1963-72. Chairman: Belfast Hospitals Management Cttee, 1950-62; Northern Ireland Poisons Board, 1956; Member: Pilkington Cttee on Broadcasting, 1961-62; Commn on the Constitution, 1969-72. *Publications:* Editor Northern Ireland Law Reports, 1947-74; papers in various legal journals. *Address:* Dolmen, Church Hill Close, Llanblethian, Cowbridge, S Wales.
[Died 10 Nov. 1976.

NEWBURGH, Countess of (10th in line, *cr* 1660); **Donna Maria Sofia Giuseppina Giustiniani Bandini;** Viscountess Kynnaird, Baroness Levingston, 1660; *b* 4 May 1889; *d* of 9th Earl and Donna Maria, *d* of Prince di Trabia e di Butera, Palermo; *S* father, 1941; *m* 1922, Count Manfredi Gravina (*d* 1932). Heir: *cousin* Prince Giulio Cesare Taddeo Cosimo Rospigliosi [*b* 26 Oct. 1907; *m* 1940, Donna Giulia Visconti di Modrone; two *s*]. *Address:* 5 Via Virginio Orsini, Rome, Italy. *T:* 350415.
[Died 30 April 1977.

NEWCOMB, Wilfrid Davison; Professor of Morbid Anatomy, University of London, 1937-54; Emeritus Professor, 1954; Morbid Anatomist, St Mary's Hospital, Paddington, 1924-54; *b* 8 June 1889; *s* of Alfred J. Newcomb, Chatham; *m* 1920, Ann G. Nash (*d* 1963); no *c. Educ:* King's School, Rochester (King's Scholar); Liverpool Coll.; Trinity Coll., Cambridge (Open Exhibitioner); London Hosp. Med. Coll. First Class Nat. Sci. Tripos, 1910; Price Entrance Schol. London Hosp. Med. Coll., 1912; Surgeon First British Field Hosp., Serbia, 1915; Surgical Specialist Deccan British War Hosp., Poona, 1916; Asst in Inst. of Pathology, London Hosp., 1919; Asst Pathologist, St Mary's Hosp., 1920. Erasmus Wilson Lecturer, RCS, 1928; Examiner in Pathology, Univ. of Cambridge, 1929; Raymond Horton Smith Prize, 1931; Examiner in Pathology, Univ. of London, 1932; Pathologist in EMS, 1939; Chm. Board of Studies in Pathology, Univ. of London, 1947. *Publications:* papers in medical press, chiefly on cancer. *Recreation:* gardening. *Address:* The Hive, Wellesley Road, Andover, Hants. *T:* Hants. *T:* Andover 3328.
[Died 15 Feb. 1971.

NEWELL, Prof. Arthur (Franklin), MA; Vice-President, formerly John G. Winant Lecturer, British-American Associates; *b* 19 Dec. 1885; *s* of Elmer Ellsworth Newell, Boston, USA, and Emma A. Newell; *m* 1st, Lena Freeman, Boston, USA; 2nd, Desiree Ames, Frome, Somerset; two *s* three *d. Educ:* Boston English High School; Colby Academy; Brown University; Harvard Graduate School. General Secretary, Brown Union, Brown University; Educational Director, War Prisoners' Aid; Executive Secretary, European Division, International YMCA; Professor of International Relations, Robert College, Istanbul, Turkey; Senior Lecturer, British-American Associates; Founder and President, American Outpost in Great Britain; President, Books-Across-The-Sea; Joint Chairman, London International Assembly; President, The Kinsmen; American Rep. Liberal International Council; American Rep. Council of Atlantic Treaty Assoc.; Vice-Pres., British Atlantic Cttee; Mem. Exec. Cttee, David Davies Institute of International Studies; Vice-Pres., Council for Education in World Citizenship; Sette of Odd Volumes (Pres. 1967-68). *Publications:* articles in various jls in Britain and USA. *Recreations:* music, backgammon and the cruder topiary arts. *Address:* The Green, Jordans, Bucks. *T:* Chalfont St Giles 3159.
[Died 17 Feb. 1976.

NEWELL, Rev. Canon John Philip Peter; Chaplain to The Queen, since 1975; *b* 4 Dec. 1911; *s* of late Joseph Newell and Edith Newell; *m* 1955, Mary, *d* of William and Alice Forbes; one *s. Educ:* Shrewsbury Sch.; Magdalen Coll., Oxford. Classical Upper Sixth Form Master, Repton Sch., 1935-36; Asst Priest, Ashbourne Parish Church, and Organizing Sec., Derby Diocesan Youth Council, 1936-39; Asst Master and Chaplain, Diocesan Coll., Rondebosch, Cape Town, 1939-43; Classical Upper Sixth Form Master and Chaplain, Sedbergh School, 1943-53; Headmaster: Bradford Grammar School, 1953-62; The King's School, Canterbury, 1962-75; Vicar of Goudhurst, 1975-80. Select Preacher, University of Oxford, 1956, 1960, 1977. Hon. Canon, Canterbury Cathedral, 1963. *Recreations:* hills and rivers and village churches. *Address:* 38 Cromwell Road, Canterbury, Kent CT1 2LE. *T:* Canterbury 53315. *Club:* East India, Devonshire, Sports and Public Schools.
[Died 7 Dec. 1980.

NEWITT, Dudley Maurice, MC 1918; FRS 1942; DSc, PhD; Professor Emeritus of Chemical Engineering in the University of London; *b* 1894. *Address:* Imperial College of Science, South Kensington, SW7. *Club:* Athenæum. *[Died 14 March 1980.*

NEWMAN, Lt-Col (Augustus) Charles, VC 1945; OBE 1957; TD; FICE; Civil Engineering and Public Works Contractor; Chairman of the Federation of Civil Engineering Contractors, 1957-58; *b* 19 Aug. 1904; *s* of A. B. and Margaret Newman, Buckhurst Hill, Essex; *m* 1929, Audrey Hickman; one *s* five *d. Educ:* Bancroft's Sch., Essex. Joined firm of W. & C. French Ltd, Civil Engineering and Public Works Contractors, in 1922; retd as Chm., 1969. Commissioned 4th Battalion Essex Regt, 1925; War of 1939-45 (despatches; VC, St Nazaire). DL Essex, 1946-48. Légion d'Honneur, Croix de Guerre (France), 1947. *Address:* Fisher Gate House, The Quay, Sandwich, Kent. *T:* Sandwich 3000. *Club:* East India and Sports.
[Died 26 April 1972.

NEWMAN, Charles; *see* Newman, A. C.

NEWMAN, Prof. Sidney Thomas Mayow, CBE 1962; MA Oxon; Hon. DMus Dunelm; FRSE; Hon. RAM 1962; FRCO; FTCL; Reid Professor of Music, University of Edinburgh, 1941-70; *b* 4 March 1906; 2nd *s* of late Julian B. Newman and Mary Clissold, Nailsworth, Glos.; *m* 1st, 1940, Joy (*d* 1943), *er d* of late J. G. Pickering, Newcastle on Tyne; one *s*; 2nd, 1946, Elizabeth, *e d* of late Dr J. D. H. Dickson, Edinburgh; three *s. Educ:* Clifton Coll.; Christ Church, Oxford; Royal Coll. of Music, London. Organ Scholar, 1924-28, Senior Scholar, 1928-30, Christ Church, Oxford; Wesley Exhibitioner, RCM, 1929. Lecturer in Music, Armstrong College (later King's College), Newcastle on Tyne, in the Univ. of Durham, 1930-41; Conductor Newcastle Bach Choir, 1930-41; Conductor Reid Orchestra, 1941-70; Cramb Lecturer, Glasgow, 1956; Choral and Orchestral Conductor various societies in Newcastle and Edinburgh; Pianoforte Recitalist. Member: Council, Edinburgh Festival Soc., 1946-68; Bd of Directors, Scottish Opera, 1962-70. *Publications:* articles in Music Review, Royal Mus. Assoc., etc. *Recreations:* chamber music; walking; collection and history of British road books and travelling maps. *Address:* Newmarket House, Nailsworth, Glos. *T:* Nailsworth 2715.
[Died 22 Sept. 1971.

NEWSOM, Rear-Adm. John Bertram, CB 1957; Senior Technical Adviser to Commander-in-Chief, The Nore, 1955-58, retd; *b* 22 Sept. 1902; *yr s* of J. A. Newsom, Epsom; *m* 1934, Edna Margaret Bowden, Plymouth; three *s. Educ:* Epsom Coll. Entered RN, 1920; completed specialist Engineering course at RN Engineering College, 1925. Served in: HMS Eagle, Curacoa, Vimiera, Duchess, Capetown, Frobisher; served War of 1939-45 in HMS Tartar, at Admiralty and in HMS Illustrious. Subsequent service: HM Dockyard, Malta; on staff of Flag Officer, Scotland and N Ireland; HM Dockyards, Sheerness and Malta. *Recreations:* all games; cricket for RN, 1933. *Address:* Blue Haze, Downderry, Cornwall. *[Died 16 June 1971.*

NEWSOM, Sir John (Hubert), Kt 1964; CBE 1954; Hon. FRIBA; Director, Longman Holdings Ltd and Longman Group Ltd; *b* 8 June 1910; *e s* of late H. N. Newsom; *m* 1931, Barbara Day; one *s* one *d. Educ:* Imperial Service Coll.; The Queen's College, Oxford (Scholar; Hon. Fellow, 1969). Varied experience in education, social work and licensed victualling (inc. Director, Community Service Council for Co. Durham), 1931-40; County Education Officer, Hertfordshire, 1940-57. Life Governor: Haileybury and ISC; St Edmund's Ware; Chairman: Central Advisory Council for Education (England), 1961-63 (Vice-Chm., 1963-66) (Council produced report Half our Future and Report on Primary Educn); Public Schools Commn, 1966-68; Harlow Development Corporation, 1966-; Educational Advisory Council of ITA, 1964-70; SRO, 1928-45; Mem. Indep. Schools Tribunal, 1960-; between 1945 and 1960 served on: Arts Council; Nathan Cttee on Charitable Trusts; Executive of Nat. Youth Orchestra; Deptl Cttee on Public Libraries, Colonial Educn, etc. Hon. LLD, University Pennsylvania. Officer, Legion of Honour. *Publications:* On the Other Side, 1930; Out of the Pit, 1936; Willingly to School, 1944; Education of Girls, 1948; Child at School, 1950; Galloway Gamble, 1951; Rogues Yarn, 1953; (as Marius Rose) The Intelligent Teacher's Guide to Preferment, 1954; AD History News Sheets, 1955. *Recreations:* cookery and conversation. *Address:* Corner House, Fair Green, Sawbridgeworth, Herts. *Club:* Athenæum. *[Died 23 May 1971.*

NEWSON-SMITH, Sir Frank (Edwin), 1st Bt, *cr* 1944; Kt, *cr* 1941; MA (Hon.); DCL (Hon.); Stockbroker; *b* 1889; *s* of Henry Newson-Smith, DL, CA, London; *m* 1904, Lilian Dorothy (*d* 1955), *d* of late Sir Henry Tozer; one *s* two *d* (and one *s* killed in action, 1944). *Educ:* University College Sch.; Paris. Mem. of London Stock Exchange since 1900; Member of Honourable Artillery Company since 1896; elected to Court of Common Council, 1911; Deputy for Ward of Broad Street, 1928, Chief Commoner, 1930; Member HM Court of Lieutenancy, City of London, 1929; Master Worshipful Company of Turners, 1933; Worshipful Company of Spectacle Makers, 1947 and 1948; Alderman of Farringdon Within Ward, 1938, removed to Bridge Without, 1954-68; Sheriff of City of London, 1939; Lord Mayor of London, 1943-44; Governor: of London House; of Sutton's Hospital in Charterhouse. Chairman Government Committee on Business Training, 1945; Pres. London Chamber of Commerce, 1946, 1947 and 1948. *Heir: s* John Kenneth Newson-Smith [*b* 9 Jan. 1911; *m* 1945, Vera Margaret Greenhouse, *d* of Dr W. G. Allt, CBE; one *s* two *d*]. *Address:* 31 Gresham Street, EC2. *T:* 01-606 7711. *[Died 23 April 1971.*

NEWTH, Brig. Arthur Leslie Walter, CBE 1938; DSO 1919; MC; TD; DL; JP; *b* 1897; *s* of late Arthur Edward Newth, Westbury-on-Trym, Bristol; *m* 1926, Ruth Buchanan, *d* of P. Steadman, JP; two *s* one *d. Educ:* Bristol Grammar School. 2nd Lieut, 4th Gloucestershire Regt, 1914; proceeded to France, March 1915; served there until transferred to Italian Expeditionary Force, Nov. 1917; returned to France, April 1918; after holding various Staff appointments, commanded 6th Bn Cheshire Regiment and 2/23rd Bn The London Regiment (DSO, MC, despatches four times); Adjutant 4th Gloucestershire Regiment, 1924-28; Captain, 1915; Major, 1917; Lieut-Colonel, 1929; Bt Colonel, 1933; Colonel, 1934; Brigadier, 1937; commanded 4th (City of Bristol) Bn Gloucestershire Regt, 1929-34; Commander 144th (Glos and Worcs) Infantry Brigade TA, 1934-38; Commander 135 Infantry Brigade, 1939-42; 1942-43 North African Campaign (despatches, Legion of Merit, Degree of Officer); Served at Allied Force HQ, 1943-45, N Africa and Italy (despatches). Chm., BEM Exports Ltd, 1965-75. DL Glos, 1950-74, Somerset, 1974; JP 1952-64. Chairman South Western Regional Board for Industry, 1956-65. Governor Bristol Grammar Sch.; Fellow Royal Commonwealth Society. Hon. Colonel 5th Bn The Gloucestershire Regiment, 1961-67. Master, Furniture Makers' Co., 1975-76. Hon. Freeman, City of London. La Médaille d'honneur d'or de l'éducation physique (France), 1946. *Recreation:* gardening. *Address:* Shepton House, Shepton Montague, Wincanton, Somerset. *T:* Bruton 2258. *Club:* Naval and Military. *[Died 27 Sept. 1978.*

NEWTON, Bernard St John, CIE 1945; retired; *b* 13 April 1890; *s* of late Rev. H. Newton; *m* 1920, Eelin Madeleine, *d* of late Percy Douglas Kirkham (Indian Police); one *d. Educ:* Haileybury; London University. ACGI, BSc (London) 1913. Appointed: to Irrigation Branch of PWD, Central Provinces and Berar (India), 1913; Inspector of Munitions, Calcutta, 1916; Asst Controller of Munitions, Calcutta, 1917; returned to PWD, 1919. Chief Engineer, PWD, CP & Berar, 1943-46; retd, 1946. *Address:* 26 Abercorn Place, NW8. *[Died 5 July 1977.*

NEWTON, Sir Charles (Henry), Kt, *cr* 1943; *b* 6 June 1882; *s* of late Henry Newton; *m* 1917, Hilda Blanche Smith (*d* 1964); (one *s* killed in action in Western Europe April, 1945). Entered GW Rly Service 1897; Asst to Comptroller Great Eastern Rly 1916; Chief Accountant, Great Eastern Rly, 1922; Chief Accountant, L and NE Rly 1928; Divisional General Manager (Southern Area) 1936; Chief General Manager London and North Eastern Railway, 1939-47, Director 1947; Holder of Brunel Medal London School of Economics, University of London; CStJ; USA Medal of Freedom with gold palm. *Publication:* Railway Accounts, 1930. *Address:* Furzefield, East Grinstead, Sussex. *T:* 25353. *[Died 23 May 1973.*

NEWTON, Sir Edgar Henry, 2nd Bt, *cr* 1924; Solicitor (admitted 1919); Consultant with legal firm of Duffield Bruty & Co., of 9 Devereux Court, Temple, WC2, and Waltham Cross and

Hoddesdon, Herts; Commissioner for Oaths; *b* 6 May 1893; *er s* of Sir Louis Arthur Newton, 1st Bt of Beckenham, Kent; *S* father, 1945; *m* 1st, 1917 Gladys Maud (*d* 1966), *d* of late Sir James Garnar; one *s* one *d*; 2nd, 1968, Mrs Alice Mary Rosser, *d* of late Henry Barber. *Educ:* Merchant Taylors' Sch. Formerly Mem. of Court of Common Council of City of London; Past Master of Feltmakers Company of London; Governor: Royal Alexandra and Albert Sch.; Royal Hosp. and Home for Incurables, Putney (Mem. Bd of Management); late comdg 1st Anti-Aircraft, RASC, TA; formerly 56th Divisional RASC. Served European War, 1914-18 (despatches), also 1939-42. *Heir:* s Lt-Col Kenneth Garnar Newton, OBE, TD [*b* 4 June 1918; *m* 1944, Margaret Isabel Blair; two *s*. *Educ:* Wellington Coll.]. *Address:* Larkshill, Harpsden Way, Henley-on-Thames, Oxon. *T:* Henley 2677. *Clubs:* Royal Automobile; Phyllis Court (Henley-on-Thames). *[Died 4 Feb. 1971.*

NEWTON, Giles Fendall, MBE 1918; BA; President, Cape Asbestos Co. Ltd; *b* 27 May 1891; *o s* of William Latham and Violet Newton, Goldington, Bedford; *m* 1921, Mary Cicely (*d* 1972), *e d* of Brig.-General Sir Frederick Meyrick, 2nd Bt, Bush, Pembroke; one *s* one *d. Educ:* Magdalen Coll. School and Lincoln College, Oxford. Open Exhib. (Hist.) Lincoln Coll., Oxford, 1910; Stillingfleet Prizewinner, 1910; BA 1914; served European War, 1914-18, Queen's Royal West Surrey Regt; commissioned, 1914; RA Adjt 29th Bde, RFA, BEF (MBE); seconded to Ministry of Munitions, 1917; Controller of Inspection (A) Ministry of Supply, 1943; Dep. Chm. London Chamber of Commerce, 1945, Chm. 1946, 1947; Dep. Chm. London Court of Arbitration, 1946, Chm., 1948; High Sheriff of Sussex, 1946-47; member of Lord Chancellor's Committee on Practice and Procedure of High Court, 1947. *Recreations:* golf, racing. *Address:* 7 Courtenay Gate, Hove 3, Sussex. *T:* Brighton 71023. *Club:* Bath. *[Died 8 April 1974.*

NEWTON, Maj.-Gen. Thomas Cochrane, CB 1940; DSO 1918; OBE 1919; JP Bedfordshire (supplementary list); *b* 1 Jan. 1885; *o surv s* of late G. O. Newton and late Lady Alice Newton, of Croxton Park, St Neots; *m* 1924, Helen (*d* 1975), *d* of late Augustus Thorne, DL, JP; one *s* one *d. Educ:* Wellington College; RM Academy, Woolwich. Served in Royal Artillery in England and India; France and Belgium, 1914-18 (despatches, DSO, OBE); Commandant, School of Anti-Aircraft Defence, 1935-39; Major-General, General Staff, 1939; retired pay, 1942. High Sheriff of Bedfordshire, 1945-46. *Address:* 9 Amhurst Court, Pinehurst, Cambridge. *Club:* Army and Navy. *[Died 16 July 1976.*

NICHOLL, Rear-Adm. Angus Dacres, CB 1950; CBE 1942; DSO 1942; *b* 17 Nov. 1896; 6th *s* of late William Nicholl, FRAM; *m* 1922, Winifred Rose Edkins; one *s* one *d* (and one *d* decd). *Educ:* Brighton Coll. Joined Navy as Special Entry Cadet, 1914; Asst Chief of Naval Staff and Dir of Naval Intelligence, RAN, 1932-34; Naval Asst Sec. Cttee of Imperial Defence, 1936-39; Capt. 1939; Naval Asst Sec. War Cabinet, 1939-41; commanded HMS Penelope in Mediterranean, 1941-42 (despatches, DSO, CBE); Dir of Operations Div. (Foreign), Admiralty, 1942-44; commanded HMS Duke of York, 1944-46; Commodore RN Barracks, Portsmouth, 1947-48; Rear-Adm. 1948; Brussels Treaty Military Cttee, 1948-49; NATO Planning Group, 1949-51; retired list, 1951. Defence Correspondent, BBC External services, 1951-66. *Address:* 4 Spice Island House, Old Portsmouth, Hants. *T:* Portsmouth 811018. *[Died 12 April 1977.*

NICHOLLS, Arthur, CBE 1941; Royal Corps of Naval Constructors (retired); *b* 16 Jan. 1880; *s* of John Nicholls and Susannah Forester; *m* 1st, 1906, Margaret Brooker (*d* 1925); one *s* three *d* (and one *s* one *d* decd); 2nd, 1927, Rhoda Brooker (*d* 1958). *Educ:* RNC, Greenwich. Joined Royal Corps of Naval Constructors, 1905; Constructor Comdr, Inter-Allied Commn, Berlin, 1920-21; Chief Constructor, Hong Kong, 1931-34; Manager Constructive Dept, Devonport Dockyard, 1936-41. *Address:* 14 Rokeby Drive, Gosforth, Newcastle upon Tyne NE3 4JX. *[Died 6 Sept. 1974.*

NICHOLLS, Bertram, Hon. RBA; landscape painter; *b* Didsbury, Lancs, 26 Sept. 1883; *s* of W. A. Nicholls and Mary Allen; *m* Mary Laura Eva (*d* 1968), *d* of late James Phillips, Malvern; one *s. Educ:* Manchester Gram. Sch. Studied at the Slade Sch. President: Royal Society of British Artists (1931, 1947), Society of Sussex Painters, Manchester Academy of Fine Arts, 1924-34. Represented at: National Gallery, Millbank, National Gallery of Canada, City of London Guildhall Gallery, Metropolitan Museum, New York; Montreal and principal municipal collections. *Publication:* Painting in Oils. *Recreation:* gardening. *Address:* Hardham House, Steyning, Sussex. *T:* Steyning 3298. *[Died 23 Dec. 1974.*

NICHOLLS, Harry, VC 1940; Head Messenger, 1947; *b* 21 April 1915; *s* of Florence Leech and John Nicholls; *m* 1937, Constance Carroll (marr. diss. 1971); one *d*; *m* 1971, Grace Nicholls. *Educ:* Bosworth Road Sch., Nottingham. Joined Army, Grenadier Guards, 1936; served War of 1939-45 (VC, prisoner). *Recreations:* most sports, boxing (won ISBA heavyweight championship of 1938 and other trophies, Army *v* Denmark, 1937); football, cricket, tennis, rugby, swimming. *Address:* Westwood, 35 Surrey Road, Cliftonville, Margate, Kent. *[Died 11 Sept. 1975.*

NICHOLLS, Maj.-Gen. Sir Leslie (Burtonshaw), KCMG 1954; CB 1945; CBE 1943 (OBE 1940); CEng; FIEE; Part-time Member, Central Electricity Generating Bd, 1957-64 (Central Electricity Authority, 1956-57); Chairman: English Telephones Ltd, 1959-69; Cable and Wireless, 1951-56 (Managing Director, 1950-51, Director, 1947-50); Shipton (Automation) Ltd, 1961-67; *b* 3 Sept. 1895; 2nd *s* of late Walter James Nicholls, Burnham, Essex; *m* 1st, 1925, Doris (marr. diss. 1948, she died 1962), *d* of late Ernest Fresson; one *s*; 2nd, 1948, Violet Ethel (marr. diss., 1955; she died 1960); 3rd, 1955, Joan Lady Douglas of Kirtleside. *Educ:* Cheltenham Coll.; University Coll., Univ. of London. Fellow of University Coll., 1948. European War, 1914-19, served with RASC and flying duties RFC and RAF in France and Belgium (twice wounded); transferred to Royal Signals 1925; Shanghai Defence Force, 1927-28; NW Frontier of India, 1936-37 (despatches, medal with clasp); War of 1939-45 in France, Persia, Middle East, N Africa, Italy, France and Germany (despatches, OBE, CBE, CB, US Legion of Merit, Degree of Commander, Legion of Honour (Officer), Croix de Guerre with palm); retired pay, 1946. Freeman of the City of London, 1954; Liveryman of the Worshipful Company of Carmen. *Recreations:* gardening and music. *Address:* Scio House, Roehampton, SW15. *Clubs:* Royal Thames Yacht, Royal Corinthian Yacht. *[Died 5 Feb. 1975.*

NICHOLS, Prof. Roy Franklin; Emeritus Professor of History, University of Pennsylvania, since 1968 (Professor of History, 1930-68; Dean of Graduate School, 1952-66; Vice-Provost, 1953-66); *b* 3 March 1896; *s* of Franklin Coriell and Anna Cairns Nichols; *m* 1920, Jeannette Paddock; no *c. Educ:* Rutgers Univ. (AM); Columbia Univ (PhD). Fellow and Instructor in History, 1920-25; Visiting Professor, 1944-45, Columbia Univ. Asst Professor of History, University of Pennsylvania, 1925-30. Visiting Professor of American History and Institutions, 1948-49, Cambridge Univ. Visiting Prof., Stanford Univ., 1952. Pres., Pennsylvania Historical Assoc., 1936-39; Member: Pennsylvania Historical Commn, 1940-43; Philadelphia Historical Commn, 1961-69 (Chm. 1966-69); Bd of Dirs, Amer. Acad. Political and Social Science, 1958-69; Pres., Genealogical Soc. of Pa, 1946-57; Vice-President: Historical Soc. of Pa, 1953-; American Historical Assoc., 1965 (Pres., 1967); Board of Directors Social Science Research Council, 1934-56; Board of Trustees Rutgers Univ., 1944-47, 1950-68; Board of Governors, 1957-69; American Philosophical Soc., 1945 (Vice-Pres., 1962-65); United States Educn Commn in Great Britain, 1948-49. Fellow of Trinity Coll., Cambridge, 1948-49 (MA). Pulitzer Prizewinner in History, 1949. Phi Beta Kappa (Senator, 1961-69). Hon. Doctorates: LittD Franklin and Marshall, 1937, Muhlenberg Coll., 1956, Univ. of Chattanooga, 1966; LHD Rutgers, 1941; LLD Moravian, 1953; Lincoln Univ., 1959; Knox Coll., 1960. DSSc, Lebanon Valley, 1961; DPed, Susquehannah, 1964; DCL, Univ. of Pennsylvania, 1966. *Publications:* Democratic Machine, 1850-1854, 1923; Franklin Pierce, a Biography, 1931 (new edns, 1958, 1969); Disruption of American Democracy, 1948; Advance Agents of American Destiny, 1956; Religion and American Democracy, 1959; The Stakes of Power, 1845-1877, 1961; Blueprints for Leviathan: American Style, 1963; Invention of the American Political Parties, 1967; A Historian's Progress, 1968; (with Jeannette P. Nichols): Republic of the United States, 1941-43, Growth of American Democracy, 1939. *Recreations:* travelling, theatre, music. *Address:* Fairfax Apartments, 43rd and Locust Streets, Philadelphia, Pa 19104, USA. *T:* 386-6630. *Clubs:* Authors'; Rittenhouse (Philadelphia); Cosmos (Washington); Century (New York). *[Died 11 Jan. 1973.*

NICHOLSON, General Sir Cameron Gordon Graham, GCB 1954 (KCB 1953, CB 1945); KBE 1950 (CBE 1943); DSO 1940; MC 1918; Governor of the Royal Hospital, Chelsea, 1956-61; Master Gunner, St James's Park, 1956-60; Colonel Commandant, Royal Artillery, 1950-60; Colonel Commandant Royal Horse Artillery, 1956-60; *b* 30 June 1898; *s* of late Brig.-General G. H. W. Nicholson, CB, CMG; *m* 1926, Evelyn Odell Westropp; one *s* two *d. Educ:* Northaw Place; Wellington; RMA, Woolwich. 2nd Lieut, RA, 1915; European War, 1915-18

(MC and Bar); RHA, 1917-27 (France, India, Iraq, Palestine, Egypt); Instructor, RMA, Woolwich, 1927-30; Staff Coll., Camberley, 1930-32; Bde Major, RA 2nd Div., 1934-36; MO War Office, 1936-37; Instructor, Staff Coll., Camberley, 1938-39; served War of 1939-45 (DSO and Bar, CBE, CB); GSO1, 45 Div., 1940; GSO1, Sickleforce, Norway, 1940; GSO1, 18 Div., 1940; DCGS Home Forces, 1941; Comd Support Group, 42 Armoured Div., 1941-42; Second-in-Command 6 Armoured Div., 1942; BGS First Army 1943; Commander 44 Indian Armoured Div., 1943-44; Commander 2 British Div., 1945-46; Director of Artillery, War Office, 1946; General Officer Commanding-in-Chief, West Africa Command, 1948-51; General Officer Commanding-in-Chief, Western Command, 1951-53; C-in-C Middle East Land Forces, 1953; Adjutant-General to the Forces, 1953-56; ADC General to the Queen, 1954-56; retired 1956. Hon. Colonel Travel Control Security Group (TA), 1955-60. Governor, Wellington Coll., 1956-68; Governor, Welbeck Coll., 1956-61. Received Order of Legion of Merit and Silver Star, USA, in North Africa. *Recreation:* gardening. *Address:* Greyhayes, St Breward, Bodmin, Cornwall.
[*Died 7 July 1979.*

NICHOLSON, Major Geoffrey, CBE 1944; MC 1917; *b* 1894; *s* of late Brig. General George Harvey Nicholson, CB, CMG; *m* 1st, 1920, Jeana Winifred Mary (*d* 1962), *d* of late Major St Andrew Bruce Warde, Chief Constable of Hants; three *d*; 2nd, 1964, Dorothy Florence, *d* of late A. E. Sedgwick, Hove, Sussex. *Educ:* HMS Conway; Imperial Service Coll.; RMC, Sandhurst. Joined 1 Bn Hampshire Regt, 1913; served in European War, 1914-19 (despatches thrice), in France and Salonika; Brigade Major, 1918; retired with rank of Bt Major, 1922; Assistant Chief Constable of Hampshire, 1922-30; Chief Constable of Surrey, 1930-46; Royal Humane Society's Bronze Medal for saving life at sea, 1912; serving brother Order of St John of Jerusalem, 1945; Officer of Star of Roumania with swords, 1919. *Recreations:* field sports and yachting.. *Address:* Mariners, 81 Haven Road, Canford Cliffs, Poole, Dorset.
[*Died 12 Nov. 1976.*

NICHOLSON, Admiral Sir Gresham; *see* Nicholson, Admiral Sir R. S. G.

NICHOLSON, Brigadier John Gerald, CMG 1961; CBE 1945; DL; retired; *b* 17 Jan. 1906; *er s* of late Lieut-Colonel Walter Adams Nicholson, RA (killed in action, 1917); *m* 1940, Emmeline Mary, *d* of late Henry Barrington Tristram; two *s* one *d* (and one *s* decd). *Educ:* Wellington Coll.; RMC, Sandhurst. Commnd into The Buffs, 1925; Adjt, 1930; Staff Coll., 1934. Served War of 1939-45 (wounded, despatches, CBE). DAAG, AHQ, India, 1939; DAAG 52 Div., 1940; AA and QMG, 15 Div., 1941; Comd 2nd Bn The Buffs, Western Desert, 1942; GSO1, Cyrenaica Dist., 1943; GSO1, GHQ, MEF, 1943; Brig. GS, Plans, AFHQ, CMF, 1944; DDI, SACSEA, 1945; seconded to Foreign Office, 1946. Retired from Army and entered Foreign Service, 1948; appointed to Political Office, MEF, 1948-51, when transferred to FO; retired, 1966. Dep. Colonel, The Buffs, 1956-58; DL Kent, 1958. Officer of the Legion of Merit (USA), 1944; Comdr Royal Danish Order of the Dannebrog, 1956. *Recreation:* horticulture. *Address:* Ashets, Stone Cross, Crowborough, East Sussex. *T:* Crowborough 61401. *Club:* Army and Navy.
[*Died 21 Oct. 1979.*

NICHOLSON, John Henry; CBE 1954; MM 1917; Hon. LLD (Leeds) 1955; Hon. LLD (Hull) 1957; *b* 21 Sept. 1889; *s* of late John Richard Nicholson; unmarried. *Educ:* Scarborough Coll.; Christ Church, Oxford. Tutorial Class Tutor, Liverpool Univ., 1913-15; served in HM Forces, RAMC and RGA, 1915-18; Tutor, Ordination Test School, Knutsford, 1919-20; Lecturer in Education, Bristol Univ., 1920-33; Director of Extra-Mural Studies, Bristol Univ., 1925-33; Professor of Education, Armstrong Coll., Newcastle upon Tyne (University of Durham), 1933-35; Principal, Hull University Coll., 1935-54; Vice-Chancellor, Hull Univ., 1954-56. Albert Khan Fellow, 1922-23. *Publications:* The Remaking of the Nations, 1925; School Care Committees, 1925; Education and Modern Needs, 1936; Help for the Handicapped, 1958; New Communities in Britain, 1961. *Recreation:* walking. *Address:* 30 Clifton, York. *Club:* Yorkshire (York).
[*Died 9 Aug. 1972.*

NICHOLSON, Otho William, TD 1942; DL; *b* 1891; *e s* of late Colonel Rt Hon. William Graham Nicholson, PC; *m* 1927, Elisabeth (who obtained a divorce, 1932), *er d* of late Frederick C. Bramwell, Clerk of the Journals, House of Commons; two *d*; *m* 1976, Joan, *widow* of Col K. F. W. Thomas. *Educ:* Harrow; Magdalene Coll., Cambridge. Served World War, 1914-19, in France with the Rifle Brigade and in the Wireless Intelligence, Royal Engineers; late Hon. Colonel 1st Anti-Aircraft Divisional Signals, Royal Corps of Signals (TA); Brigadier Comdg 40th and

51st Anti-Aircraft Brigade; Asst Comdt, School of AA Artillery, Shrivenham. LCC, 1922-25; Mayor of Finsbury, 1923-24; MP (C) Westminster (Abbey Division), March 1924-32; Chm., Finsbury Cons. Assoc. DL Mddx, 1938. CStJ. *Recreations:* cricket, shooting. *Address:* Whitecroft, Burley, near Ringwood, Hants. *Club:* Carlton.
[*Died 29 June 1978.*

NICHOLSON, Admiral Sir (Randolph Stewart) Gresham, KBE 1950; CB 1946; DSO 1940; DSC 1918; Lieutenant-Governor and Commander-in-Chief of Jersey, 1953-58; *b* 16 Dec. 1892; *s* of W. Gresham Nicholson; *m* Cicely Georgina, CStJ, *d* of the late Rev. Sub-Dean H. Mackworth Drake; one *s* one *d*. *Educ:* Royal Naval Colleges, Osborne and Dartmouth. Served European War, Harwich Force 1914-18 (DSC, despatches); took part in Zeebrugge-Ostend operation; Staff RN Coll., Dartmouth, 1919-21; first and principal ADC to Sir Laurence Guillemard, Governor Malaya and SS, 1921-23; Commander, 1929; Commander RNC, Dartmouth, 1929-31; and HMS Revenge, 1932-34; Captain, 1934; Captain D Tribal Destroyer Flotilla, 1938-40 (despatches, DSO); Commodore, RN Barracks, Chatham, 1940-43; Rear-Admiral, 1943; Dep. C-in-C, Eastern Fleet, and Flag Officer, Ceylon, 1943-45; Admiral Superintendent, HM Dockyard, Devonport, 1945-50; Vice-Admiral, 1948; retired list, 1950; Admiral (retired) 1951. KStJ. Greek Cross of Grand Officer of the Royal Order of Phœnix with Swords, 1947. *Address:* The Toll House, Bucks Green, Horsham, Sussex. *T:* Rudgwick 2314. *Club:* United Service & Royal Aero.
[*Died 28 July 1975.*

NICHOLSON-LAILEY, John Raymond, FRCS; retired as Consultant Surgeon and Gynæcologist to Taunton and Somerset Hospital (from 1930); Vice-President, British Medical Association, 1968 (Chairman Council, 1962-66); *b* 11 April 1900; *s* of Henry George and Ann Blanche Nicholson-Lailey; *m* 1932, Penelope Alice Peach, MB, BS; one *s* two *d*. *Educ:* Trowbridge High Sch.; Bristol Univ. Served with Artists Rifles, April-Aug. 1918; Royal Artillery, Aug. 1918-Jan. 1919; commissioned 2nd Lieut, RA, on demob. MRCS, LRCP, 1923; MB, ChB, Bristol 1924; FRCS 1925. Res. Surgical Officer: Royal Devon and Exeter Hospital, 1926; Salford Royal Hospital, 1927; Gloucester Royal Infirmary, 1929. Hon. Surgeon, Taunton and Somerset Hospital, 1930. Past President, Bath, Bristol and Somerset Branch, BMA; Fellow, BMA. President, South-West Obstetric Society, 1960; Vice-Chairman Council, World Medical Assoc., 1964. Hon. LLD (Manchester) 1964. FRCOG 1965. Officer, Order of Merit, Grand Duchy of Luxembourg, 1964. *Address:* Orchard Rise, Trull, Taunton, Somerset. *T:* Taunton 7270.
[*Died 29 Nov. 1979.*

NICKALLS, Guy Oliver; Hon. Vice-Chairman, Amateur Rowing Association, since 1968 (Hon. Secretary, 1946-52, Chairman, 1952-68); Senior Steward, Henley Royal Regatta (Steward, 1935; Member, Committee of Management, since 1945); Committee Member, Dogs' Home, Battersea; Past President of Leander Club; *b* 4 April 1899; *er s* of late Guy Nickalls and of Ellen Gilbey, *d* of Henry Gold; *m* 1929, Violet Rachel Pearce, *o d* of late Colonel Serocold, CMG; no *c*. *Educ:* Eton; Magdalen Coll., Oxford. Active service, Salonika, 2nd Lieut, Rifle Bde, 1918. Served in Foreign Office, 1919-20; Dip. Econ. 1921; Hons Degree Hist. 1923, MA 1964. Joined advertising firm of Alfred Pemberton Ltd, 1926 (Vice-Chairman, 1945-62). Has broadcast on numerous occasions, incl. first running commentary of Oxford and Cambridge Boat Race, 1927. *Publications:* (with Dr P. C. Mallam) Rowing, 1939. Edited and contributed to: Life's a Pudding (autobiography of late Guy Nickalls), 1938; With the Skin of Their Teeth, 1946. *Recreations:* rowed for Oxford *v* Cambridge, 1921, 1922, 1923 (President 1923); Henley: (in winning crews) Grand Challenge Cup of 1920, 1921, 1922, 1924, 1925, 1926 and 1928; Stewards' Four, 1928; Silver Goblets with R. S. C. Lucas, 1920 and 1921; in eight oar which rep. UK in Olympics of 1920 and 1928 (silver medal twice); fishing, shooting, gardening, painting (has exhibited at RA Summer Exhibition). *Address:* 30 Astell Street, Chelsea, SW3. *T:* 01-352 0693. *Clubs:* Garrick, MCC; London Rowing, Thames Rowing (Putney); Leander, Remenham.
[*Died 26 April 1974.*

NICKLIN, Hon. Sir (George) Francis (Reuben), KCMG 1968; MM 1918; retired; Premier of Queensland, 1957-68; *b* 6 Aug. 1895; *s* of George Francis Nicklin and Edith Catherine Nicklin, *née* Bond; *m* 1922, Georgina (decd), *d* of R. Fleming. *Educ:* Murwillumbah State Sch.; Highfield Coll., Turramurra, NSW. Engaged in tropical fruit culture since leaving school; took leading part in organisation of Queensland fruit industry. MLA for Murrumba, Queensland, 1932-50, for Landsborough, Queensland, 1950-68; Secretary, Parliamentary Country Party, 1935-41; Leader of the Opposition, 1941-57; Premier and Minister for State Development, Queensland, 1957-68. Hon. LLD Queensland, 1961. *Recreations:* cricket, bowls, gardening,

Surf Life Saving movement. *Address:* 13 Upper Gay Terrace, Caloundra, Queensland 4551, Australia. *T:* Caloundra 911075. *Clubs:* Queensland Cricketers', Queensland Masonic, Caloundra Services.   [*Died* 29 *Jan.* 1978.

NICKLIN, His Honour Robert Shenstone, MA; a County Court Judge, later a Circuit Judge, 1955-73; *b* 1901; *s* of late P. H. S. Nicklin, Blundellsands, Liverpool; *m* 1935, Mervyn Halley, MB, ChB, *d* of late Matthew Clark, Blundellsands; three *d. Educ:* Uppingham; University Coll., Oxford. Pte Intelligence Corps; Major JAG's department; barrister, Lincoln's Inn, 1925. Dep. Chm., Quarter Sessions: Cumberland, 1953-56; Nottingham, 1956-57; JP: Cumberland, 1953-56; Nottingham, 1956-57; Warwick, 1959. *Address:* Hercules Farm, Claverdon, Warwickshire. *T:* Claverdon 2388.   [*Died* 4 *Jan.* 1975.

NICOL, Rev. Anderson, DD (Glasgow) 1967; MA (Glasgow) Chaplain to the Queen in Scotland, since 1964 (Extra Chaplain, 1963); Minister, Dundurn Parish Church, St Fillans, Perthshire, since 1967; *b* Stevenston, Ayrshire, 17 June 1906; *s* of George Nicol and Johanna Jessiman; *m* 1932, Jane Brown Williamson, Stevenston; one *s* two *d* (and one *s* decd). *Educ:* Stevenston; High School of Glasgow; University of Glasgow MA 1927. Asst, St Michael's Parish Church, Crieff, 1931-32; Minister: Dunbarney Parish Church, 1932; Braid Church, Edinburgh, 1941. Chaplain, RN, 1943-46 (Naval General Service Medal, 1946); Minister, West Church of St Nicholas (City Church), Aberdeen, 1948-67. Governor, Robert Gordon's Colleges, 1949-67. Presbyterian preacher to USA (under British Council of Churches Interchange of Preachers), 1957 and 1969; Member Broadcasting Council for Scotland, 1958-62; Patron, Seven Incorporated Trades, 1963-. Scouting: various appointments to Asst Commissioner. *Publication:* The Story of the West Church of St Nicholas, Aberdeen, 1961. *Recreations:* reading, photography, touring. *Address:* The Manse, St Fillans, Perthshire PH6 2NF. *T:* St Fillans 267.   [*Died* 2 *Aug.* 1972.

NICOL, James Lauder, CMG 1954; OBE 1945; retired from HM Colonial Civil Service, 1954; *b* 1889; *s* of James Nicol, Balbardie House, West Lothian; *m* 1912; *o s* killed in action, 1941. *Educ:* New Coll., Edinburgh; Universities of Edinburgh and London (hons Arts and distinction Law). Served European War, 1914-18: in France as Captain, Royal Scots Regt; Reparations Commn, Vienna, 1919-20; Educational Research, 1920-22; HM Colonial Service (Malaya), 1922-36; HMI Min. of Education, and Lectr on Education, University of Cambridge, 1936-39; seconded as Chief Regional Officer, Ministry of Information, 1939-45; Chairman Regional Industrial Publicity Cttee, 1939-45; HM Divisional Inspector, NW Division, Ministry of Education, 1946-49; Educational Adviser to Comptroller, Development and Welfare in West Indies, 1949-54; Chm., Education Commn, British Guiana, 1952. *Recreations:* travel and music. *Address:* Pré Sec, Route Orange, St Brelade, Jersey, CI.   [*Died* 2 *Jan.* 1971.

NICOLL, Allardyce; *see* Nicoll J. R. A.

NICOLL, John Ramsay Allardyce, MA; Professor Emeritus of English Language and Literature in the University of Birmingham; Andrew Mellon Visiting Professor of English, University of Pittsburgh, USA, 1963-64, 1965, 1967, 1969; *b* 28 June 1894; *s* of David Binny Nicoll and Elsie Nicoll (*née* Allardyce); *m* Josephine Calina (*d* 1962); *m* Maria Dubno. *Educ:* Stirling High Sch.; Glasgow Univ. G. A. Clark Scholar in English; Lectr in English, Loughborough Coll.; Lecturer in English, King's Coll., Univ. of London; Prof. of English Lang. and Lit. in Univ. of London; Prof. of the History of Drama and Dramatic Criticism, Chm. Dept of Drama, Yale Univ.; Prof. of English, Univ. of Birmingham, 1945-61 and Dir of Shakespeare Institute, Stratford-upon-Avon, 1951-61. Attached to HM Embassy, Washington, 1942-45. Life Trustee, Shakespeare Birthplace Trust, Stratford-upon-Avon; Editor, Shakespeare Survey, 1948-65; Hon. Member: Mod. Lang. Assoc. of America; Accademia Ligure di Scienze e Lettere; Pres., Soc. for Theatre Research. Hon. DèsL: Toulouse; Montpellier. Hon. DLitt: Durham and Glasgow; Hon. DHL, Brandeis Univ. *Publications:* William Blake, 1922; Dryden as an Adapter of Shakespeare, 1922; An Introduction to Dramatic Theory, 1923; John Dryden, 1923; A History of Restoration Drama, 1923; A History of Early Eighteenth Century Drama, 1925; British Drama, 1925; Sharpham's Cupid's Whirligig, Carlell's Osmond the Great Turk and The Fool Would Be a Favourite (editor) 1926; A History of Late Eighteenth Century Drama, 1927; The Development of the Theatre, 1927; Studies in Shakespeare, 1927; The English Stage, 1928; Readings from British Drama, 1928; Eighteenth Century Comedies (editor) 1928; A History of Early Nineteenth Century Drama, 1930; The Works of Cyril Tourneur (editor) 1930; Masks, Mimes and Miracles, 1931; The Theory of

Drama, 1931; Film and Theatre, 1936; The English Theatre, 1936; Stuart Masques and the Renaissance Stage, 1937: A History of Late Nineteenth Century Drama, 1946; World Drama, 1949; A History of English Drama, 1660-1900, 6 volumes, 1952-59; The Elizabethans, 1956; Chapman's Homer (editor) 2 volumes, 1957; The World of Harlequin, A Study of the Commedia dell'Arte, 1963; Theatre and Dramatic Theory, 1963; English Drama: A Modern Viewpoint, 1968; English Drama 1900-1930, 1973; various contributions to Year's Work in English Studies, Modern Language Review, Review of English Studies, Times Literary Supplement, etc. *Address:* Wind's Acre, Colwall, Malvern. *T:* Colwall 40310. *Club:* Century, New York.   [*Died* 17 *April* 1976.

NICOLSON, Benedict; *see* Nicolson, L. B.

NICOLSON, Lionel Benedict, CBE 1971; MVO 1947; FBA 1977; Editor of The Burlington Magazine since 1947; *b* 6 Aug. 1914; *s* of late Hon. Sir Harold Nicolson, KCVO, CMG and Hon. V. Sackville-West, CH; *m* 1955, Luisa Vertova, Florence (marr. diss. 1962); one *d. Educ:* Eton Coll.; Balliol Coll., Oxford. Dep. Surveyor of the King's Pictures, 1939, resigned, 1947. Served War of 1939-45; Commn, 1942, in Intelligence Corps; Interpreter in Italian POW Camps, 1943; Middle East (Egypt, Palestine, Syria), 1943-44, Italy, 1944-45, Instr in Photo-Intelligence; Capt. 1944. Mem. Exec. Cttee, Nat. Art Collections Fund, 1972-. Hon. Dr RCA 1971. *Publications:* The Painters of Ferrara, 1950; Hendrick Terbrugghen, 1958; Wright of Derby: Painter of Light, 1968; The Treasures of the Foundling Hospital, 1972; Courbet: The Studio of the Painter, 1973; (with C. Wright) Georges de La Tour, 1974. *Recreations:* reading, travel. *Address:* 45b Holland Park, W11. *T:* 01-229 2799. *Clubs:* Brooks's, Beefsteak.   [*Died* 22 *May* 1978.

NIEBUHR, Rev. Prof. Reinhold, DD; Graduate Professor Emeritus of Ethics and Theology, Union Theological Seminary, New York City, since 1928; Editor, Bi-Weekly, Christianity and Crisis; *b* 21 June 1892; *s* of Gustave Niebuhr and Lydia Hosto; *m* 1931, Ursula Mary, *y d* of Dr Keppel-Compton, Woodhall Spa; one *s* one *d. Educ:* Elmhurst Coll.; Yale Univ. Minister, Bethel Evangelical Church, Detroit, 1915-18; Contrib. Editor of bi-weekly, Christianity and Crisis. Hon. DD: Grinnell Coll. 1932, Eden Theological Seminary (St Louis), 1933, Wesleyan Univ., 1935, Univ. of Pennsylvania, 1939, Amherst Coll., 1941, Yale Univ., 1942, Oxford Univ., 1943, Harvard Univ., 1944, Princeton Univ., 1946, Glasgow Univ., 1947, NY Univ., 1948, Hobart Coll., 1948, Dartmouth Coll., 1951, Univ. of Manchester, 1954; LLD Occidental Coll., 1945; STD Columbia Univ., 1954; LittD: New Sch. for Social Research, 1951; Hebrew Univ., Jerusalem, 1967. Presidential Medal of Freedom, 1964. *Publications:* Does Civilization Need Religion, 1927; Leaves from the Notebook of a Tamed Cynic, 1930; Moral Men and Immoral Society, 1932; Reflections on the End of an Era, 1934; Interpretation of Christian Ethics, 1935; Beyond Tragedy, 1937; Christianity and Power Politics, 1940; Nature and Destiny of Man, Vol. I, 1941, Vol. II, 1943 (Gifford Lectures); The Children of Light and the Children of Darkness, 1944; Discerning the Signs of the Times, 1946; Faith and History, 1949; The Irony of American History, 1952; Christian Realism, 1953; The Self in Its Dialogues and Dramas, 1955; The Godly and the Ungodly (Essays), 1959; The Structure of Nations and Empires, 1959: A Nation so Conceived, 1963; Man's Nature and His Communities, 1965; Faith and Politics, 1968; (with Paul E. Sigmund) The Democratic Experience, 1969. *Address:* Yale Hill, Stockbridge, Mass 01262, USA.   [*Died* 1 *June* 1971.

NIEMEYER, Sir Otto (Ernst), GBE 1927; KCB 1924 (CB 1921); Past Director: Bank of England, 1938-52; Bank for International Settlements, 1931-65 (Chairman of the Board, 1937-40; Vice-Chairman, 1941-64); Member of Council of Foreign Bondholders, since 1935 (Vice-President 1950-55; President, 1956-65); Member Advisory Committee, International Nickel Co. of Canada Ltd (Past Director); *b* 1883; *m* 1910, Sophia Benedicte, *d* of Theodor Niemeyer; two *s* one *d* (and one *s* killed on active service). *Educ:* St Paul's Sch.; Balliol Coll., Oxford. HM Treasury, 1906-27; Controller of Finance, 1922-27; Mem. of Financial Cttee of League of Nations, 1922-37 (Chm., 1927); Dir Banque des Pays de l'Europe (Paris), 1928-57; Financial Mission to Australia and NZ, 1930; Brazil, 1931; Argentine, 1933; India, 1935; China, 1941; Fellow, London Sch. of Economics (Chm. of Govs, 1941-57; Gov., 1958-65); Gov. of St Paul's Sch.; Gov. of Marlborough Coll.; Chm., Provisional National Council for Mental Health, 1943-46; Vice-Pres., National Association for Mental Health (Hon. Treas., 1947-64). High Sheriff, County of London, 1945; a Lt of the City of London. *Address:* Nash House, Lindfield, Sussex. *T:* Lindfield 3209. *Club:* Reform.
                                              [*Died* 6 *Feb.* 1971.

NIGHTINGALE, Sir Charles Athelstan, 16th Bt *cr* 1628; *b* 23 July 1902; *s* of Percy Athelstan Nightingale, MD (*g g s* of 11th Bt) (*d* 1918), and Muriel Stoughton (*d* 1955), *d* of Charles Stoughton Collison; *S* cousin, 1972; *m* 1932, Nadine, *d* of late Charles Arthur Diggens; one *s* two *d. Educ:* Harrow. *Heir: s* Charles Manners Gamaliel Nightingale, *b* 21 Feb. 1947. *Address:* 7 Victoria Street, Okehampton, Devon EX20 1NA.
[*Died 7 March* 1977.

NIGHTINGALE, Sir Geoffrey Slingsby, 15th Bt, *cr* 1628; MRCS and LRCP 1929; DPM (England) 1934; Physician Superintendent Warley Hospital, Brentwood, 1946-69; formerly Consultant Psychiatrist Oldchurch Hospital, Romford, and Ilford and Barking Hospitals; *b* 24 Nov. 1904; *s* of late Thomas Slingsby Nightingale, CMG, CBE, and Doris Elizabeth, *d* of Charles Stoughton Collison, East Bilney, Norfolk; *S* cousin, 1953; *m* 1936, Madeleine (*d* 1970), *d* of late Richard Doyle, Tramore, Co. Waterford; one adopted *s. Educ:* Marlborough; London Hospital. Served 1940-45, as Lt-Col RAMC, Command Psychiatrist, South Eastern and Western Commands and OC Div. 32nd Gen. Hospital, BLA. Formerly Asst Medical Officer, Surrey County Mental Hospital, Netherne; House Physician Skin and Light Depts, London Hospital. Member: Inst. Advanced Motorists. Warden, Essex Guild of Woodcarvers. Gold Award, High Performance Club. *Publications:* The First Hundred Years: a History of Warley Hospital, 1953; Dinghy Ownership, 1956, 4th edn, 1971; Dinghy Sailing for Boys, 1957, 4th edn 1970; (jointly) Eagle Book of Ships and Boats, 1959; chapters in The Dinghy Year Book, 1958, 1959, 1960, etc.; contributions to medical journals and yachting press. *Recreations:* fast cars, fishing, small boat sailing, sneezing. *Heir:* cousin Charles Athelstan Nightingale [*b* 23 July 1902; *m* 1932, Nadine, *d* of late Charles Arthur Diggens; one *s* two *d*]. *Address:* Gents Farm, Pilgrims Hatch, Brentwood, Essex. *T:* Coxtie Green 300. *Clubs:* BSC Master Drivers', High Performance Club of British School of Motoring.
[*Died 3 Sept.* 1972.

NIHILL, Sir (John Harry) Barclay, KBE 1951; Kt 1948; *b* 1892; *o s* of Rev. H. B. Nihill, Hastings; *m* Nuala, *e d* of late Joseph O'Carroll, MD, Past Pres. Royal Coll. Physicians, Ireland; one *s* (and one killed in action Malta Convoy, 12 Aug. 1942). *Educ:* Felsted; Emmanuel Coll., Cambridge (scholar MA). Pres. of the Union, Cambridge, 1914; served European War, 1914-18, Capt., Royal Munster Fusiliers (MC). Barrister-at-Law, Inner Temple, 1919; Sec., Joint Industrial Councils, Ministry of Labour, 1919; Colonial Civil Service, Hong Kong, 1921; Legal Sec. to High Commission, Baghdad, 1927-33; Solicitor-Gen., Uganda, 1934; KC 1936; Attorney-Gen., British Guiana, 1936; Puisne Judge, Ceylon, 1938; Legal Sec. to Govt of Ceylon, 1942-46; Chief Justice, Kenya, 1947-50 (appointed, 1946); Pres., Court of Appeal for Eastern Africa, 1950-55, retired; Speaker of the Legislative Council, Tanganyika, 1958; Chm., Admiralty Requirements Cttee, 1956; Chm., Tanganyika Sisal Industry Central Joint Consultative Council, 1959-62. Legal Mem. SW Metropolitan Mental Health Tribunal, 1962-65. *Address:* 226 Ashley Gardens, SW1. *T:* 01-828 8621. *Clubs:* United Oxford & Cambridge University; Muthaiga (Kenya).
[*Died 18 Nov.* 1975.

NILES, Emory Hamilton; retired as Chief Judge, Supreme Bench of Baltimore, Maryland, 1962; *b* Baltimore, Md, 15 Oct. 1892; *s* of Judge Alfred S. Niles and Mary Hamilton (Waters); *m* 1922, Anne Whitridge Williams; one *s* two *d. Educ:* Johns Hopkins Univ. (AB, Rhodes Scholar); Oxford Univ. (BA (1st cl.), MA, BCL (1st cl.)). Univ. of Maryland (LLB, JD). Ambulance Américaine, France, 1916; served with US Army, 313th Field Artillery, AEF, France, 1917-18 (Lt and Capt.). Amer. Commn for Relief in Near East, Turkey, 1919. Practice of Law, Baltimore, 1920-38; Assoc. Judge, 1938-54; Chief Judge, 1954-62. Lecturer: Univ. of Maryland Law Sch., 1923-59; Johns Hopkins Medical Sch., 1951-68. Chm., War Price and Rationing Boards, Baltimore, 1942-46; Maryland State Fuel Coordinator, 1948; Pres., Assoc. of American Rhodes Scholars, 1970-74 (Vice-Pres., 1956-70); Chm., Judicial Administration Section, Amer. Bar. Assoc., 1959; Governor, Amer. Bar Assoc., 1966-69; Mem. US Commn on Internat. Rules of Judicial Procedure, 1960; Pres., Maryland State Bar Assoc., 1962; Pres., Inst. of Judicial Administration, New York, 1963-66; Chm., Maryland Judicial Selection Council Inc., 1963. Editor: American Maritime Cases, 1923-; US Aviation Reports, 1928-60. Hon. Fellow, Hertford Coll., Oxford, 1961; Hon. LLD: Univ. of Maryland, 1964; Goucher Coll., 1967. Hartley Award, Amer. Judicature Soc., 1975. *Publications:* miscellaneous legal articles. *Recreations:* travel, woodworking. *Address:* 5600 Waycrest Lane, Baltimore, Md 21210, USA. *T:* 301-323-3260. *Clubs:* Hamilton Street, Johns Hopkins, Century (NY).
[*Died 8 Sept.* 1976.

NIMMO, Sir Robert, Kt 1944; JP; *b* 11 June 1894; *s* of Robert Nimmo, Brewer, Perth; *m* 1922, Dorothy Wordsworth (decd), *d* of Walter Gillies; two *s* one *d.* Lord Provost of Perth, 1935-45. Hon. Sheriff, Perth. *Address:* 8 Anderson Drive, Perth.
[*Died 22 Nov.* 1979.

NIMPTSCH, Uli, RA 1967 (ARA 1958); sculptor: *b* Berlin, 22 May 1897; of British nationality; *m* 1925, Ruth (*née* Steinhal) (*d* 1974); one *s. Educ:* studied in Berlin, Rome and Paris. One-man exhibn, RA, 1973. Works are represented in the following galleries and museums: Tate Gallery, London; British Museum; Arts Council; Museum of Leeds; Museum of Liverpool; Museum of Manchester. Statue of Lloyd George, Houses of Parliament. *Address:* 409 Fulham Road, SW10. *T:* 01-352 8679.
[*Died 2 Jan.* 1977.

NINNES, Bernard, ROI 1934; RBA 1933; Painter in oils; *b* 5 July 1899; *s* of Richard and Ellen Mary Heather Ninnes; *m* 1930, Edyth Mary Day (*d* 1963), Streatham Park. *Educ:* Slade Sch.; Univ. of London. War Service at Bristol Aeroplane Co., 1940. Painter of Architectural and Figure Compositions, Sea, and Landscape; studied art under Prof. Tonks and Wilson Steer; Mem. of St Ives art colony; represented in Stoke-on-Trent permanent collection, In for Repairs, purchased in 1932; Hereford permanent collection, The Café Born, Palma, purchased 1936; permanent collection at Royal Leamington Spa Municipal Art Gallery, The Boatbuilders' Shop, St Ives, purchased, 1937; Russell-Cotes Art Gallery, Bournemouth permanent collection, Street in Spain, purchased, 1939; Beds CC Education Cttee Purchase, Ludlow Castle, 1950; Festival of Britain 1951, prize for painting, A Cornish Village (St Ives' Permanent Collection); Picture, Drama comes to our Village, exhibited with Outstanding Pictures of the Jubilee Year, 1935; A Break in the Clouds (Albuquerque Gall., New Mexico, USA), 1957. Exhibitor at Royal Academy, Paris Salon, Royal Institute of Oil Painters, Royal Society of British Artists, New English Art Club, Royal West of England Acad., and many provincial towns; Pictures reproduced in The Times, The Artist, Illustrated Sporting and Dramatic News, Bystander, The Sketch, Oil Painting of To-day, Britain's Art Colony by the Sea, etc. Reproductions by Medici Soc., E. S. & A. Robinson, J. Salmon, Ltd, E. T. W. Dennis & Sons, Balding and Mansell, Ltd, Photochrom Co. Ltd, Mardon Son & Hall Ltd, Vivian Mansell & Solomon & Whitehead Ltd, John Arthur Dixon & Co. *Recreations:* music, garden. *Address:* Hayeswood, St Ives, Cornwall. *T:* St Ives 6499.
[*Died 28 Sept.* 1971.

NISBET, James Wilkie, MA, LLB; Professor of Political Economy, University of St Andrews, 1947-70, now Emeritus Professor; *b* 11 Dec. 1903; *s* of James Nisbet and Helen Bruce Wilkie; *m* 1927, Jean Wheatley; two *s* one *d. Educ:* Hutchesons' Gram. Sch., Glasgow; Univ. of Glasgow. MA, 1st Class Hons Econ. Science, 1925; 1st Class Hons Mental Philosophy, 1926; LLB (with distinction), 1926; Reid Stewart Fellowship and Gladstone Memorial Prize in Econ. Science, 1925; Clark Schol. and Caird Medal in Mental Philosophy, 1926; Robertson Schol. in Law, 1926; Faulds Fellowship in Fac. of Arts, 1926-29; Asst to Adam Smith Prof. of Political Econ., Univ. of Glasgow, 1926-31; Lectr in Political Econ., Univ. of Glasgow, 1935-39; Lectr in Political Econ., St Andrews Univ., 1935-39, Reader, 1939-46; Examiner in Political Economy, Universities of: Glasgow, 1946-48; Bristol, 1947-50; Aberdeen, 1953-55. Canada Council Fellow, 1958. Chm. of Scottish Consumers' Council, 1954-68. *Publications:* A Case for Laissez Faire, 1929; Banks and the Finance of Industry, 1934; Post-War Britain and Standard of Life, 1937; Britain's Economic Resources, 1941; Scottish Agriculture and Industry, 1942; The Beveridge Plan, 1943; The Triumvirate of Political Economists in St Andrews, 1947; Thomas Chalmers and Political Economy, 1964; Berlin, 1972; The Nisbets, 1972; The Wilkies, 1972; Adam Smith, 1973. *Recreations:* golf and gardening. *Address:* Balmyle, Buchanan Gardens, St Andrews, Fife. *T:* St Andrews 3631. *Club:* Royal and Ancient (St Andrews).
[*Died 26 March* 1974.

NIXON, Sir (Charles) Norman, Kt, *cr* 1946; Governor of the National Bank of Egypt until 1946; *b* 8 June 1891; *m* Catherine Marwood Ranson (*d* 1954); two *s.* Served European War, 1914-18, Indian Army (despatches). *Address:* Gaddon Leaze, Uffculme, Devon.
[*Died 11 Oct.* 1978.

NIXON, Major Sir Christopher John Louis Joseph, 3rd Bt, *cr* 1906; MC; Royal Ulster Rifles; *b* 21 March 1918; *s* of Major Sir Christopher Nixon, 2nd Bt, DSO, and Louise, *y d* of Robert Clery, JP, The Glebe, Athlacca, Limerick; *S* father, 1945; *m* 1949, Joan Lucille Mary, *d* of R. F. M. Brown, London; three *d.* Served War of 1939-45, Burma. Gurkha Bde (despatches, MC); Palestine, Egypt, 1945-48; UK, attached London Irish Rifles, 1948-50; Korea (despatches). 1950-51. *Heir: b* Rev. Kenneth

Michael John Basil Nixon, SJ. [*b* 22 Feb. 1919; in Holy Orders of Church of Rome]. *Address:* c/o Lloyds Bank Ltd, Cox's & King's Branch, 6 Pall Mall, SW1.   [*Died* 31 *Jan.* 1978.

NIXON, Sir Norman; *see* Nixon, Sir C. N.

NIXON, Rev. Robin Ernest, MA; Principal, St John's College, Nottingham, since 1975; *b* 5 Dec. 1931; *s* of Ernest Nixon and Helen Louisa Nixon (*née* Smallwood); *m* 1958, Ruth Mary, *d* of Arthur Eric Jarvis Vickers and Katherine Vickers (*née* Wood); three *d. Educ:* Ascham House Sch., Newcastle upon Tyne; Winchester Coll.; Trinity Hall, Cambridge; Ridley Hall, Cambridge. Pt I Law, Pts II and III Theol., MA 1958, Cantab. Asst Curate, Holy Trinity Church, Hull, 1957-60; Tutor, St John's Coll., Univ. of Durham, 1960-63, Sen. Tutor, 1963-75. Mem., Doctrine Commn of CofE, 1977-. Editor, The Churchman, 1972-. *Recreations:* family, reading, current affairs. *Address:* St John's College, Bramcote, Nottingham NG9 3DS. *T:* Nottingham 251114.   [*Died* 18 *Oct.* 1978.

NKRUMAH, Dr Kwame; *b* 21 Sept. 1909; *m* 1957, Madame Fathia Ritz, Egypt; one *s* two *d. Educ:* Roman Catholic Elementary Sch., Half Assini; Government Teachers' Training Coll., Accra and Achimota; Lincoln Univ., Pennsylvania (BA, STB); Univ. of Pennsylvania (BD, MAPhil, MScEd); London Univ. Schoolmaster, 1931-34; Instructor in History and Philosophy, Univ. of Pennsylvania, 1944; Gen. Sec., W African Nat. Secretariat; Jt Sec. Pan African Congress, London and Manchester; Editor of New African, London, 1945-47; Former Member and first General Secretary, United Gold Coast Convention (UGCC); arrested and detained, Feb. 1948; resigned from UGCC, demanded "Self-Government Now" and formed Convention People's Party (CPP), 1949; his party staged Positive Action, 1950; imprisoned for inciting illegal strikes, 1950; elected to Legislative Assembly under new Constitution, Feb. 1950; released from prison on being elected first Municipal Member for Accra; Leader of Government Business in the Assembly, Feb. 1951; Prime Minister of Gold Coast, 1952-57, of Ghana, 1957-60; Minister of External Affairs, 1957-58, of the Interior, 1958-59; First President of the Republic of Ghana, 1960-66; Head of State and Supreme Commander of the Armed Forces, 1960-66. Attended Commonwealth Prime Ministers' Conference, June 1957, the first African Prime Minister to do so. Convened Conference of eight Independent African States (Chairman), April 1958, and did tour of these, May-June 1958; paid Official Visits to United States and Canada, July 1958. Addressed UN Assembly, 1960, 1961. Has since visited many countries and attended or convened conferences with regard to Africa. Past Chancellor: Univ. of Ghana; Kwame Nkrumah University of Science and Technology. Resident in the Republic of Guinea, 1966-. PC (Great Britain) 1959 (entitling him to prefix "Rt Hon."); Lenin Peace Prize, 1962. Has many hon. doctorates from universities. Holds several foreign Orders. *Publications:* Towards Colonial Freedom, 1946; What I Mean by Positive Action, 1950; Ghana (autobiography), 1957; I Speak of Freedom, 1961; Africa Must Unite, 1963; Consciencism, 1964; Neo-colonialism: the Last Stage of Imperialism, 1965; Challenge of the Congo, 1966; Axioms of Kwame Nkrumah, 1966; Dark Days in Ghana, 1968; Handbook of Revolutionary Warfare: A Guide to the Armed Phase of the African Revolution, 1968; Class Struggle in Africa, 1970. *Recreations:* tennis, swimming, collection of animals. *Address:* Conakry, Guinea.   [*Died* 27 *April* 1972.

NOEL-BUXTON, 2nd Baron, *cr* 1930, of Aylsham; **Rufus Alexander Buxton;** writer and painter; *b* 13 Jan. 1917; *s* of 1st Baron Noel-Buxton and Lucy Edith (MP (Lab) North Norfolk, 1930-31, Norwich, 1945-50; *d* 1960), *e d* of late Major Henry Pelham Burn; *S* father, 1948; *m* 1st, 1939, Nancy (marr. diss. 1947; she *d* 1949), *yr d* of late Col K. H. M. Connal, CB, OBE; two *s* ; 2nd, 1948, Margaret Elizabeth (*d* 1978), *er d* of Stephanus Abraham Cloete, Pretoria, SA; one *s* one *d.* Assumed names of Rufus Alexander Buxton in lieu of those of Noel Alexander Noel-Buxton, 1944. *Educ:* Harrow; Balliol Coll., Oxford (BA). Invalided from 163 OCTU (the Artists Rifles), 1940; Research Asst, Agricultural Economics Research Inst., Oxford, 1941-43; Lecturer to Forces, 1943-45; Producer, BBC North American Service, 1946-48; editorial staff of The Farmer's Weekly, 1950-52. *Publications:* The Ford, 1955; Westminster Wader, 1957. *Heir: s* Hon. Martin Connal Noel-Buxton (assumed by deed poll, 1964, original surname of Noel-Buxton) [*b* 8 Dec. 1940; *m* 1964, Miranda Mary (marr. diss. 1968), *er d* of H. A. Chisenhale-Marsh, Gaynes Park, Epping, and Lady Buxton, Woodredon, Waltham Abbey; *m* 1972, Sarah Margaret Surridge, *d* of N. C. W. Barrett; one *s* one *d*]. *Address:* House of Lords, SW1.   [*Died* 14 *July* 1980.

NOKES, Gerald Dacre; Professor Emeritus, University of London; Fellow of King's College, London; *b* 26 Aug. 1899; *s* of Walter Frederick and Emma Nokes. *Educ:* Stationers' Sch.; King's Coll., London. 2nd Lieut, RFC and RAF, 1918-19. LLB 1921, LLD 1927 (London); Barrister, Middle Temple, 1922. In practice, England, 1922-33; Judge, High Court, Travancore, S India, 1933-47; on deputation as Public Service Comr, Travancore, 1935-40; Senior Lecturer, 1947, Reader in English Law, 1948, Professor of Law, 1955-66, King's Coll., London; Dean of Faculty of Laws, University of London, 1958-62. *Publications:* Law relating to Mortgages and Receiverships, 2nd edn, 1931; Law relating to Sales by Auction, 1925; History of the Crime of Blasphemy, 1928; Travancore Service Recruitment Manual, 1937; Introduction to Evidence, 1952, 4th edn, 1967. *Address:* 14 Wetherby Gardens, SW5. *T:* 01-373 9123. *Club:* Royal Commonwealth Society.   [*Died* 15 *Nov.* 1971.

NORFOLK, 16th Duke of, *cr* 1483; **Bernard Marmaduke Fitzalan-Howard,** KG 1937; PC 1936; GCVO 1946; GBE 1968; TD 1969; Royal Victoria Chain, 1953; Earl of Arundel, 1139; Baron Maltravers, 1330; Earl of Surrey, 1483; Baron Herries, 1490; Baron FitzAlan, Clun, and Oswaldestre, 1627; Earl of Norfolk, 1644; Earl Marshal and Hereditary Marshal and Chief Butler of England; Premier Duke and Earl; Lord-Lieutenant of West Sussex since 1974 (Lord Lieutenant of Sussex, 1949-74); Reserve of Officers; late 2nd Lieut Royal Horse Guards; Major Royal Sussex Regt; President, T&AVR Association, since 1970 (Chairman of Council, 1956-69); Elder Brother, Trinity House, since 1965; *b* 30 May 1908, *s* of 15th Duke and Hon. Gwendolen Constable-Maxwell, 12th Baroness Herries; *S* father, 1917; *m* 1937, Hon. Lavinia Mary Strutt (CBE 1971), *o d* of 3rd Baron Belper; four *d.* Mayor of Arundel, 1935-36; Jt Parly Sec. to Min. of Agriculture, 1941-45. Mem., W Sussex CC, 1937-71. Pres., Council, Protection of Rural England, 1945-71; formerly Pres., Animal Health Trust. Pres., MCC, 1957-58; Manager, MCC team to Australia and New Zealand, 1962-63. HM Representative at Ascot, 1945-72; Past Steward of the Jockey Club; Vice-Chm., Turf Bd, 1965-68. A Vice-Pres. of St Dunstan's, 1970-. *Heir:* (to *Dukedom*); *c* Baron Beaumont and Howard of Glossop, *qv* ; (to *Herries Barony*): *d* Lady Anne Elizabeth Fitzalan-Howard, *b* 12 June 1938. *Address:* Arundel Park, Arundel, West Sussex; (Seat) Arundel Castle. *Club:* Turf.   [*Died* 31 *Jan.* 1975.

NORIE-MILLER, Sir Stanley, 2nd Bt, *cr* 1936; MC 1918; MA; DL; JP; Governor (late Chairman and Managing Director), General Accident Fire and Life Assurance Corporation Ltd; *b* 4 Aug. 1888; *s* of Sir Francis Norie-Miller, 1st Bt, and Grace Harvey Day; *S* father, 1947; *m* 1921, Grace Janet Euphrosyne Berrangé, *d* of late J. B. Eagar, Somerset East, S Africa; no *c. Educ:* Rugby; Hertford Coll., Oxford, Hon. Fellow, 1968. Called to Bar, 1912. Served European War, 1914-18, in The Black Watch (RH), Captain, 1915 (despatches, MC). Freeman, City of Perth; DL, Hon. Sheriff and JP for County of Perth. *Heir:* none. *Address:* Murrayshall, near Perth, Scotland. *T:* Scone 51254. *Club:* Bath.   [*Died* 21 *Dec.* 1973 (*ext*).

NORMAN, Vice-Admiral Alfred Headley, CMG 1919; retired; *b* 27 Aug. 1881; *s* of Alfred Reynolds Norman; *m* 1906, Beatrix Mabel Godfrey (*d* 1970); four *s. Educ:* King's Sch., Rochester; Dover Coll. Joined Royal Navy, 1896; Lieut, 1903; Commander, 1914; Captain and Master of the Fleet, 1919; Rear-Adm. and retired list, 1931; ADC to King George VI, 1931; Vice-Adm., retired, 1936; served European War (despatches, Battle of Jutland, CMG); awarded Gold Medal of the Royal United Services Institution, 1923. *Address:* White House Nursing Home, Church Crookham, Fleet, Hants. [*Died* 21 *April* 1973.

NORMAN, Sir Charles, Kt 1964; CBE 1951; Director of Joseph Rank Ltd, 1952-65; *b* 22 July 1892; *e s* of late Harry Norman, JP, City of Worcester; *m* 1918, Dorothy Mary, 2nd *d* of Thomas Hayes, Worcester; two *s* one *d.* Chm., CIF Buyers (London) Ltd, and Chm., COMPRO Ltd, 1939-45; Chm., Working Party on Millable Wheat and Feeding Barley, 1965-71; Dep. Chm., Home Grown Cereals Authority, 1965. Pres., Corn Exchange Benevolent Company, 1953; Pres., National Assoc. of Compound Manufacturers, 1955-56. Liveryman of The Worshipful Company of Farmers. *Address:* 21 Cornmeadow Lane, Worcester WR3 7NY. *T:* Worcester 53841. *Club:* Farmers'.   [*Died* 9 *Dec.* 1976.

NORMAN, Maj.-Gen Charles Wake, CBE 1943; DL; *b* 13 Feb. 1891; *e s* of late Archibald Norman, The Rookery, Bromley Common, Kent; *m* 1925, Nora, *d* of Lt-Col William Beadon, 51st Sikhs; two *s* two *d. Educ:* Eton; Trinity Coll., Cambridge (MA). Joined 9th Lancers, 1913; served France, 1914 (despatches, wounded and prisoner); commanded 9th Lancers, 1936-38; Colonel, 1938; commanded 1st Armoured

Reconnaissance Brigade, France, 1940 (despatches); Maj.-Gen. 1941; Comdr, 8th Armoured Div.; retired, May 1946. Colonel, 9th Lancers, 1940-50. High Sheriff of Kent, 1950-51; Member Kent County Council, 1949-55; DL Kent. *Address:* West Farleigh Hall, Maidstone, Kent. *Club:* Cavalry.
[Died 4 Aug. 1974.

NORMAN, Duncan Thomas, MC; MA, LLD; JP Liverpool; Hon. President, Owen Owen Ltd, and associated Companies (retired as Chairman and Managing Director, 1964; 40 years service); *b* 27 June 1889; *s* of A. R. Norman, Runcorn, Cheshire, and Agnes, *d* of Duncan McKechnie, St Helens, Lancs; *m* 1918, Dilys, *d* of Owen Owen, Liverpool and Machynlleth; one *s* three *d* (*er s* killed in action, 1942). *Educ:* Shrewsbury; Emmanuel Coll., Cambridge (MA). Served European War, 1914-18 with 55th Division British Expeditionary Force, Captain, RE (TF) (MC, Chevalier Order of Leopold, Croix de Guerre). Member Council, 1942-63 (retiring as Senior Pro-Chancellor). University of Liverpool; Governor, Shrewsbury Sch., 1943-60 (Chairman, 1956-60). High Sheriff of Cheshire, 1943-44. Hon. LLD: McMaster Univ., Hamilton, Ontario, 1958; Liverpool, 1964. *Address:* Greysfield, Great Barrow, Chester. *T:* Tarvin 40219; Cwmrhaiadr, Machynlleth, Montgomeryshire. *T:* Machynlleth 2258. *Clubs:* University (Liverpool); Hamilton (Ontario).
[Died 8 Nov. 1972.

NORMAN, Brig. Hugh Ronald, CBE 1970; DSO 1944; *b* 17 Oct. 1905; *e s* of late R. C. Norman; *m* 1937, Margaret, *d* of late Scott Griffin, Toronto; three *s* one *d. Educ:* Eton; RMC, Sandhurst. Joined Coldstream Guards, 1925; served in China, 1927, Palestine, 1936; Adjutant, 3rd Bn, 1934-37; War of 1939-45, on staff of AA Command, 1939; 128 Inf. Bde, 1940; GHQ Home Forces, 1941; HQ London District, 1942; Comd 2nd Bn Coldstream Guards, Africa, 1943, and Italy, 1944 (wounded); Comd 201 Guards Bde (UK), 1945-46, and Victory Parade Camps; retired (from disability), 1947. Kent County Cadet Comdt, 1948-52; Chairman: Territorial Assoc., 1962-68; South East TA&VR Assoc., 1968-69. Member Kent Agricultural Exec. Cttee, 1952-58 (Vice-Chm., 1957); Chm., Kent Branch Country Landowners Assoc. (CLA), 1958-62, Pres., 1967-72. JP 1949; DL 1952; High Sheriff of Kent, 1957. *Address:* Lower St Clere, Kemsing, Sevenoaks, Kent. *T:* Sevenoaks 61250. *Club:* Cavalry and Guards.
[Died 9 July 1979.

NORRIE, 1st Baron, *cr* 1957, of Wellington, New Zealand, and of Upton, Glos; **Lt.-Gen. (Charles) Willoughby (Moke) Norrie,** GCMG 1952 (KCMG 1944); GCVO 1954; CB 1942; DSO 1919; MC 1915, and bar; Chancellor, Order of St Michael and St George, 1960-68; Governor General and Commander-in-Chief of New Zealand, 1952-57; *b* 26 Sept. 1893; *s* of late Major G. E. M. Norrie; *m* 1st, 1921, Jocelyn Helen (*d* 1938), *d* of late R. H. Gosling; one *s* one *d* ; 2nd, 1938, Patricia Merryweather (DStJ), *d* of late Emerson Bainbridge, MP; one *s* two *d. Educ:* Eton; Sandhurst. Joined 11th Hussars, 1913; Captain, 1918; Major, 1924; Lt-Col, 1931; Col, 1935; served European War, 1914-19, Staff Captain 73rd Inf. Brigade, GSO3 XVIII Army Corps, Bde Major 90th Inf. Bde, Bde Major 2nd Tank Bde, GSO2 Tank Corps HQ (wounded four times, despatches twice, MC and bar, DSO); psc; Bde Major, 1st Cavalry Bde, Aldershot, 1926-30; commanded 10th Royal Hussars, 1931-35; Comdr 1st Cavalry Bde, 1936-38; Comdr 1st Armoured Bde, 1938-40; Inspector RAC, 1940; GOC 1st Armoured Div., 1940-41; GOC 30 Corps (Middle East), 1941-42; Comdr RAC, 1943; Colonel, 10th Royal Hussars (PWO), 1945-49; Governor of the State of South Australia, 1944-52. Hon. Colonel, 10th Inf. Bn (The Adelaide Rifles), 1949-57. FRSA 1948. Member: National Hunt Cttee, 1935-68; Jockey Club, 1969. Vice-Patron, Combined Cavalry Old Comrades, 1959-74. Prior of the Venerable Order of St John in New Zealand, 1952-57. KStJ. *Heir: s* Major Hon. George Willoughby Moke Norrie, late Royal Hussars; Dir, Fairfield Nurseries, Hermitage, Berks [*b* 27 April 1936; *m* 1964, Celia Marguerite, *d* of Major John Mann, MC, and Mrs Mann, Horsemoor House, Chievely, Berks; one *s* two *d. Educ:* Eton; Royal Military Academy, Sandhurst]. *Address:* The Ham, Wantage, Oxon. *T:* Wantage 2110. *Club:* Cavalry and Guards.
[Died 25 May 1977.

NORRIS, Oswald Thomas, CBE 1957; *b* 1 July 1883; *s* of Arthur James and Dora Norris; *m* 1911, Evelyn Mary Seth-Smith (*d* 1969); one *d* (and one *d* decd). *Educ:* Charterhouse. Ex-Chairman of Council, National Federation of Young Farmers' Clubs. A Governor of Charterhouse, London, 1951, and member of the Governing Body of Charterhouse School, 1957. *Address:* Tilgate Forest Lodge, Crawley, Sussex. *T:* Handcross 391.
[Died 22 March 1973.

NORRIS, Rev. Canon Walter Edward, Chaplain to the Queen since 1962; Vicar and Rural Dean of Romsey, 1952-April 1971;

Assistant Curate, S Bartholomew's, Hyde, Winchester, since 1971; Chairman, Diocesan Advisory Committee for the Care of Churches, since 1968; *b* 8 Dec. 1905; 3rd *s* of late Hugh Littleton Norris and Mabel Grace Norris. *Educ:* Durnford Sch., Langton Matravers; Winchester Coll.; Trinity Coll., Oxford; Cuddesdon Theological Coll. Assistant Curate: Hemsworth, 1930-34; Dewsbury, 1934-36; Vicar: St John's, Huddersfield, 1936-44; St Luke's, Bournemouth, 1944-52; Hon. Canon of Winchester Cathedral, 1955; Proctor in Convocation, 1957-70; Sub Chaplain, Order of St John of Jerusalem, 1957. Secretary 1946-62, Vice-Chm. 1962-68, Diocesan Adv. Cttee for the Care of Churches. *Recreations:* travel, archæology. *Address:* 32 Cheriton Road, Winchester, Hampshire. *[Died 31 Aug. 1971.*

NORRISH, Ronald George Wreyford, FRS 1936; ScD, PhD (Cantab); FRIC; Professor Emeritus of Physical Chemistry; Director of Department of Physical Chemistry, Cambridge University, 1937-65; Fellow of Emmanuel College, Cambridge; *b* 9 Nov. 1897; *e s* of Herbert Norrish; *m* 1926, Annie, *e d* of Albert E. Smith, Heaton Mersey, near Manchester; two *d. Educ:* Perse Sch.; Malvern Girls' Coll.; Emmanuel Coll., Cambridge (Foundation Scholar, 1915); 1st Class Hons Natural Sciences Tripos, I and II, 1920, 1921. Served European War, 1916-19 (POW 1918). Research Fellow of Emmanuel Coll., 1925-31; Humphrey Owen Jones Lecturer in Physical Chemistry, Cambridge Univ.; Meldola Medal of Institute of Chemistry, 1926; Leverhulme Research Fellow, 1935; Council of Chem. Soc. and of Faraday Soc., 1933-36; Council of Senate, Univ. of Cambridge, 1938-41; Scientific Adv. Council of the Min. of Supply, 1942-45; Pres., Faraday Soc., 1953-55; Vice-Pres., Royal Inst. of Chemistry, 1957-59; Liverside Lecture and Medal, Chem. Soc., 1958; Davy Medal, Royal Soc., 1958; Lewis Medal of Combustion Inst., 1964; Faraday Memorial Lecture and Medal, Chem. Soc., 1965, Longstaff Medal, Chem. Soc., 1969; Bakerian Lecture, Royal Soc., 1966. Nobel Laureate (Jt) for Chemistry, 1967. Pres. British Assoc., Section B (Chemistry), 1960-61. Liveryman, Worshipful Company of Gunmakers, 1961. Hon. Ddel'U Sorbonne (Paris), 1958; Hon. Member Polish Chemical Soc., 1959; Corr. Mem. Acad. of Sciences, Göttingen, 1960; Corr. Mem., Royal Soc. of Sciences, Liège, 1960; Foreign Mem. Polish Acad., of Sciences, 1962; Hon. Member: Royal Soc. of Sciences, Uppsala, Sweden, 1964; Faraday Soc., 1966; NY Acad. of Sciences, 1968; Bulgarian Acad. of Sciences, 1970; Société de Chimie Physique, Paris; Belgian Acad of Sciences, 1975. Hon. DSc: Leeds, Sheffield, 1965; Liverpool, Lancaster, 1968; British Columbia, 1969. Hon. FRSE 1972. Chevalier Commandeur de la confrèrie des Chevaliers du Tastevin, 1971; Knight's Cross, Order of Polonia Restituta, 1974; Order of Cyril and Methodius of Bulgaria, 1974. *Publications:* Scientific papers in Proceedings of Royal Society, Journal of Chemical Soc., Transactions of Faraday Soc., etc. *Recreations:* recollections of tennis and golf. *Address:* Emmanuel College, Cambridge. *T:* Cambridge 65411; Department of Physical Chemistry, Lensfield Road, Cambridge. *T:* Cambridge 66499; 7 Park Terrace, Cambridge. *T:* 55147. *Club:* Savage.
[Died 7 June 1978.

NORTH, Rev. Christopher Richard, DLit (London), Hon. DD (Aberdeen); Methodist Minister; Emeritus Professor of Hebrew at University College of North Wales, Bangor; *b* 1888; *e s* of Richard and Gertrude North; *m* 1st, Dorothy May Atkinson (*d* 1931); one *s* three *d* ; 2nd, Helen Ramsay Winter; one *s. Educ:* Reed's Sch.; Didsbury Coll.; School of Oriental Studies. Minister in Bangor, Burnley, Worthing, Egham, Leeds, Malvern; short term as missionary in North India; Victoria Chair of Old Testament Languages and Literature, Handsworth Coll., Birmingham, 1925-40; Visiting Professor at Drew Univ. Madison, NJ, 1931; Joint Hon. Secretary Society for Old Testament Study, 1928-48; President, 1949; Treasurer, 1952-57; Examiner to Universities of London, Birmingham, Bristol, Wales; Fernley-Hartley Lecturer, 1946. Dean of Faculty of Theology, University College of North Wales, Bangor, 1948-53; Select Preacher, Cambridge Univ., 1952-53; Acting Head of Dept of OT Literature and Theology, New Coll., Edinburgh, 1962. Member, OT Panel for New English Bible, 1948-62. *Publications:* The Old Testament Interpretation of History, 1946; The Suffering Servant in Deutero-Isaiah, 1948; Isaiah 40-55: Introduction and Commentary, 1952; The Second Isaiah, 1964; articles on Old Testament Subjects in British and foreign journals. *Recreations:* philately, travel. *Address:* 7 Belmont Drive, Bangor, Gwynedd LL57 2HS. *T:* Bangor 53668.
[Died 29 July 1975.

NORTH, Brig. Francis Roger, CB 1942; MC and Bar, 1918; ED 1937; Solicitor, Member of firm of Roberts Leu & North, Solicitors, Townsville, N Queensland; *b* 13 April 1894; *s* of Robert Dundas North, Brisbane; *m* 1929, Margaret May, *d* of Robert Lawrence Craddock; two *d. Educ:* The Southport

School. Served War of 1914-18 (wounded twice, despatches twice); commissioned 1914, served 9th, 15th and 47th Inf., AIF, Egypt, Gallipoli, France and Flanders; Captain, 1916, Major, 1927, 31st Bn, Lt-Col, 1927; comd 31st Bn, 1924-29 and 1933-40. War of 1939-45; comd 11th Inf. Bde, 1940-42 (temp. Brig.); comd 1st Australian L of C Sub Area, 1942-45; Col R of O 1945; Brig., retired. Chancellor to Bishop of North Queensland, 1928-70; Chancellor to Bishop of Carpentaria, 1930-70; Pres., N Qld br., RSSAILA, 1932-39; Alderman of Townsville City Council, 1936-39. Pres., N Qld Golf Assoc., 1928-38; Trustee Scartwater Trust; Vice-Consul for Sweden. Knight of the Royal Order of Vasa (Sweden), 1953. *Address:* Roberts Leu and North, 54 Denham Street, Townsville, North Queensland 4810, Australia. *Clubs:* North Queensland, RSSAILA (Townsville); United Services (Brisbane). *[Died 1 Nov. 1978.*

NORTH, Sir George (Cecil), Kt 1956; CB 1949; MC 1917; Hon. LLD (Dublin) 1945; *b* 23 March 1895; *e s* of Matthew North and Harriet Evelyn Mitchell, Blackrock, Co. Dublin; *m* 1928, Winifred Margaret (*née* McKillop), widow of Captain Paget l'Estrange Clayton; one *s* one *d* and one step *d*. *Educ:* St Andrews Coll. and Trinity Coll., Dublin (First Scholar, Senior Moderator and Gold Medallist, LLD). Called to Bar (Lincoln's Inn). Home Civil Service, 1921; Private Secretary to Sir Edward Forber and to Susan Lawrence, MP; Sec. or Mem. of various Commns, Cttees, etc., including National Radium Trust and first Governing Body of British Postgrad. Medical Sch.; Chairman, Central Dental War Cttee, 1939-40; Asst Secretary, Ministry of Health, 1937; Director of Public Relations, 1938-40; Head of Water, etc., Division, 1940-45. Registrar General, 1945-58. A Parliamentary Boundary Commissioner for England and for Wales, 1947-57. Member Court of Governors London School of Economics and Political Science, 1947-64. Chairman, standing Interdepartmental Cttee on Social and Economic Research, 1947-62; a Governor, Nat. Inst. for Economic and Social Research; Alternate or Adviser, Sessions Economic and Social Council of UN, 1946-48; Deleg. to First World Health Assembly, 1948. Donnellan Lectr, Univ. of Dublin, 1951. Hon. MInstWE; Hon. Fellow Soc. Med. Officers of Health. Served RA France, Belgium, Germany, 1916-19 (MC, Major). *Recreations:* travel, languages, Commonwealth relations. *Address:* 2 Corner Green, Ringmer, Lewes, Sussex. *Clubs:* Athenæum; University (Dublin). *[Died 28 Jan. 1971.*

NORTH, Major John, BA, LLB; Author and Barrister-at-Law; *b* 30 Sept. 1894; *s* of late C. A. North, Leeds; *m* 1923, Freda, *d* of late Ernest H. Lawrence, Librarian of Hertford; one *d*. *Educ:* early youth devoted to musical training; Downing Coll., Cambridge (Historical Scholar, Honours in History and Law), 1913. Lieut, 4th Batt., Northampton Regt; served in France and Belgium with the Northamptonshire and Suffolk Regiments; returned to Cambridge from the Army of Occupation in Germany, 1919; founded and edited a University weekly, The Old Cambridge, 1920; called to Bar, Gray's inn, 1921; joined London Press Exchange, 1922; Director, 1937; General Staff, War Office, 1939; Allied Force HQ, North Africa, 1943; War Office, 1944; missions to Belgium, Holland, Germany, Greece, and Italy, 1944-45; appointed by War Office to write NW Europe volume in HMSO series of short military histories of Second World War. *Publications:* Girl or Boy: A Satire and a Diversion, 1925; A Comedy of Women, 1926; A Daughter of Twenty, 1926; Patricia Lacked a Lover, 1927; Unmarried Life, 1928; St Peter and the Profile, 1930; A Shade Byronic, 1933; Gallipoli: The Fading Vision, 1936 (repr. 1967); North-West Europe, 1944-45; The Achievement of 21st Army Group, 1953; (ed) Men Fighting: Battle Stories, 1958; (ed) The Alexander Memoirs, 1940-45, 1962. *Recreations:* cricket, lubricating the car, visiting the Gallipoli Peninsula. *Address:* Four Winds, Beaconsfield, Bucks. *T:* Beaconsfield 3276; 01-836 2424. *Clubs:* Army and Navy, United and Cecil, Arts Theatre. *[Died 11 Feb. 1973.*

NORTHAMPTON, 6th Marquess of, *cr* 1812; **William Bingham Compton;** DSO 1919; Earl of Northampton, 1618; Earl Compton, Baron Wilmington, 1812; *b* 6 Aug. 1885; *e* surv. *s* of 5th Marquess and Hon. Mary Florence Baring (*d* 1902), *o d* of 2nd Lord Ashburton; *S* father, 1913; *m* 1st, 1921, Lady Emma Thynne, OBE 1943 (marr. diss., 1942), 2nd *d* of 5th Marquess of Bath, KG, PC, CB; 2nd, 1942, Virginia (marr. diss., 1958), *d* of Lt-Col David Heaton, DSO, two *s* two *d*; 3rd, 1958, Elspeth, Lady Teynham (*d* 1976). *Educ:* Eton; Balliol Coll., Oxford. BA. Northamptonshire Yeomanry, 1903-06; 2nd Lieut, Royal Horse Guards, 1907; Captain and Adjutant, 1913; served European War, 1914-19 (DSO, wounded, despatches twice); commanded Warwickshire Yeomanry, 1933. JP Northants; DL Northants; late Chairman Northants CC; resigned, 1955. Owns about 10,000 acres. *Heir: s* Earl Compton. *Address:* Chadstone Old Rectory, Castle Ashby, Northampton. *Club:* Turf. *[Died 30 Jan. 1978.*

NORTHCOTT, Captain Ralph William Frank, CBE 1960; DSO 1942; RN, retired; *b* 1 July 1907; *s* of late Major F. L. Northcott, Royal Norfolk Regt and of late E. E. Northcott (*née* Badnall); *m* 1934, Molly, *d* of Brig.-General C. H. P. Carter, CB, CMG, CBE; one *s. Educ:* Osborne; Dartmouth. Joined Navy, 1921; served mainly in small ships; War of 1939-45, commanded HMS Acheron, Lance and Bicester; served with Army in Tunisian campaign, Sicily, Salerno and Normandy landings. Joint Services Staff Coll. and NATO Defence Coll.; Chief of Staff, Amphibious Warfare, 1955-58; Commodore, Naval Drafting, 1958-60; ADC to the Queen, 1960-61; Asst Gen. Manager (Staff) Rediffusion Television, 1961-69. *Address:* Border Cottage, Rowledge, Farnham, Surrey. *T:* Frensham 2946. *[Died 22 Feb. 1976.*

NORTHCROFT, Ernest George Drennan, CBE 1949; Chairman, Employers' Side, Southern Provincial Council for Local Authorities' APT&C Services, 1970-74; Member, National Joint Council for Local Authorities' APT&C Services, 1970-74; *b* 27 Jan. 1896; *s* of late G. A. Northcroft, Jersey, CI; *m* 1st, 1946, Phyllis Kathleen (*d* 1963), *d* of late H. F. Parsons, Portskewett, Mon; 2nd, 1970, Marcia Elizabeth, *d* of late A. W. Gatrall, Southampton. *Educ:* Sherborne Sch.; University Coll., Oxford. Served European War, 1914-18; Bedfordshire Regt, 1917-19; with BEF, 1917 (despatches), with Salonika Force, 1918-19. With Messrs Anglo-Iranian Oil Co. in Iran, 1919-51; Chief Representative Tehran, Anglo-Iranian Oil Co. Ltd, 1945-51. Chm., New Forest Conservative Assoc., 1958-61. Pres., 1962-65; Chm., New Forest RDC, 1964-65, 1971-73 (Chm. Finance and Gen. Purposes Cttee, 1960-63; Chm. Housing Cttee, 1965-70); Member: Hampshire CC, 1962-74; New Forest Consultative Panel, 1971-73; Southern Gas Consultative Council, 1959-66. *Recreations:* gardening, travelling. *Address:* The Splash, Minstead, Lyndhurst, Hants. *T:* Cadnam 3173. *Clubs:* East India, Sports and Public Schools, Royal Commonwealth Society. *[Died 18 April 1976.*

NORTHESK, 12th Earl of, *cr* 1647; **John Douglas Carnegie;** Baron Rosehill and Inglismaldie, 1639; *b* 16 Feb. 1895; *o* surv. *s* of late Lieut-Colonel Hon. Douglas George Carnegie, 2nd *s* of 9th Earl; *S* cousin, 1963; *m* 1920, Dorothy Mary (*d* 1967), *er d* of late Colonel Sir William Robert Campion, KCMG, DSO, DL, Hassocks, Sussex; one *s* two *d* (and one *s* decd). *Educ:* Gresham's Sch., Holt; King's Coll., Cambridge (BA). Served European War, 1914-18 (despatches); Captain (temp. Major) 95th (Hants Yeomanry) Brigade, Royal Field Artillery (TA). *Heir: s* Lord Rosehill. *Address:* Fair Oak, Rogate (Co. Sussex), Petersfield, Hants. *T:* Rogate 8. *[Died 22 July 1975.*

NORTHFIELD, Douglas William Claridge, MS; FRCS; FRCP. Formerly: Surgeon in charge of Neuro-Surgical Department, London Hospital; Neurological Surgeon, Queen Elizabeth Hospital for Children, Hackney Road; Hunterian Professor, RCS; Surgical Registrar and Demonstrator of Anatomy, Guy's Hospital; Past President: Neurology Section, RSM; Electro Encephalographic Society; British Section, International League against Epilepsy; Past President and Past Secretary, Society of British Neurological Surgeons; Past Secretary, International Congress, Neurological Surgery. MB, BS (Gold Medal) 1930; MS London 1931; FRCS 1928 (MRCS 1925); FRCP 1966 (LRCP 1925); FRSM. *Publications:* The Surgery of the Central Nervous System, 1973; contrib. medical journals. *Address:* London Hospital, Whitechapel, E1. *[Died 18 July 1976.*

NORTON, Sir Charles; see Norton, Sir W. C.

NORTON, Roger Edward, CMG 1948; OBE 1943; *b* 15 June 1897; *s* of late Henry Turton Norton; *m* 1924, Priscilla Anne Mary, *d* of late J. R. C. Deverell; one *s* two *d. Educ:* Eton College. Served European War, 1914-18, with BRCS (despatches, OStJ, Cav. Order of Crown of Italy, Italian Croce di Guerra). Started farming in E Africa, 1919. Joined Kenya Govt Service, 1938, as Sec. Standing Board of Economic Development; Chm. E African War Supplies Board, 1942; Dir Produce Disposal, 1943; Dep. Chm. EA Production and Supply Council, 1944; East African Comr in London, 1945-51; Regional Controller, East Africa, Colonial Development Corporation, 1951-59, retired. *Address:* 23 Ashley Gardens, SW1. *T:* 01-834 6731. *[Died 5 Oct. 1978.*

NORTON, Sir (Walter) Charles, Kt 1956; MBE 1944; MC 1916; *b* 24 May 1896; *s* of late Walter Percy Norton and Louisa May Norton (*née* Kershaw); *m* 1st, 1920, Bertha Hope Smith (*d* 1921); one *d*; 2nd, 1926, Bridget Elizabeth Greenwell (marr. diss. 1948); one *s*; 3rd, 1948, Olive Penelope Wood (*née* Murray). *Educ:* Winchester. Served European War in Army, 1914-19; Captain, 9th Bn Royal Sussex Regt; Staff Captain, 1918-19. Admitted Solicitor, 1921. Consultant with Norton,

Rose, Botterell & Roche (formerly Senior Partner); Chairman: Electronic Rentals Group Ltd; Europleasure International Ltd. President, Law Society, 1955-56. Mayor of the City of Westminster, 1957-58; first Lord Mayor of new City of Westminster, 1965-66. Master, City of London Solicitors' Co., 1963-64. *Address:* 4/23 Hans Place, SW1. *T:* 01-584 5315. *Clubs:* Garrick, Hurlingham (President). *[Died 22 Oct. 1974.*

NORTON, Wilfrid, ARCA; retired as Pottery Sculptor, Lecturer in Design, and Architecture, Camberwell School of Arts and Crafts; *b* Shropshire, 8 Oct. 1879; *s* of Edwin and Mary Norton; *m* 1915, Lily Holden Harley. *Educ:* Royal College of Art; abroad. Studentship in Training Scholarship, Royal College of Art; Exhibitor, Royal Academy, Arts and Crafts Society, International exhibitions in Paris, Leipzig and America, and various shows in Bond Street. *Recreations:* Philosophy and walking in unfrequented places. *Address:* Flat 3, 59 Mount Ararat Road, Richmond, Surrey. *[Died 2 Sept. 1973.*

NORWOOD, Christopher Bonnewell Burton; *b* 17 Dec. 1932; *s* of Harold Norwood and Grace (*née* Bonnewell); *m* 1955, Beryl Goldwyn; one *s. Educ:* Hawes Down Elementary Sch., W Wickham, Kent; Whitgift Sch., S Croydon; Gonville and Caius Coll., Cambridge. BA 1953, MA 1957. Trainee with Evans Medical Supplies, Liverpool, 1954-55. Admin. Asst, National Coal Board, 1955-58; then in Marketing Dept (worked underground in Lancs, certificate of competence at coal-face); Asst Economist, Central Electricity Generating Board, 1960-64. Contested: Sutton Coldfield, 1955, Bromsgrove, 1959; MP (Lab) Norwich South, 1964-70. *Recreations:* reading, swimming, squash. *Address:* 115 Great Portland Street, W1. *[Died 14 Nov. 1972.*

NOSWORTHY, Lt-Gen. Sir Francis Poitiers, KCB 1944 (CB 1938); DSO 1918; MC; Colonel Commandant RE, 1940-50; Colonel Comdt RIE, 1946; *b* 21 Sept. 1887; 2nd *s* of late Richard Nosworthy, CMG, and Beatrice (*née* Michelin), Constant Spring, Jamaica; *m* 1925, Audrey, 2nd *d* of T. R. Davey, JP, Wraxall Court, Somerset; one *s* one *d. Educ:* Exeter School. Entered Army, 1907, Captain, Royal Engineers, 1914; Bt Major, 1916; Bt Lieut-Colonel, 1921; local Colonel, 1926; Lieut-Colonel and Colonel, 1932; Maj.-General, 1937; Lieut-General, 1940; Mishmi Abor Expedition, 1912-13; European War (France), 1914-18, 3rd Afghan War, 1919 (DSO, with bar, MC with bar, Croix de Guerre avec palme, despatches six times); Instructor, Staff College, 1919-22. War Office, General Staff, 1922-26; Chief Staff Officer and Second-in-Command, Sudan Defence Force, 1926-30; Imperial Defence Coll., 1931; General Staff Officer, 1st Grade, the British Troops in China, 1932-35; Commander, 5th Infantry Brigade, 1935-38; Deputy Chief of General Staff, Army Headquarters, India, 1938-40; a Corps Commander, 1940; Commander-in-Chief, West Africa, 1943. *Address:* 70 Wellsway, Bath, Somerset. *T:* Bath 64591. *Clubs:* Lansdowne; Bath and County (Bath). *[Died 9 July 1971.*

NOTT, Commander Sir James Grenvile P.; *see* Pyke-Nott.

NOTT-BOWER, Sir Guy; *see* Nott-Bower, Sir W. G.

NOTT-BOWER, Sir John (Reginald Hornby), KCVO 1953 (CVO 1937); Kt 1950; Commissioner Metropolitan Police, 1953-58, retired; *b* 1892; 2nd *s* of late Sir William Nott-Bower, KCVO; *m* 1928, Kathleen Manners Beresford, *d* of late Major Buck, DLI; two *s* one *d. Educ:* Cheltenham; Tonbridge. Indian Police, 1911-33; Chief Constable, Metropolitan Police, 1933; Assistant Commissioner, 1940; Deputy Commissioner, 1946-53; Inspector-General Public Safety, Austria (Allied Commission), 1945-46. King's Police Medal, 1931. *Recreations:* fishing, golf. *Address:* Shady Cottage, Trinity, Jersey, CI. *[Died 3 Oct. 1972.*

NOTT-BOWER, Sir (William) Guy, KBE, *cr* 1946 (CBE 1937); CB 1942; *b* 9 Oct. 1890; *e s* of late Sir John William Nott-Bower, KCVO; *m* 1914, Frances Winifred (*d* 1966), *d* of late William Macdonald Matthews, Broadwater Downs, Tunbridge Wells; one *s* two *d. Educ:* Cheltenham Coll. (Class. Scholar); Brasenose Coll., Oxford. BA 1913 (Litt Hum) MA 1962; entered Ceylon Civil Service, 1914; transferred to Inland Revenue Dept, 1916; to Home Office, 1919; to Ministry of Labour, 1919; to Mines Dept, 1920; to Air Ministry, 1939; Deputy Under-Secretary for Mines, 1941-42; Under-Secretary for Mines, 1942; Deputy Secretary, Ministry of Fuel and Power, 1942-48; Director of Public Relations, NCB, 1948-54. OStJ. *Address:* Laurel House, Bishop's Hull, Taunton, Somerset. *[Died 19 July 1977.*

NOWELL, Ralph Machattie, CB 1947; retired; *b* 3 June 1903; *e s* of late Walter Salmon Nowell and Anita Mary Machattie; *m*

1927, Mary McGregor; one *s* one *d. Educ:* Marlborough; Brasenose Coll., Oxford. George Webb Medley Junior Scholar, 1924; BA 1926. Retired as Under-Secretary and Tariff Adviser, Board of Trade, 1963. *Address:* 77 Albert Drive, Wimbledon Park, SW19. *T:* 01-788 4951. *Club:* United Oxford & Cambridge University. *[Died 9 Oct. 1973.*

NUGENT, 1st Baron, *cr* 1960, of West Harling; Terence Edmund Gascoigne Nugent, GCVO 1952 (KCVO 1945; CVO 1937; MVO 1927); MC; late Irish Guards; *b* 11 Aug. 1895; 2nd *s* of late Brig.-General G. C. Nugent, MVO; *m* 1935, Rosalie, *o d* of late Brig.-General Hon. Charles Willoughby, CB, CMG. *Educ:* Eton; Sandhurst. Joined Irish Guards, 11 Nov. 1914; served European War, France (MC); Adjutant, 1st Bn Irish Guards; employed as GSO3, War Office, 1924-26, as Personal Assistant to the Chief of the Imperial General Staff; accompanied the Duke and Duchess of York on their Australian and New Zealand Tour, 1927; retired pay, 1936, Lt-Col. Comptroller, Lord Chamberlain's Dept, 1936-60; extra Equerry to King George VI, 1937-52, to the Queen, 1952-; a Permanent Lord-in-Waiting to the Queen, 1960-. President MCC, 1962-63. *Heir:* none. *Address:* 21 Chelsea Square, SW3. *Clubs:* Guards, White's, Turf. *[Died 27 April 1973 (ext).*

NUGENT, Major-General John Fagan Henslowe, CB 1942; DSO 1916; *b* 1 July 1889; *e s* of late John Nugent, ICS, of Grenan, Thomastown, Co. Kilkenny, and Florence Henslowe; *m* 1st, 1919, Violet Gwendolen, *o d* of Lionel Cox, Colombo, Ceylon; 2nd, 1939, Helena Norah, *er d* of Captain J. V. and the Hon. Mrs Saunderson, Honeybottom, Newbury, Berks. *Educ:* Downside Sch., near Bath; Sandhurst. Joined Indian Army, 28th Punjabis; Major, 1925; Bt Lieut-Colonel 1931; Colonel, 1935; Maj.-General, 1941; ADC to Governor of Ceylon, 1914-15; served European War in Mesopotamia, 1915 (wounded, despatches, DSO); Afghanistan, 1919; Commandant 2nd Bn 2/7th Rajput Regt, 1934-35; AA and QMG Lahore District, 1935-38; Commander of a Brigade in India, 1938-40; ADC to the King, 1940-41; Maj.-General, i/c Administration HQ, North Western Army, India, 1941; retired, 1944. *Address:* La Hougue, St Peter, Jersey, CI. *T:* Western 555. *Club:* United Service & Royal Aero. *[Died 5 July 1975.*

NUNBURNHOLME, 3rd Baron, *cr* 1906; Charles John Wilson; Hon. Captain, QO York Dragoons; *b* 25 April 1904; *s* of 2nd Baron and Lady Marjorie Wynn-Carrington (*d* 1968), *d* of 1st Marquess of Lincolnshire; *S* father, 1924, *m* 1st 1927, Lady Mary Thynne (from whom he obtained a divorce, 1947; she *m* 2nd, 1947, Rt Hon. Sir Ulick Alexander, GCB, GCVO, CMG, OBE); *y d* of 5th Marquess of Bath, KG, PC, CB; two *s* one *d*; 2nd, 1953, Alex, *o d* of Captain D. Hockly, Kent; one *s. Educ:* Eton. Served War of 1939-45 (wounded El Alamein); discharged 1943. *Heir: s* Captain Hon. Ben Charles Wilson, RHG [*b* 16 July 1928; *m* 1958, Ines Dolores Jeanne Walravens; four *d* (including twin *d*]. *Address:* Priory Lands, Appledore, Kent. *T:* Appledore 228. *[Died 1 Jan. 1974.*

NUNN, William, FRHistS; *b* 1879; *m* 1905, Mary (decd), *d* of John Fowler, Aberdeen; one *s. Educ:* King's Coll., London. Entered Civil Service, 1899; Adviser on Customs and Excise, Siamese Government, 1909-24; MP (C) Whitehaven Division of Cumberland, 1931-35; MP (C) Newcastle West Division, 1940-45. *Address:* Gillgrass, Gosforth, Cumberland. *T:* Gosforth 237. *Club:* Junior Carlton. *[Died 16 Dec. 1971.*

NUNNS, Hector Matthew, MBE 1976; Member, West Yorkshire Metropolitan County Council, since 1973 (first Chairman of Council, 1973-75); *b* 9 Nov. 1905; *s* of George Thomas Nunns and Susan Ethel (*née* Ellis); *m* 1930, Gladys, (*née* Whimpenny); two *d. Educ:* Thornhill Sch., Dewsbury. Mem. Dewsbury Co. Borough Council, 1945-74; Mem., Nat. Exec., Union of Shop, Distributive and Allied Workers, 1959-71. Hon. Freeman of Dewsbury, 1972. JP Dewsbury, 1949-76 (Chm., Dewsbury Bench, 1972-76). *Address:* Ash Grove, Overthorpe Road, Dewsbury, W Yorkshire. *T:* Dewsbury 463192. *Clubs:* Thornhill Edge Working Men's; Dewsbury Textile. *[Died 21 April 1979.*

NUSSEY, Sir Thomas Moore, 2nd Bt, *cr* 1909; JP for N. Riding of Yorkshire; *b* 19 July 1898; *s* of Sir William Nussey, 1st Bt, and Edith (*d* 1934), *d* of E. M. Daniel, MD, Fleetwood, and Mrs Daniel, Saxfield, Scarborough; *S* father, 1947; *m* 1941, Viva Frances, *yr d* of late Benjamin Talbot. *Educ:* Eton; RMC, Sandhurst; King's Coll., Cambridge (BA). Lieut, 17th Lancers. Served European War, 1914-18, 1917-22. *Heir:* none. *Address:* Rushwood, East Tanfield, Ripon. *Clubs:* Brooks's, Leander. *[Died 25 Oct. 1971 (ext).*

NUTT, Arthur E. W.; *see* Woodward-Nutt.

NUTT, Albert Boswell, FRCS; Ophthalmic Surgeon, United Sheffield Hospitals, 1948-63; *b* 7 July 1898; *s* of late Ernest Smith Nutt; *m* 1926, Olive Margaret Robson; two *s* one *d*. *Educ:* King Edward VII Sch., Sheffield; University of Sheffield; University of London. MSc Sheffield, 1922; MB, ChB Sheffield (Clinical Gold Medal in Medicine and Surgery), 1923; MB, BS London, 1923; FRCS 1949. Formerly Ophthalmic Registrar, House Surgeon and Senior Ophthalmic House Surgeon, Sheffield Royal Infirmary; Hon. Ophthalmic Surgeon, 1927-48; Hon. Ophthalmic Surgeon to Children's Hospital, Sheffield, 1938-48, Opth. Surgeon, 1948-63; Hunterian Professor, RCS, 1954; Member: Council, RCS, 1953-58 (Rep. of Ophthalmology); Standing Ophth. Advisory Cttee to Min. of Health; Council of Faculty of Ophthalmology, 1947-68 (Pres. 1963-65, Vice-Pres. 1951-53, Treasurer 1949-51); Council of Ophthalmic Soc. of UK, 1941-44 (Vice-Pres. 1950-53); Member Court of Examiners, RCS, 1957-63; External Examiner to University of Belfast, 1960-63; Chairman, British Orthoptic Board, 1958-70; Vice-Chm., British Orthoptists' Bd, 1966-70. Hon. Lecturer in Ophthalmology, Univ. of Sheffield, 1960-61; Master of Oxford Ophthalmol. Congress, 1961-62; Mem. Council, Court, and Convocation Univ. of Sheffield (Chm. of Convocation, 1964-67); Mem. Court, Univ. of Bradford. Mem. Sheffield Town Trust. Fellow: Royal Society of Medicine; Hunterian Society; Mem. Soc. Franc. d'Ophthalmologie; Hon. Mem., Australian Coll. of Ophthalmology (Guest Lecturer, 1954, 1963). Past Pres., Sheffield Medico and Chirurgical Soc. Liveryman, Soc. of Apothecaries of London; Freeman, City of London. OStJ. Hon. LLD Sheffield, 1974. *Publications:* contributions to medical journals, including BMJ, Trans. Ophth. Soc. of UK, Trans. Ophth. Soc. of Australia, British Orthoptic Journal, The Practitioner, etc. *Recreations:* masonry, golf, gardening. *Address:* 249 Glossop Road, Sheffield S10 2GZ. *T:* Sheffield 24876. *Clubs:* Sheffield (Sheffield); Lindrick Golf; Royal and Ancient (St Andrews).   [*Died 27 Feb. 1978.*

NUTTING, Sir Harold Stansmore, 2nd Bt, *cr* 1902; DL; Lt-Col Commanding Leics Bn Home Guard; late Captain 17th Lancers; *b* 14 Aug. 1882; *s* of 1st Bt and Mary Stansmore, *d* of Restel R. Bevis, Manor Hill, Claughton, Cheshire; *m* 1913, Enid Hester Nina (*d* 1961), *d* of late F. B. Homan-Mulock, Bellair, King's County; one *s* (two killed on active service); *S* father, 1918. Late ADC to Governor-General, Australia; served in France during European War, 1914-18; Master North Shropshire Hounds, 1919-20; Master of Meynell Hounds, 1920-29; Master of Quorn Hounds, 1930-40. *Heir:* *s* Rt Hon. Harold Anthony Nutting, PC. *Address:* Quenby Hall, Leicester. *T:* Hungerton 234; Achentoul Lodge, Kinbrace, Sutherland. *Clubs:* Turf, Cavalry, Bath, Royal Automobile.   [*Died 1 May 1972.*

NYE, Sir Geoffrey (Walter), KCMG 1960 (CMG 1953); OBE 1944; Chairman, Cotton Research Corporation; *b* 5 September 1902; *e s* of Stanley Nye and Gertrude Maude Kate Nye (*née* Baker); *m* 1929, Jean Etheline Stone; one *s* two *d*. *Educ:* Forest School; Wye College (BSc); Imperial Coll. of Science and Technology; Cambridge Univ.; Imperial Coll. of Tropical Agriculture, Trinidad. Dept of Agriculture, Uganda: Cotton Botanist, 1924; Senior Botanist, 1932; Deputy Director of Agriculture, 1940. Director of Agriculture, Nyasaland, 1945; Asst Agricultural Adviser, Colonial Office, 1947; Dep. Agric. Adviser, 1948-56; Agric. Adviser to: Sec. of State for the Colonies, 1956-61; Dept of Tech. Co-op., 1961-64; Min. of Overseas Develt, 1964-66. Director, Overseas Service Unit, Reading Univ., 1966-67. Mem., Governing Body, Wye College, Hon. Fellow, 1960. Awarded Silver Acorn by Chief Scout, 1944. *Recreations:* gardening, philately. *Address:* Barnabas, Brittenden Lane, Waldron, Heathfield, East Sussex. *T:* Heathfield 2843.   [*Died 1 April 1976.*

NYHOLM, Prof. Sir Ronald (Sydney), Kt 1967; FRS 1958; DSc; PhD; FRIC; Head of the Department of Chemistry, University College, London, since 1963, Professor of Chemistry since 1955; Fellow of University College, London, since 1959; *b* Broken Hill, NSW, 29 Jan. 1917; *s* of Eric Edward Nyholm, formerly of Goodwood, S Aust., and Gertrude Mary Nyholm (*née* Woods), Marryatville, SA; *m* 1948, Maureen Richardson, Sydney; one *s* two *d*. *Educ:* Broken Hill High School; Sydney and London Universities. BSc (1st Cl. Hons), Sydney, 1938, MSc 1942. Lecturer in Chemistry, Sydney Technical College, 1940; ICI Fellowship, London Univ., 1947; PhD (Lond.), 1950; DSc (Lond.) 1953; Assoc. Prof. of Inorganic Chemistry, NSW Univ. of Technology, 1952; Pres. Roy. Soc. of NSW, 1954. Corr. Member Finnish Chemical Soc., 1959; Mem., Academia Peloritana (Sicilian Acad.), 1971. Fellow Royal Australian Chemical Institute (Russell-Grimwade Lectr, 1969); Peter C. Reilly Lecturer, Univ. of Notre Dame, USA, 1957; F. P. Dwyer Medallist and Lectr, 1960; Archer D. Little Lectr, MIT, 1969. Pres., Chem. Soc. of London, 1968-70 (Tilden Lectr 1960,

Liversidge Lectr, 1968, of the Soc.); Mem. Science Research Council, 1967-68; President: Assoc. for Science Educn, 1967-; XII Internat. Conf. on Coordination Chemistry. Trustee, British Museum, 1968-. Hon. ScD East Anglia, 1968, City Univ., 1968; Univ. of NSW, 1969. Corday-Morgan Medal and Prize, Chem. Soc. London, 1950; H. G. Smith Meml Medal, Royal Aust. Chem. Inst., 1955; Roy. Medal, Roy. Soc. of NSW, 1963; Gold Medal of Italian Chem. Soc., 1968; Sigillum Magnum, Univ. of Podogna, 1969. *Publications:* approx. 250 research papers dealing mainly with chemistry of complex compounds in Jl Chem. Soc. of Lond., Proc. Roy. Soc. of NSW, Inorganic Chemistry, etc. Recent Progress in Stereochemistry (part author), Vols I and II, 1954, 1958. *Recreations:* cricket, tennis, and walking. *Address:* Chemistry Department, University College, WC1; 21 Manor Road South, Hinchley Wood, Esher, Surrey. *T:* 01-398 5338. *Club:* Athenæum. [*Died 4 Dec. 1971.*

O

OAKESHOTT, Keith Robertson, CMG 1967; Assistant Under-Secretary of State, Foreign and Commonwealth Office, since 1970; *b* 9 Feb. 1920; *s* of Harold Alan and Cecil Robertson Oakeshott, JP; *m* 1946, Eva Jill Clutterbuck; one *s* four *d*. *Educ:* Royal Grammar School, High Wycombe; Corpus Christi Coll., Oxford (MA). Served in RAF, 1940-46. Joined Foreign (now Diplomatic) Service, 1946; 3rd Sec., FO, 1946; Vice-Consul, Shanghai, 1947; 2nd Sec., FO, 1949; 1st Sec., 1951; Head of Chancery, Rangoon, 1953; FO, 1956; Head of Chancery, Moscow, 1959; Counsellor, Havana, 1962; HM Consul-General, Hamburg, 1962-67; Home Inspector, 1967-70; Asst Under-Sec. of State, seconded to CS Commn, 1970-71 and 1973. *Recreations:* fruit-growing, bee-keeping. *Address:* Little Coltstaple Farm, near Horsham, Sussex. *T:* Southwater 730385. *Club:* Royal Commonwealth Society.   [*Died 15 Dec. 1974.*

OAKLEY, Rev. Austin; Vicar of St John's, Ladbroke Grove, London, W11, 1944-62; Secretary, Anglican and Eastern Orthodox Churches Association, 1945-53, Chairman of Committee, 1953-69, Hon. President, since 1969; *b* India, 1890; *e s* of Rev. E. S. Oakley, MA, KHM, Almora, United Provinces, India; *m* 1928, Mary Alice, MB, BS, DPH (*d* 1963), *o d* of Charles Fraser van Ingen, Indian Telegraphs. *Educ:* School for the Sons of Missionaries, Blackheath; King's College School, Wimbledon; King's College, London; House of the Sacred Mission, Kelham, Newark-on-Trent. Ordained 1915; went out to South Africa, 1920; Director of St Barnabas, Masite, Basutoland, and Principal of Masite Training School, 1922; in charge of Ingwavuma Mission, Zululand, 1925; Priest-in-charge of St Mark's, Limon, Costa Rica, and Archdeacon in Central America, in the diocese of British Honduras, 1928-34; Scout Comr, Costa Rica, 1930-34, Hon. Comr, 1934-; Chaplain to HBM Embassy in Turkey and Crimean Memorial Church, Istanbul, 1934-43. Mem., Archbishop's Council for Foreign Relations, 1945-69. Order of Patriarchal Cross of St Andrew, 1965. *Publications:* The Orthodox Liturgy; articles on Orthodoxy and the Near East. *Recreations:* gardening, painting. *Address:* Freeland House, Freeland, Oxon. *Club:* Reform.

[*Died 2 April 1977.*

OAKLEY, Prof. Cyril Leslie, CBE 1970; MD; FRS 1957; Brotherton Professor of Bacteriology, University of Leeds, 1953-72, now Professor Emeritus; *b* 20 June 1907; *er c* of George and Ellen Oakley; *m* 1933, Emily Meadows; two *d*. *Educ:* St Mary's Rd School, Portsmouth; Westminster City School; Chelsea Polytechnic; University College, London; University College Hospital. MRCS, LRCP 1930; MB, BS (London), 1930; BSc (London) 1st Cl. Hons Zoology, 1930. Graham Scholar in Pathology, University Coll. Hosp. Med. Sch., 1930-33; MD (London), 1933; DSc (London), 1953. Experimental Pathologist, Wellcome Research Laboratories, 1934-47; Head, Immunology and Experimental Pathology Dept, Wellcome Research Laboratories, 1947-53. Fellow University Coll. London, 1950. President Association of Scientific Workers, 1956-59. Member of Council, 1963-64, 1965-68, Founder Fellow, Coll. Pathologists; First Cameron Lecturer, 1965; Hon. Archivist, 1963-. Mem. Agricultural Research Council, 1963-73. Editor: Jl of Pathology and Bacteriology, 1956-68 (Asst Editor, 1950-55); Jl of Medical Microbiology, 1968-71; Jl of Pathology, 1969-72. *Recreations:* parasitic copepods, spiders; mediæval churches. *Address:* 4 Otley Old Road, Leeds LS16 6HD. *T:* Leeds 673390.   [*Died 27 March 1975.*

OAKSEY, Lord; *see under* Trevethin and Oaksey.

OAKSHOTT, Baron, *cr* 1964, of Bebington (Life Peer); **Hendrie Dudley Oakshott,** MBE 1942; Bt *cr* 1959; *b* 8 Nov. 1904; *s of* Arthur John Oakshott, JP, Bidston, Cheshire, and Elizabeth Strathearn, *d* of Matthew Leggat, Hamilton, Ont.; *m* 1928, Joan, *d* of Marsden Withington, London and Buenos Aires; two *s*. *Educ:* Rugby; Trinity Coll., Cambridge. Served in Middle East and Italy, 1940-44 (despatches); retired, 1945, Lieutenant-Colonel. MP (C) Bebington, 1950-64. An Assistant Whip (unpaid), 1951-52; a Lord Commissioner of the Treasury, 1952-55; Comptroller of HM Household, 1955-57; Treasurer of HM Household, 1957-59. Parliamentary Private Secretary: to Foreign Secretary, 1959-60; to Chancellor of the Exchequer, 1960-62; a Dep. Speaker and Dep. Chm. of Cttees, House of Lords, 1967-68. Deleg., Council of Europe, Strasbourg, 1952-58. Member, Totalisator Board, 1964-73. Hon. Fellow, Inst. of Building. *Recreation:* racing. *Heir:* (to Baronetcy): *s* Hon. Anthony Hendrie Oakshott [*b* 10 Oct. 1929; *m* 1965, Mrs Valerie de Pret-Roose, *d* of Jack Vlasto, Hans Place, SW1]. *Address:* The Mount, Broxton, Cheshire. *T:* 215; 42 Eaton Square, SW1. *T:* 01-235 2107. *Clubs:* Turf, Pratt's, Boodle's.
[Died 1 Feb. 1975.

OATEN, Edward Farley, MA, LLB; *b* 24 Feb. 1884; *e s* of Samuel Oaten, Tunbridge Wells; *m* 1st, 1914; one *s* one *d*; 2nd, 1931, Kathleen Mary, *step-d.* of late T. Mullett Ellis, Shepperton; one *d. Educ:* Skinners' School, Tunbridge Wells; Tonbridge School; Sidney Sussex College, Cambridge (Scholar); twice Le Bas Cambridge University Prizeman. Appointed to Indian Educational Service as Professor of History, Presidency College, Calcutta, 1909; Calcutta Light Horse to 1916; thence to 1919 in IARO attached 11th KEO Lancers on North-West Frontier and in Punjab, including Waziristan Campaign, 1917; Lt 1917; Acting Captain, 1919; Officiating Assistant Director, Muhammadan Education, Bengal, 1919; Assistant Director of Public Instruction, Bengal, 1921; Officiating Deputy Secretary to Government of Bengal, 1924-25; Director of Public Instruction, Bengal, 1924; retired 1930; nominated Member, Bengal Legislative Council; Fellow, Calcutta Univ.; Major, Auxiliary Force, India, and Commandant, 2nd (Calcutta) Battalion, University Training Corps, 1927; called to Bar (Middle Temple), 1932. *Publications:* A Sketch of Anglo-Indian Literature; European Travellers in India; Glimpses of India's History; Song of Aton and other verses; contributed to Cambridge History of English Literature. *Recreation:* genealogy. *Address:* 9 Beech Close, Walton-on-Thames, Surrey. *T:* Walton-on-Thames 24477. *[Died 17 April 1973.*

OBERG, Olof David August, CMG 1953; Deputy Chairman, Commonwealth Immigration Advisory Council, since 1945; President, Area Council Boy Scouts' Association of New South Wales; Chairman: Timber Mutual Assurance Ltd; Timber Trade Mutual Assurance Ltd; Timber Tallying Association Ltd; Lumber Operators Pty Ltd; *b* 24 September 1893; *s* of Joseph Nathaniel Oberg, Gevie, Sweden, and Jane Hannah, Ballarat, Australia; *m* 1917, Dulcie Sutton Druce; two *s* two *d* (and one *s* decd). *Educ:* Sydney High School. Early life spent in timber industry, ultimately becoming Gen. Man. Davies & Fehon Ltd, 1921; JP 1924. Formed own Company, Thatcher & Oberg Pty Ltd, 1930; Chairman, retd, 1963. Mem. Council, Sydney Chamber of Commerce, 1928-40; Mem. Unemployment Relief Council of NSW, 1931-34; Pres. Sydney and Suburban Timber Merchants' Assoc., 1936-40; Foundation Pres. (1938-48) of Timber Devel. Assoc. of Austr.; Foundation Pres., Building Industry Congress, 1938-40; Pres. Employers' Federation of New South Wales, 1940-43; Pres. Australian Council of Employers' Fedns, 1943-48. Member Austr. Deleg. to S Francisco World Conf., 1945; led Austr. Employers' Deleg. to Internat. Labour Organisation Conf., Paris, 1945, and Asian Regional Conf., Tokio, 1953. Member Commonwealth Immigration Advisory Cttee, 1945; Member Rotary International Cttees, 1948-56; Dir, Rotary International, 1954 (first Vice-Pres., 1955-56); Vice-Pres. YMCA Jubilee Medal, 1935; Coronation Medal, 1937. Coronation Medal, 1953. *Recreations:* motoring, gardening, fishing. *Address:* 2 Clanville Road, Roseville, NSW, Australia. *Clubs:* Royal Sydney Yacht Squadron, New South Wales, Savage, Rotary (Sydney).
[Died 15 Feb. 1975.

OBERON, Merle, (Estelle Merle O'Brien Thompson); Film Actress; *b* Tasmania, 19 Feb. 1911; British; *m* 1st 1939, Sir Alexander Korda (*d* 1956) (marr. diss.); 2nd, 1945, Lucien Ballard (marr. diss. 1949); 3rd, 1957, Bruno Pagliai (marr. diss. 1973); one *s* one *d* adopted; 4th, 1975, Robert Wolders. *Educ:* La Martinere College, Calcutta; France. Films include: Henry VIII, Wuthering Heights, Night in Paradise, Temptation, Night Song, Berlin Express, Dark Angel, Song to Remember, Of Love and Desire, Hotel, Interval. *Recreations:* riding, swimming, fishing, and reading. *Address:* c/o Allan & Ingersoll, 1901 Avenue of Stars, Los Angeles, Calif 90067, USA. *[Died 23 Nov. 1979.*

OBERT de THIEUSIES, Vicomte Alain; Grand Officer de la Couronne; Grande Croix de l'Ordre de Léopold II; Grand Cordon de la Couronne de Chêne, etc.; Comdr de la Légion d'Honneur; *b* 10 March 1888; *s* of Vicomte Obert de Thieusies and Vicomtesse Obert de Thieusies (*née* Comtesse de Ribaucourt); *m* 1927, Yolanda, *d* of Baron Romano-Avezzana; two *s* (and one *s* decd). *Educ:* Maredsous Abbey; Stoneyhurst College (Doctor of Law). Entered diplomatic service, 1911, as Attaché de Légation; Secrétaire de Légation, Madrid, 1912; Chargé d'Affaires, ad interim, Belgrade, 1913, Sofia, 1913; Secrétaire de Légation (1st Cl.), 1915, Rio de Janiero, 1919; Counsellor, Paris, 1921; Minister Plenipotentiary, 1930; Consul General, Tangiers, 1930; Minister, Prague, 1932, Belgrade, 1938-41; Directeur Général du Commerce Extérieur in London, 1941; Chairman of Liquidation Cttee of Belgian Govt Service in London, 1944; Head of Belgian Economic Mission, 1945; Belgian Ambassador to the Court of St James's, 1946-53. *Recreations:* golf, shooting. *Heir:* gs Amaury, *b* 18 Aug. 1959. *Address:* Château de Thoricourt, Hainaut, Belgium.
[Died 15 April 1979.

OBEY, André; Licencié ès-lettres, Licencié en droit; Playwright; administrateur de la Comédie française, 1945-46; officier de la Légion d'Honneur; *b* 8 May 1892; *s* of Oscar Obey and Elisabeth Hisette; *m* 1st, 1919, Jane Moreau Dupuy; one *d*; 2nd, 1962, Josie Grégoire. *Educ:* Lycée de Douai. Won a first prize for piano, at the Conservatoire of Douai, his native town; when European war of 1914 was declared was going through the period of his military service; wounded twice very seriously; after the war, came to Paris; for several years belonged to the staff of divers newspapers, as reporter for sporting news, and musical and theatrical critic; his last novel awarded Prix Théophraste Renaudot, 1928; since then he has written exclusively for the stage. *Publications: novels:* Le Gardien de la Ville; L'Enfant inquiet; Savreux Vainqueur; Le Joueur de Triangle; *essays:* L'Orgue du Stade; l'Apprenti Sorcier; *plays:* Noé; Le Viol de Lucrèce; Bataille de la Marne; Vénus et Adonis; Loire; Richard III; Don Juan; Henri IV; Revenu de l'Etoile; Ultimatum; Maria; La nuit des temps, l'Homme de Cendres; Lazare; Une fille pour du vent; Orestie; Les Trois Coups de Minuit. *Recreations:* motoring, angling. *Address:* L'Hirondelle, 49730 Montsoreau, France. *[Died 12 April 1975.*

O'BRIEN, Brian; Solicitor and Legal Adviser to Ministry of Health, to Ministry of Housing and Local Government, and to Registrar-General, 1952-57, retired; *s* of late Hon. W. J. O'Brien, OBE, JP, PhD and late Mrs O'Brien, Dunkerrin, Pietermaritzburg, Natal, SA; *m* 1918, Adelaide Mone Johnson (*d* 1948), Woldingham, Surrey; one *d*. *Educ:* Pietermaritzburg College; Natal University; Trinity College, Cambridge; MA, LLB Cantab 1914 (1st Class Honours. Part II Law Tripos). Called to Bar, Inner Temple, 1915; read in chambers, Hon. Sir Malcolm Macnaghten, 1914-15; Ministry of Munitions, 1915-20; Established Civil Servant. Treasury Solicitor's Dept, 1920; transferred Ministry of Health, 1929; seconded to Ministry of Food, as Asst Sec., 1940-45; Assistant Solicitor, 1945, Principal Assistant Solicitor, 1951, Ministry of Health. Chm. and Hon. Sec. Frank Merrick Society. Order of Orange Nassau (Holland), 1952. *Recreations:* gardening (FRHS); devotee of music (Fellow Royal Philharmonic Soc.) and the arts, letters. *Address:* 26 Cottesmore Court, Kensington, W8. *T:* 01-937 4258. *Club:* United Oxford & Cambridge University. *[Died 21 Jan. 1973.*

O'BRIEN, Bryan Justin, CMG 1950; *b* 21 Jan. 1902; *s* of late Rev. G. E. O'Brien, Bosley Vicarage, Cheshire; *m* 1937, Maro, *d* of late Cleanthis Constantinides, Famagusta, Cyprus; one *s*. *Educ:* Uppingham; Queen's College, Oxford. First class honour Mods, second class literæ humaniores; Laming Fellow. Assistant Secretary, Colonial Secretary's Office, Cyprus, 1927; Commissioner, 1936; Assistant Colonial Secretary, Mauritius, 1939; Principal Assistant Colonial Secretary, 1943; Under-Secretary, Trinidad, 1943-47; Colonial Secretary, Gibraltar, 1947-53; Chief Secretary, North Borneo, 1953-56; retired. Mem. Commn on Salaries and Wages, Ghana, 1956-57. Jt Editor, Handbook of Cyprus, 1930 edn. *Club:* Travellers'.
[Died 24 May 1978.

O'BRIEN, Sir (Frederick) Lucius, Kt 1949; first Chairman (Government appointment) Northern Ireland Housing Trust, 1945-60, Member of Trust, 1960-67; *b* 1896; *s* of Louis Frederick O'Brien; unmarried. *Educ:* Friends' School, Lisburn; Bootham School, York. Honorary Secretary, Belfast Charitable Society, 1935-62, President 1962-71; Chairman, Belfast Savings Bank, 1939 and 1951; Custodian Trustee; NI Rep. Exec. on Trustee

Savings Bank Assoc., 1952-62, Vice-Pres. 1962-; Chief Welfare Officer 1941 and Member (Govt App.) of Belfast Civil Defence Auth., 1941-45; Member: ITA, 1960-65; NI Govt Commn on Charities, 1956; Exec. Belfast Council of Social Welfare; NI Council of Social Service, etc. Mem. of Senate, The Queen's Univ. of Belfast, 1950-73; Hon. LLD QUB, 1974. *Address:* c/o Midland Bank Ltd, 84 Highgates, PO Box 7, Kendal, Cumbria.
[Died 13 Oct. 1974.

O'BRIEN, George, DLitt (NUI), Hon. LittD (Dublin); Professor of Economics, University College, Dublin, 1926-61; Representative of National University of Ireland in Seanad Eireann, 1948-65; Director: Ashtown Tin Box (Ireland) Ltd; Ryan's Tourist Holdings Ltd; Ryan Traders Distribution Ltd; Phœnix Estates Ltd; *b* Dublin, 1892. *Educ:* St George's Coll., Weybridge; Univ. Coll., Dublin. Called to Irish Bar, 1913; member of Agricultural Commission, 1922, of Fiscal Inquiry Committee, 1923, of Economic Committee, 1928, of Derating Commission, 1930, of Banking Commission, 1934; and of Commission on Agriculture, 1939. President of Statistical and Social Inquiry Society of Ireland, 1942-46; Vice-President of Royal Irish Academy, 1944; Trustee of National Library of Ireland; Vice-Pres., Royal Dublin Society; mem. Pontifica Accademia Degli Arcadi; Chairman Board, Economic and Social Research Institute of Ireland; editorial consultant, The Irish Banking Review. *Publications:* The Economic History of Ireland (3 vols); An Essay on Mediæval Economic Teaching; The Economic Effects of the Reformation; Labour Organisation; Agricultural Economics; Notes on Theory of Profit; The Four Green Fields; The Phantom of Plenty; (ed) The Bank of Ireland 1783-1946 (by F. G. Hall); contrib. Encyc. Britannica, Encyc. of Social Sciences, Economic Journal, Eng. Historical Review, Economica, Camb. Jl, etc. *Address:* 3 Burlington Road, Dublin. *Clubs:* Kildare Street, Dublin University (Dublin); Royal Irish Yacht. *[Died 31 Dec.* 1973.

O'BRIEN, Kate; Playwright, Novelist; *b* 3 Dec. 1897; *d* of Thomas O'Brien and Catherine Thornhill, Boru House, Limerick, Ireland. *Educ:* Laurel Hill Convent, Limerick; University College, Dublin. *Plays:* Distinguished Villa, at Aldwych Theatre, 1926, afterwards, 1926, at Little Theatre; The Bridge, at Arts Theatre Club, 1927; The Ante-Room (dramatised from novel, with W. A. Carot and Geoffrey Gomer), Queen's Theatre, 1936; The Schoolroom Window, produced by Manuscript Theatre Club, 1937; The Last of Summer (dramatised from novel, with John Perry), Phoenix Theatre, 1944; That Lady (dramatised from novel), USA, 1949. *Publications:* novels: Without My Cloak, 1931 (Hawthornden Prize 1931 and James Tait Black Memorial Prize); The Ante-Room, 1934; Mary Lavelle, 1936; Pray for the Wanderer, 1938; The Land of Spices, 1941; The Last of Summer, 1943; That Lady, 1946; The Flower of May, 1953; As Music and Splendour, 1958; Presentation Parlour, 1963; *travel:* Farewell Spain, 1937; English Diaries and Journals, 1943; My Ireland, 1962. *Address:* 177 The Street, Boughton, Faversham, Kent.
[Died 13 Aug. 1974.

O'BRIEN, Sir Lucius; *see* O'Brien, Sir (F). L.

O'BRIEN, Rt. Rev. Mgr. Michael Joseph; Principal Chaplain (RC), Royal Air Force, 1967-71; *b* 13 April 1913; *s* of John O'Brien and Anastasia (*née* Corbett). *Educ:* De La Salle, Waterford; Rockwell Coll., Cashel; St John's Coll., Waterford. Ordained, 1936; Curate: Corpus Christi, Weston-super-Mare, 1936-40; St John the Evangelist, Bath, 1940-41; joined RAF Chaplain's Branch, 1941. *Recreation:* golf. *Address:* Lisieux, 25 Rockfield Park, Waterford, Ireland. *T:* Waterford 3117. *Club:* Royal Air Force. *[Died 16 Feb.* 1978.

O'BRIEN TWOHIG, Brig. Joseph Patrick, CBE 1945; DSO 1943, Bar 1944; *b* 30 May 1905; 4th *s* of J. O'Brien Twohig, Dunowen House, Clonakilty, Co. Cork; *m* 1st, 1933, Barbara, *e d* of W. E. Tower; one *s*; 2nd, 1944, Mary, *e d* of J. P. Blake; two *d*. *Educ:* privately and Trinity Coll., Dublin (MA). Called to Irish Bar, 1926. 2nd Lieut, KOYLI, 1926; Adjutant, 2nd Gold Coast Regt, 1933; Captain, Royal Inniskilling Fusiliers, 1937; Lieut-Colonel, 1946; CO 2nd Inniskillings, 1943-44. Brigade Commander: Adriatic, 1944-45; 2nd Parachute Bde, 1946; 28 Inf. Bde, 1949; retired, 1951. Dep. Inspector-General Malayan Home Guard, 1952-54. Chairman and Managing Director, London and Kano Trading Co., 1955-60; Dir, Hooker Craigmyle Ltd, 1967-69. *Address:* Brontë House, St James Street, Ryde, Isle of Wight. *[Died 17 Aug.* 1973.

O'BRIEN-TWOHIG, Colonel Michael Joseph, OBE 1957; *b* 6 Aug. 1893; *e s* of late John Patrick O'Brien-Twohig, Mawgan Porth, Cornwall, and Dunowen House, Clonakilty, Co. Cork, and Ellen O'Brien, Tullaneasky, Co. Cork; *m* 1st, 1919, Eileen (*d*

1958), *d* of late John Lawlor, DL, JP, Irishtown House, Clondalkin, Co. Dublin; one *d*; 2nd, 1958, Margaret Elizabeth, *o d* of late George Agnew Main, Mansfield, Wemyss Bay, Renfrewshire. *Educ:* Trinity Coll., Cambridge; King's Inns, Dublin. Barrister-at-Law. 2nd Lieut Royal Munster Fusiliers, 1913; served European War, 1914-18, Gallipoli and France; Staff Captain and DAQMG; Captain, 1916; Temp. Major, 1918. ADC, Kenya, 1921-24; Transferred KSLI, 1922. Commanding Gold Coast Defence Force, 1931-34; Staff, GHQ, BEF, 1939; Mil. Comdt "Queen Elizabeth" and "Queen Mary", 1942-44; Acting King's Messenger, 1944; appointed a King's Foreign Service Messenger, 1948; Senior King's Foreign Service Messenger, 1951; Superintending Queen's Foreign Service Messenger, 1952-57, retired. French and Belgian Croix de Guerre. *Publications:* Diplomatic Courier, 1960; contrib. to Encyclopædia Britannica. *Recreations:* yachting, painting. *Address:* Four Chimneys, High Ham, near Langport, Somerset. *T:* Langport 367. *Clubs:* Pratt's, Royal Automobile, Naval; Royal Irish Yacht, Royal Alfred Yacht (Dun Laoghaire).
[Died 9 April 1971.

O'CALLAGHAN, Most Rev. Eugene, DD; Titular Bishop of Britonia, since 1969; *b* Lisseraw, Camlough, Co. Armagh, 6 Jan. 1888. *Educ:* Drumilly NS; St Colman's Coll., Newry; St Patrick's Coll., Armagh; St Patrick's Coll., Maynooth; Post-Graduate Course in Dunboyne House, Maynooth, STL, BCL, BA. Ordained, 1913; Diocesan Inspector of Schools, Diocese of Armagh, 1913-21; Curate in Armagh, 1921-32; Administrator of Armagh, 1932-38; PP of St Peter's, Drogheda, 1938-43, and also Vicar-Gen. of the Diocese, 1938-43; Bishop of Clogher, 1943-69. *Address:* c/o Bishop's House, Monaghan. *[Died 21 May* 1973.

O'CARROLL SCOTT, Maj.-Gen. Anthony Gerald; *see* Scott.

O'CONNELL, Prof. Daniel Patrick, RD; LLD; DCL; QC 1977; Chichele Professor of Public International Law, Oxford University, since 1972, and Fellow of All Souls; *b* 7 July 1924; *s* of Daniel Patrick O'Connell, Howick, New Zealand, and of Magdalen Roche; *m* 1957, Renate von Kleist, Drenow; three *s* two *d*. *Educ:* Auckland Univ.; Trinity Coll., Cambridge (PhD, LLD). Comdr, RNR. Barrister-at-Law, Middle Temple; Reader in Law, 1952-62, Prof. of International Law, 1962-72, Univ. of Adelaide. Dir of Studies, Internat. Law Assoc., 1973-. Pres., Assoc. of Aust. and NZ Law Schools, 1964; Rapporteur, State Succession Cttee, Internat. Law Assoc., 1961-72; Rockefeller Fellow, Harvard Univ., 1957; Visiting Prof.: Georgetown Univ., 1960; Inst. Hautes Etudes Internat., Geneva, 1965; Associé de l'Institut de Droit Internat., 1967; Legal Adviser to several Commonwealth Govts. Mem., St John's Council, S Aust. FRHistS. Kt of Grace and Devotion, Order of Malta, 1958. *Publications:* The Law of State Succession, 1956; International Law, 1965 (2nd edn 1970); International Law in Australia, 1966; State Succession in Municipal Law and International Law, 1967; Richelieu, 1968; Opinions on Imperial Constitutional Law, 1972; The Influence of Law on Seapower, 1975; numerous articles in British, US and foreign, legal, political, literary and historical jls. *Recreations:* art, music, history, sailing. *Address:* All Souls College, Oxford. *T:* Oxford 722251; Powder Hill House, Youlbury, Boar's Hill, Oxford. *T:* Oxford 730148; 2 Katoomba Road, Beaumont, Adelaide, Australia. *Clubs:* Athenæum; Naval, Military and Air Force of SA (Adelaide).
[Died 8 June 1979.

O'CONNELL, Captain Donal Bernard, CBE 1943; Royal Navy, retired; *b* 3 June 1893; 2nd *s* of Sir Morgan Ross O'Connell, 4th Bt, Lakeview, Killarney, Eire, and Mary Pauline, *e d* of Col J. F. Hickie, Slevoyre, Borrisokane, Eire; unmarried. *Educ:* St Anthony's, Eastbourne; Royal Naval Colleges. European War, Destroyer Service, as Sub-Lieut and Lieut, RN; commanded HMSS Teal (Yangtse, 1926-28) and Gannet (Yangtse, 1932-34); Commander, 1929; retired, 1936; Captain, retired, 1938; Served War of 1939-45. Founded Kerry Archæological Survey, 1936. Fellow Royal Society Antiquaries of Ireland, 1937; MRIA, 1938; Irish National Monuments Commission, 1938. Chevalier de Malte, 1938; VP Cork Hist. and Archæological Society, 1938. *Publication:* Kerry Archæological Survey Publication No. 1. *Recreations:* Local Archæology, Ambulance work (Order of Malta). *Address:* Maulagh, Killarney, Co. Kerry, Eire. *TA:* Beaufort-Kerry Eire. *Club:* Hibernian, United Service (Dublin).
[Died 22 Oct. 1971.

O'CONNOR, James Malachy; Professor of Physiology, University College, Dublin, 1920-56; *b* 9 Feb. 1886; *s* of Dr M. R. O'Connor, Limerick; *m* 1919, Genevieve McGilligan; three *s* (and one *s* decd). *Educ:* Crescent Coll., Limerick; University Coll., Dublin. MB 1909, MD 1913. Assistant at Pharmacological Institute, Heidelberg, 1911-12; Assistant to Professor of Physiology, University College, Dublin, 1912-20;

Irish Representative on General Medical Council, 1945-60. *Publications:* contributions to Physiology. *Address:* 7 Palmerston Villas, Dublin 6, Eire. *[Died* 4 *Dec.* 1974.

Ó DÁLAIGH, Cearbhall; Uachtarán na hÉireann (President of Ireland), 1974-76; *b* 12 Feb. 1911; *m* 1934, Máiríin Nic Dhiarmada. *Educ:* National Sch., Bray; Scoil naLeanbh sa Rinn; Christian Brothers' Sch., Synge Street, Dublin; University College Dublin. BA (Celtic Studies); BL King's Inns 1934. Studied Irish, An Rinn, An Blascaod, Dún Chaoin, Comineoil; studied Italian, Università per stranieri, Perugia. Irish Editor, Irish Press, 1931-40; called to Bar, 1934; admitted to Inner Bar, 1945; Attorney General of Republic of Ireland, 1946-48, 1951-53; Judge of the Supreme Court, 1953, Chief Justice and Pres. Supreme Court, 1961-73; Judge of Court of Justice of European Communities, Luxembourg, 1973, Pres. First Chamber of Court of Justice of European Communities, 1974. Formerly Chairman: Commn on Industrial Taxation; Commn on Income Tax; Commn on Accommodation Needs of Constituent Colls of NUI; Commn on Higher Education; Cultural Relations Cttee of Dept of Foreign Affairs; Irish Nat. Council on Alcoholism; Council for Overseas Students; special interest in refugee problems. MRIA. Hon. FRSCI. Hon. LLD Dublin; Hon. DLittCelt NUI. *Recreations:* Irish literature, Italian and French languages, art, education, theatre, horse-riding, bird-watching. *Address:* Caoindroim, Cill Chomhaid, Baile O gCearnaigh, An Chloch Liath, Ireland. *[Died* 21 *March* 1978.

ODGERS, Lindsey Noel Blake, MC 1916; *b* 21 Dec. 1892; *s* of late William Blake Odgers, KC, LLD, and Frances (*née* Hudson); *m* 1923, Constance Attneave (*d* 1969). *Educ:* Rugby; St John's Coll., Cambridge. Served European War in Middlesex Regt, 1914-18, and Royal Engineers, 1918-19. Entered Home Office, 1919; seconded to Chief Secretary's Office, 1920-22; Principal, Home Office, 1926; Assistant Secretary, 1937; Assistant Under Secretary of State, Home Office, 1949-54. *Recreation:* gardening. *[Died* 19 *Nov.* 1979.

ODLUM, Maj.-Gen. Victor Wentworth, CB 1918; CMG 1917; DSO 1915 and Bar 1916; VD; LLD; former Canadian Ambassador to China and Turkey; *b* Cobourg, Ontario, 21 Oct. 1880; *s* of Prof. E. Odlum, MA, BSc, and Mary Powell; *m* 1904, Sada Eugenie Tressa, *d* of Isaac and Margaret Rogerson; three *s.* *Educ:* Toronto Univ. Served South African War with 1st Canadian Contingent (2nd RCR), and afterwards in 3rd Canadian Mounted Rifles (medal 3 clasps); Colonial long service medal; served European War, 1914-18 (wounded thrice, despatches 7 times, DSO and bar, CMG, CB); originally commanded 7th Canadian Infantry Batt. (1st British Columbia) CEF, afterwards GOC 11th Canadian Inf. Bde, 1916-19; Order of Danilo, 3rd Class, 1917; Liberal Member for Vancouver City in Provincial Legislature, 1924-28; Governor and Vice-Chairman, Canadian Broadcasting Corporation, 1932-40; Governor University of British Columbia, 1936-40; Publisher of Vancouver Daily Star, 1924-32; commanded 2nd Division Canadian Active Service Force, 1940-41; Canadian High Commissioner to Australia, 1941-42; Canadian Ambassador to China, 1942-46, to Turkey, 1947-52. *Address:* 1509-935 Marine, West Vancouver, BC, Canada. *Clubs:* Vancouver (Vancouver), West Vancouver Yacht, Vancouver Arts. *[Died* 4 *April* 1971.

O'DOHERTY, Most Rev. Eugene; *b* 4 Feb. 1896. Ordained priest, 1921. Formerly President of St Columb's College, Londonderry; Bishop of Dromore (RC), 1944-76. *Address:* 58 Armagh Road, Newry, Co. Down, N Ireland.
[Died 24 *March* 1979.

O'DONOGHUE, Geoffrey Charles Patrick Randal, (The O'Donoghue of the Glens); *b* 8 Oct. 1896; *e s* of late Geoffrey Charles Patrick O'Donoghue and Annie Matilda Deighton (*d* 1921), *y d* of W. Charlton of Clonmancnoise, King's County; *m* 1935, Kathleen, *d* of Patrick Finnegan, Co. Carlow; two *s* one *d.* *Educ:* Blackrock Coll., Dublin; Stonyhurst. Served European War 1914-19, as Lieut, The Connaught Rangers. *Address:* Glas Choille, Screggan, Tullamore, Offaly, Ireland.
[Died 9 *Jan.* 1974.

O'DONOGHUE, John Kingston, CBE 1956 (OBE 1947; MBE 1932); *b* 6 October 1894; *s* of Thomas and Elizabeth O'Donoghue; *m* 1925, Mary Carmela Burrell (*d* 1965); two *s* one *d.* *Educ:* St Vincent's College, Castleknock, Dublin. Appointed to Foreign Office, 1915; served European War with 18th London Regt, 1917-19; returned to Foreign Office, 1919; attached to British Delegation to Disarmament Conference, Washington, 1921-22; Archivist to HM Embassy, Berlin, 1924; Foreign Office, 1939; Allied Commission, Germany, 1944-46; Actg Consul-General, Rio de Janeiro, March 1947; Consul, New York, Oct. 1947; Assistant in Personnel Department, Foreign

Office, 1950; Consul-General for the States of Pennsylvania, Delaware, etc., 1953-56; retired, 1956. Life member Philadelphia Chamber of Commerce, 1956. *Recreations:* golf, walking. *Address:* Merrow, Park Close, Winchester, Hants. *T:* Winchester 67348. *[Died* 31 *Oct.* 1976.

O'DONOGHUE, Richard John Langford, DSO 1918; MA (TCD); MB, BS (London University); MRCP London; DMRE (Cambridge); *b* 22 August 1889; *s* of Cooper Charles O'Donoghue and M. H. Matthews. *Educ:* Campbell Coll., Belfast; Trinity College, Dublin; Guy's Hospital. Served France 1914-18 (DSO, despatches); late Egyptian Civil Service; Private Secretary to the Financial Adviser to the Egyptian Government; Assistant to Controller-General Central Administration Ministry of Finance, Cairo, and Controller of Pensions (Order of the Nile, 4th class). *Recreations:* walking, swimming, music. *Address:* 55 Rotherwick Road, NW11. *T:* 01-455 7150.
[Died 10 *March* 1972.

O'FERRALL, Rt. Rev. Ronald Stanhope More, MA, DD; *b* 1890; *s* of late J. E. O'Ferrall; *m* 1934, Ann Molesworth, *o c* of late J. M. Kindersley; one *s* one *d.* *Educ:* Charterhouse; Trinity Coll., Cambridge; Ely Theological Coll. BA 1913; MA 1916; DD (Lambeth), 1926. Deacon, 1914; Priest, 1915; Curate at Chesterfield Parish Church, 1914-18; With EEF, 1918-19; Asst Priest at St George's Cathedral and House Master at St George's School, Jerusalem, 1919-23; UMCA, Mission Priest in N Rhodesia, 1923-26; Bishop in Madagascar, 1926-40; Rector of Walton on Trent, 1940-44; Vicar of Repton and Foremark, 1944-47; Divinity Master Repton School, 1944-47; Assistant Bishop of Derby and Hon. Canon of Derby Cathedral, 1941-53; Provost of Derby and Proctor in Convocation, 1947-53. Examining Chaplain to Bishop of Derby, 1948-53; Rector of Cranham, Glos, 1953-56; Assistant Bishop of Gloucester, 1955-56; Vicar of Hyde, Fordingbridge, 1956-58, retd. Commissary for the Bishops in Madagascar. *Recreations:* archæology, gardening. *Address:* Glebefield, 130 Lower Road, Bemerton, Salisbury, Wilts SP2 GNW. *T:* Salisbury 22337.
[Died 10 *Oct.* 1973.

O'FLYNN, Surgeon Rear-Adm. Joseph Aloysius, CB 1948; MD, DTM & H; retired; *b* 7 Jan. 1889; *s* of late Edmond O'Flynn, JP and late Mary O'Callaghan, Cork, Ireland; *m* 1929, Linda Avis Leonard; two *s.* *Educ:* Clongowes Wood College, Kildare; Queen's College, Cork. Joined RN, 1912; Surg. Lt-Comdr, 1918; Surg. Comdr, 1924; Surg. Capt., 1936; Surg. Rear-Adm., 1944. Employed on initial anti-malarial work at RN Base, Singapore, 1925-26; Work on Active Immunisation against Diphtheria, 1932-33 (Medical Research Council Special Report Series No 195). Late Medical Officer in Charge, RN Hospital, Haslar, Gosport. Formerly KHP. *Recreation:* golf. *Address:* 3 Loch Lomond Crescent, Burraneer, NSW 2230, Australia. *T:* 523 9094. *[Died* 28 *March* 1976.

OGG, Sir William Gammie, Kt 1949; Director of Rothamsted Experimental Station, 1943-58, retired; *b* 2 Nov. 1891; *s* of late James Ogg, Cults, Aberdeenshire, farmer; *m* 1922, Helen, *y d* of late Henry Hilbert, Halifax; one *s* one *d.* *Educ:* Robert Gordon's College; Aberdeen University; Christ's College, Cambridge. MA, BSc, BSc (Agr.), Aberdeen Univ., PhD Cantab, LLD Aberdeen, FRSE. Res. Fellow, Bd of Agr. for Scotland, studying in Canada and USA, 1919-20; Researcher, Christ's College, Cambridge, 1920-24; Advisory Officer in Soils, Edinburgh, and East of Scotland College of Agriculture, 1924-30; first Director of the Macaulay Institute for Soil Research, Craigiebuckler, Aberdeen, 1930-43, and research lecturer in Soil Science in the University of Aberdeen; Pres. Soc. of Chem. Industry, 1953-55. Hon. Fellow of the Royal Agric. Soc. of England; For. Corresp. of French Acad. of Agriculture; For. Member of Roy. Acad. of Agriculture of Sweden; Foreign Member of All-Union Academy of Agric. Sciences of the USSR. Hon. Coun. Consejo Superior de Investigaciones Cientificas, Spain. Raffaele Piria medal of Societa Chimica Italiana, 1958. *Publications:* articles on soil chemistry, soil surveys, land reclamation and peat. *Address:* Arnhall, by Edzell, Angus. *T:* Edzell 400. *[Died* 25 *Sept.* 1979.

OGILVIE, Sir (William) Heneage, KBE 1946; Consulting Surgeon, Guy's Hospital; Editor of the Practitioner since 1946; formerly Examiner in Surgery, Universities of Oxford and Cambridge; *b* Chile, 1887; *e s* of William Ogilvie, Valparaiso and Harrow Weald; *m* 1915, Vere Magdalen, *e d* of Harry Quilter; one *s* two *d.* *Educ:* Clifton Coll.; New Coll., Oxford; Guy's Hospital. First Class Honours Oxford, 1910; MRCS, LRCP, 1913; MB, BCh Oxon, 1913; FRCS Eng., MCh Oxon, 1920; MD Oxon, 1924; FACS (Hon.) 1938; FRCSC (Hon.) 1943; MS Fouad I (Hon.), 1944; FRACS (Hon.) 1947; FRSM (Hon.) 1957; LLD Witwatersrand (Hon.), 1943; Hunterian Prof. RCS, 1924; Surgeon Urgency Cases Hosp., France, 1915-17; RAMC,

1917-20; Surgical Registrar, Guy's Hospital, 1920; Senior Demonstrator of Anatomy, 1922; Assistant Surgeon, 1925; Temp. Gen., Army Medical Service; Consulting Surgeon Expeditionary Force, 1940-45; Fellow Royal Society of Medicine; member Association of Surgeons. Upper Warden, Feltmakers' Co., 1957; Master, 1958. *Publications:* Recent Advances in Surgery; Treatment of Fractures; Forward Surgery in Modern War, 1944; Surgery, Orthodox and Heterodox, 1949; No Miracles among Friends, 1959; Hernia, 1959; Fifty, 1962; The Tired Business Man, 1963; chapters in The Operations of Surgery, and Postgraduate Surgery; contributions to professional periodicals. *Recreation:* sailing. *Address:* 18 Clifton Road, SW19. *TA:* (Monomark) BM/OPRS. *Clubs:* Athenæum; Royal Corinthian; Imperial Poona Yacht. *[Died* 15 *April* 1971.

OGILVY-WEDDERBURN, Comdr Sir (John) Peter, 12th and 6th Bt, *cr* 1704 and 1803; RN (retired 1961); *b* 29 Sept. 1917; *o s* of Sir John Andrew Ogilvy-Wedderburn, 11th and 5th Bt, and Aileen Meta Odette *(née* Grogan); *S* father 1956; *m* 1946, Elizabeth Katharine, *e d* of late John A. Cox, Drumkilbo; one *s* three *d. Educ:* The Nautical College, Pangbourne. Entered RN as cadet, 1935; Midshipman, 1936-38; Sub-Lt, 1938-40; Lt, 1940-48; Lt-Comdr, 1948-55; Comdr, 1955; psc 1956; Exec. Officer, Woolwich, 1956; Boom Defence and Marine Salvage Officer, Clyde, 1958. *Recreations:* shooting, forestry, Loch Ness monster hunting. *Heir: s* Andrew John Alexander Ogilvy-Wedderburn *[b* 4 Aug. 1952; commissioned The Black Watch, 1971]. *Address:* Silvie, Alyth, Perthshire. *T:* Alyth 362.
[Died 13 *Aug.* 1977.

OGMORE, 1st Baron, *cr* 1950, of Bridgend; **Lt-Col David Rees Rees-Williams,** PC 1951; TD; *b* 22 November 1903; *o c* of late Wm Rees Williams, FRCVS, and late Jennet Williams, Bridgend, Glamorgan; *m* 1930, Constance Wills (JP), *o d* of W. R. Wills, Lord Mayor of Cardiff, 1945-46; two *s* one *d. Educ:* Mill Hill School; University of Wales. Honoursman Law Society, 1929; practised in Straits Settlements, where he was admitted to Straits Settlements Bar; MP (Lab) Croydon, South, 1945-50; Parliamentary Under-Secretary of State: Colonial Office, 1947-50; Commonwealth Relations Office, 1950-51; Minister of Civil Aviation, June-Oct. 1951. On active service Aug. 1939-Oct. 1945, Lt-Col RA; Presided over first Gen. Military Court held in Berlin; Staff Officer, 1st Grade. Patron Bridgend Rugby Football Club; Member Government Mission to Sarawak, 1946; Chairman Burma Frontier Areas Committee of Enquiry, 1947; Pres. Bridgend YMCA; UK Deleg. to UN Gen. Assembly in NY, 1950; Leader of UK Deleg. and Chm. of African Defence Facilities Conf., Nairobi, 1951. Director: Property Owners' Building Soc. (Chm., 1971-); Leo Laboratories Ltd; Pres., Liberal Party, 1963-64; Member: Standing Group of Privy Counsellors on Official Histories; Investiture Cttee and carried the Coronet, Investiture of HRH The Prince of Wales, 1969; Departmental Cttee to examine operations of Section 2 of Official Secrets Act 1911, 1971. President: Kidney Res. Unit for Wales Foundn; Elizabeth House Assoc. (Drug Rehabilitation). Order Agga Maha Thray Sithu, Union of Burma, 1956. Panglima Mangku Negara (Hon.) in Order Pangkuan Negara (Fedn of Malaya), 1959. *Heir: s* Hon. Gwilym Rees Rees-Williams *[b* 5 May 1931; *m* 1967, Gillian Mavis, *d* of M. K. Slack, Hindley, Lancs; two *d*]. *Address:* 48 Cheyne Court, Royal Hospital Road, Chelsea, SW3 5TS. *T:* 01-352 6131.
[Died 30 *Aug.* 1976.

OGUNDIPE, Brig. Babafemi Olatunde; River Benue Star (Nigeria), 1965; High Commissioner for Nigeria in the UK, 1966-70; *b* 6 Sept. 1924; *s* of S. O. Ogundipe; *m* Elizabeth Omowunmi, *d* of T. R. P. Phelan, Lagos; three *s* four *d. Educ:* elem. and sec. schs, E. Nigeria. Enlisted Pte. Soldier, 1943; served in India and Burma, 1944-46; commnd, 1953; Comdr 5th Bn, 1961; Comdr, 3rd Bde, 1962; Chief of Staff, UN Forces, Congo, 1963; Comdr 2nd Bde, 1964; Imp. Def. Coll., 1965; Mil. Adviser to Nigerian High Comr in UK, Jan.-Feb. 1966; Chief of Staff, Supreme Mil. HQ, Nigeria, Feb.-July 1966. *Recreations:* swimming, hockey. *Address:* c/o Ministry of External Affairs, Lagos, Nigeria. *Club:* Beacon Golf.   *[Died* 20 *Nov.* 1971.

OHLIN, Prof. Bertil Gotthard, PhD; Commander with the Great Cross, Royal North Star, Sweden, 1961; *b* 23 April 1899; *s* of Elis and Ingeborg Ohlin; *m* 1931, Evy Kruse; one *s* two *d. Educ:* Univ. of Lund; Univ. of Stockholm (PhD 1924); Harvard Univ. (AM 1923). Professor: Univ. of Copenhagen, 1924; Stockholm Coll. of Business, 1929. Vis. Professor: Univ. of Calif, Berkeley, 1937; Univ. of Virginia, Charlotteville, 1959. MP, Sweden, 1938-70; Minister for Trade, 1944-45; Leader of Liberal Party, 1944-67; Mem., Pres. and Vice-Pres., Nordic Council, 1955-70; Mem., Council of Europe, 1949-60, 1969-70. Member: Acad. of Engrg Sciences, 1956; Swedish Acad. of Science, 1948. Hon. Member: Amer. Econ. Assoc., 1948; Amer. Acad. of Arts and Sciences,

1973; Académie des Sciences Politiques et Morales, Paris, 1977; Academia Nazionale dei Lincei, Rome, 1951. Hon. Dr polit. Aarhus, Denmark; Hon. Dr of hum. lett. Columbia, USA; Hon. Dr oekon. Helsinki; Hon. Dr en droit: Grenoble; Sorbonne. Nobel Meml Award in Economic Science (jt), 1977. Comdr, First Order of the Dannebrogen, Denmark. *Publications:* The Course and Phases of the World Economic Depression, 1931 (2nd edn 1932); Interregional and International Trade, 1933 (2nd edn 1967); International Economic Reconstruction, 1936; The Problem of Employment Stabilization, 1949 (2nd edn 1976); papers in Econ. Jl (London), Weltwit. Archiv. (Kiel), and Ekon. Tidskrift (Uppsala). *Address:* N Mälarstrand 72, 11235 Stockholm, Sweden. *T:* 08-535085.   *[Died* 3 *Aug.* 1979.

OISTRAKH, David (Fyodorovich); Russian concert violinist and teacher of violin; conductor; *b* Odessa, 1908; father amateur violinist, mother sang in Odessa Opera; *m* Tamara Ivanovna; one *s. Educ:* Odessa Musical-Dramatic Inst. under Stoliarsky. Played with orchestras throughout the USSR from 1926; made debut with orchestras in Moscow and Leningrad, 1928; 1st place in Ukrainian violin competition, Kharkov, USSR, 1930; Lecturer at the Moscow Conservatory, 1934; won prizes in International Wieniawski Violin Concours, Warsaw, 1935, etc.; travelled to Turkey; made debut in Brussels and Paris, 1937; Professor at the Moscow Conservatory, 1939; awarded Stalin Prize, 1942; there followed numerous appearances in Europe, including Florence Music Festival, 1951, and Palais de Chaillot, Paris, 1953; in Japan and Germany, 1955; toured USA, 1955-56, 1959-60; appearances in London since 1954; concert tours with his son, Igor Oistrakh, every year in different countries; first performances in the West of Shostakovitch's violin concertos I and II, his violin sonata, and many other works dedicated to him by different composers. Hon. RAM London, 1959; Hon. Mem. other foreign academies, 1961-. Lenin Prize, 1960. Hon. MusD Cambridge, 1969. Holds Order of Lenin and other orders and medals. *Address:* c/o State Conservatoire, Herzen Street, Moscow, USSR.   *[Died* 24 *Oct.* 1974.

OKEDEN, Richard Godfrey Christian P.; *see* Parry-Okeden.

OKORO, Godfrey; *see* Benin, Oba of.

OLDFIELD, Prof. Richard Charles; Director, Medical Research Council Speech and Communication Unit, Edinburgh University, since 1966; Hon. Professor, Edinburgh University, since 1967; *b* 26 Sept. 1909; *o s* of late Sir Francis du Pré Oldfield, ICS, and of Frances Sophia Henrietta *(née* Cayley); *m* 1933, Lady Kathleen Constance Blanche, 5th *d* of 2nd Earl of Balfour, PC; two *d. Educ:* Marlborough; Peterhouse, Cambridge. 2nd Class Nat. Sci. Tripos Pt I, 1930, BA 1931, MA 1935, Cambridge; MA Oxon, 1946. Exhibitioner in Moral Sciences, Peterhouse, 1931; Arnold Gerstenberg Student in Philosophy, Cambridge Univ., 1934; Leverhulme Research Student in Industrial Psychology, 1936; Rockefeller Research Fellow in Psychology, 1938; Univ. Lectr in Gen. Psychology, Univ. of Oxford, 1946, in Experimental Psychology, 1948; Prof. of Psychology, Reading Univ., 1950-56; Fellow of Magdalen College, Professor of Psychology and Director of the Institute of Experimental Psychology, Oxford University, 1956-66; Hon. Director, Medical Research Council, Psycholinguistics Research Unit, 1963-66; Founder-member Experimental Psychology Group, 1947, Pres. 1956-57; Mem., Experimental Psychology Soc., 1959; Sir Frederic Bartlett Lecturer, 1966. Pres. Section J. British Assoc., 1960; Mem. Roy. Soc. of Medicine; Corr. Mem. Sociedad Española de Psicologia; Assoc. Mem., Société de Psychologie Française. Ed. Quarterly Jl of Exptl Psych., 1947-49, Assoc. Ed. 1949-63. Served RAFVR (Radar Br.), 1941-46 (despatches). *Publications:* The Psychology of the Interview, 1941. Papers in scientific jls. *Recreations:* gardening, flowers, fishing. *Address:* MRC Speech and Communication Unit, Edinburgh University; Woodhall Cottage, Pencaitland, East Lothian. *Club:* Royal Automobile.
[Died 27 *April* 1972.

OLDHAM, Alan Trevor; CBE 1959; retired from Foreign Service, 1960 (HBM Consul-General, Dakar, 1956-59); *b* 20 June 1904; *s* of A. E. and H. Oldham; *m* 1944, Megan, *d* of Rev. James Evans. *Educ:* Bolton Sch.; Emmanuel Coll., Cambridge (Chancellor's Medal for English Verse, 1926). Entered HM Consular Service in Siam, 1927, later assimilated in HM Foreign Service; Consul, 1935; acting Consul-Gen., 1932, 1933, 1934, 1937, and 1943; Consul-General, 1949. Served at: Bangkok, Batavia, Saigon, Chiengmai, Nakawn Lampang, Songkhla, Basra, Port Said, Maymyo, Rangoon, Osaka/Kobe, Dakar, with Portuguese Guinea and Togo. Coronation Medal, 1953. *Address:* c/o Foreign and Commonwealth Office, SW1.
[Died 3 *Feb.* 1971.

OLDHAM, James Bagot, CBE 1964; VRD 1942; FRCS; retired as Consulting Surgeon, Liverpool United Hospitals, and Lecturer in Clinical Surgery, University of Liverpool (1925-65), and Consulting Surgeon to the Royal Navy (1944-65); QHS 1952-55; *b* 7 Nov. 1899; *s* of Samuel Charles Oldham; *m* 1931, Kathleen Longton Hicks. *Educ:* Birkenhead Sch.; Liverpool Univ. MB, ChB, 1921; MRCS, LRCP 1924, FRCS 1925. Surgeon Captain, RNVR, retired, 1955. Member Court of Examiners, Royal College of Surg. England, 1943-49; Member Council of RCS, 1947-55; Hunterian Prof., RCS, 1944 and 1951; Past President: Liverpool Medical Institution, 1954; Association of Surgeons of Great Britain and Ireland, 1963. *Publications:* chapters in various text books and papers on surgical subjects in medical journals. *Recreation:* gardening. *Address:* Cyfnant Ganol, Llanarmon-yn-Ial, near Mold, Clwyd CH7 4QD. *T:* Llanarmon-yn-Ial 233.   *[Died* 1 *March* 1977.

OLIPHANT, Patrick James, TD 1945; Deputy Keeper of Her Majesty's Signet, 1964-75; *b* 19 March 1914; 2nd *s* of Kenneth M. Oliphant, MC, WS, and Florence Agnes, *d* of late Abram Lyle; *m* 1938, Margaret Kemp, *er d* of late James Brown, Ironfounder, Stirling; no *c. Educ:* Edinburgh Academy; Trinity Coll., Oxford (BA); Edinburgh Univ. (LLB). Admitted WS, 1938. Served RA, 1939-45 (US Bronze Star, 1945). Commanded 278 (City of Edinburgh) Regt RATA, 1948-51; Hon. Colonel, 1961-64. Director: Royal Bank of Scotland Ltd; Scottish American Investment Co. Ltd. *Recreations:* shooting, fishing, golf. *Address:* 79 Ravelston Dykes Road, Edinburgh EH4 3NU. *T:* 031-337 3091. *Clubs:* Caledonian; New (Edinburgh).
                                                      [Died 1 *Jan.* 1979.

OLIVER, Dame Beryl, GBE 1948 (DBE 1920; CBE 1919); RRC 1916; *b* 20 Aug. 1882; *o d* of Francis Edward Carnegy and Mrs Carnegy of Lour, Angus; *m* 1914, Rear-Admiral Henry Francis Oliver, later Admiral of the Fleet Sir Henry Oliver, GCB, KCMG, MVO (*d* 1965). *Educ:* privately, in England and France. St John Ambulance Brigade, 1910; 2nd in Command Joint Women's VAD Dept, BRCS and Order of St John, 1916-18 (RRC, despatches). DStJ 1916. Head of VAD Dept, BRCS, 1919; Director of Education, BRCS, 1946; Archivist, BRCS, 1956. Order of Mercy, 1908; Coronation Medals, 1911 and 1937; Jubilee Medal, 1935. War Medal, 1914-18; Voluntary Medical Service Medal (7 clasps); Civil Defence Medal, 1939-45; Médaille d'Argent de la Croix Rouge Française, 1945. *Publications:* The British Red Cross in Action; The Church of St Mary the Virgin, Aldermanbury. *Address:* 20 South Eaton Place, SW1. *T:* 01-730 7370. *Club:* VAD Ladies'.
                                                      [Died 13 *July* 1972.

OLIVER, Admiral Sir Geoffrey (Nigel), GBE 1955; KCB 1951 (CB 1944); DSO 1941; *b* 22 Jan. 1898; *er s* of late Prof. F. W. Oliver; *m* 1933, Barbara, *o d* of late Sir Francis Jones, KBE, CB; one *s* (and one *s* one *d* decd). *Educ:* Rugby. Cadet, 1915; Mid. and Sub-Lieut, HMS Dreadnought, 1916; HMS Renown, 1917-20; specialised in Gunnery, 1923; HMS Carlisle, China Station, 1925-27; HMS Rodney, 1930-32; Commander, 1932; commanded HMS Diana and HMS Veteran, 1st Destroyer Flotilla, Mediterranean, 1934-36; Captain, 1937; served War of 1939-45 (DSO and two Bars, CB); commanded HMS Hermione, 1940-42, Western Mediterranean, Malta, Madagascar, Eastern Mediterranean; Commodore, 2nd class, 1942; Senior Officer Inshore Squadron, North Africa, 1942-43; British Assault Force Commander, Salerno, 1943; Commodore, 1st class, 1944; Commander, Force J, Assault Force, Normandy, 1944; 21st Aircraft Carrier Squadron, 1944-45; Rear-Admiral, 1945; Admiral (Air), 1946; a Lord Comr of the Admiralty and Asst Chief of Naval Staff, 1947-48; Vice-Admiral, 1949; President, RN Coll., Greenwich, 1948-50; Commander-in-Chief, East Indies Station, 1950-52; Admiral, 1952; Commander-in-Chief, the Nore, 1953-55; retired, Dec. 1955. *Address:* Batts, Henfield, West Sussex.   *[Died* 26 *May* 1980.

OLIVER, Henry John Callard, BSc; Assistant Master, Kingsmead School, Hoylake, since 1974; Member, Headmasters' Association; *b* 28 April 1915; *s* of late H. J. Oliver, Master Mariner, Wallington, Surrey; *m* 1939, Megan Eluned, *d* of late D. J. Edwards; two *s* one *d. Educ:* Sutton County School; King's Coll., London. 1st class Hons Physics, 1936. Physics Master, St Paul's Sch., 1936; Scientific Officer, MAP, 1940; Senior Science Master, Warwick Sch., 1951; Headmaster, Maidenhead Grammar Sch., 1954; Headmaster, Wallasey Grammar Sch., 1960; Headmaster, Northampton Grammar Sch., 1965-74. *Recreation:* dinghy sailing. *Address:* Hesny, 88 Birkenhead Road, Meols, Wirral, Merseyside. *T:* Hoylake 4203.
                                                      [Died 1 *March* 1978.

OLIVER, Prof. Raymond; Professor of Medical Physics, University of London, at Royal Postgraduate Medical School,

since 1971; *b* 14 Jan. 1921; *s* of Laurence F. Oliver, Birmingham, teacher; *m* 1945, Lucy Leslie Williams; two *s. Educ:* Town and County Sch., Northampton; London Univ. (Battersea Polytechnic). BSc Gen. 1940, BSc Special Physics 1945, MSc 1951, London; MA 1961 (Keble); DSc Oxon 1970. FInstP, FIEE, FIBiol. National Physical Laboratory, Teddington, 1938-45; Physicist, London Hosp., 1945-50; Chief Physicist, Churchill Hosp., Oxford, 1950-71. FRSocMed. *Publications:* (with L. A. W. Kemp) Basic Physics in Radiology, 1959; Radiation Physics in Radiology, 1966; Principles of the Use of Radio-isotope Tracers in Clinical and Research Investigations, 1971; papers in Brit. Jl of Radiology, Physics in Medicine and Biology, Nature, Health Physics, etc. *Address:* 46 Pitts Road, Headington, Oxford. *T:* Oxford 61506.   *[Died* 5 *March* 1976.

OLIVER, Vice-Admiral Robert Don, CB 1948; CBE 1942; DSC 1918; DL; *b* 17 March 1895; *s* of Colonel William James Oliver, CBE, and Margaret Christie Don; *m* 1928, Torfrida Lois Acantha Huddart (*d* 1961); no *c; m* 1965, Mrs M. J. Glendinning van der Velde. *Educ:* Osborne and Dartmouth Naval Colleges. Commander, 1930; Captain, 1936; Commanded: HMS Iron Duke, 1939; HMS Devonshire, 1940-42; HMS Excellent, 1943; HMS Swiftsure, 1944; Rear-Admiral, 1945; Asst Chief of Naval Staff (Weapons), 1945-46; Dep. Chief of Naval Staff, 1946-47; Flag Officer Commanding 5th Cruiser Squadron, 1947-48; Vice-Admiral, retired list, 1948. DL Roxburghshire, 1962. *Address:* Lochside House, Kelso, Roxburghshire. *T:* Yetholm 275.   *[Died* 6 *Oct.* 1980.

OLIVIER, George B.; *see* Borg Olivier.

OLORENSHAW, Leslie; Deputy Chairman, Taylor Woodrow Ltd, since 1967; Chairman: Westview Investment Corporation Ltd, Canada; Octavius Atkinson & Sons Ltd; Taylor Woodrow Homes Ltd; *b* 16 Feb. 1912; *m* 1939, Gladys Beatrice Dean; one *s.* Director: Taylor Woodrow International Ltd; Taylor Woodrow of Canada Ltd; Monarch Investments Ltd, Canada. Formerly Deputy Chairman, BNEC Africa Cttee. *Address:* 27 Linksway, Northwood, Middlesex. *T:* Northwood 24643.
                                                      [Died 20 *Aug.* 1972.

OLSON, Sven Olof; His Honour Judge Olson; a Circuit Judge since 1972 (Judge of County Courts, 1971); *b* 22 July 1916; *s* of late Sven Ragnar Olson and Elsa Juliana Olson; unmarried. *Educ:* Mill Hill Sch.; Balliol Coll., Oxford (MA). Called to Bar, Middle Temple, 1938; Bencher, 1968. Served War, 1941-46: 2nd Lieut, Oxf. and Bucks LI, 1941; Captain, Intell. Corps, 1943. *Address:* 21 Well Walk, NW3 1BY. *T:* 01-435 9928; 9 Knighton Lane, Broadmayne, Dorchester, Dorset. *Club:* Travellers'.
                                                      [Died 22 *April* 1977.

O'MALLEY, Rt. Hon. Brian Kevin, PC 1975; MP (Lab) Rotherham since March 1963; Minister of State, Department of Health and Social Security, since 1974; *b* 22 Jan. 1930; *s* of Frank and Eva O'Malley, Mexborough, Yorks; *m* 1959, Kathleen Sylvia Curtiss; one *d. Educ:* Mexborough Grammar Sch.; University of Manchester. BA (Hons) History, 1952; Teaching Diploma, 1953. Assistant Government Whip, 1964-66; Dep. Chief Govt Whip and a Lord Comr of the Treasury, 1967-69; Parly Under-Sec. of State, Dept of Health and Social Security, 1969-70; Opposition Spokesman on Pensions and Social Security, 1970-74. *Recreations:* walking, music. *Address:* 29 Hall Avenue, Mexborough, South Yorks. *T:* Mexborough 3535.   *[Died* 6 *April* 1976.

O'MALLEY, Sir Owen St Clair, KCMG 1943 (CMG 1927); *b* 4 May 1887; *s* of late Sir Edward O'Malley; *m* 1913, Mary Dolling (*see* Ann Bridge), *d* of James Harris Sanders; two *d* (one *s* decd). *Educ:* Hillbrow, Rugby; Radley; Magdalen Coll., Oxford (MA). Entered Foreign Office, 1911; Counsellor HBM Legation, Peking, 1925; Counsellor, Foreign Office, 1933-37; Envoy Extraordinary and Minister Plenipotentiary to the United States of Mexico, 1937-38; in charge of British Embassy to Spain at St Jean de Luz, 1938-39; British Minister to Hungary, 1939-41; British Ambassador to Poland, 1942-45; British Ambassador to Portugal, 1945-47; retired from Foreign Service, 1947. *Publications:* The Phantom Caravan, 1954; historical articles in Journal of Galway Archæological and Historical Society, 1950, 1951, 1952. *Address:* 27 Charlbury Road, Oxford.
                                                      [Died 16 *April* 1974.

OMAN, Carola Mary Anima, (Lady Lenanton), CBE 1957; FSA; FRSL; FRHistS; Writer; *b* 11 May 1897; *d* of late Sir Charles Oman, KBE, *m* 1922, Sir Gerald Lenanton (*d* 1952). *Educ:* Wychwood Sch., Oxford. Served BRCS, 1916-19 and 1938-58 (Co. President, Hertfordshire Branch, 1947-58). *Publications:* The Menin Road (poetry); Britain Against Napoleon (history); Ayot Rectory; *historical novels:* The Road Royal; Princess

Amelia; Crouchback; The Empress; King Heart; Major Grant; The Best of His Family; Over the Water; Miss Barrett's Elopement; *children's books:* Ferry the Fearless; Robin Hood; Johel; Alfred, King of the English; Baltic Spy; *historical biographies:* Prince Charles Edward; Henrietta Maria; Elizabeth of Bohemia; Nelson (awarded Sunday Times annual prize for English literature, 1948); Sir John Moore (James Tait Black Memorial Prize for biography, 1953); David Garrick, 1958; Mary of Modena, 1962; Napoleon's Viceroy; Eugène de Beauharnais, 1966; The Gascoyne Heiress, Diaries of 2nd Marchioness of Salisbury, 1968; The Wizard of the North: The Life of Sir Walter Scott, 1973; *autobiography:* An Oxford Childhood 1892-1914, 1976. *Address:* Bride Hall, Welwyn, Hertfordshire AL6 9DB. *T:* Wheathampstead 3160. *Club:* VAD Ladies. *[Died 11 June 1978.*

OMMANNEY, Francis Downes; *b* 22 April 1903; *s* of Francis Frederick Ommanney and Olive Caroline Owen; unmarried. *Educ:* Aldenham Sch.; Royal College of Science. ARCS, PhD (London), FLS, FRSL, FRSA. Polar Medal (Bronze), 1942. Lecturer in Zoology, Queen Mary Coll., 1926-29; Scientific Staff of Discovery Cttee, 1929-39; RNVR, 1940-46; British Council, 1946-47; Mauritius-Seychelles Fisheries Survey, 1947-49; Colonial Research Service, 1951-57; Reader in Marine Biology in the Univ. of Hong Kong, 1957-60. *Publications: scientific:* Discovery Reports, 1932, 1933, 1936; Colonial Office Fishery Publications, Vol. I, Nos 3, and 18; *non-scientific:* South Latitude, 1938; North Cape, 1939; The House in the Park, 1944; The Ocean, 1949; The Shoals of Capricorn, 1952; Isle of Cloves, 1955; Eastern Windows, 1960; Fragrant Harbour, 1962; A Draught of Fishes, 1965; The River Bank, 1966; Collecting Sea Shells, 1968; Lost Leviathan: Whales and Whaling, 1971. *Club:* Travellers'. *[Died 30 June 1980.*

ONASSIS, Aristotle Socrates; shipowner; company director; pioneer in super-tanker construction; *b* Smyrna, Ionia, 1906, an Argentine subject of Greek origin; *s* of Socrates and Penelope Onassis; *m* 1946, Athina (Tina) Livanos (marr. diss., 1961; she *d* 1974); one *d* (one *s* decd); *m* 1968, Mrs Jacqueline Lee Kennedy, widow of John F. Kennedy. *Educ:* Evangeliki Scholi, Smyrna. Aged 16 left Smyrna for Greece as refugee; emigrated to Buenos Aires, 1923; revived family tobacco business; later, became Greek Consul in Buenos Aires. Negotiated purchase of his first ships in Canada, 1932-33; ordered his first tanker in Sweden, 1936; has built numerous super-tankers in USA, France, Germany and Japan since 1945; also bulk carriers in Japan; and now has under construction several other ships. Whaling fleet sold to Japanese, 1956; among other businesses, founded Olympic Airways, a Greek company, 1957. Dag Hammarskjoeld Gold Medal for Industrial Merit, 1969. *Recreations:* nautical sports (owner yacht Christina). *Address:* 1668 Alvear Avenue, Buenos Aires, Argentina; c/o Olympic Maritime, SA, 17 Avenue d'Ostende, Monaco.
[Died 15 March 1975.

O'NEILL, Sir (Matthew) John, Kt 1971; CBE 1968; BA, LLB; FAIM; Chairman, City Mutual Life Assurance Society, since 1960; *b* 19 June 1914; *s* of Matthew John O'Neill. *Educ:* St Ignatius Coll., Sydney; Sydney Univ. Solicitor, 1938. Served War of 1939-45, AIF. Senr Partner, Murphy & Moloney, Solicitors; Chairman: Boral Ltd; City Mutual Life Assurance Soc.; City Mutual General Insurance Ltd; Vice-Chm., Trans City Ltd; Director: Bank of New South Wales; ICI Australia Ltd. Vice-Chm., United Charities Fund; Hon. Treasurer, Civic Reform Assoc. of Sydney; Chm., Lewisham Hosp. Adv. Bd. Trustee, Nat. Parks and Wildlife Foundn, NSW. KCSG 1971; Kt of Malta, 1976. *Recreations:* golf, travel, theatre. *Address:* 60 Hunter Street, Sydney, NSW 2000, Australia; Glencourt, 19 Sutherland Crescent, Darling Point, NSW 2027. *Clubs:* Australian Golf, Elanora Country, American National, Tattersall's (Sydney). *[Died 30 June 1976.*

O'NEILL, Michael; *b* 7 Oct. 1909; *s* of Michael and Sarah O'Neill; *m* 1936, Kathleen O'Connor, Ballinasloe, Co. Galway; three *s* three *d*. *Educ:* Dromore NS; Bellisle Academy. Draper's Asst, 1923-29; Haulage Contractor, 1929-31; Tillage Contractor, 1931-45; Farmer, 1945-52. Mem. Exec. Ulster Farmers' Union, 1945-48; Exec. Irish Anti-Partition League, 1946-57; Omagh RDC, 1945-57; Tyrone CC, 1950-57; Tyrone Co. Educ. Cttee, 1950-52; Tyrone Co. Health Cttee, 1950-52; Tyrone Co. Welfare Cttee, 1950-52; Entertainments Officer, Tyrone and Fermanagh Hosp., 1960-74. MP (Irish Republican) Mid-Ulster, 1951-55. *Recreations:* amateur dramatics, Gaelic football. *Address:* 24 Centenary Park, Omagh, Co. Tyrone, N Ireland. *T:* Omagh 2461. *[Died 4 Oct. 1976.*

O'NIEL, Colette; *see* Malleson, Lady Constance.

ONIONS, Mrs Oliver; *see* Ruck, Berta.

ONSAGER, Prof. Lars; Distinguished University Professor, Center for Theoretical Studies, University of Miami, since 1972; *b* Oslo, Norway, 27 Nov. 1903; *s* of Erling Onsager and Ingrid Onsager (*née* Kirkeby); *m* 1933, Margarete Arledter; three *s* one *d*. *Educ:* Norges Tekniske Högskole, Trondheim, Norway; Eidgenössische Technische Hochschule, Zürich, Switzerland; Yale Univ. (PhD). Went to USA, 1928 (naturalised, 1945). Associate in Chemistry, Johns Hopkins Univ., 1928; Instr in Chem., Brown Univ., 1928-33; Sterling and Gibbs Fellow, Yale Univ., 1933-34; Asst Prof. of Chem., Yale, 1934-40; Associate Prof., 1940-45; J. Willard Gibbs Prof. of Theoretical Chem., 1945-72. Fulbright Scholar, Cambridge, England, 1951. Visiting Prof. in US and abroad. In 1931, he showed that past-future symmetry of the laws which govern molecular motion implies a set of reciprocal relations for coupled irreversible processes; the reasoning as much as the results proved helpful in the subsequent development of kinetic theories. Among other consequences, he clarified the status of Kelvin's theory (1851) for thermoelectric phenomena and Rayleigh's "principle of the least dissipation of energy", and he showed just how far these could be generalized. Hon. DSc Oxon, 1971. Rumford Medal, 1953; Lorentz Medal, 1958; G. N. Lewis Medal 1962; John G. Kirkwood Medal, 1962; Willard Gibbs Medal, 1962; T. W. Richards Medal, 1964; Debye Award, 1965; Belfer Award, 1966; Nat. Science Medal, 1968. Nobel Chemistry Prize for 1968. FAAAS; Fellow, Amer. Phys. Soc.; Member: Amer. Philos. Soc.; Amer. Chem. Soc.; Nat. Acad. of Sciences, and of many other institutions in the USA and abroad; Foreign Mem., Royal Society, 1975. Holds hon. doctorates in science and technology. *Publications:* contrib. articles to learned jls on: electrical properties of ice, crystal statistics, electrolytes, dipole moments in liquids, reciprocal relations in irreversible processes, etc. *Address:* Center for Theoretical Studies, University of Miami, PO Box 249055, Coral Gables, Fla 33124, USA; (home) 4851 Biltmore Drive, Coral Gables, Fla 33146.
[Died 5 Oct. 1976.

ONSLOW, 6th Earl of, *cr* 1801; **William Arthur Bampfylde Onslow,** KBE 1960; MC; TD 1949; Bt 1660; Baron Onslow, 1716; Baron Cranley, 1776; Viscount Cranley, 1801; Colonel RAC (Yeomanry); late Lt Life Guards; Captain of HM Bodyguard of the Yeomen of the Guard, 1951-60; Asst Chief Conservative Whip in House of Lords, 1951-60; High Steward of Guildford; *b* 11 June 1913; *e s* of 5th Earl of Onslow, PC, GBE; *S* father 1945; *m* 1st, 1936, Hon. Pamela Dillon (marriage dissolved, 1962), *o d* of 19th Viscount Dillon, CMG, DSO; one *s* one *d*; 2nd, 1962, Nina Sturdee, MBE, *y d* of Thomas P. Sturdee. *Educ:* Winchester; Royal Military College. Served Middle East, 1941-43 (MC); Italy, 1943; Normandy, 1944 (prisoner). Member: LCC, 1940-49; Surrey CC, 1949-52; Chm., Surrey Agricultural Exec. Cttee, 1956-58. CStJ. *Publication:* Men and Sand, 1961. *Heir: s* Viscount Cranley. *Address:* Temple Court, Clandon Park, Guildford. *Clubs:* Beefsteak, Brooks's, Royal Yacht Squadron. *[Died 3 June 1971.*

ONSLOW, Sir Geoffrey Henry H.; *see* Hughes-Onslow.

ONSLOW, Adm. Sir Richard (George), KCB 1958 (CB 1954); DSO 1942 (1st and 2nd Bars, 1942, 3rd Bar, 1944); DL; *b* 15 April 1904; *e s* of Major G. A. Onslow, and the late Mrs Onslow; *m* 1932, Kathleen Meriel Taylor, *er d* of late E. C. Taylor, JP; two *s*. *Educ:* RN Colleges Osborne and Dartmouth. Entered RN, 1918. Served in destroyers almost continuously from 1926 until end of War of 1939-45. Staff College, 1935. Commander, 1938; Plans Division, Admiralty, 1939; HMS Ashanti, 1941; Capt. 1942; HMS Osprey, 1943; Capt. (D) Fourth Dest. Flot. in HMS Quilliam, 1944; idc 1946; Senior Naval Officer, Northern Ireland, 1947; Dir Tactical Div. Naval Staff, 1948; HMS Devonshire, 1951; Rear-Adm., 1952; Naval Secretary to First Lord of the Admiralty, 1952-54; Vice-Adm., 1955; Flag Officer (Flotillas), Home Fleet, 1955-56; Flag Officer Comdg, Reserve Fleet, 1956-57; Admiral, 1958; Commander-in-Chief, Plymouth, Feb. 1958-Nov. 1960. DL Salop, 1962. *Recreations:* country pursuits. *Address:* Ryton Grove, Dorrington, Shrewsbury.
[Died 16 Dec. 1975.

OPIE, Air Vice-Marshal William Alfred, CB 1955; CBE 1951; retired; *b* 4 Dec. 1901; *s* of late William Opie, Redruth, Cornwall; *m* 1950, Phyllis Constance Chalk, *d* of late Frederick George Crampton, Sissinghurst, Kent. *Educ:* RAF College, Cranwell. Flying Duties and Engineer Staff Duties, 1923-36; RAF Staff College, 1937; Comdg No 2 Sqdn, 1938; Comdg No 18 Sqdn, 1939; Engineer Staff Duties, HQ Bomber Comd, 1940; Dep. Dir Repair & Maintenance (Aircraft), Min. of Aircraft Prod., 1941; Dir Servicing and Maintenance, Air Min., 1944; Comdg RAF Station, St Athan, 1947; STSO, Far East Air

Force, 1948; Base Comdr, RAF Maintenance Base, Far East Air Force, Seletar, Singapore, 1951-52; Assistant Controller of Aircraft, Ministry of Supply, 1953-56; AOC No 41 Gp, RAF, 1956-59. *Address:* Santa Eulalia Del Rio, Ibiza, Baleares. *Club:* Royal Air Force.   *[Died 14 Oct. 1977.*

ORBACH, Maurice; MP (Lab) Stockport South since 1964; General Secretary Trades Advisory Council since 1940; *b* 13 July 1902; *s* of late Hiam M. and Millicent Orbach, Cardiff and New York; *m* 1935, Ruth Beatrice Huebsch; one *s* one *d. Educ:* Cardiff; New York City. Engineer. Member St Pancras Board of Guardians, 1924; Member, South West St Pancras, LLC, 1937-46; MP (Lab) Willesden East, 1945-Sept. 1959. Governor, Central Foundation Schools; Mem. London Town Planning Committee; Governor, St Paul's, St Peter's, St Barts and St Philip's Hospitals, 1969-; Chm., British Emigrants Families Assoc. Lecturer on Industry and Commerce and the American Scene. *Publication:* Mission to Madrid, Austria, 1946. *Address:* 76 Eton Hall, Eton College Road, NW3. *T:* 01-722 4696, 01-452 8287.   *[Died 24 April 1979.*

ORCHIN, Frederick Joseph, CB 1948; OBE 1941; FCIT; *b* 28 May 1885. Late Under Secretary Ministry of Transport; Chief Financial Officer, Road Haulage Exec., BTC, 1948-50; Deputy Chairman, Road Haulage Disposal Board, 1953-56. *Address:* 2 Raith Avenue, N14. *T:* 01-886 2366.   *[Died 20 Dec. 1971.*

ORD JOHNSTONE, Morris Mackintosh, CB 1960; Chairman, Tobacco Advisory Committee, 1968-77; Independent Member, Home Grown Timber Advisory Committee; *b* 10 Oct. 1907; *s* of late James Ord Johnstone and Emily Morrison; *m* 1935, Violet Springett; one *d. Educ:* Uppingham; Wadham Coll., Oxford. Board of Trade, 1941-67; Under-Secretary, 1955-67. *Address:* 5 Campden Grove, W8. *T:* 01-937 7654.   *[Died 26 Sept. 1978.*

ORDE, Sir Charles William, KCMG 1940 (CMG 1931); *b* 25 Oct. 1884; *s* of late William Orde, DL, of Nunnykirk, Morpeth, Northumberland; *m* 1914, Frances Fortune (*d* 1949), *o d* of James Davidson, Dunedin, New Zealand; two *s* two *d. Educ:* Eton; King's College, Cambridge. Minister to Baltic States, 1938-40; Ambassador to Chile, 1940-45. *Recreations:* fishing, music. *Address:* Nunnykirk, Morpeth, Northumberland NE61 4PB. *T:* Hartburn 250.   *[Died 7 June 1980.*

ORDE, Sir Percy Lancelot, Kt 1941; CIE 1927; retired; formerly Inspector-General of Police, Punjab; *b* 19 Jan. 1888; *s* of Col W. Orde, Nunnykirk, Northumberland; *m* 1st, Noëlle, *d* of Lt-Col A. C. Elliott; 2nd Eileen, *d* of Edward Probst; one *s* two *d. Educ:* Malvern. *Recreations:* fishing, racing. *Address:* Aldings, Wherwell, Andover, Hants. *T:* Chilbolton 316.   *[Died 18 March 1975.*

ORDE, Brig. Reginald John, CBE 1945; QC (Dominion); Commander Order of Orange-Nassau (Netherlands); formerly Judge Advocate-General, Department of National Defence, Canada; *b* 15 May 1893; *s* of late Hon. Mr Justice J. F. Orde and Edith C. M. Orde; *m* 1919, Dorothy Cook; no *c. Educ:* Ashbury College; Univ. of Toronto, Osgoode Hall Law School. Royal Artillery and Royal Canadian Artillery, European War; Service in France, Mesopotamia, India, Canada; Assistant Judge Advocate-General, 1918; attended Imperial Defence College, London, 1931. KC (Dominion), 1950. CD (with 2 clasps), 1950; retired from Cdn Army, 1951. KStJ; Legal Adviser, Priory of Canada. *Recreations:* golf, fishing. *Address:* 425 Daly Avenue, Ottawa, Canada. *Clubs:* Rideau (Ottawa); University (Toronto).   *[Died 3 June 1975.*

ORENSTEIN, Maj.-Gen. Alexander Jeremiah, CB 1943; CMG 1919; CBE 1941; LLD (Hon.); DSc; MD; MRCS, FRCP; FRSH; late Director of Pneumoconiosis Research, South African Council of Scientific and Industrial Research; Hon. Fellow: Royal Society of Tropical Medicine and Hygiene; Institute of Water Pollution Control; RSocMed; Emeritus Fellow, American College of Chest Physicians; Fellow, American Public Health Association; Hon. Member, South African Institute of Mechanical Engineers, 1967; Chevalier Ordre de la Couronne, Belgium; Medical Consultant, Rand Mines Ltd; Gold Medallist, Medical Association of South Africa (BMA); Gold Medal: Institute of Mining and Metallurgy; Mine Medical Officers, 1968; Bernard Nocht Medal (for services to tropical medicine) 1965; *b* 26 September 1879; *m* 1916, Kate Bradbury; one *d*. Acting Director of Medical Services, Col, S African Medical Corps, 1917-19. Panama Canal Medical Services, 1905-12; Special Work in East Africa, 1913-14; Belgian Congo and S West Africa Mandated Territory; Director of Medical Services, East Africa, 1940-41 (CBE); Director of Medical Services UDF in Middle East (despatches, CB), 1941; Director-General of Medical Services, Union of S Africa

Defence Force, 1939, and again 1943-Sept. 1945; Delegate to International Labour Conference, Geneva, 1925 and 1928; late President, Federal Council Medical Association of South Africa (BMA); Vice-Pres. and Fellow British Medical Assoc.; Union Leprosy Advisory Council; several other Govt Councils and Cttees; Committee on Industrial Hygiene, International Labour Office; late President Associated Scientific and Technical Societies of South Africa; late President South African Red Cross Society. Fellow, SA Inst. of Mining and Metallurgy. *Publications:* Numerous professional. *Address:* PO Box 1032, Johannesburg, SA. *Clubs:* Rand, Transvaal Automobile, Scientific and Technical (Johannesburg).   *[Died 6 July 1972.*

ORGILL, Tyrrell Churton, CIE 1937; MA; Flight Lieutenant, late RAFVR; late Indian Educational Service; *b* 7 June 1884; *s* of Bernard Churton Orgill; *m* 1910, Josephine (*d* 1971), *d* of W. T. Scruby, Cambridge; one *s* one *d* (and one *s* decd). *Educ:* Dulwich College; Trinity College, Cambridge. Entered Indian Educational Service, 1913; served European War, 1915-21, NWFP of India, German East Africa, and as political officer in Mesopotamia; Provincial Commissioner Scouts Association, NWFP, 1931; Director of Public Instruction, NW Frontier Province, India, 1931-39; retired, 1939. *Recreations:* gardening and sailing. *Address:* The Anchorage, Summercove, Kinsale, Co. Cork, Eire.   *[Died 27 March 1975.*

ORMEROD, Rt. Hon. Sir Benjamin, PC 1957; Kt 1948; *b* 7 Sept. 1890; *er s* of John Aspden Ormerod, JP, North Bank, Blackburn; *m* 1916, Kathleen May Carter (*d* 1968); one *s* two *d. Educ:* Queen Elizabeth's Grammar Sch., Blackburn; Manchester Univ. Hon. LLD Manchester Univ., 1949. Solicitor, 1913. Called to bar, Lincoln's Inn, 1924; Northern Circuit: Judge of County Courts, Circuit No 14 jointly with His Hon. Judge Stewart, 1944-46; Circuit No 5, 1946-48; Bencher of Lincoln's Inn, 1948; Judge of High Court of Justice, Probate, Divorce and Admiralty Division, 1948, King's Bench Division, 1950-57; Lord Justice of Appeal, 1957-63. Vice-President and Hon. Fellow, Royal Academy of Music. Served 4th Batt. East Lancs Regt, Sept. 1914-Jan. 1919, Captain. *Address:* 16 Old Buildings, Lincoln's Inn, WC2. *T:* 01-405 1325.   *[Died 21 Sept. 1974.*

ORMOND, Maj.-Gen. Daniel Mowat, CMG 1919; DSO 1917; Canadian Infantry; Barrister-at-Law; Permanent Force Reserve, Ottawa, Canada; *b* Pembroke, Ontario, 1885; *s* of Daniel Ormond and Frances Hudson; *m* 1910, Ann Laura, *d* of J. O. Cadham; one *s* four *d*. Served European War, 1915-18 (wounded, despatches three times, CMG, DSO and bar, Russian Order of St Stanislas with swords, Croix de Guerre). *Address:* 80 Rideau Terrace, Apartment 55, Ottawa 2, Ontario. *Clubs:* Larimac (Quebec), etc.   *[Died 19 Nov. 1974.*

ORMONDE, 6th Marquess of, *cr* 1825; **James Arthur Norman Butler,** CVO 1960; MC 1918; Lieut-Colonel, retired; Earl of Ormonde *cr* 1328; Earl of Ossory, 1526; Viscount Thurles, 1537; Baron Ormonde (UK), 1821; 30th Hereditary Chief Butler of Ireland; High Steward of Wokingham, 1956; *b* 25 April 1893; *yr s* of 4th Marquess and Ellen (*d* 1951), *d* of General Anson Stager, US Army; *S* brother, 1949; *m* 1924, Jessie, (*d* 1969), *y d* of late Charles Carlos Clarke, of Welton, Sunninghill; two *d. Educ:* Harrow; RMC, Sandhurst. Commanded 17th/21st Lancers, 1931-35; served European War, 1914-19; re-employed, 1940-45. HM Hon. Corps of Gentlemen-at-Arms, 1936-63, Lieut, 1957-63. DL Kent, 1952-56. *Heir: cousin,* James Hubert Theobald Charles Butler, MBE [*b* 19 April 1899; *m* 1935, Nan, *d* of Garth Gilpin; two *d*]. *Address:* Cantley, Wokingham, Berks. *T:* Wokingham 107. *Clubs:* Cavalry, St James'; Kildare Street (Dublin).   *[Died 17 April 1971.*

O'RORKE, (Edward) Brian, RA 1956 (ARA 1947); MA (Cantab); FRIBA; RDI 1939 (Master of the Faculty, 1961-63); Architect; *b* New Zealand, 14 June 1901; *s* of E. Dennis and Amy O'Rorke; *m* 1929, Juliet Wigan; one *s* three *d. Educ:* Wellington Coll., Berks; Jesus Coll., Cambridge; Architectural Association School of Architecture. Dawnay Scholar and Bronze Medallist, RIBA, 1926. Work includes interiors of passenger liners, aircraft and trains; Orient Line Building, Sydney, Australia (RIBA Bronze Medal, 1947); Port Line Building, Sydney, Australia; Agriculture Building, Festival of Britain; New Royal Observatory Buildings, Hurstmonceux; Office Building, Three Quays, Tower Hill (Civic Trust Award for City of London, 1961); new Berkeley Hotel, Knightsbridge; university buildings, factories, houses, etc. *Address:* Rock House, River Common, Petworth, Sussex. *TA* and *T:* Lodsworth 243. *Clubs:* Athenæum, Arts, Leander.   *[Died 1 March 1974.*

O'RORKE, Lt-Col Frederick Charles, CMG 1916; resigned appointment in Gibraltar, 1941, owing to War conditions; *b* 16 April 1879; *m* Dorothy Violet (*d* 1963), 2nd *d* of late J. Whitaker, Rainworth Lodge, Notts; one *s*. *Educ:* Nottingham High Sch.; Royal Veterinary Coll., London. Gazetted Royal Army Veterinary Corps, 1904; in India, 1905-10; Remount duty at Arborfield Cross Remount Depôt, near Reading, 1911-14; Executive Veterinary Officer at the Base at beginning of European War; joined HQ 3rd Army Corps, Oct. 1914 (despatches); Dep. Assistant Director of Veterinary Services at Headquarters, Inspector-General of Communications, 1915 (despatches twice, CMG); Assistant Director of Veterinary Services, Headquarters, Guards Division, BEF, 1915; Acting Lieut-Colonel, 1918; commanding No. 8 Veterinary Hospital, British Army of Rhine, 1919; Principal, Army Veterinary Sch., Ambala, 1920; Dep. Assistant Director of Veterinary Services, AH, India, 1921; Principal, Army Veterinary Sch., Poona, 1922-25; Aldershot Command, 1926; Lieut-Colonel, 1931; ADVS Northern Command 1931-34; retired pay, 1934; re-employed as VO in charge RHA Newport (Mon.), 1937; Government Veterinary Officer, Gibraltar, 1937-41. *Address:* Oatlands Park Hotel, Weybridge, Surrey. *[Died 27 April* 1976.

ORR, John Boyd; *see* Boyd Orr, Baron.

ORR, Sir Samuel, Kt 1953; builder and engineering contractor, retired; *b* 1886; *s* of late William Orr, Londonderry; *m* 1907, Annie, *d* of William Henry Platt; three *s* three *d*. *Educ:* First Derry PE Sch. Mem., Corp. of Londonderry, 1938- (Mayor, 1952-53). Chm., Londonderry Welfare Cttee; Member: NW Gp Hosps Cttee; NI Superannuation Cttee; Borough Welfare Cttee. Formerly JP City of Londonderry. *Address:* Orrington, 7 Rossdowney Park, Londonderry. *Club:* Northern Counties (Londonderry). *[Died 13 Aug.* 1972.

ORR-LEWIS, Sir (John) Duncan, 2nd Bt, *cr* 1920; Major RASC; *s* of 1st Bt and Maud Helen, *o d* of William Booth, London, Ontario, Canada; *b* 21 Feb. 1898; *S* father, 1921; *m* 1st, 1921 Marjory (*née* Milne) (*d* 1926); one *d*; 2nd, 1929, Doris Blanche (*née* Lee); 3rd, 1940, Phyllis Ann Maitland (*née* Bibby); 4th, 1950, Anna (*née* Filipoff); 5th, 1965. *Educ:* Eton; Cambridge. Military Service: 10th Army, Persia MEF, 1942-43; 2nd Army, France, Germany, Aug. 1944-45. *Heir:* none. *Address:* 8 rue Du Bois, 77 Cély-en-Bière, France; Ir-Razzett, Malta. *Clubs:* White's; Travellers' (Paris). *[Died 13 Nov.* 1980 (*ext*).

ORTCHESON, Sir John, Kt 1967; CBE 1954; Judge of the High Court of Judicature, Lahore, Pakistan, 1954-65; *b* 6 Dec. 1905; *s* of Robert Inches Ortcheson; *m* 1933, Norah Eileen, *d* of late Frank A. Connor; two *d*. *Educ:* Perth Academy; Edinburgh University (MA 1928); Cambridge Univ.; Sorbonne, Paris. Legal Advr, W Pakistan Water and Power Develt Authority, 1966-71. Coronation Medal, 1953. *Recreation:* golf. *Address:* 10 Stileman Way, Sharnbrook, Bedford MK44 1HX. *[Died 5 Sept.* 1977.

ORTON, Prof. Harold; Emeritus Professor of English Language and Medieval English Literature, University of Leeds (Professor, 1946-64); *b* 1898; *y s* of Thomas Orton and Emily Blair, Byers Green, Co. Durham; *m* 1925, *y d* of Rev. R. Burnham, Trimley St Mary's Rectory, Suffolk; one *d*. *Educ:* King James I Grammar Sch., Bishop Auckland; Hatfield Coll., University of Durham; Merton Coll., Oxford; Royal University of Uppsala, Sweden. BA 1921, University Research Schol. in English Philology, 1922, BLitt 1923, MA 1924, Oxford. Lektor in English, University of Uppsala, 1924-28; Lecturer in English, King's Coll., Newcastle upon Tyne in the University of Durham, 1928-39, and Senior Research Fellow, 1938-39; Lecturer in charge of Dept of English Language, University of Sheffield, 1939-46; Dep. Education Director, British Council, 1942-44 and Acting Education Director, 1944-45; Dean of Faculty of Arts, Leeds, 1947-49; Chairman, Board of Faculties of Arts, Economics and Commerce and Law, Leeds Univ., 1954-56. Visiting Lecturer, Summer Session, College of Literature, Science and the Arts, University of Michigan, 1954; Visiting Professor: Kansas and Michigan Universities, 1965; Iowa Univ., 1966, 1969; Kansas Univ., 1967, 1968; Tennessee Univ., Knoxville, 1970, 1972, 1973; Belmont Coll., Nashville, Tenn, 1971. Lieut, the DLI (TF), 1917-19 (severely wounded 1918, invalided 1919). Re-commissioned General List (TA), 1940; Acting Captain and Comdg Officer, Sheffield Univ. Sen. Training Centre, 1945-46. Consultant Member, BBC's Advisory Cttee on Spoken English, 1934-40; Member British Council's Advisory Cttee on English Overseas, 1940-44; President, Yorkshire Society for Celtic Studies, 1951-53; Hon. Member: Linguistic Society of America, 1964; Linguistic Soc. of Canada, 1965. Fil. Dr hc Univ. of Uppsala, 1969; Hon. DLitt Dunelm, 1970. Joint Editor, Trans of Yorkshire Dialect Soc., 1947-61 (Hon. Vice-Pres., 1963-; Hon. Life Mem., 1968-); Joint Editor,

Leeds Studies in English and Kindred Languages, 1952-64. *Publications:* The Phonology of a South Durham Dialect, 1933; (with late W. L. Renwick) The Beginnings of English Literature to Skelton, 1939; (with late Prof. E. Dieth, Zürich) A Questionnaire for a Linguistic Atlas of England, 1952; (with late Prof. E. Dieth, Zürich) Survey of English Dialects, 1962-71; (with Dr W. J. Halliday) The Basic Material of the Six Northern Counties and the Isle of Man, Vol. I, Part 1, 1962, Parts 2 and 3, 1963; (with M. Wakelin) The Basic Material of the Southern Counties, Vol. IV, Parts 1 and 2, 1967, Part 3, 1968; (with M. V. Barry) The Basic Material of the West Midland Counties, Vol. 2, Part 1, 1969, Part 2, 1970, Part 3, 1971; (with P. M. Tilling) The Basic Material of the East Midland Counties and East Anglia, Vol. 3, Part 1, 1969, Part 2, 1970, Part 3, 1971; (with Prof. N. Wright): Questionnaire for the Investigation of American Regional English, 1972, Word Geography of England, 1975; (ed jtly) The Linguistic Atlas of England, 1978 (posthumous publication); various articles on English Language and especially its dialects, in scientific journals. *Recreation:* gardening. *Address:* 11 Harrowby Crescent, Leeds LS16 5HP. *T:* 755451. *[Died 7 March* 1975.

ORTON-JONES, Harry, CBE 1955 (OBE 1948; MBE 1945); Foreign Service, retired; *b* 24 July 1891; *s* of Charles Newborn Jones and Harriet Hemingway; name changed to Orton-Jones, 1963; *m* 1957, Gwendolen Muriel, *e d* of Ernest MacBeath Kidd, Peterhead, Scotland. *Educ:* Bemrose Sch., Derby. Entered Home Civil Service, 1913; Foreign Office, 1914; released for active service, 1917, 2nd Lieut Northants Regt; returned to Foreign Office, 1919; assimilated to Foreign Service, 1946; Counsellor and Consul General, British Embassy, Washington, 1950-57. *Publication:* (with G. M. Orton-Jones) Jonathan Warner, 1728-1810: a man of parts. *Recreations:* music, photography. *Address:* The Barn, Goose Hill Road, Chester, Conn 06412, USA. *[Died 26 Sept.* 1976.

OSBORN, Sir Frederic (James), Kt 1956; Hon. FRTPI; Hon. FRIBA; Hon. Member: American Institute of Planners; Community Planning Association of Canada; Mark Twain Society, USA; President, Town and Country Planning Association; Hon. Vice-President, Royal Town Planning Institute; Vice-President and Hon. Member, International Federation for Housing and Planning; Corresponding Member, Akademie für Raumforschung und Landesplanung, Hannover; *b* 26 May 1885; *e s* of T. F. Osborn; *m* 1st, 1916, Margaret Paterson Robb, Glasgow (*d* 1970); one *s* one *d*; 2nd, 1974, Shirley Catherine Stephens. *Educ:* London private and Council Schools. Estate Manager, Welwyn Garden City, 1919-36; Hon. Sec. and Chm., Town and Country Planning Assoc., 1936-61; Director, Murphy Radio Ltd, 1936-60; Member New Towns Cttee, 1946. Hon. Editor, Town and Country Planning, 1949-65; Chairman, Welwyn Drama Festival, 1929-65. Silver Medal, American Society of Planning Officials, 1960; Gold Medal, Town Planning Institute, 1963; Ebenezer Howard Memorial Medal, 1968. *Publications:* New Towns after the War, 1918, 1942; Green-Belt Cities, 1946, 1969; Can Man Plan? and Other Verses, 1959; New Towns: The Answer to Megalopolis (with A. Whittick), 1963, 1974, 1977; Transatlantic Dialogue (with Lewis Mumford), 1971, etc. *Recreations:* literature, drama, music, gardening, travel. *Address:* 16 Guessens Road, Welwyn Garden City, Herts AL8 6QR. *T:* Welwyn Garden 22317.
[Died 1 Nov. 1978.

OSBORN, Theodore George Bentley, MA, DSc; FIBiol; Professor Emeritus, Oxford and Adelaide Universities; *b* 2 Oct. 1887; *o surv c* of John Ashton Osborn; *m* 1st, 1918, Edith May Kershaw (*d* 1958), Uppermill, Yorks; two *s* (one *s* killed in action); 2nd, 1960, Marjorie Hope Sabine, Adelaide. *Educ:* Burnley Grammar Sch.; University of Manchester. Lecturer in Economic Botany, Manchester Univ., 1908-12; Professor of Botany, Adelaide Univ., and Consulting Botanist to the S Australian Government, 1912-27; Professor of Botany, Sydney Univ., 1928-37; Sherardian Professor of Botany, Oxford Univ., and Fellow of Magdalen Coll., Oxford, 1937-53, Emeritus Fellow, 1970. Member Agricultural Research Council, 1945-49. *Publications:* various scientific, chiefly on fungi and ecology. *Address:* 15a Ayr Avenue, Torrens Park, South Australia 5062, Australia. *[Died 3 June* 1973.

OSBORNE, Lithgow; President, Auburn (NY) Cablevision; *b* 2 April 1892; *s* of Thos Mott Osborne and Agnes Devens; *m* 1918; three *s*. *Educ:* Harvard Class of 1915. US Diplomatic Service, 1915-19 (Berlin, Copenhagen, Paris Peace Conference); Assistant Secretary, General Conference on Disarmament, 1921-22; Editor Auburn (NY) Citizen-Advertiser, 1922-33; Conservation Commissioner, State of New York, 1933-42; Delegate-at-large, NY State Constitutional Convention, 1938; Office of Foreign Relief and Rehabilitation, Washington, 1942-

43; Deputy Director-General, Dept of Services and Areas, UNRRA European Regional Office, 1943-44; American Ambassador to Norway, 1944-46. *Recreation:* fishing. *Address:* 32 Owasco Street, Auburn, NY 13021, USA. *Clubs:* Harvard, Century (NY). *[Died 10 March 1980.*

OSTRER, Isidore; Poet, Economist; Chairman Lothbury Investment Corporation Ltd; Chairman Premier Productions Ltd. Late Senior Partner Ostrer Brothers, Merchant Bankers. Was President and Chairman of Gaumont-British Picture Corporation Ltd for many years. *Publications:* Poems, 1957; Conquest of Gold: Ostrer's Law of Interest; Ostrer's Commodity Gold Standard; Modern Money and Unemployment; has written extensively on economics and general subjects. *Address:* 8/9 Buckingham Place, SW1. *[Died 3 Sept. 1975.*

O'SULLIVAN, Dennis Neil; Stipendiary Magistrate, Kingston-upon-Hull, 1952-72; *b* 20 July 1899; *s* of Dennis O'Sullivan, Barrister-at-Law, late District Judge, Burma, and Laura O'Sullivan; *m* 1926, Eva Stewart, MA, MB, ChB, *d* of A. K. Stewart, Edinburgh; two *s* one *d. Educ:* India; Dulwich College. Barrister, Gray's Inn, 1920; practised at Bar in Prov. of Sind, India, 1921-43. Member Indian Legislative Assembly (Bombay European Non-official), 1932-33; Public Prosecutor and Govt Advocate for Sind, 1937-43; Judge of Chief Court of Sind, 1943-48; Judge, and later Chief Judge, of Control Commission Supreme Court (latterly called Allied High Commission Supreme Court) British Zone, Germany, 1949-52. Served European War, Artists' Rifles, 1917-18 (France); Indian Army, 1940-41; DAAG 10 Ind. Div., 1941. *Address:* Cedar Lodge, 54 Southfield, Hessle, E Yorks. *Club:* Reform.
[Died 15 Feb. 1973.

O'SULLIVAN, Most Rev. Joseph Anthony, DD, LLD; Titular Archbishop of Maraguia; Archbishop of Kingston, Ontario, (RC), 1944-66; retired; *b* Hamilton, Ontario, 29 Nov. 1886. *Educ:* St Jerome's College, Kitchener, Ontario; Grand Seminary, Montreal, PQ. Ordained priest, Hamilton, 1911; consecrated Bishop of Charlottetown, PEI, Hamilton, 1931. Assistant at Pontifical Throne, 1956. *Address:* c/o Archbishop's House, Kingston, Ontario, Canada. *[Died 6 June 1972.*

OTTAWAY, Prof. Christopher Wyndham, PhD, FRCVS; Research Professor of Veterinary Science, University of Bristol, 1973-75, now Emeritus; Chairman, Board of Veterinary Studies, 1955-59, 1965-67; *b* 6 June 1910; 3rd *s* of W. H. Ottaway; *m* 1938, Grace, *d* of E. Luckin, JP; two *s* one *d. Educ:* Owen's Sch.; Roy. Vet. Coll., London; King's College, Cambridge (Senior Wellcome Scholar). Veterinary Practitioner, 1931-34; Department of Anatomy, Royal Veterinary College, London: Demonstrator, 1934-38; Lecturer, 1938-41; Reader, 1941-45; Wellcome Scholar, 1945-48; Lecturer in Zoology, Cambridge University, 1949; Prof of Veterinary Anat., Bristol Univ., 1949-73. *Publications:* ed, Anatomy of the Horse (1938 edn); Locomotion, in Phys. Farm Animals (ed Hammond), 1955; scientific papers. *Recreations:* music, walking. *Address:* 59 High Kingsdown, Bristol BS2 8EP. *T:* Bristol 23330.
[Died 14 Feb. 1978.

OTTER-BARRY, Rt. Rev. Hugh Van Lynden, CBE 1951; Assistant Bishop to the Bishop of Peterborough since 1960; Vicar of Norton and Rector of Whilton since 1960; *b* 7 March 1887; 5th *s* of Robert Melvil Barry Otter-Barry, Horkesley Hall, Colchester. *Educ:* Marlborough; Trinity College, Cambridge; Wells Theological Coll. BA 1908 (2nd class Classical Tripos); MA 1912; ordained, 1910; curate of St Luke, Chelsea, 1910-15; Charleville Bush Brotherhood (Queensland), 1915-19; Vicar of Brill with Boarstall, Bucks, 1920-26; Archdeacon of Mauritius, 1926-31; Bishop of Mauritius, 1931-59. *Address:* Dee House, Hawkhurst, Kent. *Club:* Royal Commonwealth Society.
[Died 9 May 1971.

OTTER-BARRY, William Whitmore, BA, JP Essex; late General Manager Sun Insurance Office Ltd; late Director Sun Insurance Office Ltd; Sun Life Assurance Society; Planet Assurance Co. Ltd; *b* 6 March 1878; *s* of late Robert Melvil Barry Otter-Barry of Horkesley Hall, Essex, BA and Isabel Louisa, *d* of Rev. Francis Henry Wolryche-Whitmore of Dudmaston, Salop, JP; *m* 1905, Edith Wrey (*d* 1959), *d* of late Frederick Jaques Myers, of Charlton, Northants, JP; one *s* one *d* (and one *s* decd). *Educ:* Marlborough; Trinity College, Cambridge. Called to Bar, 1901; practised in London and Northern Circuit until 1912; became Assistant Secretary to Fire Offices Committee; Sub-Manager and Assistant Secretary Sun Insurance Office, Ltd, 1919; General Manager, 1923; Pres. Insurance Institute of London, 1926; Chairman London Salvage Corps, 1927-28; Chairman Insurance Clerks' Orphanage, 1930; President Chartered Insurance Institute, 1932; Chairman British Insurance

Association, 1936; Member of the Board of Trade Committee on Compulsory Insurance, 1936; High Sheriff of Essex, 1946. *Publication:* Law relating to Fire Insurance, 1911, 3rd edition. *Recreations:* shooting, fishing. *Address:* Horkesley Hall, Colchester, Essex. *T:* Great Horkesley 259. *Club:* United Oxford & Cambridge University. *[Died 2 Sept. 1973.*

OUDENDYK, Dame Margaret, DBE 1949 (Hon. DBE 1918); *b* 29 Sept. 1876; *d* of Edmond Fuller; *m* 1911, Willem Oudendyk (*d* 1953) (William J. Oudendyk, Hon. KCMG). Order of the Sun 2nd Class (Persia), 1913. *Address:* Pound Hall, Long Melford, Suffolk. *T:* Long Melford 285. *Club:* Sesame Imperial and Pioneer. *[Died 1 Nov. 1971.*

OULSNAM, Sir (Samuel) Harrison (Yardley), Kt 1947; CSI 1946; CIE 1937; MC; late ICS; *b* 17 Jan. 1898; *Educ:* Newcastle-under-Lyme; St John's College, Cambridge, BA. Joined Indian Civil Service, 1921; held appts of Deputy Commissioner, Under Sec. to Central Provs Govt, Reforms Officer to C. P. Govt; Sec. to Eastern Group Supply Conf., 1940; Joint Sec. to Govt of India; Sec. to Govt of India, Dept of Health, 1945-47; retired, on transfer of power, 1947. *Address:* c/o Lloyds Bank, 39 Threadneedle Street, EC2. *[Died 2 April 1972.*

OVENDEN, Harry, CBE 1945 (OBE 1941); Fellow of Chartered Surveyors' Institution; *b* 14 Feb. 1876; *s* of Charles Ovenden; *m* 1911, Gladys Winifred Searle (*d* 1948); one *d. Educ:* Albemarle College. District Valuer Inland Revenue, 1910-23; Superintending Valuer to 1941; Chief Technical Adviser War Damage Commission, 1941-49. *Recreation:* golf. *Address:* Hollybank House, Ninfield, Sussex. *T:* 466.
[Died 16 Jan. 1974.

OVERTON, Sir Arnold (Edersheim), KCB 1943; KCMG 1939 (CMG 1932); MC; *b* 8 Jan. 1893; *s* of late Canon F. A. Overton and Ella Edersheim; *m* 1920, Bronwen Cecilie (*d* 1974), *d* of late Sir Hugh Vincent; three *s* one *d. Educ:* Winchester; New College, Oxford. Served European War in France, Macedonia and Palestine; entered Board of Trade, 1919; private secretary to successive Presidents, 1921-25; on secretariat of Ottawa Conference, 1932; Delegate of United Kingdom Government to negotiate Anglo-American Trade Agreement, in Washington, 1937-38; Permanent Secretary Board of Trade, 1941-45; Head of British Middle East Office, Cairo, 1945-47; Permanent Secretary, Ministry of Civil Aviation, 1947-53; Member Board of BEA, 1953-63. *Address:* 41 Upper Addison Gardens, W14. *Club:* United Oxford & Cambridge University.
[Died 10 Sept. 1975.

OVERY, Sir Thomas (Stuart), Kt 1954; late Senior Partner Allen & Overy, Solicitors; *b* 13 June 1893; *s* of Henry James Overy, Mascalls Court, Brenchley; *m* 1923, Frances Hilda, (*d* 1970), *d* of W. F. Richardson; three *s* one *d. Educ:* Kent Coll., Canterbury. Served European War, 1914-18; enlisted Royal Fusiliers, Aug. 1914; 2nd Lieut, The Buffs, 1915; went to France, 8th Bn The Buffs 24th Div., Oct. 1915; Capt. The Buffs, 1918 (despatches); Staff Capt. 92nd Bde, 31st Div. 1918; Staff Capt. QMG, GHQ, 1918-19. Admitted a Solicitor, 1921. *Address:* Cossins House, Downside Road, Cobham, Surrey.
[Died 18 July 1973.

OWEN, Sir Alfred George Beech, Kt 1961; CBE 1954 (OBE 1946); DL; Chairman, Owen Organisation, Darlaston, since 1929; *b* 8 April 1908; *e s* of Alfred Ernest Owen and Florence Lucy Beech; *m* 1932, Eileen Kathleen Genevieve McMullan; three *s* two *d. Educ:* Oundle; Emmanuel College, Cambridge University. Took over Rubery, Owen & Co., Ltd, on the death of his father, 1929. Chairman or Director of several companies. Hon. Treasurer, Dr Barnardo's; formerly: President of National Sunday School Union; Former Chm., Staffordshire County Council; Former Mayor of Sutton Coldfield. Mem. Governing Body, Univ. of Birmingham. A Vice-Chm.: Nat. Savings Movement, 1960-73; Nat. Road Safety Advisory Council (Chairman 1965-67). Freeman of Borough of Sutton Coldfield. DL, County of Warwick, 1967. Ferodo Gold Trophy, 1962. Gold Medal of Brit. Automobile Racing Club, 1963. Hon. DSc, Keele, 1965. OStJ. *Address:* New Hall, Walmley, Sutton Coldfield, West Midlands. *T:* Sutton 021-354 2020. *Clubs:* National, Royal Automobile; Union (Birmingham).
[Died 29 Oct. 1975.

OWEN, Sir (Arthur) Douglas, KBE 1958; CB 1952; Commissioner, HM Customs and Excise, 1949-65; Deputy Chairman Board of Customs and Excise, 1952-65; Chairman, Customs Co-operation Council, Brussels, 1955, re-elected 1956, Président d'Honneur, 1957; Civil Service Selection Bd, 1965-68; *b* 24 Nov. 1904; *s* of late William Owen and Mrs B. J. Owen, Swansea; *m* 1934, Janet Mabel Morton, MB, ChB, DPH; one *s*.

Educ: Swansea Grammar School; Wrekin College; Downing College, Cambridge (Exhibitioner). First Class History Tripos; MA. Administrative Class, Home Civil Service, 1928; HM Customs and Excise (Private Sec. to Chm., Sir Edward Forber), Principal, 1933; Assistant Secretary, 1942. *Address:* 30 Foxes Dale, Blackheath, SE3.   *[Died 26 April 1977.*

OWEN, Sir Douglas; *see* Owen, Sir Arthur D.

OWEN, Edwin Augustine, MA, ScD (Cantab), DSc (London), MSc (Wales), FInstP; Professor of Physics, University College of North Wales, Bangor, 1926-54, Professor Emeritus since 1954; Member of Grand Council British Empire Cancer Campaign; Member of Scientific Advisory Committee National Gallery; Chairman, Board of Governors, Bangor Grammar Schools; Member, Board of Governors, Rydal School; Fellow: Physical Society; Cambridge Philosophical Society; Hon. Member: Institute of Quarrying; Association of Hospital Physicists; Member: Institute of Metals; British Institute of Radiology; *b* 5 Aug. 1887; *s* of late John and Ellen Owen, Blaenau Festiniog; *m* 1915, Julia May, *o d* of late Robert Vallance, Bangor; one *s. Educ:* Festiniog County School; University College, Bangor; Trinity Coll., Cambridge; University College, London. Open Scholarship (UCNW), 1905; BSc Wales (Honours in Mathematics and in Physics) 1909; 1851 Exhibition Scholar, 1910-12; Research Student at Cavendish Laboratory, Cambridge, 1910-12; Assistant in Metrology Dept, National Physical Laboratory, 1912-15; engaged on Standardisation of Instruments for Ministry of Munitions, 1915-19; Head of Radiology Division, National Physical Laboratory, 1919-26; Hon. Secretary, Röntgen Society, 1920-24; Hon. Secretary British Institute Radiology, 1924-25; Röntgen Award, 1927; Vice-President, Physical Society of London, 1926-28; Hon. Secretary, International Cttee for Radiological Units, 1925-37; Vice-President, British Institute of Radiology, 1939-42; Silvanus Thompson Medallist, 1945; Chairman North Wales District WEA, 1946-56; Member of Welsh Regional Hospital Board and Chairman Hospital Planning Cttee, 1948-62; Vice-President, Institute of Physics, 1957-59. *Publications:* original papers in Proceedings of the Royal Society, Proceedings of the Physical Society, Philosophical Magazine, Mineralogical Magazine, Journals of the Röntgen Society, the British Institute of Radiology, the Iron and Steel Institute and the Institute of Metals, Zeitschrift für Krist, American Chemical Society, on radiology, X-rays and crystal structure of metals and alloys. *Recreations:* golf, angling. *Address:* Penbre, College Road, Bangor, N Wales. *T:* Bangor 3773.   *[Died 31 July 1973.*

OWEN, Frank, (H. F. Owen), OBE (mil.); Journalist, Author, Broadcaster and Public Relations Consultant; *b* 1905; *s* of Thomas and Cicely Owen, Hereford; *m* 1939, Grace Stewart McGillivray (*d* 1968), Boston, USA. *Educ:* Monmouth Sch.; Sidney Sussex Coll., Cambridge (Schol.); 1st class hons, History Tripos. South Wales Argus, 1928-29; MP (L) Hereford Division, 1929-31; Daily Express, 1931-37; Editor, Evening Standard, 1938-41; served Royal Armoured Corps, 1942-43; South-East Asia Command, 1944-46; Lieut-Colonel (OBE); Editor, Daily Mail, 1947-50. Freeman of the City of London. *Publications:* (with Cemlyn Jones) Red Rainbow, 1931, novel; (with R. J. Thompson) His was the Kingdom, An Account of the Abdication, 1937; (with Michael Foot and Peter Howard) Guilty Men: an attack on Neville Chamberlain, Halifax, etc for collaboration with Hitler, 1938; The Three Dictators, 1940; The Campaign in Burma, 1946; Tempestuous Journey: Lloyd George, His Life and Times, 1954; The Eddie Chapman Story, 1956; Peron: His Rise and Fall, 1957; The Fall of Singapore, 1960. *Address:* 132 Elgin Avenue, W9. *T:* 01-289 1440. *Clubs:* Savage, Press.   *[Died 23 Jan. 1979.*

OWEN, George Sherard, CB 1946; *b* 20 June 1892; *s* of late Rev. E. C. E. Owen (late Master at Harrow School) and Rose Dora Ashington; *m* 1920, Doris Winifred Lyall Haynes, Barbados, BWI. *Educ:* Orley Farm Sch., Harrow; Rossall Sch. (Scholar); University College, Oxford (Lodge Exhibitioner). European War, 1914-16, despatch-rider RE Signals; commissioned RE Signals, 1916-19 (Mons Star, despatches). Ministry of Labour (1928-29 Imperial Defence Coll.), 1919-34; Unemployment Assistance Board, 1934-40; Board of Trade, 1940-42; Ministry of Production, 1942-45; Under-Secretary, Board of Trade, 1945-52; retired, 1952. *Recreations:* gardening, "Times" crossword. *Address:* Flat 5, 36 Belsize Park, NW3. *T:* 01-794 4518. *Club:* United Oxford & Cambridge University. *[Died 30 April 1976.*

OWEN, Captain Hilary Dorsett, CMG 1944; RN, retired; *b* 25 Aug. 1894; *s* of late J. D. Owen, JP, Plas-yn-Grove, Ellesmere, Shropshire; *m* 1924, Eileen Amy Hamilton (*d* 1952), *e d* of W. B. Dunlop, Seton Castle, Longniddry; one *s. Educ:* Belvedere, Brighton; RN Colleges, Osborne and Dartmouth. Midshipman,

1912; served at sea, War of 1914-18; Commander, 1930; Naval Attaché, Lisbon, 1938-44; SHAEF 1944-45; retired list, 1944.
[Died 18 April 1980.

OWEN, Humphrey Frank; *see* Owen, Frank.

OWEN, Sir John Arthur, 4th Bt, *cr* 1813; *b* 5 Feb. 1892; *s* of 3rd Bt and Martha Roberts Lewis; *S* father, 1909; *m* 1914, Lucy Fletcher, *e d* of Dr Pilkington, Kencot House, nr Lechlade, Glos; two *s. Educ:* Llandovery Coll.; St John's Coll., Oxford. Ex-Captain, Somerset Light Infantry. *Recreations:* football, cricket, hockey. *Heir: s* Hugh Bernard Pilkington Owen [*b* 28 March 1915. *Educ:* Chillon Coll., Switzerland]. *Address:* Cross House, Fishguard, Pembs.   *[Died 20 Sept. 1973.*

OWEN, John Glendwr, CB 1971; Under-Secretary, HM Treasury, 1959-73; Treasury Historical Section, 1973-76; *b* 12 May 1914; *s* of George Cecil Owen; *m* 1943, Caroline Gweneth Bough; no *c. Educ:* Bedford Sch.; Balliol Coll., Oxford. Entered War Office, 1937; transferred to Treasury, 1938. Served in Grenadier Guards, 1942-45. *Address:* c/o National Westminster Bank, 47 Carfax, Horsham, West Sussex RH12 1EJ.
[Died 14 Feb. 1977.

OWEN, Sir Leonard; *see* Owen, Sir W. L.

OWEN, Commodore Trevor Lewis, OBE 1942; RD 1938; RNR, retired; *b* 21 Dec. 1895; 4th *s* of D. H. Owen, Wainhams, Shrewsbury; *m* 1920, Freda, 4th *d* of Rev. Prof. John Ramsey, Ballymoney, Co. Antrim; three *d. Educ:* Arnold House Sch., Chester. Joined Merchant Service, Oct. 1911; Sub-Lieut, RNR, 1918; Master's Certificate, 1919. Commander RNR, 1937; Captain, RNR, 1942; Commodore RNR (Acting), 1942 and served in Atlantic Convoys until 1943. Elder Brother of Trinity House, 1943-62 (Nether Warden 1958); retired as an Active Elder Brother, Aug. 1962. Vice-President, Marine Society, 1961 (Chairman 1960). *Recreations:* gardening, sailing. *Address:* Sevenstones, Stoke Gabriel, Totnes, Devon. *T:* Stoke Gabriel 350.   *[Died 4 June 1980.*

OWEN, Rt. Hon. Sir William Francis Langer, PC 1963; KBE 1957; Justice of High Court of Australia since 1961; Justice of the Supreme Court of New South Wales, 1936-61; *b* 21 Nov. 1899; *s* of Sir Langer Owen and May Dames Longworth; *m* 1923, Joan Rolin; one *d. Educ:* Sydney Church of England Grammar Sch., Sydney, NSW. Served European War with AIF, 1915-19; admitted to Bar, 1923; KC 1935; Chairman of Commonwealth of Australia Central Wool Cttee, 1942-45. *Recreations:* fishing, golf. *Address:* High Court of Australia, Sydney, NSW 2000, Australia. *Clubs:* Union, Royal Sydney Golf (Sydney); Melbourne (Melbourne). *[Died 30 March 1972.*

OWEN, Sir (William) Leonard, Kt 1957; CBE 1950; MEng; FICE; FIMechE; MIChemE; Hon. DSc Manchester, 1962; former Chairman: Scottish Aviation Ltd; Cammell Laird & Co. (Shipbuilders and Engineers); Cammell Laird (Anglesey) Ltd; former Director, Cammell Laird & Co.; Consultant, United Gas Industries (lately Director); *b* 3 May 1897; *s* of Thomas John and Levina Owen; *m* 1923, Phyllis Condliff; two *s. Educ:* Liverpool Collegiate Sch.; Liverpool Univ. (MEng, 1924). Served European War, 6th King's Liverpool Regt, 1915-18. Brunner, Mond & Company, later ICI (Alkali) Ltd, designing new Chemical Plants and additions to existing Chemical Plant, 1922; loaned to Ministry of Supply as Engineering Director of Royal Filling Factories, 1940-45; Director of Engineering, Ministry of Supply, Dept of Atomic Energy Production, 1946; Asst Controller, Dept of Atomic Energy Production, 1947; Director of Engineering and Dep. Managing Director, Industrial Group, UK Atomic Energy Authority, 1954; Managing Director, United Kingdom Atomic Energy Authority, Industrial Group, Risley, 1957; Member for Production, UKAEA, 1959 and for Engineering also, 1961, ceasing to be full-time June 1962; Member (part-time), 1962-64. *Recreations:* yachting and gardening. *Address:* Eyarth, Rosemary Lane, Beaumaris, Anglesey. *T:* Beaumaris 396. *Clubs:* Royal Automobile; Royal Anglesey Yacht (Beaumaris).
[Died 25 March 1971.

OWLES, Captain Garth Henry Fyson, DSO 1941; DSC 1940; RN (retired); *b* 25 Aug. 1896; *s* of Henry Beaumont Owles and Emma Harriet Fyson; *m* 1923, Catherine Noel Banham (*d* 1969); one *s* one *d. Educ:* Felsted. Passed into Royal Navy through special entry, 1914; trained at RN Coll., Keyham; served in HMS Princess Royal, 1915-17; Battle of Jutland, 1916; HMS Raglan, 1917-18, sunk by Goeben, Jan. 1918 (despatches); in destroyers till Sept. 1918; joined Submarines Sept. 1918; Trinity Coll., Cambridge, 1919; in Submarines 1918-33, having first command in 1924; this period broken by 3 months in command special service vessel in Pearl and West Rivers, China, during anti-foreign trouble, 1925; also in Caledon, Ramillies and Malaya, 1927-29; Erebus, 1934-37; Staff of Tactical Sch., Portsmouth, 1937; Hawkins and Effingham (Reserve Fleet Flagships), 1937-40; took part in blocking of Zeebrugge harbour, commanding Atlantic Guide, and Dunkirk harbour, commanding Pacifico in May and June 1940 (DSC); Senior Officer Channel Mobile Balloon Barrage, 1940-43 (despatches, DSO); Senior Officer 9th LST Flotilla, 1943-44, Italy, India (despatches), Invasion of Normandy (despatches); Senior Officer LST SE Asia, 1944-46; retired Sept. 1946. Encyclopædia Britannica Ltd, 1946-56. *Address:* Anglesea Cottage, Auckland Road West, Southsea. *T:* Portsmouth 23074.

[Died 17 July 1975.

OXBORROW, Brigadier Claud Catton, CMG 1954; CBE 1945; MC 1917, and Bar 1918; retired; *b* 24 July 1898; *o s* of Arthur J. Oxborrow; *m* 1928, Joy Meredith McDougall (*d* 1965); one *s*. *Educ:* Portsmouth; Sandhurst. Served European War (MC and Bar): commissioned Royal Hampshire Regt, 1916, France and Italy. Adjutant, 1922-25; ADC to GOC-in-C, Middle East, 1926-28; retired, 1928. War of 1939-45 (CBE): rejoined from RARO, 1939; Lieut-Colonel 1941, Brigadier 1943, France, Normandy, Germany. Temp. Asst Secretary, Foreign Office, 1946-53. US Legion of Merit, 1944. *Recreations:* cricket, shooting. *Address:* Mill Street, Polstead, Suffolk. *T:* Nayland 306. *[Died 16 Oct. 1972.*

OXLEY, D. G. R.; *see* Rice-Oxley.

OXLEY, Maj.-General Walter Hayes, CB 1947; CBE 1941; MC 1916; *b* 2 Jan. 1891; *s* of late Edward Hayes Oxley and Bessie Eleanor Paton; *d* of late J. P. Hindley; *m* 1921, Margaret, *d* of late W. James Smith, JP, Gibraltar and Villa Viega, Algeciras; one *d*. *Educ:* Eastbourne Coll.; RMA, Woolwich. 2nd Lieut, RE, 1911; served European War, 1914-18, in Egypt, Palestine and Macedonia (despatches, MC, Bt Major); Egyptian Army, 1918-19; psc; Military Attaché HM Legations, Belgrade and Prague; Bt Lieut-Colonel, 1931; AQMG British Military Mission to Egyptian Army; Order of Nile, 3rd Class; Brigadier, i/c Admin., Malta; War of 1939-45, commanded 2nd Inf. Bde, Malta, then 7th Inf. Bde 3rd Division in UK; GOC Malta, 1943-44; Commissioner British Military Mission, Bulgaria, 1944-47. Acting Maj.-General, 1943; Temp. Maj.-General, 1944; ADC to the King, 1943-48; retired pay, 1948. *Recreations:* shooting, fishing and golf. *Address:* Charminster House, Dorchester, Dorset. *T:* Dorchester 238. *Club:* Naval and Military.

[Died 23 Jan. 1978.

P

PACE, George Gaze, CVO 1971; FRIBA; Architect in Private Practice since 1949; *b* 31 Dec. 1915; *s* of George Henry and Alice Barbara Pace, Croydon; *m* 1941, Ina Catherine, *d* of Harvey Sheridan Jones; three *s* two *d*. *Educ:* privately; articled James Ransome, FRIBA, London; School of Architecture, Polytechnic, London. Lecturer, School of Architecture, Polytechnic, London, 1939-41. Queen's Royal Regt, RE, 1941-42; Superintending Valuer, WO (Major, Gen. List), 1942-49. Surveyor to Dio. of Sheffield, 1949-56; Cons. Architect to Cathedrals of: Lichfield, 1949; Llandaff, 1949; Sheffield, 1953-61; Durham, 1954; Peterborough, 1956; Chester, 1961; Liverpool (Anglican), 1962; Newcastle, 1966; Southwark, 1971; Surveyor, St George's Chapel, Windsor Castle, 1969. Cons. Architect to Dioceses of: Wakefield, 1948, Bradford, 1949, Sheffield, 1956, York, 1957, Llandaff, 1967, and Monmouth, 1969; Hon. Cons. Architect: Historic Churches Preservation Trust; Yorks Architectural and York Archæological Society; Mem., Dio. Adv. Cttees, York, Sheffield and Liverpool; Vice-President: New Churches Research Group; Council York Civic Trust. RIBA Pugin Student, 1936; Robert Mitchell Gold Medallist, 1936; RIBA Ashpitel Prizeman, 1938; MA Lambeth, 1961. FRIBA 1949; FSA 1950. *Work includes:* rebuilding Llandaff Cathedral, 1949-63; Chapel of the Resurrection, University of Ibadan, 1951-62; completion schemes Sheffield Cathedral, 1955-61; Holy Trinity, Newport, Mon, 1958; All Saints', Doncaster, 1958; Scargill Religious Centre, 1958; The Chapel, St Michael's Theological Coll., Llandaff, 1959; New Cathedral, Ibadan, 1960-; St Mark's, Sheffield, 1963; St Mark's, Chadderton, 1963; Caer Eirthin Church, Swansea, 1963; Chapel Complex, Keele Univ., 1965; William Temple Memorial Church, Wythenshawe, 1965; St John's Coll., York Chapel,

1966; Durham Univ. Library, 1966; St Andrew's, Rushmere, 1968; (in association with Paul Paget) King George VI Memorial Chapel and Tomb, Windsor Castle, 1969; Woolston Church, 1970; St Mark's, Thornaby, 1970; James the Deacon, York, 1971; Bransholme Church Centre, 1973; *restorations include:* Castle Howard; Bramham Park; parish churches of: Boston; Louth; St Mary's, Beverley; Selby Abbey; Doncaster; Branston; Holy Trinity, Hull; *alterations etc to churches include:* Armagh Cathedral; Great St Mary's, Cambridge; Luton; Pershore Abbey; Wycliffe Hall, Oxford; St Martin's, Birmingham; Bramhall; St Aidan's Theological Coll. Chapel; St Michael's, Cambridge; St Martin le Grand, York, 1968; S Mary's Church, Luton, 1969; Organcase, New Coll., Oxford, 1969; King's Coll. Chapel, Cambridge; Treasury, Ely and Durham Cathedrals; The Chapel, Trinity Coll., Dublin. Townscape analysis Skipton: Bishophill, York and Skipton. *Publications:* contributions to: Chambers's Encyclopædia, 1948 and 1963; Collins' Guide to English Parish Churches, 1958, 1968; The Church and the Arts, 1960; Making the Building Fit the Liturgy, 1962; The York Aesthetic, 1962; The Modern Architectural Setting of the Liturgy, 1964; Bishophill: York, appraisal and renewal, 1974; contributions to technical, archæological and ecclesiological journals. *Recreations:* walking, looking at old buildings. *Address:* 18 Clifton Green, York. *T:* York 55029. *Clubs:* Athenæum, Art Workers' Guild.

[Died 23 Aug. 1975.

PACK, Captain Stanley Walter Croucher, CBE 1957; RN, 1927-60; author since 1927; *b* 14 Dec. 1904; *s* of Walter Edward Pack and Beatrice Eleanor (*née* Croucher); *m* 1934, Dorothea Edna Mary (*née* Rowe); one *s* one *d*. *Educ:* St John's, Malta; Imperial College of Science. Whitworth Scholar, 1924; John Samuel Scholar, 1925; 1st class hons BSc (Engineering) 1926; ACGI 1926; MSc 1927; DIC 1927. Served War of 1939-45: HMS Formidable, 1940-41; British Commonwealth Secretary, Combined Meteorological Cttee, Washington, 1941-43; Chief Naval Met. Officer to SACSEA, 1945. Dep. Director, Naval Weather Service, Admiralty, 1951-54; Dep. Director, Naval Education Service, Admiralty, 1956-58; ADC to the Queen, 1957-60; retired RN, 1960. Sen. Lectr, Britannia RNC, Dartmouth, 1963-69. Member: Soc. of Authors; Council, Navy Records Soc.; Cttee, Old Centralians Assoc.; MIEE 1946; FRMetS 1950. Boyle Somerville Memorial Prize for Meteorology, 1938. Officer, Legion of Merit, USA, 1948. *Publications:* Anson's Voyage, 1947; Weather Forecasting, 1948; Admiral Lord Anson, 1960; Battle of Matapan, 1961; Windward of the Caribbean, 1964; The Wager Mutiny, 1965; Britannia at Dartmouth, 1966; Sea Power in the Mediterranean, 1971; Night Action off Cape Matapan, 1972; The Battle for Crete, 1973; Cunningham the Commander, 1974; The Battle of Sirte, 1975; The Allied Invasion of Sicily, 1977; contributions to Blackwood's Magazine, 1937- and to Daily Telegraph, Sunday Times, The Field, The Navy, etc. *Recreations:* music, painting. *Address:* Blossom's Pasture, Strete, Dartmouth, Devon. *T:* Stoke Fleming 254. *Club:* Royal Ocean Racing (Life Mem.; first qualified Fastnet Race, 1929, and Santander Race, 1930).

[Died 7 Dec. 1977.

PACKER, Sir (Douglas) Frank (Hewson), KBE 1971 (CBE 1951); Kt 1959; Managing Director, Australian Consolidated Press Ltd, since 1936; *b* 3 Dec. 1906; *s* of Robert Clyde and Ethel Maud Packer; *m* 1934, Gretel Joyce (*d* 1960), *d* of Dr H. H. Bullmore; two *s*; *m* 1964, Florence A., *d* of Edmond Porges, OBE, Paris, France. *Educ:* Sydney Church of England Grammar Sch., New South Wales. Cadet Reporter, Daily Guardian, 1923; Asst Business Manager, 1926; Director and Gen. Advertising Manager, Daily Guardian, and Smith's Weekly, 1927. One of founders of Australian Women's Weekly, 1933; President, Australian Newspapers Conf., 1939-40; AIF, 1941-42; Director of Personnel, Allied Works Council, 1942-44; returned to AIF, 1944-45; President, Australian Associated Press Pty Ltd, 1951; Director: Reuters Ltd, 1954-56 and 1962-; News International, 1972-; Chairman TV Corp. Ltd, 1955; Chairman General TV Corp. Pty Ltd, Melbourne, 1960. Head of Australian Syndicate which challenged for America's Cup, 1962 and 1970 (Australian boat won one race in 1962, and crossed finishing line first in two races in 1970, losing one on a protest). Councillor, Royal Agricultural Soc., 1963. Cttee Mem., Austr. Jockey Club, 1963. *Publications:* Daily Telegraph, 1936; Sunday Telegraph, 1939; Australian Women's Weekly, 1933; Bulletin, 1960. *Recreations:* polo, golf, yachting. *Address:* (home) 76/8 Victoria Road, Bellevue Hill, NSW 2023, Australia. *T:* Sydney 36-5685; (business) Australian Consolidated Press Ltd, Box 4088, GPO, Sydney, NSW 2001, Australia. *T:* Sydney 20-666. *Clubs:* Devonshire, Savage (London); Australian, University, Australian Golf, Royal Sydney Golf, Royal Sydney Yacht Squadron (Sydney); New York Yacht. *[Died 1 May 1974.*

PACKER, Joy, (Lady Packer); Author; *b* S Africa, 11 Feb. 1905; *d* of late Dr and Mrs Julius Petersen, Cape Town; *m* 1925, Lieut-Commander Herbert Packer, RN (Admiral Sir Herbert Packer, *d* 1962); one *s*. *Educ:* St Cyprian's Sch., Cape Town; University of Cape Town. Free-lance journalist Cape Town, 1924; News Reporter, Daily Express (London), 1931-32; Hongkong Radio Women's Features, 1932-35; in Balkans, 1936-39, contributing articles to various British publications; in London, 1939-43, writing for various War organisations and broadcasting to S Africa for the BBC, London. Lent to Ministry of Information (Egypt), 1943; Psychological Warfare Branch of Allied HQ, Italy, 1944-45. *Publications:* Quintette (travel autobiographies): Pack and Follow, 1945; Grey Mistress, 1949; Apes and Ivory, 1953; Home from Sea, 1963; The World is a Proud Place, 1966; Deep as the Sea, 1975; *fiction:* Valley of the Vines, 1955; Nor the Moon by Night, 1957; The High Roof, 1959; The Glass Barrier, 1961; The Man in the Mews, 1964; The Blind Spot, 1967; Leopard in the Fold, 1969; Veronica, 1970; Boomerang, 1972; The Dark Curtain, 1977. *Recreations:* travel and the study of wild life. *Address:* 101 Grosvenor Square, Rondebosch, Cape Peninsula, S Africa. *Club:* Western Province Sports.
[Died 6 Sept. 1977.

PADWICK, Surgeon-Captain Harold Boultbee, DSO 1917; RN, retired; MA, MB, BCh, DMRE (Cambridge), LMSSA (London); retired radiologist; late Hon. Radiologist, Bedford County Hospital; Radiologist, St Peter's Hospital, Bedford; Consulting Radiologist, Kettering General Hospital; Member of British Institute of Radiology; *b* 1889; *o s* of late F. H. Padwick, CBE, of Thorney Manor and West Ashling, Sussex; *m* 1921, Edith Gwendolen Carr (*d* 1971); one *s* two *d*. *Educ:* Sherborne; Emmanuel Coll., Cambridge; London Hospital. Served European War, 1914-19 (despatches, DSO); retired as Surgeon Captain RN, 1932; Gilbert Blane medal, 1924. *Recreation:* fly-fishing. *Address:* Swallowfield Park, Swallowfield, near Reading.
[Died 29 July 1972.

PAGE, Sir Denys (Lionel), Kt 1971; LittD 1960; FBA 1952; Master of Jesus College, Cambridge, 1959-73, Hon. Fellow, 1976; Regius Professor of Greek, Cambridge University, 1950-73; Hon. Student of Christ Church, Oxford; Hon. Fellow of Trinity College, Cambridge; *b* 1908; *s* of F. H. D. Page, OBE, and late Elsie Page, MBE; *m* 1938, Katharine Elizabeth, *d* of late Joseph Michael and Edith Hall Dohan, Philadelphia, Pa, USA; four *d*. *Educ:* Newbury; Christ Church, Oxford (Schol.). 1st Cl. Hons Class. Mods, Chancellor's Prize for Latin Verse, Gaisford Prize for Greek Verse, de Paravicini Schol., Craven Schol., 1928; 1st Cl. Lit. Hum., Derby, Univ. and Goldsmiths' Company's senior Schols, 1930. Vienna Univ., 1930-31; Lecturer of Christ Church, 1931-32; Student and Tutor, 1932-50; Senior Proctor, 1948-49. Lectures: Dean West, Princeton Univ., US, 1939; Flexner, Bryn Mawr, 1954; Sather, Univ. of California, 1957-58; Jackson, Harvard, 1972. Dept of Foreign Office, 1939-46. Head of Command Unit, Intelligence Division, HQ South-East Asia, 1945-46. Pres., British Academy, 1971-74. Foreign Member: Academy of Athens; Amer. Acad. of Arts and Scis; Amer. Philosophical Soc.; Hon. Fellow: Archæological Soc. of Athens; Hellenic Soc. of Humanities. Kenyon Medal, British Academy. Hon. LittD: Trinity Coll., Dublin; Newcastle; Hull; Bristol; Hon. DLitt Oxon. Comdr, Order of Merit, Poland. *Publications:* Actors' Interpolations in Greek Tragedy, 1934; Euripides' Medea, 1938; Greek Literary Papyri, 1941; Alcman, 1951; Corinna, 1953; Sappho and Alcaeus, 1955; The Homeric Odyssey, 1955; (co-editor), Poetarum Lesbiorum Fragmenta, 1955; (co-editor), Aeschylus, Agamemnon, 1957; History and the Homeric Iliad, 1959; Poetae Melici Graeci, 1962; The Oxyrhynchus Papyri, vol. xxix, 1964; (co-editor), The Greek Anthology: Hellenistic Epigrams, 1965; The Garland of Philip, 1968; Melica Graeca Selecta, 1968; The Santorini Volcano and the Destruction of Minoan Crete, 1971; (ed) Aeschylus, 1972; Folk Tales in the Odyssey, 1973; (ed) Supplementum Lyricis Graecis, 1975; (ed) Epigrammata Graeca, 1975; Rufinus, 1978. *Address:* Thorneyburn Lodge, Tarset, Northumberland. *T:* Greenhaugh 40272.
[Died 6 July 1978.

PAGE, Harold James, CMG 1951; OBE 1947 (MBE 1919); BSc, FRIC; Fellow of University College, London; *b* 29 May 1890; *s* of James William Page and Alice (*née* Jones); *m* 1915, Gladys Isabel (*d* 1969); *d* of E. E. Shepperd, Chelsfield, Kent; one *s* one *d* (and one *s* killed on active service). *Educ:* Southend High School; University College, London (Andrews Scholar and University Exhibitioner; Tuffnell Scholar, 1851 Science Research Scholar); Berlin; Paris; Bsc 1910. Lecturer in Biochemistry, University College, London, 1910-12; served Royal Artillery, France, 1914-16, Royal Arsenal, Woolwich, 1917-19 (despatches thrice, Captain); Head of Chemistry Department, Royal Horticultural Society's Laboratories, Wisley, 1919-20; Chief Chemist and Head of Chemistry Department, Rothamsted Experimental Station, 1920-27; Head of ICI Agricultural Research Station, Jealotts Hill, 1927-32; Controller of Agricultural Research of Imperial Chemical Industries, Ltd, 1932-36; Director Rubber Research Institute of Malaya, Kuala Lumpur, Malaya, 1936-46; interned in Sumatra Camp, Mar. 1942 to Aug. 1945; Principal, Imperial College of Tropical Agriculture, Trinidad, 1947-52; on staff of Food and Agriculture Organization of the United Nations, 1952-55; Editor, Empire Journal of Experimental Agriculture, 1955-64. Member of various scientific societies. *Publications:* papers and articles in scientific journals on the results of research in chemistry, soil science, and agriculture. *Recreations:* photography, gardening. *Address:* Northbrook, West Ashling, Chichester, Sussex. *Club:* Farmers'.
[Died 27 Jan. 1972.

PAGE, Sidney John, CB 1949; MC 1917; retired as Adviser (on Transport Charges) Ministry of Transport and Civil Aviation (1951-59, retaining rank of Under-Sec. until 1952); *b* 12 January 1892; *s* of late George Arthur and late E. Page, Douglas, IoM; *m* 1919, Doris Mary (*d* 1968), *d* of late Arthur Binns, CBE; one *s*. *Educ:* Douglas High School; London University (LLB). 1st Class Clerk, Estate Duty Office, Inland Revenue, 1911; London Univ. OTC, 1914; commissioned Manchester Regt, 1915; transferred to Machine Gun Corps, 1917; served European War, France, 1916-18. Asst Inspector of Taxes, 1919; Sec., Railway Rates Tribunal, 1921-36. Min. of Transport: Asst Princ., 1919; Asst Sec. 1937; Principal Asst Sec., 1941; Under-Sec., 1946-52. *Recreations:* golf, motoring, travel. *Address:* 16 The Glen, Green Lane, Northwood, Middlesex. *T:* Northwood 25879.
[Died 9 March 1973.

PAGE, William Frank, CMG 1946; *b* 26 June 1894; *s* of late W. T. Page, civil engineer, Worcester; *m* 1932, Kathleen Margaret (*d* 1978), *d* of late Rev. C. A. Stooke, Combe Down, Bath. *Educ:* Clifton. South Wales Borderers, 1914-19, Gallipoli and France, temp. commission, Capt.; farming (War Settlement) Southern Rhodesia, 1919-21; Provincial Administration, Tanganyika Territory, 1922-47; Provincial Commissioner, 1944; Director of Man Power, 1942-46; retired, 1947. *Address:* Le Douit, Sous l'Eglise, St Saviour's, Guernsey, CI. *T:* Guernsey 63955.
[Died 24 Feb. 1980.

PAGE-JONES, Frederick Herbert, CMG 1955; Executive Officer, International Egg Commission, since 1965; Administrative Director, Export Research Group, since 1968; *b* 29 Dec. 1903; *s* of late Frederick Thomas Page-Jones and Louise Mary Young; *m* 1933, Joan, *d* of late Francis John Edward Bagshawe, CMG, MBE; one *s* two *d*. *Educ:* Manchester Grammar School; Brasenose Coll., Oxford (BA). Colonial Administrative Service, Tanganyika Territory, 1925; Provincial Comr, Tanganyika Territory, 1948; Senior Provincial Comr, 1950; Mem. for Local Govt, 1953; Minister for Local Govt, and Admin., 1957; retired, 1958; Chairman, Tanganyika Broadcasting Corporation, 1958-61. Trustee and Man. Director Tanganyika National Newspapers Co., 1958-61; Manager, latterly Managing Director, Market Research (Tanganyika) Ltd, 1961-63; London representative, Marco Surveys (Marketing Research) Group, Kenya, Tanganyika (now Tanzania), Nigeria, 1963-66. *Address:* Ashton, 35 Redstone Hill, Redhill, Surrey. *T:* Redhill 62477. *Club:* Royal Commonwealth Society.
[Died 10 Nov. 1972.

PAGET, Most Rev. Edward Francis, CBE 1950; DD (Lambeth); an Assistant Bishop of Natal since 1961; *b* July 1886; *s* of Right Rev. Francis Paget, sometime Bishop of Oxford; *cousin* and *heir-pres.* of Capt. Sir James Paget, 3rd Bt; *m* 1932, Rosemary, *d* of Auriol and Rose Sealy Allin. *Educ:* Summerfields, Oxford; Shrewsbury; Christ Church, Oxford; Cuddesdon, MA (Oxford), 1911; DD (Lambeth), 1950. Ordained, 1911; Curate at the Christ Church (Oxford) Mission (St Frideswide's, Poplar); went to Transvaal, 1914 as Vicar of Benoni; served as Chaplain in East Africa during European War (MC); Chaplain-General to SR Forces, 1925-56 (resigned); Bishop of Southern Rhodesia, 1925-52; Bishop of Mashonaland, 1952-57; Archbishop of Central Africa, 1955-57; retired, 1957. Chaplain, Order of St John of Jerusalem, 1952. Comdr of Royal Order of the Phœnix (Greek), 1950. *Address:* Auriol, Everton Road, PO Box 3 Gillitts, Natal, South Africa. *T:* Durban 77802. *Club:* Royal Commonwealth Society.
[Died 21 April 1971.

PAGET, Captain Sir James (Francis), 3rd Bt, *cr* 1871; RN retired; *b* 25 Sept. 1890; *e s* of Sir John Rahere Paget, 2nd Bt, and Julia Norrie (*d* 1926), *d* of George Moke, New York; *S* father, 1938; *m* 1943, Frances Alexandra Hamilton (who *m* 1932, Frederick David Stewart Sandeman, *d* 1938), *d* of late Sir Hugh Fraser, Stromeferry, Ross-shire. Joined RN 1906; served European War, 1914-19; Comdr, 1925; Capt. ret., 1937; rejoined RN 1940 (despatches thrice); served 1940-45. *Heir: cousin,*

Julian Tolver Paget [b 11 July 1921; m 1954, Diana Frances, d of late F. S. H. Farmer; one s one d]. Address: Balgonie, Ballater, Aberdeenshire. Club: Naval and Military. [Died 5 June 1972.

PAGNOL, Marcel; Grand Officier de la Légion d'Honneur; Member, French Academy, since 1946; author and film producer; b 28 Feb. 1895; m 1916, Simone Collin; two s one d. Films include: Marius, 1931; Fanny, 1932; Topaze, 1932, new version 1950; Le gendre de M Poirier, 1933; Joffroi, 1933; Angèle, 1934; Merlusse, 1934; Cigalon, 1934; Tartarin de Tarascon, 1934; César, 1936; Regain, 1937; La femme du boulanger, 1938; Monsieur Brotonneau, 1939; La fille du puisatier, 1940; Naïs, 1945; La belle meunière, 1948; Le rosier de Madame Husson, 1950; Manon des sources, 1952; Carnaval, 1953; Les lettres de mon moulin, 1954. Publications include: La petite fille aux yeux sombres, 1919; Pirouettes, 1919; Le premier amour; La gloire de mon pere, 1958; Le château de ma mere, 1960 (trans. by Rita Barisse, The Days Were Too Short); Le temps de secrets, 1960 (trans. by Rita Barisse, The Time of Secrets); L'eau des collines, 1963; Le masque de fer, 1965; plays: Jazz, 1926; Topaze, 1928; Marius, 1929; Fanny, 1932; César, 1936; Judas, 1953; Fabien, 1956; translations: Bucoliques de Virgile; Hamlet; Midsummer Night's Dream. Address: Villa La Lestra, Monte Carlo; 16 square du Bois-de-Boulogne, Paris 16e, France.   [Died 18 April 1974.

PAIN, Arthur Bernard, TD 1946; ChM; FRCS; Senior Clinical Lecturer in Orthopædic Surgery, University of Leeds, 1944-Sept. 1969; Consultant Surgeon in charge Orthopædic Department, United Leeds Hospitals, 1955-July 1969; Dean of Faculty of Medicine, University of Leeds, 1960-Sept. 1969; b 13 July 1904; e s of late Reverend A. T. Pain; m 1933, Irene Allison, o d of late William Webb, Harrogate; one s. Educ: Central High School, Leeds; University of Leeds; St Bartholomew's Hospital, London. MB, ChB (Leeds) Hons, 1927; FRCS 1931; ChM (Leeds), 1932. Resident posts in hospital, 1927-34; Hon. Asst Orthopædic Surgeon, General Infirmary at Leeds, 1934; Consultant Orthopædic Surgeon, United Leeds Hosps, 1948. Lt-Col RAMC (TA) retd. Fellow, British Orthopædic Assoc.; FRSocMed; Member: Soc. Internationale de Chirugie Orthopédique et Traumatique; Bd of Governors, United Leeds Hosps, 1955-69; Leeds Regional Hospital Board, 1962-69; General Medical Council, 1960-69. Publications: articles in medical journals and in medical text book. Recreations: enjoyment of wine and food and of first-class cricket. Address: Rowley Cottage, Scarcroft, Thorner, Leeds. T: Thorner 305.
[Died 17 May 1973.

PAINE, Sir (Herbert) Kingsley, Kt 1953; CMG 1944; b 26 Jan. 1883; s of Herbert Paine, Gawler, South Australia; m 1912, Amy Muriel, d of James Ford Pearson, Malvern, South Australia; one s one d (and one s and one d decd). Educ: St Peter's Collegiate Sch., S Aust. LLB, Adelaide University, 1904; admitted to South Australian Bar, 1905; Stipendiary Magistrate, 1922; Judge in Insolvency and Local Court Judge, Adelaide, South Australia, 1926; retired from Local Court Judgeship, 1948; Acting Puisne Judge, Supreme Court, 1949-50, 1951-52. Address: No 1 Flat, Buxton Court, 38 Buxton Street, North Adelaide, SA 5006, Australia. Club: Adelaide (Adelaide).   [Died 3 Nov. 1972.

PAINTER, Robert John; Under Secretary (Home Finance), HM Treasury, since 1970; b 15 Dec. 1927; s of late Edward Lawrence Painter, Norwich; m 1952, Kathleen Edith Gummer; five s. Educ: City of Norwich School; Downing College, Cambridge. BA (History). Entered HM Treasury as Assistant Principal, 1951; Principal, 1956; Assistant Secretary, 1966. Recreation: gardening. Address: 21 Priory Close, Totteridge, N20. T: 01-445 9817.   [Died 4 Oct. 1972.

PALEY, Maj.-Gen. Sir (Alexander George) Victor, KBE 1960 (CBE 1951; OBE 1940); CB 1958; DSO 1945; DL; b 30 April 1903; s of late Major George Paley, Rifle Brigade, Freckenham, Suffolk; m 1936, Susan, d of late Lt-Col Albert Ingraham Paine, CMG, DSO, 60th Rifles, Bledington, Kingham, Oxon; two d. Educ: Cheam School; Eton College; RMC, Sandhurst. 2nd Lt, Rifle Bde, 1923; Adjt London Rifle Bde, 1929-31; at Staff College, 1932-33; Brigade Major 2 London Infantry Brigade, 1935-37; Bde Major 8 Inf. Bde, 1937-39; GSO2, HQ British Troops, Egypt, 1939-41; OC 3 Libyan Arab Battalion, Senussi, 1941-42; British Military Mission, Iraq, 1942-43; OC 1st Battalion Rifle Brigade, 1943-45; Brig. "A", HQ 8 Corps District, Germany, 1945-46; Head Army Branch Combined Services Division, CCG, 1946-48; Brigadier A/Q AA Comd, 1948-51; Commander 47 London Inf. Bde, Dec. 1951-54. ADC to the Queen, 1954-57, Comdr Gold Coast Dist, 1954; GOC, Ghana Army, 1956, and Chief of Defence Staff, Ghana, 1958. Retired, June 1960. Hon. Col: London Rifle Brigade Rangers (Prince Consort's Own), TA, 1960-67; 5th Territorial Bn Royal

Greenjackets, 1967-69; London Cadre Royal Greenjackets, 1969-70. High Sheriff of Suffolk, 1967; DL Suffolk, 1968. Governor, Milton Abbey Sch., 1961-73. Address: Great Barton, Bury St Edmunds, Suffolk. Clubs: Army and Navy, Royal Automobile; West Suffolk County.   [Died 10 April 1976.

PALFREY, William John Henry, CBE 1970 (OBE 1966); QPM 1960; DL; b 1 March 1906; s of late W. H. Palfrey, Exminster, Devon; m 1927, Dorothy, d of Henry Cowell, Kenton, Devon; one s. Educ: Hele's Sch., Exeter. Portsmouth City Police, 1926; Chief Constable, Accrington, 1940; seconded to Army, 1943-47; served with 1st American Army, Chief Public Safety Officer, Cherbourg, later Paris; Lt-Col i/c Central Register of War Criminals, 1945; War Crime Investigation, Germany, 1946-47; Asst Chief Constable (Operations), Lancs Constabulary, 1951; seconded to Thai Govt to carry out survey of Thai Police, 1955; Chief Constable, Lancs, 1969-72 (Dep. Chief Constable, 1962-69). Dep. Sec.-Gen., Internat. Fedn of Senior Police Officers, 1966-72. Lectured at Internat. Traffic Confs throughout Europe. Chm., Lancs Youth Clubs Assoc. DL Co. Palatine of Lancaster, 1971. Bronze Star (US) and Certif. of Merit (US Army), 1944. Publications: contribs to police jls throughout Europe. Recreations: motor sport, cinephotography, travel. Address: Netherside, Green Lane, Whitestake, Preston, Lancs.
[Died 17 Sept. 1979.

PALING, Rt. Hon. Wilfred, PC 1944; b Marehay, near Ripley, Derbyshire, 1883. A colliery checkweighman at Bulcroft Colliery; MP (Lab): Doncaster Division of West Riding Yorks, 1922-31; Wentworth Division of Yorks, 1933-50; Dearne Valley Division, W Riding Yorks, 1950-59. A Junior Lord of the Treasury, 1929-31; Lord Commissioner of the Treasury, 1940-41; Parliamentary Secretary, Ministry of Pensions, 1941-45; Minister of Pensions, 1945-47; Postmaster-General, 1947-50. Member of West Riding County Council, 1919-23 (resigned); Member of Bentley with Arksey UDC, 1919 (resigned); formerly Trustee of Yorkshire Mineworkers' Assoc. Address: Scawthorpe, Doncaster, Yorks. T: Doncaster 3892.
[Died 17 April 1971.

PALMER, Maj.-Gen. George Erroll P.; see Prior-Palmer.

PALMER, Hon. Lewis; see Palmer, Hon. W. J. L.

PALMER, Maj.-Gen. Peter Garwood, MBE 1944; FIMechE; MBIM; Deputy Secretary, Institution of Mechanical Engineers, since 1971; b 2 March 1914; s of H. G. Palmer, Great Yarmouth, Norfolk; m 1945, Isabel Mary Kinsley Boucher; one s. Educ: Haileybury College, Herts; Sheffield University (BEng). Petters Ltd, Yeovil, Som: Graduate Apprentice, 1933-35; Development Engineer, 1935-38. Regular Army Officer: RAOC, 1938-42; REME, 1942-71 (MBE); Dep. Dir of Electrical and Mechanical Engineering (Army), MoD, 1965-68; Comdt, Technical Gp, REME, Woolwich, 1968-71. Col Comdt, REME, 1973-78. Recreations: gardening, photography, sport. Address: 127 Claygate Lane, Hinchley Wood, Esher, Surrey. Club: St Stephen's.   [Died 20 June 1979.

PALMER, Hon. (William Jocelyn) Lewis, FLS; Treasurer, the Royal Horticultural Society, 1953-65; b 15 Sept. 1894; 3rd s of 2nd Earl of Selborne; m 1922, Hon. Dorothy Loder, d of 1st Baron Wakehurst; one s one d. Educ: Winchester; Christ Church, Oxford. MA (Oxon) 1919. Served European War, 1914-19, with Roy. Hampshire Regt. Employed first in shipping, then in industry, 1919-48; Manager and Vice-Chm. Forestal Land Timber and Railways Co., 1942-48; retired, 1948. JP Hants 1941, CC 1945. CA 1957. Master of The Mercers' Company, 1950-51 and 1956-57; Member of Council of Roy. Horticultural Soc. 1937, Vice-Chm. 1952. Victoria Medal of Honour, 1964. Recreation: gardening. Address: St Michel, Rue à l'Or, St Saviour's, Guernsey, CI. Club: Brooks's.   [Died 6 June 1971.

PANKHURST, Albert Stanley, CBE 1952; b 27 September 1897; 2nd s of William Pankhurst, Eltham; m 1920, Nellie, d of late Captain Walter Palmer, MC, KRRC; two s one d. Educ: Simon Langton School, Canterbury. Entered Ministry of Agriculture (Boy Clerk), 1913; Min. of Labour (Finance Dept and Unemployment Insurance Dept), 1920-34; seconded for service with Commissioner for Special Areas (England and Wales), Dec. 1934-Mar. 1937; International Board for non-Intervention in Spain (successively Chief Clerk, Dir of Accounts, Dep. Sec.), 1937-39; returned to Home Civil Service (Home Office, then Min. of Home Security, Chief Exec. Officer), 1940-42; Asst Chief Admin. Officer, London Civil Defence Region, 1940-42; Asst Sec., 1941; Min. of Production (Establishment Officer, then Dep. Head of Regional Div.), 1942-45; Board of Trade Regional Div., 1945-47. Principal Asst Sec., 1943; Under-Secretary, HM Treasury, 1947-52; Mission to India, 1952; UN Public Administration

Adviser: to Govt of Hashemite Kingdom of Jordan, 1953-56; to Govt of Union of Burma, 1956-58; to Govt of Chile, 1959-60. Served European War (first in ranks, then commissioned), 1915-19, RA and RASC. Order of Star of Jordan, Second Class, 1956. *Recreations:* gardening, chess. *Address:* 14 Hartfield Road, Cooden, Bexhill-on-Sea, East Sussex TN39 3EA. *T:* Cooden 3268. *Clubs:* East India, Sports and Public Schools, Civil Service.   *[Died 3 March 1975.*

PANNELL, Baron *cr* 1974 (Life Peer), of the City of Leeds; **Thomas Charles Pannell,** PC 1964; *b* 10 Sept. 1902; *s* of James William and Mary Jane Pannell; *m* 1929, Lilian Maud Frailing; one *d.* Hon. Secretary, Trade Union Group Parliamentary Labour Party, 1953-64; Member AEU, 1918-; Member Walthamstow Borough Council, 1929-36, Chief Whip of Labour Group; Chairman: Rating and Valuation Cttee; Municipal Entertainments Cttee; Erith Borough Council, 1938-55. Leader of Council and Chairman of Finance and General Purposes Cttee, until 1949; responsible Chairman during whole of War of 1939-45, for post-blitz services; Mayor, 1945-46, Alderman, 1944-55. Chairman of NW Kent Divisional Exec. for Education, 1944-55; Member and Dep. Leader,Kent County Council Labour Group, 1946-49. Member Labour Party, 1918-; Past Chairman Dartford Divisional Labour Party. MP (Lab) W Leeds, 1949-74. Parliamentary Delegations, Inter-Parliamentary Union: Berne, 1951; Belgium, 1952; NATO Conference of Parliamentarians, 1955-56-57; Poland, 1958; W Germany, 1960; Singapore, 1966 (Leader); NZ CPA, 1971; UAR, 1973 (Leader); Deleg. Atlantic Congress, 1959. Member Select Cttee on: Accommodation, 1953-54; Procedure, 1958-59; Law of Privilege, 1967; Member Joint Select Cttee, Lords and Commons, on House of Lords Reform, 1962; Minister of Public Building and Works, 1964-66; British Delegate, CPA Conference, Ottawa, 1966; Member, Cttee of Privileges, 1968-74. Vice-Pres., Assoc. of Municipal Corporations. Hon. LLD Leeds, 1975. *Address:* 159 Glenview, Abbey Wood, SE2. *T:* 01-310 4180.   *[Died 23 March 1980.*

PANNELL, Norman Alfred; *b* 17 April 1901; 4th *s* of Arthur Harry Pannell and Minnie (*née* Bradberry); *m* 1932, Isabel Morris; two *s* (one *d* decd). *Educ:* Sir George Monoux Grammar Sch., London. Various commercial posts, London and Paris, 1917-30; John Holt & Co. (Liverpool) Ltd; West Africa, 1930-45; Member Nigerian Legislative Council, 1944-45; Finance Manager, Liverpool, 1945-50. Member Liverpool City Council, 1952-57, 1967-70; Chairman, Liverpool Education Cttee, 1967-70; Member: Cheshire County Council, 1970-74; Merseyside Metropolitan County Council, 1973-. Governor, Liverpool Bluecoat Sch., 1953-. MP (C) Kirkdale Division of Liverpool, 1955-64. FCIS 1937. *Publication:* (with Lord Brockway) Immigration-What is the Answer?, 1965. *Address:* Thaxted, Mill Lane, Heswall, Merseyside L60 2TQ. *T:* Heswall 1309. *Club:* Athenæum (Liverpool).   *[Died 8 March 1976.*

PANTIN, William Abel, MA; FBA 1948; Keeper of the University Archives, 1946-69; Fellow and Lecturer in History, Oriel College, Oxford, 1933-69, Hon. Fellow, 1971; University Lecturer in Mediæval Archæology and History, 1937-69; *b* Blackheath, 1 May 1902; *s* of Herbert Pantin and Emilie, *d* of late Charles D. Abel, Blackheath. *Educ:* Westminster; Christ Church, Oxford. 1st Class hons, Modern History, 1923; Bryce Research Student, 1924-25; Alexander Prize Essay, 1927; Asst Lecturer in History and Bishop Fraser Lecturer in Ecclesiastical History in the University of Manchester, 1926-33; Birkbeck Lecturer in Ecclesiastical History, Trinity Coll., Cambridge, 1948. Mem., Royal Commn on Historical Monuments, 1963-. *Publications:* Documents illustrating the activities of the General and Provincial Chapters of the English Black Monks, 1215-1540 (Camden Series, 1931-37); Canterbury College, Oxford (Oxford Historical Society), 1947; Durham Cathedral, 1948; The English Church in the Fourteenth Century, 1955; Oxford Life in Oxford Archives, 1972; articles and reviews contributed to the English Historical Review, History, Trans. of Royal Historical Society, Bulletin of John Rylands Library, Oxoniensia. *Recreations:* travel, archæology, architectural history. *Address:* Oriel College, Oxford. *Club:* Athenæum.
                                              [Died 10 Nov. 1973.

PARC-LOCMARIA, Marquis du, (Alain); Hon. CVO; Belgian Diplomat, retired; Commander, Ordre de Léopold (glaives); Grand Officier, Ordre de la Couronne (glaives); Grand Officier, Ordre de Léopold II (glaives et palme); Croix du Feu; Croix de Guerre (Belgian) (2 palmes); etc; *b* Brussels, 27 Oct. 1892; *m* Comtesse Elisabeth de Grunne (*d* 1972); one *s* one *d.* *Educ:* Oratory Sch., Edgbaston; Louvain University (Doctor of Laws). Served War of 1914-18, Belgian Army (seriously wounded). Entered Diplomatic Service, 1920; Second, then First Secretary, Belgian Embassy, Paris, 1922-28; Dept of Foreign Affairs,

Brussels, 1928-39; Couns., 1930; Minister, 1937; Minister to Rumania, 1939; Minister and Commerc. Couns., Belgian Embassy, US, 1942; President, etc; Belgian delegations, including those to FAO, UNRRA, and International Conferences, 1943-45; Minister to Sweden, 1946-48; Ambassador to Canada, 1949-53; Ambassador to Court of St James's, 1953-57, retired. Grand Cordon, Polar Star (Sweden); Officier de la Légion d'Honneur, Medaille Militaire, and Croix de Guerre (France), etc. *Recreation:* shooting. *Heir: s* Comte du Parc Locmaria. *Address:* Château de Thieusies, Hainaut, Belgium. *Club:* Beefsteak.   *[Died 26 March 1973.*

PARE, Rev. Canon Clive Frederick, MA Cantab; Canon Residentiary since 1963 and Precentor since 1966, of Gloucester Cathedral; *b* 27 April 1908; *s* of Frederick William Pare, Nottingham, and Florence May Pare (*née* Hodson), Loughborough; *m* 1954, Hilda Clare, *d* of Thomas Dewsbury Parson, Cape Town; two *s.* *Educ:* Nottingham High Sch.; King's Coll., Cambridge (Choral Scholar); Cuddesdon Theological Coll. Housemaster, Bishop Cotton Sch., Simla, India, 1931. Deacon, 1933; Priest, 1935; Asst Curate, Gillingham with Milton, Dorset, 1934-36; Senior Curate, St John, E Dulwich, 1936-37; Asst Master and Minor Canon, Canterbury, 1937-38; Headmaster, Canterbury Cathedral Choir Sch., 1938-63. Hon. Secretary, Canterbury Dio. Advisory Cttee for the Care of Churches, and Member Central Council for Care of Churches, 1947-63. Private Chaplain to Archbishop of Canterbury (Lord Fisher) for tour of Australia and New Zealand, 1950. Member Canterbury City Council, 1954; Sheriff of Canterbury, 1961-62; Mayor of Canterbury (JP), 1962-63. *Recreations:* music, gardening, walking, camping, local government. *Address:* 7 Miller's Green, Gloucester. *T:* 23695.   *[Died 3 July 1973.*

PARHAM, Hedley John, CBE 1955; MA, LLB (Cantab); JP; *b* 29 Oct. 1892; *s* of late Leonard Parham, JP, Gosport, Hants; *m* 1921, Irene, *d* of late H. E. Phillips, JP, Kintbury, Berks; two *s.* *Educ:* Leys Sch., Cambridge; Trinity Hall, Cambridge. Served European War (RE), 1914-19 (despatches). Called to the Bar (Inner Temple), 1919. Joined Department of Director of Public Prosecutions, 1920; Asst Director of Public Prosecutions, 1949-56; retired. JP Glos, 1957. *Address:* 4 The Mead, Cirencester, Glos GL7 2BB.   *[Died 19 Jan. 1978.*

PARHAM, Maj.-Gen. Hetman Jack, CB 1949; CBE 1943; DSO 1940, and Bar 1943; late Royal Artillery; *b* 27 July 1895. 2nd Lieut, Royal Artillery, 1914; served European War, 1915-19, in France, Belgium, and the Balkans (despatches twice, 1914-15 star, two medals); Major, 1934; served War of 1939-45, in North Africa and North-West Europe (despatches, DSO and Bar, CBE); Brigadier, 1942; Colonel, 1944; Maj.-Gen., 1945. ADC to the King, 1946-47; commanding No 3 Anti-Aircraft Group, 1946-49; retired pay, 1949. Officer of Legion of Merit (USA). *Address:* Hyntle Place, Hintlesham, Ipswich, Suffolk.
                                              [Died 29 Dec. 1974.

PARK, Alexander Dallas, CMG 1932; JP; FIANZ; FRANZ; Company Director; *b* Waitaki, Otago, New Zealand, 1882; *s* of George Park, Merchant; *m* Ada Emily, *d* of J. C. Mercer, Nelson; one *s.* *Educ:* Waitaki; Waimate. Joined Public Works Dept, 1900; served South African War, 1902; Senior Accountant, Dept of Agriculture, 1918; Inspector for Public Service Commissioner and Treasury, 1919; Secretary for Marine, 1922; Asst Public Service Commissioner, 1924; Asst Secretary to Treasury, 1926; Secretary to Treasury, 1930-35; Chairman, Local Government Loans Board, 1930-35; Deputy Chairman, Stores Control Board, 1930-35; Financial Adviser to Government, 1931-35; Foundation Member Reserve Bank of New Zealand Board, 1934-35; Chairman: Soldiers' Financial Assistance Board, 1940-46; State Advances Corporation of New Zealand, 1936-49. *Recreations:* golf, fishing. *Address:* 14 Park Avenue, Titahi Bay, Wellington, NZ. *T:* Titahi Bay 7414. *Club:* Wellington (Wellington).   *[Died 28 June 1971.*

PARK, Air Chief Marshal Sir Keith Rodney, GCB 1946 (KCB 1945; CB 1940); KBE 1942; MC; DFC; DCL, MA (Oxon); *b* 1892; *s* of late Professor J. Park; *m* 1918, Dorothy Margarita (*d* 1971), *d* of Lieut-Col Woodbine Parish, CMG, CBE; one *s* (and one *s* killed on active service, 1951). *Educ:* King's Coll., Auckland, NZ; Otago Boys' High Sch., Dunedin. Commanded No 11 Fighter Group during Battle of Britain; commanded RAF Egypt; AOC, RAF, Malta, 1942-43; AOC-in-C Middle East, 1944; Allied Air C-in-C South-East Asia, 1945-46. *Recreation:* sailing. *Address:* Blue Waters, Lucerne Road, Remuera, Auckland, NZ.   *[Died 5 Feb. 1975.*

PARKER OF WADDINGTON, Baron (Life Peer), *cr* 1958, of Lincoln's Inn; **Hubert Lister Parker,** PC 1954; Kt 1950; Lord Chief Justice of England, 1958-71; *b* 28 May 1900; 3rd *s* of Lord

Parker of Waddington, PC (d 1918), a Lord of Appeal in Ordinary; m 1924, Loryn, d of O. Tilton Bowser, Kentucky, USA. *Educ:* Rugby Sch.; Trinity Coll., Cambridge (Senior Scholar). Called to Bar, 1924. Junior Counsel in Common Law: to Admiralty, 1934; to the Treasury, 1945-50; Judge of High Court of Justice, King's Bench Division, 1950-54; a Lord Justice of Appeal, 1954-58. *Address:* Pile Oak Lodge, Donhead St Andrew, Shaftesbury, Dorset. [Died 15 Sept. 1972.

PARKER, Albert, CBE 1946; DSc; FRIC; FIChemE; Hon. FInstGasE; Hon. FInstFuel; Consulting Chemical Engineer; *b* 2 May 1892; *s* of late John Albert and Alice Parker, Manchester; *m* 1922, Lilian Maud (*d* 1972), *d* of late Albert Edward Midgley, Birmingham; one *d* (and one *d* decd). *Educ:* Manchester Grammar Sch.; Manchester Univ. First Class Hons Chemistry, Manchester, 1912; Grad. Schol. and Beyer Research Fellow, Manchester, 1912-14; DSc Birmingham, 1916. Lecturer in Phys. Chem. and Thermodynamics, Birmingham Univ., and Chemist Inspector on manufacture of high explosives for Midland area, 1914-19. Research Chem. to University of Leeds and Instn of Gas Engineers, 1919-28. Asst Director Water Pollution Research, DSIR, 1928-39, Director, 1939-43; Director of Fuel Research, DSIR, 1943-56. Lt-Col in charge of team of British and American experts investigating synthetic oil, etc in Germany, March-April 1945. Osborne Reynolds Medal, IChemE, 1941; Melchett Medal, Inst. of Fuel, 1955; Telford Premium, 1942, and Chadwick Medal, 1955, ICE; Mitchell Gold Medal, Stoke-on-Trent Assoc. of Engineers, 1956; Thomas Hawksley Lectr, IMechE, 1949; Cantor Lectures, RSA, 1960. Pres., Fuel Luncheon Club, 1953-55; Hon. Secretary, British National Cttee, World Power Conference, 1951-64, and Chm., Consultative Panel on Survey of Energy Resources, 1958-68; Chm. Council, RSH, 1955-56; Chm., Expert Cttee on Air Pollution, WHO, 1958; Pres., National Society for Clean Air, 1963-65 (Clean Air Award, 1973). *Publications:* Control of Industrial Air Pollution, 1977; contrib. various scientific and technical journals and books. *Recreation:* music. *Address:* Stanway, Wellesley Avenue, Northwood, Middlesex HA6 3HZ. *T:* Northwood 26435. *Club:* Athenæum. [Died 1 April 1980.

PARKER, Cecil; actor, stage and films; *b* Hastings, 3 Sept. 1897; *m* 1927, Muriel Ann Randall Brown; one *d. Educ:* St François Xavier Coll.; Bruges, Belgium. Served European War, 1914-18. First stage appearance as Lorenzo in Merchant of Venice, Eastbourne; continued in Charles Doran's company until 1924; leading parts at Liverpool Repertory, 1924-26; first London appearance, Everyman Theatre, 1925; London stage appearances include: The Constant Nymph, Wonder Bar, Mademoiselle, Reunion in Vienna, The Rats of Norway, Little Ladyship, Bonnet over the Windmill, Blithe Spirit (Charles Condamine, 1941-44), Skin of our Teeth. Entered films, 1933; *films include:* Ships with Wings, Cæsar and Cleopatra, The Magic Bow, Hungry Hill, Captain Boycott, The First Gentleman, Quartet, The Weaker Sex, The Chiltern Hundreds, I Believe in You, Isn't Life Wonderful?, Dear Mr Prohack, The Man in the White Suit, Father Brown, For Better for Worse, The Constant Husband, The Court Jester, The Lady Killers, It's Great to be Young, Twenty-three Paces to Baker Street, True as a Turtle, A Tale of Two Cities, Happy is the Bride, Indiscreet, I Was Monty's Double, A French Mistress, The Pure Hell of St Trinian's, A Study in Terror. *Address:* 1 Dyke Road Place, Brighton, Sussex. [Died 20 April 1971.

PARKER, Rt. Rev. Clement George St Michael; *b* 29 Sept. 1900; *s* of late Rev. W. H. Parker, Vicar of S Peter, Birmingham. *Educ:* Christ Church, Oxford. Ordained 1923; Asst Curate. S Bartholomew and S Jude, Birmingham; Vicar of King's Heath, 1939-61; Rural Dean, King's Norton, 1943-61; Hon. Canon of Birmingham, 1944-61; Archdeacon of Aston, 1946-54; Bishop Suffragan of Aston, 1954-61; Bishop of Bradford, 1961-71. *Address:* 22 Hillmorton Road, Rugby, Warwickshire CV22 5AA. [Died 5 March 1980.

PARKER, Geoffrey Edward, DSO 1945; MA, MD, FRCS; late Senior Surgeon to French Hospital in London and Woolwich Group of Hospitals; Surgeon to the Italian Hospital in London and to St Nicholas' Hospital (Woolwich), 1962-June 1972; *b* 24 June 1902; *s* of late Geoffrey Leslie Parker and of Gertrude Clara Pook; *m* 1st, 1930, Kathleen Hewlett Johnson (marr. diss.); two *s* one *d*; 2nd, 1968, Lois Margaret Wilsdon. *Educ:* Marlborough; Trinity Hall, Cambridge. Resident and non-resident appointments at St Thomas's Hosp. (Grainger Prize, 1928), W London Hosp., St Peter's Hosp., St Mark's Hosp., Woolwich Memorial Hosp. Mem. Roy. Soc. Med. and Assoc. of Surgeons of Gt Brit. First Chm., 1948-51, Med. Advisory Cttee Woolwich Gp of Hosps; Chm. Med. Cttee, French Hosp. Corr. Member: French Assoc. of Surgeons; French Assoc. of Urol. Surgeons; Mem. Brit. Cttee of Internat. Soc. of Surgery; Hon.

Mem., Faculty of Surgery, Univ. of Lyon. Liveryman of Worshipful Soc. of Apothecaries; Freeman, City of London. Commandeur de la Légion d'Honneur, 1968; Croix de Guerre with Palm, and Croix de Guerre with Silver Star (France), 1945; Officier de l'Ordre de Leopold (Belgium), 1956; Commendatore Al Merito della Repubblica Italiana. *Publications:* Surgery of Abdominal Trauma, 1944; The Black Scalpel, 1968; Surgical Cosmopolis, 1969; contrib. on surgery and surgical practice to Br. and continental surgical jls. *Recreations:* painting, writing, swimming; formerly boxing (welter-weight, Cambridge Blue, 1924). *Address:* 5 The Green, Great Horwood, near Winslow, Milton Keynes MK17 0RH. *T:* Winslow 2831. *Club:* Savile. [Died 5 Dec. 1973.

PARKER, Gordon, CBE 1972; MM 1916; TEM 1924; Chairman: Favor Parker Ltd, since 1921; Stoke Ferry, since 1921; Felixstowe Dock & Railway Co., 1951-76, Life President since 1976; *b* 1892; *m* 1915 and 1925; two *s* two *d* (and one *s* decd). *Educ:* Thetford Grammar School. Farming, seed merchant, 1910-22; War Service, 1914-19; grain merchant, farming, fertiliser manufacturer, 1922-51; subseq. grain merchanting, Britain and overseas, with Felixstowe Dock & Rly Co., manufacturer animal feed. *Recreations:* earlier, everything. *Address:* Stoke Ferry Hall, Kings Lynn, Norfolk. *T:* Stoke Ferry 360. [Died 26 July 1980.

PARKER, Sir Harold, KCB 1949 (CB 1943); KBE 1946; MC 1918; *b* 27 May 1895; *s* of W. G. Parker; *m* 1926, Kathleen Maud Gibbs; two *s. Educ:* Haberdashers' School. Exchequer and Audit Department, 1914; Treasury, 1919; Principal Assistant Secretary, 1938; Deputy Secretary, Ministry of Pensions, 1941-45; Secretary, Ministry of Pensions, 1946-48; Permanent Secretary to the Ministry of Defence, 1948-56, retired; Chairman: Corp. of Insurance Brokers Society of Pension Consultants, 1958-70; Member, United Nations Civil Service Advisory Board, 1957-70. President Amateur Swimming Association, 1958. Served European War, 1914-18, Temporary Captain RFA. *Recreations:* golf, swimming. *Address:* 90 Rivermead Court, SW6. *T:* 01-736 6945; 9 Upper Third Avenue, Frinton, Essex. *T:* Frinton 4783. *Club:* Hurlingham. [Died 5 Feb. 1980.

PARKER, Henry Gordon; *see* Parker, G.

PARKER, Henry Michael Denne, CB 1954; CBE 1950; *b* 31 Dec. 1894; *s* of Henry Parker; unmarried. *Educ:* Edinburgh Academy; Hertford College, Oxford (open scholar). Served 7th Battalion The King's (Liverpool) Regiment, Lieutenant, 1915-18. BA and MA, 1921; Tutor and Dean of Keble Coll., Oxford, 1921-26; Fellow and Tutor 1926-45, Senior Dean of Arts, 1928-33, Vice-Pres., 1938-40, Magdalen College, Oxford; Emeritus Fellow, 1970. Univ. Lecturer in Roman History, 1928-33; Junior Proctor, Oxford Univ., 1927-28; Member of Hebdomadal Council, 1928-41. Temp. Principal and Asst Sec., 1941-45, Established Asst Sec., 1945, Min. of Labour and National Service; Under-Secretary, Ministry of Labour and National Service, 1950-56. *Publications:* The Roman Legions, 1928; History of the Roman World, AD 138-337, 1935 (2nd edn, 1958); articles in Oxford Classical Dictionary, 1949. Volume on Manpower, in Civil History of the War, 1957. *Recreations:* gardening and walking. *Address:* Thistle House, St Catherine's, Argyll. *T:* St Catherine's 209. [Died 2 Dec. 1971.

PARKER, Lt-Col John Oxley, TD; MA; *b* 28 June 1886; *e s* of Christopher William Parker and Helen Cecilia, *d* of Sir William J. Farrer, Faulkbourne Hall, Essex; *m* 1916, Mary Monica (*d* 1958), *d* of Arnold F. Hills, Hammerfield, Penshurst; one *s* two *d. Educ:* Eton; Oriel Coll., Oxford. Local Director (retired) Barclays Bank; President Essex Agricultural Society, 1959. Served European War, 1914-18, Essex Yeo., Major, France (Croix de Guerre Belge); HG, 1940-45 (Lt-Col). Essex: JP 1921; DL 1926-72; High Sheriff, 1948-49. *Publication:* The Oxley Parker Papers, 1964. *Recreations:* shooting, estate management, gardening and forestry. *Address:* The Old Rectory, Faulkbourne, Witham, Essex. *T:* Witham 513221. *Club:* United Oxford & Cambridge University. [Died 27 Nov. 1979.

PARKER, Roger Henry, CBE 1960; MC; Formerly: Director, Head Office, Barclays Bank Ltd; Local Director, Local Head Office, Cambridge; *b* 1889; *s* of Edmund Henry Parker, MA, LLD, DL, JP, of Thorneycreek, Cambridge; *m* 1922, Helen Mary Finch Foster; three *s* one *d. Educ:* Eton; Trinity Coll., Cambridge (MA). Served European War, 1914-19, Captain SR 5 Dragoon Guards, 1917; Captain, TAR of O, 1931; Lt-Col, 4th Cambridgeshire Bn Home Guard, 1941-45. High Sheriff of Cambridgeshire, 1942; Alderman of Cambridgeshire CC till 1965, of Cambridgeshire and Isle of Ely CC, 1964-67. Vice-Chm., Cambs CC, 1949-52, Chm., 1952-55. Vice-Chm., Bd of

Govs, United Cambridge Hosps, 1948-55; Chm., 1955-63; DL Cambridgeshire, 1932-58, Lord Lieutenant, 1958-65. *Recreation:* Joint Master Cambridgeshire Foxhounds, 1935-53, Master 1953-57, Joint Master 1957-60. *Address:* Lyndewode, Grantchester, Cambridge. *T:* Trumpington 2212.
[Died 6 Oct. 1973.

PARKER, Rt. Rev. T. Leo; retired 1967; Bishop of Northampton, emeritus; *b* 21 Dec. 1883; *s* of George Parker, Birmingham. *Educ:* St Bede's, Manchester; Ushaw; University, Durham. Ordained, 1915; Secretary to Bishops of Salford, 1915-36; Parish Priest of Higher Broughton, Salford, 1936-40; Bishop of Northampton, 1941-67. *Address:* Fox Den, Dorney Wood Road, Burnham, Bucks. *T:* Burnham 5057.
[Died 25 March 1975.

PARKER, Sir William Lorenzo, 3rd Bt, *cr* 1844; OBE 1919; DL; late Captain 1/9 Hants Regiment; *b* 9 Jan. 1889; *s* of 2nd Bt and Kathleen Mary, *e d* of L. K. Hall of Holly Bush, Staffs; *S* father 1902; *m* 1915, Ruth Margaret Sillery (*d* 1971), *d* of A. B. Hanbury-Sparrow, Hillside, Church Stretton; two *s* one *d. Educ:* Eton; New College, Oxford. DL (1948), Vice-Lieutenant, County of Brecknock, 1957; Lord Lieutenant, 1959-64; DL 1965. *Heir: s* William Alan Parker [*b* 20 March 1916; *m* 1946, Sheelagh Mary, *o d* of Dr Sinclair Stevenson; one *s* one *d*]. *Address:* 4 Garscube Terrace, Edinburgh EH12 6BQ.
[Died 27 Oct. 1971.

PARKES, Sir Roderick Wallis, KCMG 1960 (CMG 1956); OBE 1945; Ambassador to Jordan, 1962-66; retired; *b* 2 Apr. 1909; *o s* of late Llywelyn Childs Parkes; *m* 1939, Eileen Mary Ernestine, *o c* of late Major Nevile Gardner; two *s. Educ:* St Paul's School; Magdalen Coll., Oxford. Entered ICS, 1932; served in Punjab until 1935; Indian Political Service, 1935-47; Asst Political Agent, South Waziristan, 1935; Sec. and later Counsellor, British legation, Kabul, 1936-39; Political Agent, Eastern Kathiawar, 1941-42; served in Rajputana and Baroda, 1943; Kolhapur, 1944; Punjab States, 1945; attached to Food Dept, Govt of India, as Liaison Commissioner (States), 1946-47; retired from Indian Political Service and entered Foreign Service, 1948; Counsellor (Information) British Embassy, Cairo, 1949; Head of Information Div., Brit. Middle East Office, Beirut, 1952; Head of Information Services Dept, FO, 1953; Counsellor, Brit. Embassy, Djakarta, 1954, Chargé d'Affaires, 1954; Ambassador to Saudi Arabia, 1955-56; to Viet Nam, 1957-60; to Sudan, 1961; seconded to Civil Service Commn as Group Chm. Civil Service Selection Bd, Jan. 1962. Chairman: Aquamarine International (Fisheries & Ocean Development) Ltd; Allied Associates Ltd, IoM; Castletown Developments Ltd. *Address:* The Old House, Castletown, Isle of Man. *T:* Castletown 2384. *Club:* Athenæum. *[Died 2 Nov. 1972.*

PARKIN, Sir Ian (Stanley Colston), Kt 1953; CBE 1946; *b* 12 Sept. 1896; *e s* of George Treble Parkin, Ashford, Devon; *m* 1920, Gertrude Watkins; three *s* one *d. Educ:* Bristol. Secretary Port of Bristol Employers' Association, 1919-40; Technical Adviser on Dock Problems to Minister of Labour, 1940-41; Gen. Man., Nat. Dock Labour Corp., Ltd, 1941-47. Member: Nat. Council of Port Employers, 1920-40; Nat. Jt Council for Dock Labour, 1927-40; Standing Advisory Cttee on Registration and Decasualisation, 1931-40; Nat. Jt Conciliation Bd for Road Motor Transport Industry (Goods), 1934-38; General Manager and Secretary, National Dock Labour Board, 1947-55, retired. *Address:* Anchorage, 15 Carlyon Road, Playing Place, Truro, Cornwall. *T:* Devoran 862720. *[Died 28 Dec. 1971.*

PARKINSON, Maj.-Gen. (Retd) Graham Beresford, CBE 1945; DSO and Bar; *b* 5 Nov. 1896; *s* of Henry Ainslie Parkinson, MA, and Ethel Constance Young, Hobart, Tasmania; *m* 1925, Barbara Waiohine Howe. *Educ:* Wellington College, NZ, Royal Military College of Australia, Duntroon (graduated 1915). Proceeded overseas and served in France until the Armistice, proceeding to Germany. Internal security expedition to Fiji in 1920; various staff appts until attended Gunnery Staff Course, Woolwich, 1924; various staff appts until appointed Director of Artillery Army HQ, Wellington, 1936; proceeded overseas with 2 NZ Div. on outbreak of war and continued to serve until conclusion of hostilities with Germany; appointments included: Comdr 4th Field Regt; Comdr 6 Inf. Bde; Comdr RA 2 NZ Div.; GOC 2 NZ Div. for a period under NZ Corps; Quartermaster-General, Army HQ, NZ, 1946; NZ Jt Liaison Staff (London), Dec. 1946-Sept. 1949. Legion of Merit Degree of Officer (USA). *Recreation:* horticulture. *Address:* 27 Clifford Avenue, Fendalton, Christchurch, New Zealand.
[Died 10 July 1979.

PARKINSON, Sir Harold, KBE 1955 (OBE 1942); Kt 1946; JP; Vice-President, Building Societies Association; *b* 2 July 1894; *m*

1921, Evelyn Green; no *c.* Chm., Lancs Chamber of Commerce, 1937-39; Vice-Chm, 1941-58, Vice-Pres., 1958-72, Nat. Savings Cttee. Chm., Shirley Institute, 1945-49; Pres., NW Assoc. Building Socs, 1951-68; Chm., NW Housing Production Board, 1952-54. Pres., Royal Lancs. Ag. Soc., 1948. High Sheriff of Lancs, 1950-51. *Address:* Old Vicarage, Hornby, near Lancaster. *T:* Hornby 21297. *Clubs:* National, Lansdowne.
[Died 26 Aug. 1974.

PARKINSON, Sir John, Kt 1948; MD London; FRCP; Hon. LLD Glasgow 1951; Hon. DSc NUI 1952; Hon. FRCPE 1953; Hon FACP 1951; Hon. FRCPS Glasgow 1959; Hon. FRCPI 1962; Hon. FRSM 1966; Consultant Physician to Cardiac Department of London Hospital; Consulting Physician to the National Heart Hospital; Consulting Cardiologist to the Royal Air Force, 1931-56; hon. corresponding member French Society of Cardiology; foreign correspondent French Academy of Medicine; Hon. Member International Society of Cardiology; Hon. President European Society of Cardiology; ex-President Association of Physicians of Great Britain and Ireland (1950); President British Cardiac Society, 1951-55; *b* 10 Feb. 1885; *s* of John Parkinson, JP, of Thornton-le-Fylde, Lancs.; *m* 1917, Clara Elvina (*d* 1974), *d* of late Alfred Le Brocq, St Heliers; four *d* (one *s* decd). *Educ:* Univ. Coll., London; the London Hosp.; the Univ. of Freiburg. Medical Registrar to the London Hospital, 1911-12; Chief Assistant to Sir James Mackenzie in the Cardiac Department of the London Hospital, 1913-14; served European War, 1914-19; Medical Officer, Casualty Clearing Station, BEF, France, 1914-16; Divisional Officer, Military Hospital for Research on Heart Cases, Hampstead, 1916; Major, RAMC, in charge of Military Heart Centre, Rouen, 1917-19. Fothergill Gold Medal, Medical Soc. of London, 1947; Moxon Medal, RCP, 1957; Gold Stethoscope Award, Internat. Cardiology Foundn, 1966. *Publications:* Harveian Oration, Royal College of Physicians, London, 1945; Lumleian Lecture, RCP, 1936; St Cyres Lecture, 1938; Address in Medicine, Canadian Medical Association, Ottawa, 1924; Address to Czechoslovak Cardiological Soc., Prague, 1935, and California Heart Association, 1946; Convocation Address, American College of Physicians, 1951; Laubry Lecture, International Congress of Cardiology, Washington, 1954; Articles on Diseases of the Heart and Vessels in the Index of Treatment, 1948; various papers on medical and cardiological subjects in the Quarterly Journal of Medicine, Heart, the Lancet, and the British Heart Journal. *Recreation:* gardening. *Address:* 4f Portman Mansions, Chiltern Street, W1M 1LF. *T:* 01-486 2246.
[Died 5 June 1976.

PARKINSON, Dame Nancy (Broadfield), DCMG 1965; CBE 1946 (OBE 1938); Leverhulme Research Fellow, since 1968; *b* 23 Jan. 1904; 2nd *d* of Frank Parkinson, Manchester. *Educ:* The College, Harrogate; Bedford Coll., Univ. of London. BSc Hons. Hospitality Secretary, National Union of Students, to 1939; Controller, Home Div., British Council, 1939-68. Member: Court, Univ. of Manchester, 1967-; Council, Inst. of Study of Internat. Organisation, Sussex Univ., 1968-. Governor, Bedford Coll., University of London; Hon. Pres., Student Cooperative Dwellings, 1972- (Chm., 1968-72). Hon. LLD Manchester, 1968. *Recreations:* walking, reading, golf. *Address:* 6 Hanover Terrace, Regent's Park, NW1 4RJ. *[Died 10 Dec. 1974.*

PARLBY, Joshua, CIE 1942; OBE; Military Accountant-General in India, 1939-45; *b* 3 March 1889; *s* of Joshua Parlby, Hanley, Staffs; *m* 1926, Elizabeth Scott, *d* of Donald Fyfe Stuart; one *s* one *d. Educ:* Manchester Grammar School; Victoria University, Manchester; Trinity College, Cambridge. Military Accounts Dept (India), 1913; Mesopotamia Expeditionary Force, 1917-21; Civil Administration of Iraq, 1921-25; Comptroller and Auditor-General in Iraq, 1925-35. Order of Rafidain (Iraq), 1935. *Recreations:* walking, shooting, and fishing. *Address:* Richmond Lodge, 7 Shorton Road, Paignton, Devon. *T:* Paignton 57017. *[Died 7 July 1975.*

PARMOOR, 2nd Baron, *cr* 1914, of Frieth; **Alfred Henry Seddon Cripps;** *b* 27 Aug. 1882; *e s* of 1st Baron and Theresa (*d* 1893), *d* of Richard Potter; *S* father, 1941; unmarried. *Educ:* Winchester; New Coll., Oxford. Called to Bar, Middle Temple, 1907; contested (U) Wycombe Division, 1906; Bursar, Queen's Coll., Oxford, 1928-45; Fellow, 1929-. Captain Lincolnshire Yeomanry during war. *Heir: b* Hon. Frederick Heyworth Cripps, DSO, TD. *Address:* 44 Admirals Walk, West Cliff, Bournemouth. *T:* Bournemouth 27688. *Club:* Brooks's.
[Died 12 May 1977.

PARMOOR, 3rd Baron *cr* 1914; **Frederick Heyworth Cripps,** DSO 1918; TD; DL; 2nd *s* of 1st Baron Parmoor, PC, KCVO, KC, and Theresa (*d* 1893), *d* of Richard Potter; *S* brother, 1977; *b* 4 July 1885; *m* 1927, Violet, Duchess of Westminster (marr.

diss. 1951), *d* of Sir William Nelson, 1st Bt; one *s*. *Educ*: Winchester; New Coll., Oxford. Dir of Russian and English bank in Petrograd until 1914; Royal Bucks Hussars Yeomanry, 1904; served European War, Gallipoli (wounded); Senussi campaign, Palestine (DSO and bar) and France (Belgian croix de guerre); commanded regt from Aug. 1917. War of 1939-45, Lieut-Comdr RNVR, 1939. DL Bucks, 1929. *Publication*: Life's a Gamble, 1958. *Recreations*: shooting and fishing. *Heir*: s Hon. (Frederick Alfred) Milo Cripps, [*b* 18 June 1929. *Educ*: Ampleforth; Corpus Christi Coll., Oxford]. *Club*: White's.
[Died 5 Oct. 1977.

PARNALL, Robert Boyd Cochrane; His Honour Judge Parnall; a Circuit Judge (Judge of County Courts), since 1971; *b* 26 Oct. 1912; *s* of R. H. B. Parnall, Glanmor, Newport, Mon; *m* 1937, Wilma Brooks, ward of Lt-Col F. L. Scott-Kerr, Ashby, Melrose, Roxburghshire; no *c*. *Educ*: Marlborough; Oriel Coll., Oxford. Called to Bar, Middle Temple, 1936; joined Oxford Circuit, 1936. Served in South Wales Borderers, 1940-43; in Judge Advocate-General's dept, 1943-46. Recorder of Hereford, 1956-71; Dep. Chm., Monmouthshire QS, 1956-71. Elected to Bar Council, 1956. *Address*: 83 Bickenhall Mansions, W1. *T*: 01-935 9306; 2 Harcourt Buildings, Temple, EC4. *T*: 01-353 8549.
[Died 12 Nov. 1976.

PARNELL, Valentine Charles; *b* 14 Feb. 1894; *s* of Thomas Frederick Parnell, OBE (Fred Russell) and Elizabeth White; *m* 1938, Helen Howell; *m* 1966, Aileen Cochrane; one adopted *s*. *Educ*: Godwin Coll., Cliftonville. Began career as office boy with late Sir Walter de Frece, 1907; later, Booking Manager to Variety Theatre Controlling Co. and retained this position with General Theatre Corporation Ltd from 1928 until this Company amalgamated with Moss' Empires Ltd, 1931, when appointed General Manager; Director, Moss' Empires Ltd, 1941-60 (Managing Director, 1945-58); Director of Associated Television Ltd, 1955-66 (Managing Director, 1957-62); retired. *Address*: Le Semiramis, 06 Cannes, France.
[Died 22 Sept. 1972.

PARR, Sir Robert, KBE 1950 (OBE 1927); CMG 1943; DèsL (*hc*) University of Lyons, 1956; *b* 15 May 1894; *e s* of Rev. Robert Edmund Parr (*d* 1938), Medomsley, Co. Durham, and of Harriet, *d* of Alfred William Nicholson; *m* Cicely Emily (*d* 1964), *d* of Henry David Shaw, Hadnall, Salop; one *d* (one *s* Robert Philip, Lieut, Grenadier Guards, killed in action at Minturno, 1944; and one *d* decd). *Educ*: Durham; Magdalen Coll., Oxford. Entered Levant Consular Service, 1919; Vice-Consul, 1926; Consul, 1933; Consul-General, 1940; retired, 1956. Chevalier Serbian Order of White Eagle (Mil.); Serbian Gold Medal for Valour and Alexander I Medal; Freedom of City of Lyons, 1945, of Villefranche-en-Beaujolais, 1949, of Tournus, 1951, of City of Dijon, 1952, of Vienne, 1954, of Grézieu-la-Varenne, 1955, and of La Mulatière, 1958; Médaille d'Honneur of City of Dijon, 1950, Médaille Bimillénaire of City of Lyons, 1958; Associate Member Acad. of Lyons, 1950, Acad. of Mâcon, 1955; Mem. various other learned societies in France; Hon. Dean of Consular Body of City of Lyons; Hon. President: Lyons Fédération des Amicales Régimentaires et d'Anciens Combattants; Union des Jouteurs et Sauveteurs de La Mulatière; Association des Rescapés de Montluc; The Lyons English Club. *Address*: c/o Mrs Michael Livingstone-Learmonth, Minchinhampton, Glos. *Clubs*: Brooks's; Salop (Shrewsbury); Rotary of Chalon-sur-Saône (Hon.). *[Died 1 Nov. 1979.*

PARRY, Rear-Adm. Cecil Ramsden Langworthy, CB 1952; DSO 1944; retired 1953; *b* 3 Sept. 1901; *s* of late Colonel P. E. Langworthy Parry, DSO, OBE; *m* 1931, Alison Fielding Blandford; one *s* one *d*. *Educ*: RNC, Osborne and Dartmouth. Midshipman, HMS Tiger, 1917; qualified as Torpedo Officer; Commander, 1935; Tactical School, 1939, in command HMS Vivacious, subsequently HMS Montrose; assistant Naval Attaché and Liaison Officer with US Pacific Fleet, Hawaiian Waters, 1941-42; Captain 1941; Captain (D), 21st Destroyer Flotilla (DSO); Admiralty, 1944-46; Captain of Dockyard, Portsmouth, 1947-48; Captain, HMS Duke of York, 1949; in command HMS Euryalus, Mediterranean, 1949-50; Rear-Admiral, 1951; Flag Officer Ground Training, Lee-on-Solent, 1951-53; retired Sept. 1953. Secretary, Commonwealth Trans-Antarctic Expedition, 1955-59. Secretary, British National Appeal, World Wildlife Fund, 1961-64. *Address*: Coachmans, Westbourne, Emsworth, Hants. *Clubs*: Army and Navy, Royal Automobile. *[Died 31 March 1977.*

PARRY, Claude Frederick, CIE 1947; OBE 1943; Indian Police (retired); Secretary, The Athenæum, 1951-62; *b* 9 March 1896; *s* of late F. W. Parry; *m* 1930, Sylvia Nancy Irene Kingsley; two *s* one *d*. *Educ*: St Bees Sch. Served European War, 1914-19 (Mons Star). Joined Indian Police, 1919; Principal, Police Coll., Saugor,

CP, 1933-36; Inspector General of Police, Central Provinces, 1946; retired, 1947. Indian Police Medal, 1943; King's Police Medal, 1945. *Address*: Gambrel West, East Street, Coggeshall, Essex. *Club*: Athenæum. *[Died 16 Nov. 1980.*

PARRY, Captain Cuthbert Morris, CVO 1952; OBE 1947; Captain, RN (retired); *b* 24 April 1907; *s* of late Major and Mrs M. V. Parry; *m* 1943, Joan Stanton Iles; three *s*. *Educ*: RN Colleges, Osborne and Dartmouth. *Recreations*: various. *Address*: Gardener's Cottage, Titchfield Lane, Wickham, Hants. *T*: Wickham 832224. *Club*: Army and Navy.
[Died 21 June 1980.

PARRY, Sir David Hughes, Kt 1951; QC 1955; BA (Wales); MA, LLM (Cantab); Professor Emeritus in the University of London since 1959; Professor of English Law, University of London, 1930-59; Director of University of London Institute of Advanced Legal Studies, 1947-59; President, University College, Aberystwyth, 1954-64; *b* Llanaelhaiarn, Caerns, 3 Jan. 1893; *e s* of late John Hughes Parry, JP, and Anne Hughes Parry, Penllwyn, Pwllheli, North Wales; *m* 1923, Haf (*d* 1965), *o d* of late Sir Owen Edwards. *Educ*: Pwllheli County Sch.; UCW, Aberystwyth (1st Class Hons Economics); Peterhouse Cambridge (Class I, Law Tripos Part II; College Prizeman); called to Bar (Certificate of Honour), Inner Temple, 1922; in practice at Lincoln's Inn, 1924-46; War Service in RWF, 1915-19 (France, 1917-18); demobilised with rank of Lieut, 1919; Lecturer in Law, Aberystwyth, 1920-24; Lecturer in Law, London School of Economics, 1924-28; Editor Solicitors' Journal, 1925-28; Reader in English Law, University of London, 1928-30; Examiner, Universities of Cambridge, London, Manchester, Liverpool, Bristol and Wales; Senator of University of London, 1930-70; Member of Court of University of London, 1938-70 (Deputy Chairman, 1958-62; Chm., 1962-70); Chairman of Academic Council of University of London, 1939-45; Deputy Vice-Chancellor, 1940-45; Vice-Chancellor, 1945-48; Member of Council of Hon. Society of Cymmrodorion since 1934; Chairman of Standing Conference of National Voluntary Youth Organisations, 1944-45; Chairman 18-30 Conference, 1947-49; Dep. Chairman National Council of Social Service, 1948-62; Member Colonial Universities Grants Cttee, 1948-53; Chairman Colonial Social Science Research Council, 1951-55; Chairman Cttee of Vice-Chancellors and Principals, 1947-48; Member of University Grants Cttee, 1948-54 (Vice-Chairman, 1951-54); President of Society of Public Teachers of Law, 1948-49; a Vice-President of the Selden Society, 1956-59; Member of Advisory Council on Post-War Reconstruction in Wales; Member War Works Commission, 1944-64; Member Royal Commission on Remuneration of Doctors and Dentists, 1957-60; Member Inter-Departmental Cttee on Business of Criminal Courts, 1958-60; Chairman Cttee of Enquiry on New Zealand University, 1959; Dep. Chairman Caernarvonshire Quarter Sessions, 1950-66; Vice-President National Council of Social Service, 1962-; Chairman, Inter-Departmental Cttee on Legal Status of Welsh Language, 1963-65; Moderator, Presbyterian Church of Wales, 1964-65. Lionel Cohen Lecturer, at Hebrew University of Jerusalem, 1956; Hamlyn Lecturer, 1958; Bencher, Inner Temple, 1952; Hon. Fellow: Peterhouse, Cambridge Univ., 1956; LSE, 1961. Hon. LLD Wales, 1947; Hon. DCL McGill, 1949; Hon. LLD West Ont., 1948, British Columbia, 1949, New Brunswick, 1950, Birmingham, 1952, Cambridge, 1953, Hull, 1955, Exeter, 1960, London 1963. Cymmrodorion Medal, 1958. *Publications*: Law of Succession 1937 (6th edn 1972); 11th edn of Wolstenholme and Cherry's Conveyancing Statutes, 1927 (with late Sir Benjamin L. Cherry and late John Chadwick); 12th edn of Williams on Executors, 1930 (with John Cherry); 12th edn of Wolstenholme and Cherry's Conveyancing Statutes, 1932 (with late Sir Benjamin L. Cherry and J. R. P. Maxwell); 13th edn Williams on Executors, 1953; Changing Conception of Contracts in English Law; Sanctity of Contracts in English Law (Hamlyn Lectures), 1958; contributions to the Law Quarterly Review, Journal of the Society of Public Teachers of Law, Modern Law Review, Cambrian Law Journal, Annual Survey of English Law, Solicitors' Journal, Toronto Law Journal, Canadian Bar Review, Journal of Legal Education; Cambridge Law Jl; Times Educational Supplement, etc. *Recreation*: gardening. *Address*: Neuadd Wen, Llanuwchllyn, Bala, Merioneth. *T*: Llanuwchllyn 255. *Club*: Athenæum. *[Died 8 Jan. 1973.*

PARRY, Admiral Sir Edward; see Parry, Admiral Sir (William) E.

PARRY, Maj.-Gen. Michael Denman G.; see Gambier-Parry.

PARRY, Adm. Sir (William) Edward, KCB 1950 (CB 1939); *b* 8 April 1893; *s* of late Sir Sydney Parry, KBE, CB; *m* 1922, Maude Mary Phillips (*d* 1971); one *s* one *d* (twins). *Educ*: RNC Osborne

and Dartmouth. Joined RN 1905; Lieut, 1914; served afloat throughout War of 1914-18; Captain, 1934; commanded Anti-Submarine Establishment (HMS Osprey), 1936-37; Imperial Defence Course, 1938; lent to New Zealand Division, in Command of HMS Achilles, 1939; commanded HMS Achilles in Battle of River Plate, 13 Dec. 1939 (CB); First Naval Member of NZ Naval Board, 1940-42; Command of HMS Renown, 1943; Rear-Admiral, 1944; Naval Commander Force "L" in Invasion of France, 1944; Deputy Head of Naval Division, Control Commission for Germany, Berlin, 1945-46; Director of Naval Intelligence, 1946-48; Vice-Admiral, 1948; Commander-in-Chief, Indian Navy, 1948-51; Admiral, 1951. retired list, 1952.
[Died 21 Aug. 1972.

PARRY-OKEDEN, Richard Godfrey Christian, CMG 1964; CBE 1961; JP; Director, John Lysaght (Australia) Ltd, 1936-70 (Chairman, 1946-67, Managing Director, 1946-65); *b* Blandford, Dorset, 25 Dec. 1900; *s* of Lt-Col U. E. Parry Okeden and Carolina Susan Hambro; *m* 1930, Florence, *d* of E. E. Brown, Pymble, Sydney, NSW; one *s* two *d. Educ:* Eton College. President: Chamber of Manufactures of NSW, 1951-53; Associated Chambers of Manufactures of Australia, 1952-53. JP New South Wales, 1934. Hon. DSc Sydney, 1957. FAIM; FInstD. *Recreation:* enjoying old age. *Address:* 1985 Pittwater Road, Bayview, NSW 2104, Australia. *T:* Sydney 99.2863. *Club:* Union (Sydney).   [Died 16 Dec. 1978.

PARRY-WILLIAMS, Sir Thomas (Herbert), Kt 1958; MA, DLitt (Wales), DLitt (Oxon), PhD (Freiburg), Hon. LLD Wales; Professor Emeritus; Professor of Welsh Language and Literature, University College of Wales, Aberystwyth, 1920-52; *b* 21 Sept. 1887; *s* of late Henry and Ann Parry-Williams, Schoolhouse, Rhyd-ddu, Caerns; *m* 1942, Amy Thomas. *Educ:* Portmadoc County Intermediate Sch.; University College of Wales, Aberystwyth; Jesus Coll., Oxford; Univ. of Freiburg; Sorbonne, Univ. of Paris. Fellow, University of Wales, 1911-14; Hon. Fellow, Jesus Coll., Oxford, 1968; Member of Staff, University College of Wales, Aberystwyth, 1914-19; President: Hon. Society of Cymmrodorion, 1961-69; National Library of Wales, 1966-69; Court of National Eisteddfod, 1955-67; National Eisteddfod Chair and Crown, both in 1912 and 1915; Medal of the Hon. Society of Cymmrodorion, 1951; Fellow of National Eisteddfod, 1968. Warden of University of Wales Guild of Graduates, 1953-56; Chairman of Advisory Council (BBC, Wales), 1947-52; Member Editorial Board Geiriadur Prifysgol Cymru (A Dictionary of the Welsh Language); O'Donnell Lecturer (Oxford), 1957. *Publications:* Welsh and Breton, 1913; Ystoriau Bohemia, 1921; The English Element in Welsh, 1923; Ysgrifau, 1928; Cerddi, 1931; Llawysgrif Rd Morris o Gerddi, 1931; Carolau Rd White, 1931; Sonnets, 1932; Canu Rhydd Cynnar, 1932; Llawysgrif Hendregadredd (joint), 1933; Elfennau Barddoniaeth, 1935; Olion, 1935; Pedair Cainc y Mabinogi, 1937; Synfyfyrion, 1937; Ystoriau Heddiw, 1938; Hen Benillion, 1940; Lloffion, 1942; O'r Pedwar Gwynt, 1944; Libretto Cymraeg Faust (Gounod), 1945; Welsh Poetic Tradition (The Sir John Rhys Memorial Lecture, British Academy), 1947; Y Bardd yn ei Weithdy, 1948; Islwyn, 1948; (Ed.) Caniadau Isgarn, 1949; Ugain o Gerddi, 1949; Libretto Cymraeg Elijah (Mendelssohn), 1950; Libretto Cymraeg Samson (Handel), 1951; ed. Awdlau Cadeiriol Detholedig, 1926-50, 1953; ed. Rhyddiaith Gymraeg, 1954; Sir John Rhŷs 1954; ed. National Eisteddfod Transactions, 1954; co-ed. Newydd a Hen, 1954; Myfyrdodau, 1957; Ymhêl â Phrydyddu (Annual Radio Lecture, BBC Wales), 1958; Y Ddinas (privately), 1962; Sant Pedr (trans. of Libretto, Daniel Jones's Oratorio, Saint Peter), 1965; Y Goresgynwyr (trans. of D. Fraser's The Invaders), 1966; Pensynnu, 1966; Detholiad o Gerddi, 1972. *Address:* Wern, North Road, Aberystwyth, Dyfed SY23 2EE.
[Died 3 March 1975.

PARSELLE, Air Vice-Marshal Thomas Alford Boyd, CB 1962; CBE 1950; psa; *b* 15 July 1911; *s* of late John Parselle, Salisbury, S Rhodesia; *m* 1st, 1936, Daphne (*d* 1970), *d* of late Lt-Col H. G. Lewis-Hall; two *s* one *d*; 2nd, 1974, Patricia Cato Catherine Duncan. *Educ:* Cheltenham Coll.; RAF Coll., Cranwell. Served Egypt, 208 Squadron, 1932-34; 601 Squadron, RAuxAF, 1935-36 and Japan, 1937-39. Middle East and E. Africa, 1940-42; Bomber Command, 1943 (POW). Staff Coll., 1946-47; Comd RAF Scampton, Hemswell, 1948-50; Air Ministry, 1951-53; Comd RAAF Staff Coll., Point Cook, Australia, 1954-56 (exchange posting); Commandant Royal Air Force College and Air Officer Commanding RAF Cranwell, Lincolnshire, 1956-58; Commander, Task Force "Grapple", 1958-59; Senior Air Staff Officer, Bomber Command, 1959-61; Deputy Air Secretary, Air Ministry, 1961-64. Air Commodore, 1956; Air Vice-Marshal, 1958; retired, 1964. *Address:* Casa Holanda, Mojacar, Almeria, Spain.   [Died 28 June 1979.

PARSEY, Edward Moreland, CBE 1953; Vice-President, London Rent Assessment Panel, 1966-72; Chairman, Paddington, St Marylebone and Westminster Rent Tribunals, 1964-72; *b* 12 Jan. 1900; *o s* of late Edward William Parsey, MA, MB, BCh Cantab, and Sarah Janet Parsey; *m* 1927, Margaret, 2nd *d* of late Erle Victor Shakespeare, King's Norton; one *s* one *d. Educ:* King Edward's Sch.; privately; Peterhouse, Cambridge. Served European War, 1914-18, with RMA. BA 1921, MA 1925, Cambridge; Barrister, Inner Temple, 1924. Asst Solicitor, Bd of Trade, 1945-63. Chm., Civil Service Legal Soc., 1949-50; Mem. Bar Council, 1950-54; Chm., Peterhouse Soc., 1963-66. *Recreations:* travelling, gardening. *Address:* Westwood, 5 Frithwood Avenue, Northwood, Mddx HA6 3LY. *T:* Northwood 25673. *Clubs:* United Oxford & Cambridge University; Union (Cambridge).   [Died 19 June 1976.

PARSONS, Ian Macnaghten, CBE 1971 (OBE 1944); Joint Chairman, Chatto, Bodley Head and Jonathan Cape Ltd; President, Society of Bookmen, since 1969; *b* 21 May 1906; *s* of late Edward Percival and Mabel Margaret Parsons, Pont Street, SW; *m* 1934, Marjorie Tulip Ritchie; no *c. Educ:* Winchester Coll.; Trinity Coll., Cambridge. Senior Scholar; 1st Class Eng. Lit. Joined Chatto & Windus, 1928, Partner, 1930-53; Dir, Chatto & Windus Ltd, 1953, Chm., 1954-74; Chm., Sprint Productions Ltd, 1969-80; Director: The Geographical Magazine, 1935-56; Scottish Academic Press, 1969-76; Sussex University Press, 1971-76. President, The Publishers Association, 1957-59. Court Asst, Stationers' and Newspaper Makers' Co., 1977-. Hon. DLitt St Andrews, 1975. *Publications:* Shades of Albany, 1928; (with George Spater) A Marriage of True Minds, 1977. Editor: The Progress of Poetry, 1936; Poetry for Pleasure, 8 vols, 1952-56, anthology 1977; Men Who March Away, 1965; Poems of C. Day Lewis, 1977; The Collected Works of Isaac Rosenberg, 1979. *Recreations:* reading, gardening. *Address:* Juggs Corner, Kingston, Lewes, East Sussex. *T:* Lewes 4707. *Clubs:* Garrick, Beefsteak, Royal Automobile, MCC, Blackheath Rugby Football.
[Died 29 Oct. 1980.

PARSONS, Rev. Canon Laurence Edmund; Hon. Canon of St George's Cathedral, Capetown, 1937, Hon. Provincial Canon since 1946; *b* 22 July 1883; *s* of late Hon. Richard Clere Parsons and Agnes Elizabeth, *d* of late J. F. la Trobe-Bateman, FRS; *g s* of 3rd Earl of Rosse; *m* 1911, Lydia Dorothy (*d* 1964), *yr d* of late Frederic Foster la Trobe-Bateman, and *g d* of late J. F. la Trobe-Bateman, FRS, of Moor Park, Surrey; one *d. Educ:* Winchester; Christ Church, Oxford; Cuddesdon Theological College. Curate of St Bartholomew's, Leeds, 1908-11; chaplain to Bishop Burge of Southwark, 1911-14; missionary in Shantung, N China, 1914; Curate of Wimbledon, 1915-16; Vicar of Chippenham, Wilts, 1916-25; Dean of Cape Town, 1925-28; Vicar of Coleman's Hatch, 1931-32; Director of South African Church Institute, 1932-45; General Secretary of SPCK, 1945-54. *Recreations:* travel, photography, gardening. *Address:* 21 Cheyne Walk, SW3. *T:* 01-352 1707.   [Died 17 Dec. 1972.

PARSONS, Sir Maurice (Henry), KCMG 1970; Kt 1966; Chairman: Billing & Sons Ltd, 1971-73; London Regional Industrial Committee National Savings Group, 1971-73; Director, Globtik Tankers Ltd, 1971-73; *b* 19 May 1910; *s* of late G. H. C. Parsons; *m* 1937, Daphne I. Warner; one *s* one *d. Educ:* University College School. Entered Bank of England, 1928; Private Secretary to Governor (Montagu Norman), 1939-43; Alternate Exec. Director for UK on International Monetary Fund, 1946-47; International Bank, 1947; Director of Operations International Monetary Fund, 1947-50; Dep. Chief Cashier, Bank of England, 1950; Asst to Governors, 1955; Executive Director, 1957; Alternate Governor for UK of International Monetary Fund, 1957-66; Dep. Governor, Bank of England, 1966-70. Chm., Bank of London and S America, July-Dec. 1970; Dir, John Brown & Co., 1970-72. Hon. Treasurer, Soc. of Internat. Develt, 1971-74. *Address:* Clifford House, Shalford, Surrey. *T:* Guildford 61523. *Club:* National.
[Died 24 July 1978.

PARSONS, Rev. Canon Richard Edward; Governor, Moor Park College for Christian Adult Education, Farnham, Surrey, since 1961 (Founder Warden, 1949-61); *b* 16 Feb. 1888; 5th *s* of late Hon. Richard Clere Parsons and Agnes Elizabeth, *d* of late J. F. La Trobe-Bateman, FRS; *m* 1917, Hester Katherine (*d* 1954), *y d* of late Major John Drummond, Scots Guards; one *s* four *d. Educ:* Wellington College; Trinity Coll., Cambridge (Mechanical Sciences Tripos (Hons. 3rd Class), 1910, BA 1910, MA 1923). Great Northern Railway (Engineer's Dept), 1910-14; served European War, 1914-18. Lt-Col RE; Personal Assistant, Chief Engineer GNR, 1918-21; King's Coll., London (Theological), 1921-23, AKC, 1923; Ely Theological College, 1923; Curate of St Paul's, Bedford, 1923-27; Vicar of Oxhey,

Watford, 1927-36; Director of Religious Education, Central Council of C. of E. for Religious Education, 1936-41; Hon. Secretary, Joint Conference Anglicans and Free Churchmen, 1937-41; Secretary Churches' Cttee for Religious Education among Men in HM Forces, 1941-48; Rector of Wotton, Surrey, 1943-49. Member, The Adult Education Cttee, British Council of Churches, 1950; Canon, York Minster, 1941, Canon Emeritus, 1968. Select Preacher, University of Cambridge, 1943. *Publications:* Re-educating Adults; The Spirit of the Christian Cell. *Address:* 19 Adam's Row, South Audley Street, W1. *T:* 01-499 7695. *Club:* Athenæum. *[Died 21 Oct. 1971.*

PARTRIDGE, Eric Honeywood; Author; *b* Waimata Valley, Gisborne, New Zealand, 1894; *s* of John and Ethel Partridge; *m* 1925, Agnes Vye-Parminter; one *d. Educ:* TGS; Queensland and Oxford Universities. School-teacher, 1910-13; served as private in Australian Infantry, 1915-18; Queensland Travelling Fellow at Oxford, 1921-23 (BLitt in Anglo-French Literature); lecturer Manchester and London Universities, 1925-27; founder and managing director of the Scholartis Press, 1927-31; since 1932 author, since 1963 partly revision, and partly work on A Dictionary of Catch Phrases; Army 1940-41; RAF Dec. 1942-Aug. 1945. *Publications:* The French Romantics' Knowledge of English Literature; Eighteenth Century English Romantic Poetry; English Prose; Three Personal Records of the War (with R. H. Mottram and John Easton); Songs and Slang of the British Soldier (with John Brophy); Slang To-day and Yesterday: a History and a Study; A Dictionary of Slang and Unconventional English, revised edn, 1970; The World of Words; A Dictionary of Clichés; Usage and Abusage: A Guide to Good English; A Dictionary of Abbreviations, 1943; Journey to the Edge of Morning, 1946; Shakespeare's Bawdy (a study and a glossary), 1947; (with Wilfred Granville and Frank Roberts) Forces' Slang (1939-45), 1948; English for Human Beings, 1949; A Dictionary of the Underworld, British and American, 1950; Here, There and Everywhere: essays on language, 1950; (with Prof. John W. Clark, University of Minnesota) A History of English in the 20th Century, 1951; From Sanskrit to Brazil, 1952; You Have a Point There (punctuation), 1953; The Concise Usage and Abusage, 1954; English Gone Wrong, 1957; Origins: An Etymological Dictionary of English, 1958 (4th edn 1966); Name This Child (Christian Names), 1959; A Charm of Words (essays), 1960; Adventuring among Words, 1961; Comic Alphabets, 1961; The Gentle Art of Lexicography, 1963; Catch Phrases, 1977. *Recreations:* reading, persons. *Address:* c/o Ronald Pearsall, Landscove, near Newton Abbot, Devon. *Club:* Savile.
[Died 1 June 1979.

PARTRIDGE, Ernest, CBE 1954; *b* 10 Aug. 1895; *s* of William Thomas Partridge, DrMed; *m* 1927, Sarah Millicent, *d* of Sinclair Orr Langtry, Co. Armagh. *Educ:* Wilson's Grammar Sch., Camberwell. Private, University and Public Schools Brigade, Royal Fusiliers, 1914-15; Captain, Durham Light Inf., 1915-16; Captain, Argyll and Sutherland Highlanders (HG), 1942-44. MP (C) Battersea South, 1951-64. PPS to Parliamentary Secretary, Ministry of Transport, 1959-64; PPS to Parliamentary Under-Secretary of State for Defence for Royal Navy, 1964. *Recreations:* shooting, fishing, cricket. *Address:* Mill Cottage, Morecombelake, Bridport, Dorset. *T:* Chideock 455. *Clubs:* St Stephen's, Battersea Conservative.
[Died 20 April 1974.

PARTRIDGE, Prof. Maurice William, BPharm, BSc, PhD (London) 1940; FPS; Lord Trent Professor of Pharmaceutical Chemistry, University of Nottingham, since 1960 and Head of the Department of Pharmacy since 1967; Deputy Vice-Chancellor, since 1972; *b* 15 June 1913; *s* of William Harold Gray and Mary Ann Agnes Partridge; *m* 1940, Monica Agnes (*née* McMain), Professor of Russian Language and Literature, University of Nottingham; no *c. Educ:* Magnus Sch., Newark; University College, Nottingham. University College, Nottingham: Leverhulme Scholar, 1934; Demonstrator, 1936-38. Home Office Research Scholar, 1938-39; Research Asst to British Pharmocopœia Commn, 1939-44; Research Chemist, Boots Pure Drug Co. Ltd, 1944-47; Lecturer in Pharmaceutical Chemistry, University College (later University of) Nottingham, 1947-55; Lord Trent Reader in Pharmaceutical Chemistry, Univ. of Nottingham, 1955-60; Dean, Faculty of Pure Science, 1971-72. Examiner: Univ. of Manchester, 1956-59, 1963-66, 1969-; Univ. of Wales, 1956-59; Univ. of Glasgow, 1962-64; Univ. of Strathclyde, 1964-66, 1969-; National University of Ireland, 1967-. *Publications:* Scientific papers, mainly in Journal Chem. Society and British Journal Cancer. *Recreation:* painting (paintings exhibited in London, 1959-). *Address:* The University, Nottingham. *T:* Nottingham 56101.
[Died 12 June 1973.

PASCAL, Roy, MA, LittD; FBA 1970; Professor of German, Birmingham University, 1939-69; *b* 28 Feb. 1904; *s* of C. S. Pascal and Mary Edmonds, Birmingham; *m* 1931, Feiga Polianovska; two *d. Educ:* King Edward's Sch., Birmingham; Pembroke Coll., Cambridge (Scholar; Hon. Fellow 1976). Studied at Berlin and Munich; Fellow of Pembroke Coll., Cambridge, 1929-34 and 1936-39; Director of Modern Language Studies at Pembroke College, 1936-39; Lecturer in German in the University of Cambridge, 1934-39; President, Assoc. of University Teachers, 1944-45; Chm. Conference of Univ. Teachers of German, 1960-61. Hon. LLD Birmingham, 1974; Hon. DLitt Warwick, 1977. Goethe Medal, 1965; Shakespeare Prize, Hamburg, 1969. *Publications:* Martin Luther, The Social Basis of the German Reformation, 1933; The Nazi Dictatorship, 1934; Shakespeare in Germany 1740-1815, 1937; Ed. of the German Ideology by Marx and Engels, 1938; contributor to The German Mind and Outlook, 1944-45; Growth of Modern Germany, 1946; The German Revolution 1848, 1948; Goethe's Faust, in Essays on Goethe, 1949; The German Sturm und Drang, 1953; Moeller van den Bruck (in The Third Reich, ed Vermeil), 1955; The German Novel, 1956; The Art of Autobiography (in Stil und Formprobleme in der Literatur, ed Böckmann), 1959; Design and Truth in Autobiography, 1960; Realism (in Spätzeiten, ed Kohlschmidt), 1962; German Literature 1500-1700, 1967; From Naturalism to Expressionism, 1973; Culture and the Division of Labour, 1974; The Dual Voice, 1977; contributions to: Presentation Vols to R. L. G. Ritchie, 1949; L. A. Willoughby, 1952; H. A. Korff, 1957; J. Boyd, 1959; W. H. Bruford, 1962; K. Hoppe, 1962; P. Böckmann, 1964; Fr Martini, 1969; C. P. Magill 1974; Fr Beissner, 1974; R. H. Thomas, 1977; E. M. Wilkinson, 1978; Introduction to Nietzsche's Thus Spake Zarathustra, Everyman edition, 1958; articles in Modern Language Review, Goethe Society Publications, German Life and Letters. *Recreations:* angling, carpentry. *Address:* 102 Witherford Way, Birmingham B29 4AW. *[Died 24 Aug. 1980.*

PASKIN, Sir (Jesse) John, KCMG 1954 (CMG 1944); MC; retired Civil Servant; *b* 15 Nov. 1892; *m* 1st, 1920, Doris Blanche North; one *s* ; 2nd, 1947, Alice Marjorie, MBE 1961, *d* of late H. J. Ruston. *Educ:* King Edward's Sch., Stourbridge; St John's Coll., Cambridge (BA). Served European War, 1914-19, with 8th Bn Worcestershire Regt and Machine Gun Corps, France, Belgium, and Germany, Major 1918 (MC, French Croix de Guerre). Assistant Principal, Ministry of Transport, 1920; transferred to Colonial Office, 1921. Successively Private Secretary to Sir C. Davis, Lord Lovat, and Sir S. Wilson, and Assistant Private Sec. to Sec. of State for the Colonies (Mr L. S. Amery and Lord Passfield), 1927-29; Principal, 1929; Asst Secretary, 1939; Principal Private Sec. to Sec. of State for the Colonies (Mr Malcolm Macdonald and Lord Lloyd), 1939-40; Assistant Under-Secretary of State, 1948; retired, 1954. *Recreations:* fly-fishing, travel. *Address:* Wishford, near Salisbury, Wiltshire. *T:* Stapleford 242. *Clubs:* Athenæum, United Oxford & Cambridge University; Fly-fishers'.
[Died 16 Sept. 1972.

PASLEY, Maj.-Gen. Joseph Montagu Sabine, CB 1952; CBE 1944; MVO 1936; late RA; *b* 5 Sept. 1898; *s* of Montagu Wynyard Sabine and Grace Lillian Pasley; *m* 1st, 1926; one *d* ; 2nd, 1950, Mrs D. B. Parsons; one *s. Educ:* Christ's Hospital; RMA. Commissioned RA, 1916; served European War, France, 1918; War of 1939-45 (CBE); Maj.-Gen., 1949. Comdr, 1st Anti-Aircraft Group, 1949-52. Formerly Commissioner for Surrey, St John Ambulance Brigade. OStJ. *Address:* 1 Ryefield Close, Eastbourne, East Sussex. *T:* Eastbourne 51478. *Club:* Cavalry and Guards. *[Died 24 Feb. 1978.*

PASOLINI, Pierpaolo; film director, poet, novelist and critic; *b* Bologna, 5 March 1922; *s* of Carlalberto Pasolini and Susanna Colussi. *Educ:* Univ. of Bologna. In Friuli, 1943-49; then settled in Rome. From 1954 to 1960 collaborated on screen-plays, etc. *Films written and directed:* Accattone, 1961; Mamma Roma, 1962; La ricotta (episode of Rogopag-Laviamoci il cervello), 1963; La rabbia, 1963; Comizi d'amore, 1964; Il Vangelo secondo Matteo, 1964; Uccellacci e uccellini, 1966; La terra vista dalla luna (episode of Le streghe), 1966; Che cosa sono le nuvole? (episode of Capriccio all'italiana), 1967; La sequenza del fiore di carta (episode of Amore e rabbia), 1967; Edipo re, 1967; Teorema, 1968; Porcile, 1969; Medea, 1970; Appunti per un' Orestiade africana, 1970; Il Decamerone, 1971; I racconti di Canterbury, 1972; Il Fiore delle mille e une notte, 1974; Storie Scellerate, 1974; Salo or the 120 days of Sodom, 1975. *Publications:* poetry: Poesie a Casarsa, 1942; La Meglio Gioventù, 1954; Le ceneri di Gramsci, 1957; L'usignolo della Chiesa cattolica, 1958; La religione del mio tempo, 1961; Poesia in forma di rosa, 1964; Poesie, 1970; Trasumanar e organizzar, 1971; novels: Il ferrobedò, 1951; Ragazzi di vita, 1955; Una vita violenta, 1959; Donne di Roma, 1960; Il sogno di una cosa, 1962; Alì dagli occhi azzurri, 1965; Teorema, 1968; *plays:* Il vantone (translation of Plautus' Miles gloriosus), 1963; Pilade, 1967; Orgia, 1968; Affabulazione, 1969; *criticism:* Poesia dialettale del Novecento, 1952; Passione e ideologia, 1960; La poesia popolare italiana, 1960; Empirismo eretico, 1972; La Divina Mimesis, 1976 (posthumous); *screenplays:* Accatone, 1961; Mamma Roma, 1962; Il Vangelo secondo Matteo, 1964; Uccellacci e uccellini, 1966; Edipo re, 1967; Medea, 1970; (with S. Citti) Ostia, 1970. *Recreation:* football. *Address:* via Eufrate 9, Rome, Italy.					[*Died* 1 *Nov.* 1975.

PASSEY, Richard Douglas, MC 1917; Emeritus Professor of Experimental Pathology, University of Leeds; *b* 28 Aug. 1888; *s* of John Passey, The Hollies, Kington, Herefordshire, and Maria Ann Jenkins; *m* 1924, Agnes Pattullo Struth, East Park, Cupar, Fife; three *s* one *d* (and one *s* decd). *Educ:* Lady Hawkins Grammar School, Kington, Herefordshire; Queen's College, Taunton; Guy's Hospital, London. MBBS, 1912 (London); MD, DPH (London) 1919; House Appointments, Guy's Hospital, 1912; Junior Asst Bacteriologist, Guy's Hospital, 1912; temp. commission, RAMC, 1914-15, Gordon Highlanders, 1915-17; Captain RAMC, 1917-19; war service, 1914-19 (MC); Senior Demonstrator and Gull Student in Pathology, Guy's Hospital, 1919; Griffith's Demonstrator of Pathology, 1921-26; Lecturer in Pathology, Welsh Nat. School of Medicine, 1926; Director of Cancer Research, Univ. of Leeds, 1926-53. Lt-Col OC 12th West Riding Bn, Home Guard, 1940-44. *Publications:* medical articles in Jl of Pathology and Bacteriology, BMJ, etc. *Recreations:* painting, fishing, shooting, golf, farming, bridge. *Address:* Chester Beatty Research Institute, Fulham Road, SW3.
					[*Died* 1 *Sept.* 1971.

PASSMORE, Rt. Rev. Nicholas Wilfrid; Abbot of Downside Abbey, 1966-74; *b* 22 Nov. 1907; *s* of Nicholas Kelly Passmore, Bangkok, Siam, and Amy Mary Touche, Edinburgh. *Educ:* Ladycross; Downside; Christ's Coll., Cambridge. Law Society Schol., 1926; entered Novitiate at Downside Abbey, 1928; Scholar of Christ's College, Cambridge, 1934, First Class Historical Tripos; studied Canon Law at University of Sant Anselmo, Rome, and Louvain University, 1935-38; Priest, 1936; Superior of Downside House of Studies at Cambridge, 1938; Prior of Worth, 1939; Bursar of Downside Abbey, 1939-46; Headmaster of Downside School, 1946-62; Prior of Downside Abbey, 1962-66. *Publications:* contributions to Downside Review, etc. *Address:* Downside Abbey, Stratton-on-the-Fosse, near Bath, Avon. *T:* Stratton-on-the-Fosse 226.
					[*Died* 20 *Feb.* 1976.

PASTOR, Antonio Ricardo, PhD, BLitt; Fellow of King's College, University of London; of the Consejo Superior de Investigaciones Científicas, Madrid; a Director of Banco Pastor, FENOSA, GENOSA, and President of PALMESA, etc, Spain, and largely interested in hydro-electric industry in that country; founder and a trustee of Pastor Foundation for Classical Studies (Madrid); Trustee of The Museum and Hon. Citizen of Pontevedra; *b* 14 Sept. 1894; *e s* of late Don Ricardo R. Pastor, a director of the Bank of Spain; *m* 1927, Gabriela Marjorie Ground, painter; one *s* one *d*. *Educ:* privately in La Coruña; Lauenburgische Gelehrtenschule, Ratzeburg (Germany); Univ. of Munich; University of Madrid; Oxford University (Spanish Government Scholar); Senior Student at Balliol College, 1917-20; did research work on Plotinus and his contemporaries; a Taylorian Lecturer in Spanish and attached to Balliol College; appointed Cervantes Reader and Head of the Department of Spanish Studies in the University of London in 1921; Cervantes Professor of Spanish Language and Literature in the University of London, King's College, 1930-45; has acted as Inspector of Spanish Teaching in the Evening Institutes maintained by the London County Council and as Adviser to the Council, 1922-36; has lectured widely in England, Spain, France and the Scandinavian countries and broadcast on Hispanic subjects; assisted the Duke of Windsor, when Prince of Wales, in preparation of South American tour, 1931. Corresponding Member of Royal Academy of History, Madrid, and of Hispanic Society of America. Officier de la Légion d'Honneur, 1934; Knight Comdr of Isabella the Catholic, 1945; Knight Comdr of Order of the Phœnix (Greece), 1957; Grand Cross Alfonso X, 1965. *Publications:* Un Embajador de España en la Escena Inglesa (Count Gondomar), 1925; Letter of the Marquis of Santillana to Don Peter, Constable of Portugal (with Professor Edgar Prestage), 1927; Contemporary Spanish Literature, Spanish Chivalry, 1928; The Idea of Robinson Crusoe, 1929; Spanish Language (with Miss J. Perry) in 14th edn of Encyclopædia Britannica; Aspects of the Spanish Renaissance, 1932; Spanish Spain, 1937; Breve Historia del Hispanismo Ingles, 1948; Presentación de Arnold Toynbee, 1952; Cicerón perseguido, 1961; El Retorno De Odiseus, 1965; many articles.
W W W — 21

Recreation: yachting. *Address:* Maceda 2, Pontevedra, Spain; Serrano 107, Madrid. *Clubs:* Athenæum; Royal Corinthian; Nuevo, Puerta de Hierro (Madrid).					[*Died* 15 *Dec.* 1971.

PATCH, Sir Edmund L. H.; *see* Hall-Patch.

PATERSON, Dr Alexander Brown, CB 1979; Research Fellow, Biochemistry Department, University of Surrey, since 1979; *b* 19 Jan. 1917; *s* of Robert Paterson and Catherine Muir; *m* 1945, Margaret Birnie Paterson; one *s* two *d*. *Educ:* Woodside Sch.; Glasgow Veterinary College. DSc London, MRCVS, FRSC. ARC Research Fellow, 1942-45; Res. Officer, Biochemistry Dept, MAFF Weybridge, 1945-59; Head, Virology Dept, 1959-65; Dep. Dir, MAFF Lab., 1965-69; Dir, Veterinary Labs and Veterinary Investigation Svces, 1969-78. FRSocMed. *Publications:* papers in scientific jls. *Recreations:* tennis, geology. *Address:* Royston, 39 London Road, Guildford, Surrey. *T:* Guildford 73147.					[*Died* 25 *Nov.* 1980.

PATERSON, Sir (Alexander) Swinton, KBE 1951 (OBE 1943); CMG 1947; *b* 12 March 1893; *s* of late William Brockie Paterson, FFA, and Ethel M. Lamplough; *m* 1930, Iseult (*d* 1978), *d* of late Theodore Charles Barclay; no *c*. *Educ:* Norwich School. Served European War, North Staffordshire Regt; entered Consular Service, 1920; Vice-Consul at Monrovia, 1921-24; Antwerp, 1924-27; Beira, 1927-29; New York, 1930-35; HM Minister Resident and Consul, Santo Domingo, Dominican Republic, 1935-43; Inspector-Gen. of Consular Establishments, Foreign Office, 1945-50; Senior Inspector, HM Foreign Service Establishments, 1950-54; retd 1954. *Address:* 17 Boscombe Overcliff Drive, Bournemouth, Dorset. *Club:* Royal Motor Yacht (Sandbanks).					[*Died* 29 *Jan.* 1980.

PATERSON, Aylmer John Noel, CBE 1963; Registrar of the Privy Council, 1954-63; retired May 1963; *b* 16 April 1902; *s* of late Rev. Canon H. D. Noel Paterson, MA; *m* 1935, Kathleen Mary, *er d* of late Sir Noel Goldie, QC. *Educ:* Rugby; Clare Coll., Cambridge (Scholar, BA, LLB). Called to Bar, Middle Temple, 1926; joined Oxford Circuit. Private Secretary to the Lord Chancellor and Deputy Serjeant-at-Arms in House of Lords, 1930-34; Legal Assistant, Lord Chancellor's Office, 1934-39; Chief Clerk, Judicial Committee of the Privy Council, 1939-54. *Recreation:* lawn tennis (rep. Cambridge against Oxford, 1925). *Address:* 8 Metropole Court, Folkestone, Kent. *T:* Folkestone 54601. *Clubs:* Athenæum; Hawks (Cambridge).
					[*Died* 4 *Oct.* 1977.

PATERSON, Maj.-Gen. Herbert MacGregor, CB 1956; CBE 1954; retired; *b* 29 Nov. 1898; *s* of James Paterson, RSA; PRSW; *m* 1929, Kathleen Mary Tennent; one *d*. *Educ:* Fettes; RMA, Woolwich; Magdalene Coll., Cambridge. 2nd Lt, RA, 1918; Egypt and Palestine, 1918-20. Cambridge University, 1920-23; BA 1923; MA 1935. India, 1923-27; Military College of Science, 1927-34; War Office and Ministry of Supply, 1938-45; Comdt Military Coll. of Science, Bury, 1946-47; Director of Artillery, 1952; Director-General of Artillery, Ministry of Supply, 1953-56. Col 1946; Brig. 1952; Maj.-Gen. 1953; retired 1957. USA Medal of Freedom (Bronze Palm). *Recreation:* music. *Address:* Swan Cottage, Shillingford, Oxford.					[*Died* 10 *Aug.* 1979.

PATERSON, Captain Quentin Hunter, DSC; FIMechE; RN, retired; *b* 25 Aug. 1888; 2nd *s* of late James Paterson, RSA; *m* 1917, Dorothy Scobell, *o d* of late Captain F. H. Peyton, RN; one *s* one *d* (and one *d* decd). *Educ:* Cheltenham Coll.; HMS Britannia. DSC May 1915 (despatches, May 1918); Naval Ordnance Dept, Admiralty, 1921-38; Armaments Manuf. Beardmores, Glasgow, till 1958. *Address:* Cossins, Downside, Cobham, Surrey. *T:* Cobham 5123.					[*Died* 7 *Aug.* 1975.

PATERSON, Sir Swinton; *see* Paterson, Sir A. S.

PATERSON, William James Macdonald, CMG 1958; Secretary, Government Hospitality Fund, since 1968; *b* 13 April 1911; *s* of late Robert Duff Paterson and Isobel Findlater; *m* 1946, Eleonóra Mária, *d* of General A. P. Vattay; one *s* one *d*. *Educ:* High School of Glasgow; Glasgow University (MA, LLB). Admitted a Solicitor in Scotland, 1936. Served with HM Forces, 1939-46 (Major, Royal Artillery). Second Secretary, Foreign Office, 1946; First Secretary: Beirut, 1947-50; Damascus, 1950; Santiago, 1951-53; Foreign Office, 1953-55; Counsellor (Commercial), Baghdad, 1955-59; Counsellor, Oslo, 1959-61; British Deputy High Commissioner, Madras, 1961-65; British Consul-General at São Paulo, 1965-68. *Recreations:* golf, reading, wine. *Address:* 135 Marsham Court, Marsham Street, SW1P 4LB. *Club:* Travellers'.					[*Died* 24 *Feb.* 1976.

PATEY, David Howard, MS London 1927; FRCS 1924; Consultant Surgeon Emeritus, Middlesex Hospital, W1, since

1964; Director Surgical Studies, Middlesex Hospital Medical School, 1952-64; *b* Oct. 1899; *s* of F. W. Patey and Mrs Patey (*née* Davies); *m* 1927, Gladys Joyce, *d* of Gilbert Summers, Hounslow; two *s* one *d. Educ:* Llandovery; London University. Surgical Asst posts at Middlesex Hosp., Hampstead Gen. Hosp., St Mark's Hosp., St Peter's Hosp., Acton Hosp., 1922-32; Surgeon, Middlesex Hospital, 1930-64. Gold Medallist, London MB, 1923; Assoc. of Surgeons Schol., 1927; Jacksonian Prize, RCS, 1930; Streatfield Schol., RCP, 1930; Hunterian Prof., RCS, 1931, 1964. Pres. Section of Surgery, Roy. Soc. Med., 1951-52; Pres., Surgical Research Society, 1958-60. Hon. Fellow: American Surgical Assoc., 1964; RSM, 1974. Colles Lecturer, RCSI, 1957. *Publications:* articles on surgery and surgical pathology. *Recreation:* bird watching. *Address:* 2 Cannongate Close, Hythe, Kent CT21 4AG. *Club:* Garrick.
[Died 27 March 1977.

PATIALA, Lt-Gen. HH the Maharajadhiraj Yadavindra Singh Mahendra Bahadur of, GCIE 1946; GBE 1942; LLD; Indian Ambassador to the Netherlands, since 1971; *b* 1913; *s* of late HH Maharajadhiraj Sir Bhupindra Singh of Patiala, GCSI, GCIE, GCVO, GBE; *m* 1938, Maharani Mohinder Kaur, *d* of a Noble of Patiala State; two *s* two *d. Educ:* Aitchison College, Lahore. Was Rajpramukh of Patiala and East Punjab States Union, 1948-56. Founder and Hon. Life Pres., Asian Games Fedn; Pres., Indian Olympic Assoc., 1938-60. Chm., All India Council of Sports, 1960-65. Patron and President of many other organizations. Was Chancellor of the Chamber of Princes. Served War of 1939-45 in Malaya, Western Desert, Italy, Burma. Delegate of India to XIth Session of United Nations, New York, 1956-57; UNESCO Conference in Paris, 1958, and Leader of Indian Delegation to Food and Agriculture Organization Conference in Rome, 1959, 1961-62, 1963, 1967, 1969; Ambassador to Italy, 1965-66. Mem., Punjab Legislative Assembly, 1967-68. Chm., Horticulture Develt Council, 1970. Hon. LLD: Benares Hindu Univ. 1939, Punjab Univ., 1949. *Recreations:* mountaineering, sports, agriculture and horticulture. *Address:* Motibagh Palace, Patiala, Punjab, India.
[Died 17 June 1974.

PATNA, HH Maharaja of; Maharaja Sir Rajendra Narayan Singh Deo, KCIE 1946; *b* 31 March 1912; *S* to Gaddi 1924; *m* 1932, Kailash Kumari Devi, *d* of His late Highness Maharajadhiraj Bhupinder Singh Bahadur of Patiala; two *s* four *d. Educ:* Mayo College, Ajmer; St Columba's College, Hazaribagh (Inter-Mediate Arts Exam., 1931). Patron of All India Cattle Show Society. MP (India), 1952-56; MLA and Leader of Opposition, Orissa, 1957-59; Finance Minister, Orissa, 1959-61; MLA and Leader of Opposition, Orissa, 1961-66, 1972-; Chm., Orissa Public Accounts Cttee, 1957-59 and 1961-66; Chief Minister, Orissa, 1967-71; Minister, Political and Services, Industries and Home (Public Relation and Tourism), 1971-72; Chm., Industrial Develt Corp., Orissa, 1971-. *Recreation:* walking. *Address:* PO Balangir, Orissa, India. *TA:* Patnesh, Balangir. *T:* Balangir 5; Bhubaneswar 234; Lucknow 23213. *Clubs:* Ranchi (Ranchi); International, National Sports (New Delhi).
[Died 23 Feb. 1975.

PATON, Brig. Charles Morgan, CVO 1944; CBE 1949; psc; *b* 5 Feb. 1896; *s* of late A. H. Paton; *m* 1920, Mabel Anne, *d* of J. M. Bathgate, JP; one *s. Educ:* Berkhamsted; Royal Military College, Sandhurst. Joined Essex Regiment 1914; Captain 1917; Staff College, 1927-28; Bt Major, 1934; Major, 1935; Lt-Col 1941; Col 1944. Served European War, 1914-18, France and Belgium; GSO for Weapon Training, W Comd, 1930-32; DAA & QMG W Comd, 1932-34; DAA & QMG S Comd, 1937-38; DAAG War Office, 1939-40; AAG Mid. East, 1941-42; DA and QMG, Palestine, 1943; DAG Allied Armies in Italy, 1944; retired, 1949. Colonel, The Essex Regiment, 1950-58; Associate Colonel, 3rd East Anglian Regiment (16/44 Foot), 1958-62; Dep. Col The Royal Anglian Regt, 1965-70. DL Essex, 1954-74. CStJ 1970. *Address:* c/o Lloyds Bank Ltd, George Row, Northampton NN1 1DJ. *Club:* Army and Navy.
[Died 24 May 1979.

PATON, Florence Beatrice, JP; *d* of George Walker and Sarah Louise Widdowson, Wolverhampton; *m* 1930, John Paton, *qv. Educ:* elementary; secondary; privately. Contested Cheltenham (By-Election), 1928, Rushcliffe 1929 and 1931; MP (Lab) Rushcliffe Div. of Notts, 1945-50. First woman MP Chairman of Standing Cttees, 1947; Delegate, UN Assembly, 1947; first woman MP to preside over the whole House in Committee, 1948. Vice-Chm., Labour Parly Assoc., until 1964. Member Royal Commission on Common Land, 1955-58. *Recreations:* reading, walking, cycling. *Address:* 19 Lancaster Gardens, Penn, Wolverhampton, West Midlands. *[Died 12 Oct. 1976.*

PATON, George Pearson, CMG 1942; CBE 1924; *b* 1882; *s* of late George Paton of Baldovan, Angus; *m* 1911, Katharine, *d* of W. B. Scranton, MD; two *s. Educ:* Dundee High Sch.; St Andrews Univ.; privately. Apptd Student Interpreter in Japan, 1906; various posts: Japan, China, Korea, Formosa; attached to British High Commission in Siberia, 1918-19; Vladivostok, 1921-28; Consul at Tamsui, Formosa, 1928-30; Commercial Counsellor at Moscow, 1930-37; Consul-General, Istanbul, 1937-42; retired, 1942; Director Intelligence Div., Far Eastern Bureau, British Min. of Information, New Delhi, 1943-46. Légion d'Honneur, 1928. *Address:* Harbour Lights, Durban, South Africa.
[Died 29 Jan. 1975.

PATON, John; late General Secretary Independent Labour Party and editor of New Leader and Penal Reformer; *b* Aberdeen, 1886; working-class parents; *m* 1930, Florence (Beatrice) Paton, *qv. Educ:* Elementary School until 12 years of age. Active in Labour Movement, 1902-; Member WEA, etc. MP (Lab), Norwich, 1945-50, North Division of Norwich, 1950-64. *Publications:* Autobiography: Proletarian Pilgrimage, 1935; Left Turn!, 1936. *Address:* 19 Lancaster Gardens, Penn, Wolverhampton, West Midlands. *[Died 14 Dec. 1976.*

PATON, Robert Young, FRCS; Consulting Orthopaedic Surgeon (retired); *b* 18 Jan. 1894; 2nd *s* of Edward Ley Paton, Perth, Scotland; *m* 1st, 1923, Daphne, *y d* of Benjamin Colet Pulleyne, Headingley, Yorks (marr. diss., 1951); 2nd, 1954, Elizabeth Law Milne, *y d* of Rt Hon. Sir John Milne Barbour, 1st and last Bt, of Conway, Dunmurry, Co. Antrim. *Educ:* Perth Academy; St Andrews Univ.; Trinity Coll., Cambridge; St Mary's and St Bartholomew's Hospitals, London. MA (1st Class Hons in Mathematics and Natural Philosophy, Guthrie and Berry Schols., Tullis Medals), St Andrews Univ., 1915. Surgeon-Probationer, RNVR, 1917-18. MRCS, LRCP, 1920. BA 1918, MB, BCh, 1920, Cambridge. FRCS 1920. Casualty House Surgeon, 1921, Surg. Registrar, 1921-23, Med. Superintendent, St Mary's Hospital, Paddington; Registrar, Royal National Orthopædic Hospital, 1924-27; now Cons. Surgeon; Cons. Surgeon, Princess Louise, Kensington, Hospital for Children; Cons. Orthopædic Surgeon: LCC; Nelson Hospital, Wimbledon; Wood Green and Southgate Hospital; Hon. Cons. Surgeon to Royal Scottish Corporation. Late President: London Perthshire Assoc.; London St Andrews University Club. *Publications:* chapters on Fractures and Surgery of Nerves in Essentials of Modern Surgery; many papers and contribs to medical journals. *Recreations:* golf, gardening, foreign travel. *Address:* Gorse Hill Manor, Virginia Water, Surrey. *T:* Wentworth 2101; 9 Astell Street, Chelsea, SW3. *T:* 01-352 2611. *Club:* Wentworth (Virginia Water). *[Died 8 Aug. 1973.*

PATON, William Calder, CIE 1945; MC; Major-General IMS (retired); *b* 27 Jan. 1886; *s* of William and Isabella Paton; *m* 1st, 1915, Marian Bruce Williamson (*d* 1948); one *s* two *d*; 2nd, 1950, Isobel, MBE, *d* of R. Dean, JP, Beauly. *Educ:* Glasgow Academy; Edinburgh Univ. MB, ChB, Edinburgh, 1910; entered IMS, 1912; FRCS (Ed.), 1920; served European War, 1914-18 (MC and Brevet Major); various appointments on civil side of IMS, including Professor of Midwifery, Medical Coll., Madras, and Civil Surgeon, Delhi; Inspector-General of Civil Hospitals, N-WFP, 1939-41; Surgeon-General, Bengal, 1941-45; KHP; retired from IMS, 1945; Medical Superintendent, Royal Northern Infirmary, 1945-48; Medical Superintendent, Inverness Hospitals, 1948-54. *Publications:* articles in medical journals. *Recreations:* formerly riding, hunting; now walking, golf. *Address:* Sandymar, 5 Campbell Road, Longniddry, East Lothian EH32 0NP. *[Died 7 Feb. 1979.*

PATRICK, Sir Paul Joseph, KCIE 1946; CSI 1934; *b* 6 Oct. 1888; *s* of late Rev. John Patrick and Ellen Maria, *d* of Joseph Freeman. *Educ:* Rugby Sch.; Corpus Christi Coll., Oxford. Junior Clerk, Secretary's Office, Post Office, 1913; transferred to India Office, 1913; Lieut, Indian Army, Reserve of Officers, 1916-19, served in NW Frontier and Palestine. Assistant Under-Secretary of State, India Office, 1941, and CRO, 1947; retired, 1949. CStJ 1963. *Address:* 10 Stonehill Road, SW14 8RW. *T:* 01-876 6105. *Club:* Travellers'. *[Died 20 Aug. 1975.*

PATTERSON, Eric James; Political Education Officer, Western Area, 1947; Member of YMCA Central Education Committee for HM Forces; Special Lecturer to Allied and British Forces; *b* 9 May 1891; *s* of late George Patterson, JP, Ballasalla, Isle of Man, and Euphemia Patterson; *m* 1936, Ethel Simkins; one *s. Educ:* King William's Coll., Isle of Man; Peterhouse, Cambridge (Graduate); University of Freiburg, Germany. Late University Extension Lecturer and Tutorial Class Tutor, University of Liverpool; University Extension Lecturer, University of London, 1920-21; Head of Department of Extra-Mural Studies, University College, Exeter, 1921-38, and Head of Department of

International Politics till 1938; Principal of Bonar Law Coll., Ashridge, Berkhamsted, Herts, 1938-40; Member of Advisory Council for Adult Education in HM Forces, 1940-42; served on Cttee of World Association for Adult Education, on the Vice-Chancellors of Oxford and Cambridge Cttee on University Extension Regulations; held scholarships for the investigation of Adult Education in Germany and for the problem of Education among National Minorities; Visiting Lecturer: in Germany, CCG, 1947; Internationale Akademische Ferienkurse, Zürich, 1950; HM Navy, 1951-53; European Youth Campaign Conference Special Lecturer, 1952; Special Lecturer to RAF, 1954; Saar Plebiscite Commission Delegate, 1955; Western European Union Commission in Saar, 1955-56. Genootschap Nederland-England Lecturer, Holland, 1957; Bursary for lecturing and research, Guest Lectr, Poznan Univ., 1971. Silver Academic Laurel, Polish Acad. of Literature. *Publications:* Survey of Adult Education in Germany, 1926; Poland, 1934; Pilsudski, Marshal of Poland, 1935; Yugoslavia, 1936; Pilsudski through English Eyes, 1936 (Warsaw); The International Mind, 1937 (USA); The Saar Referendum of 1955; European Year Book, 1958. Contributions to Empire Review and St Martins Review, 1939-40; Free Europe. Central European Observer, International Affairs (Chatham House). *Recreations:* foreign travel, swimming. *Address:* Stonehedge, Alphington Cross, Exeter. *T:* Exeter 54479. *Club:* Special Forces.
[Died 4 Oct. 1972.]

ATTERSON, Sir John Robert, KBE 1945; CMG 1939; *b* 1892; *s* of G. T. Patterson; *m* 1919, Esther Margaret Sheldon (*d* 1962); two *s*. *Educ:* Cambridge Univ., BA. Asst District Officer, Nigeria, 1915; Secretary, Northern Provinces, 1935; acting Chief Commissioner, Northern Provinces, 1938-39; Acting Chief Commissioner, 1941; Chief Commissioner, Northern Provinces, Nigeria, 1943-48. *Address:* Park Holme, Eamont Bridge, Cumbria CA10 2BX. *T:* Penrith 2515.   [Died 1 Oct. 1976.]

ATTERSON, Rear-Adm. Julian Francis Chichester, OBE 1919; *b* 6 May 1884; *s* of Rev. J. E. C. Patterson; *m* 1st, 1911, Helen Frances (*d* 1950), *d* of Major C. P. Dean; one *d* (and one *d* decd); 2nd, 1952, Sina Victoria, widow of Commander John Howard, RN. *Educ:* Bedford Sch. HMS Britannia, 1899; Lieut, 1904; Commander, 1915; Captain, 1921; Rear-Admiral, 1933; served as Gunnery Officer in HMS Orion, 1914-17, present at Battle of Jutland, 1916 (OBE); retired, 1933, and joined English Steel Corporation Ltd, Vickers Works, Sheffield, retired, 1949. *Address:* 20 Sion Hill, Bath. *Clubs:* United Service & Royal Aero, Royal Yacht Squadron (Naval Member).
[Died 23 June 1972.]

ATTERSON, Thomas Redden, CBE 1954; DL; JP; Chairman, Arthur Fraser Investment Co. Ltd, Glasgow; *b* 7 May 1898; *s* of late James Patterson, Glasgow; *m* 1st, 1921, Margaret (decd), *d* of late John Malcolm Forrester, Glasgow; one *s*; 2nd, 1967, Florence Joyce, *d* of Frederick Percival Todd, Leicester. *Educ:* Whitehill Sch., Glasgow. Member: Corporation of Glasgow, 1942-59; East Kilbride Development Corp., 1951-56; Cumbernauld Development Corp., 1956-65. Chairman and Man. Director, Nicol & Andrew Ltd; formerly Chm., The Scottish Mutual Assurance Soc. DL and JP for County of City of Glasgow. OStJ 1951. *Address:* 2 Deramore Avenue, Whitecraigs, Renfrewshire. *T:* Newton Mearns 1805. *Clubs:* Conservative, Royal Scottish Automobile (Glasgow).
[Died 26 Jan. 1972.]

ATTRICK, (William) Michael (Thomas), CBE 1975; FRIBA; AADipl; Principal, Central School of Art and Design, since 1961; *b* 25 Oct. 1913; *s* of late Arthur Devereux Pattrick and late Mrs Gilson Pattrick; *m* 1943, Joan Margaret Leech. *Educ:* Oundle School. Architectural Association School of Architecture, 1931-35; RIBA Howard Colls Scholarship, 1932. AA Studentship, 1934; Lecturer, Cambridge Univ., 1937; Architectural Assoc. Staff, 1945-61. Principal, The Architectural Association School of Architecture, 1951-61. *Recreation:* sailing. *Address:* Studio 1, St Peter's Wharf, Hammersmith Terrace, W6 9TR. *T:* 01-741 2745, (office) 01-242 7230.   [Died 23 April 1980.]

ATTULLO, William Ogilvy, Advocate; Sheriff of Glasgow and Strathkelvin (formerly Lanarkshire at Glasgow), since 1962; *b* 27 Feb. 1924; *s* of late Henry Pattullo, farmer, and Jean Robbie Ogilvy; *m* 1959, Etty Hoekstra (*d* 1971), *d* of De Heer Tijs Hoekstra, Enschede, Holland; one *s* one *d*. *Educ:* Strathallan Sch.; Aberdeen Grammar Sch.; Aberdeen Univ. MA 1948; LLB (Aberdeen), 1948. Navigator, Royal Air Force Vol. Res., 1942-45. Solicitor, 1948-50; called to Scottish Bar, 1951; practised at Scottish Bar, 1951-59 and 1961-62; Senior Lecturer in Mercantile Law, Aberdeen, 1959-61; Professor of Mercantile Law, Khartoum, 1961. Member, Parole Board for Scotland,

1967-. *Recreations:* ski-ing, hill-walking, golf, curling. *Address:* Burncroft, Thorntonhall, Lanarkshire. *T:* 041-644 1887.
[Died 1 Nov. 1975.]

PAUL VI, His Holiness Pope, (Giovanni Battista Montini); *b* Concesio, Brescia, 26 Sept. 1897; *s* of Giorgio Montini and Giuditta (*née* Alghisi). *Educ:* Istituto Arici, Brescia; Lombard Seminary, Pontifical Ecclesiastical Academy and Gregorian University, Rome. Ordained Priest, Roman Catholic Church, 1920; Attaché, Apostolic Nunciature in Warsaw, 1923; called to service of Secretariat of State, Vatican City, Oct. 1924; National Ecclesiastical Assistant to Italian Federation of Catholic University Students, 1925; Professor of History of Pontifical Diplomacy, 1931-37. Named Substitute of the Secretariat of State of His Holiness, 1937; accompanied the Papal Legate, Cardinal Pacelli, to International Eucharistic Congress in Budapest, 1938. Appointed Pro-Secretary of State by Pope Pius XII, 1952; Archbishop of Milan, 1954-63. Created Cardinal, 1958. Elected Pope, 21 June 1963; solemn Coronation, 30 June 1963. *Address:* Apostolic Vatican Palace, Vatican City, Italy.
[Died 6 Aug. 1978.]

PAUL, Sir Brian Kenneth, 6th Bt *re-cr* 1821, of Rodborough; *b* 18 May 1904; *s* of Sir Aubrey Edward Henry Dean Paul, 5th Bt *re-cr* 1821, and Irene Regine (Mme Poldowski) (*d* 1932), *d* of late Henry Wieniawski, Warsaw; *S* father 1961; *m* 1937, Muriel Frances, *d* of late John Lillie, Ontario, Canada, and widow of Arthur Edward Pearse Brome Weigall. *Educ:* Downside. Subsequently mural painter and designer. *Heir:* none. *Address:* Glover & Co., 115 Park Street, W1. [Died 5 Aug. 1972 (*ext*).]

PAUL, Cedar; Singer, Author, and Translator; retired; *b* Hampstead, *née* Gertrude Mary, *d* of late F. W. Davenport, composer, and *g d* of late G. A. Macfarren, composer, principal RAM, etc. *Educ:* Paris, Genoa, and London. Independent worker since the age of fifteen, maintaining herself by tuition in Germany, Poland, and England; trained for grand opera in Dresden and Stuttgart: Cherubino, Siebel, Marguerite, Elsa, Elizabeth, etc.; Musical career interrupted by war; collaborated with late Eden Paul, in original writings and translations, among their many joint translations being: Romain Rolland's The Forerunners, 1920; Baudouin's Suggestion and Autosuggestion, 1920; Pierre Janet's Psychological Healing, 1925; Plekhanoff's Fundamental Problems of Marxism, 1929; Yugoff's Economic Trends in Soviet Russia, 1930; Treitschke's History of Germany in the Nineteenth Century, 7 vols, 1915-19; Masaryk's The Spirit of Russia, 2 vols, 1919; many works by Stefan Zweig, Emil Ludwig, and Sudermann; Frank's Trenck, 1928; Marx's Capital, 1928; Alfred Neumann's The New Cæsar, 1934; Man of December, 1937; Novikov-Priboy's Tsushima, 1936; Prawdin's Mongolian Empire, 1940; Lermontoff's Hero of Our Own Time; Nattage's Escape to Danger, 1942; Le Verrier's France in Torment, 1942; Sergei Borodin's Dmitri Donskoi, 1945; A. Chapygun's Stepan Razin, 1946; Balzac's Fatal Skin, 1948-49; after the war of 1914-18 resumed musical career, specialising in unaccompanied folk-song, and giving recitals in London and the provinces, Paris, Brussels, and the German capitals. *Address:* 5 Hillside, Tilford Road, Hindhead, Surrey.
[Died 18 March 1972.]

PAUL-BONCOUR, Joseph; Sénateur du Loir-et-Cher; barrister; *b* Saint-Aignan, 4 Aug. 1873. Docteur en droit; private secretary to Waldeck-Rousseau, 1899-1902, and Viviani, 1906-09; Republican Socialist deputy, 1909; Minister of Labour, 1911; resigned Socialist Party, 1931; War Minister, 1932; Prime Minister, Dec. 1932-Jan. 1933; Foreign Minister, Dec. 1932-Feb. 1934 and March-April 1938; Minister for League of Nations affairs, Jan.-June 1936; formerly President of Foreign Affairs Cttee of the Chamber; Permanent Delegate to the League of Nations. *Publications:* Estienne de la Boétie et les origines des libertés modernes; Le Fédéralisme économique; Un Débat sur la République et la décentralisation (with Ch. Maurras); Les Syndicats de fonctionnaires; Art et démocratie; Trois plaidoiries. *Address:* 17 rue de Téhéran, Paris VIII; Saint-Aignan, Loir-et-Cher. *T:* Laborde 19-84.
[Died 28 March 1972.]

PAUNCEFORT-DUNCOMBE, Sir Everard Philip Digby; *see* Duncombe.

PAVIÈRE, Sydney Herbert, FSA, FMA, FRSA, FAMS, ARDS; Art Adviser, Bury Corporation; Hon. Curator, Rufford Old Hall Folk Museum, 1959-61; Art Director and Curator, Harris Museum and Art Gallery, Preston, 1926-59; *b* 25 October 1891; *s* of Frederick Leslie Pavière and Edith Mary Hughes; *m* 1915, Gladys Ruth Mary Cronk. *Educ:* Oxford. Assistant to Secretary, Oxford University Museum, 1905-12; Assistant Curator, Maidstone Museum and Art Gallery, 1912-16; Fine Art Valuer, with Hurcomb and Wm Whiteley Ltd, 1921; Assistant Curator, Lady Lever Art Gallery, Port Sunlight, 1922-23; Art Sec. and Curator of Private Collections to 1st Visc. Leverhulme; Pres. North-West Federation of Museums and Art Galls, 1944-45; Leverhulme Research Grant, 1937; Exhibitor (water colours and etchings) Royal Hibernian Academy, Royal Cambrian Academy, etc.; works reproduced in Colour Magazine, The Studio, etc. *Publications:* Monograph on the Devis Family of Painters, Walpole Society Volume, 1937; The Devis Family of Painters, 1950: Dictionary of Flower, Fruit and Still Life Painters, Vol. 1, 1961, Vols 2 and 3, 1963; Vol. 4, 1964; Floral Art, 1964; Dictionary of British Sporting Artists, 1965; Jean Baptiste Monnoyer, 1966; Dictionary of Victorian Landscape Painters, 1968; articles on History of Cotton Printing in Texture Quarterly, 1957. *Address:* 91 Lawrence Avenue, New Malden, Surrey. *T:* 01-337 7039.   *[Died 7 Jan. 1971.*

PAVLIDES, Sir Paul (George), Kt, *cr* 1955; CBE 1949; Financier; Company Director; *b* 24 Jan. 1897; *m* 1923; two *d.* *Educ:* Commercial studies in Lausanne and London. Honorary posts with Cyprus Government; Member Advisory Council, 1933-36 and 1940-42; Member Executive Council, Cyprus, 1946-55. *Address:* 30 Avenue de Grande Bretagne, Monte Carlo, Monaco.   *[Died 14 Oct. 1977.*

PAWLE, Brig. Hanbury, CBE 1939 (OBE 1919); TD; DL Herts; Director McMullen and Sons Ltd, Hertford; *b* 7 June 1886; 3rd *s* of late G. S. Pawle, DL, of Widford, Ware, Herts; *m* 1915, Mary Cecil (*d* 1971), *d* of N. J. Hughes-Hallett, OBE, DL, of the Knoll, Derby; one *s* two *d.* *Educ:* Haileybury College; Caius College, Cambridge. Member of Stock Exchange, 1912-14; France, 1914-18, Hertfordshire Regt till 1916, transferred Royal Berkshire Regt; Foreign Service, Mesopotamia, Persia and India till 1924; left Royal Berkshire Regt to command the Hertfordshire Regt 1930. Commanded 161st Infantry Bde TA, 1938; 202 Inf. Bde, 1940. *Publications:* The Sacred Trust, 1930; Tactical Exercises, 1939; The Seven Locks, 1944; In Our Own Hands, 1946; Before Dawn, 1955; The Lost Path, 1962. *Address:* Home Field House, Widford, Ware, Herts. *T:* Much Hadham 2667. *Club:* Army and Navy.   *[Died 26 July 1972.*

PAWSEY, Sir Charles Ridley, Kt 1947; CSI 1945; CIE 1943; MC 1915, and bar 1917; *b* 14 July 1894; *m* 1953, Rita, widow of Hugh Ingle Halliday. *Educ:* Berkhamsted School; Wadham College, Oxford (BA). Entered ICS, 1919; served European War, 1914-18; Burma Campaigns, 1942-44 (CIE, CSI); retired. *Address:* The Priory, Badingham, Woodbridge, Suffolk.
                                          [Died 21 July 1972.

PAWSON, Prof. Henry Cecil, MBE 1946; FRSE 1949; Emeritus Professor, Universities of Durham and Newcastle upon Tyne, since 1957; *b* 17 May 1897; *s* of late Rev. D. Ledger Pawson; *m* 1927, Edith Jean Sinclair; one *s* two *d.* *Educ:* Lady Manners Grammar School, Bakewell, Derbyshire; King's College later University, Newcastle. DSc 1959. University of Newcastle upon Tyne: Lecturer in Agriculture, 1917, Senior Tutor, 1945; Prof. of Agriculture, 1948-57. Methodist Local Preacher, 1917; Vice-President Methodist Conference of Great Britain, 1951-52. *Publications:* The Study of Agriculture, 1921; Robert Bakewell, Pioneer Livestock Breeder, 1957; Cockle Park Farm, 1960; Agriculture of Northumberland, 1961; Personal Evangelism, 1968; Words of Comfort, 1968; Hand to the Plough (autobiog.), 1973; contrib. to God in Prayer, articles and papers on agricultural and religious subjects. *Address:* 56 Dunholme Road, Newcastle upon Tyne NE4 6XE. *T:* 33269. *Clubs:* University Union, YMCA (Newcastle upon Tyne).
                                          [Died 19 Dec. 1978.

PAYNE, Prof. Arthur Robert; Director, Shoe and Allied Trades Research Association, since 1968; Industrial Professor, Institute of Polymer Technology, Loughborough University of Technology, since 1972; *b* 2 Nov. 1926; *s* of late Arthur Payne and Helen (*née* Gunn); *m* 1954, Greta (*née* Shaw), BA, DipEd; one *s* two *d.* *Educ:* Archbishop Tenison's Grammar Sch., Kennington; Durham University. BSc Hons Physics 1952, MSc and DSc 1966, Durham; FInstP 1963; CEng, MIMechE 1966; MBIM 1969; FPI 1973; FPRI 1975. Royal Air Force, 1946-49. Rubber and Plastics Res. Assoc., 1952-62; Principal Physical Group Leader of Engrg Group, Natural Rubber Producers' Res. Assoc., 1962-67. Chairman: Council, IRI, 1970-72 (Mem., 1973-); C/43 Cttee, BSI, 1971-; Cttee, Dirs of Research Assocs, 1974- (Vice-Chm., 1973-74); Cttee for Establishment of London Centre for Applied Science and Professional Learned Socs, 1973-; Liberal Party Daventry Constituency, 1974-; Member: Council, British Leather Manufrs Res. Assoc.; Court, Univ. of Leicester; Adv. Bd, Inst. of Polymer Tech., Adv. Bd, Human Sciences MSc, Loughborough Univ. of Technology; R&D Cttee, Waste Adv. Council. Colwyn Medal, IRI, 1972. Governor,

Leathersellers' Coll.; FRSA. *Publications:* Engineering Design with Rubber, 1964; Rubber in Engineering Practice, 1966; Uses of Rubber in Engineering, 1967; Poromerics in Shoe Industry, 1970; numerous technical and scientific papers on polymers, engrg, vibration and shoe technology; contribs to Faraday Soc., Jl of Polymer Science, Jl of Applied Polymer Sci., Rubber Chem. and Technol. *Recreations:* gardening, music. *Address:* 37 Howard Lane, Boughton, Northampton NN2 8RS. *T:* Northampton 843560. *Clubs:* Royal Over-Seas League, National Liberal; Rotary (Northampton).   *[Died 20 Aug. 1976.*

PAYNE, Ben Iden; Professor Emeritus of Drama, State University of Texas, since 1972, Professor, 1946-72; *b* 5 Sept. 1881; *s* of Rev. Alfred Payne; *m* 1st, Mona Limerick (marr. diss.); 2nd, Barbara Rankin Chiaroni. *Educ:* Privately; Manchester Grammar School. Began his stage career with Sir Frank (then Mr F. R.) Benson's Company, 1899; organised Miss A. E. F. Horniman's Company at Gaiety Theatre, Manchester, and produced for her, 1907-11; organised the first repertory seasons in several provincial cities and toured his own companies until 1913; produced plays in New York, Chicago and Philadelphia, until 1917; was General Stage Director for Charles Frohman Inc. at Empire Theatre, New York, 1917-22; Visiting Prof. of Drama and subsequently Head of the Drama Dept, Carnegie Inst. of Technology, Pittsburgh, also producing plays in New York for various managements, until 1928; produced and acted at the Goodman Theatre, Chicago, 1928-30; Visiting Professor of Drama at Univ. of Iowa and Univ. of Washington, 1930-34; Director of Stratford-on-Avon Shakespeare Memorial Theatre, 1935-42; Visiting Prof. of Drama, State Univs of: Iowa, 1943; Washington, 1943; Missouri, 1947; Colorado, 1953; Michigan, 1954; Dir Shakespeare Summer Festival, San Diego, Calif., 1949-52, 1955, 1957, 1964; Dir at Oregon Shakespearean Festival, Summer, 1956 and 1961; Visiting Prof. of Drama, Banff School of Fine Arts, Alberta, Canada, summer sessions 1957-64. Fifth Annual Award of Amer. Nat. Shakespeare Festival and Acad. for distinguished service to the theatre, 1959; Shakespeare productions, Sch. of Fine Arts, Univ. of Alberta, Canada, 1958-60, 1962; Rodgers and Hammerstein Award for distinguished services to the theatre, 1962; Medal of Honor, Theta Alpha Phi, 1969; Consular Law Soc.'s Award of Merit, 1968; Award for distinguished services to the theatre, San Diego Nat. Shakespeare Festival, 1974; 26 May dedicated by Mayor of Austin, Texas, as B. Iden Payne Day; given certificate of recognition by Austin Circle of Theatres, of 75 years in internat. theatre. Hon. LLD Univ. of Alberta, Canada, 1963. *Address:* 2708 Carlton Road, Austin, Texas 78703, USA. *Clubs:* Savage; Players (New York).   *[Died 6 April 1976.*

PAYNE, Rev. Ernest Alexander, CH 1968; BA, BD (London), MA, BLitt (Oxon); Hon. DD St Andrews; Hon. LLD McMaster; a President, World Council of Churches, 1968-75; General Secretary of the Baptist Union of Great Britain and Ireland, 1951-67, Vice President, 1976-77, President, 1977-78; *b* 19 Feb. 1902; *er s* of late Alexander William Payne; *m* 1930, Winifred Mary Davies; one *d.* *Educ:* Hackney Downs Secondary Sch.; King's Coll., London; Regent's Park Coll.; St Catherine's and Mansfield College, Oxford; Marburg University. Bugbrooke Baptist Church, 1928-32; Headquarters Staff, Baptist Missionary Society, 1932-40; Senior Tutor, Regent's Park College, 1940-51; Lecturer in Comparative Religion and the History of Modern Missions, Oxford Univ., 1946-51; Editor, The Baptist Quarterly, 1944-50. Pres., Baptist Historical Soc. Vice-Chm., Central Cttee World Council of Churches, 1954-68 Jt Pres. 1968-75; Moderator Free Church Federal Council 1958-59; Vice-Pres., 1960-62, Chm., Executive Cttee, 1962-71 British Council of Churches (Hon. Life Pres., 1978); Vice-Pres Baptist World Alliance, 1965-70. Examiner in the Univs of Oxford, Wales, Edinburgh and Bristol. *Publications:* The Saktas 1933; The Church Awakes, 1942; The Free Church Tradition in the Life of England, 1944; The Fellowship of Believers, 1944 Henry Wheeler Robinson, 1946; The Anabaptists of the 16th Century (Dr Williams's Lecture), 1949; The Baptists o Berkshire, 1952; James Henry Rushbrooke, 1954. The Anabaptists (in New Cambridge Modern History, Vol. II), 1958 The Baptist Union: A short history, 1959; Veteran Warrior (Memoir of B. Grey Griffith), 1962; Free Churchmer Unrepentant and Repentant, 1965; The World Council of Churches (Dr Williams's Lecture), 1970; Thirty Years of the British Council of Churches, 1942-72, 1972; Out of Grea Tribulation: Baptists in the Soviet Union, 1974; contrib. to Twentieth Century Christianity, 1961; From Uniformity to Unity, 1962; The Churches and Christian Unity, 1963 and Journal of Theological Studies, Internat. Review of Missions Congregational Quarterly, etc. *Recreations:* reading, writing and travel. *Address:* 9 Murray Court, 80 Banbury Road, Oxford Club: Athenæum.   *[Died 14 Jan. 1980.*

PAYNE, Sir Reginald Withers, Kt 1962; Judge of the Family Division (formerly Probate, Divorce and Admiralty Division), High Court of Justice, 1962-79; *b* 27 Sept. 1904; 2nd *s* of late John Herbert Payne, Solicitor, Hallgate House, Cottingham, E Yorks; *m* 1940, Alice, 3rd *d* of late Ernest Armstrong, Hankham Place, Pevensey; two *s*. *Educ:* Hymers Coll., Hull. LLB (London), 1927; admitted Solicitor, 1927; called to the Bar, Inner Temple, 1937 (North Eastern Circuit). Bencher, Inner Temple, 1962. Served, 1940-45, in RAFVR (Provost Marshal's Branch for Provost and Security Duties); Deputy Assistant Provost Marshal Yorkshire, Assistant Provost Marshal: Midlands; Karachi Area; Deputy Provost Marshal, Bengal and Assam; Squadron Leader, 1943; Wing Commander, 1945. Recorder of Pontefract, 1955-57; Recorder of Huddersfield, 1957-59; Judge of the County Courts (Circuit 14), Oct. 1959-May 1960; (Circuit 12), 1960-62. Chm., Lord Chancellor's Cttee on Enforcement of Judgments, 1965. *Recreations:* golf, shooting, gardening. *Address:* Royal Courts of Justice, Strand, WC2; 12 King's Bench Walk, Temple, EC4. *T:* 01-353 3114. *Clubs:* Reform, Garrick.   *[Died 9 May 1980.*

PAYNE, Dr Sylvia May, CBE 1918; retired Psychiatrist; *b* 6 Nov. 1880; *d* of late Rev. E. W. Moore, Wimbledon and Stoke Doyle, Northants; *m* 1908, John Ernest Payne, FRCS, *s* of late John Payne, Park Grange, Sevenoaks; three *s*. *Educ:* Wimbledon High School; Westfield College (London University); London (Royal Free Hospital) School of Medicine for Women. MB BS, London, 1906; House Surgeon and Assistant Anæsthetist Royal Free Hospital, 1907-08; Commandant and Medical Officer in charge of Torquay Red Cross Hospitals, 1914-18; Psychiatrist to London Clinic of Psycho-Analysis, 1926; Hon. Sec. to Institute of Psycho-Analysis, 1929, Hon. Training Sec. 1939, Chairman of Directors, 1944-47; Fellow of the Royal Society of Medicine, Vice-President of Psychiatric Section; Pres. British Psycho-Analytical Society; Member of International Psycho-Analytical Society; Fellow British Psychological Society (Medical Section; Chairman, 1936); Hon. Member British Psycho-Analytical Society, 1962. *Publications:* Observations on The Formation and Function of the Super-Ego in Normal and Abnormal Psychological States, The British Journal of Medical Psychology, Vol. vii, Part I, 1927; The Myth of the Barnacle Goose, The International Journal of Psycho-Analysis, Vol. x, Parts 2 and 3, 1929; A Conception of Femininity, The British Journal of Medical Psychology, Vol. xv, Part 1, 1935; Post-war Activities and the Advance of Psychotherapy, The British Journal of Medical Psychology, Vol. xvi, Part I, 1936. *Address:* c/o National Westminster Bank Ltd, 154 Harley Street, W1N 2AS. *Club:* University Women's.   *[Died 30 July 1976.*

PEACEY, Rev. John Raphael, MC, MA; Residentiary Canon, Bristol, 1945-66, now Canon Emeritus; Canon Missioner, diocese of Bristol, 1956-66; Rural Dean of Hurst, since 1969; *b* 16 July 1896; *s* of Reverend Prebendary T. Peacey, Vicar of Hove, and Ellen C. Leeper; *m* 1925, M. E. Hancock; one *d*. *Educ:* Mowden Preparatory School; S Edmund's School, Canterbury; Selwyn College, Cambridge. Lt Sussex RGA, B Battery AA, France, 1915-18; Theological Tripos, Pt I.; Master at Wellington College, 1922-23; Fellow and Dean of Selwyn College, Cambridge, 1923-27; Head Master, Bishop Cotton School, Simla, 1927-35; Principal, Bishop's College, Calcutta, 1935-45. *Recreation:* gardening. *Address:* Speedwell, 88 College Lane, Hurstpierpoint, Sussex. *T:* 2378.   *[Died 31 Oct. 1971.*

PEACH, Lawrence du Garde, OBE 1972; MA, PhD; Author and Dramatist; *b* 14 Jan. 1890; *s* of Rev. Charles Peach; *m* 1915, Marianne Leeming (*d* 1972); no *c*. *Educ:* Manchester Grammar School; Manchester University; Göttingen University; Sheffield University. Lecturer in English Language and Literature, Göttingen University, 1912-14; Manchester Regiment and Staff Intelligence, 1914-19, Captain, 1917; Major, Home Guard, 1941; Lecturer in English, University College of the South West, 1922-26; began writing for Punch and other papers, 1920; Author of 400 radio plays broadcast by BBC and of many film scenarios; Contested Derby (L) 1929; Lecturer and Political speaker. Founder and Director, Great Hucklow Village Players, 1927-. Hon. LittD, Sheffield, 1964. *Publications:* Angela and I-Punch sketches; Unknown Devon; Radio Plays: Five Country Plays; The Path of Glory; Practical Plays for Stage and Classroom; The Castles of England; Famous Men of Britain; Famous Women of Britain; Plays for Young Players; Five Plays for Boys; A Dramatic History of England; Knights of the Round Table; The Story of Sigurd; Plays of the Family Goodman; Story Tellers of Britain; Napoleon couldn't do it, 1941; According to Plan, 1942; You Never Know!, 1943; Legacy at Loon, 1943; Mystery of the Mary Celeste, 1945; The White Sheep of the Family (with Ian Hay), 1948; Mate in Three, 1949; The Town that would have a Pageant, 1951; Women are like that, 1952; A Horse A Horse!, 1953; Love One Another, 1954; Speed the

Plough, 1955; Collected Plays, IV Vols, 1955; Any Old Iron, 1956; Bless the Well, 1958; Christmas Comes, 1959; The Village that would have a Dragon, 1960; Heirs and Graces, 1962; Summat Akin, 1963; The Lopotkin Inheritance, 1963; Henry Came to Tideswell, 1964; Friday's Dream, 1965; Beautiful Garden, 1966; A Knife in her Stocking, 1967; Things just so strange, 1967; The Beacon, 1968; Where Witches do Inhabit, 1969; To the Manor Born, 1970; 40 books for young readers in Adventures from History and other series; a long series of Plays for Youth Groups; and many short plays, including many on Biblical subjects, various pageant scripts, including Centenary pageants for: Sheffield, Warrington, Wolverhampton, The Isle of Man, Sheffield Youth and National Co-operative Soc. and Transport and Gen. Workers Union. *Recreations:* Village Drama, painting. *Address:* Foolow, Eyam, via Sheffield. *T:* Tideswell 258. *Club:* Savage.   *[Died 31 Dec. 1974.*

PEACOCK, Alexander David, DSc (Durham); LLD (St Andrews); FRSE; Emeritus Professor of Natural History, Queen's College (University of St Andrews), Dundee (Professor 1926-56); *e s* of James and Jane Peacock; *m* 1917, Clara Mary, *d* of William and Ellen Turner; one *s* one *d*. *Educ:* Armstrong College (University of Durham), Newcastle upon Tyne. Graduated in Science, 1908; Prize Demonstrator in Zoology, University of Durham, 1909-11; Government Entomologist, Southern Nigeria, 1911-13; Lecturer in Zoology, University of Durham, 1913-26; on military service, 1914-19; with Field Ambulance and special services, rank of Captain, RAMC (TF), 1918; principally engaged on problems of medical entomology alone or as member of War Office Trench Fever Commission working party and American Red Cross Trench Fever Commission. *Publications:* Entomological Pests and Problems of Southern Nigeria; The Louse Problem at the Western Front, and several reports on this to the War Office; Report of the American Red Cross Trench Fever Commission (part author); papers on Parthenogenesis and Pharaoh's Ant. *Recreation:* painting. *Address:* 6 St Peter's Grove, York YO3 6AQ. *T:* 55127.   *[Died 2 March 1976.*

PEACOCK, David Henry, MA (Cantab); CChem, FRIC; DSc (London); IES (retired); *b* Dec. 1889; *s* of C. G. and Catherine Peacock; *m* 1915, Catherine Tait (*d* 1971); no *c*. *Educ:* Central Foundation School, London; Trinity Coll., Cambridge (Scholar); Gordon Wigan prize for research in Chemistry. Nobel's Explosives Factory Research Department, 1913-16; British Dyes Research Department, 1916-22; Chief Assistant Technical Department, Huddersfield, 1920-22; Professor of Chemistry, University of Rangoon, 1922-40; Special Chemical Adviser to the Government of Burma, 1938-40; Chemical Adviser, Bomber and Maintenance Commands, RAF, 1942-45; Chemical Consultant in Ministry of Supply, 1945-47; Lecturer in Organic Chemistry, University of Sheffield, 1947-55, also Tutor at Stephenson Hall; Demonstrator, Chemical Labs, Univ. of Cambridge. *Publications:* Life of Joseph Priestley; various papers in Journal of the Chemical Society, Journal of Physical Chemistry, Journal of the Society of Dyers and Colourists, Encyclopædia Britannica. *Address:* 32 London Road, Harston, Cambridge CB2 5QH.   *[Died 2 July 1978.*

PEACOCK, John Atkins, CMG 1949; President, Nurdin & Peacock Ltd, Raynes Park, SW20; Director of Eggs, Ministry of Food, 1940-54; *b* 8 Sept. 1898; *s* of Thomas Peacock; *m* 1925, Phyllis Evelyn Jones; two *s* one *d*. *Address:* Bushey Road, Raynes Park, SW20; Astra, Vicarage Lane, Send, Surrey.   *[Died 24 Oct. 1979.*

PEAKE, Sir Harald, Kt 1973; AE; MA; *b* 28 Oct. 1899; *s* of late G. H. Peake; *m* 1st, 1933, Countess Resy, OBE 1946 (marr. diss., 1944), *o d* of Count de Baillet Latour, Brussels; one *s*; 2nd, 1952, Dame Felicity Hanbury, DBE, AE; one *s*. *Educ:* Eton; Trinity Coll., Cambridge. Served in Coldstream Guards during European War, and subsequently Yorkshire Dragoons Yeomanry; raised and commanded No. 609 (West Riding) Squadron, Royal Aux. Air Force, 1936; Director of the Auxiliary Air Force, Air Ministry, 1938; Director of Public Relations, Air Ministry, 1940-42; Director of Air Force Welfare, 1942-43; Special Duty List, Air Ministry, 1943-45; retired with rank of Air Commodore. Chairman: Steel Co. of Wales, 1955-62; Lloyds Bank Ltd, 1961-69 (Dep. Chm., 1961, Vice-Chm., 1947-61). Member, Nye Cttee on War Office Organisation, 1963. Chm., RAF Benevolent Fund, 1967-. Prime Warden, Goldsmiths' Company, 1958-59. *Recreations:* rowed for Eton, Cambridge and England; Master of Rufford Hounds, 1931-32; Agriculture. *Address:* 2 Shepherd's Close, Shepherd's Place, Upper Brook Street, W1Y 3RT. *T:* 01-629 1264; Court Farm, Tackley, Oxford OX5 3AQ. *T:* Tackley 221. *Club:* Brooks's.
                                        [Died 24 May 1978.

PEAKER, Alfred Pearson, MC; MA; DL; Stipendiary Magistrate, Middlesbrough, 1939-68, Teesside, 1968-69, retired; *b* 22 June 1896; *s* of late Frederick Peaker, Past President, Institute of Journalists, and Eveline Peaker, JP; *m* 1957, Audrey Beare Hall. *Educ:* Dulwich Coll.; Worcester Coll., Oxford (Senior Classical Exhibnr). Served European War in 60th Rifles, 1915-19; Captain, 1917 (MC, wounded); Honour School of Jurisprudence, Oxford, 1920; BA 1920; MA 1922. Called to Bar, Middle Temple, 1921, and practised on North Eastern Circuit; Founder Member and Chairman, Society of Stipendiary Magistrates; Captain 66th (Leeds Rifles) Anti-Aircraft Regt, RA, TA, 1936-39; Lieut-Colonel, commanding 4th Cleveland Cadet Bn, The Green Howards, 1943-48; Hon. Colonel, 1949-64; Member North Riding T&AF Assoc.; Chairman Cadet Force Cttee, 1951-58; formerly Governor, Guisborough Grammar Sch. (Chairman, 1951-62). DL, North Riding of Yorkshire, 1964. *Recreations:* golf, gentle gardening, friendship. *Address:* Priory Cottage, Guisborough, Yorks. *T:* Guisborough 2944. *Clubs:* National Liberal; Cleveland (Teesside).
[Died 13 Jan. 1973.

PEAR, Prof. Tom Hatherley, MA, BSc; Emeritus Professor of Psychology, University of Manchester, since 1951; *b* Walpole, Norfolk, 1886; *o s* of Alfred John and Mary Ann Pear; *m* Catherine, *y d* of Samuel Henry Robinson, of Whalley Range, Manchester; one *s* (and one *s* decd) two *d*. *Educ:* Wisbech Grammar Sch.; King's Coll., London; Universities of Würzburg and Giessen. BSc London; MA (Manchester); Fellow of King's Coll., London; Hon. Fellow British Psychological Society. President of British Psychological Society, 1943; Buchanan-Riddell Lecturer, University of Durham, 1936. Formerly Lecturer in Experimental Psychology, Manchester, and on staff of Maghull Military Hospital; President of Psychology Section, British Association, 1928; Member Council, Rossall School. *Publications:* Remembering and Forgetting; Skill in Work and Play; Fitness for Work; The Art of Study; Voice and Personality; The Psychology of Effective Speaking; Religion and Contemporary Psychology; The Maturing Mind, The Psychology of Conversation; English Social Differences; Personality, Appearance and Speech; The Moulding of Modern Man; Social Relations of Speaking; (ed) Psychological Factors of Peace and War; Shell Shock and its Lessons (with Professor Sir Grafton Elliot Smith); (joint) The Study of Society; Current Trends in British Psychology; The Nature of Conflict; has contributed to British Journal of Psychology and to various journals devoted to psychology, education, broadcasting and industry. *Address:* Shirkoak House, Woodchurch, Ashford, Kent. *T:* Woodchurch 368. *Clubs:* English-Speaking Union, PEN.
[Died 14 May 1972.

PEARCE, Air Commodore Frederick Laurence, CBE 1945; DSO 1940; DFC; RAF, retired; *b* 9 Aug. 1898; *s* of Reuben Frederick Pearce, 14 Adrian Square, Westgate-on-Sea, Kent; *m* 1st, 1926, Joy May Pedley; one *s* (and one *s* decd); 2nd, 1953, Marie Gwendoline, *d* of Dr G. W. Paterson, Grenada. *Educ:* Godwin Coll.; Aylesbury. HAC 1916; RFC 1917; War of 1939-45 (DSO, despatches, DFC for action over Norway, CBE); Air Officer Commanding, Air Headquarters, Ceylon, 1949-52; retired, 1952. *Address:* Clovelly Hotel, Mill Road, Salisbury, Wilts.
[Died 3 Dec. 1975.

PEARCE, Sir George (Alfred), Kt 1947; OBE 1938; KPM 1946; Indian Police; *b* 28 Oct. 1894; 3rd *s* of Harry Walter and Edith Ellen Pearce; *m* 1st, 1920, Muriel Florence Durrell (*d* 1962); one *s* one *d*; 2nd, 1964, Muriel Sorby (*née* Wright), *widow* of Lt-Col W. J. W. Sorby. *Educ:* City of Norwich Sch.; St John's Coll., Battersea. Served European War, 1914-20, Middlesex Regt and Indian Army; entered Indian Police, 1920, as Asst Superintendent of Police; posted to UP, Superintendent of Police, 1923; Supt of Police, Special Dacoity Police UP, 1926-30; Supt of Police, Aligarh, Cawnpore, Naini Tal, 1931-40; Comdt UP Military Police and Police Training School, 1940; Dep. Inspector-General of Police, 1944; on Special Duty for Police Reorganisation, 1945; Inspector-General of Police, UP, 1946; retired, 1949. Government Communications Headquarters (Foreign Office), 1949-64. *Recreation:* reading. *Address:* Copper Beech House, Malvern Place, Cheltenham, Glos. *Club:* East India and Sports.
[Died 19 July 1971.

PEARS, Sidney John, FCA; Senior Partner, Cooper Brothers & Co., 1946-70; *b* 5 Aug. 1900; *s* of Sidney Pears and Alice Ella Grossmith; *m* 1927, Molly Kathleen Wallers; three *d*. *Educ:* Rugby. Member Inst. of Chartered Accountants in England and Wales; ACA 1924; FCA 1931; Member Council, 1946-67; Vice-President, 1959-60; Preisdent, 1960-61. Member Assembly of Delegates on Union Européenne des Experts Comptables Economiques et Financiers (UEC), 1963-66; Member Exec. Cttee of UEC, 1966-67. Ministry of Supply: Director of

Contracts, 1941; Principal Controller of Costs, 1942-45; Vice-Chairman Advisory Cttee on ROF accounting, 1946-50. Ministry of Works: Member Cttee on Enquiry into Cement Industry, 1946; Member Building Working Party, 1948. Board of Trade: Dep. Chairman Wool Working Party, 1946; Director, National Film Finance Corp., 1948-52, and Festival Gardens Ltd, 1952-53; Advisory Cttee, Revolving Fund for Industry, 1953-56; Export Credits Guarantee Dept Cttee, 1955. Treasury: Investigation into Building Material prices; Board of Referees (Board of Inland Revenue), 1956-57; Accountant Adviser, 1955-60, Part-time Director, 1960-72, UKAEA. Ministry of Agriculture, Fisheries and Food Cttee on Milk Distributors' Remuneration, 1959-61. Member, Economic Development Cttee for the Electrical Engineering Industry, 1964-. Director and Governor, Cable Trust Ltd; Chairman: Cables Investment Trust Ltd; Globe Investment Trust Ltd; Corney & Barrow Ltd; Electra Finance Co. Ltd; Electra House Ltd; Electra Investments Ltd; Aberdeen Edinburgh Trust Ltd; Young Companies Investment Trust Ltd; Director: Electra Investments (South Africa) Ltd; Electra Investments (Canada) Ltd; Electra Investments (Rhodesia) Ltd; Electra Investments (Zambia) Ltd; Singer & Friedlander Ltd; Singer & Friedlander Holdings Ltd; Telephone & General Trust Ltd. Adviser to: British and Ghanaian Govts on Volta River dam and Aluminium Scheme; Rhodesian Govt on Kariba and Kafue, 1955-60; World Bank on Indus Basin, Niger River and Caroni River hydro-electric schemes. *Recreations:* tennis, golf. *Address:* (office) Electra House, Victoria Embankment, WC2; Rest Harrow, Ashurstwood, near East Grinstead, Sussex. *T:* Forest Row 2206; Arundel House, Arundel Street, WC2. *T:* 01-836 1068. *Club:* Royal Ashdown Forest Golf.
[Died 10 Oct. 1972.

PEARS, Rear-Admiral Steuart Arnold, CBE 1950; DL; retired 1956; *b* 24 Sept. 1894; *e s* of S. D. Pears, President Municipality, Madras; *m* 1916, Anne Biggins; one *s* two *d*. *Educ:* RN Colleges, Osborne and Dartmouth. Sub-Lieut, 1914; Lieut, 1916; Lieut-Commander, 1924; Commander, 1934; Captain, 1947; Rear-Admiral, 1953. Served HMS Hercules, 1911; King George V, 1913; Falmouth, 1914; Oak, 1916; Excellent, 1919; Campbell, 1922; Reserve Fleet, 1924. Executive Officer Visit of Prince of Wales to S. America, 1925; lost right leg, 1926; transf. Inspection Research Design and Experimental Duties, 1927; Research Dept, 1928; Naval Ordnance Inspection Officer, Plymouth, 1932, Mediterranean, 1936; Supt. Experimental Establishment, Pendine, 1940; Chief Inspector, 1947; Vice-President Ordnance Board, 1953; President, 1955; Master, Lord Leycester Hospital, Warwick, 1958-66. DL Warwickshire, 1959. *Recreation:* anything out-of-doors. *Address:* Chalcroft, Cliff Way, Compton, Winchester. *Club:* Royal Navy of 1765 and 1785 (United 1889).
[Died 22 April 1978.

PEARSE, Thomas L. S.; *see* Smith-Pearse.

PEARSON, Baron (Life Peer), *cr* 1965; **Colin Hargreaves Pearson**, PC 1961; Kt 1951; CBE 1946; a Lord of Appeal in Ordinary, 1965-74; *b* 28 July 1899; 2nd *s* of Ernest William and Jessie Borland Pearson, Minnedosa, Manitoba, Canada; *m* 1931, Sophie Grace, *e d* of Arthur Hermann Thomas, LLD, DLitt, FSA, Worthing; one *s* one *d*. *Educ:* St Paul's Sch.; Balliol Coll., Oxford (Classical Scholar and Jenkyns Exhibitioner); Military service, Feb.-Dec. 1918; called to Bar, 1924; Yarborough Anderson Exhibition, Inner Temple, 1925, Reader, 1973 Treasurer, 1974; Junior Common Law Counsel to Ministry of Works, 1930-49; KC 1949; Recorder of Hythe, 1937-51; Judge of High Court of Justice, Queen's Bench Division, 1951-61; Judge of Restrictive Practices Court, 1957-61 (President, 1960-61); a Lord Justice of Appeal, 1961-65. Temporary member of Treasury Solicitor's Department, 1939-45. Member: Legal Cttee on Medical Partnerships, 1948; Supreme Court Rule Cttee 1957-65; Exec. Council of the Inns of Court, 1962-65; Senate of Inns of Court, 1966-69. Chm., Royal Commn on Civil Liability and Compensation for Personal Injury, 1973-78. Chairman Cttee on Funds in Court, 1958; Law Reform Cttee, 1963-73 Chairman, Courts of Inquiry: into a dispute in the Electricity Supply Industry, 1964; into a dispute in the Shipping Industry 1966-67; into a dispute in Civil Air Transport Industry, 1967-68 into a dispute in Steel Industry, 1968; the Dock Strike, 1970 Chm. Arbitral Body on Teachers' Remuneration, 1971, 1972 Visitor, Balliol Coll., Oxford, 1965-74; President, Old Pauline Club, 1960-63; Chairman, St Paul's School Building Appeal 1966-; Member Council, Bedford Coll., University of London (Vice-Chairman, 1959-62, Chairman, 1962-63), 1958-66 President, Inc. Assoc. of Preparatory Schools, 1965-70. *Address* 2 Crown Office Row, Temple, EC4. *T:* 01-353 5391. *Clubs* Garrick, Roehampton.
[Died 31 Jan. 1980

PEARSON, Arthur, CBE 1949; JP; *b* 31 Jan. 1897; *s* of William Pearson, Pontypridd, Glamorgan. MP (Lab) Pontypridd, 1938

70, retired; Labour Whip, 1939-45; Comptroller of HM Household, 1945-46; Treasurer of HM Household, 1946-51; an Opposition Whip, 1951-64. JP 1939, CC 1928-46, Glamorgan. *Address:* 24 The Avenue, Pontypridd, Mid Glamorgan.
                                        [Died 14 April 1980.

PEARSON, Prof. Claude Edmund, MMet; Director, Durham Chemicals Group Ltd, since 1956; *b* 13 May 1903; *s* of Thomas George and Annetta Mary Pearson; *m* 1928, Olga Mary Hunt (*d* 1959); *m* 1961, Catherine Annie Benson. *Educ:* Sir William Turner's Sch., Coatham; Sheffield University. Lecturer in Metallurgy, University of Durham, 1924; Reader, 1943; Professor of Metallurgy, King's Coll., University of Durham, 1945-48. *Publications:* The Extrusion of Metals, 1944; papers to: Institute of Metals, Iron and Steel Institute, Institute of Welding. *Recreation:* angling. *Address:* Middle Drive, Woolsington, Newcastle upon Tyne.   *[Died 25 May 1971.*

PEARSON, Colin Bateman; retired as Puisne Judge; *b* 1 Aug. 1889; *s* of Samuel Pearson, MA, Independent Minister; *m* 1942, Dulcibel Hirst Corner (*née* Hillier); no *c*. *Educ:* Tynemouth Sch., Northumberland; Peterhouse, Cambridge. Durham Light Infantry, 1915-19; Captain, RARO; called to Bar, Middle Temple, 1924; Police Magistrate, Tonga, 1928; Police Magistrate, Gold Coast, 1932; Asst Judge, Nigeria, 1938; Puisne Judge, Uganda, 1942-53 (acted as Chief Justice on occasions, 1946-52); retired, 1953. *Address:* Shortlands, Cooks Lane, Axminster, Devon. *Club:* United Oxford & Cambridge University.   *[Died 19 Dec. 1974.*

PEARSON, Egon Sharpe, CBE 1946; FRS 1966; MA, DSc; Professor Emeritus, University of London; Statistical Consultant, British Standards Institution, 1932-77; *b* 11 Aug. 1895; *s* of late Karl Pearson, FRS; *m* 1st, 1934, Eileen (*d* 1949), *yr d* of Russell Jolly; two *d*; 2nd, 1967, Margaret Turner (*née* Scott) (*d* 1975), *widow* of L. B. Turner, ScD, MIEE. *Educ:* Dragon Sch., Oxford; Winchester Coll.; Trinity Coll., Cambridge. Lecturer in Statistics at University College, London, 1921-33; Reader, 1933-35, Professor, 1935-60. Managing Editor, Biometrika, 1936-66, and Editor of Auxiliary Publications, 1966-75. Attached to Ordnance Bd, Min. of Supply later MoD, 1939-46, Assoc. Mem., 1943-. President, Royal Statistical Society, 1955-57; Guy Medal in Gold of the Royal Statistical Society, 1955. Hon. Fellow, Institute of Actuaries, 1956. Medal of Freedom with Bronze Palm, USA, 1947. *Publications:* (ed) Karl Pearson's Lectures on the History of Statistics in the 17th and 18th Centuries, 1978; papers on the mathematical theory of statistics and its applications, in Biometrika and other journals; editor of several vols of Statistical Tables; pamphlet for the British Standards Institution on the application of statistical method in problems of standardisation and quality control, 1935. *Address:* University College, Gower Street, WC1E 6BT.
                                        [Died 12 June 1980.

PEARSON, Gerald Lionel, MC 1944; HM Diplomatic Service, retired; *b* 11 Nov. 1918; *e s* of late Col H. S. I. Pearson, 5th (Royal) Mahratta LI; *m* 1st, 1945, Erica Mirrington-Mainwaring (marr. diss. 1963); one *s* one *d*; 2nd, 1964, Peggy Fallows. *Educ:* Wellington Coll.; Clare Coll., Cambridge (MA). Served War of 1939-45 (MC): S Wales Borderers and Parachute Regt; Captain 1940; discharged (wounded), 1945. BoT, 1945; British Trade Comr, Dublin, 1959-67; Counsellor (Commercial), Brit. Embassy, The Hague, 1967-71; Counsellor (Hong Kong Affairs), UK Mission to UN and other Internat. Organisations, Geneva, 1971-78. *Recreations:* fishing, bird-watching. *Address:* c/o Grindlays Bank Ltd, 13 St James's Square, SW1Y 4LF. *Clubs:* Carlton, Royal Over-Seas League; Kildare Street and University (Dublin). *[Died 12 Nov. 1978.*

PEARSON, Hon. Sir Glen (Gardner), Kt 1970; JP; *b* 19 Feb. 1907; *s* of Thomas and Julia Pearson; *m* 1932, Mavis Doreen Croxton; two *s* one *d* (and one *d* decd in infancy). *Educ:* State Schs; Prince Alfred Coll., Adelaide. Sen. Public Certif., 1922. Farming: Yorke's Peninsula, 1923-35; Eyre Peninsula, 1935-. Executive, SA Wheatgrowers Assoc., 1938-51; Mem., Aust. Barley Bd, 1948-56. MHA for Flinders, SA House of Assembly, 1951-70, retd; Minister: of Agriculture and of Forests, 1956-58; of Works and Marine, 1958-65, also of Aboriginal Affairs, 1962-65, and Dep. Leader, House of Assembly, 1960-65; Dep. Leader of Opposition, 1965-68; Treasurer and Minister of Housing (with prefix Hon.) also Dep. Leader, House of Assembly, SA, 1968-March 1970, and retd from public life, May 1970. Chm., Adelaide Permanent Building Soc., 1971-. Served on many local bodies and as Pres. and Sec. of sporting bodies, also sub branch of RS League (Mem.). JP, Cockaleechie, 1948. *Recreations:* cricket, football, tennis; latterly bowls. *Address:* Cockaleechie, SA 5610, Australia. *T:* Cockaleechie 54. *Clubs:* Royal Commonwealth Society; Masonic (SA).
                                        [Died 30 Nov. 1976.

PEARSON, Joseph, DSc (Manchester, Liverpool, Tasmania); FRSE, FLS; *b* 19 April 1881; *s* of Daniel Pearson and Cecilia Parr; *m* 1st, Lilla (*d* 1941), *o d* of Thomas McConnell, Dunboyne, Larne; (two *s* died on active service, War of 1939-45); 2nd, Mavis (*d* 1961), *d* of Frank Meadowcroft, Wellington, New Zealand. *Educ:* Liverpool Coll.; University College, Liverpool; Victoria Univ. 1st class Hons, BSc, Victoria University Scholarship, 1902; MSc, Liverpool, 1905; DSc Liverpool, 1908; MSc Manchester, 1921; DSc Manchester, 1922; DSc Tasmania, 1935; Naturalist to Ulster Fisheries and Biology Assoc., 1903; Asst Lecturer in Zoology, University College, Cardiff, 1904; Lecturer in Zoology, University of Liverpool, 1905-10; Director Colombo Museum, 1910-34; Marine Biologist to Ceylon Government, 1910-34; Inspector of Pearl Banks, 1925-34; Lecturer in Biology in Ceylon Medical Coll., 1910-20; Lecturer in Zoology, University College, Colombo, 1920-24; Acting Archæological Commissioner, 1929-31; Chairman of Commission of Enquiry into the Industries of Ceylon; Director Tasmanian Museum and Art Gallery, 1934-52; Emeritus Director, Tasmanian Museum and Art Gallery, 1952; Member, Australian National Research Council; Fellow Inst. of Biology; President, Section D (Zoology) of Australian and New Zealand Assoc. for the Advancement of Science, 1946; Hon. Member, Royal Society of Tasmania; Comr of International Commission on Zoological Nomenclature, 1946-54; Lieut, RGA, European War, 1914-18; served in Ceylon and France, 1915-19. *Publications:* Editor: Ceylon Journal of Science and Spolia Zeylanica, 1910-34; Proceedings of Royal Society of Tasmania, 1934-52; has written numerous scientific papers on Marine Biology, Zoology, Comparative Anatomy of the Marsupialia, and Ecology; articles on Archæology and Dutch Colonial furniture. *Address:* c/o Mrs Amy Derksen, Brantholme, Low Langstaffe, Sedbergh, Yorks.   *[Died 20 June 1971.*

PEARSON, Rt. Hon. Lester Bowles, CC (Canada), 1968; PC 1963; PC (Canada), 1948; OM 1971; OBE 1935; MA Oxon; BA Oxon and Toronto; Chairman of the Board, International Development Research Centre, since 1970 (Chairman, Commission on International Development, 1968-69); *b* Toronto, Ont, 23 April 1897; *s* of Rev. Edwin Arthur Pearson and Annie Sarah (Bowles) Pearson; *m* 1925, Maryon Elspeth Moody, Winnipeg; one *s* one *d*. *Educ:* Collegiate Inst. Peterborough and Hamilton, Ont; University of Toronto; St John's Coll., Oxford. Lecturer in Modern History, University of Toronto, 1926-28, Asst Professor, 1926-28; 1st Secretary Dept of External Affairs, 1928; special missions to Washington, London, The Hague, Geneva and throughout Canada; 1st Secretary London Office of High Commr for Canada, 1935-39; appointed Secretary with rank of Counsellor, 1939; Assistant Under-Secretary of State for External Affairs, Ottawa, 1941; Minister-Counsellor, Canadian Embassy, Washington, 1942-45; Ambassador to Washington, 1945-46; Under-Secretary of State for External Affairs, Ottawa, 1946-48; MP (L) Algoma East Ont, Oct. 1948-68; Sec. of State for External Affairs, 1948-57; Leader of the Opposition in Parlt, 1958-63; Leader, Liberal Party of Canada, 1963-68; Prime Minister, 1963-68. One of senior advisers at San Francisco Conference, April-June 1945, that drew up UN Charter and Leader of Canadian delegations to subsequent meetings of UN General Assembly; President General Assembly of UN, 1952-53. Represented Canadian Prime Minister at meeting of Commonwealth Prime Ministers, London, 1949; Chairman, Canadian delegns: Commonwealth Meeting on Foreign Affairs, Colombo, 1950; Japanese Peace Treaty Conf., San Francisco, 1951; 9-Power Conf. on German Rearmament, London, Sept. 1954; Geneva Conference, 1954. Represented Canada at signing of North Atlantic Treaty in Washington and has headed Canadian delegations to subs. North Atlantic Council Meetings (Chairman Council, 1951-52). President: North Atlantic Treaty Assoc., 1957; Inst. for Strategic Studies, 1968-. Chancellor: Victoria Univ., Toronto, 1951-58; Carleton Univ., Ottawa, 1968-. Awarded the Nobel Peace Prize for 1957. Reith Lecturer, 1968. Holds hon. degrees of 50 universities; Hon. Fellow: St John's Coll., Oxford; Weizmann Inst. of Science, 1968. Hon. DCL, Oxford; Hon. Fellow, RAIC; Hon. Freeman, City of London, 1967. *Publications:* Democracy in World Politics (Stafford Little Lectures: publ. Canada, 1955, Great Britain, 1956); Diplomacy in the Nuclear Age, 1959; The Four Faces of Peace, 1964; Peace in the Family of Man, 1968 (Reith Lectures); Words and Occasions, 1970; The Crisis of Development, 1970 (Leffingwell Lectures); *posthumous publication:* Memoirs: 1897-1948, 1973. *Address:* (home) 541 Montagu Place, Rockcliffe Park, Ottawa, Ont, Canada; (office) Suite 907, 75 Albert Street, Ottawa K1P 5E7, Canada. *Club:* Rideau (Ottawa). *[Died 27 Dec. 1972.*

PEARSON, Rupert Samuel Bruce, DM Oxon; FRCP; Hon. Consulting Physician, King's College Hospital and Woolwich Group of Hospitals; late Senior Specialist Physician, Queen

Elizabeth Hospital, Barbados; *b* 8 Sept. 1904; *s* of late Dr Bruce Pearson, Buckingham; *m* 1939, Mary Katherine Elizabeth Aldworth (*d* 1958); one *s* one *d*; *m* 1962, Joyce Mary Barmby (*née* Strange). *Educ:* Charterhouse; Trinity Coll., Oxford; Guy's Hospital, Treasurer's Gold Medal, 1929; House Physician, Guy's Hospital, 1929; Med. Registrar, Guy's Hosp., 1930-33; Out-Patient Medical Registrar, Hosp. for Sick Children, Great Ormond St, 1933-35; Asst Clinical Research Unit, Guy's Hosp., 1935 and 1936; Asst Physician, Hampstead General Hospital, 1937. Councillor, RCP, 1962-65. Examiner in Medicine: Oxford Univ., 1959-65; RCP, 1963-70; London Univ. Member: Assoc. of Physicians of Gt Brit.; Brit. Soc. of Gastro-enterology; British Allergy Soc. *Publications:* contribs to Arch. Dis. Child, Quarterly Jl of Med., Proc. Roy. Soc. Med., BMJ, Lancet. *Recreations:* gardening, croquet. *Address:* The Spinney, Hurtmore, Godalming, Surrey. *T:* Godalming 21349.
[Died 18 Aug. 1974.

PEARSON, William, MD, MCh, FRCSI; lately Professor of Surgery, University of Dublin; *b* Cork, 7 May 1882; *er s* of late Professor Charles Yelverton Pearson; *m* 1927, Esther Margaret, *yr d* of late Arthur H. Hurford, Dublin and Belfast; one *s*. *Educ:* Cork Grammar School; Trinity College Dublin; USA; Berlin. First place in all Arts Examinations, with First Respondency at BA Degree; first place in all examinations in the School of Physic, Trinity College, Dublin; Trinity College Scholarship in Anatomy and Institutes of Medicine; Fitzpatrick Scholarship; Surgical Travelling Prize and Bennett Medal: Haughton Clinical Medal and Prize for Surgery, Sir P. Dun's Hosp.; Consulting Surgeon, Sir P. Dun's Hospital; Consulting Surgeon, Adelaide Hospital, Dublin; Past President, Royal Coll. of Surgeons in Ireland; sometime Surgeon to Meath Hospital and County Dublin Infirmary; Temporary Major, Surgical Specialist and District Consulting Surgeon RAMC; Visiting and Operating Surgeon, British Ministry of Pensions Special Surgical Hospital, Co. Dublin; holds several Honorary Surgical appts. *Publications:* Numerous contributions to Surgical Journals, especially in connection with the Surgery of Bone and the Thyroid Gland. *Recreations:* yachting, fishing, (salmon and trout). *Address:* 24 Lakelands Park, Terenure, Dublin. *T:* Dublin 900066. *Clubs:* Kildare Street (Dublin); Royal St George Yacht (Kingstown).
[Died Nov. 1976.

PEAT, Charles Urie, MC; MA, FCA; *b* 1892; *s* of late Sir Wm Barclay Peat, CVO; *m* 1914, Ruth Martha (*d* 1979), *d* of Rev. Henry John Pulley; two *s* four *d*. *Educ:* Sedbergh; Oxford. Served European War, 1914-19; MP (U) Darlington, 1931-45; Parliamentary Private Secretary to Mr Oliver Lyttelton, President of Board of Trade, 1941; Joint Parliamentary Secretary, Ministry of Supply, 1942-45; Parliamentary Secretary, Ministry of National Insurance, April 1945. Pres. Inst. of Chartered Accountants in England and Wales, 1959-60. *Address:* Wycliffe Hall, Barnard Castle, Co. Durham DL12 9TS. *T:* Teesdale 27241. *Club:* Carlton. *[Died 27 Oct. 1979.*

PECHELL, Lt-Col Sir Paul, 8th Bt, *cr* 1797; MC; late Essex Regt and Royal Pioneer Corps; *b* 10 Dec. 1889; *s* of Sir Augustus Brooke-Pechell, 7th Bt; *S* father, 1937; *m* 1st, 1920, Helen Gertrude (*d* 1959), 2nd *d* of Rev. J. D. Todd, Newton, Lincs; 2nd, 1971, Doris Margery Green, *y d* of T. D. Lobb, Bromley, Kent. *Educ:* Malvern; RMC, Sandhurst. Served European War, 1914-19 (wounded, MC, Bt Major) and War of 1939-45; Pres. Hampshire, I of W and Channel Isles Golf Union, 1951-63. *Recreations:* golf, gardening. *Heir presumptive:* kinsman Ronald Horace Pechell [*b* 4 June 1918; *m* 1949, Dora, *d* of John Crampthorne]. *Address:* Flat 1, 35 Talbot Avenue, Winton, Bournemouth, Hants. *T:* Bournemouth 55553. *Club:* Golfers'.
[Died 16 Feb. 1972.

PECK, Arthur Leslie, MA, PhD; Fellow of Christ's College, Cambridge, since 1926, Librarian, 1945-71, Vice-Master, 1957-61; Governor of Perse School since 1929 (Chairman, 1967-72); Member Committee, GBA, 1966-70; Vice-President Hymn Society of Great Britain and Ireland; *b* 1902. *Educ:* Perse School; Christ's College, Cambridge (scholar). Craven Univ. Scholar, 1923; Chancellor's Classical Medal, 1924; Prendergast University Student, 1924; Univ. Lectr in Classics, 1930-70, Public Orator, 1965-66, Univ. of Cambridge. Temp. appt with Ministry of Food, 1942-45. Mem., Inst. for Advanced Study, Princeton, NJ, 1963-64. Pres., Morris Ring (Fedn of Morris Men's Clubs), 1947-50; Mem. Exec. Cttee, English Folk Dance and Song Soc., 1947-51. *Publications:* Papers, etc., in classical periodicals and in journals of the English Folk Dance and Song Soc.; Aristotle, De partibus animalium, revised text and trans. (Loeb Library), 1937, revised edns 1945, 1957; Aristotle, De generatione animalium, revised text and translation (Loeb Library), 1943, revised edn, 1953; Aristotle, Historia animalium, vol. i, revised text and translation (Loeb Library), 1965, vol. ii,

revised text and translation, 1970; The Church in Barnwell (a centenary memorial), 1939; This Church of Christ, 1955; Anglicanism and Episcopacy, 1958; The Book of Hours (Eng. verse trans. of R. M. Rilke's Stundenbuch), 1961. *Address:* Christ's College, Cambridge. *T:* Cambridge 59601.
[Died 26 Feb. 1974.

PECK, Jasper Augustine, CMG 1965; *b* 14 July 1905; *s* of late John Herbert Peck, Lt-Col Indian Army, and late Margaret Jane Ada Batt; *m* 1939, Olwen, *d* of late Eliot Crawshay-Williams; no *c*. *Educ:* Westminster (King's Scholar); Univ. Coll., Oxford. Called to Bar, Inner Temple, 1930; practised, 1930-39. War Service, Gunner, 86th (HAC) HAA Regt, RA, TA, Major (DAAG), Mil. Dept., Judge Advocate-General's Office, 1939-45. Entered Colonial Office, Sept. 1945; Asst Legal Adviser, Colonial Office, 1950-65, retd. *Recreations:* ornithology, music. *Address:* 50 Saxmundham Road, Aldeburgh, Suffolk. *T:* Aldeburgh 2429. *Club:* Garrick. *[Died 18 Oct. 1980.*

PEDDIE, Baron *cr* 1961, of City and County of Kingston upon Hull (Life Peer); **James Mortimer Peddie**, MBE 1944; JP; Chairman, National Board for Prices and Incomes, 1970-71 (Member, 1965-71, Deputy Chairman, 1968-70); Chairman, Agrément Board, since 1967; Director: TU Unit Trust, since 1965; Mid-Kent Water Board, since 1971; *b* 4 April 1905; *s* of Crofton and Ethel Peddie; *m* 1931, Hilda Mary Alice Bull; one *s* one *d* (and one *d* decd). *Educ:* St Paul's Church Sch.; Hull Technical Coll.; London Sch. of Economics. Lecturer in Economics and Industrial Admin., Coll. of Commerce, 1928-39; Dir and Publicity Manager, Hull Co-operative Soc. Ltd; Min. of Information, 1940-45. Director (1945-65): CWS Ltd and Co-op. Insurance Soc. Ltd.; Co-op. Permanent Building Soc.; West Norfolk Fertiliser Co.; British Luma Lamp Co.; Travco Hotels Ltd; Education Sciences Ltd, 1974; Chairman: Technical Laboratory Services Ltd, 1974; Enalon Plastics Ltd, 1975 (Dir, 1973-). Governor, British Film Institute, 1948-54; Member, Colonial Office Adv. Cttee, 1950-62; Member Exec. Cttee, Co-op. Union, 1957-65; Chairman, Brit. Co-op. Political Party, 1958-65; Pres., Brit. Co-op. Congress, 1958; Mem., Nat. Coun. of Labour, 1958-65; Vice-Chm., Reith Commn on Advertising, 1965. Trustee and Exec. Mem., Civic Trust for Manchester and the North West, 1961-; Gov., Manchester Coll. of Commerce, 1962-; Industrial Arbitrator, Film Industry, 1964; Chairman: Adv. Cttee, Dept of Technical Co-operation, 1962-65; Adv. Cttee, Min. of Overseas Development, 1965; Post Office Users Nat. Council, 1969-; Member: Consumer Council, 1963-68; Advertising Standards Authority, 1972-; Nat. Consumer Council, 1977-. Trustee: Denton Foundn, 1972; Attlee Meml Trust, 1967-; Chm., Attlee Meml Foundn, 1975; President: Industrial Police and Security Assoc., 1972; Yorkshire Kidney Res. Fund, 1974; Vice-Pres., British Waterworks Assoc., 1972. Member: Council of Europe, 1974; WEU, 1974; Budget Cttee; Parly Statutory Instruments Cttee, 1973. Led Jt Parly delegations: Sweden, 1965; Finland, 1968. JP Cheshire, 1959-. LLD Manchester University, 1966. Hon. Citizen, Forth Worth, Texas, 1963; Freeman, City of London, 1972. *Publications:* Pricing in the Public Sector, 1975; frequent contributor to jls on Economics and Political subjects. *Recreation:* golf, as an excuse for walking. *Address:* House of Lords, SW1. *Clubs:* Royal Automobile; (Vice-Pres.) Springhead Park Golf (Hull).
[Died 13 April 1978.

PEDDIE, John Ronald, CBE 1937 (MBE 1918); MA 1909; DLitt 1927; FRSE 1942; FEIS 1947; Hon. LLD Glasgow, 1958; lately Secretary and Treasurer of the Carnegie Trust for the Universities of Scotland; retired December 1957; *b* 5 January 1887; *e s* of late Richard Dawes Peddie, Grangemouth; *m* 1914, Euphemia Scott Houston. *Educ:* Grangemouth High School; Glasgow University. Lecturer in English, Glasgow Univ., 1911-19; Official Adviser of Studies, Glasgow Univ. 1919-25; Executive Officer, National Committee for the Training of Teachers in Scotland, 1925-41; OC Glasgow University Contingent, Officers Training Corps, 1916-19; Examiner in English since 1911; a Governor of Heriot-Watt Univ., Edinburgh, 1957-68; Hon. Treas. Roy. Soc. of Edinburgh, 1957-67; a Governor of Merchiston Castle School; Trustee of the Cross Trust. Trustee of National Library of Scotland, 1942-73; Vice-President and Trustee of Society of Scottish Artists; former Chairman: Sir J. Donald Pollock Trust; Edinburgh Assoc. for the Provisions of Halls of Residence for Women Students. *Publications:* The Carnegie Trust; The First Fifty Years (1901-1951); Papers on literary and educational subjects. Editor, Glasgow University Roll of Honour. *Recreation:* gardening. *Address:* 7 Bruntsfield Terrace, Edinburgh EH10 4EX. *T:* 031-229 6055. *Club:* Mortonhall Golf. *[Died 11 Nov. 1979.*

PEDLEY, John Edward, CSI 1946; CIE 1939; MC; *b* 4 Dec. 1891; *s* of Dr T. F. Pedley; *m* 1928, Effie, *d* of Dr James Craig.

Educ: Repton; Trinity College, Oxford. Served European War, 1914-19 (MC). Entered Indian Civil Service, 1920. Retired as Member Board of Revenue, UP, 1947. Regional Food Officer, Eastern Region, 1950-51. *Address:* Walden, Ballasalla, Isle of Man. [Died 12 April 1972.

PEDLEY, Richard Rodman; Headmaster, St Dunstan's College, since 1967; *b* 23 Sept. 1912; *s* of F. W. and B. M. Pedley; *m* 1938, Jeanie M. M. Evans; one *s* one *d. Educ:* Foster's Sch., Sherborne; Downing Coll., Cambridge (Schol.; MA 1937). RA, 1940-46 (Major). Asst Master: City of Leicester Boys' Sch., 1934-40, 1946; St Olave's Sch., 1946-50; Headmaster: City of Leicester Boys' Sch., 1950-54; Chislehurst and Sidcup Gram. Sch., 1954-67. Pres., Headmasters' Assoc., 1963; Chm., 3rd Four Secondary Assocs., 1966-67; Sponsor, Nat. Council for Educnl Standards, 1972-. *Publications:* (ed) Paradise Lost Bks I and II, 1956; contribs to The Fight for Education (Black Papers), 1969-71. *Recreations:* literature, polemics, watching cricket, gardening. *Address:* Headmaster's House, St Dunstan's College, Catford, SE6. *T:* 01-690 0159. *Clubs:* MCC, East India, Sports and Public Schools. [Died 17 March 1973.

PEEBLES, Allan Charles Chiappini, CVO 1956; Secretary of The Athenæum, since 1962; *b* 18 Nov. 1907; *s* of late Lt-Colonel Arthur Stansfeld Peebles; *m* 1930, Jean Ilvira Naish (*d* 1972). *Educ:* Charterhouse; Royal Military College, Sandhurst. 2nd Lt Suffolk Regiment, 1927-30; Nigeria Police, 1931-56; Queen's Own Nigeria Regt, 1940-44, Major. Commissioner of Police, Northern Region, Nigeria, 1953-56. Ministry of Aviation, 1958-62. Queen's Police Medal, 1953; Colonial Police Medal, 1951. *Address:* The Athenæum, Pall Mall, SW1. *T:* 01-930 4843; 507 Hawkins House, Dolphin Square, SW1. *T:* 01-834 3800, Ext. Hawkins 507. *Club:* MCC. [Died 1 April 1974.

PEEL, Captain Sir (Francis Richard) Jonathan, Kt 1959; CBE 1943; MC; KPM; *b* 10 Dec. 1897; *s* of late Walter Peel, CBE, JP; *m* 1932, Daphne Margaret Holwell, *d* of Commander A. McC. Pakenham, Bath; one *s* one *d. Educ:* Malvern College; Pembroke College, Cambridge. RFA, European War, 1915-19; Liverpool City Police, 1920-31; Chief Constable of Bath, 1931-33; Chief Constable of Essex, 1933-62, retired. DL County of Essex, 1959-72. King's Police Medal, 1952. CStJ 1959. *Address:* Cedarholme, 9 Lexden Road, Colchester, Essex. [Died 6 Dec. 1979.

PEEL, Sir Jonathan; *see* Peel, Sir F. R. J.

PEEL YATES, Lt-Gen. Sir David, KCB 1966 (CB 1963); CVO 1965; DSO 1943, and Bar, 1944; OBE 1943; DL; JP; *b* 10 July 1911; *er s* of late Lt-Col Hubert Peel Yates, DSO, late South Wales Borderers, and Gertrude Loetitia Molyneux (*née* Sarel); *m* 1947, Christine Hilary, *er d* of late Horatio Stanley-Williams, DSO, Irthlingborough, Northants; one *s* one *d. Educ:* Haileybury College; RMC Sandhurst. Commissioned S Wales Borderers, 1931; Waziristan operations, 1937; active service in N Africa, Italy and Greece as GSO1 HQ First Army, Comdg 6 Bn Lincolnshire Regt, GSO1 4th Div. and BGS (Ops) AFHQ, 1942-46. OC 1st Bn S Wales Borderers, 1953-55; Comdr 27 Infantry Bde, Hong Kong, 1955-57; Asst Commandant, Staff College, 1957-60; Chief of Staff, Eastern Command, 1960-62; GOC, Berlin (British Sector), 1962-66; GOC-in-C: Eastern Command, 1966-68; Southern Comd, 1968-69; retd 1969. Colonel: The South Wales Borderers, 1962-69; Royal Regt of Wales (24th/41st Foot), 1969-77. DL and JP Breconshire, 1970. Breconshire CC, 1970-74. Chm., ICP Ltd, 1973-. Legion of Merit, USA, 1946. *Recreations:* shooting, fishing, ski-ing. *Address:* Glyn Pedr, Llanbedr, Crickhowell, Breconshire. *T:* Crickhowell 810333. *Club:* Army and Navy.
[Died 8 Oct. 1978.

PEERS, Robert, CBE 1955 (OBE 1946); MC; Hon. DLitt (Nottingham); JP; Professor Emeritus, Nottingham University; Professor of Adult Education, 1922-53; Professorial Research Fellow, 1954-55; Deputy Vice-Chancellor, 1948-53; *b* Liverpool, 1888; *m* 1st, 1916, Gladys, *d* of C. H. Cundy; one *d* (one *d* decd); 2nd, 1945, Eileen Marjorie, *d* of A. Clayton. *Educ:* University of Liverpool; University of Heidelberg. Henry Warren Meade King Scholar, 1911, BA First Class Hons Economics, 1913, University Post-graduate Scholar; Stanley Jevons Research Scholar, 1914; MA, 1919; served in King's Liverpool Regiment and Army Signal Service, 1915-19 (Captain, MC); Lecturer in Economics, University College, Exeter, 1919-20; Director of Extramural Studies, University College, Nottingham, 1920; Albert Kahn Fellow, 1928-29; Asst Regional Controller, Ministry of Labour and National Service, 1941-43; Labour Adviser to the Minister Resident, Middle East, 1943-44; Vice-Principal, University College Nottingham, 1946-47; Acting Principal, 1947-48; Lecture tours, West Indies, 1949, Australia,

1950, East Africa, 1955 and several in Germany; Smith-Mundt award for advanced research, Columbia Univ., 1953. Chm. Central Cttee for Adult Educ. in HM Forces, 1949-57; Chm. Transport Users' Consultative Cttee for the East Midlands, 1951-65; JP Nottingham. *Publications:* many contributions in Journals and Transactions on the theory and practice of Adult Education; Section on Adult Education in The Schools of England (Ed. J. Dover Wilson); Adult Education in Practice (edited with introductory and other chapters), 1934; Consumers' Co-operation in Great Britain (Joint), 1938; Labour and Employment in the Middle East (Report to the Minister), 1945; Adult Education: A Comparative Study, 1958, with German translation in part, 1963; Fact and Possibility in English Education, 1963. *Recreation:* gardening. *Address:* 21 Cator Lane, Chilwell, Beeston, Nottingham. *T:* Nottingham 255457. *Club:* University (Nottingham). [Died 29 Nov. 1972.

PEGG, Arthur John, OBE 1951 (MBE 1946); AFRAeS 1953; Chief Test Pilot, Bristol Aeroplane Co., 1947-56; General Service Manager of Weston Works, retired; *b* 5 June 1906; *s* of Major S. Pegg, RAOC; *m* 1933, Eileen Mary Page; one *s* one *d. Educ:* Skinners, Tunbridge Wells. Joined Royal Air Force, 1921; learned to fly, 1925; granted permanent commission, 1930, and appointed test pilot at aeroplane and armament experimental establishments; resigned commission and appointed Asst Chief Test Pilot, Bristol Aeroplane Co., 1935. *Publication:* Sent Flying (autobiography), 1959. *Address:* Craigfoot No 1, 55 South Road, Weston-super-Mare, Avon. *T:* Weston-super-Mare 3884. [Died 8 March 1978.

PEIRCE, Lt-Col Harold Ernest, CBE 1960 (OBE 1950); JP; Director of Public Companies, since 1929; *b* 7 Nov. 1892; *s* of Harry and Elizabeth Peirce. *Educ:* Croydon, Surrey. Served European War 1915-19, (Surrey Yeomanry, Queen's Royal W Surrey Regt). Joined Hall & Co. Ltd, 1907; Director, 1929; Managing Director, 1944. Director, Hall & Ham River Ltd, Holding Board, 1962; Chm., MPR Ltd; Director, Hall Aggregates Ltd, 1968, RMC Pension Nominees Ltd, 1968 (mems of Ready Mixed Concrete Gp of Cos). Founder Member, Ballast, Sand and Allied Trades Assoc. (now called Sand and Gravel Assoc. Ltd), 1930 (Chairman, 1943); Founder Member, National Council of Building Material Producers (Vice-President, 1955; Chairman Council, 1956; President, 1965); Member Indust. Development Mission to WI, 1952; Member Board of Trade Bankruptcy Acts Amendment Cttee, 1955. Appointed Member, Dollar Export Delegation to Canada, 1957. Comdr Bn of Home Guard, War of 1939-45, and also when later reformed. Chairman, Croydon Playing Fields Assoc. JP, Croydon, 1941-. *Recreations:* cricket and squash. Captain of Addiscombe Cricket Club for 26 years, now President of the Club. *Address:* Selsdon Park Hotel, Sanderstead, Surrey CR2 8YA. *T:* 01-657 8811. *Clubs:* RAC, MCC; Surrey CCC (a Vice-Pres.). [Died 12 Nov. 1979.

PEIRSE, Sir Henry Campbell de la Poer B.; *see* Beresford-Peirse.

PEIRSON, David Edward Herbert, CBE 1965; *b* 18 May 1915; *s* of Herbert Sidney and Edith Peirson; *m* 1940, Norah Ellen Corney; one *s* two *d. Educ:* Wallasey Grammar Sch.; King's Coll., London. LLB 1937; LLM 1938; Passed 5th in Civil Service 1st Division Examination, 1939. Asst Principal, Board of Trade, 1939; Private Secretary to Lord Beaverbrook, MAP, 1941-42; Principal, Ministry of Supply, 1942; Asst Secretary, Ministry of Supply, 1946; idc 1951; Sec., UKAEA, 1955-71; General Manager, Centec GmbH, Bensberg, Germany, 1971-73. *Recreation:* music. *Address:* 37 Fordington Road, N2. *T:* 01-883 5605. *Club:* Athenæum. [Died 21 March 1976.

PELLETIER, Hector Rooney; retired; formerly General Manager, BBC Radio Enterprises; *b* 18 Oct. 1911; *s* of Achille Joseph Pelletier and Helen Louise Rooney. *Educ:* University of Ottawa; Queen's Univ., Kingston, Ont. Teaching, followed by journalism with Le Droit (Ottawa) and The Canadian Press (Toronto and Montreal). Freelance writing included poetry and art criticism. Announcer and Head of Quebec programmes for Canadian Broadcasting Corporation; Commentator, Royal Tour of Canada, 1939; War reporter and European Representative, CBC, 1941. BBC posts since 1938 include: Features and Drama producer; Asst Editor, Radio Newsreel; Head of N. American Service; Asst Head, Television Talks; Chief Instructor, Staff Training School; Asst Controller and Controller, Light Programme; Controller Programme Planning (Sound); Chief of Presentation (Sound). *Recreations:* painting; collecting Victorian ephemeral publications. *Address:* Little Dingleden, Benenden, Kent. *T:* Benenden 645. [Died 12 Nov. 1976.

PELLY, Air Chief Marshal Sir Claude (Bernard Raymond), GBE 1959 (CBE 1943); KCB 1954 (CB 1950); MC 1932; *b* 19 Aug.

1902; *e s* of late Rev. D. R. Pelly, DSO; *m* 1930, Margaret Ogilvie Spencer; two *s* one *d. Educ:* Rugby; RAF Coll., Cranwell. Directing Staff, Imperial Defence Coll., 1952-53; C-in-C, MEAF, 1953-56; Controller of Aircraft, Ministry of Supply, 1956-59, ADC (Air) to the Queen, 1957-59; retired 1959. Member for Weapons, Research and Development, UK, AEA, 1959-64. Gold Cross, Order of King George I of Hellenes. *Address:* Green Lane House, Orford, Suffolk. *Club:* Army and Navy.   *[Died 12 Aug. 1972.*

PELLY, Sir Kenneth (Raymond), Kt 1961; MC 1918; Director, Wm France Fenwick & Co. Ltd since 1919 (Chairman, 1941-66); *b* 9 Nov. 1893; *m* 1919, Elspeth Norna Grant; one *s* one *d. Educ:* Charterhouse. Served European War, 1914-18, Captain, RASC. Joined Wm France Fenwick & Co. Ltd, 1912; Director, 1918-; Managing Director, 1926-57. Member of the Port of London Authority, 1952-61; President of the Chamber of Shipping of the United Kingdom, 1956-57; Chairman General Council of British Shipping, 1956-57; Chairman (Member 1938) General Cttee, Lloyd's Register of Shipping, 1957-63. *Recreations:* farming, shooting, fishing. *Address:* Newstead Ghyll, Colgate, Horsham, Sussex. *T:* Faygate 233.
[Died 30 Sept. 1973.

PELLY, Rear-Adm. Peter Douglas Herbert Raymond, CB 1958; DSO 1942; *b* 24 Sept. 1904; *s* of Rev. Douglas R. Pelly, DSO, and Verena Noellie (*née* Herbert); *m* 1932, Gwenllian Violet Edwardes; three *d. Educ:* RNC Osborne and Dartmouth. Joined Navy, 1918; normal peace-time services, except for appointment to Royal Yacht, 1939; served War of 1939-45; Commander, 1940; Comd Destroyer Windsor until 1940; 15th Cruiser Squadron, 1940-43; Plans Divison, Admiralty, 1943-45; Comd: Aircraft Carrier Ameer, 1945; HMS Raleigh, 1945-47; Captain, 1947; Admiralty, 1947-49; Reserve Fleet, Harwich, 1950; Captain (D) in Battleaxe, 1951-52; Chief Staff Officer, Gibraltar, 1952-54; Director of Ops Division, Admiralty, 1954-56; Rear-Admiral, 1956, Admiral Superintendent, HM Dockyard, Rosyth, Sept. 1956-Nov. 1957; Director-General of the Department of Dockyards and Maintenance, Admiralty, 1958-59; retired 1960. Sec., Assoc. of Consulting Engineers, 1960-69. Hon. Member, Smeatonian Society of Civil Engineers, 1965-70. Officer, Order of Orange Nassau (Holland), 1940. *Recreations:* normal. *Address:* Lowmersland, Les Rochers, Alderney, Channel Islands.   *[Died 13 Feb. 1980.*

PELLY, Rev. Canon Richard Lawrence; Canon of Salisbury, 1952, Canon Emeritus, since 1966; *b* 18 July 1886; *s* of Canon R. A. Pelly; *m* 1927, Dr Salome Wordsworth; two *s* four *d. Educ:* Marlborough; Clare Coll., Cambridge. Lecturer, Ridley Hall, Cambridge, 1913-15; ACF 1915-18; Vice-Principal, Bishop's College, Calcutta, 1918-26; Rector, St Paul's Sch., Darjeeling, 1928-33; Vicar of Shoreditch, 1934-37; Canon of Newcastle Cathedral, 1937-45; Rector of Trowbridge, Wilts, 1945-54; Vicar of Farley and Pitton, 1954-57; Master of St Nicholas's Hospital, Salisbury, 1957, retd. *Publications:* St Paul to the Romans; Katha Upanishad; Aspects of Holy Communion; Makers of the New Testament. *Address:* 20 Middle Street, Salisbury, Wilts. *T:* 22967.   *[Died 7 April 1976.*

PELLY MURPHY, John; *see* Murphy, J. P.

PEMBERTON-PIGOTT, Alan Desmond Frederick, CMG 1965; Senior Civilian Member of Directing Staff, Royal College of Defence Studies, since 1972; *b* 3 May 1916; *s* of late Maj.-General A. J. K. Pigott, CB, CBE; *m* 1940, M. C. Tallents; one *s* three *d. Educ:* Shrewsbury Sch.; Queen's Coll., Oxford. Served Armed Forces, 1939-46. HM Diplomatic Service, 1946-. HM Consul-General, Hargeisa, Somali Republic, 1960-61; Foreign Office, 1961-64; Minister, HM Embassy, Ankara, 1964-68; Dep. UK Representative to NATO, 1969-71. *Address:* 17 Moore Street, SW3. *T:* 01-584 1832. *Club:* Travellers'.
[Died 21 Aug. 1972.

PENFIELD, Dr Wilder Graves, OM 1953; CC (Canada) 1967; CMG 1943; FRCS(C); FRSC; FRS 1943; Hon. Consultant, Montreal Neurological Institute and Hospital, since 1960; President, Vanier Institute of the Family, 1965-68; *b* Spokane, Washington, USA, 26 Jan. 1891; *s* of Dr Charles Samuel Penfield and Jean Jefferson; Naturalised Canadian Citizen in 1934; *m* 1917, Helen Katherine Kermott; two *s* two *d. Educ:* Princeton Univ. (LittB, DSc); Oxford (BA, MA, BSc, DSc); Johns Hopkins Univ. (MD). Rhodes Scholar, Oxford, 1914 and 1918-20; Beit Memorial Res. Fellow, 1920. Served in Hosp. Militaire VR 76, Ris Orangis, France, 1915, and at No 2 American Red Cross Hospital, Paris, 1917. Junior attending surgeon, Presbyterian Hospital, New York City, 1921-28; Asst Prof. of Surgery, Columbia Univ., 1924-28. Founded Laboratory of Neurocytology, Presbyterian Hospital, 1924; Study of

neurohistology, Madrid, 1924, of neurosurgery, Germany, 1928; Neurosurgeon to Royal Victoria and Montreal General Hospitals, Montreal, 1928-60; Professor of Neurology and Neurosurgery, McGill Univ., 1934-54; Director of Montreal Neurological Institute, 1934-60; retired, 1960. President, Royal College of Physicians and Surgeons of Canada, 1939-41; Chairman of Sub-Cttee on Surgery, National Research Council, Canada, 1941-45. Hon. Fellow Association Surg. of Great Britain and Ireland; FRSocMed (London) (Visiting Lecture Series, 1947-67); Hon. FRCS; Hon. FRCP; Hon. FRCSE; Hon. FRCPE. Chevalier Légion d'Honneur, 1950. Hon. Fellow, Merton College, Oxford. Hon. DCL (Oxford), 1953; Hon. LLD Wales, 1953; Hon. DSc: Leeds, 1954; RMC Canada, 1970; Hon. LLD: Edinburgh, 1959; Johns Hopkins, 1970; several other hon. doctorates from Canada, USA and Europe. Lister Medal, RCS England, 1961, and other awards. *Publications:* Cytology and Cellular Pathology of the Nervous System, 1932; Epilepsy and Cerebral Localisation (with T. C. Erickson), 1941; Manual of Military Neurosurgery, 1941; (with T. B. Rasmussen) The Cerebral Cortex of Man, 1950; (with K. Kristiansen) Epileptic Seizure Patterns, 1950; (with H. H. Jasper) Epilepsy and the Functional Anatomy of the Human Brain, 1954; No Other Gods, 1954; The Excitable Cortex in Conscious Man, 1958; (with L. Roberts) Speech and Brain-Mechanisms; The Torch, 1960; The Second Career, 1963; The Difficult Art of Giving, 1967; Man and His Family, 1967; Second Thoughts: science, the arts and the spirit, 1970; The Mystery of the Mind, 1976; contributions to medical journals. *Recreations:* farming, sailing, ski-ing, travel. *Address:* c/o Montreal Neurological Institute, 3801 University Street, Montreal H3A 2B4, Canada. *T:* 842-1251; C-33 Gleneagles Apartments, 3940 Côte des Neiges, Montreal H3H 1W2. *T:* We. 5-1889. *Clubs:* Athenæum; University, Mount Royal, Mount Stephen (Montreal); Princeton (New York).   *[Died 5 April 1976.*

PENNELL, Vernon Charles, FRCS; Senior and Life Fellow, Pembroke College, Cambridge, since 1914; Consulting Surgeon and Director of Cancer Bureau, Addenbrooke's Hospital, since 1954; *b* 30 Sept. 1889; *s* of C. W. Pennell, Lincoln; *m* 1st, 1915, Alberta Sanders (*d* 1960); one *s* ; 2nd, 1960, Catherine Margaret Nesbitt. *Educ:* Harrow School; Pembroke Coll., Cambridge. Exhib. and Schol., Pembroke Coll., Cambridge, 1908; 1st Class Nat. Sci. Tripos, 1911; Fellow, 1914; MA (Cantab), 1915; MB, BChir (Cantab) 1916; FRCS 1920; Univ. Schol., St Thomas' Hosp., 1912. Lecturer and Director of Med. Studies, Pembroke Coll., Cambridge, 1920-54; Supervisor in Surgery to Cambridge University, 1946-61; Hon. Surgeon and later Cons. Surgeon, Addenbrooke's Hospital, 1927-54. Member, Court of Examiners, RCS England, 1945; Examiner in Surgery to Cambridge Univ., 1934; Member Moynihan Chirurgical Club; Fellow Assoc. of Surgeons of Great Britain; Member British Assoc. of Urological Surgeons. *Publications:* numerous medical. *Recreation:* cricket. *Address:* 10 Gurney Way, Cambridge. *T:* 50544. *Club:* County (Cambridge).   *[Died 2 March 1976.*

PENNEY, José Campbell, CMG 1944; OBE 1942; MC 1917; *b* 1893; *e s* of late J. Campbell Penney, Accountant of Court for Scotland; *m* 1920, Joan (*d* 1970), *d* of Kenneth Mackinnon Douglas, MD; one *s* one *d. Educ:* Fettes College, Edinburgh; Oriel Coll., Oxford (Classical Scholar; BA 1918). Served European War, 1914-18 with 51st Division (7th Black Watch), France and Flanders; Egyptian Civil Service, 1919-25; Sudan Government Service, 1925-46; Director of Public Security, 1930; Commissioner Police and Prisons, 1940; Political Assistant to Civil Secretary, 1944-46; Political Adviser to British Administrations in ex-Italian colonies in Africa, 1946-50; UK representative on United Nations Council for Libya, 1950-51; British Member of Electoral Commission on Anglo-Egyptian Sudan, 1953; Supervisor of Elections, Zanzibar, 1956-57. War of 1939-45, Lieut-Colonel, 'I' Branch HQ Troops Sudan and Eritrea, 1940-41 (despatches). Order of the Nile (Officer) 1935, Commander, 1944. *Recreations:* fishing, golf. *Address:* c/o Bank of Scotland, 103 George Street, Edinburgh EH2 2HR.
[Died 24 May 1976.

PENNY, Sir James Downing, KCIE, *cr* 1943 (CIE 1937); CSI 1939; *b* 25 May 1886; *s* of late Edward Penny, MD, Medical Officer, Marlborough Coll.; *m* 1917, Margaret Mary Wilson (*d* 1962); one *d. Educ:* Marlborough Coll.; Magdalen Coll., Oxford (Classical Demy); 1st Class Classical Mods, 1907; 1st Class Lit. Hum. 1909; ICS 1910; Captain, IA Reserve of Officers, 1918; Deputy Secretary Government of India Finance Dept, 1926; Finance Secretary, Punjab Government, 1927-30; Officiating Commissioner, Multan Div., 1934, Lahore, 1935, Rawalpindi Div., 1936; Chief Secretary, 1937-41; Financial Commissioner, Development Dept and Secretary to Government of Punjab, 1941; retired, 1945. *Address:* 19 Five Mile Drive, Oxford.
[Died 23 May 1978.

PENROSE, Lionel Sharples, FRS 1953; MA, MD; FRCP 1962; Director, Kennedy-Galton Centre, Harperbury Hospital, St Albans, since 1965; *b* 11 June 1898; *m* 1928, Margaret Leathes; three *s* one *d. Educ:* Leighton Park School, Reading; St John's College, Cambridge. Res. Dir Royal Eastern Counties Institution, Colchester, 1930; Director of Psychiatric Research, Ontario, Canada, 1939; Galton Professor of Eugenics, University College, London, 1945-65, Emeritus Professor, 1965. Hon. DSc: McGill, 1958; Newcastle, 1968, Edinburgh, 1970; Hon. MD Gothenburg, 1966. *Publications:* The Influence of Heredity on Disease, 1934; The Biology of Mental Defect, 1949 (3rd edn 1963); The Objective Study of Crowd Behaviour, 1951. *Recreation:* chess. *Address:* 1 Rodborough Road, Golders Green, NW11. *T:* 01-455 1457.   [*Died* 12 *May* 1972.

PENSON, John Hubert, CB 1953; CMG 1942; MC; *b* 21 Jan. 1893; *s* of late Arthur A. Penson, formerly of Cirencester, Glos; *m* 1st, 1929, Marjorie Doreen (*d* 1971), *d* of late Col F. H. Crawford, Belfast; one *s* two *d*; 2nd, 1974, Ellen Mary, *d* of late James Cumming, Glasgow. Served European War, 1916-19 (Lieut 1918) RE (despatches, MC and bar). Commissioner for Finance, Commission of Government, Newfoundland, 1937-41. Secretary General, British Supply Mission in Washington, USA, 1944-45; Attaché British Embassy, Washington, 1947-53, Executive Secretary, International Materials Conference, Washington, 1953. *Address:* 173 Nithsdale Road, Glasgow G41 5QR. *T:* 041-423 1805.   [*Died* 1 *June* 1979.

PENSTON, Norah Lillian, DPhil; FLS; Principal of Bedford College, University of London, 1951-64, retired; *b* 20 Aug. 1903; 2nd *d* of late Andrew Joseph and Louise Mary Penston; unmarried. *Educ:* The Bolton School; St Anne's College, Oxford. BA, 1927; DPhil Oxon 1930. University Demonstrator in Botany, Oxford, 1928-29; Demonstrator in Botany, 1929-33, Assistant Lecturer, 1933-36, Lecturer, 1936-45, Actg Head of the Botany Dept 1940-44, University of London, King's College; Vice-Principal of Wye College, University of London, 1945-51 and Head of Dept of Biological Sciences, 1947-51. Member Academic Sub-Cttee of British Federation of University Women, 1944-72, Mem. Exec. Cttee, 1953-55; Council Member, Women's Farm and Garden Assoc., 1947-51; Member Senate of University of London, 1951-64; Member Committee of Management of Sister Trust, 1952-; Gov., Thomas Wall Trust, 1952-; Exhibition Trustee of Hilda Martindale Educational Trust, 1953-70; Mem. Cttee for Award of International Fellowships of Internat. Fed. of Univ. Women, 1953-58, and 1959-64; Univ. of London Rep. on Council of Roedean School, 1953-64; on Council of Dartford College of Physical Education, 1953-64; Chm., Collegiate Council, Univ. of London, 1957-59; Mem. Marshall Aid Commemoration Commn, 1957-60; Governor, Dominion Students' Hall Trust, 1965-. Hon. Fellow, Wye Coll., Univ. of London. *Publications:* contribs to scientific jls. *Address:* 29 Byron Court, Mecklenburgh Square, WC1N 2AF. *T:* 01-837 8147. *Club:* United Oxford & Cambridge University (Ladies' Annexe).   [*Died* 1 *Feb.* 1974.

PENTLAND, Norman; MP (Lab) Chester-le-Street Division of County Durham since Sept. 1956; *b* 9 Sept. 1912; *s* of William Henry Pentland, Fatfield, County Durham; *m* 1937, Ethel Maude, *d* of Charles Coates, Chester-le-Street, County Durham; two *s. Educ:* Fatfield School. Checkweighman, Harraton Miners' Lodge; Member Durham Miners' Executive Committee, 1952-53; Member Chester-le-Street Rural District Council, 1946-56 (Chairman, 1952-53). Jt Parly Sec., Min. of Pensions and Nat. Insce, 1964-66, Min. of Social Security, 1966-68; Jt Parly Under-Sec. of State (Social Security), Dept of Health and Social Security, 1968-69; Parly Sec., Min. of Posts and Telecommunications, 1969-70. *Address:* House of Commons, SW1; Great Lumley, Chester-le-Street, County Durham.
                    [*Died* 28 *Oct.* 1972.

PEPLOE, Mrs J. R.; *see* Stevenson, D. E.

PEPPERELL, Elizabeth Maud, (E. M. Brewin), OBE 1966; Assistant Director, The Industrial Society, since 1952; *b* 21 June 1914; *d* of late Edward John Pepperell and Mary Anne Pepperell; *m* 1951, Paul Kingsley Brewin, *s* of Rev. G. H. Brewin and Mabel Brewin; two *s* and one step *s. Educ:* Thomas Street Central School; Toynbee Hall; London School of Economics. Awarded Mary Macarthur Scholarship, 1938; Dip. Soc. Science, 1940. With Bryant and May Ltd, 1930-38; Chief Personnel Officer, Carreras Ltd, 1940-51. Member: King Edward Hospital Fund, Domestic Staff Cttee, 1946-; Newsom Cttee, Central Adv. Council, Min. of Education; Nat. Youth Employment Council, 1963-; CBI Working Party on Women in Employment; Min. of Labour's Nat. Jt Adv. Cttee Working Party on Part VI of the Factories Act; Bd, Nat. Inst. for Housecraft (Employment and Training) Ltd; Hon. Sec., Mary

Macarthur Scholarship Fund; Trustee, Mary Macarthur Educational Trust. USA Lecture Tours, 1949 and 1964, on Human Relationships at Work. FIPM 1949. *Publications:* Office Staff: Selection and Training, 1959; School to Work: Guide to Supervisors, 1960; What They Expect from Work, 1960; Using Secretarial Services, 1962; You and Your Secretary, 1969; articles on general management subjects; broadcasts. *Recreations:* country life, youth work, home entertaining. *Address:* Carisbrooke, 17 Aldersbrook Road, Wanstead, E12. *T:* 01-989 4314; Avishays, Shaftesbury, Dorset.
                    [*Died* 24 *May* 1971.

PEPYS, Rt. Rev. George Christopher Cutts; Bishop Suffragan of Buckingham, since 1964; *b* 29 June 1914; *s* of late Rev. Charles Sidney Pepys and Adelaide Mary Elizabeth (*née* Cutts); *m* 1947, Elizabeth Margaret Ekin; one *s* four *d. Educ:* Winchester; Oriel College, Oxford; Cuddesdon Theological College, Oxford. Assistant Curate, St John the Divine, Kennington, 1939-46; Chaplain, RNVR, 1941-46; Rector of Hartfield, Sussex, 1946-51; Vicar of St Mark, Portsea, 1951-58; Hon. Canon of Portsmouth, 1956; Rector of Liverpool and Rural Dean of Liverpool, 1958-64; Hon. Canon of Liverpool, 1959. *Recreation:* rowing. *Address:* Sheridan, Great Missenden, Bucks. *T:* Gt Missenden 2173. *Club:* Leander (Henley-on-Thames).
                    [*Died* 4 *April* 1974.

PERCEVAL-MAXWELL, Mrs P.; *see* King-Hall, Magdalen.

PEREIRA, Pedro T.; *see* Theotonio Pereira.

PERELMAN, S(idney) J(oseph); author; *b* 1 Feb. 1904, New York; *s* of Joseph and Sophia Perelman; *m* 1929, Laura West (*d* 1970); one *s* one *d. Educ:* Brown Univ. Cartoonist and writer: Judge, 1925-29; College Humor, 1929-30; New Yorker, 1935-. Member: Screen Writer's Guild; Dramatist's Guild; Nat. Inst. Arts and Letters. Writer, 1930-: *film scripts:* Monkey Business, 1931; Horsefeathers, 1932; Sweethearts, 1938; Ambush, 1939; Around the World in Eighty Days (Best Screen Writer Award, NY Film Critics Award), 1956; *sketches for reviews:* Third Little Show, 1931; Walk a Little Faster, 1932; *plays:* (with Laura Perelman) All Good Americans, 1934; Night Before Christmas, 1941; (with Ogden Nash) One Touch of Venus, 1943; (with A. Hirschfield) Sweet Bye and Bye, 1946; The Beauty Part, 1962. *Publications:* Dawn Ginsbergh's Revenge, 1929; Parlor, Bedlam and Bath, 1930; Strictly from Hunger, 1937; Look Who's Talking!, 1940; The Dream Department, 1943; Crazy Like a Fox, 1944, new edn 1973; Keep it Crisp, 1946; Acres and Pains, 1947; The Best of S. J. Perelman, 1947; Westward Ha!, 1948; Listen to the Mockingbird, 1949; Swiss Family Perelman, 1950; A Child's Garden of Curses, 1951; Ill-Tempered Clavichord, 1952; Perelman's Home Companion, 1955; The Road to Miltown, 1957; The Most of S. J. Perelman, 1958; The Rising Gorge, 1961; Chicken Inspector No 23, 1966; Baby, It's Cold Inside, 1970; Vinegar Puss, 1976; Eastward Ha!, 1978. *Club:* Century Association (New York).   [*Died* 17 *Oct.* 1979.

PEREN, Sir Geoffrey Sylvester, KBE 1959 (CBE 1953); BSA (Tor.); Brigadier (retired); Emeritus Professor of Agriculture, Massey University; *b* England, 1892; *m* 1923, Violet Essex, *d* of R. J. Surman, Worcester; one *s* one *d. Educ:* Toronto University. Four years Ontario Agric. Coll., Guelph; seven years mixed farming in Ontario and British Columbia; served European War with Canadian Field Artillery and RFA (despatches, Croix de Guerre); subsequently on staff of E Malling Agricultural Research Station, Kent; Inspector under Ministry of Agriculture; later at Agricultural and Horticultural Research Station, Long Ashton, Bristol; Prof. of Agriculture, Victoria Univ. Coll., Wellington, NZ, 1924-28; Principal, Massey Agricultural Coll., Univ. of NZ, 1928-59. During war of 1939-45 commanded 2nd Infantry Bde Group and later 4th NZ Division with rank of Brig. Colonel Comdt, 2 Armoured Regt, NZ Forces, 1954-56. Comr for Civil Defence, Central Region NZ, 1960-65. Hon. Life Member: Royal Agric. Soc. of NZ; Cheviot Sheep Soc. of NZ; Galloway Cattle Soc. of NZ; Perendale Sheep Soc. of NZ. DSc (*hc*) Massey, 1977. Silver Jubilee Medal, 1935; Coronation Medals, 1937, 1953. *Address:* 14 Collingwood Street, Palmerston North, NZ.   [*Died* 20 *July* 1980.

PERKIN, (Edwin) Graham; Editor-in-Chief, David Syme & Co. Ltd, since 1973 (Deputy, 1969-73); Editor, The Age, Melbourne, since 1966; Director: Australian Associated Press, since 1966; Reuters Ltd, London, 1971-74; *b* 16 Dec. 1929; *e s* of Herbert E. Perkin and Iris L. Perkin; *m* 1952, Peggy Lorraine Corrie; one *s* one *d. Educ:* Warracknabeal High Sch.; Univ. of Melbourne. Joined The Age as cadet, journalist, 1955-56; subseq. London Office of The Age; Canberra Office, 1957-59; Walkley Nat. Award for Journalism, 1959; Dep. News Ed., 1959; News Ed., 1963; Asst Ed., 1964.

Lectr in Journalism, Univ. of Melbourne, 1961-63; Mem., Advanced Session, Australian Admin. Staff Coll., 1963. *Recreations:* reading, golf, cricket, tennis, swimming. *Address:* 28 Gladstone Street, Sandringham, Victoria 3191, Australia. *Clubs:* Caledonian (London); Royal Auto (Victoria); Savage (Melbourne); Melbourne Scots; Melbourne Cricket; Victoria Golf. *[Died 16 Oct. 1975.*

PERKINS, Alan Hubert Banbury, MVO 1953; MBE 1936; retired as HM Consul General, Salonika, Greece (1957-59); *b* 9 Aug. 1898; *s* of late Lewis Banbury Perkins and Mary Thérèse Lawrence; *m* 1946, Gertrude Ellen Munton. *Educ:* British Schools in Argentina; Hurstpierpoint Coll., Sussex. Served with RAF, 1918-19. Has also held Consular Appointments at Buenos Aires, 1919-47; Barranquilla, 1947-49; Bahia, 1949, Valparaiso, 1949-51; Leopoldville, 1951-52; Colon, 1953-56; Athens, 1956-57. *Recreations:* tennis and golf. *Address:* Cuesta los Alvarados 31, Monte Coello, Las Palmas, Canary Islands. *T:* 351603. *[Died 15 June 1977.*

PERKINS, Sir (Albert) Edward, KCVO 1973 (CVO 1972; MVO 4th cl. 1960; MVO 5th cl. 1952); Police Officer to HM the Queen, 1954-73; *b* 1 July 1908; *s* of James Albert Perkins, Studley, Warwicks; *m* 1932, Mercy Frew (*d* 1976), *d* of Rev. A. G. Edgerton, Winchester. *Educ:* Alcester Grammar Sch. Joined Metropolitan Police Force, 1927: Police Officer to HM the Queen, later HM Queen Elizabeth the Queen Mother, 1941-54; Comdr, 1969. Order of Menelik II, Officer Class IV (Ethiopia), 1965; Officer, Cruzeiro do Sul (Brazil), 1968; 3rd Class, Order of Crown of Thailand, 1972; Officer, Ordre National du Mérite (France), 1972; Order of Yugoslav Star on Necklace, 1972; etc. *Recreations:* fishing, gardening, sport. *Address:* Studley House, 1a Bolton Avenue, Windsor, Berks. *T:* Windsor 65257. *[Died 20 May 1977.*

PERKINS, Rev. Benson; see Perkins, Rev. E. B.

PERKINS, Sir Edward; see Perkins, Sir A. E.

PERKINS, Rev. E(rnest) Benson, MA (Manchester); Hon. LLD; FSS; Hon. CF; Associate Secretary, World Methodist Council, since 1961; Hon. Secretary Department for Chapel Affairs, Methodist Church; Director, Methodist Insurance Co.; *b* 14 July 1881; *s* of George Perkins, Leicester; *m* 1910, Alice Elsie (*d* 1964) *d* of Arthur J. Bull, Leicester; one *d.* *Educ:* Alderman Newton's School, Leicester; Handsworth Theological Coll., Birmingham. Asst Sec., Christian Citizenship Dept of Methodist Church, 1920-25; Supt Minister, Birmingham Central Mission, 1925-35; Supt Minister, Sheffield Mission and Chm. Sheffield Dist, 1935-39; General Secretary Department for Chapel Affairs of the Methodist Church, 1939-52; Chm. Manchester Dist, 1941-49; Gen. Sec. World Methodist Council, 1951-61; Pres. Methodist Conference, 1948-49. Guest Preacher, Metropolitan Church, Toronto, 1932. Member: Stockholm Conf. on Life and Work, 1925; World Council of Churches, Amsterdam, 1948, Fraternal Delegate, General Council, United Church of Canada, 1950, and Quadrennial Conference, Methodist Church of America, San Francisco, 1952, Vice-President British Council of Churches, 1952-54; Moderator, National Free Church Federal Council, 1954-55; Fraternal Delegate, World Council of Churches, Evanston, Illinois, USA, 1954. Hon. LLD (Centenary, LA, USA), 1956. *Publications:* The Problem of Gambling, 1917; Betting Facts, 1924; Gambling and Youth, 1932; With Christ in the Bull Ring, 1935; (jointly) The Methodist Church Builds Again, 1946; Serving the Church, 1948; Gambling in English Life (Beckly Lecture), 1950 (revised, 1958, 1962); Methodist Preaching Houses and the Law (Wesley Hist. Soc. Lecture), 1952; So Appointed: an autobiography, 1963; Discipline, 1966. *Recreations:* travel, music, photography; special interests: sociology, church architecture, church law. *Address:* 38 Belle Walk, Moseley, Birmingham B13 9DB. *T:* 021-449 1919. *Clubs:* National Liberal; Reform (Manchester). *[Died 23 Sept. 1974.*

PERKINS, Rev. Canon Frederick Howard, MA; Canon Residentiary and Treasurer of Liverpool Cathedral, 1955-63, Canon Emeritus since 1964; Vicar of St Matthew and St James, Mossley Hill, Liverpool, 1936-63. *Educ:* St Catharine's College, Cambridge (MA); Ridley Hall, Cambridge. Lieut, RASC, 1915-19. Ordained deacon, 1922; priest, 1923. Curate: St John, Ladywood, Birmingham, 1922-26, St Martin, Birmingham, 1926-28; Vicar: St Christopher, Springfield, Worcs, 1928-36; Canon of Liverpool, 1951. Rural Dean of Childwall, 1947-63; Proctor in convocation, Liverpool, 1948-59; Chaplain, Ministry of Pensions Hosp., Mossley Hill, 1936-63; Bishop's Chaplain, Univ. of Liverpool, 1945-55; Examining Chaplain to Bishop of St Edmundsbury and Ipswich, 1960-65. *Address:* Abinger Lodge, Abbey Road, Worthing, West Sussex BN11 3RW. *[Died 2 Dec. 1977.*

PERKINS, Prof. George, MC; MCh; FRCS; Consultant Surgeon, Rowley Bristow Hospital, Pyrford. BA (1st cl. Hons), 1914; MA Oxon, 1921; MB, BCh 1916; MCh 1921; FRCS 1921. Formerly Professor of Surgery, St Thomas's Hospital Medical School, University of London; Consultant Orthopædic Surgeon, St Thomas' Hospital. Ex-president British Orthopædic Association. *Publications:* The Foundations of Surgery, 1954; Fractures and Dislocations, 1958; Orthopaedics, 1961; Ruminations of an Orthopaedic Surgeon, 1970. *Address:* Thorpe Lee, Denne Park, Horsham, W Sussex. *T:* Horsham 63759. *[Died 22 Oct. 1979.*

PERKINS, Col George Forder, CBE 1941; DSO 1918; late The Royal Hampshire Regiment; Aide-de-Camp to the King, 1934-36; *b* 1884; *s* of late Sir Edwin K. Perkins, CBE, DL; *m* Nora Christine, *d* of late Allen Shuttleworth, Indian Navy; one *s* one *d.* *Educ:* Cheltenham College. Served European War, 1914-18 (despatches, DSO, Brevets Major and Lieut-Col); retired pay, 1936. *Address:* 19 Kingsbury Square, Wilton, Salisbury, Wilts. *[Died 5 Jan. 1972.*

PERKINS, Norman Stuart, OBE 1962; JP; FRAgS 1970; Landowner and Farmer; Member: Pigs Cttee, Meat and Livestock Commission; Agricultural Land Tribunal; Director: NFU Mutual Insurance Society Ltd; Avon Insurance Co. Ltd; *b* 16 May 1904; *s* of David Perkins; *m* 1926, Helen Irene, *d* of Capt. R. E. James, Trinity Service; two *s.* *Educ:* Clifton Coll. Member: Pig Marketing Bd, 1937-57 (Chm. 1956 and 1957); Bacon Development Bd, 1939-57; Founder Mem., Pig Industry Develt Authority, 1957-68; Chm. Pemb. Branch NFU, 1940; Mem. Pemb. CC; Council Royal Welsh Agricultural Soc.; Vice-Chm. Pembs Conservative Assoc.; Chm. Pembs Red Cross Agric. Fund; Mem., Pembs War Agric. Exec. Cttee (Chm. Dist Cttee and Chm. Animal Husbandry Cttee); Chm. Welsh Regional Cttee, Wool Marketing Scheme. 2nd in Comd Bn HG. Mem. Council Central Landowners' Assoc. and Mem. Exec. Cttee; Mem. Min. of Agriculture Livestock Improvement Cttee. JP 1951 (Chm. Bench, 1960-); High Sheriff of Pembrokeshire, 1956. *Address:* St Lawrence, Fishguard, Pembs. *T:* Fishguard 2858. *Clubs:* Farmers'; Pembrokeshire County (Haverfordwest). *[Died 27 Jan. 1972.*

PERKS, Sir (Robert) Malcolm (Mewburn), 2nd Bt, *cr* 1908; retired Public Works Contractor, one time Chairman of Sir John Jackson Ltd, and Ford & Walton Ltd; *b* 29 July 1892; *s* of Sir Robert Wm Perks, 1st Bt, and Edith (*d* 1943), *y d* of late Wm Mewburn, DL; *S* father 1934; *m* 1917, Neysa Gilbert, *o c* of late Rev. Dr Cheney, New Rochelle, USA; two *d.* *Educ:* Leys Sch., Cambridge. Served European War, Lieut RNVR, Captain RAF. Director of Building Construction, Ministry of Supply, 1941-43. *Heir:* none. *Address:* 9 Esplanade Court, Worthing, Sussex. *[Died 23 Sept. 1979 (ext).*

PERREN, Edward Arthur, CB 1962; PhD; FRIC; *b* 13 June 1900; *s* of late Arthur Perren, London; *m* 1925, Muriel Davidge, Palmers Green; one *s* one *d* (and one *s* decd). *Educ:* Stationers' Sch., Hornsey; Imperial Coll., University of London. BSc Hons (London) 1919; PhD (London) 1922. Joined scientific staff of War Dept, 1922. Chief Superintendent, Suffield Experimental Station, Canada, 1949-51; Superintendent Research Division, CDEE, Porton, 1951-55; Director, CDEE, Porton (Chief Scientific Officer), 1955-61. *Publications:* various papers on Organic Chemistry. *Address:* Larchfield, Appleshaw, Andover, Hants. *T:* Weyhill 2434. *[Died 5 Feb. 1978.*

PERRY, Alan Cecil, MS, FRCS; retired as Senior Surgeon, London Hospital and Poplar Hospital; *b* 26 Nov. 1892; *s* of Major H. Perry, Ware, Herts; *m* 1922, May Alice, *d* of late Captain C. H. Palmer, RN; no *c.* *Educ:* London Univ. Price Entrance Scholar, Medical Scholarship, Andrew Clark Prize, Anatomy and Biology Scholarship, Anatomy and Physiology Scholarship, Letheby Prize, London Hospital; Begley Studentship, Royal College of Surgeons; Gold Medal, MB, BS (London) 1922 with distinction in Surgery, Medicine, Anatomy, Physiology, Pharmacology, and Organic Chemistry. *Publications:* Practice of Surgery, and House Surgeons Vade Mecum (with Russell Howard); General Nursing (with D. Harvey). *Address:* Dorney Manor Gardens, Beaminster, Dorset. *T:* Beaminster 234. *[Died 1 April 1971.*

PERRY, Edward William, CSI 1946; CIE 1930; *b* 12 June 1891; *s* of Sir William Payne Perry, CB, and Constance Gower Perry; *m* 1930, Mary Thrift, *d* of G. Reavell, Ewhurst, Sussex; three *s* two *d.* *Educ:* St Paul's Sch.; Caius Coll., Cambridge. Entered ICS, 1915; Indian Army Reserve of Officers, 1917-19, served in Palestine; Collector, Bombay suburban district, 1925-26; Bombay, 1926-27; Private Secretary to Governor, 1927; Assistant Secretary, Indian Statutory Commission, 1927-30;

Collector, Poona, 1930-31; Secretary, Bombay Reorganisation Cttee; Secretary to Government, 1935-39; Commissioner, 1939-47; Colonial Office, 1948-50. *Address:* The Clock House, Ewhurst, Robertsbridge, Sussex. *T:* Staplecross 324.
[Died 13 June 1971.

PERRY, Sir (Thomas) Wilfred, Kt 1978; CMG 1966; Director, Thomas Perry & Sons Ltd, since 1916; *b* 3 March 1899; *s* of Thomas and Florence Perry; *m* 1st, 1922, Winifred Newey Lucas (*d* 1960); four *s*; 2nd, 1962, Ada May Lucas. *Educ:* Technical Coll., Christchurch, NZ. Entered family business, 1916. Director and Chairman of many public companies, 1930-60. *Recreations:* farming, fishing. *Address:* 5 Coldstream Court, Fendalton, Christchurch, New Zealand. *T:* 517-817. *Club:* Canterbury (Christchurch). *[Died 12 July 1979.*

PERRY, Sir Wilfred; *see* Perry, Sir T. W.

PERSE, St John; *see* Leger, M.-R. A. St-L.

PERTINAX; *see* Géraud, C. J. A.

PERTWEE, Captain Herbert Guy, CBE 1949; DSO 1919; RN, retired; *b* 28 July 1893; *s* of H. A. Pertwee, Great Yarmouth; *m* 1921, Carmen (*d* 1959), 2nd *d* of late T. Waddon-Martyn, Stoke, Devonport; two *s* one *d*. *Educ:* Gresham's Sch., Holt. Joined Royal Navy, 1911; Falkland Islands action in HMS Carnarvon, 1914; joined staff of Commodore Tyrwhitt in HMS Arethusa, 1915; subsequent flagships of the Harwich Force for 3 years (clasps); secretary to Commodore, Persian Gulf and Mesopotamia Division, and later the Caspian Naval Force, 1918-19 (clasps, DSO, Russian Order of St Anne, 3rd class, Russian Order of Stanislaus, 2nd class, with swords); naval secretary of Naval and Military Commission to Persia, 1920-21 (Naval GS medal and clasp); Staff of C-in-C, The Nore, 1921-24; Naval Staff, Admiralty, 1924-26; secretary to Rear-Admiral, First Battle Squadron, 1926-27; Staffs of Cs-in-C, Portsmouth, Atlantic Fleet, and Mediterranean Fleet, 1928-31; secretary to Vice-Admiral, Commanding Battle Cruiser Squadron, 1932-34, to Deputy Chief of Naval Staff, 1935-38, and to C-in-C, Portsmouth, 1939-42; Staff Supply Officer, West Africa, 1943-44; ADC to the King, 1948; retired list, 1949. Chief Supplies Officer to the Groundnuts Scheme, 1949-51; Comdt, Government Hostel, Dar es Salaam, and Hon. ADC to the Governor, 1951-54; Divisional Comdt, Devon Special Constabulary, 1956-68. *Recreations:* gardening, local government. *Address:* Bickington, near Barnstaple, N Devon. *T:* Barnstaple 4360. *[Died 6 July 1978.*

PESHALL, Samuel Frederick, CBE 1951; MC 1916; Director, N. Corah and Sons, Leicester, since 1922; *b* 18 Nov. 1882; *s* of Rev. S. Peshall, Oldberrow, Warwickshire; *m* 1919, Mabel Eleanor Whitehurst (*d* 1966), Beaudesert Park, Henley in Arden; no *c*. *Educ:* Rossall; Caius Coll., Cambridge (MA). Served European War, 1914-18, KRRC. President National Federation of Hosiery Manufacturers, 1943; President, Leicester Chamber of Commerce, 1945; High Sheriff of Leicestershire, 1945; Chairman Regional Board for Industry in North Midlands, 1945-63; Companion, Textile Institute, 1956; Vice-President, Clothing Institute, 1957. *Address:* Quorn Grange, Loughborough, Leics. *T:* Quorn 2167. *Clubs:* Leicestershire (Leicester); Notts County (Nottingham). *[Died 25 Aug. 1977.*

PETERS, Adm. Sir Arthur Malcolm, KCB 1946 (CB 1943); DSC; *b* 1 June 1888; *o surv. s* of Maj.-Gen. W. H. B. Peters and of Hon. Mrs Peters, *d* of 24th Baron Dunboyne; *m* 1912, Agnes Vivien (*d* 1965), *d* of Colonel A. V. Payne, CMG; one *d*; *m* 1966, Mrs Sophie Maude Magnay (*d* 1976), *widow* of Brigadier A. D. Magnay. *Educ:* Stubbington House, Fareham, Hants; HMS Britannia. Went to sea 1904, served in North Sea throughout European War in HMS Southampton and Orion, present at Battle of Heligoland Bight, Dogger Bank, and Jutland (DSC, despatches); Captain, 1930; commanded HMS Southampton, 1936-38; Commodore in Charge of Naval Establishments, Hong Kong, 1939-40; Rear-Admiral, 1940; Naval Secretary to First Lord of the Admiralty, 1941-42; Mediterranean, 1943; Vice-Admiral, 1943; Flag Officer Commanding West Africa, 1943-45; retired, 1945; Admiral (retired), 1946. Since retirement interested in local affairs; Mem. for many years, St Thomas RDC and Lympstone Parish Council; formerly Chm., Sea Cadet Cttees of Exeter and Exmouth; President: Exmouth Branch, RNLI; Governors, Exeter Royal National Sch. for the Deaf; Devon Br., CLA; E Devon Hunt Cttee; Haldon Race Cttee; Chm., Ermsborough Nursing Home, Exeter, etc. *Address:* Somerton Lodge, Sidmouth, Devon EX10 8UH. *T:* Sidmouth 3927. *Club:* Naval and Military. *[Died 23 Sept. 1979.*

PETERS, Augustus Dudley, MA; Literary agent; *b* 1892; *m* 1st, Helen MacGregor; (only son killed on active service, Feb. 1945) one *d*; 2nd, Margaret Lucy Mayne; one *d*; 3rd, Margot Grahame. *Educ:* private; St John's Coll., Cambridge. Served European War, France, 1916-18; Editor of the World, 1920; dramatic critic of Daily Chronicle; established own literary and dramatic agency, 1924; began to produce plays, 1930, and continued to be active in theatrical production at The Duchess and other London theatres. War of 1939-45: Head of Public Relations Division, Ministry of Food, and later Deputy Controller, Factory and Storage, Board of Trade. *Films:* Last Holiday, 1952; An Inspector Calls, 1953; Series of television films, 1955, 1956. *Recreations:* golf, bridge. *Address:* 10 Buckingham Street, WC2. *TA:* Litteristic Rand Lond. *T:* 01-839 2556. *Clubs:* Savile, MCC. *[Died 3 Feb. 1973.*

PETERS, Sidney John, LLD; *b* Cambridge, 2 Dec. 1885; *s* of late Herbert Peters, Cambridge, and Annie M. Wright; *m* 1912, Essie, *d* of late Ald. F. W. Mills, Cambridge; one *s* one *d*. *Educ:* Cambridge County High Sch.; Cambridge and Dublin Universities. MA, LLB, Cambridge, MA, LLD, Dublin. Secretary and Legal Adviser to Central Council Forage Department for Civil Supplies during European War, 1914-18, and Executive Officer, Controlling Department, for same under Board of Trade; formerly Member of Ecclesiastical Cttee; MP (L) Huntingdonshire, 1929-31, (L Nat) 1931-45; formerly Parly Private Secretary to Minister of Mines, and Parliamentary Private Secretary to Minister of Labour to 1940. Retired from practice as a Solicitor. *Address:* Hilton House, Hilton, Cambs. *T:* Papworth St Agnes 289. *[Died 9 Jan. 1976.*

PETERSON, John Magnus, MA (Oxon); *b* 18 Feb. 1902; *yr s* of late Rev. M. F. Peterson; *m* 1938, Rosemary (*d* 1944), *yr d* of late A. M. McNeile; two *s* one *d*. *Educ:* Shrewsbury Sch.; Oriel Coll., Oxford. Scholar of Shrewsbury School, 1915, and Oriel College, 1921; 1st Cl. Classical Mods, 1923; 1st Cl. Lit. Hum., 1925. Oxford Univ. Assoc. Football XI, 1924 and 1925 (Capt.); OU Authentics. Asst Master, Eton College, 1925-50, House Master, 1938-50; Headmaster of Shrewsbury School, 1950-63. *Address:* Lower Farm, Easton Royal, Pewsey, Wilts. *T:* Burbage 343. *Club:* Vincent's (Oxford). *[Died 6 April 1978.*

PETFIELD, Sir Arthur (Henry), Kt 1968; Chairman of Directors since 1958, United Packages Ltd; *b* 10 Sept. 1912; *s* of Arthur Petfield and Florence Jane Petfield (*née* Mott); *m* 1937, Elsie Emily Mylchreest; three *s* one *d*. *Educ:* Milton State School, Brisbane; State Commercial High School, Brisbane. Joined Queensland Can Company Ltd (now United Packages Ltd), 1929; Secretary, 1934; Director and General Manager, 1948. Chairman: Overseas Telecom. Commn; Perpetual Trustees Aust. Ltd; Queensland Trustees Ltd. Director: Queensland Insurance Co. Ltd; National Mutual Life Assoc. of A/asia Ltd; Member: Industries Assistance Bd; Greater Brisbane Town Planning Adv. Cttee; Queensland Chamber of Manufactures (Pres., 1955-57); Canmakers Inst. (Pres., 1953-57); Queensland Spastic Welfare League. *Recreations:* boating, fishing, surfing. *Address:* 21 Spica Street, Coorparoo, Brisbane, Qld 4151, Australia. *T:* 973241. *Clubs:* Queensland, Masonic, Brisbane (Brisbane); Rotary of S Brisbane (Pres., 1956-57).
[Died 30 Oct. 1974.

PETIT, Rt. Rev. John Edward; *b* 22 June 1895; *s* of Edward John Petit and Mary Bridget O'Dowd. *Educ:* English Coll. and Pontifical Univ., Valladolid, Spain; St Edmund's Coll., Ware; Christ's Coll. and St Edmund's House, Cambridge. BA 1921; Historical Tripos; ordained Diocese of Brentwood, 1918; Curate, St anne's, Victoria Docks, London, 1921; Bishop's Sec., 1921; Parish Priest, Maldon, Essex, 1923; Vice-Rector, English Coll., Valladolid, 1924; Parish Priest, N Dagenham, 1930; Parish Priest, Grays, Essex, 1931; Master, St Edmund's House, Cambridge, 1934 (Hon. Fellow, 1968); Rector, St Hugh's Seminary, Tollerton, Notts, 1946; Bishop of Menevia, 1947, resigned, 1972. *Address:* Nazareth House, Wrexham, Denbighshire. *T:* Wrexham 2585. *[Died 2 June 1973.*

PETO, Brig. Sir Christopher (Henry Maxwell), 3rd Bt *cr* 1927; DSO 1945; *b* 19 Feb. 1897; 2nd *s* of Sir Basil Peto, 1st Bt, and Mary Matilda Annie (*d* 1931), *d* of Captain T. C. Baird; *g s* of Sir Morton Peto, 1st Bt (*cr* 1855); *S* brother, 1971; *m* 1935, Barbara, *d* of E. T. Close, Camberley, Surrey; two *s* one *d*. *Educ:* Harrow. Joined 9th Lancers, 1915 (wounded, despatches); commanded 9th Lancers, 1938; War of 1939-45 (wounded, despatches thrice, DSO); Brig. 1941; Chief Liaison Officer 21 Army Group, 1944; retd pay, 1946. Col, 9th Lancers, 1950-60. MP (C) for North Div. of Devonshire, 1945-55. Chm., Wilts TA and AFA, 1957-61. Pres. Conservative Association of Devizes Division of Wilts, 1958-66. Legion of Honour, Croix de Guerre, Orders of Leopold I, Belgian Croix de Guerre. DL Devon, 1950-55; DL Wilts,

1956-79; High Sheriff of Wiltshire, 1966. *Recreations:* shooting, fishing. *Heir: s* Michael Henry Basil Peto [*b* 6 April 1938; *m* 1st, 1963, Sarah Susan (marr. diss. 1970), *y d* of Major Sir Dennis Stucley, 5th Bt; one *s* two *d*; 2nd, 1971, Lucinda Mary, *yr d* of Major Sir Charles Douglas Blackett, 9th Bt; two *s*]. *Address:* The Well House, Cliddesden, Hants RG25 2JE. *T:* Basingstoke 65452. *Club:* Cavalry and Guards. [*Died 19 May* 1980.

PETO, Dorothy Olivia Georgiana, OBE 1920; *b* 15 Dec. 1886; *d* of Morton Kelsall Peto and Olivia Georgiana Elizabeth Maude; unmarried. *Educ:* privately at home. Hon. Sec., New Forest North Div. St John Ambulance Bde, 1912-14; Dep. Director (Director from 1916) Bristol Training School for Women Patrols and Police, 1915-20; Detective Inquiry Officer, Birmingham City Police, 1920-24; Organiser, British Social Hygiene Council, 1925-27; Director, Liverpool Women Police Patrols, 1927-30; Supt Women Police, Metropolitan Force, 1930-46; King's Police Medal, 1945. Member Executive Cttee, Josephine Butler Society, 1947. *Publications:* A Pilgrimage of Truth, 1907; various articles, etc dealing with women police. *Recreation:* gardening. *Address:* The Lawn, Holybourne, Alton, Hants. [*Died 26 Feb.* 1974.

PETO, Comdr Sir Francis; *see* Peto, Comdr Sir (Henry) F. M.

PETO, Gladys Emma; Black and White and Poster Artist; *b* Cannon Court, Maidenhead, Berkshire, 19 June 1890; *o d* of William Peto and Mary J. Reeves; *m* 1922, Colonel C. L. Emmerson, RAMC (*d* 1977), *o s* of Dr J. B. Emmerson of Biggleswade, Beds. *Educ:* Harvington College, Ealing. Commenced to study art at the Maidenhead Art School in 1908 and at the London School of Art, Kensington, in 1911; illustrated Simple Simon, by A. Neil Lyons, 1913; the works of Louisa Alcott, 1914; humorous drawings appeared weekly in the Sketch, 1915-26, also numerous illustrations in various periodicals and advertisement drawings and posters; has designed fabrics, pottery, costumes, and scenery; exhibitions of water colour drawings: (Cyprus), Abbey Galleries, London, 1929; (India and Ireland), Magee Gallery, Belfast, 1939; lived abroad in Malta, Egypt and Cyprus, 1924-28 and in India, 1933-38. *Publications:* Gladys Peto's Children's Annual; Gladys Peto's Children's Book; The China Cow, 1928; Malta and Cyprus, 1928; Egypt of the Sojourner, 1928; Gladys Peto's Bedtime Stories, 1931; Gladys Peto's Twilight Stories, 1932; Gladys Peto's Girls' Own Stories, 1933; Gladys Peto's Sunshine Tales, 1935; The Four-Leaved Clover, 1938. *Recreations:* books and gardening. *Address:* Leeke, Limavady, Co. Derry, N Ireland. [*Died 21 May* 1977.

PETO, Comdr Sir (Henry) Francis (Morton), 3rd Bt, *cr* 1855; RN, retired; *b* 18 Nov. 1889; *s* of late Morton Kelsall Peto and Olive Georgiana Elizabeth, *d* of late Hon. Francis Maude; *S* uncle 1938; *m* 1919, Edith (*d* 1945), *d* of late George Berners Ruck Keene; two *s*; *m* 1948, Rosemary Grizel (*d* 1976), *d* of late Rear-Adm. Archibald Cochrane, CMG, and *widow* of Major Thomas Clapton, DLI; one *s*. *Heir: s* Henry George Morton Peto [*b* 29 April 1920; *m* 1947, Frances Jacqueline, *d* of late Ralph Haldane Evers, Milan, and of Mrs Evers, Stow-on-the-Wold; two *s*]. *Address:* Balbeg, Straiton, Maybole, Ayrshire. [*Died 28 May* 1978.

PETO, Lt-Col Sir (James) Michael, 2nd Bt, *cr* 1927; *b* 8 May 1894; *e s* of Sir Basil Peto, 1st Bt; *S* father, 1945; *m* 1920, Frances, *e d* of late Canon W. H. Carnegie, sub-Dean of Westminster; one *d*. *Educ:* Summer Fields, Oxford; Harrow School; Balliol College, Oxford; RMC, Sandhurst. 2nd Lt Coldstream Guards, 1915; served European War, France and Flanders, 1915-18 (despatches); Staff appointments HQ, London District, and HQ, East Anglian Area; retired as Major, 1931. Re-employed April 1939, as a DAQMG, HQ, London District; Lieut-Col and AQMG(M), HQ, London District, 1940; Military Liaison Officer, and ADTn(M), Ministry of War Transport, 1942-45; retired as Lieutenant-Colonel, 1945. *Publications:* Accidental Poems, 1947; Pebble Ridge, 1948. *Recreations:* travel and gardening. *Heir: b* Brigadier Christopher Henry Maxwell Peto, DSO. *Address:* The Manor House, Yatton Keynell, near Chippenham, Wiltshire. *T:* Castle Combe 375. [*Died 24 March* 1971.

PETRE, Prof. Edward Oswald Gabriel T.; *see* Turville-Petre.

PETRE, Maj.-Gen. Roderic Loraine, CB 1940; DSO 1917; MC; *o s* of late F. Loraine Petre, OBE; *b* 1887; *m* 1922, Katharine, *o d* of Herbert Bryans, Bradford Priory, Wilts; one *s* one *d*. *Educ:* Downside; Sandhurst. Joined S Wales Borderers, 1908; served siege and capture of Tsingtau, 1914, Gallipoli Campaign, 1915, Mesopotamia and capture of Baghdad, 1916-18 (despatches seven times, DSO, MC); Afghanistan, 1919; Operations in

France, 1940 (CB); Bt Major, 1918; Major, 1928; Bt Lt-Col 1929; accelerated promotion into Dorset Regiment as Lt-Col 1932; commanded 2nd Bn The Dorset Regiment, 1932-35; Col 1935; Staff Officer, Sudan Defence Force, 1935-38; Comdt Senior Officers' School, Sheerness, 1938-39; Maj.-Gen., 1939; commanded 12th and 48th Divs and "Petreforce" (BEF), 1939-42; District Comd, 1942-44; retired pay, 1944. *Address:* c/o Williams & Glyn's Bank Ltd, Kirkland House, Whitehall, SW1. *Club:* Army and Navy. [*Died 21 July* 1971.

PETRIE, Sir Charles (Alexander), 3rd Bt of Carrowcarden, *cr* 1918; CBE 1957; MA Oxon, FRHistS; *b* 28 Sept. 1895; *s* of 1st Bt and Hannah, *d* of late William Hamilton; *S* brother, 1927; *m* 1st, 1920, Ursula Gabrielle (marr. diss., 1925; decd), *er d* of late Judge Dowdall, QC; one *s*; 2nd, 1926, Cecilia (*née* Mason); one *s*. *Educ:* privately; Corpus Christi College, Oxford. Historian; Corresponding Mem. of the Royal Spanish Academy of History; Pres. of Military Hist. Soc. of Ireland. Foreign Editor of the English Review, 1931-37; Associate Editor of Empire Review, 1940-41, Editor, 1941-43; Managing Editor, New English Review, 1945-50; Editor, Household Brigade Magazine, 1945-76. Served with RGA, 1915-19; attached War Cabinet Office, 1918-19; Official Lecturer to HM Forces, 1940-45. Corresp. Member: Institución Fernando el Católico, Zaragoza; Hispanic Soc. of America. Doctor (*hc*) Valladolid University, 1964; Hon. LittD Nat. Univ. of Ireland, 1971. Comdr Order of Isabella the Catholic (Spain); Knight of Order of Civil Merit (Spain); Commendatore Order of Crown of Italy; Commander Order of George I (Greece). *Publications:* The History of Government, 1929; George Canning, 1930, new edn 1946; The Jacobite Movement, 1932, new edn, 1959; History of Spain (with Louis Bertrand), 1934 (new edn 1957); The Four Georges: A Revaluation, 1935; The Stuarts, 1937; Life and Letters of Sir Austen Chamberlain (2 vols), 1939-40; Diplomatic History, 1713-1933, 1946; Earlier Diplomatic History, 1492-1713, 1949; Chapters of Life, 1950; The Marshal Duke of Berwick, 1953; The Carlton Club, 1955; Wellington: a Reassessment, 1956; The Spanish Royal House, 1958; The Powers Behind the Prime Ministers, 1959; The Victorians, 1960; The Modern British Monarchy, 1961; Philip II of Spain, 1963; King Alfonso XIII, 1963; Scenes of Edwardian Life, 1965; Don John of Austria, 1967; Great Beginnings, 1967; The Drift to World War, 1900-1914, 1968; King Charles III of Spain, 1971; A Historian Looks at his World, 1972; The Great Tyrconnel: a chapter in Anglo-Irish Relations, 1973; (ed) King Charles, Prince Rupert, and the Civil War, 1974; A Short History of Spain, 1976; contribs to Illustrated London News, 1958-. *Heir: s* Charles Richard Borthwick Petrie [*b* 19 Oct. 1921; *m* 1962, Jessie Ariana Borthwick Campbell]. *Address:* 190 Coleherne Court, SW5. *Clubs:* Carlton, 1900, Authors' (Pres.), Cavalry and Guards, Hurlingham; Kildare Street and University (Dublin). [*Died 13 Dec.* 1977.

PFEIFFER, Rudolf, MA Oxon, DPhil Munich; DPhil *hc* Vienna and Thessalonika; FBA 1949; Professor of Greek, University of Munich, 1929-37, and from 1951, Emeritus 1957; *b* 28 September 1889; *s* of late Carl Pfeiffer and late Elizabeth (*née* Naegele); *m* 1913, Lili (*d* 1969), *d* of late Sigmund and Mina Beer. *Educ:* Benedictine Abbey, St Stephan, Augsburg; Universities of Munich and Berlin. Sub-librarian, University Library, Munich, 1918; Lecturer, University of Munich, 1921; Professor extraordinarius, University of Berlin, 1923; Professor of Greek: Hamburg, 1923; Freiburg i. Br., 1927; Corpus Christi College, Oxford, 1938-51, University Lecturer, 1946, Senior Lecturer, 1948, Reader in Greek Literature, 1950. Ordinary Member of Bavarian Academy; Hon. Mem., Austrian Academy; For. Corresp. Member: Académie des Inscriptions et Belles-Lettres; Academy of Greece, 1973; Hon. Fellow of Athenian Scientific Society; Hon. Fellow Corpus Christi College, Oxford, 1959; Hon. Fellow Hellenic Society, 1961. Kenyon Medal, British Acad., 1977. Bavarian Order of Merit, 1959; Greek Order of Phoenix, 1959; Grand Cross of the Federal Republic of Germany, 1964. *Publications:* Augsburger Meistersinger und Homerübersetzer J. Spreng, 1914 and 1919; Callimachi Fragmenta nuper reperta, 1921, editio maior, 1923; Kallimachos-Studien, 1922; Humanitas Erasmiana, 1931; Die griechische Dichtung und die griechische Kultur, 1932; Die Diktyulkoi des Aischylos und der Inachos des Sophokles, 1937; Callimachus (complete edn) vol. I Fragmenta, 1949 (reprinted 1965), vol. II Hymni et Epigrammata, 1953 (repr. 1966); Von der Liebe zu den Griechen, 1958; Ausgewählte Schriften: Aufsätze und Vorträge zur griechischen Dichtung und zum Humanismus, 1960; Philologia Perennis, 1961; History of Classical Scholarship: From the Beginnings to the End of the Hellenistic Age, 1968; Von der Liebe zur Antike; zum 80 Geburtstag von R.P., 1969; History of Classical Scholarship 1300-1850, 1976. Editor: U. von Wilamowitz, Kleine Schriften II, 1940. Numerous articles in periodicals on Greek and Latin literature, Erasmus, humanism. *Recreations:* music, walking. *Address:* Hiltenspergerstrasse 21, München 40, Germany. *T:* 372185. *[Died 6 May 1979.*

PHILIP, Alexander; General Manager, Scottish Region, British Railways, 1971-74; Chairman, British Transport Ship Management (Scotland) Ltd, 1971-74; *b* 4 June 1911; *s* of Alexander Philip and Elizabeth Milne Philip; *m* 1939, Isobel Thomson Morrison; one *s. Educ:* Robert Gordon's Coll., Aberdeen. FCIT, MIPM. Joined LNER, 1927; occupied various positions mainly on personnel and movements aspects of railway business in Aberdeen, Edinburgh and Glasgow. Mem., Lanarkshire Health Bd. *Recreations:* reading, golf, gardening. *Address:* 12 Dalmorglen Park, Stirling. *T:* Stirling 3672. *[Died 22 March 1979.*

PHILIPS, Lt-Col John Lionel, DSO 1917; late RA; *b* 1878; 3rd *s* of late G. H. Philips, MA, DL, JP, of Abbey Cwmhir, Radnorshire; *m* 1st, 1911, Nora (decd), *d* of late J. Fitzmaurice, ICS; one *s* one *d*; 2nd, 1941, Shearme Van Kaughnet, *d* of late G. Wolferstan Thomas, Montreal, and late Mrs F. E. Meredith, London, England. *Educ:* Eton; New College, Oxford. Served European War, France, Mesopotamia, and Palestine, 1914-18 (DSO, despatches 4 times, Bt Lt-Col); retired pay, 1929. Sheriff, Radnorshire, 1935; JP 1933, DL 1938 Powys (formerly Radnorshire). *Address:* Little Abbey, Venns Lane, Hereford. *Club:* Army and Navy. *[Died 9 Feb. 1975.*

PHILIPSON-STOW, Sir F. L.; *see* Stow, Sir F. L. P.

PHILLIMORE, Rt. Hon. Sir Henry Josceline, PC 1968; Kt 1959; OBE 1946; a Lord Justice of Appeal, 1968-74; *b* 25 Dec. 1910; *s* of Charles Augustus Phillimore and Alice Campion; *m* 1938, Katharine Mary, *d* of late Lieutenant-Commander L. C. Maude-Roxby, Royal Navy and Mrs Maude-Roxby; two *d. Educ:* Eton; Christ Church, Oxford. Called to Bar Middle Temple, 1934; QC 1952; Bencher, 1959; enlisted TA, July 1939; Commissioned, December 1939; served War of 1939-45; Colonel 1945; demobilised, 1945, and appointed Continental Secretary British War Crimes Executive; Junior Counsel Nuremberg, 1945-46; Recorder of Poole, 1946-54; Recorder of Winchester, 1954-59; Judge of High Court of Justice, Probate Divorce and Admiralty Division, 1959-62, Queen's Bench Division, 1962-68; Chm., Oxfordshire QS, 1962-68. Member, Royal Commn on Assizes and Quarter Sessions, 1967-69; Chm., Cttee to consider law relating to contempt of court, 1971-. Fellow of Eton College, 1971-. *Recreations:* fishing, shooting. *Address:* Queen Elizabeth Building, Temple, EC4. *Clubs:* Brooks's, Pratt's. *[Died 4 June 1974.*

PHILLIPS, Col Alan Andrew, CIE 1946; VD; retired; *b* 18 Aug. 1889; *s* of Charles Addison Phillips and Annie Phillips (*née* Kerr); *m* 1st, 1915, Lucy Osborn (*d* 1952); two *s* two *d* (and one *s* killed on active service); 2nd, 1965, Peggie Crabtree, *o d* of late Charles Bell, Hexham. *Educ:* St Peter's School, York; Queen's College, Oxford. Indian State Railways, 1912-44, Chief Commercial Manager, North Western Railway, 1940-42; Government of India, War Transport Department, as Chief Controller of Railway Priorities, 1942-46. Auxiliary Force (India), 1912-46; Lt Col 1938; Hon. Col 1942; Hon. ADC to the C-in-C, India, 1936-46; retired, 1946. *Publications:* technical papers and magazine articles on Railway and Auxiliary Force matters. *Recreations:* shooting, fishing and natural history. *Address:* Kilncleuch, Langholm, Dumfriesshire. *T:* Langholm 341. *[Died 19 July 1972.*

PHILLIPS, Prof. Alban William Housego, MBE 1946; Emeritus Professor in the Australian National University since 1970; *b* 18 Nov. 1914; *s* of Harold Housego Phillips; *m* 1954, Beatrice Valda Bennett; two *d. Educ:* New Zealand State Schools; London School of Economics. Various posts in electrical engineering, 1930-40; served Royal Air Force (Technical Branch), 1940-46. Assistant Lecturer in Economics, London School of Economics, 1950-51; Lecturer in Economics, 1951-54; Reader in Economics, in the University of London, 1954-58; Tooke Prof. of Economic Science and Statistics, Univ. of London, 1958-67; Prof. of Economics, ANU, 1967-70. *Publications:* articles in various economic journals. *Address:* 11 Kirkmay Place, St Heliers, Auckland 5, New Zealand. *[Died 4 March 1975.*

PHILLIPS, Sir Charles; *see* Phillips, Sir Edward Charles.

PHILLIPS, Maj.-Gen. Sir Edward, KBE 1946 (CBE 1943); CB 1945; DSO 1919; MC; *b* 19 Dec. 1889; *s* of Edward Phillips, MB, Coventry. *Educ:* St Paul's Sch.; London Hospital; Durham Univ.; MB, BS; MRCS, LRCP, 1913. Entered RAM Corps, July 1914; Major, 1926; Lieut-Col, 1933; Colonel, 1941; Maj.-Gen.,

1944; served France, 1914-18 (MC, DSO, despatches four times, Acting Lieut-Col); NW Frontier India, 1919; War of 1939-45 (CBE, CB, KBE); retired pay, 1949. Légion d'Honneur; Croix de Guerre; Ordre de la Couronne; Legion of Merit (USA). *Address:* c/o Williams & Glyn's Bank Ltd, Whitehall, SW1. *[Died 14 May 1973.*

PHILLIPS, Sir (Edward) Charles, Kt 1954; CBE 1946; Member of the East Africa Central Legislative Assembly, 1948-59; *b* 10 March 1888; *s* of Edward C. Phillips, Teddington, Middlesex; *m* 1st, 1915, Sylvia Maud Schunke (*d* 1944); one *s* one *d* (one *d* decd); 2nd, 1951, Audrey Jane Prytz; one *d. Educ:* privately. British-American Tobacco Co. Ltd, 1907-45; President: Mombasa Chamber of Commerce, 1935; Dar es Salaam Chamber of Commerce, 1938 and 1939; Member and later Chairman, Economic Control Board of Tanganyika, 1941-48; Member, Makerere College Council, 1941-49; Chairman: Tanganyika Packers Ltd, 1947-; Director: Savings & Loan Society Ltd, 1950-65; Wigglesworth & Co. (Africa) Ltd, 1949-64; Member of: East African Airways, 1940-61; Land Bank of Tanganyika, 1949-58; East African Industrial Council, 1948-59. MLC, 1940-59, MEC, 1940-58, Tanganyika. *Recreations:* previously: tennis, golf. *Address:* Belabbey, 41 Abbots Ride, Farnham, Surrey. *T:* Farnham 3118. *Clubs:* Lansdowne; Mombasa. *[Died 10 Aug. 1974.*

PHILLIPS, Surgeon Rear-Adm. George, CB 1961; retired 1961; *b* 1902; *s* of Dr G. Phillips; *m* 1930, Ernestine S., *d* of Surgeon Captain J. S. Orwin; one *s* one *d. Educ:* Dover Coll.; Edinburgh Univ. MB, ChB (Edinburgh), 1926; DLO England, 1936. Joined RN 1926; Surgeon Commander, 1938; MO i/c RN Hospital, Malta, 1943; Surgeon Captain, 1950; Surgeon Rear-Admiral, 1958; MO i/c RN Hospital, Trincomalee, 1950; MO i/c RN Hospital, Haslar, 1958; QHS 1958-61. CStJ 1960. *Recreations:* golf, fishing. *Address:* Whinacre, Yelverton, Devon. *T:* Yelverton 2519. *[Died 14 Jan. 1980.*

PHILLIPS, John Henry Hood, MA; *b* 18 Aug. 1902; *e s* of late Surgeon-Captain J. E. Hood Phillips, RN, Portsmouth; *m* 1931, Winifred, *y d* of late S. T. Shovelton, CBE; two *s* one *d. Educ:* Weymouth Coll.; Keble Coll., Oxford (Modern History Exhibitioner, 1921); Oxford Univ. Dept of Education. Asst Master, King Edward VI School, Southampton, 1926-28; Divisional Education Officer, Middlesex CC, 1930-34; Asst Education Officer, Surrey CC, 1934-40; Dep. Education Officer, 1940-45; Sec. to Senate, Univ. of London, 1945-66. Mem. of Council, Boy Scouts' Assoc., 1947-68; Chm., Education Advisory Panel, 1945-58. Almoner, Christ's Hospital, 1947-74 (Chm., Education Cttee, 1966-74); Governor by special vote, 1975); Chairman: Raynes Park Schools' Governors, 1949-58; Council, St Gabriel's Coll. of Educn, Camberwell, 1968-73. *Publications:* The Heart of a Schoolboy, 1919; Hurrying Feet, 1924. *Address:* 7 St Cross Court, Kingsgate Road, Winchester, Hants. *T:* Winchester 65162. *[Died 17 Jan. 1977.*

PHILLIPS, Leonard George, FRCS; Hon. Consulting Surgeon: Hospital for Women, Soho Square; Queen Charlotte's Hospital; Willesden General Hospital; Emeritus Consulting Surgeon, Croydon General Hospital; Examiner: London University; RCOG; *b* Dec. 1890. MRCS, LRCP, 1915; MB, BS 1916; BSc London, MS, FRCS, 1919; FRCOG 1938. Fellow, Royal Society of Medicine and Medical Society, London. *Publications:* contributions to medical journals and to Queen Charlotte's Practice of Obstetrics. *Recreations:* shooting, golf, gardening. *Address:* 39 Harley House, Regents Park, NW1. *T:* 01-935 3686; The Grove, Godmanchester, Hunts. *Clubs:* Devonshire; Melbourne (Melbourne). *[Died 22 June 1975.*

PHILLIPS, Patrick Edward, TD 1955; RP 1954; RWS 1975; Artist, Portrait Painter; *b* 17 March 1907; 2nd *s* of late Lionel Charles Whitehead Phillips, Unsted Park, Godalming; *m* 1932, Susannah Catherine, *d* of late General Sir Reginald Byng Stephens, KCB, CMG, Church House, Lechlade, Glos; one *s* two *d. Educ:* Eton; Byam Shaw School of Art. Lieut, 98 (Surrey and Sussex Yeomanry) Field Bde, 1926; served War of 1939-45 (despatches); Major, RE, 1941; TARO retired, 1957. Principal of The Byam Shaw School of Drawing and Painting, 1946-55. *Address:* Gannets, Tolleshunt D'Arcy, Maldon, Essex. *T:* Tolleshunt D'Arcy 221. *Club:* Arts. *[Died 28 Aug. 1976.*

PHILLIPS, Patrick Laurence; Joint Managing-Director (Director, 1938) of Ernest Brown & Phillips Ltd, proprietors of the Leicester Galleries, London, since 1960; *b* 1 July 1912; *e s* of late Cecil Laurence Phillips, co-founder of the Leicester Galleries, 1902, and Eileen Christina (*née* Slattery); *m* 1945, Margaret Elinor, *d* of late Ernest Lewin Chapman; two *s. Educ:* Stonyhurst. Art studies in Paris and in Museums of Europe. Joined Leicester Galleries, 1931. Served War, 8th Army, in

Western Desert and Italy, 1940-45; Staff Officer, HQ, AA Command, 1945-46. Organizer of Festival Exhibition "Henry Moore at King's Lynn", held in open air sites throughout the town, 1964. Specialist in 19th and 20th century British and French pictures, drawings, prints, sculpture. *Recreations:* the Arts, travel, walking. *Address:* 164 Coleherne Court, SW5. *T:* 01-373 0304; Brandon House, Horn Hill, Dartmouth.
[Died 5 Nov. 1980.

PHILLIPS, Hon. Sir Rowland (Ricketts), Kt 1964; Chief Justice of Jamaica, 1963-67; *b* 30 Sept. 1904; *s* of George Augustus Phillips, Montego Bay, Jamaica, WI; *m* 1947, Enid Daphne Limonius; two *s* two *d. Educ:* Cornwall Coll., Jamaica. Called to Bar, Inner Temple, 1941; Crown Counsel, Jamaica, 1943; Resident Magistrate, Jamaica, 1946; Puisne Judge: British Guiana, 1954-59; Jamaica, 1959-Oct. 1962; Judge, Court of Appeal, Jamaica, Oct.-Dec. 1962. *Address:* 8 Grosvenor Terrace, Kingston 8, Jamaica, West Indies.
[Died 11 Oct. 1976.

PHILLIPS, Rt. Rev. Samuel Charles, MA, LTh Durham; retired; *b* 6 May 1881; *s* of late Rt Rev. C. Phillips, DD, and Mrs Marianne Phillips; *m* 1923, Ayodele Pearse; one *s* three *d. Educ:* The CMS Grammar Sch., Freetown, Sierra Leone; Fourah Bay Coll., Sierra Leone. Tutor, CMS Grammar Sch., Lagos, 1905-06; Tutor, St Andrew's Coll., Oyo, 1907-08; Vice-Principal, Abeokuta Grammar Sch., 1908-14; Principal, Ijebu Ode Grammar Sch., 1914-18; Superintendent and Chairman Ondo Church District and Canon of the Cathedral, 1919-30; Pastor of St Paul's Cathedral, Breadfruit, Lagos, 1930-31; Canon Res. Cathedral Church of Christ, Lagos, Archdeacon of Lagos and Chairman of six District Church Councils, 1931-44; consecrated Asst Bishop of Lagos, 1944; resigned, 1956; Vicar-General, Dio. Lagos, 1952-56. Subsequently Organising Secretary, Nigeria Temperance Society. *Publications:* Christ or Mohammed (Lenten Addresses), 1944; Science Handmaid to the Bible; Corruption, 1971; Gambling is Rob me I rob you, 1972; Yoruba Culture Numeration, 1973; The Heathen Secret Cult called Reformed Ogboni Society, 1974. *Address:* PO Box 105, Oshogbo, Nigeria.
[Died 1 Oct. 1974.

PHILLIPS BROCKLEHURST, Charles Douglas Fergusson, DL; *b* 17 March 1904; *o* surv. *s* of late Lieut-Colonel R. W. D. Phillips Brocklehurst, DL, JP, Hare Hill, Macclesfield, and late Ida E., CBE, *d* of late Sir Patrick Heron Watson; unmarried. *Educ:* Eton; Christ Church, Oxford (MA). Served War of 1939-45 with Cheshire Yeo., Palestine and Syria, and 10 Armoured Division, Western Desert and Alamein; GSO1, Military Liaison, Albania; retired with hon. rank of Lt-Col, 1945. A Trustee of: Wallace Collection, 1955 (Chm. 1972-76); Lady Lever Art Gallery; a Governor of Whitworth Art Gallery; Mem., Arts Panel, Nat. Trust. DL 1952, Cheshire; High Sheriff of Cheshire, 1957. *Address:* Hare Hill, Macclesfield, Cheshire; 3 West Eaton Place, SW1. *T:* 01-235 4677. *Clubs:* White's, Beefsteak.
[Died 31 July 1977.

PHILLIPSON, Prof. Andrew Tindal; Professor of Veterinary Clinical Studies, Cambridge University, and Fellow of Churchill College, since Oct. 1963; *b* 19 Aug. 1910; *s* of late John Tindal Phillipson and Cicely Gough Paterson; *m* 1936, Rachel Margaret Young; three *s. Educ:* Christ's Coll., Finchley; St Catharine's Coll., Cambridge; Royal Veterinary Coll., London. BA Cambridge 1931, MA 1937; MRCVS London, 1936; Clement Stephenson Schol., 1936-39 (Award of Royal Veterinary College); Miss Aleen Cust Schol., 1938 and 1939 (Award of Royal College of Vet. Surg.); PhD Cambridge, 1941. Scientific Officer, Inst. of Animal Pathology, Cambridge, 1939-42; seconded to Agric. Res. Council's Unit of Animal Physiology, 1941, and taken on Council's Staff, 1942, to continue previous work on Physiol. of Digestion of the Ruminant; Head of Physiol. Dept, Rowett Research Institute, 1947, and Dep. Director of Institute, 1952. FRSE 1953; Hon. Dr Vet. Sci., Royal Veterinary and Agricultural Coll., Copenhagen, 1958; Hon. DVM Univ. of Ghent, 1968; Hon. DVM and Surg Edinburgh, 1970. Dalrymple Champneys Cup and Medal, British Veterinary Assoc., 1959; Research Medal, Royal Agricultural Society of England, 1962. *Publications:* The Alimentary Tract of the Ruminant (with D. Benzie), 1957; Physiology of Digestion and Metabolism in the Ruminant, 1970; various chapters contrib. to scientific books. Papers in: Journal Exper. Biology, Journal of Physiol., Quarterly Journal of Physiol., British Journal of Nutrition. Reviews in Biolog. Reviews, Annual Review of Biochem., Nutrition Abstracts and Review, etc. *Address:* Dene House, 96 High Street, Caxton, Cambridgeshire.
[Died 10 Jan. 1977.

PHILP, Lieut-Colonel Robert, MC, TD; DL; *b* 12 July 1896; *s* of Major J. Philp, TD, JP; *m* 1924, Jane Black Adamson; one *d.*

Educ: Dollar Academy. Served War 1914-18 (France), 1939-45 (India and Burma). Hon. Sheriff, Clackmannanshire, 1962-, DL 1959; Vice-Lieutenant, County of Clackmannan, 1966-73. *Address:* 1 Castlepark, Tulliallan, Kincardine, Alloa, Clackmannanshire. *[Died 6 April 1980.*

PHIPPS, Gerald Hastings; *b* 1882; *s* of late Eccleston A. E. Phipps; *m* 1912, Aline Maclean, yr *d* of Frank P. Purvis, formerly Professor of Naval Engineering, Tokyo Imperial Univ.; two *s* one *d. Educ:* Felsted School. HM Consular Service in Japan, 1903; Vice-Consul, 1915; Consul at Tamsui, Formosa, 1920; Honolulu, 1925; Kobe, 1932; HBM Consul-General, Seoul, Korea, 1934-41; retired, 1943. *Address:* St Mary's House, Kingsmead, Seaford, Sussex. *[Died 21 Nov. 1973.*

PHIPPS, Maj.-General Herbert Clive, CB 1951; DSO 1945; late RA; retired; *b* 3 Aug. 1898; *s* of Walter Tudway Phipps, Shepton Mallet, Somerset; *m* 1929, Rosalie Osborn, *d* of A. W. Marshall, Pinner, Middlesex; one *s* one *d. Educ:* Wellington; Royal Military Academy, Woolwich. Served European War, 1914-19, Royal Artillery; 2nd Lieut, 1916. Served War of 1939-45, France and British Liberation Army; Lieut-Colonel, 1940; Colonel, 1947; Maj.-General, 1951. Commander Royal Artillery, Guards Armoured Division, 1944; Commander 2nd AA Group, 1951-54; retired 1954. Colonel Comdt RA, 1955-64. *Address:* Dalton House, Hurstbourne Tarrant, Andover, Hants. *Club:* Army and Navy. *[Died 3 Nov. 1975.*

PHIPSON, Col Edward Selby, CIE 1935; DSO 1916, MD (London) (Gold Medal), FRCP, FRSH, DPH, DTM&H; OStJ; Indian Medical Service, retired; *b* 10 March 1884; *s* of Ernest Thring Phipson and Ada Mary Yeats; *m* 1913, Mary, *d* of late Colonel Hugh Scott, JP, Lewes, Sussex; two *d. Educ:* King Edward's Sch., Birmingham; Birmingham Univ.; University College, London. Entered Indian Medical Service, 1908; served European War, 1914-17, Egypt and Gallipoli (despatches, DSO); afterwards held appointments of Assistant Health Officer, City of Bombay, 1917-18; Health Officer, Simla, 1918-23 and 1941-45 (re-employed); Port Health Officer, and Medical Officer in charge European General Hospital, Aden, 1923; Senior Medical Officer, Colony of Aden, 1937; Inspector-General of Civil Hospitals and Prisons, Assam, 1937-41. *Publications:* A Medical Survey of Aden, 1933, 1934; various contributions to Medical periodicals principally on Public Health and Tropical Diseases. *Address:* Greenwood Cottage, Heathcote Road, Camberley, Surrey. *T:* Camberley 21687.
[Died 25 May 1973.

PIAGET, Jean; Professor of Child Psychology, Geneva University, since 1929; Director, International Centre of Genetic Epistemology, Geneva, since 1955; *b* Neuchâtel, 9 Aug. 1896; *s* of Prof. Arthur Piaget; *m* ; three *c. Educ:* Neuchâtel, Zürich and Paris Univ. Dr ès Sc. naturelles, Neuchâtel, 1918. Chef de travaux, Institut J. J. Rousseau, Geneva, 1921-25; Prof. of Psychology, Sociology and Philosophy of Science, Univ. of Neuchâtel, 1925-29; Prof. of History of Scientific Thought, Geneva Univ., 1929-39; Dir, Institut universitaire des Sciences de l'Education, Geneva, 1933-71; Professor of Psychology and Sociology, Univ. of Lausanne, 1938-51; Sociology, Geneva Univ., 1939-52; Experimental Psychology, Geneva Univ., 1940-71; Genetic Psychology, Sorbonne, 1952-63. Dir. Internat. Bureau of Educn, Geneva, 1929-67; formerly: Pres., Swiss Commission UNESCO; Co-Dir, Dept of Educn UNESCO; Mem., Exec. Council UNESCO. Established, with the help of the Rockefeller Foundn and Swiss Nat. Foundn for Scientific Res., Internat. Centre of Genetic Epistemology, Geneva Univ., 1955. Formerly President: Swiss Soc. of Psychology; Assoc. de Psychologie scientifique de langue française; Internat. Union of Scientific Psychology, 1954-57; Mem., 20 Academic Socs. Editor: Revue Suisse de Psychologie; Archives de Psychologie, Geneva; Enfance, Paris; Acta Psychologica, Amsterdam; Methodos, Milan; Synthese, Dordrecht/Holland; Dialectica, Neuchâtel and Paris; Linguistic Inquiry, Cambridge/Mass. Dr *hc* Harvard Univ.; Hon. ScD Cambridge; 33 other Hon. Degrees; 12 Scientific Prizes. *Publications:* Recherche, 1918; Le Langage et la Pensée chez l'enfant, 1923 (Eng. trans. 1926); Le Jugement et le raisonnement chez l'enfant, 1924 (Eng. trans. 1928); La Représentation du monde chez l'enfant 1926 (Eng. trans. 1929); La Causalité physique chez l'enfant, 1927 (Eng. Trans. 1930); Le Jugement moral chez l'enfant, (and Eng. trans.), 1932; La Naissance de l'intelligence chez l'enfant, 1936 (Eng. trans. 1952); La Construction du réel chez l'enfant, 1937 (Eng. trans. 1954); (with A. Szeminska) La Genèse du nombre chez l'enfant, 1941 (Eng. trans. 1952); Classes, relations et nombres, 1942; Développement des quantités physiques chez l'enfant (Eng. trans. 1974); La Formation du symbole chez l'enfant, 1946 (Eng. trans. 1951); Le Développement de la notion de temps chez l'enfant, 1946 (Eng. trans. 1969); Les Notions de mouvement et de vitesse chez l'enfant, 1946 (Eng. trans. 1970); La Psychologie de l'intelligence, 1947 (Eng. trans. 1950); (with B. Inhelder) La Représentation de l'espace chez l'enfant, 1948 (Eng. trans. 1956); (with B. Inhelder and A. Szeminska) La Géométrie spontanée de l'enfant, 1948 (Eng. trans. 1960); Traité de logique, 1949; Introduction à l'épistémologie génétique, 1950; (with B. Inhelder) La Genèse de l'idée de hasard chez l'enfant, 1951; Essai sur les transformations des opérations logiques, 1952; Logic and Psychology, 1953; (with B. Inhelder) De la Logique de l'enfant à la logique de l'adolescent, 1955 (Eng. trans. 1958); La Genèse des structures logiques élémentaires, classifications et Sériations, 1959 (Eng. trans. 1964); Les Mécanismes perceptifs, 1961 (Eng. trans. 1969); Six Etudes de psychologie, 1964 (Eng. trans. 1967); Etudes sociologiques, 1965; Sagesse et illusion de la philosophie, 1965 (Eng. trans. 1971); (with B. Inhelder) L'Image mentale chez l'enfant, 1966 (Eng. trans. 1971); (with B. Inhelder) Psychologie de l'enfant, 1966 (Eng. trans. 1969); Biologie et connaissance, 1967 (Eng. trans. 1971); On the development of memory and identity, 1968; Logique et connaissance scientifique, 1967; Genetic Epistemology, 1970; Le Structuralisme, 1968 (Eng. trans. 1970); (with B. Inhelder and H. Sinclair-de Zwart) Mémoire et intelligence, 1968 (Eng. trans. 1973); Psychologie et pédagogie, 1969 (Eng. trans. 1970); L'Epistémologie génétique (and Eng. trans.), 1970; Psychologie et épistémologie, 1970 (Psychology and Epistemology, 1971); Epistémologie des sciences de l'homme, 1972; Où va l'éducation?, 1972 (Eng. trans. 1973); Problèmes de psychologie génétique, 1972 (Eng. trans. 1973); La Prise de conscience, 1974 (Eng. trans. 1977); Adaptation vitale et psychologie de l'intelligence, 1974; Réussir et comprendre, 1974; L'équilibration des structures cognitives, 1976 (Eng. trans. 1978); (ed) Etudes d'épistémologie génétique, 1957- (36 vols by 1978); (ed with P. Fraisse) Traité de psychologie expérimentale, 1963-65; and 500 publications in scientific periodicals. *Address:* Centre d'Epistémologie Génétique, l'Université, 1211 Geneva 4, Switzerland.   [*Died* 16 Sept. 1980.

PIATIGORSKY, Gregor, Doctor of Music; Concert Artist (Violoncellist); *b* Ekaterinoslav, Russia, 17 April 1903; *s* of Paul and Marie Piatigorsky; *m* 1936, Jacqueline, *d* of Baron Edouard de Rothschild; one *s* one *d. Educ:* Moscow Conservatory. Studied 'cello with Prof. de Glen. Concerts throughout Russia at age of nine. Left Russia in 1921, and has toured extensively in Europe, United States, Canada, South America, Mexico, Japan. Sonata Recitals with Rachmaninoff, Schnabel, Horowitz. Professor, Curtis Institute, Philadelphia until 1949; Doctor of Music Northwestern Univ., 1950. Director of Chamber Music, Berkshire Festival Music Center, USA. Introduced many first performances of Concertos and Sonatas by contemporary composers; founded Piatigorsky Scholarships for composition and violoncellists at Conservatoire de Paris, University of Chicago, and Peabody Conservatory, Baltimore. Has appeared in recitals and as soloist with all major Symphony Orchestras in England. Numerous recordings of Concerti, and Chamber Music. Holds hon. degrees in music and humanities. Hon. Mem. Royal Phil. Soc., London; Hon. RAM. Brandeis Gold Medal, 1954; Legion of Honour, France, 1955. *Publications:* Cellist, 1965; transcriptions of classics and modern works for 'cello and piano. *Address:* 400 South Bundy Drive, Los Angeles, Calif 90049, USA. *Club:* Lotus (New York).   [*Died* 6 *Aug.* 1976.

PICASSO, Pablo Ruiz; Spanish painter and worker in Ceramics; *b* Malaga, Spain, 25 Oct. 1881; *m* 1st, 1918, Olga Koklova (separated 1935, she *d* 1955); one *s* ; (also one *s* two *d*); *m* 2nd, 1961, Jacqueline Roque. Has worked in Paris, 1901-; founder and leader of the Cubist School. Designer for Diaghilev Ballet, 1917-27; Director, Prado Gallery, Madrid, 1936-39; painted murals for Spanish Pavilion, Paris Exhibition, 1937. Lenin Prize, 1950; Lenin Peace Prize, 1962. Exhibitions all over the World; British Exhibitions include: Gravures sur linoléum, Hanover Gallery, 1960; Paintings: Tate Gallery, 1960; Gimpel Fils, 1964; Paris, Grand Palais and Petit Palais, 1966; Sculpture, Tate Gallery, 1967. *Paintings:* Les Arlequins, L'Aveugle, La famille du singe, Femme à la mandoline, Guernica, Massacre in Korea, War and Peace; portraits of well-known people; still-life in galleries in London, Paris, Berlin, Philadelphia, Leningrad; *decorations for Russian ballets:* Parade, 1917; Tricorne, 1918; Pulcinella, 1919; *Publications:* The Dream and Life of General Franco, 1937; *plays:* Les Quatre Petites Filles, 1965 (Four Little Girls, 1970); Le Désir attrapé par la Queue, 1945 (Desire Caught by the Tail, 1970). *Address:* Villa Californie, Cannes, France; Galerie Louise Léris, 29 bis, Rue d'Astorg, Paris.
                                   [*Died* 8 *April* 1973.

PICKARD, Alexander, CBE 1942; Town Clerk and Deputy-Judge and Registrar of Tolzey Court, Bristol, 1945-58, retired; *b* 27 Sept. 1897; *m* 1924 (wife *d* 1954); two *s. Educ:* King's School, Peterborough. Solicitor, 1924; Solicitor with Bradford Corpn,

1924-25; Senior Assistant Solicitor, Hull, 1925-30; Deputy Town Clerk, Hull, 1930-34; Town Clerk, Hull, 1934-45. Served Royal Navy, 1916-19. *Recreation:* gardening. *Address:* 7 Wedgwood Close, Northwood, Mddx. *T:* Northwood 27286.
                                   [*Died* 6 *Sept.* 1972.

PICKERING, Sir George Hunter, Kt 1932; BA Oxon; Barrister-at-law (Inner Temple); *b* 7 Nov. 1877; 2nd *s* of George Pickering, Stone, Staffs; *m* 1917, Phyllis Mary Stubbs (*d* 1955); one *s* one *d. Educ:* Forest School; Hertford College, Oxford. Called to Bar, 1903; Member of the Western Circuit until 1907, when joined Mr O. Tonks, practising advocate in the BEA Protectorate; Town Magistrate, 1910; acted Judge of the High Court of Kenya, 1915-17, when appointed Judge and member of the Court of Appeal for Eastern Africa; Chief Justice of HBM's Court, Zanzibar, 1928-32; retired 1932. *Address:* South Cross, Bodicote, Banbury, Oxon.   [*Died* 13 *April* 1974.

PICKERING, Sir George White, Kt 1957; FRS 1960; MD, FRCP; Master of Pembroke College, Oxford, 1968-74; Hon. Fellow, 1974; *b* 26 June 1904; *s* of George and Ann Pickering, Whalton, Northumberland; *m* 1930, Mary Carola, *y d* of late Sir A. C. Seward, FRS; one *s* three *d. Educ:* Dulwich College; Pembroke College, Cambridge (Scholar); St Thomas' Hospital (Scholar). 1st Class Honours Nat. Sci. Tripos, Pts I, 1925 and II, 1926; MB 1930; MD 1955; FRCP 1938. Formerly Asst in Dept of Clinical Res. and Lectr in Cardio-vascular Pathology, UCH, and Mem., Scientific Staff MRC; Herzstein Lectr, Stanford Univ. and Univ. of California, 1938; Sims British Commonwealth Travelling Prof., 1949; subsequently Vis. Prof. in many American and Canadian Univs. Member: UGC, 1944-54; MRC and Clinical Res. Bd, 1954-58; Prof. of Medicine, Univ. of London and Dir of Medical Clinic. St Mary's Hosp., London, 1939-56; Regius Prof. of Medicine, Oxford Univ., Student of Christ Church, Master of God's House in Ewelme, and Physician to the United Oxford Hospitals, 1956-Dec. 1968; Pro-Vice-Chancellor, Oxford Univ., 1967-69; Emeritus Student of Christ Church, 1969, Hon. Student 1977. Member: Lord Chancellor's Cttee on Legal Educn, 1967-71; Council for Scientific Policy, 1968-71; Trustee: Beit Memorial Fellowship; Ciba Foundation. Pres. BMA, 1963-64. Stouffer Prize (jtly), 1970. Hon. degrees: DSc: Durham, 1957, Dartmouth (US), 1960, Hull, 1972; ScD, Trinity Coll., Dublin, 1962; MD: Ghent, 1948, Siena, 1965, Univ. W Aust., 1965; LLD: Manchester, 1964, Nottingham, 1965; DUniv 1969. Hon. Fellow: Pembroke College, Cambridge, 1959; Pembroke College, Oxford, 1974; American College of Physicians; American Medical Association; RCP Edinburgh; RCP Ireland; Acad. of Medicine of Mexico; Royal Soc. of Uppsala; Hon. FRSM; Hon. Member: Assoc. of American Physicians; American Gastro-enterological Assoc.; Swedish Medical Soc.; Australian Med. Assoc.; Argentine Medical Assoc.; Corresp. Mem., Deutschen Gesellschaft für Innere Medizin, 1970; Membre correspondant étranger, Soc. Med. des Hôpitaux de Paris; Foreign Hon. Member: Amer. Academy of Arts and Sciences; Czechoslovakian Med. Soc.; Hellenic Cardiac Soc.; Royal Belgian Acad. of Medicine; Danish Soc. for Internal Medicine; Foreign Associate, Amer. Nat. Acad. of Sciences, 1970. *Publications:* High Blood Pressure, 1955 (2nd edn, 1968); The Nature of Essential Hypertension, 1961; The Challenge to Education, 1967; Hypertension: Causes, Consequences and Management, 1970; Creative Malady, 1974; Quest for Excellence in Medical Education, 1978; papers relating to vascular disease, high blood pressure, peptic ulcer, headache and education. *Recreations:* gardening, fishing. *Address:* 5 Horwood Close, Headington, Oxford. *T:* Oxford 64260. *Club:* Athenæum.
                                   [*Died* 3 *Sept.* 1980.

PICKERING, Hon. Wilfred Francis; Hon. Mr Justice Pickering; Justice of Appeal of the Supreme Court of Hong Kong, since 1976; barrister-at-law (formerly solicitor); *b* 4 Dec. 1915; *o s* of late Wilfred Clayton Pickering and Catherine Pickering (née Pender); *m* 1939, Dorothy Adamson; two *d* (one *s* decd). *Educ:* Panton Coll.; Victoria Univ. of Manchester (LLB triple prizeman). Admitted to the Rolls, solicitor, 1938; called to Bar, Gray's Inn, 1963. Served War, RAF, 1940-46 (Flt Lt). Head of German Courts Dept, Land Niedersachsen, 1946-51; Mem., Supreme Restitution Court (internat.), 1951-55. Stipendiary Magistrate, Hong Kong, 1955-57; Chm., Cttee of Review, and Pres., Tenancy Tribunal, Hong Kong, 1957-60; Actg District Judge, 1960-62; District Judge, 1962; Judicial Comr, State of Brunei, 1967; Judge of Supreme Court, Hong Kong, 1970. *Recreations:* swimming, walking. *Address:* Supreme Court, Hong Kong. *Clubs:* Royal Over-Seas League; Hong Kong, LRC (Hong Kong).   [*Died* 2 *May* 1980.

PICKFORD, Mary; actress; sometime partner in three producing companies in Hollywood: Comet, Triangle and Artists Alliance, and part owner, with others, of United Artists Corporation; sold holdings in United Artists, 1956; *b* Toronto, Canada, 8 April 1893 (family name Smith); mother a character actress; *m* 1st, Owen Moore (divorced, 1919); 2nd, 1920, Douglas Fairbanks (divorced, 1935); 3rd, 1937, Charles Buddy Rogers; one adopted *s* one adopted *d*. Debut on stage at 5; first marked success was in motion pictures, in Hearts Adrift; returned to stage in A Good Little Devil and Warrens of Virginia. Returned to motion pictures as star; best known pictures: Tess of the Storm Country, Stella Maris, Daddy Long Legs, Pollyanna, Rebecca of Sunny Brook Farm, Poor Little Rich Girl, Little Lord Fauntleroy, My Best Girl, etc.; also talking pictures Coquette (Academy of Motion Picture Arts and Sciences award), Taming of the Shrew, Kiki and Secrets. Mem. Bd Directors, Thomas Alva Edison Foundation; Mem. Edison Pioneers; Director, American Society for the Aged, Inc. Apptd Mem. Nat. Advisory Cttee for White House Conf. on Aging, 1959. Holds several awards both American and foreign, for public and political service and for war work. Holds Hon. Degrees. *Publications:* Why not try God?, 1934; The Demi Widow, 1935; My Rendezvous With Life, 1935; Sunshine and Shadow, 1956; many magazine articles. *Address:* 9350 Wilshire Boulevard, Beverly Hills, Calif 90212, USA. *[Died 29 May 1979.*

PICKLES, Sir John (Sydney), Kt 1958; BSc, MIEE; *b* 2 August 1898; British: *m* 1925, Mary (*d* 1961), *d* of Bradford Pickton. *Educ:* Manchester University. The Yorkshire Electric Power Co., Leeds, 1921-31; County Electrical Engineer, Dumfries County Council, 1931-47; Chairman, South of Scotland Electricity Board, 1955-62. *Publications:* papers on Rural Electrification, read before Inst. of Electrical Engineers, 1937, 1946. *Club:* Royal Scottish Automobile (Glasgow).
[Died 4 Nov. 1972.

PICKLES, Wilfred, OBE 1950; Radio Actor; *b* 13 Oct. 1904; *s* of Fred Pickles and Margaret Catterall; *m* 1930, Mabel Myerscough; *o s* decd. *Educ:* Parkinson Lane Sch., Halifax, Yorks. First broadcast, 1927, in Children's Hour; became regular broadcaster from the North; apptd N Regional Announcer, 1938, News Reader in London, 1942. First broadcast of Have a Go series, 1946. First Appearance on West End Stage The Gay Dog (comedy), Piccadilly Theatre, in 1952; first film, The Gay Dog, 1954; Television Series, Ask Pickles, 1954; Ride a Cock Horse, Comedy, Blackpool Season, 1957; Billy Liar (film), 1963; The Family Way (film), 1966. *Publications:* Between You and Me (autobiography), 1949; Personal Choice (poetry anthology), 1950; Sometime Never (Reminiscences), 1951; Ne'er forget the people (Portraits of the new Elizabethans), 1953; My North Countrie (anthology of North Country poems, prose, rhymes, jingles and stories), 1954; For Your Delight (anthology of poetry), 1960. *Recreations:* tennis, golf. *Address:* 19 Courcels, Arundel Street, Brighton, East Sussex. *T:* 680613. *[Died 27 March 1978.*

PICKTHORN, Rt. Hon. Sir Kenneth (William Murray), 1st Bt, *cr* 1959; PC 1964; LittD Cantab 1936; Fellow of Corpus Christi College, Cambridge since 1914; *b* 23 April 1892; *e s* of late Charles Wright Pickthorn, master mariner, and late Edith Maud Berkeley Murray; *m* 1924, Nancy Catherine, *d* of late Lewis Matthew Richards, barrister-at-law; two *s* one *d*. *Educ:* Aldenham School; Trinity College, Cambridge. 15th London Regiment and RAF in France and Macedonia; Dean of Corpus, 1919-27; Tutor, 1927-35. Pres., 1937-44. MP (C) Cambridge University, 1935-50, Carlton Division of Nottinghamshire, 1950-66. Parliamentary Sec., Ministry of Education, 1951-Oct. 1954. *Publications:* History of the Peace Conference, vol. i. ch. ii, The German Revolution and the Conditions which Prepared It, 1920; History of the British People, vol. vii., From 1914 to 1922, 1924; Some Historical Principles of the Constitution, 1925; Early Tudor Government, 1934; contributions to various periodicals. *Heir: s* Charles William Richards Pickthorn [*b* 3 Mar. 1927; *m* 1951, Helen, *d* of late Sir James Mann, KCVO; one *s* two *d*]. *Address:* Quay Street, Orford, near Woodbridge, Suffolk. *T:* Orford 273. *Clubs:* Carlton, Army and Navy; University Pitt (Cambridge). *[Died 12 Nov. 1975.*

PICOT, Francis Raymond, CMG 1946; *b* Wellington, NZ, 7 June 1893; *s* of late John Picot; *m* 1917, Mavis, *d* of late Col George Hall, CMG, CBE, VD; one *s* one *d*. Bank of NSW, Wellington, 1910-17; Director of Internal Marketing, New Zealand, 1937; NZ Member Eastern Group Supply Council, India, 1940-41; Pacific Supply Council, Australia, 1941-42; late Commissioner of Supply, New Zealand. *Address:* 16 Benbow Street, St Heliers, Auckland, New Zealand. *[Died 17 July 1971.*

PIDCOCK, Air Vice-Marshal Geoffrey Arthur Henzell, CB 1948; CBE 1946; *b* 6 Nov. 1897; *s* of Arthur Pidcock, Eastbourne; *m* 1st, 1929, Evelyn Catherine (*d* 1965), *d* of

William Hardacre, Hellifield, Yorks; one *d*; 2nd, 1965, Winifred Iris (Christine), *d* of late Walter Humphry, Sudbury, Suffolk. *Educ:* Haileybury; Imperial Coll. of Science, City & Guilds Branch. Joined RFC 1916; service in France with Nos 1, 60 and 73 Squadrons; RAF 1918; service in India, Iraq and Middle East; specialised in Armament, 1924; Wing Comdr, 1937; service with Ordnance Bd, 1940-41; Dir of Armament Development, Ministry of Aircraft Production, 1941-44; Temp. Air Vice-Marshal, 1944; first RAF Pres., Ordnance Bd, 1945-47; Subst. Air Vice-Marshal, 1947; last Dir-Gen. of Armament, Air Ministry 1947-51; retired 1951; Head of Controls Division, Agence de Contrôle des Armements, Western European Union, Paris, 1955-63; Comdr USA Legion of Merit, Croix de Guerre (France), 1918. *Recreations:* reminiscence and travel. *Address:* Poynings, Winchester Road, Andover, Hants. *Club:* Royal Air Force. *[Died 12 Feb. 1976.*

PIERSON, Warren Lee; Chairman, All America Cable and Radio; Director: Vertientes-Camaguey Sugar Co., Cuba; Molybdenum Corporation of America; The Commercial Cable Co.; ITT World Communications Inc.; Twin Fair, Inc., etc; *b* Princeton, Minn, 29 Aug. 1896; *s* of Louis W. and Hilda Pearson Pierson; *m* 1927, Eleanor Mehnert; no *c. Educ:* Univ. of California (AB); Harvard Univ. (LLB). Pres. and Gen. Counsel, Export-Import Bank, 1936-45; Special Counsel, Reconstruction Finance Corp., 1933-34; Mem. Nat. Emergency Council, 1934-36; Adviser to US Delegation: at 3rd meeting, Consultation of Ministers, Amer. Republics, Rio de Janeiro, 1942; at UN Monetary Conf., Bretton Woods NH, 1944; at Inter-American Conf. on Problems of War and Peace, Mexico City, 1945. US Member of Tripartite Commission on German Debts, 1951-53; Pres., International Chamber of Commerce, 1955. Has several Orders of foreign countries. *Address:* (office) 320 Park Avenue, New York, NY 10022. *T:* Plaza 2-6000; Further Lane, East Hampton, Long Island. *T:* (516) 324-1066. *Clubs:* Brook (New York); Maidstone, Devon Yacht (Long Island).
[Died 12 Jan. 1978.

PIGGOTT, Colonel Joseph Clive, CBE 1944; MC; DL; *b* 2 February 1892; *s* of George Thomas Piggott; unmarried. *Educ:* Greenhill School, Moseley, Birmingham. Business career with Williams Brothers and Piggott Ltd, Birmingham, Brassfounders and Manufacturers of Brass and Copper Tubes. Commission with Coldstream Guards, 1915-19, and served in France with unit, Aug. 1915-Jan. 1919. Home Guard Comdr Warwickshire (Birmingham) Home Guard, 1941-45. DL Warwickshire, 1945. *Recreations:* motoring and walking. *Address:* 35 Park Hill, Birmingham B13 8DR. *T:* 021-449 0347. *[Died 6 Nov. 1975.*

PIGOT, Brig.-Gen. Sir Robert, 6th Bt, of Patshull, *cr* 1764; DSO 1916; MC; Brevet Lieutenant Colonel Rifle Brigade, retired; *b* 3 May 1882; *s* of Sir G. Pigot, 5th Bt, and Alice, *d* of Sir James Thompson Mackenzie, 1st Bt, of Glen Muick; *S* father, 1934; *m* 1913, Norah Beatrice Oakley, *y d* of C. Reginald Hargreaves, Remenham, Bucks; three *d*. Served European War 1914-18 (despatches, DSO, MC, Bt Maj.); Flying Officer RAFVR, 1939; resigned commn with rank of Wing Comdr, 1944. *Publication:* Twenty-five Years' Big-Game Hunting, 1928. *Heir: n* Maj.-Gen. Robert Anthony Pigot, CB, OBE. *Address:* Yarlington Lodge, Wincanton, Somerset. *[Died 27 Dec. 1977.*

PIGOTT, Alan Desmond Frederick P.; *see* Pemberton-Pigott.

PIGOTT, Brig. Frank Borkman, CB 1954; CIE 1946; late RE; *b* 1894. Served European War, 1914-18, in France, Belgium and the Balkans (wounded, despatches); War of 1939-45 (Burma star, medal). Formerly Deputy Engineer-in-Chief and Director of Works, Army Headquarters, India. Member of the Institution of Engineers, India; Associate Member of the Institution of Mechanical Engineers; Associate Member of the Institution of Electrical Engineers; Associate of City and Guilds of London Institute. *Address:* c/o Lloyds Bank, 6 Pall Mall, SW1.
[Died 17 Dec. 1971.

PIGOTT, Rt. Rev. Harold Grant, CBE 1969; *b* 20 Aug. 1894; *s* of Robert and Rosalind Pigott. *Educ:* Antigua Gram. Sch.; Codrington Coll., Barbados. BA 1916, MA 1918. Head Master Parry Sch., Barbados and Curate St Lucy, 1917-21. St Vincent: Curate, Cath., 1921; then Rector of Barrouallie, 1921-26, and of Calliaqua, 1926-33. Archdeacon of St Vincent and St Lucia, 1929-45; Canon of Cath. St Vincent, 1929-62, and Rector of Georgetown, 1933-37, Grenada. Rector: St Andrew, 1937-45, St George, 1945-62; Archdeacon of Grenada, 1945-62. Bishop of Windward Islands, 1962-69. Coronation Medal, 1953. *Publication:* Daily Meditations on the Lenten Epistles, 1939. *Address:* c/o PO Box 128, Sion Hill, St Vincent, Windward Islands. *[Died 26 Aug. 1979.*

PIGOTT, Harry, MB, ChB; a Member of the National Assistance Board, 1957-66. *Educ:* Manchester University. MB, ChB, Manchester, 1926. Member of Manchester Corporation; Member, Management Committee, Regional Hospital Board, 1953. *Address:* Greenacre, Fletsand Road, Wilmslow, Cheshire. *T:* Wilmslow 25848.   *[Died 10 Dec. 1974.*

PIGOTT, Group Captain Joseph Ruscombe Wadham S.; *see* Smyth-Pigott.

PIKE, Prof. Douglas Henry; General-Editor, Australian Dictionary of Biography, 1962; Professor, Australian National University, 1964; *b* 3 Nov. 1908; *s* of Douglas and Louise Pike; *m* 1941, Olive Hagger; two *s. Educ:* China Inland Mission School, Chefoo, N China; University of Adelaide. BA 1947 (First Class Hons), MA 1951, DLitt 1957. Lecturer, 1948; Lecturer in History, Univ. of Western Australia, 1949-50; Reader in History, Univ. of Adelaide, 1951-60; Prof. of History, Univ. of Tasmania, 1961-63. Commonwealth Fellow, St John's Coll., Cambridge, 1969-70. Ernest Scott Prize, Univ. of Melbourne, 1969; Enc. Britannica Award for Literature, 1971. *Publications:* Paradise of Dissent: South Australia, 1829-1857, 1957, 2nd edn 1967; Australia: The Quiet Continent, 1962, 2nd edn 1970; Charles Hawker, 1968; General Editor, Australian Dictionary of Biography, 1788-1850: vol. 1, A-H, 1966; vol. 2, I-Z, 1967; 1851-1891: vol. 3, A-C, 1969; vol. 4, D-J, 1972. *Address:* Australian National University, Canberra, ACT 2600, Australia.   *[Died 19 May 1974.*

PIKE, Most Rev. Robert Bonsall, MA (Dublin), Hon. DD Dublin; Bishop of Meath, since 1959; *b* 19 Oct. 1905; *s* of Rev. Canon William Pike and Harriet Florence (*née* Surridge); *m* 1938, Helen Kathleen Joan Moffat-Wilson; two *s* two *d. Educ:* Trinity Coll., Dublin. Deacon, 1929; Priest, 1930; Curate, Drumcree, 1929-35; Curate-in-charge, Aghavilly, 1935-36; Incumbent, Maryborough with Dysart Enos (with Ballyfin, 1950-57), 1936-57; Rural Dean of Aghade, 1942-57; Prebendary of Tullomagimma in Leighlin Cathedral and Aghour in St Canice's Cathedral, Kilkenny, 1951-57; Diocesan Sec., Diocese of Leighlin, 1952-59; Incumbent of Kilkenny-Freshford Group. Dean of Ossory, Canon of Aghold (Leighlin) and Rural Dean of Aghour, 1957-59. Examining Chaplain to Bp of Ossory, 1958. *Address:* Bishop's House, Killucan, Westmeath, Ireland. *T:* Killucan 74144. *Clubs:* University, Royal Irish Automobile (Dublin).   *[Died 27 Dec. 1973.*

PILDITCH, Sir Denys, Kt 1944; CIE 1941; 2nd *s* of Frank Slater Pilditch; *m* 1919, Phyllis Charsley (*d* 1938), *d* of late John Roberts, Hinton Charterhouse, Somerset; one *d* (and one *s* decd); *m* 1948, Mary Joyce (*d* 1975), widow of Arthur Yencken and *er d* of George Russell, Langi Willi, Linton, Vic, Aust. *Educ:* Tonbridge School. Joined Indian Police, UP, 1912; Temp. Commission, Indian Army, 1918-19; Superintendent, 1924; Central Intelligence Officer, Govt of India, 1936; Deputy Director, Intelligence Bureau, 1936; Director, Intelligence Bureau, 1939-45; Adviser to Secretary of State for India, 1947. King's Police Medal, 1933, Bar to Medal, 1935.
                                             [Died 4 Sept. 1975.

PILE, Gen. Sir Frederick Alfred, 2nd Bt, *cr* 1900; GCB 1945 (KCB 1941; CB 1938); DSO 1918; MC; LLD (Hon.) Leeds 1946; late Royal Tank Corps; *b* 14 Sept. 1884; *e s* of Sir T. D. Pile, 1st Bt, and Caroline Maude (*d* 1948), *d* of John M. Nicholson, JP, Dublin; *S* father, 1931; *m* 1st, 1915, Vera Millicent (whom he divorced, 1929), *d* of Brig.-Gen. Lloyd; two *s*; 2nd, 1932, Hester (*d* 1949), *o d* of late George Phillimore, BCL, Shedfield, Hants; 3rd, 1951, Molly Eveline Louise Mary (late Chief Comdr, ATS), *o d* of late Ralph Smyth, Newtown, Drogheda, County Louth, Ireland, widow of Brigadier Francis Wyville Home. RA 1904; Capt., 1914; Major, 1916; Bt Lt-Col, 1919; Lt-Col, 1927; Colonel, 1928; Maj.-Gen. 1937; Lieut-Gen, 1939; General 1941; served European War, 1914-18 (despatches, DSO, MC); Asst Dir of Mechanisation, War Office, 1928-32; Commander, Canal Brigade, Egypt, 1932-36; Commander, 1st Anti-Aircraft Division TA, 1937-39; GOC-in-C, Anti-Aircraft Command, 1939-45; Dir-Gen. Ministry of Works, 1945; Col-Comdt RA, 1945-52; Chairman: Cementation Co. Ltd, 1961-63 (Director, 1945-61); Fothergill & Harvey Ltd, 1956-64; Katherine Low Settlement, Battersea, 1951-63; Chartered Nurses' Soc.; Management Cttee, Herts Training School, 1950-67 (Mem. 1958-). *Heir: s* Frederick Devereux Pile, MC 1945; Col late Royal Tank Regt [*b* 10 Dec. 1915; *m* 1940, Pamela, *d* of late Philip Henstock, Falkland Garth, Newbury; two *d*]. *Address:* Broom Manor, Cottered, Herts. *T:* Cottered 298.
                                             [Died 14 Nov. 1976.

PILKINGTON, Margaret, OBE 1956; Deputy Chairman, Whitworth Art Gallery, and Hon. Director, 1935-59; Founder Red Rose Guild of Craftsmen, 1920; Member of Manchester City Art Galleries Committee, since 1925; *b* 25 Nov. 1891; *d* of Lawrence Pilkington and Mary Gavin Stevenson. *Educ:* Croham Hurst School, South Croydon; Slade School of Art. President: Manchester Luncheon Club, 1963; Manchester Literary and Philosophical Society, 1964, 1965. JP Manchester, 1945. Hon. MA Manchester Univ., 1942. *Address:* Firwood, Alderley Edge, Cheshire. *T:* Alderley 2309. *Club:* University Women's.   *[Died 2 Aug. 1974.*

PILKINGTON, Captain Sir Richard Antony, KBE 1961; MC 1940; *b* St Helens, 10 May 1908; *s* of Arthur Richard Pilkington and Marjorie, *d* of Sir Arthur Cope, KCVO, RA; *m* 1946, Rosemary (*née* Russell-Roberts); three *d. Educ:* Charterhouse; Oxford. Worked in Canada on a farm in 1928; joined Coldstream Guards in 1930; resigned Commission in 1935. Served War of 1939-45 (MC). Subsequently R of O, Coldstream Guards. MP (C) for Widnes, 1935-45, for Poole, 1951-64; PPS to Mr O. Stanley, Pres. Bd of Trade, 1939; Civil Lord of the Admiralty, 1942-45. Has travelled in Europe, Asia, Africa and America. *Recreations:* history, walking Roman roads, family genealogies, motor cars. *Address:* 1 Ilchester Place, W14; Rainford Hall, St Helens, Lancs.   *[Died 9 Dec. 1976.*

PILKINGTON JACKSON, Charles d'Orville; *see* Jackson.

PILLING, Tom Sharpley; Under Secretary, Department of Industry, since 1975; *b* 17 July 1921; *s* of George Frederick Pilling and Annie Pilling; *m* 1947, Alice Evelyn Buchan; two *d. Educ:* Roundhay Sch., Leeds; Leeds Univ. (BCom Hons 1942). Asst Principal, Treasury, 1944-46; Economist/Statistician, UK/Dominion Wool Disposals Ltd, 1946-51; Statistician, BoT, 1951-60; Central Statistical Office: Chief Stat., 1960-66; Asst Dir (Under-Sec.), 1966-71; Under-Sec., DTI, 1971-72; Asst Dir, Cent. Statist. Office, 1972-75. *Recreations:* mountain walking, industrial archaeology. *Address:* 19 Starts Close, Orpington, Kent BR6 8NU. *T:* Farnborough (Kent) 53570.
                                             [Died 9 Jan. 1977.

PING, Aubrey Charles, FCIT; Industrial and Transport Consultant, since 1970; *b* 2 Dec. 1905; *s* of Thomas Walton Ping, Middleton Cheney, Oxon, and Hester Louisa (*née* Barden), Banbury, Oxon; *m* 1936, Constance, 2nd *d* of John and Rose Bryant, Finchley; three *s. Educ:* Manor Lane LCC School; Brockley County School. Railway clerk and official, 1922-43; various hon. Trade Union offices, 1926-43; broadcasting to French Transport Workers, 1941-43. Served War of 1939-45, Captain, Allied Commission, Italy, 1944; Major Exec. Officer and Chief Operations Branch, Allied Commission, Italy, 1945, Lt-Col Asst Director, Rome European Central Inland Transport Organisation, 1946; special purposes asst to Continental Supt, British Rlys (Southern), 1947; Lecturer, International Transport, Southern Railway Training College, 1947-49. International Transport Consultant, Central Engineering Co. Ltd, 1951-70; Chairman: Air Terminals Ltd, 1958-69; British Air Services Ltd, 1966-69; Dep. Chm., BEA Helicopters Ltd, 1967-70. Director: Gibraltar Airways, 1952-70; Cyprus Airways, 1953-58; Jersey Airlines Development Corporation, 1961; Cambrian Airways, 1963-69; BKS Air Transport, 1964-69; Schreiner BEA Helicopters NV, 1968-70; HTS Management Holdings and HTS Management Consultants, 1970-72. Mem. Bd, BEA, 1949-70; Chm. Jt Council for Civil Aviation, 1956. Dep. Chm., Airways Housing Trust, 1965-70; Chm. BEA Housing Assoc. and BEA Silver Wing Club, 1957-69. MInst Traffic Administration, 1953; FCIT 1955. *Recreations:* reading, gardening, writing. *Address:* 39a Claremont Road, Seaford, East Sussex. *Club:* Special Forces.   *[Died 12 July 1978.*

PINK, Ven. Hubert Arthur Stanley, MA; Archdeacon of Hampstead, 1964-74, Archdeacon Emeritus since 1974; Rector of St Andrew Undershaft, 1965-74; Examining Chaplain to the Bishop of London, 1964-74; *b* 22 Jan. 1905; *s* of Arthur Penrhyn Stanley and Edith Mary Pink. *Educ:* Ipswich Sch.; Selwyn Coll., Cambridge; Westcott House Theological Coll. Asst Master, Ipswich Sch., 1927-33; Chaplain, 1931-33; Asst-Curate: S Augustine, Ipswich, 1928-31; Whittlesford, 1933-35; Vicar of Canvey Island, 1935-38; Rector of Little Ilford, 1938-46; Dir of Religious Educn, Dio. Chelmsford, 1945-47; Gen. Sec., Nat. Soc. for Religious Educn, and Sec., C of E Sch. Council, 1947-51; Rector of Hackney, 1951-65; Prebendary of St Paul's, 1963-64. *Recreations:* walking, reading. *Address:* 8 The Beeches, Horringer, Bury St Edmunds, Suffolk.   *[Died 22 Dec. 1976.*

PINNELL, Leonard George, CIE 1938; *b* 10 June 1896; *s* of Charles John Pinnell and Clara Matilda Wills; *m* 1924, Margaret Blake (*d* 1976), *d* of Dr C. F. Coxwell; two *s. Educ:* City of London School; Balliol Coll., Oxford (Exhibitioner). Served European War, 1915-18, 10th Bedfordshire Regt, later

Machine Gun Corps, Salonica; British Military Mission to USA (1917) and France; entered Indian Civil Service, 1920; served in Bengal, Survey and Settlement, Chief Manager Dacca Nawab Estate, and Districts; Private Sec. to the Governor of Bengal, 1935; Sec. to the Governor, 1937-40 and 1945; Supervisor ICS Training, 1940-42; Acting PSV 1942; Dir Civil Supplies, Bengal, 1942; Comr Chittagong and Presidency Divs, 1943-44; Principal Officers' Training Course, 1944-45; Develt Comr and *ex officio* Addl Chief Sec., 1946; Chief Admin Officer Industrial and Commercial Finance Corp. Ltd, 1948-51; advisory mission to Greece, 1951; Domestic Bursar, St John's Coll., Oxford, 1953-60. *Address:* c/o Lloyds Bank Ltd, High Street, Winchester, Hants.   *[Died* 11 *May* 1979.

PINNOCK, Frank Frewin, CMG 1948; late Overseas Supplies Commissioner, Ministry of Food; *b* 28 Sept. 1902; *s* of Charles George and Florence Pinnock; *m* 1928, Rosalind Mary (*née* Scott); three *d. Educ:* City of London Sch. Formerly Director of several companies engaged in export and import of foodstuffs. Commissioned RAF, 1940; lent to Ministry of Food at Washington, 1941, and continued as Temporary Civil Servant until Oct. 1952. *Address:* The Small House, Lavant, West Sussex.   *[Died* 2 *Feb.* 1977.

PINSENT, Gerald Hume Saverie, CB 1949; CMG 1935; Comptroller-General, National Debt Office, 1946-51; *b* 25 May 1888; *s* of Ross and Alice Mary Pinsent; *m* 1st, 1915, Katharine Kentisbeare (*d* 1949), *d* of late Sir George Radford, MP; two *d* ; 2nd, 1939, Margot (*d* 1950), *d* of Johann Georg von Bonin; 3rd, 1972, Luba, *widow* of Sir Lionel Fletcher. *Educ:* King's Sch., Canterbury; Trinity Coll., Cambridge (Senior Scholar). BA 1910; MA 1912; 2nd Class Clerk in Treasury, 1911; Assistant Secretary, Treasury, 1931; Financial Adviser, HM Embassy, Berlin, 1932-39, HM Embassy, Washington, 1939-41; British Food Mission, Ottawa, 1942, 1943; Principal Assistant Secretary, Board of Trade, 1943. Principal Assistant Secretary, Treasury, 1944. *Address:* The Mews Flat, 15 London Road, Saffron Walden, Essex.   *[Died* 27 *Feb.* 1976.

PINSENT, Sir Roy, 2nd Bt, *cr* 1938; *b* 22 July 1883; *e s* of Sir Richard Alfred Pinsent, 1st Bt, and Laura Proctor (*d* 1931), *d* of Thomas Ryland; *S* father, 1948; *m* 1918, Mary Tirzah (*d* 1951), *d* of Dr Edward Geoffrey Walls, Spilsby, Lincs; two *s* one *d. Educ:* Marlborough; University College, Oxford (BA). Admitted Solicitor, 1909; served European War, 1916-19, Lieut, RE. *Heir: s* Christopher Roy Pinsent [*b* 2 Aug. 1922; *m* 1951, Susan Mary, *d* of John Norton Scorer, Fotheringhay; one *s* two *d*]. *Address:* 5 St George's Square, SW1. *T:* 01-828 7282.
                                                    [Died 16 *Dec.* 1978.

PIPER, Air Marshal Sir Tim, (Thomas William), KBE 1968 (CBE 1958; OBE 1950); CB 1964; AFC 1941; *b* 11 Oct. 1911; *s* of late Thomas Edward Piper, Ackleton Hall, Worfield, Shropshire; *m* 1947, Betty Bedford, *d* of late William Bedford Mitchell, Irwin, Western Australia; no *c. Educ:* Trent College. Joined RAF, 1936; served War of 1939-45, in Bomber Command (UK) (despatches thrice); pow, 1941-45; OC, RAF Schwechat, Austria, 1946-47; Germany (Berlin Air Lift), 1948-49, Middle East, 1950-53; OC, RAF Dishforth, 1953-55; Group Captain, Plans, Transport Command, 1955-58; Director of Operational Requirements, Air Ministry, 1958-60; Chief of Staff, Near East Command, 1960-62; AOC No 38 Group, RAF, 1962-64; Comdt, RAF Staff Coll., 1965-66; UK Mem., Permanent Military Deputies Group, Central Treaty Organisation, 1966-68; retd, 1968. Group Capt., 1953; Air Cdre, 1959; Air Vice-Marshal, 1960; Air Marshal, 1966; psa, 1947; jssc, 1950. *Recreations:* shooting, fishing. *Address:* Chirton Cottage, Chirton, Devizes, Wilts. *T:* Chirton 289. *Clubs:* Army and Navy, Royal Air Force.   *[Died* 1 *Jan.* 1978.

PIPON, Vice-Admiral Sir James Murray, KBE 1937 (OBE 1919); CB 1935; CMG 1924; MVO 1921; Royal Navy, retired; *b* 25 Oct. 1882; *e s* of late Captain John P. Pipon, CB, CMG, RN; *m* 1921, Bertha Louisa Victoria, 2nd *d* of 1st Baron Roborough; one *s* two *d. Educ:* HMS Britannia. Comdr 1915; Captain 1920; Rear-Admiral, 1932; Naval Attaché to British Embassies at Paris, Brussels, etc., 1925-28; Chief of Staff to Commander-in-Chief, Plymouth, 1929-30; HMS Royal Sovereign, 1930-32; Commodore of RN Barracks, Devonport, 1932-34; Rear-Admiral in charge and Admiral Superintendent, HM Dockyard, Gibraltar, 1935-37; retired list, 1936; Senior British Naval Officer, Suez Canal, 1940-42; Flag Officer in charge Southampton, 1942-45. *Address:* Shepherds Crown, Compton Down, Winchester, Hants. *T:* Twyford (Hants) 3253. *Club:* United Service.   *[Died* 14 *Jan.* 1971.

PIRIE, Air Chief Marshal Sir George Clark, KCB 1951 (CB 1943); KBE 1946 (CBE 1942); MC; DFC; LLD; RAF retired,

formerly a Barrister-at-law; *b* 28 July 1896; *m* 1926, Dora Kennedy; one *s* one *d*. Served European War, 1914-18; Deputy Director Operations, Air Ministry, 1936-37; Air Attaché, Washington, 1937-40; Middle East, 1941-43; Director-General Organisation, Air Ministry, 1943-45; Allied Air Commander-in-Chief, SE Asia, 1946-47; Inspector-General, RAF, 1948; Member, Air Council for Supply and Organisation, 1948-50; Head of Air Force Staff, British Joint Services Mission to US, 1950-51; retired RAF, 1951. Chairman, Air League of the British Empire, 1955-58. *Address:* Cottage 13, Headbourne Worthy, Winchester SO23 7JG. *Club:* Royal Air Force.
                                                    [Died 21 *Jan.* 1980.

PIRIE-GORDON of Buthlaw, Christopher Martin, CMG 1967; OBE 1949; HM Diplomatic Service, retired; *b* 28 Sept. 1911; *er s* of late Harry Pirie-Gordon of Buthlaw, OBE, DSC, and late Mabel Alicia, *d* of George Earle Buckle, sometime Editor of The Times; unmarried; *S* father as 14th Laird of Buthlaw, 1969. *Educ:* Harrow; Magdalen Coll., Oxford. Palestine Admin Service, 1935; First Secretary and Consul, British Legation, Amman, 1946 (on secondment from Colonial Service); resigned, 1949; a Secretary to Order of St John of Jerusalem, 1950-51; entered Foreign Service, 1951; Asst Political Agent, Kuwait, 1952; Political Agent, Trucial States at Dubai, 1953; Eastern Dept, FO, 1955; Chargé d'Affaires, the Yemen, 1958; Consul, Innsbruck, 1960; Consul, Florence, and Consul-General, San Marino, 1963-70, retired 1970. Mem., Queen's Body Guard for Scotland, The Royal Co. of Archers. Lay Administrator, Dio. of Gibraltar, 1971-. CStJ 1967. Order of Merit, Italy, 1973. *Recreations:* dining, wining and talking. *Address:* Via Palestro 3, 50123 Florence, Italy. *T:* Florence 29.87.59. *Club:* Athenæum.
                                                    [Died 16 *July* 1980.

PISTON, Walter, AB, MusDoc; Professor of Music, Harvard University, 1944-Aug. 1960, retired; now Professor of Music Emeritus; *b* Rockland, Maine, USA, 20 Jan. 1894; *s* of Walter Piston and Leona Stover; *m* 1920, Kathryn Nason; no *c. Educ:* Harvard Univ., chiefly. Graduated Harvard Coll., 1924 (AB). Member faculty of music department at Harvard since 1926; John Knowles Paine Fellowship, 1924-26; studied in Paris with Nadia Boulanger; Guggenheim Fellowship; Member of American Academy of Arts and Letters and of American Academy of Arts and Sciences; numerous awards and commissions for compositions (Pulitzer prize, 1948, for Symphony No. 3); second Pulitzer prize, 1961, for Symphony No. 7; appointed to new Chair of Music at Harvard; Walter W. Naumberg Professor of Music, 1948. Hon. Doctor of Music, Harvard Univ., 1952. *Publications:* music: 8 Symphonies, 5 string quartets, ballet, orchestral works, various chamber music works, violin concerto, etc., all published, some recorded; books: Harmonic Analysis, 1933; Harmony, 1941; Counterpoint, 1947; Orchestration, 1955. *Address:* 127 Somerset Street, Belmont, Mass 02178, USA. *Club:* Harvard.   *[Died* 12 *Nov.* 1976.

PITMAN, Captain Charles Robert Senhouse, CBE 1950; DSO 1917; MC; Indian Army (retired); Game Warden, Uganda Protectorate, 1925-May 1951; retired; Acting Game Warden, N Rhodesia (seconded for two years from Uganda), 1931-33; Member of Uganda Defence Force, 1940-44; OC Uganda Defence Force, 1941-44; seconded from Game Department as Director, Security Intelligence, Uganda, 1941-46; *b* Bombay, 19 March 1890; *o s* of late C. E. Pitman, CIE; *m* 1924, Marjorie Fielding, *yr d* of late M. M. A. Duncan, Alpha, OFS. *Educ:* Royal Naval Sch., Eltham; Blundell's Sch., Tiverton; Royal Military Coll., Sandhurst (King's India Cadet). Gazetted to Indian Army as 2nd Lieut unattached, 1909; attached for one year to Royal Warwickshire Regt, 1st Bn; posted to 27th Punjabis, 1910; Lieut, 1911; Captain, 1915; served in Egypt, 1914-15; France, 1915; Mesopotamia, 1916-18 (wounded, despatches twice, MC, DSO); Palestine, 1918-20; resigned commn IA, 1921; Scientific Fellow, Zoological Soc. of London; Life Mem. and Vice-Pres. Fauna Preservation Soc. (representative, Rare Breeds (Domestic) Survival Trust); Life Member: E Africa Natural History Soc.; Uganda Soc.; Nigerian Field Soc.; S African Ornithological Soc.; Wildfowl Trust; Wig and Pen Club; British Ornithologists' Union; British Ornithologists Club; Hon. Life Mem., Game Rangers' Assoc. of Africa; Member: St George's (Hanover Square) Branch of British Legion; Officers' Assoc.; Jersey Wildlife Preservation Trust; RHS; Royal Nat. Lifeboat Instn. *Publications:* A Game Warden among his Charges, 1931 (Penguin Edition, 1943); A Report on a Faunal Survey of Northern Rhodesia, 1934; A Guide to the Snakes of Uganda, 1938, rev. edn 1974; A Game Warden Takes Stock, 1942; Common Antelopes, 1956; (monograph) Ethology and Ecology of the Giant Eagle Owl (Bubolacteus) of Africa, 1975; contributor to: A New Dictionary of Birds, 1964, and to Bulletin, British Ornithologists' Club; Uganda Journal, etc. *Recreation:* natural science. *Address:* c/o

National Westminster Bank Ltd, Exeter Bank Branch, 65 High Street, Exeter, Devon EX4 3DR; Leicester Court Hotel, 41 Queen's Gate Gardens, SW7 5NB.   *[Died 18 Sept. 1975.*

PITMAN, Clement Fothergill, MA; FMA 1952; Curator and Art Director, Nottingham Castle Museum and Art Gallery, Nottingham, 1929-59; *b* 1894; *er s* of late W. Hayward Pitman, one of HM's Lieutenants for City of London; *m* 1930, Nora Irene Greenwood (*d* 1966). *Educ:* privately; St John's Coll., Oxford. Private Sec. to the Sec. of the War Trade Intelligence Dept, 1919; sometime Official Lecturer at the National Gallery; (Univ. of London) Extension Lecturer on the History of European Art, 1926-30. Member of Nottingham University Court, 1948-59. *Publications:* Contributor to: Chambers's Encyclopædia, Vol. III, of The Concise Encyclopædia of Antiques; The Connoisseur. *Address:* Newhouse, St John's Road, Haywards Heath, Sussex. *T:* Haywards Heath 2186.
[Died 11 July 1973.

PITT, Colonel Robert Brindley, CBE 1938; MC; TD; JP, DL; formerly Managing Director of Stothert and Pitt, Ltd, Engineers, Bath; *b* 18 April 1888; *m* 1920, Norah Helen Jacomb-Hood; three *s* one *d*. *Educ:* Rugby Sch.; Clare Coll., Cambridge. Served European War, France, Salonika and Russia, 1914-19. MIMechE. *Recreation:* farming. *Address:* 14 Royal Crescent, Bath. *Clubs:* Junior Carlton; Bath and County (Bath).
[Died 15 April 1974.

PITTS, William Ewart, CBE 1963; QPM 1956; Chief Constable, Derbyshire County Police, 1953-67; *b* 18 Sept. 1900; *s* of William Pitts and Albenia Elizabeth (*née* Nicholls), Swansea; *m* 1923, Doris, *d* of Herbert Whiteley, Wakefield, Yorks; one *d*. *Educ:* Rowsley, Derbyshire. Served European War, Royal Navy, 1914-18. Liverpool City Police: Constable to Chief Superintendent, 1919-49; Bootle County Borough Police, Chief Constable, 1949-53. *Recreations:* golf, fishing, swimming. *Address:* Burre Close Cottage, Station Road, Bakewell, Derbyshire. *T:* Bakewell 2600.   *[Died 1 Oct. 1980.*

PLAMENATZ, John Petrov, FBA 1962; Chichele Professor of Social and Political Theory, University of Oxford, since 1967; Official Fellow of Nuffield College, 1951-67; *b* Cetinje, Montenegro, 16 May 1912; *s* of Peter Plamenatz and Ljubica Matanovitch; came to England, 1919; *m* 1943, Marjorie Hunter; no *c*. *Educ:* Clayesmore Sch.; Oriel Coll., Oxford Univ. MA 1937. University Lecturer in Social and Political Theory, Oxford, 1950-67. Fellow of All Souls Coll., Oxford, 1936-51, and 1967-. *Publications:* Consent, Freedom and Political Obligation, 1938; English Utilitarians, 1950; Revolutionary Movement in France, 1815-71, 1952; From Marx to Stalin, 1953; German Marxism and Russian Communism, 1954; On Alien Rule and Self-Government, 1960; Man and Society, Vols I and II, 1963; Ideology, 1970; Democracy and Illusion, 1973; contributions to Political Studies, British Journal of Sociology, American Political Science Review, etc. *Recreation:* walking. *Address:* All Souls College, Oxford; Scotland Mount, Hook Norton, Banbury, Oxon.   *[Died 19 Feb. 1975.*

PLANT, Sir Arnold, Kt 1947; Economist; Emeritus Professor, University of London; *b* London, 29 April 1898; 2nd *s* of late William C. Plant, FLA; *m* 1925, Edith Render, BA, London; two *s*. *Educ:* Strand Sch.; London School of Economics, University of London. Gerstenberg Scholar in Economics and Political Science, 1921; Bachelor of Commerce, 1922; BSc (Econ.), 1923; previously in engineering; Professor of Commerce and Dean of the Faculty of Commerce in the University of Cape Town, 1924-30 (Hon. LLD, 1968); Professor of Commerce in the University of London, at London School of Economics, 1930-65 (Hon. Fellow, 1967). Vice-Pres., Council, Royal Economic Society; Mem., Cinematograph Films Council, 1938-69; Chairman: Industrial Injuries Advisory Council, 1955-67; Advertising Standards Authority, 1962-65; Colonial Social Science Research Council, 1955-62; Member, Overseas Research Council, 1959-64; Organiser for Ministry of Information, and first Director of Wartime Social Survey, 1940; Chairman, National Service Deferment Cttee for the Cinematograph Industry, Ministry of Labour, 1942-45; temporary civil servant, 1940-46 as Adviser to Ministerial Chairman of Interdepartmental Materials Cttee and Central Priority Cttee under Production Council (1940), Production Executive (1941), Min. of Production (1942-45), and on special duties in Cabinet Office, 1945-46; Member: BoT Cttee on a Central Institute of Management, 1945-46; Min. of Works Cttee on Distribution of Building Materials, 1946; Min. of Education Cttee on Commercial Education, 1946; Board of Trade Cttee on Film Distribution, 1949 (Chm.); Monopolies and Restrictive Practices Commission, 1953-56; Chm., Min. of Agriculture Cttee on Fowl Pest Policy, 1960-62. *Publications:* contributor to:

London Essays in Economics in honour of Edwin Cannan, 1927; Tariffs: the Case Examined, 1931; Cambridge History of British Empire (South Africa Volume, 1936); Some Modern Business Problems (editor), 1937; The Population Problem, 1938; Selected Economic Essays and Addresses, 1974; the scientific economic journals. *Address:* 19 Wildwood Road, NW11. *T:* 01-455 2863.   *[Died 19 April 1978.*

PLASKETT, Harry Hemley, FRS 1936; MA (Oxon); Savilian Professor of Astronomy, Oxford, 1932-60, now Emeritus; *b* Toronto, 5 July 1893; *s* of John Stanley Plaskett, Victoria; *m* 1921, Edith Alice, *d* of John James Smith, barrister, Ottawa; one *s* one *d*. *Educ:* Ottawa Collegiate; Toronto Univ. (BA). Served CFA, France, 1917-18; Astronomer, Dominion Astrophysical Observatory, Victoria, 1919-27; Professor of Astrophysics, Harvard, 1928-32. Served anti-aircraft battery, 1939-40, and worked on experimental navigation for MAP, 1940-44 inc. Gold Medal, Royal Astronomical Society, 1963. Hon. LLD St Andrews, 1961. *Publications:* Papers on observational astrophysics in various journals and observatory publications. *Address:* 48 Blenheim Drive, Oxford OX2 8DQ.
[Died 26 Jan. 1980.

PLATNAUER, Maurice, BLitt, MA; Hon. Fellow of Brasenose College, Oxford, since 1960; Hon. Fellow of New College since 1957; *b* 18 June 1887; *s* of Henry Maurice Platnauer and Marian Platnauer (*née* Wilson); unmarried. *Educ:* Shrewsbury Sch.; New Coll., Oxford. Assistant Master, Winchester Coll., 1910-15 and 1919-22. Fellow of Brasenose Coll., 1922, Vice-Principal, 1936-56, Principal, 1956-60. Editor of Classical Quarterly, 1936-47. *Publications:* Septimius Severus, 1918; Claudian (Loeb Translation), 1922; (ed) Euripides, Iphigenia in Tauris, 1938; Latin Elegaic Verse, 1951; (ed) Aristophanes, Peace, 1964; Contributions to The Mind of Rome, 1926; New Chapters in Greek Literature, 1933; Greek Poetry and Life, 1938; Some Oxford Compositions, 1949; More Oxford Compositions, 1964. (ed) 50 Years of Classical Scholarship, 1954; articles in Classical Review, Classical Quarterly, etc. *Recreations:* travel, books, and music. *Address:* Brasenose College, Oxford. *T:* 48641.
[Died 19 Dec. 1974.

PLATT, Baron, *cr* 1967 (Life Peer), of Grindleford; **Robert Platt**, 1st Bt, *cr* 1959; MSc (Manchester); MD (Sheffield); FRCP; Professor of Medicine, Manchester University, and Physician, Royal Infirmary, Manchester, 1945-65; President of the Royal College of Physicians, 1957-62; *b* London, 16 April 1900; *s* of William Platt and Susan Jane Willis; *m* 1st, 1922, Margaret Irene Cannon, MB, ChB, DPM (marr. diss. 1974); one *s* two *d*; 2nd, 1974, Sylvia Jean Haggard (*née* Caveley), ARCM (viola). *Educ:* private schools; Sheffield Univ. Physician, Royal Infirmary, Sheffield, 1931-45; Lt-Col, 1941-44, Brig., 1944-45, RAMC. Editor Quarterly Jl of Medicine, 1948-58. Member: Medical Research Council, 1953-57; Central Health Services Council; Cttee of Hallé Concerts Soc., 1947-53; Council Royal Manchester Coll. of Music; Medical Research Soc.; Chm., Clinical Research Board of Medical Research Council, 1964-67; Member: Medical Advisory Board, RAF; Royal Commn on Medical Educn, 1965; President: Eugenics Soc., 1965-68; ASH, 1978-; Vice-President: British Assoc. Adv. Science, 1962; Family Planning Assoc., 1971- (Pres, 1968-71); Nat. Soc. for the Abolition of Cruel Sports, 1972-; Chm., Manchester Chamber Concerts Soc., 1952-65; Membre d'honneur de la Société de Pathologie Rénale; Hon. Member: Assoc. of Physicans; The Renal Assoc.; Assoc. of American Physicians; Hon. FACP; Hon. FRCGP; Hon. FRSocMed; Hon. Fellow, Manchester Med. Soc.; Hon. FRACP; Hon. FRCPsych; Mem. Soc. of Authors; Membre Correspondant étranger, Soc. Med. des Hôpitaux de Paris; Hon. Freeman, Worshipful Co. of Barbers; Fellow-Commoner, Christ's Coll., Cambridge. Lectures: Lumleian, RCP, London, 1952; Doyne Memorial, Oxford, 1956; Watson Smith, RCP Edinburgh, 1958; Galton, London, 1961; Lilly, Amer. Coll. Physicians, 1961; Linacre, St John's Coll., Cambridge, 1963; Arthur Hall, Sheffield, 1965; Wiltshire, London, 1965; Oslerian Orator, 1963; Rock Carling Fellow, 1963; Harveian Orator, RCP, 1967. Hon. LLD: Sheffield, 1959; Belfast, 1959; Manchester, 1969; Hon. MD Bristol, 1959. *Publications:* Nephritis and Allied Diseases, 1934; Private and Controversial, 1972; numerous papers to Quarterly Journal of Med., Clinical Science, etc., mostly on renal disease and genetics. *Recreations:* talking with Sylvia; String Quartet playing ('cello). *Heir:* (to father's Btcy) *s* Hon. Peter Platt, Prof. of Music at Univ. of Sydney (previously at Otago Univ., NZ) [*b* 6 July 1924; *m* 1948, Jean Halliday Brentnall; one *s* two *d*]. *Address:* 53 Heathside, Hinchley Wood, Esher, Surrey KT10 9TD. *T:* 01-398 1732.   *[Died 30 June 1978.*

PLATT, James Westlake, CBE 1965; *b* 13 June 1897; *s* of Rev. W. T. Platt, Auckland, NZ; *m* 1927, Veronica Norma Hope Arnold;

four s. *Educ:* Auckland Grammar School; Balliol College, Oxford. Joined Royal Dutch/Shell Gp of Oil Cos, 1922; served in China and Argentine, 1922-45; Managing Director, Eagle Oil & Shipping Co., 1945-49; a Managing Director, Royal Dutch/Shell Group, 1949-57; Member, Drogheda Cttee on British Inf. Services Overseas, 1952-53; Chairman: Salaries Commission, Hong Kong Government, 1959; UK Advisory Council on Education for Management, 1960-67; Foundn for Management Educn, 1960-68; OECD. Internat. Gp to examine Develt of Management Studies in Europe, 1961-68; Governor, School of Oriental and African Studies, 1962-68. Hon. Fellow, Balliol Coll., 1963-. Hon. DSc City Univ., 1969. *Address:* Anneville Lodge, Archirondel, Gorey, Jersey, CI. *T:* Jersey East 782. *Clubs:* Brooks's, United Oxford & Cambridge University.
[*Died* 17 *Dec.* 1972.

PLATT, Gen. Sir William, GBE 1943; KCB 1941 (CB 1939); DSO 1908; *b* 14 June 1885; *s* of late John Platt and Margaret Oudney Graham, 74 Whitehall Court, SW1; *m* 1921, Mollie Dendy *yr d* of late Dendy Watney; two *s. Educ:* Marlborough College; RMC Sandhurst. Entered Northumberland Fusiliers, 1905; Captain, 1914; Major, 1924; Lieut-Col, 1930; Col 1933; Maj.-Gen., 1938; Lt-Gen., 1941; General, 1943; served NW Frontier, India, 1908 (despatches). European War, 1914-18 (despatches, Bt Major, Bt Lt-Col on promotion to substantive rank of Major); commanded 2nd Bn Wiltshire Regt, 1930-33; General Staff Officer, 1st Grade, 3rd Division, Bulford, 1933-34; Commander 7th Infantry Brigade, 1934-38; ADC to the King, 1937-38. Commanded Troops in the Sudan and Commandant Sudan Defence Force, 1938-41; GOC-in-C East African Command, 1941-45; retd pay, 1945. Col, The Wiltshire Regiment, 1942-54. *Address:* 61/Fifteen, Portman Square, W1. *Club:* Athenæum.   [*Died* 28 *Sept.* 1975.

PLAYFAIR, Maj.-Gen. Ian Stanley Ord, CB 1943; DSO 1918; MC; *b* 10 Apr. 1894; *s* of late Col F. H. G. Playfair, Hampshire Regt; *m* 1930, Jocelyn, *o d* of Col L. N. Malan, OBE; two *s. Educ:* Cheltenham College. Served European War, 1914-18 (despatches, MC and Bar, DSO); General Staff Officer, 2nd Grade, Staff College, Quetta, 1934-37; at Imperial Defence College, 1938; Commandant, Army Gas School, 1939; Director of Plans, War Office, 1940-41; Maj.-Gen. GS 11th Army Group, SE Asia Comd, 1943; retired pay, 1947. *Publication:* (official history) The Mediterranean and Middle East 1939-42: vol. 1, 1954; vol. 2, 1956; vol. 3, 1960; vol. 4, 1966. *Address:* 6 Park Road, Hythe, Kent.   [*Died* 21 *March* 1972.

PLAYFAIR, Air Marshal Sir Patrick Henry Lyon, KBE 1940; CB 1931; CVO 1935; MC; *b* Edinburgh, 22 Nov. 1889; *s* of late John Playfair, MD, FRCPE; *m* 1937, Kate, *y d* of late Hayward James Strudwick; one adopted *s. Educ:* Cheltenham Coll.; Royal Military Acad., Woolwich. Entered RFA, 1910; seconded RFC (Military Wing), 1912; served European War in RFC and RAF; Air Officer Commanding No. 1 (Bomber) Group RAF, Abingdon, 1938-39; commanded Advanced Air Striking Force in France, 1939-40; AOC-in-C, India, 1940-42; retired list, 1942. DSM (USA); Legion of Honour (France). *Address:* St Mary's House, 56 Whiting Street, Bury St Edmunds, Suffolk. *Club:* Army and Navy.   [*Died* 23 *Nov.* 1974.

PLENDERLEITH, Air Vice-Marshal Brian William; Department of Air Member for Personnel, Ministry of Defence (Air), since Jan. 1978; *b* 14 June 1927; *s* of William Noble Plenderleith and Dorothy (*née* Passmore); *m* 1953, Evelyn Margaret (*née* Barker); two *d. Educ:* Rendcomb Coll., Cirencester; Emmanuel Coll., Cambridge. MA; CEng, MRAeS, MBIM. Flying training, 1950-51; QFI, 1952-53; CFS Examining Wing, 1954; Flt Comdr, 115 Sqdn, 1955; Vulcan ground instruction, 1956-57; Bloodhound (Trials Wing), 1957-60; RCAF Staff Coll., Toronto, 1960-61; OC 139 (J) Sqdn (Victor 2), 1962-63; Junior DS, IDC, 1964-66; Gp Captain Ops, RAF Germany, 1967-70; OC RAF, Topcliffe, 1970-71; DS, RAF Staff Coll., 1972; Air Cdre Plans, Strike Comd, 1973-75; Asst Comdt, Dept Air Warfare, Cranwell, 1976-77. *Recreations:* golf, gliding; Pres. RAF Fencing Union. *Address:* Woodview, The Green, Pirbright, Woking, Surrey GU24 0JT. *T:* Brookwood 4405. *Club:* Royal Air Force.   [*Died* 22 *Dec.* 1978.

PLOMER, William Charles Franklyn, CBE 1968; FRSL; writer; *b* 10 Dec. 1903. Served at Admiralty, 1940-45. President: The Poetry Society, 1968-71; The Kilvert Society, 1968-. Hon. DLitt Durham. Queen's Gold Medal for Poetry, 1963. *Publications:* Turbott Wolfe, 1926; I Speak of Africa, 1927; Paper Houses, 1929; Sado, 1931; The Fivefold Screen, 1932; The Case is Altered, 1932; Cecil Rhodes, 1933; The Child of Queen Victoria, 1933; The Invaders, 1934; Ali the Lion, 1936; Visiting the Caves, 1936; (ed) Japanese Lady in Europe, by Haruko Ichikawa, 1937; (ed) Kilvert's Diary, 1938-40; Selected Poems, 1940; Double

Lives, 1943; The Dorking Thigh, 1945; (ed) Curious Relations, by William D'Arfey, 1945; Four Countries, 1949; Museum Pieces, 1952; (with Benjamin Britten) Gloriana, 1953; A Shot in the Park, 1955; At Home, 1958; Collected Poems, 1960; (ed) A Message in Code, the Diary of Richard Rumbold, 1932-61, 1964; (with Benjamin Britten) Curlew River, 1964; (with Benjamin Britten) The Burning Fiery Furnace, 1966; Taste and Remember, 1966; (with Benjamin Britten) The Prodigal Son, 1968; Celebrations, 1972; (with Alan Aldridge) The Butterfly Ball, 1973. *Address:* c/o Jonathan Cape, 30 Bedford Square, WC1.   [*Died* 21 *Sept.* 1973.

PLUMBE, William John Conway, CB 1971; HM Chief Inspector of Factories, 1967-71; *b* 17 Mar. 1910; *s* of Charles Conway Plumbe and Lilian Plumbe (*née* Lynham); *m* 1938, Margaret, *y d* of A. E. Paine, Sevenoaks; three *d. Educ:* King Edward VII, Sheffield; Sevenoaks School; Imperial College, London University. BSc, ACGI. Appointed HM Inspector of Factories, 1935. Service in HM Forces, 1943-46. HM Superintending Inspector of Factories, 1960-63; HM Deputy Chief Inspector of Factories, 1963-67. *Recreations:* gardening, country walking. *Address:* Woodmans, Fishpond, Wooton Fitzpaine, near Bridport, Dorset. *T:* Hawkchurch 253.   [*Died* 9 *Nov.* 1979.

PLUMMER, Baroness, *cr* 1965 (Life Peeress); **Beatrice Plummer;** *b* 14 April 1903; *d* of Meyer Lapsker; *m* 1923, Leslie Arthur Plummer (later Sir Leslie Plummer, MP; *d* 1963). JP Essex, 1947, Member: Independent TV Authority, 1966-71; British Agricultural Export Council. *Recreation:* politics. *Address:* Berwick Hall, Toppesfield, Halstead, Essex; House of Lords, SW1; 31 Dorset Square, NW1.   [*Died* 13 *June* 1972.

PLUMMER, Alfred, BLitt Oxon; MSc (Econ.) London; MA, LLD Dublin; Hon. Librarian to the Worshipful Company of Weavers; *b* London, 2 Nov. 1896; *o s* of Alfred Plummer; *m* 1st, 1919, Minnie D. Goodey; 2nd, 1973, Elsie Evelyn May Fellingham. *Educ:* Christ Church Sch., Brondesbury. Univ. training in Economics, Law and History at Trinity Coll., Dublin, London Univ. (London Sch. of Economics) and Oriel Coll., Oxford; enlisted in Honourable Artillery Company, 9 June 1915; active service in France, 1916-17; Lecturer in the Dept of Commerce in University Coll., Southampton, 1920-25; Vice-Principal of Ruskin Coll., Oxford, 1925-37; Head of Dept of Economics and Social Studies, City of Birmingham Commercial Coll., 1937-38; Head of Dept of Commerce, Languages and Social Studies, SW Essex Technical Coll., 1938-43; Vice-Principal of SW Essex Technical Coll. and Headmaster of the County Technical Sch., 1944-45; Dir, Forest Training Coll., 1945-49; Inspector of Further Education, LCC, 1949-60; Staff Inspector, 1960-63. *Publications:* Exercises in Economics, 1929; Labour's Path to Power, 1929; The World in Agony-An Economic Diagnosis, 1932; The Witney Blanket Industry, 1934; International Combines in Modern Industry, 1934; New British Industries in the 20th Century, 1937; Raw Materials or War Materials?, 1937; (with Richard Early) The Blanket Makers, 1669-1969, a history of Charles Early and Marriott (Witney) Ltd, 1969; Bronterre: a political biography of Bronterre O'Brien, 1971; The London Weavers' Company, 1600-1970, 1972; various articles; contributor to the Encyclopædia of the Social Sciences. *Address:* Warmington, Black Heath, Wenhaston, Suffolk.   [*Died* 10 *April* 1978.

PLUMMER, Norman Swift, MD, FRCP; retired as Senior Physician, and Physician in charge of Chest Clinic, Charing Cross Hospital (1935-73); as Physician to London Chest Hospital (1947-73), to Bromley Hospital (1948-72), to Edenbridge Hospital (1946-72); *b* 10 June 1907; *s* of late Walter James Plummer and late Marianne Evelyn Clarence; *m* 1939, Helen Niven Wilson; one *s* three *d. Educ:* Kingswood Coll. Grahamstown; Guy's Hosp., Univ. of London; Amsterdam. Gold Medal in Medicine (Guy's), 1930; MD (London) 1933; FRCP 1941. Clin. Asst, Asst Ho. Surg., Out-Patient Officer, Ho. Phys. and Medical Registrar, Guy's Hosp., 1930-32; Post-Graduate Student, Kliniek Prof. Snapper, Amsterdam, 1932-33; Medical Registrar, Charing Cross Hosp., 1933-35. Examr in Materia Medica, Soc. of Apothecaries of London, 1947-50; Lectr and Examr in Medicine, Univ. of London; Examr in Med., Conjt Bd, and MRCP. In RAMC, 1941-46; Brig. RAMC, Cons. Phys. to MEF. Royal Coll. of Physicians: Mem. Council 1965, Censor 1966, Senior Censor and Vice-Pres., 1970. Member: Association of Physicians; Thoracic Society; Fellow American Coll. of Chest Physicians. *Publications:* contributed to British Encyclopædia of Medical Practice, 2nd edn, 1952. Various medical papers on fungal and other diseases especially on Aspergillosis in Thorax, 1952. *Address:* 118 Harley Street, W1. *T:* 01-486 2494; Jesmond, Goring Road, Steyning, West Sussex BN4 3GF. *T:* Steyning 814174.   [*Died* 3 *April* 1978.

PLUNKET, 7th Baron, *cr* 1827; **Patrick Terence William Span Plunket,** KCVO 1974 (CVO 1963; MVO 1955); Lt-Col Irish Guards; Equerry to the Queen since 1952 (Equerry to King George VI, 1948-52); Deputy Master of HM Household, since 1954; *b* 8 Sept. 1923; *s* of 6th Baron and Dorothé Mabel (*d* 1938), *widow* of Capt. Jack Barnato, RAF; *S* father, 1938. *Educ:* Eton; Cambridge. A Trustee of the Wallace Collection and National Art Collections Fund. *Heir: b* Hon. Robin Rathmore Plunket, Captain Rifle Brigade [*b* 3 Dec. 1925; *m* 1951, Jennifer, *d* of late Bailey Southwell, Olivenhoutpoort, South Africa]. *Address:* St James's Palace, SW1. *Club:* White's.
[*Died 28 May 1975.*

PLURENDEN, Baron *cr* 1975 (Life Peer), of Plurenden Manor, Kent; **Rudy Sternberg,** Kt 1970; Chairman, Sterling Group of Companies; President, British Agricultural Export Council (Chairman, 1968-75); *b* 17 April 1917; *s* of George Sternberg, Germany, and Paula (*née* Michel); *m* 1951, Dorothée Monica, *d* of Major Robert Bateman Prust, OBE, Vancouver; two *d. Educ:* in Germany. Freeman, City of London, 1960; Liveryman, Worshipful Company: of Farmers, 1963; of Horners, 1960. *Recreations:* farming, yachting. *Address:* 79b Elizabeth Street, SW1; Plurenden Manor, High Halden, Kent. *Club:* City Livery.
[*Died 5 Jan. 1978.*

POCHIN, Victor Robert, CBE 1957; *b* 10 Sept. 1879; *o s* of late George William Pochin, DL, JP, Barkby Hall. *Educ:* Wellington; Trinity Coll., Cambridge. Barrister, Lincoln's Inn, 1907; Leicestershire CC 1913, County Alderman 1938-, Vice-Chm., 1924-60, Chm., 1960-61; JP 1906, DL 1925, Leicestershire; High Sheriff of Leicestershire, 1941; served European War, 1916-19, Leicestershire Yeomanry and First Life Guards. *Recreations:* fishing and shooting. *Address:* Barkby Hall, Leicestershire. *T:* Syston 2247. *Club:* United Oxford & Cambridge University.
[*Died 5 Sept. 1972.*

POCOCK, Carmichael Charles Peter, (Michael Pocock), CBE 1967; Chairman: Shell Transport and Trading Co., since 1976; Committee of Managing Directors, Royal Dutch/Shell Group, since 1977; *b* 25 March 1920; *s* of late Lt-Col Joseph Albert Pocock; *m* 1943, Nina Alice Hilary (*née* Hearn); one *s* two *d. Educ:* Rossall School; Keble Coll., Oxford. Joined Royal Dutch/Shell Group in 1946 and served in Venezuela and London. Pres., Compania Shell de Venezuela, 1964; Regional Co-ordinator, East and Australasia, 1968; Man. Dir, Royal Dutch/Shell Gp of Cos, 1970. Chm., Council of Industry for Management Education, 1972-; Mem. Council, BIM, 1975-; Chm., London Graduate Sch. of Business Studies, 1976-. *Recreations:* sailing and mountain walking. *Address:* Shell Centre, SE1. *T:* 01-934 5866. *Club:* Buck's.
[*Died 12 Oct. 1979.*

POCOCK, Michael; *see* Pocock, C. C. P.

POLANYI, Prof. Michael, FRS 1944; Hon. DSc: Princeton, 1946; Leeds, 1947; Manchester, 1966; Cambridge, 1969; Hon. LLD: Aberdeen, 1959; Notre Dame, 1965; Wesleyan, 1965; Toronto, 1967; Loyola, 1970; Professor Emeritus at Victoria University, Manchester, (Professor of Social Studies, 1948-Sept. 1958, retired); *b* 12 March 1891; *m* 1921, Magda Kemeny; one *s* (and one *s* decd). *Educ:* Budapest; Karlsruhe. Privatdozent Technische Hochschule, Berlin, 1923; Member of Kaiser Wilhelm Institute für Physikalische Chemie, 1923; Life Member, 1929, resigned 1933; Prof. of Physical Chemistry, Victoria Univ., Manchester, 1933-48; Former Member National Society of Science, Letters and Arts in Naples, 1933; Riddell Lectr, Univ. of Durham, 1945; Lloyd Roberts Lectr, Manchester, 1946; Member of Max Planck Society, 1949; Alexander White Visiting Professor, Univ. of Chicago, 1950; Gifford Lectr, 1951-52, Univ. of Aberdeen; Visiting Prof., Univ. of Chicago, 1954. Lindsay Memorial Lectr, Keele, 1958; Eddington Lectr, Cambridge, 1960; Gunning Lectr, Edinburgh, 1960; Senior Research Fell., Merton Coll., Oxford, 1959-61; Distinguished Research Fell., Univ. of Virginia, 1961; McEnnerny Lectr, Berkeley, 1961; Foreign Hon. Member American Academy of Arts and Sciences, 1962; Terry Lectr, Yale, 1962; Member Internat. Acad. of Philosophy of Science, 1962; Fellow of Center for Adv. Study Behav. Sciences, Stanford, 1962-63; James B. Duke Vis. Prof., Duke Univ., 1964; Senior Fellow, Center of Advanced Studies, Wesleyan Univ., 1965; Alexander White Vis. Prof., Univ. of Chicago, 1967, 1968, 1969; Nuffield Lectr, RSM, 1970. *Publications:* Atomic Reactions, 1932; USSR Economics, 1935; Money and Unemployment (a diagrammatic film), 1939; The Contempt of Freedom, 1940; Patent Reform, 1944; Full Employment and Free Trade, 1945; Science Faith and Society, 1946; The Logic of Liberty, 1951; Personal Knowledge, 1958; The Study of Man, 1959; Beyond Nihilism, 1960; The Tacit Dimension, 1966;

Knowing and Being, 1969; articles on plasticity, adsorption, crystal structure, chemical reaction kinetics, bond energies and polymerisation in German and British Journals; *posthumous publication:* (with H. Prosch) Meaning, 1976. *Address:* 22 Upland Park Road, Oxford. *T:* Oxford 58288. *Club:* Athenæum.
[*Died 22 Feb. 1976.*

POLLARD, (Henry) Graham; author; *b* 7 March 1903; *e s* of Albert Frederick Pollard, first director of the Institute of Historical Research, London, and Catherine Susannah Lucy. *Educ:* Shrewsbury Sch.; University College, London; Jesus Coll., Oxford. Partner in Birrell & Garnett (Antiquarian Booksellers), 1924-38; Leverhulme Research Fellow, 1934-37; Reader in the History of Newspapers, Univ. of London, 1939-42; Board of Trade, 1942-59; Sandars Reader in Bibliography, Cambridge Univ., 1959; Lyell Reader in Bibliography, Univ. of Oxford, 1960-61; President, Bibliographical Society, London, 1960-61. Gold Medal, Bibliographical Soc., 1969. *Publications:* Catalogue of Type founders' Specimens, 1928; (with John Carter) An Inquiry into the Nature of Certain Nineteenth Century Pamphlets, 1934; (with John Carter) The Firm of Charles Ottley, Landon, & Co., 1948; T. J. Wise Centenary Studies, 1960; (with A. Ehrman) The Distribution of Books by Catalogue, Roxburghe Club, 1965. Contrib.: The Cambridge Bibliography of English Literature, 1940; The Library; The Fleuron; New Paths in Book Collecting, 1934; The Times Literary Supplement; The Book Collector; Bodleian Library Record; Oxoniensia. *Recreation:* book collecting. *Address:* Barton Manor, Barton Village Road, Headington, Oxford.
[*Died 15 Nov. 1976.*

POLLARD, Lt.-Gen. Sir Reginald (George), KCVO 1970; KBE 1961 (CBE 1955); CB 1959; DSO 1942; psc; idc; retired; *b* 20 Jan. 1903; *s* of late Albert Edgar Pollard, Bathurst, NSW; *m* 1925, Daisy Ethel, *d* of late A. H. Potter, Strathfield, NSW; two *s. Educ:* Bathurst High Sch.; Royal Military Coll., Duntroon. Lieut, Aust. Staff Corps, 1924; served War of 1939-45, France, Middle East, Syria (despatches), SE Asia, SW Pacific; Lieut-Colonel, 1941; Colonel, 1942; ADC to The King, 1951, to The Queen, 1952; Brigadier, 1953; Comd Aust. Army Component, British Commonwealth Forces, Korea, 1953; Maj.-General, 1954; QMG, AMF, 1954-57; Lt-Gen., 1957; GOC, Eastern Command, Australia, 1957-60; Chief of the General Staff, Australian Army, 1960-63; retired, 1963; Hon. Colonel, 1965, Col Comdt, 1968-71, The Royal Australian Regt. Australian Secretary to The Queen, 1969; Dir-Gen., Royal Visit, 1970. *Address:* Duntroon, Wyrallah, NSW 2480, Australia. *T:* Wyrallah 288202.
[*Died 20 Sept. 1978.*

POLLOCK, Sir Ronald (Evelyn), Kt 1947; *b* Kamptee, CP, India, 17 April 1891; *s* of Colonel E. Pollock, CBE, RA; *m* 1st, 1921, Margery (*d* 1959), *d* of late S. A. Fitze; one *d*; 2nd, 1963, Mrs Pamela Stent, *widow* of P. J. H. Stent, CIE, ICS, and *d* of late F. W. A. Prideaux, OBE. *Educ:* Harrow; Pembroke Coll., Cambridge. MA Cambridge. Called to Bar, Gray's Inn; ICS (retired). Judge of High Court, Nagpur, 1936-48; Acting Chief Justice, 1947; Chairman, Medical Appeal Tribunal, Southern Region, 1948-63. *Address:* 17 South Drive, Wokingham, Berks.
[*Died 9 March 1974.*

POLLOK, Maj.-Gen. Robert Valentine, CB 1940; CBE 1919; DSO 1917; late Irish Guards; *b* 14 Feb. 1884; 4th *s* of late John Pollok of Lismany, Ballinasloe, Co. Galway; *m* 1916, Sylvia Bettina (*d* 1977), *d* of late George Fellows, Beeston Fields, Notts; one *s* died on active service, 1945. *Educ:* Eton; Royal Military Coll., Sandhurst. Joined 15th Hussars, 1903; ADC to Lieutenant-Governor, United Provinces, India, 1908-12; ADC Governor-Gen. Australia, 1913-14. Served European War, 1914-18 (CBE, DSO, despatches, four times wounded): employed Australian Forces, Gallipoli (Adjutant and Staff Captain), 1914-15; transferred Irish Guards, 1916; Acting Major, 1917; Acting Lt-Col, 1917; Lt-Col, 1926; Bt Col, 1929; Col, 1930; Maj.-Gen., 1938; commanded 1st Bn Irish Guards, 1917-18, and 1926-30; Staff Coll., 1921; Brigade Major 1st Guards Brigade, 1922-25; Officer Commanding Regt and Regimental District, 1930-31; Commander 1st Guards Brigade, 1931-35; Commandant Senior Officers' Sch., Sheerness, 1935-38; General Officer comdg Northern Ireland District, 1938-40; Comdr 43rd (Wessex) Div. (TA); retired pay, 1941; re-employed as Colonel, General Staff, 1941; reverted to retired pay, 1941. *Address:* The Bridge House, Rathkeale, Co. Limerick, Eire. *T:* Rathkeale 11. *Club:* Cavalry and Guards. [*Died 29 Sept. 1979.*

POLSON, Milson George, QC 1964; **His Honour Judge Polson;** a Circuit Judge, since 1972; *b* 3 June 1917; *s* of Caleb George Polson, Senghenydd, Glamorganshire; *m* 1939, Ida, *y d* of George Stephens, late Chief of Police, GW Railway Co.; one *s* one *d. Educ:* Caerphilly, Glam; London Univ. Glamorganshire

County Council, 1935-37; Fulham Metropolitan Borough Council, 1937-39. Served War of 1939-45 (Defence and other Medals): Flt-Lt, Meteorologist, RAF; Europe, India, Burma, and China, 1939-46 (Burma Star). Called to the Bar, Lincoln's Inn, 1947; joined Inner Temple, *ad eundem,* 1961. Recorder of Exeter, 1966-71; Hon. Recorder of Exeter, 1972-; Chm., IoW QS, 1967-71, Dep. Chm., 1964-67; Comr of Assize, Western Circuit, 1970-71; Member: General Council of the Bar, 1967-70; Council of Exeter Univ., 1967; Chm., Devon Br., Magistrates' Assoc., 1973. *Recreations:* travel, books, sailing. *Address:* Monk's Wall Cottage, Otterton, near Budleigh Salterton, Devon. *T:* Colaton Raleigh 374; 2 Crown Office Row, Temple, EC4. *T:* 01-353 9272. *Clubs:* Royal Over-Seas League; Exeter and County (Exeter); Royal Western Yacht (Plymouth).
[Died 5 Oct. 1977.

POLTIMORE, 6th Baron, *cr* 1831; **Hugh de Burgh Warwick Bampfylde;** Bt 1641; *b* 1888; *yr b* of 5th Baron Poltimore; *S* brother, 1967; *m* 1918, Margaret Mary, *d* of 4th Marquis de la Pasture; one *s* (and one *s* decd). *Educ:* Winchester; New Coll., Oxford. MA. Served East Africa, 1914-18. *Heir: g s* Mark Coplestone Bampfylde, *b* 8 June 1957. *Address:* The Ancient House, Peasenhall, Saxmundham, Suffolk. *Club:* Brooks's.
[Died 27 March 1978.

POMPIDOU, Georges Jean Raymond, Grand Croix de la Légion d'Honneur; President of the French Republic, since June 1969; *b* 5 July 1911; *s* of late Prof. Léon Pompidou and of Marie-Louise (*née* Chavagnac); *m* Claude Cahour; one *s*. *Educ:* Lycée d'Albi; Lycée Louis le Grand; Ecole Normale Supérieure; Ecole Libre des Sciences Politiques (Dipl. Agrégé des Lettres). Taught Literature: Lycée St Charles, Marseille, 1935-39; Lycée Henri IV, Paris, 1939-44. Infantry Officer, 1939-40. Chargé de Mission, Gen. de Gaulle's Cabinet, 1944-46; Dep. Director, Tourism, 1946-49; Member Council of State, 1946-54; Maître des Requêtes honoraire, 1957; Dir, Gen. de Gaulle's Cabinet, 1958-59; Mem., Constitutional Council, 1959-62; Prime Minister of France, 1962-68; Mem., Nat. Assembly, 1968-69; elected Pres. of Republic, 16 June 1969. Dir-Gen., Rothschild Bank, and several cos, 1956-62. *Publications:* Studies of Britannicus, 1944; Taine, 1947; Malraux, 1955; Anthologie de la Poésie Française, 1961. *Recreation:* hunting. *Address:* Palais de l'Elysée, Paris 8e, France.
[Died 2 April 1974.

PONCET, André F.; *see* François-Poncet.

PONS, Lily; Opera, concert, radio, film and recording star; of French birth; *m* 1938, André Kostelanetz, conductor (marr. diss. 1958). *Educ:* Paris Conservatoire. Soprano. Past Member, Metropolitan Opera, Colon Teatre (Buenos Aires), Paris, Covent Garden, San Francisco, Rome, Chicago and Monte Carlo Opera Companies. *Radio:* Guest star on such popular air shows as Telephone Hour, Voice of Firestone, etc. *Moving Pictures:* Starred in RKO films: That Girl from Paris, I Dream Too Much, Hitting a New High. Officer, the French Legion of Honor; Chevalier of the Order of the Royal Crown of Brussels; Gold Medal of City of Paris; Order of Cross of Lorraine; Official Daughter LeClerc Div. *Recreation:* collection of Modern paintings. *Address:* Dallas, Texas.
[Died 13 Feb. 1976.

PONSONBY OF SHULBREDE, 2nd Baron, *cr* 1930, of Shulbrede; **Matthew Henry Hubert Ponsonby;** *b* 28 July 1904; *s* of 1st Baron and Dorothea (*d* 1963), *d* of Sir Hubert Parry, 1st Bt and Lady Maud Parry; *S* father, 1946; *m* 1929, Hon. Elizabeth Bigham, *o d* of 2nd Viscount Mersey, PC, CMG, CBE; one *s* three *d*. *Educ:* Leighton Park School, Reading; Balliol College, Oxford. *Heir: s* Hon. Thomas Arthur Ponsonby. *Address:* Shulbrede Priory, Haslemere, Surrey. *T:* Fernhurst 249.
[Died 29 April 1976.

PONSONBY, Arthur Gordon; *b* 14 June 1892; 2nd *s* of late Rev. Stewart Gordon Ponsonby; *m* 1938, Jacqueline, 2nd *d* of late Karl Kirdorf, Krefeld, Germany; one *s*. *Educ:* Marlborough; Trinity College, Cambridge. Interned in Ruhleben during the war, 1914-18; joined HM Consular service in 1920. HM Chargé d'Affairs, Monrovia, 1938-40; Consul-General at Rio de Janeiro, 1947-51; retd from HM Foreign Service, 1951. *Recreation:* gardening. *Address:* 26 Upper High Street, Thame, Oxon. *Club:* Royal Commonwealth Society.
[Died 8 April 1978.

PONSONBY, Col Sir Charles Edward, 1st Bt *cr* 1956; TD; DL; *b* 2 Sept. 1879; *e s* of late Hon. Edwin Ponsonby; *m* 1912, Hon. Winifred Gibbs, *d* of 1st Baron Hunsdon; one *s* four *d*. *Educ:* Eton; Balliol College, Oxford. BA 1901; admitted a solicitor, 1904; Director of Companies; Chm. Royal Commonwealth Soc., 1954-57; President Royal African Soc., 1962-71; Past-Pres. Glass Manufacturers Federation; Mem. Council Joint African Board, Commonwealth Producers Organization, etc.; a Beit

Trustee. Served European War, 1914-18, West Kent (QO) Yeomanry and 10th (Yeomanry) Battalion The Buffs in Gallipoli, Egypt, Palestine, and France (Croix de Guerre avec Palmes); commanded 97th (Kent Yeomanry) Brigade RA (T), 1930-36; Hon. Col 97th (Kent Yeomanry) Field Regt RA, 1942; and 297th (Kent Yeomanry) Lt AA Regt RA, 1942-49. MP (C) Sevenoaks, 1935-50; Parliamentary Private Sec. to Secretary of State for War and Secretary of State for Foreign Affairs (Rt Hon. Anthony Eden), 1940-45; Member Parly Delegs to Russia, 1945, Austria, 1948, Burma, 1950; Member Industrial Relations Mission to Nigeria, 1950. Vice-Pres., British Red Cross, Oxon, 1950-; Chm., Victoria Co. History Cttee, 1954-68; Vice-Chm. and Chm., Nuffield Orthopaedic Centre, 1954-68; Pres., Oxon Playing Fields Assoc., 1962-75; Mem., Oxon Pastoral Cttee, 1966-72. DL Oxon 1944. *Publications:* West Kent (QO) Yeomanry and 10th (Yeomanry) Bn The Buffs, 1914-19; History of Wootton; Ponsonby Remembers (autobiography); Wootton: anatomy of an Oxfordshire village, 1968; Ponsonby Family, 1929-70. *Recreations:* archæology, writing, etc. *Heir: s* Ashley Charles Gibbs Ponsonby, *qv. Address:* Woodleys, Woodstock, Oxfordshire. *T:* Woodstock 811422; 6 Eresby House, Rutland Gate, SW7. *T:* 01-589 3060. *Club:* Brooks's.
[Died 28 Jan. 1976.

PONTING, Brig. Theophilus John, CSI 1947; CIE 1940; MC; psc; idc; IA, retired; *b* 1886. Served NW Frontier of India, 1908; European War, 1916-18, in Mesopotamia and Egypt (despatches, MC, French Croix de Guerre); retired, 1940. *Address:* Walldown, Whitehill, Bordon, Hants.
[Died 6 Oct. 1972.

POOL, Bernard Frank, CB 1957; CBE 1951 (OBE 1944); Director of Navy Contracts, Admiralty, 1948-60, retired; Hon. Treasurer, Navy Records Society, 1960-71, Councillor, 1972, and since 1976, Vice-President, 1973-75; Councillor, Society for Nautical Research, 1968-72; *b* 17 July 1896; *s* of late Augustus Frank Pool, CBE, and 1st wife, late Harriette Maude Mary Smith; *m* 1932, Hazel Violet (*d* 1975), *d* of late Charles Ambrose; one *s* one *d*. *Educ:* Colfe Grammar School. LLB, BCom (London). Barrister-at-Law, Middle Temple, 1921. Assistant Contract Officer Admiralty, 1915; Assistant Director of Contracts, 1936; Deputy Director, 1940. *Publications:* Navy Board Contracts, 1660-1832, 1966; The Croker Papers (ed.), 1967; articles in The Mariner's Mirror, History Today. *Recreation:* naval history. *Address:* 81 Bromley Road, Shortlands, Bromley, Kent BR2 0AA. *T:* 01-460 6492. *Clubs:* Royal Commonwealth Society; Samuel Pepys.
[Died 3 March 1977.

POOLE, John Hewitt Jellett, MA, MAI, ScD; FTCD; Professor of Geophysics, University of Dublin, since 1934; *b* Dublin, 19 March 1893; *s* of T. H. Poole, Mayfield, Bandon, Co. Cork, and Maria Emily, *d* of Rev. J. H. Jellett, FRS, Provost of Trinity College, Dublin; unmarried. *Educ:* Mountjoy School, Dublin; Trinity College, Dublin. Pupil and Assistant on the GNR (I), 1916-19; served with Railway Corps in France, 1917; Research Assistant to Prof. John Joly, 1919; Assistant to Prof. W. E. Thrift, 1921-29; Lecturer in Physics, Dublin University, 1929; Commissioner of Irish Lights, 1927; Member: Royal Irish Academy, 1931; Physical Society, London, 1933; Council, Royal Dublin Society, 1933; Emergency Research Bureau, Ireland, 1941-45. Boyle Medallist, Royal Dublin Soc., 1947. *Publications:* papers in the Philosophical Magazine, Scientific Proceedings of Royal Dublin Society, etc., on radioactivity of rocks, Theories of earth history, photo-electricity, etc. *Address:* Trinity College, Dublin; Ashbrook, Clontarf, Dublin.
[Died 15 Oct. 1976.

POOLE, Vice-Adm. Sir Richard Hayden Owen L.; *see* Lane-Poole.

POPE, Lt-Gen. (retd) Maurice Arthur, CB 1944; MC; CD; *b* Rivière du Loup, PQ, 29 Aug. 1889; *s* of late Sir Joseph Pope, KCMG, CVO, ISO, sometime Under-Secretary of State for External Affairs, Ottawa, and late Henriette Taschereau; *m* 1920, Comtesse Simonne du Monceau de Bergendal (Belgium); three *s* one *d*. *Educ:* Locally Ottawa; McGill University, BSc (Civil Engineering, 1911). Civil Engineer, Canadian Pacific Railway, 1911; European War, 1914-18 (MC, despatches); Cdn Battlefields Memorials Commission, Belgium and France, 1920-21; Staff College, Camberley, 1924-25; Staff Appts, Canada, 1926-31; War Office, 1931-33; Canada, 1933-35; Imperial Defence College, 1936; Sec., Chiefs of Staff Committee, Ottawa, 1938; Director Military Operations and Intelligence, Ottawa, 1939; Brigadier, General Staff, Cdn Military HQ, London, 1940; Vice-Chief of the General Staff, Ottawa, 1941; Chairman, Canadian Joint Staff Mission, Washington, DC, 1942-44; Military Staff Officer to the Prime Minister and Military Sec.,

Cabinet War Cttee, 1944-45; Head of Canadian Military Mission to Allied Control Council, Berlin, 1945-50; Ambassador to Belgium, 1950-53; Ambassador to Spain, 1953-56, retired. Hon. LLD. *Publication:* Soldiers and Politicians (memoirs), 1962. *Address:* 216 Manor Avenue, Ottawa, K1M 0H4, Canada.
[Died 20 Sept. 1978.

POPE, Brig. Ronald James, CMG 1969; Commander, Abu Dhabi Defence Force, since 1973; *b* 5 Aug. 1924; *s* of Albert Thomas Pope; *m* 1957, Charlotte Pflanz; one *d. Educ:* Llandaff School. Commissioned S Wales Borderers, 1943; Served D-day landings and NW Europe, 1944; subsequently Palestine, Eritrea, Cyprus; Instructor, Officer Cadet School, 1954-55; Staff Coll., 1956; Joint Services Staff Coll., 1961; Bde Major, 11 Infantry Brigade Group, 1962-65; CO 1st Bn, Guyana Defence Force, 1965-67; Chief of Staff, Guyana Defence Force, 1967-69; Senior Directing Staff, JSSC, later Nat. Defence Coll., 1970-73. *Recreations:* riding, fishing. *Address:* c/o HQ Abu Dhabi Defence Force, PO Box 309, Abu Dhabi, Arabian Gulf.
[Died 14 April 1976.

POPE-HENNESSY, James, CVO 1960; writer; *b* 20 Nov. 1916; *yr s* of late Major-General L. H. R. Pope-Hennessy, CB, DSO and late Dame Una Pope-Hennessy, DBE. *Educ:* Downside Sch.; Balliol College, Oxford. Editorial Assistant, Sheed and Ward, publishers, 1937-38; private sec. to Governor of Trinidad and Tobago, 1939. War Office, 1940-44; British Army Staff, Washington, USA, 1944-45. Literary Editor, The Spectator, 1947-49. *Publications:* London Fabric, 1939; West Indian Summer, 1943; The Houses of Parliament, 1945; America is an Atmosphere, 1947; Monckton Milnes, The Years of Promise, 1950; Monckton Milnes: The Flight of Youth, 1851-1885, 1952; Aspects of Provence, 1952; The Baths of Absalom, 1953; Lord Crewe: The Likeness of a Liberal, 1955; Queen Victoria at Windsor and Balmoral, 1959; Queen Mary, 1959; Verandah, 1964; Sins of the Fathers, 1967; Half-Crown Colony, 1969; Anthony Trollope, 1971 (Whitbread Award); *posthumous publication:* Robert Louis Stevenson, 1974. *Recreation:* travel. *Address:* 9 Ladbroke Grove, W11. *T:* 01-727 6203.
[Died 25 Jan. 1974.

POPPLEWELL, Baron *cr* 1966 (Life Peer), of Sherburn-in-Elmet; **Ernest Popplewell,** CBE 1951; *b* 10 Dec. 1899; *s* of J. W. and Alice Popplewell, Selby; *m* 1922, Lavinia Rainbow; one *s. Educ:* elementary. Railway signalman; NUR Trade Union Branch Secretary. Eighteen years membership Local Government Bodies. JP WR of Yorks. MP (Lab) Newcastle upon Tyne, West, 1945-66; Asst Whip (unpaid), 1946; Vice-Chamberlain of HM Household, 1947-51; an Opposition Whip, 1951, Deputy Chief Whip, 1955-Oct. 1959. Chairman: Labour Parly Transport Gp, 1959-65; Parly Nationalised Industries Cttee, 1964-66. JP W Riding of Yorks, 1934. Served War of 1914-18 with RMA (Belgian Croix de Guerre). *Address:* North View, Moor Lane, Sherburn-in-Elmet, nr Leeds. *T:* South Milford 213.
[Died 11 Aug. 1977.

PORGES, Waldo William, QC 1952; *b* 20 Sept. 1899; *s* of late Gustave Porges and Alice (*née* Pressfield); *m* 1926, Ann Forsyth McKechnie; one *d. Educ:* Eton; Christ Church, Oxford. Called to Bar, Lincoln's Inn, 1927. Bencher, 1957. *Publication:* Joint Editor, Temperley's Merchant Shipping Acts. *Address:* The Old Parsonage, Munslow, Craven Arms, Salop SY7 9ET. *T:* Munslow 655.
[Died 8 June 1976.

PORTAL OF HUNGERFORD, 1st Viscount, *cr* 1946, of Hungerford; 1st Baron, *cr* 1945; **Marshal of the Royal Air Force Charles Frederick Algernon Portal,** KG 1946; GCB 1942 (KCB 1940; CB 1939); OM 1946; DSO 1917; MC; Chairman, British Aircraft Corporation, 1960-68; *b* 21 May 1893; *s* of late E. R. Portal, Sulham, Pangbourne; *m* 1919, Joan Margaret, *y d* of Sir Charles Glynn Welby, 5th Bt; two *d. Educ:* Winchester; Christ Church, Oxford. Served European War, 1914-18 (despatches, DSO and bar, MC); Commd British Forces, Aden, 1934-35; Instructor Imperial Defence Coll., 1936-37; Director of Organization, Air Ministry, 1937-38; Air Member for Personnel on the Air Council, 1939-40; AOC-in-C Bomber Command, 1940; Chief of the Air Staff, 1940-45. Controller, Atomic Energy, Ministry of Supply, 1946-51. Director: Barclays Bank DCO, 1946-69; Barclays Bank Ltd, 1947-69; Portals Holdings Ltd, 1959-69; Whitbread Investment Co., 1962-. Chairman: King Edward VII Hospital, Midhurst, 1950-68. President, MCC, 1958-59. *Recreations:* fishing, stalking. *Heir: d* Hon. Rosemary Ann Portal, *b* 12 May 1923. *Address:* West Ashling House, Chichester, Sussex. *T:* West Ashling 216. *Club:* Travellers'.
[Died 22 April 1971.

PORTEOUS, Douglas Archibald, CB 1950; retired; *b* 1891; *y s* of late Archibald Porteous, Glasgow. *Educ:* Glasgow High School.

Fellow of the Faculty of Actuaries, 1920; Principal Actuary, Government Actuary's Dept, 1936; Deputy Government Actuary, 1946-53; retired, 1953. *Publication:* Pension and Widows' and Orphans' Funds, 1936. *Recreation:* golf. *Address:* Tusker House, 14 Godwin Road, Hastings, Sussex. *Club:* Reform.
[Died 8 Dec. 1974.

PORTER, Mrs Adrian; *see* Heaton, Rose Henniker.

PORTER, Air Vice-Marshal Cedric Ernest Victor, CBE 1944; psa; *b* 12 Nov. 1893; *s* of late Joseph Francis Porter, OBE, JP, Helmsley, Yorks; *m* 1925, Vera Ellen, *d* of late Frank Baxendale, Framfield Place, Sussex; one *s. Educ:* Harrow Sch.; Cambridge Univ. Commissioned Essex Regt, Aug. 1914; Captain, 1916; RFC and RAF since May 1916; France, 1914-18; Palestine and Iraq, 1920-23; RAF Staff Coll., 1931; RAF Coll., Cranwell, 1932-34; Senior Air Staff Officer, Palestine and Transjordan, 1937-40; commanded RAF Sudan, 1940, Andover, 1941, 70 Group, 1941-43; 22 Group, 1943-46 (CBE, despatches twice); retired, 1946. *Recreations:* shooting, fishing, golf. *Address:* Pigeons Farm, Greenham, Newbury, Berks. *T:* Newbury 1214. *Club:* Royal Air Force.
[Died 17 April 1975.

PORTER, George, *b* 29 July 1884; *s* of George Ellis Porter, Leeds; *m* 1914, Florence Annie Pickburn; three *d. Educ:* Liverpool Elementary and Technical Schools. Labour Supply Inspector, Min. of Labour, 1939-45. Mem., Huyton UDC, 1941-45. Pres., Liverpool Trades Council and Labour Party, 1940-44. MP (Lab) Central Division of Leeds, 1945-55. JP Liverpool, 1953-59. *Address:* 61 Stockbridge Lane, Huyton, Liverpool. *T:* 051-489 1094.
[Died 25 Sept. 1973.

PORTER, Sir George Swinburne, 3rd Bt, *cr* 1889; *b* 14 Dec. 1908; *o s* of Sir William Porter, 2nd Bt, and Mary Bousfield (*d* 1915), *d* of J. Steains; *S* father, 1935. *Educ:* Eton. *Heir:* none. *Address:* Orchard House, 6 Fairfield Close, Lymington, Hants.
[Died 8 Feb. 1974 (ext).

PORTER, Maj.-General John Edmund L.; *see* Leech-Porter.

PORTER, Katherine Anne; author, lecturer and teacher to students of writing, in Colleges and Universities in USA, Mexico and Europe; *b* Texas, USA, 15 May 1890, family American (originating in Virginia) since 1648; *d* of Harrison Boone Porter, born in Kentucky, and Mary Alice Jones, Texas; *m* 1933, Eugene Dove Pressly (divorced); *m* 1938, Albert Russel Erskine, jun. (divorced); no *c. Educ:* private schools for girls in Louisiana and Texas. Guggenheim Foundn Fellowship, 1931-33; Gold Medal, Soc. for the Libraries of NY Univ., 1940; Fellow of Library of Congress, 1944 (Fellow of Regional American Literature). Lectr to students of writing, Stanford Univ., California, 1948-49; Vice-Pres., Nat. Inst. of Arts and Letters, NY, 1950; guest lectr on Literature, Spring Semester, Univ. of Chicago, 1951; one of reps of American Lit. to Internat. Festival of the Arts, Paris, 1952; Vis. Lectr in Contemporary Poetry, Univ. of Michigan, 1953-54; Fulbright Grant, Vis. Lectr, Univ. of Liège, 1954-55; Writer-in-residence, First Semester, Univ. of Virginia, 1958-59; Glasgow Prof., Second Semester, Washington and Lee Univ., Va, 1959; Ewing Lecturer, University of California, Los Angeles (UCPA), 1960; Dept State grants (USIA) Lecturer on American Literature, Mexico, 1960, 1964; first Regents' Lectr, Univ. of California, Riverside, 1961. Appointed by President Lyndon B. Johnson as Member Commn on Presidential Scholars, 1964. Poetry Consultant, Library of Congress, 1965-70. Hon. DLit Woman's Coll., Univ. of North Carolina, 1949; Hon. DLitt Hum, Univ. of Michigan, 1954; Hon. DLitt: Smith Coll., 1958, Maryville Coll., 1968; Sladmore Coll., 1976; Howard Payne Univ., 1976; Hon. DHL, Univ. of Maryland, 1966; Hon. Phi Beta Kappa, Univ. of Maryland, 1966. Doctor of Fine Arts, La Salle Coll. Emerson-Thoreau Bronze Medal for Service to Literature, American Academy of Arts and Sciences, 1962; Nat. Book Award for Fiction, 1966; Pulitzer Prize for Fiction, 1966; Gold Medal for Literature, National Inst. of Arts and Letters, 1967; Edgar Allan Poe Award Mystery Writers of America, 1972. *Publications: books:* Flowering Judas, 1930; Pale Horse, Pale Rider, 1939; The Leaning Tower, 1944; Ship of Fools, 1962; Collected Stories, 1965; A Christmas Story, 1967; *essays:* The Days Before, 1952; Collected Essays and Occasional Writings, 1969; *history:* The Never-Ending Wrong, 1977; *translations:* Katherine Anne Porter's Old French Song Book, Paris, 1933; The Itching Parrot (from the Spanish), 1942. *Recreations:* old music, medieval history, reading, cookery; growing camellias, roses, irises.
[Died 18 Sept. 1980.

PORTER, Keith Ridley Douglas, MBE 1944; FRCP, FFCM, DPH, LDSRCS; Regional Medical Officer, SE Thames Regional Health Authority, since 1973; *b* 27 March 1913; *s* of

Douglas David Porter and Olive Lucia (*née* Deck); *m* 1939, Elsie Grace, *d* of Captain Hartley Holmes, OBE, RA, and Elsie (*née* Walker); two *s* one *d*. *Educ:* Monkton Combe Sch., Bath; Guy's Hosp. Served War of 1939-45 (despatches twice, MBE). Sen. Admin. MO: N Ireland Hosp. Authority, 1964-69; SE Metrop. Regional Hosp. Bd, 1969-73. Council Member: London Sch. of Hygiene, 1970-75; Guy's Hosp. Med. Sch., 1971-75; Mem., Council for Professions Supp. to Medicine, 1971-75. Fellow, WHO, 1963. Mem. Court, Kent Univ., 1977-. QHP, 1977-. *Publication:* (jtly) Challenges for Change, 1971. *Recreations:* gardening, swimming, travel. *Address:* Knowle Orchard, Cuckfield, Sussex RH17 5ES. *T:* Haywards Heath 54088.
[Died 5 Dec. 1977.

PORTLAND, 7th Duke of, *cr* 1716; **William Arthur Henry Cavendish-Bentinck,** KG 1948; Earl of Portland, Viscount Woodstock, and Baron of Cirencester, 1689; Marquess of Titchfield, 1716; Baron Bolsover, 1880; Lord Lieutenant of Nottinghamshire, 1939-62; Chancellor of Nottingham University, 1954-71; *b* 16 March 1893; *e s* of 6th Duke and Winifred, DBE 1935 (*d* 1954), *d* of late Thomas Yorke Dallas-Yorke; *S* father 1943; *m* 1915, Hon. Ivy Gordon-Lennox (DBE 1958; Maid of Honour to Queen Alexandra, 1912-15), *o d* of late Lord Algernon Gordon-Lennox; one *d* (and one *d* decd). *Educ:* Eton. Lieutenant Royal Horse Guards; MP (U) Newark Division Notts, 1922-43; an Asst Whip, 1927; Junior Lord of the Treasury (unpaid), 1928-29 and 1931; commanded Notts Yeomanry (Sherwood Rangers), 1933-36. Hon. LLD, Nottingham, 1955. *Heir: kinsman* Major Sir Ferdinand William Cavendish-Bentinck, KBE, CMG. *Address:* Welbeck Woodhouse, Worksop, Notts. *T:* Worksop 2460; Welbeck Abbey, Worksop; Langwell, Berriedale, Caithness.
[Died 21 March 1977.

PORTLAND, 8th Duke of, *cr* 1716; **Ferdinand William Cavendish-Bentinck,** KBE 1956; CMG 1941; Earl of Portland, Viscount Woodstock, Baron Cirencester, 1689; Marquess of Titchfield, 1716; Member: East African Production and Supply Council; East African Advisory Council on Agriculture, Animal Industry and Forestry; East African Agricultural, Forestry and Veterinary Research Organisations Committee; Chairman and Founder of Kenya Association, 1932; *b* 4 July 1889; *s* of (William George) Frederick Cavendish-Bentinck (*d* 1948) (*g g s* of 3rd Duke) and Ruth Mary St Maur (*d* 1953); *S* kinsman, 1977; *m* 1st, 1912, Wentworth Frances Hope-Johnstone (marr. diss.); 2nd, 1950, Gwyneth, MBE, *widow* of Colonel D. A. J. Bowie, RA. *Educ:* Eton; RMC, Sandhurst; Germany. Late 60th Rifles (KRRC); served Malta, India and European War, 1914-18 (severely wounded, despatches); GSO War Office; Company Comdr, and later Asst Adjutant RMC, Sandhurst; worked for Vickers Ltd on Continent with HQ Brussels, 1923-24; Private Secretary to Governor of Uganda, 1925-27; Hon. Secretary Kenya Convention of Associations, 1930. Member for Agriculture and Natural Resources in Kenya Government, 1945-55; Speaker of Kenya Legislative Council, 1955-60 (MLC, and MEC, Kenya, 1934-60). Chairman: Tanganyika League and African Defence Federation, 1938; Agricultural Production and Settlement Board, Kenya, 1939-45; Timber Controller for East Africa, 1940-45; Member of East African Civil Defence and Supply Council, 1940-45; a Delegate to Delhi Conference, 1940; contested South Kensington, 1922; Member of many Commissions and Select Cttees. Officier de la Couronne (Belgium). *Publications:* articles on African subjects. *Heir: b* Lord William Cavendish-Bentinck, CMG. *Clubs:* Turf, Bath, Beefsteak; Muthaiga (Nairobi). *[Died 13 Dec. 1980.*

PORTWAY, Col Donald, CBE 1957; TD; DL; JP; MA; FICE; Hon. MIMI; Dean, Faculty of Engineering and Professor of Mechanical Engineering, University of Khartoum, 1957-61, retired; Hon. Fellow: Downing College, Cambridge; St Catharine's College, Cambridge; Emeritus Fellow Trumbull College, Yale University, USA; *b* 28 June 1887; *s* of late Ald. H. H. Portway, JP, Halstead, Essex; *m* 1919, Sophia Maud Grace, *niece* and adopted *d* of late J. A. Bezant, JP, Mettingham, Suffolk; one *d*. *Educ:* Felsted Sch.; Downing Coll., Cambridge (Senior Scholar). 1st Class Hons Mech. Sci. Tripos; Research in Mechanical Engineering, Cambridge Univ., 1911; Asst Master at RN Coll., Dartmouth, 1912; BEF 1914, 2nd Lieut to Major, RE; Fellow of St Catharine's Coll., Cambridge, and Lecturer in Engineering Dept, Cambridge Univ., 1919, subsequently Tutor, Senior Tutor and President of St Catharine's Coll., 14 years Proctor or Motor Proctor. Master of St Catharine's Coll., 1946-57. BEF 1939, as Bt Lieut-Colonel, RE (despatches), subsequently Colonel, General Staff. Army Cadet Comdt for Cambridgeshire and Isle of Ely, 1945-51; Sector Comdr, Home Guard, 1951-54. Joint Hon. Colonel University OTC Cambridge, 1950-57. *Publications:* Examples in Elementary Engineering, 1937; Science and Mechanization in Land Warfare,

1938; Military Science To-day, 1940; Talks to Future Officers, 1941; The Quest of Leadership, 1945; Korea, the Land of Morning Calm, 1953; Militant Don, 1963; Memoirs of an Academic Old Contemptible, 1971. *Recreations:* swimming, gardening; formerly winner 4 years running of Inter-Varsity Middleweights. *Address:* 33 Millington Road, Cambridge. *Clubs:* Royal Automobile; Hawks (Cambridge).
[Died 19 March 1979.

POSTGATE, Raymond William, OBE 1966; Writer; *b* Cambridge, 6 Nov. 1896; *s* of Prof. J. P. Postgate, MA, DLitt, FBA; *gs* of Dr John Postgate; *m* 1918, Daisy, *d* of Rt Hon. George Lansbury; two *s*. *Educ:* Perse Sch., Cambridge; Liverpool Coll.; St John's Coll., Oxford. Eight years in Fleet Street, chiefly as Foreign sub-editor on the old Daily Herald; edited several Socialist journals; Departmental Editor, xivth edn, Encyclopædia Britannica; Civil Servant, 1942-50; European representative, Alfred A. Knopf Inc., NY, 1930-49; President, Good Food Club since 1949. *Publications:* The International During the War, 1918; The Bolshevik Theory, 1920; Revolution from 1789 to 1906, 1920; The Workers' International, 1920; The Builders' History, 1923; Out of the Past, 1922; History of the British Workers, 1926; Murder, Piracy and Treason, 1925; Pervigilium Veneris (ed. and trans. 1924); That Devil Wilkes, 1930; The Conversations of Dr Johnson, 1930; Robert Emmet, 1931; No Epitaph, 1932; Karl Marx, 1933; How to Make a Revolution, 1934; What to Do with the BBC, 1935; (with G. A. Vallance) Those Foreigners, 1937; Verdict of Twelve, 1940; Somebody at the Door, 1943; (with G. D. H. Cole) The Common People, 1746-1946, 1946; Life of George Lansbury, 1951; Plain Man's Guide to Wine, 1951 (15th rev. edn, 1970); The Ledger is Kept, 1953; The Story of a Year, 1848, 1955; An Alphabet of Wine, 1955; Mitsou by Colette (trs. 1957); Every Man is God, 1959; Outline of History, by H. G. Wells (latest revised edn 1970); Home Wine Cellar, 1960; Portuguese Wine, 1969; The Story of a Year, 1798, 1969; (ed and trans.) The Agamemnon of Aeschylus, 1970. Author and Editor, Good Food Guide, annually 1951-54; biennially since 1955 (latest edition, for 1969-70, 1969). *Recreation:* walking. *Address:* Red Lion Cottage, Blean, Kent. *T:* Blean 474. *Club:* Savile.
[Died 29 March 1971.

POSTILL, Ronald, TD 1943; MA; Tutor for admissions, Millfield School; *b* 7 Feb. 1907; *er s* of late Harry Postill, Bridlington, Yorks, and S. Elizabeth Postill; *m* 1st, 1932, Nathalie Grace (marr. diss. 1938); one *d*; 2nd, 1939, Yvonne D. P. Ebdy; one *s*. *Educ:* Bridlington Sch.; Trinity Coll., Cambridge. Open Exhibitioner in Natural Sciences; BA 1928; MA 1944. Asst Master: Aldenham Sch., 1928-30; Tonbridge Sch., 1930-39 and 1945; Headmaster, Victoria Coll., Jersey, 1946-67; Tutor, Millfield Sch., 1967. Commissioned TA General List, 1928; comd Tonbridge Sch. OTC 1938-39; served War of 1939-45, Royal Signals; Comdt Royal Signals OCTU, 1944-45. King Haakon VII Liberty Cross (Norway), 1945. *Recreations:* criticising cricket (played for Hertfordshire, 1930-34); crosswords and cryptic puzzles. *Address:* Lavender Cottage, Charlton Adam, Somerton, Som. *T:* Charlton Mackrell 328.
[Died 24 March 1980.

POTEZ, Andrew Louis; Special Commissioner of Income Tax, since 1977; *b* 23 June 1920; *s* of Marcel Potez and Geraldine (*née* Mackenzie); *m* 1948, June Rosemary, *d* of Sydney Avila; three *s*. *Educ:* Ampleforth Coll.; Oriel Coll., Oxford (BA). Called to the Bar, Middle Temple, 1948. Served War, Army, 1940-46 (Burma Star; Temp. Major). Office of Solicitor of Inalnd Revenue, 1949-55; Legal Adviser, C&A Modes Ltd, 1955-60; Schweppes Ltd, 1960-69 (Legal Manager; Sec., Schweppes Overseas; dir of gp cos); in practice at the Bar, 1969-76. *Recreations:* living in Dedham Vale, ecumenism. *Address:* Knights Manor, Dedham, Colchester, Essex. *T:* Colchester 323355; 95 Campden Hill Towers, Notting Hill Gate, W11. *T:* 01-727 1678.
[Died 10 Oct. 1977.

POTT, Col Douglas, CIE 1929; DSO 1917; MC; Indian Army, retired; late 6th DCO Lancers; *b* 1888; *s* of late Colonel William Pott of Springfields, Steyning, Sussex. *Educ:* Wellington Coll. Served NW Frontier of India, 1908 (medal and clasp); European War, 1914-18 (despatches, DSO, MC); Instructor, Senior Officers' Sch., Belgaum, 1936-39; retired, 1939. *Address:* Thurston Old Vicarage, Bury St Edmunds, Suffolk. *Club:* Cavalry.
[Died 22 Nov. 1974.

POTTER, David Morris; Coe Professor of American History, Stanford University, since 1961; Harold Vyvyan Harmsworth Professor of American History, and Fellow of Queen's College, Oxford, 1947-48; *b* Augusta, Georgia, 6 Dec. 1910; *s* of David Morris and Katie Brown Potter; *m* 1948, Dilys Mary Roberts (*d* 1969); one *d*. *Educ:* Emory (AB); Yale (MA, PhD). Instructor in

History, University of Mississippi, 1936-38, and at Rice Inst., 1938-42. Yale Univ., Asst Professor, 1942-47; Associate Professor, 1947-49; Professor, 1949-50; Coe Prof., 1950-61. Editor, Yale Review, 1949-51; Fellow, Timothy Dwight Coll., 1942-61. Commonwealth Fund Lecturer, University College, London, 1963. *Publications:* Lincoln and his Party in the Secession Crisis, 1942; Trail to California; The Overland Journal of Vincent Geiger and Wakeman Bryarly, 1945; (with Jas H. Croushore) A Union Officer in the Reconstruction, 1948; (with T. G. Manning) Nationalism and Sectionalism in America, 1949; (with T. G. Manning) Government and the American Economy, 1949; People of Plenty: Economic Abundance and the American Character, 1954; The South and the Sectional Conflict, 1968. *Address:* Department of History, Stanford University, Stanford, California, USA. *[Died 18 Feb. 1971.*

POTTER, Sir Henry (Steven), KCMG 1956 (CMG 1948); MA (Cantab); retired as British Resident, Zanzibar (1954-60); *b* 7 March 1904; *er s* of late Charles Edward Potter, MD; *m* 1929, Ruth Newton; one *s* one *d. Educ:* Shrewsbury Sch.; Queens' Coll., Cambridge. Colonial Administrative Service, District Officer, Kenya, 1926-44; Deputy Financial Secretary, Kenya, 1944-45; Financial Secretary, Uganda, 1945-48; Chief Secretary, Uganda, 1948-52; Chief Secretary, Kenya, 1952-54. KStJ 1958; Order of Brilliant Star of Zanzibar (1st Class), 1959. *Recreation:* gardening. *Address:* Pen Pits, Penselwood, Wincanton, Somerset. *Club:* Nairobi (Kenya). *[Died 14 Nov. 1976.*

POTTER, Prof. Simeon, PhD (Prague); FRSL; Professor Emeritus, Liverpool University; *b* London, 19 Jan. 1898; *y s* of George Potter and Matilda Holdsworth; *m* 1936, Doris Clara Mackay. *Educ:* Kilburn Grammar Sch.; Queen Mary Coll. and University Coll., London (MA); St John's Coll., Oxford (BLitt). Served European War in Royal Navy, Atlantic and Mediterranean, 1916-19; Asst Master, Harrow County Sch., 1921-24; Lecturer in English, University of Brno, 1924-31; broadcast frequently for Prague Radio, 1927-31; Lecturer in English and Adviser to Overseas Students, Univ. of Southampton, 1931-45; Lecturer in Linguistics, Univ. of Aarhus, 1934-35; Baines Prof. of English Language and Philology, Univ. of Liverpool, 1945-65. Guest Prof., Westfield Coll., London, 1967-68. Member Council, Philological Society, 1933-61; Hon. Fellow, Inst. of Linguists; Jubilee Medal, 1973; Jt Editor, The Language Library. *Publications:* Everyday English, 1927; An English Vocabulary, 1930; An English Grammar, 1932; The Winchester Bede, 1935; The Outlook in English Studies, 1946; Our Language, 1950; Cheshire Place-Names, 1955; Modern Linguistics, 1957; (ed) Goad: Language in History, 1958; Language in the Modern World, 1960; English Life and Speech, 1964; (ed) Bradley, The Making of English, 1968; Changing English, 1969; essays and reviews contributed to Philologica Pragensia, Anglia, Erasmus, Encyclopædia Britannica, Essays and Studies, etc. *Address:* Maze Cottage, Hampton Court Road, East Molesey, Surrey KT8 9BY. *T:* 01-977 2953. *[Died 6 Aug. 1976.*

POULETT, 8th Earl *cr* 1706; **George Amias Fitzwarrine Poulett;** Baron Poulett, 1627; Viscount Hinton of Hinton St George, 1706; *b* 23 June 1909; *s* of 7th Earl; *S* father, 1918; *m* 1st, 1935, Oriel Ross (whom he divorced in 1941); 2nd, 1941, Lorraine Lawrence (*d* 1961), of Svendborg, Denmark, and England; 3rd, 1968, Margaret Christine Ball. *Educ:* Eton. Served pupil apprenticeship as mechanical engineer at GWR Locomotive Works, Swindon, and Signal Factory, Reading. Technical Asst: to Chief Mechanical Engr, Woolwich Arsenal, 1940-41; to Director of Ordnance Factories (Small Arms), 1941-43. Assoc. Inst., Railway Signal Engineers; Assoc. Mem. Inst., British Engineers. Coronation Medal, 1953. *Heir:* none. *Address:* Lille Hus, Gorey, Jersey, Channel Islands. *T:* Jersey East 2270. *Club:* Carlton. *[Died 1 March 1973 (ext).*

POULTON, Lt-Col Henry Mortimer, CIE 1942; late IA; Indian Political Service (retired); *b* 23 April 1898; *m* 1926, Phœbe, *d* of late Charles Frederick Howell. First commission, 1917; joined Political Dept, 1922; Resident, Central India, 1946; retd, 1947. *Address:* Folly End, Milford on Sea, Hants. *T:* 3244. *[Died 1 Sept. 1973.*

POUND, Sir Derek Allen, 4th Bt, *cr* 1905; *b* 7 April 1920; *o s* of Sir Allen Leslie Pound, 3rd Bt, LLB; *m* 1942, Joan Amy, *d* of James Woodthorpe, Boston, Lincs; one *s* one *d. Educ:* Shrewsbury. Commissioned Royal Artillery, 1941. *Heir:* *s* John David Pound [*b* 1 Nov. 1946; *m* 1968, Heather Frances O'Brien (marr. diss.), *o d* of Harry Jackson Dean; one *s*; *m* 1978, Penelope Ann, *er d* of Grahame Rayden]. *Address:* Saham Grove Hall, Shipolham, Thetford, Norfolk.
[Died 23 Dec. 1980.

POUND, Ezra, PhB, MA, DLitt; American poet and composer; Fellow, Academy of American Poets, 1963; *b* 30 Oct. 1885; *s* of H. L. and Isabel Weston Pound; *m* 1914, Dorothy Shakespear; one *s* one *d. Educ:* University of Pennsylvania (MA, Fellow in Romanics); Hamilton College (PhB). Travel and study in Spain, Italy, and Provence, 1906-7; informally, literary executor for the late Ernest Fenollosa, work on the Japanese Noh drama and on Japanese and Chinese poetry, 1914; London Editor of The Little Review, 1917-19; formerly editor of the Exile. Contributor to Rassegna Monetaria, Criterion, Action, British Union Quarterly, Townsman, Hudson Review. A follower of Confucius and Ovid. Continued to speak on Rome Radio after Pearl Harbour on condition that he never be asked to say anything contrary to his conscience or contrary to his duties as an American citizen; a condition observed by the Italian Government. Is now resident in Italy. *Publications: Poems:* A Lume Spento, 1908; Personæ, 1909; Exultations, 1909; Provença, 1910; Canzoni, 1911; Ripostes, 1912; Cathay, 1915; Lustra, 1916; Quia Pauper Amavi, 1919; Umbra (collected early poems), 1920; Hugh Selwyn Mauberley, 1920; Cantos I-XVI, 1925; Personæ (The Collected Poems), 1926; Cantos XVII-XXVII, 1928; XXX, 1930; Cantos 31-41, 1934; Fifth Decad of Cantos, 1937; Cantos 52-71, 1940; Pisan Cantos, 74-84, 1948; Section Rock-Drill, 85-95, 1955; Thrones 96-109 de los cantares, 1959; Selected Cantos, 1967; Collected Shorter Poems, 1968. *Music:* two operas, Le Testament, 1919-21, partial performance, Paris, 1926; Guido Cavalcanti, 1931-32. *Prose:* The Spirit of Romance, 1910; Gaudier Brzeska, 1916; Pavannes and Divisions, 1918; Instigations, 1920; Indiscretions, 1923; Antheil and the Treatise on Harmony, 1924; Imaginary Letters, 1930; How to Read, 1931; Prolegomena, Vol. I, 1932; ABC of Economics, 1933; ABC of Reading, 1934; Make it New, 1934; Social Credit, an Impact, 1935; Jefferson and/or Mussolini, 1935; Polite Essays, 1936; Digest of the Analects, 1937; Guide to Kulchur, 1938; What is Money for?, 1939; Literary Essays, 1954; Pavannes and Divagations, 1958. A number of these have been trans. into several languages. *Translations:* The Sonnets and Ballate of Guido Cavalcanti, 1912 and 1913; Certain Noble Plays of Japan, from the Fenollosa MSS, with Introduction by W. B. Yeats 1916; Noh, or Accomplishment, 1917; 12 Dialogues of Fontenelle, 1917; Gourmont's Physique de l'amour; The Ta Hio (Amer. version), 1928; Cavalcanti complete, definitive Text, 1932; The Classic Anthology defined by Confucius, 1954; Sophokles' Women of Trachis; Pea, Moscardino, 1956. *Written in Italian* (some trans. by others into English, etc): Confucio; Studio Integrale; L'Asse che non vacilla; Lavoro ed Usura; Natura Economica degli Stati Uniti; and numerous essays. German vols include: Masken; Frauen von Trachis. *Editor:* Catholic Anthology, 1915; Letters of John Butler Yeats, 1917; Profile, Active Anthology, 1933; The Chinese Written Character, by Ernest Fenollosa (ed with notes), 1936, etc. *Relevant publications:* The Letters of Ezra Pound (ed by D. D. Paige), 1951; The Translations of Ezra Pound, 1953; (by Charles Norman) Ezra Pound, 1969; (by Mary de Rachewiltz) Discretions, 1971. Art books Scheiwiller Series: La Martinelli, 1956; Gaudier-Brzeska, Brancusi, 1957; *posthumous publication:* Selected Prose 1909-1965, 1973. *Recreation:* the public taste. *Address:* c/o Bircham & Co., 1 Dean Farrar Street, Westminster, SW1H 0DY. *[Died 1 Nov. 1972.*

POWELL, Alan Richard, FRS 1953; retired; Research Manager, Johnson, Matthey and Co. Ltd, 1918-54; Research Consultant, 1954-59; *b* 6 March 1894; *s* of Alfred Powell and Ellen Brown; *m* 1st, 1914, Marguerite Tremmel (*d* 1956); one *s* three *d*; 2nd, 1960, Mildred Mary, *widow* of Arthur John Coleman. *Educ:* City of London School. Analytical chemist with G. T. Holloway & Co., Ltd, Poplar, 1913-18; Chief Chemist, 1916-18; started Research Laboratory with Johnson, Matthey and Co. Ltd, Hatton Garden, EC1 1918; more extensive Research Laboratories built at Wembley, 1938, extended, 1948, 1954. FIM 1947; FRIC 1948. *Publications:* Analysis of Ores and Minerals of the Rarer Elements (with late W. R. Schoeller), 1st edn 1918, 2nd edn 1940, 3rd edn 1954. Articles on Platinum Group Metals, etc. in Thorpe's Dictionary of Chemistry; articles on Rare Metals in Scott's Standard Methods of Chemical Analysis, 6th edn 1962. Chapter on Platinum Group Metals in Wilson's Comprehensive Analytical Chemistry, Vol. 10, 1961. Contributor to The Analyst, Journal of Applied Chemistry, Jl Chem. Soc., Bulletin Inst. Min. Met. Jl Inorg. Nucl. Chem. *Recreation:* gardening. *Address:* Red Roofs, Sycamore Road, Amersham, Buckinghamshire HP6 6BB. *T:* Amersham 6308.
[Died 11 Oct. 1975.

POWELL, Frank John; Metropolitan Police Magistrate, 1936-63; *b* 15 March 1891; *e s* of late Francis Cox Powell; *m* 1st, 1915, Irene Hesse (*d* 1955), *er d* of Arthur Wyatt; two *s* one *d*; 2nd, Joan (*d* 1965), *yr d* of F. L. Selley, MBE; 3rd, Betty Edelson (*d* 1971). *Educ:* Rutlish; Inns of Court. Called to Bar, Middle

Temple, 1921; contested (L) Kingston-on-Thames, 1929 and 1935; Queen's Westminster Rifles, 1910-14; King's Own Yorkshire LI, 1914-18; gassed Loos, 1915; Captain and Adjutant. Magistrate: Greenwich and Woolwich, 1936-40; Tower Bridge, 1940-42; Clerkenwell, 1942-63. Member Chairmen's Panel, Metropolitan Juvenile Courts, 1946-52. Hon. Legal adviser New Malden Citizens Advice Bureau, 1939-46. Chm. 1950-53. Mem. House of Laity of Church Assembly, 1950-64. Chm. Nat. Assoc. of Homes and Hostels, 1955-60; Pres. Probation Officers Christian Fellowship, 1954-66; Mem. Council of Magistrates Association, 1942-60. JP Surrey, 1937. *Publications:* The trial of Jesus Christ; Justice in Magistrates' Courts; The Roots of Crime (jointly), 1954. *Recreation:* golf. *Address:* 42 Queen's Park, West Drive, Bournemouth, Hants. *T:* Bournemouth 36730. *[Died 31 Oct. 1971.*

POWELL, Rear-Adm. James, DSO 1919; RN (retired); *b* 1887; *s* of late James Powell, of Lower Lockhams, Botley, Hants; *m* 1914, Gertrude Eileen, *d* of late Lt-Col F. Blenkinsop, IMS; one *s* three *d. Educ:* Eton; HMS Britannia. Lieut 1908; Lieut-Commander, 1916; Commander, 1922; Captain, 1929; served European War, 1914-19 (despatches, DSO); Captain-in-charge and King's Harbour Master, Portland, 1936-38; Captain-in-charge, Bermuda, 1938-40; Rear-Admiral, 1940; retired list, 1940; Commodore-in-charge, Bermuda, 1940-42; Commodore RNR of Convoy, 1942-43; Commodore Superintendent of Taranto Dockyard and other Italian Ports, 1944-45. Citizen and Merchant Taylor; Younger Brother of Trinity House. *Address:* Roman Villa, Twyford, Hants. *[Died 7 Sept. 1971.*

POWELL, Lawrence Fitzroy, MA Oxon; Hon. DLitt Oxford, 1969; Hon. DLitt Durham; FRSL; Librarian of the Taylor Institution, Oxford University, 1921-49; *b* 9 Aug. 1881; *y s* of H. Powell and Anne Budd; *m* 1909, Ethelwyn Rebecca Steane (*d* 1941), a member of the staff of the Oxford Dictionary; one *s. Educ:* a London Board School and privately. Junior member of staff of Bodleian Library; member editorial staff of Oxford English Dictionary, 1902-16, 1919-21; served during European War at Admiralty, 1916-19; Examiner in Literary History for Library Association, 1930-33; Leverhulme Research Fellow, 1936; Lamont Lecturer, Yale University, 1961. Vice-President Bibliographical Soc.; Vice-Pres. Edinburgh Bibliographical Society; Member of Johnson Club; Pres. Johnson Society of London; Pres. Johnson Society of Lichfield; Hon. Mem. Mod. Lang. Assoc. of America; Hon. Fellow: Pembroke Coll., Oxford; St Catherine's Coll., Oxford; Australian and S Pacific Soc. for Eighteenth Century Studies. *Publications:* Boswell's Life of Johnson, 4 vols, 1934; Boswell's Journal of a Tour to the Hebrides and Johnson's Diary of a Journey into North Wales, 2 vols, 1950 (new edition of vols 5 and 6, 1965); Boswell: Journal of a Tour to the Hebrides, 1958; (with W. J. Bate) an edition of Johnson's Adventurer, 1963 (Vol. 2 of the Yale Edition of Johnson's works), and other Johnsonian publications, etc; articles and reviews chiefly on 18th-century subjects. *Recreations:* formerly walking, chess. *Address:* The Tracey Nursing Home, Broughton Road, Banbury, Oxon. *Club:* Union Society (Oxford). *[Died 17 July 1975.*

POWELL, Dame Muriel (Betty), DBE 1968 (CBE 1962); Chief Nursing Officer, Scottish Home and Health Department, 1970-76; *b* 30 Oct. 1914; *d* of late Wallace George Powell and late Anne Elizabeth Powell, Cinderford, Glos. *Educ:* East Dean Grammar Sch., Cinderford; St George's Hosp., London. SRN 1937; SCM 1939; Sister Tutor Dipl., Battersea Coll. of Techn., 1941; Dipl. in Nursing, London Univ., 1942. Formerly: Ward Sister and Night Sister, St George's Hosp.; Sister, Co. Maternity Hosp., Postlip Hall, Glos. (War Emerg. Hosp.); District Nurse, Glos; Sister Tutor, Ipswich Borough Gen. Hosp.; Princ. Tutor, Manchester Royal Infirmary; Matron, St George's Hosp. London, 1947-70. Pres., Assoc. of Hosp. Matrons, 1958-63; Pres., Nat. Assoc. of State Enrolled Nurses, 1965-67; Dep. Pres., Royal Coll. of Nursing, 1963-64. Mem., Central Health Services Coun.; Chm., Standing Nursing Adv. Cttee, Min. of Health, 1958-69. *Publication:* Patients are People, 1975. *Recreation:* music. *Address:* Quay House, Newnham-on-Severn, Glos GL14 1BH. *T:* Newnham 510. *[Died 8 Dec. 1978.*

POWELL, Ray Edwin; *b* Table Grove, Illinois, 7 December 1887; *s* of late Joseph D. Powell and Sarah E. (*née* Anderson). *Educ:* Monmouth College; University of Illinois. Entered aluminium industry, 1909. Served War, in US Army, 1917-19; Captain. Settled in Canada, 1929. Hon. Chm. and Director, Aluminium Co. of Canada, Ltd; formerly director: Aluminium Ltd; Bell Telephone Co. of Canada; Bank of London and Montreal; Dominion Bridge Company, Ltd, etc, including many subsidiaries of Aluminium Ltd. Member Board of Governors: McGill Univ.; Univ. of Laval; Past Chancellor, McGill University, Montreal. Hon. DLitt, Monmouth Coll.; Hon. Dr of

Laws, Univ. of Laval; Hon. LLD: McGill Univ., Queen's Univ. *Address:* 1336 Redpath Crescent, Montreal 25, Quebec, Canada. *Clubs:* Mount Royal, St James's, Mount Bruno (Montreal); Seigniory, Montebello (Quebec); University, Links (New York). *[Died 9 Nov. 1973.*

POWELL, Major Sir Richard George Douglas, 3rd Bt, *cr* 1897; MC 1944, Bar 1945; Welsh Guards; Director: Bovis Ltd; Pierson, Heldring & Pierson (UK) Ltd; F. English Group Ltd; BUPA Medical Centre Ltd; The TH inc. Group (UK) Ltd; *b* 14 Nov. 1909; *o s* of Sir Douglas Powell, 2nd Bart, and Albinia Muriel, *e d* of W. F. Powell of Sharow Hall, Ripon; *S* father, 1932; *m* 1st, 1933, Elizabeth Josephine (*d* 1979), *o d* of late Lt-Col O. R. McMullen, CMG; one *s* two *d*; 2nd, 1980, Alice Maria, *e d* of Wilhelmus den Bode, Utrecht. *Educ:* Eton College. Served War of 1939-45 (MC and Bar). Croix Militaire 1st Class (Belgium), 1945; Assistant Military Attaché, British Embassy, Brussels, 1945-48. Dir-Gen., Inst. of Directors, 1954-74. *Heir: s* Nicholas Folliott Douglas Powell [*b* 17 July 1935; *m* 1960, Daphne Jean, *yr d* of Major and Mrs George Errington, Monkton Ranch, Figtree, Southern Rhodesia; one *s* one *d*]. *Address:* Mackney, Brightwell-cum-Sotwell, Oxon OX10 0SJ. *T:* Wallingford 37245. *Club:* Buck's. *[Died 16 July 1980.*

POWER, Beryl Millicent le Poer; *b* Dunham Massey, Cheshire, 17 Sept. 1891. *Educ:* Oxford High School for Girls; Girton College, Cambridge. Organiser and speaker for National Union of Women's Suffrage Societies, 1912-14; Investigator appointed under the Trade Boards Act, Board of Trade and Ministry of Labour, 1915-22; Deputy Chief Inspector of Trade Boards, 1923-29; holder of Laura Spelman Rockefeller Memorial Fellowship, studying technique of enforcement of Labour Laws in the United States of America, 1926-27; Member of Royal Commission on Indian Labour, 1929-31; Sec. Central Register of Persons with Scientific, Technical, Professional and Higher Administrative Qualifications, 1939-40; Asst Sec., Housing and Welfare, Ministry of Supply, 1941-45; UNRRA (China) Consultant in administration and welfare policies to Chinese National Relief and Rehabilitation Administration, 1945-47; seconded to ILO as Adviser on Employment and Youth Training to Chinese Ministry of Social Affairs, 1947-48; seconded to Economic Commission for Asia and the Far East, Thailand, 1949; retired from Civil Service (Min. of Labour and Nat. Service), 1951; Chm. Over Forty Assoc. for Women Workers, 1955-62. *Address:* 42 Clarendon Road, W11. *[Died 4 Nov. 1974.*

POWER, Lieut-Col Gervase Bushe, CIE 1916; MC; *b* 1883; *s* of late R. H. Power, Lismore, Co. Waterford; *m* 1953, Audrey Mary, *d* of Lt-Col E. M. A. Hogan, Indian Army (retired). *Educ:* Clifton Coll.; Royal Indian Engineering Coll., Coopers Hill. Indian Telegraphs Dept, 1905; Assistant Director Army Signals NW Frontier, 1919; served European War, Mesopotamia, 1915-19 (CIE, MC); Fourth Afghan War, 1919; resigned commission, 1919; Director of Telegraph Engineering, India, 1932-34; officiating Postmaster General, Madras, 1934; Postmaster General, Burma, 1935-36; retired, 1936. *Recreation:* gardening. *Address:* The Oast House, Tinley Lodge, Hildenborough, Kent. *T:* 3268. *[Died 26 Sept. 1974.*

POWERSCOURT, 9th Viscount, *cr* 1743; **Mervyn Patrick Wingfield;** Baron Wingfield, 1743; Baron Powerscourt (UK), 1885; Major, Royal Irish Fusiliers; late Lt 8th Hussars; *b* 22 Aug. 1905; *o s* of 8th Viscount Powerscourt and Sybil (*d* 1946), 2nd *d* of Walter Pleydell-Bouverie; *S* father 1947; *m* 1932, Sheila Claude, *o d* of Lt-Col Claude Beddington, 33 Grosvenor Street, W1; two *s* one *d. Educ:* RMC Sandhurst. Served War of 1939-45. *Heir: s* Hon. Mervyn Niall Wingfield [*b* 3 Sept. 1935; *m* 1962, Wendy Anne Pauline, *er d* of R. C. G. Slazenger; one *s* one *d*]. *Address:* Tarabeg, Dunsany, Co. Meath, Ireland. *T:* Tara 41. *Clubs:* Royal Thames Yacht; Royal Yacht Squadron (Cowes); Kildare Street (Dublin). *[Died 3 April 1973.*

POWIS, 5th Earl of, *cr* 1804; **Edward Robert Henry Herbert**, CBE 1945 (MBE 1938); TD; DL; psc; Viscount Clive, Baron Herbert, Baron Powis, 1804; Baron Clive, 1794; Baron Clive of Plassey in Ireland, 1762; Lieut-Colonel (Hon. Colonel) late Comdg 5th Bn KSLI, TA; late Major, KRRC; retired; *b* 19 May 1889; *e s* of Colonel Edward William Herbert, CB (*d* 1924), and *g g s* of 2nd Earl of Powis; *S* cousin, 1952; *m* 1932, Ella Mary, *d* of late Colonel W. H. Rathborne, Dublin. *Educ:* Eton; Christ Church, Oxford (MA). Joined KRRC 1909; served European War, 1914-19, France, Belgium; Staff Capt., 1917-18; DAQMG 1918; Iraq Ops, 1920-21. Captain, 1915; Major, 1927; retired, 1933; War of 1939-45 (CBE); Lieut-Colonel KSLI (TA) 1939; AAG War Office, Colonel, 1940. CC Salop, 1947-58, DL Salop, 1953. CStJ. *Heir: b* Hon. Christian Victor Charles Herbert [*b* 28 May 1904. Major late RAOC]. *Address:* 4 Green Street, W1. *T:*

01-499 8451; (Seat) Powis Castle, Welshpool. *T:* 3360. *Clubs:* Brooks's, United Service & Royal Aero. *[Died* 15 *Jan.* 1974.

POYNTER, (Frederick) Noel (Lawrence), BA, PhD, FLA, FRSL; Director, Wellcome Institute of History of Medicine, 1964-73; *b* 24 Dec. 1908; *s* of late H. W. Poynter; *m* 1st, 1939, Kate L. R. Marder (*d* 1966); no *c*; 2nd, 1968, Mrs Dodie Barry (*née* McClellan). *Educ:* King's and Univ. Coll., University of London. Asst Librarian, Wellcome Hist. Med. Lib., 1930; Chief Librarian, 1954. RAF, 1941-46. Founder Member, 1958, Fac. of Hist. of Medicine, Society of Apothecaries of London, Chm., 1971- (Hon. Sec. 1958-71); Member, Council, Bibliographical Society, 1960-64, 1965-72; President: Internat. Acad. of Hist. of Med., 1962-70; British Society of Hist. of Med., 1971-; XXIII Internat. Congress, Hist. of Med., London, 1972; Gideon Delaune Lecturer, Society of Apothecaries, 1964. Has given Memorial lectures, in USA; Hon. Lecturer in History of Medicine, University of British Columbia, 1966-; Henry Cohen Lecturer in Medicine, University of Jerusalem, 1968, Univ. of Liverpool, 1973; Vicary Lectr, RCS, 1973; Annual Orator, Med. Soc. London, 1974. Hon. Member, Royal Society of Medicine (Hist. Section); also Hon. Member various foreign societies, Fellow, Internat. Acads of the Hist. of Science, Medicine and Pharmacy; Hon. DLitt, California; Hon. MD Kiel; Hon. Fellow: Huguenot Society of London; Medical Society of London. *Publications:* Selected Writings of William Clowes (1544-1604), 1948; A Seventeenth Century Doctor and his Patients: John Symcotts (joint), 1951; Bibliography, some Achievements and Prospects, 1961; A Short History of Medicine (joint), 1961; The Journal of James Yonge (1647-1721), 1963; Gideon Delaune and his Family Circle, 1965; The Evolution of Medical Education in Britain, 1966; Medicine and Culture, 1968; Medicine and Man, 1971. Ed. several medical works; Ed., Medical History (quarterly) also Current Work in the History of Medicine (quarterly); also numerous articles in periodicals. *Recreations:* painting, chamber music, French literature. *Address:* 46600 Montvalent, Lot, France. *Club:* Athenæum.
[Died 12 *March* 1979.

PRATT, Sir Bernard; *see* Pratt, Sir E. B.

PRATT, Rear-Adm. Charles Bernard, CB 1961; retired; *b* 20 Feb. 1907; *s* of Rev. Charles Edward Pratt, Rector of Warbleton, Sussex, and Mrs Louisa Pratt; *m* 1945, Alice Margery, *d* of Charles Keeling, Sutton Coldfield, Warwicks; one *step d. Educ:* The King's Sch., Canterbury. Entered Navy, Special Entry cadet, 1925; Lieut, 1930; Lieut-Commander, 1938; Senior Engineer, HMS King George V, 1939-42; Commander, 1941; Captain, 1951; Commanding HMS Nuthatch, 1951-53; Chief of Staff to Flag Officer Reserve Aircraft, 1953-56; Naval Attaché, Rio de Janeiro, 1956-58; Rear Admiral, 1959; ADC to the Queen, Feb.-July 1959; Chief Staff Officer (Technical) to Flag Officer Air (Home), 1959-62; retired, 1962. *Address:* Christmas Lodge, Yapton, near Arundel, Sussex. *T:* Yapton 524.
[Died 1 *Aug.* 1973.

PRATT, Sir (E.) Bernard, Kt 1941; *b* 4 July 1889; *s* of Edmund Hustwayte Pratt and Sophie Gertrude Goodall; *m* 1st, 1944, Florence Ellen Mary Adeline Spurgin (*née* Rideal) (*d* 1967); 2nd, 1968, D'Arcy La Roche Gatehouse, Cheltenham. *Educ:* Nottingham High Sch. *Address:* Lake Cottage, Prestbury, Glos. *T:* Cheltenham 20673. *Clubs:* Oriental, Royal Automobile.
[Died 10 *Dec.* 1975.

PRATT, Rev. Canon Francis William; *b* 1900; *s* of Eliezer and Frances Elizabeth Pratt, Dunstable, Beds; *m* 1934, Phyllis May, *d* of Alexander and Kate Swift, Loughborough, Leics; three *s* (one *d* decd). *Educ:* St John's Coll., Durham; St Aidan's Coll. LTh 1927; BA 1928. Deacon, 1928; priest, 1929. Curate: St Margaret's, Leicester, 1928-30, Loughborough, 1930-34; Vicar, St Barnabas, New Humberstone, Leicester, 1934-44; Officiating Chaplain, Leicester City Mental Hospital, 1934-44; Vicar of Birstall, 1944-54; Rector of Wanlip, 1944-54; Curate-in-Charge, St John the Divine, Leicester, 1954-58; Chaplain, Leicester Cathedral, 1954-58. Hon. Chaplain to Bishop of Leicester, 1955-58; Surrogate, 1956; Second Canon Residentiary and Canon Treasurer, Leicester Cathedral, 1958-68; Master of Wyggeston Hospital, Leicester, 1957-68; retired, 1968. *Recreations:* walking and gardening. *Address:* Weybourne, Norfolk.
[Died 19 *Oct.* 1971.

PREM, Dr Dhani Ram; Padmashri, 1977; Lecturer on Hinduism, since 1979; Chairman, Federation of Indian Organisations (UK), since 1976; Founder-President, Asian Standing Conference, since 1973; Member, Liberal Party National Council, since 1973; Deputy Chairman, Joint Council for Welfare of Immigrants, since 1972; *b* 26 Sept. 1904; *s* of Jamna Das and Dalo Devi; *m* 1928, Ratan Prem; one *d. Educ:* National

Univs, Delhi and Banaras, India; Edinburgh Univ.; King's Coll. Hosp. Med. Sch.; Sch. of Tropical Med., London. MRCS, LRCP, DTM&H. Gandhi Movement (imprisoned), 1921; Sec., Indian Nat. Congress, Aligarh, India, 1923; Editor, Chand, Allahabad, India, 1931; Lectr, Nat. Med. Coll., Bombay, 1932; Mem., Birmingham CC, 1946; Mem. Nat. Cttee for Commonwealth Immigrants, 1965. Chm., Commonwealth Welfare Council, Midlands, 1965; Vice-Chm., Community Relns Council, Birm., 1968; Mem., PEP Adv. Cttee, 1973; President: W Midlands Indian Council; Nat. Council of Hindu Associations (UK), 1977-; Vivekanand Centre, 1977-; Hon. Dir, Indian Adv. Council; Trustee, Uganda Asian Relief Trust, 1973; Contested (L), Coventry SE, Feb. 1974; Mem., Gandhi Centenary Cttee (UK), 1970; Mem., BBC Radio Council, 1970. Scenario writer and Dir of Indian films, Bombay, 1932-38. Hon. DSc Aston, 1977. *Publications:* Heart of a Fallen Woman (novel), 1931, 2nd edn 1939; Darling (play), 1932; Vallari (short stories), 1933; Joan of Arc, 1934; Reawakening of Russia, 1934; Injection Therapy, 1937, 2nd edn 1938; Indian National Congress, 1942; Colour and British Politics, 1965, 2nd edn 1966. *Recreations:* reading detective novels, cine photography, being with children; Chm. Asian Music Circle, 1966. *Address:* 13 Harland Avenue, Croydon, Surrey CR0 5QB. *T:* 01-656 9159. *Club:* (Pres. 1964) Indian Social (Birmingham).
[Died 11 *Nov.* 1979.

PRESCOTT, Hilda F. M.; FRSL; *b* 22 Feb. 1896; *d* of late Rev. James Mulleneux Prescott and Margaret Prescott. *Educ:* Wallasey High Sch., Cheshire; Lady Margaret Hall, Oxford. MA Oxon; MA Manchester; research under late Prof. T. F. Tout. Jubilee Research Fellow at Royal Holloway Coll., 1958-60. Hon. DLitt Dunelm, 1957. *Publications:* The Unhurrying Chase, 1925; The Lost Fight, 1928; Flamenca, 1930; Son of Dust, 1932; Dead and not Buried, 1938; Spanish Tudor, 1940 (James Tait Black prize, 1941); The Man on a Donkey, 1952; Jerusalem Journey, 1954; Once to Sinai, 1957. *Address:* Orchard Piece, Charlbury, Oxon. *T:* Charlbury 342. *[Died* 5 *May* 1972.

PRESCOTT, Sir Stanley (Lewis), Kt 1965; OBE 1957; MSc (Manchester); Chairman, Board of Management, Royal Perth Hospital, since 1976 (Member since 1955, Deputy Chairman, 1972-76); Member Senate, Murdock University, 1973-76; *b* 21 March 1910; *s* of J. Prescott, JP, Tetbury, Glos, England; *m* 1937, Monica M., *d* of Rev. H. A. Job; two *s* two *d. Educ:* Tetbury Grammar Sch.; University of Manchester; Lancashire College. Wild Prizeman in Pharmacology, University of Manchester, 1934. Professor of Physiology, Cheeloo Univ., Tsinan, North China, 1936. Commissioned Royal Australian Air Force, 1941; Sqdn Leader, and appointed CO, No 1 Flying Personnel Research Unit, 1943-46. Master of Ormond Coll., Univ. of Melbourne, Australia, 1946-53; Vice-Chancellor, Univ. of W Australia, 1953-70. Chm., Aust. Vice-Chancellors' Cttee, 1964-65. Mem., Aitken Commn on University of Malaya, 1957; Chm., Commn on Nanyang Univ., Singapore, 1959; Commonwealth Consultant on Inter-University Council for Higher Education Overseas, 1960-70. Hon. LLD Western Australia. *Address:* 31 Esplanade Court, The Esplanade, South Perth, Western Australia 6151. *T:* 67-6963.
[Died 14 *July* 1978.

PRESLAND, John; (Gladys Bendit); author and lecturer; *b* Melbourne, Australia; *d* of John Frederick Williams, Cape Colony and London, and Alice Emily Presland; *m* 1st, John Herbert Skelton (*d* 1942); two *s*; 2nd, 1943, Francis Edmund Bendit (*d* 1953). *Educ:* Queen's Coll., London; Girton Coll., Cambridge. BA (Cantab). Honours in Medieval and Modern Languages; Director of YMCA Employment Bureau for Disabled Soldiers, 1919; in charge of Women's Section of Central Council for Economic Information, also Lecturer, 1920-24; London University Extension Lecturer in Literature, 1924-27; Member of Seafarer's Education Service, 1924-48; one-time Lecturer for League of Nations Union, Ashridge Park, Empire Marketing Board, etc; Member of Home Office Advisory Cttee on Aliens, 1940; Member of Council and Chairman of Foreign Relief and Rehabilitation Cttee, Save the Children Fund; Member of Council of British Societies for Relief Abroad, 1942-45. *Publications:* Joan of Arc, 1909; Mary Queen of Scots, 1910; Manin and the Defence of Venice, 1911; The Deluge, Marcus Aurelius, 1912; Songs of Changing Skies; King Monmouth, 1915; Poems of London, 1918; Dominion, 1925; Frustration, 1926; Barricade, 1927; Escape Me-Never, 1928; Mosaic, 1929; Satni, 1930; Albatross, 1931; Vae Victis: The Life of Ludwig von Benedek; Women and the Civilized State, 1934; Deedes Bey: A Study of Sir Wyndham Deedes, 1942; The Shaken Reed, 1945; Selected Poems, 1960. *[Died* 29 *Sept.* 1975.

PRESTON, Prof. George Dawson, MA, ScD; Harris Professor of Physics at Queen's College, Dundee, in the University of St

Andrews, 1943-66; now Emeritus; *b* 8 Aug. 1896; *s* of late Professor Thomas Preston, FRS, and Mrs K. M. Preston. MA, of Dublin; *m* 1923, Margaret Chrystal, MA; two *s* two *d*. *Educ:* Oundle Sch.; Gonville and Caius Coll., Cambridge. Served European War 7th Bn Alexandra Princess of Wales' Own Yorkshire Regt, 1914-18. Metallurgy Division, National Physical Laboratory, 1921-43. FRSE; FInstP; FPhysS. *Publications:* papers on X-ray analysis of metals and alloys, electron diffraction and electron microscopy in Phil. Mag., Proc. Royal Society, Proc. Physical Society, etc. *Address:* Craigellie, Alyth, Perthshire. *T:* Alyth 325. *[Died 22 June 1972.*

PRESTON, Kerrison; writer; *b* 21 May 1884; *s* of late Donald Preston, Solicitor, Bournemouth; *m* 1912, Evelyn Preston (second cousin) (*d* 1968); one *s* four *d* (and one *s* killed on active service, Tobruk, 1942). *Educ:* Rugby School. Practised as a family solicitor at Bournemouth, 1909-1949; held literary executorships, and many trusteeships. Founder and Governor Stanbridge School. Gave Blake Library to Westminster City, 1967. *Publications:* Blake and Rossetti, 1944; The Blake Collection of W. Graham Robertson, 1952; Letters from Graham Robertson, 1953; Blake's Fourfold Man; contributions to art magazines, etc. *Recreations:* books, pictures and grandchildren. *Address:* The Georgian House, Merstham, Surrey. *T:* Merstham 2647. *Clubs:* Authors'; Arts Theatre. *[Died 16 Jan. 1974.*

PRESTON, Adm. Sir Lionel (George), KCB 1934 (CB 1916); *b* 27 Sept. 1875; *m* 1st, Emily Elizabeth Bryant, Bridgwater, Somerset; 2nd, Ivy Lilian Record, Sheppey, Kent. *Educ:* Stubbington House, Fareham. Entered Britannia, 1888; Lieut, 1897; served in Rosario, Boxer Rebellion, 1900; specially promoted to Commander, 1907, for seamanlike handling of HMS Bruiser in heavy weather off Malta, and on a dark night, when, by taking his ship alongside HMS Ariel, which was rapidly sinking, the majority of the officers and crew were saved; served European War, 1915-16 (CB, Officer of Legion of Honour, despatches, for proceeding at once in HMS Skipjack to the assistance of two trawlers which had been mined off Scarborough, and anchoring the ship in the mine-field to destroy several mines which the trawlers had swept up); Captain, 1914; Commanded Grand Fleet Mine-Sweeping Flotilla, 1914-17; Director of Mine-Sweeping Division, Admiralty, 1917-19; in charge of the direction of the clearance of Mines in British areas after war; in command of the Patrol, Mine-Sweeping Training and Fishing Protection Flotilla, 1919-20; CO, RN Signal School, Portsmouth, 1920-22; Comd HMS Eagle, 1923-25; Rear-Admiral, 1925; ADC, 1925-26; Comd Third Cruiser Squadron, 1926-28; Vice-Admiral, 1930; Fourth Sea Lord and Chief of Supplies and Transport, 1930-32; Comdt Imperial Defence Coll., 1933-34; Admiral, 1934; retired 1935; recalled to service Sept. 1939 as Adviser on Mine Sweeping; Director Small Vessels Pool (which organised a list of small craft, largely used later in Dunkirk operation), 1940-45; reverted to retired list, 1945. *Publication:* Sea and River Painters of the Netherlands in the XVII Century. *Address:* Murrel House, Dunstable, Beds. *[Died 21 Sept. 1971.*

PRESTON, Sir Thomas (Hildebrand), 6th·Bt, *cr* 1815; OBE 1934; *b* 2 June 1886; *s* of William Thomas Preston, Gordon Highlanders, 2nd *s* of Sir Jacob Preston, 2nd Bt, Beeston Hall, Norfolk; *S* cousin, 1963; *m* 1913, Ella Henrietta v. Shickendantz; one *s* one *d*. *Educ:* Westminster; Trinity Hall, Cambridge. Conducted mining expeditions to Siberia and Caucasus; held many consular and diplomatic posts in Russia, Italy and Lithuania. One of HM Counsellors at Cairo, 1941; late Minister to Republic of Lithuania; seconded, 1947, as Resident Representative in Middle East, of Intergovernmental Committee on Refugees; retired, 1947; re-employed by FO on secretariat of Council of Foreign Ministers, 1948. Joined Messrs Thos de la Rue and Co., 1949. Associate and Official lecturer, Brit. Atlantic Cttee (NATO). Commander with star, Polonia Restitua, Poland, 1974. *Publications:* Before the Curtain, 1950; Composer of 2 ballets (performed publicly in London and elsewhere) and many other musical works. *Recreations:* tennis, golf, swimming. *Heir: s* Ronald Douglas Hildebrand Preston [*b* 9 Oct. 1916; *m* 1972, Pauleen, *d* of late Paul Lurcott. *Educ:* Westminster; Trinity College, Cambridge]. *Address:* Beeston Hall, Beeston St Lawrence, Norwich, Norfolk. *Club:* Royal Automobile. *[Died 30 Dec. 1976.*

PRETTY, Air Marshal Sir Walter (Philip George), KBE 1962 (CBE 1950; OBE 1942); CB 1957; *b* 2 May 1909; *s* of William Pretty; *m* 1940, Betty Finlayson Methven, *d* of late Sir Harry Methven, KBE; one *s* three *d*. *Educ:* Alleyns Sch.; RAF Coll., Cranwell. Served War of 1939-45 (despatches twice, OBE); Director-General of Navigational Services, Min. of Civil Aviation, 1948; Dir of Electronics Research and Development,

Min. of Supply, 1953; Director-General of Organisation, Air Ministry, 1958; Air Officer Commanding-in-Chief, Signals Command, 1961-64; Deputy Chief of the Defence Staff (Personnel and Logistics), Ministry of Defence, 1964-66. *Recreations:* gardening, fishing. *Address:* Chippings, Icklingham Road, Cobham, Surrey. *Club:* Royal Air Force. *[Died 17 Jan. 1975.*

PREVETT, Comdr Harry, OBE 1942; RN retired; Clerk to the Worshipful Company of Haberdashers, 1950-66; *b* 9 July 1900. Entered RN, 1917; Secretary to late Admiral Sir H. D. Pridham Wippell, KCB, CVO, 1936-47; retired, 1950. *[Died 2 March 1972.*

PRICE, Prof. Albert Thomas, DSc; FRAS; Professor of Applied Mathematics, University of Exeter (previously the University College of the South-West) 1952-68, now Emeritus; *b* 30 Jan. 1903; *e s* of Albert Thomas Price and Marie Lavinia (*née* Light); *m* 1947, Rose Ann Waterman; no *c*. *Educ:* Monmouth Sch.; Manchester University. Asst in Pure Mathematics, QUB, 1925-26; Asst Lecturer, 1926-30, Lecturer, 1930-46, and Asst Professor and Univ. Reader in Applied Mathematics, 1946-51, Imperial Coll. of Science and Technology, London; Professor and Head of Mathematics Dept, Roy. Technical Coll., Glasgow, 1951-52. Consultant to Admiralty, 1942-45. Guest investigator at Dept of Terrestrial Magnetism, Carnegie Instn, Washington, and at Inst. of Geophysics, Univ. of Calif, Los Angeles, 1952; Dean, Faculty of Science, Exeter Univ., 1954-58; Research Fellow, Univ. of Exeter, 1968-69. Internat. Geophysical Year Research Associate, Nat. Acad. of Sciences, Washington, DC, 1961-62. Consultant, Rand Corporation, Santa Monica, 1963. Chairman, Commn IV Internat. Assoc. Geomagnetism and Aeronomy, 1964-68; Member: Council of Royal Astronomical Soc., 1956-60; National Cttee for Geomagnetism and Aeronomy, 1946-; National Advisory Council on Education for Industry and Commerce, 1957-65; Regional Council for Further Educn for the South-West, 1953-65. Gold Medal, Royal Astronomical Soc., 1969. *Publications:* chapters in collected works include: The Earth's Mantle (ed T. Gaskell), 1967; Physics of Geomagnetic Phenomena (ed S. Matsushita and W. H. Campbell), 1967; The Earth in Space (ed A. H. Cook and T. F. Gaskell), 1968; contribs to Philosophical Transactions and Proc. Royal Soc., Jl of Royal Astron. Soc., Jl of Geophys. Res., Physics of Earth and Planetary Interiors, Space Science Reviews. *Recreation:* gardening. *Address:* 14 Corinium Gate, Cirencester, Glos. *T:* Cirencester 4271. *[Died 13 Dec. 1978.*

PRICE, Sir A(rchibald) Grenfell, Kt 1963; CMG 1933; DLitt (Adelaide), MA (Oxon); FRGS; MHR for Boothby, S Australia, 1941-43; Master, St Mark's College, University of Adelaide, 1925-57; University Lecturer in Geography, 1949-57; *b* Adelaide, 28 Jan. 1892; *s* of Henry Archibald Price, Banker, and Elizabeth Jane Price; *m* Kitty Pauline, *d* of C. W. Hayward, Solicitor, Adelaide; two *s* one *d*. *Educ:* St Peter's College, Adelaide, Magdalen College, Oxford. Housemaster St Peter's College, Adelaide, 1922-24; Member of Council, University of Adelaide, 1926-63; Macrossan Lecturer, University of Queensland, 1930; Chairman of Emergency Committee of S Australia, 1931-32; Research Fellowship, Rockefeller Foundation, 1932-33; Chm. SA Libraries Inquiry, 1936; Chm. Adv. Bd, Commonwealth Literary Fund, 1952-71; Hon. Sec. Australian Humanities Research Council, 1956-59, Hon. Treasurer, 1959-71; Chm. Council, Nat. Library of Australia, 1960-71; Cttee for Libraries, Austr. Adv. Cttee for Unesco, 1964-71. *Publications:* Causal Geography of World, 1918; South Australians and their Environment, 1921; The Foundation and Settlement of South Australia, 1924; (with Sir D. Stamp) Longmans' Geography of the World (Australasian edition), 1928; Founders and Pioneers of South Australia, 1929; History and Problems of Northern Territory, Australia, 1930; White Settlers in the Tropics, 1939; Australia Comes of Age, 1945; White Settlers and Native Peoples, 1949, repr. 1973; The Explorations of Captain James Cook in the Pacific (New York), 1957 and 1958, repr. 1969; The Winning of Australian Antarctica: Sir Douglas Mawson's BANZARE Voyages 1929-30, 1962; The Western Invasions of the Pacific and its Continents, 1963; The Importance of Disease in History (Syme Oration, RACS), 1964; The Challenge of New Guinea: Australian Aid to Papuan Progress, 1965; A History of St Mark's College, University of Adelaide, 1967; The Skies Remember: the story of Ross and Keith Smith, 1969; Island Continent: aspects of the historical geography of Australia and its territories, 1972; ed, The Humanities in Australia, 1959; contributed to Cambridge History of the British Empire. *Recreation:* fishing. *Address:* 33 Buxton Street, North Adelaide, SA 5006, Australia; University House, Canberra. *Clubs:* Adelaide (SA), Commonwealth (Canberra); Australasian Pioneers (Sydney). *[Died 20 July 1977.*

PRICE, Aubrey Joseph; *b* 29 October 1899; *s* of Joseph and Louise Price; *m* Margaret, *y d* of Capt. J. Roberton Harvey, RN; one *s* (and one *s* decd). *Educ:* City of Oxford School; Jesus College, Oxford (Ewelme Exhibitioner, Honours School of Nat. Science). House-master, Denstone Coll.; Sen. Science Master, Berkhamsted Sch.; Officer Commanding OTC; Headmaster, St Peter's Sch., York; Headmaster: Wellington School, Somerset, 1938-45; Royal Hospital Sch., Holbrook, 1945-47; Principal, Wymondham Training College, Norfolk, 1947-50; Warden, London Univ. Goldsmiths' Coll., 1950-53; Principal, Chester College, 1953-65, retd. Lieut Royal Naval Air Service, 1917-19. *Address:* 19 Durland Close, New Milton, Hants BH25 6NJ. *T:* New Milton 616950.   *[Died 29 May 1978.*

PRICE, Maj.-Gen. Charles Basil, CB 1945; DSO 1919; DCM 1915; VD; CD and Bar; retired from active management Canadian business; *b* 12 Dec. 1889; *s* of Charles Edward Burman Price, ARCO, and Catherine Durham Rogers; *m* 1915, Marjorie Meredith Holden Trenholme; one *s* (and one *s* killed in 1942 while serving with RCAF) four *d. Educ:* Montreal High School; Ottawa Collegiate Institute. Entered Bank of Montreal, Montreal, as junior clerk, 1905; with firm Evans & Evans, Ltd (Manufacturers' Agents), 1910-24; joined Elmhurst Dairy Ltd as Managing Director, 1924; joined Victoria Rifles of Canada Non-Permanent Active Militia, 1905; served in Flanders, 1914-19, with Royal Montreal Regt as CSM, Lieut, Captain, Major; Command Royal Montreal Regt Non-Permanent Active Militia, 1920-24, 1927-29; commanded 12th Inf. Bde Non-Permanent Active Militia, 1931-34; Commanded Duke of York's Royal Canadian Hussars, Non-Permanent Active Militia, Jan.-Oct. 1939; Command 3rd Inf. Bde Canadian Active Service Force, Sept. 1939; GOC 3rd Canadian Div. 1941; seconded to Canadian Red Cross Society as Overseas Commissioner, 1942; demobilised, 1945. President Canadian Club of Montreal, 1935-36; President Montreal Military Institute, 1937-38. Dominion President Canadian Legion, British Empire Service League, 1946-48 (Hon. Pres. 1948-61); Pres. Montreal Branch Royal Empire Society, 1946-49; Hon. Col Royal Montreal Regt, 1943-56; Hon. Col Comdt, Royal Canadian Infantry Corps, 1956-61. Patron, Montreal Br., Royal Commonwealth Soc., 1957-; Hon. Pres. Royal Canadian Legion, 1962-. Centennial Medal, 1967. *Recreation:* gardening. *Address:* Fayremead, Knowlton, PQ, Canada. *T:* Knowlton 243-6629. *Club:* United Services (Montreal).   *[Died 15 Feb. 1975.*

PRICE, Sir (Charles) Roy, KCMG 1950 (CMG 1942); *b* 1 May 1893; *s* of late W. Sydney Price, Wellington, Somerset; *m* 1947, Nora Sara, *o d* of late Alexander Henderson, Edinburgh. *Educ:* Wellington School, Somerset; Univ. Coll., London. Unattached List TF 1915; Royal Garrison Artillery, 1915-18; served in France, 1916-18; entered Colonial Office, 1921; transferred to Dominions Office, 1925; Assistant Secretary, Imperial Wireless and Cable Conference, 1928; on Staff of UK Delegation to London Naval Conference, 1930, to Disarmament Conference, 1932-34, and to League of Nations Assembly, 1928, 1932-34, and 1939; Joint Secretary, Oversea Settlement Board, 1937-39; Assistant Secretary, Dominions Office, 1939; Deputy High Commissioner for UK in Union of South Africa, 1940-42; Deputy High Commissioner for UK in Australia, 1948-49; High Commissioner for UK in New Zealand, 1949-53. Fellow of University College, London. *Address:* c/o Lloyds Bank Ltd, 31 Fore Street, Taunton, Somerset.   *[Died 6 Nov. 1976.*

PRICE, Dennis; Actor, since 1936; *b* 23 June 1915; *s* of Brig.-Gen. T. Rose Price and Mrs Dorothy Rose Price; *m* 1939, Joan Schofield; two *d. Educ:* Radley College, Berks; Worcester College, Oxford. Actor: Croydon and Oxford Repertory Theatres; appearances in several London theatre productions, also in USA. Has had numerous parts in films, and in television plays and programmes. *Recreation:* riding. *Address:* c/o ALS Management Ltd, 67 Brook Street, W1Y 1YD. *Club:* Lord's Taverners.   *[Died 6 Oct. 1973.*

PRICE, Rt. Rev. Dudley William Mackay, OSB, MA; Headmaster, Ampleforth Preparatory School, since 1966; Titular Abbot of St Mary's, York, since 1969; *b* 19 July 1899; 2nd and *e surv s* of late Sir Charles W. M. Price, DL. *Educ:* Radley College; Corpus Christi College, Oxford. History Scholar, 1917. Served European War, 1918-19, in France as 2nd Lt, Queen's Roy. Regt; called to Bar, Lincoln's Inn, 1923; South Wales Circuit, 1923-25; Director and Legal Adv., British-American Tobacco Co. (China) Ltd, and associated companies in Shanghai, 1925-33; entered Benedictine Order at Ampleforth Abbey, 1933; Priest, 1940; Senior History Master, 1943. House Master, 1951, Headmaster, 1954-64, Ampleforth College. *Address:* Gilling Castle, Gilling East, York. *T:* Ampleforth 328.   *[Died 2 Jan. 1971.*

PRICE, (Edith) Mary, CBE 1956; Senior Land Registrar, HM Land Registry, 1953-58; *b* 14 Nov. 1897; *d* of late William Arthur Price and Edith Octavia, *d* of late William Smoult Playfair. *Educ:* Central Newcastle High School; Girton College, Cambridge. Post-Graduate Scholar, Bryn-Mawr College, Pennsylvania, USA, 1919-20; Social and Police Work in Boston and Detroit, USA, 1920-22. Called to the Bar, 1924; Member of the Inner Temple. *Address:* Penridge, Blewbury, Oxfordshire. *Club:* Voluntary Aid Detachment Ladies'. *[Died 15 May 1980.*

PRICE, Herbert Spencer, CBE 1956 (OBE 1946); Chief Constable of Bradford, 1940-57; *b* 19 Oct. 1892; *s* of Charles and Ann Price; *m* 1918, Florence (*d* 1948), *d* of Robert and Appaline Butterworth; one *s. Educ:* Skerton Council School; Storey Institute, Lancaster. Constable, Bradford, 1912; promoted through the ranks to Chief Constable; retired, Nov. 1957. King's Police Medal, 1951. *Address:* 421 Halifax Rd, Bradford. *T:* Bradford 676615.   *[Died 25 Aug. 1976.*

PRICE, Rt. Rev. Hetley; *see* Price, Rt Rev. S. H.

PRICE, (Joseph) Thomas; MP (Lab) Westhoughton Division of Lancashire since June 1951; *b* Pendlebury, Lancs, 9 Oct. 1902; *e s* of William and Elizabeth Price; *m* 1933, Muriel Anna Wilcock; one *s* one *d. Educ:* St Peter's, Swinton; Salford Grammar School. Central Administration Staff, Distributive Workers Union (USDAW), 1921-51; Chief Legal Officer; Council Member, Association of Superannuation and Pension Funds, 1937-68; sometime secretary and treasurer, Labour Party organisation in Eccles Div. of Lancashire. Opposition Whip, 1953-64. *Publications:* numerous press articles and pamphlets. *Address:* House of Commons, SW1; 12 Rudyard Grove, Sale, Cheshire. *T:* Sale 5248.   *[Died 1 Feb. 1973.*

PRICE, Mary; *see* Price, E. M.

PRICE, Morgan Philips, MA; JP; FRGS; landowner and farmer, Taynton, near Gloucester; *b* Hillfield, Gloucester, 29 Jan. 1885; *s* of Major William Edwin Price, of Tibberton, landowner, MP Tewkesbury (1868-80), and Margaret, 2nd *d* of Robert Needham Philips, merchant, The Park, Prestwich, Manchester, MP Bury; *m* 1919, Elisa, *d* of Friedrich Balster, Halberstadt, Germany; one *s* one *d. Educ:* Harrow; Trinity College, Cambridge (Hons Science). Travelled in Central Asia, Siberia, Persia, Turkey, 1908-14; Liberal Candidate for Gloucester (City), 1911-14; correspondent of Manchester Guardian in Russia, 1914-18; joined ILP and Labour Party, 1919; correspondent of Daily Herald in Berlin, 1919-23; Parliamentary Labour Candidate for Gloucester (City), General Elections, 1922, 1923, and 1924; MP (Lab) Whitehaven Div. of Cumberland, 1929-31; Forest of Dean Div. of Glos, 1935-50; West Div. of Glos, 1950-59; PPS to Sir Charles Trevelyan, 1929-31; Forestry Commissioner 1942-45; Parliamentary Charity Comr, 1945-50. *Publications:* Siberia, 1912; Diplomatic History of the War, 1914; War and Revolution in Asiatic Russia, 1918; My Reminiscences of the Russian Revolution, 1918; Germany in Transition, 1923; Economic Problems of Europe, 1928; America after sixty years, 1936; Hitler's War and Eastern Europe, 1940; Russia through the Centuries, 1943; Russia Red or White, 1947; Through the Iron-Laced Curtain, 1949; A History of Turkey, 1956; Russia, Forty Years On, 1961; My Three Revolutions, 1969. *Recreations:* walking, shooting, hunting, study of agriculture and forestry. *Address:* The Grove, Taynton, near Gloucester. *T:* Tibberton 200. *Club:* Reform.   *[Died 23 Sept. 1973.*

PRICE, Sir Rose (Francis), 6th Bt, *cr* 1815; *b* 15 March 1910; *e s* of Sir Francis Price, 5th Bt, and Marjorie (*d* 1955), *d* of Sir W. Russell Russell, Hawkes Bay, NZ; *S* father, 1949; *m* 1949, Kathleen June, *yr d* of Norman W. Hutchinson, Melbourne, Australia; two *s. Educ:* Wellington; Trinity College, Cambridge. BA 1931. Served War of 1939-45, Captain 4/11th Sikh Regt, 1940-45. *Heir: s* Francis Caradoc Rose Price [*b* 9 Sept. 1950; *m* 1975, Marguerite, *d* of R. S. Trussler; two *d*]. *Address:* Dormer Cottage, Park Road, Stoke Poges, Bucks. *[Died 21 Sept. 1979.*

PRICE, Sir Roy; *see* Price, Sir (Charles) R.

PRICE, Rt. Rev. (Stuart) Hetley; Bishop of Ripon, since 1976; *b* 14 June 1922; *s* of F. L. Price, Loughborough; *m* 1952, Pamela Mary Cooper; one *s* one *d. Educ:* Loughborough Gram. Sch.; Corpus Christi Coll., Cambridge; Westcott House, Cambridge. Asst Curate, St Michael and All Angels, Bournemouth, 1945-48; Domestic Chaplain to Bp of Manchester, 1948-52; Asst Gen. Sec., SCM and Asst Curate, St Luke, Chelsea, 1952-55; Exam. Chaplain to Bp of Manchester, 1952-72; Rector, Emmanuel Church, Didsbury, 1955-60; Residentiary Canon, Manchester Cathedral, 1960-72; Archdeacon of Manchester, 1966-72; Bishop Suffragan of Doncaster, 1972-76. Church Comr and

Dep. Chm. Houses Cttee, 1973-. *Publication:* (with G. S. Wakefield) Unity at the Local Level, 1964. *Address:* Bishop Mount, Ripon, N Yorks HG4 5DP. *[Died* 15 March 1977.

PRICE, Thomas; *see* Price, J. T.

PRICE, Brig. Thomas Reginald, DSO 1917; MC; *b* Woburn Sands, 15 Sept. 1894; *s* of Rev. T. J. Price, BA; *m* 1st, 1931, Christian Farquharson Gordon (*d* 1960), *yr d* of James Leask and Mrs M. E. Fraser; 2nd, 1969, Gwendolen (*d* 1977), *e d* of E. S. Wicks. *Educ:* Kingswood School, Bath. Special Reserve Com. Northants Regt, 1915; Lt regular army, 1916; Captain 1923; Major, 1935; Lt-Col 1941; Brig. 1941; Royal Tank Corps, 1917; served in France, 1915-18 (DSO, MC 1917, bar to MC 1918, despatches thrice, wounded Loos, 1915. Somme, 1917, and German advance, 1918); in Nigeria, 1921-32; Lt-Col Commanding 1st Bn Nigeria Regiment, 1931-32; served War of 1939-45: Commandant Gold Coast, 1940; Commanded 31st Tank Bde, 1941-42; Commanded 1st Tank Bde, 1942-44; Brig. General Staff, Washington, 1945-48. *Recreations:* all outdoor games and sports. *Address:* Old Timbers, Dora's Green Lane, Dippenhall, Farnham, Surrey. *Club:* Naval and Military.
[Died 11 Feb. 1978.

PRICE, Major Vincent Walter, QC 1933; MA; Barrister-at-Law; Past National President, United Nations Association in Canada; Past Vice-President, World Federation, UNA; *b* 22 Aug. 1890; *s* of Rev. William Frederick and Sarah Penwarden Price; *m* 1924, Ruth Jeanette, *d* of late George Johnson Green and Laura Lawson Green, McAdam, New Brunswick; one *d. Educ:* McMaster University; Osgoode Hall, Toronto. Lecturer, Woodstock College, Woodstock, 1911-12; Master, Appleby Sch. (now Appleby Coll.), Oakville, 1913-14; served Overseas with Canadian Expeditionary Force, 1915-18, rank of Lieutenant and Captain and Acting Adjutant, 123rd Battalion Royal Grenadiers, and Captain and Adjutant 4th Battalion Canadian Engineers (despatches twice), served with Royal Grenadiers, Toronto, 1920-27, and as Major, 2nd i/c Royal Regt of Canada (2nd Bn), 1940-44, now Major, Reserve; called to Bar of Ontario, 1920. President: English-Speaking Union of British Empire (Ontario Branch), 1932-47; UNA (Toronto Branch), 1945-47; Member National Executive UN Assoc. in Canada (Chm. 1947-48); Nat. Pres. Alliance Canadienne (AC-CA), 1957-58; Former Nat. Chm., Canadian Council for Reconstruction through UNESCO; Canadian Deleg. to 11th Gen. Conf. of UNESCO, Paris, 1960. Coronation Medal, 1937. KLJ 1972. *Publication:* Canada and World Security, 1945. *Recreations:* riding, fishing. *Address:* Wishwood, PO Box 159, Rockwood, Ontario N0B 2K0, Canada. *Clubs:* University (Hon. Life Mem.), Empire, Royal Canadian Military Institute (Hon. Life Mem.), also Cricket, Skating and Curling (Hon. Life Mem.) (Toronto). *[Died* 17 April 1976.

PRICE, William James, CMG 1943; MInstCE; *b* 1884; *m* 1915, Margaret Restarick; one *s* one *d. Educ:* Ceylon PWD 1909-43; was Director of Public Works and Civil Aviation, Ceylon; retired, 1943. *Address:* Holcombe Hotel, 92 Heene Road, Worthing, Sussex. *[Died* 1 Aug. 1973.

PRICE THOMAS, Sir Clement, KCVO, 1951; LLD; Hon. FRSocMed (1960); Hon. FACS; Hon. FRCSI; Hon. FRCSE; Honorary Consulting Surgeon to Westminster Hospital; Joint-Lecturer in Surgery at Westminster Hospital Medical School; Hon. Consulting Surgeon to Brompton Hospital for Diseases of the Chest; Consulting Surgeon to King Edward VII Sanatorium, Midhurst; Civilian Consultant in Thoracic Surgery, RAF, to Army, 1946-63; Adviser for Thoracic Surgery to Ministry of Health, 1946-63; President Welsh National School of Medicine, 1958-70; President Medical Protection Society; *b* Abercarn, Mon, 22 Nov. 1893; *m* 1925, Ethel Doris, *d* of Mortimer Ricks, Paignton, South Devon; two *s. Educ:* Caterham Sch.; University College of South Wales; Westminster Hospital (Scholar). Hughes Medal in Anatomy, Cardiff, Medical Sch.; MRCS; LRCP, 1921; FRCS, 1923; FRCP 1960; held all resident appointments, Westminster Hospital and Surgical Registrar, three years; Consulting Surgeon, Metropolitan Asylums Board (Mental Service), three years; served European War, 1914-18, RAMC, Gallipoli, Macedonia, and Palestine. President Royal Society Med., 1956-58; Tudor Edward's Memorial Lectr, RCP and RCS, 1959; Vicary Lecture, 1960; Bradshaw Lectr, RCS, 1963. Royal College of Surgeons: Mem. Council, 1952-64; Vice-Pres., 1962-64; ex-Mem., Court of Examiners. Hon. Fellow, American Assoc. for Thoracic Surgery; Member: Royal Norwegian Med. Society; Argentine Med. Society; Argentine Thoracic Society; Brazilian Tuberculosis Society; For. Member Académie de Chirurgie; Hon. Member: Internat. Surgical Society; Union Internationale Contra la Tuberculose; Polish Association of Surgeons; Ex-President Association of Surgeons

of Great Britain and Ireland; Thoracic Society and Society of Thoracic Surgeons; Ex-President Royal Society Med. Hon. LLD Wales, 1953; Queen's Univ., Belfast, 1962; Hon. MD: Paris; Lisbon; Karachi, 1966; Athens, 1970. President: BMA, 1965-66; World Med. Assoc., 1965-66. Warsaw Decoration, 1960. *Publications:* Chapter on Chest in Malignant Disease and its Treatment by Radium, by Stanford Cade, 1940; Assoc. Editor and Contributor to "British Surgical Practice"; numerous articles on diseases of the chest and radium treatment in hospital reports and medical journals. *Recreations:* golf, photography. *Address:* Court Green, St Ann's Hill, Midhurst, Sussex.
[Died 19 March 1973.

PRICE-WHITE, Lt-Col David Archibald, TD 1945; solicitor; Principal, Price White & Co., Solicitors, Colwyn Bay; *b* 5 Sept. 1906; *s* of Price Foulkes White and Charlotte Bell; *m* 1934, Gwyneth Harris; one *s* one *d. Educ:* Friars School; University College of North Wales. Admitted Solicitor (Hons), 1932; practised Solicitor, Bangor, 1933-39. Joined TA (RA), 1928; served 1939-45, France 1940, Middle East, Sicily, Italy, East Africa. MP (C) Caernarvon Boroughs, 1945-50. *Address:* Dolanog, Pwllycrochan Avenue, Colwyn Bay, N Wales. *T:* Colwyn Bay 30758. *[Died* 6 March 1978.

PRICHARD, Sir John, Kt 1952; CBE 1941 (OBE 1927); JP; *b* 27 Jan. 1887; *s* of late W. Prichard, Wick, Glamorganshire; unmarried. Solicitor. Major, Royal Field Artillery, Territorial. First commission in RFA (T), 1911; served European War, Gallipoli, 1915, Mesopotamia, 1916-18 (despatches twice). Judge in Iraqi Courts, 1919-51; President Iraqi Supreme Court and Chief Justice, Iraq, 1938-51; retired, 1951. JP Co. Glamorgan, 1956. *Address:* West House, Wick, Glamorgan. *Club:* East India and Sports. *[Died* 13 April 1971.

PRICHARD, Sir Norman (George Mollett), Kt 1968; Member: Greater London Council; Inner London Education Authority; Vice-Chairman, Greater London Conference on Old People's Welfare, since 1966; Hon. Superintendent, Battersea Special Services, (a mission founded by Rev. A. G. Prichard, 1908). *b* 14 April 1895; *er s* of late Rev. Alfred George Prichard and Mrs Margaret Prichard; *m* 1921, Winifred, *d* of late Thomas Edmund Just, Middlesbrough and London; one *s* one *d. Educ:* East Ham Grammar Sch.; Henry Thornton Sch.; King's Coll., London. Civil Servant, 1910-55. Religious and social work, 1908- (President, Wandsworth Free Church Federal Council, 1965-66). Called to Bar, Lincoln's Inn, 1924. MSc (London) in Psychology (Lecturer WEA, etc., 1929-46); Member Battersea Borough Council, 1927-65 (Mayor, 1935-36); Chairman of LCC, 1955-56, and of Finance, Housing and other LCC Cttees, 1953-65; Alderman LCC, 1950-52; Member LCC (N Hammersmith), 1952-65; Chairman, London Boroughs Association, 1964-68; Member Greater London Council (Wandsworth), 1964-67, 1970- (Chairman, Establishment and Supplies Cttee, 1964-65); Member, Wandsworth London Borough Council, 1964-68; Chairman, Metropolitan Boroughs Standing Jt Cttee, 1949-65 (Organisation and Methods Cttee, 1950-61). Chairman of Governors: Hammersmith County Sch., 1956-67; Henry Thornton Sch., 1969-; Kennington Coll., 1971-; Governor, Battersea Grammar Sch., 1967-. Member: Local Government Manpower Cttee; Advisory Cttee on Recruitment for Civil Defence Services; Minister of Transport's Special Cttee on Parking. President, Bermondsey Band of Hope Union, 1967-; Hon. Treas., Nat. Peace Council. Lecture Tours on London Local Government in Holland (1957), USA and Canada (1957, 1959, and 1961), which included visits to leading American Universities. Radio and TV interviews at home and abroad on local government subjects. Freeman, London Borough of Wandsworth, 1968. JP 1950. *Publications:* sections on psychology in various popular works, and contributions to legal and local government journals and to newspapers. *Recreations:* reading, gardening. *Address:* 4 Rusham Road, SW12. *T:* 01-673 5048. *Club:* Civil Service. *[Died* 10 April 1972.

PRICHARD, Rev. Canon Thomas Estlin, MA; Residentiary Canon of Canterbury, since 1968; Archdeacon of Maidstone, 1968-72; *b* 20 Dec. 1910; 3rd *s* of Edgar and Eleanora Prichard; *m* 1937, Mildred Celina Frances Leale; four *d. Educ:* Clifton Coll.; Exeter Coll., Oxford. Curate of: Lambeth, 1934; Ashford, Kent, 1938; Vicar of: Boxley, 1943; St Peter in Thanet, 1954. *Recreation:* music. *Address:* 22 The Precincts, Canterbury, Kent. *T:* Canterbury 63056. *Club:* Vincent's (Oxford).
[Died 8 Aug. 1975.

PRICKARD, Thomas Francis Vaughan, CVO 1935 (MVO 1926); late Surveyor-General and Deputy Receiver-General of the Duchy of Lancaster; *s* of late Rev. Wm Edward Prickard of Dderw, Radnorshire; *b* 1879; *m* 1905, Margaret Taunton (*d* 1968), *d* of late R. Taunton Raikes, Treberfydd, Breconshire;

one d. Educ: Marlborough; King's Coll., Cambridge. JP Radnorshire, 1907; Sheriff of Radnorshire, 1933. Recreations: shooting, fishing. Address: Dderw, Rhayader, Radnor. Club: Leander. [Died 4 July 1973.

PRIDEAUX-BRUNE, Sir Humphrey Ingelram, KBE 1943 (OBE 1931); CMG 1938; b 16 Nov. 1886; m 1920, Adah Louisa Anne (d 1947), d of late W. Montague Pollard-Urquhart, Castle Pollard, Co. Westmeath. Educ: Marlborough; University Coll., Oxford. Student Interpreter in China, 1911; one of HM Consuls in China, 1931; acting Chinese Counsellor, British Embassy, China, 1938-39; China Relations Officer in India, 1943; retired, 1945. Address: Compton House Nursing Home, Lindfield, West Sussex. [Died 12 Dec. 1979.

PRIDHAM, Vice-Admiral Sir (Arthur) Francis, KBE 1946; CB 1940; b 3 June 1886; 2nd s of Edward Prideaux Brune Pridham; m 1911, Miriam Vidal (d 1969), d of Rev. Arthur Lewis; three d. Joined RN, 1901; served European War, 1914-19 as: Gunnery Officer of HMS Weymouth, Shannon and Marlborough; Captain, 1926; Imperial Defence Coll., 1927; commanded HM Ships Concord, Calliope, Curlew, Excellent, and Hood; ADC to the King, 1937; Rear-Admiral, 1938; Flag Officer, Humber Area, 1939-40; Vice-Admiral (retired), 1941; President of the Ordnance Board, 1941-45. Member of General Board, National Physical Laboratory, 1943-48. Imperial Russian Order of St Stanislas (2nd Class with Swords). Commander Legion of Merit (USA), 1946. Publication: Close of a Dynasty, 1956. Address: Woodhayne, Burley, Ringwood, Hants. T: Burley 2310. Club: United Service & Royal Aero. [Died 27 Jan. 1975.

PRIDIE, Sir Eric (Denholm), KCMG 1953 (CMG 1941); DSO 1918; OBE 1931; MB, BS, London, MRCS, FRCP; Chief Medical Officer, Colonial Office, 1948-58, retired; b 10 Jan. 1896; s of Dr John Francis and Florence Pridie. Educ: St Bees Sch.; University of Liverpool. Served European War, 1914-18; France, 1915-16; Mesopotamia, 1917-18, with 6th and 7th Battalions King's Own Royal (Lancaster) Regt; Captain, 1917 (despatches, wounded, DSO); joined Sudan Med. Service, 1924; served in Kassala and Blue Nile Provinces; Asst Director, 1930; Director Sudan Medical Service, 1933-45; Member of Governor General's Council, 1934-45; President Central Board Public Health, Sudan, 1933-45, and Chairman School Council, Kitchener School of Medicine, 1933-45; Brigadier, Royal Army Medical Corps; DDMS Troops, Sudan and Eritrea, Middle East Forces, 1940-43 (despatches twice); Health Counsellor, British Embassy, Cairo, 1945-49, and Health Adviser British Middle East Office, 1946-49. Order of Nile 3rd Class. Clubs: Athenæum, Royal Commonwealth Society. [Died 3 Sept. 1978.

PRIESTLEY, Sir Gerald William, KCIE 1946 (CIE 1943); b 12 Nov. 1888; s of James Henry Priestley; m 1919, Isobel Macleod Millar (d 1958); four d; m 1959, Evelyn May Ledward, Kloof. Educ: West Monmouthshire Sch., Pontypool; Trinity Coll., Cambridge. Entered ICS, 1912, in Madras; investigated Upper Bhavani and Tunga-bhadra Irrigation Projects, 1926 and 1934; Commissioner of Coorg, 1927; Member Board of Revenue, 1939; Chief Secretary to the Government of Madras, 1942; Adviser to Governor of Madras, 1945; retired, 1947. Address: 7 Park Lane, Kloof, Natal, South Africa. [Died 6 Jan. 1978.

PRIESTLEY, Sir Raymond Edward, Kt 1949; MC; MA (Cambridge); DSc, Melbourne, New Zealand and West Indies; LLD (St Andrews, Natal, Dalhousie, Birmingham); DLitt (Malaya); retired; b Tewkesbury, 20 July 1886; 2nd s of late J. E. Priestley, Tewkesbury; m 1915, Phyllis Mary (d 1961), d of late W. B. Boyd; two d. Educ: Tewkesbury Grammar Sch.; Bristol, Sydney and Cambridge Universities. Geologist, Shackleton Antarctic (Nimrod) Expedition, 1907-09; Scientist, Northern Party, Scott Antarctic Expedition, 1910-13; Adjutant, Wireless Training Centre, 1914-17; 46th Divisional Signal Company, France, 1918; Asst CSO 1st Army, 1919; SD 6 War Office, 1919, for writing History of Signal Service; Fellow of Clare Coll., Cambridge, 1923-34; Secretary General of the Faculties, Cambridge Univ., 1934; Vice-Chancellor Melbourne Univ., 1935-38; Principal and Vice-Chancellor, University of Birmingham, 1938-52. Chairman, Royal Commn on Civil Service, 1953-55; President of the British Association for the Advancement of Science, 1956. Director Falkland Islands Rear Base, 1955-59; President, Royal Geographical Society, 1961-63. Hon. Fellow of Clare Coll., Cambridge. Chevalier of the Belgian Crown. Publications: Geological Report, Shackleton Antarctic Expedition (with T. W. E. David); Antarctic Adventure; Scott's Northern Party; Breaking the Hindenburg Line (story of 46th Division); History of the Signal Service in France; Physiography and Glaciology Reports, Scott's Last Expedition, and other papers. Address: Barn Hill, Bredon's Norton, Tewkesbury, Glos. [Died 24 June 1974.

WWW—22

PRIMROSE, Sir John Ure, Kt 1951; DL; JP; Lord Provost of Perth, 1945-54; Hon. Sheriff for Perth and Perthshire; Chairman: Scottish Motor Traction Co. Ltd, and of Subsidiary Companies, 1956; First Scottish American Trust, 1969-73; Second British American Trust, since 1969; Third Scottish American Trust, since 1969; Northern American Trust, 1969-73; Camperdown Trust, since 1969; b 22 Feb. 1900; s of Rev. Robert Primrose, Minister of Parish Church of Burnbank, Glasgow, and Catherine Wingate; m 1922, Helen Victoria Baker. Educ: Kelvinside Academy, Glasgow; Stanley House, Bridge of Allan, Perthshire. Served European War, Lieut in Royal Navy, 1914-18, demobilised 1919. Sgt.-Major Intelligence Corps, War of 1939-45. Took up farming, 1921; Chairman, Perth Branch NFU for 1935. Director: General Accident Fire & Life Assurance Corp. Ltd, General Buildings, Perth, 1948. Chairman, Board of Management for Perthshire General Hospitals, 1948-58. Aviation: ATC Scottish Consultative Cttee and Scottish Representative on ATC Consultative Cttee in London; Member: Aerodrome Owners Association of Great Britain (Chairman, 1939-43); Air Transport Advisory Council; Chairman, Scottish and Northern Ireland Cttee of the White Fish Authority, 1956-. Member Nyasaland Inquiry Commission, 1959. Formerly Member Scottish Advisory Council for Civil Aviation. Recreations: Rugby, yachting, golf, tennis. Address: Thistle Cottage, Lower Largo, Fife. T: Lundin Links 456. Clubs: Royal Perth Golfing Society (Perth); Clyde Corinthian Yachting (Glasgow). [Died 14 Jan. 1974.

PRINGLE, Prof. J(ohn) Seton (Michael), FRCS, FRCSI; Regius Professor of Surgery, University of Dublin, 1961-66; Visiting Surgeon, Royal City of Dublin Hospital and Drumcondra Hospital; Consulting Surgeon: Rotunda Hospital; Stewart's Hospital; Royal Hospital for Incurables; b 12 July 1909; s of J. A. Pringle, KC; m 1st, 1939, B. Odlum; one s two d; 2nd, Mrs N. W. Cornwall (née Chaloner). Educ: Haileybury; Gonville and Caius Coll., Cambridge; Trinity Coll., Dublin. MB, BCh, BAO, Dublin, 1933; MB, BChir, Cambridge, 1933; FRCSI 1935; FRCS England 1937. Served with Royal Army Medical Corps, 1942-45 (Major). Visiting Surgeon, Mercer's Hospital, Dublin, 1938-45. Publications: contribs to Irish Journal of Medical Science, BMJ, etc. Recreations: sailing, shooting. Address: Rathmore House, Rathmore, Naas, Co. Kildare, Ireland. T: Naas 7453. [Died 22 May 1975.

PRINSEP, Col Evelyn Siegfried MacLeod, CIE 1945; OBE 1923; retired; b 23 April 1892; er s of late Captain James Frederick MacLeod Prinsep, 56th Foot and Egyptian Army; m 1921, Clavdia, d of Ivan Komarov, Samara Province, Russia; one s one d. Educ: Wellington; RMC Sandhurst. 2nd Lieut IA, 1911; joined 11th KEO Lancers (Probyn's Horse), 1912; served European War, 1914-19 (despatches), in France, Belgium, Mesopotamia, Siberia; Knox's Mission, Siberia, 1919-20; Special Mission, Far East, 1921-22; GSO3 AHQ India, 1923-25; Private Secretary to Governor of Punjab, 1931; operations, North-West Frontier, 1936-37; Lt-Col, 1937; Commandant Probyn's Horse, 1938-41; AA and QMG Lucknow District, 1941-45; Colonel, 1941; retired, 1945. 1st class interpreter in Russian (1922 and re-qualified 1931). Publications: Freshwater Gates, 1946 (miscellany of own verse and prose stories); contrib. at various times to newspaper and quarterlies. Recreations: literature, languages; golf, tennis, skating. Address: 7 Park Mansions, Knightsbridge, SW1. T: 01-589 2290. Clubs: Cavalry; Roehampton. [Died 7 June 1973.

PRIOR, Sir (Charles) Geoffrey, KCIE 1943 (CIE 1936); FRGS; retired Governor; b 9 Dec. 1896; o s of Richard Delabere Prior. Educ: Shrewsbury (Folliot Sandford English Prize, 1913, 1914); RMC, Sandhurst (Prize Cadetship). Battalion Commander, 1919-21; transferred to Indian Political Service, 1923; Under-Sec., Rajputana Agency, 1924-26; Sec., Persian Gulf Residency, 1927; Political Agent, Bahrain, 1929-32; received thanks: of Sec. of State for Air for services (exploration of E Arabian Air Route); of Govt of India for services (Bahrain Riots). Dep. Sec., FO, Delhi-Simla, 1933; Prime Minister, Alwar State, 1936-38; Polit. Resident, Persian Gulf, 1939-46; Mem., ME War Council, 1941-42; raised Persian Gulf Fighter Fund which presented ten Spitfires to HM Govt; represented India at Foreign Ministers Conf., 1945; Governor, Baluchistan, 1946, retired 1949; Resident Dir, British Bank of Iran and the Middle East; resigned, 1951. Lecture tour to US on behalf of HM Govt, 1953. Built Church of the Epiphany, Bushire. Pres., SA Nat. Equestrian Fedn, 1964-67. Jubilee Medal, 1935; Coronation Medal, 1937. Address: c/o Barclays Bank, Adderley Street, Cape Town, S Africa. Clubs: Travellers', United Service & Royal Aero; Civil Service (Capetown). [Died 11 Oct. 1972.

PRIOR, Sir Geoffrey, see Prior, Sir C. G.

PRIOR-PALMER, Maj.-Gen. George Erroll, CB 1952; DSO 1945; *b* 1903; *s* of Spunner Prior-Palmer, Co. Sligo and Merrion Square, Dublin, and Anne Leslie Gason, Kilteelagh, Co. Tipperary; *m* 1st, 1935, Katherine Edith, *d* of Frank Bibby; one *d*; 2nd, 1948, Lady Doreen Hersey Winifred Hope, *y d* of 2nd Marquess of Linlithgow, KT, GCSI, GCIE; one *s* one *d*. *Educ:* Wellington; RMC. 2nd Lt, 9th Lancers, 1923; Capt. 1930; Lt-Col 1941; Col 1946; Brig. 1943. Served in NW Europe, 1940 (despatches), and 1944-45. Mil. Attaché, British Embassy, Washington, 1946-48. Maj.-General, 1951; Commanding 6th Armoured Division, 1951-53; Commander British Army Staff and Military Member, British Joint Services Mission, Washington, 1953-56; Pres. Regular Commissions Board, 1956-57; retired, 1958. Joined British & Commonwealth Shipping Co. Ltd, 1958; Southampton Area Director, Union Castle Mail Steamship Co. Ltd, 1959-64; Manager, Cayzer Irvine & Co. Ltd, and Special Adviser to the British Commonwealth Group, 1964-65; Man. Dir, Overseas Containers Ltd, 1965-69; Dir, J. A. Peden Ltd, 1973-. Pres., Wessex Rehabilitation Assoc., 1962-. Patron, League of Venturers, 1972-. Legion of Honour, 1945; Croix de Guerre avec Palme, 1945. *Address:* Appleshaw House, Andover, Hampshire. *T:* Weyhill 2333. *Clubs:* Cavalry and Guards, Royal Ocean Racing. *[Died 18 Aug. 1977.*

PRITCHARD, Brig. Charles Hilary Vaughan; *see under* Vaughan, Brig. C. H. V.

PRITCHARD, Sir E. E. E.; *see* Evans-Pritchard.

PRITCHARD, Prof. John Joseph, DM, MA; FRCS; Professor of Anatomy in The Queen's University, Belfast, and Consultant in Anatomy to Northern Ireland Hospitals Authority, and Eastern Area Board, since 1952; *b* 9 Feb. 1916; *s* of Leonard Charles and Isobel Violet Pritchard, Adelaide, SA; *m* 1940, Muriel Rachel Edmunds; three *s* one *d*. *Educ:* St Peter's College, Adelaide; St Mark's College (University of Adelaide); Magdalen College, Oxford; St Bartholomew's Hospital, London. Rhodes Scholar, SA, 1934; BSc Adelaide, 1934; BA Hons Oxford, 1936; MRCS, LRCP 1940; MA Oxon, BM, BCh Oxon, 1941; DM Oxon, 1951; FRCS 1964. Ho. Phys., Mill Hill Emergency Hosp. and St Bartholomew's Hosp.; Demonstrator in Anatomy, University Coll., London, 1940; Asst Lectr, Lecturer, then Reader in Anatomy at St Mary's Hosp. Med. School, University of London, 1941-52. Pres., Anatomical Society of Great Britain and Ireland, 1967-69. Visiting Professor of Anatomy, Univ. of Illinois, 1965-66. Chm. NI Br., Multiple Sclerosis Soc., 1975-. Fellow, British Assoc. of Orthopaedic Surgeons, 1973. Editor, Jl of Anatomy, 1973-. *Publications:* articles on placental structure and function and bone growth and repair, chiefly in Jl of Anatomy, London. *Recreation:* country cottaging. *Address:* 75 Osborne Park, Belfast, Northern Ireland. *T:* 667206.
[Died 10 April 1979.

PRITCHARD, Leslie Francis Gordon, MBE 1955; TD 1946; Managing Director, Gallaher Ltd, since 1976; *b* 10 May 1918; *o s* of Lt-Col H. R. N. Pritchard, CIE, OBE, and Letitia de la Cloche (née Snell); *m* 1941, Diana Edmée, *yr d* of Sir Trevor Wheler, 13th Bt; four *d*. *Educ:* Blundell's Sch.; Guy's Hosp. Med. Sch. Commissioned, Royal Fusiliers, TA, 1939; war service, 1939-46, Lt-Col 1945. Colonial Administrative Service, Kenya, 1946-59: Private Sec. to Governor, 1952-55; Permanent Sec. for African Affairs, 1955-58; Secretary of the Cabinet, 1958-59. Gallaher Ltd, 1959-: Director, 1967; Jt Man. Dir, 1975. *Recreations:* travel, gardening, fishing. *Address:* The Garden House, Dewhurst, Wadhurst, Sussex TN5 6QB. *T:* Wadhurst 3179. *Club:* MCC. *[Died 9 Sept. 1977.*

PRITT, Denis Nowell, QC 1927; *b* 1887; *s* of late Harry Walter Pritt, Billericay, Essex; *m* 1914, Marie Frances, *d* of Walter Gough; one *d*. *Educ:* Winchester; London University; Germany; Switzerland; Spain; LLB London. Called to Bar, Middle Temple, 1909, retired from practice, 1960; MP (Soc.) N Hammersmith, 1935-50; Professor of Law, University of Ghana, 1965-66. Late Chm. of Howard League for Penal Reform and of Bentham Committee for Poor Litigants; President, Society for Cultural Relations with USSR; Pres., British Rumanian Friendship Assoc.; Joint Pres., Soc. for Friendship with Bulgaria; Hon. Pres. Internat. Assoc. of Democratic Lawyers; late Pres. Brit. Peace Cttee; Member of World Peace Council. Freedom of the city of Leipzig, 1957. Hon. LLD: Charles Univ., Prague, 1957; Sofia Univ., 1960; Humboldt Univ., Berlin, 1960; Moscow Univ., 1961. Lenin Peace Prize, 1954; Order of Georgi Dimitrov, 1964; Star of Internat. Friendship, 1965; Gold Medal of Czechoslovak Soc. for Internat. Relations, 1968. *Publications:* Light on Moscow, 1939; Must the War Spread?, 1940; Federal Illusion, 1940; Choose your Future, 1940; The Fall of the French Republic, 1940; USSR Our Ally, 1941; India Our Ally?; Revolt in Europe; A New World Grows; Star-Spangled Shadow, 1947;

The State Department and the Cold War (New York), 1948; The Truth about the USSR; Russia is for Peace; Spies and Informers in the Witness-box, 1958; Liberty in Chains, 1962; The Labour Government, 1945-1951, 1963; Neo-Nazis, the Danger of War, 1966; The Autobiography of D. N. Pritt, Part 1, From Right to Left, 1965; Part 2, Brasshats and Bureaucrats, 1966; Part 3, The Defence Accuses, 1966; The Sale of Goods Act and the Partnership Act (India), 1966; Unrepentant Aggressors, 1969; Law, Class and Society, Book I: Employers, Workers, and Trade Unions, 1970; The Apparatus of the Law, Book I, 1971; Law and Politics, and, Law in the Colonies, 1971; many pamphlets; pt author of Twelve Studies in Soviet Russia, 1933; joint author of The Law versus the Trade Unions, 1958. *Address:* Barn End, Pamber Heath, Basingstoke, Hants. *T:* Silchester 319.
[Died 23 May 1972.

PROBERT, Arthur Reginald; *b* 1909; *s* of Albert John Probert, Penylan, Aberaman, Aberdare; *m* 1938, Muriel, *d* of late William Taylor, Abercwmboi, Glam; two *d*. *Educ:* elementary and grammar schools, Aberdare. Entered local government service, 1928; Housing Assistant, Aberdare Urban District Council. Secretary of Aberdare Trades and Labour Council, 1949-54; Member of the Executive Committee of Glamorgan Federation of Trades Councils, 1951-54; member of local employment and old age pensioners' welfare committees. MP (Lab) Aberdare, Oct. 1954-Feb. 1974; Opposition Whip (Welsh), Oct. 1959-Feb. 1961; PPS to Minister of Technology, 1965-66; one of Mr Speaker's Chairmen of Cttees, 1966-. Served in Scotland, Germany and Denmark with Royal Air Force Volunteer Reserve, 1941-46. *Address:* Allt Fedw, Abernant, Aberdare, Mid Glamorganshire. *[Died 14 Feb. 1975.*

PROBERT, Rhys Price; CB 1972; Director, Royal Aircraft Establishment, since 1973; *b* 28 May 1921; *s* of late Reverend Thomas and Margaret Jane Probert; *m* 1947, Carolyn Cleasby, Lancaster, NH, USA; three *s* one *d*. *Educ:* Jones' West Monmouth School; St Catharine's College, Cambridge. FEng 1978. Royal Aircraft Establishment, 1942-44; Power Jets (Research and Development) Ltd, 1944-46; Applied Physics Laboratory, Johns Hopkins Univ., 1946-47; National Gas Turbine Establishment, 1947-63 (Dep. Dir, 1957); Director-General of Scientific Research/Air, Min. of Aviation, 1963-68; Dep. Controller of Aircraft A, Min. of Technology, later MoD, 1968-72. Pres., RAeS, 1979-80. *Publications:* contribs to various scientific and technical jls. *Recreations:* squash, reading. *Address:* Fourways, Avenue Road, Farnborough, Hants. *Clubs:* Athenæum; Leander (Henley). *[Died 15 Aug. 1980.*

PROBY, Major Sir Richard George, 1st Bt *cr* 1952; MC 1917; landowner and farmer; Vice-Lieutenant of Huntingdonshire, 1957-66; *b* 21 July 1886; *s* of late Col D. J. Proby, Elton, and of Lady Margaret Proby (née Hely Hutchinson), *d* of 4th Earl of Donoughmore, PC; *m* 1st, 1911, Betty Monica (*d* 1967), *d* of late A. Hallam Murray; two *s* three *d* (and one *s* decd); 2nd, 1972, Mrs Yvonne Harris. *Educ:* Eton; Royal Military Acad., Woolwich. Lieutenant RFA, 1906-10; Captain Essex Yeomanry, 1913; Major 1919; served European War, 1914-19 (MC). Private sec. to Lord Ailwyn, 1st Chm. Agricultural Wages Bd, 1918. Chm. Hunts War Agric. Exec. Cttee, 1939, liaison officer to Min. of Agriculture, 1941-44 and 1952-55. Chm. Country Landowners' Assoc., 1943-46, Pres., 1947-51; an hon. Vice-Pres. Land Agents' Soc.; Mem. Coun. RASE; Chm. Forestry Cttee of Gt Britain, 1959; Chm. Eastern Provincial Area Conservative Assoc., 1938, Pres. 1960; Chm. Ex. Cttee of National Union of Conservative and Unionist Associations, 1943; Chm. National Union, 1946; Pres. National Union, 1958. Chm. Real Estate Panel of Eton College, 1952. Member Wilson Agricultural Reorganisation Cttee, 1955; JP Hunts; CC for Hunts; DL Hunts, 1952; High Sheriff, Hunts, Cambs, and the Isle of Ely, 1953; Pres. Roy. Forestry Society of England, Wales and Northern Ireland, 1955; Chm. Timber Growers Organization of England and Wales, 1959-, Pres. 1961; Mem. Exec. of Irish Landowners' Convention; Bledisloe Gold Medal for distinguished service to Agriculture, 1967. *Publications:* articles and letters on agricultural and forestry matters contributed to the Times, the Quarterly Review, etc. *Recreations:* riding, travelling, forestry. *Heir:* *s* Captain Peter Proby [*b* 4 Dec. 1911; *m* 1944, Blanche Harrison, *o d* of Lt-Col Henry Harrison Cripps, DSO; one *s* three *d* (and one *s* decd)]. *Address:* The Dial House, Elton, Peterborough. *T:* Elton 572. *Clubs:* Travellers', Constitutional, Roxburghe. *[Died 15 Jan. 1979.*

PROCTER, Rev. Arthur Herbert, VC 1916; retired; *b* 11 Aug. 1890; *s* of Arthur Richard Procter and Ellen Cumpsty; *m* 1917; three *s*. *Educ:* St Aidan's College, Birkenhead. Clerk in provision trade, 1904-14; served in 5th King's Liverpool Regt, 1914-18; salesman in provision trade, 1918-26; ordained, 1927; Curate, Prescot Parish Church; Vicar of Bosley; Vicar of St

Stephen's, Hyde, 1933-43; RAF Chaplain, 1941; Rector of St Mary's, Droylsden, 1946-51; Vicar of St Peters, Claybrooke, Rugby, 1951-63; Vicar of St John the Baptist, Bradworthy, 1963-65. *Recreations:* golf, cricket. *Address:* 1 Cherry Tree Close, Sheffield S11 9AF. *T:* Sheffield 53108.
[*Died 26 Jan.* 1973.

PROCTER, Dod, RA 1942 (ARA 1934); Artist; *d* of Doctor Frederick Charles Shaw and Eunice Mary Richards; *m* 1912, Ernest Procter, ARA (*d* 1935); one *s. Educ:* Newlyn; Paris. *Works:* Tate Gallery, etc. *Address:* North Corner, Newlyn, Penzance, *T:* Penzance 2620. [*Died 31 July* 1972.

PROCTER, Evelyn Emma Stefanos, MA; *b* 6 June 1897; *y d* of late Harold and Ada Louisa Procter. *Educ:* Cheltenham Ladies' College; Somerville College, Oxford (Hon. Fellow, 1978). Hons Mod. Hist. Cl. 1, 1918; Mary Somerville Research Fellow, Somerville College, 1921-25; Tutor in History (1925) and Fellow of St Hugh's College, Oxford, 1926-46; University Lecturer in Medieval European History, 1933-39; Norman Maccoll Lecturer, University of Cambridge, 1948-49; Principal, St Hugh's College, Oxford, 1946-62, retd. Hon. Fell. St Hugh's College, Oxford, 1962. FRHistS. Chevalier de la Légion d'Honneur. *Publications:* Alfonso X of Castile; Patron of Literature and Learning, 1951; contributor to: Oxford Essays in Medieval History, presented to H. E. Salter, 1934; Homenaje a Rubió i Lluch, 1936; articles in Transactions of Royal Historical Society, Revue Hispanique, English Historical Review and Modern Language Review. *Recreation:* water-colour sketching. *Address:* Little Newland, Eynsham, Oxford OX8 1LD. *T:* Oxford 881394. [*Died 22 March* 1980.

PROCTER-GREGG, Humphrey, CBE 1971; Emeritus Professor; *b* Kirkby Lonsdale, 31 July 1895; *s* of Oliver Procter-Gregg, JP, and Florence Annie (*née* Hoare). *Educ:* King William's College; Peterhouse, Cambridge (Hist. and Organ Schol.); Royal College of Music (Opera Schol. and studentship to La Scala, Milan). MusB, MA. Hon. ARCM, FRCM. Became opera manager to Royal Coll. of Music, and stage-manager and/or producer to the Covent Garden, BNOC, and Carl Rosa Opera companies, also to Royal Manchester College of Music and BBC Opera Section; Dir, Carl Rosa Opera Company, 1958, Touring Opera, 1958. Professor of Music, University of Manchester, 1954-62, retired. Dir, London Opera Centre, 1962-63. Compositions include violin, viola, oboe, horn and clarinet sonatas, pianoforte music, songs and translations of operas. *Publications:* Sir Thomas Beecham: impresario and conductor, 1973, reissued, 1976, as Beecham Remembered; numerous opera versions. *Recreation:* painting. *Address:* 3 Oakland, Windermere, Cumbria LA23 1AR. [*Died 13 April* 1980.

PROCTOR-BEAUCHAMP, Rev. Sir Ivor Cuthbert; *see* Beauchamp.

PROSSER, David Russell, FJI; retired; Editor of the Western Mail, Cardiff, South Wales, 1942-56; *b* 30 October 1889; 2nd *s* of late John Lewis and Hannah Sowden Prosser; *m* 1913, Florence, 2nd *d* of Edwin Harris, Newport. *Educ:* Cardiff Technical College; University College of South Wales and Monmouthshire. Served on staffs of South Wales Echo, South Wales Daily News, Merthyr Express, Daily Dispatch, Manchester; active service European War, 1914-18, with Artists' Rifles OTC, Lieut 1st Bn Monmouthshire Regt (T); with 5th Bn South Wales Borderers in France; Publicity Officer, Ministry of Labour (Appointments Dept) Wales, 1919-22. OStJ. *Publications:* The British Newspaper Press in Mid-Century, 1957; A National Trust for Promoting the Arts in Wales, 1959; articles and reviews on history, economics and politics; investigated social conditions in South Wales for Third Winter of Unemployment Report (1922). *Recreations:* golf, angling, music. *Address:* 81a Station Road, Llanishen, Cardiff. *T:* Cardiff 752582. [*Died 27 Aug.* 1974.

PROUD, Sir George, Kt 1973; Chairman and Managing Director, Prouds (Fiji) Ltd, since 1972; Director, Electrical Equipment of Australia Ltd; *b* 6 Oct. 1910; *s* of late W. J. Proud; *m* 1934, Eileen E., *d* of Sir Walter Carpenter; two *d. Educ:* Sydney Grammar Sch. Councillor, Retail Traders' Assoc. of NSW (Pres. RTA, 1965-67); Pres., Retail Jewellers Assoc. of NSW, 1946-47; Pres., Australian Council of Retailers, 1967-. FID 1954. Associate of the Wardens and Commonalty of the Mystery of Goldsmiths of the City of London, 1965. Cavaliere, Order Al Merito Della Repubblica Italiana, 1964. *Recreations:* golf, boating, fishing. *Address:* 4 Nyora Street, Killara, NSW 2071, Australia. *T:* 498-2451. *Clubs:* No 10; Rotary, RTA (Sydney); Avondale Golf; Prince Alfred Yacht.
[*Died 12 May* 1976.

PROUDFOOT, James, RP 1947; ROI 1937; *b* 3 March 1908; *m* 1929, Editha May Gosman (marr. diss. 1936); one *s*; *m* 1945, Ellen Pollock. *Educ:* Perth Academy; St Andrews. Studied Heatherleys (First Prize for a Still Life, all schools competing); Goldsmiths College, Paris. Elected National Society, 1932; United Artists, 1946; two one-man shows Scotland, one in London. Portrait of Peter Ustinov awarded Mention Honorable, Paris Salon, 1957. Produced some thousands alleged "silly drawings" mostly for private circulation. Illustrated two books poetry: one anthology, one humorous. Served War of 1939-45 as Sapper in Camouflage. *Recreations:* squash, snooker, table-tennis, walking, theatre-going. *Address:* 28 Tedworth Square, SW3. *Clubs:* Chelsea Arts, Savage. [*Died 15 July* 1971.

PROUDMAN, Joseph, CBE 1952; MA, DSc, LLD; FRS 1925; Professor Emeritus, University of Liverpool; Member Norwegian Academy of Science and Letters; Correspondant du Bureau des Longitudes, Paris; *b* 1888; *s* of John Proudman; *m* 1st, 1916, Rubina (*d* 1958), *d* of Thomas Ormrod; two *s* one *d*; 2nd, 1961, Mrs Beryl Gould. *Educ:* Widnes; University of Liverpool; Trinity College, Cambridge. Wrangler with Distinction, 1912; Smith's Prizeman, 1915; Adams Prizeman, 1923; Fellow of Trinity College, Cambridge, 1915-21; Professor of Applied Mathematics in University of Liverpool, 1919-33; Professor of Oceanography, 1933-54; Director of Liverpool Tidal Inst., 1919-45; Pro-Vice-Chancellor, Univ. of Liverpool, 1940-46; Pres. Internat. Assoc. of Physical Oceanography, 1951-54, Sec., 1933-48; Chairman of Advisory Committee on Research on Coastal Flooding, Ministry of Agriculture, Fisheries and Food, 1954-66; Chairman Sub-Committee on Growing Demand for Water, 1959-62 (Min. of Housing and Local Govt). JP Liverpool, 1941-54. A. Agassiz Medal of United States National Academy of Sciences, 1946; Hughes Medal of Royal Society, 1957. *Publications:* The Elements of Mechanics (with F. S. Carey) 1925; Dynamical Oceanography, 1953; scientific papers, mainly on Tides. *Address:* Edgemoor, Dewlands Way, Verwood, Dorset BH21 6JN. *T:* Verwood 2285.
[*Died 26 June* 1975.

PRUNTY, Prof. Francis Thomas Garnet, FRCP; Professor of Chemical Pathology, University of London, at St Thomas's Hospital Medical School, 1954-75, now Emeritus; Honorary Consulting Physician, St Thomas' Hospital; *b* 5 Jan. 1910; *s* of Frank Hugh Prunty, and Una Elizah Newnham (*née* Marsden); *m* 1933, Rita Hepburn Stobbs (marr. diss. 1971); one *s* one *d*; *m* 1972, Jean Margaret Maxwell-Moore. *Educ:* St Paul's Sch.; Trinity Coll., Cambridge; St Thomas's Hospital Medical Sch. Senior Scholar, Trinity Coll., 1932; MA, Cambridge, 1936; MB, BChir, 1940; MD, 1944; Raymond Horton-Smith Prize, Cambridge, 1944; FRCP 1950. Research Fellow in Medicine, Harvard, USA, 1946-47; Asst in Medicine, Peter Bent Brigham Hospital, Boston, 1946-47; Rockefeller Travelling Fellow, 1946-47; Humphrey Rolleston Lecturer, RCP, 1956; Late Examr, Univ. of London. Late President: Section of Endocrinology, Royal Society Med.; International Society of Endocrinology. Life Governor, Imperial Cancer Research Fund (late Mem. Council); Hon. Member: Soc. for Endocrinology; British Nuclear Medicine Soc.; Sociedad Medica de Occidente (Guatemala); Romanian Soc. of Endocrinology; Emeritus Mem., Biochemical Soc. *Publications:* The Chemistry and Treatment of Adrenocortical Diseases, 1964; A Laboratory Manual of Chemical Pathology (jointly), 1959; various articles in Medical and Biochemical journals. *Recreations:* travel, sailing. *Address:* Little Croft, Kilmorie Close, Torquay, Devon TQ1 2PE. *Club:* Royal Torbay Yacht. [*Died 24 Sept.* 1979.

PRYCE, Prof. Daniel Merlin; Professor of Morbid Anatomy, St Mary's Hospital Medical School, University of London, 1954-67, now Emeritus; *b* 17 April 1902; *s* of Richard and Rachel Pryce, Troedyrhiw, S. Wales; *m* 1934, Mary Whelan; one *s* two *d. Educ:* Welsh National School of Medicine; St Mary's Hospital Medical Sch. St Mary's Hospital: Research Schol., Inoculation Dept, 1927; 2nd Asst Pathologist, 1928; Asst Chemical Pathologist, 1930; 1st Asst Pathologist, 1933; Reader in Morbid Anatomy, 1949. EMS Pathologist, Harefield and Amersham, 1939. *Publications:* (jointly) Ross's Post-Mortem Appearances, 6th edn, 1963; scientific papers in morbid anatomy, bacteriology and haematology. *Recreations:* sketching, the garden. *Address:* 11 Blomfield Road, W9. *T:* 01-286 5796. [*Died 8 Feb.* 1976.

PRYCE, Edward Calcott, CBE 1957 (OBE 1940); BA, LLB; Captain; Solicitor; retired; Sheriff, City of London, 1954; *b* 1885; *s* of David Pryce, Guilsfield, Mont; *m* 1911, Sylvia Middleton, Arbroath, Scotland (*d* 1967); no *c. Educ:* Welshpool and Aberystwyth. Qualified Solicitor, 1909. Served European War, 1914-18, and War of 1939-45. High Sheriff, Montgomeryshire, 1956. *Recreations:* gardening, shooting. *Address:* Bod Isaf, Guilsfield, Welshpool, Montgomeryshire. *T:* Guilsfield 362.
[*Died 20 Oct.* 1972.

PRYDE, James Richmond Northridge, CBE 1944; formerly General Manager of Poonmudi Tea and Rubber Co. Ltd, retired 1956; *b* 14 Aug. 1894; *s* of James Oliphant and Bessie Anne Pryde, Leighinmohr, Ballymena, N Ireland; *m* 1921, Katharine (*d* 1973), *d* of T. M. McNeil, St John's, Newfoundland; three *s* one *d*. *Educ:* St Bees Sch., Cumberland. Planting (entirely) since 1912. President, United Planters' Assoc. of Southern India, 1940-44.   [*Died 2 Oct.* 1980.

PRYNNE, Brig. Harold Gordon Lusby, CBE 1943 (OBE 1942); MC 1918; TD; *b* 8 May 1899; *s* of late William Henry Gordon Prynne; *m* 1950, Doris Elizabeth (*d* 1976), *d* of Harry James Gully. *Educ:* University College Sch., London. Director of various private companies at home and abroad. Served European War, France, 1915-19 (MC), Kensington Regt (Territorial), Pte, Lieut, Captain, Major; DAQMG 56th Division; Regular Commn, 1919; DAQMG Rhine Army, 1919; Reserve of Officers, 1920; Brevet Major for services to Territorial Army, 1925; War of 1939-45 with Royal Pioneer Corps (despatches); Major, 1939; Lieut-Colonel, 1940; Colonel, 1942; Brigadier, 1942; Area Commandant, Middle East, 1942; Director of Pioneers and Labour Persia/Iraq, 1942-43; Middle East, 1943-44; Central Mediterranean Force, 1944-45. *Recreation:* travel. *Address:* Seven Coastguards, Kingsdown, Deal, Kent. *Club:* East India, Sports and Public Schools.
[*Died 13 May* 1976.

PRYNNE, Maj.-Gen. Michael Whitworth, CB 1966; CBE 1962 (OBE 1944); *b* 1 April 1912; *e s* of late Lt-Col Alan H. L. Prynne and late Jeannette Annie (*née* Crosse); *m* 1940, Jean Violet (*d* 1977), *d* of late Captain Geoffrey Stewart; one *s* three *d*. *Educ:* Bedford Sch.; RMA, Woolwich; St John's Coll., Cambridge. Commissioned into RE 1932. Served War of 1939-45: Persia and Iraq, North Africa and Italy (despatches); GSO1, HQ Eighth Army; Colonel, GS, HQ, ALFSEA; Joint Services Staff Coll., 1948; Military Attaché, Moscow, 1951-53; OC 39 Corps Engineer Regt, East Africa, 1953 (despatches); Colonel GS, HQ Northern Army Group, 1956; idc 1959; Dep.-Director War Office, 1960; Ministry of Defence, 1965-66. Chief of Staff, Headquarters Southern Command, 1964-65, and 1966-67; retired, 1967. Sec., Assoc. of Consulting Engrs, 1969-77. *Address:* The Grange, Brinton, Melton Constable, Norfolk NR24 2QH. *Club:* Royal Ocean Racing. [*Died 27 Sept.* 1977.

PRYOR, Prof. Robert Nelson, CEng, FIMM, FICE, FIMinE; Professor of Mining, Royal School of Mines, Imperial College London, since 1968; *b* 19 July 1921; *s* of Thomas Pryor and Esperanza Nelson; *m* 1945, Patricia Aloysia McMahon; three *s* one *d*. *Educ:* Oundle Sch.; Imperial Coll. (Royal Sch. of Mines) (BSc). Ingeniero Jefe de Minas, CiiaEspañola de Minas de Rio Tinto, Spain, 1955; Mining Engr, Head Office, RTZ, 1960; Gen. Man., Rio Tinto Patiño, SA, Spain, 1966. Mem. Bd, 1975, Mem. Exec. Cttee, 1977, CEI; Pres., Instn of Mining and Metallurgy, 1978; Socio de Honor, Assoc. Ing. de Minas de España, 1977. *Publications:* Trans Instn of Mining and Metallurgy. *Address:* Royal School of Mines, Imperial College of Science and Technology, SW7 2AZ. *T:* 01-589 5111 (ext. 1500).
[*Died 14 July* 1979.

PUCKRIDGE, Geoffrey Martin, CMG 1949; ED 1938; Colonial Administrative Service (retired); *b* 3 Oct. 1895; *s* of Rev. Oliver Puckridge. *Educ:* Exeter Sch. Devon Regt (TF) and RFC, 1914-20. Colonial Administrative Service, Gold Coast, 1921; Financial Secretary, Gold Coast, 1945-49. *Recreation:* golf. *Address:* Avon Cottage, Worton, Devizes, Wilts. *T:* Devizes 2824.   [*Died 7 March* 1974.

PUDNER, Anthony Serle, MBE 1952; Director, Engineering, Cable & Wireless Ltd, 1969-74; *b* 10 Jan. 1917; *s* of late Engr Captain W. H. Pudner, RN, and late Betty Macfarlane; *m* 1952, Jonie Johnson; one *s* one *d*. *Educ:* Imperial Service College. Joined Cable & Wireless Ltd, 1934; foreign service, 1938-60: Bermuda, CS Cable Enterprise, Greece, Haifa, Korea, Hong Kong, West Indies; Engr-in-Chief, 1965; Director: E African External Telecommunications Co., 1969; Trinidad & Tobago External Telecommunications Co., 1970. CEng; FIEE; FIERE (Vice-Pres. 1969); MIEEE; FRSA. *Recreations:* music, tennis. *Address:* Bass Point House, The Lizard, Cornwall.
[*Died 30 April* 1980.

PUDNEY, John Sleigh; Poet, fiction writer, dramatist and journalist; *b* 19 Jan. 1909; *o s* of H. W. Pudney, farmer, and Mabel Elizabeth, *d* of H. C. Sleigh; *m* 1934, Crystal (marr. diss., 1955; she *m* 1955, L. R. Hale), *d* of Sir Alan Herbert; one *s* two *d*; *m* 1955, Monica Forbes Curtis, *d* of J. Grant Forbes. *Educ:* Gresham's Sch., Holt. Producer and writer on staff of BBC, 1934-37; Correspondent of News Chronicle, 1937-41; RAF, 1941-45. Book Critic Daily Express, 1947-48; Literary Editor,

News Review, 1948-50; Director of Putnams, publishers, 1953-63. Contested (Lab) Sevenoaks Division, 1945. *Publications: verse:* Ten Summers, 1944; Selected Poems, 1945; Sixpenny Songs, 1953; Collected Poems, 1957; The Trampoline, 1959; Spill Out, 1967; Spandrels, 1969; Take This Orange, 1971; Selected Poems, 1973; For Johnny (War Poems), 1976; Living in a One-Sided House, 1976; *collected stories:* It Breathed down my Neck, 1946; The Europeans, 1949; *novels:* Jacobson's Ladder, 1938; Estuary, 1947; Shuffley Wanderers, 1949; The Accomplice, 1950; Hero of a Summer's Day, 1951; The Net, 1952; A Ring for Luck, 1953; Trespass in the Sun, 1957; Thin Air, 1961; The Long Time Growing Up, 1971; *non-fiction:* The Green Grass Grew All Round, 1942; Who Only England Know, 1943; World Still There, 1945; The Thomas Cook Story, 1953; The Smallest Room, 1954; Six Great Aviators, 1955; The Seven Skies, 1959; Home and Away (autobiographical), 1960; A Pride of Unicorns, 1960; Bristol Fashion, 1960; The Camel, a monograph, 1964; The Golden Age of Steam, 1966; Suez, De Lesseps' Canal, 1968; Crossing London's River, 1972; Brunel and his World, 1973; London's Docks, 1975; Lewis Carroll and his World, 1976; *official:* The Air Battle of Malta, 1944; Atlantic Bridge, 1945; Laboratory of the Air, 1948; also books for boys and girls; *film scripts, etc.:* script writer for Travel Royal, 1952; Elizabeth is Queen, 1953; Welcome The Queen, 1954; May Wedding, 1960; joint author of screen play, Conflict of Wings, 1954; The Stolen Airliner, 1955; Blue Peter, 1955; The Concord, 1966; Mission of Fear, 1966; Ted, TV play, 1972; The Little Giant, musical play, 1972; Thomas Cook & Son, BBC TV documentary, 1978. *Recreation:* bonfires. *Address:* 4 Macartney House, Chesterfield Walk, SE10 8HJ. *T:* 01-858 0482.
[*Died 10 Nov.* 1977.

PUGH, Sir Alun; *see* Pugh, Sir J. A.

PUGH, His Honour Sir (John) Alun, Kt 1959; Judge of County Courts, retired; *b* 23 Jan. 1894; *o c* of Dr J. W. Pugh and Margaret Evans, Brighton; *m* 1915, Kathleen Mary, JP (*d* 1970), *o d* of late T. Edward Goodyear, Bromley, Kent; three *d* (one *s* decd). *Educ:* Brighton Coll.; Queen's Coll., Oxford (Open History Scholar). Welsh Guards, 1915-19, Lieut (wounded). Called to Bar, 1918, Inner Temple; joined South Wales Circuit. President, Hardwicke Society, 1924; Junior Editor, Butterworth's Workmen's Compensation Cases, 1927-39; Sole Editor 1939-42; Member Co. Court Rule Cttee, 1937-44, 1947-66, Chairman, 1963-66. Legal Adviser Ministry of Pensions, 1939-42; Judge of Circuit 32 (Norfolk), 1944-46, Circuit 37 (West London), 1947-48; Circuit 40 (Bow), 1948-50; Circuit 42 (Bloomsbury), 1950-66. Chairman, Norwich Licensing Area Planning Cttee, 1945-48; Member of Cttee on County Court Procedure, 1947-49; Member of Cttee on Funds in Court, 1958-59; President, Commn of Inquiry into Bahamas Police Force, 1962. *Address:* The Old Rectory, Dunsfold, Surrey. *T:* 444. *Club:* Reform.   [*Died 24 Nov.* 1971.

PUGH, Leslie Mervyn; Stipendiary Magistrate for Liverpool, 1965-76, and for Merseyside, 1974-76; *b* 19 Nov. 1905; *s* of late Joseph and Harriette Pugh; *m* 1931, Elizabeth Gwladys Newcombe; two *d*. *Educ:* Wellington (Somerset). Admitted to Roll of Solicitors, 1928; Clerk: to Gower (Glam), RDC, 1931-40; to Swansea Justices, 1940-46; to Sheffield City Justices, 1946-57; to Hallamshire (WR), Justices, 1947-57; Stipendiary Magistrate, Huddersfield, 1957-65. President Justices' Clerks' Society, 1955-56; Member: Home Office Probation Advisory and Training Board, 1953-62; Departmental Cttee on Summary Trial of Minor Offences, 1954-55. Chm., Liverpool City Justices, 1971-76. *Publications:* Matrimonial Proceedings before Magistrates. *Recreations:* walking, gardening. *Address:* 17 St George's Road, Formby, near Liverpool L37 3HH. *T:* Formby 73426. *Club:* Athenæum (Liverpool).   [*Died 4 Feb.* 1978.

PUGH, Rev. Canon T(homas) Jenkin, TD 1946; Chaplain to the Queen, 1962-73; *b* 15 Nov. 1903; seventh *s* of Rees and Margaret Ann Pugh; *m* 1932, Marjorie Window (*d* 1970). *Educ:* Universities of Wales and London. Ordained, 1931. Vicar of Acton and Little Waldingfield, Suffolk. Chaplain, TA, with BEF, France, 1939-40; Far East, 1941-45; New Zealand, 1945-46; Sen. Chaplain in Butlin Organisation, on staff of Archbishop of Canterbury, 1947-71. Canon of Lincoln Cathedral and Prebendary of Bedford Minor, 1955; Canon Emeritus, 1977. Dir, Archbishop's Mission to Holiday Camps and Caravan Sites, 1969-71. MA Lambeth 1959. Member, Governing Body of the Church in Wales. *Recreation:* fishing. *Address:* Modwenna, Criccieth, N Wales. *T:* 2808. *Club:* Reform.
[*Died 27 March* 1980.

PUGH, Sir William (John), Kt 1956; OBE; FRS; BA, DSc (Wales), MSc (Manchester); Hon. DSc (Nottingham); Hon. LLD (Wales); MIME, FGS; lately Director, Geological Survey of Great Britain and Museum of Practical Geology (1950-60); Emeritus Professor of Geology, University of Manchester, since 1951; Fellow, Imperial College of Science and Technology, University of London, since 1960; *b* 28 July 1892; *s* of John and Harriet Pugh of Westbury; *m* Manon Clayton (*d* 1973), 2nd *d* of J. Davies Bryan, LLD, Alexandria, Egypt; four *s. Educ:* Coppin Sch., Welshpool; University College of Wales, Aberystwyth. Served European War with the Royal Welch Fusiliers, and attached to the General Staff 2nd and 4th Army HQ's, BEF, and GHQ British Army of the Rhine (OBE, French Croix de Guerre, despatches twice). Univ. Coll. of Wales, Aberystwyth: Prof. of Geology, 1919-31; Dean of Faculty of Science, 1929-31. University of Manchester: Prof. of Geology, 1931-50; Dean of the Faculty of Science, 1939-41; Pro-Vice-Chancellor, 1941-43; and Deputy Vice-Chancellor, 1943-50. Chairman University of Manchester Joint Recruiting Board, 1939-47; Manchester Educ. Cttee, 1947-50; Board of Governors, United Manchester Teaching Hospitals, 1948-50; Inter-University Council for Higher Education in the Colonies, 1946-50; Member Commission on Higher Education in Malaya, 1947. Late External Examiner, Universities of Birmingham, Cambridge, Dublin, Leeds, Oxford and Wales. President Section C (Geology), 1948; Member: Council British Assoc., 1951-57; Council Geological Society of London, 1933-38, 1947-50, 1957-62; Murchison Medal, 1952. Nature Conservancy, 1952-57. Council Royal Society, 1952. Geological Survey Board, 1940-44, 1946-50; Court and lately Council University College of Wales, Aberystwyth; Gov. Body Imperial College of Science and Technology, 1951-71. *Publications:* Papers dealing with the stratigraphy and tectonics of the Lower Palaeozoic rocks principally of Wales and published mainly in the Quarterly Journal of Geological Society of London. *Address:* 171 Oakwood Court, Kensington, W14. *T:* 01-602 2151. *Club:* Athenæum.   [*Died* 18 *March* 1974.

PUGSLEY, Sir Reuben (James), Kt 1954; OBE 1939; JP; *b* 3 March 1886; *m* 1907, Dora Gwendoline Owens; two *s. Educ:* St Monica's, Cardiff. Entered Flour Milling Industry, 1901. JP, City of Cardiff, 1926. *Recreation:* golf. *Address:* Summermead, Llandennis Avenue, Cyncoed, Cardiff. *T:* Cardiff 52478. *Club:* Cardiff and County (Cardiff).   [*Died* 12 *March* 1975.

PULLAN, Ayrton George Popplewell, MA; *b* 9 June 1879; *s* of Colonel Ayrton Pullan, Indian Staff Corps; *m* 1906, Kathleen Elizabeth Love (*d* 1968), *d* of G. D. Kempson; one *s* one *d. Educ:* Malvern Coll.; Trinity Coll., Oxford; Goldsmiths' Company Exhibitioner, 1899. 1st Class Classical Moderations, 2nd Class Lit Hum. Passed 7th Civil Service Examination, 1902; Assistant Collector, United Provinces, 1903; District Judge, 1918; Judge, Chief Court of Oudh, 1929; Judge, High Court of Judicature, Allahabad, India, 1931-33; barrister, Middle Temple; practised before Privy Council, 1935-52; Ministry of Labour and National Service, 1940-43. *Publications:* A Glossary of Indian Law Terms (Middle Temple Library); Index to Criminal Appeal Reports, Vols 1-34, 1952; (with D. W. Alcock) The Commercial Dictionary, 1953. *Recreations:* gardening, chess, embroidery. *Address:* The Dene, Forest Way, Tunbridge Wells, Kent. *T:* Tunbridge Wells 26579.   [*Died* 31 *Aug.* 1973.

PURCELL-BURET, Captain Theobald John Claud, CBE 1942; DSC 1917; retired Commodore of Royal Mail Fleet; *b* London, 18 June 1879; *s* of John Claud Buret, London and Geneva, and Alice Maria, *e d* of late John Theobald Purcell, Kilkenny, Eire; assumed by royal licence 1941 additional surname of Purcell; *m* 1st, 1907, Maud (*d* 1936), *y d* of late Leonard Huckle, Bristol; one *d*; 2nd, 1941, Hon. Winifred Elspeth Guthrie (*d* 1965), *o d* of 1st Baron Forres, PC. *Educ:* Victoria Coll., Jersey. Entered Merchant Service, 1894; master mariner, 1916; Commodore Royal Mail Fleet, 1939-42; retired 1942. Younger Brother of Trinity House. *Publications:* The Wanderer, and other Poems, 1951 (Dublin). *Address:* Ballyfoyle, Christchurch Road, Winchester, Hants. *Club:* Royal Commonwealth Society.
                                                [*Died* 15 *April* 1974.

PURCHAS, Rev. Canon Alban Charles Theodore, MA; Licenced Preacher, Diocese of Christchurch, 1955-58, and since 1963; Chaplain to St George's Church Hospital, 1958-60; Hon. Canon of Christchurch Cathedral, 1949-58; *b* 8 Oct. 1890; *s* of Canon Henry T. Purchas, MA, and Lily E. Cox; *m* 1917, *d* of Rev. C. A. Tobin, Vicar of Burwood, Christchurch; two *s* three *d* (and one *s* killed in action, Italy, 1944). *Educ:* Christ's College, Christchurch, NZ. Deacon, 1914; Priest, 1915; Assistant Curate Parish of Geraldine, 1914-17; Chaplain, Christ's College, 1917-19; Vicar, Kumara, 1919-24, and with Hokitika, 1921-24; Akaroa, 1924-28; Holy Trinity, Lyttleton, 1928-32; Rangiora, 1932-39; Cashmere Hills, 1939-44; Fendalton, 1947-51; Vicar of Methven, Christchurch, 1951-55, retired. Archdeacon of Rangiora and Westland, 1934-44; Canon Missioner and Youth

Organiser for Dio. Christchurch, NZ, 1944-47; Archdeacon of Christchurch, 1944-49. *Recreation:* gardening. *Address:* The Hospice, Churchill Courts, 73 Stapleton's Road, Christchurch I, New Zealand.   [*Died* 10 *Aug.* 1976.

PURDIE, Rev. Albert Bertrand, OBE; MA, PhD; *b* 27 Aug. 1888; 3rd *s* of Arthur Purdie, London. *Educ:* St Edmund's, Ware; Christ's College, Cambridge. Priest, 1914; Hons Classical Tripos, 1921; Diploma of Classical Archæology, 1922; PhD (Fribourg) 1934; Army Chaplain, 1914-19; in France with 48th Divn 1915-16; Senior Catholic Chaplain of the British Salonika Force at Salonika and Constantinople, 1918-19 (despatches, OBE, Order of St Sava); Housemaster at St Edmund's, Ware, 1922-33; Assistant Headmaster, 1926-29; Headmaster, 1929-36; Chaplain, RAF, 1940-44. *Publications:* A Pilgrim-Walk in Canterbury, 1910; Poems, 1918; Life of Blessed John Southworth, 1930; Latin Verse Inscriptions, 1935; contributions to various journals. *Address:* 3 Thakeham Close, Goring-by-Sea, Worthing, West Sussex.   [*Died* 30 *May* 1976.

PURNELL, David Cuthbert; Chairman, County Council of South Glamorgan, 1978-79; *b* 14 July 1932; *s* of Oliver Cuthbert Purnell, CBE, DL, JP, and Pauline Purnell; *m* 1959, Helen Marie Croke; two *s* two *d. Educ:* The Oratory Sch., Woodcote, near Reading, Berks. Managing Dir, Augustine J. Stone Ltd, and Sen. Partner, Wm Hamm & Co. Member: Cardiff City Council, 1958-; S Glamorgan CC, 1974-; S Wales Police Authority, 1977-; Welsh Sports City Jt Building Cttee, 1976-78; New Theatre Trust; Court of Governors: National Museum of Wales, 1977-; University Coll., Cardiff. Lord Mayor of Cardiff, 1977-78. Contested (C) Parly Elecs, Rhondda East, 1964, Aberdare, 1970. *Recreation:* boating. *Address:* 32 Church Road, Whitchurch, Cardiff. *T:* Cardiff 66525; Ebens Lane, Cardigan.
                                                [*Died* 17 *Feb.* 1979.

PURSEY, Comdr Harry; RN, retired; journalist and lecturer; *b* 1891; *e s* of late G. Pursey, Sidmouth, Devon; *m* 1944, Dorothea Middleton (marr. diss. 1954), BSc, PhD, *e d* of A. Mowat, Inverness; *m* 1954, Lillian Maria Adler. *Educ:* elementary school; Royal Hosp. School, Greenwich (Navy's orphanage). Joined Navy as seaman boy, HMS Impregnable, Devonport, 1907, and first naval officer from lower deck to become MP. Specialised in torpedo and mining. Served European War, 1914-18, Dover Patrol, Grand Fleet, HMS Revenge (Battle of Jutland), Eastern Mediterranean (despatches). Commissioned 1917. Black Sea and Turkish operations, 1919-20; Mad Mullah campaign, Somaliland, 1920 (Africa General Service Medal and clasp); Mesopotamia, 1920. Serving in HMS Eagle when Spanish trans-Atlantic flying-boat salved in mid-Atlantic, 1929. HMS Hood, 1931-33; retired list, 1936. Press correspondent in Spain during Civil War, 1937. Ministry of Information National Speaker, 1940-41. MP (Lab) Hull East, 1945-70. Contributed to The Times, Brassey's Naval Annual, British, Dominion and American Press. *Address:* 43 Farnaby Road, Shortlands, Bromley, Kent. *T:* 01-460 0361.   [*Died* 13 *Dec.* 1980.

PURVES, Sir Raymond (Edgar), Kt 1971; CBE 1967; FCA; Principal, Raymond E. Purves & Co., Chartered Accountants; *b* 15 June 1910; *s* of late Albert E. Purves; *m* 1951, Betty Jacques, *d* of late T. A. Field; one *s* one *d. Educ:* N Sydney Boys' High Sch. Chm. and Man. Dir, Clyde Industries Ltd, and subsidiaries; Chairman: Australian Equitable Insurance Co. Ltd; Fruehauf Trailers (Australasia) Pty Ltd; Director: Fairey Australasia Pty Ltd; CAF Mechanical Handling Equipment Ltd (UK); Bowling Centres (Hldgs) Ltd. Member: Aust./Japan Business Co-operation Cttee; Pacific Basin Economic Co-operation Council. Underwriting Mem. of Lloyds. Life Governor: Royal Life Saving Soc. of Aust.; Science Foundn for Physics; Hon. Life Governor: Austr. Postgrad. Fedn in Medicine; Austr. Inst. of Management; Governor, Postgrad. Med. Foundn. *Recreations:* boating, golf. *Address:* 18 Bangalla Street, Warrawee, NSW 2074, Australia. *Clubs:* Australian, Jockey, University, Tattersall's, American National, Royal Motor Yacht, Royal Automobile, Australian Golf, Avondale Golf (Sydney); Commonwealth (Canberra).   [*Died* 18 *Sept.* 1973.

PUTTICK, Lt-Gen. Sir Edward, KCB 1946 (CB 1942); DSO 1918; idc; *b* 26 June 1890; *s* of John Prior Puttick, London, and Rachel Orpen, Kilgarvan, Kenmare, Ireland; *m* 1919, Irene Lillian Dignan (*d* 1964), Auckland; three *d. Educ:* Waitaki Boys' High School, Oamaru, NZ. Served European War, 1914-18: Capt. to Lt-Col, Samoa, Egypt, France, Belgium; Commander (temp.) 3rd New Zealand Rifle Brigade, 1917 (severely wounded); Commandant NZRB Reserve Depot, Brocton Stafford, 1918; Asst Quartermaster-General, New Zealand, 1919-29; Commandant Special Expedition to Fiji during Indian riots, 1920; Staff Officer in charge No 1 Regtl District Auckland, 1929-33; GSO Christchurch, 1933-34, Lt-Col, 1933;

Quartermaster-General, NZ Military Forces, Wellington, NZ, 1934-36; at Imperial Defence College and Imperial Conference, 1937; Colonel, 1937; ADC (addit) to the King, 1938-41; Adjutant and Quartermaster-General and 2nd Military Member of the Army Board, Army Headquarters, Wellington, NZ, 1938-39; Officer Commanding Central District, Wellington, NZ, 1939; Comdr 4th NZ Infantry Brigade, NZ Expeditionary Force, Egypt, 1940-41; Operations Greece, 1941; Comd NZ Forces, Crete, May 1941; GOC New Zealand Forces, 1942-45, and Chief of New Zealand General Staff, 1941-45 (Greek Military Cross, 1st Class, Bar to DSO, Commander Legion of Merit (USA)); Prime Ministers' Conf. (London), 1944; Maj.-Gen. 1941; Lt-Gen. 1942. Commanded New Zealand Contingent in Victory March, London, 1946; retired, 1946. Gold Staff Officer at Coronation of King George VI, 1937. *Publication:* 25 Battalion: Official History of New Zealand in the Second World War, 1939-1945, 1960. *Recreations:* cricket, shooting, fishing. *Address:* Ardtully, Wallis Street, Raglan, NZ.
[Died 25 July 1976.

PYKE, Air Commodore Alan, CB 1961; OBE 1951; Royal Air Force (Retired); *b* 5 September 1911; *s* of late Arthur Oakley Pyke, Gillingham, Kent. *Educ:* Ashton-under-Lyne; Royal Air Force College, Cranwell. Joined RAF, 1927. Served War of 1939-45, Fighter Command and Maintenance Command; jssc; psa; CEng, FIMechE. *Recreations:* golf, gardening. *Address:* Oakley, Bate's Lane, Helsby, Cheshire. *Club:* Royal Air Force.
[Died 11 March 1977.

PYKE, Cyril John, CMG 1951; *b* 1892; *s* of Richard John Pyke, Midgham, Berks; *m* 1917, Gladys, *e d* of F. W. Pote, Exeter; two *d* (and two *s* decd). *Educ:* King's College, London; Trinity Hall, Cambridge. Civil Service Administrative Class, 1921; Assistant Secretary, Ministry of Supply, 1939; Deputy Director of Finance, Ministry of Supply, 1940; Principal Assistant Secretary, 1942; Economic Adviser to Government of Malaya, 1945; Head of Finance and Economics Department, Foreign Office Administration of African Territories, 1949. *Address:* Stobshaw Place, Tweedbank, Galashiels. *[Died 11 Dec. 1976.*

PYKE-LEES, Walter Kinnear; Registrar, General Medical Council, 1951-70; *b* 17 Dec. 1909; *m* 1944, Joan Warburton, *d* of G. F. Stebbing, FRCS, FFR, and Margaret Warburton Stebbing; two *d*. *Educ:* Liverpool College; Wadham College, Oxford. Clerk of the Council's Dept, LCC, 1933-37; Asst Sec., GMC, 1937; seconded to HM Treasury, 1940-45; Asst Sec., GMC, 1945-51. Lectr, Extra-Mural Dept, Univ. of London, 1972-. Mem. Exec. Cttee, English Assoc., 1950-62. Mem. Council, Britain-Burma Soc., 1968-77. *Publications:* History and Present Work of the General Medical Council, 1958; *as Peter Leyland:* The Naked Mountain (verse), 1951; The English Association Book of Verse (anthology, with M. Alderton Pink), 1953. *Recreations:* golf, travel. *Address:* 7 Burghley Road, Wimbledon, SW19. *T:* 01-946 5727. *[Died 15 Nov. 1978.*

PYKE-NOTT, Comdr Sir James (Grenvile), Kt 1952; CMG 1949; RN (retired); *b* 28 April 1897; *s* of John Möels Pyke-Nott, Mill House, Dumbleton, nr Evesham, Worcs and Dora Florence Geraldine, *d* of Bennet Rothes Langton, Langton Hall, Langton, Spilsby, Lincs; *m* 1949, Joan Mary Lee, *d* of late Rev. W. M. L. Evans. *Educ:* Orleton Preparatory School, Scarborough; Royal Naval Colleges, Osborne and Dartmouth. Served in Royal Navy in European War, 1914-18, and in War of 1939-45. Appointed to Colonial Administrative Service, 1924; served in Nigeria; Chief Commissioner, Eastern Provinces, 1948-52, Lieut-Governor, Eastern Region, 1952, Nigeria; retired, 1952. *Recreations:* shooting and golf. *Address:* 7 Carroll Avenue, Merrow, near Guildford, Surrey. *[Died 13 April 1972.*

PYM, Barbara Mary Crampton, FRSL 1978; novelist; *b* 2 June 1913; *d* of Frederic Crampton Pym and Irena Spenser (*née* Thomas). *Educ:* Huyton Coll., Liverpool; St Hilda's Coll., Oxford. Editorial Secretary, Internat. African Inst., London, 1958-74. *Publications:* Some Tame Gazelle, 1950; Excellent Women, 1952; Jane and Prudence, 1953; Less than Angels, 1955; A Glass of Blessings, 1958; No Fond Return of Love, 1961; Quartet in Autumn, 1977; The Sweet Dove Died, 1978. *Address:* Barn Cottage, Finstock, Oxford OX7 3EY.
[Died 11 Jan. 1980.

PYM, Sir Charles (Evelyn), Kt 1959; CBE 1939 (OBE 1919); DL; *b* 11 Jan. 1879; 2nd *s* of late Horatio Noble Pym, Foxwold, Kent, and Sarah Juliet, *d* of Edmund Backhouse, MP; *m* 1905, Violet C. (*d* 1927), *o d* of Frederick Lubbock, Emmetts, Kent; three *s* one *d*. *Educ:* Eton; Magdalen College, Oxford. Late Captain 5th Lancers, Major Suffolk Yeo.; served S African War, 1901-02; Gallipoli and Egypt, 1915-16; France, 1917-19 (despatches twice, OBE); JP, DL Kent; Kent County Council, 1925-65;

County Alderman, 1935-; Vice-Chairman, 1936-49; Chairman, 1949-52. Comdr St John of Jerusalem. *Recreations:* shooting, walking. *Address:* Foxwold, Brasted, Kent. *T:* Westerham 3724. *Clubs:* Junior Carlton, Bath; Kent County (Maidstone).
[Died 13 Sept. 1971.

PYMAN, Gen. Sir Harold (English), GBE 1963 (CBE 1944; MBE 1941); KCB 1958 (CB 1946); DSO 1942; MA; *b* 12 March 1908; *yr s* of late H. E. Pyman, W Hartlepool; *m* 1933, Elizabeth McArthur; two *s* one *d. Educ:* Fettes Coll.; Clare Coll., Cambridge (MA). Gazetted to Royal Tank Regiment, 1929; North-West Frontier Campaign, 1937; Capt. 1938; student at Staff College, Quetta, 1939; Instructor at Staff College, Quetta, 1939-41; psc†; Western Desert, 1941 (despatches); GSO1, 7 Armoured Division (DSO); CO 3rd Royal Tank Regt (bar to DSO); Brigadier General Staff, Home Forces, 1943-44; Brigadier General Staff 30 Corps for Normandy invasion (CBE); Chief of Staff Second Army, 1944-45 (despatches); Chief of General Staff ALFSEA and Acting Maj.-Gen., 1945-46 (CB, US Legion of Merit, Commander); Chief of Staff, GHQ, MELF, 1946-49; Maj.-Gen., 1949; GOC 56 (London) Armoured Division TA, 1949-51; Director-General, Fighting Vehicles, Ministry of Supply, 1951-53; GOC 11th Armoured Division, BAOR, 1953-55; Director of Weapons and Development, War Office, April 1955-May 1956; Lieut-General, 1957; General Officer Commanding 1st Corps, BAOR, 1956-58; Deputy Chief of the Imperial General Staff, 1958-61; General, 1961; Commander-in-Chief, Allied Forces, Northern Europe, 1961-63; retired 1964. Late Hon. Col, Berkshire and Westminster Dragoons (2nd Company of London Yeo.) TA; Col Comdt: The Royal Tank Regt, 1958-65; The Royal Armoured Corps, 1963-66. *Publication:* Call to Arms, 1971. *Recreations:* books, his garden and his writing; horticultural exhibitor. *Address:* Chitterwell, Sampford Arundel, Wellington, Somerset. *Club:* Somerset County (Taunton). *[Died 9 Oct. 1971.*

Q

QUARONI, Pietro, Grand Cross of Order of Merit (GCOM, Italy); Grand Cross Crown (GCCI, Italy); MC (British); President-General, Italian Red Cross; *b* 3 October 1898; *s* of Giuseppe Quaroni and Sofia Pia von Seitz; *m* 1928, Larissa Cegodaeff; two *s. Educ:* Rome University. Began Italian Diplomatic career, 1920. Appointments: Constantinople, 1920; Buenos Aires, 1923; Moscow, 1925; Tirana, 1928; Ministry of Foreign Affairs, Rome, 1932; expert at Stresa Conference, 1935; Consul-General, Salonika, 1935; Italian Minister, Kabul, 1936; Ambassador, Moscow, 1944; Member of Italian Delegation at Peace Conf.; Ambassador, Paris, 1947-58; Ambassador, Bonn, 1958-61; Ambassador, London, 1961-64. Pres., Italian Radio Television, 1964-69. Grand Cross Légion d'Honneur (France), 1958; Grand Cross, Order of Merit (Germany), 1961. *Publications:* Memoirs of an Ambassador, 1954; Diplomatic Bag, 1956 (Eng. trans. 1966); The World of an Ambassador; Problems of Foreign Policy; Europe at the Crossway; Russia and China; Editor, Affari Esteri (quarterly). *Address:* Via Alberico II 4, Rome, Italy; Italian Red Cross, via Toscana 12, Rome, Italy. *Club:* Circolo Caccia (Rome); Jockey (Paris).
[Died 12 June 1971.

QUARTERMAINE, Sir Allan (Stephen), Kt 1956; CBE 1943; MC; BSc; FICE; *b* 9 November 1888; *s* of late Charles Stephen Quartermaine; *m* 1914, Gladys E. H. Siddons (*d* 1956); one *s. Educ:* University College, London (Hons Graduate, Chadwick Scholar, and Fellow). Hertfordshire CC, Surveyor's Department; Tees Side Bridge and Engineering Works; Great Western Railway; Royal Engineers, Egypt and Palestine, 1915-19 (despatches, MC); Commanded No. 1 Bridging Company, RE, SR, 1925; Director-General, Aircraft Production Factories, 1940; Chief Engineer, Great Western Railway and Western Region, British Railways, 1940-51; President Institution of Civil Engineers, 1951-52; Mem. Departmental Cttee on Coastal Flooding, 1953-54; Mem. Royal Fine Art Commission, 1954-60; Chm. Council for Codes of Practice, British Standards Institution, 1954-58; Mem. Hydraulics Research Board, DSIR, 1954-58. Hon. Member Institution of Royal Engineers; Chm. Civil Engineering Scholarship Trust, 1958-64. *Address:* 53 Westminster Gardens, SW1P 4JG. *T:* 01-834 2143. *Club:* Athenæum. *[Died 17 Oct. 1978.*

QUAYLE, Richard William, OBE 1948; Member, London Rent Assessment Panel, since 1967; *b* 9 Aug. 1901; *o s* of late Richard

Smith Quayle; *m* 1926, Ursula Mary Heron Ryan (*d* 1971), *o d* of Arthur Heron Ryan Tenison, FRIBA; one *d. Educ:* Charterhouse; Magdalen College, Oxford. Called to Bar, Inner Temple, 1925. Entered Office of Solicitor of Inland Revenue; Assistant Solicitor of Inland Revenue, 1950; Special Comr of Income Tax, 1953-66. *Recreation:* fishing. *Address:* St Peter's Cottage, Westcott, Dorking, Surrey. *T:* Dorking 5311. *Clubs:* United Oxford & Cambridge University, MCC.
[Died 30 Nov. 1973.

QUEEN, Rt. Rev. Carman John; Bishop of Huron, since 1970; *b* 10 Aug. 1912; *s* of John James Cumberland Queen and Ethel Maud Queen (*née* Eden); *m* 1938, Audrey Dardanelle Bell; one *s* one *d. Educ:* Univ. of Western Ontario (BA); Huron Coll. (LTh.). Deacon, 1936; Priest, 1937; Asst Curate: All Saints', London, Ont, 1936; Burford, 1937; Rector: Princeton, 1938; Ridgetown, 1940; Tillsonburg, 1944; Ingersoll, 1946; Domestic Chap. to Bishop Luxton, 1950; Diocesan Comr, Dio. Huron, 1956; Canon, St Paul's Cath., 1956; Archdeacon of Huron, 1958; elected Area Suffragan Bp, 1966; consecrated (title of Bishop of St Clair), 1967; installed as Bp of Huron, Nov. 1970. Hon. DD Huron Coll., 1961. *Recreations:* gardening, fishing. *Address:* Box 308, London, Ontario, Canada. *T:* (office) (519) 434-6893. *Clubs:* London, London Hunt and Country (both in London, Ont).
[Died 23 Feb. 1974.

QUENNELL, (Mrs) Marjorie, Hon. ARIBA; illustrator; *b* Bromley Common, Kent; *d* of Allen Courtney; *m* 1904, Charles Henry Bourne Quennell, Architect (*d* 1935); one *s* (one *d* decd, and one *s* decd, War of 1939-45). *Educ:* Oakhurst, Shortlands; various art schools. Curator of the Geffrye Museum till 1941. *Publications:* (with C. H. B. Quennell) A History of Everyday Things in England, Part I, 1918; Part II, 1919; Part III, 1933; Part IV, 1934; Everyday Life in the Old Stone Age, 1921; New Stone, Bronze, and Early Iron Ages, 1922; Roman Britain, 1924; Anglo-Saxon Viking and Norman Times, 1926; Everyday Things in Homeric Greece, 1929; Everyday Things in Archaic Greece, 1931; Everyday Things in Classical Greece, 1932; The Good New Days, 1936. *Recreation:* painter. *Address:* 6 Wallands Crescent, Lewes, Sussex.
[Died 2 Aug. 1972.

QUIGLEY, Hugh, MA; Economist and Farmer; *b* Stirling, 6 Aug. 1895; *e s* of James and Catherine Quigley, Stirling, afterwards Lanark; *m* Marion Sommerville (*d* 1974), *y d* of Joseph Dyer, Kilbank, Lanark; one *s* one *d. Educ:* Lanark Grammar Sch.; Glasgow Univ.; Naples Univ.; Munich Univ. War Service, 1915-18; MA, 1st Class Hons in French, German, Italian, Glasgow Univ., 1919; Carnegie Research Fellow in Modern Languages, 1919-21; Economist in Research Department of Metropolitan-Vickers Electrical Company, 1922-24; Head of Economic and Statistical Department of the British Electrical and Allied Manufacturers' Assoc., 1924-30; Chief Statistical Officer, Central Electricity Board, 1931-43. *Publications:* Lombardy, Tyrol, and the Trentino, 1925; The Land of the Rhone, 1927; Passchendaele and the Somme, 1928 (revised edn, 1965); Lanarkshire in Prose and Verse, 1929; Electrical Power and National Progress, 1925; Towards Industrial Recovery, 1927; Republican Germany (with R. T. Clark), 1928 (repr. 1968); German History from 1900 to 1931 (chap. in German Studies ed. Jethro Bithell), 1932; Part translator of R. Liefmann: Cartels, Concerns and Trusts, 1932; Power Resources of the World (for World Power Conference), 1929; Combines and Trusts in the Electrical Industry, 1927; The Electrical Industry of Great Britain, 1929; (both for the British Electrical and Allied Manufacturers' Association); Housing and Slum Clearance in London (with I. Goldie), 1934; Italian Criticism in the 18th Century; The Influence of English Philosophy and the Development of Aesthetics, based on Imagination; Antonio Conti (chapter in Mélanges Hauvette); The Highlands of Scotland, 1936; A Plan for the Highlands, 1936; End Monopoly Exploitation, 1941; New Forest Orchard, 1947; A Small Community, 1970; Melchet, 1971. *Recreation:* forestry. *Address:* Melchet Park, Romsey, Hants.
[Died 30 Jan. 1979.

QUINN, Most Rev. Austin, DD; *b* Brookley, Co Armagh, 15 March 1892. *Educ:* St Patrick's Coll., Armagh; Maynooth Coll. Ordained, 1915; DD (Maynooth) 1920. Prof. in All Hallows Coll., Dublin, 1917-26; Curate in Archdiocese of Armagh, 1926-40; Administrator, Cathedral, Armagh, 1940-43; Parish Priest of St Peter's, Drogheda, Archdeacon of Cathedral Chapter, and Vicar General of Archdiocese of Armagh, 1943-50; Bishop of Kilmore, 1950-72. *Address:* c/o Bishop's House, Cullis, Cavan, Ireland.
[Died 24 Sept. 1974.

QUIRK, Ronald Charles, OBE 1955; Member of Council, Stock Exchange, London, since 1950 (Deputy Chairman, 1964-67); *b* 11 Jan. 1908; *s* of George Henry Quirk and Ethel Jane Sargent;

m 1932, Joan Reed; one *s* two *d. Educ:* Whitgift. Joined Geo. D. Atkin & Co. (stockjobbers), 1923; admitted into partnership, 1931; Director, Akroyd & Smithers Ltd, 1970. Joined RNVR 1940; served in Combined Operations until 1946. *Address:* White Lodge, Hillcroft Avenue, Purley, Surrey. *T:* 01-660 2685. *Clubs:* City of London; Island Sailing (Cowes); Royal Yachting Association; Lee-on-Solent Sailing.
[Died 5 May 1973.

R

RADCLIFFE, 1st Viscount, *cr* 1962; **Cyril John Radcliffe,** PC 1949; GBE 1948 (KBE 1944); FBA 1968; Baron (Life Peer) *cr* 1949; a Lord of Appeal in Ordinary, 1949-64; *b* 30 Mar. 1899; *s* of Alfred Ernest Radcliffe and Sybil Harriet Cunliffe; *m* 1939, Antonia, *d* of 1st Baron Charnwood. *Educ:* Haileybury; New College, Oxford (Hon. Fellow, 1949). Fellow of All Souls College, Oxford, 1922-37; Eldon Law Scholar, 1924; called to Bar, Inner Temple, 1924; Bencher 1943. QC 1935. Appts at Ministry of Information, 1939-41; Director General, Ministry of Information, 1941-45; Vice-Chairman Gen. Council of the Bar, 1946-49; Chairman: Departmental Cttee, British Film Inst., 1946-47; Punjab and Bengal Boundary Commissions, 1947; Royal Commission on Taxation of Profits and Income, 1952; BBC General Advisory Council, 1952-55; British Commonwealth International Newsfilm Agency Trust, 1957-75; Constitutional Commissioner, Cyprus, 1956; Chairman: Cttee of Inquiry into the Monetary and Credit System, 1957-59; Cttee of Inquiry into Security Procedures and Practices, 1961; Tribunal of Inquiry into the Vassall Case, 1962; Privy Councillors' Inquiry into Daily Express and D Notices, 1967; Privy Councillors' Cttee on Memoirs of ex-Ministers, 1975. Chm., Bd of Trustees, British Museum, 1963-68 (Trustee, 1957-69); Trustee, British Museum (Natural History), 1963-69; Chancellor of University of Warwick, 1966-; Life Trustee: Shakespeare Birthplace Trust; Sir John Soane's Museum; Mem. Court of Univ. of London, 1958-63; Chm. Bd of Governors, SOAS, London Univ., 1960-75. Lectures: Reith, BBC, 1951; Montagu Burton, Glasgow University, 1953; Lloyd Roberts, RSM, 1955; Rosenthal Foundn, 1960; Rede, Cambridge, 1961; Romanes, Oxford, 1962; Oration, LSE, 1965; Carr-Saunders, Inst. of Race Relations, 1969. Hon. MICE; Hon. Fellow: Inst. of Bankers; SOAS. Hon. LLD: Univ. of Wales, 1957; Univ. of St Andrews, 1959; Northwestern Univ., Illinois, USA, 1960; Univ. of Sussex, 1963; Univ. of Manchester, 1965; Hon. DCL, Oxford, 1961. Hon. DLitt, Univ. of Warwick, 1967. *Publications:* The Problem of Power (Reith Lectures, 1951); The Law and its Compass (Rosenthal Foundation Lectures), 1960; Not in Feather Beds, 1968. *Heir:* none. *Address:* 5 Campden Hill Gate, Duchess of Bedford Walk, W8. *T:* 01-937 0321; Hampton Lucy House, Warwick.
[Died 1 April 1977 (ext).

RADCLIFFE, Sir Everard; *see* Radcliffe, Sir Joseph B. E. H.

RADCLIFFE, Sir (Joseph Benedict) Everard (Henry), 6th Bt *cr* 1813; MC 1945; Captain, late 60th Rifles; *b* 10 March 1910; *s* of Sir Everard Joseph Radcliffe, 5th Bt and Daisy (*d* 1943), *d* of Captain H. Ashton Case; *S* father, 1969; *m* 1st, 1937, Elizabeth (marr. diss. 1968), *e d* of Gilbert Butler, Utica, New York; one *d* (one *s* decd); 2nd, 1968, Marcia Anne Helen, *y d* of Major David Turville Constable Maxwell, Bosworth Hall, Husbands Bosworth, Rugby; one *s. Educ:* Downside; RMC, Sandhurst. ADC to Governor and C-in-C, Bermuda, 1936-39. Served War of 1939-45 (MC, prisoner-of-war). *Heir:* *s* Sebastian Everard Radcliffe, *b* 8 June 1972. *Address:* Le Château de Cheseaux, 1033 Cheseaux, Vaud, Switzerland. *Clubs:* Brooks's, Army and Navy.
[Died 7 Feb. 1975.

RADFORD, Adm. Arthur William, DSM (US); Legion of Merit; US Navy, retired; Director: Molybdenum Corporation of America; US Freight Company; Chairman of Board, Imodco, USA; *b* Chicago, Ill, 27 Feb. 1896. *Educ:* Naval Acad. Commissioned Ensign, 1916; served with Atlantic and Pacific Fleets, 1918-19; Flt Trg, 1920; with Bureau of Aeronautics, Navy Dept, 1921-23; Aircraft Sqdns, Battle Fleet, and air units attached to USS Colorado and Pennsylvania; Naval Air Station, San Diego, 1927-29; with USS Saratoga, 1929-30; on staff, Comdr Aircraft, Battle Sqdn, US Fleet, 1931-32; Bureau of Aeronautics, 1932-35; served USS Wright (navigator), 1935, Saratoga, 1936-37; in comd Naval Air Stn, Seattle, 1937-40; served USS Yorktown, 1940-41; Director of Aviation Trg, Bureau of Aeronautics, Navy Dept, 1941-43; served in Pacific, 1943-44; Asst Dep. Chief of Naval Operations for Air, 1944; C-in-C, US Pacific Fleet, 1949-53; Chairman of the Joint Chiefs of Staff, 1953-57, retd. *Address:* Apartment S-501, 550 N Street, SW, Washington, DC 20024, USA.   *[Died* 17 *Aug.* 1973.

RADHAKRISHNAN, Sir Sarvepalli, OM (Hon.) 1963; Kt 1931; FBA 1939, Hon. Fellow 1962; FRSL 1951; MA (Madras 1909; Oxford 1936); DCL (Hon.) 1952, Oxford; LittD (Hon.) 1953, Cambridge; LLD (Hon.) 1948, London, etc; President, the Republic of India, 1962-67; *b* 5 September 1888; *m* S. Sivakamamma; one *s* five *d. Educ:* Madras Christian College. Asst Professor of Philosophy, Presidency College, Madras, 1911-16; Prof. of Philosophy, Presidency College, 1916-17; University Prof. of Philosophy, Mysore, 1918-21; George V Prof. of Philosophy, Calcutta Univ., 1921-31 and 1937-41; Vice-Chancellor, Andhra Univ., Waltair, 1931-36, and of Benares Hindu Univ., 1939-48; Spalding Prof. of Eastern Religions and Ethics, Oxford, 1936-52; Professor Emeritus, 1952; Hon. Fellow of All Souls College; Hon. Prof. Moscow University, 1956; Indian Ambassador to USSR, 1949-52; Vice-Pres. of the Republic of India, 1952-62. Upton Lectr, Manchester Coll., Oxford, 1926 and 1929-30; Haskell Lectr in Comparative Religion, Univ. of Chicago, 1926; Gen. Pres. Third Session Indian Philosophical Congress, Bombay, 1927; Chairman Executive Council Indian Philosophical Congress, 1925-37; Pres. Post Graduate Council in Arts, 1927-31; Hibbert Lecturer, 1929; Member: International Committee on Intellectual Co-operation of the League of Nations, Geneva, 1931-39; Constituent Assembly of India, 1947-49; Leader of Indian Deleg. to UNESCO, 1946-52, and member Exec. Board UNESCO, 1946-51 (Chm. 1948-49), Pres. Gen. Conf., 1952-54, 1958; Chm. Univs. Commn, Govt of India, 1948-49. Hon. Fell. Roy. Asiatic Soc. of Bengal; Pres. Indian PEN 1949-, Vice-President, International PEN 1956-; President, Sahitya Akademi (National Academy of Letters), 1964-68; Chancellor of Delhi University, 1953-62. Hon. Member Rumanian Academy of Science. German Order pour le mérite, 1954; Goethe Plaquette, 1959; German Booksellers' Peace Prize, 1961; Templeton Prize for Religion, 1975. *Publications:* The Philosophy of Rabindranath Tagore, 1918; The Reign of Religion in Contemporary Philosophy, 1920; Indian Philosophy in the Library of Philosophy, vol. i 1923; vol. ii 1927; 2nd edn 1930 and 1931; The Philosophy of the Upanishads, 1924, 2nd edn 1935; The Hindu View of Life, 1927, translated into French and German, etc; The Religion we Need, 1928; Kalki, or The Future of Civilization, 1929, 2nd edition, 1934: An Idealist View of Life, 1932; East and West in Religion, 1933; (ed jtly) Contemporary Indian Philosophy, 1936; Eastern Religions and Western Thought, 1939, 2nd edn; (ed) Mahatma Gandhi, 1939; India and China, 1944; Education, Politics and War, 1944; Religion and Society, 1947; Is this Peace?, 1945; The Bhagavadgitā, 1948; Dhammapada, 1950; The Principal Upanishads, 1953; Recovery of Faith, 1955; East and West: Some Reflections, 1955; (ed jtly) A Source Book of Indian Philosophy, 1957; Brahma Sūtra, 1960; Fellowship of the Spirit, 1961; Religion in a Changing World, 1967; The Radhakrishnan Reader, 1969; article on Indian Philosophy in Ency. Brit., 14th edn, and others on Philosophy and Religion in Mind, International Journal of Ethics, Hibbert Journal, etc. *Recreation:* light reading. *Address:* 30 Edward Elliot Road, Mylapore, Madras 4, India.   *[Died* 16 *April* 1975.

RADLEY, Oswald Alfred, CBE 1945; MC 1918; *b* 18 June 1887; *s* of A. W. Radley, Congleton, Cheshire; *m* 1929, Joan, *d* of James Laithwood, Alcumlow Hall, Congleton, Cheshire; one *s* one *d. Educ:* Trent Coll. Served European War, 1914-19, 7th Bn Cheshire Regt and as Staff Capt. (wounded, despatches). ARP Controller, Leeds, 1941-45. President: Leeds Law Society, 1937; Town Planning Institute, 1940; Soc. of Town Clerks, 1948-50; Town Clerk of Leeds, 1938-52. *Address:* 1 Oatlands Drive, Harrogate. *T:* Harrogate 83515. *Club:* Leeds (Leeds).
          [Died 23 *July* 1977.

RAE, Sir Alexander (Montgomery) Wilson, KCMG 1960 (CMG 1945); MD; Chief MO Colonial Office, 1958-60; *b* 31 Jan. 1896; *s* of late Rev. Robert Rae and Kate Wilson; *m* 1924, Elizabeth Harper, MB, ChB, DPH; one *d. Educ:* George Heriot's School; Univ. of Edinburgh. MB, ChB 1921; MD 1929; Resident Medical Officer, North Wales Sanatorium, 1922; West African Medical Staff, 1924-45; Senior Medical Officer, Gambia, 1935-37; Deputy Director of Medical Services, Gold Coast, 1938; Deputy Director of Medical Services, Nigeria, 1939; Deputy Medical Adviser to Secretary of State for the Colonies, 1944. Lieut, Scottish Horse and Imperial Camel Corps, 1914-18. Retired, 1960. *Address:* Field House, Ramsey, Isle of Man. *T:* Ramsey 813414.   *[Died* 14 *Sept.* 1978.

RAE, Sir Robert, Kt 1958; CB 1952; BAgr, CDA (Edinburgh); retired as Director of National Agricultural Advisory Service,

(1948-59); *b* 9 June 1894; *s* of late Rev. Robert Rae and Kate Wilson; *m* 1926, Constance Alma (*d* 1965), *e d* of late George King; no *c. Educ:* George Heriot's School, University, Edinburgh; East of Scotland College of Agriculture, Edinburgh. Trooper, Scottish Horse, 1914-15; Lieutenant, 1915-16; attached 21st (E of I) Lancers, 1917-19; Lecturer in Agriculture, East Anglian Institute of Agriculture, Chelmsford, Essex, 1920-21; Vice-Principal and County Advisory Officer, Hertfordshire Institute of Agriculture, St Albans, 1921-25; Lecturer in charge of Department of Crop and Animal Husbandry, The Queen's University, Belfast, 1925-32; Professor of Crop and Animal Husbandry, The Queen's University of Belfast, 1932-33; Head of Crop and Animal Husbandry Research Division, Ministry of Agriculture, Northern Ireland, 1925-33; Joint Director of the Agricultural Research Institute, Hillsborough, Co. Down, 1926-33; Professor of Agriculture, University of Reading, 1933-44; Agricultural Attaché, British Embassy, Washington, 1944-45; Under Secretary, Ministry of Agriculture, Fisheries and Food, 1946. *Publications:* articles in agricultural journals. *Address:* Brendon, Lezayre Road, Ramsey, Isle of Man. *T:* Ramsey 3461.
          [Died 10 *Dec.* 1971.

RAE, Lt-Col William, DSO 1916; CD 1971; VD 1921; retired; *b* 15 Jan. 1883; *s* of William Rae, MA, Advocate, Aberdeen, and Joan Anderson; *m* 1936, Edith Marion, *e d* of late Lt-Col L. St John Brodrick; two *s. Educ:* Aberdeen University (MA, BL). Went to Canada, 1907; Capt. Seaforth Highlanders of Canada, Vancouver, BC, on organisation, 1910; Canadian Expeditionary Force, 1914-19 (despatches 4 times; wounded). Lt-Col Comdg 4th Canadian Inf. Bn, 1916, GSO1. Hon. Overseas Director, Canadian Legion War Services, 1940-45 (Dominion Award of Merit). Hon. Lt-Col, The Canadian Scottish (Princess Mary's), Victoria, BC, 1967-. Man. Dir, The Commonwealth Trust Ltd, retired 1949. Master, Worshipful Company of Plumbers, City of London, 1945 and 1953. French Croix de Guerre, 1918. *Recreations:* gardening, rifle-shooting (Canadian Rifle Team, Bisley, 1919). *Address:* 3065 Surrey Road, Victoria, BC, Canada. *Clubs:* Athenæum; Vancouver (Vancouver, BC); Union (Victoria, BC).   *[Died* 11 *Nov.* 1973.

RAEBURN, Sir Edward Alfred, 3rd Bt, *cr* 1923; Sub Postmaster, Wadhurst; Chairman: Raeburn Developments Ltd; Nina Breddal Ltd; *b* 18 May 1919; *s* of Sir W. Norman Raeburn, 2nd Bt, CBE, KC, and Mary Irene Lennard; *S* father, 1947; *m* 1950, Joan, *d* of Frederick Hill, Boston, USA, formerly of Bexley, Kent; one *s. Educ:* Uppingham School; Christ Church, Oxford. Served War of 1939-45, RA 1939-46, taking part in N and E African campaigns; final rank Captain. Liveryman of Worshipful Company of Shipwrights. *Recreations:* gardening, fishing. *Heir: s* Michael Edward Norman Raeburn, *b* 12 Nov. 1954. *Address:* The Post House, High Street, Wadhurst, East Sussex. *T:* Wadhurst 2930.   *[Died* 21 *April* 1977.

RAEBURN, Walter Augustus Leopold, QC 1947; MA (Oxon); LLM (London); Occasional Additional Judge, Central Criminal Court, since 1959; Recorder of West Ham, 1949-65; *b* London, 5 Jan. 1897; *s* of late H. L. Regensburg, of London Stock Exchange (who emigrated to England, 1881, naturalised British 1887); *m* 1925, Dora, *y d* of Hedley Williams, Hastings; four *s* three *d. Educ:* University College School; Charterhouse; Christ Church, Oxford. Studied at London Univ., 1947-49. Assumed present surname on leaving school, 1915; Queen's (Royal West Surrey) Regt and RAF, 1915-19 (wounded on Somme, 1916); read History at Oxford, 1919-21; called to Bar, 1922; Bencher, Middle Temple, 1955; joined Labour Party, 1923; Prospective Parly Candidate, 1925-27; foundation member Soc. of Labour Candidates (now Labour Parly Assoc.); London Press Exchange, 1928-30; foundation member of Haldane Club (now Haldane Soc.), Chm. 1935-37; resigned 1949, to found and join Soc. of Labour Lawyers; Past Chm. Tribunal of Inquiry under Prevention of Fraud (Investments) Act, 1939 (now Licensed Dealers Tribunal); Chairman: Mental Health Review Tribunal for NE Metropolitan Region, 1960-63; Performing Right Tribunal, 1958-69; Med. Appeal Tribunal, London, 1960-65, London North, 1966-1969; on panel of Chairmen for NE Metropolitan Region, 1963-. Frequently appointed to sit as Special Commissioner in Divorce, 1954-; Mem. General Cttee of Rainer Foundation (formerly London Police Court Mission); Mem., two Cttees concerned with welfare of discharged prisoners; Foundn Mem., Nat. Bureau for Co-operation in Child Care (now Nat. Children's Bureau); Mem., Howard League; Mem., Executive Cttee of the Grotius Soc., 1949-60; Mem., British Institute of International and Comparative Law, 1960-; Mem., Probation Advisory and Training Board, 1953-62; Vice-President Royal Philanthropic Society's School; President Surrey Branch, Nat. Assoc. of Probation Officers, 1953-; Manager, Mayford (LCC) Approved School, 1954-65; Vice-Chm. Govs. Isaac Newton (LCC) Comprehensive School, 1958-

67; Governor, Port Regis Preparatory Sch., 1947-. Manager, Trinity Church (Hampstead) Primary School, 1967-. *Publications:* articles in legal and social sci. jls. *Recreations:* voluntary activities shown above. *Address:* 2 Crown Office Row, Temple, EC4. *T:* 01-583 2681; 30 Maresfield Gardens, NW3. *T:* 01-435 2570.   [*Died 16 Feb.* 1972.

RAFFRAY, Sir Philippe, Kt 1946; CBE 1942; QC; London Representative, Mauritius Chamber of Agriculture, 1946-55, retired; Member of Executive Council, Mauritius, 1943-46; Elected member of Legislative Council 1916-46; *b* Mauritius, 1888; 4th *s* of late O. Raymond Raffray; *m* 1918, Marguerite, *d* of Victor de K/vern, KC (Mauritius); one *s* three *d. Educ:* Royal College, Mauritius. Called to Bar, Middle Temple, 1912; Licentiate-in-Law, Paris, 1912. Mauritius Volunteer Artillery, 1915-18. KC (Mauritius), 1932. Member Mauritius Delegation to London, 1932; Special Delegate to Colonial Office *re* Sugar Industry, 1945. FRSA 1949. *Address:* 129 Promenade des Anglais, 06 Nice, France. *Clubs:* Athenæum, Curepipe (Mauritius).   [*Died 28 April* 1975.

RAGG, Air Vice-Marshal Robert Linton, CB 1949; CBE 1945; AFC 1927; RAF retired; *b* 9 April 1901; *o s* of Robert Stewart Ragg, MA (Oxon), and Margaret Elizabeth Christie; *m* 1928, Louie Margaret Moir. *Educ:* Dragon School, Oxford; Dulwich College. Pilot Officer, RAF, 1921; served in Iraq, 1922-24; Experimental Pilot at Royal Aircraft Establishment, Farnborough, 1925-29; Pilcher Memorial Prize, RAeS, 1926; graduated RAF Staff Coll., Andover, 1937; Command Navigation Officer, Bomber Comd, 1939-40; SASO No 15 Gp, 1943-44 (despatches); Deputy AOC No 222 Gp 1944-45 (despatches); AOA, BAF, SEA (later Air HQ India), 1945-46 (despatches); AOC No 63 Gp, RAF, 1946-48; SASO, Transport Command, RAF, 1948-49; Senior Air Staff Officer, Far East Air Force, 1949-51; Director-General of Personnel (II), Air Ministry, Feb.-Sept. 1952; AOC No 18 Gp, RAF (Pitreavie Castle, Dunfermline, Fife) and Sen. Air Force Officer, Scotland, and Air Comdr, Northern Sub-Area, Allied Atlantic Command, NATO, Sept. 1952-March 1955. Brigar, Gordonstoun School, 1955-57; one of HM Comrs, Queen Victoria School, Dunblane, 1955-57; County Comr for Scouts, Cornwall, 1958-62. Mem. Bd of Governors Truro Cathedral School. Order of Cloud and Banner (Chinese), 1945. *Address:* Rockbarton, Shepton Beauchamp, Ilminster, Somerset. *Club:* Royal Air Force.
                                    [*Died 19 Dec.* 1973.

RAHIMTOOLA, Sir Fazal Ibrahim, Kt 1946; CIE 1939; MLC; BA; JP; Director: Ahmedabad Advance Mill, Ltd; Tata Power Co. Ltd; Tata Iron & Steel Co., Ltd; Bharat Line, Ltd (Chairman); The Swadeshi Mills, Ltd; Overseas Communications Service (Government of India); New Swadeshi Sugar Mills Ltd; Sultania Cotton Manufacturing Co., Ltd; Dhrangadhra Chemical Works Ltd; Fazalbhai Ibrahim & Co. Prvt Ltd; *b* 21 Oct. 1895; *s* of late Sir Ibrahim Rahimtoola, GBE, KCSI; *m* 1920, Jainabai, *d* of Alimahomed Fazalbhoy. *Educ:* St Xavier's High Sch. and Coll., Bombay; Poona Law Coll. (1st LLB). Mem., Bombay Municipal Corp., 1919-30; Trustee, Bombay Port Trust, 1921-36. Appt by Govt of India on Govt Securities Cttee; Rep. of Bombay Municipal Corp. on BB & CI Rly Advisory Council till 1930; Sec. Indian Imperial Citizenship Assoc.; Mem. Standing Finance Cttee for Railways, Rly Bd; Mem. Haj Inquiry Cttee, 1929; Chm. Reception Cttee of Bombay Presidency Muslim Educ. Conf.; Pres. Urdu Newspapers Assoc.; Rep. Bombay Govt on Cttee of the Sir Harcourt Butler Technological Inst., to advise Govt of UP; Mem. Central Broadcasting Advisory Council till 1930; Mem. Standing Cttee for Haj; Elected Mem., Central Legislative Assembly, 1925-30; appt Actg Pres., Indian Tariff Bd, 1932; Pres. Indian Tariff Bd, 1935; Elected MLA, 1937. Conducted several enquiries, 1930-38, as Mem. and Pres., Indian Tariff Board. Chairman or Mem. numerous Bombay Cttees both during War of 1939-45 and later. Delegate to Indian States on Eastern Group Conf.; Mem. War Risk Insurance Claims Cttee, Govt of India; Mem. Central Food Council and its Standing Cttee; Director, National War Front; Mem. Post-War reconstruction Cttee for Agricultural Research; Chm. Indian Fisheries Cttee; Mem. Price-Fixation Cttee of Govt of India; Mem. Gregory Foodgrains Policy Cttee; Mem. Industrial Policy Cttee (Planning Dept); Mem. All-India Council for Technical Educn; Mem. Nat. Commn for India and its Science Sub-Commn (Unesco); Elected Mem. Bombay Leg. Council, 1948; Sheriff of Bombay, 1950; Deleg. to Unesco Conf., Florence, 1950; Deleg. Internat. Engineering Confs, New Delhi, 1951; Deleg. Symposium for Utilisation of Industrial Wastes; Chm. Deep-sea Fisheries Station, Bombay, Govt of India; Mem. Central Exec. Cttee, Tuberculosis Assoc. of India; Deleg. Govt of India on Fourth Commonwealth TB and Health Conf., London, 1955; Chm., Cttee of Hosts, 38th Internat. Eucharistic

Congress. Mem. East India Assoc., London; FRSA. Late Hon. Magistrate. Hon. Consul-Gen. for Thailand in Bombay. Jubilee and Coronation Medals. *Address:* Ismail Buildings, Hornby Road, Fort, Bombay, India. *Clubs:* (Pres.) Matheran, Poona (India).   [*Died 13 Dec.* 1977.

RAHMAN, Shaikh Abdur, HPk 1957; Chief Justice Supreme Court of Pakistan, 1st March-4th June 1968, retired; *b* 4 June 1903; *s* of Sh. Ghulam Ali; *m* 1934, Mumtaz Jehan Mohammad Deen; three *s* one *d. Educ:* Punjab Univ. (MA); Oxford Univ. (BA Hons). Entered ICS 1928; served as Asst Comr, Sub-divl Officer, and then as Dist and Sessions Judge in various Districts of Punjab, up to May 1945; Legal Remembrancer and Sec. Legislative Dept, Punjab, up to May 1946; Judge, High Court, Lahore, May 1946; Mem., Bengal Boundary Commn at partition of India and Pakistan, 1947; Custodian of Evacuee Properties, 1947-51; Vice-Chancellor, Punjab Univ., 1950-51; Chief Justice: Lahore High Court, 1954; High Court of W Pakistan, 1955; Judge Supreme Court of Pakistan, 1958. Chairman Agartala case Special Tribunal (latter part), 1968; finally retd Feb. 1969. Dir, Inst. of Islamic Culture, Lahore; Chm., Bd for Advancement of Literature, Punjab, Lahore; Vice-Chm., Bazme Iqbal Lahore. Holds hon. doctorates. *Publications:* Tarjuman-i-Asrar (trans. into Urdu verse of Sir Mohammad Iqbal's Persian, Asrari-Khudi), 1952; Hadith-i-Dil (collection of addresses in Urdu), 1963; Safar (collection of original poems in Urdu), 1964; Punishment of Apostasy in Islam, 1972. *Recreations:* writing and participation in cultural activities. *Address:* 65 Main Gulberg, Lahore, Pakistan. *T:* Lahore 80109. *Club:* Gymkhana (Lahore). [*Died 11 Feb.* 1979.

RAHMAN, Sheikh Mujibur; Founding Father of Bangladesh; President of Bangladesh, since Jan. 1975; *b* 17 March 1920; *m* 1940, Fazilat-un-Nessa; three *s* two *d. Educ:* Mission Sch.; Islamia Coll., Calcutta; Dacca Univ. Mem., East Bengal Assembly, 1954-58. Founded East Pakistan Students' League to fight for Bengali Nationalism, 1948; imprisoned for about 10 years and interned about 2 years for political agitation on various occasions, from 1947; Councillor, Muslim League, 1943-47; co-Founder of Awami (People's) League, in East Pakistan, 1949 (Gen. Sec., 1953-66, Pres., 1966-73). Mem. East Pakistan Assembly, and Minister, 1954; Mem., National Assembly, 1955; Minister for Commerce, Industries and Labour, Anti-corruption, Village Aid and Social Welfare, 1954, 1956-57. Leader of Parly Delegn to Peking, 1957. Delegate to world peace confs, Peking, 1952, Stockholm, 1956. Presented Six-point plan for full autonomy for East Pakistan, now Bangladesh, 1966; Political prisoner, 1966-69; won absolute majority in Constituent Assembly election, Dec. 1970; declared Independence of Bangladesh, 25 March 1971; elected President by Govt-in-Exile; charged with treason, March 1971, tried *in camera,* and sentenced to death, Aug. 1971; Bangladesh liberated, Dec. 1971; released, Jan. 1972; Prime Minister of Bangladesh, 1972-75. Awards: Bangabondhu (Friend of Bengal), by Bangalee nation, 1969; Juliet Curio Peace Medal, World Peace Council, 1973. *Address:* (office) Ganabhabon, Dacca, Bangladesh; (home) 677 Dhanmondi Residential Area, Road No 32, Dacca, Bangladesh.   [*Died 15 Aug.* 1975.

RAIKES, Maj.-Gen. Sir Geoffrey Taunton, Kt 1960; CB 1938; DSO 1916; DL, retired as Lord Lieutenant for Brecknock (1948-59); *b* 7 April 1884; 4th *s* of late Robert Taunton Raikes of Treberfydd, Breconshire, and 2nd wife, Rosa Margaret, 4th *d* of Henry William Cripps, QC, Beechwood, Gt Marlow; *m* 1923, Dorothy Amabel Wilson (*d* 1952), *o d* of late Arthur Wilson-Fox, CB, and Mrs Wilson-Fox, of Ridgeway House, Northaw; three *d. Educ:* Radley College; Sandhurst. Entered Army, 1903; employed with Egyptian Army, 1913-15; served European War, 1914-18 (despatches, DSO and two bars, Bt Major, Bt Lieutenant-Colonel, Croix de Guerre); Chief Instructor in Military History and Tactics, RMA, 1928-30; commanded 1st Batt. South Wales Borderers, 1931-34; Instructor (Class Y) Senior Officers' School, Sheerness, 1934-35; Commander 9th Infantry Brigade, 1935-37; Maj.-Gen., 1937; retired pay, 1938; Commander Territorial Army Div., 1939-40. *Address:* Treberfydd, Bwlch, Brecon, Powys; c/o Williams & Glyn's Bank Ltd, Holt's Branch, Whitehall, SW1. *Club:* Army and Navy.   [*Died 27 March* 1975.

RAILTON, Reid Antony, BSc, FIMechE; Consulting Engineer; *b* 24 June 1895; *s* of Charles W. Railton, Alderley Edge, Cheshire; *m* 1928, Margaret Audrey Hensman; one *s* one *d. Educ:* Rugby; Manchester Univ. RAeC Pilot's Certificate, 1915; served apprenticeship with Leyland Motors Ltd, 1915-17; served with RNVR Motor Boat Section, 1918; studied Factory Layout in USA, 1920; Asst to Chief Engineer Leyland Motors Ltd, 1921-23; Managing Director of Arab Motors Ltd, Letchworth, 1925-27; Designer of the first motor cars to exceed the officially-timed speeds of four, five, and six miles per minute. Designer late John Cobb's Railton car which held world's speed record for twenty-five years. As late Sir Malcolm Campbell's engineering consultant, was responsible for his boat Blue-Bird II, which for many years held world's speed record at 141 mph. In similar capacity was responsible for late John Cobb's boat, Crusader, the first boat to exceed speed of 200 mph. *Publications:* Papers before Instn Auto. Engrs, Instn Mech. Engrs and Soc. Automotive Engrs (USA). *Address:* 241 The Uplands, Berkeley, Calif 94705, USA.   *[Died* 1 *Sept.* 1977.

RAISMAN, Sir (Abraham) Jeremy, GCMG 1959; GCIE 1945 (CIE 1934); KCSI 1941 (CSI 1938); Kt 1939; Commonwealth Trust Ltd; *b* 19 March 1892; *m* 1925, Renée Mary Kelly; two *s. Educ:* Leeds High School and University; Pembroke College, Oxford. MA (1st Class Mods 1st Lit Hum); John Locke Scholar in Moral Philosophy, 1915; joined ICS 1916; served in Bihar and Orissa till 1922; Customs Department Bombay and Calcutta, 1922-28; Commissioner of Income-Tax, Punjab and NWFP, 1928-31; Joint Secretary, Commerce Department, Government of India, 1931-34; Member Central Board of Revenue, 1934; Director, Reserve Bank of India, 1938; Secretary, Finance Dept, 1938-39; Finance Member of Govt of India, 1939-45; and Vice-President, Govr-Genl's Executive Council, 1944. Chairman, British Indian delegation to International Monetary Conference, Bretton Woods, USA, June-July 1944; retired from India, 1945; led UK Treasury Mission to India and Pakistan, Jan.-Feb. 1948; adviser to Govt of Pakistan on distribution of Central and Provincial revenues, Nov.-Dec. 1951; Chairman: Fiscal Commn for Federation of Rhodesia and Nyasaland, 1952; Nigeria Fiscal Commn, 1957-58; Economic and Fiscal Commn for East Africa, 1960-61. Comr, Public Works Loans Board, 1947, Chairman, 1948-70. Vice-Chm., Lloyds Bank Ltd, 1947-53, Dep.-Chm., 1953-63. Hon. LLD Leeds. Hon. Fellow of Pembroke College, Oxford. *Address:* Fieldhead, Shamley Green, Surrey. *T:* Bramley 3128. *Clubs:* Athenæum, Reform.

[Died 20 *Feb.* 1978.

RAISTRICK, Harold, FRS 1934; ScD (Cantab); DSc (Leeds); FRIC; MChemA; formerly Professor of Biochemistry, University of London and formerly Director of Division of Biochemistry and Chemistry in relation to Public Health, London School of Hygiene and Tropical Medicine (1929-56); retired 1956; Professor Emeritus since 1956; *b* Pudsey, Yorkshire, 26 Nov. 1890; *s* of late Mark Walker Raistrick; *m* 1917, Martha Louisa (*d* 1945), *d* of Jonathan Coates, Pudsey, Yorkshire; two *d*; *m* 1947, Betty Helen, *d* of Edward Young, London. *Educ:* Central High School, Leeds; Univ. of Leeds; University of Cambridge. On Research Staff of School of Biochemistry, University of Cambridge, 1914-21; in charge of Biochemical Department, Nobel's Explosives Co. Ltd, Stevenston, Ayrshire (Imperial Chemical Industries, Limited), 1921-29. Bakerian Lecturer, Royal Society, 1949; Flintoff Medallist, Chemical Society, 1963. *Publications:* various papers on microbiological chemistry in Biochemical Journal, Journal of Chemical Society and Philosophical Transactions of Royal Society, British Journal of Experimental Pathology, and the Lancet. *Recreations:* angling, golf and walking. *Address:* Belfairs, Sea Drive, Felpham, Bognor Regis, Sussex. *T:* Middleton-on-Sea 3150.   *[Died* 8 *March* 1971.

RAJAGOPALACHARYA, Chakravarti; *b* Hosur, Salem District, India, 1878; *s* of Chakravarti Ventatārya and Singāramma; *m* 1899, Alamelamangamma; four *c. Educ:* Central Coll., Bangalore; Presidency Coll. and Law Coll., Madras. Joined Bar, 1900; practised at Salem, India, 1900-19; joined Mahatma Gandhi's Satyagraha campaign and non-co-operation movement, 1919-20; Gen. Sec. Indian Nat. Congress, 1921-22 (Mem. Working Cttee, 1922-47); Sec. Prohibition League of India, 1930; Prime Minister, Madras, 1937-39; associated with Indian Freedom Movement since 1906; induced All India Congress Cttee to offer co-operation in war effort, 1940; underwent imprisonment in connection with Indian Freedom Movement five times during 1921 to 1942; asst, Mahatma Gandhi in the Gandhi-Jinnah talks, 1944; Member Interim Govt of India, 1946-47; Governor of West Bengal, 1947-48; acted as Gov.-Gen., India, Nov. 1947; Governor-General of India (in succession to Earl Mountbatten of Burma), June 1948-Jan. 1950; retd to inaugurate Indian Union Republic; Home Minister for India, 1950-51; Chief Minister, Govt of Madras, 1952-54. Founded Swatantra Party to oppose Congress Party, defending individual freedom and private enterprise, 1959. *Publications:* Fatal Cart and other stories, Prohibition Manual, 1935; Way Out (booklet), 1942; Reconciliation (booklet), 1942; Marcus Aurelius and Socrates in Tamil, Tamil Essays, Mahabharat, Ramayana in story chapters (translated into almost all Indian languages); Upanishads for lay readers and Bhagavat Gita Selections and Notes. Hinduism, Doctrine and

Way of Life. Ed. Mahatma Gandhi's Young India during latter's incarceration, 1922. *Address:* Nowroji Road, Madras 31, India.
[Died 26 *Dec.* 1972.

RAJAPAKSE, Sir Lalita (Abhaya), Kt 1952; QC (Ceylon); BA, LLD (London); High Commissioner for Ceylon in Great Britain, 1967-69; *b* 3 May 1900; *s* of Adrian de Abrew Rajapakse and Agnes Rajapakse; *m* 1935, Rose Thelma Chrysobel Gunasekera; one *s* two *d. Educ:* St Joseph's College, Colombo; University Coll., London (BA 1922, LLB 1923, LLD 1925, Fellow, 1968). Called to English Bar, Lincoln's Inn, 1924 (Benchers' rights at Bench Table, 1968-69). Called to Ceylon Bar, 1925; Lectr, 1926, Examiner, 1927, Ceylon Law Coll. Mem. of Council of Legal Education (Ceylon), 1939; Founded Revata Coll. Balapitiya, Ceylon, 1933. KC 1944, QC 1952 (Ceylon); Member of University Council, University of Ceylon, 1946. Commissioner of Assize, Supreme Court, Ceylon, 1947; Member of Senate, Ceylon Parliament, 1947, Leader of Senate, 1949; Minister of Justice, Ceylon, 1947-53. Ambassador of Ceylon in France, 1965-66. Mem. Ceylon Delegn, Commonwealth Conf. on Foreign Affairs, 1950; Chairman Gal Oya Commission, 1956; Mem. Univ. Council: Vidyodaya Univ., Ceylon, 1959-; Vidyalankara Univ., Ceylon, 1959-; Pres., All Ceylon Buddhist Congress, 1961-64. *Recreations:* tennis, swimming, agriculture. *Address:* Lumbini, Horton Place, Colombo, Sri Lanka. *T:* Colombo 95885.   *[Died* 25 *May* 1976.

RAKE, Alfred Mordey, CBE 1953; *b* 27 March 1906; *s* of Dr H. V. Rake, Fordingbridge, Hants; *m* 1st, 1930, Gwendolen (*d* 1944), *d* of late Edward Craig-Hall, Hove, Sussex; three *s*; 2nd, 1947, Jean Mary, *d* of late F. G. Kingsland, Thornton Heath, Surrey; two *d. Educ:* King's School, Canterbury; Corpus Christi College, Cambridge. 1st Cl. Hons Classical Tripos Pt 1, 1927; Cauldwell Scholar, 1927; 1st Cl. Hons (with distinction) Classical Tripos Pt II, 1928; Asst Principal, Min. of Transport, 1930; Private Sec. to Parliamentary Sec., 1935; Principal, 1936; Asst Sec., 1941; transferred to Min. of Fuel and Power, 1946; Under Secretary, 1955; retired, 1966. *Recreation:* gardening. *Address:* The White House, Whimple, Devon. *T:* Whimple 822560.   *[Died* 30 *April* 1978.

RALFS, Maj.-Gen. Bertram George, CB 1965; Royal Marines, retired; *b* 1 June 1905; *s* of late George Spencer Ralfs; *m* 1929, Daisy Harrison; one *d. Educ:* Portsmouth Grammar Sch. Royal Marines: Probationary 2nd Lt, 1923; Capt. 1935, Bt Maj. 1940, Maj. 1942, Lt-Col 1948, Col 1953; Maj.-Gen. 1962. Served in battleships Malaya, Barham, Warspite, Queen Elizabeth, Valiant and Nelson, also in Cruiser Devonshire; Superintendent of Applied Ballistics, 1953-57; Chief Inspector of Naval Ordnance, 1959-62; President, Ordnance Board, 1964-65; retd 1965. Pres., Instn of Engineering Inspection, 1964-66. Chairman: NATO Ballistics Group, 1953-58; NATO Standardisation of Ballistic Atmosphere Cttee, 1956-58; National Council for Quality and Reliability, 1964-66. *Address:* Greengates, Old Coach Road, Kelsall, Cheshire. *Club:* Naval and Military.   *[Died* 16 *April* 1977.

RALPHS, Sir (Frederick) Lincoln, Kt 1973; PhD; Chief Education Officer, for Norfolk, 1950-74; Chairman of Schools Council, 1972-75; Hon. General Secretary, British Association, 1973-78; Chairman of Board, Homerton College, Cambridge, since 1970; *b* 17 Feb. 1909; *s* of Frederick and Elizabeth Anne Ralphs; *m* 1938, Enid Mary Cowlin; one *s* two *d. Educ:* Firth Park Grammar Sch.; Univ. of Sheffield. MSc, PhD, LLB, DipEd, FCP. Leader, Univs debating team to USA, 1933; Past Pres.: Student Union, Sheffield, 1934; NUS, 1935-37; Internat. Confedn of Students (Vice Pres., 1935-37, Pres. 1937-38). Dep. Regional Officer for London and SE, MOI, 1942. Town Trustee Research Fellow, Univ. of Sheffield, 1936-38; Teacher and Lectr, 1938-; Life Vice-Pres., Assoc. of Educn Cttees. Pres., Nat. Adv. Council on Educn for Industry and Commerce. Vice-Pres., WEA, 1967-. Past Pres.: County Educn Officers Soc.; Assoc. of Chief Educn Officers; Educn Section of British Assoc.; Nat. Sunday Sch. Union. DUniv Surrey, 1975; Hon. DSc Lancaster, 1976. Gold Medal, Phys. Educn, Paris, 1935; Officier d'Académie, Paris. *Publications:* Young Minds for Old, 1938; many articles in various jls. *Recreations:* gardening, travel. *Address:* Jesselton, 218 Unthank Road, Norwich, Norfolk. *T:* Norwich 53382. *Club:* English-Speaking Union.
[Died 16 *Oct.* 1978.

RALSTON, Col Alexander Windeyer, CMG 1918; DSO 1917; Hon. Colonel, Retired; List Barrister-at-law (non-practising); Chairman War Pensions Entitlement Appeal Tribunal for Commonwealth of Australia, 1929-42; JP for NSW; *b* Croydon, Sydney, NSW, 27 Nov. 1885; *s* of late A. G. Ralston, KC; *m* 1927, Florence Mary, *o d* of late H. G. Currie, London; two *s* three *d. Educ:* Sydney Grammar School; University of Sydney;

BA, LLB and Diploma in Military Science. Admitted to Bar, 1909; joined Australian Naval and Military Expeditionary Force as Capt. 1914; present at capture of Rabaul, Herbertshohe, Madang, Quieta, and in command of expedition to southern end of New Ireland; joined AIF March 1915 as Major and was in Gallipoli, 1915, to evacuation, becoming 2nd in command of 19th Batt. in Oct. 1915; arrived in France March 1916; promoted Lt-Col and to command 20th Batt. 16 June 1916; 2nd Australian Machine Gun Batt., March 1918 to Aug. 1919 (despatches 4 times, CMG, DSO); Hon. Col, Retired List, 1943. Colonial Auxiliary Forces Officers Decoration, VD. *Recreations:* fishing, reading. *Address:* Knowle, 489 New South Head Road, Double Bay, Sydney, NSW. *T:* 36 5153. *Clubs:* Imperial Service, Royal Sydney Golf (non-playing) (Sydney).
[Died 29 Sept. 1971.

RAMAGE, Sir Richard (Ogilvy), Kt 1958; CMG 1943; *b* 5 Jan. 1896; *s* of John T. Ramage, Shipbuilder; *m* 1932, Dorothy Frances Broome; no *c. Educ:* Edinburgh Academy. Royal Engineers, 1914-19; Administrative Service, Nigeria, 1920-35 (Dep. Resident, 1934); Assistant to Lieutenant-Governor, Malta, 1935-39; Under-Sec. Gold Coast, 1939-42; Colonial Secretary, Sierra Leone, 1942-50; Acting Governor, Sierra Leone, on various occasions; retired 1951. Employed on special duties, 1951-55 (British Honduras, Mauritius, Aden, Gambia, Western Pacific High Commission, Kingdom of Tonga and Jamaica); Chairman: Public Service Commn, Uganda, 1955-59, Police Service Commn, 1957-59, retired; Member ILO Cttee of Experts on Social Policy in Non-Metropolitan Territories, 1951-58. Post Election (Constitution) Cttee, Tanganyika, 1959; Chm. Economy Commission, Uganda, 1960; Comr to examine arrangements for localisation in E African Post and Telecommunications Administration, and East Africa High Commission, 1961; reported on Civil Services of Basutoland, Bechuanaland and Swaziland, 1961; advised on the public service in relation to constitutional development, Aden and South Arabian Federation, 1962 and 1963; a UK Observer, Malta Referendum, 1964. Reported on the Public Service, State of Brunei and British Honduras, 1965. Arbitrator, Aden Port Trust and Senior Staff and Pilots, 1965. Salaries Commissioner for the Seychelles, 1967; Adviser on localisation of Civil Service, Fiji, 1968; Adviser on salaries etc, Civil Service, Kingdom of Tonga, 1969. OStJ. *Recreations:* golf, travel. *Address:* Spilsby House, Ottery St Mary, Devon. *Clubs:* East India and Sports, Royal Commonwealth Society.
[Died 4 Aug. 1971.

RAMSAY, Maj.-Gen. Sir Alan (Hollick), Kt 1961; CB 1946; CBE 1942; DSO 1943; retired as Director of Education, Victoria, Australia, 1960; *b* 12 March 1895; *s* of Charles Ramsay and Frances Hollick; *m* 1924, Edna Mary Watson; one *s* one *d. Educ:* Melbourne High School; University of Melbourne (BSc, DipEd). Served with 1st AIF: Egypt and France, 1915-18; with 2nd AIF: Middle East, New Guinea and New Britain (CBE, DSO, CB). *Recreations:* fishing, bowls. *Address:* 45 Allenby Avenue, East Malvern, Vic 3145, Australia. *T:* 25.3585. *Club:* Naval and Military (Melbourne).
[Died 19 Sept. 1973.

RAMSAY, Adm. Hon. Sir Alexander Robert Maule, GCVO 1938 (KCVO 1932); KCB 1937 (CB 1934); DSO 1916; *b* 29 May 1881; *s* of 13th Earl of Dalhousie and Ida, *d* of 6th Earl of Tankerville; *m* 1919, Princess Victoria Patricia Helena Elizabeth (*see* Lady Patricia Ramsay), *d* of 1st Duke of Connaught, KG; one *s* (Alexander Arthur Alfonso David Maule Ramsay of Mar; *b* 21 Dec. 1919; *m* 1956, Hon. Flora Fraser, *o d* and *heiress* of 19th Lord Saltoun; three *d*). *Educ:* Royal Naval College, Dartmouth. Served Dardanelles, 1914-15 (DSO, promoted Captain); Naval ADC to the King, 1931; late Naval Attaché in Paris; Rear-Adm., 1931; Commodore of Royal Naval Barracks at Portsmouth, 1929-31; Rear-Admiral Aircraft Carriers, 1933-36; Vice-Admiral, 1936; Commander-in-Chief East Indies, 1936-38; Fifth Sea Lord and Chief of Naval Air Service, 1938-39; Admiral, 1939. *Recreation:* sport and games. *Address:* Ribsden Holt, Windlesham, Surrey. *Club:* United Service & Royal Aero.
[Died 8 Oct. 1972.

RAMSAY, Clyde Archibald, CMG 1969; MBE 1960; JP (Barbados); Chief Establishments Officer, 1962-72, and Head of the Civil Service, 1967-72, Barbados; *b* 8 April 1914; *s* of late Alan C. and Wilhelmina Ramsay; *m* 1943, Thelma Ione, *d* of Alfred and Rowena Pragnell; two *s. Educ:* Combermere Secondary Sch., Barbados. Joined Civil Service, 1932; Asst Auditor-Gen., 1957; Local Govt Comr, Chief Registering Officer and Supervisor of Elections, 1959; Chief Establishments Officer and Chm. of Whitley Council, Barbados, 1962. Vice-Pres., Barbados Boy Scouts' Assoc. JP 1961. *Recreation:* swimming.
[Died 13 June 1974.

RAMSAY, Comdr Hugh Malcolm, CBE 1941; Royal Australian Navy (retired); *b* 28 Feb. 1884; *s* of late James and late Mary Margaret Ramsay, Melbourne, Australia; *m* 1911, Gertrude Emily, *d* of late Godfrey Leslie, Melbourne; two *s* two *d.* War of 1914-18, served in HMA ships Pioneer and Brisbane, in Australian, East African, and Mediterranean waters. Held various senior administrative posts in Department of Navy, Melbourne, 1920-48. *Club:* Naval and Military (Melbourne).
[Died 17 Feb. 1975.

RAMSAY, The Lady Patricia, (Victoria Patricia Helena Elizabeth), CI 1911; VA 1902; RWS, RWA, NEAC; *b* 17 March 1886; *y d* of TRH The Duke and Duchess of Connaught and Strathearn; *m* 1919, Admiral The Hon. Sir Alexander Ramsay, *qv*; one *s.* On her marriage she renounced, by Royal permission, the style and title of "HRH" and "Princess", and adopted that of "Lady", with precedence before Marchionesses of England. Colonel-in-Chief, Princess Patricia's Canadian Light Infantry. DGStJ. *Address:* Ribsden Holt, Windlesham, Surrey GU20 6HT. *T:* Bagshot 72157.
[Died 12 Jan. 1974.

RAMSAY, Robert Anstruther, MA, MChir, MB Cantab; FRCS; Consulting Surgeon to Metropolitan Hospital and to Belgrave Hospital for Children; *b* Montreal, Canada, 18 Feb. 1887; *s* of Robert Anstruther Ramsay and Catherine Hamilton Duff; *m* 1914, Marguerite Renée de Miniac; two *s* one *d. Educ:* Caius College, Cambridge; St Bartholomew's Hospital. *Publications:* various papers on surgical subjects. *Address:* 9 Place des Ternes, 75 Paris 17. *T:* Carnot 8340; *c/o* Bank of Montreal, 9 Waterloo Place, SW1.
[Died 17 Oct. 1975.

RAMSAY, Sir William (Clark), Kt 1971; CBE 1963; director of eight public companies; *b* 13 Jan. 1901; *s* of Dr Alexander Ramsay, DD, sometime Moderator of Presbyterian Church of England; *m* 1930, Sarah Nora, *d* of Captain A. Evans, Newquay, Cards; one *s. Educ:* Mill Hill School. Worked in Singapore, 1920-24; Partner, Lamont & Warne, Coal Factors, 1924. Chief Warden, Borough of Hendon, 1940-45. Governor, Mill Hill Sch., 1935-. Member: Byers Cttee on Athletics, 1969; CCPR Bisham Abbey Centre Cttee, 1971; Sports Council, 1972-. Chevalier, Légion d'Honneur (France), 1968; Officier de l'ordre de la Couronne (Belgium), 1971. *Recreations:* Rugby football (played for Singapore, Malaya, Old Millhillians and Mddx; Mem. RFU, 1945- (Pres. 1954-55 and 1970-71; Hon. Treas. 1950-70); Pres. Mddx, 1951-52); fishing. *Address:* 65 Warwick Square, SW1V 2AL. *T:* 01-834 0404. *Clubs:* Royal Automobile, East India, Sports and Public Schools, Old Millhillians; Radnor (Folkestone).
[Died 23 March 1973.

RAMSBOTTOM, John, OBE 1919; MA; *b* Manchester, 25 Oct. 1885; *m* 1917, Beatrice (*d* 1957), *d* of Henry Westwood Broom; one *d. Educ:* Emmanuel Coll., Cambridge; Manchester University. Asst, Brit. Mus. (Nat. Hist.), 1910, Dep. Keeper, 1928-30, Keeper of Botany, 1930-50. Protozoologist (civilian) HM Salonika Forces, 1917-19, Capt. attached RAMC, 1918 (despatches thrice; MBE, 1918, OBE 1919). Hon FRHS, 1912; Veitch Memorial Medal, 1944, VMH 1950; Dean Hole Medal (Nat. Rose Soc.), 1950. Gen. Sec. Brit. Mycological Soc., 1923-45, Pres. 1924, 1946; Botanical Sec., Linnean Soc., 1923-38, Pres. 1938-41; Linnean Gold Medal, 1965. President: Sect. K, Brit. Assoc., 1936, Sect. X, 1947; Mycology and Bacteriology, Internat. Botanical Congress, 1950, Protection of Nature, 1954; Medical Mycology, Internat. Congress of Microbiology, 1950; S London Botanical Inst., 1938-68; Soc. Bibliography Nat. Hist., 1942-; British Soc. for Mycopathology, 1964-67; Member: Lawes Agricultural Trust Cttee, 1938-; Internat. Office for Protection of Nature, 1948. Hon. Mem. of various societies and academies. Holds hon. doctorates: Coimbra, 1938; Uppsala, 1957. Grande Médaille, Geoffrey-St Hilaire, 1949. *Publications:* Handbook of the Larger British Fungi, 1923 (often repr.); Enemies of the Rose, 1925 (1956); A Book of Roses, 1939; Fungi: An Introduction to Mycology, 1929; Edible Fungi, 1943 (1948); Poisonous Fungi, 1945; Mushrooms and Toadstools, 1953. *Address:* 49 Nassau Road, Barnes, SW13; British Museum (Natural History), Cromwell Road, SW7.
[Died 14 Dec. 1974.

RAMSEY, Rt. Rev. Ian Thomas; Bishop of Durham, since 1966; *b* Kearsley, Bolton, 31 Jan. 1915; *o c* of late Arthur Ramsey and of May Ramsey; *m* 1943, Margretta, *y d* of late John and Janeanna McKay, Coleraine, Co. Londonderry; two *s. Educ:* St John's Sch., Farnworth, near Bolton; Farnworth Gram. Sch.; Christ's Coll., Cambridge (Scholar); Ripon Hall, Oxford. First Classes in Mathematical Tripos Part I, 1936, Moral Sciences Tripos Part IIa, 1938, and with distinction in Theological Tripos Part II, Section V (Old Regulations), 1939; Burney Prizeman 1938, Burney Student 1939; MA 1940. Asst Curate of Headington Quarry, Oxford, 1940-43; Chaplain of Christ's Coll., Cambridge, 1943-49; Coll. ARP and Fire Officer, 1943-45;

Fellow of Christ's Coll., Cambridge, and Dir of Studies in Theology and Moral Sciences, 1944-51, Tutor, 1949-51; University Lecturer, 1944-51; Stanton Lecturer in Philosophy of Religion, Cambridge, 1947-50, Hulsean Preacher, 1950. Canon Theologian of Leicester Cathedral, 1944-66. Nolloth Prof. of the Philosophy of the Christian Religion in University of Oxford, and Fellow of Oriel Coll., 1951-66; Dir, Lambeth Diploma in Theology, 1964-67. Select Preacher: University of Cambridge, 1944, 1949, 1956; University of Oxford, 1951; Forwood Lecturer, University of Liverpool, 1957; F. D. Maurice Lecturer, KCL, 1961; Whidden Lecturer, McMaster Univ., Hamilton, Ont., 1963; Visiting Prof. Colgate Rochester Div. Sch., New York, and South Calif. Univ., 1963; Riddell Lecturer, Newcastle upon Tyne Univ., 1963; Stephenson Lecturer, Sheffield, 1964; Zenos Lecturer, Chicago, 1966; Hon. Librarian, Faculty of Theology, 1952-65; General Board of Faculties, Oxford, 1953-59. Examining Chaplain to Bishop of Bradford, 1947-55; to Bishop of Portsmouth, 1952-59, 1960-66; to Bishop of Sheffield, 1954-62, 1963-66; to Bishop of Norwich, 1960-66; Governor of Ripon Hall, Oxford, 1946-, Treasurer, 1952-66; Governor of Westminster Coll., Oxford, 1959-66; Governor: Aldenham Sch., 1961-66; William Temple Coll., 1964- (Chm. 1967-); Member: Archbishop's Commission on Divine Healing, 1953-57; Warneford and Park Hosps Management Cttee, 1954-66 (Chm. 1960-66). Church Assembly Board for Social Responsibility, 1958-. Chairman: Archbishops' Commn on Doctrine, 1967-; Commn on Religious Education, 1967-70; Central Religious Adv. Cttee (BBC/ITA), 1971-. Pres., Northumbria Tourist Bd, 1971-. Chaplain and Sub-Prelate, Order of St John of Jerusalem, 1969. Hon. DD: Oxford, 1966; Durham, 1967; Glasgow, 1968. Hon. Fellow: Oriel Coll., Oxford, 1967; Christ's Coll., Cambridge, 1967. *Publications:* Miracles: an exercise in logical mapwork, 1952; Religious Language, 1957; Freedom and Immortality, 1960; On Being Sure in Religion, 1963; Models and Mystery, 1964; Science and Religion: conflict and synthesis, 1964; Christian Discourse, 1965; ed.: Reasonableness of Christianity (John Locke), 1958; Prospect for Metaphysics, 1961; Biology and Personality, 1965; Christian Ethics and Contemporary Philosophy, 1966; (ed) Words about God, 1971. *Recreations:* family and home; reading maps and (once) Bradshaw. *Address:* Auckland Castle, Bishop Auckland, Co. Durham. *T:* Bishop Auckland 2576. *Club:* Athenæum. *[Died 6 Oct. 1972.*

RANCE, Maj.-Gen. Sir Hubert (Elvin), GCMG 1948; GBE 1946 (OBE 1940); CB 1946; Colonel Commandant Royal Corps of Signals, 1953-62; *b* 17 July 1898; *s* of Frederick Hubert Rance; *m* 1927, Mary Noël Guy; one *s* one *d. Educ:* Wimbledon College; RMC, Sandhurst. Worc. Regiment, 1916-26. 4th Bn Worcs Regiment, BEF, France, Oct. 1916-April 1917; R Signals, 1926-44; Adjt 2 Div. Signals, 1927-30; GSO3 War Office (Military Training), 1936-38; Instructor Staff College, Camberley, 1938-39; Asst Dir BEF and GSO1, BEF, France, 1939-40; OC 4 Div. Signals, BEF, France, April-June 1940, evacuated Dunkirk, continued in command till Oct. 1940 (despatches, OBE); GSO1 War Office (Military Training), 1940-41; Deputy Director Military Training (Brig.), 1941-42; Director of Technical Training WO (Brig.), 1942-43; Brig. General Staff, Western Command, 1943-45; Director of Civil Affairs, Burma (Maj.-Gen.), 1945-46 (CB); Deputy Commander South-Western District, Taunton, 1946; Governor of Burma, 1946-48; retired pay, 1947. Chairman Standing Closer Assoc. Cttee, British West Indies, 1948-50; British co-Chairman Caribbean Commission, 1948-50; Governor and C-in-C of Trinidad and Tobago, 1950-55. *Recreations:* cricket, tennis, and shooting. *Address:* The Old Farm, Frensham, Surrey. *T:* Frensham 2164. *Club:* Army and Navy. *[Died 24 Jan. 1974.*

RANDALL, Sir Alec Walter George, KCMG 1949 (CMG 1944); OBE 1920; Delegate to International Conference on Atomic Energy Agency, 1956, and International Conference on Law of the Sea, 1958; *b* 27 July 1892; *s* of George and Clara Randall; *m* 1915, Dr Amy Jones (*d* 1966); one *s* two *d* (and one *d* decd). *Educ:* Queen Elizabeth's Grammar Sch., Barnet; University Coll., London. Entered Foreign Office, 1920; 2nd Sec. HM Legation to Holy See, 1925-30; 1st Secretary HM Legation, Bucharest, 1930-33; served in Foreign Office, 1933-35; 1st Secretary HM Legation, Copenhagen, 1935-38; Counsellor in Foreign Office, 1938-45; Ambassador to Denmark, 1947-52 (Minister, 1945-47); retired from Foreign Service, 1953. Alternate Delegate to UN Assembly and Economic and Social Council, New York and Geneva, 1953-57. Fellow of UCL, 1948. Grand Cross, Order of Dannebrog, 1946. *Publications:* Vatican Assignment, 1956; Discovering Rome, 1960; The Pope, the Jews and the Nazis, 1963. *Address:* 9 Master Close, Oxted, Surrey. *T:* Oxted 2276. *Club:* Reform. *[Died 4 Aug. 1977.*

RANDALL, Harry Enos, OBE 1972; *b* 1899; *s* of Henry Randall, Penge; *m* 1925, Rose Nellie, *d* of Joseph Nicholson, Isle of Man; one *s* two *d.* Served on executive of Workers' Educational Association. Joined Post Office, 1914. Organising Secretary of Union of Post Office Workers, 1940-55. MP (Lab) Clitheroe Division of Lancashire, 1945-50, Gateshead West, Dec. 1955-1970; Asst Govt Whip (unpaid), 2-23 Feb. 1950; British Delegate to Council of Europe and Western European Union, 1958-60; UK Representative, Exec. Cttee, UN High Commission Programme for Refugees, 1965-70. Standing Conf. of British Organisations for Aid to Refugees: Mem., Exec. Cttee, 1958-73; Chm., European Cttee, 1970-73. *Address:* Hillside, Arundel Road, Newhaven, East Sussex. *T:* Newhaven 4542. *[Died 28 Aug. 1976.*

RANDALL, John William, CBE 1963; Hon. President, The Dickinson Robinson Group Ltd, since 1968 (Chairman, 1966-68); Chairman, John Dickinson & Co. Ltd, 1955-68; Hon. President, The Dickinson Robinson Group Africa (Pty) Ltd; *b* 20 May 1891; *s* of late John T. and late Ellen A. Randall; *m* 1st, 1921, Lillian Anne Reeves (*d* 1973); no *c*; 2nd, 1977, Elma Cruise. *Educ:* Hemel Hempstead Church of England School. John Dickinson & Co. Ltd: Secretary, 1928; Financial Director, 1936; Managing Director, 1945. *Recreation:* farming. *Address:* Hawridge Court, Chesham, Bucks. *T:* Cholesbury 240. *[Died 9 Feb. 1979.*

RANDALL, Terence George, CBE 1959 (OBE 1946); Deputy Clerk of the LCC, 1947-65, Children's Officer, 1962-65, retired; *b* 5 May 1904; *s* of George Arthur and Kate Amelia Randall; *m* 1928, Ivy Diana Allen (*d* 1973); two *s. Educ:* St Bonaventure's Grammar School, Forest Gate; City of London School; Birkbeck College, London University. BA 1927. Entered clerical staff of London County Council, 1921; promoted to administrative grade, 1926. Was concerned with all sides of the Council's work, especially with housing, town planning, civil defence, staff management, the coordination of work involving several departments, and latterly child care. *Recreations:* reading, gardening. *Address:* 9 Willow Close, Hutton, Essex. *T:* Brentwood 211242. *[Died 2 March 1979.*

RANDALL LANE, Henry Jerrold; *see* Lane, H. J. R.

RANDLE, Herbert Niel, CIE 1947; FBA 1950; MA 1909; DPhil 1926; *b* 1880; *o s* of Nathaniel Randle; *m* 1915, Edith Joan (*d* 1967), *o d* of William Chaffey Whitby; (one *s,* VC posthumous 1944) two *d. Educ:* Dulwich Coll.; Hertford Coll., Oxford (Scholar). 1st Class Classical Mods, 1901; 1st Class Lit Hum 1903; Indian Educational Service, 1905-27; Prof. of Philosophy, University of Allahabad, 1926; Asst Librarian, India Office, 1927; Librarian, India Office, 1933-45; re-employed until 1949. *Publications:* Sense-data and Sensible Appearances (Mind, 1922); Fragments from Dinnāga (Royal Asiatic Society), 1926; Indian Logic in the Early Schools, 1930; articles in Orientalist publications. *Address:* 1 Denbigh Gardens, Richmond, Surrey. *T:* 01-940 3592. *[Died 8 July 1973.*

RANDOLPH, Peter, CBE 1966; Chairman, Wilkinson Sword Ltd, since 1966; *b* 21 April 1920; *s* of Harry Beckham Randolph and Margaret Isabel (*née* Adams); *m* 1943, Edith Ripley; four *s. Educ:* St Paul's School; London University. Started in law before War. Wilkinson Sword Ltd: joined as accountant, 1946; Director and Secretary, 1948; Marketing Dir, 1949; Administration Dir, 1952; Asst Man. Dir, 1954; Jt Man. Dir, 1957; Man. Dir, 1960; Dep. Chairman, 1965. FBIM. *Recreations:* travelling, meteorology, yachting. *Address:* Diss Park, Gerrards Cross, Bucks. *Clubs:* Arts, City Livery, Little Ship; Tamesis. *[Died 4 June 1971.*

RANGANATHAN, Shiyali Ramamrita, MA, DLitt, LT, FLA; Padmasri, National Research Professor in Library Science since 1965, and Hon. Professor Documentation Research and Training Centre, Bangalore 3, since 1962; President Indian Library Association, 1944-53; Professor of Library Science, University of Delhi, 1947-53; *b* Shiyali, India, 9 Aug. 1892; *e s* of N. Ramamritam and D. Sitalakshmi; *m* 1929, Sarada; one *s. Educ:* Hindu High School, Shiyali; Madras Christian College; Teachers' Coll., Saidapet; University Coll., London. Hon. DLitt: Delhi Univ., 1948; Pittsburgh Univ., 1964. Margaret Mann Award of ALA, 1970. Lectr in Maths in Govt Colls of Madras, 1917-20; Asst Prof. of Maths, Presidency Coll., Madras, 1920-23; Univ. Librarian, and Head of Library School, Madras, 1924-44; Univ. Librarian and Professor of Library Science, Banares Hindu Univ., 1945-47. Sec., Maths and Science Section, Madras Teachers' Guild, 1922-24; Treas., Indian Math. Soc., 1928-34; Sec. Madras Library Assoc., 1928-57 (Pres., 1957-67); Sec., Indian Adult Educn Assoc., 1949-52 (Vice-Pres., 1953); Sec., Library Service Section, All Asia Educnl Conf., 1930; Hon.

Vice-Pres. Brit. Library Assoc.; Hon. Fellow, Internat. Fed. for Documentation, Hon. Chm., FID/CR; Travel in Europe, 1924-25 and in Europe, America and Asia, 1948 onwards. Member: Nat. Central Library Cttee of Government of India; Chairman, Lib. Committee, University Grants Commission, Lib. Sc. Course Cttee, India; Internat. Advisory Cttee of Library Experts of UN; Internat. Bibliog. Cttee UNESCO, 1951-54; Faculty of UNESCO's Internat. School of Librarianship, 1948; Indian National Commn for UNESCO. Founder: Sarada Ranganathan Professorship in Lib. Scis, Univ. of Madras, 1957; Sarada Ranganathan Endowment for Lib. Scis, 1963. *Publications:* Five Laws of Library Science, 1931, 2nd edn, 1957; Colon Classification, 1933, 6th edn, 1960; Classified Catalogue Code, 1934, 5th edn, 1964; Library Administration, 1935, 2nd edn, 1959; Prolegomena to Library Classification, 1937, 3rd edn 1967; Theory of Library Catalogue, 1938; Reference Service and Bibliography, 1940; Bibliography of Reference Books and Bibliographies, 1941; School and College Libraries, 1942; Library Classification: Fundamentals and Procedure, 1943; Elements of Library Classification, 1945; 3rd edn, 1961; Dictionary Catalogue Code, 1945, 2nd edn, 1952; Education for Leisure, 1945, 4th edn, 1961; Library Organisation, 1946, 3rd edn, 1963; Library Development Plan for the Allahabad University, 1947; Classification and International Documentation, 1948; Preface to Library Science, 1948; Library Development Plan for India, 1950; Library Catalogue: Fundamentals and Procedure, 1950; Library Tour, 1948, Europe and America, 1950; Classification, Coding and Machinery for Search, 1950; Classification and Communication, 1951; Library Manual, 1951, 2nd edn, 1960; Documentation Problems, 1951; Philosophy of Library Classification, 1951; Library Book-Selection, 1952, 2nd edn 1966; Social Bibliography, 1952; Social Education Literature, 1952; Union Catalogue of periodicals in South Asia, Vol. I Science, 1953; Depth Classification, 1953; Library Legislation, 1953; Heading and Canons, 1955; Classification of Management, 1956; Library Plan for Bengal, 1958; Library Plan for Kerala, 1960; Social Science Research and Libraries, 1960; Reference Service, 1961; Documentation and its Facets, 1963; Colon Classification: A Descriptive Account, 1965; National Grid of Public Library System: a comparative library legislation (India, Nepal, Sri Lanka, England, USA), 1972. Ed. of Library Science with a slant to Documentation. *Address:* Sarada, 100 Main Road 4, Bangalore 3, India. *T:* 3657.   [*Died 27 Sept. 1972.*

RANGER, James; *b* 1889; *s* of Richard H. and Mary S. Ranger; *m* 1915, Mabel Annie Thorogood; three *d. Educ:* Stock Street Council School, Plaistow, E. MP (Lab) Ilford South, 1945-50. *Address:* 79 Penge Road, South Norwood, SE25.
[*Died 26 April 1975.*

RANK, 1st Baron *cr* 1957, of Sutton Scotney; **Joseph Arthur Rank,** JP; Hon. Life President, Ranks Hovis McDougall Ltd, since 1969 (Chairman, 1952-69); President, The Rank Organisation Ltd, since 1962 (Chairman, 1941-62); Vice-President Animal Health Trust; *b* 22 Dec. 1888; *s* of late Joseph and Emily Voase Rank; *m* 1917, Hon. Laura Ellen Marshall (*d* 1971), *d* of 1st and last Baron Marshall of Chipstead; two *d. Educ:* Leys School, Cambridge. Hon. LLD, Southampton, 1967. *Recreations:* golf and shooting. *Heir:* none. *Address:* Sutton Manor, Sutton Scotney, Hants. [*Died 29 March 1972 (ext).*

RANKIN, John, MA; MP (Lab-Co-op) Govan Division of Glasgow, since 1955 (Tradeston Division of Glasgow, 1945-55); Teacher; *s* of George Rankin and Henrietta Henderson; *m* 1st, Jessie Roy Turnbull (*d* 1965), Barrhead; two *s* three *d*; 2nd, 1968, M. C. Parsons. *Educ:* Allan Glen School; Glasgow University (MA). Propagandist and Lecturer for Scottish Labour College, Co-operative Movement and Labour Party. Chairman of Glasgow ILP, 1925-28; Vice-Chairman, Eastwood Parish Council, 1928-29. *Recreations:* golf, Eastwood Golf Club (Captain, 1942), swimming. *Address:* 55 Holeburn Road, Glasgow S3. *T:* 041-637 2625; 122c New Kent Road, SE1.
[*Died 8 Oct. 1973.*

RANKIN, John Eric, CMG 1972; Deputy Chairman, David Jones Ltd, since 1974 (Managing Director, 1958-74); Grazier, Australia; *b* 6 July 1905; *s* of Robert Rankin; *m* 1942, Enid Elizabeth Duffecy; two *s*. Joined David Jones Ltd, 1933. *Recreation:* golf. *Address:* 3 Minnamurra Road, Northbridge, NSW 2063, Australia. *T:* 95 2744. *Club:* Pennant Hills Golf.
[*Died 11 Oct. 1976.*

RANKIN, John Mitchell, QC 1969; a Recorder of the Crown Court, since 1977; *b* 20 April 1924; *yr s* of late Very Rev. Provost H. M. Rankin, St Ninian's Cathedral, Perth, Scotland and of late Mrs Ethel Tod Rankin (*née* Dixon); *m* 1949, Heather Hope, *o d* of late H. K. Cox, Snaigow, Perthshire; two *s* two *d. Educ:*

Trinity Coll., Glenalmond; Keble Coll., Oxford. Served in Royal Navy, 1942-46 (Lt RNVR, 1945). BA Oxon 1949; MA 1975; called to Bar, Middle Temple, 1950; Bencher, 1975. Dir, Norland Nursery Training Coll., Ltd. Dep. Chm., Local Govt Boundary Commn for England, 1972-; Chm., Cttees of Investigation for GB and England and Wales (Agricl Marketing Act), 1978-. Member: BBC Programmes Complaints Commn, 1979-; Wine Standards Bd of Vintners' Co., 1973-. *Recreations:* painting, music, gardening. *Address:* Carpmael Building, Temple, EC4. *T:* 01-353 5537. *Club:* Travellers'.
[*Died 8 Aug. 1980.*

RANKIN, William Brian, CBE 1975; Senior Partner, Cleaver, Fulton & Rankin, Solicitors, Belfast; General Solicitor for Northern Ireland, since 1954 and Official Solicitor to Supreme Court of Judicature of Northern Ireland, since 1963; *b* 18 Feb. 1915; *s* of William James and Winifred Mabel Rankin; *m* 1940, Margaret Christine, *yr d* of James Glasgow and Margaret Boswell Crawford; three *s* (and one *s* decd). *Educ:* Royal Belfast Academical Instn; Queen's Univ. of Belfast. LLB 1936. Solicitor, N Ireland, 1936. Mem. Council, Incorp. Law Soc. of NI, 1948-72 (Pres. 1963). Mem., NI Standing Adv. Commn on Human Rights, 1973-; Member: Cttee on Supreme Court of NI, 1949; Cttee on Law of Family Inheritance, 1953; Cttee on Registration of Title to Land, 1958; Cttee on Legal educn in N Ire., 1972; Senate, QUB, 1954-; NI Housing Trust (a Statutory Housing Authority), 1957 (Vice-Chm. 1960; Chm. 1970 until merger of Trust in NI Housing Exec. 1971); Cttee, Belfast Charitable Soc., 1945- (Chm. 1972-74); NI Cttee of Nat. Trust, 1970-; NI Community Relations Commn, 1972-74 (Chm.); Central Personal Social Services Adv. Cttee; NI Health and Social Services Council, 1975- (Vice-Chm.). Chm., Belfast County Scout Council, 1949-69. *Address:* Glenard, 123 Marlborough Park South, Belfast BT9 6HW. *T:* Belfast 667359. *Club:* Ulster (Belfast). [*Died 26 Aug. 1976.*

RANSFORD, Col Sir Alister John, Kt 1946; CIE 1936; RE (retired); CStJ; Bursar, Loretto School, Musselburgh, 1948-59; *b* 5 Jan. 1895; *s* of late T. D. Ransford, FRCS, LRCP, Bath; *m* 1927, Lucy Torfrida, 4th *d* of late William Walford, Greens Norton Park, Towcester; one *s* one *d. Educ:* Fettes College; Royal Military Academy, Woolwich. 2nd Lieut RE, 1914; served European War, France and Belgium (despatches, 1914-15 star, two medals); India, Military Engineering Services, 1922; Finance Dept., Govt of India, HM's Mint, Bombay, 1924; Mint Master, His Majesty's Mint, Bombay, 1931-47; Major, 1929; Lt-Col, 1937; Col, 1940; retired, 1949. *Address:* 9 Swanston View, Edinburgh EH10 7DG. *T:* 031-445 2779. [*Died 25 Nov. 1974.*

RANSOME, Prof. Sir Gordon (Arthur), KBE 1972 (CBE 1962); FRCP; Professor Emeritus of Medicine, University of Singapore, since 1972; late Senior Consultant to General Hospital, Singapore; Senior Consultant to Singapore AntiTuberculosis Association, since 1947; Hon. Consultant Physician to the Sultan of Kelantan; *b* 6 May 1910; *s* of late Rev. Maurice John Ransome, St John's Coll., Cambridge, and Rector of Pulverbatch, Salop; *m* 1st, 1940, Eryl Arundel; one *d*; 2nd, 1955, Daphne Mary, *d* of Col Lawrence George Beach, RE; two *s* one *d. Educ:* Dauntsey's Sch.; London University; St Bartholomew's Hosp.; Charing Cross Hosp.; London Sch. of Tropical Medicine. MRCS, LRCP 1933; MRCP 1935; FRCP 1947. War of 1939-45: Lt-Col, IMS; Adv. in Med., 12th Army; Adv. in Neurology, SEAC; Staff Officer, British Mil. Admin (Malaya), 1945 (despatches twice). Hon. Consultant to Army, Far East, 1947-71, and to ANZUK Hosp., 1971. Formerly: Sen. Med. Registrar, Charing Cross Hosp.; Chief Asst Med., Royal Westminster Ophthalmic Hosp.; Associate Prof. of Med., King Edward VII Coll. Med., Singapore; Prof. Clin. Med. and Prof. Med., Univ. of Malaya, Singapore; Prof. Med., Univ. of Singapore, Acad. Med. (AM), Singapore, 1957, Hon. AM 1977; Hon. MD 1969; Meritorious Service Medal, PJG, Singapore, 1967; Datoship by Sultan of Kelantan, DJMK (Order of the Life of the Throne), 1969; SPMJ, 1973; Datuk; Grand Comdr, Order of the Throne, Johore. *Publications:* contribs to scientific jls. *Recreations:* shooting, fly fishing, history. *Address:* The Grove, New Radnor, near Presteigne, Powys. *T:* New Radnor 276. *Clubs:* Royal Over-Seas League; Tanglin (Singapore).
[*Died 18 June 1978.*

RATHBONE, Monroe Jackson; Chairman, Standard Oil Co. (NJ), 1961-65 (President, 1954-61, Director, 1949-65), retired; *b* Parkersburg, W Va, 1 March 1900; *s* of Monroe Jackson Rathbone and Ida Virginia (*née* Welch); *m* 1922, Eleanor Groves; one *s* one *d. Educ:* Parkersburg High School; Lehigh University, Bethlehem, Pa (Chem. E.). Served US Army (2nd Lieut), 1918-19. Joined Standard Oil Co. of Louisiana, 1921; Chemical Engineer, asst to Gen. Superintendent, 1926-31; Gen. Superintendent, 1931-33; Asst Gen. Manager, Manufacturing

Dept, 1933-36; Vice-Pres. and Gen. Manager i/c manufacturing operations, 1935-36; President, 1936-44; President and Director, Esso Standard Oil Co., 1944-49; Director: Triangle Industries, Nuclear Systems; Tropigas International; La National Bank. Hon. Director American Petroleum Institute; Mem., Bd of Trustees, Lehigh Univ. Director: Nat. Fund for Medical Educn; Deafness Research Foundation. Comdr, Order of St Olaf, Norway; Comdr, Order of Orange-Nassau, Netherlands; Kt, Order of Leopold, Belgium; Palladium Medal, Soc. Industrielle du Chemie; Gold Medal, Amer. Petroleum Inst.; Gold Medal, Wharton Alumni Assoc., Univ. of Pennsylvania; Award of Merit, Amer. Inst. Consulting Engineers; Humanitarian Award, Deafness Research Foundation; Gold Medal, Good Citizenship Sons of Amer. Revolution. Holds numerous hon. degrees. *Address:* 7315 Richards Drive, Baton Rouge, La 70809, USA; 1 Rockefeller Plaza, NYC 10020, USA. *Clubs:* University, River (New York); Baton Rouge; Baltusrol Golf; Gulf Stream Golf.
[*Died* 2 *Aug.* 1976.

RATTERAY, Hon. Sir George Oswald, Kt 1975; CBE 1968; Commission Merchant and Wholesaler; President, Legislative Council of Bermuda; Chairman, Bermuda Library Committee; *b* Somerset, Bermuda, 30 Sept 1903; *m* 1927, Kate Cecilia Louise (*née* Trott); two *s* one *d. Educ:* Hunty Sch., Sandys Parish, Bermuda; DipEd (external), Bennett Coll., England. Missionary, N Rhodesia (now Zambia), 1932-39; MCP Sandys North, 1953-68; Chm., Treatment of Offenders Commn; Govt Spokesman on Prisons; Mem., Bd of Immigration, 1956-60; Mem., Delegn to London for Constitutional Changes, 1966. Founder, Proprietor and Manager, Ratteray's Commission Agency. *Address:* Mutende, Sound View Road, Somerset, Bermuda; King Street, Hamilton, Bermuda.
[*Died* 19 *Feb.* 1980.

RATTIGAN, Sir Terence (Mervyn), Kt 1971; CBE 1958; *b* 10 June 1911; unmarried. *Educ:* Harrow (Scholar); Trinity College, Oxford (Scholar in Modern History). Playwright. First Episode, Comedy, London, 1934, and New York; French without Tears, Criterion, London, 1936, and New York; After the Dance, St James's, London, 1939; Flare Path, Apollo, London, 1942, and New York; While the Sun Shines, London, 1943, and New York; Love in Idleness, Lyric, London, 1944; (O Mistress Mine, New York, 1945); The Winslow Boy, Lyric, 1946, and USA, 1947, New, 1970; Playbill (The Browning Version and Harlequinade), Phoenix, 1948, New York, 1949; Adventure Story, St James's, 1949; French Without Tears (revived), Vaudeville, 1949; Who is Sylvia?, Criterion, 1950; The Deep Blue Sea, Duchess, 1952, New York, 1952, Guildford, 1971; The Sleeping Prince, Phoenix, 1953, New York, 1956, St Martin's, 1968; Separate Tables, St James's, 1954, New York, 1956; Variation on a Theme, Globe, 1958; Ross, Haymarket, 1960, New York, 1961; Man and Boy, Queen's, 1963, New York, 1963; A Bequest to the Nation, Haymarket, 1970; In Praise of Love, Duchess, 1973, New York, 1975; Cause Célèbre, Her Majesty's, 1977. *Films:* French without Tears, Quiet Wedding, The Day will Dawn, Uncensored, Way To The Stars, Journey Together, While The Sun Shines, The Winslow Boy, The Browning Version, The Sound Barrier, The Final Test, The Deep Blue Sea, The Prince and the Showgirl, Separate Tables, The VIP's; The Yellow Rolls-Royce; Conduct Unbecoming; A Bequest to the Nation; *television films:* High Summer, The Final Test, Heart to Heart, Nelson; *radio play:* Cause Célèbre. *Publications:* above plays. *Recreation:* watching cricket. *Address:* c/o Dr Jan Van Loewen Ltd, 81-83 Shaftesbury Avenue, W1. *Clubs:* Royal and Ancient; MCC.
[*Died* 30 *Nov.* 1977.

RAVEN, Martin Owen, MA, MD, MRCP; retired; Hon. Consulting Physician, Ramsgate General Hospital; *b* 4 July 1888; *s* of Thomas F. and Margaret M. Raven; *m* 1920, Sibyl (*d* 1969), *d* of Sherwood Mockett, St Peter's, Kent; one *s* two *d. Educ:* Uppingham; Trinity College, Oxford. House Surgeon, House Physician, St Mary's Hospital; Naval Surgeon, 1914-18; Physician, Ramsgate Hospital, 1926; Physician at Southport Emergency Hospital, 1941-45; Physician, Ramsgate and Margate General Hospital, 1949. *Publications:* Treatment of Rheumatism in Childhood (Modern Technique in Treatment, vol. ii); Diabetes Mellitus in Childhood, 1924; Rheumatic Diseases of Childhood, 1926; Medical Treatment in the Welfare State, 1951; Intradermal injection of influenza virus vaccine in Herpes Zoster, 1965; Reflections on Retirement, 1969, etc. *Address:* East Cliff House, Broadstairs, Kent. *T:* Thanet 63700.
[*Died* 27 *Jan.* 1976.

RAWCLIFFE, Prof. Gordon Hindle, MA, DSc; FRS 1972; FIEE; FIEEE; consulting electrical engineer; Professor of Electrical Engineering, University of Bristol, 1944-75, now Emeritus; *b* Sheffield, 2 June 1910; *e s* of late Rev. J. Hindle Rawcliffe, Gloucester; *m* 1st, Stella Morgan (marriage dissolved); two *d*;

2nd, 1952, Sheila Mary Wicks, MA Oxon; two *d. Educ:* St Edmund's School, Canterbury; Keble College, Oxford, Hon. Fellow 1976; Pres., Keble Assoc., 1978. 1st Class Hons Engineering Science, 1932. Metropolitan-Vickers Electrical Co. Ltd, Manchester (now GEC Ltd), 1932-37; Lecturer in Electrical Engineering, University of Liverpool, 1937-41; Head of Electrical Engineering Department, Robert Gordon's Technical College, Aberdeen, and Lecturer-in-charge of Electrical Engineering, Univ. of Aberdeen, 1941-44. Instn of Electrical Engineers: Chairman Western Centre, 1956-57; Council, 1956-58, 1966-69; Utilization Section Committee, 1960-62; Power Divisional Board, 1963-65, and 1969-72; Hunter Meml Lecture, 1970; Vice-Pres., 1972-75; Hon. Fellow, 1978. Many patents and inventions relating to Electrical Machinery, including multi-speed P.A.M. induction motor. Mem., several official cttees on electrical machinery. Consultant to: GEC Machines Ltd; Brush Electrical Eng. Co. Ltd, 1955-69; Lancashire Dynamo Co. Ltd, 1958-67; Westinghouse Electric Corp., E Pittsburgh, USA; Lawrence-Scott & Electromotors; Parsons-Peebles and other organisations. Lecture and Consulting tours in USA, 1961, 1967, 1970, 1972, 1974, 1977, Canada, 1961, 1971, Hungary, 1962, Turkey, 1963, Australia and NZ, 1964, Japan and Far East, 1965, S Africa (Bernard Price Meml Lecture), 1965, Czechoslovakia, 1966, Far East, Australia, 1967, Middle and Far East, 1968, Bulgaria and Poland, 1968, Germany, 1969, Italy, 1971, 1975, France, 1972, 1976. Lectures: Marcus Greenhorne, Univ. of Aberdeen, 1976; Clifford Paterson, Royal Soc., 1977. S. G. Brown Medal, Royal Soc., 1978. Hon. DTech Loughborough, 1974; Hon. DSc Bath, 1976. *Publications:* numerous papers in Proceedings of Institution of Electrical Engineers (Premiums 1938, 1940, 1956, 1963, 1964, 1966) and other scientific and technical jls, etc. *Recreations:* exploring the West of England; travel, reading and music. *Address:* 28 Upper Belgrave Road, Clifton, Bristol BS8 2XL. *T:* Bristol 37940. *Club:* Athenæum. [*Died* 3 *Sept.* 1979.

RAWLINS, Evelyn Charles Donaldson, CMG 1932; CBE 1930; *b* 27 Feb. 1884; *s* of W. Donaldson Rawlins, KC, White Waltham Grove, Bucks; *m* 1908, Suzanne (*d* 1971), *d* of E. Kappes; one *s. Educ:* Eton; Trinity College, Cambridge. Acting Consul-General, Beirut, 1907; HM Vice-Consul at Adana, 1910; Acting Consul-General in Crete, 1911, and at Beirut, 1913; Consul at Canea, 1915; Member of International Consular Commission on Foreign Claims in Crete; attached to AHQ Salonica Expeditionary Force, 1915; active service with Navy, 1915-17; attached to Serbian Commercial Mission, 1918, and Greek Commercial Mission, 1918; Chief Commissioner on British Commercial Mission to Morocco, 1918; Commercial Secretary (Grade I) for Greece and Serbia, 1919; in charge of British Economic Mission to Jugoslavia, 1919; Commercial Secretary (Grade I) at Berne, 1922; transferred to Prague, 1923, and to Budapest, 1924; transferred to Rome with rank of Comerical Counsellor, 1926; Director of Exhibitions Division, Department of Overseas Trade, 1930; Commissioner-General to HM Government at International Exhibition, Antwerp, 1930, and British Empire Trade Exhibition, Buenos Aires, 1931; Commercial Counsellor, British Legation, Vienna, 1932-34; British Embassy, Berlin, 1934-37; Minister to Bolivia, 1937-40; Retired from Diplomatic Service; Greek Order of Redeemer (Gold Cross). *Address:* c/o Standard Bank, Northumberland Avenue, WC2. [*Died* 4 *Aug.* 1971.

RAWLINS, His Honour Percy Lionel Edwin, MA, LLB, Cantab; County Court Judge, 1947-67; Circuit No 36 (Berks Glos & Oxon), 1962-67; *b* 14 April 1902; *s* of F. P. F. M. Rawlins, Solicitor, and F. Rawlins; *m* 1930, Katharine M. E. Fearnley-Sander; one *s* one *d. Educ:* Highgate School; Selwyn College, Cambridge. Honours Law Tripos, Cambridge, 1924; called to Bar, 1926, Midland Circuit; Major attached ACA, 1944-46; Legal Officer, Villach, Austria, 1945-46; VP European Interchange Council, 1950; Fellow, Corporation of SS Mary and Nicolas, 1951. *Recreation:* gardening. *Address:* Izods Close, Broad Campden, Gloucestershire. *T:* Evesham 840329.
[*Died* 27 *April* 1977.

RAWLINSON, Sir Joseph, Kt 1962; CBE 1953; MEng, FINstCE, FIMechE, FIMunE; Chief Engineer and County Surveyor, London County Council, 1947-62; *b* 16 April 1897; *m* 1923, Gertrude Moseley Maggs; one *s* one *d. Educ:* Liverpool University. Served European War, 1914-18, with Liverpool Scottish and RAF; Engineer with Public Works Contractor on Construction of Roads and Sub-aqueous Tunnels; Asst City Engineer, Liverpool, 1930-35; City Engineer, Westminster, 1936-47. Hon. Citizen, City of Winnipeg, Canada, 1959. *Publications:* Reclamation of Mersey Foreshore for Promenade at Otterspool (Proceeding of Royal Sanitary Inst.), 1933; (with W. R. Davidge) City of Westminster Plan. *Recreations:* motoring and golf. *Address:* 26 Sanderstead Hill, Sanderstead, Surrey. *Club:* Royal Automobile. [*Died* 20 *Sept.* 1971.

RAWSON, Maj.-Gen. Geoffrey Grahame, CB 1941; OBE; MC; *b* 2 Dec. 1887; *s* of Edward Creswell Rawson, ICS, and Marion Duffield; *m* 1919, Ella Cane (*d* 1967); one *s* (and one *s* decd). *Educ:* Cheltenham Coll.; RMA Woolwich. Commissioned Royal Engineers, 1908; transferred Royal Corps of Signals, 1920; DAAG War Office, 1921; Chief Instructor School of Signals, 1932; Deputy Director Staff Duties, War Office, 1937; Director of Signals, War Office, 1941; Inspector of Signals, 1942; Colonel Comdt Royal Signals, 1944-50. Lt-Col, Royal Signals, 1928; Colonel, 1931; Brigadier, 1937; Major-General, 1941; served European War, 1914-18, with BEF in France and in Salonika (Brevet Major, Legion of Honour 5th Class, OBE, MC, despatches five times); ADC to the King, 1938-41; retired pay, 1944. *Address:* 15 Collingham Road, SW5.
[*Died* 14 *Jan.* 1979.

RAWSON, Sir Stanley Walter, Kt 1953; *b* 9 October 1891; *s* of Frank H. Rawson, Sheffield; *m* 1922, Phyllis (*d* 1967), *d* of Arthur Freer Bargate; two *s*. *Educ:* King Edward's School, Sheffield; Queen's Coll., Oxford, 1st Cl. Hon. Mods, 1911, Lit Hum 1913, History, 1914. Fellow of All Souls, 1914-21. Asst Sec., Bolckow Vaughan & Co. Ltd, 1916; Comptroller: Dorman Long & Co. Ltd, 1929; John Brown & Co. Ltd, 1934 (Vice-Chairman, 1953-59). Director-General Machine Tools, Ministry of Supply, 1951-53. Chm., Robert Fraser and Partners, 1960-61. *Publications:* contributions to Journal of Royal Economic Society. *Recreations:* golf and reading. *Address:* 23 Down Street, W1. [*Died* 17 *March* 1973.

RAWSTHORNE, Alan, CBE 1961; Composer; *b* Haslingden, Lancashire, 2 May 1905; *s* of Hubert Rawsthorne, MRCS; *m* 1st, 1934, Jessie Hinchliffe, violinist; 2nd, 1955, Isabel Lambert. *Educ:* Sandringham School, Southport, Lancs; Royal Manchester College of Music (Fellow, 1943). Did not begin serious study of music till the age of 20, owing to parental opposition; previously a student of dentistry and architecture; entered Royal Manchester Coll. of Music 1926, and subsequently spent some time abroad. Taught at Dartington Hall, 1932-34, and worked as musician to the School of Dance-mime there; returned to London, 1934. Compositions performed at International Soc. for Contemporary Music festivals, London 1938 and 1946; Warsaw 1939; Brussels 1950; contributed articles on Music to Life and Letters, 1934-35. Joined the Army (Royal Artillery) March 1941. Hon. Fellow, Downing College, Cambridge, 1969. Hon. DMus: Belfast, 1969; Liverpool, 1969. *Publications:* Variations for 2 Violins, 1938; Symphonic Studies, 1939; String Quartet No 1, 1939; Piano Concerto, 1942; The Creel (piano duet), 1942; Street Corner Overture, 1944; Cortèges (Fantasy-Overture), 1945; Violin Concerto, 1948; Quartet for Clarinet and strings; Sonata for cello and piano; Sonatina for piano; Concerto for String Orchestra; Concerto for oboe and strings; symphony; 2nd piano concerto; A Canticle of Man (chamber cantata); Sonata for viola and piano; Practical Cats (for Speaker and Orchestra); String Quartet No 2; Madame Chrysanthème (ballet); 2nd Violin Concerto, 1956; Sonata for violin and piano, 1957; symphony No 2, 1959; Overture, Hallé, 1958; Concerto for 10 Instruments, 1961; Improvisations on a theme by Constant Lambert, 1961; Mediaeval Diptych (for Baritone and Orchestra); Trio (for piano, violin and cello); Divertimento for Chamber Orchestra; Lament for a Sparrow (for tenor, chorus and harp), 1962; Quintet for Piano and Wind; Carmen Vitale (Cantata for soprano, chorus and Orchestra); Elegiac Rhapsody (for String Orchestra), 1964; Symphony No 3, 1964; Tankas of the Four Seasons, 1965; Suite for Brass Band; String Quartet No 3, 1965; Cello Concerto, 1966; The God in the Cave (for Chorus and Orchestra), 1966; Ballade (for piano), 1967; Concerto for two pianos and orchestra, 1968; Quintet for piano and strings, 1968; Suite for harp, flute and viola, 1968; Triptych for full orchestra, 1969; Quartet for oboe and strings, 1970; Quintet for violin, cello, horn, flute and piano, 1971; some songs and piano music. *Recreation:* chess. *Address:* c/o Oxford University Press, 44 Conduit Street, W1. [*Died* 24 *July* 1971.

RAY, Reginald Edwin Anthony, CIE 1941; *b* 15 May 1891; *s* of late George Anthony Ray, East Dulwich; *m* 1920, Marion Huggan, Pudsey, Yorks; two *s* one *d*. *Educ:* City of London School. Joined Indian Police, 1910; Deputy Inspector General, Intelligence Branch, Bengal, 1937-43; Comr of Police, Calcutta, 1943-46; retired 1946. Indian Police Medal, 1933; King's Police Medal, 1944. *Address:* Woodthorpe, Wray Common Road, Reigate, Surrey. *T:* Reigate 42647. [*Died* 13 *Nov.* 1972.

RAY, Ted; Theatrical and BBC Entertainer; *b* 21 Nov. 1905; *s* of Chas Olden, comedian, and of Margaret Ellen Kenyon; *m* 1933, Dorothy Sybil Stevens; two *s*. *Educ:* Liverpool Collegiate School. Became successively clerk, ship's steward and dance band violinist. First stage appearance, Palace Theatre, Prescot, Lancs, 1927. First London appearance, London Music Hall,

Shoreditch, 1930. Toured South Africa thrice; Royal Command Performances: London Palladium, 1948; London Coliseum, 1949; Empire, Leicester Sq., 1950; London Palladium, 1952. Interested in theatre charities (King Water Rat, 1949 and 1950). Began 1st radio series, Ray's a Laugh, 1949; Resident MC of BBC Calling All Forces, 1950. Television: The Ted Ray Show, BBC, 1955; I Object, Jackanory; Jokers Wild, 1969-70. *Films:* Meet Me To-night, 1952; Escape by Night, 1953; My Wife's Family, 1956; The Crowning Touch, 1957; Carry on Teacher, 1959; Please Turn Over, 1959. *Publications:* Autobiography: Raising the Laughs, 1952; My Turn Next, 1963; Golf—My Slice of Life, 1972. *Recreations:* golf, swimming, motoring, boxing. *Address:* 30 Broad Walk, N21. *Clubs:* Crews Hill Golf; Temple Golf. [*Died* 8 *Nov.* 1977.

RAYBOULD, Clarence, Hon. DMus, FRCO, Hon. RAM, FBSM; Hon. FTCL; Bard of Wales; Past Director of Senior Orchestra, Royal Academy of Music; *b* 1886, English; *m* 1940, Evelyn Brodhurst Vaughan. *Educ:* King Edward's School, and University, Birmingham. Conductor Beecham Opera Co. and Royal Opera, Covent Garden, for nine years; Musical adviser and conductor, Columbia Gramophone Co. 1927-31; composed, arranged and conducted for the first British film to have its own music, and a number of other early British documentaries; Chief Asst Conductor of BBC Symphony Orch., 1936-45; has conducted much British music, some for the first time, in many European cities, and in America. Hon. DMus, Univ. of Wales, 1954. *Works:* an opera and a number of pianoforte, violoncello and clarinet works, chamber music and part-songs, some of which published. *Address:* Crannies, 12 North Street, Northam, N Devon. *T:* Bideford 2517. [*Died* 27 *March* 1972.

RAYBOULD, Emeritus Prof. Sidney Griffith, PhD; Professor of Adult Education, 1952-69 (now Emeritus Professor), and Director of Extra-Mural Studies, 1946-69, University of Leeds; *b* 10 Nov. 1903; *s* of Albert and Margaret Raybould; *m* 1933, Nina Marjorie (*née* Calvert); two *s* two *d*. *Educ:* Middlesbrough High School; University College, Nottingham. Teacher, Middlesbrough Local Education Authority, 1925-35; Staff Tutor, Univ. of Leeds, 1936-46. Visiting Director of Extra-Mural Studies, Univ. Coll., Ibadan, Nigeria, 1954-55; Visiting Director of Extra-Mural Studies, University Coll. of the West Indies, 1960-61; Vis. Dean of Degree Studies in Extension, McMaster Univ., Hamilton, Ontario, 1969-70. New Zealand Prestige Fellow, 1964, 1966. Member: Central Advisory Council for Education (England), 1950-61; General Advisory Council, BBC, 1952-59; Inter-University Council for Higher Education Overseas, 1955-69; Council on Overseas Colleges of Arts, Science and Technology, 1955-62; Vice-President of the WEA, 1949-57. Hon. LLD, McMaster University, 1962. William Pearson Tolley Medallist, Syracuse Univ., 1970. *Publications:* The WEA: The Next Phase, 1949; The English Universities and Adult Education, 1951; Adult Education at a Tropical University, 1957; (with A. M. Parker) University Studies for Adults, 1972; (ed) Trends in English Adult Education, 1958; (contributor): Universities in Adult Education, 1952; University Extramural Education in England, 1945-62, 1964; Encyclopædia Britannica; British JI of Educational Studies. *Recreations:* reading, biography, watching cricket. *Address:* 49 Kent Road, Harrogate, North Yorks. *T:* Harrogate 68719.
[*Died* 1 *Oct.* 1977.

RAYMOND, Ernest, OBE 1972; novelist; Knight Officer of the Order of Merit of the Italian Republic; FRSL; President, Dickens Fellowship, 1971; *b* 31 December 1888; *s* of William Bell Raymond; *m* 1st, Zoe Irène Maude (marriage dissolved), *d* of late Capt. Doucett, RNR, Younger Brother of Trinity House; one *s* one *d*; 2nd, Diana Joan, *o d* of late William Thomas Young, Professor of Literature, University of London; one *s*. *Educ:* Colet Court; St Paul's School; Chichester Theological College; LTh Durham University, 1914; 1st Class, Universities Preliminary to Holy Orders, 1914. Assistant Master at Glengorse, Eastbourne, 1908-11; at St Christopher's, Bath, 1911-12; ordained, 1914; resigned Orders, 1923; attached to 10th Manchester Regiment, 1915-17; 9th Worcester Regiment, 1917-19; served in Gallipoli, Egypt, France, Mesopotamia, Persia, and Russia; demobilised, 1919; Awarded gold medal of Book Guild, 1936, for novel: We, the Accused. *Publications:* Tell England, 1922; Rossenal, 1922; Damascus Gate, 1923; Wanderlight, 1924; The Shout of the King, 1924, Daphne Bruno, I, 1925; Daphne Bruno, II, 1926; Morris in the Dance, 1927; The Old Tree Blossomed, 1928; Through Literature to Life, 1928; The Berg (play), 1929; A Family that Was, 1929; The Jesting Army, 1930; Mary Leith, 1931; The Multabello Road (play), 1932; Once in England (trilogy), 1932; Newtimber Lane, 1933; Child of Norman's End, 1934; We, the Accused, 1935; Don John's Mountain Home, 1936; The Marsh, 1937; In the Steps of St Francis, 1938; The Miracle of Brean, 1939; A Song of the Tide,

1940; The Last to Rest, 1941; Was There Love Once?, 1942; The Corporal of the Guard, 1943; For Them that Trespass, 1944; Back to Humanity (with Patrick Raymond), 1945; The Five Sons of Le Faber, 1945; The Autobiography of David-, (edited), 1946; The Kilburn Tale, 1947; In the Steps of the Brontës, 1948; Gentle Greaves, 1949; The Witness of Canon Welcome, 1950; A Chorus Ending, 1951; Two Gentlemen of Rome, The Story of Keats and Shelley, 1952; The Chalice and the Sword, 1952; To the Wood no more, 1954; The Nameless Places, 1954; The Lord of Wensley, 1956; The Old June Weather, 1957; The City and the Dream, 1958; The Quiet Shore, 1958; The Visit of Brother Ives, 1960; Paris, City of Enchantment, 1961; Mr Olim, 1961; The Chatelaine, 1962; One of our Brethren, 1963; Late in the Day, 1964; The Tree of Heaven, 1965; The Mountain Farm, 1966; The Bethany Road, 1967; autobiography: The Story of My Days, 1968; Please You, Draw Near, 1969; Good Morning, Good People, 1970; A Georgian Love Story, 1971; Our Late Member, 1972; Miryam's Guest House, 1973; poems and articles in periodicals; *posthumous publication:* Under Wedgery Down, 1974. *Recreations:* climbing, watching cricket, travelling. *Address:* 22 The Pryors, East Heath Road, Hampstead, NW3. *T:* 01-435 3716. *Club:* Garrick.   *[Died* 14 *May* 1974.

RAYMOND, Harold, OBE, MC, MA; *b* 1887; *s* of Cuthbert and Ellen Martha Raymond, Rose Lawn, Worcester; *m* 1920, Vera, *d* of Rev. T. M. Everett, Vicar of Ruislip, and *widow* of Captain R. G. Tasker, Worcestershire Regiment; one *s. Educ:* Worcester King's School; Pembroke College, Oxford (Scholar, Hon. Mods and Lit Hum). Assistant Master, Oundle School, 1912-14; served European War, 1914-18; 2nd Lieut 10 Worc. Regt, 1914; Captain, 1915; Staff Captain 58 Brigade, 1916-17; Major, General Staff, DAAG, 19 Division, 1918-19 (despatches thrice, OBE, MC); partner in Chatto & Windus, 1919-53; Chairman of Chatto & Windus Ltd, 1953-54; originated, and in 1926 proposed, the Book Tokens scheme, which was finally adopted by the British Book Trade in 1932; retired 1956. *Address:* Great Maytham Hall, Rolvenden, Kent. *Club:* Athenæum.
                                                                [Died 17 *July* 1975.

RAYMONT, Prof. John Edwin George, OBE 1978; Professor of Biological Oceanography, University of Southampton, since 1964; Deputy Vice-Chancellor, 1966-68; *b* 6 April 1915; *s* of Walter and Ellen Raymont; *m* 1945, Joan Katharine Brigit Sloan; one *s* two *d. Educ:* Hele's School and University College, Exeter. First Class Hons London External Degree in Zoology, 1936. Henry Fellow, Harvard Univ., USA, 1937-38. AM Harvard 1938; DSc Univ. of Exeter, 1960. Assistant Lecturer in Zoology, University College, Exeter, 1938-39; Lecturer in Zoology, University of Edinburgh, 1939-46; Prof. of Zoology, Univ. of Southampton, 1946-64. Mem. Wessex Regional Hosp. Bd, 1959-74; Chm. Planning and Development Cttee, 1959-74; Southampton Univ. HMC, 1959-74; Vice-Chm., Hants Area AHA, 1974-. Fellow, Indian Acad. of Sciences. *Publications:* Plankton and Productivity in the Oceans, 1963; on physiology of copepods, marine fish cultivation and marine benthos in Proc. Roy. Soc. of Edin., Biological Bulletin, Jl of Marine Biolog. Assoc., Limnol. and Oceanogr., Int. Revue ges. Hydrobiol., Deep-Sea Research, etc. *Address:* 246 Woodlands Road, Southampton.   *[Died* 30 *Aug.* 1979.

RAYNER, Vice-Admiral Herbert Sharples, DSC 1941, Bar 1944; CD 1946 (on institution); Royal Canadian Navy, retired; Chief of Naval Staff (Canada), 1960-64; *b* 16 Jan. 1911; *s* of Harold Rayner and Annie May (*née* Suitter); *m* 1936, Betty Bachelier Graham (*née* Snook); three *s* three *d. Educ:* Hutton Grammar School, Preston, Lancs; St Catharine's Collegiate Institute, St Catharine's, Ont. Cadet, RCN, 1928; Capt. 1948; Rear-Adm., 1955; Vice-Adm., 1960. Served War of 1939-45 (DSC and Bar, despatches twice); Comd HMCS St Laurent, 1940-42; SO Operations to CO Atlantic Coast, 1942-43; i/c destroyer Huron, 1943-44; Dir of Plans, Naval HQ, 1944-45; Capt. (D) Halifax, 1945; Comd destroyer Nootka, 1946; Comd RCN Air Section, Dartmouth, NS, 1947; Commandant, Canadian Services Coll., BC, 1948-49; Imperial Defence College, UK, 1950; Sec., Chiefs of Staff Cttee, Nat. Defence HQ, Canada, 1951; Co-ordinator of Joint Staff, 1951; Comd HMCS Magnificent, 1953; Chief of Naval Personnel, 1955; Flag Officer, Pacific Coast, 1957. Chevalier, Legion of Honour; Croix de Guerre, 1946. *Recreations:* walking and climbing; photography. *Address:* 9 Loch Isle Road, Ottawa, Ontario K2H 8G5, Canada. *T:* 828-0101. *Clubs:* Canadian Alpine, Adirondack Mountain, University (Ottawa).   *[Died* 30 *May* 1976.

RAYNER, Brigadier Sir Ralph, Kt 1956; DL; *s* of Reverend George Rayner, Bradshaw, near Queensbury, Yorks; *m* 1931, Elizabeth, *d* of late S. A. Courtauld; three *s* one *d.* Served France, 1915; Afghan War, 1919 (despatches); British Mission to Kabul, 1920; NW Frontier, 1924; France, 1939 (despatches);

Germany, 1945; Hon. Col Wessex Signals, 1948. Chairman: Western Area, Conservative Assoc., 1955-61; Royal Soc. St George, 1954-64. MP (U) Totnes Division of Devonshire, 1935-55. Chairman: Devon and Exeter Trustee Bank, 1970-; Haldon Racecourse, 1963-73. Freeman of the City of London. DL Devon, 1952; High Sheriff of Devon, 1958; Mem., Devon CC, 1964. *Address:* Ashcombe Tower, near Dawlish, Devon. *T:* Dawlish 3178; 1 Egerton Gardens, SW3. *T:* 01-584 6208. *Clubs:* Carlton, Pratt's, Pilgrims.   *[Died* 17 *July* 1977.

RAZAK bin Hussein, Hon. Tun Haji Abdul, *see* Abdul Razak.

REA, Lorna; (The Lady Rea); Writer; *b* Glasgow, 12 June 1897; *d* of late Lewis O. Smith, merchant; *m* 1922, Philip Russell Rea, later 2nd Baron Rea, PC, OBE; one *d* (one *s* decd). *Educ:* St James's, West Malvern; Newnham College, Cambridge (Hons). WVS (London Region), 1940-45. *Publications:* Six Mrs Greenes, Rachel Moon, The Happy Prisoner, First Night, The Armada, Six and Seven, and other publications. *Address:* 5 St John's House, Smith Square, Westminster, SW1. *T:* 01-222 6106.
                                                                [Died 11 *Dec.* 1978.

REA, Robert Lindsay-, BSc, MD, MCh FRCS; *b* 1881; *s* of Robert Rea, Belfast; *m* Mary Eleanor, *d* of late James Waddell, Glasgow; two *s* two *d. Educ:* Belfast Model Sch. and Belfast Technical Sch.; Queen's Univ., Belfast; Middlesex Hospital; Université de Paris. Fellow of Royal Society of Medicine; Hon. Member of Ophthalmological Society of United Kingdom; supervised X-ray work of 4th Army, BEF, in France, 1918. Consulting Surgeon to Western Ophthalmic Hospital; Consulting Surgeon to West End Hosp. for Neurology and Neuro-Surgery, London; retired 1966. *Publications:* Affections of the Eye in General Practice; Neuro-ophthalmology; various papers on Ophthalmic subjects in medical journals. *Recreation:* golf. *Address:* 7 Tenby Mansions, W1. *T:* 01-935 2357. *Club:* Moor Park (Rickmansworth).   *[Died* 28 *April* 1971.

READ, Alfred Burgess, RDI 1940; ARCA; FSIA; Design Consultant; Sqdn Ldr RAFVR, Italy (despatches twice); *b* 29 May 1899; *s* of late I. Read, Willingdon, Sussex; *m* 1924, Phyllis Barbara Walker, Harrogate, Yorks; two *s* one *d. Educ:* Eastbourne Grammar School; Eastbourne School of Art; Royal College of Art, South Kensington. 2nd Lieut, Welsh Guards, 1918-19; Royal College of Art, South Kensington, 1920-23; Diploma of Royal College of Art, 1923; Rural Industries Bureau Travelling Scholarship to Italy, 1924; Ayrton Premium from Institution of Electrical Engineers, 1933. *Publication:* Lighting the Home, 1938. *Recreation:* painting. *Address:* West Riding, Milton Abbas, Blandford Forum, Dorset. *T:* Milton Abbas 410. *Club:* Chelsea Arts.   *[Died* 11 *Oct.* 1973.

READ, Col Alfred Howard, CB 1952; OBE (mil.) 1939; TD; MEng; CEng, FIEE; *b* 25 Aug. 1893; *er s* of Alfred Read, Huyton, Lancs. *Educ:* Birkenhead Institute; Liverpool Univ. Served European War with RE, 1914-19; transf. Roy. Corps of Signals, 1921; served War of 1939-45, in France and Belgium; Col 1942. Mil. Member, Middx T and AFA, 1936-54. DL Greater London, 1965-76 (Middx, 1948-65). Director of Overseas Telecommunications, Post Office, 1950-54; retired, 1954; Telecommunications Attaché, British Embassy, Washington, 1954-60. *Address:* Thatched House, Thurne, Norfolk. *T:* Potter Heigham 316.   *[Died* 14 *Jan.* 1977.

READ, Vice-Adm. Arthur Duncan, CB 1944; *b* 1889; *m* 1922, Hon. Rosamond Vere, *d* of late W. H. Monckton; three *d.* Joined Royal Navy, 1904; Captain, 1932; Rear-Admiral, 1942; Flag Officer, Ceylon, 1942-43; commanded a Cruiser Squadron, 1943-45; retired, 1945. *Address:* Brewers Wood, Shorne Ridgeway, near Gravesend, Kent. *T:* Shorne 2328.
                                                                [Died 29 *Oct.* 1976.

READ, John Erskine, OC 1967; BA Dalhousie; BA, BCL, Oxon; QC (Nova Scotia); Hon. Fellow, University College, Oxford; Hon. Master of the Bench, Gray's Inn; Judge, International Court of Justice, 1946-58; retired; Lecturer on Constitutional Law, University of Ottawa; Member, Appeals Committee Opium Protocol, since 1963; *b* Halifax, NS, 5 July 1888; *s* of Dr H. H. Read; *m* 1915, Diana Willes, *d* of late Sir Thomas Willes Chitty, 1st Bt, KC; two *s. Educ:* Halifax City Schs; Halifax County Acad.; Dalhousie University; Columbia Univ. New York; University College, Oxford (Rhodes Scholar). Served with Canadian Field Artillery, 1914-18 (despatches, wounded and invalided from service in rank of Captain and acting Major, 1918). Admitted to the Bar of Nova Scotia, 1913; KC 1925; practised law with Harris, Henry, Rogers & Harris, later with Henry, Rogers, Harris & Stewart, until 1920. Lectr, 1914, Prof. of Law, 1920, Dalhousie Law School; Dean of the Dalhousie Law School and George Munro Professor of Law, Dalhousie

University, 1924; Legal Adviser Department of External Affairs, Canada, 1929; member of the Conference of Commissioners on Uniformity of Legislation in Canada, 1924-46. Hon. LLD: Dalhousie; McMaster; Alberta; Hon. DCL: Oxon; Acadia. *Publications:* The Rule of Law on the International Plane; Cases on Canadian Constitutional Law; Documents relating to Dominion and Provincial Constitutions; various articles in law publications. *Recreation:* golf. *Address:* Apartment 117, 71 Guildwood Parkway, West Hill, Ont, Canada M1E 1P2. *Club:* University (Ottawa). [*Died 23 Dec.* 1973.

READ, Prof. Thomas Talmage, MChD; FRCS; FDSRCS; HDD; LRCP; Professor Emeritus of Clinical Dental Surgery and Warden of Dental School and Hospital, University of Leeds (Professor 1931); Consultant, United Leeds Teaching Hospitals and Leeds Regional Hospital Boards; Consulting Oral Surgeon, Leeds Education Committee; *b* 22 Nov. 1893; *s* of Robert Patrick Read and Rachel Read (*née* Macmillan); *m* 1950, Pamela Margaret Robinson; two *s* two *d*. *Educ:* Shawlands Academy; Glasgow High School; Anderson's College; Glasgow Royal Infirmary and University; Glasgow Dental School and Middlesex Hospital. John Burns Gold Medal, Wallace Prize and Dall Prize, and medals in many branches of medicine and dentistry, and in metallurgy. From 1918-31: Res. Surg., Glasgow Royal Infirmary; Res. Surg. Officer, Glasgow Eye Infirmary; Res. MO, Roy. Samaritan Hosp.; Visiting Dental Surgeon, Glasgow Dental Hosp.; Lectr in Special Anatomy, Materia Medica and Bacteriology, Glasgow Dental School; Hon. Sec., Glasgow Odontol Soc. and W Scotland Branch, British Dental Assoc. From 1931: Founder Pres. Leeds Scientific Film Soc.; former Pres. Pathology Club and Leeds sect. British Dental Assoc.; Founder Pres. Oral Surgery Club. During War of 1939-45, Cons. i/c Maxillo-Facial Centre, St James's Hosp., Leeds; MO i/c First Aid Post 21, Leeds and mem. Manpower War Cttee. Member Dental Educ. Advisory Council, Br. Dental Hosps Assoc., United Leeds Hosp. Bd and General Dental Council; Chm. of Advisory Technical Panel, Leeds Regional Hosp. Bd; Pres. Dental Implant Soc.; Vice-Pres. Inst. of Br. Surgical Technicians; Member: BMA; Br. Dental Assoc.; Assoc. of Plastic Surgeons; West Riding Medico-Chirurgical Soc.; Royal Soc. Med. Vice-Dean, Founder Fellow and Mem. Bd of Dental Faculty, Royal Coll. of Surgeons. Former External Examiner, Univs of Manchester, Bristol, Liverpool, Durham and RCS; now External Examiner, Univ. of Glasgow and Queen's Univ. Belfast. Hon. Fell. British Assoc. of Oral Surgeons. Has produced several original films. *Publications:* Dental Operations (Demonstrations of Operative Surgery), 1954; numerous articles in medical and dental journals on various aspects of Maxillo-Facial and Oral Surgery, Oral Bacteriology and Pathology. *Recreation:* golf. *Address:* Fairlands, Foxhill Drive, Leeds 16. *T:* Leeds 52906. *Clubs:* Leeds, Alwoodley Golf (Leeds). [*Died* 12 *Jan.* 1974.

READING, 3rd Marquess of, *cr* 1926; **Michael Alfred Rufus Isaacs**, MBE 1945; MC 1940; Earl of Reading, *cr* 1917; Viscount Erleigh, *cr* 1917; Viscount Reading, *cr* 1916; Baron, *cr* 1914; Member of The Stock Exchange since 1953; *b* 8 March 1916; *o s* of 2nd Marquess of Reading, PC, GCMG, CBE, MC, TD, QC, and Eva Violet, CBE (*d* 1973), *d* of 1st Baron Melchett, PC, FRS; *S* father 1960; *m* 1941, Margot Irene, *yr d* of late Percy Duke, OBE; three *s* one *d*. *Educ:* Eton; Balliol College, Oxford. Served 1939-46, Queen's Bays and Staff (Major). *Heir: s* Viscount Erleigh. *Address:* The Old Prebendal House, Shipton-under-Wychwood, Oxfordshire OX7 6BQ. *T:* Shipton-under-Wychwood 830210; Flat 1, 28/29 Ormonde Gate, SW3. *T:* 01-332 5602. *Club:* City of London. [*Died* 2 *July* 1980.

READING, Eva Marchioness of; (Eva Violet), CBE 1957; JP; Past President National Council of Women (Vice-President, 1953-57; President Oct. 1957-59); *b* 6 Aug. 1895; *e d* of 1st Baron Melchett, PC, FRS; *m* 1914, 2nd Marquess of Reading, PC, GCMG, CBE, MC, TD, QC (*d* 1960); one *s* two *d*. *Educ:* private schools. Chm. Sun Babies Day Nursery, Hoxton, 1929-39; Mem. General Nursing Council, 1935-37; Chm. Council Nat. Soc. of Day Nurseries, 1939; Advisor to Min. of Health on Child Care, 1940-45; Chm. Violet Melchett Mothercraft Home and Infant Welfare Centre, 1946-68; Member Exec., World Jewish Congress, 1941- (Pres., British Section); Committee of Honour, International Council of Women, 1957. FRSH. Hon. Fellow, Hebrew Univ., Jerusalem, 1971. *Publications:* Little One's Log; In the Beginning; For the Record, 1973. *Recreation:* gardening. *Address:* Flat 8, 30 Cadogan Place, SW1. *T:* 01-235 7755; Cumberland House, Thakeham, W Sussex. *T:* West Chiltington 2103. [*Died* 14 *Aug.* 1973.

READING, Dowager Marchioness of; (Stella), Baroness (Life Peer), *cr* 1958, under title of Baroness Swanborough, GBE 1944 (DBE 1941); CStJ 1939; Chairman and Founder of Women's Royal Voluntary Service (formerly WVS), since 1938; Member: Factory and Welfare Board, 1940; National Savings Central Cttee, 1941-48; Central Housing Advisory Cttee; National Advisory Committee on Employment of older men and women; *b* 6 Jan. 1894; *d* of Charles Charnaud; *m* 1931, 1st Marquis of Reading (*d* 1935); Governor of the BBC, 1946; Vice-Chm., 1947-51; Chm., Personal Service League, 1932-38; Vice-Chm., Imp. Relations Trust, 1936-68; Member: Broadcasting Commission, 1935; Council of the Freedom from Hunger Campaign; Chairman Advisory Council on Commonwealth Immigration, 1962-65; Mem., Council of the University of Sussex. JP Deal and Walmer, 1932-37. Hon. DLit Reading, 1947; Hon. Dr of Laws: Smith Coll., USA, 1956; Yale Univ., USA, 1958; Univ. of Manitoba, Canada, 1960; Hon. LLD Leeds, 1969. American National Achievement Award for Women, 1948; American Red Cross Civilian Service Bar and Silver Medal. Dame of Justice and Grace, Order of St John, 1951. Grand Officer in the Order of Orange Nassau, 1952. *Address:* 16 Lord North Street, SW1; Swanborough Manor, Lewes, Sussex. [*Died* 22 *May* 1971.

READING, Major-General Arnold Hughes Eagleton, CBE 1946; DL; *b* 3 April 1896; *s* of Rev. M. A. Reading, Heilbron, OFS, S Africa; *m* 1933, Phoebe Ruth Elisabeth Powell. *Educ:* Cranleigh School. 2nd Lieut Royal Marines, Aug. 1914; Maj.-Gen. 1946; retired list 1947. DL Somerset, 1955. *Address:* The Stone House, Sellicks Green, Taunton, Som. *T:* Blagdon Hill 280. [*Died* 4 *Jan.* 1975.

READING, Joseph Lewis, CMG 1963; *b* 5 Aug. 1907; *s* of J. W. Reading, New Malden, Surrey; *m* 1934, Dorothy Elaine, *d* of Reginald Fitch, Esher and London Stock Exchange; three *s* one *d*. *Educ:* King's College School, Wimbledon; London University, BSc (Eng.) 1929; ACGI 1929. Entered Civil Service as Consular Cadet in Dept of Overseas Trade, 1932; British Embassy, Washington, 1938-39; Principal, Min. of Economic Warfare, 1939-44; Asst Secretary, Min. of Production, 1944-45; Board of Trade, 1945-64; Director, British Industries' Fair, 1952-55; Establishment Officer (Overseas), 1955-63; Economic Adviser to British High Comr and Senior British Trade Comr in NZ, 1963-67. Sec., Internat. Freight Movement EDC, NEDO, 1970-76. *Recreations:* gardening, fishing. *Address:* Forest Gate, Bourton, Gillingham, Dorset. *T:* Bourton (Dorset) 233. [*Died* 2 *March* 1980.

READMAN, Maj.-Gen. Edgar Platt, CBE 1942 (OBE 1939); TD 1939; RAOC Retd; retired as Managing Director English Steel Corporation Tool Co., Manchester, 1958; *b* 12 Aug. 1893; *s* of Ernest W. Readman, Sheffield; *m* 1919, May, *d* of Marriot Stillwell, Leeds; one *d*. *Educ:* Sheffield Central School. Served European War, 1914-19, with Tank Corps; transferred RAOC, 1923, TA; Lt-Col 1934; Brigadier, 1940; Subs. Major-General, 1944; retired, 1951. Returned to industry, 1945. *Address:* Cedarcroft, Blackford Hill, Henley-in-Arden, Warwickshire. [*Died* 18 *April* 1980.

REAVELL, (James) Arthur, MSc, MIMechE, MIChemE, FInstF, FIM; centenarian; retired from business, 1963, as President (late Chairman, Founder) of Kestner Evaporator and Engineering Co., Ltd; *b* 10 June 1872; *s* of George and Martha Rose Reavell; *m* 1898, Emma Mabel Clowes (*decd*); two *s* one *d* (and one *s* decd); *m* 1941, Winifred Ethel Haydon. *Educ:* Alnwick Gram. Sch.; Silcoates Coll., Wakefield. Engineering experience in England and USA; Gen. Manager of Blake Knowles Pump Works, Ltd, and Wheeler Condenser and Engineering Co.; for many years member of Council of Society of Chemical Industry, a founder of Chemical Engineering Group and Chairman 1920-24, also 1932-33; a founder of Institution of Chemical Engineers, President 1929-31; an original member of Chemical Plant Manufacturers' Association, Chairman 1927-30; President of Combustion Appliance Makers' Association, 1937-39; Vice-President British Coal Utilisation Research Association, 1939; FCS; Member of Executive of National Physical Laboratory, 1931-36; Chairman of Chemical Engineering Industry Section of British Standards Institution since its inception in 1931-52. Hon. MSc Witwatersrand Univ., 1964. *Publications:* Many technical papers in transactions of Institution of Chemical Engineers, of Society Chemical Industry, Chemical Engineering Group, and other technical bodies. *Recreations:* gardening, fishing and shooting. *Address:* Pollards, Four Elms, near Edenbridge, Kent. *T:* Four Elms 218. [*Died* 26 *Aug.* 1973.

REAY, George Adam, CBE 1958 (OBE 1949); Director, Torry Research Station, Department of Scientific and Industrial Research, 1958-64; retd; *b* 31 May 1901; *er s* of Adam Reay and Helen Glass Cownie, Aberdeen; *m* 1928, Tina Mary Margaret, *d* of Sinclair Pottinger Shewan and Ann Law, Fetlar, Shetland;

one s one d. *Educ:* Robert Gordon's College, Aberdeen; University of Aberdeen; Emmanuel College, Cambridge. MA, BSc (Aberdeen), 1921, 1923; PhD (Cantab) 1927; FRIC 1948; FRSE 1955; Senior Kilgour Schol., Aberdeen; Carnegie Research Fellow, Cambridge. Research Officer of Food Investigation Organisation, of DSIR, 1927-57; at Torry Research Station, 1929-64; Officer in Charge, 1937, Superintendent, 1946. Hon. Research Lecturer in Fish Technology at Aberdeen Univ., 1946-64; Chairman, FAO Liaison Cttee on Fishery Products Technology, 1950-64; Mem., Food Science Cttee of Roy. Coll. of Science and Technology, Glasgow, 1957-64; Mem., FAO Panel of Fisheries Experts, 1962-; Mem., White Fish Authority Research and Development Policy Committee, 1962-64. *Publications:* scientific and technical papers, reviews, reports, etc, concerning handling, processing, transport and preservation for food, of fish, from catching to consumption. *Recreations:* music, fishing, walking. *Address:* 27 Salisbury Terrace, Aberdeen. *T:* Aberdeen 20842.
[Died 20 Jan. 1971.

RECKNELL, George Hugh; retired as Actuary and Manager, and Director National Mutual Life Assurance Society, 1956; *b* 17 Oct. 1893; *s* of George Samuel Recknell; *m* 1st, Eileen Mary (*d* 1961), *y d* of late Dr Walter Paterson; 2nd, 1962, Jean Addison, lately Matron, Guy's Hosp. *Educ:* Christ's Hosp. Fellow of the Faculty of Actuaries, 1915 (Vice-Pres., 1950-53); Lt 12th Cameronians attached Royal Engineers Signals Service, France, 1916; Palestine and Syria, 1917-19; Fellow Institute of Actuaries, 1923 (Vice-Pres. 1941-45); Chm. for many years of Harrow Nat. Savings Cttee; Governor of Guy's Hosp., 1954-63; Investment Adviser to BOAC and BEA Jt Pension Fund, 1955-67; Chm. First Irish Investments Ltd. Director City General Insurance Co. Ltd, 1958-65. *Publications:* Contributions on Actuarial and Financial subjects in various jls; A History of King Street and Cheapside; A History of the Actuaries Club; Steyning: History and Descriptive Survey. *Recreations:* reading and showing my house to visitors. *Address:* Chantry Green House, Steyning, West Sussex. *T:* Steyning 2239. *Clubs:* Actuaries; West Sussex Golf. *[Died 7 July 1975.*

REDDICK, Ven. Percy George, MA Oxon; Archdeacon of Bristol, 1950-67; Canon Residentiary, Bristol Cathedral, 1955-62; Hon. Canon, 1962-67, now Emeritus; *b* 9 November 1896; *s* of Henry Reddick and Elisabeth (*née* Powell); *m* 1st, 1922, Edith Annie Cropper, one *d*; 2nd, 1944, Elsie Maud Thomas. *Educ:* St Edmund Hall and Wycliffe Hall, Oxford. Served European War, King's Royal Rifles, 1915-17 (General Service and Victory Medal); invalided. Oxford, 1919-23. Curate: St Michael's, Southfields, 1923-25; Holy Trinity, Sydenham, 1925-30; Vicar: St Saviour, Herne Hill, 1930-40; Downend, 1940-43; Diocesan Secretary, Bristol, 1943-50; Chaplain to Bishop of Bristol and Diocesan Chaplain, 1943-50; Hon. Canon Bristol Cathedral, 1946-50; Examining Chaplain to Bishop of Bristol. *Recreation:* woodwork. *Address:* Cowlin House, 26 Pembroke Road, Bristol BS8 3BB. *[Died 17 March 1978.*

REDDISH, Sir Halford (Walter Lupton), Kt 1958; FCA; Chairman and Chief Executive, The Rugby Portland Cement Co. Ltd and subsidiary companies, 1933-76; Director: Granada Group Ltd; Meldrum Investment Trust Ltd; Warburg Investment Management Ltd; Underwriting Member of Lloyd's; Patron, Rugby Conservative Association; Member of Council, Imp. Soc. of Knights Bachelor; Freeman of the City of London in the Livery of the Pattenmakers; *b* 15 Aug. 1898; *s* of Henry Lupton Reddish; *m* Valerie (*d* 1971), *e d* of Arthur Grosart Lehman Smith, MRCS, LRCP. *Educ:* Rugby School. Served European War, 1914-18. Gold Medallist and Inst. Prizeman, Inst. Chartered Accountants, 1920. Hon. FRCP, 1977. *Recreations:* business, chess. *Address:* Welton House, near Daventry, Northants. *T:* Daventry 2525; Dorchester Hotel, W1. *T:* 01-629 8888; (office) Rugby. *T:* Rugby 2244. *Club:* Carlton. *[Died 12 Oct. 1978.*

REDMAN, Sir (Herbert) Vere, Kt 1961; CMG 1951; OBE 1943; HM Foreign Service, retired; *b* 14 Oct. 1901; 2nd *s* of Charles D. Redman, Brockley, London; *m* 1925, Madeleine Aline (*d* 1970), *e d* of Colonel François Mathieu, Rouen, France. *Educ:* St Dunstan's College, Catford; University of London. Lecturer in English, Tokyo University of Commerce, 1927-33; Editorial Associate, Japan Advertiser, 1930-35; Associate Editor, Japan Advertiser, 1935-38; Tokyo Correspondent: Daily Mail (London), 1933-39, The Sun, Baltimore, USA, 1935-39; Press Attaché, British Embassy, Tokyo, 1939-41; Director, Far East Div., Ministry of Information, London, 1942-46; Counsellor (Information), British Embassy, Tokyo, Japan, 1946-61; retired from HM Foreign Service, 1962. Officier d'Académie (French), 1938; Order of the Rising Sun 3rd Cl. (Japan), 1964. *Publications:* Japan in Crisis, 1935; The Problem of the Far East,

(with Sobei Mogi), 1936; This Language Learning Business (with H. E. Palmer), 1934. *Recreation:* swimming. *Address:* Le Rocher, Goult, Vaucluse, France. *T:* Goult 46. *Clubs:* Tokyo, American, Josui Kai (Tokyo). *[Died 26 Jan. 1975.*

REDMAN, Roderick Oliver, FRS 1946; MA, PhD; Professor of Astrophysics and Director of the Observatories, Cambridge University, 1947-72, Professor Emeritus, 1972; *b* 17 July 1905; *s* of Roderick George Redman and Elizabeth, *née* Stone; *m* 1935, Annie Kathleen, *d* of J. A. Bancroft, Annapolis Royal, NS, Canada; three *s* one *d. Educ:* Marling School, Stroud; St John's Coll., Cambridge. Asst Astronomer, Dominion Astrophysical Observatory, Victoria, BC, 1928-31; PhD 1929; Asst Director, Solar Physics Observatory, Cambridge, 1931-37; University Lecturer in Astrophysics, 1933-37; Fellow of St John's College, Cambridge, 1932-39, 1947-; Chief Assistant, Radcliffe Observatory, Pretoria, South Africa, 1937-47. President of the Royal Astronomical Society, 1959-61. *Publications:* scientific papers. *Recreations:* music, gardening. *Address:* 29 Gough Way, Cambridge CB3 9LN. *T:* Cambridge 57501.
[Died 6 March 1975.

REDMAN, Sir Vere; see Redman, Sir H. V.

REDWOOD, Sir Thomas Boverton, 2nd Bt, *cr* 1911; TD; *b* 15 October 1906; *s* of late Bernard Boverton Redwood (*d* 1911) and Gladys Dora (*d* 1965), *d* of William J. P. Sherwen, Hensingham, Whitehaven (she *m* 2nd, 1914, Esmond Robinson); *S* grandfather, 1919; *m* 1933, Ruth (from whom he obtained a divorce, 1943), *y d* of late Mrs Creighton; one *s*; *m* 1944, Ursula, *d* of late Rev. H. P. Hale; two *s* one *d* (and one *s* decd). *Educ:* Harrow. *Heir: s* Major Peter Boverton Redwood, KOSB [*b* 1 Dec. 1937; *m* 1964, Gilian, *d* of J. L. Waddington Wood; three *d*]. *Address:* Dolphin Cottage, 37 Kersey Road, Flushing, Falmouth, Cornwall. *[Died 11 April 1974.*

REECE, Francis Bertram, CBE 1958; Metropolitan Magistrate, 1943-61 (Bow St, 1948-61); *b* 1888; *s* of late Rev. Canon J. F. Reece; *m* 1st, 1914, Gladys Catherine (*d* 1939), *d* of late Ephraim Wood, DL, JP, Pabo Hall, Conway; one *d*; 2nd, 1940, Dorothy Alice Macbeth, *widow* of Captain W. A. Low, 19th Hussars, *d* of Dr A. Macbeth Elliot. *Educ:* Rossall; St John's Coll., Cambridge (Classical Exhibitioner). Barrister, Inner Temple, 1914. Contested (C) Aberavon Div. of Glam., 1929. Chairman: Poisons Bd (Home Office), 1946-58; Preventive Detention Adv. Bd. Recorder of Birkenhead, 1935-43. *Address:* Snowdenham Cottage, Bramley, Surrey. *T:* 3145. *Clubs:* Garrick, Carlton, Oxford and Cambridge University; Royal and Ancient (St Andrews); Royal Mid-Surrey Golf.
[Died 4 April 1971.

REED, Sir Alfred Hamish, Kt 1974; CBE 1962 (MBE 1948); author of New Zealand historical and travel works, also publisher and bookseller; *b* England, 30 Dec. 1875; *s* of James William and Elisabeth Reed; *m* 1899, Isabel, *d* of Samuel and Mary E. Fisher. *Educ:* London Board Sch. and NZ State Sch. Arrived in NZ 1887; began as gumdigger; self-taught shorthand writer; Manager, Typewriter Co., Dunedin, 1897; bookseller, 1907; Founder of A. H. & A. W. Reed, 1907; Publisher, 1932; author, 1935. Founded Alfred and Isabel and Marian Reed Trust, 1938. *Publications:* (in NZ unless indicated otherwise): Early Maori Adventures (J. W. Stack, 1835-1919) (ed with a Memoir) 1935; More Maoriland Adventures (ed) 1936; Further Maoriland Adventures (ed) 1938; Marsden of Maoriland, pioneer and peacemaker, 1938; For Boys and Girls: The Blue Book, The Orange Book, The Red Book (all with A. W. Reed), 1945; The Story of New Zealand, 1946 (11th edn, 1965); Farthest East: afoot in Maoriland byways, 1946; Farthest North, 1946; Great Barrier, Isle of Enchantment, 1946; The Story of Otago, 1947; Gumdigger: the story of Kauri gum, 1948; The Story of Canterbury, 1949; (with A. Eccles) John Jones of Otago, 1949; (with A. W. Reed) Farthest West, afloat and afoot, 1950; Everybody's Story of New Zealand, 1950 (new edn, London, 1954); Captain Cook in New Zealand (ed with A. W. Reed), 1951 (new edn NZ, 1969); Coromandel Holiday, 1952; Farthest South, 1953 (also London); The Story of Kauri, 1954 (also London); The Four Corners of New Zealand, 1954 (new edn London 1959); The Story of Early Dunedin, 1956; The Story of Northland, 1957; The Story of Hawke's Bay, 1958; Heroes of Peace and War in Early New Zealand, 1959; Walks in Maoriland Byways, 1959; The Historic Bay of Islands, 1960; From North Cape to Bluff, on foot at 85, 1961; From Cape East to Cape Egmont, on foot at 86, 1961; Marlborough Journey, 1961; The Friendly Road: on foot through Otago, Canterbury, Westland and the Haast, 1964; The Footslogger: Sydney to Melbourne on foot at 89, 1964; The New Story of Kauri, 1966; The Milford Track, 1965; Nelson Pilgrimage, 1966; A. H. Reed—An Autobiography, 1967; (with T. W. Collins) New

Zealand's Forest King: the Kauri, 1967; (ed) With Anthony Trollope in New Zealand, 1969; Ben and Eleanor Farjeon, 1973; Annals of Early Dunedin, chronicles of the Sixties, 1973; The Happy Wanderer, 1974, etc. Also numerous booklets. *Recreations:* walking (see his books; Sydney to Melbourne at 89), climbing Mt Ruapehu at 83, etc; building up Alfred and Isabel Reed book collection for Dunedin Library. *Address:* 153 Glenpark Avenue, Dunedin, New Zealand. *[Died 15 Jan. 1975.*

REED, Sir Carol, Kt 1952; film producer and director; *b* 30 December 1906; *m* 1943, Diana Wynyard (marr. diss., 1947; she *d* 1964); *m* 1948, Penelope Dudley Ward; one *s. Educ:* King's School, Canterbury. First appearance on the stage Dec. 1924 at Empire Theatre, Leicester Square; acted small parts until joined Edgar Wallace as actor and stage-director in 1927; left theatre and went into Film Production, 1930. Has directed Midshipman Easy, Laburnum Grove, A Girl in the News, Bank Holiday, Penny Paradise, Who's Your Lady Friend, Talk of the Devil, Climbing High, A Girl Must Live, The Stars Look Down, Night Train to Munich, Kipps, The Young Mr Pitt, The Way Ahead, A Letter from Home, The New Lot, (British Acad. Award for Best Picture of the Year for following 3 films) Odd Man Out, The Fallen Idol, The Third Man, An Outcast of the Islands, The Man Between, A Kid for Two Farthings, Trapeze, The Key, Our Man in Havana, The Running Man, The Agony and The Ecstasy, Oliver! (Acad. of Motion Picture Arts and Sciences Award for Best Film of the Year), The Indian, Follow Me! Joined Army in 1941; directed film for SHAEF, Anglo-American Picture of the War from "D" Day to "VE" Day, entitled The True Glory. Golden Thistle Award, 1967. *Address:* 213 Kings Road, Chelsea, SW3.   *[Died 25 April 1976.*

REED, Douglas; writer; *b* London, 11 March 1895. Relatively unschooled. At 13 publisher's office-boy, at 19 bank clerk; infantry and air force war service, 1914-18 (wounded twice, despatches); newspaper clerk, 1921; sub-editor The Times, 1924; Assistant Berlin Correspondent of The Times, 1929-35; The Times Central European Correspondent, 1935-38; subsequently independent writer; War Correspondent, Normandy, 1944; Foreign Editor, Kemsley Newspapers, 1945; travelling in Africa, US and Canada, 1947-74. *Publications:* The Burning of The Reichstag, 1934; Insanity Fair, 1938; Disgrace Abounding, 1939; A Prophet at Home, 1941; All Our Tomorrows, 1942; Lest We Regret, 1943; From Smoke to Smother, 1948; Somewhere South of Suez, 1950; Far and Wide, 1951; The Battle for Rhodesia, 1966; *novels:* Galanty Show, 1947; Reasons of Health, 1949; Rule of Three, 1950. *Address:* c/o Jonathan Cape Ltd, 30 Bedford Square, WC1.   *[Died 26 Aug. 1976.*

REED, Maurice Ernest, CBE 1951 (MBE 1948); The Deputy Master in Lunacy, The Court of Protection, 1950-71; *b* 27 Feb. 1908; *yr s* of late Mr Justice Haythorne Reed, Chief Justice, Nyasaland; *m* 1932, Isabel Sidonie Lincoln-Reed; one *d. Educ:* King's College School, Wimbledon; Emmanuel College, Cambridge. Called to Bar, Gray's Inn, 1932; Legal Assistant, Law Officers Dept, 1935-48; Legal Secretary, 1948-50. *Address:* The White Cottage, Towersey, Oxon. *T:* Thame 229.
                          [Died 21 May 1975.

REES, David Morgan, CBE 1956; CEng; JP; *b* 29 March 1904; *s* of late Rees Rees, JP, Pencoed, Glam.; *m* 1935, Marjorie Griffith; one *s* one *d. Educ:* Llandovery Coll.; Birmingham University. Mining Engineer, qualified Birmingham University. Mining in Wales, 1930-36; Agent, BA Colliery, 1936-46. Area General Manager, East Midlands Division, 1947-52; Chairman South Western Division, National Coal Board, 1952-61. Mem., Council for Wales and Mon., 1953-56. Commander (Brother), Order of St John. JP Newcastle, Ogmore, and Bridgend, Glam. *Address:* Tynewydd, Abergolech, Dyfed. *T:* Talley 443. *Clubs:* Cardiff and County (Cardiff); Royal Porthcawl Golf (Porthcawl).   *[Died 16 May 1980.*

REES, Sir Frederick (Tavinor), Kt 1954; CBE 1950; MC 1917; TD 1938; *b* 24 Feb. 1890; *s* of late I. Rees, Maesteg, Glam. *Educ:* Queen's Coll., Taunton; Univ. of Wales (BSc 1912); St Bartholomew's Hospital, London. MRCS, LRCP, 1914; House Physician, St Bartholomew's Hosp., 1914; served European War, 1914-18, Major RAMC (MC immediate award); Territorial Army, Lieut-Col, 1921; Colonel, AMS (TA), 1932; ADMS 53rd (Welsh) Division, 1932-36; Hon. Colonel Medical Units, 53rd (Welsh) Division, 1938-45. Ministry of Pensions Medical Staff, 1919; Commissioner of Medical Services, Wales Region; Director of Medical Services HQ, 1941; Dep. Director-General, 1942-49; Director-General of Medical Services, Ministry of Pensions, 1949-53. CStJ 1927. *Recreations:* gardening, fishing. *Address:* 30 Gordon Road, Ealing, W5. *T:* 01-997 2435.   *[Died 7 Feb. 1976.*

REES, Goronwy; see Rees, Morgan Goronwy.

REES, Sir Hugh Ellis; see Ellis-Rees.

REES, (Morgan) Goronwy; *b* 29 Nov. 1909; *yr s* of Rev. Richard Jenkyn Rees and Apphia Mary James; *m* 1940, Margaret Ewing Morris; three *s* two *d. Educ:* High School for Boys, Cardiff; New Coll., Oxford. Fellow of All Souls, 1931; Leader Writer, The Manchester Guardian, 1932; Asst Editor, The Spectator, 1936. War of 1939-45: Gunner, 90 Field Regt RA, 1939; commissioned Royal Welch Fusiliers, 1940. Director of a firm of general engineers and coppersmiths, 1946. Estates Bursar, All Souls College, Oxford, 1951. Principal, University College of Wales, Aberystwyth, 1953-57. *Publications:* The Multi-Millionaires: Six Studies in Wealth, 1961; The Rhine, 1967; St Michael: a history of Marks & Spencer, 1969; A Chapter of Accidents, 1972; Brief Encounters, 1974; *novels:* A Summer Flood, 1932; A Bridge to Divide Them, 1937; Where No Wounds Were; *translations:* (with Stephen Spender) Danton's Death, by Georg Büchner, 1939; Conversations with Kafka, 1939, new edn, 1971; *reminiscences:* A Bundle of Sensations, 1960; The Great Slump, 1970; (ed) McVicar By Himself, 1974. *Address:* 16 Queen Anne's Gardens, W4. *T:* 01-995 7495.
                          [Died 12 Dec. 1979.

REES, Thomas Ifor, CMG 1942; Hon. LLD, BA (University of Wales); *b* 16 Feb. 1890; *s* of John Thomas Rees and Elizabeth Davies; *m* 1918, Betty Phillips; one *s* two *d. Educ:* Aberystwyth (County School and University College). Graduated, 1910; passed competitive examination and appointed Vice-Consul in the Consular Service, 1913; appointed to Marseilles same year; Acting Consul-General there, 1914; transferred to Caracas, 1914; acting as Chargé d'Affaires, 1916; Consul at Managua, Nicaragua, 1921; given rank of Chargé d'Affaires *ad interim,* 1922; transferred to Bilbao, Spain, 1925; transferred to Mexico City in 1932, with local rank of Consul-General; transferred with same rank to Havana, 1934; Chargé d'Affaires at Havana, 1934. 1935, and 1936; HM Special Envoy for inauguration of President Gomez, 1936; HM Consul-General, Milan, 1937-38; Mexico City, 1938-43; Special Ambassador for inauguration of President Hertzog, 1947; British Minister to Bolivia, 1944-47, Ambassador, 1947-49. Hon. LLD (Wales), 1950; retired, 1950. *Publications:* In and Around the Valley of Mexico, 1953; Sajama, 1960; Illimani, 1964. *Recreations:* photography and gardening. *Address:* Bronceiro, Bowstreet, Ceredigion, Dyfed SY24 5AD. *T:* 229.   *[Died 11 Feb. 1977.*

REES, Professor William; Emeritus Professor of the History of Wales and Head of Department of History at University College, Cardiff; *b* 14 Dec. 1887; *s* of Daniel and Margaret Rees; *m* 1914, Agnes Price; no *c. Educ:* Brecon County School; Univ. Coll., Cardiff; LSE, University of London. BA Hons (Wales), 1909; MA (Wales), 1914; DScEcon (London), 1920; Hon. DLitt (Wales), 1969; FSA; FRHistS; formerly Vice-Principal and Mem. of Council; formerly Fellow of Univ. of Wales and Prof. of the History of Wales and Head of the Department of History, University College, Cardiff; O'Donnell Lecturer in Celtic Studies, Univ. of Wales, 1957 and Univ. of Oxford, 1959-60; President: Cambrian Archæological Assoc., 1960-61; Cardiff Naturalists' Soc., 1949-50; Member Acad. Bd and Board of Celtic Studies, University of Wales; former Mem. Ancient Monuments Board for Wales; Member of Court and Council: National Museum of Wales; Welsh Folk Museum; Mem. Court, Nat. Library of Wales; Editor S Wales and Monmouth Record Soc.; Mem. various Editorial Boards; former Mem. Exec., Standing Conference of Local History. Chairman Exec., Welsh National Council of UNA, 1945-56. Mem., UNESCO Nat. Co-operating Body for the Social Sciences, 1952-62. KStJ 1963. *Publications:* South Wales and the March, a Social and Agrarian Study, 1924, repr. 1974; The Making of Europe; Historical Map of South Wales and the Border in the Fourteenth Century, 1933; An Historical Atlas of Wales, 1951, reprints; Caerphilly Castle (repr. 1974); The Union of England and Wales; The Order of St John of Jerusalem; The Charters of Newport (Mon), The Duchy of Lancaster Lordships in Wales, 1954; A Breviat of Glamorgan, 1954; Cardiff, A History of the City, 1962, repr. 1969; Survivals of Ancient Celtic Custom in Mediæval England, in, Angles and Britons, 1963; The Black Death in Wales, in, Essays in Mediæval History, 1968; Industry before the Industrial Revolution, 2 vols, 1968; Ancient Petitions relating to Wales, 1975; contributor to Dictionary of National Biography, Encyclopædia Britannica, Encyclopædia Americana, and Chambers's Encyclopædia; numerous papers, cartographical and bibliographical studies. List of published works in Mediæval Lordship of Brecon, Brecknock Museum, Brecon, 1968. *Address:* 2 Park Road, Penarth, S Glam CF6 2BD. *T:* Cardiff 701465.   *[Died 9 Sept. 1978.*

REES-THOMAS, Mrs William; see Darwin, Ruth.

REES-THOMAS, William, CB 1950; MD (London); FRCP (England); DPM (Cantab); Medical Senior Commissioner Board of Control, 1932, retired; *b* Bailea, Senny, Breconshire, S Wales, 15 June 1887; *m* 1st, 1917, Muriel (*decd*), *o d* of Rev. F. Hodgson Jones; one *s* one *d* ; 2nd, 1948, Ruth Darwin, CBE (*d* 1972). *Educ:* County School, Brecon; Cardiff University; Charing Cross Hospital. MB, BS (hons) London, 1909; MD (London), 1910; MRCP 1913; FRCP, 1933; DPM (Cantab), 1914; Alfred Sheen Prize, 1906; Alfred Hughes Memorial Medal, 1907; Llewelyn Prize, 1909; Murchison Scholar (RCP), 1912; Gaskell Prize and Gold Medal, 1913; Certificate Psychiatry Royal Medico Psychological Association; Distinguished Psychiatry RCP; Fellow Royal Society of Medicine; Member BMA and Royal Medico-Psychological Association; late House Physician Charing Cross Hospital; Deputy Superintendent East Sussex Mental Hospital; Medical Superintendent Rampton State Institution; KHP, 1944-47. *Publications:* various. *Recreations:* golf, photography. *Address:* 20 Haleswood, Four Wents, Cobham, Surrey. *T:* Cobham 2240.
[Died 13 April 1978.

REEVES, Rt. Rev. Ambrose; see Reeves, Rt Rev. R. A.

REEVES, James, MA; FRSL; free-lance author, editor and broadcaster since 1952; *b* 1 July 1909; *er s* of Albert John and Ethel Mary Reeves; *m* 1936, Mary (*née* Phillips) (*d* 1966); one *s* two *d. Educ:* Stowe; Cambridge. Schoolmaster and lectr in teachers' training colleges, 1933-52. *Publications:* The Wandering Moon, 1950; The Blackbird in the Lilac, 1952; English Fables and Fairy Stories, 1954; Pigeons and Princesses, 1956; The Critical Sense, 1956; Prefabulous Animiles, 1957; Mulbridge Manor, 1958; Teaching Poetry, 1958; The Idiom of the People, 1958; Exploits of Don Quixote, 1959; The Everlasting Circle, 1960; Collected Poems, 1960; A Short History of English Poetry, 1961; Ragged Robin, 1961, repr. 1972; Fables from Æsop, 1961; (ed) A Golden Land, 1958; (ed) Great English Essays, 1961; (ed) Penguin Book of Georgian Poetry, 1962; Sailor Rumbelow and Britannia, 1962; The Strange Light, 1964; Three Tall Tales, 1964; The Questioning Tiger (poems), 1964; The Pillar-Box Thieves, 1965; Understanding Poetry, 1965; (ed) Cassell Book of English Poetry, 1965; The Road to a Kingdom, 1965; The Secret Shoemakers, 1966; Selected Poems, 1967; The Cold Flame, 1967; (ed jtly) A New Canon of English Poetry, 1967; Rhyming Will, 1967; (ed jtly) Homage to Trumbull Stickney, 1968; The Trojan Horse, 1968; (ed) The Christmas Book, 1968, repr. 1972; (ed) One's None, 1968; Subsong, 1969; Poems, 1969; Commitment to Poetry, 1969; Heroes and Monsters, 1969; The Angel and the Donkey, 1969; Mr Horrox and the Gratch, 1969; (ed) The Poets and Their Critics, Vol. III, 1969; (ed jtly) Selected Poems of Andrew Marvell, 1969; (jtly) Inside Poetry, 1970; (ed) Chaucer: lyric and allegory, 1970; Maeldun the Voyager, 1971; How to Write Poems for Children, 1971; How the Moon Began, 1971; The Path of Gold, 1972; Poems and Paraphrases, 1972; (ed) Complete English Poems of Thomas Gray, 1973; (ed) A Vein of Mockery, 1973; The Voyage of Odysseus, 1973; The Forbidden Forest, 1973; Complete Poems for Children, 1973; The Lion That Flew, 1974; Collected Poems 1929-1974, 1974; Two Greedy Bears, 1974; (ed) Five Late Romantic Poets, 1974; More Prefabulous Animiles, 1975; The Shadow of the Hawk, 1975; The Reputation and Writing of Alexander Pope, 1976; The Springtime Book, 1976; The Ballad, 1976; The Clever Mouse, 1976; Quest and Conquest, 1976; Arcadian Ballads, 1977; The Autumn Book, 1977; The Closed Door, 1978. *Recreations:* music, Venice. *Address:* Flints, Rotten Row, Lewes, East Sussex. *T:* Lewes 2579. *[Died 1 May 1978.*

REEVES, Rt. Rev. (Richard) Ambrose; Assistant Bishop in the Diocese of Chichester, since 1966; *b* 6 Dec. 1899; *m* 1931, Ada Margaret van Ryssen; one *s* two *d* (and one *s* decd). *Educ:* Sidney Sussex Coll., Cambridge. 2nd class Historical Tripos, Part I, 1923, BA (2nd class Moral Science Tripos, Part II), 1924, MA 1943. College of the Resurrection, Mirfield, 1924; Gen. Th. Seminary, New York, 1926. Deacon, 1926; Priest, 1927; Curate of St Albans, Golders Green, 1926-31; Rector of St Margaret, Leven, 1931-35; licensed to officiate in the Diocese of Gibraltar and permission to officiate in the Diocese of London (N and C Eur.), 1935-37; Vicar of St James Haydock, 1937-42; Rector of St Nicholas City and Dio. Liverpool, 1942-49; Canon of Liverpool Cathedral, 1944-49; Proctor in Convocation, Liverpool, 1945-49; Bishop of Johannesburg, 1949-61; Assistant Bishop of London, 1962-66; Priest in Charge of St Michael's, Lewes, 1966-68, Rector, 1968-72. General Secretary, Student Christian Movement of Great Britain and Ireland, 1962-65; Secretary, World Student Christian Federation, Geneva, 1935-37. Sub-Prelate Ven. Order of St John of Jerusalem, 1953; STD,

Theological Seminary, NY, 1954, Pres., Anti-Apartheid Movement, 1970-. Fellow, Ancient Monuments Soc., 1957; Hon. Fellow, Sidney Sussex Coll., Cambridge, 1960. Hon. DLitt Sussex, 1975. *Publications:* Shooting at Sharpeville: the Agony of South Africa, 1960; South Africa-Yesterday and Tomorrow, 1962; Let the facts speak (Christian Action), 1962; Calvary Now, 1965. *Address:* Whitefriars, Church Street, Shoreham-by-Sea, East Sussex BN4 5DQ. *T:* Shoreham 62555.
[Died 23 Dec. 1980.

REID, Baron (Life Peer), *cr* 1948, of Drem; **James Scott Cumberland Reid,** PC 1941; CH 1967; QC 1932; LLD Edinburgh; FRSE; a Lord of Appeal in Ordinary, 1948-74; *b* 1890; *s* of late James Reid, WS, Drem, East Lothian; *m* 1933, Esther May, *d* of late C. B. Nelson and *widow* of G. F. Brierley. *Educ:* Edinburgh Acad.; Jesus Coll., Cambridge. Admitted to Scots Bar, 1914; served European War, 1914-19, 8th Royal Scots and Machine Gun Corps; in practice in Advocate since 1919; MP (U) Stirling and Falkirk Burghs, 1931-35; Hillhead division of Glasgow, 1937-48; Solicitor-General for Scotland, 1936-41; Lord Advocate, 1941-45; Dean of Faculty of Advocates, 1945-48. Chairman, Malaya Constitutional Commission, 1956-57. Hon. Fellow Jesus College, Cambridge. Hon. Bencher, Gray's Inn. Hon. DCL Oxon, 1971. *Address:* Danefold, West Grinstead, Horsham, Sussex; 4 South Square, Gray's Inn, WC1. *Club:* Athenæum. *[Died 29 March 1975.*

REID, Capt. Alec S. C.; see Cunningham-Reid.

REID, Colonel A(ndrew) McKie, MC 1916; TD 1942; FRCS; Hon. Ophthalmic Surgeon United Liverpool Hospitals; late Lecturer in Ophthalmology, University of Liverpool; Lecturer, School of Tropical Medicine, Liverpool; *b* 14 April 1893; *s* of late James Reid and late Janet McKie; *m* 1st, 1927, Clodagh (*d* 1945), *d* of late Major R. Wyman, TD, JP; one *s* one *d* ; 2nd, 1966, Jessie, JP Liverpool 1968, *d* of late Prosper Marsden, MSc. *Educ:* Liverpool (Pres. Guild of Undergraduates, Univ. of Liverpool, 1920); London; Vienna. Served European War, 1914-18 (wounded, MC immediate award), in King's Regiment and Machine Gun Corps, France and Italy, 1915-19; POW 1918. MB, ChB (distinction in Public Health), Liverpool, 1921; House Physician, Liverpool Roy. Infirmary; House Surgeon, London Hosp.; Clin. Asst, Moorfields Eye Hosp.; Dip. Ophth. Med. and Surgery, 1923; FRCS 1925; post-grad. study, Vienna, 1925-26; Cons. Ophth. Surgeon, Liverpool, 1926-39. Commanded Liverpool Univ. OTC, 1932-38. Formed 1st W Gen. Hosp. RAMC, 1939; served: Norway (ADMS), 1940; Africa and India 1942-45; resumed consulting practice, 1946. Member: Univ. Court, 1930, and Faculty of Med., 1945, Univ. of Liverpool; Court of Examiners, RCS, 1949; Examiner, QUB, 1948; Pres.: Section of Ophth., BMA, 1950; N of England Ophth. Soc., 1948; Liverpool Med. Institution, 1958-59; Vice-Pres., Section of Ophth., RSM, 1951-54; Vice-Pres. Ophth. Soc. of UK; Member: Faculty of Ophthalmologists (Treas.), 1954; Med. Advisory Council Regional Bd, 1950-53; Bd of Governors, United Liverpool Hosps, 1956; Governor: Liverpool Blue Coat Hospital, 1952-; Liverpool Coll. of Art; Hon. Treas. Liverpool Cons. Assoc., 1956 (Dep. Chm. 1959); Mem., Liverpool City Council, 1961-71; Chm. Health Cttee, 1962; Vice-Pres., Roy. Liverpool Philharmonic Soc., 1971- (Chm., 1967-71). OStJ 1961. *Publications:* chapters in: Well's Surgery for Nurses, 1938; Manson's Tropical Medicine, 16th edn, 1966; Rob and Smith's Clinical Surgery, 1964; articles in British Jl Ophthal., BMJ, Practitioner. *Recreations:* music, travel, fishing. *Address:* 86 Rodney Street, Liverpool L1 9AR. *T:* 051-709 3030. *Clubs:* Athenæum; Racquet (Liverpool). *[Died 15 Feb. 1973.*

REID, Professor Donald Darnley, MD; DSc; FRCP; Professor of Epidemiology, London School of Hygiene and Tropical Medicine, University of London, since 1959, and Director of Department of Medical Statistics and Epidemiology since 1961; *b* 6 May 1914; *s* of late Donald Reid and Mary Darnley; *m* 1939, Christine Macleod, MA, *d* of late Dr D. J. Macleod, OBE; two *d. Educ:* Royal Academy, Inverness; Universities of Aberdeen and London. House appointments Roy. Northern Infirmary, Inverness, 1937-38; served War of 1939-45, in Med. Branch RAF, first in Bomber Command then in research section, Directorate-Gen. of Med. Services, 1939-46. Lecturer, 1946-50; Reader in Epidemiology and Vital Statistics, London Sch. of Hygiene and Trop. Med., 1956-59. Vis. Assoc. Prof. of Biostatistics, Univ. of California, 1948-49; Milroy Lectr, RCP, 1958; Sydney Watson Smith Lectr, RCPE 1962; Cutter Lectr, Harvard, 1969; John Matheson Shaw Lectr, RCPE, 1975; Marc Daniels Lectr, RCP, 1976. Past Pres., section of Epidemiology and Preventive Med., RSM; (former Chm. Med. sect.) Roy. Stat. Society; Consultant in Epidemiology to RAF; Member: Environmental Med. Res. Policy Cttee, MRC; Public Health Lab. Service Bd, 1974-; consultant panel for WHO on Cardiovascular Diseases. *Publications:* contrib. to medical text books, also journals on epidemiological methods, especially in mental and cardiorespiratory diseases. *Recreations:* photography, music. *Address:* 20 Ormond Crescent, Hampton, Mddx. *T:* 01-979 1050.   [*Died 26 March 1977.*

REID, Sir Douglas Neilson, 2nd Bt, *cr* 1922; JP; farmer; Member Royal Company of Archers (Queen's Body Guard for Scotland); *b* 12 Feb. 1898; *s* of Sir Hugh Reid, 1st Bt, and Marion Maclune (*d* 1913), *y d* of late John Bell, Shipowner, Craigview, Prestwick, Ayrshire; *S* father 1935; *m* 1926, Margaret Brighton Young Maxtone; one *s* one *d*. *Educ:* Loretto; Clare College, Cambridge. Served European War, 1916-18 with HLI and RFC; served as Flying Officer in RAFVR, 1939-41. *Recreations:* shooting, fishing, natural history, etc. *Heir: s* Hugh Reid, *b* 27 Nov. 1933. *Address:* Tullich, Lochcarron, Ross-shire. *T:* Lochcarron 216; Auchterarder House, Perthshire. *T:* 2632. *Clubs:* Royal Scottish Automobile (Glasgow); Shikar.   [*Died 31 Aug. 1971.*

REID, Sir Edward (James), 2nd Bt, *cr* 1897; KBE 1967 (OBE 1946); a Director of the Bank of Scotland, 1967-71; Hon. President, Clan Donnachaidh Society; *b* 20 April 1901, godson of King Edward VII; *er s* of Sir James Reid, 1st Bt, and Hon. Susan Baring (*d* 1961), formerly Maid of Honour to Queen Victoria, *d* of 1st Baron Revelstoke; *S* father, 1923; *m* 1930, Tatiana, *d* of Col Alexander Fenoult, formerly of Russian Imperial Guard; one *s* one *d*. Page of Honour to the King, 1911-17; Scholar, King's College, Cambridge; Browne Medallist, 1920, 1921 and 1922; First Class Pt II Classical Tripos, 1922. Director of Baring Bros & Co. Ltd, 1926-66; Chairman of Provident Mutual Life Assurance Association, 1963-66 (Director 1938-66); Chairman of British and Chinese Corporation Ltd, 1946-66; Member of London Committee of Hongkong and Shanghai Banking Corp., 1946-66; (Director 1941-46 while Head Office was in London); Chairman, Accepting Houses Committee, 1946-66; Chairman Directors, Royal Caledonian Schools, Bushey, 1947-66; Commissioner for Income-Tax, City of London, 1938-66. Governor of Guy's Hosp., 1937-48. Member Executive Cttee Finland Fund, 1939-40. Treasurer of the Infants Hosp., Vincent Square, 1938-46. Chairman, British Banking Committee for German Affairs, 1948-62. President, Institute of Bankers, 1962-64; Hon. Fellow 1967; Pres., Overseas Bankers' Club, 1964-65. A Vice-Pres., Liverpool Sch. Trop. Medicine and Highland Soc. of London; Mem. Council, Scottish Craft Centre, 1966-71. FSA Scot., 1967. Order of the Rising Sun (Second Class), Japan 1964. *Heir: s* Alexander James Reid [*b* 6 December 1932; *m* 1955, Michaela Ann, *yr d* of Olaf Kier, CBE; one *s* three *d*]. *Address:* 16 Buckingham Terrace, Edinburgh EH4 3AD. *Clubs:* Caledonian; Scottish Arts (Edinburgh).   [*Died 23 Feb. 1972.*

REID, Harold Alexander, CIE 1944; retired; *b* 31 Dec. 1891; *s* of Alexander Reid, Rutherglen, Lanarkshire, Scotland; *m* 1922, Ella, *d* of Robert Gray, Bishopbriggs, Glasgow; one *d*. *Educ:* Royal Technical College, Glasgow. Assistant Locomotive Superintendent, South Indian Railway, 1914; Chief Mechanical Engineer, South Indian Railway, 1932-45. *Recreation:* golf. *Address:* 6 Montpellier Court, Lansdown Road, Cheltenham, Glos. *T:* 23655. *Club:* New (Cheltenham). [*Died 25 Oct. 1974.*

REID, Adm. Sir (John) Peter (Lorne), GCB 1961 (KCB 1957; CB 1946); CVO 1953; Vice-Lieutenant, East Lothian, 1964 and since 1967; Vice-Admiral of the United Kingdom and of the Admiralty, 1966-73; *b* 10 Jan. 1903; 2nd *s* of Sir James Reid, 1st Baronet of Ellon, and of Susan, *d* of 1st Baron Revelstoke; *m* 1933, Jean (*d* 1971), *o d* of Sir Henry Dundas, 3rd Bt of Arniston, and of Beatrix, *d* of 12th Earl of Home; one *s* one *d*. *Educ:* Royal Naval Colleges, Osborne and Dartmouth. Lieut 1925; Comdr 1935; Captain 1941; Rear-Adm. 1951; Vice-Adm. 1954; Adm. 1958. Served War of 1939-45 (CB despatches twice); commanded HMS Dido, 1947, HMS Cleopatra, 1948-49; Chief of Staff to the C-in-C Portsmouth, 1951-53. Rear-Adm. (Review) on Staff of C-in-C Portsmouth, 1953; Flag Officer (Air) Mediterranean, and Flag Officer Second in Command, Mediterranean Fleet, 1954-55; Third Sea Lord, and Controller of the Navy, 1956-61, retd, 1961. Rear-Admiral of the United Kingdom and of the Admiralty, 1962-66. President, Royal British Legion, Scotland. DL, East Lothian, 1962; Vice-Convener, E Lothian CC, 1969-. *Address:* Membland, Haddington, East Lothian. *T:* Gifford 207. *Clubs:* Army and Navy, Caledonian.   [*Died 26 Sept. 1973.*

REID, May, CBE 1920; *b* Bombay, 1 May 1882; *e d* of late Edward Jervis Reid. *Educ:* privately; Bedford College. Assistant and Acting County Secretary, London Branch British Red Cross Society, 1914-23; Secretary to Lord Queenborough, 1923-28; Assistant Sec. National Christian Council of India, 1932-41. *Address:* 4 Bywater Street, SW3. *T:* 01-589-3270.
                                    [*Died 22 Feb. 1980.*

REID, Admiral Sir Peter; *see* Reid, Sir J. P. L.

REID, Robert, QC (Scotland) 1961; Sheriff Principal, Glasgow and Strathkelvin, since 1977; *b* 5 Sept. 1922; *s* of late Robert Reid and of Mary Forsyth, Inverness; *m* 1946, Sheila Stuart Fraser (*d* 1951); *m* 1962, Jane (late Lynch or Thomson); one *s*. *Educ:* Inverness Royal Academy; Edinburgh University (BL). Passed Advocate, 1949. Sheriff Principal: Ayr and Bute, 1973-75; South Strathclyde, Dumfries and Galloway, 1975-77. Sen. Counsel to Sec. of State under Private Legislation Procedure (Scotland) Act, 1971-75. Pres., Industrial Tribunals for Scotland, 1965-71. Dir, Royal Lyceum Theatre Co. Ltd, Edinburgh. *Recreations:* poetry, gardening. *Address:* 33 Regent Terrace, Edinburgh. *T:* 031-556 1783. *Clubs:* Edinburgh University Staff (Edinburgh).   [*Died 30 Sept. 1980.*

REITH, 1st Baron, *cr* 1940, of Stonehaven; **John Charles Walsham Reith,** KT 1969; PC 1940; GCVO 1939; GBE 1934; Kt 1927; CB (Mil) 1945; TD 1947; DCL, Oxford, 1935; LLD, Aberdeen, 1933, Manchester, 1933 and Glasgow, 1951; Hon. Fellow, Worcester College, Oxford, 1962; CEng, FICE; Hon. FRIBA; Hon. MRICS; Hon. MTPI; Hon. FIMunE; Hon. FILA; Member, Queen's Body Guard for Scotland, The Royal Co. of Archers; Lord Rector of the University of Glasgow, 1965-68; Lord High Commissioner, General Assembly of Church of Scotland, 1967, 1968; *b* 1889; 5th *s* of Very Reverend George Reith, DD of Aberdeen and Glasgow, and Adah Mary Weston, London; *m* 1921, Muriel Katharine, *y d* of late John Lynch Odhams; one *s* one *d*. *Educ:* Glasgow Acad.; Gresham's Sch., Holt; Royal Tech. Coll., Glasgow; MSc (Lafayette). Served five years' engineering apprenticeship in Glasgow; London, engineer with S. Pearson & Son, Ltd, 1913; to the Front with 5th SR (Cameronians), 1914; Major RE, 1915 (wounded); America, in charge of contracts for munitions for Great Britain, 1916-17; Admiralty, Department of Civil Engineer-in-Chief, 1918; in charge of liquidation of ordnance and engineering contracts for Ministry of Munitions, 1919; General Manager, Wm Beardmore & Co., Ltd, Coatbridge, 1920; first General Manager, BBC, 1922; Managing Director, 1923; Director-General, 1927-38; Chairman, Imperial Airways, 1938-39, and first Chairman of British Overseas Airways Corporation, 1939-40; Minister of Information, 1940; Minister of Transport, 1940; first Minister of Works, 1940-42, leading to Ministry of Works and Planning; Lieutenant-Commander, RNVR, Coastal Forces, 1942; Extra Naval Assistant to 3rd Sea Lord, 1943; Captain, RNVR, Director of Combined Operations Material Dept, Admiralty, 1943-45. 45,000 miles air tour of Commonwealth and Empire, Chairman: Commonwealth Telecom. Conf., 1945; Commonwealth Telecom. Board, 1946-50; New Towns Cttee, 1946; Hemel Hempstead Development Corp., 1947-50; National Film Finance Corp., 1948-50; Colonial Development Corp., 1950-59; State Building Soc., 1960-64; Vice-Chm., British Oxygen Co. Ltd, 1956-66; Dir, Phœnix Assurance Co. Ltd, 1953-68. MP (Nat) Southampton, 1940. *Publications:* Into the Wind, 1949; Wearing Spurs, 1966. *Heir: s* Hon. Christopher John Reith, MA (Agric) [*b* 1928; *m* 1969, Penelope Margaret Ann, *er d* of late H. R. Morris, Beeston, Notts; one *s*. *Educ:* Eton; Worcester Coll., Oxford. Royal Navy, 1946-48]. *Clubs:* Athenæum; New (Edinburgh), Western (Glasgow).
                                    [*Died 16 June 1971.*

REITLINGER, Gerald Roberts, BLitt; Writer on contemporary history and the history of art; Editor and publisher of Drawing and Design, 1927-29; *b* London, 2 March 1900; 3rd *s* of Albert Reitlinger; *m* 1945; one *d*. *Educ:* Westminster School; Christ Church, Oxford. Studied art, Slade School and Westminster School of Art; exhibited paintings at New English Art Club; London Group, British Artists exhibitions; National Society, etc; directed with Professor D. Talbot Rice, Oxford Univ. Expedition to Hira, Iraq, 1931-32; served RA, 1939-41; lectr to HM Forces, 1942-45. *Publications:* A Tower of Skulls, 1932; South of the Clouds, 1939; The Final Solution, 1953 (rev. edn, 1967); The SS, Alibi of a Nation, 1956; The House built on Sand; Conflicts of German policy in Russia, 1939-45, 1960; The Economics of Taste: vol. 1, The Rise and Fall of Picture Prices 1760-1960, 1961; vol. 2, The Rise and Fall of Objets d'Art Prices since 1750, 1963; vol. 3, The Art Market in the 1960s, 1970; book reviews and articles, Daily Telegraph, Observer, Commentary, Connoisseur, Antiques Year Book, Financial Times, New York Times, etc; numerous archæological monographs in Iraq; Ars Islamica, Royal Central Asian Society Journal, The Burlington Magazine, Ars Orientalis, OCS Bulletin, etc. *Address:* Woodgate House, Beckley, Rye, East Sussex. *Club:* Savile.   [*Died 8 March 1978.*

RELTON, Rev. Herbert Maurice, DD; Curate-in-Charge, Sibton, Saxmundham, Suffolk, 1953-58, retired; *b* 15 August 1882; *s* of late Rev. Frederick Relton, FKC, FRHistS; *m* 1911, Grace

Lydia, (d 1965), d of late John Parkhouse, of Mayfield, Pinner, Middlesex. Educ: City of London School; King's Coll., Univ. of London. BD 1907; with Hons, 1910; DD 1916; Deacon, 1907; Priest, 1908; Curate of St John Baptist, Pinner, 1907-10; Lecturer in Dogmatic Theology, King's Coll. for Women, 1911-12; Curate of Christ Church, Brondesbury, 1910-15; S Andrew Undershaft, 1915-17; Vicar of Isleworth, Middlesex, 1917-27; Vicar of All Saints, Ennismore Gardens, 1930-51; Assistant Diocesan Inspector of Church Schools, London Diocese, 1915-19; Lecturer in Dogmatic Theology, KCL, 1918-24; Prof. of Dogmatic Theology, KCL, 1925-48; Hon. Secretary, Board of Studies in Theology, London University, 1923-27; Chairman of the Board, 1934-35; Dean of the Faculty of Theology, 1935; Professor of Biblical and Historical Theology, University of London, 1931-48; Examiner in Theology, Universities of London, Manchester, Durham, etc; Proctor in Convocation for Diocese of London, 1930-36 and for Univ. of London, 1936-50. Fellow of King's College, London, 1922. Publications: A Study in Christology, 1916; The Catholic Conception of the Incarnation, 1924; Some Postulates of a Christian Philosophy, 1925; messages from a Troubled Church to a World in Trouble, 1933; Church and State, 1936; Religion and the State, 1937; Cross and Altar; 1947; Studies in Christian Doctrine, 1960; contributor to King's College Lectures on Immortality; contributor to Psychology and the Church; contributor to Confirmation, vol. i, 1926; editor of and contributor to the New Prayer Book, King's College Lectures, 1927; contributor to Dogma, 1929; numerous articles, reviews, etc, on Theological subjects and the Philosophy of Religion. Recreations: chess, fishing. Address: The Old Vicarage, Bramfield, Halesworth, Suffolk. T: Bramfield 210.   [Died 30 Nov. 1971.

RENDEL, Sir George William, KCMG 1943 (CMG 1932); b 1889; y s of George Wightwick Rendel, Civil Engineer and Professional Civil Lord of the Admiralty; m 1914, Geraldine, OBE 1943 (d 1965), d of Gerald Beresford FitzGerald; two s one d (and one d decd). Educ: Downside; Queen's College, Oxford (Classical scholar, 1st Class, Mod. Hist. 1911). Entered Diplomatic Service, 1913; served in Berlin, Athens, Rome, Lisbon and Madrid; Head of the Eastern Department, Foreign Office, 1930-38; HM Envoy Extraordinary and Minister Plenipotentiary to Bulgaria, 1938-41; British Minister and (later) Ambassador to the Yugoslav Govt in London, 1941-43; Employed in Foreign Office and UK Representative on European Cttee of UNRRA, 1944-47; attended UNRRA Confs, Atlantic City, Montreal, Geneva, etc; UK Representative for Refugee questions on Econ. and Social Council of UN and on various other confs and UN Cttees in London, New York, Geneva, Lausanne, etc, 1945-47; British Ambassador to Belgium, 1947-50 (also Minister to Luxembourg, 1947-49); Chief United Kingdom Delegate on Austrian Treaty Commission in Vienna, 1947, and for negotiation of Treaty of Brussels, 1948; Montreux Straits Conference, 1936; crossed Arabia from the Persian Gulf to Red Sea (with Lady Rendel), visiting Hasa and Riyadh at the invitation of King Ibn Saud, 1937; negotiated agreement with Italy on Red Sea and Middle East, March 1938; visited the Belgian Congo, officially (with Lady Rendel), returning via East Africa, 1948. Retired on pension, 1950. Re-employed by the Foreign Office as Leader of UK Deleg. to Internat. High-frequency Broadcasting Conf., Rapallo, 1950, and as UK Mem. (and Chm.) of Tripartite Commn on German Debts, 1951-53; UK Mem. Commission on Constitutional Development in Singapore, 1953-54; UK Mem. of Saar Referendum Commission, 1955; Special Ambassador to Lima and La Paz for inaugurations of Presidents of Peru and Bolivia, 1956. Re-employed by the Foreign Office in connection with the Anglo-Egyptian Financial Agreement, 1959-64. Chm., Singer & Friedlander Ltd, 1957-68. Publication: The Sword and the Olive; Recollections of Diplomacy and the Foreign Service, 1913-54, 1957. Recreations: travelling, sketching, music. Address: Flat 5, 24 Lennox Gardens, SW1. Club: Travellers'.
                                              [Died 6 May 1979.

RENFREW, Thomas, CBE 1952 (MBE 1943); Chief Inspector of Constabulary for Scotland, 1965-66; b 18 June 1901; s of late Thomas Renfrew, and late Hannah Lennox; m 1928, Agnes Dunbar Allan (decd); three d. Educ: Eastbank Academy, Glasgow; Glasgow University (BL). Joined City of Glasgow Police, 1919; transferred to Lanarkshire Constabulary, 1926; Inspector, 1928; Superintendent, 1938; Chief Constable of Lanarkshire, 1945-58, and of Hamilton, 1949-58; Inspector of Constabulary for Scotland, 1958-65. Address: 4 Hillpark Gardens, Edinburgh 4. T: 031-336 2629.   [Died 17 Jan. 1975.

RENNELL, 2nd Baron, cr 1933, of Rodd, Herefordshire; **Francis James Rennell Rodd**, KBE 1944; CB 1943; JP; MA (Oxon); retired as Director, Morgan, Grenfell & Co., and other public bodies; b 25 Oct. 1895; e s of 1st Baron and Lilias (d 1951), d of J.

A. Guthrie, Craigie, Forfar; S father, 1941; m 1928, Mary Constance Vivian, d of 1st Baron Bicester; four d. Educ: Eton; Balliol Coll., Oxford. Served in RFA in France, 1914-15; Intelligence Officer in Italy, 1916; Staff Officer in Libya, Egypt, Sinai, Palestine, and Syria, 1917-18 (despatches, Italian Order of St Maurice and Lazarus); entered Diplomatic Service, 1919; served in Rome, Sofia, where was Chargé d'Affaires, and Foreign Office; resigned, 1924; Stock Exchange, 1926-28; Bank of England, 1929-32; Manager, Bank for International Settlements, 1930-31. Served 1939-44 (despatches, CB, KBE); Major-General, Civil Affairs Administration in Middle East, E Africa, and Italy. Visiting Fellow, Nuffield Coll., Oxford, 1947-59. Exploration in S Sahara during 1922 and 1927, for which RGS awarded Cuthbert Peake Grant and Founder's Medal, 1929. Mem. Bd, BOAC, 1954-65. President, RGS, 1945-48; Hon. Vice-Pres. and Hon. Mem., RGS; Mem. Council, Brit. School in Rome; Mem. Council, British Association for Advancement of Science; Conservative. DL 1948, Vice-Lieutenant 1957-73, Herefordshire. Hon. LLD (Manchester), 1962. Publications: People of the Veil; General William Eaton; British Military Administration of African Territories, 1940-45; Valley on the March; and articles in periodicals. Recreations: geography and farming. Heir: nephew (John Adrian) Tremayne Rodd [b 28 June 1935; m 1977, Phyllis, d of T. D. Neill; one s]. Address: 23 Great Winchester Street, EC2; The Rodd, near Presteigne, Powys. T: Presteigne 362. Club: Beefsteak.
                                             [Died 14 March 1978.

RENNERT, Guenther, Dr jur; Opera and Theatre Producer; Director, Bavarian State Opera, Munich, since 1967; b 1 April 1911; m 1956, Elisabeth Rennert (née Abegg); one s three d. Educ: Germany. Asst Prod., films, operas and plays, 1933-35; Producer in Frankfurt, 1935-37; Wuppertal, 1937-39; Head Producer: Charlottenburg Opera House, 1942-45, Munich, 1945-46; Dir of Opera and Dir State Opera House, Hamburg, 1946-56; Artistic Counsellor and Head of Production of Glyndebourne Festival Opera, 1959-67. Productions (Opera): Mozart, Wagner, Verdi, Rossini, Britten, Berg, Stravinski; Productions at: Salzburg Festival, 1948-; Edinburgh Festival, 1952-; Glyndebourne Festival, 1959-; New York Metropolitan Opera; Metropolitan National Company; San Francisco; London (Covent Garden); Hamburg; Stuttgart; Milan (Scala), 1954-; Munich (Staatsoper), 1962-. Prodns (Theatre): Shakespeare, O'Neill, Gogol, Schehade, Giraudoux, Brecht, MacLeish, Frisch, Hauptmann; Prodns in: Vienna (Burg Theater); Berlin (Schillertheater); Stuttgart (Staatstheater). Mem., Akademie der Künste, Berlin, 1961-. Brahms-Medaille, Hamburg, 1956; Decoration of Honour for Science and the Arts, Austria, 1970; Federal Republic of Germany, 1972; Bavaria, 1973. Publications: Bearbeitungen der Opern: Iphigenia in Aulis (Gluck), 1960; Der Türke in Italien (Rossini); Die Liebesprobe (Rossini), 1962; Jephta (Handel), 1958; Verlobung im Kloster (Prokoviev), 1962; translations of Puccini and Rossini; Opernarbeit, 1974. Address: 8033 Krailling, Schwalbenweg 11a, Germany. Club: Rotary.   [Died 31 July 1978.

RENNY, Brig. George Douglas, CBE 1959; DSO 1945; b 30 Dec. 1908; s of late Lt-Col G. S. Renny and late Mrs E. M. P. Renny; m 1937, Mary Helen Louise (née Wortham); three d. Educ: Cheltenham; RMC Sandhurst. Commissioned in Kings Own Scottish Borderers, 1928; served in India, 1930-37, with Regt and as ADC; Camberley Staff College; Brigade Major with 51st Highland Div. in France, 1940 (despatches); Lt-Colonel Gen. Staff, War Office, 1943; landed in Normandy 6 June, 1944, comdg 1st Bn Kings Own Scottish Borderers (wounded, despatches); comd 5/7 Bn Gordon Highlanders, 51st Highland Div., France and Holland; comd 156 West Scottish Bde (52 Lowland Div.) in operations ending at Bremen, 1945; Chief Secretary in British Military Government Land North Rhine/Westphalia, 1946; Brig.-General Staff, Eastern Command, 1949; student Imperial Defence College, 1952, comd 2nd Inf. Brigade (Suez Canal Zone & UK), 1953-56; Deputy Director Personnel Services, War Office, 1957-59; Group Staff Adviser, The Morgan Crucible Co, 1959-69; Consultant, Robert Lee & Partners, 1970-. Recreations: fishing, sailing, genealogy, reading. Address: Maybury Wood Cottage, The Ridge, Woking, Surrey. Club: Army and Navy.   [Died 21 Feb. 1971.

RENOIR, Jean; Chevalier de la Légion d'Honneur; Croix de Guerre; Commandeur de l'Ordre des Arts et Lettres; Film director, producer and writer, since 1924, and Stage, since 1953; b Paris, 15 Sept. 1894; s of Pierre Auguste Renoir, painter, and Aline (née Charigot); m 1944, Dido Freire; one s (by previous marriage). Educ: Sainte-Croix College, Neuilly; The University, Aix-en-Provence. Served War of 1914-18 (Croix de Guerre), Cavalry Officer and Air Force Pilot. Served one semester as Regents' Professor, University of California, Berkeley, USA, 1960. Subsequently concerned with ceramics, Motion pictures, and stage (directed, Shakespeare's Julius Caesar at Arles, 1954; author and dir, Orvet, French adaptation Clifford Odets Le Grand Couteau). Numerous films including: La Chienne; La Bête Humaine; La Grande Illusion (one of 12 best films of all times, Brussels Fair, 1958); La Règle du Jeu; The Southerner; The River; The Golden Coach; French Can-Can; Elena et Les Hommes; Le Testament du Dr Cordelier; Le Déjeuner sur l'Herbe, Le Caporal Epinglé, 1962; Le petit théâtre de Jean Renoir, 1969. Louis Delluc Prize, 1937; NY Critics award, 1941; Golden Lion awards, 1937, 1946, 1951; Golden Laurel Trophy, 1958; Osella d'oro, Venice, 1968; Grand Prix de l'Académie du Cinéma, 1956; Acad. of Motion Picture Arts and Sciences Special Award for lifetime achievement, 1974. Hon. Dr of Fine Arts, Univ. of California, 1963; Fellow American Acad. of Arts and Sciences, 1964; Sociétaire, Soc. des Auteurs et Compositeurs Dramatiques; Mem., Federazione Internazionale dei Cavalieri del Cinema; Hon. Mem. Royal Acad. of Arts; Hon. Dr RCA 1971. *Publications:* Orvet, 1953; Renoir, My Father, 1962 (Prix Charles Blanc, Académie Française 1963); The Notebooks of Captain Georges, 1966; My Life and My Films, 1974. *Recreation:* Art collector. *Address:* 1273 Leona Drive, Beverly Hills, Calif 90210, USA. [Died 12 Feb. 1979.

RENOUF, Vice-Adm. Edward de Faye, CB 1944; CVO 1931; RN; *b* 1888; *s* of late Edward Binet Renouf, Jersey, CI. *Educ:* HMS Britannia. Joined RN 1903; served European War, 1914-19; Naval Attaché, Buenos Aires, 1930-33; commanded HMS Orion, 1934-36; on Staff of RN War Coll. Greenwich, 1936-38; commanded HMS Sheffield, 1938-40; commanded Cruiser Squadron, 1940-41; retired, 1943. *Address:* Manleys, St Peters, Jersey, CI. [Died 15 Sept. 1972.

RENOUVIN, Pierre; Membre de l'Institut de France, 1946; Grand Croix de la Légion d'honneur; Croix de guerre; Hon. Professor Faculté des Lettres de Paris; Doyen, Faculté des Lettres, 1955-58; *b* 9 Jan. 1893; *s* of Georges Renouvin and Marguerite Dalican; *m* 1918, Marie-Thérèse Gabalda; one *s* two *d. Educ:* Lycée Louis le Grand and Sorbonne, Paris. Agrégé d'histoire et de géographie, 1912; L en droit, 1913. Served European War, 1914-18, as Lt Infantry (twice wounded). On staff, Lycée d'Orléans, 1919-20; Docteur ès Lettres, 1921; Lecturer on History of 1914-18 War, Sorbonne, 1922; Professor of Contemporary History, Sorbonne, 1932-65; Professor: Ecole libre des Sciences politiques, 1938; Institut d'Études politiques, 1944. Dir, Revue historique, 1940. Pres. Fondation nationale des Sciences politiques, 1959-71; President de la Commission de publication des documents diplomatiques français (1932-1939); Vice-Pres.: Commission des Archives diplomatiques; Dr *hc* Univs of Rome, Liège, Padua and Cambridge. Corresp. Member: British Acad., 1952; Acad. nac. de la Historia (Buenos-Aires); Membre associé: Académie royale de Belgique, 1961; Accademia nazionale dei Lincei, 1966. *Publications:* Les Assemblées provinciales de 1787, 1921; Les Formes du gouvernement de Guerre 1914, 1925; La crise européenne et la première guerre mondiale, 1934 (6th edn 1973); La Question d'Extrême-Orient, 1840-1940, 1946; Le XIXe Siècle (I L'Europe des Nationalités et l'éveil de nouveaux mondes; II L'apogée de l'Europe); Les crises du XXe Siècle: la première guerre mondiale; la seconde guerre mondiale (ces volumes forment les tomes V, VI, VII et VIII, de l'Histoire des relations internationales), 1954-58; (jt) Introduction à l'histoire des relations internationales, 1964; L'armistice de Rethondes (Nov. 1918), 1968; articles in Revue d'histoire de la guerre mondiale, Revue historique, etc. *Address:* 2 Boulevard Saint-Germain, Paris 5, France. *T:* 326 77.07. [Died 8 Dec. 1974.

RENSHAW, Sir (Charles) Stephen (Bine), 2nd Bt, *cr* 1902; *b* 9 Dec. 1883; *s* of 1st Bt and Mary Home (*d* 1937), *d* of A. F. Stoddard, Broadfield, Renfrewshire; *S* father, 1918; *m* 1st, 1911, Edith Mary (marr. diss. 1939), 4th *d* of late Rear-Adm. Sir Edward Chichester, 9th Bt of Youlston, Devonshire; one *s* two *d*; 2nd, 1939, Mace Caroline, *d* of late Major and Mrs Wynn-Tetley. *Heir: s* Charles Maurice Bine Renshaw [*b* 7 Oct. 1912; *m* Isabel Popkin (marr. diss. 1947); one *s* one *d* (and one *s* decd)]. *Address:* The Old Rectory, Great Fransham, East Dereham, Norfolk. *T:* Wendling 206. [Died 1 Nov. 1976.

RENTON, Brigadier (Hon. Maj.-Gen.) James Malcolm Leslie, CB 1948; DSO 1941; (Bar 1942) OBE 1927 (MBE 1925); JP; DL; *b* 18 March 1898; *s* of late Major Alexander Leslie Renton; unmarried. *Educ:* Eton Coll.; RMC, Sandhurst. 2nd Lt Rifle Brigade, 1916; severely wounded, 1917; DAAG Iraq Levies, 1922-27; commanded 2nd Batt. Rifle Brigade, 1940-41 (DSO); 7th Motor Brigade Group, 1942 (Bar to DSO); 7th Armoured Division, 1942; Senior Officers' School, 1943-44; Head of the British Military Mission to the Iraq Army and Inspector-General, 1944-48; retired 1948. Iraqi Order of the Rafidain, 3rd Class, 1945, 2nd Class, 1948, JP West Sussex, 1949; DL Sussex,

1956; Dep. Comr for Sussex, St John's Ambulance Bde, 1950, Comr, 1952-54. Mem. Brit. Deleg. to Coronation of King Feisal II of Iraq, 1953. Chm. Council, Anglo-Iraqi Soc., 1954-58. KStJ 1961 (CStJ 1951). *Recreations:* travelling and music. *Address:* Rowfold Grange, Billingshurst, Sussex. *T:* Billingshurst 2067. *Club:* Army and Navy. [Died 11 Jan. 1972.

RENWICK, 1st Baron *cr* 1964, of Coombe; **Robert Burnham Renwick,** Bt *cr* 1927; KBE 1946; Partner W. Greenwell & Co., Stockbrokers; Chairman or Director of several companies; Chairman, Institute of Directors; *b* 4 Oct. 1904; *s* of Sir Harry Renwick, 1st Bt, and Frederica Louisa (*d* 1927), *d* of Robert Laing, Stirling; *S* father, 1932; *m* 1st, 1929, Dorothy Mary (marriage dissolved, 1953), *er d* of late Major Harold Parkes, The Dial House, Alveston, Stratford-on-Avon; one *s* three *d*; 2nd, 1953, Mrs John Spencer, *widow* of Major J. O. Spencer, *o d* of late Sir Reginald Clarke, CIE. *Educ:* Eton; Trinity College, Oxford. Controller of Communications, Air Ministry, 1942-45; Controller of Communications Equipment, Min. of Aircraft Production, 1942-45; late Chm. Co. of London Electric Supply Co. and its Group of Companies. *Heir: s* Hon. Harry Andrew Renwick [*b* 10 Oct. 1935; *m* 1965, Sally, *d* of late Capt. K. S. B. Lucking and of Mrs M. P. Stormonth-Darling, Lednathie, Glen Prosen, Angus; two *s*]. *Address:* W. Greenwell & Co., Bow Bells House, Bread Street, EC4M 9EL; Herne's Cottage, Windsor Forest, Berks. *T:* Winkfield Row 2832. *Club:* White's. [Died 30 Aug. 1973.

RENWICK, Sir Eustace Deuchar, 3rd Bt *cr* 1921; Shipowner, retired; *b* 27 Nov. 1902; *s* of Sir John Renwick, 2nd Bt, and Ethel (*d* 1971), *d* of James Deuchar; *S* father, 1946; *m* 1934, Diana Mary, *e d* of Col Bernard Cruddas, DSO; two *s* one *d. Educ:* Uppingham. Served War of 1939-45, RAFVR 1940-45, Sqdn-Ldr 1942 (despatches). *Recreations:* golf, hunting. *Heir: s* Richard Eustace Renwick [*b* 13 Jan. 1938; *m* 1966, Caroline Anne, *er d* of Major Rupert Milburn; two *s*]. *Address:* Whalton, nr Morpeth, Northumberland. *T:* Whalton 215. *Clubs:* Army and Navy; Northern Counties (Newcastle). [Died 3 Nov. 1973.

RESTON, Clifford Arthur; Principal Chief Clerk, Inner London Magistrates Courts, and Clerk to the Committee of Magistrates for Inner London, since 1976; *b* 29 Aug. 1928; *s* of Percival and Ethel May Reston; *m* 1955, Joyce Doreen (*née* Birch); two *s* one *d. Educ:* Liverpool Institute School; King's College, Univ. of London (LLB). Called to the Bar, Middle Temple, 1955. Inland Revenue, 1945-46, 1947-57. Served in RAF, 1946-47. Metropolitan Magistrates Courts (which became Inner London Courts in 1965): Dep. Chief Clerk, 1957-63; Chief Clerk, 1963, serving at North London Court until 1966; Chief Clerk (Training), 1966-70; Chief Clerk, Tower Bridge, 1970-71; Sen. Chief Clerk, Marylebone, 1971-76. *Recreations:* gardening, dog-walking, music. *Address:* c/o Inner London Magistrates Courts, 3rd Floor, NW Wing, Bush House, Aldwych, WC2. *T:* 01-836 9331; Four Winds, Hacketts Lane, Pyrford, Woking, Surrey. *T:* Byfleet 41511. [Died 24 Jan. 1979.

REX, Marcus, CMG 1941; *b* 11 Sept. 1886; *s* of A. B. Rex, Shanghai; *m* 1930, Mary Lilian (*d* 1948), *e d* of Sir Mark Sheldon, KBE; one *d. Educ:* Highgate School; Trinity Coll., Cambridge. Cadet Malayan Civil Service, 1910; Financial Adviser and Treasurer FMS, 1932; Controller of Rubber, Malaya, 1934; Acting Chief Secretary to Government, FMS, 1935; Acting British Resident, Perak, 1936; Financial Secretary FMS, 1937; British Resident, Perak, 1938; retired. *Address:* 31 Rodney Court, W9. *Club:* East India and Sports. [Died 28 Sept. 1971.

REYNARDSON, Lt-Col Henry T. Birch, CMG 1933; *b* 24 Feb. 1892; *s* of late W. J. Birch Reynardson, Adwell House, Tetsworth; *m* 1st, 1917, Diana Helen (*d* 1962), *d* of late Hon. E. Ponsonby; two *s* two *d*; 2nd, 1965, Frances Straker. *Educ:* Eton; Christ Church, Oxford. Entered Army, Oxford and Bucks Light Infantry, 1913; served in India, 1913-14; Mesopotamia, 1914-15; retired on grounds of ill-health as result of wounds 1927; Secretary to Governor-General of Union of South Africa, 1927-33. High Sheriff of Oxfordshire, 1958. *Address:* The Flat, Spread Eagle Hotel, Thame, Oxon. *T:* Thame 3874. *Club:* Army and Navy. [Died 4 Feb. 1972.

REYNOLDS, Alan Lowe, CMG 1957; OBE 1951; retired; *b* 19 Aug. 1897; *m* 1925, Hilda Quinn; two *s. Educ:* Milton School, S Rhodesia. S Rhodesian Govt Service, 1915-57; Magistrate in various places; Secretary for Justice and Defence, S Rhodesia, 1948; Secretary for Justice, Internal Affairs and Housing, S Rhodesia, 1953-57. *Recreations:* fishing, golf. *Address:* 7 Falmouth Road, Alexandra Park, Salisbury, Rhodesia. *Club:* Royal Salisbury Golf (Salisbury, Rhodesia). [Died 8 Jan. 1977.

REYNOLDS, Clyde Albert M.; see Marshall-Reynolds.

REYNOLDS, Paul Kenneth Baillie, CBE 1957 (OBE 1950); TD 1943; President, Royal Archæological Institute, 1963-66; b 28 Feb. 1896; s of late Louis Baillie Reynolds, London Stock Exchange, and late Mrs Baillie Reynolds, novelist; m 1925, Janetta (d 1945), d of Sir Louis Stuart, CIE; two s one d. Educ: Winchester College; Hertford College, Oxford (MA). Lieut RFA (TF), 1915-19; served RA (TA), 1927-39; Major RA, 1939-45. Pelham Student, British School at Rome, 1921-23; Asst Master, Winchester, 1924; Lectr in Ancient History, UCW Aberystwyth, 1924-34; Inspector of Ancient Monuments for England, Ministry of Works, 1934-54; Chief Inspector of Ancient Monuments, Ministry of Works, 1954-61. Has taken part in excavating Roman sites. FSA 1929. Publications: The Vigiles of Imperial Rome, 1926; articles on Ancient History and Excavation Reports in Journals of Hellenic and Roman Studies, Archaeologia Cambrensis, etc. Address: 58 Forest Road, Kew, Surrey. Club: United Oxford & Cambridge University.
[Died 21 Aug. 1973.

REYNOLDS, Richard S(amuel), Jr; Honorary Chairman of the Board, Reynolds Metals Co., USA, since 1977; Honorary Chairman, Robertshaw Controls Co.; Director: Central Fidelity Bank; Lawyers Title Insurance Corporation; former Director: British Aluminium Ltd; Reynolds TI Aluminium Ltd; b Winston-Salem, NC, 27 May 1908; e s of R. S. and Louise Parham Reynolds; m 1933, Virginia Sargeant; one s. Educ: Davidson College; Wharton School of Finance, Univ. of Pennsylvania (BS). Became Mem. New York Stock Exchange, 1930, and with two partners, formed banking firm of Reynolds & Co. which he left, 1938, to join Reynolds Metals Co. as asst to the President. He served as treasurer of Reynolds, 1938-44; Vice-Pres. and Treasurer, 1944-48; President, 1948-63; Chm., 1963-71; Chm. and Pres., 1971-75; Chm. Exec. Cttee, 1976-77. Member: Business Council; Bd of Univ. of Richmond; Trustee Emeritus, Univ. of Pennsylvania. Hon. Mem., Amer. Inst. of Architects. Recreation: fox hunting (formerly master of hounds, Deep Run Hunt Club). Address: Reynolds Metals Company, 6601 West Broad Street, Richmond, Va, USA. T: 281-2148. Clubs: Commonwealth, Country Club of Virginia (Richmond, Va); Farmington Country Club; Brook, Jockey, New York Yacht (New York); Metropolitan (Washington).
[Died 5 Oct. 1980.

RHINE, Prof. Joseph Banks, PhD; Executive Director of Foundation for Research on the Nature of Man, Durham, NC, USA, since 1964; b 29 September 1895; m 1920, Louisa Ella Weckesser; one s three d. Educ: Ohio Northern; Wooster; Univ. of Chicago. Research, Plant Physiology, Boyce Thompson Inst., 1923-24; Instructor, Plant Physiology, Botany Dept, West Virginia Univ., 1924-26; Duke University: Instructor, Philosophy and Psychology, 1928; Asst Prof., Psychol., 1930; Assoc. Prof., Psychol., 1934, Professor, 1937-50. Publications: Extrasensory Perception, 1934; New Frontiers of the Mind, 1937; (co-author) Extrasensory Perception After Sixty Years, 1940; The Reach of the Mind, 1947; New World of the Mind, 1953; (co-author) Parapsychology, Frontier Science of the Mind, 1957; Parapsychology, From Duke to FRNM, 1965; (co-ed) Parapsychology Today, 1968; (ed) Progress in Parapsychology, 1970. Recreations: music, nature, and family life. Address: Box 6847, College Station, Durham, NC 27708, USA.
[Died 20 Feb. 1980.

RHODES, Geoffrey William; MP (Lab and Co-op) East Newcastle since 1964; b 7 Nov. 1928; s of Harold and late Alice May Rhodes, Leeds; m 1954, Marise Evelyn, d of late Prof. H. Victor Wiseman, Exeter; one s one d. Educ: Cockburn High Sch., Leeds; Univ. of Leeds. BA Hons 1952, MA (Local Govt) 1954, Pres. of Union, 1954, Leeds University. Mem., Leeds City Council, 1953-58. Head of Dept of Business Studies, Leigh Technical Coll., Lancs, until election to Parliament. PPS to: Minister of Housing and Local Govt, 1965-66; Leader of House of Commons, 1966-67. Chairman: Parly Labour Party Educ. Cttee, 1966-67; Lab. Party Working Gp on Higher Educn, 1967-73; Mem., Consultative Cttee, Council of Europe, 1967-70. Recreations: philately, cricket, reading. Address: 33 Southlands, High Heaton, Newcastle upon Tyne.
[Died 22 June 1974.

RHODES, Brig.-Gen. Sir Godfrey Dean, Kt, cr 1934; CB 1943; CBE 1919; DSO 1917; late RE; Chief Scout for Kenya; b Victoria, BC, July 1886; s of H. Rhodes, Vancouver, BC; m 1915, M. J. Topping; two s one d. Educ: Trinity College School, Port Hope, Canada; RMC, Kingston, Canada. Commission in RE 1907; Lt 1909; Capt. 1914; Major, 1924; retired, 1926; Adjutant to Railway Construction Troops, France, 1914-15; Commanding Railway Construction Coy Peninsula and Salonika, 1915-16; temp. Major, 1916; temp. Lt-Col 1916, Asst

Director of Railways, Salonika; temp Col 1917, Director of Railways, Salonika; Brig.-Gen. 1919; served European War, 1914-19 (despatches thrice, DSO, CBE, Legion of Honour (Officer), Order of Redeemer (Greek), Order of White Eagle (Serbian), Brevet Major); War of 1939-45; Director of Transportation Persia, Oct. 1941; Brig.; Sept. 1942 DQMG (Mov. and Tn) Paiforce; Regional Port Dir, Calcutta, under Govt of India, 1945 (CB, despatches thrice). Chief Engineer and Special Comr of Works, Govt of Kenya, 1948-51; Formerly: General Manager Kenya and Uganda Rlys and Harbours; Chief Rep. Africa Office, Sir Alex. Gibb and Partners, Consulting Engineers. KStJ. Comr SJAB. Recreations: general. Address: c/o Lloyds Bank, Ltd, 6 Pall Mall, SW1; PO Box 5077, Nairobi, Kenya.
[Died 21 Feb. 1971.

RHYS, Jean, (Mrs Jean Hamer), CBE 1978; writer; b 24 Aug. 1894; d of Dr Rhys Williams, Roseau, Dominica and Mrs Rhys Williams (née Lockhart); m; one d; m 3rd, 1947, Max Hamer. Educ: The Convent, Roseau, Dominica; RADA. Left England, 1919; began to write in Paris, helped and encouraged by friends; subseq. returned to London. FRSL 1966. Publications: The Left Bank, 1927; Quartet, 1928 (as Postures, New York); After Leaving Mr Mackenzie, 1930; Voyage in the Dark, 1934; Good Morning, Midnight, 1939; Wide Sargasso Sea, 1966 (RSL Award, 1966; W. H. Smith Annual Literary Award, 1966; Arts Council Bursary, 1967); Tigers are Better Looking, 1967; Sleep It Off Lady (short stories), 1976; posthumous publication: Smile Please (autobiog.), 1979. Address: 6 Landboat Bungalows, Cheriton Fitzpaine, Crediton, Devon EX17 4HA.
[Died 14 May 1979.

RHYS-ROBERTS, Thomas Esmôr Rhys, GM 1944; QC 1972; b 22 April 1910; o s of Arthur Rhys Roberts and Hannah Elizabeth (Dilys) Jones; m 1939, Barbara Ruth Eccles; one s. Educ: Westminster; Sandhurst. Barrister-at-Law. 2nd Lieut East Lancs Regt, 1930; Lieut 1933; served India, China; Saar Plebiscite Force; resigned 1935; called to Bar, 1938; Wales and Chester Circuit; Captain (TA) Aug. 1939; Major 1942; wounded and decorated, Italy, 1943; Lt-Col 1944. Chm., Medical Appeals Tribunal (Wales), 1952. Recreations: shooting, cruising, photography. Address: Old Factory House, Llanblethian, Cowbridge, South Glam. T: Cowbridge 2522. Club: Cardiff and County (Cardiff).
[Died 6 June 1975.

RICARDO, Sir Harry (Ralph), Kt 1948; FRS 1929; LLD Birmingham, 1943; consulting engineer; Chairman and Technical Director (1919-64; retired), Ricardo and Company Ltd, Consulting Engineers; b London, 26 Jan. 1885; s of Halsey Ralph Ricardo, architect and artist, and C. J. d of Sir Alexander Rendel; m Beatrice Bertha Hale; three d. Educ: Rugby School; Trinity College, Cambridge. Joined the staff of Rendel, Palmer and Tritton, consulting engineers, as mechanical engineer, dealing with locomotives, steam plant, hydraulic and pneumatic equipment 1906-15; designed petrol engines for the Tanks and acted as Consulting Engineer to Mechanical Warfare Dept, 1916; Consulting Engineer to the Air Ministry on aero engines, 1918; engaged on research work into and the design of high-speed internal combustion engines; Pres. Institution of Mechanical Engineers, 1944-45; Hon. Fellow, Trinity Coll., Cambridge, 1968; Hon. DSc, Univ. of Sussex, 1970; Rumford Medal, Royal Soc., 1944; James Watt Medal, IMechE 1953. Publications: The High Speed Internal Combustion Engine, 2 vols, 1st edn 1923, 5th edn 1968; Engines of High Output, 1926; Memories and Machines: the Pattern of my Life, 1968; technical papers. Recreations: sailing and gardening. Address: Woodside, Graffham, nr Petworth, Sussex. T: Graffham 205. Club: Athenæum.
[Died 18 May 1974.

RICE, David Talbot, CBE 1968 (MBE 1942); TD; MA, BSc, DLitt, FSA; Hon. RSA; Watson-Gordon Professor of the History of Fine Art, University of Edinburgh, since 1934; Lieutenant-Colonel TA (retired); b 11 July 1903; s of late Henry Charles Talbot Rice and late Cecil Mary Lloyd; m 1927, Tamara Abelson; one s two d. Educ: Eton; Christ Church, Oxford. Has travelled extensively in the Near East, principally to study Byzantine and Islamic art and archæology; excavated in Constantinople, 1927-32, and 1952-54; various expeditions to Cyprus, Asia Minor, Iraq and Iran; helped with the Persian Exhibition, London, 1931; organised Byzantine Exhibition in Edinburgh and London, 1958. Lectr on Byzantine and Near Eastern art at the Courtauld Institute, London, 1932-38. Member of ITA, 1958-63; Member of Arts Council, 1963-68, and Reviewing Cttee, 1967; Vice Principal, University of Edinburgh, 1968-71. Corresp. Mem. German Archæological Inst. Publications: Byzantine Glazed Pottery, 1930; Byzantine Art, 1935; (with R. Byron) The Birth of Western Painting, 1930; edited Russian Art, 1935; (with Gabriel Millet) Byzantine Painting at Trebizond, 1936; The Icons of Cyprus, 1937; The

Background of Art, 1939; Byzantine Painting, 1948; English Art 871-1100, 1952; Teach Yourself to Study Art, 1955; The Beginnings of Christian Art, 1957; Second Report on Walker Trust excavations, Constantinople, 1958; The Art of Byzantium, 1959; Art of the Byzantine Era, 1963; Islamic Art, 1965; The Church of Hagia Sophia, Trebizond, 1968; (with Tamara Rice) Dating Icons, 1972; numerous articles in periodicals; *posthumous publication:* The Appreciation of Byzantine Art, 1973. *Recreations:* travel, country life. *Address:* 20 Nelson Street, Edinburgh. *T:* 031-556 7100; The Pigeon House, Foss Bridge, Glos. *T:* Fossebridge 230. *Clubs:* United University; Edinburgh Arts.   *[Died 12 March 1972.*

RICE, Wilfred Eric, CBE 1948 (OBE 1942); Chairman and Life Governing Director, Rice & Son Ltd, building contractors; *b* 25 May 1898; *s* of late Sir Frederick Gill Rice, one-time MP for Harwich, Essex; *m* 1923, Vera Lillian Lampard, MBE, 1944, *d* of late W. B. Lampard. *Educ:* Dulwich College. Served European War, 1914-18, Lieut 3rd London Regt (severely wounded). Entered family business of Rice & Son Ltd, 1919. Past President: London Master Builders Assoc., 1942-43; London Rotary Club, 1944-45. Chairman: Hotel and Catering Trades Advisory Cttee (Min. of Labour), 1947-60; Disabled Persons Advisory Cttee, Brixton, 1948-59; Local Employment Cttee, Brixton, 1935-47; West London Road Safety Cttee, 1946-62; Deputy Chm. Westminster Bench, 1957-67. JP London, 1943. Member Conscientious Objectors Tribunal, 1941-44. Master, Worshipful Company of Innholders; Liveryman, Worshipful Company of Paviors. Mayor of the City of Westminster, 1950-51. Comdr Royal Order of Dannebrog (Denmark); Officer of Order of Orange Nassau (Holland), 1950. *Address:* 3 Buckingham Gate, SW1. *T:* 01-834 2831; 10 The Beach, Walmer, Kent. *T:* Deal 5516.   *[Died 14 Sept. 1979.*

RICE-JONES, His Honour Benjamin Rowland, BA, LLB Hons Cambridge; retired as County Court Judge, Circuit No 56 (1952-60); *b* 19 June 1888; *s* of J. E. and E. H. Rice-Jones; *m* 1916, Nancy (*d* 1966), *d* of H. Shelmerdine; one *d.* *Educ:* Temple Grove Sch.; Clifton Coll.; Christ's College, Cambridge. Called to Bar, Inner Temple, 1912 (Certificate of Honour); joined Northern Circuit. Assistant Judge at the Liverpool Court of Passage; Judge, Circuit No. 12, 1945-52. Served in HM Forces, 1914-19, Inns of Court OTC, 2/2 Lancs Battery RGA, TF, 1/1 West Riding Battery RGA TF (wounded at Ypres). *Address:* Kinross, West Hill Lane, Budleigh Salterton, Devon. *T:* 3214.   *[Died 26 Aug. 1978.*

RICE-OXLEY, Douglas George, MC 1918; TD 1924; MB; BS(London); MRCS; LRCP (1909); Surgeon in Ordinary to late Princess Beatrice; *b* 1885; 2nd *s* of late Sir Alfred James Rice-Oxley, CBE, MD; *m* 1916, Estelle Mortimer, *d* of late Mortimer Miller and Mrs Arthur Sidgwick; two *s.* *Educ:* Dulwich College; London Hospital. Lt-Col RAMC, TA; served European War, 1914-19, 56th Div. BEF, 1916-19 (despatches, MC, Allied, Victory and Territorial War Medals); re-employed, 1939-45; Officer i/c Medical Div. 7 General Hospital, BEF, 1939-40 (1939-43 Star); Consulting Physician, Princess Louise Kensington Hospital for Children; Hon. Medical Adviser Coal Owners' Benevolent Assoc.; Ex-Pres. West London Medico-Chirurgical Society; Vice-Pres. Chelsea Clinical Society; Hon. Medical Secretary Royal British Nurses Association; late House Physician, House Surgeon, Resident Anæsthetist, and Senior Clinical Assistant London Hospital; King's Jubilee Medal, 1935; Coronation Medal, 1937. *Publications:* contributions to various medical papers. *Recreations:* gardening, bridge. *Address:* 16 Fonnereau Road, Ipswich. *T:* Ipswich 52354.
                    [Died 30 June 1972.

RICH, Prof. Edwin Ernest, MA; LittD; Vere Harmsworth Professor of Naval and Imperial History, Cambridge, 1951-70; Master of St Catharine's College, Cambridge, 1957-73 (Fellow, 1930-73, now Emeritus); Hon. Fellow: Trumbull College, Yale; Selwyn College, Cambridge; Worcester College, Oxford; *b* 4 August 1904; *s* of George Edwin and Rose Rich, Brislington, Bristol; *m* 1934, Adele (*d* 1975), *d* of Laurence Blades; one *d.* *Educ:* Colston's School, Bristol; Selwyn College, Cambridge. *Publications:* Staple Courts of Bristol, 1931; Ordinances of the Merchants of the Staple, 1935; The Hudson's Bay Company, 1670-1870, 1958-59; Gen. Ed. Hudson's Bay Record Soc., 1937-60; Montreal and the Fur Trade, 1966; The Fur Trade and the Northwest, 1967. *Recreations:* caravanning, golf. *Address:* Stryp Lynch, Heydon, S Cambs.   *[Died 7 July 1979.*

RICH, Maj.-Gen. Henry Hampden, CB 1943; Indian Army, retired; *b* 30 March 1891; *s* of late Col H. H. Rich, RA; *m* 1st, 1925, Joyce Clelie Campbell Elliott (*d* 1968); one *s* one *d*; 2nd, 1969, Margaretta, widow of Lt-Col A. G. Shea. *Educ:* Aldenham School; Royal Military College, Sandhurst. 2nd

Lieutenant 1911; joined 120th Rajputana Infantry, 1912; European War, 1914-18 (Siege of Kut-al-Amara); North-West Frontier of India; Staff College, Camberley, 1924-25; Major, 2/6th Rajputana Rifles, 1926; Instructor Staff College, Quetta, 1931-34; commanded 1st Bn Burma Rifles, DSD Army HQ India, 1937-39; commanded Nowshera Brigade, 1940-41; 14th Indian Div., 1941-42; Assam District, 1942; re-constituted Burma Army, 1943-44; retired, 1944. Maj.-Gen. 1942. Serving Brother, Order of St John of Jerusalem. *Address:* Gosfield Hall, Halstead, Essex CO9 1SF. *T:* Halstead 3683.
                    [Died 24 Aug. 1976.

RICHARDS, Ceri Giraldus, CBE 1960; painter; Member: London Group, 1937; Surrealist Group, 1937; Objective Abstraction Group, Zwemmer's, 1934; *b* Swansea, 6 June 1903; *m* Frances; two *d.* *Educ:* County School, Gowerton, Swansea; Swansea School of Art; Royal College of Art, S Kensington. Oil paintings acquired by the Tate Gallery and Public Galleries in many parts of the world. Exhibits in Marlborough New London Gallery; also in many Galleries abroad; was one of five British artists exhibited at San Paulo II Bienal, 1953-54; exhibited at Venice Biennale, 1962; Meml Retrospective Exhibn, Fischer Fine Art Galls, 1972. A Trustee of the Tate Gallery, 1958-65. *Address:* 12 Edith Grove, Chelsea, SW10. *[Died 9 Nov. 1971.*

RICHARDS, Brig. Collen Edward Melville, CBE 1944; DSO, MC; late East Lancashire Regiment; Commander Gold Coast Regiment, 1939; *m* 1927, Violet Abigail (*d* 1967), *d* of William Briggs, Stoke Bishop, Bristol. Served European War, 1914-18 (wounded, despatches thrice, DSO, MC); Middle East, 1941 (Bar to DSO); retired pay, 1946; BSc (Hons) London. *Address:* Applecot, Budleigh Salterton, S Devon.   *[Died 8 May 1971.*

RICHARDS, Prof. Dickinson Woodruff, MD; Professor of Medicine, Columbia University, New York, 1947-61; Emeritus, 1961; *b* 30 Oct. 1895; *s* of Dickinson W. Richards and Sally Richards (*née* Lambert); *m* 1931, Constance Burrell Riley; four *d.* *Educ:* Yale University (BA); Columbia University (MD). Career in practice and teaching of medicine; medical research, 1925-61. Member: Nat. Acad. of Sciences, 1957; Amer. Acad. of Arts and Sciences, 1968. Hon. Doctor of Science: Yale, 1957; Columbia, 1966. Nobel laureate in medicine and physiology, 1956. Chevalier Legion of Honour (France), 1963. *Publications:* papers on research in cardiac and pulmonary physiology, 1927-70. Ed. and co-author: Circulation of the Blood: Men and Ideas, 1964. *Address:* College of Physicians and Surgeons, 630 West 168th Street, New York, NY 10032, USA. *T:* (New York) 579-3667. *Club:* Century (New York).   *[Died 23 Feb. 1973.*

RICHARDS, Frank Roydon, MA, BMus Oxon; Hon. LLD Glasgow; retired as Rector of Glasgow Academy (1932-59); *b* 16 Jan. 1899; *s* of Frank Herbert Richards and Edith Alice Phillips; *m* 1927, Nancy Warry; one *s* two *d* (and one *s* decd). *Educ:* Christ's Hosp.; Queen's Coll., Oxford (Scholar). 1st Class Classical Mods 1920, 2nd Class Literae Humaniores, 1922; Asst Master Glasgow Acad., 1922-24; Asst Master, Christ's Hosp., 1924-28; Headmaster, Bridlington School, 1928-32; 2nd Lt RGA, France, 1918. *Recreation:* music. *Address:* 21 Learmonth Court, Edinburgh EH4 1PB. *T:* 031-332 2068.
                    [Died 1 Oct. 1978.

RICHARDS, George Edward Fugl, CBE 1949; BA, LLB Cantab; *b* 5 Dec. 1891; *s* of Ernest Adolphus Richards and Lavinia Thomson Fraser. *Educ:* Portsmouth Grammar School; Chicago University; Downing Coll., Cambridge. Private Sec. to Hon. Gideon Murray (later Lord Elibank) and R. Popham Lobb (later Nicholson), successive Administrators of St Vincent, BWI; Barrister-at-Law, Middle Temple, 1922; Acting Magistrate, Grenada, BWI, 1925-27; St Lucia, BWI, 1927-28; Magistrate, Dominica, BWI, 1928-31; Crown Attorney, Dominica, 1931-35; Chief Justice, St Lucia, 1935-40; Senior Puisne Judge of Supreme Court of Windward Is and Leeward Is, BWI, 1940-48; retired, Dec. 1948. *Address:* St Vincent, West Indies.
                    [Died Sept. 1974.

RICHARDS, Maj.-Gen. George Warren, CB 1945; CBE 1944; DSO 1942, Bar, 1943; MC 1918; DL; *b* 4 July 1898; *s* of late John Richards, Llewynderw Hall, Welshpool; *m* 1930, Gwen Laird; two *d.* *Educ:* Oswestry; Sandhurst; commissioned into RW Fus., 1916; attached to MGC, 1917; Tank Corps, 1920. Retired from Army, 1949. DL Monmouthshire, 1965. *Address:* Trewarren, Llandewi Rhydderch, near Abergavenny, Gwent.
                    [Died 23 Feb. 1978.

RICHARDS, Gilbert Stanley Nowell, CBE 1959; DL; Senior Partner, Richards Heynes & Co., since 1962; Member, West Midlands County Council, since 1973 (Chairman, 1978-79); *b* 12

June 1912; *s* of Frank Rupert Granville Richards and Anne Louise Richards; *m* 1940, Evelyn Mary Catherine Hayward; two *s. Educ:* King Henry VIII Sch., Coventry; London Univ. (LLB). Qualified as solicitor, 1935; practising in Coventry, alone, until 1962. Member, Coventry CC, 1950-. DL West Midlands, 1975. *Recreations:* youth work and politics. *Address:* 27 Stivichall Croft, Coventry CV3 6GP. *T:* Coventry 414454. *Club:* Drapers (Coventry). *[Died 27 June* 1980.

RICHARDS, Ivor Armstrong, CH 1964; MA; LittD; University Professor (Emeritus, 1963), Harvard University, Cambridge, Massachusetts, USA (Professor 1944); Fellow of Magdalene College, Cambridge, 1926, Hon. Fellow, 1964; *b* 26 Feb. 1893; *s* of late W. Armstrong Richards, Sandbach, Cheshire; *m* 1926, Dorothy Eleanor, *e d* of John J. Pilley. *Educ:* Clifton; Magdalene College, Cambridge. Class I, Moral Sciences Tripos, Part I, 1915; MA, LittD Cambridge. College Lecturer in English and Moral Sciences, 1922; Visiting Professor Tsing Hua University, Peking, 1929-30; Visiting Lecturer, Harvard University, 1931; Director, The Orthological Institute (Basic English) of China, 1936-38. Hon. LittD Harvard, 1944; Hon. LLD Cambridge, 1977; Hon. DLitt Durham, 1978. Corresponding Fellow of the British Academy, 1959. Loines Poetry Award, 1962; Emerson-Thoreau Medal, Amer. Acad. of Arts and Sciences, 1970; RSA Benjamin Franklin Medal, 1978. *Publications:* Foundations of Aesthetics (with C. K. Ogden and James Wood), 1921; The Meaning of Meaning (with C. K. Ogden), 1923; Principles of Literary Criticism, 1924; Science and Poetry, 1925; Practical Criticism, 1929; Mencius on the Mind, 1931; Coleridge On Imagination, 1934; Interpretation in Teaching, 1938; How to Read a Page, 1942; The Republic of Plato (a simplified version), 1942; Basic English and its Uses, 1943; Speculative Instruments, 1955; Goodbye Earth and other Poems, 1958; The Screens and other Poems, 1960; Tomorrow Morning, Faustus!, 1962; Why So, Socrates?, 1963; So Much Nearer: Essays Toward a World English, 1968; Design for Escape: World Education through Modern Media, 1968; Poetries & Sciences, 1970; Internal Colloquies, 1972; Beyond, 1974; Poetries: their media and ends, 1974; Complementarities, Uncollected Papers (ed J. P. Russo), 1975; New and Selected Poems, 1978. *Recreations:* mountaineering, travel. *Address:* Magdalene College, Cambridge. *Club:* Alpine. *[Died 7 Sept.* 1979.

RICHARDS, Sir Norman (Grantham Lewis), Kt 1977; OBE 1945; QC 1955; **His Honour Judge Norman Richards;** a Circuit Judge (formerly an Official Referee of the Supreme Court), since 1963; *b* 29 Dec. 1905; *s* of L. M. Richards and Gertrude E. Richards; *m* 1930, Helen Nina Colls; one *d. Educ:* Charterhouse; Trinity College, Cambridge. Called to Bar, Inner Temple, 1928, Master of the Bench, 1961. Wales and Chester Circuit. Served War of 1939-45 (despatches twice, OBE). Recorder of Merthyr Tydfil, 1960-63; Dep. Chm., Mddx QS, 1962-65. Pres., HM Council of Circuit Judges, 1973. *Recreations:* golf, cricket. *Address:* 35 Ormonde Gate, Chelsea, SW3. *T:* 01-352 7874. *Clubs:* Brooks's, Portland, MCC. *[Died 29 Dec.* 1977.

RICHARDS, Raymond, MA, FSA, FRHistS; Past Chairman, Ancient Monuments Society; Trustee: Historic Churches Preservation Trust; Historic Cheshire Churches Preservation Trust; Friends of Ancient English Churches; *b* Macclesfield, 19 July 1906; *er s* of late Thomas Edward Richards and Lucy Mary, *d* of late William Kersall Gatley, Gatley, Cheshire; *m* 1940, Monica, *y d* of late John Relf, Liverpool and Brightling, Sussex; two *s.* Chairman: Cheshire Cttee, Nat. Register of Archives (Historical Manuscripts Commission); Southport Repertory Company, in Association with Arts Council of Gt Britain, 1948-51; Past President, Macclesfield and District Field Club. Member: Chester Diocesan Faculties Advisory Committee; Central Council for Care of Churches, 1948-58; Parochial Church Libraries Sub-Cttee, 1950-51; House of Laity, Church Assembly; Patron, Living and Manor of Gawsworth, Cheshire. Mem., Court of Keele University. Hon. MA Liverpool, 1948. *Publications:* Old Cheshire Churches, 1947, rev. edn 1973; St Winifred's Chapel, Holywell, 1948; High Legh Chapels, 1950; The Lesser Chapels of Cheshire, Part 1, 1951; Part 2, 1953; The Manor of Gawsworth, 1955, rev. edn 1974. *Recreation:* yachting. *Address:* Gawsworth Hall, Gawsworth, Cheshire. *T:* North Rode 456. *Clubs:* Athenæum; Athenæum (Liverpool); Royal Mersey Yacht; Dublin University (Dublin). *[Died 17 Aug.* 1978.

RICHARDS, William James, CBE 1971; QPM 1964; Chief Constable of Greater Manchester, 1974-76 (Manchester and Salford, 1968-74); *b* 1915; *m* 1940, Beryl Ferrier, *d* of Henry Cornforth. *Educ:* Lawrence Coll., Birmingham. Dir of Studies, Dept of Law, Police Coll., Ryton-on-Dunsmore, 1958-59; Dep. Chief Constable, Manchester, 1959-66; Chief Constable,

Manchester, 1966-68. OStJ. Hon. MA Manchester, 1977. *Address:* Freshways, 24 Cecil Avenue, Sale, Cheshire. *[Died 23 Oct.* 1978.

RICHARDS, William John, CB 1956; CBE 1952; Director, Staff College for Further Education, 1961-63, retired; *b* 6 July 1903; *s* of late Stephen Richards, Solva, Pembrokeshire; *m* 1929, Nelia, *d* of Albert Porter, Preston, Lancs; one *s* one *d. Educ:* St David's Grammar Sch.; Victoria University, Manchester (BSc Eng.). On Research staff at Royal Aircraft Establishment, Farnborough, 1925-41; Head of Physics and Instruments Dept at RAE, 1937-41; Deputy Director of Scientific Research (Armaments), Ministry of Aircraft Production, 1942-46; Chief Superintendent Telecommunications Research Establishment, Ministry of Supply, Malvern, 1946-53; Director of the Royal Radar Establishment, Ministry of Aviation (formerly Supply), at Malvern, 1953-61. *Recreations:* education, architecture. *Address:* 23 Priory Road, Malvern, Worcs. *T:* Malvern 5304. *[Died 23 May* 1976.

RICHARDSON, Very Rev. Alan, KBE 1973; MA (Liverpool); MA, DD (Oxon); Dean of York since 1964; *b* 17 Oct. 1905; *s* of late William and Annie Richardson; *m* 1933, Phyllis Mary (*née* Parkhouse); no *c. Educ:* Liverpool University; Exeter College, Oxford; Ridley Hall, Cambridge. Intercoll. Secretary, Student Christian Movement, Liverpool University, 1928-31; Curate, St Saviour, Liverpool, 1928-30; Asst Chaplain, Liverpool Cathedral, 1930-31; Chaplain, Ripon Hall, Oxford, 1931-33; Tutor of Jesus Coll., Oxford, 1934; Vicar of Cambo, Northumberland, 1934-38; Study Sec., Student Christian Movement, 1938-43; Sixth Canon of Durham Cathedral, 1943-53; Sub-Dean, 1953; Professor of Christian Theology, University of Nottingham, 1953-64; Hon. Canon, Derby Cathedral, 1953-64. Visiting Professor, Berkeley Div. School, Newhaven, Connecticut, 1949. Examining Chaplain to Bishop of Sheffield, 1939-62, to Archbishop of York, 1948-61, to Bishop of Southwell, 1953-64. Bampton Lecturer, Oxford, 1962. Hon. DD (Glasgow), 1952; DUniv York, 1973. *Publications:* Creeds in the Making, 1935; Miracle Stories of the Gospels, 1941; Preface to Bible Study, 1943; Christian Apologetics, 1947; Science, History and Faith, 1950; (ed) Theological Word Book of the Bible, 1950; Biblical Doctrine of Work, 1952; Genesis I-XI, 1953; Introduction to the Theology of the New Testament, 1958; The Bible in the Age of Science, 1961; History, Sacred and Profane (Bampton Lectures), 1964; Religion in Contemporary Debate, 1966; (ed) A Dictionary of Christian Theology, 1969; The Political Christ, 1973, etc. *Recreations:* piano, fell walking, dogs. *Address:* The Deanery, York. *T:* York 23608. *Club:* Royal Commonwealth Society. *[Died 23 Feb.* 1975.

RICHARDSON, Charles Arthur; Agent General for Province of Nova Scotia in UK and Europe, since 1969; *b* 10 Oct. 1918; *s* of John Richardson, Sydney, Nova Scotia, Canada; *m* 1945, Barbara Vaughan, Newport, Monmouthshire; three *s. Educ:* Sydney Academy, Sydney, NS, Canada. Served in War of 1939-45: European Theatre, with North Nova Scotia Highlanders, Infantry, Canadian Army Third Division. Canadian Banking, 1936-69: Sen. Manager, Maritime Provinces, Toronto-Dominion Bank, Halifax, NS. *Recreations:* golf, swimming. *Address:* Province of Nova Scotia, 60 Trafalgar Square, London WC2. *T:* 01-930 6864. *Clubs:* Royal Automobile (London); Ashburn Golf (Halifax, NS). *[Died 29 Dec.* 1972.

RICHARDSON, Mrs Emily Moore; *see* Hamilton, E. M.

RICHARDSON, Colonel (Hon.) Gerald, CMG 1954; OBE 1947; *b* 27 Feb. 1907; *s* of Frederick William and Gertrude Richardson; *m* 1939, Phyllis Vida Richardson (*née* Browne); no *c. Educ:* West Bridgford High School, Nottingham. Metropolitan Police (Detective Supt), 1927-43; seconded to HM Forces (Army) with rank of Major; special police duties, Sicily and Italy, 1943-45; formerly Inspector-General of Police and Director of Public Safety, British-United States Zone, Free Territory of Trieste and Commissioner of Police (CID), Tangier. Lieut-Col, 1945; Col, 1947. US Medal of Freedom with Bronze Palm. *Recreations:* rowing and swimming. *Address:* c/o Lloyds Bank Ltd, 58 High St, NW10. *[Died 10 Aug.* 1974.

RICHARDSON, Sir Henry; *see* Richardson, Sir J. H. S.

RICHARDSON, Henry Gerald, FBA 1952; lately Secretary, Tithe Redemption Commission. *Educ:* Westminster City School; London School of Economics. MA, BSc. *Publications:* The Early Statutes, 1934; Rotuli Parliamentorum Anglie *hactenus inediti,* 1935; Select Cases of Procedure Without Writ, 1941; Parliaments and Councils of Mediaeval Ireland, 1947; The Irish Parliament in the Middle Ages, 1952; Fleta, 1956; Parliaments and Great Councils of Medieval England, 1961;

The Administration of Ireland (1172-1377), 1963; The Governance of Mediæval England from the Conquest to Magna Carta, 1963; Law and Legislation from Æthelberht to Magna Carta, 1966 (the above with G. O. Sayles); Memoranda Roll 1 John, 1943; The English Jewry under Angevin Kings, 1960; The Coronation in Mediaeval England (Traditio), 1961; Bracton, 1964; (ed) Calendar of the Plea Rolls of the Exchequer of the Jews, vol. IV, 1972; many articles in Brit. and Amer. historical and legal publications. *Address:* The Grange, Goudhurst, Kent. *T:* Goudhurst 415.   *[Died 3 Sept. 1974.*

RICHARDSON, Rt. Rev. John; Assistant Bishop of Andaman and Nicobar Islands (Bishop of Car Nicobar), 1966-77; of Car Nicobarese parentage; *m* 1st, 1913; one *s* two *d* (and two *s* one *d* decd); 2nd, 1942; one *s* two *d* (and one *d* decd). *Educ:* SPG Mission Sch., Mandalay, Upper Burma. Leader of the Nicobarese; teacher and catechist, Car Nicobar, 1912; acted as hon. third class Magistrate, Conservator of Port, 1920-33; Assistant Bishop and Commissary to Bishop and Metropolitan of Calcutta (Bishop of Nicobar Islands), 1950-66. Nominated member of House of Parliament, New Delhi, India, by the President, 1952. Hon. DD, Serampore Coll., 1965. Padma Shri Madel, India, 1965. *Recreations:* formerly: walking, cycling and fishing. *Address:* Mus, Car Nicobar, Port Blair, Andaman and Nicobar Islands.   *[Died 3 June 1978.*

RICHARDSON, Sir (John) Henry (Swain), Kt 1941; Former Director: Yule Catto & Co. Ltd, East India Merchants; The Chartered Bank; *b* 18 June 1889; *o s* of late John Richardson, Ashford, Kent; *m* 1920, Olga, 2nd *d* of George John Stavridi, of Geneva and Calcutta; one *d.* Served European War, 1914-19, in Mesopotamia and India with 5th Buffs and XIth Rajputs; Senior Deputy Chairman, Andrew Yule & Co. Ltd, 1936-41; Vice-Pres. Bengal Chamber of Commerce, 1939, and Pres., 1940; Pres. Associated Chambers of Commerce of India, 1940, Member, Council of State, Govt of India, 1939-41; Member, Legislative Assembly, Govt of India, and Leader, European Group, 1942-45. *Recreation:* music. *Address:* Fairlawn, Hall Place Drive, Queen's Road, Weybridge, Surrey. *Club:* Oriental.
                                    [Died 28 July 1980.

RICHARDSON, Prof. Leopold John Dixon, OBE 1965; MA; Professor (Hon.) of Classical Literature, TCD, 1963; Member, Royal Irish Academy, 1965; retired as Professor of Greek, University College, Cardiff, 1946-58; Research Associate (Hon.) University College, London, 1964-66; Hon. Secretary, Classical Association, 1943-63; *b* 3 Aug. 1893; *o s* of late William Hamilton Irwin Richardson and late Sara Ann Dagg; *m* 1925, Frances Petticrew Patton (*d* 1955); two *d. Educ:* The High School, Dublin; Trinity College, Dublin. Classical Sizarship, Classical Foundn Schol.; Sen. Moderatorship with Gold Medal in Classics and in Mental and Moral Science, and Univ. Studentship in Classics, 1916; Vice-Chancellor's Prizeman, Greek Prose, Greek Verse, Latin Verse; Berkeley, Tyrrell and Vice-Chancellor's Medallist; Ferrar, William Roberts, Hebrew and Sanskrit Prizeman; Fellowship Prizeman, 1929. MA 1920; MA (Wales) 1942. Member of Council: Philological Soc., 1944-50; Roman Soc., 1949-52; Hellenic Soc., 1955-58. Editor: Proc. of Classical Assoc., 1948-63; Studies in Mycenaean Inscriptions and Dialect, 1959-73. Asst to Prof. of Greek, Queen's Univ., Belfast, 1922-23; Dep. Prof., 1923-24; Lectr in Latin, Univ. Coll., Cardiff, 1925-46. *Publications:* Ta Indika, 1929; various articles in English, Irish and foreign learned journals. *Address:* 1 Howell's Crescent, Llandaff, Glam. *T:* Cardiff 561078; 75 Wellington Road, Dublin 4. *T:* 689542. *[Died 19 March 1979.*

RICHARDSON, Linetta de Castelvecchio, MA; Serena Professor of Italian at University of Birmingham, 1921-46; *yr d* of late Francesco and the Comtesse Joséphine Palamidessi de Castelvecchio; *m* 1929, Rev. Canon Robert Douglas Richardson, DD. Bronze medallist of the Regio Conservatorio di St Anna in Pisa. Lecturer and Head of Italian Department at King's College, London, 1916-21. *Publications:* (trans.) Pekin to Paris, 1907; Italian revision of W. W. Vernon's Dante, 1908; annual reports on ecclesiastical affairs for Anglican and Foreign Church Soc., 1908-15. *Address:* Corton Parva, near Warminster, Wilts. *T:* Codford St Mary 286.
                                    [Died 4 June 1975.

RICHARDSON, Maj.-Gen. Roland, CB 1944; MC; *b* 25 March 1896. 2nd Lt Indian Army, 1915; Capt. 1918; Major, 1932; Bt Lt-Col 1935; Lt-Col 1937; Col 1940; Temp. Maj.-Gen. 1943; Maj.-Gen. 1944; psc; retired 1948. *Address:* Chisaro, Cashel, Rhodesia.   *[Died 20 Nov. 1973.*

RICHARDSON, William Rowson, CMG 1948; formerly Under-Secretary, Ministry of Education; *b* 1 Jan. 1892; *s* of George and Maria Richardson, Leeds; *m* 1922, Margaret Hadfield, *d* of late

J. N. Marsden, Lisbon; one *s* (one *d* decd). Chevalier 1st Class Order of St Olaf, 1948. *Address:* Lark Rise, Stonards Brow, Shamley Green, Nr Guildford. *T:* Bramley 2114.
                                    [Died 1 Oct. 1978.

RICHARDSON, Sir William Wigham, 2nd Bt, *cr* 1929; MBE 1919; JP; *b* 12 June 1893; *e s* of Sir Philip Wigham Richardson, 1st Bt; *S* father 1953; *m* 1921, Katharine Elizabeth (*d* 1945), *d* of late Howard John Elphinstone; no *c. Educ:* Rugby School; abroad. Served European War, 1914-19. ADC to Governor and C-in-C, Barbados, 1918-20. JP (Tunbridge Wells); 1940; CC Kent, 1946; CA Kent, 1950. Freeman, Borough of Tunbridge Wells, 1970. *Heir: b* George Wigham Richardson. *Address:* 4 Calverley Park, Tunbridge Wells. *T:* 1819. *Clubs:* Union, Royal Automobile.   *[Died 15 Nov. 1973.*

RICHES, Hon. Lindsay Gordon, CMG 1967; MP, South Australian Parliament, 1933-68, Speaker, 1965-68; Mayor of Port Augusta City, South Australia, since 1936; *b* 18 Feb. 1904; *s* of F. W. Riches, Bordertown, S Austr.; *m* 1933, Evelyn Frances Higginson; one *s* two *d. Educ:* Bordertown Public School. Editor, The Transcontinental Newspaper, Port Augusta, 1928-38; Member S Austr. Parliament: for Newcastle, 1933-38; for Stuart, 1938-68. *Recreations:* football, tennis, swimming, church activities. *Address:* 76 Lake View Crescent, Highbury, SA 5089, Australia.   *[Died 7 June 1972.*

RICHMOND AND GORDON, Hilda Madeleine, Duchess of, DBE, *cr* 1946 (CBE 1919); JP; *e d* of late Henry A. Brassey, Preston Hall, Aylesford; *m* 1893, 8th Duke of Richmond and Gordon (*d* 1935); one *s* two *d.*   *[Died 29 Dec. 1971.*

RICHMOND, Oliffe Legh, MA; *b* 13 Sept. 1881; *s* of late D. C. Richmond, CB; *m* 1st, 1919, Beryl (*d* 1929), *d* of late Very Rev. C. E. T. Griffith; one *s* one *d*; 2nd, 1934, Ursula (*d* 1973), *d* of late Rev. Charles Winser. *Educ:* Fonthill; Eton (Newcastle Medallist and Wilder Divinity Prizeman); King's College, Cambridge. Sir William Browne's Medal for Latin Ode, 1902; Craven Research Student, 1904-6; Fellow of King's College, Cambridge, 1905-15; Classical Lecturer, 1911-14; Professor of Latin in the Univ. College of South Wales and Monmouthshire, 1914-19; served with His Majesty's Forces as Intelligence Officer in War Office and at Italian Headquarters, 1916-19; Professor of Humanity in Edinburgh University, 1919-48. *Publications:* The Temples of Apollo and Divus Augustus on Roman Coins (in Essays and Studies presented to William Ridgeway, 1913); The Augustan Palatium, Journal of Roman Studies, 1914, vol. 2; Propertius 1928; Rawalpindi, and other verses in wartime, 1941; Song of Freedom, and other verses in war-time, 1942; Challenge to Faith, 1945; Thames Symphony, 1947; Two Ancient Love-tales, 1949; The Farther View, 1950. *Address:* 3 Silchester Hall, near Reading, Berks. *T:* Silchester 700269.
                                    [Died 27 May 1977.

RICHTER, Gisela M. A.; Curator Emeritus, Department of Greek and Roman Art, Metropolitan Museum of Art, NY; Curator, 1925-48; *b* London, 1882; *d* of late Jean Paul Richter. *Educ:* Maida Vale High School; Girton College, Cambridge; British School of Archæology, Athens. LittD (Cambridge University and TCD); Hon. LHD (Smith College); Hon. DFA (Rochester Univ.); Hon. DLitt (Oxford Univ.); Hon. PhD (Basle Univ.). Hon. Member of Society for the Promotion of Hellenic Studies; Hon. Fellow Society of Antiquaries, London; Member: Archæological Institute of America (Executive Committee, 1944-46); President New York Soc., 1941-48; German Archæological Inst.; Soc. for the Promotion of Roman Studies; American Philosophical Soc.; Council, L'Association Internationale d'Archéologie Classique; Member: Accademia pontificia archeologica, Rome; Accademia Nazionale dei Lincei, Accademia delle Scienze, etc., Naples; Corr. Fellow British Acad.; Fellowship Awards Cttee Internat. Fedn of Univ. Women; Vis. Cttee to Dumbarton Oaks, 1952-65 and Museum of Fine Arts, Boston; Advisory Cttee, Guggenheim Foundation, 1948-52; Managing Cttee, American School of Classical Studies, Athens; Fellow American Numismatic Society; Fellow, Metropolitan Museum of Art; Hon. Fell., Somerville College, Oxford, Girton College, Cambridge; Associate Editor American Journal of Archæology; Visiting Lecturer, Columbia University; Ryerson Memorial Lecturer at Yale Univ., 1938; Mary Flexner Lecturer at Bryn Mawr Coll., 1941-42; Charles Beebe Martin lecturer at Oberlin College, 1943. Trustee American Friends of Greece. Achievement Award, Amer. Assoc. Univ. Women, 1944; Medal, Amer. Acad., Rome, 1965; Gold Medal, Archaeological Inst. of America, 1968. *Publications:* Catalogue of Greek, Roman, and Etruscan Bronzes, 1915; Catalogue of Engraved Gems of the Classical Style, 1920; Handbook of the Classical Collection of the Metropolitan Museum, 1917, 6th edn 1930; Craft of Athenian Pottery, 1923; Ancient Furniture, 1926;

The Sculpture and Sculptors of the Greeks, 1929, 4th edn 1970; Animals in Greek Sculpture, 1930; Shapes and Names of Athenian Vases (with M. J. Milne), 1935; Red-figured Athenian Vases in the Metropolitan Museum (drawings by Lindsley F. Hall), 1936; Augustan Art (with Christine Alexander), 1939; Handbook of the Etruscan Collection, 1940; Roman Portraits, I and II, 1941; Kouroi (with photographs by Gerard M. Young), 1942, 3rd edn, 1970; Ancient Gems, from Evans and Beatty Collections, 1942; Archaic Attic Gravestones, 1944; Greek Painting, 1944, 2nd edn 1949; Attic Red-Figured Vases, A Survey, 1946, 3rd edn, 1972; Roman Portraits, 1948; Archaic Greek Art against its Historical Background, 1949; Three Critical Periods in Greek Sculpture, 1951; Attic Black-Figured Kylikes (fascicule 2 of Metropolitan Museum of Art, Corpus Vasorum Antiquorum), 1952; Handbook of the Greek Collection of the Metropolitan Museum, 1953; Catalogue of Greek Sculptures in the Metropolitan Museum, 1954; Ancient Italy, 1955; Greek Portraits (Collection Latomus XX), 1955; Catalogue of Engraved Gems in the Metropolitan Museum, 1956; Catalogue of Greek and Roman Antiquities in the Dumbarton Oaks Collection, 1956; A Handbook of Greek Art, 1959, 6th edn 1969; Greek Portraits II (Collection Latomus XXXVI), 1959; Greek Portraits III (Collection Latomus XLVIII), 1960; The Archaic Gravestones of Attica, 1961; Greek Portraits IV (Collection Latomus, 1962); The Portraits of the Greeks (3 vols) 1965, Supplement, 1972; The Furniture of the Greeks, Etruscans, and Romans, 1966; Korai, Archaic Greek Maidens, 1968; The Engraved Gems of the Greeks, Etruscans and Romans: Part I, 1968; Part II, 1971; Perspective in Greek and Roman Art, 1970; Recollections of an Archæologist's life (autobiog.), 1972; The Architectural Sculptures of the Greeks, 1973; articles in archæological jls. *Address:* 81 Viale delle Mura Gianicolensi, Rome. *Clubs:* University Women's (London); English-Speaking Union (New York). *[Died 24 Dec. 1972.*

RICHTER, Hon. Sir Harold, Kt 1971; Minister for Local Government and Conservation, 1963-69; MLA for Somerset, Queensland, 1957-72; *b* 17 Jan. 1906; *s* of F. Richter; *m* 1933, Gladys, *d* of A. James; two *s* two *d. Educ:* Ipswich Gram. Sch., Qld. Minister for Public Works and Local Govt, Qld, 1961-63. Chairman: Boonah Shire Council, 1943-47; Boonah Show Soc., 1944-57. Vice-Pres., 1951-55, Pres., 1956-60, Queensland Div. Australian Country Party. *Recreation:* bowls. *Address:* 20 Wills Street, Coorparoo, Brisbane, Qld 4151, Australia. *Club:* Brisbane. *[Died 19 June 1979.*

RICKARDS, David Ayscough, CBE 1960; MA; Headmaster, Welbeck College, 1953-72; *b* 27 Sept. 1912; *s* of late G. W. Rickards, MP for Skipton, 1933-43, and Katharine Rigby; *m* 1937, Kathleen Louise Cochran; one *d. Educ:* Sedbergh School; Pembroke College, Cambridge (MA). Asst Master, Blundell's Sch., 1934-39; Housemaster, Blundell's School, 1939-40. Served War of 1939-45: commission in Duke of Wellington's Regt, 1940; Staff Captain 3rd Inf. Bde, 1940-41; student at Staff Coll., Camberley, 1942; DAQMG, South Eastern Command, HQ, 1943; DAQMG (Plans), HQ Second Army, 1944; Lt-Col Instructor, Staff College, Camberley, 1945-46. Again Housemaster, Blundell's School, 1946-53. Hon. Major TARO. *Recreations:* Cambridge Blue for cross-country running; Half-Blue for Athletics (3 miles); ocean racing, golf, shooting. *Address:* Thornborough, Grove Hill, St Mawes, Cornwall. *T:* St Mawes 376. *Clubs:* East India, Sports and Public Schools; Royal Ocean Racing; Hawks (Cambridge); Achilles.
[Died 10 April 1973.

RICKARDS, Maj.-Gen. Gerald Arthur, DSO 1918; MC; late RA; *b* 24 Oct. 1886; *s* of late A. G. Rickards, KC, 20 Southwell Gardens, SW7; *m* 1920, Stella Evelyn (*d* 1971), 2nd *d* of late Lt-Col H. G. Ricardo, DSO, Gatcombe, Minchinhampton, Glos; four *d. educ:* Eton; RMA Woolwich. 2nd Lieut RFA, 1906; Lieut 1909; Capt., 1914; Major, 1917; Lt-Col, 1935; Col., 1938; acting Maj.-Gen., 1940; Temp. Maj.-Gen., 1941; served European War (France), 1915-19 (despatches twice, MC, DSO); commanded "A" Indian Field Artillery Brigade at Bangalore, 1935-38; commanded 44th AA Brigade, 1938-40; 12th AA Division, 1940-42; retired (Hon. Maj.-Gen.), 1942; Senior Hon. Branch Visitor, SSAFA, 1944-50. Chm. Tetbury RDC, 1950-60. DL Glos, 1953. Order of Aviz (Portugal) 2nd Class, 1919. *Recreations:* all games and sports. *Address:* Elm House, Fletching, Uckfield, Sussex. *T:* Newick 2332. *Clubs:* Army and Navy, MCC. *[Died 14 July 1972.*

RICKENBACKER, Edward Vernon; retired as Chairman of Board, Eastern Air Lines Inc., USA (1953-63); *b* Columbus, Ohio, 8 Oct. 1890; *s* of Elizabeth and William Rickenbacker; *m* 1922, Adelaide Frost Durant; two *s. Educ:* Studied mechanical engineering and drafting with International Correspondence School. Engaged in automobile racing, 1910-17; served US

Army Air Corps, 1917-19 (officially credited with 26 enemy planes; Croix de Guerre, Legion of Honour, DSC with 9 Oak leaves, Congressional Medal of Honour; Medal of Merit, War of 1939-45). Vice-President Rickenbacker Motor Co., 1921-26 Cadillac Motor Car Company Sales Manager, La Salle Division 1928-29; Vice-President General Aviation Manufacturing Corp. 1929; Vice-President American Airways, 1932; Vice-President North American Aviation Inc. 1933; General Manager Eastern Air Lines, 1935; (President, 1938-53; Chairman of the Board, 1953-63). Many Hon. Degrees from Univs and Colls in USA. *Publications:* Fighting the Flying Circus, 1919; Seven Came Through, 1943; Rickenbacker: an autobiography, 1967. *Address:* 45 Rockefeller Plaza, New York, NY 10020, USA. *T.* LT 1-7576, New York City. *[Died 23 July 1973.*

RIDDELL, Prof. Athol George, MBE 1944; FRCS; Professor of Surgery, University of Bristol, since 1964; *b* 31 Jan. 1917; *s* of John Wood Riddell; *m* 1946, Valerie Constance Wiltshire; two *s. Educ:* Harvey Grammar School, Folkestone; University College Hospital, London. MB, BS, London 1940; FRCS 1948; MS London 1954. Served War of 1939-45: RAF Medical Service, 1940-46 (Squadron Leader). John Marshall Fellow, Univ. of London, 1948-49; Res. Asst Surgeon, University Coll. Hosp. 1950-52; Fellow, Harvard Coll., 1952-54; Reader in Surgery, Univ. of Manchester, 1955-64. *Publications:* Surgery for Portal Hypertension (Taylor, Recent Advances in Surgery), 1960; numerous contribs to surgical jls. *Recreations:* gardening, golf. *Address:* 26 Castle Road, Clevedon, Somerset BS21 7DE. *T.* Clevedon 2568. *[Died 11 May 1974.*

RIDDELL, Victor Horsley, MA, MD; FRCS; Hon. Consulting Surgeon, St George's Hospital, London; *b* 23 July 1905; *e s* of Robert George Riddell, MD, FRCSEd, and Annie Wilson; *m* Jeanne, *d* of J. G. Rueb, late of Java. *Educ:* Clifton; Cambridge; St George's Hospital, London (Allingham Schol. and Brackenbury prize in Surgery). Hunterian Professor, RCS; Consultant Surgical Adviser, Civil Aviation Dept (medical branch), DTI; Examiner in Surgery to Universities of: Cambridge (1952-62), Leeds (1952), Birmingham (1953), and London (1946); President: Chelsea Clinical Society, 1954-55; St George's Hosp. Medical School and Sports Club, 1954-56; St George's Hosp. Hunterian Society, 1956; Representative of RCS on Surgical Mission to USSR, 1957; Leader of British Council Surgical Mission to Near East, Cyprus, Jordan, Irak and Iran, 1960; James IV Assoc. of Surgeons Visitor to India, 1963; guest surgeon, New Delhi and Bankok, 1970. Moynihan Fellow, Assoc. of Surgeons; Treasurer (Great Britain) Internat. Soc. of Surgery, 1950-60; Fellow Assoc. of Surgeons; FRSocMed (Council, 1952); Fellow Med. Soc. London; Fellow Hunterian Soc. *Publications:* on diseases of the thyroid and breast to medical journals and books. *Recreation:* cricket (Cambridge XI, 1926). *Address:* 97 Harley Street, W1. *T:* 01-935 5259. *Clubs.* Athenæum, MCC. *[Died 9 Aug. 1976.*

RIDDELL, William John Brownlow, MD, FRCPGlas, FRSEd, DOMS; Emeritus Professor of Ophthalmology, Glasgow University; Consulting Ophthalmic Surgeon, Western Infirmary, Glasgow, since 1964; *b* 1899; *s* of late Brownlow Riddell, MD; *m* 1932, Anna Ellinor, *y d* of late John Ferguson, Lenzie; one *s* one *d. Educ:* Glasgow Academy; Glasgow Univ.; Royal London Ophthalmic Hospital (Moorfields). Midshipman, RNVR, 1917-19; Lucien Howe Lecturer, Harvard, 1946; Charles H. May Lecturer, New York Academy of Medicine, 1946; President Section of Ophthalmology, Royal Society of Medicine, 1951-53; Pres., Ophthalmological Section, BMA, 1954; Convocation Lecturer, Univ. of Cincinnati, 1961; Vice-President Ophthalmological Soc. of UK, 1951-54; Senate Assessor on University Court, 1955-63; Pres. Scottish Ophthalmological Club, 1961-63; Deputy Master, Oxford Ophthalmological Congress, 1963-65. Vice-Pres., Faculty of Ophthalmologists, 1963-65; Member: General Optical Council, 1963-71; Comité Exécutif, Assoc. Internat. de Prophylaxie de la Cécité, 1963-69. *Publications:* Papers on Ophthalmological subjects and Human Heredity. *Address:* 24 Gladstone Place, Aberdeen AB1 6XA. *Club:* Athenæum. *[Died 18 Feb. 1976.*

RIDDELL-WEBSTER, Gen. Sir Thomas Sheridan, GCB 1946 (KCB 1942; CB 1939); DSO 1915; Vice-Lieutenant of the County of Angus, 1959-67; *b* 12 February 1886; *s* of late John Riddell-Webster and Mrs Riddell-Webster of Priorsgate, St Andrews; *m* 1920, Harriet Hill, *d* of Colonel Sir Alexander Sprot, 1st Baronet; two *s. Educ:* Harrow; RMC, Sandhurst. Entered Army, 1905; Capt. 1913; Major and Brevet Lt-Col 1923; Lt-Col 1930; Colonel, 1933; Major-Gen. 1938; Lt-Gen. 1941; Gen. 1942; served European War, 1914-18 (despatches, DSO, Bt Major); commanded 2nd Bn The Cameronians (Scottish Rifles), 1930-33; AQMG, War Office, 1933-34; Commander Poona (Independent) Brigade Area, 1935-38; ADC to the King, 1936-38; Director of Movements and Quartering, War Office, 1938-39; Deputy Quarter-Master General, 1939-40; General Officer Commanding-in-Chief, Southern India, 1941; Lt-Gen. i/c Administration, Middle East, 1941-42 (despatches); QMG to the Forces, War Office, 1942-46; retd pay, 1946. Col. The Cameronians, 1946-51; DL Angus, 1946-. President British Legion (Scotland), 1949-65. *Address:* Lintrose, Coupar-Angus, Perthshire. *Club:* Army and Navy.   [*Died 25 May* 1974.

RIDE, Sir Lindsay (Tasman), Kt 1962; CBE 1944 (OBE 1942); ED (4 clasps) 1948; MA, DM, BCh Oxon, MRCS, LRCP; JP; Emeritus Professor of Physiology, University of Hong Kong, 1965; *b* 10 Oct. 1898; *s* of Rev. William and Eliza Mary Ride; *m* 1st, 1925, M. M. L. Fenety; two *s* two *d*; 2nd, 1954, V. M. Witchell. *Educ:* Scotch College, Melbourne; Ormond College, Melbourne; New College, Oxford; Guy's Hospital, London. Served Aust. Imp. Forces, 1916-19 (twice wounded). CO Hong Kong Field Amb., 1941; prisoner-of-war, escaped, 1942; Col Comdt Brit. Army Aid Gp, China, 1942-45; Brig., Comdt Roy. Hong Kong Volunteer Defence Corps, 1948-62. Victorian Rhodes Schol., 1922; Sen. Science Schol., Guy's Hosp., 1925; Prof. of Physiology, Univ. of Hong Kong, 1928-52; Dean, Medical Faculty, 1930-32, 1935-39; Vice-Chancellor, 1949-65; Research Associate, Inst. of Social Studies and Humanities, Chinese Univ. of Hong Kong, 1965-67. Foundation Member, Association of Southeast Asian Institutions of Higher Learning, 1957, Vice-Pres. 1963-64; Chm. Assoc. of Univs of Brit. Commonwealth, 1960-61; Vice-Pres., Hong Kong Br. Roy. Asiatic Soc., 1961; Chairman: Music Soc. of Hong Kong; 2nd UNESCO SE Asian Regional Meeting on Scientific Research; Life Mem. Court of Univ. of Hong Kong, 1965-; Mem., Kowloon Riots Commn of Enquiry, 1966. Hon. LLD: Toronto, 1951; Melbourne, 1957; London, 1963; Hong Kong, 1965. Hon. RAM 1962. Hon. Col, HK Regt 1968. *Publications:* Genetics and the Clinician, 1939; Robert Morrison, The Scholar and the Man, 1957; Biographical Note on James Legge, 1961; various articles on human genetics in learned journals. *Recreations:* writing, music. *Address:* 42 Chung Hom Kok Road, Hong Kong. *T:* 5-931412. *Clubs:* Athenæum; Vincent's (Oxford); Leander (Henley); Hong Kong.   [*Died 17 Oct.* 1977.

RIDEAL, Sir Eric (Keightley), Kt 1951; MBE; FRS 1930; FKC 1963; DSc London, MA Cantab; PhD Bonn; FRIC, MRI; Hon. DSc (Dublin, Birmingham, Belfast, Turin, Bonn); DTech, Brunel; Senior Research Fellow, Imperial College of Science and Technology; Fellow: King's College, London; Trinity Hall, Cambridge; *b* 11 April 1890; *s* of late Samuel Rideal; *m* 1921, Margaret (*d* 1964), *d* of late William H. Jackson, of Princeton, New Jersey; one *d*. *Educ:* Oundle Sch.; Trinity Hall, Cambridge (Scholar); Bonn. Gold Medal, Society of Engineers, 1913; visited Ecuador 1913 for Govt on Sanitation of Guyaquil and Quito; Capt. RE European War; Invalided to Munitions Inventions Board from France; research for Dept on Fixation of Atmospheric Nitrogen; Part time lecturer University College, London; Visiting Professor of Physical Chemistry, University of Illinois, USA, 1919-20; Professor of Colloid Science, Cambridge University, 1930-46; Fullerian Professor of Chemistry, the Royal Institution and Director of Davy Faraday Research Laboratory, 1946-49; Professor of Physical Chemistry, King's Coll., Univ. of London, 1950-55; Cantor Lecturer; Past President Faraday Society; Past Pres. Society of Chemical Industry; Past Chm. Chemical Council; Past Pres. Chemical Soc.; For. Mem. Spanish Roy. Soc. Physical Chemistry; Davy Medal of Roy. Soc., 1951; Chm. Advisory Council on Scientific Research and Technical Development, Min. of Supply, 1953-58. *Publications:* Water Supplies; Recent Developments in Catalytic Chemistry, 1921; Colloid Chemistry, 1924; Disinfection and Disinfectants (with S. Rideal); Electrometallurgy; Ozone; Catalysis in Theory and Practice (with H. S. Taylor); An Introduction to Surface Chemistry; Interfacial Phenomena (with L. Davies); Concepts in Catalysis, 1968; contributions to various scientific journals. *Recreation:* gardening. *Address:* 22 Westbourne Park Road, W2. *T:* 01-229 5595; The Spinney, West Runton, Cromer, Norfolk.   [*Died 25 Sept.* 1974.

RIDEHALGH, Arthur; *b* 10 April 1907; 4th *s* of late James and Amelia Ridehalgh, Oaklands, Barrowford, Lancs; *m* 1935, Ellen Dugdale Lonsdale, 2nd *d* of late Joseph and Anne Elizabeth Lonsdale, Higher Causeway, Barrowford, Lancs; one *d*. *Educ:* Terra Nova Prep. Birkdale; Sedbergh; Wadham Coll., Oxford (BA). Barrister-at-Law, Gray's Inn, 1929; joined Northern Circuit, 1929; Crown Attorney and Magistrate, St Kitts, Leeward Islands, 1935; Crown Counsel, Gold Coast, 1939; Solicitor-General, Nigeria, 1946; Attorney-General, Hong Kong, 1952; retired from HM Overseas Service, 1962; KC (Nigeria), 1949; QC (Hong Kong), 1953. *Address:* Lilac Cottage, Llanfair Talhaiarn, Abergele, Denbighshire.   [*Died 7 Sept.* 1971.

RIDLEY, Frederick Thomas, FRCS; retired from practice, 1971; *b* 14 June 1903; *s* of Frederick William Ridley and Ellen Smith; *m* 1940, Josephine Rose Ansell (marr. diss.); two *d*; *m* 1965, Pauline Cartier Bourgeois, *widow*, *d* of Arthur J. B. Cartier, Asst US Attorney, Boston, Mass. *Educ:* King Edward's, Birmingham; Univ. of Birmingham. BSc Birmingham 1922; MB, BS London 1925; LMSSA London 1925; LRCP 1926; MRCS 1926; FRCS 1928. Formerly: House Surg. (Ophth., Gynæc. and Gen.), Queen's Hosp., Birmingham; Pathologist, Central London Ophth. Hosp.; Lectr in Pathology, DO Oxon; Hon. Research Asst, Wright-Fleming Inst., St Mary's Hosp., 1930; Lectr, Inst. of Ophth., Univ. of London, 1947; Hon. Cons. Surgeon: Western Ophth. Hosp., 1926; Central London Ophth. Hosp., 1928; Cons. Surgeon, Moorfields Eye Hosp., 1928, Life Hon. Consulting Surgeon, 1968. Dir, Contact Lens Dept, 1950; Senior Surgeon, 1961, retd 1968. Pres., Section of Ophthalmology, RSM, 1963-64; Hon. Mem. 1970; Pres., 2nd Internat. Corneo-Plastic Conf., RCS, 1967. Chm., Listening Library. FRSM; Member: Ophth. Soc. of UK; Oxford Ophth. Congress. Middlemore Lectr 1951; Doyne Memorial Lecture, 1954; Edward Nettleship Prize and Gold Medal, 1963; Sight Foundn Award, Baylor Univ., 1966. *Publications:* (jt) Mayou's Diseases of the Eye, 1933; (jt) Student's Guide to Fundus Appearances, 1933; (jt) Modern Trends in Ophthalmology, 1940; many addresses, chapters in books, and papers in scientific jls. *Recreation:* formerly farming. *Address:* Pitt's Walk, Bowling Green Close, SW15. *T:* 01-788 6168.   [*Died 2 Feb.* 1977.

RIEFLER, Winfield William; retired; Assistant to Chairman, Board of Governors, Federal Reserve System, 1948-Dec. 1959; Secretary, Federal Open Market Committee 1952-Dec. 1959; *b* Buffalo, NY, 9 Feb. 1897; *s* of Philip D. Riefler and Clara Gartner; *m* 1924, Dorothy Miles Brown; two *s*. *Educ:* Amherst College (AB 1921, LHD (Hon.) 1944); Brookings Grad. School (PhD 1927). Foreign Trade Officer, Department of Commerce, Buenos Aires, Argentina, 1921; 1923; division of research and statistics Federal Reserve Board, 1923-33; Exec. Sec. Cttee on Bank Reserves, 1930-32; Chairman Central Statistical Board, 1933-35, Economic Adviser: to Executive Council, 1933-34, to National Emergency Council, 1934-35; Professor, School of Economics and Politics of Institute for Advanced Study, 1935-48; Assistant to Secretary of the Treasury, 1939; on leave of absence to Act as Minister to London (Special Assistant to Ambassador) in charge of Economic Warfare, 1942-44; Trustee, Institute for Advanced Study, 1936-41; Director, National Bureau of Economic Research, 1936-42, 1945-48; Special Adviser, US Dept of Treasury, 1937; Alternate Member Finance Cttee, League of Nations, 1937-46; Director, Foreign Policy Assoc., 1938-40; Director, Federal Reserve Bank of Philadelphia, 1941-42; Chm., League of Nations Deleg. on Economic Depressions, 1945; Chm., Social Science Research Council Com. on Social and Economic Aspects of Atomic Energy, 1945; Director, Council on Foreign Relations, 1945-50; Chm., 20th Century Fund Com. on Foreign Economic Relations, 1946; Consultant, US Select Cttee on Foreign Aid, 1947; Member, UN Sub-commn on Employment and Economic Stability, 1947-50; Member, Business Advisory Council, 1947- (Graduate Mem. 1955-61); Trustee Foreign Service Educational Foundation, 1948-60. Member: American Economic Association; American Statistical Association (Pres. 1941); Royal Economic Soc., London. *Publication:* Money Rates and Money Markets in the United States, 1930. *Address:* 430 Island Circle, Sarasota, Florida 33581, USA. *Club:* Cosmos (Washington).   [*Died 5 April* 1974.

RIEGER, Sir Clarence (Oscar Ferrero), Kt 1969; CBE 1965; FRACS, FRCSE; *b* 23 Nov. 1897; *s* of Oscar Paul Philip and Sarina Rieger; *m* 1923, Bessie Eileen, *d* of Charles Ernest Main; two *s* one *d*. *Educ:* Adelaide High Sch.; Univ. of Adelaide. MBBS Adelaide 1919; FRCSE 1932; FRACS 1957. Served War of 1939-45: Major, AAMC, AIF. Adelaide Children's Hospital: Hon. Surgeon, 1939; Hon. Cons. Surg., 1958; Pres. and Chm. Bd, 1958-. Member: Branch Council, BMA, 1946-61 (Pres., 1949-51); Med. Bd of SA, 1952-70; Fed. Council BMA, 1950-61; Fed. Council AMA, 1962-64 (Vice-Pres., 1964-67); President: First Aust. Med. Congress, 1962; AMA, 1967-70; BMA, 1968. FAMA, 1964; FBMA 1970; Hon. FACMA, 1970. Gold Medal, AMA, 1969. Hon. LLD Aberdeen, 1969. *Publications:* contrib. (1950-) to: Med. Jl Aust., BMJ, NZ Med. Jl. *Recreation:* painting. *Clubs:* Adelaide; Kooyonga Golf (Lockleys).   [*Died 22 May* 1978.

RIEU, Emile Victor, CBE 1953; Hon. LittD (Leeds) 1949; FRSL; Editor of the Penguin Classics, 1944-64; Academic and Literary Adviser to Methuen & Co. Ltd since 1936; *b* 10 Feb. 1887; *y s* of Dr C. P. H. Rieu; *m* 1914, Nelly Lewis, *d* of H. T. Lewis, Pembrokeshire; two *s* two *d*. *Educ:* St Paul's School (scholar); Balliol College, Oxford (scholar). Manager, Oxford University

Press, Bombay, 1912; 2nd Lieut 105th Mahratta Light Inf., 1918; Educational Manager, Methuen & Co., 1923, Managing Director, 1933-36. Major, Home Guard, 1943. President, Virgil Society, 1951; Vice-President, RSL, 1958; Benson Medal (RSL), 1968; Golden Jubilee Medal, Inst. of Linguists, 1971. *Publications:* A Book of Latin Poetry, 1925; Cuckoo Calling, 1933; The Penguin Odyssey, 1945; Virgil: The Pastoral Poems, 1949; The Penguin Iliad, 1950; The Four Gospels, a New Translation, 1952; A Puffin Quartet of Poets (part author), 1958; The Penguin Argonautica (Voyage of Argo), 1959; The Flattered Flying Fish and other poems, 1962. *Recreations:* carpentry, mountains, petrology. *Address:* 31 Hurst Avenue, N6. *T:* 01-340 4178. *Club:* Athenæum.   [*Died* 11 *May* 1972.

RIFAAT, Kamal Eldin Mahmoud; Ambassador of Arab Republic of Egypt to the Court of St James's, 1971-74; *b* 1 Nov. 1921; *m*; one *s* two *d*. *Educ:* Military Academy. Served Armed Forces, 1942-55; Mem. Nat. Assembly; Dep. Minister for Presidential Affairs, 1958; Minister without Portfolio, Oct. 1958; Minister of Labour, 1961; Mem. Presidential Council; Dep. Prime Minister for Scientific Affairs (Technology), 1964; Mem. Gen. Secretariat of Arab Socialist Union, 1964; Minister of Labour, 1967; appointed Ambassador, Min. of Foreign Affairs, 1970. Medal of Mil. Bravery, 1st cl., UAR, 1954; Medal of Science, Yugoslavia, 1961; Order of Merit, 2nd cl., Cameroun, 1962; Medal of Maareb, Yemen, 1964; Medal of Renaissance, 1st cl., Jordan, 1964; Grand Collar of the Republic; Medal of Mil. Star. *Address:* c/o Ministry of Foreign Affairs, Cairo, Egypt.
[*Died* 13 *July* 1977.

RIGG, Harry Sibson Leslie, QC 1960; **His Honour Judge Rigg;** a Circuit Judge, since 1972; *b* 8 Nov. 1915; *s* of Sibson Eric Rigg and Annie Louise (*née* Green); *m* 1939, Nina Marjorie (*née* Booth); one *d*. *Educ:* Charterhouse; Lincoln College, Oxford. Manchester Regiment, Staff Captain, 1939-44. Barrister, Lincoln's Inn, 1944. Master of the Bench, 1966. Recorder of Wigan, 1964-71; Comr, CCC, 1971. Contested (C) Edge Hill Division of Liverpool, May 1955. *Recreations:* art (oil painting), music, gardening. *Address:* Fern Hill, Goldrings Road, Oxshott, Surrey.   [*Died* 11 *June* 1976.

RIGG, Sir Theodore, KBE, *cr* 1938; MA, MSc, Hon. DSc, FRIC; FNZIC; FRSNZ; retired; *b* 6 April 1888; *s* of John and Hannah Rigg; *m* 1919, Esther Mary White (*d* 1959); two *d*; *m* 1966, Kathleen Maisey Curtis, DSc. *Educ:* Wellington Coll.; Victoria Univ. Coll., Wellington; Cambridge Univ. MSc 1st Class Hons Phys. Chem., Jacob Joseph Scholar, 1851 Exhibitioner; MA Cantab 1924. War Relief work, France, Serbia and Russia, 1914-19; Agricultural Chemist Cawthron Institute, 1920; Member Research Council, NZ Dept of Sci. and Ind. Research, 1926-54; Asst Dir, 1928, Director, Cawthron Institute, 1934-56; Liversidge Lecturer, ANZAAS, 1936; Chairman NZ Research Council, 1943-54; President NZ Inst. of Chemistry, 1942-43; Member Nelson Catchment Board, 1945-55; NZ Delegate Empire Science Conferences, London, 1946; Hon. DSc Univ. of W Australia, 1947; Chairman Tobacco Research and Hop Research Cttees, DSIR, 1948-56; Organising Chairman Soils, Agriculture and Forestry Div., 7th Pacific Science Conf., NZ, 1949. Fellow Royal Hort. Soc. NZ, 1950; President, ANZAAS, 1954-55. Hon. Fellow, NZIC, 1956; Hon. DSc NZ Univ., 1957. Silver Jubilee Medal, 1935; Coronation Medal, 1953. *Publications:* numerous publications dealing with soil and fertilizer research, and progress of agriculture in the Nelson Land district, 1920-69. *Address:* 5 Taupata Street, Stoke Nelson, New Zealand.   [*Died* 22 *Nov.* 1972.

RIGNOLD, Hugo Henry; conductor; Musical Director and Principal Conductor, City of Birmingham Symphony Orchestra, 1960-68; *b* 15 May 1905; *s* of Hugo Charles Rignold, conductor, and Agnes Mann, Opera singer; *m* 1st, 1934, Rita Mary Gaylor; one *d*; 2nd, 1941, Phyllis Stanley; one *d*; 3rd, 1948, Patricia Horton. *Educ:* St Mary's and Kelvin College, Winnipeg, Canada. Royal Opera House, Covent Garden, 1947-48; Liverpool Philharmonic Soc., 1948-54; Edinburgh Festival (Midsummer Night's Dream) and American Tour following, 1954-55. Guest appearances: Holland, Italy, Switzerland, etc., and important orchestras in UK, 1955; opened Festival Cape Town, S Africa, Sept. 1955, returning there for season, 1956-57; Musical Director of the Royal Ballet, 1957-60. Hon. ARAM 1949. Hon. FRAM 1952. *Recreations:* golf, cricket, motor racing; antique furniture. *Address:* 1 Holford Road, Hampstead, NW3.   [*Died* 30 *May* 1976.

RILEY, Rt. Rev. Charles Lawrence, CBE 1942 (OBE 1920); VD; retired as Bishop of Bendigo, Victoria (1938-57), and as Chaplain-General to AMF (1942-57); Hon. Canon of St George's Cathedral, Jerusalem, 1950-57; *b* 10 Oct. 1888; *s* of Most Rev. Charles Owen Leaver Riley, sometime Archbishop of Perth, and Elizabeth Merriman; *m* 1916, Lucille Mary Lefroy two *s* two *d*. *Educ:* Hale School, Perth, WA; Gonville and Caius Coll., Cambridge (Govt of W Australia Scholar, Exhibitioner) BA 1909; LLB 1910; MA 1913; Deacon 1912; Priest 1914 Curate of Stoke-on-Trent, 1912-14; Rector of St Hilda, Perth WA, 1914-21; of St Mary, West Perth, 1921-30; Archdeacon o Northam, 1930-38; Canon of St George's Cathedral, Perth 1933-38; Senior Chaplain to AIF, 1940-41. *Address:* Lennard Street, Waterman's Bay, WA 6020, Australia. *Club:* Union (Cambridge).   [*Died* 1 *April* 1971

RILEY, Norman Denbigh, CBE 1952; Keeper, Department o Entomology, British Museum (Natural History), 1932-Nov 1955; retired; *b* 1890; *m* 1920, Edith Vaughan; one *s* one *d*. *Educ* Dulwich College. Demonstrator in Entomology, Imperial College of Science, 1911; entered Museum, 1911. Served a Captain in ASC and The Queens in France, 1914-19 (despatches). Fellow Royal Entomological Society of London (Vice-Pres. 1929, 1940; Treas., 1939-40; Sec., 1926-29, 1941-51 Pres., 1951-52). *Publications:* Field Guide to Butterflies o Britain and Europe (with Lionel Higgins), 1970; Field Guide t Butterflies of the West Indies, 1975; numerous papers o Lepidoptera. *Address:* 7 McKay Road, Wimbledon, SW20.
[*Died* 26 *May* 1979

RINGHAM, Reginald, CBE 1958; MIMinE; *b* 30 April 1894; *s* o John Charles Ringham; *m* 1923, Doris Clare Fletcher; one *d* *Educ:* Oundle. Entered Mining Industry, 1913, as student unde Sir Arthur Markham, 1st Bt; joined Staveley Coal and Iron Co Ltd, 1922, and served with them in various capacities, becomin Gen. Manager of the Collieries, 1938. Since nationalisation o the mines has served in E Midlands Div. as Area Gen. Manage Production Director, and Dep. Chm.; Chm. E Midlands Div. National Coal Board, 1951-60. OStJ 1941. *Address:* Elizabeth House, Southwold, Suffolk. *T:* 3154.   [*Died* 24 *Dec.* 1973

RITCHARD, Cyril; actor; *b* Sydney, NSW, 1 Dec. 1898; *s* o Herbert Trimnell-Ritchard and Margaret (*née* Collins); *n* Madge Elliott (*d* 1955), actress. *Educ:* St Aloysius College Sydney, New South Wales; Sydney University. Various ligh comedy parts, 1917-24; went to USA, 1924; first appearance on London stage in Bubbly (revival), Duke of York's, 1925; in various productions, 1925-31, including Charlot's Revue and the Co-Optimists of 1930; Australia, 1932-36; returned to England 1936; played the leading part in Nine Sharp (Revue), Little 1938-39; The Little Review, Little, 1939; produced The New Ambassadors' Revue, Ambassadors', 1941; appeared in Big Top His Majesty's, 1942; The Importance of Being Earnes (Algernon Moncrieffe), Phœnix, 1942; The Merry Widow (Prince Danilo), His Majesty's, 1943, on tour abroad for the Forces, 1943-44, Coliseum, 1944; Gay Rosalinda, Palace, 1945 returned to Australia, taking various parts at Theatre Royal Sydney, 1946; Love for Love (Tattle), New York, 1947; The Relapse (Sir Novelty Fashion), Lyric, Hammersmith, Dec. 1947 Phœnix, Jan. 1948, and in USA 1950. Since 1948 has directed and played in USA, London, etc. Recent successes include: The Millionairess (Adrian Blenderland), New, and in New York. 1952; High Spirits, London Hippodrome, 1953; Captain Hook in Musical of Peter Pan, Winter Garden, New York, 1954 (directed) Tales of Hoffman, New York Metropolitan Opera 1955; Eisenstein in Rosalinda, Civic Light Opera Co., Los Angeles and San Francisco, 1956; (directed and played Don Andres), Offenbach's La Perichole, Metropolitan Opera House New York, 1956; (directed) Reluctant Debutante, Henry Miller Theatre, New York, 1956; (directed and played in) Visit to a Small Planet (Kreton), Booth Theatre, New York, 1957 (directed) new versions of The Marriage of Figaro and Gypsy Baron, Metropolitan Opera, 1958-59; (directed and starred in The Pleasure of his Company, USA, 1958-60, touring Australia 1960; (directed and starred in) The Happiest Girl in the World New York, 1961; The Roar of the Greasepaint-the Smell of the Crowd, New York, 1965; appeared in Half a Sixpence (film) 1967; (directed and played in) Midsummer Night's Dream Stratford, Connecticut, 1967; (directed and played Gen. Burgoyne) The Devil's Disciple, Stratford, Conn., 1969, and Hartke Theatre, Catholic Univ., Washington, 1970; (narrated Facade (Sitwell-Walton), Ottawa Symphony, Canada, 1970 (narrated) Peter and the Wolf, Balanchine Ballet, NY City Centre, 1970, and Lancaster, Ohio, 1971; Metropolitan Opera NY: (directed) Contes d'Hoffman, 1971; (directed and played Don Andres) La Perichole, 1971, and tour 1971; (directed and played Pogo Poole) The Pleasure of his Company, 1971; Osgood in Sugar, Majestic Theatre, NY 1972-73. Starred in Romulus Music Box Theater, New York; and in revival of La Perichole Metropolitan Opera House; played Phineas Fogg in musica version of Around the World in 80 days, St Louis Municipa Opera and Kansas City Starlight Theater. Has also appeared i films and starred in several TV spectaculars. *Address:* 135

Central Park West, New York City, USA.
[Died 18 Dec. 1977.

RITCHIE OF DUNDEE, 3rd Baron, cr 1905, John Kenneth Ritchie, PC 1965; Chairman of the Stock Exchange, 1959-65 (Deputy Chairman, 1954-59 and 1965-72); Director: English Association of American Bond & Shareholders Ltd (Chairman); Hutchinson Ltd; b 22 Sept. 1902; 2nd and e surv. s of 2nd Baron Ritchie of Dundee and Sarah Ruth (d 1950), 4th d of L. J. Jennings, MP; S father 1948; m 1945, Joan Beatrice (d 1963), d of late Rev. H. C. L. Tindall; no c. Educ: RNC, Osborne; Winchester; Magdalen College, Oxford. Served War of 1939-45, KRRC (Captain), 1940-45. Chairman Poplar Hospital, 1948; Chairman Bow Group of Hospitals Management Cttee, 1948-58; Mayor of Winchelsea, 1934. Heir: b Hon. Colin Neville Ower Ritchie [b 9 July 1908; m 1943, Anne Petronill, d of H. C. Burra, Rye. Educ: Trinity College, Oxford (BA)]. Address: 40 Thurloe Square, SW7. T: 01-589 9730; Lower Bosney, Iden, East Sussex. T: Iden 282. Clubs: Brooks's, City of London, All England Lawn Tennis.   [Died 20 Oct. 1975.

RITCHIE OF DUNDEE, 4th Baron cr 1905; Colin Neville Ower Ritchie; b 9 July 1908; 3rd s of 2nd Baron Ritchie of Dundee and Sarah Ruth (d 1950), 4th d of L. J. Jennings, MP; S brother, 1975; m 1943, Anne Petronill, d of H. C. Burra, Rye. Educ: Down House, Rottingdean; Trinity Coll., Oxford (BA 1929). Formerly Headmaster of Brickwall School, Northiam, Sussex. Heir: b Hon. (Harold) Malcolm Ritchie [b 29 Aug. 1919; m 1948, Anna, d of late Col Charles George Johnstone, MC, Durban; one s one d]. Address: 5 Fairmeadow, Rye Hill, Rye, Sussex. Clubs: All England Lawn Tennis, International Lawn Tennis of GB, Rye Golf.   [Died 16 Nov. 1978.

RITCHIE, Sir John (Neish), Kt 1961; CB 1955; Principal and Dean of the Royal Veterinary College, University of London, 1965-70; b 19 Jan. 1904; m 1930, Florina Margaret Drummond (d 1975); two s two d. Educ: Turriff, Aberdeenshire; Royal (Dick) Veterinary Coll., Edinburgh; Edinburgh Univ. MRCVS 1925; DVSM 1926; BSc 1927; FRSE 1957. Asst Vet. Officer, City of Edinburgh, 1927-29; Co. Vet. Officer, Midlothian, 1929-35; Sen. Vet. Officer, Dept of Agric. for Scotland, 1935-38; Suptg Inspector, Min. of Agric. and Fisheries, 1938-45; Dep. Chief Vet. Officer, 1945; Chief Veterinary Officer, Ministry of Agriculture, Fisheries and Food, 1952-65. Hon. FRCVS, 1955; Hon. degrees: DVSc (Liv.) 1961; LLD (Toronto) 1962, (Edin.) 1965; Bledisloe Vet. Award, 1961; BOCM Poultry Award, 1964. Member: ARC, 1954-73; Scientific Adv. panel to Minister of Agric., Fisheries and Food, 1965-68; Council, Roy. Coll. of Veterinary Surgeons, 1951-70 (President, 1959-61, Vice-President, 1958-59, 1961-62). Chm., European Commn for the Control of Foot-and-Mouth Disease, 1959-65; Member Gov. Body: Houghton Poultry Research Stn, 1965-68; Animal Virus Research Inst., Pirbright, 1951-65; Wye Coll., Univ. of London, 1967-71; Chairman: FAO/WHO Expert Panel on Vet. Educn; Vet. Adv. Cttee, Horse Race Betting Levy Bd, 1961-73; Mem. Horse Race Anti-doping Cttee, 1971-73. Hon. Sheriff, Co. of Banff, 1973. Publications: articles on vet. subjects in several jls. Recreation: painting. Address: St Brandons, High Street, Banff AB4 1AE. Club: Town and County (Banff).
[Died 28 Sept. 1977.

RITCHIE, Sir Thomas Malcolm, Kt 1951; Chartered Engineer; FIE Australia; Director: Crompton Parkinson (Australia) Pty Ltd; Noyes (Australia) Pty Ltd and Associated Companies, 1934-71; b 11 June 1894; s of Thomas Ritchie, Ivanhoe, Vic; m 1924, Phyllis Elizabeth Brown. Educ: Melbourne. Diplomas in Electrical and Mechanical Engineering. Man. Dir Metropolitan Vickers (Aust.) Pty Ltd, 1923-29; Gen. Mgr Australian Electrical Mfg Co. Ltd, 1929-32; Works Director, Aust. General Elec. Co. Ltd, 1932-34; Chm. and Man. Dir Noyes Bros (Sydney) Ltd, 1934-54; Chm., British Insulated Callenders Cables (Australia) Ltd, 1953-59; Business Administrator, NSW, Min. of Munitions, 1940-45; Mem. Bd of Governors, Fairbridge Farm Schools of NSW, 1945-53; Mem. of Electricity Advisory Cttee to Govt of NSW, 1935-46; Federal Pres., The Liberal Party of Australia, 1945-47 and 1949-51. Recreations: golf, bowls. Address: Trelm, Moss Vale, NSW 2577, Australia; Royal Sydney Golf Club, Rose Bay, Sydney. T: Moss Vale 321. Clubs: Union, Australian (Sydney); Johnsonian (Brisbane, Qld), etc.
[Died 22 Feb. 1971.

RITSON, Muriel; CBE 1936; Controller (Scotland) (retd) Ministry of National Insurance; b 1885; d of John Fletcher Ritson and Agnes Jane Catto. Educ: Greenock Academy; Germany. Social Worker and Rent Collector, Glasgow Workman's Dwgs Coy. Ltd, 1908-11; Secretary Women's Friendly Society of Scotland, 1911-19; Member Scottish Board of Health, 1919-29; Controller Health and Pensions Insurance,

Department of Health, Scotland, 1929-45. Member Ryan Committee of Enquiry into Health Insurance; Committee on Admission of Women to Diplomatic and Consular Service; Beveridge Comm. on Social Insurance. Address: 8 Eton Terrace, Edinburgh.   [Died 8 July 1980.

RIVERS, Alfred Peter, FCA, FCIS; Chairman, Hovis-McDougall Ltd, 1965-71 (Deputy Chairman and Managing Director, 1957-65); b 7 April 1906; s of late Peter McKay Rivers and Grace Skinner; m 1934, Louise, d of late Charles Masters; one s one d. Educ: Addiscombe New Coll. and privately. Director: Norwich Union Insurance Group (London Board), 1964; Ranks Hovis McDougall Ltd, 1962-71. Member: UK Adv. Council on Education for Management, 1961-65; Council, Chartered Inst. of Secretaries, 1957-73 (Pres., 1970); Bd of Governors, King's Coll. Hosp., 1958-74; Economics and Business Studies Bd, Council for Nat. Acad. Awards, 1965-69; NEDC for Food Manufacturing Industry, 1968-71; Council, Chest and Heart Assoc., 1968-. Chairman: Fitton Trust, 1958-; Nat. Appeal Cttee, Shaftesbury Soc., 1962-68; Appeals and Public Relations Cttee, Voluntary Research Trust of King's Coll. Hosp. and Med. Sch., 1962-; Triad Trust, 1967-77; Flour Adv. Bureau, 1968-71. Trustee, Southwark Rehearsal Hall Trust, 1973-76; Special Trustee, King's Coll. Hosp., 1974-78; Mem. Council: London Philharmonic Orchestra, 1971-76 (Vice-Chm., 1972-); King's Coll. Hosp. Med. Sch., 1973-76. Recreations: music and humour. Address: Elmcourt, Sutton Lane, Banstead, Surrey. T: Burgh Heath 56363.
[Died 7 March 1979.

RIVETT-CARNAC, Sir Henry George Crabbe, 7th Bt, cr 1836; b 18 Jan. 1889; e s of late Rev. Sir Clennel George Rivett-Carnac, 6th Bart, and Emily Louisa (d 1894), d of late Rev. George Crabbe; S father, 1932. Formerly in Burma Police. Heir: nephew Rev. Thomas Nicholas Rivett-Carnac, b 3 June 1927.
[Died 25 Dec. 1972.

RIVINGTON, Gerald Chippindale; Chairman of Rivingtons (Publishers) Ltd; Chairman of the Governors of Harrow School, 1953-64; Member of Board of Referees (Finance), 1932-69; b 13 Dec. 1893; s of Charles Robert Rivington, JP, DL, Castle Bank, Appleby, Westmorland; m 1915, Margaret Stewardson Summersby (d 1951). Educ: Harrow. Served European War, 1914-18, Border Regt, Capt. 1914; France, 1915-16; invalided, 1916. Vice-Pres., Publishers' Association, 1929-31. Liveryman, Stationers' and Newspaper Makers' Company; Renter Warden, 1920. Recreation: books. Address: 96 Rivermead Court, Hurlingham, SW6. Club: Garrick.   [Died 2 March 1977.

ROACH, Air Vice-Marshal Harold Jace, CB 1946; CBE 1944; AFC; Polonia Restituta 3rd cl. (Poland), 1944; FIMechE; b 8 May 1896; m 1927, Emilie Blanche Fuller; one d. Educ: Lower School of John Lyon, Harrow. Apprenticed Cromptons, Chelmsford; enlisted in RNAS 1915; served in France, 1916-17; Air Ministry, 1917-20; Halton, 1920-24; Henlow, 1924-26; Irak, 1927-29; No 10 Group, 1930-32; HQ Coastal Command, 1933; Grantham, 1934; Gosport, 1936; Far East, Singapore, 1937-41; 41 Group, 1942; HQ Bomber Command, 1942-46; RAF Station, St Athan, 1946-47; AOC No 43 Group, Maintenance Command, 1947-48; AOC No 41 Group, Maintenance Comd, 1948; retd 1951. Recreations: swimming, hockey. Address: Woodcot, Goodworth Clatford, Andover, Hants. T: 2885.
[Died 21 June 1977.

ROACH, Harry Robert, MA Cantab; Headmaster, Hymers College, Hull, 1951-71; b 4 Sept. 1906; m 1943, Blanche Hortense Sinner; one s one d. Educ: St Olave's Grammar School, London; Clare College, Cambridge. Assistant Master: Aldenham School, 1928-38; King's School, Canterbury, 1938-42; Eton College, 1945-46; Head Master, King Edward VI Grammar School, Five Ways, Birmingham, 1946-51. Served War of 1939-45, in Intelligence Corps, 1942-45. Publication: Six Plays of Racine, 1951. Recreations: reading and acting. Address: 26 St Nicholas Drive, Hornsea, North Humberside.
[Died 8 May 1979.

ROAD, Sir Alfred, Kt 1953; CBE 1950; Inland Revenue, retired; b 10 Jan. 1891; s of late Alfred Road, MBE; m 1915, Gladys Mabel (d 1966), d of David Rees Thomas; two s one d. Educ: Borden Grammar School. Entered Inland Revenue as Assistant Surveyor of Taxes, 1910; Surveyor, 1915; served in charge of Sudbury, Holloway, Enfield, City 6 Districts, and in charge of Departmental Claims Branch; Principal Inspector, Somerset House, 1939; Dep. Chief Inspector of Taxes, 1947-52, Chief

Inspector, 1952-56. *Recreations:* gardening, motoring. *Address:* 31 Cornwall Road, Cheam, Surrey. *T:* 01-642 8300.
[*Died* 14 *Feb.* 1972.

ROB, John Vernon, CMG 1961; Served in the Foreign and Commonwealth Office (formerly Commonwealth Office), 1967, retired 1969; *b* 17 Dec. 1915; 2nd *s* of late Dr J. W. Rob; *m* 1942, Bridget Anne Elisabeth Freeman (marr. diss., 1946); one *d.* *Educ:* Oundle Sch.; St John's Coll., Cambridge. Entered Consular Service, 1939. Served in the Army, 1940-45. Returned to Foreign Service, 1945; served in Sofia, 1949-51; attached Canadian National Defence College, 1951-52; Foreign Office, 1952-55; Counsellor, UK High Commission, New Delhi, 1955-58, Warsaw, 1959-60; Ambassador to Congo Republic, Central African Republic and Republics of Gabon and Chad, 1960-62; served in Foreign Office as HM Inspector of Foreign Service Establishments, 1962-65; British High Commissioner in Singapore, 1965-67. *Recreations:* reading and walking. *Address:* c/o Midland Bank Ltd, Walton-on-Thames, Surrey.
[*Died* 7 *March* 1971.

ROBB, Sir (George) Douglas, Kt 1960; CMG 1956; FRCS; FACS (Hon.); FRACS; Chancellor, University of Auckland, 1961-68; *b* 29 April 1899; *s* of John and Agnes Robb, Melbourne and Auckland; *m* 1935, Helen Seabrook, Auckland; one *s* two *d.* *Educ:* Auckland Grammar School; Auckland University College; Otago University. MB 1922, MD 1929, ChM 1938, Otago. Post-graduate study in London, 1923-28; FRCS (Eng.), 1926; FRS NZ, 1961. Surgical practice in Auckland, 1928; Sen. Thoracic Surgeon, Green Lane Hosp., Auckland, 1942-64, retired. Chairman, New Zealand Medical Council, 1969-72 (Mem. 1941-); New Zealand Medical Research Council, 1951-62; Vice-President, Auckland Medical Research Foundation; President BMA, 1961-62. LLD (Hon.): Queen's, Belfast, 1962; Univ. of Auckland, 1969. FRCP 1966. *Publications:* Medicine and Health in New Zealand, 1941; Hospital Reform in NZ, 1949; University Development in Auckland, 1957; Medical Odyssey, 1967. *Recreation:* sea fishing. *Address:* 1A MacMurray Road, Auckland 5, NZ. *Clubs:* Northern, University (Auckland).
[*Died* 28 *April* 1974.

ROBB, Michael Antony Moyse, CMG 1961; Deputy Director, Central Bureau for Educational Visits and Exchanges, 1970-72; *b* Cairo, Egypt, 3 April 1914; *s* of late George Robb (Ministry of Education, Cairo, and later representative of Messrs Macmillan); *m* 1943, Brenda Patience Shankland (widow, *née* Robinson); two step *s* one *s* one *d.* *Educ:* Malvern College; Germany, France, Spain. Passed into Consular Service, 1936; Probationer Vice-Consul, British Consulate-General, New York, Nov. 1936; confirmed as Vice-Consul, 1939; HBM Vice-Consul, Miami, Fla, 1941; Acting Consul, Atlanta, in 1943 and 1944. Served in Foreign Office, 1945-Dec. 1947; Foreign Service Officer Grade 7, 1945; First Secretary (Information), at British Embassy, The Hague, 1948; Counsellor (Information), at British High Commission, later British Embassy, Bonn, 1951; Foreign Service Officer Grade 6, 1953; Counsellor, British Embassy, Rio de Janeiro, 1955-59; Foreign Service Inspector, Foreign Office, 1959-61; Minister (Information) at British Embassy, Washington, 1961-65; Minister, British Embassy, Pretoria, 1965-69. *Address:* 26 Pattison Road, NW2. *T:* 01-435 5689.
[*Died* 11 *Dec.* 1977.

ROBB, Nesca Adeline, DPhil, author; *b* 27 May 1905; *d* of late Charles Robb, Managing Director, J. Robb & Co. Ltd, Belfast, and Agnes Mabel, *d* of Dr Wilberforce Arnold, Belfast. *Educ:* Richmond Lodge, Belfast; Somerville College, Oxford. BA (1st Cl. Mod. Lang.) 1927; MA 1931; DPhil 1932. Research, voluntary social work, 1928-33; coaching at Oxford, 1934-38; senior English teacher, Italian Inst., London, 1938-39. Advisory Officer and Registrar, Women's Employment Fedn, London, 1940-44. Since then has lived in N Ireland and taken varied part in local affairs: Cttee of National Trust, Northern Ireland; Internat. PEN, Belfast Centre (Chm., 1950-51, 1961-62); Pres., Irish PEN, 1968-69; Chm., USPCA, Bangor Br. Has lectured for Society for Italian Studies, British Council, Anglo-Netherlands Soc., National Trust, etc., and written poems, articles and broadcast scripts (incl. Prisoner of State, NI Radio, 1954). FRSL 1948; Lid van de Maatschappij der Nederlandse Letterkunde, 1963. *Publications:* Neoplatonism of the Italian Renaissance, 1935; Poems, 1939; An Ulsterwoman in England, 1942; Four in Exile, 1948; William of Orange: A Personal Portrait, Vol. I 1650-1673, 1962, Vol. II 1674-1702, 1966; A History of Richmond Lodge School, 1969; Ards Eclogues (verse), 1970; contribs to Encyc. Brit. (new edn). *Recreations:* travel, music, cookery. *Address:* 5 Queen's Close, Dorchester-on-Thames, Oxon. *T:* Warborough 487. *Club:* University Women's.
[*Died* 18 *May* 1976.

ROBB, Ven. Percy Douglas; Archdeacon of Kingston-upon-Thames since 1953; Vicar of St Peter with All Saints, Petersham, since 1963; *b* 7 Aug. 1902; *s* of Percy Robb and Agnes Jane Black (*née* Thomson); unmarried. *Educ:* Bedford Sch.; Pembroke Coll., Oxford; Westcott House, Cambridge. BA Oxon 1925, MA 1928. Deacon 1926, priest 1927, diocese of Southwark; Curate of Lambeth, 1926-31; Rector of St Paul with St Mark, Deptford, 1931-44; Rural Dean of Greenwich, 1941-44; Vicar of Lewisham, 1944-55; Vicar of St Andrew's, Coulsdon, 1955-63; Hon. Canon of Southwark, 1951-53. Proctor in Convocation of Southwark, 1950-51 and 1953-75. *Address:* 11 Wantage Road, Lee, SE12 8NA. *T:* 01-318 0415. *Club:* United Oxford & Cambridge University.
[*Died* 28 *Nov.* 1976.

ROBERTS, Rev. Prof. Bleddyn Jones, MA, DD; Professor of Hebrew, University College of North Wales, Bangor, 1953-73, now Emeritus; *b* 21 April 1906; *s* of late Thomas and Sophia Jones Roberts, Penycae, Wrexham, Denbs; *m* 1943, Mirian Eluned, MB, BCh, *d* of late Rev. John Davies, and Mrs A Davies (*née* David), Aberystwyth, Cards. *Educ:* Ruabon Grammar School; Univ. Coll. of N Wales; Leipzig Univ. 1st Class Hons BA (Wales), 1928; BD (Wales) 1934; MA (Wales) 1936; DD (Wales) 1953. Asst Lecturer in Hebrew, Manchester University, 1934-36; Asst Lecturer, Bangor, 1936-37; Professor of Hebrew, United (Presbyterian) Theological College, Aberystwyth, 1937-46; Senior Lecturer in Biblical Studies, Univ Coll. of N Wales, 1946-53; Past Examiner in Universities of Sheffield, Dublin, Manchester, Glasgow; Mem., Translation Panel of New English Bible, 1949-69; President, Society OT Study, 1964; Director of New Welsh Bible, 1964-74. Hon Freeman, Bangor, 1974. *Publications:* Patrymau Llenyddol y Beibl, 1950; The Old Testament Text and Versions, 1951; Some Observations on the Damascus Document and the Dead Sea Scrolls, 1952; The Dead Sea Scrolls and Old Testament Scriptures, 1953; Sgroliau'r Môr Marw, 1956; The Second Isaiah Scroll from Qumrán, 1959; The Canon of the Old Testament: A Suggestion, 1963; Diwinyddiaeth yr Hen Destament, 1964 Jeremeia, Proffwyd Gofidiau, 1967; contributor to: The Interpreter's Dictionary of the Bible; Bulletin of the John Rylands Library; Y Traethodydd; Jl of Theological Studies Diwinyddiaeth; Jl of New Testament Studies. *Address:* Pen Tyle, Meirion Lane, Bangor, Gwynedd. *T:* Bangor 4630.
[*Died* 11 *Aug.* 1977

ROBERTS, Brian Birley, CMG 1969; PhD; Research Associate Scott Polar Research Institute, Cambridge (half-time), since 1960 (Research Fellow (half-time), 1946-60); *b* 23 Oct. 1912; *s* of late Charles Michael Roberts, MB, BS; unmarried. *Educ:* Uppingham Sch.; Emmanuel Coll., Cambridge. MA 1934, PhD 1940. Leader, Cambridge Expedns to Iceland, 1932, and E Greenland, 1933; Mem., British Graham Land Expedn, 1934-37 (Polar Medal, 1940); Special adviser on cold climate equipment to Controller of Ordnance Services, WO, 1940-41; Bruce Memorial Prize of RSE, of Royal Phys. Soc. Edinburgh and RSGS, 1940; Admty, NID, 1941-43; Jt Editor, Polar Record, 1942-75; FO Res. Dept (Head of Polar Regions Section), 1944-68 (half-time 1946-68); FO Latin America Dept (half-time), 1968-75. Co-founder and Editor, Jl of Glaciology, 1947; Back Award of RGS, 1948; Mem., Op. Lyon, Canadian Arctic, 1949; Mem. Norwegian-British-Swedish Antarctic Expedn, 1950-51; exch. visit to USSR Arctic orgs, 1956; UK Deleg. to Wash. Antarctic Conf., 1959, and subseq. Antarctic Treaty Consultative Meetings: Canberra, 1961; Buenos Aires, 1962; Brussels, 1964; Santiago, 1966; Paris, 1968; Tokyo, 1970; Wellington, 1972; Oslo, 1975; Official UK Observer with US Op. Deep Freeze, 1960-61; UK Deleg. to Conf. on Conservation of Antarctic Seals, 1972. President: Antarctic Club, 1963-64; Arctic Club, 1972-73; Mem. French Expedn to sub-Antarctic islands in S Indian Ocean, 1964. Fellow of Churchill Coll., Cambridge, 1965. Founder's Medal, RGS, 1976. *Publications:* Iceland papers, 1939; Handbook on clothing and equipment required in cold climates, 1941; Organization of polar information, 1960; (ed jtly) Illustrated glossary of snow and ice, 1966; (ed) Edward Wilson's Birds of the Antarctic, 1967; The Arctic Ocean, 1971; numerous papers in scientific periodicals. *Recreations:* ornithology, glaciology, small islands. *Address:* 4 Causewayside, Fen Causeway, Cambridge. *T:* Cambridge 55506.
[*Died* 9 *Oct.* 1978.

ROBERTS, Cecil Edric Mornington, Hon. LLD; *b* 18 May 1892. *Educ:* Mundella Grammar School. Literary Editor Liverpool Post, 1915-18; Naval Correspondent with the Grand Fleet, Dover Patrol, Milford Convoy; accredited correspondent with Royal Air Force; accredited by War Office as correspondent with the British Armies on Western Front for Newspaper Society and Reuter; with Allied Armies in march to the Rhine;

Assistant Director Munitions Overseas Transport, and Statistical Officer, American Dept, British Ministry of Munitions; Examining Officer to Civil Liabilities Commission, 1919; Editor, Nottingham Journal, 1920-25; lecture tour USA and Canada, 1920, 1924, 1926, 1929, 1936, 1939; Parliamentary candidate (L) Nottingham, East Division, 1922; British Mission, USA, 1940-46. Hon. Freeman, City of Nottingham; Hon. Citizen of Alassio, Italy; Gold Medal and Diploma, City of Rome. *Publications:* The Trent, 1912; Phyllistrata and other Poems, 1913; Through Eyes of Youth; Poems, 1914; Youth of Beauty; Poems, 1915; Collected War Poems, 1916; Twenty-Six Poems; The Chelsea Cherub (novel), 1917; Charing Cross, 1918; Poems, 1918; Training the Airmen, Poems, collected American edition, 1919; edited Raemaker's Cartoons; The People's Atlas, 1920; A Tale of Young Lovers, Poetic Drama (produced Compton Comedy Company, 1921), 1922; Scissors, 1922; Sails of Sunset, 1924; The Love Rack, 1925; Little Mrs Manington, 1926; The Right to Kiss, a comedy (produced Dean Co., 1926); Sagusto; Diary of Russell Beresford, 1927; David and Diana, 1928; Indiana Jane; Pamela's Spring Song, 1929; Havana Bound, 1930; Half Way, 1931; Bargain Basement, 1931; Spears Against US, 1932; Life of Sir Alfred Fripp, 1932; Pilgrim Cottage, 1933; Gone Rustic; The Guests Arrive, 1934; Volcano, 1935, Gone Afield, 1936; Gone Sunwards, 1936; Victoria Four-Thirty, 1937; They wanted to live, 1938; Spears Against Us (a drama, produced Liverpool Rep. Co.), 1939; And so to Bath, 1940; A Man Arose, 1941; One Small Candle, 1942; So Immortal a Flower, 1944; And So to America, 1946; Eight for Eternity, 1948; And So To Rome, 1950; Terrace in the Sun, 1951; One Year of Life, 1952; The Remarkable Young Man, 1954; Portal to Paradise, 1955; Love is Like That, 1957; Selected Poems, 1960; Wide Horizon, 1962; The Grand Cruise, 1963; A Flight of Birds, 1965; autobiography: The Growing Boy, 1967; The Years of Promise, 1968; The Bright Twenties, 1969; Sunshine and Shadow, 1972; The Pleasant Years, 1974. *Recreation:* travel. *Address:* Grand Hotel, Rome, Italy. *Clubs:* Athenæum, Royal Automobile. [*Died* 20 Dec. 1976.

ROBERTS, Denys K.; *see* Kilham Roberts.

ROBERTS, Sir Gilbert, Kt 1965; FRS 1965; BScEng; Consultant, Freeman, Fox and Partners, since 1969; *b* 18 Feb. 1899; *s* of Henry William Roberts; *m* 1925, Elizabeth Nada Hora; two *d*. *Educ:* City and Guilds Coll., London. Flt-Lt 73 Sqdn RFC, 1917-18. Asst to Sir Ralph Freeman on design of Sydney Harbour Bridge; in bridge dept of Dorman Long and Co. Ltd, 1926-35; worked on design of numerous bridges, develt of welded constrn and Chromador high tensile structural steel; joined Sir William Arrol & Co. Ltd, Glasgow: in charge of constrn and develt, 1936; Dir and Chief Engnr, 1945; joined Freeman, Fox and Partners as partner responsible for design of Severn Bridge on behalf of jt consg engrs, 1949; designed Forth Road Bridge for same consultants; invented and patented design of present Severn Bridge. Designer of: Auckland Harbour Bridge; Volta Bridge, Ghana; new Maidenhead Bridge and others; also radio-telescopes for CSIRO (Aust.) and NRC (Can.). Inventor of 500-ton Goliath Crane designed for Babcock's power station work; designer of other welded crane structures. FInstW; FICE; FIStrucE; Fell., AmSocCE; Fell., Imperial College; FCGI, Telford Gold Medal, ICE, 1967; Royal Medal, Royal Soc., 1968; James Watt Medal, ICE, 1969; MacRobert Award, 1969; Churchill Gold Medal, Soc. of Engrs, 1970. *Publications:* numerous papers and articles on engineering subjects. *Address:* 42 Wynnstay Gardens, Allen Street, W8. *Club:* Athenæum. [*Died* 1 Jan. 1978.

ROBERTS, Sir Howard; *see* Roberts, Sir J. R. H.

ROBERTS, Sir James Denby, 2nd Bt, *cr* 1909; OBE 1959; JP; *b* 3 June 1904; *e s* of late Bertram Foster Roberts and Gertrude, *o d* of Sir Ellis Denby, JP; *S* grandfather, 1935; *m* 1927, Irene Charlotte D'Orsey, *yr d* of William Dunn, MB, CM, JP; two *s* one *d* (and two *s* decd). *Educ:* Rugby; University College, Oxford (MA). Member, Central Agricultural Executive Committee; Council Member, RASE. Chairman: Scottish Soc. for Research in Plant Breeding, 1958-71; Jt ARC/MRC Cttee on Biological Problems of Nuclear Physics, 1958-66; Mem., Nature Conservancy Cttee, 1965. *Recreations:* fishing, shooting. *Heir: s* William James Denby Roberts, *b* 10 Aug. 1936. *Address:* Strathallan Castle, Auchterarder, Perthshire. *T:* 2131. *Club:* Athenæum. [*Died* 10 July 1973.

ROBERTS, Sir (James Reginald) Howard, Kt 1949; CBE 1946; JP 1947, DL 1949; Solicitor; *b* 2 Jan. 1891; *s* of James Reginald Roberts, Liverpool, and Mary Barron Muir; *m* 1950, Joan Blackstone-Smith, Egham; (two *s* one *d* by former marriage). *Educ:* Reading School. Articled to Town Clerk, Sheffield, 1908;

Asst Solicitor, Stoke-on-Trent, 1913; war service, 1914-18; Assistant Solicitor, Liverpool, 1920; Asst Prosecuting Solicitor, Liverpool, 1921; Assistant Town Clerk, Liverpool, 1922; Deputy Town Clerk, Liverpool, 1927; Town Clerk, Kingston-upon-Hull, 1929; Solicitor to LCC 1934-36; Solicitor and Parliamentary Officer to LCC, 1936-47; Clerk of London County Council, 1947-56; Clerk of Lieutenancy of County of London and Hon. Clerk to Advisory Committee on JPs for County of London, 1947-56; Regional Co-ordinating Officer for Civil Defence Vehicles, London Civil Defence Region, 1939-45; Solicitor to the National Fire Service (London Region), 1941-45; Vice-President: Royal Inst. PA; Nat. Fire Service Benevolent Fund; Past President Royal Society for the Prevention of Accidents; Legal Mem. of Town Planning Inst., Pres. 1947. Mem., Surrey CC. Officer of Legion of Honour, 1950; Officer of Order of Orange Nassau, 1950; Chevalier of Order of Dannebrog, 1951; Chevalier of Royal Order of North Star, 1954; Chevalier of Order of the Star of Ethiopia, 1954; Chevalier of Portuguese Military Order of Christ. *Publications:* The National Fire Service; The Law relating to Town and Country Planning. *Recreation:* fishing. *Address:* Burford, Englefield Green, Surrey. *Club:* Savage. [*Died* 5 May 1975.

ROBERTS, John Reginald, CBE 1943; *b* 28 June 1893; *s* of William Rowe and Ada Mary Roberts; *m* 1925, Hilda Mary Redshaw; one *s*. *Educ:* Liverpool College; Ducie Avenue Secondary School, Manchester; Manchester College of Technology (Associate). European War, 1914-18; in France with Royal Engineers. Ex Engineer PWD, Nigeria, 1921; Sen. Hydraulic Engineer PWD, Gold Coast (now Ghana), 1929; Dep. Director of Public Works Gold Coast (now Ghana), 1937; Director of Public Works, 1939-45; Regional Engineer, NW Region, Ministry of Housing and Local Govt, 1946-56. *Address:* 90 Bramhall Lane South, Bramhall, Stockport, Cheshire. [*Died* 28 Jan. 1971.

ROBERTS, Kate Winifred J.; *see* Jones-Roberts.

ROBERTS, Sir Leslie, Kt 1952; CBE 1942; *s* of William Roberts; *m* 1st, 1922, Christine Marjorie Stott (*decd*); one *s* one *d*; 2nd, 1948, Marjorie Adele Gibson (*d* 1968). Has spent all his business life in shipping, first in London and later in Liverpool and Manchester. Was Asst Manager of White Star Line, Liverpool; joined Frederick Leyland & Company Ltd as one of the Joint Managers; General Manager, 1929; Rep. Liverpool Steamship Owners' Assoc. on Mersey Docks and Harbour Bd; Dep. Gen. Manager 1934, Gen. Manager 1936, Man. Dir 1950-61, Chm. 1950-72, Manchester Ship Canal Co.; Hon. President, 1972-. Chm., Bridgewater Estates Ltd, to 1975; Dir, Manchester Liners Ltd, 1947-75; former Director: Williams, Deacon's Bank Ltd (1950-70); National Boiler & General Insurance Co. Ltd and Vulcan Boiler & General Insurance Co. Ltd. *Address:* Windy How, Broadway, Hale, Cheshire. *T:* 061-980 3032. [*Died* 24 June 1976.

ROBERTS, Brig. Michael Rookherst, DSO 1944; Historian, Cabinet Office, 1956-68; *b* 24 Oct. 1894; *s* of R. G. S. Roberts, Mount Rivers, Carrigaline, Co. Cork; *m* 1st, 1919, Isabel (*d* 1974), 3rd *d* of James Fisher, JP, ship owner, Barrow in Furness; one *s* one *d*; 2nd, 1975, Mrs Doreen Logan (*née* Miles). *Educ:* West Buckland; RMC Sandhurst. Served European War, 1914-18, with Lancashire Fusiliers and 113th Inf., IA (France and S Persia); Waziristan, 1920; 2nd Lt 1914; Bt Major, 1931; Asst Mil. Sec., 1931; Comdt 2/10th Gurkha Rifles, 1937; GSO1, Nepalese Contingent, 1940; Brig. 1940; Comd bde of 7th Indian Div., Arakan, 1943-44 (despatches); Colonel, 10th Princess Mary's Own Gurkha Rifles, 1957-59. Chm. Gurkha Brigade Assoc., 1955-67; Governor, West Buckland Sch., 1954-68 (Chm., 1960-68); Chm. Canterbury Soc., 1969-72. FRHistS 1960. *Publications:* Golden Arrow (history of 7th Indian Division), 1952; joint author, Official History, War Against Japan, Vol. II, 1958, Vol. III, 1962, Vol. IV, 1965, Vol. V, 1969; completed Brian Connell's Wavell: Supreme Commander, 1969; articles to Royal United Service Institution Journal, Army Quarterly, Economist, Dictionary of National Biography. *Address:* Swallowfield Park, Swallowfield, Reading, Berks RG7 1TG. *Club:* Army and Navy. [*Died* 30 Aug. 1977.

ROBERTS, Sir Norman (Stanley), KBE 1953 (OBE 1936; MBE 1920); CMG 1950; *b* 20 July 1893; British; *m* 1st, 1921, Olga Taskin (marr. diss. 1931); one *s*; 2nd, 1945, Marie Elder (*d* 1971), *d* of General Baron de Rauch. Served European War, 1914-19, with Rifle Brigade. Entered Foreign Office, 1920; First Secretary (Commercial), Tehran, 1945, Counsellor (Commercial) 1946; Counsellor (Commercial) Stockholm, Dec. 1948; Minister, Commercial, 1950-52, Minister, 1952-53, Tokyo; retd, June 1954. Negotiated agreement with Japanese

Govt about payment of indemnity to former Allied prisoners of war, Dec. 1954. Chm., Japan Soc. of London, 1964-67. Order of the Rising Sun (2nd Class), Japan, 1959. *Address:* 46 Princes Gate, SW7. *T:* 01-589 1317. *Clubs:* United Service & Royal Aero, MCC.   *[Died 1 Nov. 1972.*

ROBERTS, Lt-Comdr Peter Scawen Watkinson, VC 1942; DSC 1942; RN retired; *b* 28 July 1917; *yr s* of George Watkinson Roberts, 82 King William Street, EC4; *m* 1940, Brigid Victoria, *yr d* of S. J. Lethbridge, Plymouth; one *s* one *d. Educ:* King's School, Canterbury. Entered Royal Navy, 1935; Sub-Lieut 1938; Lieut 1940; Lt-Comdr 1947. HMS Shropshire, 1936-38; Submarines, Sept. 1939; HMS: Tribune, 1940; Thrasher, 1941; Beagle, 1941-42; Vernon, 1943-45; Black Prince, 1945-46; Defiance, 1946-48; Eagle, 1948; Gorregan, 1950; Apollo, 1952; Cardigan Bay, 1953; Dingley, 1955; Vernon, 1956 (HM Underwater Countermeasures and Weapons Estabt, 1957); Drake, 1959. Retired list, 1962. *Address:* Grey Barn, Membland, Newton Ferrers, S Devon. *T:* Newton Ferrers 346. *Clubs:* Royal Burnham Yacht (Burnham-on-Crouch); Royal Naval Sailing Association.   *[Died 8 Dec. 1979.*

ROBERTS, Rachel; actress; *b* 20 Sept. 1927; *d* of Rev. Richard Rhys Roberts, BA, OCF and Rachel Ann Jones; *m* 1st, 1955, Alan Dobie (marr. diss. 1960); 2nd, 1962, Rex Harrison (marr. diss. 1971). *Educ:* Univ. of Wales (BA); Royal Acad. of Dramatic Art (Dipl). Stratford Meml Theatre, 1951-52; Old Vic, 1954-55; Bristol Old Vic, 1956; cabaret; Oh My Papa, Garrick; Maggie May, Adelphi; Blithe Spirit, NY; Platonov, Royal Court (Clarence Derivent Award); Alpha Beta, Apollo, 1972; films: Saturday Night and Sunday Morning (British Film Acad. Award for Best Actress), 1960; This Sporting Life (British Film Acad. Award for Best Actress), 1962; O Lucky Man!, 1973; The Belstone Fox, 1973; Murder on the Orient Express, 1974; Foul Play, 1979; Yanks (BAFTA Award, Best Supporting Actress), 1979; films, TV and theatre, America, 1970-72. *Recreations:* reading, writing, people and cats. *Address:* c/o ICM, 22 Grafton Street, W1. *T:* 01-629 8080.
                                                          [Died 26 Nov. 1980.

ROBERTS, Robert David Valpo, CBE 1971; Member, National Industrial Relations Court, since 1973; *b* 5 July 1906; *e s* of David Roberts and Jane Anne Roberts (*née* Evans); *m* 1939, Maureen Elizabeth (*née* Gresty); no *c. Educ:* Dolgellau Gram. Sch.; London Sch. of Economics and Political Science (BCom). South American Jl, 1927-35; Leonard Hill Ltd, 1935-36; Asst Sec., S Wales and Mon Council of Social Service, 1936-40; Districts Officer, Miners' Welfare Commn, 1940-48; Sec., Nat. Jt Adv. Council of Electricity Supply Industry, 1949-57; Electricity Council: Dep. Industrial Relations Adviser, 1957-60; Industrial Relations Adviser, 1960-66; Mem., 1967-72. Member: Nat. Jt Adv. Council, Dept of Employment and Productivity (formerly Min. of Labour), 1960-; Nat. Adv. Council on Educn for Industry and Commerce, Dept of Educn and Science, 1970-. Mem. Court, Univ. of Wales Inst. of Science and Technology, 1970-. *Publications:* (with Sir Ronald Edwards) Status, Productivity, and Pay: a major experiment, 1971; Booklets: Miners' Welfare Looks Forward, 1945; (with T. E. M. McKitterick) Workers and Management: The German Codetermination Experiment; articles on aspects of industrial relations in Brit. Jl of Industrial Relations and The Listener. *Recreation:* fishing. *Address:* Mynthurst, Llanddewi Rhydderch, Abergavenny, Gwent. *T:* Gobion 428. *Club:* Flyfishers'.   *[Died 6 May 1973.*

ROBERTS, Sir Stephen (Henry), Kt 1965; CMG 1956; MA, DSc (Econ.) London, LittD (Melbourne), LLD (Bristol, British Columbia, McGill); DCL (Durham); DLit (New England); Vice-Chancellor and Principal, University of Sydney, 1947-67; Challis Professor of Modern History, 1929-47; Dean of Faculty of Arts, 1941-47; Chairman of Professorial Board, 1944-45 and 1946-47; Acting Vice-Chancellor, 1947; *b* Maldon, Victoria, 15 Feb. 1901; *m* 1927, Thelma Asche, *d* of late John Asche, Toorak, Victoria; three *d. Educ:* Castlemaine; Melbourne; London; Paris. Lecturer, Research Fellow Melbourne Univ., 1920-25; Research in London and France, 1925-29 and in Germany, 1935-37 and 1953; Chairman, Australian Vice-Chancellors' Committee, 1952-53; Chairman, New South Wales State Cancer Council, 1952-68. Commander: Royal Danish Order of Dannebrog, 1950; Order of the Cedar of Lebanon, 1962; Royal Greek Order of the Phoenix, 1964; Commander, Order of Merit (Italy), 1967; Officer, Legion of Honour (France), 1967; Hon. DLitt Sydney, 1967. *Publications:* History of Australian Land Settlement, 1923; Population Problems of the Pacific, 1925; French Colonial Policy, 1870-1925, 1928; The Squatting Age in Australia, 1932; History of Modern Europe, 1933; The House that Hitler built, 1937; Problems of Modern France, 1937; Contributor to Cambridge History of the Empire, to Cyclopedia of the Social

Sciences and to Encyclopedia Britannica Year-Book; Part-author of Australia and the Far East, 1935, and The Australian Mandate in New Guinea; many writings on French regionalism. *Recreations:* travel, philately, history of wine. *Address:* 16 Wyuna Road, Point Piper, Sydney, NSW 2027, Australia.
                                                    [Died 19 March 1971.

ROBERTS, Most Rev. Thomas d'Esterre, SJ, DD; *b* 7 March 1893. Entered Society of Jesus, 1909; Priest, 1925; Rector of St Francis Xavier's College, Liverpool, 1935-37; Archbishop of Bombay, (RC), 1937-50, retired, 1950. *Publication:* Black Popes, 1954. *Relevant Publication:* Archbishop Roberts, SJ, His Life and Writings, by D. A. Hurn, 1966. *Address:* 114 Mount Street, W1. *T:* 01-493 7811.   *[Died 28 Feb. 1976.*

ROBERTS, Thomas Esmôr Rhys R.; *see* Rhys-Roberts.

ROBERTS, Col Sir Thomas Langdon Howland, 6th Bt, of Glassenbury and Brightfieldstown, Co. Cork, *cr* 1809 (claimant to 13th Baronetcy *cr* 1620); CBE 1964; RA (retd); late King's Regt, and VIth KAR; Hon. Colonel 499 (M) HAA Regiment RA (TA), 1949; Actg Col Comdr, No 4 Sector, County of London Home Guard, 1952-56; Commandant County of London ACF, 1956-63; *b* 18 June 1898; *s* of 12th Bt and Elizabeth Marie (*d* 1949), *d* of late W. T. La Roche, MD, New Jersey, USA; *S* father, 1917; *m* 1930, Evelyn Margaret, *o d* of late H. Fielding-Hall, Burma Commission; two *s* one *d. Educ:* Westminster School; RMA, Woolwich. Capt. 1928; Major, 1938; Lt-Col 1941. President, County of Kent SS&AFA, 1964-72; Hon. Col, SE London Bde, ACF, 1964-; Vice-Chm., Royal Cambridge Home for Soldiers' Widows, 1961-68; Hon. Sec. Royal Artillery Officers' Sports Fund, 1951-; Hon. Treas., Guild of St Helena, 1958-74; Hon. Treas., Officers' Families Fund, 1964-67. Pres., Kent County Small Bore Rifle Assoc., 1971-; DL, County of London (Wandsworth), 1962-78. *Recreations:* sailing, shooting, riding, stamp collecting. *Heir: s* Gilbert Howland Rookehurst Roberts, Lt TARO, BA Cambridge [*b* 31 May 1934; *m* 1958, Ines, *o d* of late A. Labunski; one *s* one *d*]. *Address:* Furzebank, Shorne Ridgeway, near Gravesend, Kent. *Clubs:* Army and Navy; RA Yacht; RE Yacht.
                                                      [Died 8 June 1979.

ROBERTS, Sir Walter St Clair Howland, KCMG 1951 (CMG 1937); MC; *b* 14 Dec. 1893; *m* 1st, 1924, Helen Cecil Ronayne (*d* 1951), *o c* of late Colonel A. W. Weekes, DSO, OBE, RE; 2nd, Cecily (*d* 1964), *widow* of H. E. Ormond. *Educ:* Winchester; Brasenose Coll., Oxford. Prisoner of War, 1914-16; served with RFA, 1917-19 (MC). Entered Foreign Office, 1919; Head of Western Europe Dept, 1936-39, and POW Dept, 1941-45; Ambassador to Peru, 1945-48; Minister to Roumania, 1949-51; Minister to Holy See, 1951-53. OStJ 1974. *Address:* Leaton Lodge, Bomere Heath, Salop.   *[Died 18 Nov. 1978.*

ROBERTS, Walter S.; *see* Stewart-Roberts.

ROBERTS, Sir William, Kt 1938; CIE 1934; BSc; LLD (hc); Member of Council of British Cotton Growing Association, Manchester; Emeritus Director BCGA Pb Ltd and Man. Dir RCA Ltd; Member Boyd Orr Agricultural Inquiry Committee Pakistan, 1951-52; *b* 17 Feb. 1884; *s* of John and Ann Roberts; *m* 1919, E. M. Jones, Llangefni; Anglesey; one *s* two *d. Educ:* Llangefni County School; UCNW Bangor; Leipzig University BSc, with 1st Class Hons in Chemistry in 1906; LLD (hc), Wales, 1952. Joined Indian Agricultural Service, 1906; Professor of Agriculture, Lyallpur, 1909-21; Principal, 1916-21. Member Indo-Japanese and Indo-British Trade Cttees, 1934 and 1938. *Publications:* Punjab Agriculture-Text Book of, revised edn 1947 and 1951. *Recreations:* tennis, fishing. *Address:* Cae Menai, Bangor, N Wales. *Clubs:* Sind (Karachi), Punjab (Lahore).   *[Died 16 June 1971.*

ROBERTS, William; RA 1966 (ARA 1958); artist; member of the London Group; *b* London, 1895. *Educ:* St Martin's School of Art; Slade School, London University. Worked at Omega Workshops under Roger Fry before 1914-18 War. Joined Vorticist Gp, 1914 (started by Wyndham Lewis). London Group, 1915. Official War Artist during European War, 1914-18 and War of 1939-45. Five paintings acquired by the Tate Gallery. Retrospective Exhibition, Tate Gallery, 1965. Exhibition, d'Offay Couper Gallery, 1969; Retrospective Exhibition, Hamet Gallery, 1971. *Address:* 14 St Marks Crescent, NW1.   *[Died 20 Jan. 1980.*

ROBERTS, Col William Quincey, CVO 1977 (MVO 1955); CBE 1958 (OBE 1952); DSO 1944 (Bar, 1945); TD; JP; DL; Land Steward, Duchy of Cornwall, 1948-77; *b* 5 Aug. 1912; *s* of late C M. Roberts, MVO, Woodland Place, Bathwick Hill, Bath; *m* 1938, Janet Finnimore Hughes, *d* of late G. E. Hughes, Bath three *d. Educ:* Tonbridge School. Asst Land Steward, Duchy of Cornwall, 1933. Commissioned Somerset LI (TA), 1933; Captain 1939; Major 1940; 2 i/c 6th Bn, 1942; served NW Europe, 1944-45; 2 i/c 4 Som. LI 1944; Lt-Col 1944; Comdr, 5 Bn Wilts Regt, 1944, 4 Bn Dorset Regt, 1944-45, and 4 Bn Somerset LI, 1947-52; Bt-Col 1952; Col 1954; Dep.-Comdr 130 Inf. Bde (TA), 1953-58. ADC to the Queen, 1956-61. Hon. Col: The Somerset Light Infantry, 1960-67; Somerset Yeomanry and Light Infantry, 1967-71; 1st Wessex Volunteers, T&AVR, 1970-75; 6th Bn LI (Volunteers), 1972-77 (Dep. Hon. Col, 1971-72). JP Avon, formerly Somerset, 1949; DL 1958; High Sheriff, 1969-70. Hon. Show Dir, Bath and West Southern Counties Soc., 1957-77 (Dep. Pres., 1977, Pres., 1979). Fellow Land Agents' Soc., 1947. *Recreations:* all field sports. *Address:* Stonewalls, Newton St Loe, near Bath, Avon. *T:* Saltford 3646. *Club:* Bath and County (Bath).   [*Died* 1 *Aug.* 1980.

ROBERTS, Col William Richter, CBE 1944; retired Civil Servant; *b* 12 Jan. 1888; *s* of William Roberts, Buckhurst Hill, Essex; *m* 1922, Alice Katharine, *d* of Major Fasson, Shoreham, Sussex; two *d. Educ:* Bancroft's School, Woodford Wells. Surveying Staff, GPO; Surveyor of Western District, England; Deputy Regional Director, Home Counties Region, GPO, 1949; served European War with Army Postal Services, 1914-19 (despatches); demobilised with rank of Lt-Col; Order of Crown of Roumania; War of 1939-45 with Army Postal Services, France, 1939-40, MEF 1941-43 (despatches, OBE, CBE); BLA 1944-45 (despatches twice, Officer, Legion of Merit, USA, French médaille de Reconaissance, en vermeil). *Recreations:* botany, fishing. *Address:* The Gables, 9 Mill Lane, Shoreham-by-Sea, Sussex. *Club:* Royal Commonwealth Society.
                                              [*Died* 7 *March* 1975.

ROBERTSHAW, Vice-Adm. Sir Ballin Illingworth, KBE 1958 (CBE 1944; OBE 1943); CB 1955; *b* 11 Sept. 1902; *s* of late Sydney Robertshaw and Gladys Gwendoline Robertshaw; *m* 1st, 1932, Hannah Catherine Luard (*d* 1948); two *s* two *d* ; 2nd, 1949, Margaret MacLaren. *Educ:* RN Colls Osborne and Dartmouth. RN Coll., Osborne, 1916; HMS Centurion, Midshipman, 1920; HMS Eagle, Sub Lt and Lt, 1924-26; specialized in Navigation at HMS Dryad, 1927; served HMS Cornflower, 1927-30; HMS Wallace, 1932; HMS Resolution, 1933-36; RN Staff College, 1936; Commander, HMS York, 1938; in command HMS Wallace, 1940; Admiralty, 1941; Staff of C-in-C Med. 1942-43; Captain, 1943; Invasion of Normandy, 1944; in command, HMS Cleopatra, 1944-46; Naval Asst to Second Sea Lord, 1949-51; in command HMS Implacable, 1952; Rear-Admiral, 1953; Chief-of-Staff to C-in-C, Portsmouth, 1953-55; Vice-Admiral, 1956; Chief of Allied Staff, Mediterranean, 1955-58; retired 1958. *Address:* Moonhills Gate, Beaulieu, Hants. *T:* Beaulieu 340. *Clubs:* United Service & Royal Aero, Royal Cruising, Royal Ocean Racing.
                                              [*Died* 14 *July* 1971.

ROBERTSHAW, Wilfrid, MA; Director of Bradford City Art Gallery and Museums, 1939-58; *b* 11 May 1893; *s* of late Jonathan and Emma Robertshaw; *m* 1920, Doris, *d* of late Edward and Janet Smith; one *d* (one *s* decd). *Educ:* Bradford; Leeds University. Librarian and Asst Keeper, Yorkshire Museum, York, 1915-19; Chief Asst, Bradford Public Libraries, 1919-26; Dep. Dir, Bradford City Art Gallery and Museums, 1926-39. Hon. Sec.: Assoc. of Assistant Librarians (Yorkshire Div.), 1922-23; Bradford Historical and Antiquarian Soc., 1926-34, Pres., 1934-35, 1955-57; Hon. Editor, The Bradford Antiquary, 1935-72; Hon. Sec., Bradford Diocesan Area Cttee, Nat. Register of Archives, 1950-70; Mem., Exec. Cttee, WR Yorks (N Section) Cttee, Nat. Register of Archives, 1954-67; Mem., Bradford Diocesan Adv. Cttee for the Care of Churches, 1965-72; Hon. Member: Bradford Arts Club; Bradford Historical and Antiquarian Soc. *Publications:* Official Handbook of Bolling Hall Museum, 1954; Centenary History of St Philip's Church School, Bradford, 1964; (ed) West Yorkshire Deeds, 1931-36; Registers of the Independent Chapel of Kipping in the parish of Bradford, 1937-54; forewords to art exhibition catalogues; reviews, articles and papers in Librarian and Book World, etc., Studio and other art jls, and periodicals and newspapers. *Recreations:* research into art, social history and genealogy; music. *Address:* 1241 Thornton Road, Thornton, Bradford, Yorks. *T:* Queensbury 881379.
                                              [*Died* 19 *March* 1974.

ROBERTSON OF OAKRIDGE, 1st Baron *cr* 1961, of Oakridge; **Gen. Brian Hubert Robertson**, Bt, *cr* 1919, of Welbourn; GCB 1952 (CB 1943); GBE 1949 (CBE 1942); KCMG 1947; KCVO 1944; DSO 1919; MC; DL; *b* 22 July 1896; *e s* of late FM Sir William Robertson, Bt (GCB, GCMG, GCVO; *S* father, 1933; *m* 1926, Edith, *d* of late J. B. Macindoe, Glasgow; one *s* two *d*. Served European War, 1914-19 (despatches, DSO, MC);

Waziristan Expedition, 1922-23 (despatches, Bt Major); retired pay, 1933; Managing Director, Dunlop South Africa Ltd, 1935; served Middle East, 1941-43 (CBE, CB); Chief Administrative Officer to General Alexander, C-in-C Italy, 1944-45; (KCVO); restored to the Active List Oct. 1945; Lt-Gen. 1946; Dep. Mil. Gov., CCG, 1945-47; Gen. 1947; C-in-C and Mil. Gov., 1947-49; UK High Commissioner, Allied High Commission, Germany, 1949-50; Commander-in-Chief, MELF, 1950-53, retd Nov. 1953. ADC Gen. to King George VI, 1949-52 and to the Queen, Feb.-June 1952. Chairman: British Transport Commission, 1953-61; ITA General Advisory Council, 1965-68. Director, Dunlop Co. Ltd, 1961-69; Vice-Pres., International Sleeping Car Co. President: Forces Help Society and Lord Roberts Workshops until 1974; Regular Forces Employment Association; Anglo-German Assoc.; Vice-President, Gloucester Association of Boys' Clubs. Colonel Commandant RE, 1950-60. REME, 1951-61; Hon. Col RE (AER, Tn), 1956-66; Hon. Col Engr and Ry Staff Corps, RE (TA), 1961-70. DL Gloucestershire, 1965; Master, Salters' Company, 1965. Hon. FIMechE, 1971; Hon. LLD Cambridge; CStJ; Comdr Legion of Honour; Comdr US Legion of Merit. *Heir: s* Major Hon. William Ronald Robertson, late Royal Scots Greys [*b* 8 Dec. 1930; *m* 1972, Celia Jane, *y d* of William R. Elworthy, Dorchester, Dorset. *Educ:* Charterhouse]. *Address:* Iles Green, Far Oakridge, Gloucestershire. *Clubs:* United Service & Royal Aero, Buck's.   [*Died* 29 *April* 1974.

ROBERTSON, Algar Ronald Ward, CMG 1953; CBE 1948; ED; FRGS; *b* 8 Sept. 1902; *s* of late Hume Robertson, Elmhurst, Wimbledon Common; *m* 1st, 1931, Carol Rhys (marr. diss., 1954), *d* of late H. R. Maunsell; one *d*; 2nd, 1955, Marjorie Mary, *d* of F. W. Lovatt Smith, Magham Down, Sussex. *Educ:* Dean Close School, Cheltenham. Assistant Treas., Gold Coast, 1929-36; Deputy Treasurer, British Guiana, 1936-39; Financial Secretary, Fiji, 1940-48, Trinidad and Tobago, 1948-53, Nigeria, 1953-54; Federation of Nigeria, 1954-56. *Recreations:* polo, golf, tennis. *Address:* Maplestone Farm, Broad Oak, near Rye, East Sussex. *T:* Brede 882261. *Club:* Naval and Military.
                                              [*Died* 27 *May* 1975.

ROBERTSON, Andrew, FRS 1940. *Educ:* Manchester Univ., DSc; Fairbairn Prize. Demonstrator in Engineering, Manchester University; Vulcan Fellow, University of Manchester; Major (Tech.), RAF; Prof. of Mechanical Engineering, Bristol Univ., 1919-46; President, Institution of Mechanical Engineers, 1945-46; Pres. Section G British Assoc., 1950; Principal of Bristol Merchant Venturers' Technical College, 1924-49. Hon. LLD Bristol, 1959; Hon. DSc Bath, 1969. *Publications:* Papers chiefly on Strength of Materials in Proc. Roy. Soc., Inst. Civil Engineers; Section G, British Association. *Address:* New Cote, Cote House Lane, Westbury-on-Trym, Bristol.
                                              [*Died* 22 *Oct.* 1977.

ROBERTSON, Maj.-Gen. Cecil Bruce, CB 1948; CBE 1946; MC 1918; DL; JP; *b* 8 March 1897; *er s* of late W. Bruce Robertson, 26 Kensington Palace Gdns, London, W, and of Mrs Bruce Robertson; *m* 1925, Sheila Mary, *d* of late Brig.-Gen. F. A. MacFarlan, CB; two *s* one *d. Educ:* Cheltenham; RMC Sandhurst. Commnd 2nd Lt The Argyll and Sutherland Highlanders, 1914. GSO2 HQ1 Corps, 1939-40; GSO1, 45 Div., 1940-41; Bde Commander 44 Div., 1941-42; DD of O (O) War Office, 1943; Director of Combined Operations (Military), 1943-45; BGS Southern Command, 1945-47; Chief of Staff Southern Command, 1947-48. Temp. Major-Gen., 1947; retired, 1948. DL Devon, 1954; JP 1955. *Address:* The Glebe House, Chudleigh, Devon. *T:* Chudleigh 2223. *Club:* Army and Navy.
                                              [*Died* 4 *Dec.* 1977.

ROBERTSON, Edith Anne; *b* Glasgow, 1883; *e d* of Robert Stewart of Clarewood, Limpsfield; *m* 1919, Rev. Professor J. A. Robertson (*d* 1955); three *d. Publications:* Songs of Pilgrimage and Battle, 1916; The Life and Letters of St Francis Xavier, Missionary, Mystic, Explorer, 1917; Poems, Second Book, 1919; Life of St Francis Xavier in the Modern Series of Missionary Biographies, 1930; He is Become My Song, 1930; Poems frae the Suddron o Walter de la Mare made ower intil Scots, 1955; Voices Frae the City o Trees, 1955; Collected Ballads and Poems in the Scots Tongue, 1967; Translations into the Scots Tongue of Poems of G. M. Hopkins, 1968; Forest Voices, and other poems in English, 1968. Author of historical play, Lady Jonet Douglas. *Address:* c/o Post Office, Dalry, Castle-Douglas, Kirkcudbrightshire, Scotland. *Club:* PEN. [*Died* 31 *Jan.* 1973.

ROBERTSON, James Cassels; Lord-Lieutenant of Dunbartonshire, since 1975; Director, Stephenson Clarke Shipping Ltd; Chairman: Robertson Research Holdings Ltd, since 1971; Tharsis Sulphur and Copper Co. Ltd; *b* 19 May 1921; *yr s* of late William Francis Robertson and of Harriett

Willis Cassels; *m* 1947, Joan, *er d* of late Lt-Comdr E. Kirkpatrick-Crockett, RN, and of Leila Bootiman; two *s* one *d*. *Educ:* Winchester. Served in RNVR, 1940-46. DL Dunbartonshire, 1965; Vice-Lieutenant, Dunbartonshire, 1968-75. Mem., Queen's Body Guard for Scotland, Royal Co. of Archers. Chm., Scottish and Ulster Area, British Shipping Fedn, 1968-73; Deacon, Incorporation of Hammermen of Glasgow, 1971. Chairman: Scottish Council, King George's Fund for Sailors, 1972-; Bd of Governors, Glasgow Coll. of Nautical Studies, 1969-75; Glasgow Veteran Seafarers Assoc., 1962-. OStJ. *Recreation:* yachting. *Address:* Cromalt, Helensburgh, Dunbartonshire. *T:* Helensburgh 6111. *Clubs:* Royal Thames Yacht; Royal Yacht Squadron (Cowes); Royal Northern Yacht (Rhu) (Cdre 1964-70). *[Died 9 Dec. 1978.*

ROBERTSON, Col John Richard Hugh, CBE 1974 (OBE 1951); consultant; Chief Inspecting Officer of Railways, Department of the Environment, 1969-73, retired; *b* 18 Nov. 1912; *s* of Col James C. Robertson, CMG, CIE, CBE, IMS, and Catherine Mary Jones; *m* 1940, Elizabeth, *d* of W. Froggatt, MC; two *s*. *Educ:* Aysgarth Sch.; Wellington Coll.; RMA, Woolwich; Trinity Hall, Cambridge Univ. RMA, Woolwich, 1931 (Prize Cadet, Cadet Schol., Army Schol., and Sword of Honour; boxing, athletics and pentathlon teams); RE, 1932; Trinity Hall, Cambridge, 1933; BA (Hons, Mech. Sci. Tripos), 1935. Served War of 1939-45: BEF, 1939; Norway, 1940; psc, 1941; AQMG MECTC, 1943; AQMG CTC, India and SORE, DCO, India, 1944; Comd 46 Ind. Beach Gp, 1945. AQMG, Malaya, Chief Instructor Transptn Trg Centre, UK, 1946; JSSC, AAG AG3, War Office, 1947; Chief Instructor, Greek Staff Coll., 1950; CO, ME Transptn Regt, RE, 1952; Chief Instr (Tactics), SME, Chatham, 1954; AAG, MPI, War Office, 1957; Inspecting Officer of Railways, 1959. FCIT (MInstT 1969); CEng, FIMechE; FICE 1975; Fellow, Instn of Railway Signal Engrs, 1969. *Recreation:* fishing. *Address:* Little Green, Frensham, Surrey. *T:* Frensham 2775. *Club:* Naval and Military.
[Died 20 Feb. 1977.

ROBERTSON, Muriel, FRS 1947; MA, DSc (Glasgow); LLD (Glasgow) 1948; Protozoologist, Lister Institute, 1915-61; *b* 8 April 1883; *d* of Robert Andrew Robertson and Elizabeth Ritter. *Educ:* privately; Glasgow Univ. Carnegie Research Sch., 1905-06; Carnegie Research Fellow, 1907-10; Asst to late Prof. Minchin, 1909-10; on Staff Lister Inst., 1910-11; Protozoologist to Uganda Protectorate, 1911-14. *Publications:* numerous papers on Protozoology and bacteriology in various scientific journals. *Recreations:* sketching and walking. *Address:* Garth, 83 Ballyquin Road, Limavady, Co. Londonderry, Northern Ireland. *Club:* Cowdray. *[Died 14 June 1973.*

ROBERTSON, Vernon Alec Murray, CBE 1943; MC 1917, Bar 1918; *b* 29 Dec. 1890; *o s* of Alexander Robertson, Calcutta; *m* 1st, 1915, Ivy Kathleen (*decd*), *y d* of C. J. Cooper, Clapham Park, SW; one *s* two *d*; 2nd, 1934, Gertrude Ruth, *widow* of C. E. H. Morton, Bank Manager. *Educ:* Dover College; Crystal Palace School of Practical Engineering. Civil Engineer on Railway Work. Articled to late D. Gravell, MInstCE, 1909-12; SE & C Rly Engineers Department, 1912-19; GE Railway District Engineer, 1919; Underground Railways of London as Civil Engineer, 1928; Chief Engineer (Civil) LPTB, 1938; Engineer-in-Chief, 1940-43; Chief Civil Engineer to Southern Rly Co., 1944-48, British Rlys, Southern Region, 1948-51, retd 1951; Partner and consultant, Sir William Halcrow & Partners, Chartered Civil Engineers, Westminster, 1951-64. Served European War as NCO in London Scottish; commissioned RE 1915; France with BEF 1915-19 (despatches, MC and Bar); demob. as Major RE 1919; Past Col Comdg Engineer and Railway Staff Corps RE. Past Pres. InstCE; Past Pres. and Fellow, Permanent Way Institution; Hon. FSE; Hon. Mem. American Railway Engineering Association. *Recreation:* fishing. *Address:* 25 Chalfont Court, NW1. *T:* 01-935 5950. *Clubs:* Athenæum, Royal Automobile. *[Died 12 Feb. 1971.*

ROBERTSON-JUSTICE, James Norval Harold; actor; Rector of the University of Edinburgh, 1957-60, 1963-66; *b* 15 June 1905; *o s* of late James Norval Justice, DSc, MIMM; *m* (marr. diss. 1968); *m* 1975, Baroness Irina von Myerndorff. *Educ:* Marlborough Coll.; Bonn University (Dr Phil, Nat. Sci.). Career undistinguished but varied, comprising some three score jobs in different parts of the world. Inventor of the rocket propelled net method of catching wildfowl for marking. LLD (Hon.) Edinburgh, 1960. *Publications:* various papers on ornithology, ecology and conservation. *Recreation:* falconry. *Address:* Tigh an Allt, Old Town of Ardgay, Easter Ross. *T:* Ardgay 342; Top House of Ashley, King's Somborne, Stockbridge, Hants. *T:* King's Somborne 488. *Clubs:* The Goat; Highland (Inverness). *[Died 2 July 1975.*

ROBESON, Paul Le Roy; concert singer and actor; *b* Princeton, New Jersey, 9 April 1898; *s* of Rev. William D. Robeson and Louisa Bustill; *m* Eslanda Cardozo Goode (*d* 1965); one *s*. *Educ:* Rutgers Coll. (Scholar), BA; Columbia Univ., New York, LLB; Rutgers University, Hon. MA. Made first appearance on stage in New York, 1921; first appearance on concert platform in New York in 1925, as singer of negro folk music which, together with his associate Lawrence Brown, he has played a leading part in developing; first appearance in London in Emperor Jones, 1925. Makes annual international concert tours with Lawrence Brown. Played the leading roles in Taboo, Emperor Jones, All God's Chillun, Black Boy, in New York; sang Ol' Man River in the Show Boat at Drury Lane, 1928; played title role in Othello at the Savoy, 1930; title role in Hairy Ape at Ambassadors, 1932; role of Jim Harris in All God's Chillun at Piccadilly, 1933; title role in film of Emperor Jones, 1933; role of Bosambo in film of Sanders of the River, 1935; title role in Stevedore at Embassy, 1935; title role in John Henry in New York, 1940; title role in Othello in USA, 1943-44 and 1944-45 and at Royal Shakespeare Theatre, Stratford-on-Avon, 1959. Hon. Dr Phil, Humboldt Univ., Berlin, 1960. Member: Phi Beta Kappa and Cap and Skull, Rutgers; Alpha Phi Alpha and Sigma Tau Sigma fraternities. *Publication:* Here I Stand, 1958.
[Died 23 Jan. 1976.

ROBIESON, Sir William, Kt 1948; MA, LLD (Glasgow); JP; Editor of the Glasgow Herald, 1937-55; Chancellor's Assessor, Glasgow University, 1956-72; *b* Fossoway, Kinross-shire, 29 May 1890; *s* of William D. Robieson, Schoolmaster; *m* 1919, Mabel Graham, *e d* of John Mackenzie, Sandbank, Argyll; one *d*. *Educ:* Dollar Academy; University of Glasgow. MA, Glasgow, 1912, First Class Honours in History; Assistant to Professor of History in the University of Glasgow, 1913-14; joined Editorial Staff of Glasgow Herald, 1914, and returned there, 1919, after serving with Cameron Highlanders and with Gold Coast Regt of West African Frontier Force; Assistant Editor of Glasgow Herald, 1926; Member of Royal Commission on Population, 1944-49; Trustee, National Galleries of Scotland, 1949-67, and National Museum of Antiquities of Scotland, 1954-66. *Address:* 9 Clarence Drive, Glasgow G12 9QL. *T:* 041-339 5964. *[Died 19 July 1977.*

ROBINS, Sir Reginald Edwin, Kt 1945; CMG 1938; OBE; MInstT; *b* 29 April 1891; *s* of Thomas Henry Robins, late of Basingstoke, Hants; *m* 1914, Adeline Annie (*d* 1964), *d* of Edward Ayling, Bentworth, Hants; one *s* one *d*. *Educ:* Queen Mary's School, Basingstoke; London School of Economics. Entered service of Great Western Railway, 1908; special training under Great Western training scheme for officers, 1920; London School of Economics, 1919-24; Brunel Medallist; entered Colonial Service, Kenya and Uganda Railways, 1925; General Manager, Tanganyika Railways and Ports Services, 1936-42; Kenya and Uganda Railways and Harbours, 1942-48; Commr for Transport, East Africa High Commission, 1948-53. *Recreation:* golf. *Address:* Kenton, Linkside West, Hindhead, Surrey. *[Died 2 Feb. 1971.*

ROBINSON, Maj.-Gen. Alfred Eryk, CB 1949; DSO 1940; JP; DL; *b* 19 Sept. 1894; *s* of late A. H. Robinson, JP, Derwent House, West Ayton, Scarborough; *m* 1942, Ailison Campbell, *d* of late P. C. Low, Dowrich House, Sandford, Crediton, and *widow* of Major S. H. Birchall Wood, R Deccan Horse. *Educ:* RMC, Sandhurst. Joined Green Howards, Aug. 1914; Lieut-Colonel, 1st Bn Green Howards, 1939; Col 1942; Temp. Maj-Gen. 1943; retired, 1948. Colonel, The Green Howards, 1949-59. N Riding of Yorkshire: DL, 1952, JP 1953. *Address:* Derwent House, East Ayton, Scarborough, N Yorks. *T:* West Ayton 2130. *[Died 4 March 1978.*

ROBINSON, Sir Arnet, Kt 1963; formerly President, Coast Lines Ltd, and Associated Companies, 1969-71 (formerly Chairman, and Chairman of Executive Committee); *b* 24 April 1898; 2nd *s* of Francis and Amy Robinson, Stanmore Middlesex; *m* 1928, Beatrice E. Baber; two *s* one *d*. *Educ:* Westminster (King's Scholar). Chm. Mersey Docks and Harbour Board, 1954-62; President Dock and Harbour Authorities Association, 1961-63; Life Vice-Pres., RNLI. Served European War, 1914-18, 60th Rifles (SR) and attached RAF; War of 1939-45, HG, Cheshire Regt. Chm. Coasting and Short Sea Shipping Control Cttee, Liverpool Area, 1939-47; Chm. Liverpool Steam Ship Owners Assoc., 1946 (Chm. Coastwise Section, 1943-44 and 1948); Vice-Chm., Gen. Council of British Shipping, 1946; Chm. Coasting Liner Sect., Chamber of Shipping, 1948-50. OStJ. *Recreation:* yachting. *Address:* White Gables, St Margarets Road, Hoylake, Cheshire. *T:* 051-632 4453. *Clubs:* Junior Carlton, MCC; Royal Yacht Squadron; Royal Liverpool Golf.
[Died 4 May 1975.

ROBINSON, Rt. Rev. Cuthbert Cooper, DD; *b* 26 May 1893; *s* of Rev. John Cooper Robinson, DD, and Betsy Poynton; *m* 1920, Jean A. Bryce, *d* of Dr P. H. Bryce, Ottawa; two *s* two *d* (one *d* decd). *Educ:* University of Toronto (BA); Wycliffe College, Toronto. Canadian Army, 1914-19 (Lieut). Deacon, 1920; Educational work in Japan, 1920-38; Priest, 1938; Rector of Geraldton, 1939-43; Rector of Forest, 1943-44; Rector of Noranda, 1944-48; Rector of Timmins, 1948-54. Canon, 1947; Dean of Moosonee, 1948; Bishop of Moosonee, 1954-63, retired. Hon. DD 1949. *Address:* 58 Catherine Avenue, Aurora, Ontario, Canada.
[Died 30 May 1971.

ROBINSON, David Morrant, CBE 1974; JP; Joint Hon. Treasurer, National Council of YMCAs, since 1957; *b* 1 July 1910; 3rd *s* of late Alfred Robinson, JP and Constance Alice Robinson (*née* Goodes). *Educ:* Malvern College. Partner, Joseph Robinson & Sons (Managers of Stag Line Ltd), Shipowners, 1933, Sen. Partner 1941; Dir and Chm. Stag Line Ltd, 1953 (when Bd of Dirs created), retd as Chm. 1975; Chm. or Dir of other Companies. Chm., North of England Shipowners Assoc., 1951 (Vice-Pres. 1963-); Pres., Chamber of Shipping of UK, 1962. Pres., World Alliance of YMCAs, 1969-73. Hon. Freeman, Trinity House, Newcastle upon Tyne, 1974. JP County Borough of Tynemouth (now North Tyneside), 1946. *Recreation:* contemplative gardening. *Address:* 27 Beverley Gardens, Cullercoats, North Shields, Tyne and Wear NE30 4NS. *T:* Whitley Bay 24608. *Club:* National Liberal.
[Died 3 March 1977.

ROBINSON, Commodore David Samuel, CBE 1941; RD; RNR (retired); *b* 20 Dec. 1888; *s* of James Samuel and Eleanor Robinson; *m* 1st; one *s* one *d*; 2nd, 1939, Margaret Gwendoline Keyes; one *s*. *Educ:* Hull Trinity House Navigation School. Master mariner (extra), 1913; joined Cunard Steamship Company Ltd, 1913; Sub-Lieut RNR, 1914; on active service throughout War of 1914-18, light cruisers; continued in Cunard Atlantic passenger service to outbreak of War, 1939, serving in Queen Mary and in new Mauretania; served War of 1939-45 (CBE); on retired list RNR, 1944; Marine Superintendent Cunard White Star Line in New York, 1944-53; retired 1953. *Address:* The Oaks, Ebford, Topsham, Devon.
[Died 2 Jan. 1972.

ROBINSON, Edward G.; Actor, Film Actor, and Radio Entertainer; *b* Rumania, 12 Dec. 1893; *s* of M. and S. Goldenberg; *m* 1st, 1927, Gladys Lloyd Cassell (marr. diss. 1956); one *s*; 2nd, 1958, Jane Adler. *Educ:* Townsend Harris High Sch.; City of New York Coll.; Columbia Univ.; American Acad. of Dramatic Arts, NY. Stage appearances include: Paid in Full, 1913; Under Fire, 1915; Under Sentence, 1916; The Pawn, 1917; The Little Teacher, 1918; Night Lodging, 1919; Poldekin, Samson and Delilah, 1920; The Idle Inn, The Deluge, Banco, 1922; Peer Gynt, The Adding Machine, A Royal Fandango, 1923; The Firebrand, 1924; Androcles and The Lion, The Man of Destiny, 1925; The Goat Song, The Chief Thing, Henry-Behave, 1926; Juarez and Maximilian, Ned McCobb's Daughter, The Brothers Karamazov, Right You Are if You Think You Are, 1926-27; The Racket, 1927; The Man with Red Hair, 1928; Kibitzer, 1929; Mr Samuel, 1930; Darkness at Noon, Season 1951-52 (toured US); The Middle of the Night (Broadway), 1956-58 (3 yrs). *Films include:* The Bright Shawl (silent film), 1923; The Hole in the Wall, The Night Ride, East is West, The Widow from Chicago, A Lady to Love, Outside the Law, Smart Money, Little Cæsar, Five Star Final, The Hatchet Man, Two Seconds, Tiger Shark, Little Giant, Silver Dollar, I Loved a Woman, Dark Hazard, Man with Two Faces, The Whole Town's Talking, Bullets or Ballots, Kid Galahad, A Slight Case of Murder, I am the Law, The Amazing Dr Clitterhouse, Blackmail, Confessions of a Nazi Spy, The Life of Dr Ehrlich, Brother Orchid, A Dispatch from Reuter's, Man Power, The Sea Wolf, Unholy Partners, Tales of Manhattan, Night before Christmas, Flesh and Fantasy, Double Indemnity, Destroyer, Mr Winkle Goes to War, Woman in the Window, Scarlet Street, The Stranger, Our Vines have Tender Grapes, The Red House, All my Sons, Key Largo, Night has a Thousand Eyes, House of Strangers, My Daughter Joy, Operation X, Actors and Sin, Vice Squad, The Big Leaguer, The Glass Web, Black Tuesday, Violent Men, Tight Spot, Bullet for Joey, Illegal, The Darkest Hour, The Ten Commandments, Nightmare, Hell on Frisco Bay, Hole in the Head, Seven Thieves, Pépé, My Geisha, Two Weeks in Another Town, Sammy Going South, The Prize, Robin and the Seven Hoods, Good Neighbour Sam, Cheyenne Autumn, The Outrage, Cincinnati Kid, The Biggest Bundle of Them All, Peking Blonde, Grand Slam, Never a Dull Moment, Mackenna's Gold, Operation St Peter, Song of Norway, The Old Man Who Cried Wolf, The Messiah on Mott Street. Served European War, 1917-18, with United States Navy; War of 1941-45, with Office of War Information (broadcasts

from England in 9 languages to Continental underground). Chevalier Légion d'Honneur, 1952; Officier de l'Instruction Publique, 1953. Townsend Harris Medal (CCNY); James K. Hackett Medal (CCNY); Eleanor Roosevelt Humanitarian Award, 1963. *Recreations:* languages, music, pipes, painting, travelling, collecting art. *Publication:* The Kibitzer (with J. Swerling), 1929. *Address:* 910 Rexford Drive, Beverly Hills, Calif, USA. *Clubs:* Lambs (NY); Masquers (Hollywood).
[Died 26 Jan. 1973.

ROBINSON, Sir Edward (Stanley Gotch), Kt 1972; CBE 1952; MA; FSA; FBA 1942; *y s* of late Edward Robinson, Sneyd Park, Bristol; *m* 1917, Pamela Comfrey, *o d* of late Sir Victor Horsley, CB, FRS; two *s* four *d*. *Educ:* Clifton College (Scholar); Christ Church Oxford (Scholar). First Class Class. Mod. and Lit. Hum.; Barclay Head Prize for Numismatics, 1910; Student of the British School at Athens, 1910; Asst in British Museum, 1912; Dep. Keeper, 1936; Keeper of Coins and Medals, British Museum, 1949-52, retired. Lt, 3rd Northants Regt, 1914; served in France, 1915-16 (twice wounded); in Home Office, 1917-19; Huntington Medallist American Numismatic Society, 1935; Medallist of Royal Numismatic Society, 1942; Hon. Curator of Greek Coins, Ashmolean Museum, Oxford; Hon. Student of Christ Church, Oxford, 1955-; Corresponding Member: Deutsches Archäologisches Institut and the American, Vienna, and Zagreb Numismatic Socs. Hon. DLitt, Oxford, 1955. *Publications:* Cyrenaica, in British Museum Catalogue of Greek Coins, 1927; Locker-Lampson (1923) and Woodward (1928) Collections of Greek Coins; (ed and part author) Sylloge Nummorum Græcorum, 1931 (in progress); contrib. archæological periodicals. *Address:* Iwerne Stepleton, Blandford, Dorset. *Club:* Athenæum.
[Died 13 June 1976.

ROBINSON, Eric, OBE 1969; Conductor and TV Personality; *b* 13 Dec. 1908; *s* of Percy and Carrie Robinson. *Educ:* Watford Grammar School; Royal College of Music. Joined BBC Theatre Orchestra (violinist), 1923. Army volunteer, 1940; latter years of service devoted to directing and recording shows for the Troops. Appointed to BBC Television Service, 1947, where he conducted shows of every type, particularly Music for You. Programmes include: (TV) Eric Robinson presents, 1967-; (Radio) Melodies for You, 1967-; Records for You, 1960-; Eric Robinson's Music Club, 1970-. Director of some 14 companies inc. IBC Sound Recording Studios. *Publication:* Conducted Personally, 1955; Adventures in Music, 1957. *Recreation:* rose growing. *Address:* IBC Studios, 35 Portland Place, W1. *T:* 01-636 0751. *Club:* Savage.
[Died 24 July 1974.

ROBINSON, Sir (Ernest) Stanley, Kt 1969; CBE 1966; President of the Barbados Senate, 1966-73 (Member, 1964-73); sugar planter; *b* 18 Jan. 1905; *s* of Samuel Stanley Robinson and Hannah Eliza Robinson; *m* 1926, Annie Carmen Yearwood; one *s* two *d*. *Educ:* Harrison Coll., Barbados; Warwick Sch., England; St John's Coll., Cambridge. MHA Barbados, 1928-32, 1937-46; MLC, 1952-64; Mem. Barbados Privy Council, 1968. Founder Mem., Barbados Sugar Producers Assoc.; Dir, West Indies Sugar Assoc.; Chm., Plantations Ltd; Bridgetown, Barbados; Director: Foursquare Sugar Estates Ltd; Foursquare Factory Ltd; Constant Estates Ltd; Barbados Light & Power Co. *Recreations:* swimming, shooting. *Address:* Constant Estates Ltd, St George, Barbados, West Indies. *Club:* Barbados Yacht.
[Died 13 Nov. 1977.

ROBINSON, Major Sir Frederick Villiers Laud, 10th Bt, *cr* 1660; MC; late 3rd Northamptonshire Regiment; *b* 4 Dec. 1880; *o s* of 9th Bt and Madeleine Caroline, *e d* of Frederick Sartoris of Rushden, Northants; *S* father, 1893; *m* 1st, 1913, Eileen (who obtained a divorce, 1933; she *d* 1965), *e d* of Harry Higham; one *s* (and one *s* killed in action North Africa, 1941); 2nd, 1933, Frances Joyce, *er d* of Arthur Tyrwhitt Drake, Crendle, Sherborne, Dorset. Served European War, 1914-18 (wounded twice, MC, Croix de Guerre). Owns about 2100 acres. *Heir: g s* John James Michael Laud Robinson, *b* 19 Jan. 1943. *Address:* Cranford Hall, Kettering, Northants. *T:* Cranford 217.
[Died 19 March 1975.

ROBINSON, Gleeson Edward, CB 1945; MC; LLD (London); Hon. Captain, RFA; *s* of Rev. John Robinson, Dudley; *m* 1945, Frances Elizabeth (*d* 1966), widow of P. J. Horsley. *Educ:* King Edward's Sch., Birmingham; London University. Solicitor, London, 1904-15; Royal Field Artillery, 1915-19, served in France (despatches, MC and Bar); Barrister-at-Law, Middle Temple, 1920; Secretary of Clearing Office (Enemy Debts), 1920-25; British Member of Anglo-German Mixed Arbitral Tribunal established under Treaty of Versailles, 1925-30; Traffic Comr (Metropolitan Area), 1931-46; Chm. Road Rail Traffic Appeal Tribunal, 1946-49. *Publication:* Public Authorities and Legal Liability. *Recreations:* golf, fishing. *Address:* La Falaise,

Noirmont Lane, Ouaisne, Jersey, CI. *T:* Central 41461.
[Died 27 June 1978.

ROBINSON, Maj.-Gen. Guy St George, CB 1945; DSO 1918; MC 1915; psc; *b* 2 April 1887; *s* of St George Charles Woodhouse Robinson, solicitor, Sligo, Ireland, and Isabella Carson, *sister* of late Baron Carson; *m* 1917, Eva Suzanne Hadra (*d* 1959). *Educ:* Malvern; Sandhurst. Joined Northamptonshire Regiment, 1907; posted to 1st Bn, 1908, Poona; went to Aden with Bn, 1908-10, and returned to England (Devonport), 1911; went to France, Aug. 1914 (wounded, MC); Adjutant 1st Northamptonshire Regt, April-Nov. 1915; 2nd in command, April-July 1917; Lt-Col in command, July 1917-April 1919 (despatches twice, DSO, MC); Instructor RMC, Sandhurst, 1919-23; Staff College, Camberley, 1924-25; Commanded Regimental Depôt, Northampton, 1926-27; Staff, 1928-31; 2nd Bn, Aldershot, 1932; Lt-Col 1933; commanded 2nd Bn Northamptonshire Regiment, 1933-35; Col 1935; Assistant Commandant, Hythe Wing, Small Arms School, 1935-37; Commander Rangoon Brigade Area, 1937-40; Brigade Commander, Home Forces, 1941; Area Commander, 1942; District Commander, 1943; Col of Northamptonshire Regt 1943-53; retired pay, 1944. *Address:* Saltwood Cottage, Hythe, Kent.   *[Died 21 March 1973.*

ROBINSON, Sir Harold (Ernest), Kt 1955; company director, Trinidad and Tobago; Member of Trinidad and Tobago Senate, 1971-76; *b* 9 Oct. 1905; *s* of Ernest Augustus Robinson and Henrietta Mabel (*née* Fitt); *m* 1929, Clarice Graeme (*née* Yearwood); two *s* three *d*. *Educ:* Lancing; Stowe; Magdalene Coll., Cambridge. Joined Staff of Usine St Madeleine Sugar Estate Ltd, San Fernando, Trinidad, 1927; joined staff of Woodford Lodge Estates Ltd, 1929, Man. Dir, 1944-61. President: Agricultural Soc. of Trinidad and Tobago; British Caribbean Citrus Assoc.; Vice-Pres., West India Cttee. MLC, 1946-61. *Recreations:* flying, fishing, horticulture. *Address:* c/o 17-19 Edward Street, Port of Spain, Trinidad, WI. *T:* 62-51482. *Club:* Union (Port of Spain, Trinidad).   *[Died 18 Nov. 1979.*

ROBINSON, Sir John (Edgar), Kt 1958; Chairman Frederic Robinson Ltd and associated companies since 1933; *b* 20 March 1895; *s* of William Robinson, Stockport and Wilmslow and Priscilla (*née* Needham); *m* 1926, Gwendolen Harriet May, *d* of Sydney Herbert Evans, London; three *s*. *Educ:* Stockport Grammar School; Manchester University (LLB). Qualified as Solicitor, 1918; entered family business of Frederic Robinson, Ltd, 1918. President Stockport Chamber of Commerce, 1947. Held various offices in Conservative Party, 1945-75; Chairman Knutsford Division Conservative Assoc., 1949-52, Deputy President, 1952-71, President, 1971-75. *Recreation:* sailing. *Address:* Wellfield, Dean Row, Wilmslow, Cheshire. *T:* Wilmslow 23384.   *[Died 21 Feb. 1978.*

ROBINSON, Sir Leslie (Harold), KBE 1957; CB 1952; Industrial Adviser to J. Henry Schroder Wagg since 1964; Vice-Chairman: George Cohen 600 Group; R.H.P. Co.; Director: Renold Ltd; Reyrolle-Parsons; Hall-Thermotank; Chairman, EDC for Electrical Engineering, since 1964; *b* 19 Oct. 1903; *s* of George and Blanche Robinson; *m* 1938, Isobel, *d* of George William Steele; no *c*. *Educ:* Owen's School; Peterhouse, Cambridge. BA 1925; teaching, 1926-37; HMI Board of Education, 1937; Ministry of Supply, 1939; Under Secretary, 1948; Deputy-Secretary, Ministry of Supply, 1953; Second Secretary, Board of Trade, 1955-63, retired. Mem., Export Guarantees Adv. Council, 1969-, Dep. Chm. 1973-. Chairman: London Univ. Halls of Residence Cttee, 1964-; Univ. of London Cttee of Student Accommodation. *Recreations:* reading, opera, drinking wine, lawn tennis. *Address:* White House, Esher Close, Esher, Surrey. *T:* Esher 63114. *Clubs:* Brooks's, Royal Automobile.   *[Died 23 April 1974.*

ROBINSON, Air Commodore Maurice Wilbraham Sandford, CBE 1943; Royal Air Force; *b* 20 Sept. 1910; *s* of late Josiah Robinson; *m* 1936, Margaret Gwendolen Phelps (*d* 1976); one *s* two *d*. *Educ:* Liverpool College. Entered RAF Cadet College, Cranwell, 1929; commissioned RAF, 1930. Retired, March 1958. *Address:* Gwern Borter, Ro Wen, Conway, Gwynedd LL32 8YL. *Club:* Royal Air Force.   *[Died 2 April 1977.*

ROBINSON, Sir Montague Arnet; *see* Robinson, Sir Arnet.

ROBINSON, Very Rev. Norman; Provost of Blackburn Cathedral, 1961-72; *b* 18 Feb. 1905; *s* of Thomas and Margaret Robinson (*née* Cullen); unmarried. *Educ:* Ulverston Grammar School; Liverpool University; Ridley Hall, Cambridge. BSc. 1st class Hons Maths, Derby Scholar, 1927; Dip. Educ. 1928. Senior Mathematics Master, Quarry Bank School, Liverpool, 1928-35. Deacon, 1934; priest, 1935; Curate: Mossley Hill, Liverpool,

1934-35; Holy Trinity, Southport, 1935-37; Lancaster Priory, 1937-40; Vicar of: Newbarns and Hawcoat, 1940-48; Penrith, 1948-59; Hon. Canon, Carlisle, 1954; Rector of West Derby, Liverpool, 1959-61. *Recreations:* music, theatre, books. *Address:* Broomfield, Preston New Road, Blackburn, Lancs. *T:* Blackburn 52502.   *[Died 27 April 1973.*

ROBINSON, Sir Norman De Winton, Kt 1958; *b* 9 March 1890; *s* of Frederick Farquhar Robinson and Caroline Margaret Turner; *m* 1916, Edna Jeanne Smibert; one *d* (and one *s* killed in action, 1943). *Educ:* Melbourne Church of England Gram. Sch. Australian Knitting Mills Ltd, 1907-23; Yarra Falls Ltd, Abbotsford, 1923-66; Chm., Norwich Union Fire Insurance Society, Melbourne, 1942. Coronation Medal, 1953. *Recreations:* racing, golf. *Address:* 2a Hopetoun Road, Toorak, Victoria 3142, Australia. *T:* UY7898. *Clubs:* Athenæum (Melbourne); Peninsula Golf; VRC, VATC, MVRC (racing clubs).   *[Died 6 Sept. 1972.*

ROBINSON, Rev. Prof. Norman Hamilton Galloway, MA (Glasgow); BD (Edinburgh); DLitt (Glasgow); DD (Edinburgh); Professor of Divinity and Systematic Theology in the University of St Andrews; *b* 7 October 1912; *e s* of late George Robinson and late Barbara Fraser, Troon, Ayrshire; *m* 1936, Mary Elizabeth, *o d* of Christopher Johnston, Portrush; two *s* two *d*. *Educ:* Ayr Academy; Universities of Glasgow, Oxford and Edinburgh. Minister of: Sandsting Parish Church, Shetland, 1939-43; South Church, Fraserburgh, Aberdeenshire, 1943-48; High Kirk of Rothesay, 1948-54; Prof. of Divinity and Dean of Faculty, Rhodes Univ., Grahamstown, SA, 1954-56; Prof. of Systematic Theology, 1956-67, of Divinity and Systematic Theology, 1967-, Univ. of St Andrews. Dean of Faculty of Divinity, Univ. of St Andrews, 1958-62; Examiner in Divinity, Universities of: Natal, 1954-55, South Africa, 1954-56, Aberdeen, 1960-62, Edinburgh, 1962-65, Newcastle upon Tyne, 1965-67, Glasgow, 1967-71, QUB, 1971-73, Durham, 1974-76; Wales, 1975-. Special Lectr in Christian Ethics: Assembly's Coll., Belfast, 1960-61; Univ. Coll. of North Wales, Bangor, 1975; Guest Lecturer: Institute of Theology, Princeton Theol Seminary, USA, 1966; Graduate Summer Session, Anglican Theol and Union Colls, Vancouver, Canada, 1966. Mem., Ct of Univ. of St Andrews, 1971-75. Gov. of Strathallan School. *Publications:* Faith and Duty, 1950; The Claim of Morality, 1952; Christ and Conscience, 1956; The Groundwork of Christian Ethics, 1971; contribs to: Theologians of Our Time, 1966; Dictionary of Christian Theology, 1969; Talk of God, 1969; Preface to Christian Studies, 1971; Sprachlogik des Glaubens, 1974; articles and reviews in Philosophy, The Philosophical Quarterly, Theology, The Expository Times, Hibbert Jl, Scottish Journal of Theology, Religious Studies, etc. *Recreation:* golf. *Address:* Byculla, 10 Trinity Place, St Andrews, Fife KY16 8SG. *T:* 2531.   *[Died 9 March 1978.*

ROBINSON, Sir Robert, OM 1949; Kt 1939; FRS; Commandeur de la Légion d'Honneur; MA, FRIC; DSc (Victoria); Hon. DSc Oxford, London, Liverpool, Wales, Dunelm, Sheffield, Belfast, Nottingham, Delhi, Bristol, Sydney, Zagreb, Strathclyde, Hokkaido; Hon. ScD Cantab; Hon. LLD Birmingham, Edinburgh, St Andrews, Glasgow, Liverpool, Manchester; Hon. DPharm Madrid and Paris; Hon. DLL Brussels; Hon. MICE; Hon. Fellow of Magdalen College, Oxford, since 1956; Hon. Fellow of Weizmann Institute of Science, Rehovot, Israel; Director: Shell Chemical Co. Ltd since 1955, Shell Research Ltd, since 1967; President, British Association for the Advancement of Science, 1955; President, Society of Chemical Industry, 1958-59; Hon. or Foreign member of many academies and scientific societies; *b* 13 Sept. 1886; *s* of W. B. Robinson, surgical dressing manufacturer, and Mrs Robinson of Field House, Chesterfield; *m* 1st, 1912, Gertrude Maud Walsh, MSc (*d* 1954), *d* of T. M. Walsh, The Hollies, Winsford; one *s* one *d* ; 2nd, 1957, Stearn Sylvia (*née* Hershey), Hillstrom, of NY. *Educ:* Fulneck School, near Leeds; University of Manchester. Prof. of Organic Chemistry (Pure and Applied), Univ. of Sydney, NSW, 1912-15; Heath Harrison Professor of Organic Chemistry, Liverpool, 1915; Director of Research, British Dyestuffs Corporation, Ltd, 1920; Professor of Chemistry, St Andrews, 1921; Professor of Organic Chemistry, Manchester, 1922-28; Professor of Organic Chemistry, University College, London, 1928-30; Waynflete Professor of Chemistry, Oxford University, 1930-55; Bakerian Lecturer, Royal Society, 1929; President Chemical Society, 1939-41; Longstaff Medallist Chemical Society; Davy Medallist of Royal Society, 1930; Royal Medallist, 1932; President of Royal Society, 1945-50; Paracelsus Medallist of the Swiss Chemical Soc., 1939; Copley Medallist 1942; Albert Gold Medal, RSA, 1947; Hofmann Medal German Chem. Society, 1957. Hon. Member Parly and Sci Committee, 1949; Hon. Member Chemists' Club of New York Member: Roumanian Academy of Sciences; Soviet Academy o

Sciences, 1966. Hon. Freeman of Borough of Chesterfield, 1947; Franklin Medal of Franklin Institute, Philadelphia, 1947; Nobel Prize for Chemistry, 1947; Priestley Medal, American Chemical Society, 1953; Flintoff Medal, Chem. Soc. 1960. Order of the Rising Sun, 2nd class (Japan). *Publications:* (with R. Edwards) The Art and Science of Chess, 1974; numerous scientific papers, mainly in the Journal of the Chemical Society. *Recreations:* mountaineering, chess. *Address:* Grimms Hill Lodge, Great Missenden, Bucks. *T:* Great Missenden 2465; Shell Chemical Co. Ltd, Shell Centre, Downstream Building, SE1. *Clubs:* Athenæum, Alpine. [Died 8 Feb. 1975.

ROBINSON, Ronald Henry Ottywell Betham, MA, MB, BCh, FRCS; retired as Senior Surgeon and Urologist, St Thomas's, SE, and Consultant Urologist, Ministry of Pensions and St Helier Hospital; *b* 16 May 1896; *s* of Henry Betham Robinson, MD, MS, FRCS; *m* Audrey, *er d* of late Col G. K. Walker, CIE, OBE; one *d. Educ:* Malvern; King's College, Cambridge (Senior Scholar); St Thomas's Hospital (University Scholar). Temporary Surgeon Lieutenant Royal Navy during European War, and Surg. Lieut Comdr RNVR (retd); Member of International Soc. of Urology; Past Pres. of the British Association of Urological Surgeons; Hon. Sec. Royal Society of Medicine (Past Pres. Urological Section, Past Vice-Pres. Surgical Section); Fellow Assoc. of Surgeons; Member Society of Thoracic Surgeons; Arris and Gale Lecturer, Royal College of Surgeons; Member Council, RCS (Eng.); late Chairman, Court of Examiners, RCS (Eng.); Examiner in Surgery, Univ. of Cambridge and Univ. of Malaya. Past Master of the Worshipful Company of Cordwainers. OStJ. *Publications:* (with W. R. Le Fanu) Lives of Fellows of College of Surgeons, 1970; articles on Surgery and Urology in Text-books and Journals. *Recreations:* golf, travel. *Address:* Lake House, Dormans Park, East Grinstead, Sussex. *T:* Dormans Park 456. *Club:* United Oxford & Cambridge University. [Died 6 Feb. 1973.

ROBINSON, Sir Stanley; *see* Robinson, Sir E. S.

ROBINSON, Sydney Allen; General President, National Union of Boot and Shoe Operatives, 1947-70, retired; Member: Monopolies and Mergers Commission, since 1966; TUC-CBI Conciliation Panel, since 1972; *b* 13 Aug. 1905; *m* 1940, Grace Mary Lack; one *s* one *d. Educ:* Clophill Elementary School, Bedfordshire. National Union of Boot and Shoe Operatives: Full-time Branch Officer, 1939; National Organiser, 1947; Assistant General Secretary, 1949. Mem., Panel of Inquiry into Beef Supplies and Prices, 1973. *Recreations:* gardening, adult education. *Address:* 45 Fourth Avenue, Wellingborough, Northants. *T:* Wellingborough 222956. [Died 10 April 1978.

ROBINSON, Rt. Rev. Walter Wade; Bishop of Dunedin, since 1969; *b* 10 Dec. 1919; *s* of Walter Maitland Robinson and Jessie Maud Robinson (*née* Wade); *m* 1946, Amy Jean Carnie; three *s. Educ:* Cathedral Grammar Sch., Christchurch; Canterbury Univ. College; College House, Christchurch; King's Coll., London. Curate, S Mary's, Timaru, 1943-45; Asst Principal, College House, 1945-46; Curate, S Gabriel's, Cricklewood, London, 1946-49; Vicar of Linwood, Christchurch, 1949-52; Curate, Suva Cathedral, 1952-55; Vicar of Viti Levu West, 1955; priest evangelist, Lambasa, 1956; Superintendent, Indian Mission, Lambasa, 1957-62; Vicar of Hornby, Christchurch, 1962-64; Gen. Secretary, NZ Anglican Board of Missions, 1964-69. *Recreations:* music, photography, gardening. *Address:* Bishop's House, 10 Claremont Street, Roslyn, Dunedin, New Zealand. *T:* 60710. [Died 6 Oct. 1975.

ROBINSON, Rev. W(illiam) Gordon, PhD; Principal, Northern Congregational College, 1958-68; Principal, Lancashire Independent College, Manchester, 1943-58; *b* 19 May 1903; *m* 1932, Phyllis King; one *s* one *d. Educ:* Universities of Liverpool (BA), Manchester (BD, PhD), Oxford (MA). Congregational minister: Gatley, Cheshire, 1929-32; Oldham, 1932-43; Tutor, Lancashire Independent College, 1929-33; Manchester University: Lecturer in New Testament, 1943-51; Lecturer in Ecclesiastical History, 1951-70; Secretary, Faculty of Theology, 1948-58, Tutor, 1958-68; Chairman, Lancashire Congregational Union, 1946 and 1956; Chairman, Congregational Union of England and Wales, 1955-56. *Publications:* Introduction to the New Testament, 1949; Our Heritage of Free Prayer, 1950; William Roby, 1766-1830, 1954; New Testament Treasure, 1954; Decision, Challenge, Victory, 1954; History of the Lancashire Congregational Union, 1955; Catchwords, Character and The Calendar, 1957; The Gospel and the Church, 1958; Jonathan Scott, 1961; Benjamin Waugh, 1961; Historians of Israel, 1962; New Testament Detection, 1964; The Bible and History (Jtly), 1968; Living Words and Their Meaning, 1968; The Literature of the New Testament, 1971; Jesus, Lord and Saviour, 1975. *Address:* Craigneish, Highfield Road, Grange-

over-Sands, Cumbria LA11 7JA. *T:* Grange-over-Sands 3214. [Died 1 Feb. 1977.

ROBSON, Air Vice-Marshal Adam Henry, CB 1949; OBE 1938; MC; MSc; PhD; RAF retd; *b* 3 Aug. 1892; *s* of J. Robson, Low Fell, Co. Durham; *m* 1917, Vera Mary (*d* 1978), *d* of late Robert Purvis, Solicitor, South Shields; two *s. Educ:* Armstrong College, Newcastle upon Tyne; King's College, University of London. Asst Sec., Dorset County Educ. Cttee, 1920-23; Entered RAF Educational Service in 1923; Dir of Educational Services, RAF, 1944-52. Mem. Exec. Cttee and Coun., Nat. Inst. of Adult Educn, 1947-52; Mem. Exec. Cttee and Coun. Nat. Foundn of Educnl Research, 1947-52; Mem. Governing Body, Sch. of Oriental and African Studies, London Univ., 1948-52; Director, Hungarian Students Resettlement, World Univ. Service, London, 1957-58. Mem., Hampshire County Youth Adv. Cttee, 1961-67. Served in Durham Light Infantry, 1914-19 (MC and bar, despatches, wounded thrice). *Address:* Cottage 9, Headbourne Worthy House, Winchester, Hants. *T:* Winchester 881864. [Died 9 Oct. 1980.

ROBSON, Prof. Sir Hugh (Norwood), Kt 1974; MB, ChB, FRCP, FRCPEd, FRSE; Principal, University of Edinburgh, since 1974; *b* 18 Oct. 1917; *s* of late Hugh and Elizabeth Robson; *m* 1942, Alice Eleanor, *o d* of late A. McD Livingstone, CIE, MC, MA, BSc, and Gladys Livingstone, Berkhamsted, Herts; one *s* two *d. Educ:* Dumfries Academy; University of Edinburgh. Surg.-Lieut RNVR, Western Approaches, Normandy, Arakan, Malaya, 1942-46. Clinical Tutor, Royal Infirmary, Edinburgh, 1946; Lecturer, Dept of Medicine, Univ. of Edinburgh, 1947-50; Sen. Lectr, Dept of Medicine, Univ. of Aberdeen, 1950-53; Prof. of Medicine, Univ. of Adelaide, S Australia, 1953-65, Prof. Emeritus, 1965; Vice-Chancellor, Univ. of Sheffield, 1966-74. Member: Nat. Health and Med. Research Council of Australia, 1957-65; New Guinea Med. Research Council, 1962-65; Australian Drug Evaluation Cttee, 1963-65; Inter-Univ. Council for Higher Educn Overseas, 1967-; Special Steels Div. Adv. Bd, BSC, 1970-72; UN Univ. Founding Cttee, 1973; Chairman: Central Cttee on Postgraduate Med. Educn, GB, 1968-70 (Mem. 1967); Council for Postgraduate Med. Educn in England and Wales, 1970-72; Adv. Council on the Misuse of Drugs, 1971-76; Cttee of Vice-Chancellors and Principals of Univs of UK, 1972-74 (Vice-Chm., 1970-71); British Cttee of Award for Harkness Fellowships (Commonwealth Fund), 1974-77 (Mem., 1968-); Scottish Health Service Planning Council, 1974-; Mem., Northwick Park Adv. Cttee, 1971-76; Trustee, Nuffield Provincial Hosps Trust, 1966-. FRSA. Hon. DSc Philadelphia; Hon. LLD Sheffield; Hon. FRCSE; Hon. Fellow Sheffield Polytechnic. *Publications:* papers on hæmatological and other subjects in Brit., Amer. and Aust. med. jls. *Recreations:* reading, carpentry and golf. *Address:* Principal's Office, University of Edinburgh, Old College, South Bridge, Edinburgh EH8 9YL. *Clubs:* Caledonian; New (Edinburgh). [Died 11 Dec. 1977.

ROBSON, Sir Kenneth, Kt 1968; CBE 1959; FRCP; Hon. Consultant Physician: St George's Hospital, SW1; Brompton Hospital, SW3; King Edward VII Hospital for Officers; King Edward VII Hospital, Midhurst; Confederation Life Insurance Co.; *b* 1909; *y s* of late John Ajmer and Katherine Robson. *Educ:* Bradfield; Christ's College, Cambridge; Middlesex Hospital. Davis and Cree Prizes in Medicine; 2nd Broderip Schol., 1933; qualified, 1933; Resident Posts and Registrarships at Middlesex and Brompton Hospitals. MA, MD, BChir Cantab; MRCP 1935, FRCP 1943; FRCPE 1975. Goulstonian Lectr, RCP, 1944; Examr, 1949-57; Censor, 1959; Registrar, 1961-75. Examr in Med.: Univs Camb., London, Durham. RAFVR Med. Br., 1938; whole time service, 1939-46; Wing Comdr-in-charge of Med. Divs at hosps in England and India; Air Cdre, Consultant-in-Medicine to RAF in India and Far East; Civil Consultant in Medicine, RAF, 1949-77; Hon. Air Cdre, RAF Central Medical Estab., 1977. Toured Medical Estabs for HM Colonial Office in N Caribbean Is and Br Honduras, 1959; Visitor for RCP and RCS to Medical Faculty, Univ. of Khartoum, 1963; RCP Visitor, Australia and New Zealand, 1965, 1975, S Africa, 1969. Chm., Jt Consultants Cttee, 1972-74; Member: Deptl Cttee on Radiological Protection; Defence Med. Services Inquiry Cttee. Mem. Assoc. of Physicians and of Thoracic Society (President 1965; Secretary 1947-60); Hon. Fellow: Amer. Coll. of Physicians; S African Coll. of Physicians; Hon. FRCPI; Hon. FRACP. *Publications:* contributions to text books and various scientific jls mostly in connection with the chest. *Recreation:* pottering about. *Address:* 34 Sydney Street, SW3. *T:* 01-352 3852; Tatham's, Danehill, East Sussex. *Clubs:* Athenæum, Royal Air Force; Crowborough Golf. [Died 7 Dec. 1978.

ROBSON, Professor William; Professor of Biochemistry, King's College, London University, 1958-60, Professor Emeritus, 1961;

b 15 Feb. 1893; *s* of William Robson, Cramlington, Northumberland; *m* 1924, Anna Wallace, *d* of Alexander Kerr, JP, Forres, Morayshire. *Educ:* Morpeth Gram. Sch.; King's Coll., London. Royal Flying Corps, 1916; commissioned and "wings" awarded, 1917. BSc (Hons) London 1920. Asst Dept. of Medical Chemistry, Univ. of Edinburgh, 1920; Research Assistant, Dept of Therapeutics, Univ. of Edinburgh, 1922; PhD Edinburgh 1924; Lecturer in Physiological Chemistry, King's College, London, 1927; Reader in Biochemistry, King's College, London, 1931; DSc London 1930. Secretary, Biochemical Society, 1942-47. Fellow Rockefeller Foundation at Rockefeller Inst., NY, 1924, FKC 1955. *Publications:* Essentials of Chemical Physiology, 11th Edn, 1929, 12th Edn, 1933; papers in Jl of Chemical Society, Biochemical Journal. *Address:* 40 Waggon Road, Hadley Wood, Barnet, Herts. *T:* 01-449 2824.
[*Died 22 Jan.* 1975.

ROBSON, William Alexander; Professor Emeritus of Public Administration in the University of London (London School of Economics and Political Science) (Professor, 1947-62); Barrister-at-law; Hon. Fellow, London Sch. of Economics; *b* 14 July 1895; *s* of late J. Robson; *m* 1929, Juliette Alvin; two *s* one *d. Educ:* Univ. of London (London School of Economics and Political Science); BSc (Economics) First Class Honours, 1922; PhD 1924; LLM 1928. Served European War, 1914-18, as Lieutenant on active service in Royal Flying Corps and RAF; called to Bar, Lincoln's Inn, 1922; Lecturer at the London School of Economics from 1926; Reader in Administrative Law, 1933-46; Visiting Professor, University of Chicago, 1933, University of N Carolina, 1951, University of Patna, 1953, and other Indian Univs, Univ. of California, Berkeley, 1957; Indian Institute of Public Administration, 1960; Internat. Christian Univ., Tokyo, 1969. Principal, Mines Department, 1940-42; Ministry of Fuel and Power, 1942-43; Asst Sec., Air Ministry, 1943-45; Ministry of Civil Aviation, 1945; Member: Council, Town and Country Planning Assoc.; Deptl Cttee on Admin. of Greater London Plan; Cttee on Training in Public Administration for Overseas Countries; Vice-President: Royal Inst. of Public Admin; Political Studies Assoc. Pres., Internat. Political Science Assoc., 1950-53. Chairman, Gr London Gp, LSE. Noranda Lectr, Expo 1967. Founder, 1930, Joint Editor, 1930-75, Chm. Editorial Bd, 1975-, The Political Quarterly. Consultant to Govts of Lebanon, Nigeria, Turkey, Tokyo Metropol. Govt, UNICEF and State Commn for New York City Charter Reform. Hon. Fellow, Jt Univ. Council for Social and Public Administration. Docteur de l'Univ. (*hc*): Lille, 1953; Grenoble, 1955; Paris, 1955; Algiers, 1959; Hon. DLitt: Dunelm, 1963; Manchester, 1964; Hon. DSocSci, Birmingham, 1970. *Publications:* From Patronage to Proficiency in the Public Service, 1922; The Relation of Wealth to Welfare, 1924; Justice and Administrative Law, 1928; Civilisation and the Growth of Law, 1935; The Town Councillor (with C. R. Attlee), 1925; contributor to London Essays in Economics, 1927; Modern Theories of Law, 1938; The Development of Local Government, 1931; The Law of Local Government Audit, 1930; A Century of Municipal Progress (contributor and Joint Editor), 1935; The British Civil Servant, (contributor and editor), 1937; Public Enterprise (contributor and editor), 1937; The Government and Misgovernment of London, 1939; The British System of Government, 1940; Social Security (contributor and editor), 1943; Planning and Performance, 1943; Population and the People, 1945; British Government since 1918 (contributor), 1950; Problems of Nationalised Industry, 1952; The Teaching of Political Science (Unesco), 1954; (ed jtly) Great Cities of the World, 1955, repr. 1973; The Civil Service in Britain and France, 1956; Nationalised Industry and Public Ownership, 1960; The Governors and the Governed, 1964; The Heart of Greater London, 1965; Local Government in Crisis, 1966; Politics and Government at Home and Abroad, 1967; (ed with B. Crick) Protest and Discontent, 1970; (ed) The Political Quarterly in the Thirties, 1971; (ed) Man and the Social Sciences, 1972; (ed with B. Crick) Taxation Policy, 1973; Welfare State and Welfare Society, 1976. Editor, Politics Section, Hutchinson University Library. *Recreations:* walking and swimming. *Address:* 48 Lanchester Road, N6. *T:* 01-883 1331. *Club:* Athenæum.
[*Died 12 May* 1980.

ROBSON BROWN, Sir William, Kt 1957; British parentage; *m* 1st, 1922, Elsie Irene Thomas (*d* 1968); two *d*; 2nd, 1969, Mrs Kay Sanders. *Educ:* Armstrong College, Newcastle upon Tyne. Served European War, 1914-18, in RFC and RAF. MP (C) Esher Division of Surrey, 1950-70. Lifetime experience in steel industry; leading authority on management labour relations in industry. Past Pres., Society of Commercial Accountants (1959-70); formerly Mem. Council, Confederation of British Industry. Governor, Twickenham Coll. of Technology; Governor Emeritus, Brooklands County Technical Coll. Life-Pres., The Marlow Foundation; President: Lest We Forget Soc., Molesey;

St John's Ambulance, Weybridge; Silver Circle for the Handicapped; Mem. Cttee, Walton and Weybridge Old People's Welfare Assoc. Past Master, Blacksmiths Co.; Freeman of City of London. *Publications:* The Tinplate Industry; Industrial Democracy at Work; Management and Society. *Address:* Churchfields, Weybridge, Surrey.
[*Died 25 Feb.* 1975.

ROBSON-SCOTT, Prof. William Douglas, MA Oxon, DrPhil Vienna; Hon. Director, Institute of Germanic Studies, 1968-73; *b* 9 Aug. 1901; *s* of late Thomas William Robson-Scott and Florence Jane (*née* Lang); *m* 1947, Elaine Davies; one *d. Educ:* Rugby Sch.; University Coll., Oxford; Univs of Berlin and Vienna. 1st cl. hons English, Oxon, 1923. Lektor, Univ. of Berlin, 1933-37; seconded to War Office, 1939-45; Birkbeck Coll., Univ. of London: Lectr in German, 1939-61; Reader, 1961-66; Prof. of German Language and Literature, 1966-68, Emer. Prof. 1968. *Publications:* German Travellers in England 1400-1800, 1953; The Literary Background of the Gothic Revival in Germany, 1965; Goethe and the Visual Arts, 1967; German Romanticism and the Visual Arts, 1970; Goethe and the Art of the Netherlands, 1971; various translations including: (with E. Robson-Scott) Sigmund Freud and Lou Andreas-Salomé: Letters, 1972; various articles in learned jls. *Recreations:* hill-walking, travel. *Address:* 19 Dorset Square, NW1. *T:* 01-262 2877; Southdean Lodge, Hawick, Roxburghshire. *T:* Bonchester Bridge 656. [*Died 12 June* 1980.

ROCHE, Sir Standish O'Grady, 4th Bt, *cr* 1838; DSO 1942; Lt-Comdr RN retd; *b* 13 March 1911; *s* of 3rd Bt and Sybil (*d* 1950), *o d* of Col Julius Dyson-Laurie, Gloucester Pl., W; *S* father, 1914; *m* 1946, Evelyn Laura, *o d* of Major W. Andon; two *s.* ADC to Gov.-General of New Zealand, 1935-37. Croix de Guerre 1945. *Heir: s* David O'Grady Roche [*b* 21 Sept. 1947; *m* 1971, Hon. (Helen) Alexandra Briscoe, *d* of 3rd Viscount Selby; (one *s* decd)]. *Address:* Monte de Cerro, Coroteto, Sao Bras de Alportel, Portugal.
[*Died 2 April* 1977.

ROCKEFELLER, John Davison, 3rd, OBE (Hon.) 1948; Hon. Chairman, Rockefeller Foundation, (Chairman, 1952-71, Trustee, 1931-71); Chairman, Commission on Population Growth and the American Future, 1970-72; *b* 21 March 1906; *s* of late John Davison Rockefeller, Jr, FRS, and Abby Greene Aldrich; *m* 1932, Blanchette Ferry Hooker; one *s* three *d. Educ:* Loomis School, Windsor, Conn.; Princeton Univ., Princeton, NJ (BS). Lt-Comdr, USNR, working with Combined Civil Affairs Cttee and State-War-Navy Co-ordinating Cttee, 1942-45. Consultant to the Dulles Mission to Japan on Peace Settlement, 1951; Adviser, US Delegation, Japanese Peace Treaty Conf., San Francisco, 1951. Established Rockefeller Public Service Awards, 1952. Chairman: Nat. Policy Panel on World Population and Quality of Human Develt; Population Council (founder); Greater New York Fund Campaign, 1949; Agricultural Development Council (founder); Asia Soc. (founder); Japan Soc. (Pres. 1952-70); President: The JDR 3rd Fund (founder); Amer. Youth Hostels, 1948-51. Trustee: Rockefeller Brothers Fund (Pres., 1940-56; Chm., Performing Arts Panel, 1963-65); Rockefeller Family Fund, 1967-; Princeton Univ. (emeritus); United Negro College Fund (Hon. Chm., 1965-69; Chm., Nat. Council, 1958-65); Colonial Williamsburg Inc., 1934-54 (Chm., 1939-53); Educational Broadcasting Corp., 1962-64; General Education Bd, 1932-71 (Chm., 1952-71); Internat. House, NYC, 1930-49; Lincoln Center for the Performing Arts (Hon. Chm., Chm., 1961-70); Riverside Church, 1930-49, now Hon. Trustee; Rockefeller Inst. (now Rockefeller Univ.), 1932-49. Director: Phelps Meml Hosp., 1935-68; Foreign Policy Assoc., 1954-61; NY Life Ins. Co., 1949-59; Rockefeller Center Inc., 1932-63. Special Tony Award, American Theater Wing, 1960; Lasker Award in Planned Parenthood, 1961; Gold Baton Award, Amer. Symphony Orch. League, 1963; Handel Medallion, NYC, 1964; Silver Plaque, Fedn of Jewish Philanthropies of NY, 1964; Presidential Citation, 1967 (for Rockefeller Public Service Awards); Margaret Sanger Award for Public Service in Family Planning, 1967; Gold Medal, Nat. Inst. of Social Sciences, 1967; Soc. for the Family of Man Award, Protestant Council, 1968. Grand Cordon, Order of Sacred Treasure, Japan, 1954; Most Noble Order of the Crown of Thailand, 1st cl, 1960; Order of Sikatuna, Philippines, 1967; Grand Cordon, Order of Rising Sun, Japan, 1968. *Recreations:* riding, golf, sailing. *Address:* 30 Rockefeller Plaza, New York City 10020. *Clubs:* Century Association, University (New York); Metropolitan (Washington, DC).
[*Died 10 July* 1978.

ROCKEFELLER, Nelson Aldrich; Vice-President of the United States of America, 1974-77; *b* 8 July 1908; *s* of late John D Rockefeller, Jr, and Abby Greene Aldrich; *m* 1st, 1930, Mary Todhunter Clark (marr. diss. 1962); two *s* two *d* (and one decd); 2nd, 1963, Margaretta Fitler Murphy; two *s. Educ:* Dartmouth College (AB). Rockefeller Center, Inc.: Director

1931-58; Pres., 1938-45, 1948-51; Chm., 1945-53 and 1956-58; Rockefeller Brothers Fund, Inc.: Pres., 1956-58; Trustee, 1940-; Museum of Modern Art (NY City): Pres., 1939-41, 1946-53; Chm., 1957-58; Trustee, 1932-. Co-ordinator of Inter-American Affairs, 1940-44; Asst Sec. of State, for Amer. Republic's Affairs, 1944-45; Chairman: Internat. Basic Economy Corp., 1958 (Pres., 1947-53, 1956-58, Dir, 1947-53, 1956-58); Internat. Develt Adv. Bd, 1950-51; Govt Affairs Foundn Inc., 1953-58 (founder); Mem., President's Advisory Cttee on Govt Organization, 1953-58; Under Secretary, Department of Health, Education and Welfare, USA, 1953-54; Special Assistant to the President, USA, 1954-55. Governor, New York State, 1958-Dec. 1973, resigned. Mem. President's Adv. Commn on Intergovernmental Relations, 1965-69. Museum of Primitive Art (NY City): Founder and Pres., 1954-, Trustee, 1954-. Holds numerous awards and medals incl. Gold Medal, Nat. Inst. of Social Sciences, 1967. Holds various Hon. Degrees in Law and Humane Letters, Awards (US) incl. Medal of Freedom, 1977, also Foreign Orders. Citation by Nat. Conf. of Christians and Jews for work in field of human relations, 1948; Thomas F. Cunningham Award for contrib. toward betterment of Inter-American Relations, 1964. *Publications:* The Future of Federalism, 1962; Unity, Freedom and Peace, 1968; Our Environment Can Be Saved, 1970. *Address:* Room 5600, 30 Rockefeller Plaza, NYC 10020, USA. *Clubs:* Century Association, Dartmouth (NY); Cosmos (Washington, DC).
[Died 26 Jan. 1979.

ROCKLEY, 2nd Baron, *cr* 1934, of Lytchett Heath; **Robert William Evelyn Cecil;** Brig. (retired) RA; *b* 28 Feb. 1901; *s* of 1st Baron and Hon. Alicia Margaret Amherst, CBE (*d* 1941), *d* of 1st Baron Amherst of Hackney; *S* father 1941; *m* 1933, Anne, *d* of late Adm. Hon. Sir Herbert Meade-Fetherstonhaugh, GCVO, CB, DSO; two *s* one *d*. *Educ:* Christ Church, Oxford; Yale, USA (Davison scholar). Engineer; formerly Director of: National Provincial Bank Ltd, Foreign & Colonial Trust; Clerical, Medical and General Life Assurance Society. Ministry of Supply, 1939-43; Military Governor 1944-45. *Recreations:* shooting, fishing. *Heir:* s Hon. James Hugh Cecil [*b* 5 April 1934; *m* 1958, Lady Sarah, *e d* of 7th Earl Cadogan, MC; one *s* two *d*]. *Address:* Lytchett Heath, Poole, Dorset; Clive House, 5 Connaught Place, W2. *Clubs:* Carlton, Pratt's.
[Died 6 Jan. 1976.

ROCYN-JONES, Arthur, MB, BS (London), FRCS; Consulting Surgeon to Royal National Orthopædic Hospital, retired; Emeritus Consultant Orthopædic Surgeon: West End Hospital for Neurology and Neurosurgery; Fulham and Kensington Hospital Group; Consulting Orthopædic Surgeon to West Suffolk General Hospital, Glan Ely Hospital and to the Prince of Wales Hospital, Cardiff; *b* Rhymney, Monmouthshire; *y s* of David and Catherine Rocyn Jones; *m* Margaret, *d* of late Rev. D. J. Llewelyn, Vicar of Beaufort; one *d*. *Educ:* Lewis' School, University College, Cardiff (Monmouth Scholar); Univ. College, London; London Hospital. House Surgeon, Royal Infirmary, Cardiff; Senior House Surgeon and afterwards Surgical Registrar, Royal National Orthopædic Hospital; Fellow Roy. Soc. Med. (Hon. Mem. and Ex-Pres. of Orthopædic Section); Emeritus Fell., Brit. Orthopædic Association; Member Société Internationale de Chirurgie Orthopédique; Member of Council Hon. Society of Cymmrodorion; Member Cambrian Archæological Assoc.; Mem. Gen. Cttee British and Foreign Bible Soc. *Publications:* The Evolution of Orthopædic Surgery in Great Britain; and other papers in scientific journals. *Address:* Bryntirion, 151 Stanmore Hill, Stanmore, Middlesex. *T:* 01-954 1788.
[Died 12 Feb. 1972.

RODGER, Thomas Ferguson, CBE 1967; FRCPGlas, FRCPEd, FRCPsych; Professor of Psychological Medicine, University of Glasgow, 1948-73; Consulting Psychiatrist, Western Infirmary and Southern General Hospital, Glasgow; Hon. Consulting Psychiatrist to the Army in Scotland; External Examiner, Edinburgh and Leeds Universities; *b* 4 Nov. 1907; *m* 1934, Jean Chalmers; two *s* one *d*. *Educ:* North Kelvinside School, Glasgow; Glasgow University. BSc, 1927; MB, ChB, with Commendation, 1929; MRCP Ed., 1939; FRCP Ed., 1947, Glas. 1962; FRFPSG 1958; FBPsS; FRCPsych, 1971, Hon. Fellow 1972. Past Pres., Royal Medico-Psychological Assoc. Asst, Dept of Psychiatry, Johns Hopkins Univ., Baltimore, 1931-32; Dep. Superintendent, Glasgow Roy. Mental Hosp., and Assistant Lecturer in Psychiatry, Glasgow Univ., 1933-40; War of 1939-45: Specialist in Psychiatry, RAMC, 1940-44; Consultant in Psychiatry, Army Medical Services, SEAC and India, 1944-45; Commissioner, General Board of Control for Scotland, 1945-48. *Publications:* (jointly) Notes on Psychological Medicine, 1962; Psychology in Relation to Medicine, 1963; articles in medical journals on psychiatric subjects. *Address:* 25 Campbell Drive, Bearsden, Glasgow. *T:* 041-942 3101.
[Died 1 June 1978.

RODGERS, Air Commodore Alexander Mitchell, CB 1957; *b* 24 July 1906; *m* 1934, Agnes Mary Collier; one *s* one *d*. *Educ:* Forfar Acad.; St Andrews Univ. BSc 1928. Commissioned in RAF, 1931; passed flying training course as pilot, 1932; passed radio course, Cranwell, 1935; in India during 1935-38; RAF Staff College, 1939; served War of 1939-45: France, 1939-40, UK 1940-41, North Africa, Sicily, Italy, 1941-45; Transport Command, 1945-46; Commanded St Mawgan, Hendon, Defford, 1946-51; Europe, 1951-53; Commandant RAF Watton, 1953-57; retired 1957; ATC Liaison Officer, RAF Flying Training Comd, 1957-70. American Bronze Star. *Recreations:* shooting, fishing. *Address:* Farnborough, near Banbury, Oxon. *T:* Farnborough 266. *Club:* Royal Air Force.
[Died 22 May 1973.

RODGERS, David John, CBE 1933; *b* 27 March 1890; *s* of Richard Broomhead Rodgers and Janet Thomson. Entered Consular Service, 1913; Vice-Consul, Buenos Aires, 1914; Vice-Consul, Strasburg, 1921; Consul, Brest, 1922, Madrid, 1923; Chargé d'Affaires, Salvador and Guatemala, 1928; Consul, Liège, 1932, Palermo, 1936; Consul-General, Barcelona, 1938, New Orleans, 1940, Mexico, 1944; appointed Minister to Nicaragua, 1947, but could not proceed thither owing to injuries in accident; retd 1949. *Address:* 27 Loughrigg Av., Ambleside, Cumbria.
[Died 17 March 1975.

RODGERS, Richard; American composer and producer; *b* New York, 28 June 1902; *m* 1930, Dorothy Feiner; two *d*. *Educ:* Columbia University; Institute of Musical Art, New York. Musical scores include: Lido Lady (London) 1926; One Dam Thing After Another (London) 1927; Evergreen (London) 1930; America's Sweetheart, 1931; Jumbo, 1935; On Your Toes, 1936; Babes in Arms, 1937; I'd Rather Be Right, 1937; I Married An Angel, 1938; The Boys From Syracuse, 1938; Too Many Girls, 1939; Higher and Higher, 1940; Pal Joey, 1940; Oklahoma, 1943 (Pulitzer Award, 1944); Carousel, 1945; Allegro, 1947. Wrote music for: Love Me Tonight (film); Ghost Town (ballet), 1939; State Fair (film), 1945. Co-producer: By Jupiter, 1942 (wrote music); I Remember Mama, 1944; Annie Get Your Gun, Happy Birthday, 1946; John Loves Mary, Show Boat, 1947; South Pacific, 1949 (wrote score) (Pulitzer Prize, 1950); The Happy Time, 1950; wrote scores for: The King and I, 1951; Pipe Dream, 1955; Flower Drum Song, 1958; The Sound of Music, 1959; No Strings, 1962 (and produced); Do I Hear a Waltz?, 1965; Two By Two, 1970; Rex, 1976; I Remember Mama, 1979. TV series: Churchill, The Valiant Years; Victory at Sea; TV Specials; Cinderella, 1957; Androcles and the Lion, 1967. President Dramatists' Guild, 1943-47. Member: Authors League of America; Nat. Assoc. for Amer. Composers and Conductors; Nat. Inst. of Arts and Letters. Hon. Degrees: Drury Coll., 1949; Columbia, 1954; Univ. of Massachusetts, 1954; Univ. of Bridgeport, 1962; Univ. of Maryland, 1962; Hamilton Coll., 1965; Brandeis Univ., 1965; Fairfield Univ., 1968; New York Univ., 1971; New England Conservatory of Music, 1976; Philadelphia Coll. of Performing Arts, 1979. *Address:* c/o Rodgers & Hammerstein, 598 Madison Avenue, New York, NY 10022, USA.
[Died 30 Dec. 1979.

RODHAM, Brig. Cuthbert Harold Boyd, CBE 1953 (OBE 1934); DSO and Bar, 1945; MC 1921; Director of Sports, Government of Pakistan, since 1963; *b* 1900; *s* of late Rear-Adm. H. Rodham, CMG. *Educ:* Dover Coll. Entered Indian Army, 2/18 Roy. Garhwal Rifles, 1919; Capt. 1925; Bt Major, 1936; Major, 1937; Lt-Col 1942; Col 1943; Brig. 1944. Served Afghanistan, 1919; NWF of India, 1919-21; Mahsud campaign, 1920 (wounded, despatches, MC); Waziristan Operations, 1922-23; Mahsud Operations, 1930. Indian Coronation Contingent, 1937. War of 1939-45 (despatches 3 times, DSO and Bar); French Indo-China Occupation Force, 1945-46; Director of Infantry, GHQ India, 1946-47; Brigade Commander, Pakistan Army, 1948-51; Director of Infantry, 1951-57; Deputy Chief of General Staff, Pakistan Army, 1957-63, retd. Order of Quaid-i-Azam, Pakistan, 1959. *Recreation:* shooting. *Address:* Flashman's Hotel, The Mall, Rawalpindi, Pakistan; c/o National and Grindlay's Bank, The Mall, Lahore, Pakistan.
[Died 16 June 1973.

RODNEY, 8th Baron, *cr* 1782; **George Bridges Harley Guest Rodney;** Bt 1764; late Captain Royal Scots Greys; *b* 2 Nov. 1891; *s* of 7th Baron; *S* father, 1909; *m* 1917, Lady Marjorie Lowther (*d* 1968), *y d* of 6th Earl of Lonsdale; two *s* two *d* (and *e s* killed in War). *Educ:* Eton: Oxford. *Heir:* s Hon. John Francis Rodney [*b* 28 June 1920; *m* 1951, Regine, *yr d* of late Chevalier Pangaert d'Opdorp, Belgium; one *s* one *d*]. *Address:* Cottesmore Lodge, Park Drive, Albert Head, Rural Route 1, Victoria, BC, Canada.
[Died 18 Dec. 1973.

RODRIGO, Prof. Joseph Lionel Christie, CMG 1956; *b* 31 July 1895; *s* of J. A. G. and Catherine Rodrigo; *m* 1922, Evelyn Fernando; two *s* three *d. Educ:* Royal and Trinity Colleges, Ceylon; Balliol College, Oxford. BA (London) 1917; BA (Oxon.) 1920; MA 1925; Barrister, Gray's Inn, 1921. Editor of Ceylon Morning Leader, 1921-26; Headmaster, Wesley College, Colombo, 1926-28; Asst Lecturer in Classics, Univ. College, Colombo, 1928, Lecturer, 1930, Reader, 1931; Prof. of Western Classics, Univ. of Ceylon, 1945-57, Emeritus Prof., 1960; Dean, Faculty of Arts, University of Ceylon, 1952-57; Education Officer Ceylon High Commn, London, 1957-59. Chm. Bd of Governors, CMS Schools in Ceylon, 1942-49, 1959-; Dir YMCA, 1922-49; President: Classical Assoc. of Ceylon; Oxford Soc., Ceylon Br., 1961-. *Recreation:* free-lance journalism. *Address:* 23/3 Guildford Crescent, Colombo, Sri Lanka. *Club:* Sinhalese Sports' (Sri Lanka).

RODRIGO, Sir (Senanathige Theobald) Philip, Kt 1953; OBE 1952; Gate-Mudaliyar 1947; Senator, Parliament of Ceylon, 1950-71; *b* 22 Aug. 1899; *s* of Chevalier Mudaliyar John Rodrigo and Helena Roslin Fernando; *m* 1st, 1920, Mary Dorothy (*d* 1929); 2nd, 1930, Elizabeth Mary, both daughters of Simon Salgado; one *s* six *d. Educ:* De La Salle Coll. and St Benedict's Coll. Merchant and Planter; Partner S. T. P. Rodrigo & Bros; Managing Director: Eastern Ocean Steamship Supply Co.; New Imperial Lighterage Co.; Senior Partner: Dominion Trading Co.; Dominion Hotel Co., Colombo; Director: Gen. Insce Co.; United Lanka Rubber & Coconut Co. Pres. etc, various organisations. JP 1938. *Recreations:* billiards, painting, gardening. *Address:* Wasala Walauwa, Rodrigo Place, Mutwal, Colombo, Sri Lanka. *T:* 4563, 3589 & 3876; Claremont, Nuwara Eliya, Sri Lanka.

ROE, Brig. William C.; *see* Carden Roe.

ROGER, Alastair Forbes; Governor, Globe Investment Trust Ltd, since 1972; *b* 11 March 1916; *s* of Sir Alexander Roger, KCIE, and Helen Stuart; unmarried. *Educ:* Loretto Sch.; Christ Church, Oxford. Telephone operating cos in Caribbean, 1935-38. Director: Temple Bar Investment Trust Ltd (Dir 1938, Chm. 1954, Dir present co. 1947-, Chm. 1960-); Cable Trust Ltd (now merged with Globe Investment Trust Ltd), 1952- (Dep. Governor, 1965-72); Globe Investment Trust Ltd, 1964- (Dep. Chm., 1965, Chm., 1972-); British Electric Traction Co. Ltd, 1953- (Dep. Chm., 1976-); Rothesay Trust Ltd (Chm., 1959-); Nineteen Twenty Eight Investment Trust Ltd, 1960-; Border and Southern Stockholders Trust Ltd, 1963-; Electra Investment Trust Ltd, 1964- (Dep. Chm., 1965, Chm., 1972-78); English Assoc. of Amer. Stock and Bond Holders Ltd, 1968-; Birmingham and Dist Investment Trust Ltd, 1972-; Hume Corp. Ltd, 1973-. Comdr, Order of Henry the Navigator, Portugal, 1968. *Recreation:* doing nothing. *Address:* 73 Addison Road, W14 8EB. *T:* 01-603 7486; Dundonnell House, Dundonnell, by Garve, Ross and Cromarty. *T:* Dundonnell 206.
[Died 18 April 1980.

ROGERS, Claude Maurice, OBE 1959; painter; Member of the London Group (President, 1952-65); Professor of Fine Art, Reading University, 1963-72, Professor Emeritus, since 1972; Fellow, University College, London; *b* 24 Jan. 1907; *e c* of late David de Sola Rogers, LDS, RCS; *m* 1937, Elsie, *e d* of late Jethro Few, Kingston, Jamaica; one *s. Educ:* St Paul's; Slade Sch. of Fine Art, London University. With Victor Pasmore and William Coldstream founded School of Drawing and Painting, 316 Euston Rd, 1937-39. Royal Engineer, 1941-43 (Corporal). Lectr, Slade Sch. of Fine Art, London Univ., 1955-63. Member: Arts Panel, Arts Council of GB, 1957-63; Nat. Council for Diplomas in Art and Design, and Chm., Fine Art Panel, 1961-69. Exhibitions: one-man exhibns: London Artists' Assoc., 1933; Leicester Galls, 1940, 1947, 1954, 1960; Fischer Fine Arts, 1975, 1978; Exhibitor UNESCO Exhib., Paris, 1946; Carnegie Internat., 1936 and 1950; with British Council in America, Canada, etc.; with Arts Council (Four Contemporary British Painters, The Euston Road School and some others, Sixty Pictures for '51, British Painting, 1974, etc); retrospective Exhibitions: Newcastle, Manchester, Bristol, Leicester, etc, 1955; (Drawings and Paintings, 1927-73) Whitechapel Art Gall., Birmingham, Reading, Southampton, Sheffield, etc, 1973; represented in Tate Gallery, British Museum, Print Room, Victoria and Albert Museum, Ashmolean Museum, Fitzwilliam Museum; Commonwealth galleries. Works also acquired by: Chantry Bequest, Contemporary Art Society. *Address:* 36 Southwood Lane, Highgate, N6. *T:* 01-348 1997; The Old Rectory, Somerton, near Bury St Edmunds, Suffolk. *T:* Hawkedon 231.
[Died 18 Feb. 1979.

ROGERS, Brig. Edgar William, CIE 1944; BSc; late Indian Army; *b* 14 July 1892; *o* surv. *s* of late Francis Rogers, Stamford,

Lincs; *m* 1920, Marjorie, *y d* of late John Harper, Ipswich; one *s. Educ:* Bracondale Sch., Norwich; King's Coll., London. 2nd Lt The Duke of Wellington's Regt, 1914; transferred IAOC, 1928; Bt Lt Col 1936; Director of Armaments, GHQ India, 1942-46; retired 1947. Hampshire CC, 1955-58; Alton UDC, 1952-58. *Address:* 29 Marley Avenue, New Milton, Hampshire. *T:* New Milton 1221.
[Died 13 Dec. 1973.

ROGERS, Graham; His Honour Judge Graham Rogers; a Circuit Judge and Judge of the Mayor's and City of London Court, since 1972; Chairman, London Licensing Planning Committee, since 1967; *b* 10 June 1907; 2nd *s* of late Alfred Rogers, Moseley; unmarried. *Educ:* Repton Sch.; King's Coll., Cambridge (BA 1929; MA 1936). Called to Bar, Inner Temple, 1930; practised Oxford Circuit and Birmingham, 1930-39; served War of 1939-45; Major, 45th AA Battalion RE (TA), 1939; transferred to RA, 1940; UK and NW Europe, 1939-46; demobilised with rank of Colonel (TD and 2 clasps). Judge of Control Commission Supreme Court (later Allied High Commn Court), Germany, 1947; Chief Judge, 1952. Recorder of Liverpool, 1954-56; Chairman, Medical Appeal Tribunals, 1956-59; Metropolitan Magistrate, 1959-61; Additional Judge of the Mayor's and City of London Court, 1961-64; Additional Judge, Central Criminal Court, 1964-69; Asst Judge of the Mayor's and City of London Court, 1969-71; a Dep. Chm., City of London QS, 1969-71. *Address:* Mayor's and City of London Court, Guildhall, EC2. *Clubs:* United Service & Royal Aero, United Oxford & Cambridge University.
[Died 17 April 1973.

ROGERS, John, OBE 1918; FRIC; *b* 24 May 1878; *s* of Richard and Sarah Rogers; *m* 1st, 1905, M. K. Allan; one *d* ; 2nd, 1939, M. K. Garnett. *Educ:* Board Sch.; Technical Coll., Glasgow. Research Chemist, Ardeer Factory, 1899; Nobel's: Technical Supt, 1908, Tech. Manager, 1918, Tech. Dir, 1920; ICI: Tech. Dir, 1926, Dep. Chm., 1940, Chm., 1951-53, retired; formerly Dep. Chm. African Explosives and Chemical Industries Ltd; formerly Director ICI (Australia and New Zealand) Ltd, Cape Explosives Works Ltd; Pres. Society of Chemical Industry, 1951-52. Hon. LLD, St Andrew's Univ., 1952. *Address:* 29 Eaton Square, SW1W 9DF. *Clubs:* Athenæum, Chemical.
[Died 3 Aug. 1975.

ROLLASON, Prof. Ernest Clarence, MSc, PhD, FIM; Hanson Professor of Metallurgy, Chairman of School of Metallurgy, since 1969, and Head of Department of Industrial Metallurgy, University of Birmingham, since 1956; *b* 16 March 1908; *m* 1935, Norah Sylvia Palmer-Whorton; one *s* (one *d* decd). *Educ:* Dudley Grammar School; University of Birmingham. Bean Cars Ltd; County Technical College, Wednesbury, Lecturer, 1930-35; Senior Lecturer, Metallurgy Dept, Univ. of Birmingham, 1935-40; Director and Research Manager, Murex Welding Processes Ltd, 1940-51; Henry Bell Wortley Professor of Metallurgy, University of Liverpool, 1951-56. Hon. FInstW. *Publications:* Metal Spraying, 1938; Metallurgy for Engineers, 1939 (3rd edn, 1961); scientific papers in technical jls. *Address:* 83 Farquhar Road, Edgbaston, Birmingham 15. *T:* 021-454 3443.
[Died 5 May 1972.

ROLLESTON, Col (retd) William Lancelot, CMG 1958; OBE 1943; *b* 25 June 1905; *s* of Hector Rolleston, Wellington, NZ; *m* 1932, Audrey Joyce Upton; one *s* one *d. Educ:* Winchester; Royal Military Academy, Woolwich. Royal Engineers, 1925-46; Colonial Service: Singapore and North Borneo, 1947-50; Tanganyika, 1950-59 (Minister for Communications and Works, 1957-59); Hon. Colonel: 6th Bn King's African Rifles, 1958-59, 2/6th Bn King's African Rifles, 1954-59. Secretary, W Africa Cttee, 1961-70. *Address:* Timberyard Cottage, Beaulieu, Hants. *T:* Beaulieu 612388.
[Died 27 July 1974.

ROLT, Lionel Thomas Caswall; author; *b* 11 Feb. 1910; *s* of Lionel Caswall Rolt and Jemima Alice (*née* Timperley). *Educ:* Cheltenham College. Mechanical Engineer, 1926-41; Ministry of Supply, 1941-45. Author, 1945-. Co-founder Inland Waterways Association, 1946; Founder and Vice-President, Talyllyn Railway Preservation Society, 1950; Chairman, Talyllyn Railway Co., 1963-68; Member: Inland Waterways Redevelopment Advisory Cttee, 1959-62; Science Museum Adv. Council, 1963-; Exec. Cttee, Soc. for the History of Technology (USA), 1969- (Mem. Adv. Council, 1963-69); York Railway Museum Cttee, 1973-; Vice-President, Newcomen Society. FRSL; CIMechE. Hon. MA Newcastle, 1965; Hon. MSc Bath, 1973. *Publications:* Narrow Boat, 1944; High Horse Riderless, 1946; Sleep No More, 1947; Worcestershire, 1948; Green and Silver, 1949; Inland Waterways of England, 1950; Horseless Carriage, 1950; The Thames from Mouth to Source, 1951; Lines of Character, 1952; Railway Adventure, 1953; Winterstoke, 1954; The Clouded Mirror, 1955; Red for Danger, 1955; Pictorial History of Motoring, 1956; Isambard Kingdom Brunel,

1957; Thomas Telford, 1958; George and Robert Stephenson, 1960; The Cornish Giant, 1960; Great Engineers, 1961; James Watt, 1962; Thomas Newcomen, 1963; A Hunslet Hundred, 1964; Tools for the Job, 1965; The Aeronauts, 1966; The Mechanicals, 1967; Navigable Waterways, 1969; Waterloo Ironworks, 1969; (ed) Best Railway Stories, 1969; Victorian Engineering, 1970; The Making of a Railway, 1971; Landscape with Machines, 1971; From Sea to Sea, the Canal du Midi, 1973. *Recreations:* motoring in vintage cars; railways and interest in history of engineering generally. *Address:* The Cottage, Stanley Pontlarge, Winchcombe, Glos. *T:* Winchcombe 594. *Clubs:* United Motor Sports, Vintage Sports Car. *[Died 9 May 1974.*

ROMAINS, Jules, de l'Académie Française; Grand Officier de la Légion d'Honneur; Homme de Lettres; *b* Saint-Julien Chapteuil, 26 Aug. 1885; *m* 1936, Mdlle Lise Dreyfus. *Educ:* Paris, Ecole Normale Supérieure. Professeur de Philosophie, pendant dix ans, dans différents lycées de la province et de Paris; depuis 1919, carrière exclusivement littéraire: poète, auteur dramatique, romancier, etc. *Publications:* La Vie Unanime; Europe; Les Copains; Mort de Quelqu'un; Lucienne; Le Dieu des corps; Quand le navire...; Les Hommes de Bonne Volonté (27 volumes, 1932-46; traduction anglaise par Gerard Hopkins); L'Homme Blanc; Une Vue des Choses; Bertrand de Ganges, Le Moulin et l'Hospice, Salsette decouvre l'Amérique, Violation de Frontières, Le Fils de Jerphanion, Une Femme singulière, Le Besoin de voir clair, Mémoires de Mdme Chauverel, Un Grand honnête Homme, Pour Raison garder, Portraits d'Inconnus, etc.; *plays:* Knock; Le Dictateur; Le Trouhadec; Musse; Cromedeyre-le-Vieil; Donogoo; Grâce encore pour la Terre! *Address:* 6 rue de Solférino, Paris, VII, France.
[Died 14 Aug. 1972.

ROMANIS, William Hugh Cowie, JP, MA, MB, MChir Cantab, FRCS, LRCP, FRS (Edinburgh), FZS, FRAS; Barrister-at-Law; Consulting Surgeon to St Thomas's Hospital; Surgeon to Royal Masonic Hospital; Consulting Surgeon to the City of London Hospital for Diseases of the Chest, Royal Masonic Institute for Girls, Wimbledon, Sevenoaks, Wrotham, Woking, Kingston, and Okehampton Hospitals; *b* Godalming, 8 Nov. 1889; *e s* of Rev. William Francis John Romanis, MA Cantab, Preacher of the Charterhouse, EC, and Annie Ellen Cowie; *m* 1916, Dorothy Elizabeth, *d* of Rev. Canon Robert Burnet, Chancellor of Ferns Cathedral, Co. Wexford; one *s* two *d. Educ:* Charterhouse (Scholar, Captain of School); Trinity College, Cambridge (Mathematical Scholar); 1st cl. Mathematical Tripos (Part I); 1st cl. Natural Science Tripos (Part I); St Thomas's Hospital. Served European War in RAMC at Casualty Clearing Stations Nos 6 and 44; Examiner in Surgery, Universities of Cambridge, London, Glasgow; Mem. Court of Examiners, RCS; Member British Acad. Forensic Sciences. JP Surrey (Chm. Godalming Petty Sessions). CStJ. *Publications:* Science and Practice of Surgery (two vols); Surgical Emergencies in Practice; Synopsis of Surgical Diagnosis; Surgery of Exophthalmic Goitre, Lancet; Surgery in the Treatment of Phthisis, Lancet; Gastric Ulcer, The Acute Abdomen, Practitioner; and other scientific papers. *Recreations:* criminology, model engineering. *Address:* 149 Harley Street, W1. *T:* 01-935 4444; The Rough, Hurtmore, Godalming. *T:* 22518. *Clubs:* United University; Guildford County. *[Died 25 Jan. 1972.*

ROMNEY, 6th Earl of, *cr* 1801; **Charles Marsham;** Bt, 1663; Baron of Romney, 1716; Viscount Marsham, 1801; DL and JP for Norfolk; *b* 9 July 1892; *o s* of 5th Earl of Romney and Anne (*d* 1936), *d* of late Sir Edward H. Scott, 5th Bt; *S* father, 1933; *m* 1918, Marie, *e d* of late Adm. Sir Colin Keppel, GCVO, KCIE, CB, DSO. *Educ:* Eton; RMC, Sandhurst. Served European War, 1914-18 (wounded); Commandant Guards Depôt, 1928-31; Lt-Col, commanding 2nd Bn Coldstream Guards 1934-36; retired pay, 1936; Commandant Guards Depôt again, 1939-44. Life Vice-Pres., National Council of YMCA's; Pres., Debtor's Relief Funds Charity. *Heir:* cousin, Michael Henry Marsham [*b* 22 Nov. 1910; *m* 1939, Frances Aileen, *o d* of late J. R. Landale, IA]. *Address:* Gayton Hall, King's Lynn, Norfolk. *T:* Gayton 259.
[Died 6 Sept. 1975.

RONALD, E. B.; *see* Barker, Ronald Ernest.

RONALD, Sir Nigel Bruce, KCMG 1946 (CMG 1934); CVO 1935; *b* 20 Dec. 1894; *s* of late Arthur Wilson Ronald. *Educ:* Winchester; Magdalen College, Oxford. Liverpool Regiment (TF) 1914-17; Grenadier Guards (SR), 1917-20; 3rd Secretary HM Diplomatic Service 1920; 2nd Secretary 1922; Private Secretary to Parliamentary Under-Secretary, 1927; Assistant Private Secretary to Foreign Secretary, 1929-34; 1st Secretary, 1930; Counsellor, 1939; Assistant Under-Secretary, 1942; Ambassador to Portugal, 1947-54. *Address:* The Lodge, Broadwindsor, Dorset. *T:* 243. *Club:* Travellers'.
[Died 15 May 1973.

RONALDS, Andrew John, CBE 1961 (OBE 1951); *b* 4 Feb. 1897; *s* of General John Romanenko and Mary (*née* Drenteln); *m* 1918, Nathalie (*d* 1975), *d* of General Nicolas Woronow and Catherine (*née* Genishta); no *c. Educ:* Imperial Corps of Pages, St Petersburg. Served European War, 1914-18, with Russian Army, 4th Guards Rifles, Imperial Family's Own (twice wounded, Major); attached British Mil. Mission in S Russia, 1919-20; served at British Vice-Consulate, Dubrovnik, 1926-29. Entered British Consular Service, 1936, established in Foreign Service, 1947; served at Belgrade, Sarajevo, Split (captured by enemy forces, 1941), Lisbon, Lourenço Marques, Athens, Naples, Venice, Beira and Bilbao; Consul General at Tananarive, Madagascar, 1956; Ambassador to Malagasy Republic (Madagascar), 1960-61; retired August 1961. On special service with Armed Forces in ME and Central Mediterranean, 1943-45 (despatches). Imperial Order of St George, 4th Class (Russia). *Recreations:* music, walking. *Address:* c/o Barclays National Bank Ltd, PO Box 471, East London 5200, South Africa. *Clubs:* Civil Service; Società Dell'Unione (Venice). *[Died 1 Nov. 1978.*

ROOKS, Major-Gen. Lowell W., CB (Hon.) 1947; US Army, retd; Fund-Raising Co-ordinator UN International Children's Emergency Fund, since 1949; *b* 11 April 1893; *s* of Albert Rooks and Ruth Naomi Richardson; *m* 1920, Martha Caroline Phillips; two *d. Educ:* University of Washington, Seattle, Washington, USA. Served European War, 1914-18, entering military service 1917; participated in fighting in Vosges Mountains and Meuse-Argonne offensive, France, 1918; later Instructor at Infantry School and Command and Gen. Staff School; War of 1939-45, Chief of Training Div., Army Ground Forces until 1942; Chief of Staff, Second Corps, UK, 1942; participated in Assualt Landings at Oran, Algeria, Nov. 1942; Asst Chief of Staff, G3, AFHQ, under Gen. Eisenhower Dec. 1942; later Dep. Chief of Staff, AFHQ; transferred to European theatre and commanded 90th Div. in final phases of Battle of the Bulge and cracking of Siegfried Line; returned to Gen. Eisenhower's Staff at SHAEF where exercised primary role in planning operations resulting in crossing of Rhine, isolation and capture of Ruhr, advance to Elbe and thrust through Bavaria into Austria; shortly after VE Day, i/c Allied Party sent to Flensburg, Germany, to establish control over self-styled Actg German Govt headed by Grand Admiral Doenitz and German High Command, headed by Field Marshal Keitel; later acted to place all members of this "Government" under arrest; returned to US 1945; Deputy Director-General, UNRRA, Jan. 1946; Director-General UN Relief and Rehabilitation Admin., 1947-48 (when organisation liquidated); Distinguished Service Medal with Oak-leaf Cluster; Silver Star Citation, Legion of Merit and Bronze Star; British Companion of the Order of the Bath; French Legion of Honour and Croix de Guerre with Palm; Brazilian Order of Military Merit; Belgian Croix de Guerre with Palm, and Belgian Commander of the Order of the Crown with Palm. *Recreations:* golf, fishing and hunting. *Address:* Box 106, Tucson Road, Nogales, Arizona, USA. *T:* 0187J5. *Clubs:* Army Navy Town, Army Navy Country (Washington, DC). *[Died 17 Jan. 1973.*

ROONEY, Major-General Sir Owen (Patrick James), KBE 1959 (CBE 1951; OBE 1943); CB 1957; *b* 1900, *s* of late Captain Owen Rooney, Royal Artillery; *m* 1924, Una Colman, *d* of Charles Guilfoyle Doran, Queenstown, County Cork; one *s* one *d. Educ:* Haberdashers' Aske's School; RMA, Woolwich. Army Officer from 1919, when commissioned in RFA; RAPC, 1924; Egypt, Sudan and Palestine, 1932-37; served War of 1939-45, France, N Africa and Italy; BAOR, 1951-54; Maj.-Gen. 1955; Paymaster-in-Chief, War Office, 1955-59; retired. Col Comdt Royal Army Pay Corps, 1960-63. *Recreation:* formerly Hon. Vice-Pres., Football Assoc., 1959-61. Army Football Assoc. (Vice-Pres.). *Address:* Flat 9, Westfield Park House, Spencer Road, Ryde, Isle of Wight. *Club:* Army and Navy. *[Died 24 March 1972.*

ROOTES, Sir Reginald (Claud), Kt 1946; *b* 20 Oct. 1896; *s* of late William and Jane Rootes; *m* 1st, 1922, Ruth Joyce, *d* of late Harding Bensted; one *s* ; 2nd, 1938, Nancy Norris, *d* of late J. C. Beadle. *Educ:* Cranbrook Sch., Kent. Civil Service, Admiralty, 1915-18. Pres. Society of Motor Manufacturers and Traders, 1945-46, Dep. Pres., 1946-50; Past Pres. Motor Industry Research Assoc. *Recreations:* various. *Address:* Polla House, Hothfield, Ashford, Kent. *T:* Ashford 21495. *Club:* Buck's.
[Died 20 Dec. 1977.

ROOTH, Ivar; *b* Stockholm, 2 Nov. 1888; two *s* two *d. Educ:* Universities of Uppsala and Berlin. Governor of Central Bank of Sweden, 1929-48; Assistant Manager and solicitor of Stockholm Mortgage Bank; Director of Bank for International Settlements; Chairman of the Board and Managing Director of the International Monetary Fund, 1951-56. Hon. PhD Uppsala, 1962. *Address:* 13 Larsbergsvagen, 518138 Lidingö 1, Sweden.
[Died 27 Feb. 1972.

ROOTS, William Lloyd, QC 1959; TD; MA (Oxon.); *b* 10 Sept. 1911; *s* of Neville Roots; *m* 1939, Elizabeth Colquhoun Gow Gray; one *s*. *Educ:* Tonbridge School; Brasenose College, Oxford. Called to Bar, Middle Temple, 1933; Master of the Bench, 1965. Surrey and Sussex Yeomanry, RA (TA), 1939-46. Alderman, Royal Borough of Kensington, 1953-59; Chairman, Fulham and Kensington Hospital Management Cttee, 1952-55; MP (C) Kensington South, 1959-67, resigned. Dep. Chm., Dorset QS 1960-. *Publications:* a number of books on Local Government Law. *Recreations:* travel, fishing. *Address:* 2 Mitre Court Buildings, Temple, EC4. *T:* 01-236 4488. *Clubs:* Carlton, 1900, United and Cecil, Hurlingham. *[Died* 14 *Aug.* 1971.

ROPER, Edward Ridgill; DSO 1918; MC; VD; QC; formerly President of Courts of Appeal for Botswana, Lesotho and Swaziland; Judge of the Supreme Court of South Africa, 1946-55; former Member of Parliament, Union of South Africa, Wynberg Division; *b* 30 Oct. 1885; *s* of late Rev. Thomas Roper, Kroonstad, Orange Free State; *m* 1919, Gladys Frances, *e d* of F. W. Farrow, Walton-on-Thames; one *s*. *Educ:* Kingswood College, Grahamstown; Victoria College, Stellenbosch; Diocesan College, Rondebosch; BA, LLB, Maynard Scholar and Ebden Prizeman, University of Cape of Good Hope. Admitted to Cape Bar, 1910; 2nd Lt Cape Garrison Artillery, 1909; Capt. 1912; temp. Capt. RFA 1915; temp. Major, 1917; Officer Commdg Cape Garrison Artillery, 1921-24; served German SW Africa, South African Rebellion, Egypt, France and Belgium, Italy (DSO, MC, VD, Croix de Guerre, despatches, wounded thrice); Officer Commanding 32nd Field Regt, South African Artillery, 1942. Pres., S Af. Red Cross, 1958, 1959, 1961, 1962; Pres., Boy Scouts Assoc. of South Africa, 1967. *Recreation:* gardening. *Address:* 1 Kent Road, Dunkeld West, Johannesburg, S Africa. *Club:* Rand (Johannesburg).
[Died 13 *May* 1974.

ROPER, Sir Harold, Kt 1945; CBE 1943; MC; MP (C) North Cornwall, 1950-59; *b* 2 Sept. 1891; *s* of Arthur Charles Roper, FRCS, MRCP, Exeter; *m* 1929, Norah Keys, Edinburgh; four *d*. *Educ:* Blundell's; Sidney Sussex College, Cambridge. Varsity Boat, 1913. European War, France and Italy, 1915-18, 8th Devons, Capt. (MC); General Manager, Burmah Oil Co. Ltd 1936-45; despatches, 1942. Member: Burma Legislative Council, 1935-36; Burma Senate, 1937-42; Chm. Burma Chamber of Commerce, 1940. Mem. Devon CC, 1961-68. *Address:* Gorse Hill, Ilsham Marine Drive, Torquay, Devon.
[Died 20 *Aug.* 1971.

ROPNER, Sir Guy; *see* Ropner, Sir W. G.

ROPNER, Colonel Sir Leonard, 1st Bt *cr* 1952; MC; TD; DL; KStJ; Director: Sir R. Ropner & Company Ltd, Shipowners; British Ship-owners' Assoc., and other cos; Member of Council of Chamber of Shipping of the United Kingdom since 1928, and of Tramp Shipping Committee since 1935; *b* 26 February 1895; *s* of William Ropner, JP, and *g s* of late Sir Robert Ropner, Bt, VD, DL, JP; *m* 1932, Esmé, *y d* of late Bruce Robertson; one *s* two *d*. *Educ:* Harrow; Clare College, Cambridge (Scholar). Commissioned RA, 1914; later commanded a battery in France for two years (MC); OC Durham Heavy Brigade RA (TA), 1919-28; rejoined RA as 2nd Lt, 1941; later Lt-Col RA, and Col HQ 21st Army Gp, Belgium and Germany. Hon. Col 426 Coast Regt RA, TA, 1928-56, Hon. Col 132 Corps Engineer Regt TA, 1956-58; Mem., Durham County T&AFA 1920-61 (Vice-Chm. 1948-52). MP (C) Sedgefield Div. of Durham, 1923-29, Barkston Ash, W R Yorks, 1931-64; PPS to Secretary of State for War, 1924-28; Temp. Chm. of Cttees, 1945-58; Hon. Treasurer, Cons. and Unionist Films Assoc., 1930-47, Chm., 1947-59; Chm., Cons. Shipping and Ship-building Committee, 1946-64; Hon. Treasurer of Primrose League, 1952-64. Member of English Consultative Committee under the Forestry Acts, 1932-36; Forestry Commissioner, 1936-45; Assistant Controller, Ministry of Supply Timber Control, Sept. 1939; Forestry Commission Timber Supply Department, 1940; Dep. Dir Home Grown Timber Production, Ministry of Supply, 1941. County Comr, St John Ambulance Bde, N Riding of Yorkshire, 1950-66. DL Durham. *Heir: s* John Bruce Woollacott Ropner [*b* 16 April 1937; *m* 1st, 1961, Anne Melicent (marr. diss. 1970), *d* of late Sir Ralph Delmé-Radcliffe; two *d*; 2nd, 1970, Auriol, *d* of Captain Mackeson-Sandbach, Caerllo, Llangernyw; two *d*]. *Address:* Thorp Perrow, Bedale, Yorkshire. *T:* Bedale 2710. *TA:* Bedale. *Clubs:* Carlton, Bath, Buck's; Durham County (Durham); Yorkshire (York). *[Died* 12 *Oct.* 1977.

ROPNER, Sir Robert (Desmond), Kt 1959; Director, Mainsforth Investments Ltd; *b* 2 July 1908; 4th *s* of William Ropner, JP, and *gs* of Sir Robert Ropner, 1st Bt, VD, DL, JP; *m* 1st, 1932, Dorothy Beecroft Sheila (marriage dissolved, 1946), *d* of Sir Edmund Beecroft Lacon, 5th Bt; two *s*; 2nd, 1947, Sibyl (*d*

1969), *d* of late Thomas O. Carter. *Educ:* Harrow; Clare College, Cambridge (BA). Mem. Ministry of Transport Ships Licensing Cttee, 1947; Chm. Tramp Shipping Sub-Cttee of Shipping Advisory and Allocations Committee, 1947; Member Council, Chamber of Shipping of the UK, and various Committees, 1941- (Pres. 1958-59; Chairman Deep Sea Tramp Section, 1951-53); Mem., General Council British Shipping, 1941-, Chm., 1958-59; Member, Shipping Advisory Panel, 1962; Past Chm. North of England Protecting and Indemnity Assoc. *Recreations:* forestry, motoring. *Address:* Camp Hill, Bedale, Yorkshire. *T:* Sinderby 262. *Club:* Boodle's. *[Died* 31 *Aug.* 1977.

ROPNER, Sir (William) Guy, Kt 1947; Director Sir R. Ropner & Co. Ltd and other companies; *b* 14 June 1896; *s* of William Ropner; *m* 1921, Margarita Gray; two *s* one *d*. *Educ:* Harrow. European War, 1914-18, joined Durham Royal Garrison Artillery, 1914, and served in France with Siege Batteries; joined Sir R. Ropner & Co. Ltd, 1919; War of 1939-45, entered Ministry of Shipping, 1939, and served in various capacities throughout war, including Dep. Director Ship Management Div., Head of Convoy Section and Minister's Rep. in Canada; President Chamber of Shipping, 1950; Chairman General Council of British Shipping, 1950; Deputy Chairman, Lloyd's Register of Shipping, 1950-60. *Recreations:* gardening. *Address:* Hillside, Patrick Brompton, Bedale, Yorks. *T:* Constable Burton 206. *Clubs:* Royal Motor Yacht; Royal Thames Yacht.
[Died 2 *May* 1971.

ROSA, John Nogueira, OBE 1947; BCom; formerly Deputy Managing Director, M. Golodetz Ltd, International Merchants, EC3, retired 1971; *b* Durban, South Africa, 17 Jan. 1903; *s* of John Michael and Maria Magdalena Nogueira Rosa; *m* 1929, Eileen, *d* of James Moncrieff Anderson; no *c*. *Educ:* South Africa; London School of Economics and Political Science. Ottoman Bank, Istanbul, 1924-28; Helbert, Wagg & Co. Ltd, Private Bankers, London, 1929-41; HM Treasury Rep. in Syria and the Lebanon, 1941-42; Colonial Office, London, 1942-47; Member Colonial Office Mission to East and Central Africa to investigate production of groundnuts, 1946; Helbert, Wagg & Co., Ltd, 1947, resigned 1947; late Member Boards Overseas Food Corp., The Queensland-British Food Corp., and Colonial Development Corporation, 1948-51. *Recreation:* travel. *Address:* 11a Troy Court, W8. *T:* 01-937 6729.
[Died 14 *Aug.* 1977.

ROSAY, Françoise; actress; *b* Paris, 19 April 1891; *d* of Gilbert Bandy; *widow* of Jacques Feyder, director; three *s*. Started career as singer, taking important rôles at National Opera in Paris. Title rôle in Madam Tic-Tac, Winter Garden, London, 1950; Trespass, Globe Theatre. Entered films in France, 1927, and had immediate successes. Went to England in 1944, having contracts with Ealing Studios. French films include: La Kermesse héroïque, Carnet de bal, Une Femme Disparaît, Drôle de Drame. Eng. Lang. films include: The Half Way House, Johnny Frenchman, Saraband for Dead Lovers, Quartet, The Naked Heart, That Lady, Me and the Colonel. *Address:* 195 Rue de l'Université, Paris. *[Died* 28 *March* 1974.

ROSE, Sir Alan (Edward Percival), KCMG 1955; Kt 1950; QC (Ceylon), 1948; MA, LLB Cantab; Chief Justice (1st) of the State of Singapore, 1958-63; *b* 8 October 1899; *yr s* of late Charles Edward James Rose; unmarried. *Educ:* Aldenham Sch.; Trinity Coll., Cambridge. 2nd Lieut 1st Bn Rifle Brigade, BEF, 1918-19; called to Bar, Inner Temple, 1923; entered Colonial Legal Service, 1929; Chief Police Magistrate, Fiji, 1929; Crown Counsel, Northern Rhodesia, 1931; Solicitor-General, Palestine, 1936; Puisne Judge, Palestine, 1939; Chm., Commissions of Inquiry into loss of SS Patria, 1940; and into corruption in Customs Dept, 1942; acted as Chief Justice, 1944; Judge of Supreme Court, Ceylon, 1945; acted as Legal Secretary, Ceylon, 1946 and 1947; Attorney-Gen. (1st) Dominion of Ceylon, 1947-51; Officer Administering Govt of Ceylon, Mar.-June 1952, July-Sept. 1953; Chief Justice of the Dominion of Ceylon, 1951-55, retired 1955. Chm. Commn of Inquiry into affairs of Nairobi City Council, 1956; Chm. Medical Appeal Tribunal, Midland Region, 1957-58, 1963-68, London (South), 1968-71. *Address:* 9 Hove Place, Hove, Sussex BN3 2RG. *T:* Brighton 733666. *Club:* Bath. *[Died* 20 *June* 1975.

ROSE, Rt. Rev. Alfred Carey Wollaston, MA; an Assistant Bishop in the Diocese of Canterbury since 1957; Sub-Prelate of Order of St John of Jerusalem; *s* of late Rev. A. Rose, Vicar of Wilstead, Beds; *m* 1920, Lois, *d* of late Charles Garton of Banstead, Surrey; four *s*. *Educ:* Marlborough; Worcester College, Oxford. Curate of St Mary, Somers Town, 1909-14; temporary Chaplain RN, 1914-19, HMS London, 1914-16, HMS Tyne, 1917-18, HMS Marlborough, 1918-19; Sub-Warden Bishops Hostel, Lincoln, 1919-20; Warden, 1921-27; Vicar of

Haigh, Lancs, 1920-21; Prebendary of Lincoln Cathedral, 1927-28; Vicar and Rural Dean of Brighton, 1928-34; Prebendary of Waltham in Chichester Cathedral, 1928; Examining Chaplain to the Bishop of Chichester, 1928-34; Chaplain to the King, 1933-34. Suffragan Bishop of Dover, 1935-56. *Recreation:* golf. *Address:* Glebe House, St Stephen's Green, Canterbury, Kent. *T:* Canterbury 63673.   *[Died 9 April 1971.*

ROSE, Lt-Col Ernest Albert, CBE 1919 (OBE 1919); BSc, FIMechE; late Honorary Colonel 2/7th Battalion Queen's Royal Regiment; *b* 1879; *m* Dula (*d* 1970), *e d* of Eliot Lewis, JP, Liverpool; two *s* one *d* (and one *d* decd). *Educ:* Liverpool College; Liverpool University. Formerly General Manager of New Arrol-Johnston Car Co. Ltd; a pioneer of motoring in England; chief Engineer to the Pioneer Motor Traction Co. formed in 1903 at Liverpool, the Road Carrying Co. Ltd; for many years Director of Delaunay Belleville Motors, Ltd; a Member of the General Council of the Royal Automobile Club; served European War, 1914-19 (despatches, OBE, CBE, Order of Crown of Italy). *Recreations:* golf and motoring. *Address:* Old Kiln, Churt, near Farnham, Surrey. *Club:* Bath.
      [Died 2 Sept. 1976.

ROSE, Sir Francis Cyril, 4th Bt, *cr* 1872; Painter and Author; *b* 18 Sept. 1909; *e s* of 3rd Bt and Laetitia, *d* of late Comte Rouy de Labadesse; *S* father, 1915; *m* 1st, 1943, Frederica Dorothy Violet (marr. diss. 1966), *d* of late General Sir Frederick Carrington, KCB, KCMG; 2nd, 1967, Mrs Beryl Davis (marr. diss.), *widow* of Squadron Leader Basil Montefiore Davis, RAF. *Educ:* St Anthony's Preparatory School, Eastbourne; Beaumont College. Served War of 1939-45; RAF 1940-42 (invalided out). Artistic Adviser Edinburgh Tapestry Co. Ltd, 1948-50; Artistic Consultant Roosen Silks Ltd. Exhibns: Paris, 1933, New York, Chicago and London, 1934; Petit Palace, Paris, 1938 (official show); represented British Modern Art (with Group), Salon d'Automne, Paris, 1939; Reid and Lefevre, London, 1944; Exhibition of Paintings organised by US Army (441st Troop Carrier Group) Gallery Pierre Colle, Paris, Feb. 1945; Wallpaper designs, History of Wallpaper Exhibition, Suffolk Gallery, London, 1945; Cotton Board Flower Painting Exhibition, Manchester, 1945; Redfern Gallery, London, 1945; Associated American Artists, NY, 1947; Gimpel Fils, London, 1949 and 1952; Passedoit Gallery, NY, 1950; Gallery Pierre Colle, Paris, 1950; Molton Gallery, 1961; Preston Gallery, Bolton, Lancs, 1964; Upper Grosvenor Galleries, 1967; retrospective exhibition, GLC London Gall. and Royal Pavilion, Brighton, 1966. Costumes and Scenery for Cupid and Psyche Ballet at Sadler's Wells, 1939; for La Peri, ballet given by Serge Lifar, Monte Carlo ballets, 1946; sets for Trigon, Arts Theatre, 1964. Textile designs for the Cotton Board, 1944; Artistic adviser for 1947-48, Mount Row Prints Ltd. *Publications:* The White Cow and other Chinese Tales, 1945; The Shadowy Pine Tree, 1945; Your Home, 1946. Illustrations; The World is Round, 1939, Paris France, 1940, by Gertrude Stein; Gertrude Stein's First Reader, and 3 plays, Maurice Fridberg, 1946; Autobiography: Saying Life, 1961; Drinking at Home, 1964; Gertrude Stein and Painting, 1968. *Heir: cousin,* Sir Julian Rose, Bt.   *[Died 19 Nov. 1979.*

ROSE, Sir Hugh, 2nd Bt, *cr* 1935; TD 1945; DL; Director, Scottish Provident Institution; *b* 16 Dec. 1902; *s* of late Sir Arthur Rose, 1st Bt, DSO, and Mary (*d* 1939), *d* of late Robert Weir, JP, DL, Edinburgh; *S* father, 1937; *m* 1930, Marjorie, *d* of T. Leslie Usher; one *d* (and two *s* decd). *Educ:* Edinburgh Academy; Harrow; Trinity College, Cambridge. Major RA, TA, 1941, Italy (despatches). Commissioner General Board of Control for Scotland, 1936-62. Chm., Securities Trust of Scotland Ltd, 1948-75. County Comr for Boy Scouts for Edinburgh and Leith, 1946-50; Mem., Council on Tribunals, 1958-62; Chm Mental Welfare Commission for Scotland, 1962-65. Captain, Royal Company of Archers (Queen's Body Guard for Scotland). DL Edinburgh, 1958. *Address:* 38 Frogston Road West, Edinburgh EH10 7AJ. *Clubs:* Caledonian; New (Edinburgh).   *[Died 28 Sept. 1976 (ext).*

ROSE, John Donald, FRS 1971; Chairman, Fulmer Research Institute Ltd, since 1974; *b* 2 Jan. 1911; *s* of Rimington Wilson Rose and Martha Ellen Minnie Rose (*née* Dawson); *m* 1941, Yvonne Valerie Evans; one *s* one *d*. *Educ:* Rotherham Grammar Sch.; Jesus Coll., Oxford (MA, BSc); Federal Technical High School, Zürich. ICI Ltd: Dyestuffs Division: Research Chemist, 1935; Associate Research Manager, 1946; Research Dir, 1951; Production Dir, 1958; Paints Division: Man. Dir, 1959; Chm., 1964; Dir (R&D), ICI Ltd, 1966-72; Director: Canadian Industries Ltd, 1968-72; Laporte Industries (Holdings) Ltd, 1972-76. Master, Worshipful Co. of Salters, 1973. Hon. DSc Salford, 1972. *Publications:* numerous articles and lectures in (chiefly) Jl of Chem. Soc., Chemistry and Industry. *Recreations:*

motoring, travel, photography, gardening. *Address:* Mount Fort, Chalfont Heights, Gerrards Cross, Bucks SL9 9UB. *T:* Gerrards Cross 83025.   *[Died 14 Oct. 1976.*

ROSE, Reginald L. S.; *see* Smith-Rose.

ROSEBERY, 6th Earl of, *cr* 1703; **Albert Edward Harry Meyer Archibald Primrose**, KT 1947; PC 1945; DSO 1918; MC; LLD 1954; FRCSE 1955; Bt 1651; Viscount Rosebery, Baron Primrose and Dalmeny, 1700; Viscount of Inverkeithing, Baron Dalmeny and Primrose, 1703; Baron Rosebery (UK), 1828; Earl of Midlothian, 1911; Viscount Mentmore of Mentmore, 1911; Baron Epsom of Epsom, 1911; Lord Lieutenant for Midlothian, 1929-64; *b* 8 Jan. 1882; *e s* of 5th Earl and Hannah, *o d* of Baron Meyer de Rothschild (*d* 1890); *S* father, 1929; *m* 1st, 1909, Lady Dorothy A. M. A. Grosvenor (whom he divorced, 1919; she *m* 2nd, Captain R. B. Brassey; 3rd, 1929, C. Hilton-Green and 4th, Commander Mack; *d* 1966), *y d* of late Lord Henry Grosvenor and Dora Mina, *e d* of James A. Erskine Wemyss, of Wemyss Castle and Torrie House, Fifeshire; one *d*; 2nd, 1924, Eva, Lady Belper (DBE 1955; LLD Edinburgh, 1957), *d* of 2nd Baron Aberdare; one *s*. *Educ:* Eton; Sandhurst. Captained Surrey XI, 1905, 1906, 1907; played for Scotland *v* Australians, 1906; late 2nd Lieut Grenadier Guards; MP (L) Midlothian, 1906-10; served European War, 1914-18 (wounded, DSO, MC). Capt. Royal Company of Archers. A Steward of Jockey Club 1929, 1945; Pres. Thoroughbred Breeders' Assoc., 1932-57. Regional Commr for Scotland, 1941-45; Secretary of State for Scotland, 1945; Member of Royal Commn on Justice of the Peace, 1946-48; Chairman Departmental Cttee on Export and Slaughter of Horses, 1949; Pres., National Liberal Party, 1945-47; Chm., The Royal Fine Art Commission for Scotland, 1952-57; Chm., Scottish Tourist Bd, 1955-65. Pres. Roy. Zoological Soc. of Scotland, 1942-64; Pres. Royal Scot Corporation, 1947-. *Heir: s* Lord Primrose, *qv*. *Address:* Dalmeny House, South Queensferry, West Lothian. *T:* 031-331 1884; Mentmore, Leighton Buzzard. *T:* Leighton Buzzard 2147; Cleveland House, Newmarket. *T:* Newmarket 2483.   *[Died 31 May 1974.*

ROSENFELD, Prof. Léon; Professor at Nordic Institute for Theoretical Atomic Physics, Copenhagen, since 1958; Editor-in-chief, Nuclear Physics, since 1956; *b* 14 Aug. 1904; *s* of Léon Rosenfeld and Jeanne Pierre; *m* 1933, Yvonne Cambresier; one *s* one *d*. *Educ:* University of Liège, Belgium. PhD, Liège, 1926; Asst Univ. of Göttingen, 1928; Lecturer, Univ. of Liège, 1930; Prof., Univ. of Liège, 1937; Prof., Univ. of Utrecht, 1940; Prof. of Theoretical Physics, Univ. of Manchester, 1947-58. Chevalier de l'Ordre de Léopold, 1938; Member: International Acad. of History of Science, 1966; (Corresp. Mem., 1947-66); Roy. Danish Acad. of Sciences and Letters, 1951; Brazilian Acad. of Sciences, 1959; Roy. Belgian Acad. of Sciences, Letters and Fine Arts, 1959; German Acad. of Sciences in Berlin, 1969; Chm., Danish National Committee for History and Philosophy of Science, 1964; Doctor, *hc*: Univ. of Brussels, 1965; Univ. of Copenhagen, 1965. Laureate of Prix Francqui, 1949. *Publications:* Niels Bohr, an Essay, (Amsterdam), 1945; De ontsluiting van de Atoomkern, (Amsterdam) 1946; Nuclear Forces, (Amsterdam) 1948; Theory of Electrons, (Amsterdam) 1951. Papers on quantum theory, nuclear physics, history of science. *Address:* Carl Plougsvej 9/II, Copenhagen V, Denmark. *T:* Vester 8987.   *[Died 23 March 1974.*

ROSENHEIM, Baron *cr* 1970 (Life Peer); **Max Leonard Rosenheim**, KBE 1967 (CBE 1955); MA, MD, FRCP; FRS 1972; Professor of Medicine, University of London, and Director, Medical Unit, University College Hospital Medical School, 1950-71, now Professor Emeritus; *b* 1908; *s* of late Ludwig Rosenheim, London. *Educ:* Shrewsbury School; St John's Coll., Cambridge; University College Hospital. Appointments on junior staff, University College and Westminster Hospitals, 1932-38; Bilton Pollard Travelling Fellowship (University Coll. Hosp.), 1939; working as Research Assistant at Massachusetts General Hospital, Boston, USA; First Assistant, Medical Unit University Coll. Hosp., 1939. RAMC, 1941-46; served in Middle East and Italy with rank of Lt-Col. Cons. Physician (local Brig.) South-East Asia Command, 1945-46; Physician, University College Hosp., 1946-50. Sir Arthur Sims Commonwealth Travelling Prof., 1958; Sir Ernest Finch Visiting Professor, Sheffield Univ. 1967. Mem. Med. Research Council, 1961-65; Pres., Royal Coll. of Physicians, London, 1966-72. Hon. Member: Assoc. of American Physicians, 1959; Swedish Med. Soc., 1968; For. Hon. Mem. Amer. Acad. of Arts and Sciences, 1961; Hon. Fellow: University Coll., London, 1967; American Coll. of Physicians, 1967; Royal Aust. Coll. of Physicians, 1968; Royal Coll. of Physicians of Edinburgh, 1968; Royal Coll. of Physicians of Canada, 1969; Royal Irish Coll. of Physicians, 1969; Royal Coll. of Gen. Practitioners, 1969; St John's Coll., Cambridge, 1969;

RCPGlas, 1971. Hon. DSc: Univ. of Wales, 1969; Birmingham, 1970; Ceylon, 1970; Southampton, 1970; Hon. LLD Liverpool, 1972. *Publications:* contribs to various medical journals. *Address:* University College Hospital, Gower Street, WC1. *T:* 01-387 5861; 39 Eton Avenue, NW3. *T:* 01-794 3320. *Clubs:* Athenæum, Savile; United Hospitals Sailing.
[Died 2 Dec. 1972.

ROSENMAN, Samuel Irving; Lawyer, US; Counsel to law firm Rosenman Colin Kaye Petschek Freund & Emil; *b* Texas, 13 Feb. 1896; *s* of Sol Rosenman and Ethel Paler; *m* 1924, Dorothy Reuben; two *s. Educ:* Columbia University. AB 1915; LLB 1919; admitted to New York Bar, 1920; Member New York State Legislature, 1922-26, Bill Drafting Commissioner, 1926-28; Counsel to Gov. Franklin D. Roosevelt, 1929-32; apptd Justice, NY Supreme Court, 1932, re-apptd, 1933; later elected for 14-year term; resigned, to be Special Counsel: to President Roosevelt, 1943-45; to President Truman, April 1945-Feb. 1946; resigned to resume practice of law. Member: Assoc. of Bar of NYC (President, 1964-66); Board of Dirs of Amer. Judicature Soc.; Amer. Bar Assoc.; NY State Bar Assoc.; Presidential Steel Industry Fact-finding Board; Presidential Maritime industry Bd, 1961; Chm. Presidential Emergency Railway Bd, 1963. Phi Beta Kappa, Delta Sigma Rho, Phi Epsilon Pi. Democrat. Jewish religion. Awarded Medal for Merit by President Truman; Officer of French Legion of Honour. *Publications:* Public Papers and Addresses of Franklin D. Roosevelt, 1928-45; Working with Roosevelt, 1952. *Address:* 575 Madison Avenue, New York, NY 10022, USA. *T:* Murray Hill 8-7800.   *[Died 24 June 1973.*

ROSEVEARE, Rt. Rev. Reginald Richard, CBE 1968; *b* 18 May 1902; 6th *c* of Rev. Canon Richard Polgreen and Mary Isobel Roseveare; unmarried. *Educ:* Sedbergh School. Clerk and Assistant Salesman to W. J. & H. Thompson, Tea and Rubber Brokers, London, 1920-24; at Kelham Theological College, 1924-29; made Profession in Society of the Sacred Mission, Kelham, 1928; Deacon, 1929; Priest, 1930; Asst Curate, St George, Nottingham, 1929-34; Chaplain, HM Borstal Inst., Nottingham, 1932-34; Tutor, Kelham Theological College, 1934-37; Priest-in-Charge of Mission District of Parson Cross, Sheffield, 1937-39; Vicar of St Cecilia, Parson Cross, Sheffield, 1939-52; Member of Sheffield City Education Committee, 1941-50; Proctor in Convocation, 1950-52; Rural Dean of Ecclesfield, 1943-52; Canon Residentiary of Sheffield Cathedral, 1945-52; Provincial SSM, S Africa, 1952-56; Bishop of Accra, 1956-67. Expelled by Ghana Govt, 13 Aug. 1962; allowed to return, 13 Nov. 1962. *Publications:* A Parish Communion Book, 1938; Getting Married in Church, 1944. *Address:* Kelham, Newark, Notts.   *[Died 9 April 1972.*

ROSMER, Milton; *b* 4 Nov. 1882; *s* of William and Miriam Lunt (father professionally known as Arthur Milton); *m* Irene Rooke (*d* 1958), actress; no *c. Educ:* Manchester Gram. School. Began with Osmond Tearle's Shakespeare Co.; toured in Drury Lane Production of The Best of Friends, Martin Harvey's Co., two years; Miss Horniman's Co., Gaiety, Manch., four years; Ben Greet Players in America, three years playing: Everyman, Romeo, Oberon, Mark Antony, Orlando, etc. Produced under own management The Fugitive (John Galsworthy), also new plays by Stanley Houghton, Harold Brighouse, etc. at Prince of Wales, Court, Criterion Theatres, etc., London. Directed Everyman Theatre, Hampstead, three years; Director Stratford-on-Avon Shakespeare Festival Company for 1943; produced number of plays in London, The Green Bay Tree, The Father, The Devil's Disciple, etc. Acted leads in many of Galsworthy's, Shaw's, Masefield's, Ibsen's plays. Starred in silent films as Heathcliff in Wuthering Heights, Jan Ridd in Lorna Doone, etc. Dir films for Gaumont Brit. (for three years), London Films, etc. Played many leading parts in BBC and TV Played as Sgt Rough in Gaslight, Apollo Theatre; Hjaimar, The Wild Duck, St James's Theatre; Cassius, Julius Caesar, St James's; Gen. Burgoyne (and prod. the play), Devil's Disciple, Piccadilly Theatre; Dr Ferguson, One Bright Day, Apollo, and a large number of leading parts in London, the Provinces, America and Canada. *Address:* Box Tree, Hawridge, Chesham, Bucks. *T:* Cholesbury (Bucks) 297.   *[Died 7 Dec. 1971.*

ROSS, Alan Strode Campbell, MA Oxon, MA Birmingham; Professor of Linguistics, University of Birmingham, 1951-74 (Professor of English Language, 1948-51); *b* 1 February 1907; *er s* of late Archibald Campbell Carne Ross, Penzance and Brecon, and Millicent Strode Cobham; *m* 1933, Elizabeth Stefanyja (*d* 1973), *yr d* of late Bronislas Olszewski, Warsaw; one *s. Educ:* Lindisfarne, Blackheath; Naish House, Burnham-on-Sea; Malvern College; Christ College, Brecon. Henry Skynner Scholarship in Astronomy, Balliol College, Oxford, 1925; First Class Hons School of English Lang and Lit., Oxford, 1929; Asst Lecturer in English Lang., Leeds Univ., 1929. Lecturer, 1936.

Foreign Office, 1940-45. Lecturer in English Lang., Univ. of Birmingham, 1946, Reader, 1947. Corresp. member of Suomalais-ugrilainen Seura. Liveryman, Grocers' Company. *Publications:* The Dream of the Rood (with B. Dickins), 1934; Studies in the Accidence of the Lindisfarne Gospels, 1937; The Numeral-Signs of the Mohenjo-daro Script, 1938; The Terfinnas and Beormas of Ohthere, 1940; Ginger, 1952; Urs Graf edn of the Lindisfarne Gospels (with others), 1956-60; Etymology, 1958; Essentials of German Grammar, 1963; (with F. G. Healey) Patience Napoléon, 1963; (with A. W. Moverley) The Pitcairnese Language, 1964; Essentials of English Grammar, 1964; (with N. F. C. Owen) I. I. Revzin, Models of Language (translated from Russian), 1966; Arts v. Science (ed), 1967; (ed) What are U, 1969; (ed jtly) The Durham Ritual, 1969; How to Pronounce It, 1970; Don't Say It, 1973; articles in Acta Philologica Scandinavica, Archivum Linguisticum, Biometrika, Englische Studien, Finnisch-ugrische Forschungen, Indogermanische Forschungen, Geographical Journal, Journal English and Germanic Philology, Journal Roy. Statistical Soc., Mathematical Gazette, Moderna Sprak, Mod. Lang. Notes, Mod. Lang. Rev., Nature, Neuphilologische Mitteilungen, Studia germanica, Zeitschrift für vergleichende Sprachforschung, Saga-Book of Viking Soc., Trans of Philological Soc., etc; contrib: Noblesse Oblige (ed N. Mitford); U and non-U Revisited (ed R. Buckle); part-editor, Leeds Studies in English (I-VI); Editor, English Philological Studies VIII-XIV. *Recreations:* land-rovering, patience, croquet. *Address:* 37 Phoenix Way, Southwick, Sussex BN4 4HP. *T:* Brighton 595027.   *[Died 23 Sept. 1980.*

ROSS, Brig.-Gen. Alexander, OC 1971; CMG 1919; DSO 1917; VD; QC; LLD (Sask); Barrister; Judge of District Court of Yorkton, Saskatchewan, 1921-55, retired; *b* Forres, Scotland, 2 Dec. 1880; *m* 1909, Harriet Beatrice Scott of Qu'Appelle, Saskatchewan, Canada; no *c. Educ:* Public and High Schools in Saskatchewan. Called to Bar of Saskatchewan, 1901; KC 1913; Lieut in Canadian Militia, 1908; went overseas as Major Second-in-Command of 28 Batt CEF, May 1915; arrived in France Sept. 1915; promoted to command Battalion, Sept. 1916, and to command 6th Canadian Infantry Brigade, Oct. 1918; served European War, 1915-18 (despatches seven times, CMG, DSO and bar); appointed to command the 21st Infantry Brigade Canadian Militia with rank Col. (Hon. Brig.-General), 1921; retired list, 1954. *Address:* 45 Darlington St, Yorkton, Saskatchewan, Canada. *T:* 32681.   *[Died 15 Oct. 1973.*

ROSS, Sir David; *see* Ross, Sir W. D.

ROSS, Hon. Frank Mackenzie, CMG 1946; MC 1918; Hon. LLD; Hon. Co-Chairman and Hon. Director, Canada Cement Lafarge Ltd; Chairman of the Board: International Paints (Canada) Ltd, Montreal; Grosvenor International Ltd, Vancouver; Grosvenor-Laing (BC) Ltd, Vancouver; Grosvenor-Laing (Langley Park) Ltd, Vancouver; President and Director, West Coast Shipbuilders Ltd, Vancouver; Director: BC Turf and Country Club Ltd, Vancouver; Canada Wire and Cable Co. Ltd, Toronto; De Laval Turbine Company Ltd, Toronto; Grosvenor Estates Advisory Board, London; Langley Greenhouses Ltd, Langley, BC; McCord Street Sites Ltd, Montreal; McDonald-Buchanan Properties Ltd, Vancouver; RCA Ltd, Montreal; Redhill Investment Corporation Ltd, Vancouver; Westcoast Transmission Company Ltd, Vancouver; *b* Glasgow, Scotland, 14 April 1891; *s* of David and Grace (Archibald) Ross, both of Ross-shire; *m* 1945, Phyllis Gregory Turner, SM 1967, CBE 1946, LLD. *Educ:* Royal Academy, Tain, Scotland. Served European War, 1914-18, with 8th Battalion, Canadian Army (MC). Formerly Dir.-Gen. of Production of Naval Armaments and Equipment, Department of Munitions and Supply, Canada. Lieutenant-Governor of the Province of British Columbia, 1955-60. Hon. degrees from Universities of: New Brunswick, 1956; British Columbia, 1958; St Francis Xavier, Nova Scotia, 1961; Aberdeen, 1961. KStJ 1956. *Address:* 2002 Robson Street, Vancouver 5, BC, Canada; (business) 1101 West 6th Avenue, Vancouver 9, BC. *Clubs:* St James's (Montreal); Vancouver, University, Faculty, Terminal City (Vancouver).
[Died 11 Dec. 1971.

ROSS, Sir Henry (James), Kt 1952; Life President, The Distillers' Company Ltd, Edinburgh; *b* 14 March 1893; *s* of William Henry Ross, OBE, and Annie Gilmour Pollok Dalgleish; *m* 1917, Blanche Alix Jowett Newbould (*d* 1950); two *s. Educ:* George Watson's College, Edinburgh; The Leys School, Cambridge; Institut Tilly, Berlin. Distillers' Company Ltd; joined as trainee, 1910; Director, 1925; Chm. Management Cttee, 1946; Dep. Chm., 1947; Chm., 1948-58. *Recreations:* yachting and fishing. *Address:* 27 Learmonth Terrace, Edinburgh.
[Died 4 April 1973.

ROSS, Sir James Paterson, 1st Bt, *cr* 1960; KCVO 1949; Surgeon to the Queen, 1952-64, retd; Professor of Surgery, University of London, 1935-60, Emeritus Professor, 1960; Director, British Post-graduate Medical Federation, 1960-66; Consulting Surgeon, St Bartholomew's Hospital; President Royal College of Surgeons of England, 1957-60; *b* 26 May 1895; *s* of James Ross and May Paterson; *m* 1924, Marjorie Burton Townsend (*d* 1978); two *s. Educ:* Christ's College, Finchley; St Bartholomew's Hospital Medical College (Entrance Scholarship in Science). Treasurer's Prize and Junior Scholarship Anatomy and Physiology, St Bartholomew's, 1914; Sergeant RAMC(T), 1914-15; Temp. Surgeon Lieutenant, Royal Navy, 1917-19; Gold Medal, University of London MB Examination, 1920; FRCS(Eng.), 1922. Associate in Surgery (Neurological Clinic) Peter Bent Brigham Hospital, Boston, USA, 1923; MS London, 1928; Jacksonian Prize Essay, Hunterian Prof., Royal College of Surgeons; Examiner in Surgery, Universities of London, Edinburgh, Glasgow, Belfast, Wales, Manchester, Bristol and Aberdeen. Sims Commonwealth Travelling Prof., 1957. FACS (Hon.), 1953, FRACS (Hon.), 1957. LLD (Hon.), Glasgow, 1957; FRCSEd (Hon.), 1959; FFR (Hon.) 1959; FRCSGlas. (Hon.) 1959; FDS (Hon.) 1964. *Publications:* The Surgery of the Sympathetic Nervous System (with G. E. Gask), 1934; (Jt Editor) British Surgical Practice (with Sir E. Rock Carling), 1947; several papers on surgical subjects in Medical Press. *Heir:* s James Keith Ross, RD, MS, FRCS [*b* 9 May 1927; *m* 1956, Jaqueline Annella Clarke; one *s* three *d*]. *Address:* Flat H, 14 John Spencer Square, Canonbury, N1 2LZ. *T:* 01-359 1122.
[*Died 5 July 1980.*

ROSS, James Stiven, CBE 1951; Principal of Westminster Training College, 1940-53; *b* Brechin, Angus, 4 Nov. 1892; *s* of James Donaldson Ross and Isabella Small Galloway; unmarried. *Educ:* Brechin High School; University College, Dundee (University of St Andrews); Dundee Training College. MA (1st Cl. Hons Maths) St Andrews, 1914; BSc St Andrews, 1915; MA Lond., 1923. Enlisted June 1915; released Oct. 1915, to take up work as Chemist at HM Factory, Oldbury (1915-18). Westminster Training College: Lecturer in Mathematics, 1919; Lecturer in Education, 1921; Vice-Principal, 1930. Fellow: British Psychological Society; The Royal Philharmonic Society; The College of Preceptors. *Publications:* Groundwork of Educational Psychology, 1930; Groundwork of Educational Theory, 1942; Basic Psychology, 1946; The Religious Basis of Education, 1948. *Recreation:* music. *Address:* Westminster, North Latch, Brechin, Angus. *T:* 2605. [*Died 14 Jan. 1975.*

ROSS, Kenneth Brebner, OBE 1952; Former Managing Director: Steels Process Plants Ltd, Eastcote, Middlesex; Archibald Low & Sons Ltd, Kirkintilloch, Scotland; retired; *b* Aliwal North, S Africa, 28 March 1901; *s* of Edward Ross and Annie Stretch Brebner; *m* 1947, Lilian Frances Powell; no *c. Educ:* Grey Coll. School, Bloemfontein; Grey University College, Bloemfontein; Exeter College (OFS Rhodes Scholar, 1923), Oxford (Hons Chem.). Joined Anglo-Iranian Oil Co., 1926; General Refineries Manager, Abadan Refinery, 1951; Director, Costain-John Brown, 1952-54; Director of Operations in Production Group of UK Atomic Energy Authority, 1954-61. *Recreation:* golf. *Address:* Little Gables, Redwood Road, Sidmouth, Devon EX10 9AB. *Club:* East India, Sports and Public Schools.
[*Died 13 Oct. 1973.*

ROSS, Prof. Peter McGregor; Professor of Engineering, University of Cambridge, since 1970; *b* 25 June 1919; *s* of William McGregor Ross and Isabel Ross (*née* Abraham); *m* 1950, Sylvia Robson Gripper; two *s* one *d. Educ:* St Christopher Sch., Letchworth; Ulverston Grammar Sch.; St John's Coll., Cambridge. Graduate Apprentice and Asst Engineer with London Power Co., 1941-46; Chief Designer, Gas Turbine Dept, John Brown & Co. (Clydebank) Ltd, 1946-54; Head of Mechanical R&D Dept, C. A. Parsons & Co. Ltd, Newcastle upon Tyne, 1954-61; Chief Development Engineer, Tube Investments, Ltd, 1962-64; Technical Dir, W. H. A. Robertson & Co., Ltd, Bedford, 1965-66; Engineering Dir, Loewy Robertson Engineering Co., Bournemouth, 1966-68; Dir of Research, Davy Ashmore Ltd, 1968-69. Visiting Prof., Univ. of Aston, 1966-68. Fellow of Wolfson Coll. (formerly University Coll.), Cambridge, 1970-. *Recreation:* sailing. *Address:* University Engineering Department, Trumpington Street, Cambridge CB2 1PZ. *T:* Cambridge 66466; 15 Clarkson Road, Cambridge. *T:* Cambridge 65924. [*Died 26 Nov. 1974.*

ROSS, Stanley Graham, DSO 1918; MC; BA, MD (McGill), FRCP; *b* Dundas, Ontario, Canada, 29 April 1888; *e s* of late James Ross, MD, and Beatrice Dudgeon Graham; *m* 1930, Jean Lesley, *d* of late Arthur L. Drummond, Montreal, Canada; two *s* one *d* (and one *s* decd). *Educ:* Hamilton Collegiate Institute;

McGill University. Resident Physician Royal Victoria Hospital 1913-14; served overseas 1915-19 CEF (despatches twice, DSO, MC, 1914-15 star, two medals); Major in CAMC 1917; postgraduate work in London 1919-20, in the Johns Hopkins Hospital, Baltimore, 1920-22; Member of the American Pediatric Society; Member of the Canadian Pediatric Society. *Address:* Mount Royal Villa, 275 Brittany Avenue, Mount Royal, Quebec 304, Canada. *Club:* University (Montreal).
[*Died 26 March 1980.*

ROSS, Mrs Thomas A.; *see* Runge, N. C.

ROSS, William Alexander, CBE 1951 (OBE 1946); FRIBA; retired, 1960; *b* 27 June 1891; *s* of William Thomson Ross, Alva, Clackmannanshire, and Louisa Jane (*née* Bevan), London; *m* 1918, Elspeth Stuart Ramsay Colquhoun (*d* 1970). *Educ:* St Michael's School, Highgate; Regent St Polytechnic London. Gold medallist (Polytechnic). Royal Academy School of Architecture, 1912-14; articled to G. A. Mitchel, ARIBA, and employed as chief architectural asst on rebuilding of Regent St Polytechnic; Architectural Asst to J. Lyons & Co. on Regent Palace Hotel, etc., 1912; Draughtsman, H. M. Office of Works, 1912; Bronze Medallist, Nat. Competition, South Kensington, for Architectural Design, 1912. Served European War, 1914-18; RNVR, 1914; Sub-Lt RNAS, 1916; Capt. RAF, 1918; demobilised, 1919. Lecturer in Architectural Design, Polytechnic, 1920-31; Asst Architect, HM Office of Works, 1919, War Office, 1927; Architect, War Office, 1928; Senior Architect, then superintending Architect, Ministry of Works, 1941; Dep. Director of Works and Services (Scotland), 1943; Director of Works and Services (Scotland), Ministry of Works, 1944-53; retired from Civil Service, 1953. Hon. Associate Instn of Royal Engineers. Silver Jubilee Medal, 1935; Coronation Medals, 1937 and 1953. *Address:* Hydro Hotel, Eastbourne, E Sussex. [*Died 1 July 1977.*

ROSS, Sir (William) David, KBE 1938 (OBE 1918); Commander, First Class, of Order of St Olav; Grand Officer, Order of Polonia Restituta; MA, DLitt; Hon. LLD (Edinburgh and Manchester); Hon. Litt D (Dublin); Hon. LHD (Columbia): Hon. DLit (London); Hon. Doctor (Paris and Oslo); Hon. Fellow of Merton, Balliol and Oriel Colleges, and of Trinity College, Dublin; FBA; Member American Philosophical Society, Académie des Sciences Morales et Politiques, and American Academy of Arts and Sciences; Provost of Oriel College, Oxford, 1929-47; Vice-Chancellor, 1941-44; Pro-Vice-Chancellor, 1944-47; *b* Thurso, Caithness, 15 April 1877; *s* of late John Ross, MA, Principal, Maharajah's Coll., Travancore; *m* 1906, Edith Helen (*d* 1953), *d* of John Ogden, Manchester; four *d. Educ:* Royal High School, Edinburgh; Edinburgh Univ., MA, 1895; Balliol College, Oxford (Exhibitioner); First Class Classical Mods, 1898; Jenkyns Exhibitioner, Balliol, 1900; First Class Lit. Hum., 1900; Lecturer of Oriel College, Fellow of Merton College, 1900-2; Fellow and Tutor, Oriel College, 1902-29; Deputy White's Professor of Moral Philosophy, Oxford University, 1923-28; Secretary of NE Coast Armaments Committee, 1915-16; served in Ministry of Munitions, 1916-19; Major, Special List, 1918-19; late Chm. several Wages Councils; Pres. Classical Assoc., 1932; Pres. of British Academy, 1936-40; Pres. of Aristotelian Society, 1939-40; Gifford Lecturer, Univ. of Aberdeen, 1935-36; Visiting Prof., Columbia Univ., 1938-39; Chairman of Council, British (now Royal) Institute of Philosophy, 1940; Pres. Union Académique Internationale, 1947; Chm. of Departmental Cttees on Woollen Textile Trade in Yorkshire, 1936, on Health of Cotton Cardroom Workers, 1937, and on the Fair Wages Clause, 1937; Member of Departmental Committee on Holidays with Pay, 1937; Member of Appellate Tribunal for Conscientious Objectors, 1940-41; Member of Nat. Arbitration Tribunal, 1941-52; Chm. of Civil Service Arbitration Tribunal, 1942-52; Chm., Royal Commission on the Press, 1947-49. *Publications:* Joint Editor, and later Editor, of Oxford Translation of Aristotle, Metaphysics, 1908; Ethics, 1925; and Select Fragments, 1952; Aristotle, 1923; edition of Aristotle, Metaphysics, 1924; Physics, 1935; Analytics, 1949; Fragmenta Selecta, 1954; Parva Naturalia, 1955; De Anima, 1956 and 1961; Politics, 1957; Topics and Sophistici Elenchi, 1958; Rhetoric, 1959; Aristotle, Selections, 1927; edition of Theophrastus, Metaphysics, 1929; The Right and the Good, 1930; Foundations of Ethics, 1939; Plato's Theory of Ideas, 1951; Kant's Ethical Theory, 1954. *Address:* 17 Bradmore Road, Oxford. *T:* Oxford 57864. [*Died 5 May 1971.*

ROSS SKINNER, Lt-Col Harry Crawley, DSO 1918; MC; Highland Light Infantry; *b* 1896; *er s* of late Sir Harry Ross Skinner; *m* 1927, Joan, *er d* of late Francis Crawley, Stockwood, Luton, Beds; one *s.* Served European War, 1914-18 (despatches, DSO, MC); retired, 1932; served War of 1939-45. *Address:* Warmwell House, Dorchester, Dorset. *T:* Warmwell 279. *Clubs:* Caledonian, Lansdowne. [*Died 30 Sept. 1972.*

ROSS WILLIAMSON, Hugh, FRSL; Writer; *b* 1901; *e s* of late Rev. Hugh Ross Williamson and Grace Winifred Walker; *m* 1941, Margaret Joan Cox; one *s* one *d.* Asst Editor, The Yorkshire Post, 1925-30; Editor of The Bookman, 1930-34; Acting Editor of the Strand Magazine, 1934-35; Director of London General Press, 1936-42, and 1968-. Anglican Priest, 1943-55; reconciled to Catholic Church, 1955. *Publications:* The Poetry of T. S. Eliot, 1932; John Hampden, 1933; King James I, 1936; Who is for Liberty?, 1939; George Villiers, Duke of Buckingham, 1940; AD 33, 1941; Captain Thomas Schofield, 1942; Charles and Cromwell, 1946; The Arrow and the Sword, 1947; The Silver Bowl, 1948; Four Stuart Portraits, 1949; The Seven Christian Virtues, 1949; The Gunpowder Plot, 1951; Sir Walter Ralegh, 1951; Jeremy Taylor, 1952; Canterbury Cathedral, 1953; The Ancient Capital, 1953; Historical Whodunits, 1955; James by the Grace of God-, 1955; The Great Prayer, 1955; The Walled Garden (autobiography), 1956; The Day they killed the King, 1957; Enigmas of History, 1957; Beginning of the English Reformation, 1957; The Sisters, 1958; The Challenge of Bernadette, 1958; The Day Shakespeare Died, 1962; Sixty Saints of Christendom, 1960; A Wicked Pack of Cards, 1961; The Flowering Hawthorn, 1962; Guy Fawkes, 1964; The Butt of Malmsey, 1967; The Marriage made in Blood, 1968; A Matter of Martyrdom, 1969; The Cardinal in Exile, 1969; The Cardinal in England, 1970; The Florentine Woman, 1970; The Last of The Valois, 1971; Paris is worth a Mass, 1971; Kind Kit, 1972; Catherine de Medici, 1973; Lorenzo the Magnificent, 1974; Historical Enigmas, 1974; Letter to Julia, 1975; The Princess a Nun!, 1978. *Plays:* In a Glass Darkly, 1932; Rose and Glove, 1934; The Seven Deadly Virtues, 1935; Monsieur Moi, 1935; Various Heavens, 1936; Mr Gladstone, 1937; Paul, a Bond-slave, 1945; Queen Elizabeth, 1946; Odds beyond Arithmetic, 1947; Fool's Paradise, 1949; The Cardinal's Learning, 1950; Gunpowder, Treason and Plot, 1951; Diamond cut Diamond, 1952; His Eminence of England, 1953; The Mime of Bernadette, 1958; Test of Truth, 1958; Heart of Bruce, 1959; Teresa of Avila, 1961; (with Ian Burford) Quartet for Lovers, 1962; Pavane for a Dead Infanta, 1968. *Club:* Savage.
[Died 13 Jan. 1978.

ROSSE, 6th Earl of, *cr* 1806; **Laurence Michael Harvey Parsons,** KBE 1974 (MBE (mil.) 1945); MRIA, FSA (London and Ireland); Bt 1677; Baron Oxmantown, 1792; Pro-Chancellor of University of Dublin since 1965 (Vice-Chancellor, 1949-65); Chairman: London Prudential Investment Trust, 1956-76; New Hibernia Investment Trust; Birr Fabrics; *b* 28 Sept. 1906; *s* of 5th Earl and Lois, *d* of Sir Cecil Lister-Kaye, 4th Bart, and Lady Beatrice Lister-Kaye (she *m* 2nd, 5th Viscount de Vesci); *S* father, 1918; *m* 1935, Anne, *o d* of Lt-Col Leonard Messel, OBE, Nymans, Staplefield, Sussex; two *s. Educ:* Eton; Christ Church, Oxford (MA). Chairman: Standing Commission on Museums and Galleries, 1956-78; Internat. Dendrology Soc.; Dep. Chm., National Trust, 1961-76; Trustee, Historic Churches Preservation Trust. President: Friends of the National Collections of Ireland; Ancient Monuments Society; Irish Architectural Records Association; Royal Hortic. Soc. of Ireland, 1959-69; Adelaide Hospital; Furniture History Soc.; Georgian Group (Chm., 1946-68); Member: Arts Council of Ireland, 1953-74; Nat. Monuments Adv. Council of Ireland; Adv. Council, Victoria and Albert Museum and Science Museum; Min. of Transport Trunk Roads Adv. Cttee, 1956-74. Pres., London Soc. FRAS; FRSA; Hon FRIBA; Hon. LLD (Dublin and Belfast). Served War of 1939-45 (MBE). *Publication:* (with Colonel E. R. Hill) The Story of the Guards Armoured Division, 1941-45, 1956. *Heir: s* Lord Oxmantown. *Address:* Womersley Park, Doncaster, S Yorks. *T:* Wentbridge 282; 18 Stafford Terrace, W8. *T:* 01-937 5857; Birr Castle, Co. Offaly. *T:* Birr 23. *Clubs:* Brooks's, Royal Automobile; Royal Irish Automobile, Kildare Street and University (Dublin).
[Died 1 July 1979.

ROSSELLI, (Ignace Adolphe) Jacques, Hon. CBE; QC 1971; Barrister-at-Law; Avocat at the Court of Appeal of Paris; Senator representing French people abroad, in the Senate of France, since 1971; Vice-President, Law Commission of the Senate, since 1973; *b* Paris, 15 Nov. 1907; French citizen; *s* of late James Rosselli, CBE, and of late Catherine Bourgas; *m* 1941, Gisèle Nelly Plez; two *s* one *d. Educ:* Lycée Janson-de-Sailly; Faculty of Law, Paris (Dr of Laws). Called to Bar, Paris, 1935; called to Bar, Lincoln's Inn, 1936. Served War of 1939-45: Liaison Officer to British Army, 1940; French Resistance, 1942-44; Captain in French Military Courts, 1945. Mem., Conseil Supérieur des Français de l'Etranger, 1958; Conseiller du Commerce Extérieur de la France, 1960; Pres., French Chamber of Commerce in Gt Britain, 1965-67; Legal Adviser to French Embassy in London, 1961. Officier, Légion d'Honneur; Croix de Guerre 1939-45; Officer, Order of Sport (France). *Recreations:* golf, tennis, squash rackets; Hon. Internat. Sec. to French Rugby

Union. *Address:* (office) 3 Stone Buildings, Lincoln's Inn, WC2A 3XL. *T:* 01-405 8358; (home) 19 Old Buildings, Lincoln's Inn, WC2. *T:* 01-405 9057; 71 Avenue Marceau, Paris 16, France. *T:* 720-52-75. *Clubs:* Bath; Stade Français (Paris); Royal Mid-Surrey Golf.
[Died 4 Feb. 1974.

ROSSLYN, 6th Earl of, *cr* 1801; **Antony Hugh Francis Harry St Clair-Erskine;** Bt 1666; Baron Loughborough, 1795; Captain King's Royal Rifle Corps; underwriting member of Lloyd's; Director of R. F. Kershaw Ltd; *b* 18 May 1917; *s* of late Lord Loughborough (*d* 1929) and Sheila (who obtained a divorce, 1926, and *m* 2nd, 1928, Sir John Milbanke, 11th Bt, 3rd, 1954, Prince Dimitri of Russia; she *d* 1969), *o d* of Harry Chisholm, Australia; *S* grandfather, 1939; *m* 1955, Athenais De Mortemart (marriage dissolved, 1962), *o d* of late Duc De Vivonne and Mme M. V. Ollivier, La Ferme Ste Barbe, Arcangues, BP, France; one *s* one *d. Educ:* Eton; Magdalen Coll., Oxford. Served with GHQ Liaison Regt (Phantom) and attached to 3rd Canadian Infantry Division (despatches). Member: Mental Health Research Fund; Pinewood Hosp. House Cttee (Windsor Group), 1952-57. A Governor, Ludgrove Sch. Trust Ltd. *Heir: s* Lord Loughborough. *Address:* Stonerwood Park, Petersfield, Hants. *T:* Petersfield 3433. *Clubs:* White's, Royal Automobile, MCC; New (Edinburgh); Royal and Ancient (St Andrews); Travellers' (Paris).
[Died 22 Nov. 1977.

ROSTAND, Jean; Biologist and Writer; *b* 30 Oct. 1894; *s* of Edmond Rostand and Rosemonde Gérard; *m* 1920, Andrée Mante; one *s. Educ:* Sorbonne. Member of the French Academy. *Publications:* Les Chromosomes; La Vie des Crapauds; Pensées d'un Biologiste; Ce que je crois; Pages d'un moraliste; L'Aventure humaine; Aux Sources de la Biologie, etc. *Recreation:* chess. *Address:* 29 rue Pradier, 92 Ville d'Avray, France. *T:* 945-5331.
[Died 3 Sept. 1977.

ROTH, Air Commodore Victor Henry Batten, CB 1959; CBE 1949; RAF, retd; *b* 7 June 1904; *s* of late Victor Roth; *m* 1948, Catherine Lang, *d* of late John McNaught Colquhoun. *Educ:* London Sch. of Economics (BCom.). Commnd into RAF, 1929; Home Aircraft Depot, 1929-31; No 2 Maintenance Unit, 1931-32; Air HQ, Iraq, 1933; Aircraft Depot, Iraq, 1934; No 2 Maintenance Unit, 1935; Equipt Staff, Air Min., 1935-43; OC No 312 Maintenance Unit, SEAC, 1943-44; Sen. Equipt Staff Officer, No 226 Gp, SEAC, 1944; HQ Base Air Forces, SE Asia, 1944-45; Mil. Staff Coll., Quetta, 1945-46; Dir of Administrative Plans, Air Min., and Mem., Jt Admin. Planning Staff, MoD, 1946-49; Equipt Staff, Air Min., 1949-51; Sen. Equipt Staff Officer, FEAF, 1951-52; Imperial Defence Coll., 1953; OC No 61 Maintenance Unit, 1954-55; Dir of Equipt (D), Air Min., 1955-59; Sen. Air Staff Officer, No 40 Gp, 1959-61; AOC No 40 Gp (acting Air Vice-Marshal), 1961; Comdt RAF Supply Control Centre, 1961-62; retired, Jan. 1963. King's Commendation, 1941. Member: Thingoe RDC, 1964-74 (Chm., Finance and Gen. Purposes Cttee, 1970-72); Suffolk and Ipswich Fire Authority, 1966-67; St Edmundsbury Borough Council, 1973- (Chm., Finance Sub Cttee, 1973-); Chm., Horringer-cum-Ickworth Parish Council, 1973-75, 1976-78; Mayor, Borough of St Edmundsbury, 1975-76, Dep. Mayor, 1976-77. Hon. Helper, RAF Benevolent Fund, 1963-; Trustee, Horringer Charities, 1964-; Pres., Bury St Edmunds Branch, RAFA, 1974-; Mem., Eastern Road Accident Prevention Fedn, RoSPA, 1974-79; Vice Chm., Bury St Edmunds Road Safety Cttee, 1977-. Mem., Suffolk Inst. Archaeology and History, 1965-. Life Mem. Convocation, Univ. of London. *Address:* 1 Sharp's Green, Horringer, Bury St Edmunds, Suffolk IP29 5PP. *T:* Horringer 332. *Club:* Athenæum (Bury St Edmunds). *[Died 6 Dec. 1979.*

ROTHERMERE, 2nd Viscount, *cr* 1919, of Hemsted; **Esmond Cecil Harmsworth,** Baron, *cr* 1914; Bt *cr* 1910; Chairman, Daily Mail and General Trust Ltd; President and Director of group finance, Associated Newspapers Ltd, since 1971 (Chairman, 1932-71); *b* 29 May 1898; *o surv. s* of 1st Viscount and Mary Lilian (*d* 1937), *d* of George Wade Share; *S* father, 1940; *m* 1st, 1920, Margaret Hunam (from whom he obtained a divorce, 1938), *d* of late William Redhead; one *s* two *d* ; 2nd, 1945, Lady O'Neill (marr. diss., 1952; she *m* 1952, late Ian L. Fleming), widow of 3rd Baron O'Neill and *e d* of Hon. Guy Charteris; 3rd, 1966, Mrs Mary Ohrstrom, *d* of Kenneth Murchison, Dallas, Texas; one *s. Educ:* Eton. Commission in Royal Marine Artillery, 1917; ADC to Prime Minister in Paris (Peace Conference), 1919; MP (U) Isle of Thanet, 1919-29. Mem., Adv. Council, Min. of Information, 1939; Chm., Newspaper Proprietors Assoc., 1934-61. Chancellor, Newfoundland Univ., 1952-61. DCL Bishop's University, PQ, 1954. *Recreations:* tennis and racquets. *Heir: s* Hon. Vere Harold Esmond Harmsworth. *Address:* 11 South Audley Street, W1. *Clubs:* White's, Beefsteak.
[Died 12 July 1978.

ROTHES, 20th Earl of, *cr* before 1457; **Malcolm George Dyer-Edwardes Leslie;** Baron Leslie and Ballenbreich, 1457; Representative Peer for Scotland, 1931-59; Deputy Chairman, British Electric Traction Co. Ltd, to 1974; Chairman, National Mutual Life Assurance Society, to 1975; *b* 8 Feb. 1902; *e s* of 19th Earl and Noel Lucy Martha (*d* 1956) (who *m* 2nd, 1927, Col Claud Macfie, DSO, *d* 1963), *d* of T. Dyer Edwardes, Prinknash Park, Gloucester; *S* father, 1927; *m* 1926, Beryl, *o d* of J. Lionel Dugdale, of Crathorne Hall, Crathorne, Yorks; one *s* two *d. Educ:* Eton. Member of Royal Coy of Archers (Queen's Body Guard for Scotland); 2nd Lt (General List), 1939-Major (General List), 1941. Director of Tyres, Ministry of Supply, 1942-45. *Heir: s* Lord Leslie. *Address:* Strawberry House, Chiswick Mall, W4 2PS. *Club:* Travellers'.
[Died 17 May 1975.

ROTHWELL, Harry, BA, PhD Cantab; Professor of History, University of Southampton, 1945-68; Emeritus, 1968; Dean of the Faculty of Arts, 1949-52; *b* 8 September 1902; *s* of Harry Rothwell and Emma Watson; *m* 1935, Martha Annabella Goedecke; two *d. Educ:* Barnsley Grammar School; Manchester University; St John's College, Cambridge. 1st Class Hons in History, Prizeman and Faulkner Fellow, Manchester, 1925; Mullinger Schol., St John's Coll., Cambridge, 1925-28; Senior Asst to Keeper of Western Manuscripts, Bodleian Library, 1928-29; Lectr in Medieval History, Univ. of Toronto, Toronto, 1929-31; Lecturer in Medieval and European History, Edinburgh Univ., 1931-45; Lieut (Sp) RNVR, 1942-45. Past Pres., Hampshire Field Club and Archæological Soc. *Publications:* The Chronicle of Walter of Guisborough, 1957; (ed) English Historical Documents 1189-1327, 1975; articles and reviews in professional journals. *Address:* Hill House, Knapp, Ampfield, near Romsey, Hants. *T:* Braishfield 68666.
[Died 27 Jan. 1980.

ROUGHTON, Francis John Worsley, FRS 1936; MA, PhD (Cambridge); Fellow (since 1923) and Lecturer (1929-47) of Trinity College, Cambridge; John Humphrey Professor of Colloid Science in the University of Cambridge, 1947-66, Emeritus Professor, 1966; *b* 6 June 1899; *s* of John Paul Roughton, MRCS, LRCP, JP, and Caroline Margaret Worsley; *m* 1925, Alice Isabella, *e d* of late Prof. B. Hopkinson, CMG, FRS; one *s* one *d. Educ:* Winchester College (Scholar); Trinity College, Cambridge (Scholar). 1st Class Nat. Sci. Tripos Part I, 1919 BA (Cantab) 1920, Michael Foster Student 1921, George Henry Lewes Student 1921, Gedge Prize 1922, Dunn Lecturer in Bio-Chemistry (Cambridge) 1923. Rolleston Prize (Oxford), 1924; Lecturer in Physico-Chemical Physiology (Cambridge), 1927; Visiting Research Fellow in War Science and Medicine at Harvard and Columbia Univs, 1942-45. Rockefeller travelling fellow in USA, 1929; Harvey Lectr, New York, 1943; Hanna Lectr, Western Reserve Univ., 1944; Norman Bauer Lectr, Logan Univ., Utah, 1962; Vis. Prof. at Univ. of Calif. and Pennsylvania, 1967. Secretary of Physiology Section of British Association, 1931-34; formerly Director of Hopkinson House Ltd and Vincent House Ltd; Mem. Cttee of Vincent Housing Assoc. Co-editor of Biochemical Journal, 1935-41. Hon. Member: Physiological Soc.; New York Acad. of Sciences; Amer. Physiological Soc.; British Gelatine and Glue Research Assoc.; Royal Danish Acad. of Sciences and Letters. Hopkins Memorial Medal, Biochemical Soc., 1969. *Publications:* Papers in Scientific Journals on Physiological, Biochemical and Physico-Chemical Subjects (especially on the Chemistry of Respiration). *Recreations:* walking, biography, genealogy, family history and fiction. *Address:* Ellerslie, 9 Adams Road, Cambridge. *T:* Cambridge 53890.
[Died 29 April 1972.

ROUGIER, George Ronald, CBE 1967; QC 1959; *b* 6 June 1900; 2nd *s* of Charles Joseph Rougier, Odessa, and Jean Crookston; *m* 1925, Georgette Heyer (*d* 1974); one *s. Educ:* RNC Osborne and Dartmouth; Marlborough Coll.; Roy. Sch. of Mines. Entered Navy as Cadet, 1913; Marlborough, 1915. Mining Engineer, 1922-31. Called to Bar, 1939; Bencher of the Inner Temple, 1966; retired from the Bar, 1968. Chm., Cambs and Isle of Ely QS, 1965-71; Dep. Chm., Essex QS, 1963-71. Chm., General Optical Council, 1961-74. *Recreations:* golf, fishing. *Address:* 28 Parkside, Knightsbridge, SW1. *Club:* Garrick.
[Died 26 Aug. 1976.

ROULLIER, Jean Georges, Commander Legion of Honour, 1958; Great Officer, Order of Merit, 1972; Chairman, Merchant Navy Social Institutions in France, since 1968; *b* 10 Dec. 1898; *s* of Jean-Baptiste Victor Roullier and Marie-Eugénie Vacher; *m* 1930, Marie-Louise Jeanne Sevestre; two *s* two *d. Educ:* Lycée Henri IV, Paris; Facultés des Lettres et de Droit, Paris (Licencié). Sec. Gen. Dept of Wartime Shipping. France, 1940; Director, Min. of Merchant Marine, 1950-63; Vice-Chm., Higher Council of Merchant Marine, 1950-63; Chairman,

Council of Intergovernmental Maritime Consultative Organization, 1959-63, Sec.-Gen., 1963-67. *Publication:* Les Transports Maritimes de la France en Guerre, 1945. *Address:* Place du Jeu de Paume, 91 Dourdan, France. *T:* 492-77-82.
[Died 23 Sept. 1974.

ROULSTON, Air Commodore Jack Fendick, CBE 1945; DSO 1943; DFC 1940; RAF; *b* 14 Jan. 1913; *s* of late H. E. Roulston; *m* 1939, Joan Redmayne, *o d* of J. A. Carman, MD, Nairobi, Kenya; two *s* one *d. Educ:* Queen's Coll. and Univ. of Capetown, SA. Commissioned in RAF, 1936; Squadron Leader comdg 223 Sqdn, 1940; Wing Commander comdg 55 Sqdn, 1942; Group Captain comdg 232 Wing, 1943; RAF Staff College, 1946; Group Capt. Opns Far East Air Force, 1952; RAF Flying College, 1954; Directorate of Operational Requirements, Air Ministry, 1955; Commander Air Task Group, Task Force Grapple, 1958-60; Commandant the Aeroplane and Armament Experimental Establishment, Boscombe Down, Wilts, 1960-65, retd. *Recreations:* golf, shooting, fishing. *Address:* Chilmark, near Salisbury, Wilts. *T:* Teffont 384. *Club:* Royal Air Force.
[Died 7 Nov. 1973.

ROUPELL, Brigadier George Rowland Patrick, VC 1915; CB 1956; DL; Colonel, The East Surrey Regiment, 1954-59; *b* 7 April 1892; *s* of late Col F. F. Roupell, CO of 1st East Surrey Regt; *m* 1921, Doris Phoebe (*d* 1958), twin *d* of late Capt. Mowbray L. Sant; one *s* one *d*; 2nd, 1959, Mrs Rachel Kennedy, *d* of late R. A. Bruce, Yeovil, Somerset. *Educ:* Rossall; Sandhurst. Entered army, 1912; Major, 1928; Lieutenant-Colonel, 1935; Colonel, 1939; served European War, 1914-18 (despatches thrice, wounded twice, VC, French Croix de Guerre, Order of St George, 4th Class); North Russia, 1919; General Staff. Officer, 2nd grade, Royal Military Coll., Kingston, Canada, 1929-31; Commanded Depot, The East Surrey Regt, Kingston-on-Thames; GSO 2nd Grade, China Command, 1934-35; commanded 1st Batt. The East Surrey Regt, 1935-39; served War of 1939-45; commanded 36 Inf. Bde and 105 Inf. Bde; retired pay, 1946; psc 1922. DL Surrey, 1953. Member of Order of St George, 4th Class (Russian). *Address:* Little Chartham, Shalford, Surrey. *T:* Guildford 62429. *Club:* Army and Navy.
[Died 4 March 1974.

ROWALLAN, 2nd Baron, *cr* 1911; **Thomas Godfrey Polson Corbett,** KT 1957; KBE 1951; MC; TD; DL; Lieutenant-Colonel (retired) Royal Scots Fusiliers; *b* 19 Dec. 1895; *o* surv. *s* of 1st Baron and Alice Mary (*d* 1942), *o d* of John Polson, of Castle Levan, Gourock; *S* father, 1933; *m* 1918, Gwyn Mervyn (*d* 1971), *d* of J. B. Grimond, St Andrews; three *s* (and two *s* decd (one killed in action, 1944)) one *d. Educ:* Eton. Served European War, 1914-18: Gallipoli, Egypt, Palestine and France (wounded, MC); also France, 1940, comdg a Bn of Royal Scots Fusiliers; retired 1944. Chief Scout British Commonwealth and Empire, 1945-59. Governor, National Bank of Scotland, 1951-59; Governor of Tasmania, 1959 until April 1963. Hon. Col Roy. Tasmania Regt, 1961-63. Mem., The Pilgrims Soc. Hon. LLD, McGill Univ., 1948, Glasgow Univ., 1952, Birmingham Univ., 1957. Freeman of the City of Edinburgh, 1957. KStJ, 1959. *Heir: s* Captain Hon. Arthur Cameron Corbett, Royal Artillery; TA [*b* 17 Dec. 1919; *m* 1945, Eleanor Mary (marr. diss. 1962), *o d* of late Capt. George Boyle, The Royal Scots Fusiliers; one *s* three *d. Educ:* Eton]. *Address:* Rowallan, Kilmarnock, Scotland. *Club:* Brooks's. *[Died 30 Nov. 1977.*

ROWAN, Sir (Thomas) Leslie, KCB 1949 (CB 1946); CVO 1947; Chairman of the British Council, since 1971; Director: Barclays Bank Ltd; Legal and General Assurance, since 1963 (Vice-Chairman since 1971); President, Overseas Development Institute, since 1967 (Chairman, 1960-67); Deputy Chairman, British National Export Council; *b* 22 February 1908; *s* of Rev. Thomas Rowan, Dromore, Co. Sligo, and Hannah Josephine Birrel, Halifax, Yorks; *m* 1944, Catherine Patricia, 3rd *d* of Brig. R. H. A. D. Love; two *s* two *d. Educ:* Panchgani (India); Tonbridge; Queens' College, Cambridge (Hon Fellow, 1954). Entered Colonial Office, 1930; Treasury, 1933; Assistant Private Secretary to Chancellor of Exchequer, 1934-37; Asst and later Principal Private Secretary to Prime Minister (Mr Churchill), 1941-45, (Mr Attlee), 1945-47; Permanent Sec., Office of Minister for Economic Affairs, 1947; Second Secretary, HM Treasury, 1947-49; Economic Minister in the Embassy, Washington, 1949-51; Second Secretary, HM Treasury, 1951-58, retired. Chm., Vickers Ltd, 1967-71 (Dep. Chm., 1966-67); Man. Dir, 1962-67). Captained England (1937, 1938 and 1947), Cambridge (1929 and 1930) and Civil Service at Hockey. *Publication:* contrib. to Action This Day-Working with Churchill, 1968. *Recreations:* games. *Address:* 16 The Vale, Chelsea, SW3. *T:* 01-352 2668. *Clubs:* United Service and Royal Aero; Hawks (Cambridge).
[Died 29 April 1972.

ROWBOTHAM, Edgar Stanley, MD, MRCP, FFARCS, DA; Retired Cons. (late Senior) Anæsthetist, Royal Free Hospital, London; *b* 8 May 1890; *s* of Dr E. J. Rowbotham and Gertrude Wootton; *m* 1915, May Levesley (*d* 1969); no *c*; *m* 1969, Beatrice Mary Howard. *Educ:* King's College, London; Charing Cross Hospital. Served European War, 1914-18, RAMC (despatches twice); served 1939-44. Bronze Star US Forces, 1945. *Publications:* Anæsthesia in Operations for Goitre, 1945; numerous in medical journals. *Recreations:* golf, sailing. *Address:* Caminho Velho da Ajuda 24, Funchal, Madeira. *T:* 2 67 18. *[Died 10 March 1979.*

ROWE, Albert Percival, CBE 1942; Medal for Merit (USA), 1946; Hon. LLD Melbourne 1955; Vice-Chancellor of the University of Adelaide, 1948-58, retired; *m* 1932, Mary Gordon Mathews. Chief Superintendent Telecommunications Research Establishment, 1938-45; Deputy Controller of Research and Development, Admiralty, 1946-47; Chairman of the Defence Advisory Committee and Defence Scientific Adviser to the Australian Government, 1947-48. FRSA. Fellow, Imperial College Sci. and Tech., 1957. Governor, Malvern Coll., 1972-. *Publications:* One Story of Radar, 1948; If the Gown Fits, 1960; Astronomy and Cosmology, 1968. *Address:* Rickstones, Colwall, Malvern, Worcs. *[Died 25 May 1976.*

ROWE, Sir Michael (Edward), Kt 1963; CBE 1946; QC 1945; President of the Lands Tribunal, 1966-73; *b* 24 December 1901; *s* of late John Tetley Rowe, Archdeacon of Rochester; *m* 1927, Elizabeth, *d* of Basil Guy, Stonaford House, Launceston; three *d*. *Educ:* Marlborough College; Trinity College, Cambridge (MA, LLB). Barrister, Gray's Inn, 1925; Bencher, 1945; Treasurer, 1961. 2nd Lt Queen's Roy. Regt, 1940; Staff Capt. 1941; released to become Asst Sec. War Damage Commission; Deputy Secretary, 1944-45; returned to practice, Jan. 1946; Member, General Claims Tribunal, 1946; Member of Council of Royal Institution of Chartered Surveyors, 1949-60; Member, Committee Inland Waterways, 1956-58; Deputy-Chairman Local Government Commission for England, 1958-65. Former Editor, Ryde on Rating. *Recreations:* gardening. *Address:* Hunter's End, S Chailey, E Sussex. *[Died 22 Dec. 1978.*

ROWELL, Sir Andrew (Herrick), Kt 1948; MA, FIA; retired as Director of Clerical, Medical and General Life Assurance Society (Deputy Chairman, 1955-66); *b* 12 March 1890; *s* of Jabez Rowell and Eliza Tooke; *m* 1922, Olive Gwendoline Bessie Coles (*d* 1956); one *s* one *d*. *Educ:* Wellingborough Sch.; St John's Coll., Cambridge. Served European War, 1915-18; Fellow of the Institute of Actuaries, 1922; President, 1946-48. *Address:* Byways, Sandy Lane, Ivy Hatch, near Sevenoaks, Kent. *T:* Plaxtol 519. *[Died 27 Aug. 1973.*

ROWELL, Lt-Gen. Sir Sydney Fairbairn, KBE 1953 (CBE 1941); CB 1946; retired; *b* 15 Dec. 1894; *s* of Col James Rowell, CB, VD, Lockleys, S Australia; *m* 1919, Blanche May, *d* of J. S. Murison, Exeter, South Australia; one *d*. *Educ:* Adelaide High School; Royal Military College, Duntroon (graduated 1914). Served with AIF, Gallipoli, 1915; Capt. Australian Staff Corps, 1920; Major, 1925; Lt-Col, 1935; attended Staff College, Camberley, 1925-26; GSO 44th (Home Counties) Division, 1935-36; attended Imperial Defence College, 1937; Director of Military Operations, Army HQ, Melbourne, 1938; Colonel and GSO 1 6th Australian Division, AIF, 1939; Brigadier and BGS 1st Australian Corps, AIF, 1940; served in Libya, Greece and Syria, 1941; Maj.-Gen. and Deputy Chief of General Staff at Army HQ, Melbourne, 1941; Lt-Gen. and Corps Comdr, April 1942; GOC New Guinea Force, Aug. 1942; GOC, AIF, Middle East and Australian Liaison Officer at GHQ, Middle East Forces, Feb. 1943; Director of Tactical Investigation, War Office, 1944-45; Chief of General Staff, Australia, 1950-54 (Vice-Chief, 1946-50); retired Dec. 1954. *Publication:* Full Circle (autobiog.), 1974. *Address:* 39 Kensington Road, South Yarra, Victoria 3141, Australia. *[Died 12 April 1975.*

ROWLANDS, Sir Alun; see Rowlands, Sir R. A.

ROWLANDS, Sir (Richard) Alun, KBE 1946 (CBE 1944; OBE 1920); MD (London); BSc and Hon. LLD (Wales); FRCP; Hon. Consulting Physician to The London Hospital, Poplar Hospital, Claybury Mental Hospital and Barnardo's Homes; Consulting Physician to Royal Navy; *b* 12 Sept. 1885; *s* of late Richard Rowlands, Bryngwran, Anglesey; *m* 1962, Mrs Lucienne Delva, *widow* of Dr J. P. Delva. *Educ:* Beaumaris Grammar School; University College of North Wales; London Hospital. Demonstrator of Physiology and Asst to Lecturer on Cardiac Research, 1911-13, and Medical Tutor, 1914-1920, London Hosp. Med. Coll.; Medical Registrar, London Hosp., 1914-20; late Examiner in Medicine for Conjoint Board and Univs of London and Liverpool; temp. Surgeon Rear-Admiral, RN,

1939-46; Regional Adviser in Medicine (EMS Region 6), 1940-46. Sen. Mem. Assoc. of Physicians of Great Britain and Ireland; Mem. Physiological Soc.; FRSocMed (Pres., Sect. of Medicine, 1951-53). *Publications:* papers in medical and scientific journals. *Recreations:* golf and walking. *Address:* 82 Campden Hill Court, Kensington, W8. *T:* 01-937 9160. *Club:* Athenæum. *[Died 1 March 1977.*

ROWLEY, Sir William Joshua, 6th Bt, *cr* 1836; late Lt-Col Lancashire Fusiliers; breeder of racehorses; *b* 15 April 1891; *s* of George Charles Erskine Rowley, 3rd Bt (*d* 1922) and his 2nd wife Amy Isabel (*d* 1961), OBE 1918, 3rd *d* of William Foster Batt, Abergavenny; *S* nephew 1953; *m* 1st, 1917, Beatrice Gwendoline Kirby (marriage dissolved, 1940); two *s* one *d*; 2nd, 1940, Margaret Sheila, *o d* of late Harold Camp, Stamford, Conn., USA; two *d*. *Educ:* Wellington College; RMC, Sandhurst. Joined Lancashire Fusiliers, 1910; served European War, 1914-19, France (wounded, 1914 star with clasp, 2 medals); War of 1939-45, Western Command, HQ (two medals). *Heir:* *s* Charles Robert Rowley [*b* 15 March 1926; *m* 1952, Astrid Pennington Cleife, *d* of Sir Arthur Massey, CBE; one *s* one *d*]. *Address:* Widdington House, Widdington, near Newport, Essex. *T:* Newport 288. *[Died 11 Nov. 1971.*

ROXBURGH, Sir James; see Roxburgh, Sir T. J. Y.

ROXBURGH, Sir (Thomas) James (Young), Kt 1954; CIE 1932; MA Cantab; *b* 2 March 1892; *y s* of T. Y. Roxburgh, London; *m* 1918, Mona Heymerdinger; one *s* one *d*. *Educ:* Merchant Taylors'; Magdalene Coll., Cambridge. Entered Indian Civil Service, 1915; served IARO, 1916-19; Chief Presidency Magistrate, Calcutta, 1923-31; Secretary, Judicial Department, and Legal Remembrancer, to Government of Bengal, 1937-39; Puisne Judge, High Court, Calcutta, retired, 1952. Chm. Medical Appeal Tribunal, under the Industrial Injuries Act, 1952-64. Called to Bar, Lincoln's Inn, 1932. *Address:* 50 Courtfield Gardens, SW5. *T:* 01-370 3454. *Club:* East India, Sports and Public Schools. *[Died 11 Feb. 1974.*

ROXBURGHE, 9th Duke of, *cr* 1707; **George Victor Robert John Innes-Ker**, Baron Roxburghe, 1600; Earl of Roxburghe and Kelso; Viscount Broxmouth; Baron Ker, 1616; Bt (Scot.) 1625; Marquess of Bowmont and Cessford, 1707; Earl of Innes (UK), 1837; Hon. Major, late RHG; *b* 7 Sept. 1913; *o s* of 8th Duke and May (*d* 1937), *o d* of Ogden Goelet; *S* father, 1932; *m* 1st, 1935, Lady Mary Evelyn Hungerford Crewe-Milnes (marriage dissolved, 1953), 4th *d* of 1st Marquess of Crewe, KG, PC; 2nd, 1954, Mrs Elisabeth Church; two *s*. *Educ:* RMC, Sandhurst. Owns about 80,000 acres. *Heir:* *s* Marquis of Bowmont and Cessford. *Address:* Floors Castle, Kelso. *Clubs:* Turf, Jockey. *[Died 26 Sept. 1974.*

ROY, Catherine Murray, CBE 1940; RRC 1918; MM; *b* 1883; *d* of Rev. John Roy, MA. *Educ:* High School for Girls, Glasgow; Esdaile, Edinburgh. Trained at the Western Infirmary, Glasgow, 1905-9; joined QAIMNS 1909; served in European War in France, 1914-19 (despatches, MM, RRC); Médaille Militaire des Epidémies, 1918; Matron-in-Chief, Queen Alexandra's Imperial Military Nursing Service, 1938-40. *Address:* 20 Ardencaple Drive, Helensburgh G84 8PS. *Club:* Royal Over-Seas League. *[Died 14 Aug. 1976.*

ROY, James Alexander; Professor Emeritus; *s* of Rev. William and Elizabeth Fisher Roy; *m* 1917, Helen Maud Mary Talbot (*née* Fair) (marr. diss. 1952); *m* 1952, Margaret Gordon Fleming (*d* 1973), Hampstead, London. *Educ:* Edinburgh and Giessen Universities. MA 1st Class Hons English Lang. and Lit. Reader in English, Giessen Univ., 1906-08; Lectr English Lang. and Literature, St Andrews Univ., 1908-20; Prof. of English, Queen's Univ., Kingston, Canada, 1920-50; Guest Prof., Giessen, 1921, Univs of Berlin, Münster, and Göttingen, 1936 and 1937; Lectr in Scottish Literature, Queen's Univ., 1944-45; Vis. Prof., Queen's Univ., 1960; Sometime Examr in English to United Free Ch. of Scotland Theol Coll. Awarded Plaque of Honour by City of Kingston, 1960. Army, 1915-19; Artillery, and Intelligence Staff, GHQ, 1918; first Intell. Officer, Capt. XVII Corps HQs; attached as Educational Officer to GHQ Peace Conf. Staff, Paris, 1919; Mem. Inter-allied Commn of Control, Teschen, Silesia, 1919 (despatches). Guest of Czechoslovakian Govt, 1946; Charter member and past Governor of Dominion Drama Festival, Ottawa; Past Chairman: Canada Club of Edinburgh; Edinburgh Br., Royal Commonwealth Soc.; Past Mem. of Council, Victoria League in Scotland. *Publications:* The Dream of the Rood, 1910; Cowper and his Poetry, 1914; Pole and Czech in Silesia, 1920; Christ in the Strand and other Poems, 1922; The Minister of Balglass (serialized), 1925; Joseph Howe: A Study in Achievement and Frustration, 1935; James Matthew Barrie, An Appreciation, 1937; Is there a Scottish Literature?, 1945; Forbes of Culloden (St Andrew's Day Lecture), 1945; (autobiography) The Heart is Highland, 1947; The Scot and Canada, 1947; Kingston: The King's Town, 1952; ("Brother André" in) Our Sense of Identity, 1954. Contributor to: Edinburgh Review, Scottish Field, Times Literary Supplement, Toronto Quarterly, Queen's Quarterly, Dalhousie Review, etc. *Recreations:* walking, motoring and book collecting. *Address:* 17 South Learmonth Gardens, Edinburgh 4. *Clubs:* Royal Commonwealth Society, English-Speaking Union; New (Edinburgh). [*Died 26 Nov.* 1973.

ROYALL, Kenneth Claiborne, DSM 1945 (US); LLD; lawyer; *b* Goldsboro, NC, 24 July 1894; *s* of George Claiborne Royall and Clara Howard Jones; *m* 1917, Margaret Best; one *s* one *d. Educ:* Univ. of North Carolina (AB); Harvard Law School (LLB). Associate Editor Harvard Law Review, 1915-17. Admitted to North Carolina Bar, 1916; law practice Goldsboro, NC, 1919-30, Raleigh and Goldsboro, NC, 1931-42, Royall, Gosney and Smith; law practice New York and Washington, DC, 1949-58, Dwight, Royall, Harris, Koegel and Caskey; Royall, Koegel, Harris and Caskey, 1958-61; Royall, Koegel and Rogus, 1961. State Senator, NC, 1927; Presidential Elector (NC), 1940. 2nd and 1st Lt Field Artillery, 1917-19, overseas, 1918-19; Col. and Brig.-Gen., 1942-45; service overseas 1944 and 1945; Under-Secretary of War, 1945-47; Secretary of War, 1947; Secretary of the Army, 1947-49. Member: N Carolina Bar Assoc. (Pres. 1929-30); New York and American Bar Assocs; American Law Institute. *Address:* 1040 Fifth Avenue, New York City, USA. *Clubs:* Links, Blind Brook, Recess (New York); Chevy Chase, Burning Tree, Army and Navy Country (Washington).
[*Died 25 May* 1971.

ROYDEN, Sir John Ledward, 4th Bt *cr* 1905; Director, Antofagasta (Chile) and Bolivia Railway Co. Ltd, since 1974; *b* 31 Dec. 1907; *s* of Sir Ernest Royden, 3rd Bt, Hill Bank, Frankby, Cheshire; *S* father, 1960; *m* 1936, Dolores Catherine Coward; two *s* two *d. Educ:* Winchester Coll.; Magdalen College, Oxford. Ministry of Economic Warfare, 1939-45; Member, Willingdon Mission to South America, 1940-41. Order of Merit (Chile), 1945. *Recreations:* gardening (rhododendrons), farming. *Heir:* *s* Christopher John Royden [*b* 26 Feb. 1937; *m* 1961, Diana Bridget, *d* of Lt-Col J. H. Goodhart, Kirby Moorside, Yorkshire; two *s* one *d*]. *Address:* Netherfield Place, Battle, Sussex. *T:* 84. *Club:* Farmers'. [*Died 30 April* 1976.

ROYLE, Baron, *cr* 1964, of Pendleton (Life Peer); **Charles Royle**, JP; *b* 23 Jan. 1896; *m* 1919, Florence Smith; one *d. Educ:* elementary; Stockport Grammar School. Served War of 1915-19 with RE, Western Front. Engaged in Retail Meat Trade; President Manchester and Salford Meat Traders' Assoc., 1942-43; Meat Agent Ministry of Food, 1939-45. Ex-Member Stockport Borough Council; Past Chairman Stockport Labour Party; Vice-President Magistrates Association. Contested Lancaster, 1935; MP (Lab) West Salford, 1945-64; a Lord Comr of the Treasury, 1950-51; one of the Opposition Whips, 1951-64; a Dep. Speaker and a Dep. Chm. of Cttees, House of Lords. Pres., Brit.-Caribbean Assoc.; Vice-Pres., Assoc. of Metropolitan Corporations; Chm., Alliance Building Society. Hon. Fellow Inst. of Architects and Surveyors. JP Brighton, 1959. *Recreation:* golf. *Address:* Abbotswell, Frogham, Fordingbridge, Hants. [*Died 30 Sept.* 1975.

ROYLE, Rev. Canon Arthur; Hon. Canon (Emeritus) Ely Cathedral, 1965; *b* 23 April 1895; *s* of Thomas White Royle, Maidstone, Kent; unmarried. *Educ:* Maidstone Grammar School; Keble College, Oxford (MA). Curate: St John Evangelist, East Dulwich, 1924-30; Vicar of St Paul, Newington, 1930-42; Rural Dean of Newington, 1935-42, Surrogate, 1935-42; Rector of Orton Longueville, Hunts, 1942-66; Rector of Alwalton, Hunts, 1943-66; Hon. Canon of Ely, 1947-54; Rural Dean of Yaxley, 1947-54; Archdeacon of Huntingdon, 1954-65. Member: Norman Cross RDC 1948-64; Huntingdon Educn Cttee, 1953-65; Huntingdon CC 1958-65. *Address:* The College of St Mark, Audley End, Saffron Walden, Essex. *T:* Saffron Walden 3127. [*Died 8 Aug.* 1973.

ROYLE, Sir Lancelot (Carrington), KBE 1944; *b* 31 May 1898; *y* *s* of Rev. Vernon Peter Fanshawe and Eleanor Agnes Royle, Stanmore Park, Stanmore, Middlesex; *m* 1922, Barbara Rachel Haldin (*d* 1977); two *s* one *d. Educ:* Stanmore Park; Harrow School; RMA Woolwich. Left Woolwich, 1918; France, 113 Army Brigade, RFA, 1918; Cologne, 1918-21; Army Champion, 100 yds, 1920; resigned commission, 1921; took up appointment with Van den Berghs, Ltd, subsequently by amalgamation, Lever & Unilever, Ltd; recalled, War of 1939-45; served with 56th Heavy Battery, RA, 1940; appointed member Macharg/Royle Committee by Treasury, 1940. Gov. of Harrow School, 1947-62. Chairman: Navy, Army and Air Force

Institutes, 1941-53; Allied Suppliers Ltd, 1947-58; Lipton Ltd, 1952-59; Lipton (Overseas) Ltd, 1959-63. Director: British Match Corp. Ltd, 1961-68; Bryant & May Ltd, 1961-71; Liebigs Extract of Meat Co. Ltd, 1961-68; Oxo Ltd, 1961-68. *Recreations:* athletics (Olympic Games, 1924), football, cricket. *Address:* 31 Elsworthy Road, Primrose Hill, NW3. *T:* 01-722 5445. *Club:* Army and Navy. [*Died 19 June* 1978.

ROYSTON, Viscount; Philip Simon Prospero Lindley Rupert Yorke; *b* 20 April 1938; *o s* and *heir* of 9th Earl of Hardwicke; *m* 1968, Virginia Anne, *d* of Geoffrey Lyon; one *s* one *d. Educ:* Eton; McGill University, Montreal. *Recreation:* shooting. *Address:* 9 Fernshaw Road, SW10. *T:* 01-352 0891. *Clubs:* Turf, White's; Puffins (Edinburgh). [*Died 1 Jan.* 1973.

RUBINSTEIN, Harold Frederick; Solicitor; Member of the firm of Rubinstein Nash & Co.; *b* London, 18 March 1891; *s* of late J. S. Rubinstein, Solicitor; *m* 1920, Lina Lowy (*d* 1939); two *s* (and one died on active service, RAF, 31 Aug. 1943). *Educ:* Cheltenham College; France and Germany. *Author of plays produced and/or published including:* Consequences, 1913; The Spirit of Parsifal Robinson, 1919; Old Boyhood, 1919; Shakespeare (with Clifford Bax), 1921; What's Wrong with the Drama? (five one-act plays), 1923; Exodus (with Halcott Glover), 1923; Peter and Paul, 1924; Churchill (with A. J. Talbot), 1925; Revanche, 1925; The House, 1926; Plays Out of Time, 1930; The Dickens of Gray's Inn, 1931; Israel Set Free (five one-act plays), 1936; Johnson Was No Gentleman, 1937; Hated Servants (eight one-act plays), 1944; The Fifth Gospel, 1946; Six London Plays (with Vera Arlett), 1950; Bernard Shaw in Heaven, 1952; Unearthly Gentleman (Trilogy of plays about Shakespeare), 1965; Shylock's End, 1971; Prospero's Farewell, 1972; Pembroke's Mother, 1974; *also published:* The English Drama, 1928; ed Great English Plays, 1928; Four Jewish Plays, 1948; (with J. C. Trewin) The Drama Bedside Book, 1966. *Recreation:* homework. *Address:* 6 Raymond Buildings, Gray's Inn, WC1. *T:* 01-242 8404. [*Died 12 June* 1975.

RUBRA, Edward John, MRCS, LRCP; Anæsthetist and General Practitioner, retired; *b* 23 July 1902; 2nd *s* of Dr H. H. Rubra, Crouch End; *m* 1927, Alice Eliza, *d* of Ernest Lindus, Dulwich; two *s. Educ:* Brighton College; King's College, London; Westminster Hospital (Guthrie Scholar). House Surgeon and Resident Medical Officer, Westminster Hospital; late Hon. Anæsthetist, University College Hospital, Westminster Hospital, Golden Square Throat Hospital, Throat Department, Brompton Hospital; late Anæsthetist, Dental Department, London Hospital and Islington Clinic; served War of 1939-45 (despatches), Lt-Col, Adviser in Anæsthetics, Southern Command, India. *Recreation:* study of Norman Architecture. *Address:* 66 Crouch Hall Road, Crouch End, N8. *T:* 01-340 2529; 6 Church End, Walkern, Herts. *T:* Walkern 313.
[*Died 29 Jan.* 1974.

RUCK, Berta, (Mrs Oliver Onions); novelist; *b* 2 Aug. 1878; *d* of Col and Mrs A. A. Ruck; *m* 1909, Oliver Onions, (George Oliver) (*d* 1961); two *s. Educ:* St Winifred's School, Bangor, Wales. Studied art at the Slade School (scholarship), and at Calorossi's, Paris. Afterwards took to writing articles and short stories, first novel published 1913. Has lectured under Adult Education for HM Forces, and has recently broadcast. TV programme Yesterday's Witness, 1970. *Publications:* over 150 books, including: His Official Fiancée; The Lad with Wings; The Girls at his Billet; Sir or Madam and many other novels, the latest being Tomboy in Lace, She Danced in the Ballet, Love and Apron-Strings, Hopeful Journey, Song of the Lark, Marriage is a Blind Date, Fantastic Holiday, The Men in Her Life, We All Have Our Secrets, Romance and a Film Star, A Wish A Day, Romantic After-thought, Love and A Rich Girl, Sherry and Ghosts, Runaway Lovers, Rendezvous at Zagarelli's, Shopping for a Husband, *autobiography:* A Storyteller Tells the Truth, A Smile for the Past, Trickle of Welsh Blood, An Asset to Wales, Ancestral Voices. *Recreations:* was an ice-breaker, and liked air travel; is now 100 but fit. *Address:* Bryntegwel, Aberdovey, Gwynedd, Wales. *T:* Aberdovey 286. [*Died 11 Aug.* 1978.

RUCK KEENE, Vice-Admiral Philip, CB 1948; CBE 1942; DSO 1945; *b* 11 Nov. 1897; *s* of Rev. E. R. Ruck Keene; *m* 1923, Marguerite Evelyn Constance Agatha Gyles; one *d. Educ:* Haileybury College. Royal Navy, mainly in submarines; Rear-Adm. 1946; ADC to the King, 1946; Flag Officer in Charge, Ceylon, 1946-47; Director of Naval Training, 1947-49; retired, 1949. Legion of Merit (USA); Order of King George of Greece. *Recreations:* mountaineering, ski-ing, fishing. *Address:* Sonnberg, Kitzbühel, Tirol, Austria. *Club:* RN Ski and Mountaineering. [*Died 28 May* 1977.

RUDD, Surgeon Rear-Adm. Eric Thomas Sutherland, CB 1958; CBE 1954; FRCSEd; *b* 19 Feb. 1902; *s* of late Rev. Canon Thomas Ernest Rudd; *m* 1930, Enid Marjorie (*d* 1968), *d* of Capt. Hubert Vaughan-Jones, CBE, RN; one *s* one *d. Educ:* Royal Sch., Armagh; Trinity Coll., Dublin. BA 1923; MB, BCh, BAO Dublin, 1925; FRCS Edinburgh, 1930. Sen. Fell. of Association of Surgeons of Great Britain and Ireland. Late Surgical Specialist, Royal Navy; Surg. Rear-Adm., 1955; Hon. Surgeon to the Queen, 1955-58; Medical Officer-in-Charge, Royal Naval Hospital, Haslar, and on Staff of Commander-in-Chief, Portsmouth, 1955-58, retd. Retired as House Governor, King Edward VII Convalescent Home for Officers, Osborne, Isle of Wight, 1965. *Recreations:* shooting, fishing, golf. *Address:* Busherstown House, Moneygall, Birr, Co. Offaly, Eire. *T:* Moneygall 6. *Club:* Royal Yacht Squadron.
[*Died* 21 *May* 1977.

RUDD, G(eoffrey) Burkitt (Whitcomb), BA; LLB; Puisne Judge, Kenya, 1951-69, retired; *b* 29 May 1908; *s* of late T. A. Rudd; *m* 1936, Guenda Mary de Clifton Parmiter; four *s* one *d. Educ:* St Columba's College; Dublin University (TCD). Called to Bar, King's Inns, 1932; Resident Magistrate, Kenya, 1936-44; Acting Chief Justice, Aden, 1944; Judge of the Supreme Court, Aden, 1945-51; has acted as Chief Justice, Kenya. *Recreations:* shooting, fishing, riding. *Address:* The Old Rectory, Clonoulty, Goolds Cross, Co. Tipperary, Ireland. [*Died* 26 *Dec.* 1975.

RUDDERHAM, Rt. Rev. Joseph Edward; *b* 17 June 1899; *s* of William Rudderham and Agnes Mary Coan. *Educ:* St Bede's Coll., Manchester; St Edmund's Coll. Old Hall, Ware; Christ's Coll., Cambridge; Ven. English Coll., Rome. Priest 1926 (by Cardinal Pompili in Rome); Curate at All Souls Church, Peterborough, 1927-32. Parish Priest, 1932-43; Administrator of Northampton Cathedral, 1943-49; Canon Penitentiary of Northampton Cathedral Chapter, 1946-49; Diocesan Inspector of Schs, 1941-49; Bishop of Clifton, 1949-74. *Address:* Nazareth House, London Road, Charlton Kings, Cheltenham, Glos GL52 6YJ. *T:* Cheltenham 56361. [*Died* 24 *Feb.* 1979.

RUDDLE, Lt-Col Sir (George) Kenneth (Fordham), Kt 1957; TD; DL; *b* 17 May 1903; *o s* of late George Ruddle; *m* 1930, Nancy Margaret, *er d* of late H. G. Allen, Woburn Sands, Beds; one *s* two *d* (and one *d* decd). *Educ:* Repton. Pres. and former Chm., of family brewing business, G. Ruddle & Co. Ltd; Mem., Exec. Cttee of National Union of Conservative and Unionist Assocs, 1951-62, 1964-67; Chm. E Midland area of Nat. Union of Cons. and Unionist Assocs, 1951-57. Alderman, Rutland CC; Chairman, 1958-70; DL Co. of Rutland 1938-; High Sheriff of Rutland, 1938. Former Vice-Chm., Leics and Rutland T&AFA; Pres. Rutland Horticultural Soc. *Recreations:* cricket, gardening. *Address:* Islington Lodge, Langham, Oakham, Rutland. *T:* Oakham 2944. *Clubs:* Carlton, MCC.
[*Died* 29 *Sept.* 1979.

RUEFF, Jacques, Grand' Croix de la Légion d'Honneur; Croix de Guerre (3 citations); French Economist; Member of French Academy and of Academy of Moral and Political Sciences; Chancellor of the French Institute; Member of Economic and Social Council; *b* 23 Aug. 1896; *m* 1937, Christiane Vignat; two *d. Educ:* Ecole Polytechnique, Paris. Inspector of Finance, 1923; Mem. Secretariat, League of Nations, 1927-30; Financial Attaché, London, 1930-34; Asst Director, later Director, Treasury, Ministry of Finance, 1934-39; Counsellor of State, 1937; Vice-Governor, Bank of France, 1939-41, resigned; Econ. Adviser to Commander-in-Chief Germany, 1945; Delegate to Reparations Commn, Moscow, and Pres., Inter-Allied Reparations Agency, 1946; Judge, Court of Justice of European Steel and Coal Community, 1952; Judge, Court of European Communities, 1958-62; Pres., Cttee for Reform of French Financial Situation, 1958; Vice-Pres., Cttee for Removal of Economic Obstacles, 1960. Foreign Associate: Nat. Acad. of Lincei, Rome; Roy. Acad. of Sciences, Letters and Fine Arts, Belgium. Grand Cross and Grand Officer of several foreign orders. *Publications:* Des Sciences physiques au Sciences morales, 1921, new edn 1969; Theorie des Phénomènes monétaires, 1927; L'ordre social, 1946; Epître aux Dirigistes, 1949; L'âge de l'inflation, 1963; Le lancinant problème des balances de paiement, 1965; Les Dieux et les Rois, 1967; Le Péché monétaire de l'Occident, 1971; Combats pour l'ordre financier, 1972; La réforme du système monétaire international, 1973; La création du monde (comédie-ballet), 1974. *Recreation:* golf. *Address:* 51 rue de Varenne, Paris 7e, France *T:* Littré 36-01; Berville, par 27 Beuzeville. *Club:* Saint-Cloud.
[*Died* 23 *April* 1978.

RUMBALL, Air Vice-Marshal Sir (Campion) Aubrey, KBE 1960 (CBE 1954; OBE 1945); FRCP; Civilian Medical Consultant to BOAC and BEA; Medical Adviser and Consultant to Civil

Aviation Authority; *b* 26 Dec. 1904; *s* of Frederick William Rumball; *m* 1931, Margaret, *d* of George Williams, Tydd St Giles, Cambridgeshire. *Educ:* Dulwich Coll.; Guy's Hosp. LDSRCS Eng 1926; MRCS Eng, LRCP Lond., 1930; DTM & H Eng. 1937; DPM 1939; MRCP 1947; FRCP Lond. 1952. Served War of 1939-45, France and Middle East (OBE); Medical Specialist to Nos 1, 2, and 5 RAF Hosps; Senior Cons. in Medicine, RAF Medical Branch, 1951-66, later Hon. Civil Consultant. QHP 1952-66 (KHP 1948-52). FRSM; Hon. Treasurer, Royal Society of Medicine, 1959-65; Member Council, 1965-66; Hon. Fellow, 1969. Cade Gold Medal, RCS, 1956. *Publications:* contributions to BMJ, Lancet, Brit. Heart Jl, etc. *Recreations:* fishing and motoring. *Address:* The Lodge, High Beech, St Leonard's-on-Sea, East Sussex.
[*Died* 14 *Dec.* 1975.

RUMBOLD, Rev. Canon Charles Robert; retired. *Educ:* Bishops' College, Cheshunt. Deacon, 1921; Priest, 1922; Assistant Priest, Rickmansworth, St Albans dio., 1922-25; Army Chaplain, Roberts Heights, S Africa, 1925-28; Rector of Arcadia, 1928-33; Dean of Pretoria, 1933-50; Chaplain, St Mary's Diocesan Sch. for Girls, 1951-66. *Address:* Irene Homes, Irene, Transvaal, S Africa. [*Died* 30 *Nov.* 1973.

RUMSEY, Harry Victor, CB 1953; Senior Lecturer in Mathematics, Royal Military Academy, Sandhurst, 1953-68; *b* 27 Nov. 1898; *s* of Edward Victor Rumsey and Mina Esler; *m* 1939, Sarah Fox. *Educ:* The King's School, Macclesfield; Selwyn College, Cambridge (MA). Served European War, 1914-18, Border Regiment, Private (MM), Royal Navy as Instructor Lieutenant, 1922; retired as Instructor Captain, 1953. *Address:* Highways, Harcombe Cross, Axminster, Devon. *T:* Axminster 2017. [*Died* 29 *May* 1971.

RUNGE, Norah Cecil, (Mrs Thomas A. Ross), OBE 1918; Alderman LCC, 1937-61; *b* London, 1884; *d* of late Lawrence Hasluck; *m* 1st, 1906, J. J. Runge (*d* 1935); one *s* one *d* (and two *s* decd); 2nd, 1939, Thomas Arthur Ross, MD, FRCP (*d* 1941). *Educ:* privately. Supt of the Soldiers' and Sailors' Free Buffet, Paddington Station, 1915-19; President of the Rotherhithe Conservative and Unionist Association, 1932-46; Vice-Chairman of Central Women's Advisory Committee of Conservative and Unionist Associations, 1941-42, of the London Conservative Union Council, 1940-47; Chm. of the London Area Women's Advisory Committee, 1938-43, Pres. 1943-45; Member of Civil Defence, Bermondsey; worked for Red Cross POW Dept., 1941-45. MP (U) Rotherhithe, 1931-35; contested Rotherhithe, 1935 and 1945. Chairman Horton Hospital Management Committee, 1948-52; Member of Board of Governors of Bethlem Royal, and Maudsley Hosp., 1948-60. Dep. Chm. LCC, 1951-52. *Address:* St John's House, Smith Square, SW1. *T:* 01-222 1563. [*Died* 6 *June* 1978.

RUSE, Prof. Harold Stanley, MA (Oxon), DSc (Edinburgh), FRSE; Professor of Pure Mathematics in the University of Leeds, 1946-70, now Professor Emeritus; Head of Department of Mathematics, 1946-68; Chairman, School of Mathematics, and Head of Department of Pure Mathematics, 1968-70; *b* 12 Feb. 1905; 3rd *s* of late Frederick and Lydia Ruse, Hastings; unmarried. *Educ:* Hastings Gram. Sch.; Jesus Coll., Oxford. Bruce of Grangehill Research Schol., University of Edin., 1927-28; Lectr in Mathematics, Univ. of Edin., 1928-37; Sen. Mathematical Schol., Oxford, 1929; Rockefeller Research Fellow, Princeton Univ., USA, 1933-34; Pres. Edinburgh Mathematical Soc., 1935-36; Keith Prize, Royal Soc. of Edin., 1935-37; Prof. of Mathematics, Univ. Coll., Southampton, 1937-46. Visiting Fellow, Princeton, 1952-53. *Publications:* (with A. G. Walker and T. J. Willmore) Harmonic Spaces, 1962; research papers on relativity, differential geometry and algebra. *Address:* The University, Leeds LS2 9JT. [*Died* 20 *Oct.* 1974.

RUSHBROOK WILLIAMS, L. F.; *see* Williams.

RUSHBROOKE, Vice-Adm. Edmund Gerard Noel, CBE 1942; DSC 1917; retired; *b* 15 Dec. 1892; *s* of Capt. William Henry Rushbrooke, JP (Cosford, Thursley, Surrey, and Whitepoint, Queenstown, Ireland), and of Mrs Margaret Mary Rushbrooke; *m* 1st, 1926, Ada Stott Moncrieff; one *d* (decd); 2nd, 1937, Marjorie Wentworth Foster (*d* 1970). *Educ:* RNC, Osborne and Dartmouth. Served War of 1914-18, in Destroyers as Sub-Lt and Lieut (DSC, Croix de Guerre, Board of Trade Life Saving Medal). Comdr. 1928; Capt., 1936. Chief of Intelligence Staff, China Station, 1937; served War of 1939-45; in Command: HMS Guardian, 1939; HMS Argus, 1940; HMS Eagle, 1941; Director of Naval Intelligence, 1942-46; Rear-Adm., 1945; retired 1947; Vice-Adm. on retired list, 1948. US Legion of Merit, 1946. *Address:* 14 Royal Crescent, Bath, Somerset. *Club:* MCC.
[*Died* 9 *Oct.* 1972.

RUSHOLME, 1st Baron, cr 1945, of Rusholme; **Robert Alexander Palmer**; Chairman, London Midland Area Board, British Railways, 1955-60; Chairman, Board of Survey, Inland Waterways, 1954; b 29 November 1890; s of William Palmer and Elizabeth Green; unmarried. Educ: St Mary's School, Ashton-on-Mersey. Late Pres. of Internat. Co-operative Alliance; JP, Manchester. Served in Manchester Regiment, 1914-18, Egypt, Belgium, France. Member: Central Price Regulation Cttee, 1939-45; Retail Trade Cttee, 1941-42; Min. of Labour Cttee for Business Training, 1944; Cttee on Proceedings in Matrimonial Causes, 1946-47; British Transport Commission, 1947-59; Central Transport Consultative Cttee, 1948-59; Road Haulage Disposal Board, 1953; Cttee on Organisation of Crown Lands, 1954-55; Chm. Coastal Shipping Advisory Cttee, 1947-56; Dir, Thos Cook & Son Ltd and associated cos, 1949-67. President: Cooperative Congress, 1945; Inst. of Travel Agents, 1961-76. FCIT. Publications: pamphlets and articles on Co-operation and allied subjects. Address: Rusholme Gardens, Manchester M14 5LR. T: 061-224 9596.   [Died 18 Aug. 1977 (ext).

RUSHTON, Sir Reginald (Fielding), Kt 1971; Life Member, Raine Medical Research Foundation; Chairman, MacRobertson Miller Airlines Ltd (MMA), 1955-69; Director, Ansett Transport Industries Ltd, since 1969. Has given outstanding service to the community in Western Australia. Hon. LLD Univ. of WA, 1977. Address: MacRobertson Miller Airline Services, 26 St George's Terrace, Perth, Western Australia 6000, Australia. T: 3212821 and 3212691; (private) 50 Jutland Parade, Dalkeith, Perth, WA 6009, Australia. T: 3862572.
[Died 28 Oct. 1979.

RUSHTON, William Albert Hugh, FRS 1948; ScD, PhD, MA, MRCS, LRCP; Fellow, Trinity College, Cambridge, since 1938 (Director of Medical Studies, 1938-63); b 8 December 1901; er s of William and Alice Rushton, Harley Street and Hampstead, London; m 1930, Marjorie, 2nd d of Norman Kendrick, Cardiff; two s two d. Educ: Gresham's, Holt; Emmanuel Coll., Cambridge; University Coll. Hosp., London; Stokes Student Pembroke Coll., Cambridge, 1927; Johnson Fellow, Univ. Pennsylvania, 1929; Research Fellow, Emmanuel Coll., 1931; Lectr in Physiology, Cambridge University, 1935-53; Reader, 1953-65; Prof. of Visual Physiology, Cambridge Univ., 1966-68, Emeritus Prof., 1977. Distinguished Res. Prof. in Psychobiology, Florida State Univ., Tallahassee, 1968-76. Vis. Prof., Univ. of Sydney, 1973-74; Vis. Fellow, ANU, 1973-74. Hon. Member: American Academy of Arts and Sciences, 1963; Swedish Royal Soc., 1968; Physiological Soc., 1973. Ferrier Lectr, Royal Soc., 1962; Silliman Lectr, Yale Univ., 1966; Waynflete Lectr, Magdalen Coll., Oxford, 1968; Fogarty Internat. Scholar, NIH, USA, 1972-73. First Prentice Medallist, Amer. Acad. Optometry, 1963; Feldberg Prize, 1967; Royal Medal, Royal Soc., 1970; Proctor Medal, USA, 1971; Kenneth Craik Award, St John's Coll., Cambridge, 1973. Hon. DSc Case Western Reserve Univ., 1969. Publications: papers in Jl of Physiology, Proc. Roy. Soc., etc. Recreation: music (viola and bassoon). Address: Trinity College, Cambridge; Shawms, Conduit Head Road, Cambridge. T: 54742.
[Died 21 June 1980.

RUSK, Robert Robertson, MA (Glasgow), BA (Cambridge), PhD (Jena); retired as Director to The Scottish Council for Research in Education, 1958; b 1879; m Florence (d 1953), e d of late Mr and Mrs George Lowe, Lurgan House, Co. Westmeath; one d. Educ: Ayr Grammar Sch.; Ayr Acad.; Univs of Glasgow, Jena, Cambridge. Formerly Lectr on Education in the University of Glasgow, retd, 1951. Publications: Experimental Education; The Doctrines of the Great Educators; The Religious Education of the Child; the Training of Teachers in Scotland; An Historical Review; The Philosophical Bases of Education; Research in Education; An Introduction; A History of Infant Education; Outline of Experimental Education. Recreation: golf. Address: Arniston, 51 Old Edinburgh Road, Inverness. T: Inverness 32643.   [Died 25 May 1972.

RUSSELL, Hon. Lord; Albert Russell, QC (Scotland) 1931; Senator of College of Justice in Scotland, 1936-60; b 1884; s of late Sir William F. Russell, Glasgow; m 1913, Florence Muir, d of late Thomas Galloway, of Auchendrane, Ayrshire; one s three d. Educ: Glasgow Academy; Glasgow University (MA, LLB). Admitted to the Faculty of Advocates, 1908; served in Royal Engineers, 1915-18; Advocate Depute, 1928-29; MP (U) Kirkcaldy Burghs, 1931-35; Solicitor-General for Scotland, 1935-36. Address: 3 Glenorchy Road, North Berwick, East Lothian. Club: Northern (Edinburgh).   [Died 12 May 1975.

RUSSELL, Albert; see Russell, Hon. Lord.

RUSSELL, Alexander Smith, MC; MA, DSc; Emeritus Student of Christ Church, Oxford, since 1955; Governor of St Paul's School and St Paul's Girls' School, 1933-61; Elder in Presbyterian Church since 1930; b Musselburgh, Scotland, 31 May 1888; 2nd s of late John Russell, HM Inland Revenue; m 1st, 1919, Mary (d 1942), 4th d of late John Higginson, Dunmurry, Co. Antrim; three d; 2nd, 1956, Norma (née Hull Lewis), Fellow and Librarian of Somerville College, widow of J. E. Hodgson. Educ: Woodside School and High School, Glasgow; Universities of Glasgow, Berlin, and Manchester. MA (Glas.) 1908 with 2nd Class Hons, in Math. and Nat. Phil., BSc 1909; carried out research work in Chemistry, especially in Radio-activity, in the laboratories of F. Soddy in Glasgow, 1909-10, of W. Nernst in Berlin, 1910-11, and of Lord Rutherford in Manchester, 1911-13; held from the University of Glasgow successively, 1908-13, the Thomson, Mackay Smith, Carnegie Research, and 1851 Exhibition Research Scholarships, and the Carnegie Research Fellowship; DSc (Glas.) 1913; Lecturer in Physics at Westminster Training College, 1913-14; Lecturer in Physical Chemistry at the University of Sheffield, 1919-20; Student and Tutor of Christ Church, Oxford, 1920-55; Censor, 1938-46; Member of Hebdomadal Council, 1943-55. Served with army in France, 1915-18, with RGA, later attached RE (Capt. RGA, wounded, despatches, MC). MA (Oxon.) 1920. Publications: many research papers in the Philosophical Magazine, Proceedings of Royal Society, Phys Zeit, etc.; literary contributions to Manchester Guardian, Quarterly Review, Nineteenth Century, The Listener, etc.; first editor of Discovery; (with S. J. Johnstone) The Rare Earth Industry, 1915; An Introduction to the Chemistry of Radio-Active Substances, 1922; (with B. H. Streeter and others) Adventure, 1927; Incandescent Electric Lamps, 1937; (with others) The Annual Report of the Chemical Society. Recreations: house-work, drawing, book collecting. Address: 12 Frenchay Road, Oxford. T: Oxford 56275.   [Died 15 March 1972.

RUSSELL, Ben Harold; Vice-President, Scientific Development Corporation, 1964-72; Chairman, SDC (GB) Ltd, 1964-72; Associate Director, The Dorchester Hotel, 1964-77; Director, Cunard House Ltd, 1962-63; b 13 Nov. 1891; o s of late John and Clara Russell; m 1926, Evelyn Scotney White (d 1967), Melbourne, Australia; one s; 2nd, 1968, Elizabeth Gertrude Boor. Educ: privately; Christ Church, Cheltenham. Served War of 1914-18 (despatches). Entered service of Cunard Steamship Co. Ltd, 1906, Dir 1947-62, Dep. Gen. Manager, 1947-56; Director: Cunard White Star Ltd, 1947-56; Cunard House Ltd, 1962-63. Member of Board, Travel Assoc., 1946-50; Member Board British Travel and Holidays Assoc. (as rep. British Liner Cttee) on formation of Board, 1950-64, first Vice-President, 1964; Member of the London Tourist Board on formation, 1962 (Vice-Chairman, 1965, Chairman, 1966-68, Vice-President, 1968-75); Rep. International Chamber of Shipping at UN Conf. on Tourism, Rome, 1963. Member Board of Governors, University College Hospital, 1951-66; Member Whitley Councils for the Health Services (GB) Medical Council, 1953-66; Vice-President, Institute of Travel Managers; Chairman, US Sect., London Chamber of Commerce, 1964-68; Vice-Chm., Exec. Assoc. of Great Britain, 1941-43; Mem. Inst. of Directors; Liveryman, Worshipful Company of Shipwrights; Freeman, City of London. Member, The Pilgrims. FRSA. Meritorious Service Medal, 1917; Chevalier Order of Orange-Nassau, 1947. Address: 11A Lincoln House, Basil Street, SW3. T: 01-589 9157. Clubs: Naval and Military, Canada, Saints and Sinners, Anchorites.   [Died 24 Sept. 1979.

RUSSELL, Professor Charles Scott, FRCSE; Professor of Obstetrics and Gynæcology, University of Sheffield, since 1950; b 27 March 1912; s of late Prof. William Russell and Mrs Beatrice Russell (née Ritchie); m 1939, Eveline Campbell; four d. Educ: Edinburgh Acad.; Edinburgh Univ. MB, ChB Edinburgh, 1935; FRCSE 1939; MRCOG 1940; MD 1950; FRCOG 1954. House Surgeon, Canterbury, 1935-36; House Physician, Edinburgh, 1936; General Practice, Dunfermline, 1937; House Surgeon: Royal Maternity and Simpson Memorial Hospital, 1937; Royal Infirmary, Edinburgh, 1938; Research Asst and First Asst, Nuffield Dept of Obstetrics and Gynæcology, Univ. of Oxford, 1939-46; Asst Director, Dept of Obstetrics and Gynæcology, Univ. of Manchester, and Resident Obstetrician and Gynæcologist, St Mary's Hosps, Manchester, 1947-49; Reader in Obstetrics and Gynæcology, Univ. of Manchester, 1949-50. Publications: Vesico-Vaginal Fistulas and Related Matters, 1962; The World of a Gynæcologist, 1968; papers in Lancet, Jl of Obst. and Gynæc. of Brit. Empire and others. Recreations: gardening, bee-keeping. Address: 6 Cavendish Road, Sheffield 11. T: 52454.   [Died 4 July 1971.

RUSSELL, Lt-Gen. Sir Dudley, KBE 1950 (CBE 1944); CB 1945; DSO 1942; MC; late IA, retired; b 1 Dec. 1896; m 1929,

Elizabeth, *d* of Sandys Birket Foster, New York, USA. Served Eritrea and Abyssinia, 1941 (OBE); Western Desert, 1942 (DSO); Italy, 1944-45 (CBE, CB, Commander Order of the American Legion of Merit); Chief British Adviser to Indian Army, 1948-54; retd 1954. *Address:* c/o Barclays Bank, Nassau, Bahamas. *[Died 4 Feb. 1978.*

RUSSELL, Maj.-Gen. George Neville, CB 1946; CBE 1943; Royal Engineers (retired); *b* 19 Oct. 1899; *m* 1st, 1927, Iris Mills, Wimbledon; two *d*; 2nd, 1946, Jocelyn Delia Harvie Bennett; one *s* two *d. Educ:* Rugby; Woolwich; Cambridge. Director of Movements, GHQ, Middle East, 1942-43; DQMG (Movements and Transportation), GHQ, New Delhi, 1944-45; Transportation Adviser to Special Commissioner in SE Asia, 1946-47; Chairman: British Road Services, 1948-59; Sutton Dwellings Trust, 1960-71. Member: Eastern Area Board, British Transport Commn, 1957-62 (Chm., 1961-62); British Railways Board, 1962-64; Institute of Transport (President, 1958-59). *Address:* Hastoe, Manor Road, Stourpaine, Blandford, Dorset. *Club:* Army and Navy. *[Died 24 Aug. 1971.*

RUSSELL, Sir Gordon; *see* Russell, Sir S. G.

RUSSELL, Admiral Hon. Sir Guy (Herbrand Edward), GBE 1953 (CBE 1943); KCB 1951 (CB 1948); DSO 1944; RN retired; *b* 14 April 1898; 2nd *s* of 2nd Baron Ampthill; *m* 1939, Hon. Elizabeth Blades, *d* of 1st Baron Ebbisham, GBE; two *s* one *d. Educ:* Osborne and Dartmouth. Served European War, 1914-18, at Gallipoli and Jutland (despatches); afterwards saw service in Black Sea, Mediterranean, East Indies, East Africa, and China Station; psc 1929; Comdr 1931; Capt. 1936; Rear-Adm. 1945; Vice-Adm. 1948; Adm. 1952; idc 1937; attached Cabinet Office, 1938 and 1939; War of 1939-45, commanded HMS Protector, HMS Cumberland, HMS Nelson, and HMS Duke of York (despatches, DSO); Chief of Staff to Field-Marshal Lord Gort, VC, at Gibraltar and Malta, 1942 (CBE). Naval Instructor, Imperial Defence College, 1946-48; FO Commanding 2nd Cruiser Squadron, 1948-49; Admiral Commanding Reserves, 1949-51; C-in-C, Far East Station, 1951-53; a Lord Commissioner of the Admiralty, Second Sea Lord, and Chief of Naval Personnel, 1953-55; Commandant Imperial Defence College, 1956-58, retired; First and Principal ADC to the Queen, 1954-58. Chairman: Nat. Assoc. of Boys' Clubs, 1958-63; Missions to Seamen, 1960-65; Radley College Council, 1965-69. *Recreations:* all games, shooting, etc. *Address:* Cleve Cottage, Wisborough Green, Sussex. *Club:* Royal Automobile.
[Died 25 Sept. 1977.

RUSSELL, Air Vice-Marshal John Bernard, CB 1964; CBE 1960 (OBE 1954); DSO 1943; UK Representative on Council of International Civil Aviation Organization, Montreal, 1969-78; *b* 13 April 1916; *m* 1937, Dorothy Mary Lucas; one *s* one *d. Educ:* Marwood's Sch., Sandwich. Commissioned, RAF, 1935; Specialist Navigator, 1939; served War of 1939-45, 502 and 172 Squadrons and Staff appointments in Coastal Comd, 1940-44; Staff Coll., 1944; Middle East, 1944-45; Directing Staff, 1945-48; British Jt Services Mission, Washington, 1948-50; Air Ministry, 1951-54; HQ No 19 Group, 1954-57; RAF Malta, 1957-59; Director of Operations (Maritime, Navigation and Air Traffic Control), 1960-63; SASO, RAF Coastal Command, 1963-66; Controller, Nat. Air Traffic Control Services, BoT, 1966-69; retired 1969. *Recreation:* golf. *Address:* 1 Stanley Road, Deal, Kent. *[Died 8 Aug. 1978.*

RUSSELL, Rt. Rev. John Keith; *b* 4 Aug. 1916; *s* of Rev. B. Russell and A. M. Russell; *m* 1941, Doreen Glen Johnston; one *s* three *d. Educ:* Shrewsbury School; Christ's College, Cambridge; Ridley Hall, Cambridge. Assistant Curate, Shirley, Southampton, 1940-45; Tutor, Buwalasi College, Uganda, and Mass Literacy Field Worker, Upper Nile Diocese, 1946-48; Rural Dean, Masaba Deanery, Upper Nile Diocese, 1948-52; Education Secretary, Mbale Archdeaconry, Upper Nile Dio., 1948-55; Asst Bishop on Upper Nile, Uganda, 1955-60; Bishop of Northern Uganda, 1961-64; Vicar, King Charles the Martyr, Tunbridge Wells, 1965-73; Asst Bishop, Dio. Rochester, 1965-78; Rector of Hever with Markbeech, 1973-78; Chm., Jt Social Responsibility Council for Canterbury and Rochester Dioceses, 1968-78. *Publication:* Men without God?, 1966. *Recreations:* cricket, football, music. *Address:* 6 Seagrove Manor, Seaview, Isle of Wight. *T:* Seaview 3253. *[Died 1 Sept. 1979.*

RUSSELL, Sir John (Weir), Kt 1958; *b* 1893; *s* of Samuel Russell, ICS, and Maud Morrison (*née* Parr); *m* 1st, 1920, Lucy Ellen Mead; one *s* one *d*; 2nd, 1932, Mary Catherine Davies (*née* Stewart). *Educ:* Winchester; New College, Oxford. European War, 1914-18; L.-Corp. King Edward's Horse, 1914; 2nd Lt, Lt, Capt., RFA. President, Oxford Union, 1920. Barrister-at-Law, Inner Temple, 1922. War of 1939-45: Major, General Staff

Intelligence, War Office; Lt-Col Comdg Special Communications Unit. Chairman, London Conservative Union, 1953-55. Registrar, Imperial Soc. of Knights Bachelor; Governor: Old Vic; Sadler's Wells; Chm., Vic-Wells Assoc.; formerly: Governor, Morley Coll.; Trustee City Parochial Foundation; Pres., Shakespearean Authorship Soc.; Pres. Fifth Army (1916-18) Old Comrades Assoc.; Chairman Osteopathic Association Clinic. *Recreations:* golf, reading, fishing. *Address:* 57 Rivermead Court, SW6. *T:* 01-736 6783; 4 Brick Court, Temple, EC4. *T:* 01-353 2725. *Clubs:* Carlton, Garrick; Hurlingham. *[Died 6 April 1978.*

RUSSELL, Leonard; Associate Editor and Chief Literary Editor, Sunday Times; Director, Times Publications Ltd; *b* 26 July 1906; 2nd *s* of Thomas and Mary Russell; *m* 1943, Elizabeth Dilys Powell; no *c. Publications:* Edited: Parody Party, 1936; Press Gang, 1937; English Wits, 1940; founded The Saturday Book, 1941, and edited it annually until 1951; (with Nicolas Bentley) The English Comic Album, 1948; The Russell Reader, 1956; (with H. Hobson and P. Knightley) The Pearl of Days: an intimate memoir of The Sunday Times, 1972. *Address:* 14 Albion Street, Hyde Park, W2. *T:* 01-723 9807.
[Died 26 Aug. 1974.

RUSSELL, Leonard James, MA, BSc, DPhil; FBA 1954; Hon LLD Glasgow; Emeritus Professor of Philosophy, Univ. of Birmingham, since 1951; *b* 1884; *s* of late Rev. E. T. Russell; *m* 1911, Alice, *d* of late Robert Green; one *s* one *d. Educ:* Univ. of Glasgow; Emmanuel Coll., Cambridge. Lecturer in Logic, Univ. Glasgow, 1910; Prof. of Philosophy, University of Bristol, 1923-25; Professor of Philosophy, University of Birmingham, 1925-50; Dean of the Faculty of Arts, 1937-40; Acting Dean, 1941-43; Acting Professor of Philosophy for the summer quarter of 1932, Stanford University, California; President of the Aristotelian Society, 1932-33; President of Mind Association, 1932-33; Nuffield Foundation Visiting Lectureship to Australia, 1951. Sponsor, University College of N Staffordshire, 1949-52; Visiting Professor of Philosophy, Emory Univ., Atlanta, Ga, 1962-63, 1966. *Publications:* An Introduction to Logic, 1914 (Japanese trans., 1950); An Introduction to Philosophy, 1929. *Address:* 50 Weoley Park Road, Selly Oak, Birmingham B29 6RB. *T:* 021-472 2148. *[Died 8 March 1971.*

RUSSELL, Brigadier Nelson, CB 1949; DSO 1943; MC 1916; *b* 7 July 1897; *s* of Nelson Russell, Strathmore, Lisburn, N Ireland; *m* 1926, Edith, *d* of A. T. Allan, Highfield, Lisburn, N Ireland; no *c. Educ:* Campbell College, Belfast. Served European War, France and Belgium, 1914-18; 2nd Lt The Royal Irish Fusiliers, 1915. Egypt, India, Sudan, Palestine, 1919-39; Bde Major, 1937-40; Lt-Col, GSO2, 1940; Tunisia, Sicily, Italy, 1939-45; Comdr: The Irish Brigade, 1942-44; Belfast Sub-Area, 1945; Belfast Garrison, 1946; Ulster Indep. Inf. Bde Gp, 1947-50; retired, 1950. Serjeant-at-Arms to Parliament of Northern Ireland, 1951-59. *Recreations:* shooting, fishing, golf and gardening. *Address:* The Manor House, Tollymore, Newcastle, N Ireland. *Club:* Ulster (Belfast). *[Died 20 Oct. 1971.*

RUSSELL, Patrick Wimberley D.; *see* Dill-Russell.

RUSSELL, Ritchie; *see* Russell, W. R.

RUSSELL, Sir Robert Edwin, Kt 1946; CSI 1941; CIE 1934; MA, DLitt; Indian Civil Service, retired; *b* 21 April 1890; *s* of Robert Russell, Fellow of Trinity College, Dublin; *m* Esther Rhona, *d* of Lt-Colonel J. G. P. Murray, IMS; one *s* two *d. Educ:* Campbell College, Belfast; Trinity College, Dublin. Entered ICS, 1912; military service, 1915-19; District Magistrate and Collector, Bihar, 1920-38; Secretary to Government, Revenue Dept, 1927-31; Chief Secretary, 1934-35, 1938-39; Adviser to the Governor of Bihar, India, 1939-45; Asst Sec., Dept of Health for Scotland, 1947-55, retd. A Vice-Pres., National Trust for Scotland. Hon. MRTPI. *Address:* 43 Grange Road, Edinburgh 9. *T:* 031-667 3386. *Club:* New (Edinburgh).
[Died 27 Nov. 1972.

RUSSELL, Robert Tor, CIE 1930; DSO 1917; Chief Architect, Government of India; retired 1941; Chief Planning Inspector, Ministry of Housing and Local Government; retired 1954; *b* 1888; *s* of S. B. Russell, Gosmore, Hitchin; *m* 1921, Ethel Frances, MBE, *d* of H. Hatch, ICS, Hitchin; one *s* one *d.* Served Mesopotamia, 1916-19 (despatches, DSO). *Address:* Millhayes, Bickleigh, Tiverton, Devon. *[Died 3 Nov. 1972.*

RUSSELL, Sir Ronald (Stanley), Kt 1964; MA Cantab; FRSA; author and journalist; *b* 29 May 1904; *s* of late J. Stanley Russell, Seahouses, Northumberland; *m* 1933, Ena Glendenning, *d* of late Alfred Forrester, FRIBA, Grove Hill, Middlesbrough; one *s* one *d. Educ:* Haileybury; Caius Coll. Cambridge. On Staff of

Newcastle Chronicle Limited, 1929-31; Reuter's Ltd, 1931-35; Lecturer on Economics of Coal Industry, 1935-39. Served War of 1939-45 in coast artillery, and as staff officer. Research Secretary Empire Economic Union, 1945-51. Mem. LCC for Norwood, 1946-52; contested (C) Shettleston Div. of Glasgow, 1935; Coatbridge Div. of Lanarkshire, 1945. MP (C) Wembley S, 1950-Feb. 1974; PPS to Rt Hon. Duncan Sandys, MP, 1951-55. Sponsored the Pet Animals Bill and piloted it through all its stages in the Commons, 1951, also Opticians Bill, 1957-58; introduced Export of Animals Control Bill, 1973. Mem. UK Delegation to Council of Europe and WEU, 1957-66. Dep.-Chairman, General Optical Council, 1959-; Chairman, Commonwealth Producers' Organisation, 1960-63 and 1964-; Member Chairman's Panel of House of Commons, 1959-74; Jt Hon. Sec., Conservative Private Member's Cttee, 1957-61; Hon. Treasurer, 1961-74; Hon. Sec. Animal Welfare Group, 1960-71. Besides Commonwealth and foreign affairs, keenly interested in transport problems; Member of London and Home Counties Traffic Advisory Cttee 1946-52. *Publications:* Imperial Preference, 1947; Government Bulk Buying, 1948; Tariff Preferences in Western Europe, 1949; Commonwealth Co-operation 1952-53, 1952. *Recreations:* riding, swimming, photography, travel. *Address:* 29 Acacia Road, St John's Wood, NW8. *T:* 01-722 5700; Crumstone, Seahouses, Northumberland. *Clubs:* Carlton, Constitutional, Press.   *[Died 6 April 1974.*

RUSSELL, Rosalind, (Mrs F. Brisson); film and stage actress; *b* 4 June 1911; *d* of James R. and Clara McKnight Russell; *m* 1941, Frederick Brisson; one *s. Educ:* Marymount College; Barnard College. Chm., Exec. Cttee, Cedars-Sinai Hosp. Women's Guild, 1967. Hon. Dr Fine Arts, Univ. of Portland, 1967. *Films include:* Craig's Wife; Night Must Fall; His Girl Friday; My Sister Eileen; Take a Letter, Darling; Roughly Speaking; Sister Kenny; Mourning Becomes Electra; The Velvet Touch; Tell it to the Judge; Woman of Distinction; Never Wave at a Wac; The Girl Rush; Picnic; Auntie Mame; A Majority of One; Five Finger Exercise; Gypsy; Oh Dad, Poor Dad, Mama's Hung You in the Closet and I'm Feeling so Sad; Life with Mother Superior; Where Angels Go... Trouble Follows; Rosie!; Mrs Pollifax-Spy; *plays:* Bell, Book and Candle; Broadway musical comedy, Wonderful Town; Auntie Mame. TV Spectacular, Wonderful Town. *Posthumous publication:* Life is a Banquet (autobiog.), 1978. *Recreations:* riding, swimming, tennis, golf. *Address:* 706 North Beverly Drive, Beverly Hills, Calif 94710, USA. *Clubs:* Bel Air Country (Los Angeles), Eldorado Country (Palm Desert, Calif).   *[Died 28 Nov. 1976.*

RUSSELL, Sir (Sydney) Gordon, Kt 1955; CBE 1947; MC; RDI; FSIA; *b* London, 20 May 1892; *e s* of late S. B. Russell, Snowshill, Glos. and Elizabeth Russell; *m* 1921, Constance Elizabeth Jane Vere, *d* of late Dr F. A. V. Denning, Sligo; two *s* one *d* (and one *s* decd). *Educ:* Campden Grammar School. Served European War with Worcestershire Regiment, 1914-19 (MC). Designer, Managing Director, Gordon Russell Ltd, 1926-40, later Director (Chm., 1967-77); Partner Russell & Sons, 1919-46, later Director (Chm., 1970-76). The Lygon Arms Ltd (Broadway). Mem. Art Workers Guild, 1926, Master, 1962; RDI, 1940, Master of the Faculty, 1947-49; Member Utility Furniture Advisory Cttee and Furniture Production Cttee (Bd of Trade), 1942 and Chm. of Bd of Trade Design Panel, 1943-47; Specialist Assessor for Nat. Diploma in Design to Min. of Educ., 1938-53; served on jury of Internat. Low-Cost Furniture Competition, Museum of Modern Art, New York, 1948; Original Member Exec. Cttee, Festival of Britain, 1951; Member: Art Panel of Arts Council, 1948-53, Fine Arts Cttee of British Council, 1948-58, Council of Roy. Soc. of Arts, 1947-49 and 1951-55; Original Mem. Council of Industrial Design (now Design Council), 1944, Dir, 1947-59, Life Mem., 1960-; Member: Council, Royal Coll. of Art, 1948-51, and 1952-63; Council, Royal Sch. of Needlework, 1951-68; Design Panel, BR Bd, 1956-66; Pres., Design and Industries Assoc., 1959-62; Member: Nat. Council for Diplomas in Art and Design, 1961-68; Crafts Adv. Cttee, 1971-74. First FSIA, 1945; FRSA, 1949; First Hon. DesRCA, 1952, Senior Fellow, 1960; Hon. ARIBA, 1953, Hon. Fellow, 1965; Hon. AILA, 1955; Hon. LLD Birmingham Univ., 1960; DUniv. York, 1969. Mem. Hon. Cttee for Internat. Exhibition of architecture and industrial design, Hälsingborg, Sweden, 1955; Mem. Higher Jury, XIIth Milan Triennale Exhibition, 1960. Officer, Swedish Royal Order of the Vasa, 1954; Commander, Norwegian Royal Order of St Olav, 1957. Gold Albert Medal, RSA, 1962. *Publications:* The Story of Furniture (Puffin), 1947; The Things We See: Furniture (Penguin), 1948; Looking at Furniture, 1964; (autobiography) Designer's Trade, 1968; and articles, lectures and broadcasts on design and country life. *Recreations:* gardening and hand-work of many kinds. *Address:* Kingcombe, Chipping Campden, Glos. *T:* Evesham 840253. *Club:* Arts.   *[Died 7 Oct. 1980.*

RUSSELL, Col (Hon. Brig.) Valentine Cubitt, DSO 1918; MC; late Suffolk Regiment; *b* 14 Feb. 1896; *y s* of late Stuart Arthur Russell, Kensington; *m* 1918, Mabel Hannah, *d* of late Alexander Brewster, Liverpool. Served European War, 1914-18 (despatches twice, DSO, MC and bar, Belgian Croix de Guerre); War of 1939-45 (despatches), temp. Brig. 1941; Col 1941; retired, 1947. *Address:* 92 Gordon Avenue, Stanmore, Middlesex HA7 3QS. *T:* 01-954 1311.   *[Died 10 Nov. 1976.*

RUSSELL, (William) Ritchie, CBE 1952; MD, FRCP; Consultant Neurologist: to United Oxford Hospitals, 1945-70; to Army, 1948-69; Professor of Clinical Neurology, Oxford Univ., 1966-70; retired; *b* 7 Feb. 1903; *s* of Professor William Russell, MD; *m* 1932, Jean Stuart Low; one *s* one *d. Educ:* Edinburgh Academy; Edinburgh Univ. MBChB, 1926; MD(Edin.), 1932; FRCPEd, 1933; FRCP, 1943; MA Oxon, 1946; DSc Oxon, 1955. Asst Physician, Royal Infirmary, Edinburgh, 1934; Lecturer in Neurology: University of Edinburgh, 1938; Oxford University, 1949-66. Served RAMC, 1940-45; Consultant Neurologist (Brig.), MEF, 1943. Editor of Jl of Neurol., Neurosurg, Psychiat., 1948-69. KStJ 1957. *Publications:* Poliomyelitis, 2nd edn 1956; Brain-Memory-Learning, 1959; Traumatic Aphasia, 1961; The Traumatic Amnesias, 1971; Explaining the Brain, 1975; research papers on neurological subjects in medical journals. *Address:* Flat 31, 380 Banbury Road, Oxford OX2 7PW.   *[Died 8 Dec. 1980.*

RUSSELL SCOTT, Charles; *see* Scott, C. R.

RUTHERFORD, Gideon Campbell, CB 1948; JP; engaged in farming; Chairman Sutherland Territorial Forces, Major; Hon. Sheriff-Substitute for Sutherland; *b* 2 April 1888; *s* of late John Rutherford, Kildonan, Sutherland; *m* 1917, Laura Gordon; two *s* two *d. Educ:* Helmsdale Higher Grade School. Farming at Kildonan Sheep Farm until 4th Aug. 1914; served European War; mobilised with 5th Seaforths in France (wounded 1916); two years in Hospital. Bought Estate of Proncy, Dornoch, 1924. *Recreation:* fishing. *Address:* Proncy, Dornoch, Sutherland. *T:* 54.   *[Died 8 Feb. 1971.*

RUTHERFORD, Dame Margaret, DBE 1967 (OBE 1961); ARCM, LRAM (Eloc.); actress; *b* London, 11 May 1892; *d* of late William Rutherford and Florence Nicholson; *m* 1945, Stringer Davis. *Educ:* Wimbledon Hill School; Raven's Croft, Seaford, Sussex. Formerly taught pianoforte and elocution. Studied for stage at Old Vic, where made first theatrical appearance, 1925. Subsequently played in repertory at Oxford and Croydon, and with Greater London Players; West End successes from 1933, notably Bijou in Spring Meeting and Madame Arcati in Blithe Spirit; toured on the Continent, Sept. 1944, for ENSA; toured USA and Canada with John Gielgud, 1947, as Lady Bracknell in the Importance of being Earnest; subsequently played Miss Whitchurch in The Happiest Days of your Life, Apollo Theatre; Madame Desmortes in Ring round the Moon, 1950; Constance Hargreaves in Miss Hargreaves, Royal Court Theatre; Lady Wishfort in The Way of the World, Lyric, Hammersmith; The White Queen in Alice Through the Looking Glass, Princes, 1954; The Duchess in Time Remembered, Lyric, Hammersmith, and New Theatre, 1954-55; Mirabelle in A Likely Tale, Globe Theatre, 1956; Lady Wishfort in The Way of the World, Saville Theatre, 1956; Lady Bracknell in The Importance of Being Earnest, Irish Festival, 1957; Australian Tour for Elizabethan Theatre Trust, 1957-58; Minerva Goody in Farewell, Farewell Eugene, Garrick Theatre, 1959; Mrs Candour in The School for Scandal, Haymarket, 1962; The Solid Gold Cadillac, Saville, 1965; The Clandestine Marriage, Chichester, 1966; Mrs Malaprop in The Rivals, Haymarket, 1966. First appearance in films, 1936, in Dusty Ermine. *Films include:* Blithe Spirit, Miranda, Passport to Pimlico, Her Favourite Husband, The Happiest Days of Your Life, The Importance of Being Earnest, Castle in the Air, Curtain Up, Miss Robin Hood, Innocents in Paris, Runaway Bus, Trouble in Store, Mad about Men, Aunt Clara, An Alligator named Daisy, The Smallest Show on Earth, Just my Luck, I'm All Right Jack, On the Double, "Murder" she Said, Mouse on the Moon, Murder at the Gallop, The VIP's, Murder Most Foul, Murder Ahoy, Chimes at Midnight, A Countess from Hong Kong, Arabella. Has also appeared on Television, notably in 3 plays repeated frequently all over the world: Day after Tomorrow; The Two Wise Virgins of Hove; The Kidnapping of Mary Smith. Awarded Gold Medallion, Ingenio et arte, Denmark, 1955. For role in film, The VIP's, awarded: Golden Globe for Best Supporting Actress (Foreign Press Assoc., Hollywood), 1964; Best Film Actress Silver Medal (Variety Club of Gt Britain), 1964; Oscar as Best Supporting Actress, 1964; Gold Medal Una Vita per il Cinema (Consorzio Stampa Cinematografica, Rome), 1967. *Publication:* Margaret Rutherford: an autobiography, 1972. *Address:* c/o Film Rights

Ltd, 113-117 Wardour Street, W1. *T:* 01-437 7151; Chalfont St Peter, Bucks. *[Died 22 May 1972.*

RUTHERFORD, Brig.-Gen. Thomas John, CBE 1945; ED; retired as National Chairman, Farm Credit Corporation (1959-63); *b* Leith, Ontario, Canada, 16 Jan. 1893; *s* of Malcolm Rutherford; *m* 1919, Helen Sibbald; three *s* one *d.* Engaged in farming at Leith, Ont.; joined Grey Regt, September 1912; proceeded overseas, 1916; served in France and Belgium with 4th Canadian Mounted Rifles (wounded, despatches); demobilised, 1919. Contested House of Commons, Grey North, 1921; Local Registrar Supreme Court and Surrogate Regist. and Sheriff, Co. Grey, 1923; Lt-Col to command Grey Regt, 1925; Col to command 22nd Cdn Inf. Bde, 1932; R of O, 1936; reverted to Major, 1939, to command a company of the Grey and Simcoe Foresters; Lt-Col to command the Grey and Simcoe Foresters (Overseas Unit), 1940; Brig. to command 1st Canadian Armoured Brigade, 1941; commanded Canadian Armoured Corps Reinforcement Units (UK) and Senior Adviser Canadian Armoured Corps, UK, 1943; Dep. Comdr, Canadian Forces, Netherlands, and Canadian Repatriation Units, UK, 1946. Dir-Gen. of Rehabn, Can., 1946; Nat. Dir, Soldier Settlement and Veterans' Land Act, 1947-62. Hon. Col, Grey and Simcoe Foresters. *Publications:* Scouts and Patrols; Production-line Farming. *Address:* RR1, Owen Sound, Ont, Canada. *Club:* Royal Canadian Military Institute. *[Died 18 July 1975.*

RUTTER, Herbert Hugh, CB 1967; *b* 25 Dec. 1905; *m* 1948, Maureen Elsie, *d* of Donald A. Gooch; one *d. Educ:* Harris Coll., Preston; Manchester Univ.; (BA), LLM London. Admitted Solicitor, 1931; Public Trustee Office, 1931; Tithe Redemption Commn, 1936; Asst Solicitor to Min. of Agric., Comrs of Crown Lands and Forestry Commn, 1948; Dep. Legal Adviser, Min. of Agric., Fsheries & Food, 1960; retd 1967. *Publications:* contrib. legal jls. *Address:* Willows, Burton Bradstock, Bridport, Dorset. *T:* Burton Bradstock 341. *Club:* Civil Service. *[Died 22 June 1975.*

RUTTER, W(illiam) Arthur, CBE 1949 (OBE 1944); FRIBA; retired; *b* Cardiff, 8 Jan. 1890; *s* of William Rutter; *m* 1915, Amy (*d* 1980), *d* of William Dyche, BA, Cardiff; one *s* three *d.* Chief Architect to the Ministry of Works, 1946-51. *Address:* 13 Manor Way, Onslow Village, Guildford, Surrey. *[Died 27 Oct. 1980.*

RYAN, Alfred Patrick, CBE 1946; *b* 1900; *s* of Frederick and Charlotte Kate Ryan; *m* 1926, Rachel Rosa, *d* of C. E. Montague; one *d. Educ:* Whitgift; Balliol Coll., Oxford. 2nd Lt RFA. Editorial Staff, Manchester Guardian and Daily Telegraph; Empire Marketing Board Secretariat; Publicity Manager, Gas, Light & Coke Co. Squadron Leader, RAFVR, 1939-40. Editor of the BBC News Services, 1940-47; joined The Times 1947; Asst Editor and Literary Editor until 1968; now writing continuation of the official History of The Times. *Publications:* Lord Northcliffe, 1953; Islands Apart (America), 1954; Mutiny at the Curragh, 1956. *Address:* c/o The Times, EC4. *Clubs:* United Oxford & Cambridge University, Garrick, Beefsteak; St Stephen's Green (Dublin). *[Died 1 July 1972.*

RYAN, Cornelius John; Writer; Roving Editor, Reader's Digest, since 1965; *b* Dublin, Ireland, 5 June 1920; *s* of John Joseph Ryan and Amelia (*née* Clohisey); naturalside US citizen, 1950; *m* 1950, Kathryn Ann Morgan (novelist; author of The Betty Tree, 1972); one *s* one *d. Educ:* Christian Brothers' Sch., Dublin; Irish Acad. Music. Reporter: Reuter's News Agency, London, 1941-42; Daily Telegraph, London, 1943; War Correspondent, Europe, Pacific, 1943-47 (war medals); Jerusalem, 1946-47; Time and Life, NY, also St Louis Post Despatch, 1946-47; Contribs Ed. Time, 1947-49; Mem. Special Projects Dept, prod. TV show Newsweek, 1949-50; Sen. Editor Collier's, NY, 1956; Staff Writer, Reader's Digest, NY, 1962-65. Consultant, Pan Amer. World Airways; Director: D. J. Ryan & Co., Dublin; Ryan Holdings Co., Dublin; State Nat. Bank of Connecticut; Nat. Bd, Boys' Clubs of America; Trustee, Correspondents Fund, Overseas Press Club. Hon. Research Fell., Econs and Social Scis, Manchester Univ., 1964. *Publications:* (with Frank Kelley) Star Spangled Mikado, 1948; MacArthur, 1951; (with Dr Von Braun and others) Across the Space Frontier, 1952; (with Dr Von Braun and others) Conquest of the Moon, 1954; One Minute to Ditch, 1957; The Longest Day, 1959; The Last Battle, 1966; A Bridge Too Far, 1974; *posthumous publication:* A Private Battle (autobiog., ed Kathryn Morgan Ryan), 1980. *Recreations:* golf, fishing, shooting. *Address:* Old Branchville Road, Ridgefield, Conn 06877, USA. *T:* 438-2335. *Clubs:* New York Athletic, Player's (New York); National Press of America (Washington, DC); Silver Spring Country (Conn); Union Interalliée (Paris). *[Died 23 Nov. 1974.*

RYAN, Most Rev. Finbar, OP, MA, DD, LLD; *b* 4 March 1882; *s* of Edward and Matilda Ryan, Cork, Ireland. *Educ:* Christian Brothers Coll., Cork; Clongowes Wood Coll., Sallins; Roy. and Nat. Univs of Ireland; Minerva Univ. Rome. Ordained 1905; Dominican Provincial, 1921-26, 1930-34; Titular Archbishop of Gabula and Coadjutor of Port of Spain, 1937-40; Archbishop of Port of Spain, 1940-66; Titular Archbishop of Villa Magna. Assistant Pontifical Throne and Vatican Count, 1950; Grand Officer Supreme Order of Christ, 1950; Trinity Cross, Trinidad and Tobago, 1969. *Address:* Bon Secours Hospital, Cork, Eire. *[Died 10 Jan. 1975.*

RYAN, Most Rev. Hugh Edward, DD; Titular Bishop of Nigizubi, since 1967; *b* Kyabram, Victoria, 25 April 1888. *Educ:* Assumption College, Kilmore, Vic.; St Joseph's College, Hunter's Hill, NSW; St Patrick's College, Manly, NSW; College of Propaganda, Rome. Ordained, 1916. Bishop of Townsville, 1938-67. *Address:* Villa Vincent, Gulliver Street, Hermit Park, Queensland 4812, Australia. *[Died 13 Nov. 1977.*

RYAN, John, CBE 1949; MC 1916; MA (Cantab), BSc (London); Chairman, Centre for Interfirm Comparison Ltd, 1969-74; Member, Board, Oversea Service Ltd, 1954-74; Past Member, Western Area Board, BTC; *b* 27 July 1894; *m* 1922, Mabel McEwen; three *s* one *d. Educ:* Wolverhampton Grammar School; Gonville and Caius Coll., Cambridge. Mathematical Tripos, 1914. Served European War, 1914-18; Major, Royal Signals; Cmd Guards Signals Company (despatches, MC). Chm. British Closures Manufacturers' Assoc., 1942-74; Fellow, Assoc. of Incorporated Statisticians; Hon. Vice-Pres. Inst. of Sheet Metal Engineering; Fellow: International Academy of Management; British Institute of Management. Chm., Lloyd Thomas Charity; Vice-Chm., Industrial Christian Fellowship; Treasurer, Ealing Civic Soc. Member: Livery of Merchant Taylors' Company; Pilgrims of Great Britain; Conseiller d'honneur, Comité Internationale d'Organisation Scientifique (CIOS); Hon. President of CECIOS (European Council of CIOS). *Address:* 30 Amherst Road, Ealing, W13. *T:* 01-997 5190. *Club:* Reform. *[Died 5 Oct. 1975.*

RYAN, John Francis, FFARCS; Consulting Anæsthetist, St Thomas' Hospital; *b* 1894; *s* of John Ryan, OBE, and Ellen Rebecca Ryan; *m* 1924, Frances Emmeline Perry; three *d. Educ:* Merchant Taylors' School; St Thomas' Hosp. MRCS, LRCP 1917; MB, BS London 1919; DA Eng. 1939; FFARCS Eng 1949. Formerly Anæsthetist, Nat. Hosp. for Paralysed and Epileptic; Evelina Hosp. for Children. European War, 1914-18, Temp. Surg. RN; War of 1939-45, Temp. Surg. Lt-Comdr RNVR, Specialist in Anæsthetics, RN. FRSocMed; Fellow Assoc. of Anæsthetists of Gt Brit. and Ire. *Publications:* contribs to med. jls. *Recreations:* gardening, golf. *Address:* The Rookery, Burton Bradstock, Dorset. *T:* Burton Bradstock 256. *Clubs:* Naval, Lansdowne. *[Died 16 Feb. 1978.*

RYAN, Patrick John McNamara; a Recorder of the Crown Court, since 1972; Director of several companies since 1950; *b* 7 March 1919; *m* 1949, Vera, *d* of W. Craven-Ellis. *Educ:* Wimbledon Coll.; Beaumont Coll. Commnd in London Irish Rifles, 1939. Solicitor, 1946. Pres., W Surrey Law Soc., 1964-65; Chm. and Pres., Esher Conservative Constituency Assoc., 1962-65; Mem., SE Circuit Adv. Cttee, 1972. Mem., NW Surrey Medical Ethical Cttee, 1976. *Recreations:* woodwork; gardener's handyman; trying to find peace! *Address:* Beaumont Lodge, St George's Hill, Weybridge, Surrey. *Clubs:* St George's Hill Golf; Weybridge Golf. *[Died 16 July 1978.*

RYDER, Sir Gerard, Kt 1969; CB 1964; Solicitor to the Department of Trade and Industry (formerly Board of Trade), 1960-72; retired; *b* 24 May 1909; *s* of late Frederick and Elizabeth Ryder, both of Manchester; *m* 1936, Eileen McCarthy; two *s* four *d* (and one *d* decd). *Educ:* Xaverian College, Manchester; Manchester University. Admitted Solicitor, 1932; private practice, 1932-42. Mines Dept (Board of Trade) and Min. of Fuel and Power, 1942-45. Board of Trade: Senior Legal Asst, 1945; Asst Solicitor, 1948; Principal Assistant Solicitor, 1957. *Address:* 1 Furze Hill, Purley, Surrey. *T:* 01-660 8525. *[Died 5 Sept. 1973.*

RYDGE, Sir Norman (Bede), Kt 1966; CBE 1955; Hon. President, The Greater Union Organisation Pty Ltd; Chairman: Carlton Hotel Ltd; Manly Hotels Ltd; Carlton Investments Ltd; Amalgamated Holdings Ltd; *b* 18 Oct. 1900; *s* of William Rydge and Margaret McSweeney; *m* 1950, Phoebe Caroline McEwing; three *s* (and one *s* decd). *Educ:* Fort Street High School. Hon. Life Governor: Royal Prince Alfred Hosp. (Sydney); Royal Children's Hosp. and Alfred Hosp. (Melb.); Australian Inst. of Management; Royal Life Saving Soc. of NSW. Founder of Rydge's Business Journal, 1927. *Publications:* Federal Income

Tax Law; Federal Land Tax Law; The Law of Income Tax in NSW; Employers' Endowment Tax; Commonwealth Income Tax Acts; Australasian Executorship Law and Accounts; The NSW Income Tax Management Act; Australasian edition of Stevens' Mercantile Law. *Recreations:* boating, gardening. *Address:* 55 Wunulla Road, Point Piper, NSW 2027, Australia. *T:* 36-6314. *Clubs:* Tattersall's, American National, Australian Golf, Royal Motor Yacht (all Sydney). *[Died 14 May 1980.*

RYLAH, Hon. Sir Arthur (Gordon), KBE 1968; CMG 1965; ED; Chief Secretary, and Deputy Premier of Victoria, 1955-71; MLA for Kew, Victoria, 1949-71; *b* 3 Oct. 1909; *s* of W. R. Rylah; *m* 1st, 1937, Ann Flora (decd) (*née* Flashman); one *s* one *d*; 2nd, 1969, Mrs Ruth Reiner. *Educ:* Trinity Grammar Sch.; Trinity Coll., Melbourne Univ. (BA, LLB). Consultant to firm of Rylah & Rylah. *Recreation:* tennis. *Address:* Ferrier Street, Mount Macedon, Victoria 3441, Australia. *Clubs:* Naval and Military, Victoria Racing, Royal South Yarra Lawn Tennis (Melbourne).
[Died 20 Sept. 1974.

RYLE, George Bodley, CBE 1960; *b* 4 March 1902; *y s* of late Reginald John Ryle, MD, JP, and Catherine Ryle (*née* Scott); *m* 1934, Margaret Bevan; one *s* three *d*. *Educ:* Brighton College; St Catherine's, Oxford. Entered Forestry Commission, 1924; Dep. Director Gen., 1963; retired 1965. Seconded as Divisional Officer, Home Timber Production Dept, Ministry of Supply, 1939-46; as Chief Control Officer, North German Timber Control, Control Commission for Germany, 1946-47; Conservator, Forestry Commission, 1947-54; Dir of Forestry for Wales, 1954-58; Dir of Forestry for England, 1958-63. Apptd Verderer of the New Forest, 1966. Fellow and 1973 Medallist, Inst. of Foresters. *Publications:* Forest Service, 1969; numerous in Forestry, Quarterly Journal of Forestry and Empire Forestry Review. *Recreations:* walking the hills, but now only up memory tracks; entomology. *Address:* 5 Whitby Court, Milford-on-Sea, Hants SO4 0WB. *[Died 14 Feb. 1978.*

RYLE, Gilbert; *b* 19 Aug. 1900; *s* of Reginald John Ryle, MD, and Catherine Scott; unmarried. *Educ:* Brighton Coll.; Queen's Coll., Oxford. 1st Classes in Classical Hon. Mods, Lit Hum, and Philosophy, Politics and Economics; Captain Queen's Coll. Boat Club; Trial Eights, 1923; Lecturer, Christ Church, Oxford, 1924; Student and Tutor in Philosophy, Christ Church, Oxford, 1925; sometime Jun. and Sen. Censor of Christ Church and Jun. Proctor of the University; Waynflete Professor of Metaphysical Philosophy, Oxford, 1945-68. Editor of Mind, 1947-71. War of 1939-45, commissioned Welsh Guards, 1940, ending as Major. Hon. Student of Christ Church; Hon. Fellow, Queen's Coll., Oxford; Hon. Fellow, Magdalen Coll., Oxford. For. Hon. Mem., Amer. Acad. of Arts and Sciences, 1968; Hon. Dr: Birmingham; Warwick; Sussex; Hull; Keele; Trinity Coll. Dublin; Trent Univ., Ontario, Canada; St Andrews. *Publications:* The Concept of Mind, 1949; Dilemmas, 1954; Plato's Progress, 1966; Collected Papers: vol 1, Critical Essays, 1971; vol 2, Collected Essays, 1971; also various articles and reviews in Mind, Aristotelian Society Proceedings and Philosophy; also Inaugural Lecture, Philosophical Arguments, 1945. *Address:* Magdalen College, Oxford; North Street, Islip, Oxon. *T:* Kidlington 3277. *Clubs:* Travellers', Leander. *[Died 6 Oct. 1976.*

S

SACHER, Harry; Director, Marks and Spencer Ltd, 1932-62, retired; *b* London, 3 Sept. 1881; *s* of Jacob and Esther Sacher; *m* 1915, Miriam (Hon. Fellow, St Hilda's College, Oxford; Hon. Fellow, Weizmann Inst. of Science), *d* of Michael and Hannah Marks, Manchester; two *s*. *Educ:* Central Foundation School, London; University Coll., London; New Coll., Oxford; Berlin Univ.; Sorbonne. Ed. Staff, Manchester Guardian, 1905-9 and 1915-19 and Daily News, 1909-15; called to Bar, 1909; practised in Palestine, 1920-30; Member of Executive of World Zionist Organisation, 1927-31. Hon. Fellow, New College, Oxford, 1958; Hon. Fellow, University College, London, 1961; Hon. Fellow, Weizmann Institute of Science, 1962; Hon. LLD Hebrew Univ. of Jerusalem, 1966. *Publications:* Israel, the Establishment of a State; Zionist Portraits; Edited Zionism and the Jewish Future; Palestine. *Address:* 37 Grosvenor Square, W1. *T:* 01-499 3720. *Club:* Savile. *[Died 10 May 1971.*

SACHS, Major-General Albert, CB 1955; CBE 1952; Hon. Consultant Pathologist, Queen Victoria Hospital, East Grinstead; *b* 18 May 1904; *s* of late John Sachs, JP, Pretoria,

South Africa; *m* 1930, Olga Alice, KIH, OStJ, *d* of late John Winter le Chasseur, Jersey, CI. *Educ:* Pretoria High School; Trinity Coll., Dublin. BA (Hons), 1926; MB, ChB, 1926; MD 1931; MSc 1935; MRCP, 1953; FRCP 1965; FCPath 1964. Joined RAMC, 1927; Lt-Col, 1942; Col., 1945; Brigadier, 1949; Major-General, 1953. Mohmand Ops, NWFP, India (Medal and Clasp), 1933; served War of 1939-45, India, Madagascar, Middle East, Persia, Iraq and Italy; Reader in Pathology, Roy. Army Med. Coll., 1949; Dir of Path., and Cons. Path. to Army, WO, 1949-53; Deputy Director Medical Services, UK Command, 1953-56; retired, 1956; Hon. Col 44 (HC) Infantry Division RAMC (TA), 1957-62; Col Commandant, RAMC, 1964-69. FRSM; Fellow, Royal Soc. Trop. Med. and Hyg.; Member: Assoc. Clin. Pathologists; Path. Soc. of Gt Britain & Ireland; Cons. Path. Group, BMA; British Society for Immunology; British Association in Forensic Medicine; Associate Member British Association of Plastic Surgeons. KHP, 1951; QHP, 1952-56. FRSA 1972. Mem., Royal Philatelic Soc., London. Liveryman, Co. of Patternmakers. Freeman of City of London. OStJ 1956. *Publications:* articles in Journals of RAMC, IAMC, Roy. United Services Inst.; Proc. Roy. Soc. Med.; Proc. Roy. Soc. Trop. Med. and Hyg.; monthly Bulletin of Min. of Health and Laboratory Service; The Practitioner. *Recreations:* swimming, tennis and philately. *Address:* The Patch, Baldwins Hill, near East Grinstead, W Sussex. *T:* East Grinstead 21570.
[Died 23 Jan. 1976.

SACHS, Rt. Hon. Sir Eric, PC 1966; Kt 1954; MBE 1941; TD; a Lord Justice of Appeal, 1966-73; *b* London, 23 July 1898; *o s* of late Edwin O. Sachs, FRS (Edinburgh), 5 Ulster Tce, Regent's Park; *m* 1934, Hon. Margaret, 2nd *d* of late Baron Goddard of Aldbourne, GCB; one *s* one *d*. *Educ:* Charterhouse; Christ Church, Oxford (Hon. Student, 1971). Served European War, 1917-19, Lieut RA (wounded); recommissioned as 2nd Lieut Aug. 1939; Capt. 1939; Major and DAAG 1940; Lt-Col and AAG 1941; Brig. (specially employed) 1942-45. Called to Bar, Middle Temple, 1921; KC 1938; QC 1952; Leader of the Oxford Circuit, 1952-54; Bencher, 1947, Treasurer, 1967; Recorder of Dudley, 1938-43; Recorder of Stoke-on-Trent, 1943-54; Commissioner of Assize, 1946 (Western Circuit), 1948 (S-Eastern Circuit) and 1953 (Birmingham); Special Commission to Gold Coast (Appeals from Enquiry into Customs, Supplies and Currency Control Depts). 1947; Mem. of Gen. Council of the Bar (Exec. Cttee), 1946-53; Mem. of Legal Aid Committees (Legal Aid Act, 1949), 1948-53; a Judge of the High Court of Justice, Probate, Divorce and Admiralty Div., 1954-60, Queen's Bench Div., 1960-66. Gresham Lecturer on Law, 1948-49. Brig. (late RA, TARO). *Publication:* Legal Aid, 1951. *Recreation:* travel. *Address:* Walland Oast, Wadhurst, E Sussex. *T:* 2080. *Clubs:* Army and Navy, Hurlingham. *[Died 1 Sept. 1979.*

SACKETT, Alfred Barrett, MC; MA Oxon; retired as Headmaster Kingswood School, Bath (1928-59); *b* 1895; *m* 1925, Dorothy E. Salter; four *s* one *d*. *Educ:* Kingswood School, Bath; Merton College, Oxford. Served European War, Gallipoli, Egypt, France, 1915-18; Capt. Northumberland Fusiliers, attached 1/5 Lancashire Fusiliers; Housemaster Christ's Hospital, 1922-28. World Methodist Cttee, 1950-66; 1951-66; Chairman of Governors, Bath Academy of Art, 1959-64. *Publications:* in Proc. of Wesley Historical Soc.: John Wesley and the Greek Orthodox Bishop, 1971-72; John Jones, first after the Wesleys?, 1972; James Rouquet, 1972; John Wesley's Preferment to St Daniel's Church near Pembroke, 1974. *Address:* Tudor Lodge, Greenway Lane, Bath.
[Died 24 Sept. 1977.

SACKS, Mrs Samuel; see Landau, M. E.

SACKVILLE, Col Nigel V. S.; see Stopford Sackville.

SAINSBURY, Air Vice-Marshal T. A. L.; see Langford-Sainsbury.

SAINT, Charles Frederick Morris, CBE 1919; MD, MS Durham, FRCS; Hon. FRACS; Hon. FRSocMed; Hon. Fellow Greek Surgical Society; Hon. FCS (SAf), 1967; Hunterian Professor, RCS England, 1949; Emeritus Professor of Surgery, University, Cape Town; retired; *b* 1886. Formerly Major RAMC; served European War, 1914-19 (despatches, CBE). *Publications:* Surgical Note Taking, 5th Edn (with Prof. J. H. Louw), 1960; (Joint) An Introduction to Surgery, 4th Edn, 1948; An Introduction to Clinical Surgery, 1945, 2nd Edn, 1940. *Address:* Sark, CI. *[Died 15 Feb. 1973.*

SAINT, Captain Peter J. J.; see Johnston-Saint.

ST AUDRIES, 2nd Baron, *cr* 1911; **Alexander Peregrine Fuller-Acland-Hood,** Bt, *cr* 1809, also Bt of Hartington, *cr* 1806; *e s* of

1st Baron, and Hon. Mildred Rose Eveleigh-de-Moleyns (*d* 1949), 2nd *d* of 4th Baron Ventry; *b* 24 Dec. 1893; *S* father, 1917. *Educ:* Eton; Magdalen Coll., Oxford (MA). Lieut Somerset LI and Grenadier Guards (during war only). JP 1923-47, CC 1937-52, Somerset. Patron of 3 livings. CStJ. *Heir:* (to Baronetcies only) *kinsman* Alexander William Fuller-Acland-Hood [*b* 5 March 1901; *m* 1925, Mary Jessup; one *d* (one *s* decd). Naturalized American citizen, 1926]. *Address:* Fairfield, Stogursey, Bridgwater. *T:* Nether Stowey 251.
[Died 16 Oct. 1971.

ST DAVIDS, Elizabeth, Viscountess; Elizabeth Frances Philipps; (Baroness Strange of Knokin, *cr* 1299, Baroness Hungerford, *cr* 1426, Baroness de Moleyns, *cr* 1445, all in her own right; *S* on termination of abeyance, 1921); *b* 19 June 1884; 2nd *d* of late Major Hon. Paulyn Francis Cuthbert Rawdon-Hastings; *m* 1916, 1st Viscount St Davids (*d* 1938); one *s* one *d*. *Heir:* (to Baronies of Strange of Knokin, Hungerford, and de Moleyns) *s* Viscount St Davids. *Address:* 15 St Mark's Crescent, Regent's Park, NW1.
[Died 12 Dec. 1974.

SAINT-DENIS, Michel Jacques (pseudonym **Jacques Duchesne**) Officier de la Légion d'Honneur; actor; dramatic author; producer; Consultant Director of the Royal Shakespeare Theatre Company, since 1966 (Director, 1962-); Co-Director, Juilliard School Drama Division, New York, since 1968; *b* Beauvais, France, 13 Sept. 1897; *s* of Charles Saint-Denis and Marguerite Copeau; *m* 1923, Marie Ostroga (marriage dissolved); one *s* one *d*; *m* Suria Magito. *Educ:* College Rollin, Paris; Lycée de Versailles. Served European War, 1914-18 (Croix de Guerre). Began career as private secretary to Jacques Copeau (his uncle by marriage), at Théâtre du Vieux Colombier, subsequently becoming stage-manager, then stage-director and asst producer at the same theatre; first appearance as an actor, 1922, as Curio in Twelfth Night; remained for ten years with Copeau and Les Copiaux in Burgundy and wrote his first plays in collaboration with Jean Villard; in 1930 founded and was director and producer for La Compagnie des Quinze; he also acted in the plays produced; made first appearance in London as Lucas in Le Médecin Malgré Lui, in 1927, at the St James's; appeared at Arts and New Theatres, 1931; toured with his company in Europe; founded the London Theatre Studio, Islington, 1935 (Managing Director); produced Noah, with John Gielgud, New Theatre, 1935; Sowers of the Hills, Westminster, 1935; The Witch of Edmonton, with Dame Edith Evans, Old Vic, 1936; Macbeth, with Sir Laurence Olivier, Old Vic, 1937; Three Sisters, with Dame Peggy Ashcroft, Sir John Gielgud, Michael Redgrave, Sir Alec Guinness, Queens, 1938; The White Guard, Phœnix, 1938; Twelfth Night, with Michael Redgrave, Phœnix, 1938; The Marriage of Blood, with Martita Hunt, Savoy, 1939; Weep for the Spring, 1939; also produced shows at the London Theatre Studio, including The Electra of Sophocles, and The Alcestis of Euripides. Served War of 1939-45 (Rosette de la Résistance): mobilised in Infanterie Coloniale, 1939-40; Officier de liaison at English GHQ; Head of French Section, BBC, under pseudonym Jaques Duchesne, 1940-44; instigation of English Service of Radiodiffusion française, 1944-45. Foundation of Old Vic Theatre Centre and School, 1946; Director-General, 1946-52. Productions for the Old Vic since 1945, include: Œdipus Rex, with Sir Laurence Olivier; A Month in the Country, with Michael Redgrave; Electra, with Dame Peggy Ashcroft; King John, etc. Supervised (with Pierre Sonrel) complete reconstruction of stage and auditorium for re-opening of Old Vic, Waterloo Road, 1951. Foundation, under French Govt auspices, of Centre National Dramatique de l'Est. Strasbourg (Dir.-Gen., 1952-57). Has visited Russia; Canada at invitation of Canadian govt, to study foundation of Canadian Theatre and Theatre-school (opening Montreal, Nov. 1960), and US at invitation of Rockefeller Foundation, 1958. Inspecteur Général des Spectacles, 1959-; Special Consultant for foundation of Repertory Theatre and Drama School, Lincoln Square, New York, 1960; Co-Director, Royal Shakespeare Theatre, Stratford-on-Avon, 1962. Produced: Œdipus Rex, Sadler's Wells, 1960; The Cherry Orchard, Aldwych, 1965; Squire Puntila and his Servant Matti, Aldwych, 1965. Internat. Award, 1969, of Internat. Theatre Inst. and Amer. Educnl Theatre. Hon. DLitt Birmingham Univ., 1962; Hon. LHD Dartmouth College, Hanover, USA, 1962. Hon. Fellow, Royal College of Art, 1963. CBE (Hon.); Chevalier de l'Ordre de Léopold. *Publications:* Theatre: The Rediscovery of Style, 1960; articles in theatrical jls, etc. *Recreations:* travelling, driving, music, fishing. *Address:* 2 Bloomfield Terrace, SW1.
[Died 31 July 1971.

ST HELENS, 1st Baron *cr* 1964; **Michael Henry Colin Hughes-Young,** MC 1944; *b* 28 Oct. 1912; *s* of late Brig.-Gen. H. G. Young, CIE, DSO; *m* 1939, Elizabeth Agnes Blakiston-Houston (*d* 1956); one *s* three *d* (and *er s* decd). *Educ:* Harrow; Sandhurst. Joined Black Watch, 1932; attached French Army,

1934; seconded King's African Rifles, 1935; Abyssinian War and Invasion of Europe, 1940 and 1944 (wounded twice); retired as Lt-Col, 1947. Contested (C) St Helens, 1951; Conservative Central Office, 1948-55; MP (C) Wandsworth Central, 1955-64; PPS to Minister of State, Board of Trade, March-April 1956; Assistant Whip (unpaid), 1956-58, a Lord Commissioner of the Treasury, 1958-62, Dep. Govt Chief Whip, 1959-64, and Treasurer of HM Household, 1962-64. *Heir:* s Hon. Richard Francis Hughes-Young, *b* 4 Nov. 1945. *Address:* Marchfield, Binfield, Berks. *T:* Bracknell 3338. *Club:* Carlton.
[Died 27 Dec. 1980.

ST JOHN of BLETSO, 19th Baron, *cr* 1558, 16th Bt, 1660; **John Moubray Russell St John;** *b* 3 Aug. 1917; *o s* of 18th Baron and Evelyn Geraldine (*d* 1918), *d* of late Captain Andrew Hamilton Russell; *S* father, 1934. *Heir: cousin,* Andrew Beauchamp St John, TD [*b* 23 Aug. 1918; *m* 1955, Katharine, *y d* of late Alfred G. Berg; one *s*].
[Died 13 April 1976.

ST JOHN OF BLETSO, 20th Baron *cr* 1558; **Andrew Beauchamp St John,** TD 1952; Bt 1660; *b* 23 Aug. 1918; 3rd *s* of Lt-Col Hon. Rowland Tudor St John (*d* 1948) (3rd *s* of 16th Baron) and Katharine Madge (*d* 1954), *d* of late Sir Frank Lockwood, QC, MP; *S* cousin, 1976; *m* 1955, Katharine von Berg; one *s*. *Educ:* Wellington College. Joined Bank of England, 1937. Served War of 1939-45 with Indian Army. Commanded Tower Hamlets Regt (TA), 1951-54. Emigrated to South Africa 1957, joining Syfret's Trust Company in Cape Town. *Recreations:* painting, golf. *Heir: s* Hon. Anthony Tudor St John, *b* 16 May 1957. *Address:* c/o Syfret's Trust Company Ltd, 24 Wale Street, Cape Town 8001, S Africa. *Clubs:* Naval and Military; City, Netherlands, Western Province Sports (Cape Town).
[Died 11 Feb. 1978.

ST JOHN, Geoffrey Robert, MC; *s* of late H. P. St John and Maud Louisa, *d* of Hon. Pascoe Charles Glyn; *b* 4 Jan. 1889; *heir pres* to 6th Viscount Bolingbroke; *m* 1st, 1914, Gwendolen I. (who obtained a divorce, 1924), *o c* of H. Okeden, Stutton House, Suffolk; 2nd, 1925, Katharine M. (who obtained a divorce, 1940; she *d* 1958), *o d* of A. S. J. Musgrave, Abbeylands, Settle, Yorks; two *s* one *d*; 3rd, 1941, Mary Violet Handley Mills (*d* 1951), *niece* and *adopted d* of late John Mills, Maffra, Vic, Australia; 4th, 1957, Brynhildr, *d* of late Harold Archdall Vicars and *widow* of W. Bryant Purkis. *Educ:* Marlborough; Magdalen Coll., Oxford. Served with Royal Fusiliers, European War, 1914-19 (despatches, MC). Secretary of the Over 45's Assoc., from 1957. *Address:* Haytos Lodge, Newport, Essex. *T:* Newport (Essex) 650.
[Died 4 Oct. 1972.

ST JOHN, Lt-Col Oliver Charles Beauchamp, CMG 1963; with Foreign Office, 1948-68; *b* 23 Oct. 1907; *s* of late Lt-Col Sir Henry Beauchamp St John, KCIE, CBE, and late Olive Amy Herbert; *m* 1935, Elizabeth Mary Lambton (*d* 1957); one *s* three *d*; *m* 1966, Mrs Mary Maxwell-Gumbleton. *Educ:* Charterhouse; RMC, Sandhurst. XXth Lancers, IA, 1928-32; Indian Political Service, 1932-47; numerous appts in IPS including Asst Private Sec. to Viceroy, 1932-34; Prime Minister, Alwar State, 1936; Political Agent, Western Kathiawar, 1937; Sec. to Governor, NWFP, 1942-46; Dep. Comr, Hazara, 1947-48. *Recreations:* shooting, fishing, riding, golf. *Address:* Curtle Cottage, Beaulieu, Brockenhurst, Hants SO4 7YF. *T:* Beaulieu 612268. *Clubs:* Naval and Military, Hurlingham.
[Died 4 April 1976.

ST JOHN PERSE; *see* Leger, M.-R. A. St-L.

ST LAURENT, Rt. Hon. Louis Stephen, CC (Canada) 1967; PC 1946; LLD, QC 1915; Prime Minister of Canada, 1948-57; Leader of Canadian Liberal Party, 1948-58; MP Quebec-East, 1942-58; *b* Compton, Que, 1 Feb. 1882; *s* of J. B. M. St Laurent and Mary Anne Broderick; *m* 1908, Jeanne (*d* 1966), *d* of P. F. Renault, Beauceville, Quebec; two *s* three *d*. *Educ:* St Charles College, Sherbrooke; Laval University, Quebec (BA). Called to Bar of Quebec, 1905; Prof. Law Faculty, Laval Univ., 1914; formerly of St Laurent, Gagne, Devlin, and Taschereau, now of St Laurent, Monast, Desmeules and Walters, advocates, 500 E Grande Allée, Quebec, Que; Pres. Canadian Bar Assoc., 1930-32, now Hon. Life Pres. Minister of Justice and Attorney-General, 1941-46 and 1948; Minister of External Affairs, 1946-48. Chairman Can. Delegation to UN General Assembly, 1946, 1947. Liberal; Roman Catholic; Hon. LLD: Laval Univ. 1915; Queen's Univ., 1930; Univ. of Manitoba, 1935; Univ. of Montreal, 1943; Bishop's Coll., 1943; Dalhousie Univ., 1947; Univ. of Ottawa, 1947; Dartmouth Univ., 1948; McGill Univ., 1949; Rensselaer Polytechnic Inst., 1949; St Louis Univ. 1950; St Lawrence Univ., 1950; Univ. of Toronto, 1950; Univ. of Western Ont, 1951; Northwestern Univ., 1951; Univ. of BC, 1952; London Univ., 1952; St Francis Xavier Univ., 1953; Peshawar

Univ., 1954; Delhi Univ., 1954; Univ. of Sask, 1963; RMC of Canada, 1964; Hon. DCL: Mount Allison, 1952; Oxford Univ., 1953. Freedom of City of London, 1955. *Address:* 201 East Grand Allee, Quebec, Canada. *Clubs:* Garrison (Quebec); Cercle Universitaire, University (Montreal); Rideau Country (Ottawa).
[Died 25 July 1973.

ST LEONARDS, 3rd Baron (*cr* 1852), **Frank Edward Sugden;** *b* 11 Nov. 1890; *o surv s* of late Hon. Henry Frank Sugden and Edith, *e d* of Abraham Bowman of Stangrove, Edenbridge; *S* uncle, 1908. *Educ:* Westminster; Christ Church Oxford. Late Lt Royal Horse Guards (Reserve). Owns about 4600 acres. *Heir: kinsman,* John Gerard Sugden, *b* 3 Feb. 1950. *Club:* St James'.
[Died 18 July 1972.

ST LEVAN, 3rd Baron *cr* 1887; **Francis Cecil St Aubyn;** Bt 1866; JP; DL; late Major Gren. Guards; Colonel Home Guard; *b* 18 April 1895; *s* of late Hon. A. J. D. Stuart St Aubyn; *S* uncle 1940; *m* 1916, Hon. Clementina Gwendolen Catharine Nicolson, *o d* of 1st Baron Carnock; three *s* two *d. Educ:* Eton; Sandhurst. Served European War, 1914-15 (wounded); rejoined Grenadier Guards 1939-42. DL for County of Cornwall, 1961. *Heir: s* Hon. John Francis Arthur St Aubyn, DSC. *Address:* Avallon, Green Lane, Marazion, Cornwall. *T:* 22. *Clubs:* Army and Navy; Royal Cornwall Yacht.
[Died 10 July 1978.

SALE, John Lewis, CIE 1930; FICE; Public Works Dept, retired 1934; *b* 24 Aug. 1885; *s* of late Sir Stephen George Sale, KCIE; *m* 1924, Helen Caroline Ommanney, *d* of late Sir Ralph Sneyd Pearson, CIE; three *s. Educ:* Marlborough; RIEC, Cooper's Hill. Served European War, 1915-19; JP (Berks); CC 1937; CA 1950. *Address:* Priors Hold, Wantage, Berks. *T:* Wantage 2161.
[Died 5 April 1973.

SALE, Brigadier Walter Morley, CVO 1952; OBE 1944; Extra Equerry to the Queen, since 1961; *b* 1903; *s* of Charles Sale, late of Aston Rowant House, Oxon; *m* 1928, Hon. Ismay Hilda Margaret FitzRoy, *d* of 4th Baron Southampton; one *s* one *d. Educ:* RN Colls, Osborne and Dartmouth; New Coll., Oxford (BA). Royal Horse Guards: joined 1924; Captain, 1930; Major, 1936; Lt-Col, 1940; Brig. 1945. Served on staff with Guards Armoured Division and in Command of 1st Household Cavalry Regt (despatches twice); Chief of Staff, London District, 1950-54. Equerry to the Queen, 1954; Crown Equerry, 1955-61. Croix de Guerre with Palm, 1945; Chevalier Order of Leopold II with Palm (Belgium), 1945. *Recreation:* shooting. *Address:* Heveningham House, Halesworth, Suffolk. *T:* Ubbeston 348.
[Died 29 Aug. 1976.

SALISBURY, 5th Marquess of, *cr* 1789; **Robert Arthur James Gascoyne-Cecil;** KG 1946; PC 1940; FRS; Baron Cecil 1603; Viscount Cranborne, 1604; Earl of Salisbury, 1605; late Lt 5th (Res.) Batt. Grenadier Guards; Chancellor, Order of the Garter, since 1960; High Steward of Hertford, since 1947; Chancellor, University of Liverpool, 1951-71; Chairman of the Royal Commission on Historical Monuments, since 1957; *b* 27 August 1893; *e s* of 4th Marquess of Salisbury, KG, GCVO, and Lady Cicely Alice Gore (*d* 1955), *d* of 5th Earl of Arran; *S* father 1947; *m* 1915, Elizabeth Vere, *e d* of late Lord Richard Cavendish, PC, CB, CMG; one *s. Educ:* Eton; Christ Church, Oxford. MP (U) South Dorset, 1929-41; Parliamentary Under-Sec. of State for Foreign Affairs, 1935-38; Paymaster-General, 1940; Secretary of State for Dominion Affairs, 1940-42; called to House of Lords as Baron Cecil of Essendon, 1941; Secretary of State for the Colonies, 1942; Lord Privy Seal, 1942-43, 1951-52; Secretary of State for Dominion Affairs, 1943-45; Leader of the House of Lords, 1942-45, 1951-57; Secretary of State for Commonwealth Relations, 1952, Lord Pres. of Council, 1952-57. Trustee, National Gallery, 1959-66. Director: Westminster Bank Ltd, 1957-68; British S Africa Co., 1957-61. *Heir: s* Viscount Cranborne. *Address:* Hatfield House, Hatfield, Hertfordshire. *T:* Hatfield 62702; Cranborne Lodge, Cranborne, Dorset. *T:* Cranborne 225; 2 Swan Walk, Chelsea, SW3. *T:* 01-352 6666. *Clubs:* Carlton, Turf, Buck's.
[Died 23 Feb. 1972.

SALISBURY, Sir Edward James, Kt 1946; CBE 1939; FRS 1933; DSc, Hon. LLD (Edinburgh and Glasgow); VMH; FLS; Director, Royal Botanic Gardens, Kew, 1943-56; Vice-Chairman, Agricultural Improvement Council, 1944-56; Chairman, Joint Committee of AIC and ARC, 1944-59; Mem. Cttee on Higher Agricultural Educn, 1944; Scientific Advisory Cttee to Cabinet, 1943-45; Vice-Pres. RHS; Hon. Adviser Ministry of Labour; Vice-Chm. Cttee on Colonial Agricultural Research, 1945; Fullerton Prof. of Physiology, Royal Instn, 1947-52; Leader of British Delegation to Australian Conference on Plant and Animal Nutrition, 1949; *b* 16 April 1886; *y s* of J. Wright Salisbury, of Limbrick Hall, Harpenden; *m* Mabel (*d* 1956), *d* of J. Elwin-Coles. *Educ:* University College School and

University College, London. Gold Medal in Botany, BSc Hons Botany, Research Medal, Quain Student University College, DSc; Senior Lecturer East London College, 1914-18; Lecturer University College, 1918; Reader in Plant Ecology, 1924; formerly Quain Professor of Botany, Univ. of London, University Coll.; Fellow of University Coll., 1920; Vice-Pres., Royal Society, 1943, 1948-55 (Biological Secretary, 1945-55); Pres. SE Union Sci. Societies, 1932; President British Ecological Society, 1928; Pres. Herts NHS, 1922-25; Pres. Norfolk and Norwich Nat. Soc., 1931; VP Linnean Society, 1928; Pres. Section K British Association, 1937; Pres. School Nature Study Union, 1938-44; Pres. Science Masters' Association, 1955; Hon. Sec. British Ecological Soc., 1917-32; Veitchian Gold Medal, 1936; Master's Memorial Lecturer, 1937, 1962; Symonds Memorial Lecturer, 1939; Amos Memorial Lecturer, 1950; Des Vœux Lecturer, 1954; Hon. Fellow Botanical Society of Edinburgh, 1938; Fellow Queen Mary College, London University, 1938; formerly Governor: Royal Holloway College; Queen Mary Coll.; East Malling Research Station; Trustee Lawes Agricultural Trust; Chm. Commonwealth Bursaries Cttee, 1953-66; Mem. of Senate, Univ. of London, 1934-44; Mem. Univ. Grants Cttee, 1944-49; Percy Sladen Trustee, 1939-66; Member of Agricultural Research Council, 1940-44; President: Sussex Naturalists' Trust, 1961-68; Bee Research Assoc., 1964. Hon. Member: Brit. Ecological Soc., 1958; Botanical Soc. of British Isles, 1968. Hon. FInstBiol. Royal Medal of Royal Society, 1945; Hon. Freeman, Worshipful Co. of Gardeners, 1951; VMH 1953. *Publications:* numerous technical papers; article Ecology, in Encyclopædia Britannica; An Introduction to the Study of Plants, 1914, 9th edn 1928; An Introduction to the Structure and Reproduction of Plants, 1920, 2nd edn 1927; Elementary Studies in Plant Life, 1915, 8th edn 1926; Botany for Medical Students, 1921, 3rd edn 1928; The East Anglian Flora, 1933; The Living Garden, 1935, 2nd edn 1942, German edn 1936, American edn 1936; Plant Form and Function, 1938-54; The Reproductive Capacity of Plants, 1942; Flowers of the Woods, 1946; Downs and Dunes, 1952; Weeds and Aliens, 1961; The Biology of Garden Weeds, 1962. *Recreations:* walking, gardening. *Address:* Croindene, Strandway, Felpham, Bognor Regis, West Sussex PO22 7LH.
[Died 10 Nov. 1978.

SALMON, Sir Julian, Kt 1969; CBE 1957 (OBE (mil.) 1943); Chairman, Luncheon Vouchers Catering Education Trust, since 1965, Research Institute, since 1966; Director: Sweetheart Plastics Ltd, since 1969 (Chairman, 1969-72); Spey Investments Ltd, since 1969; *b* 29 Aug. 1903; *s* of late Sir Isidore Salmon, CBE, MP; *m* 1930, Anne Handelman. *Educ:* Repton; Jesus College, Cambridge. BA, LLB, 1924. Served War of 1939-45, RAFVR (Wing Comdr). Hon. Catering Adviser to the Royal Air Force, 1939-71. Dir, J. Lyons & Co. Ltd, 1938-69 (Dep. Chm., 1965-69). Chm., Hotel and Catering Ind. Trng Bd, 1966-73. Fellow, Hotel and Catering Inst., 1949-71; FHCIMA 1971-73, Hon. Fellow, 1973-. Member: Corbett Cttee on Navy, Army and Air Force Insts, 1961; Deptl Cttee on Jury Service, 1963. Member: W London Hosp. Hse Cttee, 1959-73 (Vice-Chm., 1967-73); Bd of Governors, Charing Cross Hosp., 1961-73; Cassell Hosp. Management Cttee, 1972-73. Chairman of Managers, 1953-76, Chm. of Trustees, 1972-, Finnart House, Community Home, Weybridge; Mem. Management Cttee, Mathilda and Terence Kennedy Inst. of Rheumatology, 1975-. *Address:* 54 Melbury Court, W8. *T:* 01-602 3203. *Club:* Carlton.
[Died 22 Dec. 1978.

SALMON, Sir Samuel (Isidore), Kt 1960; President, J. Lyons & Company Ltd, 1968-72 (Chairman, 1965-68); *b* 18 Oct. 1900; *s* of late Sir Isidore Salmon, CBE, DL, JP, MP, and of Lady Salmon; *m* 1937, Lallah Wendy, *d* of Alexander and Hannah Benjamin; one *s* one *d. Educ:* Bedales School, Petersfield; Jesus College, Cambridge (MA). LCC Member for Cities of London and Westminster, 1949-65; Deputy Chairman, LCC, 1959-60; (elected) GLC Mem. for City of Westminster, 1964-67; Mayor of London Borough of Hammersmith, 1968-69. Chm., Metropolitan Water Bd, 1970-. Formerly: Chm., Palace Hotel Ltd; Dir, Cadogan Investments Ltd. Governor, Regent Street Polytechnic, 1950-. *Recreations:* bridge, reading. *Address:* 14 Carlos Place, W1. *T:* 01-629 6217. *Clubs:* Carlton, 1900, Leander.
[Died 10 Nov. 1980.

SALT, Dame Barbara, DBE 1963 (CBE 1959; MBE 1946); *b* 30 Sept. 1904; *d* of Reginald J. Salt, *y s* of Sir Thomas Salt, 1st Bt (sometime MP for Stafford and Chairman of Lloyds Bank) and of Maud Fanny (*née* Wigram). *Educ:* The Downs School, Seaford, Sussex; Munich Univ., Germany. Served with HM Consulate-General, Tangier, 1942-46; Principal in Foreign Office, 1946-49; First Secretary (Commercial), Moscow, 1950-51; First Secretary, Washington, 1951-55; Counsellor, Washington, 1955-57; Counsellor and Consul-General at the

British Embassy, Tel Aviv, Israel, 1957-60; HM Minister, UK Permanent Delegation to Ten Power Disarmament Committee, Geneva, 1960; British representative on the Economic and Social Council of the United Nations, 1961-62; appointed HM Ambassador to Tel Aviv, 1962 (did not proceed); Leader, UK Delegation, Anglo/Israel Financial Negotiations, 1963-64; Leader, UK delegn to Anglo-Roumanian Negotiations, London, 1966; Head of SOE Section, FCO, 1967-72. Patron, Monopeds Assoc.; co-Patron, Rowenstall Rovers Football Club. *Recreations:* reading, gardening, motoring. *Address:* 17B, Montagu Square, W1. *T:* 01-935 8624. *Club:* New Century.
[Died 28 Dec. 1975.

SALT, Sir David Shirley, 5th Bt, *cr* 1869; *b* 14 June 1930; *s* of 4th Bt and Stella Houlton (*d* 1974), 2nd *d* of Richard Houlton Jackson, MRCS, LRCP, Bakewell, Derbyshire; *S* father 1953; *m* 1st, 1955, Margaret Gillian (marr. diss. 1974), *d* of H. Alwyn Lenox, 31 Markham Square, SW3; 2nd, 1975, Freda Evelyn Blows. *Educ:* Stowe. *Heir: b* Anthony Houlton Salt [*b* 15 Sept. 1931; *m* 1957, Prudence Meath Baker; four *d*]. *Address:* c/o Lloyd's Bank Ltd, 61 Moorgate, EC2.   *[Died 3 Dec. 1978.*

SALT, Maj.-Gen. Harold Francis, CB 1932; CMG 1919; DSO 1918; late RA; psc; *b* 30 Dec. 1879; *y s* of late Sir Thomas Salt, 1st Bt; *m* 1914, Phyllis Dulce (*d* 1965), *d* of late Major E. D. Cameron, RFA; two *d. Educ:* RIEC, Coopers Hill. Joined Army, 1900; Lieut 1901; Capt. 1908; Major, 1914; Brevet Lt-Colonel, 1918; Bt-Col 1919; Col 1919; Maj.-Gen., 1931; GSO 3rd Grade, Scottish Command, 1914; Brigade Major, RA, 11th Division 1915; GSO 2nd Grade, 10th Division, 1916-17; GSO, 1st Grade, 10th Division, 1917-18; Brigadier-General, General Staff, 21st Corps, 1918-19; Instructor Senior Officers' School, Belgaum, India; Asst-Commandant, Royal Military Academy, Woolwich, 1925-29; Comdr RA 54th (East Anglian) Division, TA 1930-31; Comdr Territorial Army Air Defence Formations 1931-35; Deputy Adjutant General (Director of Organization) Army HQs, India, 1935-36; Deputy Quartermaster General, Army HQ India, 1936-39; retired pay, 1939; served European War Gallipoli (Suvla Bay), Salonika, Palestine, and Syria (despatches thrice, DSO, CMG, Order of the Nile, 3rd Class). *Address:* Saffron Gardens, Winchelsea, Rye, Sussex.
[Died 10 Aug. 1971.

SALTER, 1st Baron, *cr* 1953, of Kidlington; **(James) Arthur Salter;** PC 1941; GBE 1944; KCB 1922 (CB 1918); *b* Oxford, 15 March 1881; *s* of late James E. Salter, Oxford; *m* 1940, Mrs Arthur Bullard (*d* 1969), *widow* of Arthur Bullard, of Washington, DC. *Educ:* Oxford High School; Brasenose College, Oxford. Transport Department, Admiralty, 1904; Assistant Secretary National Health Insurance Commission, England, 1913; Director of Ship Requisitioning, 1917; Secretary of Allied Maritime Transport Council and Chairman of Allied Maritime Transport Executive, 1918; Supreme Economic Council, 1919; General Secretary Reparation Commission, 1920-22; Director Economic and Finance Section League of Nations, June 1919-Jan. 1920, and 1922-31; Missions to India, 1930, China, 1931 and 1933; Chairman Road-Rail Conference, 1932; Gladstone Professor of Political Theory and Institutions, Oxford University, 1934-44; Chairman of Railway Staff National Tribunal, 1936-39. MP (Ind) Oxford University, 1937-50; Parliamentary Secretary to Ministry of Shipping, 1939-41; Joint Parliamentary Secretary to Ministry of War Transport, 1941, and Head of British Merchant Shipping Mission, Washington, 1941-43; Senior Deputy Director-General UNRRA, 1944; Chancellor of the Duchy of Lancaster, 1945; Chairman Advisory Council of International Bank, 1947-48. MP (C) Ormskirk Division of Lancashire, 1951-53; Minister of State for Economic Affairs, 1951-Nov. 1952; Minister of Materials, Nov. 1952-53. Officier de la Couronne Belgique, 1919; Commandeur de la Légion d'Honneur, 1920; Commendatore Order of the Crown of Italy, 1922; Brilliant Jade (China), 1937; Hon. Fellow BNC and Fellow of All Souls; Hon. DCL Oxford and hon. doctorates at Manchester, Vienna, Harvard, Columbia, McGill, University of California, Amherst. *Publications:* Allied Shipping Control; An Experiment in International Administration, 1921; Recovery, 1932; The Framework of an Ordered Society, 1933; The United States of Europe, 1933; World Trade and its Future, 1936; Security, 1939; Personality in Politics, 1947; Memoirs of a Public Servant, 1961; Slave of the Lamp, 1967. *Heir:* none. *Address:* West House, 35 Glebe Place, Chelsea, SW3. *T:* 01-352 7091; All Souls College, Oxford. *Club:* Reform.   *[Died 27 June 1975 (ext).*

SALTOUN, 19th Lord, *cr* 1445, of Abernethy; **Alexander Arthur Fraser,** MC; a Representative Peer for Scotland, 1935-63; *b* 8 March 1886; *e s* of 18th Lord and Mary (*d* 1940), *o d* of Thomas Arthur Grattan-Bellew, MP; *S* father, 1933; *m* 1920, Dorothy, *e d* of Sir Charles Welby, 5th Bt; one *d* (one *s* killed in action).

Late Sub-Lieutenant Forfar and Kincardine Artillery Militia: Captain, retired, 3rd Battalion Gordon Highlanders; prisoner of war, 1914-18. Grand Master Mason of Scotland, 1934-36. Formerly Vice-Convener, RNLI for Scotland, 1945-53, Convener, 1953-59. *Heiress: d* Hon. Flora Marjory Fraser [*b* 18 Oct. 1930; *m* 1956, Captain Alexander Ramsay, Grenadier Guards, *o s* of late Adm. Hon. Sir Alexander Ramsay, GCVO, KCB, DSO, and The Lady Patricia Ramsay, CI, VA; three *d*]. *Address:* Cairnbulg Castle, Fraserburgh; Cross Deep, Twickenham. *Clubs:* Athenæum; New (Edinburgh).
[Died 31 Aug. 1979.

SALZMAN, Louis Francis, CBE 1955; MA, FSA; *b* 26 March 1878; *s* of Dr F. W. Salzman, Brighton; *m* 1904, Maud, *d* of Rev. G. M. Russell; two *s* two *d. Educ:* Haileybury; Pembroke College, Cambridge. Editor, Victoria County Histories, 1934-49; Hon. editor, Sussex Archæological Society, 1909-59 (Pres., 1954-56); Master St George's School, Harpenden and Captain 4th Herts Cadets, 1916-18. Hon. DLitt, Sussex, 1965. *Publications:* Henry II, 1914; English Industries of the Middle Ages, 1913 and 1923; Medieval Byways, 1913; More Medieval Byways, 1926; The Girdle of Venus, a play, 1922; English Life in the Middle Ages, 1926; England in Tudor Times, 1926; A Survey of English History, 1930; English Trade in the Middle Ages, 1931; A Documentary History of Building in England Down to 1540, 1951 and 1967; A Random Scrap Book, 1957; Edward I, 1968, etc. *Address:* 12 Houndean Rise, Lewes, Sussex. *T:* 4882.   *[Died 4 April 1971.*

SAMBELL, Most Rev. Geoffrey Tremayne; *b* 28 Oct. 1914; *s* of E. Sambell, Violet Town, Vic.; single. *Educ:* Melbourne High Sch.; Melbourne University. ThL 1939; BA 1946. Deacon 1940; Priest, 1941. Army Chaplain, 1942-46 and 1949-58; Dir., Melbourne Diocesan Centre, 1947-62; Archdeacon of Essendon, 1955-61; Bishop Co-adjutor, Diocese of Melbourne, 1962-69; Archdeacon of Melbourne, 1961-69; Archbishop of Perth and Metropolitan of W Australia, 1969-80. Dir, Brotherhood of St Laurence, 1956-68. Pres., Victorian Coun. of Social Services, 1956-58; Chm., Nat. Consultative Council on Social Welfare, 1976-80. Fellow, Australian Coll. of Theology (Th.Soc.), 1962. *Recreation:* golf. *Address:* c/o Archdiocese of Perth, Church Office, GPO Box W2067, Perth, Western Australia 6001. *Clubs:* Melbourne, Royal Automobile of Victoria (Melbourne); West Australia, Weld, Lake Karrinyup (all Perth).
[Died 19 Dec. 1980.

Award of CMG gazetted, 31 Dec. 1980.

SAMPSON, Jack; *see* Sampson, Jacob Albert.

SAMPSON, Jacob Albert, (Jack Sampson); President, United Drapery Stores Ltd, 1971-74 (Chairman, 1966-71); also Director of United Drapery Stores subsidiary companies; *b* 15 March 1905; *m* 1927, Cissie Okin; one *d.* Entered family shoe business, 1920; joined Great Universal Stores Ltd, 1938 (Dir, 1942); resigned, 1946, to become Managing Dir of John Blundell Ltd, a subsidiary of United Drapery Stores Ltd; Dir, United Drapery Stores Ltd, 1947 (Managing Dir, 1959; Chm., 1966). *Address:* United Drapery Stores Ltd, Marble Arch House, Seymour Street, W1.   *[Died 17 Feb. 1976.*

SAMSON, Sir Frederick; *see* Samson, Sir W. F.

SAMSON, Otto William, PhD (Hamburg), FMA, FRAS, FRGS, FRAI; Wellcome Research Fellowship, 1965-67; Curator, Horniman Museum and Library, 1947-65; *b* Hamburg, 1 March 1900; *s* of Martin Samson and Mathilde Kallmes; *m* 1948, Muriel Elizabeth Williams (*née* Richards). *Educ:* Universities of Freiburg im Breisgau, Berlin, Munich, Hamburg. Assistant Keeper, Museum of Ethnography, Hamburg, 1928-30; Keeper, Far Eastern Dept, 1930-33; Ethnographical research for Hamburg Museum in China, 1931-32; Research work, physical anthropology, Galton Lab., Univ. of London, 1933; awarded Tweedie Exploration Fellowship for archæology and anthropology, Univ. of Edinburgh, travelling in India, Tibet, Burma, 1935-37; research work on Djebel Moya osteological material, Galton Lab., Univ. of London, 1937-39; Ethnographical Dept, British Museum, 1939, temp. Asst Keeper, 1942-47. Hon. Librarian, Royal Anthropological Inst., 1942-46. *Recreations:* reading and walking. *Address:* 1a Taymount Rise, SE23. *T:* 01-699 8245. *[Died 12 March 1976.*

SAMSON, Sir (William) Frederick, Kt 1962; Mayor of Fremantle 1951-72, retired; *b* 12 Jan. 1892; *s* of Michael and Mary Samson; *m* 1935, Daphne Alice Marks; no *c. Educ:* Christian Brothers College, Fremantle and Perth; University of W Australia. On construction reservoir and sewer mains, Metropolitan Water Supply, Sewerage and Drainage Dept, Perth, 1913-18; Surveyor with Crossland and Hardy, Perth, 1919-24; Partnership with late W. H. Shields, Engineering and

Surveying, 1925-31; since 1931, Real Estate Agent. Fellow Commonwealth Inst. of Valuers. Chm., Home Building Soc. Inc.; Mem. State Electricity Commn, WA; past Pres. Rotary Club of Fremantle; Mem. WA Cricket Assoc. Cricket Cttee, 1913-47; past Pres. Fremantle Cricket Club, Fremantle Horticultural Soc.; formerly Pres., Fremantle Chamber of Commerce; Pres., WA Rifle Assoc. First Freeman, City of Fremantle. Hon. Fellow, Royal Australian Planning Inst. *Recreations:* rifle shooting, gardening, photography. *Address:* 61 Ellen Street, Fremantle, Western Australia 6160. *T:* 35-2553; (Office) 5 Queen Street, Fremantle, Western Australia 6160. *T:* 35-6322. *Clubs:* Naval, Military and Air Force (Perth); Commercial (Fremantle). *[Died 6 Feb. 1974.*

SAMUEL, 2nd Viscount, *cr* 1937, of Mount Carmel and of Toxteth, Liverpool; **Edwin Herbert Samuel,** CMG 1947; Colonial Service, retired; Principal of the Institute of Public Administration in Israel; *b* 11 Sept. 1898; *e s* of 1st Viscount Samuel, PC, GCB, OM, GBE, and Beatrice (*d* 1959), *y d* of Ellis A. Franklin; *S* father, 1963; *m* 1920, Hadassah Goor; two *s.* *Educ:* Westminster School; Balliol Coll., Oxford (BA); Commonwealth Fund Fellow, Columbia University, 1931-32. 2nd Lieut RFA and GSI, GHQ, EEF, 1917-19; District Officer: Jerusalem, Ramallah, and Jaffa, 1920-27; Assistant Secretary, Government of Palestine, 1927-30; Assistant District Comr, Galilee, 1933-34; Deputy Comr for Migration, 1934-39; Postal and Telegraph Censor, Jerusalem, 1939-42; Chief Censor and (from 1944) Press Censor, 1942-45; Director of Broadcasting, 1945-48; Visiting Professor in Middle East Govt, Dropsie College, Philadelphia, 1948-49; European Director of the Conquest of the Desert, International Exhibition, Jerusalem, 1951-53; Sen. Lectr in British Institutions, Hebrew Univ., Jerusalem, 1954-69; Visiting Lectr in Public Administration, Univ. of the Witwatersrand, 1955; Visiting Professor: in Political Science, Graduate School of Public Affairs, Albany State Univ. of New York, 1963; in Public Admin, Graduate Sch. of Public and Internat. Affairs, Pittsburgh Univ., 1970; Dept of Urban Affairs, Univ. of Miami, Fla, 1971. A Director: the Jewish Chronicle, London, 1951-70; Vallentine Mitchell (publishers), London, 1965-; Ellern Investment Corp. Ltd, Tel Aviv, 1964-; Moller Textile Corporation, Nahariya, 1965-77; Adviser to the Magen David Adom (Israel Nat. Red Cross Society) on publicity and public relations, 1957-75; Mem. of Council: Anglo-Israel Assoc., London; Anglo-Jewish Assoc., London; Labour Friends of Israel, London; (British) Friends of the Hebrew University, etc. *Publications:* A Primer on Palestine, 1932; Handbook of the Jewish Communal Villages, 1938 and 1945; The Children's Community of Mishmar HaEmek, 1942; The Theory of Administration, 1947; Problems of Government in the State of Israel, 1956; British Traditions in the Administration of Israel, 1957; Anglo-Israel Relations, 1948-1968: a catalogue, 1969; Structure of Society in Israel, 1969; A Lifetime in Jerusalem: memoirs, 1970; See How They Run: the administration of venerable institutions, 1976; Israel's Immigration Cycle, 1976; A Cottage in Galilee (short stories), 1957; A Coat of Many Colours (short stories), 1960; My Friend Musa (short stories), 1963; The Cucumber King (short stories), 1965; Capt. Noah and His Ark (illustrated children's story), 1965; His Celestial Highness (short stories), 1968; The Man Who Liked Cats (short stories), 1975; (with M. Kamrat) Roots (Hebrew-English Lexicon), 1970. *Heir: s* Prof. The Hon. David Herbert Samuel, MA, PhD [*b* 8 July 1922; *m* 1st, 1950, Esther Berelowitz (marr. diss., 1957), Cape Town; one *d*; 2nd, 1960, Mrs Rinna Dafni, *d* of late Meir Grossman, Israel; one *d*]. *Address:* House of Lords, SW1; 15 Rashba Road, Jerusalem, Israel. *T:* 33871. *[Died 14 Nov. 1978.*

SANCHEZ-GAVITO, Vicente, GCVO (Hon.) 1973; Advisor to Minister of External Relations and to National Council of Science and Technology, since 1976; *b* 25 May 1910; *s* of Vicente Sanchez Gavito and Maria P. de Sanchez Gavito. *Educ:* Nat. Univ. of Mexico (BA); Escuela Libre de Derecho, Mexico City (LLB). Min. of External Relations, Mexico: Solicitor, Gen. Commn on Claims between USA and Mexico and at Commn on Agrarian Claims, 1935-39 (Alt. Comr for Mexico, 1937); Head, N Amer. Affairs Dept, 1939-43; Dir-Gen. of Diplomatic Service, 1947-51; Mem., UN Tribunals in Libya and Eritrea, 1951-55; Pres., Jt Honduras-Nicaraguan Commn (decision of boundary controversy, 1961); Ambassador to Organisation of Amer. States, 1959-65; Pres. Council, 1959-60; Pres. Interamerican Peace Commn, 1960-61; Mem. OAS Special Cttees visiting Central Amer. 1959, Venezuela 1960, Panama 1964; Ambassador of Mexico to Brazil, 1965-70, to London, 1970-73, to Federal Republic of Germany, 1974-75. Leader or member of numerous delegations. Order of: Southern Cross, Brazil, 1960; Liberator, Venezuela, 1962; Rio Branco, Brazil, 1970. *Recreation:* chess. *Address:* c/o Secretaria de Relaciones, Mexico DF. *Club:* University (Washington, DC). *[Died 1976.*

SANDALL, Ray St Clair; retired; Member for Administration, National Bus Co., 1979; *b* 4 Sept. 1924; *s* of Reginald Sydney Sandall and Irene Moorshead Sandall (*née* Hammill); *m* 1949, Margaret Wilson Hastings; two *s.* *Educ:* Trinity School of John Whitgift; London School of Economics; BSc (Econ); FCIS, FCIT, FRSA. Rajput Regt, Indian Army, 1944-47; Assistant Secretary, 1961-67, Secretary, 1967-69, BET Federation Ltd; Secretary, Nat. Bus Co., 1969-79 (Dir of Administration, 1971-78). *Recreations:* gardening, swimming. *Address:* 18 Courtfield Gardens, Ealing, W13 0EZ. *T:* 01-997 6727.
[Died 29 July 1980.

SANDARS, John Eric William Graves, OBE 1945; TD 1944; JP, DL; Chairman, Sandars & Co. Ltd, Maltsters, Gainsborough; Director: Vaux & Associated Breweries Ltd, Sunderland; *b* 26 Feb. 1906; *s* of late John Drysdale Sandars, JP, DL, and of late Hon. Maud Evelyn Sandars (*née* Graves); *m* 1932, Margaret Mary Katherine Clare Elwes; one *d.* *Educ:* Eton; Trinity College, Cambridge. MA, Cambridge, 1965. Commissioned into Notts (Sherwood Rangers) Yeomanry TA, 1927. Served War of 1939-45; Middle East, 1939-43 (despatches twice); France and Germany, 1944-45 (American Bronze Star, 1944, OBE), with rank of Lieutenant-Colonel. Served on Lincs (Lindsey) CC, 1937, County Agricultural Executive Cttee, 1948; Pres., Lincs Agricultural Soc., 1971. JP 1936. High Sheriff of Lincolnshire, 1949; DL 1950; County Alderman, 1953. Chairman, Maltsters Association of Great Britain, 1952-55. Chm., 1928-38, Pres., 1969, Gainsborough Div., Conservative and Unionist Assoc. *Recreation:* shooting. *Address:* Gate Burton Hall, Gainsborough, Lincs. *T:* Torksey 248. *Clubs:* Boodle's, Cavalry, MCC. *[Died 8 June 1974.*

SANDARS, Vice-Admiral Sir (Reginald) Thomas, KBE 1962; CB 1959; MIMechE; *b* 20 September 1904; *s* of Canon George Russell Sandars and Mary Lambert (*née* Wyld); *m* 1935, Elizabeth Audrey Crewdson; three *s.* *Educ:* RN Colleges Osborne and Dartmouth. Joined RN as cadet, 1918; specialised in engineering, 1924; Rear-Admiral, 1956; Deputy Chief of Naval Personnel, 1957-58; Director of Fleet Maintenance, Admiralty, 1958-59; Vice-Admiral, 1960; Director-General of Dockyards and Maintenance, 1959-62; and Chief Naval Engineer Officer, 1960-62; retired, 1962. *Address:* Woodlands, Wrecclesham, near Farnham, Surrey *T:* Farnham 6076. *Club:* Army and Navy. *[Died 26 May 1975.*

SANDERS, Air Chief Marshal Sir Arthur Penrose Martyn, GCB 1955 (KCB 1952; CB 1944); KBE 1946 (CBE 1942); *b* 17 March 1898; *s* of late Rev. Preb. H. Martyn Sanders; *m* 1928, Edith Mary, *d* of late H. A. Olivier; two *d.* *Educ:* Haileybury Coll.; Royal Military College, Sandhurst. Royal Flying Corps, 1916-18; RAF 1918; Egypt, 1921-25; psa 1927; Aden, 1932-33; idc 1934; Director Ground Defence, Air Ministry, 1940-42; Asst Chief of Staff (Air), Allied Force Headquarters, for operation Torch, Sept.-Dec. 1942; AO i/c A, Bomber Command, 1943-45; Commandant, RAF Staff College, 1945-47; AOC-in-C, BAFO, Germany, 1947-48; Vice-Chief of the Air Staff, 1948-50; Deputy Chief of the Air Staff, 1950-52; Commander-in-Chief, Middle East Air Force, 1952-53; Commandant Imperial Defence College, 1954-55; ADC to the Queen, 1954-55; retired from RAF Jan. 1956. Mem., North Thames Gas Bd, 1956-64; Ind. Chm., Fiji Sugar Bd, Jan.-July, 1962; Chm., League of Remembrance, 1959-. Order of Red Star (USSR), 1944; Polonia Restituta, 2nd Class (Poland), 1945; Legion of Merit, Commander (USA), 1947. *Recreations:* fishing, gardening. *Address:* 21 St Dunstan's Road, W6. *Club:* Royal Air Force.
[Died 8 Feb. 1974.

SANDERSON OF AYOT, 1st Baron, *cr* 1960; **Basil Sanderson,** MC 1916; Director, British Maritime Trust Ltd; *b* 19 June 1894; *s* of late Harold Arthur Sanderson (Chairman 1913-29 of White Star Line and other Shipping Companies) and Maud Blood, New York; *m* Evelyn Constance (*d* 1940), *d* of J. Bruce Ismay, and Florence Schefflyn, New York; twin *s* one *d.* *Educ:* Rugby; Trinity Coll., Oxford. Served European War, 1914-18; commissioned Duke of Lancaster's Own Yeomanry, GSO3 1st Inf. Div., Bde Major 126 Inf. Bde, GSO2 41st Inf. Div. (despatches twice, Bt-Major, MC and bar, Belgian Croix de Guerre); joined White Star Line, Liverpool, 1919, thence 1921 Geo. Thompson & Co. Ltd, and finally 1927 Shaw Savill & Albion Co. Ltd as Manager; Man. Director, 1945-59; Chairman, 1947-63; Director, 1963-68. Director:' Bank of England, 1943-65; Furness Withy & Co. Ltd, 1945-65; Finance Corporation for Industry, 1953-66. Member Committee of Lloyd's Register, 1927-; Chairman: London General Shipowners Society, 1933-34; Nat. Council of Port Labour Employers, 1934-40; Shipping Fedn, 1934-50 (Pres., 1950-63); President: Internat. Shipping Fedn, 1934-51; British Employers' Confederation, 1938-39; Mem. of Economic Planning Board, 1957-62. War of 1939-45;

Dir Shipping in Port, Min. of Shipping, 1939-41; Head of Port and Transit Control, Min. of War Transport, 1941-45, when returned to City. High Sheriff, County of London, 1948-49. US Medal of Freedom with Silver Palm. *Publication:* Ships and Sealing Wax (autobiography), 1967. *Recreations:* tennis, gardening. *Heir: er* twin *s* Dr Hon. Alan Lindsay Sanderson [*b* 12 Jan. 1931; *m* 1959, Gertrude Bochsler, Zürich; one *s* three *d. Educ:* Uppingham]. *Address:* Ayot Bury, Welwyn, Herts. *T:* Welwyn 4360. *Club:* Bath.   [*Died* 15 *Aug.* 1971.

SANDERSON, Air Marshal Sir (Alfred) Clifford, KBE 1953 (CBE 1942); CB 1948; DFC; retired; *b* 19 February 1898; *s* of late Alfred Sanderson, Hayes, Kent; *m* 1923, Hazel Evelyn, *yr d* of late Capt. Bernard Daly, The Bedfordshire Regt, Templeogue, Co. Dublin; two *d. Educ:* Dulwich College. Commissioned RFC 1916; Served in France, with 16 and 46 Sqdns, 1917 and 1918; Ireland, 1919-22; India, NW Frontier, 1924-29; Palestine, 1938-40; Malta, 1940-41; Egypt, 1942-43; Director, Administrative Planning and Chm. of Jt Administrative Planning Staff, 1943-45; AOC, Burma, 1946-47; Air Officer i/c Administration at Air Command, Far East, 1947-48; Air Officer Commanding Malaya, 1948-49; Director-General of Personnel, Air Ministry, 1949-52; Commander-in-Chief, Far East Air Forces, 1952-54; retd Feb. 1955. *Address:* 24 Hovedene, Hove, East Sussex. *Club:* Royal Air Force.
                    [*Died* 28 *Jan.* 1976.

SANDERSON, Air Marshal Sir Clifford; *see* Sanderson, Air Marshal Sir A. C.

SANDERSON, His Honour Kenneth Francis Villiers, CMG 1957; retired as Judge of Local Court, Adelaide, SA (1950-58); *b* 30 March 1895; *s* of Francis V. Sanderson and Fannie A. Klingender; three *s. Educ:* St Peter's College, Adelaide. Admitted to Bar of South Australia, 1918; appointed Stipendiary Magistrate, 1927. *Recreations:* yachting and field sports. *Address:* No 3 Hexham Avenue, Myrtle Bank, South Australia 5064, Australia. *T:* 79.4880. *Club:* Royal SA Yacht Squadron (S Australia).   [*Died* 5 *April* 1973.

SANDES, Lt-Col Edward Warren Caulfeild, DSO 1919; OBE 1959; MC 1916; RE retired; *b* 13 Feb. 1880; *o s* of late Col H. T. T. Sandes, RA; *m* 1919, Sylvia Mary, *d* of late Henry Francis Sneyd-Kynnersley; one *s* one *d. Educ:* Monkton Combe Sch.; RMA, Woolwich. Commissioned, 1899; Lieut, 1902; Captain, 1908; Major, 1916; Lt-Colonel, 1925; served in military employment in India, 1902-10; Prof. of Civil Engineering, Thomason Coll., Roorkee, India, 1910-15; Principal, Thomason Coll., 1921-30; served European War (Mesopotamia), 1915-16 (DSO, MC, French Croix de Guerre with palms); was in the besieged garrison of Kut-el-Amarah (despatches thrice) and a prisoner of war in Turkey for 2+ years after the surrender of Kut; retired, 1931. Fowke Memorial Medal for Architectural Design, SME Chatham, 1901; Gold Medal, Institution of Royal Engrs, 1964. *Publications:* In Kut and Captivity, 1919; Tales of Turkey, 1924; The Military Engineer in India, Vol. I, 1933; Vol. II, 1935; The Royal Engineers in Egypt and the Sudan, 1937; The Indian Sappers and Miners, 1948; From Pyramid to Pagoda (The W Yorks Regt History), 1952; The Indian Engineers, 1939-47, 1957; Biographies; articles in RE Journal. *Address:* Ryelands, Buxton Road, Weymouth. *T:* Weymouth 6357. *Clubs:* Naval and Military; Royal Dorset Yacht (Weymouth).
                    [*Died* 23 *Feb.* 1973.

SANDFORD, Brigadier Daniel Arthur, CBE 1942 (OBE 1941); DSO 1916; late Royal Garrison Artillery; *b* 1882; *s* of late Ven. E. G. Sandford, Archdeacon of Exeter; *m* 1918, Christine, CBE 1966, *o d* of H. S. Lush, High Croft Terr., Brighton; two *s* four *d. Educ:* St Paul's; RMA, Woolwich. 2nd Lt RGA 1900; Sudan Govt Administration, 1910-13; HM Consul at Addis Ababa, Abyssinia, 1914; served Sudan, 1910 (medal and clasp); European War, 1914-18 (wounded, despatches, DSO and bar, Legion of Honour); retired pay, 1922; resident in Abyssinia, 1920-36, farming; Adviser to Governor of Maji Province, Ethiopia, 1935; resident in England during Italian occupation of Ethiopia; joined Officers' Emergency Reserve, Sept. 1939; June 1940, Head of Mission 101 (with rank of Col) which entered Ethiopia to assist patriots 6 months before British troops; Principal Military and Political Adviser to Emperor Haile Selassie with rank of Brig., Feb. 1941; reverted to Unemployed List to become Principal Adviser to the Ministry of Interior, Ethiopian Government, Apr. 1942; Personal Adviser to Emperor, 1944; Director General of Addis Ababa Municipality, 1945-48. Now resident in Ethiopia, farming and, with wife, interested in a Community Development project. Haile Selassie Medal of Ethiopia with palm, 1942; Comdr Order of Selassie, 1951. *Address:* Addis Ababa, Ethiopia; c/o Lloyds Bank, 6 Pall Mall, SW1. *Club:* Royal Commonwealth Society.
                    [*Died* 22 *Jan.* 1972.

SANDFORD, Kenneth Stuart; Reader Emeritus in Geology, University of Oxford; Emeritus Fellow, University College, Oxford; *b* 9 Dec. 1899; *y s* of Horatio Sandford, JP, and Lizzie, *d* of Jonathan Adlington; *m* 1929, Grace Audrey Rob Prestwich (*d* 1965); one *d. Educ:* King's School, Rochester; University College, Oxford (Gunsley Scholar). 2nd Lieut RFA (Temp. Regular Army); Major, RA (Y), 1936, TD 1940; BA (1st Class Honours Natural Science), Burdett-Coutts Scholar, 1921, DPhil 1923, MA 1925, DSc 1934 (Oxford); Geological Society of London: FGS, Daniel-Pidgeon Fund, 1924, Council, 1943-47, 1950-54; Oxford University Arctic Expedition and member of sledging party in North East Land, 1924; geological research in Nile Valley and adjoining deserts, 1925-33 (Brit. Sch. of Archæology in Egypt and Oriental Institute, Univ. of Chicago); Libyan Desert Expedition (Major R. A. Bagnold), 1932; Royal Geographical Society: Murchison Grant, 1932; Council, 1934-37, 1939-43, 1962-66, Vice-Pres., 1967-; University Demonstrator in Pleistocene Geology (Oxford), 1927; in Geology, 1935; Reader, 1948. Senior Treas., OU Exploration Club, 1935-47, Vice-Pres., 1947-54, 1957-65, Pres., 1954-57; Editor, Geologists' Assoc., 1948-51, 1968-; Vice-Pres., Brit. Glaciolog. Soc., 1951-61; Hon. Foreign Member: Svenska Sällskapets für Antropologi och Geografi, 1939; Société belge de Géologie, de Paléontologie, et d'Hydrologie, 1948; Corr. Mem., Fouad I Desert Inst., and of Geological Soc., Egypt, 1950. Bolitho Gold Medal, Royal Geolog. Soc. of Cornwall, 1934. *Publications:* Papers in British and foreign scientific journals, and memoirs. *Address:* Department of Geology and Mineralogy, Parks Road, Oxford and Foxcombe Corner, Boars Hill, Oxford. *T:* Oxford 35179.   [*Died* 18 *Nov.* 1971.

SANDIE, Brigadier John Grey, DSO 1940; MC; *b* 14 June 1897; *s* of late R. L. Sandie; *m* 1951, Stella Marian (*d* 1973), *d* of late Robert Ives, Erpingham House, near Norwich. *Educ:* Shrewsbury; Royal Military College, Sandhurst. Regular Army; served European War, 1916-18 (MC; despatches twice; Croix de Guerre; wounded twice); Sudan Defence Force, 1928-35 (Staff G3 1934); served War of 1939-45, took part in the Dunkirk withdrawal (despatches, DSO); Commanded 1st Bn Loyal Regiment, 1940-42; Commander 159 Inf. Bde; North West Europe Campaign; Commandant Small Arms School, Hythe, 1944-47; retired, 1947. *Recreations:* shooting, photography. *Address:* The Old Rectory, Washford Pyne, Black Dog, near Crediton, Devon. *T:* Witheridge 335. *Club:* Naval and Military.
                    [*Died* 21 *Sept.* 1975.

SANDON, Frank, MA Cantab; Life Fellow, Royal Statistical Society; Fellow, Institute of Statisticians; Fellow, Institute of Mathematics, and its Applications; Associate, British Psychological Society; *b* 3 June 1890; *e s* of late Robert Sandon, HM Examiner of Patents, and Louisa Rudkins Watts; *m* 1919, Sophie (*d* 1968), 2nd *d* of late Carl Gugenheim and of late Laura Maison; no *c. Educ:* Burghley Road Board School; Owen's School, Islington (Foundation Scholar and Leaving Exhibitioner); Corpus Christi College, Cambridge (Scholar and Prizeman. Wrangler, 1912); Diploma (with distinction) in Education, Oxford, 1925; Higher Division Clerk, Home Office, 1913-19; Friends' Ambulance Unit, BEF, 1916-19; Mathematics and Form Master, Sheffield CSS, 1919-20; Roan School, 1920-21; Highgate School, 1921-23; West Ham Secondary School, 1923-29; Devonport High School for Boys, 1937-41; Head Master: Corporation Grammar School, Plymouth, 1929-37; Millom Grammar School, Millom Technical School and Millom Commercial School (Millom County Secondary School, Millom, Cumberland), 1941-50; Principal, Millom Inst., 1942-50; Mathematics Master, King Edward's School, Aston, 1955-57; Edgbaston High School, 1957-58; Lordswood Technical School for Girls, 1958-59. Hon. Lectr, Working Men's Coll., 1914-16; Lectr in Statistics, LCC, 1920-29; Lectr, Coll. of Commerce, Birmingham, 1955-59; Examiner: NUJMB, 1927-29, 1932-33; London Univ., SEC, 1928-31, 1940-41; Oxford Locals and Cambridge Locals, 1938-40, 1945; Oxford and Cambridge Schools Examination Bd, 1941-47; Education Committees of LCC, 1930 and 1938, Birmingham, 1930-41, and Wiltshire, 1940; Civil Service Commn, 1940; Chief Examiner: Somerset, 1945-48, 1955-59; Birmingham, 1941-50; Selection Officer, Birmingham, 1951-55. Founder-Pres. Plymouth Branch, Math. Assoc. *Publications:* mathematical, statistical, and pedagogical articles, notes, reviews, etc; Every-Day Mathematics, 1920; Wightman's Mathematical Tables, 1921; Wightman's Arithmetical Tables, 1921; miscellaneous press articles on swimming, rambling, etc. *Recreations:* swimming (CUSC, Blue, 1910-12; British team, Olympic Games, Stockholm, 1912; Hon. Rep. Plymouth and Penzance, Royal Life Saving Society), fell walking, and rambling (Gen. Cttee Holiday Fellowship; Founder Pres., Plymouth Group; Founder Treasurer, Devon and Cornwall YHA). *Address:* 726 Enterprise House, King's Head Hill, Chingford, E4 7NF. *T:* 01-524 1801.
                    [*Died* 29 *May* 1979.

SANDS, Percy Cooper, MA; JP; *b* 3 Feb. 1883; *s* of John and Annie Maria Sands; *m* 1909, Olive Clara Cowley; one *s* two *d*. *Educ*: Nottingham High School; St John's College, Cambridge (Scholar, Fellow). Composition Master of the City of London School, EC, 1906-14; Headmaster, Pocklington School, 1915-44; Thirlwall Medal, Cambridge University, 1907. *Publications*: Client Princes of the Roman Empire; Gods and Heroes; Literary Genius of the Old Testament; Literary Genius of the New Testament; Forty-five Talks for Bible Classes; Modern Illustrations of the Gospel; Men of God; Sons of God; Witnesses of God; History of Pocklington School. *Address*: The Balk, Pocklington, York. *T*: Pocklington 2187. *[Died 15 May 1971.*

SANDS, Sir Stafford (Lofthouse), Kt 1964; CBE 1955; Member of the House of Assembly, Bahamas, 1937-67; Minister for Tourism and Finance, Bahamas, 1963-67; *b* 1913; *s* of late Stafford Sands, The Knowle, Montagu Foreshore, Nassau, Bahamas; *m* 1st, 1937, Winifred Maude (marr. diss., 1961), *d* of late Sir Walter Kingsbury Moore, CBE; 2nd, 1965, Ulli, *d* of late Lauri Castren, Helsinki, Finland. *Educ*: Winnwood Sch., NY, USA. Called to the Bar, Bahamas, 1935; Bd of Educn, Bahamas, 1937-38; Member: Marketing Committee, 1941; Agricultural and Marine Products Board, 1943; Health Board, 1944-46; Broadcasting Committee, 1944-45; War-Time Supplies Commission, 1944-45; Public Board of Works, 1945-46; Executive Council, 1945-46; Economic Supplies Board, 1946; Airports Board, 1947-52; Town Planning Committee, 1952; Co-ordination Committee, 1954; Chm., Development Board, 1950-63. *Address*: Hermanos Bécquer 8, Madrid 6, Spain; Villa Corner, Cavasagra, 31030 Albaredo (Treviso), Italy.
[Died 25 Jan. 1972.

SANDYS, George Owen, JP; *b* 17 July 1884; *er* twin *s* of Lieut-Col Edwin Del Sandys, 58th Northamptonshire Regt; *m* 1914, Dulcie Edythe Angela, *o d* of late Sir E. P. W. Redford, CB; one *s* one *d*. *Educ*: Bedford Grammar School; Royal Military College, Sandhurst. Served in 1st Royal Scots (The Royal Regiment), 1903-12; in the Westmorland and Cumberland Yeo., 1912-19, when was placed in the TF Reserve Class 1 as a Major. Served in 2nd County of Lancaster (North Lonsdale) Bn Home Guard, 1940, Lt-Col from 1941; succeeded in the family estates his cousin the late Col Thomas Myles Sandys (for many years MP for Bootle Division of Liverpool), 1911; High Sheriff of Lancashire, 1925-26; DL Co. Lancaster, 1925-71. *Address*: 6/9 Wilbraham Place, SW1. *T*: 01-730 7544; Graythwaite Hall, Ulverston, Lancs. *T*: Newby Bridge 333. *Clubs*: Carlton, Beefsteak.
[Died 14 March 1973.

SANGAR, Owen Jermy, CBE 1951; MC 1918; retired from Forestry Commission; *b* 20 May 1893; *s* of late Isaac Twigg and late Cordelia Charlotte Sangar, Lowestoft, Suffolk; *m* 1920, Eveline Mary, *d* of Walter Reginald Dickinson, West Wickham, Kent; one *d*. *Educ*: Felsted Sch.; Univ. of Washington, USA. British Columbia Forest Service, 1913-14. Served European War (despatches twice): Canadian Field Artillery, 1915; RGA and RA (staff appt), 1916-19; retired as Captain. Forestry Commission, 1919-58; Asst Comr, England and Wales, 1938-45; Director, England, 1946-58. Chairman, FAO's European Commission for Forestry and Forest Products, 1948-52. Pres. Soc. of Foresters of Gt Brit., 1948-49. *Publications*: various papers and articles for Forestry Conferences and in technical journals. *Address*: Gweath, Mullion, S Cornwall. *T*: Mullion 481.
[Died 12 Sept. 1972.

SANGSTER, John Young; *b* 29 May 1896; *s* of late Charles Sangster; *m* 1st, 1923, Kathleen, *d* of late Robert Burns; one *d*; 2nd, 1951, Phyllis, *d* of Frederick Hamer; 3rd, 1963, Margery, *d* of late Robert Cheney Hart. *Educ*: Hurstpierpoint Coll. Served 14th Royal Warwickshire Regt, 1914-18. The Rover Co. Ltd, 1919-23; Chairman: Ariel Motors Ltd, 1923-45; Triumph Engineering Co. Ltd, 1936-64; The Daimler Co. Ltd, 1956-60; Birmingham Small Arms Co Ltd, 1956-61 (Dir, 1951-69). Pres. Cycle & Motor Cycle Assoc., 1953-54. *Recreations*: motoring, ski-ing, yachting. *Address*: 34 Ennismore Gardens, SW7 1AE. *T*: 01-589 2561.
[Died 26 March 1977.

SANSBURY, Rev. Canon Graham Rogers, MA; Rector of Grantham, 1973-77 (Vicar, 1958-73); Chaplain to the Queen, 1969-79; Canon of Lincoln Cathedral since 1961; *b* 4 Aug. 1909; *s* of Cyril and Sophie Sansbury; *m* 1935, Cecily (*d* 1971), *d* of Prof. Bompas Smith; one *s* one *d* (and one *d* decd); *m* 1974, Marjorie, *d* of William Buckman. *Educ*: Dulwich Coll.; Peterhouse, Cambridge; Westcott House, Cambridge. Curate: St Peter St Helier, Southwark, 1932-35; Old Malden, 1935-38; Chaplain, Kolar Gold Field, South India, 1938-44; Priest i/c St Michael's, North Hull, 1945-48; Rector of Skegness, 1948-58; Proctor in Convocation for Lincoln Dio., 1955-; Rural Dean of Grantham, 1958-69. *Publications*: The Paul Report: A Study

Guide, 1964; contrib. to The Paul Report Considered. *Recreations*: cine-photography, walking, gardening. *Address*: 5 Rock House Gardens, Radcliffe Road, Stamford, Lincs PE9 1AS. *T*: Stamford 54438.
[Died 9 April 1980.

SANSOM, George Samuel, MC, DFC; DSc; Fellow of University College, London, since 1930; *b* London, 7 Aug. 1888; *s* of S. G. C. Sansom and Annie Sansom; *m* 1921, Dorothy Vivien (*d* 1973) *d* of Rev. F. V. Dodgson and *g d* of Gen. Sir David Scott Dodgson, KCB; three *s*. *Educ*: Wellington Coll.; University Coll, London. BSc 1911; Derby Scholar, Zoology, 1912. Planned and took part in many new difficult rock climbs in Cumberland, inc. Scafell Central Buttress, 1914. British Red Cross in Flanders, 1914; Royal Air Force Balloon Observer in France, 1915-18 (MC, DFC); ROC, 1939-45. Hon. Res. Asst, Dept of Embryology, UCL. *Recreations*: formerly rock-climbing, flying; now pistol shooting. *Address*: Kennel Moor, Godalming, Surrey. *T*: Godalming 6887. *Club*: (Hon. Mem.) Fell and Rock Climbing.
[Died 21 March 1980.

SANSOM, William; FRSL; author; *b* London, 18 Jan. 1912; 3rd *s* of Ernest Brooks Sansom, MINA, and Mabel Clark, Barrow; *m* 1954, Ruth, *d* of Norman Grundy, FCA, Tunbridge Wells; one *s* (and one step *s*). *Educ*: Uppingham School; and variously in Europe. Has written regularly for literary periodicals in England; books translated into many foreign languages; awarded Travel Scholarship in 1946, literary bursary in 1947, by the Society of Authors. *Publications*: Fireman Flower, 1944; Three, 1946; Westminster in War, 1947; Something Terrible, Something Lovely, 1948; South, 1948; The Equilibriad, 1948; The Body (novel), 1949; The Passionate North, 1950; The Face of Innocence (novel), 1951; A Touch of the Sun, 1952; Pleasures Strange and Simple, 1953; A Bed of Roses (novel), 1954; Lord Love Us (ballads), 1954; A Contest of Ladies, 1956; The Loving Eye (novel), 1956; Among the Dahlias, 1957; The Icicle and the Sun, 1958; The Cautious Heart (novel), 1958; Blue Skies, Brown Studies, 1960; The Last Hours of Sandra Lee (novel), 1961; The Stories of William Sansom, 1963; Away to it All, 1964; The Ulcerated Milkman, 1966; Goodbye (novel), 1966; Grand Tour Today, 1968; Christmas, 1968; Hans Feet in Love, 1971; The Birth of a Story, 1972; The Marmalade Bird, 1973; Marcel Proust and his World, 1973; A Young Wife's Tale (novel), 1974; Victorian Life in Photographs, 1974; has also composed light music, written lyrics, illustrated humorous books, and written children's books. *Recreation*: watching. *Address*: c/o The Elaine Greene Agency, 31 Newington Green, N16 9PU.
[Died 20 April 1976.

SARGEAUNT, Bertram Edward, MVO 1920; OBE 1918; FSA; Government Secretary and Treasurer, Isle of Man, 1910-44; *b* 4 Dec. 1877; *s* of late Captain F. A. Sargeaunt, Royal Navy, and Alice Caroline, *sister* of 1st Baron Fisher of Kilverstone, Admiral of the Fleet; *m* 1910, Kathleen Hamilton (*d* 1962), *e d* of late Robert Thornewill, Craythorne, Burton-on-Trent; one *d*. *Educ*: Bedford School. Royal United Service Institution, Whitehall, 1899-1910. Late Captain, 12th London Regiment. Officer of the Order of St John of Jerusalem. A trustee of Manx Museum, 1922-53, and a Church Commissioner for Isle of Man, 1943-53. Organised and presided at centenary luncheon held in London in 1955 for sons and daughters of those who served in the Crimean War, 1854-1856; also Golden Jubilee Luncheon held in London, 1958, for TA Officers who served as such in 1908; administered internment camps for 26,000 prisoners in the first World War and 16,000 in the Second World War. FRGS (Hon. Fellow 1976). *Publications*: The Royal Monmouthshire Militia; The Isle of Man and the Great War; The Royal Manx Fencibles; A Military History of the Isle of Man. *Address*: Ladymead, Hurstpierpoint, Sussex. *T*: Hurstpierpoint 2159.
[Died 2 Feb. 1978.

SARGEAUNT, Margaret Joan, MA, BLitt; Principal of Queen Elizabeth College (formerly King's College of Household and Social Science), University of London, 1947-66; *b* 29 July 1903; *d* of Rev. William Drake Sargeaunt and Florence Thursby. *Educ*: Godolphin School, Salisbury; St Hugh's College, Oxford. First Class Hons in Eng. Lang. and Lit., 1925; Diploma in Educn with distinction, 1926; BLitt (Oxon), 1931. Asst Mistress at Wycombe Abbey School, 1926-29; Lecturer in Education, Univ. of Sheffield, 1931-37; Adviser of Women Students and Warden of Masson Hall, Univ. of Edinburgh, 1937-47. Hon. Fellow, Queen Elizabeth Coll., 1966. *Publications*: John Ford, 1935, US edn, 1966; various articles and notes (Review of English Studies). *Recreation*: walking. *Address*: The Tangle, Ibstone, High Wycombe, Bucks. *T*: Turville Heath 383.
[Died 25 June 1978.

SARGENT, Rt. Rev. Douglas Noel; *b* 19 Dec. 1907; *s* of Edwin Dowdeswell Sargent, Watford, and Charlotte Elizabeth (*née*

Taylor), St Albans; *m* 1942, Imogene Grace Ward; three *s* (one *d* decd). *Educ:* Watford Grammar School; King's College, Cambridge; London College of Divinity; Union Theological Seminary, New York. Deacon, 1931; Priest, 1932; Curate of Willian, 1931-34; Missionary with CMS at Chengtu, 1934-48, and at Lingling, 1949-51; Principal of CMS Men's Training College, Blackheath, 1951-52, Chislehurst, 1952-62; Bishop Suffragan of Selby, 1962-71. *Publications:* The Making of a Missionary, 1960; jointly, The Churchman's Companion, 1964. *Recreations:* gardening, local history. *Address:* 1 Ramsey Avenue, Bishopthorpe, York.   [*Died 5 Sept.* 1979.

SARGENT, Sir John Philip, Kt 1946; CIE 1941; MA (Oxon); Hon. DLitt (Patna, Delhi, Osmania, Travancore, Jadavpur); *b* 27 Dec. 1888; *s* of George Sargent and Bertha White; *m* 1923, Ruth (*d* 1933), *d* of R. C. Taunton; one *s*. *Educ:* St Paul's School; Oriel College, Oxford. Inspector of Schools, East Riding (Yorks) CC, 1913-20; served European War, 1914-18, Royal Artillery; Assistant Education Officer, Birmingham, 1920-27; Director of Education, Southend-on-Sea, 1927-31; Director of Education, Essex CC, 1931-38; Educational Commissioner with Govt of India, 1938-42; Educational Adviser to Govt of India, 1943-48; Sec., Education Department, Govt of India, 1945-48; Director, Commonwealth II Dept, British Council, 1948-52; Warden of Missenden Abbey Adult Educn Coll., 1953-57. Pres., Association of Directors and Secretaries for Education, 1936; Pres., Education Section, British Association, 1938. *Recreation:* walking. *Address:* Bankfield Hotel, Leamington Spa, Warwicks. *Clubs:* Oriental; Vincent's (Oxford).   [*Died* 13 *Feb.* 1972.

SARGOOD, Richard; Trade Union Officer; retired; *b* 31 July 1888; *m* 1919, Sarah Lilian Deane; one *d*. *Educ:* Kennington Road LCC School; Evening Continuation School. Trade Union Official since 1919; Member Camberwell Borough Council, 1923-29; Vice-Chm. LCC, 1951-52 (Member 1934-65). Chm., Peckham Divisional Labour Party, 1932-47. MP (Lab) for West Bermondsey, 1945-50; formerly Chairman: Mental Hospitals Committee of LCC, Supplies Cttee, Parliamentary Cttee, Fire Brigade Cttee; (till 1965) Staff Appeals Committee, LCC; Camberwell Youth Employment Cttee; Vice-Chm., Finance Cttee, LCC. *Recreations:* walking, reading, keenly interested in amateur football. *Address:* 50 Lower Drive, Dawlish, Devon EX7 0AT.   [*Died* 27 *March* 1979.

SARKODEE-ADOO, Julius; Chief Justice, Republic of Ghana, 1964-66 (Judge, Supreme Court, Republic of Ghana, 1960; Puisne Judge, Ghana, 1956); *b* 18 Sept. 1908; *e s* of late Julius Sarkodee-Adoo, Merchant, Koforidua (New Juaben), and Emma Apeakorama, Afwerase, Akwapim; *m* 1941, Florence Flatteau, Akuse, Ghana; three *s* three *d*. *Educ:* Methodist Primary Sch., Koforidua; Wesleyan Boys' High Sch., Freetown, Sierra Leone; University of London, King's College. Called to Bar, Inner Temple, 1932; enrolled in Supreme Court of Gold Coast (now Ghana), 1934; Legal Practitioner, 1934-56; Chm., Cttee of Enquiry into the Ga, Akwapim, Abeadzi, Gomoa Assin, Teshie and Osu Stool Disputes; Mem. Representational and Electoral Reform Commn; Chm. Cttee of Enquiry into Mines Disputes, 1953-56; Mem. Judicial Service Commn, 1957-59. Formerly Director Ghana Commercial Bank. *Recreation:* tennis. *Address:* Florrie Villa, PO Box 283, Accra, Ghana.
[*Died* 31 *Dec.* 1971.

SARNOFF, David, Hon. DSc, Hon. DLit, Hon. DSc Comm., Hon. Dr of Laws, Hon. Dr of Humane Letters; Chairman of the Board, RCA Corporation (formerly Radio Corporation of America), 1947-70, now Hon. Chairman; *b* Uzlian, Minsk, Russia, 27 Feb. 1891; *m* 1917, Lizette Hermant; three *s*. *Educ:* New York Public Schools; Pratt Institute. Went to USA 1900. Messenger boy, Commercial Cable Co., 1906; Office boy, Marconi Wireless Telegraph Co. of America, 1906; Junior telegraph operator, Marconi Co., 1907; Wireless operator, Nantucket Island, 1908; Manager, Marconi Station, Sea Gate, 1909; Wireless operator, SS Harvard, SS Beothic in Arctic, 1910-11; John Wanamaker's, New York, 1911-12; Chief Radio Inspector, Marconi Co., 1913; Contract Manager, 1914; Asst Traffic Manager, 1915-16; Commercial Manager, 1917-19; Radio Corp. of America (later RCA Corporation): Commercial Manager, 1919-20; General Manager, 1921; Vice-Pres., 1922; Exec. Vice-Pres., 1929; Pres., 1930; Chm. and Chief Exec. Officer, 1947; Chm., 1966-70. Lt-Col Signal Corps Reserve, US Army, 1924; Col, 1931; Brig.-Gen., 1944; now Brig.-Gen. AUS, retd. Trustee: Thomas A. Edison Foundn; Educ. Alliance; Trustee Emeritus: Pratt Inst.; New York Univ.; Member: Inst. of Electrical and Electronics Engineers (Fellow); British Instn of Radio Engineers (Hon.); Newcomen Soc. of England; Roy. Soc. of Arts, London (Fellow); Weizmann Inst. of Science, Israel (Hon. Fellow); member of many other engineering and scientific institutes and societies. Collaborated with Owen D. Young in

reparations settlement in Paris, 1929. Order of Polonia Restituta Officers Grade, 1924; Cross of Chevalier of Legion of Honour (France), 1935, Cross of Officer, 1940, Cross of Comdr, 1947; Officer of Order of Oaken Crown of Grand Duchy of Luxembourg, 1935; Order of the Rising Sun, Japan, 1960; Legion of Merit, US War Dept, 1944; Medal for Merit, 1946; US Treasury's Silver Medal Award, 1946; Citation from UN, 1949. Gold Medal of French Union of Inventors, 1954. James Forrestal Memorial Medal, Nat. Security Ind. Assocn, 1956; Decoration for Exceptional Civilian Service, US Army, 1956. Commander, Order of Merit of the Italian Republic, 1959. Christopher Columbus Internat. Award, Italy, 1959; Medallion of Valor, Commendation Award, Israel, 1960. *Address:* 30 Rockefeller Plaza, New York, NY 10020, USA. *Clubs:* Army and Navy (Washington); India House (NY); Metropolitan (Washington).   [*Died* 12 *Dec.* 1971.

SARSFIELD-HALL, Edwin Geoffrey, CMG 1933; Order of the Nile 3rd class (Comdr); FRGS; DL; JP; *b* 24 April 1886; *s* of Edwin Hall, JP, DL, Blackrock, Co. Cork and Ada Georgina Shekleton; took additional family surname of Sarsfield by Deed Poll, 1908; *m* Ethel Robin, OBE, *er d* of Edward Clowes, Betchworth, Surrey; (one *s* killed on active service, 1944) one *d*. *Educ:* Clifton College; Dublin University; Cambridge University. MA, LLB, BL; Barrister, Irish Bar; joined Sudan Political Service, 1908; Settlement Officer and District Judge, Legal Dept, 1913-16; Assistant Political and Intelligence Officer, Darfur Expedition, 1916, rank of Kaimakam (Lt-Col) in Egyptian Army (despatches twice, Order of the Nile); temp. duty with Egyptian Expeditionary Force, Palestine, 1917; Dist Comr, Darfur Province, 1917-21; Deputy Governor, Kordofan Province, 1921; Governor, 1926; Governor, Khartoum Province, 1929-36; retired, 1936; District Commissioner for Special Area of West Cumberland, 1937-38. Director Workington Iron & Steel Co., 1938-51; Director West Cumberland Industrial Development Co., 1937-57. A Dep. Chm., Cumberland Quarter Sessions, 1956-61. Hon. Major Border Regiment. DL Cumbria (formerly Cumberland), 1955; JP Cumbria. *Address:* Skiddaw Lodge, Keswick, Cumbria. *Club:* Naval and Military.   [*Died* 30 *March* 1975.

SARTRE, Jean-Paul; author; *b* Paris, 21 June 1905. *Educ:* Paris; La Rochelle. Degree in Philosophy, 1930. Professor at Le Havre, French Institute at Berlin, Lycée Condorcet, Paris and Lycée Pasteur, Paris. Wrote philosophical works first, then novels and plays. Mobilised, 1939, served in Army, 1939-40, prisoner of war, 1940-41, returned from Germany and took part in resistance movement, 1941-44. Prof. of philosophy until 1944 when resigned to become founder and editor of Les Temps Modernes. Refused Nobel Prize for Literature, 1964 (saying that he had always refused to accept all official distinctions). *Publications:* Imaginaire, 1936; Imagination, 1937; Nausée, 1937; le Mur, 1938; les Mouches, Huis-Clos, l'Etre et le Néant, 1943; les Chemins de la liberté, 1944-45; Morts sans sépulture, La Putain respectueuse, 1946; The Age of Reason, 1947; Reprieve, 1947; Le Diable et le Bon Dieu, 1948; Iron in the Soul, 1950; The Psychology of Imagination, 1951; Les Mains sales, 1952; Œuvres Complètes, 1952; Nekrassov, 1953 (Edinburgh Fest., 1957); Les Sequestrés d'Altona, 1959; Critique de la Raison dialectique, 1961; Words (memoirs), 1964; Baudelaire, 1964; Saint Genet, Actor and Martyr, 1964 (Eng. trans. by B. Frechtman); Situations, 1965 (trans. B. Eisler); Literary and Philosophical Essays, 1968; The Communists and Peace, 1969; The Spectre of Stalin, 1969; L'Idiot de la famille, 1972; Politics and Literature, 1973; Sartre in the Seventies, 1978, etc. *Address:* c/o Editions Gallimard, 5 rue Sebastien-Bottin, 75006 Paris, France.   [*Died* 15 *April* 1980.

SAUDI ARABIA, HM the King of; HM Malik Faisal bin Abdul Aziz al Saud, Hon. GBE, 1932; Hon. KCMG, 1926; Viceroy of the Hejaz since 1926; *b* 1905; 2nd *s* of Abdul Aziz al Saud, King of Saudi Arabia, and *b* of King Ibn Sa'ud. Has made many visits to Europe and the US, notably in 1939 and 1946 when he represented Saudi Arabia at London discussions on Palestine. Represented Saudi Arabia at San Francisco Conf., 1945, and has subsequently attended meetings of UN Gen. Assembly in New York. On the death of his father and accession of his elder brother, he was declared Crown Prince, 1953; proclaimed King, Nov. 1964. Prime Minister and Minister of Foreign Affairs, 1953-60; was granted full control of finances and internal and external affairs also of Armed Forces of Saudi Arabia by a decree of his brother, 24 March 1958, until Dec. 1960. *Address:* Riyadh, Saudi Arabia.   [*Died* 25 *March* 1975.

SAUGMAN, Christian Ditlev Trappaud, Comdr of the Order of Dannebrog, 1961 (Kt 1948, 1st class, 1955); Hon. KBE 1955 (Hon. CBE 1948); Managing Director; barrister; Member of board of British Import Union, Copenhagen, since 1934

(President, 1945-60); *b* 16 June 1895; *s* of late Fritz Saugman and Anna Adele (*née* Hansen); *m* 1920, Vera Schmidt; one *s*. *Educ:* Herlufsholm public sch.; Univ. of Copenhagen, Bachelor of law (Copenhagen), 1918. Junior partner W. Schmidt, 1918, sole proprietor, 1921; established associated export firms, London, 1933, New York, 1936. Delegate of Danish wholesale assoc., 1930, Vice-chm., 1938-40, council member, 1947, Vice-chm. of council, 1949, Pres., 1960-65. Mem., Cttee of the Stock Exchange; Pres. British Exhibn of Copenhagen, 1948 and 1955. Chm. Danish assoc. of race-horse breeders until 1950; Member: state export cttee; Danish cttee of internat. chamber of commerce, 1951; council of the port of Copenhagen; President of Council, Freeport of Copenhagen; President, Kraks Foundation (Danish Who is Who); Member of Council Otto Mønsteds Company; several government committees. FRSA 1962. *Recreations:* farming and riding. *Address:* Sølvgade 22, Copenhagen. *Club:* Royal Danish Automobile.
[Died 15 Jan. 1976.

SAUL, Bazil Sylvester W.; *see* Wingate-Saul.

SAUNDBY, Air Marshal Sir Robert Henry Magnus Spencer, KCB 1956 (CB 1942); KBE 1944; MC 1917; DFC 1926; AFC 1919; FRES 1950; DL; *b* 26 April 1896; *s* of late Robert Saundby, MD, LLD, FRCP, and Mary Edith Spencer; *m* Joyce Mary Rees-Webbe; one *s* two *d*. *Educ:* King Edward's Sch., Birmingham. Served European War of 1914-18; 2nd Lt Royal Warwickshire Regt, 1914; transf. to Royal Flying Corps, 1915; France and Flanders, 1916-17 (MC; wounded, despatches; AFC); served in Iraq, Aden, and Egypt, 1922-26 (DFC); RAF Staff College Course, 1928; Air Staff, Wessex Bombing Area HQ, 1929-30; Air Staff, Air Ministry, 1931-32; idc Course, 1933; Instructor at RAF Staff College, 1934-36; Deputy Director of Operations, Air Ministry, 1937; Director of Operational requirements, Air Ministry, 1938-39; Asst Chief of Air Staff (T), 1940; Senior Air Staff Officer, Bomber Comd, 1941-42; Dep. AOC-in-C, Bomber Comd, RAF, 1943-45 (despatches thrice); retd, 1946; Life Vice-Pres., RAF Assoc.; Chairman Nat. Council, 1945-58; President, Metropolitan Area, British Legion, 1947-62, Patron, 1962; Chairman, Berkshire T and AFA, 1956-61; Vice-Chm. Council T and AF Assocs, 1947-60; Mem., Minister of Pensions' Central Adv. Cttee, 1948-66; Chm., Exec. Cttee, Central Council for the Care of the Disabled, 1953-55; Member Council, Air League of British Empire, 1949-62, Vice-Pres., 1962; President: Berkshire, Buckinghamshire, and Oxfordshire Naturalists' Trust; Piscatorial Soc., 1932-50; British Entomological and Nat. Hist. Soc., 1950. officer, Legion of Honour, France, 1945; Commander, Legion of Merit, USA, 1946; Grand Officer, Order of Leopold II (Belgium) and Belgian Croix de Guerre with Palm, 1947. DL County of Berkshire, 1960. *Publications:* Flying Colours, 1918; edited the Book of the Piscatorial Society, 1836-1936, 1936; A Fly-Rod on Many Waters, 1961; Air Bombardment, the Story of its Development, 1961; numerous articles in newspapers and journals. *Recreations:* fly-fishing and entomology. *Address:* Oxleas, Burghclere, near Newbury, Berkshire. *T:* Burghclere 389. *Clubs:* Royal Air Force, Flyfishers', Pathfinders'. *[Died 25 Sept. 1971.*

SAUNDERS, Rt. Rev. Charles John Godfrey; retired; *b* 15 Feb. 1888; *s* of Rev. S. T. H. Saunders, Rector of St Helen's, Bishopsgate, and M. F. Ll. Saunders; *m* 1916, Mildred Robinson, *d* of Louis Hebblethwaite, Hull; one *s* two *d*. *Educ:* Merchant Taylors' School; St John's College, Oxford (Scholar); Cuddesdon College. Pusey and Ellerton Schol. 1907; BA (3rd Cl. Th. Hon.) and Hall Houghton Septuagint (Jun.) Prize, 1909; MA 1916. Deacon, 1911; Priest, 1912, Lucknow; SPG Cawnpore, 1911-16; Chaplain, Roorkee, 1917; Cawnpore, 1918; Chakrata, 1921; Staff Chaplain, Army Headquarters, India, 1921-25; Metropolitan's Chaplain, Calcutta, 1925-28; Bishop of Lucknow, 1928-38; Rector of Uckfield, 1938-42; Barcombe, 1942-47; Vicar of West Lavington, Midhurst, 1947-53; Assistant Bishop Diocese of Chichester, 1939-53; Canon of Middleton in Chichester Cathedral, 1943-53; on staff of St Matthew's Church, Moorfields, Bristol, as Assistant to Chaplain of Bristol Royal Infirmary, Oct. 1953-Dec. 1958; Chaplain to the Lord Mayor of Bristol, 1961-65. Grand Chaplain of England, 1940. *Recreations:* Oxford University swimming team, 1909; running, tennis. *Address:* 2 Grange Road, Clifton, Bristol BS8 4EA.
[Died 16 Oct. 1973.

SAUNDERS-DAVIES, Rt. Rev. David Henry; *b* 1894; *o s* of Rev. James Davies and Mary Saunders Davies, Liverpool; *m* 1920, Catherine, *d* of John and Ellen Livingstone Price; one *s* one *d*. *Educ:* Liverpool College; Christ College, Brecon; RMC Sandhurst; Queens' College, Cambridge. Ryle Prize, 1920; BA 1920; MA 1923. Deacon, 1921, Priest, 1922. Curate of St John, Birkenhead, 1921-24; of St John, Reading, 1925-26; licensed to officiate in Diocese of Chester, 1926-28; Vicar of Hollingworth,

1928-31; Rector of Mobberley, 1931-45; Surrogate, 1931; Rural Dean of Knutsford, 1937-42; served War of 1939-45: Chaplain RAFVR, 1940-41; Assistant Chaplain-in-Chief, RAF, Middle East, 1942-45 (despatches); Hon. Canon of Chester, 1945-; Proctor in Convocation, 1945-51; Rector of Malpas, 1945-46; Rural Dean of Stockport, 1948-51; Rector of Stockport, 1946-55; Suffragan Bishop of Stockport, 1951-65; Hon. Asst Bishop of Worcester, 1965-68. Licence, Diocese of Rochester, 1968. *Recreation:* fishing. *Address:* Flat 2, 28 Boyne Park, Tunbridge Wells, Kent TN4 8ET. *T:* Tunbridge Wells 36099.
[Died 12 Aug. 1975.

SAVAGE, Sir Alfred William Lungley, KCMG 1951 (CMG 1948); Chairman, West African Currency Board, 1956-69; *b* 5 May 1903; *y s* of late Charles Savage, Gillingham, Kent; *m* 1931, Doreen, 2nd *d* of James Hopwood, OBE, Bulawayo, Rhodesia; one *s* one *d*. *Educ:* Owens School, London. Entered Home Civil Service, 1920; Asst Treasurer, Govt of N Rhodesia, 1928; Dep. Treas., Govt of Fiji, 1935; Dep. Treas., 1939, Dep. Financial Sec., 1940, Under-Sec., 1945, Govt of Palestine; Dep. Financial Sec., Govt of Nigeria, 1946; Financial Sec., 1948; Governor and C-in-C, Barbados, 1949-53; British Guiana, 1953-55; Crown Agent for Overseas Governments, 1955-63. *Address:* 19 Caledonia Place, Clifton, Bristol BS8 4DJ.
[Died 5 March 1980.

SAVILL, Sir Eric (Humphrey), KCVO 1955 (CVO 1950; MVO 1938); CBE 1946; MC, MA Cantab, FRICS; Director of the Gardens, Windsor Great Park, 1959-70, retired; architect and planter of The Savill and Valley Gardens, which were begun in 1932; *b* 20 October 1895; *s* of late Sir Edwin Savill. *Educ:* Malvern Coll.; Magdalene Coll., Cambridge. At outbreak of European War joined Univ. and Public School Corps as a Private; Commissioned to Devonshire Regt 1915, Captain 1916; served in France with 8th and 2nd Bns (wounded); joined firm of Alfred Savill & Sons, chartered Surveyors, 1920; Partner, 1926. Deputy Surveyor, Windsor Parks and Woods, 1931-59; Deputy Ranger of Windsor Great Park, 1937-59; Director of Forestry to Crown Estate, 1958-62. Mem. Bd Management: Hosp. for Sick Children, Gt Ormond St, 1926-42; King Edward VII Hosp., Windsor, 1933-46; Mem. Min. of Transport Adv. Cttee on Landscape Treatment of Trunk Roads, 1954-69 (Chm., 1962-69). Gold Veitch Memorial Medal, The Royal Horticultural Society, 1963; Gold Medal, The Royal Forestry Soc. of England, Wales and Northern Ireland, 1963. *Recreations:* gardening, fishing. *Address:* The Garden House, The Great Park, Windsor. *T:* Egham 4617. *[Died 15 April 1980.*

SAVORY, Lt.-Gen. Sir Reginald Arthur, KCIE 1947; CB 1944; DSO 1941; MC; psc; late Indian Army; *b* 26 July 1894; *s* of A. L. Savory, Bramham Gardens, London; *m* 1st, 1922, Myrtle Estelle Richardson (*d* 1965); no *c*; 2nd, 1969, Marie Nikolaevna McIlwraith (*née* Zurabova). *Educ:* Uppingham; Hanover; Sandhurst. First Commission, 1914; served European War, Egypt, Gallipoli (wounded, despatches, MC), Persia, Mesopotamia, Siberia; Kurdistan, 1923; Brevet Major, 1930; North-West Frontier, India, 1930 (despatches); Instructor, Indian Mil. Acad., 1932-34; Brevet Lt-Col 1934; Waziristan, 1937 (despatches); War of 1939-45, commanded 11th Indian Infantry Brigade, 1940-41, Middle East (DSO); GOC Eritrea, 1941 (despatches); Maj.-Gen. 1943; commanded 23rd Indian Div. 1942-43 (despatches); Director of Infantry (India), 1943-45; GOC Persia and Iraq, 1945-46; Lt-Gen. 1947. Adjutant-General in India, 1946-47; retired 1948. Col, Sikh Light Infantry, 1947-56. DL Somerset, 1952-60; JP Somerset, 1952-60; CC Somerset, 1952-59; County Alderman, Somerset, 1959-60; Chm. T & AFA, Somerset, 1953-59. *Publication:* His Britannic Majesty's Army in Germany, during the Seven Years War, 1966. *Address:* School Hill Cottage, Seale, Farnham, Surrey GU10 1HY. *Clubs:* Athenæum, Naval and Military. *[Died 14 June 1980.*

SAWYER, Charles; Senior partner, Taft, Stettinus and Hollister, Attorneys at Law; *b* 10 Feb. 1887; *s* of Edward Milton and Caroline Butler Sawyer; *m* 1st, 1918, Margaret Sterrett Johnston (*d* 1937); three *s* two *d*; 2nd, 1942, Elizabeth L. de Veyrac. *Educ:* Oberlin College, Oberlin, Ohio (BA); University of Cincinnati (LLB). Elected to City Council, Cincinnati, Ohio, 1911; Lieut Governor of Ohio, 1932; Democratic Candidate for Governor of Ohio, 1938; Ambassador to Belgium and Minister to Luxembourg, 1944; Secretary of Commerce, 1948-53. Hon. LLD: University of Cincinnati; Bryant College; Franklin and Marshall College; Miami University; Oberlin College. Hon. JD University of Cincinnati. *Publication:* Concerns of a Conservative Democrat, 1968. *Address:* Fountain Avenue, Glendale, Ohio 45246, USA. *Clubs:* Queen City, Cincinnati Country (Cincinnati); Chevy Chase (Maryland); Everglades, Bath and Tennis (Palm Beach, Fla). *[Died 7 April 1979.*

SAXTON, John Arthur, CBE 1973; DSc, PhD, FEng, FIEE, FInstP; Consultant, Directorate of Radio Technology, Home Office, since 1977; Director, Appleton Laboratory (formerly Radio and Space Research Station), Science Research Council, 1966-77; *b* 28 June 1914; *s* of late H. and L. E. Saxton; *m* 1939, Kathleen Florence Crook, BA, JP, *d* of late Alfred H. Crook, OBE, MA; one *s* one *d. Educ:* Loughborough Grammar School; Imperial Coll., London Univ. (Royal Sch.). 1st Class Hons Phys 1935; Imperial Coll., Governors' Prize for Physics, 1935. Demonstrator Physics Dept, Imperial Coll., 1936-38; Mem. Scientific Staff, DSIR, at Nat. Phys. Laboratory, 1938-52, and at Radio Research Station, 1952-64; Dep. Dir Radio Research Station, 1960-64; Director, United Kingdom Scientific Mission, Washington, DC, USA, and Scientific Counsellor at the British Embassy there, 1964-66. Admin. Staff Coll., Henley-on-Thames, 1955; Special Lectr, Imperial Coll., 1948-58; Vis. Prof. of Elec. Engrg, Univ. Texas, 1961-62; Vis. Prof. of Physics, University Coll., London, 1968-77. Mem. Council, Instn of Elec. Engrs, 1949-52, 1962-64, 1966-71 (Vice-Pres., 1978-; Chm., Elec. Div. Bd, IEE, 1969-70). Delegate to several confs of Internat. Radio Consultative Cttee and Internat. Scientific Radio Union, 1953-; Chairman: URSI Commn II, 1966-69; CCIR Study Gp 5, 1970-. Hon. DEng Sheffield, 1979. *Publications:* numerous papers in scientific jls on radio wave propagation and dielectric studies. *Address:* 106 Teddington Park Road, Teddington, Middlesex TW11 8NE. *Club:* Athenæum. *[Died 17 April 1980.*

SAXTON, Rev. William Isaac, CB 1946; OBE 1936; MA; Instructor Captain, RN (retired); *b* Cropwell Butler, Notts, 16 Nov. 1891; *s* of W. I. Saxton, Sen., and Mathilde F. E. Saxton; *m* 1920, Juliette Morton Turner; three *s. Educ:* Nottingham High School; King's College, Cambridge (Exhibitioner, Natural Science Tripos Parts I and II, 2nd Cl.). Joined Navy as Naval Instructor, 1915; HMS Indomitable, 1916-18, present at Jutland, served subsequently in HMS Warspite, RNE Coll., Keyham, Boys' Training Service; Instr Comdr 1929; Instr Capt. 1936; Fleet Education Officer, Home Fleet and Mediterranean; Deputy Director, Education Department, 1944; Director, Education Department, Admiralty, 1945-48; retired from RN, 1948; Director of Education in the Indian Navy, 1948-53. Ripon Hall, Oxford, 1953; Deacon and Priest, 1954; Vicar of West Farleigh, 1954-70. *Address:* Brook Cottage, Mill Lane, Wateringbury, Maidstone, Kent. *T:* Maidstone 812306.
[Died 8 June 1975.

SAYERS, Sir Frederick, Kt 1941; CIE 1937; KPM 1927; *b* 22 July 1885; *s* of Hugh T. Sayers, Cashel, Co. Tipperary; *m* 1909, Elizabeth (*d* 1960), *d* of J. Boyan MD. *Educ:* Foyle College, Londonderry, Trinity College, Dublin. Joined Indian Police, Madras, 1906; Acting Inspector-General, 1936 and 1937; Deputy Inspector-General of Police, and Commissioner of Police, Madras, 1936-37; Inspector-General of Police, Madras, 1937; retired, 1940; Adviser to Secretary of State for India, 1942-47. King's Police Medal (Gallantry), 1927; General Service Medal, 1921 (Malabar Rebellion). *Address:* Beaufort, Greystones, Co. Wicklow, Eire. *[Died 7 April 1977.*

SAYLE, Robert, MA; *b* 26 Feb. 1889; 2nd *s* of late John Sayle, Kirk Michael, Isle of Man; *m* 1916, Elizabeth Stewart Mackay, Liverpool; two *d. Educ:* King William's College, IOM; Chester College; St Edmund Hall, Oxford. Second Class, Honour School of English; House Master and Chief English Master, City of Oxford School; Headmaster of Coleshill Grammar School, Warwickshire, 1929-30; of the City of Bath Boys' School, 1934-39; of the Nelson School, Wigton, 1930-34, and again 1939-52. *Address:* Moanee Mollagh, Kirk Michael, Isle of Man. *T:* Kirk Michael 243. *[Died 14 Feb. 1971.*

SCAMP, Sir (Athelstan) Jack, Kt 1968; DL, JP; Director: GEC Ltd, since 1962; National Nuclear Corporation, since 1973; *b* 22 May 1913; 2nd *s* of Edward Henry and Jane Scamp; *m* 1939, Jane, *d* of John Kendall; one *s* one *d. Educ:* Birmingham. Chief Personnel Officer, Plessey Co. Ltd, 1953-58; Personnel Dir, Massey-Ferguson (UK) Ltd, 1958-62. Mem., Industrial Arbitration Bd, 1964-; Chm., Motor Industry Joint Labour Council, 1965-69; Member Lord Devlin Cttee of Inquiry Docks, Oct. 1964; seconded to Dept of Economic Affairs as Industrial Adviser, Feb. 1965-April 1966. Associate Prof. of Industrial Relations, Univ. of Warwick, 1970-75. Chm., Urwick, Orr & Partners, 1972-77 (Dir, 1969-77); Director: Fairfields (Glasgow) Ltd, 1967-68; AEI, 1967-72; New Opportunities Assoc., 1969-72; Coventry Broadcasting Ltd, 1973-; Coventry City Football Club, 1971- (Chm., 1975-77). Chairman, Courts of Inquiry: Footplate Staff, British Railways, 1965; Transporter Drivers, Longbridge Group of Delivery Agents, 1966; Transporter Drivers, Motor Vehicle Collections Ltd, 1966; Maintenance Workers, Birmingham Aluminium Castings Ltd, 1967; British Airline Pilots' Assoc., 1967; Dispute at Liverpool Docks, 1967;

Time Workers at Pressed Steel Fisher Ltd, 1968; Sewing Machinists, Ford Motor Co., 1968; Demarcation Dispute, Vickers Shipyard, Barrow-in-Furness, 1969; Chairman: Inquiry into Employment of Coal Trimmers in NE Ports, 1967; Inquiry into Employment of Coal Trimmers, Immingham, June 1970; Council Workers' Pay Dispute, Oct. 1970. Governor, William Temple College, 1967-72. CIEE, 1967; FIPM 1970; FBIM. DL Warwicks, 1967. *Recreations:* Association football, cricket and tennis. *Address:* Flax Hill, Ufton, Harbury, Leamington Spa, Warwicks. *T:* Harbury 612799. *[Died 30 Oct. 1977.*

SCANLAN, Most Rev. Mgr James Donald, Hon. DD University of Glasgow, 1967; DCL, BL; Former Archbishop of Glasgow; *b* 24 Jan. 1899; 2nd *s* of late Dr Joseph Scanlan, Glasgow. *Educ:* St Mungo's Academy and St Aloysius' Coll., Glasgow; University of Glasgow; RMC Sandhurst; St Edmund's Coll., Ware; Institut Catholique, Paris; Apollinare, Rome, Lieut 1st Highland LI. Active Service in German East Africa and Egypt. Studied medicine and law before ordination by late Cardinal Bourne, 1929; *Officialis* of Westminster, 1936; Vice-Chancellor, 1937; Privy Chamberlain to Pope Pius XI, 1937; Chancellor of Westminster, 1944; Vicar Delegate for US Forces in Britain, 1945; Titular Bishop of Cyme and Co-Adjutor Bishop of Dunkeld with right of succession, 1946; Bishop of Dunkeld, 1949-55; Bishop of Motherwell, 1955-64; Archbishop of Glasgow, 1964-74. *Address:* Archbishop's House, 19 Park Circus, Glasgow G3 6BE. *T:* 041-332 1680. *Club:* Naval and Military. *[Died 25 March 1976.*

SCARLETT, Lt-Col Henry A.; *see* Ashley-Scarlett.

SCARSDALE, 2nd Viscount, *cr* 1911; **Richard Nathaniel Curzon,** TD; Baron Scarsdale, 1761; Bt Scotland, 1636, England, 1641; Hon. Colonel Royal Artillery; Director Arthur Woolacott and Rappings Ltd, EC; *b* 3 July 1898; *s* of late Col Hon. Alfred Nathaniel Curzon; *S* uncle, Marquess Curzon, as Viscount Scarsdale, 1925; *m* 1st, 1923, Mildred Carson Dunbar (who obtained a divorce, 1946; she *d* 1969), *d* of late William Roland Dunbar of Huyton, Cheshire; four *d*; 2nd, 1946, Mrs Ottilie Margarete Julie Harris, *e d* of late Charles Pretzlik, Lowfield Park, Crawley. *Educ:* Eton; RMC, Sandhurst. Lieut Royal Scots Greys; Capt. Derbyshire Yeomanry; Major RA. Served in France, Belgium and Germany, 1918-19, and in Middle East, 1941-43. Formerly Vice-Pres. and Admin. Steward, Brit. Boxing Board of Control. A Vice-Pres., St John Ambulance Assoc. and Brigade for Derbyshire. KStJ. *Heir: cousin* Francis John Nathaniel Curzon. *Address:* Kedleston, Derby. *T:* Derby 840386. *Clubs:* Buck's, Lansdowne, MCC, Royal Automobile. *[Died 19 Oct. 1977.*

SCARTH of Breckness, Col Henry William; Lord Lieutenant of Orkney, since 1966; JP; Hon. Sheriff (formerly Sheriff Substitute) for Orkney since 1959; *b* 19 June 1899; *o s* of late Pillans Scarth and Madelena H. Sharbau; *m* 1st, 1927, Mary Beatrix Robertson (*d* 1955); one *d* (one *s* decd); 2nd, 1960, Kathleen Edgar. *Educ:* St Paul's. Served European War, 1914-18, France and N Russia, Lt (actg Capt.) Scots Guards. Succeeded as 11th Laird, 1929. Hon. Col RA (TA) Orkney and Zetland Unit. County Clerk, Roxburgh, 1935-40; Civil Defence Comr, Orkney and Zetland, 1940-44; Dep. Dir Allied Commn for Austria, 1945-47; Chairman: Orkney CC; Orkney Hosp. Bd, 1957-65; Pres. Orkney T & AVR; Mem., Highlands and Islands Consult. Coun. DL 1954, CC 1955, JP, Orkney. Vice-Lieutenant, Orkney, 1965-66. Cross of St Anne (2nd Cl.), Cross of St Stanislaus (3rd Cl.) (Russia), 1919. *Recreations:* shooting, fishing. *Address:* Skaill House, Orkney. *T:* Sandwick 501. *Clubs:* Guards; New (Edinburgh). *[Died 19 May 1972.*

SCERRI, Arthur J.; High Commissioner for Malta: in London since 1971; to Cyprus, since 1972; Ambassador to the USSR and to Iran, since 1972; *b* 31 Jan. 1921; *s* of Alfred and Carmen Lautier; *m* 1951, Ruby Howell, Wales; one *d. Educ:* St Albert's Coll.; St Mary's Coll.; HM Dockyard Technical College. Diplomas in Statistics, Work Study, English. Electrical Engr, HM Dockyard, Malta, 1937-50; Instrument Draughtsman in UK, 1950-71; Malta Rep. of Malta Labour Party in London, and London Corresp. of Voice of Malta, 1954-71. Took part in Integration Round Table Conf., 1956 and Independence Conf., 1963. *Publications:* various articles. *Recreations:* politics, reading, Maltese stamps. *Address:* 15 Upper Belgrave Street, SW1. *T:* 01-235 3931. *Clubs:* Travellers', Hurlingham, Royal Automobile. *[Died 9 Nov. 1980.*

SCHARRER, Irene, FRAM; pianist; *m* 1915, S. Gurney Lubbock, MA (*d* 1958); one *s* one *d. Educ:* Royal Academy of Music; studied under Tobias Matthay. Has appeared at Queen's Hall Symphony Concerts; London Symphony Concerts; Royal Philharmonic Concerts, London; New Symphony Orchestral

Concerts; Nikisch Symphony Concerts; Leipzig Gewandhaus; Berlin Philharmonic Orchestra; Royal Albert Hall Sunday Concerts; Liverpool Philharmonic; Norwich Philharmonic; Richter Hallé Concerts, Manchester, and in all the musical centres of Great Britain; has toured in Europe and America. *Address:* 61 Addison Road, W14. *T:* 01-937 0848.

[Died 11 Jan. 1971.

SCHIAPARELLI, Mme Elsa; couturière; *b* Rome; *m* (marriage dissolved); one *d.* Early career as film script writer and translator for an importing firm, US; later engaged in free-lance writing and gold sculpturing, Paris; became a French citizen; set up first couture establishment, Rue de la Paix, 1929; moved into larger premises, with separate perfume business, Place Vendôme, 1935. During War of 1939-45, lectured in USA; raised funds for France and worked as nurses' aid in Bellevue Hosp., New York. Reopened establishment Place Vendôme, 1945; established Schiaparelli Parfum Inc., NY, and in 1949 opened a New York branch to manufacture her creations on mass-production basis. *Publication:* Shocking Life, 1954. *Address:* 21 Place Vendôme, Paris 1e, France.

[Died 13 Nov. 1973.

SCHILSKY, Eric, RA 1968 (ARA 1957); RSA 1956 (ARSA 1952); sculptor; Head of the School of Sculpture, Edinburgh College of Art, 1946-69, retired; *b* Southampton, Oct. 1898; *m* Victorine Anne Foot, SSA, DA (Edinburgh), *d* of Major Hammond-Foot, RE; one *d. Educ:* Slade School of Art London. Formerly on teaching staff of Westminster School of Art and subsequently Central School of Arts, London. *Address:* 16a Meadow Place, Edinburgh 9. *[Died 29 March 1974.*

SCHMIDT-ISSERSTEDT, Hans, Dr phil; Generalmusikdirektor; Hon. Conductor, Symphony Orchestra, North German Radio, Hamburg, since 1971 (Chief Conductor, 1945-71); *b* Berlin, 5 May 1900; *m* Helga Swedlund; two *s* (and one *s* decd). *Educ:* Humanistisch. Gym., Berlin; Hochschule für Musik, Berlin; Univs of Berlin, Heidelberg and Münster. Sen. Conductor, Rostock, Darmstadt, Hamburg; Opera Director, German Opera House, Berlin; Chief Conductor, Stockholm Philharmonic Orchestra, 1955-64. Guest Conductor in all important orchestral societies of Old and New Worlds. Mem., Swedish Royal Academy of Music; Hon. Mem., RAM, London, 1970. Mem., Order of Crown of Bulgaria; Comdr, Order of Cross of Vasa (Sweden), 1964. *Publications:* Hassan gewinnt (three-act opera); orchestral, chamber and vocal music, etc. *Address:* 2081 Holm (Holstein), W Germany.

[Died 28 May 1973.

SCHOFIELD, Alfred Norman; CBE 1967; Town Clerk, Southampton, 1953-68, retd; *b* 2 May 1903; *s* of Alfred Schofield and Mary Schofield (née Nodes); *m* 1929, Bessie Agnes Fyfe Hartley; two *s* one *d. Educ:* Woodhouse Grove School; Sheffield University. LLM Sheffield (Frederick Clifford Post Grad. Schol.) 1926. Admitted Solicitor, 1926. Asst Solicitor, Sheffield Corp. 1927; Asst Town Clerk, Rotherham, 1929; Town Clerk: Worksop, 1932; Watford, 1940; War Service: Judge Advocate General's Dept (Army); Pres. Mil. Court, Jerusalem, 1944-46; rank Lt-Col (despatches). Past Pres. Soc. of Town Clerks; First Pres. Commonwealth Assoc. of Town Clerks. *Publications:* Bye Laws of Local Authorities, 1939; Teach Yourself Beekeeping, 1942; Local Government Elections, 1948; Parliamentary Elections, 1949; Housing Law and Practice, 1951; House Purchase through Local Authorities, 1953; The Councillor, 1950. All the above have had several editions. Consulting Editor, Local Government Forms and Precedents. *Recreations:* azalea and heather propagation, beekeeping. *Address:* Belvedere Lodge, Bassett Green Road, Southampton SO2 3NE. *T:* 69048. *Club:* Trojans (Southampton). *[Died 23 Sept. 1973.*

SCHOFIELD, Ivor Frederick Wentworth, CMG 1957; ED 1943; *b* 5 July 1904; *s* of Charles William and Jane Schofield; *m* 1937, Gladys May Powell. *Educ:* King's School, Worcester; Hertford Coll., Oxford. Cadet. Admin. Service, Nigeria, 1927; Resident, 1949; Administrative officer, Staff Grade, Nigeria (Western Region), 1954; Commissioner of Inland Revenue, Western Region, Nigeria, 1958; retired 1959; re-engaged on contract as Comr of Inland Rev. until Dec. 1960; Administrator of Income Tax, Southern Cameroons, 1960-61; Comr of Income Tax, The Gambia (UNO, Opex), 1964-66; Adviser on Income Tax, The Gambia (UNO), 1967-70. Served War of 1939-45: Royal West African Frontier Force, 1940-42; British Military Administration, Tripolitania, 1942-43; British Military Administration, Dodecanese (Temp. Lt-Col) 1943-45 (despatches). *Recreation:* gardening. *Address:* 10 Mountain View, Ballaugh, IoM. *T:* Sulby 7493. *[Died 25 Sept. 1979.*

SCHOLDERER, (Julius) Victor, CBE 1961; MA, Hon. DLitt (Durham and University of Wales); FBA 1948; *b* Putney, 9 Oct. 1880; *s* of Otto Scholderer, artist, of Frankfort-on-Main, and Luise Steurwaldt; *m* 1913, Frida Marie (*d* 1950), *d* of Wirkl. Geh. Oberbaurat Otto Semler, Berlin. *Educ:* St Paul's School; Trinity College, Oxford (scholar). Gaisford Prize (Greek verse), 1900; 1st Classical Mods; 2nd Lit. Hum.; entered British Museum, 1904; Deputy Keeper in the Department of Printed Books, 1930-45; has worked on the Catalogue of Books printed in the XVth Century now in the British Museum since 1905 and has edited parts v-viii; worked part-time on preparation of Short Title Catalogues of books printed in Italy, in Germany and in the Netherlands up to 1600 now in the British Museum; Sandars Reader in Bibliography, Univ. of Cambridge, 1930; designer of the New Hellenic Greek type; President, Bibliographical Society, 1946-48; gold medal of the Society, 1951; Hon. Member, Gutenberg-Gesellschaft; Hon. Fellow of Pierpont Morgan Library. *Publications:* Greek Printing Types, 1465-1927, 1927; Hand-list of Incunabula in National Library of Wales, 1940; Johann Gutenberg, Inventor of Printing, 1963; Fifty Essays in Fifteenth- and Sixteenth-Century Bibliography, 1966; papers and articles on early printing published in Transactions of the Bibliographical Society, The Library, Gutenberg-Jahrbuch and elsewhere; part editor of Sir William Osler's Incunabula Medica, 1923; The Avenue and other verses, 1959; Women of Troy, 1965; Reminiscences, 1970. *Address:* British Museum, Bloomsbury, WC1. *[Died 11 Sept. 1971.*

SCHÖNER, Dr Josef Andreas Carl, GCVO (Hon.) 1966; Austrian Ambassador to the Court of St James's, 1966-70; retired; *b* 18 Feb. 1904; *s* of Andreas Schöner and Lina (née Eder); *m* 1965, Henriette (née Welz); no *c. Educ:* Grammar Sch., Vienna; Univ. of Vienna; Dr jur and Dr rer pol. Entered Austrian Foreign Service, 1933; Attaché, Austr. Legation, Washington, 1934; Ministry for Foreign Affairs, Vienna, 1934-38; dismissed by German authorities after Anschluss; returned to Foreign Service, 1945; Counsellor, Austr. Leg., London, 1947; Washington, 1947-50; Chief of Austr. Liaison Offices in Germany (Bonn); Envoy Extraordinary and Minister Plenipotentiary, 1952; Head, Dept of Political Affairs, Vienna, 1953-55; Secretary-General for Foreign Affairs, Vienna, 1955-58; Austr. Ambassador, Bonn, 1958-66. Holds Austrian Grand Decoration with Star in Silver, Grand Cross of foreign Orders and other decorations. *Recreations:* sailing, photography, painting and sculpture. *Address:* 13 Seilerstaette, 1010 Wien, Austria. *Club:* Union Yacht (Austria). *[Died 9 March 1978.*

SCHONLAND, Sir Basil (Ferdinand Jamieson), Kt 1960; CBE 1945; FRS 1938; MA, PhD, MIEE (SA); Hon. ScD Cantab, Capetown, Rhodes; Hon. DSc Southampton; Hon. LLD Natal; Hon. Fellow, of Gonville and Caius College, Cambridge, 1959; *b* Grahamstown, SA, 5 Feb. 1896; *s* of late Prof. S. Schonland; *m* 1923, Isabel Marian Craib; one *s* two *d. Educ:* St Andrew's College and Rhodes College, Grahamstown; Gonville and Caius College, Cambridge. Served European War with BEF France, 1915-18, Capt. RE (Signals) (OBE, despatches); Brig. South African Corps of Signals, 1941-44; Supt, Army Operational Research Group (Ministry of Supply), 1941-44; Brig. (Scientific Adviser) to C-in-C 21st Army Group, BLA, 1944 (CBE); George Green Student and Exhibitioner Caius College, Cambridge, Research work in Cavendish Laboratory, 1920-22; Lecturer and later Professor of Physics, University of Cape Town, 1922-36; Pres., SA CSIR, 1945-50; Dir, Bernard Price Inst. of Geophysics and Carnegie-Price Prof. of Geophysics, Univ. of the Witwatersrand, Johannesburg, 1937-54; Dep. Dir, AERE, Harwell, 1954-58, Dir, 1958-60; Dir, Research Gp, UKAEA, 1960-61, retired; Halley Lecturer, University of Oxford, 1937; Chree Lecturer and Medallist, Physical Society of London, 1943; Hughes Medal of Royal Soc., 1945; Elliott-Cresson Medal of Franklin Institute, 1950; Faraday Medallist, IEE, 1962. *Publications:* Atmospheric Electricity, 1932, 2nd edn 1953; The Flight of Thunderbolts, 1950, 2nd edn 1964; The Atomists (1805-1933), 1968; papers in scientific journals on Cathode and Cosmic rays, Wireless and Lightning. *Recreation:* gardening. *Address:* The Down House, Shawford, Nr Winchester, Hants. *T:* Twyford 2221. *Club:* Athenæum.

[Died 24 Nov. 1972.

SCHREIBER, Brig. Derek, MVO 1935; late 11th Hussars; *b* 7 May 1904; 2nd *s* of late Captain C. S. Schreiber, and late Hon. Mrs Schreiber, Marlesford Hall, Woodbridge, Suffolk; *m* 1945, Viscountess Clive; one *d. Educ:* Harrow; RMC, Sandhurst. Joined 11th Hussars, 1923; Adjutant, 1930-33; Equerry to Duke of Gloucester, 1934-35; Commander 50 Indian Tank Brigade, 1943-44; Chief of Staff to Duke of Gloucester, 1944-46. *Recreations:* hunting, polo, aviation. *Address:* Bellasis House, Dorking, Surrey. *T:* Betchworth 3339; 59 Cadogan Place, SW1. *T:* 01-235 7454. *Club:* Cavalry. *[Died 19 March 1972.*

SCHREIBER, Lieut.-Gen. Sir Edmond Charles Acton, KCB 1944 (CB 1942); DSO 1914; DL; late Royal Artillery; *b* 30 April 1890; *s* of late Brigadier-General Acton L. Schreiber, CB, CMG, DSO; *m* 1916, Phyllis, *o d* of late Major C. P. Barchard; two *d*. Entered army, 1909; Capt., 1915; Bt Major, 1918; Maj., 1927; Bt Lt-Col, 1930; Lt-Col, 1937; Col 1938; Maj.-Gen. 1940; temp. Lt-Gen. 1941; Lt-Gen. 1944; served European War, 1914-18 (despatches, DSO, Bt Maj.); GSO2 Staff College, 1930-33; GSO2 War Office, 1934-37; GSO1 Senior Officers' School, Sheerness, 1938; Brigadier RA, Southern Command, 1938-39; Comdr 45 Div. 1940, 5 Corps, 1941, First Army, 1942; GOC-in-C Western Command, 1942-44; GOC-in-C South-Eastern Command, 1944; Governor and Commander-in-Chief of Malta, 1944-46; retired, 1947. National President, Old Contemptibles Association, 1960. DL Devon, 1948. KStJ, 1944. *Address:* Devoncourt Hotel, Exmouth, Devon. *Club:* Army and Navy. *[Died* 8 *Oct.* 1972.

SCHUMACHER, Ernst F(riedrich), CBE 1974; Chairman, Intermediate Technology Development Group Ltd, since 1966; *b* 16 Aug. 1911; *s* of Prof. Hermann A. Schumacher and Edith (*née* Zitelmann); *m* 1st, 1936, Anna Maria Petersen (*d* 1960); two *s* two *d*; 2nd, 1962, Verena Rosenberger; two *s* two *d*. *Educ:* New Coll., Oxford (Rhodes Schol.); Columbia Univ., NY. Econ. Adviser, CCG (British Element), 1946-50; Econ. Adviser, NCB, 1950-70, also Dir of Statistics, 1963-70; Dir, Scott Bader & Co., 1970-; Pres., Soil Assoc., 1970-. Hon. Dr rer. nat. Clausthal, 1963. Hon. Fellow UMIST, 1975. Gallantry Medal Class I for life-saving, Germany, 1935. *Publications:* Export Policy and Full Employment, 1945; Roots of Economic Growth, 1962; Small is Beautiful: Economics as if People Mattered, 1973; Es geht auch anders, 1974; *posthumous publication:* Good Work (speeches), 1979. *Recreation:* gardening. *Address:* Holcombe, Weald Way, Caterham, Surrey CR3 6EP. *T:* Caterham 42506. *[Died* 4 *Sept.* 1977.

SCHUSCHNIGG, Dr Kurt von; Professor, St Louis University, USA, 1948-67; *b* Riva (South Tyrol), 14 Dec. 1897; *s* of Dr Artur von Schuschnigg, Austrian General; *m* 1st, 1924, Herma Masera (*d* 1935); one *s*; 2nd, 1938, Countess Czernin. *Educ:* Stella Matutina College, Feldkirch; Innsbruck University. Member Austrian Parliament, 1927; Minister for Justice, 1932; Chancellor of Austria, 1934-38. *Publications:* Dreimal Oesterreich, 1937 (Farewell, Austria, 1938); Requiem in Rot-Weiss-Rot, 1945 (Zürich, Milan, New York; The Law of Peace, 1959); Im Kampf mit Hitler: die Ueberwindung der Anschussidee, 1969 (London, New York; The Brutal Takeover, 1971). *Address:* Mutters, near Innsbrück, Austria. *[Died* 18 *Nov.* 1977.

SCHWARZENBERG, Dr Johannes Erkinger, GCVO (Hon.) 1966; Minister Plenipotentiary of Sovereign Order of Malta to Italy, since 1969; *b* 31 Jan. 1903; *m* 1931, Kathleen, Vicomtesse de Spoelberch; one *s* one *d*. *Educ:* Univ. of Vienna (Doctor of Law). Civil servant, Ministry of the Interior, Austria, 1928; Attaché, Federal Chancellery, Foreign Affairs, 1930; Secretary, Austrian Legation, Rome, 1933, Berlin, 1935; left diplomatic career, 1938; Director and Delegate, Internat. Cttee of Red Cross, Geneva, 1940-46; re-entered Austrian diplomatic career as Counsellor in Paris, 1946; Austrian Minister in Rome, 1948; Austrian Ambassador: in Rome, 1950; in London, 1955-66; to Holy See, 1966-68. Commander's Cross in gold, Austrian Order of Merit, 1955, Grand Cross of the Italian Order of Merit, 1955, and other decorations. *Address:* 32 via Botteghe Oscure, 00186 Rome, Italy. *[Died* 26 *May* 1978.

SCOGINGS, Very Rev. Frank, LTh; retired as Dean of Natal, (1946-60), now Emeritus, and Vicar Gen. (1948-60). LTh, University of Durham, 1914. Deacon, 1914; priest, 1915. Curate of St Augustine, Penhalonga, 1914-16; St Michael, Salisbury, 1916-21; St John, Bulawayo, 1921-26; Priest-in-Charge of St Michael's Mission, Salisbury, 1927-28; St Faith's Native Mission, Durban, 1928-36; Vicar of St Saviour's Cathedral, Pietermaritzburg, Diocese of Natal, 1936; Sub-Dean, 1936-46; Canon of Natal, 1944. *Address:* Chapter Close, Taunton Road, Pietermaritzburg, Natal, South Africa. *[Died* 1 *May* 1976.

SCOONES, General Sir Geoffry (Allen Percival), KCB 1947; KBE 1944 (OBE 1935); CSI 1942; DSO 1917; MC; *b* 1893; *e s* of late Major Fitzmaurice Scoones, formerly Royal Fusiliers; *m* 1918, Angela Maud, *e d* of late Rev. Spencer R. A. Buller, RD; one *s* two *d*. *Educ:* Wellington College, RMC Sandhurst. Commandant 2nd Battn 8th Gurkha Rifles, Indian Army, 1935; Director of Military Operations and Intelligence, India, 1941-42; Major-General, 1942; GOC 4 Corps, Burma, 1942-44; GOC-in-C Central Command, India, 1945-46; General, 1946; Principal Staff Officer, Commonwealth Relations Office, 1947-53; ADC to the King, 1947-49; United Kingdom High Commissioner in New Zealand, 1953-57. *Address:* Ashdon Place, Ashdon,

Saffron Walden, Essex CB10 2JD. *T:* Ashdon 233. *[Died* 19 *Sept.* 1975.

SCOPES, Sir Frederick, Kt 1954; Consultant, formerly Chairman, Solid Smokeless Fuels Federation; *b* 24 Feb. 1892; *o s* of Harry and Alice D. Scopes; *m* 1st, 1916, Effie Theresa (*d* 1962); two *s*; 2nd, 1964, Ellen Frederica, *d* of late Capt. H. P. Wallis, RHA (formerly Mrs Downe). *Educ:* King Edward's Schools, Camp Hill and New St, Birmingham; Corpus Christi College, Oxford (Modern History Scholar). MA. Chairman: The Stanton Ironworks Co. Ltd, 1957-62 (Man. Dir 1942-57); Chamberlain and Hill, 1961-71. President, The Joint Iron Council, 1948-54; OStJ. Liveryman, Worshipful Company of Founders. *Publication:* The Development of Corby Works, 1968. *Address:* 6 Clarendon Terrace, Brighton BN2 1FD. *[Died* 10 *Nov.* 1978.

SCOTLAND, Rear-Adm. John Earl, CB 1964; DSC 1943; DL; Director, The Britain-Australia Society, since 1972; *b* 24 Aug. 1911; *s* of late Capt. W. R. Scotland, RN and Gwladys Lewis, Sydney, New South Wales; *m* 1940, Eileen Anne Studholme Brownrigg; one *s* two *d*. *Educ:* Cranbrook School, Sydney, New South Wales; Royal Naval Coll., Dartmouth. Qual. Gunnery Officer; in command HMS Modeste, 1946; Comdr 1946; in comd HMS Gravelines, 1951; Captain, 1953; in comd Gunnery School, Devonport, 1953; in comd HMS Vigilant and Dartmouth Training Sqdn, 1955 Naval Attaché, Rome, 1957; in comd HMS Lion, 1960; Rear-Adm. 1962; Flag Officer Middle East, 1962-64; Senior Naval Member, Ordnance Board, 1965-67, Pres., 1967-68. Chm., Governors, RN Scholarship Fund, 1973. DL Greater London, 1977. Officer, Order of Merit of the Republic of Italy. *Recreations:* painting, tennis, water ski-ing, golf. *Address:* 9 Tite Street, SW3. *Clubs:* Naval and Military; Royal Wimbledon Golf. *[Died* 27 *Feb.* 1978.

SCOTT, Maj.-Gen. Anthony Gerald O'Carroll, CB 1951; CBE 1946 (OBE 1945); *b* 22 June 1899; *s* of late Brigadier-General P. C. J. Scott, CB, and Mrs F. K. Scott (*née* Carroll); *m* 1926, Helena, *d* of Francis R. James, Hereford; one *d*. *Educ:* Wellington College; RMA, Woolwich. Gazetted 2nd Lt RFA, 1918; served European War, 1914-18, with Chestnut Troop, RHA; RFA, 1919-21; seconded King's African Rifles (local Capt.), 1921-26; Adjutant Beds Yeo., 1927-31; Instructor in Gunnery, School of Artillery, 1932; student Staff College, Camberley, psc, 1934-35; India, 1936; Staff Officer, RA, Western Comd, India, 1937; Instructor, Staff College, Quetta, 1938; BGS, 15 Indian Corps, Arakan, Burma, 1942 (despatches); CRA 25 Indian Div., 1943; Comdr 53 Indian Inf. Bde, 1944; BGS Eastern Comd, UK, 1945; Comd Sussex AA Bde, 1948; Commander Hamburg District, 1950-51; Commander, Singapore Base District, 1951-54; retired 1954. Vice-Pres., British Falconers' Club (Pres., 1956-66); MBOU. DL Bedfordshire, 1955-78; CC 1955-70. *Publications:* occasional articles in sporting papers. *Recreations:* hunting, fishing, shooting, falconry, training gun dogs, gardening. *Address:* Mill Lane, Pavenham, Bedfordshire. *[Died* 29 *Dec.* 1980.

SCOTT, Archibald Gifford, CIE 1942; *b* 21 April 1889; *s* of late William Gifford Scott, MB, and Caroline (*née* Strickland), Newton Abbot, Devon; *m* 1932, Kathleen, *d* of late H. J. Burton-Jones, Boulters, Maidenhead, Berks. *Educ:* Bromsgrove. King's Police Medal, 1931. Inspector-General of Police, Central Provinces and Berar, 1941-44. *Recreations:* fishing, shooting, golf. *Address:* Leigh Peverell, Doddiscombsleigh, near Exeter. *Clubs:* East India, Devonshire, Sports and Public Schools; Royal Bombay Yacht. *[Died* 28 *Jan.* 1980.

SCOTT, Sir (Arleigh) Winston, GCMG 1967; GCVO 1975; Governor-General of Barbados since 1967; *b* 27 March 1900; *m* 1936, Rosita May Hynam; three *d*. *Educ:* Harrison College, Barbados; Howard University, USA. BSc 1921; MD 1925; LRCP, LRCS (Edin.), LRFPS (Glas.), 1926; O et A Chir, NY Ophthalm. Hosp., 1931. Physician and Surgeon, Woodside Nursing Home, 1934-67. Member Senate, Barbados, 1964-66; appointed to Privy Council of Barbados, 1966. Hon. LLD Howard Univ., Washington DC, 1972. KStJ 1967. *Recreation:* reading. *Address:* Government House, St Michael, Barbados. *T:* 92646. *Club:* Rotary International (Barbados). *[Died* 9 *Aug.* 1976.

SCOTT, C(harles) Russell, MA Cantab; JP; Headmaster of Cranbrook School, 1929-60; retired; *b* 8 Feb. 1898; *s* of late Russell Scott and Susanna Laetitia Worthington; *m* 1923, Irene Keightley, 2nd *d* of late Harold Rankin, JP, Rochford, Essex; three *s* one *d*. *Educ:* Bedales School; Haileybury Coll.; St John's Coll., Cambridge (Exhibitioner in Science). 2nd Lt RGA, 1917; BEF France with 529 Siege Battery RGA, Lieut Nov. 1918; Asst

in Kent County Education Office, 1921-22; Asst Education Secretary, Cambridgeshire, 1922-27; first Hon. Secretary Cambridgeshire Festival of Music; Assistant Master Tonbridge School, 1927-29; Hon. Secretary Committee for *Music and the Community*, 1933 (the Cambridgeshire Report on the Teaching of Music); Chairman of Standing Conference for Amateur Music, 1946-63, Rural Music Schools Assoc., 1958-62, Kent Council of Social Service, 1958-73, Advisory Committee on Amateur Opera, 1948-63, Kent County Music Cttee, 1932-65, and Kent Rural Music School, 1964-67. *Recreations:* music, social work. *Address:* The Quarry, Wrotham, Kent. *T:* Fairseat 822453.
[*Died 16 Sept. 1979.*]

SCOTT, David Aylmer, FRS 1949; FRSC; MA, PhD; Research Member, Connaught Medical Research Laboratories, University of Toronto, 1922, retired, now Emeritus; *b* 2 Oct. 1892; *s* of James Robert Scott and Mary Ann Scott (*née* McKenzie), Kincardine, Ont.; *m* 1928, Bertha Collett Herington, BA; two *d.* Control Chemist, British Chemical Co.; Research Chemist, British Acetones; Research Chemist, Riordon Pulp and Paper Co.; Nat. Research Council Scholarship, 1921-22; worked with Sir Charles Harington at University College Hosp., London, 1928-29. Member; Biochemical Soc.; American Soc. of Biological Chemists; Canadian Physiological Soc.; Toronto Biochemical Soc. Hon. LLD Toronto, 1971. Flavelle Gold Medal, Royal Soc. of Canada, 1954; Banting Medal, American Diabetes Assoc., 1964. *Publications:* mainly concerned with Insulin, Heparin, and Carbonic Anhydrase. *Recreation:* golf. *Address:* 16 Browside Avenue, Forest Hill, Toronto, Canada. *T:* H83-1837. *Clubs:* York, University of Toronto Faculty, York Downs Golf and Country (Toronto).
[*Died 18 Nov. 1971.*]

SCOTT, Sir Donald; *see* Scott, Sir R. D.

SCOTT, Edward Hey L.; *see* Laughton-Scott.

SCOTT, Elisabeth Whitworth, AADip, FRIBA, retired; architect; *b* 1898; *d* of Bernard Scott, Surgeon; *m* 1936, George Richards. *Educ:* Redmoor School, Bournemouth; Architectural Association Schools. Won competition for designing new Shakespeare Memorial Theatre, Stratford-on-Avon, 1928. *Recreations:* music, theatre, country. *Address:* 12a Mount Pleasant Road, Poole, Dorset.
[*Died 19 June 1972.*]

SCOTT, Francis Clayton; *b* 6 Aug. 1881; *s* of Sir James William Scott, 1st Bt, and Anne Jane, *d* of John Haslam of Gilnow Hall, Bolton-le-Moors; *m* 1911, Gwendolen Frieda Martha (*d* 1973), *d* of late George Jager of Lingdale, Birkenhead; one *s* one *d*; *m* 1974, Elsa Marion Gatey, widow of Norman Gatey, Windermere, and *d* of late Edward McNaughton, The Grange, Ambleside. *Educ:* Bedales; Oriel College, Oxford (BA). Formerly Chairman of the Provincial Insurance Company Limited of Kendal and London, founded by his father. Founder and former Chairman of Brathay Hall Centre, Ambleside; High Sheriff of Westmorland, 1934. *Recreations:* shooting, fishing, yachting. *Address:* Matson Ground, Windermere, Cumbria. *T:* 3162.
[*Died 1 Jan. 1979.*]

SCOTT, His Honour Henry Cooper, QC 1961; a Circuit Judge (formerly Judge of County Courts), 1971-77; *b* 14 March 1915; *s* of late C. Paley Scott, KC, and Ruth, *d* of Rev. S. C. Scott, Chester; *m* 1947, Anne, *d* of late A. C. Bennett, Knaresborough; three *s*. *Educ:* Uppingham; Selwyn Coll., Cambridge. BA 1936; MA 1957. Called to Bar, 1939; Bencher, Inner Temple, 1968. Served War of 1939-45, Army (TA) (1939-45, Burma, Defence, etc, medals); demobilised 1946 as Major. Chm., ER Yorks QS, 1958-71; Recorder of: York, 1961-65; Kingston upon Hull, 1965-69; Sheffield, 1969-70; Leeds, 1970-71. Mem., Parole Bd, 1967-70. Chancellor, Dio. Bradford and Ripon, 1957-71. *Address:* West End, Crayke, York. *T:* Easingwold 21490.
[*Died 11 Nov. 1977.*]

SCOTT, Brig. Sir Henry (Lawrence), Kt 1947; CB 1932; DSO 1917 and Bar, 1920; MC; psc; *b* 6 April 1882; *m* Winifred Ethel (*d* 1931); one *s* (*er s* killed in action, Waziristan, 1937) two *d.* 2nd Lt Dorset Regt, 1902; Indian Army, 1903; Lt 1904; Capt. 1911; Major, 1917; Bt Lt-Col 1919; Lt-Col 1926; Col 1927; Instructor, Senior Officers School, India, 1921-23; Comd. 1st Bn 4th PWD Gurkha Rifles; AA and QMG, 1929-31; Commander Kohat Bde, 1932-35; served European War, 1914-18; Mesopotamia, 1920-21 (despatches nine times, DSO, and bar, MC); ADC to the King, 1934-35, retired 1935; Chief of Staff Jammu and Kashmir, 1936-47. *Address:* Box 187, Grahamstown, CP, S Africa.
[*Died 1 May 1971.*]

SCOTT, Sir (Henry) Maurice, Kt 1966; CBE 1957; DFC 1945; QC 1970; Speaker, Legislative Council of Fiji, 1958-66; *b* 23 July 1910; *s* of Sir Henry Milne Scott, QC; *m* 1963, Allerdina Fenna Gatty; two *s*. *Educ:* Wanganui Collegiate Sch., NZ; Magdalen Coll., Oxford. Called to Bar, Gray's Inn, 1936; joined legal firm of Wm Scott & Co., Suva, 1939. Enlisted Fiji Mil. Forces; resigned and joined 208 Sqdn RAF as pilot; served in W Desert, Palestine, Iraq, Italy. Re-joined Wm Scott & Co., 1947. Elected European Mem. for Northwestern Div. Fiji Legislative Coun.; Sen. Mem. 1956. Chairman: Burns Philp (South Sea) Co. Ltd; Fiji Times & Herald Ltd; Fiji Industries Ltd; Pacific Fishing Co. Ltd; Lepers' Trust Bd; President: Fiji Show Assoc.; Fiji Rugby Union; Returned Soldiers and Ex-Servicemen's Assoc. of Fiji; Director: Queensland Insce Co. Ltd; Fiji Tobacco Co. Ltd; Sidney Cooke Ltd, etc. Rep. Fiji: Festival of Britain, 1951; Coronation, 1953; Independence Celebrations, Malaya, 1957. Consul for Netherlands in Fiji, Tonga and Pitcairn Island. *Recreations:* swimming, fishing. *Address:* Raivolita, Tamavua, Fiji. *T:* 22084. *Clubs:* Defence, Royal Suva Yacht (Fiji).
[*Died 5 June 1976.*]

SCOTT, Major-General James Bruce, CB 1944; DSO 1942; MC 1918; late IA; *b* 25 Dec. 1892; *s* of late James Scott, CIE, Westfield, Dorking; *m* 1923, Nancy Claridge, *d* of W. R. Davies, JP; two *s*. *Educ:* Exeter School; RMC Sandhurst. 2nd Lieut, Unattached List, Indian Army, 1912; Captain 1916; Major, 1929; Bt Lieut-Colonel 1934; Lt-Col 1936; Bde Comdr, Brig., 1939; Maj.-Gen. 1941. GSO2 AHQ, India, 1931-35; Commander 1/8 Gurkha Rifles, 1935-39; Comdr 1st Burma Bde, 1939-41; Comdr 1st Burma Div., 1941-42; Inspector of Infantry (India), 1942-43; Comdr Peshawar Dist, 1943-46. Despatches 4 times. *Address:* 177 Rivermead Court, Ranelagh Gardens, SW6 3SF. *T:* 01-736 2961. *Club:* Hurlingham.
[*Died 30 May 1974.*]

SCOTT, Brig. John, DSO 1919; OBE 1958; *b* 1887; *m* 1st, 1913, Sybil, *d* of late Sir Frederic Hewitt, MVO, MD; two *s*; 2nd, 1933, Hester Mary, *d* of late Arthur Hogan. *Educ:* St Andrews University (MA 1907). Served European War, 1914-18 (despatches twice, DSO); commanding Royal Artillery 15th (Scottish) Div., 1939-40; GSO 1 Home Guard, 12th Corps 1940-41; Commander Gravesend Sub Area, 1941-42; Training Officer Inverness-shire Home Guard, 1942-44. CC Worcestershire, 1949, Alderman, 1965. Chm. S Worcestershire Conservative Assoc., 1950-56. *Recreations:* travelling, golf. *Address:* Combermere, 25 Avenue Road, Malvern, Worcs. *T:* Malvern 4601.
[*Died 3 Dec. 1971.*]

SCOTT, John Dick; Author; *b* 26 Feb. 1917; *o s* of late Alexander Scott, OBE, and of Margaret Gourlay Allardice; *m* 1941, Helen Elisabeth, *y d* of late Sir Edmund Whittaker, FRS, and Lady Whittaker; two *s*. *Educ:* Stewart's Coll., Edinburgh; Edinburgh Univ. (MA, Hons History). Assistant Principal, Ministry of Aircraft Production, 1940; attached to Cabinet Office for work on official History of the War, 1944. Literary editor of the Spectator, 1953-56; Editor, Finance and Development, 1963-74. *Publications:* The Cellar, 1947; The Margin, 1949; The Way to Glory, 1952; The End of an Old Song, 1954; (with Richard Hughes) The Administration of War Production, 1956; Life in Britain, 1956; Siemens Brothers, 1958; Vickers: A History, 1962; The Pretty Penny, 1963. *Address:* Gwyngoed Fawr, Llanddewi Brefi, Tregaron, Dyfed. *Club:* Garrick. [*Died 10 March 1980.*]

SCOTT, John Waugh, MA, DPhil, LLD (Glasgow); Professor of Logic and Philosophy, University College, Cardiff, 1920-44, Professor Emeritus since 1944; *b* 9 Nov. 1878; 2nd *s* of Gavin Stewart Scott, Hallhill, Lesmahagow, Lanarkshire; *m* 1913, Margaret Green (*d* 1956); two *d*. *Educ:* Hamilton Academy; University of Glasgow. Graduated with First-Class Honours in Mental Philosophy, 1903; Lecturer in Moral Philosophy in the University of Glasgow, 1905-20; Mills Lecturer in Philosophy, University of California, 1921-22; Contributor to Encyclopaedia Britannica; at various dates has held external examinerships in Philosophy in seven British Universities; LLD University of Glasgow, 1944. Originated and conducted "The Homecrofts" experiment, Cheltenham, 1928-56. Hon. Secretary of the National Homecroft Association, 1925-43. *Publications:* Syndicalism and Philosophical Realism; Unemployment, a Suggested Policy; Self-Subsistence for the Unemployed; Barter; Edited, from reliquiae of A. A. Bowman, A Sacramental Universe, designed and supervised A Synoptic Index to the Proceedings of the Aristotelian Society, Vol. I, 1900-49, Vol. II 1949-59, Vol. III, 1959-69; sundry articles on philosophical and social subjects; sundry notes contrib. to The New Age (under pseudonym W. D. Law). *Recreations:* long ago: walking; today: pestering modern economists for an authoritative ruling on C. B. Phipson's The Science of Civilisation. *Address:* 11 Barton Close, Cambridge.
[*Died 10 July 1974.*]

SCOTT, Colonel Sir Malcolm S.; see Stoddart-Scott.

SCOTT, Sir Maurice; see Scott, Sir H. M.

SCOTT, Prof. Norman Carson, BA, BSc; Professor Emeritus of Phonetics in the University of London, Hon. Fellow, School of Oriental and African Studies, since 1966; *b* 14 March 1899; *m* 1st, 1920, Mildred Cardew; one *s*; 2nd, 1940, Mary Simkins. *Educ:* Alleyn's School, Dulwich; King's College, London. Asst Master in grammar schools, 1925-37; part-time lecturer in Phonetics of French, Institut Français du Royaume-Uni, 1935-39; lecturer in phonetics, University Coll., London, 1937-44; lecturer in phonetics, 1944-47, Reader in phonetics, 1947-60, Professor of phonetics, 1960-66, School of Oriental and African Studies, University of London. Hon. Secretary, Philological Society, 1951-60; President, 1963-65, Vice-President, 1970-. *Publications:* (with M. Simkins) French Sentence Tables for Schools, 1939; English Conversations in Simplified Phonetic Transcription, 1942; A Dictionary of Sea Dayak, 1956; contrib. to learned journals. *Address:* 9 Gonnerston, St Albans, Herts.
[Died 8 Nov. 1975.

SCOTT, Paul Mark, FRSL; author; *b* 25 March 1920; *y s* of Tom Scott and Frances Scott; *m* 1941, Nancy Edith Avery; two *d.* *Educ:* Winchmore Hill Collegiate Sch. FRSL 1963. Co. Sec., Falcon & Grey Walls Press, 1946-50; Dir, David Higham Associates Ltd (formerly Pearn Pollinger & Higham), 1950-60. TV and radio plays: Lines of Communication, 1951; The Alien Sky, 1954; Sahibs and Memsahibs, 1956; The Mark of the Warrior, 1959; The Bender (adapted by Jeremy Paul), 1964. *Publications: novels:* Johnnie Sahib (Eyre & Spottiswoode Literary Fellowship Award), 1952 (collected edn 1968); The Alien Sky, 1953 (collected edn 1967); A Male Child, 1956 (collected edn 1968); The Mark of the Warrior, 1958 (collected edn 1967); The Chinese Love Pavilion, 1960 (collected edn 1967); The Birds of Paradise (Book Soc. Choice), 1962 (collected edn 1967); The Bender, 1963; The Corrida at San Feliu, 1964; The Jewel in the Crown, 1966; The Day of theScorpion, 1968; The Towers of Silence (Yorkshire Post Fiction Prize), 1971; A Division of the Spoils, 1975; The Raj Quartet (Omnibus volume of Jewel in the Crown, Day of the Scorpion, Towers of Silence, Division of the Spoils), 1976; Staying On, 1977 (Booker Prize, 1977); *poetry:* I, Gerontius, 1941; *play:* Pillars of Salt, 1948; contrib. The Times, Country Life. *Recreations:* coarse gardening, watching local wild-life, listening to music, long-distance travel, not working during Wimbledon fortnight. *Address:* c/o David Higham Associates Ltd, 5-8 Lower John Street, Golden Square, W1R 4HA. *T:* 01-437 7888.
[Died 1 March 1978.

SCOTT, Peter, OBE 1948; Hon. AIPI; *b* 30 Aug. 1890; *o s* of Peter Scott and Mary Harriet Wycherley; *m* 1st, 1925, Lilian Dove (*d* 1935); 2nd, 1938, Richenda Payne; no *c.* *Educ:* privately; School of Architecture, Liverpool University. Served European War, Palestine, Captain Royal Field Artillery; after demobilisation, varied business experience; Asst Sec. Home Service Committee, Society of Friends, 1926-28; Joint Sec., 1928-34; organised relief work in S Wales, 1928; originator of the Brynmawr Experiment and Subsistence Production Societies for older unemployed men in S Wales and Lancs. *Address:* The Old Coach House, East House, Adderbury, Banbury, Oxon. *T:* Adderbury 304.
[Died 3 March 1972.

SCOTT, Peter Duncan, CBE 1974; MA, MD (Cantab); FRCP, FRCPsych; Consultant Physician, Bethlem Royal and Maudsley Hospitals; Consultant Forensic Psychiatrist, Home Office; *b* 13 June 1914; *s* of Walter Scott, JP; *m* 1940, Lilian Ruth (*née* Lewis); two *d.* Served War, 1939-46: RNVR, Surg. Lt Comdr. Forensic psychiatry in the NHS (and, latterly, Home Office), 1946-. Member: Home Office Cttee on Law Relating to Young Offenders (Ingleby Cttee); Jt Home Office and Nat. Health Cttee on the Special Hospitals; Home Office Cttee on the Organization of the Prison Medical Service; Home Office Advisory Council on Penal System; Home Office Cttee on Voluntary Service (Lady Reading's Cttee). Past Pres. British Soc. of Criminology. *Publications:* numerous contribs to learned jls. *Address:* The Maudsley Hospital, Denmark Hill, SE5.
[Died 6 Aug. 1977.

SCOTT, Ralph Roylance, CMG 1939; MC; MB; MRCS; LRCP; DPH; retired; *b* 10 July 1893; *o s* of late Ernest Scott, Tynemouth. *Educ:* Blundell's School; Durham University. RAMC (SR), 1914; Active Service, 1916-19; Colonial Medical Service, 1919; Director of Medical Services, Tanganyika, 1935-45. *Publications:* Introduction to the Study of Preventive Medicine, 1939; Glossary of Scientific Terms, 1929; contrib. E African Med. Jl, 1963. *Recreation:* music. *Address:* PO Karen, Nairobi, Kenya. *Club:* Nairobi.
[Died 14 Dec. 1978.

SCOTT, Brig. Raymond Somerville, CIE 1934; OBE 1971; Indian Army, retired; Chairman, British Bloodstock Agency Ltd, since 1962; *b* 1882; *s* of A. S. B. Scott, Crondall, Hants; *m* 1911, Phyllis Freda Hildesley; one *s* one *d.* 32nd Lancers Indian Army, and Army Remount Department; Director of Remounts, India, 1930-34. *Recreations:* riding, racing. *Address:* Water Hall, Ifield, Sussex. *T:* Crawley 20002. *Club:* Cavalry.
[Died 23 Jan. 1972.

SCOTT, Sir (Robert) Donald, Kt 1955; landowner and farmer; *b* 19 May 1901; *s* of late William Scott, Newcastle upon Tyne; *m* 1930, Olive Anna Daphne, *d* of late J. J. Russell, Ballygasson House, Co. Louth; two *d.* *Educ:* Mill Hill School; Magdalene Coll., Cambridge (MA). Liaison Officer to Minister of Agriculture, 1942-46, 1955-64, for Northern Region; Member Northumberland Rivers Catchment Board, 1942-46; MP (C) Wansbeck Division of Northumberland, 1940-45; Penrith and The Border Division of Cumberland, 1950-55; Member of the Speaker's Conference on Electoral Reform, 1944; Jt Parliamentary Sec. to Min. of Agriculture and Fisheries, May-July 1945; Chm. of Ministry of Agriculture Hill Sheep Advisory Committee for England and Wales, 1945-46; Member Hill Farming Advisory Cttee for Eng., Wales and N Ireland, 1946-50; Assistant Agriculture Adviser, Ministry of Agriculture, 1945-46; Vice-Chairman Northern Area Conservative Assocs, and Chairman Northumberland County Conservative Assocs, 1945-50; Chairman Conservative Political Education Cttee, 1949-50: Member Royal Commission on Common Land, 1955-58; Governor of Conservative Coll. of the North. *Recreation:* shooting. *Address:* Caistron, Thropton, via Morpeth, Northumberland. *TA* and *T:* Hepple 218. *Clubs:* Constitutional, Farmers'.
[Died 18 June 1974.

SCOTT, Very Rev. Robert Forrester Victor, DD Univ. of Edinburgh, 1944; CF; Minister of Auchterhouse Parish, 1960-68; retired, 1968; *b* 11 August 1897; *s* of Rev. William Frank Scott and Henrietta Porteous Hardy; *m* 1924, Phyllis Lee (*d* 1969), *d* of Frank Scott Graves; one *s* two *d.* *Educ:* Morrison's Acad., Crieff; Roy. High Sch., Edinburgh; Edinburgh Univ. On leaving school, served with 13th Bn The Royal Scots, France, 1916-19; ordained to Parish of Strathmiglo, Fife, 1923; inducted to St Andrew's Parish, Dundee, 1926; inducted as Colleague and Successor to late Very Rev. John White, CH, DD, LLD, The Barony, of Glasgow, 1935; Minister of St Columba's Church of Scotland, Pont St, SW1, 1938-60; Moderator of the General Assembly of the Church of Scotland, May 1956-May 1957; Mem. Advisory Council, BBC, 1958-62; Chm. West London Cttee for Protection of Children, 1947-60. Presbyterian Chaplain, The Royal Hospital, Chelsea, 1956-60. Officer of the Order of Orange-Nassau, 1948. *Publications:* articles in newspapers and periodicals. *Recreation:* fishing. *Address:* 20 Magdala Crescent, Edinburgh EH12 5BD. *Club:* Caledonian.
[Died 1 March 1975.

SCOTT, Rev. Sidney; see Scott, Rev. (Walter) S.

SCOTT, Maj.-Gen. Thomas Patrick David, CB 1956; CBE 1945; DSO 1943, and Bar, 1945; Lord Lieutenant of County Fermanagh, since 1971; *b* 1 March 1905; *o s* of late Lieutenant-General Sir Thomas E. Scott, KCB, CIE, DSO; *m* 1936, Peggy Winifred, *d* of late Capt. Robert McGregor Bowen-Colthurst, Killinadrish, Co. Cork; three *d.* *Educ:* Blundell's; RMC Sandhurst. 2nd Lt Royal Irish Fusiliers, 1924, Adjt, 1933-36; Instructor, RMC, 1936-38; student, Staff College, 1939; OC 1st Royal Irish Fusiliers, 1942-43; Comdr, 38th Irish Brigade, 1944-47; Comdt, Senior Officers School, 1948-50; Commander 107 Ulster Bde Gp (TA), 1950-52; DAG, MELF, 1952-54; Training Adviser to Commander-in-Chief, GHQ, Pakistan, 1954-56; GOC 42 (Lancs) Div. TA and North-West District, 1956-59. Colonel The Royal Irish Fusiliers (Princess Victoria's), 1960-68; Dep. Col Royal Irish Rangers, 1968-71. Chairman, Co. Armagh TA&AFA, Dec. 1959-67. High Sheriff, Co. Tyrone, 1966. *Address:* Rossfad House, Ballinamallard, Co. Fermanagh, N Ireland. *T:* Ballinamallard 397. *[Died 30 July 1976.*

SCOTT, Rev. (Walter) Sidney; Clergyman (licensed to officiate Dioceses of London and Winchester since 1946, Portsmouth since 1953 and Guildford since 1958); Author and Lecturer; *b* 2 November 1900; *o s* of late Walter Samuel Scott, KC; *m* 1937, Margaret (*d* 1974), *o d* of John E. Jefferson Hogg, OBE, JP, DL, Norton House, Co. Durham; no *c.* *Educ:* St Columba's College, Dublin; Trinity College, Dublin (BA 1st Class and Respondent; MA); University of Alberta, Canada (BA); Université de Nancy, France, (D d'Univ., avec mention très honorable); Wells Theological College. Curate of Writtle, Essex, 1929-31; Precentor (1931-41) and Priest-in-Charge (1941-46) of St Peter's, Cranley Gardens, SW. British Chaplain of Ostend, 1937; High Sheriff's Chaplain, Sussex, 1940 and 1941; Mem. of Bd,

American Students' Center, Paris, 1955-74; Chaplain, Westminster Abbey, 1948-49; Canon of Bermuda, 1949. Served on C of E Council on Foreign Relations, 1957-64. At various times temporary Chaplain of Paris, Antwerp, Dinard, Amsterdam, Oslo, etc. Pres., Royal Martyr Church Union. Trustee, Gilbert White Museum, Selborne. Officier d'Académie (France), 1939; Officier de l'Instruction Publique (France), 1949; Chevalier de la Légion d'Honneur (France), 1958; Médaille d'Honneur (Chinon) 1963; Freedom of Vaucouleurs, France, 1949, and of Chinon, France, 1969. *Publications:* Worship and Drama, 1938; Prayers and Intercessions, 1939; A War-Time Compline, 1940; Little Chelsea, 1941; The Athenians, 1943; Harriet and Mary, 1944; Shelley at Oxford, 1944; The Fantasticks, 1945; A Clowder of Cats, 1945; John Donne, 1946; Georgian Theatre, 1946; Pride of London (with Walter Scott and Joan Stevenson) 1947; Bygone Pleasures of London, 1948; (ed) New Shelley Letters, 1948; (ed) Gilbert White's Antiquities of Selborne, 1949; A Selborne Handbook, 1950; (ed) Hogg's Alexy Haimatoff, 1952; (ed) Letters of Maria Edgeworth and A. L. Barbauld, 1953; A Journal of the Terror, 1955; Green Retreats, 1955; The Trial of Joan of Arc, 1956; L'Art du Culte selon la coutume de l'Eglise d'Angleterre, 1957; (ed) Gilbert White's Natural History of Selborne, 1962; A Crusading Dean, 1967; Jeanne d'Arc: a biography, 1973. *Recreation:* book collecting. *Address:* Shortfield House, Frensham, Surrey. *T:* 2566. *Club:* Athenæum. *[Died 12 April 1980.*

SCOTT, Maj.-Gen. Sir William (Arthur), KCMG 1959; CB 1950; CBE 1943; *b* 25 March 1899; *s* of Herbert Ernest and Jane Scott; *m* 1927, Dulcie Buchanan; two *d. Educ:* privately; RMA, Woolwich. Commissioned RE 1917; France and Belgium, 1918; transferred to Royal Signals, 1921; Waziristan, 1921-23; Razmak FF, 1923 (MBE 1924); France, 1940; N Af., 1942 (CBE); Sicily and Italy, 1943-45. Dir of Signals, War Office, 1948-52; Dir of Weapons and Development, War Office, 1952-55; retired, 1955. Late Col Comdt Royal Signals; Master of Signals, 1961-70. Princess Mary Medal, Royal Signals Instn, 1978 (awarded posthumously). *Address:* Applecot, Upper Stoneborough Lane, Budleigh Salterton, Devon. *T:* Budleigh Salterton 3123. *[Died 12 Sept. 1976.*

SCOTT, Prof. William Douglas R.; *see* Robson-Scott.

SCOTT, Sir Winston; *see* Scott, Sir A. W.

SCOTT-BATEY, Rowland William John, JP; Chairman, Tyne & Wear Passenger Transport Authority, since 1973; *b* 30 Dec. 1913; *s* of John Henry Scott-Batey and Eva (*née* Hepburn); *m* 1942, Jessie Macpherson Ross; one *s* three *d. Educ:* South Shields High Sch.; Durham Univ. Served War of 1939-45: Captain, Oxford and Bucks LI. English Industrial Estates Corp., 1946-78. Chairman: Newcastle City Labour Party, 1958-76; Northern Regional Council of the Labour Party, 1972-76. Councillor, Tyne & Wear CC 1973- (Chm. 1973-75). JP, Newcastle upon Tyne, 1958-. *Recreations:* watching cricket, reading. *Address:* 4 Folly Yard, Greenside, Ryton, Tyne and Wear. *T:* Ryton 7017. *[Died 1 March 1980.*

SCOTT-ELLIOT, Walter Travers; *b* 9 Oct. 1895; *o s* of Wm Scott Elliot, Arkleton, Dumfriesshire, and Maude, *o c* of Robert Boyle Travers, Farsid, Co. Cork; *m* 1948, Dorothy Alice (*d* 1977), *d* of late William Nunn, Calcutta. *Educ:* Eton. 2nd Lieut Coldstream Guards, Special Reserve, 1914; Capt. 1917; retired, 1919. Subsequently joined Bombay Company Ltd, East India Merchants; Managing Director, 1927. Served on Headquarters, Ministry of Labour, 1941-45; MP (Lab) Accrington, 1945-50; PPS to Sec. of State for War, 1946-47. *Recreations:* shooting and travelling. *Address:* 22 Richmond Court, Sloane Street, SW1. *Club:* Reform. *[Died 14 Dec. 1977.*

SCOTT-MONCRIEFF, Adm. Sir Alan (Kenneth), KCB 1955 (CB 1952); CBE 1952; DSO 1942, Bar 1943; *s* of Robert Lawrence Scott-Moncrieff and Victoria Troutbeck; *m*, 1st, 1923, Norah Doreen Vereker (*d* 1973); one *d*; 2nd, 1974, Winifred Titley (*née* Richards); two step *s. Educ:* RN Colleges, Osborne and Dartmouth. Joined HMS Orion, as Midshipman, 1917; Comd HMS Enchantress, 1939-40; Comd HMS Faulkner, Capt. "D" 8th Flotilla, 1942-43 (despatches twice). Imperial Defence College, 1948; Comd HMS Superb, 1949; Flag Officer Comd Fifth Cruiser Sqdn, 1951-52. Korean War (CBE, despatches); Adm. Comd. Reserves, 1953-55; C-in-C, Far East Station, 1955-57. Retired, 1958. A Younger Brother of Trinity House. Mem., Victory Services Club. King Haakon Medal (Norway), 1945; Comdr Legion of Merit (US), 1952. *Address:* 7 King's Walk, Henley-on-Thames. *T:* Henley-on-Thames 2510. *Clubs:* Naval and Military; Phyllis Court (Henley-on-Thames). *[Died 25 Nov. 1980.*

SCOTT-MONCRIEFF, Joanna Constance; *b* 7 Sept. 1920; *y d* of late Rev. C. W. Scott-Moncrieff, MA, and Constance E. H. Lunn; *m* 1961, Noel John Horne Baker; one *d. Educ:* St Swithun's Sch., Winchester; Sorbonne, Paris. Social work, 1941; Political Warfare Executive, 1941-45; joined BBC, 1945; Deputy Editor, Woman's Hour, 1950; Editor, 1956-64; Producer, Religious Broadcasting, 1964-72. Mem., Gen. Purposes Cttee and UK Grants Cttee, Help the Aged, 1972-. *Publications:* Pause for Thought, 1971; The 60 Plus Book, 1977. *Address:* Berins Hill, Ipsden, Oxon. *[Died 28 Dec. 1978.*

SCOTT-TAGGART, Wing Commander John, OBE 1975; MC; Barrister-at-law; *b* Bolton, Lancashire, 1897; *s* of Wm Scott-Taggart, MIMechE, consulting engineer. *Educ:* Bolton School; Technological Institutions; King's College, University of London; Law at University College, London. Specialised in radio engineering and patent work; served European War, 1914-19 (despatches, MC); Head of valve manufacturing, Ediswan, 1919-20; Head of the Patent Department, Radio Communication Company, Ltd, 1920; founded 1922 and later became sole proprietor of the Radio Press, Ltd; served War of 1939-45 with RAF, France, 1939-40 (despatches). Staff Officer, Air Ministry, immediately responsible for all Radar training in RAF, 1940-41; Senior Technical Officer, No 73 Wing and, as such, was technically responsible for all radar stations in two-thirds of England and Wales, 1943-45 (despatches); Admiralty Signal and Radar Establishment, 1951-59. Has acted as Patent Adviser to radio concerns on both sides of the Atlantic. Has taken out numerous patents relating to valve manufacture, radio receiving and transmitting circuits, and allied matters since 1918; CEng; Fellow of the Institute of Radio Engineers; FIEE; FIMechE; FInstP; Fellow American Institute of Electrical Engineers. Cavaliere Ufficiale of Order Al Merito della Repubblica Italiana, 1962 (for services to art); OBE (for services to radio engineering), 1975. *Publications:* Textbooks: Manual of Modern Radio; Book of Practical Radio; Thermionic Tubes in Radio Telegraphy and Telephony; Elementary Textbook on Wireless Vacuum Tubes; Radio Valves and How to Use Them; Wireless Valves Simply Explained; Practical Wireless Valve Circuits, etc; Bibliography of Italian Maiolica, 1967; Italian Maiolica, 1972; Spanish Pottery and Porcelain, 1973; over five hundred articles in technical press; papers read before learned societies (twice at Brit. Assoc.). *Recreation:* collection of paintings, sculpture and ceramics. *Address:* 96 Gregories Road, Beaconsfield, Bucks. *[Died July 1979.*

SCOVELL, Rowley Fielding; Managing Director, Currie Line Limited, 1944-67; *b* 29 Nov. 1902; *s* of late Rowland Hill Scovell; *m* 1944, Amy Stansmore Huddart, *widow* of Lieut-Comdr G. P. Huddart, RN; one *s. Educ:* Rugby; Trinity Coll., Cambridge. Joined Currie Line Ltd, 1923. Regional Shipping Representative, E Scotland, Min. of War Transport, 1940-46; Shipping Adviser to Turkish Government, June-Dec., 1943. Director Standard Life Assurance Company (Chm., 1957-60). *Address:* Hamilton Lodge, North Berwick, East Lothian. *T:* North Berwick 2746. *Clubs:* Boodle's; New (Edinburgh). *[Died 2 Nov. 1972.*

SCULLY, Vincent William Thomas, CMG 1946; United States Medal of Freedom (Bronze Palm); FCA; *b* 9 Jan. 1900; *s* of James Scully, Dist. Inspector, RIC, and Katherine Scully, New Ross, County Wexford, Ireland; *m* 1930, Sylvia, *d* of late Sir Wyly Grier; one *s. Educ:* Christian Brothers School, New Ross and Thurles, Ireland; Trinity Coll., Dublin. Chartered Accountant, Ontario, 1929; practised as Chartered Acct with Clarkson, Gordon, Dilworth and Nash, 1925-32; Director and Sec.-Treas., J. D. Woods & Co. Ltd, 1932-45; Controller and Sec. Treas., York Knitting Mills Ltd, 1932-45; Sec.-Treas, Plateau Co. Ltd (Crown Co.), 1940-41; Treas. and subsequently Pres. War Supplies, Ltd (Crown Co.), 1941-44; Pres. Victory Aircraft Ltd (Crown Co.), 1944-45; Deputy Minister of Reconstruction and Supply and Vice-Pres., Nat. Research Council, 1945-47; Deputy Minister of National Revenue (Taxation), 1948-51; Comptroller, The Steel Company of Canada Ltd, 1951, Pres., 1957, Chief Exec. Officer, 1960, Chm. Bd, 1966, retired, 1976. *Address:* 9 Deer Park Crescent, Apt 1203, Toronto, Ontario M4V 2C4, Canada. *Club:* York (Toronto). *[Died 7 June 1980.*

SEAGER, Basil William, CMG 1949; OBE 1939; HM Immigration Service, retired 1970; *b* 1898; *s* of late E. J. P. Seager, Constantinople, and L. D. Seager (*née* Sellar); *m* 1944, Heather Mildred Carmichael, *d* of late Lt-Col R. C. Bell, DSO, OBE, late Central India Horse. *Educ:* abroad. Communications Department, FO, 1926; British Agency and Consulate (now HM Embassy), Jedda, Saudi Arabia, 1926-34; seconded to Aden Govt as Political Officer, 1933-34; Colonial Administrative Service as PO (Frontier Officer), 1934; Acting Political

Secretary on various occasions, 1935-40; Political Officer in charge W Aden Protectorate, 1940; British Agent, Western Aden Protectorate, 1942; Chairman (ex-officio) Abyan (Cotton) Board, 1947-54; retired Colonial Administrative Service, 1954. Served European War 1914-18, 1916-22 (Captain); War of 1939-45, 1941-42 (Major). *Address:* 16 Broadwater Down, Tunbridge Wells, Kent. *[Died 16 Dec. 1977.*

SEAGO, Edward Brian, RWS 1959 (ARWS 1957); RBA 1946; Painter; *b* 31 March 1910; *s* of Francis Brian Seago and Mabel Reeve Woodroffe. One-man exhibitions: London, Glasgow, New York, San Francisco, Toronto, Montreal, Los Angeles, Chicago, Johannesburg, Oslo, Bergen, Brussels, Melbourne, Zürich, Tokyo. Loan Exhibition: in Norwich City Art Gallery, 1944 and 1962; of Italian War pictures in Norwich and Bristol Municipal Galleries, 1946; Loan exhibition, King's Lynn Festival, 1954; of pictures painted during the Duke of Edinburgh's world tour, at St James's Palace, 1957. Designed: colours and insignia of Airborne Forces, and modelled statuette for their HQ, 1941; stage set for William Golding's The Brass Butterfly, London, 1958. Served with Royal Engineers, 1939-45. *Publications:* Circus Company, 1933; Sons of Sawdust, 1934; Caravan, 1936; Peace in War, 1943; High Endeavour, 1944; With the Allied Armies in Italy, 1945; A Canvas to Cover, 1947; Tideline, 1948; With Capricorn to Paris, 1956; with John Masefield: Country Scene, 1936; Tribute to Ballet, 1937; A Generation Risen, 1942; (introd) The Paintings of Field Marshal Marshal Earl Alexander, 1973. *Recreations:* reading, gardening, and "messing about with boats". *Address:* The Dutch House, Ludham, Norfolk. *T:* Potter Heigham 225. *Clubs:* Athenæum, Garrick, Beefsteak. *[Died 19 Jan. 1974.*

SEAL, Sir Eric (Arthur), KBE 1955; CB 1941; Deputy Secretary, Ministry of Works, 1951-59, retired; *b* 16 Sept. 1898; *s* of Arthur John Todd Seal; *m* 1926, Gladys Mary, *d* of Frank Leadbitter, Sutton, Surrey; three *s.* RAF 1918-19; entered Patent Office, 1921; Admiralty, 1925; Principal Private Sec. to First Lord, 1938-40; Principal Private Sec. to Mr Winston Churchill, as Prime Minister, 1940-41; Deputy Secretary of the Admiralty (North America), 1941-43; Member of British Supply Council, Washington, 1943; Under-Secretary of Admiralty (London), 1943-45; Chief, Trade and Industry Div., CCG, 1946-47; Dir-Gen. Building Materials, Min. of Works, 1947-48; Deputy Under-Secretary of State, Foreign Office (German Section), 1948-51. *Address:* Seaforth, Spinney Lane, Chichester, Sussex. *Club:* Royal Thames Yacht. *[Died 31 March 1972.*

SEAMAN, Clarence Milton Edwards, CBE 1971; MA Oxon; Headmaster of Christ's Hospital, 1955-70; *b* 1908; *s* of Rev. H. W. Seaman; *m* 1936, Kathleen M. G. Askew; one *s* one *d. Educ:* Christ's Hosp.; St John's Coll., Oxford. Assistant Master, Bedford School, 1932-39; Assistant Master, Rugby School, 1939-45; Rector of The Edinburgh Academy, 1945-51; Headmaster of Bedford School, 1951-55. *Address:* Orchard End, Ickleton Road, Wantage, Oxon. *[Died 18 Nov. 1974.*

SEATON, Reginald Ethelbert; Chairman, Greater London Area Sessions (inner area), 1965-69 (Chairman, London Sessions, 1959-65); retired; *b* 27 Dec. 1899; 2nd *s* of Albert Edward and Edith Gertrude Seaton; *m* 1930, Vera Wilson Barnett; one *s* three *d. Educ:* Epsom College; Downing College, Cambridge. BA Cantab. 1923; called to Bar, Middle Temple, 1924, Bencher, 1951; Counsel to Post Office at Central Criminal Court, 1942-43; Third Junior Prosecuting Counsel to the Crown, Central Criminal Court, 1943; Dep. Chm., E Sussex QS, 1950; Recorder of Maidstone, 1951-59; Second Senior Prosecuting Counsel to the Crown Central Criminal Court, 1954-59. *Publication:* (with R. H. Blundell) Trial of Jean Pierre Vacquier. *Recreations:* golf, gardening. *Address:* Queen Elizabeth Building, Temple, EC4. *T:* 01-353 2576; Casa Maya, 2 Rudgwick Avenue, Goring-by-Sea, Sussex. *T:* Worthing 44560. *[Died 4 April 1978.*

SEAVER, Very Rev. George, MA (Oxon); BD (London); LittD (Dublin); FRGS; MRIA; Fellow Royal Society of Antiquaries, Ireland; *b* Cheltenham, Gloucestershire, 23 July 1890. *Educ:* St Edmund Hall, Oxford. Lieutenant 40th Divisional Train, transf. Connaught Rangers, attd RAF, 1914-18; Asst Native Commissioner, Northern Rhodesia, 1919-24; ordained, 1925; first Warden of Devon Home for Wayfarers and Public Preacher Diocese of Exeter, 1930; Senior Tutor and Lecturer, St Aidan's College, Birkenhead, 1933-42; War of 1939-45, member Royal Observer Corps; Bishop's Vicar, Kilkenny Cathedral, 1946; Dean of Ossory and Rector of Kilkenny, 1950-57; Canon of St Patrick's Cathedral, Dublin, 1951-57. *Publications:* Bam: The Story of an African Boy, 1925; Edward Wilson of the Antarctic, 1933; Edward Wilson: Nature Lover, 1937; Faith of Edward Wilson, 1948; Birdie Bowers of the Antarctic, 1938; Scott of the Antarctic, 1939; Sir James Cantlie (with Col N. Cantlie), 1939;

Albert Schweitzer: Christian Revolutionary, 1944; Albert Schweitzer, the Man and his Mind, 1947; Albert Schweitzer: A Vindication, 1949; Berdyaev: an Introduction to his Thought, 1950; Sir Francis Younghusband, 1952; Icelandic Yesterdays, 1957; David Livingstone: his Life and Letters, 1957; Tales of Brother Douglas (with Coleman Jennings), 1960; John Allen Fitzgerald Gregg: Archbishop, 1963; Richard Archer Houblon: a memoir, 1970; introd. to new edition of The Worst Journey in the World, 1965. *Address:* Inniskeen, Greystones, Ireland. *[Died 25 Oct. 1976.*

SEBASTIAN, Erroll Graham, CBE 1946; DSO 1917; *b* 2 August 1892; *s* of Lewis Boyd Sebastian and Henrietta Maria Lennartson; *m* 1959, Mrs Hilda Reynolds Gardner. *Educ:* Winchester; University Coll., Oxford. Served European War, 2nd Buffs in France, Salonica, and Constantinople, 1914-19 (DSO); served in Consular Service in Siam, Roumania, Belgium, Greece; Consul-General at Athens, 1940-41; attached Minister of State's Office, Cairo, 1941-42; Consul-General at Gothenburg, 1942-44; at Antwerp, 1944-50; Consul-General at Milan, 1950-52; retired 1952. *Recreations:* needlework, music. *Address:* Bridge House, Coggeshall, Colchester, Essex. *[Died 13 Sept. 1978.*

SECKER, Martin; publisher; formerly proprietor of The Unicorn Press and director of the Richards Press Ltd; *b* Kensington, 6 April 1882; *m* 1921 (marr. diss. 1938); one *s*; *m* 1954, Sylvia Hope Gibsone. Entered publishing trade, 1908, in office of Eveleigh Nash; started in business on his own account in the Adelphi, 1910, and published early work of Sir Compton Mackenzie, Sir Hugh Walpole, Francis Brett Young, and other prominent writers, and all the works of D. H. Lawrence from 1921 until that author's death in 1930; business reconstructed under style of Martin Secker and Warburg Ltd, 1935; severed his connection therewith in 1937. Is an authority on the literature of the 1890's. *Publication:* (privately) Letters from D. H. Lawrence 1910-1930, 1970. *Address:* Bridgefoot, Iver, Bucks. *Clubs:* none. *[Died 6 April 1978.*

SEDDON, Sir Herbert (John), Kt 1964; CMG 1951; DM, MA Oxon, MB, BS (London University Gold Medal); FRCS; Hon. FACS; Dr *hc* Grenoble University; Hon. MD Malta; Hon. LLD Glasgow; retired; Hon. Consulting Surgeon, Royal National Orthopædic Hospital; Member MRC, 1956-59; *b* 13 July 1903; *s* of late John Seddon and Ellen Thornton, Sutton, Surrey; *m* 1931, Mary Lorene Lytle, Marquette, Mich., USA; one *s* one *d. Educ:* William Hulme Gram. Sch., Manchester; St Bartholomew's Hospital, London. Instructor in Surgery at the Hospital of the Univ. of Michigan, Ann Arbor, Michigan, USA, 1930, Carl Badgley Lecturer, 1963; Resident Surgeon, Country Branch of Royal National Orthopædic Hospital, London, 1931-39; Nuffield Professor of Orthopædic Surgery, University of Oxford, 1940-48; Fellow of Worcester College, 1940-48 (Hon. Fellow 1966); Director of Studies, Inst. of Orthopædics, 1948-65; Prof. of Orthopædics, Univ. of London, 1965-67; Fellow, Hon. Sec. 1940-44, Pres., 1960-61, of British Orthopædic Association; Robert Jones Medal and Association Prize, 1933; Robert Jones Lecturer, 1960 and Watson-Jones Lecturer, 1962, Royal College of Surgeons; other eponymous lectures. Hon. Mem. Brit. Pædiatric Assoc.; Corr. or Hon. Mem. of a number of foreign professional socs; Hon. FRSM 1975 (Pres., Orthopædic Section, 1948-49); Worked abroad, mainly in Africa and for HM Govt; visited East Africa as Mem. of Cttee on (EA) Univ. Needs and Priorities, 1962; Chm., MRC Working Party on Tuberculosis of the Spine, 1963-73; formerly Mem. Colonial Advisory Med. Cttee, Tropical Med. Res. Bd, and of panel of colonial medical visitors. Reader, parish of St John's, Stanmore. Lawrence Poole Prize, University of Edinburgh, 1962. Officer, Order of the Cedar of Lebanon; Mérite Libanais (first class). *Publications:* Surgical Disorders of the Peripheral Nerves, 1972, 2nd edn 1975; papers in medical journals on tuberculous disease of joints, infantile paralysis and on peripheral nerve injuries. Editor and contributor MRC special report on peripheral nerve injuries. *Recreations:* gardening, photography, painting. *Address:* Lake House, 24 Gordon Avenue, Stanmore, Mddx HA7 3QD. *T:* 01-954 0827. *[Died 21 Dec. 1977.*

SEDDON-BROWN, Lt-Col Sir Norman Seddon, Kt 1936; TD; *b* 27 Aug. 1880; *s* of James Brown and Helena Elizabeth Seddon; name altered by deed poll to Seddon-Brown; *m* 1904, Gertrude Mary (*d* 1969), *d* of William Martin Martin; two *s* (and one *s* killed in action, May 1944) two *d. Educ:* Privately; Crossways, Woodspeen, Newbury. *Club:* Carlton. *[Died 28 Sept. 1971.*

SEDGWICK, Richard Romney, CMG 1945; *b* 29 May 1894; *er s* of late Prof. Adam Sedgwick; *m* 1936, Mana, *yr d* of late Prof. T. C. Hodson; one *s* one *d. Educ:* Westminster; Trinity College,

Cambridge. Fellow of Trinity Coll., 1919; Asst Under-Secretary of State, Commonwealth Relations Office, 1949-54; retired 1954. *Publications:* Lord Hervey's Memoirs, 1931; Letters from George III to Lord Bute, 1939; (ed) History of Parliament, 1715-1754, 1970. *Address:* 75 Flask Walk, NW3. *T:* 01-435 7288. *Club:* Travellers'. *[Died 20 Jan. 1972.*

SEEDS, Sir William, KCMG, *cr* 1930; *b* 27 June 1882; *s* of late Robert Seeds, Queen's Advocate-General, and Lady Kaye, of 11 Fitzwilliam Square, Dublin; *m* 1911, Arabella, *d* of Theobald Butler, of Indian Civil Service; two *s* one *d* (and one *s* killed in action, 1940). *Educ:* Rugby. Entered Diplomatic Service, 1904; served at Washington, Peking, Athens, Lisbon, Berlin and Munich; HM Minister, Bogota (Colombia), 1923-25; Caracas, 1925-26; Durazzo (Albania), 1926-28; British High Commissioner in the Rhineland, 1928-30; British Ambassador to Brazil, 1930-35; to Soviet Union, 1939-40. *Address:* 99 North Gate, NW8. *T:* 01-722 7408. *Clubs:* Travellers', St James'. *[Died 2 Nov. 1973.*

SEEL, Sir George Frederick, KCMG 1950 (CMG 1944); *b* 8 Oct. 1895; *s* of Henry Seel, Macclesfield; *m* 1923, Phyllis, *d* of Edward Eaton, JP, Macclesfield; one *s* one *d*. *Educ:* King's School, Macclesfield; Corpus Christi College, Oxford. Served European War, 1914-18, with 7th Bn Cheshire Regt, TF; Secretary, Rhodesia-Nyasaland Royal Commission, 1938; Asst Under-Sec. of State, Colonial Office, 1946-50; Comptroller for Development and Welfare in the West Indies 1950-53; Senior Crown Agent for Oversea Governments and Administrations, 1953-59; Chairman, British Leprosy Relief Assoc., 1962-71. *Address:* Rosemount, Esher Place Avenue, Esher, Surrey. *T:* Esher 63401. *Club:* Athenæum. *[Died 2 Nov. 1976.*

SEELEY, Edward Alexander; President of Industrial Tribunals (England and Wales), since 1974; *b* 30 Sept. 1913; *s* of late Alexander Anthony Szilágyi and Elisabeth (*née* Knoll); *m* 1946, Patricia, *er d* of late John Howard-Kyan; one *s*. *Educ:* St Paul's Sch.; Jesus Coll., Cambridge. Nat. Scis Tripos, MA; rowing blue, 1935. Murex Ltd, 1936; called to Bar, Lincoln's Inn, 1951; Chm. Industrial Tribunals, 1971. *Recreation:* travel. *Address:* 54 Campden Street, W8 7EL. *T:* 01-727 8635. *Clubs:* Hurlingham; Leander (Henley-on-Thames). *[Died 7 Sept. 1979.*

SEELY, Sir Victor Basil John, 4th Bt *cr* 1896; *b* 18 May 1900; *s* of Sir Charles H. Seely, 2nd Bt; *S* to Baronetcy of brother, 1st Baron Sherwood, 1970; *m* 1st, 1922, Sybil Helen (divorced, 1931), *widow* of Sir John Shiffner, 6th Bt; one *s*; 2nd, 1931, Hon. Patience (*d* 1935), *er d* of 1st Baron Rochdale, CB, and sister of 1st Viscount Rochdale; one *d*; 3rd, 1937, Mary Frances Margaret, *er d* of W. R. Collins, 31 Lennox Gardens, SW1; one *s* one *d*. *Educ:* Eton; Trinity College, Cambridge. Late Lt S Notts Yeomanry; contested (Nat L) Pontefract, 1935, (C) Derby North, 1950; War of 1939-45 Major 9th Queen's Royal Lancers DAAG 2nd Armoured Division 1940; prisoner, 1941-43, escaped; HM Legation, Berne, 1944. Dir of Cos of Drayton Corp. Ltd, 1954-72. Master of Gunmakers' Co., 1957 and 1965. *Heir: s* Nigel Edward Seely [*b* 28 July 1923; *m* 1949, Loraine, *d* of late W. W. Lindley-Travis; three *d*]. *Address:* 42 Orchard Court, Portman Square, W1. *T:* 01-935 1311. *Clubs:* White's; Royal Solent Yacht. *[Died 10 May 1980.*

SEFERIADES, George; Ambassador (Greece); Poet (pen-name George Seferis); Grand Cross Order of Phœnix; Ambassador of Greece to the Court of St James's, June 1957-August 1962; *b* Smyrna, 29 February 1900; *e s* of Stelio Seferiades, Professor of International Law, and Despo Tenekides; family settled Athens, 1914; *m* 1941, Maria Zannos. *Educ:* Athens and Paris. Entered Greek Foreign Service, 1926; Acting Consul-General, London, 1931-34; Consul, Koritza (Albania), 1936; Head, Foreign Press Service, Athens, 1938-41; with Free Greek Govt in Crete, S Africa, the Middle East and Italy; Principal, Private Sec. of Regent Archbishop Damaskinos, 1945-46; Counsellor of Embassy, Ankara, 1948-50; Minister Counsellor, London, 1951-52; Ambassador to Lebanon and Minister to Syria, Iraq and Jordan, 1953-56. Hon. LittD Camb., 1960; Nobel Prize for Literature, 1963; Hon. DPhi Thess., 1964; Hon. DLitt: Oxon, 1964; Princeton, 1965. For. Hon. Mem., Amer. Acad. of Arts and Sciences. Holds foreign orders. *Publications:* Strophi, 1931; Sterna, 1932; Mythistorema, 1935; Book of Exercises, 1940; Log Book I, 1940; Log Book II, 1944; Log Book III, 1955; Collected Poems, 1963; Essays, 1944 and 1962. *Translations:* in English: The King of Asine and other poems (London), 1948; Poems (London and Boston), 1961; Collected Poems (Princeton), 1967; Collected Poems 1924-1955, 1969; in French: Seferis (Athens), 1945; Poèmes (Paris), 1963; in Italian: Poesie (Milan), 1963; in German: Poesie (Frankfurt am Main), 1962; in Swedish: Dikter, 1963, etc. *Address:* Agras 20, Athens (501), Greece. *[Died 20 Sept. 1971.*

SEFERIS, George; *see* Seferiades, George.

SEFTON, 7th Earl of, *cr* 1771; **Hugh William Osbert Molyneux,** Viscount Molyneux, 1628; Baron Sefton (UK), 1831; DL, JP; Constable of Lancaster Castle since 1942; *b* 22 Dec. 1898; *o surv. s* of 6th Earl and Lady Helena Mary Bridgeman (*d* 1947), *d* of 4th Earl of Bradford; *S* father, 1930; *m* 1941, Josephine, OSTJ, *d* of George Armstrong, of Virginia, USA. *Educ:* Harrow; Sandhurst. Joined Royal Horse Guards, 1917, retd 1930, rejoined 1939; ADC to Governor-General of Canada, 1919; ADC to GOC Madras District, 1925-26; ADC to the Viceroy of India, 1926; Lord in Waiting to the King, 1936-37. Lord Mayor of Liverpool, 1944-45. CStJ. *Address:* Croxteth Hall, Liverpool; Grosvenor Cottage, Culross Street, W1; Abbeystead, Lancaster. *Clubs:* Buck's, White's; Jockey (Newmarket). *[Died 13 April 1972 (ext).*

SEGONZAC, André D. de; *see* Dunoyer de Segonzac.

SEGRAVE, Edmond; Editor, Journalist-Reviewer; *b* 4 Oct. 1904; *y s* of late Michael Segrave; *m* 1936, Désirée, *o d* of Dr D. G. Macleod Munro; two *d*. *Educ:* St Edwards; Upholland College; Continent. Editor of The Bookseller since 1933. *Address:* 13 Bedford Square, WC1. *T:* 01-636 4748. *Club:* Savile. *[Died 28 March 1971.*

SEKERS, Sir Nicholas (Thomas), (Miki Sekers), Kt 1965; MBE 1955; Managing Director, West Cumberland Silk Mills, Ltd, Whitehaven, 1938-70; Chairman, Sekers Fabrics Ltd, 1954-70; Director: Sekers Mills Ltd, 1954-70; M. W. Design Associates Ltd; *b* 15 Dec. 1910; *s* of Paul L. Szekeres and Jolan Szekeres; *m* 1941, Agota Anna Balkanyi; two *s* one *d*. *Educ:* Marko Real School, Budapest; Academy of Commerce, Budapest; Textile Technological College, Krefeld, Germany. Director, Adria Silk Mills Ltd, Budapest, 1931-37. Trustee: Glyndebourne Arts Trust Ltd, 1954-; Rosehill Arts Trust Ltd, 1959-; Chichester Festival Theatre, 1962-; Vice-Pres., RSA, 1968-; Vice-Chairman: London Mozart Players, 1967- (Chm., 1962-67); London Philharmonic Orchestra Council, 1967- (Chm., 1965-66); London Mozart Players; Gov., Yehudi Menuhin School, 1965-; Member of Council: Soc. of Royal Opera House, 1962-; Shakespeare Theatre Trust, 1967-; Member, Council of Industrial Design, 1966-. Duke of Edinburgh's Prize for Elegant Design, 1962; Hon. Associate Manchester College of Art and Design, 1963; Hon. MA, Univ. Manchester, 1963. FSIA; FRSA 1967-. Freeman, Worshipful Co. of Musicians, 1966-. *Recreations:* music, the theatre, reading, travel. *Address:* M. W. Associates Ltd, 33 Sloane Street, SW1. *T:* 01-235 8194; Rosehill, Moresby, Whitehaven, Cumberland. *T:* Whitehaven 2673; Flat C, 57 Princes Gate, SW7. *T:* 01-581 0368. *Club:* Garrick. *[Died 23 June 1972.*

SELBORNE, 3rd Earl of, *cr* 1882; **Roundell Cecil Palmer,** PC 1929; CH 1945; Viscount Wolmer, 1883; Baron Selborne, 1872; Major (retired) 3rd Bn Hampshire Regt; President of the Church Army, 1949-61; Chairman of House of Laity, Church Assembly, 1955-59; *b* 15 April, 1887; *e s* of 2nd Earl of Selborne and Lady Beatrix Maud Cecil (*d* 1950), *d* of 3rd Marquis of Salisbury, KG; *S* father, 1942; *m* 1st, 1910, Grace (*d* 1959), *y d* of 1st Viscount Ridley; two *s* three *d*; 2nd, 1966, Valerie Irene de Thomka de Tomkahaza et Folkusfalva (*d* 1968). *Educ:* Winchester College; University Coll., Oxford. Contested (C) Newton Division, Lancs, 1910; represented Newton Div. of Lancashire, Dec. 1910-18, and Aldershot Div. of Hampshire, Dec. 1918-40; called up to House of Lords, Oct. 1940; Assistant Director War Trade, 1916-18; Parliamentary Secretary, Board of Trade, 1922-24; Asst Postmaster-General, 1924-29; Director of Cement, Ministry of Works and Buildings, 1940-42; Minister of Economic Warfare, 1942-45; JP 1911; Member of Sea Fish Commission, 1934-36; Chm. Cement Makers' Federation, 1934-42, 1945-51; Member of House of Laymen, Province of Canterbury, 1913; Master of the Mercers' Company, 1948; Chm., National Provincial Bank, 1951-54; Dep. Chm., Boots Pure Drug Co., 1936-63. *Publication:* Post Office Reform, 1932. *Heir: g s* Viscount Wolmer. *Address:* Blackmoor House, Liss, Hants. *Club:* Turf. *[Died 3 Sept. 1971.*

SELBY-BIGGE, Sir John (Amherst), 2nd Bt, *cr* 1919; OBE 1946; Artist; *b* 20 June 1892; *s* of Sir Amherst Selby-Bigge, 1st Bt, KCB and Edith Lindsay (*d* 1939), *d* of late Rt Hon. J. R. Davison, MP; *S* father 1951; *m* 1st, 1914, Ruth (marriage dissolved, 1944), *d* of E. W. Humphries, Bradford; three *d*; 2nd, 1946, Marija (*d* 1955), *d* of Judge Martin Bacik, Vienna. *Educ:* Winchester; Christ Church, Oxford. Studied art at Slade School and became professional artist. Served European War, 1914-19, Lt RASC, Macedonian Mule Corps, Salonica, BEF; Intelligence Service, Adviser to Greek Govt on censorship. Sub-editor BBC European News Service, 1942-43; British Red Cross (Civilian

Relief Overseas) Superviser with 8th Army in Italy, Asst Comr in Austria, 1943-45 (Order of Italian Red Cross, 1945). Travelled in most of Europe and resided since 1936 in Austria, France, and Spain. Exhibited in London, Provinces, and Paris. *Recreations:* gardening, travelling. *Heir:* none. *Address:* 10 Grand'Rue, Le Bugue, Dordogne, France.
[*Died* 3 *Oct.* 1973 (*ext*).

SELBY-LOWNDES, Brigadier Montacute William Worrall, DSO 1940; Regular Army (Retired); *b* 25 June 1896; *o s* of late Henry William Selby-Lowndes, MFH; *m* 1943, Helena Olivia (who *m* 1922, 7th Earl of Radnor, marriage dissolved 1943), *y d* of C. R. W. Adeane, CB, Babraham, Cambridge. *Educ:* Oundle. Commissioned 1914, Royal Artillery; BEF, France, 1915-17; BEF, Italy, 1918 (despatches, Italian Croce di Guerra); since served Egypt, Palestine, Syria, India; BEF, France, 1940 (DSO); Acting Brigadier CRA 61 Division, 1943-45; retired pay, 1947. *Recreations:* Master and Huntsman: Sarona Vale Hounds, Palestine, 1919-22; Mhow Hounds, India, 1925-28; RA Bordon Hounds, 1929-33; Amateur Huntsman: Tedworth Foxhounds, 1933-36; Wilton Foxhounds, 1936-39; Master Newmarket and Thurlow Foxhounds, 1946; Deputy Master and huntsman Hampshire Hunt, 1947-52; Joint Master and huntsman VWH (Earl Bathurst) Foxhounds, 1952-55; Master and huntsman North Staffs Foxhounds, 1955-58. *Address:* The Beacon, Mundesley, Norfolk. *T:* Mundesley 344.   [*Died* 2 *Oct.* 1972.

SELF, Sir (Albert) Henry, KCB 1947 (CB 1938); KCMG 1942; KBE 1939; retired as Chairman Electricity Council (1957-59); *b* 18 Jan. 1890; *s* of late S. A. T. Self, London; *m* 1918, Rosalind Audrey, *d* of late Sir John Lonsdale Otter, Brighton; two *s*. *Educ:* Bancrofts School, Woodford; University of London. BSc (Gen.), 1911; BSc(Maths), 1913; BA (Classics), 1929; BD (Gen.), 1932; BD (Philosophy), 1934; MSc (Philosophy of Science), 1951; PhD (Philosophy), 1956; Hon. Fellow of Birkbeck Coll.; Comp. IEE; Barrister-at-law, Lincoln's Inn (Certificate of Honour, 1922); entered Civil Service, 1907; served in Board of Trade, Post Office, Foreign Office, War Office, and Local Government Board; seconded to War Office and Ministry of Munitions, 1914-19; Air Ministry, 1919; Principal Assistant Secretary, 1936; Deputy Under-Secretary of State, 1937; served on special Air Mission to Middle East, Africa in connection with Empire Air Mail Scheme, 1935; served on two Air Missions to USA and Canada in Spring and Autumn of 1938, in connection with placing of aircraft orders for the RAF; Head of Mission to USA and Canada in Spring of 1940, from which emerged British Air Commission in Washington; Director-General British Air Commission, Washington, USA, 1940-41; attached for special duties with the British Joint Staff Mission in Washington concurrently with establishment of the Combined Chiefs of Staff Organization, Jan.-June 1942; Permanent Secretary to Ministry of Production, 1942-43; Deputy for Minister of Production on Combined Production and Resources Board, Washington, 1943-45; Deputy-Chairman British Supply Council in Washington, 1945; UK Member Combined Raw Materials Board, 1944-45; Permanent Secretary, Ministry of Civil Aviation, 1946-47; Deputy Chairman Central Electricity Authority, 1947-57. President British Electrical Development Assoc., 1953-54; Pres. British Electrical and Allied Research Assoc., 1959. Pres. Modern Churchmen's Union, 1947-57. *Recreation:* golf. *Address:* 16 Vernon Terrace, Brighton, East Sussex. *T:* Hove 731842.   [*Died* 15 *Jan.* 1975.

SELLECK, Sir Francis Palmer, KBE 1957; Kt 1956; MC 1918; Lord Mayor, City of Melbourne, 1954-57; *b* 20 Aug. 1895; *s* of late Christopher and Emily Selleck; *m* 1923, Mollie Constance Maud Miller; one *s* one *d*. *Educ:* High School, Shepparton, Australia. Chartered Accountant; Director of Companies; Lord Mayor of Melbourne, 1954-57; Lord Mayor, Olympic Games, Melb., 1956. Served Australian Imperial Forces, Gallipoli, France, 1915-18 (despatches, MC). Served with Board of Business Administration, Australian Defence HQ, 1940-45. Chm., St Paul's Anglican Cathedral Melbourne Restoration Appeal, 1960-67. *Address:* Suite 26, 67 Queens Road, Melbourne, Vic. 3004, Australia. *T:* 51-5362; (home) 24-6780. *Club:* Naval and Military (Melbourne).   [*Died* 2 *Oct.* 1976.

SELLERS, Rt. Hon. Sir Frederic Aked, PC 1957; Kt 1946; MC; a Lord Justice of Appeal, 1957-68; *b* 14 Jan. 1893; 3rd *s* of John Shuttleworth Sellers and Elizabeth Stuart; *m* 1917, Grace, *y d* of William Malin, JP, Derby; four *s* one *d*. *Educ:* Silcoates Sch.; Univ. of Liverpool. Served with King's (Liverpool) Regt 13th Battn 1914-18 (Capt.; MC 1916, 2 Bars 1918); HG, 1940-45; called to Bar, Gray's Inn, 1919; KC 1935; sometime Mem. Bar Council; Bencher, Gray's Inn, 1938; Treasurer, 1952; Vice-Treasurer, 1953; Northern Circuit; Recorder of Bolton, 1938-46; Judge, Queen's Bench Division, 1946-57. Mem., Standing Committee on Criminal Law Revision (Chm., 1959-69). Liberal

Candidate Waterloo Div. of Lancashire, General Election, 1929, Hendon North, 1945. Chairman of Governors: Mill Hill School, 1951-68; Silcoates Sch., 1953-58. Hon. LLD Liverpool, 1956. *Address:* Highwood Lodge, Mill Hill, NW7. *T:* 01-959 3066. *Club:* Reform.   [*Died* 20 *March* 1979.

SELLERS, Peter (Richard Henry), CBE 1966; Actor; *b* 8 Sept. 1925; *s* of late William Sellers and late Agnes Marks; *m* 1951, Anne Howe (marr. diss. 1964); one *s* one *d*; *m* 1964, Britt Ekland (marr. diss. 1969); one *d*; *m* 1970, Miranda (marr. diss. 1974), *d* of Richard St John Quarry, and of Lady Mancroft; *m* 1977, Lynne Frederick. *Educ:* St Aloysius Coll., Highgate. War of 1939-45 (Burma Star, etc). Began career at the Windmill Theatre, 1948. *Radio:* Ray's A Laugh (5 years); The Goon Show (9 years); *television:* Idiots Weekly; A Show Called Fred; Son of Fred; *variety:* touring, 1949-54; appeared at Palladium, 4 times; *films:* Let's Go Crazy, John and Julie, Orders are Orders, The Case of the Mukinese Battlehorn, The Ladykillers, The Smallest Show on Earth, The Naked Truth, Tom Thumb, Carleton Browne of the FO, The Mouse That Roared, I'm Alright Jack, Up The Creek, Two Way Stretch, Battle of the Sexes, Never Let Go, The Millionairess, Mr Topaze (also Dir), The Running, Jumping and Standing Still Film (Prod), Only Two Can Play, The Waltz of the Toreadors, The Dock Brief, Lolita, The Wrong Arm of the Law, Heavens Above!, Dr Strangelove or How I Learned to Stop Worrying and Love the Bomb, The World of Henry Orient, The Pink Panther, Shot in the Dark, What's New Pussycat?, The Wrong Box, After the Fox, Casino Royale, The Bobo, The Party, I Love You Alice B. Toklas, The Magic Christian, Hoffman, There's a Girl in my Soup, Where Does it Hurt?, Alice's Adventures in Wonderland, The Blockhouse, The Optimists of Nine Elms, Soft Beds—Hard Battles, The Return of the Pink Panther, Murder by Death, The Pink Panther Strikes Again (Evening News Best Film of the Year Award), The Revenge of the Pink Panther, Prisoner of Zenda, Being There, The Fiendish Plot of Dr Fu Manchu; *stage:* Brouhaha, 1958. Has made some recordings. Awards: Best Actor for 1959 (British Film Academy Award); Golden Gate Award, 1959; San Sebastian Film Award for Best British Actor, 1962; Best Actor award, Tehran Film Festival, 1973; Evening News Best Actor of the Year Award, 1975. *Recreations:* photography, cars. *Address:* c/o Elwood Rickless, Trafalgar House, 11/12 Waterloo Place, SW1.   [*Died* 24 *July* 1980.

SELLERS, Rev. Dr Robert Victor; Prebendary of Wiveliscombe in Wells Cathedral, since 1955 (Chancellor, 1956-61; Treasurer, 1955); Fellow of King's College, London, since 1954; *b* 18 Oct. 1894; *s* of late Richard and Martha Ann Sellers, Scholes, Cleckheaton, Yorks; *m* 1931, Irene, *d* of late Rev. Preb. W. O. E. Oesterley, DD; two *d*. *Educ:* Bradford Grammar School; St Catharine's College, Cambridge (Scholar); Wells Theological College. BA, 1916, MA 1920, BD 1927, DD 1939. Assistant Master King's School, Bruton, Som., 1917-19; Deacon, 1919; Priest, 1920; Asst Curate, Ossett Parish Church (Dioc. Wakefield), 1919-24; Vicar of Mytholmroyd (Yorks), 1924-31; Warden of St Augustine's House, Reading, 1931-49; Professor of Biblical and Historical Theology, Univ. of London (King's College), 1948-54; Exam. Chap. to Bishop of Oxford, 1941-54; Lecturer Bishops' Coll., Cheshunt, 1940-43; Select Preacher, Cambridge, 1942, 1958; Hon. Lectr, Christ Church, Reading, 1931-49; Boyle Lectr, 1950-52; Proctor in Convocation, Univ. of London, 1950-55. *Publications:* Eustathius of Antioch, 1928; Two Ancient Christologies, 1939; The Council of Chalcedon: a historical and doctrinal survey, 1952; contrib. Chambers's Encyclopædia. *Address:* Slade Cottage, Maddocks Slade, Burnham-on-Sea, Somerset.   [*Died* 21 *Jan.* 1973.

SELLON, Prof. Hugh Gilbert René, MA Oxon; Professor of International Politics, University of Exeter, since 1949; *b* 1901; *s* of Anthony Gilbert and Hortense Sellon. *Educ:* University College, Oxford, BA, 1st Cl. Hons School of History, 1924; Bryce Historical Student, 1925; MA, 1934. Assistant Lecturer, later Lecturer in History, St Andrews University, 1927-35; lectured at Bonar Law College, Ashridge, on Foreign Affairs and International Relations, 1930-39; Lecturer in History and International Relations to Oxford University Delegacy for Extra-Mural Studies, and Director of Studies at Summer meetings and Vacation Courses for Foreign Students, 1935-39; Visiting Lecturer in several American and Canadian Universities, 1938; Director of British Institute in Paris, 1939-49; Prof. of French Civilization, Univ. of Reading, 1940. *Publications:* Whither England?, 1932; Democracy and Dictatorship, 1934; Europe at the Crossroads, 1937, revised ed. 1938; Articles and reviews, mainly on subjects dealing with history and international affairs. *Recreations:* walking, hill-climbing, swimming, riding, gardening. *Address:* The University, Exeter. *Clubs:* Carlton; Royal Scottish Automobile (Glasgow); Union Interalliée (Paris).   [*Died* 29 *July* 1974.

SELLS, Arthur Lytton L.; see Lytton Sells.

SELOUS, Gerald Holgate, CBE 1946 (OBE 1929; MBE 1920); *b* 14 July 1887; *o s* of late Edmund Selous, barrister-at-law and ornithologist, and late Fanny Margaret, *d* of John Maxwell, publisher, and Mary Elizabeth Braddon, novelist; *m* Camilla, *er d* of late Jay B. Lippincott and Camilla Hare, Philadelphia, Pa; one *s. Educ:* Cheltenham College; Pembroke College, Cambridge; studied at Scoones, crammers for FO exams. Student Interpreter Levant Consular Service, 1908; Vice-Consul, Saffi, Morocco, 1914-24; Consul at Casablanca, Morocco, 1924-28; Consul at Basra, Iraq, 1929-32; Commercial Counsellor at Cairo, 1933-38, and at Brussels, 1938-40; served in Dept of Overseas Trade, 1940-42; Home Guard (St James's LDV Section), 1940-42; Trade Comr at Vancouver, BC, 1942-45; Counsellor (Commercial) at Berne, 1945-47. Silver Jubilee Medal, 1935; Coronation Medal, 1937. *Publications:* Appointment to Fez, 1956; various (published) economic reports. *Recreations:* archæology, natural history. *Address:* Château d'Hauteville, 1806 St Légier, Vaud, Switzerland. *T:* 021/54.11.95. *Clubs:* Travellers', Lansdowne, Royal Automobile; Grande Société (Berne).   *[Died 28 Feb. 1978.*

SELWYN-CLARKE, Sir (Percy) Selwyn, KBE 1951; CMG 1945; MC 1918; MD, BS London, FRCP, MRCS; DPH Cambridge, DTM&H London; Barrister-at-Law, Gray's Inn; *b* 17 Dec. 1893; *m* 1935, Hilda Alice Browning (*d* 1967); one *d. Educ:* Bedales; St Bartholomew's Hospital Med. Sch.; Univ. of London. RMO and Assistant Anæsthetist, St Bartholomew's Hospital; Lieutenant RAMC, Medical Officer i/c 285th Brigade, RFA, 1916; Medical Officer i/c Queen Victoria's Rifles, Capt. RAMC, 1918; MOH, Colonial Medical Service, Gold Coast, 1919; Senior Health Officer, Gold Coast, Langley Memorial Prizeman, 1924; Médaille en Argent des Epidémies, 1928; Gold Coast delegate to Yellow Fever Conference, Dakar, 1928; Chief Health Officer, FMS, delegate Congress, Bangkok, 1930; ADMS Gold Coast, Director, Gold Coast Central Council Branch, BRCS, 1932; Dep. Director, Health Service, Gold Coast, 1933; Gold Coast delegate Pan-African Health Conference, Johannesburg, 1935; Dep. Director, Health Service, Nigeria, 1936; Director of Medical Services, Hong-Kong, 1937-47; MLC, 1938; Hong-Kong delegate Congress, Hanoi, French Indo-China, 1938; MEC, Pres. Hong-Kong and South China Branch, BMA, 1939; Governor and C-in-C of the Seychelles, 1947-51; Principal Medical Officer, Ministry of Health, 1951-56; Med. Sec., The Society of Medical Officers of Health, 1956-61; CMO, The King's Troop, RHA, 1962-69; Chm. Hampstead Div., BMA, 1959-60; Consultant Adviser, MRC, S Pacific Commission, 1960. Pres., Camden (formerly Hampstead) Div., BRCS, 1960-73, Vice-Pres., London Br., 1974-; Hon. Life Member: BRCS and Ghana Red Cross; Trustee: Chadwick Trust, 1961; Queen Elizabeth Hosp. for Children Research Appeal Fund, 1962; Prison Visitor, 1969-. CStJ 1947. *Publications:* Smallpox in Negro and Negroid Tribes of the Gold Coast, 1921; Vaccination and Smallpox, 1921; Exhibition of Acetylarsinic Acid in Treatment of Framboesia, 1926; Influence of Rainfall on Incidence of Malaria in Federated Malay States, 1931; The Bight of Benin and Beyond, 1953; Housing and Health in the Tropics and Sub-tropics, 1955; Family Doctor and Health Visitor, 1955; The British Rehabilitation Service, 1955; An ABC for Housing, 1955; Medical History of the Second World War, Civilian Health and Medical Services, Hong Kong, 1955; Old Folks at Home, 1956; Our Duty to Old Folks and the Importance of Voluntary Effort, 1956; Housing and Health in Tropical Countries, 1957; Children in Hospital, 1958; Personal Health in the Tropics, 1959; Multiple Sclerosis, 1960; Public Health Education in the South Pacific, 1961; Team Work, 1961; Round the World in Twenty-eight Days, 1961; The Seychelles, 1961; Report on Ghana Medical, Health and Research Services, 1962; History of the Seychelles, 1962; Footprints (memoirs), 1975; various Colonial Reports on tropical diseases, town planning, water supplies, medical education, colonial administration, etc. *Recreation:* Commonwealth problems and social welfare. *Address:* 3 Stirling Mansions, 12 Canfield Gardens, NW6 3JT. *Clubs:* Athenæum, Arts Theatre.
[Died 13 March 1976.

SELWYN-LLOYD, Baron cr 1976 (Life Peer), of Wirral, Merseyside; **John Selwyn Brooke Selwyn-Lloyd,** PC 1951; CH 1962; CBE 1945 (OBE 1943); TD; QC 1947; DL; *b* 28 July 1904; *s* of late J. W. Lloyd, MRCS, LRCP, Hoylake, and Rodney Street, Liverpool; *m* 1951, Elizabeth Marshall (marr. diss., 1957); one *d. Educ:* Fettes; Magdalene Coll., Cambridge. President Cambridge Union, 1927; Barrister Gray's Inn and Northern Circuit, 1930; a Master of the Bench, Gray's Inn, 1951. Service throughout War in Army, 2nd Lieut (TA) June 1939; Captain, Jan. 1940; Major, July 1940; Lieut-Colonel, 1942; Colonel, 1943; Brigadier, 1944. Served as General Staff Officer

on HQ Second Army from its formation to surrender of Germany; returned to Bar, Aug. 1945; Recorder of Wigan, 1948-51. MP (C) Wirral Div. of Cheshire, 1945-70 (when elected Speaker); MP Wirral and Speaker of the House of Commons, 1971-76; Minister of State, FO, Oct. 1951-54; Minister of Supply, Oct. 1954-April 1955; Minister of Defence, April-Dec. 1955; Secretary of State for Foreign Affairs, 1955-60; Chancellor of the Exchequer, July 1960-62; Lord Privy Seal and Leader of the House of Commons, 1963-64; Member: Commn on the Constitution, 1969-71; NEDC 1962. Director: Sun Alliance and London Insurance Ltd, 1965-71; Sun Alliance, 1962-63, 1965-71; Alliance, 1950-51, 1962-63, 1965-71; English & Caledonian Investment Co. Ltd, 1966-71; Rank Organisation Ltd, 1963, 1965-71; IDC Group Ltd, 1970-71. Produced Selwyn Lloyd Report, 1963 (for Conservative Party Organisation). President: Nat. Assoc. of Conservative Clubs, 1963-64; National Union of Conservative and Unionist Associations, 1965-66; Hansard Soc., 1971-. Chm., Young Volunteer Force Foundn, 1970-71, Pres., 1971-; Chm., Adv. Council of Task Force, 1964-; Patron: Home Farm Trust; Methodist Homes for the Aged; President: Liverpool Sch. of Tropical Medicine, 1976; British Foundn for Age Research. Dep. High Steward, Cambridge Univ., 1971-. Hon. Freeman, Borough of Ellesmere Port, 1972. DL City and County of Chester, 1963-, Merseyside, 1974-. Hon. LLD: Sheffield, 1955; Liverpool, 1957; Cambridge, 1975; Hon. DCL Oxford, 1960; Hon. Fellow, Magdalene Coll. Legion of Merit, Degree of Commander, USA, 1946. *Publication:* Mr Speaker Sir, 1976; *posthumous publication:* Suez 1956: a personal account, 1978. *Address:* 7 Gray's Inn Square, WC1; Hilbre House, Macdona Drive, West Kirby, Wirral, Merseyside L48 3JD. *Clubs:* Hon. Member: Carlton, Pratt's, Constitutional, Oxford and Cambridge; Royal Liverpool Golf (Centenary Captain, 1969).   *[Died 17 May 1978.*

SEMON, Dr Henry, MA, DM, FRCP; retired; consulting dermatologist, Royal Northern and Hampstead General Hospitals; Medical Referee Industrial Dermatitis to Ministry of National Insurance; Vice-President Xth International Congress of Dermatology, London, 1952; *b* 9 March 1881; *e s* of late Sir Felix Semon, KCVO; *m* 1935, Marjorie, *e d* of late Captain C. F. Pilcher. *Educ:* Clifton College; Magdalen Coll., Oxford. Scholarship at University College Hospital, London, WC, 1903; qualified MRCS, LRCP 1906; took first place Indian Medical Service, 1909-10; service in England and France, Sept. 1914 to March 1919, both with Indian and British Troops; Temp. Capt. IMS, RAMC, Med. d'Honneur de la Service publique (French Republic). Pres., Dermatological Section, Royal Society of Medicine, 1941-43. *Publications:* On Diseases of the Skin; The Autobiography of Sir Felix Semon, KCVO, etc. *Recreation:* gardening. *Address:* Little White House, Penn, Bucks. *T:* Penn 2341.   *[Died 16 March 1971.*

SENANAYAKE, Hon. Dudley Shelton; Prime Minister, Minister of Defence and External Affairs of Ceylon, 1965-70; also Minister of Planning and Economic Affairs, and Minister of Information and Broadcasting, to 1970; President of the United National Party, Ceylon; Barrister-at-Law and Advocate; *b* 19 June 1911; *s* of late Right Honourable Don Stephen Senanayake, Prime Minister of Ceylon, and late Emily Maud Senanayake; unmarried. *Educ:* St Thomas' College, Mt Lavinia, Ceylon; Corpus Christi College, Cambridge. Elected to State Council under Donoughmore Constitution to represent Dedigama Constituency, 1936; Minister of Agriculture and Lands in Ceylon's first Cabinet after grant of Independence, 1947; Prime Minister and Minister of Defence and External Affairs, 1952-53; Prime Minister, March-April 1960. MA (Cantab); Fellow, Corpus Christi College, Cambridge. *Recreations:* golf, photography. *Address:* Woodlands, D. S. Senanayake Mawatha, Colombo 8, Sri Lanka. *T:* 95605.   *[Died 13 April 1973.*

SERENA, Clara; dramatic contralto vocalist; *b* near Adelaide, South Australia; *m* late Roy Mellish, conductor and accompanist; no *c. Educ:* Elder Conservatorium of Music, Adelaide; Elder Scholar at Royal College of Music, London (ARCM); Germany and Italy. Debut in London, 1923; in January, 1924, created the title-rôle in Alkestis (Rutland Boughton) at Covent Garden; appeared in Vienna, Berlin, and Paris in 1926; sang at Royal Opera, Covent Garden, 1927, in Rheingold and Götterdämmerung, and in 1928 as Amneris in Aïda; also appeared on several occasions as Guest Artist with British National Opera Company in Samson et Dalila and Aïda; Sang the rôle of Solomon in the Royal Philharmic Society's production of Handel's Solomon, at Queen's Hall, conducted by Sir Thomas Beecham, 1928, in the presence of the King and Queen; has sung at principal concerts Gt Britain, India and the East. *Recreations:* riding and lawn tennis. *Address:* c/o National Bank of Australasia, Ltd, 26 King William Street, Adelaide, SA 5000, Australia.   *[Died 11 Aug. 1972.*

SERGEANT, Maj.-Gen. Frederick Cavendish H.; *see* Hilton-Sergeant.

SERVAES, Vice-Adm. Reginald Maxwell, CB 1947; CBE 1940; *b* 25 July 1893; *s* of late J. M. Servaes; *m* 1st, 1919, Hilda Edith Johnson (*d* 1956); one *s*; 2nd, 1959, Mansel, *widow* of H. V. Bond. *Educ:* Royal Naval Colleges, Osborne and Dartmouth. Sub-Lieutenant, 1914; Lieut, 1915; European War, served in HM ships Exe, Comus and Phaeton; specialised in Gunnery, 1917; RN Staff College, 1922-23; Commander, 1928; Captain, 1935; HMS Resource, 1937; Dir of Local Defence, Admiralty, 1938-40; HMS London in Comd, 1940-42; service in Home Fleet and convoys to Russia; an Assistant Chief of Naval Staff, 1943-45; ADC to King George VI, 1944-45; Rear-Adm. 1945; Rear-Admiral Commanding Second Cruiser Squadron, British Pacific Fleet, 1945-46; Flag Officer Commanding Reserve Fleet, 1947-48; retired list, 1948, Vice-Admiral. *Address:* Crocker Hill House, near Chichester, West Sussex. *T:* Halnaker 220.
[*Died 18 Nov. 1978.*

SESHADRI, Prof. Tiruvenkata Rajendra, MA; PhD; DSc (*hc*); FRS 1960 (London); Padmabhushan, 1963 (India); Emeritus Professor, Department of Chemistry, University of Delhi, since 1965; *b* 3 Feb. 1900; *s* of R. T. and N. Iyengar; *m* 1924, Kamala; three *d.* *Educ:* Srirangam, Tiruchi, Madras; Manchester; London; Edinburgh. Chemist, Agricultural Research Inst., Coimbatore, 1930-33; Reader and later Prof. and Head of Chem. Dept, Andhra Univ., Waltair, 1933-49; Prof. and Head of the Chem. Dept, Delhi Univ., 1949-65. Mem., German Acad., 1961. *Publications:* The Chemistry of Vitamins and Hormones (Andhra University, Waltair), 1st edn, 1946, 2nd edn, 1951; over 1,000 papers in chemical jls in India and Gt Britain. *Address:* Department of Chemistry, Delhi University, Delhi 7, India. *T:* 228348. [*Died 27 Sept. 1975.*

SETCHELL, Herbert Leonard, CBE 1946; *b* 4 June 1892; *m* 1920, Winifred Susan, *d* of late W. Parkinson Bennett, JP, late of Bothe Hall, Sawley, Derby; two *s.* *Educ:* Bancroft Sch., Woodford; King's Coll., London. European War, 1914-18, Lt in 3rd Essex Regt; attached 2nd Essex Regt in France (wounded); Intelligence Officer in Dept of Overseas Trade, 1918-26; HM Trade Commissioner for Victoria and South Australia, 1926-34; Commercial Secretary at HM Legation, Berne, 1934-41; Commercial Counsellor HM Embassy, Madrid, 1941-44. Commercial Counsellor HM Embassy, Stockholm, 1944-49; Minister (Commercial) as UK Commercial Representative, Cologne, 1949-52; retired July 1952. *Recreations:* yachting, golf, ski-ing. *Address:* 51 Kennedy Rise, Walesby, Newark, Notts. *T:* New Ollerton 437. *Club:* Devonshire. [*Died 3 Nov. 1976.*

SETON PRINGLE, John; *see* Pringle, J. S. M.

SETTLE, Alison, OBE 1961; *m* A. Towers Settle, barrister-at-law; one *s* one *d.* Formerly Editor of Vogue; for 22 years fashion editor of The Observer and Fashion Consultant to leading firms; regular contributor to The Lady. Member: Council of Arts and Industry; Council of Industrial Design, 1953-58; Silver Medallist, RSA. Pres. Women's Press Club, 1952-54. *Publications:* Clothes Line, 1937 (republished 1941); English Fashion (Britain in Pictures Series), 1948; Fashion as a Career, 1963; (jtly) Paris Fashion, 1972. *Address:* Fernbank, 25-27 Gratwick Road, Worthing, Sussex. [*Died 14 Sept. 1980.*

SETTLE, Charles Arthur, QC 1960; a Commons Commissioner, since 1974; *b* 26 April 1905; *s* of Theodore Settle; *m* 1st, 1936, Pamela (*d* 1938), *d* of F. N. Marcy; one *d*; 2nd, 1947, Jane Anne, *d* of Huw Jones. *Educ:* Marlborough College; Trinity College, Cambridge. Served War of 1939-45 (despatches, 1944). Called to Bar by Middle Temple, 1928; Master of Bench, 1966. Vice-Chm., Bar Council, 1968-70. Judge of Cts of Appeal, Jersey and Guernsey, 1971-75. *Recreation:* fishing. *Address:* 3 Thurloe Close, SW7. *T:* 01-589 8932. *Clubs:* Brooks's, Flyfishers'. [*Died 28 Nov. 1979.*

SEVERSKY, Major Alexander P. de; pioneer aircraft designer, aerospace consultant, ecologist, inventor, industrialist, author, lecturer; *b* Tiflis, Russia, 7 June 1894; *s* of Nicholas de Seversky and Vera (*née* Vasilieff); *m* 1925, Evelyn Olliphant. Grad. Imperial Naval Acad. of Russia, 1914; Mil. Sch. of Aviation, Naval postgrad. course in Aeronautics, Russia. Served Russian Naval Air Service; lost right leg, 1915; returned to combat duty; Insp.-Gen. and Officer i/c Aircraft Prod. for Navy, Petrograd, 1915-16; later Chief of Pursuit Aviation; credited with shooting down 13 enemy planes. Came to US, 1918 (naturalized, 1927). Apptd Vice-Chm. Russian Naval Aviation Mission to US; Asst Naval Attaché for Air, Russian Embassy, Washington, in charge of aviation matters, 1918; when office closed, offered services to US; US Govt aeronautical engr test pilot, Inspr etc; Cons. Engr

US War Dept, 1921. Founder, Pres., Gen. Man., and Dir: Seversky Aero Corp., 1922-35; Seversky Aircraft Corp. (now Republic Aviation Corp.), 1931-39; Dir, Republic Aviation Corp., 1939-40; Consultant, Chrysler Corp., 1933; Founder, Aviation Development Corp., 1940; Founder, Pres., Seversky Aviation Corp., 1948-; Founder, Pres., Dir, Seversky Electronatum Corp., 1952-. Special Consultant Sec. of War, 1945; personal rep. Sec. of War at atom bomb tests, Bikini, 1946. Inventor, Aircraft Designer: universal landing gear for sea-planes (Naval Prize), 1916; first gyroscopically stabilized synchronous bombsight, forerunner of the inertial guidance system; first in-flight refueling system, 1921; designed and built all-metal amphibious aircraft; broke many long distance and speed records in aircraft his own design; two world's speed records for Amphibians, 1933 and 1935; designer P35, P43, and prototype P47 Thunderbolt fighter aircraft, 1938 dev. wet-type electrostatic precipitator for air pollution control, 1960. Recipient numerous awards including, Knight of St George (Russia); Officer Legion of Honour, Officer Cross of Lorraine (France); Medal for Merit, 1946; Internat. Harmon Trophy, 1939 and 1946; Air Univ. Award, USAF, 1959; Soc. of Professional Engrs Award, 1965; Exceptional Service Award, USAF, 1969; elected to Aviation Hall of Fame, 1970. Mem. Bd, NY State Aviation Commn, 1942; Trustee Chm., space tech. program, NY Inst. of Technology; Official Lectr US Air Univ., 1946-; Adviser to Chiefs of Staff, USAF, 1957-; Trustee, Vice Pres., Air Force Historical Foundn, 1954; Fellow, NY Acad. of Sciences; Inst. of Electrical & Electronics Engineers; Amer. Inst. of Aeronautics and Astronautics; FRSA; Hon. Fellow, Society of Experimental Test Pilots. US and Fgn. *Publications:* Victory through Air Power, 1942 (also Walt Disney-Seversky adaptation for screen, 1943); Air Power-Key to Survival, 1950; America: Too Young to Die, 1961; numerous articles on defense, aerospace, ecology. *Address:* (office) 30 Rockefeller Plaza, New York, NY 10020, USA; (home) PO Box 598, Northport, Long Island, NY 11768, USA. *Clubs:* Engineers, Wings, Circus Saints and Sinners, Adventurers (Pres. 1965), National Press.
[*Died 24 Aug. 1974.*

SEWARD, Sir Conrad; *see* Seward, Sir S. C.

SEWARD, Sir (Samuel) Conrad, Kt 1971; OBE 1963; Director, Stone-Platt Industries Ltd, 1966-73; *b* London, 24 April 1908; *s* of Samuel Trent and Gertrude Mary Seward; *m* 1951, Barbara Mary Boyden. *Educ:* Christ Coll., London, N. With Western Electric Co. Ltd and associate cos, was involved introduction first automatic telephones and sound film develts in UK, 1926-39. Min. of Aircraft Production, 1940-45: Dep. Chm. Coventry Reconstruction Cttee, responsible restoration of public services following Coventry blitz, 14 Nov. 1940; Dep. Dir of Engine Develt and Production 1942-45. Joined Platt Bros (Sales) Ltd, 1947, Man. Dir 1959, Chm. 1963; negotiated for British machinery manufrs contract with Yugoslav Govt for rehabilitation of Yugoslav textile industry, 1950, similar contract with UN, NY, for rehabilitation South Korean textile industry, 1952; Leader, British delegn to Soviet Union, and negotiated first large post-War contract placed by Soviet Govt with consortium of British firms, 1954; as Man. Dir Polyspinners Ltd, led negotiations for £40 million synthetic fibre plant ordered by Soviet Govt, 1964; Dep. Chm., Polyspinners Ltd, 1968-74. Chm. Exec. Council, Russo-British Chamber of Commerce, 1962-74; Mem. Exec. Cttee, Hispanic and Luso Brazilian Councils, 1963-71; Mem. Exec. Cttee, Sino-British Trade Council, 1963-74; Founder Mem., East European Trade Council; Mem. Cttee of Management, Middle East Assoc., 1968-72. *Recreations:* football, cricket, gardening. *Address:* Felden, Avon Castle Drive, Ringwood, Hants. *T:* Ringwood 4144. *Club:* Royal Automobile. [*Died 1 Sept. 1976.*

SEWARD, Air Vice-Marshal Walter John, CB 1950; CBE 1944; Director, Auxiliaries, Reserves and Air Cadets, Air Ministry, since 1954: Hon. Air Commodore, 661 Air Observation Post Squadron, RAAF, since 1955: AOA, BAFO, 1949-51; *b* 17 Oct. 1898; *m* 1934, Josephine Margaret Mary O'Neill; one *s.* Commissioned RFC, 1917. Comd as Air Cdre: No 12 OT Group, Canada, 1943-44; No 54 Group, 1944-46; No 27 Group, 1948-49. Air Vice-Marshal, 1950; AOC, No 61 (Eastern) Group, Home Command, RAF, 1951-54. *Recreations:* cricket, golf, shooting. *Address:* 11 Victoria Square, Lee-on-Solent, Hampshire. *Club:* Royal Air Force. [*Died 9 Sept. 1972.*

SEXTON, Most Rev. Harold Eustace, DD; *b* 14 May 1888; *s* of late Richard James Sexton, Adelaide; *m* 1922, Mary Hodgman, *d* of Mrs H. A. Tyree, Toorak, Victoria. *Educ:* St Peter's College, Adelaide; Keble College, Oxford; Trinity College, Toronto. Deacon, 1911; Priest, 1912; Curate of St Paul's, Port Adelaide, 1911-14; All Saints, Hindmarsh, 1915-16; Chaplain with the British Expeditionary Forces, 1916-18; Vicar of St

Martin's, Hawksburn, Melbourne, 1920-23; SPG Preacher, 1923-24; Curate of St Margaret's, Westminster, 1925-27; Vicar of All Saints, Upper Norwood, 1927-35; Bishop Coadjutor of British Columbia, 1935-36; Bishop, 1936-69; Archbishop of British Columbia, 1952-69. *Address*: 3905 Scolton Road, Victoria, BC, Canada. *[Died 29 March 1972.*

SEYMOUR, Sir Horace James, GCMG 1946 (KCMG 1939; CMG 1927); CVO 1936; *b* 26 Feb. 1885; *e s* of late Hugh F. Seymour; *m* 1917, Violet, *d* of late Thomas Erskine; one *s* two *d*. *Educ*: Eton; Trinity College, Cambridge. Foreign Office and Diplomatic Service, 1908; British Minister, Tehran, 1936-39; Assistant Under-Secretary of State at Foreign Office, 1939-42; Ambassador to China, 1942-46; retired, 1947. *Address*: Bratton House, Westbury, Wilts. *T*: Bratton 231. *[Died 10 Sept. 1978.*

SEYMOUR, Leslie (George), JP; Managing Director: Improved Metallic Appliances Limited; George E. Seymour Limited; *b* 1 November 1900; *s* of late George Seymour, Birmingham; *m* 1941, Dorothy, *d* of late J. Murdoch, Redditch, Worcestershire; two *s*. *Educ*: King's Norton Secondary School; Solihull Grammar School. Started work at 14, in a Tech. School Laboratory. Served European War, 1914-18. Sergeant, Home Guard, 1941-44. Mem. Birmingham CC, 1937-46, 1947-53; Chm. Civil Defence Cttee, 1944; Chm. Rating and Valuation Cttee, 1949; Past Chm. No 8 Hosp. Group, Regional Hosp. Bd; Mem. Regional Hosp. Bd (Past Chm. Finance Cttee); Gov., Birmingham United Hosps. Chairman Coleshill Hall Hosp. Group. JP, Birmingham, 1951. Chm. Old Yardley Div. Unionist Assoc., 1945-46; contested (U) Ladywood Div. of Birmingham, 1951; MP (C) Sparkbrook Div. of Birmingham, 1959-64. Life Vice-Chm. Birmingham Young Conservatives. Past Pres. UK Commercial Travellers' Assoc. (Birmingham branch). FIE. Member: National Assoc. of British Manufacturers; Birmingham Rotary Club; Birmingham Chamber of Commerce; Institute of Directors; Engineering Industries Assoc.; Birmingham Civic Soc. Hon. Alderman, City of Birmingham, 1974. Civil Defence Medal; Coronation Medal, 1953. *Recreations*: Freemasonry and gardening. *Address*: 514 Warwick Road, Solihull, West Midlands B91 1AG. *T*: 021-705 0523; (business) 80 Cheapside, Birmingham B91 1AG. *T*: 021-772 1221-2. *Club*: St Stephen's. *[Died 15 April 1976.*

SEYMOUR, William Kean, FRSL; Poet, novelist and journalist; a Vice-President of the Poetry Society, since 1947 (Chairman, General Council, Dec. 1961-May 1964); Vice-President, Charles Lamb Society; Vice-President and Chairman, West Country Writers' Association; *b* 1887; *s* of William Seymour and Jane Kean; *m* 1st, Beatrice Mary Stapleton; 2nd, Rosalind Herschel Wade; two *s*. *Educ*: Lawrence School, London; served in RNAS and RAF, 1917-18. Conductor (with Rosalind Wade) of Writer's Craft courses, Moor Park Coll., Farnham, 1962-. DLitt hc Free Univ., Asia, 1968. Philippines Presidential Gold Medal for Poetry, Jan. 1968. *Publications*: Poems: The Street of Dreams, 1914; To Verhaeren, 1917; Twenty-four Poems, 1918; Swords and Flutes, 1919; Cæsar Remembers, 1929; Time Stands, 1935; Chinese Crackers, 1938; Collected Poems, 1946; Burns into English (translations), 1954; The First Childermas (verse play), 1959; The Cats of Rome, 1970. Parodies: A Jackdaw in Georgia, 1925; Parrot Pie, 1927. Fiction: The Little Cages, 1944; Friends of the Swallow, 1953; The Secret Kingdom, 1954; Names and Faces, 1956. Biography: Jonathan Swift: The Enigma of a Genius, 1967. Ed. of Anthologies: A Miscellany of Poetry, 1919; ditto, 1920-22; (with John Smith) The Pattern of Poetry, 1963; (with John Smith) Happy Christmas, 1968; contribs to Poetry Review, Contemporary Review, Books and Bookmen. *Recreations*: writing, gardening. *Address*: White Cottage, Old Alresford, Alresford, Hants. *T*: Alresford 2870. *Clubs*: PEN, National Liberal. *[Died 21 Jan. 1975.*

SHACKLETON, Edith; *see* Heald, E. S.

SHAKESPEARE, Rt. Hon. Sir Geoffrey Hithersay, PC 1945; 1st Bt, *cr* 1942; Barrister; Deputy Chairman, Abbey National Building Society, 1965-69, Director, 1943-77; *b* 1893; 2nd *s* of late Rev. J. H. Shakespeare; *m* 1st, 1926, Lady Fisher (*d* 1950), of 103 Sloane St, *widow* of Comdr Sir Thomas Fisher, RN; one *s* (one *d* decd); 2nd, 1952, Elizabeth, *er d* of late Brig.-Gen. R. W. Hare, CMG, DSO, DL. *Educ*: Highgate School; Emmanuel, Cambridge. MA, LLB; President of the Union; served European War; Private Secretary to Rt Hon. D. Lloyd George, 1921-23; MP (NL) Wellingborough Division of Northants, 1922-23; MP (L) Norwich, 1929-31 (L Nat.), 1931-45; Lord Commissioner of the Treasury and Chief Whip Liberal Nationals, Nov. 1931-Oct. 1932; Parliamentary Secretary, Ministry of Health, 1932-36; Parliamentary Secretary to Board of Education, 1936-37; Parliamentary and Financial Secretary to the Admiralty, 1937-40; Parliamentary Secretary to Dept of Overseas Trade, April to

May 1940; Parliamentary Under-Secretary of State, Dominions Office and Chairman Children's Overseas Reception Board, 1940-42; called to Bar, 1922; political journalist, 1924; Vice-Chairman, Board of Governors Westminster Hosp., 1948-63; Pres. Soc. of British Gas Industries, 1953-54; Chairman: Industrial Co-Partnership Assoc., 1958-68; Nat. Liberal Exec., 1950-51; Standing Council of the Baronetage, 1972-75. Hon. Chm., Diplomatic Cttee, Mark Twain Soc., 1980. *Publication*: Let Candles be brought in (Memoirs), 1949. *Recreation*: golf. *Heir*: *s* William Geoffrey Shakespeare [*b* 12 Oct. 1927; *m* 1964, Susan Mary, *d* of A. D. Raffel, Colombo, Ceylon, and of Mrs S. G. Sproule, Aylesbury, Bucks; two *s*]. *Address*: Flat 6, Great Ash, Lubbock Road, Chislehurst, Kent. *T*: 01-467 5898. *Club*: Reform. *[Died 8 Sept. 1980.*

SHANKER SHAMSHER JANG BAHADUR RANA, Gen., Hon. GBE 1949 (Hon. KBE 1946); Star of Nepal (1st Class) 1946; Om Ram Patta (1st Class) 1948; Trishakti Patta (1st Class) 1948; Dakshina Bahu (1st Class) 1941; General, Nepalese Army; *b* 1909; *s* of HH the late Maharaja Chandra Shamsher Jang Bahadur Rana, GCB, GCSI, GCMG, GCVO and HH Badamaharani Balkumari Devi; *m* 1924, Rani K. Rajya Laxmi, *e d* of Colonel Tej Bahadur Malla, of Nepal; one *s* one *d*. Acting Head of Shrestha Kousal, 1930; Head of Madesh Report Nixari and Kathmahal (Whole Terai), 1931-34; PWD, 1936-43; Head of Rail and Road Dept, 1946-47; Chief of Police, 1947-49; again Head of Madesh Report Nixari, 1947-49; Chief of Staff to HH The Maharaja, 1948-49; visited UK with Special Mission to present Nepalese honours to HM King George VI and HM Queen Elizabeth, 1946; presented, on behalf of Govt of Nepal, Insignia of Ojaswi Rajana to HRH Princess Elizabeth, 1949, to HM Queen Juliana of the Netherlands, 1949, to President Vincent Auriol of France, 1949; Nepalese Ambassador at the Court of St James's, also, concurrently, the first Nepalese Ambassador to France and Nepalese Ambassador to the USA, 1949-54. Holds Grand Cross of Order of Orange-Nassau, 1949; Grand Officer of Legion of Honour (France), 1949. *Recreations*: big game shooting, lawn tennis, golf, riding, chess. *Clubs*: Royal Automobile; Royal Mid-Surrey Golf. *[Died 4 June 1976.*

SHANKS, S(eymour) Cochrane, CBE 1958; MD, ChB; FRCP; FRCR; Consulting Radiologist to University College Hospital; late Lecturer in Radiology, University College Hospital Medical School (Dean of the Medical School, 1943-49); late Radiologist, Goldie Leigh Hosp.; late Hon. Radiologist: University College, London; Lord Mayor Treloar's Hosp., Alton; Past Adviser in Radiology to the Ministry of Health; Past Warden of Fellowship, Past President, Skinner and Knox lecturer, and Gold Medallist (1973), RCR; Member, Spens Committee on remuneration of Consultants and Specialists, 1947; Examiner in X-ray Diagnosis, 1942, and in Medicine, 1952, RCR; Examiner in Radiology, RCP, 1940-44; Fellow (Past Hon. Treas.) RSM (PP and Hon. Mem., Section of Radiology); Fellow and Lettsomian Lecturer, Medical Society of London; Hon. Fellow, Royal Inst. of Public Health and Hygiene; Hon. Mem., British Assoc. of Dermatologists; Senior Vice-President, 6th International Congress of Radiology, 1950; Vice-Pres. Emeritus, 7th International Congress of Radiology, Copenhagen, 1953; Past Pres., Medical Defence Union; Past Chm. Institute of Dermatology, British Post-Graduate Medical Federation; Member: British Institute of Radiology; BMA (Past Chm. Medico-legal Sub-Cttee); Distribution Cttee King Edward's Hosp. Fund, 1949-59; *b* 1893; 5th *s* of late William Shanks, JP, Barrhead, Renfrewshire, and late Catherine Cook McCallum, Leeds; *m* 1st, Edith Margaret Govan (*d* 1955); no *c*; 2nd, 1956, Chrisma Elsie Clara Govan, both *d* of late James Finlayson Govan of Glasgow. *Educ*: Glasgow Academy; Glasgow University (Burns and Asher-Asher Gold Medals); Western Infirmary, Glasgow; St Thomas's Hospital. House-Surgeon, Western Infirmary, Glasgow, 1915; Temp. Capt. RAMC, 1915-18; served with BEF in Egypt and France; late Medical Assessor, Ministry of Pensions; late Visiting Radiologist, Ministry of Pensions Hospital, Orpington; late Hon. Radiologist, St Mark's Hospital; Physician with charge of out-patients, Radiological Department, Charing Cross Hosp.; Radiologist, The Prince of Wales's Gen. Hosp. Hon. Member: Dutch Soc. of Radiology; Toronto Radiological Soc. Bose Gold Medal, Indian Radiological Soc. *Publications*: Jt Ed., Textbook of X-ray Diagnosis by British Authors; papers on Radiology in Med. Jls. *Recreations*: golf, motoring. *Address*: 11 Heath Rise, SW15. *T*: 01-789 3682. *Club*: Royal Wimbledon. *[Died 14 May 1980.*

SHANNON, Howard Huntley, CMG 1961; Member of House of Assembly, South Australia, 1933-68; Member of Parliamentary Standing Committee on Public Works, 1941-68, and Chairman, 1954-68; *b* 1892; *s* of John Wallace Shannon and Alice Jane

Shannon (*née* Moody); *m* 1915, Phoebe Madeline Watson; two *s* two *d*. *Educ:* Prince Alfred College, Australia. Chairman of Directors: Southern Farmers' Co-operative Ltd; Farmers' Co-operative Executors and Trustees Ltd; Co-operative Insce Co. of Australia Ltd. House of Assembly for dist of Murray, 1933-38, dist of Onkaparinga, 1938-68. Govt Whip, 1938-41. *Address:* Aldewood, Bridgewater, South Australia. *T:* 39.100.
[Died 15 Aug. 1976.

SHAPLAND, Cyril Dee, MB, BS London, MRCP, FRCS; Ophthalmic Surgeon, 1931-67, retired; Hon. Cons. Ophthalmic Surgeon: University College Hospital, London, since 1965; Moorfields Eye Hospital, since 1964; Royal Marsden Hospital, since 1959; Teacher in Ophthalmology, University of London (UCH Medical School and Institute of Ophthalmology); *b* 22 Nov. 1899; *s* of John Dee Shapland, MD, Exmouth, Devon, and Gertrude Emma Bond, Axminster, Devon; *m* 1st, 1927, Elizabeth Stratton (*d* 1971); 2nd, 1972, Gertrude Nelson Gellatly. *Educ:* Univ. Coll.; Univ. Coll. Hospital, London. House Phys. and House Surg., UCH, 1922-23; Res. Phys., Ruthin Castle, N Wales, 1924-26; Jun. and Clin. Asst Moorfields Eye Hosp., 1927-29; 3rd, 2nd and 1st House Surg., and Sen. Res. Officer, Moorfields Eye Hosp., 1929-31; Registrar and Chief Clin. Asst, Moorfields, 1931-36; Opth. Surg. Middlesex CC, 1931-42; Ophth. Surg. to Willesden Gen. Hosp., 1932-37; Pathologist and Curator, Moorfields Eye Hosp., 1936-39, Ophth. Surg. 1938-64; Senior Ophth. Surg., UCH, 1933-65; Ophth. Surg., Royal Marsden Hosp., 1932-59; Cons. Ophth. Surg., Queen Mary's Hosp., Roehampton, 1946-61. FRSocMed; Hon. Sec., Section of Ophthalmology, RSM, 1938-42, Vice-Pres. 1952-55; Hon. Sec., Sect. of Ophthalmology, BMA, Oxford, 1936, Vice-Pres. BMA, Glasgow, 1954. War Service: part-time Ophth. Surg., EMS, 1939-42; RAMC Ophth. Specialist, Royal Victoria Hospital, Netley, 1942-44; Comd Ophthalmologist, Southern Command, Jan.-Nov. 1944; Comd Ophth., London Dist, and Ophthalmic Specialist, Millbank, 1944-46; Adviser in Ophthalmology, United Kingdom, 1945-46 (rank of Lieutenant-Colonel). Pres. UCH Old Students' Assoc., 1967-68. Liverymam of Worshipful Society of Apothecaries of London, and Freeman of City of London; Mem. Council, Ophthalmological Soc. of UK, 1945-48, Vice-Pres. 1965-68. Mem., Irish Ophth. Soc.; Membre Titulaire, Soc. Franç. d'Ophthalmologie; Hon. Member Instituto Barraquer, Barcelona, Spain; Membre d'Honneur, Club Jules Gonin, Lausanne, 1966. *Publications:* contrib. to Modern Trends in Ophthalmology, 3rd Series (ed A. Sorsby), 1955, to Operative Surgery, Vol. 8 (ed Rob and Smith), 1957, to Surgical Progress, 1960; and to The Operations of Surgery, vol. 2 (ed A. Gardham and D. R. Davies), 1969; various in British Medical Jl, Lancet, Brit. Jl Ophth., Trans. Ophth. Soc., Proc. Roy. Soc. Med., Jl of RAMC, Medical World, Medical Press, etc, since 1923. *Recreations:* fishing, photography, contract bridge. *Address:* (home) Cornerways, Orley Farm Road, Harrow-on-the-Hill, Mddx. *T:* 01-422 2450. *Clubs:* Flyfishers'; Harrow Fifty (Harrow-on-the-Hill).   *[Died 18 June* 1980.

SHAPLAND, Maj.-Gen. John Dee, CB 1948; DSO 1944; MC 1918; *b* 31 July 1897; *e s* of Dr J. Dee Shapland and G. E. Bond, Exmouth, S Devon; *m* 1920, Lily Cardew Wood; one *s* twin *d*. *Educ:* Dulwich College; Royal Military Academy, Woolwich. 2nd Lieut RGA, April 1915; served European War, 1914-18, overseas with BEF and BSF (despatches twice, MC). TA Adjt 1923-25; Instructor in Gunnery, School of Artillery, 1927-29; psc 1931; Bde Major 3 Inf. Bde, India, 1934-36; Chitral Relief Column, 1932; Mohmand Operations, 1935 (despatches twice). DAAG, War Office, 1937-39; Chief Instructor in Gunnery, School of Artillery, 1941; CRA 2 Div. 1942-43; Comd 6 Inf. Bde, 1943-44 (wounded); BRA 12 Army, 1945; Maj.-Gen. 1946; Commandant Military Coll. of Science, 1946-48; Major-General i/c Administration, BAOR, 1948-51; retired, 1952. Resident Manager, Willoughbys Consolidated Co. Ltd Rhodesia (Ranching), 1952-62. *Address:* c/o National Westminster Bank Ltd, Woking, Surrey; 42 Lawley Road, Bulawayo, Rhodesia. *Clubs:* United Service; Bulawayo.   *[Died 18 April* 1971.

SHAPLEY, Harlow; Director of the Harvard College Observatory, 1921-52, Emeritus, 1952; *b* 2 Nov. 1885; *s* of Willis Harlow Shapley and Sarah Stowell; *m* 1914, Martha Betz; four *s* one *d*. *Educ:* Univ. of Missouri, AB, AM, LLD; Princeton Univ., PhD, ScD. Astronomer, Mount Wilson Observatory, 1914-21; Lecturer, Lowell Institute, Boston, 1922; Exchange Lecturer, Belgian Universities, 1926; Halley Lecturer, Oxford, 1928; Darwin Lecturer (Royal Astronomical Society, London) 1934; Arthur Lecturer, New York University, 1934; Harris Lecturer, Northwestern University, 1935; LLD, Oglethorpe; ScD: Univs of Pittsburgh, Pennsylvania, Brown, Harvard, Toronto, New York, Copenhagen, Delhi, Ireland, Hawaii, St Lawrence; D *hc* Mexico, Nat. Michoacan (Mexico); LittD, Bates; DD Chicago, 1970. Medals: Draper, Univ. of Brussels,

Rumford, Society of Arts and Sciences, Royal Astronomical, Bruce, Astronomical Society of Pacific, Janssen (Paris), Pope Pius XI Prize, Aguila Azteca (Mexico), Calcutta Science Soc.; Hon. Foreign Member French, Mexican, Indian, Swedish, Austrian, Portuguese, Norwegian, Belgian, Lombard and Italian National Academies, and Royal Irish Academy. Past President: Science Clubs of America; Science Service; American Acad. of Arts and Sciences; American Astronomical Society; American Association for Advancement of Science; Research Soc. of America; Worcester Foundation for Experimental Biology; World Wide Broadcasting Foundation; Trustee: Massachusetts Inst. of Tech.; Woods Hole Oceanographic Inst., etc. Pres., Inst. of Religion in an Age of Science, 1959-62. *Publications:* Star Clusters, 1930; Source Book in Astronomy, 1929; Flights From Chaos, 1930; Galaxies, 1943; Treasury of Science, 1943; Of Stars and Men (in seven languages); Climatic Changes, 1952; The Inner Metagalaxy, 1957; Reading in Phys Sciences; Source book in Astronomy, 1900-1950, 1960; Science Ponders Religion, 1960; The View from a Distant Star; 500 tech. papers. *Address:* Peterboro, NH, USA. *Clubs:* Century (New York); St Botolph, Saturday, Examiner (Boston).   *[Died 20 Oct.* 1972.

SHARP, Francis Everard, CIE 1942; Indian Police (retired); *b* 4 April 1890; *s* of late Benjamin Sharp, MA (Oxon); *m* 1947, Doris Mabel, *widow* of Col C. W. Stevens, RIASC, and *d* of late Ernest Hugo Robinson. *Educ:* Felsted School. Joined Indian Police, 1909; King's Police Medal, 1921. *Address:* c/o Standard Bank of SA, Adderley Street, Cape Town, South Africa. *Club:* East India and Sports.   *[Died 19 Jan.* 1972.

SHARP, Geoffrey Newton; Founder, editor and proprietor of The Music Review, 1940; Director of Newton Sharp Estates Ltd, 1951, Chairman, 1951, 1956, 1961, 1968; *b* 14 June 1914; *m* 1940, Mary Houghton. *Educ:* Uppingham; Trinity College, Cambridge. Post-graduate course with Pye Radio, Ltd, giving special attention to LF amplification and acoustics, 1935; Royal College of Music, 1937; Fellow of Royal Philharmonic Society, 1938-41; studied operatic production under Carl Ebert at Glyndebourne, 1939. Commissioned RA, Nov. 1943; resigned commission, April 1944. Life member Royal Musical Assoc., elected to Council, 1945; Music section Critics' Circle, 1945, Hon. Secretary, 1948, Chairman 1950, Vice-Pres. of Circle, 1953, Pres. 1954; LCMC Committee, 1946. *Publications:* various essays for weekly, monthly and quarterly periodicals. *Recreation:* photography. *Address:* Herons, Barnston, Dunmow, Essex CM6 3PP. *T:* Great Dunmow 820268.
[Died 29 March 1974.

SHARP, Harold Gregory, FIA, FFA; Former Manager and Actuary Scottish Widows' Fund and Life Assurance Soc., Edinburgh; *b* 18 Aug. 1886; *s* of late Isaac Sharp, formerly Secretary and Recording Clerk of the Society of Friends, and Isabella Gregory; *m* 1917, Hilda May (*d* 1966), 3rd *d* of late Arthur Harrison Clapham; no *c*. *Educ:* Quaker Schools at Ackworth, Yorks, and Sidcot, Somerset. Assistant Actuary, National Mutual Life Assurance Society, 1919-23; Secretary, Scottish Widows' Fund Society, 1924-29; Chairman of Associated Scottish Life Offices, 1936-38. *Address:* 40 Pentland Avenue, Edinburgh EH13 0HY. *T:* 031-441 2994. *Club:* New (Edinburgh).   *[Died 9 March* 1972.

SHARP, Gen. Sir John (Aubrey Taylor), KCB 1970 (CB 1969); MC 1942 and Bar 1943; Commander-in-Chief, Allied Forces Northern Europe, since 1974; ADC General to the Queen, since 1976; *b* 6 Sept. 1917; *s* of late A. T. Sharp, Nether Hall, Scraptoft, Leicestershire; *m* 1944, Wendy Ward; one *s* three *d*. *Educ:* Bilton Grange Prep. Sch.; Repton Sch.; Jesus Coll., Cambridge. MA Cantab, 2nd Class Hons, 1939. Served War of 1939-45: 5th Medium Regt, RA, BEF, 1939-40; 4th Regt RHA, 1941-43; Staff Coll., Quetta, 1944; Personal Liaison Officer to Field-Marshal Montgomery, 1945; Battery Comdr, 4th Regt RHA, 1945-46; Instructor, RMA, Sandhurst, 1947-50; War Office, 1951-52; Battery Comdr, 2nd Regt, RHA, 1953-55; Mil. Asst: to C-in-C, FARELF, 1955-56; Adj.-Gen. 1956-57; CO 1st Regt, RHA, 1959-60; Comdr, 11th Infty Bde Gp, 1961-62; Student, IDC, 1963; Comdt, School of Artillery, Larkhill, 1964-66; GOC, 2nd Div., 1966-67; Comdt, Staff College, Camberley, 1967-69; GOC1 (British) Corps, 1970-71; Military Secretary, MoD (Army), 1972-74. Colonel Commandant: Royal Regt of Artillery, 1969-; RAEC, 1970-75; RHA, 1971-; Hon. Col, Cambridge Univ. OTC, 1971-. *Recreations:* most games and field sports. *Address:* Nether Hall, Scraptoft, near Leicester. *Clubs:* Army and Navy, MCC; I Zingari; Free Foresters; Hawks, etc.   *[Died 15 Jan.* 1977.

SHARP, Noel Farquharson; Keeper, Department of Printed Books, British Museum, 1959-66; *b* 22 Dec. 1905; *o s* of Robert Farquharson Sharp, sometime Keeper, Department of Printed

Books, British Museum; *m* 1945, Rosemarie Helen, *d* of Commander E. F. Fanning, RN; one *s* one *d*. *Educ:* Haileybury College; New College, Oxford. Assistant Keeper, Department of Printed Books, British Museum, 1929-52; Deputy Keeper also Superintendent of Reading Room, British Museum, 1952-59. Hon. FLA, 1968. *Address:* 1 Tudor Cottages, Hall Street, Long Melford, Suffolk CO10 9HZ. *Club:* Travellers'.
[*Died* 27 *Dec.* 1978.

SHARP, Thomas, CBE 1951; MA, DLitt; FRIBA, FRTPI, PPILA; town and country planning consultant, architect, landscape architect, writer; *b* 12 April 1901; *s* of Francis Sharp and Margaret Beresford; *m* Rachel, *d* of Cameron Morrison. *Educ:* Council Schools. Worked in local govt offices, 1917-37; Lecturer then Reader, in Town and Country Planning, Univ. of Durham, 1937-45; Senior Research Officer, Ministry of Town and Country Planning, 1941-43; since 1945 in private practice; designer of plans for Durham, Exeter, Oxford, Salisbury, Chichester, King's Lynn, Taunton, St Andrews, Kensington, Todmorden, Minehead, Stockport, Rugby and other towns, new villages in Northumberland for Forestry Commission, new seaside village, Port-Eynon, S Wales; re-landscaping of St John's Backs, Cambridge; planning adviser, Vienna, 1955; Mellon Vis. Prof. Univ. of Illinois, 1965. President of Town Planning Institute, 1945-46; President of Institute of Landscape Architects, 1949-51; Mem. Council RIBA, 1958-60. Hon. Member: Austrian Inst. Planning, 1955; Mexican Soc. Architects, 1961; Hon. Fellow, Ancient Monuments Soc., 1969. *Publications:* Future Development of South-West Lancashire, 1930; Town and Countryside, 1932; A Derelict Area, 1935; English Panorama, 1937; Town Planning, 1940; Cathedral City, 1945; Anatomy of the Village, 1946; Exeter Phoenix, 1946; Oxford Replanned, 1948; Georgian City, 1949; Newer Sarum, 1949; Oxford Observed, 1952; Design in Town and Village (jointly), 1953; Northumberland, 1954; Dreaming Spires and Teeming Towers, 1963; Town and Townscape, 1968. *Address:* 1 Farndon Road, Oxford. [*Died* 27 *Jan.* 1978.

SHARPLES, Sir Richard (Christopher), KCMG 1972; OBE 1953; MC 1940; Governor and C-in-C of Bermuda, since 1972; *b* 6 August 1916; *s* of Richard William Sharples, OBE; *m* 1946, Pamela Newall; two *s* two *d*. *Educ:* Eton; Royal Military College, Sandhurst. 2nd Lt Welsh Guards, 1936; served War of 1939-45 with Welsh Guards and on staff, France, Italy, Far East (wounded, despatches); Major, 1948; Military Assistant to Field Marshal Viscount Montgomery of Alamein, 1951-53; MP (C), Sutton and Cheam, Nov. 1954-72; Parliamentary Private Secretary to: Minister of State for Foreign Affairs, 1955-56; Home Secretary, Rt Hon. R. A. Butler, CH, MP, 1957-59; Assistant Government Whip, 1959-60; Joint Parly Sec., Min. of Pensions and National Insurance, 1961-62; Parly Sec., MPBW, July 1962-Oct. 1964; Minister of State, Home Office, 1970-72. Vice-Chm., Conservative Party, 1968-70. KStJ 1973. Silver Star Medal (USA). *Address:* Government House, Bermuda; Southfield Farm, Chawton, Alton, Hants. *T:* Alton 83318. *Clubs:* Carlton, Turf, Pratt's. [*Died* 10 *March* 1973.

SHAW, Alexander Malcolm, CMG 1946; BSA; retired as Chairman, Agricultural Prices Support Board, Department of Agriculture, Canada; *b* Woodburn, Ont., 12 June 1885; *s* of Robert Shaw and Annie Brown; *m* 1918, Winkona Wheelock (*d* 1948), *d* of Frederic Frank, Orangeville, Ontario; one *s* one *d*. *Educ:* Niagara Falls Collegiate Inst.; Ont. Agric. Coll.; Univ. of Toronto. Formerly Prof. of Animal Husbandry, and Dean of Agriculture, Univ. of Saskatchewan. *Address:* PO Box 26, Aylmer East, PQ, Canada. [*Died* 16 *Aug.* 1974.

SHAW, Sir Evelyn Campbell, KCVO 1947 (CVO 1930; MVO 1919); LLD (Hon.) St Andrews; Fellow of the Imperial College of Science and Technology; Hon. FRIBA; Hon. Member, Royal College of Music; Hon. Fellow, British School, Rome; *b* 1882; *m* 1911, Freda, *d* of late Lieutenant-Colonel J. H. C. Whipple, MD, Coldstream Guards; two *d*. *Educ:* abroad; Dulwich College, Trinity College, Oxford. Asst Secretary, 1904-10, Secretary, 1910-47, of Royal Commission of 1851; Hon. Gen. Sec. British School at Rome, 1912-47; elected member of both bodies on retirement in 1947. Hon. Treasurer Roy. Agricultural Benevolent Inst., 1925-65. *Address:* Little Morcote, Shalford, Surrey. *Club:* Athenæum. [*Died* 23 *Jan.* 1974.

SHAW, Geoffrey Mackintosh; Convener, Strathclyde Regional Council, since 1974; *b* 9 April 1927; *s* of John James McIntosh Shaw, surgeon, and Mina Draper Shaw; *m* 1975, Sarah Dorothy Mason. *Educ:* Edinburgh Acad.; Edinburgh Univ. (MA, BD); Union Theol Seminary, NY. Boys' Leader, Church House, Bridgeton, Glasgow, 1955-57; Founder Mem., Gorbals Gp, 1957-75. Elected to Glasgow Corp., 1970, Leader, Labour Gp, 1973; elected to Strathclyde Regional Council, 1974. Mem.,

Royal Commn on Legal Services in Scotland, 1976-. *Address:* 14 Queen Mary Avenue, Glasgow G42 8DT. *T:* 041-424 3106.
[*Died* 28 *April* 1978.

SHAW, Air Commodore Gerald Stanley, CB 1952; RAF (retired); *b* 28 Oct. 1898; *s* of John Charles Shaw, JP; *m* 1935, Dorothy Margaret Dew; two *d*. *Educ:* King Edward VI School, Birmingham; University of Birmingham. Joined RNAS, 1917; transferred to RAF on formation, with commn as Lieut (Flying), 1918; graduated RAF Staff Coll., Andover, 1933; OC, No 18 (B) Sqdn, 1935; OC, RAF Station, Nairobi, E Africa, 1939; AO i/c Admin, Air HQ, E Africa, 1942-43; Director of Manning, Air Ministry, 1944-46; AOC, RAF Burma, 1947; Senior Air Liaison Officer and Air Adviser to High Commissioner, South Africa, 1948-50; Director of Personal Services, Air Ministry, 1950-52; retired, 1952. Liaison Officer Hunting Group of Companies, 1952-54. *Recreations:* tennis, swimming. *Address:* PO Box 8, Umtentweni, 4235 Natal, South Africa. *Club:* Royal Air Force. [*Died* 14 *Nov.* 1976.

SHAW, Harry Balmforth, MBE 1951; MA, MEd, FRGS; FRSA; retired as Headmaster, The Hulme Grammar School, Oldham (1931-65); *b* 28 November 1899; *s* of Rev. Harry Shaw and Mary Balmforth; *m* 1932, Joyce M. S. de la Rue, Guernsey, Channel Islands; no *c*. *Educ:* Nottingham High School; Manchester Grammar School (Scholar); King's College, University of Durham, BA (Hons History), 1922, MA (Hons) 1925; Leeds Univ. MEd 1924; Hanson Sch., Bradford, 1924-26; Roundhay Sch., Leeds, 1926-31; Fellow, RGS, 1925; AmGS, 1927; RSA 1950; Member IAHM, 1931; HMC, 1932; Lt Loyal (N Lancs) Regt, 1917-19; Durham LI, TA, 1920-25, Capt.; Sen. Inspector, City of Leeds Special Constabulary, 1925-31; Commandant, Oldham Borough Special Constabulary; Chm. No 1 Police District, Commandants' Conf., 1945-52; Pres. Rotary Club of Oldham, 1947-48, Hon. Mem., 1973; Mem., Cheadle Rotary Club. Chairman, No 5 District, RIBI, 1950-52; Vice-Pres., RIBI, 1958-59; Pres., RIBI, 1959-60; Member, European Cttee Rotary Internat., 1960-61. *Publications:* numerous articles on education and current affairs. *Recreations:* motoring, foreign travel. *Address:* Saranac, Barrington Avenue, Cheadle Hulme, Cheshire SK8 6LD. *T:* 061-485 3206. [*Died* 23 *May* 1976.

SHAW, Rev. John Mackintosh, MA; DD; Professor Emeritus of Systematic Theology and Philosophy of Religion, Queen's Theological College, Kingston; *b* Insh, Kingussie, Inverness-shire, 10 Aug. 1879; *er s* of John and Jessie Mackintosh Shaw; *m* Devena Frances, *yr d* of W. J. Rhind, Edinburgh; one *s* two *d*. *Educ:* Raining's School, Inverness (Dux); Edinburgh University; New College, Edinburgh; Universities of Marburg and Tübingen. MA (Edinburgh) with 1st Class Honours in Philosophy, 1898; John Edward Baxter and Sir David Baxter Scholar in Philosophy, Edinburgh University, 1898-1903; entered Ministry of United Free Church of Scotland, 1906; Assistant to Rev. Alexander Whyte, DD, of United Free St George's Church, Edinburgh, 1906-09; Minister at Logiepert, Forfarshire, 1909-14; Professor of Apologetics and Systematic Theology, Presbyterian College, Halifax, NS (United Church of Canada), 1914-27; Professor of Christian Theology, Auburn Theological Seminary, Auburn, NY, 1927-29. *Publications:* Christianity as Religion and Life, 1914; The Resurrection of Christ, 1920; The Christian Gospel of the Fatherhood of God, 1924; Essentials and Non-Essentials of the Christian Faith, 1928; The Belief in the Holy Spirit, 1936; The Christian Doctrine of the Trinity, 1937; Life after Death, 1945; Christian Doctrine, 1953 (paperback edn 1966); The Wonder of the Christian Gospel, 1958. *Recreations:* walking, golf. *Address:* 74 Barrie Street, Kingston, Ontario, Canada. *T:* 548.4092.
[*Died* 12 *Nov.* 1972.

SHAW, Maurice Elgie, DM (Oxon); FRCP; Senior Member, Association of Physicians and British Society of Gastroenterologists; Hon. Consulting Medical Officer, Canada Life Assurance Co.; late: Physician and Dean of Medical School, West London Hospital; President International Committee for Life Assurance Medicine; Medical Chairman, Pensions Appeal Tribunal; *b* 1 July 1894; *yr s* of Lauriston Elgie Shaw, MD, FRCP, and Maria Howard Spalding; *m* 1927, Christine, *d* of Conrad Beck, CBE; two *s* two *d*. *Educ:* Bradfield Coll.; New Coll., Oxford; Guy's Hospital. Served European War, Gloucestershire Regt, 1914-18, Gallipoli and France. Radcliffe Travelling Fellow, Univ. of Oxford, 1923-25 (Paris, Canada and US). Fellow (late member of Council) Roy. Soc. Med. Late Examiner in medicine, RCP, London Conjoint Bd and Univ. of Oxford. *Publications:* contributions to medical books and journals. *Address:* Morton House, Chiswick Mall, W4 2PS. *T:* 01-994 2230. *Clubs:* Savile, Leander. [*Died* 31 *Oct.* 1977.

SHAW, Sir Patrick, Kt 1972; CBE 1960; Australian Ambassador to the United States of America, since 1974; *b* Kew, Vic, 18 Sept. 1913; *s* of late Dr Patrick Shaw, Ballarat, Vic; *m* 1937, Catherine Helen Jeffree; two *d* (and one *d* decd). *Educ:* Ballarat Coll.; Scotch Coll., Melbourne; Univ. of Melbourne, BA (Hons), Dip. Pub. Admin Dept of External Affairs, 1939; Third Sec., Aust. Legation, Tokyo, 1940-42; Official Sec., Office of Aust. HC in NZ, 1943-45; First Sec., Aust. Legation, China, 1945-47; Head, Aust. Mission in Japan, and Mem. Allied Council for Japan, representing UK, India, Aust. and NZ, 1947-49; Aust. Mem., and Chm., UN Commn on Korea, Seoul, 1949; Aust. Consul-Gen. in Switzerland and Permanent Deleg. to UN, Geneva, 1951-53; Asst Sec., Extl Affairs Dept, 1953-56; Aust. Ambassador to Federal Republic of Germany, 1956-60, to Indonesia, 1960-62; Dep. Sec., Dept of External Affairs, Canberra, 1964-65; Aust. Ambassador to United Nations, New York, 1965-70; High Comr to India, and Ambassador to Nepal, 1970-74. *Recreations:* tennis, golf, shooting, fishing, music. *Address:* Australian Embassy, 1601 Massachusetts Avenue NW, Washington, DC 20036, USA; 8 Hotham Crescent, Deakin, Canberra, ACT 2600, Australia. *Clubs:* Commonwealth, Royal Canberra Golf (Canberra).
[Died 27 Dec. 1975.

SHAW, Robert; author and actor; *b* 9 Aug. 1927; *s* of a doctor; *m* 1st, 1952, Jennifer Bourke; four *d*; 2nd, 1963, Mary Ure (*d* 1975); two *s* two *d*; 3rd, 1976, Virginia Jansen. *Educ:* Truro Sch.; RADA. Shakespeare Memorial Theatre Co., 1949 and 1950; Rosenkrantz in Hamlet, 1951; Old Vic Co., 1951-52; Shakespeare Memorial Theatre Co., 1953. Subsequent West End plays: Tiger at the Gates; Caro William; Live Like Pigs; The Long and the Short and the Tall; One More River; A Lodging for the Bride; The Changeling; Broadway: The Caretaker; The Physicists; Old Times; Dance of Death. *Films:* The Dambusters; Hill in Korea; Sea Fury; The Valiant; Tomorrow at Ten; The Caretaker; From Russia with Love; The Luck of Ginger Coffey; The Battle of the Bulge; A Man for all Seasons; Custer of the West; The Birthday Party, 1968; Battle of Britain, 1968; Royal Hunt of the Sun, 1969; Figures in a Landscape, 1969; A Town Like Bastard, 1971; Reflections of Fear (previously called Labyrinth), 1971; Young Winston, 1972; The Hireling, 1973; The Sting, 1973; Jaws, 1974; The Judge and His Hangman, 1974; The Taking of Pelham 123, 1975; Diamonds, 1975; Black Sunday, 1976; The Swashbucklers, 1976; The Deep, 1976; Avalanche Express, 1978. *Television:* The Buccaneers (series); Luther, 1968; The Break, 1973; many television plays. *Plays:* Off the Mainland (perf. Arts Theatre, 1957); The Man in the Glass Booth (perf. St Martin's Theatre, 1967; Broadway, 1968). *Publications: novels:* The Hiding Place, 1959; The Sun Doctor, 1961 (Hawthornden Prize, 1962); The Flag, 1965; The Man in the Glass Booth, 1967; A Card from Morocco, 1969; *play:* Cato Street, 1970. *Recreations:* tennis, golf, squash. *Address:* c/o John French Artists' Agency Ltd, 26 Binney Street, WI. *Club:* Savage.
[Died 28 Aug. 1978.

SHAW, Mrs Robert; *see* Ure, Mary.

SHAW, Thomas K.; *see* Knox-Shaw.

SHAW, Prof. Trevor Ian, FRS 1971; Professor, Department of Zoology and Comparative Physiology, Queen Mary College, London University, since 1966; *b* 18 March 1928; *s* of Donovan and Mona Elizabeth Shaw; *m* 1954, Hannah Schmeltzer; two *d*. *Educ:* Bootham Sch., York; Clare Coll., Cambridge (MA, PhD). Cambridge Univ. Spitzbergen Expedn, 1953. Scientist, Plymouth Lab. of Marine Biological Assoc. of UK, 1958-66. Vis. Assoc. Prof., Dept of Zoology, Univ. of California, Los Angeles, 1963; Vis. Prof., Duke Univ., N Carolina, 1966. Scientific Medal, Zoological Soc., 1967. *Publications:* various scientific papers in JI Physiol., etc. *Address:* Oakapple House, Little Walden, Essex. *T:* Saffron Walden 7279. *[Died 26 Sept. 1972.*

SHAW, William Boyd Kennedy, OBE 1943 (MBE 1941); *b* 26 Oct. 1901; *s* of late Col. F. S. K. Shaw, CBE; *m* 1936, Eleanor, *yr d* of Maj. R. A. Dyott, Freeford, Lichfield; one *s* three *d*. *Educ:* Radley Coll.; University Coll., Oxford. Sudan Forest Service, 1924-29; later employed on archæological excavations in Near East; explorations in Libyan Desert, 1927, 1930, 1932, and 1935; awarded Gill Memorial of Royal Geographical Society, 1934; Department of Antiquities, Palestine Government, 1936-40; Land Agent, 1946-53. Military service, 1940-45 (despatches, MBE, OBE, Belgian Croix Militaire de 1ere Classe and Croix de Guerre 1940, avec palme); Officer Order of Orange Nassau, with swords. *Publications:* Long Range Desert Group, 1945; articles in periodicals on Libyan Desert. *Address:* The Guinea Garden, Elford, Tamworth, Staffs. *T:* Harlaston 279.
[Died 23 April 1979.

SHAW-STEWART, Sir Euan (Guy), 10th Bt *cr* 1667; independent; *b* 11 Oct. 1928; *s* of Sir (Walter) Guy Shaw-Stewart, 9th Bt, MC, and Diana (*d* 1931), *d* of late George Bulteel; *S* father, 1976; *m* 1st, 1953, Mary Louise Shaw (marr. diss. 1956); one *d*; 2nd, 1964, Victoria Ann Fryer (marr. diss. 1969); one *d*. *Educ:* St Peter's Court Prep. Sch.; Eton. Coldstream Guards, 1947-50; Fed. Malay Police, 1950-55; later attached War Office. *Recreations:* fishing, shooting, eating, sleeping. *Heir: b* Houston Mark Shaw-Stewart, MC, *b* 24 April 1931. *Address:* Forces Club, Sandell Street, SE1 8UJ. *T:* 01-928 6401. *Club:* Hokien and Mandarin (Taiping, Malaya).
[Died 30 Jan. 1980.

SHAW-STEWART, Lt-Col Sir (Walter) Guy, 9th Bt, *cr* 1667; MC; Lord Lieutenant of Renfrewshire, 1950-67; *b* 10 Aug. 1892; *e s* of Capt. Walter Richard Shaw-Stewart, MBE (3rd *s* of 7th Bt) and Mary Sibell, *d* of S. L. Lane and Viscountess Downe; *S* uncle, 1942; *m* 1st, 1915, Diana (*d* 1931), *d* of late George Bulteel, Pamflete, Devon; two *s* (and one *s* two *d* decd); 2nd, 1949, Elizabeth (*d* 1968), *widow* of Maj.-Gen. A. Dawnay, CBE, DSO and *yr d* of late George Bulteel, Pamflete, Devon. *Educ:* Eton. Joined Coldstream Guards, 1911, with whom he served European War of 1914-18 (wounded twice, MC); retired, 1931; commanded 5th/6th Bn Argyll and Sutherland Highldrs, 1934-41; Member TA Assoc. (Renfrewshire). JP Renfrewshire; late Convener of Renfrew County Council. *Recreations:* hunting and shooting. *Heir: s* Euan Guy Shaw-Stewart [*b* 11 Oct. 1928; *m* 1st, 1953, Mary Louise (who obtained a divorce, 1956), *d* of late Lieut-Colonel Geoffrey Reginald Devereux Shaw; one *d*; 2nd, 1962, Victoria Anne, *d* of W. Fryer]. *Address:* Ardgowan, Inverkip, Renfrewshire. *T:* Inverkip 226. *Clubs:* Guards, White's.
[Died 26 April 1976.

SHAW-ZAMBRA, William Warren, CVO 1956; CBE 1943; TD; MA; *b* London, 1898; *s* of late J. J. G. Zambra and Florence Beatrice Shaw; assumed by deed poll the addtl surname Shaw-; *m* 1st, 1925, Marjorie Anderson (marriage dissolved, 1950), *d* of late Sir John Mann, KBE, CA; two *d*; 2nd, 1958, Barbara Mary Price (*d* 1968), MA, ARIBA; 3rd, 1970, Monica M. Wingate. *Educ:* Chatham House School; Christ's Coll., Cambridge. Served War of 1914-18, 1st Battalion London Scottish; 2/1 Yorkshire Hussars; TARO, 1919; Captain, 1932. War of 1939-45, General List, spec. emp., local Maj. 1939, Lt-Colonel, 1941, Colonel, 1944-58. Grants Secretary National Playing Fields Association, 1934; Assistant Sec. 1935; Dep. Sec. 1936; Vice-Pres., 1969; Editor of Playing Fields, 1938-39; Sec. King George's Fields Foundation (King George V National Memorial), 1936-50, Trustee and Treasurer, 1951-65; Secretary Imperial Communications Advisory Committee, 1938-44; Joint-Secretary Imperial Communications Committee of the War Cabinet, 1940-44; Secretary, Commonwealth Communications Council, 1944-49; Sec. Gen. Commonwealth Telecommunications Board, 1949-61; Sec. Commonwealth Telegraph Conf., Australia, 1942; Sec. Bermuda Telecommunications Conf., 1945; Sec. UK Deleg. Moscow Telecomm. Conf., 1946; Sec. USA-Commonwealth Govts Telecomm. Meeting, London, 1949; Sec. Commonwealth Telecomm. Conf., 1958. A Governor, Royal Ballet, 1956-67, and of Royal Ballet School, 1955-67. *Address:* 18 East Hill Road, Oxted, Surrey. *Club:* Athenæum.
[Died 25 March 1971.

SHAWCROSS, Christopher Nyholm, QC; company director; *b* 20 June 1905; *y s* of John Shawcross, MA, and Hilda Shawcross; *m* 1st, 1932, Doreen Adeline (who obtained a divorce), *o d* of R. A. Burrows; no *c*; 2nd, 1949, Maridel, *o d* of Dr Maxwell Chance; one *s* one *d*. *Educ:* Dulwich College; Heidelberg; Chelsea Sch. of Art; London School of Economics; University College, Oxford. Arden Scholar of Gray's Inn and Holker (Senior) Scholar, 1929; Law Coach, 1928-30; Bar Studentship and Certificate of Honour, for 1st place in Bar Final exam, also special prize in Examination for Barstow Scholarship, 1930; called to Bar, 1931; Lecturer Mercantile and Shipping Law, City of London College, 1932; Practised Commercial and Common Law Bar, London and Midland Circuit; Counsel to RIBA and Building Trades Fedn, also to Trade Delegn of USSR, 1935-39; Bencher of Gray's Inn, 1954. Served War of 1939-45, in RNVR (Special Br.): SO (Intelligence) and Naval Liaison Officer FOIC Harwich, 1940-41; personal staff of DNI, 1941-43; Mem., Post Hostilities Planning Staff, Chiefs of Staff, 1943-44; Comdr, 1943. Temp. Legal Adviser to Chm., BOAC, 1944-45. MP (Lab) for Widnes (Lancs), 1945-50; Chm., all-party Parly Cttee for Channel Tunnel, Sec., all-party Group for European Union, 1947-49; Member Executive, British Council of European Movement; Mem. Brit. Delegation, Hague Conf., 1948. KC, 1949; QC, 1952. Retired from politics, 1950. Recorder of Nottingham, 1950-61; founded Chair of Law, London Univ. (with Sir Frederick Handley Page), 1954; Chm., Internat. Space Law Cttee, 1959; retired from practice at Bar, 1961; joined S

Eastern Circuit, 1969. Former Chm., various cos in insurance, catering, property develt, finance; Dir., Channel Tunnel Co. Travelled Europe (incl. USSR), Canada, USA, Africa and Far East. *Publications:* The Law of Motor Insurance, 2nd edn 1958; Air Law (with late K. M. Beaumont), 3rd edn 1966; title Nuisance, Halsbury's Laws of England, 3rd edn; articles in the press. *Recreation:* strenuous exercise (rowed for Thames Rowing Club; selected Olympic Eight 1924; played Rugby for Blackheath; boxed Belsize Club). *Address:* Francis Taylor Buildings, Temple, EC4. *T:* 01-353 2711; Bunker Hill Farm, Streat Lane, Westmeston, Sussex. *T:* Plumpton 494; 10a St George's Place, Brighton. *T:* Brighton 67953. *Clubs:* United Oxford & Cambridge University; MCC; Royal Naval Sailing; OUBC, OU Air Squadron (founder member), Bar (Real) Tennis (Captain, 1953-).　　　　　　　　　　　*[Died 18 Aug. 1973.*

SHEARBURN, Rt. Rev. Victor George; Assistant Bishop, Diocese of Wakefield, since 1967; Member of Community of Resurrection, Mirfield, since 1934; *b* 28 Oct. 1900; s of George Shearburn, Architect, and Rebecca Millicent (*née* Jerome). *Educ:* Felsted School; Hertford College, Oxford; Ely Theological College. Curate, All Souls, Clapton Park, London, 1924-28; S Barnabas', Pimlico, 1928-31; CR Mirfield, 1932. CF, 1939; SCF, 6th Armoured Div., 1940-42; DACG, Gibraltar, 1942-43; ACG, Eastern Command, India, 1944-45; DCG, South-East Asia, 1946-47. Bishop of Rangoon, 1955-66. *Address:* House of the Resurrection, Mirfield, W Yorks. Yorks.　　　　　　　　　　　　　　*[Died 3 Dec. 1975.*

SHEARER, Sir Bruce, Kt 1967; CMG 1962; Chairman, James Campbell & Sons Pty Ltd and Carricks Ltd 1942-49; Chairman, Queensland Division, Australian Red Cross Society, 1959-66; *b* 3 April 1888; *m* 1952, Edith Barlow. *Educ:* Maclean High School. Man. Dir, ACF & Shirleys Fertilizers Ltd, 1916-54 (Chm., 1934-54). *Recreation:* bowls. *Address:* 8 Sector Street, Coorparoo, Qld 4151, Australia. *Club:* Queensland.
　　　　　　　　　　　　　　　　[Died 13 Feb. 1971.

SHEARER, Brigadier Eric James, CB 1942; CBE 1941; MC; Underwriting Member of Lloyd's; *b* 23 Nov. 1892; *s* of late Colonel Johnston Shearer, CB, DSO; *m* 1919; one *s*; *m* 1945, Mary, *d* of late Sir O. G. Holmden, KBE, JP, DL. *Educ:* Wellington; RMC, Sandhurst; Staff College. Indian Army, 1911; European War, 1915-18, in France and Belgium (wounded twice, despatches, French Croix de Guerre); Commandant Army Technical School (Boys), Chepstow, 1935-39. War of 1939-45: Maj.-Gen. 1941; Dist Comdr, 1942-44; retd 1945. Col The Border Regt, 1947-52.　　　　　*[Died 7 March 1972.*

SHEDDEN, Sir Frederick (Geoffrey), KCMG 1943 (CMG 1941); OBE; Former Australian Civil Servant (retired 1958); *b* 8 Aug. 1893; *s* of George Shedden, Kyneton, Victoria; *m* 1927, Anne, *d* of George Edward. *Educ:* Melbourne Univ. (BComm). London Univ. Secretary to War Cabinet, 1939-46; Secretary to Advisory War Council, 1940-45; Secretary, Department of Defence, Commonwealth of Australia, 1937-56; Member of Council of Defence, 1946-56; Chm., Defence Cttee, 1948-56; Member National Security Resources Bd, 1950-56. *Address:* 448 Barker's Road, Hawthorn, Vic. 3123, Australia.
　　　　　　　　　　　　　　　　[Died 8 July 1971.

SHEEAN, (James) Vincent; Writer; *b* Pana, Illinois, USA, 5 Dec. 1899; *s* of William Charles Sheean and Susan MacDermot; *m* 1935, Diana (marr. diss. 1946), *y d* of late Sir Johnston Forbes-Robertson; two *d*. *Educ:* University of Chicago. Foreign correspondent, 1922-27, and at intervals since then in Europe and Asia; frequent contributor to magazines and reviews in England and America. *Publications:* The Tide, 1933; Personal

History, 1935; Sanfelice, 1937; The Pieces of a Fan, 1937; A Day of Battle, 1938; The Eleventh Hour, 1939 (in America, Not Peace But A Sword); Bird of the Wilderness, 1941; Between the Thunder and the Sun, 1943; This House Against This House, 1946; A Certain Rich Man, 1949; Lead Kindly Light, 1950; The Indigo Bunting, 1951; Rage of the Soul, 1952; Lily, 1955; The Amazing Oscar Hammerstein, 1956; First and Last Love (autobiography), 1957; Orpheus at Eighty, 1959; Nehru: The Years of Power, 1959 (Eng. 1960); Dorothy and Red, 1963 (Eng. 1964); Faisal: the King and his Kingdom, 1975. *Address:* c/o Curtis Brown Ltd, 60 East 56th Street, New York, NY 10022, USA.　　　　　　　　　　　　　*[Died 16 March 1975.*

SHEEHY, Hon. Sir Joseph Aloysius, KBE 1970; Senior Puisne Judge of the Supreme Court, Queensland, 1965-70; *b* Gympie, 15 April 1900; *m* 1927, Elizabeth, *d* of C. Groves; one *s*. *Educ:* Christian Brothers Colls, Gympie and Gregory Terrace, Brisbane. Clerk, Dept of Justice, Qld, 1916; Barrister-at-law, Supreme Court, Qld, 1921; Actg Crown Prosecutor, Supreme Ct, 1924; Crown Prosecutor, 1928; Judge, Supreme Ct, Qld, 1947-70, retd. *Recreations:* golf, gardening, motoring. *Address:* 35 Craigan Crescent, Aspley, Qld 4034, Australia.
　　　　　　　　　　　　　　　　[Died 22 Sept. 1971.

SHEEN, Most Rev. Fulton John, PhD, DD; Titular Archbishop of Newport, Gwent, since 1969; *b* 8 May 1895; *s* of Newton Morris and Delia Fulton Sheen. *Educ:* St Viator Coll.; St Paul Seminary; Catholic University of America; University of Louvain, Belgium; Sorbonne, Paris; Collegio Angelico, Rome. STB and JCB, Catholic Univ. of America, 1920; Univ. of Louvain: PhD 1923; Agrégé en Philosophie, 1925; Cardinal Mercier Internat. Prize for Philosophy, 1925; STD Rome, 1924. Ordained, 1919; Papal Chamberlain, 1934; Domestic Prelate, 1935; Auxiliary Bishop of New York (RC), 1951-66; National Director, Society for the Propagation of the Faith, 1950-66; Bishop of Rochester, NY (RC), 1966-69. Lectured in Westminster Cathedral, Cambridge Univ., and Santa Suzanna (Rome); Catholic Hour radio broadcasts for 25 years; started television series, Life Is Worth Living, 1952; taught in Cath. Univ. of Amer. for 25 years. Hon. LLD, LittD, LHD from various Universities and Colleges. *Publications:* about 60 books including: Freedom under God, 1940; Philosophies at War, 1943; Communism and Conscience of the West, 1948; Philosophy of Religion, 1948; Peace of Soul, 1949; Lift Up Your Heart, 1950; Three To Get Married, 1951; World's First Love, 1952; Way to Happiness, 1954; Thinking Life Through, 1955; Life is Worth Living, 1956; Life of Christ, 1958; This is the Mass (with D. Rops), 1958; This is Rome (with H. Morton), 1960; Go To Heaven, 1960; This Is The Holy Land, 1961; These Are the Sacraments, 1962; The Priest Is Not His Own, 1963; Missions and the World Crisis, 1964; The Power of Love, 1964; Walk with God, 1965; Christmas Inspirations, 1966; Footsteps in a Darkened Forest, 1967; The Quotable Fulton J. Sheen, 1967; Guide to Contentment, 1967; Children and Parents, 1970; Those Mysterious Priests, 1974; The Electronic Christian, 1979; weekly column in secular press, 1949-. *Address:* PO Box 403, Lenox Hill Station, New York, NY 10021, USA.
　　　　　　　　　　　　　　　　[Died 10 Dec. 1979.

SHEFFIELD, 6th Baron, *cr* 1783, of Roscommon (Ire.); **Edward John Stanley;** Bt 1660; Baron Stanley of Alderley (UK) 1839 (known under this title until May 1957 when assumed the style of his senior barony); Baron Eddisbury, 1848; Lieutenant-Commander RNVR; *b* 9 Oct. 1907; *er s* of 5th Baron and Margaret Evelyn (*d* 1964), *d* of H. Evans Gordon; *S* father 1931; *m* 1932, Lady Victoria Audrey Chetwynd-Talbot (who obtained a divorce, 1936), 2nd *d* of late Captain Viscount Ingestre and Lady Winifred Pennoyer; one *d*; *m* 1944, Mrs Sylvia Fairbanks, widow of Douglas Fairbanks, and formerly Lady Ashley (marriage dissolved, 1948; she *m* 1949, Clark Gable, marriage dissolved; he *d* 1960); *m* 1951, Thérèse (marriage dissolved, 1957), *d* of Gen. Husson, Toulon; *m* 1961, Lady Crane, widow of Sir Edmund Crane. *Educ:* Eton; Balliol Coll., Oxford. *Publications:* Sea Peace, articles in journals. *Recreations:* cruising under sail, physical and chemical research. *Heir: b* Hon. Lyulph Henry Victor Owen Stanley, late Lieut-Comdr RNVR, *b* 22 Oct. 1915. *Clubs:* White's, Pratt's, Beefsteak, Brooks's, Royal Cruising, RNVR.　　　　　　　　　*[Died 5 March 1971.*

SHEFFIELD, 7th Baron *cr* 1783, of Roscommon (Ire.); **Lyulph Henry Victor Owen Stanley;** Bt 1660; Baron Stanley of Alderley (UK), 1839; Baron Eddisbury, 1848; *b* 22 Oct. 1915; *s* of 5th Baron and Margaret Evelyn (*d* 1964), *d* of H. Evans Gordon; *S* brother, March 1971. *Educ:* Eton; Balliol College, Oxford. Lieutenant RNVR, 1940; Lieut-Commander, 1944. BBC Home Service Announcer, 1944-47; Public Information Officer, United Nations, 1948-57. *Heir: cousin* Thomas Henry Oliver Stanley [*b* 28 Sept. 1927; *m* 1955, Jane Barrett, *d* of Ernest George Hartley;

three *s* one *d*]. *Address:* 7 rue Carteret, Geneva, Switzerland.
[*Died* 23 June 1971.

SHEFFIELD, Edmund Charles Reginald, *b* 24 Oct. 1908; *s* of Sir Berkeley Sheffield, 6th Bt, and *b* and *heir-pres.* of Sir Robert Arthur Sheffield, 7th Bt; *m* 1931, Nancie Kidston, *d* of E. R. Soames, London; one *s* two *d. Educ:* Eton. Served War of 1939-45: Northants Yeomanry; North Africa, Italy (despatches); Captain 1941. DL 1951-72; High Sheriff of Lincolnshire, 1959. *Address:* Sutton Park, Sutton-on-the-Forest, York YO6 1DP. *T:* Easingwold 249; 56 Montagu Square, W1. *T:* 01-262 0313. *Club:* White's. [*Died* 6 March 1977.

SHEFFIELD, Sir Robert Arthur, 7th Bt, *cr* 1756; *b* 18 Oct. 1905; *s* of Sir Berkeley Sheffield, 6th Bt, and Julia (*d* 1952), *e d* of Baron de Tuyll; *S* father 1946. *Heir: nephew* Reginald Adrian Berkeley Sheffield [*b* 9 May 1946; *m* 1st, 1969, Annabel Lucy Veronica (marr. diss. 1975), *d* of T. A. Jones; two *d* ; 2nd, 1977, Victoria, *d* of late R. C. Walker]. *Address:* Laverstoke Rectory, Whitchurch, Hants. [*Died* 2 June 1977.

SHELLEY, Herbert John, CB 1953; OBE 1944; retired as Chief Inspector for Technical, Commercial and Art Education, Ministry of Education (1945-58); *b* 28 Feb. 1895; *s* of James Shelley; *m* 1921, Josephine Lamb; one *s* one *d. Educ:* Bablake School, Coventry; Victoria Univ., Manchester (BSc). Served European War, Royal Engineers, 1916-19. Senior Lecturer in Elec. Engrg, Loughborough College, 1919-20; Asst Lecturer, Faculty of Technology, Univ. of Manchester, 1920-27; HM Inspector of Technical Schools, 1927-40, Staff Inspector, 1940-45, Board of Education. CEng, MIEE. *Publication:* (with A. E. Clayton) Elementary Electrical Engineering, 1927, fifth edn, 1966. *Recreations:* drama, gardening. *Address:* Lake View, The Downs, Standlake, Witney, Oxon OX8 7SH. *T:* Standlake 447. [*Died* 28 April 1975.

SHELLEY, Sir John Frederick, 10th Bt, *cr* 1611; JP; *b* 14 Oct. 1884; *er s* of 9th Bt and Marion (*d* 1948), *d* of Richard Benyon, Englefield House, Berks; *S* father, 1931; *m* 1st, 1912, Nora (*d* 1953), *d* of F. J. Coleridge Boles, Rackenford Manor, Morchard Bishop, Devon; one *s* three *d* (and one *s* decd); 2nd, 1953, Mariamne Mee (*d* 1974). *Educ:* Winchester; Cambridge University. Sheriff of Devonshire, 1938. Chairman, Devon County Coun., 1946-55. *Heir: g s* John Richard Shelley, MA, MB, BChir, DObstRCOG [*b* 18 Jan. 1943; *m* 1965, Clare, *d* of Claud Bicknell, OBE; two *d*]. *Address:* Shobrooke House, Crediton, Devon. *TA* and *T:* Crediton 15. *Club:* Naval and Military. [*Died* 8 March 1976.

SHENSTONE, Prof. Allen Goodrich, OBE 1943; MC 1918; FRS 1950; Professor-Emeritus of Physics, Princeton University, USA, Professor 1938; *b* 27 July 1893; British; *s* of Joseph Newton Shenstone and Eliza Hara; *m* 1st, 1923, Mildred Madeline Chadwick (*d* 1967); one *s* (and one *s* one *d* decd); 2nd, 1969, Locke Tiffin Harper. *Educ:* Princeton Univ.; Cambridge Univ. Instructor in Physics, Toronto University, 1922-25; Princeton Univ.: Asst Prof., 1925-28, Assoc. Prof., 1928-38, Actg Chm. Dept of Physics, 1949-50, Chm., 1950-60, Prof. Emeritus, 1962; leave of absence, 1940-45. Special Assistant to President of National Research Council of Canada for scientific liaison, 1940-45. Served European War, Royal Engineers (2nd Lt to Capt.), 1915-19 (despatches). Member: Physical Soc. USA; Optical Soc. of America (Meggers Prize, 1970); AAAS; FPhysS. Hon. DSc York Univ., Toronto, 1972. *Publications:* many papers on physics in various scientific journals, (mainly in spectroscopy). *Recreation:* sailing. *Address:* 111 Mercer St, Princeton, NJ 08540, USA. *T:* 609-924-2389. *Club:* Athenæum. [*Died* 16 Feb. 1980.

SHEPARD, Ernest Howard, OBE 1972; MC; artist; *b* St John's Wood, 10 Dec. 1879; *s* of Henry Dunkin Shepard, architect, and Harriet Jessie, *d* of William Lee, RWS, water-colour painter; *m* 1904, Florence Eleanor Chaplin (*d* 1927); one *d* ; *m* 1944, Norah, *e d* of J. C. Carroll. *Educ:* St Paul's School. Studied at Heatherleys and Royal Academy Schools, 1897-1902; Studio, Glebe Place, Chelsea, 1901-3; first picture exhibited Royal Academy, 1901; moved to Shamley Green, Guildford, 1904; black and white drawings for illustrated papers and book illustrations, also oil paintings; exhibited in Royal Academy and Salon, Paris; started drawing for Punch, 1907; Commission in Royal Artillery, 1915; served in France with 105th Siege Battery, May 1916-Nov. 1917, Somme, Arras, Third Ypres (Captain and MC); served in Italy, Nov. 1917-April 1919, Montello, Asiago (Major); elected to Punch Table, 1921. *Publications:* Illustrations for: When We were young, 1924; Playtime and Company, 1925; Holly Tree, etc, 1925; Winnie-the-Pooh, 1926; Everybody's Pepys, 1926; Jeremy, 1927; Litte Ones Log, 1927; Let's Pretend, 1927; Now we are Six,

1927; Fun and Fantasy, 1927; The House at Pooh Corner, 1928; The Golden Age, 1928; Everybody's Boswell, 1930; Dream Days, 1930; Wind in the Willows, 1931; Christmas Poems, 1931; Bevis, 1931; Sycamore Square, 1932; Everybody's Lamb, 1933; The Cricket in the Cage, 1933; Victoria Regina (Laurence Housman), 1934; Modern Struwwelpeter, 1936; Golden Sovereign (Laurence Housman), 1937; Cheddar Gorge, 1937; As the Bee Sucks (E. V. Lucas), 1937; The Reluctant Dragon, 1939; Gracious Majesty (Laurence Housman), 1941; Golden Age, and Dream Days (Kenneth Grahame) for Book of the Month Club, New York, 1948-49; Bertie's Escapade (Kenneth Grahame), 1948-49; Enter David Garrick (Anna B. Stewart), (USA) 1951; Silver Curlew (Eleanor Farjeon), 1953; Cuckoo Clock (Mrs Molesworth), 1954; Glass Slipper (Eleanor Farjeon), 1955; Operation Wild Goose (Roland Pertwee), 1955; The Islanders (Roland Pertwee), 1956, Crystal Mountain (B. D. Rugh), 1955 (USA); Susan Bills the Wolfdog (Malcolm Saville), 1954; Frogmarton (Susan Colling), 1955; The Brownies (Mrs Ewing), 1955; The Pancake (Child's Reader), 1956; Briar Rose (Child's Reader), 1957-58; Drawn from Memory, an autobiography of early boyhood written and illustrated, 1957, repr. 1971; Old Greek Fairy Tales, 1958; Tom Brown's School Days, 1959; Noble Company (Child's Reader), 1960; Hans Andersen's Fairy Tales, 1961; Drawn from Life, a further Autobiography, 1961; Ben and Brock (for children) written and illustrated, 1965; Betsy and Jo (for children) written and illustrated, 1966; illustrations in colour for new edns of Wind in the Willows, 1969, Winnie the Pooh, 1970, House at Pooh Corner, 1970; coloured covers for The Pooh Cook Book (USA), 1969, The Pooh Party Book (USA), 1971. *Recreation:* reading. *Address:* Woodmancote, Lodsworth, Sussex. *T:* Lodsworth 212. *Clubs:* Savage, Lansdowne. [*Died* 24 March 1976.

SHEPHEARD, Rex Beaumont, CBE 1949; Director of The Shipbuilding Conference, 1952-68, later Shipbuilders & Repairers National Association; *b* 9 Aug. 1902; *s* of Harold Beaumont Shepheard, MA, solicitor; *m* 1928, Helen H. Simmers; two *s* one *d. Educ:* Gresham's School; Glasgow University (BSc, Naval Architecture). Apprenticed with Fairfield Shipbuilding & Engineering Co. Ltd, and with J. Samuel White & Co. Ltd; Ship Surveyor, Lloyd's Register: London, 1928; Glasgow, 1930; Hamburg, 1935; Liverpool, 1939; USA, 1941. Seconded to Admiralty, and appointed Superintendent of Welding Development (Merchant Shipbuilding), 1942; Chief Ship Surveyor, Lloyd's Register of Shipping, 1944-52. Hon. Vice-Pres. Royal Inst. of Naval Architects; Hon. Fellow, NE Coast Instn of Engineers and Shipbuilders; Member: Inst. of Engineers and Shipbuilders in Scotland; Inst. of Marine Engineers. Past Prime Warden, Worshipful Company of Shipwrights. *Publications:* papers to professional institutions. *Address:* 7b South Cliff Tower, Eastbourne, East Sussex. *T:* Eastbourne 23430.
[*Died* 28 Nov. 1980.

SHEPHERD, E(dwin) Colston, BA, BLitt (Oxon); air correspondent; *b* 13 Nov. 1891; *e s* of Edwin Shepherd, Bristol; *m* 1st, 1915, Edith Julia (*d* 1959), *d* of Christopher Holloway Wootton, Oxfordshire; no *c* ; 2nd, 1960, Edith Hilda Mechem. *Educ:* Merchant Venturers', Bristol; Queen's Coll., Oxford. Before European war, worked as reporter Bristol Mercury, Yorkshire Herald, Yorkshire Observer, Leeds Mercury; served four years Royal Field Artillery; joined staff of The Times, 1923; Aeronautical Correspondent and leader writer, 1929-39; Editor, The Aeroplane, 1939-43; Secretary-General of the Air League of the British Empire, 1944-50 (seconded for duty to BBC as war corr. with RAF, 1944-45). Air Correspondent: Sunday Times, 1943-61; New Scientist, 1957-71. *Publications:* Fixing of Wages in Government Employment, 1923; Great Flights, 1939; The Air Force To-day, 1939. *Address:* St Cuthman's Cottage, King's Barn Lane, Steyning, West Sussex BN4 3YR. *T:* Steyning 812289. [*Died* 30 July 1976.

SHEPHERD, His Honour Harold Richard Bowman A.; *see* Adie-Shepherd.

SHEPHERD, Henry Bryan, TD; HM Diplomatic Service, retired; *b* 9 July 1917; *o s* of late George Edward Shepherd and late Anna Dixon; *m* 1957, Elizabeth June Streatfeild; one *s* one *d. Educ:* Winchester; King's College, Cambridge. 2nd Lieut Tower Hamlets Rifles (Rifle Bde), 1939; war service, 1939-46, UK, N Africa, Italy and Austria. 2nd Sec., HM Foreign Service, 1947; 2nd Sec. and First Sec., New Delhi, 1948-50; First Sec., UK Delegn to OEEC, Paris, 1950-53; First Sec. (Economic), UK Comr-Gen.'s Office, Singapore, and UK Liaison Officer with UNO in Far East, 1953-55; transferred to Foreign Office, 1955; First Sec. and Head of Chancery, Sofia, 1958-60; Counsellor, Dec. 1964; British Consul-General, Hanoi, Dec. 1965-Oct. 1966; Counsellor, British Embassy, Copenhagen,

1967-68. *Recreations:* walking, reading, lawn tennis, bridge, chess. *Address:* The Cottage, Shipley, Sussex. *T:* Coolham 227. *Clubs:* Travellers'; Chanctonbury Ring. [*Died 9 Sept. 1974.*

SHEPHERD, Joseph Wilfrid, CBE 1920; *b* 1885; *s* of Richard Shepherd; *m* 1910, Gertrude Mary, *d* of F. Ainsworth. Rendered services in connection with War Refugees during European War. *Address:* Rosemary, Llandudno Road, Rhos-on-Sea, North Wales. [*Died 19 Jan. 1975.*

SHEPHERD, Very Rev. Robert Henry Wishart, DD; DLitt; retired, 1968; *b* 25 May 1888; *s* of Matthew Moncrieff Shepherd and Isabella MacEwen; *m* 1918, Mary Shearer Goodfellow; two *d. Educ:* St Andrews and Edinburgh Universities; New College Divinity Hall, Edinburgh. Missionary of United Free Church of Scotland to South Africa, 1918 (came under Church of Scotland at union, 1929); in Tembuland, Cape Province, 1920-26; Lovedale Missionary Institution, 1927-58: Chaplain, 1927-42; Director of Lovedale Press, 1927-58; Principal of Lovedale, 1942-55. President of Christian Council of S Africa, 1956-60. Moderator of the General Assembly of the Church of Scotland, May 1959-May 1960. Member, Advisory Commission on Central African Federation (Monckton Commission). Editor of South African Outlook, 1932-63. Hon. DD Edinburgh Univ. 1947; Hon. DD Rhodes Univ., S Africa, 1965; DLitt Witwatersrand University, Johannesburg, South Africa. Coronation Medal, 1953. *Publications:* Humanism of Jesus, 1926; Under the Oaks, 1934; Lovedale: The Story of a Century, 1940; Lovedale and Literature for the Bantu, 1943; Children of the Veld, 1937; A South African Medical Pioneer, 1950; (ed with Mrs M. M. S. Ballantyne) Forerunners of Modern Malawi; The Story of Lovedale, 1824-1955, 1970; contributions to journals dealing with missionary and African affairs. *Recreation:* walking. *Address:* Hutchinson Road, Reeston, (PO Box 3061), Cambridge, CP, South Africa. [*Died 22 June 1971.*

SHEPHERD-BARRON, Wilfrid Philip, MC, TD; LLD; FICE, FIMechE; *b* 2 May 1888; *s* of late James Barron, MInstCE, Aberdeen; *m* 1921, Dorothy Cunliffe (*d* 1953), *e d* of A. C. Shepherd; two *s. Educ:* Aberdeen Grammar School. Chief Engineer, Chittagong Port Commissioners; Chief Engineer, Karachi Port Trust. Served European War, 1914-18, France and Belgium, Royal Engineers, TF (despatches, MC); Past President, Institution of Civil Engineers; Colonel, Engineer and Railway Staff Corps, RE (TA); Chief Engineer, Port of London Authority, retired 1953. Hon. LLD Aberdeen, 1954. *Address:* 22 Ormonde Gate, Chelsea, SW3. *T:* 01-352 0170. [*Died 6 May 1979.*

SHEPPARD, Prof. Percival Albert, (Peter), CBE 1963; FRS 1964; Professor of Meteorology, University of London (at Imperial College), 1952-74, now Emeritus; *b* 12 May 1907; *s* of Albert Edward Sheppard, Box, Wiltshire, and Flora Sheppard (*née* Archard); *m* 1933, Phyllis Blanche Foster (*d* 1976), Bath; two *s. Educ:* City of Bath Boys' School; University of Bristol. First Class Hons Physics, 1927; Demonstrator, H. H. Wills Physical Laboratory, University of Bristol, 1927-29; Resident Observer, Kew Observatory, 1929-32; British Polar Year Expedition, NWT, Canada, 1932-33; Meteorologist, Chemical Defence Research Establishment, Porton, 1934-39; Reader in Meteorology, Imperial Coll., Univ. of London, 1939-52. Served Meteorological Office, Air Min., 1939-45. Vis. Prof., Univ. of California, Los Angeles, 1963. Royal Meteorological Society: Editor and Hon. Sec., 1950-53; Pres., 1957-59; Symons Gold Medal, 1963; Hon. Mem., 1976. Chm., Meteorological Research Cttee, 1958-68; Mem. Science Res. Council, 1967-71 (Chm., Space Policy and Grants Cttee, 1965-71); Vice-Chm. of Council, ESRO, 1966-68 (Chm., Scientific and Technical Cttee, 1968-71); Mem. Council, Royal Soc., 1970-72. FInstP; Fellow, Amer. Meteorological Soc., 1967; Hon. ARCS. Hon. DSc: Leningrad, 1969; Bath, 1976. *Publications:* papers on atmospheric electricity and meteorology in various journals. *Recreation:* life. *Address:* Weathering, Longbottom, Seer Green, Bucks HP9 2UL. *T:* Beaconsfield 71297. [*Died 22 Dec. 1977.*

SHEPPARD, Prof. Philip Macdonald, FRS 1965; DPhil; Professor of Genetics, University of Liverpool, since 1963; *b* 27 July 1921; *s* of late George Sheppard and of Alison (*née* Macdonald); *m* 1948, Patricia Beatrice, *d* of R. H. Lee; three *s. Educ:* Marlborough; Worcester Coll., Oxford. RAFVR, 1940-46 (POW, 1942-45). Hons Degree in Zoology, 1948; Christopher Welch Research Schol., 1948; DPhil, Oxon, 1951. Junior Res. Officer, Dept of Zoology, Oxford, 1951-56; Rockefeller Fellow, 1954. Liverpool University: Sen. Lectr in Genetics, Dept of Zoology, 1956; Reader in Genetics, 1959. Hon. FRCP, 1975. Darwin Medal, Royal Soc., 1974; Gold Medal, Linnean Soc., 1975. *Publications:* Natural Selection and Heredity, 1958; (ed) Practical Genetics, 1973; many articles in scientific jls.

Recreations: fishing, rifle shooting (Capt. OU Rifle Club, 1948), breeding butterflies. *Address:* 25 Derwent Road, Meols, Hoylake, Wirral, Merseyside L47 8XY. *T:* 051-632 4404. [*Died 17 Oct. 1976.*

SHERA, Arthur Geoffrey, MD, MA, BCh Cantab; MRCS, LRCP; FRCPath; Hon. Consultant Pathologist to Eastbourne Hospitals; *b* Sheffield, 7 Nov. 1889; *s* of H. A. Shera, MRCS and Fanny Louisa Wild; *m* 1915, Annie Louisa Davies; one *s. Educ:* Oakham School; Emmanuel Coll., Cambridge, University College Hospital, London. Fellowes Gold Medal Clinical Medicine, University of London, 1913; British Red Cross War Medal; Hon. Capt. RAMC 1915-19; Pathologist, No 1 Red Cross Hospital, Netley; RMO Fulham Hospital, 1914; Clinical Assistant Evelina Hospital for Children, 1914; Member of Council, Association of Clinical Pathologists, 1927-28, 1932-33, and 1935-36; Pres. Channel Coast and South-East Branch Association of Clinical Pathologists, 1948-49, 1949-50. Vice-Pres. Sect. of Pathology and Bacteriology, BMA, 1931, also Chm. Museum Cttee, 1931, 1956; Chm. Eastbourne Div. BMA, 1933-34; Mem. Consulting Pathologists' Group Cttee, BMA, 1939, 1942-45; Pres. Eastbourne Medical Soc., 1934. *Publications:* Vaccines and Sera, 1918; papers on medical science in the British Medical Journal, Lancet, British Journal of Surgery (last contribs, 1963), Journal of Mental Science, Practitioner, Medical World. *Recreations:* motoring, fishing. *Address:* Holme, 24 Le Brun Road, Eastbourne, Sussex. *Club:* Devonshire (Eastbourne). [*Died 13 Oct. 1971.*

SHERBROOKE, Rear-Adm. Robert St Vincent, VC 1942; CB 1953; DSO 1940; RN; Lord Lieutenant, County of Nottingham, since 1968; JP; Registrar and Secretary of the Order of the Bath, 1964-68; *b* 8 Jan. 1901; *s* of late Capt. Henry Graham Sherbrooke, DSO, RN, Oxton Hall, Newark, Notts; *m* 1929, Rosemary Neville, *d* of late Lt-Col P. N. Buckley, CBE; two *d. Educ:* RN Colleges, Osborne and Dartmouth. High Sheriff of Notts, 1958; DL Notts, 1958; JP Notts, 1960; Vice-Lieutenant Notts, 1964. KStJ 1970. *Address:* Oxton, Southwell, Notts. *T:* Woodborough (Notts) 2016. *Clubs:* Naval and Military, White's. [*Died 13 June 1972.*

SHERIDAN, Sir Dermot (Joseph), Kt 1970; CMG 1965; Hon. Mr Justice Sheridan; Puisne Judge, High Court, Kenya, since 1972; *b* 3 Oct. 1914; *s* of late Sir Joseph Sheridan; *m* 1973, Mrs Marion Donnelly. *Educ:* Downside Sch.; Pembroke Coll., Cambridge (BA, 1st Cl. Hons Law Tripos); Harmsworth Scholar, Middle Temple. Called to Bar, 1936; practised at Bar, 1936-42; Colonial Legal Service, Resident Magistrate, Uganda, 1942-48; Crown Counsel, Uganda, 1948-51; Director of Public Prosecutions, Gold Coast, 1951-55; Puisne Judge, High Court, Uganda, 1955-70, Chief Justice, 1970-72; Acting Chief Justice, Jan.-June 1963, and 1968-70. *Recreations:* music, cricket, bridge, reading. *Address:* c/o Standard Chartered Bank Ltd, 28 Northumberland Avenue, WC2. *Clubs:* MCC, East India, Devonshire, Sports and Public Schools; Muthaiga Country, Mombasa (Mombasa). [*Died 10 Oct. 1978.*

SHERMAN, Mrs Alec; see Bachauer, Gina.

SHERRIFF, Robert Cedric, FSA; FRSL; author; *b* 6 June 1896; *s* of late Herbert Hankin Sherriff, Aylesbury, Bucks, and Constance, *d* of Charles Winder, Iver, Bucks. *Educ:* Kingston Grammar School; New College, Oxford. Entered Sun Insurance Office, 1914; Captain, East Surrey Regiment, 1917; wrote first play for performance in aid of School Chapel Restoration Fund, 1921; first London Production 1929, when Journey's End was produced at Savoy Theatre. *Publications:* plays: Journey's End, 1929; Badger's Green, 1930; Windfall, 1933; St Helena (with Jeanne de Casalis), 1934; Miss Mabel, 1948; Home at Seven, 1950; The White Carnation, 1953; The Long Sunset, 1955; The Telescope 1957; Cards, with Uncle Tom (for radio), 1958; A Shred of Evidence, 1960; The Ogburn Story (television), 1963; *novels:* The Fortnight in September, 1931; Greengates, 1936; The Hopkins Manuscript, 1939; Chedworth, 1944; Another Year, 1946; King John's Treasure, 1954; The Wells of St Mary's, 1961; *motion picture screen plays* include: Invisible Man, 1933; Goodbye Mr Chips, 1936; The Four Feathers, 1938; Lady Hamilton, 1941; This Above All, 1942; Odd Man Out, 1945; Quartet, 1948; No Highway, 1950; The Dam Busters, 1955; *autobiography:* No Leading Lady, 1968. *Recreations:* archæology, farming, rowing. *Address:* Rosebriars, Esher, Surrey. *Clubs:* Athenæum, Leander. [*Died 13 Nov. 1975.*

SHERRILL, Rt. Rev. Henry Knox, DD; retired Bishop; Presiding Bishop of Protestant Episcopal Church in USA, 1947-58; a President, World Council of Churches, 1954-61; *b* Brooklyn, New York, 6 Nov. 1890; *s* of Henry Williams Sherrill, and Maria Knox Mills; *m* 1921, Barbara Harris, Brookline,

Mass; three s one d. *Educ:* Hotchkiss School; Yale University; Episcopal Theological School, Cambridge, Mass. Deacon, 1914; Priest, 1915; Assistant Minister, Trinity Church, Boston, 1914-17; Rector, Church of Our Saviour, Brookline, 1919-23; Rector, Trinity Church, Boston, 1923-30; Bishop of Massachusetts, 1930-47; Red Cross and US Army Chaplain, AEF, France, July 1917-Jan. 1919; Pres. Nat. Council of Churches of Christ in USA, 1950-52; Board of Trustees: Massachusetts General Hospital, 1928-46 (Chairman of Board, 1934-46); Fellow Corporation of Yale University; Fellow American Academy of Arts and Sciences. Hon. DD Edinburgh, Oxford; numerous doctorates in Divinity, Law, Sacred Theology, Literature and Canon Law from American Universities and Colleges. *Publications:* William Lawrence: Later Years of a Happy Life, 1943; The Church's Ministry in Our Times (Lyman Beecher Lectures, Yale Univ.), 1949; Among Friends, 1962. *Address:* 166 Main Street, Boxford, Mass 01921, USA. *Clubs:* Graduates (New Haven); Union (Boston).   [*Died* 11 *May* 1980.

SHERSTON, Brigadier John Reginald Vivian, DSO 1917; OBE 1941; MC 1915; *b* 2 Oct. 1888; *s* of Col John Sherston, Rifle Brigade; *m* 1914, Edith Adelaide, *d* of John Lockington Impey, ICS; one *d. Educ:* Wellington; RMC. Served European War of 1914-18, 4th Hussars, staff; Afghanistan, 1919; psc Camberley, 1920; retired 1926; re-employed 1939-44, Brigadier 1942. Sheep farmer, New Zealand, 1926-46, now Gloucestershire. Order of Leopold II; Croix de Guerre with Palm (Belgium). *Address:* The Thatch, Kitebrook, Moreton-in-Marsh, Glos. *T:* Barton on Heath 215.   [*Died* 21 *April* 1975.

SHERWOOD, Leslie Robert, CMG 1947; OBE 1924; *b* 1889; *m* 1911, Ella Edith Staples; one *s* one *d. Educ:* King's College Sch., London. Foreign Office, 1908; Staff Officer, Chief Clerk's Dept, 1919; also 1st Class Establishment and Accounts Officer, 1919; Senior Establishment and Accounts Officer, 1922; Deputy Finance Officer, 1938 (title changed to Financial Assistant from Dec. 1940); Head of Finance Department, Foreign Office, 1946-49, retired. *Address:* Honey Tye, Dry Sandford, Abingdon, Berks.   [*Died* 5 *May* 1974.

SHIPTON, Eric Earle, CBE 1955; *b* 1 Aug. 1907; *s* of Cecil Shipton and Alice Lilian Earle; *m* 1942, Diana Kendall (marr. diss., 1955), *yr d* of F. F. R. Channer, late Indian Forest Service; two *s.* Consul-Gen. at Kashgar, 1940-42 and 1946-48; at Kunming, 1949-51; Five expeditions to the mountains of East and Central Africa, 1929-32; climbed Kamet (25,447 ft), 1931; Member of Mount Everest Expedition, 1933; led exploratory expedition to Central Himalayas, 1934; led Mount Everest Reconnaissance Expedition, 1935; member Mount Everest Expedition, 1936; led Shaksgam Expedition, 1937; member Mount Everest Expedition, 1938; led Karakoram Expedn, 1939; led Mt Everest Reconnaissance Expedition, 1951, and British Himalaya Expedition, 1952; Expedition to Karakoram, 1957, nine expeditions to Patagonia (1958-73). President, Alpine Club, 1964-67. Patron's Medal, RGS 1938. *Publications:* Nanda Devi, 1936; Blank on the Map, 1938; Upon that Mountain, 1948; Mountains of Tartary, 1951; Mount Everest Reconnaissance Expedition, 1951, 1952; Land of Tempest, 1963; (autobiography) That Untravelled World, 1969; Tierra del Fuego, 1973. *Address:* c/o Royal Geographical Society, 1 Kensington Gore, SW7.   [*Died* 28 *March* 1977.

SHIRLAW, John Fenton; *b* 31 Aug. 1896; *s* of late Dr M. Shirlaw; *m* 1937, Leslie Hamilton, *d* of late Henry E. Wilkes, Linden House, Stowmarket, Suffolk; *m* 1967, Muriel Tait, *d* of late William D. Robinson, Corbridge, Northumberland. *Educ:* George Heriot's Sch. and University, Edinburgh. Professor of Pathology, Punjab Veterinary College, Lahore, 1927; Pathologist, Imperial Institute of Veterinary Research, Muktesar-Kumaon, UP, India, 1936; retired (from this), 1949; bacteriologist, veterinary research laboratory, Kabete, Kenya, E Africa, retired, 1963. *Address:* 31 Kingscroft Avenue, Dunstable, Beds.   [*Died* 22 *Jan.* 1975.

SHIRLEY, Evelyn Philip Sewallis, CMG 1952; OBE 1927; *b* 2 March 1900; *s* of late Ven. Archdeacon Shirley; *m* 1930, Marian Hamilton Bowen Powell; one *s. Educ:* Saint Columba's College, Dublin; Royal Military College, Sandhurst. Commissioned Royal Irish Fusiliers, 1918; served NW Persia and Iraq, 1920. Entered Somaliland Administrative Service, 1929; Chief Secretary and Commissioner for native affairs, Somaliland Protectorate, 1951-Nov. 1954; retd 1955. Military Service, 1940-45. *Address:* The Vicarage, Hempstead, Holt, Norfolk. *T:* Holt 3281.   [*Died* 1 *June* 1978.

SHOAIB, Mohammad, HPk; MBE 1941; MA, LLB; Vice President, International Bank for Reconstruction and Development, since 1966; *b* 5 Sept. 1905; *m* 1959, Hameeda Fatima Shoaib; four *s* two *d* (and one step *s* two step *d*). *Educ:* Allahabad Univ. BA 1924 (Gold Medal for distinction in economics); MA, LLB, 1926. Joined Provincial Administrative Services, 1926; Indian Military Accounts Department, 1929; Chief Controller, Army Factory Accounts, 1942; Financial Adviser for Military Finance, Pakistan, 1947; Special Delegate to Sterling Accounts Settlement Conferences; Executive Director, IBRD, 1952-63; Minister for Finance, 1958-66. Minister of Economic Co-ordination, Feb.-May 1962. Fellow: Institute of Cost and Works Accountants (London); Institute of Cost and Works Accountants (Pakistan); Institute of Cost and Works Accountants (India); Mem., National Association of Accountants, New York. Hilal-i-Pakistan, 1962. *Address:* 6218 Perthshire Court, Bethesda, Md 20034, USA; (office) 1818 H Street NW, Washington, DC 20433, USA. *Clubs:* Metropolitan, Laurel Turf (Washington); Sind, Karachi, Karachi Gymkhana, Karachi Race (Karachi).   [*Died* 13 *May* 1976.

SHORT, Rev. Frank; Minister, United Reformed Church (formerly Congregational Church), Sherborne, Dorset; General Secretary (1957-Aug. 1965), Asia Secretary (1953-Aug. 1965) Conference of Missionary Societies in Great Britain and Ireland; *b* 6 July 1895; 3rd *s* of John Richard and Louisa M. Short; *m* 1926, Irene Alice McCalla (*d* 1967); no *c. Educ:* Latymer Sch., Hammersmith; Hackney Coll., Divinity School, University of London. Ordained to the Congregational Ministry, 1923. Minister, Kingsbridge, Devon, Congregational Church, 1923-26; Missionary, London Missionary Society, 1926-53; Hong Kong, 1926-49; Sec. of China Council (LMS), Shanghai, 1949-51; Representative of Board of LMS in SE Asia, 1951-53; Mem. Board of Educn of Govt of Hong Kong, 1928-48. *Publications:* occasional articles in International Review of Missions. *Recreation:* gardening. *Address:* Heathcot, South Street, Sherborne, Dorset. *T:* 2268.   [*Died* 15 *June* 1975.

SHORT, Rev. Harry Lismer; Principal, Manchester College, Oxford, 1965-74; Tutor, 1952-74; Librarian, 1956-74; *b* 12 July 1906; *s* of Rev. H. F. Short; *m* 1930, Agatha, *d* of Rev. L. Short; three *s* one *d. Educ:* Peterhouse, Cambridge; Manchester College, Oxford; Harvard Divinity School; London University. Unitarian Minister: Rochdale, 1930-35; Brixton, London, 1935-39; Macclesfield, 1939-54; Banbury, 1954-70. Visiting Professor of Church History at Meadville Theological School, Chicago, 1963. Editor, The Hibbert Journal, 1962-68. Hon. DD Meadville, 1973. *Publications:* Dissent and the community (Essex Hall lecture, 1962); contrib. to: Essays in Unitarian Theology, 1959; The Beginnings of Nonconformity, 1964; The English Presbyterians, 1968; to Transactions of Unitarian Hist. Soc. and other jls. *Address:* 62 Rose Hill, Oxford. *T:* 77564.   [*Died* 23 *Oct.* 1975.

SHOSTAKOVICH, Dmitry Dmitrievich; Order of Lenin; Composer; People's Artist of the USSR; First Secretary of the Soviet Union of Composers, 1960-68; *b* Leningrad, 25 Sept. 1906; *m* 1st, Nina Vasilievna (*née* Varzar) (*d* 1954); one *s* one *d* ; 2nd, Irina. *Educ:* Leningrad Conservatory of Music. Graduated pianoforte, 1924, composition, 1925. Laureate of International Peace Prize; Stalin and State Prizes (6 times); Lenin Prize, for 11th Symphony, 1958. Hon. Mem. St Cecilia Acad. of Music, Rome (Dip. of Hon.), 1958; Hon. DMus Oxford, 1958; Gold Medal, RPS, 1966; Hero of Socialist Labour, 1966. *Works:* 15 symphonies (first, 1925, while student); 3 ballets; 3 operas; 4 concertos; 1 oratorio; 1 cantata; 4 suites for symphony orchestra; 8 quartets; 2 pieces for octet; 24 preludes; 24 preludes and fugues; 11 song cycles; 2 symphonic poems; music for: 28 films, 12 theatrical productions, etc. *Posthumous publication:* The Memoirs of Dmitri Shostakovich, ed by Solomon Volkov, 1979. *Address:* Mozhalski Chaussée d.37/45 kv.87, Moscow G-151, USSR.   [*Died* 9 *Aug.* 1975.

SHREWSBURY and WATERFORD, 21st Earl of, *cr* 1442 and 1446; **John George Charles Henry Alton Alexander Chetwynd Chetwynd-Talbot;** Baron of Dungarvan, 1446; Baron Talbot, 1733; Earl Talbot, Viscount Ingestre, 1784; Premier Earl of England, Hereditary Great Seneschal or Lord High Steward of Ireland; *b* 1 Dec. 1914; *s* of Viscount Ingestre, MVO (*d* 1915) and Lady Winifred Constance Hester Paget, *e d* of Lord Alexander (Victor) Paget (she *m* 1917, R. E. Pennoyer, and *d* 1965); *S* grandfather, 1921; *m* 1st, 1936, Nadine (marr. diss., 1963), *yr d* of late Brig.-Gen. C. R. Crofton, CBE; two *s* four *d* ; 2nd, 1963, Aileen Mortlock. *Educ:* Eton. A godson of King George V and Queen Mary. Served War of 1939-45; Staff Officer to Duke of Gloucester, 1940-42; Middle Eastern and Italian Theatres of Operations, 1942-45. Pres., Staffs Agricultural Soc., 1935-60. Late CC and JP Staffs. *Heir:* s Viscount Ingestre. *Address:* Au Marguery, Sentier de Priolaz 8, 1802 Corseaux, Vaud, Switzerland. *Club:* Royal Yacht Squadron.
                    [*Died* 12 *Nov.* 1980.

SHREWSBURY, Dr John F. D., DSM, MD, ChB, DPH, FRSA, Hon. FChS; retired; Professor of Bacteriology, University of Birmingham, 1937-63; Emeritus Professor, 1963; *b* 10 May 1898; *er s* of Rev. J. S. W. Shrewsbury, BA; *m* 1920, Alys Mary (*d* 1955), *yr d* of H. R. Danford, Daintree House, Upminster, Essex; three *d*; *m* Georgina, 2nd *d* of Mrs C. M. B. Hooper, Saffron Walden, Essex; one *s. Educ:* Woodhouse Grove School, Yorks; Liverpool University. RN, 1916-19 (DSM for services at Zeebrugge); University of Liverpool, 1919-22; MB, ChB, 1923; Gee Prize, 1922; DPH, 1924; MD, 1933; House Surgeon, VD Dept Liverpool Royal Infirmary, 1923-25; Lecturer in Public Health Bacteriology, 1924-25; Lecturer in Bacteriology, University of Birmingham, and Bacteriologist to the Queen's Hospital, Birmingham, 1925-33; Reader in Bacteriology, University of Birmingham, 1933-37; Mem. British Medical Association, Pathological Soc. of Gt Britain and Ireland and Soc. Applied Bact. *Publications:* The Plague of the Philistines and other Medical-Historical Essays, 1964; A History of the Bubonic Plague in the British Isles, 1970; The Genus Willia (Journal Pathology and Bacteriology, 1930, 33, 393-416); The Genus Monilia, (ibid 1934, 38, 313-354); numerous papers on medical and public health bacteriology, and medical biochemistry in medical journals. *Recreations:* gardening, photography. *Address:* Denstone, Ripple, Tewkesbury, Glos. *T:* Upton-on-Severn 2302.   *[Died 17 March 1971.*

SHUARD, Amy, (Mrs Peter Asher), CBE 1966; Principal Soprano, Covent Garden; *b* 19 July 1924; British; *m* 1954, Dr Peter Asher. *Educ:* Morden, Surrey. Has sung at Sadler's Wells Theatre, 1949-54; Covent Garden, 1954. Sang, Vienna State Opera, 1961; La Scala, Milan, 1962; San Francisco, 1963; Stuttgart, 1965. Hon. FTCL, 1957. *Address:* 23 Wood Lane, Highgate, N6. *T:* 01-883 1591.   *[Died 18 April 1975.*

SHUTTLEWORTH, 4th Baron, *cr* 1902, of Gawthorpe; **Charles Ughtred John Kay-Shuttleworth**, MC; Bt; *cr* 1850; JP; Capt. (retd) RHA; *b* 24 June 1917; *s* of late Capt. Hon. Edward James Kay-Shuttleworth (2nd *s* of 1st Baron) and Mrs Roger Fulford; *S* cousin, 1942; *m* 1947, Anne Elizabeth, *er d* of late Col Geoffrey Phillips, CBE, DSO; three *s* one *d. Educ:* Eton; Magdalene Coll., Cambridge. Served War of 1939-45 in HM's Armed Forces, 1940-42, in France and Middle East. *Heir: s* Hon. Charles Geoffrey Nicholas Kay-Shuttleworth, *b* 2 Aug. 1948. *Address:* Leck Hall, via Carnforth. *T:* Kirkby Lonsdale 71375; 73 Cranmer Court, SW3. *T:* 01-589 3983.
                                                    [Died 5 Oct. 1975.

SIDMOUTH, 6th Viscount, *cr* 1805; **Raymond Anthony Addington**; Major late 26th (KGO) Light Cavalry; *b* 24 Jan. 1887; 2nd *s* of 4th Viscount Sidmouth and Ethel Mary (*d* 1954), *o d* of late Capt. Louis Charles Henry Tonge, RN, Highway Manor, Calne; *S* brother 1953; *m* 1913, Gladys Mary Dever, *d* of late Thomas Hughes, Commissioner of Chinese Customs; six *s* three *d. Educ:* Cheltenham; RMC Sandhurst. Served France, 1914-16 (3 medals); S Persia, 1918-19 (medal and bar); Waziristan, NW Frontier, India, 1920-21 (medal and bar); retired, 1928. Served as Company Comdr, 1st Wilts Home Guard, 1940-44. *Heir: s* Hon. John Tonge Anthony Pellew Addington [*b* 3 Oct. 1914; *m* 1940, Barbara Mary Angela, *d* of Bernard Rochford; two *s* five *d*]. *Address:* Highway Manor, Calne, Wilts.   *[Died 7 Feb. 1976.*

SIEFF, Baron, *cr* 1966 (Life Peer), of Brimpton; **Israel Moses Sieff**; BCom; President, Marks & Spencer Ltd since 1967 (Chairman and Joint Managing Director, 1964, Vice-Chairman and Joint Managing Director, 1926); Farmer; Vice-President, World Jewish Congress and Chairman European Executive; Member, Executive, Jewish Agency; Hon. President, Zionist Federation of Great Britain and Ireland; *b* 4 May 1889; *s* of Ephraim Sieff, Manchester; *m* 1910, Rebecca Doro (*d* 1966), *d* of Michael Marks; two *s* one *d* (and one *s* decd). *Educ:* Manchester Grammar School; Manchester University. Joined Marks and Spencer, Ltd, 1915. Secretary, Zionist Commission, 1918; Vice-Pres., Multiple Shops Federation, 1946-61; Pres., Anglo-Israel Chamber of Commerce (Chm. 1950-65); Hon. Pres., Joint Palestine Appeal; Hon. Fellow and Mem. Bd of Govs, Weizmann Inst. of Science, Rehovoth (established Daniel Sieff Research Inst., Rehovoth, 1934); President, PEP (Chm. 1931-39, Vice-Chairman, 1939-64). Mem. Court of Patrons, RCS England; Chm. Bd of Governors, Carmel College; FRAI; FRGS; FBIM; Hon. FRCS 1968; Hon. LLD Manchester, 1969. *Publication:* The Memoirs of Israel Sieff, 1970. *Address:* Michael House, Baker Street, W1A 1DN. *T:* 01-935 4422.
                                                    [Died 14 Feb. 1972.

SIEGBAHN, (Karl) Manne (Georg), DrSc; Professor Emeritus at the Royal Academy of ,Sciences, Director Nobel Institute for Physics, Stockholm; *b* Orebro, Sweden, 3 Dec. 1886; *m* 1914,

Karin Hogbom (*d* 1972); two *s. Educ:* Hudiksvall, Stockholm. Studied mathematics, physics, chemistry, astronomy for the Master degree at the University of Lund; further work in physics for the DrSc (1911); Lecturer in Physics at Lund, 1911-20; Professor of Physics, Lund, 1920-23; Upsala, 1923-36; Member of the Royal Acad. of Science, Sweden 1922; For. Mem., Royal Society, London; Assoc. Mem., Acad. of Sciences, Paris; Member of the Academies in Moscow, Edinburgh, Copenhagen, Oslo, and Helsinki; Nobel Laureate, 1925; Hughes Medal of Royal Society, 1934; Rumford Medal of Royal Society, 1940; Duddel Medal of the Physical Society, London, 1948. Dr (hc) Univs in Paris, Oslo, Freiburg and Bucharest. *Publications:* The Spectroscopy of X-Rays, 1925; a number of scientific papers, especially on X-Rays. *Address:* Nobel Institute for Physics, 10405 Stockholm 50, Sweden.   *[Died 26 Sept. 1978.*

SIEVEKING, Captain Lancelot de Giberne, DSC; (**Lance Sieveking**); Author, Playwright, Producer, British Broadcasting Corporation, retired from BBC, 1956; Freeman: The Merchant Taylors' Company; The City of London; *b* Harrow, 1896; 3rd *s* of late Edward G. Sieveking and late Isabel de Giberne Sieveking (writer, suffragist, cousin of Gerard Manley Hopkins); *m* 1st, 1924, April, 5th *d* of late Harry Quilter; one *s*; 2nd, 1929, Natalie, *e d* of Court Denny; two *d*; 3rd, 1949, Maisie, 3rd *d* of late Max John Christian Meiklejohn; one *s. Educ:* Switzerland; St Catharine's Coll., Cambridge. Began writing at age of six; aged 13 began novel illustrated by G. K. Chesterton which was published in 1924; between ages of 16 and 18 took part in Suffragist Movement, and followed development in science of flying at Hendon; reached normal university age, but joined Artists' Rifles, 1914; was taught to fly by Claude Graham-White; commissioned RN; served in HMS Riviera, seaplane carrier, North Sea, 1915; Royal Naval Air Service under General Smuts in East Africa, 1916; France, night bombing, Jan.-Oct. 1917; shot down over Rhine, Oct. 1917; prisoner of war in Germany, 1917-18; assisted in flying arrangements for Peace Conference at Versailles; resigned commission; owned and edited The New Cambridge, co-founded The Oxford and Cambridge Miscellany, toured as actor 1919-22; Assistant Inspector of Taxes, Sussex, 1922, resigned; commnd RAF, India, 1923-24; illustrated books, wrote; joined British Broadcasting Co. as assistant to Director of Education, 1924-26; started first Running Commentaries; successfully translated colour into sound; began producing plays; produced first television play in world, 1927-31; composed music, 1932; seconded to Canadian Broadcasting Corporation, 1938-39; West Regional Programme Director, 1942-44; Drama Script Editor, 1946-50; Radio and Stage Plays: Silence in Heaven, Kaleidoscope, The Pursuit of Pleasure (with Harold Scott), The Prophetic Camera, The End of Savoy Hill, Wings of the Morning, Arrest in Africa, Seven Ages of Mechanical Music, new English version of Ibsen's Ghosts; Radio Serial plays based on Stevenson's Dr Jekyll and Mr Hyde, H. G. Wells' The Wheels of Chance, Kipps, and Mr Polly, and F. Anstey's Vice Versa, etc., 1925-46; new English version of Ibsen's The Wild Duck, based on new translation by Arthur Vivian Burbury, 1947; An Echo from the Moon, 1948-49; Tono-Bungay, based on novel by H. G. Wells; The Longest Journey, and A Passage to India, by E. M. Forster, 1957; Christmas Pudding by Nancy Mitford; Decline and Fall by Evelyn Waugh; The Polyglots, by William Gerhardi, 1960; Radio serial plays based on The First Men in the Moon, and The War in the Air by H. G. Wells, The Purple Jewel; The Shadow of the Shark based on stories by G. K. Chesterton, 1953; Around The World in Eighty Days, and Twenty Thousand Leagues Under The Sea, by Jules Verne, 1961; Eng. version of Un Carnet de Bal, 1954; A Journey to the Centre of the Earth by Jules Verne: Howards End and A Room With A View, by E. M. Forster; Scoop by Evelyn Waugh; Fertility Rite; Survival Comes First. Films: The History of Mr Polly, by H. G. Wells, 1942; The Other Side of Silence, 1948; Soul of a Heel, 1954. *Publications:* The Psychology of Flying, Dressing-Gowns and Glue, 1919; Gladstone Bags and Marmalade, 1920; The Cud, 1922; Stampede (illustrated by G. K. Chesterton), 1924; The Ultimate Island, 1925; Bats in the Belfry (with John Nash), 1926; All Children Must be Paid For, 1927; Beyond This Point (with Francis Bruguiere), 1929; Smite and Spare Not, 1933; The Woman She Was, 1934; The Stuff of Radio, 1934; The Perfect Witch, 1935; Silence in Heaven, 1936; North American Binocular, 1948; A Tomb With a view, 1950; Soul of a Heel, 1952; The Ear and the Ice-cold Seat, 1953; The Double Who Wouldn't Quit, 1954; A Private Volcano, 1955; The Eye of The Beholder, 1957; Autobiography, 1971. *Recreations:* reading old letters, and looking at the pictures of Paul Nash. *Address:* The White House, Snape, Saxmundham, Suffolk. *T:* Snape 214. *Club:* Union (Cambridge).
                                                    [Died 6 Jan. 1972.

SIKORSKY, Igor Ivan; retired as Engineering Manager Sikorsky Aircraft Division of United Aircraft Corporation, Stratford, Connecticut, 1957, now Engineering Consultant; *b* Kiev, Russia, 25 May 1889; *s* of Ivan Sikorsky, Professor of Psychology at Univ. of St Vladimir, Kiev, Russia; *m* 1924, Elizabeth Semion; four *s* one *d*. *Educ:* Naval Academy, St Petersburg; Polytechnic Institute, Kiev. Started to work in aviation by constructing a helicopter, 1909; constructed several successful airplanes, 1910-12; produced and tested in flight the first successful 4-engined airplane, 1913; produced several 4-engined bombers for Russian Govt, 1914-17; organized Sikorsky Aero Engineering Corp. in US, 1923; successful twin-engined amphibian S-38 (used extensively for pioneering several of American airlines), 1928; ship also used by Govt; trans-oceanic clipper S-42, 1934, used for pioneering of trans-Pacific and trans-Atlantic air service; first successful and practical helicopter in Western Hemisphere, 1939; during later years, until 1957, designed several other types of successful helicopters which were used by Govt and private organizations and were first and only helicopters used by US during War of 1942-45. Several Hon. Degrees from Universities. Member following Societies: Quiet Birdmen; Early Birds; Aircraft Owners and Pilots Assoc.; American Soc. of Mech. Engineers; Soc. of Automotive Engineers; Aerospace Industries Assoc. of America; Nat. Aeronautic Assoc.; OX-5 Club of America; Benjamin Franklin Fellow, RSA (England); Amer. Inst. Aeronautics and Astronautics, Inc. (Hon. Fellow); Amer. Helicopter Soc.; Hon. FRAeS, 1955. Numerous awards (over 80) including Presidential Certificate of Merit, 1948; Silver Medal from Royal Aeronautical Society of England, 1949; James Watt International Medal (London), 1955; Chevalier, Légion d'Honneur, 1960. *Publications:* The Story of the Winged S, 1938; The Message of the Lord's Prayer, 1942; The Invisible Encounter, 1947. *Recreations:* travel, photography, astronomy. *Address:* Sikorsky Aircraft, Stratford, Conn 06602, USA. *Club:* Wings (NY). [Died 26 Oct. 1972.

SILCOX, Albert Henry; retired; Editor of British Trade Journal and Export World, and of Industria Britanica, 1957-61; Editor, Directory of British Exporters, 1957-61; Editor Directorio de Industrias Britanicas, 1957-61; Director, The Press at Coombelands Ltd, 1942-61; *b* 27 July 1895; *s* of late Henry Silcox, Bath, and Clara, *d* of late Samuel Cox, Bath; *m* 1924, Violet Lucy, *d* of Matthew J. Cooke; one *d*. *Educ:* Bath. Journalist since 1913; Bath Chronicle, Bath Herald; editor Enfield Weekly Herald, 1922-30; Editor: The Hardware Trade Jl, 1932-34; The Gas World, 1934-57. Mem., Institute of Fuel, since 1935; Freeman of Worshipful Co. of Gold and Silver Wyre Drawers; Freeman of City of London; Fellow, Ancient Monuments Soc., 1959; served with Somerset LI European War in India, Mesopotamia, Afghanistan and Egypt, 1914-19; commissioned to 3rd Surrey Bn Home Guard, 1941. *Publications:* Specialist writer on iron and steel, export trade, etc. *Address:* Whytecotte, 21 Melrose Road, Weybridge, Surrey. *T:* Weybridge 47016. *Clubs:* Press, City Livery. [Died 23 July 1971.

SILKIN, 1st Baron, *cr* 1950, of Dulwich; **Lewis Silkin,** PC 1945; CH 1965; a partner in the firm of Lewis Silkin & Partners, Solicitors; *b* 1889; *m* 1st, 1915, Rosa Neft (*d* 1947); three *s*; 2nd, 1948, Mrs Frieda M. Johnson (*d* 1963); 3rd, 1964, Marguerite Schlageter. *Educ:* Elementary and secondary schools; London University. Solicitor. MP (Lab) Peckham Division of Camberwell, 1936-50; Minister of Town and Country Planning, 1945-50; Deputy Leader of the Official Opposition, House of Lords, 1955-64. Chairman of Town Planning Cttee of LCC, 1940-45. *Heir: s* (Hon.) Arthur Silkin. *Address:* 24 Victoria Road, W8. *T:* 01-937 4322; Green Shadows, Chase Lane, Haslemere. *T:* Haslemere 2285; (Office) 7 Storey's Gate, SW1. *T:* 01-839 4223. [Died 11 May 1972.

SILLERY, Anthony, CVO 1947; MA, DPhil; *b* 19 April 1903; *s* of late Lt-Col C. C. A. Sillery, Indian Army, and Edith Charlotte Sillery, Scalby, Scarborough, Yorkshire; *m* 1941, Valentine Mary Kennerly, *d* of late A. H. Goddard; two *d*. *Educ:* Perse School; St John's College, Oxford. Provincial Administration, Tanganyika Territory, 1925-42; Deputy Provincial Comr, 1944; seconded for service in Occupied Territories Administration, Madagascar, 1942; served War of 1939-45 with MEF, 1943-46, with rank of Lt-Col in British Military Administrations, Tripolitania and Cyrenaica, and in Civil Affairs Branch, GHQ Middle East; Resident Commissioner, Bechuanaland Protectorate, 1947-50; retired, 1951. Secretary Taylor Institution, Oxford, 1951-70. Compiler and Editor, St John's Coll. Biographical Register. FRHistSoc. FRSA. *Publications:* The Bechuanaland Protectorate, 1952; Sechele, 1954; Africa, 1961; Founding a Protectorate, 1965; John MacKenzie of Bechuanaland, 1971; Botswana: a short political history, 1974; articles connected with Africa, in various periodicals.

Recreations: winter sports, fishing, African studies. *Address:* 24 Walton St, Oxford. *T:* 58261. *Club:* Ski Club of Great Britain. [Died 5 March 1976.

SILLINCE, William Augustus, RWS; FSIA; RBA; Lecturer in Graphic Design, Hull Regional College of Art, 1952-72; *b* 16 Nov. 1906; *er s* of Commander W. P. Sillince, RN, and of Lucy May Sillince; *m* 1938, Muriel Theresa Wynne; one *s*. *Educ:* Osborne House, Romsey. Studied at Polytechnic School of Art, and Central School of Arts and Crafts. Designer for advertising, 1928-36. Free-lance illustrator, contributor to Punch, 1936-. Part-time teacher, Brighton College of Art, 1949-52. Designed Alice in Wonderland Room at Burton Constable Hall, 1967. Work in public collections: British Museum, Science Museum, Imperial War Museum, National Gallery of New Zealand, and in municipal galleries of Sunderland, Worthing and Hull; one-man exhibn of water-colour drawings, Senior Common Room, Hull Univ., 1966. Council nomination to FRSA, 1971. *Publications:* Comic Drawing, 1950; contrib. poems to Yorkshire Life, 1966; *collections of drawings:* We're all in it, 1941; We're still all in it, 1942; United Notions, 1943; Combined Observations, 1944; Minor Relaxations, 1945; *illustrated books include:* Wine, Water and Song, 1943; Even the Parrot, 1944; My Friend Serafin, 1949; This Merrie England, 1954; It don't cost you a Penny, 1955; Basic British, 1956; The Saint and the Boy, 1957; David John hears about Jesus, 1960; The Jet Beads, 1961; Before Jesus Came, 1963. Illustrator of: Pray Silence, 1964. Creator of BBC (North) Television series John Bull's Other Region, 1965. Contributor to Yorkshire Post, 1964-. *Recreations:* looking about, archery. *Address:* Park Farm, Sproatley, Hull, Yorks. *T:* Hull 811038. *Clubs:* Toby, Cartoonists; Archer-Antiquaries; Literary (Hull). [Died 10 Jan. 1974.

SILONE, Ignazio; Writer and Politician; *b* Pescina dei Marsi, Abruzzi, Italy, 1 May 1900; *s* of Paolo and Annamaria Delli Quadri; *m* 1944, Darina Laracy, Dublin. *Educ:* various Catholic private and public schools. One of the leaders of the Italian Socialist Youth Movement, 1917-21; member Central Committee of Italian Communist Party and editor of various newspapers, 1921-29; in 1930 left Communist Party and has since been active mainly as an independent writer; with three warrants for arrest for underground political activity issued against him by the Fascist Special Tribunal, he was forced to go into exile in Switzerland, where he lived until the autumn of 1944; Member Executive Committee of Italian Socialist Party, 1941-47; Member of Italian Constituent Assembly, 1946-48; is now non-party independent Socialist. Pres. Italian Pen Club, 1945-59; Chm. Italian Cttee for Cultural Freedom; Co-Editor of Tempo Presente. Hon. DLitt: Yale; Warwick; Toulouse. Commandeur de la Légion d'Honneur. *Publications:* Fontamara (novel), 1933; Fascism: its Origins and Growth (history), 1934; Mr Aristotle (short stories), 1935; Bread and Wine (novel), 1937; The School for Dictators (dialogues), 1938; Mazzini (essay and selected pages), 1939; The Seed beneath the Snow (novel), 1941; And He did Hide Himself (play), 1944; The God that failed (essay), 1950; A Handful of Blackberries (novel), 1953; The Secret of Luca (novel), 1959; The Fox and the Camellias (novel), 1961; Emergency Exit (essays), 1965; The Story of a Humble Christian (play), 1969. *Recreation:* watching football matches. *Address:* Via Villa Ricotti 36, 00168 Rome, Italy. [Died 22 Aug. 1978.

SILSOE, 1st Baron, *cr* 1963; **Arthur Malcolm Trustram Eve;** 1st Bt, *cr* 1943 (as Sir Malcolm Trustram Eve); GBE 1950; MC, TD; QC 1935; Gentleman Usher of the Purple Rod in the Order of the British Empire, 1960-69; Independent Chairman Cement Makers' Federation, 1951-70; President Cembureau (International Cement Makers' Association), 1952-70; Director: Yorkshire Insurance Co. Ltd, 1949-66; New River Co. Ltd, 1954-70; Governor Peabody Trust, 1957-65; Director, St Martin's Property Corp. Ltd, 1961-70; Hon. Treasurer, Royal College of Nursing, 1964-70; *b* 8 April 1894; *e s* of late Sir Herbert Trustram Eve, KBE, and late Fanny Jean Turing; *m* 1st, 1927, Marguerite (*d* 1945), *d* of late Sir Augustus Meredith Nanton, Winnipeg; twin *s*; 2nd, 1946, Margaret Elizabeth, *d* of late Henry Wallace Robertson, Ayton, Berwickshire. *Educ:* Winchester; Christ Church, Oxford, MA. Served European War, 1914-19; Gallipoli, 1915 and Egypt and Palestine, 1916-19; Capt. Royal Welch Fusiliers; GSO3 53rd Division, 1917; Brigade Major 159th Infantry Brigade, 1918-19; called to Bar, Inner Temple, 1919, Bencher, 1942. Reader, 1965, Treasurer, 1966; commanded 6th Bn Royal Welch Fusiliers, 1927-31; Col (TA) 1931; Chm. Air Transport Licensing Authority, 1938-39; AA and QMG, 1939; Brigadier, 1940; Comd 158 (Royal Welch) Brigade, 1940-45; Chairman: War Damage (1941), War Works (1945), and Local Govt Boundary (1945) Commissions until 1949; Building Apprenticeship and Training Council, 1943-47;

Central Land Board, 1947-49; Burnham Cttees on Teachers' Salaries, 1950-53; Police Council on Police Salaries, 1951; St George's Hosp. Medical School, 1948-54; Governors of St George's Hosp., 1952-54; Road Haulage Disposal Board, 1953-56; Lord Mayor's National Flood and Tempest Distress Fund, 1953; Prime Minister's Cttee on Administration of Crown Lands, 1955; First Crown Estate Commissioner, 1954-62; First Church Estates Commissioner, 1954-69 (Third Church Estates Commissioner, 1952-54). Electoral Boundaries Commission, Mauritius, 1957; Chairman, Fiji, Sugar Inquiry Commission, 1961; President, Ski Club of Great Britain, 1950-54; Member General Council of King Edward's Hospital Fund for London, 1953; Member Church Assembly, 1952-57; Commissioner, Fiji Coconut Industry Inquiry, 1963; Hon. Member: Royal Institution Chartered Surveyors; Chartered Auctioneers' and Estate Agents' Institute; Hon. Vice-Pres. Town Planning Institute; Hon. Fellow: Inst. of Municipal Treasurers and Accountants; Inst. of Building. Recreations: ski-ing (Pres. Kandahar Ski Club, 1963-68) and golf. Heir: s Hon. David Malcolm Trustram Eve, QC. Address: Lower Ballacottier, Kirk Onchan, Isle of Man. T: Douglas 5687. [Died 3 Dec. 1976.

SILVERSTONE, Arnold; see Ashdown, Baron.

SILVESTER, Victor Marlborough, OBE 1961; b 25 Feb. 1900; 2nd s of Rev. J. W. P. Silvester, sometime Vicar of Wembley, Middlesex; m 1922, Dorothy Francis Newton; one s. Educ: Ardingly College, Sussex; St John's, Leatherhead, Surrey; John Lyons, Harrow, Middlesex. Served European War, 1914-18, London Scottish and Argyll and Sutherland Highlanders, 1915-18. Started as a dancer, 1918; Winner of the World's Professional Ballroom Championship, 1922. Formed orchestra, 1935; has broadcast for the BBC, made records and televised ever since. Pres. Imperial Soc. of Teachers of Dancing Incorporated. Pres., Lord's Taverners, 1972. Italian Bronze Medal for Military Valour, 1917. Publications: Modern Ballroom Dancing, 1927 (57th edn, 1974); Theory and Technique of Ballroom Dancing, 1933; The Art of the Ballroom, 1936; Dancing is my Life, 1959. Recreation: physical culture. Address: 19 Boydell Court, St John's Wood Park, NW8. T: 01-586 1234. [Died 14 Aug. 1978.

SIM, Alastair, CBE 1953; Hon. LLD Edin. 1951; Actor-Producer; b 9 October 1900; s of Alexander Sim, JP, and Isabella McIntyre; m 1932, Naomi Plaskitt; one d. Educ: Edinburgh. Fulton Lecturer in Elocution at New College, Edinburgh, 1925-30. Rector of Edinburgh University, 1948-51. First Stage appearance as Messenger in Othello, Savoy, 1930; Cardinal in The Venetian, Little and Apollo, 1931; played same in New York Old Vic Season, 1932-33. Produced and/or played in the following plays by James Bridie in London: Holy Isle, Mr Bolfry, It Depends What You Mean, Forrigan Reel, Dr Angelus, The Anatomist, Mr Gillie; produced and played in The Brass Butterfly by William Golding, London; produced A Clean Kill by Michael Gilbert, London; produced (with George Cole) and played in The Bargain, by Michael Gilbert, London; played Prospero in The Tempest, Old Vic; Shylock in The Merchant of Venice, Nottingham Playhouse; produced and played in Windfall, by Michael Gilbert, played in: Too True to be Good, London; The Clandestine Marriage, Chichester, 1966, Savoy, 1975; Number 10, Strand, 1967; The Magistrate, Chichester and London, 1969; The Jockey Club Stakes, Vaudeville, 1970; Siege, Cambridge, 1972; A Private Matter, Vaudeville, 1973; Dandy Dick, Chichester and London, 1973; appeared several times as Captain Hook in Peter Pan. Appeared in films since 1934. Recreations: tennis, swimming, chess. Address: Forrigan, Newnham Hill, Henley-on-Thames, Oxon. Club: Garrick. [Died 19 Aug. 1976.

SIM, Sir (George) Alexander (Strachan), Kt 1956; b 18 Dec. 1905; s of late George Gall Sim, CSI, CIE and of Margaret Byers Sim; m 1938, Florence May, d of late Jesse James Smith; one d. Educ: Winchester College. CA (Edinburgh), 1930. Director, Andrew Yule and Co. Ltd (Calcutta), 1939, Dep. Chm., 1948, Chm., 1953-56; Commissioner for the Port of Calcutta, 1950-55; Vice-Pres., Bengal Chamber of Commerce and Industry, 1954-55, Pres., 1955-56; Pres., Associated Chambers of Commerce of India, 1955-56; Director: Yule Catto & Co. Ltd, 1956-76; W. T. Henleys Telegraph Works Co. Ltd, 1957-59 (Chm., 1958-59); Peirce Leslie & Co. Ltd, 1964-68; Tote Investors Ltd, 1963-70; The Cementation Co. Ltd, 1961-70 (Dep. Chm., 1963-70). Chm., Horserace Totalisator Board, 1961-70. Recreation: golf. Address: East View, Iden, Rye, Sussex. Clubs: Oriental; Rye; Royal Calcutta Turf, Tollygunge (Calcutta). [Died 28 Dec. 1980.

SIM, Sir Wilfrid (Joseph), KBE 1951; MC 1918; QC (New Zealand), 1939; b 3 Nov. 1890; s of William Alexander Sim, a

Judge of Supreme Court and Court of Appeal of New Zealand; m 1921, Hazel Dashwood Hill (d 1950), Christchurch, NZ; one s one d. Educ: Otago Boys' High School, Dunedin, NZ; Collegiate School, Wanganui, NZ; Victoria College University, NZ. Admitted to Bar, NZ, 1913. President NZ National Party, 1944-51. Served European War, 1914-18. NZ Expeditionary Force, Samoa, 1914; Argyll and Sutherland Highlanders, 1915-18 (Salonika), Médaille d'Honneur (France). Practised in Christchurch, NZ (Duncan, Cotterill and Co.), 1919-39, and, after taking silk, subsequently in Wellington. Member, Christchurch City Council, 1925-27, and Chairman, Citizens' Association, 1927-29. Trustee of Wanganui Collegiate School, 1939-70; NZ Cttee of Management for Doctor Barnardo's Homes. Director, Mount Cook Tourist Co. Member, Law Revision Cttee (now Law Revision Commission), 1936-69. Publications: Sim's Practice of Supreme Court and Court of Appeal, NZ, 11th edn 1972; Sim on Divorce, 8th edn 1970. Recreations: golf, gardening. Address: 74 Upland Road, Wellington, NZ. Clubs: Wellington (Wellington, NZ); Christchurch (Christchurch, NZ). [Died 5 Nov. 1974.

SIMES, Charles Erskine Woollard, QC 1945; MA Oxon; b 1893; s of Frederick Albert Woollard Simes, Worcester; m 1923, Catherine Harriet (d 1964), d of W. M. Hayes, Vancouver, BC. Educ: Royal Grammar School, Worcester; St John's College, Oxford. Lieut 1/7th Batt. Worcestershire Regt, 1914-17; France, 1915; Hd Qr Staff W Midland Region, Ministry of National Service, 1917-18; Barrister-at-Law, Inner Temple, 1921; Bencher, 1961; Recorder of Banbury, 1938-51; Chm. Interdepartmental Cttee on Rating of Site Values, 1947-51; Dep. Chairman, Boundary Commission for England, 1950-56; Member, Lands Tribunal, 1951-67; Chairman Harlow New Town Licensing Cttee; a Dep. Chm. Surrey QS, 1956-66; Mem. Boundary Commission for England, 1950-66. JP Surrey, 1953. Grand Registrar, United Grand Lodge of England, 1959-74. Publications: Joint Editor Lumley's Public Health (10th, 11th and 12th edns), Local Government Law and Administration. Address: Court House, Barnards Green, Malvern, Worcs WR14 3BU. [Died 24 March 1978.

SIMMONDS, Sidney, CBE 1957 (OBE 1945); retired as British Ambassador to Hayti (1955-59); b 31 Dec. 1899; 2nd s of John Simmonds, Bulwell, Nottingham; m 1st, 1928, Stella Sue (d 1948), d of Donald MacLean, St Paul, Minn., USA; one s one d; 2nd, 1951, Magda Elisabeth Kinch, d of late Civilingenior Niels Rasmussen, Copenhagen, Denmark; one step s. Educ: High Pavement Secondary School and University College, Nottingham; King's College, Cambridge. Entered Levant Consular Service, 1922, and served in Morocco, 1924-28, and Roumania, 1928-29; Commercial Secretary, Moscow, 1930-31; Vice-Consul, Hamburg, 1932; Commercial Secretary, Tehran, 1933-37, Moscow, 1937-38. Athens, 1938-41; Counsellor (Commercial) at Rome, 1944-47; Counsellor (Commercial) and Consul-General at Copenhagen, 1948-52; Counsellor (Commercial), Bagdad, 1952-55. Address: Greystones, 16 Coppice Avenue, Great Shelford, Cambridge. T: Shelford 2507. Club: Royal Automobile. [Died 30 Jan. 1977.

SIMMONS, Charles James; b Moseley, Birmingham, 9 April 1893; s of James Henry and Mary Jane Simmons; m 1st, 1915, Beatrice (d 1972), d of Matthew and Ellen Roberts; four s; 2nd, 1972, Kate Showell. Educ: Elementary. Served with Worcestershire Regt, 1914-17, France, Egypt, Gallipoli (lost leg Vimy Ridge); Editor, Birmingham Town Crier, 1940-45; Mem. of Birmingham City Council, 1921-31 and 1942-45; Chairman Public Libraries Committee, Birmingham, 1929-31; Secretary Birmingham Borough Labour Party, 1942-45; Secretary Birmingham City Council Labour Group, 1942-45; MP (Lab) Erdington Division of Birmingham, 1929-31, West Birmingham, 1945-50; Brierley Hill Division of Staffordshire, 1950-Sept. 1959; Lord Commissioner of HM Treasury, 1946-49; Parliamentary Secretary, Ministry of Pensions, 1949-51; Chairman Birmingham Group of Labour MPs, 1945-50; Vice-Chm. West Midlands Group of Labour MPs, 1952, Chm., 1954-59; Opposition Whip, 1956-59. Chairman, House of Commons Branch, British Legion, 1955; Pres. Birmingham Temperance Soc., 1961, Hon. Sec., 1962-69, Sec., 1972-74. Pres., Birmingham Christian Socialist Movement, 1962. Hon. Mem., Birmingham City Council, 1967-74; Hon. Alderman, 1974. Publication: Soap Box Evangelist (autobiog.), 1971. Address: 20 Slack Lane, Handsworth, Birmingham B20 2JL. T: 021-554 5980. [Died 11 Aug. 1975.

SIMMONS, Prof. Ernest J.; Author, Lecturer; b Lawrence, Mass, 8 Dec. 1903; s of Mark Simmons and Annie (née McKinnon); m 1940, Winifred McNamara (d 1970); one s. Educ: Harvard (AB, AM, PhD). Research work in Russia, 1928-29, 1932, 1935, 1937, 1947, 1958, 1965. Instr, Harvard,

1929-36; asst prof. and chairman of Board of English Tutors, Harvard, 1936-39; associate professor of English and Russian literature, Cornell Univ., 1941-46; Chm., Dept Slavic Languages and Literatures, Cornell, 1942-46; Executive Officer (Chairman), Department Slavic Languages, Columbia, 1946-58; Member, Department of Slavic Languages and Professor of Russian Literature, Russian Institute, Columbia University, 1946-59. Editor American Slavic and East European Review, 1947-50. Member: Exec. Council, Mod. Language Assoc., 1953-54; Joint Slavic Cttee of American Council of Learned Socs and Social Science Res. Council, 1947-59; Pres. Cttee on Educl Future of Columbia Univ., 1956-57; Trustee, Sarah Lawrence Coll., 1954-58; Academic Freedom Cttee, Amer. Civil Liberties Union, 1955-59; Phi Beta Kappa Vis. Schol., 1959-60, 1962-63, 1964-65; Danforth Vis. Lectr, 1961-62, 1964-65; Sen. Fellow, Center for Advanced Studies, Wesleyan Univ., 1963-64, 1965-66, Actg Dir, 1967. Patten Foundn Lectr, Indiana Univ., 1964. Editorial Bd Slavonic Review (Eng.); Amer. Slavic and E European Review. General editor of series Columbia Slavic Studies, 1955-59. Hon. LHD, Northwestern Univ., 1968; Hon. LLD Middlebury Coll., 1969. Publications: English Literature and Culture in Russia, 1935; Pushkin, 1937; Dostoevski: The Making of a Novelist, 1940; Outline of Modern Russian Literature 1880-1940, 1943; Leo Tolstoy, 1946; Russian Fiction and Soviet Ideology: Introduction to Fedin, Leonov and Sholokhov, 1958; Chekhov, 1962; Introduction to Russian Realism, 1965; Introduction to Tolstoy's writings, 1968; Tolstoy, 1973; (ed) USSR, A Concise Handbook, 1947; Through the Glass of Soviet Literature, 1953; Continuity and Change in Russian and Soviet Thought, 1955. Many articles and reviews in learned and literary journals. Address: Dublin, NH 03444, USA. T: Locust 3-3451. Clubs: Harvard, Century (New York).
[Died 3 May 1972.

SIMMONS, Rev. F(rederic) P(earson) Copland, MA; b 7 July 1902; 7th c of Rev. Arthur Simmons, Kingskettle, Fife, Scotland; m 1933, Kathleen (d 1968), d of Rev. Henry Norwell, Helensburgh. Educ: Gateshead Secondary School; King's College, Newcastle; Westminster College, Cambridge. BA Dunelm 1922, MA 1926. Ordained to Ministry, Ashington, Northumberland, 1925; Rutherford Church of Scotland, Glasgow, 1929; Egremont Presbyterian Church, Wallasey, 1938; St Andrew's Presbyterian Church Frognal, London, NW3, 1946; St Andrew's Presbyterian Church, Bournemouth, 1963-68; Chaplain at Scots Kirk, Nice, 1936-37. Moderator of the Free Church Federal Council of England and Wales, 1955-56; Moderator, Presbyterian Church of England, 1959-60; Minister, Monzie and Fowlis Wester Church, 1969-74. Visiting Preacher and Lectr in USA and Canada on nine occasions. Recreations: music, colour photography. [Died 22 Oct. 1978.

SIMON OF WYTHENSHAWE, Lady; Shena D. Simon; b 21 Oct. 1883; d of late John Wilson Potter and Jane Boyd Potter; m 1912, E. D. Simon (later 1st Baron Simon of Wythenshawe; d 1960); two s. Educ: home; Newnham Coll., Cambridge; London Sch. of Economics. Mem. Manchester City Council, 1924-33; Co-opted Member Education Cttee, 1934-70; formerly Member Board of Education Consultative Cttee; Member Royal Commission on Licensing, 1929; Member Departmental Cttee on Valuation of Dwelling Houses, 1938. Hon. Freeman, Manchester, 1964; Hon. Fellow, LSE, 1965. Publications: A Hundred Years of City Government (Manchester, 1838-1938), 1939; various pamphlets on Education and Rating questions. Recreations: reading detective novels; going to the cinema. Address: Broomcroft, Didsbury, Manchester 20. Club: University Women's. [Died 17 July 1972.

SIMON, Rt. Rev. Glyn; see Simon, Rt. Rev. W. G. H.

SIMON, Rt. Rev. (William) Glyn (Hughes), DD (Lambeth), 1954; b 1903; s of Canon John Simon and Margaret Caroline Simon; m 1st, 1942, Sarah Sheila Ellen Roberts (d 1963); two s one d; 2nd, 1970, Camellia, widow of Trevor Rees. Educ: Christ Coll., Brecon; Jesus Coll., Oxford; St Stephen's House, Oxford. BA 1926, MA 1931; 2nd Cl. Lit. Hum.; 1st Cl. Theol. Ordained Deacon, 1927; Priest, 1928; Asst Priest St Paul, Crewe, 1927-31; Warden Church Hostel, Bangor, Lectr University Coll. N Wales, Bangor, 1931-40; Warden St Michael's College, Llandaff, 1940-48; Canon of Llandaff Cathedral, 1943, Chancellor, 1944. Exam, Chaplain to Bishops of: Bangor, 1931-40; Swansea and Brecon, 1934-38; Llandaff, 1938-48. Dean of Llandaff, 1948-54; Bishop of Swansea and Brecon, 1954-57; Bishop of Llandaff, 1957-71; Archbishop of Wales, 1968-71. Mem., Anglican-RC Preparatory Commn, 1967-. Select Preacher, Univ. of Cambridge, 1958; Univ. of Oxford, 1965, 1966. Sub-Prelate, Order of St John, 1958. FSA 1966. Hon. Fellow Jesus Coll., Oxford, 1967. Hon. DD Wales, 1970. Publications: Torch Commentary 1 Corinthians, 1959; Bishops (ed. and contrib.),

1961; The Landmark, 1962; Feeding the Flock, 1964; contrib. to Encylopædia Britannica, 1963. Address: The Dower House, Goathurst, North Petherton, Somerset. Club: Cardiff and County (Cardiff). [Died 14 June 1972.

SIMONDS, 1st Viscount, cr 1954, 1st Baron, cr 1952, of Sparsholt; (Life Peer), cr 1944; Gavin Turnbull Simonds, PC 1944; Kt 1937; High Steward of Winchester (City) since 1951; b 28 Nov. 1881; 2nd s of late L. de L. Simonds of Audley's Wood, Basingstoke; m 1912, Mary Hope, d of late Judge F. H. Mellor, KC; (twin s ; one decd, 1951, one killed in action, 1944). Educ: Winchester College (Scholar, Fellow of Winchester, 1933, Warden, 1946-51); New Coll., Oxford (Exhibitioner, Hon. Fellow, 1944). 1st class Mods, 1902; 1st cl. Lit. Hum., 1904. Called to Bar, 1906; KC 1924; Bencher, Lincoln's Inn, 1929, Treas., 1951; Judge of Chancery Div., High Ct of Justice, 1937-44; Chairman, Nat. Arbitration Tribunal, 1940-44; a Lord of Appeal in Ordinary, 1944-51; Lord High Chancellor of Great Britain, 1951-54; a Lord of Appeal in Ordinary, 1954-62, retd. Professor of Law, Roy. Acad. of Arts, 1951. High Steward, Oxford Univ., 1954-67. Hon. FRCOG, 1954. DLitt (Reading University) 1947; Docteur en droit (Laval Univ.), 1953; Hon. DCL (Oxford Univ.), 1954. Heir: none. Address: Flat 7, 64 Rutland Gate, SW7. T: 01-584 4000. Clubs: Brooks's, Athenæum. [Died 28 June 1971 (ext).

SIMONDS, Lt.-Gen. Guy Granville, CB 1944; CBE 1943; DSO 1943; CD 1951; Canadian Army, retired; now President and Director of companies; Vice-Chairman, Commercial Life Insurance Co. Ltd; Halifax Insurance Co. Ltd; Director of Charterhouse Investments (Canada) Ltd; b Ixworth Abbey, Bury St Edmunds, 23 April 1903; s of Lieutenant-Colonel Cecil Barrow Simonds, DSO, late RA; m 1st, 1932, Katherine Lockhart, d of C. M. Taylor, Winnipeg, Canada; one s one d ; 2nd, 1960, Dorothy Flavelle Sinclair (née Harding). Educ: Ashbury Coll., Ottawa; Roy. Mil. Coll., Kingston. Lt Royal Canadian Horse Artillery, 1925; gunnery staff course in England, 1932; also at Staff College, Camberley; Brig., Gen. Staff Canadian Corps HQ, 1941-42; commanded Canadian Infantry Bde 1942-43; Brig., Gen. Staff HQ 1st Canadian Army, 1943; commanded a Canadian Division in Sicily and Italy, 1943-44; Comd 2nd Canadian Corps, Western Europe, 1944; Lt-Gen. 1944; Chief Instructor, Imp. Defence Coll., 1948-49; Chief of the General Staff, Canadian Army, 1951-55, retired 1955; late Comdt National Defence College, Kingston, Canada, and Canadian Army Staff College. Virtuti Militari (Poland), 1945; Commandeur Légion d'Honneur and Croix de Guerre avec Palme (France), 1945; Commander Legion of Merit (US); Commandeur de l'ordre Léopold and Croix de Guerre avec Palme (Belgium); Grand Officer Order of Orange Nassau (Netherlands). Address: c/o Bank of Montreal, 9 Waterloo Place, Pall Mall, SW1; Apartment 304, 10 Benvenuto Place, Toronto 190, Ontario, Canada. [Died 15 May 1974.

SIMPSON, Bertie Soutar, OBE 1954; MB; FRCSE; Vice-Lieutenant of Sutherland, since 1963; b 17 May 1896; s of James Bertie Simpson, CBE, MD, DL; m 1924, Margaret, d of James Menzies; two s one d. Educ: Merchiston Castle; Edinburgh University. MB, ChB, 1919; FRCSE 1922. Consultant Surgeon, County of Sutherland, 1933-61; retd 1961. County Director, BRCS, 1961-72. DL, Sutherland, 1958. Publications: contrib. to surgical jls. Recreations: golf, reading. Address: Blar Mhor, Golspie, Sutherland. T: Golspie 220. [Died 7 Aug. 1972.

SIMPSON, Rt. Rev. Bertram Fitzgerald, MC; DD (hon.) Durham; MA Durham; BD London; Fellow, King's College, London, 1960; b 25 Sept. 1883; s of William and Mary Ann Simpson; m 1912, Ethel Mary Penistan (d 1952); one s one d. Educ: University College, Durham; Theological Scholar, Hebrew Scholar, Barry Scholar, Gabbett prize. Deacon, 1907; priest, 1908; Curate of St Anne, Soho, 1907-11; London Diocesan Home Missioner at St Peter's, Harrow, 1911-13; TCF 1916-18; Vicar of St Peter's, Harrow, 1913-20; Boyle Lecturer, 1923, 1924, and 1925; Golden Lecturer, 1925; Rector and Rural Dean of Stepney, 1920-26; Vicar of St Peter's, Cranley Gardens, 1926-32; Suffragan Bishop of Kensington, 1932-42; Hon. Chaplain to the King, 1919-32; Rector of St Botolph, Bishopsgate, 1935-42; Bishop of Southwark, 1942-58; Preacher at Lincoln's Inn, 1959. Publication: The Prayer of Sonship. Recreation: gardening. Address: 62 Half Moon Lane, SE24. T: 01-274 8828. [Died 16 July 1971.

SIMPSON, Charles Walter, RI; b 1885; s of late Maj.-Gen. C. R. Simpson, CB; m 1913, Ruth (d 1964), d of Alister Alison; one d. Pictures in permanent collections in public galleries at Newcastle upon Tyne, Gateshead, Blackpool, Plymouth, Doncaster, Derby, Sheffield, Bournemouth, etc. Painter of famous horses and their riders; Exhibitor, Royal Academy.

Exhibition of his pictures toured Municipal Galleries, 1956-58. Awarded Gold Medal at the Panama Internat. Exposition at San Francisco, 1915, and Silver Medal, Salon, 1923; also Olympic Medal at Exhibition of sporting pictures in connection with Olympic Games, Paris, 1924. *Publications:* author and illustrator of A Pastorale, 1923, El Rodeo, 1924; Leicestershire and its Hunts, 1926; The Harborough Country, 1926; Trencher and Kennel, 1927; Emily Brontë, 1929; Composition for Photographers, 1937; Photography of the Figure in Colour and Monochrome, 1938; Animal and Bird Painting, 1939; The Fields of Home, 1948. *Address:* Stanley House, Alverton, Penzance, Cornwall.   *[Died 3 Oct. 1971.*

SIMPSON, Rev. Frederick Arthur; Fellow of Trinity College, Cambridge, since 1911; Hon. Canon, Southwark Cathedral, since 1972; *b* 22 Nov. 1883; *s* of William Frederick Simpson, Rector of Caldbeck, Cumberland, and Frances, *d* of Edward Fidler, JP, of Standing Stone, Wigton, Cumberland. *Educ:* Rossall; Queen's College, Oxford; 1st Class Modern History, 1906. Curate of Ambleside, 1909-11; CF, 1915-18 (despatches); Hon. CF, 1919. Senior Dean, Trinity Coll., Cambridge, 1919-22, Dean of Chapel, 1922-32; Univ. Lectr in History, 1926-49; Select Preacher, Univ. of Oxford, 1932, 1935, Univ. of Cambridge, 1913, 1914, 1921, 1932. Silver Medal, Royal Soc. of Literature, 1927. *Publications:* The Rise of Louis Napoleon, 1909, 6th edn, 1968; Ambassadors in Bonds, 1913; Louis Napoleon and the Recovery of France, 1923, 5th edn, 1965; A Remembrance Day Sermon, 4th edn, 1971; A Commemoration of Benefactors, 3rd edn, 1972; Lytton Strachey on Manning, 4th edn, 1972; A Fragment of Autobiography, 2nd edn, 1972; An Inaugural Sermon, 2nd edn, 1972. *Recreation:* gardening. *Address:* Trinity College, Cambridge.   *[Died 8 Feb. 1974.*

SIMPSON, Colonel George Selden, CBE 1942; DSO 1916; TD; DL; *b* 1878; *s* of late R. Kirk Simpson, JP, Glasgow; *m* 1st, 1906, Jane Ethel (*d* 1937), *d* of late Andrew J. Kirkpatrick, JP, of Lagbuie, Shandon, and 5 Park Terr., Glasgow; two *s*; 2nd, 1939, May Hawksley Hooper (*née* Walters). *Educ:* Kelvinside Academy, Glasgow. Was Secretary for Scotland to United Kingdom Provident Institution, 1902-27; thereafter Agency Manager, Scottish T and G Assurance Co. Ltd; retired, 1943. FCII; President, Insurance and Actuarial Society of Glasgow, 1921-22; served European War, 1914-18, commanding RFA Brigades, Gallipoli, Egypt, Palestine, and France (severely wounded, despatches thrice, DSO, Serbian Order of White Eagle with Swords, 1914-15 Star); organised and commanded 80th Lowland Field Regt RA (TA) (City of Glasgow Artillery), 1920; Supt Maryhill Div. of Special Constables, 1926-39; rep. Scottish Command on WO Committee for reconstruction of TA, 1943-47; Chairman, County of Glasgow TA and AFA, 1943-45; Vice-President, West Stirlingshire Unionist Association; Chairman Glasgow Branch National Association for Employment of Regular Sailors, Soldiers, and Airmen, 1922-45; was on Executive Committees of Erskine Hospital, Western Infirmary and Glasgow Branch, Brit. Red Cross Soc.; Commissioner of Income Tax, Stirlingshire, 1936-50; Colonel and Zone Commander, 1940-44, City of Glasgow Home Guard. Deacon of the Incorporation of Weavers, Glasgow, 1941-42. *Recreations:* shooting, yachting, golf. *Address:* Kirktonshade, Kirriemuir, Angus. *Club:* Conservative (Glasgow).   *[Died 16 Jan. 1971.*

SIMPSON, Rear-Adm. George Walter Gillow, CB 1950; CBE 1942; retired; *b* 6 June 1901; 2nd *s* of late Rev. R. H. B. Simpson, of Guildford, Surrey; *m* 1945, Alison, er *d* of late Capt. L. J. Hall, CBE, RNR; two *s* one *d. Educ:* RN Colleges, Osborne and Dartmouth. Served in Grand Fleet, Sept. 1917, until end of hostilities; served in submarines, 1921-54; commanded submarines, based at Malta, 1941 and 1942; Commodore "D" Western Approaches, 1943-45; First Naval Member and Chief of New Zealand Naval Staff, 1947-50; Flag Officer, Germany, and Chief British Naval Representative on Allied Control Commission, 1951; Flag Officer, Submarines, 1952-54, retired 1954. Virtuti Militari (Poland), 1942; despatches, 1943. *Publication:* Periscope View, 1972. *Recreations:* wild fowling and fishing. *Address:* 70 Kiripaka Road, Whangarei, Northland, New Zealand.   *[Died 2 March 1972.*

SIMPSON, Gerald Gordon, CMG 1967; HM Diplomatic Service, resigned; *b* 1 Sept. 1918; *s* of Major Gerald Gordon Simpson; *m* 1943, Peggy Ena Williams; one *d. Educ:* Royal Grammar Sch., Newcastle upon Tyne. Served in British and Indian Armies, 1938-46; (retd as Lt-Col). Ministry of Labour (seconded to Control Commission for Germany), 1947-48. Joined HM Foreign Service, 1948; served in: Ankara, 1950-52; Budapest, 1952-54; Foreign Office, 1954-58; Santiago de Chile, 1958-61; Washington, 1961-62; New York, 1962-65; Consul-Gen., Houston, 1965-68; seconded to Overseas Cttee of Unilever, 1969; Consul-Gen., Düsseldorf, 1970-74. *Recreations:* golf,

gardening, painting; contemplating the folly of politicians. *Address:* Furnace Place, Haslemere, Surrey. *T:* Haslemere 51739.   *[Died 19 June 1979.*

SIMPSON, Prof. Harold, MA, DSc Oxon; Professor of Mathematics, University of London, 1912-44, Professor Emeritus, 1945; Head of Mathematical Department, Bedford College, 1907-44; *b* 22 Oct. 1876; *e s* of Rev. H. G. Hilton; took name of Harold Simpson (in lieu of Harold Hilton), 1939; *m* 1st, Edith Marsley, *d* of Rev. J. Skinner Jones; no *c*; 2nd, Dorothy Mary, *d* of C. F. Elliott; no *c. Educ:* Lancing Coll.; Hertford Coll., Oxford (Scholar). Junior Mathematical Exhibitioner and Senior Mathematical Scholar, University of Oxford; Fellow of Magdalen College, Oxford, 1898-1905; MA 1902, DSc 1913; Assistant Lecturer in Mathematics, University College, Bangor, N Wales, 1902-7; member of the Councils of the London Mathematical Society, 1915-44, and the Mineralogical Society, 1908-11, 1913-16, 1918-21, 1923-30, 1939-42. *Publications:* Mathematical Crystallography, 1903; reprinted 1963; Theory of Finite Groups, 1907; Homogeneous Linear Substitutions, 1914; Plane Algebraic Curves, 1920, 2nd edn 1932; various papers on Mathematical and Crystallographic subjects. *Recreation:* chess. *Address:* 11 Staverton Road, Oxford OX2 6XH. *T:* Oxford 58793.   *[Died 4 April 1974.*

SIMPSON, Sir James Dyer, Kt 1946; *b* 21 Aug. 1888; *m* Lucy Beavan (*d* 1978); one *s*. Chief General Manager Royal Insurance Co. and The Liverpool & London & Globe Insurance Co.; retired 1949; Director General Administrative Services, Ministry of Supply, 1942. Past Chairman, British Insurance Assoc.; Insurance Institute of Liverpool. Chm., Liverpool Caledonian Assoc., 1976. JP (Liverpool) 1944-50. *Publications:* pamphlets on insurance. *Address:* Carlton Hotel, East Cliff, Bournemouth, Dorset. *Club:* Pilgrims. *[Died 31 March 1979.*

SIMPSON, John Alexander, CIE 1945; MA; *b* 25 Nov. 1892; *s* of John and Christina Simpson, Aberdeen; *m* 1925, Mary W. U. Robertson (*d* 1970); no *c. Educ:* Robert Gordon's College, Aberdeen. MA 1st Cl. Hons in Classics, Aberdeen University, 1913; served European War, 1915-19; junior clerk, India Office, 1919; Joint Sec., Military Dept, India Office (now Commonwealth Relations Office), 1934-48. *Address:* 21 Falcon Gardens, Edinburgh EH10 4AP. *T:* 031-447 3483.
                                                         [Died 5 June 1977.

SIMPSON, Sir John (Roughton), Kt 1957; CB 1948; Chairman, Timber Trade Federation of the United Kingdom, 1961-65; *b* 19 April 1899; *m* 1923, Margaret Statham; one *s* one *d*. Inland Revenue, 1916-40; Postal and Telegraph Censorship, 1940-44; Under Secretary and Director of Organisation and Methods, HM Treasury, 1944-53; Controller of HM Stationery Office and Queen's Printer of Acts, 1954-61. Served European War, Army, 1917-19. *Address:* 17 Amberley Court, Christchurch Park, Sutton, Surrey. *T:* 01-643 1501.   *[Died 14 Dec. 1976.*

SIMPSON, Maj.-Gen. Noel William, CB 1963; CBE 1956; DSO 1942 (Bar 1944); ED 1945; *b* 22 Feb. 1907; *s* of late Harry Simpson, Rossneath, Goulburn, NSW and late Annie Simpson (*née* Thomas); unmarried. *Educ:* North Sydney High Sch. Second-in-Command, 2nd/13th Bn AIF, 1940; DAAG 7th Aust. Div. 1940-41, CO 2nd/17th Bn AIF, 1944-45; Brigadier, 1945; Bde Comd 23rd Inf. Bde, Bougainville, 1945; Bde Comd 6th Inf. Bde, 1953-58; GOC 3rd Aust. Div., 1959-60; CMF Member, Military Bd, 1960-62; R of O 1962. Joined National Bank of Australasia Ltd, 1922; various staff and managerial appointments, NSW and Victoria; retired, 1966. *Recreations:* walking, swimming. *Address:* 7 Chastleton Ave, Toorak, Victoria 3142, Australia. *T:* 242947. *Clubs:* Imperial Service (Sydney); Naval and Military (Melbourne). *[Died 9 May 1972.*

SIMPSON, Rayene Stewart, VC 1969; DCM 1964; with Australian Embassy, Tokyo, since 1972; *b* Sydney, Australia, 16 Feb. 1926; Australian parents (British stock); *m* 1952, Shoko Simpson (*née* Sakai); no *c. Educ:* Carlingford Public Sch., Sydney, Australia. Served War of 1939-45 (Pacific theatre); enlisted in AIF, 1944; discharged, 1947. Seasonal worker and merchant seaman, 1947-50; enlisted in Aust. Regular Army, 1951; served in Korea, 1951-54, with 3rd Bn, The Royal Australian Regt; served in Malaya, Oct. 1955-57, 2nd Bn, The Royal Australian Regt; 1st SAS, 1957-62; Aust. Army Trg Team, Vietnam (AATTV), July 1962-63; 1st SAS, July 1963-64; Aust. Army Trg Team, Vietnam (AATTV) July-Sept. 1964 (wounded in action, DCM, in hosp. 8 mths); 1st Bn City of Sydney Regt (Commando), 1965-66 (discharged 1966); re-enlisted Aust. Regular Army in Saigon, 1967, and served with AATTV (VC), in S Vietnam, 1970 (discharged from Service, 1970, after 21 years). Sales Representative, Caldbeck-Macgrigor

& Co., Tokyo, 1970. *Recreations:* walking, reading (military history), watching boxing. *Address:* Australian Embassy, 1-14 Mita 2 Chome, Minato-Ku, Tokyo 108, Japan; No 5-30-1 Chome, Yayoicho, Nakano-ku, Tokyo 164, Japan. *T:* 373 1066. *Club:* Returned Services League (RSL), Paddington-Woollahra Sub-Branch (Sydney). [Died 17 Oct. 1978.

SIMPSON, Rev. Robert, MA, MSc; DPhil; FCP; *b* 10 November 1900; *s* of William Robert Simpson, Dungannon, Co. Tyrone, and Mary Jackson; unmarried. *Educ:* London University; Manchester University; New College, Oxford; Buckle Research Scholar in Agricultural Zoology, 1927; Egerton Hall, Manchester (Theological Coll.). Deacon, 1924; Priest, 1925; Chaplain and Science Master at Cranleigh, 1928-32; Principal, Lawrence Memorial Roy. Mil. School, Lovedale, Nilgiri Hills, 1933-37; Headmaster Ashburton School, 1937-38; Rector of Mellis, 1939-43; Head of Dept of Zoology, Achimota College (Univ. Coll. of the Gold Coast), 1943-48; Charterhouse, 1949; Headmaster of Wolmer's School, Kingston, Jamaica, 1949-53. *Publications:* Papers on Zoological and Educational subjects. *Recreations:* swimming, rowing. *Address:* c/o Messrs Falck & Co., 68 High Street, Southwold, Suffolk IP18 6DW.
[Died 15 Feb. 1977.

SIMS, Sir Alfred (John), KCB 1960; OBE 1943; Director-General Ships, Admiralty, later Ministry of Defence, and Head of RCNC, 1958-68; *b* 11 Oct. 1907; *s* of John Thomas Sims and Jessie Sims; British; *m* 1933, Barbara Mary Hunking Paul; one *s* one *d. Educ:* Regent St Higher Elementary Sch., Plymouth; HM Dockyard School, Devonport; RN Coll., Greenwich. Assistant Constructor, 1931; Mediterranean Fleet, 1932; Chatham Dockyard i/c successively of welding, submarine construction and the Constructive Drawing Office, 1933-37; Naval Construction Dept, Admiralty, 1937-38. Staff of Flag Officer Submarines, 1938-43, as Asst Constructor (Constr Lieut-Comdr) and later as Constructor (Constructor Commander). Naval Construction Dept, Admiralty, 1943-44, i/c of salvage vessels, slipways, habitability, etc; Chief Constructor in charge of submarine design, 1944-47. Professor of Naval Architecture, Royal Naval College, Greenwich, 1947-52. Naval Construction Department, Admiralty, 1952-54; i/c aircraft carrier design; Asst Dir of Naval Construction in charge of aircraft carrier and of submarine design, Oct. 1954-58, Dep. Dir, April-Sept. 1958. Hon. Research Associate, UCL. Prime Warden, Worshipful Co. of Shipwrights, 1975-76; FICE; Member NE Coast Instn of Engineers and Shipbuilders. Chm., Western Centre, RSA, 1966-71. Hon. DSc Bath, 1974. *Publications:* Thomas Gray Memorial Lecture to RSA, 1952; Andrew Laing Lecture, NE Coast, Instn of Engrs and Shipbuilders, 1960-61; James Forrest Lecture, Instn CE, 1965; Amos Ayre Lecture, RINA, 1968; rev. Attwood and Pengelly's Theoretical Naval Architecture. Papers before RINA, etc. *Recreations:* music, reading. *Address:* Rannoch, 38 Bloomfield Park, Bath BA2 2BX. *T:* Bath 310218. *Club:* Royal Commonwealth Society. [Died 25 Aug. 1977.

SIMS, Arthur Mitford, CIE 1943; Chief Engineer, North Western Railway, Lahore, retired; *b* 31 March 1889; 2nd *s* of late Sir Thomas Sims, CB; *m* 1st, 1915, Isabella May Jeffrey (*d* 1937); one *s* two *d* ; 2nd, 1940, Mary Jeffrey (*d* 1971). *Educ:* St Paul's School; Dulwich College; University Coll., London (BScEng, 1st cl. hons); MICE. Asst Engineer, Eastern Bengal Railway, 1911-16; Military Service, 1916-18, in East Africa, Capt. RE; Asst Engineer, 1918, subsequently Executive Engineer, Deputy Chief Engineer, Deputy General Manager, North Western Railway. *Publications:* railway technical papers. *Recreation:* cricket. *Address:* Whapple House, Berry Lane, Littlehampton, West Sussex BN17 5HD. *T:* Littlehampton 3308. [Died 2 March 1977.

SINCLAIR OF CLEEVE, 1st Baron, *cr* 1957, of Cleeve, Co. Somerset; **Robert John Sinclair,** KCB 1946; KBE 1941 (MBE 1919); MA; United States Medal of Freedom with Gold Palm, 1947; *b* 1893; *s* of late R. H. Sinclair; *m* 1917, Mary Shearer Barclay; one *s* (and one killed in action, Middle East, 1942). *Educ:* Glasgow Acad.; Oriel College, Oxford (Hon. Fellow, 1959). Commnd Aug. 1914, 5th Bn KOSB; served Gallipoli (wounded, despatches); seconded to Ministry of Munitions, 1916, Deputy Director of Munitions Inspection, 1917-19; Member of Prime Minister's Advisory Panel of Industrialists, January 1939; Director-General of Army Requirements, War Office, 1939-42; Member: Supply Council, 1939-42; Army Council, 1940-42. Deputy for Minister of Production on Combined Production and Resources Board, Washington, 1942-43; Chief Executive, Ministry of Production, 1943, and subsequently with Board of Trade until Nov. 1945. Chairman, Committee to enquire into Financial Structure of Colonial Development Corporation, 1959; Member, UK Permanent Security Commission, 1965-77. Director: Imperial Tobacco Co.

Ltd, 1933-67 (Chm., 1947-59, Pres., 1959-67); Bristol Waterworks Co., 1946-72 (Chm., 1960-71); Finance Corp. for Industry (Chm., 1960-64); Commonwealth Develt Finance Corp., 1953-67; General Accident Assurance Corp. Ltd, 1958-63; Debenture Corp. Ltd, 1961-73. Pro-Chancellor, Bristol Univ., 1946-71; Pres., Federation of British Industries, 1949-51; High Sheriff of Somerset, 1951-52. Hon. LLD (Bristol), 1959. *Recreations:* fishing, shooting, golf. *Heir: s* Lt-Col The Hon. John Robert Kilgour Sinclair, OBE 1963, Queen's Own Cameron Highlanders [*b* 3 Nov. 1919; *m* 1950, Patricia, *d* of Lawrence Hellyer, Lockerbie, Dumfriesshire; one *s* two *d*]. *Address:* Cleeve Court, Cleeve, Bristol BS19 4PE. *TA* and *T:* Yatton 832124. *Clubs:* United Oxford & Cambridge University, Army and Navy. [Died 4 March 1979.

SINCLAIR, Maj.-Gen. Sir John (Alexander), KCMG 1953; CB 1945; OBE 1940; Colonel Commandant Royal Artillery, 1952-62; *b* 29 May 1897; *s* of Ven. Archdeacon J. S. Sinclair; *m* 1927, Esme Beatrice Sopwith; two *s* two *d. Educ:* West Downs, Winchester; RN Colleges; RMA Woolwich. Midshipman RN, 1914-16; RMA Woolwich, 1918; commissioned RFA 1919; Adjutant HAC, 1929-31; Staff Coll., 1932-33; Bt Maj., 1936; Instructor Staff Coll., 1938-39; Bt Lt-Col 1939; Deputy Director Military Operations, 1941; BGS South-Eastern Command, 1941; CRA 1st Division 1942; DCGS Home Forces, 1942; MGGS Home Forces, 1943; Director of Military Intelligence, War Office, 1944-45. Commander, Legion of Merit (US), 1945; Commander, Order of the Crown (Belgium), 1945. *Recreations:* cricket and reading. *Address:* East Ashling Grange, Chichester, West Sussex. *T:* West Ashling 292. [Died 22 March 1977.

SINCLAIR, Captain Sir Kenneth (Duncan Lecky), Kt 1954; DL; RNR; Member, Belfast Harbour Board, 1934-70 (Chairman, 1948-67); *b* 13 June 1889; 3rd *s* of late Rt Hon. Thomas Sinclair, PC, DLitt, MA, DL, Hopefield House, Belfast; *m* 1914, Eleanor Laura, *d* of late Lieut-Col J. Jackson Clark, HM Lieutenant, Largantogher, Maghera, Co. Derry; one *s* one *d. Educ:* Rugby School; Trinity College, Cambridge. *Address:* 44 Windsor Park, Belfast. *T:* Belfast 666698. *Club:* Ulster (Belfast).
[Died 3 Oct. 1973.

SINCLAIR, Shapton Donald, CMG 1972; Chairman, New Zealand Apple and Pear Marketing Board, since 1967; Deputy Chairman, Export Shipping Council of New Zealand, 1973; *b* 13 May 1923; *s* of Alexander Grant Sinclair and Margaret Sinclair; *m* 1st, 1945, Emily Margaret Krekoski (marr. diss.); one *s* one *d* ; 2nd, 1973, Catherine Tait, of Nelson. *Educ:* Nelson Coll., New Zealand. Served RNZAF, 1942-46: Flt Lt; pilot instructor in Canada, later with Mosquito Sqdn. Joined NZ Apple and Pear Marketing Bd, 1959; Dep. Chm., 1965-67. *Recreations:* badminton, golf. *Address:* Waimea West, Nelson, New Zealand. *Clubs:* Wellesley (Wellington); Nelson (Nelson).
[Died 19 April 1974.

SINCLAIR, Sir William, Kt 1957; CBE 1955; JP; retired as Director and Chief Executive, Dunlop Rubber Co. (Scotland) Ltd and as General Commissioner of Inland Revenue; *b* 17 Jan. 1895; *s* of Rev. James Steven Sinclair and Jessie Sutherland; *m* 1919, Stephanie Patricia Laline Hunte Taylour Daniel, MB, BS, MRCS, LRCP (*d* 1966); one *s* two *d. Educ:* Wick and Glasgow. On active service, European War, 1914-18, Vice-Pres., Scottish Motor Trade Assoc., 1941-45, 1946-47, 1948-50. FIMI (Lord Wakefield Gold Medallist, 1943). Pres. Ye Jovial Tramps, Glasgow, 1941-42 (Hon. Pres., 1957-); JP, County of City of Glasgow, 1951; Member of Merchants House of City of Glasgow, 1953, Director, 1964. Contested (C and U), Glasgow Central Div., 1951; President, Scottish Unionist Association, 1956-57; Member: Livingston New Town Develt Corp., 1961-67; Nat. Health Service Exec. Council for Glasgow, 1960-67. Patron, Hutchesons Trust, Glasgow, 1968-. Hon. President, Scottish Commercial Travellers Association Ltd, 1960-61. Trustee, Sir Walter Scott Bursary Cttee, Glasgow Univ., 1971-. *Recreation:* public service. *Address:* 58 Dalziel Drive, Glasgow G41 4PA. *T:* 041-427 1602. *Clubs:* Glasgow Conservative, RNVR (Glasgow); Clydesdale Cricket. [Died 6 Feb. 1976

SINDERSON, Sir Harry Chapman, Pasha, KBE 1946 (OBE 1932); CMG 1942; MVO 1933; KStJ; Knight Commander, Order of the North Star (Sweden); Order of Istiqlal (Jordan), 2nd class; Orders of Faisal I and Rafidain (Iraq), 2nd class; Order of Nahda (Hedjaz), 2nd class; Order of Taj (Iran) 3rd class; Officer of the Order of Leopold, Belgium; Coronation and Red Crescent Medals of Iraq; Order of Polonia Restituta, 3rd Class; MB, ChB, MD, FRCPE; DTM&H (England); FRGS; late Adviser and Inspector-General of Health Services, Min. of Social Affairs, Iraq; Emeritus Professor, late Dean and Prof. of Medicine, Royal Coll. of Medicine of Iraq; Physician to HM the King and Royal Family of Iraq, 1921-46; Major, late RAMC

(Militia); *b* 9 June 1891; *s* of late William Sinderson; *m* 1920, Maude Elsie Hyde (*d* 1967), *d* of late George Walter MunGavin, MBE. Served European War, 1914-18: OC Hospital Ships Stad Antwerpen and Wandilla; accompanied TM King Faisal I and II and the Prince Regent of Iraq on many official and private visits to various countries. Fellow, Roy. Soc. of Tropical Medicine and Hygiene; Vice-Patron, formerly hon. Warden, Sackville Coll., East Grinstead (Historic Building); Vice-Patron, Brighton College; Vice-President: E Grinstead Div. Cons. Assoc.; Nat. Children's Home; Council, Royal Society of St George; Representative Governor, Imperial Cancer Research Fund; Chapter-Gen. Order of St John; Royal Central Asian Society; Guild of Freemen, City of London; Fauna Preservation Society. *Publications:* Ten Thousand and One Nights; light verse and numerous articles in various medical and other jls. *Recreations:* travel, outdoor sports and country pursuits, represented Edinburgh University at Association Football, 1909-14 (Captain, 1911-12) and cricket, 1913-14. *Address:* Little Steddings, Forest Row, West Sussex. *T:* Forest Row 3343. *Clubs:* East India, Sports and Public Schools, MCC.
[Died 20 Nov. 1974.

SINHA, Rajandhari, CIE 1943; Mayor, Patna Municipal Corporation, 1954-57; Resident Representative of Patna, Tata Iron & Steel Co. Ltd, 1954-57; *b* 3 Oct. 1893; *s* of Rai Bahadur Chandradhari Sinha, Village Dharhara, PO Paliganj (District Patna); *m* 1915, *d* of late Babu Ambikanandan Sinha, Deputy Collector, UP; one *s* one *d. Educ:* Patna (BA, BL). Sec. of Bihar Landholders' Assoc., 1937-38; Manager of Hathwa Wards Estate, Saran, Member of Dist War Committee, Saran, and Dist Leader, National War Front, 1938-44; a Governor of Patna Arts Coll.; Member of Secondary Board of Education, Bihar and Orissa; Chairman of Dist Board, Patna, 1924-33; MLC Bihar and Orissa, 1924-37 (President, 1933-37); Member of Joint Public Service Commn of Bihar, Central Provinces and Berar and Orissa, 1947-49, and Chairman of Public Service Commn for Bihar, 1949-53; Liaison Officer, Bihar, Tata Iron & Steel Co. Ltd, 1953-54; Chairman, Bihar State Financial Corporation, 1954-57. *Address:* Dharhara House, Bankipore, Patna-4, India.
[Died 30 Dec. 1976.

SINKER, Sir (Algernon) Paul, KCMG 1954; CB 1950; Chairman, Crafts Advisory Committee, since 1971; *b* 13 April 1905; *s* of late Rev. Robert Sinker; *m* 1929, Ruth Longland; two *s* two *d. Educ:* Haileybury Coll.; Jesus College, Cambridge. University of Vienna, 1927-28; Prince Consort Prize; Fellow of Jesus College, Cambridge, 1927-49; Tutor, 1929-40; University Lecturer. Civil servant at Admiralty, 1940-45 (Washington, 1941-42); Treasury, 1945-50; adviser to Egyptian Government on Civil Service questions, 1950; First Civil Service Commissioner, 1951-54; Dir-Gen., British Council, 1954-68. Chm., Council for Small Industries in Rural Areas, 1968-76. Dep. Chm., Bd of Governors, Atlantic Coll.; Mem. Council, Voluntary Service Overseas; Mem., Governing Body, Shrewsbury Sch. Hon. Fellow, Jesus College, Cambridge, 1955. Hon. LLD: Exeter, 1961; Southampton, 1967. *Publication:* Introduction to Lucretius, 1937. *Recreations:* country pursuits. *Address:* 39 Berwick Road, Shrewsbury. *[Died 26 Feb. 1977.*

SINKER, Sir Paul; *see* Sinker, Sir A. P.

SISAM, Kenneth, MA (New Zealand University); MA, BLitt Oxon; FBA 1941; Hon. DLitt Reading, 1948; Grand Kt of the Icelandic Falcon, 1948; *b* 1887; *m* 1915, Naomi (*d* 1958), *d* of R. P. Gibbons; one *s* one *d. Educ:* Auckland Grammar School; Auckland University College, NZ; Merton College, Oxford. Rhodes Scholar, 1910; Ministry of Food, 1917-22; Secretary to the Delegates of the Oxford University Press, 1942-48; formerly Fellow of Merton College, and Hon. Fellow, 1964-. *Publications:* Fourteenth Century Verse and Prose, 1921; Studies in the History of Old English Literature, 1953; (joint editor) The Salisbury Psalter, 1959; The Structure of Beowulf, 1965; (comp., with Celia Sisam) The Oxford Book of Medieval English Verse, 1970. *Address:* Middle Carn, St Mary's, Isles of Scilly. *[Died 26 Aug. 1971.*

SISSON, Marshall Arnott, CVO 1971; CBE 1959; RA 1963 (ARA 1956); FSA, FRIBA; Architect; *b* 14 Feb. 1897; *o s* of Arthur White Sisson, MIMechE, Hucclecote, Gloucestershire; *m* 1933, Marjorie (*d* 1972), *o d* of Harold Matthews, Portishead, Somerset. *Educ:* Bartlett School of Architecture, University of London. BA (Arch.) London 1923; Jarvis Rome Scholar in Architecture, 1924; Duveen Fellow, 1927. Architectural practice has included civic, collegiate, ecclesiastical, scholastic, dramatic, commercial and other buildings, and restoration of many historic buildings. Treasurer of the Royal Academy, 1965-70; Member: Ancient Monuments Board for England, 1959-76; Diocesan Adv. Cttees of Ely and Southwark; Architectural

Panel of National Trust; Cathedrals Advisory Cttee; Architectural Adv. Panel for Westminster Abbey; Hon. Technical Adviser to the Georgian Group. Hon. D Fine Arts, Westminster Coll., Missouri, 1969. *Publications:* various papers in technical and archæological journals. *Address:* Farm Hall, Godmanchester, Huntingdon, Cambs. *T:* Huntingdon 53363. *Club:* Athenæum.
[Died 26 Jan. 1978.

SITA RAM, Rai Bahadur Sir, Kt 1931; MA, LLB, DLitt; a member of the Upper House of the Provincial legislature in United Provinces (President, 1937-48); *b* 12 Jan. 1885; *m* ; two *s* six *d* (and one *s* decd). *Educ:* Meerut; Allahabad (Honours in Sanskrit). Member Meerut Municipal Board, 1910-20; Hon. Sec. All-India Vaish Maha Sabba, 1911-25; Hon. Managing Director, Meerut District Co-operative Bank, 1918-25; Member, Indian National Congress, 1906-19; Member, United Provinces Legislative Council, 1921-37, first elected Indian non-official President, 1925-37; High Commissioner for India in Pakistan, at Karachi, March 1949-Nov. 1950. Rai Sahib, 1919; Rai Bahadur, 1923; raised a Middle English School called Deva Nagri School to the High School Standard, serving as its Hon. Secretary, 1913-36; connected with the Meerut College since 1907 as a member of its Executive Committee and as Hon. Sec., 1923-34 and 1940-46; Pres. of two Girls' Colleges at Meerut; actively associated with Executive of the Allahabad and Benares (Hindu) Universities; served on a number of Committees and Boards appointed by Government. Patron-President UP Sports Control Board; Pres. Shiri Badrinath Temple Committee, 1941-43; Patron Sangit Samaj, Meerut; ex-Chm. Universities Grants Cttee, UP; Pres. UP Ethnographical Soc.; ex-Chm. UP Police Reorganisation Cttee; ex-Chm. UP Gosamvardhan Cttee. *Address:* Champa, Meerut, UP, India. *[Died 5 May 1972.*

SITWELL, Maj.-Gen. Hervey Degge Wilmot, CB 1946; CVO 1967; MC 1917; FSA 1957; Keeper of The Jewel House, HM Tower of London, 1952-68, retired; *b* 25 Oct. 1896; *s* of Hervey Wheler Sitwell, Manor House, Leamington Hastings, Warwicks, and Alice Mary, *d* of Charles Schwind, Broomfield, Co. Derby; *m* 1919, Catherine Florence Parke, *d* of Dr Eustace Olive, FRCS, LRCP, Leamington Spa; one *d. Educ:* Wellington Coll., RMA Woolwich. Commissioned RFA, 1914; Lt 1915; Capt. 1917; Major, 1933; actg Lt-Col 1939; Brig., 1941; Maj.-Gen. (local), 1942; served European War, 1914-18 (despatches, MC); served War of 1939-45 (despatches, CB); GOC Brit. Troops, Java, 1942; prisoner of war, Japanese hands, 1942-45; Dist Comdr, Canal North District, Egypt, 1946-49; Dep. Dist Comdr, East Anglian District, 1949-51; retired 1951. Hon. Major-General. Fellow, Society of Antiquaries, 1957. *Publications:* The Crown Jewels, 1953; (with Martin Holmes) The English Regalia, 1973. *Recreations:* research on crown jewels, genealogy. *Address:* Camerton, Gate Lane, Freshwater Bay, Isle of Wight. *T:* Freshwater 2395. *Clubs:* Army and Navy; Royal Solent Yacht. *[Died 28 Sept. 1973.*

SKAE, Victor Delvine Burnham; Sheriff of Lothian and Borders (formerly the Lothians) at Edinburgh, 1968-78, retired; *b* 25 Oct. 1914; *o s* of late Ernest Traill Skae, SSC and late Elsie Burnham; *m* 1939, Barbara Landale Melville; three *d. Educ:* Edinburgh Acad.; Bruges; Clifton Coll.; Peterhouse, Cambridge (BA); Edinburgh Univ. (LLB). RA, 1940-42, 652 (AOP) Sqdn; invalided out. Advocate, 1945; Advocate Depute, 1953-60; Sheriff Substitute: Falkirk, 1960-64; Linlithgow, 1964-68. *Recreations:* shooting, fishing. *Address:* 32 Garscube Terrace, Edinburgh EH12 6BN. *Club:* New (Edinburgh).
[Died 9 Nov. 1979.

SKAUG, Arne; GCVO (Hon.); Grand Cross of Order of St Olav, Norway; Ambassador of Norway to Denmark, since 1968; *b* 6 Nov. 1906. *Educ:* (Economics) Univ. of Oslo. Manager, Norwegian Social Insurance Scheme, New York, and then in Norwegian Ministry of Supply, London, 1939-44; Commercial Counsellor to Norwegian Embassy, Washington, 1944-46; Director, Central Bureau of Statistics, Oslo, 1946-48; Under-Sec. of State, Foreign Ministry, 1948; Permanent Delegate for Norway (with rank of minister), to OEEC, Paris, 1949-55, with rank of Ambassador, also concurrently Permanent Representative of Norway to NATO Council, Paris, 1953-55; Minister of Commerce and Shipping, Norway, 1955-62; Ambassador to the Court of St James's and to Ireland, 1962-68. *Address:* Royal Norwegian Embassy, Trondhjems Plads 4, 2100 København Ø, Denmark. *[Died 4 March 1974.*

SKEAPING, John (Rattenbury), RA 1959 (ARA 1950); sculptor; Professor of Sculpture, Royal College of Art, 1953-59; *b* 9 June 1901; *m* 1st, 1923, Barbara Hepworth (Dame Barbara Hepworth, DBE, *d* 1975) (marr. diss. 1933); one *s* (killed in action, RAF, 1953); 2nd, 1934, Morwenna Ward (marr. diss. 1969); three *s* ; 3rd, 1969, Margery Scott. *Educ:* Royal Academy

Schools. Rome Scholar, 1924. Exhibited: Royal Academy; Leicester Galls; Ackermann Galls. *Publications:* Animal Drawing, 1934; How to Draw Horses, 1938; The Big Tree of Mexico, 1952; Les Animaux dans l'Art, 1969 (Paris); Drawn from Life (autobiog.), 1977. *Recreations:* fishing and riding. *Address:* c/o A. Ackermann & Sons Ltd, 3 Old Bond Street, W1X 3TD; Moulin de la Taillade, Castries, Hérault, France.
[Died 5 March 1980.

SKEFFINGTON, Arthur Massey, BSc Econ. (Hons); FRGS; FREconS; MRST; MP (Lab) Hayes and Harlington (Middx), since March 1953; Chairman of the Labour Party, since 1969; Economist and Barrister-at-law; *b* 4 Sept. 1909; *s* of Arthur James and Edith Skeffington; *m* 1952, Sheila, *d* of Thomas MacKenzie, Birmingham; two *s. Educ:* Streatham Grammar School; London Univ. Lecturer in Economics and Teacher. Member: National Executive of Labour Party; Political Purposes Committee, Royal Arsenal Co-op. Society; late member Civil Service Arbitration Tribunal. Travelled widely in Europe. Visited the Soviet Union, 1938. Winner of Scholarship to Prague University. Reformed the Battersea Parliament, 1937, contested Streatham, 1935, By-Election West Lewisham, 1938. Mem. Fabian Soc., 1933, on the Exec. from 1943, Chm., 1957. Went to Bd of Trade to assist in the Concentration of Industry, 1941; transf., 1943, to Ministry of Supply, Assistant Director in charge of production of Medical Supplies. MP (Lab) Lewisham W, 1945-50; PPS to Minister of Pensions, 1947-48; Jt Parly Sec., Min. of Land and Natural Resources, 1964-67, Min. of Housing, 1967-70. Member, LCC (Peckham), 1950-58. Initiated Law Reform (Enforcement of Contracts) Act, 1954; Member of Commonwealth Parly Society's Delegn to E Africa, 1948, 1957; visited US, Oct. 1949, 1958, 1968, India, 1961, Australia, 1966. Jt President: Brit. Sect. Council of European Municipalities; Commonwealth Assoc. of Municipalities; Pres., Arboricultural Association; Chm. Cttee on Public Participation and Planning (convened 10 Woodlands confs to safeguard future live amenity); Life Member: National Trust; Council for Nature; Ramblers Assoc. *Publications:* Leasehold Enfranchisement; American Diary; Tanganyika in Transition. *Recreations:* cricket, the theatre, bee-keeping. *Address:* 2 Harcourt Buildings, Middle Temple, EC4. *T:* 01-353 7202; The Old Vicarage, Meopham, Kent. *Club:* Irish, Chelsea Arts, Surrey County Cricket.
[Died 18 Feb. 1971.

SKELMERSDALE, 6th Baron *cr* 1828, of Skelmersdale; **Lionel Bootle-Wilbraham,** DSO 1940; MC 1917; late Coldstream Guards; *b* 23 Sept. 1896, *s* of Major Lionel Bootle-Wilbraham, 87th Royal Irish Fusiliers (*gs* of 1st Baron) (*d* 1914), and Lavinia (*d* 1930), *d* of Abraham Wilson; *S* cousin, 1969; *m* 1936, Ann Quilter; one *s* three *d. Educ:* Wellington College; Cheltenham College. Served European War, 1914-18 (MC); 3 Bn Hampshire Regt, Aug. 1914, Coldstream Guards, 1915; ADC to Governor of Madras, 1924-26; Military Secretary to Governor of Madras, 1929-32; service in Turkey, 1922; China, 1927; Sudan and Egypt, 1932; Comd 126 Inf. Bde 1940, 215 Inf. Bde, 1941, 32 Gds Bde, 1941; Staff College, 1942, BGS Eastern Command, 1943; Comd 137 Inf. Bde 1945; Regtl Lt-Col Coldstream Guards, 1946-49 (DSO, despatches); retired, with rank of Brig., 1949. Dir, Brush Export Ltd and their rep. in Caribbean and Latin America, 1949-59. *Recreations:* fishing, shooting, gardening. *Heir: s* Hon. Roger Bootle-Wilbraham [*b* 2 April 1945; *m* 1972, Christine Joan Morgan]. *Address:* Trunk House, Cove, Farnborough, Hants. *T:* Farnborough 44051.
[Died 21 July 1973.

SKELTON, Robert Lumley; Chairman and Managing Director, Curzon-Grantham Advertising Ltd; *b* 4 Oct. 1896; *s* of Robert and Elizabeth Skelton. *Educ:* Rutherford Coll., Newcastle upon Tyne. European War, 1914-18: gazetted Durham Light Infantry, Oct. 1914; seconded as pilot to Royal Flying Corps, March 1918. Editor, Natal Witness, South Africa, 1928-33; Managing Editor, Daily Telegraph, 1933-48; Editor, News of the World, 1948-50. Officer's Cross, Order of Merit, 1st Class (German), 1971. *Recreations:* fishing, shooting. *Address:* Monk's Cottage, Zeal Monachorum, Devon. *Clubs:* Gresham, Naval and Military.
[Died 11 Aug. 1973.

SKEMP, Frank Whittingham; *b* 13 Dec. 1880; *s* of Rev. Thomas Rowland Skemp and Jennie, *d* of Samuel Clewis; *m* 1914, Dorothy (*d* 1965), *d* of Rev. George Frazer; two *s* one *d. Educ:* private school; Douglas Gram. Sch., IOM; University of Manchester; Peterhouse, Cambridge. Entered Indian Civil Service (Punjab Commission) 1904; 1st class Magistrate and JP 1906; Deputy Commissioner 1910-13; District and Sessions Judge, 1918-27; Additional Judge, Lahore High Court, 1927-33; Puisne Judge, High Court, Lahore, 1933-41; retired, 1941. *Publication:* Multani Stories, 1917. *Recreation:* reading. *Address:* Fairfield, 115 Banbury Road, Oxford.
[Died 4 Jan. 1971.

SKENE, Macgregor, DSc, FLS; formerly Professor of Botany, Bristol University; Professor Emeritus, 1955; *b* 20 Oct. 1889; *s* of Alexander and Margaret Skene; *m* 1915, Agnes Wallace Hamilton; two *s. Educ:* Robert Gordon's College, Aberdeen; Universities of Aberdeen, Berlin, Strasbourg and Montpellier. *Publications:* Biology of Flowering Plants; Flower Book for the Pocket; other books and memoirs on botanical subjects. *Address:* 6 Dover Court, Abdon Avenue, Birmingham 29.
[Died 8 Aug. 1973.

SKIKNE, L. M.; *see* Harvey, Laurence.

SKILLICORN, Alice Havergal, CBE 1952; MSc; Principal of Homerton College, Cambridge, 1935-60, retired; *b* 1894; *d* of Edward Skillicorn, Ramsey, Isle of Man. London Sch. of Economics. Teaching posts, London and St Hild's Coll., Durham, 1920-28; HM Inspector of Schools, 1929-35. *Recreations:* walking, foreign travel. *Clubs:* Women Graduates', English-Speaking Union (Cambridge).
[Died 3 Feb. 1979.

SKIMMING, Ian Edward Bowring; Chairman and Chief Executive, C. T. Bowring & Co. Ltd, 1965; *b* 28 Aug. 1920; *s* of Edward Hugh Bowring Skimming, Chevalier Légion d'Honneur, and Audrey Skimming, JP, Taplow House, Taplow, Bucks; *m* 1949, Anne Miriam Barbara Maude, *e d* of Aylmer Probyn Maude, Chamberlain to HH Pope Pius XI, and Vera Maude; one *d. Educ:* Eton. Commnd Coldstream Guards, Feb. 1939; demobilized 1945 (wounded twice, despatches, 1944). Member of Lloyd's, 1942. C. T. Bowring & Co.: joined 1945; Asst Dir, 1952; Dir, 1954. FRSA. *Recreations:* shooting, ski-ing. *Address:* Shotters Farm, Newton Valence, near Alton, Hampshire. *T:* Tisted 222; 87 Dovehouse Street, SW3. *T:* 01-352 4220. *Club:* Guards.
[Died 20 Jan. 1973.

SKINNER, C(harles) William, OBE 1963; Barrister-at-Law; DL; JP; Chairman of Edmonton Petty Sessional Division and of Enfield, Tottenham and Wood Green Courts, 1949-65; Chairman of Westminster, Chelsea and Holborn Rent Tribunal since constituted, 1946, and of West London Tribunal, 1958-62; *b* 5 February 1895; *s* of Harry Skinner and Lizzie, *d* of Charles Sheldon, Freeman of City of London; *m* 1923, Jennie, *g d* of Rev. John Taylor, Wolverhampton; one *s* (and one *d* decd). *Educ:* St Olave's; College of Estate Management. Assoc. RICS; formerly Legal MTPI; FAI (Silver Medallist, Final Prizeman) and MRSanI. Called to Bar, Lincoln's Inn, 1937. JP 1942, DL: Middx, 1953, Greater London, 1965; Mayor of Southgate, 1942-43, Member Borough Council, 1938-46, Chm. Civil Defence Committee, 1942; Chm. MOI Committee, 1940-45; Hon. Freeman: Southgate, 1964, Enfield, 1965; member Middlesex CC, 1945-48; member Magistrate's Courts Committee (Middlesex), 1952-62. High Sheriff of Middlesex, 1955-56. Served European War, 1914-18, France and Belgium, 1st Bn HAC, 1915-19; War of 1939-45, FO, RAFVR, 1941-44; Flight Commander and Welfare Officer, ATC; Founder-President British Legion, Palmers Green Branch and Vice-Pres. Southgate Br., 1942 and RAF Assoc.; Vice-Pres. Nat. Assoc. of Probation Officers (Middlesex Branch), 1953-; President and Founder of various organisations connected with youth and with wartime activities. *Publications:* Editor of Yearly Digest of Land and Property Cases, 1939-58; Law of Compulsory Acquisition of Land, 1939; Rent and Mortgage Emergency Legislation, 1939, 1941; Landlord and Tenant (War Damage) Cases, 1942; (joint) Merlin and Skinner's War Damage Precedents, 1941; legal columnist Estates Gazette, 1937-45. *Address:* Southgate, The Clump, Chorleywood, Herts. *T:* Rickmansworth 77822; 25 Mariners Walk, Rustington, Sussex. *T:* 4327.
[Died 22 March 1971.

SKINNER, Cornelia Otis, (Mrs A. S. Blodget); actress, authoress, monologist; radio and motion picture actress; *d* of Otis Skinner and Maud Durbin; *m* 1928, Alden S. Blodget; one *s. Educ:* Baldwin School, Bryn Mawr, Pa; Bryn Mawr College; Sorbonne, Paris; Société aire de Comédie Française and School of Jacques Copeau. Appeared in: Blood and Sand; Will Shakespeare; Tweedles; In the Next Room; The Wild Westcotts; In His Arms; White Collars. Starred in: Candida; Theatre; The Searching Wind; Lady Windermere's Fan; Major Barbara; The Pleasure of His Company (which she wrote, with Samuel Taylor; it was filmed, 1961). Author and Producer of mono-dramas: The Wives of Henry VIII; The Empress Eugénie; The Loves of Charles II; Mansion on the Hudson; and original character sketches played in America and London; dramatized and produced mono-dramas of Margaret Ayer Barnes', Edna, His Wife, and full-length solo revue, Paris '90, with music by Kay Swift. Created and prepared scripts for radio series, William and Mary; also many other radio engagements including innumerable appearances on Information Please. Officier de l'Académie, 1953. *Publications:* Tiny Garments, 1931; Excuse

It, Please, 1936; Dither and Jitters, 1937; Soap Behind the Ears (published in Eng. under title of Popcorn), 1941; Our Hearts Were Young and Gay (with Emily Kimbrough), 1942; Family Circle, 1948; omnibus publication of some of previous works, That's Me All Over, 1948; Nuts in May, 1950; Happy Family, 1950; Bottoms Up!, 1955; The Ape in Me, 1959; Elegant Wits and Grand Horizontals, 1962; Madame Sarah, 1967; Life With Lindsay & Crouse, 1976. *Recreation:* country. *Address:* 131 East 66th Street, New York, NY 10021, USA. *TA:* Courtesy. *T:* 288 5511. *Clubs:* Colony, Cosmopolitan (NY). *[Died 9 July 1979.*

SKINNER, Maj.-Gen. Frank Hollamby, (Jerry), CB 1947; CIE 1945; OBE 1942; Indian Army (retired); *b* 24 March 1897; *s* of Arthur Richard Skinner; *m* 1920, Doris Mary Fortescue Young. *Educ:* Kent Coll., Canterbury. Commnd TA, 1916; IA, 1917; 12 (KIG) Pioneers, 1917-28; 3rd Afghan War, Waziristan, 1919-21; 1st Bn, 13 FF Rifles, 1928-40; AA&QMG, Forces in Iraq and Persia, 1941-42; BGS 21 Indian Corps, 1942-43; MGA Eastern Comd, 1943; Comd 39 Indian Div., 1944-45; Comd Secunderabad Dist, 1945-47. *Address:* Herecombe Manor, Southview Road, Crowborough, Sussex. *T:* Crowborough 3476.
[Died 18 April 1979.

SKINNER, Sir Gordon; *see* Skinner, Sir T. G.

SKINNER, Lt-Col Harry Crawley R.; *see* Ross Skinner.

SKINNER, Sir (Thomas) Gordon, 3rd Bt *cr* 1912; *b* 29 Dec. 1899; *er* and *o surv. s* of Sir Thomas Hewitt Skinner, 2nd Bt, and Nellie Constance (*d* 1955), *d* of James Hay Hall, Highgate; *S* father, 1968; *m* 1st, 1926, Mollie Barbara (marr. diss., 1953; she *d* 1965), *e d* of Herbert William Girling, Frostenden, Suffolk; three *s*; 2nd, 1953, Jeanne, *o d* of François de Launoit, Brussels. *Educ:* Charterhouse; Exeter College, Oxford. Partner in Thomas Skinner & Co., 1926-37; Director and Manager, Thomas Skinner & Co. (Publishers) Ltd, 1937-51, retired. Served European War, 1914-18; France, 1918; War of 1939-45, RAF Intelligence Officer; 12 Sqdn Advanced Air Striking Force, France, 1940 (despatches); HQ 1st Corps; HQ Southern Command, 1940-41; HQ 9th American Air Force, 1941-45. Freeman, City of London; Liveryman, Worshipful Company of Merchant Taylors. *Recreations:* gardening and love of the sea. *Heir: e s* Thomas Keith Hewitt Skinner [*b* 6 Dec. 1927; *m* 1959, Jill, *d* of C. I. Tuckett; two *s*]. *Address:* Larchmont, 55 Hill Brow, Hove, Sussex BN3 6DD. *T:* Brighton 553114. *Clubs:* City of London, Little Ship; Royal Corinthian Yacht (Burnham-on-Crouch).
[Died 22 Nov. 1972.

SKIRA, Albert; Publisher; *b* Geneva, 10 Aug. 1904; *o s* of Pierre Skira and Adélaide Skira; *m* 1937, Rosabianca Venturi; three *s* one *d*. Bank clerk, Crédit Suisse, 1922-24; organizer of hotel entertainments, 1924-26; bookseller, 1926-31. Published Ovid's Metamorphoses in 1931, with etchings by Picasso; since then over 300 books on works of art and the history of art. *Address:* Editions Skira, 4 Place du Molard, Geneva, Switzerland; Dully, Vaud, Switzerland.
[Died 14 Sept. 1973.

SKOURAS, Spyros Panayiotis; Chairman, Twentieth Century Fox Film Corporation, since 1962; *b* Skourohorion, Greece, 28 March 1893; *m* Saroula Bruiglia; two *s* two *d* (and one *s* one *d* decd). *Educ:* Public Schools, Greece; Jones Commercial Coll.; Benton Law School, St Louis. Owned 37 theatres by 1926; sold to Warner Bros; joined Warner Bros as General Manager of theatre circuit, 1929; Pres. subsidiary formed to operate all Paramount Theatres, 1931; appointed head of Fox Metropolitan Theatres; with brothers Charles and George also headed Wesco Corp., 1932, which became National Theatres, 1942; Pres. Twentieth Century-Fox, 1942-62. *Recreation:* golf. *Address:* 2 Shore Road, Rye, NY, USA. *T:* Owens 8-1170. *Clubs:* Westchester Country (Rye, NY); Metropolitan (NY); Athletic (NY).
[Died 17 Aug. 1971.

SKRIMSHIRE OF QUARTER, Baroness *cr* 1979 (Life Peer), of Dunipace in the District of Falkirk; **Margaret Betty Harvie Anderson,** OBE 1955; TD 1959; PC 1974; DL; *b* Aug. 1915; *d* of of late T. A. Harvie Anderson of Quarter and Shirgarton, CB, and Mrs Harvie Anderson; *m* 1960, John Francis Penrose Skrimshire, MD, FRCP. *Educ:* St Leonard's Sch., St Andrews. CC, Stirlingshire, 1945-59; Leader, moderate group, Stirling CC, 1953-59; Member: Sec. of State for Scotland's Advisory Council on Education, 1955-59; Bd of Management Royal Scottish Nat. Instn; City of Glasgow T & AFA, 1949-51; Stirlingshire T & AFA, 1953-59; Exec. Cttee Princess Louise Scottish Hosp.; W Stirlingshire Unionist Assoc., 1938-54; Western Div. Council Scottish Unionist Assoc., 1939-59; convener Western Div. Council Women's Cttee, 1955-58; President: Scottish Young Unionists, 1955-58; St Leonard's Sch.; Chm. Scottish Assoc. of Mixed and Girls' Clubs, 1952-55. Company Comdr, ATS, 1938;

Adj. Reception Depot, 1940; Sen. Comdr, Mixed Heavy Anti-Aircraft Regt, RA, 1942-43; Chief Comdr Mixed Heavy Anti-Aircraft Bde, 1943-46. Contested (C) W Stirlingshire, 1950 and 1951, Sowerby (Yorks), 1955; MP (C) Renfrewshire East, 1959-79; Member: Exec. Cttee, 1922 Cttee, 1962-70, 1974-79; Chairman's Panel, House of Commons, 1966-70; Dep. Chm. of Ways and Means, House of Commons, 1970-73; Member: Historic Buildings Council for Scotland, 1966-; Royal Commission on Local Government in Scotland, 1966-69; Mr Speaker's Conf., 1966-68. DL Stirlingshire, 1973. *Address:* Quarter, by Denny, Stirlingshire. *T:* Denny 822271.
[Died 7 Nov. 1979.

SKRINE, Sir Clarmont (Percival), Kt 1946; OBE 1935; *b* London, 1888; *o s* of late Francis Henry Skrine; *m* 1920, Doris Forbes (*d* 1971), 2nd *d* of James Whitelaw of Nungate, North Berwick. *Educ:* Winchester; New College, Oxford. Entered Indian Civil Service, 1912; served in South Persia, 1916-19; Political Agent, Quetta, 1921; Consul-General in Chinese Turkestan, 1922-24; Consul in Seistan and Kain, 1927-29; Political Agent, Sibi, Baluchistan, 1929-31; Kalat and Chagai, 1932-35; Revenue and Judicial Commissioner, Baluchistan, 1935-36; Resident for the Madras States, 1936-39; Resident for the Punjab States, 1939-41; Consul-General at Meshed, 1942-46; Counsellor for Indian Affairs, British Embassy, Tehran, 1946-48; retired, 1948; representative at Jerusalem of the Board, Jerusalem Electric Corporation, 1949-50; awarded OBE for services connected with Quetta Earthquake, 1935; awarded Gill Memorial by Royal Geographical Society for explorations in the Chinese Pamirs in 1922-24; Chm., Permanent Cttee on Geographical Names, 1960-64. *Publications:* Chinese Central Asia, 1926; World War in Iran, 1962; (with Pamela Nightingale) Macartney in Kashgar, 1973; papers on Chinese Turkestan, Persia, Baluchistan and Israel in the Geographical and Central Asian Journals. *Recreation:* photography. *Address:* Elmbank, 38 Carlton Drive, SW15. *Clubs:* Athenæum, Alpine.
[Died 19 Sept. 1974.

SLANEY, George Wilson, (Pseudonym: George Woden); Novelist; *b* Wednesbury, Staffs, 1 Sept. 1884; *m* 1914, Edith Margaret Tomkinson, *g d* of John Tomkinson, Manchester; one *d*; *m* 1970, Dorothy Clare Sheppard. *Educ:* Queen Mary's Grammar School, Walsall; London University; France; Germany. Abandoned career as engineer; became a journalist, artist, musician; settled in Glasgow as a schoolmaster in 1909; retired. *Publications:* Sowing Clover, 1913; Paul Moorhouse, 1914; The New Dawn, 1915; Little Houses, 1919; The Money's The Thing (three-act play) Scottish National Theatre, Glasgow, 1921; The Wrenfield Mystery, 1923; Thistledown (three-act play) Play Actors, London, 1923; The Great Cornelius, 1926; The Gates of Delight, 1927; This Way to Fortune, 1929; The Parson and Clerk, 1930; Mungo, 1932; Love and Let Love, 1933; Our Peter, 1934; Upside-Turvydown, 1934; Tannenbrae, 1935; Othersmith, 1936; Perhaps Young Man, 1936; The Bailie's Tale, 1937; The Cathkin Mystery, 1937; Happiness Has No Story, 1938; Holiday Adventure, 1939; Voyage Through Life, 1940; Dusk for Dreams, 1941; The Queer Folk Next Door, 1942; The Golden Lion, 1944; Ruffy & Sons, 1945; Messenger-at-Arms, 1946; The Lover's Tale, 1948; The Puzzled Policeman, 1949; Helen Enchanted, 1950; Mystery of the Amorous Music Master, 1951; Simonetta, 1952. *Recreation:* music. *Address:* 91 Marlborough Avenue, Glasgow G11 7BT. *Club:* Scottish PEN (President, 1944-47).
[Died 17 Nov. 1978.

SLATER, Baron *cr* 1970 (Life Peer), of Ferryhill, Durham; **Joseph Slater,** BEM 1949; *b* 13 June 1904; *s* of William and Elizabeth Slater; *m* 1928, Hilda Clement; one *s* one *d* (and one *d* decd). *Educ:* Chilton Lane Council School. Miner; Lodge Official of Miners' Union since 1930; member Durham Miners' Union Executive, 1940 and 1947. Joined Labour Party, 1928; MP (Lab) Sedgefield Div. of Durham, 1950-70. Member of Durham County Council, 1944-50 (Vice-Chairman of Highways and Bridges Committee); member of Parish and District Councils, 1930. Chairman Education Divisional Executive Committee; member of Estimates Cttee, 1955, 1956, 1957, 1958, 1959, 1960; Mem. Council of Europe and Western European Union, 1958. PPS to Leader of Opposition, 1960-64; Asst Postmaster-General, 1964-69. Governor of several secondary schools; member of two hospital management committees. Methodist preacher since 1932. *Address:* House of Lords, SW1.
[Died 21 April 1977.

SLATER, Gordon Archbold, OBE 1974; MusD (Dunelm); FRCO; JP; retired as Organist of Lincoln Cathedral (1930-66); Adjudicator at Music Festivals throughout UK since 1920; Organ Recitalist (including radio and TV, since 1920; *b* Harrogate, 1 Mar. 1896; *s* of late William Henry Slater, West Park, Harrogate; *m* 1920, Mary Hanson Thistlethwaite, *d* of late

Samuel Newton, London; one *s* one *d. Educ:* privately; studied under Sir Edward C. Bairstow at York Minster, 1914-16. Served in HM Forces, 1916-19; Organist of Boston Parish Church, 1919-27; Conductor of Boston Choral Society, 1919-27; Billingborough Choral Society, 1924-27; Musical Director Holland Choirs' Triennial Festival, 1920-27; Gate Burton Players, 1925-27; Organist and Master of the Choir, Leicester Cathedral, 1927-30; Founder and Conductor Leicester Bach Choir, 1927-30; Melton Mowbray Choral Society, 1928-29; Lecturer in Singing, Leicester Univ. Coll. also in Music, Extra-Mural Dept, 1929-30; Conductor: Lincoln Musical Society, 1931-66; Symph. Orch., 1932-66; Lectr in Music, Extra Mural Dept, Nottingham Univ., 1932-59, Hull Univ., 1932-72, Sheffield Univ., 1972-74. Ferens Fine Art Lecturer, 1946-47; Adjudicated Canadian Musical Festivals, 1935, 1948. *Publications:* solo songs, choral songs, piano pieces, Church and Organ Music. *Recreation:* travelling. *Address:* 3 Pottergate, Lincoln LN2 1PH. *T:* Lincoln 26320.   [*Died 26 Jan.* 1979.

SLATER, Mrs Harriet, CBE 1965; *b* Tunstall, Staffordshire; *d* of John Edward Evans, Stoke-on-Trent; *m* 1931, Frederick Slater. *Educ:* Chell and Park Rd Council Schools; Hanley High School; Dudley Teachers' Training College. Taught at Middleport Senior Girls School. MP (Lab and Co-op) Stoke-on-Trent North, March 1953-66; a Lord Commissioner of the Treasury (Area Whip), Oct. 1964-March 1966; Member: Burslem Co-operative Management Cttee; Burslem Co-op. Soc., 1933-46; Anglesey Health Executive, 1966; Anglesey Employment Cttee, 1966. National Organiser Co-op. Party, 1942-53; City Council, Stoke-on-Trent, 1933-65; Alderman, 1949-65, Hon. Alderman, 1965; Chm. City Educn Cttee, 1952-65. *Address:* Hebor, 70 Sytch Road, Brown Edge, Stoke-on-Trent ST6 8QX.
                                                  [*Died 12 Oct.* 1976.

SLATER, Colonel Owen, CIE 1947; MC 1917; *b* 19 June 1890; *o s* of late Edward Murray Slater; *m* 1935, Genevieve Felicia, *o d* of late Rear-Adm. G. H. Hewett, CIE; no *c. Educ:* Rugby School; RMA Woolwich. Commissioned RE, 1910; served in Mesopotamia, 1915-18; Transcaspia and East Persia, 1918-20; joined Survey of India, 1920; remainder of service in India and Burma; Colonel, 1939; retired, 1947. *Address:* Ardogeena Grange, Durrus, Co. Cork, Eire.   [*Died 11 July* 1976.

SLAYTER, Adm. Sir William Rudolph, KCB *cr* 1952 (CB 1945); DSO 1944; DSC 1918; *b* 13 Feb. 1896; *er s* of John Howard Slayter, MBE, MB, CM, Halifax, Nova Scotia, and Dunsfold, Surrey; *m* 1925, Helen Justine (*d* 1969), *d* of Major Russell Hale; one *s. Educ:* RN Colleges, Osborne and Dartmouth. NOD Admiralty, 1938-41; Commanding Officer HMS Liverpool, 1941; Commanding Officer HMS Newfoundland, 1942; Chief of Staff Home Fleet, 1943; Captain HMS Excellent, 1945; Naval Representative of UK on Military Staff Committee of UN, 1947; Flag Officer Commanding, Second Cruiser Squadron, 1949-50; Admiral Commanding Reserves, 1950-52; Commander-in-Chief, East Indies Station, 1952-Aug. 1954, retired. Mem. of Cttee of Management: Royal Nat. Lifeboat Instn. Naval Vice-Pres., Combined Cadet Force Association. Served European War, 1914-18 (despatches, DSC); War of 1939-45 (despatches twice, DSO, CB). *Recreations:* gardening, golf, music. *Address:* 5 Egerton Place, SW3. *Clubs:* United Service, MCC.
                                                  [*Died 30 April* 1971.

SLEEMAN, Cyril Montagu, MA; Fellow of Queens' College, Cambridge; *b* 5 July 1883; 2nd *s* of Rev. P. R. Sleeman, Clifton, Bristol; *m* 1946, Rose Ellen, *d* of M. Paget Baxter, Hove. *Educ:* Clifton College; Christ's College, Cambridge (Scholar). Fellow Queens' College, Cambridge, 1912; Tutor and Senior Tutor, 1919-31; Lt RNVR; Wireless Officer, HM Signal School, Portsmouth, during War. *Recreations:* mountaineering, travel, swimming. *Address:* Queens' College, Cambridge; Ellergarth, Great Langdale, Westmorland. *Club:* Alpine.
                                                  [*Died 13 May* 1971.

SLEIGH, Sir Hamilton (Morton Howard), Kt 1970; a non-executive Director, H. C. Sleigh Ltd, since 1975 (Chairman, 1947-75, and Managing Director, 1947-71); *b* 20 March 1896; *s* of Howard Crofton Sleigh and Marion Elizabeth Sleigh; *m* 1st, 1926, Doris Margherita Halbert (*d* 1968); two *s*; 2nd, 1973, Brenda, *widow* of J. W. Dodds. *Educ:* Sherborne Sch., Dorset. Kt Cross, Order of White Rose of Finland; Order of Lion of Finland. *Recreation:* gardening. *Address:* 42 Wallace Avenue, Toorak, Victoria 3142, Australia. *Clubs:* Australian (Melbourne and Sydney).   [*Died 24 Nov.* 1979.

SLESINGER, Edward G., OBE 1918; MS, FRCS, MB, BSc; late Chairman, Board of Governors and Consulting Surgeon Emeritus, Guy's Hospital; Hon. Consulting Surgeon N Hertfordshire and S Bedfordshire Hospital, and Surgical Home

for Boys, Banstead; *b* London; *m* Gladys Eleanor Trench; two *s. Educ:* Dulwich College; Guy's Hosp. (Junior Science Scholar, Michael Harris Prize in Anatomy). Late Surgeon and Surgeon i/c fracture dept Guy's Hospital; Surgical Adviser EMS; BMA Research Scholar 1914 and 1919-20; Hunterian Professor, Royal College of Surgeons; Examiner in Surgery for LDS, RCS; BSc London 1st Class Hons Physiology, 1908; MB, BS (honours Medicine) 1911; MS London (University Gold Medal) 1919; President Clinical Section, Royal Society of Medicine; Temp. Surgeon-Lt RN 1914-18 (despatches, Croix de Guerre avec Palme). *Publications:* Articles-Appendicitis, Peritonitis, Intestinal Obstruction, Price's Text-book of Medicine; (joint) Surgery for Dental Students; War Wounds and Injuries; Prevention of Operative Mortality in Ex-ophthalmic Goitre, Guy's Hospital Reports 1923, and contributions to Medical Journals on abdominal and goitre surgery and on fractures. *Recreation:* reading. *Address:* Holly House, Hedgehog Lane, Haslemere, Surrey.   [*Died 18 June* 1975.

SLESSER, Rt. Hon. Sir Henry, PC 1929; Kt 1924; JP Devon; a Lord Justice of Appeal, 1929-40; *b* London, 1883; *y s* of Ernest Slesser, Gerrards Cross, Bucks; *m* Margaret (*d* 1979), *e d* of late Corrie Grant, KC. *Educ:* Oundle and St Paul's Schools; London Univ. Called to Bar, 1906, Bencher of the Inner Temple, 1924; KC, 1924; MP (Lab.) SE Leeds, 1924-29; HM Solicitor-General, 1924. Devon CC, 1946-68; Alderman, 1956; Chairman of Dartmoor Nat. Park Cttee, 1948-64. OSB (oblate); Hon. LLD Exeter, 1963. *Publications:* Trade Union Law, 1922 (3rd ed. 1928); Religio Laici, 1929; The Pastured Shire and Other Verses, 1935; Law (Heritage Series), 1936; Judgment Reserved, 1941; The Judicial Office and other matters, 1943; History of the Liberal Party, 1944; Order and Disorder, 1945; Administration of the Law, 1948; Middle Ages in the West, 1949 (2nd edn 1951); The Anglican Dilemma, 1952; The Art of Judgment and other legal studies, 1962. *Address:* Holcombe House, Moretonhampstead, Devon TQ13 8PW.   [*Died 3 Dec.* 1970.

SLESSOR, Marshal of the Royal Air Force Sir John Cotesworth, GCB, *cr* 1948 (KCB 1943; CB 1942); DSO 1937; MC 1916; DL; *b* Rhanikhet, India, 3 June 1897; *s* of late Major Arthur Kerr Slessor, Sherwood Foresters; *m* 1st, 1923, Hermione Grace (*d* 1970), *d* of Gerald Seymour Guiness, and *widow* of Lt-Col Herbert Carter; one *s* one *d*; 2nd, 1971, Marcella Florence, *widow* of Brig. R. T. Priest. *Educ:* Dragon School; Haileybury. Served European War, RFC, 1915-18: London Air Defence, France, Egypt, and Sudan (despatches, wounded, MC); served RAF India, 1921-23; RAF Staff College, 1924-25; commanded No. 4 Squadron, 1925-28; Air Staff, Air Ministry, 1928-30; Instructor, Staff College, Camberley, 1931-34; India, 1935-37: commanded No. 3 Indian Wing, Quetta, 1935; Waziristan Operations, 1936-37 (despatches, DSO); Director of Plans, Air Ministry, 1937-41; ADC to the King, 1938; Air rep., Anglo-French Conversations, 1939 and Anglo-American (ABC) Staff Conversations, 1941; AOC 5 (Bomber) Group, 1941; ACAS, (Policy), 1942-43 (Casablanca Conf.); AOC-in-C Coastal Command, 1943; C-in-C, RAF, Mediterranean and Middle East, 1944-45; Member of Air Council for Personnel, 1945-47; Commandant Imperial Defence College, 1948-49; Principal Air ADC to the King, 1948-50; Air Commodore, 1939, Air Vice-Marshal, 1941, Air Marshal, 1943; Air Chief Marshal, 1946; Marshal of the RAF, 1950. Chief of the Air Staff, 1950-52; Rep. British Chief of Staffs, NATO Confs, Brussels, Rome, Lisbon, Paris, Washington; Mem. UK Delegations, Commonwealth Relations Confs, 1954, 1959. Order of Leopold, Belgium; Légion d'Honneur, France, Order of Phœnix, Greece; Order of St Olaf, Norway; Legion of Merit, USA; Order of the Sword, Sweden; Partisan Star, Jugoslavia. Pres. the Victory (ex-Services) Club; Chairman, Star and Garter Home, 1953-67; Vice-Pres., Inst. of Strategic Studies; Gov.: Haileybury, Sherborne, King's (Bruton). JP and CC Somerset, 1963-74; High Sheriff, Somerset, 1965; DL, Somerset, 1969. *Publications:* Air Power and Armies, 1936; Strategy for the West, 1954; The Central Blue, 1956; The Great Deterrent, 1959; What Price Co-existence, 1961; These Remain, 1969. RUSI gold medal, 1936; Chesney Memorial Award, 1965. *Address:* Rimpton Manor, Yeovil, Somerset. *T:* Marston Magna 223. *Clubs:* Royal Air Force, Naval and Military (Hon. Life).   [*Died 12 July* 1979.

SLOAN, Sir Tennant, KCIE 1942 (CIE 1930); CSI 1936; *b* 9 Nov. 1884; *s* of Alexander Sloan, CA, Glasgow; *m* Gladys Hope, *d* of R. Hope Robertson, CA, Glasgow; one *d. Educ:* Glasgow Academy; Glasgow University; Christ Church, Oxford. Assistant Magistrate, 1909-13; Assistant Settlement Officer, 1913-14; Under-Secretary to Government, UP and to Government of India, 1914-19; Magistrate and Collector, 1920-21; Deputy Secretary to Government, UP and Government of India, 1921-26; Special Reforms Officer, and Secretary to Government, UP, 1927-31; Joint Secretary, Home Dept,

Government of India, 1932-36; Settlement Commissioner and Commissioner, UP, 1936-39; Adviser to the Governor, United Provinces, 1939-45. *Recreations:* golf, fishing. *Address:* 6 Greenhill Park, Edinburgh EH10 4DW. *T:* 031-447 3688. *Club:* Western (Glasgow). *[Died 15 Oct. 1972.*

SLOT, Gerald Maurice Joseph; late Lt-Col RAMC; Consulting Physician: Royal Waterloo Hospital; St Thomas' Hospital Group; Emeritus Consulting Physician, LCC, St Alfege's Hospital, Teddington Hospital and Hampton Hospital; Emeritus Consultant: Brook Hospital; Dulwich Hospital; King's College Hospital Group; Physician in charge of Rheumatism Supervisory Centre, LCC; late Physician Buchanan Hospital, and Royal Hospital, Richmond; Physician i/c Rheumatism Borough of Chiswick and Brentford; Physician NW Metropolitan and SW Metropolitan Boards; Paediatrician SE Metropolitan Board; *b* Johannesburg; *m* 1936, Mary, *d* of late J. A. Munton, Bradford. *Educ:* St Paul's School (Schol.); St John's Coll., Oxford (Exhibitioner); St Bartholomew's Hospital; Mercer's Scholar, Skynner Prizeman, MD (University of London Gold Medal), MRCP, DPH. Mem. Inner Temple; late Editor of Transactions Medico-legal Society; Editor of Medico-legal Journal and Criminological Review; late Medical Tutor Charing Cross Hospital and London Hospital; Harmsworth Research Fellow; late Chief Assistant St Bartholomew's Hospital and House Physician; Chadwick lecturer, 1930. *Publications:* Rheumatism in Childhood; Fume Diseases; Heart Disease in Childhood; Calcium Therapy; Pain in its Medico-Legal Relations; Deaths under Anæsthetics; Obesity; Treatment of Rheumatism with Gold; The Treatment of Sciatica; Medico legal aspects of Drunkenness; Street Accidents, numerous articles, etc. *Recreations:* tennis, motoring, sailing, music. *Address:* 148 Harley Street, W1. *T:* 01-935 1207; Comeragh House, 42 Marine Crescent, Worthing, Sussex. *T:* Worthing 48022. *[Died 6 April 1972.*

SLOTKI, Israel Wolf, MBE 1962; MRST, MA, LittD (Vic.); FRSL; Emeritus Director of Education, Manchester Central Board for Hebrew Education; Hon. Minister, Manchester Great Synagogue; Principal, Manchester Talmud Torah Schools, 1911-50; Hon. Superintendent of Hebrew in Manchester and Salford County Schools, 1912-50; Chaplain to HM Prisons: Strangeways, Manchester; The Castle, Lancaster; Bela River, Westmorland; Styal, Cheshire; Chaplain to Hospitals: Calderstones, Brockhall, Lancaster Moor, Manchester Royal Infirmary, Royal Eye, St Mary's, Hope, Jewish, Northern, and Langho Epileptic Colony; *b* Jerusalem, 26 Dec. 1884; *s* of late Rabbi Moses and Sarah Slotki; *m* Sarah (*d* 1960), *y d* of Rabbi Hertz and Bessie Lowenstein; one *s* two *d. Educ:* High Schools in Jerusalem; privately; Univ. of Manchester. Editor of the Hayehudi, 1908; Manchester Editor Jewish Guardian, 1919-31; Member of various committees of London social, religious and philanthropic organisations, and Hon. Sec. LCC Care Committees, 1910; Founder and Hon. Sec. Manchester Society for Hebraic Studies, 1917; Hon. Sec. Mizrachi Centre of the United Kingdom, 1926-28; of Manchester and District Hebrew Visitation Board since 1941 and Hon. Director since 1949; Examiner in Hebrew and Cognate subjects in Jewish Congregational Schools in many Lancashire towns; Hon. Sec., 1922-40, Vice-Pres. 1941, and Hon. Educational Adviser, 1942-46, of joint Jewish Education Board; Vice-Pres., 1939-41, of Jewish Ecclesiastical Council for Manchester and Salford; Hon. Life Mem. Council, Manchester and Salford Jews, 1964-; Mem. Exec. National Savings Committee, for Salford, 1939-, Dep. Chm. 1962, and Chm. 1964-; Vice-Pres., Manchester and Salford Trustee Savings Bank, 1971-; Mem. Manchester and Salford and District Cttee of Roy. National Lifeboat Instn, 1937-61; Mem. of Council of Manchester Univ. Egyptian and Oriental Soc., 1925- (Pres. 1952-54); Speaker for Ministry of Information, 1940-45. *Publications:* Stichometry and Text of the Great Hallel, 1928; Jewish Education in Manchester and Salford, 1928; Forms and Features of Ancient Hebrew Poetry, 1931; Typographic Arrangement of Ancient Hebrew Poetry, 1931; Song of Deborah, 1932; Longer and Shorter Versions of Ancient Hebrew Poems, 1933; Antiphony in Ancient Hebrew Poetry, 1936; Translations and Commentaries in the First Unabridged English Edition of the Babylonian Talmud Tractates Baba Bathra (Joint) and Horayoth, (1935), Yebamoth and (Joint) Kethuboth, (1936), Erubin and Sukkah, (1938), Niddah, Kelim, Negaim, Parah and Tohoroth (1948); Soferim, Sefer Torah, Zizith, Tefillin and Mezuzah, 1965; Grammatical Guide to the Hebrew Text of the Jewish Prayer Book (1946, 2nd edn 1947); Commentaries on Isaiah, 1949; on Kings, 1950, on the Books of Chronicles, 1952; Seventy Years of Hebrew Education, 1950; Moses Maimonidas, 1952; History of the Manchester Shechita Board, 1954; contrib. to learned journals. *Recreations:* walking, reading. *Address:* 3 Bellott Street, Manchester M8 7PQ. *T:* 061-205 4906. *[Died 2 June 1973.*

SMAIL, William Mitchell, MA Edinburgh and Oxon; FEIS; *b* Edinburgh, 1885; 3rd *s* of Adam Smail, Edinburgh; *m* Nora Maunsell (*d* 1968), 3rd *d* of Colonel W. D. Gordon, Kingston, Ontario; two *d. Educ:* Stewart's College, Edinburgh; Edinburgh University; Oriel College, Oxford (Bible Clerk, 1907-10); First Class in Literae Humaniores, 1910; Pitt Club Scholar, Edinburgh University, 1910; Assistant Master at Oundle School, 1910-11; Assistant Professor of Classics, Queen's University, Kingston, Ont., 1911-13; Professor of Latin, Rhodes University College, Grahamstown, South Africa, 1913-29; Warden of College House, Grahamstown, 1914; Rector of Perth Academy, 1929-50. *Publication:* Quintilian on Education, 1938. *Address:* 6 Abbotsford Crescent, Morningside, Edinburgh. *[Died 26 Dec. 1971.*

SMALDON, Catherine Agnes, CBE 1964; Chairman, General Nursing Council for England and Wales, 1960-65; retired as Chief Nursing Officer and Principal, Queen Elizabeth School of Nursing, United Birmingham Hospitals (1955-63); *b* 23 April 1903; *d* of William Ernest Smaldon and Catherine Smaldon (*née* Fairley). *Educ:* The Old Palace School, Croydon; Charing Cross Hospital. Ward Sister, Princess Mary's Hosp., Margate, 1928-29; Charing Cross Hospital: Ward Sister, Theatre Sister, Out Patient Dept Sister, Night Supt, Asst Matron, 1930-36. Matron: Brompton Hosp., London, 1936-40; Queen Elizabeth Hosp., Birmingham, 1940-55. *Recreations:* gardening, walking. *Address:* Higher Longparks, Sydenham, Lewdown, Devon EX20 4PU. *[Died 8 May 1980.*

SMALL, Sir Frank (Augustus), Kt 1967; CBE 1962; DL; JP; Director, National Building Agency, since 1964; *b* 3 July 1903; *s* of Austin and Sarah Small; *m* 1928, Sarah Ann Foster; no *c. Educ:* Woods Foundn C of E Sch., Woodborough, Notts. Nottinghamshire County Council: Member, 1946; Chm., County Finance Cttee, 1951-63; Chairman, 1963-67; Vice-Chm., 1967-. Mem., County Councils Assoc., 1952- (Chm., Parly. and Gen. Purposes Cttee, 1965). JP 1952, Alderman, 1957, DL 1963, Nottinghamshire. *Recreations:* football, cricket. *Address:* The Homestead, Woodborough, Notts. *T:* 2252. *[Died 18 April 1973.*

SMALL, William Watson, JP; MP (Lab) Glasgow, Garscadden, since 1974 (Glasgow, Scotstoun, Oct. 1959-1974); *b* 19 Oct. 1909; *s* of Edward Small of Lochee, Dundee; *m* 1941, Isabella Scott, *d* of Matthew Murphy of Stevenston, Ayrshire; two *d. Educ:* Calder School, Motherwell. JP Ayrshire, 1948. PPS to: Min. of Power, 1964-65; Sec. of State for Colonies, 1965; Chancellor of Duchy of Lancaster, 1966-69. *Address:* Belle Mara, 2 Diddup Drive, Stevenston, Ayrshire. *T:* Stevenston 63474. *[Died 18 Jan. 1978.*

SMALLBONES, Robert Townsend, CMG 1943; MBE; *a* Director of Panambra, SA; *b* 19 March 1884; 2nd *s* of Paul Smallbones, Schloss Velm, Austria; *m* Inga Gjertson, Kinn, Norway; one *d. Educ:* Trinity Coll., Oxford, MA. Consular Service, 1910; Vice-Consul, Portuguese West Africa, Stavanger; Consul, Munich, 1920; Bratislava, 1922; Monrovia, 1926; Loanda, 1927; Zagreb, 1931; Consul-General at Frankfort-on-Main, 1932-Sept. 1939; and at São Paulo; retired, 1945. *Address:* CP 7205, São Paulo, Brazil. *[Died 29 May 1976.*

SMALLEY-BAKER, Charles Ernest, QC (Ont); MA, LLB, LLM, (Hon.) DCL; Dean Emeritus of Osgoode Hall Law School, Ont. since 1958 (Dean, 1949-58); *b* Randolph, St John, New Brunswick, 1891; *o s* of late Charles Frederick Baker of Randolph; *m* 1921, Mary (*d* 1966), *y d* of late Samuel Hadland. *Educ:* Acadia Univ., NS (BA); Harvard University (LLB); St John's College, Oxford (Overseas Scholar and College Exhibitioner, BA 1920 MA 1924). Lieut, in Canadian Overseas Military Forces, 1915-19; organised and was Dean of Law Department of Khaki University of Canada, London, 1918-19; called to Bar, Inner Temple (Yarborough Anderson Scholarship, Certificate of Honour, 1920); practised, 1920-24; Barber Prof. of Law, 1924-49, and first Dean of Faculty of Law, 1928-49. Univ. of Birmingham; founder and now Patron of Holdsworth Club of University of Birmingham; sometime Examiner in Law to Universities of Sheffield, Liverpool, Oxford (BCL) and London (LLM); Member of Lord Chancellor's Committee on Advanced Legal Studies, 1938; Pres. Soc. of Public Teachers of Law, 1946-47; called to Bar: Ontario, 1949 (QC 1950), New Brunswick, 1953; a President-Adjoint of IVth Internat. Congress of Comparative Law, Paris, 1954. Maj. H. G. and Capt. Gen. List, TA in last war. Freedom of City of London, 1956. Hon. DCL Acadia Univ., 1962. *Publications:* (ed) Constitutional Law, English and Empire Digest; Assistant Editor, seventh edition, Grant's Law of Banking; various legal articles. *Address:* 49 St Clair Avenue West, Toronto 7, Canada. *Clubs:* English-Speaking Union; Granite (Toronto). *[Died 2 Nov. 1972.*

SMALLWOOD, Geoffrey Arthur John; Stipendiary Magistrate, Staffordshire Potteries, 1960-73, retired; *b* 27 June 1900; *o s* of Arthur and Margaret Smallwood; *m* 1931, Violet Cecil Turnour Berens (*d* 1970), Kevington, St Mary Cray, Kent; no *c. Educ:* Lancing; Christ Church, Oxford. Called to Bar, Inner Temple, 1924. Served War of 1939-45: 2nd Lt, RA, 1940; Captain 1941, Major 1944, Dept of JAG; Lines of Communication, Brussels, June-Sept. 1945. Dep. Chm., Leics QS, 1947-71. *Recreations:* racing, travelling in France. *Address:* Chapel Leasowe, Milford, near Stafford. *T:* Stafford 61078. *Clubs:* Army and Navy; British Potteries Manufacturers Assoc. (Stoke-on-Trent).
[Died 1 Sept. 1973.

SMALLWOOD, Maj.-Gen. Gerald Russell, CB 1943; DSO 1941; MC; *b* 18 Feb. 1889. 2nd Lt East Yorks Regt, 1912; served European War, 1914-18, France and Belgium (despatches twice, MC); GSO 1st Grade, British Military Mission to the Egyptian Army, 1937-39; specially employed, 1939; commanding troops in Madagascar, 1942; retired pay, 1946. *Address:* Kichaka, PO Box 24747, Karen, Kenya. *[Died 3 Feb. 1977.*

SMART, Sir Eric (Fleming), Kt 1966; OBE 1955; farmer and grazier; *b* 12 Oct. 1911; *s* of late Percival Horace Smart, Spalding, S Australia, and Lillian Lois Rogers; *m* 1938, Jean Constance, *d* of late Hubert Arthur Oliver Davis, Adelaide, S Australia; one *s* two *d. Educ:* Prince Alfred Coll., Adelaide. Mem., Wongan Hills Road Bd, 1946-49; Pres., Wongan Hills Hosp. Bd, 1947-49; Mingenew Shire Councillor, 1949-67; Councillor, Royal Agricultural Society of Western Australia. Vice-Pres., British Boys Movement; Governor of Fairbridge Farm Society, 1959-. Farms 100,000 acres; properties: Erregulla Plains, Mingenew, WA; Broadview, Mount Kokeby, WA; Wingarra, Gnowangerup, WA. *Publication:* Wastelands Transformed, 1952, rev. edn (as Western Australia's Waste Land Transformed), 1962. *Recreation:* golf. *Address:* 59 Birdwood Parade, Dalkeith, WA 6009, Australia. *Clubs:* Royal Aero, Perth (Perth, WA); Lake Karrinyup Country.
[Died 10 June 1973.

SMART, Leslie Masson, CBE 1936; *b* 22 March 1889; *s* of William Smart; *m* 1928, Annie Smith; no *c. Educ:* Glenbervie, Kincardineshire, Scotland. Kenya and Uganda Railway, 1913-27; Tanganyika Railways, 1927-33; General Manager Gold Coast Railway, 1933-37; General Manager Federated Malay States Railways, 1937-46, retired. *Address:* Bahati, PO Borrowdale, Salisbury, Rhodesia. *[Died 1972.*

SMART, William Marshall, MA, DSc, LLD, FRSE; FRAS; Regius Professor of Astronomy, University of Glasgow, 1937-59; *b* Doune, Perthshire, 9 March 1889; *s* of P. F. Smart; *m* 1919, Isabel (*d* 1974), *d* of Dr John Carswell; three *s. Educ:* McLaren High School, Callander; Glasgow Univ. (Cunninghame Medal, Breadalbane Scholar and Ferguson Scholar); Trinity Coll., Cambridge (Sheepshanks Exhibitioner, Scholar); Mathematical Tripos, Pt I, First Class; Pt II, Wrangler, Distinction, and Tyson medal; Rayleigh Prize, 1916; Instructor Lieutenant, RN, 1915-19; served in Grand Fleet in HMS Emperor of India; John Couch Adams Astronomer and Lecturer in Mathematics, Univ. of Cambridge, 1919-37; Thomson Lecturer, Aberdeen, 1934; Elder Lecturer, Glasgow; Sec. of the Royal Astronomical Soc., 1931-37; Vice-Pres., 1937-38, 1951-53; Pres., 1949-51; Halley Lecturer, Oxford, 1941; Dean of the Faculty of Science, Glasgow, 1946-49; Vice-Pres. Royal Soc. of Edinburgh, 1952-55; Fison Memorial Lectr, Guy's Hosp., 1961. Lorimer Medal, Edinburgh Astronomical Soc. *Publications:* Admiralty Manual of Navigation, 1922 (with Com. F. N. Shearme); Position Line Tables, 1924; The Sun, the Stars and the Universe, 1928; Astrophysics, 1928; Spherical Astronomy, 1931; Astronomy, 1937; Stellar Dynamics, 1938; Sea and Air Navigation, 1941; The Foundations of Astronomy, 1942; Introduction to Sea and Air Navigation, 1942; Astronomical Navigation, 1942; Handbook of Sea Navigation, 1943; John Couch Adams and the Discovery of Neptune, 1946; The Origin of the Earth, 1950; Some Famous Stars, 1950; Celestial Mechanics, 1953; Foundations of Analytical Geometry, 1956; Combination of Observations, 1958; Stellar Kinematics, 1968; The Riddle of the Universe, 1968. Papers in Memoirs and Monthly Notices of RAS and Cambridge Observations; Encyclopædia Britannica (1919 ed.). *Recreations:* watching and talking cricket. *Address:* Westbourne House, Westbourne Road, Lancaster LA1 5EF. *T:* 64742. *[Died 17 Sept. 1975.*

SMEED, Reuben Jacob, CBE 1966; Professor of Traffic Studies, University College London, since 1966; *b* 1 Sept. 1909; *m* 1938, Dorothy Antrich; one *s* one *d* (and one *d* decd). *Educ:* Central Foundation School and Queen Mary College, London. BSc London, 1st cl. Hons Maths; PhD (Eng.) 1933. Aircraft design, 1933; Demonstrator and Lectr in Mathematics, Imperial Coll.,

London, 1933-40; RAE, Farnborough, Telecommunications Research Estabt, Swanage, Operational Research Section, Bomber Comd, RAF, 1940-47; Dep. Director (Traffic and Safety), Road Research Laboratory, 1947-65; Chief Scientist, Min. of Land and Natural Resources, 1965-66. *Publications:* scientific papers. *Address:* Brookmead, 65 Windsor Road, Bray, Berks. *T:* Maidenhead 23982. *Club:* Athenæum.
[Died 3 Sept. 1976.

SMELE, William Samuel George; *b* 9 June 1912; *o s* of late C. W. Smele and Etta Smele, Bristol; *m* 1947, Edith Stella Pascoe; one *s. Educ:* Cotham School, Bristol. Journalist, special writer on industry and politics, Bristol newspapers, 1929-40. War service, 1940-46. Chief reporter, Bristol Evening World, 1946; Press Officer, SW Region, Central Office of Information, 1948; Sen. Information Officer, N Region, COI, 1951; Press Officer, HM Treasury, 1954; Chief Press and Broadcast Officer, GPO, 1957; Commonwealth Relations Office, 1958; Regional Information Officer (British Information Services), Montreal, 1958; Counsellor and Director, British Information Services, S Africa, 1960, Malaysia, 1962; Head of News Dept, CRO, 1964; Chief Information Officer, MPBW, 1966; Head of Publicity, DoE, 1971; retired, 1972. Fellow, Inst. of Public Relations. *Recreations:* motoring, reading, writing. *Address:* 103 Pentire Avenue, Newquay, Cornwall. *[Died 19 Oct. 1976.*

SMITH; *see* Abel Smith.

SMITH, Sir Allan Chalmers, Kt 1953; MC 1918; *b* 22 Feb. 1893; *e s* of late Allan Frith Smith, Colonial Treasurer, Bermuda; *m* 1920, Elsie Joyce Martin; three *s* three *d. Educ:* Warwick Academy, Bermuda; Rossall School, Lancs, England; St John's College, Oxford. Rhodes Scholarship, Bermuda, 1912. Served European War, 1914-18 (despatches thrice); Temp. Capt. RFA. Called to Bar, Gray's Inn, 1920; law practice in Bermuda, 1920-34. Police Magistrate: Western District, 1928, Central District, 1931, Bermuda; Lagos, Nigeria, 1935. Puisne Judge: Trinidad, 1938, Gold Coast, 1944; Chief Justice, Sierra Leone, 1951-55; Assistant Justice, Bermuda, 1955-65. Judicial Comr of Plan for a British Caribbean Fedn, 1955. *Recreations:* golf, gardening. *Address:* Cleeve Cottage, Paget 6.03, Bermuda.
[Died 23 May 1980.

SMITH, Lt-Gen. Sir Arthur (Francis), KCB 1946 (CB 1941); KBE 1942; DSO 1918; MC; *b* 9 Dec 1890; *s* of late Col Granville R. F. Smith, CVO, CB, and late Lady Blanche Smith; *m* 1918, Hon. Monica Crossley, *y d* of 1st Baron Somerleyton; three *d* (and one *s* decd). *Educ:* Eton; Sandhurst. Hon. LLD (Aberdeen), 1948. Joined Coldstream Guards, 1910; Adjt 3rd Batt. Coldstream Guards, Sept. 1914-Nov. 1915; Staff Nov. 1915-Aug. 1917; served European War, 1914-18 (wounded thrice, DSO, MC, Croix de Guerre); Adjutant RMC, Sandhurst, 1921-24; Comdt of Guards Depot, 1924-27; Staff of GOC London District, 1927-30; commanded 2nd Battalion Coldstream Guards, 1930-34; commanded Coldstream Guards Regiment and 4th Guards Brigade, 1934-38; Brigadier, General Staff, British Troops in Egypt, 1938-39; CGS, Middle East, 1940; GOC London District and Major-General commanding Brigade of Guards, 1942-44; GOC-in-C Persia and Iraq Command, 1944-45; GOC-in-C Eastern Command, India, 1945-46; Chief of General Staff, India, 1946; Dep. C-in-C 1947; Comdr British Forces in India and Pakistan, Nov. 1947; retired 1948; Lieutenant at the Tower of London, 1948-51. Mem. Council, Dr Barnardo's, 1943-; Vice-Pres., 1972. *Address:* Greathed Manor, Lingfield, Surrey. *T:* Lingfield 834323. *Clubs:* Cavalry and Guards, National. *[Died 8 Aug. 1977.*

SMITH, Arthur Lionel Forster, CBE 1927; MVO 1914; Iraqi Order of Al Rafidhain; Hon. LLD Edin. and St Andrews; late 9th Batt. Hants Regt; *b* 19 Aug. 1880; *s* of late Arthur Lionel Smith, Master of Balliol. *Educ:* Rugby; Balliol College, Oxford. Fellow and Tutor of Magdalen College, Oxford, 1908-20; Fellow of All Souls, 1904-8; Director of Education, Mesopotamia, 1920-21; Adviser of Education, Iraq, 1921-31; Rector of Edinburgh Academy, 1931-45. *Address:* 84 Inverleith Place, Edinburgh.
[Died 3 June 1972.

SMITH, Arthur Llewellyn, MBE 1945; MA Oxon; FSA 1964; FRIBA; Architect in private practice, 1937-70, as partner, Llewellyn Smith and Waters, now the Waters Jamieson Partnership; Consultant for historic buildings, since 1971; *b* 25 July 1903; *e s* of late Sir Hubert Llewellyn Smith, GCB, and of Edith (Maud Sophia) (*née* Weekley); unmarried. *Educ:* St Edmund's Sch., Hindhead; Winchester Coll. (Scholar); New Coll., Oxford (1st cl. Hon. Mods Oxon, 1924; 1st cl. Litt. Hum. Oxon, 1926); Bartlett Sch. of Architecture, London Univ. Asst in office of Troup & Steele, 1928-37. War service as Inspector in Passive Air Defence Div., Min. of Supply, 1939-45; seconded to

Office of Chief Adviser, Factory ARP, Govt of India, 1941-45. Was mainly engaged on housing and domestic work, social and recreational buildings, churches and vicarages, and the restoration of historic buildings in Oxford and elsewhere. Jt Founder, Crown Club Hoxton (now Crown and Manor Boys' Club), 1926; Cons. Architect to Nat. Assoc. of Boys' Clubs, 1937-70; Hon. Sec., Crown and Manor (Boys') Club, Hoxton; Vice-Pres., Winchester Coll. Mission; Dep. Chm., Devas (Boys') Club, Battersea. Sec., Brit. Inst. of Industrial Art, 1927-33; Member, Art Workers Guild, 1946, Hon. Secretary, 1954-62; Master, 1964. Member Council RSA, 1966-72. Chm. of Governors, Camberwell Sch. of Art and Crafts, 1969-. *Publications:* Buildings for Boys' Clubs, 1937; chapter in New Survey of London Life and Labour, Vol. VI, 1934; various articles and reviews in RIBA Jl, The Builder, RSA Jl, etc. *Recreation:* sketching. *Address:* 1 Ockley Road, Streatham, SW16 1UG. *T:* 01-769 2803. *Club:* United Oxford & Cambridge University. *[Died 8 Nov. 1978.*

SMITH, Bernard Joseph Gilliat; *see* Gilliat-Smith.

SMITH, Sir Carl (Victor), Kt 1964; CBE 1946; Cadbury Fry Hudson (New Zealand): Managing Director, 1932-63; Chairman, 1939-63; retired 1964; Director, several NZ companies; *b* 19 April 1897; *s* of Dr James Smith, Edinburgh; *m* 1919, Catherine Elizabeth Gettings Johnston; two *s* one *d. Educ:* George Watson's College, Edinburgh. Served European War, 1914-18: 4th Royal Scots, Captain. Pres. NZ Manufrs Fedn, 1940-43; Member: Armed Services Appeal Board, 1940-45; Economic Stabilisation Commn, 1941; Coun. and Hon. Treas., Univ. of Otago, 1946-68; Roy. Commn on Parly Salaries, 1955, 1957, 1958; Roy. Commn on NZ Rlys, 1952; NZ Univ. Grants Cttee (3 years). Hon. LLD Otago. *Publication:* From N to Z, 1947. *Address:* Rowheath, Dudley Place, Dunedin, New Zealand. *T:* Dunedin 60076. *Club:* Dunedin.
[Died 12 Feb. 1979.

SMITH, Sir Cecil Furness; *see* Furness-Smith.

SMITH, Mrs Cecil W.; *see* Woodham-Smith.

SMITH, Charles George Percy; *see* Delacourt-Smith, Baron.

SMITH, Cyril James, OBE 1971; FRCM; Professor of Pianoforte at Royal College of Music, since 1934; *b* 11 Aug. 1909; *s* of Charles Ernest Smith and Eva Mary Smith; *m* 1937, Phyllis Sellick (OBE 1971); one *s* one *d. Educ:* Middlesbrough High School; Royal College of Music. Worshipful Company of Musicians' Medal, Royal Coll. of Music, 1928; 1st Prize Daily Express Piano Contest, 1928. First Promenade Concert at age of 20; first broadcast, 1929. Toured Central Europe for British Council, 1936. Two pianos with Phyllis Sellick, Promenade season, 1941. During war toured abroad with Phyllis Sellick, for British Council, 1944, for ENSA, 1945. Also visited Europe for ENSA, 1945; went to Germany for Foreign Office to give concerts and recitals, 1949; returned to Berlin by invitation, 1950, to play with Berlin Philharmonic Orchestra; toured USSR with Phyllis Sellick, as part of Foreign Office Cultural Mission headed by Sir Arthur Bliss, 1956; toured New Zealand, 1965; Adjudicated Internat. Piano Comp., Munich, 1965, 1967. Recorded many concertos, solo works, and two-piano works. Works written for Cyril Smith and Phyllis Sellick by Vaughan Williams, Lennox Berkeley, Gordon Jacob, Arthur Bliss and Malcolm Arnold. TV Biographies, 1960, 1967. Hon. FRCM, 1958; Hon. RAM, 1962. *Publication:* Duet for Three Hands (autobiography), 1958. *Recreations:* own children; photography; formerly yachting, golf. *Address:* Oak Lodge, 33 Fife Road, East Sheen, SW14. *T:* 01-876 5143. *[Died 2 Aug. 1974.*

SMITH, Hon. David John, CBE 1964; JP Berkshire; Lord-Lieutenant of Berkshire, 1959-75; Chairman W. H. Smith & Son (Holdings) Ltd, 1949-72, Director, since 1972; Director: W. H. Smith & Son Ltd, 1935-72; Lloyds Bank Ltd; *b* 20 May 1907; 3rd *s* of 2nd Viscount Hambleden; *m* 1931, Lady Helen Pleydell-Bouverie, *d* of 6th Earl of Radnor; four *s* one *d. Educ:* Eton; Oxford. Member of Council, Bradfield College, Berkshire; High Steward of Wallingford. Chm., Delegacy, King's College, London. Hon. DLitt, Reading, 1973. *Address:* King's Copse House, Southend, Reading RG7 6JR. *T:* Bradfield 366. *Club:* White's. *[Died 26 Nov. 1976.*

SMITH, Erik (John), RWS 1971; RE 1959 (ARE 1948); RBA 1950; Lecturer in Art History, School of Art, High Wycombe College of Technology and Art, since 1948; *b* 6 Dec. 1914; *s* of James Frederick and Lily Gertrude Smith, Birmingham; *m* 1948, Lilian Mary Novello Williams, BA; one *s. Educ:* King Edward VI, Birmingham; Royal College of Art. Served War, 1940-46, Capt. Worcestershire Regt; with 1st Army in N Africa

and 21 AG in Germany, Battalion Mines Officer. Associate of the Royal College of Art with 4th year scholarship, 1947, and Engraving School Prize. Designed and wrote Book of Remembrance, High Wycombe; work includes stained glass windows: Wouldham, Kent; Turville and Long Marston, Bucks. Exhibits regularly with RA, NEAC, RWS, RBA, RE and has exhibited in South Africa, USA, Brazil and Australia; also has Etchings in Ottawa Museum, Art Gallery, Canada, VA Museum, South London Art Gallery, Ashmolean Musuem, water colours in Sheffield Art Gallery, and works in private collections. *Publications:* Articles on art in: Discovering Art; New Knowledge; The Artist; Canvas, the Old Water-Colour Society's Club Annual Vol. *Recreations:* chess, bridge, books, especially 18th century English History. *Address:* 5 Chiltern Close, Princes Risborough, Bucks. *T:* Princes Risborough 4953. *[Died 9 Sept. 1972.*

SMITH, Ernest T.; *see* Thornton-Smith.

SMITH, Brig. Ernest Thomas Cobley, CB 1955; CBE 1952; retired as Brigadier and Chief Paymaster, Royal Army Pay Corps; *b* 1895; *s* of late Herbert Smith; *m* 1920, Marie Anne, *d* of late John Hruby; one *s* one *d.* Served European War, 1915-19: France, Belgium and the Balkans (despatches, two medals, 1914-15 star); served war of 1939-45, Middle East and South-East Asia (despatches); Command Paymaster, Malta, 1942, Egypt and Sudan, 1943; Deputy Paymaster-in-Chief, SEAC, 1944; Command Paymaster, Polish Re-Settlement Corps, 1946; Deputy Paymaster-in-Chief, Middle East, 1948; Command Paymaster, Eastern Comd, 1951; Deputy Paymaster-in-Chief, BAOR, 1954. *Address:* Derry Gariff, Seaton Road, Camberley, Surrey. *T:* Camberley 64221. *[Died 25 Jan. 1977.*

SMITH, Col Sir Eustace; *see* Smith, Col Sir Thomas Eustace.

SMITH, Florence Margaret; *see* Smith, Stevie.

SMITH, Francis Edward Viney, CMG 1942; BSc; *b* 1902; *m* 1st, 1926, Winifred Nellie Nicholson (*d* 1951), Salisbury, Wilts; three *s* one *d*; 2nd, 1956, Annie McLaren, London. *Educ:* Colston's School, Bristol; Bristol University, Department of Scientific and Industrial Research, 1921; Senior Assistant Mycologist, Ministry of Agriculture and Fisheries, 1924; Government Microbiologist, Jamaica, 1927; Comr of Commerce and Industry, Jamaica, to 1944; Devel. Sec. in charge of post-war planning and reconstruction, Nigerian Govt Secretariat, 1944-46; Commissioner on Special Duty, Nigeria, 1947-53; Chm. Cameroons Development Corp., 1947-52. Services made available, by HM Govt, to Ghana, to establish National Research Council, 1958-61. *Address:* Milbourne Cottage, Malmesbury, Wilts SN16 9JB. *T:* Malmesbury 2306.
[Died 28 Sept. 1979.

SMITH, Sir Frank Edwin N.; *see* Newson-Smith.

SMITH, Sir George Bracewell, 2nd Bt *cr* 1947; MBE 1946; (known as **Sir Guy Bracewell Smith**); *b* 5 Nov. 1912; *s* of Sir Bracewell Smith, 1st Bt, KCVO; *S* father, 1966; *m* 1951, Helene Marie Hydock (*d* 1975), Pennsylvania; two *s. Educ:* Wrekin Coll., Shropshire; Emmanuel Coll., Cambridge (MA). Chm., Park Lane Hotel Ltd. Director: Arsenal Football Club Ltd; Carpac Ltd; The Ritz Hotel Ltd (Paris). Warden, Haberdashers' Co., 1957-58, 1964-65 and 1975-76. *Recreations:* golf, riding. *Heir: s* Guy Bracewell Smith, *b* 12 Dec. 1952. *Address:* Park Lane Hotel, Piccadilly, W1A 4UA. *T:* 01-499 6321. *Clubs:* City Livery, Royal Automobile; Royal and Ancient (St Andrews); Highgate Golf, Sunningdale Golf, Royal Ashdown Forest Golf. *[Died 18 Sept. 1976.*

SMITH, Sir George (Fenwick), Kt 1978; CBE 1969; General Secretary, Union of Construction, Allied Trades and Technicians (formerly Amalgamated Society of Woodworkers and Painters), since 1959; Operatives Secretary, National Joint Council for Building Industry; *b* 24 June 1914; *s* of James Guthrie Smith and Agnes Pearson Fenwick; *m* 1937, Doris Ferguson Drever; two *s* one *d. Educ:* Inverbrothock and Downfield Schs. Amalgamated Society of Woodworkers: National Organizer, 1945-48; Asst Gen. Sec., 1949-59. Member: TUC Gen. Council, 1959- (Chm. TUC, 1972); Council, Advisory, Conciliation and Arbitration Service, 1974-. *Recreations:* photography, handcrafts. *Address:* 72 Maryland Road, Thornton Heath, Surrey. *T:* 01-764 1149.
[Died 21 Nov. 1978.

SMITH, Graham Burrell; *b* 1880; *s* of H. Arthur Smith, Barrister-at-Law. *Educ:* City of London School; King's College, Cambridge. RN College, Osborne, 1906-15; Repton School, 1919-26; Eton College, 1941-48; Headmaster, Sedbergh School,

1927-36. Cornwall Education Committee. *Publications:* Scenes from European History; Outlines of European History, etc. *Address:* Riviera Hotel, Canford Cliffs, Poole, Dorset.
[*Died* 25 *May* 1975.

SMITH, Brigadier Henry Gilbertson, CB 1945; OBE 1943; MC; TD; Frihitskors Kongen Haakon VII; *b* 15 Nov. 1896; *e s* of late Sir Gilbertson Smith, TD; *m* 1st, Dorothea Joy (*d* 1931), *d* of Major N. L. Garrett; one *s* one *d* ; 2nd, Marjorie Beatrice, *d* of George Relf, Brentwood, Essex. *Educ:* Lancing College. Served European War, 1914-18, 2/25 Bn London Regt, TA, seconded Machine Gun Corps, France; War of 1939-45, Royal Artillery, TA, England and Norway; Comdr 41 AA Bde, 27 AA Bde and 303 Infantry Bde. FRMS; FLS; FRMetS; Pres. Royal Microscopical Soc., 1952, 1953. *Recreations:* microscopy, photography and science. *Address:* Ravenscourt, Sawyers Hall, Hall Lane, Brentwood, Essex. *T:* Brentwood 210270.
[*Died* 23 *July* 1977.

SMITH, Sir Henry Martin, Kt 1971; CBE 1952 (OBE 1943; MBE 1941); retired as HM Chief Inspector of Fire Services (1948-72); *b* 10 Feb. 1907; *s* of William and Helen Smith; *m* 1937, Anita Marie Sullivan; no *c.* *Educ:* Roan School, Greenwich, London. Chief Regional Fire Officer, Southern Region, National Fire Service, 1941-46; Acting Chief of Fire Staff and Inspector-in-Chief, 1947-48. *Address:* 203 Upper Woodcote Road, Caversham, Reading, Berks. *T:* Reading 473932.
[*Died* 27 *Oct.* 1979.

SMITH, Henry Roy William, MA, PhD; Professor of Latin and of Classical Archaeology, the University of California, 1931-58, Professor Emeritus since 1958; *b* 13 June 1891; *o s* of Henry Joseph Smith and Gertrude Martha Swears; *m* 1926, Mary Adele Macdonald; one *s.* *Educ:* Wimbledon College; St Paul's School (Scholar); Pembroke College, Oxford (Scholar); Princeton University. Associate Professor of Classics, Saint Francis Xavier's College, Antigonish, Nova Scotia, 1914-21 (subaltern in Manchester Regiment, 1916-19); Professor of Classics, Saint Francis Xavier's College, 1921-22; Instructor in Classics, Princeton University, 1925-26; Assistant Professor of Classics, Princeton University, 1926-28; Assistant Professor of Latin, University of California, 1928-30; Associate Professor of Latin, University of California, 1930-31; Corr. Member of German Archæological Inst., 1935, Member, 1953; Travelling Fellow of John Simon Guggenheim Memorial Foundation, 1936; Member of Advisory Bd, Am. Jour. of Archaeology, 1947. Research Fell. of Bollingen Foundation, 1962. *Publications:* New Aspects of the Menon Painter, 1929; The Origin of Chalcidian Ware, 1932; Corpus Vasorum Antiquorum, United States, V (University of California, 1), 1936 and X (San Francisco Museums), 1943; Der Lewismaler, 1939; The Hearst Hydria, 1944; Problems (Historical and Numismatic) in The Reign of Augustus, 1951; (jointly) Votive Religion at Caere, 1959. *Address:* Faculty Club, University of California, Berkeley, California, USA. *T:* Thornwall 85678. *Clubs:* Oxford and Cambridge University; Faculty (Berkeley).
[*Died* 3 *March* 1971.

SMITH, Sir Henry Wilson; *see* Wilson Smith.

SMITH, Herbert Alexander, CBE 1958; Deputy Chief Inspector of Taxes, (retired); *b* 6 July 1896; *s* of late Robert Maxwell Smith, Edinburgh; *m* 1922, Jean Murray Weir. *Educ:* Boroughmuir School, Edinburgh. Entered Inland Revenue Department, 1920; Principal Inspector of Taxes, 1948; Senior Principal Inspector of Taxes, 1953. Fellow, Inst. of Chartered Accountants of England and Wales. Served European War, 1916-19 (wounded); Artists' Rifles, King's Own Royal Lancaster Regt, Lieutenant. *Recreations:* painting, music, gardening. *Address:* 91 Canford Cliffs Road, Canford Cliffs, Dorset. *T:* Canford Cliffs 707834. *Club:* Civil Service.
[*Died* 27 *Oct.* 1976.

SMITH, Hon. Hugh Adeane Vivian, MBE; Chairman, Charter Consolidated Ltd, 1969-71 (Dep. Chm. 1966); Executive Director, British South Africa Co., 1962-66; Director, Anglo American Corp. of South Africa, 1947-70 (Managing Dir, 1948-52); *b* 25 April 1910; *s* of 1st Baron Bicester and Lady Sybil McDonnell; *m* 1933, Lady Helen Primrose, *d* of 6th Earl of Rosebery, KT, PC, DSO, MC, and his 1st wife, Lady Dorothy Grosvenor (*d* 1966); one *s* one *d.* Partner, Messrs Rowe & Pitman (stockbrokers), 1935-46. Served War of 1939-45 (despatches): in Hertfordshire Regt, then Irish Guards. *Recreation:* golf. *Address:* Souldern Manor, Bicester, Oxon OX6 9JP. *T:* Fritwell 374. *Clubs:* Brooks's, Pratt's, White's.
[*Died* 20 *March* 1978.

SMITH, Hugh W. H.; *see* Heckstall-Smith.

SMITH, Ida Phyllis B.; *see* Barclay-Smith.

SMITH, James Dury H.; *see* Hindley-Smith.

SMITH, John Forest; *see* Forest Smith.

SMITH, John Gerald, CB 1966; *b* 2 Jan. 1907; *s* of Frederick and Mary Smith; *m* 1934, Christine Mary Till; no *c.* Joined Min. of Transport, 1935, after experience and training with Consulting Engineers and local authority. Commissioned RE, 1939; served in France, Middle East and Italy (despatches) attained rank of Major. Returned to Min. of Transport, Senior Engineer, 1948; Asst Chief Engineer at HQ of Min. of Transport, 1957; Deputy Chief Engineer, 1958; Chief Highway Engineer, 1964; retired 1966. CEng, FICE. *Address:* 5 Regent's Close, Belgrave Road, Seaford, East Sussex BN25 2EB.
[*Died* 31 *March* 1979.

SMITH, John Mitchell Aitken, CBE 1968; TD 1939; Member, London Committee, Scottish Council (Chairman, 1966-71); *b* 18 Nov. 1902; *s* of William Smith, Calcutta and Aberdeen, and Barbara Gordon Smith, Aberdeen; *m* 1935, Nota Eleanor Buckland Cooper, *d* of Buckland Cooper, Montevideo and London: one *s* one *d.* *Educ:* Morrisons Academy, Crieff. Chartered Accountant, 1925; joined Ford Motor Co. Ltd, 1930: Secretary, 1939; Asst Man. Dir, 1953-61. President, Soc. of Motor Manufacturers, 1959-60. Member: Committee of Enquiry on Decimal Currency, 1961; Monopolies Commn, 1963-69; Chm., Nat. Computing Centre, 1966-70. Territorial Army, 1921-45. Served War of 1939-45; retired as Lt-Col Royal Fusiliers. Hon. LLD Strathclyde, 1971. *Recreations:* golf and chess. *Address:* Flat H, 18 Eaton Square, SW1. *T:* 01-245 9063. *Clubs:* Caledonian, Hurlingham.
[*Died* 3 *June* 1974.

SMITH, Col Kenneth, CMG 1918; Australian AMC Reserve; *b* 13 April 1885; *m* 1914, Kate, *d* of T. W. Wise. *Educ:* Brisbane Grammar School; Sydney University, MB, ChM. Served European War, 1915-19 (despatches, CMG); ADMS 4th Australian Division, 1918. Principal Medical Officer, Commonwealth Repatriation Dept, 1935-50. *Address:* Redrith, 13 Harwood Avenue, Chatswood, NSW 2067, Australia.
[*Died* 24 *July* 1971.

SMITH, Captain Norman Wesley, CBE 1960; retired as Commodore Orient Steam Navigation Co. Ltd, 1961; *b* 27 Feb. 1900; *s* of Joseph and Margaret Anne Smith; *m* 1946, Nancy Phyllis, *d* of Engineer Captain F. J. Pedrick, RN (Retd); two *s.* *Address:* Lychgate, 37 Kewhurst Avenue, Cooden, Sussex. *T:* Cooden 2234.
[*Died* 14 *Jan.* 1977.

SMITH, Lt-Col Osbert Walter Dudley, JP; Vice-Lieutenant, County of Worcester, since 1959; *b* 1 August 1898; *s* of G. D. Smith and Lady Barbara Smith, *d* of 9th Earl of Coventry. *Educ:* Eton; RMC, Sandhurst. Grenadier Guards, Dec. 1917. Served War of 1939-45; Major 3rd Bn Grenadier Guards (despatches); Lt-Colonel 4th Bn, 1940. DL and JP Worcs, 1946. High Sheriff, Worcs, 1957. *Address:* Levant Lodge, Earls Croome, Worcester. *T:* Upton-upon-Severn 2628. *Club:* Guards.
[*Died* 24 *Jan.* 1973.

SMITH, Rear-Adm. P(hilip) Sydney, CB 1952; DSO 1945; retired; *b* 25 Feb. 1899; *s* of Rev. Sydney Edward Smith; *m* 1928, Edna Vere Herbert; two *d.* *Educ:* Hill House, St Leonards on Sea; Osborne; Dartmouth. Midshipman, 1914; Lieut, 1922; Comdr, 1935; Captain, 1941; Rear-Adm., 1950. Served European War, 1914-18; served War of 1939-45 (despatches, DSO); Head of British Naval Mission to Greece, 1951-53; retired Sept. 1953. *Recreations:* mainly gardening; formerly all games: especially tennis, golf, cricket. *Address:* Forge Lodge, Bredhurst, Kent.
[*Died* 15 *Oct.* 1973.

SMITH, Phyllis B.; *see* Barclay-Smith.

SMITH, Ralph Henry T.; *see* Tottenham-Smith.

SMITH, Mrs Reginald Donald; *see* Manning, O. M.

SMITH, Col Rt. Hon. Sir Reginald Hugh D.; *see* Dorman-Smith.

SMITH, Reginald N. M.; *see* Marsh Smith.

SMITH, Prof. Richard Edwin; Professor of Ancient History, University of Manchester, 1953-74, Pro-Vice-Chancellor, 1971-74; *b* Moscow, 15 June 1910; *s* of James Ford Smith and Katherine Louise Smith (*née* Lunn); unmarried. *Educ:* Market Bosworth and Emmanuel Coll., Cambridge. Charles Oldham Classical Scholar, University of Cambridge, 1934. Assistant

Lecturer in Classics, University College, Nottingham, 1935-38; Lecturer in Ancient History, Trinity College, University of Toronto, 1938-41, Assistant Professor, 1941. Served War of 1939-45, with RCAF, 1941-45. Classical Tutor, Queens' Coll., Cambridge, 1945-46; Professor of Latin, University of Sydney, 1946-53. *Publications:* The Failure of the Roman Republic, 1955; Service in the post-Marian Roman Army, 1959; Cicero the Statesman, 1966; articles in Classical Quarterly, Classical Philology, Historia, Greece and Rome. *Address:* 113 Marlborough Park Central, Belfast, Northern Ireland BT9 6HP. *T:* Belfast 666677.   *[Died 12 April 1978.*

SMITH, Prof. Robert Allan, CBE 1960; PhD; FRS 1962; FRSE 1969; Principal Emeritus and Hon. Professor, Heriot-Watt University; *b* Kelso, Scotland, 14 May 1909; *s* of G. J. T. Smith; *m* 1934, Doris M. L. Ward; one *s* two *d. Educ:* Edinburgh Univ.; Cambridge University. Carnegie Research Fellow, St Andrews Univ., 1935-38; Lecturer, Reading Univ., 1939; Royal Radar Establishment, 1939-61 (Head of Physics Dept, 1947-61); Professor of Physics, Sheffield Univ., 1961-62; Professor of Physics, and First Director of Center of Materials, Science and Engineering, Mass Inst. of Technology, 1962-68; Principal and Vice-Chancellor, Heriot-Watt Univ., 1968-74. Hon. DSc Heriot-Watt, 1975. PRSE 1977-79. *Publications:* Radio Aids to Navigation, 1947; Aerials for Meter and Decimeter Wavelengths, 1949; The Physical Principles of Thermodynamics, 1952; The Detection and Measurement of Infra-Red Radiation, 1957; Semiconductors, 1959, 2nd edn 1978; The Wave Mechanics of Crystalline Solids, 1961, 2nd edn 1969. *Address:* 2/18 Succoth Court, Edinburgh EH12 6BZ. *Club:* New (Edinburgh).   *[Died 16 May 1980.*

SMITH, Robert Paterson; Chairman, The Burmah Oil Company Ltd, since 1965 (Managing Director, 1957-68); *b* 29 Jan. 1903; *s* of Thomas Smith; *m* 1935, Joyce Mary Whinney, *d* of F. T. Whinney; two *d. Educ:* The Ewart, Newton Stewart. Qualified Chartered Accountant, 1925; joined Asiatic Petroleum Co., Calcutta, 1926; Burmah-Shell, India, 1928-52; joined the Burmah Oil Company Ltd, London, 1952; appointed to Board of Directors, 1955; Asst Managing Director, 1956; Managing Director, 1957; Chairman, 1965. *Recreations:* fishing, gardening. *Address:* The Pound, East Blatchington, Seaford, Sussex. *T:* Seaford 3726. *Clubs:* City of London, Oriental.   *[Died 28 May 1971.*

SMITH, Sir Ross G.; see Grey-Smith.

SMITH, Samuel Harold, OBE 1943; MC 1917; Deputy-Chairman, Bucks Quarter Sessions, 1959-63; *b* 1888; 5th *s* of J. R. Smith, JP, The Priory, Windermere; *m* 1918, Gladys Leonora Smith; one *s* two *d. Educ:* The Leys Sch., Cambridge; Caius Coll., Cambridge. Scholar of Caius Coll., 1907 and Ramadge Research Student, 1911; LLB Cambridge, 1911. Called to the Bar, Inner Temple, 1913. Served European War, 1914-19 (despatches twice, MC); Major, 5th Bn Cheshire Regt; Staff Captain, 52nd Inf. Bde, 1916; DAAG XIII Corps, 1918. Lieut-Colonel, Deputy Director Army Welfare Services, 1940-44 (OBE). Rushcliffe Cttee on Legal Aid, 1943; Member of Lord Chancellor's Advisory Cttee on Legal Aid, 1950-64. Director, Legal Division, Allied Commission for Austria, 1947-48. JP Bucks, 1950; Chairman, Appeals Cttee, Bucks Quarter Sessions, 1955. Chairman, British Tin Investment Corp. Ltd, and subsidiary companies, 1953-63. French Croix de Guerre, 1917. *Address:* Highfield, Chalfont St Giles, Bucks. *T:* Chalfont St Giles 2019.   *[Died 31 Aug. 1971.*

SMITH, Sidney, LittD, FBA 1941; Professor Emeritus, University of London; *b* Aug. 1889; *m* Mary, *d* of H. W. Parker; one *s* one *d. Educ:* City of London Sch.; Queens' Coll., Cambridge (Scholar, Hon. Fellow, 1935). Director of Antiquities, Iraq, 1929-30; University of London: Prof. of Near Eastern Archæology, 1938-46; later Prof. of Ancient Semitic Languages; Hon. Fellow, School of Oriental and African Studies. Foreign Member Royal Flemish Acad. of Belgium. *Address:* Cawthorne, Barcombe, Lewes, East Sussex.   *[Died 12 June 1979.*

SMITH, Professor Stanley Alexander de; see de Smith.

SMITH, Stevie; (Florence Margaret Smith); author; *b* Hull, 20 Sept. 1902; has lived in London since the age of three; *yr d* of Charles Ward Smith and Ethel Rahel Spear. *Educ:* Palmers Green High Sch.; North London Collegiate Sch. Marchioness of Cholmondeley Poetry Award, 1966; Queen's Gold Medal for Poetry, 1969. *Publications:* novels: Novel on Yellow Paper, 1936, repr. 1969 (Penguin, 1951); Over the Frontier, 1938; The Holiday, 1949; *poems and drawings:* A Good Time Was Had By All, 1937; Tender Only to One, 1938; Mother, What is Man?,

1942; Harold's Leap, 1950; Not Waving But Drowning, 1957; Some Are More Human Than Others (Sketch-Book), 1958; Selected Poems, 1962; The Frog Prince and Other Poems, 1966; Penguin Modern Poets, No 8 (one of three poets), 1966; The Best Beast, 1969 (USA). Cats in Colour (captions and introd.), 1959; Poems for Children (anthology), 1970. Contrib. to Observer, Sunday Times, Times Literary Supplement, New Statesman, The Listener, various anthologies. Broadcasts poems on radio and TV. LP record (reading and singing her own poems), 1966; record with other poets, 1965; *posthumous publications:* Scorpion and other Poems, 1972; Collected Poems, 1975. *Address:* 1 Avondale Road, Palmers Green, N13. *T:* 01-886 4262.   *[Died 7 March 1971.*

SMITH, Stuart Hayne Granville; see Granville-Smith.

SMITH, Colonel Sir (Thomas) Eustace, Kt 1962; CBE 1956; TD 1943; DL 1955; JP 1946; Chairman, 1956-70 (Managing Director, 1952-65) of Smith's Dock Co. Ltd; *b* 8 Sept. 1900; *s* of Eustace Smith, Benton, Newcastle upon Tyne; *m* 1925, Sylvia May, *d* of late Captain W. E. Rogerson; three *d. Educ:* Eton. Served his time with R. and W. Hawthorn Leslie & Co. Ltd; joined Smith's Dock Co. Ltd, 1922, Director, 1928, Asst Managing Director, 1945, Joint Managing Director, 1948. Joined Northumberland Hussars, 1922, and in 1940 went with them to N. Africa. Later commanded 15th (Isle of Man) Light AA Regt in N. Africa and Italy and returned with them to England, 1944. Comd Northumberland Hussars for 3 years after cessation of hostilities (Hon. Colonel, 1957-62). President: NE Coast Instn of Engineers and Shipbuilders, 1952-53, and 1953-54; Shipbuilding Employers Fedn, 1953-54; Shipbuilding Conf., 1959-61; Chairman: NE Coast Ship-repairers' Assoc., 1955-56 and 1956-57; Dry Dock Owners & Repairers' Central Council, 1956-57; Tyne Shipbuilders Assoc., 1953-54 and 1954-55; Tees Conservancy Commn, 1957-67; British Ship Research Assoc., 1962-65; Tees and Hartlepools Port Authority, 1966-71. Is also Director: Cleveland Trust Ltd; North-Eastern Improved Dwellings Co. Ltd; Lloyds Bank Ltd (Newcastle upon Tyne Cttee). *Recreations:* shooting, fishing. *Address:* Barton Lodge, Barton, Richmond, Yorks. *T:* Barton 206. *Club:* Northern Counties (Newcastle upon Tyne).   *[Died 26 Nov. 1971.*

SMITH, Rev. Canon Thomas G.; see Grigg-Smith.

SMITH, Trafford, CMG 1952; HM Diplomatic Service, retired; Clerk to Hampstead Wells and Campden Trust, since 1971; *b* 1 Jan. 1912; *s* of John Frank Smith, Leicester; *m* 1937, Mary Isabel, *d* of A. Graham Smith, Cheltenham; two *d. Educ:* City of Leicester Sch.; Trinity Coll., Cambridge. Senior Scholar, State Scholar, Jeston Exhibitioner; BA 1933 (1st Class Parts I and II Mod. and Med. Langs Trip.); MA 1936. Asst Principal, Colonial Office, 1935; Asst Private Secretary to Mr Ormsby Gore (later Lord Harlech), 1937, to Mr Malcolm MacDonald, 1938; seconded to Fiji, 1938; Asst British Resident Commissioner, New Hebrides, 1940; served in British Solomon Islands, 1940, and Gilbert and Ellice Islands, 1941; Secretary, Soulbury Commn on Constitutional Reform, Ceylon, 1944-45; Asst Secretary, Colonial Office, 1945. Attached to UK Delegation to UN, New York, for Special General Assembly on Palestine, 1948; idc 1950; Lieutenant-Governor of Malta, 1953-59; Acting Governor, Malta, May-Sept., 1953, July-Sept. 1954; Assistant Under-Secretary of State, Commonwealth Office (previously Colonial Office), 1959-67; Ambassador to Burma, 1967-70. CStJ 1956. *Recreations:* chamber music, building, travel. *Address:* Flat 5, 3 Prince Arthur Road, NW3 6AX. *[Died 15 July 1975.*

SMITH, William Owen Lester, CBE 1947; *b* Llanbrynmair, Montgomeryshire, 4 Sept. 1888; *s* of late Henry Lester Smith, Halkyn Old Hall, Flintshire; *m* Rose (*d* 1970), *d* of J. Lloyd Evans, Warwick; no *c. Educ:* King's School, Chester; Merton Coll., Oxford (History Scholar); MA; Hon. LLD: Manchester, 1949; Wales, 1967. Assistant Director of Education, Warwickshire; Chief Organiser Elementary Education, Lancashire; Director of Education. Essex, 1924-31; Chief Education Officer, Manchester, 1931-49; Professor of Sociology of Education, University of London, 1949-53. *Publications:* Contributions to Encyclopædia Britannica; To Whom do Schools Belong?, 1942; Education in Great Britain, 1949; Impact of Education on Society, 1949; Education: An Introductory Survey, 1957; Government of Education, 1965. *Address:* 62 Rhos Road, Colwyn Bay, Clwyd LL28 4RY.   *[Died 4 May 1976.*

SMITH-GORDON, Sir Lionel Eldred Pottinger, 4th Bt, *cr* 1838; *b* 25 Nov. 1889; *o c* of 3rd Bt and Sophia Annie (*d* 1943), *o d* of Robert James Scott, BCS; *S* father, 1933; *m* 1st, 1913, Ellen, *e d* of late Senator Fletcher, USA (marr. diss.); no *c*; 2nd, 1933, Eileen Laura, *o c* of late Captain H. G. Adams-Connor, CVO,

DL; one *s. Educ:* Eton (KS); Trinity Coll., Oxford (MA). Served River Emergency Service (London), 1939-40; Temp. Lieut, RNVR, 1940-43. Commandeur du Tastevin, 1956. *Publications:* Rural Reconstruction in Ireland; Co-operation in Many Lands; Co-operation for Farmers; That Basilisk (novel); translations from the French: George Villiers, Duke of Buckingam (Erlanger); Mysterious Courier (Aulen). *Recreations:* travel, wine and food. *Heir: s* Lionel Eldred Peter Smith-Gordon [*b* 7 May 1935; *m* 1962, Sandra, *yr d* of late Wing Comdr W. R. Farley, DFC, and of Mrs Dennis Poore; one *s* one *d*]. *Address:* 9 Zetland House, Marloes Road, W8. *T:* 01-937 5655. *Clubs:* Naval; Vincent's (Oxford).   *[Died 6 Dec. 1976.*

SMITH-PEARSE, Thomas Lawrence, CIE 1944; MA; Indian Education Service; Principal Rajkumar College, Raipur, 1931-46; *b* 15 July 1893; *s* of late Rev. T. N. H. Smith-Pearse, MA, and late Mrs E. I. Smith-Pearse, JP, Launceston; *m* 1923, Katharine, *d* of late Brig.-General Sir Danvers Waghorn, CB, CMG, RE; one *s. Educ:* Marlborough Coll.; St John's Coll., Oxford. *Address:* White Hill, Wildhern, Andover, Hants. *T:* Hatherden 230.   *[Died 27 June 1972.*

SMITH-ROSE, Reginald Leslie, CBE 1952; DSc, PhD, FCGI, FIEE, FIRE; FIC; Director of Radio Research, Department of Scientific and Industrial Research, 1948-Sept. 1960; *b* 2 April 1894; *m* 1919, Elsie Masters; two *d. Educ:* Latymer Upper Sch., Hammersmith; Imperial College of Science, London Univ. Board of Education, Royal Schol. (1st Place) 1912; Imperial College, Governor's Prize in Physics (1st Place) 1914; London Univ.: BSc, Hons Physics, Cl. 1, 1914; PhD, Science, 1923; DSc, Science, 1926. Assistant Engineer, Siemens Bros Ltd, Woolwich, 1915-19. National Physical Laboratory: Scientific Officer, Electricity Div., 1919-33; Principal Scientific Officer, Radio Div., 1933-39; Supt Radio Div., 1939-47; acting Director, 1950 and 1956. Institution of Electrical Engineers: Chairman, Radio Section, 1942-43; Member Council, 1953-56, 1960-61; Vice-President, 1961-64; Fellow, Institute of Electrical and Electronics Engineers (USA) (Vice-President, 1948); FIEEE. Member, various scientific and technical committees of Government Departments and other Institutions; delegate to various international scientific radio conferences in various countries; President, Internat. Scientific Radio Union, 1960-63; Chairman, Study Group V, Internat. Radio Consultative Cttee, 1951-70 (CCIR Honours award at 50th anniversary celebration, June 1978, for technical contribs in radio wave propagation and leadership in work of CCIR, 1931-; Chm., CCIR Study Gp on Tropospheric Propagation, 1949-70); Secretary-General, Inter-Union Cttee on Frequency Allocations for Radio Astronomy and Space Research, 1961-73. Chairman, PMG's Frequency Advisory Cttee, 1960-; Member PMG's Cttee on Broadcasting, 1960. Coronation Medals, 1937, 1953; US Medal of Freedom with Silver Palm, 1947. *Publications:* many original papers published in Proc. of Royal and Phys. Societies, Instn Elect. Engrs, and elsewhere. *Address:* 21 Tumblewood Road, Banstead, Surrey.   *[Died 19 March 1980.*

SMITHERS, Sir Arthur Tennyson, Kt 1959; CBE 1949; company director; *b* 30 June 1894; *s* of late Frederick Smithers; *m* 1920, Constance Helen Wise, *d* of Andrew McIntosh Wise; two *d. Educ:* Eastleigh College, Prahran. Joined Victoria Treasury, 1911; proceeded through various positions till 1937, when appointed Permanent Head. Dir of Finance, Victoria, 1937-59, retd. Pres., Marine Board, 1964-69; Mem. Cttee of Management, Royal Melbourne Hosp., 1941-; Trustee, National Gallery of Victoria, 1945-; Director of the Elizabethan Theatre Trust, 1954-; Commissioner State Savings Bank of Victoria, 1955-. AASA. *Recreations:* music, golf. *Address:* 21 Sylverley Grove, Caulfield, Melbourne 3162, Australia. *T:* 53.2177. *Clubs:* Melbourne Cricket, Lawn Tennis Association of Victoria, Victoria Amateur Turf.   *[Died 28 June 1972.*

SMOLKA, H. P.; *see* Smollett, H. P.

SMOLLETT, Harry Peter, OBE 1944; author and journalist; *b* Vienna, 17 Sept. 1912; *s* of Albert V. Smolka and Vilma Wottitz; naturalised British subject since 1938; changed name to Smollett by deed poll in 1938, but continues to use Smolka as writer's name; *m* 1933, Lotte Jaeckl; two *s. Educ:* Vienna Gymnasium; University of Vienna; London School of Economics. London Correspondent Central European Newspapers and Central European Adviser to Exchange Telegraph Co. Ltd, 1934-38; Head of Foreign Dept, Exchange Telegraph Co., 1938-39; War Service, Min. of Information, 1939-45; Vienna Correspondent of The Times, 1947-49. Chairman and Managing Director: Vienna Metal Goods Manufacturing Co.; Vienna Metal Goods Trading Co.; Jt Man. Dir Tyrolia Metal and Sporting Goods Trading Co., Munich, Germany. Commercial Advisor to Pres. of Austria, 1973; Publisher of Austria Today (quarterly). Travels:

all European countries, USA, Mexico, USSR, Israel. *Publication:* 40,000 Against the Arctic. *Recreation:* chess. *Address:* Lindauergasse 9, A.1238 Vienna, Austria.
                                                  [Died 4 Nov. 1980.

SMOUT, Professor Charles Frederick Victor; Professor of Anatomy, University of Birmingham, 1948-61, retired; *b* 23 Oct. 1895; *s* of Thomas and Mary Elizabeth Smout; *m* 1923, Ethel May Butterworth; no *c. Educ:* King Edward's School, Birmingham, MB, ChB 1923; MRCS, LRCP 1923. MD (Birmingham) 1943. *Publications:* Anatomy for Students of Physiotherapy, 1943 (rev. 5th edn, Gynaecological and Obstetrical Anatomy, Descriptive and Applied, 1968); Basic Anatomy and Physiology, 1961; An Introduction to Midwifery, 1962; The Story of the Progress of Medicine, 1964; A Layman looks at life in general and at the Bible in particular, 1966. *Address:* 111 Touchwood Hall Close, off Lode Lane, Solihull, West Midlands B91 2UE. *T:* 021-704 4637. *Club:* University Staff (Birmingham).   *[Died 13 July 1978.*

SMYLY, Col Dennis Douglas Pilkington, DSO 1945; *b* 1913; *s* of late Major R. J. Smyly, OBE, Sweethay Court, Trull, Somerset; *m* 1939, Hon. Dorothy Margaret Berry, 3rd *d* of 1st and last Baron Buckland; three *s* one *d. Educ:* Sherborne; RMC Sandhurst. 2 Lt 16/5 Lancers, 1933; served War of 1939-45, North Africa, 1942-43; Italy (despatches), 1944-45; commanded 16/5 Lancers, 1944-47. Colonel 16/5 Queens Royal Lancers, 1959-69. JP Northants, 1955-67; High Sheriff Northants, 1961; DL Northants, 1965-68; JP Glos, 1969-75. *Address:* 120 Marsham Court, Marsham Street, SW1. *T:* 01-834 5276. *Club:* Cavalry and Guards.   *[Died 8 May 1979.*

SMYTH, Prof. David Henry, FRS 1967; Professor of Physiology, Sheffield University, 1946-73, now Emeritus; Pro-Vice-Chancellor, 1962-66; Chairman, Research Defence Society, since 1977; *b* 9 Feb. 1908; *s* of late Joseph Smyth, Lisburn, Co. Antrim; *m* 1942, Edith Mary Hoyle; no *c. Educ:* Royal Belfast Academical Institution; Queen's Univ., Belfast. QUB: BSc 1929; MB, BCh 1932; MSc 1934; MD 1935; PhD London, 1940. RMO Royal Victoria Hospital, Belfast, 1932; Demonstrator in Physiology, Belfast, 1933; Musgrave Student in Physiology at Göttingen, Germany, 1936; Lectr in Physiology, University Coll., London, 1937. Mem. Editorial Bd, Journal of Physiology, 1961-68 (Chm., 1966-68). Chm., British Nat. Cttee for Physiology, 1974-; Foreign Sec., Physiological Soc., 1972-. Leverhulme Emeritus Fellow, 1973-75. Robert Campbell Memorial Orator, Ulster Med. Soc., 1968. Hon. DSc Belfast, 1976. *Publications:* Alternatives to Animal Experiments, 1978; papers in Journal of Physiology, Quarterly Journal of Experimental Physiology, Biochemical Journal, British Medical Journal, 1934-73. *Recreations:* pedigree dogs, music. *Address:* The Swevic, Foolow, Eyam, Sheffield S30 1QD. *T:* Tideswell 871330. *Club:* Kennel.   *[Died 10 Sept. 1979.*

SMYTH, John Andrew, MD, BSc, DPH; Hon. Consultant Physician, formerly Physician, Royal Victoria Hospital, Belfast; *b* 27 Jan. 1893; *s* of Rev. James and Mary Frances Dill Smyth; *m* Viola May Millar; one *s* two *d. Educ:* Royal School, Dungannon; Queen's Univ., Belfast. BSc Engineering, with first place, 1914; MB, BCh, BAO with first class hons, first place, and specially awarded Exhibition, QUB, 1921; DPH first place; MD with gold medal, 1923; served European War, France, 1915-16; Life Fellow Ulster Medical Society (Pres., 1954-55); Pres. Irish Br., Assoc. of Clinical Pathologists, 1954-55; Chm. Belfast Br., Diabetic Assoc., 1954-55; Mem., Assoc. of Clinical Pathologists. *Publications:* Serum Diagnosis of Syphilis (jointly), Medical Research Council Report Series No 78; Diabetes: Past, Present and Future, Ulster Medical Journal, 1954, etc. *Address:* 23 University Square, Belfast BT7 1PB, Northern Ireland. *T:* Belfast 24061; Trench House, Ballyaughlis, Lisburn, N Ireland. *T:* Drumbo 207.   *[Died 1 June 1971.*

SMYTH, Captain Sir Philip Weyland Bowyer-, 14th Bt, *cr* 1661; RN retired; *b* 4 Feb. 1894; *s* of late Clement Weyland Bowyer-Smijth, *b* of 13th Bt, and Maud, *d* of W. Gray, Sydney, NSW; *S* uncle, 1927; *m* 1922, Margaret Joan, OBE 1952, TD (marr. diss. 1951), *o d* of late S. McCall-McCowan, Sydney; no *c*; *m* 1951, Veronica Mary, 2nd *d* of Capt. C. W. Bower, DSC, RN retd, Fordwich, Kent; one *s* one *d.* Naval Attaché at Rome, 1939-40; ADC to the King, 1946; retired list, 1946. *Heir: s* Thomas Weyland Bowyer-Smyth, *b* 25 June 1960. *Address:* La Provençale, 06870 Plascassier, France. *Club:* Royal Yacht Squadron.   *[Died 29 Nov. 1978.*

SMYTH-PIGOTT, Group Captain (Joseph) Ruscombe (Wadham), CBE 1942; DSO 1915; late RAF; *b* 1889; *y s* of late Cecil Hugh Smyth-Pigott, Brockley Court, Somerset; *m* 1919, Lady Clare Feilding (*d* 1966), 5th *d* of 9th Earl of Denbigh; one

d. Educ: Oratory School; Dartmouth. Entered RN 1905; served European War (despatches, DSO and bar, Croix de Guerre); retired list, RAF 1934; served with RAF again, 1939. *Address:* c/o National Westminster Bank, Farnborough, Hants.
[Died 8 Oct. 1971.

SMYTHIES, Evelyn Arthur, CIE 1939; *b* 19 March 1885; *s* of Arthur Smythies, IFS, and Gertrude Aston; *m* 1911, Olive Muriel Cripps (*d* 1961); two *s. Educ:* Cheltenham College; Balliol College, Oxford. Indian Forest Service, 1908; Chief Conservator of Forests, United Provinces, India, 1937-40; Forest Adviser to the Nepal Govt, 1940-46. *Publications:* books and articles on technical forestry, sport, philately. *Recreations:* gardening, bridge, philately. *Address:* Castle Morris, Tralee, Eire.   *[Died 10 Jan. 1975.*

SNAITH, Stanley, FLA; author and librarian; Borough Librarian, Bethnal Green Public Libraries, 1950-65; *b* Kendal, 16 Dec. 1903; *e s* of J. W. Snaith, JP, and Margaret Tebay. Held senior posts in the Kendal, Kingston-upon-Thames and Islington public libraries. Local Secretary, Ministry of Information, 1940-42; HM Forces (Heavy Anti-Aircraft Batteries), 1942-46. *Publications:* April Morning, 1926; A Flying Scroll, 1928; The Silver Scythe, 1933; North, 1934; Fieldfaring, 1935; London Pageant, 1935; Men Against Peril, 1936; Green Legacy, 1937; Modern Poetry (A Bibliography), 1937; At Grips with Everest, 1937; Alpine Adventure, 1944; Stormy Harvest, 1944 (chosen as an Ambassador Book to the USA); The Inn of Night, 1946; The Flowering Thorn, 1946; (with George F. Vale) Bygone Bethnal Green, 1948; The Naked Mountain, 1949; The Common Festival, 1950; The Mountain Challenge, 1952; The Siege of the Matterhorn, 1957; The Books in My Life, 1957; The Special Shelf, 1958; The Lost Road, 1968; *poems:* Nanga Parbat, awarded Shirley Carter Greenwood Prize, 1949; Homage to Rilke and The Hawthorn in the Bombed Church, awarded 1st Prize, Nat. Shakespearian Sonnets Competition, 1964; scripts for BBC, and numerous papers and pamphlets on antiquarian matters; texts for two pageants; contributor to Oxford Junior Encyclopædia, Encyclopædia Britannica, and to many anthologies and periodicals. *Recreations:* reading, music. *Address:* 17 Newton Rise, Swanage, Dorset.   *[Died 19 Dec. 1976.*

SNOW, Baron *cr* 1964 (Life Peer); **Charles Percy Snow,** Kt 1957; CBE 1943; writer; *b* 15 Oct. 1905; *m* 1950, Pamela Hansford Johnson; one *s. Educ:* Alderman Newton's Sch., Leicester; Univ. Coll., Leicester; Christ's Coll., Cambridge. Parly Sec., Min. of Technology, 1964-66. Fellow, Churchill Coll., Cambridge; Hon. Fellow, Christ's Coll., Cambridge. Foreign Mem., American Academy-Institute; hon. doctorates, and other awards, from American, Canadian, English, Scottish and Soviet universities, colleges and academies, inc. NY Univ. and Louisville, 1976, Pace, 1977, Widener, 1978, Union, 1979. *Publications: novels:* Death Under Sail, 1932; New Lives for Old, 1933; The Search, 1934 (revised and republished, 1958); occupied, 1935-70, with novel-sequence of eleven volumes (general title, Strangers and Brothers): George Passant, 1940; The Light and the Dark, 1947; Time of Hope, 1949; The Masters, 1951; The New Men, 1954 (James Tait Black Memorial Prize, awarded in conjunction with The Masters); Homecomings, 1956; The Conscience of the Rich, 1958; The Affair, 1960; Corridors of Power, 1964; The Sleep of Reason, 1968; Last Things, 1970; The Malcontents, 1972; In Their Wisdom, 1974; A Coat of Varnish, 1979; *non-fiction:* The Two Cultures and the Scientific Revolution (Rede Lecture), 1959; Science and Government (Godkin Lectures), 1961; Appendix to Science and Government, 1962; The Two Cultures and a Second Look, 1964; Variety of Men, 1967; Public Affairs, 1971; The Realists, 1978; *critical biography:* Trollope, 1975; *plays:* View over the Park, produced Lyric, Hammersmith, 1950; The Affair (adapted by Ronald Millar), Strand, 1961-62; The New Men (adapted by Ronald Millar), Strand, 1962; The Masters (adapted by Ronald Millar), Savoy, Piccadilly, 1963-64; Time of Hope (adapted by Arthur and Violet Ketels), Philadelphia, 1963; The Case in Question (adapted from In Their Wisdom by Ronald Millar), Haymarket, 1975. *Address:* 85 Eaton Terrace, SW1. *Clubs:* Garrick, Savile, MCC; Century (NY).   *[Died 1 July 1980.*

SNOW, Edgar Parks; journalist, author, US; *b* Kansas City, Mo, 19 July 1905; *s* of James Edgar Parks Snow and Anna Katherine Fogarty Edelmann; *m* 1932, Helen Foster (pen-name, Nym Wales) (marr. diss. 1949); *m* 1949, Lois Anne Wheeler; one *s* one *d. Educ:* Univ. of Missouri. Began as reporter, Kansas City Star; travelled as free-lance writer, worked as sailor; went to China, 1928, became Asst Editor China Weekly Review, Shanghai; correspondent Chicago Tribune, 1929-30; corr. Ch. Daily News-NY Sun, 1931-34; corr. Daily Herald (London), 1932-39; corr. Saturday Evening Post, 1933-51. Covered major Asiatic events,

1931-34; lecturer, Yenching Univ., Peking, 1933-35; accredited US and British war corr., 1942-46, assigned China-Burma-India, 1942; Britain, 1943; Russia, Poland, Rumania, 1943-44; France, Germany, Austria, 1945; interviewed Mao Tse-tung, 1936 (first corr. to do so), 1965, 1970. First American corr. to enter liberated Vienna. Visited India, Burma, Siam, Indo-China, Philippines, Japan, Korea, 1945-46; in Europe again, 1947. Associate Editor for Saturday Evening Post, 1943-52; Special Research Consultant, Harvard Univ., 1956-57; Special Correspondent in People's Rep. of China for Look Magazine, 1960; revisited China, 1964-65, 1970-71 (corresp. for Epoca, etc). Photogr. and prod documentary film, One Fourth of Humanity: China, 1936-69. *Publications:* Far Eastern Front, 1934; Living China, 1936; Red Star Over China, 1937; Scorched Earth, 1941; People On Our Side, 1943; Pattern of Soviet Power, 1945; Stalin Must Have Peace, 1947; Random Notes on Red China, 1957; Journey to the Beginning, 1958; The Other Side of the River: Red China Today, 1963; Talks with Mao Tse-tung and Other Rebels, 1965-71, 1972. *Recreations:* swimming, tennis, ski-ing. *Address:* Mafroi 11, Nyon, Vaud, Switzerland. *Clubs:* National Press (Washington, DC); Overseas Press (NY); Nyon Tennis.   *[Died 15 Feb. 1972.*

SNOW, Sir Frederick (Sidney), Kt 1965; CBE 1958 (OBE 1954); Founder, Frederick S. Snow & Partners, 1942; *b* 14 Feb. 1899; *s* of William Snow, London; *m* 1924, Rosetta Elizabeth, *d* of Edmund Brown, Colchester; two *s. Educ:* Brownhill Sch., Catford. Founded firm of Frederick S. Snow & Partners, Consulting Engineers, London, Newcastle and Norwich, 1942. Designer of International Airports, Jerusalem, Amman, Gatwick, Kuwait. Authority on industrial structures, heavy foundation and underpinning problems. Pres., IStructE, 1948; Pres., Sect. Britannique, Société des Ingénieurs Civils de France, 1955; President, Reinforced Concrete Assoc., 1956; 1st Pres., the Concrete Society, 1966. Member, Permanent Cttee of Internat. Assoc. for Bridge and Structural Engineering; served on all major building and civil engineering cttees of BSI. Pres., Eastbourne Saffron Sports Club, 1974. Master, Worshipful Co. of Glaziers and Painters of Glass, 1972. Governor, Hammersmith College of Art and Building; Life Vice-Pres., Guild of Surveyors. Hon. LLD Leeds, 1974. Awarded Istiqlal Medal, 1968. Chevalier Legion d'Honneur, 1969. *Publications:* Foundations of London Structures, 1936; Human Needs and the Engineer, 1942; The De Havilland Airfield, Hatfield, 1949; The Development of Gatwick Airport, 1960; Formwork for Modern Structures, 1965. *Address:* 703 Raleigh House, Dolphin Square, SW1V 3NR. *Club:* City Livery.   *[Died 5 June 1976.*

SNOW, Rt. Rev. George D'Oyly; *b* 2 Nov. 1903; *s* of Lt-Gen. Sir Thomas D'Oyly Snow, KCB, KCMG, and Charlotte Geraldine Coke; *m* 1942, Joan Monica, *y d* of late Maj. Henry J. Way, VD; three *s. Educ:* Winchester College; Oriel College, Oxford. Assistant Master at Eton College, 1925-36; ordained, 1933; Chaplain at Charterhouse, 1936-46; Headmaster of Ardingly College, Sussex, 1946-61; Prebend of Chichester Cathedral, 1959-61; Suffragan Bishop of Whitby, 1961-71; Rural Dean, Purbeck, 1973-76. Chairman National Society, 1963-73. Chaplain to retired clergy and widows in Dorset Archdeaconry, 1976-. *Publications:* A Guide to Prayer, 1932; A Guide to Belief, 1935; A School Service Book, 1936; A Guide to Confirmation, 1936; Our Father, 1938; Letters to a Confirmand, 1946; Into His Presence, 1946; The Public School in the New Age, 1959; Forth in His Name, 1964. *Recreations:* gardening, D-I-Y, caravan camping, music. *Address:* Meadow Cottage, Corfe Castle, Wareham, Dorset. *T:* Corfe Castle 589. *[Died 17 Nov. 1977.*

SNOW, Sir Harold (Ernest), Kt 1961; CBE 1952 (OBE 1946); Director (later Deputy Chairman and Managing Director) British Petroleum Co. Ltd, 1952-62, retired; *b* 8 Sept. 1897; *s* of Ernest Alfred Snow and Elizabeth Hannah Snow (*née* May); *m* 1924. Nell Dagmar Goodale; one *s* one *d. Educ:* Merchant Ventures Sch., Bristol; Bristol Univ.; St John's Coll., Cambridge. A Wrangler in the Mathematics Tripos, 1921. Joined British Petroleum Co. Ltd, 1921; Group Manager, Shell-Mex and BP Ltd, 1932-36; Sec., Petroleum Board, 1939-45; Dep. Dir, Anglo-Iranian Oil Co. Ltd, 1946; Man. Dir, Anglo-Iranian Oil Co. Ltd (now the British Petroleum Co. Ltd), 1952. British Member of Internat. Consortium Mission which negotiated Oil Agreement with Iran, 1954. *Recreations:* gardening, music. *Address:* 29a Dene Road, Northwood, Middlesex. *T:* Northwood 21552.
[Died 20 Dec. 1971.

SNOWDEN, Joseph Stanley; *b* 16 Oct. 1901; *e s* of late Joseph Snowden, JP, and late Fanny Ruth Snowden, Morecambe and Heysham; *m* 1938, Agnes Enid Mitchell; no *c. Educ:* Sedbergh; St John's Coll., Cambridge. Law Tripos (Cantab) 1923 (BA, LLB); called to the Bar, Inner Temple, 1925; joined North-Eastern Circuit, 1925; Dep. Chm., W Riding of Yorks QS, 1960-

71. Contested (L) Bradford East Div., 1945 and 1950, Dewsbury Div., 1951 and 1955, Pudsey Div., 1959. Recorder of Scarborough, 1951-71; a Recorder, and hon. Recorder of Scarborough, 1972-73. Chairman, Yorkshire and Lancashire Agricultural Land Tribunal, 1963-71. *Recreation:* politics. *Address:* Oakburn, 20 St James Road, Ilkley, West Yorkshire LS29 9PY. *T:* Ilkley 609401.   *[Died 22 Jan. 1980.*

SOAME, Sir Charles Burnett Buckworth-Herne-, 11th Bt *cr* 1697; late King's Shropshire Light Infantry; *b* 26 Sept. 1894; *s* of 10th Bt and Mary, *d* of John Edge and widow of P. B. Pring; *S* father, 1931; *m* 1924, Elsie May (*d* 1972), *d* of Walter Alfred Lloyd, Coalbrookdale, Salop; one *s* one *d.* Served European War, 1914-16 (wounded). *Heir: s* Charles John Buckworth-Herne-Soame [*b* 28 May 1932; *m* 1958, Eileen Margaret Mary, *d* of Leonard Minton; one *s*]. *Address:* Sheen Cottage, Coalbrookdale, Salop.   *[Died 20 April 1977.*

SOAR, Joseph, MBE 1947; DL; MusD Cantuar, MusB Dunelm, ARCM, FRCO, Hon. ARCM; Organist and Master of the Choristers, St David's Cathedral, 1922-54, Emeritus 1954; *b* 9 Oct. 1878; *s* of late M. Soar, MIME, Housley Park, Sheffield; *m* 1st, 1909, Mary Dulcie (*d* 1927), *e d* of late Sir Edwin Thomas Ann, JP, Derby; 2nd, 1934, Janet (*d* 1951), *d* of late Rev. David Williams, Rector of Clydey, Pembs. *Educ:* privately; Royal College of Music (twice Council Exhibitioner); Temple Church (under Sir Walford Davies). Music Master, Barnsley Grammar Sch.; Conductor: Tankersley Choral Society, Barnsley Operatic Society, and St Cecilia Choral Soc., 1904-15; Organist: Parish Church, Chapeltown, Sheffield, 1892; St John's Clapham, 1898; Derby Cathedral, 1901; Parish Church, Barnsley, 1904; Halifax, 1912; Burnham-on-Sea, 1921. Served 1915-21, Gallipoli, Western Front of Egypt, India; Lieut IARO; Officer in Charge, Supply and Transport Depôt, Poona and Trimulgherry. Examiner and Member of Council, Royal College of Organists, 1933-46; President National Eisteddfod, Abergwaun, 1936; Hon. Sec., St David's Life-Boat, 1926- (Bronze Medal, RNLBI, 1943); Hon. Life Governor, RNLI, 1960. Commandant Special Constabulary, 1940-44; County Pres., British Legion, Pembrokeshire; DL, Pembrokeshire, 1952. *Publications:* church music, songs, pianoforte pieces. *Recreations:* Life-boat and British Legion. *Address:* Swn y Mor, St David's, Pembrokeshire. *T:* 277.   *[Died 9 June 1971.*

SOBHA SINGH, Hon. Sardar Bahadur Sir Sardar, Kt, *cr* 1944; OBE 1938; landlord, millowner and contractor; Member of the Council of State, Delhi; Chairman, Nerbudda Valley Refrigeration Products Co. Ltd, Bhopal; Director: Machinery Manufacturers Corp. Ltd, Bombay, and several other leading Indian firms; *b* 1890; *m* Shrimati Wariam Kaur; four *s* one *d.* Member Indian Overseas League. *Address:* Baikunth, New Delhi 11, India. *Clubs:* Delhi Gymkhana, Chelmsford (New Delhi); Cricket Club of India (Bombay).   *[Died April 1978.*

SOKHEY, Maj.-Gen. Sir Sahib Singh, Kt 1946; Member, Panel of Scientists, Indian Planning Commission, since 1956; Adviser, Council of Scientific and Industrial Research, New Delhi, since 1961; *b* 15 Dec. 1887; *s* of Sardar Jwala Singh Sokhey; *m* 1914, Leila Roy (Menaka, celebrated Indian danseuse), *d* of P. L. Roy of East Bengal. *Educ:* Punjab Univ. (BSc 1907); Edinburgh Univ. (MB, ChB 1911, MA 1912, MD 1925); Trinity Coll., Cambridge; Johns Hopkins Univ.; Harvard Medical Sch.; Toronto Univ. Joined Indian Medical Service, 1913. Served European War, 1914-19; France, Belgium, Mesopotamia and Egypt; Rockefeller Foundation Fellow, 1923-25. Director, Haffkine Institute, Bombay, 1932-49; Asst Director-General, WHO, 1950-52; Member, Indian Parliament (Rajya Sabha), 1952-56; President, Assoc. of Scientific Workers of India, 1953-58; Founder Fellow Nat. Inst. of Sciences of India and Indian Acad. of Sciences. International Lenin Peace Prize, 1953. *Publications:* scientific papers in various journals. *Address:* Council of Scientific and Industrial Research, 2-Rafi Marg, New Delhi, India; National and Grindlays Bank, Lloyds Branch, PO Box 48, Dr Dadabhoy Naoroji Road, Bombay 1, India.   *[Died 23 Oct. 1971.*

SOMERVELL, Theodore Howard, OBE 1953; MA, MB, BCh; FRCS; medical missionary, retired; *b* 16 April 1890; *s* of William Henry Somervell of Brantfield, Kendal; *m* 1925, Margaret, *d* of Sir James Hope Simpson; three *s. Educ:* Rugby; Caius Coll., Cambridge; University College Hospital. Captain, RAMC (TF), BEF in France, 1915-18 (despatches); Kaisar-i-Hind Gold Medal, 1938; joined Mount Everest Expedition in 1922 and again in 1924; Medical Missionary, Neyyoor, Travancore, under London Missionary Society, 1923-49 and at Vellore, 1949-61; retired, 1961. *Publications:* After Everest, 1936; Knife and Life in India, 1939; The Surgery of the Stomach and Duodenum, 1948; The Good News, 1950; articles on mountaineering and

surgical subjects. *Recreations:* painting, music. *Address:* Sykefold, Ambleside, Cumbria. *T:* 3303. *Club:* Alpine.
                       [Died 23 Jan. 1975.

SONTAG, Raymond James; Ehrman Professor of History, University of California, since 1941; *b* 2 Oct. 1897; *s* of Anthony Charles Sontag and Mary Walsh; *m* 1927, Dorothea Agar (*d* 1965); three *s* one *d. Educ:* Univ. of Illinois; Univ. of Pennsylvania. BS 1920, MA 1921, Illinois; PhD Pennsylvania, 1924. Instructor to H. C. Lea Professor, and Chm., Dept of History, Princeton University, 1939-41; Chief, German War Documents Project, Department of State, US, 1946-49; Pres., American Catholic Historical Assoc., 1952; Pres., Pacific Coast Branch, Amer. Hist. Assoc., 1959. LittD Marquette, USA, 1959; LLD: Notre Dame, USA, 1960; California, 1966. *Publications:* The Middle Ages (with Dana C. Munro), 1928; European Diplomatic History, 1932; Germany and England, 1848-1894, 1938; A Broken World, 1919-1939, 1971; (ed. with J. S. Beddie) Nazi-Soviet Relations, 1939-41, 1948; Documents on German Foreign Policy, 1918-45 (American editor-in-chief), 1949. *Address:* University of California, Berkeley, Calif 94720, USA.
                       [Died 27 Oct. 1972.

SOOTHILL, Ronald Gray; Chairman, Turner and Newall Ltd, 1959-67, Hon. President, 1967-73; *b* 19 Aug. 1890; *o s* of late Rev. Alfred Soothill, BA, Headmaster of Ashville College, Harrogate, and late H. E. Soothill (*née* Gray); *m* 1926, Thelma, *e d* of late Edwin James Bird. *Educ:* Ashville College, Harrogate; Mill Hill; Jesus Coll., Cambridge (MA). Officer in Royal Artillery, 1917-18. Cadbury Bros Ltd, 1922-28; Turner and Newall Ltd, 1928-73: Dir, 1942-69; Jt Man. Dir, 1949; Dep. Chm., 1958. Director: District Bank Ltd, 1959-69; Royal Insurance Co. Ltd, 1960-71; Liverpool & London & Globe Insurance Co. Ltd, 1960-71; London & Lancashire Insurance Co. Ltd, 1962-71; Tube Investments Ltd, 1963-68; William Mallinson and Sons Ltd, 1957-70. Mem., Cttee of Inquiry into Shipping, 1967-70; Mem. Ct, Manchester Univ., 1959-72; Chm. of Governors, Ashville Coll., Harrogate, 1957-75; Vice-Pres., Nat. Assoc. for Care and Resettlement of Offenders. *Address:* Manor Beeches, Maids Moreton, Buckingham. *T:* Buckingham 2014. *Club:* Bath.   *[Died 18 Aug. 1980.*

SOPOUSHEK, Mrs Jan; see Greig, Maysie.

SORENSEN, Baron, *cr* 1964 (Life Peer); **Reginald William Sorensen;** a Lord in Waiting, 1965-68; *b* Islington, 19 June 1891; *s* of William James Sorensen, silversmith (*s* of a Dane), and Alice (*née* Peace), *d* of Sussex fisherman; *m* 1916, Muriel, JP, *d* of Rev. W. Harvey Smith; one *s* one *d* (and one *s* decd). *Educ:* Elementary Sch.; later studied for four years in a religious community. Employed in factory, office, and shop; Ex-Minister Free Christian Church, Walthamstow; experimented with Essex farming community; Vice-Pres. Leyton Labour Party; Ex-Member, Walthamstow UDC and Essex CC; Ex-Chm., Walthamstow Educn Cttee; Labour candidate for Southampton, 1923 and 1924; MP (Lab) West Leyton, 1929-31; contested (Lab) Lowestoft By-Election, 1934; MP (Lab) West Leyton, 1935-50, Leyton, 1950-64. Chairman: India League; World Congress of Faiths; STRIVE. Vice-Pres., Indo-British Forum; President: Indo-British Parly Gp; International Friendship League; Josephine Butler Soc.; Treasurer, "Help the Aged"; Mem., Parly Deputation to India, Jan. 1946; toured USA and Canada, 1948, 1952, 1957, USA 1969, Nigeria, 1949 and 1960, Far East, 1954; with Commonwealth Parly Assoc.; Deputation, the Yemen, 1958; Inter-Parly Union Delegn to Venezuela, 1960; visited West Indies and Ghana, 1960, India and Malaysia, 1961, India, 1963, Israel and Jordan, 1966. Freeman of Borough of Leyton, 1958. Grand Cross of the Order of Merit of the Federal German Republic, 1963. *Publications:* God and Bread; Men or Sheep; The New Generation; Tolpuddle; India and The Atlantic Charter; For Sanity and Humanity; My Impressions of India; Earthquake, Wind and Fire; The Liberty of the Subject; Aden, the Protectorates and the Yemen, I Believe in Man, etc. *Address:* 38 Woodside Park Avenue, Whipps Cross, Walthamstow. *T:* 01-520 5324.   *[Died 8 Oct. 1971.*

SORLEY, Air Marshal Sir Ralph Squire, KCB, *cr* 1944 (CB 1942); OBE 1936; DSC 1918; DFC 1920; FRAeS; FRSA; *b* 9 Jan. 1898; *s* of late James Graham and Ellen Merson Sorley; *m* 1925, Mary Eileen Gayford; two *d. Educ:* University School, Hastings. Joined RNAS 1914 and served in RAF in Great Britain; No 6 Squadron, Iraq; No 14 Squadron, Palestine; No 8 Squadron, Aden. Later considerably devoted to the development of aircraft. Assistant Chief of Air Staff (Technical Requirements), 1941; Controller of Research and Development, Ministry of Aircraft Production, 1943-45; Member of Air Council; Member of Aircraft Supply Council; AOC-in-C Technical Training Command, 1945-48; retd from RAF, 1948.

Man. Dir, De Havilland Propellors Ltd, Hatfield, 1948-60. *Address:* Littlecott Mill, Enford, Wilts. *Club:* Royal Air Force.
[*Died* 17 Nov. 1974.

SORRELL, Alan, RWS 1941; ARCA 1927; Chichester Diocesan Artist Craftsman, 1952; painter and designer; *b* 11 Feb. 1904; *s* of Ernest and Edith Sorrell; *m* 1947, Elizabeth Tanner; two *s* one *d. Educ:* Royal Coll. of Art; British School at Rome. Rome Scholarship in Painting, 1928; Senior Assistant Instructor of Drawing, RCA, 1931-39 and 1946-48. Served War in RAF, 1939-46. Works in permanent collections: Tate Gall., Imp. War Mus., Nat. Mus. of Wales, London Mus.; Manchester, Sheffield, Liverpool, Bradford, Ashmolean Mus., Magdalen College, Oxford, Southend, etc, and in many private collections. Exhibitor Royal Academy, Royal Watercolour Society; numerous one-man shows; mural decorations at Liverpool, Southend-on-Sea, Harlow (New Town), Bexhill, Cecil Rhodes Memorial Museum, Bishops Stortford (The Oxford Room), Warwick Oken Secondary Modern School (The Seasons), Roman House, London (Londinium Romanum), and for Festival of Britain. Progress Paintings of Hinkley Point Atomic Power Station. Drawings of Nubia, 1962; Drawings of Oxford, 1964. Exhibitions: Sorrell Family, 1970; Reading, 1973. An authority on Roman Britain, and responsible for numerous important archæological reconstructions for Ministry of Works, many Museums, and various publications. Drawings extensively used in TV programmes. *Publications:* (with Aileen Fox) Roman Britain, 1961; (with J. R. C. Hamilton) Saxon England, 1964; Living History, 1965; (with Henry Loyn) Norman Britain, 1966; (with E. B. Green) Prehistoric Britain, 1967; Roman London, 1968; (with Margaret S. Drower) Nubia: a drowning land, 1970; (with Anthony Birley) Imperial Rome, 1970; illustrations to the Bible, 1970; British Castles, 1973; Roman Towns in Britain, 1974; various essays on drawing, painting and travel. *Recreations:* reading and writing. *Address:* Thors Mead, 185 Daws Heath Road, Thundersley, Benfleet, Essex SS7 2TF. *T:* Southend-on-Sea 557431.   [*Died* 21 Dec. 1974.

SORSBY, Arnold, CBE 1966; MD, FRCS; Consultant Adviser, Ministry of Health, 1966-71; Editor, Journal of Medical Genetics, 1964-69; Research Professor in Ophthalmology, Royal College of Surgeons and Royal Eye Hospital, 1943-66; Emeritus Professor, 1966; Hon. Director, Wernher Research Unit on Ophthalmological Genetics, Medical Research Council, 1953-66; Vice-President, Internat. Organization against Trachoma, 1951-68; Member, Expert Advisory Panel on Trachoma, WHO, 1953-68; *b* 10 June 1900; *m* Charmaine Sorsby. *Educ:* Leeds Univ. Consultant, WHO, 1969-70. Hon. DSc. Sir Arthur Keith Medal (RCS), 1966; Grimshaw Award (Nat. Fedn of the Blind), 1968. *Publications:* (ed) Tenements of Clay, 1974; Diseases of the Funus Oculi, 1976; books and papers on ophthalmology, genetics and on medical history. *Address:* 52 Cardinal Court, Grand Avenue, Worthing, West Sussex BN11 5NL. *T:* Worthing 40607.   [*Died* 6 May 1980.

SOSKICE, Frank; *see* Stow Hill, Baron.

SOTHERS, Donald Bevan, CIE 1944; Chief Conservator Forests, Bombay (retired); *b* 11 March 1889; *s* of George Henry Sothers; *m* 1922, Dorothy, *d* of A. G. Edie, CIE; one *s* one *d. Educ:* Reading School; St John's College, Oxford. Joined Indian Forest Service, 1911; War Service, 1915-18, IARO attached 114th Mahrattas, Mesopotamia; Conservator Forests, 1932; Chief Conservator, 1942; re-employed as Land Development Officer, Bombay, 1944-46. *Recreations:* shooting, golf. *Address:* Pinehurst, Box Hill, near Mickleham, Dorking, Surrey.
[*Died* 4 Dec. 1979.

SOULBURY, 1st Viscount, *cr* 1954, 1st Baron, *cr* 1941, of Soulbury; **Herwald Ramsbotham;** PC 1939; GCMG, *cr* 1949; GCVO, *cr* 1954; OBE 1919; MC; *b* 6 March 1887; *s* of late Herwald Ramsbotham, of 47 Hyde Park Gate, SW7, and late Ethel Margaret, *d* of T. Bevan, DL, JP, Stone Park, Greenhithe, Kent; *g s* of James Ramsbotham, JP, Crowborough Warren, Sussex (formerly of Old Hall, Stand, Lancs), and Jane, *d* of Joshua Fielden, Waterside, Todmorden; *m* 1st, 1911, Doris Violet (*d* 1954), *d* of late S. de Stein, London, W8; two *s* one *d*; 2nd, 1962, Mrs Ursula Wakeham (*d* 1964), London, W1, *widow* of Frederick Wakeham and *d* of late Armand and Helen Jerome. *Educ:* Uppingham; University Coll., Oxford (MA). Double First in Honours School, Oxford (First Class Hon. Mods, First Class Lit. Hum.); called to Bar, 1911; served European War, 1914-18 (OBE, MC, despatches thrice); contested Lancaster Div., Dec. 1910, and by-election, 1928; MP (C) Lancaster Div., 1929-41; Parly Sec., Bd of Educn, 1931-35; Parly Sec., Min. of Agr. and Fisheries, 1935-36; Minister of Pensions, 1936-39; First Comr of Works, 1939-40; Pres., Bd of Educn, 1940-41; Chm. of Assistance Bd, 1941-48; of the Burnham Cttees, 1942-49;

Governor-Gen., Ceylon, 1949-54; Chm. of Ceylon Commn, 1944; Pres. Classical Assoc. 1948. Chm., Bd of Govs of Royal Ballet School, 1956-64. Hon. LLD University of Ceylon; Hon. Fellow, University College, Oxford. KStJ. *Recreation:* fishing. *Heir: s* Hon. James Herwald Ramsbotham [*b* 21 March 1915; *m* 1949, Anthea Margaret Wilton (*d* 1950)]. *Address:* East Lane, Ovington, near Alresford, Hampshire. *T:* Alresford 115. *Club:* Carlton.   [*Died* 30 Jan. 1971.

SOUTHCOTT, Rev. Canon Ernest William; Canon Emeritus of Southwark Cathedral; Vicar of St Peter and St Paul, Rishton, since 1970; *b* 8 May 1915; *m* 1944, Margaret Jane Carpenter; one *s* three *d. Educ:* King Edward High School; Univ. of British Columbia. BA (BC) 1935. College of the Resurrection, Mirfield, Yorks, 1936-38; Curate: St John's, Shildon, Co. Durham, 1938-40; St James's, Gateshead-on-Tyne, 1940-42; Novice, Community of the Resurrection, 1942-43; Vicar of St Wilfrid's, Halton, Leeds, 1944-61; Hon. Canon of Ripon Cathedral, 1955-61; Rural Dean of Whitkirk, 1958-61; Provost of Southwark Cathedral, and Rector of St Saviour and All Hallows, Southwark, 1961-70. *Publications:* (with S. H. Evans) Unto a Full Grown Man (Series), 1942-; Receive This Child, 1951; The Parish Comes Alive, 1956; Meditations for Lent, 1957; contribs to Theology, etc. *Recreations:* music, theatre, walking. *Address:* The Vicarage, 4 Somerset Road, Rishton, Blackburn, Lancs BB1 4BP. *T:* Great Harwood 88691.   [*Died* 17 Jan. 1976.

SOUTHEY, Air Commodore Harold Frederic George, CB 1954; HM Diplomatic Service, retired; *b* 18 Feb. 1906; *s* of Rev. William George Southey and Edith Mary Roffey; *m* 1929, Joan Mary Gordon Davies; no *c. Educ:* Downside; RAF Coll., Cranwell. Served War of 1939-45 (despatches twice); AOC No 247 Group, and Senior British Officer, Azores, 1945; Air Attaché, Brussels, 1947; West Union Defence Organisation, 1951; SASO Transport Command, 1952; AOC, RAF Maritime HQ, Chatham, 1954; retired 1957; Queen's Messenger, 1959-71. *Recreations:* fishing, shooting, and sailing. *Address:* 17 Knightsbridge Court, SW1. *T:* 01-235 6927. *Clubs:* Royal Air Force, Royal Thames Yacht.   [*Died* 16 Feb. 1979.

SOUTHGATE, Bernard Alfred, CBE 1954; PhD, DSc (Aberdeen), FRIC; Director, Water Pollution Research, Ministry of Technology, 1965-66 (Department of Scientific and Industrial Research, 1943-65); *b* 28 Aug. 1904; *s* of Alfred and Edith Southgate; *m* 1929, Marion Hope Smith; one *s. Educ:* City of Norwich Sch.; Queens' Coll., Cambridge (Scholar, BA). With Marine Biological Assoc., engaged on survey of River Tees, 1929-33; joined Department of Scientific and Industrial Research, 1933; Officer-in-Charge, Survey of Mersey Estuary, 1933-37. *Publications:* Treatment and Disposal of Industrial Waste Waters, 1948; Water Pollution and Conservation, 1969. *Address:* Langham House, Langham, Norfolk.
[*Died* 3 Sept. 1975.

SOUTHWOOD, Albert Ray, CMG 1947; ED; Cons. Physician to the Royal Adelaide Hospital; Lecturer in Public Health and Preventive Medicine, Faculty of Medicine, University of Adelaide, 1938-59; Milroy Lecturer, RCP, London, 1959; Director-General of Public Health and Chairman Central Board of Health of South Australia, 1931-59; *er s* of late J. A. Southwood, MP, and Mrs Southwood, Joslin, South Australia; *m* 1919, Elva Dillon, Toorak, South Australia; two *s* two *d. Educ:* Prince Alfred Coll., Adelaide; Adelaide Univ. MB, BS, MD, MS Adelaide; MRCP; FRACP (Foundation Fellow); Colonel, AAMC (retired). *Publications:* Heart Disease: Ways to Prevent it, 1962; medical papers in current journals, 1919-66; contrib. Lancet Milroy Lectures, 1959; Preventive Cardiology. *Address:* 170 North Terrace, Adelaide, SA 5000, Australia. *T:* 51.5123; 129 Swaine Avenue, Toorak Gardens, SA 5065, Australia. *T:* 32.2028. *Club:* Naval, Military and Air Force (Adelaide).   [*Died* 3 Jan. 1973.

SOWBY, Rev. Cedric Walter, MA Oxon, Hon. DD Wycliffe College, Toronto; Principal of Upper Canada College, Toronto, 1949-65; Principal Emeritus since 1965; *b* 29 Jan. 1902; *s* of Walter Edwin and Lily Sowby; *m* 1924, Mary, *d* of Dr F. Savery, Oxford; one *s* two *d. Educ:* King Edward VI Sch., Louth, Lincs; Keble Coll., Oxford; St Stephen's House, Oxford. Asst Curate, St John's Church, Keswick, 1925-28; Asst Master, St Edward's School, Oxford, 1928-33; Warden, St Columba's Coll., Co. Dublin, 1934-49; Member of Headmasters' Conference. Examining Chaplain to Bishop of Toronto. Member Internat. Council, United World Colleges. *Publication:* A Family Writ Large, 1971. *Address:* 16 Chestnut Park Road, Toronto M4W 1W6, Canada. *T:* 922-8611. *Clubs:* Athenæum; Kildare Street (Dublin).   [*Died* 14 March 1975.

SOWMAN, Air Cdre John Edward Rudkin, CB 1959; CBE 1957; DL; RAF, retired; *b* West Clandon, Surrey, 8 May 1902; *s* of Alfred William Rudkin Sowman and Ellen Sowman (*née* Bone); *m* 1928, Olive Rosa Trimmer; two *s* one *d. Educ:* Bedford Sch. Engineer Training, 1919-24; Pilot Officer, RAF, Oct. 1926; Flying Officer No 70 Sqdn, Iraq, 1929-30; Flt Lieut, No 33 Sqdn, Bicester, 1930-34, No 47 Sqdn, Khartoum, 1934-36; RAF Staff Coll., 1937; Air Ministry, Sqdn Leader, Wing Comdr, Group Captain, 1938-43 (responsible for provision of radio equipment); on HQ Staff, MAAF, Algiers, 1943-45; Comdr No 351 MU Algiers, 1945-46 (clearance of N Africa); Staff appts at HQ No 40 Group and Flying Training Comd, 1946-51; Air Cdre and SESO, MEAF, 1951-53; SASO, HQ No 40 Group, 1953-56; Director of Mechanical Transport and Marine Craft, Air Ministry, Sept. 1956-Nov. 1959. DL Beds 1973. *Recreation:* rifle shooting (RAF Team, 7 times, once as Captain), won Alexandra Cup at Bisley, 1949. *Address:* 58 St Michaels Road, Bedford MK40 2LU. *T:* Bedford 66415. *Club:* Royal Air Force.
[Died 23 May 1979.

SPAAK, Paul-Henri; Lawyer and Politician, former Prime Minister of Belgium and Secretary-General of NATO; *b* 1899; *m* 1965, Mrs Simone Dear. Socialist Deputy for Brussels, 1932-66. Minister of Transport, Posts and Telegraphs, Belgium, 1935-36; Minister of Foreign Affairs and Trade, 1936-38; Prime Minister, 1938-39; Minister of Foreign Affairs, 1939-46; President, UN Assembly, 1949; Prime Minister and Minister for Foreign Affairs, 1947-49; Chairman, Council for European Recovery, 1948; President of the Consultative Assembly of the Council of Europe, 1949-51; Chairman of the International Council of the European Movement, 1950-55; Minister of Foreign Affairs, Belgium, 1954-57; Secretary-General, NATO, May 1957-March 1961; Deputy Prime Minister, Minister of Foreign and African Affairs, Belgium, 1961-66; Minister of State, 1966. Charlemagne Prize, 1957. Companion of Honour, Great Britain (Hon. CH), 1963. *Publication:* Combats inachevés, 1969 (The Continuing Battle: memoirs of a European 1936-66, 1971). *Address:* c/o ITT Europe Ltd, 11 Boulevard de l'Empereur, Brussels, Belgium.
[Died 31 July 1972.

SPAATZ, General Carl, Hon. GBE 1945 (Hon. KBE 1944); retired as Chairman, Civil Air Patrol, United States Auxiliary Air Corps; *b* 28 June 1891; *m* 1917, Ruth Harrison; three *d.* United States Military Academy at West Point, 1910. Served European War, 1914-18, American Expeditionary Force, France, 1917; Second Pursuit Group, 1918; commanded Army Plane, Question Mark, 1929; graduated Command and General Staff School, 1936. War of 1939-45; observer in Britain during Battle of Britain; Chief of the Air Staff, AAF HQ, 1941; Comdr 8th Air Force and comdg General US Army Air Forces in European theater, 1942; North-West African Air Force, 1943; Comdg General Strategic Bombing Force, operating against Germany, 1944; Comdg Gen. US Strategic Air Forces in the Pacific, 1945, and supervised final strategic bombing of Japan; Comdg General US Army Air Forces, 1946-47; Chief of Staff, US Air Force, 1947-48; retired, 1948. Distinguished Service Cross, Distinguished Service Medal (3 Oak Leaf Clusters), Legion of Merit, Distinguished Flying Cross, Bronze Star medal; Grand Officer of Legion of Honor, Croix de Guerre with Palm (France); 2nd Order of Suvorov (Russia); Polonia Restituta, Commander's Cross with Star (Poland). *Address:* 5 Grafton Street, Chevy Chase, Maryland 20015, USA.
[Died 14 July 1974.

SPACKMAN, Air Vice-Marshal (retired) Charles Basil Slater, CB 1950; CBE 1945; DFC and Bar; *b* Happisburgh, Norfolk, 4 July 1895; *s* of Rev. George Spackman; *m* 1966, Anna Margareta Gunster. *Educ:* Lancing. Norfolk Regt, enlisted Aug. 1914, commnd 1/4th Bn 1915; War Service, Gallipoli and Egypt; RFC, seconded Oct. 1916, War Service Salonika Front, 41 and 150 Squadrons; RAF transf. on formation, 1918. Overseas service, Egypt, Iraq, Palestine, Sudan and Aden. Served War of 1939-45, Libya, 1941; AOC Sudan and Eritrea, 1941-42; HQ Fighter comd. 1942; Air Officer i/c Administration, 1943-45; AOC No 19 Group Coastal Comd, 1945-47; SASO, British Air Forces of Occupation, Germany, 1947-50; retired, 1950. *Recreation:* painting (exhibitor Royal Scottish and Hibernian Academies, RI, etc). *Address:* 11 Wood Grove, Cross Douglas Road, Cork, Eire. *Club:* Royal Air Force.
[Died 7 Dec. 1971.

SPARKES, Sir James; see Sparkes, Sir W. B. J. G.

SPARKES, Prof. Stanley Robert, MSc (Bristol); PhD (London); Hon. ACGI; FICE; FIStructE; Professor of Engineering Structures, University of London, at Imperial College, 1958-73, now Professor Emeritus; *b* 30 Nov. 1910; *s* of late Matthew Henry and Rosina Sparkes; *m* 1937, Gladys Muriel, *d* of late Commander James Rea, RN and Alice Maud Rea; no *c. Educ:* Cotham Sch.; Bristol Univ. 1851 Exhibitioner, 1932. Assistant Designer Dorman Long and Co., London, 1934-35; Imperial College, London: Demonstrator, Assistant Lecturer, Lecturer, 1935-39; Ministry of Supply, Technical Officer, later Research and Development Officer, Passive Air Defence, 1939-42, and 1943-44; Government of India, Structural Precautions Adviser, 1942-43; Imperial College, 1944-; Reader in Civil Engrg, Univ. of London, 1947; seconded to be in charge of Planning Office dealing with IC Expansion Scheme, 1953; Dir of Building Works, 1955-58. Chm., Imp. Coll. Cttee for Collaboration with Indian Inst. of Technology, Delhi, 1965-71; Mem., UGC Technology Sub-Cttee, 1967-70; Member of Council: IStructE, 1958-61; ICE, 1963-68; Univ. of Science and Technology, Kumasi, 1963-68; Dean, City and Guilds Coll., 1967-70; Mem. Court, Brunel Univ. DIC. Hon. DSc Delhi, 1971. *Publications:* papers in scientific and engineering journals and publications of professional engineering and architectural bodies. *Recreations:* Rugby, squash, cricket, tennis, gardening, motoring, music and architectural planning. *Address:* Imperial College, SW7. *T:* 01-589 5111; 499 High Road, Harrow Weald, Middlesex. *T:* 01-954 1954.
[Died 9 Feb. 1976.

SPARKES, Sir (Walter Beresford) James (Gordon), Kt 1970; Governing Director, Lyndley Pastoral Co., since 1958; Stud Master, Lyndley Hereford Stud and Lyndley Poll Hereford Stud; *b* 1889; *s* of James Sparkes, Barbigal Station via Dubbo, NSW; *m* 1st, 1915, Jessie (*née* Lang); one *d*; 2nd, 1920, Alice Goongarry (*née* Scott); three *s* (and one *s* decd). *Educ:* St Joseph's Coll., Sydney. Established Lyndley Hereford Stud (oldest and largest Hereford Stud still operating in Australia), 1911; estab. Lyndley Poll Hereford Stud, 1932 (a pioneer of this breed in Aust.); played a leading part in formation of Aust. Hereford Soc. (in 1918) and also at a later date Aust. Poll Hereford Soc.; Chm., Wambo Shire Council, 1922-31 and 1937-52; Pres., Local Govt Assoc. of Queensland, 1928-32; Queensland State Parlt: Mem. for Dalby, 1932-35; Mem. for Aubigny, 1941-60. Dir, Logan Downs Pastoral Co., 1969-72. Vice-Pres., Royal National Agric. and Industrial Assoc. of Queensland, 1963- (Mem. Coun. 1949-). *Recreation:* tennis. *Address:* Lyndley, via Jandowae, Queensland 4410, Australia.
[Died 15 June 1974.

SPATER, Ernest George; Chairman: Jas Thompson & Co. Ltd, Brewers, 1952-69; Hotel Metropole (Llandrindod) Ltd, 1966; President, Lombard Banking Ltd, since 1965 (Chairman, 1951-65); *b* 29 Aug. 1886; British; *m* 1912, Florence Mary (*née* Holland) (*d* 1951); one *d*; *m* 1952, Pamela May (*née* Oliver Crofts); one *d. Educ:* Charterhouse Foundation Trust; St Saviour's Grammar Sch. Clerk, Sun Fire Office, 1907; Chief Clerk, British Dominions Insurance Co., 1915. Military service, 1916-19. Eagle Star Insurance Co.: Branch Manager, Cardiff, 1925; Branch Manager, Leeds, 1927; Deputy Agency Manager, 1937; Assistant General Manager, 1940; Joint General Manager, 1948; retired, 1951. Fellow Chartered Insurance Institute (by Examination). *Publication:* Box 1299 (documentary review of insurance documents), 1947. *Recreations:* photography, antiques, travel. *Address:* Daymer, Hervines Road, Amersham, Bucks. *T:* Amersham 7614.
[Died 30 July 1975.

SPAUL, Eric Arthur, DSc, PhD (London); FZS; FIBiol; Professor of Zoology, The University, Leeds, 1933-60; Professor Emeritus, 1960; *b* 27 Aug. 1895. *Educ:* Owen's School, London; Birkbeck Coll., Univ. of London. War Service, 1915-19, Commissioned Rank, London Regt and RE; Gen. Reserve, 1942-46. Graduated BSc (London), 1921, PhD 1924, DSc, 1930; Assistant Lecturer, 1921; Lecturer, 1924; Reader in Zoology, University of London, 1930-33. *Publications:* contributed to: The Natural History of the Scarborough District, Vols I & II, 1956; Van Nostrand's Scientific Encyclopedia, 3rd edn, 1958; and to Journal of Experimental Biology, Proceedings of the Zoological Soc., etc. *Recreations:* sports, travel. *Address:* 6 Churchdown Road, Poolbrook, Malvern, Worcs.
[Died 27 Sept. 1978.

SPEAIGHT, Richard Langford, CMG 1949; Director of East-West Contacts, Foreign Office, 1960-66; *b* 12 July 1906; *s* of Richard Neville and Alice Langford Speaight; *m* 1934, Margaret Ida Hall; one *s* two *d. Educ:* Oundle Sch.; Merton Coll., Oxford. Entered HM Diplomatic Service, 1929; 3rd Secretary, Budapest, 1931; Foreign Office, 1933-35; 2nd Secretary, Warsaw, 1935-38; Foreign Office, 1938-45; 1st Secretary and later Counsellor, Cairo, 1945-48; transferred to Foreign Office, 1948, Head of Information Policy Dept, 1948-50; HM Ambassador at Rangoon, 1950-53; an Asst Under-Secretary of State, FO, 1953-56; HM Minister at Sofia, 1956-58. *Address:* Lion House, Lavenham, Sudbury, Suffolk.
[Died 17 Nov. 1976.

SPEAIGHT, Robert William, CBE 1958; MA (Oxon); FRSL; actor and author; *b* 14 Jan. 1904; *e s* of late Frederick William Speaight; *m* 1935, Esther Evelyn Bowen; one *s*; *m* 1951, Bridget Laura Bramwell; one *s* (adopted). *Educ:* Haileybury; Lincoln Coll., Oxford. Pres., Edinburgh Sir Walter Scott Club, 1971-72. Officer, Legion of Honour, 1969. Hon. Sec., OUDS, 1925; played Peer Gynt and Falstaff for the Society, 1925 and 1926; Liverpool Repertory Theatre, 1926-27; toured Egypt in Shakespeare with Robert Atkins, 1927; Hibbert in Journey's End, at the Savoy and Prince of Wales, 1929-30; First Player and Osric at the Haymarket in "All Star" Hamlet, Edmund in King Lear, at the Old Vic, Herod in Salome, Gate, 1931; Hamlet, Malvolio, Fluellen, Cassius, King John, etc, Old Vic Season, 1931-32; Becket in Murder in the Cathedral, Canterbury Festival and Mercury, 1935, Duchess, 1936, Provincial Tours, 1937, Tewkesbury Festival, 1937, USA, 1938, Lyric and Mercury, and at Edinburgh Festival, 1947. Played Shakespeare's Coriolanus and Chapman's Biron for William Poel's Elizabethan Stage Circle, 1930 and 1931; Antony in This Way to the Tomb!, Mercury, 1945-46; producer Antony and Cleopatra for Les Rencontres Internationales, Geneva, 1947; Christian in Pilgrim's Progress, Covent Garden, 1948; Seti in The First Born, Edinburgh Festival, 1948; adjudicator, Canadian Dominion Drama Finals Festival, 1948; prod., French versions of Murder in the Cathedral and Romeo and Juliet, Théâtre des Compagnons, Montreal, 1950; producer: The Madwoman of Chaillot, St James'; The Four Men, Festival of Sussex; Gerontius in The Dream of Gerontius, Scala, 1951; St Peter, in Out of the Whirlwind, Westminster Abbey; Pole, in His Eminence of England, Canterbury Festival, 1953; Hardlip and Prime Minister, The Burning Glass, Apollo and tour, 1954; Sir Claude Mulhammer, The Confidential Clerk, Paris Festival, and tour, 1954; Dom Diogo in The Hidden King, Edinburgh Festival, 1957; Guest Artist, Australian Broadcasting Commission, 1953; King Lear, Los Angeles; Becket in Murder in the Cathedral, Adelaide Festival, 1960; Bassa Selim in Die Entführung, Glyndebourne, 1961; More in A Man for All Seasons, Australia, 1962-63; Voice of Christ in The Man Born to be King; King Lear, Kansas City, 1965; Moulton-Barrett in Robert and Elizabeth, 1967. *Publications:* Mutinous Wind, 1932; The Lost Hero, 1934; The Angel in the Mist, 1936; Thomas Becket, 1938; The Unbroken Heart, 1939; Acting, 1939; Drama since 1939, 1948; George Eliot, 1954; William Poel, 1954; Nature in Shakespearian Tragedy, 1955; Hilaire Belloc, 1957; (ed) Letters from Hilaire Belloc, 1958; The Christian Theatre, 1960; William Rothenstein, 1962; Ronald Knox the Writer, 1966; The Life of Eric Gill, 1966; Teilhard de Chardin, 1967; The Property Basket: recollections of a divided life, 1970; Vanier, 1970; A Bridges-Adams Letter Book, 1972; George Bernanos, 1973; Shakespeare on the Stage, 1973; Companion Guide to Burgundy, 1975; François Mauriac, 1976; frequent articles in the weekly press; *posthumous publication:* Shakespeare, the man and his achievement, 1977. *Recreations:* walking and riding. *Address:* Campion House, Benenden, Kent. *T:* Benenden 617. *Clubs:* Garrick, Beefsteak; Puffins (Edinburgh).
[Died 4 Nov. 1976.

SPEARMAN, Sir Alexander (Bowyer), 4th Bt, *cr* 1840; Hon. Captain late 10th Bn 7th Rajputs; Director, Nabco Cape (Pty) Ltd, Incorporated Insurance Brokers; *b* 15 Feb. 1917; *S* father, 1959; *m* 1950, Martha, *d* of John Green, Naauwpoort, SA; one *s* three *d*. *Educ:* Westminster. War of 1939-45, Staff Capt., Delhi, 1941-43, Paiforce, 1943-45. FCII. *Recreation:* philately. *Heir: s* Alexander Young Richard Mainwaring Spearman, *b* 3 Feb. 1969. *Address:* 88 Camps Bay Drive, Camps Bay, Cape Town, CP, South Africa; Nabco Cape (Pty) Ltd, Broadway Building, Heerengracht, Cape Town. *T:* 23557. *Club:* Civil Service (Cape Town).
[Died 27 May 1977.

SPEARS, Maj.-Gen. Sir Edward (Louis), 1st Bt *cr* 1953; KBE 1942 (CBE 1919); CB 1921; MC; FInstD; *b* 7 Aug. 1886; *o s* of Charles McCarthy Spears and Marguerite Melicent Hack; *m* 1918, Mary Borden, (*d* 1968) (one *s* decd); *m* 1969, Nancy, *e d* of late Maj.-Gen. Sir Frederick and Lady Maurice. *Educ:* privately. Kildare Militia, 1903; gazetted 8th Hussars, 1906; transferred 11th Hussars, 1910; temporary Captain 1914; Brevet Major; Brevet Lt-Col; Hon. Brig.-Gen.; Head of British Military Mission, Paris, 1917-20; retired, 1920 (despatches 5 times, 4 times wounded, 3 times cited in French Army Orders, CB, CBE, MC, Commander Legion of Honour, Croix de Guerre with 3 palms, Etoile Noire, Grand Cross of White Eagle of Serbia, Czecho-Slovak Croix de Guerre; mentioned in Polish despatches); MP (NL) Loughborough Div. of Leicester, 1922-24; MP (U) Carlisle, 1931-45; Maj.-Gen. 1940; Prime Minister's Personal Rep. with French Prime Minister and Minister of Defence, May-June 1940; Head of British Mission to General de Gaulle, June 1940; Head of Spears Mission, Syria and the Lebanon, July 1941; First Minister to Republics of Syria and the

Lebanon, 1942-44; Hon. Maj.-Gen. 1945; Chm. of Council, Inst. of Directors until 1965 (past Chm. of Institute, and Pres., 1953-54, Chancellor, 1966); Founder and first Chm., House of Commons Motor Club. Pres., Ashanti Goldfields Ltd; Life Pres., West End Bd, Commercial Union Assurance Co. Ltd, 1972. *Publications:* Lessons of the Russo-Japanese War, 1906; Cavalry Tactical Schemes, 1914; Liaison, 1914, 1931, repr. 1968; Prelude to Victory, 1939; Assignment to Catastrophe, 1954; Two Men Who Saved France, 1966; The Picnic Basket, 1967; Fulfilment of a Mission, 1977 (posthumous publication). *Address:* 12 Strathearn Place, W2. *T:* 01-723 8849; 164 St Stephens House, SW1. *T:* 01-930 3781; St Michael's Grange, Warfield, Berks. *T:* Bracknell 5066. *Clubs:* Cavalry, Carlton, Buck's.
[Died 27 Jan. 1974 (ext).

SPEED, Sir Eric Bourne Bentinck, KCB, *cr* 1945; KBE, *cr* 1943; MC; *b* 26 Jan. 1895; *s* of late Rev. Francis Bentinck Speed and Martha Ellen Chambers; *m* 1st, Rosa Dorothy Giles (marriage dissolved); one *s*; 2nd, Ursula, *d* of Alwyn Rashleigh Phipps; one *s* one *d*. *Educ:* Christ's Hospital; Scholar-elect of St John's College, Oxford, 1914. Served European War with KOYLI, 1914-18 (MC, French Croix de Guerre avec Etoile en Vermeil, despatches). Appointed to War Office, 1920; transferred to Treasury, 1934; Private Sec. to Rt Hon. Stanley Baldwin, Prime Minister and First Lord of the Treasury, 1936-37; rejoined War Office, 1940; Permanent Under-Sec. of State for War, 1942-48; retired, Dec. 1948. *Clubs:* Constitutional, MCC.
[Died 28 June 1971.

SPEIGHT, Harold Edwin Balme; retired college dean, United States; *b* Bradford, 1887; *s* of Edwin Speight and Charlotte Hall; *m* 1911, Mabel Grant, Ballater; two *d*; *m* 1967, Victoria Mary Tapp, Montreal, Canada. *Educ:* Univ. of Aberdeen; Exeter College, Oxford. Asst, Dept of Logic and Metaphysics, Univ. of Aberdeen, 1909-10; Fellow Manchester Coll., Oxford, 1910-12; served in the ministry, 1912-27; Chaplain with US Army in France, 1918-19; DD Tufts Univ., 1925; resigned from ministry and joined Soc. of Friends, 1928. Prof. of Philosophy, Dartmouth, 1927-29 (Hon. MA 1927); Prof. of Biography and Chm. of Dept, Dartmouth, 1929-33; Dean of Men, Swarthmore Coll., 1933-38; Dean of Coll., 1938-40; Exec. Sec., Assoc. of Colls and Univs of State of NY, 1940-42; Dean of Coll., St Lawrence Univ., 1942-45, and Actg President, 1944-45; Dean of Students, Cornell University, 1945-46; Dean of the College, Elmira College, Elmira, NY, 1946-49. Pres., Scottish Club of Twin States (NH and Vt). *Publications:* Life and Writings of John Bunyan, 1928; Editor, Creative Lives Series, 1930-33; Literary Editor, Christian Leader, 1927-38, etc. *Recreations:* gardening, photography. *Address:* 2556 Wesley Place, Victoria, BC, Canada.
[Died 9 Aug. 1975.

SPEIR, Wing Comdr Robert Cecil Talbot, OBE 1945; Vice-Lieutenant of Nairn since 1970; *b* 8 Oct. 1904; *e s* of late Lt-Col Guy Thomas Speir, North Berwick; *m* 1st, 1932, Elizabeth Findlay (*d* 1958), *d* of Sir John R. Findlay, 1st Bt, KBE; two *s* two *d*; 2nd, 1961, Dolce Maria, *d* of late Henry Hanselman. *Educ:* Eton; RMC Sandhurst. Served War, 1939-45: Bomber Comd, Gps 1, 2 and 4 (despatches thrice), and War Cabinet Office; Wing Comdr 1943; RAFVR(T), 1947-51. Mem., Royal Company of Archers (Queen's Body Guard for Scotland). DL Nairn, 1951-70. *Recreation:* shooting. *Address:* Linkside, Nairn. *T:* Nairn 53357.
[Died 2 Jan. 1980.

SPENCE, Col Sir Basil H. H. N.; see Neven-Spence.

SPENCE, Sir Basil (Urwin), OM 1962; Kt 1960; OBE 1948; TD 1957; RA 1960 (ARA 1953); ARSA 1952; RDI 1960; Professor of Architecture, Royal Academy, 1961-68; Treasurer of Royal Academy, 1962-64; RIBA Council Member from 1952 (Vice-President, 1954-55; Hon. Secretary, 1956; President, 1958-60); Member Board of Trustees, Civic Trust; First Hoffman Wood Professor of Architecture, Leeds University, 1955-56; Member, Fine Art Commission, 1956-70; *b* 13 Aug. 1907; *s* of Urwin Spence, ICS, and Daisy Crisp; *m* 1934, Mary Joan Ferris; one *s* one *d*. *Educ:* George Watson's College, Edinburgh; Schools of Architecture, London and Edinburgh Univs. RIBA Silver Medallist, 1931; Arthur Cates Prizeman (Town Planning), 1932; Pugin Student, 1933; assisted Sir Edwin Lutyens, OM, in preparation of drawings for the Viceroy's House at Delhi. Served War in Army, 1939-45 (despatches twice). Has built large country houses before War of 1939-45 and, since then, housing estates, theatres, schools, university buildings, churches and factories. Festival of Britain, 1951, award (by Council for Architecture, Town Planning and Building Research) for Housing Estate at Sunbury-on-Thames; won competition for design of new Coventry Cathedral, 1951; Saltire Award for Fishermen's Houses at Dunbar, East Lothian, 1952; Newhaven, 1960. Parish Churches: Manchester, Sheffield, Leicester,

Coventry, Edinburgh, Reading, 1955-60; Crematorium, Edinburgh; apptd Architectural Cons. Trawsfynydd Nuc. Power Stn, 1960; Undergrad. Rooms, Queens' College, Cambridge; Planning Cons. Southampton Univ., 1955 (Arts, Chemistry, Physics, Engrg Bldgs, Women's Hall of Residence, Sen. Common Room); apptd architect for Brit. Embassy, Rome, 1960 (completed 1971); Household Cavalry Barracks, Knightsbridge (completed 1970); Glasgow Air Terminal, Abbotsinch; Physics Buildings, Liverpool and Durham Univs; apptd Architect for Master Plan, Univ. of Sussex (Physics, Arts, Library, Biology, Chemistry, Engrg Sciences Bldgs, College House, Meeting House); Physics and Chemistry Bldgs, Exeter Univ.; Hampstead Civic Centre; Kensington and Chelsea Civic Centre; New Hall for Salters Co. Consultant Architect: two banks in Greece; office building, Amsterdam. Architect for housing in Islington. Adviser to Bd of Trade for Brit. Industries Fair, 1947, 1948, 1949. Chief Architect: Britain Can Make It Exhibition; Enterprise Scotland, 1947 Exhibition; Scottish Industries Exhibition, 1949; Heavy Industries Exhibition, Festival of Britain, 1951; Architect, Sea and Ships Pavilion, Festival of Britain, 1951; Architect for British Pavilion, 1967 World Exhbn, Montreal; Architectural Consultant: (with Prof. Nervi) for extension to Palais des Nations, Geneva; for Internat. Airport, Baghdad. Hon. Mem., Academia di San Luca, Rome, 1973. Hon. Fellow: RCA, 1962; AIA, 1962. Hon. DLitt: Leicester, 1963; Southampton, 1965; Hon. LLD Manitoba, 1963. Bronze Medal, RIBA, for Falmer House, Univ. of Sussex, 1963; Coventry Award of Merit, 1970; Grande Médaille d'Or, Académie d'Architecture, France, 1974. *Publication:* Phœnix at Coventry, 1962. *Recreations:* painting and sailing. *Address:* 1 Canonbury Place, N1. *T:* 01-226 7175. *Club:* Travellers'.
[Died 19 Nov. 1976.

SPENCE, Robert, CB 1953; FRS 1959; Professor of Applied Chemistry, and Master of Keynes College, University of Kent at Canterbury, 1968-73, now Professor Emeritus; *b* 7 Oct. 1905; British; *m* 1936, Kate Lockwood; two *s* one *d. Educ:* King's Coll., Univ. of Durham. Commonwealth Fund Fellow at Princeton Univ., USA, 1928-31; Lecturer in Physical Chemistry, Leeds Univ., 1931-46. War of 1939-45: OC Leeds Univ. STC, Lt-Col until 1942; Chemical Warfare Adviser, HQ RAF Middle East, 1942-43 and at HQ, MAAF, Caserta, 1943-44. Member of Anglo-Canadian Atomic Energy Laboratory, Montreal, 1945; Head of Chemistry Division, Atomic Energy Research Establishment, Harwell, 1946; Chief Chemist, 1948; Dep. Director, 1960-64; Director, 1964-68. *Publications:* scientific papers in Jl of Chemical Soc., etc. *Address:* Ranger Cottage, 5 Jenning's Lane, Harwell, Didcot, Oxfordshire OX11 0EP. *T:* Harwell 393.
[Died 10 March 1976.

SPENCE, 7th Earl *cr* 1765; **Albert Edward John Spencer,** TD 1944; FSA; FRSA; Baron and Viscount Spencer, 1761; Viscount Althorp, 1765; Viscount Althorp (UK), 1905; Lord Lieutenant and Custos Rotulorum for Northamptonshire, 1952-67; Trustee of Wallace Collection, 1945-66; Member Standing Commission on Museums and Galleries, 1948-66; Chairman Sulgrave Manor Board; Chairman Area Management Hospital Committee for Northampton, 1948-66; President Roxburghe Club; President Walpole Society; Chairman Advisory Council of the Victoria and Albert Museum, 1961-69; *b* 23 May 1892; *e s* of 6th Earl Spencer and Hon. Margaret Baring (*d* 1906), *d* of 1st Baron Revelstoke; *S* father, 1922; *m* 1919, Lady Cynthia Ellinor Beatrix Hamilton, DCVO, OBE (*d* 1972), *d* of 3rd Duke of Abercorn; one *s* one *d. Educ:* Harrow; Trinity Coll., Cambridge (MA). Captain 1st Life Guards; served European War (wounded); ADC Personal Staff, 1917-19; retd 1924; Hon. Colonel: 4 Bn Northants Regt (TA), 1924-37; Northants Searchlight Regt (TA), 1937-55; 438th LAA Regt, RA (TA), 1955-61; 4/5 Bn Northants Regt (TA), 1961-67; President: Hunts and Northants Territorial Assoc., to 1967; Old Contemptibles, Northants Br. Patron: E Midlands Area, Royal Brit. Legion; Northants Br. Royal Brit. Legion; Kettering Div. Cons. Assoc., 1924-43; Northants Rural Community Council; Northampton & County Trustee Savings Bank; Northampton Town and County Assoc. for the Blind; St John's Ambulance Coun. for Northants; Northants Antiquarian Soc.; Northants Assoc. of Boy Scouts; CPRE (Northants Br.) to 1970; Roadmender Youth Club, Northampton (Jt Founder); Putney Hosp., 1938-48. Chairman: Governors of Wellingborough Sch., 1946-; Northampton and County Police Authy; Governor, St Andrew's Hosp., Northampton, 1920-67 (Pres. 1952-67); Mem. Church Assembly House of Laity, 1930-35; Trustee: Pytchley Hunt; Nicolls Charity; Sec., Soc. of Dilettanti, 1953-71; Northamptonshire: JP, 1916-67; DL 1935-52; CC 1925; CA 1952. Hon. DLitt Leicester, 1968. KStJ. *Heir: s* Viscount Althorp, MVO. *Address:* Althorp, Northampton. *T:* East Haddon 200; 24 Arlington House, SW1. *T:* 01-499 2280. *Clubs:* Brooks's, St James', Turf.
[Died 9 June 1975.

SPENCER, Rt. Hon. Countess, (Cynthia Ellinor Beatrix), DCVO 1953; OBE 1943; Lady of the Bedchamber to Queen Elizabeth the Queen Mother since 1937; *b* 16 Aug. 1897; 2nd *d* of 3rd Duke of Abercorn, KG, PC, KP; *m* 1919, 7th Earl Spencer, TD; one *s* one *d. Address:* Althorp, Northampton. *T:* East Haddon 200.
[Died 4 Dec. 1972.

SPENCER, Lt-Col Aubrey Vere, DSO 1914; MA Oxford, 1928; JP; DL; Bursar of Corpus Christi College, Oxford, 1925-46; Land Agent for Oxford University, 1939-51; late 3rd Bn Oxfordshire and Buckinghamshire Light Infantry; *b* 4 April 1886; *o s* of late Aubrey J. Spencer, JP, of Wheatfield Park, Oxfordshire, and Florence Mary, *d* of Frederick H. Janson; *m* 1926, Gwendoline Esther Hall (*d* 1968), *widow* of Capt. Claude Holdsworth Hunt, RFA and *d* of G. N. Murton, Petleys, Downe, Kent. *Educ:* Marlborough; Wye Agricultural College, Kent. Served European War, 1914 (despatches, DSO); Lieut-Col Commanding a Bn Oxfordshire Home Guard. FRICS. JP 1938, DL 1944, High Sheriff, 1959, Oxfordshire. *Address:* Wheatfield Park, Tetsworth, Oxon. *T:* Tetsworth 225. [Died 7 Jan. 1973.

SPENCER, Brig. Francis Elmhirst, DSO 1918; MC; late RA; *s* of late Lieut-Col C. F. H. Spencer, Royal Inniskilling Fusiliers, and late Emily, *d* of William Ball; *b* 25 July 1881; *m* 1916, Augusta (Vera) (*d* 1956), *y d* of late Col Arthur Tracey, late RA; one *s* one *d. Educ:* Dover College; RMA, Woolwich. RGA, 1900; psc; served China Expeditionary Force, 1900-01 (medal); Hong-Kong, Straits Settlements, 1901-02; Mountain Artillery, India, 1903-11; Tibet Field Force (advance to Lhasa), 1904 (medal and clasp); Mekran Field Force, 1911; Malay States Guides Mountain Battery, 1911-14; served with RFA European War, 1914-18, in France and Belgium (despatches 5 times, MC, DSO); Commandant (local Lt-Col) Straits Settlements Volunteer Force, 1921-25; Lt-Col 1927; Col 1931; Commander Royal Artillery, 55th (West Lancs) Division TA Liverpool, 1932-34; Brigadier i/c Administration, Western Comd, 1934-38; retired pay, 1938; Comdt AA Practice Camp, Bude, AA&QMG, 45th (West Country) Div. (RARO), 1939-40; Comdr 12th Devon Bn HG, 1940-41; Regional Officer London Civil Defence Region, 1941-43; Admiralty Service SVP, 1944-46. *Recreations:* shooting, yachting. *Address:* Underhill House, Lympstone, Devon. *Club:* United Service & Royal Aero.
[Died 6 March 1972.

SPENCER, Gilbert, RA 1959 (ARA 1950); RWS 1949 (ARWS 1943); Hon. ARCA; Member: NEAC; Society of Mural Painters; Faculty of Prix de Rome; *b* 1893; *s* of late William and Anna Spencer; *m* 1930, Margaret Ursula Bradshaw (*d* 1959); one *d. Educ:* privately and Slade School. Served War of 1914-18, RAMC and East Surrey Regt. Professor of Painting, Royal Coll. of Art, 1932-48; Head of Department of Painting and Drawing, Glasgow School of Art, 1948-50; Head of Dept of Painting and Drawing, Camberwell Sch. of Arts and Crafts, 1950-57. Exhibitions: Goupil Gall., 1922, 1926 (with Mark Gertler and John Nash, RA), 1928, 1931; Leicester Galls, 1933, 1937, 1943, 1946, 1948; work rep. in many public galleries, including: Tate Gallery, Victoria and Albert Museum, Imperial War Museum, Aberdeen, Belfast, Capetown and Durban Art Galls. Commissioned by Imperial War Museum, 1919, and War Artists' Advisory Council, 1940 and 1943. Murals, Foundation Legend of Balliol Coll.; The Scholar Gipsy Students Union, Univ. of London; An Artist's Progress, Royal Academy. *Publications:* Stanley Spencer, 1961; Memoirs of a Painter, 1974. *Address:* c/o The Lawn, Walsham-le-Willows, Bury St Edmunds, Suffolk. [Died 14 Jan. 1979.

SPENCER, Terence John Bew; Professor of English Language and Literature, Birmingham University, since 1958; Director of the Shakespeare Institute, since 1961; Member Board, Young Vic, since 1974; *b* 21 May 1915; *s* of Frederick John and Dorothy Emmie Spencer, Harrow; *m* 1948, Katharine Margaret, *d* of Francis William Walpole, Limpsfield, Surrey; three *d. Educ:* Lower School of John Lyon, Harrow; University of London (King's Coll. and University Coll.); British School at Rome. Assistant, English Department, King's Coll., London, 1938-40; Brit. Council Lectr, Brit. Inst., Rome, and Inst. of English Studies, Athens, 1939-41. Served War, 1941-46 (despatches); Cyprus Regt and Royal Pioneer Corps; commissioned 1941; Maj. 1943; actg Lt-Col 1945. Asst Lectr and Lectr in English, 1946-55, UCL; Prof. of English, QUB, 1955-58; Public Orator, Birmingham Univ., 1966-73. Turnbull Prof. of Poetry, Johns Hopkins Univ., 1968; Berg Prof. of English, NY Univ., 1974. Hon. Sec., The Shakespeare Association, 1950-; Gov., Royal Shakespeare Theatre, 1968-; Chm. Adv. Cttee, Young Vic, 1970-74; Mem. Bd, Nat. Theatre, 1968-76. Hon. Life Mem., Modern Humanities Res. Assoc., 1975. General Editor: New Penguin Shakespeare; Penguin Shakespeare Library; English Editor, Modern Language

Review, 1956-75 (General Editor, 1959-71); Editor, Year Book of English Studies, 1971-75. *Publications:* Fair Greece, Sad Relic: Literary Philhellenism from Shakespeare to Byron, 1954; (ed with James Sutherland) On Modern Literature by W. P. Ker, 1955; From Gibbon to Darwin, 1959; The Tyranny of Shakespeare, 1959; Byron and the Greek Tradition, 1960; Shakespeare: The Roman Plays, 1963; ed, Shakespeare's Plutarch, 1964; ed, Shakespeare: A Celebration, 1964; ed, Romeo and Juliet, 1967; ed, A Book of Masques, 1967; Elizabethan Love Stories, 1968; contribs to other books, and to journals. *Address:* The Shakespeare Institute, The University, Birmingham B15 2RX. *[Died 3 March 1978.*

SPENCER, Sir Thomas George, Kt 1946; CEng., FIEE; MIPE; Hon. President and Director, Standard Telephones and Cables Ltd; Director: International Marine Radio Co. Ltd; Abbey Life Assurance Co. Ltd; *b* 1888; *s* of Thomas and Mary Spencer, Beds; *m* 1st, 1914, Grace Adelaide (*d* 1949), *y d* of Joseph Player; one *s*; 2nd, 1953, Ethel Bailey (Ethel Bilsland, FRAM), *y d* of James Bilsland. *Educ:* Polytechnic; Royal Ordnance School, Woolwich. Joined engineering staff of Western Electric Co. Ltd, 1907, later became Chief Cable Engineer, Director of Cable Manufacture. In 1930 became European Director of Manufacture for International Standard Electric Corp. (later Vice-Pres.); Man. Dir of Standard Telephone & Cables Ltd, 1932-57; Chairman, 1951-65; Chm., Woolwich Equitable Building Soc., 1958-68. Founder and Chm., 1943, Chm., 1956, Hon. Life Pres., 1964, Telecommunication Engineering and Manufacturing Assoc.; Mem. Governing Body, Woolwich Polytechnic, 1939-, Chm., 1949-52; Pres., Eltham and Mottingham Hosp., 1946-48. KCSG 1958. *Recreations:* fishing, golf. *Address:* STC, 190 Strand, WC2R 1DU. *T:* 01-836 8055. *[Died 29 Feb. 1976.*

SPENCER CHAPMAN, Lt-Col Frederick, DSO 1944 (and Bar, 1946); TD 1960; MA; Warden of Wantage Hall, University of Reading, since 1966; *b* 10 May 1907; *s* of Frank Spencer Chapman, Solicitor, and Winifred Ormond; *m* 1946, Faith Mary, Flt Officer, WAAF, *d* of late Major George Harrison Townson and Violet Beatrice Birkin; three *s*. *Educ:* Sedbergh School (Kitchener Scholar); St John's College, Cambridge (Hons English and History). Member of British Arctic Air Route Expedition to Greenland, 1930-31; Member of Pan-American Arctic Airways Expedition to Greenland, 1931-32; Master at Aysgarth School, Bedale, Yorks, 1933-35; Member of Marco Pallis' Himalayan Expedition, 1935; Private Secretary to Political Officer of Sikkim and accompanied Diplomatic Mission to Lhasa, Tibet, 1936-37; made first ascent of Chomolhari (24,000 ft), 1937; Housemaster at Gordonstoun School, Elgin, Morayshire, 1938-39. Served, 1939-46, 5th Bn The Seaforth Highlanders; trained Commando troops in Scotland, 1939, in Australia, 1940, in Singapore, 1941; entered Malayan jungle Jan. 1942 in charge of Stay-behind Parties; emerged by submarine May 1945; returned by parachute Aug. 1945 to become Civil Affairs Officer, Pahang; demobilised March 1946. First Organising Secretary of Outward Bound Trust, Dec. 1946-Dec. 1947; First Headmaster King Alfred School, Plön, BAOR 6 (Germany), 1948-52; undertook Caravan Tour of Africa from Cape Town to Uganda on behalf of Outward Bound Trust, Jan.-Dec. 1953; Headmaster, St Andrew's Coll., Grahamstown, SA, 1956-62; Warden of Pestalozzi Children's Village, Sedlescombe, 1962-66. Arctic Medal 1931, Gill Memorial Medal (RGS), 1941; Mungo Park Medal (RGSS), 1948; Sunday Times Special Award and Gold Medal, 1949; Lawrence of Arabia Memorial Medal (RCAS), 1950. *Publications:* Northern Lights, 1932; Watkins' Last Expedition, 1934; Lhasa: The Holy City, 1938; Helvellyn to Himalaya, 1940; Memoirs of a Mountaineer (reprint) 1945; The Jungle is Neutral, 1948; Living Dangerously, 1952; Lightest Africa, 1955. *Recreations:* mountaineering, ski-ing, birdwatching, photography. *Address:* Wantage Hall, The University, Reading, Berks. *Clubs:* Alpine (Vice-Pres. 1967-68), Special Forces (Dep. Chm.); Harvard Travellers' (Hon. Mem.). *[Died 8 Aug. 1971.*

SPENCER-CHURCHILL, Baroness *cr* 1965 (Life Peer), of Chartwell; **Clementine Ogilvy Spencer-Churchill,** GBE 1946 (CBE 1918); *b* 1885; *d* of late Sir Henry Hozier and late Lady Blanche Hozier, *d* of 9th Earl of Airlie; *m* 1908, Rt Hon. Sir Winston Churchill, KG, PC, OM, CH, FRS (*d* 1965); two *d* (one *s* and two *d* decd). *Educ:* at home; Berkhamsted Girls' Sch.; Sorbonne, Paris. Organised Canteens for munition workers on behalf of YMCA in NE Metropolitan Area, 1914-18; Chairman of the Red Cross Aid to Russia Fund, 1939-46; President of YWCA War Time Appeal; Chairman of Fulmer Chase Maternity Hospital for Wives of Junior Officers, 1940-46; Chairman of National Hostels Committee of YWCA, 1948-51. Freedom of Wanstead and Woodford, 1945. Hon. LLD:

Glasgow University, 1946; Bristol Univ., 1976; Hon. DCL Oxford University, 1946. CStJ. *Address:* 7 Princes Gate, SW7. *[Died 12 Dec. 1977.*

SPENS, 1st Baron *cr* 1959; **William Patrick Spens,** PC 1953; KBE 1948 (OBE 1918); Kt 1943; QC 1925; *b* 9 Aug. 1885; *o surv. s* of late Nathaniel Spens; *m* 1st, 1913, Hilda Mary (*d* 1962), *e d* of Lieut-Colonel Wentworth Grenville Bowyer of Weston Manor, Olney, Bucks; one *s* (*yr s* died on active service, 1942) two *d*; 2nd, 1963, Kathleen Annie Fedden, *o d* of late Roger Dodds, Northumberland and Bath. *Educ:* Rugby; New Coll., Oxford. Barrister of the Inner Temple, 1910; Master of the Bench, Inner Temple, 1934; Treas., 1958; served European War, 1914-19; India, 1914-15; Mesopotamia, 1915-18 (despatches thrice, OBE); Captain and Adjt 5th Bn The Queen's Royal Regt, 1914-18; MP (C) Ashford Div. of Kent, 1933-43; Chief Justice of India, 1943-47; Chairman Arbitration Tribunal in India, 1947-48; MP (C) S Kensington, 1956-59. A Comr of the Imperial War Graves Commission, 1931-43 and 1949-65. Co-opted Member of Bacon Marketing Board, 1935; Director Southern Railway, 1941-43; Chief Comr in India of St John's Brigade Overseas, 1945-48. Director, Prudential Assurance Co. Ltd, 1949-61; Member of the London Cttee of The Bank of Scotland, 1949. KGStJ 1945. *Heir: s* Hon. William George Michael Spens [*b* 18 Sept. 1914; *m* 1941, Joan Elizabeth, *d* of late Josiah Montague Goodall; two *s* one *d*]. *Address:* Beacon Cottage, Benenden, Kent. *T:* Benenden 434. *Club:* Carlton. *[Died 15 Nov. 1973.*

SPICER, Hon. Sir John Armstrong, Kt 1963; Chief Judge, Australian Industrial Court, 1956; President, Copyright Tribunal, since 1968; *b* Armadale, Victoria, 5 March 1899; *m* 1924, Lavinia M., *d* of Robert S. Webster; one *s*. *Educ:* Torquay (England); Hawksburn (Victoria); University of Melbourne. Admitted as Barrister and Solicitor, 1921; KC 1948; Attorney-General, Commonwealth of Australia, 1949-56. Senator in Commonwealth Parliament, 1940-44 and 1949-56. Chairman, Senate Cttee on Regulations and Ordinances, 1940-43. *Address:* 153 Glen Iris Road, Glen Iris, Victoria 3146, Australia. *T:* 25.2882. *Clubs:* Australian, Constitutional (Melbourne). *[Died 3 Jan. 1978.*

SPICER, Lancelot Dykes, DSO, MC; *b* 22 March 1893; *y s* of Rt Hon. Sir Albert Spicer, 1st Bt; *m* 1920, Iris Cox (who obtained a divorce, 1935); (one *s* killed in action, 31 May 1944); *m* 1951, Dorothy Beverley, *d* of late Frank Edwin Gwyther, CIE. *Educ:* Rugby Sch.; Trinity Coll., Cambridge. Granted temp. Commn in Army, Sept. 1914; T/Capt., July 1916; Bde-Major, April 1918; served European War (MC Oct. 1917; bar to MC May 1918; DSO Sept. 1918). Chairman, Spicers Ltd, 1950-59. *Address:* Salisbury Place, Shipton under Wychwood, Oxford OX7 6BP. *Club:* Hurlingham. *[Died 6 Dec. 1979.*

SPINKS, Rev. Dr (Alfred George) Stephens; Vicar, St Paul's, Scouthead, Oldham, 1966-69; Examining Chaplain to Bishop of Manchester, 1967-70; *b* Cambridge, 1903; *m* 1968, Mrs Annie Nightingale. *Educ:* Cathedral Choir Sch., Rochester; Manchester College and St Catherine's Society, Oxford; University College and King's Coll., London. MA (London), PhD (London); Hibbert Research Student, 1944-45; Upton Lecturer, Manchester Coll., Oxford, 1947-48 and 1949-50. Minister of All Souls' Church, Golders Green, London, 1937-47. Editor of the Hibbert Journal, 1948-51. Rector of Great Lever, Bolton, 1952-55; Rector of Clovelly, 1955-59; Priest-in-Charge, St Swithun's, Littleham by Bideford, 1962-64. Ext. Lectr, Exeter, 1956-66. Frequent broadcast talks on BBC European Service. Exeter University Extension Lecturer; Joyce Lecturer, Dio. Exeter, 1961; Tele-Lecture (from England to W Virginia, USA), 1968. *Publications:* (with E. L. Allen and James Parkes) Religion in Britain since 1900, 1952; The Fundamentals of Religious Belief, 1961; Psychology and Religion, 1963 (also published US, Holland, Japan); Origins of Religious Experience, chapter in Encyclopedia of Psychology, vol. III, 1972; articles in periodicals in Holland, India, Japan, UK, USA. *Address:* 13 Lindale Avenue, Heaton, Bolton, Lancs. *T:* Bolton 41857. *[Died 4 Sept. 1978.*

SPOONER, Edgar Clynton Ross, DSc, BE, DPhil, CEng, FRACI, FIChemE, FIM; Consulting Engineer, since 1963; *b* 25 May 1908; British; *m* 1937; two *d*. *Educ:* Hutchins Sch., Hobart; University of Tasmania; Oxford Univ. (Rhodes Scholar from Tasmania, 1931). Academic and industrial research in various countries, 1930-35; Technical Asst to Works Director, National Smelting Co., Avonmouth, 1935-37; Technical Supt, Magnesium Metal Corp., Swansea, 1937-44; Director of Research and Development, Sutcliffe, Speakman & Co., Leigh, Lancs., 1944-47; Consultant, S. G. Warburg & Co., 1944-47; Professor of Mining, Metallurgical and Chemical Engineering, and Director of Bonython Labs, University of Adelaide, 1947-

62. Dir, Davy Ashmore (Australasia) and other companies; Consulting Engineer, 1963-68; Chief of Project, UN ILO Project, Madras, 1969-70; UNIDO expert, Iran, 1971; IBRD expert, Philippines, 1971-72; UNIDO expert, Mexico and Brazil, 1972; Dir, Pilbara Study Gp, Perth, WA, 1973-74; IBRD expert, Jordan, 1975. Nuffield Travelling Fellowship, 1951; Colombo Plan Adviser to Ceylon Govt, 1954. *Publication:* (Co-author) The Electrode Potential Behaviour of Corroding Metals in Aqueous Solutions, Oxford, 1938. *Address:* 58 Malvern Avenue, Malvern, SA 5061, Australia. *T:* 717421.
[*Died 12 Sept.* 1976.

SPOONER, Edwin George, CIE 1946; Director and General Manager, Whitehead Iron & Steel Co. Ltd, Newport, Mon, 1954-63; *b* 1898; *s* of George Henry Spooner, Birmingham; *m* Thelma Marie, *d* of Eric Albert Bibra, Melbourne, Australia. *Educ:* Secondary Sch., Birmingham. Served in France with Coldstream Guards, European War, 1914-19. Iron and Steel Controller, Dept of Supply, India, 1944-47. *Address:* Flat 8, Hartshill Court, 104 Golf Links Road, Ferndown, Dorset BH22 8DA. *T:* Ferndown 873568.
[*Died 3 Dec.* 1977.

SPRAGGETT, Col Richard William, CMG 1956; CVO 1954; CBE 1948; MC; Colonel Royal Marines, retired; *b* 1894; *s* of late G. W. Spraggett; *m* 1st, 1930, Mary Lois Cecil (marr. diss. 1961), *d* of Sir John Cecil Power, 1st Bt; one *s* one *d*; 2nd, 1972, Geraldine Mary Harrison Warner, MB, ChB, *o d* of late Dr William Paul, Wallasey, Cheshire. *Educ:* privately. Joined Royal Warwicks Regt, 1914; tranf. to RM Light Inf., 1916; Served in France and Flanders, Aug. 1917-May 1919, including Passchendaele, Cambrai and Mons (MC); served in Constantinople, 1922-23, Shanghai and Nanking, 1927-28; psc 1931; Naval Intell. Div., 1932-35; S Africa, 1936-39, Plans Div., Admiralty, 1939-46 (attended sub-cttees of War Cabinet; liaison officer with Permt Under-Sec. of State for Foreign Affairs); Col and CO, RM, Eastney, 1946-49, retired. Private Sec. and Comptroller of Household to Governor of Victoria, Australia, 1949-62. *Address:* 16A Bedford Towers, Brighton, Sussex BN1 2JG. *T:* Brighton 26528.
[*Died 23 Oct.* 1976.

SPRIGGE, Elizabeth Miriam Squire; writer, translator, lecturer and producer; *b* 19 June 1900; *er d* of late Sir Squire Sprigge (Editor of the Lancet), and Mary Moss, *d* of Sir Charles Moss (sometime Chief Justice of Ontario); *m* 1921, Mark Napier (marr. diss., 1946); two *d. Educ:* St Paul's Girls' Sch., London; Havergal Coll., Toronto; Bedford Coll., London. Lived in Sweden, 1923-25. Wrote Novels, children's books, lectured, translated from the Scandinavian languages with Claude Napier, 1927-40. Swedish Specialist at Ministry of Information, 1941-44. Director of the Watergate Theatre, 1949-52. *Publications:* novels: A Shadowy Third, 1929; Faint Amorist, 1930; The Old Man Dies, 1933; Castle in Andalusia, 1935; The Son of the House, 1937; The Raven's Wing, 1940; play: (with Katriona Sprigge) Elizabeth of Austria (produced at Garrick Theatre), 1939; children's books: Children Alone, 1935; Pony Tracks, 1936; Two Lost on Dartmoor, 1940; (with Elizabeth Muntz) The Dolphin Bottle, 1965; biographies: The Strange Life of August Strindberg, 1949; Gertrude Stein, Her Life and Work, 1957; Jean Cocteau, The Man and the Mirror, 1968 (with Jean-Jacques Kihm); Sybil Thorndike Casson, 1971; The Life of Ivy Compton-Burnett, 1973; Journal in Quest of Gertrude Stein, 1973; translations include: Six Plays of Strindberg, 1955; Five Plays of Strindberg, 1960; Mary Stuart in Scotland, Bjørnsterne Bjørnson (Edinburgh Festival), 1960; Twelve Plays of Strindberg, 1963; The Difficulty of Being, by Jean Cocteau, 1966; The Red Room, by August Strindberg, 1967. *Recreation:* re-creation. *Address:* 75 Ladbroke Grove, W11 2PD. *T:* 01-727 9630.
[*Died 9 Dec.* 1974.

SPROTT, Professor Walter John Herbert; Emeritus Professor of Psychology, Nottingham University, since 1965 (Professor, 1960-64); *b* 1897; *s* of Herbert and Mary Elizabeth Sprott. *Educ:* Felstead; Clare College, Cambridge. Demonstrator, Psychological Laboratory, Cambridge, 1922-25; Lecturer in Psychology, University College, Nottingham, 1925, Reader in Philosophy, 1928; Professor of Philosophy, Nottingham Univ., 1948-60. Public Orator to Nottingham Univ., 1948-64; Josiah Mason Lecturer, Birmingham, 1953; Charles Russell Memorial Lecture, 1955; James Seth Memorial Lecture, 1960; Hobhouse Memorial Lecture, 1962. *Publications:* Kretschmer's Physique and Character (trans.), 1925; Freud's New Introductory Lectures (trans.), 1933; General Psychology, 1937; Sociology, 1949; Philosophy and Common Sense, 1949; (with A. H. Stewart) Living in Crowds, 1949; Social Psychology, 1952; Science and Social Action, 1954; Human Groups, 1958; Sociology at the Seven Dials, 1962; Miniatures, 1964. Sundry articles. *Address:* 116 Portland Road, Nottingham. *T:* Nottingham 72871; Blakeney, Holt, Norfolk. *T:* Cley 237.
[*Died 2 Sept.* 1971.

SPROUL, Robert Gordon; President Emeritus, University of California, since 1958 (President, 1930-58); *b* 22 May 1891; *s* of Robert Sproul and Sarah Elizabeth (Moore) Sproul; *m* 1916, Ida Amelia Wittschen; two *s* one *d. Educ:* Univ. of California (BS 1913). Efficiency Dept, City of Oakland, 1913; Univ. of California, 1914-30: as cashier, asst comptroller, asst sec. of Regents, Comptroller, Sec. of Regents and Land Agent, and Vice-President. Fellow, Amer. Assoc. for Advancement of Science; Hon. Mem., Calif Academy of Sciences; Director: Internat. House, Berkeley; Belgian Amer. Educl Foundn; Founder and Treas., Save-the-Redwoods League, Calif, 1921-; Vice-Chm., Trustees, Amer. Heritage Foundn; Carnegie Foundn for Advancement of Teaching, 1939-58; Cttee for Economic Development; Gen. Educ. Bd, 1939-56; Chm. of Bd and Pres. of the Corp., Pacific Sch. of Religion, 1959-. Rockefeller Foundn, 1939-56. President's Ambassador to Inauguration of Syngman Rhee, 1956. Member: Coll. of Electors, Hall of Fame, 1949; (Sponsor) Save the Children Fedn, 1948-; Advis. Cttee, Meals for Millions, 1949-; Bd of Dirs E Bay Reg. Parks, Calif, 1958- (Pres. 1963-67); Nat. Cttee for Support of Public Schools, 1962-; (Sponsor) The Atlantic Council, 1964-; US Dept of Interior Adv. Bd on Nat. Parks, Historic Sites, Bldgs and Monuments, 1959-65; Trustee: National Fund for Graduate Nursing Education, 1960-; California Alumni Foundation, 1963. Director YMCA, California, 1943-. Hon. degrees: LLD: Occidental Coll., 1926; Univ. of Southern Calif, Univ. of San Francisco, 1930; Pomona Coll., 1931; Univ. of Oregon, 1932; Univ. of Nebraska, Yale Univ., 1935; Univ. of Maine, 1938; Univ. of New Mexico, Harvard Univ., 1940; Mills Coll., 1943; Princeton Univ., 1947; Tulane Univ., St Mary's Coll., 1949; Univ. of California, 1958; Univ. of British Columbia, 1958; Rensselaer Polytechnic Inst., 1958; Brigham Young Univ., 1959; LittD, Columbia Univ., 1938; LHD, Univ. of California, 1958; Hon. Fellow: Stanford Univ., 1941; Amer. Coll. of Dentists, 1955; Internat. Coll. of Dentists, 1964. Comdr Order of Crown of Roumania, 1936; Kt of Order of Iron Crown of Italy, 1938; Officier Légion d'Honneur (France), 1939; Roy. Order of North Star (Sweden), 1950; Commander of the Order of St Olav (Norway), 1952. *Address:* 31 Tamalpais Road, Berkeley, Calif 94708, USA. *Clubs:* Faculty, Rotary (Berkeley); Bohemian, University, Family (San Francisco); Sunset, Lincoln (Los Angeles); Burlingame Country (Burlingame); Athenian-Nile (Oakland).
[*Died 10 Sept.* 1975.

SPRULES, Dorothy Winifred; *b* 3 Dec. 1883; *d* of Alfred and Mercy Sprules. *Educ:* Sutton High School; S. Hugh's College, Oxford, BA, and MA 1922; Student Lincoln's Inn. Assistant Mistress Ware Grammar School, 1907-16; Travelling Investigation Officer, Ministry of Munitions, 1916; Headmistress, Tonbridge County School, 1917-19; Headmistress Haberdashers' Aske's Acton School, 1920-43. *Publications:* Victoria County History-contributions to Surrey Volumes. *Recreations:* country pursuits. *Address:* c/o National Westminster Bank, Wareham, Dorset.
[*Died 8 Sept.* 1972.

SPURLING, Maj.-Gen. John Michael Kane, CB 1957; CBE 1953; DSO 1944; *b* 9 May 1906; *s* of late Dr Clement and Mrs Spurling, Oundle, Northants; *m* 1930, Penelope, *d* of Rt Rev. Neville Lovett, CBE, DD, sometime Bishop of Portsmouth and subsequently of Salisbury; one *s* one *d* (and one *s* decd). *Educ:* Oundle. Commissioned Roy. Leics Regt, 1927; served India, UK and Palestine, 1927-38; Staff College, Camberley, 1938-39; served UK and Burma, 1940-43; North-West Europe, 1944-45, including command of 131 Bde, 7th Armoured Division, War Office, and command of a Parachute Bde, 1945-50; Commandant, Senior Officers' School, 1950-53; Chief of Staff, West Africa, 1953-55; Chief of Staff, HQ Northern Command, 1955-58, retired. Col, 4th (Leics) Battn, The Royal Anglian Regt, 1965-68; Dep. Col, The Royal Anglian Regiment (Leicestershire and Rutland), 1968-70. Governor, Milton Abbey Public School, 1961. *Recreation:* shooting. *Address:* The Manor, Fifehead Neville, Sturminster Newton, Dorset DT10 2AL. *T:* Hazelbury Bryan 458.
[*Died 23 Jan.* 1980.

SPURRIER, John Marston; *b* 30 March 1886; *s* of late Henry Spurrier, JP, Marston-on-Dove; *m* 1909, Margery (*d* 1966), *d* of Samuel Marsden, Buxton, Derbyshire; one *s. Educ:* Uppingham; Royal Agricultural College, Cirencester. Served European War, 1914-18, with 4th North Midland Brigade RFA(T); JP Derbyshire, 1927; High Sheriff, Derbyshire, 1944-45; Chm., Hilcrete Ltd; Lord of the Manor and patron of livings of Marston-on-Dove and of Scropton and Foston. *Recreations:* racing, breeding blood stock. *Address:* The Hall, Marston-on-Dove, Hilton, Derby. *TA:* Tutbury. *T:* Tutbury 2121. *Club:* Boodle's.
[*Died 30 Dec.* 1973.

SPURRIER, Mabel Annie, HRI; Freelance Artist; Royal Birmingham Society of Artists, 1930; *b* Moseley, Birmingham; *y*

d of late William James and Caroline Spurrier, Moseley, Birmingham; unmarried. *Educ:* The Woodroughs, Moseley; College of Arts and Crafts, Birmingham, and London. *Address:* Compton Lodge, 7 Harley Road, Hampstead, NW3.
[*Died* 10 *Feb.* 1979.

SQUIRRELL, Leonard Russell, RE 1919 (ARE 1917); RWS 1941 (ARWS 1935); artist (painter and etcher); *b* 30 Oct. 1893; *s* of Frank Squirrell and Henrietta Clemmence (both British); *m* 1923, Hilda Victoria Bird (*d* 1972); one *d* (one *s* decd). *Educ:* British School, Ipswich; Ipswich School of Art; Slade School, London. Gold and Silver Medals, Nat. Competitions of Schools of Art, 1911-15; British Institution Scholarship in Engraving, 1915; Internat. Print-Makers' Exhibs at Los Angeles: silver medal, 1923; Gold medals, 1925 and 1930. Exhibitor Roy. Acad., 1912-59; official purchases by Toronto, British Museum, Victoria and Albert Museum, Fitzwilliam Museum, Cambridge, Brighton, Derby, Rochdale, etc. and Permanent Collection, Ipswich. *Publications:* Landscape Painting in Pastel, 1938; Practice in Water-Colour, 1950. *Address:* Merrydown, Witnesham, Suffolk. *T:* Witnesham 354. [*Died* 10 *July* 1979.

STABLE, Rt. Hon. Sir Wintringham (Norton), PC 1965; Kt 1938; MC; a Judge of the High Court of Justice, Queen's Bench Division, 1938-68; *b* 19 March 1888; *s* of Daniel Wintringham Stable and Gertrude Mary Law; *m* 1916, Lucie Haden (*d* 1976), *widow* of Richard Bayly Murphy and *d* of late F. F. Freeman, Tavistock; two *s*. *Educ:* Winchester; Christ Church, Oxford (MA). 2nd Class Honours School History; Bar, Middle Temple, 1913; served with the Montgomeryshire Yeomanry and 25th Battalion Royal Welch Fusiliers, 1914-18, Egypt, Palestine and France (MC, despatches); QC 1935; Chairman of Quarter Sessions for the Counties of Shropshire, 1947-67, and Merioneth, 1944-; Chancellor of Diocese of Portsmouth, 1937-38. Hon. Student of Christ Church, Oxford, 1960. *Recreation:* country life. *Address:* Plas Llwyn Owen, Llanbrynmair, Powys.
[*Died* 23 *Nov.* 1977.

STABLEFORTH, Dr Arthur Wallace, CB 1962; retired as Project Manager, UN Special Fund Sheep Diseases Research Laboratories, Pendik, Turkey, 1964-70; *b* 15 March 1902; *s* of W. Parkinson and Florence Kate Stableforth; *m* 1926, Hilda Dorothy Allen; one *s* one *d*. *Educ:* Allhallows School; Royal Veterinary College; London University. Demonstrator, Asst, Research Institute of Animal Pathology, 1926-33; in charge of Preventive Medicine, Royal Veterinary College, 1933-39. Veterinary Laboratory, Ministry of Agriculture and Fisheries: Senior Research Officer, 1939-49, Deputy Director, 1949-50. Director of Veterinary Laboratories and Investigation Service, 1951-63; Animal Health Officer, Food and Agriculture Organisation of the UN, 1963. Hon. FRCVS, 1968. John Henry Steele Medal, 1956; Thomas Baxter Prize, 1957. Doctor Medicinae Veterinarie (*hc*), Copenhagen, 1974. *Publications:* contributions to scientific jls and books in this and other countries; Co-editor, Infectious Diseases of Animals. *Recreations:* gardening and music. *Address:* 11 The Paddock, Merrow, Guildford, Surrey. *Clubs:* Royal Society of Medicine, Royal Over-Seas League. [*Died* 31 *Aug.* 1978.

STACEY, Sir Ernest, Kt 1958; Stockbroker since 1919; *b* 1896; *s* of W. E. Stacey and Flora Stacey, Blundellsands, Lancs; *m* 1926, Mary Kathleen Taylor; one *s* one *d*. *Educ:* Oundle School; Liverpool University. Served in Army, 1914-19 (despatches 1916); invalided, result of wounds. Engineering training. Member Liverpool Stock Exchange, 1919-. Director of various Companies, 1930-44. Breeder of Shorthorns, 1941-53. Chm., Oundelian Memorial Trust. *Recreations:* gardening, stock and plant breeding, fishing. *Address:* Stone Hey, Thurstaston Road, Heswall, Cheshire. *T:* 051-342 3487. *Club:* Palatine (Liverpool).
[*Died* 7 *May* 1973.

STACEY, Prof. Reginald Stephen, MA, MD (Cambridge); Emeritus Professor of Pharmacology and Therapeutics, University of London; Consultant, Wellcome Research Laboratories, Beckenham; *b* 1 May 1905; *s* of Stephen Sutton Stacey and Agnes May Measures; *m* 1st, 1933, Margery North; one *d*; 2nd, 1951, Helen Norman Duke; one *s*. *Educ:* Aske's Haberdashers' School; Trinity Coll., Cambridge; St Thomas's Hosp. Med. School; Univ. of Vienna. BA 1927, BChir 1930, MD 1935, MA 1937. First Asst, Med. Unit, St Thomas's Hosp. Med. Sch., 1932-35; Prof. of Pharmacology and Therapeutics, Roy. Coll. of Medicine, Baghdad, Iraq, 1935-47; Reader in Therapeutics, St Thomas's Hosp. Med. Sch., 1948-58, Professor, 1958-70. *Publications:* Recent Advances in Pharmacology (with J. M. Robson); papers in Brit. Jl Pharmacology, Jl Physiology, Lancet, etc. *Address:* 21 Chepstow Villas, W11. *T:* 01-229 5815.
[*Died* 15 *Feb.* 1974.

STACY, Lt-Col Bertie Vandeleur, CMG 1919; DSO 1917; retired District Court Judge, Sydney, NSW; *b* 7 Dec. 1886. Served European War, Australian Imperial Force, 1914-18 (despatches, CMG, DSO and bar). *Address:* 26 Salisbury Road, Rose Bay, Sydney, NSW 2029, Australia. [*Died* 6 *Dec.* 1971.

STADLER, Sir Sydney Martin, KBE 1975 (CBE 1968; OBE 1947); retired from business, 1969, and supervises agricultural interests; *b* 24 May 1893; *s* of Edward Martin Stadler; *m* 1925, Maria Mercedes, *d* of Don Francisco Escobar; no *c*. *Educ:* Oliver Goldsmith Sch., Peckham Road, Camberwell, SE5. Served 1st/18th London Irish Rifles, 1909-16 (battle of Loos, etc) Platoon Sgt; RN, with 4th Battle Sqdn, Grand Fleet, 1917-18. Asst Accountant, Salvador Railway Co. Ltd, 1920-26; founded merchant firm 1926, Sydney M. Stadler, later Stadler & Co (retd 1969), San Salvador, El Salvador. Apptd Acting British Vice-Consul at San Salvador, Sept. 1926, and British Vice-Consul (Hon.), 1927; Hon. Commercial Attaché, 1946-. In charge of British Mission at San Salvador on ten occasions, covering years 1927-46. Past Pres., Friends of the Soil, El Salvador Div. Governor Mem., RASE. KStJ; Kt of Rhodes and of Malta. Comdr, Order of José Matías Delgado (El Salvador), 1971. *Publications:* It Started with an Oyster (memoirs), 1975; pamphlets (covering military career, etc). *Recreations:* afforestation, soil conservation, horticulture. *Address:* Apartado Postal 06-552, San Salvador, El Salvador. *T:* 21-80-40. *Clubs:* Constitutional, Royal Automobile, Royal Commonwealth Society, Royal Over-Seas League; Phyllis Court (Henley); Club Salvadoreno (San Salvador); Plimsol (New Orleans, USA).
[*Died* 7 *June* 1976.

STAGG, James Martin, CB 1954; OBE 1937; Director of Services, Meteorological Office, till 1960; *b* 30 June 1900; *er s* of Alex. C. and Ellen Stagg, Dalkeith, Midlothian; *m* 1940, Elizabeth Nancy Kidner; two *s*. *Educ:* Broughton Secondary Sch., Edinburgh; Edinburgh Univ. Science Master, George Heriot's Sch., Edinburgh, 1921-23; Professional Asst, Meteorological Office, 1924; Leader, British Polar Year Exped. to Arctic Canada, 1932-33; Superintendent, Kew Observatory, 1939; Chief Meteorological Adviser to Supreme Commander, Allied Forces, Europe, 1943-45. President Royal Meteorological Society, 1959. Officer Legion of Merit (US), 1945. Gauss-Weber Medal (Göttingen), 1955. *Publications:* Forecast for Overlord, 1972; miscellaneous publications on geomagnetism, aurora and meteorology. *Recreations:* gardening and walking. *Address:* 33 Carlton Road, Seaford, Sussex. *T:* Seaford 894760.
[*Died* 23 *June* 1975.

STALLARD, Colonel Hon. Charles Frampton, QC 1910; DSO 1918; MC; Minister of Mines, South Africa, 1939-45; Colonel (SA); retired; Hon. Colonel, Witwatersrand Rifles; *s* of late William Henry Stallard and late Mary Tucker; *b* London, 1871. *Educ:* St Edward's Sch. and Merton Coll., Oxford. Called to Bar, Gray's Inn (Holt Scholar); served S African War, CIV, and Paget's Horse; Member Provincial Council, Transvaal, 1910; MP Roodepoort, 1929-38; MP Maritzburg District, 1939-48 (retired); served European War, South West Africa Staff, 1914; APM 41st Division, Flanders, 1916; Captain and acting Lieut-Colonel, various battalions, Flanders, 1917-18 (wounded Messines, MC, DSO, despatches thrice). *Recreation:* farming. *Address:* PO Box 5156, Johannesburg, S Africa; Hope Woolith, Misgund, near Johannesburg. *Clubs:* Rand (Johannesburg); City (Cape Town). [*Died* 13 *June* 1971.

STALLARD, Hyla Bristow, MBE 1942; TD; MD, MChir, FRCS, Hon. LLD (St Andrews); Eye Surgeon; *b* 28 April 1901; *s* of Hyla Holden Stallard and Evelyn Walsh; *m* Gwynneth Constance Page. *Educ:* Sherborne Sch.; Cambridge Univ. (MA); St Bartholomew's Hospital (Shuter Entrance Scholarship). BCh Cantab 1925; MRCS, LRCP 1926; MB Cantab 1928; FRCS 1928; MD (Cantab), Honourable mention, 1933; MChir (Cantab), 1967; Consulting Surgeon, Moorfields Eye Hospital; Consulting Eye Surgeon, St Bartholomew's Hospital. Major RAMC TA; served War of 1939-45, Middle East (despatches, MBE); in France and in Belgium. Late House Surgeon, and Eye House Surgeon, and Chief Assistant, St Bartholomew's Hospital; late Pathologist and Curator, Moorfields Eye Hospital; formerly Eye Surgeon, Radium Inst., and Mount Vernon Hospital; formerly Consulting Eye Surgeon to: Alexandra Hosp.; Royal Sch. for Deaf Children, at Margate. Formerly Editor Trans Ophthalmological Society of UK; Assistant Editor, British Journal of Ophthalmology; Pres., RSM, Eye Section, 1967-69; Vice-Pres., Ophthalmological Soc., UK, 1957-60, Pres., 1972-; Bentley Prize, 1927; Gifford Edmonds Prize, 1932; Nettleship Medal, 1936; Wm Mackenzie Medal, 1951. Charles H. May Memorial Lecturer, New York, 1953; Hunterian Prof. RCS, 1954-55, 1960-61, 1967-68. Doyne Memorial Lecturer, Oxford, 1962; Middlemore Lecturer,

Birmingham, 1963; Craig Lecturer, Queen's Univ., Belfast, 1965. OStJ. Order of the Southern Cross (Brazil). *Publications:* Eye Surgery, 1946 (edns 1946, 1950, 1958, 1965, 1972); ed Modern Practice in Ophthalmology, 1949; Radiant energy, as a pathogenic and therapeutic agent in Ophthalmic disorders, Monograph, 1933; War Surgery of the Eye, British Journal of Ophthalmology, 1944, etc. *Recreations:* athletics, hockey, represented England in athletics, 1921-27, Great Britain at the Olympic Games, 1924, and the British Empire against the USA, 1924. *Address:* 112 Harley Street, W1. *T:* 01-935 8840.
[*Died* 21 *Oct.* 1973.

STALLWOOD, Frank, CMG 1967; OBE 1955; *b* 5 Sept. 1910; *s* of late Henry Robert Stallwood and late Ethel (*née* Cheeseman); *m* 1935, Cora Cécile Frances (*née* Brady); one *s* one *d. Educ:* Owen's Sch.; St Luke's Coll., Exeter. BA Hons London. Schoolmaster, 1932-40. Army, Captain, Intelligence Corps, Service in ME, 1940-46. Diplomatic Service, 1946-68, retired. *Recreations:* fly-fishing, conversation. *Address:* 5 Macklin Close, Hungerford, Berks. *T:* Hungerford 3584.
[*Died* 5 *Feb.* 1978.

STAMFORD, 10th Earl of, *cr* 1628; **Roger Grey;** Baron Grey of Groby, 1603; *b* 27 Oct. 1896; *s* of 9th Earl and Elizabeth Louisa Penelope (*d* 1959), 3rd *d* of late Rev. Canon Charles Theobald; *S* father, 1910. 2nd Lieut, Territorial Force Reserve, 1916; Honorary Attaché, British Legation, Berne, Oct. 1918, Feb. 1919; Parliamentary Private Secretary to Viscount Peel, Secretary of State for India, 1922; JP 1918, DL 1937-74, Cheshire; Charter Mayor of Altrincham, 1937, Mayor, 1937-38; Hon. Freeman of Altrincham, 1939. *Heir:* none. *Address:* Dunham Massey Hall, Altrincham, Cheshire. *Club:* Travellers'.
[*Died* 18 *Aug.* 1976 (*ext*).

STAMMERS, Arthur Dighton; retired; *b* 5 May 1889; *s* of late Rev. Frederick Dighton Stammers and Charlotte Christina Noble; *m* Phyllis May, *o d* of Richard George Merrifield and Beatrice Lilian Bourke. *Educ:* Dean Close Sch., Cheltenham; The London Hospital; St John's Coll., Cambridge. BA, Hons, Cambridge, 1920; MA 1934; DSc, S Africa, 1925; war service with 7th Essex Regt, 1914-18; with SA Corps of Signals, 1942-44. Demonstrator in Physiology, Cambridge, 1920; in charge of research department in Animal Nutrition, Lever Bros Ltd, Port Sunlight, 1920-21; University of the Witwatersrand, Johannesburg; Senior Lecturer in Physiology, 1921-27; Professor of Physiology, 1927-49; Dean of the Faculty of Medicine, 1948-49; Dean of the Faculty of Science, 1937-38; Member University Council, 1938-42; Professor Emeritus, 1956; Member of Government Advisory Cttee on Broadcasting, 1932-36. Organist, Anglican Cathedral, Salisbury, S Rhodesia, 1950-51; Organising Secretary, Rhodesia Univ. Assoc., 1951-53; Temp. Lecturer in Physiology, University of Cape Town, 1956-58; University of Natal, 1959-60. Acting Head of the Department of Physiology, University of Cape Town, 1961; Temp. Lecturer in Physiology, University of Natal, 1962-63; Organist, St Mark's Cathedral, George, 1965-68. *Publications:* Editor, South African Journal of Medical Sciences, 1935-42; numerous articles and papers on physiological subjects in Journal of Physiology; Biochemical Journal; Physiological Reviews; British Journal of Experimental Pathology; Proceedings of Royal Society of S Africa; S African Journal of Science, etc; (joint) The History of The Lady Margaret Boat Club. *Recreations:* rowing, fishing, music. *Address:* c/o Standard Bank, Hillbrow, Johannesburg, South Africa. *Club:* Leander.
[*Died* 21 *Feb.* 1971.

STAMPER, Thomas Henry Gilborn, CIE 1938; MC; FRICS 1906; Formerly Consulting Surveyor to the Government of Bombay; *b* 27 Oct. 1884; *m* 1923, Edith (*d* 1979), *d* of late Rev. Stephen Edward Gladstone; two *s* one *d.* Served European War, 1914-18 (despatches, MC, with two Bars, French Croix de Guerre). *Address:* Wath Cottage, Damerham, Fordingbridge, Hants. *T:* Rockbourne 250. [*Died* 20 *March* 1980.

STANFORD, John Keith, OBE 1932; MC 1919; author and journalist; *b* 29 April 1892; 2nd *s* of late Edward Stanford, Aldringham, Suffolk, and Caroline Fraser; *m* 1st, 1919, Evelyn Lushington (marr. diss. 1924); one *s* ; 2nd, 1927, Eleanor, *y d* of late J. D. Davies, Ryde, Isle of Wight; one *s* two *d. Educ:* Rugby (Scholar); St John's Coll., Oxford (Scholar, MA). Served European War, 1914-19, Suffolk Regt and Tank Corps (wounded, despatches, MC). Entered ICS Burma, 1919; Dep. Comr, 1924; Burma Rebellion, 1930-31 (OBE); Dep. Comr, Myitkyina, 1932-36; retired, 1938. With Vernay-Cutting expedition to North-East Burma Hills, 1938-39; did much ornithological research, Burma, 1927-39. Rejoined Army, 1939, and served France, 1939-40, Middle East, 1941-43; and with 21 Army Group, 1944-45; Lieut-Colonel, 1941. Chairman Edward Stanford Ltd, 1944-50. Explored bird life of Cyrenaica for British Museum, 1952. Vice-President, British Ornithologists Union, 1951-52. *Publications:* The Birds of Northern Burma, 1938; The Twelfth, 1944; Far Ridges, 1946; Mixed Bagmen, 1949; Guns Wanted, 1949; The Awlbirds, 1949; Bledgrave Hall, 1950; Last Chukker, 1951; Reverie of a Qu'hai, 1952; No Sportsman At All, 1952; Full Moon at Sweatenham, 1953; A Bewilderment of Birds, 1954; Survey of the Ornithology of Libya, 1954; British Friesians, a History of the Breed, 1956; Fox Me, 1958; Jimmy Bundobust, 1958; The Wandering Gun, 1960; Death of a Vulpicide, 1960; Broken Lanterns, 1962; Ladies in the Sun, 1962; Grouse Shooting, 1963; Partridge Shooting, 1963; The Twelfth and After, 1964; And Some in Horses, 1965; Tail of an Army, 1966; The Complex Gun, 1968; A Keeper's Country, 1968; also papers in birds in Ibis and Journal Bombay Natural History Society; The Changing Year, 1952-61 (Field); articles on sport, travel, etc. in Blackwood's Magazine, Shooting Times, etc. *Address:* c/o Lloyds Bank, 6 Pall Mall, SW1. *Club:* East India and Sports.
[*Died* 24 *Sept.* 1971.

STANIER, Robert Spenser; Master of Magdalen College School, Oxford, 1944-67; *b* 9 Aug. 1907; *s* of C. E. Stanier, Civil Engineer to the Underground Railways; *m* 1935, Maida Euphemia Kerr Burnett; two *s. Educ:* Berkhamsted School; Wadham Coll., Oxford. Assistant Master at King's School, Canterbury, 1929-35; Usher at Magdalen College School, Oxford, 1935-44. *Publications:* Selections from the Greek Lyric Poets, 1935; Magdalen School, 1940 (republished by Oxford Historical Society, 1941; augmented edition, 1958); Oxford Heraldry for the Man in the Street, 1974; articles in 'Journal of Hellenic Society' and 'Greece and Rome'. *Address:* 211 Morrell Avenue, Oxford. *T:* Oxford 40269. [*Died* 6 *Dec.* 1980.

STANLEY, Carleton Wellesley, MA Oxon, LLD Toronto and Maine, LittD Colorado, FRSC; Professor of English Literature, United College, Winnipeg, 1946-53; *b* 6 July 1886; *m* Isabel, *d* of Prof. W. J. Alexander, Toronto; one *s* one *d. Educ:* West Toronto High School; University of Toronto (matriculated 1st place Classics, Mathematics, grad. 1st place Classics, 1st General Proficiency); New College, Oxford (1st Lit. Hum.). Lecturer, English Literature, Victoria College, Toronto, 1913-16; engaged business, 1916-25; joined staff, McGill University, 1925, Professor of Greek; Assistant to the Principal, McGill University, 1930-31; President of Dalhousie University, Halifax, NS, 1931-45; Secretary, Canadian Universities Conference, 1928-32; Vice-President, 1932-34; Pres. 1934-37. *Publications:* Roots of the Tree, 1936; Matthew Arnold, 1938, reprinted 1939; many articles European and Canadian reviews; Canadian correspondent, Manchester Guardian, 1913-16. *Address:* 31 Mark Street, Aurora, Ont, Canada. *T:* 416-727-9972.
[*Died* 30 *Nov.* 1971.

STANLEY, Rev. Howard Spencer, MA; General Secretary of the Congregational Union of England and Wales, 1956-64; *b* 25 Jan. 1901; *s* of Noah and Florence Stanley, St George's, Shropshire; *m* 1950, Olive Kenyon Crowther, MA. *Educ:* Edinburgh University; Yorkshire United Theological College. Minister: Southsea, 1925-27; Basingstoke, 1927-32; Bolton, 1932-45; Hassocks, 1964-66. Sec. and Moderator, Lancashire Congregational Union, 1945-56; Chairman Congregational Union of England and Wales, 1951-52. *Recreation:* gardening. *Address:* 24 Dukes Road, Lindfield, Sussex. *T:* Lindfield 3044.
[*Died* 23 *Oct.* 1975.

STANLEY, Wendell M.; Professor of Molecular Biology and Professor of Biochemistry, University of California, since 1948 (Director of Virus Laboratory, 1948-69); *b* 16 Aug. 1904; *s* of James G. Stanley and Claire Plessinger; *m* 1929, Marian Staples Jay; one *s* three *d. Educ:* Earlham Coll.; Univ. of Illinois. PhD Ill, 1929; ScD (Hon.): Harvard, Yale, Earlham, 1938; Princeton, 1947; Illinois, 1959; Pennsylvania, 1964; DSc (Hon.): Pittsburgh, 1962; Gustavus Adolphus Coll., 1963; Toledo, 1968; Butler, 1968; LLD (Hon.); Univ. of California, 1946; Indiana, 1951; Jewish Theol. Seminary of America, 1953; Mills Coll., 1960; Dr (*hon. causa*) Univ. of Paris, 1947; awarded many prizes and medals for work on viruses; Nobel prize for Chemistry, 1946. Sigma Xi Nat. Lectr, 1938; Harvey Lectr, Harvey Society, 1938; Hitchcock Prof., Univ. of California, 1940; Visiting Prof. of Chemistry, Earlham College, 1941. Lectures: Messenger, Cornell, 1942; Vanuxem, Princeton, 1942; Bergen, Yale, 1944; Edgar Fahs Smith, Univ. of Pennsylvania, 1947; Silliman, Yale, 1947; Lower, Cleveland Acad. of Med., 1948; Biology Colloquium, Oregon State Coll., 1950; Hanau W. Loeb, St Louis Univ., 1956; Walter R. Bloor, Univ. of Rochester, 1956; Meyer Bodansky Meml, Univ. of Texas, 1957; R. A. F. Penrose Jr Meml, Amer. Philosophical Soc., 1957; John Wesley Powell Meml, Univ. of Arizona, 1957; American-Swiss Fdn for Scientific Exchange, 1957; E. C. Franklin Meml, Univ.

of Kansas, 1958; Frank Billings, Amer. Med. Asssoc., 1958; Shannon, in Medicine, San Angelo, Texas, 1959; Stanley P. Black Meml, Los Angeles Acad. of Medicine, 1960; Martin Meml, Amer. Coll. of Surgeons, 1960; Annual Distinguished Lectr, Amer. Soc. of Hematology, 1962; Arthur Holly Compton Meml, Univ. of California, 1963; Mike Hogg, Univ. of Texas, 1963; Reynolds Distinguished Lectr, Davidson Coll., 1963; Christian Herter, New York Univ. School of Medicine, 1964; James Ewing, James Ewing Soc., 1964; Donald Johnson, in Cancer Research, Univ. of Michigan, 1964. Mem., Rockefeller Inst. for Med. Research, Dept of Animal and Plant Pathology, Princeton, 1940-48; Univ. of California: Chm. Dept of Biochem., 1948-53, Chm. Dept Virology, 1958-64; Member: Nat. Acad. of Sciences; Amer. Phil. Soc.; WHO Expert Advisory Panel on Virus Diseases; Adv. Cttee, Nat. Inst. Health; Adv. Cttee, Dept of Health, Educn and Welfare. Pres., 10th Internat. Cancer Congress, Houston, 1970. Hon. Mem., Japan Assoc.; Associate For. Mem., French Acad. of Sciences; Hon. For. Mem., Academia Nacional de Medicine de Buenos Aires. *Publications:* (ed with F. M. Burnet) The Viruses, 3 vols, 1959; (with E. G. Valens) Viruses and the Nature of Life, 1961; numerous, on viruses, in scientific journals. *Address:* Virus Laboratory, University of California, Berkeley, Calif 94720, USA. *Club:* Bohemian (San Francisco). *[Died 15 June 1971.*

STANNARD, Captain Richard Been, VC 1940; DSO 1943; RD 1942; RNR, retired; Marine Superintendent for P&O-Orient Lines, Sydney, 1955-64, retd; *b* 21 Aug. 1902; *s* of late Captain George Davis Stannard, Master Mariner, and Elizabeth Jane Knowles; *m* 1928, Phyllis May Tomkin; two *d*. *Educ:* Royal Merchant Navy School. Cadet, C and D line, 1918-21; 2nd Officer, 1924-28; entered RNR, 1929, as Sub-Lieut; joined Orient Line; Lieut RNR, 1932; 2nd Officer, 1937. Orient Line: Command HMS Arab, 1939; Lieut-Comdr RNR, 1940; Comdr RNR, 1947; Capt. RNR, 1952, retired 1954. Staff Commander, Orient Line, 1949-55. Hon. Company Master Mariners. Norwegian War Cross, 1942. *Address:* 9/20 Almora Street, Balmoral Beach, NSW 2088, Australia. *T:* 969-9725.
[Died 22 July 1977.

STANTON, Lt-Col John Percy, DL; JP; *b* 1899; *s* of late Henry and Angelica Florence Stanton, Snelston. *Educ:* Harrow; Sandhurst. 2nd Lt, Roy. Scots Greys, 1919; seconded Sudan Defence Force, 1930; Palestine, 1938 (despatches); Middle East, 1939-45 (despatches). Retired, 1945. JP 1952, DL 1957, Derbyshire; High Sheriff of Derbyshire, 1954. *Address:* Snelston Hall, Ashbourne, Derbyshire. *Club:* Cavalry.
[Died 21 Aug. 1974.

STANTON, Walter Kendall, MA, DMus Oxon; Hon. RCM; Emeritus Professor of Music, University of Bristol, 1958; *b* 29 Sept. 1891; *s* of W. B. Stanton; *m* 1931, Edith Monica Leslie Wood (*d* 1956). *Educ:* Choristers' Sch., Salisbury; Lancing Coll. Organ Scholar, Merton Coll., Oxford, 1909-13. Director of Music, St Edward's Sch., Oxford, 1915-24, Wellington Coll., Berks, 1924-37; Reading Univ., 1927-37; Music Dir, Midland Region, BBC, 1937-45; Prof. of Music, Univ. of Bristol, 1947-58. President: Incorporated Society of Musicians, 1953 (Treasurer, 1959-71); Union of Graduates in Music, 1953-57. Private organist to Duke of Marlborough, 1912-14, 1918-20; City Organist, Bristol, 1956-58; Conductor, Bristol Choral Soc., 1958-60. Examiner in Music at Oxford, Durham and Edinburgh Universities and the University of Wales. Mem., Management Board, Bournemouth Symph. Orch., 1967 (Chm., 1967-68). Editor-in-Chief, BBC Hymn Book. Vice-President: Wilts Music Festival, 1974 (Chm., 1960-73); Wilts Rural Music Sch.; President: N Wilts Orchestra, 1966-; Childrens' Concerts, Salisbury, 1968-; Vice-Pres., Western Orchestral Soc., 1973-. *Address:* Hays, Sedgehill, Shaftesbury, Dorset. *T:* East Knoyle 543.
[Died 30 June 1978.

STAPLEDON, Sir Robert (de Stapledon), KCMG 1956 (CMG 1955); CBE 1953 (OBE 1944); retired as Governor and C-in-C of the Bahamas (1960-64); *b* 6 Feb. 1909; *s* of Ernest Allen Stapledon and Vivien Stapledon (*née* Garvice); *m* 1933, Marjorie Winifred Radford. *Educ:* Marlborough; Trinity Coll., Cambridge. Provincial Administration, Nigeria, 1931; Sec., West African Governors Conf., 1940; Resident Minister's Office, West Africa, 1942; Financial Secretary, Western Pacific High Commission, 1946; Economic Secretary, East Africa High Commission, 1948; Chief Secretary, Tanganyika, 1954-56; Governor, Eastern Region, Nigeria, 1956-60. KStJ 1958. *Address:* Old Rectory, Littleham, near Bideford, N Devon. *T:* Bideford 3752. *Club:* East India, Sports and Public Schools.
[Died 30 Aug. 1975.

STAPLETON, Air Vice-Marshal Frederick Snowden, CB 1961; DSO 1941; DFC 1941; FAIM; retired from the Royal Air Force,

1966; Management Consultant, Melbourne, 1967-71; *b* 4 Feb. 1912; *s* of John Gillard Stapleton; *m* 1950, Marion Wendy Thomas; two *s*. *Educ:* Eastbourne College; Downing College, Cambridge. BA 1933. Awarded University Commn, 1936; Navigation Specialist, 1939; Hornchurch Wing Leader, 1941; In Command No 42 Navigation School, S Africa, 1943; Dep. Dir Operational Requirements, Air Min., 1945; Staff Coll., 1947; Gp Capt. Ops Fighter Comd, 1948; Sector Comr Fighter Comd, 1949; Station Comr RAF Wunsdorf, 2nd TAF, 1951; Gp Capt Ops, 2nd TAF, HQ, 1952; Chief Instructor, Royal Air Force Flying College, Manby, 1953; idc 1955; Northern Sector Comr, Fighter Comd, 1956-58; SASO No 13 Group, 1958; Head of British Defence Liaison Staff, Australia, 1959-60; Senior Air Staff Officer, RAF Transport Command, 1961-64; Dir-Gen. of Manning, Min. of Defence (RAF), 1964-66. FAIM 1967. *Address:* Aquarius, c/o PO, Batehaven, NSW 2536, Australia.
[Died 19 April 1974.

STAPLETON, Major Sir Miles Talbot, 9th Bt, *cr* 1679; *b* 26 May 1893; *o s* of Richard Talbot Plantagenet Stapleton, 2nd *s* of 7th Bt, and Emma, *d* of late Rev. J. Duncombe Shafto; *S* uncle, 1899; *m* 1st, 1913, Doris (*d* 1933), *g d* of Capt. David Fender; one *d*; 2nd, 1935, Miriam Edna (*d* 1977), *d* of late H. Ludford, S Wales; one *d*. Owns about 2000 acres. *Heir:* kinsman, Henry Alfred Stapleton [*b* 2 May 1913; *m* 1961, Rosslyne Murray, *d* of late Capt. H. S. Warren, RN, Parkstone, Dorset]. *Address:* Rotherfield, Cold Ash, Newbury, Berks. *[Died 4 April 1977.*

STAREY, Captain Stephen Helps, MA Cantab; JP Beds; *b* 26 Jan. 1896; *s* of John Helps Starey and Grace Catherine Dingwall; *m* 1927, Anne Ashworth Drew; three *s* one *d*. *Educ:* Bradfield Coll.; Trinity Coll., Cambridge. Served European War; KSLI 1914; RFC, 1916; RAF, 1918 (wounded twice). Interested in all youth work; British and Tropical Agriculture. Bedfordshire: DL 1940-71; High Sheriff 1948-69. *Address:* Were Down, Bigbury, near Kingsbridge, Devon TQ7 4AL. *T:* Bigbury-on-Sea 252. *Club:* Royal Air Force.
[Died 9 June 1972.

STARK, Admiral Harold Raynsford, GBE (Hon.) 1945; US Navy, retired; *b* Wilkes-Barre, Pa, 12 Nov. 1880; *s* of Benjamin Franklin Stark and Mary Frances Warner; *m* 1907, Katharine Adele Rhoads (*d* 1970), Wilkes-Barre, Pa; two *d*. *Educ:* Naval Academy, Annapolis, Md (graduated in Class of 1903). Commissioned ensign, 1905, promoted through grades to Rear-Admiral, 1934; served on various ships and stations, 1903-7; aide on staff of Adm. Sims, comdg US Naval Forces operating in European waters, 1917-19; inspector in charge of ordnance, Naval Proving Ground, Dahlgren, Va, and Naval Powder Factory, Indian Head, Md, 1925-28; aide on staff and chief of staff, Destroyer Squadrons, Battle Fleet, 1928-30; aide to Sec. of Navy, Washington, DC, 1930-33; comdg USS West Virginia, 1933-34; chief of Bureau of Ordnance, Navy Dept, Washington, DC, 1934-37; comdg Cruiser div. US Fleet, 1937-38; Comdg Cruisers, Battle Force, 1938-39; chief of naval operations, 1939-42; Commander, US Naval Forces in Europe, 1942-45; European Campaign Ribbon; Mexican Campaign, World War, Defense, Dominican Campaign and World War II medals (US); Expeditionary Medal, DSM (USN); Order of Crown of Italy; Gold Star Citation to DSM (USN); Gold Star in lieu of third DSM (USN); National Order of the Southern Cross (Brazilian); DSM (US Army); Commander French Legion of Honour; French Croix de Guerre with Palm; Norwegian Grand Cross of the Order of St Olaf; Knight Grand Cross Order of Orange Nassau with Swords; Belgian Croix-de-Guerre with Palm; Grand Officer Belgian Order of Leopold, with Palm; Chevalier Order of Polonia Restituta, 1st Class. *Address:* 4900 Glenbrook Road NW, Washington, DC 20016, USA. *Clubs:* Army and Navy, Athenæum; Army and Navy (Washington, DC); Chevy Chase (Md); New York Yacht (New York); Westmorland, Wilkes-Barre (Pa); Sachem's Head Yacht (Conn).
[Died 20 Aug. 1972.

STARKEY, Lt-Col Sir William Randle, 2nd Bt, *cr* 1935; JP; DL; *b* 11 Dec. 1899; *o s* of Sir John Starkey, 1st Bt, and Emily, 2nd *d* of Sir Charles Seely, 1st Bt; *S* father, 1940; *m* 1935, Irene Myrtle Francklin (*d* 1965); two *s* one *d*. *Educ:* Eton; Sandhurst. Rifle Bde, 1919-35; called to Bar (Middle Temple), 1938. Served in London Irish Rifles and Reconnaiss. Corps, 1939-45. JP, DL Notts; High Sheriff of Nottinghamshire, 1954. *Heir: s* John Philip Starkey [*b* 1938; *m* 1966, Victoria Henrietta Fleetwood, *y d* of Lt-Col Christopher Fuller, Jaggards, Corsham, Wilts; one *s* two *d*]. *Address:* Norwood Park, Southwell, Notts NG25 0PF. *T:* Southwell 813117. *Clubs:* Army and Navy, MCC.
[Died 10 July 1977.

STARKIE, Walter Fitzwilliam, CMG 1954; CBE 1948; MA, LittD; MRIA; FRSA; FRSL; Hon. FTCD; Director British

Institute, Madrid, and British Council Representative in Spain, 1940-54; Special Lecturer, English Literature, Madrid University, 1948-56; FTCD, 1924-47; Professor of Spanish in Dublin University; Lecturer in Italian Literature in Dublin University, 1926-47; a Director Irish National (Abbey) Theatre, 1927-42; Member Irish Academy of Letters; Corresponding Member Spanish Academy, and of Academy of History; Knight of Order of Alfonso XII; Knight of Order of the Crown of Italy; Chevalier de la Légion d'Honneur; Commander, Order of Isabel the Catholic; LittD (Hon.) Trinity College, Hartford, USA; *b* 9 Aug. 1894; *o s* of late Rt Hon. W. J. M. Starkie, LittD, and May, *d* of late Cornelius Walsh, Dublin; *m* Itaia Augusta, 2nd *d* of Cav. Alberto Porchietti of Genoa and Buenos Aires, and Delfina, *d* of Generale Landi conte Vincenzo; one *s* one *d. Educ:* Shrewsbury; Trinity College, Dublin. Classical Foundation Scholarship; Senior Moderator and gold medallist in Classics; also in History and Political Science; Brooke Prizeman; received musical education at Royal Irish Academy of Music (winner of Vandeleur Academy Violin Scholarship, 1913), and abroad; served in the YMCA during War and attached to BEF Italy; Lecturer in Romance Languages, Trinity College, 1920; course of lectures on Modern Spanish Drama at King's College, London, 1923; course of lectures in Spanish on Modern Drama at Residencia de Estudiantes, Madrid, 1924, under auspices of Anglo-Spanish Society, and 1928; at British Institute, Florence, April 1926; on Spanish Literature at Stockholm and other cities in Sweden; Olaus Petri Foundation Lectures at University of Upsala, Sept. 1926; Lecture tours in USA and Canada, 1929, 1930, and 1931; Lectures at American and Canadian Universities; Lecture tours in France, Dec. 1931 and 1932; Visiting Professor in Romance Languages at University of Chicago, 1930; Lord Northcliffe Lectureship in Literature at University College, London, 1936; Lecture Tour: Central and South America, 1950; in USA 1956-57; Visiting Professorship in Romance Langs, Univ. of Texas, 1958; visiting Prof.: Univ. of New York, 1959; University of Kansas, 1960; University of Colorado, 1961; Sloan Professor, Menninger Foundation of Psychiatric Research, Topeka, Kansas, 1961; Professor in Residence, University of California, Los Angeles, 1961-70. *Publications:* Jacinto Benavente, 1924; Il Teatro Contemporaneo Inglese, 1926; Writers, Modern Spain, 1929; Raggle Taggle, 1933; Translation of Tiger Juan by Ramon Pérez de Ayala, 1933; Spanish Raggle-Taggle, 1934; Don Gypsy, 1936; Luigi Pirandello, 1937 (3rd edn 1965); The Waveless Plain, 1938; Grand Inquisitor, 1940; In Sara's Tents, 1953; abridgement of Don Quixote (with Prelude), 1954, complete translation, 1964; The Road to Santiago, 1957; Spain: A Musician's Journey through Time and Space, 1958; Scholars and Gypsies, 1963; Six Exemplary Novels of Cervantes; Eight Plays of the Spanish Golden Age, 1964; Translation of The Spaniards in their History, by Menendez Pidal (with Introduction); contributions to Enciclopedia Italiana; Encyclopædia Britannica; The Americana; Chambers's, Grove's Dictionary of Music, etc. *Recreations:* violin playing, wandering. *Address:* Apartamentos Melia 15/12, 25 Calle de la Princesa, Madrid VIII, Spain. *Clubs:* Athenæum, Savage; Kildare Street and University (Dublin).   *[Died 2 Nov. 1976.*

STARR, Sir Kenneth (William), Kt 1971; CMG 1956; OBE 1941; ED 1946; FRCS, FACS, FRACS; MS; Hon. Consulting Surgeon, Sydney Hospital, New South Wales, since 1958; Medical Director, NSW State Cancer Council; President, Medical Board of NSW (Member since 1962); Member, National Health and Medical Research Council of Australia, since 1963; *b* 9 Jan. 1908; *s* of Edward Starr, Cowra, NSW; *m* 1940, Alison Neville, *d* of Sir Neville Howse, VC, KCB, KCMG, FRCS; two *s* three *d. Educ:* Fort St Boys' High School; Sydney University. MB (Sydney) 1930; FRCS 1936; MS (Melbourne) 1940; FACS 1936; FRACS 1940. Hallett Prize, Jacksonian Prize, 1944, Hunterian Prof., 1952, Royal Coll. of Surgeons; Hons Award American College of Surgeons, 1937; Mayo Foundation Lecturer (Rochester, Minn), 1952; Examr and President, Royal Australian Coll. Surgeons; Examr, RCS, 1950; Mem. Bd of Governors of Amer. Coll. of Surgeons, 1953; Mem. James IV Assoc. Surgeons, 1961; Corresp. Mem., Assoc. of Surgeons of Great Britain and Ireland. Hon. Mem. Soc. Med. Consultants of Armed Forces of USA; FACS (Hon.), 1954. *Publications:* Delayed Union of Fractures (Jacksonian Prize), 1944; Choledochotomy (Mayo Foundation Lecture), 1952; Surgical Technique (British Encyclopædia of Surgery), 1949; (jointly) Recent Advances in Clinical Cancer, 1970; articles in internat. surgical jls. *Recreations:* golf, gardening. *Address:* 36 Dudley Street, Coogee, NSW 2034, Australia. *T:* 27 4563. *Clubs:* Australian, Australian Jockey (Sydney); Elanora Country.   *[Died 16 June 1976.*

STATHAM, Heathcote Dicken, CBE 1967; MusDoc Cantab; FRCO; Hon. ARCM; retired as Organist and Choirmaster,

Norwich Cathedral (1928-66); Organist Emeritus, 1967; *b* 7 Dec. 1889; *e s* of H. Heathcote Statham, FRIBA; *m* 1928, Mary Claudine, *d* of Rev. Bourchier Wrey; one *s. Educ:* St Michael's College, Tenbury (Scholar); Gresham's Sch., Holt (Scholar); Caius College, Cambridge (Scholar); Royal College of Music. Organist Calcutta Cathedral, 1913; S Michael's Coll., Tenbury, 1920; Parish Church, Southampton, 1926; Conductor Southampton Philharmonic 1927; Norwich Philharmonic, 1928-61; Norwich Triennial Festival, 1936-61; Symphony Concerts, Queen's Hall, 1943-46; conducted London Symphony Orchestra in various concerts in London and Provinces; Examiner to Associated Board of the Royal Schools of Music, 1942. FRSCM, 1963. *Publications:* organ music, songs, part-songs, operetta; Ed. Dr John Blow's Church Music (17th Cent.). *Recreation:* walking. *Address:* 11 The Close, Norwich, Norfolk. *T:* Norwich 26746.   *[Died 29 Oct. 1973.*

STAYNER, Brig. Gerrard Francis Hood, CB 1945; CBE 1943 (OBE 1941); psc; retired; late Inf.; *b* 29 July 1900; 2nd *s* of Hewlett James Stayner and Mabel Palmer, Llanstephan, Teignmouth, Devon; *m* 1927, Leslie Edna, 2nd *d* of Horace and Diana Imber; no *c. Educ:* Cheltenham College; RMC Sandhurst. 2nd Lieut Leicestershire Regiment, 1919; served with Sudan Defence Force, 1925-35; Eritrean Campaign (OBE); Malta 1942-43 (CBE); Italy 1944-45 (CB, Legion of Merit Degree of Officer, USA); seconded to UNRRA Oct. 1945; Dep. Chief of Mission for Supply and Distrib., UNRRA Greece, 1945-46. OC Troops and Brigadier i/c Administration, Fortress HQ Gibraltar, 1950-53; retd 1953. Controller, Airborne Forces Security Fund, 1962-66. *Address:* 6 Lansdowne House, Lansdowne Road, W11 3LP. *T:* 01-727 4829.   *[Died 9 July 1980.*

STEAD, Gilbert; Professor Emeritus of Physics in the University of London since 1953; Consultant Physicist Emeritus to Guy's Hospital since 1953; *b* 3 Feb. 1888; *s* of late Richard Stead, Folkestone; *m* 1916, Margaret (*d* 1976), *d* of late Thomas Gallimore, Leamington; one *s* two *d. Educ:* Bradford Grammar School; Clare College, Cambridge (Scholar). 1st Class Nat. Sci. Tripos, Pt I, 1908, Pt II, 1909; BA 1909; MA 1913; DSc (London), 1940; Assistant Demonstrator, Cavendish Laboratory, 1910; attached to HM Signal School, Portsmouth, 1915-19; Reader in Physics, Guy's Hospital Medical School, University of London, 1923-38, Professor of Physics, 1939-53; Honorary Consulting Physicist to Guy's Hospital, 1948-53; Governor of Guy's Hospital Medical School, 1948-53; University Lecturer in Physics as applied to Medical Radiology, Cambridge, 1925-38; Sec. for Cambridge Diploma in Medical Radiology, 1927-42; FInstP; FRSA; Hon. Member of Indian Radiological Assoc.; Member British Institute of Radiology, Pres., 1947-48. Hon. Mem., RCR; Fellow of Cambridge Philosophical Society; Member Hospital Physicists' Association (President, 1951-52; Hon. Member 1960). *Publications:* Elementary Physics, 1924; Notes on Practical Physics, 1939; various original papers in Proc. Roy. Soc., Philosophical Magazine, Journ. Institution of Electrical Engineers, Proc. Cambridge Philosophical Soc. *Address:* Flat 8, Coombe Court, Station Approach, Tadworth, Surrey KT20 5AL. *T:* Tadworth 2466.   *[Died 5 July 1979.*

STEAVENSON, Dr William Herbert; *b* 26 April 1894; *s* of late Rev. Frederick Robert Steavenson, Rector of Quenington, Glos. *Educ:* Cheltenham College; Guy's Hospital. LMSSA London, 1918; Civil Surgeon, Queen Alexandra Military Hospital, Millbank, 1918-19; Captain RAMC, 1919-21; served in Egypt. President: British Astronomical Assoc., 1926-28 (Goodacre Medallist, 1961); Royal Astronomical Soc., 1957-59 (Jackson-Gwilt Medallist, 1928); Member of National Committee for Astronomy, 1927-59. Gresham Professor in Astronomy, 1946-64; Astronomical corr., The Times, 1938-69. *Publications:* A Catalogue of the Instruments of Sir William Herschel (Optical Soc.); Note on Egyptian Mirage (R Met. Soc.'s Jl); (jt ed. and part author) of Splendour of the Heavens, 1923; Physical Observations of Mars, 1924 (Greenwich Observations); ed and revised Proctor's Half Hours with the Telescope; Suns and Worlds, 1933; numerous papers in the Monthly Notices of RAS and Jl of British Astronomical Assoc. *Address:* Gordon Cottage, South Marston, Swindon, Wilts. *T:* Stratton St Margaret 478.   *[Died 23 Sept. 1975.*

STEDEFORD, Sir Ivan (Arthur Rice), GBE 1961 (KBE 1954); Life President, Tube Investments Ltd, since 1963, after nineteen years as Chairman and Managing Director; *b* Exeter, 28 Jan. 1897; *s* of late Rev. Charles Stedeford, ex-Pres. United Methodist Church; *m* 1923, Gwendoline Edith Aston; three *d. Educ:* Shebbear Coll., N Devon; King Edward VI Grammar School, Birmingham. Engineer Apprentice Wolseley Motors Ltd; served European War, RNAS, 1918-19. A Deputy

Chairman, National Provincial Bank, 1964-68, and National Westminster Bank, 1968-69. Member: Television Advisory Cttee, 1949-50; Committee of Enquiry into British Broadcasting Corporation 1949-50; a Governor of the BBC, 1951-55. Member: Advisory Council, Department of Scientific and Industrial Research, 1950-52; UK Atomic Energy Authority, 1954-59; Chairman, Advisory Group on British Transport Commission, 1960. Hon. Kentucky Colonel. *Recreations:* country pursuits. *Address:* Clifford Hill Court, Clifford Chambers, Stratford-on-Avon, Warwicks. *T:* Stratford-on-Avon 2758. *Club:* Athenæum.   *[Died 9 Feb. 1975.*

STEDMAN, Edgar, FRS 1938; DSc, PhD; Reader (Emeritus) in Biochemistry in the University of Edinburgh; *b* 12 July 1890; *m* 1920, Ellen Field (*d* 1962); no *c*; *m* 1964, Martha Jefferson Taylor. *Educ:* University of London. *Publications:* Author and Joint Author of various Scientific Memoirs published chiefly in Journal of the Chemical Society, Biochemical Journal and Philosophical Transactions and Proceedings of the Royal Society. *Recreation:* gardening. *Address:* 13 Kline Boulevard, Frederick, Maryland 21701, USA. *T:* 301-663-5330.
                                                                [Died 8 May 1975.

STEEL, Anthony Bedford, OBE 1946; MA; LittD, LLD; JP; Principal, University College, Cardiff, 1949-66; Vice-Chancellor, University of Wales, 1956-58, 1959-61; *b* 24 Feb. 1900; *s* of Major Edwin Bedford Steel, RAMC; *m* 1924, Eileen M. Johnson; one *s*; *m* 1956, Elizabeth Tesni, *yr d* of Sir Wynne Cemlyn-Jones. *Educ:* Rugby; New College, Oxford (1st Class Lit. Hum.). 2nd Lt RASC, MT, 1918-19, France and Germany; Fellow, Christ's College, Cambridge, 1924-, University Lecturer in History, 1930-49; Senior Proctor, 1937-38; Steward of Christ's College, 1937-39; Tutor, 1945-49; Ministry of Information, 1939-40; British Council, 1940-45. Assistant Director-General (Overseas), St John Ambulance Association, 1952-54; CStJ. *Publications:* Jorrocks's England, 1932; Richard II, 1941; The Custom of the Room (Early Winebooks of Christ's College, Cambridge), 1951; The Receipt of the Exchequer, 1377-1485, 1954; contrib.: Cambridge History of the British Empire; Studies presented to Sir Hilary Jenkinson, 1957. *Recreations:* fishing, bridge. *Address:* Wrangbrook, Lisvane Road, Llanishen, Cardiff. *T:* Cardiff 752498. *Clubs:* United Service & Royal Aero; Cardiff and County.   *[Died 3 Oct. 1973.*

STEEL, Sir Christopher Eden, GCMG 1960 (KCMG 1951; CMG 1945); MVO 1936; *b* 12 Feb. 1903; *er s* of late Col Richard Steel and Adine, *d* of W. Acton-Adams, Tipapa, Canterbury, NZ; *m* 1932, Catherine, *er d* of late Lieut-Gen. Sir Sidney Clive, GCVO, KCB, CMG, DSO; two *s* one *d. Educ:* Wellington College (Scholar); Hertford College, Oxford (Scholar). Entered Diplomatic Service, 1927; has served at Rio de Janeiro, Paris, The Hague, Berlin and Cairo. Assistant Private Sec. to the Prince of Wales, 1935-36; British Political Officer, SHAEF, 1945; Political adviser to Commander-in-Chief, Germany, 1947, Dep. High Commissioner, 1949; Minister, British Embassy, Washington, 1950-53; UK Permanent Representative on the North Atlantic Council, 1953-57; Ambassador at Bonn, 1957-63, retired. Chairman, Anglo-German Association, 1966-73. *Address:* Southrop Lodge, near Lechlade, Glos. *Club:* Travellers'.   *[Died 17 Sept. 1973.*

STEEL, His Honour Edward, JP; a Circuit Judge (formerly County Court Judge), 1958-75; *b* 9 May 1906; *er s* of Thomas S. Steel, Solicitor, Warrington; *m* 1936, Mary Evelyn Griffith Roberts, *er d* of late Alderman R. G. Roberts, JP; two *d. Educ:* Boteler Grammar School, Warrington; Hutton Grammar School, Preston; Liverpool University (LLB). Solicitor, Nov. 1928; called to Bar, Gray's Inn, 1937; served War of 1939-45, Judge Advocate-General's Dept, (Lt-Col); Judge Advocate, Trial of War Criminals, Germany and Norway; Assistant Recorder, Liverpool City QS, 1948-56; Chancellor: Diocese of Liverpool, 1957-; Diocese of Manchester, 1971-; County Court Judge, Circuit 10 (Yorkshire), Jan. 1958, Circuit 10 (Oldham, etc), 1958-61, Circuit 5 (Salford, etc), Jan.-May, 1961; Circuit 8 (Manchester), 1961-71; Commissioner, Crown Court, Manchester, 1961-71; Dep. Chm. Lancashire County QS, 1959-71; Cheshire County QS, 1961-71. Mem. Court, Univ. of Liverpool, 1964-. Vice-President Manchester Meeting, British Association for the Advancement of Science, 1962. JP Cheshire, 1958. *Recreation:* cinematography. *Address:* Woodlands, Walton, Cheshire. *T:* Warrington 62383.   *[Died 15 Jan. 1976.*

STEELE, Mrs Alfred N.; *see* Crawford, Joan.

STEELE, Air Marshal Sir Charles Ronald, KCB 1951 (CB 1944); DFC 1918; DL; *b* 9 November 1897; *s* of late Rev. Canon Steele, Lincoln; *m* 1920, Joan Evelyn (*d* 1972), *d* of late H. M. R. Hopkins, CSI; one *s* one *d. Educ:* Oundle; Royal Military

College, Sandhurst. Gazetted to Green Howards 1916 and seconded to RFC; served in France 1916-18 with Nos 15, 20, and 48 Squadrons RFC and RAF (DFC); India with 28 Squadron, 1919-23; served on Indian Frontier, 1921-23, in Wana and Razmak Campaigns; RAF Staff College, 1926-27; No 1 Air Defence Group (HQ Auxiliary Air Force), 1927-29; No 47 Squadron, Khartoum, 1930-31; HQ, RAF, Jerusalem, 1932-33; Staff College, Camberley, 1934-35; commanded No 18 Squadron RAF, 1936-37; HQ BAFF (France), 1940 (despatches); Rhodesian Air Training Group, S Rhodesia, 1941-42; HQ No 9 Group as SASO, 1942; AOC No 10 Group RAF, 1943-44; AOC No 85 Group RAF, 1944-45; SASO, British Air Forces of Occupation (Germany), 1945-47; AOC, RAF, Malta, 1947-49; AOC-in-C, Coastal Command, 1950-51; invalided out of RAF, 1952. DL Cambridge, 1962. Order of George I of Greece, 1942; Commander Legion of Honour, Croix de Guerre (France), 1946; Commander Order of Crown of Belgium, Croix de Guerre (Belgium), 1946. *Address:* 17 Rutherford Road, Cambridge. *Club:* MCC.   *[Died 14 Feb. 1973.*

STEELE, Lt-Col Harwood (Robert Elmes), MC; FRGS; Author and Journalist; at present engaged on History of Royal Canadian Mounted Police; *b* Fort Macleod, Alberta, Canada, 5 May 1897; *o s* of late Maj.-Gen. Sir S. B. Steele, KCMG, and Lady Steele (*née* de Lotbiniere Harwood), *d* of co-seigneur of Vaudreuil, Quebec. *Educ:* England, Canada and South Africa. Served European War, 1914-18 (Capt., MC, despatches); Capt. Winnipeg Grenadiers, 1915-26; Capt. 17th DYRC Hussars 1926; Major, 1929; Lieut-Colonel and OC 1938. Historian, Canadian Govt Arctic Expedition. CGS Arctic, 1925, to Far North; Asst Press Representative, CPR, 1923-25; lectured, with Govt endorsement, on RCM Police through Canada and Eastern US, 1928-30. Served War of 1939-45 in England, Northern Ireland, NW Frontier, India, 14th Army, East of Brahmaputra and GHQ, India Command; War Subst. Major 17/21 Lancers, 1939; Temp. Lt-Col 1944 (despatches). Lectured in England and Canada on India, Canada and RCMP, 1945-63. Hon. Chief, E Kootenay Indians (Canada), and other similar honours. *Publications:* Cleared for Action (Naval Poems), 1914; The Canadians in France, 1915-18, 1920; Spirit of Iron, novel, 1923; I Shall Arise, novel, 1926; The Ninth Circle, novel, 1927; Policing the Arctic, history of RCMP in Far North, 1936; India: Friend or Foe? a political study, 1947; To Effect An Arrest, short stories of RCMP, 1947; Ghosts Returning (novel), 1950; The Marching Call, early life of Sir S. B. Steele, 1955; The Red Serge, short stories of RCMP, 1961; Royal Canadian Mounted Police: a short history, 1968; poems, short stories, broadcasts, articles. *Address:* Warenne Lodge, Pulborough, West Sussex. *Club:* Savage.   *[Died 12 June 1978.*

STEELE, General Sir James Stuart, GCB 1950 (KCB 1949; CB 1943); KBE 1946; DSO 1940; MC 1917; LLD (QUB) 1947; *b* 26 Oct. 1894; *s* of late Samuel Steele, Ballycarry, Co. Antrim; *m* 1923, Janet Gibson Gordon; two *d. Educ:* Royal Belfast Academical Instn; Queen's Univ., Belfast. 2nd Lt Royal Irish Rifles, Sept. 1914; served France and Belgium, 1915-17 (MC, despatches); NW Frontier, 1920 (despatches); commanded 1st Bn Sherwood Foresters, 1937-39; Palestine, 1939; AAG War Office, 1939; Colonel, 1939; Bde Comdr, 1939-41; France and Belgium, 1940 (DSO); Divisional Comdr 1941-42; Corps Commander 1942; DCGS and CGS, Middle East, 1942-43; DSD War Office, 1943-45; Maj.-Gen. 1944; C-in-C British Troops and High Commissioner, Austria, 1946-47; Lt-Gen. 1946; General, 1947. Col The Royal Ulster Rifles, 1947-57. Adj.-Gen. to Forces, 1947-50. ADC General to the King, 1950; retired pay, 1950. Chm. Legal Aid Cttee, N Ireland, 1958-60. Col Comdt, Royal Army Educational Corps, 1950-59; Hon. Colonel QUB Contingent OTC, 1951-59. Pres., Army Benevolent Fund, 1954-64. *Recreation:* gardening. *Address:* Churchills, Stourpaine, Blandford, Dorset. *Clubs:* Athenæum, Army and Navy.
                                                                [Died 24 July 1975.

STEELE, Norman James; Under-Secretary, Department of Agriculture and Fisheries for Scotland; *b* 6 Feb. 1918; *m* 1941, Joan Ewers; one *s* two *d. Educ:* George Heriot's, Edinburgh. Served War, RAF, 1939-46. Civil Service (Dept of Agriculture and Fisheries for Scotland), 1935-. *Recreations:* golf, curling. *Address:* 22 Winton Terrace, Edinburgh EH10 7AP. *T:* 031-445 3066.   *[Died 1 Sept. 1977.*

STEELE, Thomas; *b* 15 Nov. 1905; *s* of late James Steele, miner; *m* 1939, Helen Thomson; two *s.* Stationmaster to 1945; MP (Lab) Lanark Division of Lanarkshire, 1945-50, West Dunbartonshire, 1950-70; Parliamentary Secretary, Ministry of National Insurance, 1946-50. Member GMC, 1965-75. *Address:* Windyridge, Lesmahagow, Lanark.   *[Died 28 May 1979.*

STEEN, Marguerite; FRSL; novelist and playwright; *b* 1894; *d* of Captain George Conolly Benson, KSLI, and Margaret Jones; adopted *d* of Joseph and Margaret Jane Steen. *Educ:* privately. Taught in private sch. during war; became a dancing mistress, and left this profession for the stage; three years with Fred Terry-Julia Neilson Co.; left stage and started career as novelist, 1926. *Publications:* Gilt Cage, 1927; Duel in the Dark, 1928; The Reluctant Madonna, 1929; They That Go Down, 1930; When the Wind Blows, 1931; Unicorn, 1931; The Wise and the Foolish Virgins, 1932; Oakfield Plays, 1932; Stallion, 1933; Spider, 1933; Hugh Walpole, a study 1933; The Spanish Trilogy: Matador, 1934 (Book Society Choice England and Book of the Month, USA); The Tavern, 1935; The One-Eyed Moon, 1935; Return of a Heroine, 1936; The Lost One, 1937; Who Would Have Daughters?, 1937; The Marriage Will Not Take Place, 1938; Family Ties, 1939; The Sun is My Undoing, 1941 (Book Society Choice, England, Literary Guild, USA); William Nicholson, a biography, 1943; Rose Timpson, 1946; Granada Window, 1949; Twilight on the Floods, 1949; The Swan, 1951; Phoenix Rising, 1952; Anna Fitzalan, 1953; Bulls of Parral, 1954; The Unquiet Spirit, 1955; Little White King, 1956; The Woman in the Back Seat, 1959; The Tower, 1959; A Pride of Terrys (biography), 1962; A Candle in the Sun, 1964; Looking Glass I (autobiography), 1966; Pier Glass (autobiography), 1968. *Plays:* Matador (with Matheson Lang), prod. 1936; French for Love (with Derek Patmore), prod. 1939. *Recreation:* writing. *Address:* 42 Dibleys, Blewbury, Berks. *T:* 294.
[Died 4 Aug. 1975.

STEER, Francis William; Maltravers Herald Extraordinary since 1972; Archivist and Librarian to the Duke of Norfolk since 1956; Archivist to New College, Oxford, 1965-78, and to College of Arms, 1969-77; Librarian of Chichester Cathedral; *b* Ashingdon, 10 Aug. 1912; *s* of William Francis Steer and Edith Caroline (*née* Todd); *m* 1934, Mabel Alice Holdstock; no *c*. *Educ:* Ashingdon; Southend-on-Sea High Sch.; privately. MA, FSA, FSA (Scot.), FRHistS. Asst Archivist, Essex Record Office, 1946-53; County Archivist: E and W Sussex, 1953-59; W Sussex, 1959-69; Archivist to Bp and Dean and Chapter of Chichester, 1953-69; Hon. Sec., Essex Archaeological Soc., 1953; Mem. Council, Sussex Arch. Soc., 1954-78, Pres., 1973-78, Vice-Pres., 1978-; Editor, Sussex Archaeological Collections, 1959-73; Jt Literary Dir, Sussex Record Soc., 1958- (Mem. Council, 1943-); Hon. Sec., Marc Fitch Fund, 1956-76; Mem. Exec. Cttee, Sussex Historic Churches Trust; served as mem. various cttees concerned with archives, local history, museums, etc. Citizen and Scrivener of London; Parish Clerk of St Benet, Paul's Wharf, London; Mem., Parish Clerks' Co. Hon. MA Oxon, 1974; Hon. DLitt Sussex, 1974. OStJ 1967. *Publications:* Farm and Cottage Inventories of Mid-Essex, 1635-1749, 1950 (2nd edn 1969); History of the Dunmow Flitch Ceremony, 1951; (ed, with L. J. Redstone) Local Records, their nature and care, 1953; (with A. S. Duncan-Jones) The Story of Chichester Cathedral, 1955; John Philipot's Roll of the Constables of Dover Castle, 1956; Catalogue of the Ashburnham Archives, 1958; I am, my dear Sir, 1959; Records of the Corporation of Seaford, 1959; Catalogue of the Shiffner Archives, 1959; Catalogue of the Crookshank Collection, 1960; Samuel Tufnell of Langleys, 1960; Bibliotheca Norfolciana, 1961; Catalogue of the Mitford Archives, vol. 1, 1962, vol. 2, 1970; A Catalogue of Sussex Estate and Tithe Award Maps, vol. 1, 1962, vol. 2, 1968; The Hawkins Papers: a catalogue, 1962; Minute Book of the Common Council of Chichester, 1783-1826, 1963; The Maxse Papers: a catalogue, 1964; The Cobden Papers: a catalogue, 1964; Catalogue of the Lavington Archives, 1964; A Catalogue of the Earl Marshal's Papers at Arundel Castle, 1965; The Letters of John Hawkins and Samuel and Daniel Lysons, 1812-1830, 1966; The Wilberforce Archives: a catalogue, 1966; (with I. M. Kirby) Records of the Diocese of Chichester, vol. 1, 1966, vol. 2, 1967; Scriveners' Company Common Paper, 1357-1678, 1968; Arundel Castle Archives: a catalogue, vol. 1, 1968, vol. 2, 1973, vol. 3, 1976; (with N. H. Osborne) The Petworth House Archives, 1968; (with J. E. A. Venables) The Goodwood Estate Archives, vol. 1, 1970, vol. 2, 1972; The Life of St Philip Howard, 1971 (revised edn); Centenary of Arundel Cathedral: a monograph, 1973; History of the Worshipful Company of Scriveners, 1973; The Archives of New College, Oxford: a catalogue, 1974; An 18th Century Survey of Arundel Castle, 1976; numerous articles, reviews, monographs. *Recreations:* looking at flowers, reading, working, talking to friends. *Address:* 63 Orchard Street, Chichester, West Sussex. *T:* Chichester 83490. *Club:* Athenæum.
[Died 23 Sept. 1978.

STEIN, Leonard Jacques, OBE 1953; Vice-President: Anglo-Jewish Association (President, 1939-49); Jewish Historical Society of England (President, 1964-65); *b* London, 12 Dec. 1887; *s* of Philip Stein and Matilda, *d* of Louis Beaver, Manchester; *m* 1928, Sarah, *d* of H. B. Kitay, Paterson, NJ,
USA; one *s* (and one *s* decd). *Educ:* St Paul's School; Balliol College, Oxford; President of the Oxford Union, 1910. Called to Bar, Inner Temple, 1912; served in Army, 1914-20 (Staff-Captain, Palestine Military Administration and subsequently on Political Staff, EEF, in Jerusalem and at GHQ, Cairo, 1918-20); Political Sec., World Zionist Organisation, 1920-29; Honorary Legal Adviser, Jewish Agency for Palestine, 1929-39; contested (L) Dover, 1922, North Kensington, 1923, West Bermondsey, 1929. *Publications:* Edition of the Vicar of Wakefield, 1912; Zionism, 1925, republished in new edition, 1932; Syria, 1926; (Joint) Tax Avoidance, 1936, The National Defence Contribution, 1937, The Excess Profits Tax, 1940; The Balfour Declaration, 1961; Weizmann and England, 1965; (Jt Editor) Letters and Papers of Chaim Weizmann, Vol. I, 1968. *Address:* 1 Temple Gardens, Temple, EC4Y 9BB. *T:* 01-353 1672. *Club:* Reform.
[Died 23 April 1973.

STEIN, Prof. William Howard; Professor of Biochemistry, Rockefeller University, New York, since 1955; *b* NYC, 25 June 1911; *s* of Fred M. and Beatrice B. Stein; *m* 1936, Phoebe Hockstader; three *s*. *Educ:* Lincoln Sch. of Teachers Coll., Columbia; Phillips Exeter Acad.; Univs of Harvard and Columbia. BS Harvard, 1933; PhD Columbia, 1938. Rockefeller Inst. for Medical Research: Asst, 1939-43; Associate, 1943-49; Associate Mem., 1949-52; Mem., 1952. Member: Nat. Acad. of Sciences; Amer. Acad. of Arts and Sciences; Amer. Soc. of Biological Chemists; Biochem. Soc., London; Amer. Chem. Soc.; Amer. Assoc. for Advancement of Science; Harvey Soc. of NY; Past Member: Editorial Cttee, Jl of Biological Chemistry (Chm. 1958-61); Editorial Bd, Jl of Biological Chemistry, 1962-64 (Assoc. Editor, 1964-68; Editor, 1968-71); Council, Inst. of Neurological Diseases and Blindness of NIH, 1961-66; Chm., US Nat. Cttee for Biochemistry, 1968-69. Harvey Lectr, 1956; Phillips Lectr, Haverford Coll., 1962; Philip Schaffer Lectr, Washington Univ., 1965. Vis. Prof., Univ. of Chicago, 1961; Vis. Prof., Harvard Univ., 1964. Mem. Med. Adv. Bd, Hebrew Univ.-Hadassah Med. Sch., 1957-70; Trustee, Montefiore Hosp., 1948-74. Amer. Chem. Soc. Award in Chromatography and Electrophoresis (jtly), 1964; Richards Medal, Amer. Chem. Soc. (jtly), 1972; Kaj Linderstrøm-Lang Award (jtly), 1972; Nobel Prize in Chemistry (jtly), 1972; Columbia Univ. Graduate Faculty and Alumni Assoc. Award of Excellence, 1973. Hon. DSc: Columbia, 1973; Albert Einstein Coll. of Medicine, Yeshiva Univ., 1973. *Publications:* numerous papers in Jl Biological Chemistry, Biochemistry, Jl Amer. Chem. Soc., Analytical Chemistry, etc. *Address:* 530 East 72nd Street, New York, NY 10021, USA. *T:* 535-7022.
[Died 2 Feb. 1980.

STEINBERG, William; Conductor and Musical Director of the Pittsburgh Symphony Orchestra, Pennsylvania, USA, 1952-76, simultaneously, Music Director of the Boston Symphony Orchestra, 1969-72; *b* Cologne, 1 Aug. 1899; *s* of Julius Steinberg and Bertha Matzdorf; *m* 1934, Lotti Stern; one *s* one *d*. *Educ:* School of Higher Musical Studies, Cologne University. Studied piano with Uzielli, composition with Boelsche and conducting with Abendroth. Conductor Cologne Opera House, 1920; Opera Director, German Theatre, Prague, 1925-29; subseq. General Music Director, Frankfort Opera House, Guest Conductor, Berlin State Opera House, Conductor, Ceska Philharmonie, Prague, Museum Gesellschaft, Frankfort, and Palestine Orchestra. Went to USA, 1938; Guest Conductor with orchestras of many US cities; Conductor, San Francisco Opera, 1944-58; Musical Director: Buffalo Philharmonic Orch., 1945-52; London Philharmonic Orch., 1958-60. Has made many gramophone records. *Address:* 44 James Avenue, Atherton, Calif. 94025, USA; (Manager) Ronald A. Wilford, Columbia Artists, 165 West 57th Street, New York, NY 10019, USA.
[Died 16 May 1978.

STENGEL, Prof. Erwin; retired as Professor of Psychiatry (now Emeritus), University of Sheffield; *b* 25 March 1902; *s* of late Markus Stengel and of Franziska Stengel; *m* 1935, Anna Kohl. *Educ:* University of Vienna. MD (Vienna), 1926. Senior Lecturer in Neurology and Psychiatry, Univ. of Vienna, 1937; Research Fellow in Psychiatry, Edinburgh, 1942; Director of Research, Graylingwell Hosp., Chichester, 1947; Reader in Psychiatry Univ. of London, 1949. Cons. Physician, The Bethlem Royal and The Maudsley Hosp., 1949; Chm. Med. Section, British Psychol. Soc., 1954, now Hon. Fellow. President: Sect. of Psychiatry, Roy. Soc. Med., 1957-58; Roy. Med.-Psychol Assoc., 1966-67; Internat. Assoc. for Suicide Prevention. Hon. FRCPsych 1971. Hon. MD Sheffield, 1971. *Publications:* (with N. G. Cook) Attempted Suicide: Its Social Significance and Effects, 1958; Suicide and Attempted Suicide, 1966; articles in medical and psychological journals. *Recreations:* music, travelling. *Address:* 7 Montrose Court, Hill Turrets Close, Sheffield S11 9RF. *T:* 360267.
[Died 2 June 1973.

STENTON, Lady (Doris Mary), FBA 1953; University Reader, retired; *b* 27 Aug. 1894; *d* of Joseph and Amelia Parsons; *m* 1919, Prof. Sir Frank M. Stenton (*d* 1967), FBA. *Educ:* Abbey Sch., Reading; Univ. Coll., Reading. 1st cl. hons History (Lond.) 1916. Lectr, Univ. Coll., Reading, 1917; Reader, Reading Univ., 1955; Raleigh Lectr, 1958. Hon. Sec. and Gen. Ed., Pipe Roll Soc., 1925-62. Hon. LLD, Glasgow; Hon. DLitt, Oxford, 1968. *Publications:* The Pipe Rolls beginning with New Series, vol. I, 1925; Cambridge Medieval History, Henry II, 1926; The Earliest Lincolnshire Assize Rolls, 1926 (Lincoln Record Soc. vol. 22); The Earliest Northamptonshire Assize Rolls, 1930; Rolls of the Justices in Eyre for Lincolnshire 1218-19 and Worcestershire 1221, Selden Soc. vol. 53; Rolls of the Justices in Eyre for Yorkshire 1218-19; Rolls of the Justices in Eyre for Gloucestershire, Warwickshire and Shropshire, Selden Soc. vols 56 and 59; (with Lewis C. Loyd) Sir Christopher Hatton's Book of Seals (presented to F. M. Stenton), 1950; English Society in the Early Middle Ages, 1951; Pleas before the King or his Justices 1198-1202 (2 vols), Selden Soc. vols 67 and 68, 1952 and 1953; The English Woman in History, 1957; English Justice 1066-1215, 1964; King John and the Courts of Justice, Pleas before the King or his Justices, vols 3 and 4, Selden Soc. vols 83 and 84, 1967; (ed) The Free Peasantry of the Northern Danelaw, 1969; (ed) Preparatory to Anglo-Saxon England, the collected papers of Frank Merry Stenton, 1970; (ed) Anglo-Saxon England, by F. M. Stenton, 3rd edn, 1971. *Address:* Whitley Park Farm, Reading, Berks. *T:* Reading 81585.
[Died 29 Dec. 1971.

STEPHEN, Sir Alexander Murray, Kt 1946; MC; DL; JP; BA; Lord Lieutenant of Lanarkshire, 1955-59; *b* 1892; *e s* of late F. J. Stephen; *m* 1922, Kathrene Paton Mitchell; two *s* one *d. Educ:* Cargilfield; Fettes College; King's Coll., Cambridge (1st Class Hons Mechanical Science Tripos). Served European war, RGA, 1914-18, Major (despatches, MC); Ex-Pres.: Institution of Engineers and Shipbuilders in Scotland; Shipbuilding Employers Federation; Shipbuilding Conference; British Shipbuilding Research Assoc. JP 1955, DL 1960, Lanarkshire. LLD (Hon.) Glasgow 1957. *Recreation:* shooting. *Address:* Craigmarloch, Kilmacolm, Renfrewshire. *Club:* Western (Glasgow).
[Died 17 Dec. 1974.

STEPHEN, Sir Andrew, Kt 1972; Chairman of the Football Association, 1967-76; *b* 20 May 1906; *s* of Alexander Stephen and Margaret Martin Stephen; *m* 1934, Frances Barker; three *s. Educ:* Peterhead Academy, Aberdeenshire; Aberdeen Univ. (MB, ChB). Various hosp. appts in Aberdeen and London, as resident MO, 1928-30; Gen. Practitioner, Sheffield, 1930-66. Pres., Sheffield Div. of BMA; Pres., Sheffield Medico-Chirurgical Soc. Served on: Exec. Council, Local Medical Cttee, and Hospital Management Cttee, in Sheffield. *Recreations:* shooting activities, including game shooting. *Address:* Wisewood House, Wisewood Road, Sheffield S6 4WB. *T:* Sheffield 43177.
[Died 26 Feb. 1980.

STEPHEN, George, CBE 1960; DL; Hon. LLD (Aberdeen) 1959; Lord Provost of Aberdeen, 1955-61; Lord Lieutenant of County of City of Aberdeen, 1955-61; *b* 12 Sept. 1886; *s* of George Stephen and Helen Peters; *m* 1917, Mary Annand Turner; one *d. Educ:* Skene Square School, and Central Secondary School, Aberdeen. Postal Service, Aberdeen, 1900-47. Served with 89th Field Ambulance RAMC in Gallipoli and France, 1914-18 (despatches). Aberdeen Town Council, 1947-61; First Patron of Aberdeen Burns Club. Member: Executive Committee British Waterworks Association, 1948-51; Scottish Gas Consultative Council, 1952-57. DL Aberdeenshire, 1964. *Publications:* When the Nichts are comin' doon and other poems, 1955; A Breath o' the North-East-A Second Book of Verse, 1958; Poems at Eventide, 1959; hymn in Church of Scotland Hymn Book for Special Services, 1923. *Recreation:* gardening. *Address:* 25 Bonnymuir Place, Aberdeen. *T:* Aberdeen 20414.
[Died 17 Jan. 1972.

STEPHENS, Sir Edgar; *see* Stephens, Sir L. E.

STEPHENS, Frederick James; retired 1971; Managing Director, The "Shell" Transport and Trading Co. Ltd, 1957-71 (Director since 1951); Chairman, 1961-67); Chairman, The Shell Petroleum Co. Ltd, 1961-71 (Managing Director, 1951-61); Managing Director, Shell International Petroleum Co. Ltd, 1959-61; Director, Bataafse Petroleum Maatschappij NV (Principal Director, 1956-61, Delegate Member of Board from 1951); *b* 30 July 1903; *er s* of late Canon John Frederick Douglas Stephens and Frances Mary (*née* Mirrlees); *m* 1948, Sara Clark (*d* 1954), Dallas, Texas; no *c. Educ:* Marlborough Coll.; Grenoble Univ., France; Pembroke Coll., Cambridge. BA 1926, MA 1956, Cambridge. Joined Royal Dutch Shell Group of Companies, 1926, and served in Venezuela, London and US;

Director and Exec. Vice-Pres. of Asiatic Petroleum Corp., New York, 1946; returned to London, 1948. Hon. Fellow, University Coll., London, 1958; Visiting Fellow Nuffield Coll., Oxford, 1961; Member of Court, University of Reading, 1962. Comdr, Order of Orange-Nassau, 1968. *Recreations:* gardening, walking. *Address:* Noel House, Les Ruisseaux, St Brelade, Jersey, CI. *Clubs:* Carlton; New Zealand Golf (Byfleet); Victoria; Royal Channel Islands Yacht (Jersey).
[Died 9 Nov. 1978.

STEPHENS, Mrs George Arbour; *see* Williams, Mary.

STEPHENS, Engineer Rear-Admiral George Leslie, CB 1946; CBE 1943; CD; Royal Canadian Navy, retired; *b* 2 Jan. 1889; *s* of George Selleck and Ernestine Stephens; *m* 1913, Edna Louise Woodill; one *s* two *d. Educ:* Plympton Public School, Plympton; Stoke Public School, Devonport. Naval Engineering training, HM Dockyard, Devonport, England, 1903-10; joined Royal Canadian Navy as Engine-room Artificer, 1910. Warrant Rank, 1912; Engineer Lieut 1915; Engineer Comdr 1929; Engineer Capt. 1940; Engineer-in-Chief, Naval Service HQ, Ottawa, 1941; Engineer Rear-Adm. 1943. *Recreations:* curling and golf. *Address:* c/o Peter H. Sinclair, 21 Cedar Road, Ottawa, Ontario K1J 6L6, Canada.
[Died 13 April 1979.

STEPHENS, Sir (Leon) Edgar, Kt 1960; CBE 1945; JP; DL; formerly Clerk of the Peace and of County Council of Warwickshire, Clerk to the Lieutenancy, Registration Officer, Acting Returning Officer (1927-67); *b* 7 Jan. 1901; *s* of late W. Edgar Stephens, OBE, FSA, The Greylands, Gorleston; *m* 1st, 1928, Joan Beeching (*d* 1946), *yr d* of late Edwin H. Johnson, JP, Flixton House, near Lowestoft; three *d*; 2nd, 1947, Joan, 2nd *d* of late Captain J. G. Miles, Gorleston, Suffolk. *Educ:* Felsted; Trinity Hall, Cambridge (MA, LLB). Barrister, Middle Temple, 1924; County Controller for Civil Def., Warwicks, 1939-45, 1964-67; Clerk of War Zone Court, Midland Region, 1939-45. Hon. Sec., Soc. of Clerks of the Peace of Counties and of Clerks of County Councils, 1947-53, Chairman, 1953-56; Hon. Treas. 1956-67; Mem. Master of the Rolls Archives Cttee, 1946-56; Mem. Historical Manuscripts Commn, 1959-; Chm. Centenary (1969) Committee; FSA, 1943; DL Warwickshire, 1950; JP 1967. *Publications:* contrib. to Macmillan's Local Government Law and Administration; The Warwickshire County Book, 1933, 1939 and 1959 Editions; The Clerks of the Counties, 1360-1960. *Recreations:* golf, gardening and reading; coxed Cambridge University Boat 1921 and 1922. *Address:* Flixton House, Rowington, Warwick. *T:* Lapworth 2019. *Clubs:* United Oxford & Cambridge University; Leander; Tennis Court (Leamington).
[Died 24 Jan. 1977.

STEPHENS SPINKS, Rev. Dr G.; *see* Spinks.

STEPHENSON, Basil Ernest, CBE 1963; *b* 11 Dec. 1901; *o s* of late Basil Stephenson; *m* 1927, Edna (*née* Broderick); one *s. Educ:* Woking Co. Sch. Gen. engineering, 1918-27; aircraft engineering at Vickers, Weybridge, 1927; appointed Asst Chief Designer, 1945; Chief Designer, 1953; Chief Engineer, 1957; appointed a Director, Vickers-Armstrongs (Aircraft) Ltd, 1957; Dir of Engineering, 1959; Director of Engineering, British Aircraft Corporation, Weybridge Division, 1963-64, retd 1964. FRAeS 1953. British Gold Medal for Aeronautics, 1960. *Address:* Cedar Ridge, St John's Hill Road, Woking, Surrey. *T:* Woking 72307.
[Died 7 May 1977.

STEPHENSON, Colonel Eric Lechmere, DSO 1940; MC and two bars; *b* 18 April 1892; *s* of late Dr O. T. and Jane Marriott Stephenson; *m* 1934, Helen Joyce Marples; one *s. Educ:* King Alfred's School, Wantage. Regular Commission in Army, 1912; retired pay, 1946. *Recreations:* cricket and polo. *Address:* 2 Comptons Lea, Comptons Lane, Horsham, West Sussex. *Club:* Army and Navy.
[Died 7 July 1978.

STEPHENSON, Vice-Admiral Sir Gilbert Owen, KBE 1943; CB 1930; CMG 1919; retired; Hon. Commodore Sea Cadet Corps, 1949-58; *b* 1878; *s* of R. M. Stephenson; *m* 1903, Helen Chesney (*d* 1954), *d* of late Col Robert Frederic Williamson, CB; two *s* one *d.* Served European War, commanded Otranto Mobile Barrage Force, 1914-19 (CMG, Order of St Maurice and St Lazarus, of Crown of Italy, of Redeemer of Greece, Distinguished Service Medal, USA, Valore Militare (silver), Italy); Chief of Staff, Portsmouth, 1924; commanded Royal Naval Barracks, Portsmouth, 1926-28; Rear-Adm. and retired list, 1929; Vice-Adm., retired, 1934; General Sec. of the Navy League, 1932-35; returned to Active Service, Sept. 1939. Commanded HMS Western Isles, at Tobermory, 1940-45 (despatches). Commander, with Star, of the Royal Order of St Olaf (Norway), 1948; Officer, Legion of Honour, 1948. *Relevant publication:* The Terror of Tobermory, by Richard Baker, 1972.

Address: 27 Gold Street, Saffron Walden, Essex. *Club:* United Service & Royal Aero.   [*Died* 27 *May* 1972.

STEPHENSON, Sir Hugh (Southern), GBE 1966 (OBE 1944); KCMG 1956 (CMG 1954); CIE 1947; CVO 1957; *b* 29 Nov. 1906; *s* of late Sir Hugh Stephenson, GCIE, KCSI; *m* 1936, Patricia Elizabeth, *d* of late Maj.-Gen. Sir Arthur Mills, CB, DSO; three *s. Educ:* Winchester Coll.; Christ Church, Oxford. 1st cl. hons, Jurisprudence. Barrister-at-Law (Inner Temple). Entered Indian Civil Service, 1931; Under-Secretary to Govt of India, 1935-38; Secretary to Governor of United Provinces, 1940-44; Collector and Dist Magistrate, Cawnpore, 1944-47. HM Foreign Service since 1947; Dep. High Comr, Lahore, 1947-49; IDC 1951; Counsellor, British Middle East Office, Faiyid, 1952-54; HM Ambassador to Viet Nam, 1954-57; Consul-General in New York, 1957-60; Deputy Under-Secretary of State, Foreign Office, 1960-63; Ambassador to South Africa, 1963-66 (High Comr of Basutoland, the Bechuanaland Protectorate and Swaziland until the abolition of this office in August 1964). (First) Chancellor of the University of Basutoland, Bechuanaland Protectorate and Swaziland, 1964-66. Retired from the Foreign Service, Nov. 1966. A Director, Ernest Benn Ltd. Dir-Gen., St John Ambulance Brigade; KStJ 1970. *Address:* 2 Sloane Terrace Mansions, SW1. *Club:* Oriental.
[*Died* 23 *Sept.* 1972.

STEPHENSON, Sir Percy, Kt 1971; company director; *b* 10 April 1909; *s* of James and Elizabeth Stephenson; *m* 1934, Kathleen, *d* of James Percy Bilbie; one *s* one *d. Educ:* Aylwin College. Articled to Accountancy, 1926; entered motor industry, 1930. Served on Lancashire County Council, 1956-57; Chm., Ormskirk Constituency Conservative Assoc., 1960-65; Conservative North Western Provincial Area: Dep. Treasurer, 1964; Vice-Chm., 1965; Chm., 1966-71. Lancaster University: Chm., Buildings Cttee, 1968-; Mem. Council, 1968-; Mem. Court, 1968-; Mem., Finance Cttee; Chm., Safety Cttee, 1974-. *Recreations:* fell-walking, gardening. *Address:* Plaisance, Alderney, Channel Islands. *T:* Alderney 2466. *Club:* Carlton.
[*Died* 22 *Feb.* 1979.

STEPHENSON, Thomas, CBE 1943; retired as Clerk of the Peace, Clerk of the County Council, Clerk of Lieutenancy, for the East Riding of Yorks, 1920-60(1); *b* 17 Oct. 1889; *s* of G. A. Stephenson, Beverley; *m* 1917, Madge (decd), *d* of A. P. Bannister, Branley, Yorks. *Address:* Flat 1, The Expanse, Bridlington, Yorks. *T:* Bridlington 2015.
[*Died* 11 *March* 1974.

STERN, Gladys Bertha; author; *b* London, 17 June 1890; 2nd *d* of Albert and Elizabeth Stern; *m* 1919, Geoffrey Lisle Holdsworth. *Educ:* Notting Hill High School. Travelled in Europe; trained at the Academy of Dramatic Art for nearly two years; wrote first novel in her twentieth year-having written plays since the age of eight; has done free-lance journalism and reviewing, and published many short stories; also worked for Studios in Hollywood and Denham. *Publications:* Pantomime, 1914; See-Saw, Twos and Threes, Grand Chain, A Marrying Man, Children of No Man's Land, Larry Munro, The Room; Smoke Rings; The Back Seat, 1923; Tents of Israel, 1924; Thunderstorm, 1925; A Deputy was King, 1926; The Dark Gentleman; Bouquet; Jack a'Manory; Debonair, 1928; Petruchio, 1929; Mosaic, 1930; The Shortest Night, 1932; Long-lost Father, 1932; Little Red Horses, 1932; The Augs, 1933; Shining and Free, 1935; Monogram, 1936; Oleander River, 1937; The Ugly Dachshund, 1938; The Woman in the Hall, 1939; A Lion in the Garden, 1940; Another Part of the Forest, 1941; The Young Matriarch, 1942; Talking of Jane Austen (with Sheila Kaye-Smith), 1943; Trumpet Voluntary, 1944; The Reasonable Shores, 1946; No Son of Mine, 1948; Benefits Forgot, 1949; A Duck to Water, 1949; More Talk of Jane Austen (with Sheila Kaye-Smith), 1950; Ten Days of Christmas, 1950; The Donkey Shoe, 1952; A Name to Conjure With, 1953; Johnny Forsaken, 1954; All in Good Time, 1954; For All We Know, 1955; The Way It Worked Out, 1956; Seventy Times Seven, 1957; The Patience of a Saint, 1958; And Did He Stop and Speak to You?, 1958; Unless I Marry, 1959; Bernadette, 1960; Dolphin Cottage, 1962; Promise Not to Tell, 1964; *plays:* The Matriarch, 1929; (with Frank Vosper) Debonair, 1930; The Man Who Pays the Piper, St Martin's Theatre, 1931. *Address:* c/o A. D. Peters, 10 Buckingham Street, Adelphi, WC2. *T:* Blewbury 256.   [*Died* 19 *Sept.* 1973.

STERNBERG, Rudy; *see* Plurenden, Baron.

STEVEN, Guy Savile, MBE 1945; Chairman of Allied Ironfounders Ltd, 1960-70, retired; *b* 24 Nov. 1906; *s* of John Hugh Steven and Ernestine May Shepherd; *m* 1937, Marion Grace Mackenzie-Kennedy; one *s. Educ:* Preparatory School;

Marlborough College. Joined McDowall, Steven & Co., Ltd, Ironfounders, Falkirk, April 1925; this company became a member of Allied Ironfounders Ltd on the Group's formation, 1929. Director, Allied Ironfounders, 1947; Dep. Man. Dir, 1954; Man. Dir, 1956-67. Served War of 1939-45 (despatches): RASC in Middle East, Italy and North West Europe (Lieut-Col). *Recreations:* shooting and tennis. *Address:* Pickhurst, Chiddingfold, Surrey. *T:* Wormley 2919. *Club:* Hurlingham.
[*Died* 15 *Feb.* 1980.

STEVENS, Hon. Sir Bertram Sydney Barnsdale, KCMG, *cr* 1941; Consulting Accountant, Sydney; *b* 2 Jan. 1889; *m* 1914 (wife *d*, 1966); one *s* two *d. Educ:* Fort Street High School, Sydney. Inspector of Public Service Board; Under Secretary and Director of Finance, NSW; MLA for Croydon, New South Wales, 1927-40; Assistant Treasurer, 1927-29; Treasurer and Minister for Railways, 1929-30; Deputy Leader of Opposition, 1930-32, Leader, 1932, Premier and Treasurer, 1932-39. Australian Representative, Empire Eastern Group Supply Council, New Delhi, 1941-42. *Publications:* Planning for War and Peace; The Next Year in the Pacific; New Horizon-a study of Indo-Australian relationships. *Address:* 19 Julia Street, Ashfield, NSW 2131, Australia.   [*Died* 23 *March* 1973.

STEVENS, E. S.; *see* Drower, Lady.

STEVENS, George (Cooper); American film director and producer; *b* Oakland, California, 1905; *s* of Landers Stevens, actor, and Georgia (*née* Cooper), actress. *Educ:* Sonoma High School, California. Cameraman, Hollywood, 1921; Director, 1930. Served War, 1943-45; Major, Lt-Col; Head of special film unit, US Army Signal Corps, assigned to 6th Army; served in Africa, Middle East, Europe. President, Screen Directors' Guild, 1946; Member of Board, 1950. Films include: Alice Adams, Vivacious Lady, Gunga Din, Penny Serenade, Woman of the Year, The Talk of the Town, The More the Merrier, I Remember Mama, A Place in the Sun, Shane, Giant, The Diary of Anne Frank, The Greatest Story Ever Told, The Only Game in Town. Has received high awards for films. *Address:* Surety National Bank Building, Suite 210, 4519 Admiralty Way, Marina del Rey, California 90291, USA. [*Died* 8 *March* 1975.

STEVENS, Hon. Henry Herbert, LLD; broker and accountant, retired; formerly Chairman of Board, C. Gardiner-Johnson Co. Ltd, Vancouver Shipping Agents; *b* Bristol, England, 8 Dec. 1878; *s* of Richard Harvey and Jane Anne Stevens, Cornwall; *m* 1905, Gertrude M., *d* of George Glover, Vancouver, BC, formerly of Grimsby; two *s* two *d. Educ:* Bristol; Peterboro, Ontario; British Columbia. Came to Canada, 1887; Alderman City Vancouver, 1910-11; Chairman of the Greater Vancouver Sewage Scheme, also Chairman of Greater Vancouver Annexation Committee; MP Vancouver, Centre, BC, 1911-30; MP East Kootenay, 1930-40; Minister of Customs and Excise in Meighen Government, 1926; Minister of Trade and Commerce, Canada, 1921, and 1930-34; Chairman of Royal Commission on Price Spreads, 1934. resigned portfolio in Government and Chairmanship of Commission, 1934. Leader of Reconstruction Party, Canada, 1935-38; realigned himself with Conservative Party, 1938; candidate (C), Vancouver Centre, Gen. Elec., 1949. Member and President of Citizens Rehabilitation Council, Vancouver, 1941-49; President of Vancouver, BC, Board of Trade, 1952. Has travelled extensively, Europe, China, Japan, and South Sea Islands; Pres. of British and Foreign Bible Soc. (BC Auxiliary), 1948-. United Church of Canada. *Address:* 1676 Pine Crescent, Vancouver 9, BC. *Clubs:* Canadian, Vancouver (Mem. for over 50 years), Kiwanis (Vancouver); Rideau (Ottawa).   [*Died* 14 *June* 1973.

STEVENS, Herbert Lawrence, CBE 1952 (OBE 1936); Consulting Engineer with Messrs Sandberg, 40 Grosvenor Gardens, SW1, since 1954; *b* 26 April 1892; *s* of Thomas Waghorn Stevens and Louisa Cecillia (*née* Davis); *m* 1st, 1917, Beryl Marjorie Gentry (*d* 1949); one *s* two *d* (and one *s* killed in action); 2nd, 1950, Amelia Beatrice Paice. *Educ:* Bradfield College, Berks; Downing College, Cambridge. Schriner Schol., Downing Coll., 1911; 2nd Cl. hons, Part I Maths Trip., 1912; 2nd Cl. hons, Mech. Sci. Trip., 1914; BA Cantab, 1914. Joined Royal Aircraft Estabt, Farnborough, 1914 (became head of full-scale flying sect.); Chief Tech. Officer, Aeroplane and Armament Exper. Estab., RAF Martlesham Heath, 1927; Head of Structures Dept, RAE, 1931; Supt of Scientific Research, RAE, 1937; Dep. Dir, Brit. Air Commn, Washington, 1940; Dep. Dir, RAE, 1941; Prin. Dir Equipment Research and Develt (Air), Min. of Supply, 1950; retd from Govt service, 1953. Fellow Roy. Aeronautical Soc.; MIMechE. *Publications:* various papers to Aeronautical Research Council. *Recreations:* photography and gardening. *Address:* Kariba, 56 Copse Avenue, Weybourne, Farnham, Surrey GU9 9EA.
[*Died* 18 *July* 1978.

STEVENS, Sir John (Melior), KCMG 1967; DSO 1945; OBE 1944; TD 1950; Chairman, since 1972, and a Managing Director, since 1967, Morgan Grenfell & Co. Ltd (Executive Vice-Chairman, 1971-72); Director: Suez Finance Company, since 1967; Bank of England, since 1968; Investment Trust Corp., since 1968; Metropolitan Trust Co., since 1968; British Bank of Middle East, since 1968; Merchants Trust Ltd, since 1969; British Petroleum Ltd, since 1969; *b* 7 Nov. 1913; *s* of late Courtenay Stevens and Melior Frances Barker; *m* 1940, Frances Anne, *d* of late Christopher Douglas Hely Hutchinson, MC; one *s* two *d. Educ:* Winchester. Admitted a Solicitor, 1937. Served War of 1939-45, with HM Forces in France, Middle East, Greece and Italy (despatches thrice, DSO, OBE); demobilised with rank of hon. Col. Entered service of Bank of England as an Adviser, 1946; Director of European Department of International Monetary Fund, Washington, DC, 1954-56; Executive Director, Bank of England, 1957-64; Head of Treasury Delegation and Economic Minister in Washington, 1965-67; UK Exec. Dir, IMF and IBRD, 1965-67. Chm., E European Trade Council, 1970-; Member: Council of Foreign Bondholders, 1957-64; BBC General Advisory Council, 1963-64; High Sheriff of County of London, 1964. Fellow, University Coll., London, 1968-, Treasurer 1970-; Mem. Council, Exeter Univ., 1971-. Mem. Council, Mem. and Governor, Ditchley Foundn, 1970-. *Recreations:* fishing and shooting. *Address:* 62 Bedford Gardens, W8. *T:* 01-727 6206; East Worlington House, Crediton, Devon. *T:* Witheridge 332. *Clubs:* Carlton; MCC.
[Died 27 Oct. 1973.

STEVENS, Sir Roger Bentham, GCMG 1964 (KCMG 1954; CMG 1947); Director, British Bank of the Middle East, 1964-77; Member, United Nations Administrative Tribunal, since 1972; *b* 8 June 1906; *s* of F. Bentham Stevens, JP, and Cordelia Wheeler; *m* 1st, 1931, Constance Hallam Hipwell (*d* 1976); one *s*; 2nd, 1977, Jane Chandler (*née* Irving); two step *s. Educ:* Wellington; Queen's Coll., Oxford; Hon. Fellow 1966. Entered Consular Service, 1928; served in Buenos Aires, New York, Antwerp, Denver and FO; Secretary of British Civil Secretariat, Washington, 1944-46; Foreign Office, 1946-48; Assistant Under-Secretary of State, Foreign Office, 1948-51; British Ambassador to Sweden, 1951-54; British Ambassador to Persia, 1954-58. Adviser to First Secretary of State on Central Africa, 1962; Deputy Under-Secretary of State, Foreign Office, 1958-63; Vice-Chancellor, Leeds Univ., 1963-70; Chm., Yorks and Humberside Economic Planning Council, 1965-70; Mem., Panel of Inquiry into Greater London Develt Plan, 1970-72; Chm., Cttee on Mineral Planning Control, 1972-74. *Publication:* The Land of the Great Sophy, 1962, new edn 1971. *Address:* Hill Farm, Thursley, Surrey; Parsons Close, Giggleswick, Yorks. *Club:* Travellers'.
[Died 20 Feb. 1980.

STEVENS, William Charles, FCA; *b* 20 Jan. 1900; *s* of late Joseph William Stevens, Woodford, Essex, and late Alice Mary Eagland; *m* 1923, Ida Grace Bullivant, LRAM (*d* 1971); two *s*; *m* 1972, Violet May Patricia Rich. With Deloitte, Plender, Griffiths & Co., Chartered Accountants, 1915-29; qualified as Incorporated Accountant, 1927; Fellow, 1947; The Exchange Telegraph Co. Ltd: Secretary, 1929-49; Director, 1946; General Manager, 1949; Chairman, 1954-61. Served War, 1918-19, in HAC. *Recreations:* golf, cricket. *Address:* Clinton Brier, 38 Roslin Road South, Bournemouth, Hants. *[Died 30 Dec. 1973.*

STEVENS, Maj.-Gen. William George, CB 1944; CBE 1941; *b* London, 11 Dec. 1893; *m* 1916, Gladys Barker (*d* 1967); three *s. Educ:* Auckland Grammar Sch.; Royal Military Coll., Australia, 1912-14; served European War, 1915-19; various positions NZ Military Forces, 1920-37; Staff Coll., 1926-27; Imperial Defence Coll., 1928; Prime Minister's Dept, New Zealand, 1937-39 (Sec. of Organisation for National Security); Officer in Charge administration, Second New Zealand Expeditionary Force in Mediterranean, 1940-45; GOC NZEF, 1945-46; Official Secretary to High Commissioner for New Zealand, London, 1946-53; retd 1953. *Publications:* Problems of 2 NZEF, 1958; Bardia to Enfidaville, 1962; Freyberg, the Man, 1965. *Address:* Whareama, Stoke, Nelson, New Zealand.
[Died 6 Aug. 1976.

STEVENS, William George, CB 1943; late Principal Assistant Secretary, Ministry of Aircraft Production (retired 1943); *b* 11 Aug. 1883; *e s* of William Henry and Elizabeth Stevens, Cambridge; *m* 1926, Edith Constance Stevens (*d* 1962), *d* of late W. J. Stevens Tout, Winkleigh, Devon; one *s. Educ:* Perse Sch.; St Catharine's College, Cambridge. Various appointments in War Office, National Insurance Audit Dept, Air Board, Air Ministry, and Ministry of Aircraft Production. *Address:* Corner House, Raleigh Drive, Claygate, Esher. *T:* Esher 63974. *Club:* Oxford and Cambridge University. *[Died 19 May 1971.*

STEVENS, William Oswald, CMG 1949; Ceylon Civil Service (retired); *b* 27 Feb. 1891; *s* of late George William Stevens; *m* 1st, 1916, Joyce Garrett; two *d* (one *s* killed in action, 1940); 2nd, 1945, Gertrude Mary Langford. *Educ:* Dulwich Coll.; Trinity Coll. Oxford. Entered Ceylon Civil Service, 1914; retired 1949. *Address:* Sussex Barn, Brockhill Rd, Hythe, Kent. *T:* 67159.
[Died 6 March 1972.

STEVENSON, Alan; *see* Stevenson, D(avid) Alan.

STEVENSON, D. E.; Author; Novels, Children's Verse, Lectures and Belles-lettres; *b* 1892; *d* of D. A. Stevenson, CE, Edinburgh; *cousin* of Robert Louis Stevenson; *m* 1916, Major J. R. Peploe, Highland LI (*d* 1969); two *s* one *d. Educ:* home. *Publications:* Miss Buncle's Book, 1934; Miss Buncle Married; Mrs Tim of the Regiment; Miss Bun the Baker's Daughter; The English Air, 1941; Spring Magic, 1942; Celia's House; Listening Valley; The Two Mrs Abbotts; The Four Graces, 1944; Rosabelle Shaw; Green Money, 1939, repr. 1973; Rochester's Wife; The Empty World; Smouldering Fire; Divorced from Reality; Mrs Tim Carries On; Mrs Tim Gets a Job; Kate Hardy, 1947; Young Mrs Savage, 1948; Vittoria Cottage, 1949; Music in the Hills, 1950; Winter, and Rough Weather, 1951; Mrs Tim Flies Home, 1952; Five Windows, 1953; Charlotte Fairlie, 1954; Amberwell, 1955; Summerhills, 1956; The Tall Stranger, 1957; Anna and Her Daughters, 1958; Still Glides the Stream, 1959; The Musgraves, 1960; Bel Lamington, 1961; Fletchers End, 1962; The Blue Sapphire, 1963; Katherine Wentworth, 1964; Katherine's Marriage, 1965; The House on the Cliff, 1966; Sarah Morris Remembers, 1967; Sarah's Cottage, 1968; The English Air, 1968; Crooked Adam, 1969; Gerald and Elizabeth, 1969; The House of the Deer, 1970; also various publications in America. Works translated into Dutch, Danish, German and Spanish. Collection of papers, MSS, letters etc in Meml Lib., Boston Univ., Mass. *Address:* North Park, Moffat, Moffat. *TA:* Moffat. *T:* Moffat 44. *[Died 30 Dec. 1973.*

STEVENSON, D(avid) Alan, BSc (Edinburgh); FRSE; FICE; technical historian; *b* Edinburgh, 7 Feb. 1891; *s* of Charles A. Stevenson; *m* 1923, J. L. M. MacLellan; one *s* two *d. Educ:* Edinburgh Academy and privately. In 1912 joined family business of civil engineering and was engaged principally with lighthouses, harbours and rivers, until retiring in 1952 to study technical history. In 1914-18 carried out lighthouse work round Scottish Coast and Eastern Mediterranean and served as Captain, RME. In 1925-26 surveyed lighthouses from Siam to Aden for a report to Govt of India; has lectured on lighthouses in Canada and USA. Member Queen's Body Guard for Scotland, Royal Company of Archers. *Publications:* Lighthouse Tours of Robert Stevenson, 1946; Triangular Stamps of Cape of Good Hope, 1950 (Crawford medal, internat. award for research of Roy. Philatelic Soc.); The World's Lighthouses before 1820, 1959; and technical papers. *Recreations:* skating, golf, philately, study of Scottish sea-charts and exploring Portugal. *Address:* 22 Glencairn Crescent, Edinburgh EH12 5BT. *T:* 031-337 2832. *Clubs:* Athenæum; New (Edinburgh). Hon. Company of Edinburgh Golfers. *[Died 22 Dec. 1971.*

STEVENSON, Sir Hubert Craddock, KCMG 1942 (CMG 1938); Kt 1941; OBE 1934; MC; *b* January 1888; 2nd *s* of late Henry Thomas Stevenson; unmarried. *Educ:* Harrow. Served European War with RFA, 1915-19; appointed to Nigerian Administrative Service, 1920; Resident, 1934; Chief Commissioner Ashanti, 1936; Governor and C-in-C, Sierra Leone, 1941-47. *Recreations:* shooting, fishing. *Address:* Vorder, Bishopsteignton, S Devon. *Clubs:* Athenæum, Travellers'. *[Died 13 June 1971.*

STEVENSON, James Arthur Radford; formerly craftsman in wrought ironwork and writer and lecturer on this subject; *b* 1 Aug. 1901; *m* 1st, 1954, Enid Bannister (*d* 1969); 2nd, 1970, Feodora Joanna Winifred Eaton. *Educ:* Harrow; Trinity College, Cambridge. Short Service Commission, RAF, 1922; Commn RAFVR, 1940-43. Air Ministry "A" Licence 777; fitter in aircraft factory; free-lance journalist; reporter on London daily newspaper. Became interested in wrought ironwork, and founded the Devon Smithy, 1926, which has specialised in decorative ironwork. *Publications:* Crafty Smiths; The Din of a Smithy; Sonnets; More Sonnets. *Recreations:* reading, fishing, swimming. *Address:* Windmill Farm, Kelvedon, Essex.
[Died 9 April 1974.

STEVENSON, John Lynn; HM Diplomatic Service; Head of Computer Services Branch, Foreign and Commonwealth Office, since 1971; *b* 13 April 1927; *s* of James Stevenson and late Margaret Stevenson; *m* 1958, Winifred Mary Temple; one *s* one *d. Educ:* Royal High Sch., Edinburgh; Univ. of Edinburgh. MA Hons English. Malayan Civil Service, 1951-57; entered HM

Foreign Service, 1957; 2nd, later 1st, Sec., Peking, 1959-61 (Actg Counsellor at Shanghai, 1960); 1st Sec.: FO, 1961-65; Bonn, 1965-68; FCO, 1968-70; Counsellor, 1971. *Publication:* (ed) John Bell's Journey to Pekin, 1966. *Recreation:* angling. *Address:* 24 The Park, W5. *T:* 01-567 7969.
[Died 2 Dec. 1971.

STEVENSON, Sir Ralph Clarmont Skrine, GCMG 1949 (KCMG 1946; CMG 1938); JP; Captain of the Parish of Arbory, Isle of Man; *b* 16 May 1895; *s* of late Surg.-Gen. H. W. Stevenson, CSI; *m* 1st, 1921, Helen Barbara Izabel (marriage dissolved 1944), *d* of Jonkheer R. J. R. Boreel; one *s*; 2nd, 1946, Marjorie Josephine Wernham Bentley (formerly wife of 8th Viscount Portman), *d* of late G. B. Gerrard, Montreal, Canada. *Educ:* Wellington College, Berks; University College, Oxford. Served European War, Rifle Brigade; 2nd Lt 1914; Lt 1915; Captain, 1917; Third Secretary in HM Diplomatic Service and Foreign Office, 1919; Second Secretary, 1921; First Secretary, 1928; Acting Counsellor, 1937; Counsellor, 1938; Minister, 1941; served in Foreign Office and HM Missions at Copenhagen, Berlin, Sofia, The Hague, Cairo and Barcelona; Chargé d'Affaires with local rank of Minister Plenipotentiary, at Barcelona, Oct. 1938; mission terminated Feb. 1939; Principal Private Secretary to Secretary of State for Foreign Affairs, 1939-41; Minister at Montevideo, 1941-43; Ambassador to Yugoslavia, 1943-46; Ambassador to China, 1946-50; Ambassador to Egypt, 1950-55; retired, 1955. Mem., Legislative Council, IOM, 1955-70; Mem., Exec. Council, 1962-69. *Address:* Gardenfield, Castletown, Isle of Man. *T:* Castletown 2550.
[Died 23 June 1977.

STEWARD, Sir Harold Macdonald, Kt 1972; Chairman, Merseyside Passenger Transport Authority, 1969-72; *b* 8 Sept. 1904; *s* of late John Steward, Rainhill, Lancs; *m* 1941, Joyce Mary, *d* of late Thomas Nevison, Liverpool; one *s* three *d. Educ:* Rainhill School; Municipal Technical College, St Helen's. Consulting Engineer. Member of Liverpool City Council, 1953; Alderman, City of Liverpool, 1961-; Leader of the City Council, 1967. JP Lancashire, 1951. Contested (C) Liverpool, Edge Hill, 1951; MP (C) Stockport South, 1955-64. During War of 1939-45, was engaged in radar industrial research. Formerly Member of Inter-Services Mission to Ex-enemy Countries. *Address:* Crawfordsburn, Glenrose Road, Woolton, Liverpool L25 5JT.
[Died 3 March 1977.

STEWARD, Maj.-Gen. Reginald Herbert Ryrie, CB 1946; CBE 1945 (OBE 1938); DSO 1943; MC 1918; Maj.-Gen., retired; *b* 8 June 1898; *s* of Col R. H. Steward, OBE, and A. R. Steward, OBE; *m* 1934, Vera Beatrice, *d* of Wilson Stuckey; two *d. Educ:* Cheltenham College. First Royal Engineers, then Royal Signals. Served European War, 1917-18 (MC); Palestine, 1936-39 (despatches, OBE); War of 1939-45 (despatches, DSO and Bar, CBE, CB). ADC to King George VI, 1947, and to the Queen, 1952. *Recreations:* fishing and shooting. *Address:* The Red House, Middle Winterslow, Wiltshire.
[Died 6 Dec. 1975.

STEWARDSON, Prof. Edward Alfred; Professor of Physics, University of Leicester, 1947-69, Professor Emeritus since 1970; *b* 27 Aug. 1904; *s* of Alexander and Frances Margaret Stewardson; *m* 1937, Winefred Muriel Jones. *Educ:* Hawarden County School; Liverpool University (State Scholar and Flintshire County Exhibitioner). BSc 1st Cl. Hons Physics Liverpool, 1924, MSc 1925. Research Student, Cambridge, 1926-28; PhD Cantab 1930; Oliver Lodge Fellow, Liverpool University, 1928-30. Professor of Physics, Nat. Central Univ., Nanking, China, 1934-39; Lecturer in Charge of Physics Dept, Univ. College of Leicester, 1940-46. *Publications:* papers in scientific journals. *Recreations:* music and mountaineering. *Address:* Clatterbrune, Presteigne, Radnorshire. *T:* Presteigne 216. *Club:* Athenæum.
[Died 24 Aug. 1973.

STEWART, Alexander Bernard, MD; MRCPE; FRCP; *b* 15 June 1908; *s* of late Alexander Murray Stewart and Helen Howie Edmonds; *m* 1937, Isabelle Webster; one *s. Educ:* Grove Academy, Broughty Ferry; Univ. of St Andrews. MB, ChB 1931; DPH 1934; MD 1936. Hospital appointments, 1931-33; Asst in Bacteriology, Univ. of St Andrews, 1933-35; Lectr in Bacteriology, Univ. of St Andrews, 1935-37; Asst MOH, Tynemouth, 1937-40; Dep. MOH, Finsbury, 1940-46; MOH, Paddington, 1946-52; Deputy MOH, LCC, 1952-64, MOH, LCC, 1964-65; Med. Advr to GLC and ILEA, 1965-73. QHP 1971-. Trustee, The Chadwick Trust. Fellow: Soc. MOH; RSH (Exec. Vice-Pres., formerly Chm. Council); RIPH&H. Liveryman, Soc. of Apothecaries. *Publications:* various papers in professional journals, and annual reports, on medical and public health subjects. *Recreations:* reading, the arts. *Address:* 17 Hogarth Way, Hampton, Middlesex. *T:* 01-979 0957. *Club:* Athenæum.
[Died 21 Nov. 1974.

STEWART, Andrew, CBE 1962; President, since 1968, and Director, since 1931, Huddersfield Building Society (General Manager, 1928-67; Vice-President, 1958-68); *b* Cramond, Midlothian, 30 June 1895; *s* of late David Stewart and Jessie Peebles, Edinburgh; *m* 1933, Norah Lucy, *d* of late David Plaistowe, Highgate, N6; one *s. Educ:* Broughton and Edinburgh University. Member, Institute of Chartered Accountants in Scotland, 1918; Fell. Institute of Cost and Works Accountants, 1923 (Member Council, 1924-26); FCIS 1934. Founder Member, Council of Building Societies Institute, 1934-46 (Vice-Pres., 1946-); Member Council, Building Socs Assoc., 1932-66 (Chm. of Coun., 1946-48; Chm. Taxation Cttee, 1938-66; Vice-President, 1966-); Vice-Pres., Yorkshire County Assoc. of Building Socs, 1968- (Chm., 1937-42 and 1956-59); Mem. Coun., Internat. Union of Building Socs and Savings Assocs, 1960-66; Founder Mem., Nat. House-Builders Registration Council, 1935- (Chm. 1948-54; Vice-Pres., 1954-); Trustee, Housing Centre Trust, 1953-; Sea Cadet Council, 1958-61; Pres., St John Ambulance Brigade, SW Yorks; Mem. Council, OStJ, W Riding, Yorks. European War, 1914-18: HM Forces (invalided 1915); on staff of Accountant Gen. of the Navy, 1917-21; War of 1939-45: nominee of Min. of Supply on Board of Rendan (Great Britain) Ltd (Chm.) and John Fowler & Co. Ltd, Leeds (Dir) and Associated Companies. *Publication:* Costing for Light Castings, Ironfounders, 1923. *Recreations:* golf, fishing. *Address:* Broomfield, Fixby, Huddersfield, Yorks. *T:* Huddersfield 20276. *Clubs:* Huddersfield; Huddersfield Golf.
[Died 24 Aug. 1972.

STEWART, Andrew Charles, CMG 1955; OBE 1942; DL; Ambassador to Libya, 1962-63; *b* 22 April 1907; *s* of Frederick Naylor F. Stewart; *m* 1935, Emily Caroline Martin; two *s* one *d. Educ:* Scarborough Coll.; RMC Sandhurst. Commissioned Indian Army, 1927; transferred to Indian Political Service, 1933; appointed to Foreign Service, 1947; British Minister to Korea, 1954-56; Consul-General at Jerusalem, 1957-59; Ambassador and Consul-General, Iceland, 1959-61. DL Ross and Cromarty, 1976. *Recreation:* golf. *Address:* The Cottage, Dunvegan, Skye. *T:* Dunvegan 213. *Club:* East India, Devonshire, Sports and Public Schools.
[Died 1 Jan. 1979.

STEWART, Donald, CIE 1944; OBE 1937; MA, BSc; *b* 14 March 1894. Joined Indian Forest Service, 1921; Dep. Dir Gen., Directorate-General of Supply, New Delhi, India, 1943-45; President Forest Research Institute and Colleges, Dehra Dun, India, 1945-47; retired, 1949. *Address:* c/o Lloyds Bank Ltd, Douglas, Isle of Man.
[Died 22 July 1976.

STEWART, Edith Anne; *see* Robertson, E. A.

STEWART, Sir Euan Guy S.; *see* Shaw-Stewart.

STEWART, Maj.-Gen. Herbert William Vansittart, CBE 1940; DSO 1914; *b* 15 Aug. 1886; 4th *s* of late Lt-Gen. J. M. Stewart; *m* 1919, Doreen Evelyn, *y d* of late J. G. Ohlenschlager, Ashurst, Fernhurst, Sussex; one *s* one *d*. Joined Royal Scots Fusiliers, 1906; Captain, 1914; Major, The Seaforth Highlanders, 1924; Lt-Col 1930; Col 1933; Temp. Maj.-Gen. 1943; served European War, 1914-18 (despatches, DSO); commanded 1st Batt. The Seaforth Highlanders, 1930-33; Instructor Senior Officers' School, Sheerness, 1934-36; Commander 152nd (Seaforth and Cameron) Infantry Brigade, 1936-40; ADC 1941-44; France, 1940 (wounded); Middle East, 1943-44; retired for age, 1944. Hon. Sheriff Substitute for Moray and Nairn, Inverness and Ross and Cromarty, 1948. *Address:* Minerva, Nairn, Scotland.
[Died 26 Jan. 1975.

STEWART, Brig. James Crossley, CBE 1944; DSO 1918; CD with clasp, 1951; Retired Canadian Army, 1947; *b* Kingston, Ontario, 17 Feb. 1891, Scotch Canadian; *m* 1915, Florence Bemrose Valleau (*d* 1951); two *s* two *d*; *m* 1953, Nancy Barbara Alleyn. *Educ:* Kingston Public Schools; Kingston Collegiate; Royal Military College. Lt 4th Hussars, 1911; Capt. Canadian Field Artillery, 1914; served European War, 1914-18 (wounded, despatches thrice, DSO, 1914-15 Star, General Service and Victory Medals). Brig. and District Officer Commanding MD 1, London, Ontario, 1936-38; District Officer Commanding MD 11 1938-39; served War of 1939-45 (Canadian Volunteer Service Medal with Maple Leaf, Italy Star, France and Germany Star, War Medal): CRA 1st Canadian Division, Dec. 1939, and proceeded overseas; CCRA 7th British Corps 1940; CCRA 1st Cdn Corps June 1941; Served Italy and NW Europe; District Officer Commanding MD6, Halifax, 1945; retired, 1947; retd as Manager, Industrial Assoc. of BC (1947-60). Jubilee Medal, 1935; Coronation Medals, 1937, 1953. *Address:* 501 Hampton House, 2155 West 38th Avenue, Vancouver 13, BC. *Club:* Vancouver.
[Died 11 June 1972.

STEWART, John Alexander; Partner, Kerr MacLeod & Co., CA, Glasgow, since 1953; *b* 4 Oct. 1915; *s* of John Stewart and Mary Cruickshanks; *m* 1944, Mary Scott Welsh; one *s. Educ:* Paisley. Inst. of Chartered Accountants of Scotland: admitted, 1949; member, General Examining Board, 1960-65; Vice-President, 1967-68; President, 1968-69. *Recreations:* gardening, walking, fishing. *Address:* (home) Lagnaha, Lochwinnoch Road, Kilmacolm, Renfrewshire. *T:* Kilmacolm 2666; (office) 100 Wellington Street, Glasgow C2. *T:* 041-221 6933. *Club:* Conservative (Glasgow).   [*Died* 24 *Nov.* 1974.

STEWART, Captain John Christie, CBE 1947; DL; JP; Lord Lieutenant of Lanarkshire, 1959-63; Chairman Red Cross Council for Scotland, 1956-59; *b* 1 Aug. 1888; *o* surv. *s* of late Sir Robert King Stewart, KBE; *m* 1928, Agnes Violet Averil, JP Lanarks (*d* 1975), *d* of Brig.-Gen. Douglas Campbell Douglas, CB, and Hon. Mrs Douglas. *Educ:* Eton; University Coll., Oxford. MA Oxon, 1912. Served 1914-21 with HLI, and on general staff as Captain. Member of Royal Company of Archers (Queen's Body Guard for Scotland). Chairman Red Cross Exec. Cttee for Scotland, 1942-56. Grand Master Mason of Scotland, 1942-46. JP 1926, DL 1933, VL, 1957-59, Lanarkshire. *Recreations:* shooting and travelling. *Address:* Murdostoun Castle, Newmains, Lanarkshire. *T:* Wishaw 4757. *Clubs:* United Oxford & Cambridge University; New (Edinburgh).
[*Died* 31 *May* 1978.

STEWART, Maj.-Gen. Sir Keith (Lindsay), KBE 1958 (CBE 1945; OBE 1935; MBE 1919); CB 1947; DSO 1941; retired list of the New Zealand Army; *b* 30 Dec. 1896; *m* 1922, Rita Moss; one *s* one *d. Educ:* Wanganui Collegiate School, NZ. Served European War, 1914-18, Wellington Mounted Rifles and DAAG, NZEF; War of 1939-45, GSO 1, NZ Div.; BGS Creforce, Crete; DCGS, New Zealand; Commander: 4 NZ Armoured Bde; 5 NZ Infantry Bde; NZEF in British Commonwealth Occupation Force, Japan; Adjutant-General, 1946-49; Chief of General Staff, 1949-52. Greek Military Cross, 1941; Officer, Legion of Merit, USA, 1943. *Recreations:* golf, sea fishing. *Address:* Kerikeri, Bay of Islands, New Zealand.
[*Died* 13 *Nov.* 1972.

STEWART, Sir Kenneth (Dugald), 1st Bt *cr* 1960; GBE 1950 (KBE 1927); *b* 29 March 1882; 4th and *y s* of late H. D. Stewart, Strathgarry, Blair Atholl; *m* Noel (*d* 1946), *y d* of Kenric Brodribb, Melbourne, Australia; two *s* two *d. Educ:* Trinity Coll., Glenalmond. In the service of Maitland & Co., Ltd, in Shanghai, 1903-19; President Trustee Savings Banks Association, 1966 (Chairman, 1946-66); Vice-Pres. National Savings Cttee, 1958; Delegate to the Special China Tariff Conference of 1925-26; *Heir: s* David Brodribb Stewart [*b* 20 Dec. 1913; *m*; no *c*]. *Address:* Newton House, Alderley Edge, Cheshire. *T:* Alderley Edge 2117. *Club:* St James's (Manchester).   [*Died* 21 *May* 1972.

STEWART, Major Oliver, MC, AFC; CompRAeS; writer and broadcaster; *b* 26 Nov. 1895; *m* 1921, Odette Suzanne Le Lay; one *d. Educ:* Copthorne Sch.; Bradfield; Royal Coll. of Music. 2nd Lt 9th Mddx, Oct. 1914; Flying Officer, RFC, 1915; Ferry Pilot, 1916; No. 54 Squadron (single-seat fighters), 1917; Major (Technical), April, 1918; Major (Flying), June 1918; permanent commission, Capt. 1919; gazetted out, Major, 1921; test pilot Orfordness and Martlesham Heath; aeronautical correspondent, Morning Post, 1924-37; The Times, 1939; Evening Standard, 1940; The Manchester Guardian, 1941-58; Editor: The Motor, 1937; Aeronautics, 1939-62. Official commentator, Farnborough air displays, 1948-62. *Publications:* Aerobatics, 1928; Aeolus, or the Future of the Flying Machine; Cross-Country Flying, 1931; (with L. Bridgman) The Clouds Remember, 1936, 2nd edn 1972; Air Power and the Expanding Community, 1944; First Flights, 1957; Danger in the Air, 1958; of Flight and Flyers, 1964; Aviation: The Creative Ideas, 1966; Bad Sailing Made Good, 1971. *Address:* Osborne, Seaview, Isle of Wight. *Clubs:* Naval and Military, Royal Aero, Seaview Yacht, Island Sailing.   [*Died* 22 *Dec.* 1976.

STEWART, Brigadier Thomas G.; *see* Grainger-Stewart.

STEWART, Sir Walter Guy Shaw; *see* Shaw-Stewart.

STEWART, William, MC; MA; Master of Haileybury, since 1963; *b* 5 April 1916; *er s* of late Mr and Mrs W. A. Stewart, Allerton, Liverpool; *m* 1942, Betty Hele Sandeman, *er d* of late Colonel and Mrs J. Sandeman Allen, Birkenhead, Cheshire; three *s* one *d. Educ:* Liverpool College; Trinity College, Cambridge (Choral Schol.). Sixth Form History Master, Brighton College, 1937-39. Commissioned in 96th (Royal Devon Yeomanry) Field Regiment RA, 1940; Battery Commander in 61st Field Regiment RA, 1944; fought in NW Europe, 1944-45.

Returned to Brighton College as Housemaster, 1945; Headmaster of Brighton College, 1950-63. *Recreations:* reading, music, all games. *Address:* The Master's Lodge, Haileybury, Hertford. *T:* Hoddesdon 62352. *Clubs:* East India, Sports and Public Schools; Union (Cambridge).   [*Died* 22 *Feb.* 1975.

STEWART-CLARK, Sir Stewart, 2nd Bt, *cr* 1918; JP; *b* 4 July 1904; *s* of 1st Bt and Marie Gertrude (*d* 1937), *d* of Major Marcell Conran of Brondyffryn, Denbigh; *S* father, 1924; *m* 1927, Jane, *d* of late Major Arundell Clarke, Fremington House, North Devon; one *s* one *d. Educ:* Eton. Served War of 1939-45 (Lieutenant, RA). A Member of the Royal Company of Archers (HM Body Guard for Scotland). *Recreations:* squash-rackets (represented Scotland *v* England and Ireland, 1937-38, and against Ireland in 1946, twice runner-up in Scottish Squash Rackets Championships), lawn tennis (has played for East of Scotland), shooting, and fishing, golf and billiards. *Heir: s* John Stewart-Clark [*b* 17 Sept. 1929; *m* 1958, Lydia F., *d* of W. Loudon, Valkenhorst, Valkenswaard, Holland; one *s* three *d*]. *Address:* Dundas Castle, South Queensferry, West Lothian. *T:* S Queensferry 364. *Clubs:* MCC, Queen's; Hon. Company of Edinburgh Golfers (Muirfield); Royal Burgess Golfing Society (Edinburgh); North Berwick Golf.   [*Died* 1 *Dec.* 1971.

STEWART-ROBERTS, Walter Stewart, CBE 1948; *b* 24 March 1889; *s* of late Rev. Ernest Stewart Roberts, Master of Gonville and Caius College, Cambridge; *m* 1928, Elizabeth Marie Errol, CStJ, *d* of late Errol Kerr, New York City, USA; one *s* one *d. Educ:* Eton College; Gonville and Caius College, Cambridge, 1912-24. Egyptian Civil Service: Ministry of the Interior, Inspector of Interior, and ultimately Director of Personnel of the Ministry; retired 1924. Member of the London Stock Exchange, 1924-40 and 1951-74. Foreign Office, 1940-48: Director of Finance and Admin, 1940-46, Dep. Director-Gen., 1946, Political Intelligence Dept.; Asst Sec., Head of Estab. and Finance Dept (Information), 1946-48; retired 1948. Order of the Nile, 4th Class, 1919. *Recreation:* gardening. *Address:* Pond House, South Chailey, near Lewes, East Sussex. *T:* Barcombe 240; 7 Birchin Lane, EC3. *T:* 01-626 5644. *Club:* Leander (Henley-on-Thames).   [*Died* 5 *March* 1975.

STEYN, Hon. Lucas Cornelius, LLD; Chief Justice of Union of South Africa, 1959-71; *b* Geluksdam, Orange Free State, 21 Dec. 1903; *s* of late Christiaan Louwrens Steyn; *m* 1928, Huibrecht Magdalena, *d* of C. B. van Schoor; one *s* one *d. Educ:* Kroonstad Secondary School; Stellenbosch University. Lecturer in Roman Dutch Law at Stellenbosch University, 1926-28; Attorney-General, South-West Africa, 1931; Senior Law Adviser, Union Government, 1944; Judge of Transvaal Provincial Division, 1951-55; Judge of Appeal, 1955-59. *Publication:* Uitleg van Wette. *Address:* 009 Van Der Stel Hof, Won Sien Glen, Bloemfontein, 9301 S Africa. *Club:* Constantia (Pretoria).
[*Died* 28 *July* 1976.

STIEBEL, Victor Frank; formerly couturier; now writer and journalist; *b* South Africa, 14 March 1907; *s* of late Frank Stiebel, Durban, Natal, S Africa. *Educ:* South Africa; Jesus College, Cambridge. Opened own couture business, 1932. Army, 1940-45. Has designed clothes: for the Princess Margaret, Countess of Snowdon; for the Princess Alice, Duchess of Gloucester; for the late Princess Marina; for the Princess Alexandra, the Hon. Mrs Angus Ogilvy. Chm. and Vice-Chm., Incorporated Society of London Fashion Designers for many years. Retd, 1963. *Publication:* South African Childhood (vol. 1 of autobiography), 1968. *Recreations:* people, music, literature. *Address:* 22 Hyde Park Gardens, W2 2LY. [*Died* 6 *Feb.* 1976.

STIKKER, Dirk Uipko, Hon. GCVO 1958; Hon. GBE 1951; Grand Cross, Order of Orange Nassau; Knight, Order of Netherlands Lion; former Director: Friesch-Groningsche Hypotheekbank; Wm H. Müller & Co.; Deli-Maatschappij, and other companies; *b* 5 Feb. 1897; *s* of Uipko Obbo Stikker and Ida Meursing; *m* 1922, Catherina Paulina van der Scheer; two *s. Educ:* Latin-grammar school; University of Groningen (Doctor of Law, 1922). Manager, Lissense Bank Vereniging, Lisse, 1931; Man. Dir, Heinekens Bierbrouwerijen, 1935; Bd of Directors, Nederlandse Bank en Nederlandse Handel Maatschappij; Organiser and Pres., Netherlands Labour Foundation, 1945; Organiser and Chm., Party of Freedom, later known as People's Party for Freedom and Democracy (liberal), 1946. Member Netherlands Govt Delegation to Round Table Conf. on political status of Netherlands West-Indies, 1946; Round Table Conf. with reps of Indonesia and preparation for Independence of Indonesia, 1948; Netherlands Minister of Foreign Affairs, 1948-52; Member Political Purging Council, 1945; Netherlands rep., Council, OEEC, 1950; Chairman OEEC, 1950-52; Netherlands Envoy Extraordinary and Minister Plenipotentiary to Icelandic Republic, 1954-56; Netherlands Ambassador at the Court of St

James's, 1952-58; Netherlands Ambassador to the Icelandic Republic, 1956-58. Chairman Netherlands Delegation to Economic and Social Council, UN, 1955-56. Netherlands Permanent Representative on the North Atlantic Council and to the Council of OEEC in Paris, 1958-61; Secretary-General of NATO, 1961-64; Consultant to Unctad, 1966. Holds Grand Cross of several orders in Europe, South America, etc. *Publications:* Men of Responsibility, 1966; (for UNCTAD) The role of private enterprise in investment and promotion of exports in developing countries, 1967; many articles. *Recreation:* golf. *Address:* Stoeplaan 11, Wassenaar, Netherlands.
[Died 26 Dec. 1979.

STIRLING, Carl Ludwig, CBE 1943; QC; *b* 10 Nov. 1890; *yr s* of late Professor William Stirling, Victoria University of Manchester; *m* 1915, Fenna Kemp Fenn-Smith; one *s* one *d*. *Educ:* Norman House School; Victoria University of Manchester (LLB). Called to Bar, Middle Temple, 1913; Western Circuit, 1915-18, in the Forces (Capt.); entered office of the Judge Advocate-General, 1924; KC 1946; Deputy Judge Advocate-General of the Forces, 1938-52; retired, 1952. *Address:* Newlands, Bishop's Lydeard, near Taunton, Somerset. *T:* Bishop's Lydeard 392. [Died 6 July 1973.

STIRLING, Hon. Sir James; *see* Stirling, Hon. Sir R. J. L.

STIRLING, Sir John, KT 1956; MBE 1919; Lord Lieutenant of Ross and Cromarty, 1964-68; Member, County Council of Ross and Cromarty, 1919-70 (Convener, 1935-61); Forestry Commissioner, 1948-62; Chairman, Scottish National Committee of Forestry Commission, 1950-59; Freeman, Royal Burgh of Dingwall; *b* Sept. 1893; *e s* of William Stirling, Fairburn; *m* 1915, Marjory Kythe (*d* 1971), *d* of Sir Kenneth Mackenzie, 7th Bt of Gairloch; one *s* three *d* (and one *s* decd). *Educ:* Harrow; Magdalen College, Oxford. Served with Lovat Scouts, 1914-35. *Address:* Fairburn, Muir of Ord, Ross-shire. *T:* Urray 208. *Club:* New (Edinburgh). [Died 21 March 1975.

STIRLING, Hon. Sir (Robert) James (Lindsay), Kt 1964; Hon. Mr Justice Stirling; Judge of the High Court of Justice, Family Division (formerly Probate, Divorce and Admiralty Division), since 1964; *b* 18 Oct. 1907; *s* of Robert Stirling, MD, FRCSE, and Mary Elizabeth Martin. *Educ:* Fettes Coll.; Worcester Coll., Oxford (Hon. Fellow, 1969). Called to Bar 1931; QC 1955. Served War of 1939-45 with RA; commissioned, Dec. 1939; served in Middle East, 1941-June 1945; Staff of Judge Advocate General, 1942-Dec. 1945; Lt-Col, 1945. Vice-Pres. and Chm. Council, Worcester Coll. Soc.; Chm. Council, London Acad. of Music and Dramatic Art. Hon. Fellow, Worcester Coll., Oxford, 1969-. *Recreations:* golf, music. *Address:* Whiteacre, Coldharbour, Cray's Pond, near Reading, Berks. *T:* Pangbourne 2318. *Club:* Garrick. [Died 6 Feb. 1974.

STIRLING, Brig. Walter Andrew, DSO 1918; MC; late RFA; *b* 5 Aug. 1883; 3rd *s* of late Gen. Sir William Stirling, KCB, Col Comdt, Royal Artillery; *m* 1914, Louie, 2nd *d* of late J. V. Faber, KCD, Consul-General for Denmark; one *s* two *d*. *Educ:* Wellington College; RMA, Woolwich. Received commission in RFA, 1902; France, Feb. 1915; Brigade-Major RA 18th Div. Feb. 1917-March 1919; RA Mid. Div. Army of Rhine, March-April 1919; Brigade Major 4th Division, Colchester, 1919-22; retired pay, 1923; recalled, 1939; raised 119th AA Battery; Comd 30th LAA Regt, 1939-40; 40th AA Bde, 1941; Worcester Sub-Area, 1942-43; retired for age, 1943. Director Red Cross and St John Civilian Relief, France and Belgium, 1944; Red Cross HQ 1945. Hon. Commissioner, Boy Scouts, Suffolk; DL Suffolk 1958-72. *Address:* Nussteads, Polstead, Suffolk. *T:* Boxford 255. *Club:* Army and Navy. [Died 18 Dec. 1972.

STIRLING, Gen. Sir William (Gurdon), GCB 1965 (KCB 1961; CB 1957); CBE 1952; DSO 1945; psc; idc; Gentleman Usher to the Sword of State since 1967; ADC General to the Queen, 1964-66; Commander-in-Chief, British Army of the Rhine and Commander NATO Northern Army Group, 1963-66, retired; late Royal Artillery; *b* 25 May 1907; *s* of Major Charles Stirling and Hon Mrs Stirling; *m* 1941, Frances Marguerite, OStJ, *d* of J. Wedderburn Wilson, Burley Bushes, Ascot; three *d*. *Educ:* Wellington College; RMA Woolwich. Commissioned, 1926; CRA 1 Div., Palestine, 1947-48; Chief of Staff, AA Comd, 1950-52; Comd 27 Inf. Bde, 1952-55; Principal Staff Officer to Chairman of Chiefs of Staffs, 1956-58; GOC 6th Armoured Div., 1958; General Officer Commanding 2 Division, 1958-60; General Officer Commanding-in-Chief, Western Command, 1960-61; Military Secretary to the Sec. of State for War, 1961-63. Colonel Commandant, Royal Artillery, 1962-72. Officer, Legion of Merit (USA). *Recreation:* shooting. *Address:* Saxham Hall, Bury St Edmunds, Suffolk. *T:* Barrow 259. *Clubs:* Army and Navy, Boodle's. [Died 29 Aug. 1973.

STOCK, Col Philip Graham, CB 1918; CMG 1947; CBE 1919; FRCP; Hon. FRCSE; formerly: Medical Consultant, World Health Organisation; Senior Medical Officer and Medical Adviser, Ministry of Health; Director of Medical Services, Union of South Africa; *b* 1876; *y s* of Granger Stock, Clifton, Glos; *m* 1934, Frances, *o d* of Hugh Feuchelle, Piazza Di Spagna, Rome. *Educ:* Clifton; Bristol University (Suple Prize and Gold Medal, 1899). Formerly Captain RAMC; served South African War, 1900-02 (Queen's medal three clasps, King's medal two clasps); DDMS South African Contingent to Europe; DMS German S West African Campaign (despatches, CB, CBE). Médaille (d'Argent) de la Reconnaissance Française. *Publications:* various scientific papers. *Address:* Tankard Cottage, Ramsbury, Wilts SN8 2PJ. *T:* Ramsbury 273. *Clubs:* Athenæum; Rand (Johannesburg). [Died 27 Dec. 1975.

STOCKDALE, Maj.-Gen. Reginald Booth, CB 1963; CMG 1975; OBE 1945; BSc (Eng); CEng; FIMechE; retired; *b* 12 Jan. 1908; *s* of late Reginald Hind Stockdale, Preston, Lancs; *m* 1940, Betty Celia, *d* of late William Alexander Tucker, Bromley, Kent; two *s* one *d*. *Educ:* Bedford Modern School. psc. Lieut, RAOC, 1931. Served War of 1939-45: BEF, 1939-40; UK, 1940-42; transferred to REME as Major, 1942; MEF, 1942-43; CMF, 1943-45. MELF, 1945-46; East Africa, 1946-48; Lt-Col, 1948; BAOR, 1948-50; Colonel, 1951; BAOR, 1952-53; DDME, Southern Command, 1953-56; DEME, BAOR, 1956-59; Commandant, Technical Group, REME, 1960-63. Brigadier, 1958; Major-General, 1960. Col Comdt, REME, 1963-68. An internat. official with WEU, Paris, 1963-74. *Address:* 9 St Ann Street, Salisbury, Wilts SP1 2DP. *T:* Salisbury 28168. *Club:* Army and Navy. [Died 12 April 1979.

STOCKLEY, David Dudgeon, BSc (Engineering, London 1st Class Hons 1921); Principal, Aston Technical College, 1936-60; *b* 2 July 1900; *s* of Charles Rennie Stockley and L. Dudgeon; *m* 1928, Elizabeth Nina Baty; no *c*. *Educ:* Sunderland Technical College. Industrial posts, 1921-25; Lecturer Huddersfield Technical College, 1925-27; Sunderland Technical College, 1927-30; Head of Engineering Department, School of Engineering and Navigation, Poplar, 1930-32; Head of Dept of Engineering and Building, Borough Polytechnic, SE1, 1932-36. *Publications:* Papers on technical and educational subjects. *Recreation:* fishing. *Address:* 15 South Grange Road, Ripon, North Yorks HG4 2NH. [Died 8 Feb. 1980.

STOCKS, Baroness *cr* 1966 (Life Peeress), of the Royal Borough of Kensington and Chelsea; Mary Danvers Stocks, BSc (Econ.); LLD, LittD; Vice-President: Central School of Speech and Drama; Association of Joint Sewerage Boards; *b* 1891; *d* of Dr R. D. Brinton; *m* 1913, J. L. Stocks (*d* 1937), Fellow of St John's College, Oxford, Vice-Chancellor of Liverpool University; one *s* two *d*. *Educ:* St Paul's Girls' Sch.; London School of Economics. Asst Lecturer, London School of Economics, 1916-19; Lecturer on Economics, King's Coll. for Women, 1918-19; Extension Lecturer and Extra-Mural tutor, Manchester Univ., 1924-37; JP Manchester City, 1930-36; General Sec. London Council of Social Service, 1938-39; Principal of Westfield College, University of London, 1939-51. Member of the Unemployment Insurance Statutory Committee and various other Government committees. *Publications:* Fifty Years in Every Street, 1945; Eleanor Rathbone, 1948; History of the Workers' Educational Association, 1953; A Hundred Years of District Nursing, 1960; Ernest Simon of Manchester, 1963; Unread Best-Seller, 1967; Where is Liberty?, 1968; My Commonplace Book (autobiog.), 1970; Still More Commonplace, 1974; *play:* Hail Nero!. *Recreations:* reading, attending the House of Lords. *Address:* Aubrey Lodge, Aubrey Road, W8. *Club:* BBC.
[Died 6 July 1975.

STOCKS, Charles Lancelot, CB 1936; *b* 6 March 1878; *s* of late John Edward Stocks, Archdeacon of Leicester, and Emily Jane Mallam; *m* 1926, Olive Gwendolen Law, of Hawksworth Hall, Bradford; (one *s* decd). *Educ:* Rossall School (Schol.); Wadham Coll., Oxford (Schol.). Master at Eton; Treasury, Whitehall, 1901-34; Secretary of the Royal Commission on Oxford and Cambridge Universities, Crown Estate Comr, 1934-41; Headmaster, Betteshanger Sch., Kent, 1941-67. *Publications:* Future Evolution, 1969; People and Places (prose and verse), 1970. *Recreations:* played football for the Casuals, and hockey for Oxford University and England; sang for many years in Oriana Madrigal Soc. and Philharmonic Choir. *Address:* Old Rectory, Betteshanger, near Deal, Kent. *T:* Eastry 287. *Club:* Athenæum. [Died 15 Feb. 1975.

STOCKS, Percy, CMG 1948; MA, MD, BCh, FRCP, DPH; *b* 5 Nov. 1889; *s* of John and Margaret Ann Stocks; *m* 1914, Augusta Griffiths; no *c*. *Educ:* Manchester Grammar Sch.; King's Coll., Cambridge (Foundation Scholar); Victoria Univ.,

Manchester; Sch. of Tropical Medicine, Liverpool. Nat. Sci. Tripos, Cambridge, 1st Cl. hons, 1910; MB, ChB (2nd Cl. hons, distinctions in Medicine and Surgery), Manchester, 1913; MB, BCh Cambridge, 1914; MD 1917, DPH 1918, MA 1920, Cambridge; FRCP 1948; Jenner medal, Royal Society of Medicine, 1956; Bisset Hawkins medal, Royal College of Physicians, 1959. House Physician, Manchester Royal Infirmary, 1913; House Surgeon, Oldham Royal Infirmary, 1914; Temp. Lt RAMC, Asst in General Practice and Bacteriologist, 1914-18. Asst School Medical Officer, Bristol, 1918-21; Reader in Medical Statistics, Galton Laboratory, University Coll., London, 1921-33; Chief Medical Statistician, General Register Office, London, 1933-50; Sen. Research Fellow, Brit. Empire Cancer Campaign, 1951-57. Chm., Expert Cttee on International Classification of Diseases, World Health Organisation, 1946-48; Member, Expert Cttee on Health Statistics, World Health Organisation, 1949-50; Member: Statistical and Medical Committees, Royal Commission on Population, 1945. Hon. Fellow Amer. Public Health Association. *Publications:* Blood Pressure in Early Life, 1924; Hereditary Disorders of Bone Development, 1925; Biometric investigation of Twins and their brothers and sisters, Annals of Eugenics, 1930 and 1933; (with N. East and H. P. Young) The Adolescent Criminal, 1942; numerous papers on Cancer, Tuberculosis, Measles, Whooping Cough, Diphtheria, Vital Statistics. *Recreations:* music, philately, foreign travel. *Address:* Arrochar, 34 Brompton Avenue, Rhos-on-Sea, Denbighshire. *T:* Colwyn Bay 48477.   *[Died 18 Dec. 1974.*

STODDART, Alexander Frederick Richard, CMG 1952; *b* 25 Aug. 1904; *s* of Alexander Reid Stoddart and Agnes Ferguson McBain. *Educ:* St Peter's, York; Loretto; Trinity College, Oxford. Colonial Administrative Service: Nigeria, 1927-42; Chief Assistant Colonial Secretary, Sierra Leone, 1942-49; Colonial Secretary, Fiji, 1949-57. *Address:* Mount Lodge, Nightingale Lane, Storrington, Sussex.   *[Died 6 Nov. 1973.*

STODDART-SCOTT, Colonel Sir Malcolm, Kt 1957; OBE 1945; TD 1943; DL; MD; ChB; MP (C) Ripon Division of West Riding since 1950 (Pudsey and Otley, 1945-50); *b* 23 Sept. 1901; *o s* of John and Jemima Stoddart-Scott, Friarwood House, Pontefract; *m* 1940, Elsie Mary, JP, *o d* of late B. Parkinson, JP, Creskeld Hall, Arthington, nr Leeds; one *s* one *d. Educ:* Elmfield College, York; Ashville College, Harrogate; University of Leeds. On Medical Staff of Leeds General Infirmary 1926-39; in RAMC, 1939-45; ADMS 48th Division, 1943-45; Hon. Col 18th (West Riding) Bn Mobile Defence Corps, 1957-60. Past Chairman British Rheumatic Asssoc. Chairman: British Group of the Inter-Parly Union, 1951-59; Yorkshire Conservative Assoc., 1957-65; Parly Medical Cttee, 1959-62. Member, General Synod (formerly Church Assembly). Chairman of Governors of Charterhouse Rheumatism Clinic; Chairman: Hospital Saturday Fund, 1964; Yorkshire Br., Heart Foundn; Vice-Chairman, Yorkshire Cancer Campaign, 1963. DL, W Riding, Yorks, 1967. *Address:* Creskeld Hall, Arthington, near Leeds, Yorks. *T:* Arthington 2222.   *[Died 15 June 1973.*

STOKES, Adrian Durham; writer; *b* 27 Oct. 1902; *m* 1947, Ann Mellis, *d* of Rev. David Mellis Mellis; two *s* one *d. Educ:* Rugby School; Magdalen College, Oxford. Trustee, Tate Gallery, 1960-67. *Publications:* The Thread of Ariadne, 1925; Sunrise in the West, 1926; The Quattro Cento, 1932; Stones of Rimini, 1934; Tonight the Ballet, 1934; Russian Ballets, 1935; Colour and Form, 1937; Venice, an Aspect of Art, 1945; Inside Out, 1947; Cézanne, 1947; Art and Science, 1949; Smooth and Rough, 1951; Michelangelo: A Study in the Nature of Art, 1955; Raphael, 1956; Monet, 1958; Greek Culture and the Ego, 1958; Three Essays on the Painting of our Time, 1961; Painting and the Inner World, 1963; The Invitation in Art, 1965; Venice, 1965; Reflections on the Nude (with J. Piper), 1967; The Image in Form: selections from Adrian Stokes, ed Richard Wollheim, 1972; Penguin Poets 23, 1973. *Address:* 20 Church Row, NW3. *T:* 01-435 4640.   *[Died 15 Dec. 1972.*

STOKES, Sir Harold (Frederick), Kt 1974; CBE 1966; Director, Stokes (Australasia) Ltd, since 1936; *b* 7 Jan. 1899; *m* 1936, Ruth Alison Baird Good; one *s* three *d. Educ:* Melbourne Grammar Sch.; Trinity Coll., Univ. of Melbourne. BSc and BEE (Melb.). Served War of 1939-45: Aust. Corps of Electrical and Mechanical Engrs, Captain (ex RofO) to Lt-Col, serving HQ, then N Australia, New Guinea, and then Dep. Dir at Aust. AHQ, 1941-45. Joined William Adams & Co. Ltd (Engineers), 1923, Manager Engrg Dept, 1927-51; joined Stokes (Australasia) Ltd, 1952. Mem. Bd of Management, Austin Hosp., Heidelberg, Melbourne, 1947-74; Pres., Bd of Management, 1952-74 (Teaching Hosp. Univ. of Melb., 1966-). Mem. Bd, Cancer Inst., 1949 (Chm., 1952-); Mem. Anti-Cancer Council (Vic.). *Recreations:* golf, sailing, farming. *Address:* 10 Nareeb Court,

Toorak, Victoria 3142, Australia. *T:* (03) 202624. *Clubs:* Australian, Melbourne, Naval and Military, Royal Melbourne Golf (all Melbourne); Barwon Heads Golf. *[Died 4 Aug. 1977.*

STOKES, (Hon.) Brig. Ralph Shelton Griffin, CBE 1942 (OBE 1919); DSO 1917; MC 1916; *b* 31 July 1882; *s* of Francis Griffin Stokes, BA Oxon; *m* 1921, Lora Mary Bradford; four *d. Educ:* St Mark's, Windsor and privately. Served Anglo-Boer War, Paget's Horse, 1901-02, with Methuen's Columns in W Transvaal; European War, 1914-18 (DSO, MC, despatches thrice); Field Company, RE; Tunnelling Companies; Lieut-Col, Controller of Mines, First Army; Colonel, Chief Engineer, Allied Forces, Archangel, North Russia, 1918-19 (OBE, despatches twice); War of 1939-45: with RE; France, 1939-40; Narvik 1940 (despatches); CE Xth Corps, 1940; Brig. CE Airfields, Middle East, 1941-43 (CBE; despatches twice); War Office, 1943-44; has record of active service in the three wars of the century. Field Engineer, International Nickel Co., New York, 1912-14; Superintendent of Mines, De Beers Consolidated, Kimberley, 1920-28; Consulting Engineer and Manager, Central Mining & Investment Corporation, 1928-44, Director, 1944-59. Chairman of Trinidad Leaseholds Ltd, 1944-47. Past President: Geological Soc. of S Africa; SA Inst. of Mining and Metallurgy; Instn of Mining and Metallurgy, London; Past Vice-Pres., Royal African Soc. *Publication:* Mines and Minerals of the British Empire, 1908. *Address:* Highfield, Leweston, Sherborne, Dorset DT9 6EL. *T:* Holnest 425. *Clubs:* Army and Navy; Rand (Johannesburg).   *[Died 24 Feb. 1979.*

STOKES, William Henry, CBE 1950; JP 1950; Personnel Manager, Armstrong Siddeley Motors Ltd, Coventry, 1954-59; Member, Coventry Pre-Retirement Committee, since 1968; *b* 18 Nov. 1894; *s* of William Henry Stokes, Coventry, and Annie Maria (*née* Jenkins); *m* 1918, Frances Emily Beckett; no *c. Educ:* Coventry. Chm. Midland Regional Bd for Industry, 1945-50; Vice-Chm. Midland Regional Production Bd, 1940-45; Member: Nat. Production Advisory Council, 1940-50; Local Employment Cttee; BBC Advisory Cttee, Midland Region; Divisional Organiser, Amalgamated Engineering Union (Coventry area), 1937-50; Iron and Steel Corporation of Great Britain, 1950-53; (part-time), East Midlands Electricity Board, 1959-65; former Chm., Coventry Pre-Retirement Cttee; Mem., Coventry Probus. *Recreations:* interest in Rugby football (a Vice-Pres. Coventry RFC); golf, pottery, sculpture. *Address:* 57 Rochester Road, Coventry CV5 6AF. *T:* Coventry 72860.   *[Died 6 Dec. 1977.*

STOKOWSKI, Leopold (Boleslawowicz Stanislaw Antoni), FRCM; BMus Oxon; DMus University of Pennsylvania; LLD University of California; Hon. Fellow Queen's College, Oxford; *b* London, 18 April 1882; *s* of Boleslaw Kopernik Stokowski, Lublin, Poland; *g s* of Leopold Stokowski; *m* 1st, 1911, Olga Samaroff (marr. diss. 1923); one *d*; 2nd, 1926, Evangeline Brewster Johnson (marr. diss. 1937); two *d*; 3rd, 1945, Gloria Vanderbilt di Cicco (marr. diss. 1955); two *s. Educ:* Royal Coll. of Music, London; France; Germany. Organist and Choirmaster: St James's, Piccadilly, London, 1902-05; St Bartholomew's, NY, 1905-08. Conductor Cincinnati Orchestra, 1909-12; Conductor Philadelphia Orchestra, 1912-36; Organiser and Conductor, All-American Youth Orchestra, 1940-41; Co-conductor, NBC Symphony Orchestra, 1941-43; Founder and Conductor, NY City Symphony Orchestra, 1944-45; Conductor, Hollywood Bowl Symphony Orchestra, 1945-46; conducted New York Philharmonic Orchestra, 1947-50; Music Director, Houston Symphony Orchestra, Texas, 1955-60; Founder and Music Director, American Symphony Orchestra, NY, 1962-72. Film, A Hundred Men and a Girl, 1937; appeared in: The Big Broadcast of 1937; Fantasia, a feature picture with music with Walt Disney, 1940; Carnegie Hall, 1946. Many symphonic transcriptions of the works of Bach. Has made records for: RCA Victor Co., Columbia Recording Co., Capitol Records, Everest Records, Vanguard Records, United Artists Records, London Records (Decca), Unicorn Records, Desmar Records. *Publication:* Music for All of Us, 1943. *Address:* c/o H. Muller, 555 Madison Avenue, New York, NY 10022, USA.   *[Died 13 Sept. 1977.*

STONE, Alan Reynolds; *see* Stone, Reynolds.

STONE, Bertram Gilchrist, OBE 1955; *b* 3 June 1903; *s* of late Reverend William Arthur Stone, Warden of St Thomas' Coll., Colombo, and of Clare Frances Stone; *m* 1933, Dorothy Kneale, *y d* of late D. E. McCracken, OBE, Liverpool; two *s. Educ:* Bromsgrove School; Sidney Sussex College, Cambridge (Scholar), Classical Tripos, BA 1925, MA 1929. District Officer, Colonial Administrative Service, Nigeria, 1925-36; Administrative Officer, Nat. Council of Social Service, 1937-43; Midland Regional Officer, 1944-47; Colonial Office, 1947; official visits to Nigeria, 1955 and 1959, Aden and Somaliland,

1957; Head of Students Branch, Colonial Office and Ministry of Overseas Development, 1956-65. Foundn Fellow, Univ. of Surrey. *Publications:* contrib. to educational journals. *Recreations:* gardening, reading. *Address:* Manor Barn, Kingston, Lewes, East Sussex. *T:* Lewes 4569. *Club:* Royal Commonwealth Society.   [*Died* 23 *Feb.* 1978.

STONE, Sir (John) Leonard, Kt 1943; OBE 1943; QC 1948; *b* 6 Nov. 1896; *s* of late John Morris Stone, Blackheath and Lincoln's Inn, and late Edith Emily Stone, *d* of Alderman Edward Hart; *m* 1923, Madeleine Marie, *d* of late Frederick Scheffler, New York; one *s. Educ:* Malvern College. Served European War, 1914-22, commissioned Worcester Regt, Oct. 1914, Gallipoli, Army of the Black Sea, Control Officer Eskishehir, 1919-20; Inter-Allied Commission of Inquiry Turco-Greek War, 1921 (despatches, thrice). Called to Bar, Gray's Inn, 1923; joined Lincoln's Inn, 1931; Bencher, Gray's Inn, 1942, Treas., 1956. Pres., Commission of Inquiry, Bombay Explosions, 1944; Chief Justice High Court, Bombay, 1943-47; Vice-Chancellor, County Palatine of Lancaster, 1948-63. Chairman of Departmental Committee on Hallmarking, 1956-58. Mem. Council, Imp. Soc. of Knights Bachelor. *Address:* 2 Gray's Inn Square, WC1. *Clubs:* MCC; Cheltenham Croquet.
[*Died* 3 *Jan.* 1978.

STONE, Sir Leonard; *see* Stone, Sir J. L.

STONE, Reynolds, CBE 1953; RDI 1956; FRSA 1964; Designer and Engraver; Fellow of Magdalene College, Cambridge; *b* 13 March 1909; *s* of Edward Wellington and Laura Neville Stone; *m* 1938, Janet Woods; two *s* two *d. Educ:* Eton; Magdalene College, Cambridge. Studied printing at the University Press, Cambridge, after taking degree in History Tripos, 1930. Worked in a printing house, Barnicott & Pearce of Taunton, for two years, then as a free-lance designer and engraver. Served in RAF (photo interpretation), 1941-45. Designs for printers and publishers chiefly, and has decorated a number of books and produced many devices and book labels with an emphasis on lettering. Also designs and executes memorial tablets and engraves glass. Designed 3d Victory Stamp 1946, seal and device for The Arts Council, book-labels for National Trust and The British Council and an engraving of the Royal Arms for HM Stationery Office, 1956, Five Pound and Ten Pound Notes. Designed and executed the Winston Churchill Memorial for Westminster Abbey, 1965. One-man exhibn of water colours, New Grafton Gall., London, 1972; Prints in Ashmolean Museum, Oxford. *Publications:* Engravings, 1977; among the books decorated are: A Shakespeare Anthology, 1935; Rousseau's Confessions, 1938; Old English Wines and Cordials, 1938; The Praise and Happiness of the Countrie Life, Guevara, 1938; Apostate, Forrest Reid, 1946; The Open Air, Adrian Bell, 1949; Omoo, 1967; St Thomas Aquinas, 1969. *Recreations:* hunting in second-hand bookshops; interest in trees and 19th century wood-engraving. *Address:* Litton Cheney Old Rectory, Dorchester, Dorset. *T:* Long Bredy 383. [*Died* 23 *June* 1979.

STONE, Richard Evelyn, CMG 1962; HM Overseas Civil Service, retired; Administrator, Agricultural Economics Institute, Oxford University, since 1967; *b* 20 Dec. 1914; 2nd *s* of late R. G. and late A. L. Stone, Yetminster, Dorset; *m* 1948, Mavis, 2nd *d* of late E. D. Tongue, OBE, and late E. E. Tongue. *Educ:* Blundell's School; Wadham College, Oxford. MA (Hons jurisprudence). Served War of 1939-45 (despatches): Adjt 34th Bn KAR; Staff Captain, 21st (EA) Inf. Bde; qualified Staff Coll., Quetta, 1945. Dist Comr, Uganda, 1948-55; Permanent Sec. of various Mins; Dep. Resident, Buganda, 1959, Resident, 1960-62. Retd 1963, on Independence of Uganda. Farmed in Devon, 1963-67. Sen. Treasurer, Oxford Univ. Cricket Club, 1972-78. *Recreations:* fishing, cricket. *Address:* Brackenhurst, Boars Hill, Oxford. *Clubs:* MCC; Vincent's (Oxford). [*Died* 8 *April* 1980.

STONE, Lt-Gen. Robert Graham William Hawkins, CB 1942; DSO 1919; MC; FRGS; *b* Dover, 16 Jan. 1890; *o s* of late Brig.-Gen. F. G. Stone, CMG; *m* 1928, Ena, *yr d* of late W. H. Rowe. *Educ:* Wellington Coll.; RM Academy, Woolwich. Served in District Mounted Troop, Aliwal North, during last six months of South African War, 1902; passed into RMA, Woolwich, 1908; awarded Pollock Medal on passing out 1st; 2nd Lieut in RE 1909; served at Chatham and Aldershot; throughout European War in France as a regimental officer and on the staff (DSO, MC, despatches five times); Brigade Major to 32nd Infantry Brigade, 1917; Staff Coll., 1922-23; GSO2, War Office, 1930-33; Bt Lt-Col 1931; Lt-Col 1933; CRE Deccan District, India, 1934-35; Col 1935; Military Attaché, Rome, 1935-38; Brigadier, 1938; Assistant Commandant and Chief of Staff, Sudan, 1938-40; Chief of British Mission to Egyptian Army, 1940-42; GOC British Troops in Egypt, 1942-44 (CB, despatches four times). Temp. Maj.-Gen. 1941; Acting Lt-Gen. 1942; Maj.-Gen. 1943;

Temp. Lt-Gen. 1943-44; retired with rank of Lt-Gen., 1947. *Recreations:* lawn tennis, golf. *Address:* 14 Mallord Street, Chelsea, SW3. *Clubs:* United Service & Royal Aero; All England Lawn Tennis; Royal Mid-Surrey Golf.
[*Died* 27 *June* 1974.

STONEHEWER BIRD, Sir Hugh, KCMG 1945 (CMG 1939); OBE 1929; *b* 13 Nov. 1891; *s* of late Frank Stonehewer Bird; *m* 1918, Françoise, *d* of Jean Laczynski; one *s* one *d. Educ:* Berkhamsted School; Pembroke College, Cambridge. Student Interpreter, Levant Consular Service, 1913; HM Vice-Consul, 1917; served at Skoplje, Jassy, Bucarest, Belgrade, Mogador, Rabat; HM Agent and Consul at Jedda, 1927; Consul, Casablanca, 1930-36; acting Consul-General, Rabat, 1936-37; Consul-General, Addis Ababa, 1937-39; Minister at Jedda, 1939-43; Consul-General for French Zone of Morocco, 1943-45; HM Ambassador to Iraq, 1945-48; retired 1948. UK rep. on UNO Council for Libya, 1950. *Recreations:* television, bridge. *Address:* Northfield Hotel, Castle Cary, Somerset. *T:* Castle Cary 638.   [*Died* 7 *Dec.* 1973.

STONELEY, Robert, FRS 1935; MA, ScD Cantab; Emeritus Reader in Theoretical Geophysics, formerly Stokes Lecturer in Mathematics, University of Cambridge; Fellow of Pembroke College; *b* 14 May 1894; *s* of Robert Stoneley and Fanny Bradley; *m* 1927, Dorothy, *d* of Gayford Duge Minn and Annie Okey; two *s* (one *d* decd). *Educ:* Parmiter's School; City of London School; St John's Coll., Cambridge (Foundation Scholar; Taylor Research Studentship). Asst Lecturer in Mathematics, Sheffield University, 1920-23; Curator of University Observatory, 1922-23; at The University of Leeds, 1923-34: Assistant Lecturer in Applied Mathematics, 1923; Astronomical Observer, 1924; Lecturer in Applied Mathematics, 1927; Hon. Reader in Geophysics, 1933; Lecturer in Mathematics, Univ. of Cambridge, 1934; Lecturer and Dir of Studies in Mathematics, Pembroke Coll., Cambridge, 1935-61. Pres., Internat. Assoc. of Seismology, 1946-51; Visiting Professor: Institute of Geophysics, Univ. of Calif., 1948; Amer. Univ. Washington, DC, 1955-56. Research Fellow in Geophysics, Calif. Inst. of Technol., 1956. Geophysicist (Seismology), Office of R&D, US Coast and Geodetic Survey, 1961-63; Prof. of Geophysics, Univ. of Pittsburgh, Pa, 1964-68. Mem. Council, Royal Soc., 1951-53; Pres., Section A, British Association, 1960-61. Chairman: British Nat. Cttee for Geodesy and Geophysics, 1949-54; British Assoc. Cttee on Seismological Investigations, 1946-. Hon. Dir, Internat. Seismological Summary, 1957-63. Chm., Cttee for Internat. Seismological Summary, 1948-67. Nat. Corresp. for Seismology and Geodesy, UK Cttees: for Internat. Geophysical Year, 1953-60; on Antarctic Research, 1958-; on Co-operation in Geophysics, 1961-68; Sub-Cttee for Seismology and the Physics of the Earth's Interior. UNESCO Senior Consultant, Internat. Inst. of Seismology and Earthquake Engineering, Tokyo, 1963-67; Mem., UNESCO Consultative Cttee on Seismology and Earthquake Engineering, 1965-. Fellow, Amer. Geophysical Union, 1967; Mem., Pontifical Acad. of Sciences, 1970; Hon. Mem., Seismological Soc. of Amer., 1973. *Publications:* Papers on geophysical subjects, mainly on earthquake waves. *Address:* 4 Croftgate, Fulbrooke Road, Cambridge CB3 9EE.
[*Died* 2 *Feb.* 1976.

STONHAM, Baron, *cr* 1958 (Life Peer); **Victor John Collins,** PC 1969; OBE 1946; *b* 1 July 1903; *s* of Victor and Eliza Sarah Collins; *m* 1929, Violet Mary Savage; one *s. Educ:* Regent St Polytechnic; London Univ. Entered family business of J. Collins & Sons, Ltd, London, E1, 1923, subseq. Gov. Dir until 1964, when in office. Joint Parly Under-Sec. of State, Home Office, 1964-67, Minister of State, 1967-69. Pres. Employers Fedn of Cane and Willow Workers Assocs, 1932; Pres. National Willow Growers Assoc., 1945; Chairman: National Basket and Willow Trades Advisory Cttee, 1942-64; National Council on Inland Transport, 1962-64; National Soc. for Mentally Handicapped Children, 1963-64; Youth Ventures, 1959-64; Advisory Council on Probation and After-Care, 1970-. MP (Lab) for Taunton Div. of Somerset, 1945-50, for Shoreditch and Finsbury, 1954-58; Minister of State, Home Office, 1967-69. *Address:* House of Lords, SW1. *T:* 01-930 8100.   [*Died* 22 *Dec.* 1971.

STOPFORD, Gen. Sir Montagu George North, GCB 1948 (KCB 1947; CB 1943); KBE 1944; DSO 1940; MC 1917; DL; Vice-President Army Cadet Force Association, since 1961 (Chairman, 1951-61); *b* 16 Nov. 1892; *m* 1921, Dorothy, *d* of late Lt-Col H. F. Deare. *Educ:* Wellington College; RMC, Sandhurst. 2nd Lt Rifle Brigade, 1911; Maj.-Gen. 1941; Lt-Gen. 1944; Gen. 1946; served European War, France and Belgium, 1914-18 (despatches twice, MC); War of 1939-45 (despatches, DSO, CB, KBE); Comd 17 Inf. Bde, BEF, 1939-40; GOC 56 (London) Div. 1941; Comdt Staff College, 1942; GOC 33rd Ind.

Corps, Burma, 1943-45; GOC-in-C 12th Army, Burma Command and Allied Forces, Netherlands East Indies, 1945-46; C-in-C Allied Land Forces, SE Asia, 1946-47; GOC-in-C, Northern Command, 1947-49; ADC General to King George VI, 1947-49; retired, 1949; Col Comdt The Rifle Bde, 1951-58. DL Oxford, 1962. Commander Legion of Merit (USA), 1946. *Address:* Rockhill House, Chipping Norton, Oxon. *Club:* United Service. [*Died* 10 *March* 1971.

STOPFORD, Robert Jemmett, CMG 1946; Commander of the Order of Orange Nassau; US Medal of Freedom; Vice-Chairman, Imperial War Museum, 1954-68; *b* 19 May 1895; *s* of late Jemmett J. Stopford, Dublin; unmarried. *Educ:* St Paul's Sch.; Magdalene Coll., Cambridge. Served European War, 1914-18; Banking, 1921-38. Private Sec. to Chm., Indian Statutory Commission, 1928-30; Member of Runciman Mission to Czechoslovakia, 1938; Liaison Officer for Refugees with the Czechoslovakian Govt, 1938-39; Financial Counsellor, British Embassy, Washington, 1940-43; War Office, 1943-45. Formerly Chairman National Film Finance Corporation. *Address:* Oyles Mill Cottage, Iwerne Minster, Blandford, Dorset. *Club:* Athenæum. [*Died* 20 *Sept.* 1978.

STOPFORD, Rt. Rev. and Rt. Hon. Robert Wright, PC 1961; KCVO 1973; CBE 1949; FKC 1965; DD (Lambeth) 1957; Bishop of Bermuda, since 1976; Vicar-General, Episcopal Church in Jerusalem and the Middle East, 1974-75; *b* 20 Feb. 1901; *s* of John William Stopford; *m* 1st, 1935, Winifred Sophia (who *d* by enemy action, 1942), *d* of William Morton; two *s*; 2nd, 1945, Kathleen Mary (*d* 1973), *d* of Harold Holt; one *d*. *Educ:* Liverpool Coll.; Hertford Coll., Oxford (Scholar); 1st Class Hons Classical Mods, 1922; BA 1st Class Hons School Mod. Hist. 1924, MA 1927; Hon. Fellow, 1956. Asst Master, Highgate Sch., 1924-25; Senior History Master, Oundle Sch., 1925-34, and Housemaster, 1926-34. Ordained, 1932; Asst Chaplain, 1932-34; Principal: Trinity Coll., Kandy, Ceylon, 1935-41; Achimota Coll., Gold Coast, 1941-45; Chm., Africa Cttee of Adv. Cttee on Educn in the Colonies, 1945-55; Rector of Chipping Barnet, 1946-48; Moderator of the Church Training Colls, 1947-55; Gen. Sec. of the National Soc. and Sec. of the Church Assembly Schs Council, 1952-55; Suffragan Bishop of Fulham, 1955-56; Bishop of Peterborough, 1956-61; Bishop of London, 1961-73. Chaplain to the Queen, 1952-55; Hon. Canon of Canterbury, 1951-56; Episcopal Sec., Lambeth Conference, 1958; Chm., Church of England Board of Education, 1958-73; Jt Chairman, Anglican-Methodist Unity Commission, 1967-69; Select Preacher, Oxford, 1959, Cambridge, 1963. Dean of HM Chapels Royal, 1961-73; Prelate of the Order of the British Empire, 1961-73; Prelate, Imperial Soc. of Knights Bachelor, 1967-73; Episcopal Canon, St George's Cathedral, Jerusalem, 1971-75. Chm., D'Oyly Carte Trust, 1972-. Hon. FCP 1965. ChStJ 1976. Freeman, City of London, 1965; Hon. Freeman, Grocers' Company, 1967. Churchill Fellow, Westminster Coll., Fulton, Mo, 1969. Hon. DCL, Durham, 1951; Hon. DD: London, 1965; Westminster Coll., Fulton, Missouri, 1966; College of William and Mary, Virginia, 1968. *Publications:* Play Production (with M. V. C. Jeffreys), 1927; The Anglican Communion (with others), 1948; Church, School and Life, 1949; No Man Liveth unto Himself, 1964. *Address:* Upper House, Up Somborne, Stockbridge, Hampshire SO20 6RD; PO Box 769, Hamilton, Bermuda. *Clubs:* Athenæum, Royal Over-Seas League. [*Died* 13 *Aug.* 1976.

STOPFORD SACKVILLE, Colonel Nigel Victor, CBE 1963 (OBE 1945); TD 1945; DL; JP; CA; *b* 27 Jan. 1901; *s* of late Col Lionel Stopford Sackville, Rifle Brigade; *m* 1st, 1929, Beatrix, *d* of late Col H. A. Pakenham, CMG; one *s* one *d*; 2nd, 1946, Lilah, *d* of Capt. Percy Hare. *Educ:* Repton; Royal Military College, Sandhurst. Lieut 14th/20th Hussars 1921; Northamptonshire Yeomanry: Capt. 1930; Lt-Col 1940; Hon. Col 1952-67. Col comdg RAC Tactical School, 1942; Col 2nd i/c 9th Armoured Bde, 1943; served in Middle East and Italy (despatches). Chm. Northants Agric. Exec. Cttee, 1953-68; Personal Liaison Officer to Minister of Agriculture, 1955. Chm., Northants. T & AFA, 1952-66. JP 1933, CC 1931, CA 1945, Northants; DL County of Northampton, 1965. *Publication:* (privately) Drayton, History of Drayton House, 1939. *Recreation:* shooting. *Address:* Drayton House, Lowick, Kettering, Northants. *T:* Thrapston 3202. *Club:* White's. [*Died* 1 *Dec.* 1972.

STOREY, (Mary) Gladys, OBE 1919; authoress; *b* Hampstead; *d* of Prof. G. A. Storey, RA, and Emily Hayward, London. *Educ:* Allen-Olney Sch., Hampstead. On stage, ingénue parts with Sir George Alexander, gave up stage for war-work; pioneer of Women's Services; commenced recruiting on own initiative, gaining approval of Lord Roberts; became only female recruiter at HQ Recruiting Depot, Whitehall, 1914; ran fund (under own

name) for providing Bovril to soldiers in trenches in every theatre of War, 1914-18; donations, King George V; grant from the Army Council; supplied British Military Mission in N and S Russia (by special request of GOC), 1919-20; transferred from Recruiting HQ to supervise staff at HQ National Registration, London, 1915-17; Sept. 1939, re-inauguration of Great War Fund (under own name) providing Bovril for HM Forces in all war and other areas; continuation of supplies after European War by request of Field-Marshal Montgomery to British Army of the Rhine, 1945-47, and British Troops, Jerusalem, 1946-47. Fund supported by King George VI and War Office. *Publications:* Humorous Stories of Famous People, 1916; All Sorts of People, 1929; Dickens and Daughter (at her request), 1939; made drawing (1925) of Mrs Perugini (Kate Dickens) bound in at beginning of vol. containing Charles Dickens' letters to his wife, Br. Museum, 1934. [*Died* 20 *Nov.* 1978.

STOREY, Samuel; *see* Buckton, Baron.

STORM, Lesley; playwright; (*née* Margaret Cowie), *d* of Rev. William Cowie, MA, and Christian Ewen; *m* James Doran Clark, MB, ChB, DPM (*d* 1955); two *s* two *d*. *Educ:* Peterhead Academy; Aberdeen University (MA). *Publications:* Plays: Black Chiffon, 1949; The Day's Mischief, 1952; The Long Echo, 1956; Roar Like a Dove, 1957; The Paper Hat, 1965; Three Goose-quills and a Knife, 1967; Look, No Hands, 1971. *Recreation:* travel. *Address:* c/o Royal Bank of Scotland, 115 Regent Street, W1A 3DD. [*Died* 19 *Oct.* 1975.

STORRS, Rt. Rev. Christopher E., MA, ThDoc (Australia); *b* 4 Feb. 1889; *s* of John Storrs, Dean of Rochester; *m* 1939, Joan Williams, Perth, Western Australia; two *s* two *d*. *Educ:* Malvern College (Senior Scholar); Pembroke College, Cambridge (Senior Scholar, 1st Class Classical Tripos); Leeds Clergy School. Boxed Cambridge v Oxford, 1908; Deacon, 1912; Priest, 1915; Leeds Parish Church, 1912-15; CF 1916-19; Macedonia, Palestine, Egypt; Chaplain and Assistant Master, Malvern College, 1915-30; St George's College, Perth, Western Australia, 1930-39; Archdeacon of Northam, W Australia, 1939-46; Bishop of Grafton, New South Wales, 1946-55; Warden of St John's Theological College, Morpeth, NSW, 1955-60; Rector of Hazelbury Bryan, Dorset, 1960-64. *Publications:* edited pamphlets The Christian and the War Series by Australian authors, 1941; Mr Valiant for Truth: an Anthology, 1942; Many Creeds One Cross (Moorhouse Lectures 1943, USA, 1944). *Recreations:* chess, golf, music, reading, talking. *Address:* 37 Westgate, Chichester, West Sussex. [*Died* 19 *Feb.* 1977.

STOTT, May, Lady, (May B. Lee); RMS; *b* Lahore, India; *e d* of late John Bridges Lee, MA Cantab, Barrister-at-Law, Inner Temple, Advocate of High Courts of Calcutta, Allahabad and Lahore; *m* Sir Philip Stott, 1st Bt, as his second wife. *Educ:* in England; studied Art at Lambeth School of Art. Exhibited Royal Academy 34 years (46 portraits), Salon Artistes Français 32 times, also occasionally Royal Scottish Academy, Walker Art Gallery, Liverpool. Mem. of Soc. of Women Artists, Royal Soc. of Miniature Painters, Sculptors and Gravers, Society of Miniaturists and Ridley Art Club; Portrait Painter in oils, water colours and miniatures. Has painted numerous portraits of well-known people (including sons of the Princess Royal) and been commissioned to paint many presentation large portraits and miniatures. Mention honorable, Salon 1950 (Section de Peinture), Société des Artistes Français. *Recreations:* reading, dancing, travelling, friends. *Address:* 20 FitzJames Avenue, W14 0RP. *T:* 01-603 3078. [*Died* 2 *Jan.* 1977.

STOTT, Sir Philip Sidney, 3rd Bt *cr* 1920; ARIBA, AIAA; Senior Architect in private practice; *b* 23 Dec. 1914; *e s* of Sir George Edward Stott, 2nd Bt, and Kate (*d* 1955), *o d* of late George Swailes, Oldham; *S* father 1957; *m* 1947, Cicely Florence, *widow* of V. C. W. Trowbridge and *o d* of Bertram Ellingham; two *s*. *Educ:* Rossall; Trinity Hall, Cambridge. Registered Chartered and Incorporate Architect; ARIBA 1947; AIAA 1950. *Recreations:* astronomy, chess, music and tennis. *Heir:* *s* Adrian George Ellingham Stott, *b* 7 Oct. 1948. [*Died* 9 *Dec.* 1979.

STOUGHTON, Raymond Henry, ARCS; DSc (London); Hon. LLD (Toronto); retired as Principal, University College of Ghana, 1957-61; *b* 8 Jan. 1903; *yr s* of Arnold Stoughton-Harris and Mary Townsend Jefferis; *m* 1925, Audrey Milne Rennie (*d* 1950); three *s*. *Educ:* St Peter's Sch., York; Imperial Coll. of Science and Technology, ARCS, 1923; BSc London 1924; DSc London 1932; Mycologist, Rubber Research scheme, Ceylon 1924-26; Assistant Mycologist, Rothamsted Experimental Station, 1926-33. Professor of Horticulture, University of Reading, 1933-57. Victoria Medal of Honour, RHS, 1955, Vice-Pres., RHS, 1976 (formerly Mem. Council). *Publications:*

various on plant pathology and bacterial cytology in Proceedings of the Royal Society, Annals of Applied Biology, etc., and on physiology and horticulture in various journals. *Recreations:* philately and art history. *Address:* Lane's Corner, North Warnborough, Basingstoke, Hants. *T:* Odiham 2783.
[Died 9 Nov. 1979.

STOUT, Sir Duncan; *see* Stout, Sir T. D. M.

STOUT, Sir (Thomas) Duncan (Macgregor), Kt 1962; CBE 1943 (OBE 1919); DSO 1917; ED; MB, MS London; FRCS; FRACS; FACS; Hon. Cons. Surgeon, Wellington Hospital; Past Member Council and past Chancellor, Victoria University of Wellington; Past Member: Senate, University of New Zealand; Council, Massey Agricultural College; Trustee, NZ Cancer Societies; Past President, Wellington Branch (NZ) British Empire Cancer Campaign; *b* 25 July 1885; *s* of late Rt Hon. Sir R. Stout, KCMG; *m* 1919, Agnes I. Pearce; three *s* one *d. Educ:* Wellington College, NZ; Guy's College and Hospital. Consultant Surgeon, Wellington Hospital (NZ); served European War, 1914-18, Samoan Force (OBE, DSO); attached to No 1 NZ Stationary Hospital at Port Said, Salonica, and France; Divisional Surgeon at Brockenhurst (NZ Hospital in England); War of 1939-45 (England, Middle East and Italy); Consultant Surgeon 2nd NZEF (CBE). Editor NZ Medical War History, 1939-45; President, NZ Branch BMA, 1937-38. Hon. LLD: Victoria Univ. of Wellington; Univ. of NZ. *Recreations:* golf and bowls. *Address:* 9 Kotare Street, Waikanae, New Zealand. *Club:* Wellington (Wellington, NZ).
[Died 27 Feb. 1979.

STOW, Sir Frederic Lawrence Philipson-, 3rd Bt, *cr* 1907; *b* 19 Sept. 1905; *e s* of Sir Elliot Philipson Philipson-Stow, 2nd Bt and Edith (*d* 1943), *y d* of late E. H. Pery-Knox-Gore, DL, JP, of Coolcronan, Ballina, Co. Mayo; *S* father 1954; *m* 1st, 1932, Daphne Morriss (marr. diss.; she *d* 1960), *e d* of late W. G. Daffarn; 2nd, 1951, Cynthia Yvette, *d* of late W. R. Jecks, Johannesburg. *Educ:* Eton. *Heir: b* Edmond Cecil Philipson-Stow, MBE 1946, *b* 25 Aug. 1912. *Address:* Apartado 211, Mahon, Menorca, Spain.
[Died 9 Jan. 1976.

STOW HILL, Baron *cr* 1966 (Life Peer), of Newport; **Frank Soskice,** PC 1948; Kt, *cr* 1945; *b* 23 July 1902; *m* 1940, Susan Isabella Cloudesley Hunter; two *s. Educ:* St Paul's School; Balliol College, Oxford. Called to Bar, Inner Temple, 1926; Bencher, 1945. MP (Lab) for Birkenhead East, 1945-50, for Neepsend Div. of Sheffield, (April) 1950-55, for Newport (Monmouthshire), (July) 1956-66; Solicitor-General, 1945-51; Attorney-General, April-Oct. 1951; Home Secretary, 1964-65; Lord Privy Seal, 1965-66. UK Delegate to UN General Assembly, 1950. Treasurer, Inner Temple, 1968. *Address:* House of Lords, SW1.
[Died 1 Jan. 1979.

STOWELL, Gordon William, ARCA; journalist and encyclopedist, retired 1967; *b* 6 September 1898; *yr s* of Rev. Arthur Knight Stowell, Leeds, and Elizabeth Ann Finlinson; *m* 1st, 1921, May Fairbrother (*d* 1926); 2nd, 1929, Millicent Louise Dods. *Educ:* Leeds Modern School; Leeds School of Art; Royal College of Art (Diploma of Associateship in Decorative Painting). Principal, Weston-Super-Mare School of Science and Art, 1923-26. Joined British Broadcasting Corporation on Staff of Radio Times, 1932; Deputy Editor, 1933; Editor, 1941-44. With Fleetway Publications 1944-64, edited New Universal Encyclopedia, The Book of Knowledge, Practical Knowledge for All, Children's Encyclopedia (30th edn), etc; Founder-Editor: Waverley Encyclopedia, 1952; The Book of Words, 1962; Junior Year Book, 1964. Served in ranks of London Territorials, 1916-18, France (wounded). *Publications:* The History of Button Hill (novel) 1929; many articles and reviews. *Address:* 113 Howard's Lane, Putney, SW15. *T:* 01-788 4754.
[Died 5 Sept. 1972.

STOWERS, Arthur, BSc (Eng), London; ACGI, FIMechE, MICE, FMA; retired; *b* 24 Jan. 1897; *yr s* of James H. Stowers, MD; *m* 1929, Freda, *d* of Richard Hall, FRIBA; two *s. Educ:* Haileybury; City and Guilds (Engineering) College, South Kensington. Contracts Engr, after 3 yrs pupilage, at W. H. Allen, Sons & Co., Bedford, 1923; Asst Keeper, Science Museum, South Kensington, 1930. Min. of Aircraft Production, 1940; Keeper, Science Museum, Department of Mechanical and Civil Engineering, 1950-62. Jt Hon. Sec. Newcomen Soc., 1933-48, Pres., 1955-57; Dickinson Memorial Medal, 1962. *Address:* 27 Woodgavil, The Drive, Banstead, Surrey SM7 1AA.
[Died 30 Nov. 1977.

STRACEY, Sir Michael (George Motley), 8th Bt, *cr* 1818; *b* 7 July 1911; *s* of Sir Edward Stracey, 7th Bt, and Mary Elizabeth Brinsley, *e d* of late Algernon Sheridan, Frampton Court,

Dorchester; *S* father, 1949. *Educ:* Harrow; Queen's College, Oxford. *Heir: cousin* John Simon Stracey [*b* 30 Nov. 1938; *m* 1968, Martha Maria, *d* of late Johann Egger; one *d*]. *Address:* c/o Barclays Bank, Goodenough House, 33 Old Broad Street, EC2.
[Died 25 Sept. 1971.

STRACHAN, Hon. Lord; James Frederick Strachan; Senator, College of Justice in Scotland, 1948-67; *b* 11 October 1894; *s* of James K. Strachan, Glasgow; *m* 1926, Irene Louise, *d* of Timothy Warren, LLD, Glasgow; two *s* one *d. Educ:* Glasgow Academy; Glasgow Univ. MA, LLB; admitted Faculty of Advocates, 1921; Advocate Depute, 1936-38; KC 1938; Vice-Dean Faculty of Advocates, 1941-48; Procurator Church of Scotland, 1938-48. Sheriff of Argyll, 1942-45; Sheriff of Perth and Angus, 1945-48. Hon. LLD Glasgow, 1961. *Address:* Woodville, Canaan Lane, Edinburgh EH10 4SG. *Club:* New (Edinburgh).
[Died 15 May 1978.

STRACHAN, Sir Andrew (Henry), Kt, *cr* 1953; CBE 1947; FCA; Director of Companies; *b* 28 August 1895; *s* of late A. Strachan, Co. Antrim, N Ireland; *m* 1929, Barbara Marian Celia, *d* of Sir Bourchier Wrey, 12th Bt, CBE; one *s* one *d. Educ:* mainly at Rathmines College, Dublin. Articled clerk to John Mackie & Co. (now Craig, Gardner & Co.), Chartered Accountants, Dublin and Belfast; qualified as Chartered Accountant. Served European War, 1914-18, throughout with Royal Dublin Fusiliers, Gallipoli and France. Joined British South Africa Company's Administration, 1921; Commissioner of Taxes, 1933; Secretary to the Treasury, S Rhodesia, 1941-53, Federation of Rhodesia and Nyasaland, 1953-55. Chm., Rhodesia Railways Board, 1954-59; Chm., Rhodesia Television Ltd, 1960-64. *Address:* 20 Hurworth Road, Highlands, Salisbury, Rhodesia. *T:* Salisbury 42662. *Club:* Salisbury (Rhodesia).
[Died 27 May 1976.

STRACHAN, James Frederick; *see* Strachan, Hon. Lord.

STRACHEY, Prof. Christopher; Professor of Computation, Oxford University, since 1971; *b* 16 Nov. 1916; *s* of late Oliver Strachey, CBE and Ray Strachey. *Educ:* Gresham's Sch.; King's Coll., Cambridge (MA). Physicist, Standard Telephones & Cables, 1937; Asst Master: St Edmund's Sch., Canterbury, 1944; Harrow Sch., 1948; Technical Officer, Nat. Research Develt Corp., 1951; Consultant in Electronic Computers, 1958; Sen. Research Fellow, Churchill Coll., Cambridge, 1962; Vis. Lectr, MIT, 1965; Reader in Computation, Oxford Univ., 1966; Fellow of Wolfson Coll., 1966. Distinguished Fellow, British Computing Soc., 1972. *Publications:* papers in technical jls. *Recreations:* music, talking, finding out how things work. *Address:* 18 Worcester Place, Oxford. *T:* Oxford 59411.
[Died 18 May 1975.

STRACHIE, 2nd Baron, *cr* 1911; **Edward Strachey,** Bt, *cr* 1801; *b* 13 Jan. 1882; *o s* of 1st Baron and Constance (*d* 1936), *o c* of late C. B. Braham; *S* father, 1936; *m* 1933, Mrs William Ethelred Jennings (*d* 1962). *Educ:* Harrow. JP Somerset; late Lt-Col 4th Somerset Light Infantry; late Lt Grenadier Guards; served European War, 1914-20. *Heir:* (to Barony) none; (to Baronetcy) *cousin* Charles Strachey, *b* 20 June 1934. *Address:* Sutton Court, Pensford, Somerset. *TA:* Bishop-Sutton, Somerset. *T:* Chew Magna 2407.
[Died 17 May 1973.

STRAHAN, Frank, CVO 1934; CBE 1928; resigned from Commonwealth Government Service, 1949; late Secretary to Cabinet; *b* 2 July 1886; *s* of late Richard Strahan; *m* 1914, Ella, *d* of William Moore, Bendigo. *Educ:* Melbourne University, BA, LLB. Assistant Secretary Prime Ministers' Dept 1921-35; Director Amalgamated Wireless (Australasia) Ltd, 1930-62. Secretary Prime Minister's Department, 1935-49; Secretary to Australian Delegation to Imperial Conferences, 1923 and 1937; Secretary, British, Australian and New Zealand Antarctic Research Expedition; Secretary of Australian tour of Duke of Gloucester (CVO). *Address:* c/o Amalgamated Wireless (Australasia) Ltd, Miles Street, Mulgrave, Vic 3170, Australia.
[Died 5 May 1976.

STRAHAN, Lt-Col Geoffrey Carteret, CIE 1944; OBE 1920; *b* 17 Sept. 1886; *y s* of H. Strahan, MA, JP, Hythe, Kent; *m* 1916, Eileen Olivia, *e d* of Col St G. L. Steele, CB; two *d. Educ:* King's School, Canterbury; Keble College, Oxford. 1st commission, 1909, Indian Army; Recruiting Officer for Gurkhas, 1937-45; retired to IRRO, 1940; re-employed, 1940. Served European War (despatches twice, OBE, Bt Major); War of 1939-45 (CIE). *Address:* Kelston, Graffham, Petworth, Sussex.
[Died 7 July 1973.

STRAIGHT, Whitney Willard, CBE 1944; MC; DFC; Legion of Merit (USA); Norwegian War Cross; Deputy Chairman, Post

Office Corporation, 1969-74; Chairman: Arran Trust Ltd; Rolls-Royce Realizations Ltd, since 1976; Director, Midland Bank Ltd; Hon. Companion, Royal Aeronautical Society; *b* 6 Nov. 1912; *e s* of late Maj. W. D. Straight and Mrs Dorothy Whitney Elmhirst; *m* 1935, Lady Daphne Finch-Hatton, *d* of 14th Earl of Winchilsea and Nottingham; two *d*. *Educ:* Lincoln Sch., USA; Dartington Hall; Trinity Coll., Cambridge. Became professional motor car driver and won many International races and held speed records. Gave up motor racing in 1934 to enter Civil Aviation. Started a number of Companies and was appointed to Govt and other National Cttees. Served War of 1939-45, in RAF; Fighter Comd, Transport Comd, Air Cdre 1942 (despatches, MC, DFC, CBE, Norwegian War Cross, American Legion of Merit). Air ADC 1944. Chm., Straight Corp. and subsidiary cos, 1935-39; Dep. Chm. BEA, 1946-47; Man. Dir (Chief Exec.), BOAC, 1947-49, Dep. Chm., 1949-55; Exec. Vice-Chm., 1956-57, Dep. Chm., 1957-71, Chm., 1971-76, Rolls-Royce Ltd. Member: Aerodrome Owners Assoc., 1936; Air Registration Bd, 1939-42, 1947-54; Council, RCA, 1955-58; Council, Business Aircraft Users Assoc., 1962; CoID, 1957-66; Council, UK S African Trade Assoc., 1969; Nat. Adv. Council on Art Educn, 1959-65; Cttee, RGS; former Chm., Contemporary Art Soc.; Vice-Pres., British Light Aircraft Centre; Chm., 1946-51, Vice-Pres., 1951-68, Royal Aero Club; Pres., PO Art Club of GB, 1969; Vice-Pres., Geoffrey de Havilland Flying Foundn, 1966; Chairman: Govt Adv. Cttee on Private Flying, 1947; Exec. Cttee, Alexandra Day, 1957. Royal Air Forces Assoc.: Pres., Ealing Br., 1965. Member: Inst. Transport; Inst. of Navigation; British Air Line Pilots Assoc.; Fellow: Royal Soc. for Protection of Birds; Brit. Inst. of Management; FRSA; FRGS (Vice-Pres., 1974); FZS. Liveryman: Guild of Air Pilots and Navigators; Worshipful Co. of Goldsmiths; Worshipful Co. of Coachmakers and Coachharnessmakers. *Publications:* numerous articles on aviation subjects. *Recreations:* ski-ing, music, art, industrial design. *Address:* The Aviary, Windmill Lane, Southall, Middlesex UB2 4NG. *T:* 01-574 2711. *Clubs:* Buck's; Royal Yacht Squadron, Cruising Association; International des Anciens Pilotes de Grand Prix FI (Lausanne); Corviglia Ski (St Moritz).   [*Died 5 April 1979.*

STRANDERS, Michael O'Connell, QC 1960; a National Insurance Commissioner, since 1971; *b* 25 March 1911; *s* of late Vivian Stranders, MA and late Patricia O'Connell Stranders; *m* 1944, Anne Mary, *d* of late Col Richard L. Winton-Wiener and of Marguerite Winton-Wiener, Montreal, Canada; two *s* one *d*. *Educ:* Henry Thornton Sch.; University Coll., London; Sch. 1930, Joseph Hume Schol. (Jurisprudence), 1934, University Coll., London; LLB (London) (1st Cl. Hons and Univ. Schol.), 1934; Barrister, Lincoln's Inn, 1934 (Tancred and George V Coronation Studentships, Buchanan Prize); Bencher, 1969. *Recreations:* foreign travel, languages, the theatre. *Address:* 5 New Square, Lincoln's Inn, WC2. *T:* 01-405 6171, 01-242 3436; 27 Park Drive, East Sheen, SW14. *T:* 01-876 2021.
[*Died 20 Feb. 1973.*

STRANG, 1st Baron, *cr* 1954, of Stonesfield; **William Strang,** GCB 1953 (KCB 1948; CB 1939); GCMG 1950 (KCMG 1943; CMG 1932); MBE 1918; Chairman, National Parks Commission, 1954-66; Member Nature Conservancy, 1954-66; Chairman Food Hygiene Advisory Council, 1955-71; Chairman, Royal Institute of International Affairs, 1958-65; a Deputy Speaker and Deputy Chairman of Committees, House of Lords, 1962; *b* 1893; *e s* of late James Strang, Englefield, Berks; *m* 1920, Elsie Wynne (*d* 1974), *y d* of late J. E. Jones; one *s* one *d*. *Educ:* Palmer's School; University Coll., London; Sorbonne. BA (London), 1912; Quain Essay, 1913; served European War with 4th Bn Worcestershire Regt, and HQ, 29th Div. (MBE); entered Foreign Office, 1919; 3rd Sec., Belgrade, 1919; 2nd Sec., 1920; Foreign Office, 1923; 1st Sec., 1925; acting Counsellor of Embassy at Moscow, 1930; Counsellor, 1932; Asst Under-Sec. of State in Foreign Office, 1939-43; UK Representative on European Advisory Commission, with rank of Ambassador, 1943-45; Political Adviser to C-in-C, British Forces of Occupation in Germany, 1945-47; Permanent Under-Sec., FO (German Section), 1947-49; Permanent Under-Sec. of State, Foreign Office, 1949-53; retired 1953. Fellow University College, London, 1946; Chairman College Committee, 1963-71. Hon. LLD (London), 1954. *Publications:* The Foreign Office, 1955; Home and Abroad, 1956; Britain in World Affairs, 1961; The Diplomatic Career, 1962. *Heir: s* Hon. Colin Strang [*b* 12 June 1922; *m* 1955, Barbara Mary Hope (*see* Prof. Barbara Strang); one *d*]. *Address:* 14 Graham Park Road, Gosforth, Newcastle upon Tyne NE3 4BH. *Club:* Travellers'.
[*Died 27 May 1978.*

STRANGE OF KNOKIN, Baroness; *see* St Davids, Elizabeth, Viscountess.

STRANGMAN, James Gonville, QC 1950; *b* 1 Dec. 1902; *s* of Sir Thomas Strangman, QC; *m* 1935, Eileen, *d* of J. S. Mallam, FCA; one *s* two *d*. *Educ:* Charterhouse; Trinity Hall, Cambridge. Called to Bar by Middle Temple, Jan. 1927. Elected Bencher, Middle Temple, 1958. *Recreation:* horticulture. *Address:* 13 Old Square, Lincoln's Inn, WC2; Brook House, Crowborough, Sussex.   [*Died 3 June 1977.*

STRANGMAN, Sir Thomas (Joseph), Kt, *cr* 1920; QC 1938; Bencher, Lincoln's Inn, 1944; *b* 7 Jan. 1873; *s* of Joseph Strangman; *m* 1896, Winifred (*d* 1955), *d* of Capt. W. J. J. Warneford; two *s* two *d*. *Educ:* Charterhouse; Trinity Hall, Cambridge. Called to Bar, Middle Temple, 1896; Advocate-General and Member of the Legislative Council, Bombay, 1908-15, and 1916-22; contested (C) Crewe Division of Cheshire, Dec. 1923, and East Wolverhampton, Oct. 1924. *Address:* 24 Hans Court, Hans Road, SW3. *T:* 01-589 8336. *Clubs:* Brooks's, City of London.   [*Died 8 Oct. 1971.*

STRATFORD, Esmé C. W.; *see* Wingfield-Stratford.

STRATH, Sir William, KCB 1959 (CB 1951); MA; Chairman, British Aluminium Co. Ltd, 1962-72; Director: Tube Investments Ltd (Non-executive Deputy Chairman, 1972-74, a Deputy Chairman, 1968-72, a Group Managing Director, 1961-72); Legal and General Assurance Society Ltd; *b* 16 Nov. 1906; *s* of J. G. and Elizabeth Strath; *m* 1938, Vera Lucy Brown; no *c*. *Educ:* Girvan High Sch.; Glasgow University. Served in following Government Departments: Inland Revenue, 1929-38; Air Ministry, 1938-40; Ministry of Aircraft Production, 1940-45; Ministry of Supply, 1945-47; Central Economic Planning staff, 1947-55; Treasury, 1948-55; Member, Economic Planning Board, 1949-55; Full-time Member Atomic Energy Authority, 1955-59; Permanent Secretary: Ministry of Supply, 1959; Ministry of Aviation, 1959-60. Pres., British Mech. Engrg Confedn, 1971-72. Mem. Steering Bd, Strathclyde Business Sch. Hon. LLD Strathclyde, 1969. *Recreations:* mountaineering, golf. *Address:* C6, Albany, Piccadilly, W1V 9RF. *T:* 01-734 2452. *Clubs:* United Service & Royal Aero, Alpine.
[*Died 8 May 1975.*

STRATHALMOND, 2nd Baron *cr* 1955, of Pumpherston, Co. Midlothian; **William Fraser,** CMG 1967; OBE 1945; TD 1955; Director: Prudential Assurance Co., since 1973; Burmah Oil Co., since 1975; Newarthill Ltd, since 1976; *b* 8 May 1916; *o s* of 1st Baron Strathalmond, CBE, and Mary (*d* 1963), *d* of Thomson McLintock, Glasgow; *S* father, 1970; *m* 1945, Letitia, *d* of late Walter Krementz, New Jersey, USA; one *s* one *d*. *Educ:* Loretto; Clare Coll., Cambridge. Barrister-at-Law, 1946-50; British Petroleum Co. Ltd, 1950-59; Managing Dir, Kuwait Oil Co. Ltd, 1959-62; Dir, BP Co. Ltd, 1962-74 (a Managing Dir, 1962-72); Chm., Govan Shipbuilders, 1972-74. KStJ 1961. Bronze Star, USA, 1945. *Recreation:* racing. *Heir: s* Hon. William Roberton Fraser [*b* 22 July 1947; *m* 1973, Amanda Rose, *d* of Rev. G. C. Taylor]. *Address:* Hillfields Farm, Lower Basildon, Berks. *T:* Upper Basildon 216. *Club:* Boodle's.
[*Died 27 Oct. 1976.*

STRATHMORE and KINGHORNE, 16th Earl of, *cr* 1677; Earl (UK), *cr* 1937; **Timothy Patrick Bowes-Lyon,** Baron Glamis (Scotland), 1445; Earl of Kinghorne, Lord Lyon, Baron Glamis, 1606; Earl of Strathmore and Kinghorne, Viscount Lyon, Lord Glamis, Tannadyce, Sydlaw, and Strathdichtie, 1677; Baron Bowes (UK), 1887; late 2nd Lieutenant Black Watch; *b* 18 March 1918; *o surv s* of 15th Earl of Strathmore and Lady Dorothy Osborne (*d* 1946), 3rd *d* of 10th Duke of Leeds; *S* father, 1949; *m* 1958, Mary (Bridget) Brennan, Leix, Eire (*d* 1967); one *d* decd. *Educ:* Stowe. Served War of 1939-45, Black Watch; retired (ill-health), 1944. *Recreation:* shooting. *Heir-pres: cousin,* Fergus Michael Claude Bowes-Lyon [*b* 31 December 1928; *m* 1956, Mary Pamela, *yr d* of Brig. N. D. McCorquodale, MC; one *s* two *d*]. *Address:* Glamis Castle, Angus, Scotland. *T:* Glamis 244; Holwick Hall, Middleton-in-Teesdale, Barnard Castle, Co. Durham. *T:* Middleton-in-Teesdale 212. *Clubs:* Bath, Turf.   [*Died 13 Sept. 1972.*

STRATTEN, Thomas Price; Hon. President, Union Corporation Limited (Managing Director, 1954-67; Chairman, 1962-72; President, 1972); *b* Kimberley, Cape Province, S Africa, 4 June 1904; *m* 1930, Mary A. Morris, New York, USA; two *s* one *d*. *Educ:* University of Cape Town; Balliol College, Oxford (Rhodes Scholar). Dir of War Supplies, S Africa, 1940-45. Director: Charter Consolidated Ltd, 1972; South African Reserve Bank, 1966-72; Comr, Electricity Supply Commission, 1954-69. Past President, Associated Scientific and Technical Societies of South Africa; Past President and Hon. Member, S African Inst. of Electrical Engrs. Hon. LLD, Univ. of Witwatersrand, 1966. *Recreation:* golf. *Address:* (home) 16

Pallinghurst Road, Westcliff, Johannesburg, 2001, South Africa; (office) 74-78 Marshall Street, Johannesburg. *Clubs:* Rand, Johannesburg Country, Royal Johannesburg Golf (Johannesburg). *[Died 2 Jan. 1980.*

STRATTON, Sir (Francis) John, Kt 1968; CBE 1948; Chairman, FMC Ltd, 1957-April 1974, President and Consultant since 1974; retired 1975 as Chairman: FMC (Meat) Ltd; FMC Products Ltd; Fatstock Finance Ltd; Marsh & Baxter Ltd; C. & T. Harris (Calne) Ltd Groups; Chairman: British Bacon Curers' Federation, 1966-75; Farm Buildings Committee, Design Council, since 1961; *b* 18 Jan. 1906; *o s* of Ernest William Stratton, Great Stukeley, Hunts; *m* 1936, Christine, *d* of Edward Harrison; one *d. Educ:* Fitzwilliam House, Cambridge. MA Cantab (BA Honours English Tripos, Part I, Archæological and Anthropological Tripos). Eastern Associated Telegraph Co., Ltd; Lewis's Ltd. Served War of 1939-45, Royal Artillery (TA), Major, 1939-47; Dir of Service Footwear and Leather Equipment; Controller of Service and Civilian Footwear and finally Controller of Leather and Footwear. Chairman Stratton Mission to Germany, on Hides, Skins, Leather, Footwear, Leather Substitutes and Ancillary Machinery, 1945. Chairman: 1952-57 (Man. Dir, 1947-57), Dolcis Ltd, and its associated Cos; Dolcis (Canada) Ltd, 1947-57. FRSA (Mem., Council, 1963-; Chm., 1971-73; a Vice-Pres., 1974-); Fellow, National Instn of Boot and Shoe Industry; FBIM (Mem. Council, 1954-60); Independent Mem., National Advisory Council for Motor Manufacturing Industry, 1947-59; Member: Council of Industrial Design, 1947-59; Inst. of Personnel Management; Staff Management Assoc.; Footwear Distributors' Fedn (Chm. 1951-56, Pres., 1956-57); Multiple Shoe Retailers' Assoc. (Chm. Exec. Council, 1953-56); Council of Multiple Shops Fedn, 1947-57; Exec. Cttee of Dollar Exports Board, 1950-51; Exec. Cttee British Productivity Council; Guild of Cordwainers, Master, 1956, 1957. Amer. Medal of Freedom with Palm, 1947. *Recreation:* farming. *Address:* Rotherwood, Fittleworth, West Sussex. *T:* Fittleworth 396. *Clubs:* United Oxford & Cambridge University, Brooks's. *[Died 14 Oct. 1976.*

STRAUSS, Lewis Lichtenstein, DSM, (US) 1952; Legion of Merit, 1943; Medal of Freedom (US); Secretary of Commerce (US), 1958-59; Special Assistant to President (US), 1953; *b* Charleston, West Virginia, 1896; *s* of Lewis Strauss and Rosa (née Lichtenstein); *m* 1923, Alice Hanauer; one *s* (and one *s* decd). *Educ:* Public schools, Richmond, Virginia. Private Secretary to Herbert Hoover, 1917-19; Kuhn Loeb & Co., 1919-46. Served War of 1939-45, Rear-Adm., USNR. Past Pres., Institute for Advanced Study. Chairman of the United States Atomic Energy Commission, 1953-58 (Mem., 1946-50). Various hon. degrees and foreign decorations. *Publication:* Men and Decisions, 1963. *Address:* Brandy Station, Virginia 2274, USA. *[Died 21 Jan. 1974.*

STRAVINSKY, Igor; composer; *b* Oranienbaum, near St Petersburg, 5 (18) June 1882; American citizen, 1945; *m* 1940, Vera de Bosset. *Works:* L'Oiseau de Feu, 1910; Petrouchka, 1911; Le sacre du Printemps, 1913; Rossignol, 1914; Renard, 1916; Les Noces, 1917-23; L'Histoire du Soldat, 1918; Pulcinella, 1919; Symphonies d'Instruments à vent, 1920; Mavra, 1922; Octuor, 1923; Concerto pour piano et orchestre, 1924; Oedipus-Rex, 1927; Apollon Musagete, 1928; Le Baiser de la Fée, 1928; Capriccio pour piano et orchestre, 1929; Symphonie de Psaumes, 1930; Concerto pour violin et orchestre, 1931; Duo Concertant pour violin et piano, 1932; Perséphone, 1934; Concerto pour deux pianos-solo, 1935; Jeu de Cartes, 1937; Symphony in C, 1940; Danses Concertantes, 1942; Scènes de Ballet, 1944; Symphony in 3 movements, 1945; Orpheus, 1947; Mass, 1948; The Rake's Progress (opera), 1951; Cantata, 1952; Septet, 1953; Three Songs from Shakespeare, 1953-54; In Memoriam Dylan Thomas, 1954; Canticum sacrum ad honorem Sancti Marcis nominis, 1956; Agon, ballet for twelve dancers, 1957; Threni, 1958; Movements, 1959; Gesualdo Monumentum, 1960; A Sermon, A Narrative, and A Prayer, 1961; The Dove Descending, 1962; The Flood, 1962; Abraham and Isaac, 1964; Elegy for J. F. K., 1964; Variations in Memory of Aldous Huxley, 1965; Requiem Canticles, 1966; Fanfare for a New Theatre, 1964. Awards: Gold Medal, Royal Philharmonic Society, 1954; Sibelius Gold Medal, 1955; Sibelius Prize, Wihuri International Prize Foundation, 1963. *Publications:* (with Robert Craft) Themes and Episodes, 1966; (with Robert Craft) Retrospectives and Conclusions, 1969; rev. edns in one vol., as Themes and Conclusions, 1972 (posthumous publication); *Relevant Publications:* Stravinsky, by Roman Vlad, 1958 (English trans. 1960); Conversations with Igor Stravinsky, Vol. I, 1959, Vol. 2, 1960, Vol. 3, 1962, Vol. 4, 1968; Stravinsky: chronicle of a friendship 1948-1971, by Robert Craft, 1972. *Address:* 1218 North Wetherly Drive, Hollywood, California 90069, USA. *[Died 6 April 1971.*

STREAT, Sir (Edward) Raymond, KBE 1957 (CBE 1930); Kt 1942; Member, Court of Governors, Manchester University (Member Council, 1943-72, Chairman, 1957-65, Treasurer, 1951-57); Hon. Fellow, Nuffield College, Oxford (Visiting Fellow, 1944-59); Vice-President, Lancashire and Merseyside Industrial Development Association, 1946-75; Trustee, John Rylands Library, 1960-75; *b* 7 Feb. 1897; *s* of late Edward Streat, Prestwich; *m* Doris (*d* 1976), *d* of late Amos Davies, JP; two *s* (and one *s* died of wounds, 1944). *Educ:* Manchester Grammar School. Lt 10th Manchester Regiment (TA), 1915-18; Assistant Secretary, Manchester Chamber of Commerce, 1919; Director and Secretary, 1920-40; Hon. Director, Lancashire Industrial Development Council, 1931-40; Chairman, The Cotton Board, Manchester, 1940-57; President, Manchester Statistical Soc., 1936-38; President, Association of Technical Institutions, 1944-45; Secretary, Export Council, Board of Trade, Jan.-June 1940; Member, Advisory Council, DSIR, 1942-47; President, Manchester Luncheon Club, 1946-47; Pres., the Textile Institute, 1946-48; Chairman: Manchester Joint Research Council, 1948-51; N-Western Electricity Consultative Council, 1960-68; Member, Gen. Advisory Council, BBC, 1947-52. Hon. LLD, Manchester University, 1963. Commander of Order of Orange Nassau (Netherlands). *Address:* 4 Mill Street, Eynsham, Oxford. *T:* Oxford 881562. *[Died 13 Sept. 1979.*

STREATFEILD, Sir Geoffrey Hugh Benbow, Kt 1947; MC; Judge of the High Court of Justice, Queen's Bench Division, 1947-66; *b* 28 July 1897; *yr s* of late Maj. H. S. Streatfeild, Ryhope, Co. Durham, and Barlay, Balmaclellan, Kirkcudbrightshire; *m* 1918, Marjorie, *yr d* of late Charles Booth, Sunderland; three *d. Educ:* Rugby School. Served with 4th Batt. Durham Light Infantry and Royal Flying Corps and RAF, 1914-19, Capt. 1917 (MC); called to Bar, Inner Temple, 1921; KC 1938. Joined North Eastern Circuit, 1922; Recorder of Rotherham, 1932-34; Huddersfield, 1934-43; Kingston-upon-Hull, 1943-47; Solicitor-General and Attorney General of the County Palatine of Durham, 1939-47; Bencher of the Inner Temple, 1945; Major (Deputy Judge Advocate), 1940; Lt-Col Asst Judge Advocate-General, 1942-43; Comr of Assize, Western Circuit, 1946. Chairman, Inter-Departmental Cttee on the Business of the Criminal Courts, 1958-60; Deputy Chairman, Somerset Quarter Sessions. Hon. DCL Durham Univ., 1957. *Address:* Cheddon Corner, Cheddon Fitzpaine, Taunton, Somerset. *T:* Kingston St Mary 277.
[Died 7 Oct. 1979.

STREET, John Hugh, CB 1965; Lecturer, Department of Town and Regional Planning, Sheffield University, since 1976; *b* 24 Aug. 1914; *s* of Hugh W. Street and Augusta Street; *m* 1938, Alicia, *d* of Oscar Kumpula, Wakefield, Mich., USA; two *d. Educ:* Aldenham School; Pembroke College, Cambridge. Home Office, 1937-46; Ministry of Town and Country Planning, 1946-47; Central Land Board, 1947-53; Treasury, 1953-54; Ministry of Housing and Local Government, 1955-70 (Under-Sec., 1956); Dept of the Environment, 1970-74. *Recreations:* looking at pictures, gardening, travel. *Address:* 43 Teignmouth Road, NW2. *T:* 01-452 5337. *[Died 30 Dec. 1977.*

STREET, Hon. Sir Kenneth (Whistler), KCMG 1956; Lieutenant-Governor of New South Wales, 1950-72; Chief Justice of New South Wales, 1950-60; *b* Sydney, NSW, 28 Jan. 1890; *e s* of late Hon. Sir Philip Street, KCMG; *m* 1916, Jessie Mary Grey (*d* 1970), *e d* of C. A. G. Lillingston, Yulgilbar, Clarence River, NSW; two *s* two *d. Educ:* Sydney Grammar School; Sydney University (BA, LLB (honours), Harris Scholarship, Wigram Allen Scholarship, Pitt Cobbett Prize). Called to Bar, 1915; held position as lecturer, Sydney University Law School in Legal Interpretation; Contracts, Mercantile Law and Torts, Legal Ethics; a member of the industrial Commission of NSW with the rank and title of a Supreme Court Judge, 1927; Puisne Judge of Supreme Court, 1931-50; held Commission in 1914 in Duke of Cornwall's Light Infantry, discharged medically unfit active service; served in Australia, 1915-19, at German Concentration Camps, NSW District HQ Staff, and General Staff, Army HQ, Melbourne; Hon. LLD, Sydney Univ. KStJ 1952. *Address:* 2 Greenoaks Avenue, Darling Point, Edgecliff, Sydney, NSW 2027, Australia. *T:* 32-2203. *Club:* Union (Sydney). *[Died 16 Feb. 1972.*

STRICKLAND, Lady; (Barbara), DBE 1923; *b* 2 April 1884; *d* of Martin W. B. and Wilhelmine M. E. ffolkes; *m* 1st, 1911, Francis Joseph Cresswell, Norfolk Regt (*d* 1914); two *d*; 2nd, 1918, General Sir E. P. Strickland, KCB, KBE, CMG, DSO (*d* 1951); one *d. Address:* The Old Hall, Snettisham, Norfolk. *T:* Snettisham 213. *[Died 20 March 1977.*

STRICKLAND, Henry; see Hornyold-Strickland.

STRICKLAND-CONSTABLE, Sir Henry Marmaduke, 10th Bt, *cr* 1641; *b* 4 Dec. 1900; *s* of late Lt-Col Frederick Charles Strickland-Constable and Margaret Elizabeth (*d* 1961), *d* of late Rear-Adm. Hon. Thomas Alexander Pakenham; *S* cousin 1938; *m* 1929, Countess Ernestine, *d* of late Count Rex. *Educ:* Eton; Magdalen Coll., Oxford. BA, BMus. *Heir: b* Robert Frederick Strickland-Constable [*b* 22 Oct. 1903; *m* 1st, 1929 (marriage annulled, 1931), Rosaline Mary, *d* of Arthur Webster; 2nd, 1936, Lettice, *y d* of late Major Frederick Strickland; two *s* two *d*]. *Address:* Wassand Hall, Seaton, near Hull, North Humberside. *T:* Hornsea 3767. *[Died 26 March 1975.*

STRINGER, John Daniel, CMG 1960; *b* 2 May 1914; *s* of late Harold Stringer, MA, AMICE; *m* 1939, Elizabeth, *d* of Colonel S. C. Layzell, MC, Kenya; one *s* two *d*. *Educ:* Uppingham; Peterhouse, Cambridge (MA). District Officer and District Commissioner, Kenya, 1936-52; Senior District Commissioner, Zanzibar, 1953; Senior Commissioner, Zanzibar, 1956. Order of the Brilliant Star of Zanzibar, 1960. *Recreations:* squash racquets, sailing, fishing. *Address:* North House, Aldeburgh, Suffolk. *Clubs:* Lansdowne; Mombasa (Mombasa). *[Died 10 July 1971.*

STROBL, Kisfalud Sigismund de; Sculptor; Professor Royal Academy of Art, Budapest, since 1924; *b* Alsórajk, Hungary, 1884; *m* 1916, Maria Mellinger; one *d*. *Educ:* Royal Academy, Budapest; Vienna; Paris; Italy. At the age of 24 completed his first great monument; several museums own his works; worked in his vacations in London, where he completed the busts of the Duke of Kent, Earl of Athlone, G. B. Shaw, Sir Austen Chamberlain, Sir John Simon, Field Marshal Allenby, Lady Astor, etc; and later completed the busts of Princess Elizabeth, Lord and Lady Londonderry, etc.; won several gold medals; had a one-man show in London in the White Allom Gallery, 1935; exhibited several times at Royal Academy in London; historical monuments for Budapest: The Liberation, Lajos, Kossuth, Ference Rákóczi. Kossuth Prize, 1950, 1953. Order of Merit (Hungary), 1954. *Recreations:* shooting, fishing. *Address:* XIV. Népstadion ut 20, Budapest. *T:* Budapest 835-831. *Club:* Rotary. *[Died 14 Aug. 1975.*

STRODE, Warren C.; *see* Chetham-Strode.

STRODE-JACKSON, Colonel Arnold Nugent Strode, CBE 1920; DSO 1917 and 3 Bars (July 1917, May and Dec. 1918); late KRRC; *b* 1891; *s* of late Morton Strode Jackson, ISO and Diana Martin, miniaturist; *m* 1918, Dora Berryman, *d* of late W. A. Mooney, USA, and Winifred Hunter Tewson; one *s*. *Educ:* Malvern Coll.; Brasenose Coll., Oxford (BA). Called to Bar, Middle Temple. Pres. OUAC; 1500 metres record at Olympic Games, Stockholm, 1912. Capt. and Adjt 13th (S) Bn Rifles Bde and Bt Maj., Temp. Lt-Col comdg 13th (S) Bn KRRC, Actg Brig. 111th Inf. Bde, 37th Div.; served on Western Front (despatches 6 times, wounded thrice). Mem. Olympic Council, 1920. Mem. Brit. Delegn to Peace Conf., Paris, 1919-20. Directed first Kentucky Derby Festival, 1935; Colonel on Staff of Governor of Kentucky. War of 1939-45: Admin. Officer of Inspection Bd of UK and Canada in New York and Ottawa, in charge of Inspectors and Anti-Sabotage precautions. *Publication:* Kentucky Heyday, a biographical novel 1787-1827, 1956 (New York). *Recreations:* fishing, Horticulture. *Address:* Norham End, Norham Road, Oxford. *[Died 13 Nov. 1972.*

STRONGE, Brig. Humphrey Cecil Travell, CBE 1945; DSO 1919; MC; *b* London, 24 Feb. 1891; *e s* of late W. Cecil Stronge; *m* 1923, Elsie Margaret, *e d* of late Canon W. F. Burnside; one *d*. *Educ:* The Oratory School; in Germany; RMC Sandhurst. Commissioned the Buffs, 1910; seconded W African Frontier Force, 1914; served European War, 1914-18, in Cameroons, German East Africa and France (DSO, MC, despatches twice); Staff College, 1926-27; Bt Lt-Col, 1937; Mil. Attaché Belgrade and Prague, 1936-39; Col 1939; Asst Comdt Nigeria Regt 1939; served War of 1939-45; Comdr, Southern Bde, Nigeria, 1939; GSO 1, War Office, 1940; Comdr, Blackdown Sub-Area, 1940-41; Brig. 1940; Comdr L of C Area, N Africa, Sicily, 1942-43; Head of Allied Mil. Mission to Corsica, and Personal Representative of C-in-C, 1943-44; Comdr, Area in France and Holland, 1944-45 (CBE, despatches twice). Retd 1946. Rep., British Council: Sweden, 1946-48, Portugal, 1948-52. Freeman: Merchant Taylors' Co.; City of London. FRGS. *Address:* Milton Rill Cottage, Watledge, Nailsworth, Glos. *[Died 27 March 1977.*

STRUTT, Vice-Adm. Hon. Arthur Charles, CBE 1928; *b* 2 Oct. 1878; 2nd *s* of 3rd Baron Rayleigh and Evelyn, *d* of J. M. Balfour of Whittingehame, and Blanche, *d* of 2nd Marquis of Salisbury; *m* 1934, Hon. Mrs Cyril Ward. *Educ:* HMS Britannia, etc. Served as Master of the Fleet in HMS Queen Elizabeth under the Flag of Earl Beatty, 1916-18; Director of Navigation, Admiralty, 1923-25; Lieut, 1900; Comdr, 1913; Capt. 1917; Rear-Adm., 1929; retired, 1929; Vice-Adm., retired, 1933. *Address:* 3 Whitehall Court, SW1. *T:* 01-930 3160. *[Died 10 Feb. 1973.*

STRUTT, Sir Austin; *see* Strutt, Sir Henry Austin.

STRUTT, Geoffrey St John, CBE 1920; JP; *b* 28 March 1888; 2nd *s* of late Hon. Richard Strutt and Augusta, *o c* of 5th Baron Braybrooke; *m* 1912, Sybil Eyre, *d* of Sir Walpole Greenwell, 1st Bt; two *s* (and one killed in action). *Educ:* Winchester; Magdalen College, Oxford, BA. Member of the Stock Exchange, 1912-17; enlisted Sept. 1914: obtained a commission in the 2/5th Essex Regiment; served in France with 2/5th Glosters (wounded, 1917); became Private Secretary to Sir Laming Worthington Evans at the Ministry of Munitions, and went with him to the Foreign Office and Ministry of Pensions; retired to stand as a Tory for the Harwich Division, 1922; worked for the League of Nations Union, and later became first News Editor of the BBC. *Address:* St Catharine's Court, Bath, Somerset BA1 SHA. *T:* Batheaston 88159. *Club:* Bath and County. *[Died 20 Oct. 1971.*

STRUTT, Sir (Henry) Austin, KCVO 1953 (CVO 1943; MVO 1937); CB 1949; MA; JP; Extra Gentleman Usher to the Queen since 1961; Chairman: Council of Voluntary Welfare Work, 1962; Church of England Pensions Board, 1965-74; *b* 23 Jan. 1903; *er s* of late Henry Strutt and Elizabeth Maher, Rathkeale, Co. Limerick; *m* 1927, Gladys May (*d* 1974), *o d* of late Arthur Salter Holt; two *d*. *Educ:* Roan School; Magdalen College, Oxford. 1st Class Modern History, 1924; Senior Demy, 1925-26; Home Office, 1925-61; Principal Private Secretary to Mr Herbert Morrison, 1940-43; Assistant Under-Secretary of State, Home Office, 1943-57; Principal Establishment and Organisation Officer, Home Office, 1945-57; subseq. Dep. Under-Sec. of State, Home Office. Registrar of the Baronetage, 1945-61; Director, John Lewis Partnership Ltd, 1962-67. JP Bucks. KStJ. Jubilee Medals, 1935, 1977; Coronation Medals, 1937, 1953. *Address:* 51 Sussex Place, Slough, Berks. *T:* Slough 21008. *[Died 29 May 1979.*

STUART OF FINDHORN, 1st Viscount *cr* 1959; **James Gray Stuart,** PC 1939; CH 1957; MVO 1921; MC; DL; Member, Royal Commission on Working of the Tribunals of Inquiry (Evidence) Act, 1921, since 1966; *b* 9 Feb. 1897; 3rd *s* of 17th Earl of Moray; *m* 1923, Lady Rachel Cavendish, OBE, 4th *d* of 9th Duke of Devonshire; two *s* one *d*. *Educ:* Eton. Capt. 3rd Bn the Royal Scots; served European War, 1914-18 (MC and bar); Brigade-Major, 1918; Equerry to Duke of York, 1920-21. MP (U) Moray and Nairn, 1923-59; a Lord Commissioner of the Treasury, 1935-41; Joint Parliamentary Secretary to the Treasury and Government Chief Whip, 1941-45; Chief Opposition Whip, 1945-48; Secretary of State for Scotland, 1951-57. *Publication:* Within the Fringe; an autobiography, 1967. *Heir: er s* Hon. David Randolph Moray Stuart [*b* 20 June 1924; *m* 1st, 1945, Grizel Mary Wilfreda (*d* 1948), *d* of D. T. Fyfe and *widow* of Michael Gillilan; one *s*; 2nd, 1951, Marian, *d* of Gerald Wilson; one *s* three *d. Educ:* Eton. DL Caernarvon, 1963-68]. *Address:* Harthill House, Redlynch, Salisbury, Wilts. *Clubs:* White's, Buck's; New (Edinburgh). *[Died 20 Feb. 1971.*

STUART, Sir Alexander M.; *see* Moody-Stuart.

STUART, Sir Campbell, GCMG 1939; KBE 1918; one of HM's Lieutenants for the City of London; *b* 5 July 1885. *Educ:* private schools; LLD College of William and Mary, Va, and Melbourne University. Represented HQ Staff of Canadian Army on visit to Ireland of the Duchess of Connaught's Own Irish Canadian Rangers, Jan. 1917, which batt. he recruited in the Province of Quebec for service in the European War (Lt-Col Canadian Army, despatches); Assistant Military Attaché, British Embassy, Washington, 1917; Military Secretary to the British War Mission to the United States of America, 1917; Vice-Chairman of the London Headquarters of the British War Mission to the USA 1918; Deputy Director of Propaganda in Enemy Countries, 1918; Director: The Times, 1919-60 (Man. Dir, 1920-24); Times Book Co., 1920-60; Managing Editor of the Daily Mail, 1921; represented The Times at the Imperial Press Conference Canada, 1920, London, 1930, and at Conference of Press Experts of the League of Nations, Geneva, 1927; Mem. Council of Empire Press Union, 1920-54; Representative of Govt of Canada on the Pacific Cable Board, 1923-28; Representative of the Government of Canada at the Imperial Wireless and Cables Conference, 1928; Chairman: Quebec House Cttee, Westerham, 1926-50; Wolfe Memorial Cttee, Greenwich, 1930; Admiral Saunders Memorial Cttee, Westminster Abbey, 1930; Representative at different periods of

Govts of Gt Britain, N Ireland, Canada, Australia and Southern Rhodesia on the Imperial Communications Advisory Committee; Chairman of the Imperial Communications Advisory Committee, and its successor, the Commonwealth Communications Council, 1933-45; Treasurer King George's Jubilee Trust, 1935-47; Chm. of the Commonwealth Telegraph Conference (Australia), 1942. Chairman Advisory Cttee of Ministry of Information, 1939; Director of Propaganda in Enemy Countries, 1939-40; Chm. and Treas. King George's Fields Foundation (National Memorial to King George V), 1936-54; Treas. Franklin Roosevelt Memorial Cttee, 1946-48; Vice-Pres. The Pilgrims (Chm. 1948-58); Chm. Beit Cttee for Scientific Research, 1930-68; Chm. Hudson's Bay Record Soc., 1938-59; Governor of Imperial College of Science and Technology, 1925-68. KStJ, 1951. *Publications:* Secrets of Crewe House (the official record of enemy propaganda in the War of 1914-18); Opportunity Knocks Once; Memorial to a King. *Recreation:* gardening. *Address:* 4 The Grove, Highgate Village, N6 6JU. *T:* 01-340 2266. *Clubs:* Brooks's, Pratt's; Century (New York).   *[Died 14 Sept. 1972.*

STUART, Charles Russell; *b* 20 April 1895; *yr s* of late John David Stuart, advocate and solicitor, Straits Settlements; *m* 1925, Margaret, *e d* of Robert Vere Bogle, New South Wales; one *d. Educ:* Cranleigh School. Rifle Brigade, 1915-19 (despatches); Capt. 1917. Barrister-at-law, Gray's Inn, 1921; Advocate and Solicitor, Straits Settlements, 1922; Magistrate, Uganda, 1937; Chancellor, Diocese of Uganda, 1941-53; Puisne Judge, Nigeria, 1953-55; Judge of High Court, Western Region, Nigeria, 1955-57. *Address:* Hilltop, Windlesham, Surrey. *Club:* Royal Commonwealth Society.   *[Died 27 March 1975.*

STUART, Hilda Violet; Headmistress, Sherborne School for Girls, Dorset, 1930-Dec. 1949; Chairman of the Governors Foster School and Lord Digby's School, Sherborne, 1934; Central Council of School Broadcasting; Chairman English Sub-Committee, 1931; *b* Highbury, London; 4th *d* of late Canon E. A. Stuart, Canterbury. *Educ:* Notting Hill High School; Girton College, Cambridge. Assistant Classical Mistress St Leonards School, St Andrews, 1913; Assistant LCC Elementary Schools, 1917; Assistant, Darlington North Road Elementary School, 1918; Headmistress, Arthur Pease School, Darlington, 1919; Travelling scholarship, English-Speaking Union, 1925; Head of Classical Side, St Leonards School, St Andrews, 1926; Housemistress, St Leonards School, St Andrews, 1927. Retired, 1949. Nat. Council of Women: British Educational Rep., Internat. Council of Women, Athens, 1951, Montreal, 1957; Chm. Education Cttee, 1954-63; Vice-President, Women's Liberal Federation. Hon. Vice-Pres. Nat. Council of Women. *Address:* Milton Court, 68 Cromwell Road, SW7. *Clubs:* United Oxford & Cambridge University, National Liberal.
                          [Died 16 March 1975.

STUART-CLARK, Arthur Campbell, MA; Registrar, Huntingdon Research Centre, since 1970; *b* 23 Feb. 1906; *s* of late Canon Stuart H. Clark; *m* 1935, Peggy Annette, *o d* of A. Anthony; two *s. Educ:* Tonbridge School; Clare College, Cambridge. Assistant Master, Chillon College, Villeneuve (Vaud), Switzerland, 1927-31; Housemaster, Weymouth College, Dorset, 1931-37; Hon. Organising Sec. National Association of Boys' Clubs for Dorset, 1933-37; Headmaster, Steyning Grammar School, Steyning, Sussex, 1937-44; Headmaster of Brighton College, 1944-50; Senior Tutor, Hospital Administrative Staff Coll. (King Edward's Hosp. Fund for London), 1950-63; Fellow and Bursar, Darwin Coll., Cambridge, 1964-69, Emeritus Fellow, 1970. Vice-Chm. Church of England Schools Council, 1946-51; Chairman: Wandsworth Hosp. Management Cttee, 1954-57; Papworth-Huntingdon Hosp. Management Cttee, 1967; Member: E Anglian Regional Hosp. Bd, 1968. Bd of Governors, United Cambridge Hosps, 1972. Citizen and Skinner. *Publication:* Administering the Hospital Group, 1956; contribs to various jls on hospital affairs. *Recreations:* reading, gardening. *Address:* Riverside, Earith, Huntingdon. *T:* Earith 313; Huntingdon Research Centre, Huntingdon. *T:* Woolley 431. *Club:* Queen's.
                          [Died 13 May 1973.

STUART-KNILL, Sir Ian, 3rd Bt, *cr* 1893; *b* 11 April 1886; *s* of Sir John Knill, 2nd Bt, and Edith (*d* 1944), *d* of John Hardman Powell; *S* father, 1934; *m* 1st, 1910, Lucy (who obtained a divorce, 1937; she *d* 1952), *d* of Capt. T. H. Willis; one *s*; 2nd, 1941, Ruth Evelyn, *d* of Archibald Barnes; two *s* one *d.* Served European War, Machine Gun Corps, 1914-18; RAF Pilot Officer, 1940-41, then invalided. *Publication:* The Pedigree of King Arthur, 1972. *Heir: s* John Kenelm Stuart Knill [*b* 8 April 1913; *m* 1951, Violette Maud Florence Barnes; two *s*]. *Address:* 19 Rookery Close, Edingworth, Axbridge, Somerset.
                          [Died 17 April 1973.

STUART TAYLOR, Sir Richard (Laurence), 3rd Bt *cr* 1917; Managing Director, Powell Duffryn Fuels Ltd, since 1978; *b* 27 Sept. 1925; *s* of Sir Eric Stuart Taylor, 2nd Bt, OBE, MD, and Evelyn Thérèse (*d* 1946), *er d* of late James Calvert, CBE, MD, FRCP; *S* father, 1977; *m* 1950, Iris Mary, *d* of Rev. Edwin John Gargery; one *s* one *d. Educ:* Winchester; King's College, Cambridge (BA 1949, MA 1959). Served War of 1939-45 with RAC and Royal Gloucestershire Hussars. Joined Regent Oil Co., 1950; Powell Duffryn Fuels Ltd, 1961, Director, 1968. *Heir: s* Nicholas Richard Stuart Taylor, *b* 14 Jan. 1952. *Address:* White Lodge, Hambrook, Chichester, West Sussex.
                          [Died 10 Sept. 1978.

STUBBS, Stanley; Headmaster, The Perse School, Cambridge, 1945-69; *b* 19 Feb. 1906; *o s* of late James Bloor Stubbs, Smallthorne, Stoke-on-Trent; *m* 1934, Margaret Eleanor, *er d* of late William Harley Grocott, Stoke-on-Trent; one *d. Educ:* Newcastle High School, Staffordshire; Emmanuel College, Cambridge. BA 2nd Cl. Hons Mod. and Med. Languages Tripos, 1933; MA 1937; Cambridge University Certificate in Education, 1934; Manager at Royal Doulton Potteries, Stoke-on-Trent, 1924-29; Assistant Master and Housemaster of Day Boys at Gresham's School, Holt, Norfolk, 1934-39; Headmaster, Soham Grammar School, Cambs, 1939-45; Officer Commanding ATC Squadron, 1941-45. *Recreations:* cricket, football, reading. College AFC Captain. *Address:* 264 Hills Road, Cambridge CB2 2QE. *T:* Cambridge 48369. *Clubs:* East India, Sports and Public Schools; Hawks (Cambridge).
                          [Died 25 Oct. 1976.

STUDD, Sir Eric, 2nd Bt, *cr* 1929; OBE 1946; formerly Senior Partner, J. Thomas & Co., Calcutta; *b* 10 June 1887; *e s* of Sir Kynaston Studd, 1st Bt, and Hilda (*d* 1921), *d* of Sir Thomas Beauchamp, 4th Bt; *S* father, 1944; *m* 1923, Stephana Langmead, *o d* of L. J. Langmead, London; three *s* one *d. Educ:* Winchester. Went to India, 1906; MLA, India, 1930-34; MLC Bengal, 1936; MLA Bengal, 1937; retd from India, 1938. *Heir: s* Robert Kynaston Studd, formerly Captain Coldstream Guards [*b* 9 July 1926; *m* 1958, Anastasia, *d* of Lt-Col Harold Leveson-Gower; three *d*]. *Address:* Tenchleys Park, Limpsfield Common, Oxted, Surrey. *T:* Limpsfield Chart 2208. *Club:* Oriental.   *[Died 11 June 1975.*

STUDD, Sir Kynaston; *see* Studd, Sir R. K.

STUDD, Brig. Malden Augustus, DSO 1919; MC; Royal Tank Corps; *b* 29 Sept. 1887; *m*; two *s* one *d.* Joined RA 1907; Captain, 1914; Major, 1917; Bt Lt-Col 1927; Lt-Col 1928; Col 1931; served European War (DSO; despatches); Assistant Director of Mechanisation War Office, 1932-36; Brigadier i/c Administration, Malaya, 1937-40; Commanded Salisbury Plain Area, 1940-42; ADC to King George VI, 1941-43; retired pay, 1943. *Address:* c/o National Westminster Bank, 1 Stratford Place, W1.   *[Died 23 Nov. 1973.*

STUDD, Sir (Robert) Kynaston, 3rd Bt *cr* 1929; JP; farmer; *b* 9 July 1926; *s* of Sir Eric Studd, 2nd Bt, OBE, and Stephena (*d* 1976), *o d* of L. J. Langmead; *S* father, 1975; *m* 1958, Anastasia Leveson-Gower, *d* of late Lt-Col Harold Boscawen Leveson-Gower, The Green, Barnard Castle; three *d. Educ:* Winchester. Late Captain, Coldstream Guards. Sometime a Vice-Chm of Poly Travel Ltd and Dir of Sir Henry Lunn Ltd. JP Hants. *Recreations:* shooting, fishing. *Heir: b* Edward Fairfax Studd [*b* 3 May 1929; *m* 1960, Prudence Janet, *d* of Alastair Douglas Fyfe, OBE; two *s* one *d*]. *Address:* Manor Farm, Rockbourne, near Fordingbridge, Hants. *T:* Rockbourne 214. *Clubs:* Boodle's, Cavalry and Guards, Pratt's.   *[Died 27 May 1977.*

STUDDERT, Ven. Augustine John de Clare, MA; Archdeacon of Surrey, 1957-68, Archdeacon Emeritus since 1968; Rector of Busbridge, 1939-69; *b* 31 Jan. 1901; *s* of Thomas de Clare Studdert; *m* 1936, Marjorie Joyce Chettle; one *s. Educ:* Trinity Coll., Dublin. BA 1924, MA 1936. Curate of Glendermott, Londonderry, 1925-29; St Martin-in-the-Fields, London, 1929-32; Assistant Chaplain, British Embassy Church in Paris, 1932-34; Curate of Cranleigh, Surrey, 1934-39. Rural Dean of Godalming, 1950-57; Hon. Canon of Guildford Cathedral, 1956-57, 1968-69. Examining Chaplain to Bishop of Guildford, 1961-69. *Address:* Southlands, Churt Road, Hindhead, Surrey. *T:* Hindhead 4620.   *[Died 20 March 1972.*

STUDDY, Sir Henry, Kt 1951; CBE 1947; KPM 1954; retired; *b* 20 April 1894; *e s* of late Major H. E. M. Studdy; *m* 1924, Marion Stonor, *o d* of H. T. S. Forrest, ICS; one *d. Educ:* St Paul's School. Indian Police, 1914-35. Served European War, 1917-19, with Indian Cavalry, Capt. 1918 (despatches). Chief Constable: of Northumberland, 1935-43; of County Durham, 1943-44; of West Riding of Yorkshire, 1944-Oct. 1959. Mem

Police Recruiting Mission to Palestine, 1948; Mem. Advisory Council on the Treatment of Offenders, 1945-59; Mem. Board of Governors of Police College, 1948-59; Mem. Singapore Riots Inquiry Commn, 1951; Chm. Cyprus Police Commn, 1956. Vice-Pres. Royal Life Saving Society, 1956-, Dep. Grand Pres., 1968-72 (Dep. Pres., UK Branch, 1960, Pres., 1963-69); Member Road Research Board, 1959-63. Chairman, St Loye's College for Training the Disabled for Commerce and Industry, 1963-69, Pres., 1969-. *Publication:* (ed jtly) A Police Constable's Guide to his Daily Work, 1961. *Recreation:* golf. *Address:* Little Westcott, Northview Road, Budleigh Salterton, Devon. *T:* Budleigh Salterton 3264. *Club:* Royal Automobile.
[Died 10 Nov. 1975.

SUÁREZ, Dr Eduardo; Mexican Ambassador to Great Britain, 1965-70; *b* Texcoco, Mexico, 3 Jan. 1895; *s* of Eduardo Suárez and Antonia Aránsolo de Suárez; *m* 1935, Maria de la Luz Dávila; four *s* one *d* (and one *s* decd). *Educ:* Col. Municipal, Texcoco; Col. Inglés, Tacubaya; Nat. Univ. of Mexico. Supt Under Sec., State of Hidalgo; Pres., Central Conciliation and Arbitration Bd of City of Mexico; Prof. of Jurisprudence, Nat. Univ. of Mexico, at different times, 1916-48. Counsel for Mexico, in Claims between: Mexico and the US, June 1926-Aug. 1927; Mexico and Gt Britain, Aug.-Dec. 1928; Member, Arbitration Tribunal between Mexico and France. Head of Legal Dept, Min. of For. Affairs, 1929-31, 1931-34, Jan.-June 1935; Minister of Finance and Public Credit, 1935-46. Dr (*hc*) Nat. Univ. of Mexico; holds foreign decorations. *Publications:* pamphlets, articles; *posthumous publication:* Comentarios y Recuerdos (1926-1946), 1977. *Address:* Paseo de la Reforma 645, Lomas, Mexico 10, DF, Mexico. *Club:* Club de Banqueros (Mexico).
[Died 19 Sept. 1976.

SUGDEN, Maj.-Gen. Sir Henry (Haskins Clapham), KBE 1960 (CBE 1945; OBE 1941); CB 1954; DSO 1943; Member, House of Keys; *b* 15 April 1904; *s* of Dr H. C. Sugden, West House, Ramsey, IOM; *m* 1934, Joan Morgan, *d* of J. M. R. Francis, The Firs, Kingston-on-Thames; two *s. Educ:* Ramsey Grammar Sch.; King William's College, Isle of Man; RMA Woolwich. Commissioned in Royal Engineers, 1924; Captain, 1935. Served War of 1939-45 (despatches twice); Major 1940; Temp. Lt-Col 1941; Temp. Brig. 1943; Col 1948; Temp. Major-General, 1952; Major-General, 1953. Col Comdt RE, 1961-69. Engineer-in-Chief, War Office, 1957-60, retd. Mem., House of Keys, IoM, 1962-76. Grand Officer, Order of Orange Nassau, Holland. FICE. *Recreations:* sailing, shooting, gardening. *Address:* River House, Ramsey, Isle of Man. *T:* 812260. *Club:* Naval and Military.
[Died 11 March 1977.

SUGDEN, Group Captain Ronald Scott, CBE 1945; AFC 1918; DL; *b* 25 May 1896; *s* of Edward Scott Sugden, MD, Aintree, Liverpool; *m* 1928, Helen Mary, *d* of William Henry Brain, Cwrt-yr-Ala, Nr Cardiff; one *d. Educ:* Eastmans, Southsea; RN Colleges, Osborne and Dartmouth. Royal Navy 1909-19 (despatches); attached RNAS, 1915-18; transferred to RAF on its formation; retd as Group Capt., 1946. Served in Iraq, 1925-27 (medal); Palestine, 1936 (medal); War of 1939-45 (despatches). ADC to Governor of Trinidad and Tobago, 1920-21. High Sheriff of Glamorgan, 1957; DL Glamorgan, 1958. *Recreations:* golf, shooting, fishing, racing, bowls. *Address:* Merevale, Dinas Powis, Glam. *T:* Dinas Powis 2106. *Club:* Army and Navy.
[Died 26 March 1971.

SUGERMAN, Hon. Sir Bernard, Kt 1970; President, Court of Appeal, Supreme Court of New South Wales, 1970-72; *b* 5 July 1904; *s* of Solomon Reuben Sugerman and Florence Sugerman; *m* 1928, Sarah Rosenblum; two *s. Educ:* Sydney High Sch.; Univ. of Sydney (Hon. LLD 1976). Admitted to Bar, 1926; Lecturer in Law, Univ. of Sydney, 1926-43; KC 1943; Judge: Commonwealth Court of Conciliation and Arbitration, 1946-47; Land and Valuation Court, 1947-61; Supreme Court of New South Wales, 1947-; Judge of Appeal, 1966-70; Acting Chief Justice, 1970, 1971; retired 1972. *Publications:* The Australian Digest (ed), 1934-46; The Australian Law Journal (ed), 1927-46; Commonwealth Law Reports (ed), 1941-46; numerous articles in legal periodicals. *Recreations:* bowls, reading. *Address:* 9 Yamba Road, Bellevue Hill, Sydney, NSW 2023, Australia. *T:* 36-3175. *Club:* University (Sydney).
[Died 3 Nov. 1976.

SULLIVAN, Very Rev. Martin Gloster, KCVO 1979; Dean of St Paul's, 1967-77, Dean Emeritus since 1977; Dean of the Order of the British Empire, 1967-77, of the Order of St Michael and St George, 1968-77; *b* Auckland, 30 March 1910; *s* of Denis Sullivan; *m* 1st, 1934, Doris (*d* 1972), *d* of Canon C. H. Grant Cowen; 2nd, 1973, Elizabeth Roberton. *Educ:* Auckland Grammar School; St John's (Theological) College, Auckland University College. MA (NZ). Deacon 1932; Priest 1934; Asst Curate, St Matthew's, Auckland, 1932; Vicar, St Columba, Grey

Lynn, 1934; Te Awamutu, 1936-46; Exam. Chap. to Bp of Waikato, 1937-46; on staff, St Martin-in-the-Fields, London, 1945-46; Chaplain to SCM Wellington, 1946-49; CF, 1941-46; Principal, College House, Christchurch, 1950-58; Dean of Christchurch, 1951-62; Vicar-General, 1952-62; Commissary to Bp of Christchurch, 1962; Rector, St Mary's, Bryanston Square, 1962-63; Archdeacon of London and Canon Residentiary of St Paul's, 1963-67. Council of Univ. of Canterbury, 1953-62; Senate of Univ. of NZ, 1961-62; Court of Directors, Royal Humane Soc. of NZ, 1956-62; Rep. of Vice-Chancellor of Univ. of Canterbury on Assoc. of Univs of Brit. Commonwealth, 1962. Member Central Council, Royal Over-Seas League; Mem., Guild of Freemen of City of London. Governor: St Paul's Sch., 1967-77; Haileybury, 1971-75. Freeman: London, 1965; Merchant Taylors' Co., 1967; Painter-Stainers Co., 1974; Glass Sellers Co., 1976. Chaplain and Sub-Prelate, Order of St John, 1968. Hon. LittD Auckland, 1976. *Publications:* Children Listen, 1955; Listen Again, 1956; A Word for Everyman, 1956; Draw Near with Faith, 1956; On Calvary's Tree, 1957; Approach With Joy, 1961; A Dean Speaks to New Zealand, 1962; A Funny Thing Happened to me on the way to St Paul's, 1968; Watch How You Go, 1975. *Recreations:* reading, theatre. *Address:* 8 Glencoe Road, Browns Bay, Auckland 10, New Zealand. *T:* 478-6366. *Club:* Athenæum. [Died 5 Sept. 1980.

SULLIVAN, Sir Richard (Benjamin Magniac), 8th Bt, *cr* 1804; *b* 26 Oct. 1906; *s* of Capt. Richard Sullivan, RN (*d* 1928; 2nd *s* of 6th Bt) and Beatrix Evelyn (*d* 1936), *d* of Arthur Magniac, The Hermitage, Ascot; *S* uncle (Rev. Sir Frederick Sullivan, 7th Bt) 1954; *m* 1928, Muriel Mary Paget, *y d* of Francis Charles Trayler Pineo; two *s. Educ:* St Andrew's Coll., Grahamstown, South Africa. Colonial Administrative Service; Bechuanaland and Nigeria; retired 1957. *Heir: s* Richard Arthur Sullivan [*b* 9 Aug. 1931; *m* 1962, Elenor Mary, *e d* of K. M. Thorpe; one *s* three *d. Educ:* Univ. of Cape Town (BSc); MIT (SM); CEng. Man. Dir, McClelland Engineering Ltd (geotechnical consultants), Harrow, Mddx]. *Address:* 2 Knowles Close, Mount Pleasant, Rhodesia. *T:* Salisbury 38010. *Clubs:* Royal Commonwealth Society; Salisbury (Rhodesia).
[Died 22 Aug. 1977.

SULLIVAN, Sir William (John), KBE 1956 (CBE 1938); CMG 1950; HM Foreign Service, retired; *b* London, 11 Oct. 1895; *o s* of late William Charles Sullivan, MD (RUI); *m* 1922, Catherine Mary (*d* 1963), *y d* of late Hugo Meynell; one *s. Educ:* St Augustine's College, Ramsgate; St Paul's School; Trinity College, Dublin (BA). Served in European War, 1915-16 (invalided); Administrative Officer Central Control Board (Liquor Traffic) 1916-20; entered Consular Service, 1920; Vice-Consul at Tallinn, 1922, Bogota, 1924; Chargé d'Affaires and Acting Consul General there, 1925-26, Chicago, 1927, Marseilles, 1930, and Genoa, 1934; Acting Consul General in Marseilles and Genoa in each year from 1930 to 1935; temporarily attached to Commercial Secretariat at Rome, in 1935, 1939 and 1940, and to Consulate General, Marseilles, 1936; Consul at Madrid, 1936, Valencia 1936; First Secretary (temp. local rank) in HM Diplomatic Service, 1936-38; attached Imperial Defence College, 1939; Acting Consul at Trieste, 1939; attached to the Spears Mission, 1940-41; Commercial Secretary and Counsellor (local rank), Berne, 1941-45; attached UK Delegn to Paris Conf. and Council of Foreign Ministers, New York, 1946; British Political Adviser, Trieste, 1945-50; British Minister to Roumania, 1951-54; British Ambassador to Mexico, 1954-56; UK Delegation to United Nations, 1956-57; to Conf. on Law of the Sea, Geneva, 1958. Called to Bar, Inner Temple, 1921. *Address:* c/o 25 Banstead Road, Purley, Surrey.
[Died 21 June 1971.

SUMMERHAYS, Reginald Sherriff; Solicitor (retired); writer; *b* 5 April 1881, British; *m* 1st, 1906, Annie May, *d* of Arthur Owen; one *s* two *d*; 2nd, Winifred Edna (*d* 1963), *d* of Walter Varley, Doncaster, Yorks. *Educ:* Westminster Sch. Judge of light horses and other types; over 50 years judging all classes in GB, including in hand, under saddle and harness, and various classes abroad; on the Council of a number of societies connected with horses. Apptd Civilian Remount Purchasing Officer and subsequently commissioned in European War, 1914-18, and became Dep. Controller of Aircraft Contracts. *Publications:* Here's Horse Sense, 1932; From Saddle to Fireside, 1936; Elements of Riding, 1936; Elements of Hunting, 1938; Riding for All, 1939; The Book of the Pony, 1946; It's a Good Life with Horses, 1951; (ed) Handbook for Horse Owners, 5th edn, 1951; The Observer's Book of Horses and Ponies, 1951; Riding on a Small Income, 1953; Show Jumpers, 1954; Our Horses and Ponies, 1954; The Story of the International, 1955; Show Ponies, 1955; (ed) Encyclopedia for Horsemen, 1959, 6th edn 1976; The Problem Horse, 1960; Young Rider's Guide to the Horse World, 1960; A Lifetime with Horses, 1962; Country

Life Horseman's Pocket Book, 1964; (with Stella A. Walker) The Controversial Horse, 1966; The Arabian Horse in Great Britain, 1967; (with C. E. G. Hope) Horse Shows, 1969; The Donkey Owner's Guide, 1970. *Address:* 30a Arterberry Road, Wimbledon, SW20. *T:* 01-946 1445. *[Died 25 Oct.* 1976.

SUMMERS, Sir Geoffrey, 1st Bt *cr* 1952; CBE 1942; CStJ 1956; *b* Greenfield, Yorks, 2 Sept. 1891; *s* of Henry Hall Summers; *m* 1st, 1915, Doris M. (marr. diss. 1930), *d* of G. R. Edgecombe, Brenchley, Kent; one *s* one *d* (and one *s* (of twin *s*) decd); 2nd, 1931, Margaret A., *d* of H. P. Stace, Brackley, Northants; two *d.* *Educ:* Uppingham; Cambridge (MA). Joined firm of John Summers and Sons, Ltd, Steel Manufacturers, Shotton, Chester, 1912; served in HM forces, 1914-18; returned to firm, 1919; a director of the firm, 1921-67; DL, County of Flint, 1938; High Sheriff, 1939; Chairman: Flintshire County Council, 1940-42; formerly Dee and Clwyd River Authority; Steel Sheet Trade Wages Bd, 1933 now retd; Member Development Corp. for Wales, 1958-67. *Recreations:* mountaineering, golf, music. *Heir:* *s* Felix Roland Brattan Summers [*b* 1 Oct. 1918; *m* 1945, Anna Marie Louise, *d* of late Gustave Demaegd, Brussels; one *d*]. *Address:* Craig-y-Castell, Dyserth, Flintshire. *T:* Dyserth 281. *Club:* Alpine. *[Died 17 Jan.* 1972.

SUMMERS, Sir (Gerard) Spencer, Kt 1956; *b* 27 Oct. 1902; *s* of late Frank Bright Summers, Froyle Place, Alton, Hants, and late Constance Taylor; *m* 1930, Jean, adopted *d* of John Pickering; one *s* one *d* (and one *s* decd. *Educ:* Wellington Trinity College, Cambridge. Chm. of Sheet Makers' Conference, 1936-39; Dir-Gen. of Regional Organisation, Min. of Supply, 1941-44; MP (U) Northampton, 1940-45; MP (C) Aylesbury Div. of Bucks, 1950-70; Mem. Parly Delegn to Australia and NZ, 1944; Sec. Dept of Overseas Trade, 1945. Pres. International Sheet Comptoir, 1936-39; Chm. Outward Bound Trust, to 1975; Pres. British Direct Mail Advertising Assoc., 1956-64. High Sheriff of Northamptonshire, 1974. *Recreations:* shooting, golf. *Address:* Thenford House, Banbury, Oxon. *Club:* Boodle's.
[Died 19 Jan. 1976.

SUMMERS, Sir Richard (Felix), Kt 1962; Chairman, John Summers & Sons Ltd, 1938-71; Director, National Westminster Bank Ltd, 1968-72 (Chairman, North Region Board, 1970-72); *b* 10 Dec. 1902; *y s* of Henry Hall Summers; *m* 1925, Evelyn, *d* of W. F. Irvine, FSA, Bryn Llwyn, Corwen; four *s.* *Educ:* Shrewsbury; Clare College, Cambridge. Entered John Summers & Sons Ltd, 1925, Dir, 1931, Man. Dir, 1936, Chairman, 1938. Dir-in-Charge, Summers Div., Scottish and NW Gp, BSC, 1967-68. High Sheriff for County of Flint, 1944-45. Pres., British Iron and Steel Fedn, 1960. *Address:* Denna Hall, Burton Point, Wirral, Merseyside. *T:* 051-336 2117. *[Died 6 Feb.* 1977.

SUMMERS, Sir Spencer; *see* Summers, Sir G. S.

SUMMERSCALE, Sir John (Percival), KBE 1960 (CBE 1951); Retired 1960, as Minister (Commercial), British Embassy, Rio de Janeiro; Editor, Penguin Books, 1961; *b* 23 Nov. 1901; *s* of Annie and Percy Summerscale; *m* 1931, Nelle Blossom Stogsdall (*d* 1977); two *s* two *d.* *Educ:* Latymers School, Edmonton; Cambridge University. Levant Consular Service, 1926; served in Beirut, Hamadan, Shiraz, Tehran, Bagdad. Commercial Secretary (Grade II), Washington, 1938; Counsellor (Commercial) there, 1945; transferred to Board of Trade, 1946, and to Warsaw, 1948 as Commercial Counsellor; Consul-Gen., Munich, 1951; Minister (Commercial), Rio de Janeiro, 1954-60. *Address:* Crossways, Tarrant Hinton, Blandford, Dorset.
[Died 4 Aug. 1980.

SUMMERSKILL, Baroness (Life Peer), *cr* 1961, of Ken Wood, **(Edith Clara),** PC 1949; CH 1966; Member, Political Honours Scrutiny Committee, 1967-76; *b* Doughty St, London, 1901; *d* of William and Edith Summerskill; *m* 1925, Dr E. Jeffrey Samuel; one *s* one *d.* *Educ:* King's Coll., London; Charing Cross Hosp. Qualified as a doctor, 1924. Member of Middlesex County Council for Green Lanes division of Tottenham, 1934-41. Contested Parly by-election in Putney, 1934, and Bury div. General Election, 1935; MP (Lab) for West Fulham, 1938-55, for Warrington, 1955-61. Parly Sec., Min. of Food, 1945-50; Minister of National Insurance, 1950-51. Chm. of Labour Party, 1954-55. Hon. LLD Newfoundland, 1968. *Publications:* Babies without Tears, 1941; The Ignoble Art, 1956; Letters to my Daughter, 1957; A Woman's World, 1967. *Address:* Pond House, Millfield Lane, Highgate, N6. *[Died 4 Feb.* 1980.

SUMMERVILLE, Sir (William) Alan (Thompson), Kt 1968; DSc, FAIAS; Agent-General for Queensland in London, 1964-70; Chairman, Queensland Sugar Board, 1970-73; Queensland Government representative on international sugar affairs; *b* 6 Feb. 1904; *s* of W. H. Summerville, Ipswich, Queensland; *m*

1930, Ethel, *d* of T. F. Barker; two *d.* *Educ:* Ipswich Grammar School; University of Queensland. Entomological Investigations, 1930-36; Plant Physiology Research, 1937-45. Studied Agricultural Research Methods in Ceylon, Egypt, Palestine, GB, USA, Canada, Hawaii and NZ, 1936-37 and 1955. Dir, Div. of Plant Industry, Dept of Agric. and Stock, Qld, 1955-58; Dir-Gen. and Under-Sec., Dept of Agric. and Stock, Qld, 1958-64. Vice-President: Australia-Britain Soc.; Exec. Cttee, Inst. Internat. Affairs (Qld). Hon. LLD (Qld), 1963. *Publications:* various, on entomological and physiological subjects. *Recreations:* bowls, gardening. *Address:* 25 Munro Street, Indooroopilly, Queensland 4068, Australia. *Club:* Johnsonian (Brisbane). *[Died 20 Dec.* 1980.

SUMNER, John Richard Hugh, CBE 1945; DL; JP; *b* 1886; *s* of late Sir John Sumner, FSA, Ham Hill, Powick; *m* 1914, Beatrice Mary, *d* of Henry Severn Black, Frisby-on-the-Wreake, Leics; one *s* one *d.* *Educ:* privately. Pres., Typhoo Tea Ltd; Chm. of a number of charitable trusts created by his father and himself; Jt Master and Master Worcs Hounds, 1934-45; late Chm. Worcs Agric. Committee for 19 years. High Sheriff of Worcs, 1944-45; DL 1953. Mem. National Hunt Cttee, and Council of the Hunter and Light Horse Improvement Society. *Recreation:* racing. *Address:* Rashwood Lodge, Droitwich. *T:* Wychbold 251. *Club:* Worcestershire (Worcester). *[Died 12 May* 1971.

SUNLIGHT, Joseph; Architect; *b* 2 Jan. 1889; *s* of Israel and Minnie Sunlight. *Educ:* Private School, Kingston-on-Thames. MP (L) Shrewsbury, 1923-24. *Address:* 14 Victoria Square, SW1. *T:* 01-834 4734; Hallside, Knutsford, Cheshire. *T:* Knutsford 3339; Sunlight House, Manchester. *T:* 061-834 7113.
[Died 15 April 1978.

SURPLICE, Reginald Alwyn, DMus (Lambeth), BMus (Dunelm), FRCO, LRAM, FRSCM; Organist and Master of the Choristers, Winchester Cathedral, 1949-71; Professor, Royal Academy of Music; Tutor in Music, King Alfred's College, Winchester, 1950-76; *b* 20 Aug. 1906; *s* of Reginald Frank and Ethel Mary Surplice; *m* 1933, Mary Florence Coxeter; two *s* one *d.* *Educ:* Reading Collegiate and Reading University. Organist, Pangbourne Parish Church, 1922-24, Easthampstead Parish Church, 1924-26; Holy Trinity, Windsor, 1928-40; Asst Organist St George's Chapel, Windsor, 1932-45; Organist and Master of the Choristers, Bristol Cathedral, 1946-49. War of 1939-45, served 1940-45. *Address:* Rosebank, Park Lane, Twyford, Hants. *T:* Twyford 712508. *[Died 21 April* 1977.

SURTEES, Maj.-Gen. George, CB 1943; CBE 1941; MC; Colonel, The Lancashire Fusiliers, since 1945; *b* 17 Dec. 1895. Served European War, 1914-18 (wounded, despatches, MC and Bar); War of 1939-45 in ME and NW Europe (despatches five times, CBE, CB) Grand Officer of Order of White Lion of Czechoslovakia, and Czechoslovak Military Cross; Comdr of Order of Crown of Belgium; Officer Legion of Honour, and Croix de Guerre with palm (France); American Bronze Star Medal. Retired pay, 1949. *[Died 16 July* 1976.

SUSSKIND, (Jan) Walter; conductor, composer and concert pianist; music advisor, Cincinnati Symphony Orchestra, since 1978; *b* 1 May 1913; of Czech parents; *m* 1st, 1943, Eleanor Warren (marr. diss. 1954); one *s* ; 2nd, 1954, Jeanne Letcher (marr. diss. 1960); 3rd, 1961, Diane Hartman; 4th, 1970, Jane Seymour. *Educ:* Prague State Conservatorium. Conductor Prague Opera, 1934-37; Principal Conductor Royal Carl Rosa Opera Co., 1943-45; Principal Conductor Sadler's Wells Opera Co., 1946; Conductor of the Scottish National Orchestra, 1946-52; Principal Conductor Glyndebourne Opera Co. (at 1st Edinburgh Festival), 1947; Resident Conductor, Victorian Symphony Orch., Melbourne (8 mths each yr), 1954-56; Principal Conductor, Toronto Symphony Orch., 1956-65; Music Dir and Principal Conductor, St Louis Symphony Orch., 1968-75. Records for numerous companies (over two hundred records so far). Regular Guest Conductor, NYC Opera, 1961-; Guest Conductor of most leading orchestras in Europe, 1952-; many world tours as guest conductor of the world's leading orchestras; has conducted in over thirty countries on all five continents. Music Director of: Mendelssohn Choir, 1958-64; National Youth Orchestra of Canada, 1960-; Music Festival, Aspen, Colorado, 1961-68; Mississippi River Festival (St Louis Symphony's summer festival), 1968-75. Conductor and Mem. Adv. Cttee, Internat. Festival of Youth Orchestras, St Moritz, Switzerland, later at Lausanne. Dir, Amer. Inst. of Orchestral Conducting. Orchestrator of many piano works. Hon. Dr of Humanities, Univ. of Southern Illinois, 1969; Hon. Dr of Fine Arts, Washington Univ., 1975. *Address:* c/o Ingpen & Williams, 14 Kensington Court, W8. *[Died 25 March* 1980.

SUTCH, Ven. Ronald Huntley; Archdeacon Emeritus of Cheltenham since 1965 (Archdeacon 1951-65); Hon. Canon of Gloucester, 1944-69, Canon Emeritus since 1969; *b* 5 March 1890; *s* of W. F. J. Sutch; *m* 1st, 1916, Elizabeth Lang Jones (*d* 1969); two *s*; 2nd, 1970, Mrs Betty Hibbett, *widow* of Basil Hibbett, Cirencester. *Educ:* Batley Grammar School; Merton College, Oxford. Deacon, 1914; Priest, 1915; Curate of Christ Church, Glasgow, 1914-16; Rector of St Mungo, Alexandria, Scotland, 1916-17; Vicar of Ravensthorpe, 1917-25; CF, 1918-19; Rector of Slymbridge, 1925-36; Vicar of St Stephen, Cheltenham, 1936-41. Surrogate, 1936-68; Rural Dean of Cirencester, 1941-51; Vicar of Cirencester, 1941-62; Proctor in Convocation, 1943-51. *Address:* The Plough Cottage, South Cerney, Cirencester, Glos. *T:* South Cerney 326.

[Died 22 Feb. 1975.

SUTHERLAND, Sir (Benjamin) Ivan, 2nd Bt, *cr* 1921; *b* 16 May 1901; *er surv. s* of Sir Arthur Munro Sutherland, 1st Bt, KBE, and Fanny Linda (*d* 1937), 2nd *d* of Robert Hood Haggie; *S* father 1953; *m* 1st, 1927, Marjorie Constance Daniel (marr. diss. 1944; she *d* 1980), *yr d* of late Frederic William Brewer, OBE, MA, Newcastle upon Tyne; two *s*; 2nd, 1944, Margaret, *d* of Albert Owen, Chalfont St Giles, Bucks; three *s*. *Heir: s* John Brewer Sutherland [*b* 19 Oct. 1931; *m* 1958, Alice Muireall, *d* of late W. Stanford Henderson, Kelso; three *s* one *d*]. *Address:* Dunstan Steads, Embleton, Northumberland.

[Died 6 Nov. 1980.

SUTHERLAND, David Macbeth, MC; RSA 1936 (ARSA 1923); Principal, Gray's School of Art, Gordon's Colleges, Aberdeen, retired, 1948; *b* Wick, Caithness-shire, 1883; *m* 1924, Dorothy Johnstone; one *s* one *d. Educ:* Pulteneytown Academy, Wick. Studied Art at Royal Institution (Mound) Edinburgh School of Art and Life Class of Royal Scottish Academy; awarded Carnegie Travelling Scholarship, and studied in Paris and Madrid; appointed to staff of Edinburgh Coll. of Art; served European War, Capt. Royal Scots Regt (despatches, MC); retired, 1948. Hon. LLD Aberdeen, 1953. *Exhibited works:* portrait, figure subjects and landscape in principal Scottish Exhibitions of Art. *Address:* Woodhouselee, Cults, Aberdeenshire. *[Died 20 Sept. 1973.*

SUTHERLAND, Prof. Earl Wilbur, Jr, MD; Professor of Physiology, Vanderbilt University School of Medicine, USA, since 1963; *b* Burlingame, Kansas, USA, 19 Nov. 1915; *s* of Earl Wilbur Sutherland and Edith Hartshorn; *m* 1963, Claudia Sebeste Smith; two *s* two *d. Educ:* Washburn Coll.; Washington Univ. Sch. of Medicine. MO in US Army, 1943-45. Intern, Barnes Hosp., 1942; Asst in Pharmacology, Washington Univ. Sch. of Med., 1940-42; Instr in Pharmacology, 1945-46; Instr in Biochem., 1946-50; Asst Prof., 1950-52; Associate Prof. of Biochem., 1952-53; Prof. of Pharmacology and Dir of Dept, Western Reserve Univ. Sch. of Med., Cleveland, Ohio, 1953-63. Mem. Editorial Bd: Biochemical Preparations, 1951-56; Jl of Pharmacology and Experimental Therapeutics, 1957-58; Mem. Cttees of Nat. Res. Council, Public Health Service and Nat. Insts of Health, 1953-68; Career Investigator, Amer. Heart Assoc., 1967; Member: Amer. Soc. of Biological Chemists; Amer. Chem. Soc.; Amer. Soc. for Pharmacology and Experimental Therapeutics; Amer. Assoc. for the Advancement of Science; Nat. Acad. of Science. Hon. Doctorates: Yale 1970; Washington 1970. Has gained many awards, including Nobel Prize for Medicine, 1971. *Publications:* articles in Jl of Biological Chem. and other scientific jls, and book chapters, 1942-. *Recreations:* fishing, gardening. *Address:* (office) Department of Physiology, Vanderbilt University Medical School, Nashville, Tenn 37203, USA. *T:* 322-2161; (home) 1941 Otter Creed Road, Nashville, Tenn 37215, USA. *T:* 383-8417.

[Died 9 March 1974.

SUTHERLAND, Sir Gordon (Brims Black McIvor), Kt 1960; FRS 1949; Hon. LLD St Andrews, 1958; Hon. DSc, Strathclyde, 1966; Master of Emmanuel College, Cambridge, 1964-77; *b* Watten, Caithness, 8 April 1907; *y s* of late Peter Sutherland and late Eliza Hope Sutherland, Dundee, Scotland; *m* 1936, Gunborg Elisabeth, *er d* of Konstnar Filip and Anna Wahlström, Gothenburg, Sweden; three *d. Educ:* Morgan Academy, Dundee; St Andrews Univ. (MA, BSc); Cambridge Univ. (PhD, ScD). Commonwealth Fund Fellow, 1931-33; Stokes Studentship, Pembroke Coll., 1934-35; Fellow and Lectr, Pembroke Coll., Cambridge, 1935-49. Leverhulme Fellow 1939, for study in US; Asst to Director of Scientific Research, Min. of Supply, 1940-41; Head of group carrying out extra-mural research in Cambridge Univ. for Min. of Aircraft Prodn, Min. of Supply and Admiralty, 1941-45; Asst Dir of Research in Dept of Colloid Science, Cambridge, 1944-47; Foster Lecturer, Univ. of Buffalo, 1948; Univ. Proctor, Cambridge, 1943-44; Member of Council of Senate 1946-49; Reader in Spectroscopy, Cambridge,

1947-49; Prof. of Physics in the Univ. of Michigan, 1949-56; Dir, National Physical Laboratory, 1956-64; Syndic, Cambridge Univ. Press, 1965-78; Syndic, Fitzwilliam Mus., Cambridge, 1977-; Reilly Lectr, Univ. of Notre Dame, 1954-55; Guggenheim Fellow, 1956; Governor: Coll. of Aeronautics, Cranfield, 1957-63; London Sch. of Economics, 1957-65; Northampton Coll. of Advanced Technology, 1960-65. Hon. Fellow: Pembroke Coll., Cambridge, 1959; Wolfson Coll., Cambridge, 1977. Vice-Pres., Royal Soc., 1961-63; Internat. Organisation for Pure and Applied Biophysics, 1961-64; Internat. Cttee on Data for Science and Technology, 1968-72; Pres., Triple Commn for Spectroscopy, 1962-63; Vice-Pres., Internat. Union of Pure and Applied Physics, 1963-69; President: Inst. of Physics and the Physical Soc., 1964-66 (Glazebrook Medal and Prize, 1972); Section X, British Assoc., 1968; Cambridge Philosophical Soc., 1980-; Mem., Council for Scientific Policy, 1965-68. A Trustee of the National Gallery, 1971-78. Fellow, Center for Advanced Study in Behavioral Scis, Stanford, 1972; For. Mem., Amer. Philosophical Soc.; For. Hon. Member: Amer. Acad. of Arts and Sciences, 1968; Société Royale des Sciences de Liège, 1960. *Publications:* Infra-Red and Raman Spectra, 1935. Scientific papers and articles on Infra-red Spectroscopy, Molecular Structure and Science Policy. *Recreation:* golf (Pres. Cambridge Univ. Golf Club, 1966-). *Address:* 38 Courtyards, Little Shelford, Cambridge CB2 5ER. *[Died 27 June 1980.*

SUTHERLAND, Graham (Vivian), OM 1960; Painter; Designer; *b* London, 24 Aug. 1903; *e s* of late G. H. V. Sutherland, Civil Servant, and E. Sutherland; *m* 1928, Kathleen Frances Barry; one *s* (died in infancy). *Educ:* Epsom Coll.; Goldsmiths' College School of Art, Univ. of London. Retrospective Exhibitions: XXVI Biennale Venice, 1952; Musée Nationale d'Art Moderne, Paris, 1952; Stedelijk Museum, Amsterdam, 1953; Kunsthaus, Zürich, 1953; Tate Gallery, London, 1953; New London Gallery, 1962; Galleria d'Arte Moderna, Turin, 1965; Basel, Munich, The Hague and Cologne, 1966-68; Marlborough Fine Art Gallery, 1968, 1973, 1977, 1979; Milan, 1973; first exhibn of portraiture, Nat. Portrait Gall., 1977. Rep. permanent collection: Tate Gallery; British Museum; Victoria and Albert Museum; Nat. Museum of Wales; Museum of Mod. Art, New York; Musée de l'Art Moderne, Paris; Musée des Beaux-Arts, Brussels; The Albertina, Vienna; Museum des 20 Jahrhunderts Künstmuseum, Basel; New Pinaleotok, Munich. Trustee of Tate Gallery, 1948-54. Graham Sutherland Gallery (now Graham and Kathleen Sutherland Foundn), Pembrokeshire, established under the Picton Castle Trust, 1976. Designed tapestry, "Christ in Majesty", hung in Coventry Cathedral, 1962. Hon. Member: Inst. of Arts and Letters; Acad. of Arts and Letters, USA. Hon. DLitt: Oxford, 1962; Leicester, 1965; Cardiff, 1979. Museum of Modern Art, São Paulo, Prize; Foreign Secretary's Prize, Tokyo; Shakespeare Prize, Hamburg, 1974. Citoyen d'honneur, Ville de Menton. Commandeur des Arts et Lettres, France. *Relevant publications:* The Work of Graham Sutherland, by Douglas Cooper, 1961; Sutherland by Francesco Arcangeli, 1976; Sutherland: Complete Graphic Work, by R. Tassi, 1978. *Address:* La Villa Blanche, Route de Castellar, 06 Menton, France. *Clubs:* Athenæum, Curzon. *[Died 17 Feb. 1980.*

SUTHERLAND, Sir Ivan; *see* Sutherland, Sir Benjamin Ivan.

SUTHERLAND, Dame Lucy Stuart, DBE 1969 (CBE 1947); DLitt Oxon 1955; Principal, Lady Margaret Hall, Oxford, 1945-71, Hon. Fellow, 1971; Pro-Vice-Chancellor, Univ. of Oxford, 1960-69; *b* 21 June 1903; *d* of Alexander Charles Sutherland, MA, MCE, and Margaret Mabel Goddard. *Educ:* Roedean School, South Africa; University of the Witwatersrand, S Africa (Herbert Ainsworth Scholar, MA (Distinction), 1925); Somerville College, Oxford (BA (Hons) Modern History Cl. I, 1927; MA 1931). Fellow and Tutor of Somerville College, Oxford, 1928-45; first Temp. Principal, then Temp. Assistant Secretary, Board of Trade, 1941-45; Chm. Lace Working Party, 1946; Pres. GPDST; Member: Cttee of Enquiry into Distribution and Exhibition of Cinematograph Films, 1949; Royal Commission on Taxation of Profits and Income, 1951; Committee of Enquiry into Grants for Students, 1958; Hebdomadal Council, Oxford Univ., 1953-71; Sponsoring Body, Univ. of Kent, Canterbury; UGC, 1964-69; Editorial Bd, The History of Parliament Trust. Governor, Administrative Staff Coll., Henley, 1964-69. FRSA 1950; FBA 1954. Hon. LittD: Cantab, 1963; Kent, 1967; Hon. LLD Smith College, Northampton, Mass, 1964; Hon. DLitt: Glasgow, 1966; Keele, 1968; Hon. DLit Belfast, 1970; Hon. DCL Oxon, 1972. Foreign Hon. Member, Amer. Acad. of Arts and Sciences, 1965. *Publications:* A London Merchant (1695-1774), 1933; edited (with M. McKisack) Mediaeval Representation and Consent, by M. V. Clarke, 1936, and Fourteenth Century Studies, by M. V. Clarke, 1937; edited (with H. Cam and M. Coate) Studies in Manorial History, by A. E. Levett, 1938; (joint) Report of the

Lace Working Party, 1947; The East India Company in Eighteenth Century Politics, 1952; edited The Correspondence of Edmund Burke, Vol. II, 1960; The University of Oxford in the Eighteenth Century, 1973; contributions to English Historical Review, Economic History Review, Economic History, Transactions of the Royal Historical Society, etc. *Address:* 59 Park Town, Oxford. *T:* Oxford 56159. *[Died 20 Aug. 1980.*

SUTHERLAND, Mary Elizabeth, CBE 1949; MA; Chief Woman Officer, Labour Party, 1932-60. *Educ:* elementary and secondary schools; Aberdeen University. MA Hons History, Aberdeen. Trade Union Organiser, 1920-22; Labour Party Women's Organiser, Scotland, 1924-32; Member, Women's Consultative Cttee, Ministry of Labour, 1941-65; Director National Institute of Houseworkers, 1946-66; UK representative, United Nations Commission on Status of Women, 1947-52; Secretary, National Joint Cttee of Working Women's Organisations, 1932-61. Chairman, International Council of Social Democratic Women, 1959-61. *Address:* 63 Dunlop Tower, East Kilbride, Glasgow. *[Died 19 Oct. 1972.*

SUTTIE, Col Hubert Francis Grant-, CBE 1940; DSO 1918; MC; RA; *b* 15 Dec. 1884; *e s* of late Robert Grant-Suttie and Hon. Edith Mary Dawnay, *d* of 7th Viscount Downe; *m* 1920, Torfrida Alianore (*d* 1971), *er d* of Sir Wroth Lethbridge, 5th Bt, and Hon. Mrs Walter Yarde-Buller of Marchington Hall, Staffs; one *s* one *d.* Served European War, 1914-18 (despatches four times, DSO, MC); Lt-Col 1933; Col 1936; AQMG War Office, 1936-39; retired pay, 1939; served War of 1939-45 (CBE); Command Welfare Officer, Scotland, 1943-47; CStJ, 1953 (OStJ, 1948). Member Royal Co. of Archers, Queen's Body Guard in Scotland. *Address:* 31 Whitelands House, Chelsea, SW3. *Club:* Caledonian. *[Died 3 June 1973.*

SUTTON, Brigadier George William, CBE 1939; DSO 1918; TD; *b* 10 Jan. 1893; *y s* of late Charles William Sutton; unmarried. *Educ:* Kersal School, 2nd Lt 8th Lancashire Fusiliers (TF) from Manchester Univ. OTC, Aug. 1914; Lt 1915; Capt. 1916; served European War, Egypt, 1914-15; Gallipoli; 1915 (wounded); Sinai Peninsula, 1916; France, 1917-18 (severely wounded; DSO, despatches); attached General Staff Adjutant OTC Universities of Manchester, Leeds, Sheffield, Liverpool, and University College, Nottingham, 1919-20; Adjutant 8th Lancashire Fusiliers 1920-23 and commanded that unit, 1932-38; Col (TA), 1938; commanded 125th Infantry Brigade, 1938-40 (France, etc.), GSO 1 (HG) Canadian Corps and Sussex and Surrey District, 1941-44; Personnel Director, Cook's of St Paul's, 1948-52. *Address:* c/o Lloyds Bank Ltd, 6 Pall Mall, SW1. *[Died 19 May 1971.*

SUTTON, Sir Graham; *see* Sutton, Sir O. G.

SUTTON, Sir (Oliver) Graham, Kt 1955; CBE 1950; FRS 1949; BSc, Oxon, DSc Wales; JP; Vice-President, University College of Wales, Aberystwyth, since 1967; *b* 4 Feb. 1903; *s* of Oliver Sutton, late of Cwmcarn, Mon, and Rachel, *d* of William Rhydderch, Brynmawr, Brecon; *m* 1931, Doris, *e d* of T. O. Morgan, Porthcawl; two *s. Educ:* Pontywaun Grammar School; University College of Wales, Aberystwyth (Scholar); Jesus Coll., Oxford (Scholar); Hon. Fellow, 1958. Lectr, University College of Wales, Aberystwyth, 1926-28; Professional Assistant, Meteorological Office, 1928-41; Superintendent of Research, CDEE, Porton, 1942-43; Superintendent, Tank Armament Research, 1943-45; Chief Superintendent, Radar Research and Development Estab., Malvern, 1945-47; Bashforth Prof. of Mathematical Physics, 1947-53 and Dean, 1952-53, RMCS; Dir-Gen., Meteorological Office, 1953-65. Chm., Atmospheric Pollution Research Cttee, 1950-55; Scientific Adviser to the Army Council, 1951; President: Royal Meteorological Soc., 1953-55, Hon. Fellow, 1976; IPCS, 1957-61; Chm., NERC, 1965-68; Member: Nature Conservancy, 1956-59; Council of University Coll. of Wales, Aberystwyth, 1958-64. Hon. Mem., Amer. Met. Soc.; Hon. Life Mem., NY Acad. of Sci. Hon. FSE. Hon. DSc Leeds; Hon. LLD Wales. President's Gold Medal, Soc. of Engineers, 1957; Symons Gold Medal, RMetS, 1959; Internat. Met. Organization Prize, 1968; Frank A. Chambers Award, Air Pollution Control Assoc., 1968. *Publications:* Atmospheric Turbulence, 1949; The Science of Flight, 1950; Micrometeorology, 1953; Mathematics in Action, 1953; (with D. S. Meyler) Compendium of Mathematics and Physics, 1957; Understanding Weather, 1960; The Challenge of the Atmosphere, 1961; Mastery of the Air, 1965; The Weather, 1974; scientific papers in various journals. *Address:* Hafod, 4 The Bryn, Sketty Green, Swansea, West Glam.
[Died 26 May 1977.

SUTTON, Stanley Cecil, CBE 1961; *b* 23 Sept. 1907; *s* of John Archibald and Margaret Sutton; *m* 1935, Elizabeth, *y d* of Bruce and Bessie Sinclair; two *s* two *d. Educ:* County Sch., Tottenham; London Sch. of Economics; University Coll., London. BSc Econ, Graham Wallas Prizeman LSE 1930, MSc Econ 1937; DipLibr 1931, Sir John MacAlister Medallist UCL. Joined Staff of British Library of Political and Economic Science, 1931; Sub-librarian, India Office Library, 1935; Asst Keeper 1937; Keeper 1946; Librarian, India Office Library, 1949-71; Keeper, India Office Records, 1954-71; Director, India Office Library and Records, 1971-72. Cnsltnt on S and SE Asia, Nat. Library of Aust., 1973-74. Chm., British South Asia Library Group, 1967-72; Corresp. Mem., Indian Hist. Records Commn, 1975-. Sir Percy Sykes Memorial Medallist, RCAS, 1969. FSA 1970. *Publications:* Guide to the India Office Library, 1952 (2nd edn 1967); South and South East Asia: a policy for the National Library of Australia, 1974; articles and reviews in librarianship jls. *Recreations:* music, golf. *Address:* 24 Stanley Hill Avenue, Amersham, Bucks. *T:* Amersham 3516. *[Died 6 May 1977.*

SWABEY, Christopher, CMG 1962; Chief Forestry Adviser to Government of Ethiopia, since 1971; *b* 6 April 1906; *s* of late Reverend M. R. Swabey and Mrs Swabey; *m* 1947, Gabrielle Patricia (*née* Markham); one *d. Educ:* Winchester College; Edinburgh University (BSc). MA Oxon 1966. Assistant Conservator of Forests, Trinidad, 1928; Conservator of Forests, Jamaica, 1937; Conservator of Forests, British Guiana, 1946; Chief Conservator of Forests, Uganda, 1951; Forestry Adviser: Colonial Office, 1957-64; Ministry of Overseas Development, 1964-65; Dir, Commonwealth Forestry Bureau, 1965-70. *Publications:* bulletins, reports and papers on tropical forestry problems. *Address:* c/o Commonwealth Forestry Bureau, South Parks Road, Oxford. *T:* Oxford 57185. *Club:* Royal Commonwealth Society.
[Died 11 April 1972.

SWABY, Rt. Rev. John Cyril Emerson, CBE 1968; Bishop of Jamaica, since 1968; *b* St Andrew, 11 Dec. 1905. *Educ:* Munro Coll.; St Peter's Theological Coll., Jamaica. BA, MA, Univ. of Durham. Deacon and Priest, 1929; Curate, Brown's Town, 1929-32; Actg Rector, St Cyprian's Highgate, Jamaica, 1932-38; Rector of St Matthew's, Kingston, Jamaica, 1938-57; Archdeacon of South Middlesex, Jamaica, 1951. Member: Kingston School Board, 1938-57; Diocesan Council; St Peter's Theological College; Hon. Visiting Chaplain, Kingston Public Hosp., 1938-57; Rector of Mandeville Parish Church, 1957-61; Suffragan Bishop of Kingston, Jamaica, 1961-68. *Address:* Bishop's Lodge, 8 Clieveden Avenue, Kingston 6, Jamaica, W Indies. *[Died 21 April 1975.*

SWAIN, Thomas Henry; MP (Lab) Derbyshire North-East since Oct. 1959; *b* 29 Oct. 1911; *s* of late Thomas Henry Swain, Burton-on-Trent; *m* 1931, Ruth Hannah (*d* 1969), *d* of Frank Wootton, Staveley, Derbyshire; six *s* four *d*; *m* 1969, Rosemary Fischer. *Educ:* Broadway School, Burton-on-Trent. Miner. Member: Staveley UDC, 1944-56; Derbyshire CC, 1946-49. Vice-Pres., Derbyshire Area Exec., and Branch Sec., National Union of Mineworkers. *Address:* House of Commons, SW1; Rosemarie, 165 Clowne Road, Stanfree, Chesterfield, Derbyshire S44 6AR. *[Died 2 March 1979.*

SWAN, Harold Couch, CMG 1948; OBE 1934; *b* 1 April 1890; *s* of late Henry Edwin Swan and Mary Westcott Couch; *m* 1916, May Augusta (*d* 1971), *d* of late Henry James Hollier; two *d. Educ:* Swansea Grammar School; German High School, Genoa. British Pro-Consul at Venice, 1913; Temp. British Vice-Consul, 1916-20; transferred to Milan and granted a Civil Service Certificate as HM Vice-Consul in the Consular Service; transferred to Savona, 1922; to New Orleans, 1924; HM Chargé d'Affaires at San Salvador, 1925; HM Consul at Havre, 1928, HM Consul-General at Leopoldville (Belgian Congo), 1932; British Sub-Agent, Malaga, Spain, 1938-39; Consul-General for the Republic of San Marino and Consul at Florence, Italy, 1939; Consul at Trieste, 1939-40; Consul at Seattle, 1940-44; Consul-General at Naples, 1944-45; HM Consul-General at Genoa (Italy), 1945-50; retired, 1951. Member Caterham and Warlingham UDC, 1954-63. Coronation Medal, 1937. *Recreations:* golf, shooting, motoring. *Address:* 7 Clareville Road, Caterham, Surrey. *T:* Caterham 43734.
[Died 15 Aug. 1972.

SWAN, Lt-Comdr Sir Kenneth Raydon, Kt 1949; OBE 1919; QC 1936; RNVR; *b* Lowfell, Gateshead-on-Tyne, 13 March 1877; 3rd *s* of Sir Joseph Wilson Swan, FRS; *m* 1919, Emily Louisa, *o d* of Edward Robert Tatchell; (one *d* decd). *Educ:* Rugby School; Balliol College, Oxford. 2nd Hon. Mods, 2nd Hon. Law; called to Bar, 1902; served European War in RNVR, 1914-19, in HMS Cyclops and at Naval Barracks, Buncrana; Board of Education (Ó Branch), 1919-20; resumed practice at Bar, 1920; Bencher, Middle Temple, 1943. Chairman: Board of Trade Patents Cttee, 1944; Dep. Chairman of Royal Commission on Awards to

Inventors, 1946; Chairman of Special Cttee Southern Province under Reorganization Areas Measure (1944), 1947; President of British Sailors' Soc., 1959 (Chairman, 1940-59); President, Royal Skating Club, 1955. *Publications:* Patents, Designs and Trade Marks; Memoir of Sir Joseph W. Swan, FRS. *Recreations:* lawn tennis, golf, skating, ski-ing, music, chess. *Address:* Cobwood, Woolton Hill, Newbury. *T:* Highclere 436. *Clubs:* Athenæum, Ski Club of Great Britain (Pres., 1911-13).
[*Died 14 Oct.* 1973.

SWANBOROUGH, Baroness (Life Peer); *see under* Reading, Dowager Marchioness of.

SWANN, Rev. Canon Sidney Ernest; Hon. Canon of Bristol Cathedral, 1938, Canon Emeritus since 1951; *b* 24 June 1890; *s* of late Rev. Sidney Swann and Josephine Anderson; *m* 1st, 1917, Marjorie (*d* 1972), *e d* of late Rt Rev. C. T. Abraham; one *s* one *d*; 2nd, 1972, Ethel Margaret Forster. *Educ:* Rugby; Trinity Hall, Cambridge. Rowed in Cambridge crews of 1911, 1912, 1913 and 1914, being president in the last year; coached the Cambridge crews of 1920, 1921, 1922, 1924, and 1946; was a member of the Leander crew which won the Eights at the Olympic Games of 1912 and was second in 1920; twice won the Goblets at Henley, with his brother, Alfred Swann; a member of the Leander crew which won the Grand, in record time, at Henley in 1913; won the Colquhoun Sculls at Cambridge, at his first attempt, in 1910, and the Visitors and Wyfolds, at Henley the same year; President National Amateur Rowing Assoc. 1938-56; Hon. Life Mem. Amateur Rowing Assoc., 1956. Served European War, 1914-18, Chaplain to the forces, 1916-19; Chaplain of Trinity Hall, Cambridge, 1920-24; Archdeacon of Nairobi, Kenya Colony, 1926; Archdeacon in Egypt and subdean of the pro Cathedral at Cairo, 1928-33; Vicar of Leighton Buzzard, 1933-36; Vicar of St Mary Redcliffe, Bristol, 1937-51; Vicar of Timberscombe, Minehead, 1951-56. A mem. of the Mission of Help to India in 1922 and 1923; Select Preacher, Cambridge University, 1939; Rural Dean of Bedminster, 1940-49; Chaplain to the Queen, 1952-65 (to King George VI, 1941-52); Archbishop's Visitor to RAF, 1943-44. *Address:* 9 Marsh Street, Dunster, Somerset.
[*Died 19 Sept.* 1976.

SWANSON, John Leslie; *b* 29 Nov. 1892; *s* of late John Swanson, Edinburgh; *m* 1915, Frances Mary, *e d* of late Edwin John Thompson, Dudley, Worcs; one *s* (and a son killed on active service) one *d*. *Educ:* Edinburgh Academy. Member of the Inst. of Chartered Accountants of Scotland; Lieut 2/7th Battalion Worcestershire Regiment, 1915-19, France, 1916-17; President, Wolverhampton Chamber of Commerce, 1929-31; Chairman, Tettenhall Urban District Council, 1932-40 and 1943-45; High Sheriff of Staffordshire, 1941. *Recreation:* fishing. *Address:* The Orchard, Compton, Wolverhampton, Staffs. *T:* Wolverhampton 751640.
[*Died 31 Jan.* 1974.

SWEENEY, Very Rev. Canon Garrett Daniel; *b* 30 Sept. 1912; *s* of Daniel Sweeney and Margaret Helen Sweeney (*née* Payne). *Educ:* Derby Sch.; Cotton Coll.; Ven. English Coll., Rome; Christ's Coll. and St Edmund's House, Cambridge. Priest (RC), 1937; BA (London) 1940; MA (Cantab) 1952. Asst Priest, Leicester, 1937-41; Parish Priest, Shirebrook, Derbys, 1941-46; Asst Master, 1948-56, and Headmaster, 1956-64, St Hugh's Coll., Tollerton, Nottingham; Master, St Edmund's House, Cambridge, 1964-76 (Hon. Fellow, 1976); Hon. Prelate to Pope Pius VI, 1975; Parish Priest, Shelthorpe, Loughborough, 1976-77, retired. *Publications:* (jtly) Bishops and Writers, 1977; articles in theological and historical jls. *Address:* St Hugh's College, Tollerton Hall, Nottingham NG12 4FZ. *T:* Plumtree 2334.
[*Died 15 June* 1979.

SWINDELL, Rev. Frank Guthrie, MA Oxon; Permission to Officiate, diocese of Exeter and diocese of Truro; *b* 18 Dec. 1874; *s* of Rev. T. G. Swindell; *m* 1910, Gladys Dorothy (*d* 1975), *d* of S. Wells Page, Penn House, Wolverhampton. *Educ:* Pocklington Sch., Yorks; St Catherine's Society, Oxford University. Deacon, 1898; Priest, 1899; Curate of Boxley, Maidstone, 1898-1902; Chaplain of Selangor (St Mary's Church, Kuala Lumpur), FMS 1902-06; Colonial Chaplain of Malacca and Negri Sembilan, 1906-16; acting in Singapore, 1907 and 1911, and in Penang, 1912; Colonial Chaplain of St Andrew's Cathedral, Singapore, 1914-29; Archdeacon of Singapore, 1916-29 (retired); Rector of Isfield, diocese of Chichester, 1930-50 (resigned). *Publication:* A Short History of St Andrew's Cathedral, Singapore. *Address:* Rhylla, Townlake, Tavistock, S Devon. *T:* Milton Abbot 263.
[*Died 22 Dec.* 1975.

SWINDELLS, Rev. Bernard Guy, SJ; BSc (London), BSc (Liverpool), ARCSc; *b* 24 May 1887. *Educ:* Stonyhurst College. Rector of Stonyhurst College, 1945-52; Rector of St Ignatius'

College, 1953-59; Spiritual Father at Beaumont College, 1959-61; Rector of Manresa College, Roehampton, 1961-62; Rector of Harlaxton Manor, 1962-65. *Address:* St Ignatius' Presbytery, South Tottenham, N15 6ND. *T:* 01-800 2121.
[*Died 2 July* 1977.

SWINDLEHURST, Joseph Eric, OBE 1951; CEng, FInstCE, FIStructE; Borough Engineer and Surveyor, Hampstead, 1924-55; *b* 2 Aug. 1890; *s* of late Joseph Eaves Swindlehurst, MInstCE, and E.I. Artis; *m* 1928, Gwendolen (*d* 1964), *d* of late Ernest Spencer Warne; no *c. Educ:* King Henry VIIIth School, Coventry; Gonville and Caius College, Cambridge, MA. Articled to J. E. Swindlehurst, .MInstCE, City and Water Engineer, Coventry; served in various capacities the Municipalities of Coventry, Eastbourne, and Preston; served with commission in RE 1914-19. President Association of Metropolitan Borough Engineers and Surveyors, 1936 and 1949; Pres. Inst. of Highway Engineers, 1937 and 1938; Pres. Incorporated Association of Architects and Surveyors, 1939-40; Vice-Pres. Royal Soc. of Health, 1945-; Pres. Instn Struct. E, 1950-51; Pres. Brit. Sect., Soc. des Ingénieurs Civils de France, 1952 and 1953; Member of Building Technical Advisory Cttee of Min. of Home Security; Mem. of Architecture and Public Utilities Committee and of Civil Engineering Committee of Ministry of Labour and Nat. Service Central Register Advisory Council, 1939; Director, Bituminous Roads Development Group, 1957. Fellow: Inst. of Municipal Engrs; Inst. of Highway Engrs. Freeman of City of London; Freeman and Liveryman of Worshipful Company of Painter Stainers; Registered Architect; James Forrest Medallist and Miller Prizeman, InstCE. *Publications:* various papers. *Recreations:* motoring, foreign travel. *Address:* The Moorings, The Avenue, Bushey, Herts. *Club:* United Oxford & Cambridge University.
[*Died 24 Dec.* 1972.

SWINFEN, 2nd Baron, *cr* 1919, of Chertsey; **Charles Swinfen Eady;** Barrister-at-Law, Inner Temple; *b* 2 Feb. 1904; *s* of 1st Baron and Blanche, (*d* 1946), *y d* of S. W. Lee; *S* father, 1919; *m* 1st, 1937, Mary Aline (from whom he obtained a divorce, 1945), *yr d* of late Col H. Mynors Farmar, CMG, DSO; two *s*; 2nd, 1950, Averil Kathleen Suzanne Knowles, *er d* of late Maj. W. M. H. Humphreys, Eire. *Educ:* Eton; Christ Church, Oxford. *Heir:* *s* Hon. Roger Mynors Swinfen Eady [*b* 14 Dec. 1938; *m* 1962, Patricia Anne, *o d* of F. D. Blackmore, Doone, Highfield Park, Dundrum, Co. Dublin; one *s* three *d*]. *Address:* Medina House, Spanish Point, Co. Clare, Ireland. *Club:* Carlton.
[*Died 19 March* 1977.

SWINTON, 1st Earl of, *cr* 1955; **Philip Cunliffe-Lister,** PC 1922; GBE 1929 (KBE 1920); CH 1943; MC; DL; Viscount Swinton, 1935; Baron Masham, 1955; *b* 1 May 1884; *y s* of late Colonel Y. G. Lloyd-Greame of Sewerby House, Bridlington; *m* 1912, Mary Constance, *o d* of late Rev. Ingram Boynton, Barmston, Yorks; *er s* died of wounds received in action, 1943, *yr s* decd; assumed name of Cunliffe-Lister, 1924. *Educ:* Winchester; University Coll., Oxford. Called to Bar, 1908; served in Army, 1914-17; Joint Secretary of Ministry of National Service, 1917-18; MP (U) Hendon Division of Middlesex, 1918-35; Parliamentary Secretary to Board of Trade, 1920-21; Secretary of Overseas Trade Department, 1921-22; President of the Board of Trade, 1922-23, 1924-29 and in 1931; Secretary of State for the Colonies, 1931-35; Secretary of State for Air, 1935-38; Chairman UK Commercial Corp., 1940-42; Cabinet Minister Resident in West Africa, 1942-44; Minister for Civil Aviation, 1944-45; Chancellor of the Duchy of Lancaster, and Minister of Materials, 1951-52; Secretary of State for Commonwealth Relations, Dec. 1952-Apr. 1955. Deputy Leader of the House of Lords, 1951-55; Chairman of Permanent Labour Committee of War Cabinet War Priorities Committee, 1918; Member of Select Committee on National Expenditure and Select Committee on High Prices and Profits, 1919; Chairman Imperial Economic Conference, 1923. Pres. Nat. Union of Conservative and Unionist Associations, 1949; Chairman of Governors of Swinton Conservative College, 1958-. DL North Riding, Yorkshire. Hon. Fellow University College, Oxford. Hon. LLD Liverpool University. Grand Officier, Order of Leopold. Hon. Air Commodore 608 Squadron RAF. *Publications:* I Remember, 1948; Sixty Years of Power: Some Memories of the Men Who Wielded it, 1966. *Recreations:* shooting and fishing. *Heir:* *g s* Lord Masham. *Address:* 16 Kingston House, SW7. *T:* 01-589 0994; Swinton, Masham, Yorks. *T:* Masham 310. *Club:* Carlton.
[*Died 27 July* 1972.

SWINTON, Brig. Alan Henry Campbell, MC 1915; FSA (Scotland) 1956; late Scots Guards; *b* 15 March 1896; *s* of late Capt. G. S. C. Swinton; *m* 1923, Mariora Hankey (who obtained a divorce, 1944); one *s*; *m* 1945, Mrs J. E. A. Best, *d* of Charles Baker, Southampton; one *s* one *d*. *Educ:* University College

School; RMC, Sandhurst. A Member of the Queen's Body Guard for Scotland, The Royal Company of Archers (retd list). Hon. Sheriff (formerly Hon. Sheriff Substitute), Berwickshire, 1954-; County Councillor, 1949-. *Address:* Kimmerghame, Duns, Berwickshire. *T:* Duns 3277. *Clubs:* Pratt's; New (Edinburgh).   *[Died 21 April 1972.*

SWYNNERTON, Maj.-Gen. (Hon.) Charles Roger Alan, CB 1950; DSO 1945; retired; *b* 12 February 1901; *s* of F. Swynnerton, Isle of Man; *m* 1926, Clare Inès, *d* of T. R. Stevenson, Moor Court, Amberley, Glos.; two *s. Educ:* RMC, Sandhurst. Commissioned The North Staffordshire Regt. 1920; Capt. 1933; Major, 1938; Lt-Col 1947; Colonel, 1947; Brigadier, 1947; Temp. Maj.-Gen. 1947-49; ADC 1949-54. Served in Ireland, Mediterranean, India, West Africa and Burma; Military Attaché, HBM Embassy, Ankara, Turkey, 1950-54; ADC to King George VI and subsequently to Queen Elizabeth II, 1950-54; retd, 1954. Col Comdt, Royal West African Frontier Force, 1954-58; Col The North Staffordshire Regt, 1955-58. *Address:* Finca Las Chumberas, Alhaurin de la Torre, Málaga, Spain. *Club:* Army and Navy.   *[Died 2 March 1973.*

SYFRET, Adm. Sir (Edward) Neville, GCB 1948 (KCB 1942; CB 1941); KBE 1945; *b* 20 June 1889; *s* of Edward Ridge Syfret, Cape Town, SA; *m* 1913, Hildegarde Warner; one *s* one *d. Educ:* Diocesan College, SA; HMS Britannia. Entered RN 1904; Lieut 1909; Commander, 1922; Captain, 1929; Rear-Adm. 1940; Vice-Adm. 1943; Adm. 1946; Naval Secretary to 1st Lord, 1939-41; commanded Force "H" Sea Command, 1941-43; Vice-Chief of Naval Staff, 1943-45; Commander-in-Chief Home Fleet, 1945-48. *Address:* c/o Standard Bank, 10 Clements Lane, EC4.
                                                [Died 10 Dec. 1972.

SYKES, (Arthur) Frank (Seton), CVO 1962; CBE 1979; DL; Agricultural Adviser to the Queen at Windsor, 1950-71; *b* 4 July 1903; *e s* of late Sir Percy Sykes, KCIE, CB, CMG; *m* Barbara Godolphin, *e d* of W. H. Yeatman Biggs; one *s. Educ:* Rugby. Chm., Frank Sykes Ltd. Mem. Royal Commission on East Africa, 1953. Vice-Pres., 1970, Dep. Pres., 1979-80, RASE. Alderman, Wilts CC, 1952; High Sheriff of Wilts, 1964; DL Wilts, 1968. Gold Medal, RASE, 1974. Chevalier de la Légion d'Honneur. *Publications:* This Farming Business, 1944; Living from the Land, 1957. *Recreations:* travel, hunting, fishing. *Address:* Stockton, Warminster, Wilts.   *[Died 31 Dec. 1980.*

SYKES, Sir (Benjamin) Hugh, 2nd Bt, *cr* 1921; *b* 8 June 1893; *e s* of Sir Charles Sykes, 1st Bt, and Mary (*d* 1944), *y d* of late Benjamin Newsome; *S* father, 1950; *m* 1935, Audrey Winifred, *o d* of late F. C. Thompson, Cricklewood, NW2; no *c. Educ:* Leys School, Cambridge. *Heir: n* John Charles Anthony Le Gallais Sykes, *b* 19 April 1928. *Address:* 19 Bouverie Gardens, Harrow HA3 0RQ. *T:* 01-907 3884. *Club:* Royal Automobile.
                                                [Died 22 Dec. 1974.

SYKES, Frank; *see* Sykes, A. F. S.

SYKES, Sir Hugh; *see* Sykes, Sir B. H.

SYKES, Sir (Mark Tatton) Richard T.; *see* Tatton-Sykes.

SYKES, Lt-Col Peter Thomas Wellesley, OBE 1942; DL; farming at Chitterne since 1948; *b* 21 Dec. 1903; *s* of late Lt-Col H. P. Sykes and Winifred Charlotte Jane (*née* Wellesley); *m* 1st, 1931, Nina Violet Eyre Coote (*d* 1935); two *s*; 2nd, 1937, Violet Lavender Christie-Miller; one *s* one *d. Educ:* Rugby; Sandhurst. Joined The Queens Bays, 1924; Adjutant, 1935-38. Served War of 1939-45 (wounded twice); i/c Royal Wiltshire Yeomanry, 1942; GSO1, War Office, 1943; i/c 54th training regt, 1944; i/c The Queens Bays 1945. Retired from Army, 1947. Mem. Wilts TAA, 1950; CC 1949, DL 1963, High Sheriff 1963, CA 1964, Wilts. *Recreations:* shooting, fishing. *Address:* Chitterne House, Chitterne, Warminster, Wilts. *T:* Codford St Mary 209. *Club:* Cavalry.   *[Died 20 Nov. 1975.*

SYKES, Sir Richard (Adam), KCMG 1977 (CMG 1965); MC 1945; HM Diplomatic Service; Ambassador to the Netherlands, since 1977; *b* 8 May 1920; *s* of late Brig. A. C. Sykes, CBE, DSO; *m* 1953, Ann Georgina, *d* of late Brig. A. F. Fisher, CBE, DSO; two *s* one *d. Educ:* Wellington Coll.; Christ Church, Oxford. Served Army, 1940-46; Major, Royal Signals. Joined HM Foreign Service, 1947; served: Foreign Office, 1947-48; Nanking, 1948-50; Peking, 1950-52; Foreign Office, 1952-56; Brussels, 1956-59; Santiago, 1959-62; Athens, 1963-66; Foreign and Commonwealth Office, 1967-69; Ambassador to Cuba, 1970-72; Minister, Washington, 1972-75; Dep. Under-Sec., FCO, 1975-77. Croix de Guerre (France), 1945. *Address:* c/o National Westminster Bank Ltd, Warminster, Wilts. *Club:* Army and Navy.   *[Died 22 March 1979.*

SYLVESTER-BRADLEY, Prof. Peter Colley; Professor of Geology, University of Leicester, since 1959; *b* 21 May 1913; 2nd *s* of Lt-Col C. R. Sylvester-Bradley; *m* 1945, Joan Eveleen Mary Campbell; three *s* one *d. Educ:* Haileybury College; University of Reading. Lecturer, Seale Hayne Agricultural College, 1937-39. Served War of 1939-45, Royal Navy. Assistant Lecturer, Lecturer, and Senior Lecturer, University of Sheffield, 1946-59; Rose Morgan Professor, University of Kansas, 1955-56; Internat. Commissioner of Zoological Nomenclature, 1953-58. Vice-Pres., Palæontographical Soc. *Publications:* (ed) The Species Concept in Paleontology, 1956; (ed) The Geology of the East Midlands, 1968; papers on palæontology, stratigraphy, taxonomy, evolution and the origin of life. *Recreations:* natural history, travel, landscape gardening, photography, the gramophone, country wines. *Address:* Department of Geology, University of Leicester, LE1 7RH. *T:* Leicester 50000; Noon's Close, Stoughton, Leicester. *T:* Leicester 713764.
                                                [Died 17 April 1978.

SYMES, Maj.-Gen. George William, CB 1946; MC; *b* 12 Jan. 1896; *o s* of late George and Eliza Symes; *m* 1st, 1939, Katherine Bellairs Lucas (*d* 1961); 2nd, 1967, Kathleen Champion de Crespigny. *Educ:* Bridport Gram. Sch. Commissioned 1915, York and Lancaster Regt; served with MG Corps, 1915-19 (MC and bar); Staff College, Camberley, 1930-31; Bt Major, 1932; Major, 1938; Bt Lt-Col, 1939; Col, 1942; Acting Maj.-Gen. 1942; Temp. 1943; Subst. Maj.-Gen., 1944. Comd 8th Inf. Bde, 1940-41; Brig.-Gen. Staff, Eastern Comd, 1941-42; Comd 70th Division, 1942-43; Deputy Commander Special Force, India, 1943-44; Deputy Commander L of C 21st Army Group, May-Nov. 1944 (despatches); Comd L of C Comd, SEAC, 1944-45; Comd South Burma District, June-Dec. 1945 (despatches); Commander South-Western District, Taunton, Som., 1946-48, and 43rd (Wessex) Division TA, 1947-48; retired April 1949. Colonel, York and Lancaster Regt, 1946-48; Hon. Col, 10th Bn Adelaide Rifles, 1958-60. Dir, Santos Ltd, 1955-78; Private Sec. to Governor of S Australia, 1956-64. Founded Nat. Trust of S Australia, 1954, Vice-Pres. 1965-. Pres., S Australia Branch, RGSA, 1954-57. *Publications:* contribs. to Australian Dictionary of Biography. *Recreations:* historical research, golf. *Address:* 81 Esplanade, Tennyson, SA 5022, Australia. *T:* 356-8568. *Club:* Adelaide (Adelaide).   *[Died 26 Aug. 1980.*

SYMON, Sir Alexander (Colin Burlington), KCMG 1955 (CMG 1948); KCVO 1961; OBE 1944; retired; British High Commissioner in Pakistan, 1954-61; *b* 13 May 1902; 2nd *s* of late J. M. Symon, Hull, Yorks; *m* 1930, Doris (Dodo) Olive, *o d* of late E. J. Comfort, Harrow, Middlesex and Meopham, Kent; no *c. Educ:* Technical College, Hull. Appointed to India Office, 1921; Assistant Secretary, Indian Delegation to Disarmament Conf., Geneva, 1932-33; Sec. to Indian Delegation to London Naval Conf., 1935; Sec. to Indian Supply Mission in USA, 1941-46; Deputy High Commissioner for the United Kingdom in India, 1946-49; visited Nepal, 1947, to negotiate Agreement for British Gurkha Brigade; Asst Under-Secretary of State, Commonwealth Relations Office, 1949-52; Deputy Under-Secretary of State, Commonwealth Relations Office, 1952-54. Member, UK Deleg. to Consultative Cttee of Colombo Plan, Karachi, 1952, Delhi, 1953, Ottawa, 1954; reported on Economic Develt of Territories of Swaziland, Basutoland and Bechuanaland, 1954; Member UK delegation to SEATO Council meeting, Karachi, 1956; Member UK delegation to Bagdad Pact Council meeting, Karachi, 1957, London, 1958 and Karachi, 1959-61. President, Jockey Club of Pakistan, 1959-61; Director of Companies. *Recreation:* golf. *Address:* 33 Offington Lane, Worthing, Sussex.   *[Died 16 July 1974.*

SYMON, Mrs David; *see* Moore, Miss Jocelyn A. M.

SYMON, Harold, CB 1949; *b* 1896; *s* of Harris Zaiman, Sheffield; *m* 1st, 1917, Winifred Lilian Ashwell; one *s* one *d*; 2nd, 1968, Edith Celia Napier Boreham. *Educ:* Central School, Sheffield; King's College, Cambridge. Entrance Scholar, King's College, Cambridge, 1913; Wrangler with special distinction, 1916. Assistant Principal, Dept of Scientific and Industrial Research, 1919; Assistant to Director of Building Research, and Secretary, Building Research Bd, 1925-34; Ministry of Health: Sec., Cttee on Constructing Flats, 1934-36, Principal, 1936, Asst Sec., 1941, Principal Asst Sec., 1945, Under-Sec., 1946; Under-Secretary, Ministry of Housing and Local Govt (formerly Min. of Local Govt and Planning), 1951-55; Director and Consultant to Assoc. of Land and Property Owners, 1955-68. *Recreation:* golf. *Address:* Knowle Holt, Tilford Road, Hindhead, Surrey. *Clubs:* Reform; Hindhead Golf.   *[Died 12 Nov. 1971.*

SYMONDS, Sir Charles (Putnam), KBE 1946; CB 1944; MA, DM Oxon; FRCP, Hon. FRCPEd; Air Vice-Marshal RAFVR; Consulting Physician Emeritus for Nervous Diseases, Guy's

Hospital; Consulting Physician Emeritus, The National Hospital, Queen Square; Hon. Consulting Neurologist, RAF; *b* 1890; *s* of Sir Charters Symonds; *m* 1st, 1915, Janet Palmer Poulton (*d* 1919); 2nd, 1920, Edythe Dorton; four *s. Educ:* Rugby; New Coll., Oxford; Guy's Hospital; Entrance Scholarships Rugby and Guy's Hospital. Served European War, 1914-18 (Médaille Militaire). Held appts at Guy's Hosp., at Throat Nose and Ear Hosp., and at Nat. Hosp., Queen Square, from 1919 until retirement. Radcliffe Travelling Fellow, Oxford University, 1920; FRSM (Ex-Pres. Sections of Psychiatry and Neurology); Ex-Pres., Assoc. of British Neurologists, 1956. Hon. Visiting Neurologist, Johns Hopkins Hosp.; Sims Commonwealth Travelling Professor for 1953; Harveian Orator, RCP, 1954. Hon. Member, Amer. Neurological Assoc.; Membre Correspondant de la Société de Neurologie de Paris; Hon. Member, New York Neurological Soc. Hon. Fellow RSM 1964. *Publications:* Studies in Neurology, 1970; Section on Nervous Diseases in Taylor's Textbook of Medicine; papers on neurological subjects in scientific journals. *Recreations:* photography, bird-watching, fly-fishing. *Address:* c/o Walker Martineau & Co., 10 and 11 Gray's Inn Square, WC1R 5JL. *Club:* Royal Air Force. [*Died 7 Dec. 1978.*

SYMONDS-TAYLER, Admiral Sir Richard Victor, KBE 1951; CB 1948; DSC 1915; *b* 27 Oct. 1897; *s* of late Lt-Col R. H. Symonds-Tayler, Hereford; *m* 1925, Letitia Mary, *d* of late E. J. Gunner, IW; one *s* one *d. Educ:* Hereford Cathedral School; RNC, Osborne and Dartmouth. Joined RN as cadet, 1910; served Wars, 1914-18, 1939-45. Comdr, 1931; Capt., 1936; Rear-Adm., 1946; Vice-Adm., 1949; Adm. (retd), 1953. Graduated Naval Staff Coll., 1928; Imperial Defence College, 1938; British Naval Mission to Greece, 1929-31; commanded HMS Centurion, 1938-39; HMS Sussex, 1940; HMS London, 1942-44; Director of Training and Staff duties, Admiralty, 1940-42; Chief of Staff to C-in-C Portsmouth, 1945-46; Chief of Staff to Naval Representative of British Chiefs of Staff, Military Staff Committee, United Nations, 1946-47; Flag Officer commanding First Cruiser Squadron, 1947-48; C-in-C America and West Indies Station, 1949-51. Iraq Petroleum Company Ltd, 1952-58. *Recreations:* fishing, golf. *Address:* Copper Beeches, Worplesdon, Surrey. *Clubs:* Army and Navy. [*Died 18 Feb. 1971.*

SYMONETTE, Hon. Sir Roland Theodore, Kt 1959; Premier of the Bahamas, 1964-67; Member of HM Executive Council, Bahamas, since 1949; Leader of Government in the House of Assembly, 1955-67; MHA since 1925; shipyard owner, Bahamas; Contractor for the Construction of roads, wharfs, and harbours; *b* 16 Dec. 1898; *m* 1945, Margaret Frances Thurlew; four *s* one *d* (and one *d* decd). *Educ:* day school at Current Eleuthera, Bahama Islands. *Recreation:* yachting. *Address:* 601 Bay Street, Nassau, Bahamas. *Clubs:* Nassau Yacht (Bahamas); North American Yacht Racing Association (New York). [*Died 13 March 1980.*

SYMONS, Hubert Wallace, FRCS; Emeritus Professor of Clinical Surgery, University of Leeds; Honorary Surgeon, General Infirmary, Leeds; Honorary Consulting Surgeon: Bartholomew Hospital, Goole; District Hospital, Castleford; Selby War Memorial Hospital; *b* 24 Nov. 1890; *s* of William Wallace Symons and Mary Helen Symons (*née* Lilly); *m* 1925, Charlotta Dolores Naomi de Wilde, MRCS, LRCP; one *s* one *d. Educ:* Bradford Grammar School; Leeds University. MB, ChB Leeds, 1912; FRCS 1924. Formerly: Demonstrator in Anatomy and Surgical Tutor, University of Leeds; Resident Surg. Officer, Leeds General Infirmary; Lieutenant-Colonel, RAMC (T). *Address:* 120 Grove End Gardens, St John's Wood, NW8 9LR. *T:* 01-286 8996. [*Died 24 Feb. 1973.*

SYMONS, Ronald Stuart, CMG 1960; CIE 1945; *b* 24 July 1904; *s* of William John and Margaret Lilian Symons, Maresfield, Sussex; *m* 1st, 1930, Joan Alice (marr. diss. 1942), *d* of John Robertson, Wormley, Surrey; one *s*; 2nd, 1944, Phyllis Jane (*d* 1955), *d* of Henry Wingfield King, Reigate, Surrey; one *d*; 3rd, 1958, Christine Mary Vivien Gresty, *d* of Canon H. H. Coley, Holne Vicarage, Devon. *Educ:* Christ's Hospital, Horsham; King's College, Cambridge. Joined Indian Civil Service, 1927; Magistrate and Collector, district Pilibhit, UP, 1933-34; Revenue and Finance Minister, Rampur State, UP, 1935-37; Deputy Secretary in Finance Dept, Govt of India, 1938-40; various appointments in Military and Supply Finance Depts of Govt of India, 1940-45; Joint Secretary to Govt of India in Finance Dept, 1945-47; retired from ICS and joined Home Civil Service, 1947; Assistant Secretary, HM Treasury, 1949. Minister in UK Delegn to OECD, Paris, 1961-64; Treasury Historical Section, 1969-75. *Recreations:* golf, photography, ornithology, gardening. *Address:* Chantry Cottage, High Street, Lindfield, Sussex. *T:* Lindfield 3509. *Club:* Royal Commonwealth Society (Fellow). [*Died 5 Aug. 1977.*

SYNGE, Victor Millington, MD, DPH, FRCPI; FRCP; retired 1974 as Regius Professor of Physic, Trinity College, Dublin; formerly Visiting Physician, Royal City of Dublin Hospital; *b* 1893; *s* of Edward Synge; *m* 1919, Edith Allen; two *s. Educ:* Trinity College, Dublin (Foundation Scholar in Experimental Science, Medical Travelling Prizeman); Paris. Formerly Professor of Preventive Medicine and Medical Jurisprudence, and later Professor of Medicine in the Royal College of Surgeons, Ireland. *Publications:* Contributions on medical subjects to Irish Journal of Medical Science, and Lancet. *Address:* Killakee Cottage, Rockbrook, Dublin 14. *T:* Dublin 909797. [*Died 25 Feb. 1976.*

SYNNOT, R. V. O. H.; *see* Hart-Synnot.

SZIGETI, Joseph; violinist; *b* Budapest, 5 Sept. 1892. *Educ:* Budapest. Pupil of Hubay; made his debut at the age of 13 years; toured England several times with Busoni, McCormack, Melba, etc., between 1907 and 1914; from 1919 concertized on the Continent. Professor of the classe de virtuosité at the Geneva Conservatory, 1917-24; first American Tour, 1925-26; since then every season in USA in recital and as soloist with every major orchestra, and extensive tours in the Far East, Australia, NZ, South America, and South Africa, 1931-38; led Edinburgh Festival Quartet (Schnabel, Primrose, Fournier), 1947 and 1952; toured Japan, 1953, South America, 1954. Cross of Chevalier of the Légion d'Honneur, 1930; Officer of Légion d'Honneur, 1939; Hungarian Order of Merit, 1931; Commander of Belgian Order of Leopold, 1937; has published several violin transcriptions of contemporary works, among others by Bela Bartok and Sir Edward Elgar (Serenade and Adieu; Elgar's last completed compositions); also transcribed works by Peter Warlock, Scriabin, de Falla, Bach, Weber, Lie, Rameau, etc. Bach Seminar (the Six Solo Sonatas), Northwestern Univ., Evanston, Ill., 1955, Cycle of 20th Century Masterpieces (3 programmes) in Zürich, and USA, 1956-57. Hon. RAM London; Hon. Member, Guildhall School of Music. Film debut in Warner Bros film Hollywood Canteen. *Publications:* With Strings Attached (a volume of memoirs), (London), 1949; A Violinist's Note Book (London), 1964; The Violin Sonatas of Beethoven (Illinois), 1965; Szigeti on the Violin, 1970. *Address:* Le Crépon, Baugy sur Clarens (Vaud), Switzerland. [*Died 19 Feb. 1973.*

T

TAGGART, John S.; *see* Scott-Taggart.

TAILYOUR, General Sir Norman (Hastings), KCB 1966 (CB 1964); DSO 1945, and Bar to DSO 1956; Captain of Deal Castle, since 1972; *b* 12 Dec. 1914; *s* of late Lt-Col G. H. F. Tailyour and Mrs Tailyour (*née* Hutcheson); *m* 1st, 1941, Priscilla June Southby (*d* 1971); one *s* one *d*; 2nd, 1973, Juliet, *d* of late Col. K. N. Colvile and of Mrs K. N. Colvile, and *widow* of J. A. Greig; two step *s* one step *d. Educ:* Nautical College, Pangbourne. 2nd Lieutenant, RM 1933; seconded to Royal West African Frontier Force (Nigeria Regiment), Captain RM, 1939; 5th Battalion RM, RM Div., 1941; Staff College, Camberley, 1943; G2, HQs RM Div., 1943; OCRM, HMS Robertson, then Exec. Officer, HMS St Mathew (Landing Craft Base), 1943-44; CO 27th Bn RM, NW Europe, 1945 (despatches, DSO); OC Training Cadre, Inf. Sch., RM, 1946; Sen. Course, US Marine Corps, Quantico, USA, Major RM, 1947; Chief Instr Amphibious Sch., RM, 1948; GI Plans and Ops RN Rhine Flotilla, 1949; JSSC, Latimer, 1951; GI Amphibious Warfare HQ, London, 1952; Lieut-Col Comdg Officer 45 Commando, RM, Cyprus (Bar to DSO), Port Said (wounded, despatches), 1954; NATO Defence Coll., Paris, 1957; CO RM Barracks, Plymouth, 1957; Chief of Amphibious Warfare's Rep., BJSM, Washington, 1958; Asst Naval Mem., Mil. Staff Cttee, UN, Col RM; Comdr 3rd Commando Bde, RM, Brig. RM, 1960; Comdr Plymouth Gp, RM, Maj.-Gen., 1962; Lt-Gen. 1965; General 1967. Comdt-Gen., Royal Marines, 1965-68. Adm. in Texas Navy, 1972. Patron: Goodwin Sands and Downs RNLI; Deal Soc.; Council Member: Officers' Pension Soc.; Stoll Foundn. MBIM. *Recreation:* sailing. *Address:* West Brae, Johnshaven, by Montrose, Angus. *T:* Benholm 372. *Clubs:* Army and Navy; Royal Yacht Squadron; (Life Vice-Cdre) Royal Marines Sailing; Royal Naval Sailing Association (Rear Commodore, 1961-65). [*Died 28 Dec. 1979.*

TAIT, Sir John, Kt 1943; Director, Eastern Tractors Ltd and Subsidiaries; *b* 21 May 1890; *s* of Robert Tait, Girvan, Ayrshire;

m 1919, Sarah Turner (*d* 1946), *d* of R. Montgomery; one *d* ; *m* 1950, Nancy, *widow* of W. R. Glen, and *d* of J. Purdie, Glasgow. MLA India, 1931-32; Member of the Senate, Burma; Chairman, Burma Chamber of Commerce. *Address:* 113 Rivermead Court, SW6. *T:* 01-736 2976. *Clubs:* Oriental, Hurlingham, City of London; Mid-Surrey Golf.   *[Died 7 Aug. 1972.*

TALBOT DE MALAHIDE, 7th Baron *cr* 1831; **Milo John Reginald Talbot;** CMG 1957; Baron Talbot of Malahide, Baron Malahide of Malahide (I), 1831; Baron Talbot de Malahide (UK), 1856; Hereditary Lord Admiral of Malahide and adjacent seas (15 Edward IV); *b* 1 Dec. 1912; *o s* of Colonel Hon. Milo George Talbot, CB, RE (4th *s* of 4th Baron), and Eva, *d* of Col John Joicey, MP; *S* cousin, 1948; unmarried. *Educ:* Winchester; Trinity Coll., Cambridge. Entered Diplomatic Service, 1937; Foreign Office, 1937-39; Min. of Economic Warfare, 1939-40; Foreign Office, 1940-43 and 1947-54; Ankara Embassy, 1943-45; Beirut Legation, 1945-47; HM Ambassador to Laos, 1955-56 (Minister Sept. 1954-July 1955); resigned from HM Diplomatic Service, 1958. FLS 1968. *Recreations:* music, gardening and travel. *Heir: (to Irish Barony only*): *cousin,* Reginald Stanislaus Victor Talbot, MC [*b* 7 May 1897; *m* 1924, Cecily Elizabeth, *d* of Major Garstang Hodgson, Clevedon, Som.; one *d*]. *Address:* Malahide Castle, Co. Dublin. *Clubs:* Brooks's; Kildare Street (Dublin).   *[Died 14 April 1973.*

TALBOT OF MALAHIDE, 8th Baron *cr* 1831 (Ire.); **Reginald Stanislaus Victor Talbot,** MC 1918; Baron Malahide of Malahide (Ire.), 1831; Hereditary Lord Admiral of Malahide and adjacent seas (15 Edward IV); *b* 7 May 1897; *s* of John Reginald Charles Talbot (*d* 1909) and Maria Josephine (*d* 1939), *d* of 3rd Duc de Stacpoole; *S* to Irish barony of cousin, 7th Baron Talbot de Malahide, CMG, 1973; *m* 1924, Cecily Elizabeth, *d* of Major Garstang Hodgson; one *d*. *Educ:* Beaumont Coll., Old Windsor. Formerly Pilot Officer, RAFVR; served European War, 1914-18, Captain Royal Berkshire Regt (MC). *Heir: b* Joseph Hubert George Talbot [*b* 22 April 1899; *m* 1st, 1924, Hélène (*d* 1961), *o d* of M. Gouley; 2nd, 1962, Beatrice Bros]. *Address:* Llyswen, Brecon.   *[Died 2 April 1975.*

TALBOT, Bridget Elizabeth, OBE 1920; Croce di Guerra; National Labour Council; *d* of late Hon. Alfred Chetwynd-Talbot, *y s* of 18th Earl of Shrewsbury and Emily Louisa Augusta, *e d* of 5th Baron Walsingham. Belgian refugee committee, 1914; Anglo-Italian Red Cross, 1916-19 (Italian Medal for Valour); 1920-22, in Turkey started committee to deal with Russian refugees and later co-operative farm colony in Asia Minor; went to Russia, 1932, with Lady Muriel Paget's Mission. Sailed on 4-masted sailing ship Pamir to Finland, 1937. Started National Labour enquiry into state of Merchant Navy, 1939. Invented a watertight electric torch for lifebelts and was instrumental in getting these made compulsory by Parliament for all MN, RAF and RN personnel, and so saved hundreds of lives. In 1914 started the cultivation of co-operative gardens on waste land; Ministry of Agriculture later adopted the scheme all over the country. Was instrumental in securing Ashridge Estate to National Trust. Contested Bermondsey (L), 1950. Lord of the Manor of Scorton; hereditary Gov. Scorton Gram. Sch. Vice-Pres. Red Ensign Club; Vice-Pres. Watch Ashore Assoc. Hon. Mem., St Dunstan's Governing Cttee. Hon. Officer, Roman Grenadier Guards (apptd following battle of Monte Santo, 1917). *Publication:* treatise on co-ordinating Empire sea and air Transport. *Address:* Little Gaddesden House, Berkhamsted, Herts; Kiplin Hall, Scorton, Yorks.   *[Died 29 Nov. 1971.*

TALBOT, Lt-Gen. Sir Norman (Graham Guy), KBE 1969 (OBE 1945); TD 1950; Director-General, Army Medical Services, 1969-73, retired; *b* Hastings, 16 Feb. 1914; *s* of late Rev. Richard Talbot, MA, and late Ethel Maude Talbot (*née* Stuart); *m* 1939, Laura Winifred, *d* of late William Kilby, Donington, Lincs; two *s* one *d*. *Educ:* Reigate Grammar Sch.; King's Coll., London; King's Coll. Hosp. MRCS, LRCP 1937; MB, BS London 1938; DA England 1939; MRCOG 1951; MD London 1953; FRCOG 1960; FRCP 1973. Commission into RAMC from RAMC (TA), Aug. 1939. Served War of 1939-45 (despatches, twice, OBE): in BEF, 1939-40; Egypt, Palestine and Syria, 1941-43; Sicily and Italy, 1943-46. Consultant Adviser in Obstetrics and Gynæcology to Army, 1951-58 and 1963-66. Served in Malta, 1958-61, and in Germany, 1961-63; DDMS, 1 (Br.) Corps, 1967-68; Comdt and Dir of Studies, Roy. Army Med. Coll., 1968-69. Brig. 1967; Maj.-Gen. 1968; Lt-Gen. 1969. Comr, Royal Hosp. Chelsea, 1969-73; Med. Dir, Margaret Pyke Centre, 1974-78; Mem. Control Bd, Army Benevolent Fund, 1972-78; Vice-Pres., Finsbury Rifles OCA. FRSM; Mem. Council, Section of Obstetrics and Gynaecology of RSM, 1968-71; Vice-Pres., United Services Section, RSM, 1969-73; Examiner: RCOG; Central Midwives Board. Fellow, 1968-77, and Counsellor, 1973-74, Med. Soc. London; Mem., Anglo-German Med. Soc.; Liveryman, Soc. of

Apothecaries of London; Freedom of City of London. QHS 1968-73. CStJ 1970 (OStJ 1966). *Publications:* contribs to various medical jls. *Recreations:* gardening, travel. *Address:* The Beeches, 76 Church Road, Fleet, Hants GU13 8LB. *T:* Fleet 7727.   *[Died 27 Feb. 1979.*

TALBOT RICE, David; *see* Rice.

TAMM, Igor Evgenievich; Soviet physicist; Head of Theoretical Department of the Lebedev Institute of Physics under USSR Academy of Sciences; *b* 1895. *Educ:* Moscow University. Worked at Moscow University from 1924; produced quantum theory of acoustical vibrations and scattering of light in solid bodies, developed theory of interaction of light with electrons (1930); indicated existence of surface states (Tamm's Levels) of electrons in crystals, 1933; developed theory of nuclear forces due to exchange of electrons and neutrinos (*β*-forces), 1934, produced jointly Cherenkov Radiation theory 1937. Institute of Physics, Academy of Sciences of USSR, 1934-. Suggested, with others, a method of obtaining controlled thermonuclear reaction, 1950. Mem. Acad. of Sciences, USSR, 1953; For. Mem., Polish Acad. of Sciences, 1961; For. Mem. Amer. Acad. of Arts and Sciences, 1961. Awarded Nobel Prize for Physics (jointly with P. A. Cherenkov and I. M. Frank) for discovery and interpretation of Cherenkov effect, 1958. Hero of Socialist Labour; State Prize. *Publications:* Foundations of the Theory of Electricity, 1929, 8th edn 1966; Exchange Forces Between Neutrons and Protons, 1937; Relativistic Interaction of Elementary Particles, 1945. *Address:* Lebedev Institute of Physics, Academy of Sciences of the USSR, Leninski Prospekt 53, Moscow, B-17, USSR.   *[Died 12 April 1971.*

TANGLEY, Baron *cr* 1963 (Life Peer), of Blackheath, Co. Surrey; **Edwin Savory Herbert,** KBE 1956; Kt 1943; LLB; Hon. LLD: Montreal 1956; Leeds 1960; Solicitor; *b* 29 June 1899; *s* of Henry William Herbert; *m* 1932, Gwendolen Hilda, *d* of late Thomas Langley Judd, CBE; one *s* three *d*. *Educ:* Queen's College, Taunton; Law Society's Law School. Solicitor, Senior Partner Sydney Morse & Co.; Chairman, Ultramar Co. Ltd, 1946-70, Consultant 1970-; Chairman: The Industrial and General Trust Ltd, 1954-72; Trustees Corporation Ltd, 1954-72, and other companies. Director: Rediffusion Ltd, 1946- (Dep. Chm., 1946-47, 1954-); Rediffusion TV Ltd (Dep. Chm., 1964-70); Imperial Continental Gas Assoc., and other companies. Served at sea as Signalman RNVR, 1917-19; LLB London, 1919 (University Law Scholar); Solicitor, 1920; Mem. Council, Law Soc., 1935-58 (Pres., 1956); Mem. various Departmental Cttees; Aliens Tribunal, 1939; Chm., London Regional Price Regulation Cttee, 1939-40; Dir-Gen., Postal and Telegraph Censorship Dept, 1940-45; Member: Inter-dept Cttee on Matrimonial Causes, 1947; Inter-dept Cttee on Leaseholds, 1948; Chairman: Cttee on Intermediaries, 1949; Cttee of Inquiry into Electricity Supply Industry, 1954; Royal Commn: on Local Govt in Greater London, 1957; on Trade Unions and Employers' Assocs, 1965-68. Pres., Court of Arbitration, Internat. Chamber of Commerce, 1970-. Pres. Alpine Club, 1953-55 (Hon. Sec. 1935-40); Chm. Finance Committee, Trans-Antarctic Expedition. Hon. Fellow, 1969, and Hon. LLD, 1969, Darwin Coll., Cambridge. Medal for Merit, USA; King Haakon's Liberty Cross, 1947. *Recreations:* mountaineering, ski-ing, sailing. *Address:* Tangley Way, Blackheath, near Guildford, Surrey. *T:* Bramley 3072. *Clubs:* Athenæum, Reform, Alpine; RYS (Cowes); Royal Corinthian Yacht (Burnham-on-Crouch).   *[Died 5 June 1973.*

TANKERVILLE, 8th Earl of, *cr* 1714; **Charles Augustus Ker Bennet,** FZS; ARAeS; Baron Ossulston, 1682; JP Northumberland; Flight-Lieutenant RAFVR; late Captain RAF; *b* 16 Aug. 1897; *s* of 7th Earl and Leonora Sophie (*d* 1949), *d* of J. G. Van Marter, of New York; *S* father, 1931; *m* 1st, 1920, Roberta (marriage dissolved, 1930), *e d* of Mrs Percy Mitchell; two *s* ; 2nd, 1930, Violet, *d* of Erik Pallin, Stockholm; one *s* one *d*. *Heir: s* Lord Ossulston. *Address:* Estate House, Chillingham, Alnwick, Northumberland. *T:* Chatton 213.   *[Died 1 Dec. 1971.*

TANKERVILLE, 9th Earl of, *cr* 1714; **Charles Augustus Grey Bennet;** Baron Ossulston, 1682; Flight Lieutenant RAFVR; *b* 28 July 1921; *er s* of 8th Earl of Tankerville, and of Roberta, *d* of late Percy Mitchell; *S* father, 1971; *m* 1st, 1943, Virginia Diether (from whom he obtained a divorce, 1950), Vancouver; one *d* ; 2nd, 1954, Georgiana Lilian Maude, *d* of late Gilbert Wilson, DD, of Vancouver, Canada; one *s* two *d* (of whom one *s* one *d* are twins). Joined RAF 1941; Flight Lieut 1943. *Heir: s* Lord Ossulston. *Address:* 139 Olympia Way, San Francisco, Calif, USA.   *[Died 27 April 1980.*

TANNER, Sir Edgar (Stephen), Kt 1968; CBE 1957; ED; Member for Ripponlea, then for Caulfield, Victoria, in Victorian Legislative Assembly, since 1955, Chairman of Committees, since 1970, and Deputy Speaker, since 1973; President, Australian Olympic Federation, 1973-77 (Hon. Secretary and Treasurer, 1946-72); *b* Albany, WA, 1914; *s* of late Edgar Tanner; *m* 1938, Edna, *d* of late Miles de H. Ponsonby; one *s* one *d. Educ:* All Saints' Gram. Sch., Melbourne; Melbourne Univ. (boxing Blue). Served War of 1939-45 as Captain 2nd AIF (prisoner). Victorian Legislative Assembly: Member: Industries and Labour Cttee; Constitution Cttee; State Develt Cttee; Liberal Party Jt Policy Cttee. Hon. Sec. Organising Cttee, Olympic Games, Melbourne, 1956; Hon. Gen. Manager Australian Teams: Olympic Games, London, 1948; Commonwealth Games, Perth, 1962; Member Australian Delegn: Olympic Games, Helsinki 1952, Rome 1960, Tokyo 1964, Mexico City 1968, Munich 1972, Montreal 1976; Commonwealth Games, Auckland 1950, Edinburgh 1970, Christchurch 1973. President: Australian Commonwealth Games Assoc.; Olympians International; Australian Amateur Boxing Union; Victorian AAA; Soc. of Sen. Execs. Life Member: Aust. Commonwealth Games Assoc.; Victorian Olympic Council Commonwealth Parly Assoc. Life Governor: Vic. Amateur Boxing Assoc. (Pres.); Vic. Amateur Wrestling Assoc.; Aust. Olympic Fedn. Pres., Melbourne Univ. Boxing Club; Patron, Aust. Fireball Yacht Racing Assoc. Life Governor, Royal Children's Hosp.; Mem. Exec., Good Neighbour Council. Life Member: Caulfield Historical Soc; Nat. Parks Soc. *Address:* Parliament House, Melbourne, Victoria 3002, Australia; 190 Hawthorn Road, Caulfield, Vic. 3161, Australia. *Clubs:* Naval and Military, Victoria, Amateur Sports, Melbourne Cricket (Melbourne); Elwood Servicemen's.
[Died 21 Nov. 1979.]

TANNER, Herbert George, LLD; JP; Managing Director, E. S. & A. Robinson, Ltd and its subsidiary companies, until retirement in 1945; Director of Friends Provident and Century Life Office and Century Insurance Co. Ltd, 1940-58, retired (Chairman, 1945-55; Deputy Chairman, 1955-58); *b* 19 Nov. 1882; 2nd *s* of S. T. Tanner, JP, Bath; *m* 1906, Agatha Mary (*d* 1957), *d* of Edwin L. Gales, Bath; one *d* (two *s* decd). *Educ:* privately. Sheriff of Bristol, 1930-31; Treasurer of Bristol Univ., 1939-57, Pro-Chancellor, Nov. 1957-; JP Bristol since 1934; formerly Chairman of Justices, Bristol, and of Bristol Licensing Justices; JP Somerset, 1940; Chairman SW Reg. Hospital Board, 1947-53. Hon. LLD (Bristol), 1954. *Address:* Trinmore, Clifton Down, Bristol 8. *T:* Bristol 36409.   [Died 24 March 1974.]

TANNER, Lawrence Edward, CVO 1953 (MVO 1932, 5th cl. 1932, 4th cl. 1948); MA, FSA; Emeritus Librarian, Westminster Abbey (Librarian, 1956-72; Keeper of the Muniments, 1926-66); Secretary HM's Royal Almonry, 1921-64; *b* 12 Feb. 1890; *y s* of Ralph Tanner, Senior Assistant Master, Westminster School, and Lucy L. le G., *d* of G. L. Phipps Eyre; *m* 1945, Joan Doreen (*d* 1971), *e d* of Hon. Assheton N. Curzon. *Educ:* Westminster; Pembroke College, Cambridge. Hist. Tripos Pts I and II; Winchester Reading Prize, Cambridge University, 1912; BA, 1912; MA, 1919; Lieutenant (Gen. List), European War; Master, History Form, Westminster School, 1919-32; Clerk to Worshipful Company of Weavers, 1919-60 (Member Court, 1960); Upper Bailiff, Weavers Company, 1963-64. FSA 1926 (Vice-President, 1951-55); FRHistS, 1929 (Council, 1936-39); Vice-President, Society of Genealogists, 1939; Hon. Vice-Pres., R Arch. Inst. 1952. President, Brit. Archæological Association, 1951-56. OStJ, 1931. Gold Staff Officer, Coronations 1937 and 1953. Hon. DLitt Southampton, 1967. *Publications:* Westminster School, its Buildings and their Associations, 1923; Story of Westminster Abbey, 1932; Westminster School: A History, 1934 (2nd ed 1951); Recent Investigations regarding the fate of the Princes in the Tower, 1935; Unknown Westminster Abbey (King Penguin), 1948; The History of the Coronation, 1952; The History and Treasures of Westminster Abbey, 1953; Recollections of a Westminster Antiquary, 1969; articles and lectures on Westminster Abbey, etc. *Recreation:* fishing. *Address:* 32 Westminster Mansions, Great Smith Street, SW1P 3BP. *T:* 01-222 5753. *Club:* Athenæum.
[Died 15 Dec. 1979.]

TAPP, Norman Charles, QC 1967; a Recorder of the Crown Court, since 1976; *b* 22 May 1925; *e s* of C. Charles and late Dorothea Tapp; *m* 1951, Patricia Rose Whatmoor; three *s. Educ:* Lydgate House, Hunstanton; Bootham Sch.; Corpus Christi, Cambridge. RNVR, 1943-46. Called to Bar, Gray's Inn, 1948, Bencher 1972. *Recreations:* sailing, gardening, music. *Address:* Hamptons Farm House, Shipbourne, Tonbridge, Kent. *T:* Plaxtol 547.   [Died 9 Aug. 1977.]

TARBAT, Sir John Allan, Kt 1937; *b* 1891; *s* of late John Allan Tarbat, Arbroath, Angus, Scotland; *m* 1918, Gladys Victoria (decd), *d* of Thomas Fuller James, Melbourne; one *d*; *m* 1960, Rita Grace, *er d* of late Herbert Wallis Marsh, Beckenham, Kent. *Educ:* Queen's Park School, Glasgow. Fellow: Chartered Institute of Secretaries; Certified and Corporate Accountants; Royal Society of Arts. Member of Senate, Ceylon, 1947-55. Formerly General Manager of James Finlay & Co. Ltd, Colombo; Chairman of Ceylon Chamber of Commerce, 1932-40 and 1945-47. *Address:* Old Well Cottage, Tompset's Bank, Forest Row, East Sussex.   [Died 7 Oct. 1977.]

TARRANT, Dorothy, MA Cantab, MA, PhD London; Professor Emeritus of Greek, University of London; *b* 7 May 1885; *d* of late Rev. William George Tarrant, Wandsworth, and Alice, *d* of Henry Stanley of Manchester. *Educ:* Clapham High School (LCC Scholar); Girton College, Cambridge (Scholar). Classical Tripos, Cambridge, Part I 1907, Part II (Ancient Philosophy), 1908; London BA Hons Classics, 1906; MA 1909, PhD 1930; at Girton, Agnata Butler and Thérèse Montefiore Prizes, and Gilchrist Fellowship for research, 1908-9; Assistant Lecturer in Classics, Bedford College, 1909; in Greek, 1915; Lecturer, 1921; University Reader, 1929; University Professor and Head of Greek Department, 1936-50. Hon. Fellow: Girton Coll., 1955; Bedford Coll., 1969; Manchester Coll., Oxford, 1969. President: Unitarian Assembly, 1952-53, Hellenic Society, 1953-56, Classical Association, 1957-58. *Publications:* The Hippias Major attributed to Plato, 1928; contributions to Year's Work in Classical Studies, and to various classical and other periodicals. *Address:* 3 Alcon Court, 20 Earlsfield Road, Wandsworth, SW18 3DW. *T:* 01-870 3785. *Club:* University Women's.
[Died 4 Sept. 1973.]

TARRY, Frederick Thomas, CB 1962; CBE 1946 (OBE 1937); MM; HM Inspector of Constabulary, 1946-62; *b* 19 Dec. 1896; *m* 1922, Frances Winter (*d* 1967); two *s. Educ:* Hartfield, Sussex. Served European War, 1914-19 (despatches, MM and Bar) in Queen's Own (Royal West Kent) Regiment. Served in Brighton police force, 1919-30; chief constable, Exeter, 1930-40; chief constable, Southampton, 1941-46. Serving Brother, Ven. Order of St John, 1933. King's Gold Medal, 1932; King's Police Medal, 1941. Trustee, Police Coll. and Chm., Coll. Adv. Cttee, 1948-62; Mem., Southampton Group HMC, 1955-71; Chm., Knowle Group HMC, 1967-72. *Address:* 13 Sherwood Road, Chandlers Ford, Hants.   [Died 5 Oct. 1976.]

TASKER, Rev. Canon Derek Morris Phipps; Canon Residentiary and Treasurer of Southwark Cathedral since 1962; Director of Post-ordination Training for Diocese of Southwark, since 1965; Director of Ordinands, since 1968; *b* 15 Nov. 1916; *er s* of late Morris Bennet and Geraldine Emily Tasker. *Educ:* Sherborne Sch.; Exeter Coll., Oxford (BA, DipTheol); Westcott House, Cambridge. Curate, St Mary Redcliffe, Bristol, 1939-47; Vicar, St Stephen, Southmead, Bristol, 1947-55; King George VI Training Officer, Church of England Youth Council, 1955-62. *Publications:* The Parish and Young People, 1957; Letters to an Apprentice, 1958; Vocation and Work, 1960; Training the Youth Group, 1960. *Recreations:* English literature, contemporary theatre, cricket. *Address:* 2 Sandover House, Ormond Road, Richmond, Surrey. *T:* 01-948 0463.
[Died 26 March 1978.]

TASKER, Rev. Randolph Vincent Greenwood, MA, BD Cantab; DD Lambeth; Professor of New Testament Exegesis, King's College, London, 1953-61; Professor Emeritus since 1961; *b* 31 Aug. 1895; *s* of William Henry and Evelyn Tasker; *m* 1928, Helen, *d* of Robert Wilkinson, MD; one *s* one *d. Educ:* Rossall; Corpus Christi College, Cambridge; Westcott House, Cambridge. Curate of Christ Church, Purley, 1922-24; Domestic Chaplain to Bishop Burge, Bishop of Oxford, 1924-25; Lecturer at King's College, London, 1926; Rector of Chenies, Bucks, 1928-34; Head of Department of New Testament, King's College, London, 1934; Chaplain of Lincoln's Inn, 1936-39; Rector of Lambourne with Abridge, 1942-46; Exam. Chap. to Bp of Ripon, 1938-46, to Bp of Salisbury, 1946-58; Dean of Faculty of Theology, University of London, 1948-52, and 1956-59. DD Lambeth, 1961. *Publications:* The Nature and Purpose of the Gospels, 1944; The Old Testament in the New Testament, 1945; The Gospel in the Epistle to the Hebrews, 1950; The Biblical Doctrine of the Wrath of God, 1951; The Narrow Way, 1952; The Epistle of James, 1956; The Second Epistle of Paul to the Corinthians, 1958; The Gospel according to John, 1960; The Gospel according to Matthew, 1961; Greek New Testament, 1964; Editor Augustine. City of God (Everyman's Library), 1945; articles in Church Quarterly Review, Journal of Theological Studies, Harvard Theological Review, etc. *Address:* 42 Stafford Way, Hassocks, Sussex.   [Died 17 March 1976.]

TATTON-SYKES, Sir (Mark Tatton) Richard, 7th Bt, *cr* 1783; JP; DL; Chairman, Driffield Magistrates, 1969-75; *b* 24 Aug. 1905; *s* of Sir Mark Sykes, 6th Bt, MP, and late Edith Violet, 3rd *d* of Rt. Hon. Sir J. E. Gorst; *S* father, 1919; changed name by deed poll to Tatton-Sykes, 1977; *m* 1942, Virginia (*d* 1970), *o d* of John Gilliat and Lillian (widow of 5th Marquess of Anglesey and *d* of Sir George Chetwynd, 4th Bt); four *s* two *d*. *Educ:* Downside; Trinity Coll., Cambridge. Member East Riding County Council, 1931-70, Alderman 1946-70; President: Bridlington Div. Conservative Assoc., 1948-77; East Riding Georgian Soc., 1962-75; E Yorkshire Local History Soc. 1968-71; Northern Counties Concert Soc. Lieutenant 5th Bn The Green Howards, 1925-27; Lt 7th Bn The Green Howards, 1939; served France, 1940; Captain, 1940. Lt-Col 1952. Jt Master, E Middleton Foxhounds, 1931-39; Member, Jockey Club, 1947-; JP E Yorks and N Humberside, 1945-. High Sheriff, Yorks, 1948-49; DL Yorks, 1953, N Humberside, 1974. *Recreations:* horse breeding, coursing, organist. *Heir: s* Tatton Christopher Mark Sykes, *b* 24 Dec. 1943. *Address:* Sledmere, Driffield, North Humberside. *Club:* White's.   *[Died 24 July 1978.*

TATUM, Dr E(dward) L(awrie); Member and Professor, Rockefeller University, New York, NY, since 1957; *b* 14 Dec. 1909; *s* of Arthur L. and Mabel W. Tatum; *m* 1st, 1934, June Alton; two *d*; *m* 1956, Viola Kantor. *Educ:* University of Wisconsin. Asst Prof. of Biology, Stanford Univ., 1941-45; Assoc. Prof. of botany, 1945-46, Prof. of microbiology, 1946-48, Yale Univ.; Prof. of biology, 1948-56, Prof. of biochemistry, 1956-57, Stanford Univ. (jointly) Nobel prize for physiology and medicine, 1958. *Publications:* more than 100 papers in learned journals. *Recreations:* music (French horn); sports (swimming, skiing, etc). *Address:* 450 East 63rd Street, New York, NY 10021, USA. *T:* TE 8-5645.   *[Died 5 Nov. 1975.*

TAYLER, Admiral (retired) Sir Richard Victor S.; *see* Symonds-Tayler.

TAYLOR, Prof. Alan Carey, BA Sydney, DUP, DèsL, Lauréat de l'Académie Française; Visiting Professor of French, University of Cape Coast, Ghana, since 1972; *b* Goulburn, NSW, 11 Feb. 1905; *s* of late W. Carey Taylor; *m* Yvonne Albertine Antoinette, *d* of Ernest Le Gal, Conseiller à la Cour d'appel, Caen; two *s* one *d*. *Educ:* North Sydney High School; Univ. of Sydney, Sydney Teachers' College; University of Paris. BA 1926, Dip. Mod. Lang. 1927; French Govt Travelling Schol., 1927; DUP, 1929. Taught at North Sydney and Goulburn High Schools; Lecturer, Univ. of Sydney, 1933; Rep. Sydney Univ. at Internat. Phonetics Congress, 1935; DèsL, 1938; Lecturer and Senior Lecturer, Melbourne Univ., 1938-48; Prof. of French, Birkbeck Coll., Univ. of London, 1948-72. French Translator and Announcer, Radio Australia, 1941-48; Vice-Pres. French Australian Assoc. of Victoria, 1944-48; Hon. Pres., Assoc. of Heads of French Departments, 1973- (Hon. Sec., 1950-72); Mem. Mixed Commission under Franco-British Cultural Convention, 1957-72. Exchange Professor, University of Paris, 1959, Univ. of Moscow, 1969. Mem. Senate, Univ. of London, 1963-72, Dean of Faculty of Arts, 1968-72. Croix des Forces Françaises Libres (hon.), 1947. Médaille de la Langue Française (French Acad.), 1948; Chevalier, Légion d'Honneur, 1961. Editor, Current Research in French Departments of UK Universities, 1952-72. *Publications:* Carlyle: sa premiére fortune littéraire en France, 1929; Carlyle et la pensée latine, 1937; Le Président de Brosses et l'Australie, 1938. Annotated Edns Th Gautier: Jean et Jeannette, 1934; A Book of French Verse, 1939; Contes et nouvelles, 1942; Vingt et un Contes, 1949. Contributions to learned periodicals, mainly on 19th Century Literature. *Recreations:* walking, swimming, reading. *Address:* 29 Menelik Road, Hampstead, NW2. *T:* 01-435 6264.   *[Died 13 March 1975.*

TAYLOR, Albert Booth, MA Oxon; Professor of English Language and Literature, University of Tasmania, 1925-57, Professor Emeritus since 1957; *b* Manchester, 1896; *s* of A. Taylor, Auckland, NZ; *m* 1931, Molly, *o d* of Douglas Fitzgerald, Hobart; three *s*. *Educ:* Auckland Grammar School; Auckland University College; Merton College, Oxford (First Class Honours in English). University Scholar, University of New Zealand, 1914; Overseas Scholarship from Rhodes Trust, 1918; served in New Zealand Expeditionary Force, 1915-18; Lecturer in English, Leeds University, 1920-21; Armstrong College, Durham University, 1921-25. *Publications:* An Introduction to Mediæval Romance, 1930; The History of Long Diphthongs in Middle Kentish, Modern Language Review, Jan. 1924; edit. Floris and Blanchefleur, 1927; edit. Shakespeare's Macbeth, 1936 and Merchant of Venice, 1937. *Recreation:* bowling. *Address:* 316 Davey Street, Hobart, Tasmania. *T:* Hobart 2-2203.   *[Died 12 Sept. 1971.*

TAYLOR, Alexander Burt, CBE 1961; *b* 6 June 1904; *s* of Rev. A. B. Taylor; *m* 1st, 1935, Jean Allardice (*d* 1959); two *s* one *d*; 2nd, 1965, Elizabeth Gordon (née Hogg). *Educ:* Hamilton Academy; Kirkwall Grammar School; Edinburgh University; Columbia University. MA Edinburgh 1925; DLitt Edinburgh 1935. Inspector of Schools, Scottish Education Dept, 1933; Principal, Dept of Health for Scotland, 1939; Asst Sec., 1947; Registrar General for Scotland, 1959-66. Member of interdepartmental cttees on medical auxiliaries, 1949-51, on rehabilitation, 1953-56, and on number of doctors, 1955-57. FRSE 1961. *Publications:* Orkneyinga Saga, A New Translation with Introduction and Notes, 1938; articles on educational, historical and linguistic topics. *Recreations:* gardening, woodwork, studies in Scandinavian influences on Scottish History, study of early Scottish maps. *Address:* 35 Balgreen Road, Edinburgh 12. *T:* 031-337 3681.   *[Died 13 March 1972.*

TAYLOR, Rear-Admiral Alfred Hugh, CB 1942; OBE 1919; retired; *b* 24 Oct. 1886; 3rd *s* of late Alfred Taylor, JP, of Starston Place, Norfolk; *m* 1911, Maud Violet (*d* 1959), *e d* of late Col Sir William Bisset, KCIE; three *s* one *d*. *Educ:* HMS Britannia. Entered Navy, 1901; Rear-Adm. and retired, 1936; rejoined, 1939-45; JP, Norfolk, 1937, DL 1951. *Address:* The Manor House, Diss, Norfolk. *T:* Diss 2096. *Clubs:* United Service & Royal Aero; Norfolk (Norwich).
   [Died 16 Aug. 1972.

TAYLOR, Prof. (Alfred) Maurice, PhD, MA; FInstP; Professor of Physics, University of Southampton, 1945-68, now Emeritus Professor; *b* 6 Feb. 1903; *o s* of Alfred Ernest Taylor, MA, Clerk in Holy Orders, and Helen Caroline Georgiana (née Adams); *m* 1938, Sarah Margaret Alston, *yr d* of Edward Judge; one *s* one *d*. *Educ:* Reigate Grammar School; Trinity College, Cambridge. Sen. Schol., Alhusen and Coutts-Trotter Research Student, etc, Trinity Coll., Cambridge, 1921-27; PhD Cambridge 1927, MA 1928. Madden Prizeman, TCD, 1928; Ramsay Memorial Fellow, 1927-29. Asst Prof. of Physical Optics, Univ. of Rochester, NY, USA, 1929-34; Lectr in Natural Philosophy, Univ. of St Andrews, Scotland, 1934-45 (seconded to Southampton in 1941); Dep. Prof. of Physics, University Coll., Southampton, 1941-45; Vis. Lectr on the Tallman Foundation, Bowdoin Coll., Brunswick, Maine, USA, 1964-65; Vis. Professor: Hollins Coll., Virginia, USA, 1965-66; Bowdoin Coll., Brunswick, Maine, USA, 1968-69, 1969-70. *Publications:* (with F. I. G. Rawlins) Infra-red Analysis of Molecular Structure, 1929. Imagination and the Growth of Science (Tallman Lectures, 1964-65, given at Bowdoin College, USA), 1966. Papers in Proceedings Royal Society, Philosophical Magazine, Trans Faraday Soc., Proc. Physical Soc., Jl of Scientific Instruments, Jl of Optical Soc. of Amer., etc. *Recreations:* gardening, caravanning. *Address:* Randal's, Chilworth, Southampton SO1 7WS. *T:* Southampton 68114.
   [Died 7 May 1979.

TAYLOR, Arthur John Ernest, OBE 1968; Chairman, Skelmersdale Development Corporation, 1975-78; *b* 25 May 1913; *s* of Henry and Margaret Jane Taylor; *m* 1939, Lillian Joyce Mitchell; one *s* two *d*. *Educ:* Bootle Grammar Sch.; Liverpool Univ. (LLM). Solicitor. Royal Navy, 1941-45. Deputy Town Clerk, Bootle, 1947-63; Town Clerk and Chief Executive, Bootle, 1963-74; Chief Executive, Sefton Metropolitan District Council, 1974. SBStJ 1972. *Recreations:* gardening, travel. *Address:* Meresden, 14 St Andrews Road, Blundellsands, Liverpool L23 7UR. *T:* 051-924 2150.   *[Died 17 May 1979.*

TAYLOR, Maj.-Gen. Sir Brian; *see* Taylor, Maj.-Gen. Sir G. B. O.

TAYLOR, Desmond Maxwell; Chief Assistant to the Director-General (Regions), BBC, since 1977; *b* 1 June 1928; *s* of Alexander Taylor and Jane Bell; *m* 1958, Rosemary Anne Overfield. *Educ:* Ballymena Academy; Royal Belfast Academical Instn; Queen's Univ., Belfast. Northern Whig, 1951-53; Belfast Telegraph, 1953-54; BBC, 1954-; Editor, News and Current Affairs, BBC, 1971-77. *Address:* BBC, Broadcasting House, W1A 1AA. *T:* 01-580 4468.
   [Died 1 June 1978.

TAYLOR, Douglas, CMG 1960; Deputy Director General, Confederation of British Industry since 1966; *b* 22 May 1915; *s* of George Taylor, Oldham, Lancs; *m* 1947, Margaret Bryant; one *s* two *d*. *Educ:* Manchester Grammar School (foundn schol.); Oriel College, Oxford (schol.). Entered Ministry of Labour, 1939. Served War of 1939-45, RAF, Middle East, 1941-45. Seconded Commonwealth Department of Labour and National Service, Australia, 1948-51; Labour Attaché; British Embassy: Athens, 1954-55; Rome, 1955-59; Asst Sec., Min. of Labour, 1959-62, resigned from CS to become Internat. Sec.,

Brit. Employers' Confedn, 1962; Dep. Dir, 1963. Mem., SW Metropolitan Regional Hosp. Bd, 1970. *Address:* 14 Corkran Road, Surbiton, Surrey. *T:* 01-399 1554. *Club:* Reform.
[*Died* 24 *Nov.* 1971.

TAYLOR, (Edward) Wilfred, CBE 1946; FRS 1952; FRMS; FInstP; Hon. DSc Leeds, 1957; *b* 29 April 1891; *s* of Harold Dennis Taylor and Charlotte Fernandes Barff; *m* 1921, Winifred Mary, *d* of Edward George Hunter, Hastings; one *s*. *Educ:* Oundle School. Joined Messrs Cooke Troughton & Simms, 1908; served European War, 1914-19, Lieut RNVR Admiralty War Staff; Optical Manager, 1923; Technical Manager, 1932; Joint Managing Director, 1937-56; Director, 1956-61. Govt sponsored missions, US, 1943; Jena, 1945; Delegate, Commission Internationale d'Optique, 1948, 1950, 1953, 1956 and 1959. President Yorkshire Naturalists' Trust, 1952-70. DUniv York, 1977. *Publications:* Design and Construction of Surveying Instruments, 1938; contributions to technical and scientific journals, including Proceedings of the Royal Society, on microscopy and surveying. *Recreations:* fishing and ornithology. *Address:* Grimston Court, Hull Road, York YO1 5LE. *T:* York 489343.
[*Died* 1 *Nov.* 1980.

TAYLOR, Edwin, JP; *b* 1905; *s* of Lawrence Taylor and Elizabeth (*née* Waterhouse); *m* Sarah Elizabeth Rostron; one *s* one *d*. *Educ:* St John's School, Wingates; Bolton Technical College. Member Bolton Town Council, 1940-44 and 1947-, Alderman, 1955-74; Mayor, 1959-60, Dep. Mayor, 1960-61; Mem., Gtr Manchester Metropolitan CC, 1973-. Founder Chairman, Bolton and District Master Bakers' Assoc.; Master Baker; President Bolton Master Bakers, 1961. MP (C) Bolton East, Nov. 1960-Sept. 1964. Mem. Trade Union Gp attached to Conservative Party. Past Pres. Bolton Chamber of Trade. Pres., No 2 Area, St John Ambulance Bde, 1972-. JP Bolton 1952. SBStJ. *Recreations:* cricket and music. *Address:* 602 Tonge Moor Road, Bolton, Lancs. *T:* Bolton 51571. *Clubs:* Constitutional; Rotary (Bolton.
[*Died* 25 *Sept.* 1973.

TAYLOR, Edwin, CMG 1936; *b* 10 Nov. 1881; *m* 1912, E. M. Messom (*d* 1955); two *c*. *Educ:* Nottingham School; King's College, London. Colonial Office, 1901; served South African War, 1901; Board of Trade, 1902-05; Nyasaland, 1906-08; Asst Treasurer Uganda, 1909-16; Civil Administration German East Africa Occupied Territory, 1917-19; Treasurer, etc., Seychelles, 1919-23; Deputy Treasurer Uganda, 1923-25; President, Freetown Municipal Council, 1928; Deputy Treasurer, Sierra Leone, 1925-30; Treasurer, Hong Kong, 1931; Chairman Exchange Fund Advisory Committee, 1936; Assessor, Estate Duty Commissioner; retired, 1937. Temp. Administrative Officer Ministry Economic Warfare, 1940-42; Colonial Office, 1942-45. *Address:* 3 Cavendish Road, Bognor Regis, Sussex.
[*Died* 5 *Nov.* 1972.

TAYLOR, Elizabeth, (Mrs J. W. K. Taylor); author; *b* 3 July 1912; *d* of Oliver Coles and Elsie (*née* Fewtrell); *m* 1936, John William Kendall Taylor; one *s* one *d*. *Educ:* The Abbey School, Reading. *Publications:* At Mrs Lippincote's, 1946; Palladian, 1947; A View of the Harbour, 1949; A Wreath of Roses, 1950; A Game of Hide-and-Seek, 1951; The Sleeping Beauty, 1953; Hester Lilly and Other Stories, 1954; Angel, 1957; The Blush and Other Stories, 1958; In a Summer Season, 1961; The Soul of Kindness, 1964; A Dedicated Man, 1965; Mossy Trotter (for children), 1967; The Wedding Group, 1968; The Excursion to the Source, 1970; Mrs Palfrey at the Claremont, 1971; The Devastating Boys, 1972; *posthumous publication:* Blaming, 1976. *Address:* Grove's Barn, Penn, Buckinghamshire. *T:* Penn 3270.
[*Died* 19 *Nov.* 1975.

TAYLOR, Sir Eric Stuart, 2nd Bt, *cr* 1917; OBE; MA, MD Cantab; MRCP; Médaille des Epidémies; *b* 28 June 1889; *s* of 1st Bt and Helen Mary (*d* 1917), *d* of Frederic Manby of East Rudham, Norfolk; *S* father, 1920; *m* 1st, 1920, Evelyn Thérèse (*d* 1946), MA Oxon, JP County Gloucester, *er d* of late James Calvert, CBE, MD, FRCP; one *s* one *d*; 2nd, 1949, Lilian Rosamond (*d* 1958), widow of Mr Justice P. A. Farrer Manby, and *e d* of late E. H. Leeder, Swansea; 3rd 1959, Hope, widow of Norman Alfred Yarrow, Victoria, BC. *Educ:* Clifton; King's Coll., Cambridge (Exhibitioner), Guy's Hospital; Capt. RAMC, TF, 1914-19. Medical practice in Hong Kong, 1919-28; Cheltenham, 1928-46; City of London, 1947-53. Retired, 1953. Member Council Cheltenham Ladies' College. *Heir: s* Richard Laurence Stuart Taylor, MA Cantab. [*b* 27 Sept. 1925; *m* 1950, Iris Mary, *d* of Rev. E. J. Gargery; one *s* one *d*]. *Address:* Union Club of British Columbia, 805 Gordon Street, Victoria, BC, Canada. *Clubs:* United Oxford & Cambridge University; Union (BC).
[*Died* 25 *Oct.* 1977.

TAYLOR, Vice-Adm. Sir Ernest Augustus, Kt, *cr* 1952; CMG 1920; CVO 1919; *b* 1876; *s* of late Lt-Col F. H. Taylor, RHA; *m* 1st, 1898, Rose Isabel (*d* 1956), *d* of Louis Alexander Campbell; one *s* two *d*; 2nd, 1957, Hilda (Jill), widow of Major Horace Gough Turner. *Educ:* Stubbington. Commanded HMS Renown during Prince of Wales' tours in Canada, 1919, and Australia and New Zealand, 1920; Retired List, 1924. Served in the War, 1940-46. MP (Empire Crusade) South Paddington, 1930-31. (U), 1931-50. Member of London County Council for 3 years. Silver Medal, 1909, certificate, 1913, Royal Humane Society. Commander Crown of Italy, 1917. *Address:* Old Way House, Stogumber, Taunton, Somerset. *Club:* Royal Yacht Squadron (Cowes).
[*Died* 11 *March* 1971.

TAYLOR, Ernest Edward, CBE 1956; *b* 10 Dec. 1897; *s* of late Alfred George Taylor and Mary Taylor; *m* 1920, Dorothy Eileen (*d* 1969), *d* of Charles Henry Hardy; one *s* four *d*; *m* 1970, Elsa G. Kressig, *d* of late Robert J. Kressig, Kingston, Surrey. *Educ:* Epsom Coll. Dir, Onyx Country Estates Ltd. Dir, Brit. Sailors' Soc. *Address:* Hazelmere, 1 Chelwood Avenue, Goring by Sea, Worthing, Sussex. *Club:* City Livery.
[*Died* 1 *July* 1974.

TAYLOR, Lt-Col Eustace Trevor Neave, CIE 1943; MB, ChB; IMS, retired; *b* 8 Nov. 1894. *Educ:* Edinburgh University (MB, ChB 1917). IMS 1918-47; Lt-Col 1937; Served in France, Iraq and Burma; late Dep. Dir Gen. *Address:* Berkeley Square, Suite 40, Main Road, Rondebosch, Cape Town, South Africa.
[*Died* 7 *April* 1971.

TAYLOR, Rt. Rev. Francis John, MA Oxford; *b* 13 Nov. 1912; *er s* of late F. W. Taylor and Mrs Taylor, Hull, Yorks; *m* 1940, Margaret Emsé, *o d* of late W. H. Chapman and late Mrs Chapman, Bath; one *d* (one *s* decd). *Educ:* Hymers Coll., Hull; Queen's Coll., Oxford; Wycliffe Hall, Oxford. Scholar of Queen's Coll. Oxford; Holwell Student, Liddon Student. Deacon, 1936, priest, 1937; Curate of Walcot, Bath, 1936-38; Tutor and Lectr, 1938-42. Chaplain, 1939-42, Wycliffe Hall, Oxford; Chaplain, Corpus Christi Coll., Oxford, 1939; Actg Principal, Clifton Theol. Coll., 1942; Vicar of Christ Church, Claughton, Birkenhead, 1942-54; Vicar of St Andrew, Oxford, 1954-55. Proctor in Convocation and Member National Church Assembly: Dio. Chester, 1945-54, Dio. Oxford, 1955-62. Lectr William Temple Coll., 1947-53; Lectr St Aidan's Theol. Coll., 1950-54; WEA Lectr, 1947-54; Principal, Wycliffe Hall, Oxford, 1955-62; Bishop of Sheffield, 1962-71. Exam. Chap. to Bp of Oxford, 1955-56; Select Preacher: Univ. of Edinburgh, 1951; Univ. of Aberdeen, 1952; Univ. of Oxford, 1960-61, Governor: Dean Close School; Wrekin College; Headington School; Mem. C of E Bd of Educn. *Publications:* The Church of God, 1946; Into Thy Courts, 1947; (contrib. to) Theological Word Book of the Bible, 1950; The People of God, 1951; Becoming a Christian, 1954; The Doctrine of Justification by Faith, 1954; Scripture and Tradition, 1955; Anglo-Russian Theological Conference, 1958; Die Kirche von England, 1966. Contributor to: The Churchman, Theology, Church Quarterly Review. Editor of Parish and People, 1953-60. *Recreations:* literature, walking, ecclesiastical architecture. *Address:* Ranmoor Grange, Sheffield 10.
[*Died* 4 *July* 1971.

TAYLOR, Frank Herbert Graham, CIE 1941; *b* 17 Jan. 1890; *s* of late E. Taylor, HBM Consul, Dunkirk; unmarried. *Educ:* Haileybury College. Joined Indian Police, 1910; Director-General of Police and Jails, Hyderabad State, 1942-45; Managing Director, Sassoon J. David & Co. Ltd, Bombay, 1945-54; retired 1954. King's Police Medal, 1933. *Address:* c/o National and Grindlay's Bank Ltd, 13 St James's Square, SW1. *Clubs:* Oriental, Devonshire.
[*Died* 11 *May* 1971.

TAYLOR, Prof. Sir Geoffrey Ingram, OM 1969; Kt 1944; FRS 1919; formerly Yarrow Research Professor of the Royal Society; *b* 7 March 1886; *s* of Edward Ingram Taylor and Margaret, *d* of Dr George Boole; *m* 1925, Grace Stephanie Francis Ravenhill (*d* 1967). *Educ:* University Coll. School; Cambridge University. Elected to Fellowship at Trinity College, Cambridge, 1910; Meteorologist to Scotia Expedition to the North Atlantic, 1913; engaged in experimental aeronautics and meteorology during war of 1914-18; pilot's certificate at Brooklands, July 1915. Worked in Los Alamos, New Mexico, with group making first nuclear explosion, 1944-45. Dr (*hc*): Univ. of Paris (Fac. des Sciences), Oxford, Cambridge, London, Birmingham, Liverpool, Bristol, Edinburgh, Vancouver, Aachen, Oslo, Rice, Michigan. Royal Medal, 1933, Copley Medal, 1944, Royal Society; American Medal for Merit, 1947; Gold Medal, RAeS, 1954; Exner Medal, Oesterreichischer Gewerbeverein, 1954; de Morgan Medal, Lond. Math. Society, 1956; Internat. Panetti Prize and Medal, accad. delle Scienze di Torino (1st Award) 1958; Timoshenko Medal, Amer. Soc. of Mech. Engineers, 1958;

Kelvin Gold Medal, Instn of Civil Engineers, 1959; Franklin Medal, Franklin Inst., US, 1962; Platinum Medal, Inst. of Metals, 1964; James Watt International Gold Medal, 1965. Foreign corresponding or hon. member of numerous societies. *Publications:* papers on mathematics, meteorology, aeronautics and engineering in proceedings of learned societies. *Address:* Trinity College, Cambridge. *[Died 27 June 1975.*

TAYLOR, Maj.-Gen. Sir (George) Brian (Ogilvie), KBE 1942 (CBE 1919); CB 1940; RE; *b* 15 April 1887; *s* of late Edward Taylor and Mary Alexander; *m* Cecilia Maria Julia, *d* of late Col D. ffrench Mullen, retired IMS; one *s. Educ:* Cheltenham College; RMA, Woolwich. Served European War, 1914-19 (despatches, CBE); Asst Director of Works, BEF, Salonica, 1917-18; Dep. Director, 1918-19; Staff Officer to Chief Engineer, Aldershot, 1922-24; Deputy Assistant-Director of Fortifications and Works, War Office, 1924-26; Chief Instructor SME, Chatham, 1926-29; Chief Engineer to RAF Iraq, 1929-31. Assistant Director of Works, War Office, 1935-37; Chief Engineer, Northern Command, 1937-39; Director of Fortifications and Works, War Office, 1939-40; an Inspector-General, 1940; Director Bomb Disposal, 1941-42; Engineer-in-Chief, Persia and Iraq, 1942-43, retired pay, 1943. *Recreations:* golf, tennis, croquet, squash, badminton. *Address:* Tresillian, Durley Road, Seaton, Devon. *[Died 2 Sept. 1973.*

TAYLOR, George Francis, CBE 1943; Chairman, Bank of London and South America, 1970-71 (Deputy Chairman, 1966-70; Director, 1950); *b* 13 Jan. 1903; *s* of George Arthur Taylor and Anna Maria (*née* Ryan); *m* 1937, Vivian Judith Elizabeth, *d* of late Lt-Comdr Vivian Rose Price, RN; one *s* two *d. Educ:* Xavier Coll., Melbourne; Melbourne Univ. (MA, LLB). Served 1939-45 with Special Ops, (SOE), Middle East, Greece, Yugoslavia, India, SE Asia and SW Pacific; Chief of Staff, HQ, 1940-42; Colonel. TARO, 1945-53. FRSA 1967. *Recreation:* reading. *Address:* 20 Keane Street, Peppermint Grove, WA 6011, Australia. *Clubs:* Boodle's; Weld (WA); Melbourne (Vic.). *[Died 17 Jan. 1979.*

TAYLOR, Henry Archibald; CBE 1952; journalist; *b* 16 March 1892; *s* of George Taylor and Ellen E. Collins; *m* Mollie Little (Capt., WRAC, Retd); two *s.* After provincial experience, joined staff of Daily Chronicle; served European War, Western Front; Royal Fusiliers and Staff. Chm. Newspaper Features, Ltd, 1923-64; Editor, Empire Review, 1943-44; special political contributor, Evening Standard, 1945-46, Yorkshire Post, 1949-60; leader writer, Country Life 1956-; President Institute of Journalists, 1938; Member: Court of Bristol Univ., 1936-68; Lord Chancellor's Cttee on Law of Defamation, 1939-48. Chairman Restoration Cttee St Bride's Church, Fleet Street, 1951-57. Parliamentary Candidate (C) Doncaster, 1939-45, NE Leicester, 1949, contesting that division at General Election and subsequent by-election, 1950. *Publications:* Goodbye to the Battlefields, 1930; Smith of Birkenhead, 1931; The Strange Case of Andrew Bonar Law, 1932; Robert Donald, 1934; Jix, Viscount Brentford, 1935; Will You Be Left? (in collaboration), 1945; The British Press: a Critical Survey, 1961; (with Sir Linton Andrews) Lords and Labourers of the Press, 1970. *Address:* Oldwell House, Dummer, Basingstoke, Hants. *T:* Dummer 227. *Clubs:* Press, Whitefriars. *[Died 3 Nov. 1980.*

TAYLOR, Sir Hugh (Stott), KBE 1953; FRS 1932; DSc Liverpool, 1914; President Emeritus, Woodrow Wilson Fellowship Foundation; David B. Jones Professor of Chemistry Emeritus, Princeton University; Chairman of Chemistry Department, 1926-51; Dean of the Graduate School, 1945-58, retired; *b* St Helens, Lancashire, 6 Feb. 1890; *s* of James Taylor and Ellen Stott; *m* 1919, Elizabeth (*d* 1958), *d* of James Sawyer, Southport, Lancs; two *d. Educ:* Cowley School, St Helens; Liverpool University; Nobel Institute, Stockholm; Technische Hochschule, Hannover. From 1914 with Princeton University, Department of Chemistry; Munitions Inventions Department, London, 1917-19. Nichols Medallist, American Chemical Soc., 1928; Mendel Medallist, Villanova Coll., 1933; Franklin Medallist, Amer. Philos. Soc., 1941; Longstaff Medallist, Chem. Soc. London, 1942; Franklin Medallist, Franklin Inst., 1957; Proctor Prize, Research Soc. of Am., 1964. Francqui Professor, University of Louvain, Belgium, 1937. Member various scientific societies of USA and Europe; holds numerous Hon. degrees. Commander of Order of Leopold II of Belgium, 1938; Kt Comdr, Order of St Gregory (Papal), 1953. *Publications:* (with E. K. Rideal) Catalysis in Theory and Practice; Industrial Hydrogen; Treatise of Physical Chemistry (Editor and Part Author); Elementary Physical Chemistry; Fuel Production and Utilization; numerous articles on Physical Chemistry in various scientific journals. *Recreation:* photography. *Address:* 191 Library Place, Princeton, NJ 08540, USA. *TA:* Princeton, New Jersey. *T:* 924-2211. *Clubs:* Century, Princeton, Chemists (New York); Nassau (Princeton). *[Died 17 April 1974.*

TAYLOR, Air Vice-Marshal James Clarke, CB 1970; OBE 1953; Deputy Director General, RAF Medical Services, 1968-70, retired; *b* 6 July 1910; *s* of William and Agnes Taylor; *m* 1961, Moira Jane, *d* of late Sir Hector Macneal, KBE; no *c. Educ:* Glasgow Acad.; Glasgow Univ. Commissioned RAF, 1937; various appts; PMO, Arabian Peninsula, 1957-59; PMO, Near East Air Force, 1961-64; Officer Commanding Central Medical Estab., RAF, London, 1965-66; PMO, Bomber Command, 1967-68, Strike Command, 1968-69. QHP 1967-70. *Recreation:* golf. *Address:* Dormer Cottage, Aston Clinton, Bucks. *T:* Aylesbury 630217. *Clubs:* Royal Air Force; Royal and Ancient (St Andrews). *[Died 22 June 1978.*

TAYLOR, Sir John, Kt 1937; Solicitor; Senior Partner in Firm of John Taylor and Co., Manchester and Blackburn; *b* 28 March 1876; *s* of Joseph and Mary Berry Taylor; *m* 1904, Helen Louisa Anne (*d* 1944), *d* of John Jackson; one *s* one *d. Educ:* Whalley Grammar School; privately. Formerly Chm. and Leader of the Conservative Party in Blackburn and Leader of the Town Council; at time of resignation in 1936 Alderman of the Borough; for six years Chairman of the Finance Committee. *Publications:* many papers in connection with Factory Legislation, Yarn and Cloth Contracts-International Arbitration in the Cotton Trade and other Cotton Trade matters. *Club:* District and Union (Blackburn).
[Died 21 Jan. 1971.

TAYLOR, John Idowu Conrad; Hon. Mr Justice Taylor; Chief Justice of the High Court, Lagos, Nigeria, since July 1964; *b* 24 Aug. 1917; *s* of E. J. Alex. Taylor and Mrs R. A. Taylor; *m* 1st, 1943, Josephine Luke (*d* 1947); no *c* ; 2nd, 1949, Ivy Pratt; one *s* two *d. Educ:* Culford Sch., Bury St Edmunds; King's College, London; Brasenose College, Oxford. MA Oxford, 1944. Legal Practitioner, Dec. 1941-March 1956; Judge of High Court, W Reg. Nigeria, 1956-60; Justice of the Supreme Ct, Nigeria, 1960-64. Pro-Chancellor, Univ. of Lagos, 1967-. *Recreations:* cricket, tennis, motor sport, golf, fishing; formerly boxing (Blue for Oxford, 1936-40). *Address:* Chief Justice's Chambers, High Court, Lagos, Nigeria. *Club:* British Automobile Racing.
[Died 7 Nov. 1973.

TAYLOR, Sir John (William), KBE 1954 (MBE 1929); CMG 1947; *b* 1 Mar. 1895; *e s* of late John S. Taylor, Aberdeen; *m* 1st, Rachel (*d* 1925), *d* of late Rev. James Thomason Lang, Fellow of Corpus Christi; four *s* ; 2nd, Margaret (*d* 1961), *d* of James B. Simpson, CBE, MD Edinburgh; two *d* ; 3rd, 1961, Joan Maria Cecilia, *d* of late Bernard Hickman, Wolverhampton. *Educ:* Aberdeen University (MA). Served European War, 1914-18, in Gordon Highlanders; Captain 1916; entered HM Foreign Service, 1919; consular posts in France, Czechoslovakia, Austria, USA and Commercial Secretary for Central America; Dep. British Delegate on International Danube Commission, 1934-38; Commercial Counsellor, Prague, 1945-46; Minister (Commercial), Cairo, 1946; Minister (Commercial) British Embassy, Washington, 1948-50; British Ambassador to Mexico, 1950-54; Chm., British Mexican Soc., 1954-64; Dir Gen. Hispanic and Luso-Brazilian Councils, 1954-62. Council, Royal Geographical Soc., 1958-61; Council, Royal Soc. of Arts, 1959-65. Silver Medallist, Royal Soc. of Arts, 1958; Coronation Medal, 1953. Mexican Order of Aztec Eagle, First Class, 1958; Grand Cross, Order of Merit of Chile, 1959. *Address:* 25 Park Mansions, 141 Knightsbridge, SW1. *T:* 01-589 5648.
[Died 25 May 1974.

TAYLOR, Mrs John William Kendell; *see* Taylor, Elizabeth.

TAYLOR, Joseph Charlton, TD; Chairman, Mersey Docks and Harbour Board, since 1969 (Member since 1950); Vice-President, Docks and Harbours Authorities Association, 1969; Director, Cunard Steam-Ship Co. Ltd, and other companies; *b* 13 Aug. 1913; *er s* of late Percy James Taylor and Nancy Skelton Charlton; *m* 1948, Kathleen Margaret Williams; two *d. Educ:* Charterhouse. Served War of 1939-45, RASC (despatches 1944). Pres., Liverpool Cotton Assoc. Ltd, 1948-49. High Sheriff of Cheshire, 1971. *Recreations:* tennis, golf, gardening. *Address:* Fiddlestone Wood, Burton-in-Wirral, Cheshire. *T:* 051-336 2109. *Clubs:* Royal Thames Yacht; Racquet (Liverpool).
[Died 1 April 1971.

TAYLOR, Leonard Whitworth, OBE 1947; MA Oxon; retired; *b* 29 March 1880; *s* of Thomas Taylor, JP, CA; *m* 1904, Madeline Hills; no *c. Educ:* Warwick School; New College, Oxford. Assistant Master Stratford-on-Avon; Second Master, Bournemouth School; Headmaster Darlington Grammar School, 1913-33; Captain OTC and 5th Battalion DLI; served European War in France, 1916-18 (wounded, prisoner); Pres. IAHM, 1931; Secretary IAHM and HMC, 1934-55. *Address:* 8 Inman's Lane, Sheet, Petersfield, Hants. *Club:* National Liberal.
[Died 3 Jan. 1979.

TAYLOR, Lionel Robert Stewart; Civilian Consultant in Otolaryngology to Royal Navy, since 1962; Cons. ENT Surgeon: Charing Cross Hospital since 1950; Royal Masonic Hospital since 1962; King Edward VII Hospital for Officers, since 1963; *b* 4 Nov. 1915; *s* of Rev. Reginald Charles Taylor and Mildred Eleanor Taylor (*née* Stewart); *m* 1945, Gillian Bridget (*née* Baily); one *s* two *d. Educ:* Monkton Combe School; Emmanuel College, Cambridge; St Thomas's Hospital. BA Camb. 1937; MB, BChir 1940; FRCS Eng. 1946. Served RNVR, 1941-45. Chief Asst, ENT Dept, St Thomas's Hosp., 1948-50; Temp. Fellow in Otolaryngology, Yale Univ., USA, 1948. Mem., RAC Medical Panel, 1960. Mem., British Assoc. of Otolaryngologists (Hon. Sec. 1970). Mem. RPSL, 1970. FRSM (Hon. Treasurer 1968). Assistant Editor, Journal of Laryngology and Otology. *Recreations:* lawn tennis, gardening, philately, motor sport. *Address:* 55 Harley Street, W1. *T:* 01-580 3416. *Club:* Royal Automobile. *[Died 6 Nov. 1972.*

TAYLOR, Maurice; *see* Taylor, A. M.

TAYLOR, Peter Athol; JP; Master of the Supreme Court, Chancery Division, since 1970; *b* 12 Sept. 1926; *s* of Edward Athol William Taylor and Violet May Taylor; *m* 1951, Patricia Lois Wade; three *s* one *d. Educ:* Harrow. Lieut, Royal Berks Regt, 1945-47. Articled to father; admitted a Solicitor, 1950; Partner, T. Richards & Co., 1950-70. Mem. Board, Gardner Art Centre, Univ. of Sussex, 1970-73. JP Brighton, 1971. *Recreations:* the theatre, watching cricket. *Address:* Copthorne, 9 Radinden Drive, Hove, East Sussex. *T:* Brighton 554925. *Clubs:* MCC; Sussex County Cricket. *[Died 23 Oct. 1976.*

TAYLOR, Raymond Charles; Managing Director, Renmark Development Co. Pty Ltd, since 1976; Chairman, Waninga Pty Ltd; Director: Allumba Development Pty Ltd; South Australian Industries Assistance Corp.; Consul for the Netherlands in South Australia, since 1975; *b* 7 Nov. 1926; *s* of Frank Reeves Taylor and Doris Mills, Perth, WA; *m* 1959, Hilary Thérèse, *d* of A. J. Flanagan, Perth, WA; two *s* two *d. Educ:* James Street High Sch., Perth, WA. Asst to Gen. Manager, Western Australia Farmers Co-operative Ltd, 1948-54; Ampol Petroleum Ltd, 1954-71: Sales Manager, South Australia, 1961, Victoria, 1965; Branch Manager, South Australia, 1967-71; Agent-General and Trade Comr for S Australia in London, 1971-74; Chm., Monarto Develt Commn, 1974-76. Pres., SA Soccer Fedn Inc. *Recreation:* golf. *Address:* Renmark Development Co. Pty Ltd, 56 Carrington Street, Adelaide, S Australia 5000; 508 Greenhill Road, Hazelwood Park, S Australia 5066. *Club:* East India, Devonshire, Sports and Public Schools. *[Died 27 Feb. 1977.*

TAYLOR, Sir Reginald (William), Kt 1958; CMG 1951; MICE; Engineer-in-Chief, Crown Agents for Overseas Governments and Administrations, 1954-61; *b* 1 Dec. 1895; *y s* of John Edward Taylor, Dunkirk, France, and Mary Houldsworth (*née* Alexander); *m* 1928, Ruth du Boulay, *y d* of Dr W. J. Tyson, MD, FRCP, FRCS; two *s. Educ:* St Lawrence College, Ramsgate; University College, London (BSc). Served European War, 1914-18, France. Public Works Department: Uganda, 1921-37; Nigeria, 1938-51; Director of Public Works, Nigeria, 1947-51, Kenya, 1951-54. Fellow, UCL, 1963. *Publications:* Aerodrome Construction, 1945; Nigerian Highways, 1951. *Recreation:* sketching. *Address:* The Crown House, Great Haseley, Oxfordshire. *T:* Great Milton 226.
[Died 19 Oct. 1971.

TAYLOR, Sir Richard Laurence S.; *see* Stuart Taylor.

TAYLOR, Robert Walter, CMG 1933, CBE 1928 (OBE 1919); Controller of Exchange, Bahamas, 1947-56, retired; *b* 30 Nov. 1883; *y s* of late Joseph Needham Taylor; *m* 1930, Irene (*d* 1968), *er d* of Allister Macmillan, FRGS, FRSA. *Educ:* Emanuel Sch.; King's Coll., London. Somaliland, 1906-10; Uganda, 1910-14; Somaliland, 1914-20; Tanganyika, 1920-33; Treasury in each Territory; retired from post of Treasurer of Tanganyika in 1933; Receiver-General and Treasurer, Bahamas, 1936-42; Financial Secretary, Jamaica, 1942-47; retd, 1947. *Address:* Barclays Bank, 160 Piccadilly, W1.
[Died 21 March 1972.

TAYLOR, Stanley Grisewood, CIE 1946; Indian Police (retired); *b* 19 May 1893; *s* of Edmund Judkin Taylor, Solicitor, Bristol; *m* 1919, Coralie May, *d* of Robert Elphinstone Bradley, Indian Police; one *d* (one *s* decd). *Educ:* Clifton Coll. Appointed to Indian Police, 1913; seconded to Indian Army, 1916-19, serving in Mesopotamia, 1917-18; Principal, Police Training College, Bengal and Assam, 1936-39; Dep. Inspector-General of Police, Bengal, 1939; Inspector-General of Police, Bengal, 1945; retired 1947. Intelligence Officer, Ministry of Food, Tunbridge Wells,

1948; Deputy Chief Constable, Ministry of Civil Aviation Police, London, 1949; Commandant, Police College, Federation of Malaya, 1951-53. King's Police Medal, 1934; Indian Police Medal, 1944. *Address:* 1 Apsley Court, Ticehurst, Wadhurst, Sussex TN5 7BJ. *T:* Ticehurst 200264. *[Died 12 April 1980.*

TAYLOR, Wilfred; *see* Taylor, E. W.

TAYLOR, William, CB 1947; retired; Under-Secretary, Ministry of Labour and National Service, 1946-52; *b* 1 May 1892; *s* of late Alexander Taylor, Cullen, Banffshire; *m* 1st, 1919, Gaynor Yseult Brockbank; one *d*; 2nd, 1963, Mildred Hartley, Somerville College, Oxford. *Educ:* Fordyce Academy; Aberdeen University. MA 1st Class Hons Mental Philosophy, 1913; Hutton Prize; Bain Gold Medal. Served European War, 1914-18, 4th Battalion Gordon Highlanders (despatches, 1916; Captain). Asst Principal, Ministry of Labour, 1919; Chief Insurance Officer, 1937; Director of Services and Establishments, 1938; Vice-Chm. Civil Service Selection Board, 1945; UK Govt Deleg., Internat. Lab. Conf., Geneva, 1949; Chm. Rehabilitation Cttee, Brussels Treaty Powers, 1950; Chm. Working Party on Employment of Blind Persons, 1950-51; Mem. Bd of Management, Aberdeen Gen. Hosps, 1953-63; Chm., Jute and Bespoke Tailoring Wages Councils, 1954-59; Chancellor's Assessor, Aberdeen Univ., 1955-63; Mem., Indust. Injuries Adv. Council, 1960-64. Hon. LLD Aberdeen, 1962. *Address:* Old Post Office, Kirtlington, Oxford.
[Died 12 Feb. 1977.

TAYLOR, Sir William (Johnson), 1st Bt *cr* 1963; CBE 1951 (OBE 1943); DL; JP; is a Civil Engineer; Member of Lloyds; Director, Building, Insurance and Engineering Companies; Liveryman, Fishmongers Company; Freeman of London; Member, Air Cadet Council, Ministry of Defence; Chairman, Sheffield Diocesan Board of Finance; Commander, West Riding St John Ambulance; *b* 23 Oct. 1902; *s* of Frank and Margaret Elizabeth Taylor; *m* 1930, Mary Hall; two *d. Educ:* Archbishop Holgate's Grammar School, Barnsley; Sheffield Univ. Member, Barnsley County Borough Council, 1933-45. Major TA, R of O; raised and commanded 1st Cadet Bn, The York and Lancaster Regt, 1943-45; Capt., 72nd Bn WR Home Guard, 1941-44. Parly Sec., Min. of Supply, 1957-Oct. 1959. Chm.: Yorks ATC Assoc., 1940-46; ATC Central Council of Welfare, 1958; Member: ATC Consultative Cttee, Air Ministry, 1946-51; Air Cadet Council, 1951-; Exec. Council, Air League of British Empire, 1940-57; Air Cadet League of Canada (hon.); Exec. Council, Assoc. of British Chambers of Commerce. 1947-50; Vice-Chm., West Riding, T&AFA Air Cttee, 1946-56; Chm. Wentworth Conservative Assoc., 1940-46; Pres., Penistone Cons. and Unionist Assoc., 1965-; Pres., Mid-Yorks Cons. Fedn, 1965-; Pres., N Bradford Cons. Assoc.; Chm. Yorkshire Provincial Area Cons. and Unionist Assoc., 1956-57. Contested East Bradford (C) 1945; MP (C and Nat. L) Bradford North, 1950-64. Parliamentary Under-Secretary of State for Air, 1959-62, and Vice-Pres of The Air Council. Hon. Air Commodore, RAFVR, 1963. Mayor, Hon. Co. of Merchants of the Staple of England, 1965-66; Fellow, Inst. of Builders. DL, 1943, W Riding of Yorkshire and City and County of City of York; JP Barnsley County Borough. 1943; High Sheriff of Hallamshire, 1968-69. CStJ. *Recreations:* music, fishing. *Heir:* none. *Address:* Bentwood, Cawthorne, near Barnsley, Yorks. *T:* Silkstone 266; Flat 19b, 36 Buckingham Gate, SW1. *T:* 01-834 7959. *Clubs:* Carlton, Royal Air Force. *[Died 26 July 1972 (ext).*

TAYSIDE, Baron, *cr* 1967 (Life Peer); **David Lauchlan Urquhart,** OBE 1966; JP; Chairman, Don Brothers Buist & Co. Ltd Group, since 1966, Managing Director since 1952; Chairman, Tayside Economic Planning Consultative Group, 1969-70 (Vice-Chairman, 1966-69); *b* 13 Sept. 1912; *s* of David Urquhart, Kirriemuir; *m* 1939, Hilda Gwendoline Harris, BSc (Hons), St Andrews Univ., *d* of John Thomson Harris, Dundee; two *s* one *d. Educ:* Harris Academy, Dundee; St Andrews Univ. Member, Inst. of Chartered Accountants of Scotland (distinction), 1936. Member: Forfar Town Council, 1951-59 (Provost, 1956-59); Angus County Council, 1953-59; Chairman, Forfar Local Labour Party, 1959-65; Vice-Chm., S Angus Constituency Labour Party, 1959-70. Member: Parliamentary Labour Party, 1967-; Local Cttee Forfar Air Training Corps Sqdn, 1945-71 (Chm. 1955-71); Scottish Air Cadet Council, 1962-68; Valuation Appeal Cttee for Angus, 1957-; Scottish Economic Planning Council, 1968-70. General Commissioner for Income Tax, 1966-; Pres. Dundee Chamber of Commerce, 1967-68; Mem., North of Scotland Hydro-Electric Bd, 1966-71. Chairman: Strathmore Woollen Co. Ltd, Forfar; Don & Low Ltd, Arbroath; Director: Daniel Buchanan & Sons Ltd, Prestonpans; J. & J. Smart (Brechin) Ltd, Brechin; Low Brothers & Co. (Dundee) Ltd, Dundee; Grampian Television Ltd, Aberdeen, etc. Mem. Ct, Univ. of Dundee, 1967- (Chancellor's Assessor,

1967-73). Member: Inst. of Taxation, 1945; Inst. of Directors, 1953; Licenciate, Textile Inst., 1954. *Address:* The Manor, Forfar, Angus. *T:* Forfar 3338. *Club:* Eastern (Dundee).
[*Died* 12 *March* 1975.

TEAKLE, Prof. Laurence John Hartley, CMG 1970; Deputy Vice-Chancellor, University of Queensland, 1963-70, retired; *b* 2 Aug. 1901; *s* of David John and Bertha Teakle; *m* 1927, Beatrice Elizabeth Inch; three *s* one *d. Educ:* Perth Modern Sch., WA; Univ. of Western Australia; Univ. of California (Berkeley). Dept of Agriculture, WA: Agricultural Adviser, 1923; Research Officer, 1928-46; Comr for Soil Conservation, 1946-47; Univ. of Queensland: Prof. of Agriculture, 1947-62; Dep. Vice-Chancellor, 1963-70; Acting Vice-Chancellor, 1968-70. Hon. LLD Queensland, 1969. *Publication:* Fertilizers for the Farm and Garden (Teakle and Boyle), 1958. *Address:* 51 Goldieslie Road, Indooroopilly, Queensland 4068, Australia. *T:* 378.1502. *Clubs:* Rotary of Brisbane, University of Queensland Staff (Brisbane). [*Died* 8 *Dec.* 1979.

TEALE, Sir Edmund Oswald, Kt 1936; DSc, FGS, FRGS, MIMM; *b* Melbourne, Victoria, of British parentage, 29 Nov. 1874; *m* 1909, Charlotte W. Stalker; one *s* one *d. Educ:* Victorian State School, New College, Box Hill; Victorian Schools of Mines; Melbourne University. Science teacher at Victorian Schools of Mines; Caroline Kay Scholarship, Melbourne University; Field Geologist, Geological Survey, Victoria; Geological work in Africa, Nigeria, P E Africa, Gold Coast, Tanganyika Territory, starting in 1908; Director Geological Survey, Tanganyika Territory, 1926-35; Mining Consultant to Government of Tanganyika Territory, 1935-40. *Publications:* Geological and Geographical Papers on Australian and African Regions. *Recreations:* gardening, photography. *Address:* The Bungalow, Pirbright, near Woking, Surrey; *T:* Brookwood 2119.
[*Died* 17 *July* 1971.

TEALE, Rear-Adm. Godfrey Benjamin, CB 1962; CBE 1953; retired as Chief Staff Officer (Administration) on staff of C-in-C, Portsmouth (1960-63); *b* 27 Oct. 1908; *s* of Captain G. C. Teale; *m* 1933, Frances Evelyn Turreff; one *s* one *d. Educ:* Radley. Entered Royal Navy, 1926; Sec. to Admiral of the Fleet Sir Rhoderick McGrigor, GCB, DSO, 1938-55; Director of Manning, Admiralty, 1957-60. *Recreations:* cricket, tennis. *Address:* La Esperanza, Apartado 92, Marbella, Malaga, Spain. *Club:* Royal Naval and Royal Albert Yacht (Portsmouth).
[*Died* 19 *July* 1978.

TEARE, R(obert) Donald, MD, FRCP, FRCPath; Professor Emeritus in Forensic Medicine, University of London (Reader, 1963-67, Professor, 1967-75); Hon. Lecturer in Forensic Medicine, Charing Cross Hospital Medical School, 1976; *b* 1 July 1911; *s* of late A. H. Teare, JP, and Margaret Green; *m* 1937, Kathleen Agnes Gracey, JP; three *s* one *d. Educ:* King William's College, Isle of Man; Gonville and Caius College, Cambridge; St George's Hospital. BA 1933; MRCS 1936; MB, BCh 1937; MRCP 1937; MA, MD 1948; FRCP 1962; DMJ, FRCPath 1963. Past Consultant Pathologist, St George's Hosp.; Past Lectr in Forensic Medicine, St Bartholomew's Hosp. Med. Coll. and Metropolitan Police Coll. Examr in Forensic Medicine at various times in Univs of Oxford, London, Bristol, Nat. Univ. of Ireland, Riyadh, Soc. of Apothecaries, and in Pathology in Univ. of Cambridge. Past Pres., Med. Defence Union; Past Pres., Medico-Legal Soc.; Past Treasurer, RCPath; Past Sec. and Pres., Brit. Assoc. in Forensic Medicine; Brit. Council Lectr, Denmark, 1964. Master, Soc. of Apothecaries of London, 1976. Hon. LLD Sheffield, 1977. *Publications:* scientific papers in Lancet, BMJ, Jl of Bone and Joint Surgery, Thorax, and many forensic jls. *Recreations:* golf, gardening. *Address:* 8 Highdown Road, Putney, SW15. *T:* 01-788 6663; St George's Hospital, SW1. *T:* 01-235 6303; Ripple Cottage, Castletown, Isle of Man. *T:* Castletown 3353. *Clubs:* MCC; Royal Wimbledon Golf.
[*Died* 17 *Jan.* 1979.

TEELING, Sir (Luke) William (Burke), Kt 1962; MA; author and traveller; *b* 5 Feb. 1903; *o c* of late Luke Alexander Teeling and Margaret Mary, *o d* and *heiress* of William Burke of Ower, Co. Galway; *m* 1942, Mary Julia (*d* 1953), *e d* of late Charles H. O'Conor and *sister* of the 25th O'Conor Don. *Educ:* The Oratory School, Edgbaston; Magdalen College, Oxford. BA 1924; MA 1958. Exec. Chm., Catholic Emigration Society of Great Britain and Northern Ireland, 1929-31; represented Overseas League as Mem. Council at Melbourne Centenary, 1934; contested (C) Silvertown Division of West Ham, 1929. Served 1940-45 in RAF. MP (U) Brighton, 1944-50, Pavilion Div. of Brighton, 1950-69; Led Parliamentary Delegation to Finland, 1947; Member, Govt Parliamentary Delegation to Japan, 1947 and to Peru, 1955, and of Commonwealth Parly Delegation to British Guiana, 1965. Vice-Chairman: Parly

Anglo-Norwegian and Anglo-Danish Cttees, 1963-65; Anglo-Irish Parly Cttee, 1967-69; attended Independence Celebrations of Malta as guest of Maltese Govt, Sept. 1964. Rep. European anti-Communist organisations at opening of South Korean Freedom Centre, Seoul, Dec. 1964. Hon. Secretary: Holiday Resorts Committee in House of Commons, 1944-54; House of Commons Branch, RAF Association, 1945-62; Chairman: Essex Junior Imp. League, 1928-30; Channel Tunnel Parliamentary Committee, 1954-69; Cons. Parly Mediterranean Sub-Cttee (visited Gibraltar, 1967). President: Brighton Young Conservatives, 1961-69; UK Branch, Korean Taikwan-Do Soc.; Founder, 1946, and Vice-Pres., Regency Soc.; Mem. Council: Catholic Union, 1952-59; Japan Society, 1949-61; Anglo-Korean Society; a Governor of the Oratory School. Hon. Sec., Irish Peers Assoc., 1970-74. President: Brighton Antique Dealers' Fair, 1955-69; Hove Squash Rackets Club, 1946-69; Nat. Dog Owners Assoc. Is a Director of several companies. Freeman: City of Seoul, South Korea; City of London, 1950. Commander Order of Merit (Peru), 1957; Knight of Malta (Honour and Devotion); Order of the Brilliant Star (China). Coronation Medal, 1937, 1953; Gold Staff Officer, Coronation, 1937. *Publications:* England's French Dominion?, 1932; The Near-By Thing, 1933; American Stew, 1933 (also in Tauchnitz Edition for Europe 1934); Gods of Tomorrow, 1936; The Pope in Politics, 1937; Why Britain Prospers, 1938; Crisis for Christianity, 1939; Know thy Enemy, 1939; Corridors of Frustration, 1970. Contribs to: The Times, The Sunday Times, Daily Telegraph, The Tablet, The Tatler. *Recreations:* walking, travelling. *Address:* c/o Royal Bank of Scotland, Burlington Gardens, W1. *Clubs:* Carlton, Press, St James', Royal Air Force; Kildare Street (Dublin). [*Died* 26 *Oct.* 1975.

TELFER, Rev. Andrew Cecil, MA; FRAS; *b* 1893; 2nd *s* of Rev. A. Telfer, Faversham, Kent; *m* 1928, Dorothy, *y d* of C. J. Britton, Ford End, Essex; two *d. Educ:* King's School, Canterbury; Selwyn College, Cambridge. Deacon, 1943; Priest, 1944; served European War, 1914-19 (wounded); Captain CUH and H, 1913-20; President CUAC, 1919-20; Assistant Master Felsted School, 1920-27; Headmaster Ludlow Grammar School, 1927-33; Housemaster, Felsted School, 1933-46; retired, 1960. Co-Founder Achilles Club. *Address:* Felsted, Essex.
[*Died* 1 *June* 1978.

TEMPEL, Frederik Jan; Commander, Oranje Nassau; Kt, Order of Netherlands Lion; Chairman of Unilever NV, 1955-66, and a Vice-Chairman of Unilever Ltd, 1954-66, retired; *b* 26 Dec. 1900; Dutch nationality; *s* of Jacob Tempel and Minke Tempel (*née* van der Meulen); *m* 1925, Annie Zwartsenberg; no *c. Educ:* Gymnasium Assen, Holland; Handels HS, Rotterdam, Holland. Joined Van den Bergh's Fabr. NV, Rotterdam, 1923; Head of local Unilever companies in France, Italy and Germany, 1929-40; in Holland during the War; Germany, 1945-47; Director, Unilever NV and Unilever Ltd, 1947-66; Advisory Director, Unilever NV, 1966-72. *Recreations:* shooting, fishing, golf. *Address:* Cees Laseurlaan 1189, The Hague, Netherlands.
[*Died* 27 *Dec.* 1974.

TEMPLE, Maj.-Gen. Bertram; CB 1947; CMG 1952; OBE 1941; MC and Bar; *b* 31 July 1896; *s* of Lt-Col John Temple, RA; *m* 1924, Dulcibella Mary, *d* of Col F. W. Radcliffe, Dorset Regt; one *s* one *d. Educ:* Clifton College; Royal Military College, Sandhurst. Served European War, 1914-19, Gloucester Regiment; War of 1939-45; Bt Lt-Col, 1939; Brig. 1941 (despatches). Director of Staff Duties, General Headquarters, India, 1946 (actg Maj.-Gen.); Maj.-Gen. 1949; late Dep. Director of Quartering. ADC to the King, 1948-49; Head of British Services Mission to Burma, 1949-52. *Address:* Hayfield, Hill Crest Road, Hythe, Kent. [*Died* 27 *March* 1973.

TEMPLE-GORE-LANGTON, Comdr Hon. Evelyn Arthur Grenville, DSO 1918; RN retired; *b* 5 April 1884; 3rd *s* of 4th Earl Temple of Stowe; *m* 1922, Irene (*d* 1967), *d* of Brig.-Gen. C. W. Gartside-Spaight, Tzonhalem Ranch, Duncan, BC; one *s* one *d. Educ:* Stubbington House School; HMS Britannia. Entered Royal Navy, 1900; retired, 1911; rejoined, 1914; served in minesweeping flotilla till Feb. 1919, when demobilised (DSO). Served War of 1939-45, in RN. [*Died* 7 *June* 1972.

TEMPLEMAN, Philip George, CBE 1965; Alderman; Chairman: Wessex Regional Hospital Board, since 1959; Bournemouth and East Dorset Hospital Management Committee, since 1957; Vice-Chairman, Dorset and Bournemouth Police Authority, since 1968; *b* 2 June 1910; *s* of William James and Amelia Ruth Templeman, Bournemouth; *m* 1934, Elizabeth Kathleen, *d* of Howard Stanley Fudge, Bournemouth; three *d. Educ:* Taunton Sch., Somerset. Chm., Templeman & Son, Bournemouth, Masonry Contractors, 1942-. Mayor, 1956-57, Alderman, 1961, Leader of Council, 1963-

(Chm. 3 Cttees), Bournemouth. Chm., Bournemouth and Christchurch Bldg Soc., 1960-. Mem. Council, Southampton Univ., 1967-; Pres., Inst. Social Welfare Southern Centre, 1967-. Past Pres. various Bournemouth organisations. Freeman, Co. Borough of Bournemouth, 1970. MInstD. Hon. LLD Southampton, 1972. *Recreations:* reading, music. *Address:* The Garden House, 22a Cavendish Road, Bournemouth, Hants. *T:* Bournemouth 25476. *Club:* Constitutional (Bournemouth).
[Died 17 May 1972.

TEMPLER, Field-Marshal Sir Gerald (Walter Robert), KG 1963; GCB 1955 (KCB 1951; CB 1944); GCMG 1953 (CMG 1946); KBE 1949 (OBE 1940); DSO 1936; *b* 11 Sept. 1898; *o s* of late Lt-Col Walter Francis Templer, CBE, DL; *m* 1926, Ethel Margery, *o d* of Charles Davie, JP, Bishops Tawton, Barnstaple; one *s* one *d. Educ:* Wellington Coll.; RMC, Sandhurst. Joined Royal Irish Fusiliers, 1916; Capt. Loyals 1928; Bt Maj. 1935; Capt. Royal Irish Fusiliers 1937; Bt Lt-Col 1938; commanded between 1942 and 1944 2 Corps, 47th (London) Div., 1st Div., 56th (London) Div. and 6th Armd Div.; Dir of Milit. Govt 21 Army Group, 1945-46; Director of Military Intelligence, War Office, 1946-48; Vice-CIGS, 1948-50; GOC-in-C, Eastern Command, 1950-52; High Commissioner, and Director of Operations, Federation of Malaya, 1952-54; Chief of the Imperial General Staff, 1955-58. Colonel: The Royal Irish Fusiliers, 1946-60; Fedn Regiment of Malaya, 1954-59; 7th Gurkha Rifles, 1956-64; Royal Horse Guards (The Blues) 1963-69, The Blues and The Royals, 1969-; Gold Stick to the Queen 1963-. Served European War, 1914-18; operations in North-West Persia and Mesopotamia, 1919-21 (medal and two bars); operations in Palestine, 1936 (despatches, DSO); War of 1939-45 (wounded, OBE, CB). ADC General: to King George VI, 1951-52; to Queen Elizabeth II, 1952-54. Constable, HM Tower of London, 1965-70; HM Lieutenant of Greater London, 1967-73; Freeman, City of London, 1965; Hon. Freeman: Armourers' and Brasiers' Co., 1965; Merchant Taylors' Co., 1979; Fishmongers' Co., 1979. Trustee: Nat. Portrait Gallery, 1958-72; Imperial War Museum, 1959-66; Historic Churches Preservation Trust, 1963-. Member: Council, Outward Bound Trust, 1954-74; Exec. and Finance Cttees, National Trust, 1959-74; Exec. Cttee and Council, Voluntary Service Overseas, 1961-77; Council, Scout Assoc., 1968-; Chm. Exec. Cttee and Mem. Council, Nat. Army Museum, 1960-; President: Soc. of Army Historical Research, 1965-; British Horse Soc., 1968-70. Comr, Royal Hospital Chelsea, 1969-. Commander, Legion of Merit (USA); Commander, Order of Crown, with Palm (Belgium); Croix de Guerre (Belgium); Kt Grand Cross, Order of Orange Nassau with Swords (Netherlands); Kt Grand Cross, Most Distinguished Order of Defender of Realm (Malaya). Hon. DCL Oxon; Hon. LLD St Andrews, 1974. *Address:* Flat 7, 31 Sloane Court West, SW3 4TE. *Clubs:* Boodle's, Bucks.
[Died 25 Oct. 1979.

TEMPLETON, James Stanley; Puisne Judge, Supreme Court, Kenya, 1957; *b* 24 January 1906; *m* 1932, Elizabeth Dorothy Scott; two *s* two *d. Educ:* Bangor Grammar Sch., N Ireland. Crown Counsel, Kenya, 1949; Sen. Crown Counsel, Kenya, 1955. *Publications:* (poetry) The Young Ones, 1973; Westminster Abbey Revisited, 1975; Why Should I Mourn?, 1976. *Recreation:* photography. *Address:* 8 High Trees, Beach Road, Canford Cliffs, Poole, Dorset. *T:* Canford Cliffs 709207. *Club:* Nairobi.
[Died 24 March 1977.

TENNYSON, Sir Charles Bruce Locker, Kt 1945; CMG 1915; MA; *b* 8 Nov. 1879; 2nd *s* of late Hon. Lionel Tennyson and late Eleanor Bertha Mary, *d* of Frederick Locker (*m* 2nd, Rt Hon. Augustine Birrell); *m* 1909, Ivy Gladys (*d* 1958), OBE, *d* of late W. J. Pretious; one *s* (two having been killed on active service, 1941 and 1945). *Educ:* Eton College (King's Scholar); King's College, Cambridge (Eton Scholarship). Whewell Scholar in International Law, Cambridge University; 1st Division 1st Class, Classical Tripos, 1902; Arden Scholar, Gray's Inn, 1904; called to Bar, 1905; Junior Equity Counsel to Office of Works, 1909-11; Asst Legal Adviser to Colonial Office, 1911-19; one of the British delegates at the New Hebrides Conf., 1914; Sec., Dunlop Rubber Co. Ltd, 1928-48; Chairman of Board of Trade Utility Furniture Committee, 1943, and Furniture Production Committee, 1944; President Association of Technical Institutes, 1946, and of Union of Educational Instns, 1947. Chm. of Council, Bedford College, London Univ., 1946-53; Vice-Pres. Fedn Brit. Industries (late Dep. Dir); Fellow Bedford College, Hon. Fellow King's College, Cambridge, and Royal College of Art; FRSL. Hon. LLD Cambridge; Hon. DLitt Leicester Univ. *Publications:* Cambridge from Within, 1912; Alfred Tennyson, 1950; Life's all a Fragment, 1953; Six Tennyson Essays, 1953; Stars and Markets, 1957; (with H. Dyson) Dear and Honoured Lady, 1969; (with H. Dyson) The Tennysons: background to genius, 1974. Edited, Shorter Poems of Frederick Tennyson,

1913, The Devil and the Lady, by Alfred Lord Tennyson, 1930; Unpublished Early Poems by Alfred Tennyson, 1931. *Recreation:* represented Cambridge University against Oxford at golf, 1902. *Address:* 23 The Park, NW11. *[Died 22 June 1977.*

TENNYSON D'EYNCOURT, Sir (Eustace) Gervais, 2nd Bt, *cr* 1930; *b* 19 Jan. 1902; *o s* of Sir Eustace Tennyson-d'Eyncourt, 1st Bt, KCB, FRS, and Janet (*d* 1909), *widow* of John Burns, e *d* of Mathew Finlay, Langside, Glasgow; *S* father 1951; *m* 1st, 1926, Pamela (*d* 1962), *yr d* of late W. B. Gladstone; two *s* one *d*; 2nd, 1964, Vinnie Lorraine, *widow* of Robert J. O'Donnell and *yr d* of late Andrew Pearson, Minneapolis, Minnesota. *Educ:* Charterhouse. Pres., Shellfish Assoc. of Great Britain, 1971-. Mem., Exec. Cttee, Standing Council of the Baronetage. Member: Smeatonian Soc. of Civil Engrs; Royal Instn; The Pilgrims; Tennyson Soc. Prime Warden of the Fishmongers' Company, 1960-61. FRSA 1956. *Recreations:* golf, shooting. *Heir:* s John Jeremy Eustace Tennyson d'Eyncourt [*b* 8 July 1927; *m* 1964, Mrs Sally Fyfe-Jamieson, *e d* of Robin Stratford, QC]. *Address:* 16 Pelham Place, SW7. *T:* 01-589 1670. *Clubs:* Turf, Beefsteak, White's, Garrick; Ulster (Belfast); The Brook (NY).
[Died 21 Nov. 1971.

TERRELL, Edward, OBE 1953; QC 1955; Chairman, Chevrons Club for Non-commissioned Officers of Royal Navy, Army, Royal Air Force and Commonwealth, to 1975; Honorary Recorder of Newbury, since 1972; *b* 12 June 1902; *s* of Thomas Terrell, KC; *m* 1928, Winifred Packard Shyvers; one *s. Educ:* Berkhamsted School; London University. Called to Bar, Gray's Inn, 1924; Member of Middle Temple. Recorder of Newbury, 1935-71; a Recorder of the Crown Court, 1972-74. War Service: joined RNVR as Temp. Lieut 1940; Lieut-Comdr (acting), 1941; Comdr (acting), 1942; Capt. (acting), 1944; apptd to personal staff of First Sea Lord (Adm. of the Fleet Sir Dudley Pound) for duties on U-Boat Warfare, 1941-45; inventor of Plastic Armour (July 1940) which was fitted to 10,000 Allied War and Merchant Ships, 1940-44 (award from Royal Commission on Awards to Inventors, 1949); inventor of first Allied Rocket Bomb for attacks on U-Boat shelters. *Publications:* The Law of Running Down Cases, Edns, 1931, 1936, 1965; Admiralty Brief (an autobiography of the War), 1958. Hon. Recorder, Newbury, 1972-74. *Recreations:* tennis, yachting, inventing. *Address:* 14 Keats Grove, Hampstead, NW3. *T:* 01-435 2402; 4 Brick Court, Temple, EC4. *TA:* 77 Temple. *T:* 01-353 2725.
[Died 13 Nov. 1979.

TERRELL, Captain Sir (Thomas Antonio) Reginald, Kt 1959; *b* 1889; *y s* of late George Terrell; *m* 1923, Marjorie Ethel, 2nd *d* of late Mr O'Connor; two *d. Educ:* Harrow. Served his apprenticeship in sailing ships. Joined the London and North-Western Works at Crewe. Entered the Grenadier Guards, 1915; served European War, 1915-19; MP (C) Henley Division of Oxfordshire, December 1918-October 1924. *Address:* Cliff Lodge, Cliff Road, The Leas, Folkestone, Kent. *T:* Folkestone 51806. *Clubs:* Hon. Life Member: Carlton, Royal Thames Yacht.
[Died 5 Feb. 1979.

TERRY, Major Sir Edward Henry Bouhier I.; see Imbert-Terry.

TERRY, Phyllis N.; see Neilson-Terry.

TERTIS, Lionel, CBE 1950; FRAM; *b* W Hartlepool, 29 Dec. 1876; *m* 1st, Ada (*d* 1951), *d* of Rev. Hugh Gawthrop; 2nd, 1959, Lillian Florence Margaret, *o d* of the late H. H. Warmington and Mrs Warmington, Bournemouth. Propagandist for Viola as solo instrument. Gold Medallist, Worshipful Company of Musicians; Chevalier de l'Ordre de Couronne, Belgium. Has written numerous published articles decrying lack of facilities and opportunity for English musical talent. Is responsible for design of a viola (The Tertis Model) which is being made in seventeen countries; a "Tertis Model" Violoncello (1959) and a "Tertis Model" Violin (1962), designed on the same lines. Hon. Fellow, Trinity Coll., London, 1966. Kreisler Award of Merit, 1950; Gold Medal, Royal Philharmonic Society, 1964; Eugene Ysaye Medal and Diploma of Honour, Ysaye Foundation, Brussels, 1968. *Publications:* numerous arrangements for Viola; Beauty of Tone in string playing, 1938; Cinderella No More, an Autobiography, 1953; My Viola and I (autobiog.), 1974. *Address:* 42 Marryat Road, Wimbledon Common, SW19. *T:* 01-946 5541. *Club:* Sesame.
[Died 22 Feb. 1975.

TESTER, Air Cdre John Andrews, CB 1958; CBE 1953 (OBE 1942); BA; Royal Air Force (retired); Allied Radio Frequency Agency, NATO, since 1960; *b* Lancaster, 21 Aug. 1907; *s* of William Andrews Tester, Consultant Engineer; *m* 1932, Kathleen Blanche, *d* of Herbert Hill Parry, Heswall, Cheshire; one *d* (one *s* killed while in RAF, in an aircraft accident, 1958).

Educ: Hastings Grammar School; Downing College, Cambridge. Entered RAF, Sept. 1930; usual varied career as General Duties Officer; retired from RAF 1958. *Recreations:* most forms of sport. *Address:* 41 Square des Latins, 1050 Brussels, Belgium. *T:* 47.13.26.　　　　　*[Died 6 July 1972.*

TESTER, Leslie, CMG 1942; MC; Brilliant Star Zanzibar; late British Member of the Allied Quadripartite Directorates for Finance, Economics, Transport and Social Administration, Austria; *b* 1891; *s* of late William George Tester, JP, County Kent; unmarried. Served European War, 1914-19. York and Lancaster Regiment Special Reserve (despatches 5 times, MC). Colonial Service, Nigeria, 1919-32, Member of Exec. and Leg. Councils, Mauritius, 1932-34, Zanzibar, 1934-40, Tanganyika, 1940-41, Kenya, 1941-45. Commissioner of Currency, Mauritius; Chairman, E African Land Bank. Deputy Chief, British Finance Division, Germany, 1946-47; Austria, 1947-50. *Address:* c/o The National Westminster Bank, Ashford, Kent.
[Died 1 Dec. 1975.

TETLEY, Brig. James Noel, DSO 1944; TD; DL; President, Joshua Tetley & Son Ltd; Director, Leeds Permanent Building Society; *b* 30 Dec. 1898; *s* of Frank Tetley, Leeds; *m* 1925, Joyce Carine, *d* of C. E. Grierson, Walton-le-Dale; one *s* one *d. Educ:* St Bees School; Pembroke College, Oxford. In Brewing Industry with Joshua Tetley & Son, 1923-. Territorial Army Service, 1918-63; Comdr of Armoured Bde, in UK, N Africa and Italy, 1941-44. ADC to King George VI, 1948, to the Queen, 1952-58. Pro-Chancellor, 1956-64, Treasurer, 1964-70, Univ. of Leeds. DL 1956. Hon. LLD Leeds. *Recreations:* shooting, fishing. *Address:* Moor House, Moortown, Leeds 17. *T:* 661329. *Club:* Leeds (Leeds).　　　　　　　　　　*[Died 25 Dec. 1971.*

TEVERSHAM, Brigadier Mark Symonds, CIE 1946; MC; late Indian Army; *b* 5 April 1895; *s* of late Col R. K. Teversham, DSO, OBE, IA; *m* 1918, Evelyn Mary Ross (*d* 1954); twin *s. Educ:* Bedford School; Cheltenham College; RMC, Sandhurst. Commissioned Aug. 1914; served European War, 1914-18, France and Flanders and Iraq with 2nd Bn Lincolnshire Regt and 32nd Sikh Pioneers; Arab Rebellion, Iraq, 1920; NWF, 1922-24 and 1941; Staff College, Quetta, 1930-31; commanded 5th Bn Rajputana Rifles, 1937-40; 1st Ind. Inf. Bde, 1940-41; 62nd Ind. Inf. Bde, 1941-43; Dir of Quartering, GHQ, India, 1944-47; retd 1947. CStJ. *Address:* c/o Lloyds Bank, Emsworth, Hampshire. *Club:* United Service and Royal Aero.
[Died 15 Nov. 1973.

TEYNHAM, 19th Baron, *cr* 1616; **Christopher John Henry Roper-Curzon,** DSO 1945; DSC 1944; despatches 1944; Captain, RN (retired); King Haakon Cross of Liberty; Younger Brother of Trinity House; formerly a Deputy Speaker of House of Lords and Deputy Chairman of Committees; HM Lieutenant of the City of London; a Director of British Sailors Society; a Governor and Member of Managing Committee of Royal National Lifeboat Institute; Chairman of Prince of Wales Sea Training School, Dover; Chancellor of the Primrose League, 1948; Member, Council, Navy League; Member Post Office Advisory Board; Member of Court of Directors of Royal Exchange Assurance; *b* 6 May 1896; *e s* of 18th Baron and Mabel (*d* 1937), *d* of late Col Henry Green Wilkinson, Scots Guards, Pannington Hall, Ipswich; *S* father, 1936; *m* 1927, Elspeth Grace (marr. diss., 1954; she *m* 1958, 5th Marquess of Northampton), *e d* of late William Ingham Whitaker, Pylewell Park, Lymington; two *s ; m* 1955, Anne Rita Curzon-Howe; two *d. Educ:* Royal Naval Colleges, Osborne and Dartmouth. Served with Grand Fleet European War, 1914-18, and War of 1939-45; Naval Control Service Officer Port of London, 1939-40; commanded Destroyers HMS Campbeltown, Venomous, and Amazon and the Minesweeping Forces from HMS Ambitious in the Invasion Area North France (DSO). Chm. Automobile Association, 1953-57. Chevalier Légion d'Honneur. KStJ. A Conservative. *Heir: e s* Hon. John Christopher Ingham Roper-Curzon [*b* 25 Dec. 1928; *m* 1964, Elizabeth, *d* of late Lt-Col the Hon. David Scrymgeour Wedderburn and of the Countess of Dundee; one *s* three *d*]. *Address:* Inwood House, Sarisbury Green, Hants. *Clubs:* Carlton; Royal Yacht Squadron (Cowes).
[Died 5 May 1972.

TEYTE, Dame Maggie, (Dame Margaret Cottingham), DBE 1958; prima donna; *b* Wolverhampton, 17 April 1888; *m* 1921, W. S. Cottingham (from whom she obtained a divorce, 1931). *Educ:* Royal College of Music; Paris, under Jean de Reszke. Was for several years a member of the Opéra Comique, where she, at the age of nineteen, sang in June 1908 the rôle of Melisande in Debussy's Pelleas and Melisande; since then she has appeared in London at many concerts, and with the T. Beecham Opera Co. in Nozze di Figaro (Cherubino); Tales of Hoffmann (Antonia); Faust (Marguerite), and also Pelleas and Melisande; sang in

Philadelphia, Chicago and New York, 1911-12-13-14; touring England with Kubelik, 1914; toured America, 1915-18; returned to England for Monsieur Beaucaire and Little Dutch Girl; joined BNOC, 1922; joined Covent Garden Opera Co., 1930; sang in Pelleas and Melisande, Covent Garden, 1930. Chevalier of the Legion of Honour, 1957. *Publication:* Star on the Door, 1958. *Recreations:* motoring, golf, tennis, and all out-of-door sports.
[Died 26 May 1976.

THANT, U; Maha Thray Sithu, 1961 (Sithu, 1957); Thiripyanchi, 1953; Wunna Kyaw Htin, 1949; Secretary-General, United Nations, 1962-71 (Acting Secretary-General, 1961-62); Burmese Statesman; *b* Jan. 1909; *m* ; one *d* (one *s* decd). *Educ:* National High School, Pantanaw, Burma; University Coll., Rangoon. Sen. Master, Nat. High School, Pantanaw, 1928, Head Master, 1931, 1943-47; Sec. Education Re-organisation Cttee, Burma, 1942. Free-lance journalist. Press Director, Govt of Burma, 1947; Director of Broadcasting, 1948; Sec., Min. of Information, 1949-57; Sec. for Projects, Office of the Prime Minister, 1953. United Nations: Mem. Burmese Delegn to 7th Session of Gen. Assembly, 1952; Permanent Burmese Rep., 1957-61; Chm. Burmese Delegn, 1957-61; Chm. Asian-African Standing Cttee. on Algeria, 1957; Vice-Pres. Gen. Assembly, 1959; Chm. Cttee on a UN Development Fund, 1961; Chm. UN Congo Conciliation Commn, 1961. Hon. Mem., American Academy of Arts and Sciences, 1963. *Publications:* (in Burmese) Cities and their Stories, 1930; (in Burmese) League of Nations, 1933; (in Burmese) Towards a New Education, 1946; (in Burmese) Democracy in Schools, 1952; (in Burmese) History of Post-War Burma (3 vols), 1961; Toward World Peace, 1964; Portfolio for Peace, 1971; View from the UN, 1978 (posthumous publication). *Address:* 136 Osborn Road, Harrison, New York, NY 10528, USA.　　　　　　　　　　　　　　*[Died 25 Nov. 1974.*

THEILER, Max, MRCS, LRCP; Director of Laboratories, The Rockefeller Foundation, since 1951; *b* 30 Jan. 1899; *s* of late Sir Arnold Theiler, KCMG, and Emma Jegge; *m* 1928, Lillian Graham; one *d. Educ:* University of Cape Town; St Thomas's Hospital, London. MRCS, LRCP, DTM&H London School of Tropical Medicine, 1922. Assistant and later Instructor in Department of Tropical Medicine, Harvard Medical School, Boston, Massachusetts, 1922-30; staff member, Rockefeller Foundation, 1930-. Chalmers Medal, Royal Soc. Trop. Med. and Hygiene, England, 1939; Flattery Medal, Harvard University, 1945; Lasker Award, Lasker Foundation, 1949; Nobel Prize for Physiology and Medicine, Caroline Inst., 1951. *Publications:* scientific articles. Chapter 2 of Yellow Fever (ed by G. K. Strode). *Address:* 48 Circle Drive, Hastings-on-Hudson, New York, USA. *T:* Hastings 5-2076.　　　*[Died 11 Aug. 1972.*

THEOTONIO PEREIRA, Pedro, GCVO (Hon.) 1955; Grand Cross of Cristo of Portugal; *b* 7 Nov. 1902; *s* of João Theotonio Pereira and Dona Virginia Herrmann; *m* 1926, Isabel van Zeller Palha; one *s* two *d. Educ:* Univ. of Lisbon (high mathematics). Member Portuguese Cabinet (first Social Welfare and later Commerce and Industry), 1933-37; Ambassador to Madrid, then Rio de Janeiro and Washington, 1938-50; Ambassador to the Court of St James's, 1953-58; Minister of the Presidency, Portugal, 1958-61; Ambassador to Washington, 1961-63. Life Member of Portuguese Council of State. Grand Cross of Carlos III, Merito Naval, Merito Militar, Yugo y Flechas, of Spain; Cruzeiro do Sul, of Brasil; Grand Cross, Order of George I, of Greece. *Address:* Alameda de Algés, TP, Dáfundo, Portugal.
[Died 14 Nov. 1972.

THICKNESSE, Very Rev. Cuthbert Carroll, MA; Dean of St Albans and Rector of the Abbey Church, St Albans, 1936-55; Dean Emeritus, 1955; *b* 19 Nov. 1887; *o surv. s* of late Ven. F. N. Thicknesse and late Mary Sibylla, *d* of Rev. Joseph Walker, sometime Vice-Principal of BNC, Oxford; *m* 1916, Rhoda Oonah Marjorie, *d* of late Rev. H. Madan Pratt, JP and G. S. M., *d* of Sir Mathew Wilson, Bt; two *s* five *d. Educ:* Marlborough; Keble College, Oxford. Deacon, 1913; Priest, 1914; Curate of St John-at-Hackney, 1913-15; temporary Chaplain to Forces, attached RA, 1915-17; wounded at Ypres and invalided out; Rector of Badsworth, Yorkshire, 1917-22; Rector of Wigan, 1922-36; Proctor in Convocation for Diocese of Liverpool, 1925; Hon. Canon of Liverpool Cathedral, 1926-36; Select Preacher, Cambridge, 1935; Chaplain to the King, 1935-36; Priest-in-charge of Luccombe, 1956-63. Consulting Editor of the Church Times, 1950-54. *Address:* Heatherlands, Doverhay, Porlock, Minehead, Somerset. *T:* Porlock 440.　　*[Died 2 June 1971.*

THIMAN, Eric Harding, DMus; FRCO; Professor, Royal Academy of Music, London, since 1931; Organist to the City Temple, London, since 1958; *b* 12 Sept. 1900; *s* of Israel Phoebus Thiman and Muriel Kate Harding; *m* 1928, Clare Madeline Arnold. *Educ:* Caterham. FRCO 1926, DMus (London) 1927.

Member, professorial staff, Royal Acad. of Music, 1931, after musical training, largely private, and self-administered. Dean, Faculty of Music, Univ. of London, 1956-62. Musical pursuits: lecturer, examiner, composer, organ recitalist, adjudicator at musical festivals. Hon. RAM. *Publications:* compositions for organ and choir; school music; instrumental and orchestral works and musical textbooks. *Recreations:* walking, motoring, foreign travel. *Address:* 7 Edmunds Walk, N2. *T:* 01-883 4718.
[Died 13 Feb. 1975.

THIRKILL, Sir Henry, Kt 1951; CBE 1946; MC; Master of Clare College, Cambridge, 1939-58, retired; President of Clare College, 1930-39; Tutor, 1920-39; Lecturer, 1918-39; Fellow, 1910-39, and since 1958; *b* 8 Aug. 1886; *s* of William Thirkill and Alice, *d* of Henry Pickles. *Educ:* Clare Coll., Cambridge, MA. Late Univ. Lectr in Experimental Physics; Vice-Chancellor of Cambridge Univ., 1945-47; Deputy Vice-Chancellor of Cambridge, 1947-55, 1956-58; Member of Council of Senate, 1927-56. Served European War: RE, 1914-19. OC Wireless, East African Campaign, 1915-18. Chm., Cambridge Univ. Joint Recruiting Bd, 1940-58. *Address:* Clare College, Cambridge. *Club:* Athenæum. [Died 26 March 1971.

THOM, Herbert James, CIE 1943; CBE 1962; MC; MA; *b* 24 Feb. 1895; *s* of J. MacGillivray Thom; *m* 1922, Nan Mary, *d* of J. B. Clark, CBE, LLD; one *s* one *d*. *Educ:* Daniel Stewart's College; Edinburgh University. Served European War, 1914-19; Captain Royal Scots (MC). Indian Police, 1921-45; Principal, Police Training College; Commandant Military Police, Deputy Inspector-General CID (CIE). Transport Commissioner, United Provinces, 1945-47; Department of Health for Scotland, 1947-48; Chairman, Traffic Commn, S Wales Traffic Area, 1948-53; South Eastern Traffic Area, 1953-65, retired. Mem., Panel to hold Public Enquiries for Minister of Transport, 1965-71. Chairman, Motor Transport Commn, Northern Rhodesia, 1951. *Address:* Hillside, Brockham Lane, Betchworth, Surrey. *T:* Betchworth 2032. [Died 6 May 1972.

THOMAS, Baron *cr* 1971 (Life Peer), of Remenham, Berks; **William Miles Webster Thomas,** Kt 1943; DFC; CEng; FIMechE; MSAE; FRAeS; President, National Savings Committee, 1965-72 (also Chairman, 1965-70); Chairman: Britannia Airways Ltd; Chesham Amalgamations and Investments Ltd; Director: Sun Insurance Office, Ltd; Dowty Group Ltd; Thomson Organisation (Sunday Times, etc); Thomson Travel Ltd; *b* 2 March 1897; *s* of late William Henry Thomas and Mary Elizabeth Webster; *m* 1924, Hylda Nora Church, Kidlington, Oxford; one *s* one *d*. *Educ:* Bromsgrove School. Served as Engineering Premium Pupil at Bellis and Morcom Ltd, Birmingham; joined Armoured Car Squadron as private; served in German East African campaign as Armoured Car Driver; Commissioned to RFC in Egypt; Stunt Flying and Aerial Fighting Instructor at Heliopolis; afterwards served with RAF in Mesopotamia, Persia and Southern Russia (DFC); Demobilised, 1919; became editor on technical journals; joined Lord Nuffield (then Mr W. R. Morris) as adviser on Sales Promotion, 1924; founded Morris-Oxford Press in 1926; Director and General Sales Manager of Morris Motors Ltd, 1927; Director and General Manager of Morris Commercial Cars Ltd, Birmingham, 1934; of Wolseley Motors Ltd, Birmingham, 1935; Managing Director of Wolseley Motors Ltd in 1937; Vice-Chairman and Managing Director of Morris Motors Ltd and Subsidiary Companies, 1940-47. Chairman: Cruiser Tank Production Group and member of Advisory Panel on Tank Production, 1941; British Tank Engine Mission to US, 1942; Govt of Southern Rhodesia Development Co-ordinating Commission, 1947; Oxfordshire Council, Order of St John, 1947. President, Soc. of Motor Manufacturers, 1947-48; Director, Colonial Development Corporation, 1948-51; Chairman of BOAC, 1949-56; Dep. Chm., P. Leiner & Sons Ltd, 1961-71; President: Advertising Assoc., 1949-53; International Air Transport Assoc., 1951-52; Carbon Electric Holdings Ltd, 1971-72 (Chm. 1964-70); Neumo Ltd. Member: BBC General Advisory Council, 1952-56; Brit. Productivity Council, 1957-62 (Chm., 1959); Chairman: Monsanto Chemicals Ltd, 1956-63; Welsh Adv. Cttee for Civil Aviation, 1961-66; Development Corp. for Wales, 1958-67; Vice-Chm., Welsh Econ. Council, 1965-66. Comdr of Cedar of the Lebanon, Lebanon. *Publications:* Treatise on the development and use of multi-wheel vehicles for cross-country and military purposes, 1924; numerous articles, broadcast talks and television "Brains Trust" and "Get Ahead", 1934-64. (Autobiography) Out on a Wing, 1964. *Recreations:* modest motoring and simple gardening. *Address:* Remenham Court, Henley-on-Thames, Oxon. *T:* Henley 5400. *Clubs:* Athenæum, East India, Devonshire, Sports and Public Schools; The Links (New York).
[Died 8 Feb. 1980.

THOMAS, Arthur Hermann, MA, LLD Cantab; Hon. DLit London; FSA, FRHistSoc; CStJ; Deputy-Keeper of the Records to the Corporation of London, 1914-45; *b* Newton Heath, Lancashire, 5 April 1877; 2nd *s* of Rev. Hallowell Thomas; *m* 1902, Marie Louise Sophie (*d* 1965), *e d* of John Charles Andreae, Champion Hill, SE; one *s* three *d* (and one *s* decd, War of 1939-45). *Educ:* St Catharine's College, Cambridge (Exhibitioner); Manchester College, Oxford; University of Berlin. Sometime lecturer in ecclesiastical history in the University of Sheffield; served as a Major, Lancashire Fusiliers, 1914-17, France and Belgium (despatches twice); and in the Historical Sect. (Military Branch), Cttee of Imperial Defence, 1917-18; Pres. Brit. Archæological Assoc., 1938-45. *Publications:* A History of the Early Church: its Orders and Institutions, 1907; A History of the Great Meeting, 1908; (joint) Descriptive Catalogue of the Jackson Collection of Charters, Rolls, etc, 1913; Court and Account Rolls of Hallamshire, 1920-23; Calendar of Early Mayor's Court Rolls (1298-1307), 1924; Calendar of Plea and Memoranda Rolls (1323-1364), 1926; Calendar of P and M Rolls (1365-1381), 1929; Calendar of Select Pleas and Mem. (1381-1412), 1932; (joint) Great Chronicle of London, 1938; Calendar of P and M Rolls (1413-1437), 1943; articles on medieval history and records in historical and archæological publications. *Recreations:* walking, swimming. *Address:* 2 West Park Lane, Worthing, Sussex. *T:* Worthing 42423. [Died 25 Dec. 1971.

THOMAS, Sir Arwyn L. U.; *see* Ungoed-Thomas.

THOMAS, Sir Ben Bowen, Kt 1950; Member, Commission on the Constitution, 1969-73; Permanent Secretary to the Welsh Department, Ministry of Education, 1945-63; *b* Ystrad Rhondda, 1899; *o s* of late Jonathan Thomas and Ann (*née* Bowen); *m* 1st, Rhiannon Williams (*d* 1932), 3rd *d* of late Rev. I. Jones Williams, Llandderfel, Merion.; one *d*; 2nd, Gweneth (*d* 1963), *o d* of late Alderman Ellis W. Davies, Caernarvon. *Educ:* Rhondda Grammar School, Porth; University Coll. of Wales, Aberystwyth; Jesus Coll., Oxford. Univ. Tutorial Class Lectr, Univ. of Wales, 1922-27; Warden Coleg Harlech, Harlech, 1927-40; Director of Extra Mural Studies, University Coll. of Wales, Aberystwyth, 1940; seconded, 1941, to Ministry of Labour and National Service as Chairman, Swansea Man Power Board; Chairman, Cardiff Man Power Board, May 1945; Member Bd of Education Cttee on Training of Teachers and Youth Leaders, 1942-44. UK Deleg. 1946-62; Member: Exec. Bd, Unesco, 1954-62 (Chm. 1958-60); ITA, 1964-70; President: London Welsh Assoc., 1953-55; Nat. Inst. of Adult Education, 1964-71; University College of Wales, Aberystwyth, 1964-76; Baptist Union of Wales, 1966-67; Hon. Society of Cymmrodorion, 1969-(Cymmrodorion Medal, 1976); Cambrian Archaeol Assoc., 1977. Chm. N Wales Assoc. for the Arts, 1967-77. Dep. Chm., Christian Aid, 1967-69. Hon. Fellow, Jesus College, Oxford, 1963. Hon. LLD Wales, 1965. *Publications:* An Economic History of Wales, 1941; The Old Order, 1945; Baledi Morgannwg, 1951; Drych y Baledwr, 1958; Aber 1872-1972, 1972; (Editor) Harlech Studies, 1938; (Editor) Lleufer y Werin, 1965; articles on historical subjects relating to Wales. *Recreations:* strolling and travel. *Address:* Wern, Bodlondeb, Bangor, N Wales. *T:* Bangor 2971. *Club:* Reform.
[Died 26 July 1977.

THOMAS, Cecil, OBE 1953; FRBS; Sculptor; *b* 8 March 1885; *s* of J. Thomas, Engraver; *m* 1930, Dora Margaret (*d* 1967), *yr d* of late Alderman George Pearson, JP, Wigton, Cumberland; one *s*. *Educ:* London, Central School, Heatherly's, Slade. Served War of 1914-18, service in Belgium as Lt in Middlesex Regiment; Flying Officer, RAF, 1940-45; Master, Art Workers Guild, 1946; exhibited at RA, Salon, Walker Art Gallery, Washington, etc. Formed Dora Charitable Trust, 1970, to protect his house for benefit of RBS. Gold Medal, RBS, 1973. *Principal Works:* Relief portraits of Queen Elizabeth II for overseas coinage, Coronation Medal, the embossed stamps for UK and NZ; modelled four of the reverses of new UK coinage; decimal coinage for Ghana, 1965, with portrait of Dr Nkrumah; Recumbent memorials to Archbishop Davidson in Canterbury Cathedral; Bishop Talbot in Southwark Cathedral, Alfred Forster at Exbury and Newcastle Cathedral, Australia, the Toc H Monument; and Admiral Nelson-Ward at Boxgrove Priory, Chichester; Bronze statue, New Zealand Youth, King's College, Auckland; Peter Pan and The Darling children learning to fly, Botanical Gardens, Dunedin; Peter Pan, Wanganui, New Zealand. Lord Wakefield's portrait at Tower Hill, also two groups on The Terrace representing The Sea, children playing with porpoises; The Lees, Dundonald, Montagu, Vyner, and Prebendary Boyd memorials, etc; part of heraldic decoration of Brit. pavilion, NY World's Fair, 1939; sculpture on rebuilt Church of All Hallows by the Tower (where his meml to late Rev. Tubby Clayton was dedicated in 1976), and St John of

Jerusalem, Clerkenwell; medals for the Franklin Mint of Philadelphia, USA. *Publications:* articles and lectures on Art and Crafts. *Address:* 108 Old Brompton Rd, SW7. *T:* 01-373 5377. *Club:* Arts. *[Died 16 Sept. 1976.*

THOMAS, Cecil James, CMG 1950; *b* 14 June 1902; *y s* of late Thomas Thomas, Cardiff; *m* 1946, Ruth Christabel, *o d* of late A. W. Jeffree, West Kensington Court, W14. *Educ:* privately. Entered Colonial Service, 1930, and has served in Ceylon, Cyprus, Sarawak and Malaya. Member, Advisory Development Service, World Bank, 1962-64; Ministry of Overseas Development, 1965-67. *Address:* 7 Furze Croft, Hove, Sussex BN3 1PB. *[Died 25 June 1973.*

THOMAS, Sir Clement Price; *see* Price Thomas.

THOMAS, Rev. Canon Dennis Daven-; Vicar of St Mary-de-Lode with St Nicholas, Gloucester; since 1967; Residentiary Canon of Gloucester Cathedral, since 1968 (Hon. Canon, 1961-67); Director of Ordination Training and Chief Examining Chaplain to the Bishop of Gloucester since 1957; *b* 7 April 1913; *y s* of David and Maud Thomas, Kidwelly, Carms; *m* 1939, Joan, *o d* of Greig and May Simpson, Langland Bay, Swansea; one *s* one *d. Educ:* Christ College, Brecon; St David's College, Lampeter; Jesus College, Oxford; St Michael's College, Llandaff. Asst Curate: St Mary, Swansea, 1936-39; Oystermouth, 1939-42. Organising Secretary Waifs and Strays Soc., 1942-44; Vicar of Falfield and Rector of Rockhampton, Dio. of Gloucester, 1944-46; Chaplain, Leyhill Prison, 1945-46; Vicar of Christ Church, Gloucester, 1946-57. Chaplain, HM Prison, Gloucester, 1946-53; Rural Dean of Gloucester, 1955-57; Rural Dean of Dursley, 1962-64; Canon Missioner, 1957-60; Rector of Dursley, 1961-65; Vicar of Maisemore, 1965-67. Principal, Gloucester Theol Course, 1968. *Address:* 38 St Mary's Square, Gloucester. *T:* Gloucester 20864. *[Died 19 Oct. 1973.*

THOMAS, Ebenezer Rhys, OBE 1941; DCL, MA, MSc; retired Part-time Lecturer, Physics Department, University of Newcastle upon Tyne; *b* April 1885; *s* of late D. Thomas, Aberystwyth; *m* Mary Foster (*d* 1956), *d* of Hugh Richardson, MA, Stocksfield, Northumberland; three *s. Educ:* Aberystwyth School and University College; Emmanuel College, Cambridge. Late Headmaster Royal Grammar School, Newcastle upon Tyne; formerly Head of Science Dept, Rugby School; did work on high explosives during the European War; later DAQMG, GHQ, BEF, France (despatches). *Publications:* papers in Journal of Chemical Society and other scientific journals; articles in Listener; School Science Review; New Scientist; Editor of Classics of Scientific Method; joint author of Newton and the Origin of Colours. *Recreations:* research on singing sands, chamber music. *Address:* Clova, 2 Clothersholme Road, Ripon, North Yorkshire. *[Died 20 April 1979.*

THOMAS, Prof. Edgar, CBE 1958; BSc Wales; BLitt Oxon; Professor of Agricultural Economics, University of Reading, 1945-65, Emeritus Professor since 1965 (Dean of the Faculty of Agriculture and Horticulture, 1955-59); *b* 24 July 1900; *y s* of Henry Jones Thomas, JP, Penrhos, Llanfynydd, Carmarthenshire, and Elizabeth Lewis; *m* 1927, Eurwen Parry-Williams (*d* 1951); two *d. Educ:* Llandeilo County Scho.; University Coll. of Wales, Aberystwyth; Wadham College, Oxford; Royal Agricultural Coll., Copenhagen. Research Assistant, Agricultural Economics Research Institute, Oxford, 1926-27; Chief Advisory Officer and Lecturer in Agricultural Economics, Reading Univ., 1927-45. First Pres., Thames Valley Rent Assessment Panel, 1966-72. Vice-President, Internat. Conference of Agricultural Economists, 1952-64; Hon. Sec., Agricultural Economics Society, 1930-52, President, 1953-54; Chairman of Curators of Museum of English Rural Life, 1954-65; Corresponding Member: Accad. Economico-Agraria dei Georgofili, Florence, 1958; Scientific Agricultural Society of Finland, 1961; a Vice-President of Hon. Society of Cymmrodorion. *Publications:* The Economics of Smallholdings, 1927; An Introduction to Agricultural Economics, 1946. Contributions to Journal of Agricultural Economics, Proceedings International Conference of Agricultural Economists and to other economic journals and reviews. *Address:* 81 Elm Road, Earley, Reading, Berks. *T:* 81474. *[Died 9 May 1979.*

THOMAS, Sir George Alan, 7th Bt, *cr* 1766; late Lieutenant 6th Battalion Hampshire Regiment; *b* 14 June 1881; *s* of 6th Bt and Edith Margaret, *d* of Morgan Hugh Foster, CB, Brickhill, Bedfordshire; *S* father, 1918. *Educ:* Wellington. British Chess Champion, 1923 and 1934; All England Badminton Champion, Singles, 1920-23, Doubles nine times. *Publication:* The Art of Badminton, 1923. *Heir:* none. *Address:* Knaresborough Nursing

Home, 7 Knaresborough Place, SW5.
[Died 23 July 1972 (ext).

THOMAS, Gilbert Oliver; author and journalist; *b* 1891; *s* of late J. Oliver Thomas, Leicester; *m* 1928, Dorothy Kathleen, *y d* of late Robert Dann, Hythe, Kent; one *s* one *d. Educ:* Wyggeston School, Leicester; Leys, Cambridge. Editorial Staff, Chapman & Hall, 1910-14; Editor, The Venturer, 1919-21. *Publications:* Birds of Passage (Poems), 1912; The Wayside Altar (Poems), 1913; The Voice of Peace, and other Poems, 1914; The Grapes and the Thorns: Thoughts in War Time, 1915; The Further Goal and other Poems, 1915; Towards the Dawn, and other Poems, 1918; Things Big and Little (Essays), 1919; Poems: 1912-1919, 1920; Sparks from the Fire (Essays), 1923; Mary of Huntingdon and other Poems, 1928; Calm Weather (Essays), 1930; John Masefield (Modern Writers Series), 1932; The Master Light; Letters to David, 1932; William Cowper and the Eighteenth Century, 1935, revised edition, 1949; The Inner Shrine: anthology of the author's devotional poems, 1943; Builders and Makers (literary essays), 1944; Times May Change (essays), 1946; Autobiography: 1891-1941, 1946; Paddington to Seagood: The Story of a Model Railway, 1947; Selected Poems Old and New, 1951; Window in the West (Essays), 1954; Later Poems, 1960; Double Headed: Two Generations of Railway Enthusiasm (in collaboration with David St John Thomas), 1963; One Man Speaks (Text of broadcast poem), 1967; Collected Poems, 1969; contributor, Observer, Sunday Times, Spectator, and many others. For some years wrote regular weekly book feature for Birmingham Post. *Recreations:* music, model railways. *Address:* Queenswood, Cliffgrove, Chilwell, Nottingham. *T:* Nottingham 255328. *[Died 14 Jan. 1978.*

THOMAS, General Sir (Gwilym) Ivor, GCB 1952 (KCB 1950; CB 1944); KBE 1947; DSO 1917; MC; psc; ns; late RA; *b* 1893; *s* of late John Thomas (Pencerdd Gwalia), Harpist to Queen Victoria and King Edward VII, and late Joan Francis, *y d* of William Denny, Tralee, Co. Kerry; *m* 1949, Elliott Ellen (*d* 1971), *o d* of late Major van Kriekenbeek, 128th Pioneers, and late Mrs H. S. Wilding. *Educ:* Cheltenham College; Royal Military Academy, Woolwich. Commissioned, 1912; served European War, 1914-18 (DSO, MC and bar, despatches); Bt Major, 1929; Major, 1931; Bt Lt-Col, 1933; Col, 1936; Brigadier, 1939; Maj.-Gen., 1942; Acting Lt-Gen., 1945; Lt-Gen., 1946; Gen., 1949; commanded 43rd Div. in campaign in NW Europe, 1944-45 (despatches); Commander, 1st Corps District, BAOR, 1945-47; Administrator of Polish Forces under British Command, 1947; GOC-in-C Anti-Aircraft Command, 1948-50; Quarter-Master-General to the Forces, 1950-52. Col Comdt RA, 1947-57. Officier Légion d'Honneur, 1945; Knight Grand Officer of the Order of Orange Nassau with swords, 1946; Comdr Order of Leopold with Palm, 1950; Croix de Guerre avec palme (France), 1945; Croix de Guerre avec palme (Belgium), 1950. *Recreations:* hunting, polo. *Address:* c/o Lloyds Bank, Ltd, 6 Pall Mall, SW1. *Club:* Army and Navy.
[Died 29 Aug. 1972.

THOMAS, Herbert Percival, CIE 1933; BSc, *b* 12 Dec. 1879; *s* of John Caldwell Thomas, MD, etc, and Annie M. Calder; *m* 1907, Elsie Geard, *d* of Thos Harbottle Guenett; two *s* one *d*; *m* 1949, Esther Amelia (*d* 1956), *d* of late Alfred David Price, Melbourne. *Educ:* Melbourne Church of England Grammar School; Melbourne University; McGill University, Montreal. Erection Engineer, Allis Chalmers, Bullock, 1907; Electrical Engineer, Town of Kenora, Ontario, 1908; Manager, Public Utilities City of Nelson, British Columbia, 1912; Coates and Co., Melbourne, Australia 1920; Chief Engineer, Southland Electric Power Board, New Zealand, 1921; Superintending Engineer, Punjab PWD Hydro Electric Branch, 1926; Chief Engineer, Punjab Public Works Department Electricity Branch, 1932-39; retired, 1939. Mobilised 1942 in RANVR as Squadron Skipper Naval Auxiliary Patrol, equivalent rank Lieut RANVR; Staff Officer Coastal Craft, Jan.-July 1945; then Lieut RANVR to HMAS Moreton (additional); demobilised, 1946. *Recreations:* golf, tennis, fishing. *Address:* Rakiura, PO Box 34, Mansfield, Victoria, Australia. *[Died 25 Jan. 1972.*

THOMAS, Prof. Horatio Oritsejolomi, CBE 1963; CON 1965; FRCS; Vice-Chancellor, University of Ibadan, 1972-75; *b* 31 Aug. 1917; *s* of James Awadagin and Alero Ogiedi Thomas; *m* 1940, Dorothy Irene (*née* Williams); one *s* two *d. Educ:* Univ. of Birmingham. MB, ChB 1942; MRCS 1942, LRCP, FRCS 1949. University Coll., Ibadan (now Univ. of Ibadan): Lectr in Surgery, 1949-52; Sen. Lectr in Surgery, 1952-62; Univ. of Lagos: Prof. and Head of Dept of Surgery, Coll. of Medicine of the Univ., 1962-72; Dean and Provost, Coll. of Medicine, 1962-69; Chm., Bd of Management, Lagos Univ. Teaching Hosp., 1962-66. Hon. DSc, Univ. of Ife, 1967; Hon. FRCSI, 1970. *Publications:* contribs (chap.) to Diseases of Children in the

Subtropics and Tropics (ed Trowell and Jelliffe), 1970; also to: Lancet; Brit. Jl of Surgery; Jl of Med. Educn; W African Med. Jl. *Recreations:* gardening, water-skiing, books (reading, designing and publishing). *Address:* St Thomas's Clinic, Jathomas Estates, PO Box 1, Sapele, Nigeria. *Clubs:* Metropolitan, 400, Lagos Motor Boat (all in Lagos).   [*Died 2 July 1979.*

THOMAS, Gen. Sir Ivor; *see* Thomas, General Sir G. I.

THOMAS, Sir (James William) Tudor, Kt 1956; DSc, MD, MS, FRCS; Hon. LLD Glasgow; Hon. Ophthalmic Surgeon, United Cardiff Hospitals and Welsh Regional Hospital Board; *b* 23 May 1893; *s* of late Thomas Thomas, Ystradgynlais, Breconshire, and late Mary Thomas; *m* 1938, Bronwen Vaughan Pugh, Cardiff; two *s. Educ:* Cardiff Medical School (Alfred Sheen Prize); Middlesex Hospital (Leopold Hudson Prize). BSc Wales 1913; LRCP, MRCS 1915; MB, BCh Wales 1916; MD Wales 1929; DSc Wales 1931; MB, BS London 1916; MS London 1929; FRCS 1925. Captain RAMC (SR), 1914-18 War. Hunterian Prof. RCS, 1930-31. Assoc. Surg. i/c Corneo-plastic Dept, Central London Ophth. Hosp., 1935-40; Ophthalmic Surgeon, Cardiff Royal Infirmary, and United Cardiff Hospitals, 1921-58 and Corneo-plastic Surgeon to 1960. Member: Ophthalmological Society of UK (President, 1966-68); Master, Oxford Ophthalmological Congress, 1956-58; Vice-President, British Medical Association (President, 1953-54). President Cardiff Med. Soc., 1948-49. Hon. Pres. British Medical Students' Assoc., 1957-58. Montgomery Lectr, TCD, 1936; Middlemore Lectr, Birmingham and Midland Eye Hosp., 1933; Doyne Memorial Lectr Oxford Ophthalmological Congress, 1955. Sheriff of Breconshire, 1956. Hon. FRSM. Gold Medal in Therapeutics, Worshipful Society of Apothecaries of London, 1960. *Publications:* Contrib. on Corneal Transplantation experimental and clinical, 1930-, in BMJ, Lancet, Trans Ophthalmological Soc. UK, Proc. Roy. Soc. Med., Proc. Oxford Ophthalmological Congress, etc. *Recreations:* golf and fishing. *Address:* Oakhurst, Ty-gwyn Road, Penylan, Cardiff CF2 5JG. *T:* Cardiff 28679. *Club:* Royal Porthcawl Golf.
                    [*Died 23 Jan. 1976.*

THOMAS, Sir Leslie (Montagu), Kt 1963; MBE 1945; TD; *b* 24 April 1906; *s* of late Rt Hon. J. H. Thomas, PC; *m* 1929, Ursula Mary, *d* of late H. B. Owen; two *s* one *d. Educ:* elementary, private and Dulwich College. Great Western Railway, 1923-29; Member London Stock Exchange, 1931-. Served War of 1939-45, North Africa and Italy; demobilised with rank of Major. Member: Caterham and Warlingham UDC, 1932-35; Whitstable UDC, 1950-52. Contested (Nat Lab), Leek, Staffs, 1935. MP (C) Canterbury Div. of Kent, 1953-66, retd. *Recreations:* golf, gardening. *Address:* Dene Park, Tonbridge, Kent. *Club:* Carlton.   [*Died 27 Nov. 1971.*

THOMAS, Sir Lynn U.; *see* Ungoed-Thomas.

THOMAS, Meirion, FRS 1949; MA, FRSE; Professor of Botany, King's College, Newcastle upon Tyne, 1946-60; Professor Emeritus since 1961; *b* 28 Dec. 1894; *s* of late J. Thomas, V.-P. Normal Coll., Bangor. *Educ:* Friars' School; University College of North Wales; Trinity Hall, Cambridge. 2nd Lt South Wales Borderers, 1914-15; served with Special Companies, Royal Engineers in France, 1915-19; demobilised with rank of Capt.; at Cambridge, 1919-24; subsequently at what is now called The University of Newcastle upon Tyne, as Lecturer in Botany (1924-43), Reader in Plant Physiology (1943-46). Service with Durham University Senior Training Corps, 1940-45, and Home Guard, 1941-45. President, Section K, British Association, Belfast, 1952. Vice-President RSE, 1955-58. Hon. DSc Wales, 1964. Charles Reid Barnes Hon. Life Mem. of Amer. Soc. of Plant Physiologists, 1963. *Publications:* Textbook: Plant Physiology, 5th edn (with Ranson and Richardson), 1973; several papers on Plant Physiology. *Recreations:* formerly Association football (blue, 1922), cricket (elected to Crusaders Club, 1923), golf. *Address:* Glannant, Bryn Crug, Tywyn, Gwynedd LL36 9PH.   [*Died 5 April 1977.*

THOMAS, Lt-Col Sir Reginald Aneurin, Kt 1946; CBE 1919; late RA; Chief Inspector of Explosives, Home Office, 1931-45; *b* 1879; *s* of A. H. Thomas, Gampola, Ceylon; *m* 1st, 1910, Violet Mary (*d* 1910), *d* of H. Anderson; 2nd, 1918 Kathleen Mary, *d* of late G. C. Bliss, Glen Lyon, Ceylon; three *s* one *d. Educ:* Cheltenham College; RMA Woolwich. Served S Africa, 1900-2 (Queen's medal with three clasps, King's medal with two clasps); European War, 1914-19 (despatches, CBE). *Address:* Holmwood, Foxcombe Road, Boar's Hill, Oxford OX1 5DL. *T:* Oxford 39994.   [*Died 4 Jan. 1975.*

THOMAS, Richard, MA London; MA, DSc Wales; Principal, Normal College, Bangor, 1935-58; Member: University of Wales

Council and Court of Governors; Council and Court of Governors, University College, Aberystwyth, and University College, Bangor; *b* Trefeglwys, Montgomeryshire, 1890; *s* of John Thomas; *m* 1919, Margaret (*d* 1963), *d* of David Edwards, Aberystwyth; *m* 1969, Sarah, *d* of John S. Duffy, Liverpool. *Educ:* University College of Wales, Aberystwyth. Asst Master under LCC Educn Cttee, 1913; Served in the RA, Balkan Expeditionary Force 1915-19; Lectr in Educn, UCW, Aberystwyth, 1919; Lectr in English, 1922; Lectr in Educn, UC of S Wales and Monmouthshire, Cardiff, 1923; Master of Method, 1933; Member: Exec. Cttee, Central Welsh Bd, 1936-49; Min. of Educn Interim Cttee for Teachers, 1946-48; Welsh Jt Educn Cttee, 1949-55; Nat. Adv. Cttee on Art Exams, 1952-55; Univ. of Wales Bd for Training Colls and Educn Bd, 1935-58; Caernarvonshire Educn Cttee, 1936-74 (Chm., 1969-72). Vice Pres., UC Bangor, 1966-71. Hon. LLD Wales, 1974. *Publications:* Articles in Educational Journals. *Recreations:* golf, gardening. *Address:* 22 Kings Road, Colwyn Bay, North Wales.   [*Died 2 Feb. 1977.*

THOMAS, Ronald Hamilton Eliot, OBE 1946; Member National Coal Board 1955-60, retired (Chairman, Opencast Executive, 1957-60); *b* 12 June 1896; 2nd *s* of William Eliot and Emily Thomas, Torquay, Devon; *m* 1920, Ethel Mary Green; two *d. Educ:* St Winifred's School, Torquay. Founder of firm of Milner, Thomas & Co. Ltd, London, Coal Distributors, 1921; Deputy Director-General of Marketing, National Coal Board, 1947. *Recreation:* golf. *Address:* Belliver, 39 The Downs, Wimbledon, SW20. *T:* 01-946 1857. *Club:* Royal Wimbledon Golf.
                    [*Died 4 Feb. 1977.*

THOMAS, Stephen Peter John Quao; Hon. Mr Justice Thomas; Chief Justice of the High Court, Mid-Western Region, Nigeria, 1964; *b* 31 March 1904; *e s* of late Peter John Claudius Thomas, Freetown, Sierra Leone, and Lagos, Nigeria; *m* 1940, Margaret Amelia, *o d* of I. K. Roberts, Barrister-at-Law; one *s* four *d. Educ:* King's College, Lagos; London School of Economics and Political Science, Univ. of London. Master, King's College, Lagos, 1925-26; Mercantile Asst, 1926-29; called to Bar, Middle Temple, 1933; Sierra Leone Bar, 1935; Nigeria Bar, 1935; Magistrate, Grade I, 1941; Acting Puisne Judge, Supreme Court, 1951; Chief Magistrate, 1951; Puisne Judge, 1953-55; Judge, High Court, Western Region, 1955-63. Coronation Medal, 1953. *Recreations:* gardening, walking. *Address:* 23 Desalv Street, Ebute-Metta, Lagos, Nigeria. *Club:* Royal Commonwealth Society.

THOMAS, Terry, MA, LLB Cantab, BSc London and Wales, PhD London; Headmaster, Leeds Grammar School, 1923-53; *b* 19 Oct. 1888; *e s* of late David Terry Thomas, Cardiff; *m* 1915, Mair, *e d* of late Major Henry Davies, OBE, CC, Cardiff; two *d. Educ:* Howard Gardens; University College, Cardiff (Isaac Roberts' Science Scholar); St John's Coll., Cambridge (Foundation Scholar). First Class Honours in Physics, BSc Wales; Second Class Honours in Physics BSc, London; 1st Cl. Natural Sci. Tripos, Part II, Physics; Second Class Mathematical Tripos, Part I; Third Class Law Tripos, Part II. Chief Science Master, Inverurie Academy, 1909-11; Head of Military and Engineering Side, Haileybury Coll., 1914-22; former Mem. of Headmasters' Conference Committee; Captain OTC; Chm., Leeds XIII Discussion Club, 1929-; Pres. of the Incorporated Association of Headmasters, 1936, Hon. Treas., 1938-46; former Member Secondary School Examination Council; Member of Norwood Committee; formerly Mem. Court, Univ. of Leeds; JP, Leeds, 1937-; Chm. Visiting Magistrates, Leeds Prison, 1948-63; Chm., Leeds Medical and Legal Gp on Psychiatry and the Law, 1948-53; Dep. Chairman Leeds Group B Hospital Management Committee, 1948-54; Chm. Leeds Bench, 1950-63; Pres. W Riding Branch Magistrates' Association, 1956, 1957, and 1958; President Leeds Lit. and Philosophical Society, 1952 and 1953. Mem. Nat. Assistance Bd Tribunal; Education Adviser, RAF Benevolent Fund. Hon. LLD Leeds, 1948. *Publications:* Mathematical and Science Papers for Army Candidates; Revision Arithmetic and Mensuration; Notes on Dynamics; Outlines of the Calculus; The Leeds Intelligence Test; The Science of Marking. *Recreations:* fly-fishing, golf, painting. *Address:* Fairmount, 25 Shire Oak Road, Leeds LS6 2DD. *T:* Leeds 751895. [*Died 22 July 1978.*

THOMAS, Theodore Lynam; Headmaster, Repton School, 1944-61; *b* 17 Sept. 1900; *s* of late Canon L. W. Thomas; *m* 1931, Margaret Astbury; two *s. Educ:* Dragon School, Oxford; King William's College, Isle of Man; St John's College, Cambridge. Assistant Master Rugby School, 1923-44. *Address:* Warren Lodge, 69 Links Lane, Rowlands Castle, Hants. *T:* Rowlands Castle 2370.   [*Died 15 May 1976.*

THOMAS, Sir Tudor; see Thomas, Sir J. W. T.

THOMAS, William, CB 1951; former Director of the Council of Social Service for Wales and Monmouthshire (Inc.); retired; now farming at Trefloyne; b 1890; m 1919, Elizabeth Morgan, BSc; one s (and one s decd). Educ: University College of Wales, Aberystwyth; Royal University of Holland, Groningen; Emmanuel College, Cambridge (1851 Research Exhibitioner, Research Exhibitioner); MA Cantab, 1927; DSc Wales; PhD Aberdeen; Fellow of the University of Wales; Hon. LLD Wales, 1968. Principal, Tech. Inst., Wrexham. Army Rank, Captain. Chief Inspector of Schools for Wales, retired 1952. Member Court of Governors of: Univ. of Wales; Nat. Library of Wales; Nat. Museum of Wales; Council, Welsh Nat. Sch. of Med.; UC of Wales, Aberystwyth (Vice-Pres.). Publications: Twelve original papers in Chemical Journals; Complex Salts, 1924. Recreation: golf. Address: Trefloyne, Tenby, Dyfed.
[Died 22 Nov. 1974.

THOMAS, William Herbert Evans, CBE 1941; retired; b 28 Dec. 1886; s of late John Owen Thomas and Mary Elizabeth Evans, Llantwit Major, Glamorgan; m; two s one d. Educ: Privately; London University. Joined Chartered Bank of India, Australia and China, 1907; Manager at Peking, Tientsin and Hong Kong Branches; Inspector of Branches, 1939; British Member Stabilization Board of China, 1943. Financial Counsellor, HBM Embassy, Chungking, 1944, 1945-46. Publication: Vanished China. Address: c/o Standard Chartered Bank Ltd, 38 Bishopsgate, EC2.   [Died 17 Sept. 1979.

THOMAS, William R.; see Rees-Thomas.

THOMPSON, Lt-Col Cecil Henry Farrer, DSO 1918; OBE 1919; TD 1924; b 16 Dec. 1882; s of late Geo. Rodie Thompson, JP, DL, of Lynwood, Ascot, and Alice Howard, d of Capt. H. H. Barber, 17th Lancers; m 1915, Rachel Ellen, d of late John Holmes, of Brooke Hall, Norwich; three s. Educ: Harrow; Trinity College, Cambridge, BA. Called to Bar, Inner Temple, 1910; 2nd Lieut London Rifle Brigade, 1909; Captain, 1913; Major, 1917; served European War, 1914-19 (DSO, OBE, despatches four times; French Croix de Guerre); Bt Lt-Col, 1922; DL, JP, Cumberland; High Sheriff of Cumberland, 1940. Address: Nunwick Hall, Penrith, Cumbria. T: Langwathby 205. Clubs: Brooks's, MCC.   [Died 27 March 1975.

THOMPSON, Daniel Varney; author and columnist; Registered Professional Engineer (Massachusetts); b 29 Dec. 1902; s of Daniel Varney and Grace Randall Thompson; m 1927, Cécile de Luze Simonds (d 1972); one d (one s decd). Educ: Harvard. AB cum laude Harvard 1922; AM 1926; Instr and tutor, Harvard Univ., 1923-24, 1925-26 (Sheldon Fellow, 1922-23, 1924-25); Technical Adviser, Fogg Art Museum China Expedition 1924-25; Instructor and Assistant Professor of the History of Art in Yale University, 1926-33 (Sterling Fellow, 1931-32); Research Fellow of American Council of Learned Societies, 1933-34; Research and Technical Adviser Courtauld Institute of Art, 1934-36; Head of its Scientific Department, 1936-38; Professor of the History of the Technology of Art in University of London, 1938-46. Man. Dir, Daniel Varney Ltd, 1943-47. Technical Consultant, Head of Research and Development, E-Z Mills, Inc., 1948-50. Sen. Staff Consulting Engr, AVCO Corp. Res. and Advanced Develt, Missile Systems Div., Advanced Electronics Gp, 1956-68, retd. Member Royal Institution (Board of Visitors, 1946-48); Technical Consultant, Sylvania Electric Products, Electronics Division, 1951; Comstock & Wescott, Inc., 1952 and 1955-67; Chief Engineer, Jarrell-Ash Co., 1953-55; Vice-Pres. Swett & Sibley Co. 1955-57. Food and Garden Editor, North Shore Magazine, 1966-73. Hon. Mem. Soc. of Painters in Tempera (London). Publications: Il Libro dell' Arte 1932; The Craftsman's Handbook, 1933 (rev. 1936); De Arte Illuminandi: The Technique of Manuscript Illumination, 1933; The Practice of Tempera Painting, 1936 (1962); The Materials of Medieval Painting, 1936 (repr. as The Materials and Techniques of Medieval Painting, 1957); (introd) C. E. Francatelli's The Modern Cook, 1846, 1973; contrib. various learned and tech. jls, magazines and newspapers. Address: Box 1569, Manchester, Mass 01944, USA. Club: Athenæum.   [Died 4 Jan. 1980.

THOMPSON, Mrs E. Roffe; see Lejeune, Miss C. A.

THOMPSON, Lt-Col Edgar Hynes, OBE 1944; MA, ScD; Professor of Photogrammetry and Surveying, University College, London, since 1951; b 13 Jan. 1910; s of Edgar Thompson, OBE; m 1934, Muriel May Smith; two d. Educ: Cheltenham; Royal Mil. Acad., Woolwich; Downing College, Cambridge. Commissioned, 2nd Lt Royal Engineers, 1930; Ordnance Survey, 1938-39, 1944-47, 1950-51. Served War of 1939-45: BEF France, Middle East, Italy (despatches twice);

retired, 1951. FRAS, FRGS, FRICS. Patron's Medal, RGS, 1973. Publications: An Introduction to the Algebra of Matrices, 1969; numerous papers on geodetic and photogrammetric subjects. Address: University College, Gower Street, WC1. T: 01-387 7050.   [Died 9 April 1976.

THOMPSON, Edward Vincent, CB 1943; b 1880; s of Reginald E. Thompson, MD, and Anne Isabella, d of Prof. Augustus De Morgan; m 1912, Jessie Forbes (d 1968), d of James Cameron, Stanley, Perthshire; two s one d. Educ: St Paul's Sch.; King's College, Cambridge (MA). Solicitor, 1907; entered Treasury Solicitor's Department, 1912; Principal Assistant Solicitor to HM Treasury, 1941-49. Address: 24 High Street, Southwold, Suffolk. T: 2046.   [Died 8 April 1976.

THOMPSON, Sir Eric; see Thompson, Sir John Eric Sidney.

THOMPSON, E(rnest) Heber, RE 1939 (ARE 1923); Artist, Etcher, Painter; b 1891; s of John Brown Thompson and Victoria Marie Dyer; m 1919, Nellie Florence Gutteridge (d 1967); one d. Educ: Dunedin, New Zealand. Began as free-lance Black and White artist in Dunedin, New Zealand; served European war, 1915-17 in Egypt and France with New Zealand Expeditionary Force (wounded); after war studied at Slade School (drawing and painting) and at Royal College of Art and Central School of Arts and Crafts (etching); Finalist, Prix de Rome (engraving), 1923. Representative in London, NZ Nat. Art Gallery, 1951-66. Retrospective exhbn, Dunedin Public Art Gallery, 1970. Work represented in permanent collections of: Ashmolean Museum, Oxford, British Museum, Bradford and Harrogate Art Galleries, National Art Gallery, New Zealand, Dunedin Public Art Gallery, Hocken Library Art Gallery, Dunedin. Publications: The Sketcher, Nos 1-7, 1914-15; Light Diet, 1919. Recreations: gardening, walking. Address: Mount Warren, Upper Warren Avenue, Caversham, Reading, Berks.
[Died 13 April 1971.

THOMPSON, Estelle Merle O'Brien; see Oberon, Merle.

THOMPSON, Francis L.; see Longstreth-Thompson.

THOMPSON, Frank Charles, DMet Sheffield; MSc Manchester; BSc London; Professor of Metallurgy, University of Manchester, 1921-59, Emeritus Professor, 1959; Pro-Vice-Chancellor, 1937-41; Fellow of Institute of Metals, 1962; b 3 April 1890. Educ: Royal Grammar School, Sheffield; King Edward VII School, Sheffield; Univ. of Sheffield. Lecturer in Metallurgy, Univ. of Sheffield, 1920-21; Sorby Research Fellow, 1920-21. President, Institute of Metals, 1953-54; Pres., Institution of Metallurgists, 1955-56. Hon. Curator of Coins, Manchester Museum, 1959-76. Publications: many papers on metallurgical subjects, particularly relating to the effects of strain. Address: 45 Moss Lane, Bramhall, Stockport, Cheshire SK7 1EQ.   [Died 12 Aug. 1977.

THOMPSON, Colonel Horace Cuthbert Rees, CBE 1955; TD; JP, DL; b 11 Jan. 1893; s of Cuthbert and Ada Thompson; m 1st, 1920, Margaret (d 1946), d of T. B. R. Wilson; one s two d ; 2nd, 1956, Violet Mary, widow of John Watcyn Morgan, MC. Commissioned 1913, 1st (Rifle) Bn Monmouthshire Regt TA; seconded King's African Rifles, 1917; served in France, Belgium, Egypt, and East Africa; rejoined Monmouthshire Regt 1919; commanded it, 1929-32; late Hon. Colonel 603 HAA Regt RA, TA. High Sheriff 1944; DL 1946, Monmouthshire; late Chairman and Military Member of Monmouthshire T&AFA. Recreation: salmon fishing. Address: Oakdene, Llantarnam, Gwent. T: Cwmbran 2323.   [Died 9 June 1975.

THOMPSON, Sir (John) Eric (Sidney), KBE 1975; FBA 1959; retired from staff of Department of Archaeology, Carnegie Institution of Washington (1935-58); b 31 Dec. 1898; yr s of George W. Thompson, FRCS and Mary Thompson (née Cullen); m 1930, Florence L. Keens; one s. Educ: Winchester Coll.; Cambridge Univ. 2nd Lt Coldstream Guards, 1918. Assistant Curator, in charge of Central and South American archaeology and ethnology, Chicago Natural Hist. Mus., 1926-35. Hon. Professor, Museo Nacional de México, 1941-; Hon. curator, Middle American archæology, Chicago Nat. Hist. Mus., 1945-; President, 32nd Internat. Congress of Americanists, 1952; Consejero: Centro de Investigaciones antropológicas mexicanas, 1953-; Seminario Maya, Univ. Mexico, 1960. Hon. Fellow, Fitzwilliam Coll., Cambridge, 1973; LLD Univ. of Yucatan, 1959; DLit: Univ. of Pennsylvania, 1962; Tulane, 1972; Hon. LittD Cantab 1973. Rivers Memorial medal, R. Anthrop. Inst., 1945; Viking Fund medal for Anthropology, New York, 1955; Huxley Meml Medal, 1966; Sahagún Medal, Mexico, 1972. Encomienda de Isabel la Católica, 1964; Order of the Aztec Eagle, 1965. Publications:

Excavations at San Jose, British Honduras, 1939; Maya hieroglyphic writing; introduction, 1950; The Rise and Fall of Maya Civilization, 1954; Thomas Gage's Travels in the New World, 1958; Maya History and Religion, 1970. *Address:* Harvard, Ashdon, Saffron Walden, Essex. *T:* Ashdon 265.
[Died 9 Sept. 1975.

THOMPSON, John McLean, MA, DSc, D ès Sc; FLS; FRSE; Professor of Botany, the University, Liverpool, 1921-52; *b* Rothesay, 1887; 2nd *s* of Hugh Thompson, Rothesay; *m* 1920, Simonne Denil, MB, ChB. *Educ:* Rothesay Academy; Glasgow University. Demonstrator in Geology and Dobbie-Smith Medallist, Glasgow University, 1910-11; Robert Donaldson Research Scholar in Biology and Senior Assistant in Botany, Glasgow University, 1913-15; Protozoologist to the Military Hospitals in the West of Scotland, 1915-19; Lecturer in Plant Morphology, Glasgow University, 1918-21; Botanical Expeditions to Jamaica, 1920 and to Columbia, Dominica, Venezuela and Panama, 1930 and 1931; Neill Prize, RSE 1924. *Publications:* chiefly memoirs on Floral Structure to RSE, in Publications of Hartley Botanical Laboratories, and in Proc. Linnean Soc. *Address:* 8 Linnet Lane, Sefton Park, Liverpool. *T:* 051-727 3174.
[Died 17 April 1977.

THOMPSON, Rt. Rev. Kenneth George; *b* 7 Aug. 1909; *s* of George William Thompson, Doncaster, and Edith Thompson (*née* Pearson), Manningham Bradford; *m* 1935, Doreen May Latchford, Cambridge; one *s* two *d.* *Educ:* The Perse, Cambridge; Christ's Coll., Cambridge; Lincoln Theological College. BA 1932 (2nd cl. English, 3rd cl. Theology), Cambridge. Curate, S Mary's, Stoke Newington, 1933-37; Vicar, S Mark, Ford, Devonport, 1937-46. Chaplain RNVR, 1940-44; 13th Destroyer Flotilla, 1940-41; HMS Rodney, 1942-44 (despatches). Vicar of Hucknall Torkard, Notts, 1946-62; Hon. Canon of Southwell, 1954-62; Chm., Exec. Cttee, Southwell Diocesan Day Schools Board, 1966-. Proctor in Convocation, 1958-65. Hon. Chaplain to the Queen, 1962-65; Archdeacon of Newark, 1962-65; Bishop Suffragan of Sherwood, 1965-74. *Publication:* HMS Rodney at War, 1944. *Recreations:* reading, travel. *Address:* 76 Beresford Avenue, Skegness, Lincs. *T:* Skegness 3249.
[Died 9 Jan. 1975.

THOMPSON, Llewellyn E.; Ambassador of the United States to the Soviet Union, 1966-Jan. 1969; Foreign Affairs Consultant, since 1969; *b* 24 Aug. 1904; *m* 1948, Jane Monroe Goelet; two *d.* *Educ:* University of Colorado. Appointed Foreign Service Officer, January 1929; Vice-Consul, Colombo, March 1929; Geneva, 1933-37; Army War College, Jan. 1940; Moscow, 1940-43; London, 1944-45; Washington, 1946-47; Rome, 1950-52; US High Commissioner for Austria, 1952-55; US Ambassador to Austria, 1955-57, to USSR, 1957-62; Ambassador-at-Large, 1962-66. Medal of Freedom, 1947; President's Award for Distinguished Federal Civilian Service, 1962; Rockefeller Public Service Award, 1962. *Address:* 3915 Watson Place NW, Washington, DC 20016, USA. *Clubs:* Metropolitan, Chevy Chase (Washington, DC).
[Died 6 Feb. 1972.

THOMPSON, Sir Peile Beaumont, 4th Bt *cr* 1890; *b* 4 Feb. 1874; 2nd *s* of Sir Peile Thompson, 2nd Bt, and Jessie (*d* 1927), *d* of Joseph Beaumont, Huddersfield; *S* brother 1956; *m* 1908, Stella Mary, *d* of Arthur Harris, Heaton Grove, Bradford; one *s* one *d.* *Educ:* Sedbergh; Trinity College, Cambridge. Tomato grower, Guernsey, 1908-18. *Recreations:* travelling and gardening. *Heir:* *s* Lt-Col Peile Thompson, OBE [*b* 28 Feb. 1911; *m* 1937, Barbara Johnson, *d* of late H. J. Rampling; one *s* one *d*]. *Address:* Old Farm, Augres, Trinity, Jersey, Channel Islands.
[Died 8 Aug. 1972.

THOMPSON, Maj.-Gen. (Hon. Lt-Gen.) Sir Treffry Owen, KCSI 1947; CB 1946; CBE 1942; KHP 1944; County Patron BRCS, Devon Branch; *b* 9 Aug. 1888; *s* of late Rev. W. F. Thompson (Chaplain, India), Fyfield, Abingdon, Berks; *gs* of Sir Charles Bell, Anatomist and Surgeon; *m* 1916, Mary Emily (*d* 1958), *d* of late Rev. Canon Medd, North Cerney, Gloucester; two *s* two *d* ; *m* 1959, Vera Elaine, *d* of late E. J. F. A. Ward and Mrs Ward. *Educ:* Dragon Sch., Oxford; Priory, Repton; St John's Coll., Oxford; St George's Hosp., London. House appointments Radcliffe, Oxford; RAMC, 1914; served European War, 1914-19, with RAMC; Lt, 1914; Capt., 1915; Major, 1926; DAD Hygiene, India, 1926-29; Lt-Col, 1935; AD Hygiene and Path., India, 1933-37; AD of Hygiene, War Office, 1938-39; DD Hygiene, and Pathology, India, 1939; Col, 1941; DDMS L of C Iraq Forces; Brig., 1942; DDMS Burma, Jan.-May 1942; Acting Maj.-Gen. 1942; DDMS Cen. Command, India; DDMS Eastern Army, 1943-44; Maj.-Gen. 1944; Medical Adviser SACSEA; DMS ALFSEA, 1944-45; DMS SACSEA, 1945; DMS in India, 1946-47; Lt-Gen. (local) 1947; retd, 1948;

Col Comdt RAMC, 1950-53. Br. Red Cross Comr for relief work in India and Pakistan, 1947-49; Editor, RAMC Journal, 1950; writer for Official Medical History, Campaigns of World War, 1939-45. County Dir British Red Cross Soc. Devonshire Br., 1951-65. CStJ 1945; Special Service Cross, BRCS 1960. Italian Croce di Guerra, 1917. *Publications:* scientific (Hygiene) articles. *Recreations:* hockey (Oxford Occasionals, Oxford County, 1910-14), cricket, Rugby football, tennis, squash, fishing, bee-keeping. *Address:* Savourys, Chulmleigh, N Devon EX18 7ES. *T:* Chulmleigh 314.
[Died 1 Dec. 1979.

THOMPSON, William David James C.; *see* Cargill Thompson.

THOMPSON, Rt. Rev. William Jameson, CBE 1953; MA; *b* 27 Oct. 1885; *s* of late Robert Wade Thompson, JP, DL, and E. I. Jameson; *m* 1926, M. R. Carr; three *d.* *Educ:* Monkton Combe School, near Bath; Trinity College, Cambridge. Master on Staff of Jay Narayans' School, Benares, 1908-10; Engineer in charge of building St John's College, Agra, 1910-12; Teacher's Diploma of Education, Oxford, 1913; Lieut and Capt. Indian Army Reserve of Officers (IARO); served with the Mesopotamia Expeditionary Force, attached to RE Works Dept, 1915-19 (despatches twice); Deacon, 1920; Priest, 1921; Principal of the Stuart Memorial College, Isfahan, 1921-35; Archdeacon of Isfahan, 1933-35; Bishop in Iran, 1935-Oct. 1960. Retd, 1960. *Address:* 29 Portman Avenue, SW14. *Club:* Royal Over-Seas League.
[Died 17 Nov. 1975.

THOMPSON, William John, CB 1968; Comptroller and Auditor-General, Northern Ireland. *Address:* Exchequer and Audit Department, Arnott's Buildings, 12 Bridge Street, Belfast BT1 1LZ.
[Died 6 May 1971.

THOMPSON, Dr William Robin, FRS 1933; Director, Commonwealth Institute of Biological Control, 1947-58 (Retired); *b* London, Canada, 29 June 1887; son of late William Thompson, Editor of Canadian Agricultural Weekly (The Farmer's Advocate), and Alice Morgan; *m* 1919, Mary, *d* of late Lieut-Commander R. E. Carmody, USN, one *s* one *d.* *Educ:* London Collegiate Institute, London, Canada; Universities of Toronto (BSc 1909), Cornell (MSc 1912), Paris (D ès Sc 1921), Cambridge (Special Research, 1914-15), St Maximin (PhD 1924). Entomologist, US Dept of Agriculture, 1909-13, 1919-28; Bacteriologist, RN 1915-19; Assistant Director, Imperial Institute of Entomology, 1928-47, and Director, Imperial Parasite Service, 1940-47; FRS Canada, 1949; Hon. Member, Prof., Institute of the Civil Service of Canada, 1949; Corresp. Mem. Nat. Acad. of Bordeaux; Lauréat Société Entomologique de France (Prix Passet); Past Pres., Aquinas Society; Editor, Canadian Entomologist, 1947-58; Pres., 10th Internat. Congress of Entomology, 1956. Distinguished Vis. Prof., Michigan State Univ., 1959. Hon. FRES, London. Hon. Fellow RIA; Hon. Mem. Entomolog. Soc. Canada. Medal: Univ. Bordeaux; Nat. Academy of Bordeaux; DUniv hc Bordeaux; DSc hc Carleton. First Harry Scott Smith Award, 1967. *Publications:* Science and Common Sense, 1937; numerous on biological subjects. *Recreations:* philosophy, fishing. *Address:* Apartment 310, 150 Driveway, Ottawa, Ontario, Canada.
[Died 30 Jan. 1972.

THOMPSTONE, Sir Eric Westbury, KBE 1950; CMG 1946; MC; *b* 21 May 1897; *s* of late S. W. Thompstone, CMG, FRCS, FRCP, Deloraine, St Saviour, Jersey, Channel Islands (sometime PMO Northern Nigeria); *m* 1963, Enid Maryon, widow of J. J. A. Johnson. *Educ:* Shrewsbury School. Commissioned KSLI 1915; served France and Italy, 1916-19 (MC, Italian Silver Medal for Military Valour, wounded). Joined Colonial Administrative Service, Nigeria, 1919; Resident, 1937; Senior Resident, 1942; Chief Commissioner, NP, 1947-51; Lieutenant-Governor of Northern Region, Nigeria, 1951-52; President: Northern Region House of Assembly, 1946; Northern Region House of Chiefs, 1947-52; MEC and MLC, Nigeria, 1947-52; retired, 1952. *Recreations:* various. *Address:* Deloraine, St Saviour, Jersey, CI. *Club:* Royal Commonwealth Society.
[Died 7 Sept. 1974.

THOMSON, Hon. Lord; Alexander Thomson; a Senator of the College of Justice, Scotland, since 1965; *b* 9 Nov. 1914; *s* of James Stuart Thomson, Dunfermline, Fife; *m* 1957, Marie Wilson, *o d* of late David G. Cowan, Milngavie. *Educ:* Dunfermline High School; Edinburgh University (MA, LLB). Served War of 1939-45, Capt., RA. Mem. Faculty of Advocates, Edinburgh, 1946 (Dean, 1964-65); QC (Scotland) 1955; Sheriff of Renfrew and Argyll, 1962-64; a Judge of Nat. Industrial Relations Court, 1971-74. *Address:* 9 Moray Place, Edinburgh EH3 6DS.
[Died 2 Feb. 1979.

THOMSON OF FLEET, 1st Baron, *cr* 1964; **Roy Herbert Thomson**, GBE 1970; Chairman: The Thomson Organisation

Ltd (and subsidiaries including The Times and The Sunday Times); Thomson Newspapers Ltd, Canada; Founder, The Thomson Foundation; *b* 5 June 1894; *s* of Herbert Thomson and Alice Maud Coombs; became British citizen, 1963; *m* 1916, Edna Alice (*d* 1951), *d* of John Irvine, Drayton, Ontario; one *s* one *d* (and one *d* decd). *Educ:* Jarvis Collegiate, Toronto. Dir, Security Trust Co. Ltd; Trustee of Reuters Ltd, 1965-. Vice-Pres., Periodical Proprietors Assoc. Ltd; Hon. Life Mem., Commonwealth Press Union, 1972 (Vice-Chm. of Council, 1963-72). Vice-Pres., Publicity Club of London. Formerly Chancellor, Memorial Univ., Newfoundland. Liveryman, Worshipful Co. of Stationers and Newspaper Makers. FRSA; FBIM. Hon. DLitt St John's Memorial Univ., Newfoundland; Hon. DCL New Brunswick Univ.; Hon. LLD Northern Michigan Univ.; Hon. LHD Long Island Univ., NY. Former Hon. Col, Toronto Scottish Regt. Comdr, Royal Order of Phoenix, Greece. *Recreations:* reading Who Dunnits and balance sheets, light music. *Heir: s* Hon. Kenneth (Roy) Thomson. *Address:* Alderbourne Arches, Gerrards Cross, Bucks. *T:* Fulmer 2215; 4 Stratford Place, W1A 4YG; 65 Queen Street West, Toronto, Ont M5H 2M8, Canada. *Clubs:* Caledonian; Albany, National, Toronto, York (Toronto).
[*Died* 4 Aug. 1976.

THOMSON, A(dam) Bruce, OBE 1963; RSA 1946 (ARSA 1937); HRSW 1968 (RSW 1947, President, 1956-63), President, SSA 1937; *b* 22 Feb. 1885; *m* 1918, Jessie I. Hislop; one *s* two *d*. Served in World War I, Royal Engineers. *Address:* 65 Cluny Gardens, Edinburgh EH10 6BW. *T:* 031-447 4031. *Club:* Scottish Arts (Edinburgh). [*Died* 4 Dec. 1976.

THOMSON, Alexander; *see* Thomson, Hon. Lord.

THOMSON, Alfred Reginald, RA 1945 (ARA 1939); RP 1944; RBA 1973; *b* Bangalore, India; father, Civil Service, India; *m* ; one *s* one *d*. Farm training in Kent and Buckingham. *Murals:* Hotel, Duncannon Street; The Science Museum, London; private houses near Cannes, France; The Queen Mary; County Hall of Essex, Chelmsford; The Dental Hospital, Birmingham, etc.; official artist to Royal Air Force (portraits of the Queen and members of Royal Family for RAF Commem. Dinner). *Portraits:* King George of Greece; Cardinal Godfrey; Bishop of London, 1961; Bishop of Southwark, 1961; Lord Mayors of Liverpool, Duke of Marlborough, Lord Vansittart, Lord Trenchard, etc; other principal works: White Collar Dinner of the Pytchley Hunt at Althorp, The Houses of Parliament in Session, The Greater London Council, The Royal Yacht Squadron, Court of Grocers' Company, 40th Anniversary of RAF, mural for children's library, Darlington, 1974; book illustrations. The XIV Olympiad Gold Medallist for painting of sports, London, 1948. FSA 1948. *Recreation:* talking nonsense. *Address:* Milton House, 2 Fernshaw Road, SW10. *Clubs:* Chelsea Arts, London Sketch. [*Died* 27 Oct. 1979.

THOMSON, Sir (Arthur) Landsborough, Kt 1953; CB 1933; OBE 1919; DSc; LLD; late Second Secretary, Medical Research Council, having been second officer from 1919 (Assistant Secretary, Principal Assistant Secretary 1936, Under-Secretary 1946, Second Secretary 1949) and retiring to part-time special duties, 1957; late Chairman, Public Health Laboratory Service Board, 1950-61 (MRC), 1961-63 (statutory); President, Zoological Society of London, 1954-60 (Vice-President, 1945-48, 1950-53, 1960-64); Chairman, Home Office Advisory Committee on Protection of Birds, 1954-69; Chairman (formerly President), Council for Nature, 1964-69; Chairman of Trustees, British Museum (Natural History), 1967-69 (Trustee, 1963-71); *b* Edinburgh, 8 Oct. 1890; *e s* of late Professor Sir J. Arthur Thomson, LLD, Aberdeen; *m* 1920, Mary Moir (*d* 1969), 2nd *d* of late Professor J. W. H. Trail, MD, FRS, Aberdeen. *Educ:* Royal High School, Edinburgh; Aberdeen Grammar School; Univs of Heidelberg, Aberdeen, and Vienna. MA Aberdeen 1911; BSc (with distinction in Zoology) 1914; DSc 1920; Asst to the Prof. of Natural History, University of Aberdeen, 1914. On active service in France and Flanders, 1915-19, with Argyll and Sutherland Highlanders and on the Staff, latterly as Assistant Quartermaster-General at GHQ (despatches twice, OBE); demobilised with rank of Lieut-Col. Secretary, MRC Distemper Research Cttee, 1923-32; Sec., MRC Tropical Medical Research Cttee, 1936-41; Member, National Radium Commission, 1937-41; Member Colonial Medical Research Committee (CO and MRC), 1954-60; Chm., British Ornithologists' Club, 1938-43; Chm. British Trust for Ornithology, 1941-47; President, British Ornithologists' Union, 1948-55; President, XI Internat. Ornithological Congress, Basel, 1954; Mem., Serengeti National Park Enquiry Cttee (Govt of Tanganyika), 1957; FRSE, FRGS. Hon. Fellow Amer. Orn. Union. Hon. Member: Société Orn. de France; Deutsche Ornithologen-Ges. Hon. LLD: Aberdeen, 1956, Birmingham, 1974. Order of Golden Ark (Netherlands),

1972. Buchanan Medal, Royal Society, 1962, etc. *Publications:* Problems of Bird Migration, 1926; Birds, an Introduction to Ornithology, 1927; Bird Migration, a Short Account, 1936, 3rd edn 1949; (ed) A New Dictionary of Birds, 1964; Half a Century of Medical Research, 2 vols, 1973, 1975; various papers on migration of birds, etc. *Recreation:* travel, formerly climbing. *Address:* 42 Girdwood Road, Southfields, SW18 5QS. *T:* 01-788 8692. *Clubs:* Athenæum, Alpine. [*Died* 9 June 1977.

THOMSON, Sir Arthur (Peregrine), Kt 1959; MC, MD, FRCP; Consulting Physician to United Hospitals, Birmingham; *b* 1890; *s* of Arthur Henry Thomson, Colonial Civil Service; *m* Minnie Scott Lindsley (*d* 1960); one *d*. *Educ:* Dulwich College; University of Birmingham (Queen's Scholar, Ingleby Scholar and Russell Prizeman); RAMC, TF, 1915-19, retiring with rank of Major (Croix de Guerre, 1918). Lumleian Lectr, RCP, 1949; Linacre Lectr, St John's College, Cambridge, 1959; Harveian Orator, RCP, 1961. Member Gen. Medical Council, 1953-65. Pres. BMA, 1958-59. Chm. Birmingham Reg. Hosp. Bd, 1962-63. Sen. Fellow in Med. Hist., Birmingham Univ., 1960-65. LLD (*hc*) Edinburgh, 1959; Birmingham, 1965. *Publications:* contributions to medical journals. *Address:* 74 Richmond Hill Road, Edgbaston, Birmingham. *T:* 021-454 0735. *Clubs:* National Liberal; Union (Birmingham). [*Died* 15 July 1977.

THOMSON, Sir Daniel, Kt 1975; CB 1963; MD; FRCP; Civil Service Medical Adviser, since 1968 (Treasury Medical Adviser, 1965-68); *b* 30 May 1912; *s* of John Duncan Thomson and Janet Simpson Macfadyen, Dundee and Carradale, Argyll; *m* 1946, Dorothy Violet Coles; two *s*. *Educ:* St Andrews and Edinburgh Universities. MB, ChB 1935; DPH 1946; MD 1948; MRCP 1965. Various hospital and university appointments, 1935-39; served RAMC, 1939-46; Asst Co. MOH, Surrey CC, 1947-50; MO, Min. of Health, 1950; Dep. Chief MO, 1958-65. QHP 1962. Pres., Section of Epidemiology and Preventive Medicine, Royal Soc. of Medicine, 1964-; Milroy Lectr, 1966. *Publications:* articles on medicine and public health. *Recreations:* reading, gardening. *Address:* Langhurst, Prey Heath, Worplesdon, Surrey. *T:* Worplesdon 2078. *Club:* Athenæum.
[*Died* 29 Oct. 1976.

THOMSON, Sir Douglas; *see* Thomson, Sir J. D. W.

THOMSON, Eric Hugh, CEng, FICE, MIHE; retired; *b* 29 Jan. 1909; *s* of late Hugh Marsh Thomson; *m* 1937, Sarah Skinner Anderson, *d* of late George Anderson, St Andrews; one *s* two *d*. *Educ:* Bradfield; London Univ. (BSc(Eng)). Joined Air Min. Works Directorate, 1935; seconded to RAF Airfield Construction Br. Served War of 1939-45: Middle East, 1942-45. Germany, 1948-50; Chief Engr, Bomber Command, 1951; Dep. Dir of Works, Air Min., 1952; Air Cdre, Chief Engr, Second TAF, 1955; Head of NATO Perm. HQ Office, Paris, 1957; Dir of Works, Air Min., 1960; Dir of Works (Civil Aviation), Min. of Aviation, 1962; Regional Dir, Germany, Min. of Public Bldg and Works, 1964-67; Chief Engineer, Road Construction Units, Min. of Transport, 1967-70. *Recreations:* domestic architecture, gardening, motoring, travel. *Address:* 7 Doocot Road, St Andrews, Fife. *T:* St Andrews 4850. [*Died* 15 July 1973.

THOMSON, Sir George Paget, Kt 1943; FRS 1930; DSc Cantab; Master of Corpus Christi, Cambridge, 1952-62, retired; Emeritus Professor of Physics, London University, since 1952; Hon. Fellow: Trinity College, Cambridge; Corpus Christi College, Cambridge; Imperial College of Science and Technology; Institute of Physics; Foreign Member: American Academy of Arts and Sciences; Lisbon Academy; Corresponding Member, Austrian Academy of Sciences; Hon. degrees: DSc Lisbon; LLD Aberdeen; ScD Dublin, Sheffield, Wales, Reading, Westminster College, Mo; Dr Humane Letters Ursinus College, Pa; *b* 1892; *s* of late Sir J. J. Thomson, OM, FRS; *m* 1924, Kathleen Buchanan (*d* 1941), *d* of late Very Rev. Sir George Adam Smith; two *s* two *d*. *Educ:* Perse School, Cambridge; Trinity Coll., Cambridge. First Cl. Math. Trip. Parts I and II, Nat. Sc. Trip. Part II, Fellow and Lecturer, Corpus Christi College, Cambridge, 1914; served in France with 1st Queen's, 1914-15; attached RFC and RAF, 1915-19; worked on various problems of aeronautical research; returned to Cambridge, 1919; Member of Aeronautical Research Committee, 1937-41; Professor of Natural Philosophy in University of Aberdeen, 1922-30; Professor of Physics, Imperial College of Science, 1930-52; Chm. first British Cttee on Atomic Energy, 1940-41; Scientific Adviser: to Air Ministry, 1943-44; to Brit. Delegation Atomic Energy Commn of UN, 1946-47. President, Institute of Physics, 1958-60; President, British Assoc. for Advancement of Science, 1960. Awarded Nobel Prize for Physics, 1937; Hughes Medal, 1939, and Royal Medal, 1949, of Royal Society; Faraday Medal of Institute of Electrical Engineers, 1960. *Publications:* Applied Aerodynamics, 1919;

The Atom; Wave Mechanics of the Free Electron; The Foreseeable Future; The Inspiration of Science; J. J. Thomson, 1964; papers on Physics in Scientific Journals and on Aeronautics in Government publications; (with Sir J. J. Thomson) Conduction of Electricity through Gases, 3rd edition; (with W. Cochrane) Theory and Practice of Electron Diffraction. *Recreation:* ship models. *Address:* Little Howe, Mount Pleasant, Cambridge. *T:* 54790. *Club:* Athenæum.
[Died 10 Sept. 1975.

THOMSON, Sir (James) Douglas (Wishart), 2nd Bt, *cr* 1929; Managing Director, William Thomson & Co., Shipowners, Edinburgh; *b* 30 Oct. 1905; *s* of Sir Frederick Charles Thomson, 1st Bt, KC, MP, and Constance Margaret (*d* 1970), *yr d* of Hamilton A. Hotson, General Manager British Linen Bank, Edinburgh; *S* father 1935; *m* 1935, Bettina, *er d* of late Lt-Comdr David W. S. Douglas, RN; *two s three d*. *Educ:* Eton; University College, Oxford, BA. MP (U) South Aberdeen, 1935-46. *Heir: s* Frederick Douglas David Thomson [*b* 14 Feb. 1940; *m* 1967, Caroline Anne, *d* of Major Timothy S. Lewis; *two s*]. *Address:* Holylee, Walkerburn, Peeblesshire. *T:* Walkerburn 207. *Clubs:* Carlton; New (Edinburgh). *[Died 3 Jan. 1972.*

THOMSON, Maj.-Gen. James Noel, CB 1946; DSO 1917; MC; *b* 25 Dec. 1888; *s* of James Thomson and Margaret Stuart; *m* 1929, Lorna Carmen, *d* of late Sir Edward Buck, CBE; no *c*. *Educ:* Fettes; RMA Woolwich. Senior Under Officer RMA Woolwich, 1909; Commissioned in Royal Field Artillery, 1909; European War France and Germany, 1914-19 (DSO, MC, despatches thrice, French Croix de Guerre); Adjutant Royal Military Academy, 1919-21; Staff College, Camberley, 1921; War Office, 1922-23; Brigade Major 1st Rhine Brigade, 1923-24; General Staff Rhine Army (Operations and Intelligence) 1924-26; Staff Officer to Major-General Royal Artillery, India, 1927-30; Lieut Colonel, 1929; idc 1932; Asst Master Gen. of the Ordnance in India, 1934-37; Col, 1935; Brig. RA, N Command, India, 1938-41; Comdr 6 Ind. Div., 1941; Temp. Maj.-Gen., 1942; Dep. Master Gen. of Ord. GHQ, India, 1943. ADC to the King, 1939; retired pay, 1946, with hon. rank of Maj.-Gen. *Recreations:* horses, racing. *Address:* c/o Meerut Race Club, Meerut, UP, India. *[Died May 1978.*

THOMSON, Professor James Oliver, OBE 1919; Professor of Latin, University of Birmingham, 1919-55; Emeritus Professor, 1956; *b* 1889; *s* of J. A. Thomson, tea-planter, Tezpore, Assam, and Isabella Watt; *m* 1935, Linda Marie Kelly, Milngavie; *two s*. *Educ:* Gordon's College, Aberdeen; Univ. of Aberdeen (MA); Trinity College, Cambridge. First Cl. Hons in Classics, Fullerton Scholar, Aberdeen; Ferguson Scholar, Scottish Universities; Senior Scholar of Trinity Coll., Cambridge; Classical Tripos, Pt I, Cl. I, Div. I, 1914, Pt II, Cl. I, 1915; Chancellor's Medal; Charles Oldham Shakespeare Scholarship. Served European War, in France, in KOYLI and Intelligence, 1915-19. Croom Robertson Fell., Aberd. Bailiff of King Edward VI Foundn, Birm., 1951-52. *Publications:* History of Ancient Geography, 1948; Dent's Everyman's Classical Atlas, 1961; articles in learned journals. *Recreations:* gardening, sketching, geology. *Address:* Overdale, Baldernock Road, Milngavie, by Glasgow. *T:* 041-956 1607. *[Died 31 March 1971.*

THOMSON, Very Rev. James Sutherland, MA; Hon. DD: Toronto, 1936, Glasgow, 1946, Emmanuel College, Saskatoon, 1949, Pine Hill, Halifax, 1957; Hon. LLD: State Coll. of Washington, 1944, Queen's Univ., Kingston, Ont, 1945, Univ. of Toronto, 1945, McGill Univ., Montreal, 1946, McMaster Univ., Hamilton, Ont, 1947, Manitoba, 1948, Alta, 1949, Sask, 1951, Mount Allison Univ., Sackville, NB, 1958; FRSC 1942; *b* 1892; *s* of late John Thomson and Margaret Sutherland; *m* 1922, Margaret Stewart, *d* of late David Troup; one *s* one *d*. *Educ:* Eastbank Academy, Glasgow; Univ. of Glasgow (MA, 1st Cl. Hons Philosophy, 1914); Trin. Coll. Glasgow (Hons in Theol. 1920). John Clark (Milend) Fell., 1914-20, Univ. of Glasgow; ordained, 1920; Minister Middle Ch., Coatbridge, 1920-24; Sec. for Educ., Church of Scotland, 1924-30; Professor, Systematic Theology, Pine Hill College, Halifax, NS, 1930-37; Pres., Univ. of Saskatchewan, 1937-49; Prof. of Philosophy of Religion (Dean of Divinity) McGill Univ., 1949-59 (Emeritus Prof., 1966); Lecturer, McGill Univ., 1959-65. Served Cameron Highlanders, 1915-17; Rifle Brigade, 1917-19; Temp. Capt., later Hon. Col, Canadian OTC; Chairman, United Council Miss. Educ., 1927-29; Vice-Pres. Brit. and For. Bib. Soc. 1945; President, United Nations Soc. of Can., 1946; Pres., Sect. II, Royal Soc. of Canada, 1955-56; Swander Lecturer, Lancaster, Penn., 1934; Chancellor's Lecturer, Queen's Univ., Kingston, Ont., 1942; Nathaniel Taylor Lecturer, Yale Univ., 1943; Armstrong Lecturer, Toronto Univ., 1950; Alexander Robertson Lecturer, Univ. of Glasgow, 1952-54. Moderator, United Church of Canada, 1956-58. Canadian Centennial

Medal, 1967. *Publications:* Studies in the Life of Jesus, 1927; The Way of Revelation (with others), 1928; The Hope of the Gospel, 1955; The Divine Mission, 1957; The Word of God, 1959; God and His Purpose, 1964; Yester-Years, 1969; many articles; presented with Festschrift, The Christian in the Modern World, 1967. *Address:* 4544 Kensington Avenue, NDG, Montreal 261, Canada. *Clubs:* McGill Faculty, Royal Montreal Curling.
[Died 18 Nov. 1972.

THOMSON, John; Director, Daily Mail & General Trust Ltd, since 1968; *b* 9 June 1903; *s* of late John Thomson and Mrs Helen Thomson (*née* Reid); *m* 1930, Grace, *d* of Hugh Robertson; *two s*. *Educ:* Shawlands Academy, Glasgow. CA, 1926. John Menzies & Co. Ltd, 1926-29; Northcliffe Newspapers Ltd, 1929-32; Northcliffe Newspapers Group Ltd, 1932: Dir, 1942; Dir-in-Charge, 1944; Man. Dir, 1949; Vice-Chm., 1968; Chm., 1970-72. Dir, Press Association Ltd, 1952-59 (Chm. 1957); Trustee, Reuters Ltd, 1964-. Treasury O&M Branch (part-time), 1943-44. *Recreation:* golf. *Address:* 45 Arden Road, Finchley, N3. *T:* 01-346 4358. *Club:* Royal Automobile. *[Died 6 Oct. 1974.*

THOMSON, Sir John Mackay, Kt 1946; CB 1941; MA Edinburgh and Oxon; FRSE; (Hon.) FEIS, 1947; *b* Dunning, Perthshire, 21 March 1887; *er s* of late Rev. Peter Thomson, DD, and Margaret, *d* of John Mackay of Inveralmond, Cramond Bridge; unmarried. *Educ:* Trinity College, Glenalmond; Edinburgh University (Bruce of Grangehill Scholar, 1908; Guthrie Fellowship in Classics, 1911); Oriel College, Oxford (Scholar, 1st Classical Moderations, 1911; 2nd Lit Hum 1913). Assistant to Professor of Humanity, Edinburgh University, 1913-14; VIth Form Master, Fettes College, 1915-20; Rector of Aberdeen Grammar School, 1920-21; Scottish Education Department: HM Inspector of Schools, 1921-24; Junior Assistant Secretary, 1925-35; Senior Assistant Secretary, 1935-36; Second Secretary, 1936-39; Acting Secretary, 1939; Secretary of Scottish Education Department, 1940-52; retired 1952. Member of: Scottish Inter-Departmental Cttee on Road Safety among School Children, 1935; Scottish Cttee of Bd of Trade Council for Art and Industry, 1937-39. Chevalier, First Class, of the Order of St Olav, 1948. *Recreations:* fishing, motoring. *Address:* 14 Royal Circus, Edinburgh 3. *T:* 031-225 6845. *Club:* New (Edinburgh). *[Died 15 March 1974.*

THOMSON, J(ohn) Murray, RSA 1957 (ARSA 1939); RSW; *b* 17 Dec. 1885; *m* 1917, Ellen May Frew; one *s*. *Educ:* Morrison's Academy, Crieff. Studied art in Edinburgh and Paris; specialised in painting animals and birds; ex-President, Society of Scottish Artists. *Recreations:* fly-fishing for trout and salmon. *Address:* 7 Randolph Cliff, Edinburgh 3. *T:* 031-225 6468.
[Died 16 Oct. 1974.

THOMSON, John Stuart, CIE 1935; *b* 4 Aug. 1888; *s* of John Cunningham Thomson; *m* 1941, Mary Catherine Frances, *d* of late Maj.-Gen. W. V. Coppinger, CIE, DSO; *two d*. *Educ:* Charterhouse; Oriel College, Oxford. Joined Indian Civil Service, 1912; military duty, 1915-17; Civil Administration, Iraq, 1917-23; Deputy Commissioner in Punjab, 1923-31; Development Commissioner NWFP, 1931-32; Revenue Commissioner NWFP, 1932-36; retired, 1937. *Address:* Gunnels, The Avenue, Bucklebury, Reading, Berks.
[Died 22 March 1973.

THOMSON, Sir Landsborough; *see* Thomson, Sir (Arthur) Landsborough.

THOMSON, Leslie G.; *see* Grahame-Thomson.

THOMSON, Louis M. M.; *see* Milne-Thomson.

THOMSON, Colonel Roger Gordon, CMG 1918; DSO 1916; late RA; *b* 4 Apr. 1878; *s* of late Maj.-Gen. D. Thomson, RE; *m* 1904, Florence Lucy (*d* 1949), *y d* of late Maj.-Gen. W. E. Delves Broughton, Bengal Staff Corps; one *s two d*. *Educ:* Cheltenham College; RMA, Woolwich. Joined Army, 1898; Capt. 1905; Major, 1914; Temp. Lt-Col 1916; Col 1922; served European War, 1914-18 (DSO, CMG); retired pay, 1926; employed at the War Office, Oct. 1927-April 1942, and then at Ministry of Home Security (Home Office), June 1942-Sept. 1945. *Recreations:* hunting, rowing, cricket. *Address:* c/o Mrs F. M. G. Richardson-Bunbury, Quarrymead, Hillcrest Road, Hythe, Kent. *[Died 6 Aug. 1976.*

THOMSON, Sir Ronald (Jordan), Kt 1950; Lord Lieutenant of Peeblesshire, 1956-68; *b* 13 March 1895; *s* of William Thomson, shipowner; *m* 1919, Patricia Martha Burrell Guild (*d* 1955); one *s* (one *d* decd). Commissioned Border Regiment, 1914; served European War, 1914-18; resigned commission on account of wounds, 1917. Elected Peeblesshire County Council, 1922; Convener of Peeblesshire, 1932-58; President, Association of County Councils in Scotland, 1948-50; Civil Defence Controller, Eastern Scotland, 1954-60; Chairman, Scottish Special Housing Association, 1952-62. JP 1922-69; DL 1930, VL 1945, Peeblesshire. *Address:* Kaimes, West Linton, Peeblesshire. *T:* West Linton 413. *[Died 16 June 1978.*

THOMSON, Roy Harry Goodisson, FCA; *b* 2 Jan. 1891; *m* 1921, Margaret Hewetson Harper, *d* of James Williamson Blacklock; two *d. Educ:* Merchant Taylors' School. Joined Trinity House Service as Deputy Accountant, 1922; Secretary of the Corporation, 1946-51. Retired. Younger Brother, Trinity House, 1953. *Address:* 56 Trinity Church Square, SE1.
[Died 4 April 1974.

THOMSON, Rev. T(homas) B(entley) Stewart, MC 1918; TD 1939; Hon. DD Aberdeen 1946; Extra Chaplain to the Queen since 1959 (Chaplain to the Queen, 1952-59, to King George VI, 1951-52); *b* 1889; *s* of Rev. William Stewart Thomson, MA, FSA, FRGS, Principal of Aberdeen CS and Business Coll.; *m* 1918, Margaret Rolland Menzies, *d* of Rev. Robert Mackenzie, MA, Alloa; one *s* two *d. Educ:* Robert Gordon's College; Aberdeen University (MA Hons), BD, (Lyon Prizeman, Brown Scholar). Missioner on the Canadian prairies, 1913; Asst Minister, Glasgow Cathedral, 1914; ordained to Dalziel (Motherwell), 1919; St Stephen's, Edinburgh, 1923; Govan Old, Glasgow, 1939; Dunbarney (Bridge of Earn), 1948-59. 2nd Lieut Glasgow Hldrs, 1915; Capt., 1917; Divisional Gas Officer, 19th and 62nd Divs; CF (TA), 1922; SCF, 52nd (Lowland) Div., 1928; SCF, Scottish Comd, 1934; DACG, 10th Corps, 1940; invalided out of TA, 1941. For many years Vice-pres., British Legion; Chm., Church of Scotland Young Men's Guild, 1926-29; Convener: Cttee on Socs for Young Men and Women, 1929-31; Jewish Mission Cttee, 1931-34; Home Mission Cttee, 1945-47; Home Board, 1947-52; Cttee on Ministers' War Memorial and Orphan Funds, 1953-63; Moderator of Presbytery of Edinburgh, 1938; Moderator of Synod of Perth and Stirling, 1954-55; Moderator of Presbytery of Perth, 1957-58; Senior Past Grand Chaplain, Grand Lodge of Scotland. *Publications:* Crumbs for the Children, 1923; Preparing for the Lord's Table, 1925; The Quest of Youth, 1926; Studies in the Teaching of Jesus, 1928; Bens and Glens, 1938; Job: A dramatised version, 1939; Five Hundred Texts for Special Occasions, 1945; Guide to Govan Old Parish Church, 1947; The Chaplain in the Church of Scotland (Baird Lecture), 1947. *Recreation:* journalism. *Address:* 7 Tullylumb Terrace, Perth. *T:* Perth 21797. *Clubs:* Royal Scots (Edinburgh); Perth Conservative.
[Died 10 Aug. 1973.

THOMSON, Sir William, Kt 1970; OBE 1960; JP; Chairman: Turner & Co. (Gibraltar) Ltd, since 1946, also of Mediterranean Bank Ltd; Hon. Consul for the Netherlands, Gibraltar, since 1946; *b* 30 Aug. 1916; *s* of William J. Thomson, and Africa Ruiz; *m* 1943, Clemencia Isola; no *c. Educ:* Forest Sch., Essex; Downing Coll., Cambridge (MA). Joined Gibraltar Defence Force, 1939, Major comdg AA Battery, 1943. Director (family firm), Turner & Co. (Gib.) Ltd (founded 1831), 1940. Hon. Col, Gibraltar Defence Force, later Gibraltar Regt, 1953-58; Mem., Public Service Commn, 1959-; Speaker, Legislative Council, later House of Assembly, 1964-69; Mayor of Gibraltar, Aug.-Dec. 1969. Actively engaged since 1946 in shipping matters in Gibraltar and on Boards of various companies. JP (Gibraltar). Chevalier, Order of Orange Nassau, Netherlands, 1959. *Recreations:* shooting, yachting. *Address:* 63/65 Irish Town, Gibraltar. *T:* 5794. *Clubs:* Royal Thames Yacht; Royal Gibraltar Yacht (past Vice-Commodore), Calpe Rowing (past Vice-Pres.), Mediterranean Racing (Gibraltar).
[Died 4 June 1971.

THORBY, Hon. Harold Victor Campbell, JP; farmer and grazier; *b* Annandale, NSW, 2 Oct. 1888; 3rd *s* of late F. J. Thorby; *m* 1st, Vera Lynda (*d* 1958), 2nd *d* of late A. F. Morley; two *d*; 2nd, 1960, Alfreda Elizabeth. *Educ:* Geurie PS; Sydney Grammar School; Technical College, Sydney. President Farmers' and Settlers' Assoc., NSW, 1923-26; Member for Wammerawa, NSW Assembly, 1922-27; Castlereagh, 1927-30; Minister for Agriculture, Sydney, NSW, 1927-30; MHR Calare, 1931-40; Assistant Minister for Repatriation and War Service Homes, 1934; Asst Minister for Commerce, 1935; Acting Minister Commerce, 1936; Acting Minister for Defence, 1937; Minister for Defence and Civil Aviation, 1938; Minister of Civil Aviation and Works, 1938-39; Postmaster-General and Minister of Health, 1940; Deputy Leader Australian Country Party, 1937-40; Chairman Water Conservation and Irrigation Commission, 1927-30; Chairman River Murray Commission, 1938-39; Member Trade Delegation, London, 1935, and International Wool Conference, Berlin, 1935; Chm. Dubbo

Graziers' Assoc., 1951-53; NSW Graziers' Gen. Council, 1952-53; Exec. Cttee, 1953-54. Chm. Medical Dental Bldg Ltd, 1957-58. Trustee, Lawson and Dubbo, 1956-60. Chm. Dirs, Gibb & Beeman, Optometrists, 1957-63. Life Member: FSA, NSW; Aust. Country Party; NSW Ambulance Brigade. MEC, 1934-40. *Address:* 29 Carnarvon Road, Roseville, Sydney, NSW 2069, Australia. *[Died 1 Jan. 1973.*

THORN, Sir Jules, Kt 1964; President of THORN EMI Limited (formerly Thorn Electrical Industries), since 1976 (Chairman 1937-76, Managing Director, 1937-69); other companies are included in the Thorn Group; *b* Feb. 1899; *m* 1927, Dorothy Olive (marr. diss. 1971); two *c.* Chairman, Radio Industry Council, 1966. Hon. Master of the Bench, Middle Temple, 1969. President: British Radio Equipment Manufacturers' Assoc., 1964-68; Conf. of Electronics Industry, 1971; Mem., Sch. Council, UCH Med. Sch. FRSA; CIEE; Hon. FIES. *Recreations:* travelling, reading, music. *Address:* THORN EMI Limited, Thorn House, Upper St Martins Lane, WC2H 9ED. *T:* 01-836 2444. *[Died 12 Dec. 1980.*

THORNDIKE, (Arthur) Russell; actor and author; *b* 6 Feb. 1885; *s* of Rev. Arthur J. W. Thorndike, Hon. Canon of Rochester, and Agnes Macdonald Bowers; *m* Rosemary Benvenuta Dowson (*d* 1970). *Educ:* St George's School, Windsor; King's School, Rochester; Ben Greet's Academy. First stage appearance, Theatre Royal, Cambridge, 1904; first London appearance, Marlborough Theatre, Holloway, 1905; member of Ben Greet's company in England and America, 1905-08; in Shakespeare season, Court Theatre, 1909; toured with Matheson Lang in South Africa, India and the Far East, 1911-13; Horniman repertory, Manchester, 1913; served in Egypt and Gallipoli with 1st Westminster Dragoons, 1914-16; invalided out; with Old Vic company 1916-20, as leading man and joint-producer in 1919-20; Grand Guignol, 1920; Old Vic, 1922; played name part in his own play Dr Syn, at Lyceum, on tour, and at Strand under own management, 1926-27; lead in Ben Greet's company in America, 1929-30; in Shakespeare season, Kingsway, 1932. Since 1932 has had many parts in West End productions, notably in Shakespeare, including Open Air Seasons, also made frequent appearances as Smee in Peter Pan. Has appeared in several films. *Publications:* The Tragedy of Mr Punch (with Reginald Arkell); The Slype; Herod's Peal; Jet and Ivory; Vandekkers; The Water Witch; Sybil Thorndike, a biography; Show House Sold; The House of Jeffreys; The Master of the Macabre; In the Steps of Shakespeare; The First Englishman; also the "Dr Syn" Saga. *Address:* 5 Oaklands Road, SW14. *[Died 7 Nov. 1972.*

THORNDIKE, Dame Sybil, CH 1970; DBE 1931; LLD Manchester and Edinburgh; DLitt: Southampton, Oxford and Surrey; actress and manager; *b* Gainsborough, 24 Oct. 1882; *d* of Rev. A. J. W. Thorndike, Hon. Canon of Rochester; *m* 1908, Sir Lewis Casson, MC (*d* 1969); two *s* two *d. Educ:* Rochester High School. Shakespearian Repertory in America with Ben Greet; about 100 parts in twenty-five days, 1903-7; Miss Horniman's Co., Manchester, 1908-9; Chas. Frohman's Repertory, Duke of York's Theatre, 1910; American tour with John Drew, 1910-11; leads with Miss Horniman's Company, 1911-13; Shakespearian leads at Old Vic, 1914-18; played in numerous London productions, 1919-20; Little Theatre, 1920-22, London's Grand Guignol; about thirty parts in as many plays including Louise (The Old Women), the Model (The Medium), Judy (The Tragedy of Mr Punch), Mrs Meldon (Progress); in management various London theatres, 1922-27, productions include Saint Joan (and revivals), The Trojan Women, Medea, The Verge, Hippolytus, Henry VIII, Macbeth, The Greater Love, also took leading parts in many; played leading parts for the Old Vic season at the Lyric, Hammersmith, 1927; Nurse Cavell in Dawn (film); produced Judith of Israel, playing the title-rôle, 1928; toured South Africa for nine months; returned in Jan. 1929, and played the name part in Major Barbara, Lily Cobb in Mariners by Clemence Dane, and revived Jane Clegg and the Medea in one bill; toured with Madam Plays Nap, playing Henriette, and played at New Theatre, 1929; played Phèdre in French; Sylvette in Fire, and Mrs Alving in Ghosts, Emilia in Othello at the Savoy, 1930; Jess Fortune in Matchmaker's Arms, Eloise in Marriage by Purchase, 1931; revived Saint Joan and toured with it, 1931; toured in Egypt, Palestine, Australia, and New Zealand, 1932-33; on return to London played Evie in The Distaff Side, Victoria Van Brett (Double Door), Z in Shaw's Village Wooing; autumn 1934, The Distaff Side in New York; 1935, Grief Goes Over, London; Short Story; 1936, Kind Lady; My Son's my Son; Six Men of Dorset; Hippolytus (Nurse); 1937, Yes My Darling Daughter; 1938, Time and the Conways, New York; The Corn is Green, Duchess Theatre, 1940, Piccadilly Theatre; six war-time tours with the Old Vic under CEMA, 1940-42; 1942-43 in House of Jeffreys; Ibsen's Ghosts and Shaw's Captain Brassbound's

Conversion, Dublin; 1943, Bristol and Liverpool Season with She Stoops to Conquer and Queen Bee; Vaudeville, London, in Lottie Dundass; Alice in Wonderland, White Queen and Queen of Hearts, Old Vic Repertory, New Theatre, 1944. Old Vic Repertory, New Theatre and ENSA tour Belgium, Germany and Paris, 1945-46; Clytemnestra in Electra, and Mrs Wilson in In Time to Come, King's, Hammersmith, 1946; Mrs Fraser in Call Home the Heart, St James's, 1946-47; Mrs Linden in The Linden Tree, Duchess, 1947-48; Mrs Jackson in The Return of the Prodigal, Globe, 1948; Isobel Brocken in The Foolish Gentlewoman, Duchess, 1949; Aunt Anna Rose in Treasure Hunt, Apollo, 1949; Lady Douglas in Douglas, Edinburgh Festival, 1950; Mrs Whyte in Waters of the Moon, Haymarket, 1951; Laura Anson in A Day by the Sea, Haymarket, 1953. Recitals in Australia, New Zealand, Far East, Africa, Turkey and Israel for the British Council, 1954-56; A Family Reunion, Phœnix Theatre, 1956; film of The Prince and the Showgirl; The Potting Shed, New York; tour, Australia, in The Chalk Garden, 1957-58; Eighty in the Shade, Globe, 1959; tour of Sea Shell, 1959; film, Big Gamble; film Hand in Hand; Waiting in the Wings, tour and Duke of York's, 1960; Teresa of Avila, Dublin and Vaudeville, 1961. Toured Australia in recitals, 1962; Chichester Festival, 1962; Vanity Fair, tour and Queen's, 1962-63; Chichester Festival, 1963; The Reluctant Peer, Duchess, 1964; Season of Goodwill, Queen's, 1964; Return Ticket, Duchess, 1965; Arsenic and Old Lace, Vaudeville, 1966; The Viaduct, Yvonne Arnaud, Guildford, 1967; There Was an Old Woman, Sybil Thorndike Theatre, 1969. Has appeared on television. Freedom of Rochester, 1929. *Publications:* Religion and the Stage; Lillian Baylis (with R. Thorndike); (ed) Favourites, 1973; *relevant publications:* Sybil Thorndike Casson, by E. Sprigge, 1971; Lewis and Sybil, by John Casson, 1972. *Recreation:* piano. *Address:* 98 Swan Court, Chelsea, SW3.
[*Died* 9 *June* 1976.

THORNTON, Sir Gerard; *see* Thornton, Sir H. G.

THORNTON, Sir (Henry) Gerard, Kt 1960; DSc; FRS 1941; formerly Head of Department of Soil Microbiology, Rothamsted; *b* 22 Jan. 1892; *s* of Francis Hugh Thornton, Kingsthorpe, Northampton; *m* 1924, Gerda, *d* of Kai Norregaard, Copenhagen; one *s. Educ:* Radley; New College, Oxford. Northamptonshire Regt, 1914-19 (despatches); seconded Royal Flying Corps and RAF, served in Egypt, Sudan and Salonika; Rothamsted Experimental Station, 1919-57, researches on nitrogen-fixing and other soil bacteria. Foreign Secretary, Royal Society, 1955-60. *Publications:* Papers on researches in Proceedings of Royal Society, Journal of Agricultural Science and other periodicals. *Recreations:* gardening and geology. *Address:* 3 Romeland Cottage, St Albans, Herts. *T:* St Albans 51333. *Clubs:* Athenæum, Savile.
[*Died* 6 *Feb.* 1977.

THORNTON, Air Vice-Marshal Henry Norman, CBE 1946; retired; *b* 25 April 1896; *s* of Edward Thornton, Dersingham; *m* 1933, Lucie Marie Louise, *d* of A. Argod, Paris. *Educ:* Chatham House Sch. Northumberland Fusiliers, 1914-16; RFC, 1917-18; RAF, 1918-47. 601 Squadron, 1928-30; Staff Coll., Camberley, 1931-32; Air Attaché, Low Countries and Scandinavia, 1935-37; Stockholm, Helsinki, 1940-41; Washington, 1941-43; Bomber Command, 1944; AOC a group in SEAC, 1945; AOC a group in BAOR, 1946. *Recreation:* golf. *Address:* West Lavington Hill, Midhurst, Sussex. *T:* Midhurst 2593. *Clubs:* White's, Royal Air Force.
[*Died* 5 *Jan.* 1971.

THORNTON, Colonel Thomas Anson, CVO 1939; Order of Sword of Sweden, 1935; *b* 1887; *s* of late T. W. Thornton, JP, Brockhall, Northampton; *m* 1916, Constance Maude Stuart (*d* 1964); *d* of late Sir S. Fraser, KCSI, CIE; two *d* (*er s* killed in action, 1944; *yr s* decd 1951). *Educ:* Harrow; RMC, Sandhurst. Joined 7th Hussars, 1906; served European War, 1914-19 with 7th Hussars and in Afghanistan on Staff, 1919; Lt-Col Commanding 7th Hussars, 1927-31; re-employed, 1940-44. Equerry to Prince Arthur of Connaught, 1932-38; High Sheriff of Northamptonshire for 1946-47; DL Northamptonshire, 1947; Colonel of 7th Hussars, 1948-52. *Address:* Brockhall, Northampton. *T:* Weedon 40445. *Club:* Cavalry and Guards.
[*Died* 12 *Jan.* 1978.

THORNTON-KEMSLEY, Col Sir Colin (Norman), Kt 1958; OBE 1946; TD 1950; MA; *b* 2 Sept. 1903; *e s* of late Norman Kemsley, Woodford Green, Essex; *m* 1930, Alice Helen (*d* 1973), *o c* of late William Thornton of Thornton; assumed additional surname Thornton by Deed Poll upon marriage; one *s* two *d. Educ:* Chigwell Sch.; Wadham Coll., Oxford. Until 1969, a partner in Kemsley, Whiteley and Ferris, Chartered Surveyors, and a Director, John Lewis Properties Ltd. Chm., Thornton Farms Ltd; Hon. Treasurer, Essex and Middlesex

Provincial Area, National Union of Cons. and Unionist Associations, 1938-43. MP (U) Kincardine and West Aberdeenshire, 1939-50, North Angus and Mearns, 1950-64. Vice-Chairman Cons. Parliamentary Cttee for Agriculture and Food, 1950-53; Chairman, Scottish Unionist Members' Cttee, 1957-58; Chairman, Liberal-Unionist Parliamentary Group, 1961-62; Member Public Accounts Cttee, 1955-64. A Vice-Pres., Town and Country Planning Assoc. Trustee, Speech Therapists Union. President, Kincardineshire Scout Assoc., 1968-75. Dir, BRCS, Kincardineshire, 1968-73. Rejoined Royal Artillery from TARO, Sept. 1939; passed Staff Coll. (Sen. Wing), and held various staff appointments including AQMG (ops), Eastern Command; Colonel comdg an Area, 1945. *Publications:* (jtly) Change and Challenge, 1962; (jtly) Contemporary Problems of Land Ownership, 1963; Bonnet Lairds, 1972; Through Winds and Tides, 1974; numerous articles on planning and land policy. *Recreations:* golf, shooting, caravanning and grandchildren. *Address:* Muirside of Thornton, Laurencekirk, Kincardineshire. *T:* Fettercairn 260. *Clubs:* Caledonian (Edinburgh); Aberdeen Conservative; MCC.
[*Died* 17 *July* 1977.

THORNTON-SMITH, Ernest; Fellow of the Institute of Directors; Fellow of the Royal Society of Arts; *b* 7 March 1881. *Educ:* City of London Sch. Served with the Queen's Westminsters, 1914-16; with the Ministry of Food, 1917-19; Grand Council, Our Dumb Friends League, since 1918; Squire of Telscombe since 1933; Chairman of the National Mark Egg and Poultry Trade Cttee, 1933-36; Government Director on the National Mark Egg Central Board, 1931-36; Minister of Agriculture's representative on the Pig Marketing Board, 1935-39; London Area Officer Ministry of Food, 1939-41; Master Worshipful Company of Gardeners, 1938-39. Member Westminster City Council, 1947-53; Chairman, Hospital for Women, Soho, 1937-57; Board of Governors Middlesex Hospital, 1948-57; Hon. Treas., Blue Cross, 1962; Member Council of Educational Television, 1961; Exec. Cttee of The Friends of St Johns, 1963. Gave historic Manor House, Telscombe Village and considerable acreage of surrounding farmlands and downs to the National Trust, 1960; gave Park Head, Cornwall with a mile of coast to the Trust in connection with Enterprise Neptune, 1966. Instituted Scholarship for Royal Gardens, Kew, for annual study of tropical and botanical growth in Caribbean and S America, 1967. Coronation Medal, 1937. *Publications:* The State and Agriculture, etc. *Recreations:* chess, riding, racing (won Oaks with Chatelaine, 1933; gave stallion Jock Scot and ten brood mares to National Stud, 1952), punting, skating, paddling-mate to the Royal Canoe Club, 1909-14. *Address:* 14 Carlos Place, W1. *T:* 01-499 4338; Telscombe Village, near Lewes, Sussex. *T:* Brighton 32167. *Club:* Bath.
[*Died* 7 *Nov.* 1971.

THORPE, Prof. Harry, OBE 1976; MA, MLitt, PhD, FRGS, FSA; Professor of Geography, University of Birmingham, since 1964 (Head of Department, since 1971); *b* 2 Feb. 1913; *s* of late Harry Thorpe and of Ada Kirk; *m* 1940, Patricia Lilian, *d* of W. H. Gardiner, OBE; two *s* two *d. Educ:* Chesterfield Sch.; Bede Coll., Univ. of Durham (Maltby Prizeman, 1933). BA, 1st Cl. Hons Geog., MA, MLitt; PhD (Birmingham). Demonstrator in Geography, Univ. of Durham, 1934-39. Served War, 1939-46: RE Survey in Europe and SE Asia; GSGS (Air); Survey 3B; GSO2 14th Army. Univ. of Birmingham: Lectr in Geog., 1946-54; Reader in Historical Geog., 1955-63. Chm., Govt Cttee of Inquiry into Allotments (Min. Housing and Local Govt), 1965-69; Mem., W Midlands Archaeol. Adv. Cttee, DoE, 1975-. President: Birmingham and Warwickshire Archaeological Soc., 1970-; Nat. Soc. of Leisure Gardeners (formerly Nat. Allotments and Gardens Soc.), 1973-; Geographical Assoc., 1974; Internat. Fedn of Leisure Gardeners, 1974-. Life Fellow, RGS, 1946-; FSA, 1957-. *Publications:* The City of Lichfield: a study of its growth and function, 1950; (with P.D.A. Harvey) The Printed Maps of Warwickshire 1576-1900, 1959; Report of the Departmental Committee of Inquiry into Allotments, 1969 (HMSO); numerous articles, incl. contribs to: Trans Inst. of Brit. Geographers; Geography; Geographical Jl; Trans Birmingham and Warwickshire Arch. Soc. *Recreations:* music, motoring, shooting, swimming, gardening. *Address:* Longacre, 86 Brooklands Road, Hall Green, Birmingham B28 8JZ. *T:* 021-777 3829.
[*Died* 14 *Feb.* 1977.

THORPE, Prof. Lewis (Guy Melville), BA, L-ès-L, PhD, D de l'U, LLD; FIAL, FRSA, FRHistS, FSA; Professor of French, University of Nottingham, since 1958; *b* 5 Nov. 1913; *e s* of late Lewis Thorpe and Jessie Emily Thorpe, of Brighton, Sussex; *m* 1939, Barbara Reynolds, PhD, *d* of late Alfred Charles Reynolds; one *s* one *d. Educ:* University College, London; University of Paris. War service with Rifle Brigade, Intelligence Corps, Army Educational Corps in Algeria, Tunisia, Italy, Greece, Austria, 1940-46; 2nd Lieut, 1942, Captain, 1942,

Major, 1943, Lt-Col, 1945; despatches, 1945. Lecturer in Romance Linguistics, University College, Nottingham, 1946-54; Reader, 1955-57. Hon. Sec., British Branch, Internat. Arthurian Soc., 1951-66, Pres., 1966-, Internat. Sec., 1966-75, World Pres., 1975-; Hon. Treas. of Assoc. of University Teachers of French, 1951-52, Hon. Sec., 1953-55, Pres., 1956; Member: Calvin Editorial Cttee, World Alliance of Reformed and Protestant Churches, 1962-; Assoc. degli Scrittori Veneti, 1964-; Cttee, British Branch, Société Rencesvals, 1964-; Cttee, Assoc. Internat. des Docteurs (Lettres) de l'Université de Paris, 1965-67; Visiting Professor, French Language and Literature, University of Munich, 1965. Editor: Nottingham Mediæval Studies since inception in 1957; Nottingham French Studies, 1962-75; Bulletin Bibliographique de la Société Internationale Arthurienne, 1967-75. *Publications:* La France Guerrière, 1945; Le roman de Laurin, fils de Marques le Sénéchal: a first contribution to the study of the Linguistics of an unpublished thirteenth-century Prose-Romance, 1950; The Study of French in a Modern University, 1958; Le roman de Laurin, fils de Marques le Sénéchal: the text of MS BN f. fr. 22548, 1960, 2nd edn, 1972; Geoffrey of Monmouth: The History of the Kings of Britain, 1966, 4th edn, 1976; (with Barbara Reynolds) Guido Farina, Painter of Verona, 1896-1957, (and Italian edn) 1967; Two Lives of Charlemagne, 1969, 5th edn, 1977; Einhard the Frank: The Life of Charlemagne, 1970; Le roman de Silence: a thirteenth century verse-romance by Heldris de Cornuälle, 1972; The Bayeux Tapestry and the Norman Invasion, 1973; (ed jointly) Studies in Medieval Language and Literature in memory of Frederick Whitehead, 1973; Gregory of Tours, The History of the Franks, 1974, 2nd edn 1977; Gerald of Wales, the Journey through Wales and the Description of Wales, 1977; contribs to Encyclopaedia Britannica, Erasmus, French Studies, Modern Language Notes, Modern Language Review, Renaissance and Modern Studies, Rivista di Letterature Moderne, Romania, Scriptorium, etc. *Recreations:* travel, cricket, amateur antiquarianism. *Address:* Department of French, The University, Nottingham. *T:* Nottingham 56101, Ext. 2476. *Club:* MCC.   [*Died* 10 *Oct.* 1977.

THORPE, William Geoffrey, CBE 1970; Deputy Chairman, Derek Crouch (Contractors) Ltd, since 1972; Chairman, Northern Coasters Ltd, since 1974; Director, SKF (UK) Ltd, since 1973; *b* 14 Oct. 1909; *s* of Robert Smith Thorpe and Maude Elizabeth Taylor Thorpe, York; *m* 1940, Gwendoline Margaret Marriott; one *s*. *Educ:* Nunthorpe Grammar Sch., York. Traffic Apprentice, L&NER, 1934; series of posts in Operating Dept, 1934-39; attached to Admiralty, 1939-41; further series of posts in Operating Dept, 1942-57; Line Traffic Manager (Great Eastern), 1957-62; Asst General Manager, London Midland Region, May 1962; General Manager, Scottish Region, Oct. 1963; Chairman and General Manager: Scottish Railway Board, 1964-67; London Midland Railway Board, 1967; British Railways Board: Vice-Chm., 1968-69; Dep. Chm., 1969-72; Chief Exec. (Rlys), 1970-71. FCIT; FBIM. OStJ. *Recreation:* golf. *Address:* 14 Amhurst Court, Grange Road, Cambridge. *T:* Cambridge 59020. *Club:* Naval and Military.
[*Died* 25 *Sept.* 1975.

THORSON, Hon. Joseph Thorarinn, PC Canada, 1941; President of Exchequer Court, Canada, from 1942, retired; Barrister-at-law, Winnipeg; *b* Winnipeg, 15 March 1889; *s* of Stephen Thorson who came from Iceland, 1887; *m* 1916, Alleen B. Scarth; one *s* two *d*. *Educ:* Manitoba Coll., Winnipeg; New Coll., Oxford. BA University of Manitoba, 1910; First Class Honours and Silver Medal in Classics. Rhodes Scholar for Manitoba, 1910; BA in Jurisprudence, University of Oxford, 1912; LLB University of Manitoba, 1921; Juris Doctor (Hon.), University of Iceland, 1930; Hon. LLD University of Manitoba, 1958; called to Bar, Middle Temple, 1913; Manitoba, 1913; enlisted CEF, 1916; served in France, rank Captain; Dean of Manitoba Law School, 1921-26; MP (L) Winnipeg South Centre, 1926-30; MP (L) Selkirk, 1935-42, Canadian House of Commons; Minister National War Services, Canada, 1941-42; KC 1930; appointed one of delegates of Canada to assembly of League of Nations, Sept. 1938; Chairman, War Expenditures Cttee, House of Commons, 1941; President, International Congress of Jurists, Berlin, 1952, Athens, 1955. Awarded the Grand Cross of the Order of the Falcon, Iceland. Religion: Anglican. *Recreations:* gardening, golf. *Address:* 20 Crescent Road, Rockcliffe, Ottawa, Canada. *Club:* Canadian (Ottawa).
[*Died* 5 *July* 1978.

THROCKMORTON, Geoffrey William Berkeley, CB 1947; Clerk of the Journals, House of Commons, 1940-48, retired; *b* 3 Sept. 1883; *yr s* of Sir Richard Throckmorton, 10th Bt; unmarried. Clerk in the House of Commons, 1908-48. Served European War, 1914-19, Captain, Berkshire Yeomanry (wounded, despatches). *Address:* Spiney House, Coughton, Alcester, Warwicks. *Club:* Cavalry.   [*Died* 4 *July* 1976.

THURLOW, 7th Baron, *cr* 1792; **Maj.-Gen. Henry Charles Hovell-Thurlow-Cumming-Bruce**, CB 1961; CBE 1956 (OBE 1948); DSO 1944 (Bar 1945); *b* 29 May 1910; *e s* of 6th Baron and Grace Catherine (*d* 1959), *d* of Canon Trotter of Christ Church, Barnet; *S* father, 1952. *Educ:* Eton; RMC, Sandhurst. Commissioned 2nd Lieut, Seaforth Highlanders, 1930; ADC to High Commissioner, Palestine, 1936-39; Assistant Military Secretary, British Troops in Palestine, 1940; served with 2nd Cameron Highlanders, Eritrea, 1941; Libyan Arab Force, Western Desert, 1942; Bde Major 152nd Inf. Bde, 1942 (despatches); Instructor Senior Officers' School, 1943; OC 1st Bn Gordon Highlanders, NW Europe, 1944 (Lt-Col); Comd 44 Lowland Bde, 1944 (Brig.); Comdt, BAOR Training Centre, 1945; OC Highland Bde Training Centre, 1947; GSO 1, HQ, MELF, 1949; AA&QMG, 1st Infantry Div., 1950. Comd 39 Inf. Bde, East Africa Command, 1954 (despatches). Staff Coll., 1942. Joint Services Staff Coll., 1949. Imperial Defence Coll., 1953. Dep. Director of Infantry, War Office, 1956-59; GOC 50 (N) Division and Northumbrian Area, 1959-62; GOC Troops, Malta and Libya, 1962-63; retired, 1964. Bt Lt-Col 1950, Colonel 1952, Brigadier 1958, Maj.-Gen. 1959. Member Royal Company of Archers (Queen's Body Guard for Scotland). President: Missions to Seamen, 1965-; SSAFA Berks, 1969-. Chairman: Directors, Jerusalem and the East Mission, 1969-; St Christopher's Hospice, Beckenham, 1966-. CStJ 1968 (OStJ 1937). *Recreation:* gardening. *Heir: b* Hon. Sir Francis Edward Hovell-Thurlow-Cumming-Bruce. *Address:* The Old Vicarage, Mapledurham, near Reading, Berks. *T:* Kidmore End 3339. *Clubs:* United Service, Pratt's.   [*Died* 29 *May* 1971.

THURSTAN, Violetta, MM, FRGS; *o d* of Edward Paget Thurstan, MD. *Educ:* Ladies' Coll., Guernsey; Germany; LLA St Andrews. Honours in Aesthetics and Fine Art. Sent to Brussels in Aug. 1914 by the Order of St John of Jerusalem; and served throughout the War in Belgium and Russia (Military Medal, 1914 Star, etc); Officer WRNS, 1939-44. Late Director of Bedouin Industries Frontier Districts Administration, Egypt. Officer in Allied Commission, Austria, 1946-48. Fellow Society of Designer-Craftsmen, 1975. *Publications:* Field Hospital and Flying Column; The People Who Run, Tragedy of the Refugees in Russia; Desert Songs; The Use of Vegetable Dyes; Decorative Textiles and Tapestries, 1934; Weaving Patterns of Yesterday and To-day; History of Ancient Fabrics (republished 1954); Weaving without Tears, 1956; Stormy Petrel, 1964; The Foolish Virgin, 1966; The Lucky Mary, 1973; The Hounds of War Unleashed, 1977. *Recreations:* travelling, gardening, weaving. *Address:* Old Mill House, The Square, Penryn, Cornwall. *T:* Penryn 2339.   [*Died* 13 *April* 1978.

THURSTON, Gavin (Leonard Bourdas), CBE 1966; FRCP, FRCGP; HM Coroner, Inner West London, 1965-80 (Western District, County of London, 1956-65); Deputy Coroner to the Royal Household since 1964; *b* 26 March 1911; 4th *s* of John Bourdas Thurston, London; *m* 1st, 1935, Ione Witham (*d* 1967), *d* of J. T. Barber, JP; one *s* one *d*; 2nd, 1969, Janet Hazell, MB, ChB, LRAM. *Educ:* Dulwich Coll.; Guy's Hosp. Med. School. MRCS, LRCP 1933; MRCP, 1937; DCH, 1937; FRCP 1969; FRCGP 1969. Barrister, Inner Temple, 1952. Treasurer's Cert. in Clinical Surgery, Guy's, 1933; Res. MO, Pembury Hosp. and Belgrave Hosp., 1933-35. Served War of 1939-45, RAMC, India and NW Europe; Specialist in Medicine, Lt-Col. Asst Dep. Coroner: South Essex, 1946-56; City of London, 1950-56; Dep. Coroner: Metropolitan Essex, 1949-56; North London, 1952-56; West Ham, 1950-56; Treasury MO, 1950-56. Hon. Treasurer, Coroners' Soc., 1958-60; Lecturer in Forensic Medicine, W London Hosp. Med. Sch., 1956-60; Sen. Lectr in Forensic Medicine, Charing Cross Hosp. Med. Sch., 1969-71; Hon. Editor, Medico-Legal Journal, 1958-; Founder Member, British Acad. of Forensic Sciences, 1959; Vice-Pres., Medical Defence Union, 1960-; Hon. Sec., Coroners' Soc. of England and Wales, 1960-71, Pres. 1971-72; President: Medico-Legal Soc., 1969-71; Chelsea Clinical Soc., 1976-77; Examiner for DMJ, 1963-72; Examiner for Milburn Prize, 1961-. Chm., Authors' Club, 1967-69. DMJ (hc) 1963. *Publications:* Coroner's Practice, 1958; contrib. to Atkin's Court Forms, 1961, and 1974; contrib. to Encyclopædia of General Practice, 1963; The Great Thames Disaster, 1965; The Clerkenwell Riot, 1967; Coroners, in Halsbury's Laws of England, 4th edn, 1974; Coronership, 1977; articles on medico-legal subjects. *Recreations:* reading and writing. *Address:* Ripe, Lewes, East Sussex BN8 6AS. *Clubs:* Authors', Savage.   [*Died* 15 *June* 1980.

THWAITE, Hartley, JP; Yorkshire District Manager, Lloyds Bank Ltd, retired (Yorkshire Regional Director, 1963-70); *b* Kalutara, Ceylon, 5 Aug. 1903; *e s* of late Rev. Simon and Susannah Thwaite; *m* 1928, Alice Evelyn Mallinson; one *s*. *Educ:* Kingswood, Bath; Leeds Univ. (research). MPhil 1972; FSA 1957; FIB 1949; FSG 1973. Entered service of Lloyds

Bank, 1920. Mem. Council, Inst. of Bankers, 1950-53, Chm. Huddersfield Centre, 1950-53, Pres. Leeds Centre, 1959-60; Chm., Leeds Coll. of Commerce, Banking Adv. Sub-Cttee, 1959-60; British Bankers' Assoc. rep., BSI Cttee on documentary reproduction, 1948-49. Mem., Nat. Register of Archives, WR (North) Cttee, 1952-75. Pres., Huddersfield Union Discussion Soc., 1958-59; Chm., Scarcroft Conservative Assoc., 1964-68. Yorkshire Archaeological Soc.: Sen. Vice-Pres.; Mem. Council, 1954-; Hon. Treas., 1955-59; 11 yrs Chm., Parish Register Section; Chm., Family Studies Section, 1973-76. Member: Leeds Library Cttee; Leeds Watch Cttee, 1966-68; Chm., Leeds Parole Cttees, 1971 and 1972; Chm., Leeds Prison Bd, 1973 and 1974 (Dep. Chm., 1970-72). Dir, Northern and Scottish Bd, Legal & General Assce Soc. Ltd, 1963-73. Dir, Kirkstall Lodge Ltd (ex-prisoners' hostel), 1970-77. Pres., Kingswood Old Boys' Assoc., 1969-70. JP Leeds City, 1962 (Court Chm.; Chm. Betting and Gaming Licensing Cttee). Frequent lectr on genealogy, parish registers, the history of probate and admin, etc. *Publications:* Parish Register of Wensley, Yorks, 1701-1837, 1967; Abstracts of Abbotside Wills, 1552-1688, 1968; contrib. Genealogists' Magazine. *Recreations:* genealogy, archaeology, local history. *Address:* Rose Cottage, Manor Park, Scarcroft, Leeds LS14 3BW. *T* Leeds 892367. *Clubs:* East India, Devonshire, Sports and Public Schools; Leeds (Leeds); Huddersfield and Borough (Huddersfield).   *[Died 21 Feb. 1978.*

THYNE, William, OBE 1969; President, William Thyne (Holdings) Ltd, since 1973 (Chairman, 1948-73); Director, Clydesdale Bank Ltd, 1948-78 (Chairman, 1969-75); *b* 23 March 1901; *e s* of late William Thyne and late Christian Seton Watt; *m* 1931, Virginia Neeb Williams (*d* 1968); two *s* two *d*. *Educ:* George Watson's Coll., Edinburgh; CIT, Pittsburg. Director: Clydesdale Bank Finance Corp. Ltd, until 1978 (Chm., 1969-75); Clydesdale Bank Insurance Services Ltd, until 1978 (Chm., 1969-75); Midland Bank Ltd, 1970-75; Henry Ballantyne & Sons Ltd; Man. Dir, A. & R. Scott Ltd, 1941-54. Pres., Edinburgh Chamber of Commerce and Mfrs, 1950-52; Chm., Council of Scottish Chambers of Commerce, 1964-66; Pres., Grocers' Inst., 1957-60; Past Convener of Commerce Advisory Cttee, Edinburgh Univ., and Past Mem., Industrial Liaison Cttee, Edinburgh Univ.; Mem., Scottish Nat. Cttee, English-Speaking Union; Mem., Scottish Tourist Board, 1965-69. *Recreations:* fishing, shooting. *Address:* The Yair, by Galashiels, Selkirkshire. *T:* Clovenfords 212.   *[Died 24 Aug. 1978.*

TIARKS, Rt. Rev. John Gerhard; *b* 5 April 1903; *s* of late Rev. Hope Charles Tiarks, lately Rector of Donington, Salop, and late Evelyn Louisa, *d* of Capt. Charles Oakes Blackwood Hall, RN; *m* 1927, Gwyneth Mary, 2nd *d* of Rev. Griffith Mathews, BA; one *s* one *d*. *Educ:* Westminster (King's Scholar); Trinity Coll., Cambridge (Class. and Theological Triposes, BA 1925, MA 1929); Ridley Hall, Cambridge. Curate of Christ Church, Southport, 1926-29; 1st Vicar of Christ Church, Norris Green, Liverpool, 1930-34; Vicar of St Paul, Widnes, 1934-37; Vicar of St Helens, Lancs, 1937-44; Proctor in York Convocation, 1944; Vicar of Bradford and Provost of Bradford Cathedral, 1944-62; Bishop of Chelmsford, 1962-71. *Recreations:* motoring, walking. *Address:* 128d Oxford Road, Moseley, Birmingham 13.   *[Died 2 Jan. 1974.*

TIBBITS, Sir (Jabez) Cliff, Kt 1948; JP; Managing Director of Jabez Cliff & Co.; *b* 15 Sept. 1884; *s* of Frederick and Mary Tibbits, Aldridge; *m* 1914 (she *d* 1971); two *d*. *Educ:* Queen Mary's School, Walsall. *Address:* Cedar Court, Aldridge, Walsall, Staffs. *T:* (home) Aldridge 52132; (business) Walsall 21676. *Club:* National Liberal.   *[Died 31 Jan. 1974.*

TIBBLE, Prof. John William, MA, MEd; Professor of Education, University of Leicester, 1946-66; Emeritus since 1967; Academic Secretary, Universities Council for Education of Teachers, since 1967; *b* Skelton in Cleveland, Yorks, 3 April 1901; *s* of the late Henry Tibble, Redcar, Yorks; *m* 1928, Anne, *d* of F. Northgrave, Rounton, Northallerton; one *s* one *d*. *Educ:* Guisborough Grammar School; Leeds University. Assistant Master, Deacon's School, Peterborough, 1924-32; Lecturer in Education, University Coll. of the South West, Exeter, 1932-46. Visiting Asst Professor of Education, Teachers' College, Columbia Univ., New York, 1936-37. Past Dir, Univ. of Leicester Sch. of Educn. Editor, Education for Teaching, 1963-68; Gen. Editor, Students' Library of Education, 1966-. *Publications:* (with Anne Tibble) John Clare, A Life, 1932; The Poems of John Clare, 1935; (with Anne Tibble) The Letters of John Clare, 1951; (with Anne Tibble) The Prose of John Clare, 1951; The Rôle of the Teacher in Modern Society, 1950; Physical Education and the Educative Process, 1953; (ed) The Study of Education, 1966; W. B. Curry: A Pioneer of Education, 1967; (ed) The Extra Year, 1970; (with Anne Tibble) John Clare: a life, 1972; (ed) The Future of Teacher Education, 1972;

contrib. on educational topics to books and periodicals. *Address:* Clare Cottage, Guilsborough, Northants. *T:* Guilsborough 396.   *[Died 23 Jan. 1972.*

TICKELL, Maj.-Gen. Sir Eustace Francis, KBE 1945 (CBE 1941); CB 1942; MC; Officer of Legion of Honour (France), 1944; *b* 10 Dec. 1893; *s* of late Charles Tickell, Indian Public Works Department, and late Alice Esther Francis; *m* 1921, Mary Violet, *d* of Marston Clarke Buszard, KC; two *s* one *d*. *Educ:* Bedford; RMA, Woolwich. Entered Royal Engineers, 1913; various regimental and staff appointments with 6th, 28th, 26th, 54th and 15th Divisions in France, Salonica, and Palestine, 1914-18; Chatham, 1919; Instructor at RMA, Woolwich, 1924; North China, 1928; in charge of RE officers at Cambridge University, 1932; Commander RE, York, 1936; Commander RE, 5th Division, Catterick, 1938; Chief Engineer, British Troops in Egypt, 1939; General Headquarters Middle East Forces, Director of Works 1940, Engineer-in-Chief 1944; BLA Director of Works, 1944, Chief Engineer, 1945; Engineer-in-Chief, War Office, 1945-48; retired pay, 1949. Colonel Comdt, Corps of Royal Engineers, 1950-58; Hon. Col, Resources Units, RE, Army Emergency Reserve, 1953-59. President, Institution of Royal Engineers, 1948-51; Chairman RE Assoc., 1954-56. *Address:* Wood End, Silvermere, Cobham, Surrey. *T:* Cobham 3056. *Club:* Army and Navy.   *[Died 28 Dec. 1972.*

TIERNEY, Michael, DLitt (Hon.) NUI and Queen's University Belfast; President, University College, Dublin, 1947-64; Professor of Greek, 1923-47; Vice-Chairman Seanad Eireann (representing National University), 1938-44; Member, Council of State, 1940-44; Member Royal Irish Academy; *b* 20 Sept. 1894; *s* of Michael Tierney, of Esker, Castleblakeney, Co. Galway and Bridget Finn; *m* 1923, Eibhlin, *e d* of Professor Eoin MacNeill; five *s* one *d* (and one *d* decd). *Educ:* St Joseph's College, Ballinasloe; University College, Dublin; Sorbonne, Athens, Berlin. BA degree First Class Hons. Classics, 1914; Travelling Studentship NUI 1917; Student British School of Archaeology, Athens, 1919; Member of Dail Eireann for North Mayo, 1925-27; for National University, 1927-32; Member Gaeltacht Commission, 1925; Second Chamber Commission, 1936; Commission on Vocational Organisation, 1939. KSG 1955. *Publications:* (ed) A Tribute to Newman, 1945; (ed) Daniel O'Connell, 1949; (ed) Struggle With Fortune, 1954; articles in Studies, Classical Quarterly, Journal of Hellenic Studies, etc. *Address:* Alloon, Taney Road, Dundrum, Co. Dublin.   *[Died 10 May 1975.*

TIFFANY, Stanley, CBE 1967; Hotelier and Caterer; *b* 1908. *Educ:* Leeds Modern School; Technical College. Trained as electrical engineer. Lately Director Peterborough and District Co-operative Soc. Ltd and Leeds Co-operative Soc. MP (Lab) Peterborough Division of Northamptonshire, 1945-50. Councillor (Leader of Council), Wakefield County Borough, 1952-67. Has been member of several Parliamentary delegations to European countries. *Address:* Alexandra Hotel, Bridlington, Yorks.   *[Died 19 March 1971.*

TIGHE, Rear-Adm. Wilfred Geoffrey Stuart, CB 1961; *b* 29 July 1905; *yr s* of late Wilfred Tighe and of Mrs Tighe, Rossanagh, Co. Wicklow; *m* 1935, Dorothea Rosemary, *yr d* of late Julius Benedict Simpson and Mrs Simpson, Claremont, Weymouth; one *s* one *d*. *Educ:* Arnold House; Haileybury Coll. Joined Royal Navy as Paymaster Cadet, 1923; Comdr 1942; Captain 1952; Rear-Admiral 1959. Qualified as Interpreter in Italian, 1931, and in Russian 1934. Member of Institute of Patentees, 1933, and granted British Letters Patent in that year for invention and design of the electric razor. Staff of C-in-C East Indies Squadron, 1935-37; specialised in Communications Security and attached to Foreign Office, 1938-39. Served during War of 1939-45 in the Home Fleet and as Assistant Director of Signal Division, and Intelligence Division, of the Naval Staff. Assistant Director of Plans, Admiralty, 1953-55; Supply Officer, HMS Raleigh, 1955-57; Base Supply Officer at Chatham, 1957-59; Rear-Admiral (Personnel), Home Naval Air Command, Lee-on-Solent, 1959-62, retired. *Recreations:* fishing and shooting. *Address:* Haddon, The Avenue, Fareham, Hants. *T:* 80297; River Lodge, Inistioge, Co. Kilkenny. *T:* Kilkenny 29423. *Clubs:* Naval and Military; Royal Southern Yacht (Hamble); Kildare Street (Dublin).   *[Died 17 July 1975.*

TILEA, Viorel Virgil, CBE 1938; LLD; Roumanian politician, diplomat and industrialist; *b* Sibiu, 6 April 1896; *s* of O. Tilea, MSc, and Emilia Ratiu; *m* 1921, Eugenia Pop (*d* 1947); one *s* three *d*; *m* 1951, Mrs Manuela Munroe; one *s* one *d*. *Educ:* Univs of Bratislava, Vienna, and Cluj; London School of Economics. Founded in Sibiu, students' club, Britannia, for English language, literature and institutions, 1913; Secretary Roumanian National Council, 1918; Delegate Roumanian

National Council for Transylvania to Bern and Paris, 1918-19; PS to Pres. Transylvanian Reg. Govt, 1919; Attaché and Secretary to Roumanian Legation in London, 1920; founded first Anglo-Roumanian Soc. (cultural) in Roumania-Cluj, 1923; entered Politics and Industry, 1923; head of timber concern and dir various industrial concerns, 1924-38; candidate for Cluj county, 1925; Leader National Peasant Youth of Transylvania, 1926; co-founder Central Anglo-Roumanian Society in Bucharest, 1927; MP, Sec. Foreign Affairs Committee, Member Delegation and Delegate to LON Assemblies, Tariff Conference and Inter-parliamentarian Conferences, 1928-33; Head of Roumanian Commercial Delegation and signatory Anglo-Roumanian Commercial Treaty, 1930, and Roumanian-Hungarian Com. Tr., 1931, 1932; Under Sec. of State to Presidency of Council, Press and Information, 1930-33; Vice-Pres. and Acting Pres. Anglo-Roumanian Soc. in Roumania, 1931-39; Pres. Federation of Association Football Clubs, 1932-39; Roumanian Minister at Court of St James's, 1938; recalled by Hitler's order but stayed in England and started Free Roumanian Movement, July 1940 (dissolved as Roumania broke with Axis, Aug. 1944); nationality taken and property seized by Antonescu pro-Nazi govt, Jan. 1941, restored 1944, re-confiscated by Communist Regime, 1947; kept contact with opposition in Roumania; several broadcasts, articles and lectures in England and Scotland, 1940-44; against Communist domination in Roumania, but favours the more independent policy from Russia. Capt. in Reserve Roumanian Horse Guard; Grand Crosses of St Sava and Skander Beg; Grand Officer St Sylvester and Polonia Restituta; Comm. Carol I; Knight of Ferdinand; Knight Ord. of Malta, etc. Publications: Le Désarmement de la Haine, 1924; The New Slovakia (trans.), 1925; Roumania's Diplomatic Action, 1925; Iuliu Maniu, Der Mann und das Werk, 1927; Articles in Periodicals and Daily Papers, Roumanian and Foreign. Address: 28 Redcliffe Square, SW10. T: 01-373 8246.   [Died 20 Sept. 1972.

TILLEY, Cecil Edgar, FRS 1938; BSc; PhD Cantab; Hon. DSc Manchester, Sydney; Professor of Mineralogy and Petrology, Cambridge, 1931-61; Fellow of Emmanuel College, Cambridge, 1931; Vice-Master, 1952-58; b 14 May 1894; m 1928, Irene Doris Marshall; one d. Educ: Univs of Adelaide and Sydney. Demonstrator in Geology and Mineralogy, Univ. of Sydney, 1916; Chemist to Dept of Explosives Supply, Queensferry, 1917-18; 1851 Exhibition Scholar, 1920-22, and Senior 1851 Exhibition, 1922-24, University of Cambridge; Wollaston Fund, Geological Society of London, 1924; Lecturer in Petrology, Cambridge, 1928-31; Sedgwick Prize, 1931; Bigsby Medal, 1937; Roebling Medal, 1954; Wollaston Medal, 1960. Pres., Mineralogical Soc., 1948-51, 1957-60; Pres., Geological Soc. of London, 1949-50, William Smith Lectr, 1957; Vice-Pres. Royal Soc., 1949; Royal Medal, Royal Soc., 1967; Hon. FRSE; Foreign Associate, Nat. Acad. of Sciences, USA; Hon. Fellow, Geological Soc. of America; Foreign Mem.: Geological Soc. of Sweden; Mineralogical Soc. of America; Roy. Swed. Acad. of Sciences, 1966; Hon. Member, Royal Society, New Zealand; Foreign Hon. Mem. Amer. Acad. of Arts and Sciences, 1966; Research Associate, Carnegie Institution of Washington, 1956-67; President International Mineralogical Association, 1964-70. Sen. Vis. Fellow in Dept of Geology, Manchester Univ., 1967-. Publications: Contributions to igneous, metamorphic and experimental petrology. Address: 30 Tenison Avenue, Cambridge; Emmanuel College, Cambridge. T: 52234.
[Died 24 Jan. 1973.

TILMAN, Harold William, CBE 1973; DSO 1945; MC; FRGS (Founder's Medal); LLD; late RA; b 14 Feb. 1898; s of late John Hinkes Tilman. Educ: Berkhamsted School; Royal Military Academy, Woolwich. Commissioned Royal Artillery, July 1915; served on Western Front with RFA and RHA until end of War (MC and bar); resigned, 1919; Reserve of Officers; Farming in Kenya, 1919-33; expeditions to Mts Kenya, Kilimanjaro, and Ruwenzori; various expeditions to Himalaya; Mt Everest Reconnaissance, 1935; Nanda Devi, 1934-36; Leader Mt Everest, 1938; two journeys to Sinkiang, 1947, 1948; two journeys to Nepal, 1949-50; annual voyages to sub-antarctic, antarctic and arctic islands, 1955-76. Served with Royal Artillery in France (despatches), Syria, Irak, Western Desert, Tunisia, 1939-43; with Albanian partisans, 1943-44, and with Italian partisans, 1944-45 (DSO, Freeman of City of Belluno, N Italy). Hon. LLD University of St Andrews, 1954. Blue Water Medal of Cruising Club of America, 1956. Publications: Ascent of Nanda Devi, 1937; Snow on the Equator, 1938; When Men and Mountains Meet, 1947; Mount Everest, 1938, 1948; Two Mountains and a River, 1949; China to Chitral, 1951; Nepal Himalaya, 1952; Mischief in Patagonia, 1957; Mischief Among the Penguins, 1961; Mischief in Greenland, 1964; Mostly Mischief, 1966; Mischief goes South, 1968; In Mischief's Wake, 1972; Ice with Everything, 1974; Triumph and Tribulation,

1976. Address: Bodowen, near Barmouth, Gwynedd. T: Barmouth 280630. Clubs: Alpine, Naval and Military, Ocean Cruising, Royal Cruising.
[Died at sea, between Nov. 1977 and April 1978.

TILTMAN, H(ugh) Hessell, OBE 1959; Author and Journalist; b 2 February 1897; s of Frank Tiltman, Rye, Sussex, and Ada Wood Rose; m 1925, Marjorie (author of Quality Chase, 1940; Born a Woman, 1951, etc), e d of Sydney Hand; no c. Educ: privately. Newspaper correspondent in Europe, United States and Far East, 1934-51. War Correspondent in Sino-Japanese hostilities in China, 1937-38; in Nationalist Spain, 1938-39; and accredited to United States Forces in Japan, 1945-63; Japan Correspondent of The Guardian, 1951-63; special writer on Japanese affairs for the Washington Post, 1948-62; Contributing Editor and Adviser on Japanese Affairs to Encyclopædia Britannica (Japan) Inc., 1967-72. Japanese Order of the Sacred Treasure, 1959. Publications: James Ramsay MacDonald: an Authentic Life, 1929; The Terror in Europe, 1930; Peasant Europe, 1934; The Far East comes nearer, 1936; Uncensored Far East, 1937; Nightmares must End, 1940; (with Col P. T. Etherton)-The Pacific: A Forecast, 1928; Manchuria: The Cockpit of Asia, 1932; Japan: Mistress of the Pacific?, 1933. Recreation: travel. Address: Foreign Correspondents Club of Japan, 1 Shimbun Alley, Marunouchi, Tokyo, Japan. Club: Savage.   [Died 10 Aug. 1976.

TIMOSHENKO, Stephen; Professor Emeritus of Theoretical and Applied Mechanics at Stanford University since 1944; b 23 Dec. 1878; s of Prokop Timoshenko and Jezefina Sarnavskaja; m 1902, Alexandra Archangelskaya; one s two d. Educ: Institute of Engineers of Ways of Communication; St Petersburg. Laboratory of testing materials, Inst. of Engineers of Ways of Communication, 1902-3; Asst Prof., Petersburg Polytech. Inst., 1903-6; Prof. Kiew Polytechn. Inst., 1907-11; Prof. Inst. of Engrs of Ways of Communication and also Prof. Polytech. Inst. Petersburg, 1912-18; Consulting Engr, Russian Navy, 1912-18. Member Acad. of Sciences, Kiew, 1918-20; Prof. Polytechn. Inst., Zagreb, Yugoslavia, 1920-22; Research Engr Vibration Speciality Co., Philadelphia, USA, 1922-23; Research Engr Westinghouse El. and Mfg Co., Pittsburgh, USA, 1923-27; Prof. Michigan Univ., USA, 1927-36; Prof. Stanford Univ., 1936-44. Corresp. de l'Acad. des sciences, Paris, 1939-; Member Nat. Acad. of Sciences, Washington, DC, 1941; For. Mem. Royal Soc. London, 1944-; Foreign member Accademia Nationale dei Lincei, Rome, 1948-. Publications: books and papers published in Russian until 1920; since leaving Russia, following books published in English: Applied Elasticity, 1924; Theory of Vibrations, 1928; Strength of Materials (Vols 1 and 2), 1930; Theory of Elasticity, 1934; Theory of Elastic Stability, 1936; Theory of Plates, 1940; (with Prof. D. H. Young) Statics and Dynamics, 1936, Theory of Structures, 1945; Advanced Dynamics, 1948; History of Strength of Materials, 1953; The Collected Papers of Stephen P. Timoshenko, 1953; Engineering Education in Russia, 1959. Address: Böcklin Str. 35, 56 Wuppertal E, Germany.   [Died 29 May 1972.

TINKER, Brian; TD; JP; b 4 Apr. 1892; s of Charles Shaw Tinker, JP, CC, Meal Hill, Hepworth, Yorks; m Helen Violet Brameld, d of Frank Johnson, Scarborough; no c. Educ: Repton; Magdalene College, Cambridge. Studied Mining Engineering with H. St John Durnford at Doncaster; entered Tinker Bros Ltd, 1913; joined QO Yorks Dragoons, 1912; served with them during European War; retired with rank of Major, 1930; commanded the Huddersfield and Wakefield Squadron. JP WR Yorks, 1928. Recreations: hunting, Master, Rockwood Harriers, 1927-31, Master, Badsworth Hounds, 1931-34; Master, Grove Hounds, 1937-39. Address: Meal Hill, New Mill, Huddersfield, West Yorks. TA: New Mill. T: Holmfirth 3170.
[Died 15 Aug. 1977.

TISELIUS, Professor Arne (Wilhelm Kaurin); Head, Nobel Institute, Royal Swedish Academy of Sciences, Stockholm, since 1968; Professor of Biochemistry, University of Uppsala, Sweden, 1938-68, retired 1968; President, Nobel Foundation, 1960-64; b 10 Aug. 1902; s of Dr Hans A. Tiselius and Rosa Kaurin; m 1930, Greta Dalén; one s one d. Educ: Uppsala Univ. DSc Uppsala, 1930; Docent of Chemistry, Uppsala Univ., 1930-38; Nobel Prize in Chemistry, 1948. Hon. Degrees: Stockholm, 1948 (MD); University of Paris, 1948; University of Cambridge, 1949; University of Bologna, 1955; University of Glasgow, 1956; University of Madrid, 1957; University of Oxford, 1958 (DSc); University of Oslo, 1961; University of Lyon, 1962; Gustavus Adolphus Coll., Minnesota, 1963; University of California, 1964; University of Michigan, 1967; Charles Univ., Prague, 1968. Hon. Member: Harvey Society of New York, 1939; New York Academy of Sciences, 1943; New York Academy of Medicine, 1947; Royal Institution of Great Britain, 1947; Chem.

Society, London, 1949; Real Sociedad Española de Física y Química, 1952; Consejo Superior de Investigaciones Científicas, Madrid, 1953; Finnish Society of Science, 1953; Royal Dutch Chemical Society, 1953; Swiss Chemical Society, 1955; Nat. Acad. of Sciences of India, Allahabad, 1956; Franklin Institute, 1956; French Chem. Society, 1957; American Society of Biol. Chemists, 1961; Acad. Republ. Populare Romine, Bucarest; Soc. for Electrophoresis, Tokyo. Hon. Foreign Member: Society of Chemical Industry, London, 1951; Royal Inst. of Chemistry, London, 1952; American Academy of Arts and Sciences, 1953; Czechoslovak Acad. of Sciences, 1965; World Acad. of Art and Science, 1965; Deutsche Akad. d. Wissenschaft, Berlin, 1969. Member: several Swedish Academies; National Academy of Sciences, Washington; Royal Danish Scientific Society; Accademia Nazionale Dei Quaranta, Rome; Corresp. Member Acad. of Sciences, Lissabon, 1953; Corresp. Member Académie des Sciences, Paris, 1955; Member Pontificia Scientiarum Academia, Vatican, 1955; Foreign Member: Royal Society, 1957; Polish Acad. of Sciences, Warsaw, 1959; Inst. Chem. of India, 1959; Hon. Member Society Swedish Physicians, 1959. Chairman, Nobel Cttee for Chemistry, 1945-; Vice-President Nobel Foundation, 1947-60. Chairman Swedish Natural Science Research Council, 1946-50; President International Union of Pure and Applied Chemistry, 1951-55; Member Science Advisory Council to the Government, 1962-68; Hon. Member, Amer. Soc. Biol. Chemists, 1962; Foreign Member, American Philosophical Society, 1964. *Publications:* various papers, mostly in scientific journals, about protein chemistry, electrophoresis and adsorption. *Recreation:* birdwatching. *Address:* Thunbergsvägen 22, 75238 Uppsala, Sweden. *T:* 135554.
[Died 29 Oct. 1971.

TISSERANT, His Eminence Cardinal Eugène; Dean of Sacred College of Cardinals, since 1951; Cardinal Bishop of Ostia, 1951-66; Cardinal Bishop of Porto and Santa Rufina, 1946-66; *b* Nancy, 24 March 1884; *s* of Hippolyte Tisserant, Veterinary Surgeon and Octavie Connard. *Educ:* Collège Saint-Sigisbert; Grand Séminaire de Nancy; Ecole Biblique Saint-Etienne de Jérusalem; Ecole des Langues Orientales vivantes, Ecole des Hautes Etudes, Ecole du Louvre; Institut Catholique de Paris. Ordained Priest, 1907; Curator of Oriental MSS, Vatican Library, 1908; Professor of Assyrian, Apollinarian Univ., Rome, 1908-13. Served European War of 1914-18 in French Army. Asst Prefect, Vatican Library, 1919-30; Adviser of the Sacred Congregation for Eastern Church Affairs, 1926; Prelate of His Holiness, 1929; Pro-Prefect, Vatican Library, 1930-36; Protonotary Apostolic, 1936; Cardinal-Deacon, 1936; Cardinal-Priest, 1937; Sub-Dean, Sacred College of Cardinals, 1948. President, Commn Biblique, 1938; Member: Institut de France; Académie Française. Grand Croix de la Légion d'Honneur. *Publications:* Ascension d'Isaïe, 1909; Codex Zuquinensis Rescriptus Veteris Testamenti, 1911; Specimina Codicum Orientalum, 1914; Codices Armeni Bybliothecae Vaticanae, 1927; Codices Aethiopici Bybliothecae Vaticanae, 1936; Luigi Maria Grignion de Montfort: le Scuole di Carità e le Origini dei Fratelli di San Gabriele, 1949; Saint Louis Marie Grignion de Montfort, les écoles charitables et les origines des Frères de Saint Gabriel, 1960. *Address:* Via Giovanni Prati 4, Rome, Italy.
[Died 21 Feb. 1972.

TITMAN, Sir George (Alfred), Kt 1954; CBE 1948 (OBE 1937); MVO (4 cl.) 1942; Secretary, Lord Chamberlain's Office, 1939-54, retired; *b* 12 July 1889; *o s* of late George Titman, Lewisham; *m* 1914, Eva Ellen, *e d* of late Charles Comfort, Cheltenham; one *s* one *d* (twins). Clerk, Duchess of Albany's Household, 1910-16; served in The King's (Liverpool) Regt, 1916; Clerk in Queen Mary's Household, 1916-19; Central Chancery of Orders of Knighthood, 1919-22; entered Lord Chamberlain's Office, 1922; First Clerk, 1932; Asst Secretary, 1936; a Sergeant-at-Arms to King George VI, 1946-52, to the Queen, 1952-54. Order of St John; Officer Legion of Honour; Chev. Order of Dannebrog (Denmark); Officer House of Orange (Netherlands); Chevalier (Cl. IV), Order of Vasa (Sweden); Cav. Crown of Italy; Order of Menelik II (Cl. IV); Star of Ethiopia (3). *Publication:* Dress and Insignia Worn at Court, 1937. *Address:* 42 Chadacre Road, Stoneleigh, Epsom, Surrey. *T:* 01-393 1683.
[Died 10 June 1980.

TITMAS, Air Commodore John Francis, CB 1950; CBE 1946; CEng; AFRAeS; psa; retired; *b* 20 Aug. 1898; *s* of late W. R. Titmas, Anerley, Kent; *m* 1925, Doris Maude, *d* of late Captain F. W. Young, JP; one *d*. *Educ:* Whitgift School. Served European War, 1914-19, Lieut, RFC, 1917. Air Commodore, RAF, 1944; AOC, RAF Station, Halton, Bucks, 1946-49; Senior Technical Staff Officer, HQ Bomber Command, 1949-50; Director of Aeronautical Inspection Services, Air Ministry, 1951-54; retired 1954. JP Kent, 1956. *Address:* St Ronans, Anerley Road, Anerley, SE20. *T:* 01-778 3065. *Club:* RAF Reserves.
[Died 28 April 1973.

TITMUSS, Professor Richard Morris, CBE 1966; FBA 1972; Professor of Social Administration, University of London, London School of Economics, since 1950; Deputy Chairman, Supplementary Benefits Commission, since 1968 (Member, 1967-68); *b* 1907; *m* 1937, Kathleen Caston Miller; one *d*. *Educ:* private school, to age of 15. Industrial and commercial experience, 1922-42; historian, Cabinet offices, 1942-49; Social Medicine Research Unit of Medical Research Council, 1949-50. Mem., Community Relations Commn, 1968-71. Hon. DSc University of Wales, 1959; Hon. LLD: Edinburgh, 1962; Toronto, 1964; Chicago, 1970; Hon. DTech Brunel, 1971. *Publications:* Poverty and Population, 1938; (with F. Le Gros Clark) Our Food Problem, 1939; (with K. C. Titmuss) Parents Revolt, 1942; Birth, Poverty and Wealth, 1943; Problems of Social Policy (official War History), 1950; (with B. Abel-Smith) The Cost of the National Health Service, 1955; The Social Division of Welfare, 1956; Essays on the Welfare State, 1958; Health in Law and Opinion in England in the Twentieth Century (ed M. Ginsberg), 1959; (with B. Abel-Smith and T. Lynes) Social Policy and Population Growth in Mauritius, 1961; Income Distribution and Social Change, 1962; The Health Services of Tanganyika (ed); Choice and the Welfare State, 1967; Commitment to Welfare, 1968; The Gift Relationship, 1970. Various papers in The Lancet, British Journal of Sociology, Political Quarterly, etc. *Address:* 32 Twyford Avenue, W3.
[Died 6 April 1973.

TITO, President (Josip Broz); Marshal of Yugoslavia since 1943; Prime Minister and Minister of National Defence, Yugoslavia, since 1945; President of Yugoslavia, since 1953, Life President, since 1974; Life President of the League of Communists of Yugoslavia; Supreme Commander of the Yugoslav Army; *b* 7 May 1892; *s* of Franjo and Marija Broz; a Croatian; *m* 1st, 1918 (wife decd); one *s*; 2nd, 1939 (marr. diss.); one *s*; 3rd, 1952, Jovanka Budisavljevic. Served in Austro-Hungarian Army, 1913-15; war prisoner, Russia, 1915-17; fought with Red Army, 1917-20; returned to Yugoslavia, worked as machinist and mechanic, and became Croatian Labour leader working with Metal Workers' Union; was imprisoned for five years for conspiracy after taking part in illegal Communist activities, 1928; left the country, on release, and recruited Yugoslavs for the International Brigades in Spanish Civil War, 1936-37; became Member of Central Committee, 1934; Secretary General of the Yugoslav Communist Party, 1937; returned to Yugoslavia before War of 1939-45, during which, at head of Yugoslav Communist Party, led general people's uprising and revolution in occupied Yugoslavia; Supreme Commander of Yugoslav National Liberation Army. Elected Marshal of Yugoslavia and President Nat. Liberation Cttee, 1943. Elected President of the Yugoslav Government, 1945; elected President of the Republic, 1953, re-elected 1954, 1958, 1963, 1967 and 1971. Decorations: Grand Star of Yugoslavia; Order of Liberty; 3 orders of National Hero; Hero of Socialist Work; National Liberation; War Flag; Great Cordon of Yugoslav Flag; Partisan Star with Golden Wreath; Merit for the People with Golden Star; Fraternity and Unity with Golden Wreath; Outstanding Courage; Order of the October Revolution; Hon. GCB 1972; in all about 70 high foreign decorations. *Publications:* twenty-three volumes of articles, speeches and other documents covering the period 1941-68. *Address:* Užička 15, Belgrade, Yugoslavia.
[Died 4 May 1980.

TIWANA, Al-Haj Lt-Col Nawab Sir Malik Khizar Hayat Khan, KCSI 1946; OBE 1931; Member of Legislative Assembly; *b* 7 Aug. 1900. *Educ:* Aitchison Chiefs' Coll., Lahore. Minister of Public Works, Punjab, 1937-42; Premier of the Punjab, 1942-47. Attended the Jubilee Celebrations in London, 1935; as Premier, Punjab, attended Victory Celebrations, London, 1945, and Paris Peace Conf., 1945, representing India. Hon. DCL Oxford 1945. Jubilee Medal, 1935; Coronation Medal, 1937. *Address:* Kalra, District Sargodha, Pakistan; 47 Wellington Mall, Lahore Cantonment, Pakistan.
[Died 20 Jan. 1975.

TIZARD, Prof. Jack, CBE 1973; Professor of Child Development, University of London, Institute of Education, 1964-71; Research Professor since 1971; Director, Thomas Coram Research Unit, since 1973; *b* 25 Feb. 1919; *s* of John Marsh Tizard; *m* 1947, Barbara Patricia Parker; two *s* one *d* (and one *d* adopted). *Educ:* Timaru Boys' High Sch.; Canterbury University Coll., NZ; Universities of Oxford and London. MA NZ 1940; BLitt Oxford 1948; PhD London 1951. Army Service, 2 NZEF, MEF, and CMF, 1940-45. Lecturer in Psychology, St Andrews, 1947-48; Sci. Staff, MRC, Social Psychiatry Research Unit, 1948-64. Bartholomew Lecturer, University of Keele, 1966; Emanuel Miller Lecture, Assoc. for Child Psychology and Psychiatry, 1973; Dorothy Gardner Lecture, 1975. Kennedy International Scientific Award, 1968. Member, Social Science Research Council and Chm. of its Educational Research Board,

1969-71; Consultant Adv. in Mental Subnormality, Dept of Health and Social Security, 1965-75; Consultant to Home Office Res. Unit, 1975-78; Chairman: Spastics Soc. Educational Adv. Cttee, 1966-; Sec. of State's Adv. Cttee on Handicapped Children, 1970-73; Assoc. of Child Psychology and Psychiatry, 1964-65; Member: Chief Scientist's Res. Cttee, DHSS, 1973-77; Child Health Services Cttee; WHO Expert Cttee on Mental Health. Pres., British Psychological Soc., 1975-76. Consultant: OECD Project on the Handicapped Adolescent; Centre for Educnl Res. and Innovation; Consultant on Mental Subnormality, WHO. Hon. Mem., British Paediatric Assoc. FBPsS, FRSM. Res. Award, Amer. Assoc. on Mental Deficiency, 1973. Publications: The Social Problem of Mental Deficiency (with N. O'Connor), 1956; The Mentally Handicapped and their Families (with J. C. Grad), 1961; Community Services for the Mentally Handicapped, 1964; Education, Health and Behaviour (with M. L. Rutter and T. K. Whitmore), 1970; Patterns of Residential Care (with R. D. King and N. V. Raynes), 1971; (with R. Clarke and I. Sinclair) Varieties of Residential Experience, 1975; (with P. Moss and J. Perry) All Our Children, 1976; articles on mental retardation and child development. Address: 4 The Gables, Vale of Health, NW3. T: 01-435 4475.   [Died 2 Aug. 1979.

TOBIAS, Rt. Rev. George Wolfe Robert; retired; b 30 Sept. 1882; s of late Canon Charles Frederick Tobias, Cape Town; m 1933, Edith Anne Perkins; one s one d. Educ: University of Cape of Good Hope, BA 1902; Sidney Sussex Coll., Cambridge (Scholar), BA 1906, MA; Cuddesdon Coll., 1906-07. Deacon, 1907; priest, 1908; Curate, King Cross, Halifax, 1907-10; Priest-in-Charge, All Saints, Roodebloem, Cape, 1910-23; served in South African Medical Corps, 1915-17; Temp. CF, 1917-19 (MC); priest-in-charge of St Mary's Mission, Ovamboland, 1924-39; Bishop of Damaraland, 1939-49, resigned, 1949; Rector of Simonstown, 1949-54; Priest-in-Charge, Hout Bay, Cape, 1954-56, retired. Address: 8 Rubicon Road, Rondebosch, Cape, South Africa.   [Died 3 May 1974.

TOCHER, Rev. Forbes Scott, CBE 1928; MC; DD (Aberdeen University, 1934); b 9 Feb. 1885; s of James Tocher, Whitehills, Banffshire; m 1917, Johanna, MA (d 1957), d of John Forbes, Cullen, Banffshire; one d; m 1965, Helen Dickie Wilson. Educ: Fordyce Academy; Aberdeen Univ.; Edinburgh Univ. Ordained Missionary of the Church of Scotland at Ichang, China, 1909-15 and 1920-48; in the Army, Royal Field Artillery, at first as gunner and after as Commissioned Officer, 1916-19. Held by Japanese in Shanghai from Sept. 1940; Relief Work among destitute Britons in Shanghai from Dec. 1941; interned in Lunghwa Civilian Assembly Centre near Shanghai, June 1943; released from internment Aug. 1945; returned direct to work at Ichang; retired, 1948. Minister of the Parish of Botriphnie, Banffshire, 1948-55. Recreation: gardening. Address: 9 Scotstown, Banff. T: Banff 2163.   [Died 15 Aug. 1973.

TOD, Marcus Niebuhr, OBE, MA; FBA 1929; Hon. LittD Dublin, 1938; Hon. LLD Edinburgh, 1948; Hon. DLitt Birmingham, 1953, Oxford, 1967; Fellow of Oriel College, Oxford, 1903-47, Hon. Fellow, since 1947; Tutor, 1914-40; Vice-Provost, 1934-45; Hon. Member of Staff, Birmingham University, 1952; b Highgate, 24 Nov. 1878; 2nd s of John Tod, Highgate, and Gertrude von Niebuhr; m 1909, Mabel Bowker, 3rd d of George F. Byrom, Manchester; one s one d. Educ: Merchant Taylors' Sch., London; St John's Coll., Oxford (Scholar); First Class Classical Mods, 1899, First Class Lit Hum 1901; Senior Student of British School at Athens, 1901; Senior Scholar of St John's Coll., Oxford, 1902; Craven Travelling Fellow, 1902; Assistant Director and Librarian of British School at Athens, 1902; Fellow of Oriel Coll., 1903; Corresponding Member of Imperial German Archæological Institute, 1906; University Lecturer in Greek Epigraphy at Oxford, 1907; University Reader, 1927-49; Secretary to Cttee for Classical Archæology, Oxford, 1907; Conington Prize, 1912; Captain, Intelligence Corps (Croix de Guerre, despatches thrice); Secretary to Oxford Cttee of the Royal Commission on Oxford and Cambridge Universities, 1919; Hon. Fellow St John's Coll., Oxford, 1946. Hon. Life Governor of British and Foreign Bible Society, 1945. Publications: Catalogue of the Sparta Museum (with Mr A. J. B. Wace), 1906; International Arbitration amongst the Greeks, 1913; Sidelights on Greek History, 1932 (German trans. 1968); A Selection of Greek Historical Inscriptions, 1933 (2nd edition, 1946), Vol. 2, 1948; assistant editor of Supplementum Epigraphicum Græcum, vols I-XXIV; numerous articles on Greek Epigraphy, Archæology and History in The British School Annual, Journal of Hellenic Studies, Classical Quarterly, etc. Address: 64 Elizabeth Road, Moseley, Birmingham 13. T: 021-449 0763.   [Died 21 Feb. 1974.

TOD, Murray Macpherson, RSW 1953; Artist; b 15 Jan. 1909; 2nd s of William Tod, Glasgow; m 1938, Marjorie A. Lucas, ARCA, d of Stanley B. Lucas, London; one s two d (and one er s decd). Educ: Kelvinside Academy, Glasgow, Glasgow School of Art, 1927-31; Royal College of Art, London, 1932-35; Rome Schol. in Engraving, 1935-37; Teacher of Art, Dalbeattie High Sch., 1940-47; Part-time Assistant (etching), School of Drawing and Painting, Edinburgh College of Art, 1949-59. RE 1953, retired 1966. Member: Society of Scottish Artists; Royal Glasgow Institute of Fine Arts; FRSA. Chairman, Edinburgh Branch of Muscular Dystrophy Group, 1957-69, Hon. Pres. 1969. Recreations: music (listening), watching sport, reading. Address: 3 Seton Place, Edinburgh EH9 2JT. T: 031-667 5930.   [Died 13 Aug. 1974.

TODD, Alan Livesey Stuart, CBE 1958; MA Oxon; JP; Barrister-at-Law; Executive Director, National Association of Drop Forgers and Stampers, 1948-69; Member of Worcestershire County Council since 1938; Alderman since 1953; b 3 June 1900; s of late Richard Stuart Todd of Eastcliffe, Budleigh Salterton, Devon; m Cynthia, d of H. Sanders, Paignton, Devon; one s. Educ: Wellington Coll.; Magdalen Coll., Oxford. MP (U) Kingswinford Division of Staffordshire, 1931-35; Regional Commissioners Staff, Midland Civil Defence Region, 1940-45; Asst Regional Controller, Board of Trade Midland Region, 1945; Chairman, Brierley Hill Petty Sessional Div. (Staffs), 1958-67; Dep. Chm. Seisdon Div. (Staffs), 1967-; President, Bromsgrove Div. Cons. Assoc., 1962-67. JP Staffordshire 1939. Publication: Indian Constitutional Reform, 1934. Recreation: gardening. Address: Clent House Lodge, Clent, Stourbridge, West Midlands. T: Hagley 2633. Clubs: Carlton, Royal Automobile.   [Died 14 Aug. 1976.

TODD, Arthur James Stewart; retired; b 12 Feb. 1895; s of George Todd, ISO, and Emily Mary Ellerman; m 1927, Marjorie Elizabeth Moughton; one d. Educ: St Paul's Sch.; University of Lausanne. Served at home and abroad during the European War in the Army from the outbreak to end 1916 and the Naval Auxiliary Services during 1918 (Mons medal, Army medal, Allied medal, Naval medal). Home Guard, 1940-44; Staff Captain, 1943-44. Joined family shipping co. (nephew of Sir John Ellerman, 1st Bt, CH) after World War I; Dir, Westcott & Laurance Line, Ellerman's Wilson Line and other subsidiary cos; Dir, 1929, Alliance Assce Co., later Sun Alliance & London Insce Gp; retired after 40 years. Recreations: rugby commentator, philately. Address: Flat 42, 4 Grand Avenue, Hove, East Sussex. Clubs: Sussex County Cricket, St James' Cricket, Brighton Rugby.   [Died 8 June 1978.

TODD, Ronald Ruskin; Colonial Administrative Service, retired; b 23 March 1902; er s of late A. E. Todd, Histon, Cambridge; m 1947, Madge, yr d of late Captain H. Griffiths, Wallasey; one s. Educ: Cambridge and County High School; Emmanuel Coll., Cambridge (Scholar). Colonial Administrative Service, Hong Kong, 1924; various administrative posts, 1927-41; Acting Financial Secretary, 1941; interned by Japanese, 1942-45; Secretary for Chinese Affairs, Hong Kong, 1946-55, and Member of Executive and Legislative Councils. Acting Colonial Secretary various occasions, 1946-53. Recreation: tennis. Address: Manston, Kippington Road, Sevenoaks, Kent. T: Sevenoaks 51582. Club: Royal Commonwealth Society.   [Died 25 April 1980.

TODD, Thomas Robert Rushton, MD, FRCPEd; b 23 Dec. 1895; s of Robert Todd; m 1951, Mary Isabel Johnston, Auckland, New Zealand. Educ: Edinburgh Institution (now Melville College); Edinburgh University. Lieut, 8th Bn, Seaforth Highlanders, France, 1916-17; graduated MB, ChB, Edinburgh Univ., 1919; gold medal for MD thesis, Edinburgh Univ., 1925. House Physician, Edinburgh City Hospital; House Physician, Clinical Tutor, Asst Pathologist, Asst Physician, Royal Infirmary, Edinburgh; Physician, Leith Hospital; Physician in Charge, Royal Infirmary, Edinburgh, 1941-61; Senior Physician, Queensberry House Hosp., Edinburgh, 1961-70. President: Edinburgh Medical Missionary Society, 1952-68; Scottish Soc. of History of Medicine, 1971-74. Publications: contributions to medical journals. Recreations: motoring, photography. Address: 13 Lansdowne Crescent, Edinburgh EH12 5EH. T: 031-337 2966.   [Died 24 June 1975.

TODD-JONES, Sir (George) Basil, Kt 1957; b 18 Feb. 1898; s of Edgar William Todd-Jones and Theodora, d of Captain David Anderson; m 1st, 1928, Margaret Helen (d 1950), d of Sir Alexander Mackenzie, KCSI; no c; 2nd, 1954, Anne Elizabeth, d of William Scott Adie. Educ: Sherborne; University College, Oxford. Served European War, 1914-18; RFA, 1916-19, France 1917 and 1918. Called to Bar, 1922, Midland Circuit. Office of Solicitor of Inland Revenue, 1928-36; Special Commissioner of

Income Tax, 1945-63; Presiding Commissioner, 1953-63. Retired, 1963. *Address:* 93 Rivermead Court, Ranelagh Gardens, SW6. *T:* 01-736 1654. *Club:* Hurlingham.
[*Died 10 June 1980.*

TODHUNTER, Brig. Edward Joseph, TD 1944; JP; *b* 4 Oct. 1900; *e s* of late Benjamin Edward Todhunter, OBE, and late Ethel Christine Todhunter, Kingsmoor, Harlow, Essex; *m* 1927, Agnes Mary (*d* 1975), *yr d* of John Swire, Hillingdon House, Harlow, Essex; one *s* three *d*. *Educ:* Rugby. 2nd Lieut Essex Yeo., 1922; Lt-Col, 1938. Served War of 1939-45: Palestine, Western Desert, Italy, India (despatches, POW 1941-43); CRA 2nd Armd Div., 1941; Comdr Transit Command Calcutta, 1945. Colonel, 1945; Brigadier, 1946. Comdr 97 Army Group Royal Artillery (TA), 1946-50. Military Member, Essex T&AFA, 1938-65; Chairman Essex ACF Cttee, 1959-65; Chairman Essex Assoc. of Boys' Clubs, 1959-64. CC 1952-55, DL 1949-68, JP 1946-68, High Sheriff 1964, Essex; JP Wilts, 1968. *Recreation:* shooting. *Address:* The Glebe House, Great Bedwyn, near Marlborough, Wilts. *T:* Great Bedwyn 351. *Club:* Cavalry and Guards.
[*Died 6 June 1976.*

TOLANSKY, Samuel, FRS 1952; DSc, PhD, DIC, FRAS, DThPT; Professor of Physics, Royal Holloway College (University of London), Egham, Surrey, since 1947; *b* 17 Nov. 1907; *s* of B. Tolansky; *m* 1935, Ethel Pincasovich; one *s* one *d*. *Educ:* Rutherford Coll. and King's Coll., Newcastle upon Tyne; Imperial Coll., London. Fellow of Armstrong Coll., 1929; Earl Grey Fellow, 1931; 1851 Exhibition Senior Student, 1932; Asst Lecturer, Physics, 1934, Lecturer 1937, Senior Lecturer 1945, Reader 1946, Manchester Univ. Research work conducted in Optics and in Spectroscopy; research work carried out in connection with Atomic Energy during war years; principal investigator to NASA Lunar Project. Member: Scientific Adv. Cttee, National Gallery; Senate, London Univ.; Council, RSA. Hon. Fellow, Royal Microscopical Soc., 1970. Awarded C. V. Boys Prize for contributions to optics by London Physical Society, 1948; Silver Medallist, RSA, 1961. *Publications:* Introduction to Atomic Physics (5th edn), 1963 (Spanish and Italian Translations, 1950); Hyperfine Structure in Line Spectra and Nuclear Spin (2nd edn), 1947; High Resolution Spectroscopy, 1947 (Russian Translation, 1955); Multiplebeam Interferometry of Surfaces and Films, 1948, repr. 1971; Introduction to Interferometry, 1955; Microstructure of Diamond Surfaces, 1955; Surface Microtopography, 1960; History and Use of Diamond, 1962; Optical Illusions, 1964 (Russian trans.); Curiosities of Light Rays and Light Waves, 1964 (Russian trans.); Interference Microscopy for the Biologist, 1968; The Strategic Diamond, 1968; Microstructures of Surfaces, 1968; Revolution in Optics, 1968 (German, Russian and Japanese trans); over 300 scientific papers in optics and spectroscopy. *Recreations:* gardening, music, reading in folklore and psychology. *Address:* Physics Department, Royal Holloway College, Egham, Surrey. *T:* Egham 4455. *Club:* Athenæum.
[*Died 4 March 1973.*

TOLKIEN, John Ronald Reuel, CBE 1972; MA Oxon; Hon. DLitt: University College, Dublin; Nottingham; Oxon; Hon. Dr en Phil et Lettres Liege; FRSL; Merton Professor of English Language and Literature, 1945-59; Emeritus Fellow, Hon. Fellow 1973, Merton College; Hon. Fellow, Exeter College, Oxford; *b* 3 Jan. 1892; *e s* of late Arthur Reuel Tolkien, of Birmingham, and Bloemfontein, South Africa; *m* 1916, Edith (*d* 1971), *d* of late F. Bratt; three *s* one *d*. *Educ:* King Edward VI School, Birmingham; Exeter Coll., Oxford. Served with Lancashire Fusiliers, 1915-18; Reader in English Language, University of Leeds, 1920; Professor of the English Language, University of Leeds, 1924-25; Rawlinson and Bosworth Professor of Anglo-Saxon, Oxford, 1925-45; Fellow of Pembroke College, 1926-45. Leverhulme Research Fellow, 1934-36; Andrew Lang Lecturer, St Andrews, 1939; W. P. Ker Lecturer, Glasgow, 1953; Vice-President Philological Society; Hon. Member of Hid Islenzka Bókmennta-félag. Benson Medal (RSL), 1966. *Publications:* A Middle-English Vocabulary, 1922; Sir Gawain and the Green Knight (edited with E. V. Gordon), 1925; Chaucer as a Philologist (Philological Society), 1934; Beowulf: the Monsters and the Critics (British Academy), 1936; On Fairy-stories, 1938; The Homecoming of Beorhtnoth (Essays and Studies, Eng. Assoc.), 1953; Ancrene Wisse (EETS), 1962; Tree and Leaf (reprint of On Fairy Stories, 1938, and Leaf by Niggle, 1945), 1964; also The Hobbit, 1937; Aotrou and Itroun (Welsh Review), 1945; Farmer Giles of Ham, 1949; The Lord of the Rings: The Fellowship of the Ring (vol. i), 1954; The Two Towers (vol. ii), 1954; The Return of the King (vol. iii), 1955; The Adventures of Tom Bombadil, 1962; Smith of Wootton Major, 1967; (with Donald Swann) The Road Goes Ever On, 1968; *posthumous publication:* (ed Christopher Tolkien) The Silmarillion, 1977. *Address:* c/o George Allen and Unwin Ltd, 40 Museum Street, WC1.
[*Died 2 Sept. 1973.*

TOLLEMACHE, 4th Baron, *cr* 1876; John Edward Hamilton Tollemache, MC 1940; DL; Chairman, Tollemache & Cobbold Breweries Ltd, 1972-74; formerly Chairman, General Reinsurance Co. Ltd; Director, New London Reinsurance Co. Ltd; *b* 24 April 1910; *o s* of Maj.-Gen. E. D. H. Tollemache, DSO, MC (*d* 1947), *g s* of 1st Baron, late Coldstream Guards, of Devenish House, Sunningdale, Berks, and of Violet (*d* 1970), *d* of late Rt Hon. Sir (Joseph) West Ridgeway, GCB, GCMG, KCSI; *S* cousin 1955; *m* 1939, Dinah Susan, *d* of late Sir Archibald Auldjo Jamieson, KBE, MC; four *s*. *Educ:* Eton; Royal Military College, Sandhurst. 2nd Lieut, Coldstream Guards, Jan. 1930; served War of 1939-45 (wounded, MC); Major Reserve of Officers, Coldstream Guards, 1945. DL Suffolk, 1958; Cheshire, 1970. *Recreations:* shooting, ornithology. *Heir: s* Hon. Timothy John Edward Tollemache [*b* 13 Dec. 1939; *m* 1970, Alexandra, *yr d* of late Col Hugo Meynell and of Mrs Meynell, Hollybush Park, Burton-on-Trent; one *d*. *Educ:* Eton. Lieut, Coldstream Guards, 1961]. *Address:* Helmingham Hall, Stowmarket, Suffolk. *T:* Helmingham 217; Home Farm, Peckforton, Tarporley, Cheshire. *T:* Bunbury 301; 43 Belgrave Mews North, SW1. *T:* 01-235 1767. *Clubs:* Guards, MCC.
[*Died 27 May 1975.*

TOLLEY, Major Cyril James Hastings, MC; Councillor (Conservative), County Borough of Eastbourne, 1958-62; *b* London, 14 Sept. 1895; *yr* and *o* surv. *s* of late James T. Tolley and late Christiana Mary Pascall. *Educ:* University College, Oxford. Served European War, Royal Tank Corps, 1915-19 (MC); Prisoner of War, 1917-18; Royal Sussex Regt, 1940-45. Liberal Candidate South Hendon, Feb. 1950; Hon. Treasurer London Liberal Party, 1950-51. Pres., Eastbourne Downs Golf Club; former Pres., Eastbourne Society of Artists; Vice-President Eastbourne Downs Artisans' Golf Club. British Amateur Golf Champion, 1920 and 1929; French Open Golf Champion, 1924 and 1928; Welsh Open Amateur Golf Champion, 1921 and 1923; Captain Royal and Ancient, St Andrews, 1948; Captain, Oxford and Cambridge Golfing Society, 1946-48. London Stock Exchange, 1921-29, and 1933-39. *Publication:* The Modern Golfer, 1924. *Recreations:* golf, bowls, croquet; apiarist; philately. *Address:* Pommern Lodge, Eastbourne, East Sussex. *Clubs:* Royal Automobile; Vincent's, Bullingdon (Oxford); Royal and Ancient (St Andrews); Oxford and Cambridge Golfing Society; Royal Eastbourne Golf; Woking; Pine Valley Golf (Pa, USA), etc; Eastbourne (Saffrons) Bowling, Preston (Brighton) Bowling, Compton Croquet.
[*Died 18 May 1978.*

TOLLINTON, Richard Bartram Boyd, CBE 1955 (OBE 1947); *b* London, 28 Aug. 1903; *o s* of Rev. Canon Tollinton, DD, DLitt, and Minnie Tollinton (*née* Boyd Carpenter); *m* 1931, Mary Judith Paulina (*d* 1977), *d* of late Judge Harold Chaloner Dowdall. *Educ:* Rugby; Balliol Coll., Oxford. Levant Consular Service, 1926; Acting Vice-Consul, Tehran, 1928; Bushire, 1929; Vice-Consul, Rotterdam, 1931; Consul (local rank) and Commercial Secretary (local rank), Sofia, 1934; Vice-Consul, Casablanca, 1938; seconded to British Council, London, 1939-40; Vice-Consul and Second Secretary (local rank), Washington, 1940; Acting Consul, Boston, 1941, Consul 1944; First Secretary and Consul, Sofia, 1944; Acting Political Rep., Sofia, 1946-47; Consul, Oporto, 1947; Consul-General, 1948; Consul-General, Leopoldville, 1952; HM Ambassador to Nepal, 1955-57; HM Foreign Service, Levant Dept, Foreign Office, 1957-60, HM Ambassador to Honduras, 1960-63, retired. *Publications:* Economic Conditions in Bulgaria, 1935 and 1937. *Recreations:* hill scrambling, tennis, amateur theatricals. *Clubs:* Royal Automobile; Oxford Union; Himalayan. [*Died 21 April 1978.*

TOLSTOY, Alexandra; Farmer, Speaker, Writer; President, Tolstoy Foundation Inc. (for Russian Welfare and Culture), New York, since 1939; *b* Yasnaia Poliana, Russia, 1 July 1884; *d* of Leo and Sophia Tolstoy. *Educ:* Moscow; Home. Secretary to Tolstoy, 1901-10; in 1911, fulfilled Tolstoy's will, edited his posthumous works; bought land of father's estate with money secured and distributed it among Yasnaia Poliana Peasants (1800 acres); 1914 went to war first as a nurse, then as representative for refugees at the Western front; worked as a chief of a sanitary detachment at the Western Front; in 1918 organised a society in Moscow to study and work on a complete edition of Tolstoy's works (91 volumes); organised Museums, several schools in Yasnaia Poliana, kindergartens, a hospital; worked in Russia till 1929; compelled to leave because the Soviets instilled anti-religious propaganda in Tolstoy's museums and schools; in 1929 went to Japan, lectured there; entered USA 1931; lectured all over America, now lives on a farm (Resettlement Center of Tolstoy Foundn; Nursing Home and Homes for the Aged, etc, of the Tolstoy Foundation Inc. of which she is Chairman Emeritus); in 1941 became an American citizen. Hon. DHL, Hobart and William Smith Colleges, USA,

1962. *Publications:* Tragedy of Tolstoy (numerous trans.); I Worked for the Soviet, 1934; Tolstoy-a Life of My Father, 1953 (numerous trans.); The Real Tolstoy, 1968; contrib. magazines. *Address:* Tolstoy Foundation Inc., 250 West 57th Street (Room 1101), New York, NY 10019, USA; (home) Valley Cottage, Tolstoy Foundation Resettlement Center, New York 10989, USA.   *[Died 26 Sept. 1979.*

TOMES, Brigadier Clement Thurstan, CBE 1940; DSO 1918; MC; *b* 28 Aug. 1882; *s* of Lt-Col A. Tomes, IMS; *m* 1912, Edith Gladys (*d* 1947), *d* of late Lt-Col W. P. Newall, Indian Army; two *s* one *d*; *m* 1948, Clare, widow of Lt-Col Rev. T. E. H. Taylor. *Educ:* Marlborough Coll.; RMC, Sandhurst. Joined The Royal Warwickshire Regt, 1901; served in the operations on the North-West Frontier of India, 1908; France and Belgium, 1914-18 (twice wounded, DSO, MC, Legion of Honour); passed the Staff Coll., 1919; Brigadier in charge of Administration, British Troops in Egypt, 1935-39; retired pay, 1939; Colonel, The Royal Warwickshire Regt, 1935-46. *Address:* Minson's Common, Charmouth, Dorset. *T:* 323. *Club:* United Service & Royal Aero.
                                                     [Died 6 Oct. 1972.

TOMKINSON, Charles, CMG 1947; retired Colonial Administration, Kenya; *b* 4 Aug. 1893; 8th *s* of late Michael Tomkinson, JP, DL, Franche Hall, near Kidderminster; *m* 1922, Hyacinthe Gabrielle, *d* of M. Bally, Calais. *Educ:* Winchester Coll. Asst District Commissioner, 1915; served European War, 1914-18, Turkana Expedition, 1915 (African General Service Medal and clasp); Provincial Commissioner, Central Province, Kenya, 1938-46, and Official Member of Legislative Council. *Recreation:* fishing. *Address:* Nyeri, Kenya. *Club:* East India, Sports and Public Schools.   *[Died 18 Oct. 1976.*

TOMKINSON, Vice-Adm. Wilfred, CB 1918; MVO 1919; RN retired; *b* 1877; 4th *s* of Michael Tomkinson, Franche Hall, Kidderminster; *m* 1907, Edith Joan, *d* of Colonel G. H. Bittleston, Royal Artillery; one *s* four *d*. *Educ:* Stubbington House, Fareham. Entered HMS Britannia, 1891. Served China War, 1900; European War; took part in operations against Zeebrugge and Ostend, 1918; a Naval ADC to the King, 1926; Chief of Staff to Admiral Sir Roger Keyes, Bt, Commander-in-Chief of Mediterranean Fleet, 1927; Rear-Admiral, 1927; Assistant Chief of Naval Staff, 1929-31; in command of Battle Cruiser Squadron, 1931-32; Vice-Admiral, 1932; retired list, 1935; Flag Officer in Charge, Bristol Channel, 1940-42; officer of the Orders of St Maurice and Lazarus of Italy and Leopold of Belgium; French Croix de Guerre; awarded gold medal of Royal Humane Society, 1913. *Address:* Stert House, near Devizes, Wilts. *T:* Devizes 3713.   *[Died 7 Oct. 1971.*

TOMLINSON, Reginald Robert, OBE 1959; RBA (Hon. Mem., 1971); ARCA; Senior Inspector of Art to the LCC, 1925-51; *b* Overton, Hants, 10 Oct. 1885; *s* of F. C. Tomlinson; *m* 1914, Emily E., *d* of A. E. Mullins; two *s* one *d*. *Educ:* Farnham Grammar Sch. Apprentice Designer to Minton, Hollins & Co.; Pottery Painter and Designer for Bernard Moore, 1906-09; Royal College of Art; Art Director to the Crown Staffordshire China Co. Ltd, 1913-19; Principal of Cheltenham Coll. of Arts and Crafts, 1922-25; Acting Principal, Central School of Arts and Crafts, London, 1935-36 and 1939-46; President English Speaking Nations International Art Congress, Brussels, 1935; Chairman British Cttee for International Art Congress, Paris, 1937; awarded two international Gold Medals for Design and Craftsmanship, in collaboration with Bernard Moore, at Ghent and Turin; exhibited at Principal Exhibitions and Art Galleries. Chm., Bd of Examiners for ATD, Univ. of London. Hon. Fellow, Institute of British Decorators; Hon. Fellow, College of Handicrafts. Liveryman of Company of Goldsmiths; Freeman of City of London; Past President Royal Drawing Society; President Artists Annuity and Benevolent Fund; Master Art Workers' Guild, 1955. *Works purchased:* Pottery in Museums in this country and abroad; *Portraits:* Lady Arkell, Sir Aylmer Firebrace, J. J. Mallon, CH, Sir Arthur Middleton, Sir William Houghton, Lord Alexander, etc. *Publications:* Lettering for Arts and Crafts; Memory and Imaginative Drawing; Picture Making by Children, 1934; contributed Encyclopædia Britannica, Art in General Education; Crafts for Children, 1935; Children as Artists (King Penguin), 1945; Picture and Pattern Making by Children, 1950; (with J. F. Mills) Growth of Child Art, 1966. *Recreation:* gardening. *Address:* Chestnut Cottage, The Drive, Chichester, West Sussex. *T:* Chichester 527551.
                                                     [Died 6 Nov. 1978.

TOMLINSON, Miss Ruth, CBE 1960 (MBE 1928); UK representative at 12th, 13th, 14th Sessions (1958, 1959, 1960) of United Nations Status of Women Commission; Vice-President, International Federation of Business and Professional Women, 1956-62; Lecturer. *Educ:* Liverpool. Secretary, Federated

Assocs of Boot and Shoe Manufacturers of Great Britain and Ireland (London), 1922-37; Secretary, Nat. Institute of Boot and Shoe Industry (Technical Education), 1927-37; Consultant Administration, 1937-39; Director Domestic Bureau for Refugees, 1939-42; Ministry of Labour and National Service, Man Power Board, 1943-48; Rep. at UN Commissions and Confs for International Federation of Business and Professional Women, 1949-58. *Recreations:* walking, reading. *Address:* Woodfield, Sparkbridge, Ulverston, Lancs.
                                                     [Died 15 Sept. 1972.

TOMONAGA, Dr Sin-itiro; Professor Emeritus, since 1969, Tokyo Kyoiku University (Tokyo University of Education); *b* 31 March 1906; *s* of Sanjuro and Hide Tomonaga; *m* 1940, Ryoko Sekiguchi; two *s* one *d*. *Educ:* Kyoto Imperial University. Research Student, Institute of Physical and Chemical Research, 1932-39; studied at University of Leipzig, Germany, 1937-39; Asst, Inst. of Physical and Chemical Research, 1939-40; Lecturer, Tokyo Bunrika Univ. (absorbed into Tokyo University of Education, 1949), 1940; Prof. of Physics, Tokyo Bunrika Univ., 1941; studied at Inst. for Advanced Study, Princeton, USA, 1949-50; Prof. of Physics, Tokyo Univ. of Educn, 1949-69 (President, 1956-62); Director, Inst. for Optical Research, 1963-69; Pres., Science Council of Japan, 1963-69. Japan Academy Prize, 1948; Order of Culture, Japan, 1952; Lomonosov Medal, USSR, 1964; Nobel Prize for Physics (jointly), 1965. *Publications:* Quantum Mechanics, Vol. I, 1962, Vol. II, 1966. *Recreation:* rakugo. *Address:* 3-17-12 Kyonan-cho, Musashinoshi, Tokyo, Japan.   *[Died 8 July 1979.*

TONG, Sir Walter (Wharton), Kt 1955; JP; MSc; *b* 26 February 1890; *e s* of William Tong and Bertha Tong (*née* Wharton), both of Bolton; *m* 1919, Anne (*d* 1972), 2nd *d* of Alfred Glaister, Bolton; three *d*. *Educ:* Bolton School; Giggleswick Sch.; Manchester Univ. Mem. Bolton Town Council, 1925-52; Alderman 1941; Mayor of Bolton, 1940-41; Chm. Housing Cttee, 1931-41; Chm. Finance Cttee, 1941-46 and 1948-52; Leader of Conservative Party in Town Council, 1942-52. Past Governor: Canon Slade Grammar Sch.; Bolton School; Bolton County Grammar School. Pres. Bolton Rotary Club, 1942-43; formerly Pres. and Trustee, Bolton Trustee Savings Bank. Formerly: Pres., Bolton Amateur Operatic Soc.; Chm., Bolton Little Theatre. JP, Bolton, 1935. Contested (C) Bolton West Division, 1950. *Address:* Greenleaves, Bromley Cross, Bolton BL7 9LZ. *T:* Bolton 53892.   *[Died 18 May 1978.*

TONGE, George Edward, CBE 1960; JP; Chairman: Exmouth Docks Transit Co. Ltd; Devon Dock Pier and Steamship Co. Ltd; Exmouth Docks Co; Director, Westbrick Products Ltd; *b* 30 April 1910; bachelor. Member: Council, Nat. Council of Social Service; Nat. Dock Labour Bd, 1964-72; Council, CBI, 1965-72. Chairman: Trade Assoc. Management Services Ltd; London Port Employers, 1957-64; Nat. Assoc. of Port Employers, 1965-72; Pres., Oxford and Bermondsey Boys' Clubs; Warden, St Olave's and St Saviour's Grammar School Foundation and Schools; Trustee, Marshall's Charity; Treasurer, Royal Society of Arts, 1958-62. JP London, 1965. *Recreations:* sailing, gardening, the arts. *Address:* Sherbrook Dene, Budleigh Salterton, Devon. *T:* Budleigh Salterton 3148. *Clubs:* Garrick, Royal Thames Yacht, Little Ship; Exe Sailing (Exmouth).   *[Died 23 Oct. 1979.*

TOOKEY, Geoffrey William, QC 1949; *b* 26 Nov. 1902; *er s* of late William Alfred Tookey, Bromley, Kent; *m* 1933, Rosemary Sherwell, *y d* of late Arthur Henry Clogg; two *s* two *d*. *Educ:* St Dunstan's College, Catford; City and Guilds College, Imperial College of Science and Technology. FCGI. Mem. Delegacy of C and G College. Called to Bar, Gray's Inn, 1924; Bencher, 1952; Treasurer, 1967; Vice-Treasurer, 1968. Member: Inns of Court Senate, 1966-69; Council of Law Reporting, 1958-74. Appointed, 1955-68, to exercise appellate jurisdiction of Board of Trade under Trade Marks Act; Member British Delegation, Lisbon Diplomatic Conference 1958. Chairman, Board of Trade Advisory Group on European Patents and Unification of Patent Laws, 1961-66. Membre d'Honneur, International Association for Protection of Industrial Property (President, British Group, 1954-64). Hon. Mem., Chartered Inst. of Patent Agents, 1969. General List TA, 1922-27 (Captain); War of 1939-45: Royal Air Force Volunteer Reserve, 1940-45, Squadron Ldr (despatches). *Address:* 4 Russell Close, Wickham Road, Beckenham, Kent BR3 2QL. *T:* 01-650 4469. *Club:* Royal Air Force.
                                                     [Died 15 Aug. 1976.

TOOSEY, Sir Philip (John Denton), Kt 1974; CBE 1955 (OBE 1946); DSO 1945; TD 1944; DL; JP; Director, Liner Holdings Ltd; *b* 12 Aug. 1904; *s* of C. D. Toosey; *m* 1932, Muriel Alexandra Eccles; two *s* one *d*. *Educ:* Gresham's Sch., Norfolk. Baring Brothers & Co. Ltd, 1927-64. JP Cheshire, 1947; DL

Merseyside (formerly County Palatine of Lancaster), 1961; High Sheriff, County Palatine of Lancaster, 1964. Hon. Col, West Lancs Regt, RA (Territorials), T&AVR, 1967-69. Hon. LLD Liverpool, 1974. *Recreations:* shooting and gardening. *Address:* Heathcote, Oakfield Road, Ellesmere Port, Wirral, Merseyside L66 7NU. *T:* 051-339 2225. *Club:* Racquet (Liverpool).
                                                    [Died 22 Dec. 1975.

TOPP, Brig.-Gen. Charles Beresford, CBE 1945; DSO 1919; MC and Bar; Member Canadian Pension Commission since 1956; *b* 7 December 1893; *s* of Richard Ussher Topp, MD, FRCS, and Mary Eliza Beley; *m* 1919, Constance Christine Helliwell; one *s* one *d*. *Educ:* Public Schools; Toronto University. Reporter, Toronto Globe and Toronto Mail and Empire; sent to London, England, as correspondent for Toronto Mail and Empire, 1914; resigned to enlist for war service, May 1915; served in France with 42nd Battalion Royal Highlanders of Canada (thrice wounded, despatches thrice, DSO, MC and Bar, three service medals); on discharge held rank of Major; served with the Governor-General's Foot Guards, Canadian Militia, Ottawa, since 1920; commanded the 1st Battalion with rank of Lt-Col, 1925-30; commanded 4th Canadian Inf. Bde, 2nd Canadian Division Overseas, 1940-42; Staff appts 1942-45; Hon. ADC to Lord Willingdon, Gov.-Gen. of Canada; served in various capacities in admin of Canadian Pension law since war of 1914-18; mem. special committee appointed by Canadian Government to Revise Pension Law, 1932. Past Pres. Ottawa Branch, Canadian Legion, British Empire Service League. *Publications:* History of the 42nd Battalion Royal Highlanders of Canada; various short stories and articles principally on hunting and fishing topics. *Recreations:* hunting, fishing, golf. *Address:* 635 Blair Road, Ottawa K1J 7M3, Ontario, Canada. *Clubs:* Royal Commonwealth Society; (Hon. Pres.) University (Ottawa); Lake Bernard Fish and Game (Lascelles, Quebec).
                                                    [Died 29 Oct. 1976.

TOPP, Wilfred Bethridge, CMG 1949; retired; formerly London Technical Advisor to Diamond Producers Association; *b* 29 Aug. 1891; *s* of Joseph Bethridge Topp, Kimberley, S Africa; *m* 1918, Beatrice Maud Matthews, Port Elizabeth, S Africa. *Educ:* Kimberley, S Africa. Joined De Beers Consolidated Mines Ltd, 1909. Served with 7th S African Inf., 1914-17. Joined Consolidated Diamond Valuation Staff, 1920; one of valuators for famous Hans Merensky diamond finds at Orange River mouth, 1926; taken over by Union Govt for valuations of State Alluvial Diamonds, 1928. At amalgamation of all S African Diamond producers sent to Kimberley Central Office, until sent to England in 1934. At outbreak of War of 1939-45 joined a board of experts to control export of diamonds; after termination of hostilities examined all diamonds for export and import on two days each week (duties for the State honorary since 1939). *Recreations:* rifle shooting, golf. *Address:* Laughing Waters, Valley Road, Kenilworth, Cape, South Africa.
                                                    [Died 29 Sept. 1978.

TOPPING, Rt. Hon. Walter William Buchanan, PC (NI) 1957; QC (NI) 1946; **Rt. Hon. Judge Topping;** Recorder of Belfast, since 1960; Judge of County Court, Antrim, since 1960; *b* 13 Jan. 1908; *m* 1933, Maureen Gallaher; three *s*. *Educ:* Rossall School; Queen's University, Belfast. Called to Bar, NI, 1930; QC 1946. MP Larne Div. of Co. Antrim, Parliament of Northern Ireland, 1945; Chief Government Whip, Northern Ireland Parliament, 1947-56; Minister of Home Affairs, 1956-59. *Address:* Windy Ridge, Dunmurry, County Antrim, Northern Ireland.
                                                    [Died 26 July 1978.

TORPHICHEN, 13th Lord *cr* 1564; **John Gordon Sandilands;** *b* 8 June 1886; *s* of 12th Baron and Ellen, *d* of Lt-Gen. Charles Edward Park Gordon, CB; *S* father, 1915; *m* 1st, 1916, Grace Douglass (*d* 1948), 2nd *d* of Winslow Pierce, Bayville, Long Island, NY; one *s*; 2nd, 1950, Isabel Fernandez Phillips, 2nd *d* of Mrs Barnett, North Berwick and Monte Carlo. *Educ:* Eton; Birmingham Univ. *Heir:* *s* Master of Torphichen. *Address:* Calder House, Mid-Calder, Midlothian EH53 0HN. *T:* Mid-Calder 319. *Club:* New (Edinburgh).   *[Died 1 July 1973.*

TORPHICHEN, 14th Lord *cr* 1564; **James Bruce Sandilands;** *b* 26 Oct. 1917; *o s* of 13th Baron Torphichen, and Grace Douglass (*d* 1948), 2nd *d* of Winslow Pierce, Long Island, NY; *S* father, 1973; *m* 1st, 1943, Mary Thurstan Vaudrey (marr. diss. 1952); one *s* one *d*; 2nd, 1955, Margaret Jane (marr. diss.), *d* of George Dawson, New York City; 3rd, 1973, Mrs P. M. Hodson Pressinger, *d* of late Howard Snow. *Educ:* Eton; Balliol College, Oxford. *Heir:* *s* Master of Torphichen. *Address:* c/o History Department, Franklin Pierce College, Rindge, NH, USA; Calder House, Mid-Calder, Midlothian. *[Died 12 July 1975.*

W W W — 27

TORRES BODET, Jaime; Mexican writer; *b* Mexico City, 17 Apr. 1902; *m* 1929, Josefina Juarez. *Educ:* Escuela Normal; Univ. of Mexico (Faculty of Philosophy and Letters). Head of the Libraries Department, Ministry of Education, Mexico, 1922; Professor of French Literature, Univ. of Mexico, 1924-28; Sec. Mexican Legation, Spain, 1929, France, 1931; Mexican Chargé d'Affaires, Netherlands, 1932; Head of Diplomatic Dept, Min. of Foreign Affairs, Mexico, 1936; Mexican Chargé d'Affaires, Belgium, 1938-40; Under-Sec. for Foreign Affairs, Mexico, 1940-43; Minister of Education, 1943-46; Minister for Foreign Affairs, 1946-48; Director-General, Unesco, Dec. 1948-Nov. 1952; Mexican Ambassador in Paris, 1954-58; Minister of Education, 1958-64. Holds numerous foreign orders. Gold Medal of Pan-American League (US). Doctor *hc* of several univs both in Mexico and abroad. *Publications:* Fervor, (Mexico) 1919; La casa, (Mexico) 1923; Los dias, (Mexico) 1923; Poemas, (Mexico) 1924; Biombo (Mexico) 1925; Poesía, (Madrid) 1926; Margarita de Niebla, (Mexico) 1927; La educación sentimental, (Madrid) 1929; Destierro, (Madrid) 1930; Proserpina rescatada, (Madrid) 1931; Estrella de dia, 1933; Primero de enero, 1934; Sombras, 1937; Cripta, (Mexico) 1937; Nacimiento de Venus y otros relatos, (Mexico) 1941; Sonetos, (Mexico) 1949; Fronteras, (Mexico) 1954; Tiempo de Arena, 1955; Essays: Contemporáneos, 1928; Educación Mexicana, 1944; Educación y concordia internacional, 1948; Balzac, 1960; Maestro venecianos, 1961; Obras escogidas, 1961; Tolstoi, 1965; Poesía de Jaime Torres Bodet, 1965; Discursos, 1965; Rubén Darío, 1966; Tiempo y Memoria en la Obra de Proust, 1967; Obra Poética, 1967; *memoirs:* Años contra el tiempo, 1969; La victoria sin alas, 1970; El desierto internacional, 1971; La tierra prometida, 1972. *Address:* Vicente Güemes 326, Mexico 10, DF.
                                                    [Died 13 May 1974.

TOSELAND, Charles Stephen, CBE 1955 (MBE 1934); *b* 1 Sept. 1894; *s* of late Stephen Charles and Charlotte Toseland; *m* 1924, Kathleen Muriel (*née* Coombs); no *c*. *Educ:* Owen's School; King's College, London. Entered Civil Service, 1910; British Vice-Consul, Norway, 1917-19; Department of Overseas Trade, 1920-39 and 1945-47; Asst Sec. and Principal Asst Sec., Ministry of Food, 1939-45; Secretary-General, British Tourist and Holidays Board, 1948-50; Under Secretary, Board of Trade, Jan. 1949-55, retired. Mem. (Chm. 1958) Epping Urban District Council, 1956-59. *Recreation:* motoring. *Address:* The Willows, Beulah Road, Epping, Essex. *T:* Epping 2113.
                                                    [Died 14 Sept. 1971.

TOTTENHAM, Rear-Adm. Edward Loftus, CB 1952; OBE 1937; DL; *b* 12 May 1896; 3rd *s* of Rev. C. F. B. Tottenham, sometime Rector of Castletownroche, Co. Cork; *m* 1924, Florence Luise (*d* 1974), *d* of W. Gates, Oldcastletown, Kildorrery, Co. Cork; one *s* one *d*. *Educ:* Bishop Foy School, Waterford; Dean Close School, Cheltenham. Entered RN, 1913. Served European War, 1914-18, various ships in Grand Fleet. Sec. to Adm. Sir Hugh D. R. Watson in various appts, 1920-28; HMS Triad, Persian Gulf, 1930-33; Naval Sec. and mem. NZ Naval Board, 1935-39; HMS Fiji, 1939-41; HMS Illustrious (despatches), 1942-44; Asst Director of Air Equipment, Admiralty, 1945-46; Captain (S) 1945; Fleet Supply Officer, E Indies Station, 1946-47; HMS Ceres, Supply Br. Trg Establishment in Command, 1948-50. Rear-Adm (S) 1950. Retired 1963. DL Hampshire, 1965. *Address:* Struan, Links Lane, Rowlands Castle, Hants. *T:* Rowlands Castle 310. *Club:* Naval and Military.
                                                    [Died 31 Aug. 1974.

TOTTENHAM, Sir (George) Richard (Frederick), KCIE 1946 (CIE 1930); Kt 1937; CSI 1936; *b* 18 Nov. 1890; 2nd *s* of late Lt-Col F. St L. Tottenham, DL, JP, of Mount Callan, Inagh, Co. Clare; *m* 1917, Hazel Joyce (*d* 1955), 2nd *d* of late Major J. H. Gwynne; one *s* one *d*. *Educ:* Harrow; New College, Oxford. Entered ICS 1914; Sec. to the Government of India, Defence Department, 1932-37; Addtl Secretary and Secretary Home Department, 1940-46; retired, 1948. *Address:* Weston Farm House, Totland Bay, IOW. *T:* Freshwater 2722.
                                                    [Died 11 Jan. 1977.

TOTTENHAM, Percy Marmaduke, CBE 1919; *b* 17 Aug. 1873; *e s* of late Capt. Francis Loftus Tottenham of Coolmore, Crowboro', and Cicell, *d* of late Colonel C. Grimston, of Grimston Garth, Yorkshire; *m* 1909, Angel (*d* 1973), *o d* of Rt Hon. Sir Edward M. Archdale, 1st Bt; two *s* one *d*. *Educ:* Repton; RIEC, Coopers Hill. Entered the Egyptian Public Works Ministry, 1895; Inspector-General of Irrigation in the Sudan, 1909-14, and Member of Governor-General's Council, 1910-14; Inspector-General of Irrigation for Lower Egypt, 1914-16; Inspector-General of Public Works, 1917-19; Under-Secretary of State for Public Works, Egypt, 1919-25; Agent to Egyptian Government, London, 1925-37. Grand Cordon Nile, 2nd Ismail, 2nd Medjidie and 4th Osmania. *Address:* 4 Croft Lodge, Crowborough, Sussex.   *[Died 27 Jan. 1975.*

TOTTENHAM, Sir Richard; *see* Tottenham, Sir G. R. F.

TOTTENHAM, Richard E., MD, BA, DPH, FRCPI, FRCOG; *s* of late Edward Tottenham, Mallow, County Cork, Ireland; *m* Norah Margaret (*d* 1965), *d* of late H. J. Daly, Dublin. *Educ:* Trinity College, Dublin. Late Professor of Obstetrics and Gynæcology, University of Hong Kong; Consultant to the Hong Kong Government; Assistant Master, Rotunda Hospital, Dublin; Surgeon Lieut, Royal Navy; Obstetric Physician and Gynæcologist, Steevens' Hospital; Obstetrician and Gynæcologist, City and County Hospital, Londonderry; Rockefeller Travel Grant for USA and Canada, 1924; Medical Tour, Europe, 1930. Member Royal Dublin Society. King's Jubilee Medal, 1935. *Publications:* A Handbook of Midwifery; A Handbook of Practical Midwifery (in Chinese); A Short Practice of Gynæcology (Jellet and Tottenham); Aids to Gynæcology, 6th, 7th and 8th edns; Impressions of Continental Clinics; A New Pelvimeter; Articles on Irish History, etc. *Recreations:* fishing, historical research, carpentry, golf. *Address:* Gortmore, 169 Strand Road, Merrion, Dublin 4, Ireland.
[Died 31 May 1971.

TOTTENHAM-SMITH, Ralph Henry, CBE 1946; FRGS; *b* 21 Sept. 1893; *o s* of Robert Tottenham-Smith, Johannesburg, South Africa; *m* 1917, Alice Geneviève Marie, *d* of René Martin, Rouen; one *s* one *d. Educ:* Johannesburg College; Clifton College; Trinity College, Dublin. Served European War, France, 1914-17 (prisoner); entered Consular Service, 1919; Vice-Consul: Valparaiso, 1919; Constanza, 1922; Cettinje, 1925; Dubrovnik, 1926; Paris, 1927; Consul and Chargé d'Affaires, Asuncion, 1931; Special Envoy there for inauguration of President, 1932; Consul, Turin, 1937; Lisbon, 1940; Commercial Secretary, Lisbon, 1944; Counsellor of Embassy and HBM Consul-General, Paris, 1944, Minister, 1948. Chairman of British Charitable Fund, Paris, 1945-48; Member, Cttee of Management of Hertford British Hosp., Paris, 1945-50; Coronation Medals, 1937, 1953. Special Ambassador for inauguration of President of El Salvador, 1950; Minister to El Salvador, 1950-53; retired 1953. *Recreations:* tennis (Pres. Paraguaya LT Assoc., 1936), motoring, golf, bridge, reading. *Address:* Clareen, 9 Marina Drive, Parkstone, Poole, Dorset. *T:* Parkstone 3255. *Clubs:* Royal Over-Seas League; Parkstone Golf.
[Died 20 Dec. 1971.

TOUCHE, Rt. Hon. Sir Gordon (Cosmo), 1st Bt, *cr* 1962; PC 1959; Kt 1952; *b* 8 July 1895; *s* of Sir George Touche, 1st Bt; *m* 1926, Ruby Anne Hume-Purves, *d* of late Sir Duncan Macpherson, CIE; one *s* one *d. Educ:* Marlborough; University College, Oxford, MA. Served in Army, 1915-19; Barrister-at-Law, Inner Temple; Director: Trustees Corp. Ltd; City National Investment Trust, Ltd; Cedar Investment Trust Ltd; Chm. Surrey Conservative and Unionist Club, 1950-57; Chairman United Club, 1938-42; contested (C) Ashton-under-Lyne, 1928, and North Islington, 1929; MP (C) Reigate Division of Surrey, 1931-50, Dorking Division, 1950-64. Dep. Chm. of Ways and Means, Nov. 1956-Oct. 1959; Chm. of Ways and Means, 1959-Jan. 1962. Hon. Freeman of Reigate, 1942. *Publications:* The Law of Parliamentary Elections; The Law of Criminal Procedure. *Heir:* s Rodney Gordon Touche [*b* 5 Dec. 1928; *m* 1955, Ouida Ann, *er d* of F. Gerald MacLellan, Moncton, New Brunswick; one *s* three *d*]. *Address:* Gable End, Mill Road, Holmwood, near Dorking, Surrey. *T:* Dorking 6444. *Club:* Royal Automobile.
[Died 19 May 1972.

TOUCHE, Sir Norman George, 2nd Bt, *cr* 1920; barrister; Director of Industrial and General Trust, Ltd, 1921-67; *b* 11 May 1888; *s* of Sir George Touche, 1st Bt, and Jessie (*d* 1917), *d* of late Isaac Brown; S father, 1935; *m* 1923, Eva Maitland, *e d* of P. E. Cameron, Salachan, Ardgour, Argyllshire; two *d. Educ:* Marlborough; Univ. College, Oxford, MA, BCL. Called to Bar, Lincoln's Inn, 1914; served European War, 1915-19. *Heir:* n Anthony George Touche [*b* 31 Jan. 1927; *m* 1961, Hester Christina, *er d* of Dr Werner Pleuger, Leek, Staffs; three *s* one *d*]. *Address:* Nenthorn, 1 Broomfield Park, Westcott, near Dorking, Surrey. *Club:* United Oxford & Cambridge University.
[Died 18 May 1977.

TOVEY, 1st Baron, *cr* 1946, of Langton Matravers; **Adm. of the Fleet John Cronyn Tovey,** GCB 1943 (KCB 1941; CB 1937); KBE 1941; DSO 1919; *b* 1885; *s* of late Lieutenant-Colonel Hamilton Tovey, RE; *m* 1916, Aida (*d* 1970), *d* of John Rowe. Served European War, 1914-19 (despatches, DSO); Capt. 1923; Naval Assistant to the Second Sea Lord, 1930-32; commanded HMS Rodney, 1932-34; ADC to the King, 1935; Commodore RN Barracks, Chatham, 1935-37; Rear-Adm. 1935; Rear-Admiral Destroyers, Mediterranean, 1938-40; Vice-Admiral, 1939; Vice-Admiral Second-in-Command Mediterranean Fleet, 1940; C-in-C Home Fleet, 1940-43; Admiral, 1942; Admiral of

the Fleet, 1943; Commander-in-Chief, the Nore, 1943-46; First and Principal Naval ADC to the King, 1945-46. Third Church Estates Commissioner, 1948-52. *Recreations:* golf, fishing. *Address:* House of Lords, SW1. *[Died 12 Jan. 1971 (ext).*

TOWELL, Brig. Rowland Henry, CBE 1940; MC; *b* 4 Feb. 1891; *o surv. s* of late H. J. Towell, Great Missenden; *m* 1940, Joan Margaret, *o d* of James S. Lacy, Burwash Place, Sussex; one *s* one *d. Educ:* Clifton Coll.; RMA, Woolwich. Served War of 1914-18, France and Flanders (MC and Bar, despatches twice, 1914 Star, wounded twice); commanded Chestnut Troop RHA, 1935-38; Brigadier, 1939; CRA, 3rd Division, France and Belgium, 1939-40 (CBE); CCRA 9 Corps, 1941-42; Commandant School of Artillery, 1942-45; retd pay, 1946. King Haakon VII Liberty Cross (Norway). *Club:* Army and Navy.
[Died 24 Nov. 1973.

TOWERS, Graham Ford, CC (Canada) 1969; CMG 1944; LLD; Governor, Bank of Canada, Ottawa, Ontario, 1934-54; *b* Montreal, Quebec, 1897; *s* of William Crawford and Caroline Towers (*née* Auldjo); *m* 1924, Mary Scott, *d* of C. H. Godfrey, Montreal. *Educ:* Montreal High Sch.; St Andrew's Coll.; McGill Univ. (BA). Joined Royal Bank of Canada, Montreal, 1920; Accountant, Havana Branch, 1922; Inspector, Foreign Dept, 1924; Chief Inspector, 1929; Asst Gen. Man., 1933; Chm., Foreign Exchange Control Bd, 1939-51; Chm., Nat. War Finance Cttee, 1943-45; President, Industrial Development Bank, 1944-54; Alternate Governor, International Monetary Fund, Washington, DC, 1946-54. Lieut, Canadian Army, 1915-19. Hon. LLD: McGill Univ., 1944, Queen's Univ., 1954; Hon. DCL Bishop's Univ., 1961. *Address:* 260 Park Road, Rockcliffe, Ontario, Canada. *Clubs:* Rideau, Country, Anglican (Ottawa).
[Died 4 Dec. 1975.

TOWN, Sir (Hugh) Stuart, Kt 1947; retired; Director, 1925-47, of: Binny & Co. (Madras) Ltd, Madras; Buckingham & Carnatic Co. Ltd, Madras; Bangalore Woollen, Cotton & Silk Mills Ltd, Bangalore; *b* 19 April 1893; *s* of Christopher Edward and Mary Town; *m* 1920, Christine Mary, K-i-H (silver), OStJ, *d* of Richard Lewis and Mary Tucker, New Barnet; one *s. Educ:* privately. Served European War, 1914-18, with RAMC. Joined Binny & Co. (Madras) Ltd, 1920. Mem. Income Tax Bd of Referees; Trustee Madras Port Trust, 1937-47; MLA (Central), 1938; MLA Madras, 1939-47; Chm. S India Branch of European Assoc., 1939-40; Chm. Nat. Service Advisory Cttee, 1940 and 1945; Mem. Income Tax Appellate Tribunal, 1940; Chm. Employers' Federation of S India, 1940, and again, 1945; served on ARP and Governor's War Fund Cttee; Treasurer St John Ambulance, Madras, 1941-47; Chm. Madras Presidency Electric Licencees Assoc., 1944-45; Chm. Madras Chamber of Commerce, 1945 and 1946; Local Board Imperial Bank of India, 1945. Senate Madras Univ., 1945; Sheriff of Madras, 1946. OStJ. *Address:* 15 Langton Avenue, Ewell, Surrey.
[Died 23 June 1972.

TOWNEND, Sir Harry (Douglas), Kt 1947; Director, 1948-70 (Chairman, 1955-61), R. G. Shaw & Co. Ltd, 19 Leadenhall Street, London, EC3; *b* 29 Dec. 1891; *s* of late Rev. A. J. Townend, CF, and Margaret Wiseman Townend, *d* of Hon. William James Stairs, Halifax, Nova Scotia; *m* 1925, Mary Winifred Edwards, *d* of late Rev. E. Stanley Edwards and of Kathleen Mary Edwards; one *d* (one *s* decd). *Educ:* King's Sch., Canterbury; Queens' College, Cambridge (MA). Joined Shaw Wallace & Co., Eastern Merchants, 1913, Senior Partner India, 1942-47; Member Local Board, Reserve Bank of India, 1943-46; Pres. Bengal Chamber of Commerce and Associated Chambers of Commerce of India, 1946-47; Member Council of State, India, 1946-47. *Address:* Parkgrove, Lye Green, Crowborough, East Sussex. *T:* Crowborough 2088. *Clubs:* Oriental, City of London, Royal Commonwealth Society; Bengal (Calcutta).
[Died 9 Jan. 1976.

TOWNER, Major Edgar Thomas, VC 1918; MC; on Army retired list; grazier; *b* Glencoe, near Blackall, Central Queensland, 19 April 1890; *s* of E. T. and Greta Towner; unmarried. *Educ:* Blackall State Sch.; private tuition. Engaged in pastoral pursuits from an early age; enlisted for service in European War, 2 Jan. 1915, at Blackall, Central Queensland; served in Egypt and France (wounded, VC and MC, despatches twice); served War of 1939-45 until Jan. 1942, in Australia. Life Member Returned Soldiers', Sailors' and Airmen's Imperial League of Australia; Fellow, Royal Geog. Society of Australia (Queensland); Thompson Gold Foundation Medal, RGS, Australia. Member Royal Historical Society of Queensland. *Publication:* Lake Eyre and its Tributaries. *Recreations:* riding, shooting, tennis, literature. *Address:* Kaloola, Longreach, Qld 4730, Australia. *T:* 62K Isisford. *Clubs:* Longreach; Blackall; United Service (life Hon. Member) (Brisbane); Imperial Service

(Sydney); Town and Country Cricket (Vice-President) (Longreach). *[Died 18 Aug. 1972.*

TOWNESEND, Air Cdre Ernest John Dennis, CBE 1947; BA, CEng; FRAeS; RAF (retired); *b* 21 March 1896; *e s* of late Charles John Henry Fyler Townesend, late a civil engineer in India; *m* 1929, Ethel Aiken; one *s* one *d. Educ:* Royal Grammar Sch., Lancaster; Dulwich Coll.; University Sch., Victoria, British Columbia; RMC, Kingston, Canada; Jesus Coll., Cambridge; Imperial College of Science and Technology, London. Served European War, 1914-18, in RFA, RFC, and RAF as observer (No. 21 Sqdn) and pilot (No. 60 Sqdn); at Air Ministry, 1918-20; RAF Engineer Specialist Course, 1920-23; Assistant to Chief Technical Officer, A&AEE, Martlesham Heath, 1923-25; Iraq Aircraft Depot and AHQ, Baghdad, 1925-27; Station Engineer Officer, Upper Heyford, 1928-32; HQ Wessex Bombing Area, 1932, DDRM, Air Ministry, 1932-35; HQ Western Area, 1935; served in Iraq Aircraft Depot, 1935-37; OC No 3 School of Tech. Training, Manston, 1937-39; HQ No 41 Group, 1939-41; transferred to Tech. Branch, 1940; OC No 30 Maintenance Unit and RAF Station, Sealand, 1942-43; Air Commodore, 1944; OC 13 Maintenance Unit and RAF Station, Henlow, 1943-46; retired as Air Commodore, 1946; Engineer I, Directorate of Engine Production, Ministry of Supply, 1946-56. R. M. Groves Aeronautical Research Prize, 1926; Order of Polonia Restituta. *Address:* 30 Watcombe Road, Southbourne, Bournemouth BH6 3LU. *T:* Bournemouth 49075.
[Died 13 Oct. 1975.

TOWNLEY, Rt. Rev. George Frederick, MA; an Assistant Bishop, Diocese of Peterborough, since 1970; *b* 15 April 1891; *s* of Frederick William and Emily Louisa Townley; *m* 1915, Charlotte Catherine Whiting; no *c. Educ:* Lincoln Coll., Oxford (MA); Ripon Hall, Oxford. Served European War, 1914-18, Gallipoli and Egypt, in Northamptonshire and Bedfordshire Regts. Curate of Keighley, 1922-25; Curate in Charge of Harden, Bingley, 1925-27; Vicar of Lidget Green, Bradford, 1927-32. Vicar of St Barnabas, Linthorpe, Middlesbrough, 1932-44; Canon and Preb. of York, 1939-57; Vicar and Rural Dean of Scarborough, 1944-47; Archdeacon of Cleveland, 1947; Archdeacon of York and Secretary to the York Diocesan Board of Finance, 1947-57; Suffragan Bishop of Hull, 1957-65. *Publication:* The Great Ambition, Mystery Play, 1933. *Recreation:* golf. *Address:* Orchard Gate, 16 Park Street, Earls Barton, Northampton. *T:* Northampton 810182.
[Died 9 March 1977.

TOWNSEND, Brigadier Edward Philip, CBE 1957 (OBE 1951); DSO 1950; retired; *b* 24 July 1909; 2nd *s* of late Lt-Col E. C. Townsend, Indian Army; *m* 1952, Imogen Martin; two *d. Educ:* Haileybury; RMC, Sandhurst. Commissioned, 1929; joined 5th Royal Gurkha Rifles, 1930; Commanded: 2nd Bn 5th RGR, 1944-47; 1st Bn 6th Gurkha Rifles, 1948-51; 48th Gurkha Infantry Brigade, Aug. 1953-Feb. 1955; 99th Gurkha Infantry Brigade, Oct. 1955-Nov. 1957; British Gurkha L of C Nepal, July 1958-April 1961; retired, 1961. *Address:* Copleston, Peterstow, Ross-on-Wye, Herefordshire HR9 6LD.
[Died 28 May 1978.

TOWNSHEND, Hugh, CB 1947; Assistant Secretary-General (retired), International Telecommunication Union, 1950-57; *b* 17 Nov. 1890; *s* of late Colonel G. R. Townshend, RA; *m* 1920, Winifred Dora Mary Higham (*d* 1972); one *s* two *d. Educ:* King's Sch., Canterbury; Trinity Coll., Cambridge. Civil Servant (General Post Office), 1914-49. Served European War, 1914-18: Royal Engineers, 1916-18. *Publication:* (with Myra Curtis) Modern Money, 1937. *Address:* 6 Lyric Road, SW13.
[Died 8 July 1974.

TOYNBEE, Arnold Joseph, CH 1956; Hon. DLitt (Oxon, Birmingham and Columbia), LittD (Cambridge), DCL (Princeton); FBA, 1937; Director of Studies in the Royal Institute of International Affairs, 1925, and Research Professor of International History in the University of London, both on the Sir Daniel Stevenson Foundation; retired, 1955; Professor Emeritus, 1955; Associate Member, Academy Moral and Political Sciences, Institut de France, 1968; *b* 14 April 1889; *m* 1913, Rosalind (marr. diss. 1946), *d* of late Professor Gilbert Murray, OM; two *s* ; *m* 1946, Veronica Marjorie, *d* of Rev. Sidney Boulter. *Educ:* Winchester (Scholar); Balliol Coll., Oxford (Scholar). Fellow and Tutor, Balliol Coll., Oxford, 1912-15; various Government work in connection with the War, 1915-19; Political Intelligence Dept, Foreign Office, April 1918; Member of Middle Eastern Section, British Delegation, Peace Conference, Paris, 1919; Koraes Professor of Byzantine and Modern Greek Language, Literature, and History at London Univ., 1919-24; War Work: Director, Foreign Research and Press Service, Royal Institute of International Affairs, 1939-43;

Director, Research Department, Foreign Office, 1943-46; member of British Delegation, Peace Conference, Paris, 1946. Hon. Fellow Balliol Coll., Oxford, 1957. *Publications:* Nationality and the War, 1915; The New Europe, 1915; The Western Question in Greece and Turkey, 1922; Greek Historical Thought, 1924; Greek Civilisation and Character, 1924; The World after the Peace Conference, 1925; A Survey of International Affairs for 1920-23, 1924, 1925 (vol. i: The Islamic World since the Peace Settlement), etc, to 1938, vol. i; Joint Editor with V. M. Toynbee, of vols covering 1939-46; (with K. P. Kirkwood) Turkey, in the Nations of the Modern World Series, 1926; A Journey to China, 1931; Editor, British Commonwealth Relations, 1934; A Study of History, Vols i-iii, 1934, Vols iv-vi, 1939 (Abridgement of Vols i-vi, 1946); Vols vii-x, 1954; Vol. xi, 1958; Vol. xii, 1961; Civilisation on Trial, 1948; War and Civilisation, 1951; The World and the West (1952 Reith Lectures), 1953; An Historian's Approach to Religion (Edinburgh Gifford Lectures, 1953 and 1954); Christianity Among the Religions of the World, 1958; East to West: a Journey Round the World, 1958; Hellenism, 1959; Between Oxus and Jumna, 1961; (with T. P. Toynbee) Comparing Notes: a Dialogue across a Generation, 1963; Between Niger and Nile, 1965; Hannibal's Legacy, 1965; Change and Habit, 1966; Acquaintances, 1967; Between Maule and Amazon, 1967; (co-author) Man's Concern with Death, 1968; (ed) The Crucible of Christianity, 1968; Cities of Destiny, 1969; Experiences, 1969; Some Problems of Greek History, 1969; Cities on the Move, 1970; (with Kei Wakaizumi) Surviving the Future, 1971; Constantine Porphyrogenitus and his World, 1972; illustrated abridgement of A Study of History, 1972; (ed) Half the World, 1973. *Address:* Chapel Cottage, Ganthorpe, Terrington, York YO6 4QD. *Club:* Athenæum. *[Died 22 Oct. 1975.*

TOZER, Col William, CBE 1938; TD; Stockbroker; *b* 11 Feb. 1894; *er s* of Major William Tozer, VD, Tapton Edge, Sheffield; *m* 1919, Eileen Nanciebel (*d* 1958), *er d* of Lt-Col Herbert Higginson Sykes, VD, Briar Court, Lindley, Huddersfield; one *s* one *d. Educ:* Malvern Coll.; Clare Coll., Cambridge. Now a Governor of Malvern Coll. Served The Hallamshire Battalion, The York and Lancaster Regt, 1914-38; European War, 1914-19, France and Belgium (despatches, 1914-15 Star); Lt-Col Commanding, 1931-38; Brevet Colonel, 1935; Colonel, 1939; War of 1939-45; AA and QMG; a Member of West Riding of Yorks TA Assoc., 1931-39; Master of Cutlers Company of Sheffield, 1936. Councillor of East Grinstead UDC, 1955-58. *Address:* Wye House, Courtlands Estate, Sharpthorne, Sussex; c/o Gerald Hodgson, Andreae & Co., 2 Copthall Buildings, EC2. *T:* 01-628 9991. *[Died 20 March 1971.*

TRAFFORD, Rt. Rev. Ralph Sigebert, OSB; Manager Downside Settlement; *b* 18 Oct. 1886; 4th *s* of late E. S. and late Hon. Mrs E. S. Trafford of Wroxham Hall, Norfolk. *Educ:* Downside. Priest, 1912; Headmaster of Downside, 1918-34; Prior of Worth, 1934-38; Abbot of Downside, 1938-46; Abbot-Pres. of English Benedictine Congregation, 1939-41; Abbot of St Alban's, 1953. *Address:* Mount St Benedict, Gorey, Co. Wexford, Ireland. *T:* Holyfort 4. *[Died 22 Nov. 1976.*

TRAIL, Richard Robertson, CBE 1953; MC, MA, MD, FRCP; late Medical Director, Papworth and Enham-Alamein Village Settlements; Hon. Consultant to the RAF (Air Commodore, RAFVR Medical Service); Past-Master, Society of Apothecaries; Member, Medical Research Council Committee on Tuberculosis in War-time; late Medical Superintendent, King Edward VII Sanatorium, Midhurst; *b* 25 May 1894; *m* 1924, Marion Dawson McAfee; one *s. Educ:* Robert Gordon's Coll., Aberdeen; King's College and Marischal College, Aberdeen Univ. Matriculated 1911; served European War, Captain RA (SR). MA (Hons), MB, ChB (Hons), MD Aberdeen, Simpson Gold Medallist, FRCP. Resident Officer Aberdeen Maternity Hospital; House Physician, later Assistant RMO, later RMO, Brompton Hosp., London; Mitchell Lectr, RCP, 1936; Fitzpatrick Lectr, RCP, 1964-65; Sydenham and Gideon de Laune Lectr, Faculty of History, Soc. of Apothecaries, 1964. Life Member, BRCS. Chevalier of the Legion of Honour; Officier de l'Ordre de la Santé Publique; Order of Merit, first class, of Czechoslovakia; CStJ. *Publications:* Pulmonary Tuberculosis: A report upon the experience of the Patients of King Edward VII Sanatorium, Midhurst, 1931; Inaugural Lecture of the Varrier-Jones Memorial Lectureship; The Early Diagnosis of Pulmonary Tuberculosis, 1942; Mass Miniature Radiography (with Trenchard and Kennedy), 1943; Chest Examination: Physical Signs and X-Ray Findings correlated through Pathology, 1943; numerous articles on Tuberculosis in leading medical journals. *Address:* 82b Ashley Gardens, Westminster, SW1. *T:* 01-828 8897. *[Died 15 June 1971.*

TRAILL, Air Vice-Marshal Thomas Cathcart, CB 1948; OBE 1940; DFC 1918; Royal Air Force, retired; *b* 6 Aug. 1899; *s* of Edmund Bernard Traill, Chirú, Traill, Argentine, and Gertrude Ann (*née* Dickinson); *m* 1931, F. M. Harvey; two *d*; *m* 1945, W. B. Reeves; one *s*. *Educ:* RN Colleges, Osborne and Dartmouth; St Catharine's Coll., Cambridge (MA). Joined HMS Lord Nelson, 2nd Aug. 1914; served European War, 1914-19, Dardanelles Campaign; transferred to RFC 1917, and joined No. 20 Sqdn, France, May 1918 (temp. Captain, DFC). Asst Air Attaché, Washington, 1919-20; Cambridge, BA, MA, 1922-24. Served Iraq, Trans-Jordan and Egypt. In War of 1939-45 served in Bomber Command, N Africa and Air Ministry. Retired, 1954. US Legion of Merit, 1944, when he was serving on the Staff of General Spaatz. *Address:* Flat 4, Garrick's Villa, Hampton, Middx. *Club:* Royal Air Force. *[Died 1 Oct.* 1973.

TRAPPES-LOMAX, Michael Roger; Somerset Herald, 1951-67, retired; *b* 16 Oct. 1900; 3rd *s* of late Richard Trappes-Lomax, Allsprings, Great Harwood, Lancashire, and late Hon. Alice Mary Wilhelmina Fitzherbert, sister of 13th Baron Stafford. *Educ:* Stonyhurst; New Coll., Oxford. Major, late R. of O., Scots Guards. Rouge Dragon Pursuivant of Arms, 1946-51; Admiralty Adviser on Heraldry, 1954. Librarian, College of Arms, 1960. FSA 1960. Kt Grand Cross, Order of Malta. *Publications:* One of These Days, 1926; Pugin, 1933; Bishop Challoner, 1936. *Address:* Pamments, Great Hockham, Thetford, Norfolk. *Clubs:* Pratt's, Royal Ocean Racing. *[Died 24 Nov.* 1972.

TRATMAN, Edgar Kingsley, OBE 1949; retired; *b* 23 Feb. 1899; *s* of J. F. W. and E. S. Tratman. *Educ:* Clifton Coll.; University of Bristol. Prof. of Dental Surgery: King Edward VII College of Medicine, Singapore, 1929-49; University of Malaya, 1949-50; University of London (University College Hospital Med. Sch.), 1950-51. FDS, RCS 1949; MD University of Malaya, 1950; FDS, RCSE, 1951. FSA 1938. Hon. DSc Bristol, 1976. *Publications:* many contributions to dental and archæological journals. *Recreations:* cave exploring and prehistoric archæology. *Address:* Penrose Cottage, Burrington, Bristol BS18 7AA. *T:* Blagdon 62274. *[Died 21 Aug.* 1978.

TRAVERS, Ben, CBE 1976; AFC 1920; dramatist and novelist; *b* 1886; *e s* of W. F. Travers; *m* 1916, Violet (*d* 1951), *o c* of D. B. W. Mouncey; two *s* one *d*. *Educ:* Abbey Sch., Beckenham; Charterhouse. Served in RNAS, 1914-18, Squadron Commander; transferred RAF as Major, 1918; received Air Force Cross, 1920; rejoined RAF for War Service, Nov. 1939; Sqdn Leader, 1940; Prime Warden of Fishmongers' Company, 1946. Evening Standard special award for services to the theatre, 1976. *Publications: Plays, Novels and Films:* The Dippers, 1922; A Cuckoo in the Nest, 1925 (revived, 1964); Rookery Nook, 1926 (revived, 1941, 1979) (as musical, Popkiss, 1972); Mischief, 1926; Thark, 1927 (revived 1965); Plunder, 1928 (revived 1973 and 1976); The Collection To-day, 1928; A Cup of Kindness, 1929; A Night Like This, 1930; Turkey Time, 1931; The Chance of a Night-time, 1931; Dirty Work, 1932; Just My Luck, 1932; A Bit of a Test, 1933; Hyde Side Up, 1933; Up to the Neck, Lady in Danger, 1934; Fighting Stock, 1935; Stormy Weather, 1935; Foreign Affairs, 1935; Pot Luck, 1936; Dishonour Bright, 1936; O Mistress Mine, 1936; For Valour, 1937; Second Best Bed, 1937; Old Iron, 1938; Banana Ridge, 1938 (revived 1976); Spotted Dick, 1939; She Follows Me About, 1943; Outrageous Fortune, 1947; Wild Horses, 1952; Nun's Veiling, 1956; Vale of Laughter (autobiography), 1957; Corker's End, 1969; The Bed Before Yesterday, 1975; A-sitting on a Gate (autobiog.), 1978; After You with the Milk, 1980; 94 Declared (posthumous publication), 1981; Television Play, Potter, 1948. *Recreation:* watching cricket. *Address:* c/o Fishmongers' Company, Fishmongers' Hall, London Bridge, EC4R 9EL. *Clubs:* Garrick, Beefsteak, MCC. *[Died 18 Dec.* 1980.

TREACY, Rt. Rev. Eric, MBE 1945; *b* 2 June 1907; *s* of George Treacy, Rangoon; *m* 1932, Mary Leyland, *d* of J. A. Shone, JP, Hoylake; no *c*. *Educ:* Haberdashers' School; King's Coll., London; St Aidan's, Birkenhead. Deacon, 1932, Priest, 1933; Curate of Liverpool Parish Church, 1932-34; Shrewsbury School Missioner, 1930-36; Vicar of Edge Hill, Liverpool, 1936-40; Chaplain to the Forces (EC), 1940-45; Senior Chaplain (NW Europe), 1944 (despatches, MBE); Rector of Keighley, 1945-49; Hon. Canon: of Bradford Cathedral, 1946; of Wakefield Cathedral, 1949; Rural Dean of South Craven, 1946; Proctor in Convocation, 1949; Examining Chaplain to Bishop of Wakefield, 1949; Canon of Wakefield Cathedral, 1956; Archdeacon of Halifax, 1949-61; Vicar and Rural Dean of Halifax, 1950-61; Bishop Suffragan of Pontefract, 1961-68; Archdeacon of Pontefract, 1961-68; Bishop of Wakefield, 1968-76. Hon. Chaplain, Duke of Wellington's Regt, 1961. Church Commissioner, 1963. Introduced House of Lords, 1972. Hon.

Freeman, Co. Borough of Halifax, 1973. Hon. LLD (Leeds) 1968. *Publications:* Main Lines over the Border, 1960; The Lure of Steam, 1966; Portrait of Steam, 1967; Glory of Steam, 1969; Spell of Steam, 1973; Roaming the Northern Rail, 1975. *Recreations:* fell walking, photography, railways preservation. *Address:* The Ghyll, Applethwaite, Keswick, Cumbria. *Club:* Army and Navy. *[Died 13 May* 1978.

TREDENNICK, Rev. John Nesbitt Ernest, MA; *b* 23 Sept. 1892; *e s* of late Canon G. N. H. Tredennick; *m* 1931, Marjorie Phyllis, *y d* of Henry Currie; two *d*. *Educ:* King Edward's School, Birmingham; Trinity Hall, Cambridge (Scholar), BA 1914; MA 1921 (Hons in Classics and Theology); Ridley Hall, Cambridge, 1919-21. Served European War, 1914-19, as Captain (R War. Regiment and General List); wounded in 1st Battle of the Somme, July 1916; Deacon, 1921; Priest, 1922; Curate of St James's, Paddington, 1921-24; Principal of Bishop Wilson Theological College, Isle of Man, and Domestic Chaplain to the Bishop of Sodor and Man, 1924-31; Vicar of Emmanuel Church, Southport, 1931-52; Vicar of Crockham Hill, Kent, 1952-68. *Recreations:* fishing, sailing, motoring. *Address:* 111 Dean Court Road, Rottingdean, Sussex. *T:* Brighton 36423. *[Died 14 Aug.* 1976.

TREDGOLD, Rt. Hon. Sir Robert Clarkson, PC 1957; KCMG 1955 (CMG 1943); Kt 1951; QC; *b* 1899; *s* of Sir Clarkson Tredgold, KC; *m* 1st, 1925, Lorna Doris Keilor (*d* 1972); no *c.*; 2nd, 1974, Margaret Helen Phear. *Educ:* Prince Edward School, Salisbury, Rhodesia; Rondebosch High School; Hertford College, Oxford. Hon. Fellow, Hertford College, Oxford, 1961. On Military Service, 1918; called to Bar, Inner Temple, 1923; practised in Southern Rhodesia and Northern Rhodesia with Headquarters at Bulawayo; acted Judge in N Rhodesia; MP for Insiza District, 1934-43; KC (S Rhodesia), 1936; Minister of Justice and Defence, S Rhodesia, 1936-43; also Minister of Natives, 1941, 1942-43; High Court Judge, Southern Rhodesia, 1943-50; Chief Justice, SR, 1950-55; Chief Justice, Federal Supreme Court, Federation of Rhodesia and Nyasaland 1955-60, resigned. Acted as Governor of S Rhodesia and Gov.-Gen. of Federation, on a number of occasions. LLD (Hon.) Witwatersrand Univ., 1953. *Publications:* The Matapos, 1956; The Rhodesia That Was My Life, 1968; Xhosa, 1973. *Recreation:* the veld. *Address:* 43 Jelliman Avenue, Marandellas, Rhodesia. *T:* Marandellas 3348. *Clubs:* Bulawayo (Bulawayo); Salisbury (Salisbury). *[Died 8 April* 1977.

TREDGOLD, Roger Francis, MD; Physician to Department of Psychological Medicine, University College Hospital; *b* 23 Oct. 1911; *s* of late Alfred Frank Tredgold, FRCP, FRSE; *m* 1938, Verity Micheline, *d* of late Sir Gilbert Walker, CSI, FRS; one *s* one *d*. *Educ:* Winchester Coll.; Trinity Coll., Cambridge; University Coll. Hosp. Medical School. MA Cantab, 1939; MD 1947; DPM 1939; MRCP 1965; FRCP 1971; FRCPsych 1971. Asst MO, Brentwood Mental Hosp., 1937-40. RAMC, 1940-46; served in S India and SE Asia Commands, as Adviser in Psychiatry, with rank of Lt-Col; also Reader in Psychiatry, RAM College, Millbank. Boots Lectr in Industrial Health, Roffey Park Rehabilitation Centre, 1946-48. Regional Psychiatrist, South East Metropolitan Regional Hosp. Bd, 1948-56. Hon. Consultant in Psychiatry to the Army at Home. *Publications:* Human Relations in Modern Industry, 2nd edn 1963; (jtly with late A. F. Tredgold) Manual of Psychological Medicine, 3rd edn 1953; (jtly with K. Soddy) Mental Retardation, 11th edn 1970; (jtly with H. H. Wolff) UCH Handbook on Psychiatry, 1975. *Recreations:* fencing, chess, bird-watching. *Address:* White Cottage, Old Heathfield, East Sussex TN21 9BP. *T:* Heathfield 3258. *[Died 24 Dec.* 1975.

TREE, Ronald; *o s* of Arthur Tree and late Countess Beatty; *m* 1920, Nancy, 2nd *d* of Moncure Perkins, Richmond, Virginia, and widow of Henry Field, of Chicago; two *s*; *m* 1947, Mrs Mary Endicott Fitzgerald, *o d* of Rt Rev. Malcolm Peabody, Syracuse, NY; one *d*. *Educ:* Winchester. Served war of 1914-18, in Italy and France, 1917-18. Managing Ed. of Forum Magazine, NY, 1922-26; Joint Master Pytchley Hounds, 1927-33; MP (C) Harborough division of Leicestershire, 1933-45; Parliamentary Private Secretary to R. S. Hudson when Minister of Pensions and when Secretary to Overseas Trade Dept, 1936-38; to Sir John Reith, Minister of Information, to Rt Hon. Alfred Duff-Cooper and to Rt Hon. Brendan Bracken, 1940-43; Parliamentary Secretary, Ministry of Town and Country Planning, 1945; a Trustee of the Wallace Collection. Formerly Mem., Council, Univ. of the West Indies; Pres., Barbados National Trust. *Publications:* A History of Barbados, 1972; When the Moon was High, 1975. *Recreations:* golf, swimming, yachting. *Address:* Heron Bay, Barbados, WI; 123 East 79 Street, New York City, USA. *Clubs:* Turf, White's; Century (New York). *[Died 14 July* 1976.

TREMAYNE, Air Marshal Sir John Tremayne, KCB 1942 (CB 1939); CBE 1934; DSO 1915; DL, JP; *b* 20 July 1891; *s* of C. H. Babington, 47 Lennox Gdns, SW1; renounced surname of Babington, 1945; *m* 1916, Cicely (*d* 1953), *y d* of Philip Beresford-Hope, Bedgebury; two *d*. Served European War, 1914-15 (DSO, Chevalier Legion of Honour); Air Representative to League of Nations, 1929-34; Air Officer Commanding RAF Halton, 1934-36; No 24 (Training) Group, 1936-38; Far East, 1938-41; Air Officer Commanding-in-Chief, Technical Training Command, 1941-43; Head of RAF Mission in Moscow, 1943; retired 1944. Cornwall: DL 1945, JP 1948, High Sheriff 1954. *Address:* Croan, Wadebridge, Cornwall. *T:* St Mabyn 368. *Club:* Army and Navy. *[Died 20 March 1979.*

TREMELLEN, Norman Cleverton; FCIB; FRSA; *b* 8 March 1895; *s* of Henry Josiah and Elizabeth Tremellen; *m* 1923, Lorna, *o d* of Dr John McKeague and *g d* of Judge Purcell, Dublin. *Educ:* Villa Longchamp, Lausanne, Switzerland. Served European War, 1914-18 (4 General Service Medals). Former Member Common Council, City of London; Founder Chm. and Hon. Treas., City of London Sheriffs Society. Insurance Broker and Underwriting Member of Lloyd's; Fellow of the Corporation of Insurance Brokers; Past President, London Cornish Association. Past Governor of: The Bridewell and Bethlem Royal Hospitals; Archbishop Tenison's Grammar Sch. Pres., Insurance Debating Society. Sheriff of the City of London, 1953-54. Mem., Court, Worshipful Co. of Weavers; Mem. Worshipful Co. of Shipwrights; Past President: City Livery Club; Bishopsgate Ward Club; United Wards Club; Past Master, Lime Street Ward Club; Past Chm., Langbourn Ward Club; Mem., Three Rooms Club, Lloyd's; Governor (for 18 years), Bishopsgate Foundn. Past Dep. Gov. The Hon. The Irish Soc.; Fellow, Royal Soc. for Protection of Birds; FAMS. Mem. Anglo-Ethiopian Soc. Comdr Roy. Order of the North Star (Sweden). *Address:* Burlington, Orchehill Avenue, Gerrards Cross, Bucks. *T:* 83047. *Club:* City Livery.
[Died 30 March 1979.

TREMLETT, Col Colin Percy, CBE 1919; TD; DL; *b* 1880; *s* of late W. W. Tremlett, JP, Exeter; *m* Dorothy, *d* of late Percy Gray, MBE, Indian Civil Service; three *s* two *d*. *Educ:* Inverness College. DL Devonshire. *Address:* Highlands, Littleham Cross, Exmouth, Devon. *T:* Exmouth 2016. *[Died 20 Feb. 1972.*

TRENCH; see Chenevix-Trench.

TREVELYAN, Sir Willoughby John, 9th Bt, *cr* 1662; *b* 16 April 1902; *s* of 8th Bt and Alice Edith Money, *y d* of late W. J. Money, CSI; *S* father, 1931. *Heir:* kinsman Norman Irving Trevelyan [*b* 29 Jan. 1915; *m* 1951, Jennifer Mary, *d* of Arthur E. Riddett, Burgh Heath, Surrey; two *s* one *d*]. *Address:* Old Manor House, Salisbury, Wilts. *[Died Dec. 1976.*

TREVETHIN, 3rd Baron *cr* 1921 **AND OAKSEY, 1st Baron,** *cr* 1947; **Geoffrey Lawrence,** PC 1944; Kt 1932; DSO 1918; TD; (to be known as Lord Oaksey); Vice-Lieutenant of Wiltshire, since 1949; *b* 1880; *y s* of 1st Baron Trevethin; *S* brother 1959, in Trevethin Barony, and assumed double title; *m* 1921, Marjorie, *yr d* of late Comdr Chas. N. Robinson, RN, retd; one *s* three *d*. *Educ:* Haileybury; New Coll., Oxford (Hon. Fellow, 1944). Hon. DCL 1947. Barrister, Inner Temple, 1906; KC 1925; Attorney-General to the Prince of Wales and a member of the Council, 1928-32; Recorder of Oxford, 1924-32; Judge of High Court of Justice, King's Bench Division, 1932-44; a Lord Justice of Appeal, 1944-47; a Lord of Appeal in Ordinary, 1947-57; Counsel to the Jockey Club, 1922-32; Examiner in Ecclesiastical Causes, 1927-32; JP Wilts, 1924; DL Wilts, 1945; Chairman Quarter Sessions, 1945-55; served Herts RFA European War, 1914-18 (despatches twice, DSO); commanded 86th Bde RA, TA, 1919-26; Bt Col, 1925; Col, 1926. British President of International Tribunal Nuremberg, 1945. President, British Dairy Farmers' Assoc., 1953; Treasurer, Inner Temple, 1955. *Heir: s* Hon. John Geoffrey Tristram Lawrence [*b* 21 March 1929; *m* 1959, Victoria Mary, *er d* of Major John Dennistoun, Letcombe Regis, Berkshire; one *s* one *d*]. *Address:* Flintham Cottage, Oaksey, Malmesbury. *T:* Crudwell 214. *Club:* Brooks's.
[Died 28 Aug. 1971.

TREVOR, Sir Cecil Russell, Kt 1950; CIE 1946; retired; *b* 20 Feb. 1899; *s* of James and Isabel Mary Trevor. *Educ:* St Xavier's College, Bruges, Belgium. Served European War, 1914-18, as Lieut King's Liverpool Regt; joined Imperial Bank of India, 1921; Chief Accountant, Reserve Bank of India, 1935; Deputy Governor, Reserve Bank of India, 1943-50. *Recreations:* golf, bridge. *Clubs:* Oriental; Bengal (Calcutta); Royal Bombay Yacht (Bombay). *[Died 5 Sept. 1971.*

TREVOR JONES, Alan; see Jones.

TRILLING, Lionel; American Author; University Professor, Columbia University, USA, 1970-74, now University Professor Emeritus; *b* 4 July 1905; *s* of David W. and Fannie Cohen Trilling; *m* 1929, Diana Rubin; one *s*. *Educ:* Columbia Univ. AB, MA, PhD. Instructor: University of Wisconsin, 1926-27; Hunter Coll., 1927-32; Columbia University: Instructor, 1932-39, Asst Professor, 1939-45, Assoc. Professor, 1945-48, Professor, 1948-65, George Edward Woodberry Prof. of Literature and Criticism, 1964-70. George Eastman Vis. Prof., Oxford, 1964-65; Charles Eliot Norton Vis. Prof. of Poetry, Harvard Univ., 1969-70; Vis. Fellow, All Souls Coll., Oxford, 1972-73. Member: Nat. Inst. of Arts and Letters, 1951; American Acad. of Arts and Sciences, 1952. Hon. DLitt: Trinity Coll., Hartford, Conn., 1955; Harvard Univ., 1962; Case Western Reserve Univ., 1968; Durham, 1973; Leicester, 1973; Hon LHD Northwestern Univ., 1963; Brandeis, 1974; Yale 1974. Creative Arts Award, Brandeis Univ., 1968. *Publications:* Matthew Arnold, 1939, repr. 1975; E. M. Forster, 1944; The Middle of the Journey, 1948, repr. 1975; The Liberal Imagination, 1950; The Opposing Self, 1955 (all dates of English publications); Freud and the Crisis of Our Culture, 1955 (US); A Gathering of Fugitives, 1956 (US), 1957 (England); Beyond Culture, 1965 (US), 1966 (Eng.); Sincerity and Authenticity, 1972 (US and Eng.); Mind in the Modern World, 1972 (US); edited: The Portable Matthew Arnold, 1949; The Letters of John Keats, 1950; The Experience of Literature, 1967 (US); (with others) The Oxford Anthology of English Literature, 1973 (US and Eng.); stories and essays to Partisan Review, Kenyon Review, The Nation, etc. *Address:* Hamilton Hall, Columbia University, New York, NY 10027, USA; 35 Claremont Avenue, New York, NY 10027. *Clubs:* Athenæum; Century (New York).
[Died 5 Nov. 1975.

TRIMMER, Sir George (William Arthur), Kt 1937; MInstCE; FIMechE; FCIT; Ministry of Supply, retired; *b* 12 Feb. 1882; *e s* of late Rev. G. J. Trimmer, Ceylon, and Caroline Elizabeth, *d* of late Rev. W. S. Bestall; *m* 1939, Phyllis Primrose, widow of Colonel B. H. Beaumont-Checkland, MC, Sherwood Foresters, and *d* of Edward Hodgson, Beverley, Yorks. *Educ:* Harrogate Coll., Yorks; Kingswood Sch., Bath. Pupil of Pulsometer Engineering Co., Reading; Engineer in charge Mugra Hat. Bengal and Mon Canals Burma Irrigation construction, 1904-10; Construction of Empire Dock and reconstruction Wharves Singapore with Topham Jones and Railton, 1911-18; Assistant General Manager and Local Chairman Singapore Harbour Board, 1919; Chairman, General Manager and Chief Engineer Singapore and Penang Harbour Boards, Straits Settlements, 1923-39; Director of Building Construction, 1940-43; Controller Building Construction, 1943-47, Adviser Building Constr. (part time), 1947-56, Ministry of Supply. *Recreations:* riding, golf, and tennis. *Address:* Croft Point, Links Road, Bramley, near Guildford, Surrey. *T:* Bramley 2389. *Clubs:* Junior Carlton, East India, Sports and Public Schools, Royal Automobile.
[Died 16 Oct. 1972.

TRITTON, Arthur Stanley, MA, DLitt; *b* 1881; *s* of late Rev. William Tritton and Eliza Squire. *Educ:* Mansfield Coll., St Catherine's Society, Oxford; Göttingen. Teacher in the Friends' Sch., Brumana, Mt Lebanon; Assistant in Universities of Edinburgh and Glasgow; Professor of Arabic, Aligarh, UP, India; Professor of Arabic at the School of Oriental and African Studies, University of London, 1938-46; Hon. Fellow, School of Oriental and African Studies, 1946; Professor Emeritus since 1947. Hon. Vice-Pres., Royal Asiatic Soc., 1969. *Publications:* Rise of the Imams of Sanaa, 1925; Caliphs and their Non-Muslim Subjects, 1930, reprinted 1970; Arabic Self Taught, 1943; Muslim Theology, 1947; Islam, Beliefs and Practices, 1951; Materials on Muslim Education in the Middle Ages, 1957; articles in various encyclopædias and journals. *Address:* 11 Rusthall Road, Tunbridge Wells, Kent. *Club:* Athenæum.
[Died 8 Nov. 1973.

TRITTON, Major Sir Geoffrey Ernest, 3rd Bt *cr* 1905; CBE 1958 (MBE 1945); DL; Rifle Brigade (TA); *b* 3 Nov. 1900; *s* of Sir Alfred Ernest Tritton, 2nd Bt, and Agneta Elspeth (*d* 1960), *d* of W. M. Campbell; *S* father, 1939; *m* 1925, Mary Patience Winifred, *y d* of late J. Kenneth Foster; one *s* one *d*. *Educ:* Eton; Trinity Coll., Cambridge. Served War of 1939-45 (MBE, French Croix de Guerre, US Bronze Star, Czech. Medal of Merit 1st Class). DL Wiltshire, 1956; High Sheriff of Wiltshire, 1958. *Heir: s* Anthony John Ernest Tritton [*b* 4 March 1927; *m* 1957, Diana, *d* of Rear-Admiral St J. A. Micklethwait, CB, DSO; one *s* one *d*. *Educ:* Eton. Major, 3rd KO Hussars]. *Address:* Stanton House, Highworth, Wiltshire. *T:* Highworth 762923.
[Died 15 Nov. 1976.

TRITTON, Julian Seymour, FICE, FIMechE, MConsE; Consulting Engineer; retired from practice in the firm of Rendel, Palmer & Tritton (Partner, 1929-55; Consultant, 1955-65); *b* Calcutta, 31 Oct. 1889; *er s* of late Sir Seymour Tritton, KBE; *m* 1918, Theodora, *er d* of late Canon W. G. Kerr, Truro; one *s* one *d. Educ:* Rugby Sch.; King's Coll., University of London. Served European War, 1914-18; commissioned RE, in Transportation Branch at WO, and later in Afghanistan Campaign; War of 1939-45: Technical Adviser to India Supply Mission in Washington. Was in charge of firm's Calcutta Branch, 1929-32. President, Instn of Locomotive Engineers, 1947 and 1951; Chairman, Assoc. of Consulting Engineers, 1953-54 and 1955-56; President International Federation of Consulting Engineers (FIDIC), 1955-63 (Hon. Member, 1963); President, Diesel Engineers' and Users' Association, 1962-63; Fellow and Silver Medallist, Royal Society of Arts. *Publications:* Presidential addresses and technical papers before Instn of Locomotive Engineers, Royal Society of Arts, and British Assoc. for Advancement of Science. *Recreations:* golf, bowls. *Address:* Westfield, Steels Lane, Oxshott, Surrey. *T:* Oxshott 2469. *Clubs:* Athenæum, Royal Automobile.   *[Died 13 May 1979.*

TROTT, George Henry, CBE 1946; Director: Blue Star Line Ltd, since 1945; Albion Insurance Co. Ltd, since 1957; *b* 7 May 1889; *m*; one *s* three *d. Educ:* private. Secretary, 1916-20, Manager, 1920-39, Blue Star Line Ltd; Director of Refrigerator Tonnage, Ministry of Food, Sept. 1939-March 1945. *Address:* 17 Newnham House, Loughton, Essex. *T:* 01-508 1119.
                         [Died 24 Jan. 1972.

TROTT, Hon. Sir (William James) Howard, Kt 1943; CBE 1937; President of Frascati Hotel Company Ltd; *b* 1 Feb. 1883; *s* of Thaddeus Trott and Margaret Pearman; *m* 1910, Elmina Morrison Hutchings, Paget, Bermuda; two *s* (and one *s* decd), two *d. Educ:* Whitney Institute; Ontario Business Coll. *Recreations:* golf and tennis. *Address:* Hamilton, Bermuda. *TA:* Trottmore, Bermuda. *T:* 1-2164. *Clubs:* Royal Bermuda Yacht, Hamilton Dinghy; Mid Ocean; Riddell's Bay Golf.
                         [Died 25 July 1971.

TROTTER, Alexander Cooper, CBE 1958; JP; Editor, Scottish Daily Express, 1934-59; Chairman, Beaverbrook newspaper interests in Scotland, 1959-70; *b* 31 Dec. 1902; *s* of A. E. Trotter, Edinburgh; *m* 1925, Sarah Sherry, Portobello; one *s* two *d. Educ:* St Mary's Cathedral Choir School, Edinburgh. Former Vice-Chm., Scottish Tourist Board (Mem. 1946-69); Mem., Countryside Commn, 1969-74. JP: Glasgow 1948; Edinburgh 1975. *Recreation:* newspapers. *Address:* 14 Swanston Cottages, Swanston, Edinburgh EH10. *T:* 031-445 4350. *Clubs:* Press; Royal Scottish Automobile, Arts (Edinburgh); Western (Glasgow).   *[Died 10 Oct. 1975.*

TROTTER, His Honour Richard Stanley; a Circuit Judge (formerly County Court Judge), 1961-73; *b* 29 June 1903; *s* of Thomas Ashton and Alice Howe Trotter; *m* 1946, Ruth Elizabeth Pierce; three *s* one *d. Educ:* Shrewsbury Sch.; Magdalen Coll., Oxford. BA Oxon 1925. Called to the Bar, 1926; practised on Northern Circuit, 1927-61. *Address:* Corner House, Acre Lane, Heswall, Cheshire. *T:* 051-342 2632.
                         [Died 17 Jan. 1974.

TROUGHTON, John Frederick George, CMG 1948; MBE 1936; *b* 24 May 1902; *o s* of late Charles A. J. Troughton and Ellen Troughton; *m* 1st, 1927, Margaret Walker Pike (marr. diss. 1957); three *s* one *d*; 2nd, 1957, Beryl Rose Froome. *Educ:* Rathmines, St Andrews and Trinity Colleges, Dublin. Senior Moderatorship in Mental and Moral Philosophy; Administrative Cadet, Kenya Colony, 1926; LLB (Dublin), 1929; Clerk to Executive and Legislative Councils, 1933; seconded to BBC as Empire News Editor, 1936-38; Deputy Financial Secretary, Kenya, 1939; Economic Secretary, 1944; Financial Secretary, Member for Finance, 1946-49; MLC, 1943-49; Member East Africa Central Legislative Assembly, 1948-49; Controller of Finance in E Africa, Overseas Food Corp., 1949-50, retired; Barrister-at-law, Gray's Inn, 1952; private legal practice, Uganda, 1953-61. Magistrate, Swaziland, 1961-70; Acting Chief Justice, 1965 and subsequent occasions; Puisne Judge and Chairman and Member of various public bodies. *Address:* PO Box 229, Manzini, Swaziland.
                         [Died 22 Jan. 1975.

TROUP, Vice-Adm. Sir James Andrew Gardiner, KBE 1943; CB 1936; *b* Broughty Ferry, Angus, 7 March 1883; 2nd *s* of late Rev. G. E. Troup; *m* 1946, Kathleen Phyllis Simpson, *d* of late William Melvin, Glasgow. *Educ:* Dundee High School; Ascham House, Bournemouth. Battles of Colenso, Spion Kop, Vaalkrantz, Tugela Heights, Relief of Ladysmith, 1899-1900; Boxer War Tientsin and Relief of Pekin, 1900; specially promoted, 1903, for services in South African War; Commander, 1916; Master of the Fleet, 1920-22; Captain, 1922; Captain HM Navigation School, 1928-30; Flag Captain, HMS Revenge, 1930-32; Director of Tactical School, 1933-35; ADC to the King, 1934; Rear-Admiral, 1935; Director of Naval Intelligence, 1935-39; Vice-Admiral, 1938; retired, 1939; Flag Officer in charge Glasgow and District Shipyard Controller, 1940-46. Order of Polonia Restituta, 2nd class, 1944; Commander Legion of Honour and Croix de Guerre with Palm, 1946. *Publication:* On the Bridge, 1934, 4th edn 1952. *Address:* Broom, Auchterarder, Perthshire. *T:* Auchterarder 2254. *Club:* United Service & Royal Aero.   *[Died 11 May 1975.*

TROUT, Sir H(erbert) Leon, Kt 1959; FASA; Director of several Companies; Solicitor; *b* 12 Feb. 1906; *s* of late Walter John Trout and Margaret Alice Trout; *m* 1936, Peggy Elaine Hyland. *Educ:* Brisbane Grammar Sch. Fed. President, Australian Automobile Assoc., 1946; President, Brisbane Chamber of Commerce, 1953-56; Fed. President, Associated Chambers of Commerce of Australia, 1956-59; Member of Exports Payment Insurance Corporation, 1958; Member of Manufacturers' Industries Advisory Council, 1958. President, Liberal Party of Queensland, 1953-57. President, Queensland National Art Gallery Society, 1951-54; Chairman of Trustees, Queensland Art Gallery; President, Queensland Musical Literary self-aid Society for the Blind, 1938-45. Active service overseas with RAAF, War of 1939-45; commissioned rank, Queensland Cameron Highlanders. *Recreations:* golf and bowls. *Address:* Everton House, Dargie Street, Everton Park, Brisbane, Queensland 4053, Australia. *Clubs:* Brisbane (President, 1955, 1956); Royal Queensland Yacht; (Hon. Life Member) Royal Automobile of Queensland (President, 1946, 1947, 1948).
                         [Died 6 March 1978.

TROUTBECK, Sir John Monro, GBE 1955; KCMG 1948 (CMG 1939); *b* 2 Nov. 1894; *s* of John Troutbeck and Harriet Elizabeth Monro; *m* 1924, Katherine Morley; one *d* (and *er d* decd). *Educ:* Westminster Sch.; Christ Church, Oxford. Served European War, 1914-19; entered Foreign Office, 1920; 2nd Secretary, Stambout, 1927; 1st Secretary, Addis Ababa, 1930; Imperial Defence College, 1932; 1st Secretary, Rio de Janeiro, 1933; 1st Secretary, Foreign Office, 1935; 1st Secretary, Prague, 1937; seconded to Ministry of Economic Warfare, 1939-43; Counsellor, Foreign Office, 1943; Assistant Under-Secretary, Foreign Office, 1946-47; Head of British Middle East Office, Cairo, 1947-50; HM Ambassador to Iraq, 1951-54, retired 1954. UK Member of Saar Referendum Commission, 1955. Chairman of Save the Children Fund, 1956-62. *Address:* 28 The Causeway, Horsham, Sussex. *T:* Horsham 5263.   *[Died 28 Sept. 1971.*

TRUETA, Joseph, MA Oxon; MD Barcelona; DSc (*hc*) Oxford, Bogotá; MD (*hc*) Gothenburg, Buenos Aires, Rio de Janeiro; FRCS England; FRCS (Hon.) Canada; FACS (Hon.); (Hon.) FRFPS(G); Hon. Member, National Academy of Medicine, Buenos Aires; Nuffield Professor of Orthopædic Surgery, University of Oxford, 1949-66 (now Emeritus); Fellow, Worcester College, Oxford (Hon. Fellow, 1966); President Congress of International Society of Orthopædic and Traumatic Surgery; Officier de la Légion d'Honneur, 1963; Commander, Order of Southern Cross, Brazil, 1957; Hon. Surgeon, Nuffield Orthopædic Centre; *b* 27 Oct. 1897; *m* 1923, Amelia Llacuna (*d* 1975); three *d. Educ:* Barcelona Institute and Univ. Licentiate in Medicine, 1921; Dr, 1922; Auxiliary Prof. of Surgery, University of Barcelona, 1932; Director of Surgery, General Hospital of Catalonia, University of Barcelona, 1935; Acting Surgeon-in-Charge, Accident Service, Radcliffe Infirmary, Oxford, 1942-44; Member Catalan Society of Surgery, 1928; Founder Spanish Orthopædic Assoc., 1934; Member, Association Française de Chirurgie, 1933; Vice-President, Soc. Internat. de Chirurgie Orthopédique et de Traumatologie, 1954; Hon. Member: British Orthopædic Assoc.; Società Italiana di Ortopedia e Traumatologia; Société Pathologie Renale; Soc. française d'Orthop. et de Traumat.; Deutschen Orthop. Gesellschaft; Soc. Orthop. Scandinavia; Soc. Latino-Americana de Ortop. y Traumat.; Soc. Brasileira de Orthop. e Traumat.; Soc. Argen. de Ortop. y Traumat; Soc. Portuguesa de Ortop.; Soc. Colombiana de Cirugia Ortop. y Traumat.; Soc. Venezolana de Ortop. y Traumat.; Hon. Member Section of Orthopædics, RSM. Visiting Prof. University of Pittsburgh, Ohio State Univ. Coll. of Medicine, 1958, University of Padua, 1960, Univ. of British Columbia, 1970. Associé Etranger, 1949, Académie de Chirurgie, Paris; Hon. Mem., Real Academia de Medicina, Barcelona, 1970; Corresp. Mem., Spanish Orthop. Soc.; Mem. Institut d'Estudis Catalans, 1972. Prix Laborie, 1948; Gold Medal, Univ. of Mérida, 1956; Prix Robert Danis, 1963; Premi Virgili, 1971. *Publications:* Els tumors malignes primitius dels ossos, Barcelona, 1933; La Hidatidosi ossia, Barcelona, 1936; Tractament de les Fractures de Guerra, 1938; Treatment of War

Wounds and Fractures, London, 1939; Principles and Practice of War Surgery, London-St Louis, 1943; The Spirit of Catalonia, 1946; (in collaboration) Studies of the Renal Circulation, 1947; An Atlas of Traumatic Surgery, Oxford, 1949; (in collaboration) A Hand Book of Poliomyelitis, 1956; Studies of the Development and Decay of the Human Frame, 1968; Gathorne Robert Girdlestone, 1971. *Address:* Rambla de Cataluña 74, Barcelona, Spain.   [*Died* 19 *Jan.* 1977.

TRUMAN, Harry S.; President of USA, April 1945-Jan. 1953; *b* Lamar, Barton County, Mo., 8 May 1884; *s* of John Anderson Truman (*d* 1914) and Martha Ellen Young (*d* 1947); *m* 1919, Bess Wallace; one *d*. *Educ:* Public schools in Independence; Field Artillery Sch. (Ft Sill. Okla.), 1917-18; Kansas City Sch. of Law, 1923-25. Operated family farm, 1906-17. First Lieut, Battery F and Captain, Battery D, 129th Field Artillery, 35th Division, US Army, in European War and served in Vosges operations, St Mihiel and Meuse-Argonne offensives, 18 Aug. to 11 Nov. 1918; discharged with rank of Major, USARC, 1919; Colonel, USARC, since 1927; Judge, Jackson County (Mo.) Court, 1922-24, Presiding Judge, 1926-34; elected to United States Senate from Missouri, 1934, and re-elected 1940; served on Appropriations, Enrolled Bills, Military Affairs, Printing, Interstate Commerce, and Public Buildings and Grounds Cttees and as Chairman of the Special Committee to Investigate the National Defense Program; elected Vice-President, 7 Nov. 1944, and took office 20 Jan, 1945; acceded to Presidency, 12 April 1945, on death of President Roosevelt; elected for second term, Nov. 1948-Jan. 1953. Democrat. Member of the Baptist Church; Past Grand Master of Masons of Missouri. *Publications:* Autobiography: Vol. I, Year of Decisions, 1955; Vol. II, Years of Trial and Hope, 1956; Mr Citizen, 1961; *relevant publication:* Harry S. Truman, by Margaret Truman 1973. *Address:* Independence, Mo, USA.   [*Died* 26 *Dec.* 1972.

TRUSCOTT, Sir Eric Homewood Stanham, 2nd Bt, *cr* 1909; MA; *b* 16 Feb. 1898; *o surv. s* of Sir George Wyatt Truscott, 1st Bt, Lord Mayor of London, 1908-09, and Jessie Guthrie (*d* 1921), DGStJ, *e d* of late Geo. Gordon Stanham, architect; *S* father, *m* 1st, 1924, Mary Dorcas (*d* 1948), *d* of late Rev. Canon T. H. Irving, MA; one *s* one *d* ; 2nd, 1950, Marjorie Berta (*d* 1951), *y d* of late Prof. Leonard Trelawny Hobhouse, MA, LittD, and widow of Alfred William Sutton; 3rd, 1953, Renée Franklin, *y d* of John William Marshall, and former wife of William Archibald Redgrave (from whom she obtained a divorce, 1947). *Educ:* Rugby; Trinity Coll., Cambridge. BA 1920; MA 1925; served European War, 1916-18, and War of 1939-45. *Heir:* *s* George James Irving Truscott [*b* 24 Oct. 1929; *m* 1962, Yvonne Dora Nicholson; one *s* one *d*]. *Address:* 27A The Square, Latimer, Chesham, Bucks.   [*Died* 11 *May* 1973.

TRYHORN, Frederick Gerald, CBE 1963; *b* 1893; *s* of Frederick George Tryhorn, Salisbury; *m* 1919, Beryl, *e d* of R. V. Marwood, Ambleside. *Educ:* Liverpool Univ. BSc 1st Hons Chemistry, 1914; DSc 1928. FRIC; Sub-Lt, RNVR, 1917; Lieut, RAF, 1918; Assistant Lecturer, Liverpool Univ., 1919-20; Lecturer on Physical Chemistry, University of Sheffield, 1920-28; Professor of Chemistry, University College, Hull, 1928-46; Director, Forensic Science Laboratories: Nottingham, 1946-52; Wakefield, 1952-54; Harrogate, 1954-58; Forensic Science Adviser, Home Office, 1958-63, retired. *Publications:* contribs to scientific journals; contribs to police science and criminological studies. *Address:* c/o Midland Bank Ltd, Baxtergate, Whitby, Yorks.   [*Died* 17 *April* 1972.

TRYON, 2nd Baron, *cr* 1940; of Durnford; **Charles George Vivian Tryon,** PC 1972; GCVO 1969 (KCVO 1953); KCB 1962; DSO 1945; DL; Brigadier, retired, Grenadier Guards; Keeper of the Privy Purse and Treasurer to the Queen, 1952-71 (Assistant Keeper, 1949-52); a Permanent Lord in Waiting to the Queen, since 1971; *b* 1906; *s* of 1st Baron and Hon. Averil Vivian (*d* 1959), 2nd *d* of 1st Lord Swansea; *S* father, 1940; *m* 1939, Etheldreda Josephine, *d* of late Sir Merrik Burrell, 7th Bt, CBE; one *s* one *d*. *Educ:* Eton. ADC Governor-General of Canada, 1933-34; Commanded 5th Guards Brigade, 1945-46. DL Wilts 1972. Commander, Legion of Honour, 1960. *Heir:* *s* Captain Hon. Anthony George Merrik Tryon, Wessex Yeomanry, T&AVR [*b* 26 May 1940; *m* 1973, Dale Elizabeth, *d* of Barry Harper, Melbourne, Australia; one *s* one *d*]. *Address:* Church Farm House, Great Durnford, near Salisbury, Wilts. *T:* Middle Woodford 281. *Club:* White's.   [*Died* 9 *Nov.* 1976.

TUBB, Carrie, (Mrs A. J. E. Oliveira); singer; *b* Westminster, 17 May 1876; *d* of John Tubb and Anne Bardon; *m* Alexander John Ede Oliveira (*d* 1936). *Educ:* Guildhall School of Music. Made début Covent Garden, 1910 but after a short operatic spell sang mostly on the concert platform, specialising in Mozart and Wagner operatic rôles. Also sang at several festivals, mostly in

oratorios. Retired from singing about 1930 and became a Professor at the Guildhall School of Music until 1958. Made FRCM 1976 on her 100th birthday.   [*Died* 20 *Sept.* 1976.

TUBBS, Francis Ralph, CBE 1960; VMH 1977; MSc, PhD, ARCS, DIC, FIBiol; *b* 8 Oct. 1907; *s* of William Edward and Elizabeth Clara Tubbs; *m* 1939, Helen Beatrice Alice Green; two *s* two *d*. *Educ:* Hackney Downs School; Imperial College of Science. Forbes Medallist, 1928; Research at Rothamsted, 1928-30; Plant Physiologist, Tea Research Institute of Ceylon, 1930-48; Dir, East Malling Research Station, 1949-69. On active service, 1939-45, Lt-Col RARO, The Durham Light Infantry. Officer Order of Orange Nassau, 1946; Chevalier Order of Leopold II, avec Palme, 1946; Croix de Guerre, 1940, avec Palme, 1946. *Publications:* in scientific journals. *Recreations:* gardening and sailing. *Address:* Hayletts, Barton Turf, Norwich NR12 8AZ.   [*Died* 21 *Dec.* 1980.

TUCKER, Baron (Life Peer), *cr* 1950; **Frederick James Tucker,** PC 1945; Kt 1937; a Lord of Appeal in Ordinary, 1950-61; *b* 1888; *s* of Frederick Nugent Tucker and Alice Green; *m* 1918, Benedicta (*d* 1972), *d* of Rev. C. P. Berryman. *Educ:* Winchester; New College, Oxford. Called to the Bar (Inner Temple), 1914; KC 1933; Treasurer of the Inner Temple, 1960. Served as Lieut (General List), European War; Member of General Council of the Bar, 1930-37; Recorder of Southampton, 1936-37; Justice of High Court of Justice, King's Bench Division, 1937-45; a Lord Justice of Appeal, 1945-50; Hon. Fellow New College, Oxford, 1946. *Address:* Fairfield House, Great Bookham, Surrey.   [*Died* 17 *Nov.* 1975.

TUCKER, Prof. Archibald Norman; Professor of East African Languages, School of Oriental and African Studies, University of London, 1951-71, now Emeritus Professor; *b* Cape Town, 10 March 1904; *s* of Norman Tucker and Gertrude Sarah Tucker (née Matthews); *m* 1931, Elizabeth Berthe Hills; four *s* one *d*. *Educ:* South African College School; University of Cape Town; University of London. MA Cape Town 1926; PhD London 1929; DLit London 1949. Linguistic research in Basutoland and Transvaal for Univ. of Cape Town, 1926; Linguistic Expert to Sudan Govt for non-Arabic langs, 1929-31; joined staff of School of Oriental Studies, 1932; Linguistic Research in S Sudan and S Africa on Internat. African Inst. Fellowship, 1932-33; Dinka orthography unification for Sudan Govt, 1938. Conscientious objector during War of 1939-45; foundation member of Peace Pledge Union; served in Pacifist Service Unit in E End Hosp.; subseq. active Mem., Campaign for Nuclear Disarmament. Orthographic Research for Uganda and Kenya Govts in Luganda, Kikuyu and Nilotic langs, 1946-47; launched 1949 (and supervised, 1950-51) Bantu line expedition in Belgian Congo for Internat. African Inst.; research in Uganda, Kenya, and in Southern Sudan, 1949, 1950-51; organized and directed orthography conference, W Uganda, 1954; Vis Prof., Lovanium Univ., Kinshasa, 1963; research expedition in Tanzania, Kenya, Uganda, 1965-66, in which discovered grammatical resemblances between Ik (North Uganda) and Ancient Egyptian; visited and lectured at Univs and Instns in Cape Town, Pretoria, Salisbury, Nairobi, Jerusalem, 1973; Lecture tour, Nairobi and Khartoum Univs, for Inter-Univ. Council, 1975; research in Maltese, 1978. Mem., Exec. Council, Internat. African Inst., 1951-71; Chm., Subcommission on Place-names in Africa south of Sahara. Hon. Fellow, SOAS, 1973. *Publications:* Comparative Phonetics of Suto-Chuana, 1929, rev. and expanded edn, 1969; Primitive Tribal Music and Dancing in the Southern Sudan, 1933; The Disappointed Lion and other stories from the Bari of Central Africa, 1938; The Eastern Sudanic Languages, Vol. I, 1941; (with Mrs E. O. Ashton) Swahili Phonetics, 1943; (with Ashton, Mulira, Ndawula) a Luganda Grammar, 1954; (with J. T. Mpaayei) a Maasai Grammar, 1955; (with M. A. Bryan) Handbook of African Languages, Vol. III, 1956, Linguistic Survey of Northern Bantu Borderland, Vol. IV, 1957; Linguistic Analyses, 1966; (with P. E. Hackett), Le groupe linguistique zande, 1959; numerous articles in Bulletin School of Oriental and African Studies, Africa, African Studies, Kongo-Overzee, Afrika und Übersee, etc. *Recreations:* photography, African music. *Address:* 76 Granville Road, Sevenoaks, Kent TN13 1HA. *T:* Sevenoaks 52572.   [*Died* 16 *July* 1980.

TUCKER, Norman Walter Gwynn, CBE 1956; a Governor of The Royal Ballet since 1957; *b* 24 April 1910; *s* of Walter Edwin and Agnes Janet Tucker. *Educ:* St Paul's School; New College, Oxford. Solo pianist, 1935-39. Civil servant, Treasury, 1939-45 (private sec. to Sir Kingsley Wood, Sir John Anderson (later *cr* Visc. Waverley) and Hugh Dalton). Director of Opera, Sadler's Wells, 1947; Director of Sadler's Wells Theatre, 1951-66. *Recreations:* playing the piano, squash racquets.
                                    [*Died* 10 *Aug.* 1978.

TUDOR DAVIES, William; see Davies, W. T.

TUGENDHAT, Georg, LLD, MSc (Econ.); a founder of the Manchester Oil Refinery Group of Companies, Petrocarbon Ltd and Petrochemicals Ltd; lately one of their Managing Directors; Independent Consultant on energy, chemical and industrial problems; *b* 17 February 1898; *s* of Samuel Tugendhat, Vienna, and Gabriele (*née* Schick); *m* 1934, Maire, *d* of late Major Arthur Charles Littledale, RFA; two *s* two *d*. *Educ:* Vienna University (LLD); London School of Economics (MSc). First Lt KK Schützenregiment 24, Imperial Austrian Army, 1916-18. Arrived in England, 1921. 1922-28: London representative Neue Freie Presse, Vienna; Deutscher Volkswirt, Berlin. Acting Financial Adviser to Austrian Legation in London, 1924-28; London representative of Reichskredit Gesellschaft AG of Berlin, 1930-33. A Gov. and Hon. Fell., London School of Economics and Political Science; Fell. of Royal Economic Soc.; Foreign Mem. Association Française des Techniciens du Pétrole. *Publications:* Sources of Energy; Wanted-A Policy for Fuel; Freedom for Fuel and Dilemma of the State Monopolies; contrib. to: The Times; American, French, German and Belgian economic periodicals. *Recreations:* writing, travelling, music. *Address:* 6 Rutland Court, Knightsbridge, SW7. *T:* 01-589 3015. *Clubs:* Reform, Political Economy.   [*Died 6 April 1973.*

TUKE, Anthony William; Director, Barclays Bank Ltd, 1947-71, retired (Chairman, 1951-62); Fellow of Winchester College, 1956-72 (Warden, 1962-70); Trustee: D'Oyly Carte Opera Trust Ltd; Historic Churches Preservation Trust; *b* 24 Feb. 1897; *s* of William Favill Tuke (*d* 1940) and Eva Marian (*d* 1919), *d* of Martin Nockolds; *m* 1919, Agnes Edna (*d* 1966), *d* of late Henry George Gannaway; one *s* (and two *s* decd). *Educ:* Winchester. Joined Barclays Bank on demobilisation, 1919; Local Dir of Luton Dist, 1923-31; Gen. Man. 1931-46; Vice-Chm., 1946-47; Dep. Chm., 1947-51; Pres. British Bankers' Assoc. 1952-54; Hon. Treas. of St Dunstan's, 1947-57. OSt.J. *Publications:* History of Barclays Bank Ltd (with P. W. Matthews), 1926; Barclays Bank Ltd, 1926-69 (with R. J. H. Gilman), 1972. *Recreations:* fishing, gardening. *Address:* Freelands, Wherwell, Hampshire. *Clubs:* Brooks's, Flyfishers'. [*Died 12 June 1975.*

TULLOCH, Maj.-Gen. (Donald) Derek (Cuthbertson), CB 1955; DSO 1944; MC 1940; late RA; Game Farmer; *b* 28 April 1903; *s* of late Lt-Col D. F. Tulloch, DSO, late RA, and late Diana Mary Tulloch; *m* 1927, Mary, *e d* of late Jonathan Formby, Firwood, Formby, Lancs; two *s*. *Educ:* Temple Grove, Eastbourne; Imperial Service College; Royal Military Academy, Woolwich. 2nd Lt RA 1923; ADC to GOC-in-C, Southern Command, Salisbury, 1926; GSO2, GHQ, BEF, 1939-40; evacuated Dunkirk, 1940; BGS to Maj.-Gen. Wingate, Chindit Operation Burma, 1943-44; BRA Southern Command, 1952-54; General Officer Commanding Singapore Base District, Far ELF, 1954-57, retired. ADC to The Queen, 1953-55. Commissioner, St John Ambulance Brigade, Wiltshire, 1961-66; CStJ. Testimonial of Royal Humane Society on Vellum, 1927. *Publication:* Wingate in Peace and War, 1972. *Recreations:* shooting and fishing. *Address:* The Old Rectory, Rushall, Pewsey, Wiltshire. *Club:* Army and Navy. [*Died 3 July 1974.*

TUNNARD, John (Samuel), ARA 1967; ARCA, NRD; Hand block printer of fabrics; Painter and Designer; teaching at Penzance School of Art; *b* Cæsar's Camp, Sandy, Beds, 7 May 1900; *s* of John Charles and late Nina Tunnard; *m* 1926, Mary May Robertson (*d* 1970); no *c*. *Educ:* Charterhouse; Royal Coll. of Art. Diploma, ARCA 1921; designer on retaining fee to Messrs Tootal, Broadhurst, Lee Co., Textile Manufacturers, 1924-27; art adviser to H. & M. Southwell, Carpet Manufacturers, 1927-29; selector to John Lewis & Co., Oxford Street, 1929-30; visiting teacher in Design to Central School of Arts and Crafts, Southampton Row, 1930. Then gave up all commercial work to paint, and retired to Cornwall; first one-man show of landscapes and still life, Redfern Gallery, 1932; one-man show of abstract painting, Guggenheim Jeune, Cork Street, W1, 1939; one-man show of non-representational painting, Redfern Gallery, 1942; one-man show of gouaches, Nierendorf Gallery, New York, 1945; one-man show, McRoberts and Tunnard Gall., Curzon St, W1, 1959, 1961 and 1964; Durlacher Gallery, New York, 1961; Galleria l'Attico, Rome, 1962; also exhibited at Leicester Galleries, Lefevre Gallery, Leger, Redfern, etc.; pictures purchased by Tate Gallery, Museum of Modern Art, NY, San Francisco, Manchester, Glasgow, Leicester City, Hull, Birmingham, Nat. Gallery of Australia, Melbourne, etc. Member of The London Group. *Recreations:* field botany, bug hunting, bird watching, boating. *Address:* 2 Custom House Lane, Lamorna, Penzance, Cornwall.   [*Died 18 Dec. 1971.*

TUNNICLIFFE, Charles Frederick, OBE 1978; RA 1954 (ARA 1944); RE 1934; ARCA; *b* 1 Dec. 1901; *s* of William and Margaret Tunnicliffe; *m* 1929, Winifred Wonnacott, ARCA (*d* 1969). *Educ:* St James School, Nr Macclesfield; Macclesfield and Manchester Schools of Art; Royal Exhibition Scholarship to Royal College of Art, 1921; Diploma of RCA in Painting, 1923; occupied in painting, engraving, book illustrating. Gold Medal, RSPB, 1975. *Publications:* My Country Book, 1942; Bird Portraiture, 1945; Shorelands Summer Diary, 1952; illustrated Orieltton, by Ronald Lockley, 1977. *Address:* Shorelands, Malltraeth Bay, Bodorgan, Gwynedd.   [*Died 7 Feb. 1979.*

TUPLIN, Prof. William Alfred, DSc, FIMechE, AILocoE; Emeritus Professor of Applied Mechanics, Sheffield University, since 1969 (Professor of Applied Mechanics, and in charge of Post Graduate Dept of Applied Mechanics, 1951-68); formerly Chief Engineer David Brown and Sons (Huddersfield) Ltd and Head of Engineering Research and Development, David Brown Group of companies. DSc Manchester 1939. *Publications:* Torsional Vibration, 1934 (1966); Gear Design, 1962; Involute Gear Geometry, 1962; Great Western Steam, 1958; North Western Steam, 1963; Great Central Steam, 1967; British Steam since 1900, 1969; North Eastern Steam, 1970; Great Northern Steam, 1970; Great Western Saints and Sinners, 1972; Midland Steam, 1973; The Steam Locomotive, 1974. *Address:* Beech Dell, Collegiate Crescent, Sheffield S10 2BA.
          [*Died 7 March 1975.*

TUPOLEV, Andrei Nikolaevich; Hero Socialist Labour (twice); Order of Lenin; aeronautical engineer and designer; *b* 11 Nov. 1888. *Educ:* studied Prof. Zhukovsky, Moscow. Higher Technical Institute. Became a Lieut-General in the Engineering-Technical Service. Helped to found Central Aerodynamical Institute, Moscow, 1918; Asst Director, 1918-35; Head of Designing Bureau, 1922; Chief Engineer, 1923-38; designed first aeroplane to fly from Moscow to New York, 1927; designed TU types and many other airliners. Deputy of the Supreme Soviet; Mem. Acad. of Sciences of USSR; President, Soviet-Bulgarian Friendship Soc., 1957. Hon. FRAeS, 1970. Honoured Worker of Science and Technology, Russian Soviet Federative Socialist Republic, 1933; State Prizes, 1943, 1948; Orders of Lenin, 1947, 1949; Lenin Prize, 1957; Gold Medal, Internat. Aviation Federation, 1959. *Address:* Academy of Sciences of the USSR, Moscow, USSR.   [*Died 23 Dec. 1972.*

TURLE, Henry Bernard, CBE 1958 (OBE 1954); Member Capital Issues Committee, 1946; *b* 18 Sept. 1885; *s* of Edward and Jessie Elizabeth Turle; *m* 1922, Alison Lee Rabett; three *d*. *Educ:* Wellington Coll. In business in India, 1907-16; Indian Army Reserve of Officers, 1916-19; Stockbroker in Calcutta, 1919-28; Stockbroker in London, 1929-56. *Publications:* plays: Miss Smith, 1936; The Old Master, 1938; Marie Antoinette, 1953. *Recreations:* golf, bridge. *Address:* Cedars, Sunninghill, Berks.   [*Died 25 Jan. 1974.*

TURNBULL, Brig. Douglas John Tulloch, CBE 1945; DSO 1941; Regular Army Officer, Royal Horse Artillery; *b* 12 Dec. 1901; *s* of Lt-Col W. J. Turnbull, VD, MICE, and Margaret Stuart Tulloch; *m* 1927, Adelia Brackenbury; three *s*; *m* 1948, Mrs Andrea Warren (*d* 1966), *d* of late Admiral Sir Ernest Troubridge, and late Una, Lady Troubridge; *m* 1968, Mrs Marjorie Benge. *Educ:* Cheltenham Coll.; RMA, Woolwich. Regular Army: India, Egypt, at home, also in Ethiopia (Local Maj.-Gen.); first commission, 1921; served in War of 1939-45: France and Belgium, 1939 till Dunkirk evacuation; Egypt and Libya campaigns, 1940-43 (wounded); Aegean Sea, 1943-45; retired 1954. Kt Commander Royal Order of the Phœnix (Greece), 1945. *Recreations:* hunting, polo, shooting. *Address:* Vine Cottage, Filkins, Lechlade, Glos. *Club:* MCC.
          [*Died 9 Aug. 1973.*

TURNBULL, Lt-Col Sir Hugh Stephenson, KCVO 1937; KBE 1929; KPM; Commissioner of Police for the City of London, 1925-50; *b* 25 Aug. 1882; 3rd *s* of late Maj.-Gen. P. S. Turnbull, IMS, Hon. Surgeon to the King, and late Mary Oliver of Borthaugh, Hawick; *m* 1909, Jean, *d* of late John Grant, MD, of Grantown-on-Spey, Scotland; two *s* one *d*. *Educ:* Merchiston Castle Sch., Edinburgh; Royal Military Coll., Sandhurst. Indian Army; Royal Irish Constabulary; Chief Constable of Argyllshire; Chief Constable of Cumberland and Westmorland; Major, 8th Argyll and Sutherland Highlanders, 1914-16; Lt-Col, 7th Gordon Highlanders, 1916-19; Member, Queen's Body Guard for Scotland (The Royal Company of Archers); Liveryman of Fanmakers' Company; Mem., Highland Society of London. KJStJ, Mem., Scottish Priory, Order of St John of Jerusalem; Officer, Order of House of Orange (Holland); Commander, Legion of Honour (France); Grand Cross, Order of Etoile Noire (France); 2nd class Order of Leopold II

(Belgium), and other Foreign Orders. King's Police Medal, 1936. *Address:* Reidhaven, Grantown-on-Spey, Morayshire. *T:* Grantown 61. *Club:* United Service & Royal Aero.
[Died 9 Jan. 1973.

TURNBULL, Ven. John William; *b* 29 Aug. 1905; 2nd *s* of William and Elizabeth Turnbull; *m* 1938, Alice Trewick Atkinson; one *s* one *d. Educ:* Durham Univ.; Edinburgh Theological Coll. Deacon 1934, Priest 1935, Newcastle Cathedral. Curate of Horton, Northumberland, 1934-36; Curate of Alnwick, 1936-41; Vicar of Longbenton, 1941-48; Vicar of All Saints', Gosforth, 1948-62; Hon. Canon of Newcastle Cathedral, 1958-62; Canon Residentiary of Ripon Cathedral, 1962-72; Archdeacon of Richmond, 1962-76, now Archdeacon Emeritus. *Address:* St Anne's, High Saint Agnesgate, Ripon, North Yorkshire. *T:* Ripon 3270.   *[Died 20 Aug.* 1979.

TURNBULL, Sir Winton (George), Kt 1972; CBE 1968; *b* 13 Dec. 1899; *s* of Adam Turnbull, Winninhorn, Coleraine, and Georgiana Drummond; *g g s* of Adam Turnbull of Campbell Town, Tas; *m* 1947, Beryl Bradley; no *c. Educ:* being resident in country area, was chiefly tutored. Primary Producer until 1922; Live-stock Auctioneer, 1922-40. Served War: AIF (chiefly Malaya) 1940-46 (POW Selerang and Changi, 3½ years). MHR for Wimmera, 1946-49, for Mallee, 1949-72; Australian Govt Dep. Whip, 1956-72; Aust. Parly Country Party Whip and Secretary, 1956-72. Holds undisputed world record for Parliamentary attendance, House of Representatives, Canberra, ACT, Australia, of 26 years and 8 months without missing one sitting day; retired 1972. *Recreations:* various sports; now chiefly retired from football, cricket, show riding etc. *Address:* 41 Putnam Avenue, Bendigo, Victoria 3550, Australia. *T:* (054) 438104. *Clubs:* Australian country clubs only.
[Died 15 Jan. 1980.

TURNER, Sir Alfred Charles; *see* Turner, Sir Victor A. C.

TURNER, Arthur James, CBE 1950; MA, DSc, FTI; Director, 1940-56, of Linen Industry Research Association, Lambeg, Co. Antrim; retired, 1956; *b* 30 Sept. 1889; *s* of A. A. Turner, Camberwell, SE; *m* 1st, 1916, Winifred (*d* 1945), *y d* of Alfred Fisher, Streatham, SW; three *s* one *d* ; 2nd, 1959, Winifred Doris (*d* 1970), *er d* of late Sir Frederick (Joseph) and Lady West, Wilmslow. *Educ:* Wilson's Grammar Sch., Camberwell, SE. Gonville and Caius Coll., Cambridge (Scholar and Research Student). Assistant at National Physical Laboratory, 1912-15; Head of Experimental Fabrics Laboratory, Royal Aircraft Establishment, 1915-19; Prof. of Textile Technology, Manchester Univ., and College of Technology, Manchester, 1919-23; Director, Technological Research Laboratory, Indian Central Cotton Cttee, Bombay, 1924-30; Head of Spinning Dept, British Cotton Industry Research Assoc., Manchester, 1931-40; Member of Flax Development Cttee, Northern Ireland, 1940-56; Member of Flax Cttee, Ministry of Supply, 1942-50; Chairman, Flax Utilisation Sub-Cttee, 1943-50; Member of Council of Textile Institute, 1941-48, Vice-President, 1948-52, President, 1952-54; Adviser to Bombay Textile Research Assoc., 1958. Hon. Assoc. College of Technology, Manchester, 1951. Hon. Liveryman, 1923, and Member of Court, Worshipful Company of Weavers, Upper Warden, 1946, Upper Bailiff, 1962. *Publications:* Quality in Flax, 1955; Technological Reports on Standard Indian Cottons; numerous scientific and technical papers. *Recreations:* gardening, walking, cricket, chess. *Address:* Springfield, 12 Lumley Road, Kendal, Westmorland. *T:* Kendal 22324.   *[Died 30 Sept.* 1971.

TURNER, Maj.-Gen. Cecil Douglas Lovett, CIE 1946; OBE 1943; retired; *b* 25 Feb. 1898; *s* of G. D. Pitt Turner, Bristol; *m* 1928, Frances Joan, *d* of T. W. Morcom-Harneis, Urchfont, Wilts; two *s. Educ:* Denstone; RMC and Staff Coll., Camberley. Joined 5th Royal Mahrattas, 1917; served European War, 1917-18, India; Afghanistan and Waziristan, 1919-22; Brig. Q Plans Ops. and Admin. Co-ordination, GHQ India Command, 1939-46; Lt-Col, 1941; Brigadier, 1943; Maj.-Gen., 1949. *Recreation:* gardening. *Address:* Herbsland House, Hurstbourne Tarrant, Andover, Hants. *T:* Hurstbourne Tarrant 295.
[Died 17 June 1976.

TURNER, Douglas William, JP; *b* 8 Dec. 1894; *m* 1922, Mary Kathleen (*d* 1971), *d* of Alfred Rogers; one *s. Educ:* Repton. Served European War, 1914-18, Warwickshire Yeomanry. Governor of Birmingham Univ. JP Birmingham. *Recreation:* golf. *Address:* Home Lea, Woodbourne Road, Edgbaston, Birmingham. *T:* 021-454 3740. *Clubs:* Conservative, Edgbaston Golf, Moseley Golf (Birmingham).   *[Died 2 Sept.* 1977.

TURNER, Eric, CBE 1968; FCA; Director: Iron Trades Employers Insurance Association Ltd; Iron Trades Mutual

Insurance Co. Ltd; English & Scottish Investors Ltd; Underwriting Member of Lloyd's; *b* 18 July 1918; *o s* of William Edmund and Elsie Turner, Staveley, Derbyshire; *m* 1st, 1943, Zena Doreen Schellenberg (decd); 2nd, Eileen Laura Svrljuga; one *s* one *d. Educ:* Chesterfield Sch. Served India and Burma, War of 1939-45; demobilised, 1946, Lt-Col. Chairman (1955-59) and Managing Director (1951-59), The Blackburn Group; Chairman: BSA, 1961-71 (Chief Exec., 1960-71); Economic League, 1967-72. Member: Malta Industrial Development Board, 1959-65; Advisory Council, Export Credits Guarantee Dept, 1965-70; Pres., Birmingham Chamber of Commerce and Industry, 1971-72. Hon. Treasurer and Chairman of Finance Cttee, University of Aston, 1968-76. Hon. DSc Aston, 1976. *Recreation:* golf. *Address:* Lennoxwood, Windlesham, Surrey. *T:* Ascot 22404. *Club:* Brooks's.   *[Died 21 Sept.* 1980.

TURNER, Vice-Admiral Sir Frederick Richard Gordon, KCB 1943 (CB 1942); OBE 1918; *b* 29 March 1889; *e s* of R. J. Turner, Solihull, Warwickshire; *m* 1914, Emily A. Gregory; one *s* three *d. Educ:* RNE Coll., Keyham. Engineer-in-Chief of the Fleet, 1942-45; retired list, 1945. *Address:* The Friary, 19 St Cross Road, Winchester, Hants.   *[Died 9 Feb.* 1976.

TURNER, Sir George Wilfred, KCB 1950 (CB 1942); KBE 1944; Director: ITT Creed; Goodyear Tyre and Rubber Co. (Great Britain) Ltd; *b* 22 Jan. 1896; *s* of John W. Turner, Rotherham, Yorks; *m* 1921, Elizabeth, *d* of late P. T. Chirgwin, Penzance; one *s.* War Office, 1911-39; Ministry of Supply, 1939-48; Principal Asst Secretary, 1939; Under-Secretary, 1941; Second Secretary, 1942; Permanent Under-Secretary of State for War, 1949-56, retired. Member, Royal Commission on the Police. Served European War in ranks with Grenadier Guards, 1916-19. *Address:* Pentreeve, Gulval, Penzance, Cornwall. *Club:* Reform.
[Died 10 May 1974.

TURNER, H(enry) F(rederic) Lawrence; *b* 30 Dec. 1908; *s* of G. F. Turner, Goring; *m* 1938, E. M. Hartley (marr. diss. 1966); one *s* one *d. Educ:* Radley; Reading Univ.; Exeter Coll., Oxford. Served War of 1939-45, at first in the ranks and later commissioned, RA; served Thailand (prisoner-of-war, Burma Road); lectured on politics during captivity. Contested (C) North Paddington, by-election, 1946, and general election, 1950; MP (C) Oxford, 1950-59; Information Officer, Central Office of Information, 1961-64; later General Manager, Amalgamated Developers Ltd.   *[Died 17 Dec.* 1977.

TURNER, Sir Henry Samuel Edwin, Kt 1946; *b* 18 Aug. 1887; *s* of Samuel Turner and Lillian, *d* of Henry Thorne; *m* 1912, Edith (*d* 1948), *d* of William Rose; two *d* ; *m* 1959, Louise (*d* 1975), *d* of late Ernest Kirk, Batley, Yorks, and *widow* of Marshal Shaw Lodge. *Educ:* Lower School of John Lyon, Harrow. English Civil Service, 1907-19; Board of Education, Ministry of Food; British Economic Section, Peace Conference, Paris; London Manager, NZ Refrigerating Co. Ltd, 1919-22; NZ Manager, NZ Refrigerating Co. Ltd, 1923-39; Controller of Meat and Livestock, Ministry of Food, London, 1940-50; Chairman, Towers & Co. Ltd, 1950-66; former Dir, Express Dairy Co. Ltd; Past President, Canterbury Chamber of Commerce, NZ; Past Vice-President, Associated Chambers of Commerce of NZ. *Recreations:* reading and watching cricket. *Address:* White Lodge, 6 Oliver's Battery Road, Winchester, Hampshire. *Club:* Junior Carlton.   *[Died 28 May* 1978.

TURNER, Herbert Arthur; Assistant Under-Secretary of State, Department of Health and Social Security, since 1968; *b* 9 March 1912; *s* of Thomas Stewart Turner, Rochester, Kent, and Ellen Spice, Bapchild, Kent; *m* 1937, Paule Felicia Gerardine Delecroix, Douvrin, France; two *s* one *d. Educ:* High Storrs Grammar Sch., Sheffield; Sidney Sussex Coll., Cambridge (Scholar). Ministry of Transport: Asst Principal, 1935; Principal, 1939; Asst Secretary, 1944; HM Treasury, 1946-49; Central Economic Planning Staff, 1949-50; Under-Secretary, 1961; Secretary, Forestry Commission, 1950-65; Under-Secretary: Ministry of Land and Natural Resources, 1965-67; Ministry of Social Security, 1967-68. *Recreations:* various. *Address:* 71 Stanley Road, SW14. *Club:* Medway Cruising.
[Died 26 May 1972.

TURNER, Dr J(ohn) W(illiam) Aldren, MA, DM Oxon; FRCP; Neurologist, St Bartholomew's Hospital, since 1946; Neurologist, St Alban's City Hospital and Finchley Memorial Hospital; *b* 13 Feb. 1911; *s* of W. Aldren Turner, CB, MD, FRCP; unmarried. *Educ:* Clifton Coll.; New Coll., Oxford; St Bartholomew's Hospital Medical Coll. BA (Oxon) 1932 (1st class honours Final School of Natural Science); Theodore Williams Scholarship in Anatomy and Gotch Medal in Physiology, University Entrance Scholarship, St Bart's. Walsham Prize in Pathology and Brackenbury Scholarship in

Medicine; BM, BCh (Oxon), 1935; MRCP 1937; DM 1940; FRCP 1946. Resident house appointments at St Bart's, and at National Hospital for Nervous Diseases, Queen Square. Served War of 1939-45, Temp. Lt-Col, RAMC (adviser in Neurology, Southern Command, India). Sub-dean, St Bart's Medical Coll., 1946-50. Examiner in Neurology: University of London; Manchester and Conjoint Board. *Publications:* (joint) Clinical Neurology, 1952; papers on neurological subjects in medical journals. *Recreations:* philately, travel. *Address:* 149 Harley Street, W1. *T:* 01-935 4444; (home) 23 Malvern Court, Onslow Square, SW7. *T:* 01-589 1086. *Club:* Athenæum.
[Died 12 Oct. 1980.

TURNER, Lawrence; *see* Turner, H. F. L.

TURNER, Sir Mark; *see* Turner, Sir Ronald Mark Cunliffe.

TURNER, Sir Michael (William), Kt 1961; CBE 1957; Colonial Police Medal 1956; formerly Chairman and Chief Manager of The Hong-Kong and Shanghai Banking Corporation, retired 1962; *b* 25 April 1905; *s* of late Sir Skinner Turner, HBM Supreme Court at Shanghai, and late Lady Turner; *m* 1938, Wendy Spencer, *d* of late Morris Stranack, Durban, SA; three *s*. *Educ:* Marlborough Coll.; University Coll., Oxford (MA). Joined The Hong-Kong and Shanghai Banking Corporation, 1926. Served in: Hong Kong, Shanghai, Singapore. Interned at Singapore, 1942-45. Former Dir, National Westminster Bank Ltd (Chm.), W Midlands and Wales Regional Bd, 1973-75); Member, London Cttee, The Hong Kong and Shanghai Banking Corp., 1962-. Skinner and Citizen of the City of London; Master of the Skinners Company, 1967-68. FZS (London). Hon. LLD (Hong Kong), 1959. CStJ 1960; Commander, Order of Prince Henry the Navigator (Portugal), 1963. *Recreations:* shooting, fishing, walking, formerly hockey (Oxford Univ., Hockey XI, 1925, 1926). *Address:* Flat 6, 39 Egerton Gardens, SW3. *T:* 01-581 1865. *Clubs:* Overseas Bankers; Vincent's (Oxford); Hong Kong (Hong Kong). *[Died 27 Sept. 1980.*

TURNER, Lt-Col Ralph Beresford, CMG 1919; DSO 1917; *b* 1879; 4th *s* of late E. J. Turner, MA, JP, Hants; *m* 1st, 1908, Ailsa (*d* 1949), *d* of late W. J. and Mrs Scudamore Smith; 2nd, 1950, Maude, *widow* of late Sir Edward Denham, GCMG, KBE. *Educ:* Winchester. Served South African War, 1899-1902, Royal Engineers (despatches, Queen's Medal 2 clasps, King's Medal 2 clasps); Asst Dir Repatriation and Farming in Transvaal, 1903-14; served European War, SW Africa and E Africa, 1914-19, DAQMG 3rd Div. and AQMG GHQ, East Africa Expeditionary Force (despatches 7 times, DSO, CMG); investigating sisal industry, E Africa and Yucatan, 1919-20; investigating inter-trade, South Africa and East Africa, 1922-23; Comr for the Union of South Africa in East African Territories, 1924-39; Kenya Information Officer, 1939-40; DAQMG L. of C. East African Comd, 1940-41; Chief Evacuation Officer, Occupied Territories Administration HQ, Civil Affairs Branch, East African Comd, 1941-47 (despatches); Nairobi Agent, Civil Affairs Directorate, War Office, 1947-49. *Address:* Little Park House, Brimpton, Berks. *T:* Woolhampton 3236.
[Died 29 April 1972.

TURNER, Vice-Adm. Sir Robert Ross, KBE 1946; CB 1937; DSO 1916; Royal Navy, retired; *b* 13 Oct. 1885; *s* of Thomas Turner, Sheffield, and Jessie Alice Ross, Cape Town; *m* 1910, Mabel (*d* 1976), *d* of James Fisher, Barrow-in-Furness; three *s* three *d*. *Educ:* Dulwich Coll. Joined Navy, 1900; Lieut 1906; joined Submarine service; served in HMS Argyll, 1912-14; outbreak of war commanded C 15; transferred to comd D 3, Oct. 1914; commanded E 23, Jan. 1916; Comdr 1917; Captain, 1923; comd First Flotilla, 1924-26; Captain Submarine Depot at Fort Blockhouse, 1927-29; Dep. Dir of Operations Div., 1929-31; idc 1932; Comd HMS Leander, 1933-35; Adm. Supt, Portsmouth Dockyard, 1935-40; Vice-Adm. 1939; retired list, 1939; on active service abroad, 1940; Dir-Gen. of Shipbuilding and Repairs, India, Dec. 1941-44; Senior British Naval Officer, Greece, 1945-46. Kt Comdr Cross of King George I of Greece with crossed swords, 1946; Grand Officer of Order of Orange Nassau, 1949. *Address:* Park Cottage, East Malling, Kent.
[Died 26 June 1977.

TURNER, Sir (Ronald) Mark (Cunliffe), Kt 1946; Chairman, Rio Tinto-Zinc Corporation, since 1975 (Chief Executive, 1975-78); Director: Kleinwort, Benson, Lonsdale Ltd (Deputy Chairman, 1969-77); Whitbread Investment Co. Ltd, and other companies; *b* 29 March 1906; *s* of Christopher Rede Turner and Jill Helen Pickersgill Cunliffe; *m* 1st, 1931, Elizabeth Mary Sutton (marr. diss. 1936); one *d* decd; 2nd, 1939, Margaret Wake; three *s* two *d*. *Educ:* Wellington Coll., Berks, 1924, with M. Samuel & Co. Ltd, Merchant Bankers; Nov. 1934 until outbreak of war with Robert Benson & Co. Ltd, Merchant Bankers; with

Ministry of Economic Warfare, 1939-44; Foreign Office, 1944-45; Under-Secretary Control Office for Germany and Austria, 1945-47. Chairman: Mercantile Credit Co. Ltd, 1957-72; British Home Stores Ltd, 1968-76; Dep. Chm., Kleinwort, Benson Ltd, 1966-71. Dir, Sotheby Parke Bernet Gp Ltd. *Address:* 3 The Grove, Highgate, N6. *T:* 01-340 3421. *Club:* Brooks's.
[Died 13 Dec. 1980.

TURNER, Sir Victor (Alfred Charles), Kt 1947; CSI 1946; CIE 1941; MBE; MA; JP; late ICS; assumed additional Christian name of Victor on receiving knighthood; *b* 12 March 1892; *y s* of late W. C. Turner, Kensington; *m* 1927, Gladys Blanche Hoskins (marr. diss. 1950); one *s* one *d*; *m* 1957, Winifred Bessie Howarth. *Educ:* Emmanuel Coll., Cambridge. Wrangler, 1914; War service, 1914-19, Royal Fus., and Inspector Propellant Explosives, Inspection Dept, Woolwich Arsenal, rank of Captain; arrived in India, 1920, and posted to Lucknow as Asst Comr; Settlement Officer Rae Bareli, 1926-29; Census Supt, UP, 1930-33; Revenue Sec. to UP Govt, 1935; Finance Sec., UP Govt, 1936; Additional Sec., Finance Dept, Govt of India, 1941; Financial Comr for Railways, Govt of India, 1945; Prin. Sec., Finance Dept, 1947; Sec., Min. of Finance, Govt of Pakistan, 1947-50; Financial Adviser to High Comr for Pakistan in London, 1950-54. Economic Adviser to The De La Rue Co. Ltd, 1954-64. *Publications:* Settlement Report of Rae Bareli District, UP, 1929; Census Report of the UP, 1931. *Recreations:* fishing, shooting, etc. *Address:* 4 Windacres, 27 Warren Road, Guildford, Surrey. *[Died 16 Oct. 1974.*

TURNER, Lt-Col Victor Buller, VC 1942; CVO 1966; late Rifle Brigade; *b* 17 Jan. 1900; *s* of late Major Charles Turner, Royal Berkshire Regt; unmarried. *Educ:* Wellington Coll., Berks; RMC Sandhurst. Commnd Rifle Bde, 1918; Iraq, 1919-20 (medal with clasp); War of 1939-45, Middle East, 1941-42 (wounded, VC); retired, 1949. Exon of the Yeomen of the Guard, 1950, Ensign, 1953, Clerk of the Cheque and Adjutant, 1955-67, Lieutenant, HM Body Guard, 1967-70. *Recreation:* shooting. *Address:* Ditchingham Cottage, Bungay, Suffolk. *T:* Bungay 2303. *Club:* Naval and Military. *[Died 7 Aug. 1972.*

TURNER, William Hovell, CIE 1947; CBE 1957; MC 1918; MA; Director of Audit, Indian Accounts in the UK, 1943-56; *b* 10 Sept. 1891; *s* of George Turner, OBE, JP, and Bertha, *d* of W. Eaden Lilley, Cambridge; *m* 1920, May Calder Scott, *d* of Mrs M. C. Turner, Godstowe Sch.; two *s* one *d*. *Educ:* Perse School and Christ's Coll., Cambridge; State Coll. of Washington, USA; Jena Univ., Germany. Served European War, 1914-19, RFA, Major (despatches twice). Junior clerk, India Office, 1919; Private Sec. to Earl of Lytton, Parly Under-Sec. of State, 1920-22; Sec. of Indian Delegn to League of Nations Assembly, 1932 and 1933; Asst Sec. Burma Office, 1940, Min. of Supply, 1943. Head of Indian Home Accounts for many years. *Address:* 26 Connaught Avenue, Loughton, Essex. *T:* 01-502 1108.
[Died 6 March 1979.

TURQUET, Gladys, DLit, MA (London); Professor Emeritus of French Language and Literature, University of London, since 1952 (Professor of French Language and Literature, at Bedford College, 1934-52); *d* of late Alfred Milnes, DLit; *m* 1912, André Turquet, CBE (*d* 1940); one *s* decd. *Educ:* privately; University College, London. Head of French Dept, Westfield College (Univ. of London), 1916-34; Univ. Reader in French, 1921; Dep. Chm. of Convocation, 1936; Mem. Senate, 1936-46. *Publications:* The Influence of Baudelaire in France and England; Some Modern Belgian Writers; Some Modern French Writers (a study in Bergsonism); From Pascal to Proust; Introduction to Mallarmé in English Verse; Poems; Paul Valéry; The Defence and Illustration of the French Language by Joachim du Bellay; Apples I have Picked; contribs to reviews, etc. *Recreation:* music. *Address:* The Ingle Nook, Pound Road, West Wittering, near Chichester, West Sussex. *T:* West Wittering 3012. *[Died 17 Jan. 1977.*

TURVILLE-PETRE, Prof. Edward Oswald Gabriel, FBA 1973; Professor of Ancient Icelandic Literature and Antiquities, Oxford University, 1953-75, now Professor Emeritus (Reader, 1941-53); Student of Christ Church, 1964-75; *b* 25 March 1908; *s* of late O. H. P. Turville-Petre and Margaret Lucy (*née* Cave); *m* 1943, Joan Elizabeth Blomfield; three *s*. *Educ:* Ampleforth; Christ Church, Oxford (MA, BLitt). Studied Icelandic language and literature in Iceland, Scandinavia and Germany. Lecturer, University of Iceland, 1936-38; Hon. Lectr in Modern Icelandic, Univ. of Leeds, 1935-50; Vis. Prof., Univ. of Melbourne, 1965. Corr. Mem. Icelandic Acad. of Sciences, 1959. Hon. DPh Univ. of Iceland, 1961. Kt of Falcon (Ice.), 1956, Comdr, 1963. *Publications:* Víiga-Glúms Saga, 1940 (enlarged edn, 1960); TheHeroic Age of Scandinavia, 1951; Origins of Icelandic Literature, 1953 (2nd edn 1967); Hervarar Saga, 1956; Myth and

Religion of the North, 1964; Nine Norse Studies, 1972; Scaldic Poetry, 1976; (ed jtly) Iceland and the Mediaeval World, 1976; numerous articles in learned journals. *Address:* The Court, Old Headington, Oxford. *T:* Oxford 62502.   *[Died* 17 *Feb.* 1978.

TWEEDDALE, 12th Marquis of, *cr* 1694; **David George Montagu Hay,** GC; Baron, 1488; Earl of Tweeddale, 1646; Earl of Gifford, Viscount Walden, 1694; Baron (UK), 1881; regular attender at House of Lords; *b* Oct. 1921; *s* of Col Lord Edward Hay and Bridget Barclay; *S* kinsman, 1967; *m* 1st, 1946, Sonia Peake (marr. diss. 1958); three *s* (inc. twin *s*); 2nd, 1959, Nella Doreen Dutton; two *s* (twins). *Educ:* Eton. Merchant Service, 1939; Royal Naval Reserve, 1941; retired 1947. Worked in London various private enterprise jobs. Local Director, Martins Bank Ltd, 1955; retired, 1965. Albert Medal, 1941; Lloyd's Medal, 1942; Royal Life Saving Medal, 1943. *Recreations:* philately, entomology, ornithology; striving to exist after dynamic Socialism. *Heir: s* Earl of Gifford. *Address:* Tweeddale House, Gifford, East Lothian. *T:* Gifford 217. *Club:* Puffins (Edinburgh).   *[Died* 23 *Jan.* 1979.

TWEEDSMUIR, Susan, Lady; *d* of Hon. Norman Grosvenor; *m* 1907, John Buchan, author (1st Baron Tweedsmuir, PC, GCMG, GCVO, CH); two *s* one *d* (and one *s* decd). *Educ:* at home. George V Jubilee, George VI Coronation medals. DStJ 1936. Hon. DLitt: McGill Univ., Montreal; Univ. of Toronto. *Publications:* Sword of State; Canada (Britain in Pictures Series); John Buchan by his Wife and Friends; The Lilac and the Rose (autobiography); Winter Bouquet (essays); Cousin Harriet (novel); Dashbury Park (novel); A Stone in the Pool (novel); The Edwardian Lady (social history); *children's books:* Freedom of the Garden, etc; *one act plays:* The Vision at the Inn; The Wife of Flanders. *Recreation:* gardening. *Address:* Hill House, Burford, Oxfordshire. *T:* Burford 2218. *Club:* VAD Ladies'.
          [Died 21 *March* 1977.

TWEEDSMUIR OF BELHELVIE, Baroness *cr* 1970 (Life Peer), of Potterton, Aberdeen; **Priscilla Jean Fortescue Buchan,** PC 1974; *b* 25 Jan. 1915; *d* of late Brig. Alan F. Thomson, DSO; *m* 1934, Major Sir Arthur Lindsay Grant, 11th Bt, Grenadier Guards (killed in action, 1944); two *d*; 2nd, 1948, 2nd Baron Tweedsmuir, CBE, CD; one *d*. *Educ:* England, Germany, France. Contested (C) N Div. of Aberdeen, July 1945; MP (C) Aberdeen South, 1946-66; Delegate Council of Europe, 1950-53; Mem. Commonwealth Parliamentary Delegation, West Indies, 1955; UK Delegate to UN General Assembly, 1960-61; Jt Parly Under-Sec. of State, Scottish Office, 1962-64; Minister of State: Scottish Office, 1970-72; FCO, 1972-74; Principal Dep. Chm. of Cttees, 1974-77; Chm., Select Cttee on European Communities, 1974-77; a Deputy Speaker. Director: Factoryguards, 1966-70; Cunard Steam-ship Co., 1966-68; Cunard Line, 1968-70; Member, Cttee for Exports to Canada. Hon. Col (316 Scottish Command) Bn WRAC/TA, 1958-61. *Publications:* writes for TV and newspapers. *Recreations:* swimming, gardening, bee-keeping. *Address:* 40 Tufton Court, Westminster, SW1. *T:* 01-222 6997; Potterton House, Balmedie, Aberdeenshire. *T:* Balmedie 230.   *[Died* 11 *March* 1978.

TWINING, Richard Haynes, CBE 1959; Member of Council of Foreign Bondholders, 1948-75; *b* 3 Nov. 1889; *s* of Herbert Haynes Twining; *m* 1915, Ellen Irene Rosalind Tweed (*d* 1961); one *s* (killed in Tunisia, 1943). *Educ:* Eton; Magdalen Coll., Oxford. Served European War, 1914-18, in Queen's Royal West Surrey Regt; served War, 1939-46, Home Guard and Civil Defence. Deputy Chairman, The Stock Exchange, London, 1949-58. Trustee of MCC, President, 1964-65, Hon. Life Vice-President, 1969. *Recreations:* cricket (Eton XI, 1907-09, Captain 1909; Oxford University XI, 1910-13, Captain 1912); golf. *Address:* 114 Gloucester Road, SW7. *T:* 01-373 2320. *Clubs:* Buck's, MCC; I Zingari; Free Foresters.   *[Died* 3 *Jan.* 1979.

TWINN, Frank Charles George, CMG 1943; *b* 1 Sept. 1885; *m* 1913, Lilian May Tomlinson (*d* 1971); two *s*. *Educ:* St Olave's Grammar School, London; St John's College, Cambridge. Entered Post Office, 1910; Director of Postal Services and Director of Army Postal Services, 1939-40; Regional Director, South Western Region, GPO, 1940-46. *Recreations:* walking, reading. *Address:* 13 Jordans Close, Boxgrove Road, Guildford, Surrey. *T:* 70076.   *[Died* 22 *Sept.* 1972.

TWOHIG; *see* O'Brien Twohig and O'Brien-Twohig.

TYNAN, Kenneth Peacock, FRSL; Literary Consultant of the National Theatre, 1969-73 (Literary Manager, 1963-69); *b* 2 April 1927; *s* of late Sir Peter Peacock and Letitia Rose Tynan; *m* 1951, Elaine Brimberg (marr. diss. 1964); one *d*; *m* 1967, Kathleen Halton; one *s* one *d*. *Educ:* King Edward's Sch., Birmingham; Magdalen Coll. Oxford. Dramatic Critic of:

Spectator, 1951; Evening Standard, 1952-53; Daily Sketch, 1953-54; Observer, 1954-63; New Yorker, 1958-60. Script Ed., Ealing Films, 1955-57; Ed., TV programme Tempo, 1961-62; Film Critic of Observer, 1964-66. Member Drama Panel, British Council. *Co-produced:* Soldiers, New, 1968. *Devised and part-wrote revues:* Oh, Calcutta!, NY, 1969, London, 1970; Carte Blanche, Phoenix, 1976. *Publications:* He That Plays the King, 1950; Persona Grata, 1953; Alec Guinness, 1954; Bull Fever, 1955; The Quest for Corbett, 1960; Curtains, 1961; Tynan Right and Left, 1967; A View of the English Stage, 1975; The Sound of Two Hands Clapping, 1975; Show People, 1980; edited books on National Theatre productions of The Recruiting Officer, 1965, and Othello, 1966. *Recreations:* sex, eating. *Address:* 20 Thurloe Square, SW7.   *[Died* 26 *July* 1980.

TYNDALL, Sir Arthur, Kt 1955; CMG 1939; MInstCE; FASCE; FNZIE; ACA; Solicitor of the Supreme Court; Judge, Court of Arbitration, New Zealand, 1940-65; *b* Dunedin, Otago, NZ, April 1891; *s* of late A. W. Tyndall, Dunedin; *m* 1916, Gladys Muriel (*d* 1973), *d* of Col A. Stoneham, Gisborne, NZ. *Educ:* Blue Spur Sch.; Lawrence District High Sch.; Otago Univ., Dunedin; Massachusetts Institute of Technology. Joined New Zealand Public Works Dept, 1909; Under-Secretary, Mines Dept, 1934-40; also Director Housing Construction, 1936-40. Hon. LLD Victoria Univ. of Wellington, 1973. Jubilee Medal, 1935; Coronation Medal, 1937 and 1953. *Address:* 5 Gilmer Terrace, Wellington, C1, New Zealand.   *[Died* 27 *June* 1979.

TYNDALL, Rt. Rev. Charles John, DD; *b* 30 May 1900; *m* 1924, Alice O., *d* of Canon R. J. Mitchell, MA, Rector of Cashel and Rathclyne; one *s* one *d*. *Educ:* King's Hospital Sch. (Blue-coat), and Trinity Coll., Dublin. Ordained, 1924; priest, 1925; Hon. Clerical Vicar, Christ Church, 1927; Asst Curate: Clontarf, 1924-29; Leeson Park, 1929; Rector: Enniscorthy, Co. Wexford, 1930-36; Drumcondra with North Strand, 1936-45; Rural Dean of Fingal, 1943; Rector of Calry, Sligo (Elphin and Ardagh), 1945; Archdeacon of Elphin and Ardagh, 1951-55; Bishop of Kilmore and Elphin and Ardagh, 1956-58; Bishop of Derry and Raphoe, 1958-69. DD (Jure Dignitatis), TCD, 1956. *Publications:* The Ancient Parish and Church of St John the Baptist, Sligo; Cavalcade of History. *Recreations:* golf, fishing, gardening, walking, reading. *Address:* c/o Diocesan Office, London Street, Londonderry, N Ireland. *[Died* 3 *April* 1971.

TYNDALL, Maj.-Gen. William Ernest, CB 1946; CBE 1943; MC 1918; BA, MB, DPH England; *b* 27 May 1891; *s* of J. P. Tyndall; *m* 1918, Helen O'Connell Bianconi (*d* 1958); one *s*. *Educ:* Castleknock Coll., Dublin; Trinity Coll., Dublin. Served European War, RAMC, France, 1914-19 (MC); India; BAOR; West Africa; China. Specialist in Pathology; Instructor Anti-gas, SAS, 1929-32. Served War of 1939-45 (despatches, CBE, CB): Norway; ADMS 11th Armoured Div.; DMS, GHQ, Home Forces; Dep. Director-General, AMS War Office; DMS, GHQ, ALFSEA; DDMS, GHQ, Southern Command, UK; KHS, 1948-51; retired, Major-General, 1951. Surgeon, Furness Withy & Co., New York, 1951-56; Adviser, Public Health, GHQ Civil Affairs, 2nd Br. Corps, 1956. Dep. Dir.-Gen., St John Assoc., 1957. CStJ. *Address:* c/o Williams & Glyn's Bank Ltd, Kirkland House, Whitehall, SW1.   *[Died* 20 *March* 1975.

TYSON, Dorothy Estelle Esmé W.; *see* Wynne-Tyson.

TYSON, Geoffrey (William), CIE 1941; Adviser, India, Pakistan, Burma Association, 1953-69 (Secretary, 1953-68); *b* Reigate, 14 June 1898; *s* of Thomas William Tyson and Annie Irwin Smith; *m* Kathleen Corbett; one *s*. *Educ:* Lancaster Royal Grammar Sch.; London School of Economics (University of London). RN Reserve (afloat), 1914-18; Editorial Staffs, Northern Whig, News Agencies; Editor, Capital. Chairman, Public Relations Cttee, Bengal, 1940-45; Publicity Adviser to Bengal Government, 1942-46; Member, Indian Legislative Assembly, 1944-47. Adviser on Public Relations to Indian Jute Mills Assoc., 1947-52. Editor of Capital, Calcutta, 1932-52. *Publications:* Danger in India, 1930; India Arms for Victory, 1942; Forgotten Frontier, 1945; The Bengal Chamber of Commerce, a Centenary Survey, 1953; 100 Years of Banking in Asia and Africa, 1963; Nehru: The Years of Power, 1966; contribs on India and economic topics to reviews, etc; short stories, occasional magazine articles under pseudonym Geoffrey Irwin. *Club:* Oriental.   *[Died* 27 *Aug.* 1971.

TYSON, George Alfred, CMG 1952; FRICS; Consultant to Tysons Ltd, Nairobi (Land, Estate and Managing Agents); *b* 4 Sept. 1888; *m* 1942, Ann (*d* 1958), *d* of late James Macdonald and of Mrs Macdonald, Hill House, Portree, Isle of Skye; two *s*; *m* 1961, Elaine Violet Pryor. Went to Kenya, 1921. Member Nairobi City Council, 1933-; Alderman, 1946; Mayor, 1947-48. Nominated MLC, Kenya, 1953-60. Pres., Associated Chambers

of Commerce of Eastern Africa, 1948. Is a Director of several commercial and financial companies operating in East Africa. *Address:* Mansion House, PO Box 228, Nairobi, Kenya. *T:* (office) 22011, (house) 23675. *Club:* Nairobi (Nairobi).
[*Died* 12 *March* 1972.

TYSON, Sir John (Dawson), KCIE 1947; CSI 1945; CBE 1933; *b* 25 April 1893; *s* of Rev. Henry Tyson and Eliza Baird; *m* 1930, Dorrice (*d* 1965), *d* of A. D. Yuill, Durban; two *d. Educ:* Aldenham; Magdalen Coll., Oxford (MA). Commissioned in Argyll and Sutherland Highlanders (Special Reserve), Aug. 1914; served in France 1915 and 1917; Captain, 1917; entered Indian Civil Service, 1920; Chief Presidency Magistrate of Calcutta, 1926-27; Secretary to Agent of Govt of India in South Africa, 1927-29, and Acting Agent, 1930; Private Sec. to Governor of Bengal, 1930-35, Sec., 1938 and 1945-47; Adviser, Cooch Behar State, 1936; represented Govt of India before West India Royal Commn, 1939; officiated as Sec. to Govt of India, Communications Dept, 1939; Sec., Govt of India, Dept of Education, Health and Lands, 1940-45; Pres., Himalayan Club, 1943-45. *Recreations:* mountain and big game photography. *Address:* Lloyds Bank, 6 Pall Mall, SW1; 462 Musgrave Road, Durban, South Africa. *Clubs:* East India, Sports and Public Schools; Durban Country. [*Died* 1 *July* 1976.

TYZACK, Group Captain John Edward Valentine, CBE 1944; Chairman: John Tyzack & Partners Ltd, 1959-71; Dollar Land Holdings Ltd, 1970-72; *b* 11 Jan. 1904; *s* of late Ernest and Mildred Tyzack; *m* 1935, Carol, *d* of late Alfred and Caroline Davidson; two *s* one *d. Educ:* Harwich High Sch. RAF, 1929-46: served in Aden and Sudan, 1932-36; DAQMG, Palestine, 1936-37; Staff Coll., psa, 1938; HQ British Air Forces in France (despatches), 1939-40; Dep. Dir of Admin. Plans, Air Min., 1940-44; Dep. Dir, of Movements (Air), Air Min., 1944-45; retd at own request, 1946. Dir of Admin. Services, BEA, 1946-52; Man. Dir, Concrete Development Co. Ltd, 1953-56; Chm., Incomes Data Services Ltd, 1965-75. FBIM. *Recreations:* work, enjoyment of all the arts, gardening. *Address:* 50A Davenant Road, Oxford. *Club:* Savile. [*Died* 10 *Dec.* 1979.

U

UHR, Sir Clive Wentworth, Kt 1972; CBE 1961; ChM, FRCA; Senior Radiologist, Brisbane General Hospital, Queensland, since 1938; *m* 1933, Marie J., *d* of T. M. Barry; four *s* two *d.* Chairman: Brisbane Amateur Turf Club, 1952-; Albion Park Trotting Club, 1968-; *Recreations:* racing, watching league football. *Address:* Radiology Department, Brisbane General Hospital, Brisbane, Queensland, Australia; 67 Enderley Road, Ascot, Qld 4007, Australia. *Clubs:* BATC, Tattersall's, Johnsonian, QTC (all in Qld). [*Died* 19 *Sept.* 1974.

ULLMAN, Maj.-Gen. Peter Alfred, CB 1946; OBE 1940; *b* 14 June 1897; *s* of Percy David Ullman; *m* 1929, Elinor Agnes Bradshaw (marr. diss. 1942); one *s* one *d. Educ:* Cheltenham Coll.; RMA Woolwich; Trinity Coll., Cambridge. First commission, 1915, in Royal Engineers; European War, 1914-18, served in France and East Africa (despatches): North-West Frontier, 1923-29 (medal and clasp); War Office, 1934-38; Palestine, 1938-39 (medal and clasp, despatches); Lt-Col 1939; Col 1942; Brigadier, 1947; MEF, 1939-41 (OBE, despatches); Home Forces, 1942-43, CE 2 Corps; Persia and Iraq Command, 1943-44, Chief Engineer; 21 Army Group, 1944-45 (despatches). War Office (Deputy Engineer-in-Chief), 1945; Chief Engineer, South East Asia, 1946-48; retired pay, 1948. *Address:* Rowan Tree Cottage, Effingham Common, Leatherhead, Surrey. *Club:* Army and Navy. [*Died* 12 *Aug.* 1972.

ULLMANN, Prof. Stephen, MA, PhD, DLitt; Professor of the Romance Languages, Oxford University, and Fellow of Trinity College, since 1968; *b* 13 June 1914; *s* of late Dr and Mrs István Ullmann; *m* 1939, Susan Gáspár; one *s* two *d. Educ:* Teachers' Training Coll.; Univ. of Budapest. PhD Budapest, 1936; DLitt Glasgow, 1949; MA Oxford, 1968. Employed by BBC Monitoring Service, 1940-46. Lecturer, from 1950 Senior Lecturer, in Romance Philology and General Linguistics, University of Glasgow, 1946-53; Professor of French Language and Romance Philology, University of Leeds, 1964-68 (Professor of Romance Philology, 1953-64). Visiting Professor: Toronto, 1964, 1966; Michigan, 1965; Canberra, 1974; Sir D. Owen Evans Meml Lectr, UC Wales, 1971-72. Joint Editor of jl Archivum Linguisticum, 1949-64; President: Philological Soc.,

1970-76; Modern Language Assoc., 1973. Hon. FIL 1968. Diamond Jubilee Medal, 1972. *Publications:* Words and their Use, 1951; The Principles of Semantics, 1951, 2nd edn 1957; Précis de sémantique française, 1952, 4th edn 1969; Style in the French Novel, 1957; The Image in the Modern French Novel, 1960; Semantics: An Introduction to the Science of Meaning, 1962; Language and Style, 1964; Meaning and Style, 1973; Words and Their Meanings, 1974; articles and reviews in learned journals. *Address:* 128 Evans Lane, Kidlington, Oxford. *T:* Kidlington 4979. [*Died* 10 *Jan.* 1976.

UNBEGAUN, Prof. Boris Ottokar, MA, DLitt Oxon, D ès L; Professor of Slavic Languages, New York University, since 1965; Professor Emeritus, University of Oxford; *b* 23 Aug. 1898; *s* of late Henri Unbegaun and Gabrielle Koehler; *m* 1928, Helena, *d* of late Ivan Maksouroff; one *d. Educ:* Reformed Church School, Moscow; Constantine Artillery School, St Petersburg; University of Ljubljana, Yugoslavia; Sorbonne; Ecole des Langues Orientales Vivantes, Paris. Served European War, Russian Artillery (twice wounded), 1917-20. Librarian, Institut d'Etudes Slaves, University of Paris, 1925-37; Chargé de Cours, 1936-45 and Professor of Slavonic Philology, 1946-53, Institut de Philologie et d'Histoire Orientales et Slaves, Univ. of Brussels; Maître de Conférences, 1937-45, and Professor of Slavonic Philology, 1946-53, University of Strasbourg; Director of the Slavonic Institute, University of Strasbourg, 1937-53; Prof. of Comparative Slavonic Philology, University of Oxford and Fellow, Brasenose Coll., 1953-65, Emeritus Fellow, 1965. Vis. Prof., Columbia Univ., NY, Yale Univ., Aust. National Univ., Canberra. Hon. Prof., Univs of Brussels and Strasbourg. Associate Mem., Royal Belgian Acad.; Corresp. Member, Akademie der Wissenschaften und der Literatur, Mainz. Chevalier de l'Ordre de Léopold (Belgium), 1948; Commandeur de l'Ordre de la Couronne (Belgium), 1955; Chevalier de la Légion d'Honneur, 1965. *Publications:* Catalogue des Périodiques Slaves des Bibliothèques de Paris, 1929; La Langue russe au XVIe siècle, 1935; Les Débuts de la langue littéraire chez les Serbes, 1935; (ed) Pushkin, Tales of the late I. P. Belkin, 1947; La Religion des anciens Slaves, 1948; Grammaire russe, 1951; A Bibliographical Guide to the Russian Language, 1953; Russian Versification, 1956; Russian Grammar, 1957; Russische Grammatik, 1969; Selected Papers on Russian and Slavonic Philology, 1969; (ed) Drei russische Grammatiken des 18. Jahrhunderts, 1969; Russian Surnames, 1972; various papers in learned journals. *Recreation:* walking. *Address:* 1 Washington Square Village, New York, NY 10012, USA.
[*Died* 4 *March* 1973.

UNDERWOOD, Edgar Ashworth, MD; DLitt; FRCP, FLS, FSS; Chevalier de la Légion d'Honneur; Hon. Research Fellow, formerly Hon. Lecturer, Department of History and Philosophy of Science, University College, London; Member of Board of Studies in the History and Philosophy of Science, 1947-77, and formerly Examiner, University of London; Hunterian Trustee, Royal College of Surgeons, since 1953; President British Society for History of Science, 1957-62; Fellow, Royal Society Medicine (President, 1948-50, and Hon. Secretary, 1942-48, Section of History of Medicine, late Hon. Secretary Section of Epidemiology and Community Medicine; Member, Library Committee, 1938-77); Hon. Fellow, American Medical Association; Corresponding Member of numerous foreign societies for history of medicine, etc; *b* Dumfries, 9 March 1899; *s* of David Underwood and Janet Milligan Grierson; *m* 1928, Embling Halliday, MA (marr. diss.); *m* 1949, Nancy W. Singer; two *d. Educ:* Dumfries Acad. (Modern dux, 1917); Univs of Glasgow (MA 1924; BSc 1924; MB, ChB (Commend.), 1924; DPH, 1926; MD (High Commend.), 1936; Hon. DLitt, 1970; Cullen Medal in materia medica, Hunter Medals in midwifery and in clinical surgery (Sir William Macewen); Vice-Pres., Glasgow Univ. Medico-Chirurgical Soc., 1923-24) and Leeds. Served European War (France), 1917-19, Cameron Highlanders. Hospital and public health posts in Glasgow and County of Lanark, 1925-29; Dep. MOH, Co. Borough of Rotherham, and Med. Supt of Oakwood Hall Sanatorium, 1929-31; Dep. MOH, City of Leeds, and Lectr in Public Health, Univ. of Leeds, 1932-34; MOH, Metrop. Borough of Shoreditch, 1934-37; MOH and Chief Sch. MO, Co. Borough of West Ham, 1937-45; Dir of the Wellcome Inst. of History of Medicine, 1946-64. Thomas Vicary Lectr, RCS, 1946; Guest Lectr, Centenary Meeting of Amer. Med. Assoc., 1947; Fielding H. Garrison Lectr, Amer. Assoc. for History of Medicine, 1947; 2nd John Ash Lectr, Univ. of Birmingham, 1969; FitzPatrick Lectr, RCP, 1971, 1972. *Publications:* A Manual of Tuberculosis, Clinical and Administrative, 3rd edn, 1945; Science Medicine and History, Essays in honour of Charles Singer, 2 vols (ed), 1953; A Short History of Medicine (jt), 1962; memoir on Charles Creighton, the Man and his Work, 1965; (trans. and adapted) Pollak, The Healers (Die Jünger des Hippokrates), 1968; Boerhaave's Men

at Leyden and After, 1977; The Irish Medical Students at the University of Leyden, in Essays in Honour of J. D. H. Widdess, 1978; individual essays on work of 21 Nobel Prizewinners in Encyclopedia of World Biography, 1973; contribs to Chambers's Encyclopædia and the Encyclopædia Britannica; publications on History of Society of Apothecaries of London, 1963 and in progress; papers on historical, epidemiological and statistical subjects in Proc. RSM, Annals of Science, and in other jls. *Recreations:* books, music, mountains. *Address:* Glenmerle, 36 Burwood Park Road, Walton-on-Thames, Surrey KT12 5LH. *T:* Walton-on-Thames 25725. *Club:* Athenæum.
[Died 6 March 1980.

UNDERWOOD, Prof. Eric John, AO 1976; CBE 1963; FRS 1970; FAA 1954; FTS; Emeritus Professor since 1971, and Hon. Research Fellow since 1976, University of Western Australia; *b* London, England, 7 Sept. 1905; 2nd *s* of James and Elizabeth Underwood; *m* 1934, Erica Reid Chandler; two *s* two *d. Educ:* Perth Modern Sch.; Univ. of Western Australia; Cambridge Univ.; Univ. of Wisconsin. Research Officer in Animal Nutrition, Dept of Agriculture, WA, 1931; Hackett Prof. of Agriculture, Dean of Faculty of Agric., and Dir, Inst. of Agric. in Univ. of Western Australia, 1946-70. Part-time Mem. Executive, CSIRO, 1966-75. Hon. degrees: DRurSci New England, 1967; DScAgric Western Australia, 1969; DAgricSc Melbourne, 1973; DSc Wisconsin. *Publications:* Principles of Animal Production, 1946; Trace Elements in Human and Animal Nutrition, 1956, 4th edn 1977 (NY); The Mineral Nutrition of Livestock (CAB Pubn), 1966 (Aberdeen), 2nd edn 1980; about 130 pubns in Agricultural, Veterinary and Biological Research jls. *Recreations:* reading, gardening. *Address:* 3 Cooper Street, Nedlands, WA 6009, Australia.
[Died 19 Aug. 1980.

UNDERWOOD, Leon; artist, sculptor, painter, engraver, writer, inventor; *b* London, 25 Dec. 1890; *m* 1917, Mary Louise Coleman; two *s* one *d. Educ:* Hampden Gurney School; Royal College of Art; Slade School. Studied Holland, Germany, Russia, 1914; served European War, 1914-18, Captain, RE (Camouflage Section); Civil Defence camouflage, 1939, 1942; travelled Iceland, Canada, USA; Mexico, West Africa (1945). Exhibitions: Alpine Gallery, 1923; Chenil Gallery (etchings), 1924; New York, Weyhe Gallery, 1928; Leicester Gallery, 1934; Beaux Arts Gallery, 1936, 1953; Zwemmer Gallery, 1939; Kaplan Gallery, 1961, 1963; Acquavella Galleries, New York, 1962; The Minories, Colchester, 1969; Archer Gall. (sculpture) 1970, (painting) 1971; Agnew Gallery (sculpture and engravings), 1973. Official purchase by Chantrey Bequest, 1964. FRAI. Hon. FRBS, 1962. *Publications: written and illustrated:* Animalia, 1926; The Siamese Cat, 1927 (New York); Art for Heaven's Sake, 1934; Figures in Wood of West Africa, 1947, rev. edn 1973; Masks of West Africa, 1948, rev. edn 1973; Bronzes of West Africa, 1949, rev. edn 1973; *illustrated:* The Music from Behind the Moon (New York), 1926; John Paul Jones (New York), 1927; Red Tiger; Travels in Yucatan and Lesser Known Mexico (New York), 1929. *Address:* 12 Girdlers Road, Brook Green, W14. *T:* 01-603 3517. *[Died 9 Oct.* 1975.

UNGOED-THOMAS, Hon. Sir (Arwyn) Lynn, Kt 1951; QC 1947; **Hon. Mr Justice Ungoed-Thomas;** Judge of Chancery Division, High Court of Justice, since 1962; *b* Carmarthen, 29 June 1904; *s* of late Rev. Evan Ungoed-Thomas and Katherine Howells; *m* 1933, Dorothy, *d* of Jasper Travers Wolfe, Skibbereen, County Cork; two *s* one *d. Educ:* Haileybury Coll.; Magdalen Coll., Oxford (Demy). Reserve Welsh Rugby International XV, 1924. Called to Bar, Inner Temple, 1929; Profumo Prizeman and Yarborough Anderson Exhibitioner of Inner Temple; Member Lincoln's Inn (Bencher, 1951; Treasurer, 1968); Member Gen. Council of the Bar, 1946; Chairman, Chancery Bar Assoc. Served throughout War of 1939-45; Major RA. MP (Lab) Llandaff and Barry Div. of Glamorgan, 1945-Feb. 1950; contested (Lab) Carmarthen, Feb. 1950; MP (Lab) North East Leicester, 1950-62; Solicitor-General, April-Oct. 1951. Member: Cttee on Leasehold Reform (Chm. Lord Uthwatt) appointed by the Lord Chancellor, 1948, and signed Minority Report recommending Leasehold Enfranchisement; Cttee on Naval Courts Martial (Chm. Mr Justice Pilcher) appointed by the First Lord of the Admiralty, 1949; Statute Law Revision Cttee (Chm. Lord Chancellor), 1950; British delegate to Council of Europe, Strasbourg, 1949. *Address:* Royal Courts of Justice, Strand, WC2.
[Died 4 Dec. 1972.

UNMACK, Randall Carter, MA, Docteur de l'Université, Sorbonne, Paris; Headmaster of King's College, Taunton, 1937-65, retired; *b* West Horsley, Surrey, 26 Aug. 1899; *s* of late Rev. E. C. Unmack, DD, formerly Rector of W Horsley, and of Emily, *d* of late Dean West, Ardagh, Ireland; *m* 1933, Anne Roberta (*d* 1972), *d* of late Dr Robert Stuart, Durham; one *s* one *d. Educ:* King's College Sch., Wimbledon; Queen's Coll., Oxford; Sorbonne, Paris. Served in RNAS and RAF, 2nd Lieut; Airship Pilot on Anti-submarine Patrol, 1918-19; taught at Oakham Sch., Rutland, Ecole Normale, Laval, Bristol Grammar Sch. and Mill Hill Sch. between 1921 and 1928; Senior Modern Language Master at Lancing Coll., 1928-33; Headmaster of Doncaster Grammar Sch,, 1933-37. Member Adv. Cttee on Religious Broadcasting, Western Region, 1952-56. Member, Governing Body St Audries Sch., 1960-66. Hon. Fellow, Woodard Corp., 1966; Governor, Cathedral School, Exeter, 1969-73. Order of Menelik II (Ethiopia), class IV, 1953. *Publications:* Education et Décentralisation, Paris, 1927; The Family and Education, London, 1962; articles on education and religious teaching. *Recreations:* travelling, sailing. *Address:* c/o Mrs Hill, Arundel, Victoria Road, Barnstaple, Devon EX32 9HP. *[Died 12 April* 1978.

UNTERMEYER, Louis; author, lecturer, editor; *b* New York City, 1 Oct. 1885; *s* of Emanuel Untermeyer and Julia Michael; *m* 1948, Bryna Ivens; no *c* ; (by previous marriages: three *s*, and one *s* decd). *Educ:* privately and abroad. Contributing Editor to The Masses and The Liberator. Editor of Publications at Office of War Information and Associate Editor of The Armed Services Editions during War of 1939-45. Lectr at various Univs throughout USA, including Michigan, Amherst, Knox, etc. Editor of Decca Records, 1945-58. Consultant in Poetry at Library of Congress in Washington, 1961-63. *Publications:* by 1969 author and editor of more than ninety volumes of prose and verse, including: Challenge, 1914; Roast Leviathan, 1923; Moses, a novel, 1928; Food and Drink, 1932; The Book of Living Verse, 1932; Rainbow in the Sky, 1935; Selected Poems and Parodies, 1935; Heinrich Heine: Paradox and Poet (2 vols), 1937; Play in Poetry, 1937; Modern American Poetry (10th edn 1969); Modern British Poetry (9th edn 1969); A Treasury of Great Poems, 1942; The Wonderful Adventures of Paul Bunyan, 1945; A Treasury of Laughter, 1946; The New England Poets, 1948; The Inner Sanctum, Walt Whitman, 1949; The Best Humor of 1949-50, 1950-51, 1951-52; The Magic Circle, 1952; Makers of the Modern World, 1955; A Treasury of Ribaldry, 1956; Lives of the Poets, 1959 (USA), 1960 (Eng.); The Golden Treasury of Poetry for Young People, 1959; The Britannica Library of Great American Writing, 1960; Collins Albatross Book of Verse, 1962; Long Feud: Selected Poems, 1962; An Uninhibited Treasury of Erotic Poetry, 1963; The Letters of Robert Frost to Louis Untermeyer, 1963; The World's Great Stories, 1964; Labyrinth of Love, 1965; Bygones: An Autobiography, 1965; The Paths of Poetry: Twenty-five Poets from Chaucer to Frost, 1966; Tales of the Ballets, 1968; The Firebringer and other Stories, 1968; The Pursuit of Poetry, 1969; Cat O'Nine Tales, 1971; A Treasury of Great Humor, 1972; 50 Modern American and British Poets, 1973. *Recreations:* piano-playing, gardening and cats. *Address:* Great Hill Road, Newtown, Conn 06470, USA. *[Died 19 Dec.* 1977.

UPJOHN, Baron, *cr* 1963 (Life Peer), of Little Tey; **Gerald Ritchie Upjohn,** PC 1960; Kt 1951; CBE 1945; DL; a Lord of Appeal in Ordinary since 1963; Bencher of Lincoln's Inn, 1948, Treasurer, 1965; *b* 25 Feb. 1903; *y s* of late William Henry Upjohn, KC, and Lucy Upjohn; *m* 1947, Marjorie, *y d* of late Major E. M. Lucas. *Educ:* Eton; Trinity College, Cambridge. Exhibitioner, 1924; 1st Class Mechanical Sciences Tripos, 1925; 1st cl. Pt II Law Tripos, 1926; called to Bar, 1929 (Certif. of Honour); KC 1943; Attorney-General, Duchy of Lancaster, 1947-51; Deputy Chairman Board of Referees, 1946-51; member panel of Chairmen of Tribunal, Coal Industry Nationalisation Act, 1947-51; Judge of Chancery Division, High Court of Justice, 1951-60; Judge of the Restrictive Practices Court, 1956-60; a Lord Justice of Appeal, 1960-63. Member, Statute Law Committee, 1966-70. Hon. Treasurer Gen. Council of Bar, 1946-51. Joined Welsh Guards, 1939; Captain and Technical Adjt 2nd Armoured Bn Welsh Guards, 1941-43; Col 1943-44; Brig. 1944-45; Chief Legal Adviser, Allied Control Commission (Italy), 1943; Vice-Pres. Allied Control Commn, 1944-45 (despatches). Fellow of Eton; Governor of Felsted School. Chm. St George's Hosp. Med. Sch., 1954-64. Hon. Fellow, Trinity College, Cambridge. DL Essex. Officer Legion of Merit, 1946. *Recreation:* fishing. *Address:* 309 Hawkins House, Dolphin Square, SW1. *T:* 01-834 9237; The Old Rectory, Little Tey, Colchester, Essex. *T:* Marks Tey 410. *Clubs:* Athenæum, United University, Pratt's; New Forest Hunt. *[Died 27 Jan.* 1971.

UPJOHN, Howard Emlyn, RDI 1973; FSIAD; Joint Senior Partner, London and Upjohn, since 1960; *b* 26 Dec. 1925; *m* 1953, Hilary Newton; one *d. Educ:* Southgate County Grammar Sch.; Central School of Art (NDD). Designer: Rank Precision Ltd, 1953-55; Thorn Electrical Ltd, 1955-57; Industrial Liaison Officer, Design Council, 1957-60; established design partnership

with Noel London, 1960-; part-time Tutor, Royal College of Art, 1967-. FRSA 1965. *Recreations:* fishing, gardening, furniture restoration. *Address:* Greenbanks, King's Road, Berkhamsted, Herts HP4 3BP. *T:* Berkhamsted 2903. *Club:* (Senior Common Room) Royal College of Art.
[*Died 16 May* 1980.

UPJOHN, Sir William George Dismore, Kt 1958; OBE 1919; ED 1976; MD, MS, FRCS, FRACS, LLD (Melbourne), 1962; Hon. Surgeon to Inpatients and Clinical Lecturer in Surgery, Royal Melbourne Hospital, since 1927; Consulting Surgeon Royal Children's Hospital, Melbourne and Royal Melbourne Hospital; *b* Narrabri, NSW, 16 March 1888; *s* of George Dismore Upjohn; *m* 1927, Norma S., *d* of John Withers; two *s* two *d. Educ:* Wesley Coll.; Melbourne Univ.; Middlesex Hosp. Medical Sch.; London Hosp. Med. Sch. RMO, Clinical Asst and Hon. Surgeon to Outpatients, Melbourne Hosp., 1910-27; Lectr in Surgery and Stewart Lectr in Anatomy, Melbourne Univ., 1912-18. Served in both world wars: Dep. Chm. Central Coordination Cttee, War of 1939-45 (despatches). Lt-Col Australian Army Medical Corps, R of O. Chancellor, Melbourne Univ., 1966-67 (Council, 1958-74; Dep. Chancellor, 1962-66). Mem. Cttee, Greenvale Geriatric Centre, 1959- (Pres., 1959-77); Pres., Royal Melbourne Hosp., 1960. *Publication:* Human Osteology, 1913. *Recreations:* art, music, literature. *Address:* 12 Collins Street, Melbourne, Australia. *Club:* Melbourne (Melbourne). [*Died 19 Jan.* 1979.

UPTON, James Bryan, MBE 1945; TD 1945; JP, DL; Major, retired, Hon. Colonel, 1964; sometime Director of Reckitt & Colman Holdings Ltd (Chairman from firm's formation in 1953 until 1966), retired 1968; *b* 18 Dec. 1900; *e s* of Colonel E. J. Upton, DL and Mary Kathleen Upton (*née* Reckitt), Coptfold Hall, Margaretting, Essex; *m* 1931, Guendolene Price; three *s* one *d. Educ:* Harrow; Trinity College, Cambridge. Westinghouse Airbrake Co., Pittsburgh, USA, 1922; Reckitt & Sons Ltd, 1925, Director, 1930; Director, Reckitt & Colman Ltd, on formation, 1938. Served War of 1939-45, Major (Essex Yeomanry) RHA (prisoner of war 1941-45). Sometime Mem., E. Riding of Yorks TA&VRA (Chm. E Riding TA&AFA, 1956-65). Member: Yorkshire Electricity Board, 1961-71; Council, Hull Univ., 1966-; Past Pres., Hull Chamber of Commerce. JP Kingston-upon-Hull, 1951; DL E Yorks, 1953; High Sheriff, Yorks, 1960. Hon. Colonel: E Riding Yorks Army Cadet Force, 1955-67; 129 Corps Engineer Regt TA, 1964-67. *Recreation:* shooting. *Address:* Hotham House, Hotham, York. *T:* North Cave 2244. *Clubs:* Cavalry and Guards, Lansdowne, MCC.
[*Died 15 Dec.* 1976.

UPTON, Leslie William Stokes, CBE 1967 (MBE 1954); JP; retired as Registrar of the Privy Council (1963-66); Barrister-at-law, Gray's Inn, 1952; *b* 29 June 1900; *yr s* of late Alfred Charles Upton; *m* 1927, Frances, *yr d* of late Richard John Snowden Jesson; one *s. Educ:* Coopers' Company's School. Served with Hon. Artillery Company, 1918; Asst Clerk, War Office, 1918; transferred to Treasury, 1921; 3rd Clerk, 1925; 2nd Clerk, 1937, to the Judicial Cttee of the Privy Council; Chief Clerk, Judicial Cttee of the Privy Council, 1954-63. JP Kent, 1956. *Publications:* contribs to legal jls. *Recreations:* music, motoring. *Address:* 114 Copse Avenue, West Wickham, Kent. *T:* 01-777 3162. *Clubs:* Civil Service, Royal Commonwealth Society.
[*Died 3 Jan.* 1979.

URE, Mary (Eileen), (Mrs Robert Shaw); actress; *b* Glasgow, 18 Feb. 1933; *d* of Colin McGregor Ure and Edith Hannah Eileen (*née* Willis Swinburne); *m* 1st, 1957, John James Osborne, dramatist; 2nd, 1963, Robert Shaw, actor; two *s* two *d. Educ:* The Mount School, York; Central School of Speech Training and Dramatic Art. First stage appearance in Simon and Laura, Opera House, Manchester, 1954; first London appearance in Time Remembered, Lyric, Hammersmith, 1954; other plays include: Hamlet (Ophelia), Brighton, 1955; View from the Bridge, New Watergate, 1956; Look Back in Anger, New York, 1958; Othello (Desdemona) and A Midsummer Night's Dream (Titania), Stratford-on-Avon, 1959; Duel of Angels, New York, 1960; The Crucible, Royal Court, 1960; The Changeling, Royal Court, 1961; Old Times, New York, 1971-72; The Exorcism, Comedy, 1975. Films include: Windom's Way; Look Back in Anger; Sons and Lovers; The Mindbenders; The Luck of Ginger Coffey; Custer of the West, 1966; Where Eagles Dare, 1968; Reflections of Fear, 1971. Has appeared on television in US and England. *Recreations:* travelling, reading, sailing.
[*Died 3 April* 1975.

URLING CLARK, Sir Henry (Laurence), Kt 1950; *b* 2 Jan. 1883; *s* of Edward Clark, JP, Lapsewood, Sydenham Hill; *m* 1910, Norah Ferrand Hooper; one *s* three *d* (and two *s* decd); assumed by Deed Poll, 1950, the surname of Urling Clark. *Educ:* Harrow. Member Stock Exchange, 1904-67; Mem. Hatry Crisis Cttee,

1929; Stock Exchange Benevolent Fund: Chm., 1930-34; Trustee and Manager, 1933-47; Dep. Chm. of Council, 1945-47; Chm. of Council, 1947-49. *Recreation:* gardening. *Address:* Borrowdale, Blanford Road, Reigate, Surrey. *T:* Reigate 43666.
[*Died 15 April* 1975.

URQUHART, David Lauchlan; *see* Tayside, Baron.

UTLEY, Clifton Maxwell; commentator, television and radio newspaper columnist, USA; *b* 31 May 1904; *m* 1931, Frayn Garrick; three *s. Educ:* Univs of Chicago, Munich, and Algiers. Director, Chicago Council on Foreign Relations, 1931-59; commentator, NBC, USA, 1941-59; American commentator, British Broadcasting Corporation, 1945-53. Dupont award for TV and radio commentaries, 1957. Hon. DHL, Illinois Coll., 1946; Hon. LLD, Lawrence Coll., 1945. *Address:* SR Box 110, Hana, Hawaii 96713, USA. *Clubs:* Quadrangle, Commonwealth, Wayfarers' (Chicago). [*Died 19 Jan.* 1978.

UTTERSON-KELSO, Maj.-Gen. John Edward, CB 1943; DSO 1918; OBE 1936; MC; Chairman of Ayrshire T&AFA, 1952-57; *b* 1893; *m* 1915, Florence Mary (*d* 1955), *d* of Rev. Francis Henry Payne-Gallwey; two *d* (one *s* killed 1944). RSF 1912-36; served European War, 1914-18 (DSO and bar, MC and bar, wounded, despatches); Instructor, Netheravon Wing, Small Arms School, 1928-32; Commander, Lines of Communication Troops Palestine and Transjordan, 1936; operations in Palestine, 1936 (OBE); commanded 2nd Bn The Devonshire Regt, 1937-39; Area Commander, 1939; Infantry Brigade Commander, 1939-41; Commander of a Division, 1941; retired pay, 1946. *Address:* Bryn, Clynnog Road, Caernarvon, N Wales.
[*Died 2 Oct.* 1972.

UTTLEY, Alison; *b* 17 Dec. 1884; *d* of Henry Taylor and Hannah Dickens, Castle Top Farm, Cromford, Derbyshire; *m* 1911, James A. Uttley, MSc, MInstCE (*d* 1930); one *s. Educ:* Bakewell Grammar School; Manchester University. BSc Hons Physics. Hon. LittD Manchester, 1970. *Publications:* The Country Child, 1931; Moonshine and Magic, 1932; Candlelight Tales, 1936; Ambush of Young Days, 1937; Adventures of No Ordinary Rabbit, 1937; Mustard, Pepper and Salt, 1938; High Meadows, 1938, new edn 1967; A Traveller in Time, 1939, new edn 1963; Tales of Four Pigs and Brock the Badger, 1939; Adventures of Sam Pig, 1940; Sam Pig goes to Market, 1941; The Farm on the Hill, 1941; Sam Pig and Sally, 1942; Sam Pig at the Circus, 1943; Cuckoo Cherry-tree, 1943; Country Hoard, 1943; When all is done, 1945; The Weathercock, 1945; Country Things, 1946; The Washerwoman's Child (a play), 1947; John Barleycorn, 1948; Carts and Candlesticks, 1948; Buckinghamshire (in the County series), 1950; Sam Pig in Trouble, 1948; Macduff, 1950; The Cobbler's Shop, 1950; Yours ever, Sam Pig, 1951; Plowmen's Clocks, 1952; The Stuff of Dreams, 1953; Sam Pig and the Singing Gate, 1955; Here's a New Day, 1956; A Year in the Country, 1957; Magic in my Pocket, 1957; Tim Rabbit and Company, 1959; The Swans fly over, 1959; Snug and Serena count Twelve, 1959; Snug and Serena go to Town, 1961; Something for Nothing (Essays), 1960; John at the Old Farm, 1960; Sam Pig goes to the Seaside, 1960; The Little Knife who did all the work (Coll. fairy tales), 1962; Wild Honey (Essay), 1962; The Country Child (Penguin), 1963; Cuckoo in June (Essays), 1964; Tim Rabbit's Dozen, 1964; The Sam Pig Story Book, 1965; A Peck of Gold (Essays), 1966; Recipes from an Old Farmhouse, 1966; The Button-Box (Essays), 1968; Lavender Shoes, 1970; A Ten O'Clock Scholar and other essays, 1970; Secret Places (Essays), 1972; Hare and the Rainbow, 1975; Grey Rabbit Books; Brown Mouse books; Little Red Fox books; Cowslip books. *Recreations:* reading, music. *Address:* Thackers, 10 Ellwood Road, Beaconsfield, Bucks. *T:* 3059.
[*Died 7 May* 1976.

UVEDALE OF NORTH END, 1st Baron *cr* 1946, of North End, in the County of Middlesex; **Ambrose Edgar Woodall,** Kt 1931; Resident Surgeon, Manor House Hospital, NW11, 1920-58; *b* 24 April 1885; *2nd s* of late Rev. S. R. Woodall; *m* 1949, Joyce Eleanor, JP, 2nd *d* of late S. H. Holman, Highgate and St Margarets Bay, and *widow* of Rt Hon. H. B. Lees-Smith, PC, MP. *Educ:* Univ. of Manchester. BSc 1905; MB, ChB (Hons), 1908; MSc 1909; MD 1911; FRCS 1916; Civil Surgeon and Capt. RAMC, 1915-19; Surgical Specialist Ministry of Pensions, 1921-24; Medical Adviser, National Union of Railwaymen and other Trade Unions, 1922-58. Member Central Medical War Cttee, 1940-46. *Heir:* none. *Address:* No 1 The Park, NW11. *T:* 01-458 3636. [*Died 28 Feb.* 1974 (*ext*).

UWINS, Cyril Frank, OBE 1943; AFC 1937; FRAeS; retired as a Director; *b* 2 August 1896; *e s* of late Frank Uwins; *m* 1st, 1919, Joyce Marguerite Boucher (*d* 1950); two *d*; 2nd, 1955, Naomi Scott Short, *widow* of Capt. E. D. Short, King's Regt, and *d* of late H. A. Scott-Barrett. *Educ:* Whitgift Sch., Croydon. Served War of 1914-18 in RFC; seconded as Test Pilot to Bristol Aeroplane Co. Ltd, 1918; demobilised 1919; joined Bristol Aeroplane Co. as Chief Test Pilot. Set up World Altitude Record of 43,976 ft in Vickers Vespa, 1932; awarded Britannia Trophy, 1932; British Silver Medal for Aeronautics; Hon. MSc Bristol Univ., 1964. President SBAC, 1956-58; Board Member, Air Registration Board, 1959-64. *Address:* 7 Bathwick Hill, Bath, Som. *Clubs:* United Service & Royal Aero; Bath and County (Bath). *[Died* 11 *Sept.* 1972.

V

VAGHJEE, Sir Harilal Ranchhordas, Kt 1970; Speaker, Legislative Assembly, Mauritius, since 1960; *b* 10 Jan. 1912, Mauritius; *s* of Ranchhordas Vaghjee. *Educ:* Port Louis High Sch., Mauritius. Called to Bar, Middle Temple, 1937. MLC, Mauritius, 1948-59; Vice-Pres., Legislative Council, 1951-57; Minister of Educn and Cultural Affairs, 1957-59. Hon. DCL Mauritius, 1975. Officer, Legion of Honour (France), 1977. *Address:* Government House, Port Louis, Mauritius.
[Died 25 *May* 1979.

VALANTINE, Louis Francis, CBE 1964 (MBE 1956); JP; High Commissioner for The Gambia in London, 1965-68; *b* 7 July 1907; *s* of late René Charles Valantine, JP, Banjul; *m* 1940, Priscilla Ellen, *d* of late Sir John Mahoney, OBE, JP, Banjul; three *s* two *d. Educ:* Hagan St Sch.; Boys' High Sch., Banjul; Fourah Bay Coll., Sierra Leone. BA (Durham), 1930. Joined The Gambia Civil Service, 1933; Administrative Officer, 1949-59; Asst Postmaster General, 1959-60; Postmaster General, 1960-62; Chm. of Public Service Commn, 1962-64; Gambia Comr in London, 1964. JP Banjul, 1960. *Recreations:* reading, walking. *Address:* 9 Picton Street, Banjul, The Gambia.
[Died 1977.

VALE, Brig. Croxton Sillery, CMG 1960; CBE 1946; MC 1918; psc; retired; *b* 23 Feb. 1896; *s* of Dr Charles Sillery Vale of Mathon, and Martha Elizabeth (*née* Crabtree); *m* 1927, Emily (*d* 1956), *d* of John Graham, Belfast; two *d. Educ:* Brighton Coll.; RMC Sandhurst. 2nd Lieut, RASC, 1914. Served European War of 1914-18: France, 1914-18; N Russia, 1919; DADST, N Russia, 1919 (despatches twice). GSO3, WO, 1932; Staff Captain, 44 Div. and HC Area, 1934; Military Attaché, Riga, 1936; DDMI, 1942; Brigadier i/c Admin. and Deputy Fortress Comdr, Gibraltar, 1944; Director of Prisoners of War and Director Graves Registration and Enquiries, War Office, 1947; retired, 1949; Regional Director, Commonwealth War Graves Commission, 1948-61. 4th Class, Order of St Anne, Russia. *Recreation:* golf. *Address:* Flat 65, Furze Croft, Furze Hill, Hove, East Sussex. *T:* Brighton 731805. *[Died* 1 *Nov.* 1975.

VALENTINE, Sir Alec, (Alexander Balmain Bruce), Kt 1964; MA; OStJ; *b* 22 Dec. 1899; *o s* of late Mr and Mrs Milward Valentine (and *g s* of late Prof. A. B. Bruce, DD, of Glasgow); *m* 1936, Beryl, *o c* of late Eng. Capt. F. Barter, RN, and Mrs Barter; one *s* two *d. Educ:* Highgate School; Worcester Coll., Oxford (Scholar, 1918). Dep. Editor, British Commercial Gas Assoc., 1922-27; entered service of Underground Group of Companies, 1928; transferred to London Passenger Transport Board, 1933; Personal Asst to late Frank Pick, 1928-36; Chief Supplies Officer, 1943-47; Chief Commercial Officer, 1945-47; Operating Manager (Railways), 1946-47; Member: Railway (London Plan) Cttee, 1946-48; Railway Executive Cttee, 1947; London Transport Executive, 1947-54; British Transport Commission, 1954-62, and its Southern Area Board, 1955-59; Chairman: London Transport Executive, 1959-62; London Transport Board, 1963-65. Mem., Supervisory Cttee, Channel Tunnel Study Group, 1957-62; Dir, Channel Tunnel Co., 1956-69. Colonel (Commanding) Engineer and Railway Staff Corps, RE, 1963-64. Mem., Oxford University Appointments Cttee, 1955-69. Governor of Highgate School, 1963-69. Pres., Design and Industries Assoc., 1963-64. FCIT (Pres., 1951-52). *Publication:* Tramping Round London by "Fieldfare" (of the Evening News), 1933. *Recreations:* exploring wild country, bird watching, fishing. *Address:* Balmain, Borders Lane, Etchingham, E Sussex TN19 7AE. *T:* Etchingham 220. *Club:* United Oxford & Cambridge University. *[Died* 1 *Dec.* 1977.

VALON, Maj.-Gen. Albert Robert, CB 1943; OBE 1919; MC

1916; CEng, FIMechE; WhE; retired; *b* 9 June 1885; *s* of E. J. D. Valon; British; *m* 1st, 1909, Nellie Hildred Worke (decd); one *s* one *d*; 2nd, 1951, Muriel Irene Hope Potten. *Educ:* University College, London. Commissioned, 1906. Served European War, 1914-18, BEF, France, 1915-19 (OBE, MC); Col RAOC, 1936; Principal Ord. Mech. Engineer, War Office, 1937-40; Dir of Ord. Services (Engrg), WO, 1940; Inspector of Army Ord. Workshop Services, WO, 1940-42; transferred to REME, 1942; Inspector, REME, WO, 1942-43; Col Comdt REME, 1942-51. With British Council, 1945-49. A Director, Plint and Partners, Wargrave-on-Thames, 1955-63; Past President, Whitworth Society. *Address:* Flat 1, Gordon House, 8A Carew Road, Eastbourne, Sussex. *[Died* 2 *June* 1971.

VANDERBILT, Cornelius; author, lecturer, radio commentator, columnist; *b* 30 April 1898; *s* of late Cornelius Vanderbilt and late Grace Graham Wilson; *m* 1st, 1919, Rachel Littleton (div. 1927); 2nd, 1927, Mary Weir Logan (div. 1931); 3rd, 1935, Helen Varner Anderson (div. 1940); 4th, 1946, Maria Pablos (div. 1947); 5th, 1948, Patricia Murphy Wallace (div. 1953); 6th, 1957, Ann Needham (div. 1960); 7th, 1967, Mrs Gardner Bristol; no *c. Educ:* private and public schools in Europe and USA. 27th Division (USA) HQ Troop, AEF, 1917-19, private; Lieut; Captain; Major MI, US Army Reserve Corps, 1919-41; Inspector-General Army Transports, 1941-42; Croix de la Croix Rouge (France); FBI Distinguished Service Cross (US); Abdon Cauldron (Ecuador); invalided Walter Reed Army Hospital, Washington, DC, Nov. 1942-July 1943, retired US Army, Aug. 1943. Reporter NY Herald, 1918-20; political correspondent NY Times, Albany, NY, March-Oct. 1920; congressional correspondent, NY Times, Washington, DC, Nov. 1920-June 1921; Washington correspondent, Universal News Service, 1921-23; editor and publisher, Los Angeles Illustrated Daily News, 1923-27; editor and publisher, San Francisco Daily Herald and Miami, Florida, Daily Tab., 1923, 1927; associate editor, NY Daily Mirror, 1927, 1929; roving correspondent, United Press, 1929, 1930; editorial staff, Liberty Weekly, 1931-41; Washington Columnist, New York Post Syndicate, Aug. 1943-Aug. 1945; national survey chief of the Roosevelt party, April-Nov. 1932; national survey man for Democratic National Cttee, 1932-33, 1936-37 and 1940-41. Edited and published Vagabonding with Vanderbilt Inc., 1952-65. Vice-President, American Film Prod., Inc., 1960-65. *Publications:* Lines from the Front Lines, 1918; The Gas Attack, 1919; Experiences of a Cub Reporter, 1920; Experiences of a Legislative Correspondent, 1921; Experiences of a Washington Correspondent, 1922; The Far West, 1923; Symposium on Japanese-American Relations, 1925; Reno, 1927; Park Avenue, 1928; Palm Beach, 1929; Farewell to Fifth Avenue, 1935; A Woman of Washington, 1936; Filthy Rich, 1939; The Vanderbilt Feud, 1957; Man of the World, 1959. *Recreations:* horseback-riding, shooting, motoring, chess. *Address:* Box 654, Reno, USA. *[Died* 7 *July* 1974.

van der BYL, Major Hon. Pieter Voltelyn Graham, MC; MA Cantab; LLD; JP; farmer and landowner; Deputy Chairman, South African Mutual Life Assurance Society; Director: Mortgage Investment Corp. Ltd; Fire & General Insurance Co. Ltd; Investment Corp.; Rhodesia Corp., and other companies; *b* 21 Feb. 1889; *m* 1922, Joy Clare, *d* of late Colonel and Mrs S. Fleming; two *s. Educ:* Diocesan Coll., Rondebosch; Pembroke Coll., Cambridge (Rowing "Blue" 1911). SW African Campaign, 1914-15; E African Campaign, 1916-17; GHQ Royal Air Force, 1918-19 (despatches twice, MC, Chevalier Légion d'Honneur (France), Cross of Merit of Netherlands Red Cross). Entered Parliament, 1929; Cabinet Minister, 1939-48; Minister of Native Affairs, 1943-48; retired from politics, 1966. Leader South African Delegation International Affairs Conference on Commonwealth Relationships at Sydney, 1938; Past President, Western Province Agric. Society. Hon. Colonel, UCT Regt. Hon. LLD Rhodes. *Publications:* From Playgrounds to Battlefields; Tophat to Velskoen; The Shadows Lengthen. *Address:* Fairfield, Caledon, South Africa. *Clubs:* Royal Air Force, Leander (England); (President) Civil Service, Olympic Sports, Western Province Sports, SA Turf, Cape Turf (Cape Town); Country (Johannesburg) and others.
[Died 21 *Jan.* 1975.

van RHYN, Albertus Johannes Roux, MSc, PhD; *b* 7 July 1890; *s* of Gerhardus Petrus van Rhyn and Aletta (*née* Roux); *m* 1917, Miriam Héléne de Villiers; one *s* two *d. Educ:* Univ. of Stellenbosch, S Africa; Frankfurt A/M, Germany. Stellenbosch, 1910-20 (BA, MSc); Frankfurt A/M, 1921 (PhD). Lecturer in Chemistry, University of Stellenbosch, 1919-20; Principal, High School, Calvinia, 1921-25; Editor in Chief, Volksblad, 1925-48; Member of Parliament, 1948-51; Administrator of South West Africa, 1951-53; Minister of Mines and Economic Affairs, S

Africa, 1953-58; High Comr in London, Dec. 1958-61. *Recreations:* hunting, tennis. *Address:* 43 Paul Roux Street, Bloemfontein, OFS, S Africa.   *[Died 31 Dec. 1971.*

VAN RYNEVELD, Gen. Sir Pierre, KBE 1920; CB 1945; DSO 1919; MC; *b* Orange Free State, 2 May 1891; *s* of late D. J. Van Ryneveld, JP, Theunissen; *m* 1931, Edith S. (*d* 1971), *yr d* of late Rev. E. K. Graham, MA, Warwickshire. *Educ:* Grey College School and Grey Univ. Coll., South Africa; Imperial Coll., Univ. of London. BA Cape of Good Hope, 1909; BSc London, 1914. FCGI, Fellow Imperial College of Science. Commissioned Loyal North Lancashire Regt, 2 Sept. 1914; transferred RFC April 1915; served Egypt (Western Frontier and Palestine), Salonika, France, Army Occupation; SA Liaison at Air Ministry (with the RFC and RAF); Pioneer Flight from London to Cape Town via Cairo, 1920; Commandant, SA Military Coll., 1929; Officer Commanding Troops, Roberts' Heights, 1929; Chairman, Civil Air Board, 1931; Chief of the General Staff, Union Defence Forces, 1933-49; retired, 1949. *Address:* Spitzkop, Bronkhorstspruit, Transvaal, South Africa. *Clubs:* Pretoria (Pretoria); Bulawayo (Bulawayo).   *[Died 2 Dec. 1972.*

VAN VLECK, Prof. John Hasbrouck; Hollis Professor of Mathematics and Natural Philosophy, Harvard University, 1951-69, now Professor Emeritus; *b* 13 March 1899; *s* of Edward Burr Van Vleck and Hester Raymond Van Vleck; *m* 1927, Abigail Pearson; no *c. Educ:* Wisconsin Univ.; Harvard Univ. AB Wisconsin, 1920; AM 1921, PhD 1922, Harvard. Instructor, Harvard Univ., 1922-23; Asst Prof., then Prof., Minnesota Univ., 1923-28; Prof., Wisconsin Univ., 1928-34; Harvard Univ.: Assoc. Prof., 1934-35; Prof., 1935-69; Head of Theory Group, Radio Res. Lab., 1943-45; Dean of Engineering and Applied Physics, 1951-57. Guggenheim Fellow, 1930; Lorentz Visiting Prof., Leiden Univ., 1960; Eastman Prof., Oxford Univ., 1961-62; Visiting Lecturer, various universities; member numerous scientific societies; President, American Phys. Soc., 1952-53; MNAS; Member: Amer. Philosoph. Soc.; Amer. Acad. of Arts and Sciences; Internat. Acad. of Quantum Chem.; Foreign Member: Royal Society, London; Royal Netherlands Acad. of Science; Royal Swedish Acad. of Science; Royal Uppsala Acad. of Science; Foreign Associate, Académie des Sciences, France; Hon. Member, Phys. Soc. of France. Hon. ScD: Wesleyan, 1936; Wisconsin, 1947; Maryland, 1955; Oxford, 1958; Rockford Coll., 1962; Harvard, 1966; Chicago, 1968; Minnesota, 1971; Dr *hc*: Grenoble, 1950; Paris, 1960; Nancy, 1961. Michelson Prize, Case Inst. of Technology, 1963; Langmuir Award, American Phys. Society, 1965; National Medal of Science, US, 1966; Cresson Medal, Franklin Inst., 1971; Lorentz Medal, Netherlands Acad., 1974; (jtly) Nobel Prize for Physics, 1977. Chevalier, Légion d'Honneur, 1970. *Publications:* Quantum Principles and Line Spectra, 1926; The Theory of Electric and Magnetic Susceptibilities, 1932. *Address:* Lyman Laboratory of Physics, Harvard University, Cambridge, Mass 02138, USA. *T:* 547-1427. *Clubs:* Harvard (New York and Boston).
[Died 27 Oct. 1980.

van ZEELAND, Paul, (Vicomte); Croix de Guerre avec Palme; Médaille de la Victoire; Médaille Commémorative; Croix Civique; Grand Cordon de l'Ordre de la Couronne; Ministre D'Etat Belgium; Hon. Président de la Banque Belge d'Afrique; Professor Émérite at Louvain University; *b* Soignies, 11 Nov. 1893; *m* 1926, Renée, *o d* of Gen. Baron Dossin de St Georges; two *s* two *d. Educ:* Louvain University (Doctor at Law, Doctor in Political and Diplomatic Sciences, PhB); Princeton Univ., USA (MA Econ), Hon. LLD, Princeton and Brown; Hon. DCL Wesleyan; Hon. Doctor, Costa Rica; Docteur (*hc*) en Sciences Sociales de la Faculté de Philosophie et Lettres, Juiz de Fora, Brésil; Mem., American Philosophical Soc. of Philadelphia; Membre de l'Académie Méditerranéenne; Membre de l'Institut de France. Formerly: Prime Minister; President Assembly of the League of Nations; Minister of Foreign Affairs and Foreign Trade; Member of Cabinet; Senator. Pres. Belgian Commission pour l'Etude des Problèmes d'Après-Guerre; Director Institute of Economic Sciences of Univ. of Louvain; Vice-Governor Banque Nationale de Belgique; Deputy Director Bank for International Settlements; Belgian commissioner for Repatriation; President: Co-ordinating Foundation for Refugees; OEEC; Cttee of Ministers of Council of Europe. Council of Governors, Atlantic Institute; Founder and Hon. Pres., European League of Economic Co-operation; Conseillier Général, Administrateur de la Banque de Bruxelles. Holds numerous foreign decorations and orders. *Publications:* La Réforme bancaire aux Etats-Unis d'Amérique de 1913 à 1921, 1922; Réflexions sur le plan quinquennal, 1931; Regards sur l'Europe 1932, 1933; Report to the Governments of the United Kingdom and France on the Possibility of Obtaining a General Reduction of the Obstacles to International Trade, 1938;

numerous articles. *Address:* La Maison Flamande, 7 Avenue Charles Albert, 1170 Brussels.   *[Died 22 Sept. 1973.*

VARIN, René Louis; Croix de Guerre, 1916; Médaille de la Résistance, 1945; Comdr, Légion d'Honneur, 1958; Inspector-General of English Teaching in State Schools, France, 1959; *b* 13 Feb. 1896; *s* of Edouard Varin and Sophie de Vignacourt; *m* 1921, Germaine Bessé; one *s* four *d. Educ:* La Sorbonne (Agrégé d'Univ.); University Coll., London. Lecturer in French: Nevers, 1920; Rambouillet, 1922; Versailles, 1926; Inspector General of Education, 1946; Dep. Director of Cultural Relations, Ministry of Foreign Affairs, 1940. Served European War, 1914-18, in Infantry and French Air Force, 1915-19; Major, French Air Force, 1939-40; French Rep. at Air Executive Cttee, London, 1940; Cultural Counsellor, The French Embassy, 1945-59. CBE (Hon.) 1946; DCL (Hon.) Oxford, 1952; KCSG 1955. *Publications:* articles in reviews, literary and linguistic magazines. *Recreations:* art, book collecting. *Address:* 25 bis, rue Alexis Fourcault, Versailles, Seine-et-Oise, France. *Club:* Athenæum.   *[Died 23 April 1976.*

VAUGHAN, Brig. (Charles) Hilary (Vaughan), DSO 1944; DL; JP; late Royal Welch Fusiliers and Adjutant 60th AT Regiment RA (TA); *b* 29 Oct. 1905; *e s* of Col C. H. Pritchard, Indian Political Service; *m* 1935, Hon. Mary Patricia Monck, *yr* sister of 6th Viscount Monck, OBE; four *d. Educ:* Sherborne: Trinity Hall, Cambridge (BA). Changed name by deed poll from Pritchard to Vaughan (his mother's maiden name) on inheriting the Nannau Estates in N Wales, Nov. 1956. Joined Royal Welch Fusiliers, 1927; ADC to Gov. and C-in-C, Gibraltar, 1931-32; Adjt, Depot RWF, 1933-34. Staff College, Camberley, 1939; served War of 1939-45: N Africa, Italy, S France, Greece, Palestine; MO4, War Office, 1940-42; 2nd in Comd 70th Bn RWF, Temp. Lt-Col, 1942; Comd 6th (Royal Welch) Bn The Parachute Regt, Temp. Col, 1943; Brig. 1943; Comd 2nd Indep. Parachute Bde Group, 1943-46; Comdr Airborne Establishments, 1946-48; Comdg Officer 10th Cadet Bn RWF; retd 1949. DL, JP 1950; High Sheriff, Merioneth, 1956-58. Now engaged in farming and running his estate. Commander, Royal Order of George I with Swords (Greece). *Address:* Nannau Home Farm, Dolgellau, Gwynedd. *T:* 674.
[Died 28 March 1976.

VAUGHAN, Brig. Hilary; *see* Vaughan, Brig. C. H. V.

VAUGHAN, (John) Keith, CBE 1965; painter, designer, illustrator; Tutor at Slade School of Art, London; *b* 23 Aug. 1912; *e s* of E. G. S. Vaughan, civil engineer, and Gladys Regina Marion (*née* Mackintosh); unmarried. *Educ:* Christ's Hospital. Mem. Faculty of Painting, British School at Rome, 1962; Advisory Cttee for Painting, Gulbenkian Foundation, 1964; Hon. Fellow Royal Coll. of Art, 1964. First exhibited at Lefevre Gallery, 1942. One-man shows at following galleries: Lefevre, 1944, 1946, 1948, 1951; Redfern, 1950, 1952; Hanover, 1951; Durlacher, New York, 1948, 1952, 1955, 1957, 1966; Inst. of Modern Art, Buenos Aires, 1950; Leicester Galls, London, 1953, 1955, 1956, 1958, 1959; Matthiesen Gall., London, 1960; Whitechapel Art Gall., 1962; Sao Paulo Bienal, 1963; Marlborough Gall., London, 1964, 1965, 1969; Waddington Galls, 1973, 1974. Works in public collections: Tate Gall., Arts Council, British Council, Contemporary Art Society; Balliol College, Oxford; Fitzwilliam Museum, Cambridge; Nat. Gall. of Scotland, Edinburgh; Municipal Galleries of Leeds, Manchester, Wakefield, Birmingham, Leicester, Newcastle, Bristol, Huddersfield, Aberdeen, Bolton; Univ. of Kent; Phillips Collection, Washington DC; Stuyvesant Collection; Art Inst. of Chicago; Norwich Castle Museum; Glynn Vivian Gall., Swansea; NSW Gallery; Nottingham Museum; Christ Church College, Oxford; V&A Museum, London; Whitworth Museum, Manchester; Museum of Modern Art, New York; Albright Museum, Buffalo; Toronto Art Gallery; Wadsworth Athenæum, Connecticut; Tel Aviv Museum; City of Auckland Gallery, New Zealand; State University of Iowa, USA. Executed central mural in Dome of Discovery, Festival of Britain, 1951; mural for Aboyne Estate, Wandsworth, 1963 (LCC Commn). Member of Arts Panel, Arts Council of Great Britain, 1956, 1959. *Publications:* books illustrated: Tom Sawyer, 1947; Rimbaud, Une Saison en Enfer, 1949; Journal and Drawings, 1939-65, 1966. *Address:* 9 Belsize Park, NW3; Harrow Hill, Toppesfield, Halstead, Essex.   *[Died 4 Nov. 1977.*

VAUGHAN, Keith; *see* Vaughan, John Keith.

VAUX OF HARROWDEN, 9th Baron *cr* 1523; **Rev. Peter Hubert Gordon Gilbey,** OSB, MA; Rector of St Mary's Catholic Church, Warrington, since 1962; *b* 28 June 1914; *e s* of William

Gordon Gilbey and Grace Mary Eleanor, 8th Baroness Vaux of Harrowden; *S* mother, 1958. *Educ:* Ampleforth College; St Benet's Hall, Oxford. Became a Benedictine monk at Ampleforth, 1932; ordained at Ampleforth, 1940; Asst Master at Ampleforth College, 1939-53; Asst Priest at St Mary's Catholic Church, Cardiff, 1953-57; subseq. at St Alban's, Warrington. *Heir: b* Hon. John Hugh Philip Gilbey [*b* 4 Aug. 1915; *m* 1939, Maureen Pamela Gilbey; three *s* one *d*]. *Address:* St Mary's Priory, Buttermarket Street, Warrington, Cheshire WA1 2NS. *T:* Warrington 35664.   [*Died* 1 *Nov.* 1977.

VEALE, Sir Douglas, Kt 1954; CBE 1929; Hon. LLD Melbourne; Hon. DCL Oxford; Registrar of University of Oxford, 1930-58, retired; Fellow of Corpus Christi College, 1930-58; Hon. Fellow of Corpus Christi College; Hon. Fellow (formerly Trustee) of St Edmund Hall, 1958; Secretary, Oxford Preservation Trust, 1958-62, Trustee, 1962; *b* 2 April 1891; 3rd *s* of Edward Woodhouse Veale and Maud Mary Rootham; *m* 1914, Evelyn Annie (*d* 1970), *d* of J. A. Henderson; one *s* two *d*. *Educ:* Bristol Grammar Sch.; Corpus Christi Coll., Oxford (1st Mods 1912, 2nd Greats, 1914, MA 1930). Second Class Clerk, Local Government Board, 1914; Private Sec. to Permanent Sec., Ministry of Health, 1920; Private Secretary to Dr Addison and successive Ministers of Health, 1921-28; Principal, 1926. Served European War, France and Belgium, with 4th Bn Gloucester Regiment (1915); subsequently Adjutant of Reserve Battalion. *Address:* 94 Lonsdale Road, Oxford. *T:* 55199. *Club:* United Oxford & Cambridge University.   [*Died* 27 *Sept.* 1973.

VEALE, Hon. Sir Geoffrey, Kt 1961; **Hon. Mr Justice Veale;** Judge of the High Court of Justice (Queen's Bench Division) since 1961; *b* 12 Jan. 1906; *s* of late Dr Henry Veale, Clifford House, Ilkley; *m* 1937, Elizabeth Patricia Barrow; one *d*. *Educ:* Rugby; Oriel College, Oxford. BA, BCL Oxon. Called to the Bar, 1929; Bencher, Inner Temple, 1959; KC 1951. Chairman Ilkley UDC, 1936; Recorder of Scarborough, 1950-51; Recorder of Sunderland, 1951-54; Recorder of Kingston upon Hull, 1954-57; Recorder of Leeds, 1957-61. Dep. Chm.: NR Yorks Quarter Sessions, 1949-54; WR Yorks Quarter Sessions, 1954-61; Solicitor-General of the County Palatine of Durham, 1955-57; Attorney-General of the County Palatine of Durham, 1957-61. Served War of 1939-45, 4 years' service Middle East (despatches); Colonel, Deputy Judge Advocate General to Middle East forces, 1944. Hon. LLD Leeds, 1966. *Recreation:* shooting. *Address:* West House, Wetherby, Yorks. *T:* Wetherby 2130; 26 Montpelier Walk, SW7. *T:* 01-589 6965. *Club:* Oxford and Cambridge University.   [*Died* 29 *Dec.* 1971.

VEITCH, Allan, CBE 1960 (OBE 1953; MBE 1947); *b* 23 May 1900. Served at Hankow, 1927; Kunming, 1930; Shanghai, 1938; Chungking, 1942. Higher Executive Officer, 1943; Nanking, 1946; Actg Consul-Gen., Kunming, 1946; Consul and Actg Consul-Gen., Hankow, 1946; Consul-Gen., Chungking, 1947; Consul, Los Angeles, 1948; Consul, and Consul-General, Shanghai, 1950-54; Counsellor, HM Embassy, Bonn, 1955-57; HM Consul at Tamsui, 1958-60; retired, 1960. *Address:* c/o Lloyds Bank Ltd, Cox's & King's Branch, 6 Pall Mall, SW1.   [*Died* 21 *May* 1971.

VEITCH, Marian, (Mrs Donald Barnie); National Woman Officer, General and Municipal Workers Union, 1960-70; *b* 8 July 1913; *d* of Arthur Edward and Elizabeth Veitch; *m* 1965, Donald Barnie, MA. *Educ:* Huntsman's Gardens Sch., Sheffield; Ruskin Coll., Oxford. Clerk up to 1956; Yorkshire Dist Official, G&MWU, 1957-60. Member: Sheffield City Council, 1945-56; Food Standards Cttee, 1965-68; Confedn Shipbuilding and Engineering Unions Exec. Cttee, 1962-70; Internat. Metal Workers Fedn Women Workers' Cttee, 1962-70; Internat. Union of Food and Allied Workers Assoc., 1964-70; Internat. Fedn of Industrial Organisations Women's Cttee (Chairman, 1969-70); Engrg Trg Bd, 1964-70; Food, Drink and Tobacco Trg Bd, 1968-70. *Recreations:* gardening, reading. *Address:* 12 Rosehill, Claygate, Esher, Surrey. *T:* Esher 62357.
                    [*Died* 24 *July* 1973.

VENABLES, Sir Peter (Percy Frederick Ronald), Kt 1963; PhD, BSc, FRIC; *b* 5 Aug. 1904; British; *m* 1932, Ethel Craig Howell, MSc (PhD 1956); two *s* two *d*. *Educ:* Liverpool University. BSc 1st Cl. Hons, 1925; Education Diploma, 1926; PhD 1928; Research Fellowship, 1928-30. Lectr and Sen. Lectr, Leicester Coll. of Technology, 1930-36; Head of Science Dept, SE Essex Tech. Coll., 1936-41; Principal: Municipal Coll., Southend-on-Sea, 1941-47; Royal Technical College, Salford, 1947-56; Coll. Advanced Technology, Birmingham, 1956-66; Vice-Chancellor, 1966-69, Univ. Fellow, 1969-72, Univ. of Aston in Birmingham; Chm., Planning Cttee to establish Open Univ., 1967-69; Pro-Chancellor and Chm. of Council, Open Univ., 1969-74. Leverhulme Research Fellowship, 1955-56. Commonwealth

Senior Visiting Fellowship, Australia, 1960. President: Assoc. of Principals of Technical Instns, 1952-53; Manchester Literary and Philosophical Soc., 1954-56; Birmingham and Midland Inst., 1969-71; Vice-Pres., BACIE, 1969-73; Pres., Nat. Inst. of Adult Educn, 1971-77; Chairman: Council of Assoc. of Technical Institutions, 1953-54; ITA Adult Education Adv. Cttee, 1965-69; BBC Further Education Adv. Council for the UK, 1965-69; Member: Central Advisory Council for Education (England), 1956-60; Adv. Council on Scientific Policy, 1962-64; Cttee on Manpower Resources, 1965-68; Northern Ireland Cttee on Univ. and Higher Tech. Educn, 1963-64; West Midlands Economic Planning Council, 1965-68; Midlands Electricity Board (part-time), 1967-73. Hon. Fellow: UMIST, 1970; Chelsea Coll., 1973. Hon. DSc: Aston, 1969; Sussex, 1971; DUniv Open Univ., 1973. *Publications:* Technical Education, 1956; Sandwich Courses for training Technologists and Technicians, 1959; British Technical Education, 1959; The Smaller Firm and Technical Education, 1961; Higher Education Developments: the technological universities 1956-1976, 1978; papers in educational jls. *Recreations:* varied. *Address:* 15 Forest Road, Moseley, Birmingham B13 9DL. *T:* 021-449 3462. *Club:* Athenæum.   [*Died* 17 *June* 1979.

VENABLES-LLEWELYN, Brig. Sir (Charles) Michael Dillwyn-, 3rd Bt, *cr* 1890; MVO 1937; Lieutenant of Powys, since 1974 (Lord Lieutenant of Radnorshire, 1949-74); *b* 23 Feb. 1900; 2nd and *o* surv. *s* of Sir Charles Leyshon Dillwyn-Venables-Llewelyn, 2nd Bt, CB; *S* father, 1951; *m* 1934, Lady Delia Mary Hicks-Beach, *o d* of Viscount Quenington (killed in action, 1916) and *sister* of 2nd Earl St Aldwyn, PC, KBE, TD; one *s* one *d*. *Educ:* Eton; RMC Sandhurst. Joined Grenadier Guards, 1918; Captain, 1927; Lt-Col, comd 2nd Bn Gren. Gds, 1941; Brigadier, 1943; retired, 1946, with rank of Hon. Brig. Commanded 159 Inf. Bde TA, 1947-49. JP 1946, DL 1947, County of Radnor. *Heir: s* John Michael Dillwyn-Venables-Llewelyn [*b* 12 Aug. 1938; *m* 1963, Nina (marr. diss. 1972), *d* of late Lt J. S. Hallam and of Mrs E. L. Thomas; two *d*]. *Address:* Llysdinam, Newbridge-on-Wye, Llandrindod Wells, Powys. *T:* Newbridge-on-Wye 200. *Clubs:* Guards, Naval and Military.
                    [*Died* 15 *March* 1976.

VENTER, Gen. Christoffel Johannes, CB 1944; DFC and bar; retired as Director, English Electric Company of South Africa; *b* 1892; *s* of Sarel Johannes Venter; *m* 1918, Catherine Josephine Clarke, Liverpool (decd); two *d*; *m* 1972, Esmé Marjorie Bailey, Leics. *Educ:* Middelburg Cape Public School. Served SA Forces, 1914-16; RFC and RAF, 1916-19; foundn Mem., SA Air Force, 1922; OC Wit. Comd, 1936, Cape and Cape Fortress Comd, 1939; Maj.-Gen. and Dir Gen., SA Air Force, 1940-45. Formerly Manager, SA Airways; Member: Civil Aviation Adv. Cttee, 1946-55; Exec. Cttee, IATA, 1947-55. *Address:* Clubview, Transvaal.   [*Died* 20 *Feb.* 1977.

VERDIN, Lt-Col Sir Richard Bertram, Kt 1962; OBE 1954; TD; DL; JP; Deputy Chairman, Meat and Livestock Commission, 1967-73; *b* 1912; *e s* of late Lt-Col Richard Norman Harrison Verdin, DL, JP, Garnstone, Weobley, Herefordshire; *m* 1950, Helen Margaret, *e d* of Sir Watkin Williams-Wynn, 8th Bt; one *s*. *Educ:* Harrow; Magdalen Coll., Oxford. Barrister, Inner Temple 1937. Liaison Officer, Ministry of Agriculture, Fisheries and Food, 1958-71; Chairman: Pig Industrial Develt Authority (PIDA), 1962-69; Lawes Trust Cttee, Rothamstead, 1964-. Served with Cheshire Yeomanry, 1931-54; Lt-Col 1952. Chm., County Agric. Exec. Cttee, 1955-72; Pres., Country Landowners' Assoc., 1959-61. DL, JP, Cheshire, 1955. *Publication:* History of the Cheshire (Earl of Chester's) Yeomanry, 1971. *Address:* Stoke Hall, Nantwich, Cheshire.
                    [*Died* 16 *Aug.* 1978.

VERE HODGE, John Douglass; *see* Hodge.

VEREKER, Sir (George) Gordon (Medlicott), KCMG 1948 (CMG 1942); MC; *b* 11 Dec. 1889; *s* of late George Medlicott Vereker, Sharpitor, Salcombe, South Devon; *m* 1945, Roxana Wentworth van Rensselaer, NYC, USA (*d* 1968). *Educ:* Eton; Trinity Coll., Cambridge. Amateur Epée Champion, 1913. Served European War, 1914-18; HQ 8th Div. 1914; 2nd Bn Grenadier Guards, 1915-19; entered Diplomatic Service, 1919; Cairo, 1919-23; Peking, 1923-27; Budapest, 1927-30; Foreign Office, 1930-32; Warsaw, 1932-34; Stockholm, 1934-36; Foreign Office, 1936-37; Counsellor British Embassy, Moscow, 1937-39; Minister in Finland, 1940-41, till rupture of relations; special service at Gibraltar, 1942. Minister in Uruguay, 1943; British Ambassador to Uruguay, 1944-49; retired, 1949. *Address:* Domaine de Beaumont, Valbonne, Alpes Maritimes, France. *Clubs:* Carlton, Guards, White's.   [*Died* 14 *March* 1976.

VERITY, Sir Edgar (William), KBE 1954; CB 1948; *b* 21 Oct. 1891; *s* of late William Verity, Bradford, Yorkshire; *m* 1937, Dorothy, *d* of late William Hobson, Heysham, Lancashire; one *d. Educ*: Bradford Grammar School; Brasenose College, Oxford. Entered Civil Service (Inland Revenue Dept), 1914; Assistant Secretary, 1936; Commissioner of Inland Revenue, 1945; Deputy Chairman, Board of Inland Revenue, 1951-54. *Address*: 3 Lyme View Court, Lansdowne Road, Budleigh Salterton, Devon EX9 6AH. *T*: Budleigh Salterton 2222.
[Died 22 Feb. 1975.

VERNER, Sir Edward Derrick Wingfield, 6th Bt, *cr* 1846; *b* 28 May 1907; *s* of 5th Bt, of Corke Abbey, Bray, Co. Wicklow, and Agnes Dorothy (*d* 1951), *y d* of late Henry Laming; *S* father 1936; *m* 1948, Angèle Becco (*d* 1973), Menton. *Educ*: Greshams, Holt; Magdalen College, Oxford (BA 1928). *Address*: c/o Williams & Glyn's Bank Ltd, 67 Lombard St, EC3.
[Died 27 March 1975 *(ext).*

VERNEY, Sir Harry (Calvert Williams), 4th Bt, *cr* 1818; DSO 1918; MA (Oxford); Lt-Colonel; *b* 7 June 1881; *s* of 3rd Bt and Margaret, *e d* of Sir John Hay Williams and Lady Sarah, *d* of 1st Earl Amherst; *S* father, 1910; *m* 1911, Lady Rachel Bruce (*d* 1964), *d* of 9th Earl of Elgin; five *s* three *d. Educ*: Harrow; Balliol College, Oxford. Assistant Private Secretary to Secretary of State for the Colonies, Lord Elgin, 1907-08, Lord Crewe, 1908-1910; MP (L) North Bucks, 1910-18; Parliamentary Private Secretary to the Chief Secretary for Ireland, 1911-14; Parliamentary Secretary to the Board of Agriculture, 1914-15; served European War, 1915-18 (despatches twice, DSO). CC Anglesey, 1949-55. *Publications*: (ed) The Verneys of Claydon, 1969; Florence Nightingale at Harley Street, 1971. *Recreation*: old letters. *Heir*: *s* Sir Ralph Bruce Verney, KBE. *Address*: Ballams, Middle Claydon, Bletchley, Bucks. *T*: Steeple Claydon 321. *Club*: St James'.
[Died 23 Dec. 1974.

VERNEY, Air Commodore Reynell Henry, CBE 1937; DL; RAF (retired); *b* Lighthorne, Warwickshire, 12 Jan. 1886; 2nd *s* of late Rev. Hon. Walter R. Verney; *m* 1942, Hon. Dorothy Ceciley Tollemache, *er d* of 3rd Baron Tollemache. *Educ*: Seafield Park Coll.; Imperial Service Coll. 2nd Lieut, ASC, 1910; seconded RFC, 1914; transferred RAF, 1918; retired list, 1938; employed Supply Dept (Aircraft), Government of India, 1943-46. DL Warwickshire, 1952. *Address*: Stone House, Bishop's Hill, Lighthorne, Warwick. *T*: Moreton-Morrell 246. *Club*: United Service & Royal Aero.
[Died 27 Oct. 1974.

VERNON, Sir Wilfred (Douglas), Kt 1960; JP; President of Spillers Ltd, 1965-69 (Chairman, 1953-65); *b* 27 April 1897; 4th *s* of late William Allen and Elizabeth Vernon; *m* 1923, Nancy Elizabeth, *d* of late Tom Jackson, JP, Bolton; one *s* (and one *s* killed on active service, 1944). *Educ*: Sedbergh; Trinity Coll., Cambridge. Served European War, 1915-18: London Regt, Royal Fusiliers, 1915; attached RFC, 1917-18. Director of Spillers Ltd, 1930. President, Nat. Assoc. of British and Irish Millers, 1947-48; JP, 1952-; High Sheriff of Surrey, 1960-61. *Recreation*: shooting. *Address*: Anningsley Park, Ottershaw, Surrey. *T*: Byfleet 45088.
[Died 17 July 1973.

VERNON, Major Wilfrid Foulston; *b* 1882; *s* of George Thomas Vernon, Islington, London, and Rebecca Clark, Nottingham; *m* 1st, 1907, Josephine Mary, *d* of Joseph Jervis, Stafford; two *s*; 2nd, 1918, Laura Gladys Adeline (*d* 1972), *d* of Dr H. Meade, Bradford. *Educ*: Stationers Company's Sch.; City and Guilds Technical Coll. Apprenticed to Electrical Engineering Siemens, Woolwich; Assistant Engineer Siemens, Stafford, Designer and Engineer Humphrey Pump Co. European War, Lieut and Lieut-Commander, RNVR, Squadron Comdr RNAS, Major RAF, technical assistant to Comdr Porte, pioneer flying boat designer at Felixstowe Air Station. Chief draughtsman Bristol Aeroplane Co., 1923; Technical Officer Royal Aircraft Establishment, 1925-37. War of 1939-45, associated with Tom Wintringham in founding Osterley Park Home Guard Sch.; Lecturer and Demonstrator No. 1 War Office Home Guard Sch., Denbies, Dorking; Lecturer to Forces and Civil Defence Workers; Workers Educational Association Tutor and Organiser. MP (Lab.) Dulwich Division of Camberwell, 1945-51; LCC Member for Dulwich, 1952-55, Borough Councillor, Camberwell, 1953-56. *Address*: Wyngarth, Easter Compton, Bristol BS12 3RA. *T*: Pilning 2329.
[Died 1 Dec. 1975.

VERSCHOYLE, Derek Hugo; Wing Commander, RAFO; Managing Director, Derek Verschoyle (Publishers) Ltd; *b* 24 July 1911; *e s* of late William Denham Verschoyle, Tanrago House, County Sligo, Ireland, and late Iole MacDonnell; *m* 1956, Moyra, *o d* of late James Sutherland, Knockbrex,

Kirkcudbright; one *s* one *d. Educ*: Malvern; Trinity Coll., Dublin; Paris. Literary Editor of Spectator, 1932-40. Served in Royal Air Force, 1939-46. First Secretary HM Embassy, Rome, 1946-50. Man. Dir, Grower Pubns, and Man. Editor, The Grower, 1960-66; Man. Dir, Deben Bookshop, Woodbridge, and Ancient House Bookshop, Ipswich, 1967-69. *Publications*: XXX Poems, 1931; Spectator's gallery (with Peter Fleming), 1933; The English Novelists, 1936; The Balcony, 1949. *Recreations*: travel, reading, music. *Address*: 26 Market Hill, Framlingham, Suffolk. *T*: Framlingham 723923. *Club*: Garrick.
[Died 16 Dec. 1973.

VERSTONE, Philip Eason, FJI; author and journalist; *b* 13 Nov. 1882; *s* of late Joseph Verstone, Liverpool; *m* Ethel Yathé (*d* 1947), *e d* of late Max Mandelbom; three *d. Educ*: Dr Tate's Laboratory, Liverpool; Liverpool Univ. Educated for analytical chemistry, but entered journalism, 1901; London correspondent of New York Dramatic Mirror, 1903-06; alternated between play writing, dramatic criticism and technical journalism from 1906; joined Fleet Street Volunteers, 1915; 2nd City of London Volunteer Regt, 1916-17; adjutant, 7th City of London Cadet Regt, The Royal Fusiliers, to 1919; Founder, and Editor until 1959, of The Paper Container, 1919; The Paper Sampler, 1929; The Fibreboard Container, 1934; Year Book of British Paper Box Industry, 1952; Councillor of the Institute of Journalists, 1924-53; Chairman, Establishment Cttee of the Institute, 1929-37; Chairman, Post-War Conditions Cttee, 1941-46; Chairman, London District, 1934; President of Institute, Jubilee Year, 1940; President, Press Golfing Society, 1958 (Hon. Treasurer, 1933-54; Captain, 1952; Vice-President, 1955); Asst Hon. Social Secretary Press Club, London, 1935-46. Is a Freemason. Commendatore dell' Ordine Capitolare e Militare della Libertà, 1948. *Publications*: The Manufacture of Paper Containers, 1922, 2nd edn 1932, 3rd edn 1949, 4th edn 1960; How to be Natural, a three-act play, 1927; Technical articles and dramatic criticism. *Recreations*: theatre, golf. *Address*: Flat 1, Osborn Lodge, 8 West Parade, West Worthing, Sussex BN11 3QP. *T*: Worthing 32539. *Club*: Press.
[Died 19 Sept. 1973.

VERULAM, 6th Earl of, *cr* 1815; **John Grimston**, DL; Bt 1628; Baron Forrester (Scotland), 1633; Baron Dunboyne and Viscount Grimston (Ireland), 1719; Baron Verulam (Great Britain), 1790; Viscount Grimston (UK), 1815; *b* 17 July 1912; 2nd *s* of 4th Earl of Verulam (*d* 1949) and *b* of 5th Earl; *S* brother, 1960; *m* 1938, Marjorie Ray, *d* of late W. Duncan; one *s* four *d. Educ*: Oundle Sch.; Christ Church, Oxford. RAFO, 1930-36; AAF 1937; Chairman Enfield Rolling Mills, 1960, Director and General Manager, 1938, Managing Director, 1953; Dir, Delta Metal Co. Ltd, 1968- (Chm. 1968-72). MP (C) St Albans and Mid Herts Div., 1943-45, 1950-Sept. 1959. Hon. Air Commodore, No 1 (County of Hertford) Maritime Headquarters Unit, RAAF, 1963. President: London Chamber of Commerce, 1963-66; International Wrought Non-Ferrous Council, 1963. DL Herts 1963. *Recreation*: shooting. *Heir*: *s* Viscount Grimston. *Address*: Gorhambury, St Albans, Herts. *T*: St Albans 55000. *Club*: Bath.
[Died 15 April 1973.

VESEY, General Sir Ivo Lucius Beresford, KCB 1935 (CB 1921); KBE 1923; CMG 1919; DSO 1917; late The Queen's Regiment; *b* 11 Aug. 1876; 2nd *s* of Maj.-General George H. Vesey and Constance, 2nd *d* of George Marshall; *m* 1913, Geraldine (*d* 1963), *e d* of Vice-Admiral Francis J. Foley; two *s* decd. Served S. African War, 1899-1901; European War, 1914-18 (CMG, DSO); Director of Recruiting and Organisation, War Office, 1919-23; Director of Organisation and Staff Duties, Air Ministry, 1923-29; Maj.-Gen. 1928; commanded 48th South Midland Division, TA, 1930-31; Director of Staff Duties, War Office, 1931-34; Lt-Gen. 1934; GOC-in-C, Western Command, India, 1935-36; Southern Command, India, 1936-37; General, 1937; Chief of General Staff, India, 1937-39; retired pay, 1939; Colonel of Queen's Royal Regt, 1939-45; Officer Legion of Honour and of the Order of the Crown, St Michael and Lazarus, Croix de Guerre. *Address*: Gosfield Hall, Halstead, Essex CO9 1SF.
[Died 19 Feb. 1975.

VICARY, Col. Alexander Craven, CB 1945; DSO and Bar, 1918; MC 1915; late Gloucestershire Regiment; *b* 2 Jan. 1888; *m* 1919, Kathleen Hamilton (*d* 1942), *d* of late F. Hilton Green, JP; one *d* (one *s* killed in action, 1943); *m* 1947, Bridget, *widow* of Commander J. B. W. Hale, RNVR, and *d* of late John L. Hunter, Larkbeare, Talaton, Devon. *Educ*: Newton Coll.; RMA, Woolwich. Entered Army, 1908; Lieut and Adjutant, 2nd Batt., Gloucestershire Regt, 1914; Captain, 1914; acting Lt-Col, 1917-19; Major, 1925; Bt Lt-Col, 1929; Adjutant, 1919; Passed Staff Coll., Camberley, 1921; held Staff appointments GSO 3, Scottish Command, Bde Major Small Arms Sch., GSO 1, War Office; served European War, 1914-19, France,

Macedonia, Russia (DSO and bar, Bt-Major, MC, Knight of Legion of Honour, despatches six times); retired pay, 1930; Hon. Col, 1946. Served War of 1939-45: GSO 1, 51st Div. Comdg SAS Italy and Burmah (despatches, CB). Lord of the Manor of Gidleigh. *Address:* Scorhill, Gidleigh, near Chagford, Devon.
[Died 30 June 1975. \

VICK, Reginald Martin, OBE; TD; MA; MChir, FRCS; Consulting Surgeon to St Bartholomew's Hospital, London; *s* of Richard William Vick, JP, West Hartlepool, Co. Durham; *m* 1920, Mary Kate, *d* of Sir Reginald Neville, 1st Bt; four *d. Educ:* Leys Sch., Cambridge; Jesus Coll., Cambridge; Saint Bartholomew's Hospital. Served in Territorial Army, 1912-20; European War, France and Salonika, 1914-18 (despatches four times); Warden of St Bartholomew's Hospital, 1920-36; Consulting Surgeon to several hospitals (Walton, Bexhill-on-Sea, etc); late Asst Surgeon to Metropolitan Hospital; late Officer i/c Surgical Division Friern War Emergency Hospital; late Director of Cancer Records Bureau, S Western Area of England. *Publications:* medical. *Address:* Old Schoolhouse, Baas Manor, Broxbourne, Herts. *T:* Hoddesdon 62559. *Club:* United University.
[Died 18 Dec. 1971.

VICKERS, William John, CMG 1950; MRCS, LRCP, DPH Cambridge; DTM&H Cambridge; Barrister-at-Law (Inner Temple); Deputy Coroner for East Staffordshire and County Borough of Burton-on-Trent, 1959-74; *b* 21 March 1898; *s* of late William Vickers; *m* 1939, Elizabeth Rachel, *d* of late S. Vernon Jackson; one *s* one *d. Educ:* Privately; Birmingham Medical Sch. Served European War, 1917-19, 2nd Lieut, RFA; resident Staff, General Hospital, Birmingham, 1923-25; Colonial Medical Service, 1925-54 (retired 1954); Malaya, 1925-38; Medical Officer, Health Officer, Acting Senior Medical Officer, Kedah; Palestine, 1938-44: Senior Medical Officer, Acting Dep. Director of Medical Services; British West Indies, 1944-45: Adviser on Human Nutrition to Development and Welfare Organisation. British Military Administration, Singapore (Temporary Colonel), 1945-46; gazetted Hon. Colonel. Director of Medical Services, Colony of Singapore, 1946-54; MLC, Colony of Singapore, 1948-54. CStJ, 1951. *Publications:* (Government): (jointly) Health Survey of the State of Kedah, 1936; A Nutritional Economic Review of War-Time Palestine, 1944. *Address:* 174 Ashby Road, Burton-on-Trent, Staffs DE15 0LG. *T:* Burton-on-Trent 68899.
[Died 8 Nov. 1979.

VILLIERS, Brig. Richard Montagu, DSO 1944 (Bar 1945); Secretary, Royal Hospital and Home for Incurables, Putney, 1951-68, retired; *b* 10 Sept. 1905; *s* of late John R. Villiers and of Grace E. Villiers; *m* 1932, Nancy Godwin, *d* of late Lt-Gen. Sir C. A. C. Godwin, KCB, CMG, DSO; one *s* three *d. Educ:* Winchester; RMC Sandhurst. Commissioned, The Cameronians, 1923; retired, 1949. *Recreations:* fishing and shooting. *Address:* Nutwood, Strathpeffer, Ross-shire.
[Died 8 Aug. 1973.

VINAVER, Eugène, MA, DLitt, D ès L; Emeritus Professor in the University of Manchester; *b* St Petersburg, 18 June 1899; *s* of Maxime Vinaver; *m* 1939, Alice Elisabeth Malet Vaudrey; one *s. Educ:* Univs of Paris and Oxford. Lectr in French Language and Literature at Lincoln College, Oxford, 1924-28; Lecturer in French, 1928-31, Reader in French Literature, Univ. of Oxford, 1931-33; Professor of French Language and Literature, Univ. of Manchester, 1933-66; Gregynog Lectr, Univ. of Wales, 1957; Zaharoff Lectr, Univ. of Oxford, 1960; Alexander White Professor, Univ. of Chicago, 1960; Visiting Professor of French, Stanford Univ., 1962; Herbert F. Johnson Professor, Univ. of Wisconsin, 1964-65; Phi Beta Kappa Visiting Scholar, 1967-68; Visiting Professor: Univ. of Wisconsin, 1966-70; Northwestern Univ., 1970-74; Univ. of Victoria, BC, 1972-73, 1974-75; Univ. of Toronto, 1975-76; Univ. of Texas, 1977; Hon. Prof. of French, Univs of Hull and Kent, 1977-; Lord Northcliffe Lectr in Literature, London Univ., 1971. President: Soc. Study of Medieval Langs and Lit., 1939-48; Modern Language Assoc., 1961; Modern Humanities Research Association, 1966; Internat. Arthurian Soc., 1966-69 (Hon. Pres., 1969-). BLitt 1922. MA 1927, Oxford; Docteur ès Lettres at Paris, 1925; DLitt, Oxford, 1950; Hon. DHL, Chicago, 1960; Hon. DLitt: Hull, 1964; Univ. of Wales, 1969; Manchester, 1978; Hon. LLD Univ. of Victoria, 1976; Hon. Fellow, Lincoln College, Oxford; Corresp. Fellow: British Academy, 1972; Medieval Acad. of America, 1973; Laureate, French Acad. (Prix Broquette-Gonin, 1971); Foreign Mem. Belgian Roy. Acad. of French Language and Literature; Hon. Mem., Modern Language Assoc. of America; Chevalier of the Legion of Honour. *Publications:* The Love Potion in the Primitive Tristan Romance, 1924; Le Roman de Tristan et Iseut dans l'œuvre de Malory, 1925; Etudes sur le Tristan en prose, 1925; Malory, 1929, 2nd imp. 1970; Principles

of Textual Emendation, 1939; Hommage à Bédier, 1942; Le Roman de Balain (Introduction) 1942; Racine et la poésie tragique, 1951 (Eng. trans. 1955; revised French edn, 1963); L'Action poétique dans le théâtre de Racine, 1960; Tristan et Iseut à travers le temps, 1961; Form and Meaning in Medieval Romance, 1966; A la Recherche d'une poétique médiévale, 1970; The Rise of Romance, 1971; critical editions of Renan, Prière sur l'Acropole (with T. B. L. Webster), 1934; Racine, Principes de la Tragédie, 1944, 2nd edn, 1951; The Works of Sir Thomas Malory, 3 vols, 1947 (reprinted 1948; one vol. edn, 1954, 1970; 2nd rev. edn 1967); Malory's Tale of the Death of King Arthur, 1955, 1967; King Arthur and His Knights, 1956, 1968, 1975; articles in Medium Aevum, French Studies, Bulletin of the John Rylands Library, Revue d'Histoire littéraire de la France, Cahiers de Civilisation médiévale, etc.; Editor of Arthuriana, 1929-31. *Address:* 20 Fordwich Road, Sturry, Canterbury, Kent; 4 Rue des Eaux, Paris, 16e.
[Died 21 July 1979.

VINCENT, Prof. Eric Reginald Pearce, CBE 1947; LittD; DPhil; MA; Professor Emeritus of Italian, Cambridge University, since 1962 (Professor, 1935-62); Fellow of Corpus Christi College, Cambridge; President, 1954-59; *b* 10 Dec. 1894; *s* of Charles Vincent, MusDoc Oxon., and Hannah Phillips; *m* 1923, Ivy, 3rd *d* of Lt-Col W. Barrow-Simonds, JP; one *d. Educ:* Berkhamsted School; Christ Church, Oxford (Heath-Harrison travelling scholar. First class honours in the School of Modern and Medieval languages, 1921. Studying in Germany at outbreak of war, 1914, and interned as a civil prisoner of war in Ruhleben Camp until Nov. 1918. Lecturer in Italian at King's College, University of London, 1922; Univ. Lecturer in Italian language and literature at Oxford, 1927-34; Assistant Dir in a Department of Foreign Office, 1939-45. British Academy Serena Medal, 1973. Commendatore, Order Al merito della Repubblica Italiana, 1955. *Publications:* Ardengo Soffici, Six Essays on Modern Art, Preface and Notes, 1922; The Italy of the Italians, 1927; R. B. Adam Library Publication, trans. and editing of Italian MSS in this collection, 1930; Enciclopedia Italiana, many articles, 1932-34; Machiavelli, Il Principe, Preface and revision of text 1935; Gabriele Rossetti in England, 1936; The Commemoration of the Dead (Foscolo's Sepolcri), 1936; British Academy Lecture on Dante, 1945; Byron, Hobhouse and Foscolo, 1949; Ugo Foscolo, An Italian in Regency England, 1953; contributions to learned periodicals; translations, etc. *Address:* Sandhills Cottage, Salcombe, S Devon; Corpus Christi College, Cambridge.
[Died 13 Dec. 1978.

VINCENT, Air Vice-Marshal Stanley Flamank, CB 1945; DFC; AFC; DL; *b* 7 April 1897; *s* of Dr Charles Vincent, MusDoc Oxon and Hannah Phillips; *m* 1921, Elisabeth Ursula Peyton; two *s* one *d. Educ:* King's College Choir School, Cambridge; Lancing College. Commission RFC Dec. 1915; France, 60 Sqdn, 1916-17; instructing and hospital, England, to 1919; taught Prince of Wales, Croydon, early 1919 (AFC); instructor Cadet College Cranwell, 1920-23; 30 Sqdn Iraq, 1923-25; 2 Arm. Car Coy., Palestine, 1926-27; 1 Sqdn Tangmere, 1928-31; CO 41 Sqdn Northolt, 1931-33; Sqdn Ldr 1931; CO 84 Sqdn Shaibah, Iraq, 1933-35; armament course, 1936; CO Air Fighting Development Estabt, 1937; Stn Comdr Northolt, end 1937; Wing Comdr, 1937; Air Ministry, 1938; Naval Staff College, 1939; Stn Comdr Northolt and North Weald, 1940 and 1941; Group Capt., 1940 (DFC); Singapore, Sumatra, Java, Australia, NZ, USA, England, 1942-43; Air Commodore, 1941; Fighter Command and AOC 13 Group Scotland, 1943; AOC 221 Group SE Asia Air Forces, Burma, 1944-45 (CB); Actg Air Vice-Marshal, 1944; Air Vice-Marshal, 1947; SASO Fighter Command, 1945-48; AOC No. 11 (F) Group, 1948-50; retired, 1950; Commandant Eastern Area, Royal Observer Corps, 1954-65. DL, Suffolk, 1962. Comdr Legion of Merit (USA), 1945. *Publication:* Flying Fever, 1972. *Recreation:* golf. *Address:* 10 Angel Hill, Bury St Edmunds, Suffolk IP33 1UZ. *T:* Bury St Edmunds 3110.
[Died 13 March 1976.

VINDEN, Brig. Frederick Hubert, CIE 1945; *b* 3 Dec. 1898; *o s* of F. W. Vinden, Mt Radford, Exeter; *m* 1st, 1918, Eva (decd) *y d* of T. Beynon Thomas, Newcastle Emlyn; one *s*; 2nd, 1971, Rose Jeanne, *d* of J. Porrovecchio, Palermo, Sicily. *Educ:* Exeter School; the Sorbonne. Commissioned, 1917, Suffolk Regt; Staff College, Camberley, 1929-30. General Staff, War Office, Malaya and China, 1931-40; AAG Infantry, 1940; Director of Selection of Personnel, India, 1943; retired, 1945; Home Dept, Govt of India, 1945-47; special appointment with UNESCO, 1951-62; Mission to Pakistan for World Veterans Federation, 1954; Consultant, OECD, 1962-64; National Foundation for Educational Research, 1964-. *Address:* 8 rue de la Ronce, 92 Ville d' Avray, Paris, France. *T:* 222.7280. *Club:* Army and Navy.
[Died 2 Feb. 1977.

VINE, Rev. Aubrey Russell, DD, MA, BA, BSc; General Secretary, Free Church Federal Council, 1957-69, General Secretary Emeritus, since 1970; *b* 11 July 1900; *yr s* of Rev. C. H. Vine, Ilford, Essex; *m* 1924, Constance Ida Brand; one *s* one *d*. *Educ:* Cranbrook Park School, Ilford; Trinity College, Dublin (MA); New College, London (DD). Minister: Maze Hill Congregational Church, Greenwich, 1924-27; Broad Street Congregational Church, Reading, 1927-51; Professor, Yorkshire United Independent Coll., Bradford, 1951-57; Director, Independent Press Ltd, 1950-; Review Editor, Congregational Quarterly, 1951-58; Member Congregational Council, 1934-; Deleg. to Internat. Congregational Councils, 1949, 1954, 1958, 1962, 1966; Pres., Berks, Bucks and Oxon Free Church Federation, 1950-52; Chairman Yorkshire Congregational Union, 1957-58; Free Church Representative, Atlantic Congress, 1959; President, Congregational Church in England and Wales, 1967-68. *Publications:* The Nestorian Churches, 1937; An Approach to Christology, 1948; The Free Churches and the State, 1953; Thine is the Kingdom, 1954; Free Church Unity, 1957; contrib. to Expository Times, Congregational Quarterly, Encyclopædia Britannica, London Quarterly and Holborn Review. *Recreations:* foreign travel; chess. *Address:* 26 Newlands Avenue, Radlett, Herts. *Club:* Athenæum.
[*Died 6 June 1973.*

VINEY, Lt-Col Horace George, CMG 1918; CBE 1919; DSO 1917, French Croix de Guerre (with palms); psc 1921; Australian Staff Corps (retired); journalist; *b* Parkside, S Australia, 8 June 1885; *s* of George Viney, JP; *m* 1st, 1918, Gwendoline Darragh (decd), *d* of John O'Neill, of Holywood, County Down, Ireland; one *s*; 2nd, Margaret Jane Lillian, *d* of Robert Browne of Melbourne, Australia. *Educ:* Adelaide High School; Adelaide University; Royal Staff College, Camberley. Commissioned in Australian Permanent Forces, 1912; Adjutant 3rd Light Horse Regiment (Australian Imperial Forces), Aug. 1914, and subsequently served (1914-18) war as Brigade Major, 5th Austn Inf. Brigade; AA and QMG 1st Austn Division; AQMG Australian Corps (despatches five times, DSO, CMG, CBE); returned to Australia on demobilisation, Sept. 1919; resigned from Australian Permanent Forces and posted to Citizen Forces, 1922. *Recreations:* represented Adelaide University at rowing, lacrosse and athletics. *Address:* Gracedale, 42 Bee Farm Road, Springwood, NSW 2777, Australia.
[*Died 7 March 1972.*

VINEY, Col Oscar Vaughan, TD; DL; *b* 16 March 1886; *s* of Joseph Elliott Viney; *m* 1912, Edith (*d* 1951), *d* of C. P. Merriam; three *s* (and one *s* and one *d* decd). *Educ:* Mill Hill School; Germany. Master Printer. Bucks Bn Oxford and Bucks Light Infantry, TA, 1914-34; commanded, 1930-34. High Sheriff of Buckinghamshire, 1950; Chm. Hazell Sun Ltd, Printers, 1950-58. Governor, Mill Hill School, 1929-65 (Vice-Chairman, 1951-61). DL Bucks, 1938. *Recreations:* travel, books. *Address:* Green End House, Aylesbury, Bucks. *T:* Aylesbury 82186. *Club:* Garrick.
[*Died 7 June 1976.*

VIRTANEN, Artturi Ilmari, PhD, MedD (*hc*) University of Lund, 1936; DTechn (*hc*) Finland Institute of Technology, Helsinki, 1949, and Tekniska Högskolan, Stockholm, 1949, University of Paris, 1952; DAgric (*hc*) University of Helsinki, 1955, Justus-Liebig University, Giessen, 1955; Nobel Laureate; Emeritus Member, Academy of Finland (President, 1943-63); Director, Biochemical Research Institute, Helsinki (Director of the Laboratory of Valio, Finnish Co-operative Dairies' Assoc., 1921-70, and Director of Laboratory of Foundation for Chemical Research since 1931); *b* Helsinki, 15 Jan. 1895; *s* of engine-driver Kaarlo Virtanen and Serafiina Isotalo; *m* 1920, Lilja Moisio, MSc; two *s*. *Educ:* Classical Lyceum in Viipuri (grad 1913); Univ. of Helsinki (MSc 1916, PhD 1919); Univ. studies in Zürich, Münster and Stockholm. First assistant of the Central Laboratory of Industry, 1916-17; chemical assistant of the Government Butter and Cheese Control Station, 1919; chemist of the Laboratory of Valio, Finnish Co-operative Dairies' Assoc., 1919-20; Docent in Chemistry, Univ. of Helsinki, 1924-39; Prof. of Biochemistry at Finland Inst. of Technology, 1931-39; Professor of Biochemistry at University of Helsinki, 1939-48. Member: Finnish Chemical Soc., 1919; Finnish Acad. of Sciences, 1927; Swedish Acad. of Agriculture, 1933; British Assoc. for the Advancement of Science, 1935; Finnish Acad. of Agriculture, 1939; Royal Scientific Soc. of Uppsala, 1939; Royal Scientific Acad. of Sweden, 1939; Swedish Acad. of Engineering Sciences, 1945; Danish Acad. of Technical Sciences, 1947; Amer. Soc. Microbiology, 1966; German Soc. Quality Res.; Fellow: Amer. Assoc. for Advancement of Science, 1948; Royal Soc. of Arts, 1948; Royal Flemish Acad. of Sciences (Belgium), 1949; Bavarian Acad. of Sciences, 1949; Norwegian Acad. of Sciences, 1950; Pontifical Acad. of Sciences, 1955;

German Acad. Leopoldina, 1963; Accad. Pugliese delle Scienze (Bari), 1964; US Nat. Acad. of Sciences, 1969. Hon. Member: European Nutritionists, 1965; Biochemical Soc. of Stockholm, 1943; Finnish Medical Soc. Duodecim, 1945; Finnish Technical Soc., 1946; Finnish Chemical Soc., 1946; Finnish Academy of Sciences, 1968; Austrian Chemical Society, 1952; Royal Society of Edinburgh, 1959; American Institute of Nutrition, 1960; American Society of Biological Chemists, 1961; Deutsche Gesellschaft für Ernährung, 1963; Deutsche Gesellschaft für Milchwissenschaft, Kiel, 1971; Foreign Mem., Orden pour le Mérite für Wissenschaften und Kunst, 1971 (Gold Medal); Hon. Councillor, Higher Council for Scientific Research (Madrid), 1964. Friesland Prize, Holland, 1967; Atwater Prize, 1968; Siegfried Thannhauser Medal, 1969; first Fundación F. Cuenca Villoro Lecture, Prize and Gold Medal (Spain), 1972; Uovo d'oro (Italy), 1973. *Publications:* Cattle Fodder and Human Nutrition, 1938; AIV-järjestelmä karjanruokinnan perustana (AIV-system as the basis of cattle-feeding), Helsinki, 1943 (3rd edition 1945); AIV-systemet såsom grundval för husdjurens utfodring, Stockholm, 1945; *c* 800 essays on various biochemical problems; biochemistry of bacteria, symbiotic nitrogen fixation and related agricultural problems, vitamins, antimicrobial substances in cultivated plants, amino acids, etc. *Recreation:* fishing. *Address:* Biochemical Research Institute, 00180 Helsinki 18, Kalevank 56 b, Finland. *TA:* Virtanen, Valio. *T:* 646211.
[*Died 11 Nov. 1973.*

VISCONTI, Luchino; stage and film director; *b* 2 November 1906. Produced plays by Chekov, Shakespeare, Miller, Williams, Goldoni, Anouilh, Sartre, Beaumarchais, etc. Plays include: 'Tis a Pity She's a Whore, Paris; La Monaca di Monza, Rome. Operas by Verdi, Bellini, Donizetti, Strauss, etc. produced at: La Scala, Milan; Royal Opera House, Covent Garden; Festival, Spoleto; Rome Opera House; Vienna State Opera. Directed films: Ossessione; La Terra Trema; Bellissima; Senso; Le Notti Bianche; Rocco e i suoi Fratelli; Boccaccio 70 (Dir of 1 of 4 sequences); The Leopard; Vaghe stelle dell' orsa, (English title) Of a Thousand Delights; The Witches; The Stranger; Götterdämmerung; Death in Venice (Cannes 25th Anniversary Prize, 1971, Golden Globe Prize, 1971); Ludwig, 1973; Conversation Piece, 1974; The Innocent, 1976. Prod ballets: Marathon, Berlin State Opera House; Mario e il Mago, La Scala. Director of Morelli-Stoppa Company; produced with it La Locandiera, The Impresario from Smyrna, Figli d' Arte, at Paris International Drama Festival.
[*Died 17 March 1976.*

VIVIAN, Graham Linsell, CSI 1946; CIE 1944; *b* 1 Aug. 1887; *s* of late Richard Thomas Vivian; *m* 1923, Norah, *d* of late E. H. Ashworth; two *s* one *d*. *Educ:* Epsom Coll.; Selwyn Coll., Cambridge. Entered Indian Civil Service, 1911; held various administrative posts in United Provinces, rising to Commissioner, 1941; Adviser to the Governor, 1945; retired, 1946. *Address:* Middlemead, Rectory Close, Burwash, Sussex. *T:* Burwash 882436.
[*Died 18 Feb. 1978.*

VIVIAN, Richard P. G.; *see* Graham-Vivian.

VLASTO, Michael, MB, BS, FRCS; Officier de l'Instruction Publique; late Consulting Throat and Ear Surgeon to West London Hospital and Consulting Surgeon to Throat and Ear Departments of Queen's Hospital for Children; Fellow of Royal Society of Medicine; *b* 1888; *o s* of Ernest and Helen Vlasto; *m* 1919, Chrissy Mitchell Croil, Aberdeen; three *d* (one *s* decd). *Educ:* Winchester Coll.; University College Hospital. Surgeon-Lieut, 1914-19; late Surgeon-in-Chief of Ear, Nose and Throat Dept of Royal Naval Hospitals of Portsmouth and Malta; Registrar Golden Square Nose and Throat Hospital. *Publications:* Diseases of the Ear, Nose, Throat, for Nurses, and various papers in medical journals. *Recreation:* chess. *Address:* Gresham Lodge, Limpsfield, Oxted, Surrey. *T:* Oxted 3961.
[*Died 29 May 1979.*

von BRAUN, Wernher (Magnus Maximilian); Corporate Vice-President for Engineering and Development, Fairchild Industries, 1972-77; *b* 23 March 1912; *s* of late Magnus and of Emmy von Braun; *m* 1947, Maria L. von Quistorp; one *s* two *d*. *Educ:* University of Berlin (PhD). Experimented with liquid fuel rockets from 1930; Technical Director Liquid Fuel Rocket and Guided Missile Centre at Peenemuende, 1937-45. After coming to America, worked, Sept. 1945-April 1950 as project director of Guided Missile Develt, Fort Bliss, Texas, and simultaneously, advisor for V-2 test firings at White Sands Proving Ground, New Mexico; Tech. Director, Guided Missile Dev. Div., Redstone Arsenal, April 1950-Nov. 1952; Chief, Guided Missile Dev. Div. there, Nov. 1952-Feb. 1956; Director: Development Ops Div. Army Ballistic Missile Agency, Redstone Arsenal, 1956-60; Director, George C. Marshall Space Flight Center,

NASA, Huntsville, Alabama, 1960-70; Dep. Associate Administrator, NASA, 1970-72. Member: Internat. Acad. of Astronautics; Nat. Acad. of Engineering; Fellow, American Astronautical Society Inc.; Hon. Fellow: American Inst. for Aeronautics and Astronautics; various foreign interplanetary societies. Langley Medal (Smithsonian) 1967. Holds hon. degrees, awards, etc. *Publications:* The Mars Project, 1953; Across the Space Frontier, 1952; Conquest of the Moon, 1953; The Exploration of Mars, 1956; First Men to the Moon, 1960; A Journey through Space and the Atom, 1962; (with F. I. Ordway) History of Rocketry and Space Travel, 1966, rev. edn 1975; Space Frontier, 1967, rev. edn 1971. *Recreations:* boating, scuba diving, flying. *Address:* Fairchild Industries, Germantown, Maryland 20767, USA. *Club:* Explorers (New York).
[*Died* 16 *June* 1977.

VON DER HEYDE, Brig. John Leslie, CMG 1960; CBE 1943 (OBE 1941); MC 1918; *b* 1 Oct. 1896; *s* of Major J. L. Von der Heyde, Brighton; *m* 1930, Sybil Marjorie Buckwell; one *d. Educ:* Trescoe House Sch., Brighton TA 1914-17; Regular Army, 1917; substantive promotions: Captain, 1929; Major, 1938; Lieut-Colonel, 1944. Adjut Regular Army twice, TA once; Temp. Colonel, 1941; Temp. Brigadier, 1943. Served European War, 1914-18 (MC, despatches); Palestine (medal); War of 1939-45 (OBE, CBE, despatches); retired pay, 1949 (Hon. Brigadier). Foreign Office, 1948-54; Chairman, Public Service Commission, Tanganyika, 1955-60. Surrey County Councillor, 1965. Coronation Medal, 1953. *Recreation:* golf. *Address:* Beechcroft, Wonersh Road, Shamley Green, near Guildford, Surrey. *T:* Bramley 2412. *Clubs:* Royal Over-Seas League, Army and Navy.
[*Died* 4 *March* 1974.

VONWILLER, Oscar Ulrich; Professor of Physics in the University of Sydney, 1923-46, Emeritus Professor, 1946; *b* 18 Feb. 1882; *s* of late J. U. Vonwiller, Merchant, Sydney; *m* 1st, 1907, Vera Bennett (*d* 1920); one *s* ; 2nd, 1925, Elsie Taylor (*d* 1961); one *s. Educ:* Paddington Public Sch.; Sydney Boys' High Sch.; University of Sydney. Lecturer in Physics, 1903; Assoc. Professor, 1920; Dean of Faculty of Science and Fellow of Senate, 1939-41; Fellow of Institute of Physics, 1927; Vice-President, Australian Branch, 1942; President, Royal Society of New South Wales, 1930-31 (Medal 1950); Hon. Treasurer, Australian National Research Council, 1934-42; Foundation President, Science Teachers Assoc. of NSW, 1919-22, then Hon. Life Vice-President; Member of Board of Visitors, Sydney Observatory, 1930-61; Vice-President, NSW Branch of British Astronomical Association, 1928-58; Member of Board of Visitors, Commonwealth Observatory, Chairman 1944-55; Member of Commonwealth Optical Scientific Instruments and Panel; Director Optical Munitions Annex, University of Sydney, 1940-46; Fellow, Australian Inst. of Physics, 1963. Hon. Life Member, Teachers' Guild of NSW, 1960. *Publications:* Practical Physics (with late Professor J. A. Pollock); various papers in scientific journals. *Recreation:* gardening. *Address:* Rathkells, Kangaroo Valley, NSW 2577, Australia. *Clubs:* University, High (Sydney, NSW).
[*Died* 30 *July* 1972.

VULLIAMY, Colwyn Edward; author; *b* 20 June 1886; *s* of Edwin Papendiek Vulliamy and Edith Jane Beavan; *m* 1916, Eileen (*d* 1943), *d* of Harry H. Hynes; one *s* one *d. Educ:* privately. Studied art under Stanhope A. Forbes at Newlyn, 1910-13; served in France, Macedonia and Turkey, European War; active interest in field archæology for many years; contributor to Spectator and other periodicals. *Publications:* Charles Kingsley (Fabian Tract), 1914; Prehistoric Forerunners, 1925; Unknown Cornwall, 1925; Immortal Man, 1926; Letters of Tsar Nicholas II, 1929; Red Archives, 1929; The White Bull (trans.), 1929; Archæology of Middlesex and London, 1930; Voltaire, 1930; Rousseau, 1931; John Wesley, 1931; The Vicar's Experiments, 1932; Lobelia Grove, 1932; James Boswell, 1932; William Penn, 1933; Family Matters, 1934; Fusilier Bluff, 1934; Scarweather, 1934; Judas Maccabeus, 1934; Aspasia (Life and Letters of Mrs Delany), 1935; Mrs Thrale of Streatham, 1936; Royal George (Life of George III), 1937; Outlanders; Imperial Expansion in South Africa, 1938; Crimea: The Campaign of 1854-55, with an Outline of Politics, etc., 1939; Calico Pie, an Autobiography, 1940; A Short History of the Montagu-Puffins, 1941; The Polderoy Papers, 1943; Doctor Philligo: His Journal and Opinions, 1944; English Letter Writers, 1945; Edwin and Eleanor, 1945; Ursa Major: Dr Johnson and his Friends, 1946; Man and the Atom, 1947; Byron, 1948; Prodwit's Guide to Writing, 1949; Henry Plumdew, 1950; The Anatomy of Satire, 1950; Rocking Horse Journey, 1952; Don among the Dead Men, 1952; The Onslow Family, 1953; Jones: A Gentleman of Wales, 1954; The Proud Walkers, 1955; Body in the Boudoir, 1956; Cakes for your Birthday, 1959; Justice for Judy, 1960; Little Arthur's Guide to Humbug, 1960; Tea at the Abbey, 1961;

Floral Tribute, 1963. *Address:* c/o National Westminster Bank, Guildford, Surrey.
[*Died* 4 *Sept.* 1971.

VULLIAMY, Maj.-Gen. Colwyn Henry Hughes, CB 1945; DSO 1938; Director: Standard Telephones and Cables, 1949-67; Creed & Co., 1949; *b* 22 April 1894; *s* of Colwyn Williams Vulliamy, Lieut-Colonel Her Majesty's 17th Foot, and Lilian Isobel Gosling; *m* Veronica Mary, *y d* of Rev. John Ellis; two *s* one *d. Educ:* Cheltenham Coll.; Royal Military Academy, Woolwich. Commissioned RE, 1913; transferred to Royal Signals in 1926; served European War, France and Flanders, 1914-18 (despatches thrice); service in India, 1921-30 and 1935-38, including Waziristan, 1922-23, 1936-37, Mohmand, 1935 (despatches twice, DSO); has held appointments on Rhine Army HQs, 1919, and in War Office, 1931-34; Chief Signal Officer, Anti-Aircraft Command, 1939-40; Signal Officer in Chief, Middle East, 1943 (despatches); at Supreme HQ, NW Europe, 1943-45 (CB, Commander US Legion of Merit, Officer Légion d'Honneur, Croix de Guerre avec palme); GHQ, India, 1945-46; Director of Signals, War Office, 1946. Retired pay, 1949. Colonel Comdt, RCS, 1949-58, Rep. 1951 and 1955. *Recreation:* golf. *Address:* Dunimarle, Dunmow Hill, Fleet, Hants. *T:* Fleet 4233.
[*Died* 30 *Sept.* 1972.

VYSE, Charles, ARCA; sculptor and potter; *b* 16 March 1882; *s* of Charles Vyse, of Stoke-on-Trent; *m o d* of John Edwards, Sanderstead; one *s* one *d. Educ:* Royal College of Art; Italy. Double Gold Medallist; National Scholarship; Royal College of Art Scholarship; Travelling Scholar. *Address:* Cheyne Cottage, Crown Court, 14 Middle Street, Deal, Kent. *Club:* Chelsea Arts.
[*Died* 10 *June* 1971.

VYVYAN, Jennifer (Brigit), FRAM 1955; soprano; *b* 13 March 1925; *d* of late Major Cecil Albert Vyvyan and of late Mrs Brigit Sinclair; *m* 1962, Leon Crown, FCA; one *s. Educ:* Kensington High Sch.; St Paul's Girls' Sch., London; Talbot Heath, Bournemouth. Joined Royal Academy of Music as pianoforte student and gained LRAM (performer's degree), also LRAM (teacher's degree) for singing; Fred Walker Scholarship; studied singing with Roy Henderson; Boise Foundation travelling Sch. (studies with Fernando Carpi, and also in Milan, and Rome); studied with David Keren, London; 1st prize, Concours Internat. de Genève, 1951 (1st British singer to receive an award). Appeared as Donna Anna in Don Giovanni and as Constanze in Die Entführung by Mozart with Sadler's Wells Opera, 1952; appeared with Glyndebourne Opera as Electra in Mozart's Idomeneo, Edinburgh Festival, 1953. Visited Russia with group led by Sir Arthur Bliss, 1956; visited S Africa and S Rhodesia, recital and concert tour, 1958; first visit to USA for 4 perfs of Britten's Spring Symphony with New York Philharmonic Orchestra, etc., 1963. Created roles of: Lady Rich in Britten's Coronation opera, Gloriana, Covent Garden; Governess in Britten's opera, The Turn of the Screw, Venice Festival, 1954 (subseq. in European cities, Canada and London, and on TV); Miss Hargreaves in The Spur of the Moment, an opera written for TV by Guy Halahan; Tytania, in Britten's opera, A Midsummer Night's Dream, at Aldeburgh Festival and Holland Festival (subseq. in London and San Francisco); Countess of Serendin in The Violins of St Jacques (Malcolm Williamson), Sadler's Wells; Agnes in The Growing Castle (Malcolm Williamson), Dynevor Castle, 1968 (subseq. at Australia House and in Sweden); series of comedy cameos in Lucky Peter's Journey (Malcolm Williamson), Sadler's Wells, 1969. Other roles include: Miss Wordsworth in Britten's Albert Herring; Thérèse in Poulenc's Les Mamelles de Tirésias; Polissena in Handel's Radamisto; Armida in Handel's Rinaldo; Mrs Julian in Owen Wingrave. Large repertoire of works by Bach (3 visits Bethlehem Bach Festival, USA), solo cantatas, etc; has sung in Beethoven's 9th Symphony with many distinguished Conductors. Many European Concerts and Festivals, including Britten's Les Illuminations (Prague Festival, Bratislava and Budapest, 1968, with Giulini and New Philharmonia Orch.; London and Bath Festival, 1969; Reykjavik, 1973); concert performances, Aldeburgh, Brussels and Lucerne Festivals, Purcell's Fairy Queen; Flanders Festival, 1970. Numerous recordings and appearances on TV. Santley Meml Gift Award, Worshipful Co. of Musicians, 1973. *Recreations:* the theatre, reading, painting. *Address:* 59 Fitzjohn's Avenue, NW3. *T:* 01-435 2342.
[*Died* 5 *April* 1974.

VYVYAN, Major-General Ralph Ernest, MBE 1944 (MBE 1923); MC; *b* 1891; *s* of late Captain H. R. Vyvyan, sometime Devonshire Regt and Chief Constable of Devon, 1907-31; *cousin* and *heir-pres.* to Sir Richard Philip Vyvyan, 11th Bt; *m* 1st, 1915, Vera Grace (from whom he obtained a divorce), *er d* of late Robert Arthur Alexander, Portglenone, Co. Antrim; one *s* ; 2nd, 1930, Kathleen Antonia, *o d* of Haskett Farquhar Haskett-Smith, Starcross, S Devon; one *d. Educ:* Stubbington; Exeter;

RMC, Sandhurst. 2nd Lieut, Worcestershire Regt, 1910; served European War, 1914-19, with Regt, Army Signal Service and Staff (despatches, MC); transferred to R Signals, 1920; Lieut-Colonel, 1931; Colonel, 1934; Brig., 1941; temp. Maj.-Gen., 1942-45; Chief Signal Officer: Eastern Command, India, 1932-35; Western Command, India, 1935-39 (Quetta Earthquake, 1935, thanks of Viceroy); Northern Command, India, 1939-40; Signal Officer-in-Chief and Director of Signals, India (including for periods Burma, Ceylon and Iraq), 1941-45; retired 1946, hon. rank of Maj.-Gen. Editor Journal of RUSI, 1950-57, and Registrar of the Museum, 1948-58. *Address:* Limes Well, Streatley-on-Thames, Berks. *T:* Goring-on-Thames 2364. *Clubs:* Army and Navy, MCC. *[Died 31 Jan. 1971.*

VYVYAN, Sir Richard Philip, 11th Bt, *cr* 1645; *b* 21 Nov. 1891; *s* of late Major Richard Walter Comyn Vyvyan, 2nd *s* of 9th Bt; *S* uncle, 1941. *Heir:* cousin John Stanley Vyvyan [*b* 20 Jan. 1916; *m* 1st, 1941, Joyce Lilia (marr. diss. 1946), 2nd *d* of late Frederick Marsh; one *d* ; 2nd, 1948, Marie (marr. diss. 1958), *o d* of late Dr O'Shea; 3rd, 1959, Jonet Noël, *e d* of Lt-Col Alexander Barclay, DSO, MC; one *s* one *d*].
[Died 15 May 1978.

W

WACE, Ernest William Cornish, CSI 1946; CIE 1941; Indian Police (Retired); *b* 11 May 1894; *s* of late Colonel E. C. Wace, DSO, RA; *m* 1921, Irene Marguerite Sant; one *s* one *d* (*er d* killed on active service, Burma, 1945). *Educ:* Felsted Sch., Essex. Appointed to Indian Police, 1914; served in Indian Army, 1915-17, till invalided; held charge of the Police in several Punjab districts and in the Delhi Province; Deputy Inspector-General, 1936; Deputy Inspector-General CID, 1941-45; Inspector-General, Police, Punjab, 1945; Indian Police Medal, 1933. Security Officer, Ministry of Supply, 1948, retired. *Recreation:* gardening. *Address:* Pays Meadow, South Harting, Petersfield, Hants. *T:* Harting 278. *[Died 5 Nov. 1977.*

WADDAMS, Rev. Canon Herbert Montague, MA (Cantab); Canon Residentiary of Canterbury Cathedral and Examining Chaplain to the Archbishop of Canterbury since 1962; *b* 15 Nov. 1911; *s* of William Henry Waddams, CBE, and late Ruby Waddams; *m* 1940, Margaret Mary Burgess; one *s* one *d*. *Educ:* King's Sch., Bruton; King's Coll., Cambridge; Cuddesdon College; Lund Univ., Sweden. Deacon, 1935; Priest, 1936, Dio. of Southwark; Asst Missioner, Corpus Christi Coll., Cambridge Mission, 1935-37; Asst Priest, Grosvenor Chapel, and Chaplain of Liddon House, 1937-41; CF (TA), 1938-41; Priest Vicar and Sub-Dean of Chichester Cathedral, 1941-42; Religious Div., Ministry of Information, 1942-45; Hon. Chaplain, Bishop of Gloucester, 1943-46; Gen. Secretary, C. of E. Council on Foreign Relations, 1945-59; Guild Vicar of St Michael, Paternoster Royal, 1954-59; Hon. Canon of Canterbury, 1955-62; Rector of Manotick, Ont., Canada, 1959-62; Lecturer in Ascetical Theology, General Theological Seminary, New York, 1964; Select Preacher, Oxford Univ., 1965. Chm., Hansard Soc. for Parly Govt, 1970-. Mem., Ct, Univ. of Essex, 1971-. Knight of Order of Orange Nassau, 1954; Vardapet's Cross from Armenian Patriarch of Jerusalem, 1955; Archpriest's Cross from Orthodox Patriarch of Rumania, 1958. *Publications:* The Swedish Church, 1946; Communism and the Churches, 1950; Believing, 1958; Meeting the Orthodox Churches, 1964; Life and Fire of Love, 1964; A New Introduction to Moral Theology, 1964; Companion to the Book of Common Prayer, 1966; The Church and Man's Struggle for Unity, 1968; Illustrated Guide to Canterbury, 1968; Basic Questions of Life and Death, 1968; The Life of the Spirit, 1969; Illustrated Life of St Thomas Becket, 1969. Contributor: Christian Counter Attack, 1943; English Church and the Continent, 1959; The Church in the 60's, 1962; numerous articles. *Recreations:* hearing and making music. *Address:* 15 The Precincts, Canterbury, Kent. *T:* Canterbury 64764. *Club:* Athenæum. *[Died 13 May 1972.*

WADDILOVE, Douglas Edwin, MBE 1945; **His Honour Judge Waddilove;** a Circuit Judge, since 1973; *b* 27 May 1918; *er s* of late Lt-Col E. Waddilove, OBE, and late Dorothy Waddilove; *m* 1949, Heather Jane Fleming; one *s* one *d. Educ:* Rugby; Gonville and Caius Coll., Cambridge (MA, LLB). Cambridge, 1937-39 and 1945-47. Served War (despatches): Coldstream Gds, 1940-45, serving with 3rd Bn in Egypt, North Africa; also with Raiding Forces, SAS, in Aegean, 1943-45. Called to Bar, Middle

Temple, 1947; Barrister: London, 1947-54; Norwich, 1960-73; a Recorder, 1972-73. Dir of Provident Clothing and Supply Co. Ltd, 1954-60. *Recreations:* golf, gardening, snooker. *Address:* The Old Rectory, Snailwell, Newmarket, Suffolk. *T:* Exning 222. *Clubs:* Norfolk (Norwich); West Suffolk County (Bury St Edmunds). *[Died 28 April 1976.*

WADDINGTON, Prof. Conrad Hal, CBE 1958; MA; ScD; FRS 1947; Buchanan Professor of Animal Genetics, University of Edinburgh, since 1947; *b* 8 Nov. 1905; *s* of Hal Waddington, Coimbatore, S India; *m* 1st, 1926, Cecil Elizabeth Lascelles; one *s* ; 2nd, 1934, Margaret Justin Blanco White; two *d. Educ:* Clifton Coll.; Sidney Sussex Coll., Cambridge. 1st Class, Nat. Sc. Trip. Part II (Geology) 1926; Gerstenberg Studentship in Philosophy, 1927; Senior Student, Exhibition of 1851; Travelling Fellow, Rockefeller Foundation, 1932 and 1938; Lecturer in Zoology and Embryologist, Strangeways Research Laboratory, Cambridge, 1933-45; Fellow of Christ's Coll., Cambridge, 1934-45; Hon. Fellow, 1966. Vis. Einstein Prof., State Univ. of New York at Buffalo, 1969-71. President, International Union of Biological Sciences, 1961-67. Albert Brachet Prize for embryology, awarded by Royal Academy of Belgium, 1936; Foreign Hon. Member: American Academy of Arts and Sciences, 1960; Finnish Acad., 1967. Hon. DSc: Montreal, 1958; Dublin, 1965; Prague, 1966; Geneva, 1968; Hon. LLD: Aberdeen, 1966; Cincinnati, 1971. Operational research in Coastal Command, Royal Air Force, 1942-45; Scientific Adviser to Commander-in-Chief, 1944-45. *Publications:* Introduction to Modern Genetics, 1939; Organisers and Genes, 1940; The Scientific Attitude, 1941; Science and Ethics (ed), 1942; Epigenetics of Birds, 1952; Principles of Embryology, 1956; The Strategy of the Genes, 1957; The Ethical Animal, 1960; The Nature of Life, 1961; New Patterns in Genetics and Development, 1962; Principles of Development and Differentiation, 1966; (ed) Towards a Theoretical Biology, Vol. I, 1968, Vol. II, 1969, Vol. III, 1970; Behind Appearance, 1970; Operational Research in World War Two, 1973; (with Kenny, Longuet-Higgins and Lucas) Gifford Lectures, The Nature of Mind, 1972, The Development of Mind, 1973; The Evolution of an Evolutionist, 1975; many articles in scientific journals. *Recreation:* painting. *Address:* Institute of Animal Genetics, West Mains Road, Edinburgh EH9 1RJ. *T:* 031-667 1081. *Club:* Athenæum. *[Died 26 Sept. 1975.*

WADE, Emlyn Capel Stewart, QC 1959; JP; MA, LLD (Cantab); Hon. DCL (Durham); FBA; Downing Professor of the Laws of England, Cambridge University, 1945-62, Professor Emeritus, since 1962; Fellow of Gonville and Caius College since 1931; Reader in Constitutional Law, Council of Legal Education, 1945-66; Member of the Law Reform Committee, 1952-63; Hinkley Visiting Professor, Johns Hopkins University, Baltimore, 1962-63; Barrister-at-Law; Hon. Bencher, Inner Temple; *b* 31 Aug. 1895; *er s* of late Charles Stewart Douglas Wade; *m* 1924, Mary Esmé, *yr d* of late Rev. W. B. Cardew; four *d. Educ:* St Lawrence Coll., Ramsgate; Gonville and Caius Coll., Cambridge. Served with British Salonika Force, and in France, 1916-19; Temp. Major, RA (TA), 1940-42; employed in offices of War Cabinet and Home Office, 1942-45; Lecturer-in-Law, Armstrong Coll., University of Durham, 1923-24; Vice-Principal, 1924-26, Principal, 1926-28. Law Society's School of Law; Fellow of St John's Coll., Cambridge, 1928-31; Member of the Council of the Senate, Cambridge Univ., 1936-40; Hon. Secretary, Society of Public Teachers of Law, 1925-38, President, 1950-51. Member of Lord Chancellor's Committees on Law of Defamation and Limitation of Actions; Cttee on Electoral Law Reform. JP Cambridge, 1946. *Publications:* (with late G. Godfrey Phillips) Constitutional Law, 1931, 8th edn (with A. W. Bradley), 1970; edited Dicey, Law of the Constitution, 10th edn, 1959; articles in Law Quarterly Review, and various legal publications. *Address:* 17 Sculthorpe Road, Fakenham, Norfolk. *T:* Fakenham 2565. *[Died 28 April 1978.*

WADE, Rt. Rev. (Sydney) Walter; a Bishop Suffragan of Cape Town since 1970; *b* 21 March 1909; *s* of late John and Ada Wade; *m* 1940, Henrietta Glover; two *s* one *d. Educ:* King Edward's Sch., Stafford; Kelham. Deacon, 1933; Priest, 1934; Curate, St George's Ch., Nottingham, 1934-39; Rector: St Albans, Kimberly, South Africa, 1940-41; Holy Trinity, Upington, 1941-50; St Matthews, Kimberly, 1950-63. Archdeacon of: Bechuanaland, 1954-58; Kimberly, 1958-63; Dean of Umtata, 1963-67; Archdeacon of Western Transvaal, 1967-70. ChStJ 1975. *Publication:* Afrikaans Gesangboek, 1948. *Recreation:* football. *Address:* Bishop's House, 79 Kildare Road, Newlands, Cape, South Africa. *[Died 10 March 1976.*

WADE-GERY, Henry Theodore, MC; MA; FBA 1941; Hon. Litt D (Dublin); Wykeham Professor Emeritus, Oxford University;

Hon. Fellow of Wadham and New Colleges, Oxford; *b* 2 April 1888; *y s* of Arthur Staunton Wade-Gery, Campton Grange, Shefford, Beds; *m* 1928, Vivian, *yr d* of Richard Whitfield, Kilcormac, King's Co.; one *s*. *Educ:* Winchester; New Coll., Oxford. 1st Class Classical Mods. 1909 and Greats 1911; Home Civil Service (Admiralty), 1912-13; Assistant Master, Sherborne School, 1913-14; Fellow of Wadham, Oxford, 1914-39; served European War in France and Belgium, 1915-18, with 19th Lancs Fusiliers; Member of Institute for Advanced Study, Princeton, USA, 1937-38, 1947-48, 1956-58, 1960-61; Fellow of New College and Wykeham Professor of Ancient History, Oxford Univ., 1939-53; Fellow of Merton Coll., Oxford, 1953-58. Corr. Member, German Archæological Inst. *Publications:* (with C. M. Bowra) Pindar's Pythian Odes, 1928; (with B. D. Meritt and M. F. McGregor) The Athenian Tribute Lists, Vols 1-4, 1939-53; The Poet of the Iliad, 1952; Essays in Greek History, 1958; chapters in Cambridge Ancient History II (1st edn) and III (1st edn), 1924-25. *Address:* The Cottage, Upton, Didcot, Berks. *T:* Blewbury 277. *[Died 2 Jan. 1972.*

WADHAM, Sir Samuel (MacMahon), Kt 1956; Hon. LLD; Professor of Agriculture, University of Melbourne, 1926-56, now Professor Emeritus; *b* Ealing, 31 Oct. 1891; *s* of Samuel Thomas Wadham; *m* 1919, Dorothy Fanny Baylis; one *s*. *Educ:* Merchant Taylors' Sch., London; Christ's Coll., Cambridge. Cambridge Agricultural Diploma and First Class Hons Nat. Science Tripos, Parts I (1912) and II (1914); Agricultural Department Scholar (England and Wales), 1914; in Signal Service and Durham LI (T) during War; Junior Demonstrator in Botany, Cambridge, 1919; Senior, 1920-26; Member Australian Commonwealth Royal Commission on Wheat Flour and Bread Industries, 1934-35; Member Australian Advisory Council on Nutrition, 1936-38; Member: Rural Reconstruction Commission under Australian Ministry of Post-War Reconstruction, 1943-46; Commonwealth Council Scientific and Industrial Research, 1944-55 and 1959-63; Australian Commonwealth Immigration Planning Council, 1949-62; Commonwealth Council on Tertiary Education, 1961-65; Lay Canon, St Paul's Cathedral, Melbourne, 1954-61; President, ANZAAS, 1960-61. Farrer Memorial Medallist, 1947; Medallist Australian Inst. Agric. Science, 1948. *Publications:* Land Utilization in Australia, with Professor G. L. Wood, 4th edn with Dr R. U. Wilson; Farming in Australia, 1788-1965, 1967; various papers in scientific journals. *Recreation:* talking. *Address:* 220 Park Street West, West Brunswick, Victoria 3055, Australia. *Club:* Australian (Melbourne). *[Died 18 Sept. 1972.*

WADSWORTH, Sir Sidney, Kt 1946; ICS (retired); *b* 21 Dec. 1888; *s* of late Rev. H. Wadsworth and late Alice Nelstrop; *m* 1916, Olive Florence, MBE 1946 (*d* 1962), *d* of late Sir Robert Clegg, KCIE, Indian Civil Service; one *s* two *d*. *Educ:* Loughborough Grammar Sch.; Sorbonne, Paris; Jesus Coll., Cambridge; Middle Temple. Joined ICS 1913; Sub-Collector; Under-Secretary to Government, Madras; Secretary to Board of Revenue; Registrar, High Court, Madras; District Judge; Judge, High Court, Madras, 1935-47. *Recreations:* gardening, crossword puzzles, bridge. *[Died 2 March 1976.*

WAINWRIGHT, (Edward) Desmond; Executive Chairman, Army and Navy Stores Ltd, 1959-72; *b* 27 Jan. 1902; *s* of late Ernest Harold Wainwright; *m* 1st, 1928, Iris (*d* 1959), *d* of late Rev. Herbert Sheppard; one *s* one *d*; 2nd, 1960, Leonora (*d* 1972), widow of Maj.-Gen. P. J. Mackesy. *Educ:* Haileybury College; Trinity College, Cambridge. MA, LLB Cantab. 1924; qualified as solicitor, 1927. Lecturer, Law Society's School of Law, 1929-39. *Recreation:* gardening. *Address:* 6 Gretton Court, Girton, Cambridge CB3 0QN. *[Died 23 Feb. 1976.*

WAIT, Air Vice-Marshal George Enoch, CBE 1945; CD; RCAF (retired); *b* 26 May 1895; *s* of late Frank Goodell Wait, Ottawa; *m* 1923, Doris Lilian Browne (*d* 1968); one *s*. *Educ:* University of Toronto; Royal College of Science, London. RFC, RAF and RCAF from 1916. *Address:* PO Box 175, St Andrews, NB, Canada. *[Died 6 Oct. 1972.*

WAITE, Clifford, CMG 1959; Chairman, International Tin Research Council, since 1963; Director: Malayan Tin Dredging Ltd; Southern Malayan Tin Dredging Ltd; Southern Kinta Consolidated Ltd; Kamunting Tin Dredging Ltd; *b* 12 Oct. 1896; *s* of late Jasper and Mary Waite; *m* 1920, Mary Isabel Davey; two *s*. *Educ:* Guiseley. Served European War with Royal Engineers, 1914-18. *Recreation:* fishing. *Address:* 61 Albany Manor Road, Bournemouth, Hants. *T:* Bournemouth 23981. *Club:* Oriental. *[Died 7 May 1974.*

WAITE, Air Commodore Reginald Newnham, CB 1949; CBE 1946; RAF, retired; *b* 30 June 1901; *s* of Alderman Richard Waite, JP, Duffield, Derbyshire; *m* 1940, Jessamy, *d* of late C. F. Lowenthal, KC, Treasurer Middle Temple; one *s* two *d*. *Educ:* Repton; RAF Cadet College, Cranwell. Commissioned, 1921; served War of 1939-45 in First Lord's Operations Room, Admiralty, and Air Ministry, and commanded Coastal Comd Stations at St Eval and Nassau, Bahamas. Supreme Headquarters Allied Exped. Force, 1944; HQ Control Commn, Berlin, for Air matters, until 1949. Conducted Anglo-Russian enquiry into Viking-Yak disaster, 1948. Devised and organised the Air Lift to Berlin in 1948. Assistant Chief of Staff, Allied Air Forces, Central Europe, 1951-53; retd 1953. *Recreations:* yachting, farming. *Address:* Foyers, Woodlands, Southampton. *[Died 7 May 1975.*

WAKE, Joan, CBE 1960; FRHistS; FSA; *b* 29 Feb. 1884; 5th *c* of Sir Herewald Wake, 12th Bt, and of Catherine, *d* of Sir Edward St Aubyn, 1st Bt. *Educ:* at Courteenhall, mainly by Rachel Forester Forbes; London School of Economics (1913-15). Hon. Sec. Northamptonshire District Nursing Assoc., 1916-19. Hon. Sec., Northants Record Society, 1920-63; member of Council and/or committees of British Records Association for 25 years, 1932-55. Hon. MA Oxon, 1953; Hon. LLD, University of Leicester, 1959. Editor, Northamptonshire Past and Present, 1948-59. *Publications:* How to Compile a History and Present-day Record of Village Life; Northampton Vindicated, or Why the Main Line missed the Town; St Peter, Himself a Married Man; A Northamptonshire Rector, The Life of Henry Isham Longden; The Brudenells of Deene, 1953. Editor (for the Northamptonshire Record Society) of: Northamptonshire Quarter Sessions Records, 1630, 1657-8; Musters, Beacons and Subsidies in the County of Northampton, 1586-1623; The Montagu Musters Book, 1602-1623; (with D. C. Webster) The Letters of Daniel Eaton to the Third Earl of Cardigan, 1972. *Address:* 11 Charlbury Road, Oxford. *T:* Oxford 55397. *[Died 15 Jan. 1974.*

WAKEFIELD, Arthur John, CMG 1942; BSc, NDA, NDD; *b* 28 Jan. 1900; *s* of John and Mary Elizabeth Wakefield, Brewood, Staffs; *m* 1927, Winifred Blanche Cook; no *c*. *Educ:* Brewood Grammar School; Harper Adams Agricultural Coll.; Edinburgh University; Reading University. Artists Rifles, 1918; Stock-Inspector, Veterinary Dept, Northern Rhodesia, 1923; Agricultural Officer, 1924, Deputy Director of Agriculture, 1935, Directory of Agriculture, 1938, Tanganyika Territory; Member of Legislative Council, Tanganyika Territory, 1933 and 1938-40; Member of Makerere College Council; Inspector-General of Agriculture and Agricultural Adviser to Comptroller for Development and Welfare in the West Indies, 1940-46; Acting Director of Agriculture, Jamaica, 1945; Member Anglo-American Caribbean Commission, 1943-45, and Caribbean Research Council, 1944-45; leader East African Groundnuts Mission, 1946; Member Overseas Food Corporation, 1948-49. Member Colonial Advisory Council on Agriculture, Animal Health, and Forestry, 1946-50; Resident Rep. of UN Tech. Assistance Board, Haiti, 1950-52, Burma, 1953-56. *Recreation:* gardening. *Address:* The Croft, Marchamley, Shrewsbury. *T:* Hodnet 282. *[Died 5 June 1973.*

WAKEFIELD-HARREY, Cyril Ogden, CMG 1953; HM Foreign Service (retired); *b* 16 Sept. 1894; *s* of Captain A. Harrey and Hannah Ogden, Manchester; *m* 1922, Margaret (*d* 1971), *d* of late J. H. Wakefield, York, and Elizabeth Curthoys, Bristol; one *s*. *Educ:* Manchester Grammar School; Caius College, Cambridge (Scholar). Served European War, 1914-18, Manchester Regiment, and Intelligence Corps (French Croix de Guerre). Entered Consular Service, 1920; HM Consul at Florence, 1936; Commercial Secretary, Budapest, 1939-41; Consul at Port Said, 1944-45; Consul-Gen., Zagreb, Yugoslavia, 1945. Permanent UK Representative to the Council of Europe at Strasbourg, 1951-52; Consul-General at Algiers, Oct. 1952-May 1955, retired. *Publications:* The Golden Chain (Poems), 1944; The Everlasting Quest, 1948. *Recreations:* music, travel. *Address:* 98 St Augustine's Avenue, Thorpe Bay, Essex. *T:* Southend-on-Sea 88673. *[Died 5 Aug. 1971.*

WAKEFORD, Edward Felix, ARA 1968; *b* 1914; *s* of Rev. Robert Wakeford and Felicia Wakeford; *m* 1945, Aileen Mary Rivett-Carnac. *Educ:* King William's Coll., Isle of Man. Studied at Chelsea Sch. of Art, and Royal Coll. of Art. *Exhibitions:* Brook Street Gall., 1946; Hanover Gall., 1953; Wildenstein & Co. (gp exhibns, 1947-62); Ware Gall., 1966. Visiting Teacher at: Chelsea Sch. of Art, 1946-64; West of England Coll. of Art, 1964-66. Represented in public and private collections in: England; USA; Australia; work purchased by Chantrey Bequest, 1971. Lord Mayor's Art Award, 1966; Austin Abbey Award, 1971. *Publications:* (autobiography) A Prize For Art, 1961.

Poetry contributed to: The Observer, The Listener, Poetry Review, etc. *Address:* 108 Beaufort Street, Chelsea, SW3. *T:* 01-352 1618.   [*Died* 29 *Jan.* 1973.

WAKEFORD, Major Richard, VC 1944; MA; JP; Master of Supreme Court of Judicature, Chancery Division, since 1964; late Hampshire Regiment; Solicitor; *b* 23 July 1921; 2nd *s* of late V. D. C. Wakeford, MB, BS, and of Mary Kite; *m* 1951, Denise Elizabeth Corlson. *Educ:* Westminster; Trinity College, Oxford. Governor Haberdashers' Aske's Hatcham Schools, 1961. JP Co. Surrey, 1963. Mem. Civil Judicial Statistics Cttee, 1966-. *Recreation:* shooting. *Address:* Weavers, Elm Drive, Leatherhead, Surrey. *Club:* Leander.   [*Died* 27 *Aug.* 1972.

WAKELEY, Sir Cecil (Pembrey Grey), 1st Bt *cr* 1952; KBE 1946; CB 1941; DSc (London); MCh; Consulting Surgeon: King's College Hospital; Belgrave Hospital for Children; West End Hospital for Nervous Diseases; Royal Masonic Hospital; Petersfield Hospital; Senior Consulting Surgeon, Royal Navy; Senior Lecturer in Anatomy, King's College, University of London, since 1919; *b* Rainham, Kent, 5 May 1892; *s* of Percy and Mary Wakeley, West Dulwich; *m* 1925, Elizabeth Muriel, *d* of James Nicholson-Smith, Blackheath; three *s*. *Educ:* Dulwich Coll.; King's Coll. Hosp. (Tanner Prizeman, Jelf Medal for surgery and other surgical prizes). Temp. Surgeon, RN, 1915-19, and 1939-46 (Rear-Adm.); Mem., War Wounds and Burns Cttee, MRC. President: Bible League; Chartered Soc. of Physiotherapy; RCS, 1949-54 (formerly Vice-Pres. and Mem. Court of Examiners); Med. Soc. of London; Hunterian Soc. Past President: Harveian Soc. of London; Listerian Soc.; Clinical, United Services and Children's Sections of Roy. Soc. Med.; Royal Life Saving Soc.; Alleyn Club. Vice-President: British Empire Cancer Campaign (also Chm. Council) Imperial Cancer Research Fund, 1949-67. Past Vice-Pres., Council, Med. Defence Union. Chairman: Med. Sickness Finance Corp.; Internat. Wine Soc.; Wakeley Bros, Rainham, Kent. Pres., Med. Sickness Soc. Member: Cttee of Management, Conjoint Bd, 1942-54; Council (also Treas.), Gen. Med. Council, 1942-55; Council, Med. Defence Union. Treas., Assoc. of Independent Hospitals. Examiner in Surgery to Univs of London, Cambridge, Durham, Sheffield, Glasgow, Wales and Dublin. Royal College of Surgeons: Hunterian Prof., 1929, 1934, 1937, 1940, 1942; Arris and Gale Lectr, 1924, 1925; Erasmus Wilson Lectr, 1928, 1930-33, 1935-36; Bradshaw Lectr, 1947; Hunterian Orator, 1955; Thomas Vicary Lectr, 1957; Arnott Demonstrator, 1934. Harveian Lectr, Harveian Soc., 1934; Sheen Memorial Lectr, Cardiff, 1953. Legg Lectr, King's Coll. Hosp. Med. Sch., 1957; Sir Thomas and Lady Edith Dixon Memorial Lectr, Queen's Univ. of Belfast, 1957. Past Grand Warden, United Grand Lodge of England; Past Master and Mem. Court of Assistants: Worshipful Co. of Barbers; Worshipful Soc. of Apothecaries. Hon. Convener, Professional Nurses and Midwives' Yearly Conference. Pres., St John's Ambulance Cadets, Chatham. FRSE, FRCS, FRSA, FKC, FZS. Hon. FRCSE, Hon. FRFPS, Hon. FFR, Hon. FRCSI, Hon. FRACS, Hon. FACS. Hon. LLD: Glasgow; Leeds; Lahore. Hon. DSc: Delhi; Colombo. KStJ; Mem., Chapter Gen., Order of St John; Order of the Nile, 2nd Class, 1938; Legion of Merit (USA), 1946; Chevalier, Légion d'honneur, 1950; Order of Southern Cross, Brazil, 1951. Editorial Sec., British Jl of Surgery, 1940-72. *Publications:* A Textbook of Surgical Pathology; The Life of Sir George Buckston Browne; ed Rose and Carless' Manual of Surgery, 1922-; ed Surgical Diagnosis; ed Treeves' and Wakeley's Handbook of Surgical Operations; ed Aids to Surgery; ed The Pineal Gland; ed Neuro-radiology; ed Synopsis of Surgery; ed Medical Dictionary; ed Surgery for Nurses; ed Annals of Roy. Coll. of Surgeons, 1947-69; ed Medical Press, 1932; articles in surgery, cancer and cancer research, and surgical subjects, in med. and sci. jls. *Recreations:* gardening and photography. *Heir:* *s* John Cecil Nicholson Wakeley. *Address:* 240 Maidstone Road, Chatham, Kent. *T:* Medway 45946.   [*Died* 5 *June* 1979.

WAKELY, Sir Clifford Holland, KBE 1945; *b* 1891; *s* of Charles Wakely. *Educ:* Merchant Taylors' School; St John's College, Oxford. Entered Civil Service, 1914; Deputy Chairman, Board of Inland Revenue, 1942-51. *Address:* The Homestead, Upper Cumberland Walk, Tunbridge Wells, Kent. *T:* Tunbridge Wells 27872.   [*Died* 12 *Aug.* 1976.

WAKEMAN, Captain Sir Offley, 4th Bt, *cr* 1828; CBE 1957; JP; late Grenadier Guards; *b* 19 Oct. 1887; *s* of 3rd Bt and Catherine Mary (*d* 1925), *d* of Sir Charles Henry Rouse Boughton, 11th Bt; *S* father, 1929; *m* 1st, 1920, Winifred (*d* 1924), 2nd *d* of late Col C. R. Prideaux-Brune; one *s*; 2nd, 1929, Josceline Ethelreda, *widow* of Comm. Walter Leeke, RN, and *e d* of late Maj.-Gen. Bertram Mitford, CB, CMG; one *s*. *Educ:* Eton; Christ Church, Oxford (MA). Served European War, 1914-15 (wounded); ADC to Governor, New South Wales, 1914; ADC to Viceroy of India,

1918-19; sometime Private Sec. to Sec. for Mines; Member of LCC, 1922-25; Co-opted Member of LCC Education Committee, 1925-30; Member of Shropshire Education Committee, 1926-70, Chm., 1938-40, 1945-67; Mem. Salop County Council since 1928-70 (CA, 1940-70; Chm., 1943-63); Chairman Salop CC Finance Committee, 1940-45; Vice-President County Councils Association (Chairman CCA Education Cttee, 1948-62). Formerly Member Central Board of Finance of Church of England. JP Shropshire, 1927-, Sheriff, 1934; Vice-Lieutenant, for Salop, 1950-69. *Heir:* *s* Offley David Wakeman [*b* 6 March 1922; *m* 1946, Pamela Rose Arabella, *d* of late Lt-Col C. Hunter Little, DSO, MBE]. *Address:* Grafton Lodge, Montford Bridge, Shrewsbury SY4 1HE. *T:* Montford Bridge 262. *Club:* Shropshire (Shrewsbury).
                                    [*Died* 17 *Sept.* 1975.

WAKSMAN, Prof. Selman Abraham; Professor Emeritus, 1958, Professor of Microbiology, 1940-58 and (first) Director of Institute of Microbiology, 1949-58, Rutgers University; Nobel Prize in Physiology and Medicine, 1952; *b* Priluka, Ukraine, 22 July 1888; *s* of Jacob and Fradia Waksman; became naturalized US citizen, 1916; *m* 1916, Deborah B. Mitnik; one *s*. *Educ:* Fifth Gymnasium, Odessa; Rutgers Coll. BSc 1915, in Agr., MSc 1916 (Rutgers); PhD 1918, in Biochem. (Univ. of California). Rutgers Univ.: Lectr in Soil Microbiology and Microbiologist at Expt. Station, 1918; Assoc. Prof. 1925; Prof. 1930. Has also served at Woods Hole Oceanographic Instn and is now a Trustee. For limited periods has held industrial positions and been consultant to Govt Organizations. Has isolated (with associates) many antibiotics (streptomycin, neomycin, etc.). Fellow Hon. Mem. and Mem. various scientific socs. Holds several hon. degrees, both Amer. and foreign, in Medicine, Science, Laws, and Hebrew Letters. Has received numerous awards and medals from scientific and other socs. Comdr Legion of Honour (France). *Publications:* My Life With the Microbes (autobiography); has written, alone or with others, 25 books on Soil Microbiology, Actinomycetes, Antibiotics, etc, and over 400 scientific papers. *Address:* c/o Crown Tower, Apt 17G, 123 York Street, New Haven, Conn 06511, USA.
                                    [*Died* 16 *Aug.* 1973.

WALCH, Sir Geoffrey (Archer), KBE 1954 (CBE 1943); CVO 1954; JP Tasmania; Chairman of J. Walch & Sons Pty Ltd, Publishers and Manufacturing Stationers, Hobart; *b* 8 May 1898; *s* of Richard Crosby and Elvie Mary Walch; *m* 1922, Thelma Fleming; one *s* one *d*. *Educ:* Hutchins School, Hobart; Clemes College, Hobart. Director of Civil Defence for State of Tasmania, 1940-45. Ex-Pres. of Returned Soldiers' Assoc., Hobart and Hobart Legacy Club; Chairman Tasmanian Veterans Trust; Director: Perpetual Trustees and National Executors Co. Ltd. of Tasmania, 1948; Tasmanian Television Ltd, 1958; Chairman of: Derwent and Tamar Assurance Co. Ltd, Hobart; Oldham, Beddome and Meredith Pty Ltd, Hobart; J. C. McPhee Pty Ltd, Hobart; Australian Landtrusts (Tas.) Ltd; Director: Tasmanian Finance & Agency Co. Ltd; Associated Securities (Tasmania) Ltd. Tasmanian Representative Australian Commonwealth Jubilee Council, 1951; Tasmanian State Director, Commonwealth Jubilee Celebrations, 1951-; State Director, 150th Anniversary Celebrations Committee, 1951-54; Deputy Director for Tasmania Royal Visit, 1954. *Recreation:* gardening. *Address:* 654 Sandy Bay Road, Hobart, Tasmania. *T:* 5-1244. *Club:* Tasmanian (Hobart).   [*Died* 6 *Feb.* 1971.

WALDEN, Stanley Arthur, CMG 1956; FRPS(L) 1960; MA Cantab; Member: Committee, Overseas Service Pensioners' Benevolent Society; Council, Overseas Service Pensioners' Association, since 1969 (Secretary, 1960-71); *b* 17 June 1905; *s* of late Alfred Walden, Rotherfield, Henley-on-Thames; unmarried. *Educ:* Royal Grammar Sch., Henley-on-Thames; Selwyn College, Cambridge. Cadet, Colonial Service, Tanganyika, 1929; Assistant District Officer, 1931; District Officer, 1941; Deputy Provincial Comr, 1948; Provincial Commissioner, 1951; Sen. Provincial Commissioner, 1953-59; Provincial Comr in charge of Lake Province, 1954-59. Mem., House of Laity, General Synod of Church of England, 1970-75; Chm. Wage Structure Cttee of Joint Council of Sisal Industry, Tanganyika, 1960. *Recreations:* philately, music, rowing. *Address:* Laund, Henley-on-Thames, Oxon RG9 1NG. *T:* 4715. *Clubs:* Royal Commonwealth Society; Leander.
                                    [*Died* 4 *March* 1980.

WALDEN, Trevor Alfred, CBE 1974; Director, City of Glasgow Museums and Art Galleries, since 1972; *b* 15 April 1916; *s* of Alfred Walden, Peterborough; *m* 1941, Annie Chalmers Nicoll, Dundee; two *s*. *Educ:* Wyggeston Sch., Leicester. Trained Leicester Museums, 1934-38; Asst Keeper, Halifax Museums, 1938-41; War Service, Royal Navy, 1941-46; Leicester

Museums: Keeper of Biology, 1947-49; Dep. Dir, 1949-51; Dir, 1951-72. Chm. of Educn, Museums Assoc., 1959-64, Pres. 1970. Hon. MSc Leicester 1965. *Publications:* papers in Museums Jl, etc. *Address:* Machrimore, Manse Road, Bowling, Glasgow G60 5AA. *T:* Duntocher 72747. *Clubs:* Glasgow Art, Royal Scottish Automobile (Glasgow).   *[Died* 12 *March* 1979.

WALDER, (Alan) David; ERD 1965; MP (C) Clitheroe since 1970; Barrister and Author; *b* 13 Nov. 1928; *o s* of late James Walder, Chailey, Sussex, and of Helen Walder (*née* McColville); *m* 1956, Elspeth Margaret, *y d* of late Rt Hon. Lord Milligan; one *s* three *d* (including twin *d*). *Educ:* Latymer School; Christ Church, Oxford (Scholar), MA. Served Malaya, 1948-49; AER of 4th Queen's Own Hussars until 1958, of Queen's Royal Irish Hussars until 1965. Served as a Reservist in Germany, Aden and Borneo, Major. Called to the Bar, Inner Temple, 1956; Forster-Boulton Prize; Paul Methven Scholar; Midland Circuit. Chairman, Wembley South Conservative Assoc., 1959. Contested (C) Leicester SW Division, 1959. MP (C) High Peak Division of Derbyshire, 1961-66. PPS to Jt Under-Secs of State, Scottish Office, 1963-64; PPS to Minister for Trade, 1970-72; an Asst Govt Whip, 1973-74. Mem., UK Parly Delegn to Chinese Republic, 1972; UK Parly Deleg. to Council of Europe and Assembly of WEU, 1972, 1973; Vice-Chm., Cons. Home Affairs Cttee, 1973. Vice-Chm., Conservative Defence Cttee; Mem. Exec., 1922 Cttee. Exec., National Book League, 1976-. *Publications:* Stability and Survival (with Julian Critchley), 1961; Bags of Swank, 1963; The Short List, 1964; The House Party, 1966; The Gift Bearers (USA), 1967; The Fair Ladies of Salamanca, 1967; The Chanak Affair, 1969; The Short Victorious War, 1973; Nelson, 1978; (contrib.) Purnell's History of the First World War. *Recreations:* shooting, ornithology, opera. *Address:* The White House, Grimsargh, near Preston, Lancs PR2 5JR. *T:* Longridge 3618; 45 Courtenay Street, SE11 5PH. *T:* 01-735 8281. *Club:* Cavalry and Guards.
                [*Died* 26 *Oct.* 1978.

WALDMAN, Milton; FRSL; author and publisher; *b* USA, 4 Oct. 1895; *s* of Benjamin Waldman and Ida Spire; *m* 1934, Marguerite David (*d* 1969); one *s* two *d. Educ:* Yale University, USA. Journalist. In USA War Service, 1917-19. Assistant Editor London Mercury, 1924-27. Literary Adviser Longmans Green & Co. Ltd, 1929-34; William Collins Sons & Co. Ltd, 1939-52; Joint Managing Director, Rupert Hart-Davis, Ltd, 1952-55; Literary Adviser, William Collins Sons & Co. Ltd, 1955-69. Contributor to various periodicals, anthologies, etc. Editor The Golden Hind Series. *Publications:* Americana, 1925; Sir Walter Raleigh, 1928; The Disinherited (a novel), 1929; King, Queen, Jack, 1931; Elizabeth of England, 1933; Joan of Arc, 1935; Biography of a Family, 1936; Three English Dictators, 1940; Elizabeth and Leicester, 1944; Queen Elizabeth (Brief Lives Series), 1952; The Lady Mary: a biography of Queen Mary I, 1972. *Address:* 79 Dorset House, Gloucester Place, NW1. *Club:* Savile.   [*Died* 6 *March* 1976.

WALDMAN, Ronald Hartley; Managing Director, Visnews Ltd, 1963-77; Trustee, International Institute of Communications, since 1975; *b* 13 May 1914; *e s* of late Michael Ernest Waldman, OBE, JP; *m* 1953, Lana Morris; one *s. Educ:* Owen's School; Pembroke College, Oxford. Actor and Producer, 1935-38. Producer, BBC Variety Dept, 1938; wartime service in RAFVR. Assistant Head of Variety (Productions), 1948; Senior Producer, Television Light Entertainment, 1950; Head of Light Entertainment, BBC Television, 1950; Business Manager, BBC TV Programmes, 1958-60; General Manager, BBC TV Enterprises, 1960-63. *Recreations:* music, cricket, watching and listening to experts being expert. *Address:* 60 Wolsey Road, Moor Park, Mddx. *Clubs:* MCC, Lord's Taverners'.
                [*Died* 10 *March* 1978.

WALDRON, Sir John (Lovegrove), KCVO 1966 (CVO 1959); Commissioner, Metropolitan Police, 1968-72; *b* 5 Nov. 1909; *s* of late Frederick Waldron, Wargrave, Berkshire; *m* 1937, Joan Elsie, *d* of late P. G. Osborne; two *d. Educ:* Charterhouse; Clare College, Cambridge (BA). Joined Metropolitan Police, 1934; seconded Ceylon Police, 1943-47. Acted as Dep. Inspector-Gen., CID, 1944-47. Asst Chief Constable, Lancashire, 1951-54; Chief Constable, Berkshire, 1954-58; Asst Commissioner, Metropolitan Police, 1959-66; Dep. Commissioner, 1966-68; Governor, Sutton's Hosp. in Charterhouse. Chm., Council for Vehicle Servicing and Repair, 1974. *Address:* 110 Priory Lane, Roehampton, SW15 5JL. *T:* 01-876 2020. *Clubs:* Buck's, MCC.
                [*Died* 24 *Aug.* 1975.

WALKER, Hon. Lord; James Walker; one of the Senators of the College of Justice in Scotland since 1954; Chairman Law Reform Committee for Scotland, 1954-64; President of Scottish Universities Law Institute, 1960; *b* Wigtown, 1890; *s* of late A.

D. Walker, solicitor; *m* 1918, Ella (*d* 1972), *d* of late John Grieve; one *s. Educ:* Ewart Acad., Newton Stewart; Glasgow and Edinburgh Universities. Advocate, 1914; Royal Scots and Machine-Gun Corps in Egypt and France, 1915-19; Member of Rules Council, 1933-48; Junior Counsel to Scottish Office, 1934-36; Advocate-Depute, 1937-40; Clerk of Justiciary, 1940-48; Vice-Dean of the Faculty of Advocates, 1948-54; Member of Royal Commission on Marriage and Divorce, 1951-55; Sheriff of Inverness, Moray, Nairn and Ross and Cromarty, 1949-53; Sheriff of Aberdeen, Kincardine and Banff, 1953-54. QC (Scotland) 1944. Hon. LLD (Edinburgh), 1961. *Publications: Intestate Succession in Scotland, 1927. Recreations:* fishing, shooting. *Address:* 14 Dalrymple Crescent, Edinburgh. *T:* 031-667 1822. *Clubs:* New, Scottish Arts (Edinburgh).
                [*Died* 11 *June* 1972.

WALKER, Sir Alan, Kt 1975; President, Bass Charrington Ltd, since 1976 (Chairman, 1967-76); Member, British Railways Board, since 1969 (Chairman, Western Region Advisory Board, since 1977); a Deputy Chairman, Midland Bank, since 1977; Director: Bass Charrington Vintners (Chairman, 1974-76); Crest Hotels Ltd; Eagle Star Insurance Co. Ltd; Standard Broadcasting Corp. (UK) Ltd; Capital Radio; Hogg Robinson Group Ltd; Chairman, Thos Cook Group Ltd, since 1976; *m* 1938, Evelyn Melissa, *d* of Harold Alexander de Pass; one *s* two *d.* Chm., Midland Western Region, BR, 1972-77. Trustee, Glyndebourne Festival. Liveryman, Shipwrights' Co.; Liveryman, Ct, Brewers' Co. *Recreations:* fishing, ballet, opera. *Address:* 7 Grosvenor Gardens, SW1. *T:* 01-834 3121; Poachers, Alcester Heath, Warwickshire. *T:* Alcester 2291. *Clubs:* Brooks's, MCC.   [*Died* 3 *Jan.* 1978.

WALKER, Alexander Neilson Strachan, CMG 1974; Director, International Office, Conservative Party, since 1979; *b* 8 March 1921; *s* of Col W. O. Walker, IMS and Janet Cormack (*née* Strachan); *m* 1947, Elizabeth Anne (*née* Ireland); two *s* three *d. Educ:* Oundle Sch.; Gonville and Caius Coll., Cambridge (BA). Royal Artillery, 1941-46 (despatches twice); served Africa, France, Italy and SE Asia. HM Foreign (subseq. Diplomatic) Service, 1949-77; served in Paris, 1950; FO, 1952; Düsseldorf, 1954; Rangoon, 1957; Singapore, 1959; FO, 1961; Brussels, 1964; FCO, 1968; Rome, 1971; Washington, 1973; FCO, 1975-77. Croix de Guerre with Palm 1944. *Recreations:* fishing, gardening. *Address:* Puck Hill, Wadhurst, East Sussex. *T:* Wadhurst 2586. *Club:* Travellers'.   [*Died* 10 *May* 1980.

WALKER, Col Charles William Garne, CMG 1933; DSO 1918; *b* 2 July 1882; *s* of late Charles Walker, Bridgend; *m* 1915, Dorothy Frances (*d* 1965), *e d* of late F. Hughes-Gibb, JP, Manor House, Tarrant Gunville, Dorset; one *s. Educ:* King's Sch., Canterbury; Sandhurst. 2nd Lieut, 1902; joined Indian Army, 1903; Captain, 1911; Staff Coll., Camberley, 1912-13; served European War, 1914-18 (despatches twice, DSO, Bt Lt-Col); Col, 1923; Asst Sec. Cttee of Imperial Defence, 1921-25; retired, 1927; Secretary to the Conference of Governors of the East African Dependencies, 1925-36; employed HM Treasury, 1936-40; Principal Officer Southern Civil Defence Region, 1940-42; War Cabinet Office, 1943-47; Secretary: Lord De La Warr's mission to Ethiopia, 1944; Assoc. of Consulting Engineers, 1948-60. *Address:* The Old Vicarage, South Cerney, Cirencester. *Club:* Travellers'.   [*Died* 7 *Nov.* 1974.

WALKER, Eric Anderson, MA (Oxon, Cape Town, Cantab); Fellow of St John's College, Cambridge, 1936-68; Vere Harmsworth Professor of Imperial and Naval History, Cambridge, 1936-51, now Emeritus; *b* Streatham, SW, 6 Sept. 1886; *e s* of William and Jessie Walker; *m* 1913, Lucy Stapleton, *d* of late James Walker. *Educ:* Mill Hill Sch.; Merton Coll., Oxford (History Exhibitioner). Lecturer in History in the University of Bristol, 1908-11; King George V Professor of History in University of Cape Town, 1911-36. Hon. DLitt, Witwatersrand, Cape Town. *Publications:* Historical Atlas of South Africa, 1922; Lord de Villiers and his Times, 1925; A Modern History for South Africans, 1926; A History of South Africa, 1928 (2nd edn, 1940, rep. with corrs., 1947); The SA College and the University of Cape Town, 1929; The Frontier Tradition in South Africa, 1930; The Great Trek, 1934, 4th edn, 1960; W. P. Schreiner: A South African, 1937 (shortened edn, 1960); South Africa, 1940 and 1941; Britain and South Africa, 1942; The British Empire, 1943 (2nd and extended edn, 1953); Colonies, 1944; A History of Southern Africa, 1957 (5th reprint 1968); South African Adviser to the Editors of the Cambridge History of the British Empire, Vol. VIII (South Africa); Joint Editor of the Cambridge History of the British Empire, Vol. III and Vol. VIII (2nd edn). *Recreations:* rowing, painting. *Address:* 76 Manning Road, Durban, South Africa. *Club:* Leander (Henley-on-Thames).   [*Died* 23 *Feb.* 1976.

WALKER, George Edward Orr, MBE 1943; TD 1952; QC (Scotland) 1955; Treasurer of the Faculty of Advocates, 1949-70 (admitted 1936); *b* 16 Sept. 1909; *s* of Archibald Walker, DL, and Adelaide Orr Thomson; *m* 1935, Margaret Sybil, *d* of George Simpson Orr; one *s* two *d* (and one *s* decd). *Educ:* Winchester Coll.; Trinity Coll., Oxford (BA); Edinburgh Univ. (LLB). Standing Counsel to Scottish Home Dept and to Nat. Art Galleries, 1951-55; Chairman of Medical Appeal Tribunal (Scotland), 1956-70. 2nd Lieut, Ayrshire (ECO) Yeomanry, 1931; served War of 1939-45: Lt-Col North West Europe Campaign, 1945 (despatches). Contested (U) Kilmarnock Burghs, 1945 and 1946. *Recreations:* golf and (formerly) hunting. *Address:* Newark Castle, Ayr. *T:* Alloway 41204. *Clubs:* New (Edinburgh); Western (Glasgow).
[*Died* 21 *Feb.* 1973.

WALKER, Major Sir George Ferdinand Forestier-, 4th Bt, *cr* 1835; Coldstream Guards, retired; *b* 20 May 1899; *o s* of 3rd Bt and Georgina (*d* 1910), *y d* of late Robert D. Chamberlain, 1st Regt; *S* father, 1933. *Educ:* Wellington Coll.; RMC, Sandhurst. *Heir: cousin* Clive Radzivill Forestier-Walker [*b* 30 April 1922; *m* 1948, Pamela Mercy, *d* of Clifford Leach; three *d*]. *Address:* Monks Mill, Pilton, Shepton Mallet, Somerset. *T:* Pilton 228.
[*Died* 1 *Oct.* 1976.

WALKER, Col George Gustavus, CBE 1958; MC and Bar 1917; TD; *b* 4 July 1897; *e s* of Captain George Laurie Walker, Crawfordton, Dumfriesshire; *m* 1924, Sybilla Catherine, 2nd *d* of Charles Hyslop Maxwell, Dalruscan, Dumfriesshire; one *d* decd. *Educ:* Sandroyd; Repton. Joined 3 KOSB, 1914; transferred to Scots Guards, 1916; Captain, 1918; Lt-Col comdg 5 KOSB (TA), 1934; Bt-Col, 1938; Commanded 9 KOSB, 1940-41; Commanded No. 10 Infantry Training Centre, 1942-45. Chairman, Dumfriesshire T&AFA, 1949-62. Hon. Sheriff Substitute of Dumfries and Galloway, 1938. Hon. Colonel, 5 KOSB (TA), 1949-61. DL 1947, JP 1920, County of Dumfries. *Address:* Morrington, Dumfries, Scotland. *T:* Dunscore 349.
[*Died* 2 *June* 1972.

WALKER, Adm. Sir Harold Thomas Coulthard, KCB 1946 (CB 1944); *b* 18 March 1891; *yr s* of late Lt-Gen. Sir H. B. Walker, KCB, KCMG, DSO, and late Lady Walker; *m* 1931, Olive Marjory, *yr d* of Major J. A. Berners, Woolverstone Park, Ipswich; one *s* one *d*. *Educ:* St Christopher's, Bath; Royal Naval Colleges, Osborne and Dartmouth. Midshipman, 1908; Sub-Lt, 1911; Lieut, 1913; served European War (wounded, despatches twice); Comdr, 1926; Captain, 1931; Commanded HMS Canterbury, 1932; HMAS Canberra, 1934-36; HMS Hood, 1938-39; HMS Barham, 1939-40; Deputy Director Training and Staff duties, Admiralty, 1936-38; Commodore RNB Portsmouth, 1940-41; Rear-Admiral, 1941; Director of Personal Services, Admiralty, 1941-43; Commanded 5th Cruiser Squadron, 1944; 3rd Battle Squadron, and 2nd in Comd, East Indies Station, 1944-45; Vice-Admiral, 1944; Commanded British Naval Forces in Germany, 1946-47; retired, 1947; Admiral (retired), 1948. *Address:* Pin Mill, Heathfield Road, Woking, Surrey. *T:* Woking 63390. *Club:* Naval and Military.
[*Died* 25 *Dec.* 1975.

WALKER, Sir (Horace) Alan; *see* Walker, Sir Alan.

WALKER, James; *see* Walker, Hon. Lord.

WALKER, James Arthur H.; *see* Higgs-Walker.

WALKER, John Henry; Assistant Secretary, Home Office, 1950-73; *b* 14 May 1915; *s* of late Edwin Walker, Nelson, Lancs; *m* 1957, Norma, *d* of late Arthur Griffiths, Hamilton, Ontario, Canada. *Educ:* Grammar Sch., Nelson, Lancs; St John's Coll., Cambridge. Asst Principal, Home Office, 1937. Served War of 1939-45, Captain, East Lancashire Regt, 1940-45. Principal, Home Office, 1945; Asst Secretary, Home Office, 1950; UK Delegate to: UN Narcotics Commission, 1952-56 (Chairman 1956); UN Opium Conference, 1953; Prison Commissioner, 1955-62; Secretary, Prison Commission, 1955-62. *Address:* 12 Oakcroft Road, SE13. *T:* 01-852 7925.   [*Died* 9 *Aug.* 1974.

WALKER, Malcolm Thomas, CBE 1964; HM Diplomatic Service, retired; *b* 8 April 1915; *s* of late Major Herbert Thomas Walker and Caroline Dorothy Clerk; *m* 1949, Jean Rosemary Edith Mair; two *s* one *d*. *Educ:* Sherborne Sch.; Worcester Coll., Oxford. Entered HM Foreign Service, 1938; served at Beirut, 1938; Jedda, 1940; Bagdad, 1943; First Secretary in Foreign Office, 1947; Benghazi, 1949; Amman, 1950; Foreign Office, 1953; Counsellor at Khartoum, 1956; Consul-General, Hanoi, 1958; Consul-General, Seville, Spain, 1960-63; British Ambassador in Liberia, 1963-67; Consul-General, Cape Town, 1967-70; retd. Mem., West Dorset DC, 1977-. *Recreations:*

sailing and gardening. *Address:* The Manor House, Plush, Dorchester, Dorset DT2 7RJ. *T:* Piddletrenthide 280. *Club:* Royal Ocean Racing.   [*Died* 1 *Jan.* 1980.

WALKER, Norman Macdonald Lockhart, CBE 1960; Sheriff-Substitute of Lanarkshire at Glasgow, 1942-62, retired; *b* 1889; *s* of late Sir Norman Walker, MD, LLD; *m* 1925, Alison, *d* of late Walter W. Blackie, Publisher, Glasgow; two *s*. *Educ:* Edinburgh Academy; St Andrews Univ.; Balliol Coll., Oxford. Glasgow Univ. Served European War, 1914-19; called to Scottish Bar, 1920; Advocate Depute, 1934-36; Sheriff-Substitute of Lanarkshire at Hamilton, 1936-42. Hon. LLD Glasgow, 1955. *Publications:* co-author Walker on Evidence, 1963; co-editor 6th edn of Gloag and Henderson's Introduction to the Law of Scotland, 1956; Digest of Sheriff Court Practice, 1932. *Address:* Castlelea, East Scores, St Andrews, Fife. *T:* St Andrews 4153. *Clubs:* Western (Glasgow); Royal and Ancient (St Andrews).
[*Died* 25 *Jan.* 1975.

WALKER, Patrick Chrestien G.; *see* Gordon-Walker, Baron.

WALKER, Raymond St John, (Henry), CBE 1970; Secretary, Science Research Council, 1972-78 (Director, Establishment and Finance, later Administration, 1965-72); *b* 11 April 1917; *o s* of late William and Sybil Mary Walker; *m* 1941, Eva Mary, *e d* of late Walter Lionel and Ethel Marion Dudley; three *s*. *Educ:* Leeds Grammar Sch.; St Peter's Coll., Oxford. Royal Artillery, 1939-46. Min. of Supply, 1947-58 (Private Sec. to Minister, 1950-53); Imperial Defence Coll., 1959; Min. of Aviation, 1960-61; DSIR, 1962-64. *Recreation:* sailing. *Address:* The Grove, Cordy's Lane, Trimley St Mary, Ipswich, Suffolk. *T:* Felixstowe 2315. *Club:* Athenæum.   [*Died* 2 *June* 1980.

WALKER, Sir Ronald Fitz-John, Kt 1953; Chairman, James Walker & Sons Ltd, Mirfield; Chairman, Dewsbury Reporter Group, since 1951; and other directorships; Income Tax Commissioner, 1925-65; Liberal Party (President, 1952); *b* 24 Nov. 1880; *s* of John Ely and Mary Elizabeth Walker; *m* 1916, Edith Mary (*d* 1966). *Educ:* Mill Hill School. On leaving school went into family blanket manufacturing business. Liberal speaker and worker since 1900 and thereafter continually in office; Chairman, Central National Exec., 1932. Contested (L) NE Leeds, 1922 and 1923, Colne Valley, 1924, Dewsbury, 1929, Royton, 1931 and 1935. First Hon. Life Pres. Yorkshire Liberal Party, 1960 (President, 1947-60). *Publications:* pamphlets on Free Trade, and (against) transport nationalisation. *Recreations:* formerly cliff climbing and golf; now bridge (family type). *Address:* Fir Cottage, Mirfield, Yorks. *T:* Mirfield 2143. *Club:* National Liberal.   [*Died* 26 *March* 1971.

WALKER, Air Cdre Sidney George, CB 1965; OBE 1945; RAF (Retired); *b* 6 Aug. 1911; *s* of late Capt. S. G. Walker, The Sherwood Foresters, and late Katie Rowena (*née* Worley), both of Nottingham; *m* 1939, Laura, *d* of Edward Craig Gorton and of Laura Harriet Matilda (*née* Hayden), Hull; one *s* one *d*. *Educ:* St Edmund's Coll., Shillong, Assam; Nottingham High School. Nottingham City Police, 1929-34; granted perm. commn, Cranwell, on direct entry to Equipment Branch, RAF, 1935; Aden, 1936-38; Arabic Interpretership, Baghdad, 1938; Air Min., 1938-41; Brit. Air Commn, USA, 1941-43; HQ, 2 TAF, 1943-45; HQ, BAFO, 1945-46; RAF Staff Coll., 1946; comd RAF Kemble, 1946-47, and RAF Edzell, 1947; Directing Staff, RAF Staff Coll., 1948-50; Jt Services Staff Coll., 1950-51; Dep. Chief Logistics Div., HQ, Allied Air Forces Central Europe (Fontainebleau), 1951-53; comd RAF Marlebury, 1953-55; Dep. Dir of Organisation (Aircraft), Air Min., 1955-58; Imp. Def. Coll., 1959; Dep. Dir of Movements, Air Min., Jan.-Oct. 1960; Dir of Movements (RAF) in Min. of Defence (Air), Oct. 1960-July 1965, retd at own request. *Publication:* RUSI Trench Gascoigne Prize Essay, 1947. *Recreations:* Rugby football (RAF representative; founded Ranji Walker's XV), cricket, track athletics. *Address:* 265 Turleigh, Bradford-on-Avon, Wilts. *Clubs:* Royal Air Force; (Life Mem.) Wanderers Football (Dublin); (Life Mem.) Swansea Football (St Helen's).
[*Died* 29 *July* 1975.

WALKER LEE, Rev. William; *see* Lee, Rev. W. W.

WALKLEY, Sir William (Gaston), Kt 1967; CBE 1961; *b* 1 Nov. 1896; *s* of Herbert and Jessie Walkley; *m* 1945, Theresa May Fisher. *Educ:* Wellington, New Zealand. Founder of: Ampol Petroleum Ltd (Dir, 1939-67); Ampol Exploration Ltd (Man. Dir, 1955-67), retired. FCIS Australia; FCANZ. *Publication:* Solicitors' Accounts and Audits, 1922. *Recreation:* fishing. *Address:* 3 King Avenue, Balgowlah, NSW 2093, Australia. *T:* 94.6242. *Clubs:* Royal Sydney Yacht Squadron, American National (Sydney).   [*Died* 12 *April* 1976.

WALL, Baron *cr* 1976 (Life Peer), of Coombe in Greater London; **John Edward Wall**, Kt 1968; OBE 1944; Director: Laporte Industries (Holdings) Ltd, since 1968; The Exchange Telegraph Co. (Holdings) Ltd, 1972-78; Grundy (Teddington) Ltd, since 1972; Chairman: Charterhouse Development Capital Ltd, since 1976; Nurdin and Peacock, since 1977; *b* 15 Feb. 1913; *s* of late Harry Arthur Fitzgerald and Marie Louise Wall; *m* 1939, Gladys Evelyn (*née* Wright); two *s* one *d*. *Educ:* Wandsworth School; London School of Economics, BCom 1933, Hon. Fellow, 1970. O. T. Falk & Co., 1933-39; Min. of Food, 1939-52; Under-Sec., 1948-52. Dep. Head, Finance Dept, Unilever Ltd, 1952-56; Head of Organisation Div., Unilever Ltd, 1956-58; Man. Dir, Electric & Musical Industries, 1960-66 (Dir, 1958); Dep. Chm., Post Office Board, 1966-68; Chairman: International Computers (Holdings) Ltd and International Computers Ltd, 1968-72; Burrup Mathieson (Holdings) Ltd, 1973-76. Mem. (part-time), Sugar Bd, 1964-77. Officer, Order of Orange Nassau, 1947. *Recreation:* golf. *Address:* Wychwood, Coombe End, Kingston-upon-Thames, Surrey. *T:* 01-942 3873. *Club:* Royal Automobile.   [*Died 29 Dec.* 1980.

WALL, Rt. Rev. Bernard Patrick, DD; Titular Bishop of Othona; *b* 15 March 1894; *s* of Daniel and Elizabeth Wall. *Educ:* St John's Seminary, Wonersh, Guildford; Institut Catholique, Paris; Collegio Angelico, Rome (DD). Ordained July 1918; curate at English Martyrs' Church, Walworth, SE, 1918-20; postgraduate studies Paris and Rome, 1920-23; Prof. of Humanities, Southwark Junior Seminary, 1923-27; Prof. of Dogmatic Theology, St John's Seminary, Wonersh, 1927-35; Parish Priest of Anerley, SE, 1935-45; of Reigate, 1945-49; Rector of St John's Seminary, Wonersh, 1949-55; Canon of Southwark, 1950; Bishop of Brentwood, 1956-69. Domestic Prelate to HH The Pope, 1952. *Address:* 18 Bressey Grove, South Woodford, E18 2HP.   [*Died 18 June* 1976.

WALL, Sir (George) Rolande (Percival), Kt 1946; MC 1917; President Lovell & Christmas Ltd; *b* West Kirby, Cheshire, 9 March 1898; *s* of late Percy T. Wall; *m* 1923, Dorice Katharine Whineray, Neston, Cheshire; one *s* one *d*. *Educ:* Lockers Park; Winchester College. Served European War, 1914-18. RFA (wounded, MC). Served with Min. of Food from Oct. 1939, starting Asst Dir Imports Dairy Products; Dep. Sec. and Head Supply Dept until 31 Dec. 1946; Hon. Commercial Adviser to Ministry of Food, 1947-55. *Address:* Fairmead, Greenways, Haywards Heath, Sussex. *Club:* Royal Automobile.
                          [*Died 5 June* 1972.

WALL, Sir Rolande; see Wall, Sir G. R. P.

WALLACE, Harry Wright, CBE 1950; Member of Lambeth Borough Council, 1936-56; Mayor, 1952-53; *b* 11 Sept. 1885; *m* 1924, Margaret Gardiner, BA, *e d* of Edward Gardiner, Laburnum House, Llansamlet, S Wales; one *s*. *Educ:* Public Elementary School. MP (Lab) East Walthamstow, 1929-31 and 1945-55. *Address:* 1 Voss Court, Streatham Common, SW16. *T:* 01-764 5701.   [*Died 30 April* 1973.

WALLACE, Air Cdre James, DSO 1944; MVO 1962; DFC 1942; AFC 1953; *b* 28 July 1918; *s* of late Frederick George Wallace and late Isobel May (*née* Wickham), Limerick, Ireland; *m* 1948, Irene Maria (*née* Heilbuth), Copenhagen (marr. diss. 1971); one *s* one *d*. *Educ:* Mountjoy School; Kilkenny College, Ireland. Joined RAF, 1938; served in: Middle East, 1939-41; Desert Air Force, 1941-43; psa 1942; Italy, 1943-44; NE Europe, 1944-48; Fighter Comd, OC 41 Sqdn, 1949-51; Fighter Comd, Duxford wing, 1951-53; jssc 1953; British Joint Staff, Washington, DC, 1954-56; NATO (France), 1956-58; Fighter Comd, 1958-60; Deputy Capt. The Queen's Flight, 1960-63; Director of Public Relations (RAF), Ministry of Defence, 1964-67; retired. Spitfire Productions Ltd, 1967-70; Director, Promotor (Europe) Ltd, 1970-73. Area Warden, Wilts Nat. Trust, 1974-75. Walsh Security Service, London Hilton, 1976-77. Légion d'Honneur, Croix de Guerre (French), 1945. *Recreations:* military history, swimming, walking. *Address:* c/o National Westminster Bank, 14 Minster Street, Salisbury, Wilts. *Clubs:* London Irish Rugby, Lord's Taverners'.   [*Died 17 Sept.* 1980.

WALLACE, Air Vice-Marshal John Brown, CB 1963; OBE 1945; RAF retired; Deputy Director-General of Medical Services, Royal Air Force, 1961-66; *b* 4 Sept. 1907; *s* of late James Wallace, Cambuslang, near Glasgow; *m* 1937, Gwendolen Mary Shorthouse; two *d*. *Educ:* Hamilton Academy; Glasgow University. MB, ChB (Glasgow), 1931, MD (Glasgow), 1940. Joined RAF, 1936; served in Southern Rhodesia, 1941-45. Dep. Principal MO, Coastal Command, 1950, appointment in USA, 1950-54; Dep. Principal MO, Home Command, 1955; Principal MO: Fighter Command, 1958; Near East Air Force (Cyprus), 1961. QHS, 1962-66. *Recreation:* gardening. *Address:* 3

Wakehams Hill, Pinner, Mddx. *T:* 01-866 8345.
                          [*Died 16 Jan.* 1980.

WALLACE, John Madder, CBE 1963; lately Chairman Board Royal Marsden Hospital, London; Director of Companies; *b* 22 July 1887; *s* of late James and Mary Wallace; *m* 1914 (wife *decd* 1949); one *s* two *d*; *m* 1958, Gertrude Florence Mitchell. *Educ:* George Heriot's, Edinburgh. Entered Royal Bank of Scotland, 1904; Toronto-Dominion Bank, 1912; Vice-President: Equitable Trust Co. of NY, 1923; Chase Manhattan Bank, 1930. *Recreations:* golf, fishing. *Address:* Kirklands, Derby Road, Haslemere, Surrey. *T:* Haslemere 2148. *Clubs:* Athenæum, Carlton, City of London.   [*Died 17 Jan.* 1975.

WALLACE, Sir Martin (Kelso), Kt 1963; *b* 3 May 1898; *s* of William Henry and Mary May Wallace; *m* 1926, Eileen Bertha (*née* Marshall), OBE, BA, LLB, HDipEd. *Educ:* Methodist College, Belfast. Served RNVR European War, 1914-18 (General Service and Victory Medals). High Sheriff, 1960, Lord Mayor, 1961-63, Belfast. Rep. Windsor Ward as Councillor, later Alderman, in Belfast Corporation, for 19 years. Served on various boards, hospital cttees, etc. *Recreation:* angling. *Address:* 23 Cranmore Avenue, Belfast, Northern Ireland BT9 6JH. *T:* Belfast 665531.   [*Died 12 Feb.* 1978.

WALLACE, Philip Adrian H.; see Hope-Wallace.

WALLACE, William, CBE 1954; MCom; Member: Joseph Rowntree Memorial Trust, 1933-66 (Chairman, 1951-63); Joseph Rowntree Social Service Trust, 1959-69 (Emeritus Trustee, 1969); Acton Society Trust; National Birthday Trust; Court of York University; Vice-President, British Society for International Health Education; resigned as Chairman of Rowntree and Co. Ltd, 31 October 1957; Vice-President, Industrial Co-Partnership Association (Chairman 1954-57); Founder Member, British Institute of Management; *b* 10 May 1891; *s* of late James Wallace; *m* 1918, Nancie E. Hancox; one *s* two *d*. *Educ:* Argyle House Sch.; legal articles; London Univ. Qualified as Solicitor Clements Inn, Daniel Reardon and Clabon prizeman, Scott Scholar, 1912. Ministry of Reconstruction: Secretary of Housing (Rent Restrictions), Housing (Financial Assistance), and Neutral Tonnage Cttees and Asst Secretary Local Government Cttee, 1917-19; an industrial adviser and director, Ministry of Food, 1940-45. Rowntree & Co., Ltd: Executive, 1919; Secretary, 1929-31; Director, 1931-57; Dep.-Chm., 1944-52; Chairman, 1952-57. President, Cocoa, Chocolate and Confectionary Alliance Ltd, 1951-53 (Vice-Pres., 1948-51). Mem. Grand Council, FBI, 1950-57; Lay Member, Restrictive Practices Court, 1958-60. Coronation Medal, 1953. *Publications:* Business Forecasting and its Practical Application, 1927; We Can Conquer Unemployment, 1929; Enterprise First, 1946; Prescription for Partnership, 1959. Associated with: The Agricultural Dilemma, 1935; British Agriculture, 1938. *Recreations:* travel, gardening and social economics. *Address:* Windrush, Strensall, York. *T:* Strensall 327. *Club:* Reform.
                          [*Died 21 Oct.* 1976.

WALLACE-COPLAND, Harold; Captain late RFA; HM Lieutenant for the County of Stafford, 1949-68; Hon. Colonel; *b* 30 May 1893; *s* of William Wallace-Copland, MVO, and Caroline Sarah Wallace-Copland; *m* 1918, Winifred Hester Sutton (*d* 1961), JP Staffordshire, *d* of Thomas Sutton Lones; one *s*. *Educ:* Coatham, Redcar, Yorks. Solicitor, 1919; Stafford Borough Council, 1922-34 and 1938-49; Staffordshire CC, 1940-50; Mayor of Stafford, 1944-46; Chairman Staffordshire CC, 1946-49. managing Director Duke & Dudley Ltd, Copeway Ltd. KStJ 1949. *Recreation:* golf. *Address:* Cotteswold, Rowley Park, Stafford. *T:* Stafford 2892.   [*Died 7 June* 1973.

WALLER, Vice-Adm. John William Ashley, CB 1946; *b* 17 Jan. 1892; *s* of John Ashley Waller, Beenham Court, Kingsclere, Hants, and Margaret Priscilla Lavinia Waller; *m* 1918, Adye Campbell Russell, Melbourne; one *s* one *d*. *Educ:* Naval Colleges. Midshipman, 1909; Sub-Lt 1912; Lieutenant 1913; Served in Grand Fleet, 1914-18, King Edward VII, Royal Oak and Marlborough; qualified in torpedoes, 1918; staff college, 1928; Comdr 1926; Capt. 1934; Chief of Intelligence Staff Far East, 1935-36; commanded HMAS Sydney, 1937-39; Naval Assistant to First Sea Lord, 1941-42; commanded HMS Malaya, 1942-44; Rear-Adm. 1944; Red Sea and Suez Canal Area, 1944-45; Washington, USA, 1945-46, on Lend Lease and Administration; Naval Adviser to Netherlands Ministry of Marine, 1946-47; Vice-Admiral, retired list, 1947. *Recreations:* riding, fishing, ornithology. *Address:* Es Mastay, San Cristobal, Menorca, Baleares, Spain; c/o National Westminster Bank Ltd, South Kensington Station, 18 Cromwell Place, SW7.
                          [*Died 9 Jan.* 1975.

WALLER, Mervyn Napier, CMG 1959; OBE 1953; mural painter, stained-glass and mosaic artist; *b* 19 June 1893; *s* of late William and Sarah Waller; *m* 1958, Lorna Marion Reyburn. *Educ:* National Gallery Art School, Melbourne. Served European War, 1914-18 in AIF, 111th Howitzer Battery (loss of right arm at Bullecourt). Served as Trustee, National Art Gallery, Melbourne. Recent works: stained-glass and mosaic, Hall of Memory, Australian War Memorial, Canberra; stained-glass, in churches in Melbourne, incl. St Mark's, St Stephen's, St Peter's; mosaics, Temple Court, State Electricity Commn, Monash House, Melbourne. *Address:* 9 Crown Road, Ivanhoe, Victoria 3079, Australia. *T:* 491014. *Club:* Savage (Melbourne).
[Died 27 March 1972.

WALLINGER, Sir Geoffrey (Arnold), GBE 1963; KCMG 1953 (CMG 1947); *b* 2 May 1903; *s* of late William A. Wallinger, OBE, IFS; *m* 1st, 1939, Diana Peel Nelson; one *s*; 2nd, 1950, Alix de la Faye Lamotte (*d* 1956); 3rd, 1958, Stella Irena, *d* of late Konni Zilliacus. *Educ:* Sherborne; Clare Coll., Cambridge. Entered Diplomatic Service, 1926; Secretary: at Cairo, 1927-29, at Vienna, 1929-31, at Foreign Office, 1931-34; Political Sec. to UK High Comr in S Africa, 1935-38; First Sec., Buenos Aires, 1938-42; First Sec., Foreign Office, 1943; Counsellor in China, 1943-47 (Minister-local rank, 1945); Counsellor in Foreign Office, 1947-49; Minister to Hungary, 1949-51; Ambassador: to Thailand, 1951-54, to Austria, 1954-58, to Brazil, 1958-63; retired from Foreign Service, 1963. Director: Lloyds Bank International, 1972-75; Bank of London and South America, 1963-75. *Address:* 10 Baskerville Road, SW18. *T:* 01-870 4474. *Club:* Brooks's. *[Died 5 July 1979.*

WALLINGFORD, Air Cdre Sidney, CB 1951; CBE 1944; RNZAF, retired; *b* 12 July 1898; *s* of late Major Jesse Alfred Wallingford, MC, and Alice Wallingford; *m* 1929, Kathleen Matilda Jamieson; one *s* one *d. Educ:* Auckland Grammar Sch., New Zealand. Served European War, 1916-20, with Artists' Rifles, Rifle Brigade, and RAF; First Commissioned, Dec. 1916; Fiji Constabulary, 1921-23; Royal Air Force, 1924-29; NZ Permanent Air Force, 1929; PSA 1937; NZ Liaison Officer, Air Ministry, 1938-40; Air Force Member for Personnel, Air Dept, Wellington, NZ, 1941-42; RNZAF Staff Officer to Commander Aircraft South Pacific and AOC No. 1 (Islands) Group, RNZAF, 1942-43; AOC Northern Group, RNZAF, 1944; Air Member for Supply at Air Dept, Wellington, NZ, 1945-46; idc 1947; Air Member for Personnel at Air Dept, NZ, 1948-52; AOC HQ Task Force, RNZAF at Hobsonville, Auckland, NZ, 1952-53; retired 1954. Pres. Nat. Rifle Assoc. of NZ, 1954-58. US Legion of Merit (Degree of Officer). *Recreations:* trout fishing, rifle and pistol shooting; winner Queen Mary's Prize at Bisley in 1928; RAF Rifle Championship, 1927, 1929. *Address:* Opito Bay, Whitianga, New Zealand. *Club:* Officers' (Auckland, NZ). *[Died 25 July 1978.*

WALLIS, Sir Barnes (Neville), Kt 1968; CBE 1943; FRS 1945; Hon. DSc Eng London and Bristol; Hon. ScD Cambridge; Hon. DSc Loughborough, Oxford and Heriot-Watt; FICE; Hon. MIMechE; Hon. FRAeS; FRSA; FSE; RDI, 1943; Chief of Aeronautical Research and Development, British Aircraft Corporation Ltd, Weybridge Division, Weybridge, Surrey, 1945-71; *b* 26 Sept. 1887; *s* of Charles George Wallis, BA (Oxon), MRCS, LRCP, and Edith Eyre Ashby; *m* 1925, Mary Frances, *d* of Arthur George Bloxam, FIC; two *s* two *d. Educ:* Christ's Hospital. Trained as Marine Engineer at J. S. White & Co. Ltd, Cowes, 1905-1913; Designer, Airship Dept, Vickers Ltd, 1913-15; served European War, Artists' Rifles and RNVR, 1915; Chief Designer, Vickers Ltd, Airship Dept, Barrow-in-Furness, 1916-22; Chief Engineer, Airship Guarantee Co., London and Howden, Yorks, 1923-30; Chief Designer, Structures, Vickers Aviation Ltd, Weybridge, 1930-37; Asst Chief Designer, Vickers-Armstrongs Ltd, Aviation Section, 1937-45. Designer of HMA R100; Inventor of Geodetic Construction; Inventor of weapon which destroyed Moehne and Eder Dams, and penetration bombs, 1940-45; Inventor of Variable Geometry Aircraft. Vice-Pres., Bath Inst. of Medical Engineering, 1968-. Master of Faculty, RDI, 1965-67. Hon. Fellow, Churchill Coll., Cambridge, 1965-; Senior Fellow, RCA, 1966; Hon. Fellow: UMIST; Manchester Coll. Art and Design. Hon. FRAeS 1967; Hon. Life Mem. and Fellow, Inst. of Patentees and Inventors, 1968. Treasurer, Christ's Hosp., and Chm., Council of Almoners, 1957-70. Freeman and Liveryman, Worshipful Co. of Shipwrights and Guild of Air Pilots and Navigators; Freeman of City of London. Founders' Medal, Air League, 1963; Kelvin Gold Medal, ICE, 1968; Albert Medal, RSA, 1968; Royal Medal, Royal Society, 1975. *Publications:* Some Technical Aspects of the Commercial Airship (Lloyd's Register of Shipping, 1925); The Design and Construction of HMA R100; *relevant publication:* Barnes Wallis, by J. E. Morpurgo, 1972. *Address:* White Hill House, Effingham,

Surrey. *Clubs:* Athenæum, Royal Air Force.
[Died 30 Oct. 1979.

WALLIS, Claude (Edgar), MBE 1944; retired as Chairman and Managing Director Associated Iliffe Press Ltd (1945-60) and Chairman Kelly's Directories Ltd (1954-60); *b* Madras, India, 21 Jan. 1886; *s* of late Charles and Constance Walder-Wallis. *Educ:* City of Westminster and Emanuel Schools. Associated with motoring journalism for 60 years; joined late Lord Montague in 1905 on staff of Car Illustrated and transf. to Iliffe & Sons Ltd, publishers of The Autocar, Automobile Engineer, and other motoring and aviation journals, 1911; Managing Director Associated Iliffe Press, 1939. Special Reserve of Officers, 1912-20, rank Captain. Served European War: 1st Bn Loyal North Lancashire Regt during retreat from Mons (wounded, prisoner, Sept. 1914; despatches, 1914 Star, GS and Victory Medals); War of 1939-45 (MBE); served on numerous government cttees relating to publishing, paper rationing, etc.; was instrumental in organising special appeals in motor and other industries which raised £250,000 for BRCS. President: Motor & Cycle Trades Benevolent Fund, 1947-48; Periodical Proprietors Assoc., 1953-56; Fellowship of the Motor Industry. *Recreations:* motoring, sailing. *Address:* 25 Manchester Square, W1. *T:* 01-935 9375. *Clubs:* Royal Automobile; Royal Motor Yacht (Poole). *[Died 25 May 1980.*

WALLIS, Leonard G. C.; *see* Coke Wallis.

WALMSLEY, Air Commodore John Banks, CBE 1946; DFC 1918; QC 1955; retired; *b* 9 Oct. 1896; *s* of Thomas James Walmsley; *m* 1926, Dorothy Maud Bleasdale; two *d. Educ:* Shrewsbury Sch.; RMC, Sandhurst. Called to Bar, Gray's Inn, 1924. Served European War, 1915-18, as pilot in RFC and RAF. Practised as barrister on Northern Circuit, 1924-33; joined RAF Legal Branch in Office of The Judge Advocate General, 1933; Dep. Judge Advocate General of Army and RAF in Middle East, 1936-40; served in RAF Legal Branch in office of The Judge Advocate General, 1940-48; Director of Legal Services, Air Ministry, 1948-57. Greek Military Cross, 1918. *Recreations:* golf, gardening. *Address:* Littledene, Church Lane, Oxted, Surrey. *T:* Oxted 2942. *[Died 28 Oct. 1976.*

WALMSLEY, Kenneth Maurice, CMG 1959; OBE 1953; *b* 26 Jan. 1914; *s* of late George Walmsley, Clonskeagh, Dublin, and Ventnor, IoW; *m* 1941, Kathleen Margaret, *d* of late J. R. Patterson, Skeagh House, Brookeborough, Co. Fermanagh; one *s. Educ:* St Columba's Coll., Rathfarnham, Co. Dublin; Trinity Coll., Dublin; Christ's Coll., Cambridge. Cadet in Colonial Administrative Service, Nigeria, 1937; District Officer, Nigeria, 1946; Financial Secretary, Somaliland, 1950; Colonial Secretary of the Bahamas, 1956; retired, 1964. *Recreations:* golf and riding. *Address:* Las Yucas I, Primero C, Limonar Alto, Málaga, Spain. *[Died 26 Feb. 1977.*

WALPOLE, George Frederick, CBE 1953; Director-General Department of Lands and Surveys, 1940, Director of Irrigation, 1948, Director of Forests, 1952, in the Jordan Government, retired from the service of the Jordan Government, 1954; *b* 8 Jan. 1892; *o s* of W. J. Walpole, JP, and E. M. Walpole (née Russell); *m* 1928, Agnes Letitia Blount-Dinwiddie (*d* 1974); two *d. Educ:* Bootham Sch., York; Trinity Coll., Dublin (BA, BAI). Served European War, 1914-18, France and Cameroons; commissioned RA, 1914; retired, 1919. Joined Egyptian Civil Service as Inspector of Surveys, 1921; carried out extensive surveys in Sinai, Eastern and Western Deserts of Egypt, 1921-30; discovered and mapped the Qattara Depression, 1926-29; prepared and published the 1/500,000 map of Egypt, 1930-36; resigned from Egyptian service, 1936; Assistant Director of Lands and Surveys, Trans Jordan Government, 1936-40. FRICS 1950; Founder's Medal, Royal Geographical Society, 1950. *Publications:* An Ancient Aqueduct West of Mersa Matruh, 1929; Land Settlement in Trans Jordan, 1942; Land Problems in Trans Jordan, 1947. *Recreation:* gardening. *Address:* Rust Hall, Bridge Road, Helen's Bay, Bangor, Co. Down.
[Died 18 Jan. 1975.

WALSH, Prof. Arthur Donald, MA, PhD (Cantab); FRS 1964; FRSE, FRIC; Professor of Chemistry, University of Dundee, since 1967 (University of St Andrews, 1955-67); *b* 8 Aug. 1916; *s* of Arthur Thomas and Amy Florence Walsh; *m* 1945, Elin Frances Woolley, MA, *er d* of H. C. Woolley, London; two *s* two *d. Educ:* Loughborough Grammar Sch.; Corpus Christi Coll., Cambridge (Mawson Schol.). Research and teaching: Cambridge Univ., 1938-49; Univ. of Leeds, 1949-54; Visiting Prof., Univ. of California, 1950-51; Reader in Physical Chemistry, Univ. of Leeds, 1953-55. *Publications:* numerous papers in scientific journals. *Recreations:* gardening, bird-watching. *Address:* Department of Chemistry, University of

Dundee, Dundee DD1 4HN. *T:* Dundee 23181; Groom's Garth, 26 Glamis Drive, Dundee DD2 1QP.   *[Died* 23 *April* 1977.

WALSH, Rt. Hon. Sir Cyril Ambrose, PC 1971; Justice of High Court of Australia since 1969; *b* 1909; *s* of late Michael J. and Mary E. Walsh, Sydney; *m* 1942, Mary Agnes Smyth; three *s.* *Educ:* Parramatta High Sch.; Univ. of Sydney. BA 1930, LLB 1934, Sydney. Admitted Bar of NSW, 1934; Judge of Supreme Court of NSW, 1954; Judge of Appeal, Supreme Court of NSW, 1966. *Address:* 13 Mandolong Road, Mosman, NSW 2088, Australia. *T:* 960-2296. *Club:* University (Sydney).
[Died 29 *Nov.* 1973.

WALSH, Rt. Rev. Francis, DD, DPh; retired Bishop of Aberdeen (RC); *b* 15 Sept. 1901. *Educ:* Fordyce Academy, Banffshire; Blairs Coll., Aberdeen; Scots Coll., Rome. DPh 1921; DD, 1925. Parish work, Inverness, 1925-29. Joined White Fathers Society (Missionaries of Africa), 1929; founded St Columba's Coll., Newtown St Boswells, 1934; Superior of White Fathers, Heston, Mddx, 1949-51. Bishop of Aberdeen, (RC), 1951-63; Titular Bishop of Birta, 1963. Resigned formally from White Fathers Society, 1974. *Address:* (temporarily) c/o Bishop Foylan, 156 King's Gate, Aberdeen, Scotland.   *[Died* 27 *Oct.* 1974.

WALSH, Maj.-Gen. George Peregrine, CB 1944; CBE 1943; DSO 1942; late Royal Artillery; *b* 30 June 1899; *s* of late Charles Peregrine Walsh; *m* 1944, Ruth Vaughan Ashe, *yr d* of R. A Holmes a Court, MC; two *s* one *d. Educ:* Felsted; RMA, Woolwich. 2nd Lieut, RA, 1918; served European War, France and Belgium, 1918; Waziristan, 1921-24; Palestine, 1936-39 (despatches); War of 1939-45 (despatches, DSO, CBE, CB); Maj.-Gen., 1944; Chief of Staff; 8th Army, 1944; ALFSEA 1945; Southern Comd, 1948-49; Director of Weapons and Development, War Office, 1949-52; retired 1954. Assistant Controller of Munitions, Ministry of Supply, 1954-60. *Address:* The Old Rectory, Warmwell, Dorchester, Dorset.
[Died 5 *Feb.* 1972.

WALSH, Rt. Rev. Gordon John; Assistant Bishop of Ely since 1942; *b* 1880; *s* of late John Edward Walsh, BL, JP, Dublin; *m* 1909, Edythe (*d* 1956), *d* of late Archdeacon Spence, DD, Belfast; no *c. Educ:* Sutton Valence Sch., Kent; Trinity Coll., Dublin; BA 1902, MA 1909, DD 1927; MA Jesus Coll., Cambridge, 1945. Ordained, 1903; Curate, Trinity Church, Belfast, 1903, and St Mary's, Belfast, 1905; Association Secretary of the Colonial and Continental Church Society for Ireland, 1909; Rector of St Peter's, Athlone, 1910-13; missionary under the Church Missionary Society at Tokushima, 1914-22; Hakodate, 1922-23; Asahigawa, 1923-27; Secretary to the CMS Hokkaido Mission and Examining Chaplain to the Bishop of the diocese, 1922-27; Bishop in Hokkaido, 1927-40; Vicar of Eastry and Tilmanstone, Kent, 1941-42; Residentiary Canon of Ely Cathedral, 1942-67; Vice-Dean, 1956-67. *Address:* 3 Bishop Wynn Close, Broad Street, Ely, Cambs. *T:* Ely 2764. *Clubs:* Royal Societies, Royal Over-Seas League. *[Died* 19 *Nov.* 1971.

WALSH, Henry Francis Chester, OBE 1936; *b* 10 May 1891; *s* of late Richard Walter Walsh and Ismay Chester, Williamstown House, Castlebellingham, Co. Louth; *m* 1st, 1924, Carla (*d* 1955), *d* of Colonel Holger Hedemann, Copenhagen; three *d;* 2nd, 1956, Violet Mary, *d* of late Lt-Col A. T. S. Magan, CMG. *Educ:* Stonyhurst; Exeter Coll., Oxford (MA Mod. Languages); Inner Temple. Vice-Consul, Surabaya, 1924; Consul at Batavia, 1931; acted at various Consular posts in Siam, French Indo-China and Netherlands East Indies; Acting Consul-General at Batavia in 1935 and 1936; Consul-General at Saigon, 1938-39; at Batavia, 1939-42; Consul-General for Texas and New Mexico, 1942-45; Political Adviser to C-in-C Allied Forces, Netherlands East Indies, 1945-46; retired Oct. 1946. *Recreations:* tennis and golf. *Address:* Williamstown House, Castlebellingham, Co. Louth, Ireland. *Club:* Royal Irish Automobile (Dublin).
[Died 16 *Sept.* 1977.

WALSH, Most Rev. Joseph, DD, MA; Titular Archbishop of Tubernuca; *b* Newport, Mayo, 1888. *Educ:* St Jarlath's Coll., Tuam; Maynooth. Graduated RUI, 1909; MA 1911; priest, 1914; Prof. of Classics, St Jarlath's Coll., Tuam, 1914-18; Secretary to Archbishop of Tuam, 1918-26; Canon and Vicar General, 1924; Administrator, Tuam, 1926-29; President, St Jarlath's Coll., Tuam, 1929-40; titular Bishop of Cela and Auxiliary to Archbishop of Tuam, 1938; Archbishop of Tuam, 1940-69. *Address:* Shrine House, 6 St Jarlath's Place, Tuam, Eire.   *[Died* 20 *June* 1973.

WALSH, William Joseph; National Secretary, Association of Clerical, Technical and Supervisory Staffs, 1961-78; *b* 28 Aug. 1919; *m* 1942, Doreen Mary Garton; three *s. Educ:* Tonysguboriau Sch., Llantrisant, Glam. Regional Officer,

Assoc. of Clerical, Technical and Supervisory Staffs, 1951. Member: Nat. Jt Council for Local Authorities APT&C Grades, 1961-; TUC Non-Manual Adv. Cttee, 1962-; TUC Steel Cttee, 1964-; Nat. Jt Council for Non-Manual Staff of National Bus Co., 1968-; Petroleum Trng Bd, 1970-; Nat. Council for Passenger Transport Exec. Staff, 1970-; Business Studies Bd, British Educn Council, 1976-. *Recreations:* Rugby Union football, cricket, National Hunt racing. *Address:* 171 Clapham Road, SW9. *T:* 01-274 5906.   *[Died* 17 *June* 1978.

WALSHE, Sir Francis (Martin Rouse), Kt 1953; OBE 1919; FRS 1946; MD, DSc, FRCP; Hon. DSc National University of Ireland; Hon. DLittHum University of Cincinnati, USA; Hon. Consulting Physician to University College Hospital and to the National Hospital for Nervous Diseases, Queen Square, WC; Fellow University College, London; *s* of late M. C. Walshe, JP, London; *m* Bertha (*d* 1950), *d* of late Charles Dennehy, FRCSEd, St Lucia, BWI, and Lismore, Co. Cork; two *s. Educ:* Prior Park Coll.; University College Sch. and University College and Hospital. Major, RAMC and Consulting Neurologist, MEF and EEF, 1915-19 (despatches, OBE); Welch Lecturer Clinical Physiology, University of Oxford, 1921; Visiting Neurologist Johns Hopkins Hospital, Baltimore, Md, USA, 1925; Oliver Sharpey Lecturer, Royal College of Physicians, 1929; Victor Horsley Lecturer, 1946; Harveian Orator, RCP, 1948; Editor of *Brain,* 1937-53. Hon. Member Neurological Societies of America, Canada, Denmark, France, Germany, New York, Spain, Uruguay, and of American Academy of Neurology. Thayer Lecturer, Johns Hopkins Hospital, Baltimore, 1952. President: Assoc. British Neurologists, 1950-51; RSM, 1952-54; Royal Soc. Hygiene and Public Health, 1962-64. Fothergillian Gold Medallist, Medical Society of London, 1951; Ferrier Lecturer, Royal Society, 1953; Hughlings Jackson Lecturer and Medallist, 1952, Gowers' Lecturer and Medallist, 1956, RSM, Nuffield Lecturer and Medallist, 1961; Harben Lecturer and Medallist, 1966. *Publications:* Textbook of Nervous Diseases, 11th edn; Critical Studies in Neurology, 1948; Further Critical Studies in Neurology, 1965; On the Structure of Medicine and its Place among the Sciences (Harveian Oration, RCP), 1948; Humanism, History and Natural Science in Medicine (Linacre Lecture); papers on physiology and diseases of nervous system. *Address:* Manor Cottage, Brampton, Hunts.
[Died 21 *Feb.* 1973.

WALTARI, Mika; Author since 1928, Finland; Member of Academy of Finland since 1957; *b* 19 Sept. 1908; *s* of Toimi Armas Waltari and Olga Maria (*née* Johansson); *m* 1931, Marjatta Luukkonen; one *d. Educ:* Helsinki Univ. (MA). Literary critic for Maaseudun Tulevaisuus, 1932-42; Literary reviewer for Finnish Broadcasting Company, 1937-38; Editor for Suomen Kuvalehti, weekly illustrated magazine, 1936-38; with editorial office of Finnish State Information Bureau, 1939-40 and 1941-44. DrPhil *hc* Turku Univ., 1970. Awarded literary prizes, Finland 1934, 1935, 1950 and 1954; Pro Finlandia, 1952; Commander of Finnish Lion, 1960. *Publications:* The Egyptian, 1949; Michael the Finn, 1950; The Sultan's Renegade, 1951; The Dark Angel, 1953; A Nail Merchant at Nightfall, 1954; Moonscape, 1955; The Etruscan, 1957; The Secret of the Kingdom, 1961; The Roman, 1966. *Recreation:* detective stories. *Address:* Tunturikatu 13, Helsinki 10, Finland. *Club:* PEN (Finland).   *[Died* 16 *Aug.* 1979.

WALTER, Keith McNeil C.; *see* Campbell-Walter.

WALTER, W(illiam) Grey, MA, ScD; Scientific Consultant, Burden Neurological Institute, Bristol, 1939-76, now Emeritus Consultant; *b* Kansas City, Mo, USA, 19 Feb. 1910; *s* of Karl Walter and Margaret Hardy; *m* 1st, 1934, Monica Ratcliffe (divorced, 1947); two *s;* 2nd, 1947, Vivian Joan Dovey; one *s;* 3rd, 1960, Lorraine Josephine Aldridge (*née* Donn) (divorced, 1974). *Educ:* Westminster Sch.; King's Coll., Cambridge. BA Hons 1st class Part II Physiology, 1931; Harold Fry and Michael Foster Student, 1931; MA 1934; ScD 1947; Rockefeller Fellow, Maudsley Hosp., 1935. Founder and Foreign Sec., Electroencephalographic Soc., 1942; Co-Founder and Hon. Pres., Internat. Fedn of Socs for Electroencephalography and Clinical Neurophysiology, 1947; Co-founder and Co-Editor of Electroencephalography and Clinical Neurophysiology, 1947. Maudsley Lectr, Royal Medico-Psychological Assoc., 1949. Mem. WHO Study Group on Psychobiological Develt of the Child, 1953-56. Co-Founder and Council Mem. Internat. Assoc. of Cybernetics, 1956. Adolf Meyer Lectr, American Psychiatric Assoc., 1959. Prof. and Dr *hc*, Univ. of Aix-Marseille, 1949. *Publications:* The Living Brain, 1953; Further Outlook (The Curve of the Snowflake), 1956; papers on neurophysiology, electronics and cybernetics in Jl of Physiology, EEG Jl, Jl of Mental Science, Proc. Royal Soc. Medicine, etc. *Recreations:* tennis, skin diving. *Address:* 20 Richmond Park Road, Bristol BS8 3AP. *T:* Bristol 312702.   *[Died* 6 *May* 1977.

WALTERS, Rev. David John, MC, MA; *b* Ammanford, Carmarthenshire, 13 Jan. 1893; *s* of T. Watkyn Walters, Tirydail, Neath; *m* 1917, Frances, *d* of Mrs F. Atkinson, Daleside, Sleights, Yorks; one *s* one *d. Educ:* Christ College, Brecon; Brasenose College, Oxford (Junior Hulme Scholar), 2nd Class Hons School of Natural Science. Assistant Master at Haileybury College, 1914-19; Assistant Master and Housemaster at Uppingham School, 1919-31; Headmaster of Bromsgrove School, 1931-53; Vicar of Lindridge, dio. of Worcester, 1953-57; Rector of All Saints', Worcester, 1957-64; Rural Dean of Worcester, 1960-64. On active service as Lieutenant in RGA, 1915-18 (despatches, MC). *Publications:* (Joint) History of 135th Siege Battery, RGA, 1921; Bromsgrove in Exile, 1971. *Recreation:* walking. *Address:* 138 Graham Road, Malvern, Worcs. *[Died 11 Dec. 1979.*

WALTERS, Francis Paul; *b* 1888; *s* of late Rev. F. B. Walters, King William's College, Isle of Man, and Cecilia Beales; *m* 1921, Louise Roux-Bourgeois; two *d. Educ:* Eton; University Coll., Oxford. Fellow and Tutor of University Coll., Oxford, 1912, Hon. Fellow, 1938; served European War, in Oxford and Bucks Light Infantry (Special Reserve) (Captain) and General Staff; joined Secretariat of League of Nations, 1919; Deputy-Secretary-General of the League of Nations, 1939-40. *Publication:* A History of the League of Nations, 1951. *Address:* 10 Rue Cortot, Paris 18. *[Died 14 April 1976.*

WALTHER, Prof. David Philippe; Professor of Orthodontics, University of London, since 1961; Director and Head of Orthodontic Department, Royal Dental Hospital School of Dental Surgery; Hon. Consultant in Orthodontics to Hospital for Sick Children, Great Ormond Street and to St George's Hospital Group; *b* 18 Sept. 1909; *s* of Dr David Walther and Miriam Walther; *m* 1939, Barbara Brook; one *s* one *d. Educ:* St Edward's School, Oxford; Guy's Hospital Medical and Dental School. LDS; RCS 1934; MRCS, LRCP, 1941; DOrth, RCS 1954; MDS Univ. London, 1964; FDS, RCS 1965. House Surgeon in Children's Dentistry, including Surgery and Orthodontics, Guy's Hospital, 1934-35; private practice, Hampstead, 1935-49. Served War of 1939-45, Captain, RAMC, 1942-46. Registrar in Dental Department for Children and Orthodontics, Guy's Hospital, 1946-48; half-time Senior Orthodontic Registrar, Hospital for Sick Children, Gt Ormond St, 1948-50. Sen. Hosp. Dental Officer, Orthodontist in Charge of Orthodontic Clinic Dept, Eastman Dental Hosp., 1949-54; Consultant in Orthodontics, Eastman Dental Hosp., and Hosp. for Sick Children, Gt Ormond St, 1952-54. Reader in Orthodontics, Univ. of London and Director and Head of Orthodontic Dept, Royal Dental Hosp. of London School of Dental Surgery, 1954-61. *Publications:* Orthodontic Notes, 1960; (ed) Current Orthodontics, 1966; contrib. to scientific journals. *Recreations:* gardening, farming. *Address:* Cantreyn, Bridgnorth, Salop. *[Died 21 Dec. 1973.*

WALTON, Brig. Sir George (Hands), KBE 1958 (CBE 1937); CB 1953; TD 1942; DL; JP; Chairman: Newcastle Board, Commercial Union Assurance Co. Ltd; Industrial Management Research Association, 1954-63; Durham County T&AF Association, 1948-58; North Region Re-settlement Committee (Regular Services); *s* of James Walton, JP, North Shields; *m* Winifred (*d* 1972), *d* of W. J. Arkle, Stocksfield; one *s* one *d.* Chartered Accountant; served European War, 1914-18; served in Territorial Army between wars and commanded 50th Divisional Signal Regiment, 1930-36. Colonel 1934; Deputy Chief Signal Officer, Northern Command, 1937-39. Served throughout War of 1939-45 as Chief Signal Officer, Northern Command, York; also 10th Corps and 13th Corps, and BTE; Brig. 1942 (despatches twice); 4 years Middle East Command; in 1943 seconded by Army to serve as a Director on Middle East Board of the United Kingdom Commercial Corporation, Ltd (British Government war organisation); 1945, released to return to civil occupation. Hon. Colonel 50th Divisional Signal Regt TA, 1953-58; Chm. Finance Cttee, Member, Corps Cttee, Royal Corps of Signals, 1949-69. DL Co. Durham, 1942; JP Northumberland, 1950. OStJ. *Recreations:* shooting, hunting, golf, etc. *Address:* Letton Lodge, Alnmouth, Northumberland. *T:* 270. *Clubs:* Army and Navy; Union (Newcastle upon Tyne); County (Durham). *[Died 25 Nov. 1976.*

WALTON, Col Granville, CMG 1953; OBE 1919; late Royal Engineers; DL 1950; JP 1942, CC 1931; *b* 1888; *s* of late F. T. G. Walton, CIE, MInstCE, 34 St George's Ct, SW7; *m* 1924, Isabel Joan (MFH Old Berks Hunt 1939-42), *y d* of late Sir Robert McCraken, 23 Kensington Palace Gardens, W8; three *s. Educ:* Marlborough; RMA, Woolwich. 2nd Lieut RE 1907; NW State Railway of India, 1912-14 and 1920-28; retd as Asst Chief Operating Supt and Lt-Col, RE, 1928. RE Railway Troops in France and Greece, and on War Office Missions to Middle East,

Russia and Rumania (despatches twice), 1914-20. Hon. Sec. World Scout Jamboree, 1929; Member Council Scouts Assoc. 1929-; HQ Commissioner Boy Scouts Assoc., 1929-40; Group Comdr (Col) Berks HG, 1940-43. Re-employed War Office Directorate of Transportation, 1943-45; Overseas Comr, Boy Scouts Assoc., 1945-54. Chairman Faringdon RDC, 1948-50; High Sheriff of Berkshire, 1949; Transport Users Consultative Committee (SE Area), 1951-53; Member Thames Conservancy Board, 1951-57; Chairman, Faringdon Bench, 1951-57; CA 1949-63; Vice-Chairman Berkshire Standing Joint Cttee, 1955-63; Chairman County Council of Royal County of Berkshire, 1957-60; Chief Scout's Commissioner, 1954-59. Silver Wolf (British Scouting), 1929; Bronze Wolf (International Scouting), 1955. Officier L'Instruction Publique (France); St Anne and St Stanislas with swords (Russia); Commander Crown and Officer Star, with swords (Rumania). *Address:* Longworth Manor, near Abingdon, Berkshire. *T:* Longworth 223.
[Died 19 March 1974.

WALTON, James Ratcliffe, CBE 1943; *b* 12 July 1898; *m* 1925, Daisy Elizabeth Outram, Wanstead, Essex; no *c. Educ:* King Henry VIII, Coventry. Pupil with Alfred Herbert Ltd, Machine Tool Makers, Coventry; in India for same company, 1919-23; in 1924 joined staff of John Brown & Co. Ltd, Sheffield and Clydebank (now Thos Firth & John Brown Ltd, Sheffield) as Special Representative in India and the East; seconded to Govt of India as Controller of Steel Imports, 1940-46. *Recreation:* golf. *Address:* 4 Nelson House, Birkdale, Bexhill-on-Sea, Sussex. *T:* Cooden 3598. *Clubs:* Royal Bombay Yacht; Punjab, Lahore, etc. *[Died 14 March 1973.*

WALTON, John, MA, ScD (Cantab); DSc (Manchester); Hon. LLD (McMaster University); Hon. DèsSc (Universities of Montpellier and Lille); FRSE; Regius Professor of Botany, University of Glasgow, 1930-62, retired; Dean of Faculties, University of Glasgow, 1967-70; *b* London, 1895; *s* of late E. A. Walton, PRSW, RSA; *o s* of late Sir Albert C. Seward, FRS; one *s* one *d. Educ:* Daniel Stewart's College, Edinburgh; St John's College, Cambridge (Hutchinson Research Student). Junior Demonstrator in Botany, Cambridge University, 1922-23; Lecturer in Botany, University of Manchester, 1923-30; Botanist to 1st Oxford Expedition to Spitsbergen, 1921; Forestry Commissioner, 1949-54; Member of Scottish Cttee, Nature Conservancy, 1949-54; Pres. Botanical Soc. of Edinburgh, 1962-64. Corresp. mem., Botanical Soc. of America, 1957-, and Geological Soc. of Belgium, 1963-; Foreign mem., Botanical Soc. of Poland, 1961. *Publications:* An Introduction to the Study of Fossil Plants and various on Palæobotany in the Trans. Royal Soc. London and Edinburgh and in Annals of Botany; Editor and part-author, four Scottish National Forest Park Guidebooks, since 1938. *Address:* 9 Windsor Street, Dundee, Angus. *T:* Dundee 68411.
[Died 13 Feb. 1971.

WALTON, Prof. Kenneth, FRSE, FRSGS; Professor of Geography, since 1965, Vice-Principal, since 1977, University of Aberdeen; *b* 9 March 1923; *s* of Albert Walton and Annie Constance (*née* Burton); *m* 1949, Sheila Burrows; two *s. Educ:* King's Sch., Macclesfield; Univ. of Edinburgh. Univ. of Edinburgh, 1941-42. Commissioned in RA, 1942-46. Univ. of Edinburgh, 1946-48. Grad. 1st Class Hons with MA in Geography. Univ. of Aberdeen: Research Fellow, 1948; Lectr, 1949 (PhD 1951); Sen. Lectr, 1960; Reader, 1965. Murchison Award, RGS, 1978. *Publications:* The Highlands and Islands of Scotland, 1961; The Arid Zones, 1969; papers in Scottish Geographical Magazine, Trans. Inst. British Geographers, etc. *Recreations:* compulsive sailor, watching the family gardening, photography. *Address:* 23 Baillieswells Road, Bieldside, Aberdeen AB1 9BL. *T:* 48387. *[Died 2 Jan. 1979.*

WALTON, Sir Richmond, KBE 1946; CB 1944; *b* 16 May 1888; *s* of late Rev. Octavius F. Walton; *m* 1912, Emily Gladys Dibben (*d* 1962); one *s* three *d. Educ:* Wolverhampton; Caius Coll., Cambridge (scholar). First Class Classical Tripos, 1910; entered Admiralty, 1911; Assistant Secretary, Admiralty, 1932; Principal Assistant Secretary, Admiralty, 1941; Under-Secretary, Admiralty, 1943; Deputy Secretary of the Admiralty, 1944-48. *Address:* North Lodge, Matfen, Northumberland.
[Died 8 Aug. 1971.

WALTON, Prof. (William) Stanley, GM; MD, BHy; Emeritus Professor of Public Health, London School of Hygiene and Tropical Medicine, University of London; *b* 9 Nov. 1901; *s* of William and Mary Walton; *m* 1930, Anne Dorothy Margaret, *e d* of Edward Robson, Hexham. *Educ:* Gateshead Grammar Sch.; Univ. of Durham. MB, BS, Durham, 1925; BHy and DPH, 1927; MD (Commend.), 1932. Medical Officer of Health, West Bromwich; Dep. Medical Officer of Health for the City and Port

of Plymouth; Dep. MOH, Middlesbrough; Medical Officer and School Medical Officer for the City of Newcastle upon Tyne, and Head of Department of Public Health, Durham University; also sometime External Examiner in Public Health to 12 British universities; Consultant to WHO; Fellow of the Society of Medical Officers of Health; Member Soc. Middle Temple. *Publications:* (joint) A Thousand Families in Newcastle upon Tyne, 1954; One Hundred Years in History of The Society of Medical Officers of Health, 1956; (joint) Growing up in Newcastle upon Tyne, 1960. *Recreation:* sylviculture. *Address:* Kingstreet End, Little Missenden, Amersham, Bucks HP7 0RA. *T:* Great Missenden 2857. *Club:* Athenæum.
[*Died* 8 *Feb.* 1979.

WALWYN, Lady; (Eileen Mary), DBE 1947; DStJ; *d* of late Maj.-Gen. T. van Straubenzee, CB, Spennithorne House, Leyburn, Yorks; *m* 1912, Vice-Adm. Sir Humphrey Walwyn, KCSI, KCMG, CB, DSO (*d* 1957), Governor and C-in-C of Newfoundland, 1936-46; one *s. Educ:* privately. *Address:* 42 Jubilee Place, SW3.
[*Died* 11 *June* 1973.

WALZER, Richard Rudolf, MA (Oxford); Dr phil (Berlin); FBA 1956; Reader in Arabic and Greek Philosophy, University of Oxford, 1960-70, now Emeritus; Fellow, St Catherine's College, Oxford, 1962-70, now Emeritus; *b* 14 July 1900; *s* of M. Walzer, Berlin; *m* Martha Sofie, *d* of Bruno Cassirer, Berlin. *Educ:* Werner Siemens Realgymnasium, Berlin-Schoeneberg; Univ. of Berlin. Asst, Berlin Univ., 1927; Privatdocent in Classics, 1932; Lectr in Greek Philosophy, Univ. of Rome, 1933-38; Lectr in Medieval Philosophy (Arabic and Hebrew), Univ. of Oxford, 1945; Senior Lectr in Arabic and Greek Philosophy, 1950. Hon. Prof., Univ. of Hamburg, 1952; Member Inst. for Advanced Study, Princeton, New Jersey, 1953-54; Corr. Mem., Academy of Science and Literature, Mainz, 1962; Hon. Mem., Amer. Assoc. for History of Medicine, 1972; Hon. Mem. Deutsche Morgenländische Gesellschaft, 1974. *Publications:* Magna Moralia und Aristotelische Ethik, 1929; Aristotelis Dialogorum Fragmenta, 1934; Eraclito, 1939; (with F. Rosenthal) Plato Arabus II, 1943; Galen on Medical Experience, 1944; Galen on Jews and Christians, 1949; (with P. Kraus) Plato Arabus I, 1951; Greek into Arabic, 1961; L'eveil de la philosophie islamique, 1971; articles on Greek and Arabic subjects in periodicals. *Address:* 2 Bladon Close, Oxford.
[*Died* 16 *April* 1975.

WAND, Rt. Rev. and Rt. Hon. (John) William (Charles), PC, KCVO 1955; MA, Hon. DD Oxford and London; Canon and Treasurer of St Paul's 1956-69; Editor Church Quarterly Review 1956-69; Dean of the Chapels Royal, 1945-56; Chaplain and Sub-Prelate Order of St John of Jerusalem, 1936; Prelate Order of British Empire, 1946-57; Prelate Emeritus, 1957; STP (Columbia), 1947; STD (Tor.), 1947; DLitt (Ripon, USA), 1949; DD (W Ontario), 1957; *b* 25 Jan. 1885; *s* of Arthur James Henry Wand and Elizabeth Ann Ovelin Turner; *m* 1911, Amy Agnes Wiggins (*d* 1966); one *d* (one *s* decd). *Educ:* King's Sch., Grantham; St Edmund Hall, Oxford; Bishop Jacob Hostel, Newcastle upon Tyne. BA (1st Class Theology), 1907; MA 1911; Curate of Benwell, 1908-11; Lanc., 1911-14; Vicar-Choral of Sarum, 1914-19; TCF, 1915-19; Hon. CF, 1919-22 and 1925-; Hon. Chaplain, RNVR, 1947; Vicar of St Mark, Sarum, 1919-25; Chaplain RAF, 1922-25; Lectr, Sarum Theol. Coll., 1914-20; Tutor, 1920-24; Fellow, Dean and Tutor Oriel Coll. Oxford, 1925-34; Lectr in Theol. St Edmund Hall, Oxford, 1928-31; Select Preacher, Oxford, 1930-32; Univ. Lectr in Church History, 1931-34; Examr, Hon. Sch. Theology, Oxford, 1932-34; Archbishop of Brisbane and Metropolitan of Queensland, 1934-43; Bishop of Bath and Wells, 1943-45; Bishop of London, 1945-55, retired 1955; Senior Chaplain (Anglican) 1st Military District, Australian Military Forces, 1935-43; Warburton Lectr, Lincoln's Inn, for 1956-58; Hon. Fellow, St Edmund Hall, Oxford, and Oriel Coll. Oxford; Hon. Fellow, King's Coll., London. *Publications:* The Golden String, 1926; Development of Sacramentalism, 1928; History of the Modern Church, 1930; The Old Faith and the New Age, 1933; Westminster Commentary on I, II Peter and Jude, 1934; History of the Early Church, 1937; First Century Christianity (Moorhouse Lectures), 1937; New Testament Letters, 1944; God and Goodness, 1947; The Spirit of Church History, 1948; The Latin Doctors, 1948; The Authority of the Scriptures, 1949; White of Carpentaria, 1949; The Church, its Nature, Structure and Function, 1949; The Greek Doctors, 1950; The Four Councils, 1950; The High Church Schism, 1951; What the Church of England stands for, 1951; What St Paul said, 1952; The Second Reform, 1953; The Mystery of the Kingdom, 1953; The Life of Christ, 1954; The Four Heresies, 1955; The Road to Happiness, 1957; True Lights, 1958; The Church To-day, 1960; Anglicanism in History and Today, 1961; Atonement, 1962; Seven Words, Seven Virtues, 1962; St Augustine's City of God, 1963; Reflections on the Collects, 1964; The Temptation, 1964;

Changeful Page (Autobiography), 1965; Reflections on the Epistles, 1966; Transfiguration, 1967; What St Paul Really Said, 1968; Reflections on the Gospels, 1969; Christianity: a historical religion?, 1971; Letters on Preaching, 1974; (ed) The Anglican Communion, 1948; (jointly) Oxford and the Groups, 1934; (jointly) European Civilisation, 1937; (jointly) Union of Christendom, 1938; (jointly) Promise of Greatness, 1968. *Recreations:* reading and writing. *Address:* Homes of St Barnabas, Lingfield, Surrey. *Club:* County (Bath).
[*Died* 16 *Aug.* 1977.

WANSBROUGH, George, MA; CompIEE; *b* Oxford, 23 April 1904; *s* of Rev. H. A. Wansbrough, Rector of South Warnborough, and of Uliana, *d* of Bishop Tufnell; *m* 1st, 1928, Elizabeth (marr. diss. 1938), *d* of Sir George Lewis, 2nd Bt; one *s* one *d*; 2nd, 1939, Kathleen Barbara Rawdon (marr. diss. 1955), *d* of C. G. H. R. Macnamara, Indian Civil Service; one *s*; 3rd, 1955, Nancy, *d* of F. D. H. Joy, Marelands, Bentley, Hampshire. *Educ:* Cheam School; Eton (King's Scholar, Capt. of the School); King's College, Cambridge (Minor Scholar). Class I Mathematical Tripos Part I, 1924; Class II Div. I Economics Tripos Part II, 1926; Second Winchester Reading Prize, 1926; stroked Cambridge VIII, 1925; with Selfridge & Co. Ltd, intermittently, 1923-27; played rôle of The Poet in Anmer Hall's production of Sierra's Cradle Song, Little Theatre and Fortune Theatre, 1926-27; Robert Benson & Co. Ltd, Merchant Bankers, 1927-35, Dir, 1932-35; Sec., Anglo-French Timber Production Cttee, 1939-40; Member of Pottery Working Party, 1946; Cttee of Inquiry into Tudor Aircraft, 1947; Cttee to advise Govt on methods of purchase of aircraft for airways corporations, 1948; Director: A. Reyrolle & Co. Ltd, 1934-49, Chm. 1945-59; Mercantile Credit Co. Ltd, 1934-75; Bank of England, 1946-49; Chm., Morphy-Richards Ltd, 1943-54; investment consultant, 1952-73. Member: National Advisory Council for Motor Manufacturing Industry, 1946-49; Development Areas Treasury Advisory Cttee, 1945-49; Public Works Loan Bd, 1946-49; Mem. Council, Institution of Electrical Engineers, 1946-49. Member: St Marylebone Borough Council, 1934-37; Holborn Borough Council, 1937-38. Financial Adviser to New Philharmonia Orchestra, 1968-69. Joint Treas. Fabian Soc., 1936-37; contested (Lab) West Woolwich, 1935. Mem. Governing Body, Bedales Sch., 1965-74. MSAE 1967. *Publications:* various articles, reviews, etc, signed and unsigned in The Times, Economist, Economic Journal, motoring and yachting press, etc. *Recreations:* reading, writing, arithmetic. *Address:* Udimore Cottage, Otterbourne Hill, Winchester. *T:* Chandler's Ford 66525. *Club:* Leander, Political Economy (Hon. Member).
[*Died* 14 *July* 1979.

WANSBROUGH-JONES, Maj.-Gen. Llewelyn, CB 1946; CVO 1966; CBE 1944; FCIT; *b* 2 July 1900; 2nd *s* of late A. Wansbrough-Jones, BA, LLB, Long Stratton, Norfolk; *m* 1939, Laura Skelton, *d* of late J. J. Prest, JP, Hardwick Hall, Castle Eden, Co. Durham; one *s. Educ:* Malvern College; RMA, Woolwich. 2nd Lieut Royal Engineers, 1920; served in England, 1920-27; Singapore, 1927-30; Nigerian Survey, 1930-31; Johore Colonial Survey, 1932-33; India, QVO Madras Sappers and Miners, 1934-40 (Waziristan Campaign, 1936-38); War Office, 1940-42; British Joint Staff Mission, Washington, 1942-43; War Office, 1943-44; DQMG (Movements and Transportation) 21 Army Group, 1944-46; DQMG BAOR, 1946-47 (despatches thrice); Dir of Administrative Planning, WO, 1947-48; Chief Admin Officer and Chief of Staff CCG, 1948-51; Chief of Staff, Western Command, 1951-52; Principal Staff Officer to Deputy Supreme Allied Comdr, SHAPE, 1952-54; Maj.-Gen., 1949. Sec.-Gen. to British Transport Commn, May 1955-Dec. 1962, Sec. to British Railways Bd, 1963-65; Gen. Manager, Nat. Assoc. for Employment of Regular Sailors, Soldiers and Airmen, 1965-71. US Legion of Merit (Officer) and Bronze Star; Croix de Guerre (France). *Recreations:* sailing, shooting, ski-ing. *Address:* Goat Hall, Galleywood, Chelmsford, Essex. *T:* Chelmsford 52809. *Club:* United Service & Royal Aero.
[*Died* 8 *March* 1974.

WARBEY, William Noble; Executive Director, Organisation for World Political and Social Studies, since 1965; Secretary, World Studies Trust, since 1966; Chairman, Rossetti House Group, since 1968; *b* 16 August 1903; *s* of Charles Noble Warbey and Alice May Symons; *m* 1931, Audrey Grace Wicks; no *c. Educ:* Grocers' Company's School, Hackney Downs; King's College, London; London School of Economics. Language Teacher and Interpreter, France and Germany, 1925-26; Secondary School Master, Derby Municipal Secondary School, 1927-28; Secretary and Tutor, University Tutorial College, London, 1929-37; Tutor-Organiser, National Council of Labour Colls, 1937-40; Chief English Press Officer to Norwegian Govt (London), 1941-45. MP (Lab) for Luton Div. of Beds, 1945-50; Broxtowe Div. of Notts, (Sept.) 1953-55; Ashfield Div. of Notts, 1955-66, resigned. Travel organiser, 1950-51; Editor of Look and Listen, 1952-55. *Publications:* Look to Norway, 1945; (jt) Modern Norway, 1950; Vietnam: The Truth, 1965; Ho Chi Minh: Life and Achievements, 1970. *Recreations:* music, travel, organic horticulture. *[Died 6 May 1980.*

WARD OF NORTH TYNESIDE, Baroness *cr* 1974 (Life Peer), of North Tyneside; **Irene Mary Bewick Ward,** CH 1973; DBE 1955 (CBE 1929); JP; *b* 1895; *d* of late Alfred Ward, London, and late Elvina Mary Ward. Contested (C) Morpeth, 1924 and 1929, Wallsend, 1945; MP (C) Wallsend-on-Tyne, 1931-45; MP (C) Tynemouth, 1950-Feb. 1974. Hon. Fellow, Lucy Cavendish Collegiate Soc., Cambridge, 1972; Hon. FRSA, 1972. JP Newcastle upon Tyne, 1949. *Publication:* FANY Invicta, 1955. *Address:* 4 Roseworth Terrace, Gosforth, Newcastle upon Tyne NE3 1AA. *T:* 51863. *Club:* Sloane. *[Died 26 April 1980.*

WARD, Basil Robert, FRIBA; Hon. FRCA; Hon. FNZIA; first Lethaby Professor of Architecture, Royal College of Art, 1950-53; in private practice, The Basil Ward Partnership; Consultant to Mills Group Architects; Hon. Fellow, Visual Arts Centre, University of Lancaster; *b* Wellington, New Zealand, 1902; 2nd *s* of late Louis Ernest Ward, Civil Servant New Zealand Government and Secretary Geographic Board, and Theresa Kilgour; *m* 1928, Beatrix Douglas, *d* of late Nigel Douglas Connell, Taranaki, New Zealand; two *d. Educ:* Napier Boys High School, New Zealand. Served as architect's pupil; studied London University Atelier of Architecture; studied and travelled extensively abroad, 1924-28; worked way round Cape Horn; Henry Jarvis Studentship (2nd prize Rome Scholarship), 1927; studied at British School at Rome, and was employed in carrying out works for Government of Burma, 1928-31; from 1931 until outbreak of war, 1939, in practice in London in firm of Connell & Ward, and Connell, Ward & Lucas; principally concerned with modern forms of planning and construction. Recent practice includes: High Altitude Test Facilities bldgs for Rolls Royce; Plan for new science area, Oxford Univ.; numerous laboratories for Oxford Univ.; Electrostatic generator bldg for Cambridge Univ.; HQ Offices for Provincial Insurance Co. Ltd, Kendal; premises for Soc. for Chemical Industries, London; Linear Accelerator, Cyclotron and Radiobiology bldg, Hammersmith, for MRC; Inst. of Experimental Surgery, laboratories and offices, Hammersmith, for Postgrad. Medical Sch., London Univ.; Metabolic Ward, Refectory, laboratories for Hammersmith Hosp.; extensions and alterations for various depts of Royal Coll. of Art, Kensington; cricket pavilion for E Molesey Cricket Club. Lecture Tour, USA, Fiji, NZ, Australia, Singapore, Hong Kong, 1973. Lt-Comdr, RNVR (Special Branch), retired. *Publications:* contrib. Architectural Jls. *Relevant publications:* Bibliog. in Sources of Modern Architecture, 1967; Planning and Architecture, 1967; A Visual History of Twentieth Century Architecture, 1972; Sir Banister Fletcher's History of Architecture, 18th edn 1975. *Recreations:* food and travel. *Address:* Over Beachwood, Arnside, via Carnforth, Lancs LA5 0AU. *T:* Arnside 761218; Lancaster University, Bailrigg, Lancaster. *T:* Lancaster 65201. *Club:* Oriental. *[Died 2 Aug. 1976.*

WARD, Rt. Rev. James; Bishop-Auxiliary of Glasgow, (RC), since 1960; Vicar General of Glasgow; Protonotary Apostolic; *b* Dumbarton, 4 Sept. 1905; *s* of James Ward and Catherine (*née* Bell). *Educ:* St Aloysius' Coll., Glasgow; St Peter's Coll., Bearsden, Glasgow. Ordained 1929; Secretary, Archdiocese of Glasgow, 1929; Chancellor, Archdiocese of Glasgow, 1947; Vicar General, Archdiocese of Glasgow, Diocesan Treasurer and Member of Diocesan Curia, 1948; Titular Bishop of Sita, 1960; Vicar Capitular, 1963. *Address:* Holy Cross, 113 Dixon Avenue, Glasgow, S2. *T:* 041-423 0105. *[Died 21 Oct. 1973.*

WARD, Leslie M.; *see* Ward, Philip Leslie M.

WARD, Commander Sir Melvill Willis, 3rd Bt, *cr* 1914; DSC; RN, retired; *b* 25 May 1885; 2nd *s* of 1st Bt, and Florence Caroline, *d* of H. M. Simons; *S* brother, 1930; *m* 1st, 1907, Alice Sophia (marr. diss. 1944), *d* of William Cobbett; 2nd, 1944, Helene (*d* 1962), *d* of Isaac Guggenheim; 3rd, 1965, Mrs Margaret Mary Risley, *widow* of Captain Ralph Risley, USN (author of House of Healing, 1962). *Heir:* none. *Recreation:* racing. *Address:* Post Office Box 276, Southport, Connecticut 06490, USA. *Clubs:* St James'; Travellers' (Paris). *[Died Sept. 1973 (ext).*

WARD, Sir Michael B.; *see* Barrington-Ward.

WARD, (Philip) Leslie Moffat, RE 1936 (ARE 1916); artist; formerly Senior Assistant, Southern College of Art, Bournemouth; retired, 1953; *b* 2 April 1888; *s* of Charles James and Charlotte Ward, Worcester; *m* 1st, 1925, Nellie Ethel Robinson; one *s*; 2nd, 1939, Eleanor Glassford Roberts. Gold Medallist (Pictorial Composition and Illustration) National Competition of School of Art, 1909-10. Hon. Member Society of Graphic Art; exhibitor at RA in most years since 1915. Pictures in public art galleries: Southampton, Rochdale, Bournemouth, Eastbourne, Hastings; also at Worcester, Mass, USA, and at Los Angeles, California, USA. One man shows, Red House Art Gallery, Christchurch, Hants, and Eastbourne and Hastings Municipal Galleries, 1956. Senior Fellow, Royal Society of Painter Etchers, 1963. *[Died 16 Nov. 1978.*

WARD, Ronald, FRIBA; PPIArb; FRSH; AIStructE; architect; *b* 20 April 1909; *o s* of Elisha Ward and Elsie M. (*née* Broadway); *m* 1939, Muriel Pemberton (actress, as Muriel Walker). *Educ:* Peter Symonds' Sch., Winchester; Royal Acad. Schools, London. Served War of 1939-45: Lt-Col, RE, France and Africa. Created Ronald Ward & Partners, 1936; architects of works for: Assurance cos: Legal & General; Norwich Union; Pearl; Phœnix; Royal Exchange; Banks: Barclays; Glyn Mills; Martins; Pakistan; Standard of W Africa; Burston Group; Guinness Peat Group; English Industrial Estates Corp.; Barham Court Housing Assoc.; Borough Councils of Ilford, Islington, and Reigate; County Councils of London and Herts; Develt Corps of Basildon, Hatfield, Harlow, and Welwyn; HM Comr for Office of Works; Governments of Gambia, Germany, and Portugal; Metropolitan Regional Hosp. Bds (NE, SW and SE); British Transport Commn; Church Comrs of England; Corp. of Trinity House; Inst. of Marine Engineers; Livery cos: Cutlers; Plaisterers; Cooks; Associated-Rediffusion Ltd; British-American Tobacco Ltd; British & Commonwealth Shipping Co. Ltd; Diamond Corp. of Sierra Leone; Daily Mirror Group; NFU; Nestle Co. Ltd; Remploy Ltd; United Africa Co. Ltd; Vickers Ltd, and many private cos in British Isles, Eire and W Africa. Consultant Architect, Royal Borough of Kingston upon Thames; Hon. Architect to: Church of St Peter-upon-Cornhill; Albert Hall. Director: Abbey Nat. Bldg Soc. 1963-; W End London Dir, Phoenix Assurance Co., 1963-73; Underwriting Mem. of Lloyd's, 1963-. Member: Housing Study Mission for GB to Canada, 1967; Eurosound Mission to USA, 1971; Adviser, Timber Research and Develt Assoc., 1968-; Nat. Assoc. of Property Owners, (Mem. Council, 1964-71); World of Housing Property Trust (Mem. Central Council, 1971-); W Africa Cttee (Mem. Council, 1957-60); British Humane Assoc. (Hon. Dir, 1960-63); Internat. Cultural Exchange (Mem. Central Council, 1960-62); Inst. of Hosp. Administrators (Examiner, 1955-57); St John Ambulance Assoc. (Founder Chm., City of Westminster Branch, 1957-60); Inst. of Royal Engrs (Lt-Col); Hon. Soc. of Knights of Round Table, 1938- (Keeper of Muniments and Chattels of the Knights); Guild of Freemen (Master, 1963-64); Queenhithe Ward Club (Chm., 1950-51 and 1954-55); United Wards Club (Mem. Governing Body, 1950-53); City Pickwick Club (Angelo Cyrus Bantam); City of London Soc.; Old Symondians Assoc.; Winchester City FC (Life Mem.). Hon. Mem., Bldg Societies Assoc. Freeman, City of London, 1935. Liveryman, Worshipful Co. of Horners (Plastics Lectr, 1957; Master, 1967-68); Hon. Liveryman, Worshipful Co. of Plaisterers, 1973; Past Asst Grand Supt of Works, 1969. Governor, Hythe Cricket Club, 1962-. *Publications:* Design and Equipment of Hospitals, 1949; Historical Survey 1769-1969 of the Royal Athelstan Lodge No 19, 1969; Historical Diary 1914-64 of City Livery Club, 1974; regular contribs to jls and press. *Recreations:* science of building, gardening, writing. *Address:* 29 Chesham Place, Belgrave Square, SW1X 8HB. *T:* 01-235 3361; The Martello Tower, Hythe, Kent. *T:* Hythe 66246. *Clubs:* City Livery (Pres., 1958-59); Hythe Imperial Golf. *[Died 30 Sept. 1973.*

WARD, Ronald Ogier, DSO 1919; OBE 1940; MC 1918; TD; MCh (Oxon); FRCS; retired as Consulting Surgeon to Miller General Hospital, Greenwich; late Surgeon: St Peter's and St Philip's Hospitals; *b* 6 March 1886; *s* of Alan Ogier Ward; *m* 1928, Elsie Antoinette, *e d* of David Jones; two *s. Educ:* Magdalen College Sch. and Queen's Coll., Oxford; St Bartholomew's Hospital. Fellow, Royal Society of Medicine; Ex-President of Section of Urology; Ex-President British Assoc. of Urological Surgeons; served as Surgeon with British Red Cross in Balkan War, 1912-13; European War, HAC Artillery, 1914-18 (DSO, MC, despatches); Officer i/c Surgical Division, BEF, 1939-40 (OBE) and MEF, 1940-42; Consulting Surgeon, East Africa Command, 1942-44. Hon. DSc, Leeds. *Address:* Cuckmere Cottage, Seaford, Sussex. *T:* Seaford 2147. *[Died 4 April 1971.*

WARD, Prof. Stacey George; Emeritus Professor, Department of Minerals Engineering, University of Birmingham; *b* 3 Sept. 1906; *s* of George Richard Ward; *m* 1950, Helen, *d* of Samuel Thomas Windsor. *Educ:* Queen Elizabeth's Grammar Sch., Kingston-upon-Thames; Imperial College of Science, London.

PhD, MSc, ARCS, DIC. Research Dept, Powell Duffryn Associated Collieries Ltd, 1930-34; Field Research and Liaison Officer, British Iron and Steel Federation, 1935-37; University of Birmingham: Lecturer, Mining Dept, 1937-42; Acting Prof. of Mining, 1942-46 and 1947-48; Prof. of Chemical Engineering, 1946-48; Prof. and Head of Dept of Minerals Engineering, 1948-73; Prof. and Senior Fellow, 1973-74; Dean of the Faculty of Science, 1960-63. *Publications:* various technical papers connected with coal, fuel, minerals Engineering, extractive metallurgy and rheology of suspensions. *Address:* 5 Birnam, 56 Harborne Road, Edgbaston, Birmingham B15 3HE.
[Died 2 Sept. 1980.

WARD, Sir (V.) M. B.; *see* Barrington-Ward.

WARDE, Rt. Rev. Geoffrey Hodgson; *b* 23 Aug. 1889; *s* of Rev. Henry John and Eleanor Harriett Warde; *m* 1915, Eileen Margaret (*d* 1957), *er d* of Rev. F. K. Hodgkinson; no *c*. *Educ:* Tonbridge Sch.; Keble Coll., Oxford; Oxford House, Bethnal Green; Cheshunt Theological Coll. Deacon, 1914; Priest, 1915; Curate of St Pancras, 1914-16; Temp. CF 1916-19. Hon CF 1919; Priest-in-Charge All Saints, Grosvenor Road, Pimlico, 1919-24; Vicar of St Mark's, Regent's Park, 1924-28; Deputy Priest-in-Ordinary to the King, 1922-28; Dean of Gibraltar, 1928-33; Vicar of Grantham, Rural Dean of North Grantham, 1933-39; Vicar of Brighton and Rural Dean, 1939-44; Archdeacon of Carlisle and Canon of Carlisle, 1944-46; Suffragan Bishop of Lewes, 1946-Oct. 1959; Hon. Canon of Chichester, 1947-63. *Recreations:* cricket, golf, lawn tennis. *Address:* The Lodge, Southdown Road, Seaford, Sussex. *T:* Seaford 3355.
[Died 20 May 1972.

WARDLAW, Rear-Admiral A. L. P. M.; *see* Mark-Wardlaw.

WARING, Sir (Arthur) Bertram, Kt 1960; DL; first Hon. President, Joseph Lucas (Industries) Ltd, electrical engineers, Birmingham, since 1969 (Chairman, 1951-69); Past Director of Lloyds Bank Ltd; *b* 12 June 1893; *s* of B. M. Waring, Manchester; *m* 1927, Muriel, *d* of E. H. Collumbell, Derby; one *s.* Chartered Accountant, 1920. Past President: Motor Industry Research Assoc.; Inst. Industrial Supervisors; Soc. of Motor Manufactureres and Traders; Birmingham and district Engineering and Allied Employers' Assoc.; Birmingham Chamber of Commerce; Past Chm., British Productivity Council; Vice-Pres., Engineering and Allied Employers' National Federation; Past Pres., Institution of Works Managers; Pres., Birmingham Productivity Assoc.; Life Mem. Court of Governors, Birmingham Univ. Hon. Colonel, TA; Mem. Warwickshire TA Assoc.; Past-President Birmingham CC British Legion. Hon. LLD Birmingham, 1963. DL Warwickshire, 1952. *Address:* Heath Lodge, Ullenhall, Warwickshire. *T:* Tanworth-in-Arden 2227. *Club:* Royal Automobile.
[Died 2 March 1974.

WARING, Sir Bertram; *see* Waring, Sir A. B.

WARING, Sir Douglas (Tremayne), Kt 1957; CBE 1953; retired; *b* 16 April 1904; *s* of late Rev. C. T. Waring, Oxted, Surrey. *Educ:* Rossall Sch. Chartered Accountant, 1927. Joined London Tin Corp., London, 1927; Director, Anglo-Oriental (Malaya) Ltd, 1934; Chairman of Anglo-Oriental (Malaya) Ltd, 1952-59, and of other Tin Mining Companies operating and registered in Malaya. Pres., FMS Chamber of Mines, Ipoh, Malaya, 1952, 1955, and 1956. Served with FMS Volunteer Force, 1939-46 (POW Malaya and Siam, 1942-45). MLC and Mem. Exec. Council, Federation of Malaya, 1948-59; Chairman: London Tin Corporation, 1961-72 (Dep. Chm., 1958); Malayan Chamber of Mines, London, 1963-73; Amalgamated Tin Mines of Nigeria (Holdings), Ltd, 1961-74; Southern Kinta Consolidated Ltd, 1961-74; Kamunting Tin Dredging Ltd, 1966-74. Past Pres., Overseas Mining Assoc. Hon. Panglima Mangku Negara (Malaya), 1961. *Recreation:* retirement. *Address:* 93 Whitehall Court, SW1. *T:* 01-930 5073. *Clubs:* City of London, Farmers'; Roehampton.
[Died 5 March 1980.

WARNER, Sir George (Redston), KCVO 1934; CMG 1927; *b* 18 July 1879; *s* of late Sir Joseph Warner; *m* 1910, Margery Catherine (*d* 1963), *e d* of late W. E. Nicol, Ballogie, Aberdeenshire; three *s. Educ:* Eton; Balliol College, Oxford. Entered Foreign Office, 1903; served at HM Legations at Tangier and Oslo; Minister at Berne, 1935-39. *Address:* Inholmes, Cliff Way, Compton Down, near Winchester, Hants. *Club:* Travellers'.
[Died 23 June 1978.

WARNER, Oliver; writer; *b* 28 Feb. 1903; *s* of Richard Cromwell and Grace Rankin Warner; *m* 1st, 1925, Dorothea Blanchard (*d* 1937); one *d*; 2nd, Elizabeth Strahan; one *s* one *d. Educ:* Denstone; Caius College, Cambridge. Gold Medal, Royal

Asiatic Society, 1920. BA (Cantab), 1925, MA 1946. Reader to Chatto and Windus, 1926-41, and again temp., 1964-65; Admiralty, 1941-47; Secretary, Naval Honours and Awards Committee, 1946-47; War Artists Advisory Committee, 1944-46; British Council, Deputy Director of Publications, 1947-63. Member: Council of Soc. for Nautical Research, 1955-60, 1970-71 (Vice-Pres., 1973); Coun. of Navy Records Soc., 1960-63, 1967-68, 1970-72; Advisory Board, Buckler's Hard Maritime Museum, 1964-70. Book Critic, the Tatler, 1964-65. FRSL Society of Bookmen, 1949-62. *Publications:* A Secret of the Marsh, 1927; Hero of the Restoration, 1936; Uncle Lawrence, 1939; Captains and Kings, 1947; An Introduction to British Marine Painting, 1948; Joseph Conrad, 1951; The Crown Jewels, 1951; Captain Marryat, 1953; Battle Honours of the Royal Navy, 1956; A Portrait of Lord Nelson, 1958; Trafalgar, 1959; Emma Hamilton and Sir William, 1960; The Battle of the Nile, 1960; Great Seamen, 1961; The Glorious First of June, 1961; Wilberforce, 1962; A History of the Inn-holders' Company, 1962; Great Sea Battles, 1963; A History of the Tin-Plate Workers' Company, 1964; English Literature: a Portrait Gallery, 1964; The Sea and the Sword, the Baltic, 1630-1945, 1965; (ed) Best Sea Stories, 1965; Portsmouth and the Royal Navy, 1965; Nelson's Battles, 1965; Cunningham of Hyndhope, Admiral of the Fleet, 1967; Marshal Mannerheim and the Finns, 1967; The Navy, 1968; The Life and Letters of Lord Collingwood, 1968; A Journey to the Northern Capitals, 1968; Admiral of the Fleet: the Life of Sir Charles Lambe, 1969; (ed) Nelson's Last Diary, 1971; With Wolfe at Quebec: the Path to Glory, 1972; Great Battle Fleets, 1973; The Life-boat Service: a history of the RNLI 1824-1974, 1974; Nelson, 1975; The British Navy: a concise history, 1975; Command at Sea, 1976; Great Naval Actions, 1976; Introduction to Centenary History of Chatto and Windus, 1955, rev. new edn 1973; (with Margaret Meade-Featherstonhaugh) Uppark and its People, 1964; Fighting Soil, 1979 (completed by Victoria Howard-Vyse; posthumous publication), 1979. *Recreation:* numismatics. *Address:* The Old Manor Cottage, Haslemere, Surrey. *T:* Haslemere 2691. *Club:* Travellers'.
[Died 14 Aug. 1976.

WARNER, Sydney Jeannetta, CBE 1946 (OBE 1918); Director, Dominion and Foreign Relations Department British Red Cross, retired 1949; *b* 13 June 1890; *d* of Frederick Ashton Warner, FRCS, and Sydney Anne Grove. *Educ:* home and in Germany. British Red Cross Commandant, 1910-17; Area VAD Commandant in France, 1915-17; Dep. Asst Dir Personnel in WRNS (OBE), 1917-19. Worked for LNU, rep. them at Geneva at various cttees of the League of Nations, 1919-28; Mem. staff of Internat. Office of World Assoc. of Girl Guides and Girl Scouts, 1928-36; rejoined British Red Cross for the War, 1939. 1st Class Knight of Order of St Olav (Norwegian), 1946; Chevalier de la Légion d'Honneur, 1946; Danish Médaille Royale de Récompense de première classe avec couronne, avec l'autorisation de la porter dans le ruban de l'ordre de Dannebrog, 1947; Commander of Order of Orange Nassau (Netherlands), 1948; Commander of Order of Phœnix (Greece), 1950. *Recreation:* travelling. *Address:* 33 Moore Street, Chelsea, SW3. *T:* 01-589 6816.
[Died 25 March 1979.

WARNER, Sylvia Townsend, FRSL; Hon. AAAL; Author; *b* 1893. Prix Menton, 1969. *Publications:* The Espalier, 1925; Lolly Willowes, 1926 (repr. 1978); Mr Fortune's Maggot, 1927; Time Importuned, 1928; The True Heart, 1929; Opus 7, 1931; The Salutation, 1932; Whether a Dove or Seagull (with Valentine Ackland), 1934; Summer Will Show, 1936; After the Death of Don Juan, 1938; A Garland of Straw, 1943; The Museum of Cheats, 1947; The Corner That Held Them, 1948, repr. 1972; The Flint Anchor, 1954; Winter in the Air, 1956; (with Reynolds Stone) Boxwood, 1960; The Cat's Cradle Book, 1960; A Spirit Rises, 1962; A Stranger with a Bag, 1966; T. H. White: a biography, 1967; The Innocent and the Guilty, 1971; Kingdoms of Elfin (short stories), 1977. *Address:* c/o Chatto & Windus, 40 William IV Street, WC2.
[Died 1 May 1978.

WARNOCK, Rt. Hon. Edmond, PC (N Ireland) 1944; QC 1932; DL Belfast; *b* 8 May 1887; *m* 1913, Jessie M. Cleland; three *d. Educ:* Methodist College, Belfast; Trinity College, Dublin. Called Irish Bar, 1911. MP St Anne's Div. of Belfast, NI Parliament, 1938-69; Parliamentary Secretary to Minister of Home Affairs, 1939-40; Minister of Home Affairs, 1944-49; Attorney-Gen., 1949-56, resigned. *Address:* The Glebe House, Ballee, Downpatrick, Co. Down, N Ireland. *Club:* Ulster Reform (Belfast).
[Died 19 Dec. 1971.

WARNOCK, Prof. Frederick Victor, OBE 1955; PhD (QUB), MSc (NUI), FRScI, CEng; FIMechE; Professor of Mechanical Engineering, Queen's University, 1955-59, now Emeritus Professor (Professor of Mechanical Engineering, College of Technology, Belfast, 1937-55); *b* 11 Feb. 1893; *s* of Samuel and

Margaret Warnock; *m* 1920, Mary Ferguson; two *s. Educ:* Coll. of Technology, Belfast; Royal Coll. of Science, Ireland. Apprenticeship with Messrs Portadown Foundry Co., Ltd 1909-13; student, Royal Coll. of Science, Dublin, 1914-18; Lecturer in Mechanical Engineering, Londonderry Tech. Coll., 1918-20; Senior Lecturer in Mechanical Engineering, Queen's Univ. and College of Technology, Belfast, 1920-37. *Publications:* Strength of Materials, 1927; (with P. P. Benham) Mechanics of Solids and Strength of Materials, 1965; contribs to: Proc. Iron and Steel Inst., Engrg, and Instn of Mech. Engrs. *Address:* 43 Balmoral Avenue, Belfast BT9 6NX. *T:* 667324.   *[Died 17 Oct. 1976.*

WARNOCK, Rt. Hon. (John) Edmond; *see* Warnock, Rt Hon. Edmond.

WARNOCK, William Robertson Lyon; Chartered Accountant; Chairman, Charterhouse Group Ltd, since 1968; *b* 27 July 1916; *s* of Robert Baillie Lyon Warnock, East India Merchant, and Elizabeth Warnock; *m* 1940, Beryl Atkinson, *d* of Shera Atkinson, LLD and Agnes Atkinson; one *d. Educ:* University College Sch. With Brown, Fleming & Murray, CA, 1934-39. Served Royal Artillery (Captain), 1940-44. Lines Brothers Ltd, 1945-48; Charterhouse Group Ltd (and subsidiaries), 1948-. *Recreation:* golf. *Address:* Flat 5, 3 Templewood Avenue, NW3. *T:* 01-435 7377. *Club:* Junior Carlton.   *[Died 8 July 1971.*

WARREN, Douglas Daintry, CSI 1947; CIE 1945; MC 1918; late ICS; *b* 17 Jan. 1897; *s* of Charles Warren, Royston, Herts; *m* 1922, Nora Mary, *d* of Major J. O'C. Phelan; one *s. Educ:* King's School, Worcester; Corpus Christi College, Cambridge. Served in European War with Bedfordshire Regt, 1915-19 (MC); entered ICS 1920; Secretary to Govt of Madras, Public Works Dept, 1940-43; Joint Sec. to Govt of India, Transport Dept, 1943, Sec. in 1946 and 1947. *Address:* 18 Cedar Crescent, Royston, Herts.   *[Died 15 Aug. 1972.*

WARREN, Earl; Chief Justice of the United States, 1953-69; *b* Los Angeles, Calif, 19 March 1891; *s* of Methias H. Warren and Chrystal Hernlund; *m* 1925, Nina E. Meyers; three *s* three *d. Educ:* public schools, Bakersfield, Calif; University of California, Berkeley, Calif (Bachelor of Letters, 1912; JD 1914). Admitted to California Bar, 1914; practised in San Francisco and Oakland, Calif, 1914-17; Deputy City Attorney, Oakland 1919-20; Dep. Dist Attorney, Alameda County, Calif, 1920-25, Dist Attorney, 1925-39; Attorney-Gen. of Calif, 1939-43; President Nat. Assoc. of Attorneys-General, 1940-41. Alternate Delegate, Republican Nat. Convention, 1928, deleg., 1932; Chm. Republican State Central Cttee, 1934-36; Republican nat. cttee-man from Calif, and member nat. exec. cttee, 1936-38; Governor of California, 1943-53; temp. chm. and keynote speaker, Republican National Convention, 1944; Republican nominee for US vice-presidency, 1948; Candidate for Republican nomination for US Presidency, 1952. Special US Ambassador to Coronation, 1953. Chm., President's Commn on the Assassination of President Kennedy, 1963-64. Hon. Chm., World Association of Judges, 1969-. Entered US Army, as private, 1917, discharged as 1st Lt 1918 (Capt. Reserve until 1935). Hon. Master of the Bench, Gray's Inn, 1965. *Hon. degrees:* LLD University of California and other universities and colleges. Holds various foreign decorations. *Publications:* various articles on legal subjects. *Recreations:* hunting, fishing. *Address:* Supreme Court Building, Washington, DC 20543, USA. *Clubs:* Olympic, Bohemian (San Francisco); Athens Athletic, Claremont Country (Oakland).   *[Died 10 July 1974.*

WARREN, Brig. Edward Galwey, CBE 1940; *b* 3 May 1893; *y s* of Deputy Inspector-General T. R. Warren, RN, and Harriet Lavinia Warren, Kylenahoory, Ballyhooly, Co. Cork; *m* 1914, Gwendolyn Agnes (*d* 1967), *yr d* of Brooke Brasier, JP, Ballygarrett, Mallow, Co. Cork. *Educ:* Royal Naval School, Eltham; RMC, Sandhurst. Gazetted to Northamptonshire Regt 1912; Commanded 2nd Northamptonshire Regt 1939; 4th Inf. Bde 1940-41; has served in BEF France, 1914, Sudan, Sierra Leone, Iraq, India, and BEF France, 1939-40; retired 1946. *Address:* Stradbally, Castle Connell, Co. Limerick, Ireland.   *[Died 10 Aug. 1975.*

WARREN, Lt-Col John Leighton Byrne L.; *see* Leicester-Warren.

WARREN, Rev. Dr Max Alexander Cunningham; *b* 13 Aug. 1904; *s* of Rev. J. A. F. Warren; *m* 1932, Mary Collett; two *d. Educ:* Marlborough College; Jesus College, Cambridge (Rustat Scholar). BA 1926; CMS Missionary, Northern Nigeria, 1927; MA 1931; deacon 1932, priest 1933, Winchester Diocese; Curate of St John's, Boscombe, and Joint Secretary for Youth Work in Diocese of Winchester, 1932-36; Vicar of Holy Trinity Church, Cambridge, and Secretary of the Cambridge Pastorate, 1936-42;

General Secretary, Church Missionary Society, 1942-63; Sub-Dean and Canon of Westminster, 1963-73. Hon. Fellow, Jesus College, Cambridge, 1967. Hon. DD: Wycliffe Coll., Toronto, 1944; St Paul's Univ., Tokyo, 1959; Glasgow Univ., 1963; Huron College, Ontario, 1963; Univ. of Sierra Leone, 1969. *Publications:* Loyalty, 1935; Interpreters, 1936; Master of Time, 1943; The Calling of God, 1944; Strange Victory, 1946; The Truth of Vision, 1948; The Christian Mission, 1951; (Ed.) The Triumph of God, 1948; Revival, 1954; The Christian Imperative, 1955; Caesar the Beloved Enemy, 1955; The Gospel of Victory, 1955; Partnership, 1956; Challenge and Response, 1959; Letters on Purpose, 1963; Perspective in Mission, 1964; The Missionary Movement from Britain in Modern History, 1965; Social History and Christian Mission, 1967; To Apply the Gospel, 1971; A Theology of Attention, 1971; Crowded Canvas, 1974; I Believe in the Great Commission, 1976. *Recreations:* reading, travel, stamp collecting. *Address:* 30 Michel Dene Road, East Dean, East Sussex BN20 0JR. *[Died 23 Aug. 1977.*

WARREN, Sir Mortimer (Langton), Kt 1959; FCA; Director: Trustees Corporation Ltd, Great Portland Estates Ltd, Ellis (Kensington) Ltd, Achille Serre, and other companies; *b* 27 Oct. 1903; *o c* of late Mortimer Warren and Mary (*née* Langton); *m* 1929, Dorothea Ann Burns; one *d. Educ:* Cranleigh. Chartered Accountant, 1927; Queen Anne's Bounty: Asst Accountant, 1927; Asst Sec. and Finance Officer, 1942; Church Commissioners for England: Financial Secretary, 1948-54; Secretary, 1954-64, retired. A Governor of Guy's Hospital, of Cranleigh School and of Francis Holland Schools. *Publication:* Investment for the Ordinary Man, 1958. *Address:* 7 Strathearn Place, Hyde Park, W2. *T:* 01-262 9715. *Club:* Athenæum.   *[Died 18 Feb. 1972.*

WARTER, Sir Philip Allan, Kt 1944; President, Associated British Picture Corporation Ltd and associated companies; formerly Chairman: Thames Television; Transport Holding Co.; Director Thomas Cook and Son; *b* 31 Dec. 1903; 3rd *s* of W. H. Warter, Folkestone; *m* 1929, Katherine Scott Maxwell; one *d* (decd). *Address:* 30 Golden Square, W1. *[Died 14 April 1971.*

WATERER, Sir (Robert) Bernard, Kt 1955; CB 1951; JP; *b* 12 Feb. 1891; *s* of late Robert Waterer, Chertsey, Surrey; *m* 1937, Hilda Constance, *d* of late E. T. Griffiths, Glanyrannell Park, Carmarthenshire. *Educ:* Eastbourne Coll. Enlisted RE, 1914; commissioned, RE, Feb. 1915; invalided out, Oct. 1916. Entered Treasury Solicitor's Dept, 1920; transferred to Solicitor's office, Inland Revenue, 1925. Principal Assistant Solicitor of Inland Revenue, 1946-52; Solicitor of Inland Revenue, 1952-56. Chairman, Standing Cttee under Merchandise Marks Act, 1926 (agricultural etc produce), 1960. JP Hants, 1956; Glos, 1958. *Address:* Parkside, Hatherley Court Road, Cheltenham, Glos. *T:* 54504.   *[Died 3 Nov. 1971.*

WATERHOUSE, Captain Rt. Hon. Charles, PC 1944; MC; *b* 1893; 2nd surv. *s* of Thomas Crompton Waterhouse, Lomberdale Hall, Bakewell; *m* 1917, Beryl (*d* 1970), 2nd *d* of Thomas Ford, New South Wales; two *s* one *d. Educ:* Cheltenham; Trinity Hall, Cambridge; MA Economics Tripos, 1914. Served European War, France, 1914-18, 1st Life Guards; contested (C) NE Derbyshire, 1922 and 1923, South Leicester, 1945; MP (C) South Leicester, 1924-45, South-East Division of Leicester, 1950-57. Parliamentary Private Secretary to President of Board of Trade, 1928; to Minister of Labour, 1931-34; Assistant Whip, 1935-36; Junior Lord of the Treasury, 1936; Comptroller of HM Household, 1937-38; Treasurer of HM Household, 1938-39; Assistant Postmaster-General, 1939-41; Parliamentary Secretary Board of Trade, 1941-45; Chairman: East Midlands Area of Conservative and Unionist Associations, 1946-51; Public Accounts Cttee, 1951; Nat. Union of Conservative and Unionist Assocs, 1952; Estimates Cttee, 1953. Chairman, Tanganyika Concessions, 1957-66. DL, JP Derbyshire. *Recreation:* fishing. *Address:* Middleton Hall, Bakewell, Derbyshire. *Clubs:* Carlton, Buck's.   *[Died 2 March 1975.*

WATERHOUSE, Eben Gowrie, CMG 1976; OBE 1962; MA, Officier d'Académie; Cavaliere of the Order of the Crown of Italy; Professor of German, Sydney University, 1937-46, now Emeritus Professor; *b* 29 April 1881; *s* of Australian parents; *m* 1912, Janet Frew Kellie, MA (*d* 1973), Kilmarnock, Scotland; four *s. Educ:* Sydney Grammar Sch.; Sydney Univ.; Leipzig Univ.; Paris. BA (Sydney) with First Class Honours in English, French, German, and MacCallum prize for English; MA with First Class Honours in French; Master of Modern Languages at Sydney Grammar Sch. (for 4 years); Senior Lecturer in Modern Languages at Teachers' Coll., Sydney (for 11 years); acting Professor of French at Sydney Univ., 1921; Associate Professor of German and Comparative Literature, 1925-37; President of the Sydney University Union, 1928; Trustee Art Gallery of New South Wales, 1938-62. President Internat. Camellia Society, 1975. Gold Medal of Goethe Institute, 1957. *Publications:* The Teaching of the French Verb by the Direct Method; (with J. A. Snowden) The Initial Stages in French by the Direct Method, Parts I and II; French Phonetic and Fluency Exercises; Goethe (Centenary lecture), 1932; Camellia Quest, 1947; Camellia Trail, with 21 colour plates, 1952; (with Norman Sparnon) The Magic of Camellias, 1968. *Recreations:* landscape gardening; special hobby: the propagation and cultivation of camellias. *Address:* Eryldene, 17 McIntosh Street, Gordon, Sydney, NSW 2072, Australia. *T:* 498-2271.   *[Died 17 Aug. 1977.*

WATERHOUSE, Maj.-Gen. George Guy, CB 1939; MC; *b* 12 June 1886; 3rd *s* of late Thomas Crompton Waterhouse of Lomberdale Hall, Bakewell, and Sarah, *d* of late Jonathan Holden of Reims; *m* 1st, Katherine Louise (*d* 1930), *d* of late Charles Birks, Adelaide; no *c* ; 2nd, 1932, Eileen Dendy, *d* of late Dendy Watney. *Educ:* Cheltenham Coll.; RMA, Woolwich. 2nd Lieut, Royal Engineers, 1905; employed on survey in Nigeria, 1910-13; served European War in France and Salonika (wounded, despatches twice, MC, brevets of Major and Lieut-Colonel, Chevalier of the Legion of Honour, White Eagle of Serbia); passed Staff Coll., Camberley, 1919; Instructor of English, Ecole Supérieure de Guerre, Paris, 1922-23; passed Royal Naval Staff Coll., Greenwich, 1928; commanded Training Bn, RE, 1930-31; Military Attaché, Paris, 1931-32; with British Military Mission, Iraq, 1934-37; Maj.-General, 1938; Inspector-General and Head of British Advisory Military Mission, Iraq Army, 1938-41; District Commander UK, 1941-44; retired pay, 1945; Deputy Commissioner, British Red Cross and St John War Organisation, at HQ, SEAC, 1945. Order of Rafidain 3rd Class. *Address:* 9 Hamston House, Kensington Court Place, W8 5BL. *T:* 01-937 3397.   *[Died 22 Aug. 1975.*

WATERHOUSE, Gilbert, LittD (Dublin), MA (Cambridge and Dublin); MRIA; FRGS; Professor of German, Queen's University, Belfast, 1933-53; *b* Hipperholme, Yorks, 15 July 1888; *s* of late Harold Waterhouse, Tarleton, Lancs; *m* 1920, Mary Elizabeth, *e d* of late Sir Robert Woods, MCh; three *d*. *Educ:* Manchester Grammar Sch.; St John's Coll., Cambridge; University of Berlin. First Tiarks University German Scholar, Cambridge, 1910; Asst Lecturer in English in the University of Leipzig, 1911-14; Asst Master, Manchester Grammar Sch., 1914-15; Professor of German, University of Dublin, 1915-32; served European War as Lieut TF Unattached List and Lieut, RNVR; Administrator, Government Scheme of Grants to ex-Service Students (Ireland), 1919-25; Secretary, Royal Commission on the University of Dublin, 1920. Dep. Chief Welfare Officer, Belfast Civil Defence, 1941-45. Exchange Professor of German, University of Illinois, 1950, and University of California (Los Angeles), 1951. Trustee, Magee University College, Londonderry, 1953-67. *Publications:* The Literary Relations of England and Germany in the Seventeenth Century, 1914; The War and the Study of German, 1917; Grillparzer: Weh' dem, der lügt, 1923; The Prince of Peace, 1927; German Literature, 1928; (trans.) Clara Viebig: The Sleeping Army, 1929; (trans.) Gen. v. Seeckt: Thoughts of a Soldier, 1930; Simon van der Stel's Journal of his Expedition to Namaqualand, 1932, Supplement: Addenda et Corrigenda, 1953; A Short History of German Literature, 1942, 3rd edn, 1959. Editor of Year-Book of Modern Languages, 1920. *Address:* 92 Malone Road, Belfast.   *[Died 25 July 1977.*

WATERLOW, Sir Philip Alexander, 4th Bt, *cr* 1873; retired as Chairman and Managing Director of Waterlow & Sons Ltd, 1960; *b* 17 March 1897; *s* of Sir Edgar Lutwyche Waterlow, 3rd Bt and Martha (Ruth), *d* of late Robert Carter; *S* father, 1954; *m* 1st, 1923, Gwendoline Iris (marr. diss., 1937), *d* of late Charles Rupert Butler, New Place, Sunningdale; (one *s* decd); 2nd, 1937, Annie (marr. diss.), *e d* of late Léon and Winifred Balanché. *Educ:* Harrow; RMC, Sandhurst. Formerly Lieut, 3rd King's Own Hussars; served in Ireland and European War, 1914-18, 1916-18; ADC to Military Governor of Cologne, BAOR, 1919-20, RARO; served War of 1939-45 as Captain, Home Guard. Governor of Christ's Hospital and Lloyd Memorial (Caxton) Home, Deal; Liveryman Stationers' and Newspaper Manufacturers' Company; Freeman, City of London. *Heir: g s* Christopher Rupert Waterlow, *b* 12 Aug. 1959. *Address:* Chapel Cottage, Nuthurst, Horsham, West Sussex. *Club:* Cavalry.   *[Died 18 July 1973.*

WATERS, Frank George, OBE 1963; HM Diplomatic Service, retired; Secretary, Schoolmistresses and Governesses Benevolent Institution; *b* 14 April 1911; *m* 1938, Dulcie Georgina (*née* Burden); two *d*. *Educ:* Woolwich Polytechnic Secondary Sch. Business (Swift & Co. Ltd) London, 1928; Royal Ordnance Factories, Woolwich, 1938; HM Customs and Excise, 1939; entered FO, 1942; British Embassy, Washington, 1945-48; Foreign Office, 1949; HM Consul, Leopoldville, 1950-51; First Secretary, Paris, 1952-53; Foreign Office, 1954-58; HM Consul-General, Berlin, 1959-63; Deputy Consul-General, Los Angeles, 1963-66; HBM Consul-General, Alexandria, UAR, 1966-68; Counsellor, FCO, 1968-71. *Recreations:* golf, tennis, philately, fishing. *Address:* 5 Stainmore Close, Chislehurst, Kent. *Clubs:* Royal Automobile; British United Services (Los Angeles).   *[Died 4 Nov. 1974.*

WATERSON, Hon. Sidney Frank; *b* 4 June 1896; *er s* of late John Waterson, FRIBA, and Louisa Waterson; *m* 1924, Hilda Maude, *d* of late Major J. A. E. Markus; one *s* one *d. Educ:* St Clare, Walmer; Westminster (King's Scholar). Served European War, 1915-19: 2nd Lieut, 3rd (Spec. Res.) Royal Sussex Regt attached Machine Gun Corps, Salonika, 1916, France, 1917-18; MP (Union of S Africa) for South Peninsula Division, 1929-38; Envoy Extraordinary and Minister Plenipotentiary for the Union of South Africa to France, 1939; High Commissioner for Union of S. Africa in London, 1939-42; Minister of Economic Development, 1943-48, of Mines, 1945-48; Minister of Transport, South Africa, 1948. MP Constantia Division, 1943-70. *Recreations:* golf, fishing. *Address:* Blairbuoy, Summerley Road, Kenilworth, CP, South Africa. *Clubs:* Beefsteak; City, Civil Service (Capetown).   *[Died 8 Aug. 1976.*

WATHERSTON, Sir David (Charles), KBE 1956; CMG 1953; Hon. PMN (Malaya), 1958; *b* 26 Feb. 1907; *s* of late Charles Fell Watherston, CB; *m* 1933, Maude, *d* of W. Hobkirk Noble, Aldwick, Sussex; two *s* two *d. Educ:* Westminster Sch. (King's Schol.); Christ Church, Oxford. Cadet, Malayan Civil Service, 1930; seconded to Colonial Office, 1939-44. Malayan Planning Unit, 1944-45. British Military Administration, Malaya, 1945-46. Secretary Constitutional Working Cttee which negotiated Federation of Malaya Agreement, 1946-48; Secretary for Defence and Internal Security, Federation of Malaya, 1948; Chief Secretary, Federation of Malaya, 1952-57 (administered the Government on various occasions); Special Counsellor, Malayan High Commission in the United Kingdom, 1957-59. Dir of Personnel and Gp Personnel Advr, Tube Investments Ltd, 1959-74. Member of the Commission of Enquiry, North Borneo and Sarawak, 1962. Mem. Council, City University; Chairman: Electricity Supply Industry Trng Bd, 1969-74; Cttee for the Diploma in Management Studies, 1971-; Vice-Chm., Council of Foundn for Management Educn; Mem. Council of Industry for Management Educn. Liveryman of the Goldsmiths' Company. KStJ 1975 (CStJ 1956). Hon. DSc: Aston, 1968; City, 1971. Burnham Medal, BIM, 1975. *Address:* Harbury House, Harbury, Warwickshire. *T:* Harbury 612158. *Clubs:* East India, Sports and Public Schools, Royal Commonwealth Society.   *[Died 16 Jan. 1977.*

WATKINS, Brig. Bernard Springett, CBE 1946; JP; Ecclesiastical Secretary to the Lord Chancellor, 1950-65; *b* 8 April 1900; *o s* of late Rev. H. S. Watkins, Rector of Morchard Bishop, Devon; *m* 1926, Sybil Eugene, *o d* of late Col A. E. Berry, CIE, IMS; three *d. Educ:* King's School, Worcester; RMC, Sandhurst. Joined Indian Army, 1918; transferred Royal Signals, 1929; Capt., 1924; Major, 1938; Lieut-Col, 1944; Col, 1946; Temp. Brig., 1944-46; served, India, 1914-18; served with Royal Signals as Chief Signals Officer, Air Force South East Asia and Air Force Germany, 1942-47; AAG War Office, 1947-50; retired, 1950. JP Kent 1952. *Recreations:* gardening, shooting and fishing. *Address:* Highfield, 26 Pennington Road, Southborough, Tunbridge Wells. *T:* Tunbridge Wells 29089.   *[Died 11 June 1977.*

WATKINSON, Sir (George) Laurence, KBE 1949; CB 1944; MC; *b* 29 Jan. 1896; *s* of late G. L. Watkinson, Battenhall, Worcester; *m* 1919, Doris, *d* of late Richard Pilling, Bolton; one *d. Educ:* Port Charlotte School, Islay, NB; Royal Grammar School, Worcester. Served with Worcs Regt 1915-19, in France and Italy (MC and Bar); Board of Inland Revenue, 1919-31; Board of Trade, 1931-46; Deputy Secretary, Ministry of Fuel and Power, 1947-55. Vice-Chm., Harris Lebus Ltd, 1955-57, and Chairman, 1958-61. Mem. Council, RCVS, 1960-65; Chm., London Electricity Consultative Council and Mem., London Electricity Board, 1960-65; Mem. Monopolies Commn, 1960-68. Hon. ARCVS, 1966. *Recreation:* fishing. *Address:* 15 Newnham House, High Road, Loughton, Essex. *T:* 01-508 7141. *Club:* United Service and Royal Aero.   *[Died 23 March 1974.*

WATSON, Very Rev. Alan Cameron, CMG 1968; retired; *b* 16 March 1900; *s* of Thomas Watson and Marion Thomson; *m* 1928, Eileen Ballantyne; two *s* one *d. Educ:* Otago Univ., Dunedin, NZ (MA). Minister: East Taieri, NZ, 1927-32; St Paul's, Christchurch, NZ, 1932-41; Toorak, Melbourne, Aust.,

1942-67. Moderator-General, Presbyterian Church of Australia, 1959-62. President, Australian Council of Churches, 1962-63. *Address:* 35 Herbert Street, Mornington, Victoria 3931, Australia. *T:* 5.3666. *Club:* Melbourne (Aust.).
[Died 15 Jan. 1976.

WATSON, Benjamin Philp, MD, Hon. LLD, Edinburgh University, 1951; FRCSE, FACS, FRCOG; Professor Emeritus of Obstetrics and Gynæcology, Columbia University, New York; *b* Anstruther, Scotland, 1880; 2nd *s* of David Watson, Largo, Scotland; *m* 1917, Angèle, *d* of Paul Hamendt, St Nicolas, Belgium. *Educ:* Waid Academy, Anstruther; Universities of St Andrews and Edinburgh. MB, ChB, University of Edinburgh, 1902; awarded Ettles and Buchanan Scholarships; MD Edinburgh, 1905; Gold Medal for Thesis; University Tutor in Gynæcology, 1905-10; Lecturer in School of Medicine, Royal College, Edinburgh, 1910-12; Professor of Obstetrics and Gynæcology, University of Toronto, 1912-22; Professor of Midwifery and Diseases of Women, University of Edinburgh, 1922-26; Professor of Obstetrics and Gynæcology, Columbia University, 1926-58; Head, Sloane Hosp. for Women, NY. President, Acad. of Medicine, NY, and other socs throughout America. Served with the CAMC in England and Salonika with rank of Captain, 1915-16. *Publications:* Gynecological Pathology and Diagnosis; Chronic Endometritis; New System of Gynecology; many articles in medical and scientific journals. *Recreations:* golf and travel. *Address:* 21 Long Ridge Road, Danbury, Conn 06810, USA. *Club:* Century (New York).
[Died 7 Aug. 1976.

WATSON, Vice-Adm. (retd) Bertram Chalmers, CB 1938; DSO 1917; RN; *b* 1887; *s* of Charles Watson, Slateford; *m* 1915, Isabel, *d* of John Buist, Broughty Ferry; one *s* two *d. Educ:* Merchiston; Temple Grove. In Harwich Force throughout European War, 1914-18; HMS Valiant, 1933-34; Dir, RN Staff Coll., 1934-36; Rear-Adm., 1936; Rear-Adm. (Submarines), 1938-40; Flag Officer, Greenock, 1940-42; Commodore of Convoys, 1942-43; Admiral Commanding Iceland, 1943-45. *Recreations:* hunting, fishing, astronomy. *Address:* The Court House, Hambledon, Portsmouth. *T:* Hambledon 727. *Clubs:* Army and Navy.
[Died 22 July 1976.

WATSON, David Archibald Beverley; Chairman, Johannesburg Consolidated Investment Company, since 1963 (Joint Managing Director, 1963-71); Director: Argus Printing & Publishing Co. Ltd; Rand Selection Corp. Ltd; Standard Bank of SA Ltd, and of numerous S African Companies; Chairman, Rustenburg Platinum Mines, etc; *b* 7 Sept. 1905; *s* of late Archibald Watson and late Beatrice Mary Watson; *m* 1930, Christine Margaret (*née* Innes); two *d. Educ:* Oundle; Birmingham University (BSc Hons). Associated with Johannesburg Consolidated Investment Company and its allied companies, 1926-. *Recreation:* gardening. *Address:* Flint Farm, Sandton, PO Box 590, Johannesburg, South Africa. *Clubs:* Rand, Country (Johannesburg).
[Died 28 Oct. 1971.

WATSON, David Meredith Seares, FRS 1922; LLD, DSc; *b* 18 June 1886; *s* of David Watson, DSc; *m* Katherine (*d* 1969), *d* of Rev. I. Parker; two *d. Educ:* Manchester Grammar School; Manchester University. Lecturer in Vertebrate Palæontology, UC, 1912-21; Jodrell Prof. of Zoology and Comparative Anatomy, UC, Univ. of London, 1921-51, Emeritus, 1951-. Alexander Agassiz Prof., Harvard Univ., 1952. Lt RNVR 1916-18; Croonian lecturer, Roy. Soc., 1924; Romanes lecturer, Oxford, 1928; Silliman lecturer, Yale University, 1937; Member Agricultural Research Council, 1931-42; Secretary Scientific Food Policy Committee, 1940. Rainer Medal, 1928; Lyell Medal, Geological Soc. of London, 1935; Thompson Medal, National Academy of Sciences of the USA, 1941; Darwin Medal, Royal Society, 1942; Linnean Medal, Linnean Society, 1949; Darwin Wallace Medal, Linnean Soc., 1958; Wollaston Medal, Geological Soc. of London, 1965. Trustee of the British Museum, 1946-63. Hon. LLD, Aberdeen, 1943; Hon. DSc: Cape Town, 1929; Manchester, 1943; Reading, 1948; Wales, 1948; Witwatersrand, 1949. Hon. Mem. of various foreign scientific societies. *Publications:* many papers on Vertebrate Palæontology and connected subjects in Phil. Trans., Proc. Zoo. Soc., Journ. of Anat., etc. *Recreation:* travel. *Address:* Pendean Convalescent Home, Midhurst, Sussex.
[Died 23 July 1973.

WATSON, Dennis George, CIE 1945; KPM; *s* of late G. E. Watson; *m* 1934, Dawn, *d* of late Lieutenant-Colonel F. O. Bowen, DSO; one *s* one *d. Educ:* Blundell's School. Indian Army (Reserve of Officers), 1917-19; Inspector-General of Police, Indore State, 1929-32 and 1937-41; Inspector-Gen. of Police, CP and Berar, 1944-46. *Address:* c/o Grindlay's Bank, Ltd, 13 St James's Square, SW1. *Club:* East India, Sports and Public Schools.
[Died 24 Jan. 1977.

WATSON, Maj.-Gen. Gilbert France, CB 1945; DSO 1915; OBE 1942; Chairman Board of Governors, Bristol United Hospital, 1962-65; *b* 6 May 1895; *s* of late Charles France Watson, of Banchory, Kincardine; *m* 1st, 1917, Marjorie Wyndham (*d* 1962), 2nd *d* of Dr J. Lewis, Roath, Cardiff; one *s*; 2nd, 1964, Evelyn Gaynor, *widow* of Charles Lund. *Educ:* Berkhampstead; Colchester. Served with Royal Engineers in France, 1915-19 (DSO, despatches twice); entered Royal Welch Fusiliers, 1921; graduated Staff College; Director of Manpower Planning, War Office, 1943-46. Bt Major, 1936; Bt Lt-Col, 1939; Temp. Brig., 1940; Col, 1942; Acting Maj.-Gen., 1943; Temp. Maj.-Gen. 1944, retired pay, 1946. Principal Regional Officer, Min. of Health, SW Region, 1946-60. Officer Fr. Légion d'Honneur. *Address:* Knowle, Edward Road, Walton St Mary, Clevedon, Avon. *T:* Clevedon 3568.
[Died 5 March 1976.

WATSON, G(ordon) G(raham) Gibbes, CMG 1957; Barrister; Chairman of Directors of several New Zealand financial and industrial companies; *b* 21 Oct. 1891; *yr s* of Clement and Ruth Watson, Wellington, NZ; *m* 1929, Edith Jessie, *d* of Harry Beloe Crawford, Barrister, Oamaru, NZ; no *c. Educ:* Wellington Coll. and Victoria Univ. Coll., Wellington (MA, LLB). Practice as barrister, 1915; Lecturer in Law, Victoria Univ. Coll., 1915-28; Pres. Wellington Law Society, 1932; Mem. Council NZ Law Society, 1932-46. Acted for many years as Counsel for various companies and financial instns in NZ. Mem. Royal Commission on Banking and Monetary System in NZ, 1955-56; Pres. NZ Acad. of Fine Arts, 1938-49; Chm. Management Cttee, National Art Gallery, NZ, 1944-; Pres. Overseas League, Wellington Br., 1949-56. *Recreations:* Horticulture (Pres. Hutt Valley Hort. Soc.), art, travel. *Address:* Wicklow, 335 Waterloo Road, Lower Hutt, New Zealand. *T:* Wellington 63861. *Club:* Wellington (NZ).
[Died 6 June 1971.

WATSON, Hon. Sir (Henry) Keith, Kt 1968; FCIS; Public Accountant at Perth, WA, since 1921; Director since 1933, and Chairman since 1951, of Perth Building Society; Director of various companies; *b* 22 Aug. 1900; *s* of W. H. Watson, Cottesloe, WA; *m* 1926, Edith, *d* of Edwin Symonds; one *s* (one *d* decd). *Educ:* Cottesloe and Claremont State Schs, W Australia. Chairman of Building Societies Assoc. of WA, 1951-68. Mem. of Secession Delegn from people of WA to Parlt of UK, 1934-35; MLC of Western Australia (Metropolitan Province), 1948-68. *Publication:* (jtly) Western Australia's Case for Secession, 1934. *Recreation:* bowls. *Address:* 85 Tyrell Street, Nedlands, Western Australia 6009. *Clubs:* Dalkeith Bowling, Nedlands Golf.
[Died 13 Jan. 1973.

WATSON, Brig. Henry Neville Grylls, DSO 1919; OBE 1922; late RASC; *b* Worthing, Sussex, 9 Sept. 1885; *s* of late Rev. Wm Grylls Watson, MA Oxon, Rector of St Margaret's, Canterbury; *m* 1946, Dorothy Marian Jones (*née* Boyton). *Educ:* Dover College. In the City, 1904-8; 2nd Lt 3rd Royal Sussex Regt, 1908; joined RASC 2nd Lt 1909; Lt 1912; Capt. 1915; temp. Major, 1915; Major, 1929; Bt Lt-Col 1932; Lt-Col 1937; Colonel, 1935; served European War (Mons Star, British and Allied War Medals): France, 1914-15; North Russia EF, 1918-19; Adj. 1st Cavalry Div. RASC 1914; Adj. 1st London Div. Train. TF 1915; DADT War Office, 1918; DADST North Russia EF 1918-19 (DSO, brevet Major, despatches thrice, one mention by Secretary of State for War, 2nd class Order of St Stanislaus with swords, 3rd class Order of St Anna with swords); Adjutant North Midland Div. Train. TF 1920; seconded for duty on the staff of Police Adviser to RIC, 1920-22; Adjutant No 1 Corps Depôt, 1923; Adjutant RASC Training College, 1924; Assistant Director of Supplies and Transport, British Forces in Palestine and Transjordania, 1938-40 (despatches, General Service Medal); War of 1939-45 (1939-45 Star, Africa Star, Defence Medal, War Medal 1939-45); Acting Brig. Feb. 1940; Temp. Brig. Aug. 1940; Dir of Supplies and Transport, GHQ, Middle East, 1940-41; retired pay, 1942. A Governor of Dover Coll., 1924. Coronation Medal, 1937. *Recreations:* Rugby football and golf. *Address:* Barclays Bank Ltd, Aldershot, Hants. *Club:* East India, Sports and Public Schools.
[Died 30 May 1976.

WATSON, Herbert A. G.; *see* Grant Watson.

WATSON, Herbert Edmeston, DSc (London); FRIC; FIChemE; Emeritus Professor of Chemical Engineering, University of London; *b* 17 May 1886; *s* of late A. E. Watson, London; *m* 1st, 1917, Margaret Kathleen (*d* 1951), *d* of late William Rowson, Liverpool; one *s* one *d*; 2nd, 1955, Eileen Elsie, *widow* of Col W. J. Norman and *d* of late Robert H. Moore. *Educ:* Marlborough College; London, Berlin, Geneva, Cambridge Universities. BSc 1st Class Hons Chemistry, 1907; DSc 1912; 1851 Exhibition Scholar, 1909; Fellow University College, London, 1914; Assistant Professor Indian Institute of Science, 1911-16;

Professor of Inorganic and Physical Chemistry, Indian Institute of Science, Bangalore, 1916-34; Professor of Chemical Engineering, University College, 1934-51 (services lent to Admiralty, 1939-45); invented neon glow lamp, 1911. *Publications:* numerous papers in scientific journals. *Recreation:* Fluoride research. *Address:* Westside, Knowl Hill, Woking, Surrey GU22 7HL. *T:* Woking 5411. [*Died* 24 *Sept.* 1980.

WATSON, John Arthur Fergus, CBE 1965; PPRICS; JP; Member, Lands Tribunal, 1957-69; retired Juvenile Court Magistrate; *b* 24 July 1903; *s* of late Capt. J. G. Maitland Watson, Royal Artillery, and Mabel (*née* Weir); *m* 1948, Joan, *d* of late Claude Leigh; one *s* one *d*. *Educ:* Uppingham. Passed into RMA, Woolwich, 1921, but declined cadetship. Chartered surveyor, 1926; partner in Ferris & Puckridge, 1928-47; and in Alfred Savill & Sons, 1947-56. A Chm., Inner London Juvenile Courts, 1936-68. Member: Central Housing Advisory Cttee to Minister of Health, 1936-47; Inter-departmental Cttee on New Towns, 1945-46; Prime Minister's Cttee on Regent's Park Terraces, 1946-47; Pres., RICS, 1949-50; Mem., Stevenage Development Corp., 1952-56. Worked voluntarily for some years in prisons and borstals; Vice-Pres., Nat. Assoc. of Prison Visitors, 1938- (Hon. Sec., 1928-38; Chm., 1941-44); Mem. Youth Advisory Council to Minister of Education, 1942-45; advised CCG on problems of juvenile delinquency in British Zone, 1947-48; Mem., Royal Commission on Justices of the Peace, 1946-48; Mem. Nat. Adv. Council on Training of Magistrates, 1967-73. JP Inner London Area (formerly County of London) 1935. *Publications:* The Housing Act 1935, 1936; Meet the Prisoner, 1939; The Child and the Magistrate, 1942 (revd 1950, 1965); British Juvenile Courts, 1948; Which is the Justice?, 1969; The Juvenile Court-1970 Onward, 1970; Nothing but the Truth: expert evidence in principle and practice, 1971 (rev. edn 1975); The Incompleat Surveyor, 1973; (with P. M. Austin) The Modern Juvenile Court, 1975; Savills: a Family and a Firm 1652-1977, 1977. *Address:* Elmdon Old Vicarage, Saffron Walden, Essex. *T:* Chrishall (via Cambridge) 346.
[*Died* 5 *Feb.* 1978.

WATSON, Hon. Sir Keith; *see* Watson, Hon. Sir (Henry) K.

WATSON, Maj.-Gen. Norman Vyvyan, CB 1945; OBE 1940; late Royal Artillery; Managing Director, Army Kinema Corporation, 1957-67, Vice-Chairman since 1967, General Manager since 1952; *b* 26 January 1898; *m* 1927, Maud (decd), *d* of R. P. Randall; one *s*; *m* 1962, Vera, *d* of W. P. Tracy. 2nd Lt RA 1915; served European War, France and Belgium, 1916-18 (despatches); Iraq Operations, 1919-20. Director of Staff Duties, GHQ India, 1943-47; Deputy Quarter-Master-General, War Office, 1949-52; retired pay, 1952. *Address:* Games' Farmhouse, Peldon, Essex. *T:* Peldon 326. [*Died* 4 *Oct.* 1974.

WATSON, Robert, CMG 1947; OBE 1944; Country Representative, Ethiopia, Food and Agriculture Organisation of United Nations, 1957-62; *b* 9 June 1894; *s* of T. Watson; *m* 1926, E. M. S. Armstrong (*d* 1973); one *s* one *d*. *Educ:* Gordon Schools, Huntly; Aberdeen Univ. County Organiser on staff of North of Scotland Coll. of Agriculture, 1915-21 (including war service 1915-19); joined Indian Agric. Service, 1921; Dir of Agriculture, Burma, 1941; held commission in Army Reserve, 1927-41, and as Colonel (agriculture) in Civil Affairs Service (Burma), 1945; Dir of Agriculture, Burma, and (from 1946) Commissioner for Agricultural Rehabilitation; Mem. East Africa Rice Mission, April-Oct. 1948; Department of Agriculture for Scotland, 1949; Dir of Agriculture, Cyrenaica, 1950. *Address:* 18 Charleston, North Kessock, Inverness-shire.
[*Died* 11 *Sept.* 1977.

WATSON, Sir Stephen (John), Kt 1969; CBE 1959; MSc, DSc (Dunelm); FRSE; FRIC; FRAgS; Professor of Agriculture and Rural Economy, Edinburgh University and Principal, Edinburgh and East of Scotland College of Agriculture, 1944-68, now Emeritus Professor; *b* 24 March 1898; *e s* of William Watson, Accountant, Newcastle on Tyne, and Lima, Peru; *m* 1925, May, *yr d* of late Joseph Robinson, JP, Newcastle on Tyne; one *s*. *Educ:* Tynemouth School, Northumberland; Armstrong College, University of Durham. Scottish Horse and 1st King Edward's Horse, 1915-19; Demonstrator, Armstrong College, 1920-22; Lecturer in Agricultural Chemistry, Cheshire School of Agriculture, 1922-23; East Anglian Institute of Agriculture, 1923-27; Head of Biochemistry and Animal Nutrition Section and Deputy Head of Research Laboratories, ICI, Agricultural Research Station, Jealott's Hill, 1927-36; Head of Research Laboratories, 1937-44. Member Ministry of Agriculture Advisory Panel (grass and fodder conservation), 1939. Director, Central Agricultural Control, Imperial Chemical Industries Ltd, 1944. Mem., ARC, 1951-61 (Dep. Chm., 1953-58). Member: Scottish Agricultural Improvement Council, 1945-68; Scottish

Adv. Council, 1945-48; Hill Farming Adv. Cttee for Scotland, 1947-50; Hill Farming Res. Cttee, 1947-54; Scottish Standing Cttee for Calculation of Residual Value of Fertilizers and Feeding Stuffs, 1949- (Chm., 1965-); Conditional Aid (Agric.) Adv. Cttee, 1953-56; Adv. Cttee on Revolving Loan Fund for Agric., 1953-58; Bd of Dirs, Scottish Soc. for Res. in Plant Breeding, 1946-49. Member Board of Management: Oatridge Agric. Coll., West Lothian (Chm., 1967-75); Edinburgh Centre of Rural Econ. (Dep. Chm., 1948-68); Hill Farming Res. Orgn, 1954-68 (Chm., Finance Cttee); Mem., Council of Management, Macaulay Inst. of Soil Res., 1945-69; Member Governing Body: Nat. Vegetable Res. Station, 1947-52; Grassland Res. Inst., 1949-63; Scottish Horticultural Res. Inst., 1953-67; Nat. Coll. of Agricultural Engrng, 1964- (Chm., 1970). *Publications:* Silage and Crop Preservation, 1938; The Science and Practice of Conservation, 1939, revised 1961; Feeding of Livestock 1949; Grassland and Grassland Products, 1951; Silage (with Dr A. M. Smith), 1951; many papers in various chemical and agricultural journals on the results of research in animal nutrition, and the conservation and utilization of grassland herbage. *Address:* 18 Cluny Drive, Edinburgh. [*Died* 25 *June* 1976.

WATSON-JONES, Sir Reginald, Kt 1945; FRCS, FACS (Hon.), FRACS (Hon.), FRCSE (Hon.), FRCSC (Hon.); MChOrth, BSc; Orthopædic Surgeon Extra to The Queen, 1952 (Orthopædic Surgeon to King George VI, 1946-52); Consultant in Orthopædic Surgery, RAF; Hon. Consultant in Orthopædic and Accident Department, London Hospital; British Editor, Journal of Bone and Joint Surgery, since 1947; Hon. Consultant, Robert Jones and Agnes Hunt Hospital, Shropshire; Hunterian Professor of Surgery, Royal College of Surgeons of England, 1945; Arthur Sims Commonwealth Travelling Professor of Surgery, 1950; President, British Orthopædic Assoc., 1952-53; Senior Vice-President, Royal College of Surgeons of England, 1953-54; Member Court of Examiners, Hunterian Orator, 1959; President Orthopædic Section, Royal Society of Medicine, 1956; Hon. Orthopædic Surgeon, Liverpool Royal Infirmary; *b* 1902; *m* 1930, Muriel Cook (*d* 1970); one *s* one *d*; *m* 1971, Miss Wallace Robertson. Senior Lyon Jones Scholar, 1921; Mitchell Banks Medallist, 1920; George Holt Medallist, 1921; Robert Gee Prizeman, 1923; George Holt Fellow in Physiology, 1923; Samuel's Research Scholar in Surgery, 1926; Robert Jones Fellow in Orthopædic Surgery, 1928; Gold Medallist in Orthopædic Surgery, 1926; Demonstrator in Anatomy and Physiology, 1923; Senior Surgical Tutor and Registrar, Liverpool Royal Infirmary, 1926-27; House Surgeon, Royal National Orthopædic Hospital, and Clinical Assistant, Great Ormond Street Hospital, 1926; formerly Lecturer in Orthopædic Pathology and Orthopædic Surgery, University of Liverpool; Hon. Lecturer, War Surgery, British Post-Grad. Med. Sch., London; FRSM. Hon. Member: American Orthopædic Assoc., American Acad. Orthopædic Surg., Société Française d'Orthopédie et Traumatologie. Societa Italiana di Ortopedia e Traumatologia Canadian Med. Assoc., Belgian, Swedish, Latin-American, Ecuadorian and Brazilian Orthop. Societies; Australian and NZ Orthop. Associations, etc; Assoc. of Surgeons of E Africa. KStJ. *Publications:* Fractures and Joint Injuries: 1st edn 1940; fifteen reprints; 5th edn 1969; trans.: Italian, Spanish, Portugese, German, Russian, Greek, French; Pye's Surgical Handicraft, 1938, 15th edn 1953; (British edn) Medicine and Surgery for the Attorney, 1959. *Address:* 82 Portland Place, W1. *T:* 01-580 1378 and 1379. *Club:* Garrick.
[*Died* 9 *Aug.* 1972.

WATSON-WATT, Air Chief Commandant Dame Katherine (Jane Trefusis), DBE 1944 (CBE 1941); *b* 21 March 1899; *d* of late Edmund Forbes, AMICE, and *g d* of late Principal James David Forbes, DCL, LLD, FRS; *m* 1966, Sir Robert Watson-Watt, *qv*. *Educ:* London. Women's Volunteer Reserve, European War, 1916-18; Founder, 1922, and later Managing Director of Bell Mead Kennels Ltd; retired, 1938; Manager of Building Estate, 1932; retired, 1939; Member of Council of Emergency Service, 1935-39, a Service which undertook the training of women as officers, in preparation for the foundation of Women's Services; Chief Instructor to the Auxiliary Territorial Service, School of Instruction for officers, with rank of Company Comdr, 1938; attached to No. 20 Royal Air Force Company ATS, 1939; Director, Women's Auxiliary Air Force, 1939-43; Missions to North America and Far East, 1943-44; retired 1944; Director/Dep. Director of Welfare for CCG, 1946-48. RAF Association: Vice-President; Member Council; Dep. Chairman Exec. Cttee; Chairman and Member, various sub-cttees. Chairman: Draydonne Properties; Disabled Adv. Cttee, Hammersmith; Member: Nat. Adv. Council for Employment of Disabled; Disabled Training and Employment Cttee; Central Adv. Cttee, Ministry of Social Security; Council, RAF Benevolent Fund; Joint Cttee, Service and Ex-Service Organisations. Hon. LLD St Andrews Univ., 1968. *Address:* 7

Crescent Place, SW3. *T:* 01-589 9982; The Shed, Pitlochry, Perthshire. [*Died* 18 *June* 1971.

WATSON-WATT, Sir Robert (Alexander), Kt 1942; CB 1941; LLD (St Andrews) 1943; DSc (Toronto) 1943; DSc (Laval) 1952; FRS 1941; scientific adviser, author and lecturer; *b* 13 April 1892; *s* of Patrick Watson Watt, Brechin, Angus, Scotland, and Mary Matthew; *m* 1st, 1916, Margaret (marr. diss. 1952), *d* of David Robertson, Perth; 2nd, 1952, Jean (*widow* of Prof. George M. Smith) (*d* 1964); one *step s* one *step d*; 3rd, 1966, Air Chief Commandant Dame Katherine Jane Trefusis Forbes, DBE (*d* 1971). *Educ:* Brechin High Sch.; UC, Dundee, in University of St Andrews. Asst to Professor of Natural Philosophy, UC, Dundee, 1912-21; various posts in meteorology, radio and radar in Met. Office, DSIR, Air Ministry, Ministries of Aircraft Prod., Supply, Civil Aviation and Transp., 1915-52. Dep. Chairman Radio Board of War Cabinet, 1943-46; US Medal for Merit, 1946. Ex-President, Royal Met. Society for Inst. of Navigation; Ex-Vice-President, Inst. of Radio Engineers, New York. Hughes Medal of Royal Society, Elliott Cresson Medal of Franklyn Institute, etc. *Publications:* The Cathode Ray Oscillograph in Radio Research, 1933; Through the Weather House, 1935; Three Steps to Victory, 1958; The Pulse of Radar, 1959; Man's Means to His End, 1961; various communications to learned societies, etc. *Address:* c/o Miss J. Williamson, Black Mill, Kincraig by Kingussie, Inverness-shire. *Club:* Athenæum.
[*Died* 5 *Dec.* 1973.

WATT; *see* Watson-Watt.

WATT, Francis Clifford, QC (Scotland) 1946; Sheriff of Stirling, Dunbarton and Clackmannan since 1961 (Caithness, Sutherland, Orkney and Zetland, 1952-61); *b* 20 July 1896; *s* of late Rev. Charles James Watt, Polwarth, Berwickshire; *m* 1945, Theresa Dorothy (*d* 1971), *d* of John M'Quaker, Edinburgh; one *s. Educ:* Berwickshire High Sch.; Edinburgh Univ. Served European War, Argyll and Sutherland Highlanders and King's Own Scottish Borderers; called to Scottish Bar, 1925; Junior Counsel to Treasury for Scotland, 1940-46; MP (C) Central Division of Edinburgh, 1941-45. *Recreation:* golf. *Address:* 52 Inverleith Place, Edinburgh. *T:* 031-552 2932. *Clubs:* Caledonian; Caledonian (Edinburgh). [*Died* 8 *April* 1971.

WATT, Rt. Hon. Hugh, PC 1974; Member, Accident Compensation Commission, New Zealand, since 1976; *b* 19 March 1912; *m* 1st, 1935; 2nd, 1968; two *s* two *d. Educ:* Remuera Primary Sch.; Techn. College. Engineer. Founded own engineering business, 1947. MP for Onehunga, New Zealand, 1953; Minister of Works, also Minister of Electricity, 1957-60; Deputy Prime Minister, 1972-74; Minister of Works, Development and Labour, 1972-74; High Comr for NZ in UK, 1975-76. *Recreations:* football, racing, swimming, fishing. *Address:* c/o Accident Compensation Commission, Private Bag, Wellington, New Zealand. [*Died* 4 *Feb.* 1980.

WATT, Prof. John Mitchell, ED; MB, ChB (Edinburgh), Hon. LLD (Witwatersrand); FRCP (Edinburgh), FRSE, FLS, FRSSAf; CStJ; Emeritus Professor of Pharmacology and Therapeutics, University of the Witwatersrand, Johannesburg; Priory Surgeon-in-Chief (Reserve), St John Ambulance Brigade, Southern Africa; *b* Port Elizabeth, South Africa, 1 Dec. 1892; Scottish parentage; *m* 1st, 1920, Yelena T. Nikonova; two *s* two *d*; 2nd, 1942, Betty Gwendoline Lory; one *s* one *d. Educ:* Grey Institute High Sch., Port Elizabeth; Stirling High Sch., Scotland; University of Edinburgh. Graduated MB, ChB 1916; commissioned in the RAMC (Special Reserve) 4 Aug. 1914; on Active Service until 1919; Assistant in Materia Medica to Professor Cushny of Edinburgh Univ.; medical author, and member various medical societies; Foreign Corresponding Member, Royal Flemish Academy of Medicine, Belgium. Twice President of the Royal Medical Society of Edinburgh. Selected by Universities' Bureau of British Empire for a Carnegie Corporation Grant, 1933-34. Served as Head of Section M3 on the staff of Medical Headquarters, Union Defence Forces, South Africa, 1941-45; Major, RAMC (Militia) (retired); Colonel, South African Medical Corps (Retired List). *Publications:* numerous articles on medical and natural history subjects in medical and scientific journals; The Medicinal and Poisonous Plants of Southern and Eastern Africa (with Maria G. Breyer-Brandwijk), 2nd edn, 1962. Editor, Formulary of the South African Railways and Harbours Sick Fund, 1st edn, 1935, 2nd edn, 1943, 3rd edn, 1952; Practical Notes on Pharmacology, Therapeutics, and Prescription Writing, 1940. Editor with F. J. Todd of The South African Pharmaceutical Formulary, 1943; Practical Pharmacology and Prescription Writing (with Margaret Brown), 1949. *Recreations:* gardening, ornithology, philately. *Address:* 36 Ludlow Street, Chapel Hill, Qld 4069, Australia. [*Died* 23 *April* 1980.

WATTIE, Sir James, Kt 1966; CBE 1963; Chairman and Managing Director, J. Wattie Canneries Ltd, since 1934 (Founder, 1934); *b* 23 March 1902; 3rd *s* of late William John Wattie and late Annie Elizabeth; *m* 1925, Gladys Madeline Henderson; two *s. Educ:* Public Schools, Blenheim and Hastings, NZ. Post Office Messenger, 1916; Junior Clerk, HB Farmers Meat Co. Ltd, 1917, Asst Accountant, 1919-24; Accountant, Roachs Ltd, 1924-25; Secretary, H. B. Fruitgrowers Ltd, 1926-27, Manager, 1927-34. Member: Hastings Chamber of Commerce; Hawke's Bay Medical Research Foundation (Life Member); NZ Trade Promotion Council. Fellow: Royal Arts Soc., NZ, 1970; Inst. of Directors, 1970. *Recreations:* trout fishing, horse racing and breeding, horticulture. *Address:* Mangapapa, PO Box 439, Hastings, Hawke's Bay, New Zealand. *T:* Hastings 85-401. *Clubs:* Wellesley (Wellington); Auckland (Auckland); Poverty Bay (Gisborne); Havelock (Havelock North); Hawke's Bay, Napier (Napier); Hastings, County (Hastings). [*Died* 8 *June* 1974.

WATTS, Arthur Francis, CMG 1964; OBE 1959; Assistant High Commissioner, Aden, 1964-66; retired; *b* 15 Aug. 1916; *s* of Frank Godley Watts; *m* 1939, Barbara Mills; four *s. Educ:* Trent Coll. Served War of 1939-45. Famine Relief Officer, Eastern Aden Protectorate, 1944-46; Political Officer (Asst Adviser), E Aden Prot. and W Aden Prot., 1946; Dep. Adv. and British Agent, E Aden Prot. 1955, W Aden Prot., 1958; Resident Adviser and British Agent E Aden Prot. until 1960. *Address:* Ashleigh, Mark Cross, Crowborough, Sussex. *T:* Rotherfield 2570. [*Died* 5 *Dec.* 1972.

WATTS, Gordon Edward, CBE 1960; MA, PhD (Cantab); BSc (London); FRIC; FRSA; Adviser on Technical Education to Overseas Development Administration, Foreign and Commonwealth Office (formerly Ministry of Overseas Development), 1967-72; *b* 6 Dec. 1902; *s* of Edward Watts, Dulwich, SE; *m* 1929, Nancy Margaret, *d* of Alfred Charles Playne, Looe, Cornwall; one *s* one *d. Educ:* Alleyn's Sch., Dulwich; Magdalene Coll., Cambridge. Res. Chemist, ICI, 1927-30; Lectr in Chem. and Head of Dept, Brighton Tech. Coll., 1930-39; Adviser on Tech. Educn, Anglo-Iranian Oil Co., 1939-41; Vice-Principal, Brighton Tech. Coll., 1941-44; Principal: Brighton Tech. Coll., 1944-62; Brighton Coll. of Technol., 1962-67. Pres., Assoc. of Principals of Techn. Instns, 1953-54; Chm., Council, Assoc. of Techn. Instns, 1959-60; Vice-Chm., Nat. Adv. Council for Educn for Industry and Commerce, 1959-67; Member: Adv. Cttee on Educn in the Colonies, 1959-62; Council for Overseas Colls of Arts, Sci. and Technol., 1959-62; Council for Techn. Educn and Trg for Overseas Countries, 1962-74; Ashby Commn on Higher Educn in Nigeria, 1959-60; British Delegation to Commonwealth Education Confs; Oxford, 1959, New Delhi, 1962, Lagos, 1968, Canberra, 1971. Chm., Commonwealth Conf. on Educn and Trg of Technicians, Huddersfield, 1967, Member: CNAA, 1964-67; Governing Body, Imperial Coll. of Science and Technology, 1970-72. Hon. Mem., City and Guilds of London Inst., 1972. Hon. DSc Sussex, 1968. *Recreations:* travel, photography, gardening. *Address:* 1 The Green, Barrowfield, Hove, East Sussex BN3 6TH. *T:* Brighton 554894. [*Died* 8 *Dec.* 1974.

WATTS, John Hylton; President: United Transport Company Ltd, since 1968 (Chairman, 1959-68; Managing Director, 1937); United Transport Overseas Ltd, since 1969 (Chairman, 1949-68); *b* Lydney, 14 March 1890; 2nd *s* of late Joseph Stephen Watts, Lydney, Glos.; *m* 1926, Iris Dyne, *er d* of late W. E. Birt; no *c. Educ:* Wycliffe Coll., Stonehouse. director: Bulwark United Transport Ltd; Cambrian Airways Ltd, 1949-71 (Chm. 1949-59); Watts of Lydney Ltd; Lydney Industrial Holdings Ltd; Chepstow Racecourse Co. Ltd; Member S. Wales Cttee of Lloyds Bank Ltd, 1959-67. Chairman, St Pierre Golf and Country Club Ltd. Served European War, 1915-19, 14th Siege Battery and Motor Transport Section (four years in France and Belgium). President 1935-65, now Life Patron, Lydney Branch of British Legion; Governor of Wycliffe Coll., 1952-66, now President; Member, Worshipful Company of Carmen, 1948; Freeman City of London, 1957; Verderer and Inclosure Commissioner of the Royal Forest of Dean, 1961. Member of Inst. of Directors, 1949; FCIT (MInstT 1950). *Recreations:* croquet, cricket, tennis. *Address:* The Rocklands, Lydney, Glos. *T:* Lydney 2827. *Clubs:* County (Cardiff); St Pierre Golf and Country (Chepstow). [*Died* 1 *May* 1972.

WATTS, Rev. Sidney Maurice, DD (St Andrews); BD (London); Minister of Union Church, Mill Hill, NW7, 1942-61, retired; Moderator, International Congregational Council, 1953-58; *b* Bishops Stortford, 1892; *y s* of James Watts, Lowestoft; *m* 1917, Winifred Chambers; one *s* two *d. Educ:* Lowestoft; Hackney Coll. (University of London). President, London University Debating Society, 1915; Asst Minister, Bromley Congregational

Church, 1916-18; Supt Minister (Congregational), Whitefield's Central Mission, Tottenham Court Road, W1, 1918-24; Minister of Warwick Road Congregational Church, Coventry, 1924; of Elgin Place Congregational Church, Glasgow, 1937-42. Chairman Congregational Union of England and Wales, 1948-49; Moderator Free Church Federal Council, 1952-53. *Publications:* The Garden of God, a volume of Sermons; Liberty to the Captives, a short history of Slavery; Thinking Again About the Future Life, 1948. *Recreation:* gardening. *Address:* Fen Place, Turner's Hill, Crawley, East Sussex.
[*Died* 30 *May* 1979.

WATTS, Weldon Patrick Tyrone, AFC 1918; Hon. Surgeon, Royal Victoria Infirmary, since 1963; Consultant Surgeon: Royal Victoria Infirmary, 1947; Princess Mary Maternity Hospital, 1945; Shotley Bridge General Hospital, 1940; Hospital for Sick Children, 1927; retired, 1962; *b* 30 Oct. 1897; *s* of Joseph Patrick Weldon Watts, Dublin, and Kate Crisp, The Elms, Sunderland; *m* 1933, Sarah Bruce Allan, MB, BS; one *s. Educ:* Lake House Preparatory Sch., Bexhill; Sherborne Sch., Dorset; College of Medicine, Durham Univ. Served European War, 1914-18, RFC, 1916; RAF, 1917. MB, BS Durham, 1922; MS Durham, 1928; FRCS Edinburgh, 1927. Resident appointments, Royal Victoria Infirmary, Newcastle upon Tyne, 1922-33; general practice, 1924; Resident Med. Officer, 1925-26, Surgical Registrar, 1926-35, Asst Surgeon, 1935-47, Royal Victoria Infirmary. British Medical Association: joined 1922; Secretary, Newcastle Div., 1936-52; Chairman, Newcastle upon Tyne Div., 1953; President, North of England Branch, 1954; Member Council, 1940-59; President, 1957. Member, General Medical Council, 1961-66. *Publications:* contrib. Newcastle Med. Journal and BMJ. *Recreations:* golf, fishing, shooting, natural history. *Address:* Fenham Hill, Beal, Berwick-on-Tweed. *T:* Beal 234. *Club:* Northumberland Golf (Gosforth).
[*Died* 23 *Oct.* 1972.

WAVERLEY, Ava, Viscountess; *b* Dec. 1896; *o d* of late J. E. C. Bodley and Evelyn (*née* Bell); *m* 1st, 1925, Ralph Wigram, CMG, Counsellor in HM Diplomatic Service (*d* 1936); one *s* decd; 2nd, 1941, Sir John Anderson, PC, GCB, GCSI, GCIE, FRS, MP (*cr* Viscount Waverley of Westdean, 1952; awarded OM 1957) (*d* 1958). *Educ:* in France. Member of Governing Body, Dockland Settlement; Trustee of Royal Ballet Benevolent Fund; Member of Council, "Friends of Covent Garden"; Bloodhound breeder. *Address:* 4 Lord North Street, Westminster, SW1. *Club:* Kennel (Ladies' Branch).
[*Died* 22 *Dec.* 1974.

WAY, Andrew Greville Parry, CMG 1963; Assistant Commissioner, Metropolitan Police, 1963-69, retired; *b* 9 Dec. 1909; *s* of late Preb. Charles Parry Way, and Ethel Mary (*née* Danks); *m* 1939, Maureen Molyneux; two *s. Educ:* St Edward's and Christ Church, Oxford. Joined Metropolitan Police, 1934; Metropolitan Police Coll., 1934-35. Army (General List), 1943-49. Seconded Police Force of Free Territory of Trieste, 1947-52. Seconded: Montreal Police Dept (Canada), 1961-62; Anguilla Police Unit, 1969. *Recreations:* supporting those sports which gave great pleasure in the past. *Address:* Ponda Rosa, Lerryn, near Lostwithiel, Cornwall. *Club:* Royal Fowey Yacht.
[*Died* 8 *Sept.* 1974.

WAY, Christine Stella; *b* 26 July 1895; *o c* of late Captain C. M. S. Humphreys, JP, Garthmyl Hall, Montgomeryshire; *m* 1932, Captain H. Bromley Way (*d* 1968); one *s* one *d. Educ:* Tudor Hall, Chislehurst. County Secretary of Girl Guides for County of Montgomeryshire, 1919; County Commissioner (Girl Guides), 1930-47; Hon. Treasurer, Wales Girl Guides since 1945; JP 1934; High Sheriff of Montgomeryshire, 1943. Chairman of House Cttee for Broneirion (The Welsh Training Centre for Girl Guides), 1947. VAD nurse through European War. *Address:* Garthmyl Hall, Montgomery, Powys. *T:* Berriew 283.
[*Died* 27 *Jan.* 1975.

WEARING, John Frederick; India Office Library and Records, since 1973; *b* 5 Oct. 1922; *s* of Walter and Elsie Wearing; *m* 1945, Rose Vacher; one *d* (one *s* decd). *Educ:* Whitehaven Grammar Sch.; St Edmund Hall, Oxford. RAF, 1942-46. Asst Principal, Colonial Office, 1948; Foreign Office, 1949; 2nd Secretary, British Legation, Helsinki, 1950; HM Vice-Consul, Amsterdam, 1953; HM Consul, Hanover, 1955; FO, 1956; 1st Secretary, British Embassy, Djakarta, 1959; FO, 1961; 1st Secretary, UK Delegation to OECD, Paris, 1963; Counsellor and Head of Economic General Department, Commonwealth Office, 1966; UK Alternate Governor, Internat. Atomic Energy Agency, 1967-69, and UK Permanent Rep. to UN Industrial Develt Org., Vienna, 1968-69; Graduate Sch. of Contemporary European Studies, Reading Univ., 1969-70; Counsellor and Dep. Head of UK Delegn to OECD, Paris, 1970-71; retired from HM

Diplomatic Service, 1972, and re-employed in unestablished capacity. *Recreations:* gardening, amateur dramatics, debating. *Address:* c/o India Office Library and Records, Orbit House, 197 Blackfriars Road, SE1; 42 The Mead, Beckenham, Kent. *T:* 01-658 6837. *Club:* Travellers'.
[*Died* 24 *March* 1974.

WEATHERBURN, Prof. Charles Ernest, MA, DSc, Hon. LLD; Emeritus Professor of Mathematics, University of Western Australia since 1950 (Professor of Mathematics 1929-50); Chairman of the Professorial Board, 1934 and 1942-43; *b* Sydney, NSW, 18 June 1884; *s* of Henry Weatherburn, formerly of Leicester, England; *m* 1909, Lucy May Dartnell, Sydney, NSW; three *s. Educ:* Sydney University (post-graduate travelling scholarship); Trinity College, Cambridge (Major Scholarship). First Class Mathematical Tripos. Lecturer in Mathematics and Natural Philosophy for Ormond College, University of Melbourne, 1911-23; Trinity College, 1916-23; Professor of Mathematics at Canterbury University College, Christchurch, New Zealand, 1923-29; President of Section A, Australian and NZ Association for the Advancement of Science, 1932; awarded Hector Medal and Prize by the Royal Society of New Zealand, 1934. Hon. LLD (Glasgow), 1951. *Publications:* Vector Analysis; Differential Geometry; Riemannian Geometry; Mathematical Statistics, and a large number of original memoirs in Pure and Applied Mathematics. *Recreations:* bowling, motoring, gardening. *Address:* 34 Dalkeith Road, Nedlands, WA 6009, Australia.
[*Died* 18 *Oct.* 1974.

WEATHERHEAD, Rev. Leslie Dixon, CBE 1959; MA (Manchester); PhD (London); Hon. DD (Edinburgh and California); Hon. DLitt (University Puget Sound, Washington); Minister of The City Temple, London, 1936-October 1960, now Minister Emeritus; President of the Methodist Conference, July 1955-56; Hon. Chaplain to Forces; Freeman of City of London; Hon. Member, Association of Psychotherapists; Member: Society for Psychical Research; Churches' Fellowship for Psychical Study; President Institute of Religion and Medicine, 1966-67; *b* London, 1893; *s* of Andrew Weatherhead, a Scottish Presbyterian, and Elizabeth Mary Weatherhead, London; *m* 1920, Evelyn (*d* 1970), *er d* of Rev. Arthur Triggs, formerly Missionary in Ceylon; two *s* one *d. Educ:* Newton Secondary School Leicester; Richmond Theological Coll.; London Univ.; Manchester Univ. Served European War as 2nd Lieut IARO; Mesopotamian Campaign as Staff Capt.; after the Armistice with Turkey served as Chaplain to 1/4 and 1/6 Devon Regts, took charge of English Methodist Church, Madras, 1919; returned England in 1922; Oxford Road Wesleyan Church, Manchester, 1922-25; Brunswick Methodist Church Leeds, 1925-36; specialized in Psychology; Lecturer in Psychology for the Workers' Educational Association; Certificated Teacher of Psychology under Board of Education; Formerly Examiner in Psychology for Ordination Candidates in Wesleyan Methodist Church. *Publications:* After Death; The Afterworld of the Poets; Psychology in Service of the Soul; Psychology and Life; The Mastery of Sex through Psychology and Religion; The Transforming Friendship; Jesus and Ourselves; His Life and Ours; Discipleship; How can I find God?; Why do men Suffer?; It Happened in Palestine; A Shepherd Remembers; The Eternal Voice; Thinking aloud in Wartime; This is the Victory; Personalities of the Passion; In Quest of a Kingdom; The Will of God; A Plain Man looks at the Cross; The Significance of Silence; When The Lamp Flickers; The Resurrection and the Life; Psychology, Religion and Healing; That Immortal Sea; Over His Own Signature; Prescription for Anxiety; A Private House of Prayer; The Resurrection of Christ in the Light of Modern Science and Psychical Research; Key next Door; The Case for Re-incarnation; Salute to a Sufferer; Wounded Spirits; The Christian Agnostic; Time for God; Life Begins at Death; The Busy Man's Old Testament. *Recreation:* bird-watching. *Address:* 20 Richmond Grove, Bexhill-on-Sea, East Sussex. *T:* Bexhill 211719.
[*Died* 3 *Jan.* 1976.

WEATHERSTONE, Sir Duncan (Mackay), Kt 1965; MC 1918; TD 1945; DL; Lord Provost of the City of Edinburgh, May 1963-May 1966; *b* Edinburgh, 10 May 1898; *s* of R. M. Weatherstone and Harriet Mackay; *m* 1st, 1920, Janet Pringle Brunton (*d* 1966); one *s* one *d*; 2nd, 1968, Elizabeth Anne, *d* of late Rev. David S. Evans. *Educ:* Daniel Stewart's College, Edinburgh. Entered Life Assurance 1916; joined Army, 1917; returned to Life Assurance, 1919; Branch Manager, Belfast, 1922; Agency Manager and Executive, Head Office, holding position of second in command of the Company, 1933; retired, 1961. ACII 1922. Hon. DLitt, Heriot-Watt Univ., 1966; Hon. LLD, Edinburgh, 1966. Order of The Two Niles (Sudan), 1964. DL, Edinburgh, 1967. *Recreations:* golf, art and culture. *Clubs:* Scottish Conservative; Royal Scots (Edinburgh).
[*Died* 31 *Jan.* 1972.

WEAVER, Warren; Medal for Merit (US), 1946; Vice-President, Alfred P. Sloan Foundation until 1964, when resigned, but continues as consultant on scientific affairs; *b* 17 July 1894; *s* of Isaiah and Kittie Belle Stupfell Weaver; *m* 1919, Mary Hemenway; one *s* one *d*. *Educ:* Univ. of Wisconsin. 2nd Lieut Air Service, 1917-19. Asst Prof. Mathematics: Throop Coll., 1917-18; Cal. Inst. of Technology, 1919-20; Univ. of Wisconsin, 1920-25, Assoc. Prof. Mathematics, 1925-28, Prof. of Mathematics and Chairman of Dept, 1928-32; Lecturer, Univ. of Chicago, summer, 1928; Dir, Div. of Natural Sciences: Gen. Educn Bd, 1932-37; Rockefeller Foundation, 1932-55; Vice-Pres., Rockefeller Foundation, 1955-59. Chief, Applied Mathematics Panel, Office of Scientific Research and Devel., 1943-46; Chm., Naval Research Adv. Cttee, 1946-47. Sloan-Kettering Inst.: Trustee, 1954-67; Chairman Board, 1959-60; Vice-President, 1958-59; Trustee: Eastman Fund; Alfred P. Sloan Foundation, 1956-67; Member: Nat. Science Board, Nat. Science Foundation, 1956-60; Board of Directors, Coun. on Library Resources, 1956-59; Nat. Advisory Cancer Council, US Public Health Service, 1957-60; Councillor, Amer. Philos. Soc., 1957-60; Bd of Managers, Memorial Center for Cancer and Allied Diseases, 1958-60; Mem. Bd of Managers and Exec. Cttee, Mem. Hosp. for Cancer and Allied Diseases, 1960-67; Mem. and Vice-Chm., Health Res. Council, C., NY, 1958-60; Mem. Gov. Coun., Courant Inst. of Mathematical Sciences, 1962-72; Bd of Dirs, Scientists' Inst. for Public Information, 1963-67; Mem., Gov. Rockefeller's Cttee on Hosp. Costs, 1964-65. Fellow Amer. Acad. of Arts and Scis., 1958-; Assoc. Trustee, Univ. of Pennsylvania, 1959-63; Acad. of Religion and Mental Health (Mem. Bd of Trustees, 1959-63); Vice-Pres., 1961-63, Hon. Vice-Pres., 1963-); Memorial Sloan-Kettering Cancer Center (Vice-Chm. of Board, 1960-67; Chm. Cttee on Scientific Policy); Public Health Research Inst. of City of New York, Inc. (Pres. 1961-63); Salk Inst. for Biological Studies, San Diego, Calif. (Trustee, Chm. Bd, Non-Res. Fellow, 1962-). Holds several hon. degrees and awards. King's Medal for Service in Cause of Freedom (Gt Brit.), 1948; Public Welfare Medal, National Academy of Sciences, USA, 1957. Kalinga Prize, 1964; Arches of Science Award, 1964. Officer, Legion of Honor (France), 1950. *Publications:* (with Max Mason) The Electromagnetic Field, 1929; (with Claude Shannon) Mathematical Theory of Communication, 1949; Lady Luck-The Theory of Probability, 1963; Alice in Many Tongues, 1964; US Philanthropic Foundations: Their History, Structure, Management and Record, 1967; Science and Imagination, 1967; Scene of Change (autobiography), 1970. Editor: The Scientists Speak, 1947; mathematical and general articles, on science, in journals. *Recreation:* collector of Lewis Carroll. *Address:* 40 Lillis Road, RR3, New Milford, Conn 06776, USA. *T:* New Milford, Elgin 4-4177. *Club:* Century Association (NY City).
[Died 28 Nov. 1978.

WEBB, Cecil Richard, OBE 1926; MC; *b* 17 Aug. 1887; *y s* of Rev. S. G. M. Webb, late Rector of Newton Kyme, Yorkshire; *m* 1922, Beatrice Helen Gordon, *y d* of late Charles Gulland Ballingall; one *s* one *d*. *Educ:* St John's School, Leatherhead; North Eastern Railway, 1904-14; Assistant Traffic Manager, Uganda Railway, 1914; war service, British and German East Africa, 1914-19 (despatches, MC); Traffic Manager, Tanganyika Railway, 1919-23; General Manager and Traffic Manager, Sierra Leone Railway, 1923-30; General Manager, Palestine Railways, 1930-42; Ministry of War Transport, Cape Town, 1943-45; Ministry of Transport (London), Railways Maintenance Division, 1945-47. *Address:* 1 Stokes House, Sutherland Avenue, Bexhill-on-Sea, Sussex. *T:* Bexhill 2790.
[Died 4 April 1974.

WEBB, Clifford, RBA 1936; RE 1948; Illustrator and Engraver; *b* 14 Feb. 1895; *m* 1924, Ella Monckton; two *s* one *d*. Apprenticed as lithographer in City of London. Served European War, 1914-18, Army. Studied Westminster School of Art. Specializes in animal drawing. Illustrated books for Golden Cockerel Press and many others. Member of Wood Engraving Society, Royal Society of Painters Etchers and Royal Society of British Artists. Author and illustrator of children's books. *Publications:* The Story of Noah; The Thirteenth Pig; Butterwick Farm; Animals from Everywhere. *Recreation:* gardening. *Address:* Dormers, Abinger Hammer, Surrey. *T:* Dorking 730172.
[Died 29 July 1972.

WEBB, Dr Robert Alexander, AB (Southwestern, Tenn); MD (Johns Hopkins); MRCS; LRCP; PhD (Cambridge); Demonstrator in Bacteriology, Oxford University; Hon. Consultant Pathologist, Royal Free Hospital; Professor Emeritus University of London since 1956; *b* Charleston, SC, USA, 26 July 1891; *s* of Robert A. Webb, Prof. of Theology, Presbyterian Theological Seminary of Kentucky, and Roberta C. Beck; *m* 1918, May Barrow, Edgbaston; one *s* two *d*.

Demonstrator in Pathology, University of Manchester, 1921-22; University Demonstrator in Pathology and MRC. Research Grant, Cambridge University, 1922-29; Lecturer in Pathology, Cambridge University, 1929-33; Capt. US Medical Corps (attached RAMC, England and BEF), 1917-18. *Publications:* various papers in scientific journals. *Recreations:* golf, tennis, squash. *Address:* Wyck Rissington, Glos GL54 2PN. *T:* Bourton-on-The-Water 20262; Dunn School of Pathology, Oxford University. *T:* Oxford 57321. *[Died 27 June 1978.*

WEBB, Lt-Col Wilfred Francis, CIE 1944; late Indian Political Service; *b* 20 Feb. 1897. Dewan, Bundi State, 1932; Political Agent, Orissa States, Sambalpur, 1937; Chhaltesgarh, Raipur, 1938; Punjab Hill States, 1939; Dewan Gutch, Western India, 1939-41; Political Agent, Malwa and Bhopal States, Central India, 1941-45; Resident in Kashmir, 1945-47. *Address:* c/o Lloyds Bank Ltd (Cox's and King's Branch), 6 Pall Mall, SW1; Odstock Farm, PO Box 304, Umtali, Rhodesia.
[Died 28 Jan. 1973.

WEBB, Hon. Sir William Flood, KBE 1954; Kt 1942; LLD (Hon.) Queensland; Justice of the High Court of Australia, 1946-58, retired; Chairman of Electric Power Transmission Pty Ltd, since 1958; *b* 1887; *m* Beatrice (*d* 1970), *y d* of George Agnew, formerly MP, Queensland; two *s* four *d*. *Educ:* Catholic Schs; Qld Univ. Admitted to Bar 1913; Crown Solicitor of Queensland, 1917-22; Solicitor-General of Queensland, 1922-25; visited England on Privy Council Appeals in 1919 and 1924; Judge of Supreme Court, 1925-46; Chief Justice of Queensland, 1940-46; Pres.: Board of Trade and Arbitration, 1925-30; Industrial Court, 1930-46; Chairman, Central Sugar Cane Prices Board, 1926-42; Chairman, Royal Commission on Transport, 1936, and Sugar Industry, 1939; Chairman, Australian Industrial Relations Council, 1942; Japanese Atrocities Commissioner, 1943; Chm. War Crimes Commn, 1944-46, visited England as such in 1944-45 to appear before United Nations War Crimes Commission presided over by Lord Wright; Communication Censorship Commissioner, 1944 (under National Security Regulations); Member Senate of the University of Queensland, 1944-46; President of the International Military Tribunal for the Far East for the trial of major Japanese War Criminals (incl. 4 former Prime Ministers of Japan: Tojo, Hirota, Hiranuma and Koiso), 1946-48; Chm. of Cttees to advise on Ministerial and Parliamentary allowances in Tasmania (1960) and Queensland (1961, 1963). *Clubs:* Queensland, Johnsonian, Tattersall's (Brisbane); University of Qld. *[Died 11 Aug. 1972.*

WEBSTER, Sir David (Lumsden), KCVO 1970; Kt 1960; BA; FRCM; (Hon.) RAM; General Administrator, Royal Opera House, Covent Garden, Ltd, 1946-70; *b* 3 July 1903; *s* of Robert Lumsden and Mary Webster. *Educ:* Holt Sch.; Liverpool Univ.; Oxford Univ. Pres., Liverpool Guild of Undergraduates, 1924-25. Gen. Man. Bon Marché (Liverpool) Ltd, 1932-40; General Manager Lewis Ltd (Liverpool), 1940-41; Ministry of Supply Ordnance Factories, engaged on special methods of developing production, 1942-44; Administrator Covent Garden Preliminary Committee, 1944-46; Chairman Liverpool Philharmonic Society Ltd, June 1940-Aug. 1945. Chairman Orchestral Employers' Assoc., 1948-65; Governor and Treasurer Royal Ballet, 1957-; Governor and General Administrator of the London Opera Centre, 1962-. Director: Southern Television Ltd, 1957-; Commonwealth Arts Festival Ltd, 1961-; Chairman, London Concerts Board, 1965-. Rockefeller Foundation Lectr, Bristol University, 1955-56; Shute Lecturer, Liverpool University, 1958. Officier de la Légion d'Honneur, France, 1960; Commander: Order of the North Star, Sweden, 1954; Military Order of Christ, Portugal, 1955; Order of Merit, Italy, 1965. *Recreations:* theatre-going, talking, travelling, eating and drinking. *Address:* 39 Weymouth Street, W1. *T:* 01-935 1636.
[Died 11 May 1971.

WEBSTER, Prof. James Mathewson, CBE 1951; MD, FRCSEd; lately Director, West Midland Forensic Science Laboratory, Birmingham. Home Office; Professor of Forensic Medicine and Toxicology, Birmingham University; *b* 1898. *Educ:* St Andrews University. MA, BSc; MB, ChB St Andrews, 1923; FRCSEd 1926; MD Birmingham, 1943. Hon. LLD St Andrews, 1960. *Address:* c/o The University, Birmingham B15 2TT; Clovelly, Beacon Hill, Rubery, Worcestershire. *T:* Rubery 110.
[Died 17 Nov. 1973.

WEBSTER, John Henry Douglas, MD, ChB, FRCPEd, FRCR; Emeritus Consultant, Middlesex Hospital; formerly University Lecturer (late Examiner) in Radiology; *b* Edinburgh, 22 June 1882; *e s* of late Arthur Douglas Webster, OBE, MD, FRCPEd, Edinburgh; *m* Siri Björnström-Steffanson, of Ruda, Sweden; two *d*. *Educ:* Royal High School; University, Edinburgh; Prague.

Late Hon. Director Meyerstein Institute of Radiotherapy, Middlesex Hospital; Captain RAMC; served as Radiologist, British Salonika Army; FRSM (late Pres. Section of Radiology); Mem. Royal Medico-Psychol. Assoc., Mem. Committee of Foundation; for Study of Cycles, Pittsburg; New York; Mem. Soc. for Biol. Ryth. Research, Stockholm; Mem. Brit. Astron. Assoc.; Mem. Cttee, Norman Lockyer Observatory, Sidmouth (Univ. of Exeter); Member: Soc. of Authors; Horatian Soc.; Osler Club. Engaged in research on periodicity in nature, life, mind and diseases. *Publications:* The Periodicity of the Psychoses, 1968; Periodic Inspiration in Poetry and Music (Poetry Rev. 1943); Golden Mean Form in Music (Music and Letters, 1950); The Periodicity of the Sevens in Mind, Man and Nature (Brit. Jour. Med. Psychol., 1951); Poems (Pen-name Colin Tolly): Horizons, 1918; Knowledge and Dream, 1926; Janus-Man, 1935. *Address:* 23 Hertford Street, W1. *T:* 01-499 7362. *Clubs:* Athenæum; University (New York).
[Died 13 *Sept.* 1975.

WEBSTER, Margaret; Theatrical Producer, Director and Actress; *b* New York City, 15 March 1905; *d* of late Ben Webster and late Dame May Whitty (Dame May Webster), DBE. *Educ:* Burlington School, London; Queen Anne's School, Caversham; London Univ. Comes of old theatre family; first professional engagements with Sybil Thorndike in Trojan Women, 1924, and with John Barrymore in Hamlet, 1925; subsequently with Dame Sybil in many productions; with the Macdona Players, 1926; J. B. Fagan's Oxford Company, 1927; Ben Greet Players, 1928; Old Vic. Co., 1929-30; played in many London productions, notably with John Gielgud in Musical Chairs, Richard of Bordeaux and Queen of Scots, 1931-34; several productions in London at the Gate, Embassy, Q, St James's and other theatres; came to America, 1936, to produce Richard II with Maurice Evans, and remained to do a notably successful series of Shakespearian revivals with Evans and others, including Hamlet, Henry IV, Twelfth Night, Macbeth, Othello (with Paul Robeson), The Tempest, etc; Managing Director of Am. Rep. Theatre, which did six classic revivals in repertory, NY, 1946-47; directed and played in many other productions in NY; initiated Margaret Webster Shakespeare Company, 1948, playing Shakespearean repertoire through schools and colleges of US; staged Verdi's Don Carlos, Metropolitan Opera House, NY, 1950; produced Richard II and Taming of the Shrew, City centre, 1951; played in High Ground, NY, 1951; staged Saint Joan, Cort Theatre, NY, 1951; Aida, Metropolitan Opera House, 1951; An Evening with Will Shakespeare, 1952; The Strong Are Lonely, 1953, London, 1955-56; Troilus and Cressida (opera by William Walton), New York City Opera Co., 1955; The Merchant of Venice, Stratford-on-Avon, 1956; Measure for Measure, Old Vic, 1957; Back to Methuselah, NY, 1958; Simone Boccanegra, Metropolitan Opera House, 1960; Prod. The School for Scandal, Birm. Rep., 1960; Prod. Waiting in the Wings, Duke of York's, 1960. Made two visits to S Africa, 1961, 1962, representing the US Dept of State, producing and lecturing. Prod The Aspern Papers, NY, 1962; 12 Angry Men, London, 1964; wrote and performed one-woman show, The Brontës, London, NY and US Tour, 1963-64. Hon. LittD Lawrence College, 1942, Russell Sage Coll., 1944, and Rutgers Univ., 1947; DHL: Smith College, 1945, Fairfield University, 1964; was member of original Coun. of Brit. Actors' Equity; Coun. mem. of American Actors' Equity Ass., and Board member of American National Theatre and Acad.; elected one of ten outstanding Women of the Year for 1946 by Women's Nat. Press Club of America. *Publications:* Shakespeare Without Tears, 1942 (revised and re-issued, 1955); Shakespeare Today, 1957; The Same Only Different, 1969; Don't Put Your Daughter on the Stage, 1972; many articles and essays in New York Times, Good Housekeeping, Theatre Arts Monthly, etc. *Recreations:* gardening, swimming. *Address:* c/o Spotlight, 43 Cranbourne Street, WC2.
[Died 13 *Nov.* 1972.

WEBSTER, Thomas Bertram Lonsdale, FBA 1965; Professor of Classics, Stanford University, 1968-70, Emeritus since 1970; *b* July 1905; *s* of Sir T. Lonsdale Webster, KCB, and Esther Dalton; *m* 1944, Amy Marjorie Dale, FBA (*d* 1967). *Educ:* Charterhouse; Christ Church, Oxford; Leipzig University. Ireland Scholar, 1924; Student and tutor of Christ Church, Oxford, 1927-31; Derby Schol., 1928, Cromer Prize, 1929; Hulme Prof. of Greek at Manchester Univ., 1931-48; Prof. of Greek, UCL; 1948-68, Prof. Emeritus, 1968, Hon. Fellow, 1969. Prof. of Ancient Literature, Royal Acad. of Arts and Hon. RA, 1955. FSA 1934. President: Hellenic Soc., 1950; Classical Assoc., 1959 (Vice-Pres., 1948); Jt Assoc., Classical Teachers, 1965. Chm., Gilbert Murray Trust, 1959. Corresp. Mem., German Archæological Inst., 1935, Ord. Mem., 1954; Member: Vetenskapsoc. i Lund, 1949; Norwegian Acad. Science and Letters, 1958; Royal Soc. Arts and Sciences, Gothenburg, 1958; For. Mem., Royal Danish Acad. Sciences and Letters; Corresp.

Member: Austrian Acad. Sciences, 1967; Royal Soc. of Humane Letters, Lund, 1970. Hon. DLitt: Dublin, 1958; Manchester, 1965. *Publications:* Cicero: pro Flacco, 1931; Forum Romanum (with A. S. Owen), 1930; An Anthology of Greek Prose (with E. S. Forster), 1933; Renan: Prière sur l'Acropole, (with E. Vinaver), 1934; Der Niobidenmaler, 1935; An Anthology of Greek Verse (with E. S. Forster), 1935; An Introduction to Sophocles, 1936, 2nd edn, 1969; Greek Art and Literature, 530-400 BC, 1939; Greek Interpretations, 1942; Political Interpretations in Greek Literature, 1947; Studies in Menander, 1950; Greek Terracottas, 1951; Studies in Later Greek Comedy, 1952, 2nd edn, 1970; Art and Literature in Fourth Century Athens, 1955; Greek Theatre Production, 1956, 2nd edn 1970; From Mycenae to Homer, 1958; Greek Art and Literature, 700-530 BC, 1959; Monuments illustrating Old and Middle Comedy, 1960; Monuments illustrating New Comedy, 1961; Monuments illustrating Tragedy and Satyr Play, 1962; 2nd edn of A. W. Pickard-Cambridge, Dithyramb, Tragedy and Comedy, 1962; Griechische Bühnenaltertümer, 1963; Hellenistic Poetry and Art, 1964; Hellenistic Art, 1967; Tragedies of Euripides, 1967; Everyday Life in Classical Athens, 1968; Sophocles, Philoctetes, 1970; The Greek Chorus, 1970; Illustrations of Greek Drama (with A. D. Trendall), 1971; Potter and Patron in Classical Athens, 1972; Athenian Culture and Society, 1973; articles in classical journals, etc. *Recreation:* walking. *Address:* Department of Classics, Stanford University, Stanford, California 94305, USA. *Club:* Athenæum. *[Died* 31 *May* 1974.

WEBSTER, Gen. Sir Thomas Sheridan R.; *see* Riddell-Webster.

WEDDERBURN, Sir (John) Peter; *see* Ogilvy-Wedderburn.

WEDGWOOD, Dame Ivy Evelyn, DBE 1967; JP; Senator for Victoria, Australia (first woman elected to the Senate for Victoria), 1950-June 1971; *m* Jack Kearns Wedgwood. Member: Senate House Cttee, 1950-55, 1965-71; Jt Cttee of Public Accounts, 1955-71; Australian Delegn to Commonwealth Parly Assoc. Conf., New Delhi, 1957; Jt Select Cttee on New and Permanent Parliament House, 1965-71 (Mem. Overseas Delegn, 1968-71). Temporary Chm. of Cttees, 1962-71; Chairman: Select Cttee on Medical and Hosp. Costs, 1968-70; Senate Standing Cttee on Health and Social Welfare, 1970-71. Mem. Council, Duke of Edinburgh's Third Commonwealth Study Conf., 1968. *Address:* Whitehall, 16 Woorigoleen Road, Toorak, Victoria 3142, Australia. *Clubs:* Lyceum, Soroptimist (Melbourne).
[Died 24 *July* 1975.

WEEDON, Air Marshal Sir Colin Winterbotham, KBE 1952 (CBE 1943); CB 1946; MA; *b* 2 July 1901; *s* of H. W. Weedon, Durban, South Africa; *m* 1926, Gladys Frances Marian (*d* 1968), *d* of Col T. P. Lawrenson; two *d. Educ:* Royal Naval Colleges, Osborne and Dartmouth; Royal Air Force College, Cranwell; Christ's College, Cambridge (Hons Degree Mechanical Sciences). Royal Navy (serving in HMS Royal Sovereign and HMS Walker), 1915-19; Royal Air Force, 1920; 20 Squadron India, 1923-28; 111 Fighter Squadron, Northolt, 1934-35; RAF Staff College, 1936; Director-General Repair and Maintenance, Ministry of Aircraft Production, 1940-44; HQ Air Command, SE Asia, 1944-46; AOC 41 Group, 1946-48. SASO, HQ Technical Training Command, Brampton, Huntingdon, 1948-50; Dir-Gen. of Technical Services, 1950-51; Controller of Engineering and Equipment, Air Ministry, 1951-52; retired, 1952. Director and Gen. Man. (Commercial), Aero Div., Rolls Royce, 1952-61. *Address:* Hedges, South Stoke Road, Woodcote, Reading, Berks. *T:* Checkendon 461.
[Died 16 *Feb.* 1975.

WEIR, 2nd Viscount *cr* 1938; **James Kenneth Weir,** CBE 1944; BA (Cantab); Director: The Weir Group Ltd (Chairman, 1955-72); Dunlop Holdings Ltd; International Nickel Co. of Canada Ltd; *b* 10 Sept. 1905; *s* of 1st Viscount Weir and Alice Blanche MacConnachie (*d* 1959); *S* father 1959; *m* 1st 1929, Lucy (*d* 1972), *o d* of late James F. Crowdy, MVO; four *s* one *d* (and one *d* decd); 2nd, 1973, Mrs Dorothy Dear Hutton, New York. *Educ:* Oundle School; Trinity College, Cambridge. Hon FRCOG. Hon. LLD Strathclyde, 1967. *Recreations:* golf, fishing, shooting. *Heir: s* Hon. William Kenneth James Weir, *qv. Address:* Montgreenan, Kilwinning, Ayrshire. *T:* Kilwinning 2666; 28 Roebuck House, Palace Street, SW1. *T:* 01-828 2442. *Clubs:* Boodle's, Carlton; Western, Royal Scottish Automobile (Glasgow).
[Died 16 *Aug.* 1975.

WEIR, James George, CMG 1918; CBE 1919; Hon. President, formerly Chairman, Cierva Rotorcraft, Ltd; *b* 1887; *s* of late James Weir, Over Courance, Dumfriesshire; *m* 1915, Mora Morton, *d* of late James Christie, Craigearn, Tayport; one *d* (one *s* decd). *Educ:* Dollar Academy; Glasgow University. Served European War, 1914-19; Major, 77th Highland Brigade, Royal

Field Artillery (TF), 1916-21. Was Air Commodore Royal Air Force Reserve. Formerly Director of the Bank of England; one of HM's Lieutenants for the City of London from 1936. FRAeS. Officer of Legion of Honour; Order of Crown of Italy. *Address:* 20 Roebuck House, Palace Street, Westminster, SW1. *T:* 01-828 2949; Skeldon, Dalrymple, Ayrshire. *T:* Dalrymple 223. *Club:* United Service and Royal Aero.   [*Died* 7 *Nov.* 1973.

WEIR, Sir John, GCVO 1939 (KCVO 1932; CVO 1926); Royal Victorian Chain, 1949; Knight Grand Cross of Royal Order of St Olav, 1938; MB, ChB Glasgow, FFHom; Physician to the Queen, 1952-68; Honorary Consulting Physician to Royal London Homœopathic Hospital; *b* 1879; *s* of late James Weir, Glasgow; Physician-in-Ordinary to Prince of Wales, 1923-36; Physician to late Queen of Norway, 1928-38; Physician-in-Ordinary to Duke and Duchess of York, 1936, to late King George VI, 1937-52, and to late Queen Mary, 1936-53. *Address:* Flat 11, 96/100 New Cavendish Street, W1. *T:* 01-935 3491. *Club:* Royal Automobile.   [*Died* 17 *April* 1971.

WEIS-FOGH, Prof. Torkel; Professor of Zoology, University of Cambridge, since 1966; Fellow of Christ's College, Cambridge; *b* 25 March 1922; *s* of S. Weis-Fogh and Dagmar (*née* Foldager Larsen), Aarhus, Denmark; *m* 1st, 1946, Hanne (*d* 1971) (*née* Heckscher); 2nd, 1972, Shirley E. M. Stevenson. *Educ:* Aarhus Kathedralskole; Univ. of Copenhagen. *Magister scientiarum* in Zoology, 1947, Gold Medal, 1944, *Dr phil* 1952, Univ. of Copenhagen. Asst in Research to late Prof. August Krogh, Denmark, 1947-49; Head of his private laboratory, 1949-53; Assoc. Lectr, Copenhagen Univ., 1953-54; Fellow of Rockefeller Foundn, 1954-55; Balfour Student of Univ. of Cambridge (Dept of Zoology) and Member of Trinity Coll., 1956-59; Prof. of Zoophysiology and Head of Zoophysiological Laboratory B, Univ. of Copenhagen, 1958-66; Head of Dept of Zoology, Univ. of Cambridge, 1966-74. Prather Lectr in Biology, Harvard Univ., 1961. Mem., Danish State Research Foundn, 1962, Chm. Nat. Sci. Sect., 1963. Fellow, Royal Danish Acad., 1961; Fell., Acad. of Techn. Scis, 1965; Foreign Hon. Mem., Amer. Acad. of Arts and Sciences, 1974. *Publications:* articles in learned journals. *Recreations:* travel, mountain walking. *Address:* Department of Zoology, Downing Street, Cambridge CB2 3EJ. *T:* 58717; 7 Almoners' Avenue, Cambridge CB1 4NZ. *T:* 45783.   [*Died* 13 *Nov.* 1975.

WEISBERG, Hyman, CMG 1942; retd; *b* 1890; *m* 1930, Ester Riva Cernjack; one *s* one *d. Educ:* Cambridge (Wrangler, mathematical tripos). Cadet, FMS, 1914; Treasurer, SS, 1935; Financial Sec., 1937. Director Finance Div., Allied Commission Austria (British Element), 1946; Finance Dept., Foreign Office (German Section), 1947. *Recreations:* music, chess. *Address:* 21 Hillcroft Crescent, Wembley Park, Mddx. *T:* 01-902 0652.   [*Died* 21 *July* 1976.

WEISS, Prof. Joseph J., DEng (Vienna), PhD (London); Professor of Radiation Chemistry in the University of Newcastle upon Tyne (formerly King's College, University of Durham), 1956-70; *b* 30 August 1907; *s* of Sandor Simon Weiss and Ernestine (*née* Steinhardt); *m* 1942, Frances Sonia Lawson; two *s* one *d. Educ:* Technische Hochschule, Vienna; University of Vienna. Head of Chemistry Department, Textile Institute, Sorau, Germany, 1928-30; Assistant to Professor F. Haber, Kaiser Wilhelm Institut für Physikalische Chemie and Elektrochemie, 1930-33; Research work at University of Cambridge, 1933-34; Research at University College, London, 1934-39; Assistant Lecturer, King's College, University of Durham, 1939-44; Lecturer, King's College, University of Durham, 1944-48; Reader in Mechanism of Chemical Reactions, University of Durham, 1948-55. Marie Curie Medal, 1970; J. J. Weiss Medal, Assoc. of Radiation Research, 1971. Hon. DSc Tech. Univ. of Berlin. *Publications:* scientific papers in: Z physikal. Chemie, Naturwissenschaften, Proceedings of the Royal Society, Nature, Transactions of the Faraday Society, Journal of the Chemical Society, Annual Reviews of the Chemical Society, Advances in Catalysis, etc. *Recreations:* music, cycling, sailing. *Address:* 12 Glastonbury Grove, Newcastle upon Tyne 2. *T:* Newcastle 810658.   [*Died* 9 *April* 1972.

WELBY, Sir Oliver Charles Earle, 6th Bt, *cr* 1801; TD; *b* 26 Jan. 1902; *o surv. s* of Sir Charles G. E. Welby, 5th Bt, and Lady Maria Louisa Helen (*d* 1920), *e d* of late Lord Augustus Hervey, and *sister* of 5th Marquess of Bristol; *S* father, 1938; *m* 1927, Barbara Angela Mary Lind, *d* of late John Duncan Gregory, CB, CMG; one *s* (and one *s* decd). *Educ:* Eton; Christ Church, Oxford (MA). Addtl Assistant Private Secretary to Home Sec. (Sir W. Joynson-Hicks), 1925-26; JP parts of Kesteven, Lincs, 1931; High Sheriff of Lincolnshire, 1953; Hon. Capt. RA, TA. *Heir: s* Richard Bruno Gregory Welby [*b* 11 March 1928; *m*

1952, Jane Biddulph, *y d* of late Ralph Wilfred Hodder-Williams, MC; three *s* one *d*]. *Address:* Denton Manor, Grantham, Lincs. *TA* and *T:* Knipton 256; 76 Burton Court, SW3. *T:* 01-730 8575. *Club:* Leander.   [*Died* 6 *Oct.* 1977.

WELCH, Sir Cullum; see Welch, Sir G. J. C.

WELCH, Col Sir (George James) Cullum, 1st Bt, *cr* 1957; Kt 1952; OBE 1944; MC 1918; Alderman of City of London, Ward of Bridge Within, 1947-70; *b* 20 Oct. 1895; *o s* of late James Reader Welch, Beckenham and Croydon, and late Harriet Welch; *m* 1st, 1921, Gertrude Evelyn Sladin (*d* 1966), *o d* of late John William Harrison, Stubbins, Lancs and Eastbourne, and late Evelyn Harrison; one *s* one *d*; 2nd, 1969, Irene Avril, *d* of late John Foster, OBE. *Educ:* Alleyn's School, Dulwich. Served European War, 1914-18, in France in Royal Berkshire Regt and on Staff of 18th Div. Admitted Solicitor, 1920. Member of Court of Common Council (Ward of Candlewick), 1931-47; Chief Commoner, 1946; Sheriff of the City of London, 1950-51; Lord Mayor of London, 1956-57. War of 1939-45 commanded 3rd HGAA Regt; Member City of London TA&AFA, 1941-65 and City Lieutenancy; Hon. Colonel City of London Battalion Royal Fusiliers (TA), 1956-65; and City of London Army Cadet Force, 1953-65; Liveryman and Member, Court of Assistants, Co. of Haberdashers (Warden, 1963, 1964, 1965, 1966; Master, 1966-67); Liveryman: Co. of Spectaclemakers; Co. of Solicitors of the City of London (Past Master); Co. of Parish Clerks (Past Master); Co. of Paviors (Past Master); Member Council, Law Society, 1951-63; Registrar Archdeaconry of London, 1953-67; Chairman, Florence Nightingale Hosp., 1954-63; Vice-Chm. Bd of Govs, Bethlem Royal Hosp. and Maudsley Hosp., 1953-66; Chm. Lord Mayor of London's Nat. Hungarian and Cent. European Relief Fund, 1956-60; Dep. Chm. George VI Foundn Exec. Cttee; Pres., London Homes for the Elderly; Governor, Irish Soc., 1967-70; Hon. Treas., UK Cttee, UN Children's Fund, 1963-67; Trustee: Morden Coll., 1960-79 (Chm., 1966-79); Wakefield (Tower Hill Trinity Sq.) Trust, to 1972; Pres. City Livery Club, 1943-44. Freedoms: Bangor, County Down, 1957; Chard, Somerset, 1957; London, Ontario, 1957; Granby, Canada, 1957; New Orleans, 1957. KJStJ, Order of Mercy; Officer of Orange Nassau (Netherlands); Commander Dannebrog (Denmark). Commander (1st Class) of Order of The Lion of Finland; Grand Ufficiale Al Merito Della Repubblica Italiana. *Heir: s* John Reader Welch, MA Oxon, OStJ, Mem. Ct of Common Council [*b* 26 July 1933; *m* 1962, Margaret Kerry, *o d* of K. Douglass, formerly of Killara, NSW; one *s* twin *d*]. *Address:* 43 St Margarets, Rottingdean, East Sussex BN2 7HS; 16 Bedford Street, Covent Garden, WC2E 9HF. *Club:* City Livery.   [*Died* 28 *July* 1980.

WELCH, William Tom, OBE 1973; JP; Vice-Chairman, Co-operative Wholesale Society Ltd, 1973-75; *b* 13 June 1910; *s* of Alfred Henry Welch and Mary (*née* Topp); *m* 1935, Audrey D. Moxham; one *s. Educ:* Queen Elizabeth Grammar Sch., Wimborne. Gen. Man., Bournemouth Co-operative Soc., 1947; Dir, Co-operative Wholesale Soc. Ltd, 1957; Chm., Shoefayre Ltd, 1966-75; Dir, Co-operative Insce Soc., 1962-75. Member: EDC for Distributive Trades, 1966-76; Industrial Tribunal, 1978-; Gen. Comr for Income Tax, 1977-. JP Dorset 1951. *Recreations:* music (especially church organs), Dorset history, gardening, angling. *Address:* Stourton, Redcotts Road, Wimborne, Dorset BH21 1ET. *T:* Wimborne 882667.   [*Died* 29 *Jan.* 1979.

WELDON, Sir Anthony Edward Wolseley, 7th Bt, *cr* 1723; Squadron Leader, AAF, RAF Regiment; *b* 1 Dec. 1902; *e s* of 6th Bt and Winifred, *d* of late Col Varty Rogers of Broxmore Park, Romsey, and late of the Royal Dublin Fusiliers and HM Bodyguard of Gentlemen-at-Arms; *S* father, 1917. *Heir: b* Thomas Brian Weldon [*b* 19 May 1905; *m* 1942, Marie Isobel, *d* of Hon. W. J. French; one *s* one *d.*]. *Club:* White's.   [*Died* 9 *Jan.* 1971.

WELDON, Sir Thomas (Brian), 8th Bt *cr* 1723; retired; *b* 19 May 1905; 2nd *s* of Col Sir Anthony Arthur Weldon, 6th Bt, CVO, DSO, and Winifred Bruce Blakeney (OBE) (later Mrs. Wilfred Fitzgerald) (*d* 1951), *d* of Col Varty Rogers; *S* brother, 1971; *m* 1942, Marie Isobel, *d* of Hon. William Joseph French; one *s* one *d. Recreations:* shooting, fishing. *Heir: s* Anthony William Weldon, *b* 11 May 1947. *Address:* The Fighting Cocks, West Amesbury, Salisbury, Wilts SP4 7BH. *T:* Amesbury 2239. *Club:* White's.   [*Died* 5 *Aug.* 1979.

WELLESZ, Egon Joseph, CBE 1957; FBA 1953; MA (by decree 1939); Hon. Mus. Doc. Oxon 1932; Fellow of Lincoln College, Oxford and Music Tutor, since 1939; University Reader in Byzantine Music, 1948-56; late Professor of Music, University of Vienna; Editor of the Monumenta Musicæ Byzantinæ (publ.

Royal Danish Academy, 1932-); Co-Editor of The New Oxford History of Music, since 1947; Corresponding Member American Musicological Society, 1947-; Vice-President, canonised Consociatio Internationalis Musicae Sacrae, 1963; *b* 21 October 1885; *s* of S. J. Wellesz and Ilona Lövenyi; *m* Emmy Franziska Stross; two *d. Educ:* Vienna Hegel-gymnasium; Summer ext., Cambridge; Univ. of Vienna. Dr 1908, Vienna; Privat-Dozent of History of Music, 1913; first performance of his opera, Die Prinzessin Girnara, at Frankfurt, 1921; first performance of Alkestis, Mannheim, 1924; lectures on music at the Hochschule f. Musik, Köln, 1926; Prof. of History of Music, Univ. Vienna, 1929-38; Director of the "siège scientifique" of the Monumenta Musicae Byzantinae at Vienna, 1931-38; Vice-Pres., Osterreichischer Komponistenbund, 1928-38; first performance of Bacchants, State-opera, Vienna, 1931; Lecturer on Byzantine music, London, Cambridge, Oxford, 1932; on Opera, Univ. of London, 1933. RCM London and Univ. of Cambridge, 1938; lecturing on the History of Music, Univ. of Oxford, since 1940; Univ. Lecturer in the History of Music, 1944-48; Member of Board of Faculty of Music, Univ. of Oxford, since 1944; Chm. of Faculty, 1955-56; Fellow Royal Danish Academy of Science and Letters, 1946; Harvard Visiting Scholar, 1954; Pres. Oxford Univ. Byzantine Soc., 1955-66; Gunning Lecturer, University of Edinburgh, 1956; Harvard Visiting Scholar, 1956; Music Prize of City of Vienna, 1953; Grand Silver Medal of City of Paris, 1957; Austrian Order of Merit, Pro Musica Austriaca Medal, Silver Medal of Honour of City of Vienna, 1960; Austrian Great State Prize for work as a composer, 1961; Fellow (formerly Mem.) Serbian Acad. of Science and Letters, 1972; Apostolic KCSG 1961; Austrian Order Litteris et Artibus, 1971. *Publications: music, operas-* Die Prinzessin Girnara, 1921; Alkestis, 1924; Die Opferung des Gefangenen, 1926; Scherz, List und Rache, 1928; Die Bakchantinnen, 1931; Incognita, 1951; chamber music, songs, Cantata, 1932; Concerto for piano, op. 49, 1934; Amor timido, Cantata 1933, Mass for choir and organ, 1934; Sonette der Elisabeth Barrett-Browning for soprano and string quartet, 1934; Prosperos Beschwörungen, 1934-35; Mass for female voices and orchestra, 1937; Fifth String quartet op. 60, 1943; Cantata op. 61; Symphony in C op. 63, 1945; Sixth String Quartet op. 67, 1947; Symphony in E flat op. 65, 1948; Seventh String Quartet op. 66, 1948; Octet, 1949; Symphony in A, op. 68, 1951; Symphony in G, op. 70, 1953; Fifth Symphony, 1956; Eighth String Quartet, 1957; Clarinet Quintet, 1959; Violin Concerto, op. 84, 1961; Laus Nocturna, op. 88, 1962; Missa brevis, op. 80, 1963; Duineser Elegie, 1963; Music for Strings, 1964; Sixth Symphony, op. 95, 1965; Ninth String Quartet, op. 97, 1966; Vision for Soprano and orchestra, op. 99, 1966; Magnificat, op. 100, 1967; Mirabile Mysterium, op. 101, 1967; Seventh Symphony, op. 102, 1968; Canticum Sapientiae, op. 104, 1969; Divertimento, op. 107, 1969; Symphonic Epilogue, op. 108, 1970; String Quintet, op. 109, 1970; Eighth Symphony, op. 110, 1970; Ninth Symphony, op. 111, 1971; *books:* Biography on A. Schönberg, 1921, English versions, 1924, 1969, 1971; Aufgaben u. Probleme auf d. Gebiet der byzantin. u. oriental. Kirchenmusik, 1923; Byzantinische Musik, 1927, Spanish version, 1930; Die neue Instrumentation, 2 vols, 1929-30; Trésor de musique byzantine, Vol. I, 1934; Monumenta Musicae Byzantinae, Vol. I, Cod. theol. gr. 181 Palat Vindob. (with H. J. W. Tillyard), 1934; Monumenta Musicae Byzantinae, Transcripta I, Hymni mensis Septembris, 1936; Transcripta VII, The Akathistus Hymnus, 1956; articles for Grove's Dictionary of Music, 1939; Eastern Elements in Western Chant, 1947, 2nd edn 1968; A History of Byzantine Music and Hymnography, 1949, 4th edn 1971; Essays on Opera, 1950. Ed. Vol. I on The New Oxford History of Music, 1957; The Music of the Byzantine Church, Anthology of Music, Vol. I, 1959; J. J. Fux, 1965; (ed) Studies in Eastern Chant, vol. 1 1966, vol II, 1970. *Address:* 51 Woodstock Road, Oxford; Lincoln College, Oxford. *T:* 59857.   [*Died* 9 *Nov.* 1974.

WELLINGTON, 7th Duke of, *cr* 1814, **Lt-Col Gerald Wellesley,** KG 1951; Baron Mornington, 1746; Earl of Mornington; Viscount Wellesley, 1760; Viscount Wellington of Talavera and Wellington, Somersetshire; Baron Douro, 1809; Earl of Wellington, Feb. 1812; Marquess of Wellington, Oct. 1812; Marquess Douro, 1814; Prince of Waterloo, 1815, Netherlands; Count of Vimeiro, Marquess of Torres Vedras and Duke of Victoria in Portugal; *b* 21 Aug. 1885; 3rd *s* of 4th Duke of Wellington; *S* nephew, 1943; *m* Dorothy Violet (*d* 1956), *d* of late Robert Ashton, Croughton, Cheshire, and late Countess of Scarborough; one *s* one *d. Educ:* Eton. Entered HM Diplomatic Service, 1908; retired, 1919, having been Sec. at Petrograd, Constantinople, and Rome; 2nd Lt (Temp. Lt-Col) Grenadier Guards, Sept. 1939; Served with BEF, France, 1939-40; MEF 1942; CMF 1943; Lord Lt of County of London, 1944-49; Lord Lt of Hampshire, 1949-60; a Trustee of National Gallery, 1950-57; Chancellor of the Univ. of Southampton, 1951-62; Governor of the Isle of Wight, 1956-65. *Publications:* The Iconography of

the First Duke of Wellington, 1935; (ed, with Francis Bamford) The Journal of Mrs Arbuthnot, 1820-1832 (2 vols), 1950; (ed) The Conversations of the First Duke of Wellington with George William Chad, 1956; (ed) Wellington and his Friends: Letters of the First Duke, 1965. *Heir: s* Marquess Douro. *Address:* Stratfield Saye House, near Reading, Berks. *T:* Turgis Green 218; Apsley House, 149 Piccadilly, W1. *T:* 01-499 1953.
[*Died* 4 *Jan.* 1972.

WELLINGTON, Rt. Rev. John; retired; *b* 28 December 1889; *s* of late Reverend G. Wellington. *Educ:* Wimborne Grammar School; Salisbury Theological College. BDLond; Curate S Martin's, Salisbury, 1913-16; SPG Missionary, Shantung, China, 1917-35; Vicar Holy Trinity, Bedford, 1936-40; Bishop of Shantung, 1940-50. Interned by Japanese in China; released, 1945. Assistant Bishop of Truro and Vicar of St Germans, Cornwall, 1951-60; Hon. Canon of St Constantine in Truro Cathedral, 1951-60. Archdeacon of Bodmin, 1953-56. *Address:* 23 East Street, Wareham, Dorset BH20 4NN. *T:* Wareham 2740.   [*Died* 11 *Sept.* 1976.

WELLOCK, Wilfred; *b* Nelson, Lancs, 2 Jan. 1879; *s* of John Wellock, Nelson, Lancs, and Thirza Punt Barker, Norfolk; *m* 1913, Frances, *d* of James Wilson, Colne, Lancs. *Educ:* Elementary school; night schools; Edinburgh University. Journalist and lecturer; MP (Lab) Stourbridge, 1927-31; member of Select Committee on Future Government of East Africa; spent eight months, 1919-20, in Holland, Germany and Austria investigating economic and other conditions; four months, 1925, lecture tour in America and Canada, on Peace and Socialism; lecture tours in USA, 1946 and 1949; tour of Gandhi Ashrams, India, 1949-50; lecture tours in America, 1954 and 1956. *Publications:* The Spiritual Basis of Democracy, (out of print) India's Awakening, The Way Out, Pacifism, A Modern Idealist (novel); War as viewed by Jesus and the Early Church; Money has Destroyed Your Peace; Which Way, Britain?, 1942; A Mechanistic or a Human Society?, 1944; The Third Way, 1947; Rebuilding Britain, 1949; Power or Peace, Gandhi as a Social Revolutionary, 1950; Annihilation or Creative Revolution, 1951; The Orchard Lea papers, 1952; New Horizons, 1954; Not by Bread Alone, 1955; Which Way, America? and Which Way, Britain?, 1957; From Ghandhi to Vinoba Bhave, 1959; The Crisis in our civilization, 1962; Off the Beaten Track (autobiography), 1962; Beyond These Spiritually Barren Years, 1964; Towards One World, but shall we arrive?, 1967. *Recreations:* spinning, gardening, walking. *Address:* Orchard Lea, Saunders Lane, New Longton, Preston, Lancs. *TA:* Wellock, New Longton, Preston.   [*Died* 22 *July* 1972.

WELLS, Denys George, BEM 1941; RBA 1910; *b* 1881; 4th *s* of late George Wells, JP, of Bedford; *m* 1905; one *d. Educ:* Bedford Grammar School. Studied Art at the Slade School under Professor F. Brown and Wilson Steer. British Empire Medal, 1941; Lazlo Bronze Medal, 1943, for picture Waterloo in Wartime. Works bought by Ministry of Works, LCC, Sutherland Public Art Gallery and Borough of Southwark. Vice-President, RBA, 1955. Pension for work as an Artist, awarded by the Queen, 1968. *Address:* 45A Kingston Road, New Malden, Surrey. *T:* Malden 1312.   [*Died* 27 *June* 1973.

WELLS, Prof. Frederick Arthur, OBE 1954; Professor of Industrial Economics, University of Nottingham, 1958-67, now Emeritus; *b* 12 July 1901; *s* of Frederick Wells and Lucy Eliza Wells (*née* Hooton); *m* 1931, Dora Jean Ward; one *d. Educ:* University College Nottingham; London School of Economics. BSc (Econ) 1927; Cassel Scholarship, 1927; PhD 1931. University College, Nottingham: Staff Tutor, Department of Adult Education, 1928-32; Lecturer in Economics, 1932-45; Reader in Applied Economics, 1945; Head of Department of Industrial Economics, 1953-. Board of Trade, 1944-45. Visiting Professor: State University of Pennsylvania, 1950-51; University of Khartoum, 1962; Monash Univ., Australia, 1968. Chairman of Wages Councils, Ministry of Labour, 1952-; Member of Agricultural Wages Board, 1950-59. *Publications:* The British Hosiery Trade, 1935, new edn, The British Hosiery and Knitwear Industry, 1972; Productivity in a Printing Firm, 1958; (jt) Studies in Industrialisation: Nigeria and the Cameroons; contrib. to works on industrial economics, and articles in learned journals. *Address:* 3 Manor Court, Bramcote, Nottingham. *T:* 255131.   [*Died* 10 *Oct.* 1971.

WELLS, Lt-Gen. Sir Henry, KBE 1956 (CBE 1945; OBE 1941); CB 1954; DSO 1943; idc; psc; retired; *b* 22 March 1898; *s* of Arthur Wells, Kyneton, Victoria; *m* 1926, Lorna, *d* of Nathaniel Skippen; two *s.* Trained in England, 1920-21; 6th Cavalry Bde, 1926; RMC, Duntroon, 1927-30; Small Arms Sch., 1931-33; Staff Coll., Camberley, 1934-35; Bde Major 1 Inf. Bde, 1936-38; Instructor in Tactics, RMC Duntroon, 1939-40; seconded to 7

Australian Division, AIF, 1940; served War of 1939-45: Middle East, South West Pacific (OBE, DSO, CBE); Director of Mil. Operations, AHQ, 1946; Comdt, RMC, Duntroon, 1949-50; GOC Southern Command, 1951-52; C-in-C, British Commonwealth Forces in Korea, 1953-54; CGS, Australia, 1954-58; Chairman, Chiefs of Staffs Cttee, Department of Defence, Australia, 1958-59; retired, 1959. Hon. Col, Royal Victoria Regt, 1962-66. Commander, US Legion of Merit, 1954. *Address:* 12A Heyington Place, Toorak, Victoria 3142, Australia.   *[Died 21 Oct. 1973.*

WELLS, Sir Henry Weston, Kt 1966; CBE 1957; Chairman, The Land Commission, 1967-70; Director: Investment & Merchant Finance Corporation Pty Ltd, South Australia; Town & City Holdings (Australia) Pty Ltd; *b* 28 Feb. 1911; *s* of Sir William Henry Wells and Dorothy Kate Wells (*née* Horne); *m* 1937, Rosemary Haliday Witchurch; two *s* one *d. Educ:* Sherborne Sch., Dorset; Coll. of Estate Management. Dir of Accommodation, War Organisation, Order of St John and Brit. Red Cross Soc., 1939-41, and Dep. Dir of Hosps thereof, 1940-41; Reconstruction Officer and Chief Estates Officer, Min. of Town and Country Planning, 1943-46; Dep. Chm., Bracknell Development Corp., 1949-50; Chm., Hemel Hempstead Development Corp., 1950-62. Partner, Chesterton & Sons, Chartered Surveyors, 1934-66. Chairman: Commn for New Towns (UK), 1964-70 (Dep. Chm., 1961-64); The Land Commn (UK), 1967-70. Director: Abbey National Building Society, 1966-70; Morgan Crucible Company, 1965-70; Coll. of Estate Management, 1968-69. President: RICS, 1965-66. Hon. DLitt Reading, 1968. KStJ 1958. *Address:* (office) 33 King William Street, Adelaide, South Australia 5000; (home) Jordans, Crafers, SA 5152, Australia. *Club:* Boodle's.   *[Died 30 Nov. 1971.*

WELLS, Stanley Walter, MBE 1918; Major; owner and controller laundry businesses in Kent, since 1920; *b* 11 Nov. 1887; *s* of William Malcolm and Kate Madeleine Wells, late of High Dells, Woldingham, Surrey; *m* 1917, Violet (*d* 1972), *e d* of Edward Manwaring, late of Elm Lodge, College Road, Dulwich; one *s* one *d. Educ:* Mercers' School; Dulwich College. Freedom of City of London, 1912; Livery of Tallow Chandlers' Company, 1912, Master, 1947 and 1953; Member: Court of Guild of Freemen (Dep. Master, 1955, Master, 1956); Master The Company of Launderers, 1960; Court of Common Council for Ward of Cripplegate Within, 1949-72. Sheriff for City of London, 1949-50. Joint Honorary Treasurer of the Corporation of the Sons of the Clergy; Member of the Council of the People's Dispensary for Sick Animals; Member of the Council of the Royal London Society for the Blind. Sevenoaks Rural District Council (Mem. for Westerham) (10 years); Mem. Kent County Constabulary (21 years). Served European War, 1914-19, London Scottish and RASC Horse Transport (despatches twice, MBE); Army Cadet Force, Royal West Kent Regt, 1925-31, 1940-46. Comdr of Order of Merit (Italy); Order of Grand Cross (West German Federal Republic); Officer of Legion of Honour (France). *Recreations:* gardens and sailing. *Address:* Uplands, Westerham, Kent. *T:* Westerham 3243; Downlands, Aldwick, Sussex. *T:* Bognor Regis 21908. *Clubs:* City Livery (Pres. 1958), United Wards.   *[Died 18 Oct. 1975.*

WELLWOOD, William, MC and Bar; *b* Belfast, N Ireland, 1893; Farmed for a period. Joined Northern Ireland Civil Service, and was private secretary to late Rt Hon. Sir R. Dawson Bates, Bt, DL; late Rt Hon. William Lowry, KC, MP; Rt Hon. Edmond C. Warnock, KC, MP; Rt Hon. W. B. Maginess, KC, MP; resigned from the civil service. MP (UU) for Londonderry, at Westminster, (May) 1951-55; was returned unopposed May 1951, and again in October 1951. Member Orange Order, Lodge 1974 for fifteen years (Master for five years). Served European War, 1914-18, with Royal Marines (MC and Bar). *Address:* 90 Hawthornden Road, Belfast.   *[Died 28 June 1971.*

WENTWORTH-FITZWILLIAM; *see* Fitzwilliam.

WERE, Cecil Allan Walter, CMG 1943; *b* 16 June 1889; *e s* of late Captain Walter Were, Dublin Fusiliers; *m* 1930, Elinor Louise Rogers; one *s* two *d. Educ:* Kelly College, Tavistock; Pembroke College, Cambridge. Entered Levant Consular Service, 1913; served in Egypt (Port Said and Alexandria), 1914-22, and in Morocco, at Tetuan, Tangier, and Marrakesh, 1922-27; Consul at Constantinople, 1928, and served there and at Trebizond until 1932; Consul at Bagdad, 1932-37; Consul-General at Cairo, 1937-43, for Eritrea, 1942-43 and at Alexandria, 1943-46; Consul-Gen. at Bâle, 1946-50; retd 1950. *Address:* 6 Lauriston Road, SW19.   *[Died 5 Aug. 1977.*

WERNHER, Hon. Maj.-Gen. Sir Harold Augustus, 3rd Bt, *cr* 1905; GCVO 1949 (KCVO 1930); TD; DL; President, Electrolux, Ltd, since 1963 (Chairman, 1926-63); Past

Chairman Plessey Company; *b* 16 Jan. 1893; *s* of 1st Bt and Alice S. Mankiewicz (afterwards Lady Ludlow); *S* brother 1948; *m* 1917, Lady Anastasia (Zia) Michaelovna Torby, CBE 1956 (OBE 1946), DStJ (given precedence by royal warrant, 1917, as *d* of an Earl), *d* of Grand Duke Michael of Russia and late Countess de Torby; two *d* (one *s* killed in action, 1942). Served European War, 1914-18 (despatches); Lt-Col 5th Bn Beds and Herts Regt (TF); Col 1928, comdg; retd 1928; re-employed, 1939; Actg Brig. 1941; Actg Maj.-Gen. 1943; Hon. Major-General, 1944; Vice-Patron, University College Hospital, 1951- (Chm., 1945-51); Chairman, King Edward VII's Hosp. for Officers, 1941-69, Life Vice-Pres., 1969. DL Bedfordshire. A Knight Commander of the Swedish Order of Vasa, 1930; Knight Grand Cross of Swedish Order of the Pole Star, 1959; Legion of Merit degree of Officer, US Army, 1946. *Heir:* none. *Address:* 15 Grosvenor Square, W1; Luton Hoo, Luton, Beds.
                              [Died 30 June 1973 (ext).

WEST, Mrs Algernon; *see* Young, Gladys.

WEST, Maj.-Gen. Clement Arthur, CB 1944; DSO 1932; MC 1915; idc; psc; RE; *b* Manmad, India, 13 Aug. 1892; *o s* of late Clement West, GIPR, India and Canterbury, Kent, England; *m* Margaret Elizabeth, *o d* of late Aylward Robert O'Conor, Somerton, Co. Dublin. *Educ:* King's School, Canterbury; RMA Woolwich. Commissioned RE 1912; served European War, France and Belgium, 1914-18 (MC, despatches twice); Captain 1917; Assistant Instructor Survey, SME, Chatham, 1919-22; General Staff War Office, 1923-26; Major, 1928; Brigade-Major, India, 1930-31; Operations, NWF, 1930-31 (DSO, despatches); General Staff, AHQ, India, 1932-34; Bt Lieut-Colonel, 1933; Deputy Assistant Military Secretary, War Office, 1934-36; Lieut-Col, 1936; Col, 1938; Deputy Military Secretary to Secretary of State for War, and Assistant Secretary of the Selection Board, War Office, 1938-39; Brig., General Staff, 1940-42; Delegation to New Zealand Govt, 1941; District Commander, 1942-43; Major-General, General Staff, 1943-45; Maj.-Gen. in charge Administration, Southern Command, 1945-46; retired, Jan. 1947. Gen. Sec., Royal United Kingdom Beneficent Assoc., 1947-57. *Recreations:* gardening, fishing, golf. *Address:* Kingsmal, Cross-in-Hand, Heathfield, Sussex. *Club:* Army and Navy.   *[Died 4 Sept. 1972.*

WEST, Sir Frederick (John), Kt 1960; OBE 1952; JP; *b* 29 March 1897; *s* of Frederick Hargrave and Martha West; *m* 1926, Frances (*née* Taylor); one *s* one *d. Educ:* William Morris School, Walthamstow. Member of London Stock Exchange, 1933; Director of companies. Diocesan Reader (Church of England) for Diocese of Chelmsford; JP Essex. Freeman of City of London; Mem. Bakers' Company and Gold and Silver Wire Drawers' Company. *Recreations:* walking, music, reading. *Address:* 75 Theydon Grove, Epping, Essex. *T:* 01-375 3304. *Clubs:* St Stephen's, City Livery.   *[Died 11 Jan. 1971.*

WEST, Rt. Rev. George Algernon, MM; MA; *b* 17 Dec. 1893; *s* of George Algernon and Marion West; *m* 1st, 1923, Helen Margaret Scott Moncrieff (deceased); 2nd, 1943, Grace Hay (*d* 1980). *Educ:* S Bees School; Lincoln College, Oxford. Served in Serbia with Serbian Relief Fund, 1915; in France with Royal Garrison Artillery, Corporal; MM 1918. Went to Burma under SPG 1921; Bishop of Rangoon, 1935-54. Asst Bishop of Durham, 1965-68, resigned. *Publications:* Jungle Folk (with D. C. Atwool); Jungle Friends, 1937; The World that Works, 1944. *Address:* Lever Flat, Sherburn House, Durham.
                                     [Died 25 May 1980.

WEST, Col John Milns, CBE 1960; TD 1938; DL; Vice-Chairman, Combined Cadet Force Association, since 1950; *b* 30 May 1897; *s* of John Henry West; *m* 1934, Katherine Mary, *d* of Robert Scott, Toronto; two *d. Educ:* Shrewsbury; King's College, Cambridge (choral scholar). Served European War, 1914-19 with Rifle Brigade (SR); Adjutant 2nd Bn Rifle Bde, 1918. Assistant Master, Shrewsbury School, 1922; Housemaster, 1945, retired 1957. Staff Capt. OTC Camps, 1924-28; comd Shrewsbury Sch. OTC, 1928-38. Served War of 1939-45: 9th Bn Royal Welch Fusiliers; comd 70th Bn RWF; Lt-Col 1941; comd Infantry NCOs' Sch., 1942-45; Col 1944; comd NCOs' Wing Sch. of Infantry, 1945. Chm. Shrewsbury Branch, British Legion, 1927-34; Vice-Chm., Shropshire Committee, British Legion, 1930-34, Chm., 1959-61; Comr St John Amb. Bde (Salop), 1956-67; Governor: Royal Normal School for the Blind, 1958-; Shrewsbury School, 1961-. Mem. Salop T&AFA, 1947-68. Mem. Shrewsbury Borough Council, 1930-66; Alderman, 1949; Mayor, 1952; DL Salop, 1955. KStJ. *Recreation:* gardening. *Address:* Dorrington House, Dorrington, Shropshire. *T:* Dorrington 396.   *[Died 6 Feb. 1973.*

WEST, Gen. Sir Michael (Montgomerie Alston Roberts), GCB 1964 (KCB 1959; CB 1951); DSO and Bar 1945, 2nd Bar, 1953; *b* 27 Oct. 1905; *s* of Capt. H. C. J. Alston-Roberts-West, RN; *m* 1935, Christine Sybil Oppenheim; one *d. Educ:* Uppingham; Royal Military College, Sandhurst. 2nd Lt Oxford and Bucks Light Infantry, 1925. Served War of 1939-45; Brigade Major, 165 Brigade; Commanding 2nd South Lancashire Regt; Dep. Comdr 72 Indian Infantry Brigade; Commander 5 Infantry Brigade; Commandant, School of Infantry, 1946-48; Dep. Director, Man Power Planning, War Office, 1949-50; GOC-in-C British Troops in Austria, 1950-52; Commander, Commonwealth Division, Korea, 1952-53; Director, Territorial Army, War Office, 1955-57; Commander 1st British Corps, BAOR, 1958-59; GOC-in-C, Northern Command, 1960-62; Head of British Defence Staff, Washington, and UK Representative on the NATO Standing Group, 1962-65. Commander, US Legion of Merit, 1954. *Recreations:* undisclosed. *Address:* The Garland, Bembridge, Isle of Wight. *Clubs:* White's, Ronnie Scott's.   *[Died 14 May 1978.*

WESTAWAY, Katharine Mary, MA (Cantab), DLit (London); Headmistress, Bedford High School, 1924-49; retd 1949; *b* 1893; *d* of late F. W. Westaway, formerly HMI Secondary Schools. *Educ:* Bedford High School; Newnham College, Cambridge (Open Classical Scholar); Classical Tripos, Parts I and II. University of Leyden. Classical Mistress, Cheltenham Ladies' College, 1917-19; Marion Kennedy Research Student, Newnham College, 1919-20; Staff Lecturer in Classics, Royal Holloway College, University of London; member of University Boards of Studies in Classics and History; University Examiner in Classics, 1920-24; Member of the Bedford Borough Education Committee, 1924-45; Lectr Yorks Fedn of Women's Institutes, 1951-65. *Publications:* Original Element in Plautus; Educational Theory of Plutarch; Selections from Plautus; A History of the Bedford High School (editor and contributor); Old Girls in New Times; Unwillingly to School?; A Year in our Village; Cloudy Summits; A Wonderful Town; Seventy-five Years (editor and contributor). *Recreations:* photography, music. *Address:* 128 Foster Hill Road, Bedford.   *[Died 16 June 1973.*

WESTBROOK, Trevor Cresswell Lawrence, CBE 1945; FRAeS; MIPE; MInstM; Production Consultant since 1945; Chairman: Amorvale Construction; Kenure Development Ltd; Action Engineering Ltd (since inception, 1965); Director of a number of companies; *b* 14 January 1901; *s* of late Dr Ernest Westbrook; *m* 1942, Shielah Gillham (marr. diss.); one *s* one *d* ; *m* 1950, Carmel Stewart. *Educ:* Epsom College. Gen. Man. Vickers Supermarine, 1929-36; Gen. Man. Vickers Aviation Section, 1937-40; joined MAP 1940, Director of Aircraft Repairs and all American Aircraft Purchases and later in charge of Aircraft Programme; Member of Minister's Council, June 1941; Adviser to Intendant-General, Sept. 1941; Production Adviser to Ministry of Supply, Sept. 1941-Jan. 1942; Member first Churchill mission to USA, 1942; Production Controller de Havilland Aircraft, 1942-45; responsible for production of Schneider Spitfire and Wellington aircraft; also Mosquito; Production adviser to De Havillands Canada, temporary war assignment. *Address:* Little Brockhurst, Lurgashall, near Petworth, W Sussex. *Clubs:* Royal Thames Yacht, Royal Air Force.   *[Died 8 Sept. 1978.*

WESTLAKE, Alan Robert Cecil, CSI 1947; CIE 1943; *b* 18 July 1894; *s* of late Robert Hole and of Gertrude Westlake; *m* 1916, Dorothy Louise Turner (*d* 1966); one *s* three *d* ; *m* 1966, Isabel Flora Beck. *Educ:* at a Council School; University College School; Brasenose College, Oxford. DCLI (TF), 1914-18, retiring with rank of Capt.; Political Dept, Iraq, 1919-21; entered ICS 1921. Collector and District Magistrate. Director of Agriculture, 1948. Secretary Revenue, Development Depts. Member Board of Revenue, Madras; retd. *Address:* Chanctonbury, Fuller's Road, Rowledge, Farnham, Surrey. *T:* Frensham 2658.   *[Died 14 Nov. 1978.*

WESTLAKE, Sir Charles (Redvers), Kt 1954; *b* 25 April 1900; *s* of Capt. H. Westlake; *m* 1st, 1929, Winifred Lucy Luxton (*d* 1965), *d* of F. W. Western, Biggleswade, Beds; two *d* ; 2nd, 1968, Evelyn Isabel, *d* of Christian Aistrup, Capetown. County Electrical Engineer, Dumfriesshire, 1929; Chief Engineer and Manager, Electricity Board for N Ireland, 1931; General Manager and Engineer, Finchley Corporation Electricity Dept, 1936. Member Council IEE 1936-39. GSO1, War Office, 1943-44. Member, Uganda Legislative Council, 1954-55; Chairman Uganda Electricity Board, 1947-55; Chairman: Metal Industries Ltd, 1956-64; Williams & Williams (Reliance Holdings) Ltd, 1963-68; S. W. Wood Group Ltd, 1968-70. *Recreation:* golf. *Address:* Avenue Bartolomeu Dias 131, Cascais, Portugal. *T:* 28.3610. *Clubs:* Athenæum; Royal British (Lisbon).   *[Died 17 Feb. 1972.*

WESTMEATH, 12th Earl of *cr* 1621, **Gilbert Charles Nugent; Baron Delvin**, by tenure temp. Henry II; by summons, 1486; *b* 9 May 1880; 3rd *s* of 10th Earl and Emily, *d* of Andrew William Blake, JP, DL, Furbough, Co. Galway; *S* brother, 1933; *m* 1915, Doris (*d* 1968), 2nd *d* of C. Imlach, Liverpool; one *s* one *d. Heir:* *s* Lord Delvin. *Address:* Golden Meadow, Gulval, Penzance, Cornwall. *T:* Penzance 2049.   *[Died 20 Nov. 1971.*

WESTMINSTER, 5th Duke of, *cr* 1874; **Robert George Grosvenor**, TD, DL, JP; Bt 1622; Baron Grosvenor, 1761; Earl Grosvenor and Viscount Belgrave, 1784; Marquess of Westminster, 1831; Lord-Lieutenant of Co. Fermanagh, since 1977; *b* 24 April 1910; *yr s* of Captain Lord Hugh William Grosvenor, 1st Life Guards (killed in action, 1914), and Lady Mabel Hamilton-Stubber, MBE (*d* 1944); *S* brother, 4th Duke of Westminster, 1967; *m* 1946, Hon. Viola Maud Lyttelton, *e* surv. *d* of 9th Viscount Cobham, KCB, TD, Hagley Hall, Worcestershire; one *s* two *d. Educ:* Eton. 2nd Lt City of London Yeo., 1938; served 1939-45 with RA (Middle East), Lt-Col, 1943; Maj., City of London Yeo., 1946-49; Maj. North Irish Horse, 1949, Lt-Col, 1953-56, Hon. Col, 1971-75. MP (UU) Fermanagh and South Tyrone, 1955-64; PPS to the Foreign Secretary (Mr Selwyn Lloyd), 1957-59; Senator, NI Parlt, 1964-67. Chm., Maritime Trust, 1970-75, Vice-Pres., 1975-. Freeman: The Goldsmiths' Company; City of London; City of Chester. A Younger Brother of Trinity House, 1970-. Joint Master, Fermanagh Harriers, 1959-62. JP 1950, DL 1953, Vice-Lieutenant, 1971-76, Co. Fermanagh; High Sheriff, 1952; DL Cheshire, 1970. Hon. ADC to Governor of N Ireland, 1953-55. KStJ 1976; Kt Comdr, Commandery of Ards (Order of St John). *Heir: s* Earl Grosvenor. *Address:* Eaton Hall, Chester. *T:* Chester 674489; Ely Lodge, Enniskillen, Co. Fermanagh, Northern Ireland. *T:* Springfield 224. *Clubs:* Cavalry and Guards; MCC, Royal Ocean Racing; Royal Yacht Squadron; Ulster (Belfast); Vancouver (BC).   *[Died 19 Feb. 1979.*

WESTON, Rev. Arthur Ernest, MM 1917; ThL 1922; Dean of Adelaide, 1957-66; Honorary Chaplain to Bishop of Adelaide, 1966; *b* New South Wales, 22 Jan. 1890; *s* of Thomas Whitney and Mary Eliza Weston; *m* 1925, Mary E., *d* of Richard Zouch, Moss Vale, New South Wales; one *s. Educ:* Gilgandra Public School; St John's College, Armidale (ThL). In business, 1902-16; entered Brotherhood of the Good Shepherd, 1916. Served European War, AIF, 1916-19; 33rd Bn France (MM); commissioned 1918. Deacon and Priest, 1922; Curate of All Saints' Cathedral, Bathurst, 1922-23; locum tenens, George's Plains, 1923-24; Rector of Parkes, 1924-34; Rector of South Bathurst, Archdeacon of Bathurst, and Registrar, 1934-36; Rector of St Bartholomew's, Norwood, SA, 1936-47; Archdeacon of Strathalbyn, 1939-53; Honorary Canon of Adelaide, 1939-53; Rector of St Peters, Glenelg, SA, 1947-57; Archdeacon of Adelaide, 1953-57. *Recreations:* cricket and tennis. *Address:* 100 Farrer Brown, Nuffield Village, Castle Hill, NSW 2154, Australia. *Club:* Commonwealth (Adelaide).
                    [Died 2 July 1971.

WESTON, Sir Eric, Kt 1954; *b* 8 Dec. 1892; *s* of W. J. Weston, South Shields; *m* 1919, Georgina, *d* of W. J. Cork, Hampstead; three *d. Educ:* South Shields High School; St John's Coll., Cambridge. Math. Tripos, Part I, 1912; Part II, 1914; ICS Exam. 1915; Assistant Collector and Judge of various districts Bombay Presidency and Sind District, 1916-29; Judge, 1929; Judge, Aden, 1931; Judicial Commissioner, Rajkot and Ajmer, 1934-35 and 1937-38; Judge Chief Court of Sind, 1938-42; Judge High Court, Bombay, 1943-50; Chief Justice, Punjab High Court, Simla, 1950-52; retired, Dec. 1952. *Recreations:* tennis, golf. *Address:* c/o National Westminster Bank Ltd, Sevenoaks, Kent; 66 Kippington Road, Sevenoaks, Kent.
                    [Died 20 Oct. 1976.

WESTON, Garfield; *see* Weston, W. G.

WESTON, Maj.-Gen. Gerald Patrick Linton, CB 1962; CBE 1960; DSO 1945; *b* 21 August 1910; *s* of late Donald Weston, ICS (retd) and of Ethel Linton Weston, Clent, Worcs; *m* 1938, Moira Olive Hale, *d* of Major D. B. Hale, RA (retd); one *s* one *d. Educ:* Haileybury; RMC Sandhurst. Commnd Middlesex Regt, 1931; seconded RAF, 1936-40; served War of 1939-45; comdg: 18 (Bomber) Sqdn, RAF France, 1939-40; 2nd Bn, Middlesex Regt, France and Germany, 1943-45 (despatches); 161 Indian Infantry Brigade, Burma and Java, 1945-46; 6 Parachute Brigade TA, 1947-49; jssc, 1949; AAG War Office, 1949-52; Senior Operations Officer, Malaya, 1952-53 (despatches); idc, 1954; Asst Comdt School of Land/Air Warfare, 1955-57; Commandant, Army Air Corps Centre, 1957-60; Director of Land/Air Warfare, War Office, 1960-64, retd. Order of Leopold and Belgian Croix de Guerre, 1945. *Recreations:* cricket and skiing. *Address:* Whitewater Cottage, North Warnborough, Hants. *T:* Odiham 2113.   *[Died 26 Oct. 1977.*

WESTON, Air Vice-Marshal Sir John (Gerard Willsley), KBE 1964 (OBE 1942); CB 1947; *b* 15 Nov. 1908; *e s* of late Col Edward Thomas Weston and Constance Alice Weston (*née* Turpin); *m* 1932, Eileen Margaret Gwendoline (*d* 1966), *o d* of late H. E. Rose, Bristol; one *s* one *d*. *Educ:* Cranbrook Sch.; RAF Coll., Cranwell. 207 (B) Sqdn, 1929; 60 (B) Sqdn, 1930-32; Signals Specialist Course, 1932-33; 99 (B) Sqdn, 1934; seconded RCAF, 1935-36; Air Ministry staff duties, 1938-41 (despatches, 1940); Chief Signals Officer, Ferry Command, 1941; Dep. Director Signals, Air Ministry, 1942-43; Director of Signals, Air Ministry, 1943-45; Comdt Central Signals Establishment, 1946-47; idc, 1948; Director of Policy (AS), Air Ministry, 1949-51; Commandant RAF, Halton, 1952-53; AOC No 90 (Signals) Group, 1954-55; Assistant Chief of Air Staff (Signals), Air Ministry, 1956-59; Senior Directing Staff, Imperial Defence College, 1959-61; Director-General of Manning, Air Ministry, 1961-64, retd. Chm., National Small-bore Rifle Assoc., 1965-68. *Recreations:* cricket, shooting. *Address:* c/o Williams & Glyn's Bank Ltd, Whitehall, SW1. *Club:* Royal Air Force.
[Died 13 June 1979.

WESTON, Kenneth Southwold, CMG 1956; OBE 1951; Assistant Secretary, HM Treasury, retired, 1962; *b* 9 Nov. 1899; *s* of late Benjamin Samuel Weston, Bromham, Wilts; *m* 1935, Kathleen Elizabeth, *d* of Arthur Leach, Huntingdon; one *s*. *Educ:* Southend-on-Sea High School. Served War of 1914-18, Lieut Wilts Regt; Home Civil Service from 1921; Financial Adviser, HM Embassy, Madrid, 1943-45; HM Treasury Representative in Canada, 1951-53. *Address:* 5 Lancaster Gardens, SW19.
[Died 27 Dec. 1971.

WESTON, Laurence; Hon. Mr Justice Weston; Puisne Judge, Malawi, since 1969; *b* 1909. *Educ:* Pembroke College, Oxford. Called to the Bar (Middle Temple), 1942. Asst Custodian of Enemy Property, Palestine, 1939-43. War Service, 1943-46 (Lt-Col). Magistrate, Nigeria, 1950 (Crown Counsel 1951); Assistant Attorney General, North Borneo, 1952; Attorney-General, The Gambia, 1955; Puisne Judge in Tanganyika, 1961-65; Chief Justice, Botswana (formerly Bechuanaland Protectorate), 1965-68. *Address:* High Court, Blantyre, Malawi.
[Died 29 Oct. 1972.

WESTON, Brig.-Gen. Spencer Vaughan Percy, DSO 1917; MC; Member of the Stock Exchange; *b* 1883; *m* 1913, Henrietta Valerie, *d* of W. Compton-Smith; five *s* four *d*. Served European War (Despatches four times, DSO two bars, MC, French and Belgian Croix de Guerre); rejoined from Officers' Emergency Reserve, 1940-46. FRGS. *Address:* Bente, Carters Hill, Sevenoaks, Kent. *T:* Sevenoaks 61082. *Clubs:* Carlton, City of London; Wildernesse (Sevenoaks).
[Died 3 Dec. 1973.

WESTON, (Willard) Garfield; Chairman: George Weston Holdings, Ltd and its associated companies; Weston Foods, Ltd; Fortnum & Mason Ltd; Director of other companies in Britain; President, Associated British Foods Ltd; Chairman of George Weston Ltd, Toronto, and of its associated companies; also of Weston Bakeries Ltd, Toronto; Wm Paterson, Ltd, Brantford, Ontario, and Weston Biscuit Co., Passaic, New Jersey, USA; *b* Toronto, Ontario, 1898; *e s* of George and Emma Maude Weston; *m* 1921, Reta Lila Howard (*d* 1967); three *s* six *d*. *Educ:* Harbord Collegiate Inst., Toronto. Joined Canadian Engrs on leaving sch. and served in France during European War; with George Weston Ltd (Toronto) since 1919, becoming Vice-President in 1921 and Manager in 1922; came to Great Britain in 1934; founded the Weston Biscuit Companies and erected new plants in many parts of the country; founded Allied Bakeries, Ltd. MP (Nat U) for Macclesfield Division, 1939-45. *Recreations:* riding, tennis. *Address:* Weston Centre, 40 Berkeley Square, W1. *T:* 01-499 8931. *TA:* Garwest, London. *Club:* Carlton.
[Died 22 Oct. 1978.

WESTON, William Guy, CMG 1945; *b* 30 Jan. 1907; *s* of late W. H. Weston, Quorn Lodge, Melton Mowbray; *m* 1st, 1930, Joan (marr. diss. 1953), *d* of J. P. Chettle, RBA; three *s* one *d*; 2nd, 1955, Evelyn Mary, *er d* of late T. G. Marriott. Lightfoot Scholar in Ecclesiastical History, Cambridge, 1929; Historical Tripos, 1929-30. Dep. Sec. Minister of Transport, 1946-48; General Manager Marine Dept Anglo-Saxon Petroleum Co., 1948-52; Governing Director, W. G. Weston Ltd, 1953-78. Comdr, Order of St Olaf (Norway); Comdr, Order of Orange Nassau (Netherlands). *Recreation:* painting. *Address:* Little Langford, Stoke Row, Oxon RG9 5PS. *T:* Checkendon 680015. *Club:* Travellers'.
[Died 2 Dec. 1980.

WESTROP, Brigadier Sidney Albert, CBE 1946; DSO 1917; MC 1915; FIMechE; Consulting Engineer, retired; *b* 20 May 1895; *s* of A. W. Westrop; *m* 1918, Eileen M. Alton; one *s* three *d*. *Educ:* Bridgnorth Grammar School; Birmingham Univ. (BSc). Served

European War, 1914-18 (despatches twice, MC, DSO); on active service in France, England, Iraq, India and Burmah, 1939-46 (despatches twice, CBE); Chief Engineer and Brig. 1943; was Director of Open Cut Coal Mining for India, 1944-45. *Recreations:* fishing, shooting. *Address:* Old Rectory, Brattleby, Lincoln, *T:* Scampton 221. *Club:* East India, Devonshire, Sports and Public Schools.
[Died 28 March 1979.

WESTROPP, Maj.-Gen. Victor John Eric, CB 1947; CBE 1943; *b* 24 May 1897; *s* of late Brig.-Gen. H. C. E. Westropp and M. F. A. Lowndes; *m* 1923, E. A. Lynch (*d* 1940); one *s* one *d*; *m* 1944, Elspeth, *yr d* of Lt-Col H. A. Duncan, one *s* (one *d* decd). *Educ:* Bradfield; RMA, Woolwich. Commissioned Regular Army, RE, 1916; France, 1917-18; transferred to Royal Signals, 1921; Instructor RMA, Woolwich, 1926-29; Staff College, Quetta, 1931-32; NW Frontier, 1930 and 1933-34 (Frontier Medal); War Office 1934-36; Palestine 1936, and 1938-39 (Palestine medal); War of 1939-45 (CBE, Africa Star, 1939-45 Star, Italian Star, Defence Medal, Commander Legion of Merit, USA); late Deputy Adj.-Gen., India; Dep. Chief of Staff, CCG; UK Commissioner, Military Security Board, CCG, 1947-51; retired, 1951. *Address:* Tenacres, Bracknell, Berks.
[Died 8 June 1974.

WESTRUP, Sir Jack (Allan), Kt 1961; MA, BMus, FRCO; Hon. DMus Oxon, 1944; FBA 1954; Hon. RAM, 1960; FRCM, 1961; FRSCM, 1963; Heather Professor of Music in the University of Oxford, and Fellow of Wadham College, Oxford, 1947-71, Fellow Emeritus, 1971; *b* 26 July 1904; *s* of George Westrup and Harriet Sophia Allan; *m* 1938, Solweig Maria, *d* of Musikdirektör Per Johan Rösell, Linköping, Sweden; three *s* one *d*. *Educ:* Dulwich College (scholar); Balliol College, Oxford (Nettleship scholar). President, Oxford University Musical Club and Union, 1926, 1947; Musical Director, Oxford Opera Club, 1927, 1947-62; Asst Master (Classics), Dulwich College, 1928-34; Assistant Music Critic, Daily Telegraph, 1934-40; Editor, Monthly Musical Record, 1933-45; Lecturer in History of Music, RAM, 1938-40; Collard Fellow, Company of Musicians, 1940-43 (Master, 1971-72); Lecturer in Music, King's College, Newcastle upon Tyne, 1941-44; Conductor, Newcastle on Tyne Bach Choir, 1942-44; Peyton and Barber Professor of Music, University of Birmingham, 1944-46. Pres., Union of Graduates in Music, 1949-51; Ferens Lecturer in Fine Art, University College, Hull, 1950-51; President Royal Musical Assoc., 1958-63; President, Incorporated Society of Musicians, 1963; President, Royal College of Organists, 1964-66; Member, BBC General Advisory Council, 1963-68; Editor, Music and Letters, 1959-; Edited for performance Monteverdi's Orfeo (Oxford, 1925, Royal College of Music, London, 1926, Scala Theatre, London, 1929), Monteverdi's L'Incoronazione di Poppea (Oxford, 1927), Locke's Cupid and Death (Scala Theatre, London, 1929). Conducted at London Opera Festival, 1929-30, London Theatre Concerts, 1938, Barber Institute Chamber Concerts, Birmingham, 1946, etc; Conductor: Oxford Univ. Orchestra, 1954-63; Oxford Bach Choir, 1970-71; Oxford Orchestral Soc., 1970-71. Hon. FTCL 1946. *Publications:* Purcell, 1937; Handel, 1939; Liszt, 1940; Sharps and Flats (essays on music), 1940; When Israel came out of Egypt (motet for double choir), 1940; British Music, 1943; The Meaning of Musical History (Deneke lecture), 1946; 3rd edn of Ernest Walker's History of Music in England, 1952; Introduction to Musical History, 1955; The Nature of Recitative, 1957; Collins Music Encyclopedia (with F. Ll. Harrison), 1959; Bach Cantatas, 1966; Schubert Chamber Music, 1969; Fellowes' English Cathedral Music, 5th edn, 1969; Musical Interpretation, 1971; (ed) Everyman's Dictionary of Music, 5th edn, 1971; songs, organ music, arrangements, etc; contributions to: Oxford History of Music, 2nd edn, 1932; Grove's Dictionary, 4th edn, 1940, 5th edn, 1954; Musical Education, 1946; British Music of our Time, 1946; The Character of England, 1947; Schubert-a Symposium, 1947; Die Musik in Geschichte und Gegenwart, 1949-67; Bach-Gedenkschrift, 1950; The Heritage of Music, vol. iii, 1951; New Oxford History of Music, 1954; Fanfare for Ernest Newman, 1955; Music and Western Man, 1958; The Decca Book of Ballet, 1958; Riemann Musiklexikon, 12th edn, 1959; Fellerer Festschrift, 1962; Jeppesen Festschrift, 1962; Blume Festschrift, 1963; Wellesz Festschrift, 1966; La Musica, 1966; Grout Festschrift, 1968; Haydon Festschrift, 1969; Lenaerts Festschrift, 1969; Szabolcsi Festschrift, 1969; Proc. Musical Association, various musical periodicals. *Address:* Maycroft, Hurland Lane, Headley, Bordon, Hants GU35 8NQ. *T:* Headley Down 2274.
[Died 21 April 1975.

WETHERALL, Lt-Gen. Sir (Harry) Edward de Robillard, KBE 1946 (OBE 1937); CB 1941; DSO 1917; MC; *b* 22 Feb. 1889; 2nd *s* of late Major H. A. Wetherall, Coldstream Guards; *m* 1923, Vera G., *o d* of George de Lisle Bush, of Eastington Park, Stonehouse, Gloucestershire. Gloucester Regt; served European

War, 1914-18 (wounded, despatches, MC, DSO); accelerated promotion, Captain to Major, 1927; GSO for Weapon Training, Scottish Command, 1930-34 (Brevet Lt-Col); commanded 1st Bn York and Lancaster Regiment, 1936-38; Commander 19th Infantry Brigade, 1938-40; Commander 11th African Div. in Abyssinia, 1941; GOC-in-C E Africa, 1941; GOC Ceylon, 1943-45; C-in-C Ceylon, 1945-46; retired pay, 1946. Colonel, The Gloucestershire Regiment, 1947-54. *Address:* Littlecourt, Bagborough, Taunton, Somerset. *Club:* Army and Navy.
[*Died* 18 *Nov.* 1979.

WETHERED, His Honour Ernest Handel Cossham, OBE; MA, LLB; Special Commissioner for Matrimonial Causes, 1947; *b* 18 July 1878; *s* of Edward Bestbridge Wethered, JP, and Mary Ellen Wright; *m* 1904, Jessie Marian Ward (*d* 1956); one *s* one *d*. *Educ:* Cheltenham Coll.; Pembroke Coll., Cambridge. Barrister-at-law called at Lincoln's Inn, 1899; Tancred Student; Western Circuit; practised at Bristol and in London, 1899-1934; Judge of County Courts, Circuit 57, 1934-37; Circuit 54, 1938-50; retired from County Court Bench, 1950; Chairman of Court of Referees under Unemployment Insurance Acts at Bristol, 1912-34; Chairman of Trade Boards, 1919-34; Hon. Member of National Council of Pottery Industry, 1918-46; Chairman SW Tribunal under National Service (Armed Forces) Acts, 1939-47 and re-appointed 1951-60; Training Officer, Fire Guard Service, Clifton Division, Bristol, 1943-45. Vice-Pres. British Red Cross Bristol Branch, 1946-49; County Civil Defence Officer, 1949-54; Hon. Vice-Pres. Bristol Branch, 1954; Civil Defence Corps, General Instructor (Falfield Special), 1950. Pres., Internat. Brotherhood of Magicians, 1949-50. *Address:* Gort Lodge, 11 The Avenue, Clifton, Bristol 8. *T:* Bristol 33695.   [*Died* 17 *April* 1975.

WHARTON, Baroness (Barony *cr* 1544-5, called out of abeyance, 1916) (10th in line); **Elisabeth Dorothy**; *b* 4 May 1906; *d* of 8th Baron Wharton and Dorothy (*d* 1944), *y d* of late Maj.-Gen. Sir Arthur Edward Augustus Ellis, GCVO, CSI; *S* brother, 1969; *m* 1st (marr. diss. 1946); two *d*; *m* 2nd (marr. diss. 1958). *Co-heiresses: d* Hon. Myrtle Olive Felix Robertson [*b* 20 Feb. 1934; *m* 1958, Henry MacLeod Robertson; three *s* one *d*] and *d* Hon. Caroline Elizabeth Appleyard-List [*b* 28 Aug. 1935; *m* 1970, Commander Jonathon Appleyard-List; one *d*].
[*Died* 4 *May* 1974.

WHARTON, Sir (George) Anthony, Kt 1977; CBE 1969 (MBE 1944); TD 1946; DL; solicitor; Under Sheriff of Nottingham and Nottinghamshire, since 1952; *b* 22 Sept. 1917; *s* of George Leslie Wharton and Beatrice Alice Wharton. *Educ:* Oakham; E Midlands Law Sch. (University Coll., Nottingham). Solicitor, 1947. Clerk of the Peace, Nottingham, 1956-74. Chairman: Notts T&AFA, 1956-68; E Midlands TA&VRA, 1968-; a Vice-Chm. Council, TA&VRAs, 1972-79. Pres., RFU, 1977-78 (formerly Vice-Pres.). DL Notts 1958. *Recreations:* Territorial Forces, Rugby football, young people. *Address:* The Old House, Edwalton, Notts. *T:* (office) Nottingham 42042. *Clubs:* Brooks's, Army and Navy, Naval and Military.
[*Died* 31 *March* 1980.

WHEARE, Sir Kenneth Clinton, Kt 1966; CMG 1953; FBA 1952; DLitt (Oxon); Fellow, All Souls College, Oxford, 1944-57, and since 1973; Chancellor of Liverpool University, since 1972; *b* Warragul, Vict., Australia, 26 March 1907; *e s* of Eustace Leonard Wheare and Kathleen Frances Kinahan; *m* 1st, 1934, Helen Mary Allan; one *s*; 2nd, 1943, Joan Randell; two *s* two *d*. *Educ:* Scotch College, Melbourne; University of Melbourne; Oriel College, Oxford. BA Univ. of Melbourne, 1929, MA, 1949; Rhodes Scholar from Victoria, Australia, 1929; Oriel College, Oxford, 1929-32; 1st class Hons, School of Philosophy, Politics and Economics, 1932; BA Oxford, 1932, MA 1935, DLitt 1957; Lecturer, Christ Church, Oxford, 1934-39; Beit Lecturer in Colonial History, Oxford, 1935-44; Fellow of University Coll., Oxford, 1939-44, and Dean, 1942-45; Gladstone Prof. of Government and Public Administration, Univ. of Oxford, 1944-57; Fellow of Nuffield College, 1944-58; Rector, Exeter Coll., Oxford, 1956-72; Vice-Chancellor, Oxford Univ., 1964-66, Pro-Vice-Chancellor, 1958-64, 1966-72. Hon. Fellow of Nuffield, Oriel, University, Wolfson and Exeter Colls, Oxford. Member of Oxford City Council, 1940-57. Member of Hebdomadal Council, 1947-67; Constitutional Adviser to Nat. Convention of Newfoundland, 1946-47, and to Confs on Central African Federation, 1951, 1952, 1953; a Rhodes Trustee, 1948-77; Chm. Departmental Ctee on Children and the Cinema, 1947-50; Member: Franks Ctee on Administrative Tribunals and Inquiries, 1955-57; University Grants Committee, 1959-63; Governing Body, Sch. of Oriental and African Studies, Univ. of London, 1970-74; Nuffield Trustee, 1966-75; Pres. Brit. Acad., 1967-71. Rede Lectr, Cambridge, 1967; Hamlyn Lectr, 1973. Hon. Admiral, Herring Fishery Fleet, IOM, 1973-75. Hon. LHD Columbia, 1954; Hon. LittD Cambridge, 1969; Hon.

LLD: Exeter, 1970; Liverpool, 1972; Manchester, 1975. Queen's Silver Jubilee Medal, 1977. *Publications:* The Statute of Westminster, 1931, 1933; The Statute of Westminster and Dominion Status, 1938 (5th edn 1953); Federal Government, 1946 (4th edn 1963); Abraham Lincoln and the United States, 1948; Modern Constitutions, 1951, 2nd edn 1978; Government by Committee, 1955; The Constitutional Structure of the Commonwealth, 1960; Legislatures, 1963; Maladministration and its Remedies, 1973; Walter Bagehot (lecture), 1974. *Recreations:* walking, cooking. *Address:* 55 Park Town, Oxford. *T:* Oxford 53775. *Clubs:* Vincent's (Oxford); Athenæum (Liverpool).   [*Died* 7 *Sept.* 1979.

WHEATCROFT, Harry; Consultant, Harry Wheatcroft Roses Ltd; *b* 24 Aug. 1898; *s* of George Alfred and Sarah Elizabeth Wheatcroft; *m* 1929, Dorothy Averill; three *s* two *d*. *Educ:* Nottingham High Sch.; Grosvenor Sch. Started rose growing, on one acre of land, 1919; business increased to 500,000 roses by 1937; ploughed and destroyed all roses at outbreak of War, 1939, and started farming; re-started rose growing after War. Producing yearly 1,500,000 roses. Has travelled widely, lecturing and searching the world for new roses, and has introduced many of the outstanding roses in commerce today into this country; varieties such as: Peace, Queen Elizabeth, Fragrant Cloud, Super Star, Sir Harry Pilkington; and continues to do so. Vice-Pres., Royal Nat. Rose Soc. Liveryman, Worshipful Co. of Gardeners. VMH 1972, DHM 1974. *Publications:* My Life with Roses, 1959; In Praise of Roses, 1970; How to Grow Better Roses, 1974; The Root of the Matter, 1974. *Recreations:* reading, theatre, rose growing. *Address:* The Paddock, Melton Road, West Bridgford, Notts. *T:* Nottingham 232610. *Club:* Chelsea Arts.   [*Died* 8 *Jan.* 1977.

WHEATLEY, Dennis Yates, Bronze Star (Mil., US), 1945; FRSA; FRSL; Novelist, Inventor (with J. G. Links) of Crime Dossier Murder Fiction; *b* 8 January 1897; *o s* of late Albert David Wheatley and Florence, Lady Newton; *m* 1st, 1923, Nancy Madelaine Leslie Robinson; one *s*; 2nd, 1931, Joan Gwendoline, *d* of late Hon. Louis Johnstone. *Educ:* HMS Worcester; Germany. Entered his father's Mayfair wine business, 1914; Commissioned RFA (T), Sept. 1914 (City of London Brigade); President, Old Comrades Association, 1961; transferred to 36th (Ulster) Division, 1917; invalided from the Service, 1919; re-entered his father's business; became sole owner, 1926; bought and dispersed many famous cellars; director of numerous companies; sold business, 1931; commenced writing, 1932. Toured England as member of Sir John Anderson's panel of voluntary speakers on National Service, 1939. Recommissioned in RAFVR Dec. 1941 to fill specially created post; only non-regular officer to be commissioned direct to Joint Planning Staff; worked for following three years in Offices of the War Cabinet; Wing Comdr, 1944. Invented war games, Invasion, 1938, Blockade, 1939, Alibi, 1953. Livery of Vintners' Company, 1918, and of Distillers' Company, 1922. Pres. New Forest Agricultural Show, 1968. *Publications:* The Forbidden Territory (filmed); Such Power is Dangerous; Old Rowley (a Private Life of Charles II), 1933; Black August; The Fabulous Valley, 1934; The Devil Rides Out (filmed); The Eunuch of Stamboul (filmed), 1935; They Found Atlantis; Murder Off Miami (with J. G. Links); Contraband, 1936; The Secret War; Who Killed Robert Prentice (with J. G. Links); Red Eagle (story of the Russian Revolution), 1937; Uncharted Seas (filmed as The Lost Continent); The Malinsay Massacre (with J. G. Links); The Golden Spaniard, 1938; The Quest of Julian Day; Herewith the Clues! (with J. G. Links); Sixty Days to Live; Those Modern Musketeers, 1939; Three Inquisitive People; The Scarlet Impostor; Faked Passports; The Black Baroness, 1940; Strange Conflict; The Sword of Fate; Total War, 1941; V for Vengeance; Mediterranean Nights (Short Stories), 1942; Gunmen, Gallants and Ghosts (Short Stories), 1943; The Man Who Missed the War, 1945; Codeword Golden Fleece; Come into my Parlour, 1946; The Launching of Roger Brook, 1947; The Shadow of Tyburn Tree; The Haunting of Toby Jugg, 1948; The Rising Storm; The Seven Ages of Justerini (privately printed for bi-centenary of firm of Justerini & Brooks), 1949; The Second Seal, 1950; The Man Who Killed the King, 1951; Star of Ill Omen, 1952; To the Devil a Daughter (filmed); Curtain of Fear, 1953; The Island where Time Stands Still, 1954; The Dark Secret of Josephine, 1955; The Ka of Gifford Hillary, 1956; The Prisoner in the Mask, 1957; Traitors' Gate, 1958; Stranger than Fiction; The Rape of Venice, 1959; The Satanist, 1960; Saturdays with Bricks, 1960; A Vendetta in Spain, 1961; Mayhem in Greece, 1962; The Sultan's Daughter, 1963; Bill for the Use of a Body, 1964; They Used Dark Forces, 1964; Dangerous Inheritance, 1965; The Wanton Princess, 1966; Unholy Crusade, 1967; The White Witch of the South Seas, 1968; Evil in a Mask, 1969; Gateway to Hell, 1970; The Ravishing of Lady Mary Ware,

1971; The Devil and all his Works, 1971; The Strange Story of Linda Lee, 1972; The Irish Witch, 1973; (ed) Dennis Wheatley's Library of the Occult, 1974; Desperate Measures, 1974; The Time Has Come (memoirs), vol. 1, 1977, vol. II, 1978. Writings published in 31 languages. *Recreations:* collecting books, stamps, coins, Georgian furniture and Oriental rugs; travel, building. *Address:* 60 Cadogan Square, SW1. *Clubs:* White's, Pratt's, Saintsbury, Paternosters.   [Died 11 Nov. 1977.

WHEATLEY, Major (Hon. Lt-Col) Sir Mervyn James, KBE 1952 (CBE 1928; OBE 1918); DL; retired; *b* Kinson, Dorset, 24 April 1880; 3rd *s* of Lieutenant-Colonel F. G. Wheatley, VD, JP, Ravenshoe, Poole, Dorset; *m* 1909, Mary Irene (*d* 1952), *er d* of Arthur Cox; one *s* one *d*; *m* 1952, Mrs Eileen Shelley, widow of K. J. Shelley, Trentham. *Educ:* Sutton Valence School. Entered Dorset Regt from 1st V/B Dorset Regt 1900; retired, 1918; served South African War, 1900-2; European War, 1914-18; operations in the Sudan, 1917 (despatches twice); Egyptian Army and Sudan Defence Force and Sudan Political Service, 1907-28; Private Sec. Sirdar & Governor-General, 1916-20; Governor and OC District Bahr-el-Ghazal Province, Sudan, 1921-28; Clothworker and Freeman City of London; Hon. Freeman of Poole; Army Welfare Officer, 1939-45; raised 2 Bns Home Guard, and was Comdg Officer 3rd Dorset Bn Home Guard; was Alderman Borough of Poole; JP, Poole; Mayor of Poole, 1936-37; was Alderman County of Dorset; MP (C) East Dorset, 1945-50, Poole, 1950-51; Conservative Whip, 1948-51. Chm.: E Dorset Conservative Assoc., 1940-45; Wessex Area Conservative and Unionist Assoc., 1944-46; Pres. W Regional Assoc. for the Blind, 1945-62. Pres., Poole Conservative Assoc., 1953-67. DL Dorset, 1952. CStJ 1964. 3rd Class Order of the Nile; 3rd Class Nahda; 4th Class Osmanieh. *Publications:* contributions to Geographical Journal and Journal of the African Society. *Recreations:* winner Army quarter-mile, 1907; played hockey, County of Dorset, 1903, 1904, 1905. *Address:* 65 Compton Avenue, Parkstone, Poole, Dorset BH14 8PX. *T:* Canford Cliffs 708453.   [Died 26 Oct. 1974.

WHEATLEY, Maj.-Gen. Mervyn Savile, CB 1953; CBE 1945 (OBE 1941); CEng, FIEE; retired 1957; *b* 18 April 1900; *s* of late Major S. G. Wheatley and Mrs Savile Wheatley, Parkstone, Dorset; *m* 1936, Iris Veronica Margaret Kenyon; one *d* (by previous marriage). *Educ:* Blundell's; RMC Sandhurst. 2nd Lt Dorset Regt, 1918; Malabar, 1921-22; Lt Royal Signals, 1925, Adjutant, Captain 1926-29; Instructor, RMA, Woolwich, 1929-33; DAAG War Office (Major), 1939-40; Commander, Royal Signals, 1st Armoured Division (Lieutenant-Colonel), 1940-41; Chief Signal Officer, SE Comd (Colonel), 1941-42; GSO1 Home Forces and 21 Army Group (Colonel), 1942-43; Chief Signal Officer, 13 Corps, Italy (Brig.), 1943-44; DD Signals, War Office, 1944-46; Comdr STC, 1946-47; Comdr Canal South District, 1947-49; Dep. Comdr Mid West District, 1949-51; Maj.-Gen. 1951; Chief Signal Officer, MELF, 1951-54; Signal Officer-in-Chief, War Office, 1954-57. Col Comdt Royal Signals, 1957-62. Hon. Col 41st Signal Regt (Princess Louise's Kensington Regt TA), 1957-62. *Recreations:* tennis, golf, sailing. *Address:* 5 Heathfield Court, Fleet, Hants. *Club:* Army and Navy.   [Died 13 Nov. 1979.

WHEELDON, Edward Christian, CBE 1959; *b* 12 May 1907; *s* of Edward Wheeldon, Manchester; *m* 1935, Alice Willan (*d* 1975); one *s*. *Educ:* Openshaw Technical College; Manchester College of Technology. Served apprenticeship at Metropolitan-Vickers Ltd, Manchester, 1923-28; Process Engineer, 1928-34; Group Production Engineer, Parkinson and Cowan, 1934-38; joined Westland Aircraft Ltd as Planning Engineer, 1938; Works Supt, 1939; Works Manager, 1943; Works Dir 1944; Dep. Man. Dir, 1946; Man. Dir, 1950; Dep. Chm. and Man. Dir, 1960; Dep. Chm. and Chief Executive, 1965; Chm., 1968-70. Pres., Soc. of British Aerospace Cos Ltd, 1964-65, Treasurer, 1968-72. FIProdE; FRAeS; FInstD. *Recreations:* golf, Association football. *Address:* 88 Ilchester Road, Yeovil, Somerset. *T:* Yeovil 24799. *Clubs:* Golf (Yeovil); Golf (Sherborne).
                    [Died 20 Dec. 1980.

WHEELER, Burton Kendall; *b* Hudson, Mass, 27 Feb. 1882; *s* of Asa Leonard Wheeler and Mary Elizabeth Tyler; *m* 1907, Lulu White; three *s* two *d*. *Educ:* Public Schools; Business College; University of Michigan. LLD 1905; elected to Montana Legislature, 1910 (2-year term); US District Attorney, 1913-19; elected US Senate, 1922--1928-1934-1940; Chm. Indian Cttee (3-year); Chm. Interstate Commerce Committee (12-year); nominated Vice-Pres. on progressive ticket, 1924, with Elder Senator Robt M. La Follette. Practising Law, Southern Bldg, Washington, DC. *Recreations:* golf, fishing. *Address:* 704 Southern Building, 15th & H Streets, Washington, DC 20005, USA. *T:* District 7-7117. *Clubs:* Mason, Burning Tree Golf, Metropolitan, Elks (Washington, DC).   [Died 6 Jan. 1975.

WHEELER, Sir Charles (Reginald), KBE 1966 (CBE 1946); Chairman, Sheerness Steel Co. Ltd, since 1969; *b* 5 December 1904; *s* of late Henry Wheeler and Nellie Bowdler (*née* Healing); *m* 1st, 1929, Frieda Close (*d* 1972); one *s* two *d*; 2nd, 1973, Marcelle Ades. *Educ:* St Paul's School. Joined Baldwins Ltd, 1922, and continued with this and associated Cos. Iron and Steel Control, Min. of Supply, 1939-45, Controller, 1945. Jt Man. Dir, Guest Keen Iron and Steel Co. Ltd, 1946-59; Chairman, 1959-60. Chairman, AEI Ltd, 1964-67; Dir, Rudolf Wolff Steel Ltd. President: British Electrical and Allied Manufacturers' Association, 1965; Electrical Research Association, 1966; British Iron and Steel Federation, 1961; Iron and Steel Institute, 1958-59. Vice Pres., British Olympic Assoc.; Mem. Bd of Governors, and Jt Hon. Treasurer, English-Speaking Union; Governor: St Paul's Sch.; St Paul's Girls' Sch.; Pangbourne Coll. High Sheriff, Co. of Glamorgan, 1955. Officier Légion d'Honneur, 1966. Hon. DSc Salford, 1967. *Recreations:* beagling, rowing, golf. *Address:* Flat 7, 34 Chesham Place, SW1X 8HB. *Clubs:* Garrick, Leander, London Rowing.
                    [Died 25 Nov. 1975.

WHEELER, Sir Charles (Thomas); KCVO 1958; CBE 1948; PPRA (RA 1940; ARA 1934); FRBS 1935 (President, 1944-49); Hon. FRIBA; Hon. RSA; Hon. RE; Hon. RWS; Hon. RI; sculptor: President of the Royal Academy, 1956-66; *b* Codsall (Freedom of Wolverhampton, 1958), 1892; *s* of S. P. Wheeler; *m* Muriel, *yr d* of A. W. Bourne; one *s* one *d*. *Educ:* South Kensington Royal Exhibitioner. A trustee, Tate Gallery, 1942-49. Exhibited at Royal Academy since 1914; executed sculptures on Winchester College War Memorial Cloisters, 1924; Bishop Jacob Memorial Church, Ilford; Indian Memorial at Neuve Chapelle, India House, South Africa House, Rhodes House, Oxford, Haileybury College Chapel, Royal Empire Society, The Bank of England, Church House, Jellicoe Memorial Bust and Fountain, Trafalgar Sq., RAF Memorial, Malta, English Electric House, Barclay's Bank, Queens Park, Invercargill, NZ, etc; Bust, Infant Christ, purchased for nation under Chantrey Bequest, 1924; also Bronze Statue, Spring, 1930; Aphrodite II, 1944; Earth and Water, 1952; Merchant Navy Memorial, Tower Hill; Statue of Gen. Katoka, Accra; Poseidon Fountain, George Yard, EC. Member Royal Fine Art Commission, 1946-52. Hon. Corresp. Academician, Royal Acad. of San Fernando, Madrid. Gold Medal Royal Soc. Brit. Sculptors for Distinguished Services to Sculpture, 1949; Gold Medal, USA National Academy of Design, 1963. Hon. DCL (Oxon), 1960; Hon. LLD (TCD) 1961; Hon. DLitt Keele, 1971. Officier de la Légion d'Honneur; Knight Comdr of the Crown of Siam; Commendatore Al Merito della Repubblica Italiana. *Publication:* (Autobiography) High Relief, 1968. *Address:* Garden Studio, 22 Cathcart Road, South Kensington, SW10. *T:* 01-352 8234; Woodreed Farmhouse, Five Ashes, Mayfield, Sussex. *T:* Hadlow Down 303. *Clubs:* Athenæum, Arts, Chelsea Arts, Savage.   [Died 22 Aug. 1974.

WHEELER, Dr Denis Edward, CBE 1965; BSc, PhD, FRIC; Consultant to the Wellcome Foundation, since 1970 (Managing Director, 1948-67, Deputy Chairman, 1967-70); *b* 6 Sept. 1910; *s* of late Edward James Wheeler; *m* 1938, Dilys Mary, *d* of late Alfred Evans; one *d*. *Educ:* Queen Elizabeth's, Bristol; University of Bristol (BSc, PhD); Princeton Univ., USA (Salters Fellow). ICI (Explosives), 1935-40; Research and Development Dir, Hardman & Holden Ltd, 1940-45; Asst Managing Dir, The Wellcome Foundation Ltd, 1946. Member: Economic Development Cttee for Chemical Industry; Council CBI; Mem., Trade Affairs Bd of Chemical Industries Assoc.; Vice-Pres., Spastics Soc., 1967 (Chm. 1963-66); Pres., Assoc. of Brit. Pharmaceutical Industry, 1963 and 1964. Master, Salters' Co., 1969-70. *Recreation:* golf. *Address:* Penilee, Four Marks, Alton, Hants.   [Died 24 Jan. 1977.

WHEELER, Sir Mortimer; *see* Wheeler, Sir R. E. M.

WHEELER, Brig. (retd) Ralph Pung, CBE 1952; late RE; (formerly Deputy Director-General, Ordnance Survey); *b* 21 Nov. 1898; *s* of Charles William Wheeler, Speenhamland, near Newbury; *m* 1931, Norah Cordukes Kitchin, *d* of Frederick Hyland Kitchin, Harrogate; two *s*. *Educ:* Owen's School; RMA Woolwich; Peterhouse, Cambridge. Egypt and Palestine, 1917-18; Waziristan, 1920-23; Gold Coast, 1926-28; France and Belgium (despatches), 1939-40; Tunisia, Sicily and Italy, 1943-44; Palestine, 1945-46; seconded to Ordnance Survey, 1935-39 and 1946-. Capt., 1927; Major, 1937; Lt-Col, 1940; Col 1946; Brigadier, 1950. *Recreation:* gardening. *Address:* Woodbine Farm, Brent Knoll, Somerset. *T:* Brent Knoll 388.
                    [Died 23 June 1977.

WHEELER, Sir (Robert Eric) Mortimer, CH 1967; Kt 1952; CIE 1947; MC, TD; SPk (Sitara-i-Pakistan) 1964; MA, DLit

(London), Hon. DLitt (Bristol, Delhi, Ireland, Wales, Oxford and Liverpool); Hon. DSc (Bradford); Hon. Brigadier; FRS 1968; FBA 1941 (Sec., 1949-68); FSA (Pres., 1954-59; Vice-Pres., 1935-39; Sec., 1939; Dir, 1940-44 and 1949-54; Gold Medal, 1944); Commissioner, Royal Commission on Historical Monuments (England), 1939-58; Chairman, Ancient Monuments Board for England, 1964-66; Trustee, British Museum, 1963-73; Professor of Ancient History to Royal Academy, since 1965; Fellow of University College, London, since 1922; b 1890; m 1st, 1914, Tessa Verney, FSA (d 1936); one s ; 2nd, 1939, Mavis de Vere Cole (marr. diss. 1942; she d 1970); 3rd, 1945, Margaret Norfolk. Franks Student in Archæology, 1913; on staff of Royal Commission on Historical Monuments (England), 1913; Major, Royal Field Artillery, 1917, France, Italy, Germany (MC, despatches); Keeper of the Archæological Department, National Museum of Wales, 1920-24; Lecturer in Archæology, University of Wales, 1920-24; Director National Museum of Wales, 1924-26; Keeper and Secretary of the London Museum, 1926-44; Lecturer in British Archæology, University College, London; Hon. Director Institute of Archæology, London University, 1934-44; Dir-Gen. Archæology, India, 1944-48; Adviser in Archæological matters to Dominion of Pakistan, 1948-50; Prof. of the Archæology of the Roman Provinces, University of London, 1948-55. Lieutenant-Colonel RA, TA, 1939, raised and commanded a regiment RA, Brig., 1943 (8th Army in Africa, El Alamein to Tunis; 10th Corps in Italy, Salerno landing). Rhys Lecturer (British Academy), 1929; Norman Lockyer Lecturer (British Association), 1937; Rhind Lecturer (Edinburgh), 1951; Norton Lecturer (Arch. Inst. of America), 1952; Hobhouse Lecturer, Univ. of London, 1955; nominated Queen's Lectr in Berlin, 1968; President: Cambrian Archæological Assoc., 1931; South Eastern Union of Scientific Societies, 1932; Conf. of Delegates, British Assoc., 1933; Museums Assoc., 1937-38; Indian Museums Assoc., 1947-48; Pakistan Museums Association, 1949-50; Royal Archæological Institute, 1951-53; Section H Brit. Assoc., 1954. Hon. MRIA; Hon. Mem., Archæological Inst. of America. Hon. Life Mem., NY Acad. of Sciences, 1963; Corres. Mem., German Archæological Inst. Hon. Fellow, School of Oriental and African Studies, 1970. Led Govt Missions from India to Iran and Afghanistan, 1945-46. Directed archæological excavations at: Colchester, 1917 and 1920; Carnarvon, 1921-23; Brecon, 1924-25; Caerleon, 1926-27; Lydney, 1928-29; St Albans, 1930-33; Maiden Castle (Dorset), 1934-37; Brittany, 1938; Normandy, 1939; India, 1944-48; Pakistan, 1950 and 1958; Stanwick (Yorks) 1951-52, etc. Petrie Medal, Univ. of London, 1950; Lucy Wharton Drexel Medal, Pennsylvania Univ., 1952. OStJ. *Publications:* books on Segontium and the Roman Occupation of Wales, 1924; Prehistoric and Roman Wales, 1925; The Roman Fort near Brecon, 1926; Prehistoric and Roman Site at Lydney, 1932; The Belgic and Roman Cities of Verulamium, 1936; Maiden Castle, 1943; 5,000 Years of Pakistan, 1950; The Indus Civilisation, 1953, 1962 and 1968; Archæology from the Earth, 1954; Rome beyond the Imperial Frontiers, 1954; The Stanwick Fortifications, 1954; Hill-forts of Northern France, 1957; Early India and Pakistan, 1959; Charsada, 1962; Roman Art and Architecture, 1964; Still Digging (autobiog.), 1955; (ed) Splendours of the East, 1965, repr. 1970; Alms for Oblivion (collected essays), 1966; Roman Africa (with R. Wood), 1966; Civilizations of the Indus Valley and Beyond, 1966; Flames over Persepolis (Alexander in the East), 1968; The British Academy, 1949-68, 1970; and papers on European and Indian archæological subjects. *Address:* British Academy, Burlington House, W1V 0NS. *T:* 01-734 0457. *Club:* Athenæum.
[Died 22 July 1976.

WHEELER-BENNETT, Sir John (Wheeler), GCVO 1974 (KCVO 1959); CMG 1953; OBE 1946; MA Oxon (by decree) 1946; FBA 1972; FRSL 1958; FZS 1973; Hon. Fellow, St Antony's College, Oxford, 1961; Historian; Historical Adviser, Royal Archives, since 1959; Trustee, Imperial War Museum; b Keston, Kent, 13 Oct. 1902; 2nd surv. s of late John Wheeler Wheeler-Bennett, CBE, JP, and Christina Hill McNutt, of Truro, Nova Scotia; m 1945, Ruth Harrison Risher, Charlottesville, Va. *Educ:* Wellington House, Westgate-on-Sea; Malvern Coll. Travelled extensively; Asst Publicity Secretary, League of Nations Union, 1923-24; Founder and Hon. Secretary of the Information Service on International Affairs, 1924-30; Hon. Information Secretary, RIIA, 1927-31; Founder and Editor, 1924-32, Bulletin of International News; Lecturer in International Law and Relations, University of Virginia, 1938-39; attached British Library of Information, New York, 1939-40; Assistant-Director, British Press Service, New York, 1940-41; Special Assistant to Director-General of British Information Services in the United States, 1941-42; Head of New York Office of British Political Warfare Mission in the United States, 1942-44; European Adviser to Political Intelligence Dept of Foreign

Office, 1944, Assistant Director-General, 1945; Assistant to British Political Adviser to SHAEF, 1944-45; attached to British Prosecuting Team at War Criminal Trial, Nuremberg, 1946; British Editor-in-Chief of captured German Foreign Ministry Archives, 1946-48; Historical Adviser to Foreign Office Project for publishing GFM Archives, 1948-56; Lecturer in Internat. Politics, New College, Oxford, 1946-50; Fellow of St Antony's College, Oxford, 1950-57; Governor: Radley College, 1955-67; Cuddesdon Theol Coll., 1955-72; Lord Williams's Grammar Sch., Thame; Member Council: RIIA, 1930-38, 1959-67; Ditchley Foundn 1961-72 (Chm., 1961-63); Malvern Coll., 1955-72 (Chm., 1964-67). Leslie Stephen Lecturer, Cambridge University, 1955; Dance Memorial Lecturer, Virginia Military Inst., Lexington, Virginia, 1960; Visiting Lecturer in Politics and History, Univ. of Arizona, 1964, 1966, 1968-70, 1972-76; Page-Barbour Lectr, Univ. of Virginia, 1966; Vis. Prof. of Modern Hist., NY Univ., 1967, 1968-69, 1969-70, 1971; Scholar-in-Residence, Univ. of Virginia, 1967-68, 1971-72. Hon. Mem., Soc. of Fellows, Univ. of Virginia, 1971. Hon. Citizen of New Orleans, USA, 1949. MA Christ Church 1949; Hon. DCL Oxon, 1960; Hon. DLitt: New York, 1973; Birmingham, 1973; Arizona, 1974. *Publications:* Information on the Reduction of Armaments, 1925; Information on the Problem of Security (with F. E. Langermann), 1927; Information on the Renunciation of War, 1928; Information on the World Court, 1918-28 (with Maurice Fanshawe), 1929; Information on the Reparation Settlement (with H. Latimer), 1930; Disarmament and Security since Locarno, 1932; The Wreck of Reparations, 1933; the Disarmament Deadlock, 1934; Hindenburg, the Wooden Titan, 1936; Brest-Litovsk; The Forgotten Peace, March 1918, 1938; Munich, Prologue to Tragedy, 1948; Nemesis of Power: the German Army in Politics, 1918-45, 1953; King George VI, his Life and Reign, 1958; John Anderson, Viscount Waverley, 1962; A Wreath to Clio, 1967; (ed) Action this Day, Working with Churchill, 1968; Semblance of Peace (with Anthony Nicholls), 1972; (ed and contrib.) The History Makers, 1973; Knaves, Fools and Heroes, 1974; Special Relationships, 1975; contributor to Foreign Affairs, Virginia Quarterly Review, History Today, New York Review, Dictionary of National Biography, Encyclopædia Britannica, Virginia Magazine of History and Biography. *Address:* Garsington Manor, near Oxford. *T:* Garsington 234. *Clubs:* Beefsteak, Brooks's, Pratt's; Colonnade, University of Virginia (Charlottesville, Va); The Brook, Century.
[Died 9 Dec. 1975.

WHETTON, Prof. John Thomas, DSO 1943; OBE 1941; MC 1919; TD 1951; Professor of Mining, University of Leeds, 1945-60, now Emeritus; Private Consultant, Mining, Surveying, Geophysical Surveying, since 1960; b 27 Oct. 1894; m Effie Rickerby; no c. Educ: Universities of Leeds and Durham. MSc (Leeds); MSc (Durham); 1st Class Colliery Manager's Certificate. Practical Mining experience West and South Yorks, Durham, Northumberland, Germany, France, Belgium, Poland and Canada. Visited oil fields of the Middle East, Venezuela and Trinidad. Army service France and Russia, 1914-19. Reader in Mining, King's Coll., Univ. of Durham, 1924-39. Comd 4th Survey Regt RA TA, 1937-48; service in Balkans, Middle East, North Africa, Sicily and NW Europe. Mining Advr (Tech.), Ruhr, Germany, 1945. Pro-Vice-Chancellor, University of Leeds, 1955-57. Founder Member, International Organising Mining Committee, 1957. Nuffield Foundn and Research Coun. of Canada Lectr, 1960; Engineers Jt Coun., Lectr, American Inst. of Mining Engineers, 1964. Hon. Col, Leeds Univ. Officers' Training Corps T & AVR, 1968-69. President, Midland Institute of Mining Engineers, 1960-61. Russian Order of St Stanislav 2nd class with swords, 1919; Belgian Order of the Crown with Palm, 1945; Belgian Croix de Guerre, 1945. *Publications:* contrib. Prospecting, Boring, and Sinking sections in Coal Mining Practice, 1958; numerous research and general papers on mining and allied sciences to technical press and instns in UK, Canada, USA, Holland, Poland and Czechoslovakia, from 1925. *Recreations:* cricket and bowls. *Address:* Westbourne House, 16 Westbourne Grove, Scarborough, North Yorks. *T:* Scarborough 72432.
[Died 23 Sept. 1979.

WHINNEY, Margaret Dickens, FBA 1967; DLitt; b 4 Feb. 1897; d of Thomas Bostock Whinney and Sydney Margaret Dickens. *Educ:* private schools. Academic Diploma in Hist. of Art, Univ. of London, 1935; DLit, Univ. of London, 1940. Reader in the History of Art, Courtauld Inst. of Art, 1950-64. Hon. Sec. and Ed., Walpole Soc., 1957-72; Trustee, Sir John Soane's Museum, 1960-71; Mem., Adv. Coun., Victoria and Albert Museum, 1966-71; FSA 1944; Vice-Pres., Soc. of Antiquaries, 1960-64. Hon. FRIBA 1969. *Publications:* English Art, 1625-1714 (Oxford History of English Art) (with Oliver Millar), 1957; Sculpture in Britain, 1530-1830 (Pelican History of Art), 1964; Catalogue of Models by John Flaxman at University Coll., London (with late Rupert Gunnis), 1967; Early Flemish

Painting, 1968; Home House, 1969; Wren, 1971; English Sculpture 1720-1830, 1971; articles in Walpole Soc., Jl of Warburg and Courtauld Insts, Archæological Jl, etc. *Address:* 58 Marlborough Court, Pembroke Road, W8 6DF. *T:* 01-602 6568. *Club:* (Lady Assoc. Mem.) United Oxford & Cambridge University.   *[Died 29 Aug. 1975.*

WHIPPLE, Prof. George Hoyt; Professor of Pathology, University of Rochester School of Medicine and Dentistry, 1921-55; now Emeritus; Dean, 1921-53, now Emeritus; *b* 28 Aug. 1878; *s* of Ashley Cooper Whipple, MD, and Frances Anna Hoyt; *m* 1914, Katherine Ball Waring; one *s* one *d. Educ:* Yale University, AB, MA 1927; Johns Hopkins University, MD, Hon. LLD 1947. Assistant in Pathology, Johns Hopkins Medical School, 1905-06; Instructor, 1906-07; Pathologist, Ancon Hospital, Panama, 1907-08; Associate in Pathology, Johns Hopkins Medical School, 1909-11; Associate Professor, 1911-14; Resident Pathologist, Johns Hopkins Hospital, 1910-14; Professor of Research Medicine, Univ. of California Medical School, and Director of the Hooper Foundation for Medical Research, University of California, 1914-21; Dean of the Univ. of California Medical School, 1920-21; Board of Scientific Directors, The Rockefeller Institute for Medical Research since 1936 and Bd of Trustees, 1939-60, Emer., 1960-; Member: Nat. Acad. of Sciences, American Philosophical Society; Hon. Member: Pathological Society of Gt Brit. and Ireland; Internat. Assoc. for Dental Research; Foreign Corresponding Mem., BMA, 1957. Nobel Prize in Medicine, joint award, 1934; Charles Mickle Fellowship, Univ. of Toronto, 1938; Kober Medal Georgetown Univ., 1939; Gold-Headed Cane Award (Amer. Assoc. of Pathologists and Bacteriologists), 1961; Kovalenko Medal (National Acad. of Sciences), 1962; Distinguished Service Award, Amer. Med. Assoc., 1973; President's Medal, Univ. of Rochester, 1975. Hon. LLD Glasgow, 1951; numerous other hon. doctorates in science and laws from American and foreign universities. *Publications:* 270 medical publications. *Recreations:* fishing, hunting, all outdoor recreation. *Address:* 601 Elmwood Avenue, Rochester, NY 14642, USA.   *[Died 2 Feb. 1976.*

WHISHAW, Sir Ralph, Kt 1958; CBE 1957; Consulting Physician, Royal Hobart Hospital, Tasmania, 1955-71, retired; Consulting Physician, Repatriation Commission, Tasmania, 1936-71; *b* Croydon, 29 March 1895; *s* of late Reginald Robert Whishaw, Croydon; *m* 1921, Violet Mary, *d* of G. Beckley; one *d. Educ:* Friends' High School, Hobart; Sydney University. MB, ChM 1918; MRCP 1935; FRACP 1938; FRCP 1954. Physician Royal Hobart Hospital, 1930-55. President BMA, Tasmania Br., 1938; Vice-Pres., Royal Australasian Coll. of Physicians, 1949. Served European War, 1914-18, AIF, 7th Field Ambulance, Gallipoli; served Middle East, 1940-42 (Major). *Publications:* contrib. to Medical Jl of Australia. *Recreations:* cabinet making and photography. *Address:* 650 Sandy Bay Road, Hobart, Tasmania 7005, Australia.   *[Died 13 July 1976.*

WHITAKER, Ernest Gillett, CBE 1967; FCIT; Chairman, Central Transport Consultative Committee, 1962-68; Transport Adviser to the Board of Unilever Ltd, 1958-65; *b* 8 May 1903; *s* of Frederick and Bessie Whitaker; *m* 1929, Cissie Mucklow; one *s* one *d. Educ:* Knowbury Sch., Salop. After apprenticeship in motor engrg started own business as haulier and motor repairer, 1924. Later merged with Gupwell Gp of Cos, Birmingham; Dir, 1936-47. Ministry of Food: Area Meat and Livestock Forwarding Officer, Apr.-Dec. 1940; Asst Dir of Transport, Dec. 1940. Joined Unilever Ltd, 1947. Deputy Transport Adviser, Unilever Ltd, 1954; Director, SPD Ltd, 1954 (Chairman, 1956-58); Member: Channel Tunnel Study Gp; Rochdale Cttee of Inquiry into Major Ports of Gt Britain, 1961-62; Transport Advisory Council, 1965; National Ports Council, 1962-67; Founder Member (former Dep. Chm.), Inst. of Materials Handling; Pres. Inst. of Transport, 1962-63. *Recreations:* gardening, music, photography. *Address:* 21 Cliff Road, Worlebury, Weston-super-Mare, Avon BS22 9SE. *T:* Weston-super-Mare 28211.   *[Died 24 March 1975.*

WHITAKER, Mrs Geoffrey Charles Francis; *see* Love, Enid Rosamond.

WHITBY, Anthony Charles; Controller, BBC Radio 4, since 1969; *b* 19 Nov. 1929; *o s* of Charles Thomas Whitby and Ethel May Whitby (*née* King); *m* 1954, Joy Field; three *s. Educ:* Bristol Cathedral Sch.; St Edmund Hall and Nuffield Coll., Oxford. National Service (Gloucestershire Regt and Intell. Corps), 1947-49. Asst Principal and Principal, Colonial Office, 1954-59. Joined BBC as Radio Current Affairs Producer, 1959; transferred BBC Television, 1961; Producer of Gallery, 1963-65; Dep. Editor of 24 Hours, 1965-67, Editor, 1967-68; Secretary of the BBC, 1969. *Recreation:* writing plays. *Address:* 20 Brunswick Gardens, W8. *T:* 01-229 1181. *[Died 25 Feb. 1975.*

WHITBY, Sir Bernard James, Kt 1947; Chartered Accountant; Partner, A. F. Ferguson & Co., Chartered Accountants, Bombay and elsewhere; *b* 8 March 1892; *s* of late Frank Freeman Whitby, Bridgwater, and Louisa, *d* of late Rev. R. James, Yeovil; *m* 1st, 1919, Louey (*d* 1925), *e d* of late Rev. W. T. Soper, Croyde, Devon; 2nd, 1935, Kathleen Mary, *d* of late Metford Rowe, Bridgwater, Som.; two *s. Educ:* Taunton School. Mem. Indian Accountancy Board, 1934-47. JP Bombay, 1930-47. *Recreations:* music, sailing. *Address:* Villa Capri, Daddyhole Road, Torquay, Devon TQ1 2ED. *T:* 27959. *Club:* Royal Bombay Yacht (Bombay).   *[Died 26 June 1973.*

WHITBY, G. Stafford, PhD, DSc, ARCS; FRSC; LLD (Hon.); ScD (Hon.); Professor Emeritus of Rubber Chemistry and Director of Rubber Research, Univ. of Akron, Ohio, USA; *b* 26 May 1887; *s* of late Stafford B. Whitby, MBE, Hull; *m* 1915, Wynne Atkinson (*d* 1955; author of Pilgrim Soul, London, 1961), Hampstead; one *s* one *d*; *m* 1964, Claire Newman. *Educ:* The Royal Coll. of Science, London. Demonstrator, Imp. Coll. of Sci. and Technology, 1906-10; in the rubber-growing countries of the East, as Chief Chemist to the Société Financière des Caoutchoucs, 1910-17; Department of Chemistry, McGill University, Montreal, 1917-29; Professor of Organic Chemistry, 1923-29; Director, Division of Chemistry, National Research Laboratories, Ottawa, 1929-39; Director of Chemical Research Laboratory, Teddington, 1939-42; Chm., Canadian Synthetic Rubber Technical Advisory Committee, 1942-44; Pres. Canadian Chemical Association, 1928-29; Pres. Canadian Institute of Chemistry, 1927-28; Officier d'Académie, 1928; Editor, Rubber Section, International Critical Tables; First Colwyn Gold Medallist, Institution of the Rubber Industry, 1928; Charles Goodyear medal, Amer. Chem. Soc., 1954; Foundn Lectr, Inst. of the Rubber Industry, 1962; Jt Editor, Series on High Polymers, 1941; Editor (with H. Mark), Scientific Progress in the Field of Rubber and Synthetic Elastomers, 1946; Editor-in-Chief, Synthetic Rubber, 1954. Dunlop Lect. Award for Macromolecular Science, Chem. Inst. of Canada, 1971. *Publications:* Plantation Rubber and the Testing of Rubber, 1920; numerous scientific papers dealing with the chemistry of rubber, colloid chemistry, etc. *Recreations:* reading, walking. *Address:* University of Akron, Akron, Ohio 44304, USA. *Club:* University (Akron, O).
                        [Died 10 Jan. 1972.

WHITE, Alexander Hay, CBE 1959; Director, Lithgows (Holdings) Ltd, Kingston Shipbuilding Yard, Port Glasgow; Part-time Member, Iron and Steel Board, 1962-67; *b* 1898; *m* 1929, Louisa Rowan, *d* of late William Cherry Hay, Jordanhill. Assistant Director of Merchant Shipbuilding, Admiralty, 1941-45. Director: Tontine Hotel (Greenock) Ltd; Ferguson Bros (Port Glasgow), Ltd. Past President of the Shipbuilding Conference (1961-63). FBIM. *Recreation:* golf. *Address:* Thorndene, Kilmacolm, Renfrewshire.   *[Died 4 Jan. 1975.*

WHITE, Anne Margaret Wilson, CBE 1971; District Nursing Officer, Liverpool Area Health Authority (Teaching), Central/Southern District, since 1974; *b* 1916; *d* of Alexander Rankin and Elizabeth White. *Educ:* Rothesay Acad. SRN, SCM, RFN. Nursing Sister, QARANC, 1942-46; Area Organiser for Scotland, Royal Coll. of Nursing, 1946-48; Registrar and Sec., Joint Nursing and Midwives Council for Northern Ireland, 1948-53; Chief Nursing Officer, Northern Ireland Hospitals Authority, 1953-61; Matron, Royal Southern Hosp. Liverpool and Liverpool Royal Infirmary, 1961-68; Dir of Nursing and Chief Nursing Officer, United Liverpool Hosps, 1968-74. *Publications:* contrib. Nursing Times, District Nurse, Internat. Nursing Jl. *Recreations:* ornithology, fishing, reading. *Address:* 1 Ibbotson's Lane, Liverpool L17 1AL. *T:* 051-724 3251.   *[Died 25 Jan. 1976.*

WHITE, Antonia, FRSL; author; *b* 31 Mar. 1899; *d* of Cecil George Botting, MA, and Christine Julia Botting (*née* White); *m* 1930, H. T. Hopkinson (marr. diss., 1938); two *d. Educ:* Convent of the Sacred Heart, Roehampton; St Paul's Girls' School. Copywriter, W. S. Crawford Ltd, 1924-31; Assistant Editor, Life and Letters, 1928-29; Freelance Journalist, 1931-34; Copywriter, J. Walter Thompson, 1934-35; Fashion Editor, Daily Mirror, 1935-37; Fashion Editor, Sunday Pictorial, 1937-39; BBC 1940-43; Political Intelligence Dept (French Section), FO, 1943-45. Occupied in writing novels, short stories and occasional critical articles and reviews, also translating from the French. Denyse Clairouin prize for translation, 1950. Visiting Lecturer in English, St Mary's College, Notre Dame, Indiana, 1959. *Publications:* Frost in May, 1933; The Lost Traveller, 1950; The Sugar House, 1952; Beyond the Glass, 1954; Strangers (short stories), 1954; Minka and Curdy, 1957; The Hound and the Falcon, 1966; Life with Minka and Curdy, 1970; over 30 trans from the French including Maupassant's Une Vie, 1949,

Colette's La Chatte, 1953, Claudine à L'Ecole, 1956, Claudine à Paris, 1958, Claudine en Ménage, 1960; Claudine s'en va, 1961; Le Tendron (Selected Short Stories), 1959; L'Entrave, 1964; L'Ingénue Libertine, 1968; Loys Masson, Le Notaire des Noirs, 1962; H. Fabre-Luce, Haute Cour, 1963; Christine Arnothy, Le Cardinal Prisonnier, 1964; Mémoires du Chevalier d'Eon, 1970; Simenon, La Cage de Verre, 1973; Paul-Gabriel Boucé, Les Romans de Smollett, 1974; Voltaire, Histoire de Charles XII, 1976. *Recreations:* reading, seeing friends, crosswords. *Address:* 42D Courtfield Gardens, SW5. *T:* 01-370 2661.
[*Died* 10 *April* 1980.

WHITE, Col Archie Cecil Thomas, VC, MC, BA; *b* 1891; *s* of Thomas White and Jean Finlayson; *m* Jean G. Will, MA (*d* 1960); three *d. Educ:* Harrogate Grammar School; King's College, London (Univ. Scholar in English Literature, 1912). Served with the Green Howards, 1914-19; with Army Educational Corps, 1920-47. Principal, City Literary Institute, 1948-56; Member of Senate, University of London, 1953-56. Deputy Colonel-Commandant, Royal Army Educational Corps, 1960-69. Officier d'Académie; FKC. *Address:* Brucklay, Upper Park Road, Camberley. *Club:* Naval and Military.
[*Died* 20 *May* 1971.

WHITE, Cyril Grove C.; *see* Costley-White.

WHITE, Cyril Montgomery, CMG 1972; QC 1946; MA; Chairman, Foreign Compensation Commission, 1958-72; *b* 10 August 1897; *o s* of William Montgomery White and Mary Augusta Mourilyan; *m* 1950, Jessie Thompson (OBE 1945), *d* of late James Kidd of Linlithgow; one *d. Educ:* Colet Court; St Paul's School; Corpus Christi College, Oxford. Served in European War (Royal Flying Corps and Royal Air Force) July 1916-Jan. 1919. Called to Bar, Lincoln's Inn, 1923; Bencher, 1952; Treasurer, 1971. Served War of 1939-45 (RAFVR) Aug. 1939-Jan. 1944; Pres. (except for Scottish Proceedings) Transport Arbitration Tribunal, 1947-57. *Publications:* The Conveyancers' Year Book 1947. Senior Editor, Underhill on Trusts and Trustees, 10th edn, 1950, 11th edn, 1959. Has contributed to Halsbury's Laws of England, 3rd edition (Titles: Landlord and Tenant, 1958; Real Property, 1960). *Recreation:* reading. *Address:* Bartlemas, 7 Dover Road, Sandwich, Kent. *T:* Sandwich 613336; 2 Stone Buildings, Lincoln's Inn, WC2. *T:* 01-242 7637. *Club:* United Oxford & Cambridge University.
[*Died* 27 *Sept.* 1980.

WHITE, Lt-Col David A. P.; *see* Price-White.

WHITE, (Elizabeth) Evelyne (McIntosh); *d* of late J. A. Jardine and Alexandrina, *d* of Alexander McIntosh, Manchester; *m* 1st, 1924, W. Bertram White (*d* 1960); 2nd, 1965, Ernest James Battey. *Educ:* Harris Acad., Dundee; University of Liverpool, BSc, MA. Mathematics Mistress, Runcorn Grammar School; Mathematics Mistress, Wallasey High School for Girls; Vice-Principal, Mistress of Method and Lecturer in Education, National Society's Training College for Teachers of Domestic Subjects, London; Editor of The Schoolmistress, 1926-35 (Director, Schoolmistress Newspaper Co.); Lecturer for the Ministry of Information, 1940; Chairman, YWCA Committee, Mansfield; Member of Panel and Executive of Ministry of Information Anglo-American Panel; Member of Mansfield Hospital Board; Governor of Mansfield Technical College; and of Mansfield Queen Elizabeth's Grammar School for Girls; Chairman of Mansfield Juvenile Court; Chm. of Probation Case Committee; Member Notts Combined Probation Cttee; First Woman Chairman, Mansfield Borough Bench, 1957 (formerly Deputy Chairman); Vice-Chm., Women's Sub-Cttee, Mansfield and Dist Employment Cttee. JP Mansfield, 1942-62. *Publications:* Practical Science for Girls, 1920, now in 4th ed.; Practical Courses in Housecraft, 1924; Section on Domestic Science in Girls' Book of Careers, 1925; Housecraft, Vol. VI of Modern Teaching, 1929; The Household from A-Z, 1931; The White-Watson Menu and Recipe Book, 1937; Teach Yourself to Cook, 1938 (6th new edition, 1951); The Russell Dramatic Readers, 1938; Practical English Revision, 1938; Winifred Holtby as I knew her, 1938; Practical Everyday English for Juniors, Books I and II, 1941; The End Crowns All, 1943; Practical Modern English, Pts I, II, and III, 1947; Full Tide, 1946; Love's Enough; Mock Marriage; Love's Conquest; The Lady Entertains; (joint) Essential Everyday Arithmetic for Girls, 1950; Production Notes for The Russell Dramatic Readers; Second Series, 1951; Twenty Time-Tests in English, 1951; Cook Without Fears, 1951; Come Cooking with me, 1953; The Russell Literary Readers, Bks I, II and III, 1953; Twenty Time Tests in Arithmetic, 1954; English for the Primary School, Books 1-4, 1956; Poetry for the Primary School, Books 1-4, 1957; Women of Devotion and Courage, 6 Books, 1957; Poetry for Today (Books 1-4) 1960; Good Everyday English (books 1-4)

1962; Etiquette for the Teen-ager, 1967; English for Junior Forms, Books 1-5, 1968; Poetry for Junior Forms, Books 1-5, 1968; ed (with E. James Battey), The Spanish Cook Book, 1969, and several other foreign cookery books; short stories to various magazines; books reviewer and contributor to newspapers and magazines. *Recreations:* golf, dancing, fishing, motoring, foreign travel. *Address:* Flat 2, 8 The Leas, Folkestone, Kent. *T:* Folkestone 55718. *Clubs:* Royal Commonwealth Society, National Book League, Vanity Fair.   [*Died* 16 *Jan.* 1972.

WHITE, Sir Eric (Henry) W.; *see* Wyndham White.

WHITE, Sir (Eric) Richard Meadows, 2nd Bt, *cr* 1937; *b* 29 June 1910; *s* of Sir Robert Eaton White, 1st Bt, and Rose Dorothy (*d* 1967), *d* of Charles Pearce-Serocold, Taplow Hill, Bucks; *S* father, 1940; *m* 1939, Lady Elisabeth Mary Gladys Townshend (marr. diss. 1947; she *d* 1950), *o d* of 6th Marquess Townshend; one *s*; *m* 1947, Ann Heron, *d* of A. G. Eccles, 16 Sussex Mansions, Old Brompton Rd, SW7. *Educ:* Eton. *Heir: s* Christopher Robert Meadows White [*b* 26 Aug. 1940; *m* 1962, Anne Marie Ghislaine, *yr d* of late Major Tom Brown and of Mrs R. W. Taggart-Browne, Hove, Sussex]. *Address:* The Vine, Presteigne, Radnorshire.   [*Died* 26 *April* 1972.

WHITE, Brig. Eric Stuart, DSO 1918; OStJ; late RASC; *b* 15 Nov. 1888; *o s* of late W. W. White of Lee, Kent; *m* 1st, 1914; one *d*; 2nd, 1939, Ysobel Dora (*d* 1959), *d* of Lt-Col W. P. Murray, DSO, Farnham. *Educ:* Felsted; Sandhurst. Served European War, 1914-18, NW Persia, Iraq (DSO, despatches, Officer, Order of Crown of Belgium; Belgian Croix de Guerre, with two palms); retired, 1944. *Address:* The Cottage, Donnington, Chichester, West Sussex.   [*Died* 25 *June* 1979.

WHITE, Ethelbert, RWS; Artist; *b* 26 Feb. 1891; *s* of Bernard Richard White; *m* 1911, Elizabeth Crofton-Dodwell. *Educ:* St George's College, Weybridge, Surrey. Became a Member of the New English Art Club, 1921, Royal Society of Painters in Water-colours, 1930. Exhibited at Venice International Exhibition, 1929. Work purchased by: Tate Gallery; Contemporary Art Society; Municipal Galleries throughout England and Ireland. *Publications:* Fine Art Prints: 1931, 1936, 1940. *Recreation:* music. *Address:* The Pink Cottage, 14 Hampstead Grove, NW3.   [*Died March* 1972.

WHITE, Evelyne; *see* White, E. E. M.

WHITE, Lt-Col Harold Fletcher, CMG 1919; DSO 1917; *b* 13 June 1883; *s* of F. J. White, Saumarez, Armidale, NSW; *m*; two *s* two *d*. Served European War, 1915-19 (despatches, DSO, Croix de Guerre, CMG); MLC New South Wales, 1932-34. *Address:* Bald Blair, Guyra, NSW 2365, Australia.
[*Died* 20 *Feb.* 1971.

WHITE, Sir Headley Dymoke, 3rd Bt *cr* 1922; *b* 15 April 1914; *s* of Sir Dymoke White, 2nd Bt and Isabelle, *yr d* of James G. MacGowan; *S* father, 1968; *m* 1943, Elizabeth Victoria Mary, *er d* of Wilfrid Wrightson; one *s* two *d. Educ:* Winchester; Trinity Coll., Cambridge. *Heir: s* John Woolmer White, *b* 4 Feb. 1947.
[*Died* 25 *Feb.* 1971.

WHITE, Surg. Rear-Adm. Sir Henry Ellis Yeo, KCVO 1947 (CVO 1927; MVO 1922); OBE 1925; late RN; *b* 1888; *s* of late W. H. White, MD, Airton, Yorks; *m* 1921, Adelaide Beatrice, *d* of late Lt-Col G. F. Napier; one *s* one *d. Educ:* Edinburgh Univ. (MB, ChB); MD, FRCS Edinburgh. Accompanied Prince of Wales, Canada, 1919, Australasia, 1920, the East, 1921-22 in HMS Renown, and Africa and S America in HMS Repulse, 1925, Duke and Duchess of York to New Zealand and Australia, 1927; and the King and Queen to Canada and the United States, 1939, and South Africa, 1947; HMY Victoria and Albert, 1927-39; retired list, 1948. CStJ 1948. *Address:* 36 Lourensford Road, Somerset West, CP, South Africa.   [*Died* 18 *July* 1976.

WHITE, Hugh Fortescue Moresby, CMG 1943; *b* 15 Sept. 1891; *s* of Lt-Col R. F. Moresby White, OBE, VD, Grantham; *m* Betty Sophia Pennington, *d* of Capt. Frank Brandt, RN; one *s. Educ:* Malvern College; St John's College, Oxford. Administrative Service, Nigeria, 1915-45; Acting Chief Commissioner, Southern Provinces, 1938, Western Provinces 1939 and 1944; Senior Resident, Oyo Province, 1940-44. *Address:* Le Clos D'Avranche, St Mary, Jersey, Channel Islands. *T:* Central 61631.   [*Died* 23 *Jan.* 1979.

WHITE, Leslie Gordon, CBE 1949; retired; *b* 1889; *s* of late Henry Tom White; *m* 1919, Dorothy Morgan (*d* 1961). *Educ:* Eastbourne Grammar School; Entered Inland Revenue Department, 1908; Dep. Chief Inspector of Taxes, 1947-50; retired 1950. *Address:* 35 Neville Close, Basingstoke, Hants.
[*Died* 14 *Jan.* 1979.

WHITE, Margaret B.; *see* Bourke-White.

WHITE, Norman Lewis, MD, FRCS, FRCOG; retired as Obstetrician, University College Hospital; Gynæcological Surgeon, Royal Northern Hospital; Gynæcologist, Ministry of Pensions Hospital, Roehampton, and West Herts Hospital. *Educ:* University of Cambridge; University College Hospital, London. MRCS, LRCP 1923; BA Cambridge (1st Cl. Nat. Sci. Tripos), MA, BChir, 1929; FRCS 1929; MD 1933; FRCOG 1943. Examiner in Midwifery, Society of Apothecaries; Fellow of the Royal Society of Medicine. Formerly: Associate Examiner in Obstetrics and Gynæcology, University of London; First Assistant, Obstetrical Unit, University College Hospital; Examiner, Midwives Conjoint Board. *Address:* Fern Cottage, Norton Green, Freshwater, Isle of Wight PO40 9RY.
[Died 3 Oct. 1978.

WHITE, Paul Dudley; American physician; cardiac specialist since 1913; *b* Roxbury, Mass, 6 June 1886; *s* of Herbert Warren White; *m* 1924, Ina Reid; one *s* one *d. Educ:* Roxbury Latin School; Harvard College. AB Harvard, 1908; MD, 1911. Intern. Mass. General Hosp., Boston, 1911-13; Sheldon travelling fellowship, Univ. Coll. Hospital Medical School, London, 1913-14; teaching fellow, Harvard Medical Sch., 1914-20, to Clin. Prof. Med., Harvard, till 1949. Resident in medicine, Mass. General Hospital, 1914-16; served as medical officer, BEF, France, 1916; Capt. US Army Medical Corps, 1917; with AEF, 1917-19; medical officer, Amer. Red Cross, Macedonia, 1919; returned to Mass. Gen. Hosp., 1919, physician in charge cardiac clinics and laboratory, until 1949, subseq. Consultant in Medicine. A founder of American Heart Assoc., 1923; Vice-Pres., 1939-40; Pres., 1940-42; Sec., section pharmacol. and therapeutics, Amer. Med. Assoc., 1921-24, Chm. 1924-25; Chm. subcttee on cardiovascular diseases, National Research Council, 1940-46; Exec. Dir, Nat. Advis. Heart Coun., 1948-56. Vice-Pres. Internat. Soc. of Cardiology, 1950, Pres., 1954; Pres., Internat. Cardiology Foundation. Member: Amer. Acad. Arts and Sciences, RCP (Eng.), 1962; Roy. Soc. Med. (Eng.); Nat. Acad. of Med. of France; Soviet Academy of Medical Sciences, 1961, etc. Distinguished Service Medal, Amer. Med. Assoc., 1952; Albert Lasker award, 1953; Freedom Medal (USA), 1964. Holds honorary degrees from American and European universities and many decorations. *Publications:* Heart Disease (1st edition, 1931, revised and re-issued 1932, 1937, 1944 and 1951); Heart Disease in General Practice, 1937; (jointly) Electrocardiography in Practice (1st edn, 1941, 3rd, 1952); (jointly) Coronary Heart Disease in Young Adults: A Multidisciplinary Study, 1954; Clues in the Diagnosis and Treatment of Heart Disease, 1955; Hearts: their long follow-up, 1967; (trans., with Prof. Alfred Boursy) Lancisi, De Subitaneis Mortibus, 1971; Autobiography, 1971; contribs to medical jls. *Address:* 264 Beacon Street, Boston, Mass, USA; 115 Juniper Road, Belmont, Mass. *Clubs:* Harvard, St Botolph, Saturday (Boston).
[Died 31 Oct. 1973.

WHITE, Sir Richard; *see* White, Sir E. R. M.

WHITE, Robert George, CBE 1949; MSc; *b* 30 April 1885; *m* 1919, Iola (*d* 1975), 2nd *d* of late E. O. Price, MD, Bangor; two *s* two *d. Educ:* Archbishop Holgates School, York; Leeds University. Lecturer University College, Bangor, 1905-10; County Agricultural Organiser, Edinburgh and East of Scotland Agricultural College, 1910-12; Ministry of Agriculture, 1912; Professor of Agriculture, University College of North Wales, 1913-45; Director of Animal Breeding and Genetics Research Organisation of the Agricultural Research Council, 1945-50, retired 1950. Gold Medal, Royal Welsh Agricultural Society, 1965. Hon. DSc Univ. of Wales, 1967. *Address:* c/o G. R. White, 2 Smeaton Grove, Inveresk, Musselburgh, Midlothian.
[Died 16 June 1976.

WHITE, Rt. Rev. Russell Berridge; MA (Oxon), Dipl. Theology (Oxon); *b* 13 Dec. 1896; *yr s* of late Benjamin Beeson, Poplar, London; *m* 1926, Sarah Margaret, *e d* of Rev. J. A. Bunch, Manby, Lincs; two *s* one *d* (and one *s* decd). *Educ:* City of Oxford School; St Edmund Hall, Oxford (1919-22); Wycliffe Hall, Oxford (1922-23). Served European War, 1914-18 (Mons Star, etc.); Queen's Own Oxfordshire Hussars. Curate St Philemon, Toxteth, 1923-27; Clerical Supt, Liverpool CE Scripture Readers Society, 1927-29, Secretary from 1932; Vicar of St Chrysostom, Everton, 1929-33; Secretary, Evangelical Churchmen's Ordination Council, 1933-59; Curate of St Mary Woolnoth, London and offg Chap. Mercer's Co., 1934-37; Vicar of St Stephen, E Twickenham, 1937-45; Vicar of Tonbridge, 1945-59; Rural Dean of Tonbridge, 1946-59; Suffragan Bishop of Tonbridge, 1959-68. Proctor in Convocation, 1947-64. *Recreations:* music, gardening. *Address:* 11 Sondes Place Drive, Dorking, Surrey. *T:* Dorking 3445. *[Died 10 Dec. 1978.*

WHITE, William Lindsay; Journalist; *b* 17 June 1900; *s* of William Allen White and Sallie Lindsay; *m* 29 April 1931, Kathrine Klinkenberg; one *d. Educ:* Harvard University. Elected to Kansas State Legislature, 1930, and served a term. Staff of Washington Post, 1935, Fortune Magazine, 1937. War Correspondent for various American Newspapers and Columbia Broadcasting System (European correspondent), 1939-40; Roving Editor, Readers Digest, 1942; Editor the Emporia Gazette, 1944. Mem. Board of Overseers of Harvard Univ., 1950-56; Member: American Society of Newspaper Editors; Internat. Press Inst.; Inter-American Press Inst. Director: Theodore Roosevelt Memorial Assoc.; American Cttee for Liberation; American Assoc. of Indian Affairs; American Friends of the Middle East; Freedom House; Member National Committee, American Civil Liberties Union; Fellow American Numismatic Society. *Publications:* What People Said, 1938; Journey for Margaret, 1941 (filmed); They were Expendable, 1942 (filmed); Queens Die Proudly, 1943; Report on the Russians, 1945; Report on the Germans, 1947; Lost Boundaries, 1948 (filmed); Land of Milk and Honey, 1949; Bernard Baruch: Portrait of a Citizen, 1950; Back Down the Ridge, 1953; The Captives of Korea, 1957; The Little Toy Dog, 1962; Report on the Asians, 1969. *Address:* 160 East 66th Street, New York, NY 10021, USA. *Clubs:* Century, Harvard, Overseas Press, Dutch Treat (NY); National Press (Washington). *[Died 26 July 1973.*

WHITEFOORD, Maj.-Gen. Philip Geoffrey, OBE 1940; MC 1918; DL; *b* 24 September 1894; *e s* of late Rev. Philip Whitefoord and late Gertrude Relton Whitefoord; *m* 1930, Helen Marjorie (*d* 1969), *d* of late Arthur Edward Lord, The Mount, Hallow, Worcs; one *d. Educ:* Realgymnasium, Stuttgart; St John's, Leatherhead; Staff College, Camberley; Imperial Defence College. 2nd Lt, 3rd Bn Lincolnshire Regt, SR, 1912; 2nd Lt, Royal Field Artillery, 1914. Served European War of 1914-18 (despatches twice): France and Belgium, 1915-19. Barrister-at-Law, Gray's Inn, 1930. Bt Major, 1931; Bt Lt-Col, 1935. Served War of 1939-45: France, 1939-40; GSO1 (Intelligence), GHQ, BEF, 1939-40; GSO1 5 Div., 1940; Col, 1940; Brig., Dep. Dir Mil. Intelligence, War Office, 1941; BGS 8 Corps, 1942; Maj.-Gen. Intelligence COSSAC, 1943; Actg Maj.-Gen., 1943; BGS, GHQ, W Africa, 1944; BGS Scottish Comd and Chief of Staff, Allied Forces, Norway, 1944-45; retired (Hon. Maj.-Gen.), 1945. Contested (C) Lowestoft Div., General Election, 1950. West Suffolk County Council: Mem. Council, 1946; CA 1958; Chm. of Council, 1957-65; DL Suffolk, 1962. Comdr with Star, Order of St Olav, Norway, 1946. *Recreation:* shooting. *Address:* Falkland House, Long Melford, Sudbury, Suffolk. *T:* Long Melford 456. *Club:* Army and Navy.
[Died 28 Oct. 1975.

WHITEHEAD, Sir Edgar Cuthbert Fremantle, KCMG 1954 (CMG 1952); OBE 1944; *b* 1905; *s* of late Sir James Beethom Whitehead, KCMG. *Educ:* University College, Oxford (BA 1926, MA 1929). Served War, 1939-45: W Africa (OBE) and with Air Despatch in United Kingdom. Member of the Legislative Assembly for Southern Rhodesia, 1939-40, 1946-53, 1958-65; Acting High Commissioner for S Rhodesia in the UK, 1945-46; Ministry of Finance, and of Posts and Telegraphs, Southern Rhodesia, 1946-53, retd; Member Council University of Rhodesia and Nyasaland, 1955-58; Minister for the Federation of Rhodesia and Nyasaland in Washington, 1957-58. Elected MP for Salisbury North constituency (United Federal Party) in Southern Rhodesia General Election, June 1958. Minister of Native Affairs, 1958-60; Prime Minister of Southern Rhodesia, Feb. 1958-Dec. 1962; Leader of the Opposition, 1962-65 (United Federal Party); returned to England on retirement, 1965. *Address:* Gardeners Cottage, Newtown, Newbury, Berks.
[Died 22 Sept. 1971.

WHITEHEAD, Commander Edward, CBE 1967 (OBE 1961); on board of Bahamas Development Corporation and other Bahamian companies; *b* 20 May 1908; *s* of Walter and Amy Whitehead; *m* 1940, Adinah (known as Tommy) (*d* 1976); one *s* one step *d. Educ:* Aldershot County High School. General Accident Assurance Company, 1925-39. Served RNVR, 1939-46. General Secretary, British Assoc. for Commercial and Industrial Educn, 1946; HM Treasury, 1947-50; joined Schweppes Ltd, 1950; Pres., Schweppes (USA) Ltd, 1953-67, later Chm. Former Director: Cadbury Schweppes Ltd; Cunard Steam-Ship Co. Ltd; General Cigar Co. Inc., etc. *Publications:* How to Live the Good Life, 1977; various articles. *Recreations:* sailing, swimming, walking, beagling, fox hunting, ski-ing. *Address:* Lyford Cay Club, PO Box N7776, Nassau, Bahamas. *Clubs:* Lansdowne; RN Sailing Assoc.; Lyford Cay (Nassau).
[Died 16 April 1978.

WHITEHEAD, Comdr Walter Edward; *see* Whitehead, Comdr E.

WHITEHORN, Rev. Roy Drummond, MBE 1918; MA (Cambridge; Oxford by incorporation); Hon. DD: Glasgow, 1946; Knox College, Toronto, 1950; *b* 4 Aug. 1891; *s* of late Joseph Hammond Whitehorn, MVO, Past Prime Warden of the Goldsmiths' Company, and late Jane Elizabeth, *d* of Rev. R. S. Drummond, DD; *m* 1921, Constance Margaret, MA Cambridge (*d* 1976), *d* of late J. A. Ryley, Birmingham; two *s* one *d. Educ:* St Paul's Sch., London; Trinity Coll. (Scholar) and Westminster College, Cambridge (Barnes, Browne, Waddington, Univ. Classical Scholarships). Class I Div. I Classical Tripos Pt I, 1912; Class II Moral Sciences Tripos Pt II, 1914; Secretary, Army Department, YMCA of India, Burma and Ceylon, 1915-19; Lieut 37th (Presidency) Battn Indian Defence Force; Asst Secretary, Student Christian Movement of GB and I, 1921-23; Ordained, 1923, Presbyterian Church of England; Minister, Selangor, Federated Malay States, 1923-27; York, 1928-33; Presbyterian Chaplain and Minister, St Columba's, Oxford, 1933-38; Balliol and Christ Church, Oxford; Moderator, Free Church Federal Council, 1943-44; Moderator, General Assembly of Presbyterian Church of England, 1950; member of Central Cttee, World Council of Churches, 1948-54; Select Preacher, Cambridge University, 1945, 1949, 1951, 1961 and 1963; Sen. Proctor, 1945-46. Editor: Cambridge Review, 1913-14; Journal of Presbyterian Historical Soc. of England, 1940-47. Liveryman of the Goldsmiths' Company. Principal, Westminster College, Cambridge, 1954-63; Professor of Church History, 1938-63. *Publications:* Hibbert Lecture, Beginnings of Nonconformity, 1964; articles in Chambers's Encyclopædia and various periodicals. *Recreations:* formerly swimming (CUSC 1912-14, Capt. 1913), Rugby football (Old Paulines, Middlesex, Selangor). *Address:* Flat 5, Fenners Lawn, Gresham Road, Cambridge CB1 2EH. *T:* Cambridge 68487. *Clubs:* Union Society, Hawks, Rotary (Cambridge). *[Died 14 Nov. 1976.*

WHITELAW, David; *b* 1876; Inventor of Games, Lexicon, Alfa-Cubes, Cross-Sums, 1936, Carlette, Sokka, Picture-Rummey, Drafts, 1938, Les Rois de France (Paris), 1952, and Monarchy. *Publications:* M'Stodger's Affinity, 1896; The Gang; Moon of the Valleys; Princess Galva; The Man with the Red Beard; The Secret of Chauville; Girl from the East; The Little Hour of Peter Wells; The League of Saint Louis; A Castle in Bohemia; The Mystery of Enid Bellairs; The Imposter, 1915; A Flutter in Kings, 1916; The Madgwick Affair, 1917; The Master of Merlains; The Valley of Bells, 1918; Man on the Dover Road, 1919; Ballet-scene Carmagnole (music by Herman Finck); Pirates' Gold, 1920; Little Lady of Arrock, 1922; The Stones of Khor, 1923; For Conduct Unbefitting, 1925; The Villa Petroff, 1926; The Man from Mexico City, 1927; Mystery at Furze Acres; Spanish Heels; Number Fifteen; The Roof; Murder Calling; Hotel Sinister, 1936; Wolfs Crag; The Big Picture; Corpus Delicti; The Feud, 1937; The Face; A Bonfire of Leaves, 1938; Frame-Up, 1939; Blackmail-de-Luxe, 1939; Girl Friday, 1940; The Jackal, 1941; Horace Steps Out, 1941; Black-Out Murder, 1942; The Lexicon Murders, 1944; The Ryecroft Verdict, 1945; Lovers-in-Waiting, 1946; Garments of Repentance, 1948; The Moor, 1949; The House in Cavendish Square, 1950; The Yellow Door, 1951; Legacy in Green, 1953; Murder Besieged, 1953; Presumed Dead, 1955; I Could a Tale Unfold, 1957; *plays:* Murder Calling, Theatre Royal, Norwich; The Yellow Book, BBC; Ships That Pass (Television); The Feud; Murder Calling; late Editor, London Magazine. *Address:* The Old Stables, Courtlands Avenue, Esher, Surrey. *T:* Esher 6344. *Clubs:* Savage, Crimes. *[Died 8 Sept. 1971.*

WHITELEY, Captain Sir (Herbert) Maurice H.; *see* Huntington-Whiteley.

WHITEMAN, George W., MA Oxon; Consultant, The Antique Collector, since 1973 (Editor, 1930-71); *b* 28 Nov. 1903; *m* 1931, Mary Vernon, *d* of Rowland Walker; three *s* one *d. Educ:* Highgate School; Queen's College, Oxford. Asst Editor, The Bazaar, Exchange and Mart, 1926; Editor, 1927-29; editorial posts on The Clarion, 1930, and The Friend, 1932-36. Chief Billeting Officer, Saffron Walden Borough, 1940-42; Personnel Secretary, Friends Service Council, 1945-68. *Publications:* Some Famous English Country Homes, 1951; Halls and Treasures of the City Companies, 1970; The Collector's Round, 1971. *Address:* Dykes End, Gibson Close, Saffron Walden, Essex. *[Died 10 March 1974.*

WHITFIELD, Maj.-Gen. John Yeldham, CB 1945; DSO 1943 and bar 1944; OBE 1942; psc; retired; Colonel, The Queen's Royal Regiment, 1954-59; *b* 11 October 1899; *y s* of late Rev. F. W. G. Whitfield, Caerleon, Mon. and Roehampton; *m* Sheelagh Norah Dundas, *y d* of late H. C. Quin, Inch, County Wexford, Ireland; no *c. Educ:* Monmouth School; RMC Sandhurst. 2nd Lt The Queen's Regt 1918; Capt. 1934; Major, 1938; Temp. Lt-Col 1940; Col 1945; Maj.-Gen. 1946. Employed with Royal

West African Frontier Force, 1924-30; employed King's African Rifles (Bde Major), 1937-39; served War of 1939-45 (OBE, DSO and Bar, CB); Commander Legion of Merit (US), Order of Red Star (Russia); Comd 15 Inf. Bde, 1944; GOC 56 (London) Div., 1944-46; GOC 50 Div. and Northumbrian District, 1946-48; Chief of Staff, Northern Command, 1948-51; Inspector of Recruiting, War Office, 1952-55, retired 1955. *Address:* Marden Well, Chiddingfold, Surrey. *T:* Wormley 2027. *Club:* Army and Navy. *[Died 23 Sept. 1971.*

WHITING, Winifred Ada, MA (London); retired, 1958; *b* 6 Jan. 1898; *d* of Harry Whiting and Ada Elizabeth Kent. *Educ:* County School, Putney; King's College, London. Teaching posts at Kesteven and Sleaford High School, Lincs; William Gibb's School, Faversham, Kent; St Paul's Girls' School; Headmistress, Girls' County Grammar School, Bromley, Kent; Principal, CF Mott Training College, Liverpool; Principal, Nonington Coll. of Physical Educn, near Dover, Kent, retd. *[Died 16 May 1979.*

WHITLEY, Very Rev. Dr Henry Charles, CVO 1974; MA (Edinburgh), PhD (Edinburgh), Hon. DD (Glasgow); HRSA, 1971; Minister of the High Kirk of Edinburgh, St Giles' Cathedral, 1954-72, now Emeritus; Chaplain to the Queen in Scotland, 1963-76, Extra Chaplain since 1976; Chaplain to Royal Scottish Academy, since 1971; Dean of the Order of the Thistle, 1969-74; *b* 20 March 1906; 2nd *s* of W. E. Whitley; *m* 1939, Elizabeth Young Thom; two *s* two *d* (and one *s* decd). *Educ:* Daniel Stewart's College; George Heriot's School; Edinburgh University; Glasgow University. Parish Minister, Newark Parish Church, 1935-50; Member of Port Glasgow Town Council, 1945-49; Parish Minister, Old Partick Parish Church, 1950-54. Served War of 1939-45 (wounded) as Chaplain with 7th Seaforth Highlanders. Chaplain to: Kingston Shipyard, Port Glasgow, 1945-50; High School, Glasgow, 1950-54; the Waverley Station; the Edinburgh Evening News; Company of Merchants of the City of Edinburgh, 1969-; Royal Coll. of Surgeons of Edinburgh, 1969-; Pontifex Maximus, Harveian Soc. of Edinburgh, 1970-. Gov. of Fettes Coll., 1957; Mem. Managing Board of Edinburgh Royal Infirmary, 1959; Hon. Chaplain to Society of High Constables of Edinburgh. Trustee, National Library of Scotland; Trustee, Iona Abbey. *Publications:* Blinded Eagle-An Introduction to the Life and Teaching of Edward Irving, 1954; A Pictorial Guide to St Giles' Cathedral, 1959; Laughter in Heaven, 1962. *Address:* The Glebe, Southwick, by Dumfries. *Club:* New (Edinburgh).
[Died 8 May 1976.

WHITMORE, Francis; Financial Director, Daily Telegraph; *b* 11 Nov. 1903; *y s* of late Charles Whitmore; *m* 1941, Mary, *e d* of late Charles Cubitt Cooke; one *s* one *d. Educ:* Merchant Taylors' Sch., Crosby; Manchester Univ. BCom 1923. Financial News, 1924-28; Evening Standard, 1930-33. City Editor, Daily Telegraph, 1938-66. *Publication:* The Money Machine, 1928. *Recreations:* music, books. *Address:* New Mills, Whitebrook, Monmouth. *T:* Trelleck 269. *Clubs:* Reform, Authors'. *[Died 12 June 1975.*

WHITNEY, William Dwight; international lawyer, retired; *b* 26 Aug. 1899; *s* of Mr Justice Edward B. Whitney, New York Supreme Court and Josepha Newcomb; *m* 1939, Adrianne Allen; two *d. Educ:* Taft Sch.: Yale Univ., USA; New College, Oxford. Cadet for Pilot RAF, 1918; 2nd Lt (Acting Major) Scots Guards, 1940-41. Various Missions for US Government in Liaison with UK, 1941-45. Called to Bar, Inner Temple. *Publication:* Who are the Americans?, 1941. *Address:* 48 avenue de Sully, La Tour-de-Peilz, Switzerland. *T:* (021)54-03-37. *[Died 28 Dec. 1973.*

WHITTALL, Lionel Harry; Foreign Books Buyer, Globe Book Shops, Washington DC, USA; *b* 1907; *s* of H. A. Whittall; *m* 1937, Elizabeth Morris; no *c. Educ:* privately, in W Europe; Oxford (MA); Inst. of Education, London; Agric. Dept Grad. Sch. HM Foreign Service, 1929-56; latterly Consul-Gen., Berlin. Translations for World Bank, Berlitz, Govt of Chile, Sec. of Treasury, etc. *Publications:* contrib. to official surveys of foreign press; unsigned trans. for official use: Rumanian Forces Uniforms; Surinam Pilot, and other manuals. *Recreations:* reading, travel. *Address:* 5410 Connecticut Avenue, Washington, DC 20015, USA. *Clubs:* Old Greshamian (Holt); Union (Oxford). *[Died 31 Oct. 1977.*

WHITTINGTON, Sir Richard, KCMG 1958; CBE 1949 (OBE 1945); *b* 22 June 1905; *o s* of Ernest Storrs Whittington, Manchester; *m* 1937, Muriel Elizabeth Fisher (*d* 1972). *Educ:* Manchester Grammar School; Brasenose College, Oxford. Som. Thornhill Schol., BA 1927, MA 1959. Joined Consular Service, 1928; Acting Vice-Consul at Batavia, 1929; one of HM Vice-Consuls in Siam, 1931; in charge of HM Consulate, Chiengmai,

1934; Acting Consul-Gen., Bangkok, 1935; in charge of HM Consulate at Songkhla, 1936-38; Consul (Grade II) and 1st Sec., Bangkok, 1939-42; Consul at Algiers, 1942-44; Actg Consul Gen., Algiers, 1944; Consul at Atlanta Ga, 1945-46; Actg Consul-Gen., Bangkok, 1946, Counsellor and Consul-General Bangkok, 1947-51; Chargé d'Affaires in 1948, 1950 and 1951; Inspector, 1952-54; HM Senior Inspector of Foreign Service Establishments, 1954-57; British Ambassador to Thailand, 1957-61, retired. Order of White Elephant of Thailand, First Class, 1960. *Address:* Overbrow, Upavon, Pewsey, Wilts. *T:* Upavon 263. [*Died* 18 *Aug.* 1975.

WHITTINGTON-INCE, Captain Edward Watkins, CBE 1943; Royal Navy (retired); *b* 3 Oct. 1886; *s* of late Rev. E. J. C. Whittington-Ince, late of Marrick Abbey, Yorks; *m* 1919, Rosalind Mary, *er d* of E. L. Baker, Rochester, Kent; one *s* one *d. Educ:* Eastman's, Southsea; Burney's, Gosport. Joined RN 1904; served on staff of Admiral Commanding Eastern Mediterranean during Dardanelles Campaign, 1915-16, in Harwich Force, 1917, staff of C-in-C Mediterranean, 1917-19; Secretary to C-in-C East Indies, 1925-27. Paymaster Capt. 1936; Command Supply Officer, Nore Command, 1941-43; retired, 1941. *Address:* Shorne House, Lyme Road, Axminster, Devon. *T:* Axminster 32133. [*Died* 5 *June* 1976.

WHITTOME, Sir Maurice (Gordon), Kt 1961; CB 1955; Solicitor for the Customs and Excise, 1951-63; *b* 15 Dec. 1902; 3rd *s* of late John Whittome; *m* 1934, Angela Nadine, *yr d* of late A. H. Copeman, MD, DL; two *s. Educ:* Eton (King's Scholar); Corpus Christi College, Cambridge (Classical Scholar); 1st Cl., Law Tripos (Part II); MA; LLB. Called to the Bar, Gray's Inn, 1928; entered HM Customs and Excise, 1932. *Address:* Freshfield Place Farm, Scaynes Hill, Sussex. *T:* Scaynes Hill 231. [*Died* 15 *July* 1974.

WHITTON, Charlotte Elizabeth, OC 1967; CBE 1934; MA; DCL King's College, Halifax, NS, 1939, Acadia, Wolfville, Nova Scotia, 1948; LLD Queen's University, 1941; LLD University of Rochester (NY) 1952; LLD Smith College (Mass), 1955; *b* 8 March, 1896; *d* of John and Elizabeth Langin Whitton. *Educ:* Queen's Univ., Kingston, Ont. Assistant Secretary, Social Service Council of Canada, 1918-22; Asst Editor, Social Welfare; Private Secy to the Minister of Trade and Commerce for Canada, 1922-26; Executive Director, The Canadian Welfare Council, 1926-41; Delegate, Advisory Commission on Social Questions of the League of Nations; Editor, Canadian Welfare, Canadian Welfare Council Publications, 1926-41; now lecturer, writer, and consultant on welfare questions and general historical and literary subjects. Elected Controller, City of Ottawa, 1950; on death of Mayor, 1951, became first woman Mayor of a Canadian City; re-elected, 1952, 1954, 1960, 1962; elected Alderman, in 1966, for 1967-68-69; re-elected 1969, as Alderman and Regional Councillor for 1970-71-72. *Publications:* A Hundred Years A-Fellin', 1942; The Dawn of Ampler Life, 1943; pamphlets on various forms of social work; regular contributor several periodicals. *Recreations:* paddling, ski-ing. *Address:* 1 Renfrew Avenue, Ottawa, Canada. *Clubs:* Women's Press; Ladies (Toronto); Chelsea (Ottawa); Rideau Curling. [*Died* 25 *Jan.* 1975.

WHITWORTH, Arthur; late Director, Bank of England; Lieutenant of City of London; *b* 17 June 1875; *e s* of late William Whitworth, Barrister-at-Law; *m* 1914, Monica, *y d* of late Lt-Col E. M. Dansey. *Educ:* Shrewsbury; New Coll., Oxford (MA). High Sheriff County of London, 1924. *Address:* 38 Normandy House, The Drive, Hove 3, Sussex. *T:* Brighton 773617. *Clubs:* Boodle's, Leander. [*Died* 29 *March* 1972.

WHITWORTH, Brig. Dysart Edward, CBE 1943; MC; Indian Army (retired); *b* 13 July 1890; *s* of Major A. W. Whitworth, Royal Warwickshire Regt, Earls Barton, Northants, and Isabel Hunter, Antons Hill, Berwickshire; *m* 1916, Helena Margherita Powell (*d* 1963); one *s. Educ:* Shrewsbury; RMC, Sandhurst. Commn, 1910. Served in 2nd Royal Lancers (Gardner's Horse), 1911-35; European War, France, 1917 (MC); Palestine, 1920 (Bar to MC, despatches); War of 1939-45 (CBE); commanded E Bengal and Assam Area, 1940-42; North Assam Bde 1942; Honorary Commissioner Boy Scouts Assoc., Sussex. *Club:* Cavalry. [*Died* 2 *Jan.* 1974.

WHITWORTH, Eric Edward Allen, MC; Headmaster, Tonbridge School, 1939-July 1949; 3rd *s* of late Prebendary Allen Whitworth, sometime Fellow of St John's Coll., Cambridge, and Vicar of All Saints, Margaret Street; *m* Evelyn (*d* 1966), *d* of late Capt. B. H. Chevalier, RN, The Lodge, Great Beelings, Suffolk; two *s. Educ:* Radley; Trinity College, Cambridge (Exhibitioner). History Tripos, Part I, 1st Class, 1911; Part II, 1st Class, 1912; Lightfoot University Scholar,

1912; Assistant Master Rugby School, 1913-28; House Master, 1924-28; Headmaster, Bradfield College, Berks, 1928-39; Officer Commanding Rugby School OTC, 1919-24; served War of 1914-18 with 2nd and 12th Bns of South Wales Borderers in 29th and 40th Divisions (MC, Croix de Guerre, despatches twice, wounded). *Address:* Long Close, Lyddington, Swindon, Wilts. *Club:* Oxford and Cambridge. [*Died* 6 *Jan.* 1971.

WHITWORTH, Air Commodore John Nicholas Haworth, CB 1960; DSO 1941; DFC and bar 1940; RAF retired; *b* Buenos Aires, 1912; *er s* of late Walter Haworth Whitworth (killed in action, 1918); *m* 1945, Joan Prevett; one *s* one *d* (both adopted). *Educ:* Oundle; RAF College, Cranwell. Served as Flight Comdr in Bomber Command, 1939-43 (DFC and bar, DSO, MC (Czechoslovakia), despatches); RAF Staff Coll., Haifa, 1946 (psa); AHQ, New Delhi, 1947; HM Air Attaché, Bangkok, 1948; AOC and Comdt Central Flying Sch., Little Rissington, Glos, 1958; Air Chief of Staff, Ghana Air Force, during 1961; AOC, RAF, Hong Kong, 1962-64. *Address:* The Old Rectory, Rodmarton, near Cirencester, Glos. *T:* Rodmarton 223. *Club:* Royal Air Force. [*Died* 13 *Nov.* 1974.

WHITWORTH, Thomas; Master of Hatfield College, Durham, since 1956; *b* 7 April 1917; *o s* of late Leonard and Elizabeth Whitworth, Oldham, Lancs; *m* 1941, Joan Mohene, *er d* of late Sir Clifford Agarwala; one *s* two *d. Educ:* Manchester Grammar School; Oriel College, Oxford. Royal Engineers, 1939-45. Burdett-Coutts Scholar, Oxford University, 1947-49. MA (Oxon) 1947, DPhil (Oxon) 1950. University Demonstrator in geology at Oxford and Lecturer of Oriel College, 1949-56. *Publications:* in various scientific journals. *Recreations:* painting; refereeing (Rugby Union); geological expeditions to East Africa. *Address:* The Master's Lodging, Hatfield College, Durham. *T:* Durham 65008. [*Died* 18 *Dec.* 1979.

WHITWORTH, Admiral Sir William Jock, KCB 1941 (CB 1938); DSO 1918; *b* 29 June 1884; *s* of late Major A. W. Whitworth, Earls Barton, Northants; *m* 1910, Marguerite (*d* 1970), *d* of late Lieut-Col A. H. Maclean, RA; one *s* one *d* (and one *s* one *d* decd). Served European War, 1914-18 (despatches, DSO); commanded the Physical and Recreational Training School, Portsmouth, 1926-28; in command of HMS Stuart and Second Destroyer Flotilla, Mediterranean Fleet, 1928-31; Capt. (D) Reserve Destroyer Flotilla, 1931; Dir of Physical Training and Sports, and Head of the Naval Personnel Committee, 1931-33; Captain of the Fleet to Commander-in-Chief, Mediterranean, 1933-35; commanded HMS Rodney, 1936; Rear-Admiral, 1936; Naval Secretary to First Lord of the Admiralty, 1937-39; Vice-Admiral commanding Battle Cruiser Squadron, 1939-41; in command in Warspite, 2nd Battle of Narvik, 1940; Second Sea Lord of the Admiralty, 1941-44; Commander-in-Chief, Rosyth, 1944 to July 1946; Admiral, 1943; retired list, 1946. Grand Cross Order of St Olav (Norway). [*Died* 25 *Oct.* 1973.

WHYATT, Sir John, Kt 1957; *b* 13 April 1905; *o s* of late George Whyatt; *m* 1936, Margaret (*d* 1976), *er d* of Kenneth Stewart; one *s. Educ:* Stonyhurst; Balliol Coll., Oxford. Entered Colonial Legal Service, 1937; Crown Counsel, Hong Kong; Hong Kong Deleg. to Eastern Group Conference, New Delhi, 1940; Secretary, Eastern Group Supply Council, New Delhi, 1941; Adviser to British Representative, UNRRA Council Meeting, Sydney, 1945; Attorney-General, Barbados, 1948; Attorney-General and Minister for Legal Affairs, Kenya, 1951-55; Chief Justice of Singapore, 1955-58, retd. Judge of the Chief Court for the Persian Gulf, 1961-66; Director of Studies, Overseas Government Legal Officers Course, 1966-67. KC (Barbados) 1949; QC (Kenya) 1952. *Recreations:* travel, fishing, walking. *Address:* Boxwood, Amberley, Arundel, West Sussex. *Club:* Travellers'. [*Died* 14 *March* 1978.

WHYTE, Angus H.; *see* Hedley-Whyte.

WHYTE, Air Commandant Dame Roberta (Mary), DBE 1955; RRC 1949; *b* 6 June 1897; *d* of Robert Whyte and Mary Whyte (formerly Lumsden). Trained at King's College Hospital, SE5, 1923-28. Princess Mary's Royal Air Force Nursing Service, 1929-56; Matron-in-Chief Princess Mary's Royal Air Force Nursing Service, 1952-56, retired; QHNS 1952. *Club:* United Nursing Services. [*Died* 25 *Jan.* 1979.

WHYTE, William Hamilton, MA; *b* 15 Jan. 1885; *s* of John Whyte and Elizabeth Alexander; *m* 1925, Janet, *d* of late Dr Williamson, Exmouth; two *s. Educ:* Woodside School, Glasgow; Universities of Glasgow and Leeds. Stock Exchange, Glasgow; served European War, Lieut RNVR; Staff of University College of the South-West, Exeter, 1921-25; Professor of Economics, University of Bristol, 1925-50 (Dean, Faculty of Arts, 1939-46);

Director, Institute of Social and Economic Research, University Coll., Ibadan, Nigeria, 1950-53; Member Nigerian Government Western Region, Overseas, Public Service Board, 1953-60. Ex-Chairman of following Wages Councils: Wholesale Mantle and Costume; Corset; Coffin; Industrial Canteens; Hairdressers. *Publications:* The Stock Exchange; Decasualisation of Dock Labour; Drink and Industrial Efficiency. *Recreations:* golf, tennis. *Address:* Amberley Court 3, Amberley, near Stroud, Glos. *T:* Amberley 2282. *Club:* National Liberal.
[*Died* 31 *Jan.* 1973.

WICKHAM, Lt-Col Sir Charles (George), KCMG 1952; KBE 1945; Kt 1922; DSO 1900; DL; late Norfolk Regiment; *b* 11 Sept. 1879; 4th *s* of W. W. Wickham of Chestnut Grove, Yorks; *m* 1st, 1916, Phyllis Amy (*d* 1924), 2nd *d* of Edward G. Rose; two *d*; 2nd 1925, Fanny Desirée Dyott (*d* 1946), 2nd *d* of Howard Paget, Elford Hall, Tamworth. *Educ:* Harrow; Royal Military College, Sandhurst. Entered Army, 1899; Captain, 1906; Major, 1915; served South Africa, 1900-02 (wounded, despatches, Queen's medal 5 clasps, King's medal 2 clasps, DSO); European War, 1914-16 (despatches thrice, Bt Major); AQMG and GSO1, 1918-20 (Bt Lieut-Col); temp. Lieut-Col with General Knox's Military Mission, Siberia; Divisional Commissioner Royal Irish Constabulary, 1920; Inspector-General Royal Ulster Constabulary, 1922-45; Maj.-Gen. (HG). Head of British Police-Prisons Mission to Greece, June 1945-52. Formed: Ulster Special Constabulary, 1920; Royal Ulster Constabulary, 1922; Ulster Home Guard, 1940. High Sheriff, County Down, 1960; DL Co. Down, 1962. French Legion of Honour; Order of Crown of Italy; Czechoslovak War Cross. *Address:* Ashdene, Comber, Co. Down. *T:* Comber 206. *Clubs:* Army and Navy, United Service & Royal Aero.
[*Died* 20 *July* 1971.

WICKINS, Brevet-Col (Temp. Brig.) George Cradock, CB 1945; CBE 1939; TD; DL Greater London Council; Royal Signals, TA; *b* 1884; *s* of George Cradock Wickins; *m* 1918, Mabel English. Served European War, 1914-19, and War of 1939-45. Chief Signal Officer Anti-Aircraft Command until Feb. 1945; on return to Post Office appointed Public Relations Officer, 1945-46; Chm. Cadet Committee, County of London, 1945-49. *Address:* 8 Alderton Court, West Parade, Bexhill-on-Sea, Sussex.
[*Died* 4 *Feb.* 1973.

WICKLOW, 8th Earl of, *cr* 1793; **William Cecil James Philip John Paul Howard**; Baron of Clonmore; Captain Royal Fusiliers; Director, Sun Insurance Company, Dublin; *b* 30 Oct. 1902; *o s* of 7th Earl of Wicklow and Lady Gladys Mary Hamilton (*d* 1917), *y d* of 2nd Duke of Abercorn; *S* father, 1946; *m* 1959, Eleanor, *d* of Prof. R. M. Butler. *Educ:* Merton College, Oxford (BA Hons). A convert to the Roman Catholic Church. Editor, Dublin Review, 1937-40. *Publications:* Pope Pius XI and World Peace, 1937; More about Dom Marmion, 1949; Fireside Fusilier, 1959; and various translations. *Heir:* cousin Cecil Aymar Forward-Howard, *b* 13 Sept. 1909. *Address:* Sea Grange, Sandycove, Dun Laoghaire, Co. Dublin. *Club:* Royal Irish Yacht (Dun Laoghaire).
[*Died* 8 *Feb.* 1978.

WIGAN, Sir Frederick Adair, 4th Bt, *cr* 1898; *b* 13 April 1911; *e s* of Sir Roderick Grey Wigan, 3rd Bt, and Ina (*d* 1977), *o c* of late Lewis D. Wigan, Glenalmond, Perthshire; *S* father 1954. *Educ:* privately. *Heir:* *b* Alan Lewis Wigan [*b* 19 Nov. 1913; *m* 1950, Robina, *d* of Lt-Col Sir Iain Colquhoun, 7th Bt, KT, DSO; one *s* one *d*. *Educ:* Eton; Magdalen Coll., Oxford. Captain, King's Royal Rifle Corps (Reserve of Officers); served War of 1939-45 (prisoner)]. *Address:* Borrobol, Kinbrace, Sutherland.
[*Died* 24 *Jan.* 1979.

WIGGIN, Sir Charles (Douglas), KCMG 1976 (CMG 1968); DFC 1944; AFC 1945; HM Diplomatic Service; Ambassador to Spain, since 1974; *b* 26 Sept. 1922; *s* of late Arthur Francis Holme Wiggin, CMG, and late Carmen (*née* Fernandez Vallin); *m* 1948, Marie Thérèse Elizabeth, *e d* of late Sir John H. Leche, KCMG, OBE, Carden, Chester; three *d*. *Educ:* Eton; Christ Church, Oxford. RAFVR, 1941-46 (Flt-Lt). Joined Foreign Service (now Diplomatic Service), 1946; FO, 1946-47; Third Sec., Santiago, 1947-49; Third/Second Sec., Stockholm, 1949-52; FO, 1952-53; Second/First Sec., Tehran, 1953-56; First Sec., Washington, 1956-61; Private Sec. to Lord Privy Seal, FO, 1961-63, and to Lord Carrington, 1963; IDC, 1964; Counsellor, Tehran, 1965-69; Head of American Dept, FCO, 1969-71; Under-Sec., FCO, 1971-74. *Address:* c/o Foreign and Commonwealth Office, SW1; 16 Regents Park Terrace, NW1. *T:* 01-485 1647.
[*Died* 8 *March* 1977.

WIGGIN, Sir Charles Richard Henry, 3rd Bt, *cr* 1892; TD; JP; DL; *b* 21 March 1885; *s* of 2nd Bt and Annie Sarah, *d* of C. R. Cope of Kinnerton Court, Radnors; *S* father, 1917; *m* 1916,

Mabel Violet Mary (*d* 1961), *d* of late Sir William Jaffray, 2nd Bt; one *s*. *Educ:* Eton; Trinity Coll., Cambridge; BA 1907. Served in European War, 1914-18; in Egypt, Palestine and Syria, 1915-18 (despatches). Lt-Col and Bt-Col comdg Staffs Yeomanry, 1921-25; Hon. Col Staffs Yeomanry, 1951-54. DL 1931, High Sheriff 1942, Warwickshire. *Heir:* *s* John Henry Wiggin, MC, Major (retired), Grenadier Guards [*b* 3 Mar. 1921; *m* 1st, 1947, Lady Cecilia Evelyn Anson (marriage dissolved, 1961; she *d* 1963), *yr d* of 4th Earl of Lichfield; two *s*; 2nd, 1963, Sarah, *d* of Brigadier Stewart Forster; two *s*. *Educ:* Eton; Trinity College, Cambridge]. *Address:* Honington Hall, Shipston-on-Stour, Warwickshire. *T:* Shipston 61434. [*Died* 16 *Sept.* 1972.

WIGGINS, William Denison Clare, CMG 1968; OBE 1957; Director of Overseas Surveys and Survey Adviser to Minister of Overseas Development, 1965-68, retired; *b* 7 Feb. 1905; *s* of late Dr Clare Aveling Wiggins and Mrs Ethel Beatrice Wiggins; *m* 1933, Mary Isabel Macnair; two *d*. *Educ:* Dragon Sch., Oxford; King's Sch., Canterbury; Univ. Coll., London. Surveyor, Survey Dept, Nigeria, 1928; Mil. Service, RE, 1939-46 (Lt-Col). Overseas (Geodetic and Topographic) surveys: Asst Dir, 1946; Dep. Dir, 1948. Pres., Brit. Cartographic Soc., 1966-68; Chairman: (Royal Society's) Cartography Sub-Cttee of Brit. Nat. Cttee for Geography, 1966-; Jt Cttee, Nat. Certs in Surveying, Cartography and Planning, 1969-. Murchison Award (of RGS), 1952. *Publications:* contrib. to: Antarctic Research, Empire Survey Review, Geographical Jl, etc. Professional papers at Commonwealth Survey Officers' Confs. *Recreation:* golf. *Address:* Rosemary Cottage, Watersfield, Pulborough, Sussex. *T:* Bury 543. *Club:* West Sussex Golf.
[*Died* 22 *Jan.* 1971.

WIGGLESWORTH, Air Marshal Sir (Horace Ernest) Philip, KBE 1946 (CBE 1942); CB 1943; DSC; *b* 11 July 1896; *s* of late George and Mary Wigglesworth; *m* 1963, Florence Elizabeth Hills (*d* 1973), widow of Alec Percy Hills, Hove. *Educ:* Chesterfield. Served European War, 1914-19, commissioned RNAS 1915. Instructor RAF Staff College, Andover, 1933-36; Deputy Director of Intelligence, Air Ministry, 1936-39; Group Captain, 1939; Combined Planning Staff, ME 1939; Air Commodore, 1941 (despatches); Acting Air Vice-Marshal, 1941; SASO ME Command, 1941-42; AOC E Africa, 1942; Dep. C-in-C Allied Air Forces Mediterranean Command, 1943; SASO AEAF, 1943 (despatches); Dep. Chief of Staff (Air) Supreme Headquarters, AEF (acting Air Marshal), 1944; Air Vice-Marshal, 1945; Deputy Air C-in-C, Germany and Dep. Chief of Air Division, British Control Commission, 1945; AOC-in-C British Air Forces of Occupation (Germany) and Chief of Air Division, CCG (BE), 1946; Air Marshal, 1948; retired, 1948. President, Renault Ltd (British company). Comdr Legion of Merit (USA); Comdr Legion of Honour (Fr.); Croix de Guerre (Fr.); Knight Spanish Order Military Merit; Comdr Order King George of Greece. *Address:* 65 Hove Park Road, Hove 4, East Sussex. *T:* Brighton 552524.
[*Died* 31 *May* 1975.

WIGGLESWORTH, Walter Somerville, QC 1971; Vicar-General of Province of York since 1944; Dean of the Arches Court of Canterbury, Auditor of the Chancery Court of York, and Master of the Faculties, since 1971; Member of General Synod of Church of England and its Legal Advisory Commission; *b* 14 April 1906; *yr s* of late Francis William and Florence Mary Wigglesworth, Marple, Cheshire; unmarried. *Educ:* Clifton Coll. (Scholar); Magdalene Coll., Cambridge (Exhibitioner). BA 1928; LLB 1929; MA 1931; Called to Bar, 1930, Inner Temple and Lincoln's Inn; Bencher, Lincoln's Inn, 1960. Squadron Leader, RAFVR (Air Staff Intelligence, 1940-45). Bronze Star Medal (USA), 1949. Chancellor, Dioceses of: Portsmouth, 1940-70; Exeter, 1941-70; Bath and Wells, 1942-70; Derby and York, 1944-70; London, 1954-70; Commissary to the Dean and Chapter of St Paul's Cathedral, 1961-. Conveyancing Counsel to: BoT 1956-71; Supreme Court, 1970-71. DCL (Lambeth) 1961. *Address:* 54 Swan Court, SW3. *T:* 01-352 8751; 24 Old Buildings, Lincoln's Inn, WC2. *T:* 01-405 1124 and 7515. *Clubs:* Athenæum, United Service and Royal Aero, United University.
[*Died* 27 *May* 1972.

WIGHT, Prof. (Robert James) Martin; Professor of History, University of Sussex, since 1961; Dean of School of European Studies, 1961-69; *b* 26 Nov. 1913; 2nd *s* of late Dr Edward Wight, Brighton; *m* 1952, Gabriele, *d* of Peter-Erich Ritzen, Rolandia, Brazil; two *s* four *d*. *Educ:* Bradfield; Hertford College, Oxford (open scholar). 1st class hons Modern History, 1935. On Staff of Chatham House, 1936-38; assistant master, Haileybury Coll., 1938-41; on staff of: Nuffield College Colonial Research, Oxford, 1941-46; Chatham House, 1946-49; The Observer, 1946-47; Reader in International Relations in Univ. of London, 1949-61. Member, Council of Roy. Inst. of Internat. Affairs, 1952-; Vis. Professor, Univ. of Chicago, 1956-57; Mem.

Academic Planning Bd, Univ. of Kent. *Publications:* Power Politics, 1946; Development of the Legislative Council, 1946; Gold Coast Legislative Council, 1947; (joint) Attitude to Africa, 1951; British Colonial Constitutions, 1952; (joint) The World in March 1939, 1952; (jt editor with Herbert Butterfield) Diplomatic Investigations, 1966. *Recreations:* gardening, bookshops, travel. *Address:* Harwarton, Speldhurst, Kent. *T:* Langton 3131; University of Sussex, Brighton.
[Died 15 July 1972.

WIGHTMAN, Ralph; Free-lance Journalist and Broadcaster since 1948; associated with programme Any Questions; *b* 26 July 1901; *s* of Tom Wightman, Farmer and Butcher, Piddletrenthide, Dorchester, Dorset; *m* 1924, Margaret Dorothy Wiggins. *Educ:* Beaminster Grammar Sch.; Durham University. Lectr in Agriculture, Devon CC, 1923-27; Lecturer in Agriculture, Wilts CC, 1927-30; Senior Agricultural Adviser, Dorset CC, 1930-48. *Publications:* Moss Green Days, 1948; My Homeward Road, 1950; Arable Farming, 1951; Watching the Certain Things, 1951; Livestock Farming, 1952; Days on the Farm, 1952; The Seasons, 1953; The Wessex Heathland, 1953; Rural Rides with Ralph Wightman, 1957; Abiding Things, 1962; Portrait of Dorset, 1965; Take Life Easy, 1968; The Countryside Today, 1970. *Recreations:* retired-hockey and cricket. *Address:* Tudor House, Puddletown, Dorchester, Dorset. *T:* Puddletown 464. *[Died 28 May 1971.*

WILBRAHAM, Sir Randle (John) Baker, 7th Bt, *cr* 1776; FRICS; DL; JP; Consultant partner in firm of John German Ralph Pay, Land Agents; *b* 31 March 1906; *o s* of Sir Philip W. Baker Wilbraham, 6th Bt, KBE, DCL; *S* father 1957; *m* 1930, Betty Ann, CBE (*d* 1975), *e d* of W. Matt Torrens, The Grove, Hayes, Kent; one *s* one *d*. *Educ:* Harrow; Balliol College, Oxford. Entered the Land Agency profession, 1928; served War of 1939-45 as Squadron-Leader, Royal Auxiliary Air Force; resumed practice, 1945. President of the Chartered Land Agents' Society, 1958-59; High Steward of Congleton, 1957-; High Sheriff, 1953, JP 1954, DL 1959, Cheshire. *Heir: s* Richard Baker Wilbraham, late Lieut Welsh Guards [*b* 5 Feb. 1934; *m* 1962, Anne Christine Peto Bennett; one *s* three *d*. *Educ:* Harrow. A Dir, Schroder Wagg & Co.]. *Address:* Rode Hall, Scholar Green, Cheshire. *T:* Alsager 3237. *Clubs:* MCC, United Oxford & Cambridge University. *[Died 24 Feb. 1980.*

WILCOCKS, C(harles), CMG 1952; retired; *b* 10 April 1896; *s* of late F. W. Wilcocks; *m* 1921, Frances Gertrude Bullough, MB, ChB, DPH. *Educ:* Wigan Grammar School; Manchester University. Military Service: Lt, Lancs Fusiliers, attached Northamptonshire Regt, Egypt and Palestine Campaign, 1915-19, wounded Gaza, April 1917. MB, ChB, 1924; MD 1932; DTM&H 1941; FRCP 1950. East African Med. Service, 1927; Tuberculosis Res. Officer, Tanganyika, 1930; Asst Dir, Bureau of Hygiene and Tropical Diseases, 1938-42; Dir, Bureau of Hygiene and Tropical Diseases, London, 1942-61. Editor, Tropical Diseases Bulletin and Bulletin of Hygiene, 1938-61; Bulletin of War Medicine, 1942-46. Pres., Royal Society of Tropical Medicine and Hygiene, 1963-65, Hon. Sec., 1951-63; Editor, Trans. Roy. Soc. Trop. Med. and Hyg., 1964-70; Mem., Court of Governors, London School of Hygiene and Tropical Medicine, 1963-71; Mem., Bd of Governors, University College Hospital, 1953-56; Examr, DTM&H (apptd by Royal College of Physicians), 1959-63; Heath Clark Lectr, Univ. of London, 1960; Consultant, The Counties Public Health Laboratories, London, 1962-76. *Publications:* Tuberculosis in Tanganyika Territory, 1938; Health and Disease in the Tropics, 1950; Aspects of Medical Investigation in Africa, 1961; Medical Advance, Public Health and Social Evolution, 1965; (with P. E. C. Manson-Bahr) Manson's Tropical Diseases, 17th edn, 1972; articles in medical journals. *Address:* 24 Randalls Road, Leatherhead, Surrey KT22 7TQ. *T:* Leatherhead 72928. *Club:* Athenæum. *[Died 6 March 1977.*

WILCOX, Bernard Herbert, OBE 1967; HM Diplomatic Service, retired; Consul-General, Lille, France, 1973-77; *b* 4 May 1917; *s* of late Herbert Wilcox, and of Elsie May Wilcox; *m* 1946, Mary Cameron Rae; one *d*. *Educ:* King Edward's High Sch., Birmingham; Birmingham Univ. (BA). Served War, with S Staffords, RA, and British Mil. Mission to Italian Army, 1939-46. British Vice-Consul, Lisbon, 1947-49; Pro-Consul, Berlin, 1949-50; 2nd Sec., British Embassy, Belgrade, 1950-52; Vice-Consul: Los Angeles, 1952-54; Kansas City, 1954-56; Consul, Philadelphia, 1956-58; FO, 1958-60; 1st Sec., British Embassy, Rangoon, 1960-63; Consul, Los Angeles, 1963-67; 1st Sec., British Embassy, Paris, 1967-72; Consul-General, Casablanca, 1972-73. *Recreations:* tennis, chess, gardening. *Address:* 4 Randolph Close, Stoke D'Abernon, Cobham, Surrey KT11 2SW. *[Died 16 July 1980.*

WILCOX, Herbert, CBE 1951; Film Producer, Director, and Author; *b* 19 April 1890; *s* of Joseph John and Mary Healy Wilcox; *m* 1st, Maude Bower; one *s* three *d*; 2nd, 1943, Florence Marjorie (Dame Anna Neagle, DBE), *d* of late Herbert William Robertson. *Educ:* Brighton. Began as journalist. Served European War, 1914-18: 2nd Lieut, East Kent Regiment; Pilot and Flight-Lieut, Royal Flying Corps, then Royal Air Force. Films prod. and Dir.: Good Night Vienna, The Little Damozel, The Wonderful Story, Bitter Sweet, Chu Chin Chow, Decameron Nights, The Only Way, The Scarlet Pimpernel, Madame Pompadour, Carnival, Walls-Lynn Aldwych Farces, Sorrel and Son, The Speckled Band, Paddy the Next Best Thing, Flames of Passion, Escape Me Never, Brewsters Millions, The Blue Danube, Wolves, Black Waters, Nell Gwyn, Peg of Old Drury, Victoria the Great, Sixty Glorious Years, They Flew Alone, Yellow Canary, I Live in Grosvenor Square, Piccadilly Incident, The Courtneys of Curzon Street, Spring in Park Lane, Elizabeth of Ladymead, Maytime in Mayfair, Odette, The Lady With a Lamp, Derby Day, Trent's Last Case, The Beggar's Opera, Laughing Anne, Trouble in the Glen, Lilacs in the Spring, King's Rhapsody, My Teenage Daughter, Yangtse Incident, These Dangerous Years, The Man Who Wouldn't Talk, The Lady is a Square. In Hollywood: Nurse Edith Cavell, Irene, Sunny, No No Nanette. Hon. Mem., Amer. Inst. Cinematography. Gold Cup, Venice. Nat. Film Award 4 times. Hon. Fellow, British Kinematograph Soc. *Publication:* Twenty Five Thousand Sunsets, 1967. *Recreations:* theatre and work. *Address:* 117B Hamilton Terrace, NW8. *Clubs:* Garrick, City Livery. *[Died 15 May 1977.*

WILD, Albert, DL; JP; Chairman, Co-operative Insce Soc. Ltd, 1962-64, retd; *b* 21 Aug. 1899; *m* 1927, Ella Siddall; one *d*. *Educ:* Manchester High School of Commerce. Director: CWS, 1941-64; CIS, 1944-64; Bridgewater Estates, 1948-; Russo-Brit. Chamber of Commerce, 1949-64; Member: Postmaster General's Advisory Council, 1949-64; Min. of Labour, Transp. Tribunal Gen. Panel, 1949-64; Dir, Co-op. Dental Assoc., 1954-64; Dir, Internat. Co-op. Petroleum Assoc., 1954-64. Mem. Coun., Lancaster Univ. (Vice-Chm. Finance Cttee, 1964-71); Mem. Coun. (Lancs) Order of St John (Chm. Appeals and Publicity Cttee, 1964-), Pres., Lancaster Area; Mem. Management Cttee, Mary MacArthur Holiday Homes, 1948-. DL Lancs 1967; High Sheriff, County Palatine of Lancaster, 1968-69. *Recreations:* reading, gardening, fishing. *Address:* 8 Marlton Way, Lancaster, Lancs. *T:* Lancaster 67451.
[Died 29 Aug. 1971.

WILD, Rt. Hon. Sir (Herbert) Richard (Churton), PC 1966; GBE 1978; KCMG 1966; Chief Justice of New Zealand, 1966-78; *b* 1912; *s* of Dr L. J. Wild; *m* 1940, Janet Grainger; two *s* two *d*. *Educ:* Feilding High Sch.; Victoria Univ. Private practice, 1939-57 (absent on War Service with NZ Div. in ME, 1940-45). Apptd Judge Advocate Gen., 1955; QC 1957. Solicitor-Gen., 1957-65. Hon. LLD, Victoria Univ., 1969. Hon. Bencher, Inner Temple, 1969. *Club:* Wellington (NZ). *[Died 22 May 1978.*

WILD, Ira, CB 1952; CMG 1947; OBE 1939; *b* 23 May 1895; *s* of Leonard Holt Wild and Mary Hopkinson; *m* 1922, Edith Mary Barbour; one *d*. *Educ:* Bury Grammar School; London School of Economics. Exchequer and Audit Dept, 1914-34; Comptroller and Auditor-General of Newfoundland, 1934-38; Colonial Office and Ministry of Home Security, 1939; HM Treasury, 1940; Commissioner for Finance, Newfoundland, 1941-46; Director of Finance, Ministry of Transport and Civil Aviation, 1948-57. *Address:* Bella Vista, Whitchurch Road, Bunbury, Cheshire. *[Died 10 Sept. 1974.*

WILD, Rt. Hon. Sir Richard; *see* Wild, Rt Hon. Sir H. R. C.

WILDER, Thornton Niven; author; *b* Madison, Wisconsin, 17 April 1897; *s* of Amos Parker Wilder and Isabella Niven. *Educ:* Schools in California, China and Ohio; BA Yale Univ. 1920; MA Princeton, Univ., 1926. Schoolmaster, Lawrenceville, NJ, USA, 1921-28; Faculty Univ. of Chicago, 1930-36; C. E. Norton Professor, Harvard Univ., 1950-51. Hon. degrees: New York Univ., 1930; Yale Univ., 1947; Kenyon Coll., 1948; Coll. of Wooster, 1950; Harvard Univ., 1951; Northeastern Univ., 1951; Northwestern Univ., 1951; Oberlin Coll., 1952; Univ. of New Hampshire, 1953; Goethe Univ., 1957; Brandeis Univ., 1960; Univ. of Zurich, 1961, Beloit Coll., 1975. Mem., American Acad. of Arts and Letters; Corresp. Mem.: Bayrische Akademie der Schönen Künste; Akademie der Wissenschaften und der Literatur (Mainz). Served European War and War of 1939-45, commnd in Air Corps, Capt. 1942, advanced through grades to Lt-Col, 1944; served overseas, 1943-45 (Legion of Merit). Chevalier Légion d'Honneur, 1951; Hon. MBE (United Kingdom); Order of Merit (Peru); Pour le Mérite (Bonn), 1957; Gold Medal for Fiction, Amer. Inst. of Arts and Letters, 1952;

Peace Prize des Deutschen Buchhandels (Frankfurt-a-M), 1957; Goethe-Plakette der Stadt (Frankfurt-a-M), 1959; Ehrenmedaille, of Austria, 1959; US Presidential Medal of Freedom, 1963; National Medal of Literature, 1965. *Publications:* The Cabala, 1926; The Bridge of San Luis Rey (awarded Pulitzer Prize), 1927; The Angel that Troubled the Waters, 1928; The Woman of Andros, 1930; The Long Christmas Dinner (made into opera, music by Hindemith, 1961), and other Plays in one act, 1931; Heaven's My Destination, 1935; Our Town (awarded Pulitzer Prize), 1938; The Merchant of Yonkers, 1938; Skin of Our Teeth (Pulitzer Prize), 1942; The Ides of March, 1948; The Matchmaker (Edinburgh Festival), 1954; The Alcestiad, presented as A Life in the Sun (Edinburgh Festival), 1955; The Long Christmas Dinner (opera), 1961; Plays for Bleecker Street, 1962; Hello Dolly (musical based on The Matchmaker), 1964; The Eighth Day, 1967 (Nat. Book award 1968); Theophilus North, 1974. *Address:* 50 Deepwood Drive, Hamden, Conn 06517, USA. *[Died 7 Dec. 1975.*

WILDING, Michael; Actor (stage and films); *b* Westcliff-on-Sea, Essex, 23 July 1912; *s* of late Henry Wilding, MBE and Ethel Thompson; *m* 1937, Kay Young (marr. diss. 1952); *m* 1952, Elizabeth Taylor (marr. diss. 1957); two *s*; *m* 1958, Mrs Susan Nell (marr. diss.); *m* 1964, Margaret Leighton, CBE (*d* 1976). *Educ:* Christ's Hospital. Began career painting portraits and working at commercial art in Brussels. First West End appearance, Daly's, 1935; toured with Fay Compton in Australia and New Zealand, playing leading parts in Victoria Regina, To-Night at 8-30, and George and Margaret; played Denys Royd in Quiet Week-End, Wyndham's, 1941-43; went to Gibraltar and Malta, with John Gielgud and Company, entertaining HM Forces, Jan. 1943; succeeded John Mills as Lew in Men in Shadow, Vaudeville, 1943; played the Earl of Harpenden in While the Sun Shines, Dec. 1943 until 1945; succeeded Sir John Gielgud in Nude With Violin, 1957; Mary Mary, Broadway, 1961. First appeared in films, 1940. Films include: Piccadilly Incident, Carnival, The Courtneys of Curzon Street, An Ideal Husband, Spring in Park Lane, Maytime in Mayfair, Under Capricorn, Stage Fright, The Law and The Lady, The Lady With a Lamp, Derby Day, Trent's Last Case, Torch Song, The Law and the Lady, The Egyptian, The Glass Slipper, The World of Suzie Wong, The Naked Edge, The Two Enemies, Waterloo, Lady Caroline Lamb, Dr Frankenstein. *Address:* c/o Green & Underwood, 11 Garrick Street, WC2. *[Died 8 July 1979.*

WILDISH, Engineer Rear-Adm. Sir Henry William, KBE 1946 (CBE 1939); CB 1942; *b* 25 June 1884; *s* of late J. G. Wildish, Naval Architect; *m* 1911, Elfrida Phyllis, *d* of late H. G. Bryant, Milton Regis, Kent; one *s* one *d*. *Educ:* King's School, Rochester; RNE College, Devonport. Joined Navy, 1900; Eng. Commander 1921; in charge Haslar Fuel Experimental Station, 1926-28; Eng. Capt. 1930; Staff of C-in-C Mediterranean, 1934-36; Eng. Rear-Adm. 1936; Staff of C-in-C Nore, 1937-40; Staff of C-in-C Western Approaches, 1940-45. *Address:* Queensberry Lodge, Hayling Island, Hants. *T:* Hayling Island 3604. *[Died 9 July 1973.*

WILENSKI, Reginald Howard, Hon. MA (Manchester), 1938; artist and art critic; Special Lecturer in the History of Art, Victoria University of Manchester, 1933-46; Special Lecturer in Art, Bristol University, 1929 and 1930; *b* London, 1887; *m* Marjorie Harland, BA (*d* 1965). *Educ:* St Paul's Sch.; Balliol Coll., Oxford. Exhibitor, International Society Sculptors, Painters, and Gravers, Royal Society Portrait Painters, ROI, Paris Autumn Salon, etc. Chevalier, Legion of Honour, 1967. *Publications:* The Modern Movement in Art, 1927 (revised 1957); Dutch Painting, 1929 (revised 1955); French Painting, 1931 (revised 1974); The Meaning of Modern Sculpture, 1932; John Ruskin, 1933; English Painting, 1933 (revised 1963); The Study of Art, 1934; Modern French Painters, 1940 (revised 1963); Flemish Painters (2 vols), 1960; Editor: The Faber Gallery. *Address:* Maldah, Marlow, Bucks. *Club:* Savile. *[Died 19 April 1975.*

WILES, Reid; *b* 11 Nov. 1919; *s* of Richard S. Wiles and Miamah Gbenni; *m* 1946, C. Louise Wiles (*née* Pratt); one *s* two *d*. *Educ:* Coll. of West Africa (Cl. of 1940); Liberia Coll. (BA, Cl. of 1944). Attorney-at-Law. In Mercantile and Law Firms of Hon. William E. Dennis, 1938-43; Cadet, Bureau of Audits, 1937-38; transf. to Bureau of Revenues, 1938; Cadet, Dept of State, 1943 (Clerk, 1944); Private Sec. to Sec. of State of Liberia, 1944-46; Commercial Business (Private), 1946-51; Second Sec., Liberian Embassy, Washington, DC, 1952; First Sec., Liberian Embassy, Madrid, 1956; Ambassador to: W Germany, 1960; Sweden, 1961; Norway and Denmark, 1964-68; UK, 1972-75. Attended: Internat. Coffee Conf., as observer of Liberian Govt, Mexico City, 1956; ICAO, as observer, Madrid, 1957; WHO Conf.,

1967; Anniv. of Coronation of Pope John XXIII, as Special Rep. of President of Liberia. Past Pres., Les Amis Club (Monrovia). Holds Grand Cross, etc. of various foreign orders. *Recreations:* football, tennis, reading. *Address:* c/o Ministry of Foreign Affairs, Monrovia, Liberia. *[Died 23 June 1975.*

WILKINS, Charles Timothy, OBE 1952; CEng; FRAeS; Director of Hawker Siddeley Dynamics Limited, in charge of Space Projects, 1963; *b* 26 Nov. 1905; *s* of G. C. A. Wilkins and A. N. Berg; *m* 1940, Gladys Marie Alexander; one *s* one *d*. *Educ:* Cordwalles; Brighton College. With Vickers Armstrongs Ltd, Weybridge, 2 years Shops and 1 year Drawing Office; Drawing Office, de Havilland Aircraft Co. Ltd, 1928-30; Drawing Office of Cierva Autogiro Co. for 1½ years and of Handley Page Ltd for six months; rejoined de Havilland Aircraft Co. Ltd, Drawing Office, 1932; appointed Director, 1958. "A" Licence (Pilot's), 1929. FRAeS 1950. Fellow, British Interplanetary Society. *Address:* Brook Hill Cottage, Brook Hill, Woodstock, Oxon. *T:* Woodstock 812071. *[Died 6 Feb. 1979.*

WILKINSON, Rev. Arthur Henry, BA, BD; *b* 8 Sept. 1885; *s* of John Wilkinson, Whitworth, Co. Durham; *m* Edith McQuhae; one *s* one *d*. *Educ:* Privately; Balliol College, Oxford; Egerton Hall, Manchester. Secretary of the Student Christian Movement in Manchester University, 1910; Ordained, 1911; Curate at Christ Church, Bradford, Manchester, 1912; Holy Trinity, Rusholme, 1914; CMS Missionary, 1918; Principal of CMS College in West China University, 1924; Vicar of Poynton, Cheshire, 1929. Formerly Chief Secretary, British and Foreign Bible Society. Travelled extensively. *Recreation:* gardening. *Address:* 1 Spring Court, Church Road, W7. *T:* 01-567 5542. *[Died 18 March 1973.*

WILKINSON, Rt. Rev. (Charles Robert) Heber; Assistant Bishop of Niagara, 1960-70; *b* 28 Dec. 1900; *s* of late Rev. Frederick Wilkinson; *m* 1926, Rowena Victoria Stringer; two *s* one *d*. *Educ:* University of Toronto Schools; University of Toronto. MA (Toronto) and grad. Wycliffe Coll., Toronto, 1926. Priest, 1926, and appointed to Kangra Mission, Punjab Missionary Society, C of E in Canada. Secretary-Treasurer, Kangra Mission, 1930; Canon, Lahore Cathedral, 1942; Archdeacon, East Punjab, 1949; Assistant Bishop of Lahore, 1950; first Bishop of Amritsar, 1953-59. Hon. DD: Wycliffe Coll., 1946; Huron Coll., 1962. Jubilee Medal, 1935; Coronation Medal, 1937; Kaisar-i-Hind (Silver), 1942. *Address:* 2211 New Street, Burlington, Ont, Canada. *[Died 11 Aug. 1979.*

WILKINSON, Sir David; see Wilkinson, Sir L. D.

WILKINSON, Edgar Riley, CMG 1956; FIMechE; FIEE; *b* 14 April 1898; *s* of late James Driver Wilkinson, Ashton-on-Ribble, Preston, Lancashire; *m* 1945, Frances Elizabeth, *d* of late Dr George Lambright, Shaker Heights, Ohio, USA; two *d*. *Educ:* Technical College, Preston. Power Station design engineer, English Electric Co., 1919-24; Cons. Engineer, Merz and McLellan, 1924-28; Deputy Commercial Manager, Central Electricity Board, 1928-37. Commercial Manager, 1937-48; Commercial Manager, British Electricity Authority, 1948-55. Dep. Chm. Balfour Beatty & Co. Ltd, 1956-67; Dir, Power Securities Corp. Ltd, 1956-68; Deputy Chairman (London Board): East African Power & Light Co., 1966-72; Kenya Power Co. Ltd, 1966-72. Pres. Assoc. of Supervising Electrical Engineers, 1944-46; Technical Adviser, Four-Power Conf., Paris, 1946; Chm. Br. Electrical Develt Assoc., 1950-51; Special rep. of IBRD (Mexico), 1954-55. *Address:* 2 Alington House, Lilliput, Poole, Dorset. *T:* Canford Cliffs 708038. *Club:* Reform. *[Died 20 Dec. 1977.*

WILKINSON, Prof. Frank Clare, CBE 1956; LLD; MD; ChB, BDS, DDSc, MSc; FRCS, FDS; Hon. Consultant Dental Surgeon, Eastman Dental Hospital, 1959-64, retired; Dean and Dir of Studies of Institute of Dental Surgery in British Postgraduate Medical Federation, Univ. of London, and Dir of Eastman Dental Hospital, 1950-59; Prof. of Dental Surgery, London Univ., 1952-57; Consultant Dental Surgeon to the Royal Navy, 1944; Member, Board of the Faculty of Dental Surgery, Roy. Coll. of Surgeons, 1947, Dean, 1953-56; *b* Cheshire, 31 Aug. 1889; *s* of Frank Wilkinson and Annie A. Clare; *m* 1917, Gladys Eveline Tweedie; one *d*. *Educ:* Wallasey Grammar School; Univ. of Liverpool. Prizes in Operative Dental Surgery and in Orthodontia; House Surgeon, Liverpool Dental Hospital, 1912; Senior Demonstrator in Operative Dental Surgery, University of Liverpool, 1919-23; Dental Tutor, University of Liverpool, 1923; Hon. Dental Surgeon, David Lewis Northern Hospital; Lecturer for the Dental Board of UK; Member, Board Dental Studies University of Liverpool; Professor of Dental Science, Dean of the Faculty of Dental Science, and Director Dental Research Depart, University of

Melbourne; Principal of the Australian College of Dentistry, 1925-33; Captain RAMC, attached Liverpool Merchants Mobile Hosp., France, 1915-19; Hon. Major AMC, 1928-33; Professor of Dental Surgery, Dean of the Turner Dental School, and Director of Dental Hospital, Manchester University, 1933-50; Hon. Adviser in Dental Surgery, Manchester Royal Infirmary, 1934-50, and St Mary's Hospitals, 1946-50; Hon. Consultant Dental Surgeon Christie Hospital and Holt Radium Institute, 1934-50; Director, Maxillo-facial Centre, NW Area, 1939-50; Surgical Specialist, EMS; Member: Dental Advisory Cttee, MEd. Research Council, 1947-60; Standing Dental Services Advisory Cttee, Central Health Council, 1948-60; Medical Sub cttee of Univ. Grants Cttee, 1952-60; Inter-departmental Cttee on Recruitment of Dental Students, 1955; Council Roy. Soc. Med. (Pres. Odont. Sect. 1959-60); General Dental Council (Chm. Educ. Cttee), 1956-59; Mem. NW Metropolitan Regional Hospital Board, 1954-60. Colyer Gold Medal, 1965. Hon. FRACDS. *Publications:* numerous articles in British Dental Journal, etc. *Recreation:* yachting. *Address:* 33 Craigmore Tower, Guildford Road, Woking, Surrey. *[Died 22 Aug. 1979.*

WILKINSON, Frederick, OBE 1968; MA; Head Master, Latymer Upper School, Hammersmith, 1937-57; *b* 18 Apr. 1891; *m* 1924, Edith Mary Previté (*d* 1968), *e d* of Professor Kennedy Orton, DSc, FRS. *Educ:* Grammar School, Dudley; Sidney Sussex College, Cambridge. Historical Tripos, Second Class; Assistant Master, Laxton School, Oundle; Senior History and House Master, Liverpool College, 1920-26; Head Master, Grammar School, Wallasey, 1927-34; Polytechnic School, W1, 1934-37; Active Service 1914-19 in France, Egypt and Italy; Captain 5th South Staffs Regt, Captain and Wing Adjutant RAF (Observers' Badge, R Aero Club Certificate, despatches); Producer of plays and operas to various Societies-specialised in the work of Purcell and Holst. Hon. Fellow, Roy. Commonwealth Society. *Publications:* various articles in English and foreign periodicals on subjects connected with education, drama and film. *Recreation:* walking. *Address:* 5 The Mall, East Sheen, SW14. *T:* 01-876 6186.   *[Died 24 Sept. 1978.*

WILKINSON, Rt. Rev. Heber; *see* Wilkinson, Rt Rev. C. R. H.

WILKINSON, Hector Russell, CIE 1927; *b* 11 March 1888; *s* of late Rev. G. G. Wilkinson; *m* 1920, Theodora, *d* of late Robert Daintree, Horam, Sussex; one *s* (and two *s* one *d* decd). *Educ:* Clifton Coll.; Queen's Coll., Oxford. Indian CS 1912-39, Dist Magistrate, Chittagong, 1928-30, Sec., Educn Dept, Bengal, 1931-35, Comr, Dacca Div., 1937-38; Ministry of Food, 1939-45. *Address:* Grange Cottage, Hadlow Down, Uckfield, Sussex. *T:* Hadlow Down 252. *Club:* East India, Sports and Public Schools.   *[Died 26 Nov. 1972.*

WILKINSON, Brig. John Shann, CB 1939; DSO 1918; MC; psc; retired; *b* 1884; *s* of Rev. Christopher George Wilkinson, MA Cantab, Bubwith, E Yorks; *m* 1st, 1918, Gwendoline Mary Brooke Bailey (*d* 1962); 2nd, 1965, Katharine Hutton Wanklyn, *widow* of Endell Wanklyn, Christchurch, New Zealand. Sherwood Foresters, 1906; served East Africa, 1913 (medal with clasp); European War, 1914-18 (despatches, DSO, MC); Somaliland, 1920 (despatches, Bt Lt-Col, clasp, Somaliland 1920); GSO2, Staff Coll., Camberley; Dep. Dir of Movements, War Office; retired pay, 1938. Re-employed, 1939, in charge Administration Aldershot Command, then as DA and QMG 2nd AA Corps. *Recreation:* fishing. *Address:* 13 Highgate Avenue, Christchurch, New Zealand.   *[Died 27 Feb. 1977.*

WILKINSON, Sir (Leonard) David, 2nd Bt *cr* 1941; DSC 1943; *b* 18 Jan. 1920; *o s* of Sir George Henry Wilkinson, KCVO, 1st Bt and of Lady Wilkinson (*née* Volland); *S* father, 1967; *m* 1946, Sylvia Ruby Eva Anne Gater (marr. diss. 1967); one *s* one *d*. *Educ:* Eton; Christ Church, Oxford. Joined RNVR 1939; served Mediterranean, North Sea, Atlantic and Southern reaches with Fleet Air Arm; comd 801 Sqn, 1944, 803 1st RCN Air Sqn, 1945; Lt-Comdr 1946. Hon. Dir, Thermega Ltd, 1947-56; Hon. Treas., Ex-Services Welfare Soc., 1947-56; Mem. Council, Music in Hospitals, 1948-54; a Governor, Bridewell Royal Hosp., 1958-; Assistant Dir-Gen, St John Ambulance Assoc., 1964-68, Director, 1968-. OStJ 1956, CStJ 1965, KStJ 1968, Mem. of Chapter General 1969-. *Recreations:* ski-ing, sailing. *Heir:* *s* David Graham Brook Wilkinson [*b* 18 May 1947. *Educ:* Millfield; Christ Church, Oxford]. *Address:* Brook, near Godalming, Surrey.   *[Died 1 Nov. 1972.*

WILKINSON, Leslie, OBE 1969; DLitt 1970; FRIBA; (Life) FRAIA; Emeritus Professor of Architecture, University of Sydney (Professor, 1918-47); in practice; *b* London, 12 Oct. 1882; *s* of Edward Henry and Ellen Wilkinson; *m* 1912, Alice Dorothy Ruston; one *s* two *d*. *Educ:* St Edward's School, Oxford. Articled to J. S. Gibson, FRIBA, 1900; Gold and Silver medallist Royal Academy School; Travelling Student RA Schools; Silver medallist, RIBA; Assistant Professor, School of Architecture, University College, London, 1908; RAIA Gold medallist, 1961. *Publications:* papers on architectural subjects. *Address:* 24 Wentworth Road, Vaucluse, Sydney, NSW 2030, Australia.   *[Died 20 Sept. 1973.*

WILKINSON, Norman, CBE 1948 (OBE 1918); Order of the Crown of Belgium; ROI; Hon. RWS; Past President, Royal Institute of Painters in Water Colours; Lieut-Commander, RNVR; Marine Painter to Royal Yacht Squadron; *b* Cambridge, 24 Nov. 1878; *m* 1st, 1918, Evelyn (*d* 1967), *y d* of Rev. Murdo C. Mackenzie; one *s* one *d*; 2nd, 1968, Joyce Jervis. *Educ:* Berkhamsted School; St Paul's Cathedral Choir Sch. Adviser on Camouflage to Air Ministry, 1939-42 (with rank of Hon. Air Cdre). Originator of Dazzle painting adopted by all the Allied Nations in the European War, 1914-18, for the protection of merchant vessels against submarine attack. Seconded to US Navy to advise on dazzle painting of ships. Presented fifty-four pictures of The War at Sea to the Nation, 1944, now at Imperial Maritime Museum, Greenwich. One-man show, Tryon Gallery, 1970. *Publications:* The Dardanelles; Colour Sketches from Gallipoli, 1915; Ships in Pictures, 1945; Water Colour Sketching out of doors, 1953; A Brush with Life (memoirs), 1969. *Address:* The Studio, Winchfield, near Basingstoke, Hants. *T:* Hartley Wintney 2968; (summer) Seaview House, Seaview, Isle of Wight. *T:* Seaview 3160. *Clubs:* Arts; (Hon. Member) Royal Thames Yacht; (Hon. Member) Royal Yacht Squadron; (Hon. Member) RNVR.   *[Died 30 May 1971.*

WILKINSON, Reginald Warren Hale, QC; *b* Leamington Spa, Warwicks, 1882; *s* of late Rev. Dr Edward Wilkinson; *m* 1928, Catherine, Countess Troyanovsky (*née* de Danilkiewicz) (*d* 1966). *Educ:* abroad; Leamington Coll.; Balliol Coll., Oxford; BA (Hons in Classics and Modern History), 1904; MA 1911. Barrister-at-law, Inner Temple, 1907; and of Sierra Leone Bar, 1909; Assistant District Commissioner, Sierra Leone, 1909; Assistant Colonial Secretary and JP, Sierra Leone, 1912; Senior Crown Counsel, Gold Coast, 1914; Solicitor-General, Gold Coast, 1915; attached to Colonial Office (Legal Adviser's Department), 1915; acted for prolonged periods as Attorney-General, Gold Coast, and as legal adviser to the British Military Administration in Togoland, 1915-20; Judge of the Supreme Court of the Gold Coast Colony, 1920; Acting Governor and C-in-C, Gold Coast, 1921, Attorney-General, 1921-28; KC 1924; retired, 1928. Formerly Hon. Corr. Secretary, Royal Empire Society (which is now Royal Commonwealth Society). *Address:* c/o Barclays Bank (France), Ltd, Monte Carlo, Monaco.
                                              [Died 30 Jan. 1973.

WILKINSON, Richard Edward, CBE 1966; British Consul-General at Izmir, Turkey, 1960-69, retired; *b* 11 Nov. 1901; *s* of Charles Crosbie Wilkinson and Madeline La Fontaine; *m* 1924, Thelma de Cramer; two *s*. *Educ:* privately. Appointed Vice-Consul at Izmir, 1933; Consul, 1950; Consul-General, 1960. *Recreation:* archæology. *Address:* 16 Hürriyet Caddesi, Bornova, Izmir, Turkey. *T:* 81179.   *[Died 8 Nov. 1972.*

WILKINSON, William Dale, CB 1949; CBE 1942; DSO 1917; MC; *b* 1893; *e s* of late Rev. W. Wilkinson; *m* 1st, 1924, Margaret Frances (*d* 1932), *e d* of late J. E. Bunting; 2nd, 1934, Mary Devas, *e d* of late R. Marshall. *Educ:* Bradford Grammar Sch.; Magdalen Coll., Oxford; MA. Gazetted to 7th Battalion Yorkshire Regt (The Green Howards); 1914; Captain, 1916; served in France, 1915-18 (MC, DSO, despatches); in India (seconded to Indian Army), 1918-19; entered the Treasury, 1919; Private Secretary to the Financial Secretary, 1921-22; to Controller of Finance, 1922-30; Seconded to Cabinet Offices, 1930-34 and 1935-39; to Imperial Defence College, 1934; transferred to Cabinet Offices, 1939; transferred to Ministry of Aircraft Production, afterwards amalgamated with Ministry of Supply, 1942; Principal Assistant Secretary, 1944; Principal Establishment Officer, 1945; Under Secretary, 1946; retired 1954. *Address:* Hanover House, Curry Rivel, Somerset. *T:* Curry Rivel 372.   *[Died 31 Jan. 1973.*

WILLAN, Sir Harold Curwen, Kt 1947; CMG 1946; MC 1917; Commissioner, Foreign Compensation Commission, 1962-68, Vice-Chairman, 1967-68; *b* 29 Feb. 1896; *s* of late Richard Willan, Kendal, Westmorland; *m* 1922, Marjorie Rigg; one *s*. *Educ:* Kendal School; Jesus Coll., Oxford (BA). Barrister-at-Law, Inner Temple (Cert. of Hon.); Inns of Court OTC 1915; Lieut, RA, 1916; BEF France, 1916-17 (MC); Cadet, Malayan Civil Service, 1920; District Judge, Straits Settlements, 1932; Deputy Legal Adviser, Federated Malay States, 1934; Solicitor-General, Kenya, 1937; Attorney-General, Zanzibar, 1940 (Brilliant Star of Zanzibar); Legal Adviser, Civil Affairs, East Africa Command, and acted as Chief Political Officer, 1941;

President, High Court, Ethiopia, 1942; Deputy Chief Civil Affairs Officer, Malay Peninsula, with rank of Brigadier, 1945 (despatches twice); Chief Justice, Malayan Union, 1946, Fed. of Malaya, 1948-50; Chief Justice of the United Kingdom High Commission Territories in S. Africa, 1952-56. *Publications:* Digest of Reported Law Cases, Federated Malay States, 1936; High Commission Territories Law Reports. *Recreations:* golf and bowls. *Address:* 6 Squirrels Way, Epsom, Surrey. *T:* Epsom 21185. *Club:* East India and Sports. *[Died* 11 *Dec.* 1971.

WILLERT, Sir Arthur, KBE 1919; *b* 19 May 1882; *s* of late P. F. Willert of Headington Hill, Oxford; *m* 1908, Ethel Florence McKay (*d* 1955), *er d* of Sir Walter Simpson, 2nd Bt of Balabraes, Ayton, Scotland; one *s. Educ:* Eton; Balliol Coll., Oxford. Joined staff of The Times, 1906; worked in Paris, Berlin, and Washington Offices of The Times, 1906-08; Member editorial staff of The Times in London, 1909, and also London correspondent of New York Evening Post; Chief correspondent of The Times in USA, 1910-20, except in 1917-18 when served as Secretary in Washington of the British War Mission in the USA, and as Washington representative of the Ministry of Information; joined the Foreign Office, 1921, where he became head of the News Department and Press Officer; Member of the United Kingdom Delegations to the Washington Naval Conference, 1921-22, to the London Economic Conference, 1924, to the London Naval Conference, 1930, to the Geneva Disarmament Conference, 1932-34, and to meetings of the League of Nations, 1929-34; resigned from Foreign Office, 1935; Head of Ministry of Information Office for the Southern Region, 1939-45. *Publications:* Aspects of British Foreign Policy, 1928; The Frontiers of England, 1935; (joint) The Empire in the World, 1937; The Road to Safety, 1952. *Address:* 37 Eaton Place, SW1. *T:* 01-235 6452. *Clubs:* Brooks's, Beefsteak, National Press; Washington (hon. member).
[Died 11 *March* 1973.

WILLETT, Comdr William (Basil), OBE 1964; MVO 1969; DSC 1942; RN; Private Secretary to The Duke of Edinburgh, since 1970; *b* 24 Feb. 1919; *s* of late Captain B. R. Willett, CBE, DSC, RN, and of Mrs Willett, OBE; *m* 1946, Anne, *d* of late C. R. Rolland, Montreal, Canada, and of Mrs Rolland; one *s* two *d. Educ:* Winchester. Royal Navy, 1937. Served War of 1939-45 (despatches, DSC). Sailing Master, Royal Yacht, Bloodhound, 1967-68. Officier, Légion d'Honneur; Comdr, Mil. Order of Christ (Portugal). *Address:* c/o National Westminster Bank, 74 Sloane Street, SW1. *[Died* 3 *Jan.* 1976.

WILLEY, Prof. Basil, MA (Cantab); FBA 1947; FRSL 1950; Hon. LittD (Manchester), 1948; King Edward VII Professor of English Literature, University of Cambridge, 1946-64; Hon. Fellow, Pembroke College, 1964 (Fellow, 1935); President, 1958-64; *b* 25 July 1897; *s* of William Herbert Willey and Alice Ann Le Gros; *m* 1923, Zélie Murlis Ricks; two *s* two *d. Educ:* University College Sch., Hampstead. History Scholarship at Peterhouse, 1915; Lieut, West Yorkshire Regt, 1916-18; 1st Class Historical Tripos, 1920; 1st Class English Tripos, 1921; Hugo de Balsham Student at Peterhouse and Le Bas Prize, 1922; Lecturer in English at Cambridge from 1923; University Lecturer, 1934. Visiting Professor: Columbia Univ., New York, 1948-49; Cornell Univ., 1953; Vis. Fellow, University Coll., Cardiff, 1970-71; Chairman, Dove Cottage Trustees, 1961-72; Lectures: Hibbert, 1959; Ballard Mathews, UC N Wales, 1964; Drew, New Coll., Univ. of London, 1967. *Publications:* Tendencies in Renaissance Literary Theory (Le Bas Prize Essay), 1922; The Seventeenth Century Background, 1934; The Eighteenth Century Background, 1940; Collected Essays and Studies by Members of the Eng. Assoc., Vol. XXXII, 1946; XLIV, 1958; Coleridge on Imagination and Fancy (British Acad. Warton Lecture, 1946); Chapter on English Thought in The Character of England (ed Sir Ernest Barker, 1947); Richard Crashaw Memorial Lecture, 1949; Nineteenth Century Studies, 1949; Introduction to Thoreau's Walden, 1951; Christianity Past and Present, 1952; (ed) Bacon and Donne in Major British Writers (New York), 1953; More Nineteenth Century Studies, 1956; The Religion of Nature (Essex Hall Lecture), 1957; Darwin and Butler: Two Versions of Evolution, 1959; The English Moralists, 1964; Centenary Introductions to Newman's Apologia and Quiller-Couch's Troy Town, 1964; Spots of Time, 1965; Cambridge and Other Memories, 1920-1953, 1969; Introduction to Mark Rutherford's Autobiography and Deliverance, 1969; Religion Today, 1969; Samuel Taylor Coleridge, 1972; various articles and reviews. *Relevant publication:* The English Mind (essays presented to Basil Willey, ed by H. S. Davies and G. Watson), 1964. *Recreations:* music; the English countryside. *Address:* 18 Adams Road, Cambridge. *Club:* Athenæum. *[Died* 3 *Sept.* 1978.

WILLIAMS; *see* Lloyd-Williams.

WILLIAMS, A. Franklyn, CMG 1960; Member, Welsh Council, since 1971; *b* 5 Feb. 1907; *s* of Benjamin Williams and Katherine Williams (*née* Thomas); *m* 1st, Doris May (marr. diss., 1952), *d* of David I. and Sarah Jane Munro; one *s* decd; 2nd, 1952, Nancy, MBE, *d* of Evan John and Edith David. *Educ:* Ferndale Secondary Sch., Rhondda; University College, Cardiff. BSc University of Wales, 1927. HM Inspector of Taxes, Inland Revenue, 1929-45; Ministry of Power, 1946-. Chairman, Coal Cttee of Economic Commn for Europe (ECE), 1952-55. Petroleum Attaché, HM Embassy, Washington, 1956-60; Senior Officer for Wales, Ministry of Power, 1960-61; Chairman, Welsh Bd of Health, 1962-69. Mem., General Optical Council, 1974-. CStJ 1968. *Recreation:* wood turning. *Address:* 45 Cyncoed Road, Cardiff. *T:* Cardiff 32334. *Clubs:* Royal Air Force; Cardiff and County (Cardiff). *[Died* 15 *Nov.* 1978.

WILLIAMS, Sir Alan (Meredith), KCMG 1963 (CMG 1958); Ambassador to Spain, 1966-69; *b* 22 Aug. 1909; *s* of Thomas Charles Williams and Margaret Williams (*née* McGregor); *m* 1946, Masha Poustchine; one *s* one *d. Educ:* Berkhamsted Sch.; Pembroke Coll., Cambridge. Entered HM Consular Service, 1932, and served at San Francisco, Reykjavik, Leopoldville, Vienna, Panama, Hamburg, Rotterdam, Baghdad, Tunis and at the Foreign Office; Consul-General, New York, 1960-64; also for St Pierre amd Miquelon, 1961-64; Ambassador and Consul-General to Panama, 1964-66. *Recreations:* reading, watching, listening. *Address:* 1 Morland Close, NW11; Cae Ffynnon, Llangystenin, Caernarvonshire. *Club:* Travellers'.
[Died 2 *Dec.* 1972.

WILLIAMS, Alfred Cecil, CB 1961; Permanent Secretary, Ministry of Education for Northern Ireland, 1958-64; *b* 11 May 1899; *er s* of Owen R. Williams, Dublin and Holyhead; *m* 1926, Eileen Mary, *o d* of Alexander Poole Wilson, Dublin and Birkenhead; one *s* two *d. Educ:* St Andrew's Coll., Dublin; Trinity Coll., Dublin. Sizarship in Maths, 1st Place (TCD); Kidd Entrance Schol. 1st Place (TCD); Foundation Schol. (TCD); Senior Moderatorship in Maths, 1st Place; Senior Moderatorship in Experimental Science, 1st Place in Physics; University Studentship in Maths; Fitzgerald Schol. in Physics; BAI, 1st Place, Alexander Prize. Lecturer in Mathematics, Magee University Coll., Londonderry, 1922; Inspector of Schools, Ministry of Education for Northern Ireland, 1924; Senior Inspector of Schools, 1929; Senior Chief Inspector, 1943. Civil Service Commissioner for Northern Ireland, 1958-64. Hon. LLD (*jure dignitatis*) Dublin University. *Recreations:* gardening, music. *Address:* Delgany, 37 Hawthornden Road, Belfast BT4 3JW. *T:* Belfast 653078. *[Died* 1976.

WILLIAMS, Rt. Rev. Anthony Lewis Elliott, MA; DD; Sub-Prelate, Order of St John of Jerusalem, since 1956; *b* 5 Feb. 1892; *s* of George Robert Williams, MD, and Adelaide Frances Williams (*née* Murray); *m* 1922, Mary Freeman; one *s* three *d. Educ:* King's Sch., Worcester; Exeter Coll., Oxford; Salisbury Theological Coll. Curate: St John, Kidderminster, 1915-18; Christchurch, Harrogate, 1918-20; Vicar, North Stainley, Ripon, 1921-25; Rector, Kirkby Wiske, Thirsk, 1925-31; Vicar: Banbury, 1931-46; Bournemouth, 1946-56. Chaplain to the Bishop of Ripon, 1921-31; Dep. Priest-in-Ordinary to: King George VI, 1945-52; Queen Elizabeth II, 1952-56. Chaplain, Order of St John of Jerusalem, 1953-56. Bishop of Bermuda, 1956-62, resigned. Hon. Canon: Christchurch, Oxford, 1940-46; Winchester, 1950-56. *Publications:* The Two Ways, 1937; The Happy Heathen, 1938; From A to B, 1972. *Recreations:* painting in oils, motoring, walking. *Address:* 7 Park Street, Woodstock, Oxon. *Clubs:* Athenæum; Oxford Union. *[Died* 31 *Aug.* 1975.

WILLIAMS, Ven. Arthur Charles; Archdeacon of Bodmin, 1962-68; Archdeacon Emeritus and Prebendary Emeritus of St Endellion, since 1969 (Rector, 1965-68); *b* 8 July 1899; *s* of Thomas John and Belle Williams, Truro; *m* 1929, Jessie Lucretia Boggia; one *d. Educ:* Truro Cathedral Sch.; College of the Resurrection, Mirfield. Joined Army, 1917 (PoW 1918). College of Resurrection, 1919-22. Curate of S Clements, Barnsbury, London, 1922-26; Curate of S Mary, Penzance, 1926-32; Vicar of Stratton, 1932-45; Rural Dean of Stratton, 1934-39 and 1943-45. CF, 1939-43, SCF 1940, Hon. CF 1943 (TA). Vicar of S Mary the Virgin, Penzance, 1945-62; Rural Dean of Penwith, 1959-62. Hon. Canon of Truro Cathedral, 1952-74, Canon Emeritus, 1974; Fellow of Woodard Corporation, 1945-74, Hon. Fellow, 1974; Vice-Provost of the Western Division, 1962-74; Proctor in Convocation, 1957. *Address:* 4 Clarence Place, Penzance. *T:* Penzance 2798. *[Died* 23 *Sept.* 1974.

WILLIAMS, Arthur de Coetlogon, CSI 1946; CIE 1938; *b* 27 Sept. 1890; *s* of late E. de C. Williams; *m* 1919, Bethea Helen

Field; one *s* two *d. Educ:* Winchester; Marlborough; Balliol Coll., Oxford. Entered ICS 1915. Army Service, 1916-19. Legislative Secretary and Legal Remembrancer, Bengal, 1935; Secretary, Viceroy's Executive Council, 1936; Secretary to the Governor-General and Government of India, Defence Co-ordination, 1938; Secretary to the Governor of Bengal, 1942; Chief Secretary, Bengal, 1943; Civil Supplies Commissioner, Bengal, 1945; Adviser to Governor of Bengal, retired, 1949. *Address:* Glencoe, Les Camps, St Martin's, Guernsey. *Clubs:* East India, Sports, and Public Schools; Bengal (Calcutta).
[Died 20 Feb. 1973.

WILLIAMS, A(rthur) Emlyn, VRD 1945; BSc, MB, BCh, FRCS; Consultant Surgeon, Royal Free Hospital, since 1949; Consultant Surgeon, Hampstead General Hospital, since 1948; Teacher in Surgery, Royal Free Hospital Medical School, since 1958; *b* 11 April 1910; *o s* of late Obadiah and Ruth Williams, Cardiff; *m* 1940, Zoë Irene, *d* of late Major Richard Ralph Baldwin Wall, RA, Omagh, Co. Tyrone; four *s. Educ:* Cardiff High Sch.; University College, Cardiff; Welsh National School of Medicine; University of London (St Bartholomew's Hospital). Demonstrator and Tutor in Anatomy and Physiology, University College, Cardiff, 1935-36; House Surgeon, British Postgraduate Medical School, London, 1937-38. Surgical Specialist, RN, 1940-46 (Surgeon Lieut-Commander RNVR). Surgical Registrar, Hampstead General Hospital, 1946-48; Clinical Asst, St Peter's Hospital and St Mark's Hospital, London, 1946-50; Tutor in Surgery, Royal Free Hosp. Med. Sch., 1964-67. Marsden travelling professorship to USA, 1953. Examiner in Surgery, London Univ. FRSocMed., Fellow: Med. Soc. London; Hunterian Society; Assoc. of Surg., Great Britain. Freeman, City of London, 1952. *Publications:* contributions to learned journals and Societies; contrib. to official Naval Medical History of the War. *Recreations:* golf, sailing. *Address:* 112 Harley Street, W1. *T:* 01-935 1956; 3 Turner Drive, NW11. *T:* 01-458 1646; Pantyrhedd, Newport, Dyfed. *Club:* Savile.
[Died 5 April 1976.

WILLIAMS, Sir (Arthur) Leonard, GCMG 1968; GCVO 1972; Governor-General of Mauritius, since 1968; *b* 22 Jan. 1904; *o s* of late George Williams; *m* 1930, Margaret Wiggins. *Educ:* Holy Trinity C of E Elementary Sch., Birkenhead; The Labour Coll., London. Member Liverpool & N Wales District Council, NUR, 1920-21; Secretary, Birkenhead & District Joint Cttee, NUR, 1923-24; Staff Tutor, Liverpool Labour Coll., 1924-26; Tutor-Organiser, National Council of Labour Colleges, 1926-36; contested (Lab) Southport, 1929; Winchester, 1935. Secretary Leeds Labour Party, 1936-42; joined Labour Party Head Office Staff, 1942; Reg. Organiser, E and W Ridings of Yorks, 1942-46; Asst National Agent, 1946-51; National Agent, 1951-59; Nat. Agent and Dep. General Secretary, 1959-62; General Secretary, 1962-68. Editor, Leeds Weekly Citizen, 1937-44; Editor, Labour Organiser, 1952-62. *Recreations:* reading, walking, talking. *Address:* Government House, Le Réduit, Mauritius.
[Died 27 Dec. 1972.

WILLIAMS, Maj.-Gen. Aubrey Ellis, CBE 1944; DSO 1918; MC; *b* 19 May 1888; *s* of late Lieut-Colonel D. E. Williams, VD, JP, of Griffithstown, Mon; *m* 1922, Sybil (*d* 1966), *d* of late Dr J. R. Essex, The Woodlands, Pontypool, Mon; one *s* one *d. Educ:* Monmouth Grammar Sch.; Sandhurst. 2nd Lieut, South Wales Borderers, 1907; Lieut, 1909; Captain, 1914; Bt Major, 1918; Major, 1925; Bt Lieut-Colonel, 1930; Lieut-Colonel, 1934; Colonel, 1938; Maj.-General, 1940; served European War, 1914-19 (MC, DSO, Croix de Guerre, despatches five times); Waziristan, 1937 (Bar to DSO, despatches twice); War of 1939-45 (CBE); retired pay, 1941; re-employed, 1941-44; retired pay, 1944. Civil Defence Officer, Isle of Wight, 1950-60. *Address:* Blackbridge House, Freshwater Bay, IoW PO40 9QR. *T:* Freshwater 2159; Williams & Glyn's Bank Ltd, Kirkland House, Whitehall, SW1. *Club:* Naval and Military.
[Died 25 March 1977.

WILLIAMS, Barbara M.; *see* Moray Williams.

WILLIAMS, Lt-Col Brian Robertson; *b* 1 May 1909; *s* of Wellington Archbold Williams and Helena Worsley Williams; *m* 1st, 1938, Hilary Charmian (marr. diss. 1953), *d* of David Charles; 2nd, Amanda Elizabeth, *d* of Geoffrey Spence; one *s* one *d. Educ:* Eton. 2nd Lieut The Life Guards, 1931; Captain 1938; Major 1946; served War of 1939-45 with 2nd Household Cavalry Regt, Normandy, Belgium, Holland and Germany; temp. Lt-Col Comdg Household Cavalry Trng Regt and Depot, 1947-48; APM, London Dist, 1951; Lt-Col The Life Guards (Employed List 1), 1953; retd 1957. *Recreation:* racing. *Address:* 17 Montpelier Square, SW7 1JR. *T:* 01-584 1065; The Manor Cottage, Thruxton, Hants. *T:* Weyhill 2270. *Clubs:* Turf, Beefsteak, White's, Buck's, MCC. *[Died 5 March 1980.*

WILLIAMS, Charles Garrett, DSc; Director, Ricardo & Co.; *b* 20 October 1901; *s* of Rev. John Williams; *m* 1926, Winifred, *d* of James Doody; one *s* one *d. Educ:* Mundella Sch., Nottingham; Manchester University. BSc London 1922; BSc Manchester 1922; DSc Manchester 1941. Research Engineer with Research Association of British Motor and Allied Manufacturers, 1923-29, Technical Sec., 1929-31; Research Manager of Instn of Automobile Engineers, 1931-34, Dir of Research, 1934-40; Dir of Research of Shell Thornton Aero-Engine Laboratory, 1940-48; Dir of Research of Thornton Research Centre, 1948-52; Director of Research, Shell Petroleum Co. Ltd, London, 1952-54; Director and General Manager, Shell Research Ltd, 1955-61. Chairman Automobile Div., IMechE, 1955-56; Member Council, University of Surrey. DUniv Surrey, 1972. *Publications:* collected researches on Cylinder Wear, 1940; numerous papers to Instn of Automobile Engineers, IMechE, Institute of Petroleum, etc. on internal combustion engine, fuels, lubricants, wear, etc., and on organisation of industrial research. *Address:* Shortlands, 7 Downside Road, Guildford, Surrey. *T:* Guildford 4775. *Club:* Athenæum. *[Died 21 May 1976.*

WILLIAMS, Captain Charles Shrine; *b* 27 Sept. 1895; *s* of William and Wilhelmina Williams; unmarried. *Educ:* Liverpool Institute. Commenced seafaring career, 1913; joined Cunard Steamship Co. Ltd, 1919; Captain of "Queen Elizabeth" from Nov. 1957; retired from active service, September 1958, as Commodore. *Address:* 64 Higher Road, Hunts Cross, Woolton, Liverpool. *T:* 051-486 1505. *[Died 8 Sept. 1973.*

WILLIAMS, Clarence Faithfull M.; *see* Monier-Williams.

WILLIAMS, Sir (Daniel) Thomas, Kt 1958; OBE 1953; JP 1942; FCIS; Lloyd's Underwriter; *y s* of late D. T. Williams, Civil Servant; *m* 1934, Bertha Mary (*d* 1969) *d* of David Morgan, Monmouthshire. Lord Mayor of Cardiff, 1956-57 (Deputy, 1951-52); Vice-Chairman, Wales and Monmouthshire Conservative Association and Chairman, Glamorgan Conservative Association, 1949-60. Member, Council for Wales and Monmouthshire, 1956-59; Past Chairman: Cardiff Bench of Magistrates; Cardiff and Barry Post Office Advisory Committee; Member, Central Executive Committee, NSPCC; Past President: Cardiff and District Society of Incorporated Secretaries; Cardiff Incorp. Chamber of Commerce. KStJ; Past Pres. Welsh Amateur Boxing Assoc., and many other public bodies. Served War, 1914-18, RFC and RAF. Chevalier de la Légion d'Honneur. DL Glamorgan, 1955-68. *Address:* Freshwinds, Pleinmont, Guernsey, Channel Islands.
[Died 26 March 1973.

WILLIAMS, Prof. David; Sir John Williams Professor of Welsh History, University College of Wales, 1945-67, retired, 1967; *b* 9 Feb. 1900; *y s* of David and Anne Williams, Llan-y-cefn, Pembrokeshire; *m* 1st, 1930, Irene Muriel Fothergill (*d* 1942); 2nd, 1952, Hilarie Margaret Waddington. *Educ:* University of Wales; Columbia University; Paris and Berlin. AM (Columbia); MA, DLitt (Wales). Lecturer, University College, Cardiff, 1930-45. Served European War of 1914-18, army; War of 1939-45, Man Power Officer for south-east Wales, Min. of Labour. *Publications:* John Frost: A Study in Chartism, 1939; A History of Modern Wales, 1950; The Rebecca Riots, a Study in Agrarian Discontent, 1955; John Penry: Three Treatises concerning Wales, 1960; contrib. Eng. Hist. Rev., American Hist. Rev., etc. *Address:* 2 Laura Place, Aberystwyth. *T:* Aberystwyth 7407. *[Died 24 Feb. 1978.*

WILLIAMS, David Gwynne, MA; Headmaster, The Crypt School, Gloucester, 1920-50, retired; *b* 4 Jan. 1886; *s* of Rev. John Alexander Williams and Louisa Jane Jones; *m* 1910, Henny (*d* 1972), *d* of August Felbecker, Colmar, Alsace; two *s. Educ:* Llandovery College; Corpus Christi College, Oxford (Classical Scholar). 1st Class Lit. Hum. 1909; Classical VIth Form master at Reading, 1910; Durham, 1914; Bradford, 1915. *Publications:* Existentialist Sonnets, 1953; The Ascension of Man, 1966; Love in Escalation, 1968. *Recreation:* gardening. *Address:* 153 Finlay Road, Gloucester. *T:* Gloucester 24028.
[Died 30 Jan. 1975.

WILLIAMS, David James; Executive Council Member, South Wales Miners' Federation; *b* 3 Feb. 1897. *Educ:* Elementary School; Central Labour College. Colliery Checkweighman. MP (Lab) Neath Division of Glamorgan, 1945-64. *Publication:* Combination in the Coal Industry, 1924. *Address:* Delfryn, Penscynor, Cilfrew, Neath, Glam. *T:* Neath 832.
[Died 12 Sept. 1972.

WILLIAMS, Captain Douglas, MC; Special Correspondent of the Daily Telegraph; *b* 7 Oct. 1892; 2nd *s* of late G. D. Williams, Chief Editor of Reuters Agency, and *gs* of late W. J. Skerrett,

DL, Finavara, Co. Clare; *m* 1948, Anna Wrenn Fulton, *o d* of late Everts Wrenn, Chicago, USA. *Educ:* Benedictine College, Ealing; privately in France and Germany. Joined Reuters, 1910; served in France, 1915-17, Royal Artillery (wounded); Staff Captain on Murmansk Expedition, 1918-19. Chief Editor of Reuters, 1922; joined Daily Telegraph Staff, 1933, as American Correspondent. War Correspondent for Daily Telegraph, 1939-40, and 1943-45; Lieut RA, July 1940; Director American Division of Ministry of Information, 1940-41; Press Adviser to Minister of State at Cairo, 1941-42. *Clubs:* White's; Racquet and Tennis (NYC). *[Died 21 June 1975.*

WILLIAMS, E. C., DSc London, and MSc Manchester; now retired; Industrial Scientist; *b* 1892; *s* of late T. R. Williams, OBE, Newcastle upon Tyne; *m* 1918, Lilian (*d* 1966), *d* of J. H. Baxter, Crewe; two *s* one *d*. *Educ:* Christ's Hospital; (Grecian and Univ. Exhibr, 1911); Manchester University (Mercer Scholar 1914, Dalton Research Scholar 1917). University Rugby XV, 1911-14 and Lancs County Rugby XV, 1913-14; Capt. East Yorks Regiment, 1914-16; Research Staff and head of Intermediate Products Dept, British Dyestuffs Corporation (later Imperial Chemical Industries), 1916-21; Research Chemist to Joint Research Committee of National Benzole Association and University of Leeds, 1921-23, and member of that committee 1923-27; First Ramsay Memorial Professor of Chemical Engineering, University College, London, 1923-28; Director of Research, 1928-40, and Vice-President, 1935-40, Shell Development Co., California; originated supplies of 100 octane aircraft fuels to RAF and USAF prior to World War II, and took leading part in devel't of petrochemical industry; scientific and technical adviser to Air Reduction Company, US Industrial Chemical Co., and American Cyanamid Co., 1940-41; Vice-President and Director of Research, General Mills, Inc., Minneapolis, 1941-42; Director, Distillation Products, Inc., 1941-42; Vice-Pres. and Director of Research, General Aniline and Film Corpn, New York (IG Farben's Chemical and Photographic Industry in USA), one of four directors appointed by US Government to reorganise and operate this industry after seizure, 1942-45; Director US Industrial Chemical Co., 1942-45; Vice-President and Director of Research, Schenley Industries Corpn, New York, 1945-50; member of first Council of the Institution of Chemical Engineers, London, also of councils of other British and American societies; member of committees of National Research Council, USA, and American Association for the Advancement of Science; Walker Medallist of American Institute of Chemical Engineers, 1942; Chm. Joint-Engineering Societies' Council Advisory Cttee (Fuels) to US Dept of State on industrial disarmament of Germany. *Publications:* scientific and technical papers. *Recreations:* riding, fishing, gardening. *Address:* Belden Hill, Wilton, Conn 06897, USA. *Clubs:* Athenæum; Century Association (NY). *[Died 30 May 1973.*

WILLIAMS, Brig. Edward Stephen Bruce, CBE 1943; MA by decree Oxon 1934; *b* 2 Nov. 1892; *s* of late Maj.-Gen. Sir Hugh B. Bruce-Williams, KCB, DSO; *m* 1st, 1925, Elizabeth Frances Chadwyck-Healey (*d* 1934); 2nd, 1938, Evelyn Agnes Clay; two *s* two *d*. *Educ:* Winchester Coll.; (Inf. Coy) RMA Woolwich. 2nd Lt Rifle Bde, 1911; Capt. 1915; served France, Belgium, 1914 and 1917, Gallipoli, Egypt, 1915-16 (wounded twice, despatches, Legion of Honour 5th Class); Iraq operations, 1919-20; Bt Major, 1930; Lt-Col, Cmdg Oxford Univ. OTC, 1930-34; Bt Lt-Col 1934; Comd 2nd Bn Rifle Brigade, 1938-40; Palestine Ops 1939; Col 1940; Temp. Brig. 1940; BGS Scottish Command, 1941-42; BGS East Africa Command, 1943-46; psc; ns; retired pay, 1946. *Address:* The Old Rectory, Bramdean, Alresford, Hants. *T:* Bramdean 208. *[Died 20 Jan. 1977.*

WILLIAMS, Eric Charles, CB 1969; Chief Inspector of Nuclear Installations, 1971-75; *b* 15 May 1915; *s* of Charles Henry Williams and Agnes (*née* Turner); *m* 1946, Elisabeth Ruby Alice Bryan; one *s* one *d*. *Educ:* King Edward VI School, Stratford upon Avon; University of Birmingham. BSc (Hons 1st Cl.) 1935, MSc 1936. Joined Civil Service, 1936, at Bawdsey Research Station, Air Ministry; Hon. Wing Commander, RAF, 1943-45; attended Imperial Defence Coll., 1947; Asst Scientific Adviser, Air Ministry, 1948-49; Director of Operational Research, Admiralty, 1949-54; Scientific Adviser, Intelligence, Min. of Defence, 1955-60; Director, SHAPE Technical Centre, 1960-64; Chief Scientific Adviser, MoT, 1964-67; Chief Scientist, Min. of Power, then Chief Scientist (Energy), Min. of Technology (later DTI), 1968-74. *Recreations:* cricket, gardening. *Address:* 4 Sandringham Drive, Bangor, Co. Down, N Ireland. *T:* Bangor 55261. *Clubs:* Royal Air Force; Royal Ulster Yacht.
[Died 8 Jan. 1980.

WILLIAMS, Prof. Sir Frederic (Calland), Kt 1976; CBE 1961 (OBE 1945); FRS 1950; FIEE 1950; FIRE 1957; Professor of Electrical Engineering at Manchester University since 1946;

Director, Granada Television Ltd, since 1968; *b* 26 June 1911; *s* of F. Williams and E. A. Williams (*née* Smith); *m* 1938, Gladys Ward; one *s* one *d*. *Educ:* Stockport Grammar School; Manchester University; Magdalen College, Oxford. Manchester Univ., 1929-33, BSc 1932, MSc 1933; Metropolitan Vickers Elec. Co. Ltd, College Apprentice, 1933-34; Oxford Univ., 1934-36, DPhil 1936. Assistant Lecturer, Manchester University, 1936-39; DSc 1939. Scientific Civil Service, Bawdsey and Telecommunications Research Estab., Malvern, 1939-46. Rank, on leaving, Principal Scientific Officer. First holder of the Benjamin Franklin Medal, Royal Society of Arts, 1957; John Scott Award, City of Philadelphia, 1960; Hughes Medal, Royal Society, 1963; Faraday Medal, IEE, 1972; Pioneer Award, IEEE Aerospace and Electronics Systems Soc. of America, 1973. Hon. DSc: Durham, 1964; Sussex, 1971; Wales, 1971; Hon. DEng Liverpool, 1966. *Publications:* (Collab. ed.) Vols 19 and 20 of Radiation Laboratory Series. Scientific papers in: Jl of IEE; Proc. IMechE; Proc. Royal Soc.; Wireless Engineer; Post Office Electrical Engineers' Journal; Proc. Cambridge Philosophical Society. *Address:* Spinney End, The Village, Prestbury, Cheshire. *T:* Prestbury 48154. *[Died 11 Aug. 1977.*

WILLIAMS, Gilbert Milner, CB 1956; CBE 1950; retired from Civil Service, 1961; *b* London, 27 May 1898; *o s* of late H. Noel Williams; *m* 1927, Vera, *y d* of Carl Salling; one *d* (one *s* one *d* decd). *Educ:* Merchant Taylor's School. Barrister-at-law (Gray's Inn). Served European War, 1915-19 (RE); Admty, 1919-28; Min. of Labour, 1928-44; Assistant Secretary, Ministry of National Insurance, 1945-53; Under-Secretary for Finance and Accountant-General, Ministry fof Pensions and National Insurance, 1953-57, and Director of Establishments and Organisation, 1957-61. Public Inquiries for Min. of Transport, 1962-70. *Address:* 61 The Avenue, Watford, Herts. *T:* Watford 26761. *Club:* Royal Commonwealth Society.
[Died 24 Jan. 1979.

WILLIAMS, Sir Griffith Goodland, KBE 1949; CB 1945; retired; *b* 20 Sept. 1890; *o surv. s* of late Alfred Augustus Williams and late Mrs E. F. Ambrose; unmarried. *Educ:* Westminster; Christ Church, Oxford. Assistant Master at Wellington and Lancing; European War, 1914-18, Captain 4th Dorsets, General Staff Officer AHQ India, Poona Brigade, and GHQ Mes. Exp. Force; Board of Education, 1919; Principal Private Secretary to Earl of Halifax, 1935, Colonel Oliver Stanley, 1935-37; Deputy Secretary Ministry of Education, 1946-Dec. 1953. Comr for Boy Scouts, City of Westminster, 1925-35. Governor of Eastbourne College. Secretary, Churches Main Cttee, 1954-70. KSG 1971. *Recreation:* music. *Address:* 52 Cranmer Court, Sloane Avenue, SW3. *T:* 01-589 4347. *Club:* Athenæum.
[Died 19 April 1974.

WILLIAMS, Harley; *see* Williams (J. H.) H.

WILLIAMS, Lt-Gen. (Hon.) Sir Harold, KBE 1956 (CBE 1946); CB 1953; FICE, MIE (Ind.), MIS (Ind.); Major-General (Hon.) late Corps of Royal Engineers, retired; Lieutenant-General (Hon.) Indian Army; Colonel Commandant, Corps of Engineers, IA. 1951-55; *b* 1 June 1897; *e s* of late Hillas Williams. *Educ:* Mountjoy Sch., Dublin; RMA, Woolwich; Gonville and Caius Coll., Cambridge. Joined 1st KGO Bengal Sappers and Miners, 1918. Served European War, 1914-18 Aden Field Force; Adj. King George's Own Bengal Sappers and Miners, 1929-33; Ind. Mil. Acad., 1933-36; Bt Major, 1934; Professor of Civil Engineering, Roorkee Coll., 1936-38; CRE 1st Armd Div., 1940-41; Brig. Eng. Staff, GHQ, India, 1942-43; Chief Engineer, 4 Corps, Assam and Burma (despatches), 1943-44; Comdt SME India, 1945-47; Chief Engineer, Southern Command, 1947; Engineer-in-Chief, Indian Army, 1948-55. Retired from Regular Army, 1956. Director, Central Building Research Institute, India, 1955-62; Adviser to Council of Scientific and Industrial Research, India, 1962-64; Consultant, Planning Commn, Government of India, 1965-67. Member Council, Inst. CE, 1951-54, 1958-61. President Inst. of Engineers (Ind.), 1954-55; President, Inst. of Surveyors (Ind.), 1954-55. MBOU. Hon. DEng Roorkee, 1970. *Publications:* various papers in scientific and technical journals. *Address:* 5 Greenhill Court, Sherborne, Dorset. *T:* Sherborne 3383. *Clubs:* United Service and Royal Aero, Alpine; Himalayan (Calcutta; President, 1960-64). *[Died 17 Oct. 1971.*

WILLIAMS, Ivor M. B.; *see* Bankes-Williams.

WILLIAMS, (John Hargreaves) Harley, OBE 1950; MD; Physician and Author; Barrister-at-Law; *s* of John and Lilian Williams; *m* 1941, Elizabeth Mackay Pascoe. *Publications:* A Century of Public Health, 1929; Northern Lights and Western Stars, 1938; The Inheritors, 1939; Fingal's Box, 1941; At Cape Faithful, 1943; Doctors Differ, 1946; Men of Stress, 1948; The Healing Touch, 1949; Between Life and Death, 1951; The

Conquest of Fear, 1952 (Swedish trans. 1953); Don Quixote of the Microscope, 1954 (Spanish trans. 1955); A Doctor looks at Miracles, 1959; Great Biologists, 1961; The Will to Health, 1961; Your Heart, 1970; Requiem for a Great Killer, 1973. *Recreations:* the arts. *Address:* Cloisters, Temple, EC4. *Club:* Reform.   *[Died* 12 *April* 1974.

WILLIAMS, John Haulfryn; Hon. Secretary, Honourable Society of Cymmrodorion, since 1973; *b* 1 Nov. 1908; *s* of Morgan and Elizabeth Williams; *m* 1938, Mary Gertrude Snowden; one *s. Educ:* Rhondda Grammar Sch.; Univ. of Wales (University Coll., Cardiff). BA (Hons Classics). Entered Inland Revenue Dept as Asst Inspector of Taxes, 1930; retd as Sen. Principal Inspector of Taxes, 1973. Mem. Council, Honourable Soc. of Cymmrodorion, 1973-. Mem., Ct of Governors, and Council, Nat. Library of Wales, 1978. *Publications:* contribs to Qly Jl of HM Inspectors of Taxes on Taxation of Insurance Companies and on Double Taxation. *Recreations:* music, archaeology, bookbinding, walking. *Address:* 52 Harrow Road, Carshalton, Surrey SM5 3QQ. *T:* 01-642 6393.
[Died 2 *Nov.* 1980.

WILLIAMS, Lieut-Col Kenneth Greville, OBE 1920; *b* 30 Jan. 1892; *s* of Lewis Greville Williams, *g s* of Charles Greville Williams, FRS; *m* Elia Mary, *d* of Major Cecil Howard, Royal Horse Artillery; one *s* three *d. Educ:* Royal Military Coll., Sandhurst. Commissioned Royal Northumberland Fusiliers, 1912; France, Flanders, Salonika, 1915-18; Mesopotamia, Brigade Major, 1919-20 (despatches twice, OBE); Bt Major 1918; retired, 1927. Recalled to Colours, 1939; Sen. Movement Control Officer, Cherbourg, 1939-40 (despatches); Glider Pilot Regt, 1942-45; Lieut-Colonel; President: NE Hants Agricultural Assoc., 1936-39; Gillingham and Shaftesbury Agricultural Society, 1952. High Sheriff of Dorset, 1959. *Recreations:* yachting, racing, coaching. *Address:* Stock Hill, Gillingham, Dorset. *T:* Gillingham, Dorset 206. *Clubs:* Royal Thames Yacht; Coaching; Royal Yacht Squadron (Cowes).
[Died 4 *April* 1972.

WILLIAMS, L(aurence) F(rederic) Rushbrook, CBE 1923 (OBE 1919); MA, BLitt; JP; formerly Chairman of Petty Sessions and a Commissioner for Income Tax (Basingstoke); Adviser to Maharao of Kutch; Membre Associé de l'Académie Diplomatique Internationale; Corresponding Hon. Member of the Institut Historique et Heraldique de France; Vice-President, Indo-British Historical Association; Editorial Adviser, Pakistan Society; *b* 10 July 1890; *m* 1923, Freda May, *d* of Frederick H. Chance, of Coward, Hawksley Sons and Chance; two *s* one *d. Educ:* private; University College, Oxford. Linton Exhibitioner at University College, 1909; Leicester Exhibitioner, 1910; Plumptre Prizeman, 1912; Gladstone Memorial Prizeman, 1912; 1st Class Final Honour School of Modern History, 1912; BLitt 1913; Lecturer in Medieval History at Queen's University, Canada, 1913-14; Fellow of All Souls Coll., Oxford, 1914-21; University Professor of Modern Indian History in the Universities of Allahabad and Delhi, India, 1914-25; Royal Society of Arts Silver Medal, 1937; on Special Duty in connection with the Indian Constitutional Reforms, 1918; on Special Duty in the Home Department, Government of India, 1919; Director, Bureau of Public Information, 1920-26; Secretary to the Indian Delegation at the Imperial Conference, 1923; Political Secretary to the Maharaja of Patiala, and Substitute-Delegate, League of Nations Assembly, 1925; Secretary to the Chancellor of the Chamber of Princes, 1926-30; Foreign Minister of Patiala State, India, 1925-31, MLA 1924-25; Joint Director, Indian Princes' Special Organisation, 1929-31; Adviser to Indian States Delegn, Round Table Conf., 1930-31; Delegate Round Table Conf., 1932; CO 1935-38; FO 1938-39; Adviser, ME Affairs, MOI 1939-41; Eastern Service Dir, BBC, 1941-44; Editorial Staff, The Times, 1944-55. LFRSA. JP Hants, 1935. *Publications:* (with J. K. Fotheringham, DLitt) Marco Sanudo, or The Conquest of the Archipelago; History of the Abbey of St Albans; Four Lectures on the Handling of Historical Material; Students' Supplement to the Ain Akbari: A Sixteenth-Century Empire-Builder; A Primer of Indian Administration; Moral and Material Progress Reports of India (Parliamentary Papers), 1917-25; Report of Lord Chelmsford's Administration (Official Document); History of the Tour of the Prince of Wales (Official Document); India's Parliament, Vols I-IV *et seq*; A History of India under the Company and the Crown; What About India?; India (Oxford Pamphlet); The State of Israel (World Jewish Congress Book of the Year for 1957); The Black Hills: Kutch in History and Legend; The State of Pakistan, 1962, 1966; The East Pakistan Tragedy, 1972; Sufi Studies East and West, 1973; Pakistan under Challenge, 1975; (ed) A Handbook for Travellers in India, Pakistan, Nepal, Bangladesh and Sri Lanka, 1975; contribs to: The Times; The Times Literary Supplement; The Round Table; Encyclopædia

Britannica; Asian Affairs. *Recreation:* colour photography. *Address:* Bodgers Chance Mews, Great Kimble, Aylesbury HP17 9TN. *T:* Princes Risborough 5256. *[Died* 1 *Oct.* 1978.

WILLIAMS, Sir Leonard; *see* Williams, Sir A. L.

WILLIAMS, Leonard John; Director, National Provincial Bank Ltd, 1956-69; Vice-President, Institute of Bankers, 1956-69; Director: Ranks Hovis McDougall Ltd, 1956-72; City of London Real Property Co. Ltd and its subsidiaries, 1956-69; *b* 7 Aug. 1894; *s* of late Charles and Lily Williams; *m* 1923, Doris (*d* 1965), *d* of late Arthur Mayall; two *s. Educ:* Bideford Grammar Sch. Entered National Provincial Bank, 1911, retired as Chief General Manager, 1956. Member Court of Patrons, Royal College of Surgeons; Hon. FRCS 1968. *Recreations:* music, reading. *Address:* 4 Woodfield Road, Ealing, W5. *T:* 01-997 4219.   *[Died* 18 *Dec.* 1975.

WILLIAMS, Leslie Harry; Member, British Railways Board, 1962-66 (Member, British Transport Commission, 1961-62); *b* 30 July 1909; *s* of late Harold Williams; Cosham, Hants, and of late Ivy Williams, Reigate, Surrey; *m* 1946, Margaret, *o d* of late H. T. Gerrard, Goring-by-Sea, Sussex; one *s. Educ:* Portsmouth Grammar Sch.; Jesus Coll., Cambridge. Joined Shell Petroleum Co., 1930; served Kenya and Uganda, 1931-41; Adviser on oil supplies to Occupied Enemy Territories Administration, Addis Ababa, 1941; West Africa, 1942-45; General Manager, Shell Chemicals, Johannesburg, 1948-50; Managing Director, Petrochemicals Ltd and Shell Chemical Co. Ltd, London, 1955-60. *Recreations:* fishing, gardening, music. *Address:* 18 Woodland Rise, Sevenoaks, Kent. *T:* Sevenoaks 61166. *Clubs:* MCC, Catalysts.   *[Died* 6 *April* 1978.

WILLIAMS, Leslie Herbert Whitby, MD, MS, FRCS, FRCOG; Medical Inspector in Nullity to the High Court, retired; formerly: Consulting Gynæcological Surgeon, St Mary's Hospital, Paddington; Consulting Obstetric Surgeon, Queen Charlotte's Hospital; Consulting Gynæcological Surgeon, Samaritan Hospital for Women; Sometime Obstetric Consultant to LCC, etc; sometime Examiner in Gynæcology and Obstetrics to The University of London, the Conjoint Board, Universities of Cambridge, Durham, Wales, etc; *b* 27 Feb. 1893; *s* of late T. Gill Williams, Newport (Mon); *m* 1930, Patrice, *er d* of late Hatton Ronayne Conron, Douglas, County Cork; two *s one d. Educ:* University College, Cardiff; University College Hospital, London. Served European War, RAMC, 1914-20; Commanded 110 Indian Field Ambulance, 1919; House appointments at University College Hospital, 1920, 1921; Obstetric Registrar, Radium Registrar and Chief Assistant on Obstetric Unit at University College Hospital, 1921-30; Obstetric Registrar St Mary's Hospital, 1930; appointed to Honorary Staff, 1931; President of Section of Obstetrics and Gynæcology of Royal Society of Medicine, 1949-50 (Secretary, 1935-37); Member of Council, RCOG. First William McIlrath Guest Professor to University of Sydney, 1949. *Publications:* Aids to Obstetrics; Recent Advances in Obstetrics and Gynæcology (with Aleck Bourne); Chapters in Fleming's Penicillin; Surgery by Handfield-Jones and Porritt, etc; various contributions to Medical Journals. *Recreations:* golf, photography, travel. *Address:* 27 Cottenham Park Road, Wimbledon, SW20. *T:* 01-946 7844. *Clubs:* Berkshire (Ascot); Royal Wimbledon (Wimbledon).   *[Died* 1 *Jan.* 1972.

WILLIAMS, Leslie Thomas Douglas, CMG 1962; *b* 20 Jan. 1905; *s* of late Herbert Douglas and Alice Williams, St Aubyns, Hove, Sussex; *m* 1927, Anne Irene de la Bere (*d* 1954); no *c. Educ:* Brighton College. Royal College of Science Chemical Defence Research Department, 1925-54; Director, Explosives Research and Development Establishment, Ministry of Supply, 1954-58. Attended Imperial Defence Coll., 1958. Director-General, Defence Research Staff, Washington, DC, USA, 1959-62; Director-General of Space Activities, Ministry of Aviation, 1963-66. Retired from public service, June 1966. *Publications:* Some contributions to Journal of Chemical Society. *Address:* 20 Cleveland Terrace, W2. *T:* 01-723 1957. *Club:* Royal Commonwealth Society.   *[Died* 3 *Jan.* 1976.

WILLIAMS, Mary; *b* June 1882; *e d* of Rev. John Williams, Aberystwyth; *m* Dr G. Arbour Stephens (*d* 1945). *Educ:* Frances Mary Buss Schools, London; University College, Aberystwyth; Sorbonne (University of Paris); National University of Ireland; Scholar of the University of Wales, BA (Honours Double First); MA; Research Fellow of the University of Wales, Docteur de l'Université de Paris; Officier d'Académie; Chevalier de la Légion d'Honneur; FRAI; Assistant Lecturer in French, University of Manchester; Reader in French and Romance Philology in the University of London; Professor of French Language and Literature, University College, Swansea, until 1948; Acting Professor of French Language and Literature, University of Durham, 1948-52. President, Folk-lore Society, 1961-63. *Publications:* Essai sur le Roman Gallois de Peredur; Mabinogi Iesu Grist-3 unpublished MSS in Revue Celtique, T. XXXIII; Life in Wales in Mediæval Times; Perceval le Gallois (mediæval French poem by Chrestien de Troyes); Studies in Romance Languages and Literatures (with J. A. de Rothschild); The Dying God in Welsh Literature (Revue Celtique, T. L, 1929); contributor to Speculum, Etudes Celtiques, Folklore, Man, etc. *Recreations:* music, archæology, anthropology, folklore, letter-writing. *Address:* Morven, St David's Road, Aberystwyth, Dyfed.   *[Died 17 Oct. 1977.*

WILLIAMS, Neville John; Secretary of the British Academy, since 1973; *b* 31 Aug. 1924; *o s* of late John James Williams and May Sworn, Chalfont St Peter; *m* 1953, Betty King; one *s* three *d. Educ:* Cathedral Choir Sch., Oxford; Merchant Taylors' Sch.; St Edmund Hall, Oxford (MA, DPhil). RNVR, 1943-46. Asst Keeper, Public Record Office, 1950-66; Sec., Adv. Council on Public Records, 1959-63; Records Administration Officer, 1967-69; Dep. Keeper of Public Records, 1970-73. Registrar, Royal Literary Fund, 1965-; Treas., Pipe Roll Soc., 1969-74. FRHistS 1952; FSA 1957. *Publications:* Contraband Cargoes, 1959; Knaves and Fools, 1959; Tradesmen in Early-Stuart Wiltshire, 1960; Thomas Howard 4th Duke of Norfolk, 1964; (with H. C. Johnson) Warwickshire Quarter Sessions Records Vol. IX, 1964; Chronology of the Modern World, 1966; Elizabeth I, Queen of England, 1967; Chronology of the Expanding World, 1969; Henry VIII and His Court, 1971; The Life and Times of Elizabeth I, 1972; All the Queen's Men, 1972; The Life and Times of Henry VII, 1973; Sir Francis Drake, 1974; The Cardinal and the Secretary, 1975; The Sea Dogs, 1975; (ed) Calendar of Patent Rolls, Elizabeth I, Vols III-VI, 1961-72; articles and reviews. *Recreations:* writing, music. *Address:* 57 Rotherwick Road, NW11 7DD. *T:* 01-455 3427. *Clubs:* Athenæum, United Oxford & Cambridge University.
                    [Died 29 Jan. 1977.

WILLIAMS, Sir Reginald (Lawrence William), 7th Bt, *cr* 1798; MBE 1944; ED 1945; mining engineer, retired; *b* 3 May 1900; *s* of Colonel Lawrence Williams and Catherine Elizabeth Anne Phibbs; *S* kinsman, Sir Hugh Grenville Williams, 6th Bt, 1961; *m* 1936, Elinor Meriol Enriqueta Trevor; two *d. Educ:* Malvern Coll.; Camborne School of Mines. Joined Royal Tank Corps (temp. commn), 1918; Camborne School of Mines, 1919; Mining Engineer, N Nigeria, 1922-40 (mining in all W African Colonies). Commnd in W African Frontier Force, 1932; War service: in Nigeria, 1940-42; in Burma and India, 1942-45, Major. Commandant, Army Leave Station, N Nigeria, 1946-48, when demobilized and returned to tin mining his own property until retiring in Oct. 1957. High Sheriff of Caernarvonshire, 1968-69. *Recreations:* shooting, racing. *Heir:* *b* Francis (John Watkin) Williams. *Address:* Penrhos, Caeathraw, Caernarvon. *T:* Caernarvon 2109. *Club:* Grosvenor (Chester).
                    [Died 30 Jan. 1971.

WILLIAMS, Air Marshal Sir Richard, KBE 1954 (CBE 1927; OBE 1919); CB 1935; DSO 1917; RAAF (retired); Director-General of Civil Aviation in Australia, 1946-56, retired; *b* 1890; *s* of late Richard Williams, Grant Avenue, Rose Park, Adelaide; *m* 1st, 1915, Constance Esther Griffiths; 2nd, 1950, Lois V. Cross. Served European War, 1914-19 (despatches, DSO, OBE, Order of El Nahda of the Hedjaz). Formerly Chief of Air Staff, RAAF, and later RAAF Representative, Washington, DC. *Publication:* These are Facts (autobiog.), 1977. *Address:* 5 Ardgour Street, North Balwyn, Victoria 3104, Australia.
                    [Died 7 Feb. 1980.

WILLIAMS, Richard Tecwyn, FRS 1967; (first) Professor of Biochemistry at St Mary's Hospital Medical School (University of London), 1949-76, now Emeritus Professor; Deputy Dean, St Mary's Hospital Medical School, 1970-76; sometime Examiner, Universities of Wales, the West Indies, and Royal Veterinary College, Universities of Glasgow, Liverpool, St Andrews, Ibadan, Nigeria, Ghana, London, King Abdulaziz Univ. Jeddah, and Royal College of Physicians; *b* Abertillery, Mon, South Wales, 20 Feb. 1909; *e s* of Richard and Mary Williams, North Wales; *m* 1937, Josephine Teresa Sullivan; two *s* three *d. Educ:* Abertillery County Sch.; University College, Cardiff. BSc (Wales) 1929; Research Assistant to Dr J. Pryde at Physiology Institute, Cardiff, 1930-34; PhD (Wales) 1932; Lecturer in Biochemistry, University of Birmingham, 1934-42; DSc (Birmingham) 1939; Senior Lecturer in Biochemistry, University of Liverpool, 1942-48. Visiting Scientist, National Institutes of Health, Bethesda, Md, USA, 1956; Member: IUPAC/WHO Expert Cttee on Food Additives, Geneva, 1961; WHO Sci. Gp on safety of food additives, Geneva, 1966; Food Additives and Contaminants Cttee, Min. of Agriculture, 1965-

72; Horserace Anti-Doping Cttee, 1970-; Toxicity Sub-Cttee of Cttee on Med. Aspects of Chemicals in Food and Environment, 1972-. Vis. Professor: NY Univ. Med. Sch., 1965-66; Indian Inst. of Science, 1975; Howard Fox Meml Lectr, NY Univ. Med. Sch., 1969. Hon. Member: Society of Toxicology (USA), 1966; Societé Française de Toxicologie, 1976; Hon. Life Member, Pan American Medical Assoc., 1968. DUniv Paris, 1966; Hon. MD Tübingen Univ., 1972; Hon. DSc: Univ. Ibadan, Nigeria, 1974; Wales, 1976. Merit award, Society of Toxicology (USA), 1968; CIBA Medal and Prize, Biochem. Soc., 1972; 1922 Medal, Univ. of Turku, Finland, 1975; Medal of Acad. de Pharmacie, Paris, 1970. *Publications:* Detoxication Mechanisms-The Metabolism of Drugs and Allied Organic Compounds, 1947 (2nd edn, 1959). Ed. Biochemical Society Symposia, 1947-55. Numerous research papers published mainly in Biochemical Journal and Journal of Chemical Society. *Recreations:* gardening, Welsh Culture and History. *Address:* 95 Vernon Drive, Stanmore, Mddx. *T:* 01-427 5554.   *[Died 29 Dec. 1979.*

WILLIAMS, Sir Robert (Ernest), 9th Bt, *cr* 1866; *b* 6 June 1924; *e s* of late Ernest Claude Williams and of Theresa Gertrude, *d* of R. Graefer; *S* kinsman Sir William Law Williams, 8th Bt, 1960; *m* 1948, Ruth Margaret, *d* of C. Butcher, Hudson Bay; two *s* one *d* (and one *s* decd). Employed by Canadian National Railways, 1944-60. *Heir:* *s* Donald Mark Williams, *b* 7 Nov. 1954. *Address:* Upcott House, Barnstaple, N Devon. *T:* Barnstaple 2498.   *[Died 26 May 1976.*

WILLIAMS, Rt. Rev. Ronald Ralph, MA, DD; *b* 14 Oct. 1906; *s* of Rev. Ralph Williams and Mary, *d* of Joseph Sayers; *m* 1934, Cicely Maud, FRGS, *o d* of Edward Glanville Kay, Enfield; no *c. Educ:* Judd Sch., Tonbridge; Gonville and Caius Coll., Cambridge; Ridley Hall, Cambridge. 2nd Class, Division I, English Tripos Part I, Cambridge, 1926; 1st Class Theological Tripos, Part I, 1927; 1st Class with distinction, Part II, 1928; Carus Greek Testament Prize, 1927; Scholefield Greek Testament Prize, 1928; Archbishop Cranmer Prize, 1932; Hulsean Preacher, 1934. Tutor, St Aidan's Coll., Birkenhead, 1928-29; Curate, Leyton Parish Church, 1929-31; Chaplain, Ridley Hall, Cambridge, 1931-34; Examining Chaplain to Bishop of Chelmsford, 1931; Home Education Secretary, CMS, 1934-40; Religious Division, Ministry of Information, 1940-45 (Director, 1943-45); Lieut MOI Home Guard; Commissary to Bishop of Tasmania, 1944; Examining Chaplain to Bishop of Durham, 1945; Principal, St John's Coll., Durham, 1945-53; Bishop of Leicester, 1953-78. Hon. Canon Durham Cathedral, 1953-54; Proctor in Convocation of York, 1950. President, Queen's Coll., Birmingham, 1957-63; Visitor, Ridley Hall, Cambridge, 1957. Trustee, Historic Churches Preservation Trust, 1960-. C of E Rep. to Brussels Ecumenical Centre, and Mem., Consultative Cttee of Churches of European Community, 1973-; Chairman: C of E Bd for Social Responsibility, 1961-76; C of E Council for Foreign Relations; Pres., European Christian Industrial Movement, 1975-. Entered House of Lords, 1959. Hon. Fellow, St Peter's Coll., Oxford, 1961. FRSA 1972. DD Lambeth, 1954; Hon. DD Cantab, 1974; Hon. LLD Leicester, 1976. *Publications:* Religion and the English Vernacular, 1940; The Strife Goes On, 1940; The Christian Religion, 1941; Authority in the Apostolic Age, 1950; The Perfect Law of Liberty, 1952; The Acts of the Apostles, 1953; Reading Through Hebrews, 1960; The Word of Life, 1960; Take thou Authority, 1961; The Bible in Worship and Ministry, 1962; Letters of John and James (Commentary), 1965; What's right with the C of E, 1966; I Believe—and why, 1971; Faith and the Faith, 1973; The Well is Deep, 1978. *Recreations:* golf, walking, climbing. *Address:* 15 Sandringham Court, Maida Vale, W9. *T:* 01-286 1477. *Clubs:* Alpine, English-Speaking Union, MCC; Leicestershire (Leicester).   *[Died 13 Feb. 1979.*

WILLIAMS, Major Ronald Samuel Ainslie; *b* 1890; 2nd *s* of late Frank Williams of Brasted Hall, Kent; *m* 1918, Cicely, 3rd *d* of late Henry Monro; one *s* two *d. Educ:* Repton; RMA, Woolwich. MP (L) Sevenoaks, 1923-24. JP, 1936-64, Alderman, 1945-52, Co. Wilts. *Address:* Little Bridge House, West Chinnock, Crewkerne, Somerset. *Club:* United Service and Royal Aero.   *[Died 10 Dec. 1971.*

WILLIAMS, Sir Roy E. H.; *see* Hume-Williams.

WILLIAMS, Lt-Col Stanley Price, CIE 1930; *b* 1885; *s* of C. A. Williams, Ashfield, Builth Wells; *m* 1913, Winifred de L. (*d* 1976), *d* of late Col E. A. Young, Wykeham Close, Steyning; (only son killed in action in Burma, Mar. 1945), two *d. Educ:* Leys School; Sandhurst. Commissioned in 1st Bn Middlesex Regt 1905; transferred to 51st Sikhs FF 1907; during European War served on NWF in Frontier Militia; 3rd Afghan War, 1919; Commandant, South Waziristan Scouts, 1924-29; commanded 2nd Bn 14th Punjab Regt (DCO) (Brownlow's), 1930-34; retired

1935; RAFVR, 1939-41; recalled to IA, Nov. 1941, and sent to India; reverted to retired list, 1944. *Address:* 15c Hyde Park Mansions, NW1. *T:* 01-723 2850. *[Died 29 Oct. 1977.*

WILLIAMS, Sir Thomas; *see* Williams, Sir Daniel T.

WILLIAMS, Thomas Christopher, CBE 1970; QPM 1966; Chief Constable of Sussex since 1968; *b* 14 Dec. 1913; *s* of Sidney Herbert Williams and Dorothy (*née* Roth); *m* 1939, Peggy Katherine Ellen (*née* Orr); one *s* one *d*. *Educ:* Dulwich Coll. Prep. Sch.; Bromsgrove Sch.; University Coll., London. Served with RAFVR, Bomber Comd, 1942-45. Called to Bar, Gray's Inn, 1952. Metropolitan Police, 1937-57; Metropolitan Police Coll., Hendon, 1938-39; Dir of Studies, Police Coll., Ryton-on-Dunsmore, 1950-53; Comdt, No 2 District Police Trng Centre, 1954-57; Chief Constable: Hunts and Isle of Ely, 1957-64; W Sussex, 1964-67. FRGS. *Publications:* Prosecuting Officer, 1956; numerous articles in legal jls. *Address:* Little Manor, Ringmer, Lewes, Sussex. *T:* Ringmer 777; Troedrhiwnawpant, Cwrt-y-Cadno, Pumpsaint, Carms. *[Died 9 Sept. 1972.*

WILLIAMS, Sir Thomas Herbert P.; *see* Parry-Williams.

WILLIAMS, Maj.-Gen. Walter David Abbott, CB 1946; CBE 1944 (OBE 1940); Principal of Staff College for Higher Management, at Woking, 1959-65; *b* 31 December 1897; *c* of late Walter Charles Williams; *m* 1925, Eunice Florence Longley; one *s* one *d*. *Educ:* Brighton College; Royal Military Academy; Emmanuel College, Cambridge. Commissioned Royal Engineers, 1917; Scholar of Emmanuel College, Cambridge, 1923; graduated, 1924; Graduate of Staff College, Camberley, 1933; Actg Maj.-Gen. as a WO Director, 1943; Director of Movements, WO, 1945-49; retd pay, 1949. Commander, US Legion of Merit, 1945. Formerly Director of Port Emergency Planning, Ministry of Transport; Commissioner for Transport, East Africa High Commission, 1954-58. *[Died 24 Jan. 1973.*

WILLIAMS, Sir William Emrys, Kt 1955; CBE 1946; BA; Arts Adviser, Institute of Directors; Penguin Books (Chief Editor and Director), 1935-65; Secretary-General, Arts Council, 1951-63 (Founder Member, 1946); *b* 5 Oct. 1896; *m* 1919, Prof. Gertrude Williams, CBE (*née* Rosenblum); no *c*. *Educ:* elementary and secondary schools in Manchester; Univ. of Manchester. Staff Tutor, University of London Extra-Mural Dept, 1928-34. Sec. of British Institute of Adult Education, 1934-40; Director Army Bureau of Current Affairs, 1941-45. Director Bureau of Current Affairs, 1946-51; a Trustee of the National Gallery, 1949-56; a Trustee of Shakespeare's Birthplace, 1953-68; Sec., Nat. Art-Collections Fund, 1963-70; Chm., Arts Council Theatre Enquiry; Hon. Member of the Architectural Association. American Medal of Freedom, 1946. Hon. DLitt Wales, 1963. *Publications:* Allen Lane: a personal portrait, 1973; Official Historian of Army Education, 1939-46; regular contributor to several national newspapers, 1937-67. *Address:* Grenville Paddock, Haddenham, Aylesbury, Bucks. *T:* Haddenham 219464. *Club:* Garrick. *[Died 30 March 1977.*

WILLIAMS, Lt-Col Sir William (Jones), KCVO 1969; OBE 1953; QPM 1959; DL; Chief Constable, Gwynedd Constabulary, 1967-70; *b* 31 May 1904; *s* of Thomas Williams, Towyn, Merioneth; *m* 1st, 1930, Margaret Enid (*d* 1957), *d* of John Pugh, Aberdovey; one *s* one *d*; 2nd, 1970, Myra Hughes, Towyn, Merioneth. *Educ:* Bala and Towyn Grammar Schs; Aberystwyth and Birmingham Univs. BSc Aberystwyth 1926, LLB Birmingham 1933. Birmingham City Police, 1926-46. Served War of 1939-45, Lt-Col, Gen. List, 1945. Chief Constable, Caernarvonshire Constabulary, 1946-50; Chief Constable, Gwynedd Constabulary: Counties of Anglesey, Caernarvon and Merioneth, 1950-67; Counties of Anglesey, Caernarvon, Denbigh, Flint and Merioneth, 1967-70. DL Caernarvon 1971. KStJ 1969. *Publications:* (as Asst to late Dr C. C. H. Moriarty): Police Procedure and Administration, 6th edn 1955; also (jointly with him) Police Law, 15th edn 1959; (since the death of Dr Moriarty in 1958) Editor of Moriarty's Police Law, 16th edn, 1961, to 22nd edn, 1974. *Recreation:* golf (Captain Royal St David's Golf, Harlech, 1963). *Address:* Coed-y-Glyn, South Road, Caernarvon, Gwynedd. *T:* Caernarvon 3015. *Club:* Royal Welsh Yacht (Caernarvon).
[Died 26 March 1976.

WILLIAMS-DRUMMOND, Sir W. H. D. W.; *see* Drummond.

WILLIAMS-ELLIS, Sir (Bertram) Clough, Kt 1972; CBE 1958; MC; JP; FRIBA; architect; Past-President Design and Industry Association; Vice-Pres., Council for the Preservation of Rural Wales; Member Town Planning Institute; Member National Parks Committee; Chairman Glass Industry Working Party; Member National Trust Committee for Wales; Member Government Committee on Art and Industry; Member of Art Committee, University of Wales; Member Grand Council, British Travel Association; Vice-President Institute Landscape Architects; Member Advisory Council for Welsh Reconstruction; First Chairman First New Town Development Corporation (Stevenage); Member Festival of Britain 1951 Committee (Wales); Member Trunk Road Advisory Committee; late Welsh Guards, served in France, 1915-18 (despatches); *b* 28 May 1883; *m* 1915, Amabel, author and journalist, *o d* of late J. St Loe Strachey, Newlands Corner, Surrey; (son Christopher, killed in action—Welsh Guards—1944) two *d*. *Educ:* Oundle; Trinity College, Cambridge. Larger works include sections of the Wembley Exhibitions, Llangoed and Bolesworth Castles, Moynes Park, Oare House, Caversham Place, Kilve Court, Stowe School, Hurtwood School, Bishop's Stortford College Chapel, Great Hundridge Manor, Cornwell Manor and Village, conversion of Ashridge Park (Bonar Law College), Lloyd George Mausoleum, Museum, Westminster Abbey Memorial and Memorial County College, Rhiwlas, Voelas, Nantclwyd Hall, Dalton Hall, etc; other works include churches, schools and village schemes in England, Ireland and Wales, a number of smaller houses, hotels, monuments and gardens, several London houses, including Dartmouth House and Ladies' Carlton Club, Oxford and Cambridge Club Annexe, also residences in China, S Africa and New Zealand; owns and is designer and builder of the new model resort of Portmeirion, North Wales; Town Planning Consultant to various Municipalities. Hon. LLD Wales, 1971. *Publications:* Cottage Building; England and the Octopus; The Architect; The Face of the Land; Sir Laurence Weaver (with his wife); The Tank Corps (a War History); The Pleasures of Architecture; (with John Summerson) Architecture here and now; (ed) Britain and the Beast, 1937; (with Lord Rosse) The Protection of Ancient Buildings, 1939; Plan for Living, 1941; The Adventure of Building, 1947; On Trust for the Nation, 1949; (2 Vols) An Artist in North Wales; Town and Country Planning, 1951; Portmeirion, 1963, Portmeirion—the place and its meaning, rev. and updated edn 1973; Trunk Roads in the landscape; Architect Errant (autobiog.), 1971; Around the World in Ninety Years, 1978. *Recreations:* travelling, building. *Address:* Plâs Brondanw, Penrhyndeudraeth, Gwynedd. *T:* Penrhyndeudraeth 292. *Clubs:* Athenæum, Lansdowne; Royal Welsh Yacht (Caernarvon). *[Died 8 April 1978.*

WILLIAMSON, Alec, CMG 1944; late Indian Civil Service; *b* 7 Nov. 1886; *s* of late T. Williamson; *m* 1937, Jessie Cunningham Hofford (decd), *d* of J. Hartley Welsh; no *c*. *Educ:* Kirkcudbright Academy; Edinburgh Univ.; Balliol College, Oxford. Asst Commissioner, Burma, 1910; Lt 3/70th Burma Rifles, 1918; Deputy Commissioner and Settlement Officer, 1919; Dep. Comr., Rangoon Develt Trust, 1925; Chm., Rangoon Develt Trust and Collector of Rangoon, 1933; Excise Comr, 1934; Comr of Settlements and Land Records, 1936; Comr of Arakan, 1938; Financial Comr, Burma, 1940. Now retired. *Recreations:* golf, shooting. *Address:* c/o Chartered Bank of India, Australia and China, 38 Bishopsgate, EC2.
[Died 14 Aug. 1975.

WILLIAMSON, Sir Alexander, Kt 1952; CBE 1941; BSc, MInstCE. *Educ:* Greenock Collegiate School; Glasgow University. Master of the Cutlers' Company of Hallamshire, 1934-35. Chairman of the Gun Forgings Committee, 1940-45. *Recreation:* golf. *Club:* Sheffield (Sheffield).
[Died 29 June 1971.

WILLIAMSON, Mrs Catherine Ellis; for 35 years Director and Manager in the family business of J. J. Williamson & Sons (Canterbury) Ltd, Tanners and Leather Manufacturers (Sales Manager, 1948-58); *b* 1 May 1896; *d* of Lewis Goodbody, Dublin Solicitor, and Edith Lisetta (*née* Pim); *m* 1921, Stephen Williamson, Canterbury; two *s* one *d*. *Educ:* Cheltenham Ladies Coll.; St Germain-en-Laye, Paris. War of 1914-18: First Aid and Home Nursing; Teacher of Braille, St Dunstans, London. Mem. (Lab), Canterbury CC 1935-43; wide experience of Health Services, homes for the aged and mental health and industrial welfare; Chm. Canterbury Mental Hosp. for 5 years; Mayor, 1938-39 and 1939—40 (first woman in 750 years of Canterbury civic life to hold this office). War of 1939-45: Chm., Wartime Emergency Cttee for Civil Defence, etc; Mem., Price Regulation Control Cttee, SE Div., BoT. Contested (Common Wealth) Ashford, Kent, 1943 and Canterbury, 1945; contested (Lab) E Grinstead, 1950 and Hastings, 1951; also local elections in Canterbury, Dover, and Bridge Blean. Widely travelled, espec. since 2nd World War; countries visited incl. China (personal acquaintance with Chm. Mao Tsetung and Premier Chou En-lai, and is indebted to Bishop K. H. Ting for much of her knowledge of the People's Republic); has also visited Japan (twice), USSR, India, Ceylon, USA, South, Central and W Africa, Egypt, Israel, and all Europ. countries; on her return, always lectured on her experiences and knowledge gained. Founded Travel Bursary for students, Nottingham Univ., 1968; benefactor to restoration work of Canterbury Cath., following 2nd World War damage. Mem., C of E, Holy Catholic Ch. of China, Soc. of Friends, Franco-Brit. Soc. *Publications:* Though the Streets Burn, 1949, 2nd edn 1966; The Crimson Dawn, 1963; Come Along With Me, 1971; Death and Its Aftermath, 1975. *Recreations:* cello (1st and 2nd Medals, Feis Ceoil, Dublin, 1912, 1914) and piano playing, speaking with people from other countries in their tongue. *Address:* 2 Lady Wootton's Green, Canterbury, Kent. *T:* Canterbury 65997. *[Died 25 April 1977.*

WILLIAMSON, Colin Martin, CBE 1920; FRPS; *b* 1887; *s* of J. Williamson; *m* 1912, Gertrude, *d* of F. Parsons, Hove, Sussex. Rendered service to RAF in connection with Photography during European War, 1914-18. *Address:* Abney Thatch, Bourne End, Bucks SL8 5DH. *T:* Bourne End 20440.
[Died 26 Sept. 1976.

WILLIAMSON, David, OBE 1971; QPM 1968; Chief Constable of Renfrew and Bute Constabulary, 1967-75, retired; *b* 16 Jan. 1916; *s* of Walter Williamson, fisherman, Havera, Shetland and Margaret Ann Fraser, Havera; *m* 1944, Mary Gwendoline Price, Warley, Staffs; one *s*. *Educ:* Anderson Educational Inst., Lerwick. Joined Greenock Burgh Police, 1937; Flt-Lt, RAF Bomber Comd, 1941-45; rejoined Greenock Burgh Police, 1945; Chief Constable, Greenock Burgh Police, 1958. *Recreations:* gardening, cabinetmaking, reading. *Address:* Havera, Lawmarnock Crescent, Bridge of Weir, Renfrewshire. *T:* Bridge of Weir 612121. *[Died 8 Sept. 1980.*

WILLIAMSON, Sir George (Alexander), Kt 1953; DL; Consultant, Messrs Paull & Williamsons, Advocates in Aberdeen, since 1970 (Partner, 1928-69); *b* Aberdeen, 5 Jan. 1898; *e s* of late Robert M. Williamson, CBE, LLD, of Aberdeen, and late Katharine H. Macrae; *m* 1931, Lucie, *yr d* of late Alexander J. Cran, Aberdeen; two *d*. *Educ:* Aberdeen Gram. Sch.; Clifton Bank, St Andrews; RMC, Wellington, S India; Aberdeen Univ. Indian Army: Nov. 1916-; Capt. Nov. 1920; resigned, 1923. BL (Aberdeen) 1926; Scottish Solicitor, 1927. Lt Aberdeen Univ. OTC, 1927-37. ROC, 1939-; Observer Capt. and Scottish Area Comdt, 1950-58. Scottish Unionist Assoc.; Convener Eastern Divl Council, 1950-51; Pres., 1951-52. Aberdeen Savings Bank: Manager, 1932; Trustee and Mem. of Cttee of Management, 1945; Chm. 1953-70. Director, Scottish Northern Investment Trusts, 1938-71 (Chm. 1943); Dir Aberdeen Local Bd, Bank of Scotland, 1947-70. Mem. Aberdeen City Council, 1934-37. Mem. Aberdeen T&AFA, 1935-56; Hon. Col 501 (Mob.) HAA Regt RA (TA), 1949-55. DL Aberdeen, 1948. *Recreation:* philately. *Address:* 6 Union Row, Aberdeen. *T:* Aberdeen 26262. *Clubs:* United Service & Royal Aero; Royal Northern (Aberdeen); Adelaide. *[Died 23 June 1975.*

WILLIAMSON, Henry; author and journalist; *b* 1 Dec. 1895; *o s* of late William Williamson, Parkstone, Dorset; *m* 1st, Ida Loetitia, *o d* of late Charles Calvert Hibbert, Chalfont Park, Bucks, and Lancross, N Devon; four *s* two *d*; 2nd, Christine Mary (marr. diss. 1968), *o d* of late Hedley Duffield, Keswick, Cumberland; one *s*. The author lives in N Devon. *Publications:* The Beautiful Years, Dandelion Days, The Dream of Fair Women, The Pathway which form a tetralogy called The Flax of Dream, and were first published respectively in 1921, 1922, 1924 and 1928; also The Lone Swallows, 1922, The Peregrine's Saga (Sun Brothers in USA), 1923; The Old Stag, 1926; Tarka the Otter, 1927 (Hawthornden Prize); The Wet Flanders Plain, 1929; The Patriot's Progress, 1930; Tales of a Devon Village, and Life in a Devon Village, 1932; The Gold Falcon, 1933 (recast and rewritten in 1943); Salar the Salmon, 1935; Selections from Richard Jefferies, 1937; Hodge and his Masters, by Richard Jefferies (a new edition re-arranged by Henry Williamson, 1945); The Children of Shallowford, 1939; The Story of a Norfolk Farm, 1941; T. E. Lawrence, Genius of Friendship, 1941; The Phasian Bird, 1948; Scribbling Lark, 1949; Tales of Moorland and Estuary, 1953; A Clear Water Stream, 1958; The Henry Williamson Animal Saga, 1959; Collected Nature Stories, 1970; A Chronicle of Ancient Sunlight, a novel of 15 volumes, comprising: The Dark Lantern, 1951; Donkey Boy, 1952; Young Phillip Maddison, 1953; How Dear is Life, 1954; A Fox Under My Cloak, 1955; The Golden Virgin, 1957; Love and the Loveless, 1958; A Test to Destruction, 1960; The Innocent Moon, 1961; It was the Nightingale, 1962; The Power of the Dead, 1963; The Phoenix Generation, 1965; A Solitary War, 1966; Lucifer before Sunrise, 1967; The Gale of the World, 1969; The Scandaroon, 1972. *Clubs:* Savage, National Liberal, Chelsea Arts.
[Died 13 Aug. 1977.

WILLIAMSON, Group Captain Hugh Alexander, CMG 1919; AFC; *b* 1885; *s* of Andrew Williamson. Served European War, 1914-19 (despatches, CMG); Iraq command, 1923-24; retired 1928. Calshot Pembroke Dock and Air Ministry, 1939-43. *Address:* Mill Park House, Witheridge, Tiverton, Devon.
[Died 15 Nov. 1979.

WILLIAMSON, Hugh R.; *see* Ross Williamson.

WILLINGDON, 2nd Marquess of, *cr* 1936, **Inigo Brassey Freeman-Thomas;** Earl of Willingdon, *cr* 1931; Viscount Ratendone of Willingdon, *cr* 1931; Viscount Willingdon, *cr* 1924; Baron Willingdon of Ratton, *cr* 1910; *b* 25 July 1899; 2nd and *o* surv. *s* of 1st Marquess and Lady Marie Adelaide (*d* 1960) (Marie, Marchioness of Willingdon, CI, GBE), *d* of 1st Earl Brassey; *S* father, 1941; *m* 1943, Daphne, *er d* of late Seymour Cadwell. *Educ:* Eton. President of: St John's, Berkshire; The Fauna Preservation Society; The Feathers Clubs Association. Late Capt. 3rd Skinners Horse, Indian Cavalry; Major Sussex Yeomanry; Sqdn Ldr RAFVR. KStJ. *Address:* Kilbees Farm, Windsor Forest. *T:* Winkfield Row 2645. *Clubs:* Turf, White's.
[Died 19 March 1979 (ext).

WILLINK, Rt. Hon. Sir Henry Urmston, 1st Bt, *cr* 1957; PC 1943; MC; QC 1935; DCL (Lambeth); MA; Master of Magdalene College, Cambridge, 1948-66, Hon. Fellow since 1966; Vice-Chancellor of the University of Cambridge, 1953-55; Dean of the Arches, Master of the Faculties, Vicar-General of the Province of Canterbury and Auditor of the Chancery Court of York, 1955-70; *b* 7 March 1894; *s* of William Edward Willink, FRIBA, and Florence Macan, *d* of Col H. B. Urmston; *m* 1st, 1923, Cynthia Frances (*d* 1959), *d* of H. Morley Fletcher, MD, FRCP; two *s* two *d*; 2nd, 1964, Mrs Doris Campbell Preston, *d* of William Campbell Sharman. *Educ:* Eton College (King's Scholar); Trinity College, Cambridge. Served in RFA (TF), 1914-19, Captain (a/Major) (MC despatches; French Croix de Guerre avec Palme). Called to Bar, Inner Temple, 1920; Bencher, 1942. A Special Commissioner for London Region, 1940-43; MP (Nat C) Croydon (North Divn) 1940-48; Minister of Health, 1943-45. Chancellor of Dioceses of Norwich and St Edmundsbury and Ipswich, 1948-55; High Bailiff of Westminster, 1942-67; Member of the Council of the Senate, Univ. of Cambridge, 1951-60. Chairman: Royal Commn on Betting, etc., 1949; Departmental Cttee on Medical Manpower, 1955; Commn of Enquiry to Examine Problems of Minorities in Nigeria, 1957; Royal Commn on the Police, 1960. Mem., Eastern Area Bd, British Transport Commn, 1955-61; Mem., Archbishops' Commn on Crown Appointments, 1962. A Governor of Wellington Coll., 1955-61; Fellow of Eton Coll., 1946-56; Steward of the Courts, Eton Coll., since 1961. Hon. FRCGP; Hon. FRIBA; Hon. LLD, Liverpool and Melbourne. Officier de la Légion d'Honneur. *Heir: s* Charles William Willink [*b* 10 Sept. 1929; *m* 1954, Elizabeth Andrewes; one *s* one *d*]. *Address:* 51 Madingley Road, Cambridge. *T:* Cambridge 53539. *[Died 1 Jan. 1973.*

WILLIS, Adm. of the Fleet Sir Algernon Usborne, GCB 1947 (KCB 1943; CB 1940); KBE 1945; DSO 1920; DL; *b* 17 May 1889; *s* of late Herbert Bourdillon Willis; *m* 1916, Olive Christine, CBE, *d* of late Henry E. Millar, Hampstead; two *d*. *Educ:* Eastbourne College; HMS Britannia. Entered Royal Navy, 1904; Midshipman, 1905; Lt 1909; served European War, 1914-18, present at Battle of Jutland HMS Fearless, took part in operations in Baltic, 1919, HMS Wallace (despatches, DSO); HMS Renown with Prince of Wales to Australia and New Zealand, 1920; Commander, 1922; commanded HMS Warwick, 1927-29; Captain, 1929; Staff RN War College, 1930-32; Flag Captain, HMS Kent, China Fleet, 1933-34; Flag Captain, HMS Nelson, Home Fleet, 1934-35; Capt. HMS Vernon, Torpedo School, Portsmouth, 1935-38; Captain HMS Barham, 1st Battle Squadron, 1938-39; Commodore 1st Class, 1939; Chief of Staff, Med. Fleet, HMS Warspite, 1939-41; Rear-Admiral, 1940; Acting Vice-Admiral, 1941; Commander-in-Chief, South Atlantic Station, 1941-42; Vice-Admiral 2nd in Command, Eastern Fleet, 1942-43; Vice-Admiral, 1943; Flag Officer commanding Force H, Mediterranean, 1943 (despatches twice); Commander-in-Chief, Levant Station, 1943; a Lord Commissioner of the Admiralty and Chief of Naval Personnel (Second Sea Lord), 1944-46; Admiral, 1945; C-in-C Mediterranean Fleet, 1946-48; Commander-in-Chief, Portsmouth Command, 1948-50; Admiral of the Fleet, 1949; KStJ 1948; DL Hampshire, 1952. Grand Cross, Order of Phoenix (Greece), 1946; Greek War Cross, 1944. *Address:* Monks Lea, Petersfield, Hants. *[Died 12 April 1976.*

WILLIS, Anthony Armstrong, OBE 1944; MC 1916; late Squadron-Leader, RAFVR; late Captain RE; author and playwright (writing as Anthony Armstrong); *b* 2 Jan. 1897; *er s* of late Paymaster Captain G. H. A. Willis, CB, RN; *m* 1926, Monica, *o d* of Dr A. L. M. Sealey; one *s* two *d. Educ:* Uppingham Sch.; Trinity College, Cambridge. Entered Royal Engineers, 1915; served with 34th Div. in France, 1916-19 (despatches, MC, wounded); retired to RERO, 1925; began to write for Punch, 1924, and contributed every week (as "A.A."), 1925-33; contributor (articles and short stories): New Yorker; Strand; Daily Mail; Sunday Chronicle; Country Fair; Evening News, etc; invalided out of reserve, 1939; joined RAFVR 1940; and founded Tee Emm, the RAF Training Memorandum. Creator (with Raff) of Pilot Officer Prune. *Plays:* Well Caught, 1929; Full House, 1930; In the Dentist's Chair, 1931; At the Coach and Horses, 1932; Brains and Brass, 1932 (prod. as Sitting on a Fence, 1939); (with Ian Hay) Orders are Orders, 1932; Eleventh Hour, 1933; Ten Minute Alibi, 1933; (with Harold Simpson) Without Witness, 1933; Business with Royalty (adapted from the German), 1934; Mile Away Murder, 1936; Postal Service, 1937; (with Ronald Crossley) The Three Pigeons, 1938; (with Arnold Ridley) The Running Man, 1949; Horatius (3 plays for WO), 1950; (with Philip King) Here We Come Gathering, 1951; (with Arnold Ridley) Bellamy, 1959; Jumble Warfare, 1952; *radio plays:* For Love of a Lady, 1948; The Black King, 1951; Return, 1953; At Squinty Abbott's, 1953; Death Set to Music, 1953; The Case of Mr Pelham, 1954; The Wide Guy, 1961 (filmed as Never Come Back, 1948); *radio adaptations:* Ten Minute Alibi, 1947; Without Witness, 1948; Mile Away Murder, 1949; *scripts:* (with Richard Murdoch and Kenneth Horne) Over to You (series), 1951; These Radio Times (compère), 1951; (with David Climie) Home and Away, 1954; *film work:* OHMS (treatment), 1936; Young and Innocent (treatment), 1948. Radio broadcasts; TV: Armstrong's Garden (weekly prog. on Southern TV), 1958. *Publications:* The Lure of the Past, 1920; The Love of Prince Rameses, 1921; The Heart of a Slave Girl, 1922; When Nile was Young, 1923; Wine of Death, 1925; Warriors at Ease, 1926; Warriors Still at Ease, 1926; Patrick Undergraduate, 1926; Jimmy Rezaire, 1927 (2nd edn as The Trail of Fear, 1928); Patrick Engaged, 1927; Percival and I, 1927; Patrick Helps, 1928; The Secret Trail, 1928; How to Do It, 1928; Livestock in Barracks, 1929; No Dragon, No Damsel, 1929; Percival at Play, 1929; The Trail of Lotto, 1929; Two Legs and Four, 1930; Taxi, 1930; Me and Frances, 1930; Apple and Percival, 1931; The Trail of the Black King, 1931; Yesterdailies, 1931; Selected Warriors, 1932; The Poison Trail, 1932; Easy Warriors, 1932; Britisher on Broadway, 1932; The Prince Who Hiccuped, 1932; While You Wait, 1933; Selections, 1934; (with Herbert Shaw) Ten Minute Alibi (the story of the play), 1934 (filmed 1935); Thoughts on Things, 1935; Captain Bayonet and Others, 1937; Cottage into House, 1937; The After Breakfast Book, 1937; The Laughter Omnibus: a Punch anthology, 1937; Warriors Paraded: a military omnibus, 1938; We Like the Country, 1940; Nothing to do with the War, 1940; Laughter Parade: an anthology of humour, 1940; Warriors at War, 1941; Village at War, 1941; The Pack of Pieces, 1942 (2nd edn as The Naughty Princess, 1945); (with Raff) Pilot Officer Prune's Progress, 1942; Plonk's Party, 1942; (with Raff) Nice Types, 1943; (with Bruce Graeme) When The Bells Rang, 1943; The Garden, 1943; (with Raff) More Nice Types, 1944; (with Fred Robinson) Good Egg, 1945; Prangmere Mess and other Tales, 1945; (with Raff) Whiskers Will Not Be Worn, 1945; (with Raff) Goodbye, Nice Types, 1946; We Keep Going, 1946; (with Treyer Evans) England, Our England, 1948; My Friend Serafin, 1949; Sappers at War (for WO), 1949; No Higher Mountain, 1951; He Was Found in the Road, 1952 (filmed as Man in the Road, 1955); The Year at Margaret's, 1953; Spies in Amber, 1956 (Room at the Hotel Ambre, USA, 1956); Saying Your Prayers (a book about learning to pray), 1957; The Strange Case of Mr Pelham, 1957 (filmed as The Man Who Haunted Himself, 1970); One Jump Ahead, 1972. *Recreations:* talking, gardening, reading. *Address:* Sadlers End, Three Gates Lane, Haslemere, Surrey. *T:* Haslemere 2066. *Club:* Savage.   *[Died 10 Feb. 1976.*

WILLIS, Charles Armine, CBE 1930; MA (Oxon); Sudan Political Service (retired); *b* 1881; *s* of John Armine Willis, late Fellow of King's College, Cambridge, and Senior Inspector HM Education Department; *m* 1st, 1919, Clare (*d* 1935), *y d* of 1st Lord Holmpatrick and *g-gd* of 1st Duke of Wellington; one *s*; 2nd, 1937, Katharine Winifred Nutcombe Barnett (*d* 1960), 3rd *d* of late James Nutcombe Gould. *Educ:* Eton (Scholar, 1894); Newcastle Select, 1899; Magdalen Coll., Oxford (Exhibitioner). Eton Eight, 1899 and 1900; won Ladies Plate, 1899; 2nd Captain of boats, and keeper of wall, 1899-1900; Editor Eton College Chronicle, 1899-1900; rowed in trials, Oxford, 1900-01-02; rowed for Oxford, 1903; President, 1904, but did not row; won Ladies' Plate, 1904, rowing for Magdalen, Grand Challenge in Leander crew, 1901; Sudan Political Service, 1905; various appointments in that service till attached to Intelligence Dept, 1914; Director of Intelligence, 1919-26; Governor, Upper Nile Province, 1926-31; Member of Mui Tsai Commission (Colonial

Office), 1936; delegate for the Sarawak Government on the Rubber Regulation Cttee, 1937, 1938; Chairman of Royal London Society for Aid of Discharged Prisoners, 1941-47. JP Berks, 1942-49. *Address:* 69 St James's Street, SW1. *Clubs:* Carlton, Beefsteak, Leander.   *[Died 4 Dec. 1975.*

WILLIS, Sir Frank; *see* Willis, Sir Z. F.

WILLIS, Rt. Rev. Frederick Roberts, DD; *b* 10 June 1900; *s* of late Ven. J. R. Willis, BD, Church of Ireland; unmarried. *Educ:* Trinity Coll., Dublin. BA 1923; DipEd 1928; MA 1946; DD (jure dignitatis), 1951. Curate of Sandford Parish, Dublin, 1924-28; Missionary to Chota Nagpur (Dublin University Mission), Hazaribagh, India, 1928-51; Head of the DU Mission, 1946-51; Bishop of Delhi, 1951-66. Retired, and now assisting Rev. Canon R. F. G. Jenkins (Vicar of All Saints' Church, Grangegorman, Dublin). Canon of St Patrick's Cathedral, Dublin, 1966-75. *Address:* c/o All Saints' Vicarage, 30 Phibsborough Road, Dublin 7, Eire.   *[Died 13 Nov. 1976.*

WILLIS, Prof. Rupert Allan, DSc, MD, FRCP, FRCS; FRACP; Consultant Pathologist, Imperial Cancer Research Fund, London; Emeritus Professor and Research Fellow in Pathology, University of Leeds; *b* 24 Dec. 1898; Australian; *m* 1924, Alice Margaret Tolhurst; one *s* one *d. Educ:* Melbourne Univ. Medical Superintendent, Austin Hospital, Melbourne, 1927-30; Pathologist: Alfred Hospital, Melbourne, 1930-45; Royal College of Surgeons, London, 1945-48; Royal Cancer Hospital, London, 1948-50. Professor of Pathology, University of Leeds, 1950-55; Macfarlane Professor of Experimental Medicine, University of Glasgow, 1963-64. Hon. LLD Glasgow, 1962; Hon. MD Perugia, 1975. *Publications:* The Spread of Tumours in the Human Body, 1934; Pathology of Tumours, 1948; Principles of Pathology, 1950; Borderland of Embryology and Pathology, 1958; Pathology of Tumours of Children, 1962; contrib. to Journal Path. Bact., Medical Journal Australia, etc. *Recreation:* gardening. *Address:* Inverdee, Delavor Road, Heswall, Wirral, Merseyside.   *[Died 26 March 1980.*

WILLIS, Sir (Zwinglius) Frank, Kt 1947; CBE 1942 (OBE 1918); General Secretary of the National Council of YMCAs, 1939-55, retired; Hon. Consultant to World Council of YMCAs on Ecumenical Questions and YMCA-Church Relationships; Chairman of Council of Voluntary Welfare Work 1956-62; Chairman of Committee for Overseas Travel Parties for Youth of the South African Aid to Britain Fund, 1948-58; Member Executive Committee, National Council of Social Service, 1941-70; *b* 1890; *s* of late Rev. R. Elgar Willis, Ipswich; *m* 1918, Helen Frances, *d* of late Sir Frederick Walker Mott, KBE, FRS, MD. *Educ:* Northgate Grammar Sch., Ipswich, Ipswich Sch. (Foundation Scholar); King's Coll., Cambridge (Drapers' Exhibitioner). Dep. Organising Secretary, YMCA Services, W. Front, 1915-18; Sen. Tutor, YMCA Training Coll., London, 1919-21; Secretary for Personnel, Training, and Programme, Nat. Council of YMCAs, 1921-30; Commonwealth Representative on staff of World Alliance of YMCAs and Co-Director of YMCA Training Coll., Geneva, 1930-34; Asst General Secretary, Nat. Council of YMCAs, 1934-39. Member World Council of YMCAs and several of its main Cttees and Commissions, 1955-65; Member Exec. Cttee, 1948-55, and Vice-Chairman, Internat. Dept, 1951-55, of British Council of Churches; Member, Adult Education Cttee, Board of Education, 1921-28; Member British Inst. of Adult Education, 1921-39; Chairman of Social Hygiene Cttee, British Social Biology Council, 1935-39; Member Standing Conf. of Nat. Voluntary Youth Organisations, 1936-55. Comdr, Order of Polonia Restituta (1918), 1973. *Address:* 165 West Heath Road, NW3 7TT. *T:* 01-455 8544.   *[Died 8 Nov. 1974.*

WILLMOTT, Sir Maurice (Gordon), Kt 1956; MC; Master of the Supreme Court (Chancery Division) since 1931 (Chief Master, 1950-59); *b* Ealing, Middlesex, 25 Feb. 1894; *s* of James William Willmott, Ealing; *m* 1934, Joan Barbara, *o d* of Gervase Edward Newby, OBE, FRCS; two *d. Educ:* Privately. Qualified as Solicitor, 1915; Inns of Court, OTC, 1915; 2nd Lieut, KRRC, 1916; Captain, 1917; served in France in European War (wounded, despatches); demobilised, 1919; admitted Solicitor, 1919. *Recreation:* gardening. *Address:* Old Beams, Blackford, Yeovil, Somerset. *T:* North Cadbury 397. *[Died 14 Oct. 1977.*

WILLOCK, Air Vice-Marshal (retired) Robert Peel, CB 1943; *b* 17 Dec. 1893; *s* of Canon R. P. Willock; *m* 1919, Dorothy York Liversidge; one *d. Educ:* Marlborough Coll. Oxford and Bucks LI and RFC 1914-18; RAF 1918; Staff Coll., Camberley, 1928-30; Air Attaché to British Embassy, China, 1933-36; Imperial Defence Coll., 1937; Director of Staff Duties, Air Ministry, 1938; AOC No. 21 Group RAF, 1940-43; AOC Iraq and Persia, 1943-44. Deputy Head of RAF Delegation, Washington, 1944-

46; retired list, 1946; Civil Air Attaché to British Embassy, Washington, 1946-47; Overseas Representative of Minister of Civil Aviation, 1947-49; Civil Aviation Adviser to High Commissioner for UK, Australia, 1949-59. Commander USA Legion of Merit, 1946. *Recreation:* shooting. *Address:* c/o Lloyds Bank Ltd, 6 Pall Mall, SW1. *Club:* Royal Air Force.
[Died 22 March 1973.

WILLOUGHBY, Leonard Ashley, MA, DLitt (London), PhD (Vienna); Fellow of University College, London; Hon. Director Institute of Germanic Languages and Literatures, University of London, 1950-53; Emeritus Professor of the University of London; President, English Goethe Society; Founder and Editor of German Life and Letters, 1936-56; a Freeman of the City of London; *b* Bonby, Lincs, 4 June 1885; 2nd *s* of W. H. and F. A. Willoughby; *m* 1916, Lucie Edith, 2nd *d* of H. E. Berthon; one *s*. *Educ:* Lycée Carnot, Paris; Realschule, Ohligs, Germany; City of London Sch.; University College, London; Universities of Vienna and Bonn. Lecturer in English in the University of Cologne, 1908-10; Senior Taylorian Lecturer in German in the University of Oxford, 1910-19; Lecturer in charge of German in the University of Sheffield, 1919-30; Henry Simon Professor of German Language and Literature in the University of Manchester, 1930-31; Fielden Professor of German, University College, London, 1931-50; visiting Professor in the University of Toronto, 1949, and Columbia Univ., New York, 1953; Advisory sub-editor, Chambers's Encyclopædia. Member Mixed Commission for cultural relations with Austria, 1953-55. Corr. Member of Deutsche Akademie, Darmstadt, 1956. Served European War as 2nd Lieut, in the 2/4 Loyal North Lancs Regt; Lieut, RNVR in the Naval Intelligence Department; for a few months on the Reparation Commission in Paris, 1920. *Publications:* D. G. Rossetti and German Literature, 1912; Samuel Naylor and Reynard the Fox, 1914; Von dem jungesten Tage, 1918; Schiller's Die Räuber, 1922; The Classical Age of German Literature, 1926; The Romantic Movement in Germany, 1930; Letters of Kerner to Alexander of Württemberg, 1938; Urfaust and Faust ein Fragment, 1943; Kabale und Liebe, 1945; (with E. M. Wilkinson) Goethe, Poet and Thinker, 1962; Schiller's Aesthetic Letters, 1967. Articles and Reviews in literary and linguistic journals, English and foreign. *Recreations:* music, travelling. *Address:* Angle Place Cottage, Montague Road, Berkhamsted, Herts. *T:* 3736.
[Died 5 Oct. 1977.

WILLS, John Joseph, CB 1941; CBE 1933; *b* 1877; *s* of John William Thomas Wills and Mary, *d* of Joseph Barrett; *m* 1905, Mary (Lillie) Clark (*d* 1960). *Educ:* St John's Coll., Cambridge, 14th Wrangler, Mathematical Tripos, 1899. Entered Board of Trade, 1901; Secretary of Miners' Eight Hour Day Cttee, 1906; Secretary of Royal Commission on Railway Conciliation Scheme, 1911; Director of Petroleum Department, 1924-28; Member of Cttee on Registration of Accounts, 1930; Member of Cttee on Industrial Life Assurance, 1931; Comptroller of the Companies Department, 1928-32; Member of UK delegation in numerous commercial treaty negotiations and international conferences; Head of Commercial Relations and Treaties Department, 1935; retired from Board of Trade, 1942; Chairman of certain Local Appeal Boards under Essential Work Orders, 1943-47. *Address:* c/o National Westminster Bank, 10 St Martin's Place, WC2. *[Died 13 Sept. 1971.*

WILLS, Brigadier Sir Kenneth Agnew, KBE 1960 (CBE 1946; OBE 1941); MC; ED; *b* Adelaide, 3 March 1896; *s* of late Richard J. H. Wills; *m* 1st, 1920, Viola Ethel (*d* 1956), *d* of late Albert Crossland, Egyptian Civil Service, Cairo; one *s* one *d*; 2nd, 1959, Mavis Catherine, *d* of late H, H. Marsh, Adelaide, widow of Dr W. Gilfillan. *Educ:* University College School, London. Served European War, 1914-18 (despatches, MC); Captain, Royal Northumberland Fusiliers; served in France, Salonika, Palestine and Egypt. Served War of 1939-45 (despatches, OBE, CBE): Brigadier, 2nd AIF; DDMI, and Controller, Allied Intelligence Bureau GHQ, SW Pacific Area; served in N Africa, Greece, Crete, Syria and SW Pacific. Member Australian Universities Commission, 1959-65; Chancellor, Adelaide Univ., 1966-68. Hon. Colonel, Adelaide University Regt, 1955-64. KStJ. *Recreation:* fishing. *Address:* 3 Kingston Terrace, North Adelaide, SA 5006, Australia. *Clubs:* Naval and Military; Adelaide. *[Died 13 May 1977.*

WILLS, Leonard Johnston; MA, ScD (Cambridge), PhD (Birmingham); FGS; Emeritus Professor, formerly Professor of Geology and Geomorphology, Birmingham University (1932-49); *b* 27 Feb. 1884; *s* of W. Leonard Wills; *m* 1910, Maud Janet (*d* 1952), *d* of late Sir Alfred Ewing, KCB; one *s* one *d*. *Educ:* Uppingham Sch.; King's Coll., Cambridge. Hon. Member: East Anglian Geol Soc., 1964; Yorkshire Geol Soc., 1975. Hon. Fellow, Geolog. Soc., 1975. *Publications:* The Physiographical

Evolution of Britain, 1929; Palaeogeography of the Midlands, 1948; Palæogeographical Atlas, 1951; Concealed Coalfields, 1956; Palæogeological Maps, 1973, 1978, and scientific papers. *Address:* Brockencote, Romsley, Halesowen B62 0LY.
[Died 12 Dec. 1979.

WILLS, Philip Aubrey, CBE 1945; President, George Wills & Sons (Holdings) Ltd, since 1977 (Chairman, 1959-77); *b* 26 May 1907; *s* of C. P. Wills; *m* 1931, Katharine Fisher; three *s* one *d*. *Educ:* Harrow. Learnt to fly 1928, owned a light aeroplane and in 1932 took up gliding. Took part in rapid development of British sail-flying from that date; second British holder of international "Silver C" in 1934, held British records for height and distance on and off since 1934. First British holder of International Gold Badge (No. 3) for flights of over 3000 metres and 300 kms distance on a sailplane. Senior pilot British team at seven World Gliding Championships; World Champion, 1952 (single-seaters), Madrid. Joined ATA in 1939, became 2nd in command and Director of Operations. Qualified to ferry all types of single-, twin and multi-engined aircraft. General Manager (Technical) British European Airways Corporation, 1946-48; President of the British Gliding Association; Chm., Royal Aero Club, 1975-77. AFRAeS; Coronation Medal, 1953; British gold medal for aeronautics, 1960. *Publications:* On Being a Bird, 1953; Where No Birds Fly, 1961; Free as a Bird, 1973; The Inevitability of Confrontation, Part 1, 1974, Part 2, 1975; contributions to the technical and non-technical press on motorless flight, aircraft accident prevention, etc. *Recreation:* sail-flying. *Address:* 54 Holland Park Mews, W11.
[Died 16 Jan. 1978.

WILLSON, Thomas Olaf, CBE 1918; MA; Chevalier de l'Ordre de la Couronne; Director of Education for the County of Oxford, 1920-45; *b* 1880; *er s* of late Rev. Dr. T. B. Willson; *m* 1st, 1919, Constance Horsburgh (*d* 1946), *d* of late Walter Basil Cowan, St Kilda, Sidmouth; one *s* three *d* (and one *s* decd); 2nd, 1948, Joan, *d* of late A. J. Livesey, Leyland, Lancs. *Educ:* Westminster Sch.; Keble Coll., Oxford. 2nd Class Hons Modern History, 1901. Assistant Secretary, Higher Education for Berkshire, 1905-19; HAC 1914-15; seconded for duty with Foreign Office, Department and Ministry of Information, 1915-18; Asst Secretary, for Education for Oxfordshire, 1919-20. *Publications:* articles on Scandinavian and educational subjects; radio scripts, etc; hon. editor Norwegian Club Year-book, 1907-39. *Address:* 93 Aynho, near Banbury, Oxon. *[Died 5 July 1973.*

WILLWAY, Brig. Alfred Cedric Cowan, CB 1953; CBE 1944; TD 1940; Chairman, Surrey Quarter Sessions, 1955-69; *b* 1898; *o s* of late Rev. A. P. Willway and late Laura Elizabeth (*née* Cowan); *m* 1922, Frances Mary, *y d* of late C. A. Crane; one *s* one *d*. *Educ:* privately; Oriel Coll., Oxford (BA 1921, 2nd Class Honours Mod Hist.). Barrister, Inner Temple, 1924; practised till 1932; Deputy Clerk of the Peace (Surrey), 1932-46; Member, Social Services Committee (Home Office), 1934-36; Probation Advisory Committee and Probation Training Board, 1936-39; Chm. Surrey Probation Cttee, 1948-69, Magistrates Courts Cttee, 1957-69; Vice-Chm. Surrey Standing Jt Cttee JP (Surrey) 1946; Chairman, Surrey Quarter Sessions (formerly Deputy Chairman), 1955; DL (Surrey) 1950-72; CC (Surrey) 1952-59. Mem. Standing Cttee on Criminal Law Revision, 1959-69. Vice-Pres., Magistrates' Assoc., 1969. Served European War (2nd Lt RE), Palestine; commissioned R Signals TA, 1922; War of 1939-45, comd 56 Div. Signals, 1936-41; Dep. CSO, SE Command, 1941; CSO, 5 Corps (N Africa and Italy), 1942-44 (despatches, CBE); CSO, Northern Command, 1945-46; Hon. Col 56 (Lond.) Armd Div. Sig. Regt, 1945-56; Chairman Surrey T&AFA, 1949-52. *Publication:* Willway's Quarter Sessions Practice, 1940 (Supplement, 1952). *Recreation:* gardening. *Address:* Wilgate, Orchard Drive, Wye, near Ashford, Kent. *T:* Wye 812651.*Club:* Carlton. *[Died 25 March 1980.*

WILMOT, Sir Robert Arthur, 8th Bt, *cr* 1759; *b* 8 Oct. 1939; *s* of Major Sir Arthur Wilmot, 7th Bt (killed in action at Alamein, 1942), and Pamela Vera (who *m* 2nd, 1955, Lt-Col Charles Frederick Cathcart, (*d* 1971), twin *d* of Major Garrard, Welton Place, Daventry; *S* father, 1942; *m* 1965, Juliet Elvira, *e d* of Capt. M. N. Tufnell, RN; two *s* one *d*. *Educ:* Eton. Commissioned Scots Guards, 1958; Capt. retd, 1966. Apptd Equerry to HRH the Duke of Gloucester, 1966. *Heir:* s Henry Robert Wilmot, *b* 10 April 1967. *Address:* Pitcairlie, Newburgh, Fife. *T:* Auchtermuchty 464. *Clubs:* Turf, MCC.
[Died 14 Nov. 1974.

WILSON OF HIGH WRAY, Baron *cr* 1976 (Life Peer), of Kendal, Cumbria; **Paul Norman Wilson,** OBE 1959; DSC 1945; MA (Cantab); FSA; FICE; FIMechE; JP; Lieut-Commander RNVR (retired); HM Lieutenant of Cumbria, since 1974 (Lord Lieutenant of Westmorland, 1965-74); *b* 24 Oct. 1908; *y s* of late

Norman Forster Wilson, CE, Kendal, and H. G. M. Wilson (née Harris); *m* 1935, Valerie Frances Elizabeth, *d* of late William Baron Fletcher, Cape Town; no *c. Educ:* Gresham's Sch.; Clare Coll., Cambridge. MA (Mech. Sci.) Cantab, 1934. Served War of 1939-45: mainly at sea in capital ships; temp. Lt-Comdr RN. Worked in S Africa, 1930-34; Gilbert Gilkes & Gordon Ltd, Water Turbine & Pump Manufacturers, Kendal: Man. Dir, 1934-67; Chairman, 1954-78. Chairman: Kendal & District Local Employment Cttee, 1954-69; Westmorland Youth Employment Cttee, 1946-69; Mem., Nat. Youth Employment Council, 1959-69; Member Council: Newcomen Soc., 1958-77 (Vice-Pres., 1968-77, Pres, 1973-75); and Patron, Cumberland & Westmorland Antiquarian and Archaeological Soc., 1965- (Pres., 1975-78); Dep. Chm., Exec. Cttee, British Hydromechanics Res. Assoc., 1973-75; Science Museum: Mem. Adv. Council, 1968-72, 1973-78; Chm., Fund for Preservation of Technol and Scientific Material, 1973-78. Chairman of Governors, Kendal Coll. of Further Educn, 1958-74; Governor, Sedbergh Sch., 1965-74; Chairman of Trustees and Governors: Lake District Museum Trust, 1968-78; Heron Corn Mill Beetham Trust, 1973-78; Governor of BBC, 1968-72. JP 1958, DL 1964, Cumbria, formerly Westmorland. KStJ 1966. *Publications:* Watermills, an introduction, 1956, 2nd edn 1973; Watermills with Horizontal Wheels, 1960; Water Turbines (Sci. Mus. Pubn), 1974; Water and other forms of Motive Power, in History of Technology, 1900-1950, 1977; contributions to journals on history of water power, local history and technical matters. *Recreation:* industrial archæology (especially water power). *Address:* Gillinggate House, Kendal, Cumbria LA9 4JB. *T:* Kendal 20209. *Clubs:* Army and Navy, Beefsteak.
[Died 24 Feb. 1980.

WILSON, Alexander; MP (Lab) Hamilton since 1970; Member, Scottish National Union of Mineworkers; *b* Wilsontown, Lanarkshire, 5 June 1917; *s* of James and Elizabeth Wilson; *m* 1941; one *s* one *d. Educ:* Forth Grammar School. Became a Miner. Joined Labour Party, 1946. Member, 3rd District Council, Lanarkshire, 11 years. Contested (Lab) Hamilton, by-election 1967. Especially interested in welfare of the disabled, sick and elderly persons, and in Trade Unionism. *Address:* House of Commons, SW1. *[Died 23 March 1978.*

WILSON, Prof. Andrew, CBE 1971; MD, PhD, FPS, FRCP, FRCPGlas; Professor of Pharmacology, University of Liverpool, 1951-74, now Emeritus; Consultant Physician, Liverpool Regional Hospital Board; *b* 13 July 1909; *s* of late Hugh and Sarah Wilson, Stepps; *m* 1939, Margaret Hope, *d* of late Rev. Thos Paterson, MA; two *d. Educ:* Muirkirk Sch.; Royal Technical Coll. and University, Glasgow. Weir Assistant in Materia Medica, Univ. of Glasgow, 1933-37; Lecturer in Pharmacology and Therapeutics, Univ. of Sheffield and Clinical Assistant, Sheffield Royal Infirmary, 1939-46; Lecturer in Applied Pharmacology, University College, London, and University College Hospital Medical School, 1946-48; Reader in University of London, 1948-51. Chm., Adv. Cttee on Pesticides and other Toxic Chemicals; Member, Medicines Commn, and of other scientific cttees of Government Depts; Member of British Pharmaceutical Codex Revision Cttee; Past Chairman: British National Formulary Cttee; Prescribers' Jl Cttee. Examiner in Universities of Aberdeen, Belfast, Birmingham, Bristol, Cambridge, Cardiff, Durham, Glasgow, Leeds, Liverpool, London, Manchester, Sheffield; Privy Council Visitor to Examinations of Pharmaceutical Society. *Publications:* (jointly) Applied Pharmacology, 10th edn, 1968; original papers in Nature, Jl Physiol., Jl Clinical Invest., Quart. Jl Med., Lancet, BMJ, Amer. Jl Med., Brit. Jl Pharmacol. *Recreations:* climbing, ski-ing, golfing. *Address:* 3 Weston Court, Burbo Bank Road South, Blundellsands, Liverpool 23. *T:* 051-924 4664. *Club:* Authors'. *[Died 2 Oct. 1974.*

WILSON, Sir Arton, KBE 1948; CB 1946; retired from Civil Service; *b* 16 July 1893; *m* 1920, Enid Beatrice Barnard; two *s* one *d. Educ:* Central Foundation School, London. Service in General Post Office and later in Ministry of Agriculture; entered Ministry of Labour, 1919; Chief Inspector, 1938-40; Director of Establishments in Ministry of Economic Warfare, 1940; Director of Organisation and Establishments, Ministry of Labour and National Service, 1941-48; Permanent Secretary, Ministry of Pensions, 1948-53. President, Civil Service Pensioners' Alliance, 1961-76; Chairman: Roehampton Hospital Trust; Chaseley Trust for Disabled Men, Eastbourne. *Recreations:* tennis, country life. *Address:* The White House, Newdigate, Dorking, Surrey. *T:* Newdigate 281. *Club:* Royal Commonwealth Society. *[Died 19 Sept. 1977.*

WILSON, Sir Bertram, Kt 1952; FRICS; JP; *b* 14 March 1893; *s* of Thomas and Emma Wilson, Hazel House, Tadcaster; *m* 1918, Doris (*d* 1948), *d* of J. Walter Harrison, Tadcaster; one *s. Educ:*

Tadcaster Grammar School. Articled as Civil Engineer and Surveyor to Bromet and Thorman, Tadcaster. LRIBA 1935. Dir (Past Pres.), Leeds Permanent Building Soc. Mem. of W Riding CC, 1940-55; County Alderman, 1945-55; many local govt and public offices. JP WR Yorks, 1940. *Recreations:* music and reading. *[Died 19 Sept. 1974.*

WILSON, Maj.-Gen. Bevil Thomson, CB 1941; DSO 1918; RE; *b* Toronto, 12 December 1885; *s* of Alexander Wilson, FRCS, DL Manchester; *m* 1918, Florence Erica, *d* of Sir John Starkey, 1st Bt; one *s* one *d. Educ:* Clifton; RMA, Woolwich. Entered RE, 1905; Captain, 1914; Major, 1922; Lt-Col, 1930; Bt Col, 1932; Col, 1934; Maj.-Gen., 1939; served India, 1907-12; Egyptian Army, 1912-14; European War, 1914-18, Egypt, Gallipoli. France, Italy (despatches, DSO, Italian Silver Medal), General Staff, War Office, 1922-25; DAA and QMG West Riding Div. York, 1927-29; Chief Staff Officer, Sudan Defence Force, 1929-33; Commander Lahore Brigade Area, India, 1935-37; Commander Nowshera Brigade, NWFP, India, 1937-39; Commander 53rd (Welsh) Division, 1939-41; retired pay, 1941. Employed, 1944-50, with UNRRA and CCG in Germany, Member of Council Royal National Institute for the Blind, 1952-65. *Address:* 9 Hasker Street, Chelsea, SW3. *T:* 01-589 8945. *[Died 30 Oct. 1975.*

WILSON, Col Campbell Aubrey Kenneth I.; *see* Innes-Wilson.

WILSON, Charles Edward; American Industrialist; *b* 18 Nov. 1886; *s* of George H. Wilson and Hannah Rebecca Stiles; *m* 1907, Elizabeth Maisch; one *d. Educ:* public schools of New York City. Sprague Works, Gen. Electric Co., Sept. 1899; Gen. Electric Co.: served successively in accounting, production, engineering, manufacturing and marketing depts; Vice-Pres., 1930-37; Exec. Vice-Pres., 1937-39; President, 1940-42 and 1944-50. Appointed by President Roosevelt as Vice-Chm. War Production Bd, 1942; then Exec. Vice-Chm. until 1944; apptd by President Truman as Director, Office of Defense Mobilization, Dec. 1950-Apr. 1952. Director and Consultant, W. R. Grace & Co., 1952; Chm. Exec. Cttee, 1953-55; Chm. Bd of Directors, 1955-56; Pres., People-to-People Foundation, 1956-58. Has various medals and awards for public service; holds hon. degrees. *Address:* (office) 437 Fifth Avenue, New York City, USA; (residence) 7 Hampton Road, Scarsdale, NY 10583, USA. *[Died 3 Jan. 1972.*

WILSON, Clyde Tabor; retired Metropolitan Police Magistrate, 1962 (South-Western Police Court, 1935, subsequently Marlborough Street Magistrates Court); *b* 21 September 1889; *s* of Dr Foden Wilson, The Wood, Shrewsbury Road, Birkenhead; unmarried. *Educ:* Rugby School; Trinity College, Cambridge. Called to Bar, Inner Temple, 1913, and practised on North Wales and Chester Circuit; served European War with 5th London Brigade RFA (T); MP (U) West Toxteth Division, Liverpool, 1931-35; Recorder of Birkenhead, 1934-35; member for Central Wandsworth on the London County Council, 1925-35. *Address:* Flat 20, Pearl Court, Eastbourne, Sussex. *Club:* Carlton. *[Died 13 Nov. 1971.*

WILSON, Rt. Rev. Douglas John, MA; *b* 22 June 1903; *e s* of late Canon J. K. Wilson, Vicar of Bromley, Kent, and late Mrs E. L. Wilson; *m* 1946, Mary Theodora, *er d* of late Rev. A. F. Bliss; one *s* one *d. Educ:* King's School, Rochester; Haileybury College; Queens' College, Cambridge; Westcott House, Cambridge. Hist. Tripos, BA Cantab 1924; MA Cantab 1928; ordained 1927, to Curacy of Dartford Parish Church; Curate Walsall Parish Church, 1931; Vicar of Kingswinford, Staffs, 1935; Asst Bishop of British Honduras, 1938-44; Archdeacon in Central America, 1939-44; Asst Bishop of Southwell, 1944-45; Bishop of British Honduras, 1945-50; Bishop of Trinidad, 1950-56; Asst Bishop of Bath and Wells and Canon Residentiary and Treasurer of Wells Cathedral, 1956-73; Proctor in Convocation for Dean and Chapter, Wells Cathedral, 1961-63. Fellow of Woodard Corporation (Western Division), 1958, Vice-Provost, 1976-80, Hon. Fellow, 1980. Chairman of Governors, King's Coll., Taunton, 1958-75. Coronation Medal, 1953. *Recreation:* reading, travel. *Address:* 3 St Mary Well Street, Beaminster, Dorset. *T:* Beaminster 862616. *[Died 30 Nov. 1980.*

WILSON, Edmund; writer; *b* Red Bank, New Jersey, 8 May 1895; *s* of Edmund Wilson and Helen Mather Kimball; *m* 1st, 1923, Mary Blair; one *d*; 2nd, 1930, Margaret Canby; 3rd, 1938, Mary McCarthy; one *s*; 4th, 1946, Elena Thornton; one *d. Educ:* Hill School, Pottstown, Pa; Princeton Univ. (AB 1916). Reporter on New York Evening Sun, 1916-17; Managing Editor. Vanity Fair, 1920-21; Associate Editor, New Republic, 1926-31. US Presidential Medal of Freedom, 1963. *Publications:* The Undertaker's Garland (with John Peale Bishop), 1922; Discordant Encounters (dialogues and plays), 1926; I Thought

of Daisy (novel), 1929; Poets, Farewell! (verse), 1929; Axel's Castle (literary criticism), 1931; The American Jitters—A Year of the Slump, 1932; Travels in Two Democracies, 1936; This Room and This Gin and These Sandwiches (plays), 1937; The Triple Thinkers, 1938; To the Finland Station, 1940; The Boys in the Back Room, 1941; The Wound and the Bow, 1941; Note-Books of Night, 1942; The Shock of Recognition (anthology), 1943; Memoirs of Hecate County, 1946; Europe Without Baedeker, 1947 (new edn 1967); The Little Blue Light (play), Classics and Commercials, 1950; The Shores of Light, 1952; Five Plays, 1954; The Scrolls from the Dead Sea, 1955; Red, Black, Blond and Olive, 1956; A Piece of My Mind, 1956; The American Earthquake, 1958; Apologies to The Iroquois, 1960; Wilson's Night Thoughts, 1961; Patriotic Gore, 1962; The Cold War and the Income Tax; a Protest, 1964; The Bit between my Teeth, 1966; A Prelude, 1967; The Duke of Palermo, and Other Plays, 1969; The Dead Sea Scrolls: 1947-1969, 1969; Upstate: Records and Recollections of Northern New York, 1972. *Address:* Wellfleet, Cape Cod, Mass, USA.
[*Died* 12 *June* 1972.

WILSON, Prof. Edward Meryon, FBA 1964; MA, PhD; Professor of Spanish, Cambridge University, 1953-73; Vice-Master of Emmanuel College, 1961-65; *b* Kendal, 1906; *s* of Norman F. Wilson, Kendal, and Henrietta Gwendolen Meryon Harris. *Educ:* Windermere Grammar School; Trinity Coll., Cambridge. Modern Languages Tripos, Part II, 1928; Esmé Howard Studentship at Residencia de Estudiantes, Madrid, 1929-30; Rouse Ball Studentship at Trinity College, Cambridge, 1930-31; Jane Eliza Proctor Visiting Fellowship at University of Princeton (NJ), 1932-33; PhD Cambridge, 1934; Assistant Lecturer in Spanish at Cambridge, 1933-39; University Lecturer there, 1939-45 (absent on national service, 1941-44); Cervantes Prof. of Spanish, Univ. of London, 1945-53. Fellow of Emmanuel College, Cambridge, Jan.-Sept. 1945. Visiting Professor: Indiana Univ., Bloomington, 1966; Univ. of Calif, Berkeley, 1968-69; Univ. of Texas, 1975; Johnson Prof., Inst. of Res. in Humanities, Univ. of Wisconsin, 1977. Pres. Assoc. of Hispanists of Great Britain and Ireland, 1971-73; Provisional Pres. First Internat. Congress of Hispanists, Oxford, 1962; Pres., Internat. Assoc. of Hispanists, 1971-74; Pres., Cambridge Bibliographical Soc., 1975-. Corresp. Member: Hispanic Soc. of America, 1963; Royal Spanish Acad., 1964; Royal Acad. of Good Letters, Barcelona, 1974. Hon. DLitt Southampton, 1972. *Publications:* The Solitudes of Don Luis de Gongora, 1931, 2nd edn, 1965; (with Jack Sage) Poesías líricas en las obras dramáticas de Calderón1964; (with F. J. Norton) Two Spanish Verse Chap-books, 1968; Entre las jarchas y Cernuda, 1977; also articles in various reviews. *Address:* Emmanuel College, Cambridge CB2 3AP.
[*Died* 21 *Nov.* 1977.

WILSON, Brig. Edward William Gravatt, CBE 1943; MC; *b* 14 April 1888; *s* of Rev. Alfred Wilson; *m* 1926, Edith Margaret Smith; one *s* one *d*. *Educ:* Charterhouse; RMA, Woolwich. 2nd Lt RA 1908; served in RFA till 1936, then Anti-Aircraft; peacetime service in UK, South Africa, and India; European War, 1914-18, France and Salonika; War of 1939-45, A-A Brigade Commander UK, and A-A Defence Commander, Egypt; retired pay, 1944. *Address:* The Firs, Selkirk. *Club:* United Service.
[*Died* 31 *Jan.* 1971.

WILSON, Edwin J. B.; *see* Boyd-Wilson.

WILSON, Eleanora Mary C.; *see* Carus-Wilson.

WILSON, Sir Garnet Douglas, Kt 1944; LLD (St Andrews); JP; Hon. Sheriff-Substitute at Dundee; Chairman; Sir James Caird's Travelling Scholarships Trust; Armitstead Lectures Trust; Deputy Chairman, Dundee Savings Bank, 1949-75; Lord Provost of Dundee, 1940-46; Lord Lieutenant of County of City of Dundee, 1940-46, now DL; *b* 24 March 1885; 2nd *s* of Gavin Laurie Wilson, JP, and Jessie Dunlop McCulloch; *m* 1st, 1925, Gladys Margery Johnson (*d* 1953); two *s* one *d*; 2nd, 1953, Mrs Marguerite Lawson (*d* 1975), *widow* of J. Douglas Lawson, and *d* of late Rev. J. H. Morrison, Kirkmichael, Perthshire. *Educ:* Bell Baxter School, Cupar; Newport School, Fife; High School of Dundee. Dundee Education Authority, 1919-30; Newport (Fife) Town Council, 1919-29; Town Council of Dundee, 1929-35 and 1937-46; Chairman of Education Committee, 1930-35, 1937-40; President, University College, Dundee, 1946-52 (Mem., Coll. Council, 1940-53); Member: Nat. Youth Employment Council, 1948-62; Queen's College (now University of Dundee) Council, 1953-67; Chairman: National Camps Association of Scotland, 1941-65; Advis. Committee on Youth Employment (Scotland), 1946-62; Youth Employment Cttee, 1931-62 and Local Employment Cttee, 1936-62; Glenrothes Develt Corp., 1952-60. Hon. FEIS 1943; Vice-Chm. Adv. Council on Education in Scotland, 1942-46; 1947-51;

Member, St Andrews University Court, 1940-49; Rector's Assessor, 1946-49. Chairman, Scottish Special Housing Assoc., 1944-46; Mem., Building Apprenticeship and Training Council (MPBW), 1943-56. Formerly Senior Partner, G. L. Wilson, Dundee (Drapers). Freeman, City of Dundee, 1972. Order of Finnish Lion, 1952. *Publications:* Bachelor's Buttons (privately), 1921; The Making of a Lord Provost, 1966; Overspill, 1970; articles and addresses on Scottish education (advocated Pre-Vocational Courses for Secondary Schools). *Recreations:* reading, football (fan). *Address:* St Colmes, Perth Road, Dundee. *T:* Dundee 67454.   [*Died* 18 *Sept.* 1975.

WILSON, Geoffrey; *see* Wilson, (H.) G. (B.).

WILSON, Sir George, KBE 1959; Kt 1944; Hon. LLD; Chairman of Governors of West of Scotland Agricultural College, 1942-71; *b* 24 Nov. 1900; 3rd *s* of Sir David Wilson, 1st Bt of Carbeth, Killearn; unmarried. *Educ:* Harrow; Trinity College, Cambridge (MA, Nat. Sci. Tripos). Hon. LLD (Glasgow), 1950; DUniv Stirling, 1973. Post-graduate study, then farming. Member: Scottish Milk Marketing Bd, 1935-50 (Chm.); Balfour of Burleigh Committee on Hill Sheep Farming in Scotland, 1941-44; Herring Industry Bd, 1945-63; Director British Linen Bank, 1950-71. Mem., Stirling CC, 1930-75. *Recreations:* fishing, walking. *Address:* King's Mile, Killearn, by Glasgow. *TA:* King's Mile, Killearn. *T:* Killearn 50363. *Club:* Athenæum.   [*Died* 25 *May* 1979.

WILSON, George Ambler, CBE 1967; CEng, FICE, FIMechE; Consultant Engineer and Director of Land Reclamation and Development; *b* 16 May 1906; *s* of Frederick Coe Wilson and Betsey Alice (*née* Pickles), Halifax, Yorks; *m* 1950, Audry Beryl (*née* Vernon); two *d*. *Educ:* Wrekin Coll.; Liverpool Univ. MEng 1932, FICE 1944, FIMechE 1951. Leyland Motors Apprentice; Anglo-Iranian Oil Co.; MoT, Bridge Section; Admty, Civil Engr-in-Chief's Dept; Port of London Authority, 1948-69 (Dir, 1965-69). Pres., Council of Instn of Civil Engrs, 1971-72; Hon. Member: Perm. Internat. Assoc. of Navig. Congresses; Hydraulic Research Bd, Wallingford (Chm., 1959-63); British Hydromechanics Research Assoc. (Vice-Chm., 1968); Thames Survey Cttee, 1948-63; Nat. Economic Develt Cttee for Civil Engrg Industry, 1965-70; Smeatonian Soc. of Civil Engineers. Pres., Société des Ingénieurs Civils de France, 1969. OC, Engr and Rly Staff Corps, RE T&AVR, 1964-69. *Recreation:* a little gardening. *Address:* Amblers, Lanchard Lane, Shillingstone, Dorset. *Clubs:* Athenæum, Royal Automobile.
[*Died* 20 *Dec.* 1977.

WILSON, Maj.-Gen. (Hon. Lt-Gen.) Sir Gordon, KCSI, *cr* 1946; CB 1944; CBE 1940 (OBE 1928); MC; MB, ChB, DPH; *b* 1 Feb. 1887; 3rd *s* of late John Wilson, Cheltenham; *m* Ethel Marian (*d* 1970), 4th *d* of late John Loring, Doddington, Nantwich; two *s*. *Educ:* Edinburgh Univ. Joined RAMC 1911; Lt-Col 1934; Bt-Col 1937; Subst 1938; Brig. 1941; Maj.-Gen. 1941; local Lt-Gen. 1943; Hon. Lt-Gen., 1946; retired list 1946. Served European War, 1914-18, Mesopotamia; served in India, Burma, NWF, France, Middle East; DADGAMS WO, 1929-33; DADMS Waziristan Dist, 1934-36; DADMS HQ N Command, India, 1936-38; OC Royal Victoria Hospital, Netley, 1938-39; Commandant Dieppe Sub-Area, 1939-40; DDMS X Corps, 1940-41; DDMS Southern Army, India, 1941-43; DMS India, 1943-46; KHS, 1941-46. CStJ. *Address:* c/o Williams & Glyn's Bank Ltd, Whitehall, SW1.   [*Died* 17 *July* 1971.

WILSON, Prof. Graham Malcolm; Regius Professor of Medicine, University of Glasgow, since 1967; *b* 16 April 1917; *er s* of Dr Malcolm Wilson; *m* 1949, Elizabeth Stanfield, *er d* of Dr J. T. Bell Nicoll; two *s* four *d*. *Educ:* Edinburgh Academy. MB, ChB, Edinburgh (hons), 1940; Ettles Scholar; MD (gold medal), 1950; DSc 1964; FRCP, 1956; FRCPE, 1947; FRCPG 1967; FRSE 1969. Royal Air Force Medical Service, 1941-46; Assistant Medical Unit, St Mary's Hospital, 1947-49; Lecturer in Therapeutics, University of Sheffield, 1950-54; Professor of Pharmacology and Therapeutics, 1954-67. Eli Lilly Research Fellow, Harvard Univ. Med. School, 1952-53; Visiting Professor of Medicine, Univ. of Adelaide, 1960; Edwin Tooth Vis. Prof., Royal Brisbane Hosp., 1971. Bradshaw Lectr, RCP, 1962. Former Member: British Pharmacopoeia Commn; Royal Commn on Medical Educn; Nat. Council for Educn Technology; British Nat. Formulary Cttee; Prescriber's Journal Cttee. Managing Trustee, Nuffield Foundn, 1967-; Chm., Safety of Medicines Cttee, 1976; Chm., Editorial Bd, Brit. Jl Clinical Pharmacology, 1975-. *Publications:* articles in med. and scientific journals dealing chiefly with the peripheral circulation and with metabolic problems. *Recreations:* boating, fishing. *Address:* 11 Westbourne Gardens, Glasgow G12 9XD. *T:* 041-334 3287. *Club:* Athenæum.   [*Died* 15 *April* 1977.

WILSON, Rev. Canon Harold, MA (Cantab); DD; Canon Residentiary and Chancellor of St Paul's Cathedral, since 1973; *b* 17 Dec. 1919; *s* of late John William and Ada Wilson; unmarried. *Educ:* Bradford Regional Coll. of Art; Selwyn Coll., Cambridge. Served RAMC, 1940-46. Deacon, 1951; Priest, 1952. Curate, St Augustine, Sheffield, 1951-54; Chaplain to Bishop of Sheffield and Diocesan Youth Organiser, 1954-59; Sec., C of E Bd of Educn, 1959-65; Principal, Salisbury and Wells Theological Coll., 1971-73 (of Salisbury Theol Coll., 1965-71); Canon Residentiary of Sarum, 1968-73 (Canon 1965, Chancellor 1971-73, Prebendary of Netherbury in Terra). Examining Chaplain to Bishops of Bradford, Chelmsford, Kensington and London; Commissary to Bp of Newcastle, Aust. Chm., Adult Educn Cttee, British Council of Churches, 1964. Member: Bd of Management, World Council of Christian Education; Archbishop of Canterbury's Commn on Roman Catholic Relations, 1969; World Council of Churches Educn Renewal Fund, 1970; Churches Commn on Broadcasting, 1971; Central Religious Adv. Cttee for Broadcasting, 1971; Proctor in Convocation, 1970; Governor: SPCK, 1971; Whitelands Coll. of Education, 1974. Du Bose Lectr, Univ. of the South, Tennessee, 1969; Bradner Lectr in Educn, Virginia, 1969. DD Univ. of the South, USA, 1971. *Publications:* The Parish Youth Club, 1960; Reading the Bible Together, 1960; Living the Liturgy Together, 1962. *Recreations:* painting, music, theatre. *Address:* 1 Amen Court, EC4M 7BU. *T:* 01-248 4518. *Club:* Royal Commonwealth Society. *[Died 2 Nov. 1975.*

WILSON, Henry Wilcox, QC 1941; BA; LLB; *b* 19 Jan. 1895; *s* of Cornelius Wilcox and Julia Adèle Wilson; *m* 1931, Muriel Gough Wickenden (*d* 1959). *Educ:* Uppingham; Trinity Coll., Cambridge. Barrister-at-law (Inner Temple) South Eastern Circuit; Kent Sessions; Magistrate, Tanganyika, 1929; Legal Secretary, British Somaliland, 1935; Attorney-General: N. Rhodesia, 1937-44; Trinidad and Tobago, 1944-50; Puisne Judge, Federation of Malaya, 1950-56; first Speaker, Nyasaland Legislative Council, 1958-61. *Club:* Bath. *[Died 1 June 1974.*

WILSON, Sir Horace John, GCB 1937 (KCB 1924; CB 1920); GCMG 1933; CBE 1918; Hon. LLD (Aberdeen, 1934, Liverpool, 1939); *b* 23 Aug. 1882; 2nd *s* of late Harry Wilson, Bournemouth; *m* 1908, Emily, *d* of late John Sheather, Beckley; one *s* two *d. Educ:* Kurnella Sch., Bournemouth; London School of Economics. Entered Civil Service, 1900; Principal Assistant Secretary, Ministry of Labour, 1919-21; Permanent Secretary, Ministry of Labour, 1921-30; Chief Industrial Adviser to HM Government, 1930-39; seconded to the Treasury for service with the Prime Minister, 1935; Permanent Secretary of HM Treasury and official Head of HM Civil Service, 1939-42. Independent Chairman, National Joint Council for Local Authorities' Administrative, Professional, Technical and Clerical Services, 1944-51. Hon. Fellow, LSE, 1960. *Address:* 8 Byron Road, Boscombe, Bournemouth, Hants. *T:* Bournemouth 33752. *[Died 19 May 1972.*

WILSON, Sir Hubert Guy M. M.; *see* Maryon-Wilson.

WILSON, (Hugh) Geoffrey (Birch), CBE 1973; *b* 11 June 1903; *s* of late F. J. Wilson, CIE, Sidmouth, and of Mary Phoebe, *d* of late Colonel E. Birch, IMS; *m* 1935, Daphne Violet Nona, *d* of late Gordon Astley Wake; two *s* five *d. Educ:* Clifton College; Pembroke College, Cambridge (MA). Admitted Solicitor, 1928; Solicitors Department, GWR, 1928-47, finishing as senior Solicitor Assistant, Parliamentary and General section; assistant solicitor, Railway Executive, Western Region, 1948-49; resigned Jan. 1949, for political reasons; MP (C) Truro, 1950-70. Chm., Cons. Party Transport Cttee, 1955-63; Cons. Jt Chm., All Party Roads Study Gp; Sec., All Party Channel Tunnel Gp. Now a partner in a London firm. Associate Inst. Transport. *Address:* 36 Cleaver Square, SE11. *T:* 01-735 7566. *[Died 11 April 1975.*

WILSON, Hon. Sir Ian; *see* Wilson, Hon. Sir T. I. F.

WILSON, James Thomas Pither, CBE 1955; *b* 16 Aug. 1884; *e s* of Alfred Thomas Wilson; *m* 1913, Netia Ling, *o d* of William James Welch, St Peter's Port, Guernsey, CI; one *s* (and one *s* decd). HM Land Registry, 1900; High Court of Justice in Bankruptcy, 1910; Registrar Companies Court and in Bankruptcy, 1947-53; Chief Registrar in Bankruptcy of the High Court of Justice, 1953-57. Served European War, 1914-18, in France. *Address:* Leiston Old Abbey, Leiston, Suffolk. *[Died 26 July 1976.*

WILSON, Sir John Mitchell Harvey, 2nd Bt, *cr* 1920; KCVO 1957 (CVO 1950); Barrister; late 2nd Lieutenant Coldstream Guards; Keeper of the Queen's Philatelic Collection, 1952-69; President, Royal Philatelic Society, London, 1934-40; *b* 10 Oct. 1898; *e surv. s* of 1st Bt and Susan Main (*d* 1944), *d* of Rev. J.

Mitchell Harvey, DD; *S* father, 1930; *m* 1927, Mary Elizabeth, *er d* of William Richards, CBE; three *s. Educ:* Harrow; New Coll., Oxford. Keeper of the King's Philatelic Collection, 1938-52. An Extra Gentleman Usher to the Queen, 1969-. *Publication:* The Royal Philatelic Collection, 1952. *Heir:* s David Wilson [*b* 30 Oct. 1928; *m* 1955, Eva Margareta, *e d* of Tore Lindell, Malmo, Sweden; two *s* one *d*]. *Address:* Carbeth, Killearn, Stirlingshire. *TA:* Killearn. *Club:* Arts. *[Died 6 Feb. 1975.*

WILSON, Joseph Vivian; retired as New Zealand Ambassador to France, 1959; *b* 14 July 1894; *s* of J. H. Wilson; *m* 1929, Valentine, *d* of H. van Muyden, Geneva; two *s. Educ:* Christchurch Boys' High Sch.; Canterbury University College, NZ; Trinity Coll., Cambridge (MA). Craven Scholar and Porson Prizeman, Cambridge. Served in first New Zealand Expeditionary Force, 1915-18. International Labour Office, Geneva, 1921-23; Secretariat, League of Nations, Geneva, 1923-40 (Chief of Central section, 1933-40); Assistant Director of Research, Chatham House, London, 1940-44; Member NZ delegation to San Francisco Conference, 1945, and to several sessions of the General Assembly of the United Nations; Assistant Secretary of External Affairs, New Zealand, 1944-56; HM New Zealand Minister at Paris, 1956, Ambassador, 1957. *Address:* 2 Mahina Road, Eastbourne, NZ. *Club:* United Oxford & Cambridge University. *[Died 29 Dec. 1977.*

WILSON, Sir Leonard, KCIE 1945; Kt 1941; BEng; MICE; *b* Birkenhead, 12 March 1888; *s* of late G. R. Wilson, Birkenhead; *m* 1919, Muriel (*d* 1926), *d* of John Smethurst; two *s*; *m* 1947, Annis, *d* of late Rev. J. C. Abdy. *Educ:* Birkenhead Sch.; Liverpool Univ. Went to India, 1910; employed GIP Railway, Chief Engineer, 1930-34; General Manager, 1934-40; Chief Commissioner of Railways, India, 1940-46. *Address:* Lowbury, Compton, Berks. *Club:* East India, Devonshire, Sports and Public Schools. *[Died 13 April 1980.*

WILSON, Rev. Richard Mercer, MA; Rector of St George the Martyr, Queen Square, Holborn (with St Bartholomew and Holy Trinity Gray's Inn Road) and Anglican Chaplain, Hospital for Sick Children, Great Ormond Street, 1944-66, resigned; *b* 9 Dec. 1887; *s* of David Wilson and Jane Mercer; *m* 1914; one *s* (and two killed in action, 1939 and 1944) one *d. Educ:* St Patrick's Cathedral and Trinity Coll., Dublin. Curate of Christ Church, Delgany, 1910; Mariners Church, Kingstown, 1913; Incumbent, St John's Church, Cork, 1916; Clerical Secretary, Irish Church Missions, London, 1922; Professor of Church History, Wycliffe Coll., Toronto, 1927; General Secretary United Society for Christian Literature and Lutterworth Press, 1931-40; Vicar of St Philip's, Arlington Square, Islington, 1940-43. *Publications:* Before the Reformation, 1929; Vital Themes, 1932; Protestantism: Its Fundamental Basis, 1932; Fourfold Aspect, 1933; The Book of Books, a fresh translation of the New Testament, 1938; Editor: Lutterworth Library, vols i-xiii; Tyndale Commemoration Volume, etc. *Recreations:* swimming and walking. *Address:* 188 Court Lane, SE21. *T:* 01-693 2864. *[Died 26 Nov. 1976.*

WILSON, Hon. Sir Robert (Christian), Kt 1966; CMG 1952; Chairman: Australian Guarantee Corporation Ltd; Country Television Services Ltd; Sydney Board, Union Fidelity Trustee Co. Ltd; a Director of other companies; *b* 11 Nov. 1896; *s* of late Henry Christian Wilson, Blayney; *m* 1932, Gertrude, *d* of Clayton K. Brooks, Boston, Mass., USA; one *s* two *d. Educ:* Fort Street High School, Australia. Served European War, 1914-18; on active service, 1st LH Regt, AIF in Palestine, 1915-18. MLC New South Wales, 1949-61. General Manager, Grazcos Co-op. Ltd, 1924-61; Chm., Tooheys Ltd, 1962-72; formerly Director: Bank of NSW; Scottish Australian Co. Ltd. *Address:* 25 Bushlands Avenue, Gordon, Sydney, NSW 2072, Australia. *Club:* Australian, Elanora Country (Sydney). *[Died 21 Aug. 1973.*

WILSON, Stanley Reginald; Portrait Painter; *b* Camberwell, 27 May 1890; *yr s* of late Alfred Wilson; unmarried. *Educ:* Aske's School, Hatcham; University of London. Goldsmiths' College, School of Art; Inns of Court Officers Training Corps; Royal Staff College, Camberley; Gazetted 2/Lt to 3rd 6th Battalion (Territorial) Duke of Wellington's Regt (West Riding), attached 10th Service Bn Duke of Wellington's Regt (West Riding), 23rd Division, on Active Service in Flanders, France and Italy (despatches); represented by works in British Museum, Imperial War Museum, South Kensington Museum, The Museums of Leeds, Liverpool, Manchester, Salford, Charlton, Bradford, Rotherham, Whitworth, National Gallery of Sports and Pastimes, Brooklyn, New York, etc. *Address:* c/o Barclays Bank Ltd, 1 Pall Mall East, SW1. *[Died 25 April 1973.*

WILSON, Sydney Ernest, MA Cantab; retired as Principal of King William's College, Isle of Man (1935-58); b London; s of late Arthur Wilson and late Emily Ellen Percival; m 1923, Barbara Isabel Ross, d of late H. J. Davis, LRAM, Bath; two s. Educ: Christ's Hospital; Trinity College, Cambridge (Major Scholar). 1st Class, Mathematical Tripos, Part 1, 1920; 1st Class, Part II, 1922, Wrangler; Sixth Form Master, Blundell's School, 1922-30; Headmaster, Burton-on-Trent Grammar School, 1930-35; served European War, Lieut RGA in France and Flanders. Recreations: woodwork, gardening, tapestry, watching TV. Address: Keristal House, Port Soderick, Isle of Man. T: Douglas 3816.   [Died 20 Dec. 1973.

WILSON, Sir T. George; see Wilson, Sir George.

WILSON, Hon. Sir (Tom) Ian (Findlay), KBE 1963; CMG 1957; Politician and Farmer, Rhodesia; b 15 Jan. 1904; m 1952, Jacqueline Primrose, d of J. G. Robinson, Salisbury, S Rhodesia; one s one d. Educ: Morrison's Academy, Crieff, Scotland. MP, S Rhodesia, 1940-52. Elected Speaker, Legislative Assembly, S Rhodesia, 1950-53; first Speaker, Fedn of Rhodesia and Nyasaland, 1953, re-elected, 1959, 1962-63. Address: Zengeni Farm, Penhalonga, Rhodesia. Clubs: Salisbury, Umtali (Rhodesia).   [Died 3 March 1971.

WILSON, William; HM Diplomatic Service; Minister, Rome, since 1972; b 10 March 1920; s of Major Noel Wilson, Norton Manor, Malmesbury, Wiltshire and of late Hilda Margaret Wilson (née Wiggin); m 1st, 1944, Sylvia McLachlan (marriage dissolved, 1961); one s one d; 2nd, 1961, Monica (née Dehn); one step s one step d. Educ: Eton. Joined Foreign Office, 1942; 3rd Sec., Rome, 1945; Information Officer, Venice, 1947; Foreign Office, 1949; Military Govt, Berlin, 1952; Consul, Jerusalem, 1954; FO, 1958; Consul, Elisabethville, 1963; Ambassador and Consul-Gen. to Togo and Dahomey, 1965-66; Head of British Interests Section, Dar-es-Salaam, 1966; Head of W and Central African Dept of FO, 1968; Head of Central and Southern Africa Dept, FCO, 1969-72. Recreations: gardening, riding, tennis, shooting. Address: c/o Foreign and Commonwealth Office, SW1; Ash, Stedham, Midhurst, Sussex.
[Died 25 Nov. 1972.

WILSON, William Combe; Regius Professor of Surgery, University of Aberdeen, 1939-62, now Emeritus; b 8 Sept. 1897; s of John Wilson and Janet Combe; m 1939, Ivy Marian Allan; three s. Educ: Royal High Sch., Edinburgh; Univ. of Edinburgh. MB, ChB Edinburgh 1924; FRCSE 1927. Served Army, 1915-19: Private, Argyll and Sutherland Highlanders, 2nd Lieut Black Watch. rockefeller Travelling Fellow in USA; Carnegie Foundation Research Fellow; Surgeon Royal Hospital for Sick Children, Edinburgh, 1935-39; Director, Edinburgh Surgical Research Unit of Medical Research Council, 1938-39; Lt-Col RAMC i/c No 1 Medical Research Section in Middle East, 1942-43. Hon. LLD (Aberdeen), 1963. Publications: papers in surgical and scientific journals. Address: 3 Burnside Gardens, Aberdeen AB2 4QW. T: Aberdeen 50198.
[Died 12 March 1974.

WILSON, Group Captain William Proctor, CBE (mil.) 1943; (RAFVR); b 14 Jan. 1902; e c of late Canon C. E. Wilson, MA, BD; m 1st, 1926, Evelyne Christiana Cornet-Auquier; two s; 2nd, 1947, Agnes Christian Gillan, OBE, MB, ChB (d 1975); one s. Educ: St Lawrence College, Ramsgate; City and Guilds; Imperial Coll. (University of London). BSc (Eng); FCGI; CEng, FIEE; RAF (Signals Branch), 1939-45; RAF Supplementary Reserve (Signals Branch), 1946-54; Head of Research Department, BBC, 1950-64. Member, Radio Research Board, 1962-64; Mullard Ltd, 1964-72. Hon. Research Fellow, Dept of Electrical Engineering, University College, London, 1964-73. Address: c/o Barclays Bank, Langham Place, W1. Club: Athenæum.   [Died 25 Oct. 1980.

WILSON SMITH, Sir Henry, KCB 1949; KBE 1945; Director: Guest Keen and Nettlefolds Ltd, 1951-72 (Deputy Chairman, 1962-72); Powell Duffryn Ltd, 1951-69 (Chairman, 1957-69); Doxford & Sunderland Ltd, 1961-72; HAT Group Ltd, 1969-74; b 30 Dec. 1904; e s of J. Wilson Smith, Newcastle upon Tyne; m 1931, Molly, d of A. W. G. Dyson, Wylam, Northumberland; two s. Educ: Royal Grammar School, Newcastle upon Tyne; Peterhouse, Cambridge. 1st Class, 1st Div. History Tripos, Parts I and II; Administrative Class, Home Civil Service, 1927; Secretary's Office, General Post Office, 1927-29; HM Treasury, 1930; Asst Private Secretary to Chancellor of Exchequer, 1932, Prin. Private Sec., 1940-42; Under-Sec., HM Treasury, 1942-46; Permnt Sec., Min. of Defence, 1947-48; addtl Second Sec., HM Treasury, 1948-51. Chm. Doxford and Sunderland Shipbuilding & Engineering Co. Ltd, 1962-68; Formerly Part-time Mem. Nat. Coal Board; Dir, Bank of England, 1964-70. A Vice-Chm.,

Council BIM, 1963-67. Address: 68 Colinas Verdes, Bensafrim, Lagos, Algarve, Portugal. Club: United Oxford & Cambridge University.   [Died 28 March 1978.

WIMBLE, Ernest Walter, CBE 1946; b 23 Sept. 1887; 4th s of Charles Wimble, Old Romney, Kent, and Annie Elizabeth Wimble (née Aylward); m 1912, Daisy Edith Robarts (d 1961); one s one d. Educ: Elementary Sch.; St Dunstan's, Catford; King's College, London. 4 years Civil Service, 1903-06; 6 years Commercial, 1906-12; served European War, 1914-19; 11 years WEA, 1912-23; 25 years Secretary and Gen. Man. Workers' Travel Assoc. Ltd, 1923-47; Dir of Students Bookshops Ltd, 1924-65; Member Management Committee Travel Assoc. of Great Britain and Northern Ireland, 1945-49; Member British Tourist and Holidays Board, 1947-50. Chm. Creative Tourist Agents Conf., 1947-48; Chm. Home Holidays Division British Tourist and Holidays Board, 1947-50; Pres. International Union of Official Travel Organisations, 1948-49; Chm. Olympic Games (Overseas) Visitors Accommodation Bureau, 1948; Member: Hotels Executive (British Transport), 1948-52; British Travel and Holidays Assoc., 1950; National Parks Commission, 1950-51; Founder-member of Youth Hostels Assoc. Publications: European Recovery, 1948-51 and the Tourist Industry, 1948; Western Europe's Tourist Trade, 1948, 1949, 1950. Editor and founder of The Travel Log. Recreation: travel. Address: Flat 5, 67 St Aubyns, Hove BN3 2TL.   [Died 17 Nov. 1979.

WINCHELL, Walter; TV-Radio Commentator; Columnist, New York Morning Telegraph; b New York, 7 April 1897; m 1919, Elizabeth June Magee; one d (and one s one d decd). Appeared in own act in Vaudeville, 1917; served European War, 1914-18, with USNR; joined staff of Vaudeville News, 1922; with NY Mirror, Journal-American, World-Journal-Tribune, as columnist, dramatic critic, and dramatic editor; syndicated column in over 100 US papers and in 11 foreign lands; broadcasts talks. Founder-Treasurer, Damon Runyon Cancer Fund. Comdr USNR. Publications: contributions to magazines. Address: (office) 33 W 56th Street, New York City, USA.
[Died 20 Feb. 1972.

WIND, Edgar, MA, DPhil; Professor Emeritus of the History of Art in the University of Oxford and Honorary Fellow of Trinity College, Oxford; b Berlin, Germany, 14 May 1900; s of late Maurice Delmar Wind; m 1942, Margaret Kellner. Educ: Kaiser Friedrich Schule, Berlin; Universities of Berlin, Freiburg, Vienna, Hamburg. DPhil (summa cum laude) in History of Art, 1922. Kegan Fellow, Instructor, Assistant Professor of Philosophy, Univ. of N Carolina, 1925-27; Research Asst Bibliothek Warburg, Hamburg, 1928-33; Privatdozent, Univ. of Hamburg, 1930-33; Dep. Dir, Warburg Inst., London, and Hon. Lecturer in Philosophy, University Coll., London, 1934-42; Vis. Lectr, Pierpont Morgan Library and Inst. of Fine Arts, NY Univ., 1940-42; Prof. of Art, Univ. of Chicago, 1942-44; William Allan Neilson Research Prof., 1944-48; Prof. of Philosophy and of Art, 1948-55, Smith Coll.; Prof. of History of Art, Univ. of Oxford, 1955-67; Fellow, Trinity Coll., Oxford, 1955-67. Fellow, American Academy of Arts and Sciences, 1951-; Chichele Lecturer, Oxford, 1954; Rede Lecturer, Cambridge, 1960; Reith Lecturer, BBC, 1960. Serena Medal, British Academy, 1967. Grosses Verdienstkreuz der Bundesrepublik Deutschland, 1966. Publications: Aesthetischer und kunstwissenschaftlicher Gegenstand, 1924; Humanitätsidee und heroisiertes Porträt in der englischen Kultur des 18. Jahrhunderts, 1932; Das Experiment und die Metaphysik, 1934; Bellini's Feast of the Gods, 1948; Pagan Mysteries in the Renaissance, 1958; 3rd edn enl. 1967; Art and Anarchy, 1963; Michelangelo's Prophets and Sibyls, 1967; Giorgione's Tempesta, 1969. Jt Editor: K. B. McFarlane's Hans Memling, 1971; A Bibliog. on the Survival of the Classics, 1934, 1938; Jl of Warburg Inst., 1937-42; articles on philosophical and iconographic subjects. Address: Trinity College, Oxford.   [Died 11 Sept. 1971.

WINDHAM, Sir Ralph, Kt 1960; Commissioner, Foreign Compensation Commission, 1965-77, Vice-Chairman, 1969, Chairman, 1972-77; b 25 March 1905; er s of Major Ashe Windham and Cora E. S. Middleton, Waghen Hall, East Yorkshire; heir pres. to baronetcy of Bowyer-Smyth; m 1946, Kathleen Mary, o d of Captain Cecil Henry FitzHerbert, DSC, Latimerstown, Wexford, Eire; two s two d. Educ: Wellington Coll.; Trinity Coll., Cambridge, 1st class Part II, Law Tripos; MA, LLB, 1928; Barrister-at-Law, Lincoln's Inn (Buchanan Prizeman), 1930. Legal Draftsman, Government of Palestine, 1935; Judge of Dist Court, Palestine, 1942; Puisne Judge, Supreme Court, Ceylon, 1947; Puisne Judge, Supreme Court, Kenya, 1950-55; Chief Justice, Zanzibar, 1955-59; Justice of Appeal, Court of Appeal for Eastern Africa, 1959-60; Chief Justice, Tanganyika (later Tanzania), 1960-65; Actg Gov.-Gen., Tanganyika, Feb.-May 1962. Order of the Brilliant Star of

Zanzibar (2nd class), 1959; Grand Commander, Star of Africa (Liberia), 1964. *Recreations:* music and tennis. *Address:* Hook's Cottage, Kingscote, near Tetbury, Gloucestershire.
[*Died 6 July* 1980.

WINDHAM, William Evan; *b* 1 May 1904; *o s* of late Sir William Windham, CBE; *m* 1932, Constance (*d* 1939), *d* of late J. H. Loudon, Olantigh, Wye, Kent; two *d*; *m* 1962, Dorothy Muir, *widow* of Carl Davis (MInstMM, Gold Medallist), Villa Berg, Bishopscourt, Cape Town. *Educ:* Wellington Coll.; London University. Barrister at Law, Gray's Inn, 1936. Served AAF, 1928. Administration, Fiji and Western Pacific, 1930-34; practised on South Eastern circuit, 1936-39. Served War of 1939-45 in Fighter Command, RAFVR (despatches), Sqdn Leader. Sen. Res. Magistrate, N Rhodesia, 1952; Commissioner, Emergency Regulations, 1956-57; Puisne Judge, High Court of Northern Rhodesia, 1956-63; Chief Justice, St Helena and Dependencies, 1969-71. *Recreations:* tennis, golf. *Address:* De Goede Verwachting, Cavalcade Road, Green Point, Cape, S Africa. *Clubs:* Royal Air Force, Royal Commonwealth Society.
[*Died 28 Sept.* 1977.

WINDLEY, Sir Edward (Henry), KCMG 1958 (CMG 1953); KCVO 1961; Director, Yuills Ltd; Chairman, Exchange Travel Agency Ltd, since 1965; *b* 10 March 1909; *s* of late E. C. Windley, S Rhodesia, and late Vicomtesse de Toustain; *m* 1939, Patience, *d* of Lieut-General Sir B. Sergison-Brooke, KCB, KCVO, CMG; one *s* three *d*. *Educ:* Repton; Cambridge Univ. District Officer, Kenya, 1931; Dep. Provincial Commissioner, 1947; Provincial Commissioner, 1948; Chief Native Comr and Min. for African Affairs, Kenya, 1953 (despatches 1957). Governor and Commander-in-Chief of the Gambia, 1958-62. Chairman: Guarantee Fund, Deans Yard, 1962-69; Save the Children Fund, 1962-68. *Recreations:* tennis, fishing, shooting, ski-ing, mountaineering. *Address:* 5 Regency Terrace, Elm Place, SW7. *T:* 01-373 5070; Mawley House, Quenington, Glos. *Clubs:* Turf, Travellers'.
[*Died 5 Jan.* 1972.

WINDSOR, Bt-Col Arthur Herbert, CMG 1916; TD 1923; *b* 1880; *s* of late Geo. Patrick Windsor, Salisbury; Served S Africa, 1900 (Queen's medal 5 clasps); European War, 1914-19 (despatches, CMG); commanded 11th Batt. London Regt, TA, 1917-23; Brevet Colonel, 1924; Member of the National Trust; Fellow of Royal Society of St George. Freeman of the City of London. *Address:* 23 Bruton Street, W1. [*Died 10 Aug.* 1972.

WINDSOR, Robert, CB 1974; Assistant Under Secretary of State, Department of Health and Social Security (formerly Ministry of Social Security), 1966-76, retired; *b* 9 April 1916; *s* of late Henry and Alice Windsor; *m* 1939, Eleanor Malone; two *s* one *d*. *Educ:* Liverpool Collegiate Sch.; University of Liverpool. BA 1937, MA 1940. Served in S Lancs Regt and Intelligence Corps, 1940-45. Asst Principal, Assistance Board, 1947; Principal, National Assistance Board, 1949; Asst Secretary, National Assistance Board, 1962; Under-Secretary, National Assistance Board, 1965. *Recreation:* listening to music. *Address:* Berfra-Mont, Armscote, Stratford-upon-Avon, Warwickshire CV37 8DE. *T:* Ilmington 302.   [*Died 31 July* 1980.

WINEGARTEN, Asher, CBE 1968; Director General, National Farmers' Union, 1978; *b* 26 March 1922; *s* of Emanuel and Sally Winegarten; *m* 1946, Renee Cecile Aarons. *Educ:* Highbury County Secondary Sch.; London Sch. of Economics. 1st cl. hons BCom and BScEcon; Farr Medallist 1942; FSS. Admty, 1942-47: Sec., Chain Cable Control (Temp. Admin. Asst). Chief Economist, NFU, 1947; Dep. Dir-Gen., NFU, 1970-78. Vis. Prof. of Agricl Policy, Wye Coll., London Univ., 1973-78. Employer Mem., Agricultural Wages Bd, 1957-77; a Mem. for NFU on Council of CBI; Mem. Council for Internat. Develt, 1977-. Hon. FRAgSs. *Publications:* (contrib.) Agriculture and the British Economy, 1956; (contrib.) Economic Change and Agriculture, 1967; (contrib.) US Agriculture in a World Context, 1974; various lectures and papers; contrib. Jls of Ag. Econ. Soc., Royal Soc. of Arts, Farmers' Club, etc. *Recreations:* opera, theatre, travel, gardening. *Address:* 12 Heather Walk, Edgware, Mddx HA8 9TS. *T:* 01-958 9365. *Clubs:* Reform, Farmers'.   [*Died 19 Sept.* 1979.

WINGATE, Sir Ronald (Evelyn Leslie), 2nd Bt, *cr* 1920; CB 1959; CMG 1952; CIE 1931; OBE 1945; ICS, retired; *b* 30 Sept. 1889; *o surv. s* of Sir F. Reginald Wingate, 1st Bt, GCB, GCVO, GBE, KCMG, DSO; *S* father 1953; *m* 1916, Mary Harpoth, *d* of Lady Vinogradoff, Oxford. *Educ:* Bradfield; Balliol Coll., Oxford (MA). Entered ICS 1912; Indian Political Service; retired, 1939; served Mesopotamia, 1917-19 (despatches). Served War of 1939-45, in Africa, South-East Asia and with Joint Planning Staff in Offices of the War Cabinet. *Publications:* Wingate of the Sudan, 1955; Not in the Limelight, 1959; Lord

Ismay, 1970. *Recreations:* shooting, fishing, golf. *Heir:* none. *Address:* Barford Manor, Barford St Martin, Salisbury, Wilts. *T:* Wilton 2252. *Club:* Brooks's.   [*Died 31 Aug.* 1978 (*ext*).

WINGATE-SAUL, Bazil Sylvester; His Honour Judge Wingate-Saul; a Circuit Judge (formerly Judge of County Courts), since 1959; *b* 15 June 1906; *s* of late Sir Ernest Wingate-Saul, KC, and late Violet Annie Wingate-Saul; *m* 1942, Cecily Mary Kingston; two *s* two *d*. *Educ:* Rugby; St John's Coll., Oxford. Called to the Bar, 1928; Recorder of Oldham, 1950-59; Junior Counsel to Ministry of Agriculture, Fisheries and Food, Forestry Commission and Commissioners of Crown Lands, 1949-59; Master of the Bench of the Inner Temple, 1958. Served War of 1939-45 in Army (Royal Berkshire Regt), 1940-45. *Address:* Wrayswood, Horsehills, Horley, Surrey. *T:* Norwood Hill 862589.   [*Died 4 Oct.* 1975.

WINGFIELD-STRATFORD, Esmé Cecil, DSc, MA; *b* 20 Sept. 1882; *s* of late Brig.-Gen. C. V. Wingfield-Stratford, CB; CMG; *m* 1915, Barbara Elizabeth, *d* of Lieut-Colonel F. H. L. Errington and Hon. Mrs Errington; one *d*. *Educ:* Eton; King's Coll., Cambridge. BA, 1904. Research Studentship London School of Economics, 1904; MA and Fellowship King's Coll., Cambridge, 1907; DSc (Econ) University of London, 1913; Gazetted to QORW Kent Regt, Aug. 1914; Captain, 1916. *Publications:* The Call of Dawn, 1908; The History of English Patriotism, 2 vols, 1913; An Appeal to the British People, 1914; India, 1920; The Reconstruction of Mind, 1921; Facing Reality, 1922; Life, 1923; The Reconstruction of Life, 1923; Parent or Pedagogue, 1924; The Grand Young Man, 1926; Until it doth Run Over, 1927; The History of British Civilization, 2 vols, 1928; If Labour Wins, 1929; The Victorian Tragedy, 1930; They that take the Sword, 1931; The Victorian Sunset, 1932; The Victorian Aftermath, 1933; New Minds for Old, 1934; The Harvest of Victory, 1935; Good Talk, 1936; King Charles and the Conspirators, 1937; The Making of a Gentleman, 1938; The Foundations of British Patriotism, 1939; Crusade for Civilization, 1940; Churchill, The Making of a Hero, 1942; The New Patriotism and the Old, 1943; The Price of Liberty, 1944; Before the Lamps went out, 1946; Charles King of England, 1949; King Charles and King Pym, 1949; This was a Man, 1949; King Charles the Martyr, 1950; Truth in Masquerade, 1951; The Unfolding Pattern of British Life, 1953; The Squire and his Relations, 1956; The Lords of Cobham Hall, 1959; Beyond Empire, 1964. *Recreations:* golf, travel. *Address:* The Oaks, Berkhamsted, Herts. *T:* Berkhamsted 433. *Clubs:* Constitutional, MCC.   [*Died 20 Feb.* 1971.

WINN, Rt. Hon. Sir (Charles) Rodger (Noel), PC 1965; Kt 1959; CB (Mil); OBE; a Lord Justice of Appeal, 1965-71. *b* 22 Dec. 1903; *s* of Ernest Winn and Joan Winn (later Martino); *m* 1930, Helen Joyce, *d* of late Colonel E. V. Sydenham, DSO, TD, DL; one *d*. *Educ:* Oundle; Trinity Coll., Cambridge (Classics I; Law II; LLB, firsts). Davison Scholar, Yale Univ., 1925; Choate Fellow, Harvard Univ., 1927; MA, LLM, Cambridge, 1928. Called to Bar (Cert. Hon.), Inner Temple, 1928; Bencher, 1953; formerly Counsel to GPO (common law); Junior Counsel to the Treasury (Common Law), 1954-59; Judge of High Court of Justice, Queen's Bench Div., 1959-65. Lord Chancellor's Law Reform Cttee, 1963-; Criminal Law Revision Cttee, 1964-; Chairman: Permanent Security Commn, 1964-71; Cttee on Personal Injury Litigation, 1966-68 (Cmnd 3691). Served War of 1939-45, Naval Intelligence Div., Captain, RNVR. Officer, US Legion of Merit, 1945. Governor of St Thomas' Hospital and Chairman of Council of Medical School, 1965-70. *Address:* 11 Groom Place, SW1. *T:* 01-235 3454. *Club:* Pratt's.
[*Died 4 June* 1972.

WINN, Godfrey (Herbert); author, broadcaster, and lecturer; *b* Edgbaston, Birmingham, 15 Oct. 1908; *s* of Ernest Winn and Joan Winn (later Martino); unmarried. *Educ:* St Christopher's, Eastbourne; King Edward's, Birmingham. Started career as a boy-actor in Galsworthy's Old English, Haymarket Theatre, followed by St Joan and Noel Coward's The Marquise, Criterion. First novel published, Dreams Fade, 1928; switched after several more novels to freelance journalism, and became star columnist of Daily Mirror, 1936-38, and Sunday Express, 1938-42. Was first British war correspondent to enter Maginot Line (Autumn 1939); later served in RN on Russian run as Ordinary Seaman. After war, lectured twice across United States, and continued to publish books. Appears on sound radio and television. At present under exclusive contract to International Publishing Corporation and Associated Newspapers. Member of Lloyd's. *Publications:* numerous including: PQ 17, Home from Sea, This Fair Country, The Infirm Glory (autobiog.); The Positive Hour (autobiog.), 1970. *Recreations:* lawn tennis, contract bridge, travelling. *Address:* 115 Ebury Street, SW1; The Mill House, Falmer, Sussex. *Clubs:* Queen's, Crockford's.   [*Died 19 June* 1971.

WINN, Rt. Hon. Sir Rodger; *see* Winn, Rt. Hon. Sir C. R. N.

WINTER, James Alexander, CMG 1942; QC Newfoundland, 1933; Chief Clerk and Registrar of Supreme Court, Newfoundland, 1941-63; retired; *b* St John's, Newfoundland, 20 Dec. 1886; *s* of late Sir James Spearman Winter, KCMG; *m* 1915, Mary Evangeline, *d* of late Elias De Barbazan Arnaud; one *s* two *d* (and one *s* killed in action, in Africa, 1943). *Educ:* Bishop Feild Coll., St John's; Rossall Sch., Lancs. Solicitor, 1910; called to Bar, St John's, 1911; Speaker House of Assembly, Newfoundland, 1933-34; Comr for Home Affairs and Education, Newfoundland, 1936-61. *Address:* 6 Riverview Avenue, St John's, Newfoundland, Canada.
[*Died 29 June* 1971.

WINTER, Robert Pearson, CBE 1958; MC 1918; TD 1934; President of the Institute of Chartered Accountants in England and Wales, 1963-64 (Member, 1921, Vice-President, 1962); *b* 4 March 1897; *s* of Robert Pearson Winter, Newcastle upon Tyne; *m* 1937, Nora Margaret, *d* of Harry Hunter Blair, Newcastle upon Tyne; two *s* (and one *s* decd). *Educ:* Mill Hill Sch. 2nd Lieut, Royal Engineers, TA, 1915; served UK, France, Belgium and Italy, 1915-19. Commanded Regt of Royal Engineers, TA, 1934-38 and served on Staff, 1939-42. Member T&AFA of Northumberland, 1934-64, Vice-Chairman 1950-64. Hon. Colonel, Tyne Electrical Engineers (TA), 1952-60. *Recreation:* walking. *Address:* Old Prior Manor, Corbridge, Northumberland. *T:* Corbridge 2185. *Clubs:* Northern Counties, Union (Newcastle upon Tyne). [*Died 13 June* 1973.

WINTRINGHAM, Col John Workman, CBE 1943; MC; DL, JP; *b* 24 Sept. 1894; *s* of late John Fibbes Wintringham, LLB, and of late Eliza Mapson; *m* 1920, Caroline Howe; two *s* one *d. Educ:* Mill Hill Sch. Lincs Yeomanry, 1913-19, Egypt and Palestine (MC, despatches); retired as Hon. Colonel. Asst County Commissioner, Lincs Boy Scouts, 1934; HG, 1940, Zone Commander, 1941, Lincs. JP Lindsey (Lincs) 1929; DL Lincs 1944. *Recreation:* Boy Scouts Association. *Address:* 63 Humberstone Avenue, Humberstone DN36 45R. *T:* Grimsby 812134. [*Died 1 Jan.* 1980.

WIPPELL, Rev. Canon John Cecil, MA; BD; Hon. DD; Chaplain to Deaconess House, Farquharson House and Nuttall Hospital, 1957-63; Warden, St Peter's Theological College, West Indies, 1961-63 (Tutor, 1956-59); retired; *b* 6 June 1883; *s* of late William Joseph Wippell. *Educ:* Exeter Sch. (Oxford and Cambridge Higher Certificate); Exeter Coll., Oxford (2nd Class Hons Theology); BD (London) Pass 1911, 1st Class Hons, 1913. Tutor of St Boniface Coll., Warminster, 1905-11; Deacon, 1907; Priest, 1908; Assistant Curate of Warminster, 1907-10; Prof. of Theology, Codrington Coll., Barbados, 1911-18; Principal of Codrington Coll., 1918-45; Principal Rawle Training Institute for Elementary Teachers; Chaplain of SPG Estates, Barbados; CF to 4 BWI Regt, France, 1917-18; Hon. CF; Examining Chaplain to the Bishop of Barbados, 1918-45, and to the Bishop of the Windward Islands; Canon of Barbados, 1932. General License, Diocese of Jamaica, 1945; Canon Emeritus of Barbados, 1946; Rector of Brown's Town, 1947-49; Rector of St Michael's, Kingston, 1949-52; Asst Master, Kingston Coll., 1952-53; Asst Master and Chaplain, Jamaica Coll., 1954-56. Hon. Chaplain to Univ. of WI, 1960-; Lectr, United Theol Coll. of WI, 1967-70. Hon. DD Trinity Coll., Toronto, 1934; Hon. LLD Univ. of West Indies, 1972. Coronation Medal, 1937. *Address:* 16 Phoenix Avenue, Kingston 10, Jamaica.
[*Died 27 Aug.* 1978.

WISE, Lt-Col Alfred Roy, MBE 1941; TD 1943; Queen's Royal Regiment (West Surrey); *b* 7 July 1901; *s* of late Alfred Gascoyne Wise, Puisne Judge, Supreme Court of Hong Kong, and Augusta Frances, *d* of A. N. C. R. Nugent; *m* 1942, Cassandra Noel, *o d* of Lt-Col B. E. Coke, OBE; one *s. Educ:* Repton; Oriel College, Oxford. Asst District Commissioner, Kenya Colony, 1923-26; MP (C) Smethwick Division of Staffordshire, 1931-45; contested Smethwick Division, Staffs, 1929; MP (C) Rugby Division of Warwickshire, 1959-66. Served with British Intelligence Organization (Germany), 1946-54. Westminster City Council, 1956-59. Upper Warden, Worshipful Company of Pattenmakers, 1967, Master, 1968. *Address:* 43 Boscobel Place, SW1. *T:* 01-235 2565. *Club:* Carlton.
[*Died 21 Aug.* 1974.

WISEHAM, Sir Joseph (Angus Lucien), Kt 1967; Chief Justice of the Supreme Court in the Gambia 1957-68; retired; *b* 13 Dec. 1906; *s* of Osmond Wiseham; *m* 1931, Olive Bell. *Educ:* University Coll., University of London. Called to the Bar, Gray's Inn, 1928. Practised at Rangoon High Court, Burma, 1932; Parliamentary Sec. to Premier and to Judicial Minister, Burma, 1937-42; practised in India, 1942-46; Asst Custodian of

Enemy Property, Tanganyika, 1946-51; Resident Magistrate, 1951-56; Senior Resident Magistrate, 1956-57. *Address:* Mabruk, Vicarage Lane, East Preston, Littlehampton, Sussex.
[*Died 3 May* 1972.

WISEMAN, Prof. Stephen, MEd, DSc, PhD, FBPsS; Director, National Foundation for Educational Research; *b* 1 Sept. 1907; *s* of Stephen Wiseman and Nellie Wiseman (*née* Wilcox); *m* 1934, Winifred Agnes Rigby, MA; two *s. Educ:* Hatfield College, University of Durham. Teaching in various elementary, central and technical schools, 1929-42. War of 1939-45, RAF education service, 1942-46. Senior Lecturer, Univ. of Manchester, 1946; Reader, 1956; Professor, 1961. Vis. Prof., Univ. of Surrey, 1969-. *Publications:* Reporting Research in Education, 1952; The Devon Interest Tests, 1955; The Manchester General Ability, Reading and Arithmetic Tests, 1959; Preparation for Teaching, 1960; Examinations in English Education, 1961; Education and Environment, 1964; Intelligence and Ability, 1967; contrib. to educational and psychological journals. *Address:* 7 Little Buntings, Windsor, Berks. *T:* Windsor 63040.
[*Died 24 July* 1971.

WISKEMANN, Elizabeth, MA, DLitt; writer on modern and contemporary history; *b* 1901; *d* of Hugo Wiskemann and Myra Burton. *Educ:* Notting Hill High Sch., London; Newnham Coll., Cambridge (First Class Hons in Historical Tripos), Historical Research and Tutoring at Cambridge; from 1932 travelled in Europe as free lance writer; worked for Royal Institute of International Affairs in Czechoslovakia collecting material for book, 1937; lecturing in USA, 1938; Asst Press Attaché, British Legation, Berne, 1941-45; Rome Correspondent of The Economist, 1946-47; Montague Burton Professor of International Relations, Edinburgh Univ., 1958-61; Tutor in Modern European History, Univ. of Sussex, 1961-64; Former Associate of Newnham College. Hon. DLitt (Oxford), 1965. *Publications:* Czechs and Germans, 1938 (new edn 1967); Undeclared War, 1939 (new edn 1967) (American Title-Prologue to War); Italy (World To-day Series), 1947; The Rome-Berlin Axis, 1949 (rev. edn 1966); (joint) Central and South East Europe, 1945-48, 1950; (joint) Hitler's Europe, 1954; Germany's Eastern Neighbours, 1956; (joint) The Initial Triumph of the Axis, 1958; A Great Swiss Newspaper: the Story of the Neue Zürcher Zeitung, 1959; (joint trans. with Marian Jackson) The Kremlin since Stalin (by W. Leonhard), 1962; Europe of the Dictators, 1966; The Europe I Saw, 1968; Fascism in Italy, 1969. *Address:* 41 Moore Street, SW3. *T:* 01-589 2560.
[*Died 5 July* 1971.

WITTEWRONGE, Sir J. C. B. L.; *see* Lawes, Sir J. C. B.

WITTKOWER, Rudolf, FBA 1958; Slade Professor of Fine Art, Cambridge, 1970-71; Professor of Fine Arts, Columbia University, New York, 1965-69, now Avalon Foundation Professor Emeritus in the Humanities; Member, Institute for Advanced Study, Princeton, 1971-72; *b* 22 June 1901; *er s* of late Henry Wittkower; *m* 1923, Margot Holzmann; one *s. Educ:* Munich and Berlin Univs. Asst, Bibliotheca Hertziana, Rome, 1923-27; Research Fellow, Bibl. Hertziana, 1928-33; Lecturer, Cologne Univ., 1932-33; Staff Member, Warburg Institute, London, 1934-56; Reader in the History of Classical Tradition in Art, Univ. of London, 1946; Durning Lawrence Professor in the History of Art in the University of London, 1949-56. Co-Editor: Jl of Warburg and Courtauld Institutes, 1937-56; Studies in Architecture, 1958-; Editor, Columbia Univ. Studies in Art and Archæology, 1962-. Visiting Prof., Harvard Univ., 1954 and 1955, Columbia University, 1955-56; Kress Prof., Nat. Gallery, Washington, 1969-70. Member Accademia Olimpica, Vicenza; For. Corresp. Mem. Max-Planck-Inst. Bibl. Hertziana, Rome; Hon. Fellow Warburg Inst., London, 1958; FIAL 1958; Fellow American Academy of Arts and Sciences, 1959; Hon. Fellow Accademia di Belle Arti, Venice, 1959; Fellow Accademia dei Lincei, Rome, 1960; Hon. FRIBA, 1965; FRSA 1971; Felow, Amer. Philosophical Soc., 1971; Fellow, Accademia delle Scienze, Turin, 1971, etc. MA Cantab, 1970; Hon. Dr of Fine Arts, Duke Univ., 1969; Hon. Dr of Humane Letters, Columbia, 1970; Hon. LittD Leeds, 1971. Serena Medal of the British Academy, 1957; medal of Gallerie Nazionali, Naples, 1957. *Publications:* (with E. Steinmann) Michelangelo Bibliographie, 1927; Die Zeichnungen des G. L. Bernini, 1931; (with T. Borenius) Sir Robert Mond's Collection of Drawings, 1935; (with F. Saxl) British Art and the Mediterranean, 1948. Architectural Principles in the Age of Humanism, 1949; The Artist and the Liberal Arts, 1952; The Drawings of the Carracci in the Royal Collection at Windsor Castle, 1952; Gian Lorenzo Bernini, 1955; Art and Architecture in Italy 1600-1750, 1958; (with Margot Wittkower) Born under Saturn: The Character and Conduct of Artists, 1962; Disegni de le Ruine di Roma, 1963; (with Margot Wittkower) The Divine Michelangelo: The

Florentine Academy's Homage on his Death in 1564, 1964; La Cupola di San Pietro, 1964. Contrib. to: Journal of the Warburg and Courtauld Inst., Art Bulletin, Burlington Mag., Archeological Journal, Town Planning Review, Daedalus, etc. *Address:* 7a Crediton Hill, London, NW6. *T:* 01-435 9329.
[*Died* 11 *Oct.* 1971.

WODEHOUSE, Sir Pelham (Grenville), KBE 1975; author; *b* 15 Oct. 1881; 3rd *s* of late Henry Ernest Wodehouse, CMG; *m* 1914, Ethel, *widow* of late Leonard Rowley of Dee Bank, Cheshire. Became an American Citizen in 1955. Hon. LittD Oxon, 1939. *Educ:* Dulwich College. *Publications:* The Pothunters, 1902; A Prefect's Uncle, 1903; Tales of St Austin's, 1903; The Gold Bat, 1904; William Tell Told Again, 1904; The Head of Kay's, 1905; Love among the Chickens, 1906, rev. edn 1921; The White Feather, 1907; (with H. Westbrook) Not George Washington, 1907; (with H. Westbrook) The Globe By the way Book, 1908; The Swoop, 1909; Mike, 1909; Psmith in the City, 1910; A Gentleman of Leisure, 1910; The Prince and Betty, 1912; The Little Nugget, 1913; The Man Upstairs, 1914; Something Fresh, 1915; Psmith, Journalist, 1915; The Man with two Left Feet, 1917; Uneasy Money, 1917; Piccadilly Jim, 1918; My Man Jeeves, 1919; A Damsel in Distress, 1919; The Coming of Bill, 1920; The Indiscretions of Archie, 1921; Jill the Reckless, 1921; The Clicking of Cuthbert, 1922; The Girl on the Boat, 1922; The Adventures of Sally, 1922; The Inimitable Jeeves, 1923; Leave it to Psmith, 1923; Ukridge, 1924; Bill the Conqueror, 1924; Carry on Jeeves, 1925; Sam the Sudden, 1925; The Heart of a Goof, 1926; The Small Bachelor, 1927; Meet Mr Mulliner, 1927; Money for Nothing, 1928; Mr Mulliner Speaking, 1929; Summer Lightning, 1929; Very Good Jeeves, 1930; Big Money, 1931; If I were You, 1931; Dr Sally, 1932; Hot Water, 1932; Louder and Funnier, 1932; Mulliner Nights, 1933; Heavy Weather, 1933; Thank you Jeeves, 1934; Right Ho Jeeves, 1934; Enter Psmith, 1935; Blandings Castle, 1935; The Luck of the Bodkins, 1935; Young Men in Spats, 1936; Laughing Gas, 1936; Lord Emsworth and Others, 1937; Summer Moonshine, 1938; The Code of the Woosters, 1938; Uncle Fred in the Springtime, 1939; Eggs, Beans and Crumpets, 1940; Quick Service, 1940; Money in the Bank, 1946; Joy in the Morning, 1947; Full Moon, 1947; Spring Fever, 1948; Uncle Dynamite, 1948; The Mating Season, 1949; Nothing Serious, 1950; The Old Reliable, 1951; Barmy in Wonderland, 1952; Pigs have Wings, 1952; Mike at Wrykin (rev. reissue of Mike), 1953; Mike and Psmith (rev. reissue of Enter Psmith), 1953; Ring for Jeeves, 1953; Performing Flea (autobiography), 1953; (with G. Bolton) Bring on the Girls, 1954; Jeeves and the Feudal Spirit, 1954; French Leave, 1956; Something Fishy, 1957; Over Seventy (autobiography), 1957; Cocktail Time, 1958; A Few Quick Ones, 1959; Jeeves in the Offing, 1960; Ice in the Bedroom, 1961; Service with a Smile, 1962; Stiff Upper Lip, Jeeves, 1963; Frozen Assets, 1964; Galahad at Blandings, 1965; Plum Pie, 1966; The World of Jeeves, 1967; Company for Henry, 1967; Do Butlers Burgle Banks?, 1968; (ed, with S. Meredith) A Carnival of Modern Humour, 1968; A Pelican at Blandings, 1969; A Girl in Blue, 1970; Much Obliged Jeeves, 1971; Pearls, Girls and Monty Bodkin, 1972; Bachelors Anonymous, 1973; The Golf Omnibus, 1973; Aunts Aren't Gentlemen, 1974; part author, also writer of lyrics, 18 musical comedies, mostly produced in America; best known in England: Kissing Time, The Golden Moth, 1921; The Cabaret Girl, 1922; (with Ian Hay) Leave it to Psmith, play produced 1930; (with Guy Bolton) Who's Who (adptd from his book, If I were You) and Anything Goes, plays produced 1934 and 1935; *posthumous publications:* The World of Blandings, 1976; Sunset at Blandings, 1977; *relevant publication:* Wodehouse at Work, by Richard Usborne, 1961. *Recreations:* golf, swimming, motoring. *Address:* c/o Barrie & Jenkins Ltd, 24 Highbury Crescent, N5 1RX. *Club:* Coffee House (New York).
[*Died* 14 *Feb.* 1975.

WODEN, George; *see* Slaney, G. W.

WOFINDEN, Prof. Robert Cavill, FRCP; Medical Officer of Health, City and County of Bristol, 1956-74; Professor of Public Health, University of Bristol, 1956-74; *b* 25 Jan. 1914; British; *m* 1938, Eileen Frances Rachel Sinnamon; one *s* two *d. Educ:* Rotherham Grammar School; St Mary's Hospital Medical School, Paddington; London School of Hygiene and Tropical Medicine. County Major Schol. to St Mary's Hosp. Med. School, 1931-37; MD London, MB, BS London (Hons); MRCS, LRCP, 1937, MRCP 1967, FRCP 1972; FFCM 1972; DPH London (Hons); DPA London. House Physician, Med. Teaching Unit, St Mary's Hosp.; Asst MOH, Rotherham, 1939-42; Dep. MOH and Sen. Sch. MO, Rotherham, 1943-46; Deputy MOH: Bradford, 1946-47; Bristol, 1947-55. Consultant, WHO; Mem., Internat. Epidemiological Assoc.; Mem. various Govt and Nat. Cttees, etc. FRSH; FRIPH; Hon. Fellow: Soc. of Community Health; Social Med. Soc., Eugenics Soc.; Smith

Award for Public Health, RIPH. OStJ. *Publications:* Health Services in England, 1947; Problem Families in Bristol (Eugenics Soc.), 1950; contrib. to Public Health, Medical Officer, Lancet, BMJ and foreign journals. *Recreations:* golf, gardening. *Address:* 2 Church Road, Stoke Bishop, Bristol BS9 1JS. *T:* Bristol 682053.
[*Died* 7 *Nov.* 1975.

WOLFF, Hon. Sir Albert (Asher), KCMG 1959; Chief Justice of Western Australia, 1959-69; Lieutenant-Governor of Western Australia, 1968-74; *b* 30 April 1899; *s* of Simon and Bertha Clara Wolff; *m* 1st, 1924, Ida Violet Jackson (*d* 1953); one *s* one *d* ; 2nd, 1956, Mary Godwin. *Educ:* Perth Modern School. Admitted Bar Supreme Court of Western Australia, 1921; Crown Prosecutor, 1926; Crown Solicitor and Parliamentary Draughtsman, 1929; KC 1936; Justice Supreme Court of Western Australia, 1938. President Public Library, Museum and Art Gallery Trust, WA, 1954-58. Author and draughtsman W Aust. Matrimonial Causes Code and Rules. Official Visitor Harvey Internment Camp, War of 1939-45. *Address:* c/o Home of Peace, Thomas Street, Subiaco, WA 6008, Australia.
[*Died* 27 *Oct.* 1977.

WOLFF, Michael, JP; *b* 24 Oct. 1930; *m* 1956, Rosemary Langley Clarkson; two *d. Educ:* Cheltenham; Wadham Coll., Oxford. Served with Royal Fusiliers in Korean War, 1952-53 (Captain). Editorial staff of: The Sphere; John Bull; Truth (Dep. Editor); Daily Express (Chief American Corresp.); Sunday Telegraph; Editor, Crossbow, 1964-66. Organised and led research for official biography of Winston Churchill, 1961-66; ed first companion vol. of documents, 1967. Conservative Research Dept, 1966-70 (special duties with Leader of the Opposition); Special Adviser to Govt, 1970-74; Dir-Gen., Conservative Party Organisation, 1974-75. JP Inner London, 1967; Dep. Chm., West London bench; Lord Chancellor's Advisory Cttee on Justices of the Peace for Inner London. Council of Francis Holland (C of E) Schools Trust. *Publications:* The Unquiet Peace (contrib.), 1957; (with John Vidler) If Freedom Fail, 1964; (ed) The Conservative Opportunity, 1965; Prison, 1967; Winston Churchill as Nobel Prizewinner, 1970. *Address:* 13 Holland Park, W11 3TH. *T:* 01-727 9051. *Clubs:* Garrick, MCC.
[*Died* 13 *May* 1976.

WOLFF, Mrs Nat; *see* Best, Edna.

WOLLASTON, Vice-Adm. Herbert Arthur Buchanan-, CMG 1919; *b* 13 Oct. 1878; *s* of late S. G. Buchanan-Wollaston and C. E. Harper; *m* 1908, Dora Caroline Chambers (*d* 1961); one *d. Educ:* Park House, Reading; Cordwalles, Maidenhead; HMS Britannia. Served European War, 1914-18 (despatches four times); Rear-Adm. and retired list, 1928; Vice-Adm., retired, 1932. *Address:* Woodcote House, Ottery St Mary, Devon EX11 1NS. *T:* Ottery 2385.
[*Died* 24 *March* 1975.

WOLVERSON, William Alfred, CB 1954; a Deputy Director General of the Post Office 1960-65, retired; *b* 13 Oct. 1905; *s* of William Alfred Wolverson and Mary (*née* Johnston); unmarried. General Post Office: Asst Traffic Superintendent, 1928; Asst Surveyor, 1932; Asst Principal, 1935; Principal, 1938; Asst Sec., 1946; Regional Director, N Western Region, 1950; Commandant Management Training Centre, 1951; Director External Telecommunications Executive and United Kingdom Member, Commonwealth Telecommunications Board, 1952; Director, Radio Services Department, General Post Office Headquarters, London, 1955-60; idc, 1949. *Recreation:* gardening. *Address:* 28 North Down, Sanderstead, South Croydon, Surrey. *Club:* Reform.
[*Died* 8 *Oct.* 1974.

WOMBWELL, Sir (Frederick) Philip (Alfred William), 6th Bt, *cr* 1778; MBE 1944; Captain (temporary Major) RE; *b* 6 July 1910; *s* of late Frederick Adolphus Wombwell, Capt. 16th The Queen's Lancers, and May (*d* 1948), *d* of A. Harrison-Smith, of Carlton Hall, Worksop (who *m* 2nd, Thomas Stamford Booth, of Leam Hall, Derbyshire); *S* great-uncle, 1926; *m* 1936, Ida Elizabeth, *er d* of Frederick J. Leitch, Branksome Park, Bournemouth; one *s* two *d. Educ:* Repton. Served War of 1939-45 (MBE); Major, 1946. *Heir: s* George Philip Frederick Wombwell [*b* 21 May 1949; *m* 1974, Hermione Jane Wrightson, Leyburn, Yorks]. *Address:* Bridge House, West Baldwin, Isle of Man.
[*Died* 4 *April* 1977.

WOOD, Rev. Canon Cecil Thomas; retired; *b* 1903; *s* of Henry Mathew Wood and Letitia Maud Cannon. *Educ:* Uppingham Sch.; Lincoln Coll., Oxford; Cuddesdon Theological Coll. MA (Oxford) 1926. Deacon 1927, priest 1928, Southwark diocese. Curate, St John the Divine, Kennington, 1927-32; Chaplain to Archbp of Cape Town, 1933-38; SPG Candidates Sec., 1938-41; actg Archdeacon of Bloemfontein, 1942-46; Warden of St John's Hostel, Cape Town, 1946-51; Director of South African Church

Institute, London, 1952-55; Rector of Hermanus, Cape, 1955-58; Archdeacon of Cape Town, 1958-65; Canon Emeritus, 1965; Senior Chaplain to Archbishop of Cape Town, 1965-72. Vicar General of Diocese of Cape Town, 1963, 1968. Provincial Archivist, Province of S Africa, 1957-79. Hon. Associate in Theology (SA), 1963. Hon. PhD Witwatersrand, 1978. *Publications:* Short History of Bloemfontein Cathedral, 1945; Cathedral Sermons, 1962. *Recreations:* travel, book collecting. *Address:* Taunton House, Cape Town, South Africa. *Clubs:* United Oxford & Cambridge University; Vincent's (Oxford); Leander (Henley); City and Civil Service (Cape Town).
[*Died* 20 *May* 1980.

WOOD, Eric Rawlinson, CIE 1939; MC and Bar; *b* 24 March 1893; *m* Madeline, *d* of late P. F. Campbell; (two *s* killed in action, War of 1939-45) two *d*. *Educ:* Denstone Coll.; St Catharine's Coll., Cambridge, BA. Joined Indian Civil Service, 1919; officiating Chief Secretary to Government, Orissa, 1938; Revenue Commissioner, Orissa, 1939-42; Ministry of Supply, 1943-55; retired. *Address:* 143 Barnhorn Road, Little Common, Bexhill, Sussex. *T:* Cooden 2830. [*Died* 17 *Aug.* 1977.

WOOD, Lt-Gen. Sir Ernest, KBE 1947; CB 1945; CIE 1941; MC 1917; Indian Army (retired); *b* 1894; *m* Grace, *y d* of J. F. Goodliffe; two *d*. Appointments in India: Deputy Secretary Defence Department, 1936-38; Sec. Supply Dept, 1939-40; Dir Gen. of Supply, 1940-42; Administrator Gen. Eastern Frontier Communications, 1942; Sec. Food Dept, 1943; Dir Gen. Munitions Production, 1943-45; Dep. Master Gen. of the Ordnance, 1945-46; QMG, India, 1946-47; Controller of Operations, Colonial Development Corporation, 1948-51; Chief of Staff, Defence Production Board, NATO, 1951-52; Director of Civil Defence, Eastern Region (Cambridge), Sept. 1955-60. *Recreation:* golf. *Address:* Foxton House, Via Royston, Herts. *T:* Harston (Cambs) 530. [*Died* 17 *May* 1971.

WOOD, Sir Frank, KBE 1972; CB 1960; *b* 9 Nov. 1913; *m* 1946, Olive May Wilson; two *s* one *d*. *Educ:* The College, Swindon, Wilts. Exchequer and Audit Dept; Assistant Auditor, 1932; Air Ministry; Asst Principal, 1938. Private Secretary to Secretary of State for Air, 1946; Private Secretary to Minister of Defence, 1947; Dep. Sec., Air Min., 1960-61, MoD 1961-65, Min. of Aviation, 1965-66, BoT (Civil Aviation), 1966-69; Sec., Min. of Posts and Telecommunications, 1969-74; *Address:* 16 Woodlands Road, Bickley, Kent. *T:* 01-467 6220. *Club:* Reform. [*Died* 7 *Oct.* 1974.

WOOD, Franklin Garrett, MA, MB, BCh, DMRE Cantab; Hon. Consulting Radiologist to: Hospital for Diseases of the Chest, German Hospital, London, and Black Notley Hospital; Fellow of Royal Society of Medicine; 2nd *s* of late James Wood, LLD, Grove House, Southport. *Educ:* Rydal School; Jesus Coll., Cambridge; St Thomas' Hospital, London. Late House Physician and Casualty Officer, St Thomas' Hospital; Temporary Surgeon Lt RN. *Publications:* Contributions to Medical Press. *Recreations:* riding and music. *Address:* 14 Upper Park Road, NW3. [*Died* 17 *May* 1978.

WOOD, Sir John (Arthur Haigh), 2nd Bt, *cr* 1918; MC 1915; DSC 1917; *b* 22 May 1888; *o s* of Sir John Wood, 1st Bt, of Hengrave, and Estelle, *d* of Henry Benham; *S* father 1951; *m* 1919, Hon. Evelyn Saumarez (*d* 1934), *e d* of 4th Baron de Saumarez; one *d* (and one *d* decd). Barrister, Inner Temple, 1912. Served European War, 1914-18, as Capt. in East Surrey Regt, and Lieut RNVR (despatches, DSC, MC). *Heir:* none. *Address:* The Ship Hotel, Market Place, Wisbech, Cambs.
[*Died* 5 *March* 1974 (*ext*).

WOOD, Oswald Edward; Director, Midland Bank Ltd, and Midland Bank Trust Co. Ltd, since 1962; *b* 13 December 1899; *s* of James and Flora Wood; *m* 1926, Muriel Hay, Hackensack, New Jersey, USA. *Educ:* Latymer Upper School; Gonville and Caius College, Cambridge (Open Scholar). 1st Cl. Historical Tripos, Pt I, 1920, 1st Cl. Law Tripos, Pt II, 1921; Arden Prize, Gray's Inn, 1921; Barrister, Gray's Inn, 1923. Entered Midland Bank, 1921; various appointments in London and Provinces; Asst Gen. Manager, 1940, Jt Gen. Manager (International and City), 1944; Asst Chief Gen. Manager, 1951; Chief General Manager, 1956-62, retired. Director Belfast Banking Co. Ltd, 1960-70; Vice-Chairman Forward Trust Ltd, 1962-69; Ind. Member Cinematograph Films Council, 1962-69; Pres. Manchester & District Bankers' Inst., 1962-63; Hon. Treasurer, Alexandra Rose Day, 1963-. Pilot Officer, RAF, 1918. *Recreations:* music, golf. *Address:* 65A Egerton Gardens, Knightsbridge, SW3. *T:* 01-589 0254. *Clubs:* United Oxford & Cambridge University, Hurlingham; Royal and Ancient (St Andrews); Royal Mid-Surrey (Richmond).
[*Died* 4 *March* 1974.

WOOD, Thomas Andrew Urquhart; Sheriff of Glasgow, 1961-74; *b* 26 July 1914; *s* of Victor Cartwright Wood, JP, and Barbara Forbes Urquhart; *m* 1942, Daphne Eileen Wells Weston; two *s*; *m* 1969, Ann Menzies Marshall. *Educ:* Loretto Sch.; Trinity Coll., Oxford; Edinburgh Univ. Captain, York and Lancaster Regt, War of 1939-45; served in India and Burma. Called to Scots Bar, 1947. Sheriff-Substitute of Lanarkshire at Hamilton, 1955-61. *Recreations:* music, golf, squash. *Address:* 65 Colinton Road, Edinburgh. *Clubs:* New, Hon. Company of Edinburgh Golfers (Edinburgh). [*Died* 13 *Sept.* 1975.

WOOD, Sir Wilfred William Hill H.; *see* Hill-Wood.

WOODARD, Rev. Canon Alfred Lambert; Hon. Canon of Ely since 1933; *b* 27 April 1880; *s* of late Canon L. Woodard and Emily, *d* of late Henry Perkins of Thriplow Place, Cambs; *g s* of Canon Nathanael Woodard, Founder of Schools; *m* 1905, Fanny Gertrude (*d* 1947), *d* of late Rev. Cyril FitzRoy Wilson; five *s* three *d*. *Educ:* Lancing; Trinity Coll., Cambridge; Classical Tripos. Curate of Sulhamstead, Reading, 1903-05; St James, Bury St Edmunds, 1905-10; Rector of West Stow with Wordwell; Domestic Chaplain to 5th Earl Cadogan, and Chaplain to Culford Parish, 1910-15; Hon. Chaplain to 6th Earl Cadogan, 1915-34; Rector of St Mary Stoke, Ipswich, 1915-24; Rural Dean of Ipswich, 1921-24; Hon. Canon St Edmundsbury and Ipswich, 1922-24; Vicar of Sutton, Cambs, 1924-41; Proctor in Convocation, 1924 and 1929-50; Founder and Convener Teaching Church Group, 1925; Member of Archbishop's Commission on Religious Education, 1926-29; Delegate, Society for the Propagation of the Gospel to the Episcopal Synod of the West Indies; Convener Joint Conference of Anglicans and Evangelical Free Churchmen, 1937-45; Chairman, Standing Cttee Society for the Propagation of the Gospel, 1936-38; Warden of Central Society of Sacred Study, Diocese of Ely, 1938-52; Treasurer of the Society, 1939-50; Vice-Chairman National Society, 1940-44; Envoy for Central Council of the Church of England for Religious Education, 1941-50; Vicar of St Andrew the Great, Cambridge, 1950-58. Fellow Corporation of SS Mary and Nicolas (Woodard Schools); Chairman of Council for East Anglia. *Publications:* St John in the Isle of Patmos; The Teaching Church (Editor); The Teaching Church Review (Editor); Educational Review in Official Year Book of the Church of England, 1928-44. *Recreations:* cricket, rugger, athletics. *Address:* 6 Luard Road, Cambridge. *T:* 48287. *Club:* Athenæum. [*Died* 21 *June* 1971.

WOODBURN, Rt. Hon. Arthur, PC 1947; DLitt; *b* Edinburgh, 25 Oct. 1890; *s* of Matthew Woodburn (Brassfounder) and Janet Brown Woodburn; *m* 1919, Barbara Halliday. *Educ:* Bruntsfield and Boroughmuir Public Schools, Edinburgh; Heriot-Watt Coll., Edinburgh. For 25 years in Engineering and Ironfounding Administration, specialised in languages and costing; Hon. Secretary, Edinburgh Labour College till 1932; Secretary, Scottish Labour College, till 1939; President National Council of Labour Colleges, 1937-; Lectured in History, Economics and Finance in Labour College, 1919 onwards; gave evidence before MacMillan Cttee on Finance and Industry, 1929; contested (Lab) S Edinburgh, 1929, Leith, 1931; Scottish Secretary, Labour Party, 1932-39; MP (Lab) Clackmannan and East Stirling, 1939-70; Parliamentary Private Secretary to Rt Hon. Thomas Johnston, Secretary of State for Scotland, 1941-45; Parliamentary Secretary, Ministry of Supply, 1945-47; Secretary of State for Scotland, 1947-50. Member of Select Cttee on National Expenditure and Chairman Sub-Committee on Finance and Establishments, 1939-45; Administrative Cttee and Front Bench of Parliamentary Labour Party, 1943-45; Member of Speaker's Conference on Electoral Reform, 1944; led first Inter-Parliamentary Union Delegn to West German Bundestag at Bonn; Member: Select Cttee on Clergy Disqualification, 1952-53; Select Cttee on Delegated Legislation, 1952-53; Select Cttee on House of Commons Procedure, 1956-68; Historic Buildings Council for Scotland. Trustee, Scottish National Library, 1962. Led British Inter-Parliamentary Union Delegations to Uruguay, 1957, to Spain, 1960 and House of Commons Delegn to Uganda, 1964, to Kenya, 1966; has visited numerous countries in Europe and S America; Jt Pres., Brit. Section, Council of European Municipalities, 1971-. *Publications:* Banks and the Workers, 1924; Mystery of Money, 1929; Outline of Finance, 1930 (4 editions). *Recreation:* golf. *Address:* 83 Orchard Road, Edinburgh EH4 2EX. *T:* 031-332 1961. [*Died* 1 *June* 1978.

WOODCOCK, Eric Charles, MA; Professor of Latin in the University of Durham (late Durham Colleges), 1948-66; now Professor Emeritus; *b* 20 May 1904; *s* of Charles T. Woodcock; *m* 1933, Ruth Mary Ball; two *s*. *Educ:* King Edward's Sch., Birmingham; St John's Coll., Cambridge. First class in both parts of Classical Tripos, Cambridge (Part I, 1925; Part II, 1927); Instructor in Department of Ancient Languages,

Harvard, 1927-28; Asst Lecturer in Classics, University of Reading, 1928-30; Asst Lecturer in Classics, University of Manchester, 1930-32; Lecturer in Latin, 1932-47; Senior Lecturer in Latin, 1947-48. *Publications:* Tacitus, Annals XIV (edited with Introduction and notes), 1939; A New Latin Syntax, 1959; various articles and reviews in Harvard Studies in Classical Philology, in Classical Review and in Greece and Rome. *Recreation:* reading. *Address:* 25 Dingle Road, Boscombe, Bournemouth BH5 2DP. *[Died 6 Nov. 1978.*

WOODCOCK, Rt. Hon. George, PC 1967; CBE 1953; *b* 20 Oct. 1904; 2nd *s* of Peter Woodcock, Bamber Bridge, Lancashire; *m* 1933, Laura M. McKernan; one *s* one *d. Educ:* Brownedge Elementary; Ruskin College and New Coll., Oxford. Cotton Weaver, 1916-27; 1st Class Hons Philos. and Polit. Economy, Oxford, 1933; Jessie Theresa Rowden Senior Scholarship, New Coll., 1933; Civil Servant, 1934-36; Secretary to TUC Research and Economic Dept, 1936-47; Assistant General Secretary, TUC, 1947-60, General Secretary, 1960-69. Member Royal Commn: on Taxation of Profits and Income, 1950; on Trade Unions and Employers' Assocs, 1965-68; Member British Guiana Constitutional Commission, 1954; Member Committee on the Working of the Monetary System, 1957; Vice-Chairman, National Savings Cttee, 1952-75; Mem., NEDC, 1962-69; Chm., Commn on Industrial Relations, 1969-71. Hon. Fellow, New Coll., Oxford, 1963; Hon. Fellow, LSE, 1964. Hon. LLD: Sussex, 1963; Manchester, 1968; Lancaster, 1970; London, 1970; Hon. DCL: Oxford Univ., 1964; Kent Univ., 1968; Hon. DSc Univ. of Aston in Birmingham, 1967. *Address:* Lower Hill Road, Epsom, Surrey. *T:* Epsom 22694. *[Died 30 Oct. 1979.*

WOODESON, Sir James (Brewis), Kt 1977; CBE 1972 (OBE 1945); TD; Executive Chairman, Northern Engineering Industries Ltd (a merger of Clarke Chapman and Reyrolle Parsons), since 1977; *b* 14 Oct. 1917; *s* of William Armstrong Woodeson and Ethel Margaret Woodeson (formerly Brewis); *m* 1957, Joyce Doreen Burrows; one *d* decd. *Educ:* Oundle Sch., Northants. Commenced with Clarke Chapman Ltd, 1933; Dir, 1938; Exec. Chm., 1949; Chm., Reyrolle Parsons Ltd, 1974. Mem., Engineering Industries Council, 1975-; Mem. (part time), BSC, 1976-79. Hon. DCL Newcastle upon Tyne 1971. *Recreations:* golf, shooting, ornithology. *Address:* Overcliffe, Foxton, Alnmouth, Northumberland. *T:* Alnmouth 284. *Club:* Northern Counties (Newcastle). *[Died 23 Jan. 1980.*

WOODFORD, James, OBE 1953; RA 1945; FRBS; Sculptor; *b* 25 Sept. 1893; *m* 1929, Rose Harrison; one *s. Educ:* Nottingham School of Art; Royal College of Art. Served with 11th Sherwood Foresters, France and Italy, 1915-18 (despatches). Camouflage Officer to Air Ministry, 1941-44. *Principal Works:* Bronze Doors, RIBA; 3 Main Double Leaf Bronze Doors, Norwich City Hall; Carved Stone Figures and Panels, Huddersfield New Library and Art Gallery; sculpture on Ministry of Agriculture and Fisheries, Whitehall Place; Bronze Statue Robin Hood, Groups and Reliefs, Robin Hood Lawn, Nottingham; Queen's Beasts, Coronation Annexe, Westminster Abbey; 13-ft Statue, Memorial to Rt Hon. D. S. Senanayake, First Prime Minister of Ceylon; Sculpture for Imperial War Graves Commission British Cemeteries in Italy. Carved Groups, Thor and Marlborough, RN Engineering Coll., Manadon; 13-ft Reliefs, etc. for Lloyd's New Building; Carved Doors in wood, etc., Main Hall, Carpenters' Company; Carved Panel and Keystones, Coutts Bank, Lombard Street; Memorial Bust, Canon Wylie Blue, May Street Church, Belfast; BMA War Memorial, Tavistock Place (RBS Medal, best work of year, 1955); 17-ft Royal Arms in aluminium, New Delhi, UK Diplomatic Compound Offices; 6-ft Memorial Bronze Figure, Captain Cipriani, Port-of-Spain. New design, Royal Coat of Arms, 1962. Clytie Fountain, Assembly Rooms, Norwich; Memorial Bust on granite plinth to Coxswain Henry Blogg; Cromer; Ebenezer Howard Memorial, Welwyn Garden City; Lion and Unicorn Statues, British Embassy, Teheran; Bronze Panels for Ceremonial Doors, Houses of Parlt, Swaziland; Royal Coats of Arms for Consulates; 5-ft Lion and Unicorn for Wandsworth County Ct; Aluminium Plaque, St John's Wood Barracks; Dolphin Fountain Bronze, Tonga Independence Gift, 1973; Bronze garden column for Dr Lawrence Pilkington, Frodsham, Cheshire. Many coats of arms for Govt and other buildings, UK and abroad. *Publication:* Heraldic Sculpture and the Work of James Woodford, 1972. *Recreation:* billiards. *Address:* 76 Popes Grove, Twickenham, Middlesex. *T:* 01-891 1540. *Club:* Arts. *[Died 8 Nov. 1976.*

WOODHAM-SMITH, Cecil, CBE 1960; historian and biographer; *b* 1896; *d* of Colonel James FitzGerald, late Berar Commn, and Blanche Elizabeth FitzGerald (*née* Philipps); *m* 1928, George Ivon Woodham-Smith, Solicitor (*d* 1968); one *s* one *d. Educ:* St Hilda's Coll., Oxford. Until marriage wrote articles and short stories; started research into life of Florence

Nightingale, 1941. A. C. Benson Medal for contrib. to literature, 1969. Hon. DLitt NUI, 1964; Hon. LLD St Andrews, 1965; Hon. Fellow, St Hilda's Coll., Oxford, 1967. *Publications:* Florence Nightingale, (London) 1950 (awarded James Tait Black Memorial Prize, 1950), (New York) 1951; Lonely Crusader, (New York) 1951; Lady in Chief, (London) 1953; The Reason Why, (London) 1953, (New York) 1954; The Great Hunger, (London), 1962, (New York), 1963; Queen Victoria: her life and times, vol. I (London and NY), 1972. *Address:* 44 Mount Street, W1. *T:* 01-499 7986. *[Died 16 March 1977.*

WOODHEAD, Sir John Ackroyd, GCIE 1946 (CIE 1930); KCSI 1934; *b* 19 June 1881; *m* 1908, Alice Mary, *d* of late B. S. Wadsworth; one *s* one *d. Educ:* Bradford Grammar Sch.; Clare Coll., Cambridge, BA. Entered Indian Civil Service, 1904; posted to Bengal, 1904; transferred to Eastern Bengal and Assam, 1905; Magistrate and Collector, 1909; transferred to Bengal, 1912; District and Sessions Judge, 1917; Special Land Acquisition Collector, 1918; Chairman, Calcutta Improvement Trust, 1924; Secretary, Government of Bengal, Finance Department, 1924; Joint-Secretary, Commerce Department, Government of India, 1927; Secretary, Commerce Department, Government of India, 1929; Temporary Member, Council of the Governor-General of India, 1931; Finance Member, Government of Bengal, 1932-37; Acting Governor of Bengal, Aug.-Dec. 1934; Chairman Palestine Partition Commission, 1938; Governor of Bengal, June-Nov. 1939; Adviser to Secretary of State for India, 1939-44; Chairman Famine Enquiry Commission, Aug. 1944; President, India, Pakistan and Burma Association, 1948-62. *Address:* Chevremont, Hockering Road, Woking, Surrey. *[Died 8 Jan. 1973.*

WOODHOUSE, Admiral (retired) Sir Charles (Henry Lawrence), KCB, *cr* 1949 (CB 1940); *b* 9 July 1893; *s* of Rev. A. P. Woodhouse and F. D. Woodhouse; *m* 1928, Barbara Margaret, *d* of Dr H. M. Brownfield, Petersfield; three *d. Educ:* RN Colleges, Osborne and Dartmouth. Commanded HMS Ajax in Battle of the River Plate 1939 (CB); C-in-C East Indies Station, 1948-50; retired, 1950; Admiral, retired list, 1952. *Address:* Flat 2, 98 Westhall Road, Warlingham, Surrey CR3 9HD. *[Died 23 Sept. 1978.*

WOODHOUSE, Rear-Admiral Hector Roy Mackenzie, CB 1941; OBE 1919; RN, retired; *b* 15 Feb. 1889; *s* of late Alfred Woodhouse; *m* 1920, Norah Constance Mackenzie (*d* 1967); no *c. Educ:* Bedford Sch. Entered Royal Navy, 1906; retired, 1944; Rear-Admiral, retired, 1946. Chairman, South-Eastern Division of National Coal Board, 1946-55. *Address:* 6 Pembroke Chambers, Penny Street, Portsmouth, Hants. *T:* 25322. *Club:* United Service. *[Died 5 June 1971.*

WOODING, Rt. Hon. Sir Hugh (Olliviere Beresford), TC 1969; PC 1967; Kt 1963; CBE 1957; Chief Justice, Trinidad and Tobago, 1962-68; *b* 14 Jan. 1904; *s* of late Iddo A. Reginald Wooding and late Mrs Wooding, Port of Spain, Trinidad; *m* 1928, Anne Marie, *d* of late Charles Louis P. R. Coussey, Gold Coast (now Ghana); two *s* two *d. Educ:* Queen's Royal Coll., Trinidad; Middle Temple, London. KC 1948; Hon. Master of Bench, Inner Temple, 1969. Chairman: Trinidad and Tobago Board of Furness Withy & Co., 1969-; Swan Hunter (Trinidad), 1969-; Furness and Gordon, 1969-; Continental Communications (Caribbean) Ltd, 1969-73; Insurance Brokers (West Indies), 1970-; Caribbean Development Co. Ltd, 1971-; Reed Trinidad Ltd, 1971-; Director, Texaco (Trinidad) Inc., 1969-. Mayor of Port of Spain, 1943-44. Hon. LLD University of West Indies, 1967. *Publication:* A Collection of Addresses, 1968. *Recreation:* racing. *Address:* 2 Champs Elysées, Maraval, Trinidad. *T:* 22477. *Clubs:* Royal Commonwealth Society (West Indian); Union, Maple and Arima Race (Trinidad); Jamaica (Jamaica). *[Died 26 July 1974.*

WOODLEY, Sir (Frederick George) Richard, Kt 1950; *m* 1929, Betsy Maud Hind (*d* 1961); *m* 1961, Joyce Mary Forrest, *d* of late S. O. C. Forrest. Alderman, Nairobi Municipal Council, 1947-63 (Councillor, 1944); County Councillor and Rural Dist Councillor, 1955-63; Charter Mayor and three times (1947-50) Mayor of the City of Nairobi; President of Nairobi Chamber of Commerce, 1949; Chairman, Hotel Control Authority for Kenya, 1945-53; Broadcaster for Kenya Information Office, 1942-46; Past President, Kenya Cultural Centre and of The Kenya National Theatre. Cordwainer and Citizen of London. *Address:* The Glebe House, Checkendon, Reading, Berks. *T:* Checkendon 685. *Clubs:* Royal Commonwealth Society; Surrey County Cricket; Nairobi (Nairobi). *[Died 6 Oct. 1971.*

WOODLEY, Sir Richard; *see* Woodley, Sir (F. G.) R.

WOODMAN, John, OBE 1928; BA (Oxon); retired; *b* Newcastle upon Tyne, 21 July 1888; *s* of William Hunter Woodman and Mary Ann Woodman (*née* Millican); *m* 1930, Magdeleine Louise Gardoni; no *c*. *Educ*: Royal Grammar Sch., Newcastle upon Tyne; Brasenose Coll., Oxford. Hulme Scholar, Brasenose Coll., Oxford; 2nd Class Hon. Mods and Lit. Hum.; Barrister, Inner Temple, 1914. Served as Lieut, ASC, attached S and T Corps, India, 1916-20; Afghan War, 1919-20. Judge in Iraq, 1920-28; International lawyer, Paris, 1929-40; War Damage Insurance Dept, Board of Trade, 1941-43; Chief Justice, Seychelles, 1943-47; Acting Governor, Seychelles, 1946; at times Acting Chief Justice, N Rhodesia; Member, Rhodesia and Nyasaland Court of Appeal, 1947-53; Puisne Judge, Northern Rhodesia, 1947-53; retired from Colonial Legal Service, Nov. 1953. *Recreation*: languages. *Address*: 17 rue de Téhéran, Paris 8e, France.   [*Died 26 May 1971.*

WOODNUTT, Mark, (Harold Frederick Martin Woodnutt); Chartered Secretary; Chairman, Southern Constructions (Holdings), since 1972; *b* 23 Nov. 1918; *s* of Harold Frederick Woodnutt, Cowes, IoW; *m* 1945, Gwynneth Alice Lovely; two *s* two *d*. *Educ*: Isleworth Grammar Sch. Militiaman, 1939; commissioned Royal Artillery, Dec. 1939. Served War of 1939-45: Norway, Egypt, Crete, Germany (despatches, POW). Chartered Secretary, 1945. Isle of Wight County Council, 1952-74: Alderman, 1957-74; Chairman Highways, 1953-55; Chairman Finance, 1955-61. MP (C) Isle of Wight, 1959-Feb. 1974. Chairman IOW Conservative Assoc., 1954-59; Chairman, Bembridge Lifeboat, 1960-. *Address*: Portland House, Bembridge, IOW. *T*: Bembridge 2414; 16 Dalkeith Court, Vincent Street, SW1. *T*: 01-834 0507. *Clubs*: Constitutional; Bembridge Sailing.   [*Died 6 Nov. 1974.*

WOODRUFF, Douglas; *see* Woodruff, J. D.

WOODRUFF, (John) Douglas, CBE 1962; Chairman, BOW Holdings, 1959-70; Chairman, Associated Catholic Newspapers, 1953-70; Editor of The Tablet, 1936-67; *b* 8 May 1897; *s* of late Cumberland Woodruff, BCL, FSA, of the Public Record Office, and late Emily Louisa, *d* of William Hewett, Norton Fitzwarren, Somerset; *m* 1933, Hon. Marie Immaculée, *d* of 2nd Lord Acton. *Educ*: St Augustine's, Ramsgate; Downside Sch.; New Coll., Oxford (Lothian prizeman, 1921, 1st class Hon. Modern History, 1923, President of the Union). Served under Foreign Office in Holland, 1917-19; Lecturer in History at Sheffield Univ., 1923-24; Editorial staff of The Times, 1926-38; in charge of Press Publicity for Empire Marketing Board, 1931-33; on staff of BBC, 1934-36; Dep. Chairman Burns and Oates, Publishers, 1948-62; Director, Hollis & Carter, 1948-62; Chairman of Allied Circle, 1947-62. Grand Cross, Order of St Gregory the Great, 1968. *Publications*: Plato's American Republic, 1926; The British Empire, 1929; Plato's Britannia, 1930; Charlemagne, 1934; Contributor to Early Victorian England, 1934; Great Tudors, 1935; European Civilisation, The Grand Tour, 1935; (Editor) Dear Sir, 1936; The Story of the British Colonial Empire, 1939; Talking at Random, 1941; More Talking at Random, 1944; Still Talking at Random, 1948; Walrus Talk, 1954; The Tichborne Claimant, 1957; Church and State in History, 1961; The Life and Times of Alfred the Great, 1974; contrib. to current periodicals. *Address*: Marcham Priory, Abingdon, Oxon. *T*: Frilford Heath 391260. *Club*: Athenæum.   [*Died 9 March 1978.*

WOODRUFF, Keith Montague Cumberland, MB, BS (London); MRCS; LRCP; FFARCS; *b* 18 June 1891; *s* of Rev. A. W. Woodruff and Emily (*née* Hamilton), Testwood, Hants; *m* 1934, Beatrice Evelyn, *d* of late Colonel C. C. O. Whiteley and of Mrs Whiteley; one *s*. *Educ*: Eastmans Royal Army and Navy Academy, Winchester; St Edward's Sch., Oxford; Guy's Hospital. Consulting Anæsthetist: Royal National Orthopædic Hospital, 1924; Chelsea Hospital for Women, 1925; Queen Charlotte's Maternity Hospital, 1938; Charing Cross Hospital, 1935; Royal Masonic Hospital, 1937. 1914-15 Medal, 1914-18 Medal, Victory Medal, 1914-18. *Recreations*: golf, sailing. *Address*: Mount Cottage, Rhodes Minnis, Elham, near Canterbury, Kent. *T*: Lyminge 862445.   [*Died 26 July 1978.*

WOODS, Irene Charlotte, CBE 1946; TD 1951; *b* 4 Jan. 1891; *y d* of late Thomas Pickering, Newcastle, and The Hill House, Gilsland; *m* 1918, R. Salisbury Woods, MD, FRCS; one *s* two *d*. *Educ*: privately. European War, 1914-18, trained at St George's Hospital, and became Staff Nurse. Joined ATS 1938. In War of 1939-45 served ATS, reached rank of Controller; DDATS, Scottish Comd, 1943; DDATS, 2 AA Gp, Mixed Batteries, Thames Estuary, Kent, Sussex, Hants, 1944; invalided out, 1945. Organiser, City of Cambridge, WRVS, 1954-67. Patron, Cambridge Br., Old Contemptibles Assoc. *Recreations*: bridge, golf. *Address*: 4 Manor Court, Grange Road, Cambridge CB3 9BE. *T*: 59451.   [*Died 8 Oct. 1976.*

WOODS, Oliver Frederick John Bradley, MC 1943; TD and Bar, 1947; MA; *b* 21 Nov. 1911; *o s* of late Maurice Woods and late Mrs J. L. Garvin; *m* 1956, Joan Nancy, *widow* of F. H. Waters and *d* of late Colonel C. R. Maude, OBE, MC, and Mrs Maude (Nancy Price). *Educ*: Marlborough; Geneva Univ.; New Coll., Oxford. Senior open classical schol., 1930. Joined editorial staff of The Times, 1935. Served War of 1939-45: Major, 3rd County of London Yeomanry (Sharpshooters); Western Desert, Sicily, Italy, North-West Europe (despatches). Rejoined The Times as special writer, 1946; Colonial Correspondent, 1948; Colonial Editor and Assistant Foreign Editor, 1956; Assistant Editor, 1961; Chief Asst to Editor-in-Chief, Times Newspapers, 1967-70. Member: Council, Univ. of Sussex; Commonwealth Press Union. Travelled widely, especially in Africa and the Commonwealth. *Address*: 6 Southover High Street, Lewes. *T*: Lewes 3418. *Clubs*: Travellers', Pratt's, Garrick, Royal Commonwealth Society.   [*Died 13 Dec. 1972.*

WOODS, Admiral (Retired) Sir Wilfrid (John Wentworth), GBE 1963; KCB 1960 (CB 1957); DSO 1942; Bar to DSO 1942; DL; *b* 19 Feb. 1906; *s* of late Sir Wilfrid Woods, KCMG, KBE, and late Ethel Maud Woods (*née* Palmer); *m* 1st, 1930, Murray Auriol Ruth Inglis (*d* 1956); one *d* (one *s* decd); 2nd, 1957, Joan Bridget Constance Eden. *Educ*: Seabrook Lodge, Hythe, Kent; Royal Naval Colleges Osborne and Dartmouth. Midshipman, 1924; Sub-Lieut, 1926; joined Submarines, 1927; Lieut, 1928; First Command, HMS/M Seahorse, 1935; Lieut-Commander, HMS Nelson, 1936; RN Staff Coll., 1939. Served War of 1939-45: Staff of 6th S/M Flotilla, Home Waters, 1939; HMS/M Triumph in Command, Mediterranean, 1940 (DSO and Bar, Order of White Eagle of Yugo-Slavia); Commander 1941; Staff of C-in-C, Mediterranean, 1942; HMS Centurion in Command, Normandy Landings, 1944; Staff of 3rd S/M Flotilla, Home Waters, 1944; HMS Forth in Command, and Captain 3rd S/M Flotilla, 1945. Chief Staff Officer to Flag Officer S/M's, 1947; Admiralty, as Director of Torpedo, Anti-Submarine and Mine Warfare, 1948; idc 1951; HMS Indomitable in Command, 1952; Chief of Staff to C-in-C Mediterranean as Cdre 1st Class, 1953; Rear-Admiral, 1955; Flag Officer (Submarines), Dec. 1955-Nov. 1957; Vice-Admiral, 1958; Deputy Supreme Allied Commander Atlantic, 1958-60; Admiral, 1960; Commander-in-Chief, Home Fleet, and NATO C-in-C Eastern Atlantic Area, 1960-62; Commander-in-Chief, Portsmouth, and Allied Commander-in-Chief, Channel, 1963-65; Principal Naval ADC to the Queen, 1962-65; Cdre RN Sailing Assoc., 1963-66. Member, Cttee of Management, RNLI, 1966, Chairman, 1968-72; President, Sea Cadet Corps Sports Council, 1966; Chairman, Foudroyant Trust, 1967. DL Hants 1971. Knight Commander, Order of King George the First of Greece, 1963. *Recreations*: sailing, gardening, walking. *Address*: Shappen Farm, Burley, Hampshire BH24 4AG. *T*: Burley 2256. *Clubs*: United Service & Royal Aero; Royal Naval and Royal Albert Yacht (Portsmouth); Royal Yacht Squadron (Cowes).   [*Died 1 Jan. 1975.*

WOODS, Colonel William Talbot, CB 1950; DSO 1918; MC 1915; TD; MIMinE; Mining Engineer since 1920; Umpire to Conciliation Board, SW Division, National Coal Board, 1947-60; *b* 10 Dec. 1891; *s* of William Woods, FRCVS, MSc, Wigan; *m* 1927, Enid Comer, *d* of Arthur Smith, BA, LLB, Golborne, Wigan; one *s* two *d*. *Educ*: Charterhouse. Served European War, 1914-19, Egypt, Gallipoli and France (despatches three times); comd 4th Bn Welch Regt, TA, 1927-32 (Hon. Colonel, 1953-59); Colonel, 1931; comd 15th Bn Welch Regt, 1939; comd Home Guard Bn, 1940-45; Colonel, TARO, 1932-51; Chairman, Carmarthen TA Assoc., 1945-52. JP 1938-66, DL 1935-69, Carmarthenshire. KStJ, 1957. *Address*: 17 The Fairway, Post Hill, Tiverton, Devon. *T*: Tiverton 3405. [*Died 13 Feb. 1975.*

WOODS, William Wilson, LRCP, MRCS; Assistant Director, The Pathological Institute, London Hospital, 1920, retired; Formerly Consulting Pathologist (Morbid Histologist) to the Navy; *b* 10 May 1884; 3rd *s* of late Robert Woods, JP, Stewartstown, Tyrone, and Jane Frances, *d* of late John Cowan, Annahavil, Co. Derry; *m* 1911, Stéphanie (*d* 1967), *y d* of late A. W. Bellmont, Christiania; one *s*. *Educ*: Royal Sch., Dungannon; London Univ.; London Hospital. Pathological Asst, Pathological Institute, London Hospital, 1911; Junior Assistant Director, 1912. *Recreation*: played Rugby football for London Hospital, 1906 (Inter-Hospital Cup Winners), and for Middlesex County. *Address*: Guildown, 10 Lynwood Road, Epsom, Surrey.   [*Died 10 March 1972.*

WOODS BALLARD, Lt-Col Basil, CIE 1943; MBE 1935; *b* 28 Sept. 1900; *s* of Frederick George Ballard; *m* 1931, Eileen Rose, *d* of Lt-Col Hugh Wilson Molesworth, CBE; two *s*. *Educ*: Dulwich Coll. Commissioned 5th Royal Gurkha Rifles, FF, IA, 1920; Indian Political Service, 1925; Political Agent, Loralai,

1936-39; Secretary to Resident, Punjab States, 1939-41; Political Agent, Quetta, 1941-45; Political Agent, Bhopal, 1945-47; Resident in Kolhapur, 1947; retired, Aug. 1947. Employed in Persian Gulf, 1948-53; has since served on local councils (inc. E Sussex CC), and on governing bodies of schools. *Address:* Shepherds Oak, Crawley Down, West Sussex. *T:* Copthorne 712314. *[Died 4 June 1980.*

WOODWARD, Arthur Maurice, MA, FSA; Hon. FRIBA; *b* 29 June 1883; 2nd *s* of late W. H. Woodward; *m* 1925, Jocelyn Mary, 2nd *d* of John Pybus, Newcastle on Tyne. *Educ:* Shrewsbury; Magdalen Coll., Oxford. Student at the British School, Athens, 1906-09; Asst Director, 1909-10 and 1922-23; Director, 1923-29; Assistant Lecturer, Univ. of Liverpool, 1911-12, and Leeds, 1912-22; Lecturer in Ancient History, 1931-45, and Reader in Ancient History and Archæology and Head of Dept of Ancient History, Univ. of Sheffield, 1945-47. Served in Macedonia and Bulgaria with British Salonika Force, Nov. 1915-Jan. 1919 (despatches twice). Officer, Greek Order of the Redeemer, 1924. *Publications:* numerous articles on Greek inscriptions and other archæological subjects in Journal of Hellenic Studies, Annual of the British School at Athens, Numismatic Chronicle, etc. *Recreations:* restricted. *Address:* Spa Hotel, Tunbridge Wells, Kent. *[Died 12 Nov. 1973.*

WOODWARD, Denys Cuthbert, CMG 1949; FCIT; *b* 15 March 1902; *s* of Rev. W. E. Woodward, MA, and Mrs Woodward (*née* Richardson); *m* Mary Stuart, *d* of Rev. T. H. Strong (late of Sandy, Bedfordshire); one *s*. *Educ:* St Peter's Court, Broadstairs; Christ's Hospital, Horsham. Joined L and NWR, 1918; Nigerian Railway, 1928; General Manager, 1947-Nov. 1953; Chairman of Nigeria Hotels Ltd, 1949-58. *Recreations:* cricket, sailing. *Address:* 1 Spinola Court, The Gardens, St Julians, Malta. *[Died 21 Dec. 1972.*

WOODWARD, Lieut-Colonel Edward Hamilton Everard, CBE 1949; MC 1916; TD 1931; FIEE; *b* 4 Feb. 1888; *s* of Colonel J. H. Woodward, CB, VD, JP, and Mary Alice Hamilton, *d* of Admiral T. Fisher, Clifton, Bristol; *m* 1917, Violet Ethel, *d* of Lieut-Commander A. S. Hamilton, RN; two *s* two *d*. *Educ:* Clifton Coll.; Bristol University College. BSc (Eng.) London, BSc (Eng.) Bristol. Assistant Engineer, Newcastle on Tyne Electric Supply Co. Ltd, 1909-14. Served European War, 4th Bn Gloucestershire Regt and Tyne Electrical Engineers, RE, 1914-19. North-Eastern Electric Supply Co. Ltd, 1920-48, ending as General Manager and a Director. In command of Tyne Electrical Engineers, RE, 1929-34. Appointed by Minister of Fuel and Power a member Organising Cttee for Electricity Supply Industry, May 1947, and a member British Electricity Authority, Aug. 1947-Dec. 1957. *Recreation:* flower garden. *Address:* Cherryburn, Kivernell Road, Milford-on-Sea, Hants. *T:* 2374. *[Died 2 Jan. 1976.*

WOODWARD, Sir (Ernest) Llewellyn, Kt 1952; MA; Hon. LittD, Princeton; FBA; Hon. Fellow of Worcester College, and of Corpus Christi College, Oxford; Member American Philosophical Society; *b* London, 14 May 1890; *s* of late G. E. Woodward, CBE; *m* 1917, Florence Marie (*d* 1961), *y d* of late Very Rev. R. S. O'Loughlin, DD, Dean of Dromore. *Educ:* Merchant Taylors' Sch.; Corpus Christi Coll., Oxford. Served BEF France and Salonika, 1915-18; Fellow of All Souls Coll., 1919-44 and 1962-, and formerly Lecturer in Modern History, New Coll.; Professor of International Relations, Oxford, 1944-47; Professor of Modern History, Oxford Univ., 1947-51; Professor at the Institute for Advanced Study, Princeton, 1951-62; Senior Proctor, Oxford University, 1928-29; Rhodes Travelling Fellow, 1931; Editor (with R. D'O. Butler), 1944-55, of Documents on British Foreign Policy, 1919-39. *Publications:* Christianity and Nationalism in the Later Roman Empire; Three Studies in European Conservatism; The Twelve-Winded Sky; War and Peace in Europe, 1815-70; French Revolutions; Great Britain and the German Navy; The Age of Reform (vol. xiii in the Oxford History of England); Short Journey; British Historians; History of England; British Foreign Policy in the Second World War (Official History); Great Britain and the War of 1914-18. *Address:* The Garden House, 2a Walton Street, Oxford. *[Died 11 March 1971.*

WOODWARD, Joan, (Mrs L. T. Blakeman); Professor of Industrial Sociology, Imperial College of Science and Technology, since 1969; *b* 19 June 1916; *d* of Joseph Henry Woodward and Lily Woodward (*née* King); *m* 1951, Leslie Thompson Blakeman, CBE. *Educ:* Durham and Oxford Universities (MA Durham; BA Oxon). Various Industrial Appointments, 1939-46; Administrative Class, Civil Service, 1946-48; Lecturer, Department of Social Science, Liverpool University, 1948-53; Director, DSIR Research Unit, SE Essex College of Technology, 1953-57; Special Tutor, Industrial Sociology, Dept of Social and Administrative Studies, Oxford, 1957-62; Reader in Industrial Sociology, Imperial Coll., 1962-69. Part-time Mem., Nat. Board for Prices and Incomes, 1968-71. *Publications:* include: Employment Relations in a Group of Hospitals, 1951; The Dockworker, 1954; Management and Technology, 1957; The Saleswoman, 1961; Industrial Organization: theory and practice, 1965; (with Flanders and Pomeranz) Experiment in Industrial Democracy, 1968; (ed) Industrial Organization: behaviour and control, 1970. *Recreation:* re-making houses and gardens. *Address:* 71 Roebuck House, Stag Place, SW1. *T:* 01-828 6203; Fishponds Farm, Brook, near Ashford, Kent. *T:* Wye 514. *[Died 18 May 1971.*

WOODWARD, Sir Llewellyn; *see* Woodward, Sir E. L.

WOODWARD, Prof. R(obert) B(urns), BS; PhD; Donner Professor of Science, Harvard University, since 1960; Director of the Woodward Research Institute, Basel, since 1963; Member of Corporation, Massachusetts Institute of Technology, 1966-71; *b* Boston, 10 April 1917; *s* of Arthur Chester Woodward and Margaret (*née* Burns); *m* 1st, 1938, Irja Pullman; two *d*; 2nd, 1946, Eudoxia M. M. Muller; one *s* one *d*. *Educ:* Massachusetts Institute of Technology. BS, 1936; PhD, 1937. Post-Doctoral Fellow, Harvard Univ., 1937-38; Mem., Soc. of Fellows, 1938-40; Instructor in Chemistry, 1941-44; Asst Prof., 1944-46; Assoc. Prof., 1946-50; Prof., 1950-53; Morris Loeb Prof. of Chem., 1953-60. Todd Prof. of Chem. and Fellow, Christ's Coll., Cambridge Univ., 1973-74. Consultant: Polaroid Corp., 1942-; Cttee on Medical Research, Office of Scientific Research and Development, 1944-45; War Production Bd, 1944-45; Pfizer & Co. Inc., 1951-70. Dir, CIBA-GEIGY Ltd, Basel, 1970-. Mem. Bd of Governors, Weizmann Inst. of Science, 1968-. Hon. Lecturer to many organisations in America, Europe, Australia and Asia. Member, National Academy of Sciences; Fellow, Amer. Acad. of Arts and Sciences; Foreign Member: Royal Society; Accademia Nazionale dei Lincei; Acad. of Scis of USSR; Acad. of Scis of Institute of France; Royal Acad. of Sciences of Spain; For. Fellow, Indian Nat. Sci. Acad.; Hon. Fellow: Chemical Society; Indian Academy of Sciences; Weizmann Inst. of Science; Indian Chem. Soc.; Hon. FRSE; Hon. Member: German Chemical Society; Royal Irish Academy; Belgian Chemical Society; Swiss Chemical Society; Pharmaceutical Soc. of Japan; Pharmaceutical Soc. of GB; Royal Instn of GB; Spanish Royal Soc. of Physics and Chemistry; Phi Lambda Upsilon (Nat. Hon. Chem. Soc.); Hon. Life Mem., NY Acad. of Scis; Member: American Philosophical Society; Deutsche Akademie der Naturforscher (Leopoldina); Harvey Soc. of NY; Corresponding Member: Austrian Academy of Sciences; Yugoslav Acad. of Scis and Arts. Hon. AM Harvard Univ., 1946; Hon. LLD Glasgow, 1966; Hon. Dr tech. wiss. Zurich; Hon. DSc: Wesleyan; Manchester; Bucknell; New Brunswick; Yale, Harvard; S Carolina; Chicago; New England Coll. of Pharmacy; Colby; Cambridge; Brandeis; Stonehill; Sheffield; Haifa; Brooklyn; W Ontario; Columbia; Louvain; Paris; St Andrews; London. John Scott Medal, 1945; Baekeland Medal, 1955; Ledlie Prize, 1955; Research Corp. Award, 1955; Nichols Medal, 1956; Amer. Chem. Soc. Synthetic Organic Chemistry Award, 1957; T. W. Richards Medal, 1958; Davy Medal, Royal Soc., 1959; Roger Adams Medal, 1961; Pius XI Gold Medal of Pontifical Acad. of Sciences, 1961; Scientific Achievement Medal, 1961; Priestley Medallion, 1962; Stas Medal, 1962; Gold Medal for Creative Res. in Synthetic Organic Chem., 1962; Nat. Medal of Science, USA. 1964; Nobel Prize for Chemistry, 1965; Kirkwood Medal, 1965; Willard Gibbs Medal, 1967; Lavoisier Medal, 1968; Hanbury Meml Medal, 1970; Pierre Bruylants Medal, 1970; Scientific Achievement Award, 1971; Dr B. C. Law Gold Medal, 1972; Arthur C. Cope Award, 1973; Copley Medal, Royal Society, 1978. Order of the Rising Sun, 2nd cl. (Japan), 1970. *Address:* Dept of Chemistry, Harvard University, 12 Oxford Street, Cambridge, Mass 02138, USA. *[Died 8 July 1979.*

WOODWARD-NUTT, Arthur Edgar; *b* 19 Aug. 1902; *m* 1st, 1928, Dorothy Muriel Linzell (*d* 1974); one *s*; 2nd, 1975, Gladys Alexandra MacBain. *Educ:* King Edward's, Birmingham; Gonville and Caius Coll., Cambridge (MA). Seely Prizeman, Cambridge, 1923. De Havilland Aircraft Co., 1924-25; at Royal Aircraft Estabt, Farnborough, 1925-27 and 1934-38, Aeroplane and Armament Experimental Estabt, Martlesham Heath, 1927-31, Marine Aircraft Experimental Estabt, Felixstowe, 1931-34; in charge of Air Defence Res. Section, Air Ministry, 1938-41; Sec. to Brit. Technical Mission to USA, 1940; various directing appointments at Min. of Aircraft Production and Min. of Supply, 1941-58; Dir.-Gen. of Aircraft General Services, Ministry of Aviation, 1958-65; Technical Adviser (Civil) to Ministry of Aviation, 1965-66; British Exec. Deleg. and Chm. of Central Secretariat, Commonwealth Adv. Aeronautical Res.

Council, 1957-66; retired 1966. CEng; FRAeS. *Publications:* various Reports and Memoranda of Aeronautical Research Council, and articles in Technical Press. *Recreations:* lawn tennis (until 1979), bowls, gardening (until Jan. 1980 when incapacitated by disease of nervous system). *Address:* Badgers, Woodland Way, Crowhurst, Battle, Sussex. *T:* Crowhurst 286.
[*Died* 10 *Sept.* 1980.

WOOLDRIDGE, Henry, CBE 1964 (OBE 1942); *b* 9 Jan. 1908; *o s* of Alderman Henry Wooldridge and Mrs Emma Wooldridge; *m* 1939, Marjorie, *er d* of Albert Dranfield and Mrs Annie Dranfield; two *s. Educ:* Reading Sch.; King's Coll., London. King's Schol.; Univ. Exhibr in Sci.; Sec., Coll. Union Soc., 1929-30; Captain and Vice-Pres., Coll. Boat Club; Univ. Rowing Colours, 1928; BSc (Physics, Special), 1929; AKC 1929; Teacher's Dipl. 1930. Asst Sec., British Assoc., 1930-35; DSIR Headquarters as Scientific Officer, 1935; Private Sec. to Perm. Sec., 1935-43; Princ. in Gen. Div., 1943-45; Asst, later Dep. Estab. Off., 1945-47; Head of Stations Div., 1957; Dep. Dir (Stns), 1958; Asst Controller (Stns and Res. Assocs), Min. of Technology, 1965; Head of Information and Regional Org. Div. (Chief Scientific Officer), 1965-66; Head of Productivity Services and Information Div., 1968. *Recreation:* gardening. *Address:* 29 Hewett Avenue, Caversham, Reading RG4 7EA. *T:* Reading 471501.*Club:* Athenæum. [*Died* 15 *May* 1975.

WOOLLEY, Frank Edward; cricketer, retired; *b* Kent, 27 May 1887; 4th *s* of Charles William Woolley and Louise Lewis Woolley; *m* 1st, Sibyl Fordham (*d* 1962), Ashford, Kent; two *d* (one *s* decd); 2nd, Martha Wilson Morse, Chester, NS, *widow of* Major Sydney J. Morse. *Educ:* in Tonbridge, Kent. Professional, Kent County Cricket Club, 1903; subseq. played 67 times for England in 32 years; scored over 60,000 runs in 1st cl. cricket, took over 2,500 wickets, made 1,007 catches (world record) and 156 centuries; played in 54 consecutive Test Matches (world record); scored over 2000 runs and took 100 wickets in 4 successive seasons (world record); on 8 occasions, scored over a century and took 10 wickets in same match (world record); in Tasmania, 1912, scored highest-ever (305) in 4 hrs 15 mins not out (unequalled record); played greatest innings at Lords against Australia (93-95), 1921; scored 50 runs and 5 wickets, Gravesend, 1937; captained The Players at Lords for last time, Sept. 1938, then retd. Served War of 1914-18, HMS King George V. *Publications:* The King of Games; Early Memoirs of Frank Woolley as told to Martha Woolley, 1976. *Relevant publications:* Encyclopædia Britannica (under Cricket); Woolley, the Pride of Kent, by Ian Peebles; Great Men of Kent, by A. A. Thomson; Good Days, Full Score, etc, by Neville Cardus; A Sort of Cricketer, by E. W. Swanton; Frank Woolley, by Oliver Warner; Cricket Scores of Frank E. Woolley, by A. K. Nowll. *Address:* Chester, Nova Scotia, Canada. *T:* 902 275-3866. *Clubs:* (Hon. Life Mem.) MCC; (Hon. Life Mem.) Band of Brothers; Men of Kent; Kent County Cricket; Royal Nova Scotia Yacht Squadron. [*Died* 18 *Oct.* 1978.

WOOLLEY, Howard Mark, CBE 1927; *b* 23 June 1879; *m* 1st, Margaret Marie (*d* 1926), *d* of F. Gaze; 2nd, 1932, Aline Veronica, *o d* of late Sir F. A. Van der Meulen; one *s* one *d. Educ:* London. Civil Service, Post Office, 1891; Northern Nigeria Civil Service, 1905; retired as Postmaster-General, Nigeria, 1926; served Cameroons Expeditionary Force, 1914-15; Central Electricity Board, 1928-36. *Address:* Little Barden, Speldhurst, Tunbridge Wells, Kent. [*Died* 4 *Sept.* 1971.

WOOLMER, Rt. Rev. Laurence Henry, MA; *b* 22 Feb. 1906; *s* of Alfred Henry Woolmer, actuary; *m* 1941, Ruth May, *d* of Rev. Canon W. Hanan, MA, Sligo; two *s. Educ:* King Edward's School, Birmingham. Bank of England, 1925-34; passed Intermediate Examination Chartered Institute Secretaries, 1927, Final, 1929; Hons Theology 3rd class, St Peter's Coll., Oxford, 1934-37; Wycliffe Hall, Oxford, 1937-38; Curate, S Paul's Church, Salisbury, 1938-40; Church Missionary Society, Gojra, Lyallpur District, Punjab, 1940-44; Sec., CMS Mission, Punjab, 1944-48; Archdeacon of Lahore, 1948-49; Bishop of Lahore, 1949-68; Rector of St Andrew's, Meonstoke with Corhampton with Exton, 1968-74; Asst Bishop, Dio. Portsmouth, 1968-75; Hon. Canon of Portsmouth Cathedral, 1968-76; Canon Emeritus, 1976-. Hon. Fellow, St Peter's College, Oxford, 1968-. *Address:* Flint Cottage, 53 Ridgway Road, Farnham, Surrey GU9 8NR. *T:* Farnham 5889. [*Died* 5 *Aug.* 1977.

WOOLNOUGH, Rev. Canon Howard Frank, OBE 1957; Canon of Manchester Cathedral, 1934-60, Canon Emeritus since 1960; *b* 28 Feb. 1886; *e s* of Howard James and Fanny Kate Woolnough; unmarried. *Educ:* Christ's Coll., Cambridge (MA). Army, 1914-18; Ridley Hall, Cambridge, 1918; Asst Curate St Paul, Cheltenham, 1919-26; Chaplain Christ's College, Cambridge, 1924-34; Gen. Sec., Central Advisory Council of

Training for the Ministry, 1927-34. Chairman, Chaplains' Committee, Air Cadet Council, 1941-67. *Address:* 20 Blackfield Lane, Manchester 7. *T:* 061-792 1769. [*Died* 21 *May* 1973.

WOOTTEN, Maj.-Gen. Richard Montague, CB 1940; MC; *b* 19 June 1889; *s* of William Montague Wootten, Headington House, Oxon; *m* 1st, 1915, *d* of Sir John Wormald, KBE; two *d* ; 2nd, *d* of William Percival. *Educ:* Rugby; RMC Sandhurst; Staff College, Camberley. 2nd Lieut 6th Dragoons, 1909; Major Queen's Bays, 1921; served European War, France and Belgium, 1914-18 (MC); Instructor Staff Coll., 1928-31; CO The Queen's Bays, 1932-36; Dep. Dir-Gen., TA, 1938-39, Dep. QMG for US Forces; Palestine and Egypt, 1936-39; War of 1939-45 (CB, Commander Legion of Merit, USA). Retired, 1945. *Address:* Little Court, Cromwell Gardens, Marlow, Bucks. *T:* 4246.
[*Died* 14 *May* 1979.

WORKMAN, Harold, RBA, ROI, RSMA, RCA, FPhS; Painter in oil and water colour; Lecturer on colour and pigments, and demonstrator of landscape painting; Visiting master, Sir John Cass College, and Hammersmith School of Arts and Crafts; *b* 3 Oct. 1897; 3rd *s* of Ernest Workman, Decorator and Contractor; *m* 1st, (marr. diss.); 2nd, 1958, Margaret Joan, *d* of E. J. Stokes, Darlington. *Educ:* Private School and Tutor; Oldham and Manchester Schools of Art. Exhibitor at Principal exhibitions in Europe, Toronto, and New York; International Exhibitions, Pittsburg and Ghent; numerous works in permanent collections including Manchester, Salford, Oldham, Northampton and Bournemouth; RBA 1937; ROI 1948; RSMA 1962; RCA 1950; Member Manchester Academy of Fine Arts; Pres. United Society of Artists; formerly Art Master and Lecturer at Architectural Assoc. *Publications:* Polymer Painting, 1967; series of articles on Oil Painting, 1945-46. *Recreations:* motoring, chess, billiards. *Address:* 3 Olney House, 51 Palace Road, East Molesey, Surrey. *T:* 01-979 5139. *Club:* Arts.
[*Died* 18 *May* 1975.

WORKMAN, William Thomas, CBE 1919; MC, BA (Hons); Headmaster Alleyne's Grammar School, Stevenage, retired; 2nd *s* of Charles Workman, RHA, and Elizabeth Wilkes; *m* 1919, Veronica Grace Moore; one *d. Educ:* privately; Clevedon; Paris; Rome. Schoolmaster and Journalist, USA, Canada and England; served with Canadians, European War (despatches, CBE, MC). *Recreations:* cricket and golf; first winner of The Bandit's Driver at Knebworth Golf Club. *Address:* Gaerwen, Grenville Road, Salcombe, Devon. [*Died* 15 *Dec.* 1971.

WORLEY, Sir Newnham (Arthur), KBE 1958; Kt 1950; *b* 2 March 1892; *y s* of late Charles Worley, Reigate; *m* 1919, Marie (*d* 1966), *d* of late Rev. R. R. Forlong; two *d. Educ:* Reigate Grammar Sch.; Emmanuel Coll., Cambridge (MA). Barrister-at-law, Inner Temple; Hon. Bencher, Inner Temple, 1959. Malayan CS, 1914-37; Colonial Legal Service, Solicitor General Straits Settlement, 1937; Puisne Judge, Supreme Court, Singapore, 1941-47; interned by Japanese, 1942-45; Chief Justice, British Guiana, and a Member of West Indian Court of Appeal, 1947-51; President, E. African Court of Appeal, Oct. 1955-April 1958 (Vice-President, 1951-55); retired from Overseas Judiciary, 1958; Chief Justice, Bermuda, 1958, resigned 1960. *Address:* 33 Castle Garden, Petersfield, Hants. *T:* 3857. [*Died* 13 *May* 1976.

WORMALD, Francis, CBE 1969; MA, LittD, FBA, FSA; President, Society of Antiquaries of London, 1965-70; Hon. Fellow Magdalene Coll., Cambridge, 1961; *b* 1 June 1904; *m* 1935, Honoria Mary Rosamund Yeo. *Educ:* Eton; Magdalene Coll., Cambridge. Asst Keeper, Dept of Manuscripts, British Museum, 1927-49; Prof. of Paleography, London Univ., 1950-60; Prof. of History and Dir, Inst. of Historical Research, London Univ., 1960-67. Member: Inst. for Advanced Study, Princeton, 1955-56; Royal Commn on Historical Monuments, 1957; Advisory Council on Public Records, 1965-67; Trustee, British Museum, 1967-; Governor, London Museum, 1971-. FKC 1964. Membre adhérent de la Société des Bollandistes, 1960; Corresp. Fellow, German Archæol Inst., 1962. Hon. DUniv York, 1969. *Publications:* English Kalendars before AD 1100, 1934, English Benedictine Kalendars after AD 1100, 2 vols, 1939, 1946, English Drawings of the 10th and 11th Centuries, 1952; Miniatures in the Gospels of St Augustine, 1954. Style and Design in the Bayeux Tapestry in Phaidon Press's The Bayeux Tapestry, 1957; Liturgical and Palæographical Appendixes in H. Buchthal's Miniature Painting in the Latin Kingdom of Jerusalem, 1957; with O. Pächt and C. R. Dodwell, The St Albans Psalter, 1960. Articles in Analecta Bollandiana, Archæologia, Antiquaries Journal, Proc. Walpole Society, etc. *Address:* 59 Warwick Square, SW1. *Club:* Reform. [*Died* 11 *Jan.* 1972.

WORSLEY, Rev. Richard, SJ; MA Oxon; *b* 6 Dec. 1889. *Educ:* Stonyhurst; Oxford. Taught at Mount St Mary's Coll., St Francis Xavier's Coll., Liverpool, and Wimbledon Coll.; Professor of Logic at Heythrop Coll.; Headmaster of Stonyhurst Coll., 1929-32. Served as Army Chaplain, War of 1939-45. *Address:* St Joseph's Priory, Harrow Road West, Dorking, Surrey. *T:* 2824.   *[Died 28 April 1972.*

WORSLEY, Col Sidney John, DSO 1919; MC; TD; Hon. MA Oxford; Hon. LLD Exeter; BA (London) 1923; Fellow of King's College, London, 1937; Member of Council of King's College, London, since 1939; Member of Senate, University of London, 1946-59; Chairman of External Council, 1948; *b* 1895; *m* 1924, Marie Léodine Versnel, Edgbaston; two *d. Educ:* University College, Nottingham; King's Coll., London. Served European War, 1914-19 (wounded, despatches, MC with two bars, DSO). Senior Secretary and Deputy Academic Registrar University of London, 1923-28; Warden of University College Hall, Ealing, 1923-24; Deputy Education Officer, County of Southampton, 1928-30; Academic Registrar, University of London, 1930-45; Principal, College of Estate Management, 1945-55. Colonel Comdg. University of London Contingent, Senior Division, OTC, 1938-40 and 1947-49; Acting Principal of University of London, 1936-37. Military representative Joint Recruiting Board, London University, 1939-40; General Staff, War Office, 1940-44; Chairman, Military Education Cttee, University of London, 1944-45; Chairman Board of Military Studies, 1946; Almoner, Christ's Hospital, 1946-56; Mem. SE Metropolitan Regional Hosp. Board, 1947-49. Governor: Wye Coll., 1946-55; LSE, 1955; Sec., Inter-University Council for Higher Education Overseas, 1955-59; Academic Sec., University College, Ibadan, Nigeria, 1959-60; Sec., Gilchrist Educational Trust, 1961-73; Adviser to Overseas Students, Inst. of Education, 1960-65. *Address:* 79 Cloncurry Street, SW6. *Club:* Royal Commonwealth Society.   *[Died 21 Dec. 1974.*

WORSLEY, Colonel Sir William Arthington, 4th Bt, *cr* 1838; late Green Howards; *b* 5 April 1890; *s* of Sir William Worsley, 3rd Bt, and Augusta Mary (*d* 1913), *e d* of Edward Chivers Bower, Broxholme, Scarborough; *S* father, 1936; *m* 1924, Joyce Morgan, *d* of Sir John Brunner, 2nd Bt; three *s* one *d. Educ:* Eton; New Coll., Oxford. Joined Green Howards, 1912; served European War, 1914-19 (wounded and prisoner); retired, 1922; rejoined Green Howards, 1939; retired, 1941. Lord Lieutenant, North Riding of Yorkshire, 1951-65; County Alderman N Riding of Yorks. President: Yorkshire Agricultural Society, 1959; Yorks County Cricket Club, 1960-. President of the MCC, 1961-62. Hon. LLD Leeds, 1967. *Recreations:* cricket, golf, shooting. *Heir: s* William Marcus John Worsley, MP. *Address:* Hovingham Hall, York. *TA:* Hovingham. *T:* Hovingham 206. *Clubs:* Bath, Yorkshire (York).   *[Died 4 Dec. 1973.*

WORSNOP, Bernard Lister, BSc, PhD, FInstP; *b* Bradford, 11 Nov. 1892; *s* of Julius Worsnop and Marie Aykroyd; *m* 1st, Nellie (*d* 1951), *d* of J. H. Wilkinson, Heaton, Bradford; one *s* one *d*; 2nd, Caryl Boyce Gale, *d* of late A. E. Gale, Farnham, Surrey. *Educ:* Carlton Sch., Bradford; King's Coll., London. BSc (1st Class Hons Physics), 1913; AKC 1914; Jelf Medallist, 1913; Layton Research Scholar, 1914; PhD 1927. Served in European War, 1915-19 (i/c X-ray Department, Military Hospital, Cosham, 1915-16; Sound Ranging in France, 1916-19 (Captain, RE); Lecturer in Physics, King's Coll., London, 1919; later Senior Lecturer and Sub-Dean of the Faculty of Science and Lecturer in Radiology, King's College; Head of Dept of Mathematics and Physics, The Polytechnic, Regent Street, 1933-37; Head of Quintin School, 1937-58. Major commanding LU OTC Survey Co., 1923-35; President of the Field Survey Association, 1930-31. *Publications:* Advanced Practical Physics (with H. T. Flint); X-Rays; originator and general editor of Methuen's Monographs on Physical Subjects; original papers in scientific journals. *Address:* Pennyfarthings, 11 Higher Woolbrook Park, Sidmouth, Devon. *T:* Sidmouth 2068.
                          [Died 23 Aug. 1980.

WORSTER-DROUGHT, Charles, MA, MD Cantab, FRCP, FCST (Hon.); MRCS, etc.; Hon. Consulting Physician and Neurologist to the Metropolitan Hospital; Hon. Consulting Physician West End Hospital for Neurology, and formerly Director of Department of Speech Disorders; Consulting Neurologist and formerly Lecturer in Neurology, Bethlem Royal Hospital; Hon. Consulting Physician-Neurologist to Royal Marsden Hospital, Leatherhead Hospital, National Institute for the Blind; Hon. Medical Director Moor House School for Speech Disorders, Hurst Green, Surrey; *s* of Thomas C. W. and Louise W. Drought, County Tyrone; *m* 1st, Lilian (*d* 1953), *d* of William T. Revnell; 2nd, Marjorie, *d* of Rev. A. J. Revnell. *Educ:* Merchant Taylors' Sch.; Downing Coll., Cambridge (Scholar and Prizeman). Natural Science Tripos, 1st

Class honours, 1910; Guy's Hospital; MRCS 1911; MB, ChB, 1912; MA 1912; MD Cambridge, MRCP 1919; FRCP 1925; Clinical Assistant, Department for Diseases of Nervous System, Guy's Hospital, 1911-14; Captain, RAMC, 1914-19 (European War); Consulting Neurologist, Woolwich Military District, 1917-19, also Tetanus Officer and other medical offices; Fearnsides Scholar in Organic Neurology, University of Cambridge, 1921; FRSM (sometime President, 1947-49) Neurological Section and Member of Council Neurological, Ophthalmological, Psychiatry and Children's Diseases Sections); Consultant Neurologist in EMS, 1939-44. *Publications:* papers and articles on medical subjects, speech disorders and organic diseases of the nervous system, including monographs on Cerebro-Spinal Fever, 1919, Neurosyphilis, 1941; Residential Speech Therapy, 1952, and chapters on Neurological subjects in Oxford Loose-leaf Medicine, British Encyclopædia of Medical Practice, Modern Trends in Neurology and Medical Evidence in Cases of Personal Injury, etc. *Recreations:* various. *Address:* Rider's Cottage, White Hill, Bletchingley, Surrey. *T:* Caterham 45055. *Club:* United University.   *[Died 28 Oct. 1971.*

WORT, Sir Alfred William Ewart, Kt 1939; Barrister; *b* 17 March 1883; *e s* of Alfred and Annie Elizabeth Wort; *m* 1st, Isabelle Mary (*d* 1954), 3rd *d* of Rev. E. Henderson; two *d* (one *s* decd); 2nd, Nancye, *d* of John James Simpson. Engaged in commerce, City of London; journalist until 1913; called to Bar, Middle Temple, 1914; Judge High Court, Patna, India, 1927-40; Acting Chief Justice, 1933, 1936 and 1938. President, Bihar College, University of Patna, 1928-40; President, Council, High Sch., Patna, 1927-40; Member, Diocesan Conference (Sarum), 1946; Chairman Medical Appeal Tribunal, 1949; Divorce Commissioner, 1948; now retired. *Recreations:* angling and agriculture. *Address:* 2 Paper Buildings, Temple, EC4.
                          [Died 1 Feb. 1976.

WORTHINGTON-EVANS, Sir (William) Shirley (Worthington), 2nd Bt, *cr* 1916; His Honour Judge Worthington-Evans; a Judge of the County Courts for Brentford and Uxbridge since 1957; *b* 9 June 1904; *o s* of The Rt Hon. Sir Laming Worthington-Evans, 1st Bt, GBE, MP, and late Gertrude Annie, CBE 1939, *d* of William Hale; *S* father, 1931; *m* 1st, 1928, Joan Irene (who obtained a divorce, 1943), *er d* of W. H. K. Pears, New Chapel House, Lingfield, Surrey; two *d*; 2nd, Hazel Wells, *o d* of Fearnley Wells Owen. *Educ:* Eton; Trinity Coll., Cambridge (BA). Called to Bar, 1927. Commissioned in RA, Sept. 1939. *Recreations:* golf, tennis. *Heir:* none. *Address:* 29 Eaton Square, SW1. *T:* 01-235 2870. *Club:* White's.
                          [Died 31 July 1971 (ext).

WOTHERSPOON, (George) Ralph (Howard); writer and journalist; *b* 1897; *o s* of George Wotherspoon, MA (sometime Vice-Master, King's College School) and Juliana Mary, *d* of Henry Norton, JP, Green Hill, Carmarthen, Wales; unmarried. *Educ:* Eastbourne Coll.; Merton Coll., Oxford. BA Distinction Honour School English Literature. War service, 1915-19, 5th Bn Queen's Royal West Surreys (TF) and Royal Garrison Artillery; War Service, 1940-41, AOER, Captain, General List; Embarkation Staff Officer Movement Control Southampton, Liverpool; invalided, Oct. 1941; Ministry of Supply, 1942; Ministry of Information, 1943; Regional Press Officer, London and SE Region, 1944-45; Member original Cherwell Editorial Staff, 1920-21; Editorial Staff, George Newnes & Co. Ltd, 1923; Private Secretary to late Henry Arthur Jones, Dramatist, 1923; to Colonel Hon. Angus McDonnell, 1924; Vice-Chairman Kent Federation Junior Imperial League since inception 1928 until 1933; Secretary of Primrose League, 1935-40; as a writer has contributed extensively in prose and verse to leading humorous journals, magazines, newspapers, etc.; first wrote for Punch, 1924 (Woon, 1928); Member contrib. staff of services paper Blighty, 1939-45; Director, Smith and Whiley Theatrical Productions, 1948-61 (original backer of Agatha Christie's play, The Mousetrap, 1951). *Publications:* Ready-Made Rhymes, 1927; (with Aubrey Hammond) Jack and Jill, the Underground Fairy Tale, 1932-33; (with L. N. Jackson) Some Sports and Pastimes of the English, 1937; (with L. N. Jackson) numerous broadcasts from BBC West Regional, including serial sketches, The Life We Lead; one-act play, All in The Day's Work. *Recreations:* formerly playing, now watching Rugby football; golf, fishing, motoring, railways. *Address:* Charterhouse, EC1. *Clubs:* Royal Automobile, (Senior Member) Myrmidon, Mousetrap.   *[Died 12 March 1979.*

WOTHERSPOON, Robert Andrew, DL; solicitor; Clerk of the County Council of North Riding of Yorkshire, 1960-74; Clerk to the Lieutenancy, 1962-74; *b* 18 May 1912; *s* of James A. Wotherspoon, Burnley, Lancs; *m* 1937, Mary Beryl, *d* of Robert Casson Jackson; one *s* one *d. Educ:* Burnley Sch.; Manchester

Univ. RAF, General Duties, 1940-45. Deputy Clerk of the Peace and of County Council of Derbyshire, 1951-60; Clerk of the Peace, NR Yorks, 1960-71. Pres., Yorks Parish Councils Assoc., 1975. DL NR Yorks, 1973. *Address:* Cotescue Park, Middleham, Leyburn, Yorks. *T:* Coverdale 269. *Club:* Royal Automobile. [*Died 6 Oct. 1975.*

WRAXALL, Sir Morville (William Lascelles), 8th Bt, *cr* 1813; on staff of a rubber company from 1947; *b* 11 June 1922; *o s* of Sir Charles Wraxall, 7th Bt and Marceline, *d* of O. Cauro, of Cauro, Corsica; *S* father 1951; *m* 1956, Irmgard Wilhelmina Maria Schnidrig, Basle, Switzerland; two *s* one *d*. *Educ:* St Mark's Coll., Alexandria, Egypt. RASC 1940-46 (Africa Star and clasp). *Recreations:* gardening, woodwork, stamp collecting. *Heir: s* Charles Frederick Lascelles Wraxall, *b* 17 Sept. 1961. [*Died 19 July 1978.*

WRIGHT OF ASHTON UNDER LYNE, Baron, *cr* 1968 (Life Peer), of Ashton-under-Lyne; **Lewis Tatham Wright,** CBE 1964; General Secretary, Amalgamated Weavers' Association, 1953-68; Member, Advisory Council on Technology, since 1968; *b* 11 Oct. 1903; British; *m* 1933, Kathleen (*née* Firth); two *s*. *Educ:* Elementary and Secondary Schools. Ex-Weaver; Full-Time Trades Union Official since age of 24. Chairman, TUC, 1967-68, President, 1968. Member: NBPI, 1968-71; Staff Commn for England, DHSS, 1972; CEGB, 1968-73. Pres., Textile Inst., 1969-71. CompTI, 1971. Hon. DTech Loughborough, 1968. *Recreations:* gardening, travel; Member Manchester United FC. *Address:* Brookfield Grove, Ashton-under-Lyne, Lancs. *T:* (home) 061-330 4122. [*Died 15 Sept. 1974.*

WRIGHT, Sir Andrew Barkworth, KCMG 1948 (CMG 1941); CBE 1932; MC; MA; *b* 30 Nov. 1895; *er s* of late Rev. H. L. Wright, Church Knowle Rectory, Dorset, and Emma, *d* of Rev. S. M. Barkworth, DD, and Ellen Janson; *m* Rosemary, CStJ, *o d* of late Geoffrey Barrett; one *s* one *d* (and one *d* decd). *Educ:* The Old Ride Prep. Sch.; Haileybury; Jesus Coll., Cambridge (Scholar, 1914). Served European War with Suffolk Regt, 1914-19 (immediate award of MC, Hargicourt, 1917, and of bar to MC, Battle of the Lys, 1918); Platoon Comdr, Somme, 1916; Co. Comdr, Arras, 1917; 2 i/c Bn, 1918; Major, Reserve of Officers, 1920; Civil Administration, Cyprus, from 1922 (CBE for services as acting Colonial Secretary during disturbances, 1931); Colonial Secretary, Cyprus, 1937; re-employed in Army, rank of Lieut-Colonel, and served with Middle East Forces, May 1940-Sept. 1942; Colonial Secretary, Trinidad, 1943-46; Governor and C-in-C of the Gambia, 1946-49; Governor and C-in-C, Cyprus, 1949-54. KStJ 1950. *Address:* c/o Midland Bank, Market Hill, Cambridge. *Club:* Travellers'. [*Died 24 March 1971.*

WRIGHT, A(rthur) Dickson, MS, MB, FRCS; DTM&H; Senior Consulting Surgeon St Mary's Hospital and Prince of Wales Hospital; Consulting Surgeon to Society for Propagation of the Gospel, Concert Artists Assoc. and British Railways; *s* of late Dr Edward Wright, Dublin; *m* Molly Bath (*d* 1975); one *s* three *d*. *Educ:* St Mary's Hosp. Late Assistant Dir of Surgical Unit, St Mary's Hospital; House Surgeon, Assistant in Neurological Department, and Ear, Nose, and Throat Department; House Surgeon, North Middlesex Hospital; Professor of Clinical Surgery, Singapore School of Medicine; Acting Senior Surgeon, Singapore; Hon. Surgeon, St Andrew's Hospital, Singapore. Past President: Brit. Soc. of Neurological Surgeons; Med. Soc. of London; Hunterian Soc.; Harveian Soc.; Clinical, Protological and Surgical Sections, RSM; Inst. of British Surgical Technicians; Hervey Tercentenary Congress, 1957; British Med. Reps Assoc.; Saints and Sinners Soc.; Osler Club; former Member of Council: RCS (late Vice-Pres.); BMA; Bd of Examrs, RCS; Examr, Manchester and Newcastle Univs; Bradshaw Lectr; Hunterian Orator, RCS, Hunterian Orator, Hunterian Soc.; Vice-Pres., Royal Inst. of Hygiene; Hon. Treas., Imp. Cancer Res. Fund; Hon. Member: Scandinavian Soc. of Neurosurgery; La Sociedad Luso-Española de Neurocirugia; FRSocMed; Hon. FCS(SoAf); Hon. FRCSI. *Publications:* numerous articles in Proc. RSM and medical press, also articles on Diseases of the Liver and Pancreas, Post-Graduate Surgery (Maingot); article on Infections of the Brain, Penicillin (Fleming). *Recreation:* nil. *Address:* Lister House, 12 Wimpole Street, W1. *T:* 01-580 2511. *Clubs:* Athenæum, Carlton, Garrick, Oriental, Royal Air Force. [*Died 6 Jan. 1976.*

WRIGHT, Prof. Bernard Arker; Professor Emeritus, University of Southampton; *b* 20 June 1893; *s* of Rev. James and Emily Wright (*née* Fisher); *m* 1923, Phyllis Adèle Lebus (*d* 1965); one *s*. *Educ:* Ashville Coll., Harrogate; Univ. of Manchester; Lincoln College, Oxford. Lecturer, Adult Education Department, University College, Nottingham, 1921-22; Lecturer in English, Glasgow Univ., 1922-38; Professor of English, University of Southampton, 1938-57. *Publications:* Milton's Shorter Poems,

1938; (ed) Milton's Poems (Everyman edition), 1956, Milton's Paradise Lost, 1962; contrib. to Modern Language Review, Review of English Studies, Notes and Queries, Library. *Address:* 210 Ashley Gardens, SW1. *T:* 01-828 2065. [*Died 7 June 1973.*

WRIGHT, Sir Charles Seymour, KCB 1946 (CB 1937); OBE, MC; MA; *b* Toronto, 1887; *s* of Alfred Wright, Toronto, and Katherine Kennedy; *m* 1914, Edith Mary Priestley; one *s* two *d*. *Educ:* Upper Canada College and University, Toronto; Gonville and Caius College, Cambridge University (Wollaston Student 1851 Exhibition Scholar). Research at Cavendish Laboratory 1908-10; Scientist British Antarctic Expedition 1910-13; Royal Engineers, 1914-18; Wireless 5th Corps (MC); OC Wireless II Army (Chevalier Legion of Honour); General Staff (Intelligence) GHQ (OBE); Admiralty Department of Scientific Research and Experiment, 1919-29; Superintendent, Admiralty Research Laboratory 1929-34; Director of Scientific Research, Admiralty, 1934-46; Chief of Royal Naval Scientific Service, 1946-47; Adviser, British Jt Services Mission, Navy Staff, 1948-51; Dir, Marine Physical Lab. of Scripps Instn of Oceanography, 1952-56. Contractor for Defence Research Board of Canada, 1956, retired 1969. Lecturer in Geophysics, Institute of Earth Sciences, Univ. of British Columbia, 1964-69, retired. Hon. DSc, British Columbia; Hon. LLD, Victoria. *Publications:* Scientific Reports. *Address:* Arbutus Road, Ganges, RR1, British Columbia, Canada. [*Died 1 Nov. 1975.*

WRIGHT, Dickson; *see* Wright, A. D.

WRIGHT, Ernest, CBE 1936; retired; Secretary Guildford Diocesan Board of Finance, 1940-48, thereafter working part-time at Diocesan House, Guildford, until retirement in 1967; *b* 22 April 1882; *s* of late Thomas Wright and Jane Taylor; *m* 1st, 1908, Irene Marion Bishop Ackerman (*d* 1954); two *s* one *d*; 2nd, 1959, Olive May Moody, *née* Ellis (*d* 1969). *Educ:* Privately; Kendrick Grammar School; University College, Reading. Banking: London and County Bank Ltd, 1900-03; Birmingham District and Counties Bank, 1905-06; Alliance Bank of Egypt, Cairo, 1919; Cox and Co., Cairo, Lloyds Bank Ltd, Cairo 1920-22, 1924-25; Bank of Abyssinia, Addis Ababa, 1926-31; Bank of Ethiopia, Addis Ababa (Sub-Governor and Director), 1931-36. Farming: Canada, Manitoba, 1904; Egypt, Kharga Oasis, Libyan Desert, 1910-15; South Africa, Cape Province, 1922-23; Enemy Licensing Office, Public Custodian's Office, Ministry of Finance, Cairo, 1915-19. Officier, Ordre de Menelik II, 1934. *Recreations:* golf, riding, walking. *Address:* Ludshott Manor, near Bramshott, Hants. [*Died 21 April 1974.*

WRIGHT, Frank T. W.; *see* Wynyard-Wright.

WRIGHT, Lt-Col Herbert James, CMG 1917; Company Director; *b* 1888; *s* of Thomas Wright; *m* 1910, Winifred Alice Croxon (decd); two *s* two *d*. Served War, 1914-18; War of 1939-45 as Commanding Officer, permanent Ships' Staff, 1941. *Recreation:* bowls. *Address:* 40 Fidden's Wharf Road, Killara, NSW 2071, Australia. *T:* 49.3276. [*Died 30 Nov. 1974.*

WRIGHT, Prof. John George, DSc (Hon.); Dr med. vet. (Hon.); MVSc, FRCVS, DVA; Emeritus Professor of Veterinary Surgery, University of Liverpool, since 1963 (Professor, 1941-63); Dean of Faculty of Veterinary Science, 1952-61; *b* 2 Sept. 1897; *m* 1925, Elsie Lloyd Razey (*d* 1955); one *s* one *d*; *m* 1958, Winefred Mayor Jones. *Educ:* High School, Newport, Monmouthshire; Royal Veterinary College, London. Served European War, 1915-19, RFA; France, Belgium, South Russia. Royal Veterinary College, 1919-23; general veterinary practice, 1923-28; Staff of Royal Veterinary College, ending as Professor of Surgery, 1929-41. Member Inter-Univ. Council for Higher Education in the Colonies, 1945-56; Pres. Royal College of Veterinary Surgeons, 1951 and 1952; Fellow, Royal Veterinary Coll., 1965. *Publications:* Veterinary Anæsthesia, 1941, 1946, 1952, 1956, (with L. W. Hall) 1961; Veterinary Obstetrics (with F. Benesch), 1951 and (with G. H. Arthur), 1964. Numerous contribs to veterinary literature on the subjects of surgery, anæsthesia, obstetrics and diseases of reproduction. *Recreation:* gardening. *Address:* Wendover, Overdale Road, Willaston, Wirral, Cheshire. [*Died 26 Oct. 1971.*

WRIGHT, John Moncrieff, CBE 1920; ICS retired; *b* 1884; *s* of James Moncrieff Wright; *m* 1912, Leonore Ada Beddall (*d* 1959); one *s* (and one killed in action 1944). *Educ:* Dulwich College; Jesus College, Cambridge. 1st class Honours Classical Tripos, 1906; passed Indian Civil Service Examination, 1907; Assistant Commissioner Burma, 1908; Superintendent Chin Hills, 1913-19; Political Officer Operations, 1917-18; Deputy Commissioner Burma, 1920; Port Blair, 1921-24; Burma, 1925-27; Acting Chief Commissioner Andaman and Nicobar Islands, 1927-28; Bursar Malvern Girls' College, 1929-39; JP

Worcestershire, 1938-47; Ministry of Food, 1939-48, retired as Assistant Secretary and Director, Ancillary Materials. *Address:* Brookside, Winfrith, Dorset. *T:* Winfrith 239. *Club:* Oxford and Cambridge University. *[Died 18 Aug. 1971.*

WRIGHT, Kenneth Anthony, OBE 1953; Director: Harmony Films, I. R. Maxwell Film Distributors Ltd; Norman McCann Artists' Management; British National Song and Dance Co.; London Master Players' Orchestra; writer, adjudicator and lecturer; retired as Head of Music Productions, BBC Television; *b* 5 June 1899; *o s* of William John and Elizabeth Maria Wright; *m* 1931, Helen (marr. diss., 1946), 2nd *d* of John Crichton and Jeanie Forsyth Connal, Cambuslang; no *c* ; *m* 1947, Diana (marr. diss., 1962), *o d* of Lt-Col Newton Stirrett, OBE, MC and Desirée Ellinger; two *s* ; *m* 1963, Lilian Dorothy Letitia Calleia, *o d* of John Leslie and Lilian Tompkins, two *d* by previous marriage. *Educ:* City of Norwich Sch.; Sheffield Univ. BEng (Hons Mech. and Elec.), 1920; MEng, 1921; Cadet, RFC, Pte XIX Bn The London Regt, gazetted RE, 1919; Res. Engineer Metropolitan Vickers Co., Manchester, 1920-22, while continuing to pursue music energetically as hobby; after participating in pioneer experiments in Radio Telephony he combined engineering and music as first Director of Manchester Station (2ZY) of BBC 1922; subsequent career entirely in BBC. Asst Mus. Dir of Corporation, 1937; Overseas Mus. Dir, 1940-43; Dep. Dir of Music, 1944-47; Artists' Manager, 1948; Head of Music Programmes (Television), 1951; responsible for special projects involving television and music, 1956-59; retired Oct. 1959; rep. BBC, from 1930 onwards at many internat. music festivals, confs, etc., in Europe, USA, Canada; Mem. Jury first Salzburg internat. Comp. TV Opera, 1959. Hon. FTCL; co-produced and commentated film, Musicians to Moscow, with L. Kristy in two visits to USSR, 1954 and with O. Gajic, of Filmske Novosti, Summer in Dubrovnik, 1956. Prod. Symphony of Switzerland, 1959. Chevalier de la Légion d'Honneur, 1947. *Compositions:* many works for Brass and Military Bands, including Overture, Glendalough, and Rhapsodies, Irish Merry and Peddar's Way, 1937; Suite, Pride of Race, 1935, for National Festival, Crystal Palace; Peddars' Way, for Bell Vue, Leicestershire Rhapsody, 1971, etc. Composed (1946) Scores for Heart's Beloved (Richard Fisher); Shoemaker's Holiday (Dekker-Richard Fisher); Dear Beast (Joan Murray Simpson); Suite Tobacco, commissioned for BBC Light Music Festival, 1949. Guest of Honour, representing Llangollen, at inauguration of Australian Nat. Choral Festival, Hobart, 1975. *Publications:* Gentle are its Songs (also in Welsh, as Gwaraidd fydd ei gerddi fo), 1973; contribs to Grove's Dictionary and various jls. *Address:* 77 Ashworth Mansions, W9 1LN. *T:* 01-286 7495. *[Died 15 Jan. 1975.*

WRIGHT, Rev. Leslie, CBE 1952; MA (Lambeth), 1953; Vicar of St John's, Kingston Vale, SW15, 1961-68; Hon. Canon of Southwark Cathedral, 1960-68; Emeritus Canon since 1968; *b* 19 Nov. 1899; *s* of John Wright, Carlisle; *m* 1935, Katrina, *d* of Dr T. B. Gilbart-Smith, Nottingham; two *s*. *Educ:* St Bees, Cumberland; Royal Military Academy, Woolwich. Commissioned into Royal Artillery, Dec. 1919; retired, 1926. Travelling Secretary Officers' Christian Union, 1928-35; ordained, 1935; Curate St Andrews, Nottingham, 1935-36, when commissioned in RAF Chaplains' Branch; KHC, Chaplain-in-Chief Royal Air Force, 1949-53; Prebendary of St Botolph's in Lincoln Cathedral, 1950-May 1953; retired, 1953; Vicar of Wimbledon, 1953-61; Rural Dean, 1954-60. *Recreation:* golf. *Address:* Queen Oak House, Bourton, Gillingham, Dorset. *T:* Bourton 425. *[Died 28 April 1972.*

WRIGHT, Sir Michael (Robert), GCMG 1958 (KCMG 1951; CMG 1945); HM Diplomatic Service, retired; *b* 3 Dec. 1901; *s* of late Sir Robert Wright; *m* 1934, Esther (*d* 1976), *d* of late George Long; two *s*. *Educ:* Winchester; Balliol Coll., Oxford. Entered HM Diplomatic Service, 1926; Brit. Embassy, Washington, 1926-30; FO, 1930-36; Brit. Embassy, Paris, 1936-40; Cairo, 1940-43; Brit. Embassy, Washington, 1943-46; served on staff of Special Commissioner in South-East Asia, 1946-47; Assistant Under-Secretary of State, Foreign Office, 1947-50; Ambassador to Norway, 1951-54; Ambassador to Iraq, 1954-58; UK deleg. to Conf. for Cessation of Nuclear Tests, Geneva, 1959; to 10 Power and 18 Power Disarmament Confs, Geneva, 1960 and 1962; Chm., Atlantic Trade Study. Director, Guinness Mahon Holdings Ltd, 1964-73. Mem. Bd, Internat. Movement for Atlantic Union; Founder Mem., British N American Cttee; Chm., Anglo-Norse Soc.; a Vice-Pres., Royal Geographical Soc., 1971-74. Mem., Inst. of Directors. Grand Cross, Order of St Olav (Norway) 1975. *Publication:* Disarm and Verify, 1964. *Recreations:* fishing, ski-ing. *Clubs:* St James', Norske. *[Died 10 June 1976.*

WRIGHT, Rear-Adm. Noel, CB 1946; OBE 1919; retired; *b* 24 Dec. 1890; 4th *s* of late William Wright, JP, Whitby, Yorks; *m* 1921, Phœbe, *o d* of J. Gandon, Smyrna; one *s* one *d*. *Educ:* St Helen's College, Southsea. Entered Navy, 1908; Paymaster Captain, 1939; acting Rear-Admiral (S), 1944. Fleet Supply Officer, Mediterranean and Levant 1942-43; Command Supply Officer Western Approaches, 1944-45. Sponsored British Cape Britannia Expedition, in hopes of finding a message deposited by Sir John Franklin, 1962. Gave to Prime Minister the "Resolute" bell to present to President of USA, 1965. *Publications:* Glimpses of South Africa; Sun of Memory; New Light on Franklin (privately printed); Quest for Franklin, 1959. *Recreations:* literary research and gardening. *Address:* 46 Little Green, Alverstoke, Hants. *T:* Gosport 81567. *[Died 18 April 1975.*

WRIGHT, Lt-Col Robert Ernest, CIE 1929; BA (Sen. Mod.), MD, MCh (Hon.), DPH (TCD), IMS retired; late Professor of Ophthalmology Medical College and Superintendent Government Ophthalmic Hospital, Madras, India; *b* 1884; *s* of R. Wright, JP, of Prumplestown, Carlow, Ireland; *m* 1930, Ruby Evelyn Sheldon, *d* of Dr S. T. Pruen, Cheltenham. *Educ:* Trinity College, Dublin. Graduated with Honours in 1906, taking Large Gold Medal and Senior Moderatorship in Natural Science; also Med. Travelling Prize; joined the IMS 1907; served in Burma with the Hpi-maw Expedition, 1910; Assistant Director Pasteur Institute of S India, 1912; served in Mesopotamia European War (despatches); brevet promotion to Major, 1915; Lieut-Col, 1927; retired, 1938; Member Internat. Council of Ophthalmology, 1929-39. Re-employed by W. D. as Ophth. Specialist, 1939-46. *Publications:* various papers in Medical Literature dealing chiefly Clinical Ophthalmology, biological and ophthalmological research. *Recreations:* shooting, fishing. *Address:* c/o Barclays Bank, Fleet, Hants. *Club:* East India, Sports and Public Schools. *[Died 22 Dec. 1977.*

WRIGHT, Adm. Sir Royston (Hollis), GBE 1964; KCB 1961 (CB 1958); DSC 1941 and Bar 1944; *b* 29 September 1908; *s* of Thomas Henry and Lydia Maude Wright; *m* 1945, Betty Lilian (*née* Gladstone), widow of Lieutenant (E) J. E. Ackery, DSC, RN; no *c*. *Educ:* Haileybury College, Hertford. Naval Cadet, 1927; Comdr 1940; comd HM Ships: Beagle, 1939-41; Derwent, 1942; Hurworth, 1943; Capt. 1946; commanded HM Ships: Wakeful, 1948-49; Triumph, 1953-54; Director of Manning, Admiralty, 1950-51; Imperial Defence Coll., 1952; Cdre Royal Naval Barracks, Devonport, 1955-56; Promoted Rear-Adm. 1956; Asst Chief of Naval Staff, 1956-58; Vice-Adm., 1959; Flag Officer Flotillas, Home Fleet, 1958-59; Flag Officer, Scotland, Dec. 1959-61; a Lord Comr of the Admiralty, Second Sea Lord and Chief of Naval Personnel, 1961-64; Admiral, 1962; Chief of Naval Personnel and Second Sea Lord, Ministry of Defence, 1964-65; retd 1965. Aristeon Amdrias (Greek Gold Medal for Valour), 1944. *Recreations:* fishing, shooting. *Address:* Danewell House, Downton, Wilts. *[Died 18 July 1977.*

WRIGHT, Samuel, CB 1949; JP; lately Director of Establishments, and Under Secretary, Ministry of Power, retired 1959; *b* 1895; *o surv. s* of late Samuel Wright, HM Inland Revenue; *m* 1923, Dorothy (*d* 1965), *d* of late G. P. Chapman, Wells, Somerset; one *s*. *Educ:* High Pavement Sch.; University Coll., Nottingham. Entered Civil Service, 1913; National Health Insurance Commission, England, 1913-19; Ministry of Health, 1919-40; Mines and Petroleum Depts, 1940-42; Ministry of Fuel and Power, now Ministry of Power, 1942-59. JP Surrey, 1951. *Address:* 2 Ashley Close, Walton-on-Thames. *T:* Walton-on-Thames 20820. *Club:* Reform. *[Died 1 Dec. 1975.*

WRIGHT, Samuel John, MA, retired; *b* 14 April 1899; *s* of S. J. Wright, Taunton; *m* 1924, Violet, *d* of W. S. Bond; two *s* two *d*. *Educ:* Wellington, Somerset; Emmanuel Coll., Cambridge. Served European War, 1917-19, Lieut, RE; Engineering Dept National Physical Laboratory, 1923-26 and 1927-29; Director: Institute for Research in Agricultural Engineering, 1937-42; National Institute of Agricultural Engineering, 1942-47; Consulting Engineer to Royal Agricultural Society, 1931-64; Agricultural Adviser to Ford Motor Co. Ltd, 1947-64. *Publications:* many papers on engineering research and mechanized farming. *Address:* 6 College Road, Cheltenham, Glos. *T:* Cheltenham 53158. *[Died 30 June 1975.*

WRIGHTSON, Edmund Harry Paul Garmondsway, QC 1963; a Recorder, since 1972 (Recorder of Walsall, 1965-71); *b* 31 Jan. 1919; *o s* of late Lt-Comdr E. G. Wrightson, DSO, RNR, and Mrs Rose Wrightson; *m* 1942, Mary, *o c* of late Major L. C. Dickens, MC, and of Mrs Dickens, Froxfield, Hants; three *d*. *Educ:* Marlborough Coll.; Hertford Coll., Oxford (MA). Called to Bar, Lincoln's Inn, 1942, Buchanan Prize; Bencher, 1971. Oxford Circuit. *Recreations:* wireless telegraphy, astronomy, lawn tennis, golf. *Address:* 5 Paper Buildings, Temple, EC4. *T:* 01-353 7811; 4 Milborne Grove, SW10. *Clubs:* United University, Roehampton. *[Died 22 Jan. 1972.*

WRIGLEY, Sir John Crompton, KBE 1944; CB 1941; *b* 8 Feb. 1888; *s* of George Wrigley, Bury, Lancs; *m* 1919, Jane Elizabeth Pollard; two *s* one *d. Educ:* Bury Grammar Sch., Lancs; Corpus Christi Coll., Cambridge. Entered Local Government Board, 1912; Principal, Ministry of Health, 1919; Assistant Secretary, 1930; Principal Assistant Secretary, 1936; Acting Deputy Secretary, 1941-43, Joint Dep. Secretary, 1943-51; Joint Deputy Secretary, Ministry of Housing and Local Government, 1951-52 (formerly Ministry of Local Government and Planning); retired, 1952. *Address:* Over Chess, Chorleywood, Rickmansworth, Herts WD3 5SB. *T:* Chorleywood 2146. *[Died 7 June 1977.*

WRINCH, Dorothy, BA, MA (Cantab); MSc, DSc (London); MA, DSc (Oxon); Sophia Smith Fellow of Smith College, USA, 1966 (Visiting Professor, 1954-59; Visiting Research Professor, 1959-66); *e d* of late Hugh Wrinch, MIMechE; *m* 1922, J. W. Nicholson, FRS (marr. diss., 1938; he *d* 1955); one *d*; *m* 1941, Otto Charles Glaser (*d* 1951), Prof. of Biology, Amherst Coll. *Educ:* Girton Coll., Cambridge (Scholar); Mathematical Tripos (Wrangler), and Moral Sciences Tripos; Yarrow Fellow of Girton Coll., 1920-24, Hertha Ayrton Fellow, 1930-34; University and King's Colls, Univ. of London; Univs of Oxford, Vienna and Paris. Lectr in Pure Mathematics, University College London, 1918-20, Mem., Research Staff, 1920-24, Hon. Research Associate, Biochem. Dept, 1960. Mem., Faculty of Physical Sciences, Oxford Univ., 1922-39; Sec. Mathematics sub-section, British Assoc., 1932-38; Res. Fellow, Rockefeller Foundn, 1935-41; Carlisle Res. Fellow, Somerville Coll., Oxford, 1939-41; Lectr in Chemistry, Johns Hopkins Univ., USA, 1939-41; Vis. Lectr at Amherst, Mt Holyoke and Smith Colls, 1941-42; Lectr, Smith Coll., 1942-54; Mem. Corp. of Marine Biol. Lab., Woods Hole, 1943. Fellow, Amer. Phys. Soc., 1942; Member: Amer. Chem. Soc.; Amer. Crystallographic Soc.; Peptide and Crystallography Gp, Chemical Soc., London; X-Ray Analysis Gp, Phys. Soc., London. *Publications:* Fourier Transforms and Structure Factors, 1946 (repr. 1966); Chemical Aspects of the Structure of Small Peptides: an introduction, 1960; Chemical Aspects of Polypeptide Chain Structures and the Cyclol Theory, 1965; papers on epistemology, probability, pure and applied mathematics, physics, chemistry and biology. *Recreations:* playing piano duets, swimming, conversation. *Address:* Clark Science Center, Smith College, Northampton, Mass 01060, USA; Greenhaven, Woods Hole, Mass 02543, USA. *Club:* English-Speaking Union. *[Died 11 Feb. 1976.*

WROTTESLEY, 5th Baron, *cr* 1838; **Richard John Wrottesley,** Bt 1642; MC; Major, Royal Horse Guards (Reserve); *b* 7 July 1918; *s* of Hon. Walter Bennet Wrottesley (*yr s* of 3rd Baron); *S* uncle, 1962; *m* 1st, 1941, Roshnara Barbara (marr. diss., 1949), *o d* of Captain Esmé Cecil Wingfield-Stratford; (one *s* decd); 2nd, 1949, Joyce Marion (marr. diss., 1953), *d* of late Frederick A. Wallace; one *s*; 3rd, 1955, Mary Ada Van Echten, *o d* of Edgar Dryden Tudhope; two *s. Educ:* Harrow; RMC, Sandhurst. Served War of 1939-45 (MC). Royal Rhodesia Regt, 1961-66. OStJ 1971. *Recreations:* fishing, shooting, riding. *Heir: g s* Clifton Hugh Lancelot de Verdon Wrottesley, *b* 10 Aug. 1968. *Address:* De Verdon House, Josephine Road, Claremont, Cape, South Africa. *Clubs:* Cavalry and Guards, Lansdowne, Hurlingham; Civil Service (Cape Town); Seven Seas (Simonstown). *[Died 23 Oct. 1977.*

WUNDERLY, Sir Harry Wyatt, Kt 1954; MD, FRCP; Director of Tuberculosis, Commonwealth Department of Health, Canberra, 1947-57; retired; *b* Camberwell, Vic, Aust., 30 May 1892; *s* of late James Wunderly; *m* 1919, Alice J. B., *d* of Alfred J. Barker. *Educ:* Wesley Coll., Melbourne; Queen's Coll., Melbourne. MB, ChB, Melbourne, 1915; MRCP 1925; MD Melbourne, 1927; FRACP, 1938; FRCP 1952. Formerly: Assistant Pathologist and Assistant Physician, Royal Adelaide Hospital; Member of Panel of Consultants on Tuberculosis, WHO HQ, 1957-. *Publications:* articles on tuberculosis in medical journals. *Address:* 53 Tasmania Circle, Forrest, ACT 2603, Australia. *T:* 731242. *Club:* Commonwealth (Canberra). *[Died 13 April 1971.*

WYETH, Rex; solicitor; a Recorder of the Crown Court, since 1972; *b* 11 Aug. 1914; *s* of William James and Edith Emily Wyeth; *m* 1st, 1939, Leah Nichols (*d* 1943); 2nd, 1947, Gabriele Bopst (*d* 1969); one *d. Educ:* Tolworth Council Sch.; Surbiton County Sch. Solicitor's Clerk, 1931; qual. Solicitor, 1939; served with RAOC, 1940-46; admitted Solicitor, 1946; in private practice thereafter. *Recreations:* indifferent golf and worse bridge. *Address:* 8 Stone Buildings, Lincoln's Inn, WC2A 3TA. *T:* 01-242 7588. *Club:* Golfers'. *[Died 23 Jan. 1978.*

WYLES, Lilian Mary Elizabeth, BEM 1949; retired (but lectures and broadcasts on police subjects and child welfare); *b* Bourne, Lincs, 1895; *d* of Joseph Wyles, brewer, and Julia Grylls Wyles, Bourne House, Bourne. *Educ:* Thanet Hall, Margate; privately. Joined Metropolitan Police, 1919; Sergeant, 1919; Inspector, 1922; transferred from Uniform Branch to CID, 1922; Chief Inspector, 1932. Organised Women's Branch of CID. Retired, 1949. *Publication:* A Woman at Scotland Yard (autobiography), 1952. *Recreations:* sailing, embroidery, cooking. *[Died 13 May 1975.*

WYLLIE, Lt-Col Harold, OBE 1919; VPRSMA; placed in charge of restoration of Implacable, 1932; late The Wiltshire Regt and RAF; Marine artist, sculptor and engraver; *b* 29 June 1880; *s* of late W. L. Wyllie, RA, and Marion Amy Wyllie; *m* Euphans Hilary Strain (*d* 1960), Hillhead of Dunkeld, Perthshire, portrait painter, *d* of late John Strain, Civil Engineer, Cassillis House, Ayrshire. *Educ:* Littlejohn's, Greenwich; Smythe's, Southsea. Destined for Navy; failed to pass examination; took up art; went to New York as special artist to the Graphic, 1898; received commission in the 4th Volunteer Bn, Royal West Kent Regt, 1900; South African War (Queen's Medal, 3 bars); temp. commission 2nd Bn The Buffs, 1902; exhibited in Royal Academy and Royal Institute of Painters in Water-colour; Exhibition Britain in Water Colours; Municipal Art Galleries all over England, by invitation. Served on Victory technical cttee, Council of Society for Nautical Research, and Museum Cttee of RUSI; a Vice-Pres., Soc. for Nautical Research, 1950; served in Royal Flying Corps in France, 1914-18, as pilot; granted permanent commission in Regular Army in the field and posted to Wiltshire Regt, 1916 (despatches, OBE, 1914 Star, war medal, victory medal); granted rank of Lieut-Colonel on retirement from Regular Army, 1920; served in Reserve of Air Force Officers, 1925-30, and re-qualified as Air Pilot, granted Hon. rank of Wing Commander on reaching age limit; temp. commission in RAFVR Oct. 1939; transferred to RNVR as Lieut for special duty, 1943; Acting Lieut-Commander, 1944; demobilised Nov. 1945; received RHS certificate; Hon. Marine painter to RYS, 1934; Member of Council of Society of Marine Artists, 1939, Vice-President, 1958-; Assoc. Member Instn of Naval Architects, 1959; Life Hon. Vice-President, The Navy League, 1961. *Recreation:* nautical research. *Address:* Hillhead of Dunkeld, Perthshire. *Clubs:* Royal Corinthian Yacht (Cowes); (Marine artist to), Royal Victoria Yacht (Ryde). *[Died 22 Dec. 1973.*

WYMER, Francis John, CBE 1943; *b* 6 Dec. 1898; *s* of Daniel William and Jean Renwick Wymer; *m* 1st, 1925, Dorothy Edith Kershaw (marr. diss., 1946); one *s*; 2nd, 1948, Elizabeth Mary Grisell Swanson, *yr d* of late Col J. J. C. Davidson, and Mrs Davidson, Cally, Blairgowrie, Perthshire. *Educ:* Merton Court, Sidcup; Eltham Coll., Mottingham. RGA 1917-19; entered service SE and C Ry, 1920; Asst to Traffic Manager, Southern Ry, 1932; Divisional Marine Manager, Dover, 1934; Asst Continental Supt, 1938; Asst to Gen. Manager, 1942; Asst Docks and Marine Manager, Southern Ry, 1945-47; Asst Chief Regional Officer, Southern Region, British Rys, 1951-55; Pres., Retired, Railway Officers' Soc., 1962-63; Pres., Old Southeronians. FCIT. Photography is now occupation. *Address:* East Lodge, Old Perry Street, Chislehurst, Kent. *[Died 26 March 1976.*

WYN-HARRIS, Sir Percy, KCMG 1952 (CMG 1949); MBE 1941; MA (Cantab); *b* 24 Aug. 1903; *e s* of late Percy Martin Harris, JP, and Catherine Mary Davies; *m* 1st, 1932, Mary M. Macdonald (*d* 1976), *d* of late Ranald Macdonald, CBE, Christchurch, New Zealand; one *s*; 2nd, 1976, Mrs Julie Gunning-Scheltema, *widow* of late M. F. Gunning, MRINA. *Educ:* Gresham's Sch.; Caius Coll., Cambridge. Colonial Administrative Service, 1926; District Officer, Kenya, 1926-45; Settlement Officer (Kikuyu Land Claims), 1939-40; District Commissioner, Nyeri, 1941-43; Labour Liaison Officer, Kenya, 1943; Labour Comr, 1944-46. Provincial Comr, Kenya, 1945; Chief Native Comr and Mem. for African Affairs on Executive Council, Kenya, 1947-49; Governor and C-in-C of the Gambia, 1949-58; Mem. Devlin Commn of Enquiry into disturbances in Nyasaland, 1959; Administrator, Northern Cameroons, for period of plebiscite under UN supervision, 1960-61; toured Canada, Australia, and New Zealand as Special Representative Overseas of the Duke of Edinburgh's Award, 1962-63. With E. E. Shipton, 2nd ascent of Mt Kenya, 1929; first visit to North Island, Lake Rudolf, 1931; Mem. of Mt Everest expedition, 1933, and took part in first assault with L. R. Wager, reaching height of approx. 28,000 ft; mem. Mt Everest Expedition, 1936. Circumnavigation of the world, 1962-69, in 12 ton Gunning Grundel Sloop. KStJ 1950. *Address:* Little Hawsted, Steep, Petersfield, Hants. *T:* Petersfield 3435. *Clubs:* Alpine, East India, Devonshire, Sports and Public Schools, Little Ship.
[Died 25 Feb. 1979.

WYNDHAM WHITE, Sir Eric, KCMG 1968; *b* 26 Jan. 1913; *s* of Henry Wyndham White and Helen White (*née* Peppiatt); *m* 1947, Tina Gibson Thayer, Worcester, Mass, USA; two *d. Educ:* Westminster City Sch.; London Sch. of Economics, Univ. of London. LLB first class hons. Member of the Bar, Middle Temple, 1938; Asst Lectr, LSE, 1938-39; Mem. British delegs, Internat. Chamber of Commerce Congresses, Berlin, 1937, Copenhagen, 1939; Min. of Economic Warfare, 1939-41; First Sec., HM Embassy, Washington, 1942-45; Economic Counsellor, HM Embassy, Paris, 1945-46; Special Asst to European Director, UNRRA, 1945; Sec.-Gen., Emergency Economic Cttee for Europe (EECE), 1946; Exec. Sec. Prep. Cttee for ITO, then Sec.-Gen., UN Conf. on Internat. Trade and Employment (London, Geneva, Havana, 1946-48); Exec. Sec., GATT, 1948-65, Dir-Gen., 1965-68. Advr to Canadian Govt in multilateral trade negotiations, 1978-79. Hon. Dr *rerum publicarum,* of Sch. of Economics, Business and Public Administration, St Gall (Switzerland), 1963; Hon. Dr Laws: Univ. California, Los Angeles, 1966; Dartmouth Coll., New Hampshire, 1968. *Publications:* numerous articles and addresses in various learned jls (legal and economic) in England and abroad. *Recreations:* gardening, ski-ing, music. *Address:* Case Postale 5, 1211 Geneva 19, Switzerland. *Club:* Reform.
[Died 27 Jan. 1980.

WYNN, Hon. Rowland Tempest Beresford, CBE 1949; MA; CEng; FIEE; Chief Engineer, BBC, 1952-60, retired; *b* 31 Jan. 1898; *y s* of late Hon. Charles Henry Wynn, Rhug, Corwen, N Wales, and uncle of 7th Baron Newborough; *m* 1943, Eleanor Mary Tydfil, *y d* of late A. E. Smith-Thomas and Mrs Rondolph Burden, Five Wells, Brentwood, Essex; no *c. Educ:* Uppingham Sch., Rutland; Trinity Hall, Cambridge (MA). Served European War with RFC and RAF, 1917-18. Engineer, Marconi's Wireless Telegraph Co. Experimental Establishment, Writtle, Chelmsford, 1922-26. Head of Engineering Information Dept, BBC, 1926-35; Senior Superintendent Engineer, BBC, 1935-43; Asst Chief Engineer and Dep. Chief Engineer, BBC, 1943-52. Chairman, Radio Section of Institution of Electrical Engineers, 1949-50. *Publications:* various technical articles and papers. *Recreations:* golf, sailing. *Address:* Sunningdale, The Heights, Worthing, West Sussex BN14 0AJ. *T:* Worthing 60088.
[Died 24 April 1977.

WYNNE-EDWARDS, Sir Robert (Meredydd), Kt 1965; CBE 1962 (OBE 1944); DSO 1919; MC; MA; FICE (Past President); *b* 1 May 1897; *s* of late Rev. Canon J. R. Wynne-Edwards; *m* 1924, Hope Elizabeth Day, *d* of late Francis Fletcher, Nelson, British Columbia; one *s* three *d. Educ:* Leeds Grammar Sch.; Christ Church, Oxford. Royal Welch Fusiliers, 1914-19. Chairman, Council of Engineering Institutions, 1964-66. Hon. Fellow, Manchester College of Science and Technology, 1965; Hon. DSc Salford Univ., 1966. *Address:* The Old House, Blandford Forum, Dorset. *T:* Blandford 2292.
[Died 22 June 1974.

WYNNE-JONES, Major Charles Llewelyn, JP; Vice-Lieutenant of Merioneth, since 1957; *b* 3 Oct. 1890; *s* of late Very Rev. Llewelyn Wynne-Jones, MA, Dean of St Asaph; *m* 1915, Sybil, *o c* of late Lieut-Colonel G. F. Scott, DL, JP; one *d* (two *s* killed in action). *Educ:* Eton; RMC. Commissioned in 17th Lancers, 1910; served in France, 1914-18; Captain, N Somerset Yeomanry, 1928-35; retired as Major. Re-employed, 1940-45; DAQMG War Office, 1940; DAAG London District, 1943. JP for Merioneth, 1919; High Sheriff, 1928; DL 1930. *Recreations:* fishing, shooting. *Address:* Penmaenucha, Dolgellau, Gwynedd. *T:* Dolgellau, 625.
[Died 21 Aug. 1974.

WYNNE-JONES, Tom Neville, CMG 1954; CBE 1950 (OBE 1943); Architect to the Ceylon University and Ceylon Army Cantonment, Panagode, Sri Lanka, 1953-71, retired; reemployed as Consultant Adviser and Documentator to Ministry of Buildings, to 1973; *b* 19 Nov. 1893; *m* 1920, Mabel (Phil) Phillips (*d* 1972). *Educ:* Technical Coll. and School of Arts and Crafts, Swansea. Articled pupil to Sir Charles Tamlyn Ruthen, OBE, 1909-14. War Service, France, 1914-18, commnd RE; Army of Occupation as DORE Abbeville, demobilized Nov. 1919. PWD Ceylon, 1920; Architect, various grades, to Chief Architect, 1932-53. FRIBA, CEng, FIStructE, FCIA (PP), FIE(PP) (Life Member of all). *Recreations:* settling down, reading, writing, sketching, still a student. *Address:* Long Sands, 15 Second Avenue, Frinton-on-Sea, Essex. *Clubs:* Rotary (Colombo) (longest and oldest member); Frinton-on-Sea Golf.
[Died 21 June 1979.

WYNNE-TYSON, Dorothy Estelle Esmé; *b* 29 June 1898; *d* of late H. Innes Ripper and Maude Ripper (*née* Pitt); *m* 1918, Wing Comdr Lynden Charles Wynne-Tyson, OBE (decd) (marr. diss.); one *s. Educ:* boarding schs, governess, Belgian convent.

Actress under stage-name Esmé Wynne from 1909; original Rosamund in Where the Rainbow Ends, 1911; last stage appearance, Faith in Noel Coward's I'll Leave It to You, 1920. *Plays:* first play, The Prince's Bride, prod by Charles Hawtrey at Savoy Theatre, London, when she was 13; Little Lovers, London, 1922; Security, NY, 1929, London, 1932; one-act collaborations with Noel Coward, England and America; curtain-raisers with, and lyrics for, Noel Coward. *Publications:* Security, 1926; Quicksand, 1927; Momus, 1928; Melody, 1929; Incense and Sweet Cane, 1930; Prelude to Peace, 1936; Strange Rival (with J. D. Beresford), 1940; Men in the Same Boat (with J. D. Beresford), 1943; The Riddle of the Tower (with J. D. Beresford), 1944; The Gift (with J. D. Beresford), 1947; The Unity of Being, 1949; This Is Life Eternal, 1951; The Best Years of Their Lives, 1955; Mithras: the Fellow in the Cap, 1958 (rev. edn 1972); The Philosophy of Compassion, 1962; The Dialectics of Diotima, 1970; contribs to many newspapers and jls inc., into the 1930s, Daily Telegraph, Daily Express, Daily Mail, Evening Standard, Punch, Bystander, Queen, Homes and Gardens, Westminster Gazette; later to (Manchester) Guardian; Listener; Hibbert Jl; Contemporary Review; The Aryan Path; Hindustan Times; many books and jls of comparative religion and philosophy; Editor, World Forum, 1961-70. Millenium Guild of America Award winner, 1957, 1962. *Address:* c/o Centaur Press Ltd, Fontwell, Sussex.
[Died 17 Jan. 1972.

WYNTER, Bryan Herbert; freelance artist (painter); *b* 8 Sept. 1915; *s* of James Harold Wynter and Dora (*née* Judd); *m* 1st, 1949, Suzanne Lethbridge; one *s* one *d;* 2nd, 1959, Monica Harman; two *s. Educ:* Haileybury; Slade School of Fine Art. One Man Exhibitions: 6 of paintings, Redfern Gall., 1947-57; 3 of paintings, Waddington Galls, 1959-67; Imoos kinetic works, Waddington Galleries, 1965. Work exhibited extensively in all continents. Public acquisitions include: Tate Gallery; Museum of Modern Art, NY; Victoria and Albert Museum; British Council; Arts Council; Contemp. Art Society; Gulbenkian Foundation; Stuyvesant Foundation; City Art Galleries of Bristol, Manchester, Bradford, Birmingham, Lincoln, Plymouth, Coventry; Fitzwilliam Museum, Cambridge; Towner Art Gallery, Eastbourne; Whitworth Art Gallery, Univ. of Manchester; Univ. of Warwick; Rutherstone Collection; CEMA; Ulster Museum; Arts Council of NI, Belfast. *Recreations:* white water canoeing, skin diving. *Address:* Treverven House, St Buryan, Penzance, Cornwall. *T:* St Buryan 280.
[Died 11 Feb. 1975.

WYNYARD-WRIGHT, Frank Trueman, MA; *b* 29 Jan. 1884; *s* of Rev. Frank Wynyard-Wright and Annie Grace Trueman; *m* Laura Kathleen Tweed (*d* 1964), Lincoln; one *s. Educ:* Rossall; Emmanuel Coll., Cambridge. Asst Master, Lexden House, Seaford; Headmaster, St Peter's Sch., Sheringham, for 10 years; Headmaster, Thames Nautical Training Coll., HMS Worcester; resigned, 1935. Served Malaya States Regt, 1914-18; world traveller, 1912-21. *Recreations:* photography, lecturing. *Address:* Stoneycrest Nursing Home, Churt Road, Hindhead, Surrey. *T:* 4455. *Clubs:* Penn, Alpine. *[Died 8 Sept. 1979.*

WYSE, Marjorie A. E.; *see* Erskine-Wyse, M.

Y

YAHYA KHAN, General Agha Muhammad, HPk (Hilal-i-Pakistan); HJ (Hilal-i-Jurat); President of Pakistan, and Chief Martial Law Administrator, 1969-71; *b* 4 Feb. 1917; *s* of Khan Bahadur Agha Saadat Ali Khan; *m* 1945, Begum Fakhira Yahya; one *s* one *d. Educ:* Indian Military Academy (King's Cadet). On commissioning, he was attached to 2nd Bn Worcester Regt and later to 3rd Bn Baluch Regt. War of 1939-45: 5 year tour of duty overseas with his Regt in Egypt, Sudan, Libya, Cyprus, Iraq, Italy, etc. Staff Coll., Quetta (grad. 1946); Lt-Col, 1947; Brig. 1951; Maj.-Gen. and CGS, 1957 (associated with modernisation of Army); GOC E Pakistan, Dec. 1962-Aug. 1964; commanded an infantry div. during War with India, 1965; became C-in-C of Army, Sept. 1966; President Ayub Khan called upon him to preserve the integrity of Pakistan, 24 March 1969. *Recreations:* golf, shooting, reading. *[Died 8 Aug. 1980.*

YASHIRO, Yukio; Member, The Japan Art Academy; Adviser, Museum Yamato Bunkakan, Nara; *b* Yokohama, Nov. 1890; *s* of Munekatsu Yashiro; *m* Fumi Kimura; one *s. Educ:* Tokio Imperial University. Studied art, Tokio, Florence, London, Paris, Berlin. Prof., Imperial School of Fine Arts, Tokio, 1918-

42; Director, Institute of Art Research, Tokio, 1930-42; Lectr, Harvard Univ., 1933; Consulting Prof., Stanford Univ., 1959. Socio Onorario, Ist Italiano per il Medio ed Estremo Oriente, Roma. Medaglia d'Oro ai Benemeriti della Cultura, 1957; Charles Lang Freer Medal, Freer Gall. of Art, Smithsonian Instn, 1965; Cultural Merits Prize, Japan, 1970. Commendatore Ordine al Merito della Repubblica Italiana, 1954. *Publications:* Sandro Botticelli: 3 vols, 1925; 2nd and revised edition in one volume, 1929; Japanische Malerei der Gegenwart, 1 vol. 1931; Characteristics of Japanese Art, 1943 (2nd, and supplemented edn in 2 vols, 1965); Masterpieces of Far Eastern Arts in European and American Collections, 2 vols 1943; 2000 years of Japanese Art, 1958; Art Treasures of Japan, 2 vols, 1961. *Address:* 1013 Kitahonmachi, Oiso, Kanagawa-ken, Japan.
[*Died 25 May 1975.*

YATES, Lt-Gen. Sir David P.; *see* Peel Yates.

YATES, Sir Thomas, Kt 1959; CBE 1951; retired as General Secretary, National Union of Seamen (1947-60) and Chairman of the TUC, (1957-58); Member, Southern Region Railway Board, 1963; *b* 25 Sept. 1896; *s* of William Yates, Sea View, Wallasey, Cheshire; *m* 1st, 1918, Lilian Grace (*d* 1960), *d* of William K. Church; three *s* one *d*; 2nd, 1962, Mrs Dorothy Kilpatrick. *Educ:* St Mary's Sch., Wallasey. Served European War, 1914-18, with Loyal North Lancashire Regiment. District Secretary for SW Coast, National Union of Seamen, 1940-41, and for Scottish Area, 1941-42, National Organiser, 1942-43, and Asst General-Secretary, 1943-47. Chm. of Merchant Seamen's War Memorial Soc.; Member: Seamen's Welfare Board; Merchant Navy Training Board; Management Cttee of Merchant Navy Comforts Trust; Coastal Advisory Cttee; Gen. Council of King George's Fund for Sailors; Exec. Council of Navy League; Shipping Defence Cttee; Personnel Training Cttee; National Maritime Board; International Labour Office Maritime Commission; Covent Garden Market Authority. Delegate for international seafarers to International Labour Office and World Health Organisation Joint Cttee; Representative of Trades Union Congress on Govt's Colonial Advisory Cttee and on various other Joint Bodies. *Address:* 9/84 Cronulla Street, Carlton, Sydney, NSW 2218, Australia.
[*Died 27 May 1978.*

YEAMAN, Sir Ian (David), Kt 1958; President of The Law Society, 1957-58; *b* 20 March 1889; *s* of David Yeaman and Catherine Sanger; *m* 1926, Anne Doris Wood (*d* 1975); two *s*. *Educ:* Dean Close Sch., Cheltenham. Admitted Solicitor, 1911; European War, 1914-18; enlisted Gloucestershire Regt TA, Sept. 1914; commissioned, RFA, 1915; served in France, 1916-18 (wounded); demobilised, 1919. Partner Rickerbys, Cheltenham, 1922. Member of Council of Law Society, 1936-64; Pres. Glos and Wilts Law Soc., 1952; Vice-Pres. Law Soc., 1956-57; Member of Lord Chancellor's Cttee on Land Registration, 1942. Hon. Member, American Bar Assoc., 1957. *Recreation:* gardening. *Address:* The Moat House, Uckington, near Cheltenham. *T:* Combe Hill 254. *Clubs:* East India, Sports and Public Schools; New (Cheltenham). [*Died 28 Feb. 1977.*

YELLOWLEES, Henry, OBE 1919; MD (Glasgow); FRCPGlas, FRCPE; FRCP; DPM (London); Hon. Consulting Physician, St Thomas' Hospital; *b* 11 June 1888; *yr s* of late David Yellowlees, MD, LLD, Gartnavel, Glasgow, and Federata, *d* of late Rev. H. M. Williamson, DD, Belfast; *m* 1918, Dorothy, *d* of Major A. J. Davis, Pagham, Sussex; two *s* one *d*. *Educ:* Kelvinside Academy, Glasgow; Glasgow Univ. Senior Resident and Deputy Supt Western Infirmary, Glasgow; Asst Physician and Deputy Supt, Perth District Mental Hosp., and Royal Hosp., Morningside, Edinburgh; served in France, 1915-18 as Capt. RAMC and Mental Specialist, Etaples Hospital Area (despatches twice, OBE); Lecturer and Assistant to Professor of Psychiatry, University of Edinburgh, 1919-22; Physician Superintendent of the Retreat, York, 1922-29; Physician for Mental Diseases and Lectr in Psychological Medicine, St Thomas' Hosp., 1928-48; consulting work in London since 1929, and in Bath from 1956. Examiner in Mental Diseases and Psychology, Univ. of London, 1931-35; Examiner in Psychological Medicine, Royal College of Physicians, 1936-39. Colonel, AMS, and Consulting Psychiatrist to BEF in France, 1939-40. *Publications:* A Manual of Psychotherapy, 1923; Clinical Lectures on Psychological Medicine, 1932; Out of Working Hours, 1942; The Human Approach, 1946; To Define True Madness, 1953; Frames of Mind, 1957; lectures, addresses, and papers. *Address:* 1 Lansdown Place West, Bath. *T:* Bath 60593.
[*Died 5 April 1971.*

YEO, Sir William, Kt 1964; CBE 1954; JP; farmer and grazier; President, New South Wales Council of Returned Services League of Australia, 1949-69; *b* Alectown, 1 May 1896; *s* of late Arthur Plane Yeo; *m* 1925, Eileen Theresa, *d* of Robert Golding. *Educ:* Peak Hill Public School. Served European War, 1914-18: 18th Battalion, Australian Imperial Force, Gallipoli and France. *Address:* 21 French Street, Maroubra, NSW 2035, Australia.
[*Died 9 Dec. 1972.*

YERBURY, Air Vice-Marshal Richard Olyffe, CBE 1962; Principal Medical Officer, HQ Training Command, RAF, since Sept. 1969; *b* 27 May 1914; *s* of Edgar Olyffe Yerbury and Constance Mary Kelson; *m* 1940, Drusilla Mary Dunn; one *s* two *d*. *Educ:* Epsom Coll.; Guy's Hosp. MRCS, LRCP 1937; MB, BS London 1938; DPH 1956; QHS 1970. Indian Medical Service, 1939-48; transfer to RAF (Medical Branch), 1948. Lady Cade Medal, RCS, 1969. *Address:* c/o Lloyds Bank, 6 Pall Mall, SW1. *Club:* Royal Air Force. [*Died 19 Feb. 1971.*

YOOL, Air Vice-Marshal William Munro, CB 1946; CBE 1941; RAF, retired list; *b* 26 May 1894. Director of Auxiliaries, Reserves and Air Cadets, Dec. 1951-54; Acting Air Vice-Marshal and AOA, Technical Training Command, 1944; formerly AOA, HQ, Mediterranean and Middle East; retd 1949. *Address:* Dawney Hill Cottage, Pirbright, Surrey GU24 0JB.
[*Died 19 Sept. 1978.*

YORKE, Henry Vincent; *see* Green, H.

YOUNG, Rev. Allan; Minister, St John's Kirk of Perth, since 1973; Chaplain in Ordinary to the Queen in Scotland, since 1978; *b* 15 Sept. 1925; *s* of Alexander Hackney Young and Mary Ann Mitchell Gibson; *m* 1954, Agnes Tannahill Reid; one *s* two *d*. *Educ:* Univ. of Glasgow (MA, Hons Classics); Univ. of London (BD Hons); Union Theological Seminary, New York (STM). Sen. Asst Minister, Paisley Abbey, 1952-54; Minister of Troon, Ayrshire, 1954-73, translated to St John's Kirk of Perth, 1973. Moderator of Ayr Presbytery, 1969-70; Preacher to General Assembly, 1970; Chaplain: to Perth Town Council, 1973-75; to Perth and Kinross Dist Council, 1976-. Convener of Gen. Assembly's Cttee on Parish Educn, 1974-78; Chm., C. K. Marr Educnl Trust, and Bd of Governors of Marr Coll., Troon, 1971-73. *Publications:* contrib. Art. Liturgical Rev. *Recreations:* music, literature. *Address:* The Manse of St John's Kirk, Bellwood Park, Perth, Scotland PH2 7AJ. *T:* Perth 21755. *Club:* Liberal (Edinburgh). [*Died 16 April 1979.*

YOUNG, Rev. Canon Andrew John, MA (Edinburgh) 1908; Hon. LLD (Edinburgh) 1951; FRSL; Canon of Chichester Cathedral since 1948; Vicar of Stonegate, Sussex, 1941-59; *b* 1885; *m* 1914, Janet Green; one *s* one *d*. *Educ:* Royal High Sch., Edinburgh; Edinburgh University. Queen's Medal for Poetry, 1952. *Publications:* A Prospect of Flowers, 1945; A Retrospect of Flowers, 1950; Collected Poems, 1950; Into Hades, 1952; A Prospect of Britain, 1956; Out of the World and Back (poem), 1958; The Collected Poems of Andrew Young, 1960; The Poet and the Landscape, 1962; The New Poly-Olbion, 1967; Poetic Jesus, 1972. *Relevant Publication:* Andrew Young: Prospect of a Poet (ed Leonard Clark), 1958. *Address:* Park Lodge, Church Lane, Yapton, Arundel, Sussex.
[*Died 25 Nov. 1971.*

YOUNG, Col Sir Arthur (Edwin), KBE 1971; Kt 1965; CMG 1953; CVO 1962; KPM 1952; Commissioner, City of London Police, 1950-71 (seconded 1969-70 as Chief Constable, Royal Ulster Constabulary); President, Greater London Scout County (Boy Scouts' Association), since 1972; *b* 1907; *s* of Edwin Young; *m* 1st, 1939, Ivy Ada (*d* 1956); one *s*; 2nd, 1957, Margaret Furnival Homan (*née* Dolphin), Sidmouth and Washington (*d* 1966); 3rd, 1970, Mrs Ileen Turner. *Educ:* Portsmouth Grammar Sch. Joined Portsmouth City Police, 1924. Chief Constable, Leamington 1938; Senior Assistant Chief Constable of Birmingham, 1941; Allied Control Commission for Italy (Public Safety), 1943-45; Chief Constable of Hertfordshire, 1945; Assistant Commissioner of Police of the Metropolis, May 1947. Visited the Gold Coast, 1951, to make recommendations to Govt on re-organisation of Gold Coast Police; Comr of Federation of Malaya Police, 1952; Comr of Kenya Police, 1954. Hon. Comr of Police, New York. Director, Police Extended Interviews, 1962-71; Chairman: Police Council for Great Britain, 1965-71; Council, Police Athletic Assoc., 1952-71; Life Saving Federation, 1968. Member: Advisory Council National Police Fund, 1950-71 (Chairman Educ. Committee); Board of Governors of the Police Coll. and Atlantic Coll., 1966-71; Vice-President, Police Mutual Assurance Soc., 1960-71. King Gustav VI of Sweden's medal of merit, for services to sport, 1962, 1977. Vice-Chairman, National Small-Bore Rifle Assoc., 1964. Officer (Brother) Order of St John. Holds many foreign decorations. *Recreation:* walking. *Address:* 22 Grand Court, Eastbourne BN21 4BU. *T:* Eastbourne 25905. *Club:* Athenæum.
[*Died 20 Jan. 1979.*

YOUNG, Arthur Primrose, OBE; CEng, FIEE, FIMechE, FIWM; Member, Factory and Welfare Advisory Board, Ministry of Labour, 1940-47; Founder Vice-President, Institution of Works Managers (Chairman, 1934-50); *b* 2 July 1885; 7th *s* of late William Young, Highfield, Ayrshire, and late Mary Potts, *d* of late William Walker, Culmalzie, Wigtownshire; *m* 1st, 1912, Lillie Louisa (*d* 1961), 3rd *d* of late Abel Porter, Rugby; one *d* decd; 2nd, 1962, Winifred Rose, *widow* of George Henry Young, Broadford Bridge, Billingshurst, Sussex. *Educ:* Stanley School, St Pancras; Finsbury Technical College, London. Joined BTH Co. Ltd, 1901; continuous service to retirement in 1945 except for a break of nearly two years, 1906-08, when in USA working with General Electric Co.; Engineer Coventry Works, BTH Co. Ltd, 1915-21; Engineer and Manager, 1921-28; Manager Rugby Works, British Thomson Houston Co. Ltd, 1929-45. Took out in association with Company nearly 150 patents, 1909-31; Member: Council IAE, 1928-34; Faraday Centenary Cttee, IEE, 1931; Council IEE, 1938-41; Coventry Education Cttee, 1928-38; Warwickshire National Service Cttee, 1939; visited USA, 1939 and 1945, at invitation of Episcopal Church of America to attend private conference, Washington, to survey impact of Christian principles on industrial relations; Visiting Fellow Nuffield College, Oxford, 1939-47; Director of Labour Supply Cttee, Min. of Labour, 1940-41; lent to Lord Beaverbrook, Minister of Aircraft Production, for special duties as Controller of Magneto Production, 1941; Chairman: Confederation of Management Associations, 1938-48; Midland Regional Council, UNA, 1946-53; Spencer Trust, Coventry, 1952-62; Dir, BKL Alloys Ltd, 1945-67. Governor: Birmingham College of Advanced Technology, 1956-61; Coventry Technical College and College of Art, 1960-62; Member Warwickshire Education Committee, 1950-62; Member, Management Committee, South Warwickshire Hospital Group (no 14), 1950-62. Institution of Works Managers inaugurated biennial A. P. Young Lecture, 1962. *Publications:* Magnetos, 1919, 2nd edn, revised 1920; Elements of Electrotechnics, 1921; Automobile Electrical Equipment, 1933 (8th edn rev. 1970) (with L. Griffiths); Forward from Chaos, 1933; Plan and Serve, 1938; Man at the Cross Roads, 1941; The Production Front and You, 1942; The World of Industry, 1946 (Japanese edn, 1948); Lord Kelvin, 1948; Coal, 1948; Report on American Productivity, 1949; Across the Years, 1971; The X Documents, 1974. *Recreations:* walking, reading, writing and painting. *Address:* Oakcroft, Mannings Heath, near Horsham, West Sussex. *T:* Horsham 5509; 36 Brookhurst Court, Beverley Road, Leamington Spa, Warwickshire. *T:* Leamington Spa 25271. *Club:* National Liberal.						*[Died 1 Feb. 1977.*

YOUNG, Rev. Canon Charles Edgar, AFC; MA; Vicar of Thornthwaite, 1957-65; Headmaster, Rossall School, 1937-57, retired; Hon. Canon of Carlisle Cathedral, 1962-65; Canon Emeritus, 1965; *b* Clifton, Bristol, 8 Jan. 1897; *s* of late Prof. Sydney Young; *m* 1928, Dorothy Vere, *d* of late Rt Rev. Harry Vere White, late Bishop of Limerick; one *s* two *d*. *Educ:* Charterhouse (Scholar); Exeter College, Oxford. Lieut RASC 1915-17; Lieut, RFC, 1917-18; Capt. RAF, 1918-19; Exeter College, Oxford, 1919-21; 2nd class Honours Moderations, 1921, BA 1921; MA 1928; Lower Sixth Form Master at Fettes College, Edinburgh, 1921-29; Headmaster Lincoln School, 1929-37. Served with RAF, 1940-42; Flight Lieut, 1942. JP, 1947-56. Made deacon, 1952; ordained priest, 1953. *Address:* Park House, Church Stretton, Salop.		*[Died 25 Sept. 1977.*

YOUNG, Christopher Alwyne Jack, FRS 1972; *b* 7 March 1912; *s* of Henry George and Penelope Young; *m* 1946, Wendy Gladys Henniker Heaton, *d* of Peter Edward and Ellen Mary Tyson, Alnwick, Northumberland; no *c*. *Educ:* Colston's Sch.; St Edmund Hall, Oxford (BA, BSc). Cheltenham Coll., 1934-37; Sudan Govt Service, 1937-40; ICI Ltd, Billingham Div. (incl. TA and FIDO Projects), 1940-46. Dir, ICI Central Instrument Research Laboratory, 1946-71; Technical Dir, ICI Corporate Laboratory, 1971-73. Chairman: Instrumentation and Control Panel of Engineering Equipment Users' Assoc., 1949-58; Process Control Terminology Panel of BSI, 1949-59; Instrument Adv. Cttee of City and Guilds Inst., 1949-64; Process Control Engrg Cttee, BSI, 1971-. Governor, Battersea Polytechnic, 1956-66. Member: OEEC Mission to USA on Chemical Engrg, 1950; Inst. of Measurement and Control (formerly Soc. Inst. Tech.), Council, 1951-54, Pres., 1954-57; Scientific Instrument Research Assoc., Council, 1953-56. Chm., Control Advisory Cttee, 1965-67; UK Automation Council, R&D Cttee, 1957-59; Chm., Instrumentation and Control Adv. Cttee of Assoc. of British Chemical Manufrs, 1954-58; British Council Mission to USSR on Automation, 1959; Glazebrook Cttee, Nat. Phys. Laboratory, 1966-68; Fluids and Heat Cttee, Nat. Engrg Laboratory Steering Cttee, 1966-68; Univ. of Surrey, Council, 1966-72; Council for Nat. Academic Awards, Instrumentation

and Systems Engrg Bd, 1967-; Hon. Fellow, Inst of Measurement and Control, 1973. Hon. DTech Univ. of Bradford, 1969. First Sir Harold Hartley Medal, 1969. *Publications:* Process Control, 1954; An Introduction to Process Control System Design, 1955; numerous papers on instrumentation and control. *Address:* Concord House, White Cross, Zeals, Warminster, Wilts BA12 6PH. *T:* Bourton (Dorset) 482.						*[Died 20 Jan. 1978.*

YOUNG, Sir Douglas; see Young, Sir J. D.

YOUNG, Sir Eric; see Young, Sir T. E. B.

YOUNG, Gladys, OBE 1951; Radio Artist; *b* Newcastle; *d* of William Michael Young; *m* 1916, Algernon West; one *s*. *Educ:* Sutton High Sch.; Bonn, Germany. Entered RADA, 1912; scholarship; Silver Medal, 1913; Gold Medal, 1914; under Vedrenne and Eadie management, 1914-16. War work, 1916-18; began broadcasting, 1926; BBC Rep. Co. from outbreak of war, 1939-49. Has appeared in many television plays, 1930-. *Recreation:* mountaineering. *Address:* Twitten Bend, Willingdon, Eastbourne, East Sussex.		*[Died 18 Aug. 1975.*

YOUNG, James; *b* 1 Oct. 1887; *s* of David S. Young and Henrietta Martin; *m* 1914, Margaret Cowan Smith Finlay; one *s*. *Educ:* George Heriot's Sch., Edinburgh. Apprentice Engineer and Draughtsman, 1904-13, Brown Bros, Rosebank Ironworks, Edinburgh; Draughtsman, 1913-18, John Brown & Co., Shipbuilders, Clydebank; Draughtsman, 1918-20, Barclay Curle & Co., Marine Engineers, Glasgow. Assoc. of Engineering and Shipbuilding Draughtsmen: Asst General Secretary, 1920-29; Divisional Organiser, 1929-45; General Secretary, 1945-52. Member General Council Scottish Trades Union Congress, 1932-45, Chairman, 1935-36 and 1944-45; President, Scottish Trades Union Congress, St Andrews, 1936, and Aberdeen, 1945; Member Labour Research Dept Executive, 1920-29; Regional Production Board, Scotland, 1941-45; Advisory Council of Education, Scotland, 1944-46; Executive Council, Confederation of Shipbuilding and Engineering Unions, 1944-52; Member of Commission appointed to enquire into the advancement of Africans in industry in Northern Rhodesia, 1947; Member of Tribunal set up under the constitution of the National Council for the Omnibus Industry to deal with a claim for National Conditions covering stage carriage operations, 1947; Member Court of Enquiry into Road Haulage Dispute, 1947. President, International Federation Commercial Clerical and Technical Employees, 1949-55. Member London County Council for East Woolwich, 1955-65; Chairman, Education Cttee, LCC, 1964-65; Member Greater London Council (Greenwich), 1964-67; Chairman, Education Cttee, Inner London Education Authority, 1964-67. Member Commn to inquire into causes of Trade disputes in Colony of Aden during March 1956; Member Board of Enquiry into Trade Dispute between Pilots and British West Indian Airways Ltd, 1958; part-time Member SE Gas Board, 1955-58. *Address:* Flat 11, 55 Orchard Brae Gardens, Edinburgh EH4 2HR. *T:* 031-332 8153.						*[Died 16 July 1975.*

YOUNG, Sir James Reid, Kt 1951; CA; FCIS; Chartered Accountant (Scotland); *b* 2 Dec. 1888; *s* of late Rev. Dr Young, Paisley, and Janet, *d* of late James Reid, Glasgow; *m* 1918, Margaret Boyd, *d* of late Dr Wm Walker, Grangemouth; one *d* (one *s* decd). *Educ:* Paisley Grammar Sch.; Glasgow Univ. Dir, Vickers-Armstrongs Ltd, 1936; Chm., 1952-54; Dir, Vickers Ltd, 1937-59; Man. Dir, 1952-54; Chm., International Combustion (Holdings) Ltd, 1956-67. Chm., Adv. Panel, Organisation and Methods Div. of HM Treasury, 1941-54. *Address:* 65 Eaton Square, SW1. *T:* 01-235 1088.						*[Died 6 Sept. 1971.*

YOUNG, Sir (John) Douglas, Kt 1935; Controller of Military Government Courts (President, Military Government General Court), Allied Commission for Austria (British Element), Dec. 1944-Jan. 1948; *b* Helensburgh, 7 April 1883; *s* of James Young; *m* 1912, Joyce Macewen, *d* of William Alexander Smith, Glasgow; two *s*. *Educ:* Merchiston Castle Sch., Edinburgh; Pembroke Coll., Cambridge, BA. Called to Bar, 1907; Midland Circuit; Hon Counsel to Earl Haig's Officers' Assoc.; served European War, 1915-19; contested (L) Hendon, 1922; Southend, 1923, 1924, and West Lothian, 1928; Judge of the High Court, Allahabad, 1929-34; Chief Justice, High Court of Judicature, Lahore, 1934-43. Founded the College of Physical Education and Scouting at Lahore. *Address:* Ballasalla House, Ballasalla, Isle of Man.						*[Died 13 April 1973.*

YOUNG, John Stirling, MC; Regius Professor of Pathology, University of Aberdeen, 1937-62, now Emeritus; *b* Symington, Ayrshire, 24 Sept. 1894; *s* of Matthew Young and Mary D.

Stirling; *m* 1930, Ruth Muir Whipple; three *s*. *Educ:* Kilmarnock Academy; Glasgow Univ. MA (Glasgow) 1919; BSc 1920; MB, ChB 1923; MD (Gold Medal) 1928; Reader in Experimental Pathology, University of Leeds, 1927-31; Professor of Pathology, Queen's Univ., Belfast, 1932-37; Member Agricultural Research Council, 1952-56. Hon. LLD (Aberdeen), 1963. *Publications:* various scientific papers in Journal of Pathology and Bacteriology. *Recreation:* golf. *Address:* 16 Rubislaw Den South, Aberdeen.
[*Died 16 Sept.* 1971.

YOUNG, Sir Mark Aitchison, GCMG 1946 (KCMG 1934; CMG 1931); KStJ; *b* 30 June 1886; 3rd *s* of late Sir W. Mackworth Young, KCSI; *m* Josephine Mary, CStJ, *d* of late Walter C. Price; two *s* two *d*. *Educ:* Eton; King's Coll., Cambridge. Entered Ceylon Civil Service, 1909; served European War from 1915; Principal Assistant Colonial Secretary, Ceylon, 1923-28; Colonial Secretary, Sierra Leone, 1928-30; Chief Secretary to the Government of Palestine, 1930-33; Governor and Commander-in-Chief of Barbados, 1933-38; administered Government of Trinidad and Tobago, Nov. 1937-Feb. 1938; Governor and C-in-C of Tanganyika Territory, 1938-41; assumed duties as Governor and C-in-C, Hong Kong, Sept. 1941; prisoner of war in Japanese hands, Dec. 1941-Aug. 1945; resumed duties in Hong Kong, 1 May 1946; retired, 1947. *Address:* Lang House, Winchester. *T:* Winchester 2480. [*Died 12 May* 1974.

YOUNG, Maj.-Gen. Peter George Francis, CB 1965; CBE 1958; retired 1968; *b* 15 July 1912; *s* of late Major Reginald Bradley and Mrs Young; *m* 1949, Patricia FitzGerald, *d* of late Lt-Col A. E. FitzGerald and late Mrs Ronald Beauchamp; one *s* one *d*. *Educ:* Winchester Coll.; Royal Military Coll., Sandhurst. Commissioned Oxford and Bucks Light Inf., 1932; served with Oxford and Bucks Light Inf. and RWAFF, 1932-40; served with Airborne Forces, 1941-48; comd 1st Bn Oxford and Bucks Light Inf., 1952-55; comd 44 Parachute Bde, TA, 1955-58; comd 1st Bde, Royal Nigeria Regt, 1958-61; War Office, 1961-62; GOC Cyprus District, 1962-64; Director of Infantry, MoD, 1965-67. *Recreations:* shooting, polo, bird watching. *Address:* The Lodge, Rushall, Pewsey, Wilts. *T:* Upavon 300. *Club:* Army and Navy.
[*Died 4 Nov.* 1976.

YOUNG, Stephen, JP; MB, ChB, FRCSGlas; Hon. Consulting Surgeon, Royal Infirmary, Glasgow; Lecturer, Otorhino-Laryngology, University of Glasgow; *b* 16 May 1894; *s* of James Young, Merchant, Glanderstan, Renfrewshire, and Glasgow, and Margaret MacAlister; *m* Jessica Adamson Dickie, Ayrshire. *Educ:* Privately; Allen Glen's Sch.; Glasgow Univ.; Edinburgh Univ. RSO Scottish Branch, British Red Cross, 1917-19; Resident, Dept of Medicine, Western Infirmary, 1919-20; Senior ENT Registrar, Edinburgh Royal Infirmary, 1921; ENT Surgeon, Out-Patient Dept, Royal Infirmary, Glasgow, 1922, later Senior Assistant Surgeon, ENT Dept; Surgeon-in-Charge of ENT Wards, Royal Infirmary, 1947; ENT Consultant, Corporation of Glasgow; Regional ENT Consultant, Lanarkshire; Member: Board of Management, Royal Infirmary Group of Hospitals, 1947-59; General Advisory Council, BBC. Burgess and Freeman of City of Glasgow. *Publications:* numerous scientific publications and contributions to BMJ, Glasgow Medical Jl, Jl of Laryngology and Otology, etc. *Recreations:* chess, beagling, golf, breeding and judging hounds. *Address:* 65 Kelvin Court, Glasgow W2. *T:* 041-334 2302. *Clubs:* Kennel; Royal Scottish Automobile (Glasgow).
[*Died 6 July* 1972.

YOUNG, Maj.-Gen. Thomas, CB 1951; OBE 1945; retired, 1953; *b* 4 June 1893; *s* of William Fulton Young, Kilmarnock, and Euphemia Murray Wilson, Crosshouse; *m* 1922, Alison Rowe; no *c*. *Educ:* University of Glasgow. MB, ChB (Glasgow) 1915; MD 1951; DPH (Cambridge) (Dist. in Principles of Hygiene), 1924; Lieut, RAMC (SR) 1914; served European War, Dardanelles, MEF, EEF, 1915-22 (despatches twice); India, 1925-31 and 1934-39. Major, 1927; Lt-Col, 1941; Temp. Major, 1919 and 1924; Temp. Lt-Col, 1939; Temp. Col, 1941; Dep. Dir of Hygiene, BNAF and CMF, 1942-46 (despatches twice); Col, 1945; Comdt Army School of Hygiene, 1946; Brig., 1947; Dir of Medical Services, FARELF, 1948; Maj.-Gen., 1949; KHP, 1950; QHP, 1952-53. Dir, Army Health, 1949-53; retired, 1953. Col Comdt, RAMC, 1955-61. Legion of Merit (USA) Légionnaire, 1946; Médaille de la Reconnaissance Française, 1945. *Publications:* contributions to Journal of RAMC. *Recreation:* gardening. *Address:* Penair Nursing Home, St Clement, near Truro, Cornwall TR1 1TD.
[*Died 21 Aug.* 1979.

YOUNG, Thomas, CBE 1953 (OBE 1948); TD 1955; Sheriff at Falkirk, 1964-69 and at Airdrie, 1955-64; *b* 7 Nov. 1896; *s* of Thomas Downie Young, Edinburgh; *m* 1924, Lilias Adie, *d* of

Andrew Allan, Edinburgh and Leith; one *s*. *Educ:* George Heriot's Sch. Edinburgh Univ. WS 1927; in practice until 1955. Formerly Member: Schuster Cttee on Legal Aid for the Forces; Royal Commn on Marriage and Divorce; Legal Aid Scheme Making Cttee, Central Cttee and Amending Cttee Scotland (Chm.); Legal Aid Cttee for England and Scotland (Jt Chm.); Rules Council (Court of Session); Council of Law Soc. of Scotland; WS Council; Jt Cttee of Edinburgh Legal Socs; Member of Law Reform Cttee (Scotland). Solicitor in Scotland to Ministry of Pensions; Examiner to Police Examinations (Scotland) Board. JP Edinburgh. Served in TA, 1939-52, in Royal Scots and latterly in command of various units of RA and Legal Aid Section, Scottish Command. *Address:* 90 Murrayfield Gardens, Edinburgh EH12 6DJ. *T:* 031-337 2670.
[*Died 8 March* 1977.

YOUNG, Sir (Thomas) Eric (Boswell), Kt 1949; retired; *b* 6 Feb. 1891; *s* of Dr Moffat Young; *m* 1928, Margaret Mary, *d* of Rev. A. E. Hayward, Emley, Yorks; two *s* one *d*. *Educ:* Loretto; Durham Univ. Mining Engineer with experience in Durham, Northumberland, Yorkshire, Kent, Nottinghamshire and Derbyshire Coalfields. National Production Director, Ministry of Fuel and Power, 1942-43; Member NCB, 1946-50; former Managing Director, Bolsover Colliery Co. Ltd, re-elected a Director in 1950. *Publication:* Simultaneous Cutter and Loader for Longwall Workings (Trans. Inst. Min. E.). *Recreations:* shooting, yachting. *Address:* Willow Cottage, Phyllis Road, Claremont, Cape Town, South Africa. *T:* 77-9106 Cape Town.
[*Died 12 March* 1973.

YOUNG, Sir William, Kt 1975; CBE 1960; Chairman, Scottish Milk Marketing Board, since 1962; *b* 13 June 1905; *s* of John and Jessie Young; *m* 1937, Elizabeth Clelland Smith; one *s* one *d*. *Educ:* Kilmarnock Acad.; West of Scotland Agricultural Coll. Elected Pres., National Farmers' Union of Scotland, 1945. Mem., Scottish Milk Marketing Bd, 1943- (Vice-Chm. 1950, Chm. 1962); Chm., Royal Highland and Agricultural Soc. of Scotland, 1969 (Hon. Treas., 1973). FRAgSs. *Recreations:* curling, bowling. *Address:* Kyleholm, Skerrington Mains, Kilmarnock, Strathclyde, Scotland. *T:* Kilmarnock 26021.
[*Died 19 June* 1980.

YOUNGER, Sir James (Paton), Kt 1961; CBE 1945; JP; Chairman: George Younger & Son Ltd, 1947-65; Scottish Central Glass Works Ltd, 1947-65; Western Regional Hospital Board, Scotland, 1955-63; United Caledonian Breweries Ltd, 1960-68; President, Tennent Caledonian Breweries Ltd, 1968, Hon. President, 1972; Lord Lieutenant, County of Clackmannan, 1955-66; *b* 19 June 1891; *s* of James Younger, LLD, Mount Melville, St Andrews, and Annie, *d* of J. Thomson Paton, Alloa; *m* 1921, Rachel Howard, *d* of Paul Waterhouse, Yattendon Court, Berkshire; three *s* one *d*. *Educ:* Eton; Balliol Coll., Oxford. Captain, 3rd Bn Argyll and Sutherland Highlanders; served European War, 1914-18. Dir, Brewers Food Supply Co. Ltd. Member, Royal Company of Archers (Queen's Body Guard for Scotland), 1921. JP County of Clackmannan, 1933. *Recreation:* shooting. *Address:* Arnsbrae, Cambus, Alloa, Clackmannanshire. *T:* Alloa 3516. *Club:* New (Edinburgh).
[*Died 17 Sept.* 1974.

YOUNGER, Maj.-Gen. John Edward Talbot, CB 1945; *b* 2 Nov. 1888; *yr s* of late Colonel J. Younger, Royal Artillery, Langshaw Bush, Moffat, Dumfriesshire; *m* 1919, Harriot Bisset, *d* of late Sir Robert Holmes, KCB, Rathfarnham; (one *s* one *d* decd). *Educ:* Wellington Coll.; RMA, Woolwich. 2nd Lieut, RFA, 1909; France and Belgium, 1914-18 (despatches); School of Artillery, 1919-23; Instructor in Gunnery, Southern Command, 1931-34; Dep. Asst Director of Artillery, War Office, 1934-36; Bt Lt-Col, 1936; Asst Dir of Artillery, War Office, 1938-39; Bt Col, 1938; Commander 57th AA Brigade, 1939-40; Commander 3rd AA Division, 1940-42; General Staff, Washington, USA, 1942-43; retired pay, 1944. Red Cross Comr to USSR, 1945. Sec. Ven. Order of St John of Jerusalem, 1944-50; KStJ. Founder and Vice-Pres. of the Army Ski Assoc.; Vice-Pres., Altus Climbing Club; Pres., Royal Artillery Alpine Club. American Medal of Freedom with Bronze Palm; Médaille de la reconnaissance Française en vermeil. *Recreation:* enjoying old age. *Address:* Gowrie House, Kilmington, Devon. *Clubs:* Army and Navy, Ski Club of Great Britain.
[*Died 4 July* 1974.

YOUNGER, Rt. Hon. Sir Kenneth (Gilmour), PC 1951; KBE 1972; *b* 15 Dec. 1908; 2nd *s* of 2nd Viscount Younger of Leckie, DSO; *m* 1934, Elizabeth Kirsteen Stewart; one *s* two *d*. *Educ:* Winchester; New Coll., Oxford. Barrister, Inner Temple, 1932. Served Army, 1940-45, Temporary Major, Intelligence Corps; Chairman, UNRRA Cttee of Council for Europe, 1946-47. MP (Lab) Grimsby, 1945-59; Parly Under-Sec., Home Office, 1947-50; Minister of State, 1950-51. Joint Vice-Chm., Royal Inst. of

Internat. Affairs, 1953-55, re-elected Vice-Chm., 1958-59, Director, 1959-71. Mem. Cttee of Inquiry into Security Procedures and Practices, 1961; Chm., Adv. Council on Penal System, 1966-; Chm., Cttee of Inquiry on Privacy, 1970-72; Mem., Diplock Commn on NI, 1972; Chm., Data Protection Cttee, 1976-. Chairman: Howard League for Penal Reform, 1960-73; Bd of Trustees, UN Inst. for Training and Research, 1965-; Council, St George's Hosp. Med. Sch., 1965-74; Bd of Governors, St. George's Hosp., 1966-69; Lambeth, Southwark and Lewisham AHA (Teaching), 1974-. Hon. LLD, St John's Univ., New York, 1968. *Publications:* (joint editor) Fabian International Essays, 1957; contrib. to New Fabian Colonial Essays, 1959; The Public Service in New States, 1960; Changing Perspectives in British Foreign Policy, 1964; contrib., Britain and the World of the Seventies, 1970. *Recreations:* walking, music, sailing. *Address:* 3 Clareville Grove, SW7.
[Died 19 May 1976.

YOUNGER, Sir William Robert, 2nd Bt, *cr* 1911; late Diplomatic Service; *b* 27 Oct. 1888; *s* of Sir William Younger, 1st Bt, and Helen Caroline Benyon (Nellie) (*d* 1925), *e d* of Col Sir Robert Gunter, 1st Bt, MP; *S* father, 1937; *m* 1st, 1915, Joan Gwendoline (from whom he obtained a divorce, 1923), *d* of Hon. Louis Johnstone, Lavington Hall, Ipswich; two *s* two *d*; 2nd, 1930, Nellie Archbold (*d* 1960). *Educ:* Harrow; Christ Church, Oxford. *Heir: s* Maj.-Gen. John William Younger, CBE. *Address:* 4 Belgrave Crescent, Edinburgh. *[Died 25 May 1973.*

Z

ZAEHNER, Prof. Robert Charles, FBA 1966; MA; Spalding Professor of Eastern Religions and Ethics, University of Oxford, since 1952; Fellow of All Souls College, Oxford, since 1952; *b* 8 April 1913; *s* of Edward and Maria Louisa Zaehner. *Educ:* Tonbridge School; Christ Church, Oxford (Scholar); King's Coll., Cambridge. MA Oxon Oriental Languages, First Class. Senior Scholar of Christ Church, 1937-39; Research Lectr of Christ Church, 1939; Asst Press Attaché, then Press Attaché, British Embassy, Teheran, 1943-47; received into Roman Catholic Church, 1946; Lectr in Persian, Univ. of Oxford, 1950; Acting Counsellor, British Embassy, Teheran, 1951-52; Lectures: Jordan, at SOAS, Univ. of London, 1959; Union Theological Seminary, and Columbia Univ., NY, 1962; Gifford, Univ. of St Andrews, 1968-69; Riddell, Univ. of Newcastle upon Tyne, 1969; Westcott, on Teape Foundn, St Stephen's Coll., Delhi, 1969; Santa Barbara Univ., 1972. Hon. DLitt Lancaster, 1970. *Publications:* Foolishness to the Greeks, 1953; Zurván, a Zoroastrian Dilemma, 1955; The Teachings of the Magi, 1956; Mysticism Sacred and Profane, 1957; At Sundry Times, 1958; The Concise Encyclopædia of Living Faiths (editor and two contributions), 1959; Hindu and Muslim Mysticism, 1960; The Dawn and Twilight of Zoroastrianism, 1961; Hinduism, 1962; The Convergent Spirit, 1963; The Catholic Church and World Religions, 1964; Hindu Scriptures (ed and trans.), 1966; The Bhagavad-Gītā, 1968; Concordant Discord, 1970; Evolution in Religion, 1971; Dialectical Christianity and Christian Materialism, 1971; Drugs, Mysticism and Make Believe, 1972; Our Savage God, 1974. *Address:* All Souls College, Oxford.
[Died 24 Nov. 1974.

ZAMBRA, William Warren S.; *see* Shaw-Zambra.

ZANUCK, Darryl Francis; Chairman of the Board and Chief Executive Officer, 20th Century-Fox Film Corporation, 1969-71, Chairman Emeritus since 1971; *b* 5 Sept. 1902; *s* of Frank H. and Louise Torpin Norton Zanuck; *m* 1924, Virginia Ogelsby Fox; one *s* two *d*. *Educ:* Oakdale, Nebraska; Los Angeles, Calif. Served European War, 1917-18, with 37th Div.; with Warner Bros till 1933 (Producer of Little Caesar, Public Enemy, Five Star Final, I am a Fugitive from a Chain Gang, The Jazz Singer); joined Joseph M. Schenck in 20th Century Pictures (Producer of House of Rothschild, Les Misérables, Cardinal Richelieu and others). Amalgamated 20th Century with Fox, 1935, and became Vice-Pres., later President; first winner Irving Thalberg Memorial Trophy, again winner in 1944 and 1951. Supervised production training films for defence forces, Lt-Col 1941; Col 1942 (Legion of Merit). *Films:* with 20th Century-Fox include: Wilson, How Green was my Valley, This above all, The Purple Heart, Winged Victory, Grapes of Wrath, The Razor's Edge, Forever Amber, Gentleman's Agreement, The Snake Pit, Pinky, All About Eve. D. F. Zanuck Productions: Island in the Sun, The Sun Also Rises, 1957; The Roots of Heaven, 1958.

Produced: Crack in the Mirror, 1959 (Paris); The Big Gamble, 1960 (France, Ireland, Africa); The Longest Day, 1962. Comdr Legion of Honour (France); Comdr of Order of Arts and Letters (France), 1968; Comdr in Order of Merit (Italy), 1969. *Recreations:* big-game hunting, polo, ski-ing. *Address:* c/o 20th Century-Fox Film Corporation, Box 900, Beverly Hills, California 90213, USA. *[Died 22 Dec. 1979.*

ZEPLER, Eric Ernest; Emeritus Professor of Electronics, Southampton University (Professor, 1949-63); Research Fellow, Institute of Sound and Vibration, Southampton University, 1963-73; Past President British IRE; *b* 27 Jan. 1898; *s* of Dr med. M. Zepler and F. Guttfreundt; *m* 1926, Eleanor Fischer; one *s* one *d*. *Educ:* Realgymnasium Altena (Westphalia); Univ. Bonn, Berlin, Würzburg. Dr Phil., Würzburg, 1922. Research Engineer, Telefunken, 1925; Head of Design of Receivers and Direction Finders, Telefunken, 1932-35; came to England, 1935; Research Engineer, Marconi's Wireless Tel. Co. Ltd, 1936-40; Lecturer University Coll., Southampton, 1941; seconded to Cavendish Laboratory, 1943-46. Hon. DSc Southampton, 1977. Electronics Bldg, Southampton Univ., named Zepler Building, 1978. *Publications:* The Technique of Radio Design, 1943; (contrib. 2 chapters) University Radio Conference Proceedings, 1944; Under the Spell of the Chess Problem, 1951; (co-editor with S. W. Punnett) Electronic Devices and Networks, 1963; Electronic Circuit Techniques, 1963; (with K. G. Nichols) Transients in Electronic Engineering, 1971; contrib. to Telefunken Zeitung, Wireless Engr. *Recreations:* music, chess, bridge. *Address:* 6 Saxholm Way, Southampton SO1 7GU. *T:* Southampton 768020. *[Died 13 May 1980.*

ZHUKOV, Marshal Georgi Konstantinovich; Hero of the Soviet Union (three awards); Order of Lenin (five); Order of Victory (2); Order of Suvorov (2), etc; *b* Kalinin Region, 1896. Joined Red Army, 1918; took part in Civil War; took part in Battle of Khalkin-Gol against Japanese, 1939; during War held posts as Chief of General Staff, Deputy People's Commissar of Defence, C-in-C Leningrad, Western and 1st Ukrainian Fronts, 1941-45; in charge of defence of Moscow, 1941; took part in drawing up plan for defeat of German Army at Stalingrad, 1942; co-ordinator of Leningrad and Volkhov Fronts to break blockade of Leningrad, 1943; co-ordinated activity of 1st and 2nd Ukrainian Fronts and 1st and 2nd Byelorussian Fronts, 1943-44; C-in-C 1st Byelorussian Front, 1944-45; commanded capture of Berlin, 1945; Soviet representative at capitulation of Germans, 1945; Deputy Minister of Defence, 1953-55; Minister of Defence of the USSR, 1955-57. Member of the Presidium, in 1957 (Candidate Mem. 1956). Holds several foreign awards. *Publication:* The Memoirs of Marshal Zhukov, 1971. *Address:* c/o Ministry of Defence, 34 Naberzhnaya Maurice Thorez, Moscow, USSR.
[Died 18 June 1974.

ZIEGLER, Prof. Dr Karl; Director, Max Planck Institute (formerly Kaiser Wilhelm Institute) for Coal Research, Mülheim-Ruhr, 1943-69, retired; Hon. Professor, Technische Hochschule, Aachen, since 1949; *b* 26 Nov. 1898; *s* of Karl and Luise Ziegler; *m* 1922, Maria Kurtz; one *s* one *d*. *Educ:* Marburg University. Lecturer, Marburg University, 1923-26; Assistant, Chemical Institute, Heidelberg University, 1926-36; Professor of Chemistry and Director of Chemical Institute, University of Halle-Saale, 1936-43. Visiting Professor, University of Chicago, 1936; Carl Folkers Lecturer, Madison, Wisconsin, and Urbana, Illinois, 1952. Foreign Mem., Royal Society, 1971; Hon. FRSE, 1972. Holds numerous awards, including Nobel Prize for Chemistry (jointly), 1963. *Publications:* about 180 contribs learned jls. *Recreations:* astronomy, mountain-climbing. *Address:* c/o Max-Planck-Institut für Kohlenforschung, Kaiser-Wilhelm-Platz 1, Mülheim-Ruhr, Germany. *T:* 3061 (private) 306 290. *[Died 12 Aug. 1973.*

ZINKEISEN, Anna Katrina, RP, ROI, RDI; Portrait and Mural Painter; *b* Kilcreggan, Scotland; *d* of Victor Zinkeisen and Clare Bolton Charles; *m* 1928, Colonel Guy R. N. Heseltine, MC. *Educ:* home; Royal Academy Schools. Ambulance Officer in St John Ambulance, nursing at St Mary's Hospital and doing pathological and clinical drawings for surgeons throughout the war. *Address:* 25 Cheyne Court, Chelsea, SW3; Looms Cottage, Burgh, Woodbridge, Suffolk. *[Died 23 Sept. 1976.*

ZUKOR, Adolph; Chairman of Board Emeritus, Paramount Pictures Corporation; *b* 7 Jan. 1873; *s* of Jacob Zukor and Hannah Liebermann; *m* 1897, Lottie Kaufman (*d* 1956); one *s* one *d*. *Educ:* Hungary; evening schools, New York City. Came to US 1888; engaged in hardware, upholstery and fur business; went to Chicago 1892 where he became successful in fur trade; returned to NY in 1901 and 1903 ventured with the late Marcus Loew in the penny arcade; this was the foundation of the Loew Enterprises of which Loew became the President and Zukor the

Treasurer; formed Famous Players Film Company with aid of Daniel Frohman, 1912; the first production of the new company was Queen Elizabeth with Sarah Bernhardt; this was followed by Prisoner of Zenda with James K. Hackett and these two were the first two feature pictures of multiple-reel length produced; Famous Players Film Company and Jesse L. Lasky Feature Play Combined under the name of Famous Players Lasky Corporation, 1916, then absorbed Paramount Pictures Corporation; erected theatres in the key cities of the country; this led to establishment of Publix Theatres Corporation, 1926; corporate name changed to Paramount Famous-Lasky Corporation 1927; to Paramount Publix Corporation 1930; to Paramount Pictures, Inc., 1935. *Address:* c/o Paramount Pictures Corp., 1 Gulf & Western Plaza, New York, NY 10023, USA. *Clubs:* Masons, Lambs, City Athletic (New York); Hillcrest Country (Los Angeles).   *[Died* 10 *June* 1976.